LANGENSCHEIDT'S STANDARD FRENCH DICTIONARY

French-English
English-French

by

KENNETH URWIN

Docteur de l'Université de Paris
Docteur de l'Université de Caen

Enlarged and updated edition 1988

LANGENSCHEIDT

NEW YORK · BERLIN · MUNICH · VIENNA · ZURICH

© *1968, 1988 Langenscheidt KG, Berlin and Munich*
Printed in Germany

First Part

French-English

Contents

Table des matières

Preface

Language has two faces: one looking back, one looking forward. This revised edition of the "Standard French Dictionary" has tried to take both of these aspects into account: In retaining some of yesterday's speech, it will help the user to grapple with the great 19th century authors, whether for school or for pleasure. At the same time, he will find language's path into the future staked out by such words as: *aiguilleur du ciel, alcootest, banlieue-dortoir, écologisme, microprocesseur, organigramme, rétro, télédistribution, etc., etc.*

Needless to say, a great deal of the material old and new is made up of phrases and phraselike expressions covering all registers of speech from everyday language down to slang.

A series of appendices to the dictionary proper gives a list of some common proper names, of common abbreviations, tables of numerals and weights and measures, and a list of model verbs to which the user is referred by the reference number with each verb in the vocabulary. Irregular forms of verbs have been given as separate entries.

The instructions on how to use this dictionary (pages 7–13) should be read carefully: they are intended to increase its practical value.

The phonetic transcription has been given in square brackets after each entry word, using the system of the International Phonetic Association.

It is hoped that this new dictionary will be an instrument for better understanding between peoples.

LANGENSCHEIDT

Préface

La langue a deux visages: l'un est tourné vers le passé, l'autre vers le futur. Cette nouvelle édition du «Standard French Dictionary» s'efforce de tenir compte de ces deux aspects: En gardant une certaine partie du vocabulaire d'hier, il aidera l'utilisateur dans la lecture des auteurs classiques, que ce soit à l'école ou pour son plaisir personnel; mais d'autre part, pour rendre son dû à l'aspect «futuriste» de la langue, de nombreux «mots nouveaux» ont été introduits, comme par ex.: *aiguilleur du ciel, alcootest, banlieue-dortoir, écologisme, microprocesseur, organigramme, rétro, télédistribution, etc., etc.*

Il va sans dire qu'une bonne partie de ce dictionnaire consiste en phrases et expressions idiomatiques appartenant à tous les niveaux de langue.

En complément du dictionnaire proprement dit nous donnons une liste de noms propres, une autre des abréviations les plus courantes, ainsi que des tables d'adjectifs numéraux et de poids et de mesures et une table synoptique des conjugaisons à laquelle renvoie le numéro après chaque verbe. Les formes irrégulières des verbes se trouveront dans le vocabulaire sous forme de mots-souches indépendants.

Nous recommandons aux utilisateurs de lire attentivement les indications pour l'emploi de ce dictionnaire (pages 7–13), ce qui en relevera la valeur pratique.

La prononciation figurée, placée entre crochets à la suite du mot-souche, est indiquée selon la méthode de l'Association Phonétique Internationale.

Puisse ce dictionnaire contribuer à une meilleure compréhension entre les peuples.

LANGENSCHEIDT

Directions for the use of this dictionary
Indications pour l'emploi de ce dictionnaire

1. Arrangement. The alphabetic order of the entry word has been observed throughout. Hence you will find, in their proper alphabetic order:

a) the irregular forms of nouns, adjectives, comparatives, adverbs, and those forms of irregular verbs from which the various tenses can be derived. Reflexive or pronominal verbs, however, will be found under the simple infinitive;

b) the various forms of the pronouns;

c) compound words.

2. Homonyms of different etymologies have been subdivided by exponents;

e.g. *mousse*[1] ship's boy ...
mousse[2] moss ...
mousse[3] blunt ...

3. Differences in meaning. The different senses of French words can be distinguished by:

a) explanatory additions given in italics after a translation;

e.g. *tombant* drooping (*moustache, shoulders*); sagging (*branch*); flowing (*hair*);

b) symbols and abbreviations before the particular meaning (see list on pages 10–11). If, however, the symbol or abbreviation applies to all translations alike, it is placed between the entry word and its phonetic transcription.

A semicolon is used to separate one meaning from another which is essentially different.

1. Classement. L'ordre alphabétique des mots-souches a été rigoureusement observé. Ainsi on trouvera dans leur ordre alphabétique:

a) les formes irrégulières des noms, des adjectifs, des comparatifs, des adverbes et, des verbes irréguliers, les formes, dont on peut dériver les divers temps; toutefois les verbes réfléchis ou pronominaux se trouveront après l'infinitif simple;

b) les formes diverses des pronoms;

c) les mots composés.

2. Les Homonymes d'etymologie différente font l'objet d'articles différents distingués par un chiffre placé en haut derrière le mot en question;

p.ex. *mousse*[1] ship's boy ...
mousse[2] moss ...
mousse[3] blunt ...

3. Distinction de sens. Les différents sens des mots français se reconnaissent grâce à:

a) des additions explicatives, en italique, placées à la suite des versions proposées;

p.ex. *tombant* drooping (*moustache, shoulders*); sagging (*branch*); flowing (*hair*);

b) des symboles ou des définitions en abrégé qui les précèdent (voir liste, pages 10–11). Si, cependant, les symboles ou les abréviations se rapportent à l'ensemble des traductions, ils sont intercalés entre le mot-souche et la transcription phonétique.

Le point-virgule sépare une acception donnée d'une autre essentiellement différente.

4. **The gender** of French nouns is always given. In the case of adjectives the gender is not given unless there is a danger of misunderstanding.

5. **Letters in brackets** within an entry word indicate that the word may be spelt with or without the letter bracketed;

e.g. *immu(t)abilité* immutability.

6. **Conjugations of verbs.** The number given in round brackets after each French infinitive refers to the table of conjugations at the end of this volume (pages 570–598).

4. **Le genre grammatical** des noms français est toujours indiqué. Pour les adjectifs le genre est indiqué exceptionnellement pour éviter des malentendus.

5. **Les lettres entre parenthèses** dans les mots-souches indiquent qu'il est permis d'écrire le même mot de deux manières différentes;

p.ex. *immu(t)abilité* immutability.

6. **Conjugaisons des verbes.** Les chiffres donnés entre parenthèses à la suite de chaque verbe français renvoient à la table synoptique des conjugaisons à la fin de ce dictionnaire (pages 570–598).

Key to the symbols and abbreviations
Explication des symboles et des abréviations

1. Symbols

The tilde (~, ~) serves as a mark of repetition. To save space, compound entry words are often given with a tilde replacing one part.

The tilde in bold type (~) replaces the entry word at the beginning of the entry;

e.g. **wagon** ...; **~-poste** = wagon-poste.

The simple tilde (~) replaces:

a) The entry word immediately preceding (which may itself contain a tilde in bold type), or in an illustrative example containing a feminine adjective, that part of the feminine adjective suppressed in the catchword;

e.g. **abattre** ...; s'~ = s'abattre; **aéro**...; **~statique** ...; *ballon m* ~ = ballon aérostatique; **aphteux, -euse** *adj.*: *fièvre f* ~*euse* = fièvre aphteuse;

b) within the phonetic transcription, the whole of the pronunciation of the preceding entry word, or of some part of it which remains unchanged;

e.g. **vénérable** [vene'rabl] ...; **vénération** [~ra'sjɔ̃] = [venera'sjɔ̃] ...; **vénérer** [~'re] = [vene're].

The tilde with circle (ℒ, ℒ). When the first letter changes from capital to small or vice-versa, the usual tilde is replaced by a tilde with circle (ℒ, ℒ);

e.g. **saint, sainte** ...; ℒ-**Esprit** = Saint-Esprit; **croix** ...; ℒ-*Rouge* = Croix-Rouge.

The other symbols used in this dictionary are:

1. Symboles

Le tilde (~, ~) est le signe de la répétition. Afin de gagner de la placé, souvent le mot-souche ou un de ses éléments a été remplacé par le tilde.

Le tilde en caractère gras (~) remplace le mot-souche qui se trouve au début de l'article;

p.ex. **wagon** ...; **~-poste** = wagon-poste.

Le tilde simple (~) remplace:

a) le mot-souche qui précède (qui d'ailleurs peut également être formé à l'aide du tilde en caractère gras), ou dans une expression avec adjectif féminin l'élément de l'adjectif féminin supprimé dans le mot-souche;

p.ex. **abattre** ...; s'~ = s'abattre; **aéro**...; **~statique** ...; *ballon m* ~ = ballon aérostatique; **aphteux, -euse** *adj.*: *fièvre f* ~*euse* = fièvre aphteuse;

b) dans la transcription phonétique, la prononciation entière du mot-souche qui précède ou la partie qui demeure inchangée;

p.ex. **vénérable** [vene'rabl] ...; **vénération** [~ra'sjɔ̃] = [venera'sjɔ̃] ...; **vénérer** [~'re] = [vene're].

Le tilde avec cercle (ℒ, ℒ). Quand la première lettre se transforme de majuscule en minuscule, ou vice versa, le tilde normal est remplacé par le tilde avec cercle (ℒ, ℒ);

p.ex. **saint, sainte** ...; ℒ-**Esprit** = Saint-Esprit; **croix** ...; ℒ-*Rouge* = Croix-Rouge.

Les autres symboles employés dans ce dictionnaire sont:

F	*colloquial*, familier.		🚂	*railway*, *Am.* railroad, chemin de fer.
V	*vulgar*, vulgaire.		✈	*aviation*, aviation.
†	*obsolete*, vieilli.		♪	*music*, musique.
⚘	*botany*, botanique.		△	*architecture*, architecture.
⊕	*technology*, technologie; *mechanics*, mécanique.		⚡	*electricity*, électricité.
⚒	*mining*, mines.		⚖	*law*, droit.
⚔	*military*, militaire.		Å	*mathematics*, mathématique.
⚓	*nautical*, nautique; *navy*, marine.		✔	*agriculture*, agriculture.
⚑	*commercial*, commerce; *finance*, finances.		🜍	*chemistry*, chimie.
			🜎	*medicine*, médecine.
			⊘	*heraldry*, blason.

2. Abbreviations – Abréviations

a.	*also*, aussi.		*fut.*	*future*, futur.
abbr.	*abbreviation*, abréviation.		*geog.*	*geography*, géographie.
adj.	*adjective*, adjectif.		*geol.*	*geology*, géologie.
admin.	*administration*, administration.		*ger.*	*gerund*, gérondif.
adv.	*adverb*, adverbe; *adverbial phrase*, locution adverbiale.		*gramm.*	*grammar*, grammaire.
Am.	*Americanism*, américanisme.		*hist.*	*history*, histoire.
anat.	*anatomy*, anatomie.		*hunt.*	*hunting*, chasse.
approx.	*approximately*, approximativement.		*icht.*	*ichthyology*, ichtyologie.
archeol.	*archeology*, archéologie.		*imper.*	*imperative*, impératif.
art.	*article*, article.		*impers.*	*impersonal*, impersonnel.
astr.	*astronomy*, astronomie.		*impf.*	*imparfait*, imperfect.
attr.	*attributively*, attribut.		*ind.*	*indicative*, indicatif.
bibl.	*biblical*, biblique.		*indef.*	*indefinite*, indéfini.
biol.	*biology*, biologie.		*inf.*	*infinitive*, infinitif.
box.	*boxing*, boxe.		*int.*	*interjection*, interjection.
Br.	*British*, britannique.		*interr.*	*interrogative*, interrogatif.
ch.sp.	*childish speech*, langage enfantin.		*inv.*	*invariable*, invariable.
			Ir.	*Irish*, irlandais.
cin.	*cinema*, cinéma.		*iro.*	*ironically*, ironiquement.
cj.	*conjunction*, conjonction.		*irr.*	*irregular*, irrégulier.
co.	*comical*, comique.		*journ.*	*journalism*, journalisme.
coll.	*collective*, collectif.		*ling.*	*linguistics*, linguistique.
comp.	*comparative*, comparatif.		*m*	*masculine*, masculin.
cond.	*conditional*, conditionnel.		*metall.*	*metallurgy*, métallurgie.
cost.	*costume*, costume.		*meteor.*	*meteorology*, météorologie.
cuis.	*cuisine*, culinary art.		*min.*	*mineralogy*, minéralogie.
def.	*definite*, défini.		*mot.*	*motoring*, automobilisme.
dem.	*demonstrative*, démonstratif.		*mount.*	*mountaineering*, alpinisme.
dial.	*dialectal*, dialectal.		*myth.*	*mythology*, mythologie.
dimin.	*diminutive*, diminutif.		*n*	*neuter*, neutre.
eccl.	*ecclesiastical*, ecclésiastique.		*neg.*	*negative*, négatif.
e.g.	*exempli gratia, for example*, par exemple.		*npr.*	*nom propre*, proper name.
			num.	*numeral*, numéral.
esp.	*especially*, surtout.		*oft.*	*often*, souvent.
etc.	*and so on*, et cætera.		*opt.*	*optics*, optique.
f	*feminine*, féminin.		*orn.*	*ornithology*, ornithologie.
fig.	*figuratively*, sens figuré.		*o.s.,o.s.*	*oneself*, soi-même.
foot.	*football*, football.		*p.*	*person*, personne.
Fr.	*French*, français.		*paint.*	*painting*, peinture.
			parl.	*parliament*, parlement.
			pej.	*pejoratively*, sens péjoratif.
			pers.	*personal*, personnel.

phls.	*philosophy*, philosophie.	*s.th., s.th.*	*something*, quelque chose.
phot.	*photography*, photographie.		
phys.	*physics*, physique.	*su.*	(= *f* + *m*) *substantif*, noun.
physiol.	*physiology*, physiologie.	*su./f*	*substantif féminin*, feminine noun.
pl.	*plural*, pluriel.		
poet.	*poetic*, poétique.	*su./m*	*substantif masculin*, masculine noun.
pol.	*politics*, politique.		
poss.	*possessive*, possessif.	*sup.*	*superlative*, superlatif.
p.p.	*participe passé*, past participle.	*surv.*	*surveying*, arpentage.
		tel.	*telegraphy*, télégraphie.
p.pr.	*participe présent*, present participle.	*teleph.*	*telephony*, téléphonie.
		telev.	*television*, télévision.
pred.	*predicative*, prédicatif.	*tex.*	*textiles*, industries textiles.
pref.	*prefix*, préfixe.	*thea.*	*theatre*, théâtre.
pres.	*present*, présent.	*(TM)*	*trademark*, marque déposée.
pron.	*pronoun*, pronom.	*typ.*	*typography*, typographie.
prp.	*preposition*, préposition; *prepositional phrase*, locution prépositive.	*univ.*	*university*, université.
		USA	*United States of America*, États-Unis.
p.s.	*passé simple*, past tense.	*usu.*	*usually*, d'ordinaire.
psych.	*psychology*, psychologie.	*v/aux.*	*verbe auxiliaire*, auxiliary verb.
q.	*quelqu'un*, someone.		
qch.	*quelque chose*, something.	*vet.*	*veterinary*, vétérinaire.
qqf.	*quelquefois*, sometimes.	*v/i.*	*verbe intransitif*, intransitive verb.
recip.	*reciprocal*, réciproque.		
rel.	*relative*, relatif.	*v/impers.*	*verbe impersonnel*, impersonal verb.
rfl.	*reflexive*, réfléchi.		
sbj.	*subjunctive*, subjonctif.	*v/t.*	*verbe transitif*, transitive verb.
sc.	*scilicet, namely*, c'est-à-dire.		
Sc.	*Scottish*, écossais.	*vt/i.*	*verbe transitif et intransitif*, transitive and intransitive verb.
sg.	*singular*, singulier.		
sl.	*slang*, argot.	*zo.*	*zoology*, zoologie.
s.o., s.o.	*someone*, quelqu'un.		
sp.	*sports*, sport.		

The phonetic symbols of the International Phonetic Association

Signes phonétiques de l'Association Phonétique Internationale

A. Vowels

Note: In French the vowels are "pure", i.e. there is no slackening off or diphthongization at the end of the sound. Thus, the [e] of *né* [ne] has no tail as in English *nay* [nei].

[ɑ]   back vowel, mouth well open, tongue lowered, as in English *father*: long in *pâte* [pɑːt], short in *cas* [kɑ].

[ɑ̃]   [ɑ]-sound, but with some of the breath passing through the nose: long in *prendre* [prɑ̃ːdr], short in *banc* [bɑ̃].

[a]   clear front vowel, tongue further forward than for [ɑ] and corners of the mouth drawn further back: long in *page* [paːʒ], short in *rat* [ra].

[e]   closed vowel, tongue raised and well forward, corners of the mouth drawn back, though not as far as for [i]; purer than the vowel in English *nay*, *clay*, etc.: *été* [e'te].

[ɛ]   open vowel, tongue less raised and further back than for [e], corners of the mouth drawn back but slightly less than for [e]; purer than the sound in English *bed*: long in *mère* [mɛːr], short in *après* [a'prɛ].

[ɛ̃]   [ɛ]-sound, but with some of the breath passing through the nose: long in *plaindre* [plɛ̃ːdr], short in *fin* [fɛ̃].

[ə]   rounded sound, something like the **a** in English *about*: *je* [ʒə], *lever* [lə've].

[i]   closed vowel, tongue very high, corners of the mouth well back, rather more closed than [i] in English *sea*: long in *dire* [diːr], short in *vie* [vi].

[o]   closed vowel, tongue drawn back, lips rounded: no tailing off into [u] or [w] as in English *below*: long in *fosse* [foːs], short in *peau* [po].

[ɔ]   open **o** but closer than in English *cot*, with tongue lower, lips more rounded, mouth more open: long in *fort* [fɔːr], short in *cotte* [kɔt].

[ɔ̃]   [ɔ]-sound, but with some of the breath passing through the nose: long in *nombre* [nɔ̃ːbr], short in *mon* [mɔ̃].

[ø]   a rounded [e], pronounced rather like the **ir** of English *birth* but closer and with lips well rounded and forward: long in *chanteuse* [ʃɑ̃'tøːz], short in *peu* [pø].

[œ]   a rounded open **e** [ɛ], a little like the **ur** of English *turn* but with the tongue higher and the lips well rounded: long in *fleur* [flœːr], short in *œuf* [œf].

[œ̃]   the same sound as [œ] but with some of the breath passing through the nose: long in humble [œ̃:bl], short in *parfum* [par'fœ̃].

[u] closed vowel with back of the tongue raised close to the soft palate and the front drawn back and down, and lips far forward and rounded; rather like the **oo** of English *root* but tighter and without the tailing off into the [w] sound: long in *tour* [tu:r], short in *route* [rut].

[y] an [i] pronounced with the lips well forward and rounded: long in *mur* [my:r], short in *vue* [vy].

B. Consonants

Note: the consonant sounds not listed below are similar to those of English, except that they are much more dry: thus the [p] is not a breathed sound and [t] and [d] are best pronounced with the tip of the tongue against the back of the top teeth, with no breath accompanying the sound.

[j] a rapidly pronounced sound like the **y** in English *yes*: *diable* [dja:bl], *dieu* [djø], *fille* [fi:j].

[l] usually more voiced than in English and does not have its 'hollow sound': *aller* [a'le].

[ɲ] the "n mouillé", an [n] followed by a rapid [j]: *cogner* [kɔ'ɲe].

[ŋ] not a true French sound; occurs in a few borrowed foreign words: *meeting* [mi'tiŋ].

[r] in some parts of France the [r] may be sounded like a slightly rolled English [r], but the uvular sound is more generally accepted. It has been described as sounding like a short and light gargle: *ronger* [rɔ̃-'ʒe].

[ʃ] rather like the **sh** of English *shall*, never like the **ch** of English *cheat*: *chanter* [ʃɑ'te].

[ɥ] like a rapid [y], never a separate syllable: *muet* [mɥɛ].

[w] not as fully a consonant as the English [w]. It is half-way between the consonant [w] and the vowel [u]: *oui* [wi].

[ʒ] a voiced [ʃ]; it is like the second part of the sound of **di** in the English *soldier*, i.e. it does not have the [d] element: *j'ai* [ʒe]; *rouge* [ru:ʒ].

C. Use of the sign ' to mark stress

The stressed syllable is indicated by the use of ' before it. This is to some extent theoretical. Such stress as there is is not very marked and the presence of the ' may be considered a reminder that the word should not normally be stressed in any other syllable, especially if the word resembles an English one which *is* stressed elsewhere.

Though a stress-mark is shown for each word, all the words in one breath group will not in fact carry the stress indicated: thus, though *mauvais* may be transcribed [mɔ've], in *mauvais ami* there is only one main stress, on the -*mi*.

In words of one syllable only, the stress mark is not given.

D. Use of the sign : to mark length

When the sign [:] appears after a vowel it indicates that the duration of the vowel sound is rather longer than for a vowel which appears without it. Thus the [œ] of *feuille* [fœ:j] is longer than the [œ] of *feuillet* [fœ'jɛ]. In unstressed syllables one frequently finds a semi-long vowel but this fine shade of duration has not been marked in the transcription.

A

A, a [a] *m* A, a.

a [a] *3rd p. sg. pres. of avoir* **1**.

à [~] *prp. place*: at (*table, Hastings*), in (*Edinburgh*), on (*the wall*); *direction*: to, into; *distance*: at a distance of (*10 miles*); *origin*: from, of; *time*: at (*7 o'clock, this moment, his words*); in (*spring*); *sequence*: by (*twos*); for; *agent, instrument, etc.*: on (*horseback*); with; by (means of); *manner*: in; on (*condition, the occasion*); *price*: for (*two dollars*); at, by; *dative, possession*: donner qch. *à q.* give s.th. to s.o., give s.o. s.th.; *grâce à Dieu!* thank God!; *c'est à moi* this is mine; *c'est à moi de* (*inf.*) it is for me to (*inf.*); *un ami à moi* a friend of mine; *à terre* on *or* to the ground; *de la tête aux pieds* from head to foot; *prêt à* ready *or* willing to; *au secours!* help!; *à vingt pas d'ici* twenty steps *or* paces from here; *emprunter* (*arracher*) *à* borrow (tear) from; *c'est bien aimable à vous* that's very kind of you; *à l'aube* at dawn; *à la longue* at length; *au moment de* (*inf.*) on (*ger.*); *à le voir* seeing him; *à tout moment* constantly; *à demain* till tomorrow; *int.* see you tomorrow!; *à jamais* for ever; *à partir de* ... from ... (on); *mot à mot* word for word, literal(ly *adv.*); *quatre à quatre* four at a time; *peu à peu* little by little; *bateau m à vapeur* steamer, steamboat; *maison f à deux étages* two-storied house; *♩ à quatre mains* for four hands; *verre m à vin* wineglass; *fait à la main* handmade; *à voix basse* in a low voice; *à la nage* swimming; *peinture f à l'huile* painting in oil; *aux yeux bleus* blue-eyed; *à dessein* on purpose; *à regret* reluctantly; *à merveille* excellently; *à prix bas* at a low price; *à mes frais* at my expenses; *à louer* to let; *à vendre* for sale; *à la bonne heure* well done!; fine!

abaissement [abɛs'mã] *m* lowering,

sinking; *prices, temperature, etc.*: fall; falling; dropping; *water etc.*: abatement; *ground*: dip; *fig.* humbling, abasement; **abaisser** [abɛ'se] (1b) *v/t.* lower; *fig. a.* reduce (a humble, bring low; ⚔ bring down (*a figure*), drop (*a perpendicular*), depress (*an equation*); *s'~* fall, drop, go down; *fig.* humble o.s., lower o.s.; *fig. s' ~ à* descend *or* stoop to.

abajoue [aba'ʒu] *f zo.* cheek-pouch; F flabby cheek.

abandon [abɑ̃'dɔ̃] *m* abandonment, forsaking; desertion; neglect; destitution; *rights*: surrender; lack of restraint, absence of reserve; *sp.* withdrawal; *à l'~* completely neglected; at random; *laisser tout à l'~* leave everything in confusion; **abandonner** [~dɔ'ne] (1a) *v/t.* forsake, abandon; leave; ⚔ surrender; renounce (a claim, a right); *s'~* lose heart; neglect o.s.; give way *or* vent (to, à); give o.s. up (to, à), indulge (in, à).

abasourdir [abazur'diːr] (2a) *v/t.* stun; *fig.* dumbfound.

abat [a'ba] *m*: *pluie f d'~* downpour; *~s pl.* offal *sg.*

abâtardir [abatar'diːr] (2a) *v/t.* impair; debase; *s'~* deteriorate, degenerate; **abâtardissement** [~dis'mã] *m* deterioration, degeneration.

abat-jour [aba'ʒuːr] *m/inv.* lampshade; sun-blind; △ skylight.

abattage [aba'ta:ʒ] *m* knocking down, throwing down; *tree*: felling; clearing; *animals*: slaughter; *fig.* F dressing-down; *~* urgent forced slaughter; **abattant** [~'tã] *m* counter, table: flap; trapdoor; *~ de W.-C.* lavatory seat; **abattement** [abat'mã] *m* prostration; dejection; *~ à la base* personal allowance; *Am.* exemption; **abattis** [~'ti] ⚔ abatis; *cuis.* giblets *pl.*; *sl. ~ pl.* limbs; *sl.* numéroter ses *~* take stock of o.s.; **abattoir** [~'twa:r] *m* slaughterhouse; **abattre** [a'batr] (4a) *v/t.* knock down; fell; slaughter, destroy;

⚓ bring *or* shoot down; *fig.* dishearten, depress, demoralize, wear out; ~ *de la besogne* get through a lot of work; *ne te laisse pas* ~ don't let things get you down; *s'*~ crash; fall; *s'*~ *sur* beat down on (*rain etc.*); swoop down on, pounce on; *fig.* hail down on; **abattu,e** *fig.* [aba'ty] depressed.

abat-vent [aba'vã] *m/inv.* chimney-cowl; 🪓 wind-break, cloche.

abbatial, e, *m/pl.* -aux [aba'sjal, ~'sjo] abbatial; **abbaye** [abe'ji] *f* abbey; *monks:* monastery; *nuns:* convent; **abbé** [a'be] *m* abbot; priest; *hist.* abbé; **abbesse** [a'bɛs] *f* abbess.

ABC [abe'se] *m* primer; spelling-book; *fig.* rudiments *pl.*

abcès ✂ [ap'sɛ] *m* abscess.

abdication [abdika'sjo] *f* abdication; renunciation.

abdiquer [abdi'ke] (1m) *v/i.* abdicate; *v/t.* renounce (*s.th.*).

abdomen [abdɔ'mɛn] *m* abdomen.

abécédaire [abese'dɛːr] *m* spelling-book; primer; *fig.* elements *pl.*

abeille [a'bɛːj] *f* bee; ~ *mâle* drone; ~ *mère*, *reine f des* ~s queen (bee); ~ *ouvrière* worker (bee).

aberration [abera'sjo] *f* aberration.

abêtir [abe'tiːr] (2a) *v/t.* make stupid, stupefy; *s'*~ grow stupid.

abhorrer [abɔ're] (1a) *v/t.* loathe, detest.

abîme [a'biːm] *m* abyss, chasm; **abîmer** [abi'me] (1a) *v/t.* spoil, damage, ruin; *sl.* beat up, smash; *s'*~ get spoilt *or* damaged *or* ruined; be plunged (in, *dans*).

abject, e [ab'ʒɛkt] contemptible, mean; abject; **abjection** [~ʒɛk'sjo] *f* baseness, abjection, meanness.

abjurer [abʒy're] (1a) *v/t.* abjure; retract, recant.

ablation ✂ [abla'sjo] *f* removal, excision.

able *icht.* [abl] *m*, **ablette** *icht.* [a'blɛt] *f* bleak.

ablution [ably'sjo] *f* ablution (*a. eccl.*).

abnégation [abnega'sjo] *f* abnegation, self-denial, self-sacrifice.

abois [a'bwa] *m/pl.*: *aux* ~ at bay (*a. fig.*), hard pressed; **aboiement** [abwa'mã] *m* bark(ing), bay(ing).

abolir [abɔ'liːr] (2a) *v/t.* abolish, suppress; annul; repeal; **abolition** [~li'sjo] *f* abolition, suppression; ✝ *debt:* cancelling; annulment.

abominable [abɔmi'nabl] abominable; heinous (*crime*); **abomination** [~na'sjo] *f* abomination; **abominer** [~'ne] (1a) *v/t.* abominate, loathe.

abondamment [abõda'mã] *adv. of* *abondant*; **abondance** [~'dãːs] *f* abundance; *en* ~ plentiful(ly *adv.*); *parler d'*~ extemporize; **abondant, e** [~'dã, ~'dãːt] plentiful, copious, abundant; abounding (in, *en*); **abonder** [~'de] (1a) *v/i.* be plentiful; abound (in, *en*).

abonné *m*, **e** *f* [abɔ'ne] *magazine, paper, telephone:* subscriber; *electricity, gas:* consumer; 🚋 *etc.* season-ticket holder, *Am.* commuter; **abonnement** [abɔn'mã] *m* subscription; *carte f d'*~ season-ticket, *Am.* commutation ticket; **abonner** [abɔ'ne] (1a) *v/t.*: ~ *q. à qch.* take out a subscription to s.th. for s.o.; *s'*~ *à* subscribe to; take (out) a season-ticket for.

abord [a'bɔːr] *m* approach, access (to, *de*); manner, address; ~s *pl.* approaches, outskirts; *d'*~ (at) first; *de prime* ~ at first sight; *dès l'*~ from the outset; *d'un* ~ *facile* easy to approach; *tout d'*~ first of all; **abordable** [abɔr'dabl] accessible; ✝ reasonable (*price*); **abordage** ⚓ [~'daːʒ] *m* boarding, grappling; coming alongside; collision; **aborder** [~'de] (1a) *v/i.* land, berth; *v/t.* ⚓ grapple; run down (*a ship*); *fig.* approach, tackle (*a problem*); *fig.* accost (*s.o.*); *s'*~ meet.

aborigène [abɔri'ʒɛn] **1.** *adj.* aboriginal; native; **2.** *su./m* aboriginal; ~s *pl.* aborigines.

abortif, -ve [abɔr'tif, ~'tiːv] **1.** *adj.* abortive; ✂ abortifacient; **2.** *su./m* ✂ abortifacient.

abouchement [abuʃ'mã] *m* ✝ interview; ⊕ butt-joining; **aboucher** [abu'ʃe] (1a) *v/t.* join together; ⊕, *a.* ✂ connect; ⊕ join end to end; *s'*~ confer.

aboulie *psych.* [abu'li] *f* aboulia, loss of will-power; **aboulique** *psych.* [~'lik] irresolute.

about ⊕ [a'bu] *m wood:* butt-end; **abouter** ⊕ [abu'te] (1a) *v/t.* join end to end; **aboutir** [~'tir] (2a) *v/i.* lead ([in]to, *à*), end (in, *à*); abut

(on, à); ✼ come to a head, burst
(*abscess*);*fig.* succeed;**aboutissant,
e** [ˌti'sã, ˌ'sã:t] bordering, abut-
ting; **aboutissement** [ˌtis'mã] *m*
issue, outcome; *plan:* materializa-
tion; ✼ *abscess:* bursting, coming
to a head.

aboyer [abwa'je] (1h) *v/i.* bark, bay;
aboyeur [ˌ'jœ:r] *m* yelping dog;
fig. carping critic; tout; dun.

abrasif, -ve ⊕ [abra'zif, ˌ'zi:v] *adj.,
a. su./m* abrasive; **abrasion** ✼
[ˌ'zjõ] *f* abrasion, scraping.

abrégé [abre'ʒe] *m* summary, précis;
abréger [ˌ] (1g) *v/t.* shorten, ab-
breviate.

abreuver [abrœ've] (1a) *v/t.* water;
soak; s'ˌ drink (*animal*); quench
one's thirst (*person*); **abreuvoir**
[ˌ'vwa:r] *m* horse-pond, trough,
watering place (*in a river*).

abréviation [abrevja'sjõ] *f* abbreviation; *a.* ⚖ *sentence:* shortening.

abri [a'bri] *m* shelter, cover; ✕ dug-
out; air-raid shelter; ✕ ˌ *atomique*
atomic shelter; ✕ ˌ *bétonné* block-
house, *sl.* pill-box; ⚓ ˌ *de mécanicien* cab; *à l'ˌ de* sheltered from;
screened from; *mettre à l'ˌ* shelter,
screen (from, *de*).

abricot [abri'ko] *m* apricot; **abricotier** [ˌko'tje] *m* apricot-tree.

abriter [abri'te] (1a) *v/t.* shelter,
screen, protect, shield (from *de,
contre*); s'ˌ take shelter *or* refuge.

abrivent [abri'vã] *m* ✕ sentry-box,
shelter; ✔ screen, matting.

abroger [abrɔ'ʒe] (1e) *v/t.* abrogate,
repeal, rescind.

abrupt, e [a'brypt] abrupt; steep,
sheer; *fig.* rugged (*style*); blunt
(*words*).

abruti *m, e f sl.* [abry'ti] fool, idiot;
abrutir [ˌ'ti:r] (2a) *v/t.* stupefy,
brutalize;s'ˌ become sottish;**abrutissement** [ˌtis'mã] *m* brutishness;
degradation.

abscisse ⚑ [ap'sis] *f* abscissa.

absence [ap'sã:s] *f* absence; lack;
ˌ *d'esprit* absent-mindedness; **absent, e** [ˌ'sã, ˌ'sã:t] absent; *fig.*
absent-minded;**absentéisme** [ˌsã-
te'ism] *m* absenteeism; **absenter**
[ˌsã'te] (1a) *v/t.:* s'ˌ absent o.s.,
stay away; go away from home.

abside ⚛ [ap'sid] *f* apse.

absinthe [ap'sɛ̃:t] *f* absinth; ♣
wormwood.

absolu, e [apsɔ'ly] absolute; peremptory (*voice*); ⚗ pure (*alcohol*);
phys. zéro *m* ˌ absolute zero
(—*459.4° F.*);**absolument**[apsɔly-
'mã] *adv.* absolutely, completely;
absolution [ˌ'sjõ] *f* absolution
(from, *de*); **absolutisme** [ˌ'tism]
*m*absolutism; **absolutoire** [ˌ'twa:r]
absolving.

absorber [apsɔr'be] (1a) *v/t.* absorb, soak up; imbibe; consume;
fig. engross; s'ˌ be absorbed (in,
dans); **absorption** [ˌsɔrp'sjõ] *f*
absorption (*a. fig.*).

absoudre [ap'sudr] (4bb) *v/t. eccl.,
a. fig.* absolve; exonerate; **absous,
-te** [ˌ'su, ˌ'sut] *p.p. of absoudre.*

abstenir [apstə'ni:r] (2h) *v/t.:* s'ˌ
refrain *or* abstain (from, *de*); *parl.* s'ˌ
(*de voter*) abstain (from voting); **abstention** [ˌtã'sjõ] *f* abstention (from,
de); renunciation.

abstinence [apsti'nã:s] *f* abstinence; abstention (from, *de*); *faire*
ˌ *de* abstain from (*s.th.*); **abstinent, e** [ˌ'nã, ˌ'nã:t] **1.** *adj.* abstemious, sober; **2.** *su.* total abstai-
ner, teetotaller.

abstraction [apstrak'sjõ] *f* abstraction; ˌs *pl.* vagueness *sg.*; ˌ *faite de
cela* leaving that aside; apart from
that; *faire* ˌ *de qch.* leave s.th. out
of account, disregard s.th.; *se perdre dans des* ˌs be lost in thought.

abstraire [aps'trɛ:r] (4ff) *v/t.* abstract, isolate; s'ˌ become en-
grossed (in *dans, en*); **abstrait, e**
[ˌ'trɛ, ˌ'trɛt] abstracted; abstract
(*idea*); abstruse (*problem, subject*).

abstrus, e [aps'try, ˌ'try:z] abstruse; obscure; recondite.

absurde [ap'syrd] **1.** *adj.* absurd;
2. *su./m: tomber dans l'ˌ* become
ridiculous; **absurdité** [ˌsyrdi'te] *f*
absurdity, nonsense.

abus [a'by] *m* abuse, misuse (of, *de*),
error; ˌ *de confiance* breach of trust;
faire ˌ *de* abuse; overindulge in;
abuser [aby'ze] (1a) *v/t.* mislead;
deceive; s'ˌ be mistaken; *v/i.:* ˌ *de*
misuse; take unfair advantage of;
impose upon; delude; **abusif, -ve**
[ˌ'zif, ˌ'zi:v] excessive; *gramm.* contrary to usage, improper.

abyssal, e, *m/pl.* **-aux** [abi'sal, ˌ'so]
deep-sea...; **abysse** [a'bis] *m* deep
sea.

acabit F [aka'bi] *m* quality, nature;

du même ~ tarred with the same brush.

acacia ♀ [aka'sja] *m* acacia.

académicien [akademi'sjɛ̃] *m* academician; **académie** [~'mi] *f* academy; learned society; school (*of art etc.*); *paint.* nude; *in France:* educational district; **académique** [~'mik] academic; pretentious (*style*).

acagnarder [akaɲar'de] (1a) *v/t.:* *s'*~ idle, laze.

acajou [aka'ʒu] *m* mahogany.

acanthe ♀ [a'kɑ̃:t] *f* acanthus (*a.* △), brank-ursine.

acariâtre [aka'rjɑ:tr] quarrelsome; peevish; shrewish; nagging.

accablant, e [aka'blɑ̃, ~'blɑ̃:t] overwhelming (*proof, emotions*); crushing, oppressive (*heat*); **accablement** [~blə'mɑ̃] *m* dejection; ✷ prostration; ✝ pressure; **accabler** [~'ble] (1a) *v/t.* overwhelm (with, *de*); overpower, crush.

accalmie [akal'mi] *f* ✕, ⚓, *a. fig.* lull; ✝ slack period.

accaparement [akapar'mɑ̃] *m* hoarding; *fig.* F monopolizing; **accaparer** [~'re] (1a) *v/t.* corner, hoard; *fig.* F monopolize (*the conversation*); *fig.* seize; *fig.* take up (*time, energy, etc.*); *fig.* take up the time (and energy) of (*s.o.*); **accapareur** *m*, **-euse** *f* [~'rœ:r, ~'rø:z] *supplies:* buyer-up; monopolizer; *fig.* F hoarder; grabber.

accéder [akse'de] (1f) *v/i.:* ~ *à* have access to; accede to (*a request*).

accélérateur, -trice [akselera'tœ:r, ~'tris] **1.** *adj.* accelerating; **2.** *su./m* accelerator; ~ *de particules* particle accelerator; **accélération** [~ra'sjɔ̃] *f* acceleration; *work-rhythm:* speeding up; *mot.* pédale *f* d'~ accelerator; **accélérer** [~'re] (1f) *v/i.* accelerate (*a. mot.*); *mot. sl.* step on the gas; *v/t. fig.* expedite, quicken; *s'*~ become faster.

accent [ak'sɑ̃] *m* accent; stress; emphasis; pronunciation; **accentuation** [aksɑ̃tɥa'sjɔ̃] *f* stress(ing); accentuation; **accentuer** [~'tɥe] (1n) *v/t.* stress; accentuate; emphasize; *fig.* strengthen.

acceptable [aksɛp'tabl] acceptable; satisfactory; **acceptation** [~ta'sjɔ̃] *f* acceptance (*a.* ✝); **accepter** [~'te] (1a) *v/t.* accept; agree to; **accep-**

teur ✝ [~'tœ:r] *m* drawee, acceptor; **acception** [~'sjɔ̃] *f* meaning, sense; *sans* ~ *de personne* without respect of persons; *dans toute l'*~ *du mot* in the full meaning *or* in every sense of the word.

accès [ak'sɛ] *m* access, approach; anger, *fever:* attack; fit; *par* ~ by fits and starts; **accessible** [aksɛ'sibl] accessible; approachable (*person*); **accession** [~'sjɔ̃] *f* accession; adherence; ~ *à la propriété* home ownership; ~ *du travail* rehabilitation; **accessoire** [~'swa:r] **1.** *adj.* accessory; *occupation f* ~ subsidiary occupation, side-line; **2.** *su./m* accessory; subsidiary topic *or* matter; *thea.* ~s *pl.* properties, *sl.* props.

accident [aksi'dɑ̃] *m* accident (*a. phls.*); ♪ accidental; ~ *de circulation* road accident; ~ *de personne* casualty, ~ *de terrain* unevenness, undulation; *par* ~ accidentally; **accidenté, e** [aksidɑ̃'te] **1.** *adj.* uneven, irregular (*ground*); chequered (*life*); **2.** *su.* injured person, casualty; **accidentel, -elle** [~'tɛl] accidental, unintentional, casual; **accidenter** [~'te] (1a) *v/t.* vary (*one's style*); make picturesque, give variety to (*a landscape*); injure, damage; *s'*~ have an accident; **accidenteur** [~'tœ:r] *m* party who causes an *or* the accident.

acclamation [aklama'sjɔ̃] *f* acclamation, applause; **acclamer** [~'me] (1a) *v/t.* acclaim, applaud, cheer.

acclimatation [aklimata'sjɔ̃] *f* acclimatization; *jardin m* d'~ Zoo; Botanical Gardens *sg.*; **acclimater** [~'te] (1a) *v/t.* acclimatize (to, *à*); *s'*~ become acclimatized.

accointance [akwɛ̃'tɑ̃:s] *f* oft. *pej.* intimacy, intercourse; *avoir des* ~s *avec* have dealings with; **accointer** [~'te] (1a) *v/t.:* *s'*~ *de* (*or avec*) *q.* enter into relations with s.o.

accolade [akɔ'lad] *f* embrace; accolade; F hug; *typ. a.* bracket, brace (‿); **accolage** ⚘ [~'la:ʒ] *m* fastening to an espalier; **accoler** [~'le] (1a) *v/t.* couple, brace, bracket; tie up (*a plant*).

accommodage [akɔmɔ'da:ʒ] *m* *food:* preparation, dressing; **accommodant, e** [~'dɑ̃, ~'dɑ̃:t] accommodating, easy to deal with, good-natured; **accommodation**

[⌣da'sjõ] *f* adaptation; **accommo-dement** [akɔmɔd'mã] *m* compromise, arrangement; ✝ agreement; **accommoder** [⌣mɔ'de] (1a) *v/t.* fit, adapt (to, *à*); prepare, dress (*food*); s'⌣ *à* adapt o.s. to; s' ⌣ *de* put up with, make the best of.

accompagnateur *m*, **-trice** *f* [akõ-paɲa'tœːr, ⌣'tris] ♪ accompanist; escort (of a tour); **accompa-gnement** [⌣paɲ'mã] *m* attendance; accompaniment (*a.* ♪); **accompa-gner** [⌣pa'ɲe] (1a) *v/t.* accompany; escort.

accomplir [akõ'pliːr] (2a) *v/t.* accomplish, achieve; complete; **ac-complissement** [⌣plis'mã] *m* accomplishment, achievement; completion.

accord [a'kɔːr] *m* agreement; harmony; ♪ chord; pitch; *gramm.* concordance, agreement (*a. pol.*); *pol.* treaty; ⌣ *commercial* trade agreement; d'⌣ agreed!; *d'un commun* ⌣ by common consent, by mutual agreement; *tomber d'*⌣ agree, reach an agreement; **accordable** [akɔr'dabl] reconcilable; grantable; ♪ tunable; **accordage** ♪ [⌣'daːʒ] *m* tuning; **ac-cordailles** [⌣'dɑːj] *f/pl.* † betrothal *sg.*; **accordéon** ♪ [⌣de'õ] *m* accordion; concertina; *fig.* en ⌣ crumpled (up); **accordéoniste** [⌣deɔ'nist] *m* accordion player; **accorder** [⌣'de] (1a) *v/t.* grant; match; ♪, *a. radio:* tune; s'⌣ agree (*a. gramm.*); harmonize (with, *avec*); **accordeur** *m*, **-euse** *f* ♪ [⌣'dœːr, ⌣'døːz] tuner.

accorte [a'kɔrt] *adj./f* pleasing, winsome.

accostable [akɔs'tabl] approachable; **accostage** ⚓ [⌣'taːʒ] *m* boarding; drawing alongside (of, *de*); **ac-coster** [⌣'te] (1a) *v/t.* ⚓ berth; board; ⌣ *q.* accost s.o., F go up to s.o.; greet s.o.

accotement [akɔt'mã] *m* mot., 🚗 shoulder; verge (*of road*); ⌣ *stabilisé* hard shoulder; ⌣ *non stabilisé* no hard shoulder, *Br. a.* soft verges; **accoter** [akɔ'te] (1a) *v/t.* lean, rest (against *contre*, *à*; on, *sur*); s'⌣ lean (against, *contre*); **accotoir** [⌣'twaːr] *m* armrest.

accouchée [aku'ʃe] *f* woman in childbed; **accouchement** [akuʃ-'mã] *m* confinement; ⌣ *laborieux* difficult confinement; ⌣ *sans dou-*

leur painless delivery; **accoucher** [aku'ʃe] (1a) *v/i.* be delivered (of, *de*), give birth (to, *de*); *fig.* ⌣ *de qch.* bring s.th. forth; *v/t.* deliver (*a woman*); **accoucheur** [⌣'ʃœːr] *m* obstetrician; **accoucheuse** [⌣'ʃøːz] *f* midwife.

accouder [aku'de] (1a) *v/t.:* s'⌣ lean (on one's elbows); **accoudoir** [⌣'dwaːr] *m* arm-rest, elbow-rest; balustrade, rail.

accouple [a'kupl] *f* leash; **accou-plement** [akuplə'mã] *m* coupling (*a. radio*); pairing; ⚡ connecting; ✦ copulation; ⊕ ⌣ *articulé* joint coupling; ⚡ ⌣ *en série* series connection; **accoupler** [⌣'ple] (1a) *v/t.* couple (up) (*a.* 🐕); ⚡ connect, group; *fig.* join; s'⌣ mate.

accourcir [akur'siːr] (2a) *v/t.* curtail; shorten; **accourcissement** [⌣sis'mã] *m* shortening.

accourir [aku'riːr] (2i) *v/i.* hasten (up), run up.

accoutrement [akutrə'mã] *m* dress, F get-up; **accoutrer** [⌣'tre] (1a) *v/t.* equip; rig (*s.o.*) out (in, *de*).

accoutumance [akuty'mãːs] *f* habit, use, usage; **accoutumé, e** [⌣'me] 1. *adj.* accustomed (to, *à*); *à l'*⌣e usually; 2. *su.* regular visitor; **accoutumer** [⌣'me] (1a) *v/t.* accustom (*s.o.*) (to, *à*).

accouvage [aku'vaːʒ] *m* artificial incubation.

accréditer [akredi'te] (1a) *v/t.* accredit (*an ambassador*); confirm (*a story*); credit; authorize; s'⌣ gain credence; **accréditeur** [⌣'tœːr] *m* guarantor; surety; **accréditif** [⌣-'tif] *m* ✝ (letter of) credit; credential.

accroc [a'kro] *m* clothes: rent, tear; *fig.* hitch; *fig.* impediment; *sans* ⌣s smooth(ly *adv.*).

accrochage [akrɔ'ʃaːʒ] *m* hooking; *picture:* hanging; accumulation; *box.* clinch; *radio:* picking-up; ✕ engagement; clash (*with the police*); F squabble; **accroche-cœur** [akrɔʃ'kœːr] *m* kiss-curl; **accroche-ment** [⌣'mã] *m* hooking; *fig.* difficulty; 🐕 coupling; **accrocher** [akrɔ'ʃe] (1a) *v/t.* hang (up) (on, from *à*); collide with (*a vehicle*); hook; catch; ⚓ grapple; ✕ engage; *radio:* pick up; *sl.* pawn (*a watch*); F buttonhole (*s.o.*); s'⌣ cling (to, *à*); get

caught (on, *à*); *box.* clinch; ⚓
follow closely; F have a set-to;
accrocheur, -euse [-'ʃœːr, -'ʃøːz]
tenacious, persistent; eye-catching,
catchy; *c'est un ~* he's a sticker.
accroire [a'krwaːr] (4n) *v/t.*: *(en)
faire ~ qch. à* q. delude s.o. into
believing s.th.; *s'en faire ~* over-
estimate o.s.
accroissement [akrwas'mã] *m*
growth; increase; ⚕ *function*: increment.
accroître [a'krwaːtr] (4o) *v/t.* increase; *v/i. a. s'~* grow.
accroupir [akru'piːr] (2a) *v/t.*: *s'~*
crouch (down); squat (down).
accru, e [a'kry] 1. *p.p.* of *accroître*;
2. *su./f* accretion, extension.
accu F [a'ky] *m* ⚡ accumulator; battery; *(re)charger (or régénérer) l'~*
charge the accumulator.
accueil [a'kœːj] *m* reception, greeting; ⚕ *faire (bon) ~ à une traite*
hono(u)r a bill; *faire bon ~à* welcome
(s.o.); **accueillant, e** [akœ'jã,
~'jãːt] affable; **accueillir** [~'jiːr]
(2c) *v/t.* welcome, greet, receive;
⚕ hono(u)r *(a bill)*.
acculer [aky'le] (1a) *v/t.* drive into
a corner *or* to the wall; *s'~* set one's
back (against *à*, *contre*).
accumulateur, -trice [akymyla-
'tœːr, ~'tris] *su.* hoarder; *fig.* miser;
su./m ⚡ accumulator; **accumuler**
[~'le] (1a) *v/t.* accumulate.
accusateur, -trice [akyza'tœːr,
~'tris] 1. *adj.* incriminating; accus-
ing; 2. *su.* accuser; *su./m* 🜂🜃 *hist.* ~
public Public Prosecutor; **accusation** [~za'sjõ] *f* accusation; charge;
accusé, e [~'ze] 1. *adj.* accused;
prominent *(feature)*; 2. *su.* accused;
su./m: ⚕ ~ *de réception* acknowl-
edgement (of receipt); **accuser**
[~'ze] (1a) *v/t.* accuse; *fig.* emphasize, bring out; show; ⚕ ~ *réception* acknowledge receipt (of, *de*); *s'~*
stand out; accuse o.s.
acéphale *zo.* [ase'fal] acephalous,
headless.
acerbe [a'sɛrb] tart; *fig.* sharp;
acerbité [asɛrbi'te] *f* acerbity;
tartness; sharpness.
acéré, e [ase're] sharp, keen; *fig.*
mordant *(criticism)*; **acérer** [~] (1f)
v/t. steel; *fig.* sharpen, give edge to.
acétate 🜍 [ase'tat] *m* acetate; ~
d'alumine acetate of alumina; ~ *de*

cuivre verdigris; **acéteux, -euse**
[~'tø, ~'tøːz] acetous; **acétique**
[~'tik] acetic; **acétone** [~'tɔn] *f*
acetone; **acétylène** [~ti'lɛn] *m*
acetylene.
achalandage [aʃalã'daːʒ] *m* cus-
tom(ers *pl.*); **achalandé, e** [~'de]:
bien ~ well-stocked; † *with a large
custom (shop);* **achalander** [~'de]
(1a) *v/t.* provide with custom.
acharné, e [aʃar'ne] keen; fierce;
bitter; strenuous; relentless; **acharnement** [~nə'mã] *m* tenacity; re-
lentlessness; fury; stubbornness;
acharner [~'ne] (1a) *v/t.*: *s'~ à* be
intent on; slave at; *s'~ sur (or contre)*
be implacable towards.
achat [a'ʃa] *m* purchase; purchasing; ⚕ *pouvoir m d'~* purchasing
power.
acheminement [aʃmin'mã] *m* progress, course (towards, *vers*); ⚕ *etc.*
routing; **acheminer** [~mi'ne] (1a)
v/t. put on the way; train *(a horse);* ⚕
etc. route, forward (to *sur*, *vers*); *s'~*
make one's way (towards *vers*, *sur*).
acheter [aʃ'te] (1d) *v/t.* buy, purchase; *fig.* bribe; ~ *qch. à* buy s.th.
from s.o.; buy s.th. for s.o., buy s.o.
s.th.; ~ *cher (bon marché)* buy at a
high price (cheap); **acheteur** *m*,
-euse *f* [~'tœːr, ~'tøːz] purchaser,
buyer.
achèvement [aʃɛv'mã] *m* completion, conclusion; **achever** [aʃ've]
(1d) *v/t.* finish, complete; F do for;
s'~ draw to a close; *v/i.*: ~ *de (inf.)*
finish *(ger.).*
achillée 🜎 [aki'le] *f* milfoil, yarrow.
achoppement [aʃɔp'mã] *m* stumble; knock; *pierre f d'~* stum-
bling-block; **achopper** [aʃɔ'pe] (1a)
v/i. a. ~ stumble (over *sur*; against,
à); *fig.* come to grief.
achromatique *opt.* [akrɔma'tik]
achromatic.
acide 🜍 [a'sid] 1. *adj.* sharp, tart,
acid; 2. *su./m* acid; ~ *chlorhydrique*
hydrochloric acid; ~ *sulfurique* sulphuric acid; **acidification** [asidifi-
ka'sjõ] *f* acidification; **acidimètre**
[~'mɛtr] *m* acidimeter; **acidité** [~'te]
f acidity, sourness; **acidulé, e**
[asidy'le] acidulated; *bonbons m/pl.*
~s acid drops; **aciduler** [~] (1a) *v/t.*
turn sour; acidulate.
acier [a'sje] *m* steel; ~ *à précontrainte*
pre-stressed steel; ~ *au tungstène*

tungsten steel; ~ *coulé* (*or fondu*) cast steel; ~ *doux* mild steel; ~ *laminé* rolled steel; ~ *spécial* high-grade steel; ~ *trempé* hardened *or* tempered steel; *d'~* steel(y), of steel; **aciérage** ⊕ [asje'ra:ʒ] *m* steeling; *bain m d'~* steel bath; **aciérer** [~'re] (1f) *v/t.* steel, acierate; **aciérie** ⊕ [~'ri] *f* steelworks *usu. sg.*

acné ✻ [ak'ne] *f* acne.

acolyte [akɔ'lit] *m eccl.* acolyte; *fig.* associate, confederate.

acompte [a'kɔ:t] *m* down payment, deposit, payment on account; instalment; F *fig.* foretaste; *par ~s* by instalments.

aconit ♀ [akɔ'nit] *m* aconite, monk's-hood.

acoquiner [akɔki'ne] (1a) *v/t. oft. pej.* s'~ *avec* q. take up with s.o.

à-côté [akɔ'te] *m remark:* aside; side-issue; *~s pl.* purlieus.

à-coup [a'ku] *m* jolt, jerk, sudden stop; *par ~s* by fits and starts; *sans ~s* smooth(ly *adv.*).

acoustique [akus'tik] **1.** *adj.* acoustic; *appareil m ~* hearing-aid; **2.** *su./f* acoustics *pl.*

acquéreur [ake'rœ:r] *m* purchaser, buyer; acquirer; **acquérir** [~'ri:r] (2l) *v/t.* acquire, obtain; win (*esteem, friends*); *fig. ~ droit de cité* become naturalized; *v/i.* improve; **acquerrai** [aker're] *1st p. sg. fut. of acquérir.*

acquêt ⚖ [a'kɛ] *m* acquisition; *~s pl.* common property *sg.* (*in marriage*).

acquièrent [a'kjɛ:r] *3rd p. pl. pres. of acquérir;* **acquiers** [~] *1st p. sg. pres. of acquérir.*

acquiescement [akjɛs'mã] *m* acquiescence (in, *à*); consent; **acquiescer** [akjɛ'se] (1k) *v/i.* acquiesce (in, *à*), agree (to, *à*).

acquis¹ [a'ki] *1st p. sg. p.s. of acquérir.*

acquis², e [a'ki, ~'ki:z] **1.** *p.p. of acquérir;* **2.** *adj.* acquired, gained; established (*fact*); **3.** *su./m* attainments *pl.*, experience; **acquisition** [akizi'sjɔ̃] *f* acquisition, acquiring; purchase; *fig. ~s pl.* attainments.

acquit [a'ki] *m* discharge, release; ✝ receipt (for, *de*); *~ de transit* Customs: transire; *par ~ de conscience* for conscience sake; for form's sake; F *par manière d'~* as

a matter of form; ✝ *pour ~* paid, received with thanks; **~-à-caution,** *pl.* **~s-à-caution** [akiakɔ'sjɔ̃] *m* Customs: permit; **acquittement** [akit'mã] *m debt:* discharge; ⚖ acquittal; **acquitter** [aki'te] (1a) *v/t.* unburden (*one's conscience*); ⚖ acquit; ✝ discharge (*a debt*); ✝ receipt (*a bill, a note*); fulfil (*an obligation*); ~ *q. de qch.* release s.o. from s.th.; *s'~ de* discharge (*a debt*); perform, fulfil (*a duty*).

acre ✒ [akr] *m* acre.

âcre [ɑ:kr] tart, sharp; *fig.* caustic (*remark*); **âcreté** [ɑkrə'te] *f* bitterness, acidity.

acrimonie [akrimɔ'ni] *f* acrimony; bitterness; **acrimonieux, -euse** [~'njø, ~'njø:z] acrimonious, bitter.

acrobate [akrɔ'bat] *su.* acrobat, tumbler; **acrobatie** [~ba'si] *f* acrobatics *pl.*; ~ (*aérienne*) aerobatics *pl.*

acte [akt] *m* act (*a. thea.*); deed (*a.* ⚖); ⚖ title; bill (*of sale*); ⚖ writ; *~s pl. learned society:* transactions; records; *bibl.* ♀s *pl. des Apôtres* Acts of the Apostles; ⚖ ~ *civil* civil marriage; ~ *de décès* death-certificate; ~ *notarié* notarial deed; *faire ~ de présence* put in an appearance; *prendre ~ de* take note of; **acteur** [ak'tœ:r] *m* actor.

actif, -ve [ak'tif, ~'ti:v] **1.** *adj.* active; busy; alert; **2.** *su./m* ✝ assets *pl.*, credit (side); *gramm.* active voice. [actinotherapy.\ **actinothérapie** ✻ [aktinɔtera'pi] *f]* **action** [ak'sjɔ̃] *f* action, act; exploit; *water:* effect; *machine:* working; *thea.* gesture; ⚖ action, lawsuit; ✗ engagement; ✝ share(-certificate), *Am.* stock; *eccl.* ~ *de grâces* thanksgiving; ✝ ~ *de mine* mining-share; *champ m d'~* sphere of action; **actionnaire** [aksjɔ'nɛ:r] *su.* shareholder, *Am.* stockholder; **actionnariat** [~nar'ja] *m* (~ *ouvrier,* ~ *des salariés* employee) shareholding; **actioner** [~'ne] (1a) *v/t.* ⚖ sue; ⊕ set in motion; operate (*a machine*); urge on; *s'~* bestir o.s.

activer [akti've] (1a) *v/t.* stir up, push on; expedite; *s'~* busy o.s. (with, *à*); **activité** [~vi'te] *f* activity; briskness.

actrice [ak'tris] *f* actress.

actualité [aktɥali'te] *f* actuality,

reality; topical question; ~s *pl. cin.*
news-reel *sg.*, F news *sg.*; *radio*:
current events; d'~ topical.
actuel, -elle [ak'tɥɛl] current, present.
acuité [akɥi'te] *f* acuteness (*a. */); sharpness, keenness.
acupuncteur, acuponcteur [akypɔ̃k'tœːr] *m* acupuncturist; **acupuncture, acuponcture** [~'tyːr] *f* acupuncture. [angled.]
acutangle *Ⱥ* [aky'tãːgl] acute-⌡
adage [a'daːʒ] *m* adage, saying, saw.
adamantin, e [adamã'tɛ̃, ~'tin] adamantine.
adaptabilité [adaptabili'te] *f* adaptability, adaptableness; **adaptable** [adap'tabl] adaptable; **adaptateur** *phot., telev.* [~ta'tœːr] *m* adapter; **adaptation** [~ta'sjɔ̃] *f* adaptation; adjustment; **adapter** [~'te] (1a) *v/t.* adapt, adjust (s.th. to s.th., *qch. à qch.*); s'~ *à qch.* adapt o.s. to s.th.; fit s.th.
additif [adi'tif] *m* additive; **addition** [adi'sjɔ̃] *f* addition; accretion; *restaurant*: bill, *Am.* or F check; **additionnel, -elle** [adisjɔ'nɛl] additional; *impôt m* ~ surtax; **additionner** [~'ne] (1a) *v/t.* add up, tot up; add (to, *à*); ~ *un liquide de qch.* add s.th. to a liquid, mix *or* dilute a liquid with s.th.; *additionné de sucre* with sugar added.
adénite *ⱴ* [ade'nit] *f* adenitis.
adéno... [adenɔ] glandular, adeno...
adent ⊕ [a'dã] *m* dovetail, tenon.
adepte [a'dɛpt] *su.* adept; initiate.
adéquat, e [ade'kwa, ~'kwat] adequate.
adhérence [ade'rãːs] *f* adherence; adhesion (*a. */, *phys.*); **adhérent, e** [~'rã, ~'rãːt] 1. *adj.* adhesive; adherent (to, *à*); 2. *su.* adherent, supporter; **adhérer** [~'re] (1f) *v/i.: ~ à* adhere *or* cling to; hold (*an opinion*); join, support (*a party*); *mot.* grip (*the road*).
adhésif, -ve [ade'zif, ~'ziːv] adhesive, sticky; *emplâtre m* ~ adhesive plaster; **adhésion** [~'zjɔ̃] *f* adhesion (*a. fig.*).
adieu [a'djø] 1. *int.* farewell!; goodbye!; *dire* ~ *à* say goodbye *or* farewell to; *fig.* give up *or* renounce (*s.th.*); 2. *su./m*: ~x *pl.* farewell *sg.*, leave-taking *sg.*; *faire ses* ~x (*à*) say good-bye (to); take one's leave (of).

adipeux, -euse [adi'pø, ~'pøːz] adipose, fatty; **adipose** [~'poːz] *f* adiposis; **adiposité** [~pozi'te] *f* adiposity, fatness.
adirer *ⱬⱬ* [adi're] (1a) *v/t.* lose, mislay (*documents*).
adjacent, e [adʒa'sã, ~'sãːt] adjacent, contiguous (to, *à*); *être* ~ *à* border on, adjoin; *rue f* ~e side-street.
adjectif [adʒɛk'tif] *m* adjective.
adjoindre [ad'ʒwɛ̃ːdr] (4m) *v/t.* unite, associate; appoint as assistant; enrol(l); s'~ *à* join with (*s.o.*); **adjoint, e** [~'ʒwɛ̃, ~'ʒwɛ̃ːt] 1. *adj.* assistant-...; 2. *su./m* assistant; ~ *au* (*or du*) *maire* deputy-mayor.
adjonction [adʒɔ̃k'sjɔ̃] *f* adjunction; *Ⱥ* annexe; *gramm.* zeugma.
adjudant [adʒy'dã] *m* ✕ company sergeant-major; ⚓ warrant-officer; ✕ ~-*chef* regimental sergeant-major; ⚓ ~ *de pavillon* flag-lieutenant.
adjudicataire [adʒydika'tɛːr] *m* highest-bidder; *auction*: purchaser; contractor; **adjudication** [~'sjɔ̃] *f* adjudication, award; *contract*: allocation; *auction*: knocking-down; *mettre en* ~ invite tenders for; put up for auction.
adjuger [adʒy'ʒe] (1l) *v/t.* award; *auction*: knock down.
adjuration [adʒyra'sjɔ̃] *f* adjuration; imprecation; **adjurer** [~'re] (1a) *v/t.* adjure, beseech; exorcise (*a spirit*).
adjuvant [adʒy'vã] *m* *ⱴ* adjuvant, additive; stimulus.
admettre [ad'mɛtr] (4v) *v/t.* admit; let in; permit.
administrateur [administra'tœːr] *m* administrator, manager; *bank*: director; **administratif, -ve** [~'tif, ~'tiːv] administrative; **administration** [~'sjɔ̃] *f* administration (*a. eccl.*); management; governing body; civil service; **administratrice** [~'tris] *f* administratrix; **administré m, e f** [adminis'tre] person under one's administration *or* jurisdiction; **administrer** [~] (1a) *v/t.* administer (*a. eccl.*), conduct, manage, govern; *ⱬⱬ* ~ *des preuves* furnish proof.
admirable [admi'rabl] admirable, wonderful; **admirateur, -trice** [admira'tœːr, ~'tris] 1. *adj.* admiring; 2. *su.* admirer; **admiratif, -ve**

[~'tif, ~'ti:v] admiring; **admiration** [~'sjõ] *f* admiration, wonder; **admirer** [admi're] (1a) *v/t.* admire.

admis, e [ad'mi, ~'mi:z] **1.** *p.p. of admettre;* **2.** *adj.* admitted; accepted; conventional; **admissible** [admi'sibl] admissible; eligible (to, *à*); **admission** [~'sjõ] *f* admission; ⊕ inlet; ⊕ *période f* d'~ induction stroke.

admonestation [admɔnɛsta'sjõ] *f*, **admonition** [~ni'sjõ] *f* admonition, reprimand; **admonester** [~nɛs'te] (1a) *v/t.* admonish, reprimand, censure.

ado F [a'do] *m* youth, young man.

adolescence [adɔlɛ'sã:s] adolescence, youth; **adolescent, e** [~'sã, ~'sã:t] **1.** *adj.* adolescent; **2.** *su.* adolescent; F teen-ager; *su./m* youth.

adonner [adɔ'ne] (1a) *v/t.:* s'~ *à* devote o.s. to; take to (*drink etc.*), become addicted to.

adopter [adɔp'te] (1a) *v/t.* adopt (*a child, a name, an opinion*); assume (*a name*); *parl.* pass (*a bill*); **adoptif, -ve** [~'tif, ~'ti:v] adopted; adoptive (*parent*); **adoption** [~'sjõ] *f* adoption; *bill:* passage; carrying; *fils m par ~* adopted son; *pays m* d'~ adopted country.

adorable [adɔ'rabl] adorable; charming; **adorateur, -trice** [~ra'tœ:r, ~'tris] **1.** *su.* adorer, worshipper; F great admirer; **2.** *adj.* adoring; **adoration** [~ra'sjõ] *f* adoration, worship; **adorer** [~'re] (1a) *v/t.* adore (*a. fig.*); worship (*God*); F dote on.

adossement [ados'mã] *m* leaning (against *à*, *contre*); position back to back; **adosser** [ado'se] (1a) *v/t.* lean; place back to back; s'~ *à* (or *contre*) lean one's back against.

adouber [adu'be] (1a) *v/t.* chess: adjust (*a piece*); *hist.* dub (*s.o.*) ([a] knight).

adoucir [adu'si:r] (1a) *v/t.* sweeten; tone down (*a colour*); mitigate; allay (*a pain*); pacify; ⊕ polish (*metal*), rough-polish (*glass*); s'~ soften; grow softer (*voice*); grow milder (*weather*); grow less (*pain, grief*); **adoucissement** [~sis'mã] *m* softening; alleviation; relief; sweetening.

adresse [a'drɛs] *f* address; skill, dexterity; shrewdness; **adresser**

[adrɛ'se] (1a) *v/t.* address; send; direct; refer (to, *à*); ~ *la parole à q.* adress s.o.; s'~ *à* speak to; go and see; inquire at; be intended for; appeal to.

adroit, e [a'drwa, ~'drwat] dexterous; shrewd.

adulateur, -trice [adyla'tœ:r, ~'tris] **1.** *adj.* flattering, fawning; **2.** *su.* sycophant; **adulation** [~la'sjõ] *f* adulation, sycophancy; **aduler** [~'le] (1a) *v/t.* fawn upon, flatter (*s.o.*).

adulte [a'dylt] *adj., a. su.* adult, grown-up.

adultération [adyltera'sjõ] *f* adulteration; **adultère** [adyl'tɛ:r] **1.** *adj.* adulterous; **2.** *su./m* adulterer; adultery; *su./f* adulteress; **adultérer** [~te're] (1f) *v/t.* adulterate; **adultérin, e** [~te'rɛ̃, ~'rin] adulterine; ♀ hybrid.

advenir [advə'ni:r] (2h) *v/i., a. impers.* happen, occur, turn out; *advienne que pourra* come what may.

adventice [advã'tis] adventitious, casual (*a.* ♀); **adventif, -ve** [~'tif, ~'ti:v] ♀ growing wild, chance...; accrued (*property*).

adverbe [ad'vɛrb] *m* adverb.

adversaire [advɛr'sɛ:r] *m* adversary, opponent; **adverse** [~'vɛrs] adverse, unfavo(u)rable; ⚖ opposing, other (*party*); *fortune f* ~ adversity; **adversité** [~vɛrsi'te] *f* adversity, bad luck.

aérage [ae'ra:ʒ] *m* aeration, airing; ventilation (*a.* ⚒); *puits m* d'~ air-shaft; **aération** [~ra'sjõ] airing, ventilation; **aéré, e** [~'re] airy; **aérer** [~'re] (1f) *v/t.* air, give (*s.th.*) an airing; aerate; ventilate; s'~ get some fresh air; **aérien, -enne** [~'rjɛ̃, ~'rjɛn] aerial; air-...; *chemin m de fer* ~ elevated railway; *défense f* ~enne aerial defence; *voyage m* ~ journey by air; **aérifère** [aeri'fɛ:r] air-...

aéro... [aerɔ] flying-..., air-...; **~bus** [~'bys] *m* airbus; **~drome** [~dro:m] *m* aerodrome, *Am.* airdrome; **~dynamique** [~dina'mik] **1.** *adj.* aerodynamic; streamlined; **2.** *su./f* aerodynamics *sg.*; **~gare** [~'ga:r] *f* air terminal; **~gramme** [~'gram] *m* air letter; **~modélisme** [~mɔde'lism] model aircraft making; **~modéliste** [~mɔde'list] *m* model aircraft maker; **~moteur** [~mɔ'tœ:r] *m* aero-engine;

wind-engine; ⏦**naute** [⏦'noːt] *m* aeronaut, balloonist; ⏦**nautique** [⏦no'tik] **1.** *adj.* aeronautical; **2.** *su./f* aeronautics *sg.*; ⏦**plane** [⏦'plan] *m* aeroplane, aircraft; ⏦**port** [⏦'pɔːr] *m* airport; ⏦**porté, e** [⏦pɔr'te]: *troupes f/pl.* ⏦es airborne troops; ⏦**postal, e,** *m/pl.* **-aux** [⏦pɔs'tal, ⏦'to] airmail...; ⏦**sol** [⏦'sɔl] aerosol; spray; ⏦**spatial, e** *m/pl.*, **-aux** [⏦spa'sjal, -'sjo] aerospace ...; ⏦**stat** [⏦s'ta] *m* airship, balloon; ⏦**station** [⏦sta'sjɔ̃] *f* aeronautics *sg.*; ⏦**statique** [⏦sta'tik] **1.** *adj.*: *ballon m* ⏦ balloon; **2.** *su./f* aerostatics *sg.*; ⏦**train** (*TM*) [⏦'trɛ̃] *m* hovertrain.

affabilité [afabili'te] *f* affability, graciousness (to *avec*, envers); **affable** [a'fabl] affable, gracious.

affadir [afa'diːr] (2a) *v/t.* render tasteless *or* uninteresting; *fig.* disgust; **affadissement** [⏦dis'mɑ̃] *m* loss of flavo(u)r; growing insipid.

affaiblir [afɛ'bliːr] (2a) *v/t.* weaken; *phot.* reduce (the contrasts of); *s'*⏦ grow weaker; **affaiblissement** [⏦blis'mɑ̃] *m* diminution; weakening; reducing; **affaiblisseur** *phot.* [⏦bli'sœːr] *m* reducing agent *or* bath.

affaire [a'fɛːr] *f* business, affair; question, matter; ⏦♫ case; transaction; ⏦s *pl. a.* belongings; ⏦s *pl.* étrangères foreign affairs; *avoir* ⏦ à have to deal with (*a problem etc.*); *cela fait l'*⏦ that will do (nicely); *ce n'est pas petite* ⏦ it is no trifling matter; *parler (d')*⏦s talk business; *son* ⏦ *est faite* he is done for; *voilà l'*⏦ that's it!; **affairé, e** [afɛ're] busy; **affairement** [afɛr'mɑ̃] *m* hurry, bustle; **affairer** [afɛ're] (1a) *v/t.*: *s'*⏦ busy oneself, be busy; **affairisme** [afɛ'rism] *m* racketeering; **affairiste** [afɛ'rist] *m* racketeer.

affaissement [afɛs'mɑ̃] *m* sinking; *ground:* subsidence; *strength:* breaking up; ♫ prostration; *fig.* depression; **affaisser** [afɛ'se] (1b) *v/t.* cause to sink; weigh down; *s'*⏦ sink, subside; give way; cave in; collapse (*a.* ♫).

affaler [afa'le] (1a) *v/t.* ♻ haul down; lower; *s'*⏦ ♻ be driven ashore; F drop.

affamé, e [afa'me] hungry, ravenous (for, *de*); **affamer** [⏦] (1a) *v/t.* starve.

affectation [afɛkta'sjɔ̃] *f* affectation;

pretence; ✝ appropriation; ✝ predilection; ✕ *etc.* posting, *Am.* assignment; assignment (*to a post*); **affecté** [⏦'te] affected, F put-on; **affecter** [⏦'te] (1a) *v/t.* assign; set apart; pretend; assume (*a shape*); move (*s.o.*); affect; have a predilection for; ✿ burden (*the land*); ♫ affect, attack; ✕ *etc.* post, *Am.* assign; **affectif, -ve** [⏦'tif, ⏦'tiːv] affective; **affection** [⏦'sjɔ̃] *f* affection (*a.* ♫); fondness, liking; ♫ disease, complaint; **affectionner** [⏦sjɔ'ne] (1a) *v/t.* be fond of, have a liking for; ✝ *s'*⏦ à *q.* become fond of s.o.; *s'*⏦ *q.* gain s.o.'s affections; **affectueux, -euse** [⏦'tɥø, ⏦'tɥøːz] affectionate, fond, loving.

afférent, e [afe'rɑ̃, ⏦'rɑ̃ːt] relating, relative (to, à); accruing.

affermer [afɛr'me] (1a) *v/t.* let; rent (*land*).

affermir [afɛr'miːr] (2a) *v/t.* consolidate, make firm; *fig.* strengthen.

affété, e [afe'te] affected, mincing; **afféterie** [⏦'tri] *f* affectation, mincing.

affichage [afi'ʃaːʒ] *m* bill-posting; *fig.* F show; *panneau m d'*⏦ noticeboard; **affiche** [a'fiʃ] *f* poster; **afficher** [afi'ʃe] (1a) *v/t.* post up, placard; *fig.* parade, flaunt; *s'*⏦ *pour* set up for; **afficheur** [⏦'ʃœːr] *m* bill-sticker.

affidé, e [afi'de] **1.** *adj.* ✝ trusty; **2.** *su. pej.* accomplice; secret agent.

affilage ⊕ [afi'laːʒ] *m* whetting, sharpening.

affilée [afi'le]: *d'*⏦ at a stretch, on end.

affiler [afi'le] (1a) *v/t.* sharpen, whet; ⊕ set (*a saw*); draw (*gold*).

affiliation [afilja'sjɔ̃] *f* affiliation; **affilié** *m,* **e** *f* [afi'lje] *su.* (affiliated) member, associate; **affilier** [afi'lje] (1o) *v/t.* affiliate (with, to à); *s'* ⏦ à join (*a society etc.*).

affiloir [afi'lwaːr] *m* hone; *razor:* strop; *knife:* steel; whetstone.

affinage ⊕ [afi'naːʒ] *m* refining; *fig.* improvement; *cloth:* cropping; *hemp:* hackling; *plank:* fining down; ⏦ *de surface* surface refinement; **affiner** [⏦'ne] (1a) *v/t.* refine; improve; point (*needles*); fine (*metals*); fine down (*a plank*); hackle (*hemp*); crop, shear (*cloth*); mature (*wine, cheese*).

affinité [afini'te] *f* affinity (*a.* ⚲),
relationship; *fig.* resemblance.

affirmatif, -ve [afirma'tif, ~'ti:v]
1. *adj.* affirmative; **2.** *su./f* affirmative; *dans l'*~ve in the affirmative;
if so; *répondre par l'*~ve answer yes *or*
in the affirmative; **affirmation**
[~ma'sjɔ̃] *f* assertion; **affirmer**
[~'me] (1a) *v/t.* assert.

affleurer [aflœ're] (1a) *v/t.* level;
make flush; be level *or* flush with;
v/i. be level *or* flush.

afflictif, -ve ⚖ [aflik'tif, ~'ti:v] corporal, bodily; *peine f* ~ve corporal
punishment; penal servitude; **affliction** [~'sjɔ̃] *f* affliction, sorrow,
distress; **affliger** [afli'ʒe] (1l) *v/t.*
afflict (with, *de*); distress, grieve;
s'~ grieve, be distressed (at, *de*).

affluence [afly'ã:s] *f* flow(ing);
flood; ⚙ afflux; abundance; crowd;
heures f/pl. d'~ peak hours, rush
hours; **affluent, e** [~'ã, ~'ã:t]
1. *adj.* † affluent; **2.** *su./m* tributary;
affluer [~'e] (1n) *v/i.* flow (*a.* ⚙);
abound; *fig.* crowd, flock; **afflux**
[a'fly] *m* afflux, rush.

affolement [afɔl'mã] *m* panic;
engine: racing; **affoler** [afɔ'le] (1a)
v/t. frighten, terrify, throw into a
panic; madden; *s'*~ (get in a) panic, F
get in a flap; go crazy; ⊕ *etc.* (begin
to) race (*engine etc.*).

affouragement [afuraʒ'mã] *m* fod-
der(ing); **affourager** [~ra'ʒe] (1l)
v/t. fodder (*cattle*).

affranchi, e [afrã'ʃi] **1.** *adj.* freed;
free (from, *of de*); **2.** *su./m* freed-
man; *su./f* freedwoman; **affranchir** [~'ʃi:r] (2a) *v/t.* free, emancipate; exempt; *post*: frank, prepay,
stamp; *s'*~ *de* get rid of; **affranchissement** [~ʃis'mã] *m* emanci-
pation; release, exemption; *post*:
franking, prepayment; postage.

affres [afr] *f/pl.* pangs, terrors,
throes.

affrètement ⚓ [afrɛt'mã] *m* freight-
ing; charter(ing); **affréter** ⚓
[afre'te] (1f) *v/t.* freight; charter.

affreux, -euse [a'frø, ~'frø:z] frightful, dreadful; ghastly; hideous.

affriander [afriã'de] (1a) *v/t.* entice,
allure; make attractive.

affront [a'frɔ̃] *m* affront, insult;
faire un ~ *à* insult; **affronter**
[afrɔ̃'te] (1a) *v/t.* confront, face;
fig. brave; ⊕ join face to face.

affublement *pej.* [afyblə'mã] *m* get-
up, rig-out; **affubler** *pej.* [~'ble]
(1a) *v/t.* rig out (in, *de*).

affût [a'fy] *m* hiding-place; gun-
carriage; *chasser à l'*~ stalk; *être à
l'*~ lie in wait; be on the look-out
(for, *de*); **affûter** ⊕ [afy'te] (1a)
v/t. sharpen (*a.* F *fig.*); set (*a saw*);
stock with tools; **affûteuse** ⊕
[~'tø:z] *f* grinding-machine.

afin [a'fɛ̃] **1.** *prp.*: ~ *de* (*inf.*) (in
order) to (*inf.*); **2.** *cj.*: ~ *que* (*sbj.*)
in order that, so that.

africain, e [afri'kɛ̃, ~'ken] *adj.*, *a.*
su. ♀ African.

Afrikander [afrikã'dɛ:r] *m* Afrikander.

agaçant, e [aga'sã, ~'sã:t] irritating; provocative; **agacer** [~'se]
(1k) *v/t.* irritate, annoy; *s'*~ get annoyed; **agacerie** F [agas'ri] *f* provocation, teasing, coquetry.

agapes F [a'gap] *f/pl.* feast.

agate [a'gat] *f* agate.

âge [ɑ:ʒ] *m* age; period; generation;
d'~ *à, en* ~ *de* of an age to; *enfant mf
d'*~ *scolaire* child of school age; *entre
deux* ~s middle-aged; *quel* ~ *avez-
vous?, quel est votre* ~? how old are
you?; *à ton* ~ when I was your age;
retour m d'~ change of life; **âgé, e**
[a'ʒe] old, aged; elderly; ~ *de deux
ans* 2 years old, aged 2.

agence [a'ʒã:s] *f* agency; ~ *de publicité* advertising agency; ~ *de voyages*
travel agency; ~ *générale* general
agency; ~ *matrimoniale* marriage
bureau; **agencement** [aʒãs'mã] *m*
arrangement, order; ~s *pl.* fixtures;
agencer [aʒã'se] (1k) *v/t.* arrange;
order; fit up.

agenda [aʒɛ̃'da] *m* note-book, mem-
orandum-book; appointment book;
diary.

agenouiller [aʒnu'je] (1a) *v/t.*: *s'*~
kneel (down).

agent [a'ʒã] *m* agent; middleman;
medium, agency; (*a.* ~ *de police*)
policeman, (police) constable; ~ *de
brevet* patent agent; ~ *de change*
stockbroker, exchange broker; ~ *de
liaison* liaison officer; ~ *de location*
house agent; ~ *de maîtrise* supervisor; foreman; ~ *fiduciaire* trustee; ~
provocateur agent provocateur.

agglomération [aglɔmera'sjɔ̃] *f*
agglomeration; mass; built-up area;
~s *pl. urbaines* centres of popu-

lation, urban districts *or* centres;
aggloméré [~'re] *m* patent fuel,
briquette; *geol.* conglomerate; **ag-glomérer** [~'re] (1f) *v/t.* agglom-erate; bring together; s'~ cohere;
cake.

agglutinant, e [aglyti'nă, ~'nă:t]
1. *adj.* adhesive; agglutinative;
binding; **2.** *su./m* bond; **agglutina-tif, -ve** [~na'tif, ~'ti:v] **1.** *adj. see*
agglutinant 1; **2.** *su./m* agglutinant;
agglutiner [~'ne] (1a) *v/t.* agglu-tinate; bind; s'~ cake, agglutinate.

aggravant, e [agra'vă, ~'vă:t] ag-gravating; **aggravation** [~va'sjõ] *f*
worsening; *penalty*: increase; ⚖, ⚔
aggravation; **aggraver** [~'ve] (1a)
v/t. aggravate; worsen; increase;
s'~ worsen.

agile [a'ʒil] agile, nimble; active;
agilité [aʒili'te] *f* agility, nimble-ness.

agio [a'ʒjo] *m* ⭐ agio; F jobbery;
agiotage ⭐ [aʒjɔ'ta:ʒ] *m* (stock-)
jobbing; **agioter** ⭐ [~'te] (1a)
v/i. gamble, speculate; **agioteur**
[~'tœ:r] *m* gambler, speculator.

agir [a'ʒi:r] (2a) *v/i.* act; do; operate,
work; behave; ~ *bien* (*mal*) *envers*
(*or avec*) behave well (badly) to-wards; ⚖ ~ *contre* prosecute; sue;
il s'agit de savoir si the question is
whether; s'~ *de* be a question of
(*s.th.*); **agissant, e** [aʒi'sã, ~'sã:t]
active; bustling; **agissements**
[aʒis'mã] *m/pl.* doings; machina-tions; goings-on.

agitateur, -trice [aʒita'tœ:r, ~'tris]
su. agitator, ⊕ mixer; *su./m* 🔧 stir-ring-rod; **agitation** [~ta'sjõ] *f* agi-tation (*a. fig.*); stir(ring); shaking;
tossing; disturbance; restlessness;
excitement; **agité, e** [~'te] restless;
excited; perturbed; choppy, rough
(*sea*); **agiter** [~'te] (1a) *v/t.* agitate;
wave; shake, toss; stir; disturb;
debate (*a question*); s'~ move (about);
stir; fidget.

agneau [a'ɲo] *m* lamb; **agneler**
[aɲə'le] (1d) *v/i.* lamb; **agnelet** †
[~'lɛ] *m* lambkin; **agnelin** [~'lɛ̃] *m*
fur: lambskin.

agonie [agɔ'ni] *f* death agony; être
à l'~ be at the point of death;
agonir [~'ni:r] (2a) *v/t.*: ~ *q. d'in-jures* heap abuse on s.o.; **agoniser**
[~ni'ze] (1a) *v/i.* be at the point of
death, be dying.

agrafe [a'graf] *f* hook; clasp; clamp;
clip; ⊕ dowel; ⊕ joint; **agrafer**
[agra'fe] (1a) *v/t.* hook; clasp;
fasten; clip (*papers*); ⊕ dowel; *sl.*
nab (= *capture*); **agrafeuse** [~'føːz]
f stapler.

agraire [a'grɛːr] agrarian; *réforme f*
~ agrarian reform.

agrandir [agrã'di:r] (2a) *v/t.* in-crease; enlarge; exalt; exaggerate;
s'~ grow larger; **agrandissement**
[~dis'mã] *m* enlargement; increase;
rise (in power *etc.*); *phot.* blow-up;
agrandisseur *phot.* [~di'sœːr] *m*
enlarger.

agrarien, -enne [agra'rjɛ̃, ~'rjɛn]
adj., a. su./m agrarian.

agréable [agre'abl] agreeable, pleas-ant; pleasing.

agréé [agre'e] *m commercial court*:
counsel, attorney.

agréer [~] (1a) *v/t.* accept; approve;
allow; *veuillez* ~ *l'expression de mes*
sentiments distingués Yours sin-cerely; s'~ *à* enjoy; *v/i.* be agree-able (to, *à*).

agrégat ⊕ [agre'ga] *m* aggregate;
agrégation [~ga'sjõ] *f* ⊕ binding;
⊕ aggregate; admission (*to a so-ciety*); *in France*: competitive State
examination for appointment as
teacher in a *lycée*; **agrégé, e** [~'ʒe]
1. *adj.* aggregate; *geol.* clastic (*rock*);
2. *su./m* one who has passed the
agrégation; **agréger** [~'ʒe] (1g) *v/t.*
† admit, incorporate; admit to the
title of *agrégé*.

agrément [agre'mã] *m* consent;
approval; pleasure, amusement;
charm; ~*s pl.* ornaments; trim-mings; *voyage m d'*~ pleasure-trip;
agrémenter [~mã'te] (1a) *v/t.*
adorn.

agrès [a'grɛ] *m/pl.* ⚓ tackle *sg.*,
gear *sg.*; *sp.* apparatus *sg.*, fittings.

agresseur [agrɛ'sœːr] *m* aggressor;
assailant; **agressif, -ve** [~'sif, ~'siːv]
aggressive; **agression** [~'sjõ] *f* ag-gression; attack; assault; ~*s pl.*
stresses *pl.*, strains *pl.*; **agressivité**
[agresivi'te] *f* aggressiveness.

agreste [a'grɛst] rural; rustic; un-couth.

agricole [agri'kɔl] agricultural (*la-bourer, products*); **agriculteur**
[~kyl'tœːr] *m* agriculturist; hus-bandman; farmer; **agriculture**
[~kyl'ty:r] *f* agriculture; husbandry.

agriffer [agri'fe] (1a) v/t. F claw; s'~ à claw at; clutch at.

agripper [agri'pe] (1a) v/t. F clutch (at); grab.

agronomie [agrɔnɔ'mi] f husbandry, agronomy.

agrumes [a'grym] m/pl. citrus fruit.

aguerrir [agɛ'riːr] (2a) v/t. harden, season; s'~ grow seasoned; s'~ à (or contre) become hardened to.

aguets [a'gɛ] m/pl.: aux ~ on the watch or look-out.

aguicher sl. [agi'ʃe] (1a) v/t. excite; tantalize; sl. turn (s.o.) on.

ah! [ɑ] int. oh!; ah!

ahaner [aa'ne] (1a) v/i. pant; work hard, toil; hum and haw.

ahurir F [ay'riːr] (2a) v/t. bewilder.

ai [e] 1st p. sg. pres. of avoir 1.

aï zo. [ai] m ai.

aide [ɛːd] su. assistant; help; su./f help, assistance; pol. ~ économique economic aid; à l'~ de to or with the help of; venir en~ à q., venir à l'~ de q. help s.o.; su./f: ~ ménagère home help; **~-comptable,** pl. **~s-comptables** [ɛdkɔ̃'tabl] su. assistant-accountant; **~-maçon,** pl. **~s-maçons** [~ma'sɔ̃] m hodman; **~-mémoire** [~me'mwaːr] m/inv. pocket-book; manual; pol. aide-mémoire; memorandum; **aider** [ɛ'de] (1b) v/t. help, assist, aid; s'~ de make use of; v/i.: ~ à qch. help (towards) s.th., contribute to s.th.

aie [ɛ] 1st p. sg. pres. sbj. of avoir 1.

aïeul [a'jœl] m grandfather; **aïeule** [~] f grandmother; **aïeuls** [~] m/pl. grandparents; grandfathers; **aïeux** [a'jø] m/pl. ancestors, forefathers.

aigle [ɛgl] su./m eagle; fig. genius; elephant paper; lectern; su./f 𝄞 eagle; 𝄪 standard.

aiglefin icht. [ɛglə'fɛ̃] m haddock.

aiglon [ɛ'glɔ̃] m eaglet.

aigre [ɛːgr] **1.** adj. sour, tart; bitter (wind, tone); shrill, sharp (voice, sound); crude (colour); **2.** su./m sharpness; **aigre-doux, -douce** [ɛgrə'du, ~'dus] bitter-sweet; fig. subacid; **aigrefin** [~'fɛ̃] m icht. haddock; fig. sharper, swindler; **aigrelet, -ette** [~'lɛ, ~'lɛt] sourish, tart; **aigrette** [ɛ'grɛt] f orn. aigrette (a. cost., 𝄪), egret (a. 𝄪); tuft; 𝄪 a. brush; **aigreur** [ɛ'grœːr] f sourness (a. fig.); fig. ranco(u)r; ⊕ iron: brittleness; 𝄪 ~s pl. acidity sg. (of

the stomach); heartburn sg.; **aigrir** [ɛ'griːr] (2a) vt/i. turn sour; v/t. fig. embitter.

aigu, -guë [e'gy] sharp, pointed; 𝄪, 𝄞, gramm. acute; fig. intense; bitter; piercing (sound); ♪ high(-pitched).

aigue-marine, pl. **aigues-marines** [ɛgma'rin] su./f, a. adj./inv. aquamarine.

aiguière [ɛ'gjɛːr] f ewer.

aiguillage 🚂 [egɥi'jaːʒ] m shunting, Am. switching; points pl., Am. switches pl.; **aiguille** [e'gɥiːj] f needle (a. pine, compass); clock: hand; ⚠ king-post; mountain: point; churchtower: spire; 🚂 points pl., Am. switch; **aiguillée** [egɥi'je] f needleful; **aiguiller** [~'je] (1a) v/t. 🚂 shunt, Am. switch; fig. direct, steer, orient(ate); **aiguillette** [~'jɛt] f aiguillette, aglet; ⚔, ⚓ shoulder-knot; **aiguilleur** 🚂 [~'jœːr] m pointsman, Am. switchman; ⚔ ~ du ciel air traffic controller; **aiguillier** [~'je] m needle-maker; needle-book; **aiguillon** [~'jɔ̃] m goad; wasp: sting; fig. spur, stimulus; **aiguillonner** [~jɔ'ne] (1a) v/t. goad; fig. spur on; rouse.

aiguiser [eg(ɥ)i'ze] (1a) v/t. whet (a. fig.), sharpen; set (a razor, a saw); fig. excite, quicken.

ail, pl. 🌿 **ails,** cuis. **aulx** [aːj, o] m 🌿 allium; cuis. garlic.

aile [ɛl] f wing (a. ⚔, sp.); windmill: sail; blade; eccl. aisle; F fin, arm; mot. wing, Am. fender; 𝄪 ~ en delta delta wing; ⚔ ~ en flèche swept-back wing; **ailé, e** [ɛ'le] winged; **aileron** [ɛl'rɔ̃] m pinion; small wing; shark: fin; ⚔ aileron; water-wheel: float(-board); ⚠ scroll; **ailette** [ɛ'lɛt] f ⚠ small wing; ⊕ lug; radiator: gill, fin; ventilator: vane; turbine: blade; **ailier** sp. [ɛ'lje] m wing(er).

aillade cuis. [a'jad] f garlic sauce.

aille [aj] 1st p. sg. pres. sbj. of aller 1.

ailleurs [a'jœːr] adv. elsewhere; d'~ from somewhere else; moreover, besides; nulle part ~ nowhere else.

aimable [ɛ'mabl] agreeable, pleasant; amiable, kind; nice.

aimant¹, e [ɛ'mɑ̃, ~'mɑ̃ːt] loving, affectionate.

aimant² [ɛ'mɑ̃] m magnet (a. fig.); ~ long bar magnet; ~ naturel magnetic iron ore; **aimantation** [ɛmɑ̃-

ta'sjɔ̃] *f* magnetization; **aimanter** [ˌ'te] (1a) *v/t.* magnetize; *aiguille f aimantée* magnetic needle.

aimer [ɛ'me] (1b) *v/t.* love; like; be fond of; be in love with; *v/i.* love; ~ *à* (*inf.*) like (*ger.*) *or* to (*inf.*); *j'aimerais* I would like; *j'aimerais mieux* I would prefer *or* rather *or* sooner.

aine *anat.* [ɛn] *f* groin.

aîné, e [ɛ'ne] *adj., a. su.* elder; eldest; first-born; senior; *il est mon ~ de trois mois* he is 3 months older than I; he is my senior by 3 months; **aînesse** [ɛ'nɛs] *f* primogeniture; seniority; *droit m d'~* law of primogeniture; birthright.

ainsi [ɛ̃'si] **1.** *adv.* thus; so; in this way; ~ *soit-il!* so be it!; *eccl., a. co.* amen; *pour ~ dire* so to speak; **2.** *cj.* so; ~ *que* as well as; like.

air[1] [ɛːr] *m* air; wind; atmosphere (*a. fig.*); *metall.* ~ *chaud* hot blast; ⊕ ~ *comprimé* compressed air; ~ *conditionné* air-conditioned; ~ *frais* fresh air; *courant m d'~* draught, *Am.* draft; *en l'*~ (up) into the air; *en plein* ~ in the open air; *il y a qch. dans l'*~ there is s.th. in the wind; *menaces f/pl. en l'*~ empty threats; *mettre à l'*~ place in the open; *fig.* être *en l'*~ be in disorder *or* confusion, be in a mess; *fig.* flanquer (*or* F ficher) *en l'*~ throw away; F chuck up *or* out; knock over; *fig.* mettre *en l'*~ throw into confusion; *fig.* paroles *f/pl.* en *l'*~ idle talk; *fig.* projets *m/pl.* en *l'*~ castles in the air; *fig.* vivre de *l'*~ *du temps* live on air.

air[2] [~] *m* air, look, appearance; way, manner; ~ *de famille* family likeness; *avoir l'*~ *de* look like; *avoir l'*~ *de* (*inf.*) seem to (*inf.*), look as if (*ind.*); *prendre* (*or se donner*) *des* ~s give o.s. airs.

air[3] ♪ [~] *m* air, tune, melody; aria; ~ *à boire* drinking song.

aire [~] *f* area; site; (threshing-)floor; ⚠, ⚗ area; *eagle:* eyrie; ⚓ ~ *d'atterrissage* landing strip *or* patch; *meteor.* ~ *de haute (basse) pression* high (low) pressure (area); ~ *du vent* wind direction; point of the compass.

airelle ♀ [ɛ'rɛl] *f* bilberry, whortleberry, *Am.* huckleberry, blueberry.

airer [ɛ're] (1a) *v/i.* build an eyrie *or* a nest.

aisance [ɛ'zɑ̃ːs] *f* ease; comfort;

competency; *cabinet m d'*~s public convenience, water-closet; **aise** [ɛːz] **1.** *adj.:* être bien ~ be very glad; **2.** *su./f* ease, comfort; † pleasure; *à l'*~, *à son* ~ comfortable; well-off; *adv.* comfortably; *en prendre à son* ~ take it easy; *mal à l'*~ ill at ease; **aisé, e** [ɛ'ze] easy; well-to-do, well-off (for money).

aisselle [ɛ'sɛl] *f anat.* armpit; ⚠ haunch; ♀ axilla.

ajointer [aʒwɛ̃'te] (1a) *v/t.* join (together); fit end to end.

ajonc ♀ [a'ʒɔ̃] *m* gorse, furze.

ajour [a'ʒuːr] *m* ⚠ opening; ⊕ perforation; **ajouré, e** [aʒu're] perforated; open-work.

ajournement [aʒurnə'mɑ̃] *m* postponement; adjournment; ⚔ deferment; **ajourner** [ˌ'ne] (1a) *v/t.* postpone; adjourn; defer; *pol.* table (*a bill*).

ajouter [aʒu'te] (1a) *v/t.* add; ~ *foi à* believe (*s.th.*).

ajustage ⊕ [aʒys'ta:ʒ] *m* fitting, assembly; fit; ~ *lâche* (*serré*) loose (tight) fit; **ajustement** [ˌtə'mɑ̃] *m* adjusting, adjustment; **ajuster** [ˌ'te] (1a) *v/t.* adjust, fit; adapt; settle, arrange; true up; aim (*a shot, a gun*); ~ *une montre* put a watch right; *s'*~ fit; agree; adapt o.s.; suit o.s.; **ajusteur** [ˌ'tœːr] *m* fitter.

ajutage [aʒy'ta:ʒ] *m* nozzle; jet; *water-works:* a(d)jutage.

alacrité [alakri'te] *f* alacrity; eagerness.

alaire [a'lɛːr] alar, of the wings.

alambic [alɑ̃'bik] *m* still; **alambiqué, e** *fig.* [ˌbi'ke] oversubtle, strained.

alanguir [alɑ̃'giːr] (2a) *v/t.* make languid; *s'*~ languish; flag; grow languid; **alanguissement** [ˌgis'mɑ̃] *m* languor; weakness.

alarme [a'larm] *f* alarm; *donner l'*~ sound the alarm; **alarmer** [alar'me] (1a) *v/t.* alarm, startle; disquiet; worry; *s'*~ be(come) alarmed; worry; **alarmiste** [ˌ'mist] *su., a. adj.* alarmist.

albanais, e [alba'nɛ, ˌ'nɛːz] **1.** *adj.* albanian; **2.** *su./m ling.* Albanian; *su.* ♀ Albanian.

albâtre [al'bɑːtr] *m* alabaster.

albatros *orn.*, ⚓ [alba'trɔs] *m* albatross. [albino.)

albinos [albi'noːs] *su., a. adj./inv.*⎰

Albion [al'bjɔ̃] *f* Britain; *poet.* Albion.

album [al'bɔm] *m* album; *paint.* sketch-book; picture-book.

albumine ✿ [alby'min] *f* albumin.

alcali [alka'li] *m* alkali; ~ *minéral* soda-ash; ~ *végétal* potash; ~ *volatil* ammonia; **alcalin, e** [~'lɛ̃, ~'lin] alkaline.

alchimie [alʃi'mi] *f* alchemy.

alcool [al'kɔl] *m* alcohol; F spirit(s *pl.*); ~ *dénaturé* methylated spirits *pl.*; ~ *méthylique* methyl alcohol; **alcoolique** [alkɔ'lik] **1.** *adj.* alcoholic; **2.** *su.* alcoholic; drunkard; **alcooliser** [~li'ze] (1a) *v/t.* alcoholize; fortify (*wine*); **alcoolisme** [~'lism] *m* alcoholism; **alcoomètre** [~'mɛtr] *m* alcoholometer; **alcootest** [~'test] *m* breathalyser; breath test.   [recess.]

alcôve [al'ko:v] *f* alcove; (bed-)

alcyon *orn.* [al'sjɔ̃] *m* kingfisher, halcyon.

aléa [ale'a] *m* risk, hazard; **aléatoire** [~a'twa:r] aleatory; risky; problematic(al).

alène ⊕ [a'lɛn] awl.

alentour [alɑ̃'tu:r] **1.** *adv.* around; **2.** *su./m.* ~s *pl.* neighbourhood *sg.*, surroundings.

alerte [a'lɛrt] **1.** *adj.* alert, quick; watchful; **2.** *int.* look out!; **3.** *su./f* alarm, alert; warning; ~ *au feu* fire alarm; *fausse* ~ false alarm; **alerter** [alɛr'te] (1a) *v/t.* alert; warn.

alésage ⊕ [ale'za:ʒ] *m* boring; reaming; bore; **aléser** ⊕ [~'ze] (1f) *v/t.* bore; ream.

alevin [al'vɛ̃] *m* fry; **alevinier** [~vi'nje] *m* breeding-pond.

alexandrin, e [alɛksɑ̃'drɛ̃, ~'drin] **1.** *adj.* Alexandrian; Alexandrine; **2.** *su./m prosody*: alexandrine; *su.* ♀ Alexandrian.

alezan [al'zɑ̃] *su./m, a. adj.* chestnut.

alfa ♀ [al'fa] *m* alfa(-grass), esparto (-grass).

algarade [alga'rad] *f* storm of insults *or* abuse; dressing-down; escapade; sally; ✕ † raid.

algèbre [al'ʒɛ:br] *f* algebra; **algébrique** [~ʒe'brik] algebraic.

algérien, -enne [alʒe'rjɛ̃, ~'rjɛn] *adj., a. su.* ♀ Algerian.

algue ♀ [alg] *f* alga; sea-weed.

alibi [ali'bi] *m* alibi; ~ *de fer* cast-iron alibi.

aliénable ⚖ [alje'nabl] alienable; **aliénation** [~na'sjɔ̃] *f* alienation (*a.* ⚖); ✿ mental derangement; insanity; **aliéné, e** [~'ne] *su., a. adj.* lunatic; **aliéner** [~'ne] (1f) *v/t.* ⚖ alienate; unhinge (*s.o.'s mind*).

alignement [aliɲ'mɑ̃] *m* alignment; building-line; ✕ dressing (*of line*); **aligner** [ali'ɲe] (1a) *v/t.* △ align; lay out in a line; mark out; ✕ dress, draw up in a line; *s'* ~ fall into line; ✕ dress; *non aligné* nonaligned.

aliment [ali'mɑ̃] *m* food, nutriment; ⚖ ~s *pl.* alimony *sg.*; ~s *pl. naturels* health food (*sg.*); **alimentaire** [alimɑ̃'tɛ:r] alimentary; for food; nutritional; dietary; **alimentation** [~ta'sjɔ̃] *f* feeding, alimentation; food, diet; nutrition; supplying, supply; ⊕ feed; ~ *défectueuse* malnutrition; ~ *en essence* fuelling; *magasin m d'*~ food shop (*Am.* store); *rayon m d'*~ food department; **alimenter** [~'te] (1a) *v/t.* feed (*a.* ⊕); nourish (*a. fig.*); supply with food; *fig.* keep alive (*hatred, a quarrel, etc.*); ~ *en qch.* supply with s.th.

alinéa [aline'a] *m* paragraph; *typ.* en ~ indented.

alité, e [ali'te] confined to bed; **alitement** [alit'mɑ̃] *m* confinement to bed; **aliter** [ali'te] (1a) *v/t.* confine to bed; *s'*~ take to one's bed.

alizé [ali'ze] *m* trade wind.

allaiter [alɛ'te] (1b) *v/t.* suckle.

allant [a'lɑ̃] *m* initiative; energy; F dash; *avoir de l'*~ have plenty of go.

allécher [ale'ʃe] (1f) *v/t.* entice, tempt, allure.

allé, e [a'le] **1.** *p.p. of aller 1*; **2.** *su./f* going; avenue; (tree-lined) walk; path; passage; drive(way); ~es *pl. et venues f/pl.* coming *sg.* and going *sg.*, to-and-fro *sg.*

allégation [alega'sjɔ̃] *f* allegation.

allège [al'lɛ:ʒ] *f* ♣ lighter; ♣ barge; △ breast-wall; △ balustrade.

allégement [alɛʒ'mɑ̃] *m* alleviation (of, de), relief (from, de); lightening; ~ *fiscal* tax relief; **alléger** [~le'ʒe] (1g) *v/t.* make lighter; lighten; *fig.* alleviate, relieve.

allégorie [allegɔ'ri] *f* allegory.

allègre [al'lɛ:gr] lively, brisk; cheerful; **allégrement** [~legra'mɑ̃] *adv.* of *allègre*; **allégresse** [~le'grɛs] *f* joy, cheerfulness; liveliness.

alléguer [alle'ge] (1s) v/t. allege;
state; urge; adduce (evidence etc.);
quote; cite; ~ l'ignorance plead
ignorance.

alléluia [alelɥi'ja] m hallelujah,
alleluia(h).

allemand, e [al'mã, ~'mã:d] 1. adj.
German; 2. su./m ling. German;
su. ♀ German.

aller [a'le] 1. (1q) v/i. go; depart;
~ (inf.) be going to (inf.), go and
...; a. = fut. tense; ~ à bicyclette
go by bicycle; ~ à cheval ride (a
horse); ~ bien (mal) be or be going
well (badly); ~ chercher (go and)
look for; fetch; ~ diminuant grow
steadily less; ~ en chemin de fer go
by train or rail; ~ en voiture drive,
ride (in a car), go by car; ~ se coucher
go to bed; ~ sur la cinquantaine be
going or getting on for fifty; ~ voir
q. call on s.o.; go and see s.o.;
allons! let's go!; come!; nonsense!; come along!; ce chapeau
lui va bien (mal) that hat suits
(does not suit) him; cela me va
that suits me; comment allez-vous?
how are you?; il va sans dire it goes
without saying, it is obvious; il y
va de ... it is a matter of ...; ... is at
stake; la clef va à la serrure the key
fits the lock; n'allez pas croire ...!
don't believe ...!; don't think ...!;
F on y va! coming!; s'en ~ go
away, leave, depart; va! agreed!;
believe me ...!; 2. su./m ⚓ outward journey; 🎫 single ticket; ~ et
retour journey there and back;
ticket: return; à l'~ on the outward
journey; au pis ~ if the worst comes
to the worst; le pis ~ the last resort.

allergie [aller'ʒi] f 🩹, a. F fig.
allergy; **allergique** [~'ʒik] allergic
(to, à).

alliable [a'ljabl] miscible; fig. compatible; **alliage** [a'lja:ʒ] m alloy;
🜛 alligation; **alliance** [a'ljã:s] f
alliance; marriage; union; wedding
ring; **allié, e** [a'lje] 1. adj. allied;
2. su. ally; relation by marriage;
allier [~] (1o) v/t. ally; unite; 🜛
alloy (metals); blend (colours); s'~
marry, be married.

allitération [alitera'sjõ] f allitera-
tion.

allô! [a'lo] int. hullo!, hello!

allocation [alloka'sjõ] f allocation;
allowance; grant; ~s pl. familiales

family allowances; ~ d'assistance
subsidy; ~ de chômage unemployment benefit; ~ de maternité maternity benefit; ~ vieillesse old age relief.

allocution [alloky'sjõ] f address,
speech.

allogène [alo'ʒɛn] non-native; alien.

allonge [a'lõ:ʒ] f extension; eking-
piece; table: leaf; meat-hook; box.
reach; ✝ rider; **allongement**
[alõʒ'mã] m lengthening; 🜛 elon-
gation; **allonger** [alõ'ʒe] (11) v/t.
lengthen; delay; prolong; sl. aim
(a blow); (at, à); sl. fork out (money);
s'~ stretch (out), grow longer.

allopathie 🩹 [allopa'ti] f allopathy.

allouable [a'lwa:bl] grantable; **allouer** [a'lwe] (1p) v/t. grant;
allocate.

allumage [aly'ma:ʒ] m lighting; 🜛
ignition; mot. ~ prématuré back-
fire; pinking; ~ raté misfire; couper l'~ switch off the ignition; retarder l'~ retard the spark; **allumé, e** sl. [~'me] worked-up; **allume-feu** [alym'fø] m/inv. fire-lighter;
allume-gaz [~'ga:z] m/inv. gas-
lighter; **allumer** [aly'me] (1a) v/t.
light, kindle; inflame; v/i. switch
on (the light); s'~ catch fire; light up;
allumette [~'mɛt] f match; ~ de
sûreté safety match.

allure [a'ly:r] f walk, gait; bearing;
manner; demeanour; speed; pace;
appearance; ⚓ mode of sailing,
sailing-trim; ✝ business: trend; à
toute ~ at full speed; filer (marcher) à une ~ normale travel (walk,
go) at a normal speed; forcer l'~
increase speed; fig. prendre une
bonne ~ take a promising turn;
régler l'~ set the pace.

alluvial, e, e m/pl. -aux geol. [aly-
'vjal; ~'vjo] alluvial; **alluvion**
[~'vjõ] f alluvium; alluvial (deposit).

almanach [alma'na] m almanac;
calendar; ~ du commerce commercial directory; faiseur m d'~s
weather-prophet.

aloi [a'lwa] m standard, quality (a.
fig.); fig. de bon ~ genuine; sterling;
fig. de mauvais ~ base, worthless;
monnaie f d'~ sterling money.

alors [a'lɔ:r] adv. then; at or by
that time; in that case; well (then); ~
même que even when or though; ~ que
at a time when; whereas; d'~ of that

time; *jusqu'~* until then; F *et ~?* and what then?; so what?

alouette *orn.* [a'lwɛt] *f* lark.

alourdir [alur'diːr] (2a) *v/t.* make heavy *or* dull; weigh down; *s'~* become heavy; **alourdissement** [~dis'mã] *m* heaviness.

aloyau [alwa'jo] *m* sirloin (of beef).

alpaga *zo.* [alpa'ga] *m* alpaca.

alpage [al'paːʒ] *m* pasture on the upper slopes; **alpe** [alp] *f* Alp, height; *geogr. les ~s pl.* the Alps; **alpestre** [al'pɛstr] alpine.

alphabet [alfa'bɛ] *m* alphabet; spelling-book; primer; **alphabétique** [~be'tik] alphabetical.

alpin, e [al'pɛ̃, ~'pin] alpine; ✕ *chasseur m ~* mountain infantryman; **alpinisme** [alpi'nism] *m* mountaineering; **alpiniste** [~'nist] *su.* mountaineer, F climber.

alsacien, -enne [alza'sjɛ̃, ~'sjɛn] **1.** *adj.* Alsatian, of Alsace; **2.** *su.* ♀ Alsatian, man (woman) of Alsace.

altérable [alte'rabl] liable to deterioration; *~ à l'air* which deteriorates on exposure to the air; **altérant, e** [~'rã, ~'rãːt] thirst-making; **altération** [~ra'sjɔ̃] *f* deterioration; weakening; *coinage:* debasing; *colour:* fading; *voice:* faltering; *fig.* misrepresentation.

altercation [alterka'sjɔ̃] *f* altercation; dispute.

altéré[1], e [alte're] thirsty (*fig.* for, de).

altéré[2], e [~] haggard (*face*); faded (*colour*); broken, faltering (*voice*).

altérer[1] [~] (1f) *v/t.* change for the worse; corrupt; debase (*the currency*); taint; spoil; adulterate, tamper with; inflect (*a note*); *s'~* change for the worse; deteriorate; break (*voice*); weather (*rock*).

altérer[2] [~] (1f) *v/t.* make thirsty.

alternance [alter'nãːs] *f* alternation (*a. ⚡*); *↗ ~ des cultures* crop rotation; **alternateur** *⚡* [~na'tœːr] *m* alternator; **alternatif, -ve** [~na'tif, ~'tiːv] alternate; alternative; ⊕ reciprocating; *⚡ courant m ~* alternating current; **alternative** [~na'tiːv] *f* alternation; alternative; *~s pl. saisonnières* seasonal alternation *sg.*; **alterne** [al'tɛrn] alternate (*angle*); **alterner** [~tɛr'ne] (1a) *v/i.* alternate, take turns; *v/t.* rotate (*the crops*); ⊕ break (*a joint*).

Altesse [al'tɛs] *f title:* Highness.

altier, -ère [al'tje, ~'tjeːr] haughty, proud, lofty; **altimètre** [alti'mɛtr] *m* altimeter; **altitude** [~'tyd] *f* altitude; *✈ ~ d'utilisation* cruising altitude; *✈ prendre de l'~* climb.

alto ♪ [al'to] *m voice:* alto; viola; alto saxophone.

altruisme [altry'ism] *m* altruism; **altruiste** [~'ist] **1.** *adj.* altruistic; selfless; **2.** *su.* altruist.

alumine [aly'min] *f* alumina; **aluminium** [~mi'njɔm] *m* aluminium, *Am.* aluminum.

alun [a'lɶ̃] *m* alum; **aluner** [aly'ne] (1a) *v/t.* alum; *phot.* harden (*the negative*).

alunir [aly'niːr] (2a) *v/i.* land on the moon; **alunissage** [~ni'saːʒ] *m* landing on the moon, lunar landing.

alvéole [alve'ɔl] *m* alveolus; *a.* ⊕ cell; *tooth:* socket; cavity.

amabilité [amabili'te] *f* amiability; kindness; *~s pl.* civilities.

amadou [ama'du] *m* tinder, touchwood, *Am.* punk; **amadouer** [~'dwe] (1p) *v/t.* coax, wheedle; draw, attract (*customers*).

amaigrir [amɛ'griːr] (2a) *v/t.* make thin; reduce; *s'~* lose weight, grow thin; **amaigrissement** [~gris'mã] *m* growing thin; slimming; emaciation; *soil:* impoverishment.

amalgamation [amalgama'sjɔ̃] *f* amalgamation; ✝ merger; **amalgame** [~'gam] *m* amalgam; F mixture; **amalgamer** [~ga'me] (1a) *v/t.* amalgamate.

amande [a'mãːd] *f* almond; kernel; **amandier** [~'dje] *m* almond-tree.

amant, e [a'mã, ~'mãːt] *su.* lover; *su./f* mistress.

amarante ♀ [ama'rãːt] *su./f, a. adj./inv.* amaranth.

amarrage [ama'raːʒ] *m* mooring; docking; **amarre** ⚓ [a'maːr] *f* mooring rope; hawser; *~s pl.* moorings; **amarrer** [ama're] (1a) *v/t.* moor; make fast; secure; dock; lash (*a hawser*); *s'~* moor, make fast; dock.

amas [a'mɑ] *m* heap; store; crowd; *~ de neige* snow-drift; **amasser** [amɑ'se] (1a) *v/t.* heap up; amass; accumulate.

amateur [ama'tœːr] *m* lover (*of music, sports, etc.*); admirer; amateur; **amateurisme** [~tœ'rism] *m sp. etc.* amateurism; *pej.* amateurishness.

amatir [ama'ti:r] (2a) *v/t.* mat; dull; deaden.

amazone [ama'zo:n] *f* amazon; horsewoman; (lady's) riding-habit.

ambages [ăm'ba:ʒ] *f/pl.* circumlocution; *sans* ~ forthrightly.

ambassade [ămba'sad] *f* embassy; ambassador's staff; *fig.* errand; **ambassadeur** [~sa'dœ:r] *m* ambassador; *fig.* messenger; **ambassadrice** [~sa'dris] *f* ambassadress, *a.* ambassador's wife.

ambiance [ă'bjă:s] *f* surroundings *pl.*, environment; atmosphere; **ambiant, e** [ă'bjă, ~'bjă:t] surrounding; *conditions f/pl.* ~es circumstances; environment *sg.*

ambidextre [ăbi'dɛkstr] **1.** *adj.* ambidextrous; **2.** *su.* ambidexter.

ambigu, -guë [ămbi'gy] **1.** *adj.* ambiguous; equivocal; **2.** *su./m* mixture, medley; cold collation; **ambiguïté** [~gɥi'te] *f* ambiguity.

ambitieux, -euse [ăbi'sjø, ~'sjø:z] **1.** *adj.* ambitious; *style m* ~ affected style; **2.** *su.* ambitious person; **ambition** [~'sjɔ̃] *f* ambition; **ambitionner** [~sjɔ'ne] (1a) *v/t.* covet; be eager for; *pol.* ~ *le pouvoir* aspire to power; strive for power.

amble [ă:bl] *m* amble, pace; *Am.* single-foot.

ambre [ă:br] *m* amber; ~ *gris* ambergris; **ambrer** [ă'bre] (1a) *v/t.* scent with amber. [♀ wormseed.]

ambroisie [ăbrwa'zi] *f* ambrosia;⌡

ambulance [ăby'lă:s] *f* ambulance (*a. mot.*); ✕ field hospital; **ambulancier** [~lă'sje] *m* ambulance man *or* driver; **ambulancière** [~lă'sjɛ:r] *f* ambulance woman; **ambulant, e** [~'lă, ~'lă:t] **1.** *adj.* itinerant, travelling; ambulant; strolling (*player*); **2.** *su./m post:* travelling sorter; **ambulatoire** [~la'twa:r] *ambulatory.

âme [ɑ:m] *f* soul (*a. fig.*); *fig.* feeling; ⊕ *cable etc.:* core; *girder:* web; ✕ *gun:* bore; *fig.* ~*s pl.* souls, inhabitants; *fig.* ~ *damnée* tool, F stooge; ~ *en peine* soul in Purgatory; *rendre l'*~ breathe one's last.

amélioration [ameljɔra'sjɔ̃] *f* improvement; **améliorer** [~'re] (1a) *v/t.* improve, ameliorate.

amen [a'mɛn] *int., a. su./m/inv.* amen.

aménagement [amenaʒ'mă] *m* arranging; arrangement; adjustment; ✔ parcelling out; development; ~ *du territoire* town and country planning; ~ *intérieur* interior decoration; **aménager** [~na'ʒe] (11) *v/t.* arrange; ✔ parcel out; plan (*a town*); develop (*an area etc.*).

amendable [amă'dabl] improvable; **amende** [a'mă:d] *f* fine; ~ *honorable* amende honorable; *sous peine d'*~ on pain of a fine; *mettre q. à l'*~ fine s.o.; **amendement** [amăd'mă] *m* improvement (*a.* ✔); ✔ manure; *parl.* amendment; **amender** [amă'de] (1a) *v/t.* amend; improve; *s'*~ *a.* mend one's ways.

amenée [am'ne] *f* bringing; ⊕ ~ *d'air* air-intake, air-inlet; **amener** [~] (1d) *v/t.* lead (to, *à*); pull; bring (in, up, down, out); produce; cause; throw (*a number*); ~ *pavillon* strike one's flag; ~ *une crise* force an issue; *sl.* *amène-toi!* come along!; ⚖ *mandat m d'*~ order to appear.

aménité [ameni'te] *f* amenity; charm; *usu. iro.* ~*s pl.* compliments.

amenuisement [amnɥiz'mă] *m* decrease, dwindling, lessening, diminishing; **amenuiser** [amnɥi'ze] (1a) *v/t.* thin down; pare down; *s'*~ decrease, dwindle, lessen, diminish.

amer, -ère [a'mɛ:r] bitter (*a. fig.*).

américain, e [ameri'kɛ̃, ~'kɛn] **1.** *adj.* American; **2.** *su.* ♀ American; **américaniser** [~kani'ze] (1a) *v/t.* Americanize; *s'*~ become Americanized; **américaniste** [~ka'nist] *su.* Americanist.

amerrir ✈ [ame'ri:r] (2a) *v/i.* land, alight (*on sea*); splash down; **amerrissage** [~ri'sa:ʒ] *m* alighting, landing (*on sea*); splashdown.

amertume [amer'tym] *f* bitterness (*a. fig.*).

améthyste [ame'tist] *f* amethyst.

ameublement [amœblə'mă] *m* furnishing; (suite of) furniture; *tissu m d'*~ furnishing fabric; **ameublir** [~'bli:r] (2a) *v/t.* 🏛 convert into personalty; bring (*realty*) into the communal estate; ✔ break up (*the soil*); **ameublissement** [~blis'mă] *m* conversion into personalty; *realty:* inclusion in the communal estate; ✔ *soil:* breaking-up.

ameuter [amø'te] (1a) *v/t.* form (*hounds*) into a pack; assemble; stir

up, incite (*the mob*) (against, *con-tre*); s'~ collect (into a mob); riot.
ami, e [a'mi] **1.** *su.* friend; *société f des* ~*s* Quakers *pl.*; **2.** *adj.* friendly; *fig.* kindly; **amiable** [a'mjabl] amicable; friendly; *à l'*~ amicably; *adj.* private; *vendre à l'*~ sell privately.
amiante *min.* [a'mjã:t] *m* asbestos.
amical, e, *m/pl.* **-aux** [ami'kal, ~'ko] friendly; amicable.
amidon [ami'dɔ̃] *m* starch; **ami-donner** [~dɔ'ne] (1a) *v/t.* starch.
amincir [amɛ̃'si:r] (2a) *v/t.* make thinner; make (*s.o.*) look slender; *Am.* slenderize; s'~ grow thinner; **amincissant, e** [~si'sã, ~'sã:t] slimming, *Am.* slenderizing.
amiral [ami'ral] *m* admiral; *vais-seau m* ~ flagship; **amirauté** [~ro-'te] *f* admiralship; admiralty; *l'*~ the Admiralty.
amitié [ami'tje] *f* friendship; affection; friendliness; ~*s pl.* compliments (= *greetings*); *faites-lui mes* ~*s* give him my compliments *or* regards; remember me to him; *faites-moi l'*~ *de* (*inf.*) do me the favo(u)r of (*ger.*).
ammoniac, -que [amɔ'njak] *adj.*: *gaz m* ~ ammonia; *sel m* ~ sal am-moniac; **ammonisation** *biol.* [~niza'sjɔ̃] *f* ammonification.
amnésie [amne'zi] *f* amnesia, loss of memory.
amnistie [amnis'ti] *f* amnesty; **am-nistier** [~'tje] (1o) *v/t.* pardon, grant an amnesty to.
amocher *sl.* [amɔ'ʃe] (1a) *v/t.* make a mess of; bash up.
amoindrir [amwɛ̃'dri:r] (2a) *v/t.* lessen, reduce, decrease; s'~ dimin-ish, grow less; **amoindrissement** [~dris'mã] *m* lessening, reduction, decrease. [ning amok.\
amok [a'mɔk] *m* amok; person run-\
amollir [amɔ'li:r] (2a) *v/t.* soften; *fig.* weaken; s'~ go soft; weaken; **amol-lissement** [~lis'mã] *m* softening (*a. fig.*); *fig.* weakening.
amonceler [amɔ̃s'le] (1c) *v/t.* pile up; accumulate; **amoncellement** [~sɛl'mã] *m* heap(ing); piling; ac-cumulation; pile.
amont [a'mɔ̃] *m*: *en* ~ up-stream; *fig.* beforehand, in advance; *en* ~ *de* above; *fig.* previous to, before; *voya-ge m en* ~ up journey.

amorçage [amɔr'sa:ʒ] *m* pump: priming; *shell*: capping; starting; *fish*: baiting; **amorce** [a'mɔrs] *f* bait; priming; *pump, gun*: primer; *shell*: percussion cap; ⚡ fuse; *fig.* beginning; **amorcer** [amɔr'se] (1k) *v/t.* bait; prime (*a pump*); cap (*a shell*); *fig.* begin; ⊕, *a. fig.* s'~ start; ⚡ build up (*magnetic field*); **amorçoir** ⊕ [~'swa:r] *m* auger, boring-bit; centre punch.
amorphe [a'mɔrf] amorphous; *fig.* spineless.
amortir [amɔr'ti:r] (2a) *v/t.* deaden (*a noise, a pain*); cushion, absorb (*a shock*); tone down (*a colour*); ✝ pay off, amortize; ✝ write off (*equip-ment*); △ slake (*lime*); *phys.* damp down; **amortissable** ✝ [~ti'sabl] redeemable; **amortissement** [~tis-'mã] *m* deadening; ✝ depreciation; ✝ redemption; paying-off; *shock*: absorption; **amortisseur** ⊕ [~ti-'sœ:r] *m* damping device; damper; (*a.* ~ *de choc*) shock absorber.
amour [a'mu:r] *m* love; passion; affection; ♀ Cupid, Love; ~*s f/pl.* love *sg.*, delight *sg.*; amours; *l'*~ *du prochain* love of one's neighbour; *iro. pour l'*~ *de Dieu* for heaven's sake; **amoura-cher** [amura'ʃe] (1a) *v/t.* enamour; s'~ *de* fall in love with, become enamoured of; **amourette** [~'rɛt] *f* love affair; F crush; ♀ quaking-grass; ♀ London pride; **amou-reux, -euse** [~'rø, ~'rø:z] **1.** *adj.* loving; amorous (*look etc.*); ~ *de* in love with; enamoured of; **2.** *su.* sweetheart; **amour-propre**, *pl.* **amours-propres** [amur'prɔpr] *m* self-respect; *pej.* conceit.
amovible [amɔ'vibl] removable; detachable.
ampérage ⚡ [ãpe'ra:ʒ] *m* amperage; **ampère** ⚡ [ã'pɛ:r] *m* ampere.
amphibie [ãfi'bi] **1.** *adj.* amphib-ious; ✕ *etc.* combined (*operation*); **2.** *su./m* amphibian; **amphibiens** [ãfi-'bjɛ̃] *m/pl.* amphipia *pl.*, amphibians *pl.*
amphigouri [ãfigu'ri] *m* am-phigory; rigmarole.
amphithéâtre [ãfite'a:tr] *m* am-phitheatre, *Am.* amphitheater; *univ.* lecture hall.
amphityron [ãfiti'jɔ̃] *npr./m* Am-phitryon; *fig.* host, entertainer.

34

ample [ɑ̃pl] ample; spacious, roomy; full, complete; **ampleur** [ɑ̃'plœ:r] *f* fullness; *meal*: copiousness; *style*: breadth; *appeal*: generality; ~ *du son* volume of sound; **ampliation** [ɑ̃plia'sjɔ̃] *f* certified copy; **amplificateur** [~fika'tœ:r] *m sound*: intensifier; *radio*: amplifier, booster; *phot.* enlarger; **amplification** [~fika'sjɔ̃] *f* amplification (*a. radio*); development; *phot.* enlargement; *opt.* magnification; *fig.* exaggeration; **amplifier** [~'fje] (1o) *v/t.* amplify (*a. ⚡*), develop; *opt.* magnify; *fig.* exaggerate; **amplitude** [~'tyd] *f* amplitude (*a. phys., astr.*); vastness.

ampoule [ɑ̃'pul] *f* 🕭 flask; ⚡ bulb (*a. thermometer*); *vacuum flask*: container; 🖋 blister; 🖋 ampoule; *phot.* ~ (*de*) *flash* flash; **ampoulé, e** [ɑ̃pu'le] blistered; *fig.* bombastic.

amputation [ɑ̃pyta'sjɔ̃] *f limb*: amputation, cutting off; *book*: curtailment; **amputé** *m*, **e** *f* [~'te] person who has lost a limb; **amputer** [~'te] (1a) *v/t.* 🖋 amputate; *fig.* cut down.

amulette [amy'lɛt] *f* amulet, charm.

amusant, e [amy'zɑ̃, ~'zɑ̃:t] amusing, entertaining; funny; **amuse-gueule** F [amyz'gœl] *m/inv.* appetizer (*a. fig.*); cocktail snack; **amusement** [amyz'mɑ̃] *m* entertainment; amusement; pastime; **amuser** [amy'ze] (1a) *v/t.* amuse, entertain; put off, fool (*creditors*); s'~ *a.* have fun; *amusez-vous bien!* enjoy yourself; have a good time!; s'~ *de* make fun of, laugh at; **amusette** [~'zɛt] *f* plaything; diversion.

amygdale *anat.* [amig'dal] *f* tonsil; **amygdalite** [~da'lit] *f* tonsillitis.

an [ɑ̃] *m* year; *avoir dix* ~s be ten (years old); *bon* ~, *mal* ~ taking one year with another; *jour m de l'*~ New Year's day; *par* ~ a year, per annum; *tous les trois* ~s every three years.

anabaptiste [anaba'tist] *m* anabaptist.

anachorète [anakɔ'rɛt] *m* anchorite, recluse.

anachronisme [anakrɔ'nism] *m* anachronism.

anal, e, m/pl. -aux *anat.* [a'nal, ~'no] anal.

analgésique [analʒe'zik] *adj., a. su./m* analgesic.

analogie [analɔ'ʒi] *f* analogy; *par* ~ by analogy (with, *avec*); **analogue** [~'lɔg] **1.** *adj.* analogous (to, with *à*), similar (to, *à*); **2.** *su./m* analogue; parallel.

analphabète [analfa'bɛt] *adj., a. su.* illiterate; **analphabétisme** [~be'tism] *m* illiteracy.

analyse [ana'li:z] *f* analysis (*a. ⚗, ⚕, etc.*); précis, abstract; ✝ ~ *du marché* market analysis; 🖋 ~ *du sang* bloodtest; ~ *du travail* time and motion study; **analyser** [~li'ze] (1a) *v/t.* analyse (*a. ⚗, ⚕, fig.*); make a précis of; **analytique** [~li-'tik] analytic(al).

ananas [ana'na] *m* pineapple, ananas.

anarchie [anar'ʃi] *f* anarchy; *fig.* state of confusion; **anarchique** [~'ʃik] anarchic(al), anarchist(ic); **anarchisme** [~'ʃism] *m* anarchism; **anarchiste** [~'ʃist] *adj., a. su.* anarchist.

anathème [ana'tɛm] *m* anathema; curse.

anatomie [anatɔ'mi] *f* anatomy; F *fig. une belle* ~ a nice figure (*woman*); **anatomique** [~'mik] anatomical; **anatomiste** [~'mist] *m* anatomist; **anatomiser** [~mi'ze] (1a) *v/t.* anatomize.

ancêtre [ɑ̃'sɛtr] *m* ancestor, forefather.

anche ♪ [ɑ̃:ʃ] *f* reed.

anchois [ɑ̃'ʃwa] *m* anchovy.

ancien, -enne [ɑ̃'sjɛ̃, ~'sjɛn] **1.** *adj.* ancient, old; bygone, past; former, late; senior; ~(*ne*) *élève mf* old boy (girl); *univ. Am.* alumnus (alumna); ~ *combattant* ex-serviceman, *Am.* veteran; **2.** *su./m eccl.* elder; *les* ~s *pl.* the Ancients (Greeks and Romans); **anciennement** [ɑ̃sjɛn'mɑ̃] *adv.* in days of old, formerly; **ancienneté** [~'te] *f* oldness, antiquity; length of service; *avancer à l'*~ be promoted by seniority.

ancrage [ɑ̃'kra:ʒ] *m* anchoring, anchorage; *droit m d'*~ anchorage due; **ancre** [ɑ̃:kr] *f* ⚓ anchor; ⚓ brace; *être à l'*~ ride at anchor; **ancrer** [ɑ̃'kre] (1a) *v/t.* anchor; *fig.* fix firmly.

andalou, -ouse [ɑ̃da'lu, ~'lu:z] *adj., a. su.* ♀ Andalusian.

andouille [ɑ̃'du:j] *f* chitterlings *pl.*; *sl.* duffer, mug; **andouiller** *hunt.*

[ãdu'je] *m* tine; **andouillette** [ˌ'jɛt] *f* small chitterling sausage.

androgyne [ãdrɔ'ʒin] androgynous; **androphobe** [ˌ'fɔb] **1.** *adj.* man-hating; **2.** *su.* man-hater.

âne [ɑːn] *m* ass; donkey (*a. fig.*); ⊕ bench-vice; *pont m aux* ˌs child's play.

anéantir [aneã'tiːr] (2a) *v/t.* annihilate; destroy; reduce to nothing; *fig.* overwhelm; **anéantissement** [ˌtis'mã] *m* annihilation, destruction; prostration; dejection.

anecdote [anɛk'dɔt] *f* anecdote; **anecdotique** [ˌdɔ'tik] anecdotal.

anémie ✱ [ane'mi] *f* an(a)emia; **anémier** [ˌ'mje] (1a) *v/t.* render an(a)emic; F weaken; *s'*ˌ become an(a)emic; **anémique** [ˌ'mik] an(a)emic.

anémomètre [anemɔ'mɛtr] *m* anemometer, wind-ga(u)ge.

anémone ♀ [ane'mɔn] *f* anemone.

ânerie [ɑn'ri] *f* gross blunder, stupidity; F ignorance.

anéroïde [anerɔ'id] aneroid (*barometer*).

ânesse [ɑ'nɛs] *f* she-ass.

anesthésie ✱ [anɛste'zi] *f* an(a)esthesia; an(a)esthetic; **anesthésier** [ˌ'zje] (1a) *v/t.* an(a)esthetize; **anethésique** [ˌ'zik] *adj., a. su./m* an(a)esthetic.

anfractuosité [ãfraktɥozi'te] *f* irregularity; ˌs *pl.* winding(s *pl.*) *sg.*

ange [ãːʒ] *m* angel; ˌ *gardien* guardian angel; *fig.* être aux ˌs be in the seventh heaven, be overjoyed; *faiseuse f d'*ˌs baby-farmer; **angélique** [ãʒe'lik] **1.** *adj.* angelic; **2.** *su./f* ♀, *cuis.* angelica; ♀ *sauvage* cow-parsnip; **angélus** [ˌ'lys] *m* angelus (*a. bell*).

angine ✱ [ã'ʒin] *f* angina; tonsillitis; ˌ *de poitrine* angina pectoris; **angineux, -euse** [ãʒi'nø, ˌ'nøːz] anginal, anginous.

anglais, e [ã'glɛ, ˌ'glɛːz] **1.** *adj.* English; **2.** *su./m ling.* English; ♀ Englishman; *les* ♀ *m/pl.* the English; *su./f* ♀ Englishwoman.

angle [ã:gl] *m* angle; ⊕ edge; ⋏ ˌ *aigu (droit, obtus)* acute (right, obtuse) angle; ˌ *visuel* angle of vision.

anglican, e [ãgli'kã, ˌ'kan] **1.** *adj.* Anglican; *l'Église f* ˌe the Church of England; **2.** *su.* Anglican.

angliciser [ãglisi'ze] (1a) *v/t.* anglicize; *s'*ˌ become English; imitate the English; **anglicisme** [ˌ'sism] *m* Anglicism; English idiom; **angliciste** [ˌ'sist] *su.*, **anglicisant** *m*, e *f* [ˌsi'zã, ˌ'zãːt] student of *or* authority on English language and literature.

anglo... [ãglɔ] Anglo...; ˌ**manie** [ˌma'ni] *f* anglomania; ˌ**normand, e** [ˌnɔr'mã, ˌ'mãːd] *adj., a. su.* ♀ Anglo-Norman; ˌ**phile** [ˌ'fil] *adj., a. su.* Anglophil(e); ˌ**phobe** [ˌ'fɔb] **1.** *su.* Anglophobe; **2.** *adj.* Anglophobic; ˌ**phone** [ˌ'fɔn] **1.** *adj.* English-speaking; **2.** *su.* English-speaking person; ˌ**-saxon, -onne** [ˌsak'sõ, ˌ'sɔn] *adj., a. su.* ♀ Anglo-Saxon.

angoisse [ã'gwas] *f* anguish, agony; ✱ *a.* spasm; *poire f d'*ˌ choke-pear; **angoisser** [ãgwa'se] (1a) *v/t.* cause anguish to, distress.

angora [ãgɔ'ra] *adj. a. su.* angora.

anguille *icht.* [ã'giːj] *f* eel; ˌ *de mer* conger-eel; *il y a* ˌ *sous roche* there's more in it than meets the eye; **anguillière** [ãgi'jɛːr] *f* eel-pond; eel-pot; **anguillule** *zo.* [ˌ'jyl] *f* eel-worm.

angulaire [ãgy'lɛːr] angular; angle-...; *pierre f* ˌ corner-stone; **anguleux, -euse** [ˌ'lø, ˌ'løːz] angular; rugged.

anhélation [anela'sjõ] *f* shortness of breath; **anhéler** [ˌ'le] (1f) *v/i.* gasp, pant.

anhydre ⚗ [a'nidr] anhydrous.

anicroche [ani'krɔʃ] *f* hitch, difficulty; F snag.

ânier *m*, **-ère** *f* [ɑ'nje, ˌ'njɛːr] donkey-driver, ass-driver.

aniline ⚗ [ani'lin] *f* aniline; *colorant m d'*ˌ aniline dye.

animadversion [animadvɛr'sjõ] *f* animadversion, reproof.

animal, e, *m/pl.* **-aux** [ani'mal, 'mo] **1.** *su./m* animal; *fig.* dolt; **2.** *adj.* animal, brutish; *règne m* ˌ animal kingdom; **animalcule** [ˌmal'kyl] *m* animalcule; **animalier** [ˌma'lje] *m* painter *etc.* of animals; **animaliser** [animali'ze] (1a) *v/t.* animalize; *s'*ˌ become animalized; **animalité** [ˌ'te] *f* animality; animal kingdom.

animateur, -trice [anima'tœːr, ˌ'tris] **1.** *adj.* animating; **2.** *su.* emcee, *Br. a.* compère; organizer; *fig.* driving force (*person*); **animation** [~'sjɔ̃] *f* animation; coming *or* bringing to life; **animé, e** [ani'me] spirited, lively; ✝ brisk (*market*); *cin.* dessins *m/pl.* ~s animated cartoons; **animer** [~] (1a) *v/t.* animate; liven up; impel, prompt, actuate; light up (*the features*).

animosité [animozi'te] *f* animosity, ranco(u)r, spite.

anis ♀ [a'ni] anise; aniseed; **aniser** [ani'ze] (1a) *v/t.* flavo(u)r with aniseed.

ankylose ✖ [ãki'lo:z] *f* anchylosis.

annal, e [an'nal] 1. *adj.* yearly, lasting for one year; 2. *su./f:* ~es *pl.* annals, records.

anneau [a'no] *m* ring (*a.* ⊕, *sp.*); ⊕ chain: link; hair: ringlet; ~ brisé split ring.

année [a'ne] *f* year; ~ bissextile leap year; ~ civile natural year; ~ scolaire school year, academic year, session; **~-lumière**, *pl.* **~s-lumière** [~ly-'mjɛːr] *f* light year.

anneler [an'le] (1c) *v/t.* curl (*the hair*); ring (*a pig*).

annexe [an'nɛks] 1. *su./f* annex(e), outbuilding; *document*: schedule, supplement; appendix; *letter*: enclosure; *state*: dependency; 2. *adj.* annexed; école *f* ~ demonstration school; lettre *f* ~ covering letter; **annexer** [annɛk'se] (1a) *v/t.* annex; **annexion** [~'sjɔ̃] *f* annexation.

annihiler [annii'le] (1a) *v/t.* annihilate, destroy; ⚖ annul.

anniversaire [anivɛr'sɛːr] 1. *adj.* anniversary; 2. *su./m* birthday; anniversary; ~ de mariage wedding anniversary; gâteau *m* d'~ birthday cake.

annonce [a'nɔ̃:s] *f* announcement, notice; advertisement; *cards*: call; *fig.* presage, sign; ~s *pl.* encartées inset (advertisements) *sg.*; *journ.* petites ~s *pl.* classified adds; **annoncer** [anɔ̃'se] (1k) *v/t.* announce; foretell; *fig.* indicate; s'~ promise (*well, ill, etc.*); **annonceur** [~'sœːr] *m* advertizer; **Annonciation** [~sja'sjɔ̃] *f:* l'~ the Annunciation; fête *f* de l'~ Lady Day.

annotateur *m*, **-trice** *f* [anɔta'tœːr, ~'tris] annotator, commentator; **annotation** [~ta'sjɔ̃] *f* annotating; note, annotation; ✝ inventory of goods attached; **annoter** [~'te] (1a) *v/t.* annotate.

annuaire [a'nɥɛːr] *m* year-book, annual; almanac; *teleph.* directory; ⚹ militaire Army List; **annuel, -elle** [a'nɥɛl] annual, yearly; ♀ plante *f* ~elle annual; **annuité** [anɥi'te] *f* annual instalment; (terminable) annuity.

annulable [any'labl] that can be cancelled *or* annulled; ⚖ voidable; defeasible.

annulaire [any'lɛːr] 1. *adj.* ringlike, annular; 2. *su./m* (*a.* doigt *m* ~) ring-finger.

annulation [anyla'sjɔ̃] *f* annulment; ⚖ judgment: setting aside; *sentence*: quashing; **annuler** [~'le] (1a) *v/t.* annul; cancel (*a cheque, a contract*); set aside (*a judgment, a will*); quash (*a sentence*).

anoblir [anɔ'bliːr] (2a) *v/t.* ennoble; raise to the peerage.

anode ⚡ [a'nɔd] *f* anode.

anodin, e [anɔ'dɛ̃, ~'din] 1. *adj.* anodyne; *fig.* harmless, mild; 2. *su./m* analgesic, anodyne.

anomalie [anɔma'li] *f* anomaly.

ânon *zo.* [ɑ'nɔ̃] *m* young ass, ass's foal; F ass; **ânonner** [anɔ'ne] (1a) *v/t.* stumble through; mumble through; drone through.

anonymat [anɔni'ma] *m* anonymity; **anonyme** [~'nim] 1. *adj.* anonymous; unnamed; société *f* ~ limited (-liability) company, *abbr.* Ltd., *Am.* Inc. Ltd.; 2. *su./m* anonymous writer; anonymity.

anorak [anɔ'rak] *m* anorak.

anorexie ✖ [anɔrɛk'si] *f* anorexia, loss of appetite; **anorexigène** [anɔrɛksi'ʒɛn] appetite suppressant.

anormal, e, *m/pl.* **-aux** [anɔr'mal, ~'mo] abnormal, irregular.

anse [ãːs] *f* cup etc.: handle; ear; rope: loop; geog. cove, small bay.

antagonisme [ãtagɔ'nism] *m* antagonism; **antagoniste** [~'nist] 1. *su./m* antagonist, opponent; 2. *adj.* antagonistic, opposed.

antalgique [ãtal'ʒik] *adj.*, *a.* *su./m* antalgic; anodyne.

antan [ã'tã] *adv.:* d'~ of yester year.

antarctique [ãtark'tik] 1. *adj.* antarctic; 2. *su./m* l'⚹ the Antarctic.

anté... [ãte] pre..., ante...

antébois ⚹ [ãte'bwa] *m* chair-rail.

antécédent [ãtese'dã, ~'dã:t] 1. *adj.* antecedent, preceding; 2. *su./m* ♀, ♪, gramm. antecedent;

~s *pl.* (past) records, antecedents; *sans* **~s** *judiciaires* with a clean record, not known to the police.

antéchrist [ãte'krist] *m* Antichrist.

antédiluvien, -enne [ãtedily'vjɛ̃, ~'vjɛn] antediluvian (*a. fig.*).

antenne [ã'tɛn] *f zo.* antenna, F feeler; ⚓ lateen yard; *radio*: aerial; **~** *à cadre* frame aerial; **~** *dirigée* directional aerial; **~** *extérieure* outdoor aerial.

antérieur, e [ãte'rjœ:r] anterior, prior, previous (to, *à*).

anthère ♀ [ã'tɛ:r] *f* anther.

anthologie [ãtɔlɔ'ʒi] *f* anthology.

anthracite [ãtra'sit] *m* anthracite.

anthrax ✿ [ã'traks] *m* anthrax.

anthropo... [ãtrɔpɔ] anthropo...; **~ïde** [~'id] *adj.*, *a. su./m* anthropoid; **~logie** [~lɔ'ʒi] *f* anthropology; **~logue** [~'lɔg] *m* anthropologist; **~morphe** [~'mɔrf] **1.** *adj.* anthropomorphous; **2.** *su./m zo.* anthropoid (ape); **~phage** [~'fa:ʒ] **1.** *su./m* cannibal; **2.** *adj.* cannibalistic.

anti... [ãti] anti...; ante...; **~aérien, -enne** [~ae'rjɛ̃, ~'rjɛn] anti-aircraft (*defence etc.*); **~biotique** ✿ [~bjɔ'tik] *m* antibiotic; **~brouillard** *mot.* [~bru'ja:r] *adj.*, *a. su./m/inv.* demister; **~chambre** [~'ʃã:br] *f* anteroom, waiting-room; *faire* **~** *chez* wait on, dance attendance on; **~char** [~'ʃa:r] *adj.* anti-tank (*missile*); **~choc** [~'ʃɔk] *adj./inv.* shockproof; **~chrétien, -enne** [~kre'tjɛ̃, ~'tjɛn] anti-christian.

anticipation [ãtisipa'sjɔ̃] *f* anticipation; encroachment (*on rights*); *par* **~** in advance; **~** *de paiement* advance payment; *littérature d'*~ science fiction; *roman d'*~ science fiction novel; **anticiper** [~'pe] (1a) *v/t.* anticipate; foresee; *v/i.:* **~** *sur* anticipate.

anti...: **~clérical, e,** *m/pl.* **-aux** [ãtikleri'kal, ~'ko] *adj.* anticlerical; **~conceptionnel, -elle** [~kɔ̃sɛpsjɔ-'nɛl] contraceptive; **~corps** [~'kɔ:r] *m* anti-body; **~dater** [~da'te] (1a) *v/t.* antedate; **~dépresseur** [~depre'sœ:r] antidepressant; **~dérapant, e** *mot.* [~dera'pɑ̃, ~'pɑ:t] **1.** *adj.* non-skid; **2.** *su./m* non-skid tyre; **~détonant, e** *mot.* [~detɔ'nɑ̃, ~'nɑ:t] antiknock; **~dote** ✿ [~'dɔt] *m* antidote (to, for, against *à, de*);

~éblouissant, e [~eblui'sã, ~'sãt] anti-dazzle.

antienne [ã'tjɛn] *f* antiphon; anthem; *fig. chanter toujours la même* **~** be always harping on the same string.

anti...: **~fading** [ãtifa'diŋ] *m radio*: (*a. dispositif m* ~) automatic volume control; **~gel** ⊕ [~'ʒɛl] *m* antifreeze; **~halo** *phot.* [~'lo] **1.** *adj./inv.* non-halation..., backing; **2.** *su./m* backing.

antilope *zo.* [ãti'lɔp] *f* antelope.

anti...: **~parasite** [~para'zit] *m radio*: suppressor; **~pathie** [~pa'ti] *f* antipathy (against, to *contre*), aversion (to, *contre*); **~pathique** [~pa'tik] disagreeable; **~pode** [~'pɔd] *m* antipode; *fig. the* very opposite; **~polluant, e** [~pɔlɥ'ã, ~'ãt] non-polluting; **~pollution** [~pɔly'sjɔ̃] *f* antipollution; **~pyrine** ✿ [~pi'rin] *f* antipyrin.

antiquaille [ãti'ka:j] *f* lumber; fog(e)y, F old stuff, chunk; **antiquaire** [~'kɛ:r] *m* antiquary, antique dealer; second-hand bookseller; **antique** [ã'tik] ancient; antique; antiquated; **antiquité** [ãtiki'te] *f* antiquity; **~s** *pl.* antiques.

anti...: **~rides** [ãti'rid] **1.** *adj.* anti-wrinkle; **2.** *su./m* anti-wrinkle cream or lotion; **~rouille** ⊕ [~'ru:j] *m* anti-rust (composition); **~sémite** [~se-'mit] **1.** *adj.* anti-Semitic; **2.** *su.* anti-Semite; **~septique** ✿ [~sɛp'tik] *adj.*, *a. su./m* antiseptic; **~social, e,** *m/pl.* **-aux** [~sɔ'sjal, ~'sjo] antisocial; **~solaire** [~sɔ'lɛ:r]: *crème f* ~ sun cream; **~spasmodique** ✿ [~spasmɔ'dik] antispasmodic; **~tétanique** ✿ [~teta'nik] antitetanic; **~thèse** [~'tɛ:z] *f* antithesis; direct contrary; **~tuberculeux, -euse** ✿ [~tybɛrky'lø, ~'lø:z] antitubercular; **~vol** [~'vɔl] *adj.* (*a. su./m*) anti-theft (device).

antonyme [ãtɔ'nim] **1.** *adj.* antonymous; **2.** *su./m* antonym.

antre [ã:tr] *m* cave; den, lair.

anurie ✿ [any'ri] *f* anuresis.

anus *anat.* [a'nys] *m* anus.

anxiété [ãksje'te] *f* anxiety, concern; **anxieux, -euse** [~'sjø, ~'sjø:z] anxious, uneasy; eager (to, *de*).

aorte *anat.* [a'ɔrt] *f* aorta.   [ripe.\

août [u] *m* August; **aoûté, e** [u'te]∫ (*usu. in Paris*)

apache [a'paʃ] *m* (*usu. in Paris*) hooligan, tough, hoodlum.

apaisement [apɛz'mɑ̃] *m* appease-
ment; quieting, calming; **apaiser**
[apɛ'ze] (1b) *v/t.* appease (*a. one's
hunger*); calm, pacify, soothe;
quench (*one's thirst*); lull (*a storm*);
s'~ calm down (*person*); die down.

apanage [apa'na:ʒ] *m* ap(p)anage;
prerogative, privilege; exclusive
right (to, *de*); **apanager** [~na'ʒe]
(1l) *v/t.* endow with an ap(p)anage;
apanagiste [~na'ʒist] **1.** *adj.* having
an ap(p)anage; **2.** *su.* ap(p)anagist.

aparté [apar'te] *m thea.* aside; F private conversation; en ~ aside, in a
stage-whisper.

apathie [apa'ti] *f* apathy, listlessness;
apathique [~'tik] apathetic, listless.

apatride [apa'trid] **1.** *su.* stateless
person; **2.** *adj.* stateless.

apepsie ⚕ [apɛp'si] *f* dyspepsia, indigestion.

apercevable [apɛrsə'vabl] perceivable, perceptible; **apercevoir** [~sə-
'vwa:r] (3a) *v/t.* see; s'~ de notice;
realize; become aware of; **aperçu**
[~'sy] *m* glimpse; general idea; rough
estimate.

apéritif, -ve [aperi'tif, ~'ti:v] **1.** *adj.*
appetizing; **2.** *su./m* appetizer; aperitif; *l'heure f de l'*~ cocktail time.

apéro F [ape'ro] *m* aperitif.

apesanteur [apəzɑ̃'tœ:r] *f* weight-
lessness; en état d'~ weightless.

à-peu-près [apø'prɛ] *m* approximation.

apeuré, e [apœ're] frightened.

aphasie ⚕ [afa'zi] *f* aphasia; **apha-
sique** ⚕ [~'zik] aphasic, speechless.

aphone [a'fɔn] voiceless.

aphorisme [afɔ'rism] *m* aphorism.

aphte ⚕ [aft] *m* aphtha; **aphteux,
-euse** *vet.*, ⚕ [af'tø, ~'tø:z] *adj.:*
fièvre f ~euse foot-and-mouth
disease.

apical, e, *m/pl.* -aux ♉, ♀, *gramm.*
[api'kal, ~'ko] apical.

apicole [api'kɔl] apiarian; **apiculteur** [apikyl'tœ:r] *m* beekeeper,
apiarist; **apiculture** [~'ty:r] *f*
beekeeping.

apitoiement [apitwa'mɑ̃] *m* pity,
compassion; ~ sur soi-même self-
pity; **apitoyer** [~'je] (1h) *v/t.* move
(to pity); s'~ sur feel pity for (*s.o.*);
bewail, lament (*s.th.*).

aplanir [apla'ni:r] (2a) *v/t.* level;
smooth; plane; *fig.* remove, smooth
(away).

aplatir [apla'ti:r] (2a) *v/t.* make flat,
flatten; ⊕ clench (*a rivet*); *fig.* crush;
s'~ flatten o.s.; *fig.* gravel (before,
devant).

aplomb [a'plɔ̃] *m* perpendicularity;
fig. balance, equilibrium; steadiness; coolness; self-possession; *pej.*
cheek; *d'*~ vertical(ly *adv.*), upright,
plumb; steady (steadily *adv.*); F well,
in good shape; △ *prendre l'*~ take the
plumb.

apo... [apɔ] apo...; ~**calypse** [~ka-
'lips] *f* apocalypse; *l'*♑ the Book of
Revelation; ~**calyptique** [~kalip-
'tik] apocalyptic; *fig.* obscure
(*style*); ~**cryphe** [~'krif] **1.** *adj.* apoc-
ryphal; **2.** *su./m:* ~s *pl.* the Apoc-
rypha. [footless; **2.** *su./m* apod.\
apode *zo.* [a'pɔd] **1.** *adj.* apodal,/
apo...: ~**dictique** [apɔdik'tik] apo-
dictic, indisputable; ~**gée** [~'ʒe] *m*
astr. apogee; *fig.* height, zenith,
culminating point; ~**logie** [~lɔ'ʒi] *f*
apologia; vindication; ~**logiste**
[~lɔ'ʒist] *m* apologist; ~**plexie** ⚕
[~plɛk'si] *f* apoplexy; ~**stasie**
[~sta'zi] *f* apostasy; *pol.* F ratting;
~**stasier** [~sta'zje] (1o) *v/t.* apostatize from; *v/i.* apostatize; renounce
one's faith *or* principles *or* party;
~**stat, e** [~s'ta, ~s'tat] *adj., a. su.*
apostate, F turncoat.

apostille [apɔs'tij] *f* marginal recommendation; ⚓ entry (*in log*); †
apostil, foot-note, side-note.

apostolat [apɔstɔ'la] *m* apostolate,
apostleship; **apostolique** [~'lik]
apostolic.

apostrophe [apɔs'trɔf] *f rhetoric, a.
gramm.* apostrophe; rude remark;
apostropher [~trɔ'fe] (1a) *v/t.*
address (*s.o.*) sharply.

apothéose [apɔte'o:z] *f* apotheosis;
fig. a. pinnacle; *thea.* grand finale.

apothicaire [apɔti'kɛ:r] *m: compte m
d'*~ exorbitant bill.

apôtre [a'po:tr] *m* apostle (*a. fig.*);
faire le bon ~ play the saint.

apparaître [apa'rɛ:tr] (4k) *v/i.* appear; come into sight; become
evident.

apparat [apa'ra] *m* pomp, show.

appareil [apa'rɛ:j] *m* apparatus (*a.
fig.,* ⚕, ⚙ᵐ); ⚕ *wound:* dressing;
△ bond; △ *stones:* height; *phot.*
camera; ⊕ machinery; ⊕ device;
teleph. etc. instrument; *radio:* set;
pomp, display; *anat.* ~ *digestif*

digestive system; *phot.* ~ *de petit
format* miniature camera; ~ *de projection* projector; *teleph. qui est à
l'*~*?* who is speaking?; **appareillage** [ˌrɛˈjaːʒ] *m* ⚓ getting under
way; installation; ⚒ bonding; ⚒
stones: drafting; ⚓ *etc.* equipment;
⊕ fixture; ⊕ plant.

appareillement [aparɛjˈmɑ] *m*
matching (up); pairing.

appareiller[1] [apareˈje] (1a) *v/t.*
match (up); pair.

appareiller[2] [apareˈje] (1a) *v/t.* install; ⚒ bond; ⚓ draft; ⚓ trim
(*a sail*); *v/i.* ⚓ get under way;

appareilleur [~ˈjœːr] *m* fitter,
trimmer; ⚒ house carpenter; ⚒
foreman mason.

apparemment [aparaˈmɑ̃] *adv. of
apparent;* **apparence** [~ˈrɑ̃ːs] *f* appearance, semblance; *en* ~ out-
wardly; *sauver les* ~*s* save one's
face; **apparent, e** [~ˈrɑ̃, ~ˈrɑ̃ːt]
apparent; conspicuous.

apparenter [aparɑ̃ˈte] (1a) *v/t.: s'*~
à marry into (*the nobility etc.*).

apparier [apaˈrje] (1o) *v/t.* pair (off);
mate.

appariteur [apariˈtœːr] *m* 𝕫𝕫 ap-
paritor, usher; *univ.* laboratory
assistant.

apparition [apariˈsjɔ̃] *f* appearance;
apparition; spectre; vision.

apparoir 𝕫𝕫[apaˈrwaːr] (3b) *v/impers.*
appear (from, *de;* that, *que*).

appartement [apartˈmɑ̃] *m* flat, *Am.*
apartment.

appartenance [apartəˈnɑ̃ːs] *f:* ~ *à*
belonging to; membership of; **appartenant, e** [~ˈnɑ̃, ~ˈnɑ̃ːt] belonging (to, *à*); **appartenir** [~ˈniːr] (2h)
v/i. belong (to, *à*); *il appartient à q. de
faire qch.* it is s.o.'s business *or* it rests
with s.o. to do s.th.; *v/t.: s'*~ be one's
own master.

appas [aˈpɑ] *m/pl.* charms.

appât [aˈpɑ] *m* bait; lure; *poultry:*
soft food; *mordre à l'*~ take the bait;
appâter [apɑˈte] (1a) *v/t.* lure, entice; cram (*poultry*).

appauvrir [apoˈvriːr] (2a) *v/t.* im-
poverish; *s'*~ become impoverished;
grow poor(er); **appauvrissement**
[~vrisˈmɑ̃] *m* impoverishment; deterioration; ~ *du sang* impoverished
blood.

appeau [aˈpo] *m* decoy(-bird); bird-
call.

appel [aˈpɛl] *m* call; appeal (*a.* 𝕫𝕫); ✗
roll-call, call-over, muster; ⊕~ *d'air*
indraught, intake of air; *teleph.* ~
local (interurbain) local call (trunk
call); ~ *téléphonique* (tele)phone call;
𝕫𝕫 *cour f d'*~ Court of Appeal; *faire* ~ *à*
have recourse to; ✗ *ordre m d'*~
induction order; **appeler** [apˈle]
(1c) *v/t.* call; call to; call up; send
for; ~ *l'attention de q. sur qch.* call
s.o.'s attention to s.th.; *s'*~ be called;
v/i.: à d'un jugement appeal against a
sentence; *en* ~ *à* appeal to; **appellation** [apɛlaˈsjɔ̃] *f* appellation; ✝ ~
d'origine indication of origin.

appendice [apɛ̃ˈdis] *m* appendix (*a.
✿, anat.*); ⚒ annex(e); ✗ tail; **appendicite** ✗ [~diˈsit] *f* appendicitis.

appentis [apɑ̃ˈti] *m* lean-to (roof);
penthouse; outhouse.

appert [aˈpɛːr] *3rd p. sg. pres. of
apparoir.*

appesantir [apzɑ̃ˈtiːr] (2a) *v/t.*
make heavy; weigh down; dull; *s'*~
become heavy; *s'*~ *sur* dwell upon;
appesantissement [~tisˈmɑ̃] *m* increase in heaviness *or* dullness.

appétence [apeˈtɑ̃ːs] *f* appetency,
craving (for, of, after *pour*).

appétissant, e [apetiˈsɑ̃, ~ˈsɑ̃ːt] appetizing, tempting (*a. fig.*); **appétit**
[~ˈti] *m* appetite; desire; craving;
ouvrir l'~ give an edge to the appetite.

applaudir [aploˈdiːr] (2a) *v/i.* approve (s.th., *à qch.*); *v/t.* applaud;
clap; *s'*~ *de* congratulate o.s. on;
applaudissements [~disˈmɑ̃] *m/pl.*
applause *sg.*; commendation *sg.*

applicable [apliˈkabl] applicable (to,
à); that can be applied; **application** [~kaˈsjɔ̃] *f* application; *fig.*
diligence; *broderie f* ~ appliqué
work; **applique** [aˈplik] *f* inlaid
work, inlaying; application; applied ornament; (wall-)bracket; ap-
pliqué, e [apliˈke] diligent; ⚒ *etc.*
applied; **appliquer** [~] (1m) *v/t.*
apply; ⛨ *une gifle à q.* fetch s.o.
one; *fig. s'*~ *à* work hard at; be bent
on.

appoint [aˈpwɛ̃] *m* contribution;
added portion; help, support; (*a.
monnaie f d'*~) odd money, (right)
change; *d'*~ secondary; extra; *faire
l'*~ give the right change; **appointements** [apwɛ̃tˈmɑ̃] *m/pl.* emoluments, salary *sg.*

appointer[1] [apwɛ̃'te] (1a) *v/t.* put on a salary (basis).

appointer[2] ⊕ [~] (1a) *v/t.* sharpen.

appontement ⚓ [apõt'mã] *m* gang-plank; wharf; landing-stage; **apponter** [apõ'te] (1a) *v/i.* land on an aircraft carrier.

apport [a'pɔːr] *m* ⚖ contributed property; ✝ contribution; ✝ initial share; ⚹ bringing up; ✝ *capital m d'~* initial capital; **apporter** [apɔr'te] (1a) *v/t.* bring; exercise (*care*); supply, provide; produce; *~ du retard à* be slow in; *~ du zèle à* show zeal in.

apposer [apo'ze] (1a) *v/t.* affix (to, *à*); put; set (*a seal*); **apposition** [~zi'sjõ] *f* affixing; *gramm.* apposition.

appréciable [apre'sjabl] appreciable; **appréciation** [~sja'sjõ] *f* valuation; estimate; appreciation; **apprécier** [~'sje] (1a) *v/t.* value; estimate; appreciate.

appréhender [apreã'de] (1a) *v/t.* apprehend; dread; seize; **appréhension** [~'sjõ] *f* apprehension; ⚖ arrest.

apprenant *m*, **e** *f* [aprə'nã, ~'nãt] learner, student.

apprendre [a'prãːdr] (4aa) *v/t.* learn; teach (s.o. s.th., *qch. à q.*); *~ à q. à faire qch.* teach s.o. (how) to do s.th.; *~ par cœur* learn by heart.

apprenti *m*, **e** *f* aprã'ti] apprentice; learner; ⚖ *etc.* articled clerk; **apprentissage** [~ti'saːʒ] *m* apprenticeship; ⚖ *etc.* articles *pl.*

apprêt [a'prɛ] *m* preparation; ⊕ finishing; *cuis.* dressing, seasoning; *paint.* priming, size; *fig.* affectation; **apprêtage** [aprɛ'taːʒ] *m* finishing; sizing; **apprêté, e** [~'te] affected; **apprêter** [~'te] (1a) *v/t.* prepare; ⊕ finish; size, prime; starch; *s'~* get ready; be imminent; dress; **apprêteur** *m*, **-euse** *f* [~'tœːr, ~'tøːz] finisher, dresser.

apprivoiser [aprivwa'ze] (1a) *v/t.* tame (*a. fig.*); *fig.* make sociable.

approbateur, -trice [aprɔba'tœːr, ~'tris] **1.** *adj.* approving; **2.** *su.* approver; **approbatif, -ive** [~'tif, ~'tiːv] approving; **approbation** [~'sjõ] *f* approbation, approval; ✝ certifying.

approchant, e ✝ [aprɔ'ʃã, ~'ʃãːt] **1.** *adj.: ~ de* approximating to; **2.** *appro-*

chant adv., a. prp. nearly; **approche** [a'prɔʃ] *f* approach; *les ~s de* the immediate surroundings of (*a town etc.*); **approcher** [aprɔ'ʃe] (1a) *v/t.* bring (*s.th.*) near; *s'~ de* draw *or* come near (to); *v/i.* approach; draw *or* come near.

approfondir [aprɔfõ'diːr] (2a) *v/t.* deepen; *fig.* go deeper into; investigate thoroughly; **approfondissement** [~dis'mã] *m* deepening; *fig.* thorough investigation.

appropriation [aprɔpria'sjõ] *f* appropriation; adaptation (to, *à*); embezzlement; allocation; **approprier** [~pri'e] (1o) *v/t.* appropriate; adapt (to, *à*); *s'~ à* adapt o.s. to; fall in with.

approuver [apru've] (1a) *v/t.* approve (of); consent to; agree to; confirm (*an appointment*); authorize.

approvisionnement [aprɔvizjɔn-'mã] *m* provisioning, supply(ing); stock(ing); **approvisionner** [~zjɔ-'ne] (1a) *v/t.* supply (with, *en*); provision, victual; *s'~* lay in stores.

approximatif, -ve [aprɔksima'tif, ~'tiːv] approximate; **approximation** [~'sjõ] *f* approximation.

appui [a'pɥi] *m* support (*a. fig.*); rest, prop, stay; *à l'~ in* support of this; *à l'~ de* in support of; *~(e)-livres, pl. ~s-livres, ~e-livres* [apɥi'liːvr] *m* book-rest; *~(e)-tête, pl. ~s-tête* [~'tɛːt] *m* headrest; *mot.* head-restraint; **appuyer** [apɥi'je] (1h) *v/t.* support; press; lean, rest (against, *contre*); *v/i.: ~ sur* rest on; press, push (*a button etc.*), press down; *fig.* emphasize, stress; *~ sur la* (*or ~ à*) *droite* bear to the right; *s'~ sur* lean, rest on *or* against; *fig.* rely on.

âpre [ɑːpr] rough, harsh; biting; keen; *~ à* eager for; ruthless at; *~ au gain* grasping, greedy.

après [a'prɛ] **1.** *prp. space, time:* after; behind; *idea of attack:* at, on to; *~ vous, Madame* after you, Madam; *~ quoi* after which; thereupon; *~ tout* after all; *~ Jésus-Christ* after Christ; *être toujours ~ q.* be always nagging at s.o.; *~ avoir lu ce livre* after reading this book; *d'~* according to; *~ que* after, when; **2.** *adv.* after(wards), later; next; *la semaine d'~* the following week; *une semaine d'~* one week later; *~-demain* [aprɛdə'mɛ̃] *adv.*

the day after tomorrow; ~-**guerre** [~'gɛːr] *m or f* post-war period; ~-**midi** [~mi'di] *m/inv.* afternoon; ~-**rasage** [~ra'zaːʒ] *adj.*, *a. su./m/inv.* after-shave; ~-**vente** [~'vãːt]: *service* *m* ~ after-sales service.

âpreté [ɑprə'te] *f* roughness; harshness; sharpness; bitterness; keenness.

à-propos [aprɔ'po] *m* aptness, suitability; opportuneness.

apte [apt] fit(ted) (to, for *à*); apt; **aptitude** [apti'tyd] *f* aptitude; fitness; ⚖ capacity, qualification; ✕ ~s *pl. physiques* physique *sg.*; *mot.* ~ *à conduire* fitness to drive.

apurement ✝ [apyr'mã] *m* audit (-ing); **apurer** [apy're] (1a) *v/t.* audit, pass; discharge (*a liability*).

aquafortiste [akwafɔr'tist] *su.* etcher; **aquaplane** [~'plan] *m* surfboard; **aquaplaning** *mot.* [~pla'niŋ] *m* aquaplaning; **aquarelle** [~'rɛl] *f* aquarelle, water-colo(u)r; **aquarelliste** [~rɛ'list] *su.* aquarellist, water-colo(u)rist; **aquarium** [~'rjɔm] *m* aquarium; **aquatique** [~'tik] aquatic; marshy (*land*).

aqueduc [ak'dyk] *m* aqueduct (*a. anat.*); culvert; **aqueux, -euse** [a'kø, ~'køːz] watery.

aquilin, e [aki'lɛ̃, ~'lin] aquiline; *nez m* ~ Roman nose.

aquilon [aki'lɔ̃] *m* north wind.

arabe [a'rab] **1.** *adj.* Arabian; Arab; Arabic; *chiffre m* ~ Arabic numeral; **2.** *su.* ♀ Arab; *su./m ling.* Arabic; *horse:* Arab; *fig.* Shylock, usurer.

arabesque [ara'bɛsk] *adj.*, *a. su./f* arabesque.

arabique [ara'bik] Arabic; Arabian; *gomme f* ~ gum arabic; *geog.* le *golfe* ♀ the Arabian gulf.

arable [a'rabl] arable (*land*).

arachide ♀ [ara'ʃid] *f* peanut, ground-nut.

araignée [arɛ'ɲe] *f zo.* spider; ⊕ grapnel; ⚓ clew; *vehicle:* buggy; *sl. avoir une* ~ *au plafond* have bats in the belfry; *fig. pattes f/pl. d'*~ long thin fingers; scrawl *sg.*; ⊕ grease-channels; *toile f d'*~ cobweb; spider's web.

aratoire [ara'twaːr] farming, agricultural.

arbalète [arba'lɛt] *f* cross-bow; **arbalétrier** [~letri'e] *m* cross-bowman; ⚼ principal rafter.

arbitrage [arbi'traːʒ] *m* arbitration; ✝ arbitrage; *conseil m d'*~ conciliation board; **arbitraire** [~'trɛːr] arbitrary; **arbitre** [ar'bitr] *m* ✝ arbitrator; referee (*a. sp.*); *phls: libre* ~ free will; **arbitrer** [~bi'tre] (1a) *v/t.* arbitrate; *sp.* referee.

arborer [arbɔ're] (1a) *v/t.* hoist (*a flag*); *fig.* wear, display; sport (*a garment*); **arborescence** ♀ [~rɛ'sãːs] *f* arborescence; **arborescent, e** ♀ [~rɛ'sã, ~'sãːt] arborescent; **arboriculteur** ✒ [~rikyl'tœːr] *m* arboriculturist, nurseryman; **arboriculture** ✒ [~rikyl'tyːr] *f* arboriculture.

arbre [arbr] *m* tree; ⊕ spindle, shaft, axle; ⚓ mast; arbor; ⊕ ~ *à cames* cam-shaft; ⊕ ~ *de transmission* propeller shaft; ~ *généalogique* genealogical tree; ~ *manivelle* crankshaft; ⊕ ~ *primaire* driving shaft; **arbrisseau** [~bri'so] *m* sapling; shrub.

arbuste ♀ [ar'byst] *m* bush, shrub.

arc [ark] *m* bow; ⚼ arch; ⌒, ⊕ arc; ~ *en ogive* ogival arch; ~ *plein cintre* semi-circular arch; ⚼ *avoir de l'*~ sag; ✦ *lampe f à* ~ arc-lamp.

arcade [ar'kad] *f* archway; ⊕ arch; *spectacles:* bridge; ~s *pl.* arcade *sg.*

arcanes [ar'kan] *m/pl.* arcana, mysteries.

arc-boutant, *pl.* **arcs-boutant** [arkbu'tã] *m* ⚼ flying buttress; ⌒, ⊕ stay (*a. fig.*), strut; **arc-bouter** [~'te] (1a) *v/t.* buttress; shore up.

arceau [ar'so] *m* hoop; arch.

arc-en-ciel, *pl.* **arcs-en-ciel** [arkã'sjɛl] *m* rainbow.

archaïque [arka'ik] archaic; **archaïsme** [~'ism] *m* archaism.

archange [ar'kãːʒ] *m* archangel.

arche¹ [arʃ] *f* arch; hoop.

arche² *bibl.* [~] *f* Ark; ~ *d'alliance* Ark of the Covenant.

archéologie [arkeɔlɔ'ʒi] *f* arch(a)eology; **archéologue** [~'lɔg] *m* arch(a)eologist.

archer [ar'ʃe] *m* archer; **archet** ♪, ⊕ [~'ʃɛ] *m* bow.

archétype [arke'tip] **1.** *adj.* archetypal; **2.** *su./m* archetype, prototype.

archevêché [arʃəve'ʃe] *m* archbishopric, archdiocese; archbishop's palace; **archevêque** [~'vɛk] *m* archbishop.

archi... [arʃi] arch...; extremely; to the hilt; ~**bondé, e** [~bɔ̃'de],

~**comble** [~'kɔ̃:bl] packed (full); ~**duc** [~'dyk] *m* archduke.

archipel *geog.* [arʃi'pɛl] *m* archipelago.

architecte [arʃi'tɛkt] *m* architect; ~ *paysagiste* landscape gardener; **architecture** [~tɛk'ty:r] *f* architecture; ~ *de paysage* landscape gardening *or* design.

archives [ar'ʃi:v] *f/pl.* archives, records; **archiviste** [~ʃi'vist] *su.* archivist; ✝ filing clerk.

arçon [ar'sɔ̃] *m* saddle-bow; *vider les* ~*s* be unhorsed; *fig.* become embarrassed.

arctique [ark'tik] Arctic.

ardemment [arda'mã] *adv. of ardent*; **ardent, e** [~'dã, ~'dã:t] hot, burning (*a.* ⚗), scorching; *fig.* ardent, fervent, eager; *fig.* être sur des charbons ~*s* be on tenterhooks; **ardeur** [~'dœ:r] *f* heat; *fig.* ardo(u)r; eagerness; *horse:* mettle; ⚗ ~ *d'estomac* heartburn.

ardillon [ardi'jɔ̃] *m* buckle: tongue, catch; *typ.* pin.

ardoise [ar'dwa:z] *f* slate; **ardoisé, e** [ardwa'ze] slate-colo(u)red; **ardoisière** [~'zjɛ:r] *f* slate-quarry.

ardu, e [ar'dy] steep, abrupt; arduous; difficult.

are [a:r] *m* are.

arène [a'rɛn] *f* arena; *poet.* sand.

aréole [are'ɔl] *f* ♀, ⚗, *anat.* areola; *meteor.* nimbus, halo.

arête [a'rɛt] *f icht.* (fish-)bone; ⊕, *mount., etc.* edge; *mount.* crest, ridge; ⚠, ⊕, *etc.* chamfer; beading; ♀ awn, beard; à ~*s vives* sharp-edged.

argent [ar'ʒã] *m* silver; money; ⌂ argent; ~ *comptant* cash; ~ *de poche* pocket-money; ~ *en caisse* cash in hand; ~ *liquide* ready money; *en avoir pour son* ~ have one's money's worth; *être à court d'*~ be short of money; **argentan** [arʒã'tã] *m* nickel *or* German silver; **argenté, e** [~'te] silver(ed); silvery; silver-plated; **argenter** [~'te] (1a) *v/t.* silver; **argenterie** [~'tri] *f* (silver-)plate.

argentin¹, e [arʒã'tɛ̃, ~'tin] silvery.

argentin², e [~] *adj., a. su.* ♀ Argentine.

argenture [arʒã'ty:r] *f* mirror: silvering; silver-plating.

argile [ar'ʒil] *f* clay; ~ *réfractaire*

fire-clay; **argileux, -euse** [arʒi'lø, ~'lø:z] clayey; argillaceous.

argon ⚗ [ar'gɔ̃] *m* argon.

argot [ar'go] *m* slang; **argotique** [~gɔ'tik] slangy.

arguer [ar'gɥe] (1e) *v/t.* infer, deduce (from, *de*); assert; ~ *de qch.* put s.th. forward (as a reason); ⚖ ~ *un acte de faux* assert that a document is spurious; *v/i.* argue; **argument** [argy'mã] *m* argument (*a.* ⚠, *a. of a book*); plot, summary; ⚠ variable; **argumentation** [~mãta'sjɔ̃] *f* argumentation; **argumenter** [~mã'te] (1a) *v/i.* argue (about, à propos *de*; against, *contre*; **argutie** [~'si] *f* quibble.

aride [a'rid] arid, dry; sterile; barren; **aridité** [aridi'te] *f* aridity, dryness; barrenness.

arien, -enne [a'rjɛ̃, ~'rjɛn] *adj., a. su.* Arian.

ariette ♪ [a'rjɛt] *f* arietta.

aristo *sl.* [aris'to] *m* swell; **aristocrate** [~tɔ'krat] *su.* aristocrat; **aristocratie** [~tɔkra'si] *f* aristocracy; **aristocratique** [~tɔkra'tik] aristocratic, upper-class.

arithméticien *m*, **-enne** *f* [aritmeti'sjɛ̃, ~'sjɛn] arithmetician; **arithmétique** [~'tik] **1.** *adj.* arithmetical; **2.** *su./f* arithmetic.

arlequin [arlə'kɛ̃] *m* Harlequin; *food:* scraps *pl.*; *fig.* weathercock.

armateur ⚓ [arma'tœ:r] *m* shipowner; **armature** [~'ty:r] *f* frame; brace; *brassière:* boning; ⚡ armature; ♪ key-signature; *fig.* structure.

arme [arm] *f* arm; weapon; ⚔ branch of the service; ⚔ ~*s pl. blanches* side-arms; ~ *à tir rapide* automatic weapon; ~ *automatique* light machine-gun; ~ *de choc* striking weapon; ~*s pl. spatiales* space weapons; *sp. faire des* ~*s* fence; **armé, e** [ar'me] *adj.:* béton *m* ~ reinforced concrete, ferro-concrete; poutre *f* ~*e* trussed beam; verre *m* ~ wired glass; **armée** [ar'me] *f* army; forces *pl.*; ~ *de l'air* Air Force; ~ *de mer* Navy; ~ *de métier* regular army; ~ *de terre* land forces *pl.*; ♀ *du Salut* Salvation Army; **armement** [armə'mã] *m* armament, arming; equipment; ⚓ commissioning; ⚓ manning.

arménien, -enne [arme'njɛ̃, ~'njɛn] *adj., a. su.* ♀ Armenian.

armer [ar'me] (1a) *v/t.* arm (with, *de*); equip; ♣ commission; ♣ man; cock (*a pistol*); ⊕ mount (*a machine*); ⚡ wind (*a dynamo*); ⚡ sheath (*a cable*); set (*an apparatus*); † ~ *q. chevalier* dub s.o. knight; *s'~ de* arm o.s. with, *fig.* call upon (*one's courage, patience, etc.*).

armistice [armis'tis] *m* armistice.

armoire [ar'mwa:r] *f* cupboard; wardrobe; locker; ~ *à pharmacie* medicine-chest; ~ *au* (*or à*) *linge* linen-closet.

armoiries ⌀ [armwa'ri] *f/pl.* (coat *sg.* of) arms; armorial bearings.

armorial, e, *m/pl.* -**aux** ⌀ [armɔ'rjal, ~'rjo] **1.** *adj.* armorial; **2.** *su./m* armorial, book of heraldry; **armorier** ⌀ [~'rje] (1o) *v/t.* emblazon.

armure [ar'my:r] *f* armo(u)r; ⊕ weave; *phys. magnet:* armature; ⚡ *dynamo:* pole-piece; **armurerie** [armyr'ri] *f* manufacture of arms; arms factory; gunsmith's shop; ✕ armo(u)ry; **armurier** ✕, ♣ [~'rje] *m* armo(u)rer; gunsmith.

arnica ♀ [arni'ka] *f* arnica.

aromate [arɔ'mat] *m* spice, aromatic; **aromatique** [arɔma'tik] aromatic; **aromatiser** [~ti'ze] (1a) *v/t.* give aroma *or* flavo(u)r to; *cuis.* flavo(u)r; **arome** [a'ro:m] *m* aroma; *cuis.* flavo(u)ring.

aronde ⊕ [a'rɔ̃:d] *f:* *queue f d'*~ dovetail.

arpège ♪ [ar'pɛ:ʒ] *m* arpeggio.

arpent [ar'pɑ̃] *m* (*approx.*) acre; **arpentage** [arpɑ̃'ta:ʒ] *m* (land-)surveying; survey; **arpenter** [~'te] (1a) *v/t.* survey, measure (*the land*); *fig.* pace (up and down), stride along; **arpenteur** [~'tœ:r] *m* (land-)surveyor; *orn.* great plover.

arquebuse [arkə'by:z] *f* (h)arquebus.

arqué, e [ar'ke] arched, curved; *jambes* ~*es* bow legs, bandy legs; **arquer** [~] (1m) *v/t.* bend; arch; camber.

arraché [ara'ʃe] *m sp.* snatch; *fig. à l'*~ narrow (*victory etc.*); *fig. obtenir qch. à l'*~ (just manage to) snatch s.th.; **arrache-clou** ⊕ [araʃ'klu] *m* nail claw, nail wrench; **arrache-pied** [~'pje] *adv.:* *d'*~ relentlessly; fiercely; *travaller d'*~ F work flat out; **arracher** [ara'ʃe] (1a) *v/t.* tear out *or* away (from, *à*); pull out; extract; draw (*a tooth*); extort (*a confession, money*); **arracheur, -euse** [~'ʃœ:r, ~'ʃø:z] *su.* puller; *su./f* ⚡ potato-lifter.

arraisonnement ♣ [arɛzɔn'mɑ̃] *m* boarding; examination (of a bill of health); **arraisonner** ♣ [~zɔ'ne] (1a) *v/t.* hail; board; stop and examine.

arrangement [arɑ̃ʒ'mɑ̃] *m* arrangement (*a.* ♪); settlement, agreement; ♥ composition (*with creditors*); **arranger** [arɑ̃'ʒe] (11) *v/t.* arrange (*a.* ♪); put in order; tidy, straighten; sort (*cards*); organize; settle (*a dispute, a quarrel*); suit (*s.o.*); *cela m'arrange* that suits me; F *cela s'arrangera* it'll turn out all right; *s'~* manage (with, *de*), make do (with, *de*); come to an agreement, ♥ compound (with, *avec*); dress; *s'~ pour faire qch.* see to it that one can do s.th.; **arrangeur** *m*, -**euse** *f* ♪ [~'ʒœ:r, ~'ʒø:z] arranger.

arrérager ♥ [arera'ʒe] (11) *v/i.* get in arrears; **arrérages** ♥ [~'ra:ʒ] *m/pl.* arrears; back-interest *sg.*

arrestation [arɛsta'sjɔ̃] *f* arrest; apprehension; ⚖ ~ *préventive* protective custody.

arrêt [a'rɛ] *m* stop (*a.* ⊕); ⊕ stoppage; stopping; halt; interruption; ⚖ judgment; ⚖ award; *admin.* decree; ⚖ seizure; ♣ detention; ⚖ arrest; *foot.* tackle; ⊕ *lock:* tumbler; *bus, tram, train:* stop(ping-place); ✕ ~*s pl.* arrest *sg.*; ⚖ ~ *de mort* death sentence; *chien m d'*~ pointer; *cran m d'*~ safety-catch; *dispositif m d'*~ arresting device; ⚖ *rendre un* ~ deliver judgment; ⊕ *robinet m d'*~ stop-cock; *temps m d'*~ pause, halt; **arrêté** [arɛ'te] *m* order; decree; ordinance; by(e)-law; ♥ ~ *de compte(s)* settlement; **arrêter** [~] (1a) *v/t.* stop; arrest; check; fix, fasten; draw up; decide; ♥ make up, close (*an account*); fasten off (*a stitch*); ~ *les mailles knitting:* cast off; *s'~* stop; halt, pause; cease (*noise*); *sans s'~ a.* without (a) letup; *v/i.* stop; *hunt.* point (*dog*); ~ *de faire qch.* stop doing s.th.

arrhes [a:r] *f/pl.* deposit *sg.*; earnest (money) *sg.*

arrière [a'rjɛ:r] **1.** *adv.:* *en* ~ behind; back, backward(s); in arrears; *être en*

~ be behind; *regarder en* ~ look back; *rester en* ~ lag behind; *faire un pas en* ~ step back(wards); *revenir en* ~ go back; **2.** *su./m* back (part), rear; ⚓ stern; *sp.* back; **3.** *adj./inv.* back; *mot.* feu *m* (*or* lanterne *f*) ~ rear-light; roue *f* ~ back-wheel, rear-wheel; *vent m* ~ leading wind; **arriéré, e** [arje're] **1.** *adj.* late; in arrears; backward (*child, country*); **2.** *su./m* arrears *pl.*; ✝ *faire rentrer des* ~s recover debts.

arrière...: ~**-ban** *hist.* [arjer'bã] *m* (whole body of) vassals *pl.*; ~**bouche** [~'buʃ] *f* back of the mouth; ~**-boutique** [~bu'tik] *f* back-shop; ~**-cour** [~'kuːr] *f* backyard; ~**-garde** ⚔ [~'gard] *f* rearguard; ~**-goût** [~'gu] *m* after-taste; ~**-grand'père** [~grã'pɛːr] *m* great-grandfather; ~**-main** [~'mɛ̃] *f* back of the hand; *horse:* hindquarters *pl.*; back-hand stroke; ~**-neveu** [~nə'vø] *m* grand-nephew; ~**-pensée** [~pã'se] *f* ulterior motive; mental reservation; ~**-petit-fils,** *pl.* ~**-petits-fils** [~pəti'fis] *m* great-grandson; ~**-plan** [~'plã] *m* background; ~**-point** [~'pwɛ̃] *m* backstitch.

arriérer [arje're] (1f) *v/t.* postpone; *s'* ~ fall behind (*person*); get into arrears.

arrière...: ~**-saison** [arjɛrsɛ'zõ] *f* late season *or* autumn, *Am.* late fall; ~**-train** [~'trɛ̃] *m* waggonbody; trailer; *animal:* hindquarter.

arrimer ⚓ [ari'me] (1a) *v/t.* stow; trim (*a ship*); pack (*for transit*).

arrivant *m,* **e** *f* [ari'vã, ~'vãːt] arrival, comer; **arrivée** [~'ve] *f* arrival, coming; ⊕ inlet, intake; *sp.* finish; **arriver** [~'ve] (1a) *v/t.* arrive (at, *à*), come; happen; succeed, be successful; ⚓ bear away; ~ *à* (*inf.*) succeed in (*ger.*), manage to (*inf.*); **arriviste** [~'vist] *su.* thruster, (social) climber; careerist.

arrogance [aro'gãːs] *f* arrogance; haughtiness; **arrogant, e** [~'gã, ~'gãːt] arrogant; haughty.

arroger [aro'ʒe] (1l) *v/t.*: *s'* ~ arrogate (*s.th.*) to o.s.

arrondir [arõ'diːr] (2a) *v/t.* (make) round; round off (*a. fig. a sum*); round, double; *s'* ~ fill out; become round; **arrondissement** [~dis'mã] *m* rounding off; roundness; *admin.* district; *admin. town:* ward.

arrosage [aro'zaːʒ] *m* watering; wetting; sprinkling; *cuis.* basting; *wine:* dilution; *rain:* soaking; **arroser** [~'ze] (1a) *v/t.* water; wet (*a. fig.*); sprinkle; moisten; *cuis.* baste; dilute (*wine*); F wash down (*the food*); F *ça s'arrose* that calls for a drink; **arroseur** [~'zœːr] *m* watercart attendant; **arroseuse** [~'zøːz] *f* watercart; ~**-balayeuse** combined streetwatering and sweeping lorry *or* truck; **arrosoir** [~'zwaːr] wateringcan; sprinkler.

arsenal [arsə'nal] *m* arsenal (*a. fig.*); armo(u)ry; ⚓ dockyard.

arsenic ⚗ [arsə'nik] *m* arsenic.

art [aːr] *m* art; skill; ~s *pl.* et *métiers m/pl.* arts and crafts; ~s *pl.* ménagers domestic science.

artère [ar'tɛːr] *f* artery (*a. fig.*); thoroughfare; ⚡ feeder; **artériel, -elle** [arte'rjɛl] arterial; **artériosclérose** ⚕ [~rjɔsklé'roːz] *f* arteriosclerosis.

artésien, -enne [arte'zjɛ̃, ~'zjɛn] artesian; of Artois; *puits m* ~ artesian well.

arthrite ⚕ [ar'trit] *f* arthritis; gout.

artichaut [arti'ʃo] *m* cuis. artichoke; ⚔ spiked barrier.

article [ar'tikl] *m* article (*a.* ⚥, ✝, *eccl., gramm.*); thing; *treaty:* clause; item; subject, topic; ✝ ~s *pl.* goods; ~s *pl.* de Paris fancy goods; *journ.* ~ *de fond* leader, leading article; ~ *de luxe* luxury article; ~ *documentaire* documentary report; *à l'* ~ *de la mort* at the point of death; *faire l'* ~ puff one's goods; **articlier** *journ.* [~ti'klje] *m* copy-writer, columnist.

articulaire ⚕ [artiky'lɛːr] articular, of the joints; **articulation** [~la'sjõ] *f anat., speech:* articulation; joint; ⊕ connection; ⚥ node; utterance; **articuler** [~'le] (1a) *v/t.* articulate; link; pronounce distinctly; state clearly.

artifice [arti'fis] *m* artifice; guile; stratagem; expedient; ⚔ ~s *pl.* flares; *feu m d'* ~ fireworks *pl.*; *fig.* flash of wit; **artificiel, -elle** [artifi'sjɛl] artificial; **artificier** [~'sje] *m* pyrotechnist; ⚔ artificer; **artificieux, -euse** [~'sjø, ~'sjøːz] artful, crafty, cunning.

artillerie ⚔ [artij'ri] *f* artillery, ordnance; gunnery; ~ *antiaérienne* (*or contre avions*) anti-aircraft artillery; ~ *d'assaut* assault artillery; ~ *lourde* (*or à pied*) heavy artillery; *pièce f d'*~ piece of ordnance; **artilleur** [ˌtiˈjœːr] *m* artilleryman, gunner.

artimon ⚓ [artiˈmɔ̃] *m* mizzen; mizzenmast.

artisan [artiˈzɑ̃] *m* artisan; craftsman; working-man; *fig.* creator, agent; **artisanat** [ˌzaˈna] *m* handicraft; craftsmen *pl*.

artiste [arˈtist] *su.* artist; ♪, *thea.* performer; **artistique** [ˌtisˈtik] artistic.

aryen, -enne [aˈrjɛ̃, ˌrjɛn] *adj., a. su.* ♀ Aryan, Indo-European.

as¹ [a] *2nd p. sg. pres. of avoir 1.*

as² [ɑːs] *m* ace (*a. fig.*); *sp.* crack (player *etc.*); *sl. être plein aux* ~ have stacks of money.

asbeste [asˈbɛst] *m* asbestos.

ascendance [asɑ̃ˈdɑ̃ːs] *f* ancestry; *astr.* ascent; **ascendant, e** [ˌˈdɑ̃, ˌˈdɑ̃ːt] 1. *adj.* upward (*motion etc.*); 2. *su./m* ascendant; ascendency; *fig.* influence; ~*s pl.* ancestry *sg.*

ascenseur [asɑ̃ˈsœːr] *m* lift, *Am.* elevator; F *fig. renvoyer l'*~ do a favour in return, return the favour, reciprocate; **ascension** [ˌˈsjɔ̃] *f* ascent; climb; rising; ⊕ *piston:* upstroke; *eccl. l'*♀ Ascension-day; **ascensionniste** [ˌsjɔˈnist] *su.* climber; mountaineer; balloonist.

ascète [aˈsɛt] *su.* ascetic; **ascétique** [aseˈtik] ascetic; **ascétisme** [ˌˈtism] *m* ascetism.

asepsie ✚ [asɛpˈsi] *f* asepsis; **aseptique** ✚ [ˌˈtik] aseptic; **aseptiser** ✚ [ˌtiˈze] (1a) *v/t.* asepticize.

asexué, e [asɛksɥˈe] *biol.* asexual; sexless.   [Asiatic; Asian.]

asiatique [azjaˈtik] *adj., a. su.* ♀]

asile [aˈzil] *m* asylum; retreat; shelter; † sanctuary; ~ *d'aliénés* mental hospital; ~ *pour animaux* animal home, *Am.* animal shelter.

asocial, e *m/pl.* -**aux** [asɔˈsjal, ˌˈsjo] antisocial.

aspect [asˈpɛ] *m* aspect (*a. gramm.*); sight; appearance; look; *fig.* viewpoint.

asperge ♀ [asˈpɛrʒ] *f* asparagus.

asperger [aspɛrˈʒe] (1l) *v/t.* sprinkle; spray (with, de).

aspérité [asperiˈte] *f* asperity, roughness, harshness; unevenness.

asperseur [aspɛrˈsœːr] *m* sprinkler; **aspersion** [ˌˈsjɔ̃] *f* aspersion, sprinkling; spraying; **aspersoir** [ˌˈswaːr] *m* ✝ *watering-can:* rose; *eccl.* aspergillum.

asphaltage [asfalˈtaːʒ] *m* asphalting; **asphalte** [ˌˈfalt] *m* asphalt.

asphyxie [asfikˈsi] *f* asphyxia(tion), suffocation; **asphyxier** [ˌˈsje] (1o) *v/t.* (*a. s'*~) asphyxiate, suffocate.

aspic [asˈpik] *m zo.* asp; *cuis.* aspic; ♀ aspic, French lavender; *fig. langue f d'*~ venomous tongue.

aspirant, e [aspiˈrɑ̃, ˌˈrɑ̃ːt] 1. *adj.* sucking; ⊕ suction-...; 2. *su.* aspirant, candidate; *su./m* ✕ officer candidate; ⚓ midshipman; 🚀 acting pilot-officer; **aspirateur, -trice** [ˌraˈtœːr, ˌˈtris] 1. *adj.* suction-...; 2. *su./m* ⊕ suction-conveyor; ⊕ exhaust-fan; aspirator; vacuum cleaner; **aspiration** [ˌraˈsjɔ̃] *f* aspiration (*a. gramm.*); *fig.* longing (after, à); ⊕ suction; ⊕ inspiration, inhaling; ⊕ intake; **aspirer** [ˌˈre] (1a) *v/t.* breathe in; suck in *or* up; *gramm.* aspirate; 🚀 inhale; *v/i.:* ~ *à* (*inf.*) aspire to (*inf.*); ~ *à qch.* aspire to s.th.; long for s.th.

aspirine 🚀 [aspiˈrin] *f* aspirin; *prendre un comprimé d'*~ take an aspirin.

assagir [asaˈʒiːr] (2a) *v/t.* make wiser; steady, sober (down).

assaillant [asaˈjɑ̃] *m* assailant; **assaillir** [ˌˈjiːr] (2s) *v/t.* assail, attack; *fig.* beset (with, de).

assainir [asɛˈniːr] (2a) *v/t.* make healthier; cleanse, purify; clean (up); clear (*slums, the atmosphere, etc.*); drain (*marshes*); stabilize (*the economy etc.*); reorganize (*the finances etc.*); **assainissement** [ˌnisˈmɑ̃] *m* cleansing, purifying; cleaning (up); clearing; *marshes:* draining; *economy:* stabilization; *finances:* reorganization.

assaisonnement [asɛzɔnˈmɑ̃] *m* seasoning; flavo(u)ring; *salad:* dressing; **assaisonner** [ˌzɔˈne] (1a) *v/t.* season (with, de); flavo(u)r (with, de); dress (*salads*).

assassin, e [asaˈsɛ̃, ˌˈsin] 1. *su./m* assassin; murderer; *à l'*~! murder!; *su./f* murderess; 2. *adj.* murderous; *fig.* provocative; *fig.* deadly; **assassinat** [ˌsiˈna] *m* murder; assassination; **assassiner** [ˌsiˈne] (1a) *v/t.*

murder (a. fig.); assassinate; F
pester.

assaut [a'so] m assault, attack; sp.
bout, match; faire ~ de bandy
(words, wit).

assèchement [aseʃ'mã] m drying,
draining, drainage; **assécher** [ase-
'ʃe] (1f) v/t. dry; drain.

assemblage [asã'bla:ʒ] m gathering, collection; ⊕ assembly; ⊕
joint; ⚡ connection, coupling; **assemblée** [~'ble] f assembly, meeting; congregation; gathering; ~
générale general meeting; ~ plénière plenary assembly; **assembler**
[~'ble] (1a) v/t. assemble (a. ⊕);
gather, call together; convene (a
committee); ✗ muster; ⚡ couple,
connect; join(t); s'~ assemble, meet.

assener [asə'ne] (1d) v/t. strike,
land (a blow).

assentiment [asãti'mã] m agreement, assent, consent; signe m d'~
nod.

asseoir [a'swa:r] (3c) v/t. seat,
place; pitch (a tent); lay (a stone);
establish (a tax); base (an opinion);
on le fit ~ he was asked to take a
seat; s'~ sit down; settle; ✗ pancake.

assermenté, e [asɛrmã'te] sworn,
on oath.

assertion [asɛr'sjõ] f assertion.

asservir [asɛr'vi:r] (2a) v/t. enslave
(to, à) (a. fig.); subdue; subject;
⊕ synchronize; **asservissement**
[~vis'mã] m slavery, subjection;
bondage; ⊕ control.

assesseur [ase'sœ:r] m assessor;
assistant judge.

asseyons [ase'jõ] 1st p. pl. pres. of
asseoir.

assez [a'se] adv. enough; rather;
sufficiently; fairly; ~! that's
enough!; that will do!; (en) avoir ~ de
be sick (and tired) of; j'en ai ~! a. I've
had enough of it, F I'm fed up with it.

assidu, e [asi'dy] diligent; assidu-
ous; regular; constant; attentive
(to, auprès de); **assiduité** [~dɥi'te]
f diligence, assiduity; ~s pl. constant attentions or care sg.; **assidû-
ment** [~dy'mã] adv. of assidu.

assieds [a'sje] 1st p. sg. pres. of asseoir.

assiégeant, e [asje'ʒã, ~'ʒã:t] 1. adj.
besieging; 2. su./m besieger; **assiéger** [~'ʒe] (1g) v/t. besiege (a. fig.);

surround; beset; fig. mob; fig.
dun.

assiérai [asje're] 1st p. sg. fut. of asseoir.

assiette [a'sjɛt] f plate; ⚓ trim;
horse: seat; ⊕ etc. basis; machine:
support; tax: establishment; F il
n'est pas dans son ~ he's out of
sorts, he's not up to the mark; **assiettée** [asje'te] f plate(ful).

assignation [asiɲa'sjõ] f assignation;
🏛 summons, subpoena; **assigner**
[~'ɲe] (1a) v/t. assign; allot; appoint,
fix (a time); allocate; ✝ earmark (a
sum); 🏛 summon, subpoena.

assimilable [asimi'labl] 🔬 assimilable; comparable (to, à); **assimilation** [~la'sjõ] f assimilation; ✗,
⚓ correlation, equivalence; **assimiler** [~'le] (1a) v/t. assimilate;
compare; give equal status to.

assis¹ [a'si] 1st p. sg. p.s. of asseoir.

assis², e [a'si, ~'si:z] 1. p.p. of asseoir; 2. adj. seated; sitting; être ~
be seated or sitting; 🪑 etc. place f
~e seat; 3. su./f △ foundation; △
bricks: course; cement: layer; rider:
seat; ~es pl. meetings, sessions; 🏛
assizes; 🏛 cour f d'~es Assize
Court.

assistance [asis'tã:s] f assistance,
help; audience, spectators pl.; eccl.
congregation; 🏛, eccl. attendance,
presence; ~ judiciaire (free) legal
aid; ~ maritime salvage; ~ publique
public assistance, public relief; ~
sociale (social) welfare work; **assistant, e** [~'tã, ~'tã:t] su. assistant;
usu. ~s pl. spectators, onlookers;
audience sg.; su./f: ~e sociale social
worker; **assister** [~'te] (1a) v/i.:
~ à attend, be present at; v/t.
assist, help, aid (s.o.).

association [asɔsja'sjõ] f association; ✝ partnership; society; union;
⚡ coupling, connection; ~ de bienfaisance charitable organization; ✝
~ en nom collectif (ordinary) partnership; **associé** m, e f [asɔ'sje]
partner; learned society: associate;
✝ ~ commanditaire sleeping partner; **associer** [~] (1o) v/t. associate,
unite; join up; ⚡ connect, couple;
s'~ (à or avec) associate o.s. (with);
join (in s.th.); keep company with;
✝ enter into partnership with.

assoiffé, e [aswa'fe] thirsty; fig. eager
(for, de).

assoirai F [aswa're] *1st p. sg. fut. of*
asseoir; **assois** F [a'swa] *1st p. sg.*
pres. of asseoir.

assolement ✍ [asɔl'mã] *m* (crop-)
rotation; **assoler** ✍ [asɔ'le] (1a)
v/t. rotate the crops on.

assombrir [asɔ̃'bri:r] (2a) *v/t.*
darken; make gloomy (*a. fig.*);
cloud (*a. fig.*); s'~ darken; become
cloudy (*sky*); *fig.* become gloomy.

assommant, e [asɔ'mã, ~'mã:t] F
boring; tiresome; **assommer** [~-
'me] (1a) *v/t.* fell; stun; knock on
the head; knock out; *fig.* bore; *fig.*
overcome; **assommoir** [~'mwa:r]
m † bludgeon; *fig. coup m d'*~ staggering blow.

assomption [asɔ̃p'sjɔ̃] *f* assumption; *eccl.* l'♎ the Assumption.

assonance [asɔ'nɑ:s] *f* assonance;
assonant, e [~'nã, ~'nã:t] assonant.

assorti, e [asɔr'ti] assorted; (*well-,
badly-*)matched; ✝ (*well-, badly-*)
stocked; ~ *à* matching; **assortiment** [asɔrti'mã] *m* assortment (*a.
✝*), range, variety; ⊕ set; *typ.* sorts
pl.; **assortir** [~'ti:r] (2a) *v/t.* match;
s'~ match (s.th., *à* qch.), go well
together.

assoupir [asu'pi:r] (2a) *v/t.* make
sleepy *or* drowsy; soothe, deaden,
lull (*a pain etc.*); s'~ doze off; wear
off (*pain*); **assoupissement** [~pis-
'mã] *m* drowsiness; nap, doze; *fig.*
sloth; ✼ torpor.

assouplir [asu'pli:r] (2a) *v/t.* make
supple; break in (*a horse*); *fig.* s'~
become more tractable.

assourdir [asur'di:r] (2a) *v/t.* deafen
(*a. fig.*); *fig.* deaden, damp, muffle
(*a sound*); tone down (*a light etc.*);
gramm. unvoice (*a consonant*).

assouvir [asu'vi:r] (2a) *v/t.* satiate,
appease (*one's hunger*); quench
(*one's thirst*); ✝ glut (*the market*);
s'~ gorge; become sated (with, de).

assoyons F [aswa'jɔ̃] *1st p. pl. pres.
of asseoir.*

assujetti, e [asyʒe'ti] subject, liable
(to, *à*); ~ *à l'assurance* subject to
compulsory insurance; ~ *aux droits
de douane* liable to duty, dutiable;
assujettir [~'ti:r] (2a) *v/t.* subjugate, subdue; fix, fasten; secure;
make liable (to, *à*); compel (to *inf.*,
à inf.); **assujettissement** [~tis'mã]
m subjugation; securing.

assumer [asy'me] (1a) *v/t.* assume,

take (*a responsibility*) upon o.s.;
take up (*duties*).

assurance [asy'rã:s] *f* assurance (*a.
✝*), self-confidence; certainty; security, pledge; safety; ✝ insurance;
~s *pl.* *sociales* social security *sg.*;
~-*automobile* car insurance; ~-
incendie fire-insurance; ~ *maladie*
health-insurance; ~ *maritime* marine
insurance; ~ *au tiers* third-party insurance; ~ *tous risques* comprehensive insurance; ~-*vie*, ~ *sur la vie* life
assurance *or* insurance; ~-*vieillesse*
old-age insurance; *passer un contrat
d'*~ take out an insurance policy;
assuré, e [~'re] **1.** *adj.* sure; confident; **2.** *su.* ✝ the insured; policy-
holder; **assurément** [~re'mã] *adv.*
assuredly; **assurer** [~'re] (1a) *v/t.*
assure; secure, fasten; make secure;
make steady; affirm; ensure (*a
result*); ✝ insure; provide, maintain
(*a service etc.*); carry out, undertake,
handle (*work etc.*); s'~ *a.* make sure
(of, de; that, que); s'~ *de a.* ensure;
assureur ✝ [~'rœ:r] *m* insurers *pl.*,
insurance agent; ~ *maritime* underwriter.

aster ♣, *biol.* [as'tɛr] *m* aster; **astérisque** *typ.* [~te'risk] *m* asterisk (*).

asthénie ⚕ [aste'ni] *f* debility.

asthmatique ⚕ [asma'tik] *adj.*, *a.
su.* asthmatic; **asthme** ⚕ [asm] *m*
asthma.

asticot [asti'ko] *m* maggot; F *un
drôle d'*~ a queer cove *or* chap;
asticoter F [~kɔ'te] (1a) *v/t.* plague,
worry.

astigmate ⚕ [astig'mat] astigmatic.

astiquer [asti'ke] (1m) *v/t.* polish;
smarten.   [♣, *anat.* astragalus.|

astragale [astra'gal] *m* △ astragal;|

astral, e [as'tral] *m/pl.* -**aux** [as'tral, ~'tro]
astral; **astre** [astr] *m* star (*a. fig.*).

astreindre [as'trɛ̃:dr] (4m) subject;
force, compel (to, *à*); bind; s'~ *à*
force o.s. to, keep to.

astringent, e ⚕ [astrɛ̃'ʒã, ~'ʒã:t]
adj., *a. su./m* astringent.

astro... [astrɔ] astro...; **~logie** [~lɔ-
'ʒi] *f* astrology; **~logue** [~'lɔg] *m*
astrologer; **~naute** [~'no:t] *m* astro-
naut, space traveller; **~nautique**
[~no'tik] *f* astronautics *sg.*, space
travel; **~nef** [~'nɛf] *m* space-ship;
~nome [~'nɔm] *m* astronomer;
~nomie [~nɔ'mi] *f* astronomy;
~nomique [~nɔ'mik] astronomical

(*year, a.* F *price*); ⁓**physique** [⁓fi-'zik] **1.** *adj.* astrophysical; **2.** *su./f* astrophysics *sg.*

astuce [as'tys] *f* guile, craftiness; wile, trick; **astucieux, -euse** [⁓ty-'sjø, ⁓'sjø:z] crafty, astute, artful.

asymétrique [asime'trik] asymmetrical, unsymmetrical.

asymptote [asɛ̃p'tɔt] **1.** *adj.* asymptotic; **2.** *su./f* asymptote.

atavique [ata'vik] atavistic; *biol.* *retour m* ⁓ throw-back; **atavisme** [⁓'vism] *m* atavism.

ataxie [atak'si] *f* ataxy, ataxia.

atelier [atə'lje] *m* workshop; studio; (shop *or* workroom) staff; ✂ working party; *pol.* work-group; ⊕ ⁓ *de constructions mécaniques* engine works; ⁓ *de réparations* repair-shop.

atermoiement [atɛrmwa'mɑ̃] *m* † deferment of payment; procrastination; F ⁓s *pl.* shilly-shallying *sg.*; **atermoyer** [⁓'je] (1h) *v/t.* † put off, defer (*payment*); *v/i.* temporize, procrastinate; *s'*⁓ arrange for an extension of time (*with creditors*).

athée [a'te] **1.** *adj.* atheistic; **2.** *su.* atheist; **athéisme** [ate'ism] *m* atheism.

athlète [at'lɛt] *m* (*Am.* track and field) athlete; **athlétique** [atle'tik] athletic; **athlétisme** [⁓'tism] *m* (*Am.* track and field) athletics *pl.*

atlantique [atlɑ̃'tik] **1.** *adj.* Atlantic; **2.** *su./m* ♀ Atlantic (Ocean).

atlas [at'lɑ:s] *m* atlas; *geog., myth.* ♀ Atlas.

atmosphère [atmɔs'fɛ:r] *f* atmosphere (*a. fig.*); **atmosphérique** [⁓fe'rik] atmospheric.

atoll *geog.* [a'tɔl] *m* atoll, coral island.

atome [a'to:m] *m* atom (*a. fig.*); *fig.* speck; F *fig. avoir des* ⁓s *crochus (avec q.)* have things in common (with s.o.), be on the same wavelength (with s.o.); **atomique** [atɔ'mik] atomic; *bombe f* ⁓ atom(ic) bomb; *énergie f* ⁓ atomic energy; *ère f* ⁓ atomic age; *pile f* ⁓ atomic pile; *poids m* ⁓ atomic weight; **atomiser** [⁓mi'ze] (1a) *v/t.* atomize; pulverize; **atomiseur** [⁓mi'zœ:r] *m* spray, atomizer.

atone [a'tɔn] *gramm.* atonic, unstressed; *fig.* dull; vacant; **atonie** ✍ [atɔ'ni] *f* atony, sluggishness.

atours [a'tu:r] *m/pl.* †, *a. co.* finery *sg.*

atout [a'tu] *m* trump; *fig.* asset, advantage; *jouer* ⁓ play trumps.

atoxique [atɔ'ksik] non-poisonous.

âtre [ɑ:tr] *m* hearth.

atroce [a'trɔs] atrocious, dreadful; grim; **atrocité** [atrɔsi'te] *f* atrocity; atrociousness.

atrophie ✍ [atrɔ'fi] *f* atrophy; emaciation; **atrophier** [⁓'fje] (1o) *v/i., a. s'*⁓ atrophy.

attabler [ata'ble] (1a) *v/t.*: *s'*⁓ sit down to table; *fig.* F own up, *usu. Am.* come clean.

attache [a'taʃ] *f* bond, tie, link; cord, strap; ⊕ brace, joint; paper clip; *chien m d'*⁓ house-dog; ♥ *pat m d'*⁓ home pat; **attaché** [ata'ʃe] *m pol.* attaché; **attachement** [ataʃ'mɑ̃] *m* attachment (*a. fig.*); **attacher** [ata'ʃe] (1a) *v/t.* attach; fasten (*a. fig.*); tie; *fig.* attract; *s'*⁓ *à* attach o.s. to; cling to; apply *or* devote o.s. to; ✂ *s'*⁓ *au sol* hold on to the ground; *s'*⁓ *aux pas de q.* dog s.o.'s footsteps.

attaque [a'tak] *f* attack (*a. ⚔, ✂*); assault; ⊕, *mot.* drive; être d'⁓ feel fit; **attaquer** [ata'ke] (1m) *v/t.* attack; assail; assault; ⚖ contest (*a will*), sue (*s.o.*); ⊕ operate; F begin; *s'*⁓ *à* fall upon, attack; *fig.* tackle; *v/i.* attack.

attardé, e [atar'de] **1.** *adj.* belated; backward; old-fashioned; **2.** *su.* late-comer; **attarder** [⁓] (1a) *v/t.* make late; *s'*⁓ delay, linger (over, *sur*); *s'*⁓ *à* (*inf.*) stay (up) late (*ger.*).

atteindre [a'tɛ̃dr] (4m) *v/t.* reach; attain; overtake; hit (*a target*); strike (*a. fig.*); *fig.* affect; *v/i.*: ⁓ *à* attain (to), achieve; **atteint, e** [a'tɛ̃, ⁓'tɛ̃:t] **1.** *p.p. of atteindre*; **2.** *su./f* reach; attack (*a. ⚔*), blow, stroke; touch; harm, injury; *hors d'*⁓e out of reach.

attelage [at'la:ʒ] *m* harnessing; yoke, team; ⊕ attachment; 🚂 coupling; **atteler** [⁓'le] (1c) *v/t.* harness; yoke; connect; 🚂 couple; *s'*⁓ *à* settle *or* F get down to (*a task*); **attelle** [a'tɛl] *f* ✍ splint; ⁓s *pl.* hames.

attenant, e [at'nɑ̃, ⁓'nɑ̃:t] neighbo(u)ring, adjacent (to, *à*).

attendant [atɑ̃'dɑ̃]: en ⁓ *adv.* meanwhile; *prp.* pending; en ⁓ que (*sbj.*) until, till (*ind.*); **attendre** [a'tɑ̃dr] (4a) *v/t.* wait for, await; look forward to; expect; *attendez voir!* wait and see!; *faire ~* keep s.o. waiting; *s'~ à* expect (*s.th.*).

attendrir [atɑ̃'driːr] (2a) *v/t.* soften, make tender; tenderize (*meat*); *fig.* touch, move; *s'~ sur* gush over; *se laisser ~* be moved *or* affected; **attendrissement** [~dris'mɑ̃] *m* emotion; (feeling of) pity.

attendu, e [atɑ̃'dy] **1.** *p.p. of* attendre; **2.** *attendu prp.* considering; on account of; *~ que* seeing that ...; ✞ whereas; **3.** *su./m: ~s pl.* ✞ reasons adduced.

attentat [atɑ̃:ta] *m* assassination attempt; attack; outrage; ✞ *~ à la pudeur* indecent assault; ✞ *~ aux mœurs* indecent behavio(u)r, *Am.* offense against public morals.

attente [a'tɑ̃:t] *f* wait(ing); expectation; *contre toute ~* contrary to expectations; 🚂 *salle f d'~* waiting room.   [attempt (on, *à*).]

attenter [atɑ̃'te] (1a) *v/i.* make an⌉

attentif, -ve [atɑ̃'tif, ~'tiːv] (*à*) attentive (to); heedful (of); careful; mindful; **attention** [~'sjɔ̃] *f* attention, care; *~!* look out; *faire ~* pay attention (to, *à*); take care (of, *à*); **attentisme** [~'tism] *m* wait-and-see attitude *or* policy; waiting game; **attentiste** [~'tist] **1.** *su.* partisan of a wait-and-see policy; **2.** *adj.* wait-and-see.

atténuant, e [ate'nɥɑ̃, ~'nɥɑ:t] ✞ mitigating *or* extenuating (*circumstances*); 🖋, 🎗 attenuant; **atténuer** [~'nɥe] (1n) *v/t.* mitigate; lessen, soften; *s'~ à.* die down.

atterrer [atɛ're] (1a) *v/t.* overwhelm, astound, stun.

atterrir [ate'riːr] (2a) *v/i.* ⚓ make a landfall; ⚓ land; **atterrissage** [~ri'sa:ʒ] *m* ⚓ landfall; ✈ landing; ✈ *~ forcé* forced landing; ✈ *~ sans visibilité* instrument landing; ✈ *train m d'~* undercarriage.

atterrissement [ateris'mɑ̃] *m* alluvium.

atterrisseur ✈ [ateri'sœ:r] *m* undercarriage; *~ escamotable* retractable undercarriage.

attestation [atɛsta'sjɔ̃] *f* attestation; testimonial; certificate; ✞ *~ sous serment* affidavit; **attester** [~'te] (1a) *v/t.* testify, certify.

attiédir [atje'diːr] (2a) *v/t.* cool (*a. fig.*); take the chill off; *s'~* (grow) cool (*a. fig.*).

attifer [ati'fe] (1a) *v/t. usu. pej.* dress (*s.o.*) up; *s'~* get o.s. up, rig o.s. out.

attiger F [ati'ʒe] (1l) *v/i.* exaggerate, F lay it on.

attique [a'tik] **1.** *adj.* Attic; **2.** *su./m* △ attic; *su./f:* l'~ Attica.

attirail [ati'ra:j] *m* outfit; gear; F pomp; *pej.* paraphernalia *pl.*

attirance [ati'rɑ̃:s] *f* attraction; **attirant, e** [~'rɑ̃, ~'rɑ̃:t] attractive; engaging; **attirer** [~'re] (1a) *v/t.* attract; draw; (al)lure; *s'~* win (*s.th.*).

attiser [ati'ze] (1a) *v/t.* stir up (*a. fig.*); ⊕ stoke; *fig.* fan, feed; **attisoir** [~'zwa:r] *m* poker; ⊕ pricker, fire-rake.

attitré, e [ati'tre] appointed, regular; customary.

attitude [ati'tyd] *f* attitude (towards, *envers*).

attouchement [atuʃ'mɑ̃] *m* contact (*a. ⚡*), touch(ing).

attractif, -ve [atrak'tif, ~'ti:v] attractive; gravitational (*force*); **attraction** [~'sjɔ̃] *f* attraction (*a. fig.*), pull; *~s pl.* variety show *sg.*; cabaret *sg.*, *Am.* floor show *sg.*; *phys. ~ universelle* gravitation.

attrait [a'trɛ] *m* attractiveness, charm; inclination (for, *pour*).

attrapade F [atra'pad] *f*, **attrapage** F [~'pa:ʒ] *m* tiff, quarrel; blowing-up, reprimand.

attrape [a'trap] *f* hoax, trick; *object:* joke (article); **attrape-mouches** [atrap'muʃ] *m/inv.* flypaper; 🌱 catchfly; *orn.* flycatcher; **attrape-nigaud** [~ni'go] *m* booby trap; **attraper** [atra'pe] (1a) *v/t.* catch (*a. 🐟*); trap; *fig.* trick; F scold; *se faire ~* be taken in; get hauled over the coals (for *ger.*, *pour inf.*).

attrayant, e [atrɛ'jɑ̃, ~'jɑ̃:t] attractive; engaging.

attribuer [atri'bɥe] (1n) *v/t.* attribute (to, *à*); assign; allot; *s'~* appropriate; **attribut** [~'by] *m* attribute; *gramm.* predicate; emblem; ⚔ badge; **attribution** [~by'sjɔ̃] *f* attribution; allocation; conferment; *~s pl.* competence *sg.*, powers, duties.

attrister [atris'te] (1a) *v/t.* sadden; *s'~* become sad; cloud over (*sky*).

attrition [atri'sjɔ̃] *f* abrasion; *eccl.* attrition (*a. ⚔*).

attroupement [atrup'mɑ̃] *m* ✞

unlawful assembly; *fig.* mob; **at-trouper** [atru'pe] (1a) *v/t.* gather together; s'~ flock together; assemble, crowd.

atypique [ati'pik] atypical.

aubade [o'bad] *f* ♪ aubade; F cat-calling.

aubaine [o'bɛn] *f* 🟤 right of escheat; *fig.* godsend, windfall.

aube¹ [o:b] *f* dawn; *eccl.* alb.

aube² [ʌ] *f* paddle, float; blade.

aubépine ♀ [obe'pin] *f* hawthorn; whitethorn.

auberge [o'bɛrʒ] *f* inn, tavern; ~ de la jeunesse youth hostel.

aubergine ♀ [ober'ʒin] *f* egg-plant.

aubergiste [ober'ʒist] *su.* innkeeper; *su./m* landlord; *su./f* landlady.

aucun, e [o'kœ̃, ʌ'kyn] **1.** *adj.* any; **2.** *pron.* any(one); *with* ne *or on its own:* none; d'~s some (people); **aucunement** [okyn'mã] *adv.* not at all, by no means.

audace [o'das] *f* audacity (*a. fig.*); daring; boldness; F payer d'~ face the music; **audacieux, -euse** [oda'sjø, ʌ'sjø:z] audacious, bold, daring; impertinent.

au-deçà † [odʌ'sa] *adv.* on this side; **au-dedans** [ʌ'dã] *adv.* inside, within; ~ de within; **au-dehors** [ʌ'ɔ:r] *adv.* (on the) outside; ~ de outside, beyond; **au-delà** [ʌ'la] **1.** *adv.* beyond; ~ de beyond, on the other side of; **2.** *su./m* beyond; l'~ the next world; **au-dessous** [ʌ'su] *adv.* below; ~ de below, under; beneath; **au-dessus** [ʌ'sy] *adv.* above; ~ de above; *fig.* beyond; **au-devant** [ʌ'vã] *adv.* forward, ahead; aller ~ de go to meet; anticipate; forestall; aller ~ d'un danger court danger.

audible [o'di:bl] audible; **audience** [o'djã:s] *f* attention, interest; 🟤 hearing; audience; *radio etc.:* public; **audiencier** [odjã'sje] *m* 🟤 usher; F haunter of law-courts; **audiovisuel, -elle** [odjovi'zɥɛl] audiovisual; **auditeur, -trice** [odi'tœ:r, ʌ'tris] *su.* hearer, listener; *univ.* student who attends lectures only; *su./m* 🟤, 🟤 public prosecutor; *admin.* commissioner of audits; ~s *m/pl.* audience; **auditif, -ve** [ʌ'tif, ʌ'ti:v] *anat.* auditory; *appareil m* ~ hearing aid; **audition** [ʌ'sjɔ̃] *f* hearing; recital; audition; ~s *pl. du*

jour radio: today's program(me) *sg.*; **auditionner** [ʌsjɔ'ne] (1a) *v/t.* audition (*s.o.*); *v/i.* audition, give an audition; **auditoire** [ʌ'twa:r] *m* audience.

auge [o:ʒ] *f* trough (*a.* ⊕); manger; ⊕ *water-wheel:* bucket; *geol.* ~ glaciaire glacial valley; **auget** [o'ʒe] *m* small trough; ⊕ *water-wheel:* bucket.

augmentation [ogmãta'sjɔ̃] *f* increase (*a.* ✝, ♪); *prices, wages:* rise; augmentation (*a.* ✝, ♪); *faire une* ~ *knitting:* make a stitch; **augmenter** [ʌ'te] (1a) *v/t.* increase, augment; raise (*a price, the wages*); s'~ increase; *v/i.* increase, rise; grow.

augure [o'gy:r] *m* augury, omen; augur; **augurer** [ogy're] (1a) *v/t.* augur; forecast.

auguste [o'gyst] **1.** *adj.* august, majestic; **2.** *su./m circus:* the funny man.

aujourd'hui [oʒur'dɥi] today; (d')~ en huit (quinze) today week (fortnight).

aumône [o'mo:n] *f* alms; charity; **aumônier** [omo'nje] *m* almoner; chaplain (*a.* ✂).

aunaie [o'ne] *f* plantation of alders.

aune¹ ♀ [o:n] *m* alder.

aune² [ʌ] *f* † ell; F une figure longue d'une ~ a face as long as a fiddle; **auner** [o'ne] (1a) *v/t.* measure by the ell.

auparavant [opara'vã] *adv.* before(hand); d'~ preceding.

auprès [o'prɛ] *adv.* near; close by; ~ de near, beside; compared with; in the opinion or view of, with (*s.o.*).

aurai [ɔ're] *1st p. sg. fut. of avoir 1.*

auréole [ɔre'ɔl] aureole, halo; *phot.* halation.

auriculaire [ɔriky'lɛ:r] **1.** *adj.* auricular; ear-...; *doigt m* ~ = **2.** *su./m* little finger.

aurifère [ɔri'fɛ:r] auriferous, gold-bearing; **aurification** [ʌfika'sjɔ̃] *f tooth:* filling *or Am.* stopping with gold; **aurifier** [ʌ'fje] (1o) *v/t.* fill *or* stop with gold.

aurore [ɔ'rɔ:r] **1.** *su./f* dawn (*a. fig.*), daybreak; *myth.* ♀ Aurora; ~ boréale northern lights *pl.*; **2.** *adj.* golden yellow.

auscultation 🩺 [ɔskylta'sjɔ̃] *f* auscultation, sounding (of chest); **aus-**

culter ⚕ [ˌˈte] (1a) *v/t.* auscultate, sound.

auspice [ɔsˈpis] *m* auspice, omen; ~s *pl.* protection *sg.*; auspices.

aussi [oˈsi] **1.** *adv.* also; too; as well; so; ~ ... *que* as ... as; *moi* ~ so am (do, can) I, F me too; **2.** *cj.* therefore; and so; ~ *bien* besides, moreover; **aussitôt** [osiˈto] **1.** *adv.* immediately, at once; ~ *que* as soon as; **2.** *prp.* immediately on.

austère [ɔsˈtɛːr] austere, stern; severe; **austérité** [ˌteriˈte] *f* austerity, sternness; severity.

austral, e, *m/pl.* **-als** *or* **-aux** [ɔsˈtral, ˌˈtro] southern; **australien, -enne** [ˌtraˈljɛ̃, ˌˈljɛn] *adj., a. su.* ♀ Australian.

austro... [ɔstrɔ] Austro-...

autan [oˈtɑ̃] *m* strong south wind.

autant [ˌ] *adv.* as much, as many; so much, so many; ~ *dire* practically, to all intents and purposes; (*pour*) ~ *que* as far as; *d'*~ (*plus*) *que* especially as, all the more as; *en faire* ~ do the same.

autarcie [otarˈsi] *f* autarky; **autarcique** [ˌˈsik] autarkical.

autel [oˈtɛl] *m* altar.

auteur [oˈtœːr] *m* author (*a. fig.*); *crime:* perpetrator; writer; ♪ composer; ♟ principal; *droit m d'*~ copyright; *droits m/pl. d'*~ royalties; *femme f* ~ authoress.

authenticité [otᾰtisiˈte] *f* authenticity, genuineness; **authentique** [ˌˈtik] authentic, genuine.

auto F [oˈto] *f* (motor-)car.

auto... [ɔtɔ] auto-...; self-...; motor-...; ~**bus** [ˌˈbys] *m* (motor) bus; ~**car** [ˌˈkaːr] *m* motor coach; ~**chenille** [ˌʃəˈniːj] *f* crawler tractor; half-track vehicle.

autochtone [otɔkˈtɔn] **1.** *adj.* autochthonous; aboriginal; **2.** *su.* autochthon.

auto...: ~**clave** [otɔˈklaːv] *m* sterilizer; *cuis.* pressure-cooker; ~**collant, e** [ˌkɔˈlɑ̃, ˌˈlɑ̃t] **1.** *adj.* self-adhesive; **2.** *su./m* sticker; ~**crate** [ˌˈkrat] *m* autocrat; ~**cratie** [ˌkraˈsi] *f* autocracy; ~**cratique** [ˌkraˈtik] autocratic; ~**détermination** [ˌdetermináˈsjɔ̃] *f* self-determination; ~**didacte** [ˌdiˈdakt] **1.** *adj.* self-taught; **2.** *su.* self-taught person; ~**drome** [ˌˈdroːm] *m* motor-racing

track; ~**-école** [ˌeˈkɔl] *f* school of motoring; driving school; ~**gène** [ˌˈʒɛn] autogenous; ⊕ *soudure f* ~ autogenous *or* oxy-acetylene welding; ~**gire** ✈ [ˌˈʒiːr] *m* autogiro; ~**graphe** [ˌˈgraf] *adj., a. su./m* autograph; ~**mate** [ˌˈmat] *m* automaton; ~**mation** [ˌmaˈsjɔ̃] *f* automation; ~**matique** [ˌmaˈtik] automatic, self-acting; ~**matisation** ⊕ [ˌmatisaˈsjɔ̃] *f* automation; ~**matiser** [ˌmatiˈze] (1a) *v/t.* automate.

automnal, e, *m/pl.* **-aux** [otɔmˈnal, ˌˈno] autumnal; **automne** [oˈtɔn] *m* autumn, *Am.* fall.

auto...: ~**mobile** [otɔmɔˈbil] **1.** *su./f* (motor-)car, *Am.* automobile; **2.** *adj.* self-propelling; *canot m* ~ motor boat; ~**mobilisme** [ˌmɔbiˈlism] *m* motoring; ~**mobiliste** [ˌmɔbiˈlist] *su.* motorist; ~**motrice** 🚋 [ˌmɔˈtris] *f* rail-motor, *Am.* rail-car; ~**neige** [ˌˈnɛːʒ] *m* snowmobile, snowcat; ~**nome** [ˌˈnɔm] autonomous; independent; self-governing; ~**nomie** [ˌnɔˈmi] *f* autonomy; independence; ~**portrait** [ˌpɔrˈtrɛ] *m* self-portrait; ~**propulsé, e** [ˌprɔpylˈse] self-propelled.

autopsie [otɔpˈsi] *f* autopsy.

autorail 🚋 [otɔˈraːj] *m* rail-motor, *Am.* rail-car.

autorisation [otɔrizaˈsjɔ̃] *f* authorization; permission; leave; licence; ~ *exceptionnelle* special permission *or* permit; **autorisé, e** [ˌˈze] authorized; authoritative (*source*); **autoriser** [ˌˈze] (1a) *v/t.* authorize; empower; permit; *s'*~ *de* use, rely on; refer to; **autoritaire** [ˌˈtɛːr] **1.** *adj.* authoritative; dictatorial; **2.** *su.* authoritarian; **autoritarisme** [ˌtaˈrism] *m* authoritarianism; **autorité** [ˌˈte] *f* authority; (legal) power; control; *faire* ~ be an authority (on, *en matière de*).

auto...: ~**route** [otɔˈrut] *f* motorway, *Am.* superhighway; ~**stop** [ˌˈstɔp] *m* hitch-hiking; *faire de l'*~ hitch-hike, thumb a lift; ~**stoppeur** *m*, **-euse** *f* [ˌstɔˈpœːr, ˌˈpøːz] hitch-hiker.

autour[1] *orn.* [oˈtuːr] goshawk.

autour[2] [ˌ] *adv.* round, about; ~ *de* round, about (*s.th.*).

autre [oːtr] **1.** *adj.* other; different; further; ~ *chose* something else; *d'*~ *part* on the other hand; *l'*~

jour the other day; *nous ⁓s Français* we Frenchmen; *tout ⁓ chose quite a different matter*; *un ⁓ moi-même* my other self; **2.** *pron./indef.* (an-)other; *⁓s pl.* others; *à d'⁓s! non-sense!*, tell that to the marines!; *de temps à ⁓* now and then; *l'un l'⁓* one another, each other; *ni l'un ni l'⁓* neither; *tout ⁓* anybody else; *un(e) ⁓* another; another (one), one more; **autrefois** [otrə'fwa] *adv.* formerly; **autrement** [⁓'mã] *adv.* otherwise; (or) else.

autrichien, -enne [otri'ʃjɛ̃, ⁓'ʃjɛn] *adj., a. su.* ♀ Austrian.

autruche *orn.* [o'tryʃ] *f* ostrich; *pratiquer la politique de l'⁓* stick one's head in the sand.

autrui [o'trɥi] *pron., no pl., usu. after prp.* others, other people.

auvent [o'vã] *m* penthouse; porchroof; △ weather-board; ⊕, 🏠 hood; *mot.* dash; *mot. ⁓s pl.* louvres.

auxiliaire [oksi'ljɛːr] **1.** *adj.* auxiliary; *bureau m ⁓* sub-office; **2.** *su./m* auxiliary (*a. gramm.*).

avachi, e [ava'ʃi] limp, flabby; **avachir** [ava'ʃiːr] (2a) *v/t.* make limp *or* flabby *or* sloppy; *s'⁓* go out of shape; become limp *or* flabby *or* sloppy.

aval¹, *pl.* **-s** ✝ [a'val] *m* endorsement.

aval² [⁓] *m* lower course of stream; *en ⁓* downstream; afterwards; *en ⁓ de* below; after; **avalage** [ava'laːʒ] *m* going downstream; *wine:* cellaring.

avalanche [ava'lɑ̃ːʃ] *f* avalanche; *fig.* shower.

avaler [ava'le] (1a) *v/t.* swallow; gulp down; inhale (*the cigarette smoke*); *fig.* swallow, pocket; **avaleur** *m*, **-euse** *f* [⁓'lœːr, ⁓'løːz] swallower; F guzzler.

avaliser ✝ [avali'ze] (1a) *v/t.* endorse, back (*a bill*); **avaliste** ✝ [⁓'list] *m* endorser.

à-valoir [ava'lwaːr] *m/inv.* advance (payment); down payment, deposit.

avance [a'vãːs] *f* advance; progress; lead; ⊕ *tool:* feed movement, travel; ✝ loan, advance; *mot. ⁓ à l'allumage* advance of the spark; *à l'⁓, d'⁓* in advance, beforehand; *être en ⁓* be early; be ahead (*of schedule*); *faire des ⁓s à* make up to (*s.o.*); **avancée** [avã'se] *f* projection; **avancement** [avãs'mã] *m* advancement; progress; putting forward; promotion;

avancer [avã'se] (1k) *v/t.* advance (*a.* ✝); hasten (*s.th.*); put on (*a watch*); promote; *fig.* be of help to; *s'⁓* advance; move forward; *fig.* commit o.s., F stick one's neck out; *v/i.* advance; be fast (*watch*); be ahead; △ project; *⁓ en âge* be getting on (in years).

avanie [ava'ni] *f* affront, snub.

avant [a'vã] **1.** *prp.* before (*Easter, the end, his arrival*); in front of (*the church*); within, in less than (*three days*); *⁓ peu* before long; *⁓ Jésus-Christ* before Christ, *abbr.* B.C.; *⁓ tout* above all; first of all; *⁓ de* (*inf.*) before (*ger.*); *⁓ que* (*sbj.*) before; **2.** *adv.* beforehand; previously; forward; far; *d'⁓* before, previous; *peu de temps ⁓* shortly before; *plus ⁓* further, more deeply; *bien ⁓ dans* (*la nuit, la forêt*) far into (the night, the wood); **3.** *cj.:* *⁓ que* (*sbj.*) before (*ind.*); *⁓ de* (*inf.*) before (*ger.*); **4.** *adj./inv.* front ...; *roue f ⁓* front wheel; **5.** *int.:* *en ⁓!* forward!; *ad-vance!*; *mettre en ⁓* advance (*an argument etc.*); **6.** *su./m* front; ⚓ bow; *sp.* forward.

avant-... [avã] fore...

avantage [avã'taːʒ] *m* advantage; privilege; profit, gain; benefit; *tennis:* vantage; *à l'⁓ de* to the benefit of; **avantager** [⁓ta'ʒe] (1l) *v/t.* favo(u)r; *fig.* flatter (*dress etc.*); **avantageux, -euse** [⁓ta'ʒø, ⁓'ʒøːz] *adj.* attractive (*price etc.*); profitable; favo(u)rable; conceited.

avant...: **⁓-bec** [avã'bɛk] *m* △ *bridge:* pier-head; ⚓ forepeak; **⁓-bras** [⁓'bra] *m/inv.* forearm; **⁓-centre** *sp.* [⁓'sãːtr] *m* centre forward; **⁓-corps** △ [⁓'kɔːr] *m* projecting part, projection; **⁓-coureur** [⁓ku'rœːr] **1.** *su./m* forerunner; **2.** *adj.* precursory; *signe m ⁓* premonitory sign; **⁓-dernier, -ère** [⁓dɛr'nje, ⁓'njɛːr] *adj. a. su.* last but one; **⁓-garde** [⁓'gard] *f* ✗ advance(d) guard; vanguard (*a. fig.*); **⁓guerre** [⁓'gɛːr] *m* or *f* pre-war period; *d'⁓* pre-war; **⁓-hier** [⁓'tjɛːr] the day before yesterday; **⁓-port** [⁓'pɔːr] *m* outer harbo(u)r; **⁓-poste** ✗ [⁓'pɔst] *m* outpost; **⁓-projet** [⁓prɔ'ʒɛ] *m* pilot study; **⁓-propos** [⁓prɔ'po] *m/inv.* preface, foreword; **⁓-scène** *thea.* [⁓'sɛn] *f* proscenium; stagebox; **⁓-train** [⁓'trɛ̃] *m* forecarriage;

⚔ limber; ~-**veille** [~'vɛ:j] f two days before.

avare [a'va:r] **1.** adj. miserly; stingy; **2.** su. miserly person; **avarice** [ava'ris] f avarice; stinginess; **avaricieux, -euse** [~ri'sjø, ~'sjø:z] avaricious; stingy.

avarie [ava'ri] f ⚓ average; damage; ⊕ breakdown; deterioration; F syphilis; **avarié, e** [~'rje] damaged; injured; spoiled; rotting, bad; **avarier** [~'rje] (1o) v/t. spoil; damage; s'~ go bad, rot.

avatar [ava'ta:r] m avatar; ~s pl. ups and downs; vicissitudes.

avec [a'vɛk] **1.** prp. with; for, in spite of (all his riches); ~ patience (véhémence etc.); ~ patiently (vehemently etc.); ~ l'âge with age; ~ ça into the bargain; et ~ ça, Madame? anything else, Madam?; ~ ce temps-là in this weather; divorcer d'~ sa femme divorce one's wife; distinguer l'ami d'~ le flatteur distinguish a friend from a flatterer; **2.** adv. F with it or them, F him, her, them.

avenant¹, e [av'nɑ̃, ~'nɑ̃:t] comely; à l'~ in keeping; ... to match; appropriate.

avenant² ⚖ [av'nɑ̃] m codicil, rider.

avènement [avɛn'mɑ̃] m arrival, coming; king: accession; **avenir** [av'ni:r] m future; à l'~ in (the) future; **avent** eccl. [a'vɑ̃] m Advent.

aventure [avɑ̃'ty:r] f adventure; chance, luck; love affair; à l'~ at random; dire la bonne ~ tell fortunes; parc m d'~ adventure playground; **aventurer** [avɑ̃ty're] (1a) v/t. venture, risk; s'~ venture, take a risk; **aventureux, -euse** [~'rø, ~'rø:z] adventurous; hazardous; bold (theory); **aventurier, -ère** [~'rje, ~'rjɛ:r] **1.** adj. adventurous; su./m adventurer; su./f adventuress.

avenue [av'ny] f avenue; drive.

averé [ave're] established (fact etc.); known, recognized; **avérer** [~] (1f) v/t.: s'~ be confirmed; s'~ ... turn out to be ..., prove (to be) ..., show oneself to be ...

avers [a'vɛr] m coin: obverse.

averse [a'vɛrs] f shower, downpour.

aversion [avɛr'sjɔ̃] f aversion (to, pour), dislike (of, for pour).

avertir [avɛr'ti:r] (2a) v/t. warn (of, de); notify; **avertissement** [~tis'mɑ̃] m warning; notification; foreword; ⚑ demand note; **avertisseur** [~ti'sœ:r] m warner; warning signal; thea. call-boy; 🚗 signal; mot. horn; ~ d'incendie fire-alarm.

aveu [a'vø] m confession; consent; homme m sans ~ disreputable character.

aveugle [a'vœgl] **1.** adj. blind; ~ d'un œil blind in one eye; **2.** su. blind person; en ~ blindfold; les ~s pl. the blind; **aveuglement** [avœgle'mɑ̃] adv. blindly; **aveuglement** [~glə'mɑ̃] m blindness; **aveugle-né, e** [~glə'ne] **1.** adj. blind from birth; **2.** su. person blind from birth; **aveugler** [~'gle] (1a) v/t. blind; dazzle; ⚓ stop (a leak); **aveuglette** [~'glɛt] adv.: à l'~ blindly; ✈ voler à l'~ fly blind.

aveulir [avœ'li:r] (2a) v/t. enfeeble.

avez [a've] 2nd p. pl. pres. of avoir **1.**

aviateur m, **-trice** f [avja'tœ:r, ~'tris] aviator; **aviation** [~'sjɔ̃] f aviation; flying; air force; aircraft; ~ civile civil aviation; ~ de ligne air traffic.

aviculteur [avikyl'tœ:r] m bird-fancier; poultry farmer.

avide [a'vid] greedy, eager (for, de); **avidité** [avidi'te] f greediness; eagerness.

avilir [avi'li:r] (2a) v/t. degrade, debase; lower; s'~ lower o.s., demean o.s.; lose value, fall (in price etc.); **avilissement** [~lis'mɑ̃] m debasement, degradation, depreciation, fall (in price etc.).

aviné, e [avi'ne] intoxicated, drunk, F tipsy; **aviner** [~] (1a) v/t. season (a cask); s'~ get drunk.

avion [a'vjɔ̃] m aeroplane, Am. airplane; F plane; ~ à décollage vertical vertical takeoff aircraft; ~ à réaction jet (plane); ~ bimoteur (polymoteur) two- (multi-)engined aircraft; ~ de bombardement bomber; ~ de chasse fighter; ~ de combat battle plane; ~ d'entraînement training plane; ~ de ligne airliner; ~ de reconnaissance scouting or reconnaissance plane; ~ de transport transport plane; ~-fusée rocket-plane; ~-taxi charter plane; ~ transbordeur air ferry; par ~ by air-mail; **avionette** [avjo'nɛt] f light aeroplane (Am. airplane).

aviron [avi'rɔ̃] m oar; rowing.

avis [a'vi] m opinion; notice, notification; advice; warning; ~ d'expert expert opinion; être d'~ que feel or think or be of the opinion that; être de l'~ de q., être du même ~ que q. be of or share s.o.'s opinion; à mon ~ in my opinion; jusqu'à nouvel ~ until further notice; note f d'~ advice note; sans ~ préalable without notice; ✝ suivant ~ as per advice; un ~ a piece of advice; **avisé, e** [avi'se] shrewd; prudent; bien ~ well-advised; **aviser** [~] (1a) v/t. catch sight of; notify, inform; s'~ realize, notice; s'~ de think about (s.th.); take it into one's head to (inf.); v/i. decide, take steps; ~ à see about (s.th.). [sloop.]

aviso ⚓ [avi'zo] m dispatch-boat.

avitaminose ✿ [avitami'no:z] f avitaminosis, vitamin deficiency.

aviver [avi've] (1a) v/t. revive, brighten; touch up (a colour); ⊕ put a keen edge on, sharpen; ⊕ burnish (metal); ✿ ~ les bords de refresh (a wound).

avocat¹ ⚖ [avɔ'ka] m barrister, counsel; Am. counsellor; Sc. advocate (a. fig.); ~ général (approx.) King's or Queen's Counsel.

avocat² ♀ [~] m avocado (pear).

avoine [a'vwan] f oat(s pl.).

avoir [a'vwa:r] (1) 1. v/t. have; obtain; hold; ~ en horreur abhor, detest; ~ faim (soif) be hungry (thirsty); ~ froid (chaud) be cold (hot); ~ honte be ashamed; ~ lieu happen, take place; en ~ assez be fed up; en ~ contre have a grudge against; j'ai vingt ans I am 20 (years old); qu'avez vous? what's the matter with you?; v/impers.: il y a there is, there are; il y a un an a year ago; 2. su./m property, possession; ✝ credit; ~ à l'étranger deposits pl. abroad; ~ en banque credit balance; doit et ~ debit and credit.

avoisiner [avwazi'ne] (1a) v/t. border on; be near to.

avons [a'vɔ̃] 1st p. pl. pres. of avoir 1.

avortement [avɔrtə'mɑ̃] m ✿ miscarriage (a. fig.); abortion; ♀ nonformation; **avorter** [~'te] (1a) v/i. miscarry (a. fig.); abort; ♀ develop imperfectly; faire ~ procure an abortion; **avorton** [~'tɔ̃] m abortion; F shrimp, sl. little squirt.

avouable [a'vwabl] avowable; **avoué** [a'vwe] m solicitor; attorney; **avouer** [~] (1p) v/t. admit, acknowledge, confess; s'~ coupable plead guilty.

avril [a'vril] m April; poisson m d'~ April fool.

axe [aks] m axis (a. pol.); ⊕ axle; ⚔ ~ balisé (localizer) beam; ⊕ ~ de pompe pump spindle; opt. ~ optique axis of vision.

axiome ⚗, phls., fig. [ak'sjo:m] m axiom.

axonge [ak'sɔ̃:ʒ] f lard; grease.

ayant [ɛ'jɑ̃] p.pr. of avoir 1; ~ cause, pl. ~s cause ⚖ su./m assign; executor; trustee; ~ droit, pl. ~s droit ⚖ su./m rightful claimant; beneficiary; **ayons** [ɛ'jɔ̃] 1st p.pl. pres. sbj. of avoir 1.

azalée ♀ [aza'le] f azalea.

azimut [azi'myt] m azimuth; fig. tous ~s omnidirectional.

azotate ⚗ [azɔ'tat] m nitrate; **azote** ⚗ [a'zɔt] m nitrogen; **azoté, e** [azɔ'te] nitrogenous; engrais m/pl. ~s nitrate fertilizers; **azotite** ⚗ [~'tit] m nitrite.

aztèque [az'tek] 1. adj. Aztec; 2. su. ♀ Aztec; su./m sl. little shrimp of a fellow.

azur [a'zy:r] m azure, blue; pierre f d'~ lapis lazuli; blue-spar; **azuré, e** [azy're] azure, (sky-)blue.

azyme [a'zim] 1. adj. unleavened; 2. su./m unleavened bread.

B

B, b [be] *m* B, b.

baba¹ [ba'ba] *m* baba (*sponge-cake soaked in rum syrup*).

baba² F [„] *adj./inv.* flabbergasted.

babeurre [ba'bœːr] *m* buttermilk.

babil [ba'bil] *m child*: prattle; *birds*: twittering; *brook*: babble; **babillage** [babi'jaːʒ] *m child*, *brook*: babbling; *birds*: twittering; **babillard, e** [„'jaːr, „'jard] **1.** *adj.* talkative, garrulous; **2.** *su.* chatterer; *su./f sl.* better; **babiller** [„'je] (1a) *v/i.* prattle; babble.

babine [ba'bin] *f zo.* pendulous lip; chop; F „*s pl.* lips, chops.

babiole [ba'bjɔl] *f* knick-knack, curio; toy, bauble.

bâbord ⚓ [ba'bɔːr] *m* port (side).

babouche [ba'buʃ] *f* Turkish slipper.

babouin [ba'bwɛ̃] *m zo.* baboon; F imp (= *naughty child*).

bac¹ [bak] *m* ferry(-boat); ⊕ tank, vat; ⚡ *accumulator*: container; *passer q. en* „ ferry s.o. over.

bac² F [bak] *m see baccalauréat*; **baccalauréat** [bakalɔre'a] *m* school-leaving certificate.

bacchanale F [baka'nal] *f* orgy; drinking song; **bacchante** [„'kɑ̃t] *f* bacchante; *fig.* lewd woman.

bâche [bɑːʃ] *f* ⊕ tank, cistern; ⊕ casing; ↗ forcing frame; sheet, cover; „ *goudronnée* tarpaulin.

bachelier *m*, -**ère** *f* [baʃə'lje, „'ljɛːr] holder of the school-leaving certificate.

bâcher [bɑ'ʃe] (1a) *v/t.* cover (*with a sheet*); ⊕ case (*a turbine*).

bachique [ba'ʃik] Bacchic; bacchanalian (*scene*); drinking (*song*).

bachot¹ [ba'ʃo] *m* ⚓ wherry, dinghy; ⊕ sieve.

bachot² F [ba'ʃo] *m see baccalauréat; boîte f à* „ cramming-shop, crammer's; **bachotage** F [„ʃɔ'taːʒ] *m* cramming (*for an exam*); *faire du* „ = **bachoter** F [„ʃɔ'te] (1a) *v/i.* cram (*for an exam*).

bacille [ba'sil] *m* bacillus; *porteur m de* „*s* germ-carrier.

bâcle [bɑːkl] *f* bar; **bâcler** [bɑ'kle] (1a) *v/t.* bar (*a door*); ⚓ block (*a port*); F hurry over (*one's toilet*); F scamp (*a piece of work*).

bactérie [bakte'ri] *f biol.* bacterium; *zo.* bacteria.

badaud *m*, **e** *f* [ba'do, „'doːd] stroller; gaper; *Am.* F rubber-neck.

baderne ⚓ [ba'dɛrn] *f* fender; F *vieille* „ old fog(e)y; ✗ old dug-out.

badigeon [badi'ʒɔ̃] *m* whitewash; distemper; **badigeonnage** [„ʒɔ-'naːʒ] *m* whitewashing; distempering; ✚ painting (*with iodine*); **badigeonner** [„ʒɔ'ne] (1a) *v/t.* whitewash; distemper; daub; ✚ paint.

badin¹, e [ba'dɛ̃, „'din] **1.** *adj.* playful; **2.** *su.* joker, banterer.

badin² ✈ [ba'dɛ̃] *m* air-speed indicator.

badinage [badi'naːʒ] *m* banter.

badine [ba'din] *f* cane, switch.

badiner [badi'ne] (1a) *v/i.* jest; toy (with, *avec*).

baffe F [baf] *f* slap (in the face).

bafouer [ba'fwe] (1p) *v/t.* ridicule, scoff at; **bafouillage** [bafu'jaːʒ] *m* stammering; **bafouiller** [„'je] (1a) *v/i.* stammer; *sl.* talk nonsense; *mot.* splutter.

bâfrer *sl.* [bɑ'fre] (1a) *vt/i.* guzzle.

bagage [ba'gaːʒ] *m* luggage, *Am.* baggage; ✗ kit; *fig.* stock of knowledge; „*s pl. non accompagnés luggage sg.* in advance; *plier* „ pack up and leave; *sl.* decamp; *sl.* die.

bagarre [ba'gaːr] *f* fight(ing); scuffle; brawl; riot; **bagarrer** F [„ga're] (1a) *v/t.: se* „ quarrel; fight.

bagatelle [baga'tɛl] *f* trifle, bagatelle; „! nonsense!; F *pour une* „ for a song.

bagne ⚖ [baɲ] *m* convict prison; penal servitude.

bagnole F [ba'ɲɔl] *f* motor car; *vieille* „ jalopy.

bagou(t) F [ba'gu] *m* glibness; *avoir du* „ have the gift of the gab.

bague [bag] *f* ring; *cigar*: band; ⊕ strap; ⊕ ~ *d'arrêt* set collar; **baguenauder** F [~no'de] (1a) *v/i. a. se* ~ go for stroll; stroll about; **baguette** [ba'gɛt] *f* stick, rod; stick of bread; ♪ baton; △ beading; *writing paper*: black border; *stockings*: clock; ~ *magique*, ~ *de fée* magic wand; ⚕ ~ *d'or* wall-flower; *passer par les* ~*s* run the gauntlet; **baguier** [ba'gje] *m* ring-case; ring size ga(u)ge.

bahut [ba'y] *m* † trunk, chest; low sideboard; *sl.* school.

bai, e [bɛ] *adj., a. su./m* bay.

baie[1] ♀ [~] *f* berry.

baie[2] *geog.* [~] *f* bay, bight.

baie[3] △ [~] *f* bay, opening.

baignade [bɛ'ɲad] *f* bathe, dip; **baigner** [~'ɲe] (1b) *v/t.* bathe; bath; *se* ~ bathe; take a bath; *v/i.* steep; *fig.* baigné de larmes suffused with tears (*eyes*); **baigneur, -euse** [~'ɲœːr, ~'ɲøːz] *su.* bather; bathing attendant; *su./f* bathing-wrap, *Am.* bathrobe; **baignoire** [~'ɲwaːr] *f* bath(-tub); *thea.* ground-floor box.

bail, *pl.* baux [baːj, bo] *m* lease; ~ *à ferme* farming lease; *prendre à* ~ take a lease of, lease.

bâillement [baj'mɑ̃] *m* yawn(ing); gaping; **bâiller** [ba'je] (1a) *v/i.* yawn; gape; stand ajar (*door*).

bailleur *m*, **-eresse** *f* [ba'jœːr, baj-'rɛs] *tt* lessor; ♥ ~ *de fonds* backer; sleeping *or* silent partner.

bâillon [bɑ̃'jɔ̃] *m* gag; *horse*: muzzle; **bâillonner** [~jɔ'ne] (1a) *v/t.* gag (*a. fig.*).

bain [bɛ̃] *m* bath; bathing; F *fig. dans le* ~ in the picture, informed; implicated, involved; *prendre un* ~ *de foule* go on a walkabout; *sortie f de* ~ bath-wrap, *Am.* bath-robe; ~**douche,** *pl.* ~**s-douches** [~'duʃ] *m* shower(-bath); ~**marie,** *pl.* ~**s-marie** [~ma'ri] *m* ⚗ waterbath; *cuis.* double saucepan, *Am.* double boiler.

baïonnette ⚔ [bajɔ'nɛt] *f* bayonet.

baisemain [bɛz'mɛ̃] *m* hand-kissing; **baiser** [bɛ'ze] **1.** *su./m* kiss; **2.** (1b) *v/t.*: ~ *q. à la joue* kiss s.o.'s cheek; *sl. (a. v/i.)* ~ (*q.*) make love (to *s.o.*); **baisoter** F [~zɔ'te] (1c) *v/t.* peck at.

baisse [bɛs] *f* fall (*a. prices*), going down; subsidence; *sight, prices*: decline; *tide*: ebb; *en* ~ falling (*stocks*);

baisser [bɛ'se] (1b) *v/t. usu.* lower; turn down (*the light*); drop (*a curtain*); *se* ~ bend down; *v/i.* decline; fall; abate (*flood*); ebb (*tide*); burn low (*lamp*).

bajoue [ba'ʒu] *f*: ~*s pl.* cheeks, chaps, chops.

bakélite [bake'lit] *f* bakelite.

bal, *pl.* bals [bal] *m* ball; dance; **balade** F [ba'lad] *f* stroll; ramble; **balader** F [bala'de] (1a) *v/t.* take for a walk; carry about; *se* ~ (take a) stroll; **baladeur, -euse** [~'dœːr, ~'døːz] **1.** *adj.* F wandering; **2.** *su.* wanderer, saunterer; *su./f* trailer (*of car, of tram*); street-barrow; hand-cart; ⚡ inspection lamp.

baladin *m*, **e** *f* [bala'dɛ̃, ~'din] mountebank; F clown.

balafre [ba'lafr] *f* gash, slash; scar; **balafrer** [~la'fre] (1a) *v/t.* gash, slash; scar.

balai [ba'lɛ] *m* broom; brush; *mot. windscreen-wiper*: blade; ~ *mécanique* carpet sweeper; *coup m de* ~ sweep; *fig.* clean sweep.

balance [ba'lɑ̃ːs] *f* balance (*a.* ⚕); scales *pl.*, weighing machine; ♥ balance; † hesitation; ♥ ~ *de(s) paiements* balance of payments; ~ *romaine* steelyard; ⚕ *faire la* ~ strike the (*fig.* a) balance; *faire pencher la* ~ turn the scales; *astr. la* ♎ Libra, the Balance; *fig. mettre en* ~ weigh up; **balancement** [balɑ̃s-'mɑ̃] *m* sway(ing), swing(ing); *fig.* balance; **balancer** [balɑ̃'se] (1k) *v/t.* swing; throw, fling, chuck; F chuck out; balance; *fig.* weigh up; *se* ~ rock, sway; swing; seesaw; *sl. se* ~ *de* not to care a damn about; *sl. je m'en balance a.* I couldn't care less (about it); **balancier** [~'sje] *m* balancing pole; *mot. crank-shaft*: balancer; *watch*: balance-wheel; *clock*: pendulum; *pump*: handle; ⊕ *beam-engine*: beam; ⊕ fly(-press); **balançoire** [~'swaːr] *f* seesaw; swing.

balayer [balɛ'je] (1i) *v/t.* sweep out *or* up *or* away (*a. fig.*); *fig.* clear out; scour (*the sea*); *telev.* scan; **balayette** [~'jɛt] *f* whisk; small brush; **balayeur, -euse** [~'jœːr, ~'jøːz] *su. person*: sweeper; *su./f machine*: sweeper; **balayures** [~'jyːr] *f/pl.* sweepings.

balbutiement [balbysi'mɑ̃] *m* stuttering, stammering; **balbutier**

bande

[∿'sje] (1o) v/i. mumble; stammer; v/t. stutter out, stammer out.

balcon [bal'kɔ̃] m △ balcony; *thea.* dress circle.

baldaquin [balda'kɛ̃] m canopy, baldachin.

baleine [ba'lɛn] f whale(bone); **baleinier** [balɛ'nje] m whaler (*ship, a. man*); whaling; **baleinière** [∿'njɛːr] f whale-boat; ∿ de *sauvetage* life-boat.

balise¹ ⚘ [ba'liːz] f canna seed.

balise² [ba'liːz] f ⚓ beacon; ✈ runway light; *mot.* road sign; marker; ∿ *flottante* buoy; **baliser** [∿li'ze] (1a) v/t. ⚓ beacon; ⚓ buoy; provide with runway lights *or* road signs; mark out.

balistique [balis'tik] 1. adj. ballistic; 2. su./f ballistics sg.

baliverne F [bali'vɛrn] f *mostly* ∿s pl. nonsense sg.

ballade [ba'lad] f ballad.

ballant, e [ba'lɑ̃, ∿'lɑ̃ːt] 1. adj. dangling; swinging; slack (*rope*); 2. su./m swing.

ballast [ba'last] m ⊕ ballast; ⚓ ballast-tank; **ballastière** [∿las'tjɛːr] f gravel-pit.

balle¹ [bal] f ball; bullet, shot; ✝ *cotton*: bale; *pedlar*: pack; *sl.* head; *sl.* franc; ∿ de *service tennis*: service-ball.

balle² [∿] f husk, chaff; ⚘ glume.

ballerine [bal'rin] f ballet-dancer, ballerina; **ballet** [ba'lɛ] m ballet.

ballon [ba'lɔ̃] m balloon (a. 🜍); (foot)ball; 🜍 flask; ⊕ carboy; ⚓ ball-signal; ∿ de *plage* beach ball; *fig.* ∿ d'essai feeler; ∿-sonde test *or* sounding balloon; **ballonnement** [∿lɔn'mɑ̃] m ✅ swelling; ✅ distension; ✅ flatulence; **ballonner** [∿lɔ'ne] (1a) vt/i. swell; bulge; distend (a. ✅).

ballot [ba'lo] m pack, bundle; F idiot, chump; **ballottage** *pol.* [balɔ'taːʒ] m second ballot; **ballotter** [∿'te] (1a) v/t. toss (about), shake about; *fig.* être ballotté entre be tossed *or* torn between; v/i. shake; toss; rattle (*door*).

bal(l)uchon F [baly'ʃɔ̃] m bundle.

balnéaire [balne'ɛːr] bath...; watering-...; *station f* ∿ watering-place; seaside resort.

balnéothérapie [balneɔtera'pi] f balneotherapy.

balourd, e [ba'luːr, ∿'lurd] 1. adj.

awkward; 2. *su.* awkward person; yokel; su./m ⊕ unbalance; unbalanced weight; **balourdise** [∿lur-'diːz] f awkwardness; F bloomer, stupid mistake.

baltique [bal'tik] 1. adj. Baltic; 2. su./f: la (mer) ♀ the Baltic (Sea).

balustrade [balys'trad] f balustrade; banister; (hand-)rail; **balustre** [∿'lystr] m baluster; banister.

bambin m, e f F [bɑ̃'bɛ̃, ∿'bin] little child; kid; youngster.

bamboche [bɑ̃'bɔʃ] f puppet; F spree; faire ∿ go on the spree; il est ∿ he's a bit merry; **bambocher** F [bɑ̃bɔ'ʃe] (1a) v/i. go on the spree; **bambocheur** m, -euse f F [∿'ʃœːr, ∿'ʃøːz] reveller.

bambou [bɑ̃'bu] m bamboo(-cane).

ban [bɑ̃] m ✝ proclamation; drum roll; F applause; *mettre au* ∿ banish; F send to Coventry; outlaw (from, de); *publier les* ∿s put up *or* publish the bans; *fig.* le ∿ et l'*arrière*-∿ de ses amis etc. all his friends etc.

banal, e, m/pl. **-als** *fig.* [ba'nal] commonplace, banal; vulgar; **banaliser** [∿nali'ze] (1a) v/t. popularize; vulgarize.

banane [ba'nan] f ⚘ banana; *sl.* decoration, medal; *sl.* chopper, whirlybird (= *helicopter*); **bananier** [∿na'nje] m banana-tree.

banc [bɑ̃] m bench (a. ⊕); form, seat; *eccl.* pew; *lathe, oysters, stone*: bed; *sand, mud*: bank; *sand, coral*: shoal; (*witness*-)box; *fish*: school, shoal; ⊕ ∿ d'*épreuve* testing stand, bench.

bancal, e, m/pl. **-als** [bɑ̃'kal] 1. adj. bandy(-legged); unsteady, rickety; 2. su. bandy-legged person.

bandage [bɑ̃'daːʒ] m ✅ bandaging; bandage; *mot.* tyre, *Am.* tire; ⊕ *spring*: winding up; ✅ ∿ herniaire truss.

bande¹ [bɑ̃d] f band, strip; stripe; stretch (*of land*); ✅ bandage; strap; ⊕ *spring*: compression; *cin.* reel; *post*: wrapper; ⚓ list; ∿ dessinée comic strip; strip cartoon; ∿ *magnétique* recording tape; ∿ molletière puttee; ⊕ ∿ *transporteuse* conveyor belt; *enregistrer sur* ∿ tape-record; *enregistrer sur* ∿ *vidéo* videotape; *sous* ∿ *post*: by post.

bande² [∿] f band, gang; party; flock; pack.

bandeau [bã'do] *m* headband; diadem; bandage; **bandelette** [bãd-'let] *f* strip; **bander** [bã'de] (1a) *v/t.* bandage, bind up; wind up, tighten; ⚿ key in; *fig.* ~ *les yeux de* blindfold (*s.o.*); *v/i.* be tight; **banderole** [~'drɔl] *f* streamer; pennant; ✕ *rifle:* sling; *cartoon:* balloon.

bandit [bã'di] *m* bandit; gangster; crook.

bandoulière [bãdu'ljɛːr] *f* shoulder-strap; *en* ~ slung over the shoulder.

banjo ♩ [bã'ʒo] *m* banjo.

banlieue [bã'ljø] *f* suburbs *pl.*, outskirts *pl.*; *de* ~ suburban; ~-*dortoir* dormitory suburb; **banlieusard** *m*, **e** *f* F [~ljø'zaːr, ~'zard] suburbanite.

banne [ban] *f* hamper; coal cart; awning; tarpaulin; ⚒ tub, skip; ⚓ *dredger:* bucket; **bannette** [ba-'net] *f* small hamper.

banni, e [ba'ni] 1. *adj.* banished; 2. *su.* outcast; outlaw; exile.

bannière [ba'njɛːr] *f* banner; F *être en* ~ be in shirt-tails.

bannir [ba'niːr] (2a) *v/t.* outlaw; exile (from, *de*).

banque [bãːk] *f* bank; banking; ~ *du sang* blood bank; ~ *par actions* joint-stock bank; *faire sauter la* ~ break the bank; **banqueroute** ✝ [bãˈkrut] *f* bankruptcy; failure; *faire* ~ go bankrupt.

banquet [bã'kɛ] *m* banquet, feast.

banquette [bã'kɛt] *f* bench, seat; *earth:* bank; *golf:* bunker.

banquier *m*, **-ère** *f* [bã'kje, ~'kjɛːr] banker. [ice.)

banquise [bã'kiːz] *f* ice-floe; pack-)

baptême [ba'tɛːm] *m* baptism, christening; *nom m de* ~ Christian name, *Am.* given name; **baptiser** [bati'ze] (1a) *v/t.* baptize, christen; F *fig.* water (down) (*the wine*); **baptismal,** e, *m/pl.* -aux [batis'mal, ~'mo], **baptistaire** [~'tɛːr] baptismal; *extrait m baptistaire* certificate of baptism.

baquet [ba'kɛ] *m* tub, bucket.

bar¹ [baːr] *m* (public) bar; *au* ~ in the pub.

bar² *icht.* [~] *m* bass; perch.

bar³ *phys.* [~] *m* bar.

baragouin F [bara'gwɛ̃] *m* gibberish; lingo; **baragouiner** F [~gwi'ne] (1a) *vt/i.* jabber, gibber.

baraque [ba'rak] *f* hut, shed; F dump, joint, hole; **baraquement**

[~rak'mã] *m*: ✕ ~*s pl.* hutments; **baraquer** ✕ [~ra'ke] (1m) *vt/i.* hut.

baratin F [bara'tɛ̃] *m* sweet talk; patter, *Am.* malarky; **baratiner** [~ti'ne] (1a) *vt/i.* sweet-talk; *v/t.* chat (*s.o.*) up.

barattage [bara'taːʒ] *m* churning; **baratte** [~'rat] *f* churn; **baratter** [~ra'te] (1a) *v/t.* churn.

barbacane [barba'kan] *f* ⊕ draining channel; weep-hole; △ barbican; △ loop-hole.

barbare [bar'bar] 1. *adj.* barbaric; barbarous; uncivilized; 2. *su./m* barbarian.

barbaresque [barba'rɛsk] *adj., a. su./m* Berber.

barbarie [barba'ri] *f* barbarism; barbarity, cruelty; **barbarisme** *gramm.* [~'rism] *m* barbarism.

barbe¹ [barb] *f* beard (*a.* ♆); whiskers *pl.*; mould, mildew; ⊕ burr; F bore, nuisance; ~ *à papa* candyfloss, *Am.* cotton candy; *se faire faire la* ~ get o.s. shaved; (*se*) *faire la* ~ shave.

barbe² [~] *m* barb, Barbary horse.

barbeau [bar'bo] *m* *icht.* barbel; ♀ cornflower; *icht.* ~ *de mer* red mullet; *bleu* ~ cornflower blue; **barbelé,** e [~bə'le] 1. *adj.* barbed; *fil m de fer* ~ barbed wire; 2. *su./m*: ~*s pl.* barbed wire entanglement *sg.*

barber *sl.* [bar'be] (1a) *v/t.* bore.

barbet, -ette [bar'bɛ, ~'bɛt] *su.* water-spaniel; *su./m icht.* barbel.

barbiche [bar'biʃ] *f* goatee; short beard.

barbier [bar'bje] *m* barber; **barbifier** F [~bi'fje] (1o) *v/t.* shave; bore; *se* ~ be bored.

barbiturique [barbity'rik] 1. *adj.* barbituric; 2. *su./m* barbiturate.

barbotage [barbɔ'taːʒ] *m* paddling, splashing; ⊕ splash; *gas:* bubbling; mess, mud; bran mash; *sl.* filching; *sl.* mumbling; **barboter** [~'te] (1a) *v/i.* paddle, splash (about); bubble (*gas*); *v/t.* mumble; *sl.* filch; *sl.* scrounge; **barboteur, -euse** [~-'tœːr, ~'tøːz] *su.* paddler; *sl.* scrounger; *su./m* ⊕ bubbler; ⊕ stirrer; *su./f* rompers *pl.*; washing machine.

barbouillage [barbu'jaːʒ] *m* daubing; scrawl(ing), scribble; **barbouiller** [~'je] (1a) *v/t.* daub; smear (with, *de*); sully; scribble, scrawl;

fig. botch; **se ~** dirty one's face;
barbouilleur *m*, **-euse** *f* F [~'jœːr,
~'jøːz] dauber; hack.

barbouze F [bar'buːz] *m* secret
(police) agent.

barbu, e [bar'by] bearded (*a.* ♀);
mouldy.

barbue *icht.* [~] *f* brill.

barcasse ⚓ [bar'kas] *f* launch; F old
tub.

barda *sl.* [bar'da] *m* ✗ pack, kit;
stuff, things *pl.*

bardane ♀ [bar'dan] *f* burdock.

barde[1] [bard] *m* bard.

barde[2] [~] *f* pack-saddle; *cuis.* slice of
bacon, bard.

bardeau[1] [bar'do] *m* △ shingle
(-board), *Am.* clapboard; lath; small
raft.

bardeau[2] [~] *m* hinny.

barder[1] *sl.* [bar'de] (1a): *ça barde*
sparks are flying.

barder[2] [~] (1a) *v/t.* ✗ † arm with
bards; *cuis.* bard (*with bacon*), lard (*a.
fig.*).

bardot [bar'do] *m* hinny; packmule.

barème [ba'rɛm] *m* table, (price) list;
scale; schedule; graph.

barguigner F [bargi'ɲe] (1a) *v/i.*:
sans ~ without shilly-shallying.

baril [ba'ri] *m* cask(ful); **barillet**
[~ri'jɛ] *m* keg; *revolver:* cylinder;
⊕ barrel; *anat.* middle-ear.

bariolage [barjɔ'la:ʒ] *m* motley;
gaudy colo(u)r scheme; **barioler**
[~'le] (1a) *v/t.* variegate; paint in
gaudy colo(u)rs.

barman, *pl. a.* **-men** [bar'man,
~'mɛn] *m* barman.

baromètre [barɔ'mɛtr] *m* barometer; F (weather-)glass.

baron [ba'rɔ̃] *m* baron; **baronne**
[~'rɔn] *f* baroness.

baroque [ba'rɔk] **1.** *adj.* quaint; odd;
baroque; **2.** *su./m* △ *etc.* baroque.

baroud F [ba'rud] *m* fight(ing); *~
d'honneur* gallant last stand; **barou-
der** F [baru'de] *v/i.* fight.

barouf F [ba'ruf] *m* noise, racket.

barque ⚓ [bark] *f* barge, boat.

barrage [ba'ra:ʒ] *m* barring, closing; dam(ming); *fig.* obstruction;
⊕ barrage (*a.* ✗), weir; ⚓ *harbour:*
boom; ♥ *cheque:* crossing; ✗ *tir m
de ~* curtain-fire.

barre [ba:r] *f* bar (*a.* ♬♭); ⊕ rod;
gold: ingot; ⚓ helm; stroke (*of
the pen*); *tex.* stripe; ♪ bar(-line);

(tidal) bore; *sp.* *~s pl. parallèles*
parallel bars; *sp. ~ fixe* horizontal
bar; *mot. ~ de connexion* tie-rod;
♬♭ *~ des témoins* witness-box; ✦ *~
omnibus (collectrice)* omnibus-bar;

barreau [ba'ro] *m* bar (*a.* ♬♭);
rail; *ladder:* rung; fire-bar; *être
reçu au ~* be called to the bar, *Am.*
pass the bar.

barrer [ba're] (1a) *v/t.* bar; secure
with a bar; block (up); dam (*a
stream*); close (*a road*); cross out
(*a word*); ⚓ steer; ♥ cross (*a
cheque*); *route f barrée* no thoroughfare; *sl.* **se ~** skedaddle, make off.

barrette[1] *eccl.* [ba'rɛt] *f* biretta;
cardinal's cap.

barrette[2] [~] *f* hair slide; *medal:* bar.

barreur ⚓ [ba'rœːr] *m* helmsman,
cox.

barricader [barika'de] (1a) *v/t.*
barricade; **barrière** [~'rjɛːr] *f* barrier (*a.* ✦, *a. fig.*); obstacle; *castle,*
✦ *level-crossing, town:* gate; turnpike; *sp.* starting-post.

barrique [ba'rik] *f* hogshead, cask,
butt.

barrir [ba'riːr] (2a) *v/i.* trumpet
(*elephant*).

bartavelle *orn.* [barta'vɛl] *f* rock
partridge.

bas, basse [ba, baːs] **1.** *adj. usu.*
low (*a. fig.*); mean; lower; *basse
fréquence radio:* low frequency; *au
~ mot* at the lowest estimate; *à voix
basse* in a low voice; *under one's
breath; chapeau ~* hat in hand;
chapeaux ~! hats off!; *en ~ âge* of
tender years; *les classes f/pl. ~ses*
the lower classes; *prix m ~* low price(s
pl.); **2.** *su./m* lower part; bottom;
stocking; *fig.* low state; **3.** *bas adv.*
low (down); *ici-~* here below; *là-~*
down there; over there; *à ~ ...!*
down with ...!; *en ~* (down) below.

basalte *geol.* [ba'zalt] *m* basalt.

basane [ba'zan] *f* sheepskin, basil;
basaner F [~za'ne] (1a) *v/t. a. se
~ tan.

basculant, e [basky'lɑ̃, ~'lɑ̃:t] rock-
ing, tilting; *pont m ~* drawbridge;
siège m ~ tip-up seat; **bascule**
[~'kyl] *f* weighing machine; seesaw; *cheval m à ~* rocking-horse;
weigh-bridge; *wagon m à ~* tip-
waggon, *Am.* dump-cart; **basculer** [~ky'le] (1a) *vt/i.* rock; seesaw,
Am. teeter; tip (up); topple over; *fig.*

fluctuate; *fig.* ~ *dans* get into; **basculeur** [ˌky'lœ:r] *m* rocker; ⊕ rocking-lever.

base [bɑ:z] *f* base (*a.* ⚗, ♟); *surv.* base(-line); bottom; ⊕ bedplate; *fig.* basis, foundation; ~ **aérienne** air-base; ~ *de lancement* rocket launching site; ~ *d'entente* working basis; *sans* ~ unfounded; **baser** [bɑ'ze] (1a) *v/t.* base, found (on, *sur*); *se* ~ *sur* be grounded on.

bas-fond [bɑ'fɔ̃] *m* low ground; *fig.* underworld; ♻ shallows *pl.*

basilic [bazi'lik] *m* ♀ basil; *myth.*, *a. zo.* basilisk.

basique ⚗ [ba'zik] basic.

basket(-ball) *sp.* [baskɛt('bɔ:l)] *m* basket-ball.

basque¹ [bask] *f* skirt (*of a garment*).

Basque² [~] *su.*: *tambour m de* ~ tambourine.

basse [bɑ:s] *f* ♪ *part, singer, voice*: bass; ♻ sandbank, shoal; ♻ reef; ~**-contre**, *pl.* ~**s-contre** ♪ [bas-'kɔ̃:tr] *f* deep bass; ~**-cour**, *pl.* ~**s-cours** [ˌ'ku:r] *f* farm-yard; ~**-courier**, **-ère** [ˌku'rje, ~'rjɛ:r] *su.* farm-hand; *su./m* poultry-boy; *su./f* poultry-maid; ~**-fosse**, *pl.* ~**s-fosses** [ˌ'fo:s] *f* dungeon; **bassement** [ˌ'mɑ̃] *adv.* basely, meanly; **bassesse** [bɑ'sɛs] *f* baseness; lowness; low deed, mean action.

basset *zo.* [ba'sɛ] *m* basset hound.

basse-taille, *pl.* **basses-tailles** [bas-'ta:j] *f voice*: bass-baritone.

bassin [ba'sɛ̃] *m* basin (*a. geog.*); artificial lake; ⊕ tank; ♻ dock; *anat.* pelvis; *sl.* bore; ♻ *de carénage* careening basin; ~ *de radoub* dry dock; ~ *de retenue* reservoir; ♻ *faire entrer au* ~ dock; **bassinant, e** *sl.* [basi'nɑ̃, -'nɑ̃t] boring; **bassine** [ba'sin] *f* pan; ~ *à confiture* preserving pan; **bassiner** [basi'ne] (1a) *v/t.* bathe (*a wound*); ⚡ spray; warm (*a bed*); *sl.* bore; *sl.* annoy; **bassinoire** [ˌ'nwa:r] *f* warming pan; *sl.* bore; *sl.* large watch. [bassoonist.\
basson ♪ [ba'sɔ̃] *m* bassoon; *person*:\
baste! † [bast] *int.* enough of that!

bastille ⚔ [bas'ti:j] *f* small fortress.

bastingage ♻ [bastɛ̃'ga:ʒ] *m* bulwarks *pl.*; rails *pl.*

bastion ⚔, *fig.* [bas'tjɔ̃] *m* bastion; stronghold, bulwark.

bastonnade [bastɔ'nad] *f* bastinado; † flogging.

bastringue *sl.* [bas'trɛ̃:g] *m* low dancing-hall; shindy; paraphernalia.

bas-ventre [bɑ'vɑ̃:tr] *m* lower part of the abdomen.

bât [bɑ] *m* pack-saddle; *cheval m de* ~ pack-horse.

bataille [ba'ta:j] *f* battle (*a. fig.*); *ordre m de* ~ battle formation *or* order; **batailler** [bata'je] (1a) *v/i.* (*contre*) struggle (with), fight (against); **batailleur, -euse** [ˌ'jœ:r, ~'jø:z] **1.** *adj.* quarrelsome; **2.** *su.* fighter; **bataillon** ⚔, *a. fig.* [bata'jɔ̃] *m* battalion; *chef m de* ~ major.

bâtard, e [bɑ'ta:r, ~'tard] **1.** *adj.* bastard; *fig.* degenerate; **2.** *su.* bastard; *animal*: mongrel.

bateau ♻ [ba'to] *m* boat, ship; *sl.* ~**x** *pl.* beetle-crushers; ~ *à vapeur* steamer; ~ *de sauvetage* lifeboat; F *monter un* ~ *à q.* pull s.o.'s leg; ~**citerne**, *pl.* ~**x-citernes** ♻ [bato-si'tɛrn] *m* tanker; ~**-feu**, *pl.* ~**x-feux** ♻ [ˌ'fø] *m* lightship; ~**-mouche**, *pl.* ~**x-mouches** ♻ [ˌ'muʃ] *m* small passenger steamer; ~**-phare**, *pl.* ~**x-phares** ♻ [ˌ'fa:r] *m* lightship; ~**-pilote**, *pl.* ~**x-pilotes** ♻ [ˌpi'lɔt] *m* pilot boat; ~**-pompe**, *pl.* ~**x-pompes** ♻ [ˌ'pɔ̃:p] *m* fireboat.

bateleur *m*, **-euse** *f* [ba'tlœr, ~'tlø:z] knock-about comedian; juggler.

batelier [batə'lje] *m* boatman; ferryman; ~ *de chaland* bargee; **batellerie** [batɛl'ri] *f* lighterage; inland water transport; ~ *fluviale* river fleet.

bâter [bɑ'te] (1a) *v/t.* saddle (*a pack-horse etc.*); F *c'est un âne bâté* he is a complete fool.

bath *sl.* [bat] *adj./inv.* super, posh, fab.

bâti [bɑ'ti] *m* frame(work); ⊕ bed, support.

batifoler F [batifɔ'le] (1a) *v/i.* frolic; cuddle (s.o., *avec q.*).

bâtiment [bɑti'mɑ̃] *m* building, edifice; ♻ vessel.

bâtir¹ [bɑ'ti:r] (2a) *v/t.* build, erect; ~ *un terrain* build on a site; *terrain m à* ~ building site.

bâtir² [~] (2a) *v/t.* baste, tack.

bâtisse [bɑ'tis] *f* masonry; F house, building.

batiste *tex.* [ba'tist] *f* cambric.

bâton [bɑ'tɔ̃] *m* stick; staff; truncheon; wand of office; ~ *d'encens* joss stick; ~ *de rouge à lèvres* lipstick; ⚕ ~

bec-de-cane

d'or wallflower; ~ *ferré* alpenstock; *à* ~s *rompus* by fits and starts; **bâtonner** [batɔ'ne] (1a) *v/t.* beat; **bâtonnet** [~'nɛ] *m* short stick; *cuis.* ~s *pl. de poisson* fish fingers, *Am.* fish sticks.

bats [ba] *1st p. sg. pres. of* battre; **battage** [ba'ta:ʒ] *m* beating; *butter:* churning; *corn:* threshing;✗ field of fire; ⊕ ramming; F plugging, boosting; **battant, e** [~'tã, ~'tã:t] **1.** *adj.* banging; pelting (*rain*); *porte f* ~e swing-door; folding-door; *fig. tambour* ~ briskly; F *tout* ~ *neuf* brand-new; **2.** *su./m door:* leaf; *bell:* clapper; *fig.* fighter; F *fig.* go-getter; **batte** [bat] *f* beater; beating; beetle, rammer; *cricket:* bat; **battement** [~'mã] *m* beating; clapping; palpitation; pulsation, up and down movement; **batterie** [ba'tri] *f* ♪, ✗ battery; *drum:* beat, roll; ♪ drums *pl.*, percussion; † scuffle; ⊕ ~ *de chaudières* battery of boilers; ~ *de cuisine* kitchen utensils *pl.*; **batteur** [~'tœ:r] *m* beater (*a. cuis.*); *sp. cricket:* batsman; ♪ drummer; **batteuse** ✗, ⊕ [~'tø:z] *f* thresher; **battoir** [~'twa:r] *m* (linen) beetle; bat (*a. sp.*); F *fig.* (large) hand, paw.

battre [batr] (4a) *v/t.* beat, strike; thrash; thresh; mint (*money*); defeat; scour (*the countryside*); shuffle (*cards*); ~ *q. en brèche* disparage s. o., run s.o. down; *se* ~ fight; *v/i.* throb; clap; bang; **battu, e** [ba'ty] **1.** *p.p. of* battre; **2.** *su./f* beat; *admin.* round-up; ♣ ~ *en mer* scouting cruise.

baudet [bo'dɛ] *m* donkey; ass (*a. fig.*).

bauge [bo:ʒ] *f* wallow; lair (*of wild boar*); *fig.* pigsty.

baume [bo:m] *m* balsam; balm (*a. fig.*).

bauxite ⚙ [bok'sit] *f* bauxite.

bavard, e [ba'va:r, ~'vard] **1.** *adj.* garrulous, talkative; **2.** *su.* chatterbox; gossip; F bore; **bavardage** [bavar'da:ʒ] *m* gossip; chatter; **bavarder** [~'de] (1a) *v/i.* gossip; chatter; tell tales.

bave [ba:v] *f* dribble; slobber; froth, foam; *fig.* venom; **baver** [ba've] (1a) *v/i.* dribble, slobber; run (*pen*); ⚙ ooze; F talk drivel; ~ *sur* cast a slur on; F *fig.* ~ *d'admiration* be agape with admiration; F *fig.* en ~ have a hard time (of it); F *fig.* en faire ~ à q.

give s.o. a hard time (of it); *v/t.* F *fig. en* ~ *des ronds de chapeau* gape in astonishment.

bavette [ba'vɛt] *f* bib; F *tailler une* ~ chew the fat; **baveux, -euse** [~'vø, ~'vø:z] slobbery (*mouth*); runny, wet; *typ.* blurred.

bavure [ba'vy:r] *f* ⊕ burr; ⊕ seam; *writing:* smudge.

bazar [ba'za:r] *m* bazaar; bargain stores; *sl. tout le* ~ the lot, the whole caboodle; **bazarder** *sl.* [~zar'de] (1a) *v/t.* sell off; get rid of.

béant, e [be'ã, ~ã:t] gaping, yawning, wide open.

béat, e [be'a, ~'at] **1.** *adj.* smug, complacent; **2.** *su.* smug *or* complacent person; **béatifier** *eccl.* [beati'fje] (1o) *v/t.* beatify; **béatitude** [~'tyd] *f* bliss, beatitude; complacency.

beau (*adj. before vowel or h mute* **bel**) *m*, **belle** *f*, *m/pl.* **beaux** [bo, bɛl, bo] **1.** *adj.* beautiful; fine; handsome; *au* ~ *milieu de* right in the middle of; *avoir* ~ (*inf.*) (*inf.*) in vain; *il fait* ~ (*temps*) it is fine; *le* ~ *sexe* the fair sex; **2.** *su./m hist.* beau; *le* ~ the beautiful; *être au* ~ be set fair (*weather*); *faire le* ~ sit up and beg (*dog*); *su./f* beauty; *sp.* deciding game; *la Belle au bois dormant* (the) Sleeping Beauty.

beaucoup [bo'ku] *adv.* much, a great deal; many; F *à* ~ *près* by a long chalk; *de* ~ by far.

beau-fils, *pl.* **beaux-fils** [bo'fis] *m* stepson; son-in-law; **beau-frère,** *pl.* **beaux-frères** [~'frɛ:r] *m* brother-in-law; **beau-père,** *pl.* **beaux-pères** [~'pɛ:r] *m* father-in-law; stepfather.

beaupré ♣ [bo'pre] *m* bowsprit.

beauté [bo'te] *f* beauty; *fig.* belle, beauty.

beaux-arts [bo'za:r] *m/pl.* fine arts; **beaux-parents** [~pa'rã] *m/pl.* parents-in-law.

bébé [be'be] *m* baby; doll.

bec [bɛk] *m bird:* beak, bill; ⊕ *tool:* nose; ⊕ nozzle; spout; ♪ mouthpiece; *pen:* nib; F mouth, nose; ⊕ ~ *d'âne* mortise-chisel; ~ *de gaz* gas burner, F lamp-post; F *fig. tomber sur un* ~ (*de gaz*) get be stymied.

bécane F [be'kan] *f* bike, bicycle.

bécarre ♪ [be'ka:r] *m* natural (sign).

bécasse *orn.* [be'kas] *f* woodcock.

bec-de-cane, *pl.* **becs-de-cane**

[bɛkdə'kan] *m* spring lock; slide-bolt; lever handle; ⊕ flat-nosed pliers *pl.*; **bec-de-lièvre,** *pl.* **becs-de-lièvre** [ˌ'ljɛːvr] *m* harelip.

bêchage [bɛ'ʃaːʒ] *m* digging; F disparagement.

béchamel *cuis.* [beʃa'mɛl] *f* bechamel.

bêche [bɛʃ] *f* spade.

bêche-de-mer, *pl.* **bêches-de-mer** [bɛʃdə'mɛːr] *m* bêche-de-mer; *gramm.* beach-la-mar.

bêcher [bɛ'ʃe] (1a) *v/t.* dig; F disparage, run (*s.o.*) down, pull (*s.o., s.th.*) to pieces; **bêcheur, -euse** F [bɛ'ʃœːr, -øːz] stuck-up.

bécot [be'ko] *m orn.* small snipe; F peck (= *little kiss*); **bécoter** F [beko'te] (1a) *v/t.* give (*s.o.*) a peck.

becqueter [bɛk'te] (1c) *v/t.* peck at; pick up; *sl.* eat; F kiss.

bedaine F [bə'dɛn] *f* belly; paunch.

bedeau *eccl.* [bə'do] *m* verger, beadle.

bedon F [bə'dɔ̃] *m* paunch; **bedonner** F [ˌdɔ'ne] (1a) *v/i.* grow paunchy, acquire a corporation.

bée [be] *adj./f:* bouche *f* ~ gaping, open-mouthed.

beffroi [be'frwa] *m* belfry; ⊕ *dredge:* gantry.

bégayer [bege'je] (1i) *v/i.* stammer; *v/t.* stammer out.

bègue [bɛg] **1.** *adj.* stuttering, stammering; *être* ~ stammer; **2.** *su.* stutterer, stammerer.

bégueter [beg'te] (1d) *v/i.* bleat (*goat*).

béguin [be'gɛ̃] *m* hood; baby's bonnet; F infatuation; *person:* love; **béguine** [ˌ'gin] *f eccl.* beguine; F very devout woman.

beige [bɛːʒ] **1.** *adj.* beige; **2.** *su./f* unbleached serge.

beigne *sl.* [bɛɲ] *f* blow; bruise.

beignet *cuis.* [bɛ'ɲɛ] *m* fritter; doughnut.

bel [bɛl] *see beau; ~ esprit m person:* wit; ~ *et bien* well and truly, genuinely; *le ~ âge* youth; *un ~ âge* a ripe old age.

bêlement [bɛl'mɑ̃] *m* bleating; **bêler** [bɛ'le] (1a) *v/i.* bleat (*sheep*).

belette *zo.* [bə'lɛt] weasel.

belge [bɛlʒ] *adj., a. su.* ♀ Belgian; **Belgique** [bɛl'ʒik] *f: sl. filer en* ~ bolt (*financier*).

bélier [be'lje] *m zo.* ram (*a.* ⊕), *Am.*

buck; ✂ *hist.* battering ram; *astr.* le ♀ Aries, the Ram.

belinogramme [bəlino'gram] *m* telephotograph.

bélitre † [be'litr] *m* cad, knave.

bellâtre [bɛ'lɑːtr] **1.** *adj.* foppish; **2.** *su./m* fop.

belle [bɛl] *see beau 1; à la ~ étoile* in the open; *de plus ~* more than ever; *iro. en faire de ~s* be up to s. th. pretty; *l'échapper ~* have a narrow escape; **~-dame,** *pl.* **~s-dames** [ˌ'dam] *f* ♀ deadly nightshade; *zo.* painted lady; **~-fille,** *pl.* **~s-filles** [ˌ'fiːj] *f* stepdaughter; daughter-in-law; **~-mère,** *pl.* **~s-mères** [ˌ'mɛːr] stepmother; mother-in-law; **~s-lettres** [ˌ'lɛtr] *f/pl.* belles-lettres, humanities; **~-sœur,** *pl.* **~s-sœurs** [ˌ'sœːr] *f* sister-in-law.

bellicisme [bɛlli'sism] *m* warmongering; **belligérant, e** [ˌʒe'rɑ̃, ˌ'rɑ̃ːt] *adj., a. su./m* belligerent; **belliqueux, -euse** [ˌ'kø, ˌ'køːz] bellicose, warlike.

bellot, -otte F [bɛ'lo, ˌ'lɔt] dandi-fied; pretty(-pretty). [pinocle.\

belote [bə'lɔt] *f cards:* sort of\

belvédère [bɛlve'dɛːr] *m* belvedere; summer-house; vantage-point.

bémol ♩ [be'mɔl] *m* flat.

bénédicité [benedisi'te] *m* grace (before a meal); **bénédiction** [ˌdik-'sjɔ̃] *f* blessing.

bénéfice [bene'fis] *m* ✝ profit, gain; benefit; *eccl.* living; **bénéficiaire** [ˌfi'sjɛːr] *m* ✝ payee; ⚖, *eccl., etc.* beneficiary; **bénéficier** [ˌfi'sje] (1o) *v/i.* profit, benefit (by, *de*); make a profit (on, *sur*).

benêt [bə'nɛ] **1.** *adj./m* stupid, silly; **2.** *su./m* simpleton.

bénévole [bene'vɔl] benevolent; gratuitous, unpaid; voluntary.

bénignité [beniɲi'te] *f* kindness; mildness (*a.* ✻); **bénin, -igne** [be-'nɛ̃, ˌ'niɲ] kind, benign; mild (*a.* ✻).

bénir [be'niːr] (2a) *v/t.* bless; *eccl. a.* consecrate; **bénit, e** [ˌ'ni, ˌ'nit] blessed; consecrated; *eccl.* eau *f* ~e holy water; **bénitier** *eccl.* [ˌni'tje] *m* holy-water basin.

benne [bɛn] *f* hamper; *dredger:* bucket; ✂ tub, skip; ✂ cage; *telpherway:* bucket seat; ⊕ ~ *preneuse* (mechanical) grab; clam-shell bucket; ⊕ (*camion m à*) ~ *basculante* tipping waggon.

benoît, e [bən'wa, ~'wat] sanctimonious; bland.

benzine [bɛ̃'zin] f benzine; **benzol** ♁ [~'zɔl] m benzol.

béquille [be'ki:j] f crutch; *bicycle:* stand; ♣ shore, prop; *marcher avec des ~s* walk on crutches; **béquiller** [~ki'je] (1a) v/i. walk on crutches; v/t. ♣ shore up.

bercail [bɛr'ka:j] m/sg. sheepfold; *eccl.* fold.

berceau [bɛr'so] m cradle (a. fig., a. △); ⊕ bed; ✿ bower, arbo(u)r; **bercer** [~'se] (1k) v/t. rock; lull; soothe; delude (with promises, *de promesses*); **berceuse** [~'sø:z] f cradle; rocking-chair; ♪ lullaby.

béret [be'rɛ] m (a. ~ *de Basque*) beret; ✿ *écossais* tam-o'-shanter.

berge [bɛrʒ] f *river, ditch:* bank; *mountain:* flank; ✕ rampart.

berger [bɛr'ʒe] m shepherd (a. fig.); **bergère** [~'ʒɛːr] f shepherdess; easy chair; *orn.* wagtail; **bergerie** [~ʒə'ri] f sheep-pen; *paint., prosody:* pastoral; **bergeronnette** *orn.* [~ʒərɔ'nɛt] f wagtail.

berline [bɛr'lin] f saloon (car), *Am.* sedan; † *coach:* Berlin; ✕ truck, tram.

berlue [bɛr'ly] f ✿ false vision; *fig. avoir la ~* get things all wrong.

berne ♣ [bɛrn] f: *en ~* at half-mast.

berner [bɛr'ne] (1a) v/t. laugh at, chaff; hoax.

bernique¹! *sl.* [bɛr'nik] *int.* nothing doing!

bernique² *orn.* [~] f limpet.

besace [bə'zas] f † double sack; *fig. être réduit à la ~* be reduced to beggary.

bésef *sl.* [be'zɛf] *see* bezef.

besicles *iro.* [bə'zikl] f/pl. glasses, spectacles.

besogne [bə'zɔɲ] f work; job; **besogneux, -euse** [~zɔ'ɲø, ~'ɲøːz] needy, hard-up.

besoin [bə'zwɛ̃] m need, want; poverty; *au ~* in case of need; when required; *avoir ~ de* need; *il est ~ (de inf.)* it is necessary (to *inf.*).

bestial, e, m/pl. **-aux** [bes'tjal, ~'tjo] bestial, brutish; **bestialité** [~tjali'te] f brutishness; bestiality; **bestiaux** [~'tjo] m/pl. livestock *sg.*, cattle *sg.*

best-seller [bɛstsɛ'lœːr] m best seller.

bêta, -asse [bɛ'ta, ~'tas] **1.** *adj.* stupid; **2.** *su.* blockhead, ass.

bétail [be'ta:j] m/sg. livestock, cattle.

bête [bɛːt] **1.** *su./f* animal; beast; fool; ~s *féroces* wild beasts; ~ *à cornes* horned beast; ~ *de somme* beast of burden; ~ *de trait* draught-animal; ~ *fauve* deer; ~ *noire* wild boar; *fig. chercher la petite ~* split hairs; *fig. ma~ noire* my pet aversion; **2.** *adj.* stupid, silly; **bêtifier** [bɛti'fje] (1o) v/i. play the fool; talk stupidly; **bêtise** [~'ti:z] f stupidity; blunder; nonsense; mere trifle.

béton △ [be'tɔ̃] m concrete; *fig. du ~* absolutely safe *or* reliable; **bétonnière** [~tɔ'njɛːr] f cement mixer.

bette ✿ [bɛt] f beet; **betterave** ✿ [bɛ'tra:v] f beet(root); (a. ~ *sucrière*) sugar-beet; ~ *fourragère* mangel-wurzel.

beuglant *sl.* [bø'glɑ̃] m cheap café-concert; **beuglement** [~glə'mɑ̃] m lowing, mooing; **beugler** [~'gle] (1a) v/i. low; moo.

beurre [bœːr] m butter; *au ~ noir* with browned butter sauce; *sl. c'est du ~* it is child's play; *faire son ~* feather one's nest; F *un œil au ~ noir* a black eye; **beurré** [bœ're] m butter-pear; **beurrée** [~'re] f slice of bread and butter; **beurrer** [~'re] (1a) v/t. butter; **beurrier, -ère** [~'rje, ~'rjɛːr] **1.** *su./m* butter-dish; **2.** *adj.* butter-producing.

beuverie [bø'vri] f drinking bout.

bévue [be'vy] f blunder, slip; *commettre une ~* drop a brick.

bezef *sl.* [be'zɛf] *adv.:* pas ~ not much.

bi... [bi] bi..., di...

biais, e [bjɛ, bjɛːz] **1.** *adj.* skew, oblique; **2.** *su./m* △ *etc.* skew; slant; slanting; *fig.* expedient; *de (or en)* ~ on the cross, on the slant; *regarder de* ~ look askance at; **biaiser** [bjɛ'ze] (1b) v/i. (be on the) slant; skew; *fig.* use evasions.

bibelot [bi'blo] m knick-knack, trinket.

biberon [bi'brɔ̃] m *baby:* feeding (*Am.* nursing) bottle; *invalid:* feeding-cup; F tippler; **biberonner** F [~brɔ'ne] (1a) v/i. tipple.

bibi *sl.* [bi'bi] m I, me, myself; F (woman's) hat.

Bible [bibl] f Bible.

biblio... [biblio] biblio...; **~graphie** [~gra'fi] f bibliography; **~manie** [~ma'ni] f bibliomania; book collecting; **~phile** [~'fil] m bibliophile, book-lover; **~thécaire** [~te'kɛ:r] m librarian; **~thèque** [~'tɛk] f library; bookcase; ~ de prêt lending library; fig. ~ vivante walking encyclop(a)edia.

biblique [bi'blik] Biblical.

bicarbonate ⚗ [bikarbɔ'nat] m bicarbonate; ~ de soude bicarbonate of soda, baking soda.

bicentenaire [bisɑ̃t'nɛ:r] m bicentenary, Am. bicentennial.

biceps anat. [bi'sɛps] m, a. adj. biceps.

biche zo. [biʃ] f hind, doe; ma ~ my darling.

bicher sl. [bi'ʃe] (1a) v/i.: ça biche? how goes it?; things alright with you?

bichette zo. [bi'ʃɛt] f young hind.

bichon m, **-onne** f [bi'ʃɔ̃, ~'ʃɔn] lapdog; **bichonner** [~ʃɔ'ne] (1a) v/t. spruce (s.o.) up; titivate.

bichromie [bikrɔ'mi] f two-colo(u)r printing.

bicolore [bikɔ'lɔ:r] two-colo(u)r; of two colo(u)rs.

bicoque [bi'kɔk] f shanty; F dump.

bicorne [bi'kɔrn] **1.** adj. two-pointed; **2.** su./m cocked hat.

bicyclette [bisi'klɛt] f (bi)cycle.

bidasse sl. [bi'das] m (simple) soldier.

bide sl. [bi:d] m belly; flop, washout; lies pl., rubbish, nonsense.

bidet [bi'dɛ] m nag; ⊕ trestle; hygiene: bidet.

bidoche sl. [bi'dɔʃ] f meat.

bidon [bi'dɔ̃] **1.** m tin, can, drum; ✗ canteen, water-bottle; sl. belly; sl. rubbish, pack of lies; c'est pas du ~ that's the honest truth; **2.** adj. sl. fake, mock, sham, phoney. **bidonner** sl. [bidɔ'ne] (1a) vt/i. swig; v/t.: se ~ split one's sides.

bidonville [bidɔ̃'vil] m shanty-town.

bidule F [bi'dyl] m thing(umabob).

bief [bjɛf] m canal reach; mill-race.

bielle ⊕ [bjɛl] f connecting rod.

bien [bjɛ̃] **1.** adv. usu. well; right(ly), proper(ly); quite, rather; really, indeed; adjectivally: good, nice, fine, all right; ~ de la peine much trouble; ~ des gens many people; ~ que (sbj.) (al)though; aller ~ be well; eh ~! well!; être ~ a. be on good terms (with s.o., avec q.); se porter ~ be in good health; tant ~ que mal so so; c'est ~ de lui! that's just like him!; **2.** su./m good; welfare; possession, property, wealth, estate; goods pl.; ~ public public or common weal; ✝ ~s pl. de consommation consumer goods; **~-aimé, e** [~nɛ'me] beloved; **~-dire** [~'di:r] m fine words pl., eloquence, ~-être [~'nɛ:tr] m wellbeing, comfort; **~faisance** [~fɛ'zɑ̃:s] f beneficence, charity; œuvre f ou société f ou association f de ~ charitable organization, charity; **~faisant, e** [~fɛ'zɑ̃, ~'zɑ̃:t] beneficent, charitable; salutary, beneficial; **~fait** [~'fɛ] m benefit; service; fig. blessing; **~faiteur, -trice** [~fɛ'tœ:r, ~'tris] **1.** su./m benefactor; su./f benefactress; **2.** adj. beneficent; **~-fondé** [~fɔ̃'de] m merits pl. (of claim etc.); **~-fonds**, pl. **~s-fonds** [~'fɔ̃] m real estate; landed property; **~heureux, -euse** [~nœ'rø, ~'rø:z] blissful, happy; blessed; **~-jugé** ⚖ [~ʒy'ʒe] m proper decision.

biennal, e, m/pl. **-aux** [biɛ'nal, ~'no] biennial.

bien-pensant, e [bjɛ̃pɑ̃'sɑ̃, ~'sɑ̃:t] adj., a. su. right-thinking (person).

bienséance [bjɛ̃se'ɑ̃:s] f propriety, decorum; **bienséant, e** [~'ɑ̃, ~'ɑ̃:t] seemly, decent.

bientôt [bjɛ̃'to] adv. soon, before long; à ~! so long!

bienveillance [bjɛ̃vɛ'jɑ̃:s] f kindness; goodwill; benevolence; **bienveillant, e** [~'jɑ̃, ~'jɑ̃:t] kind(ly), benevolent.

bienvenu, e [bjɛ̃vә'ny] **1.** adj. welcome (to, à); **2.** su. welcome person; soyez le ~! welcome!; su./f welcome; souhaiter la ~e à q. welcome s.o.

bière¹ [bjɛ:r] f beer; ~ blonde pale or light ale; ~ brune brown ale.

bière² [~] f coffin.

biffer [bi'fe] (1a) v/t. cross out (a word); ⚖ strike out; ~ les indications inutiles strike out what does not apply.

bifteck [bif'tɛk] m beefsteak; ~ de porc pork steak.

bifurcation [bifyrka'sjɔ̃] f road etc.: fork; ⚙ junction; **bifurquer** [~'ke] (1m) v/i. a. se ~ fork, divide; ⚙ branch off; ⚡ shunt (current).

bigame [bi'gam] **1.** adj. bigamous; **2.**

su. bigamist; **bigamie** [~ga'mi] *f* bigamy.

bigarré, e [biga're] variegated; **bigarrer** [~'re] (1a) *v/t.* variegate, mottle; **bigarrure** [~'ry:r] *f* motley, variegation.

bigle [bigl] 1. *adj.* squint-eyed; 2. *su.* squint-eyed person.

bigleux, -euse F [bi'glø, ~'glø:z] shortsighted.

bigophone F [bigo'fɔn] *m* phone.

bigorne [bi'gɔrn] *f* two-beaked anvil; *anvil:* beak; **bigorner** *sl.* [~gɔr'ne] (1a) *v/t.* smash up; se ~ fight.

bigot¹ ⚓ [bi'go] *m* mattock.

bigot², e [bi'go, ~'gɔt] *adj.* (*a. su.*) sanctimonious (person); **bigoterie** [~gɔ'tri] *f* sanctimoniousness, (religious) bigotry.

bigoudi [bigu'di] *m* (hair) curler.

bigre! *sl.* [bigr] *int.* by Jove!, bosh!; **bigrement** *sl.* [~ə'mɑ̃] *adv.* jolly (well), darn (well).

bijou, *pl.* **-x** [bi'ʒu] *m* jewel, gem; **bijouterie** [biʒu'tri] *f* jewellery, *Am.* jewelry; jeweller's shop; **bijoutier** *m*, **-ère** *f* [~'tje, ~'tjɛ:r] jeweller.

bikini [biki'ni] *m* bikini.

bilan [bi'lɑ̃] *m* ✝ balance sheet; *fig.* outcome; *fig.* consequences *pl.*; *fig.* toll; ✝ *déposer son* ~ file a petition in bankruptcy; *fig. faire le* ~ (*de*) take stock (of).

bilatéral, e, *m/pl.* **-aux** [bilate'ral, ~'ro] bilateral, two-sided.

bilboquet [bilbɔ'kɛ] *m toy:* cup-and-ball; *toy:* tumbler; *typ.* jobwork.

bile [bil] bile, gall; **biler** *sl.* [bi'le] (1a) *v/t.: ne te bile pas!* don't worry!; take it easy!; se ~ get worked up; **bilieux, -euse** [~'ljø, ~'ljø:z] bilious; *fig.* testy; morose.

bilingue [bi'lɛ̃:g] bilingual.

billard [bi'ja:r] *m* (game of) billards *pl.*; billiard table; billiard room; F operating table; **bille** [bi:j] *f* (*billiard etc.*) ball; marble; billet, block; *sl.* mug (= *face*); *sl.* nut (= *head*); *stylo m à* ~ ball-point pen.

billet [bi'jɛ] *m* note, letter; notice; circular; ticket (*a.* 🚋, *thea.*); ✝ bill; ~ *à ordre* ✝ promissory note; ⚓ single bill; ~ *blanc lottery:* blank; ~ *circulaire* tourist ticket; ✝ circular note; ~ *de banque* bank-note, *Am. a.* bill; ~ *de faire part* intimation, notice (*of death, wedding, etc.*);

~ *de faveur* complimentary ticket; ~ *doux* love-letter.

billevesée [bilvə'ze] *f* crazy notion.

billion [bi'ljɔ̃] *m* one million millions, billion; *Am.* one thousand billions, trillion.

billon [bi'jɔ̃] *m* alloy; copper *or* nickel coinage; base coinage; ✔ ridge of earth; **billot** ✔ [bi'jo] *m* block; *tethering:* clog; wheel drag.

bimbeloterie [bɛ̃blɔ'tri] *f* toys *pl.*, knick-knacks *pl.*; (cheap) toy trade.

bimensuel, -elle [bimɑ̃'sɥɛl] fortnightly.

bimoteur [bimɔ'tœ:r] *adj./m* twin-engined.

binaire [bi'nɛ:r] binary.

binard [bi'na:r] *m* (stone-)lorry, dray.

biner [bi'ne] (1a) *v/t.* ✔ hoe; dig *etc.* for a second time; *v/i. eccl.* celebrate two masses in one day; **binette** ✔ [~'nɛt] *f* hoe; *sl.* face, dial, mug.

biniou [bi'nju] *m* Breton pipes *pl.*; *sl.* horn, wind instrument.

binocle [bi'nɔkl] *m* eye-glasses *pl.*; pince-nez; lorgnette.

binôme ⚛ [bi'no:m] *adj., a. su./m* binomial.

biochimie ⚕ [biɔʃi'mi] *f* biochemistry.

biographe [biɔ'graf] *m* biographer; **biographie** [~gra'fi] *f* biography.

biophysique [biɔfi'zik] *f* biophysics *sg.*

biosphère [biɔ'sfɛ:r] *f* biosphere.

biotope [biɔ'tɔp] *m* biotope.

bipartisme *pol.* [bipar'tism] *m* coalition government.   [seater.\
biplace [bi'plas] *adj., a. su.* two-\
biplan ✈ [bi'plɑ̃] *m* biplane.

bipolaire ⚡ [bipɔ'lɛ:r] bipolar.

bique [bik] *f* F nanny-goat; *sl.* old hag; *sl.* nag; **biquet** *m*, **-ette** *f* F [bi'kɛ, ~'kɛt] kid.

biréacteur ✈ [bireak'tœ:r] 1. *adj./m* twin-jet; 2. *su./m* twin-jet plane.

bis¹, bise [bi, bi:z] greyish-brown; *à* ~ *ou à blanc* anyhow; *pain m* ~ brown bread.

bis² [bis] 1. *adv.* twice; again; encore!; *no. 9* ~ 9A (*house etc.*); 2. *su./m* encore.

bisaïeul [biza'jœl] *m* great-grandfather; **bisaïeule** [~] *f* great-grandmother.

bisannuel, -elle [biza'nɥɛl] biennial.

bisbille F [bis'bi:j] *f* bickering; en ~ at loggerheads (with, *avec*).

biscornu, e F [biskɔr'ny] mis-shapen; distorted; illogical; queer (*idea*).

biscotin [bisko'tɛ̃] *m* crisp biscuit; ship's biscuit; **biscotte** [~'kɔt] *f* rusk; **biscuit** [~'kɥi] *m* biscuit, *Am. a.* zwieback; plain cake; ✝ *ceramics*: biscuit, bisque; ~ *à la cuiller* sponge-finger, *Am.* lady-finger; ~ *de mer* ship's biscuit.

bise[1] [bi:z] *f* north wind; *poet.* winter.

bise[2] F [~] *f* (little) kiss; *faire une* ~ *à q.* give s.o. a (little) kiss.

biseau ⊕ [bi'zo] *m* chamfer, bevel; en ~ chamfered, bevelled; **biseauter** [~zo'te] (1a) *v/t.* ⊕ chamfer, bevel; bezel (*gems*); *fig.* mark (*cards*).

biser[1] [bi'ze] (1a) *v/t.* re-dye.

biser[2] ✔ [~] (1a) *v/i.* darken.

biser[3] F [~] (1a) *v/t.* kiss.

bismuth ⚗ [bis'myt] *m* bismuth.

bison *zo.* [bi'zɔ̃] *m* bison.

bisque [bisk] *f cuis.* shellfish soup; **bisquer** F [bis'ke] (1m) *v/i.*: *faire* ~ *q.* rile s.o.

bissac [bi'sak] *m* double wallet.

bissecteur, -trice ⚹ [bisɛk'tœ:r, ~'tris] bisecting; **bissection** ⚹ [~'sjɔ̃] *f* bisection.

bisser [bi'se] (1a) *v/t.* encore (*a singer, a song*); repeat; **bissextile** [bisɛks'til] *adj./f*: *année f* ~ leap year; **bissexuel, -elle** ⚹ [~sɛk'sɥɛl] bisexual.

bistourner [bistur'ne] (1a) *v/t.* wrench.

bistre [bistr] **1.** *su./m* bistre; **2.** *adj./inv.* blackish-brown, swarthy.

bistrot [bis'tro] *m* pub, café; pub- *or* café-owner.

bitume [bi'tym] *m* bitumen; **bitumer** [~ty'me] (1a) *v/t.* tar; asphalt.

biture *sl.* [bi'ty:r] *f*: *prendre une* ~ get drunk.

bivouac ⚔ [bi'vwak] *m* bivouac.

bizarre [bi'za:r] odd, curious, strange, peculiar; **bizarrerie** [~zar'ri] *f* oddness, peculiarity; whimsicality.

bizut(h) *sl.* [bi'zy] *m* first-year student; beginner.

bla-bla F [bla'bla] *m/inv.* bunkum, *Am.* blah.

blackbouler [blakbu'le] (1a) *v/t.* blackball, turn down.

blafard, e [bla'fa:r, ~'fard] wan, pale.

blague [blag] *f* F joke; trick, practical joke; F stupid mistake, blunder; F stupid thing, nonsense; (~ *à tabac*) tobacco pouch; ~ *à part* joking apart; F *sans* ~? you don't say!; really?; **blaguer** F [bla'ge] (1m) *v/i.* joke; *tu blagues!* impossible!; *v/t.* make fun of, F kid.

blair *sl.* [blɛ:r] *m* nose.

blaireau [blɛ'ro] *m zo.* badger; shaving-brush; *paint.* brush.

blairer *sl.* [blɛ're] (1a) *v/t.*: *je ne peux pas le* ~ I can't stand him.

blâmable [blɑ'mabl] blameworthy; **blâme** [blɑ:m] *m* blame; *admin.* reprimand; **blâmer** [blɑ'me] (1a) *v/t.* blame; censure; reprimand.

blanc, blanche [blɑ̃, blɑ̃:ʃ] **1.** *adj.* white; clean, pure; blank (*paper, cartridge*); pale (*ale*); *armes f/pl. blanches* side-arms; F *carte f blanche* free hand; *nuit f blanche* sleepless night; *se battre à l'arme blanche* fight with cold steel; **2.** *su.* white; white person; *su./m* blank; white wine; (egg) white; white meat; *chauffer à* ~ make white-hot; *fig.* work (*s.o.*) up, excite (*s.o.*); *saigner à* ~ bleed white; *tirer à* ~ fire blanks; (*signer un*) *chèque en* ~ (sign a) blank cheque; ~**-bec**, *pl.* ~**s-becs** F [blɑ̃'bɛk] *m* callow youth, *Am.* sucker, greenhorn; **blanchâtre** [blɑ̃'ʃɑ:tr] whitish; **blanche** ♩ [blɑ̃:ʃ] *f* minim, *Am.* half note; **blancheur** [blɑ̃'ʃœ:r] *f* whiteness; paleness; purity; **blanchir** [~'ʃi:r] (2a) *v/t.* whiten; bleach; clean; wash, launder; *v/i.* turn white; blanch; fade; **blanchissage** [~ʃi'sa:ʒ] *m* washing; laundering; **blanchisserie** [~ʃis'ri] *f* laundering; laundry; **blanchisseur** [~ʃi'sœ:r] *m* laundryman; ⊕ bleacher; **blanchisseuse** [~ʃi'sø:z] *f* laundress; washerwoman; **blancseing**, *pl.* **blancsseings** [blɑ̃'sɛ̃] *m* blank signature; *fig.* full power (*s pl.*).

blaser [blɑ'ze] (1a) *v/t.* blunt (*the palate*); surfeit; *se* ~ become indifferent (to *de, sur*).

blason [blɑ'zɔ̃] *m* coat-of-arms; blazon; heraldry; **blasonner** [~zɔ'ne] (1a) *v/t.* blazon.

blasphémateur, -trice [blasfema'tœ:r, ~'tris] **1.** *su.* blasphemer; **2.** *adj.* blasphemous; **blasphème** [~'fɛm] *m* blasphemy; **blasphémer** [~fe'me] (1f) *vt/i.* blaspheme.

blatte [blat] *f* cockroach, blackbeetle.
blé [ble] *m* corn; wheat; ~ *de Turquie*
maize, *Am.* (Indian) corn; ~ *noir*
buckwheat.
blême [blɛːm] wan, pale; ghastly,
livid; **blêmir** [blɛ'miːr] (2a) *v/i.*
blanch; grow pale.
blennorragie ✝ blɛnɔra'ʒi] *f* gonor-
rh(o)ea.
blèse [blɛːz] lisping; *être* ~ = **bléser**
[ble'ze] (1f) *v/i.* lisp.
blessant, e [blɛ'sɑ̃, ~'sɑ̃ːt] offensive
(*remark*); **blesser** [~'se] (1a) *v/t.*
wound; hurt; offend; *se* ~ *a.* take
offence; **blessure** [~'syːr] *f* wound,
injury.
blet, blette [blɛ, blɛt] over-ripe.
bleu, bleue, *m/pl.* **bleus** [blø] **1.** *adj.*
blue; *cuis.* underdone; *une colère f
bleue* a towering rage; *une peur f bleue*
a blue funk; *zone f bleue* zone of
parking restrictions in the centre of a
town; **2.** *su./m* blue; ⊕ blue print; ✝
bruise; F greenhorn; ✕ F recruit; ~*s*
pl. overalls; *de Prusse* Prussian
blue; ~ *d'outremer* ultramarine;
bleuâtre [~'ɑːtr] bluish; **bleuir**
[~'iːr] (2a) *v/t.* blue; make blue; *v/i.*
become blue.
blindage [blɛ̃'daːʒ] *m* ✕, ⚓ armo(u)r
plating; ✕ timbering; ⚡ screening;
blindé, e [~'de] **1.** *adj.* armo(u)red;
bullet-proof; F *fig.* hardened,
immune (to, *contre*), thick-skinned;
sl. drunk; **2.** *su./m* armo(u)red car;
blinder [~'de] (1a) *v/t.* ✕, ⚓
armo(u)r-plate; ⊕ shore up, timber;
F *fig.* harden, make immune *or* indifferent (to, *contre*).
bloc [blɔk] *m* block; (memo) pad;
mass; *pol.* bloc; ⊕ unit; *sl.* prison,
clink; *à* ~ tight, hard, right home; *en*
~ *in one piece; in the lump; wholesale; **blocage** [blɔ'kaːʒ] *m* blocking
(*a.* ⚡); ⚓ rubble; ⚓ cement-block
foundation; ⊕ jamming, stopping; ~
des prix freezing of prices; ~ *des
salaires* pay freeze; **bloc-cylindres**,
pl. **blocs-cylindres** *mot.* [blɔksi-
'lɛ̃ːdr] *m* cylinder-block.
blockhaus [blɔ'koːs] *m/inv.* ✕ block-
house; ⚓ conning-tower.
bloc-notes, *pl.* **blocs-notes** [blɔk-
'nɔt] *m* (memo) pad, writing pad.
blocus [blɔ'kys] *m* blockade; *hist.* ~
continental continental system; *faire
le* ~ *de* blockade; *forcer le* ~ run the
blockade.

5*

blond, blonde [blɔ̃, blɔ̃ːd] **1.** *adj.*
blond, fair; pale (*ale*); **2.** *su./m*
blond; *su./f* blonde.
blondin, e [blɔ̃'dɛ̃, ~'din] **1.** *adj.*
fair-haired; **2.** *su.* fair-haired person.
bloquer [blɔ'ke] (1m) *v/t.* block
(up); besiege; blockade; ✝ stop
(*a cheque*); ⊕ lock; ⊕ jam on (*the
brake*); ⚙ close (*a section*); ✝ freeze
(*wages, prices*); F lock up; *se* ~ get
jammed.
blottir [blɔ'tiːr] (2a) *v/t.*: *se* ~
crouch, squat; nestle.
blouse [bluːz] *f* blouse; smock;
overall; *billiards*: pocket; **blouser**
[blu'ze] (1a) *v/t.* pocket (*the ball at
billiards*); F deceive; **blouson** [~'zɔ̃]
m lumber-jacket; *Am.* windbreaker.
bluet ♀ [bly'ɛ] *m* cornflower.
bluette [bly'ɛt] *f* trivial story.
bluff F [blœf] *m* bluff; **bluffer** F
[blœ'fe] (1a) *v/t.* bluff (*s.o.*); *v/i.*
pull a fast one, try it on.
blutage [bly'taːʒ] *m* bolting, sifting;
bluter [~'te] (1a) *v/t.* bolt, sift
(*flour etc.*); **blutoir** [~'twaːr] *m*
bolting-machine; sieve.
boa *zo.*, *cost.* [bɔ'a] *m* boa.
bobard *sl.* [bɔ'baːr] *m* tall story; lie,
fib.
bobèche [bɔ'bɛʃ] *f candlestick:*
sconce; *sl.* nut, head.
bobinage ⚡, ⊕ [bɔbi'naːʒ] *m* winding; **bobine** [~'bin] *f* bobbin, reel,
spool; roll; ⚡ coil; ⊕ drum; *sl.* dial,
face; **bobiner** [bɔbi'ne] (1a) *v/t.*
wind, spool; **bobineuse** [~'nøːz] *f*
winding-machine.
bobo F [bɔ'bo] *m* hurt; sore; *ch.sp.*
bump.
bocage [bɔ'kaːʒ] *m* grove, copse.
bocal [bɔ'kal] *m* jar, bottle (*with
wide mouth and short neck*); globe,
fish-bowl; *chemist:* show-bottle.
bocard *metall.* [bɔ'kaːr] *m* ore-crush-
er; **bocarder** [~kar'de] (1a) *v/t.*
crush (*ore*).
bock [bɔk] *m* glass of beer.
bœuf [bœf, *pl.* bø] **1.** *su./m* ox; beef;
boiled beef; ~ *à la mode* stewed
beef; ~ *conservé* corned beef; **2.** *adj.*
sl. colossal, fine, *Am.* bully.
boggie ⚙ [bɔ'ʒi] *m* bogie, *Am.* truck.
bohème [bɔ'ɛm] *adj., a. su.* Bohe-
mian; **bohémien, -enne** *geog.*
[~e'mjɛ̃, ~'mjɛn] *adj., a. su.* ♀ Bo-
hemian; gypsy.

boire [bwaːr] (4b) **1.** *v/t.* drink; soak up, imbibe; *fig.* pocket (*an insult*); *fig.* drink in (*s.o.'s words*); ~ *un coup* have a drink; ~ *une goutte* take a sip; have a nip; *v/i.* drink; be a drunkard; ~ *comme un trou* drink like a fish; **2.** *su./m* drink(ing).

bois [bwa] *m* wood; timber; forest; *rifle:* stock; ~ *pl. stag:* horns, antlers; ~ *contre-plaqué* plywood; ~ *de construction* (*or d'œuvre*) timber; ~ *de lit* bedstead; ♪ *les* ~ *pl.* the woodwind *sg.*; *touchez du* ~ touch wood!; **boisage** △ *etc.* [bwaˈzaːʒ] *m* timbering; frame(work); saplings *pl.*; **boisé, e** [~ˈze] (well-)wooded; wainscoted (*room*); **boisement** [bwazˈmɑ̃] *m* afforestation; **boiser** [bwaˈze] (1a) *v/t.* panel; afforest; ⚒ timber, prop; **boiserie** [bwazˈri] *f* △ panelling; wainscoting; woodwork.

boisseau [bwaˈso] *m measure:* 13 litres (*approx. 1 peck*); ⊕ faucetpipe; △ drain-tile; **boisselier** [~sɔˈlje] *m* bushel-maker; cooper.

boisson [bwaˈsɔ̃] *m* drink; *pris de* ~ drunk, intoxicated.

boîte [bwat] *f* box (*a.* ⊕); tin, *Am.* can; ⊕ case; F place, room; F joint, dump; F company, firm; F école; *sl.* prison; *mot.* ~ *à gants* glove compartment; ~ *à ordures* litterbin, *Am.* litterbag; ~ *à outils* tool-box; ~ *aux lettres* letter-box, *Am.* mail-box; ~ *de conserves* tin, *Am.* can; F ~ *de nuit* night-club; *mot.* ~ *de vitesses* gearbox, *Am.* transmission; ~ *postale* post-office box; *en* ~ tinned, *Am.* canned; F *fig.* *mettre q. en* ~ pull s.o.'s leg.

boiter [bwaˈte] (1a) *v/i.* limp; **boiteux, -euse** [~ˈtø, ~ˈtøːz] lame; rickety (*table etc.*).

boîtier [bwaˈtje] *m* box-maker; watch-case maker; *torch, watch, etc.:* case.

boivent [bwaːv] *3rd p. pl. pres. of* **boire** 1.

bol¹ [bɔl] *m* ⚕ bole; ⚕ bolus.

bol² [~] *m* bowl; *sl.* (good) luck; *sl.* *avoir du* ~ be lucky; F *prendre un* ~ *d'air* get some fresh air; *sl.* *en avoir ras le* ~ be fed up with it.

bolchevisme [bɔlʃəˈvism] *m* Bolshevism; **bolcheviste** [~ˈvist] *adj.*, *a. su.* Bolshevist. [car.⟩

bolide [bɔˈlid] *m* bolide; *mot.* racing-⟩

bombance F [bɔ̃ˈbɑ̃ːs] *f* feast(ing); junket(ing); carouse.

bombardement [bɔ̃bardəˈmɑ̃] *m* shelling; bombing; bombardment (*a. phys.*); **bombarder** [~ˈde] (1a) *v/t.* shell; bombard; pelt (with, de) (*stones, a. fig. questions*); F *on l'a bombardé ministre* he has been pitchforked into a Ministry; **bombardier** [~ˈdje] *m* bomber.

bombe [bɔ̃ːb] *f* ⚔ bomb; (aerosol) spray; F feast; ~ *à hydrogène* H-bomb; ~ *à retardement* time-bomb; ~ *nucléaire* nuclear bomb; *en* ~ like a rocket; *faire la* ~ go on a spree; **bomber** [bɔ̃ˈbe] (1a) *v/t.* cause to bulge; curve, arch; camber (*a road*); ~ *la poitrine* stick out one's chest; ~ *le torse* throw out one's chest, *fig. a.* swagger; *v/i. a.* se ~ bulge; swell out.

bon, bonne [bɔ̃, bɔn] **1.** *adj. usu.* good; nice, kind; proper, right; fit (for, à), apt; benevolent, charitable, dutiful (*son*); ✝ sound (*firm*); witty; *typ.* stet; ~ *à manger* eatable; ~ *marché* cheap(ly); ~ *mot* witticism; *à quoi* ~? what's the use?; *à son* ~ *plaisir* at his own convenience; at his discretion; *de bonne famille* of good family; *de bonne foi* truthful, honest; *de bonne heure* early; *prendre qch. en bonne part* take s.th. in good part; *pour de* ~, *tout de* ~ in earnest; really; for good; **2.** *bon adv.* nice; good; *il fait* ~ it's nice and warm (*weather*); *il fait* ~ (*faire qch.*) it's nice (*to do s.th.*); *il ne fait pas* ~ (*faire qch.*) it's not advisable (*to do s.th.*); *tenir* ~ stand fast *or* firm, hold out; **3.** *su./m* voucher, ticket, coupon; ✝ bond, draft; I.O.U., note of hand; ~ *de caisse* cash voucher; ~ *de poste post:* postal order; ~ *du Trésor* Treasury bond.

bonace [bɔˈnas] *f* lull (*before storm*).

bon(-)à(-)rien, *pl.* **bons(-)à(-)rien** [bɔ̃aˈrjɛ̃] *m* good-for-nothing.

bonasse [~] good-hearted; simpleminded.

bonbon [bɔ̃ˈbɔ̃] *m* sweet, *Am.* candy.

bonbonne [bɔ̃ˈbɔn] *f* carboy.

bonbonnière [bɔ̃bɔˈnjɛːr] *f* sweet (-meat)box; *fig.* snug little dwelling.

bond [bɔ̃] *m* jump; bound; leap; *fig.* ~ *en avant* breakthrough; *fig.* *faire faux* ~ *à* leave in the lurch, let down.

bonde [bɔ̃ːd] *f* ⊕ plug; *barrel:* bung; bung-hole; sluice-gate; **bondé**

[bɔ̃'de] packed, crammed, chock-full.

bondir [bɔ̃'diːr] (2a) *v/i.* bound, jump; bounce; caper; **bondissement** [~dis'mã] *m* bounding, leaping; frisking.

bondon ⊕ [bɔ̃'dɔ̃] *m* bung, plug.

bonheur [bɔ'nœːr] *m* happiness; bliss; good luck; success; *par* ~ luckily; *porter* ~ bring good luck.

bonhomie [bɔnɔ'mi] *f* simple goodheartedness; simplicity; *avec* ~ good-naturedly; **bonhomme,** *pl.* **bonhommes** [bɔ'nɔm, bɔ̃'zɔm] 1. *su./m* fellow, chap; ~ *de neige* snowman; 2. *adj. inv.* good-humo(u)red.

boni † [bɔ'ni] *m* surplus; profit; **bonification** [bɔnifika'sjɔ̃] *f* improvement, amelioration; † allowance, bonus; *insurance:* ~ *pour non sinistre* no claims bonus; **bonifier** [bɔni'fje] (1o) *v/t.* improve; † make good; † allow a discount to; † credit (*s.th.*); **boniment** [~'mã] *m advertizing:* puff; *pej.* claptrap, humbug.

bonjour [bɔ̃'ʒuːr] *m* good morning; good afternoon.

bonne [bɔn] *f* maid; servant; waitress; ~ *à tout faire* maid of all work, F general; ~ *d'enfants* nursery-maid; ~**-maman,** *pl.* ~**s-mamans** *ch.sp.* [bɔnma'mã] *f* grandma, granny.

bonnement [bɔn'mã] *adv.:* tout ~ simply, plainly.

bonnet [bɔ'nɛ] *m* cap; *brassière:* cup; F *avoir la tête près du* ~ be quick-tempered *or* hot-headed; F *gros* ~ bigwig, *Am.* big shot; **bonneterie** [bɔn'tri] *f* hosiery; **bonnetier** *m,* -**ère** *f* [~'tje, ~'tjɛːr] hosier; **bonnette** [bɔ'nɛt] *f* child's bonnet; *phot.* supplementary lens.

bon-papa, *pl.* **bons-papas** *ch.sp.* [bɔ̃pa'pa] *m* gran(d)dad, grandpa.

bonsoir [bɔ̃'swaːr] *m* good evening; good night.

bonté [bɔ̃'te] *f* goodness, kindness; *ayez la* ~ *de* (*inf.*) be so kind as to (*inf.*).

bonze [bɔ̃ːz] *m* bonze (*Buddhist priest*); F bigwig, big shot; *sl. vieux* ~ old dodderer.

borax [bɔ'raks] *m* borax.

bord [bɔːr] *m* edge, border; side; seaside, shore; *river:* bank; tack; *hat:* brim; ✈ ~ *d'attaque* leading edge; ✈ ~ *de fuite* trailing edge; ⚓ *à* ~ on board; **bordage** [bɔr'daːʒ] *m*

hem(ming), border(ing); ⊕ flanging; ⚓ planking, sheathing; **bordé** [~'de] *m* edging, border; ⚓ planking; ⚓ plating; **bordée** ⚓ [~'de] *f* broadside; tack; watch; *fig. une* ~ *d'injures* a volley of abuse; *courir une* ~ ⚓ make a tack, *fig.* go on the spree.

bordel [bɔr'dɛl] *m* brothel.

bordelais, e [bɔrdə'lɛ, ~'lɛːz] of Bordeaux.

border [bɔr'de] (1a) *v/t.* hem, border (*a dress*); ⊕ flange; ⚓ plank; ⚓ ~ *la côte* keep close to the shore, hug the shore; ~ *un lit* tuck in the bedclothes.

bordereau † [bɔrdə'ro] *m* memorandum; statement; invoice; dispatch note; note, slip; list.

bordure [bɔr'dyːr] *f* border(ing); frame; edge; rim; kerb, *Am.* curb.

bore ⚗ [bɔːr] *m* boron.

boréal, e, *m/pl.* -**als** *or* -**aux** [bɔre'al, ~'o] north(ern).

borgne [bɔrɲ] 1. *adj.* one-eyed, blind in one eye; *fig.* disreputable, shady; 2. *su.* one-eyed person.

borique ⚗ [bɔ'rik] boric.

borne [bɔrn] *f* boundary, limit; boundary-stone; landmark; ⚓ bollard; ⚡ terminal; ~ *kilométrique* (*approx.*) milestone; **borné, e** [bɔr'ne] limited; narrow, restricted; **borner** [~'ne] (1a) *v/t.* set limits to; limit; mark the boundary of; *se* ~ *à* content o.s. with, restrict o.s. to; **bornoyer** [~nwa'je] (1h) *v/t.* squint along (*an edge*); *surv.* stake off.

boscot, -otte † [bɔs'ko, ~'kɔt] 1. *adj.* hunchbacked; 2. *su.* hunchback.

bosquet [bɔs'kɛ] *m* grove, thicket.

bosse [bɔs] *f* hump; bump; knob; dent; *fig. avoir la* ~ *de* have a gift for; *en* ~ in relief; **bosseler** [~'le] (1c) *v/t.* ⊕ emboss; *fig.* batter; **bosser** *sl.* [bɔ'se] (1a) *v/i.* work hard, *sl.* peg away; **bossoir** ⚓ [~'swaːr] *m* bow; davit; **bossu, e** [~'sy] 1. *adj.* hunchbacked; 2. *su.* hunchback; **bossuer** [~'sɥe] (1n) *v/t.* dent, batter.

bot, bote [bo, bɔt] *adj.: pied m* ~ club-foot.

botanique [bɔta'nik] 1. *adj.* botanical; 2. *su./f* botany.

botte[1] [bɔt] *f* high boot; *fig.* heel; ~*s pl. à l'écuyère* riding boots; ~*s pl. imperméables* waders; *fig. à propos de* ~*s* without rhyme or reason.

botte[2] [bɔt] *f* bunch; bundle, bale;

wire: coil; **bottelage** [bɔ'tla:ʒ] *m* trussing; **botteler** [~'tle] (1c) *v/t.* bundle; bunch; tie up.

botter [bɔ'te] (1a) *v/t.* put boots on, supply (*s.o.*) with boots *or* shoes; *sp.*, a. F kick; *le Chat botté* Puss-in-Boots; *sl. ça me botte* I like that; o.k.!

bottine [bɔ'tin] *f* (half-)boot; Wellington boot.

botulisme [bɔty'lism] *m* botulism.

bouc [buk] *m* he-goat; *beard*: goatee; ~ *émissaire* scapegoat, *Am.* fall guy.

boucan F [bu'kã] *m* shindy, hullabaloo.

boucaner [buka'ne] (1a) *v/t.* cure (*by smoke*); F sun-burn; *v/i.* hunt wild animals; be cured *or* smoke-dried; *sl.* kick up a row; **boucanier** F [~'nje] *m* buccaneer.

bouche [buʃ] *f* mouth; opening; ⊕ nozzle; ⚔ *canon*: muzzle; ⚔ ~ *à feu* piece of artillery; ~ *d'eau* hydrant; ⛽ water-crane; ~ *de chaleur* hot-air vent; ~ *d'incendie* fire-hydrant, *Am.* fire-plug; ~ *de métro* underground (*Am.* subway) entrance; *sl.* ta ~! shut up!; **bouche-à-bouche** [buʃa'buʃ] *m/inv.* mouth-to-mouth artificial respiration, kiss of life.

bouché, e [bu'ʃe] blocked; choked; F stupid, dense; F ~ à l'émeri absolutely blockheaded.

bouchée [~] *f* mouthful; *cuis.* patty.

boucher¹ [bu'ʃe] (1a) *v/t.* stop (up); shut up; cork (*a bottle*).

boucher² [bu'ʃe] *m* butcher; **bouchère** [~'ʃɛːr] *f* butcher's wife; **boucherie** [buʃ'ri] *f* butcher's shop; butcher's trade; slaughter (*a. fig.*).

bouche-trou [buʃ'tru] *m* stop-gap, substitute; **bouchon** [bu'ʃõ] *m* cork, stopper, plug (*a.* ⚡); *cask*: bung; *fishing*: float; F † pub; *mot.* (*a.* ~ *de circulation*) traffic jam; ~ *de paille* wisp of straw; **bouchonner** [buʃɔ'ne] (1a) *v/t.* rub down (*a horse*); † bundle up; F *fig.* coddle, cosset.

boucle [bukl] *f* buckle; ring; loop; circuit; ear-ring; *hair*: curl, lock; **boucler** [bu'kle] (1a) *v/t.* buckle; loop; curl (*one's hair*); F lock up; *v/i.* curl (*hair*).

bouclier [bu'klje] *m* shield (*a. fig.*).

bouder [bu'de] (1a) *v/i.* sulk; shirk; pass (*at dominoes*); *v/t.* be sulky with; be cool towards; **bouderie** [~'dri] *f* sulkiness; **boudeur, -euse** [~'dœːr,

~'døːz] **1.** *adj.* sulky; **2.** *su.* sulky person.

boudin [bu'dɛ̃] *m* black pudding, *Am.* blood-sausage; *tobacco*: twist; ⊕ *wheel*: flange; ~ *blanc* white pudding; ⊕ *ressort m à* ~ spiral spring; **boudiner** [budi'ne] (1a) *v/t.* ⊕ coil; F be too tight for (*s.o.*) (*garment*); F se ~ *dans* squeeze o.s. into (*a garment*).

boudoir [bu'dwaːr] *m* boudoir, lady's private room. [ment.\]

boue [bu] *f* mud; dirt; slush; sedi-⌡

bouée ⚓ [bu'e] *f* buoy.

boueur [bu'œːr] *m* scavenger; dustman, *Am.* garbage-collector; street cleaner; **boueux, -euse** [bu'ø, ~'øːz] muddy; dirty.

bouffant, e [bu'fã, ~'fãːt] **1.** *adj.* puffed (*sleeve*); full (*skirt*); ample; **2.** *su./m* puff; **bouffarde** F [~'fard] *f* pipe.

bouffe¹ [buf] comic.

bouffe² *sl.* [~] *f* food, F grub.

bouffée [bu'fe] *f* puff, whiff; ✻ attack; ✻ ~ *de chaleur* hot flush; **bouffer** [~] (1a) *vt/i.* puff out; *v/t.* F eat (greedily); blue (*money*).

bouffi, e [bu'fi] puffed (with, de), puffy, swollen; turgid (*style*); **bouffir** [~'fiːr] (2a) *vt/i.* swell; **bouffissure** [~fi'syːr] *f* swelling; *fig.* bombast.

bouffon, -onne [bu'fõ, ~'fɔn] **1.** *adj.* farcical; comical; ridiculous; **2.** *su./m* buffoon, clown, fool; **bouffonnerie** [~fɔn'ri] *f* buffoonery.

bouge [buːʒ] *m* hovel, dump; low dive; ⊕ *cask*: bilge; *wall*: bulge; ⚓ camber.

bougeoir [bu'ʒwaːr] *m* candlestick.

bouger [bu'ʒe] (1l) *v/i.* move, stir; *v/t.* F move.

bougie [bu'ʒi] *f* candle; taper; *phys.* candle-power; *mot.* (*a.* ~ *d'allumage*) sparking-plug, Am. spark plug.

bougon, -onne F [bu'gõ, ~'gɔn] **1.** *adj.* grumpy; **2.** *su.* grumbler.

bougran *tex.* [bu'grã] *m* buckram.

bougre *sl.* [bugr] **1.** *su./m* fellow, chap; ~ *d'idiot!* you blooming idiot!; **2.** *int.* gosh!; **bougrement** *sl.* [bugrə'mã] *adv.* devilishly; very; **bougresse** *sl.* [~'grɛs] *f* jade.

boui-boui, *pl.* **bouis-bouis** F [bwi-'bwi] *m* low theatre *or* music-hall; low haunt, *Am.* dive.

bouillabaisse [buja'bɛs] *f* (*Provençal*) fish-soup.

bouillant, e [bu'jã, ⁓'jã:t] boiling (*a. fig.* with, *de*); hot; *fig.* hotheaded.

bouille *sl.* [bu:j] *f* face; head.

bouilli, e [bu'ji] 1. *p.p. of* bouillir; 2. *su./m* boiled beef; *su./f* gruel; pulp;

bouillir [⁓'ji:r] (2e) *v/i.* boil; *faire* ⁓ *l'eau* boil the water; **bouilloire** [buj'wa:r] *f* kettle, *Am.* teakettle;

bouillon [bu'jɔ̃] *m* bubble; broth (*a. biol.*); soup; restaurant; ✝ unsold copies *pl.*; ⁓ *d'onze heures* poison(ed drink); *fig. boire un* ⁓ suffer a loss; **bouillonner** [⁓jɔ'ne] (1a) *v/i.* bubble; seethe (*a. fig.* with, *de*); *v/t.*: ⁓ *une robe* gauge a dress; **bouillotte** [⁓'jɔt] *f* footwarmer; hot-water bottle; *cards*: bouillotte; *sl.* head; kettle, *Am.* teakettle; **bouillotter** [⁓jɔ'te] (1a) *v/i.* simmer.

boulange F bu'lã:ʒ] bakery trade; **boulanger** [bulã'ʒe] 1. *su./m* baker; 2. (11) *v/t.* make (*bread*), bake (*bread*); **boulangerie** [bulãʒ'ri] *f* bakery; baker's shop; baking.

boule [bul] *f* ball; bowl; *sl.* head; ⁓ *de neige* snowball; ⁓*s pl. Quiès* (*TM*) earplugs.

bouleau ♀ [bu'lo] *m* birch; birchwood.

bouledogue [bul'dɔg] *m* bulldog.

bouler F [bu'le] (1a) *v/t.* send rolling; *v/i.* roll; *envoyer* ⁓ send (*s.o.*) packing; **boulet** [⁓'lɛ] *m* bullet; shot; (⁓ *de canon*) cannon-ball; ✝ *coal:* ovoids *pl.*; *horse:* pastern-joint; **boulette** [⁓'lɛt] *f* small ball; *cuis.* (⁓ *de viande*) meat ball; *sl.* blunder.

boulevard [bul'va:r] *m* boulevard.

bouleversement [bulvɛrsə'mã] *m* overthrow; confusion; **bouleverser** [⁓'se] (1a) *v/t.* upset (*a. fig.*); throw into confusion; bowl over.

boulier [bu'lje] *m billiards:* scoring board; (*a.* ⁓ *compteur*) abacus.

boulimie ✽ [buli'mi] *f* abnormal hunger.

boulin [bu'lɛ̃] *m* pigeon-hole; ⚠ putlog(-hole).

bouline ⚓ [bu'lin] *f* bowline; **bouliner** ⚓ [⁓li'ne] (1a) *v/i.* sail close to the wind; *v/t.* haul (*a sail*) to windward.

boulingrin [bulɛ̃'grɛ̃] *m* lawn, grassplot.

boulon ⊕ [bu'lɔ̃] *m* bolt; pin; **boulonner** [⁓lɔ'ne] (1a) *v/t.* bolt (down); *v/i. sl.* swot.

boulot, -otte [bu'lo, ⁓'lɔt] 1. *adj.*

dumpy; 2. *su./m sl.* work; job; **boulotter** F [⁓lɔ'te] (1a) *v/t.* eat; get through (*money*); *v/i.* jog along; *ça boulotte!* things are fine!

boumer *sl.* [bu'me] *v/i.*: *ça boume?* how's things?; *ça boume!* it's going fine!

bouquet [bu'kɛ] *m* bunch of flowers, nosegay; aroma; *wine:* bouquet; *c'est le* ⁓! that takes the cake!; **bouquetière** [buk'tjɛ:r] *f* flower-girl.

bouquetin *zo.* [buk'tɛ̃] *m* ibex.

bouquin¹ [bu'kɛ̃] *m* old he-goat.

bouquin² [bu'kɛ̃] *m* old book; F book; **bouquiner** [buki'ne] (1a) *v/i.* collect old books; pore over old books; F read; **bouquineur** [⁓'nœ:r] *m* lover *or* collector of old books; **bouquiniste** [⁓'nist] *m* second-hand bookseller.

bourbe [burb] *f* mud; mire; slime; **bourbeux, -euse** [bur'bø, ⁓'bø:z] muddy; *zo.* mud-...; **bourbier** [⁓'bje] *m* mire; *fig.* mess.

bourdaine ♀ [bur'dɛn] *f* black alder.

bourde F [burd] *f* fib; blunder.

bourdon¹ [bur'dɔ̃] *m* pilgrim's staff.

bourdon² ♪ [bur'dɔ̃] *m* drone (*bass*); tenor *or* great bell; *zo.* bumblebee; *typ.* out; *zo. faux* ⁓ drone; **bourdonner** [⁓dɔ'ne] (1a) *v/i.* hum, buzz; *fig.* murmur; *v/t.* hum (*a tune*); **bourdonneur, -euse** [⁓dɔ'nœ:r, ⁓'nø:z] 1. *adj.* humming; 2. *su./m* F hummingbird.

bourg [bu:r] *m* small market-town; borough; **bourgade** [bur'gad] *f* large village; **bourgeois, e** [⁓'ʒwa, ⁓'ʒwa:z] 1. *adj.* middle-class; homely; *pej.* narrow-minded; bourgeois; 2. *su.* citizen; middle-class person; F Philistine; *les petits* ⁓ the petty bourgeoisie *sg.*; *en* ⁓ in plain clothes; *su./f* F *la or ma* ⁓*e* my wife, F the missus; **bourgeoisie** [⁓ʒwa'zi] *f* citizens *pl.*; freemen *pl.*; middleclass; *petite* ⁓ lower middle-class, small shopkeepers *pl.*, tradespeople *pl.*

bourgeon [bur'ʒɔ̃] *m* ♀ bud; ✽ pimple; **bourgeonner** [⁓ʒɔ'ne] (1a) *v/i.* ♀ bud, shoot; ✽ break out into pimples.

bourgeron [burʒə'rɔ̃] *m* overall; ✂ fatigue jacket; ⚓ jumper.

bourgmestre [burg'mɛstr] *m* burgomaster.

bourgogne [bur'gɔɲ] *m wine:* burgundy; **bourguignon, -onne** [~gi'ɲɔ̃, ~'ɲɔn] *adj., a. su.* ♀ Burgundian.

bourlinguer [burlɛ̃'ge] (1m) *v/i.* ⚓ strain, make heavy weather; *fig.* knock about (*the world*).

bourrache ♀ [bu'raʃ] *f* borage.

bourrade [bu'rad] *f* blow; thrust; unkind word; *gun*: kick; **bourrage** ⊕ [~'ra:ʒ] *m* packing; charging; F~ *de crâne* bluff, eyewash; *media*: brainwashing.

bourrasque [bu'rask] *f* squall; gust of wind; *fig.* gust, attack.

bourre[1] [bu:r] *f* fluff; waste; padding; stuffing; *fire-arms*: plug; ⊕ ~ *de soie* floss-silk.

bourre[2] *sl.* [~] *m* cop (= *policeman*).

bourré, e [bu're] packed, crammed, stuffed (with, *de*); chock-full; *sl.* plastered (= *drunk*).

bourreau [bu'ro] *m* executioner; *fig.* tormenter.

bourrée [bu're] *f* bundle of firewood.

bourreler [bur'le] (1c) *v/t.* torture (*a. fig.*); ⊕ fit draught-excluders to (*a door*); **bourrelet** [~'lɛ] *m* pad; wad; draught-excluder; bulge; fold *or* roll (*of flesh*); **bourrelier** [~ə'lje] *m* saddler; **bourrer** [bu're] (1a) *v/t.* stuff; cram; pad; ram in; *fig.* trounce.

bourriche [bu'riʃ] *f* hamper(ful).

bourricot [buri'ko] *m* (small) donkey; **bourrin** *sl.* [~'rɛ̃] *m* horse, nag; **bourrique** [~'rik] *f* she-ass; *fig.* blockhead; **bourriquet** [~ri'kɛ] *m* ass' colt; ⊕ winch.

bourru, e [bu'ry] **1.** *adj.* surly, churlish; **2.** *su./m* curmudgeon; ~ *bienfaisant* rough diamond.

bourse [burs] *f* purse (*a. fig.*); bag; *zo.* pouch; *univ. etc.* scholarship; ✝ ♀ Stock Exchange; ♀ *du Travail* Labo(u)r Exchange; **boursicot** F [bursi'ko] *m* savings *pl.*, F nest-egg; ✝ purse; **boursier, -ère** [~'sje, ~'sjɛ:r] *su. univ. etc.* scholarship-holder; exhibitioner; *su./m* ✝ speculator; paymaster, purse-holder.

boursoufler [bursu'fle] (1a) *v/t.* puff up; bloat; **boursouflure** [~'fly:r] *f* swelling; *paint*: blister; *fig. style*: turgidity.

bous [bu] *1st p. sg. pres.* of *bouillir.*

bousculade [busky'lad] *f* hustle; scrimmage; **bousculer** [~'le] (1a)

v/t. knock (*s.th.*) over; jostle (*s.o.*).

bouse [bu:z] *f* cow-dung; **bousiller** F [buzi'je] (1a) *v/t.* botch, bungle (*a piece of work*); ruin, wreck, F bust up, goof up.

boussole [bu'sɔl] *f* compass; ⚡ galvanometer; F *perdre la* ~ lose one's head; be all at sea.

boustifaille F [busti'fɑ:j] *f* food, grub.

bout [bu] *m usu.* end (*a. fig.*); extremity; *cigarette*: tip, butt; *pen*: nib; bit, piece; *ground*: patch; *à* ~ worn out, F all in; *être à* ~ *de qch.* have run out of s.th.; *à* ~ *de course* at the end of one's resources; *à* ~ *de forces* at the end of one's tether; *à* ~ *portant* point-blank; *au* ~ de after *or* in (*a year*); *au* ~ *du compte* after all, in the end; *de* ~ *en* ~ from beginning to end; ⚓ from stem to stern; *fig. joindre les deux* ~s make both ends meet; *pousser à* ~ try to breaking point; *venir à* ~ *de* manage; (be able to) cope with.

boutade [bu'tad] *f* whim; sally; outburst.

boute-en-train [butɑ̃'trɛ̃] *m/inv.* exhilarating fellow, good company; life and soul (*of a party*).

bouteille [bu'tɛ:j] *f* bottle; ⊕ ~ *à gaz* gas cylinder; ~ *isolante* (*or thermos*) Thermos flask; *prendre de la* ~ age (*wine*); *fig.* grow old.

bouter ✝ [bu'te] (1a) *v/t.* push.

bouteroue ⚠ [bu'tru] *f* guard-stone; *bridge*: guard-rail.

boutique [bu'tik] *f* shop; booth; ⊕ set of tools; *parler* ~ talk shop; **boutiquier** *m*, **-ère** *f* [~ti'kje, ~'kjɛ:r] shopkeeper.

boutoir *zo.* [bu'twa:r] *m* snout (*of boar*); *fig. coup m de* ~ thrust; cutting remark.

bouton [bu'tɔ̃] *m* button; ♀ bud; ✽ pimple; *cost.* stud, link; *door, radio*: knob; ~ *de puissance radio*: volume control; *appuyer sur le* ~ press the bell; *tourner le* ~ switch on *or* off; ~-**d'or**, *pl.* ~**s-d'or** ♀ [~tɔ̃'dɔ:r] *m* butter-cup; **boutonner** [~tɔ'ne] (1a) *v/t.* button (up); *v/i.* ♀ bud; ✽ come out in pimples; **boutonnerie** [~tɔn'ri] *f* button trade *or* factory; **boutonnière** [~tɔ'njɛ:r] *f* buttonhole; ✽ incision; **bouton-poussoir**, *pl.* **boutons-poussoirs** [~tɔ̃pu'swa:r] *m* push-button; **bou-**

ton-pression, *pl.* **boutons-pression** [ˌtɔ̃prɛ'sjɔ̃] *m* press-stud.

bouture ✔ [bu'ty:r] *f* cutting.

bouverie [bu'vri] *f* cowshed.

bouvet ⊕ [bu'vɛ] *m* grooving-plane; tonguing-plane.

bouvier, -ère [bu'vje, ‿'vjɛ:r] *su.* cowherd; drover; F boor; *su./f* cowgirl.

bouvreuil *orn.* [bu'vrœ:j] *m* bullfinch.

bovin, e [bɔ'vɛ̃, ‿'vin] bovine; *bêtes f/pl.* ‿es horned cattle.

box, *pl.* **boxes** [bɔks] *m* horse-box; *mot.* lock-up (garage); *dormitory:* cubicle; ⚖ ‿ *des accusés* dock.

boxe *sp.* [‿] *f* boxing.

boxer[1] [bɔk'se] (1a) *vt/i.* box.

boxer[2] [bɔk'sœ:r] *m dog:* boxer.

boxeur [bɔk'sœ:r] *m* boxer, prize-fighter.

boyau [bwa'jo] *m* hose-pipe; bowel, gut; ✂ communication trench; *fig.* narrow passage.

boycottage [bɔjkɔ'ta:ʒ] *m* boycotting; **boycotter** [‿'te] (1a) *vt/t.* boycott.

bracelet [bras'lɛ] *m* bracelet; bangle; armlet; ♀ node; ‿ *de montre* watch-strap; **‿-montre,** *pl.* **‿s-montres** [‿lɛ'mɔ̃:tr] *m* wristwatch.

brachial, e, *m/pl.* **-aux** *anat.* [bra'kjal, ‿'kjo] brachial.

braconnage [brakɔ'na:ʒ] *m* poaching; **braconner** [‿'ne] (1a) *v/i.* poach; **braconnier** [‿'nje] *m* poacher.

bractée ♀ [brak'te] *f* bract.

brader [bra'de] (1a) *v/t.* sell off cheap(ly), undersell.

braguette [bra'gɛt] *f trousers:* fly, flies *pl.*

brai [brɛ] *m* tar, pitch.

braillard, e [brɑ'ja:r, ‿'jard] **1.** *adj.* brawling; shouting, obstreperous; **2.** *su.* bawler; brawler; **brailler** [‿'je] (1a) *vt/i.* bawl; **brailleur, -euse** [‿'jœ:r, ‿'jø:z] **1.** *adj.* brawling; shouting; **2.** *su.* bawler; brawler.

braire [brɛ:r] (4c) *v/i.* bray (*ass*); F cry; *sl.* squeal.

braise [brɛz] *f* glowing embers *pl.*; live charcoal; cinders *pl.*; *sl.* cash; **braiser** [brɛ'ze] (1b) *v/t.* *cuis.* braise; *v/i. sl.* pay; **braisière** *cuis.* [‿'zje:r] *f* braising-pan.

brait [brɛ] *p.p. of braire.*   [(*stag*).]

bramer [bra'me] (1o) *v/i.* bell)

brancard [brɑ̃'ka:r] *m* stretcher; hand-barrow; ⊕ *carriage:* shaft; **brancardier** [‿kar'dje] *m* stretcher-bearer.

branchage [brɑ̃'ʃa:ʒ] *m coll.* branches *pl.*; **branche** [brɑ̃:ʃ] *f* branch (*a. fig.,* ♀, ♥); bough; *spectacles:* side; *propeller:* blade; *compass:* leg; *sl.* vieille ‿ old pal; **branchement** [brɑ̃ʃ'mɑ̃] *m* branching; ⚡ lead, branch-circuit; ⚡ tapping (*of main*); 🚋‿ (*de voie*) junction; **brancher** [brɑ̃'ʃe] (1a) *v/t.* ⚡ plug in(to *sur*); ⊕, *a. fig.* connect *or* link (up) (with *sur*); *fig.* être branché en direct sur qch. be in immediate touch *or* in close contact with s.th.; F *fig.* être branché be in the know; be well up on things.

branchies *zo.* [brɑ̃'ʃi] *f/pl.* gills.

branchu, e [brɑ̃'ʃy] branchy.

brande ♀ [brɑ̃:d] *f* heather; heath.

brandebourg *cost.* [brɑ̃d'bu:r] *m* frogs *pl.* and loops *pl.*

brandiller [brɑ̃di'je] (1a) *vt/i.* dangle.   [dish, wave.]

brandir [brɑ̃'di:r] (2a) *v/t.* bran-)

brandon [brɑ̃'dɔ̃] *m* (fire-)brand; *fig.* ‿ *de discorde* troublemaker.

branlant, e [brɑ̃'lɑ̃, ‿'lɑ̃:t] tottering; shaky; loose (*tooth*); **branle** [brɑ̃:l] *m* swing; shaking; impulse, start; *en* ‿ in action, going; **branle-bas** [brɑ̃l'bɑ] *m/inv.* ⚓ clearing the decks, pipe to quarters; *fig.* commotion; **branler** [brɑ̃'le] (1a) *vt/i.* shake, move; swing; *v/i. a.* rock, be unsteady; be loose (*tooth, tool, etc.*).

braquage [bra'ka:ʒ] *m car etc.:* steering; *gun:* aiming, pointing; *car: rayon de* ‿ turning circle.

braque [brak] **1.** *su./m* pointer; F mad-cap; **2.** *adj.* F silly, *sl.* daft.

braquer [bra'ke] (1m) *v/t.* aim, point (*a gun etc.*); *mot. etc.* change the direction of; *v/i. mot.* turn the wheel.

bras [brɑ] *m* arm; ⊕ handle; ⊕ leg; ⊕ *crane:* jib; ⊕‿ *pl.* workmen; hands; ‿ (*de pick-up*) *gramophone:* tone-arm; ‿ *dessus,* ‿ *dessous* arm-in-arm; *à* *tendus* at arm's length; *à tour de* ‿ with might and main; *avoir le* ‿ *long* be very influential; *couper* ‿ *et jambes à q.* dishearten s.o.; *en* ‿ *de chemise* in shirt-sleeves.

braser ⊕ [bra'ze] v/t. hardsolder.
brasero [braze'ro] m brazier; glowing fire; fig. blaze; **brasier** [~'zje] m
brazier; glowing fire; fig. blaze;
brasiller [~zi'je] (1a) v/i. sparkle
(sea); splutter (meat etc. in pan); v/t.
grill.
brassage [bra'sa:ʒ] m brewing; fig.
(inter)mixing.
brassard [bra'sa:r] m arm-band;
armlet.
brasse [bras] f ⚓ fathom; swimming:
stroke; ~ sur le dos (ventre) back-
(breast-)stroke; **brassée** [bra'se] f
armful; swimming: stroke.
brasser¹ [bra'se] (1a) v/t. ⚓ brace;
🚀 swing (the propeller).
brasser² [bra'se] (1a) v/t. brew (a.
fig.); stir up; metall. puddle; (inter-)
mix; F handle (an affair); **brasserie**
[bras'ri] f brewery; beer-saloon;
brewing; restaurant.
brassière [bra'sjɛ:r] f shoulder-
strap; (child's) bodice; ~ de sauvetage life-jacket.
brassin [bra'sɛ̃] m brew; mash-tub.
brasure [bra'zy:r] f brazed seam;
hard solder(ing).
bravache [bra'vaʃ] 1. su./m bully;
swaggerer; 2. adj. blustering, swaggering; **bravade** [~'vad] f bravado,
bluster; **brave** [bra:v] brave; good,
honest; F smart; un ~ homme a
worthy man; un homme ~ a brave
man; F faux ~ see bravache 1; **bra-**
ver [bra've] (1a) v/t. defy; brave;
bravo [~'vo] 1. su./m cheers pl.;
2. int. ~! bravo!; well done!; hear,
hear!; **bravoure** [~'vu:r] f bravery.
brayer [brɛ'je] 1. su./m 🩹 truss;
2. (1i) v/t. ⚓ tar; ⚓ sling.
break mot. [brɛk] m estate (car), Am.
station wagon.
brebis brɔ'bi] f ewe; sheep; fig. ~
galeuse black sheep.
brèche [brɛʃ] f breach; gap; ⚓ hole;
blade: notch; fig. battre en ~ disparage; ~-**dent** [~'dã] 1. adj. gap-
toothed; 2. su. gap-toothed person.
bredouille [brɔ'du:j] unsuccessful;
empty-handed; se coucher ~ go sup-
perless to bed; **bredouiller** [~du'je]
(1a) vt/i. mumble.
bref, brève [brɛf, brɛ:v] 1. adj. brief,
short; 2. su./m eccl. (papal) brief; 3.
bref adv. in short, briefly.
bréhaigne † zo. [brɛ'ɛɲ] barren
(mare etc.).

brelan [brɔ'lã] m cards: brelan;
cards: pair royal; gambling den.
breloque [brɔ'lɔk] f (watch-)charm;
🎖 dismiss; F battre la ~ go erratically.
brème [brɛm] f icht. bream; sl. playing card.
brésilien, -enne [brezi'ljɛ̃, ~'ljɛn]
adj., a. su. ♀ Brazilian.
bretailler F [brɔta'je] (1a) v/i. fight
on the slightest provocation; fence.
bretelle [brɔ'tɛl] f (shoulder-)strap;
mot. link road; mot. ~ de contournement bypass; ~s pl. braces, Am.
suspenders.
breton, -onne [brɔ'tɔ̃, ~'tɔn] 1. adj.
Breton; 2. su./m ling. Breton; su. ♀
Breton.
bretteur † [brɛ'tœ:r] m swashbuckler; duellist.
breuvage [brœ'va:ʒ] m beverage,
drink; 🐴 draught.
brève [brɛ:v] f gramm. short syllable;
♪ breve; tel. dot; orn. short tail.
brevet [brɔ'vɛ] m patent; † warrant;
certificate, diploma; 🎖 commission;
~ de capacité school: lower certificate;
⚓ ~ de capitaine master's certificate;
🎖 ~ de pilote pilot's licence; prendre
un ~ take out a patent; **breveté, e**
[brɔv'te] certificated (teacher etc.),
commissioned (officer); **breveter**
[~] (1c) v/t. patent; grant a patent to;
fig. license.
bréviaire eccl. [bre'vjɛ:r] m breviary.
bréviligne [brevi'liɲ] thick-set,
squat.
bribes [brib] f/pl. scraps; fragments.
bric-à-brac [brika'brak] m/inv.
odds pl. and ends pl.; curios pl.;
curiosity shop.
brick ⚓ [brik] m brig.
bricole [bri'kɔl] f strap; breast-
harness; rebound; F ~s pl. odds
and ends, odd jobs; **bricoler** F
[~kɔ'le] (1a) v/i. do odd jobs; v/t.
arrange; **bricoleur** [~kɔ'lœ:r] m
handy man, Am. putterer; pot-
terer.
bride [brid] f bridle; rein (a. fig.);
⊕ tie, strap; ⊕ flange; ⊕ ~ de
serrage clamp(ing) piece; à ~ abat-
tue, à toute ~ at full speed; lâcher
la ~ à l'émotion give free rein to
one's feelings; fig. laisser à q. la ~
sur le cou give s.o. his head; fig.
tenir la ~ haute à keep a tight rein
on; be high-handed with; **brider**

[bri'de] (1a) v/t. bridle; curb; tie (up); ⊕ flange; cuis. truss (fowl); cost. bind (a buttonhole).

bridger [brid'ʒe] (1l) v/i. play bridge.

bridon [bri'dɔ̃] m snaffle.

brie [bri] m Brie (cheese).

brièvement [briɛv'mɑ̃] adv. briefly, succinctly; **brièveté** [~'te] f brevity; concision.

brigade [bri'gad] f ✕ brigade; workers: gang; workers: shift; police: squad; **brigadier** [~ga'dje] m ✕ corporal; ⊕ foreman; police: sergeant.

brigand [bri'gɑ̃] m brigand; robber; F ruffian; **brigandage** [~gɑ̃'da:ʒ] m highway robbery; plunder.

brigue [brig] f intrigue; cabal; **briguer** [bri'ge] (1m) v/t. seek, aspire to or after; court (favour); canvass for (votes).

brillant, e [bri'jɑ̃, ~'jɑ̃:t] 1. adj. shining, brilliant, bright; 2. su./m brilliance, brightness; gloss; shine; diamond: brilliant; **briller** [~'je] (1a) v/i. shine, glisten, sparkle; F ~ par son absence be conspicuous for one's absence.

brimade [bri'mad] f rag(ging), Am. hazing.

brimbaler [brɛ̃ba'le] (1a) v/i. dangle; wobble; v/t. F carry about.

brimborion [brɛ̃bɔ'rjɔ̃] m bauble.

brimer [bri'me] (1a) v/t. rag, Am. haze; bully.

brin [brɛ̃] m grass: blade; tree: shoot, ⚓, rope: strand; fig. bit; touch; **brindille** [~'di:j] f twig.

bringue[1] F [brɛ̃:g] f spree, F binge, bust; faire la ~ be or go on a spree.

bringue[2] F [~] f: grande ~ tall (and ugly) woman, F beanpole.

brioche [bri'ɔʃ] f brioche; bun; F blunder.

brique [brik] f △ brick; ✝ soap: bar; ~ de parement facing brick; ~ hollandaise clinker; ~ tubulaire hollow brick; sl. bouffer des ~s not to have a bite; **briquet** [bri'kɛ] m cigarette-lighter; tinder-box; battre le ~ strike a light; **briqueter** [brik'te] (1c) v/t. brick; face with bricks or with imitation brickwork; **briqueterie** [~'tri] f brick-yard; **briquetier** [~'tje] m brick-maker; **briquette** [bri'kɛt] f briquette.

bris [bri] m breaking (a. 🕮); ⚓ wreckage; **brisant, e** [bri'zɑ̃, ~'zɑ̃:t] 1. adj. high-explosive; 2. su./m reef; breaker (wave).

brise ⚓ [bri:z] f breeze.

brise-bise [briz'bi:z] m/inv. draught-excluder.

brisées [bri'ze] f/pl. tracks; hunt. broken boughs; fig. aller sur les ~ de q. trespass s.o.'s preserves.

brise...: **~-glace** [briz'glas] m/inv. ice-breaker; ice-fender; **~-jet** ⊕ [~'ʒɛ] m/inv. anti-splash nozzle; **~-lames** ⚓ [~'lam] m/inv. break-water; groyne.

briser [bri'ze] (1a) v/t. break; shatter; fig. a. crush; v/i. break (with, avec); brisons là! let's leave it at that!; **brise-tout** F [briz'tu] su./inv. esp. destructive child; **briseur** m, -euse f [bri'zœ:r, ~'zø:z] breaker; ~ de grève strikebreaker.

brisure [bri'zy:r] f break; shutter: folding-joint; ⌧ brisure.

britannique [brita'nik] 1. adj. British; Britannic (majesty); 2. su.: les ~s m/pl. the British.

broc [bro] m jug, pitcher.

brocanter [brɔkɑ̃'te] (1a) v/i. deal in second-hand goods; v/t. sell (to a second-hand dealer); barter; **brocanteur** m, -euse f [~'tœ:r, ~'tø:z] second-hand dealer; broker.

brocard[1] ✝ [brɔ'ka:r] m lampoon.

brocard[2] hunt. [~] m yearling roedeer.

brocart ✝ [~] m brocade.

broche [brɔʃ] f spit; skewer; ⊕ spindle; ⊕ pin; tent-peg; brooch; F knitting-needle; zo. boar: tusk; **brocher** [brɔ'ʃe] (1a) v/t. stitch; brocade; emboss; livre broché paper-bound book.

brochet icht. [brɔ'ʃɛ] m pike.

brochette [brɔ'ʃɛt] f skewer; ⊕ pin.

brocheur, -euse [brɔ'ʃœ:r, ~'ʃø:z] su. stitcher, sewer (of books); su./f stitching-machine; stapling-machine; **brochure** [~'ʃy:r] f booklet, brochure; pamphlet; stitching (of books); tex. inwoven pattern.

brodequin [brɔd'kɛ̃] m half-boot; ✕ ammunition-boot; F thea. chausser le ~ take to comedy.

broder [brɔ'de] (1a) v/t. embroider (a. fig.); **broderie** [~'dri] f embroidery (a. fig.); fig. embellish-

brodeur

ment; **brodeur** *m*, **-euse** *f* [ₛ'dœːr, ₛ'døːz] embroiderer.

broie [brwa] *f tex.* brake; ✗ brakeharrow; **broiement** [ₛ'mã] *m* crushing, pulverizing; *tex.* braking.

brome ⚗ [broːm] *m* bromine; **bromique** ⚗ [brɔ'mik] bromic; **bromure** ⚗ [ₛ'myːr] *m* bromide.

bronche *anat.* [brɔ̃ːʃ] *f* wind-pipe; bronchus; ₛs *pl.* bronchi(a).

broncher [brɔ̃'ʃe] (1a) *v/i.* stumble; trip; move; *fig.* falter, flinch; *sans* ~ without flinching.

bronchite ⚕ [brɔ̃'ʃit] *f* bronchitis.

bronze [brɔ̃ːz] *m* bronze; *fig.* cœur *m de* ~ heart of steel; **bronzer** [brɔ̃'ze] (1a) *v/t.* bronze; tan; *fig.* harden.

brosse [brɔs] *f* brush; paint-brush; ₛs *pl.* brushwood *sg.*; *cheveux m/pl.* en ~ crew-cut *sg.*; *fig. passer la* ~ *sur* efface; **brosser** [brɔ'se] (1a) *v/t.* brush; scrub; F thrash; F *se* ~ *(le ventre)* go without; *sl.* have an empty belly; **brosserie** [brɔs'ri] *f* brush-ware; brush-trade; brushfactory; **brossier** [brɔ'sje] *m* brushmaker; dealer in brushes.

brou [bru] *m* husk; ~ *de noix* walnut stain; walnut liqueur.

brouet [bru'ɛ] *m* (thin) gruel, F skilly; ~ *noir* black broth.

brouette [bru'ɛt] *f* wheelbarrow; **brouetter** [ₛɛ'te] (1a) *v/t.* convey in a (wheel)barrow.

brouhaha [brua'a] *m* hubbub; hullabaloo; uproar.

brouillage [bru'jaːʒ] *m radio:* jamming; interference.

brouillamini F [brujami'ni] *m* muddle.

brouillard [bru'jaːr] **1.** *su./m* fog; smog; ⳿ waste-book; **2.** *adj./m:* *papier m* ~ blotting-paper; **brouillasser** [ₛja'se] (1a) *v/impers.* drizzle.

brouille F [bru:j] *f* disagreement; quarrel; *être en* ~ *avec* be at loggerheads with; **brouiller** [bru'je] (1a) *v/t.* mix up; confuse; *radio:* jam; *radio:* interfere with *(a broadcast)*; shuffle *(cards)*; scramble *(eggs)*; *fig.* create dissension between; set at variance; ~ *du papier* scribble over paper; **brouillerie** [bruj'ri] *f* disagreement; **brouilleur** [ₛ'jœːr] *m radio:* jammer.

brouillon¹, -onne [bru'jɔ̃, ₛ'jɔn] **1.**

adj. unmethodical; muddle-headed *(person)*; *avoir l'esprit* ~ be muddleheaded; **2.** *su.* muddler; muddlehead.

brouillon² [bru'jɔ̃] *m* draft, rough copy; scribbling paper; **brouillonner** [ₛjɔ'ne] (1a) *v/t.* botch *(an essay etc.)*; draft, make a rough copy of.

broussailles [bru'saːj] *f/pl.* brushwood *sg.*, scrub *sg.*, bush *sg.*; *en* ~ shaggy, unkempt *(hair)*; **brousse** [brus] *f the* bush *(in Australia etc.)*.

brout [bru] *m* tender shoots *pl.*; browse(-wood); **brouter** [bru'te] (1a) *v/t.* browse (on), graze; *v/i.* ⊕ jump *(tool)*; **broutille** [ₛ'tiːj] *f* twig; F trifle.

broyage [brwa'jaːʒ] *m* pounding, crushing; grinding; *tex.* braking; **broyer** [ₛ'je] (1h) *v/t.* pound, crush; grind; *tex.* brake; **broyeur** *m*, **-euse** *f* [ₛ'jœːr, ₛ'jøːz] pounder; grinder; *tex.* hemp-braker.

brrr! [brrr] *int.* ugh!

bru [bry] *f* daughter-in-law.

bruine [brɥin] *f* drizzle, Scotch mist; **bruinement** [ₛ'mã] *m* drizzling; **bruiner** [brɥi'ne] (1a) *v/impers.* drizzle; **bruineux, -euse** [ₛ'nø, ₛ'nøːz] drizzly.

bruire [brɥiːr] (4d) *v/i.* rustle; hum *(machine)*; murmur *(brook etc.)*; **bruissement** [brɥis'mã] *m* rumbling; rustling; humming; murmuring; **bruit** [brɥi] *m* noise; clatter, din; rumble; *metal:* clang; *gun:* report; ✗ murmur; *fig.* rumo(u)r, report; ₛs *pl. parasites radio:* interference *sg.*; ~ *de fond radio etc.:* background noise; ~ *sourd* thud; *le* ~ *court que* ... rumo(u)r has it that ..., it is rumo(u)red that ...; **bruitage** *thea.*, *cin.* [brɥi'taːʒ] *m* sound effects *pl.*; **bruiteur** *m*, **-euse** *f* [ₛ'tœːr, ₛ'tøːz] sound-effects engineer.

brûlé [bry'le] *m* smell of burning; **brûle-gueule** F [bryl'gœl] *m/inv.* nosewarmer; **brûle-pourpoint** [ₛpur'pwɛ̃] *adv.: à* ~ point-blank; **brûler** [bry'le] (1a) *v/t.* burn *(a. fig.)*; scorch; ✗ cauterize; overrun *(a signal)*; ✗ nip; 🚂 not to stop at; *sl.* unmask, detect; *fig.* ~ *ses vaisseaux* burn one's boats; *se* ~ *la cervelle* blow one's brains out; *v/i.* burn *(a. fig.)*, be on fire; catch *(milk)*; *fig.* be consumed; F be hot,

bureau

be roasting; ~ de (*inf.*) be eager to (*inf.*); **brûleur, -euse** [~'lœːr, ~'løːz] *su. person*: burner; *coffee*: roaster; *brandy distiller*; *su./m gas etc.*: burner; **brûloir** [~'lwaːr] *m machine*: coffee roaster; blowlamp; **brûlot** [~'lo] *m* ⚓ flare; F *pol.* fire-brand; **brûlure** [~'lyːr] *f* burn; scald; ✒ frost-nip; ✱ ~s *pl. d'estomac* heartburn *sg.*

brume [brym] *f* thick fog; (sea-) mist; **brumeux, -euse** [bry'mø, ~'møːz] foggy; *fig.* hazy.

brun, brune [brœ̃, bryn] **1.** *adj.* brown; dark (*complexion*); dark-haired; **2.** *su./m* brown; *su./f* brunette; nightfall; **brunâtre** [bry-'naːtr] brownish; **brunir** [~'niːr] (2a) *vt/i.* brown; tan; *v/t.* ⊕ burnish, polish; **brunissage** [~ni-'saːʒ] *m* burnishing; polishing; (sun)tan.

brusque [brysk] blunt, brusque, abrupt; sudden; rough; sharp; **brusquer** [brys'ke] (1m) *v/t.* be blunt with (*s.o.*); hurry; hustle; precipitate (*s.th.*); **brusquerie** [~kə'ri] *f* abruptness, brusqueness.

brut, brute [bryt] raw; crude (*oil*); unrefined (*sugar*); uncut (*diamond*); undressed (*stone*); ♥ *poids m* ~ gross weight; **brutal, e,** *m/pl.* **-aux** [bry-'tal, ~'to] brutal; savage, fierce; harsh (*colour*); brute (*force*); unfeeling; plain, unvarnished (*truth*); **brutaliser** [~tali'ze] (1a) *v/t.* ill-treat; bully; **brutalité** [~tali'te] *f* brutality; *sp.* rough play; *fig.* suddenness (*of an event etc.*); **brute** [bryt] *f* brute (*a. fig.*); lout.

bruyant, e [brɥi'jɑ̃, ~'jɑ̃ːt] noisy, loud; boisterous; *fig.* resounding (*success*).

bruyère [brɥi'jeːr] *f* heather; heath; briar; *orn. coq m de* ~ grouse.

bu, e [by] *p.p. of boire 1.*

buanderie [bɥɑ̃'dri] *f* wash-house.

bubonique ✱ [bybɔ'nik] bubonic; *peste f* ~ bubonic plague.

buccal, e, *m/pl.* **-aux** [byk'kal, ~'ko] buccal, of the mouth.

bûche [byʃ] *f* log; block; *cuis.* Swiss roll; F blockhead; *ramasser une* ~ have a fall, come a cropper.

bûcher¹ [by'ʃe] *m* wood-shed; pile of firewood, wood-stack; pyre.

bûcher² [~] (1a) *v/t.* ⊕ rough-hew; *sl.* thrash; F swot at, work hard at

or for, *Am.* grind; *v/i.* F work hard; swot, *Am.* grind.

bûcheron [byʃ'rɔ̃] *m* woodcutter, *Am.* lumberjack; **bûcheronne** [~'rɔn] *f* woodcutter's wife.

bûchette [by'ʃɛt] *f* stick.

bûcheur *m*, **-euse** *f* F [by'ʃœːr, ~'ʃøːz] plodder; swotter, *Am.* grind.

budget [byd'ʒɛ] *m* budget; *admin.* estimates *pl.*; F *boucler son* ~ make ends meet; **budgétaire** [~ʒe'teːr] budgetary; financial (*year etc.*); **budgétisation** [~ʒetiza'sjɔ̃] *f* budgeting.

buée [bɥe] *f* steam, vapo(u)r.

buffet [by'fɛ] *m* sideboard; dresser; cupboard; buffet; ⛟ refreshment room; F *danser devant le* ~ have a bare cupboard; **buffetier** [byf'tje] *m* refreshment-room manager; **buffetière** [~'tjeːr] *f* refreshment-room manageress.

buffle [byfl] *m zo.* buffalo; buffalo-hide; ⊕ buff-stick; **buffleterie** [~'tri] *f* leather equipment.

bugle¹ ♪ [bygl] *m* saxhorn.

bugle² ♀ [~] *f* bugle.

buis ♀ [bɥi] *m* box-tree; box-wood; **buisson** [bɥi'sɔ̃] *m* bush; spinney, thicket; **buissoneux, -euse** [bɥi-sɔ'nø, ~'nøːz] bushy; **buissonnier, ère** [~'nje, ~'njeːr] *adj.*: *faire l'école* ~ère play truant, *Am.* play hooky.

bulbe ♀ [bylb] *m* bulb; **bulbeux, -euse** [byl'bø, ~'bøːz] bulbous; ♀ bulbed.

bulldozer [buldɔ'zœːr] *m* bull-dozer.

bulle [byl] *f* bubble; blister; *cartoon*: balloon; *eccl.* papal bull; *faire des* ~s blow bubbles.

bulletin [byl'tɛ̃] *m* bulletin; form; voting-paper; report; ⛟ ~ *de bagages* luggage-ticket, *Am.* baggage-check; ♥ ~ *de commande* order-form; ~ *d'expédition* way-bill; ~ *de santé* health report.

bulleux, -euse [by'lø, ~'løːz] bubbly; ♀ bullate; ✱, *geol.* vesicular.

bungalow [bœ̃ga'lo] *m* bungalow.

buraliste [byra'list] *su.* tax collector; tobacconist; clerk.

bure¹ *tex.* [byːr] *f* rough homespun.

bure² ⚒ [~] *f* shaft (*of a mine*).

bureau [by'ro] *m* writing-table, desk; bureau; office; *admin.* department; board of directors, governing body; *thea.* ~x *pl.* fermés sold out; 🚌 ~ *ambulant* travelling post office; ~ *central* head post office, G.P.O.; *teleph.* exchange; ~ *de bienfaisance* relief committee; ~ *de douane* custom-house; *thea.* ~ *de location* box-office; ~ *de placement* labo(u)r exchange; (private) employment bureau; ~ *de poste* post office; ~ *de renseignements* information bureau; ~ *de tabac* tobacconist's (shop); ~ *ministre* kneehole desk; ⚔ *deuxième* ~ Intelligence (Department); ⚓ Naval Intelligence Division; **bureaucrate** [byro'krat] *m* bureaucrat; F blackcoated worker; **bureaucratie** [~kra'si] *f* bureaucracy, F red tape; **bureaucratiser** [~krati'ze] (1a) *v/t.* bureaucratize.

burette [by'rɛt] *f* cruet (*a. eccl.*); ⊕ oil-can, oiler; 🔧 burette.

burin ⊕ [by'rɛ̃] *m* burin, etching-needle, graver; cold chisel; engraving; **buriner** [~ri'ne] (1a) *v/t.* engrave; chisel; *v/i.* F swot.

burlesque [byr'lesk] burlesque; comical, ridiculous.

bus [by] *1st p. sg. p.s. of boire 1*.

buse[1] [by:z] *f orn.* buzzard; F blockhead, fool.

buse[2] [~] *f* ⊕ pipe; nozzle; ⚒ air-shaft; *mot.* choke(-tube).

busqué, e [bys'ke] arched, curved; *nez m* ~ hook nose.

buste [byst] *m* bust; *en* ~ half-length.

but [by(t)] *m* target; aim; goal (*a. sp.*); purpose; *avoir pour* ~ aim at, intend;

de ~ *en blanc* bluntly; *droit au* ~ (straight) to the point; *marquer un* ~ score a goal.

buté, e [by'te] obstinate, mulisk; **buter** [~] (1a) *v/i.:* ~ *contre* stumble over (*a. fig.*); bump *or* bang against *or* into, hit; *fig.* ~ *contre or sur* meet with, come up against (*a difficulty etc.*); *v/t.* prop (up); *fig.* make (*s.o.*) obstinate; se ~ be(come) obstinate; **buteur** [by'tœ:r] *m foot.* striker; *sl.* killer.

butin [by'tɛ̃] *m* booty, spoils *pl.*; **butiner** [~ti'ne] (1a) *vt/i.* † plunder; *v/i.* gather honey (*bee*); *v/t.* gather honey from (*a flower*).

butoir [by'twa:r] *m* ⊕ stop; catch; 🚌 terminal buffer.

butor [by'tɔ:r] *m orn.* bittern; F lout, clod.

butte [byt] *f* mound, hillock; bank; ⚔ butts *pl.*; *fig. en* ~ *à* exposed to; **butter** 🌱 [by'te] (1a) *v/t.* earth up; **buttoir** 🌱 [~'twa:r] *m* ridging-plough, *Am.* ridging-plow.

buvable [by'vabl] drinkable; *sl.* acceptable; **buvard** [~'va:r] *m* blotting-paper; **buvette** [~'vet] *f* refreshment bar; *spa:* pump-room; **buveur** *m*, **-euse** *f* [~'vœ:r, ~'vø:z] drinker; toper; ~ *d'eau* teetotaller; **buvons** [~'vɔ̃] *1st p. pl. pres. of boire 1*; **buvoter** F [~vɔ'te] (1a) *v/t.* sip (*wine*); *v/i.* tipple.

byzantin, e [bizɑ̃'tɛ̃, ~'tin] Byzantine.

C

C, c [se] *m* C, c.

ça [sa] F *abbr. of cela; c'est ~!* that's right!; *et avec ~?* anything else?

çà [~] 1. *adv.* here; hither; *~ et là* here and there; 2. *int.* (*ah*) *~!* now then!

cabale [ka'bal] *f* cabal; intrigue; clique, faction; **cabaler** [kaba'le] (1a) *v/i.* intrigue; **cabaleur, -euse** [~'lœːr, ~'løːz] 1. *adj.* intriguing; 2. *su.* intriguer.

caban [ka'bã] *m* oilskins *pl.*; duffle-coat.

cabane [ka'ban] *f* hut, shed; cabin; *rabbit:* hutch; *dog:* kennel; **cabanon** [~ba'nõ] *m* small hut; *prison:* cell; *lunatic:* padded cell.

cabaret [kaba'rɛ] *m* night club; † pub(lic house), tavern; **cabaretier** *m*, **-ère** *f* † [~barə'tje, ~'tjɛːr] inn-keeper; publican.

cabas [ka'bɑ] *m* basket.

cabestan ⊕, ⚓ [kabɛs'tɑ̃] *m* capstan, winch.

cabillau(d) *icht.* [kabi'jo] *m* fresh cod.

cabine [ka'bin] *f* cabin; (*~ téléphonique*) telephone-box, telephone-booth; ▓ (*a. ~ d'aiguillage*) signal-box; *cin. ~ de projection* projection room; **cabinet** [~bi'nɛ] *m* small room; office; consulting room; practice; ⚖ chambers *pl.*; ministry; *~(s pl.) (d'aisances)* water-closet, lavatory; *~ de groupe* joint practice; *~ de toilette* dressing-room; *~ (de travail)* study; *phot. ~ noir* dark room.

câble [kɑːbl] *m* cable (*a.* F = *cablegram*); ⚓ *~ de remorque* hawser; *~ métallique* wire rope; stranded wire; **câbler** [kɑ'ble] (1a) *v/t.* cable (*a message*); ⚡ wire up; **câblogramme** [~blɔ'gram] *m* cablegram.

caboche [ka'bɔʃ] *f* (hob)nail; ⊕ clout-nail; F head, pate.

cabosse F [ka'bɔs] *f* ⚑ cacao-pod; ⚙ bump, bruise; **cabosser** F [~bɔ'se] (1a) *v/t.* ⚙ bump, bruise; dent.

cabotage ⚓ [kabɔ'taːʒ] *m* coastal navigation; **caboter** [~'te] (1a) *v/i.* coast.

cabotin, e [kabɔ'tɛ̃, ~'tin] 1. *adj.* theatrical, histrionic, affected; 2. *su.* *thea.* ham (actor, *f* actress); *fig.* show-off, play-actor (*f* -actress); **cabotinage** [~ti'naːʒ] *m* *thea.* hamming; *fig.* showing-off, play-acting; **cabotiner** [~ti'ne] (1a) *v/i.* *thea.* ham; *fig.* show off, playact.

cabrer [kɑ'bre] (1a) *v/t.* ✈ elevate; *se ~* rear (*horse*); ✈ rear, buck; *fig. se ~ contre* jib at, rebel against.

cabri *zo.* [ka'bri] *m* kid; **cabriole** [kabri'ɔl] *f* caper, leap; **cabrioler** [~ɔ'le] (1a) *v/i.* caper; **cabriolet** [~'lɛ] *m* *mot.* cab(riolet).

cabus [ka'by] *adj./m*: *chou m ~* headed cabbage.

cacahouète ⚑ [kaka'wɛt] *f*, **cacahuète** ⚑ [~'ɥɛt] *f* peanut.

cacao [kaka'o] *m* ⚑ cacao; ⚑ cocoa; **cacaotier** [~ɔ'tje] *m*, **cacaoyer** [~ɔ'je] *m* cacao-tree.

cacarder [kakar'de] (1a) *v/i.* cackle (*goose*).

cacatoès *orn.* [kakatɔ'ɛs] *m* cockatoo; **cacatois** ⚓ [~'twa] *m* royal (-sail).

cachalot *zo.* [kaʃa'lo] *m* sperm-whale, cachalot.

cache [kaʃ] *su./f* hiding-place; *su./m* *phot.* mask; ⊕ panel, plate; **~-cache** [~'kaʃ] *m* hide-and-seek (*a. fig.*); **~-col** [~'kɔl] *m/inv.* scarf; **~-nez** [~'ne] *m/inv.* muffler; **~-poussière** [~pu'sjɛːr] *m/inv.* dust-coat.

cacher [ka'ʃe] (1a) *v/t.* hide, conceal; *~ sa vie* live in retirement; *esprit m caché* reserved person; sly person; *se ~* hide; **cache-sexe** [kaʃ'sɛks] *m/inv.* G-string; **cachet** [ka'ʃɛ] *m* seal; stamp; ⚑ trade-mark; mark; F fee; ⚙ cachet; *courir le ~* give private lessons; **cacheter** [kaʃ'te] (1c) *v/t.* seal; **cachette** [ka'ʃɛt] *f* hiding place, hideout; *en ~* secretly; by stealth; under the counter (*sale*); **cachot** [~'ʃo] *m* dungeon; ⚓ cell; prison; **cachotterie** [~'tri] *f* mysterious ways *pl.*; *faire des ~s* be secretive; act secretevely; **cachottier,**

cacique

-ère F [ʌˈtje, ʌˈtjɛːr] 1. adj. secretive; 2. su. sly person.
cacique F [kaˈsik] m candidate who has obtained first place; fig. (big) boss, big chief.
caco... [kako] caco...; **ʌphonique** [ʌfɔˈnik] cacophonous, discordant.
cactus ⚥ [kakˈtys] m, **cactier** ⚥ [ʌˈtje] m cactus.
cadastre [kaˈdastr] m cadastral survey; (public) register of lands; survey.
cadavéreux, -euse [kadaveˈrø, ʌˈrøːz] cadaverous, deathlike; deathly pale; **cadavérique** anat. [ʌˈrik] cadaveric; rigidité f ʌ rigor mortis; **cadavre** [kaˈdɑːvr] m corpse, Am. a. cadaver; animal: carcase; sl. dead man (= empty winebottle).
cadeau [kaˈdo] m present, gift.
cadenas [kadˈnɑ] m padlock; clasp; ʌ à chiffres combination-lock.
cadence [kaˈdɑ̃ːs] f cadence (a. ♪), rhythm; step; march: time; à la ʌ de at the rate of, fig. to the tune of.
cadet, -ette [kaˈdɛ, ʌˈdɛt] 1. adj. younger; 2. su. (the) younger, junior; il est mon ʌ he is my junior (by 3 years, de 3 ans), he is younger than I; su./m ✗ cadet; golf: caddie.
cadran [kaˈdrɑ̃] m dial; clock: face; ʌ solaire sun-dial; **cadre** [kɑːdr] m usu. frame; fig. a. framework, context; fig. setting, surroundings pl.; fig. scope, limits pl.; personnel: executive, manager; ✗ officer; les ʌs a. the managerial staff; ʌ (de réception) radio: frame aerial; ʌ orienté radio: directional aerial; **cadrer** [kaˈdre] (1a) v/i. tally, agree; fit in.
caduc, -que [kaˈdyk] decrepit, decaying; feeble (voice); ♂ null, lapsed; ♂ time-barred; ⚥ deciduous; **caducité** [ʌdysiˈte] f dilapidated state; decrepitude; ♂ nullity; ♂ lapsing; ⚥ caducity.
cafard¹ [kaˈfaːr] m zo. cockroach; F avoir le ʌ be down in the dumps.
cafard², e [kaˈfaːr, ʌˈfard] 1. adj. sanctimonious; 2. su. school: sneak; su./m ✗ sl. spy; **cafarder** [ʌfarˈde] (1a) v/i. school: sneak.
café [kaˈfe] 1. su./m coffee; café; ʌ complet continental breakfast; ʌ crème white coffee; ʌ nature (or noir) black coffee; 2. adj./inv. coffee-colo(u)red; ʌ-concert, pl. ʌs-concerts [ʌfekɔ̃ˈsɛːr] m, F **caf'conc'**

[kafˈkɔ̃ːs] m café with a cabaret show.
cafetier, -ère [kafˈtje, ʌˈtjɛːr] su. café-owner; su./f coffee-pot; sl. head.
cafouillage F [kafuˈjaːʒ] m muddle; **cafouiller** F [ʌˈje] (1a) v/i. not to work properly, F be on the blink (machinery etc.); fig. muddle things up, get into a muddle, flounder (person); fig. get or turn into a shambles; **cafouillis** F [ʌˈji] m muddle.
cage [kaːʒ] f bird: cage; hen-coop; ⚿ frame; cover, casing; F prison; ʌ d'ascenseur lift (Am. elevator) shaft; ʌ d'escalier stair-well; anat. ʌ thoracique chest.
cagne sl. [kaɲ] f school: class preparing to compete for entrance to the École normale supérieure.
cagneux, -euse [kaˈnø, ʌˈnøːz] knock-kneed; **cagnotte** [ʌˈnɔt] f pool, kitty.
cagot, e [kaˈgo, ʌˈgɔt] 1. adj. sanctimonious; 2. su. bigot; hypocrite; **cagoterie** [kagɔˈtri] f cant; **cagotisme** [ʌˈtism] m false piety.
cahier [kaˈje] m paper-book; exercise-book; ⚓ defaulters' book; ✝ ʌ des charges specifications pl.
cahin-caha F [kaɛ̃kaˈa] adv. so-so; middling.
cahot [kaˈo] m vehicle: jolt, jog; **cahoter** [kaɔˈte] (1a) v/t./i. jolt along; toss; vie f cahotée life of ups and downs; **cahoteux, -euse** [ʌˈtø, ʌˈtøːz] bumpy (road).
cahute [kaˈyt] f hut; cabin; hovel.
caïd F [kaˈid] m (big) boss, big chief; gangster boss.
caille orn [kɑːj] f quail.
caillé [kɑˈje] m curds pl., curdled milk.
caillebotis [kajbɔˈti] m duck-board(s pl.); ⚓ grating.
caillebotte [kajˈbɔt] f curds pl.; **cailler** [kɑˈje] v/t./i. curdle, clot; congeal (blood); sl. be cold; ça caille it's freezing.
caillette¹ [kɑˈjet] f zo. ruminants: fourth stomach; cuis. rennet.
caillette² F [ʌ] f flirt; tart.
caillot [kɑˈjo] m clot.
caillou, pl. **-x** [kɑˈju] m pebble; cobble; **cailloutage** [kajuˈtaːʒ] m ⚿ rough-cast, pebble-dash; ⛏ gravel; road-metal; pebble paving; **caillouter** [ʌˈte] (1a) v/t. ballast,

metal (*a road, a railway-track*); pave with pebbles; **caillouteux, -euse** [\ˈtø, \ˈtøːz] stony; pebbly, shingly (*beach*); **cailloutis** [\ˈti] *m* gravel; road-metal; pebbled surface; cobbled pavement; rubble.

caisse [kɛs] *f* case, box; ✝ cash-box; ✝ till; (pay-)desk; *thea.* pay-box; ✝ fund; ♪, *anat.* drum; ⊕ body; ✖ *sl.* prison, cells *pl.*; ~ *à eau* water-tank; ✝ ~ *d'amortissement* sinking-fund; depreciation; ~ *d'épargne* savings-bank; ~ *de prêts* loan bank; ~ *enregistreuse* cash-register; ⚡ ~ *nationale de l'énergie* national grid; *argent m en* ~ cash in hand; *fig. battre la grosse* ~ advertize; boost a product; *faire la* ~ balance the cash; *grosse* ~ *instrument:* bass *or* big drum; *person:* bass drummer; *tenir la* ~ be in charge of the cash; **caissier** *m*, **-ère** *f* [kɛˈsje, ~ˈsjɛːr] cashier; treasurer; **caisson** [\ˈsõ] *m* box; ⊕ caisson; ✖ ammunition-waggon; locker; *mot.* boot; ✗ bunker.

cajoler [kaʒɔˈle] (1a) *v/t.* coax, wheedle; **cajolerie** [\ʒɔlˈri] *f* coaxing, wheedling; **cajoleur, -euse** [\ʒɔˈlœːr, ~ˈløːz] **1.** *adj.* wheedling; **2.** *su.* wheedler.

cal, *pl.* **cals** [kal] *m* callosity; ♀, ♂ callus.

calamité [kalamiˈte] *f* calamity, disaster; **calamiteux, -euse** [\ˈtø, ~ˈtøːz] calamitous.

calandre [kaˈlãːdr] *f* mangle; *tex.* calender, roller (*a. for paper*); *mot.* shell; *mot.* radiator grill; **calandrer** [\lãˈdre] (1a) *v/t.* mangle; *tex. etc.* calender; surface.

calcaire [kalˈkɛːr] **1.** *adj.* calcareous, chalky (*soil*); hard (*water*); **2.** *su./m* limestone; **calcification** ♂ [\sifika'sjõ] *f* calcification; **calcination** [\sinaˈsjõ] *f* calcination; *metall.* oxidation; *ores:* roasting.

calciner [kalsiˈne] (1a) *v/t.* char; burn (to cinders *or* ashes); ⊕ *etc.* roast; ⚗ calcine.

calcul [kalˈkyl] *m* reckoning, calculation; estimate; ⚕ calculus; ⚕ arithmetic; ♂ calculus, stone; ~ *biliaire* gall-stone; ~ *mental* mental arithmetic; **calculateur, -trice** [kalkylaˈtœːr, ~ˈtris] **1.** *adj.* scheming; **2.** *su. person:* calculator, reckoner; *su./f machine:* calculator; **cal-**culer** [\ˈle] (1a) *v/t.* reckon, calculate; ~ *de tête* work (*s.th.*) out in one's head; **calculette** [\ˈlɛt] *f* pocket *or* desk calculator; **calculeux, -euse** ♂ [\ˈlø, ~ˈløːz] **1.** *adj.* calculous; **2.** *su.* sufferer from stone.

cale[1] ♨ [kal] *f* hold; *quay:* slope, slip; ~ *sèche* drydock.

cale[2] [kal] *f* ⊕ wedge; ⊕, ✗ chock; ⊕ prop, strut; ⊕ tightening-key; **calé, e** F [kaˈle] clever, bright; difficult, tough, tricky.

calebasse [kalˈbɑːs] *f* ♀ calabash; gourd; *metall.* small ladle; *sl.* head.

calèche [kaˈlɛʃ] *f* barouche, calash.

caleçon [kalˈsõ] *m* (pair of) underpants *pl.*; ~ *long* long johns *pl.*; ~ *de bain* bathing-trunks *pl.*

calembour [kalãˈbuːr] *m* pun.

calembredaine F [kalãbrəˈdɛn] *f* nonsense; quibble.

calendrier [kalãˈdrje] *m* calendar; almanac; ~ *à éffeuiller* tear-off calendar.

cale-pied *cycl.* [kalˈpje] *m* toe-clip.

calepin [kalˈpɛ̃] *m* notebook.

caler[1] [kaˈle] (1a) *v/t.* ♨ strike (*the sail*); ♨ house (*a mast*); *v/i.* ♨ draw water; F climb down.

caler[2] [\] (1a) *v/t.* prop up (*a. fig.*); wedge (up), chock (up); ⊕ jam; *mot.* stall (*an engine*); ⊕, ⚡ adjust; F *se* ~ *les joues, se les* ~ have a good feed; *v/i. mot.* stall; F idle.

calfat ♨ [kalˈfa] *m* caulker; **calfater** [\faˈte] (1a) *v/t.* caulk.

calfeutrer [kalføˈtre] (1a) *v/t.* stop up the chinks of (*a window etc.*); F *se* ~ shut o.s. up.

calibrage [kaliˈbraːʒ] *m* tube: calibrating; ⊕ ga(u)ging; *phot.* trimming; **calibre** [\ˈlibr] *m* ✗ calibre (*a. fig.*); bore; size; ⊕ *tool:* ga(u)ge; template; ⊕ ~ *pour filetages* thread ga(u)ge; *compas m de* ~ callipers *pl.*; **calibrer** [\liˈbre] (1a) *v/t.* ⊕ ga(u)ge; calibrate; *phot.* trim; *typ.* cast off [cup; ♀ calyx; *anat.* calix.]

calice [kaˈlis] *m eccl.* chalice; *fig.*)

calicot [kaliˈko] *m tex.* calico; *sl.* counter-jumper, sales assistant, *Am.* sales-clerk.

califourchon [kalifurˈʃõ] *adv.:* à ~ astride.

câlin, e [kɑˈlɛ̃, ~ˈlin] **1.** *adj.* cajoling, coaxing; caressing, winning (*ways*); **2.** *su.* wheedler; **câliner** [\liˈne] (1a) *v/t.* wheedle; caress; pet.

calleux, -euse [ka'lø, ~'lø:z] horny, callous.

calligraphie [kaligra'fi] f calligraphy, penmanship.

callosité [kalozi'te] f callosity.

calmant, e [kal'mɑ̃, ~'mɑ̃:t] **1.** adj. calming; soothing (a. 🞲); **2.** su./m 🞲 sedative.

calme¹ [kalm] m calm(ness); stillness; fig. composure.

calme² [kalm] calm, still, quiet; **calmer** [kal'me] (1a) v/t. calm, still, quiet; fig. soothe; se ~ calm down.

calomniateur, -trice [kalɔmnja'tœːr, ~'tris] **1.** adj. slanderous, libellous; **2.** su. slanderer, calumniator; **calomnie** [~'ni] f calumny, slander, libel; **calomnier** [~'nje] (1o) v/t. slander, libel.

calorie phys. [kalɔ'ri] f calorie; **calorifère** [kalɔri'fɛːr] **1.** adj. heat-conveying; **2.** su./m central heating installation; **calorifique** phys. [~'fik] calorific, heating; **calorifuge** [~'fyːʒ] **1.** adj. heat-insulating; **2.** su./m heat-insulator; ⊕ non-conduction; **calorifugeage** ⊕ [~fy'ʒaːʒ] m heat-insulation; **calorifuger** ⊕ [~fy'ʒe] (11) v/t. insulate.

calot [ka'lo] m ✂ forage-cap; ⊕ small wedge; ⊕ quarry: block of stone; sl. eye; ribouler des ~s be flabbergasted; **calotin** sl. [~lɔ'tɛ̃] m ardent church-goer; sky-pilot (= priest); **calotte** [~'lɔt] f skull-cap (a. eccl.); ✂ undress cap; watch-case; F box on the ears; sl. clergy; **calotter** [~lɔ'te] (1a) v/t. F cuff (s.o.); golf: top (the ball).

calque [kalk] m tracing; F copy; **calquer** [kal'ke] (1m) v/t. trace (from, sur); needlework: transfer (a pattern); copy; papier m à ~ tracing-paper; se ~ sur q. copy s.o., model o.s. on s.o.

calumet [kaly'me] m 🞲 reed; pipe (of a Red Indian); le ~ de la paix the pipe of peace, the calumet.

calvaire [kal'vɛːr] m eccl. stations pl. of the Cross; eccl. calvary; fig. martyrdom; le ♀ (Mount) Calvary.

calvinisme eccl. [kalvi'nism] m Calvinism.

calvitie [kalvi'si] f baldness.

camail cost. [ka'maːj] m cape (a. eccl., a. orn.), cloak.

camarade [kama'rad] su. comrade, fellow, mate, F chum; ~ de classe

classmate; **camaraderie** [~ra'dri] f comradeship, friendship; clique.

camard, e [ka'maːr, ~'mard] **1.** adj. snub-nosed; **2.** su./f: la ~e Death.

cambouis [kɑ̃'bwi] m dirty oil; cart-grease.

cambré, e [kɑ̃'bre] bent; cambered, arched; bow-legged; **cambrement** [~brə'mɑ̃] m bending, cambering; **cambrer** [~'bre] (1a) v/t. bend; camber; arch; se ~ throw out one's chest; warp (wood).

cambriolage [kɑ̃briɔ'la:ʒ] m house-breaking; burglary; **cambrioler** [~'le] (1a) v/t. break into (a house), burgle; **cambrioleur** [~'lœːr] m housebreaker; burglar.

cambrure [kɑ̃'bry:r] f curve, camber; foot: arch.

cambuse [kɑ̃'by:z] f ⚓ store-room; canteen; sl. hovel; low pub(lic house); glory-hole; **cambusier** ⚓ [~by'zje] m store-keeper; steward's mate.

came¹ [kam] f cam; arbre m à ~s cam-shaft.

came² sl. [~] f drug; sl. junk; **camé, e** sl. [ka'me] adj., a. su. drug-addicted (person); su. sl. a. junkie.

caméléon zo. [kamele'ɔ̃] m chameleon.

camélia ♀ [kame'lja] m camelia.

camelot [kam'lo] m street hawker; newsvendor; ~ du roi young royalist; **camelote** [~'lɔt] f cheap goods pl.; junk, trash; de ~ gimcrack.

caméra [kame'ra] f cine-camera.

camérier eccl. [kame'rje] m chamberlain.

camériste [kame'rist] f lady's maid; chamber-maid.

camion [ka'mjɔ̃] m waggon; lorry, Am. truck; (a. ~ automobile) motor lorry; **~-citerne**, pl. **~s-citernes** [~mjɔ̃si'tɛrn] m lorry: tanker; **~grue**, pl. **~s-grues** [~mjɔ̃'gry] m breakdown lorry, Am. wrecker; **camionnage** [kamjɔ'na:ʒ] m cartage; carting, Am. trucking; **camionner** ✝ [~'ne] (1a) v/t. cart, carry; truck; **camionette** [~'nɛt] f small lorry, Am. light truck; **camionneur** [~'nœːr] m lorry-driver, Am. truck driver.

camisole [kami'sɔl] f sleeved vest; woman: dressing jacket; ~ de force strait jacket.   [mile.)

camomille ♀ [kamɔ'miːj] f camo-⌡

camouflage [kamuˈflaːʒ] *m* disguising; ⚔, ⚓ camouflage; **camoufler** [∼ˈfle] (1a) *v/t.* disguise; ⚔, ⚓ camouflage; **camouflet** F [∼ˈflɛ] *m* insult; snub.

camp [kɑ̃] *m* camp (*a. fig.*); party; *fig.* side; ∼ de *réfugiés* refugee camp; ∼ de *vacances* holiday camp; ∼ *volant* temporary shelter; F *ficher* (*or sl. fouter*) *le* ∼ clear out; **campagnard, e** [kɑ̃paˈnaːr, ∼ˈnard] 1. *adj.* country; rustic; 2. *su.* rustic; *su./m* countryman; *su./f* countrywoman; **campagne** [∼ˈpaɲ] *f* open country; countryside; ⚔, ⚓, *pol.*, ✝ *etc.* campaign; *à la* ∼ in the country; *en pleine* ∼ in the open; **campagnol** *zo.* [∼paˈnɔl] *m* vole.

campanile ⌂ [kɑ̃paˈnil] *m* belltower; **campanule** ♀ [∼ˈnyl] *f* campanula.

campé, e [kɑ̃ˈpe] (*bien* ∼) (well) established; well-constructed; wellbuilt; firmly fixed; **campement** ⚔ [kɑ̃pˈmɑ̃] *m* camping; encampment, camp; camp party; **camper** [kɑ̃ˈpe] (1a) *vt/i.* encamp; *v/t.* F place; *fig.* arrange; *se* ∼ *devant etc.* plant o.s. in front of *etc.*; *v/i.* camp; **campeur** *m*, **-euse** *f* [∼ˈpœːr, -ˈpøːz] camper; **camping** [∼ˈpiŋ] *m* camping; (*terrain de*) ∼ camping site; *faire du* ∼ go camping.

campos F [kɑ̃ˈpo] *m* holiday.

camus, e [kaˈmy, ∼ˈmyːz] snubnosed; pug-nosed.

canadien, -enne [kanaˈdjɛ̃, ∼ˈdjɛn] 1. *adj.* Canadian; 2. *su.* ♀ Canadian; *su./f* sheepskin jacket.

canaille F [kaˈnɑːj] 1. *adj.* low, base; cheap; 2. *su./f* bastard; rascal; ✝ rabble.

canal [kaˈnal] *m* canal (*a.* ♀, *a. anat.*); channel; ⚓ passage; ⊕ pipe, conduit; ⊕ culvert; ⚓ fluting; *anat.* duct; ⊕∼*-tunnel* underground canal; **canalisation** [∼nalizaˈsjɔ̃] *f* river: canalization; ⊕ pipeline; ⊕ mains *pl.*

canapé [kanaˈpe] *m* couch, sofa; *cuis.* canapé, fried slice of bread; ∼*-lit*, *pl.* ∼*s-lits* [∼peˈli] *m* bed-settee.

canard [kaˈnaːr] *m* duck; drake; F hoax; F false news; sensationalist newspaper, rag; F brandy- *or* coffeesoaked lump of sugar; ♪ wrong note; **canardeau** [kanarˈdo] *m* duckling; **canarder** [∼ˈde] (1a) *v/i.* ⚓ pitch; ♪ play *or* sing a wrong note; *v/t.* F snipe

at; **canardière** [∼ˈdjɛːr] *f* duckpond; *duck-shooting*: screen; duckgun; ⚔ loop-hole.

canari *orn.* [kanaˈri] *m* canary.

canasson *sl. pej.* [kanaˈsɔ̃] *m* horse; nag.

cancan[1] [kɑ̃ˈkɑ̃] *m dance*: cancan.

cancan[2] [kɑ̃ˈkɑ̃] *m* piece of gossip; ∼*s pl.* tittle-tattle *sg.*; **cancaner** [kɑ̃kaˈne] (1a) *v/i.* gossip; talk scandal; **cancanier, -ère** [∼ˈnje, ∼ˈnjeːr] 1. *adj.* tale-bearing; 2. *su. person*: gossip.

cancer [kɑ̃ˈsɛːr] *m* ⚕ cancer; malignant growth; *astr. le* ♋ Cancer (*a. geog.*), the Crab; **cancéreux, -euse** ⚕ [kɑ̃seˈrø, ∼ˈrøːz] 1. *adj.* cancerous; 2. *su.* cancer patient; **cancérigène** ⚕ [∼riˈʒɛn] carcinogenic, carcinogenous; **cancérologie** ⚕ [∼rɔlɔˈʒi] *f* cancer research; **cancre** [kɑ̃ːkr] *m* crab; F dunce, dud.

candeur [kɑ̃ˈdœːr] *f* artlessness.

candi [kɑ̃ˈdi] 1. *adj./m* candied; 2. *su./m*: ∼*s pl.* crystallized fruit.

candidat *m*, **e** *f* [kɑ̃diˈda, ∼ˈdat] candidate; **candidature** [∼daˈtyːr] *f* candidature; *poser sa* ∼ *à* apply for (*a position*).

candide [kɑ̃ˈdid] artless, ingenuous.

cane [kan] *f* (female) duck; **caner** *sl.* [kaˈne] (1a) *v/i.* funk it, chicken out; **caneton** [kanˈtɔ̃] *m* duckling.

canette[1] [kaˈnɛt] *f orn.* duckling; teal.

canette[2] [∼] *f* ⊕ faucet; can; bottle; *tex.* spool.

canevas [kanˈva] *m* canvas; outline.

caniche *zo.* [kaˈniʃ] *m* poodle.

caniculaire [kanikyˈlɛːr] sultry; *jours m/pl.* ∼*s* dog-days; **canicule** [∼ˈkyl] *f* dog-days *pl.*; *astr.* dogstar. [knife.)

canif [kaˈnif] *m* penknife, pocket-)

canin, e [kaˈnɛ̃, ∼ˈnin] 1. *adj.* canine; *exposition f* ∼*e* dog-show; *avoir une faim* ∼*e* be as hungry as a wolf; *dent f* ∼*e* = 2. *su./f* canine (tooth).

caniveau [kaniˈvo] ⊕ gutter; ⚡ *cables*: conduit; ⚡ main.

canne [kan] *f* ♀ cane, reed; walkingstick; ∼ *à pêche* fishing rod; ∼ *à sucre* sugar-cane; *sucre m de* ∼ cane-sugar; **canneler** [∼ˈle] (1c) *v/t.* groove; ⌂ flute; corrugate.

cannelle[1] [kaˈnɛl] *f* ♀ cinnamon; *fig.* small pieces *pl.*

cannelle² [~] f faucet.

cannelure [kan'ly:r] f groove, channel; △ fluting; corrugation; **canner** [ka'ne] (1a) v/t. cane-bottom; **cannette** [~'nɛt] f see cannelle¹; canette².

cannibale [kani'bal] m cannibal, man-eater.

canon¹ [ka'nɔ̃] m ✂, ⚓ gun, cannon; coll. artillery; key, rifle, watch, etc.: barrel; measuring-glass; sl. glass of wine; ~ à électrons electron gun.

canon² [ka'nɔ̃] m ♫, eccl. canon; **canonial, e**, m/pl. -aux [kanɔ'njal, ~'njo] canonical; of a canon; **canonique** [~'nik] canonical (book, age); F respectable, proper; **canoniser** eccl. [~ni'ze] (1a) v/t. canonize.

canonnade ✂ [kanɔ'nad] f gun-fire; cannonade; **canonner** [~'ne] (1a) v/t. cannonade; batter (a fortress); **canonnier** ✂ [~'nje] m gunner; **canonnière** [~'njɛ:r] f ⚓ gunboat; △ drain-hole; toy: pop-gun.

canot [ka'no] m boat; dinghy; ~ automobile motorboat; ~ de sauvetage lifeboat; ~ glisseur speedboat; ~ pliable folding boat; ~ pneumatique rubber dinghy; **canotage** [kanɔ'ta:ʒ] m rowing, boating, canoeing; faire du ~ row; **canoter** [~'te] (1a) v/i. row; go (in for) boating; **canotier** [~'tje] m boatman; oarsman; cost. straw-hat, boater.   [singer, vocalist.)

cantatrice [kɑ̃ta'tris] f (professional))

cantharide zo. [kɑ̃ta'rid] f Spanish fly; poudre f de ~s cantharides pl.

cantine [kɑ̃'tin] f ✂ restaurant: canteen; soup-kitchen; equipment-case; **cantinier, -ère** [~ti'nje, ~'njɛ:r] su. canteen-attendant; su./m canteen-manager; su./f canteen-manageress.

cantique eccl. [kɑ̃'tik] m canticle; hymn; sacred song; bibl. le ♀ des ♀s the Song of Songs.

canton [kɑ̃'tɔ̃] m admin. canton, district; ▤, road: section.

cantonade thea. [kɑ̃tɔ'nad] f wings pl.; thea. parler à la ~ speak to s.o. behind the scenes, speak off; crier à la ~ shout for everybody to hear.

cantonnement [kɑ̃tɔn'mɑ̃] m ✂ quarters pl.; ✂ billeting; **cantonner** [kɑ̃tɔ'ne] (1a) v/t. ✂ billet, quarter; v/i. ✂ be billeted; **cantonnier** [~'nje] m district road-surveyor; roadman; ▤ permanent-way man.

canule [ka'nyl] f ✂ nozzle; cannula; sl. bore.

caoutchouc [kau'tʃu] m india-rubber; mackintosh, raincoat; mot. etc. tyre; ~s pl. galoshes, Am. rubber overshoes; ~ durci vulcanite; ~ mousse foam rubber; gant m de ~ rubber-glove.

cap [kap] m geog. cape, headland; ⚓, ✈ head; de pied en ~ from head to foot; mettre le ~ sur head for; ⚓, ✈ suivre le ~ fixé be on one's course.

capable [ka'pabl] capable, able; **capacité** [~pasi'te] f capacity (a. ✂); ability; ✂ legal competence.

cape [kap] f cape, cloak; hood; cigar: outer leaf; ⚓ être à la ~ be hove to; rire sous ~ laugh up one's sleeve.

capeline [kap'lin] f sun-bonnet; wide-brimmed hat.

capillaire [kapil'lɛ:r] 1. adj. capillary; artiste m ~ tonsorial artist; 2. su./m ♣ maidenhair fern; **capillarité** phys. [~lari'te] f capillary attraction, capillarity.

capilotade cuis. [kapilɔ'tad] f hash; fig. en ~ bruised; F mettre q. en ~ beat s.o. to a pulp.

capitaine [kapi'tɛn] m captain (a. fig.); ⚓ a. master; ✂, gang, team: leader; sp. ~ d'equipe team captain.

capital, e, m/pl. -aux [kapi'tal, ~'to] 1. adj. capital; fundamental, essential; deadly (sin); peine f ~e capital punishment, death penalty; 2. su./m ✝ capital, assets pl.; ~ d'apport initial capital; ~ d'exploitation working capital; ✝ ~ et intérêt principal and interest; su./f geog. capital; typ. capital (letter); **capitaliser** [~tali'ze] (1a) v/t. ✝ capitalize; v/i. save; **capitalisme** [~ta'lism] m capitalism.

capitation [kapita'sjɔ̃] f poll-tax.

capiteux, -euse [kapi'tø, ~'tø:z] heady (wine); sensuous, F sexy.

capiton [kapi'tɔ̃] m silk waste; **capitonner** [~tɔ'ne] (1a) v/t. upholster; cost. quilt.

capitulaire [kapity'lɛ:r] capitular(y); **capitulation** [~la'sjɔ̃] f capitulation, surrender; **capituler** [~'le] (1a) v/i. ✂ surrender; capitulate; fig. yield; fig. compromise (with, avec) (one's conscience).

capoc ✝ [ka'pɔk] m kapok.

capon, -onne [ka'pɔ̃, ~'pɔn] 1. adj.

cowardly, afraid; **2.** *su.* coward; *school*: sneak.

caporal [kapɔ'ral] *m* ✕ corporal; F *tobacco*: shag; ✕ ~ *chef* lance-sergeant; **caporalisme** [ˌra'lism] *m* narrow militarism.

capot [ka'po] **1.** *su./m mot.* bonnet, *Am.* hood; ⚓ cowling; *cards*: capot; ⚓ companion(-hatch); **2.** *adj./inv. fig.* nonplussed; **capotage** [ˌpɔ-'ta:ʒ] *m mot.* hooding; ⚓, *mot.* overturning; ⚓ noseover; **capote** [ˌ'pɔt] *f* greatcoat; bonnet; *mot.* hood, *Am.* convertible top; *chimney*: cowl; *sl.* ~ *anglaise* French letter (= *contraceptive*); **capoter** [ˌpo'te] (1a) *v/i.* capsize, overturn; *fig.* fail, founder.

câpre ♀ [kɑ:pr] *f* caper.

capricant, e ♣ [kapri'kɑ̃, ~'kɑ̃:t] bounding; caprisant (*pulse*).

caprice [ka'pris] *m* caprice, whim; impulse; *geol.* offshoot; ♪ caprice, capriccio; **capricieux, -euse** [ˌpri'sjø, ~'sjø:z] capricious; whimsical; wayward (*child*).

capricorne [kapri'kɔrn] *m* capricorn beetle; *astr.* le ♌ Capricorn, the Goat.

capsule [kap'syl] *f* capsule; *bottle*: cap, crown-cork; ✕ percussioncap; ⚡ à ~ dished (*electrode*); **capsuler** [ˌsy'le] (1a) *v/t.* seal, cap (*a bottle*).

captage [kap'ta:ʒ] *m* water-catchment; collecting (*of waters*); ⚡ picking up; ⊕ recovery (*of by-products*); **captateur** *m*, **-trice** *f* ⚖ [ˌta'tœ:r, ~'tris] inveigler; **captation** [ˌta'sjɔ̃] *f* ⚖ inveiglement; ⚡ collecting; collection; *tel., teleph.* tapping; **capter** [ˌ'te] (1a) *v/t.* ⚡ collect; catch (*waters*); ⊕ recover (*waste*); *radio*: pick up (*a station*); *tel., teleph.* tap, intercept; captivate (*s.o.*); win by insidious means; **capteur** [ˌ'tœ:r] *m* ⚓ captor; ⊕ collector; ~ *solaire* solar energy collector; **captieux, -euse** [ˌ'sjø, ~'sjø:z] fallacious, specious.

captif, -ve [kap'tif, ~'ti:v] **1.** *adj.* captive; **2.** *su.* prisoner; **captiver** [ˌti've] (1a) *v/t.* captivate, charm; master (*one's feelings*); **captivité** [ˌtivi'te] *f* captivity.

capture [kap'ty:r] *f* capture; seizure; ⚓ *a.* prize; **capturer** [ˌty-'re] (1a) *v/t.* capture; ⚓ seize; arrest.

capuchon [kapy'ʃɔ̃] *m cost.* hood; *eccl.* cowl; *lamp, pen, etc.*: cap.

capucin [kapy'sɛ̃] *m* Capuchin friar; **capucinade** F [ˌsi'nad] *f* dull sermon *or* address; **capucine** [ˌ'sin] *f* Capuchin nun; ♀ nasturtium; △ drip-stone; *vehicle*: hood; *rifle*: band.

caque [kak] *f* keg; herring-barrel; **caquer** [ka'ke] (1m) *v/t.* cure and barrel (*herrings*).

caquet [ka'ke] *m, caquetage* [kak-'ta:ʒ] *m hens*: cackling; F gossip, chatter; *rabattre le caquet de q.* show s.o. up; make s.o. sing small; **caqueter** [ˌ'te] (1c) *v/i.* cackle (*hen*); F gossip, chatter; gabble; **caqueteur** *m*, **-euse** *f* [ˌ'tœ:r, ~-'tø:z] *person*: gossip.

car¹ [ka:r] *m* ➍, tram: car; *police*: van; motor-coach.

car² [ˌ] *cj.* for, because.

carabe *zo.* [ka'rab] *m* carabid (beetle).

carabin *sl.* [kara'bɛ̃] *m* medic.

carabine ✕ [kara'bin] *f* rifle; carbine; **carabiné, e** [ˌbi'ne] sharp, violent; ⚓ strong; **carabinier** [ˌbi'nje] *m* † carabineer; *Italy*: soldier of the police militia, constable; *Spain*: customs officer.

caracole [kara'kɔl] *f horsemanship*: caracole, half-turn; *fig.* caper; **caracoler** [ˌkɔ'le] (1a) *v/i. horsemanship*: caracole; *fig.* caper, gambol.

caractère [karak'tɛ:r] *m* character; nature; temperament; feature, characteristic; letter; *typ.* type; *mauvais* ~ bad temper; **caractériel, -elle** [ˌte'rjɛl] **1.** *adj.* (of) character; (emotionally) disturbed; **2.** *su.* problem child, (emotionally) disturbed child; **caractériser** [ˌteri'ze] (1a) *v/t.* characterize; *se* ~ *par* be distinguished by; **caractéristique** [ˌteris'tik] **1.** *adj.* characteristic (of, de), distinctive; typical (of, de); **2.** *su./f* characteristic.

carafe [ka'raf] *f* decanter; waterbottle; carafe; ⚓ *avoir la* ~ make a forced landing; *rester en* ~ be left in the lurch; **carafon** [ˌra'fɔ̃] *m* small decanter *or* carafe; *wine*: icepail.

carambolage [karɑ̃bɔ'la:ʒ] *m billiards*: cannon, *Am.* carom; *mot.* crash, pileup; **caramboler** [ˌbɔ'le] (1a) *v/i.* cannon, *Am.* carom; *v/t.* hit, crash into; *se* ~ crash (into each other), collide; **carambouilleur** [~bu'jœ:r] *m* swindler (*who buys things on credit and sells or pawns them at once*).

caramel [kara'mɛl] *m* caramel, burnt sugar; gravy-browning; **caraméliser** [~meli'ze] (1a) *v/t.* caramel(ize) (*sugar*); mix caramel with.

carapater *sl.* [karapa'te] (1a) *v/t.*: se ~ decamp, scram.

carat [ka'ra] *m* carat.

caravane [kara'van] *f* caravan; *mot.* caravan, *Am.* trailer; **caravanier** [~va'nje] *m* caravaneer; **caravansérail** [~vãse'ra:j] *m* caravanserai.

carbonate ⚗ [karbo'nat] *m* carbonate; *sl.* washing soda; **carbonater** ⚗ [~bɔna'te] (1a) *v/t.* carbonate; **carbone** [~'bɔn] *m* ⚗ carbon; *papier m* ~ carbon paper; **carbonique** ⚗ [~bɔ'nik] carbonic; **carboniser** [~bɔni'ze] (1a) *v/t.* carbonize, char; *fig.* burn to death.

carburant [karby'rã] *m* motor fuel; **carburateur** *mot.* [~byra'tœ:r] *m* carburettor; **carbure** ⚗ [~'by:r] *m* carbide; **carburé, e** [~by're] carburetted; vaporized (*fuel*).

carcan [kar'kã] *m hist.* iron collar; *fig.* yoke, restraint.

carcasse [kar'kas] *f* carcass; frame(-work); ⚙ shell, skeleton.

carcinome ✚ [karsi'nɔm] *m* carcinoma.

cardage *tex.* [kar'da:ʒ] *m wool:* carding; *cloth:* teaseling, raising.

cardamine ♀ [karda'min] *f* cardamine; ~ *des prés* mayflower.

cardan ⊕ [kar'dã] *m* universal joint; *arbre m à* ♀ Cardan shaft.

carde [kard] *f* ♀ bur, teasel; ♀ chard; *tex.* carding-brush; ⊕ ~ *métallique* wire-brush; **carder** *tex.* [kar'de] (1a) *v/t.* card, comb (*wool*); teasel (*cloth*); **cardeuse** *tex.* [~'dø:z] *f* carding-machine.

cardiaque ✚ [kar'djak] **1.** *adj.* cardiac; *crise f* ~ heart attack; *être* ~ have a heart condition; **2.** *su.* sufferer from heart trouble, F heart-case.

cardinal, e, m/pl. -aux [kardi'nal, ~'no] *adj., a. su./m* cardinal.

carême [ka'rɛm] *m* Lent; fast; *comme mars en* ~ without fail; ~-**prenant, pl. ~s-prenants** [~rɛmprə'nã] *m* Shrovetide; *person:* Shrovetide reveller.

carénage [kare'na:ʒ] *m* ⚓ careening;

careening-place; docking; ✈, *mot.* stream-lining.

carence [ka'rã:s] *f* ⚖, ✚ insolvency; defaulting; ✚, *a. fig.* deficiency (of, in *de*); incompetence, inadequacy; *maladie f par* ~ deficiency disease.

carène [ka'rɛn] *f* ⚓ hull; ✈, *mot.* stream-lined body; *pompe f de* ~ bilge-pump; **caréner** [~re'ne] (1f) *v/t.* ⚓ careen; ✈, *mot.* stream-line.

caresse [ka'rɛs] *f* caress; endearment; **caresser** [~rɛ'se] (1a) *v/t.* caress, fondle; *fig.* cherish (*hopes*).

cargaison ⚓ [kargɛ'zõ] *f* cargo; shipping (*of cargo*); **cargo** ⚓ [~'go] *m* cargo-boat, tramp; **carguer** ⚓ [~'ge] (1m) *v/t.* take in (*sail*).

caricature [karika'ty:r] *f* caricature; cartoon; *fig.* travesty.

carie [ka'ri] *f* ✚ caries; *trees:* blight; ✿ *corn:* stinking smut; **carier** [~'rje] (1o) *v/i. a. se* ~ rot, decay.

carillon [kari'jõ] *m* carillon, chime(s *pl.*); peal; ♪ tubular bells *pl.*; F row; **carillonner** [~jɔ'ne] (1a) *vt/i.* chime; sound; *fête f carillonnée* High Festival; **carillonneur** [~jɔ'nœ:r] *m* carillon player; bell-ringer; change-ringer.

carlin, e [kar'lɛ̃, ~'lin] *adj., a. su.* pug.

carlingue [kar'lɛ̃:g] *f* ⚓ keelson; ✈ fuselage; F cockpit.

carme [karm] *m* Carmelite, White Friar; ~ *déchaussé* discalced Carmelite; **carmélite** [karme'lit] *f nun:* Carmelite.

carmin [kar'mɛ̃] *su./m, a. adj./inv.* carmine.

carminatif, -ve ✚ [karmina'tif, ~'ti:v] *adj., a. su./m* carminative.

carnage [kar'na:ʒ] *m* slaughter; **carnassier, -ère** [karna'sje, ~'sjɛ:r] **1.** *adj.* carnivorous; **2.** *su./f* game bag; *su./m* carnivore; **carnation** [~'sjõ] *f* flesh tint(s *pl.*).

carnaval, pl. -als [karna'val] *m* carnival; King Carnival.

carne *sl.* [karn] *f* tough meat; old horse; bad-tempered person; wastrel; slut.

carnet [kar'nɛ] *m* notebook; (*cheque-, ticket-, etc.*) book; ~ *de bal* card; ✚ ~ *de commandes* order book.

carnier [kar'nje] *m* game-bag.

carnivore [karni'vɔ:r] **1.** *adj.* carnivorous; **2.** *su./m:* ~s *pl.* carnivora.

carotte [ka'rɔt] **1.** *su./f* ♀, ✿ carrot;

tobacco: plug; *sl.* trick, swindle; **2.** *adj./inv.* carroty, ginger; **carotter** F [ʌrɔ'te] (1a) *v/t.* steal, F pinch; cheat, F do.

caroube ♀ [ka'rub] *f* carob; **caroubier** ♀ [ʌru'bje] *m* carob-tree.

carpe¹ *anat.* [karp] *m* carpus, wrist.

carpe² *icht.* [karp] *f* carp; **carpeau** *icht.* [kar'po] *m* young carp.

carpette¹ [kar'pɛt] *f* rug.

carpette² *icht.* [ʌ] *f* young carp.

carquois [kar'kwa] *m* quiver.

carre [kaːr] *f plank*: thickness; *hat*: crown; *boot*: square toe; **carré, e** [ka're] **1.** *adj.* square; squared (*stone*), *fig.* plain, blunt; **2.** *su./m* square; ✎ patch; *staircase*: landing; *anat.* quadrate muscle; *cuis.* loin; ⚓ ~ *des officiers* ward-room; mess-room; *su./f sl.* room, digs *pl.*; **carreau** [ʌ'ro] *m* small square; *flooring*: tile, flag; floor; (window-) pane; *cards*: diamonds *sg.*; ⚒ *mine*: head; (tailor's) goose; † bolt; *à* ~*x* checked (*material*); F *se garder* (*or tenir*) *à* ~ take every precaution; **carrefour** [kar'fur] *m* crossroads *pl.*; intersection; square (*in town*).

carrelage [karla'ʒ] *m* tiling; **carreler** [ʌ'le] (1c) *v/t.* tile, pave with tiles; square (*paper*); checker; **carrelet** [ʌ'lɛ] *m* square dipping-net; ⊕ large needle; sewing-needle (*of boatmen*); **carreleur** [ʌ'lœːr] *m* tile-layer.

carrément [kare'mã] *adv.* square (-ly); *fig.* bluntly; straight (out); **carrer** [ka're] (1a) *v/t.* square; *se* ~ swagger; loll (*in a chair*).

carrier [ka'rje] *m* quarryman.

carrière¹ [ka'rjɛːr] *f* quarry.

carrière² [ʌ] *f* course; career; *donner* ~ *à* give free rein to.

carriériste [karje'rist] *su.* careerist.

carriole [ka'rjɔl] *f* light cart.

carrossable [karɔ'sabl] carriageable, passable (*for vehicles*); **carrosse** [ʌ'rɔs] *m* † coach; *fig.* rouler ~ live in style; **carrosserie** [ʌrɔs'ri] *f* mot. body, coachwork.

carrousel [karu'sɛl] *m* merry-go-round; ⚔ tattoo.

carrure [ka'ryːr] *f* breadth of shoulders.

cartable [kar'tabl] *m* satchel; writing-pad; cardboard portfolio.

carte [kart] *f* card; *restaurant*: menu; map, ⚓ chart; ticket; *fig.* ~ *blanche*

full powers *pl.*; a free hand, a blank cheque; ⚔ ~ *d'accès au bord* boarding pass; ~ *d'alimentation* ration book; ~ *de lecteur* reader's ticket; ~ *d'identité* identity card; *mot.* ~ *grise* car licence; ~ *postale* postcard; *mot.* ~ *verte* insurance document, *Br.* green card; *battre les* ~s shuffle (the cards); *faire les* ~s deal (the cards); *jouer* ~s *sur table* be above-board.

carte-lettre, *pl.* **cartes-lettres** [kartə'lɛtr] *f* letter-card.

cartellisation ⊕ [karteliza'sjõ] *f* cartelization.

carter [kar'tɛːr] *m mot.* crank-case; *bicycle*: gear-case.

cartilage [karti'laːʒ] *m anat.* cartilage, F gristle; **cartilagineux, -euse** [ʌlaʒi'nø, ʌ'nøːz] *anat.* cartilaginous, F gristly; ♀ hard.

cartographe [kartɔ'graf] *m* map-maker, chart-maker; cartographer; **cartographie** [ʌgra'fi] *f* cartography; mapping; map collection; **cartomancie** [ʌmã'si] *f* cartomancy, fortune-telling (by cards).

carton [kar'tõ] *m* cardboard; pasteboard; cardboard box; cardboard portfolio; *art*: cartoon; *phot.* mount; *typ.* cancel; *geog.* inset map; ...*en* ~ *a.* paper...; ~ *bitumé* roofing felt; ~ *ondulé* corrugated cardboard; *fig.* *homme m de* ~ man of straw; **cartonner** [ʌtɔ'ne] (1a) *v/t.* bind in boards, case; *cartonné* hardback (*book*); **cartonnerie** [ʌtɔn'ri] *f* cardboard manufactory; cardboard trade; **cartonnier** [ʌtɔ'nje] *m* (cardboard) file; **carton-pâte,** *pl.* **cartons-pâtes** [ʌtõ'paːt] *m* papier mâché.

cartothèque † [kartɔ'tɛk] *f* card index.

cartouche¹ [kar'tuʃ] *m* ⚓, *art*: cartouche.

cartouche² [kar'tuʃ] *f* ⚔ cartridge; refill (*of ball-pen*); **cartouchière** [ʌtu'ʃjɛːr] *f* ⚔ cartridge-pouch; ~ *d'infirmier* first-aid case.

carvi ♀ [kar'vi] *m* caraway.

cas [ka] *m* case (*a.* ✚ = *disease*, *patient*; *a. gramm.*); instance, circumstance; affair; ~ *limite* borderline case; *au* (*or dans le*) ~ *où* (*cond.*) in case *or* in the event of (*ger.*); *au* ~ *où* (*cond.*), *en* ~ *que* (*sbj.*) in case ... should (*inf.*); *dans tous les* ~, *en* *tout* ~ in any case; *en aucun* ~ in no circumstances; *en ce* ~ if so; *faire grand* ~ *de* think highly of (*s.th.*); *faire peu de* ~ *de* set little value on; *le* ~ *échéant* if needed; *selon le* ~ as the case may be.

casanier, -ère [kaza'nje, ~'njɛːr] *adj., a. su.* stay-at-home.

casaque [ka'zak] *f* coat, jacket; jumper (*of woman*); F *tourner* ~ turn one's coat; **casaquin** [~za'kɛ̃] *m* dressing-jacket; jumper.

cascade [kas'kad] *f* waterfall, falls *pl.*, cascade; F gay time; F piece of reckless folly; **cascader** [~ka'de] (1a) *v/i.* cascade; **cascadeur** [~ka-'dœːr] *m* stuntman; acrobat.

case [kɑːz] *f* hut, small house; compartment; pigeon-hole; *chessboard*: square; ~ *postale* Post Office box, P.O. box.

caséeux, -euse [kaze'ø, ~'øːz] cheesy, caseous.

casemate ✕ [kaz'mat] *f* casemate.

caser [kɑ'ze] (1a) *v/t.* break; † put (*papers*); marry off; find a job for; put (*s.o.*) up; *se* ~ settle down; find a home (with, *chez*).

caserne ✕ [ka'zɛrn] *f* barracks *pl.*; **caserner** ✕ [~zɛr'ne] (1a) *v/t.* quarter, billet; *v/i.* live in barracks.

casier [kɑ'zje] *m* compartment; locker; pigeon-hole; filing cabinet; rack, bin; ᵗᵗ ~ *judiciaire* police record; *avoir un* ~ *judiciaire vierge* have a clean record.

casino [kazi'no] *m* casino.

casque [kask] *m* helmet; ~*s pl. d'écoute* ear-phones; ~ *blindé* crash helmet; **casqué, e** [kas'ke] helmeted; **casquer** F [~'ke] (1m) *v/i.* foot the bill; *v/t.* fork out (*a sum*); **casquette** [~'kɛt] *f* (peaked) cap.

cassable [kɑ'sabl] breakable; **cassant, e** [~'sɑ̃, ~'sɑ̃ːt] brittle (*china etc.*); crisp (*biscuit*); curt, short (*manner, voice*); F knife-edge (*crease*); *metall.* short; *sl. ce n'est pas* ~, *ça n'a rien de* ~ it's not exactly tiring work; F it's not so hot, it's nothing to write home about; **cassation** [~sa'sjɔ̃] *f* ᵗᵗ reversing, quashing, setting aside; ✕ reduction to the ranks; ᵗᵗ *cour f de* ~ Supreme Court of Appeal.

casse¹ [kɑːs] *f* breakage, damage; *fig.* break; F row.

casse² [~] *f typ.* case; ⊕ ladle; *metall.*

crucible; *typ.* haut (*bas*) *de* ~ upper (lower) case.

casse³ [~] *f* ♀ cassia; senna.

casse...: ~**-cou** [kas'ku] *m/inv.* dangerous spot; ~**-croûte** [~'krut] *m/inv.* snack; snack-bar; ~**-noisettes** [~nwa'zɛt] *m/inv.*, ~**-noix** [~'nwa] *m/inv.* nutcrackers *pl.*; ~**-pieds** F [~'pje] **1.** *su/inv.* bore, F pain in the neck; **2.** *adj./inv.* boring; ~**-pipe(s)** F [~'pip] *m/inv.* war; front.

casser [kɑ'se] (1a) *v/t.* break, smash; crack; F punch (*s.o.'s* nose, *le nez à q.*); ✕ reduce to the ranks; ᵗᵗ set aside, quash, reverse; F ~ *sa pipe* kick the bucket (= *die*); *v/i. a. se* ~ break, give way; wear out (*person*).

casserole [kas'rɔl] *f* saucepan, stewpan.

casse-tête [kas'tɛt] *m/inv.* life-preserver (= *loaded stick*); club, truncheon; *fig.* puzzle, head-ache; *fig.* din, uproar.

cassette [ka'sɛt] *f* (jewel-)casket; case; money-box; cassette.

casseur, -euse [kɑ'sœːr, ~'søːz] **1.** *adj.* destructive, aggressive (*look etc.*); **2.** *su.* breaker; *cars:* scrap dealer; F ~ *d'assiettes* truculent person.

cassis¹ [ka'sis] *m* ♀ black currant; *sl.* head.

cassis² ⊕ [ka'si] *m* cross-drain.

cassonade [kasɔ'nad] *f* brown sugar.

cassure [kɑ'syːr] *f* break; fragment.

caste [kast] *f* caste; *esprit m de* ~ class consciousness.

castel † [kas'tɛl] *m* (small) castle.

castillan, e [kasti'jɑ̃, ~'jan] *adj., a. su.* ♀ Castilian.

castor *zo.*, ✝ [kas'tɔːr] *m* beaver.

casuel, -elle [ka'zɥɛl] **1.** *adj.* accidental, fortuitous, casual; *gramm.* case-...; ᵗᵗ contingent; **2.** *su./m* perquisites *pl.*

casuistique [kazɥis'tik] *f* casuistry (*a. fig.*).

cataclysme [kata'klism] *m* cataclysm, disaster; **catalepsie** ✱ [~lɛp'si] *f* catalepsy; **catalogue** [~-'lɔg] *m* catalogue, list; *faire le* ~ *de* run over the list of; **cataloguer** [~lɔ'ge] (1m) *v/t.* catalogue, list; **catalyser** [~li'ze] (1a) *v/t.* catalyse; **catalyseur** ⚗ [~li'zœːr] *m* catalyst; **cataphote** *mot.* [~'fɔt] *m* road: cat's eye, *Am.* reflector; **cataplasme** ✱ [~'plasm] *m* poultice; **catapulter**

[~pyl'te] catapult; **cataracte** [~'rakt] *m* cataract (*a. 🗲*).

catarrhe 🗲 [ka'taːr] *m* catarrh; F ~ *nasal* cold in the head; **catarrheux, -euse** [~taˈrø, ~ˈrøːz] catarrhous.

catastrophe [katasˈtrɔf] *f* catastrophe; disaster; **catastrophique** [~trɔˈfik] catastrophic.

catch *sp.* [katʃ] *m* catch-as-catch-can.

catéchiser [kateʃiˈze] (1a) *v/t.* *eccl.* catechize; *fig.* coach; lecture; reason with (*s.o.*).

catégorie [kategɔˈri] *f* category, class; **catégoriser** [~riˈze] (1a) *v/t.* classify.

caténaire 𝄢 [kateˈnɛːr] 1. *adj.* catenary; 2. *su./f* trolley-wire.

cathédrale [kateˈdral] *f* cathedral.

cathode 𝄢 [kaˈtɔd] *f* cathode; **cathodique** 𝄢 [~tɔˈdik] cathodic; *tube m à rayons* ~s cathode-ray tube.

catholique [katɔˈlik] 1. *adj.* (Roman) Catholic; F *pas (très or bien)* ~ (a bit) fishy *or* shady, not (quite) straight; 2. *su.* (Roman) Catholic.

catimini F [katimiˈni] *adv.*: *en* ~ stealthily; on the sly.

catin F [kaˈtɛ̃] *f* prostitute.

catir *tex.* [kaˈtiːr] (2a) *v/t.* press, gloss.

cauchemar [koʃˈmaːr] *m* nightmare; *fig.* pet aversion.

causal, e [koˈzal] causal, causative.

cause [koːz] *f* cause, motive; reason; 🏛 case, trial; *à* ~ *de* on account of; *fig.* *en* ~ at stake; involved; *mettre en* ~ question (*s.th.*); *pour* ~ for a good reason; 🏛 *sans* ~ briefless (*barrister*).

causer[1] [koˈze] (1a) *v/t.* cause.

causer[2] [koˈze] (1a) *v/i.* talk (*a. fig.* = *blab*), chat; **causerie** [kozˈri] *f* talk, chat; **causette** F [koˈzet] *f* little chat; **causeur, -euse** [~ˈzœːr, ~ˈzøːz] 1. *adj.* talkative, chatty; 2. *su.* talker; *su./f* settee for two.

causticité [kostisiˈte] *f* 🜍 causticity; *fig.* caustic humo(u)r; biting quality (*of a remark etc.*); **caustique** [~ˈtik] 1. *adj.* 🜍, *a. fig.* caustic; 2. *su./m* 🜍 caustic; *su./f* *opt.* caustic.

cautèle [koˈtɛl] *f* cunning, craftiness; **cauteleux, -euse** [kotˈlø, ~ˈløːz] cunning, crafty; wary.

cautère 🗲 [koˈtɛːr] *m* cautery; **cautériser** 🗲 [~teriˈze] (1a) *v/t.* cauterize.

caution [koˈsjɔ̃] *f* security, guarantee; 🏛 bail; ✝ deposit; *être* (*or se porter*) ~ go bail; ✝ stand surety; *fournir* ~ produce bail; *sujet à* ~ unreliable, unconfirmed; **cautionnement** [~sjɔnˈmɑ̃] *m* surety; **cautionner** [~sjɔˈne] (1a) *v/t.* stand surety for (*s.o.*); 🏛 go bail for; *fig.* support, back.

cavalcade [kavalˈkad] *f* cavalcade; procession; **cavale** *poet.* [~ˈval] *f* mare; **cavaler** *sl.* [~vaˈle] (1a) *v/i.* run; *v/t.* pester (*s.o.*); *se* ~ do a bunk (= *run away*); **cavalerie** [~valˈri] *f* cavalry; **cavalier, -ère** [~vaˈlje, ~ˈljɛːr] 1. *su.* rider; *su./m* horseman; *dancing:* partner; *chess:* knight; ✕ trooper; *su./f* horsewoman; 2. *adj.* haughty; off-hand; jaunty; 𝄢 *perspective f* ~ère isometric projection.

cave [kaːv] 1. *su./f* cellar (*a. fig.*); vault; ⊕ *coke-oven:* wharf; *cards:* stake(s *pl.*); 2. *adj.* hollow; *anat. veine f* ~ vena cava; **caveau** [kaˈvo] *m* cellar, vault; burial vault; **caver** [~ˈve] (1a) *v/t.* hollow (out), undermine; put up (*money at cards*); *v/i.* put up a sum of money; **caverne** [~ˈvɛrn] *f* cave, cavern; (thieves') den; 🗲 cavity; **caverneux, -euse** [~vɛrˈnø, ~ˈnøːz] cavernous; *fig.* hollow, sepulchral (*voice*); **caviste** [~ˈvist] *m* cellarman; **cavité** [~viˈte] *f* cavity, hollow.

ce[1] [s(ə)] *dem./pron./n* it; this; that; these, those; *ce qui* (*or que*) what, which; *c'est pourquoi* therefore; *c'est que* the truth is that; *c'est moi* it is I, F it's me.

ce[2] (*before vowel or h mute* **cet**) *m*, **cette** *f*, **ces** *pl.* [sə, set, se] *dem./adj.* this, that, *pl.* these, those; *ce ...-ci* this; *ce ...-là* that.

céans [seˈɑ̃] *adv.* F here(in); *maître m de* ~ master of the house.

ceci [sɔˈsi] *dem./pron./n* this; ~ *étant* this being the case *or* so.

cécité [sesiˈte] *f* blindness.

cédant, e ✝, 🏛 [seˈdɑ̃, ~ˈdɑ̃ːt] 1. *su.* assignor, grantor, transferor; 2. *adj.* assigning, granting, transferring; **céder** [~ˈde] (1f) *vt/i.* give up, yield; surrender; *v/t.* 🜍 give off; transfer; sell (*a lease*); ~ *le pas à* give way to; ~ *le passage* give way; *le* ~ *à q.* be inferior *or* second to s.o. (*in, en*).

cédille *gramm.* [seˈdiːj] *f* cedilla.

cèdre [sɛːdr] *m tree or wood:* cedar.
cédule [se'dyl] *f* script, note; *admin. taxes:* schedule; summons *sg.*
cégétiste [seʒe'tist] *m* trade-unionist (= *member of the C.G.T.*).
ceindre [sɛ̃ːdr] (4m) *v/t.* (de, with) gird; bind; surround; wreathe.
ceinture [sɛ̃'tyːr] *f* belt (*a. fig. of fortifications, hills, etc.*); girdle; waist; waistband; enclosure, circle; ~ (de sécurité) seat *or* safety belt; ~ de sauvetage lifebelt; ~ verte green belt; 🚇 ligne *f* de ~ circle line; **ceinturer** [sɛ̃ty're] (1a) *v/t.* seize (*s.o.*) round the waist; *fig.* surround; *foot.* collar (*s.o.*) low; **ceinturier** [~'rje] *m* belt-maker; **ceinturon** [~'rɔ̃] *m* waist-belt, sword-belt.
cela [s(ə)la] **1.** *dem./pron./n* that; à ~ près with that exception; ~ fait thereupon; c'est ~ that's right, that's it; comment ~? how?; et ... avec tout ~? and what about ...?; **2.** *su./m psych.* id.
céladon [sela'dɔ̃] *su./m, a. adj./inv.* celadon, parrot-green.
célébration [selebra'sjɔ̃] *f* celebration; **célèbre** [~'lɛbr] famous, celebrated; **célébrer** [sele'bre] (1f) *v/t.* celebrate; extol; **célébrité** [~bri'te] *f* celebrity.
celer [sə'le] (1d) *v/t.* conceal.
céleri 🌿 [sel'ri] *m* celery; pied *m* de ~ head of celery.
célérité [seleri'te] *f* speed, rapidity, swiftness.
céleste [se'lɛst] heavenly, celestial; bleu ~ sky-blue; ♪ voix *f* ~ organ: vox angelica.
célibat [seli'ba] *m* celibacy; **célibataire** [~ba'tɛːr] **1.** *adj.* single; celibate; **2.** *su./m* bachelor; *su./f* unmarried woman; single girl; spinster.
celle [sɛl] *f see* celui. [cupboard.\
cellier [sɛ'lje] *m* store-room, store-\
cellulaire [sɛly'lɛːr] cellular; régime *m* ~ solitary confinement; voiture *f* ~ police-van, F Black Maria; **cellule** [~'lyl] *f* cell; F den; ⚡ ~ au sélénium selenium cell; ✈ ~ d'avion air-frame; *telev.* ~ photo-électrique electric eye; **celluleux, -euse** [sɛly'lø, ~'løːz] cell(at)ed; **celluloïd(e)** [~lɔ'id] *m* celluloid; **cellulose** 🌿, † [~'loːz] *f* cellulose.
celte [sɛlt] **1.** *adj.* Celtic; **2.** *su.* ♀ Celt; **celtique** [sɛl'tik] **1.** *adj.* Celtic; **2.** *su./m ling.* Celtic.

celui *m,* **celle** *f,* **ceux** *m/pl.,* **celles** *f/pl.* [sə'lɥi, sɛl, sø, sɛl] *dem./pron.* he (*acc.* him); she (*acc.* her); the one, that; *pl.* they (*acc.* them); those; ~-ci *etc.* [səlɥi'si *etc.*] the latter; this one; ~-là *etc.* [səlɥi'la *etc.*] the former; that one.
cément *metall.* [se'mã] *m* cement (*a.* ⚙), powdered carbon; **cémenter** [~mã'te] (1a) *v/t. metall.* case-harden (*steel*); cement (*an armour-plate*).
cendre [sãːdr] *f* cinders *pl.,* ash; mercredi *m* des ♀s Ash Wednesday; **cendré, e** [sã'dre] **1.** *adj.* ash-grey, ashy; **2.** *su./f sp.* cinders *pl.*; ⚛ lead ashes *pl.*; **cendreux, -euse** [~'drø, ~'drøːz] ash-grey, ashy; gritty; *metall.* brittle (*steel*); **cendrier** [~dri'e] *m* ash-pan; 🚂 ash-box; ash-tray.
Cendrillon [sãdri'jɔ̃] *f* Cinderella (*a. fig.*); *fig.* stay-at-home; F drudge.
Cène [sɛn] *f the* Last Supper; *protestant service: the* Lord's Supper; *the* Holy Communion.
censé, e [sã'se]: être ~ faire qch. be supposed to do s.th.; nul n'est ~ ignorer la loi ignorance of the law is no excuse; **censément** [~se'mã] *adv.* supposedly; ostensibly; to all intents and purposes; **censeur** [~'sœːr] *m* censor; *lycée:* vice-principal; *univ.* proctor; **censurable** † [~sy'rabl] open to censure; **censure** [~'syːr] *f* censure; *cin., journ., etc.* censorship; **censurer** [~sy're] (1a) *v/t.* censure; censor.
cent [sã] **1.** *adj./num.* (a *or* one) hundred; **2.** *su./m* (*inv. when followed by another number*) hundred; cinq pour ~ five per cent; je vous le donne en ~ I give you a hundred guesses; trois ~ dix three hundred and ten; trois ~s three hundred years; **centaine** [sã'tɛn] *f* (about) a hundred.
centaure *myth.* [sã'tɔːr] *m* centaur.
centenaire [sãt'nɛːr] **1.** *adj.* a hundred years old; *fig.* ancient, venerable; **2.** *su./m* centenary; *su. person:* centenarian; **centésimal, e,** *m/pl.* **-aux** [sãtezi'mal, ~'mo] centesimal; thermomètre *m* ~ centigrade thermometer.
centi... [sãti] centi...; **centiare** [sã'tjaːr] *m measure:* one square metre (*approx.* 1¹/₅ *square yards*); **cen-**

tième [~'tjɛm] **1.** *adj./num., a. su., a. su./m fraction*: hundredth; **2.** *a./f thea.* hundredth performance; **centigrade** [~ti'grad] centigrade; **centime** [~'tim] *m* ¹/₁₀₀ of a franc; **centimètre** [~ti'mɛtr] *m measure*: (approx.) ²/₅ inch; tape-measure.

central, e *m/pl.* **-aux** [sɑ̃tral, ~'tro] **1.** *adj.* central; **2.** *su./m* telephone-exchange; call-station; *su./f* ⚡ (~ électrique) powerhouse; power station (Am. plant); ⚡ ~e hydro-électrique hydro-electric generating station; ~e nucléaire (or atomique) nuclear power station (Am. plant); **centraliser** [~trali'ze] (1a) *v/t. a.* se ~ centralize; **centre** [sɑ̃tr] *m* centre, Am. center; middle; *foot.* ~s *pl.* insides; *meteor.* ~ de dépression storm centre; *phys.* ~ de gravitation (or d'attraction) centre of attraction; **centrer** [sɑ̃'tre] (1a) *v/t.* centre, Am. center; adjust; **centrifuge** [sɑ̃tri'fy:ʒ] centrifugal; essoreuse *f* ~ rotary dryer; **centripète** [~'pɛt] centripetal; **centriste** *pol.* [sɑ̃'trist] *adj., a. su.* centrist.

centuple [sɑ̃'typl] *su./m, a. adj.* hundredfold; **centupler** [~ty'ple] (1a) *vt/i.* increase a hundredfold.

cep ⚹ [sɛp] *m* vine-stock; vine-plant.

cèpe ⚘ [~] *m* flap mushroom.

cependant [səpɑ̃'dɑ̃] **1.** *adv.* meanwhile; **2.** *cj.* however, nevertheless, yet.

céramique [sera'mik] **1.** *adj.* ceramic; **2.** *su./f* ceramics *pl.*, pottery; **céramiste** [~'mist] *su.* potter.

cérat ⚕ [se'ra] *m* cerate, ointment.

Cerbère [sɛr'bɛːr] *m myth., a. fig.* Cerberus.

cerceau [sɛr'so] *m* hoop; ⚕ cradle (over bed); **cercle** [sɛrkl] *m* circle (a. fig.), ring (a. ⊕); barrel: hoop; dial; *fig.* company, group; *fig.* sphere, range; *geog.* ~ polaire polar circle; en ~s in the wood (wine); ♀ quart *m* de ~ quadrant; **cercler** [sɛr'kle] (1a) *v/t.* encircle, ring; hoop; put a tyre on (a wheel).

cercueil [sɛr'kœːj] *m* coffin; ~ en plomb (leaden) shell.

céréale ⚘ [sere'al] *su./f, a. adj.* cereal.

cérébral, e, *m/pl.* **-aux** [sere'bral, ~'bro] cerebral, brain...; fatigue *f* ~e brain-fag.

cérémonial, *pl.* **-als** [seremo'njal] *m* ceremonial; **cérémonie** [~'ni] *f* ceremony (a. fig.), pomp; formality; sans ~ informal(ly *adv.*); **cérémonieux, -euse** [~'njø, ~'njøːz] ceremonious, formal.

cerf [sɛːr] *zo.* stag, hart; *cuis.* venison.

cerfeuil ⚘ [sɛr'fœːj] *m* chervil.

cerf-volant, *pl.* **cerfs-volants** [sɛrvɔ'lɑ̃] *m zo.* stag-beetle; (paper) kite.

cerise [sə'riːz] **1.** *su./f* ⚘ cherry; *sl.* bad luck; **2.** *adj./inv.* cherry-red; **cerisette** [səri'zɛt] *f* dried cherry; ⚘ winter-cherry; **cerisier** [~'zje] *m* cherry-tree; cherry-wood.

cerne [sɛrn] *m tree*: (age-)ring; ring, circle (round eyes, wound, etc.); **cerneau** [sɛr'no] *m* green walnut; **cerner** [~'ne] (1a) *v/t.* encircle, surround; hem in; ring (a tree etc.); *fig.* delimit, define (a problem etc.); shell (nuts); avoir les yeux cernés have rings under one's eyes.

certain, e [sɛr'tɛ̃, ~'tɛn] **1.** *adj.* certain, sure; positive, definite; (before noun) one; some; **2.** *pron.* some, certain; **certes** [sɛrt] *adv.* indeed; **certificat** [sɛrtifi'ka] *m* certificate (a. ⚕); testimonial; ~ de bonne vie et mœurs certificate of good character; ~ d'origine dog etc.: pedigree; **certification** [~fika'sjɔ̃] *f* certification; signature: witnessing; **certifier** [~'fje] (1o) *v/t.* certify, attest, assure; witness (a signature); **certitude** [~'tyd] *f* certainty.

cérumen [sery'mɛn] *m* ear-wax.

céruse 🜍 [se'ryːz] *f* white lead; **cérusite** 🜍 [~ry'zit] *f* cerusite.

cerveau [sɛr'vo] *m* brain; *fig.* mind; *fig.* mastermind; ~ brûlé hothead; rhume *m* de ~ cold in the head.

cervelas *cuis.* [sɛrvə'la] *m* saveloy.

cervelet *anat.* [sɛrvə'lɛ] *m* cerebellum; **cervelle** *anat., cuis.* [~'vɛl] *f* brains *pl.*; brûler la ~ à q. blow s.o.'s brains out; se creuser la ~ rack one's brains; *fig.* une ~ de lièvre a memory like a sieve.

ces [se] *pl.* of ce³.

césarienne ⚕ [seza'rjɛn] *adj./f*: (opération *f* ~) Caesarean (operation).

cessation [sɛsa'sjɔ̃] *f* cessation, stoppage, suspension; breach (of relations); **cesse** [sɛs] *f*: n'avoir pas de ~ que not to rest until; sans ~ continually; continuously, constantly; **cesser** [sɛ'se] (1a) *vt/i.* cease; leave off; *v/i.: faire* ~ put a stop to; **cessez-le-feu** [~selə'fø] *m/inv.* ceasefire; **cessible** ⚖ [~'sibl] transferable; assignable; **cession** [~'sjɔ̃] *f* ⚖ transfer, assignment; ✝ *shares*: delivery; **cessionnaire** ✝ [~sjɔ'nɛːr] *m* transferee, assignee; *bill*: holder.

c'est-à-dire [sɛta'diːr] *cj.* that is to say, i.e.; in other words; F ~ *que* well, actually.

césure [se'zyːr] *f* caesura.

cet *m*, **cette** *f* [sɛt] *see* ce².

cétacé, e *zo.* [seta'se] 1. *adj.* cetaceous; cetacean; 2. *su./m* cetacean.

ceux [sø] *m/pl. see* celui.

chabler [ʃa'ble] (1a) *v/t.* ⊕ hoist (*a load*); ⚓ tow (*a boat*); ✒ beat (*a walnut-tree*). [*Burgundy*).\
chablis [ʃa'bli] *m* Chablis (= *white*)\
chabot *icht.* [ʃa'bo] *m* bullhead, miller's thumb; chub.

chacal, *pl.* **-als** *zo.* [ʃa'kal] *m* jackal.

chacun, e [ʃa'kœ̃, ~'kyn] *pron./indef.* each (one); everybody.

chafouin, e [ʃa'fwɛ̃, ~'fwin] sly, toxy; sly-looking.

chagrin¹, e [ʃa'grɛ̃, ~'grin] 1. *su./m* grief, sorrow; trouble; annoyance; 2. *adj.* sorry; sad; troubled (at, *de*); distressed (at, *de*); peevish.

chagrin² [ʃa'grɛ̃] *m* (*a.* peau *f de* ~) *leather*: shagreen.

chagriner¹ [ʃagri'ne] (1a) *v/t.* grieve, distress; annoy; *se* ~ fret.

chagriner² [~] (1a) *v/t.* grain (*leather*).

chahut F [ʃa'y] *m* uproar, row; rag; **chahuter** F [~y'te] (1a) *v/i.* kick up a row; *sl.* boo; *v/t.* rag (*s.o.*); give (*s.o.*) the bird; boo (*s.o.*).

chai [ʃɛ] *m* wine and spirit store.

chaîne [ʃɛn] *f* chain; link(s *pl.*); fetter; necklace; *fig.* sequence, train (*of ideas*); *tex.* warp; ⚓ chain-boom; *geog.* mountains: range; *mot.* ~*s pl.* antidérapantes anti-skid chains; ⊕ *travail m à la* ~ assembly line work, work on the conveyor belt; **chaîner** [ʃɛ'ne] (1b) *v/t.* △, *surv.* chain; △ tie; **chaînette** [~'nɛt] *f* small chain; ⚡ catenary; *point m de* ~ chain-stitch; **chaînon** [~'nɔ̃] *m* chain: link; *geog. mountains*: secondary range.

chair [ʃɛːr] *f* flesh; meat; *fruit*: pulp; *fig.* ~ *de poule* goose-flesh.

chaire [~] *f* *eccl.*, *a. univ.* chair; *eccl.* throne; *eccl.* pulpit; rostrum; tribune.

chaise [ʃɛːz] *f* chair, seat; *hist.* (*a.* ~ *à porteurs*) sedan-chair; ~ *de poste* post-chaise; ~ *longue* couch, chaise longue.

chaland¹ [ʃa'lɑ̃] *m* lighter, barge.

chaland² *m*, **e** *f* ✝ [ʃa'lɑ̃, ~'lɑ̃ːd] customer (*a. fig.*), purchaser.

chalcographie [kalkɔgra'fi] *f* engraving on metal; engraving studio.

châle [ʃɑːl] *m* shawl.

chalet [ʃa'lɛ] *m* chalet; country cottage; ~ *de nécessité* public convenience.

chaleur [ʃa'lœːr] *f* heat (*a. of animals*), warmth; ardo(u)r, zeal; ⊕ ~ *blanche* white heat; **chaleureux, -euse** [~lœ'rø, ~ø~'røːz] warm; *fig.* ardent; cordial, hearty (*welcome etc.*); glowing (*colour, terms*).

châlit [ʃa'li] *m* bedstead.

challenge *sp.* [ʃa'lɑ̃ːʒ] *m* challenge.

chaloupe ⚓ [ʃa'lup] *f* launch, long-boat.

chalumeau [ʃaly'mo] *m* drinking-straw; ♪, ⊕ pipe; ⊕ blow-lamp.

chalut [ʃa'ly] *m* trawl; drag-net; **chalutier** ⚓ [~ly'tje] *m* person, *boat*: trawler.

chamailler F [ʃama'je] (1a) *v/t.* squabble with; *se* ~ squabble (with, *avec*); be at loggerheads, bicker (with, *avec*); **chamaillerie** [~maj-'ri] *f* squabble, brawl, scuffle; **chamailleur, -euse** [~ma'jœːr, -'jøz] 1. *adj.* quarrelsome; 2. *su.* squabbler.

chamarrer [ʃama're] (1a) *v/t.* bedeck; *fig.* embroider; **chamarrure** [~'ryːr] *f* (*tawdry*) decoration.

chambard F [ʃɑ̃'bar] *m*, **chambardement** F [~bardə'mɑ̃] *m* upheaval, upset; **chambarder** F [~bar'de] (1a) *v/t.* rifle (*a room*); smash up, upset (*a. fig.*).

chambellan [ʃɑ̃bɛl'lɑ̃] *m* chamberlain.

chambranle △ [ʃɑ̃'brɑ̃ːl] *m* frame; ~ *de cheminée* mantelpiece.

chambre [ʃɑ̃:br] *f* (bed)room; chamber (*a. pol.*, ✝, ⊕); ⚖ division; ⚓ cabin; *mot.* ~ *à air* inner tube; ~ *à un lit* (*deux lits*) single (double) room; ~ *d'amis* guest *or* spare room; ✝ ~ *de commerce* chamber of commerce; *pol.* 2 *des députés* House of Commons, *Am.* House of Representatives, *France:* Chamber of Deputies; ⚓ ~ *des machines* engineroom; *phot.* ~ *noire* dark room; ~ *sur la cour* (*rue*) back (front) room; *garder la* ~ be confined to one's room; ♪ *musique f de* ~ chamber music; ⊕ *ouvrier m en* ~ homeworker; garret-craftsman; *fig.* stratégiste *m en* ~ armchair strategist; **chambrée** [ʃɑ̃ˈbre] *f* roomful; ✕ barrack-room; *thea.* house; *thea.* takings *pl.*; **chambrer** [~ˈbre] (1a) *v/t.* lock up in a room; bring (*wine*) to room temperature; **chambrière** [~ˈbrjɛːr] *f* † chambermaid; long whip; *truck etc.*: drag.

chameau [ʃaˈmo] *m zo.* camel; 🚂 shunting engine; *sl.* dirty dog *m*, bitch *f*; **chamelier** [~məˈlje] *m* camel-driver; **chamelle** *zo.* [~ˈmɛl] *f* she-camel.

chamois *zo.* [ʃaˈmwa] *m* chamois; chamois *or* shammy leather; *gants m/pl. de* ~ wash-leather gloves; **chamoiser** [~mwaˈze] (1a) *v/t.* chamois, dress (*leather*).

champ [ʃɑ̃] *m* field (*a. fig.*); open country; ground; space; *fig.* range; ⊕ side; edge; ~ *d'activité* scope *or* field of activity; *sp.* ~ *de courses* racecourse, race-track; ~ *de repos* churchyard; ~ *visuel* field of vision; *à tout bout de* ~ the whole time, at every end and turn; *à travers* ~*s* across country; ⊕ *de* ~ on edge, edgewise.

champagne [ʃɑ̃ˈpaɲ] *su./m* champagne; *su./f: fine* ~ liqueur brandy. **champenois, e** [ʃɑ̃pəˈnwa, ~ˈnwaːz] of Champagne.

champêtre [ʃɑ̃ˈpɛːtr] rural, rustic. **champignon** [ʃɑ̃piˈɲɔ̃] *m* 🍄 mushroom; 🚂 *rail:* head; F *mot.* accelerator pedal; F *mot. appuyer sur le* ~ step on¬ the gas; **champignonnière** [~ɲɔˈnjɛːr] *f* mushroom-bed. **champion** *m*, **-onne** *f* [ʃɑ̃ˈpjɔ̃, ~ˈpjɔn] *sp.*, *fig.* champion; *fig.* supporter; ~ *du monde* world champion; **championnat** [~pjɔˈna] *m* championship.

chançard, e [ʃɑ̃ˈsaːr, ~ˈsard] **1.** *adj.* lucky; **2.** *su.* lucky person; **chance** [ʃɑ̃ːs] *f* luck, fortune; chance; ~*s pl. égales* equal opportunities *or* chances; *bonne* ~! good luck; *par* ~ by good fortune; *les* ~*s sont contre lui* the odds are against him.

chanceler [ʃɑ̃sˈle] (1c) *v/i.* reel, stagger, totter; falter.

chancelier [ʃɑ̃səˈlje] *m* chancellor; *pol. embassy:* secretary; **chancelière** [~səˈljɛːr] *f* chancellor's wife; foot-muff; **chancellerie** [~sɛlˈri] *f* chancellery.   [risky; lucky.\

chanceux, -euse [ʃɑ̃ˈsø, ~ˈsøːz]∫ **chancir** [ʃɑ̃ˈsiːr] (2a) *v/i. a. se* ~ go mo(u)ldy; **chancissure** [~siˈsyːr] *f* mo(u)ld, mildew.

chancre [ʃɑ̃ːkr] *m* 🐛 ulcer; 🐛 F, *a.* 🌱 canker; **chancreux, -euse** [ʃɑ̃ˈkrø, ~ˈkrøːz] 🐛 ulcerous; cankerous (*growth*); cankered (*organ*).

chandail [ʃɑ̃ˈdaːj] *m* sweater.

Chandeleur *eccl.* [ʃɑ̃dˈlœːr] *f: la* ~ Candlemas; **chandelier** [ʃɑ̃dəˈlje] *m* candlestick; *person:* chandler; ⊕ *boiler:* pedestal; **chandelle** [~ˈdɛl] *f* candle; *cricket, tennis:* skyer, lob; ✈ stay, prop; *à la* ~ by candlelight; *fig. en voir trente-six* ~*s* see stars; *fig. le jeu n'en vaut pas la* ~ the game is not worth the candle; **chandellerie** [~dɛlˈri] *f* candleworks *usu. sg.*

chanfrein¹ [ʃɑ̃ˈfrɛ̃] *m* blaze (*on a horse's forehead*); *horse etc.:* forehead.

chanfrein² [ʃɑ̃ˈfrɛ̃] *m* bevelled edge; **chanfreiner** ⊕ [~frɛˈne] (1a) *v/t.* bevel, chamfer.

change [ʃɑ̃ːʒ] *m* † exchange; *hunt.* wrong scent; F false scent; *fig. donner le* ~ *à q.* put s.o. off, sidetrack s.o.; **changeable** [ʃɑ̃ˈʒabl] changeable; exchangeable; **changeant, e** [~ˈʒɑ̃, ~ˈʒɑ̃ːt] changing; changeable, variable; unsettled (*weather*); **changement** [ʃɑ̃ʒˈmɑ̃] *m* change, alteration; *mot.* ~ *de vitesse* gear-change, *Am.* gearshift; 🚂 ~ *de voie* points *pl.*; **changer** [ʃɑ̃ˈʒe] (1l) *v/t.* change; exchange (for, *contre*); alter; *se* ~ change (one's clothes); *se* ~ *en* change *or* turn into; *v/i.* change, alter (s.th., *de qch.*); ~ *de train* change (trains); **changeur** [~ˈʒœːr] *m* money-changer.

chanoine *eccl.* [ʃaˈnwan] *m* canon; **chanoinesse** *eccl.* [~nwaˈnɛs] *f* canoness.

chanson [ʃɑ̃ˈsɔ̃] *f* song; † ~*s pl.* nonsense; **chansonner** [ʃɑ̃sɔˈne] (1a) *v/t.* write satirical songs about (*s.o.*); **chansonnette** [~ˈnɛt] *f* comic song; **chansonnier, -ère** [~ˈnje, ~ˈnjɛːr] *su.* singer; *su./m* songbook.

chant¹ [ʃã] *m* ♪ singing; song; *eccl.* chant; canto; melody; *au ~ du coq* at cock-crow; *~ de Noël* Christmas carol.

chant² ⊕ [~] *m* edge, side; *de ~, sur ~* on edge, edgewise.

chantage [ʃã'ta:ʒ] *m* blackmail.

chantepleure [ʃãtə'plœ:r] *f* wine funnel; colander; watering-can with a long spout; *cask:* tap; △ *gutter:* spout; **chanter** [ʃã'te] (1a) *v/t.* sing; celebrate; *~ victoire* sur crow over; *iro. que me chantez-vous là?* that's a fine story!; *v/i.* sing; creak (*door*); sizzle (*butter*); crow (*cock*); *faire ~ q.* blackmail *s.o.*; F *si ça vous chante* if it suits you.

chanterelle¹ [ʃã'trɛl] *f* ♪ violin: E-string; decoy-bird; bird-call.

chanterelle² ♀ [~] *f* mushroom: cantharellus.

chanteur *m*, **-euse** *f* [ʃã'tœ:r, ~'tø:z] singer; *maître m ~ hist.* mastersinger; F blackmailer.

chantier [ʃã'tje] *m* building site; (timber- *etc.*) yard; workyard, site; F mess; *traffic sign:* roadworks; *sur le ~* in hand.

chantonner [ʃãtɔ'ne] (1a) *vt/i.* hum.

chantourner ⊕ [ʃãtur'ne] (1a) *v/t.* jig-saw; ⊕ *scie f à ~* bow saw, jig-saw.

chantre [ʃã:tr] *m eccl.* cantor; *poet.* singer, poet.

chanvre [ʃã:vr] *m* hemp; cannabis; **chanvrier, -ère** [ʃãvri'e, ~'ɛ:r] **1.** *su.* hemp-grower; **2.** *adj.* hemp-...

chaos [ka'o] *m* chaos, confusion; **chaotique** [~o'tik] chaotic.

chaparder F [ʃapar'de] (1a) *v/t.* scrounge, filch, lift.

chape [ʃap] *f eccl.* cope; covering, layer; *cuis.* dish cover; ⊕ D-joint; *mot. tyre:* tread; *mot.* patch (*on tyre*); △ *bridge:* coping; ⊕ *roller:* flange; *pulley-block:* strap; *pulley:* shell; **chapeau** [ʃa'po] *m* hat; △ *chimney:* cowl; ⊕, *a. pen:* cap; *~!* well done!, hats off!; ♪ *~ chinois* Chinese bells *pl.*; *~ haut de forme* top hat; *~ melon* bowler; F *travailler du ~* talk through one's hat.

chapelain [ʃa'plɛ̃] *m* chaplain.

chapelet [ʃa'plɛ] *m* rosary; ✝ beads, onions: string; *fig.* string, series; ✕ bombs: stick; **chapelier, -ère** [~pə'lje, ~'ljɛ:r] **1.** *adj.* hat-...; **2.** *su.* hatter, *Am.* milliner; *su./f* Saratoga trunk.

chapelle [ʃa'pɛl] *f* chapel; *~ ardente* chapel of rest.

chapellerie [ʃapɛl'ri] *f* hat-trade; hat-shop; **chapelure** *cuis.* [~'ply:r] *f* bread crumbs *pl.*

chaperon [ʃa'prɔ] *m* hood; △ *wall:* coping; *roof:* cap-stone; chaperon; *le petit ♀ rouge* Little Red Riding Hood; **chaperonner** [~prɔ'ne] (1a) *v/t.* hood (*a falcon*); chaperon (*s.o.*); △ put a coping on (*a wall*).

chapiteau [ʃapi'to] *m* ✝ capital; *windmill etc.:* cap; *circus:* big top.

chapitre [ʃa'pitr] *m* chapter (*a. eccl.*); heading, subject; **chapitrer** F [~pi-'tre] (1a) *v/t.* read (*s.o.*) a lecture, reprimand.

chapon [ʃa'põ] *m* capon; **chaponner** [~pɔ'ne] (1a) *v/t.* caponize.

chaque [ʃak] *adj.* each, every.

char [ʃar] *m* waggon; *~ à bancs* char-a-banc(s *pl.*); ✕ *~ blindé* armo(u)red car; ✕ *~ d'assaut* tank; ✕ *~ de combat* light-armo(u)red car; ♀ *~ de l'État* Ship of State; *~ de triomphe* triumphal car; *~ funèbre* hearse.

charabia [ʃara'bja] *m* gibberish.

charade [ʃa'rad] *f* charade.

charançon *zo.* [ʃarã'sõ] *m* weevil.

charbon [ʃar'bõ] *m* coal; (*a. ~ de bois*) charcoal; ✝ carbon; ✔ blight; anthrax; ✿ carbuncle; *fig.* être sur des *~s ardents* be on tenterhooks; **charbonnage** ✕ [~bɔ'na:ʒ] *m* coal mining; colliery; bunkering; **charbonner** [~bɔ'ne] (1a) *v/t.* char, carbonize; *cuis.* burn; sketch *or* blacken with charcoal; *v/i.* ⚓ coal (*ship*).

charbonnerie [~bɔn'ri] *f* coal depot; **charbonnier, -ère** [~bɔ'nje, ~'njɛ:r] **1.** *adj.* coal-...; charcoal-...; **2.** *su./m* coal-man; coal-merchant; coal-hole; ⚓ collier; *~ est maître chez lui* a(n English)man's home is his castle; *su./f* coal-scuttle; charcoal kiln; *orn.* great tit; ⚓ coal lighter.

charcuter [ʃarky'te] (1a) *v/t.* cut (*meat*) into small pieces; F mangle; ✿ F carve, operate clumsily upon (*a patient*); **charcuterie** [~'tri] *f* pork-butcher's shop *or* trade *or* meat; delicatessen; **charcutier** *m*, **-ère** *f* [~'tje, ~'tjɛ:r] pork-butcher; F sawbones *sg.* (= *surgeon*).

chardon [ʃar'dõ] *m* thistle; **chardonneret** *orn.* [~dɔn'rɛ] *m* goldfinch.

charge [ʃarʒ] *f* load, burden; ⚓

loading; ⊕, ⚒, ✎, ✕ *arms*: charge;
cost; post, office; responsibility;
exaggeration, caricature, *thea.* over-
acting; ⚖ ~ *payante* pay load; ⊕ ~
utile useful load; à ~ de |*revanche*
on condition of reciprocity; *être
à la* ~ de be dependent on *or*
depending upon; *femme f de* ~
housekeeper; *pas m de* ~ *marching*:
double time; **chargé, e** [ʃarˈʒe] **1.**
adj. loaded, laden (with, de); full (of,
de); heavy (with, de); full, busy (*day,
schedule*); ✿ coated, furry (*tongue*);
troubled, guilty (*conscience*); over-
loaded, overladen (*a. fig.*); overelab-
orate (*style etc.*); ~ de a. in charge of;
2. *su./m: pol.* ~ *d'affaires* chargé
d'affaires, ambassador's deputy;
univ. ~ *de cours* reader, senior lecturer; **chargement** [~ʒəˈmɑ̃] *m*
load; ⚓ lading; ⚓ cargo; ✂ charging;
charger [~ˈʒe] (1l) *v/t.* (de, with)
load, burden (*a. fig*); charge (*a.* ✕,
⚒, ✎); entrust; *post*: register; *thea.*
overact; ✝ inflate (*an account*); ~ q.
de coups drub s.o., belabo(u)r s.o.; *se*
~ become overcast (*sky*); become
coated (*tongue*); *se* ~ de take care
or charge of, see to; *se* ~ de (*inf.*)
undertake to (*inf.*), take it upon
o.s. to (*inf.*); **chargeur** [~ˈʒœːr]
m loader, ⚓ shipper; stoker; ✂
charger.

chariot [ʃaˈrjo] *m* waggon; cart, trolley; ⚓ cradle; ⚓ *crane*: crab; *typewriter*: carriage; *camera*: baseboard;
astr. le grand ♀ Charles's Wain.

charitable [ʃariˈtabl] charitable (to,
towards *envers*); **charité** [~ˈte] *f*
charity, love; alms(-giving) *sg.*

charivari [ʃarivaˈri] *m* din, noise,
hullabaloo.

charlatan *m*, **e** *f* [ʃarlaˈtɑ̃, ~ˈtan]
charlatan, quack; **charlatanisme**
[~taˈnism] charlatanism.

charlotte *cuis.* [ʃarˈlɔt] *f* apple charlotte; trifle.

charmant, e [ʃarˈmɑ̃, ~ˈmɑ̃ːt]
charming, delightful.

charme[1] ♀ [ʃarm] *m* hornbeam.

charme[2] [ʃarm] *m* charm (*a. fig.*);
spell; **charmer** [ʃarˈme] (1a) *v/t.*
charm (*a. fig.*); delight; **charmeur,
-euse** [~ˈmœːr, ~ˈmøːz] **1.** *adj.*
charming; **2.** *su.* charmer.

charmille [ʃarˈmiːj] *f* hedge; ar-
bo(u)r.

charnel, -elle [ʃarˈnɛl] carnal;

sensual; **charnier** [~ˈnje] *m* charnel-
house (*a. fig.*).

charnière [ʃarˈnjɛːr] *f* hinge; ⊕ ~
universelle univeral joint.

charnu, e [ʃarˈny] fleshy.

charogne [ʃaˈrɔɲ] *f* carrion; *sl.
woman*: slut; *man*: scoundrel.

charpente [ʃarˈpɑ̃ːt] *f* framework
(*a. fig.*); timber-work, steel-work;
house, ship, etc.: skeleton; **charpenter** [ʃarpɑ̃ˈte] (1a) *v/t.* frame
(*a. fig.*); **charpenterie** [~ˈtri] *f*
carpentry; carpenter's (shop);
timber-yard; **charpentier** [~ˈtje]
m carpenter; ~ *de navires* ship-
|wright.|

charpie ✿ [ʃarˈpi] *f* lint. [wright.|

charretée [ʃarˈte] *f* cartload; F *fig.*
une ~ de loads of, piles of; **charretier** [~ˈtje] *m* carter; **charette**
[ʃaˈrɛt] *f* cart; ~ à *bras* handcart,
pushcart, barrow; **charriage**
[~ˈrjaːʒ] *m* carriage; *sl.* swindling;
exaggeration; chaffing; **charrier**
[~ˈrje] (1o) *v/t.* cart, carry; *sl.*
swindle; make fun of; *v/i.* exaggerate; *sans* ~ joking apart; **charroi**
[~ˈrwa] *m* carriage, cartage; ✕ †
~*s pl.* transport *sg.*; **charron** [~ˈrɔ̃]
m wheelwright; cartwright; **char-
royeur** [~rwaˈjœːr] *m* carter, carrier.

charrue [ʃaˈry] *f* plough, *Am.* plow;
fig. mettre la ~ *devant les bœufs* put
the cart before the horse.

charte [ʃart] *f* charter; deed; *hist. la
Grande* ♀ Magna C(h)arta; *École f des*
~*s* School of Pal(a)eography; ~-
partie, *pl.* ~*s*-**parties** [ʃartəparˈti] *f*
charterparty.

chartreux, -euse [ʃarˈtrø, ~ˈtrøːz] **1.**
adj. Carthusian; **2.** *su.* Carthusian;
su./f Carthusian monastery; *liqueur*:
Chartreuse.

chas [ʃa] *m needle*: eye.

chasse [ʃas] *f* hunt(ing) (*a.* ~ *au tir*)
shooting; game, bag; shooting-
season; hunting-ground; ⊕ *wheels*:
play; ⊕ flush; ~ à *courre* (stag-)
hunting; ~ *d'eau* W.C.: flush, lavatory chain.

châsse [ʃɑːs] *f eccl.* reliquary, shrine;
spectacles: frame; *sl.* ~*s pl.* eyes.

chasse...: ~-**marée** [ʃasmaˈre] *m/inv.*
fish-cart; coasting lugger; ~-**mouches** [~ˈmuʃ] *m/inv.* fly-swatter;
horse: fly-net; ~-**neige** [~ˈnɛːʒ]
m/inv. snow-plough, *Am.* snow-
plow; *sp. ski*: stem; *virage m en* ~

stem-turn; **~-pierres** 🚂 [~'pjɛːr] *m/inv.* cow-catcher.

chasser [ʃa'se] (1a) *v/t.* hunt, pursue; drive away *or* out; expel; drive (*a nail*); *v/i.* (*usu.* ~ *à courre*) hunt, go hunting (s.th., *à qch.*); drive; *mot.* skid; ⚓ drag; **chasseresse** *poet.* [ʃas'rɛs] *f* huntress; **chasseur** [ʃa'sœːr] *m* hunter; *hotel*: page-boy, *Am.* bell-hop; ✗ rifleman; ⚓ chaser; ✗ fighter; ✗ ~ *à réaction* jet fighter; **chasseuse** [~'søːz] *f* huntress.   [bleary-eyed.\

chassieux, -euse [ʃa'sjø, ~'sjøːz]\ **châssis** [ʃa'si] *m* frame (*a. mot.*, 🚂); *mot.* chassis; window-sash; *paint.* stretcher; *trunk*: tray; ✗ slide; ✗ under-carriage; ✗ forcing frame; *typ.* chase; *thea. scenery*: flat; *phot.* plate-holder; ✗ ~ *d'atterrissage* landing gear; **~-presse** *phot.* [~si-'prɛs] *m* printing-frame.

chaste [ʃast] chaste, pure; **chasteté** [~ə'te] *f* chastity, purity.

chasuble *eccl.* [ʃa'zybl] *f* chasuble.

chat *zo.* [ʃa] *m* (tom-)cat; *le* ♀ *botté* Puss in Boots.

châtaigne [ʃa'tɛɲ] *f* ♀ chestnut (*a. horse*); **châtaigneraie** [ʃatɛ-ɲə'rɛ] *f* chestnut grove; **châtaignier** [~'ɲje] *m* chestnut(-tree, -wood); **châtain, e** [ʃa'tɛ̃, ~'tɛn] *adj.*, *a. su./m* chestnut, brown.

château [ʃa'to] *m* castle; manor, hall; palace; *fig.* ~ *de cartes* house of cards; ~ *d'eau* water-tower, 🚂 tank; ~*x pl. en Espagne* castles in the air.

chateaubriand, châteaubriant *cuis.* [ʃatobri'ɑ̃] *m* grilled steak, *Am.* porter-house steak.

châtelain [ʃat'lɛ̃] *m* castellan; lord (*of the manor*); **châtelaine** [~'lɛn] *f* chatelaine (*a. cost.*); lady (*of the manor*).

chat-huant, *pl.* **chats-huants** *orn.* [ʃa'ɥɑ̃] *m* tawny *or* brown owl.

châtier [ʃa'tje] (1o) *v/t.* punish, chastise; *fig.* refine (*one's style*); ~ *l'insolence de q.* punish s.o. for his impudence.

chatière [ʃa'tjɛːr] *f* cat-hole (*in a door*); cat-trap; ventilation hole; *fig.* secret entrance.

châtiment [ʃati'mɑ̃] *m* punishment.

chatoiement [ʃatwa'mɑ̃] *m* sheen, sparkle; glistening.

chaton¹ [ʃa'tõ] *m jewel*: setting; jewel (*in setting*).

chaton² [~] *m zo.* kitten; ♀ catkin.

chatouillement [ʃatuj'mɑ̃] *m* tickle, tickling; **chatouiller** [ʃatu'je] (1a) *v/t.* tickle (*a. fig.*); F thrash; **chatouilleux, -euse** [~'jø, ~'jøːz] ticklish; sensitive, touchy, sore (*point*); delicate (*question*).

chatoyer [ʃatwa'je] (1h) *v/i.* shimmer; glisten; *soie f chatoyée* shot silk.

châtrer [ʃa'tre] (1a) *v/t.* castrate, geld; ✗ prune.

chatte [ʃat] *f* (she-)cat; tabby; **chattemite** F [~'mit] *f* toady, sycophant; **chatterie** [ʃa'tri] *f* wheedling; ~*s pl.* dainties, goodies.

chatterton ✗ [ʃater'tõ] *m* insulating *or* adhesive tape.

chaud, e [ʃo, ʃoːd] **1.** *adj.* warm; hot; *fig.* ardent, keen; bitter (*tears*); *avoir* ~ be *or* feel warm; be *or* feel hot; *il fait* ~ it is warm *or* hot; *la donner* ~*e à* fill (*s.o.*) with dismay; *servir* ~ serve up (*a dish*) hot; *tenir* ~ keep warm; **2.** *chaud adv.* warm etc.; **3.** *su./m* heat, warmth; **chaudeau** *cuis.* [ʃo'do] *m* caudle, eggnog; **chaud-froid**, *pl.* **chauds-froids** *cuis.* [ʃo'frwa] *m* chaud-froid; ~ *de ...* cold jellied ...; **chaudière** ⊕ [ʃo'djɛːr] *f* boiler; ~ *auxiliaire* ⊕ donkey boiler; ~ *à vide* vacuum pan; **chaudron** [~'drõ] *m* ca(u)ldron; F old and tinny piano; **chaudronnier** [~drõ'nje] *m* brazier; coppersmith; ironmonger.

chauffage [ʃo'faːʒ] *m* heating; warming; ~ *à distance* long-distance heating; ~ *au pétrole* oil heating; ~ *central* central heating; *bois m de* ~ firewood; **chauffard** F [~'faːr] *m* road hog; **chauffe** ⊕ [ʃo:f] *f* heating; stoking, firing; *metall.* firechamber; ⊕ *activer la* ~ fire up. **chauffe...: ~-bain** [ʃof'bɛ̃] *m* geyser; **~-eau** [ʃo'fo] *m/inv.* water-heater; **~-pieds** [ʃof'pje] *m/inv.* foot-warmer; **~-plats** [~'pla] *m/inv.* dish-warmer, chafing-dish.

chauffer [ʃo'fe] (1a) *v/t.* warm, heat; ⊕ stoke up (*a furnace*); *fig.* boost; *fig.* cram (*s.o. for an examination*); *sl.* pinch, steal; *v/i.* get warm *or* hot; ⊕ overheat (*bearings etc.*); ⊕ get up steam (*engine*); ~ *au pétrole* burn oil; *sl. se faire* ~ get pinched (= *arrested*); **chaufferette** [~'frɛt] *f* foot-warmer; dish-warmer; *mot.* heater; **chaufferie** [~'fri] *f metall.* reheating furnace;

forge; ⚓ stokehold; **chauffeur, -euse** [ʌˈfœːr, ʌˈføːz] su. mot. driver; su./m mot. chauffeur; ⚓ stoker; sl. crammer, coach (for examination); su./f mot. chauffeuse; fireside chair; **chauffoir** [ʌˈfwaːr] m warm-room.

chaufour [ʃoˈfuːr] m lime-kiln.

chauler ⚡ [ʃoˈle] (1a) v/t. lime (the soil); lime-wash.

chaume [ʃoːm] m haulm; roof: thatch; stubble; **chaumière** [ʌˈmjɛːr] f thatched cottage; **chaumine** poet. [ʌˈmin] f cot.

chausse [ʃoːs] f wine strainer; † ʌs pl. breeches; **chaussée** [ʃoˈse] f roadway; road; causeway; geog. reef; **chausse-pied** [ʃosˈpje] m shoehorn; **chausser** [ʃoˈse] (1a) v/t. put on (shoes etc.); put shoes on (s.o.); fit (shoe); ʌ bien (large) be well-(large-) fitting; ʌ du 40 take size 40 (in shoes); se ʌ put on (one's) shoes; **chausse-trape** [ʃosˈtrap] f hunt. trap (a. fig.); fig. trick; ♀ starthistle; **chaussette** [ʃoˈsɛt] f sock; **chausson** [ʌˈsɔ̃] m slipper; ballet shoe; boxing shoe; fencing shoe; gym shoe; **chaussure** [ʌˈsyːr] f shoe, boot.

chauve [ʃoːv] 1. adj. bald; 2. su. bald person; **ʌ-souris**, pl. ʌs-souris zo. [ʃovsuˈri] f bat.

chauvin, e [ʃoˈvɛ̃, ʌˈvin] 1. adj. jingoistic, chauvinist(ic); 2. su. chauvinist warmonger; **chauvinisme** [ʌviˈnism] m jingoism, chauvinism, F flag-waving.

chaux [ʃo] f lime; ʌ éteinte slaked lime; ʌ vive quicklime; blanchir à la ʌ whitewash, limewash.

chavirer ⚓ [ʃaviˈre] (1a) vt/i. capsize; upset.

chef [ʃɛf] m head, principal; chief, chieftain; master; leader; cuis. (a. ʌ de cuisine) chef (= male head cook); ♪ conductor; fig. heading; 🚂 count; fig. authority; ⊕ ʌ d'atelier shop foreman; ʌ de bande ringleader; ✕ ʌ de bataillon major; ʌ de bureau (comptabilité) chief or head clerk (accountant); sp. ʌ d'équipe team leader, captain; ʌ d'État chief of State; 🚂 ʌ de gare station master; ✝ ʌ de rayon, ʌ de service departmental manager or head, floor manager; 🚂 ʌ de train guard, Am. conductor; au premier ʌ in the highest degree; in the first place; de mon ʌ for myself; on my own authority; ... en ʌ ... in chief; ʌ-

d'œuvre, pl. ʌs-d'œuvre [ʃɛˈdœːvr] m masterpiece; **ʌ-lieu**, pl. ʌs-lieux [ʃɛfˈljø] m chief town; county town, Am. county seat.

cheftaine [ʃɛfˈtɛn] f scout-mistress.

chemin [ʃəˈmɛ̃] m way; road; path; eccl. ʌ de croix Way of the Cross; ʌ de fer railway, Am. railroad; ʌ de table (table)runner; ʌ faisant on the way; faire son ʌ make one's way; fig. get on well; **chemineau** [ʃəmiˈno] m tramp, Am. hobo; **cheminée** [ʌˈne] f chimney; ⚓ funnel; smoke-stack; ⊕ stack; fireplace; mantelpiece; **cheminer** [ʌˈne] (1a) v/i. tramp, plod on; **cheminot** 🚂 [ʌˈno] m railwayman; platelayer.

chemise [ʃəˈmiːz] f shirt (of men); chemise (of women); book: wrapper; folder (for papers); ⊕ boiler etc.: jacket; ⊕ ʌ d'eau water jacket; **chemiserie** [ʌmizˈri] f shirt-making; shirt shop; shirt factory; haberdashery; **chemisette** cost. [ʃəmiˈzɛt] f jumper; chemisette (of women); **chemisier, -ère** [ʌˈzje, ʌˈzjɛːr] su. shirt-maker; shirt-seller; haberdasher; su./m shirt-blouse; jumper.

chênaie [ʃɛˈnɛ] f oak-grove.

chenal [ʃəˈnal] m channel, fairway; ⊕ mill-race.

chenapan [ʃənaˈpɑ̃] m scoundrel.

chêne ♀ [ʃɛːn] m oak.

chéneau [ʃeˈno] m △ eaves: gutter; mot. drip-mo(u)lding.

chêne-liège, pl. **chênes-lièges** [ʃɛnˈljɛːʒ] m cork-tree, cork-oak.

chènevière [ʃɛnˈvjɛːr] f hemp-field; **chènevis** [ʌˈvi] m hemp-seed.

chenil [ʃəˈni] m dog-kennel (a. fig.).

chenille [ʃəˈniːj] f caterpillar; caterpillar tractor: track; tex. chenille.

chenu, e [ʃəˈny] hoary (hair); snowy (mountain).

cheptel [ʃɛpˈtɛl] m (live-)stock; ʌ mort implements pl. and buildings pl.

chèque ✝ [ʃɛk] m cheque, Am. check; ʌ barré crossed cheque; ʌ de voyage traveller's cheque; ʌ sans provision cheque without cover; formulaire m de ʌ blank cheque; **chéquier** [ʃeˈkje] m cheque book, Am. checkbook.

cher, chère [ʃɛːr] 1. adj. dear, beloved; expensive; la vie f chère high prices *pl.*; *moins* ~ cheaper; *peu* ~ cheap; **2.** *su./m*: *mon* ~ my dear friend; *su./f*: *ma chère* my dear; **3.** *cher adv.* dear(ly); *acheter* ~ buy at a high price; *coûter* ~ be expensive; *payer* ~ pay a high price for (*s.th.*); *fig.* smart *or* pay for; *vendre* ~ sell dear.

chercher [ʃɛr'ʃe] (1a) *v/t.* look for, seek; search; try; *aller* ~ fetch, get; *envoyer* ~ send for; *venir* ~ call for, fetch; F *ça va* ~ *dans les ...* that'll add up to about ...; **chercheur, -euse** [~'ʃœːr, ~'ʃøːz] **1.** *adj.* enquiring; **2.** *su.* seeker; investigator; researcher; *su./m* finder; detector; *radio*: cat's-whisker.

chère [ʃɛːr] *f*: (*la*) *bonne* ~ good food.

chéri, e [ʃe'ri] **1.** *adj.* dear, cherished; **2.** *su.* darling, dear(est); **chérir** [~'riːr] (2a) *v/t.* cherish, love dearly; **chérot** *sl.* [ʃe'ro] (too) expensive, *Brit.* F pricey; **cherté** [ʃɛr'te] *f* dearness; high price; high prices *pl.*; *la* ~ *de la vie* the high cost of living.

chérubin [ʃery'bɛ̃] *m* cherub.

chétif, -ve [ʃe'tif, ~'tiːv] puny, weak; paltry (*reason*); wretched, pitiful, miserable.

cheval [ʃə'val] *m* horse; *mot.* horse-power; *sp.* ~ *de bois* vaulting horse; ~ *de course* race-horse; ✗ ~ *de frise* cheval de frise; ~ *entier* stallion; *chevaux pl. de bois* merry-go-round *sg.*; *aller à* ~ ride, go on horseback; *être à* ~ *sur* straddle (*s.th.*); F be well up in; F be a stickler for (*etiquette*); **chevalement** [~val'mã] *m* ⚒ pit-head frame; ⚔ *walls*: shoring; **chevaler** [~va'le] (1a) *v/t.* ⚔ shore up; ⊕ put (*s.th.*) on a trestle; **chevaleresque** [ʃəval'rɛsk] chivalrous; knightly; **chevalerie** [~'ri] *f* chivalry; knighthood; chivalrousness; **chevalet** [ʃəva'lɛ] *m* trestle; ♪ *violin etc.*: bridge; ⊕, *a. billiards*: rest; *paint.* easel; ⊕ saw-horse; **chevalier** [~'lje] *m* knight; *fig.* ~ *d'industrie* sharper, swindler; *faire q.* ~ knight *s.o.*; **chevalière** [~'ljɛːr] *f* signet-ring; **chevalin, e** [~'lɛ̃, ~'lin] equine; **cheval-vapeur,** *pl.* **chevaux-vapeur** ⊕ [ʃəvalva'pœːr, ~vova'pœːr] *m* horse-power; **chevaucher** [~vo'ʃe] (1a) *v/i.* ride on horseback; sit astride; overlap; *v/t.*

ride on; sit astride; *bridge*: span (*a river*).

chevelu, e [ʃə'vly] long-haired; *cuir* *m* ~ scalp; **chevelure** [~'vlyːr] *f* (head of) hair; *comet*: tail.

chevet [ʃə'vɛ] *m* bed-head; bolster; ⚧ *church*: chevet, apse; *fig.* bed-side (*of a sick person*); *lampe f de* ~ bedside lamp; *livre m de* ~ bedside book, *fig.* favo(u)rite reading.

chevêtre [ʃə'vɛːtr] *m* ⚙ (jaw-)band-age; ⚧ trimmer beam.

cheveu [ʃə'vø] *m* (single) hair; ~*x pl.* hair *sg.*; ~*x pl. à la Jeanne d'Arc* bob-bed hair (with fringe); ~*x pl.* en brosse crewcut; *sl.* avoir mal aux ~*x* have a hang-over; *fig.* couper les ~*x* en quatre split hairs; *de l'épaisseur d'un* ~ by a hair's breadth; F *se prendre aux* ~*x* have a real set-to; *tiré par les* ~*x* farfetched; *voilà le* ~! that's the snag!

cheville [ʃə'viːj] *f* peg (*a. violin*), pin (*a.* ⊕); ⊕ bolt; *fig.* padding; *anat.* ankle; ~ *ouvrière* king-pin, *fig.* main-spring; **cheviller** [~vi'je] (1a) *v/t.* pin, peg, bolt; plug; *fig.* pad.

cheviotte *tex.* [ʃə'vjɔt] *f wool, cloth*: cheviot.

chèvre [ʃɛːvr] *f zo.* (she-)goat; ⊕, ⚧ derrick; ⊕ trestle; **chevreau** *zo.* [ʃə'vro] *m* kid; *de* (*or* en) ~ kid-...; **chèvrefeuille** ⚘ [ʃɛvrə'fœːj] *m* honeysuckle; **chevrette** [ʃə'vrɛt] *f* *zo.* kid; roe-doe; ⊕ trivet; F shrimp, prawn; **chevreuil** [~'vrœːj] *m* roebuck; roe-deer; *cuis.* venison; **chevrier** [~'vrje] *m* goatherd; **chevrière** [~'vrjɛːr] *f* goat-girl; **chevron** [~'vrõ] *m* ⚧ rafter; ✗ chevron, stripe; **chevronné, e** [~'ne] expe-rienced, practised, seasoned; vet-eran ...; **chevrotement** [ʃəvrɔt'mã] *m* quavering; **chevroter** [ʃəvrɔ'te] (1a) *v/i.* quaver, quiver, tremble (*voice*); bleat (*goat*); **chevrotine** [~'tin] *f* buckshot.

chez [ʃe] *prp. direction*: to; *place*: at (*s.o.'s house or shop*); with (*my aunt*); in (*a. fig.*); *post*: care of, *abbr. c/o*; *fig.* among (*the English*); ~ *nous* in our country; ~ *Zola* in (the works of) *Zola*; *être* (*aller*) ~ *soi* be at (go) home; *être* (*aller*) ~ *le docteur* be at (go to) the doctor's; *faire comme* ~ *soi* make o.s. at home; *de* ~ *q.* from s.o.'s (house); *de* ~ *soi* from home; ~**-moi** (*etc.*) [~'mwa] *m/inv.*: *mon* ~ my home.

chialer *sl.* [ʃjaˈle] (1a) *v/i.* snivel.

chiasse [ʃjas] *f fly etc.*: dirt; *sl.* drag; *sl. avoir la* ~ have the runs; be in a blue funk.

chic [ʃik] **1.** *su./m* chic, smartness, style; *fig.* knack; **2.** *adj.* smart, stylish; F first-rate, F posh, classy; F decent *(fellow)*; *des robes f/pl. chics* smart robes.

chicane [ʃiˈkan] *f* quibbling; chicanery; ⊕ baffle(-plate); ⚔ zigzag trench; **chicaner** [ʃikaˈne] (1a) *v/i.* quibble, cavil; *v/t.* wrangle with (*s.o.*); haggle over (*s.th.*); **chicaneur, -euse** [~ˈnœːr, ~ˈnøːz] **1.** *adj.* argumentative; quibbling; **2.** *su.* quibbler, haggler; litigious person; **chicanier, -ère** [~ˈnje, ~ˈnjɛːr] **1.** *adj.* litigious; quibbling; haggling; **2.** *su.* litigious person; ⚖ barrator.

chiche [ʃiʃ] **1.** *adj.* scanty; niggardly, mean *(person)*; **2.** *su./m* ⚘ *(a. pois m* ~*)* chick-pea.

chichis [ʃiˈʃi] *m/pl.* frills *(a. fig.)*; *fig.* affected manners; *faire des* ~ put on airs; make a fuss; create difficulties.

chicorée ⚘ [ʃikɔˈre] *f* chicory; endive *(a. salad etc.).*

chicot [ʃiˈko] *m tooth, tree:* stump.

chicotin [ʃikɔˈtɛ̃] *m* aloes *pl.*; *amer comme* ~ as bitter as gall.

chien [ʃjɛ̃] *m* dog; *gun:* hammer, cock; ~ *d'aveugle* guide dog; ~ *de chasse* hound; *entre* ~ *et loup* in the twilight; ~ *méchant!* beware of the dog!; **chiendent** ⚘ [~ˈdã] *m* couchgrass; **chienloup,** *pl.* **chiensloups** *zo.* [~ˈlu] *m* Alsatian, wolfhound; **chienne** [ʃjɛn] *f* (female) dog; bitch.

chier V [ʃje] (1o) *v/i.* shit.

chiffe [ʃif] *f* rag; *fig.* weakling; **chiffon** [ʃiˈfɔ̃] *m* rag; frippery; scrap; *tex.* chiffon; F *parler* ~s talk dress; **chiffonner** [ʃifɔˈne] (1a) *v/t.* ruffle, crumple; *fig.* sully; *fig.* irritate, provoke; *v/i.* pick rags; rake through *or* comb dustbins; do some dressmaking; **chiffonnier, -ère** [~ˈnje, ~ˈnjɛːr] *su.* rag-picker; dustbin-raker; *su./m* bureau, chest of drawers.

chiffre [ʃifr] *m* figure, number, numeral; cipher, code; amount, total; mark; monogram; ~ *d'affaires* turnover; ~ *repère* reference number; **chiffrer** [ʃiˈfre] (1a) *v/i.* calculate; *v/t.* number; work out, express in figures; *f* figure; write in cipher *or* code, encipher, encode; **chiffreur** [~ˈfrœːr] *m* reckoner; cipherer.

chignole [ʃiˈnɔl] *f* ⊕ hand-drill; F jalopy.

chignon [ʃiˈnɔ̃] *m* bun, chignon; coil of hair.

chilien, -enne [ʃiˈljɛ̃, ~ˈljɛn] *adj., a. su.* ♀ Chilean.

chimère [ʃiˈmɛːr] *f* chimera; **chimérique** [~meˈrik] visionary.

chimie [ʃiˈmi] *f* chemistry; **chimique** [~ˈmik] chemical; **chimiste** [~ˈmist] *su.* chemist *(not pharmacist).*

chimpanzé *zo.* [ʃɛ̃pɑ̃ˈze] *m* chimpanzee.

chiner¹ *tex.* [ʃiˈne] (1a) *v/t.* shadow *(a fabric).*

chiner² F [~] (1a) *v/t.* make fun of, kid, rag.

chinois, e [ʃiˈnwa, ~ˈnwaːz] **1.** *adj.* Chinese; **2.** *su./m ling.* Chinese; ♀ Chinaman; *les* ♀ *m/pl.* the Chinese; *su./f* ♀e Chinese woman; **chinoiserie** [~nwazˈri] *f* Chinese curio; F trick; ~s *pl. administratives* red tape *sg.*

chiper *sl.* [ʃiˈpe] (1a) *v/t.* pinch; swipe; *tennis:* poach *(a ball).*

chipie F [ʃiˈpi] *f* sour woman; shrew.

chipoter F [ʃipɔˈte] (1a) *v/i.* nibble at one's food; haggle, quibble; waste time.

chique [ʃik] *f zo.* chigger, jigger; *tobacco:* quid.

chiqué *sl.* [ʃiˈke] *m* fake, pretence.

chiquenaude [ʃikˈnoːd] *f* flick (of the finger).

chiquer [ʃiˈke] (1m) *v/t.* chew *(tobacco)*; *v/i.* chew (tobacco).

chiragre ⚕ [kiˈragr] *f* gout in the hand; **chiromancie** [kirɔmɑ̃ˈsi] *f* palmistry; **chiromancien** *m*, **-enne** *f* [~ˈsjɛ̃, ~ˈsjɛn] palmist.

chirurgical, e, *m/pl.* **-aux** [ʃiryrʒiˈkal, ~ˈko] surgical; **chirurgie** [~ˈʒi] *f* surgery; **chirurgien** [~ˈʒjɛ̃] *m* surgeon.

chlorate ⚗ [klɔˈrat] *m* chlorate; **chlore** [klɔːr] *m* ⚗ chlorine; *sl.* calcium chloride; **chlorhydrique** [klɔriˈdrik] ⚗ *adj.: acide* *m* ~ hydrochloric acid, F spirits *pl.* of salt; **chloroforme** ⚗, ⚕ [~rɔˈfɔrm] *m* chloroform; **chlorose** [~ˈroːz] *f* ⚕, ⚘ chlorosis; ⚘ *a.* etiolation; **chlorotique** ⚕ [~rɔˈtik] chlorotic;

chlorure ⚗ [ˌ'ry:r] *m* chloride; ~ *d'ammonium* sal-ammoniac; ~ *de chaux* bleaching powder.

choc [ʃɔk] *m* shock; collision, crash; impact; *de* ~ shock-...

chocolat [ʃɔkɔ'la] 1. *su./m* chocolate; ~ *à craquer* plain chocolate; 2. *adj./inv.* chocolate; **chocolatier**, **-ère** [ˌla'tje, ˌ'tjɛːr] 1. *adj.* chocolate; 2. *su.* chocolate-maker, chocolate-seller; *su./f* chocolate-pot.

chœur [kœːr] *m* ⚖, *eccl.* choir, ⚖ *a.* chancel; ♪, *thea., etc.* chorus.

choir [ʃwaːr] (3d) *v/i.* fall.

choisi, e [ʃwa'zi] choice, select(ed); chosen, appointed (*party leader etc.*); **choisir** [ˌ'ziːr] (2a) *v/t.* choose, pick (from *entre, parmi*); *sp.* toss for (*sides*); **choix** [ʃwa] *m* choice, option; selection; *au* ~ as you wish; ♰ all one price; *de* ~ choice, *fig.* picked (*man*); ♰ *de premier* ~ best quality..., prime (*meat*).

chômage [ʃo'maːʒ] *m* unemployment; stoppage; ⊕ shut-down; ♒ (power) cut; F dole; *en* ~ out of work; *en* ~ *partiel* on part-time, on short work; **chômer** [ˌ'me] (1a) *v/i.* take a day off; be idle; be unemployed; *jour m chômé* day off; **chômeur** *m*, **-euse** *f* [ˌ'mœːr, ˌ'møːz] unemployed worker; *les* ~*s m/pl.* the unemployed.

chope [ʃɔp] *f* tankard.

choper [ʃɔ'pe] (1a) *v/t.* pinch (= *steal, a.* = *arrest*); *tennis:* chop.

chopine [ʃɔ'pin] *f* half-litre mug; ⊕ *pump:* plunger; **chopiner** F [ˌpi'ne] (1a) *v/i.* booze.

chopper [ʃɔ'pe] (1a) *v/i.* trip, stumble.

choquant, e [ʃɔ'kã, ˌ'kãːt] shocking, offensive; gross; **choquer** [ˌ'ke] (1m) *v/t.* shock; offend; bump against; clink (*glasses*); *se* ~ come into collision (with, *contre*); be shocked; take offence (at, *de*).

choral, e, *m/pl.* **-als, -aux** [kɔ'ral, ˌ'ro] 1. *adj.* choral; 2. *su./m* chorale; *su./f* choral society.

chorégraphie [kɔregra'fi] *f* choreography.

choriste [kɔ'rist] *m eccl.* chorister; *opera:* chorus-singer; **chorus** [ˌ'rys] *m* chorus; *faire* ~ chorus one's agreement; echo; repeat in chorus.

chose [ʃoːz] 1. *su./f* thing; matter, affair; property; ~ *en question* case in point; ⚖ ~ *jugée* res judicata; ~ *publique* State; *autre* ~ something else; *grand-*~ much; *peu de* ~ not much, very little; *quelque* ~ something; *quelque* ~ *de bon* (*nouveau*) something good (new); *su./m* what's-its (his, her)-name, thingumajig; *monsieur* ♀ Mr. What's-his-name; 2. *adj./inv.* F: *tout* ~ queer, out-of-sorts.

chou, -x [ʃu] *m* cabbage; *fig.* cabbage-bow; rosette; ~*x pl. de Bruxelles* Brussels sprouts; ~ *à la crème* cream puff; ~ *frisé* kale; *être bête comme* ~ be idiotic; be simplicity itself; *pej.* feuille *f de* ~ rag, gutter paper (= *newspaper of no standing*); *mon* ~! (my) dear!; darling!

choucas *orn.* [ʃu'kɑ] *m* jackdaw.

chouchou *m*, **-oute** *f* F [ʃu'ʃu, ˌ'ʃut] darling, pet; **chouchouter** [ˌʃu'te] (1a) *v/t.* pamper, pet.

choucroute *cuis.* [ʃu'krut] *f* sauerkraut.

chouette [ʃwɛt] 1. *su./f orn.* owl; 2. F *adj., a. int.* fine, splendid.

chou...: ~*-fleur*, *pl.* ~*x-fleurs* [ʃu'flœːr] *m* cauliflower; ~*-navet*, *pl.* ~*x-navets* [ˌna'vɛ] *m* swede; ~*-palmiste*, *pl.* ~*x-palmistes* [ˌpal'mist] *m* palm-cabbage; ~*-rave*, *pl.* ~*x-raves* [ˌ'raːv] *m* kohlrabi.

choyer [ʃwa'je] (1h) *v/t.* fondle, pet; *fig.* cherish.

chrétien, -enne [kre'tjɛ̃, ˌ'tjɛn] 1. *adj.* Christian; 2. *su.* Christian; *su./m fig.* good citizen; **chrétienté** [ˌtjɛ̃'te] *f* Christendom.

Christ [krist] *m* (Jesus) Christ; ♀ crucifix; **christianiser** [kristjani'ze] (1a) *v/t.* christianize; **christianisme** [ˌ'nism] *m* Christianity.

chrome [kroːm] *m* ⚗ chromium; ♰ chrome; **chromo** F [krɔ'mo] *m* colo(u)r-print.

chromo... [krɔmo] chromo..., colo(u)r-...

chronique [krɔ'nik] 1. *adj.* ♒ chronic; 2. *su./f* chronicle; *journ.* report, news *sg.*; **chroniqueur** *m*, **-euse** *f* [ˌni'kœːr, ˌ'køːz] chronicler; *journ.* reporter; par-writer, paragrapher.

chrono... [krɔnɔ] chrono...; ~*graphe* [ˌ'graf] *m* stop-watch; *phys.* chronograph; ~*logie* [ˌlɔ'ʒi] *f* chronology; ~*logique* [ˌlɔ'ʒik] chronological; ~*mètre* [ˌ'mɛtr] *m* chronometer; *sp.* ~ *à déclic* stop-watch; ~**métrer** *sp.* [~me'tre] (1f) *v/t.* time; ~**métreur** [~me'trœ:r] *m* *sp.*, *a.* ⊕ time-keeper; ~**métrie** [~me'tri] *f* chronometry, time-measurement.

chrysalide *zo.* [kriza'lid] *f* chrysalis, pupa; **chrysanthème** ⚘ [~zã'tɛ:m] *m* chrysanthemum.

chuchoter [ʃyʃɔ'te] (1a) *vt/i.* whisper; **chuchoterie** [~'tri] *f* whispering.

chut! [ʃyt] *int.* ssh!; hush!

chute [~] *f* fall; spill; *fig.* downfall, overthrow, ruin; ⊕, ⚒ shoot; *geog.* falls *pl.*; ~ *d'eau* waterfall; ✝ ~ *des prix* drop in prices; *anat.* ~ *des reins* small of the back; ~ *du jour* nightfall; *faire une* ~ (have a) fall.

chuter[1] [ʃy'te] (1a) *v/t.* hush; *thea.* hiss; *v/i.* say hush.

chuter[2] [~] (1a) *v/i.* fall; decrease, diminish; *thea.* (be a) flop; ~ *de deux levées cards:* be two tricks down.

ci [si] **1.** *adv.* here; *cet homme-*~ this man; **2.** *dem./pron.* see ceci; *comme* ~ *comme ça* so so; ~**-après** [~a'prɛ] *adv.* below.

cibiche *sl.* [si'biʃ] *f* cig, *Br.* fag (= *cigarette*).

cible [sibl] *f* target (*a. fig.*); ✝ *etc.* target group.

ciboire *eccl.* [si'bwa:r] *m* ciborium.

ciboule ⚘ [si'bul] *f* Welsh onion; **ciboulette** ⚘ [sibu'lɛt] *f* chive; **ciboulot** *sl.* [~'lo] *m* nut (= *head*).

cicatrice [sika'tris] *f* scar; **cicatriser** [~tri'ze] (1a) *v/t.* heal; *se* ~ heal (up), scar over.

ci...: ~**contre** [si'kɔ̃:tr] *adv.* opposite; ~**dessous** [~'dsu] *adv.* below, hereunder; ⚹⚹ hereinafter; ~**dessus** [~'dsy] *adv.* above(-mentioned); hereinbefore; ~**devant** [~'dvã] **1.** *adv.* formerly, previously; **2.** *su./inv.* aristocrat; F old fogey.

cidre [sidr] *m* cider.

ciel [sjɛl] **1.** *su./m* (*pl.* **cieux**) [sjø]) sky, heaven; (*pl.* **ciels** [sjɛl]) (bed-)tester; ⊕, ⚒ roof; (*pl.* **ciels** *ou* **cieux**) climate, sky; **2.** *int.* good heavens!   [taper.\

cierge *eccl.* [sjɛrʒ] *m* (wax) candle,∫

cigale *zo.* [si'gal] *f* cicada.

cigare [si'ga:r] *m* cigar; **cigarette** [~ga'rɛt] *f* cigarette; **cigarière** [~ga'rjɛːr] *f* cigar-maker.

cigogne [si'gɔɲ] *f* *orn.* stork; ⊕ crank(-lever).

ciguë ⚘, ⚘ [si'gy] *f* hemlock.

ci-inclus, e [siɛ̃'kly, ~'kly:z], **ci-joint, e** [~'ʒwɛ̃, ~'ʒwɛ̃:t] **1.** *adj.* enclosed, sub-joined (*letter, copy*); **2.** *ci-inclus, ci-joint adv.* herewith; ~ *la lettre* herewith the letter.

cil [sil] *m* (eye)lash.

cilice [si'lis] *m* hair-shirt.

cilié, e ⚘ [si'lje] ciliate; **ciller** [~'je] (1a) *v/t.* blink (one's eyes, *les yeux*).

cime [sim] *f* top, summit; *mountain:* peak.

ciment [si'mã] *m* cement; ~ *armé* reinforced concrete; **cimenter** [simã'te] (1a) *v/t.* cement (*a. fig.*); **cimenterie** [~'tri] *f* cement works *usu. sg.*; **cimentier** [~'tje] *m* cement-maker; cement-worker.

cimeterre [sim'tɛːr] *m* scimitar.

cimetière [sim'tjɛːr] *m* cemetery, graveyard; *mot.* ~ *de voitures* scrapyard.

cimier [si'mje] *m* helmet, *a.* ✂: crest; *venison:* haunch.

cinabre [si'na:br] *m* cinnabar; *paint.* vermilion.

ciné F [si'ne] *m* cinema, F films *pl.*, *Am.* movies *pl.*; **cinéaste** [~'ast] *m* cinematographer; film-producer; scenario-writer; **ciné-caméra** [~kame'ra] *f* cine-camera; **ciné-club** [~'klœb] *m* filmclub; **ciné-journal** [~ʒur'nal] *m* news-reel; **cinéma** [~'ma] *m* cinema; F films *pl.*, pictures *pl.*, *Am.* movies *pl.*; F *fig.* playacting, act, show; F *fig.* fuss; ~ *parlant* F talkie; **cinémathèque** [sinema'tɛk] *f* film-library; **cinématique** *phys.* [~'tik] **1.** *adj.* kinematic; **2.** *su./f* kinematics *pl.*; **cinématographe** [~tɔ'graf] cinematograph, F cinema; **cinématographier** [~tɔgra'fje] (1o) *v/t.* film; **cinématographique** [~tɔgra'fik] cinematographic; film-...; **cinéphile** [~fil] *su.* film enthusiast.

cinéraire [sine'rɛːr] **1.** *adj.* cinerary; **2.** *su./f* ⚘ cineraria.

ciné-roman [sinerɔ'mã] *m* film story.

cinétique *phys.* [sine'tik] **1.** *adj.* kinetic; **2.** *su./f* kinetics *pl.*

cingalais, e [sɛ̃ga'lɛ, ~'lɛ:z] *adj., su.* ♀ Cingalese.

cinglant, e [sɛ̃'glã, ~'glã:t] lashing (*rain*); bitter, biting (*cold, wind, etc.*);

cinglé 102

fig. scathing; **cinglé, e** F [ʌˈgle] **1.** *adj.* nutty, nuts (= *mad*); **2.** *su.* crackpot; **cingler** [ʌˈgle] (1a) *v/t.* lash; ♣ *v/i.* sail; scud along; steer a course.

cinq [sɛ̃:k; *before consonant* sɛ̃] *adj./ num., a. su./m/inv.* five; *date, title:* fifth; **cinquantaine** [sɛ̃kɑ̃ˈtɛn] *f* (about) fifty; *la* ʌ the age of fifty, the fifties *pl.*; **cinquante** [ʌˈkɑ:t] *adj./num., a. su./m/inv.* fifty; **cin-quantième** [ʌkɑ̃ˈtjɛm] *adj./num., a. su.* fiftieth; **cinquième** [ʌˈkjɛm] **1.** *adj./num.* fifth; **2.** *su.* fifth; *su./m fraction:* fifth; fifth, *Am.* sixth floor; *su./f secondary school:* (approx.) second form.

cintre [sɛ̃:tr] *m* △ arch, curve, bend; coat *or* clothes hanger; *thea.* ʌs *pl.* flies; **cintré, e** [sɛ̃ˈtre] arched, curved; *cost.* waisted; F nutty, nuts (= *mad*); **cintrer** ⊕ [ʌ] (1a) *v/t.* bend, curve; arch.

cirage [siˈra:ʒ] *m* waxing, polishing; *boot, shoe, floor, etc.:* polish.

circon... [sirkɔ̃] circum...; **ʌcire** [ʌˈsi:r] (4e) *v/t.* circumcise; ring (*a tree*); **ʌcis, e** [ʌˈsi, ʌˈsi:z] *p.p. of cir-concire;* **ʌcision** [ʌsiˈzjɔ̃] *f* circumcision; *tree:* ringing; **ʌférence** [ʌ-feˈrɑ̃:s] *f* circumference; perimeter; *tree:* girth; **ʌflexe** *gramm.* [ʌˈflɛks] circumflex; *accent m* ʌ circum-flex (accent); **ʌlocution** [ʌlɔkyˈsjɔ̃] *f* circumlocution; **ʌscription** [ʌs-krip'sjɔ̃] *f* A circumscribing; *ad-min.* division, district; ʌ *électorale* electoral district *or* ward; constitu-ency; **ʌscrire** [ʌsˈkri:r] (4e) *v/t.* A circumscribe (*a. fig.*); *fig.* limit; ✂ locate (*a fault*); **ʌspect, e** [ʌs-ˈpɛ, ʌsˈpɛkt] guarded, circumspect; **ʌspection** [ʌspɛkˈsjɔ̃] *f* caution, circumspection; **ʌstance** [ʌsˈtɑ̃:s] *f* circumstance; event; ʌs *pl.* atté-nuantes attenuating circumstances; ⚔ ʌs *pl. et dépendances f/pl.* appur-tenances; *de* ʌ occasional; tempo-rary; special; **ʌstancié, e** [ʌstɑ̃ˈsje] detailed; **ʌstanciel, -elle** [ʌstɑ̃ˈsjɛl] due to circumstances; *gramm.* ad-verbial (*complement*); **ʌvenir** [ʌ-vˈni:r] (2h) *v/t.* circumvent; outwit (*s.o.*); † impose on (*s.o.*); **ʌvention** † [ʌvɑ̃ˈsjɔ̃] *f* imposture, fraud; **ʌvolution** △, *anat.* [ʌvɔlyˈsjɔ̃] *f* convolution.

circuit [sirˈkɥi] *m* circuit; circuitous

route, roundabout way; circum-ference; ✂ *mettre en* ʌ connect up; ✂ *mettre en court* ʌ short-circuit; *ouvrir (fermer) le* ʌ switch on (off), ʌ *imprimé* printed circuit; ✂ ʌ *intégré* integrated circuit.

circulaire [sirkyˈlɛ:r] *adj., a. su./f* circular; **circulation** [ʌlaˈsjɔ̃] *f air,* bank-notes, blood, information, etc.: circulation; ✝, *bank-notes etc.:* cur-rency; traffic; ⚙ running; ʌ *interdite* no thoroughfare; **circulatoire** [ʌlaˈtwa:r] circulatory; *appa-reil m* ʌ circulatory system; **circuler** [ʌˈle] (1a) *v/i.* circulate, flow; ✝ turn over; ⚙ run (*train*); *circulez!* move along!; pass along!

circumnavigation [sirkɔmnaviga-ˈsjɔ̃] *f* circumnavigation.

cire [si:r] *f* wax; *eccl.* taper; ʌ *à cacheter,* ʌ *d'Espagne* sealing-wax; ʌ *à parquet* floor-polish; ʌ *d'abeilles* beeswax; **ciré, e** [siˈre] **1.** *adj.* waxed, polished; *toile f* ʌe oilcloth, Ameri-can cloth; **2.** *su./m* oilskin *pl.*; **cirer** [ʌˈre] (1a) *v/t.* wax; polish; **cireur, -euse** [ʌˈrœ:r, ʌˈrø:z] *su.* polisher; (ʌ *de chaussures*) shoeblack, *Am.* shoe-shine boy; *su./f machine:* waxer, polisher; **cirier, -ère** [ʌˈrje, ʌˈrjɛ:r] **1.** *adj.* wax...; **2.** *su./m* wax-chandler; ⚘ candleberry-tree, *Am.* bayberry.

ciron *zo.* [siˈrɔ̃] *m* mite.

cirque [sirk] *m* circus; amphithea-tre; cirque (*of mountains*).

cirrhose ✻ [siˈro:z] cirrhosis.

cirrus *meteor.* [sirˈrys] *m* cirrus.

cisaille [siˈza:j] *f metal:* clippings *pl.*; ⊕ shearing machine; ⊕ guillotine; ʌs *pl.* shears; wire-cutter *sg.*; ʌs *pl. à haies* hedge-shears, hedge-clippers; **cisailler** [ʌzaˈje] (1a) *v/t.* clip; cut; shear (*metal*); *fig.* discredit; cripple (*s.o.'s career*); **ciseau** [ʌˈzo] *m* chisel; ʌx *pl.* scissors; ✄ shears; **ciseler** [sizˈle] (1d) *v/t.* chisel; cut; chase (*silver*); tool (*leather*); *fig.* polish (*one's style*); **ciselet** [ʌˈlɛ] *m* small chisel; chasing tool; **ciseleur** [ʌˈlœ:r] *m* chiseler; engraver; chaser; tooler; **ciselure** [ʌˈly:r] *f* chiseling; chasing; tooling; **cisoires** [siˈzwa:r] *f/pl.* bench-shears.

citadelle ✕ [sitaˈdɛl] *f* citadel, strong-hold; **citadin, e** [ʌˈdɛ̃, ʌˈdin] *su.* citizen; *su./m* townsman; *su./f* townswoman.

citation [sitaˈsjɔ̃] *f* quotation; ✕

mention in dispatches; ⚖ summons *sg.*; ⚖ subpoena (*of a witness*).

cité [si'te] *f* city; (large) town; housing estate; *la ♀ London*: the City; *Paris*: the Cité; ⁓ *lacustre* lakedwelling; ⁓ *universitaire* students' residential blocks *pl.*; *droit m de* ⁓ freedom of the city; *fig. avoir droit de* ⁓ be accepted; be established; **⁓-dortoir**, *pl.* **⁓s-dortoirs** [⁓dɔrt'wa:r] *f* dormitory town; **⁓-jardin**, *pl.* **⁓s-jardins** [⁓teʒar'dɛ̃] *f* gardencity.

citer [si'te] (1a) *v/t.* quote, cite; ✗ mention in dispatches; ⚖ summon; ⚖ subpoena (*a witness*).

citerne [si'tɛrn] *f* cistern, tank; 🚊 tank-car.

cithare ♪ [si'ta:r] *f* zither; **cithariste** ♪ [⁓ta'rist] *su.* zither-player.

citoyen *m*, **-enne** *f* [sitwa'jɛ̃, ⁓'jɛn] citizen.

citrin, e [si'trɛ̃, ⁓'trin] lemon-yellow; **citrique** ♠ [⁓'trik] citric; **citron** [⁓'trɔ̃] **1.** *su./m* ♀ lemon, citron, lime; F nut (= *head*); ⁓ *pressé* lemon squash; **2.** *adj./inv.* lemon(-colo[u]red); **citronnade** [sitrɔ'nad] *f* lemonade; **citronnier** [⁓'nje] *m* ♀ lemon-tree; *wood*: lemon-wood.

citrouille ♀ [si'tru:j] *f* pumpkin.

civet *cuis.* [si've] *m* stew; ⁓ *de lièvre* jugged hare.

civette¹ *zo.* [si'vɛt] *f* civet-cat; ♣ *perfume*: civet.

civette² ♀ [⁓] *f* chive.

civière [si'vjɛ:r] *f* hand-barrow; stretcher; *coffin*: bier.

civil, e [si'vil] **1.** *su./m* ✗ civilian; *eccl.* layman; civil status or dress; *dans le* ⁓ in civil life; *en* ⁓ in mufti, in plain clothes; **2.** *adj.* civil; ✗ civilian; *eccl.* lay; civic; polite (*to*, towards *à*, *envers*); *année f* ⁓e calendar year; ⚖ *droit m* ⁓ common law; *état m* ⁓ civil status; register office; *mariage m* ⁓ civil marriage; *mort f* ⁓e civil death; **civilisateur, -trice** [siviliza'tœ:r, ⁓'tris] **1.** *adj.* civilizing; **2.** *su.* civilizer; **civilisation** [⁓za'sjɔ̃] *f* civilization; **civiliser** [⁓'ze] (1a) *v/t.* civilize; *se* ⁓ become civilized; **civilité** [⁓'te] *f* civility, courtesy; *fig.* ⁓*s pl.* compliments, kind regards; *faire des* ⁓*s à* be civil to.

civique [si'vik] civic; civil (*rights*);

patriotic (*song*); *droits m/pl.* ⁓s civic rights, *Am.* citizen rights; *instruction f* ⁓ civics *sg.*; **civisme** [⁓'vism] *m* good citizenship.

clabaud [kla'bo] *m hunt.* (long-eared) hound; F scandal-monger; **clabaudage** [⁓bo'da:ʒ] *m hunt.* babbling; F spiteful gossip; **clabauder** [⁓bo'de] (1a) *v/i. hunt.* babble; F talk scandal (about, *sur*).

claie [klɛ] *f* ✗ hurdle; fence; ⊕ screen; ⊕ grid.

clair, e [klɛ:r] **1.** *adj.* clear; bright; obvious; thin (*silk, soup, wood*); **2.** *clair adv.* clearly, plainly; thinly; **3.** *su./m* light; *garment*: thin place; *tirer au* ⁓ decant (*wine*); *fig.* clarify, bring to light; **clairet, -ette** [klɛ'rɛ, ⁓'rɛt] **1.** *adj.* pale, light; thin (*voice*); **2.** *su./m* local light red wine; **claire-voie,** *pl.* **claires-voies** [klɛr'vwa] *f* open-work; △ skylight; ⚓ decklight; *eccl.* clerestory; ⁓ *à* ⁓ thinly; **clairière** [klɛ'rjɛ:r] *f* clearing; glade; *linen*: thin place; **clair-obscur,** *pl.* **clairs-obscurs** *paint.* [klɛrɔps'ky:r] *m* chiaroscuro.

clairon ♪ [klɛ'rɔ̃] *m* bugle; *clarinet*: upper register; *person*: bugler; **claironner** [⁓rɔ'ne] (1a) *v/i.* sound the bugle; trumpet; *v/t. fig.* trumpet; *fig.* trumpet abroad.

clairsemé, e [klɛrsə'me] thinly-sown; scattered, sparse; thin (*hair, beard*).

clairvoyance [klɛrvwa'jɑ̃:s] *f* perceptiveness; clear-sightedness; **clairvoyant, e** [⁓'jɑ̃, ⁓'jɑ̃:t] perceptive; clear-sighted; clairvoyant.

clamer [kla'me] (1a) *v/t.* protest (*one's innocence etc.*); F cry (*s.th.*) out; **clameur** [⁓'mœ:r] *f* clamo(u)r, outcry; *sea, tempest*: roar(ing).

clan [klɑ̃] *m* clan; *fig.* clique.

clandestin, e [klɑ̃dɛs'tɛ̃, ⁓'tin] clandestine, secret; ✗ underground (*forces*); illicit; *fig.* underhand; stealthy; ⚓ *passager m* ⁓ stowaway; **clandestinité** [⁓tini'te] *f* secrecy; clandestineness; stealth.

clapet [kla'pɛ] *m* ⊕ valve; ⚡ rectifier.

clapier [kla'pje] *m* rabbit hutch or warren; F *fig.* dump, hole.

clapotement [klapɔt'mɑ̃] *m*, **clapotis** [klapɔ'ti] *m waves*: lapping, plashing; **clapoter** [⁓'te] (1a) *v/i.* lap, plash; **clapoteux, -euse** [⁓'tø,

~'tø:z] choppy (*sea*); plashing (*noise*). [*one's tongue*).\

clapper [kla'pe] [1a] *v/i.* click (*with*)

claque [klak] *su./f* smack, slap; *thea.* claque, hired applause; *sl.* death; golosh, *Am.* overshoe; *fig. prendre ses cliques et ses* ~*s depart* quickly, F clear off; *su./m* opera-hat, crush-hat; cocked hat; *sl.* disorderly house; **claquedent** F [~'dã] *m* starveling; **claquement** [~'mã] *m* bullet, whip: smack; *door:* slam; *hands:* clapping; *teeth:* chattering; *machine:* rattle.

claquemurer [klakmy're] (1a) *v/t.* immure; se ~ shut o.s. up.

claquer [kla'ke] (1m) *v/i.* clap; crack (*whip*); bang, slam (*door*); burn out (*lamp*); F kick the bucket (= *die*); break; snap (*string etc.*); F go bust; F go phut; F come to nothing; ~ *des doigts* snap one's fingers; ~ *des mains* clap; *il claquait des dents* his teeth were chattering; 2. *v/t.* slap, smack; slam, bang; *fig.* burst; wear out, tire out; *thea.* applaud; F blue, blow (*money*); F se ~ tire o.s. out; **claquet** [~'kɛ] *m* (mill-)clapper; **claqueter** [klak'te] (1c) *v/i.* cluck, cackle (*hen*); clapper (*stork*); **claquette** [kla'kɛt] *f eccl.* clapper; F chatterbox; (*danse f à*) ~*s pl.* tap-cance *sg.*; **claqueur** thea. [~'kœ:r] *m* hired clapper.

clarifier [klari'fje] (1o) *v/t.* clarify.

clarine [kla'rin] *f* cattle-bell; **clarinette** ♪ [~ri'nɛt] *f* clarinet; *person:* clarinettist.

clarté [klar'te] *f* light, clearness; brightness; *sun:* gleam; *glass:* transparency; *fig.* lucidity.

classe [klɑ:s] *f* class (*a. sociology; a.* 🚂 *etc.*); category; rank; kind; ⚔ annual contingent; *primary school:* standard; *secondary school:* form, *Am.* grade; class-room; lessons *pl.*; ~ *moyenne* (*ouvrière*) middle (working) class(es *pl.*); *aller en* ~ go to school; *de première* ~ 🚂 *etc.* first-class (*ticket, compartment*); *fig.* first-rate; *faire la* ~ teach; **classé, e** [kla'se] classified; listed (*building*); **classement** [klɑs'mã] *m* classification; ⚓ *etc.* filing; grading; **classer** [klɑ'se] (1a) *v/t.* classify; ⚓ *etc.* file; catalogue, *Am.* catalog; grade; **classeur** [~'sœ:r] *m* ⚓ file; filing cabinet, *Am.* file case; ⊕ sorter; sizer; ~ *à anneaux* ring binder.

classicisme [klasi'sism] *m* classicism.

classification [klasifika'sjɔ̃] *f* classification; **classifier** [~'fje] (1o) *v/t.* classify.

classique [kla'sik] **1.** *adj.* classical (*author, music, period*); classic; standard; *fig.* orthodox; **2.** *su./m* classic; classicist (*as opposed to romantic*); *les* ~*s pl.* the (*ancient, French*) classics.

clause ⚖ [klo:z] *f* clause; ~ *additionnelle* rider; additional clause.

claustral, e, *m/pl.* -aux [klos'tral, ~'tro] monastic; **claustrophobie** [klostrɔfɔ'bi] *f* claustrophobia.

claveau [kla'vo] *m* ⚠ arch-stone; *vet.* sheep-pox.

clavecin ♪ [klav'sɛ̃] *m* harpsichord.

clavette ⊕ [kla'vɛt] *f* pin, key, peg, cotter.

clavicule *anat.* [klavi'kyl] *f* clavicle, collar-bone.

clavier ♪ *etc.* [kla'vje] *m piano, typewriter:* keyboard; *organ:* manual; *wind-instrument:* range; † key-ring, key-chain.

clayon [klɛ'jɔ̃] *m* wicker-tray (*for cheese*); wattle enclosure; **clayonnage** [~jɔ'na:ʒ] *m* wicker-work; wattle fencing; ⊕ mat; **clayonner** [~jɔ'ne] (1a) *v/t.* protect with wattle fencing; mat.

clé, clef [kle] *f* key (*a. fig.*); ⚠ keystone; ⚠ *beam:* reinforcing piece; ⊕ spanner, wrench; ⚡ switch-key; ♪ clef; ♪ key-signature; ♪ key (*woodwind instrument*); *sp. wrestling:* lock; ~ *à douilles* box-spanner; ~ *à molette* adjustable spanner; ~ *anglaise* monkey-wrench; ~ *crocodile* crocodile spanner; *mot.* ~ *pour roues* wheel-brace; ⚠, *a. fig.* ~ *de voûte* keystone; ~*s en main* ready for immediate occupation (*house etc.*); *fausse* ~ skeleton key; *mettre sous* ~ lock up; *sous* ~ under lock and key.

clématite 🌿 [klema'tit] *f* clematis.

clémence [kle'mã:s] *f* clemency (*a. of weather*), leniency; mercy; **clément, e** [~'mã, ~'mã:t] clement, lenient; merciful; mild (*disease etc.*); *ciel m* ~ mild climate.

clenche [klã:ʃ] *f* (door-)latch.

clerc [klɛ:r] *m eccl.* cleric, clergyman; ⚖ clerk; F *être (grand)* ~ *en* be an expert on; *faire un pas de* ~ blunder; **clergé** [klɛr'ʒe] *m* clergy *pl.*; **clérical, e**, *m/pl.* -aux *eccl., a. pol.*

[kleri'kal, ‿'ko] *adj., a. su./m* clerical.
**clic! ** [klik] *int.* click!
clichage [kli'ʃa:ʒ] *m typ.* stereotyping; electro-typing; ⚒ caging; **cliché** [‿'ʃe] *m typ. type:* plate; *illustration:* block; *phot.* negative; *fig.* cliché, stock phrase; **clicher** [‿'ʃe] (1a) *v/t. typ.* stereotype; make electrotypes of; ⚒ cage; **clicherie** *typ., journ.* [kliʃ'ri] stereotype room; stereotyping shop.
client *m, e f* [kli'ã, ‿'ã:t] client; ⚕ customer; ✚ patient; *hotel:* guest; **clientèle** [‿ã'tɛl] *f* ✚ custom, customers *pl.*; ✚ goodwill; ✚ connection; ✚, ⚖ practice; ‿ *d'habitués* regular clients *pl.* or customers *pl.*; *donner sa* ‿ *à* patronize.
cligner [kli'ne] *vt/i.* wink; blink; *v/t.* screw up *(one's eyes)*; **clignotant** *mot.* [kliɲɔ'tã] *m* indicator, trafficator; blinker; *fig.* warning light; **clignoter** [‿'te] (1a) *v/i.* blink; flicker *(eyelids, light)*; twinkle *(star)*.
climat [kli'ma] *m* climate; region; *fig.* atmosphere; **climatérique** [klimate'rik] **1.** *su./f* climacteric; **2.** *adj.* climacteric; *a.* = **climatique** [‿'tik] climatic *(conditions)*; *station f* ‿ health-resort; **climatisation** [‿tiza'sjɔ̃] *f* air conditioning; **climatiser** [‿ti'ze] (1a) *v/t.* air-condition; **climatiseur** [‿ti'zœ:r] *m* air conditioner; **climatologie** [‿tɔlɔ'ʒi] *f* climatology; **climatologique** [‿tɔlɔ'ʒik] climatological.
clin [klɛ̃] *m:* ‿ *d'œil* wink; *en un* ‿ *d'œil* in the twinkling of an eye.
clinicien ⚕ [klini'sjɛ̃] *su./m, a. adj./m* clinician; **clinique** ⚕ [‿'nik] **1.** *adj.* clinical; **2.** *su./f* clinic; nursing home; F surgery *(of a doctor)*; teaching hospital.
clinquant, e [klɛ̃'kã, ‿'kã:t] **1.** *adj.* showy, gaudy, flashy; **2.** *su./m* tinsel; ⊕ foil; *fig.* showiness.
clip [klip] *m pen etc.:* clip.
clipper ⚓, ✈ [kli'pœ:r] *m* clipper.
clique F [klik] *f* set, clique; gang; ✖ drum and bugle band; **cliquet** ⊕ *etc.* [kli'kɛ] *m* catch; ratchet; **cliqueter** [klik'te] (1c) *v/i.* rattle; clink *(glass)*; jingle *(keys etc.)*; *mot.* pink; **cliquetis** [‿'ti] *m metall.* clang, rattle; clatter; *glasses:* clinking; *keys etc.:* jingling; *mot.* pinking.
clisse [klis] *f bottle:* wicker covering; *cheese:* drainer; ✚ splint; **clisser**

[kli'se] (1a) *v/t.* wicker *(a bottle)*; ✚ put in splints; *bouteille f clissée* demijohn.
clivage [kli'va:ʒ] *m* cleavage; gap, split; **cliver** [kli've] (1a) *v/t. a. se* ‿ split, cleave.
cloaque [klɔ'ak] *m* cesspool *(a. fig.)*; *fig.* sink *(of iniquity)*.
clochard F [klɔ'ʃa:r] *m* down-and-out; tramp, *Am.* hobo; **clochardiser** [‿ʃardi'ze] (1a) *v/t.: se* ‿ go to the dogs.
cloche [klɔʃ] *f* bell; ⚕ bell-jar; ✔ cloche; ✚ cup *(for blistering)*; dishcover; cloche(-hat); *sl.* idiot; F *la* ‿ (the) down-and-outs (in general); ‿**pied** [‿'pje] *adv.: sauter à* ‿ hop.
clocher¹ [klɔ'ʃe] *m* church tower; steeple; *fig. de* ‿ parochial; *esprit m de* ‿ parochialism.
clocher² [‿] (1a) *v/i.* F go *or* be wrong; limp, hobble.
clocheton [klɔʃ'tɔ̃] *m* bell-turret; **clochette** [klɔ'ʃɛt] *f* handbell; ⚘ bell-flower; ‿ *d'hiver* snowdrop.
cloison [klwa'zɔ̃] *f* ⚙ partition (wall); ⚓ bulkhead; *mot.* baffle-plate; *fig.* ‿ *(étanche* impenetrable) barrier; *fig. séparé(e)s par des* ‿*s étanches* in watertight compartments; **cloisonnage** [‿zɔ'na:ʒ] *m* partition (-ing); **cloisonner** [‿zɔ'ne] (1a) *v/t.* partition; divide up; compartmentalize.
cloître *eccl.* [klwɑ:tr] *m* cloister(s *pl.*); monastery; convent; **cloîtrer** [klwa'tre] (1a) *v/t.* cloister; *nonne f cloîtrée* enclosed nun.
clope *sl.* [klɔp] *f* cig, *Br.* fag (= *cigarette)*.
clopin-clopant F [klɔpɛ̃klɔ'pã] *adv.* hobbling (along); **clopiner** [‿pi'ne] (1a) *v/i.* hobble, limp.
cloporte *zo.* [klɔ'pɔrt] *m* woodlouse, *Am.* sow-bug.
cloque [klɔk] *f* ✚ lump, swelling; ✔ *corn:* rust; *tree:* blight.
clore [klɔ:r] (4f) *vt/i.* close; *v/t.* enclose *(land)*; **clos, close** [klo, klo:z] **1.** *p.p.* of *clore;* **2.** *adj.* closed; shut in; finished; **3.** *su./m* enclosure, close; vineyard; **closerie** [kloz'ri] *f* small estate; small holding; croft; pleasure garden; **clôt** [klo] *3rd p. sg. pres. of clore;* **clôture** [‿'ty:r] *f* fence, enclosure; closure, closing; end; ✚ *account:* winding up; ✚ *books:*

balancing; **clôturer** [ˌty're] (1a) *v/t.* enclose (*land*); ✝ close down (*a factory*); *pol.* apply the closure to (*a debate*); ✝ wind up, close.

clou [klu] *m* nail; *fig.* star turn, hit, highlight; ✍ boil, carbuncle; *pedestrian crossing*: stud; *sl.* pawnshop, *Am.* hock shop; *sl.* clink, jail; *sl.* old jalopy; *cuis.* ~ de girofle clove; **clouer** [klu'e] (1a) *v/t.* nail; pin down; rivet; *fig.* tie; *tapis m cloué* fitted carpet; **clouter** [~'te] (1a) *v/t.* stud; **clouterie** [~'tri] *f* nail-making; nail-works *usu. sg.*; **cloutier** [~'tje] *m* nail-dealer; nailsmith.

clown [klun] *m* clown; buffoon; **clownerie** [~'ri] *f* clownish trick; clownishness; **clownesque** [klu-'nɛsk] clownish; farcical.

cloyère [klwa'jɛːr] *f* oyster-basket.

club [klœb] *m* club.

cluse *geol.* [klyːz] *f* transverse valley.

coadjuteur *eccl.* [koadʒy'tœːr] *m* coadjutor; **coadjutrice** *eccl.* [~'tris] *f* coadjutrix.

coagulation [koagyla'sjɔ̃] *f* coagulation, congealing; **coaguler** [~'le] (1a) *v/t. a.* se ~ coagulate, clot; curdle.

coaliser *pol.* [koali'ze] (1a) *v/t. a.* se ~ unite; **coalition** [~'sjɔ̃] *f* coalition; *fig.* combine; *ministère m de* ~ coalition ministry.

coasser [koa'se] (1a) *v/i.* croak.

coassocié *m,* e *f* [koasɔ'sje] co-partner.

cobaye *zo., fig.* [kɔ'baːj] *m* guinea-pig.

cocagne [kɔ'kaɲ] *f:* mât *m de* ~ greasy pole; *pays m de* ~ land of plenty.

cocaïne [kɔka'in] *f* cocaine.

cocasse F [kɔ'kas] comical, droll.

coccinelle *zo.* [kɔksi'nɛl] *f* lady-bird.

coccyx *anat.* [kɔk'sis] *m* coccyx.

coche¹ [kɔʃ] *m* ✝ stage-coach; *faire la mouche du* ~ buzz around; be a busy-body; F *manquer le* ~ miss the boat (= *lose an opportunity*).

coche² [~] *f* nick, notch.

coche³ *zo.* [~] *f* sow.

cocher¹ [kɔ'ʃe] (1a) *v/t.* nick, notch; check off, tick off.

cocher² [kɔ'ʃe] *m* coachman, F cabby; **cochère** [~'ʃɛːr] *adj./f: porte f* ~ carriage-entrance; main gate.

cochon, -onne [kɔ'ʃɔ̃, ~'ʃɔn] **1.** *su./m*

pig, hog, porker; *fig.* filthy swine; ~ *de lait* sucking-pig; ~ *d'Inde* guinea-pig; **2.** *adj. sl.* indecent; filthy; **cochonner** [~'ʃɔ'ne] (1a) *v/i.* farrow; *v/t.* F botch (*a piece of work*); **cochonnerie** [~ʃɔn'ri] *f* filth; rubbish; foul trick; hogwash (= *bad food*); **cochonnet** [~ʃɔ'nɛ] *m* young pig; *bowls:* jack; *tex.* cylinder.

cockpit ✈[kɔk'pit] *m* cockpit.

cocktail [kɔk'tɛl] *m* cocktail; cocktail party; ~ *Molotov* Molotov cocktail.

coco [kɔ'ko] *su./m* (*a. noix f de* ~) coco(a)nut; F liquorice water; *sl.* head; F guy; F darling; F stomach; ✈ *sl.* petrol; *ch.sp.* hen; egg; *su./f* F snow (= *cocaine*).

cocon [kɔ'kɔ̃] *m* cocoon.

cocorico [kɔkɔri'ko] *m* cock-a-doodle-doo.

cocotier ♣ [kɔkɔ'tje] *m* coconut palm.

cocotte¹ [kɔ'kɔt] *f* chuck-chuck (= *hen*); F darling, ducky; *pej.* loose woman, tart.

cocotte² *cuis.* [~] *f* stew-pan.

coction [kɔk'sjɔ̃] *f* ✍ boiling, coction; ✍ digestion.

cocu F [kɔ'ky] *m* cuckold, deceived husband; **cocufier** F [~ky'fje] (1o) *v/t.* cuckold.

codage [kɔ'daːʒ] *m* (en)coding; **code** [kɔd] *m* code (*a.* 𝄪, *a. tel.*); 𝄪 ~ *civil* (*pénal, de la route*) civil (penal, highway) code; ~ *postal* postcode, *Am.* zip code; *mot. se mettre en* ~ dip (*Am.* dim) the headlights; **coder** [kɔ'de] (1a) *v/t.* code.

codétenu *m,* e *f* 𝄪 [kodet'ny] fellow-prisoner.

codifier [kɔdi'fje] (1o) *v/t.* 𝄪 codify; *tel. etc.* code.

coéducation [koedyka'sjɔ̃] *f* coeducation. [factor.\
coefficient [koefi'sjã] *m* coefficient;∫

coéquation *admin.* [koekwa'sjɔ̃] *f* proportional assessment.

coercitif, -ve 𝄪, *phys.* [koɛrsi'tif, ~'tiːv] coercive.

cœur [kœːr] *m* heart (*a. fig.*); courage; feelings *pl.*; centre; *cards:* heart(s *pl.*); ✍ ~-*poumon m artificiel* heart-lung machine; ✍ *arrêt m du* ~ heart failure; *à* ~ *joie* to one's heart's content; *avoir mal au* ~, *avoir le* ~ *sur les lèvres* feel sick; *par* ~ by heart; *cela vous (sou)lève le* ~ that makes you (feel) sick.

coexistence [koɛgzis'tã:s] *f* coexistence (*a. pol.*); **coexister** [~'te] (1a) *v/i.* coexist.

coffrage [kɔ'fra:ʒ] *m* ⚒ coffering, lining; shuttering (*for concrete work*); **coffre** [kɔfr] *m* chest, box; coffer; ⚓ moorings *pl.*; ⚓ (mooring-)buoy; case; 🔋 ballast-bed; *mot.* boot; ⚠ form, box (*for concrete work*); ⚓ *navire m à ~* well-decker; **coffre-fort,** *pl.* **coffres-forts** [~ə'fɔ:r] *m* safe; strong-box; **coffrer** [kɔ'fre] (1a) *v/t.* F imprison; ⚒ coffer, line; **coffret** [~'frɛ] *m* casket; (*tool-, work-, etc.*)box.

cogérance [koʒe'rã:s] *f* co-administration; joint management; **cogérer** [~'re] (1f) *v/i.* manage jointly; **cogestion** [~'stjõ] *f* joint management; co-management.

cogiter [kɔʒi'te] (1a) *vt/i.* cogitate; think (up).

cognac [kɔ'ɲak] *m* cognac, F brandy.

cognassier ♀ [kɔɲa'sje] *m* quincetree.

cognée [kɔ'ɲe] *f* axe, hatchet; **cogner** [~] (1a) *v/t.* hammer in; drive in (*a nail*); knock, hit; bump against; *v/i.* knock (*a. mot.*); bump.

cohabiter [koabi'te] (1a) *v/i.* live together, cohabit.

cohérence [kɔe'rã:s] *f* coherence; *avec ~* coherently; **cohérent, e** [~'rã, ~'rã:t] coherent; **cohésion** [~'zjõ] *f* cohesion; *phys. force f de ~* cohesive force.

cohue [kɔ'y] *f* crowd, throng, crush; mob.

coi, coite [kwa, kwat] quiet; *se tenir ~* keep quiet; F lie doggo.

coiffe [kwaf] *f* head-dress; cap; *hat:* lining; ⚓ cap-cover; **coiffé, e** [kwa'fe] *adj.:* *être ~* be wearing a hat; have done one's hair; *fig.* be infatuated (with, *de*); *être bien ~* have one's hair well dressed; *né ~* born lucky; **coiffer** [~'fe] (1a) *v/t.* cover (*one's head*); *hat:* suit; put on (*a hat*); do (*one's hair*); *fig.* cover (up for) (*s.o.*); *fig.* control (*an organization etc.*); *sp., a. fig.* beat (*an opponent*); *de combien coiffez-vous?* what size in hats do you take?; *~ sainte Catherine* reach the age of 25 without being married (*woman*); *sp., a. fig. ~ q. au poteau* beat s.o. at the post; **coiffeur, -euse** [~'fœ:r, ~'fø:z] *su.* hairdresser; *su./f* dressing-table;

coiffure [~'fy:r] *f* head-dress; hair-style; hairdressing; *~ à la Jeanne d'Arc* bobbed hair (with fringe).

coin [kwɛ̃] *m* corner; nook, spot; *ground:* patch; *coins:* die; ⊕ wedge, chock; *fig.* hallmark, stamp; *~ du feu* fireside; *dans tous les ~s et recoins in* every corner, everywhere; **coincement** ⊕ [kwɛ̃s'mã] *m* jamming; **coincer** ⊕ [kwɛ̃'se] (1k) *v/t.* wedge; *fig. sl.* corner; arrest; *v/i. a. se ~* jam, stick.

coïncidence [kɔɛ̃si'dã:s] *f* coincidence; ⚡ *~ d'oscillations* surging; **coïncider** [~'de] (1a) *v/i.* coincide.

coing ♀ [kwɛ̃] *m* quince.

coït kɔ'it] *m* coitus.

coke [kɔk] *m* coke; *petit ~* breeze; **cokerie** [kɔ'kri] *f* coking plant.

col [kɔl] *m* neck (*a. fig.*); *cost.* collar; *geog.* pass, col; *fig. ~ blanc (bleu)* white- (blue-)collar worker; *~ cassé* (*droit, rabattu*) wing (stand-up, turn-down) collar; *~ roulé* polo neck, *Am.* turtleneck; *à ~ Danton* open-necked (*shirt*); *faux ~* detachable *or* separate collar.

colchique ♀ [kɔl'ʃik] *m* colchicum.

coléoptère *zo.* [kɔleɔp'tɛ:r] *m* beetle; *~s pl.* coleoptera.

colère [kɔ'lɛ:r] **1.** *su./f* anger; *en ~* angry; *se mettre en ~* become angry; **2.** *adj.* angry; irascible (*person*); **coléreux, -euse** [kɔle'rø, ~'rø:z] hot-tempered, irascible; **colérique** [~'rik] choleric.

colifichet [kɔlifi'ʃɛ] *m* trinket; *~s pl.* rubbish *sg.*; 🕇 *rayon m des ~s* fancy goods department.

colimaçon *zo.* [kɔlima'sõ] *m* snail; *en ~* spiral (*staircase*).

colin *icht.* [kɔ'lɛ̃] *m* hake.

colin-maillard [kɔlɛ̃ma'ja:r] *m* game: blind-man's buff.

colique ⚕ [kɔ'lik] *f* colic; F stomach-ache; *sl. avoir la ~* have the wind up.

colis [kɔ'li] *m* packet, parcel; luggage; *par ~ postal* by parcel post.

collaborateur *m*, **-trice** *f* [kɔllabɔra'tœ:r, ~'tris] collaborator (*a. pol.*); associate; *review:* contributor; **collaboration** [~ra'sjõ] *f* collaboration (*a. pol.*); co-operation; *book:* joint authorship; **collaborer** [~'re] (1a) *v/i.* collaborate, co-operate; contribute (*to a journal etc.*).

collage [kɔ'la:ʒ] *m* pasting; gluing;

paper: sizing; F (*unmarried*) coha-bitation; *paint*. collage; **collant, e** [~'lɑ̃, ~'lɑ̃:t] **1.** *adj.* sticky, adhesive; *cost.* tight, close-fitting, skintight; *pej.* clinging; **2.** *su./m*: ~*s pl.* tights.

collatéral, e, *m/pl.* -**aux** [kɔllate'ral, ~'ro] **1.** *adj.* collateral; *eccl.* side-(*aisle*); **2.** *su.* relative, collateral; *su./m eccl.* side-aisle.

collateur *eccl.* † [kɔlla'tœ:r] *m* patron (*of a living*); **collation** [~'sjɔ̃] *f ⚜ etc.* granting, conferment; *eccl.* advowson; *typ.* checking, proofreading; *documents*: collation; light meal; **collationner** [~sjɔ'ne] (1a) *v/t.* collate, compare; check; *v/i.* have a light meal.

colle [kɔl] *f* paste, glue; gum; *paper etc.*: size; *fig.* poser, difficult question; *school*: detention; ~ *forte* glue.

collecte [kɔ'lɛkt] *f eccl. etc.* collection; collecting; *eccl. prayer*: collect; *faire une* ~ make a collection; **collecteur** [kɔllɛk'tœ:r] *m ⚡* collector; *⚡* commutator; ⊕ sewer; *mot.* ~ *d'admission* (*d'échappement*) intake (exhaust) manifold; **collectif, -ve** [~'tif, ~'ti:v] collective; **collection** [~'sjɔ̃] *f* collection; gathering; **collectionner** [~sjɔ'ne] (1a) *v/t.* collect; **collectiviser** [~tivi'ze] (1a) *v/t.* collectivize; communize; **collectivité** [~tivi'te] *f* community; group; common ownership.

collège [kɔ'lɛ:ʒ] *m* college; school; secondary grammar school; ~ *électoral* constituency; electoral body, *Am.* electoral college; *sacré* ~ College of Cardinals.

collégial, e, *m/pl.* -**aux** [kɔle'ʒjal, ~'ʒjo] **1.** *adj.* collegiate; collegial; **2.** *su./f* collegiate church; **collégialité** *pol.*, † *etc.* [~ʒjali'te] *f* collegial administration; **collégien, -enne** [~'ʒjɛ̃, ~'ʒjɛn] *su.* college-student; *su./m* schoolboy; *su./f* schoolgirl.

collègue [kɔl'lɛg] *su.* colleague.

coller [kɔ'le] (1a) *v/t.* stick; paste; glue; size (*paper*); clarify (*wine*); F put, stick (*s.th. in a place*); F plough (*a candidate*); se ~ stick; *sl.* cohabit, live (with, *avec*); *v/i.* stick; cling; *sl. ça colle!* all right!; *sl. cela ne colle pas* it is not going properly.

collerette [kɔl'rɛt] *f cost.* collarette; ⊕ *joint, pipe*: flange.

collet [kɔ'lɛ] *m* ♀, ⊕, *cost.* collar; *cost.* cape; *cuis.* neck, scrag; *tooth,*

violin, ⊕ *screw, chisel*: neck; ⊕ *pipe, etc.*: flange; snare (*for rabbits etc.*); *fig.* ~ *monté* strait-laced person; strait-laced; **colleter** [kɔl'te] (1c) *v/t.* (seize by the) collar; grapple with; *fig.* hug; *se* ~ come to grips; *v/i.* set snares (*for rabbits etc.*).

colleur *m,* -**euse** *f* [kɔ'lœ:r, ~'lø:z] paster; (*bill-*)sticker; *paper*: sizer; *sl. school*: stiff examiner; *sl.* liar.

collier [kɔ'lje] *m* necklace; collar (*a.* ⊕, ⚓, *zo., order*); ~ *de chien* dog collar; *coup m de* ~ *fig.* big effort; ⚡ sudden overload; *fig. reprendre le* ~ be back in harness.

collimateur [kɔlima'tœ:r] *m* collimator; *fig. avoir or prendre dans le* ~ train one's sights on.

colline [kɔ'lin] *f* hill.

collision [kɔlli'zjɔ̃] *f* collision.

collocation [kɔlɔka'sjɔ̃] *f ⚜* order of priority of creditors (*in bankruptcy*); *gramm.* collocation.

collodion ⚕ [kɔlɔ'djɔ̃] *m* collodion.

colloque [kɔl'lɔk] *m* conference; conversation; parley.

collusion ⚜ [kɔlly'zjɔ̃] *f* collusion; **collusoire** ⚜ [~'zwa:r] collusive.

collutoire [kɔlly'twa:r] *m* mouthwash.

collyre [kɔl'li:r] *m* eyewash.

colmater [kɔlma'te] (1a) *v/t.* seal (up *or* off); plug (up); fill in (*holes etc.*); ⚡ warp (*the soil*); ⚒ consolidate.

colocataire [kɔlɔka'tɛ:r] *su.* joint tenant; co-tenant.

colombe *orn.* [kɔ'lɔ̃:b] *f* pigeon; dove (*a. pol.*); **colombier** [kɔlɔ̃'bje] *m* dovecot(e); pigeon-house; **colombin, e** [~'bɛ̃, ~'bin] **1.** *adj.* dove-like; dove-colo(u)red; **2.** *su./m orn.* stock-dove; ⚒ lead ore; *su./f* ⚡ pigeon-dung.

colon [kɔ'lɔ̃] *m* small holder; settler, colonist.

côlon *anat.* [ko'lɔ̃] *m* colon.

colonel ⚔ [kɔlɔ'nɛl] *m* colonel; **colonelle** [~] *f* colonel's wife.

colonial, e, *m/pl.* -**aux** [kɔlɔ'njal, ~'njo] **1.** *adj.* colonial; *denrées f/pl.* ~*es* colonial produce *sg.*; **2.** *su./m* colonial; *su./f* ⚔ colonial troops *pl.*; **colonialisme** *pol.* [~nja'lism] *m* colonialism; **colonie** [~'ni] *f* colony, settlement; ~ *de vacances* holiday camp; **colonisateur, -trice** [kɔlɔ-niza'tœ:r, ~'tris] **1.** *adj.* colonizing; **2.** *su.* colonizer; **colonisation** [~za'sjɔ̃ *f* colonization, settling; **coloniser** [~'ze] (1a) *v/t.* colonize, settle.

colonne [kɔ'lɔn] *f* △, ✗, anat. column; △ pillar; ⚓ en~ line ahead; ~ Morris advertizing column *or* pillar.

colophane [kɔlɔ'fan] *f* rosin.

colorant, e [kɔlɔ'rɑ̃, ~'rɑ̃:t] **1.** *adj.* colo(u)ring; **2.** *su./m* colo(u)ring (matter); **colorer** [~'re] (1a) *v/t.* colo(u)r, stain; dye; **colorier** [~'rje] (1o) *v/t.* colo(u)r; coloris [~'ri] *m* colo(u)r(ing); *fig.* hue.

colossal, e, *m/pl.* **-aux** [kɔlɔ'sal, ~'so] colossal, gigantic; **colosse** [~'lɔs] *m* colossus; F giant.

colportage [kɔlpɔr'ta:ʒ] *m* hawking, peddling; **colporter** [~'te] (1a) *v/t.* hawk, peddle; *fig.* spread (*news*); **colporteur** *m*, **-euse** *f* [~'tœ:r, ~'tø:z] hawker; pedlar, *Am.* peddler; *fig.* newsmonger.

coltiner [kɔlti'ne] (1a) *v/t.* carry (*loads*) (on one's back); F *fig.* se ~ saddle o.s. with (*s.th., s.o.*); **coltineur** [~'nœ:r] *m* heavy porter; ~ de charbon coal-heaver.

colza ♀ [kɔl'za] *m* rape, colza; rapeseed.

coma 🐟 [kɔ'ma] *m* coma; **comateux, -euse** 🐟 [~ma'tø, ~'tø:z] comatose.

combat [kɔ̃'ba] *m* ✗ combat, battle, engagement; struggle (*a. fig.*); *fig.* contest; hors de ~ disabled; out of action; **combatif, -ve** [kɔ̃ba'tif, ~'ti:v] pugnacious; **combattant** [~'tɑ̃] *m* combatant, fighting man; fighter; *zo.* game-cock; ancien ~ ex-service man, veteran; **combattre** [kɔ̃'batr] (4a) *vt/i.* fight.

combe [kɔ̃:b] *f* coomb, dale, dell.

combien [kɔ̃'bjɛ̃] *adv.* how (many *or* much); ~ de temps how long; ~ de ... qui (*or* que) (*sbj.*) however much ... (*inf.*); F le ~ sommes-nous? what day of the month is it?

combinaison [kɔ̃binɛ'zɔ̃] *f* combination, arrangement, plan; *cost.* overalls *pl.*, boiler-suit; *cost.* combinations *pl.*; ✈ flying suit; *woman:* slip; **combinateur** ⚡ [~na'tœ:r] *m*: ~ de couplage controller; **combine** F [kɔ̃'bin] *f* plan, scheme; **combiner** [~bi'ne] (1a) *v/t.* combine, devise, concoct; se ~ combine.

comble [kɔ̃:bl] **1.** *su./m fig.* summit, height; △ roof(ing); au ~ de la joie overjoyed; de fond en ~ from top to bottom; mettre le ~ à crown; pour ~ to cap it all; c'est le *or* un ~! that beats all!; **2.** *adj.* heaped up; packed (*house, room*); **comblé, e** [kɔ̃'ble] overjoyed; **comblement** [kɔ̃blə-'mɑ̃] *m* filling in; **combler** [~'ble] (1a) *v/t.* fill (in); ✗, ✝ make good (*a deficit, casualties*); *fig.* fulfill; *fig.* gratify; *fig.* ~ q. de qch. shower s.th. on s.o.

combustibilité [kɔ̃bystibili'te] *f* inflammability; **combustible** [~'tibl] **1.** *adj.* inflammable; combustible; **2.** *su./m* fuel; **combustion** [~'tjɔ̃] *f* combustion, burning; ~ continue slow combustion.

comédie [kɔme'di] *f* comedy; *fig.* playacting; *fig.* jouer la ~ playact; **comédien, -enne** [~'djɛ̃, ~'djɛn] **1.** *su.* comedian; *su./m* actor; *su./f* actress; **2.** *adj.* theatrical.

comestible [kɔmɛs'tibl] **1.** *adj.* edible, eatable; **2.** *su./m* article of food; ~s *pl.* provisions, victuals.

comète *astr.* [kɔ'mɛt] *f* comet.

comice [kɔ'mis] *m* show; gathering; *hist.* ~s *pl.* electoral meeting *sg.*; ~ agricole agricultural show, cattle-show.

comique [kɔ'mik] **1.** *adj.* comic (*actor, author*); comical, funny; **2.** *su./m* comedian, humorist; comic actor; comedy-writer; comedy.

comité [kɔmi'te] *m* committee, board; ~ d'arbitrage arbitration board; ~ de surveillance vigilance committee; petit ~ little *or* informal meeting.

commandant [kɔmɑ̃'dɑ̃] *m* ✗, ⚓ commanding officer, commander; ✈ squadron-leader; ✗ ~ de bataillon, ~ d'escadron major; ~ en chef commander-in-chief; **commande** [~'mɑ̃:d] *f* ✝ order; ⊕, ✈ control; ⊕ lever; *mot.* drive; ✝ bulletin *m* de ~ order-form; de ~ feigned; *eccl.* of obligation; F essential; sur ~ to order; **commandement** [~mɑ̃d'mɑ̃] *m* ✗, *a. fig.* command; instruction; ⚖ summons *sg.*; *eccl.* commandment; **commander** [~mɑ̃'de] (1a) *v/t.* command (*a. fig.*), order (s.th. from s.o., qch. à q.); control; dominate; ~ à control; se ~ control o.s.; lead into each other *or* one another (*rooms*); cela ne se commande pas it does not depend upon our will; *v/i.* give orders; **commandeur** [∼'dœːr] *m* *order of knighthood*: commander.

commanditaire ✝ [kɔmɑ̃di'tɛːr] *m* sleeping *or* Am. silent partner; **commandite** [∼'dit] *f* (*a.* *société f en* ∼) limited partnership; **commanditer** ✝ [∼'te] (1a) *v/t.* finance (*an enterprise*); become a sleeping partner in.

comme [kɔm] **1.** *adv.* as, like; how; in the way of; ∼ *ça* like that; just (so); F ∼ *ci* ∼ *ça* so so; F *c'est tout* ∼ it comes to the same thing; ∼ *il faut* proper(ly *adv.*); **2.** *cj.* as, seeing that; *temporal:* just as.

commémoratif, -ve [kɔmemɔra'tif, ∼'tiːv] commemorative (of, *de*); memorial (*service*); *fête f* ∼ve festival of remembrance; **commémoration** [∼ra'sjɔ̃] *f* commemoration; **commémorer** [∼'re] (1a) *v/t.* commemorate.

commençant, e [kɔmɑ̃'sɑ̃, ∼'sɑ̃ːt] **1.** *adj.* beginning, early; **2.** *su.* beginner; **commencement** [∼mɑ̃s'mɑ̃] *m* beginning, start, outset; **commencer** [∼mɑ̃'se] (1k) *vt/i.* begin; start.

commendataire *eccl.* [kɔmɑ̃da'tɛːr] *m* commendator.

commensal *m, e f* [kɔmɑ̃'sal] companion at table, table-companion; regular guest.

commensurable ⚗ [kɔmɑ̃sy'rabl] commensurable (with, to *avec*).

comment [kɔ'mɑ̃] **1.** *adv.* how; what: **2.** *int.* what!; why!; F *et* ∼! and how!; **3.** *su./m/inv.* why; *les* ∼ *et les pourquoi* the whys and the wherefores.

commentaire [kɔmɑ̃'tɛːr] *m* commentary; *fig.* comment; **commentateur** *m, -trice* f [∼ta'tœːr, ∼'tris] commentator; **commenter** [∼'te] (1a) *v/t.* comment upon (*a.* *fig.* = *criticise*).

commérage [kɔme'raːʒ] *m* gossip.

commerçant, e [kɔmɛr'sɑ̃, ∼'sɑ̃ːt] **1.** *adj.* commercial; business...; mercantile; *très* ∼ very busy (*street*); **2.** *su./m* tradesman, merchant; *les* ∼s *pl.* tradespeople; **commerce** [∼'mɛrs] *m* trade, commerce; commercial world; ✝ dealings *pl.*; ∼ *de détail* retail trade; ∼ *d'outre-mer* overseas trade; *registre m du* ∼ Commercial Register; **commercer** [kɔmɛr'se] (1k) *v/i.*

(with, *avec*) trade, deal; *fig.* have dealings; **commercial, e**, *m/pl.* **-aux** [∼'sjal, ∼'sjo] commercial, trading, business.

commère [kɔ'mɛːr] *f* ✝ *eccl.* godmother; gossip; crony.

commettant [kɔmɛ'tɑ̃] *m* ⚖✝, ✝ principal; *pol.* ∼s *pl.* constituents; **commettre** [∼'mɛtr] (4v) *v/t.* commit.

comminatoire [kɔmina'twaːr] comminatory; *fig.* threatening.

commis, e [kɔ'mi, ∼'miːz] **1.** *p.p.* of *commettre*; **2.** *su./m* clerk; agent; (shop-)assistant; ∼ *voyageur* commercial traveller, Am. travelling salesman.

commisération [kɔmizera'sjɔ̃] *f* pity; commiseration.

commissaire [kɔmi'sɛːr] *m* commissioner; *police:* superintendent; ⚓ purser; *sp.* steward; ✝ ∼ *aux comptes* auditor; **∼-priseur,** *pl.* **∼s-priseurs** [∼sɛrpri'zœːr] *m* auctioneer; official valuer; **commissariat** [∼sa'rja] *m* commissioner's office; central police station.

commission [kɔmi'sjɔ̃] *f* commission; *admin. a.* committee, board; message; errand; *faire la* ∼ *à q.* give s.o. the message; **commissionnaire** [∼sjɔ'nɛːr] delivery boy *or* man; messenger; ✝ commission agent; ∼ *de transport* forwarding agent; ∼ *en gros* factor; **commissionner** [∼sjɔ'ne] (1a) *v/t.* commission.

commissure [kɔmi'syːr] *f* commissure; ∼ *des lèvres* corner of the mouth.

commode [kɔ'mɔd] **1.** *adj.* convenient; comfortable; handy; easygoing (*person*); good-natured; **2.** *su./f* chest of drawers, Am. *a.* highboy; **commodément** [kɔmɔde'me] *adv.* of *commode 1*; **commodité** [∼di'te] *f* convenience; comfort; ∼s *pl.* public convenience *sg.*

commotion [kɔmɔ'sjɔ̃] *f* commotion, disturbance; ⚡, ⚕ shock; ⚕ concussion.

commuer ⚖✝ [kɔ'mɥe] (1p) *v/t.* commute (to, *en*).

commun, e [kɔ'mœ̃, ∼'myn] **1.** *adj.* common; usual; joint; vulgar; ✝ average, mean (*tare*); *chose* f ∼e common cause; *faire bourse* ∼e pool resources; *sens m* ∼ common sense; **2.** *su./m* generality, common run;

common funds *pl.*; † servants *pl.*; ~s *pl.* outbuildings; conveniences; *en* ~ in common; *su./f admin.* commune, (*approx.*) parish; *hist.* ♀e Commune (*1789, a. 1871*); *parl. Chambre f des* ~es House of Commons *pl.*; **communal, e**, *m/pl.* -aux [kɔmyˈnal, ~ˈno] common; communal; parish ...; **communard** *hist.* [~ˈnaːr] *m* communard (*supporter of the 1871 Paris Commune*); **communauté** [~noˈte] *f eccl., admin., a. fig.* community; ⚹ joint estate; *pol.* ♀ French Community; ♀ *Économique Européenne* European Economic Community; ~ *de travail school:* group activity; **communément** [~neˈmɑ̃] *adv. of commun 1.*

communiant *m*, **e** *f eccl.* [kɔmyˈnjɑ̃, ~ˈnjɑ̃ːt] communicant; **communicable** [kɔmyniˈkabl] communicable; **communicatif, -ve** [~kaˈtif, ~ˈtiːv] communicative; infectious (*laughter*); **communication** [~kaˈsjɔ̃] *f* communication; message; (telephone) call; *teleph.* ~ *locale* (*interurbaine*) local (long-distance) call; *teleph. donner la* ~ put a call through; *teleph. mauvaise* ~ wrong number; **communier** *eccl.* [kɔmyˈnje] (1o) *v/i.* communicate; *v/t.* administer Holy Communion to (*s.o.*); **communion** [~ˈnjɔ̃] *f* communion (*a. eccl.*); **communiqué** [kɔmyniˈke] *m* official statement, communiqué; *radio:* news *sg.*; bulletin; ~ *de presse* press release; **communiquer** [~] (1m) *vt/i.* communicate; *v/i.* be in communication *or* connection; ~ *avec* lead into; (*faire*) ~ connect; *v/t.:* se ~ spread (to, à); be communicative (*person*).
communisant, e [kɔmyniˈzɑ̃, ~ˈzɑ̃ːt] **1.** *adj.* communistic; **2.** *su. pol.* fellow-traveller, communist sympathizer; **communisme** [~ˈnism] *m* communism; **communiste** [~ˈnist] *su., a. adj.* communist.
commutateur ⚡ [kɔmytaˈtœːr] *m* commutator; *light:* switch; **commutation** [~ˈsjɔ̃] *f* commutation (*a.* ⚹); ⚡ changing over; *de* ~ switch-...; **commutatrice** ⚡ [~ˈtris] *f* rotary transformer; **commuter** ⚡ [kɔmyˈte] (1a) *v/t.* change over.
compacité [kɔ̃pasiˈte] *f* compactness; *metal:* density; **compact, e** [~ˈpakt] compact; dense.

compagne [kɔ̃ˈpaɲ] *f* companion; wife; mate; **compagnie** [kɔ̃paˈɲi] *f* company (*a.* ✝, ✕, *a. person*); ⚓ division; society; *de ou en* ~ together; *tenir* ~ *à q.* keep s.o. company; **compagnon** [~ˈɲɔ̃] *m* companion, comrade; mate (*a.* ⊕), partner; ⊕ journeyman; ~ *de route* fellow traveller; **compagnonnage** † [~ɲɔˈnaːʒ] *m* trade-guild; time of service as journeyman.
comparable [kɔ̃paˈrabl] comparable; **comparaison** [~rɛˈzɔ̃] *f* comparison; simile.
comparaître ⚹ [kɔ̃paˈrɛːtr] (4k) *v/i.* appear; *faire* ~ *devant* bring before.
comparatif, -ve [kɔ̃paraˈtif, ~ˈtiːv] *adj., a. gramm. su./m* comparative; **comparé, e** [~ˈre] comparative (*grammar, history, etc.*); **comparer** [~ˈre] (1a) *v/t.* compare (to, with à, avec).
comparse [kɔ̃ˈpars] *m thea.* supernumerary; ⚹ super; *fig.* confederate.
compartiment [kɔ̃partiˈmɑ̃] *m* 🚂, ship, ceiling, etc.: compartment; partition; division; *draughts, chess, etc.:* square; ~ *de congélation* freezing compartment, freezer.
comparution ⚹ [kɔ̃paryˈsjɔ̃] *f* appearance.
compas [kɔ̃ˈpɑ] *m* compasses *pl.*; ⚓ etc. compass; *mot. hood:* arms *pl.*; standard, scale; *&* ~ *à pointes sèches* dividers *pl.*; *surv.* ~ *de relèvement* azimuth compass; ⚓ ~ *gyroscopique* gyro-compass; **compassé, e** [kɔ̃paˈse] formal, stiff; regular; **compasser** [~] (1a) *v/t.* measure with compasses; *fig.* consider, weigh, study; ⚓ ~ *la carte* prick the chart.
compassion [kɔ̃paˈsjɔ̃] *f* compassion, pity.
compatible [kɔ̃paˈtibl] compatible.
compatir [kɔ̃paˈtiːr] (2a) *v/i.:* ~ *à* sympathize with; bear with; **compatissant, e** [~tiˈsɑ̃, ~ˈsɑ̃ːt] (*pour, to*[*wards*]) compassionate, tender; sympathetic; indulgent.
compatriote [kɔ̃patriˈɔt] *su.* compatriot; *su./m* fellow-countryman; *su./f* fellow-countrywoman.
compensateur, -trice [kɔ̃pɑ̃saˈtœːr, ~ˈtris] **1.** *adj.* compensating; ⚡ equalizing (*current*); *phot.* compensating (*filter, screen*); *phys.* pen-

dule m ~ compensation pendulum; **2.** *su./m* compensator; ⚡ trimmer; **compensation** [~sa'sjɔ̃] *f* compensation; ⊕, ⚡ balancing; *sp.* handicapping; ✝ *accord m de* ~ barter agreement; ✝ *caisse f de* ~ equalization fund; ✝ *chambre f de* ~ clearing-house; **compenser** [~'se] (1a) *v/t.* compensate, make up for; ⊕ balance; ⚓ adjust (*a compass*); *sp.* handicap.

compère [kɔ̃'pɛːr] *m eccl.* godfather; *thea.* compère; *fig.* accomplice; F comrade, pal; *bon* ~ good fellow; **~-loriot**, *pl.* **~s-loriots** ⚡ [~pɛrlɔ-'rjo] *m* sty.

compétence [kɔ̃pe'tɑ̃ːs] *f* competence (*a.* ⚖); skill, ability; **compétent, e** [~'tɑ̃, ~'tɑ̃ːt] competent (*a.* ⚖); **compéter** [~'te] (1f) *v/i.* ⚖ be within the jurisdiction (of, *à*); belong by right (to, *à*).

compétiteur *m*, **-trice** *f* [kɔ̃peti-'tœːr, ~'tris] competitor, candidate, rival (for, *à*); **compétitif, -ve** [~'tif, ~'tiːv] competitive (*prices*); rival; **compétition** [~'sjɔ̃] *f* competition, rivalry.

compiler [kɔ̃pi'le] (1a) *v/t.* compile.

complainte [kɔ̃'plɛ̃ːt] *f* lament; ⚖ complaint; plaintive ballad or song.

complaire [kɔ̃'plɛːr] (4z) *v/i.* be pleasing; ~ *à* please, humo(u)r (*s.o.*); *v/t.*: *se* ~ take pleasure (in *ger.*, *à inf.*; in s.th., *dans or en qch.*); **complaisance** [kɔ̃plɛ'zɑ̃ːs] *f* obligingness, kindness; self-satisfaction, complacency; ✝ *effet m de* ~ accommodation bill; **complaisant, e** [~'zɑ̃, ~'zɑ̃ːt] obliging; self-satisfied, complacent.

complément [kɔ̃ple'mɑ̃] *m* complement (*a.* ✂, *a. gramm.*); *gramm.* object; **complémentaire** [~mɑ̃-'tɛːr] complementary (*a.* ⚗); supplementary; further (*information*).

complet, -ète [kɔ̃'plɛ, ~'plɛt] **1.** *adj.* complete; full (*theatre etc.*); ~! full up; *hotel*: no vacancies; *thea.* full house; *café m* ~ continental breakfast; **2.** *su./m* (*a.* ~-*veston*) suit; *au* (*grand*) ~ whole, entire; **complètement** [~plɛt'mɑ̃] **1.** *su./m* completion; ⚔ bringing up to strength; **2.** *adv.* completely, thoroughly, utterly; **compléter** [~ple'te] (1f) *v/t.* complete, fill up; ⚔ bring up to strength; replenish (*stores*).

complexe [kɔ̃'plɛks] **1.** *adj.* complex; complicated; *gramm.*, *a.* ⚕ compound; **2.** *su./m* complex; **complexé, e** [~plɛk'se] **1.** *adj.* suffering from a complex; **2.** *su.* person suffering from a complex.

complexion [kɔ̃plɛk'sjɔ̃] *f* constitution; temperament.

complexité [kɔ̃plɛksi'te] *f* complexity.

complication [kɔ̃plika'sjɔ̃] *f* complication (*a.* ⚕); complexity.

complice [kɔ̃'plis] *adj.*, *a. su.* accessory (to, *de*); accomplice (of, *de*); **complicité** [~plisi'te] *f* complicity; ⚖ aiding and abetting, abetment.

compliment [kɔ̃pli'mɑ̃] *m* compliment; congratulation; flattery; ~*s pl.* kind regards; **complimenter** [~mɑ̃'te] (1a) *v/t.* compliment, congratulate (on *de*, *sur*).

compliqué, e [kɔ̃pli'ke] complicated, elaborate, intricate; ⚕ compound (*fracture*); **compliquer** [~] (1m) *v/t.* complicate; ⚕ *la maladie s'est compliquée* complications set in.

complot [kɔ̃'plo] *m* plot, conspiracy; *former un* ~ hatch a plot; **comploter** [~plɔ'te] (1a) *v/t.* plot, scheme (to *inf.*, *de inf.*); *v/i.* conspire.

componction [kɔ̃pɔ̃k'sjɔ̃] *f* compunction; F *avec* ~ solemnly.

comportement [kɔ̃pɔrtə'mɑ̃] *m* behavio(u)r; *psych. etc. de* ~ behavio(u)ral; **comporter** [kɔ̃pɔr'te] (1a) *v/t.* consist of, be composed of; comprise, include; *fig.* involve; require; *se* ~ behave, act.

composant, e [kɔ̃po'zɑ̃, ~'zɑ̃ːt] *adj.*, *a. su.* component; **composé, e** [~'ze] **1.** *adj.* compound (*a.* ⚕, *a. gramm.*); ⚘ composite; *fig.* composed; impassive; *être* ~ *de* be made up of, consist of; **2.** *su./m* compound; **composer** [~'ze] (1a) *v/t.* make up; set up; form; compose; arrange; *typ.* set; ⚘ find the resultant of; ~ *son visage* compose one's countenance; *se* ~ *de* be made up of, consist of; *v/i.* compose music etc.; write a composition; come to terms (with, *avec*); **compositeur, -trice** [~zi'tœːr, ~'tris] *su.* ♪ composer; *typ.* compositor, type-setter; *su./m typ.* type-setting machine; **composition** [~zi'sjɔ̃] *f* making-up; setting-up; formation; composition; composing (*a. typ.*); *typ.* type-setting; *school:* essay; examination

(paper); *amener q.* à~ get s.o. to come to terms; *venir* à~ come to terms.
compost ✔ [kɔ̃ˈpɔst] *m* compost; **composter** [kɔ̃pɔsˈte] (1a) *v/t.* ✔ treat with compost; date *or* punch (*a ticket*); **composteur** [~ˈtœːr] *m typ.* composing-stick; dating stamp; dating and numbering machine.
compote [kɔ̃ˈpɔt] *f* stewed fruit; *en* ~ stewed; *fig.* to *or* in a pulp; **compotier** [~pɔˈtje] *m* compote-dish; fruit-dish.
compréhensible [kɔ̃preɑ̃ˈsibl] comprehensible, understandable; **compréhension** [~ˈsjɔ̃] *f* understanding; **comprendre** [kɔ̃ˈprɑ̃ːdr] (4aa) *v/t.* understand; include; F *je comprends!* I see!
compresse ✔ [kɔ̃ˈprɛs] *f* compress; **compresser** F [kɔ̃prɛˈse] (1a) *v/t.* pack; **compresseur** [~ˈsœːr] *m* compressor; *mot.* supercharger; road-roller; **compressible** [~ˈsibl] compressible; **compression** [~ˈsjɔ̃] *f* compression; ⊕ crushing; repression; ✔ cutback, restriction.
comprimé ✔ [kɔ̃priˈme] *m* tablet; **comprimer** [~] (1a) *v/t.* compress; *fig.* repress; hold back (*emotions etc.*); ✔ cut back (*expenses etc.*).
compris, e [kɔ̃ˈpri, ~ˈpriːz] 1. *p.p.* of *comprendre*; 2. *adj.* (*inv. before su.*): *non* ~ exclusive of; *service m* ~ service included; *tout* ~ all in; *y* ~ including.
compromettre [kɔ̃prɔˈmɛtr] (4v) *v/t.* compromise; endanger, jeopardize; *fig.* implicate; **compromis** [~ˈmi] *m* compromise (*a.* 🜨), arrangement (*a.* ✔); **compromission** [~mi'sjɔ̃] *f* compromising; compromise.
comptabilité ✔ [kɔ̃tabiliˈte] *f* bookkeeping, accountancy; counting-house; accountancy department; ~ *en partie double* (*simple*) double (single) entry book-keeping; **comptable** [~ˈtabl] 1. *adj.* accountable, responsible; 2. *su.* book-keeper, accountant; **comptant** [~ˈtɑ̃] 1. *adj./m* ready (*cash*); 2. *su./m* cash, ready money; *au* ~ (for) cash; 3. *adv.* in cash, F on the nail; **compte** [kɔ̃ːt] *m* account; count; reckoning; number; *fig.* profit, advantage; ~ *à rebours* rocket: countdown; ~ *bloqué* (*courant, ouvert*) blocked (current, open) account; ~ *de chèques postaux* postal cheque account; ~

d'épargne savings account; ~ *de virement* clearing-account; ~ *rendu* account, report; *book etc.*: review; *à* ~ on account; *fig. à bon* ~ cheap; *à ce* ~ in that case; *en fin de* ~ after all; *mettre qch. sur le* ~ *de* ascribe s.th. to; *régler un* ~ settle an account; *se rendre* ~ *de* realize; *tenir* ~ *de qch.* take s.th. into account; **compte-gouttes** [kɔ̃tˈgut] *m/inv.* dropper; ⊕ drip-feed lubricator; **compter** [kɔ̃ˈte] (1a) *v/t.* reckon, count (up); value; ✔ charge; expect; *v/i.* count, rely (on, *sur*); reckon; **compteur** [~ˈtœːr] *m* meter; register; *person:* counter; ~ *à gaz* gas-meter; ✔ ~ *de courant* electricity meter; ~ *de Geiger* Geiger counter; *mot.* ~ *de stationnement* parking meter; *mot.* ~ *de vitesse* speedometer; **comptoir** [~ˈtwaːr] *m* ✔ counter; *public house:* bar; ✔ bank; ✔ ~ *d'escompte* discount bank.
compulser [kɔ̃pylˈse] (1a) *v/t.* examine, check (*documents*).
compulsif, -ive [kɔ̃pylsif, -iːv] compulsive. [pute.]
computer [kɔ̃pyˈte] (1a) *v/t.* compute.]
comte [kɔ̃ːt] *m* earl; (non-English) count; **comté** [kɔ̃ˈte] *m* county; shire; **comtesse** [~ˈtɛs] *f* countess.
con, conne *sl.* [kɔ̃, kɔn] 1. *adj.* stupid; *il est* ~ *comme la lune* he is an absolute idiot; 2. *su.* idiot; *à la* ~ stupid, foolish; lousy.
concasser ⊕ [kɔ̃kɑˈse] (1a) *v/t.* crush, grind, break up; **concasseur** [~ˈsœːr] *m* breaker, crushing-mill.
concave [kɔ̃ˈkaːv] concave. [grant.]
concéder [kɔ̃seˈde] (1f) *v/t.* concede,]
concentration [kɔ̃sɑ̃trɑˈsjɔ̃] *f* concentration; condensation; *camp m de* ~ concentration camp; **concentré, e** [~ˈtre] 1. *adj. fig.* reserved; abstracted (*look*); 2. *su./m* extract; concentrate; **concentrer** [~ˈtre] (1a) *v/t.* concentrate (*a.* 🜋); intensify; focus (*light*); *fig.* restrain (*one's feelings*); *se* ~ *sur* be centred upon; **concentrique** ✔ *etc.* [~ˈtrik] concentric.
concept [kɔ̃ˈsɛpt] *m* concept; **conceptible** [kɔ̃sɛpˈtibl] conceivable; **conceptif, -ve** [~ˈtif, ~ˈtiːv] conceptive; **conception** [~ˈsjɔ̃] *f* conception (*a. fig.*); idea; ~ *du monde* philosophy of life.

concernant [kɔsɛr'nɑ̃] *prp.* concerning, regarding; **concerner** [~'ne] (1a) *v/t.* concern, regard; *en ce qui concerne* ... with regard to ..., as far as ... is concerned; in matters of ...

concert [kɔ'sɛːr] *m* concert; *fig.* agreement; *fig. de ~ (avec)* together (with); in unison (with); *agir de ~* take concerted action; **concertation** [kɔsɛrtɑ'sjɔ̃] *f* consultation(s *pl.*), dialog(ue); **concerter** [kɔsɛr-'te] (1a) *v/t.* (pre)arrange; plan; *se ~* concert *or* work together; **concerto** ♩ [~'to] *m* concerto.

concession [kɔsɛ'sjɔ̃] *f* concession, grant; *~ à perpétuité grave:* grant in perpetuity; **concessionnaire** [~sjɔ'nɛːr] **1.** *adj.* concessionary; **2.** *su./m* grantee (*of land*); ✝ licence-holder, concession-holder.

concevable [kɔs'vabl] conceivable; **concevoir** [~'vwaːr] (3a) *v/t.* conceive (*a. physiol., a. fig.*); understand; imagine; word (*a message*).

conchoïde ⅋ [kɔ̃kɔ'id] *f* conchoid.

concierge [kɔ̃'sjɛrʒ] *su.* door-keeper; caretaker; *su./m* porter; *su./f* portress; **conciergerie** [~sjɛrʒə'ri] *f* caretaker's lodge; post of caretaker; *a. hist.* ♀ *a prison in Paris.*

conciliable [kɔ̃si'ljabl] reconcilable; **conciliabule** [~lja'byl] *m* secret meeting; *eccl.* conventicle; F confabulation; **conciliant, e** [~'ljɑ̃, ~'ljɑ̃ːt] conciliatory; **conciliateur** *m*, **-trice** *f* [~lja'tœːr, ~'tris] peacemaker; **conciliation** [~lja'sjɔ̃] *f* conciliation; **concilier** [~'lje] (1o) *v/t.* reconcile, conciliate; *se ~ gain,* win (*s.o.'s esteem etc.*); *fig.* win (*s.o.*) (over); *se ~ avec* agree with.

concis, e [kɔ̃'si, ~'siːz] concise, terse; **concision** [~si'sjɔ̃] *f* concision, terseness, brevity.

concitoyen *m*, **-enne** *f* [kɔ̃sitwa'jɛ̃, ~'jen] fellow-citizen.

concluant, e [kɔ̃kly'ɑ̃, ~'ɑ̃ːt] conclusive; **conclure** [~'klyːr] (4g) *v/t.* conclude (*a. a treaty, a. fig.*), finish; *fig.* infer (from, de); *~ à* conclude in favo(u)r of; **conclusion** [~kly'zjɔ̃] *f* conclusion; end; inference; ⚖ finding; ⚖ *~s pl.* pleas; case *sg.*; ⚖ *déposer des ~s* deliver a statement.

concocter F [kɔ̃kɔk'te] (1a) *v/t.* concoct; work out, devise. [ber.)

concombre ⚘ [kɔ̃'kɔ̃ːbr] *m* cucum-)

concomitant, e [kɔ̃kɔmi'tɑ̃, ~'tɑ̃ːt] concomitant.

concordance [kɔ̃kɔr'dɑ̃ːs] *f* concordance (*a. bibl.*); *gramm.* agreement; **concordant, e** [~'dɑ̃, ~'dɑ̃ːt] harmonious; **concordat** [~'da] *m eccl.* concordat; ✝ bankrupt's certificate.

concorde [kɔ̃'kɔrd] *f* harmony, concord; **concorder** [~kɔr'de] (1a) *v/i.* concur, agree; ✝ compound with one's creditors.

concourant, e [kɔ̃ku'rɑ̃, ~'rɑ̃t] ⅋ *etc.* convergent; concerted (*efforts etc.*); **concourir** [~'riːr] (2i) compete; *~ à* contribute to, work towards; **concours** [~'kuːr] *m* assistance; help, aid; ✝ gathering; competition; competitive examination; show (*of agricultural products, cattle, horses, etc.*); ⅋ convergence; *~ hippique* horse show; *hors ~* not competing (for prize); *fig.* unequalled, outstanding.

concret, -ète [kɔ̃'krɛ, ~'krɛt] concrete; **concréter** [~kre'te] (1f) *v/t. a. se ~* solidify, congeal; **concrétion** [~'sjɔ̃] *f* coagulation; concretion (*a. ⚕*). [cubinage.)

concubinage [kɔ̃kybi'naːʒ] *m* con-)

concupiscence [kɔ̃kypi'sɑ̃ːs] *f* concupiscence, lust; **concupiscent, e** [~'sɑ̃, ~'sɑ̃ːt] concupiscent.

concurremment [kɔ̃kyra'mɑ̃] *adv.* jointly; ✝ in competition; ⚖ *venir ~* rank equally; **concurrence** [~-'rɑ̃ːs] *f* coincidence; competition, rivalry; *~ déloyale* unfair competition; ✝ *faire ~ à* compete with; ✝ *jusqu'à ~ de* to the amount of; *sans ~* unrivalled; **concurrent, e** [~'rɑ̃, ~'rɑ̃ːt] **1.** *adj.* co(-)operating; rival, competing; **2.** *su.* competitor; candidate (*for a post*).

concussion [kɔ̃ky'sjɔ̃] *f* misappropriation of funds; extortion; **concussionnaire** [~sjɔ'nɛːr] **1.** *adj.* guilty of misappropriation *or* extortion; **2.** *su.* official guilty of misappropriation *or* extortion.

condamnable [kɔ̃dɑ'nabl] blameworthy; criminal; guilty; **condamnation** [~na'sjɔ̃] *f* condemnation; ⚖ sentence; ⚖ conviction; ⚖ *~ à vie* life sentence; **condamner** [~'ne] (1a) *v/t.* condemn; ⚖ sentence; ⚖ convict; *fig.* blame, censure; 🏛 block up; board up (*a window*).

condensateur ⚡ *etc.* [kɔ̃dɑ̃sa'tœːr] *m* condenser; ~ *à plaques* plate condenser; **condensé** [~'se] *m journ.* digest; précis; sum-up; **condenser** [~'se] (1a) *v/t.* condense; **condenseur** ⊕ [~'sœːr] *m* condenser.

condescendance [kɔ̃desɑ̃'dɑ̃:s] *f* condescension; *avec* ~ condescending(ly *adv.*); **condescendre** [~'sɑ̃:dr] (4a) *v/i.* condescend (to *inf.*, *à inf.*); comply (with, *à*).

condiment [kɔ̃di'mɑ̃] *m* condiment; seasoning.

condisciple [kɔ̃di'sipl] *m* schoolfellow; fellow-student.

condition [kɔ̃di'sjɔ̃] *f* condition (*a. sp.*); circumstances *pl.*; rank; ~s *pl.* terms; ~s *de travail* working conditions; ~ *préalable* condition precedent; *à* ~ on condition, ✝ on approval; *à* ~ *que* provided *or* providing (that); *mettre en* ~ *sp. etc.* make fit; *fig.* condition; **conditionné, e** [kɔ̃disjɔ'ne] in ... condition; ⚡, *phls.* conditioned; **conditionnel, -elle** [~'nɛl] *adj., a. gramm. su./m* conditional; **conditionner** [~'ne] (1a) *v/t.* condition (*the air, wool, etc., a. fig.*); ✝ package.

condoléance [kɔ̃dɔle'ɑ̃:s] *f* condolence; *sincères* ~s *pl.* deepest sympathy *sg.*

conductance ⚡ [kɔ̃dyk'tɑ̃:s] *f* conductivity; **conducteur, -trice** [~'tœːr, ~'tris] 1. *adj.* ⚡ conducting; ⊕ driving; 2. *su.* leader; *mot. etc.* driver; 🚗 guard, *Am.* conductor; *su./m* ⚡ *phys.* conductor; ⚡ main; **conductibilité** ⚡, *phys.* [~tibili'te] *f* conductivity; **conductible** [~'tibl] conductive; **conduction** [~'sjɔ̃] *f* conduction; **conduire** [kɔ̃'dɥiːr] (4h) *v/t.* conduct (*a. ♪, ⊕*); lead (to *à*); *mot.* steer (*a. ♣*), drive; ✝ manage, run; *mot. permis m de* ~ driving licence, *Am.* driver's license; *se* ~ behave; **conduisis** [~dɥi'zi] *1st p. sg. p.s. of conduire;* **conduisons** [~dɥi'zɔ̃] *1st p. pl. pres. of conduire;* **conduit, e** [~'dɥi, ~'dɥit] 1. *p.p. of conduire;* 2. *su./m* conduit, pipe, passage; *anat.* duct; ~ *principal* main; ~ *souterrain* culvert; drain; *su./f* guidance; *vehicle:* driving; command, management; ⊕ pipe; *fig.* behavio(u)r; *mot.* ~ *à gauche (à droite)* left-hand (right-hand) drive; ~ *d'eau* water-main; channel; ~ *de gaz* gas-

piping; ~ *d'huile* oilduct; *mot.* ~ *en état d'ivresse* drunken driving.

cône [koːn] *m* cone; ⊕ *a.* bell; ♣ ~ *de charge torpedo:* war-head; *en* ~ tapering.

confection [kɔ̃fɛk'sjɔ̃] *f* making; manufacture; ✝ ready-made clothes *pl.*; 🪡 confection; *cost. de* ~ ready-made; **confectionner** [~sjɔ'ne] (1a) *v/t.* make (up) (*a.* ✝ *a balance-sheet*); manufacture; **confectionneur** *m,* **-euse** *f* [~sjɔ'nœːr, ~'nøːz] manufacturer; ✝ ready-made clothier.

confédération [kɔ̃federa'sjɔ̃] *f* (con-)federation; **confédéré, e** [~'re] 1. *adj.* confederate; 2. *su.* confederate; *su./m: hist. Am. les* 2s *pl.* the Confederates; **confédérer** [~'re] (1f) *v/t. a. se* ~ confederate, unite.

conférence [kɔ̃fe'rɑ̃:s] *f* conference; *univ.* lecture; ~ *avec projections* lantern lecture; ~ *de presse* press conference; *univ.* ~s *pl. pratiques* seminar *sg.*; *univ. maître m de* ~s lecturer; **conférencier** *m,* **-ère** *f* [~rɑ̃'sje, ~'sjɛːr] member of a conference; lecturer, speaker; **conférer** [~'re] (1f) *v/t.* compare (*texts*); confer (*a degree*); *typ.* check (*proofs*); *v/i.* confer (with, *avec*); ~ *de* talk about (*s.th.*); talk (*s.th.*) over.

confesse *eccl.* [kɔ̃'fɛs] *f* confession; **confesser** [kɔ̃fɛ'se] (1a) *v/t.* confess (*a. eccl.*); admit; *c'est le diable à* ~ this is the dickens of a job; *eccl. se* ~ confess, go to confession; **confesseur** *eccl., a. hist.* [~'sœːr] *m* confessor; **confession** [~'sjɔ̃] *f* confession (*a. eccl.*); admission; **confessionnal** *eccl.* [~sjɔ'nal] *m* confessional(-box); **confessionnel, -elle** [~sjɔ'nɛl] confessional, denominational.

confiance [kɔ̃'fjɑ̃:s] *f* confidence, trust, reliance; ~ *en soi* self-confidence; *avoir* ~ *en, faire* ~ *à* have confidence in, trust; *homme m de* ~ reliable man; confidential agent; **confiant, e** [~'fjɑ̃, ~'fjɑ̃:t] confident, trusting; **confidence** [~'dɑ̃:s] *f* confidence, secret; **confident** [~'dɑ̃] *m* confidant; **confidente** [~'dɑ̃:t] *f* confidante; **confidentiel, -elle** [~dɑ̃'sjɛl] confidential; **confier** [kɔ̃'fje] (1o) *v/t.* entrust; *fig.* confide; *se* ~ *à* put faith in; rely on; *se* ~ *en q.* put one's trust in s.o.; confide in s.o.

configuration [kɔ̃figyra'sjɔ̃] *f* configuration (*a. astr.*); lie (*of the land*).

confiner [kɔ̃fi'ne] (1a) *v/i.* border (on, *à*); *v/t.* shut (*s.o.*) up (in, *dans*) (*a. fig.*); se ~ seclude o.s.; **confins** [~'fɛ̃] *m/pl.* confines (*a. fig.*), limits.

confire [kɔ̃'fiːr] (4i) *v/t.* preserve (*fruit*); candy (*peels*); pickle (*in salt or vinegar*); steep (*skins*).

confirmatif, -ve [kɔ̃firma'tif, ~'tiːv] corroborative; confirmative; **confirmation** [~ma'sjɔ̃] *f* confirmation (*a. ⚖, eccl., etc.*); **confirmer** [~'me] (1a) *v/t.* confirm (*a. eccl.*); bear out, corroborate.

confis [kɔ̃'fi] *1st p. sg. pres. and p.s. of confire.*

confiscable [kɔ̃fis'kabl] liable to seizure *or* confiscation; **confiscation** [~ka'sjɔ̃] *f* confiscation; seizure, forfeiture.

confiserie [kɔ̃fiz'ri] *f* confectionery; confectioner's (shop); **confiseur** *m*, **-euse** *f* [~fi'zœːr, ~'zøːz] confectioner; **confisons** [~fi'zɔ̃] *1st p. pl. pres. of confire.*

confisquer [kɔ̃fis'ke] (1m) *v/t.* confiscate, seize.

confit, e [kɔ̃'fi, ~'fit] **1.** *p.p. of confire;* **2.** *adj. cuis.* preserved; candied; *fig.* ~ dans (*or* en) steeped in, full of; **confiture** [~fi'tyːr] *f* jam, preserve; F soft soap.

conflagration [kɔ̃flagra'sjɔ̃] *f* conflagration, blaze.

conflit [kɔ̃'fli] *m* conflict; clash; ✝ ~ salarial wages dispute; ✝ ~ social industrial dispute.

confluent, e [kɔ̃fly'ã, ~'ãːt] **1.** *adj.* ⚕, ⚘ confluent; **2.** *su./m* confluence, meeting.

confondre [kɔ̃'fɔ̃ːdr] (4a) *v/t.* confound (*a. fig.*); (inter)mingle; *fig.* confuse; *fig.* disconcert; se ~ blend; be lost; be confused.

conformation [kɔ̃fɔrma'sjɔ̃] *f* conformation, structure; **conforme** [~'fɔrm] conformable; true; consonant (with, *à*); identical (with, *à*); ⚖ pour copie ~ certified true copy; **conformément** [kɔ̃fɔrme'mã] *adv.* in accordance with, *à*); **conformer** [~'me] (1a) *v/t.* shape, form; *fig.* conform (to, *à*); ✝ ~ les écritures agree the books; se ~ à conform to, comply with; **conformité** [~mi'te] *f* conformity (with, *avec*,

to, *à*); agreement, accordance (with, *avec*).

confort [kɔ̃'fɔːr] *m* comfort; *mot.* pneu *m* ~ balloon tyre; **confortable** [~fɔr'tabl] comfortable; considerable; **conforter** [~fɔr'te] (1a) *v/t.* strengthen, reinforce; confirm.

confraternité [kɔ̃fraterni'te] *f* confraternity; (good) fellowship; **confrère** [~'frɛːr] *m* colleague; fellow (-teacher, -doctor, *etc.*); **confrérie** *eccl.* [~fre'ri] *f* confraternity.

confrontation [kɔ̃frɔ̃ta'sjɔ̃] *f* ⚖ confrontation; ⚖ identification; *texts:* comparison; **confronter** [~'te] (1a) *v/t.* confront (with *à*, *avec*); compare (*texts*).

confus, e [kɔ̃'fy, ~'fyːz] confused (*a. fig.*); indistinct (*noise, sight*); obscure (*style*); *fig.* ashamed; **confusément** [kɔ̃fyze'mã] *adv.* confusedly; indistinctly; F in a jumble; **confusion** [~'zjɔ̃] *f* confusion, disorder; *fig.* embarrassment; *dates, names, etc.:* mistake; ⚕ (*mental*) aberration.

congé [kɔ̃'ʒe] *m* leave (*a.* ✕); holiday; dismissal, notice (to quit, of dismissal, *etc.*); ✕, ⚓ discharge; *admin.* permit; △ congé; ~ de maladie sick leave; ~ de maternité maternity leave; ~s scolaires *pl.* school holidays (*Am.* vacation); ~ payé paid holidays *pl.* (*Am.* vacation); deux jours *m/pl.* de ~ two days off, two days' holiday; donner (son) ~ à q. give s.o. notice; prendre ~ de take leave of; **congédiable** [kɔ̃ʒe'djabl] due for *or* liable to dismissal; **congédier** [~'dje] (1o) *v/t.* dismiss; ✕, ⚓ discharge; ⚓ pay off; ✕ disband (*troops*).

congelable [kɔ̃ʒ'labl] freezable; **congélateur** [kɔ̃ʒela'tœːr] *m* freezer; **congélation** [kɔ̃ʒela'sjɔ̃] *f* freezing; setting; ⚕, ⚘ frost-bite; **congelé, e** [kɔ̃ʒ'le] frozen; chilled (*meat*); **congeler** [~] (1d) *v/t. a.* se ~ freeze (*a.* ✝ *credits*); congeal; F solidify.

congénère [kɔ̃ʒe'nɛːr] **1.** *adj. biol.* congeneric; *anat.* congenerous; **2.** *su./m biol.* congener; *fig.* lui et ses ~s he and his like.

congénital, e, *m/pl.* **-aux** [kɔ̃ʒeni'tal, ~'to] congenital.

congestion ⚕ [kɔ̃ʒes'tjɔ̃] *f* congestion; ~ pulmonaire pneumonia; **con-**

gestionner [ˌʒtjɔ'ne] (1a) *v/t.* 🖈 congest; *fig.* flush (*s.o.'s face*).

conglomérat [kɔ̃glɔme'ra] *m geol.* pudding-stone; ⚕ cemented gravel; **conglomération** [ˌra'sjɔ̃] *f* conglomeration; **conglomérer** [ˌ're] (1f) *v/t. a.* se ~ conglomerate.

conglutiner 🖈 [kɔ̃glyti'ne] (1a) *v/t. a.* se ~ conglutinate.

congratuler [kɔ̃graty'le] (1a) *v/t.* congratulate.

congréganiste *eccl. hist.* [kɔ̃grega-'nist] *su.* member of the Congregation; **congrégation** *eccl.* [ˌ'sjɔ̃] *f* community; *protestantism:* congregation; brotherhood; *College of Cardinals:* committee; *hist.* the Congregation.

congrès [kɔ̃'grɛ] *m* congress; **congressiste** [ˌgrɛ'sist] *su.* member of a congress; *su./m Am.* Congressman.

congru, e [kɔ̃'gry] adequate; suitable; *eccl.* congruous; *fig. portion f* ~e short allowance; bare living; **congruent, e** [ˌgry'ɑ̃, ˌ'ɑ̃:t] congruent (with, à).

conicité [kɔnisi'te] *f* conical shape; *bullet:* taper; **conifère** ♀ [ˌ'fɛ:r] **1.** *adj.* coniferous; **2.** *su./m:* ~s *pl.* conifers; **conique** [kɔ'nik] **1.** *adj.* conical; conic; ⊕ coned, tapering; ⊕ bevel (*gearing, pinion*); **2.** *su./f* Å (*a. section f* ~) conic section.

conjecture [kɔ̃ʒɛk'ty:r] *f* surmise, guess; **conjecturer** [ˌty're] (1a) *v/t.* surmise, guess.

conjoint, e [kɔ̃'ʒwɛ̃, ˌ'ʒwɛ̃:t] **1.** *adj.* united, joint; ♫ married; Å règle *f* ~e chain-rule; **2.** *su./m* spouse; ~s *pl.* husband and wife.

conjonctif, -ve [kɔ̃ʒɔ̃k'tif, ˌ'ti:v] conjunctive (*a. gramm.*); *anat.* connective; **conjonction** [ˌ'sjɔ̃] *f* conjunction (*a. gramm., astr.*); union; **conjonctive** *anat.* [ˌ'ti:v] *f* conjunctiva; **conjonctivite** 🖈 [ˌti'vit] *f* conjunctivitis; **conjoncture** [ˌ'ty:r] *f* (set *or* combination of) circumstances *pl.*; ~ (*économique*) economic situation; ✝ haute ~ boom; **conjoncturel, -le** [ˌty'rɛl] cyclical; of the economic situation.

conjugaison [kɔ̃ʒygɛ'zɔ̃] *f gramm., biol., etc.* conjugation; pairing (*of guns etc.*).

conjugal, e, *m/pl.* **-aux** [kɔ̃ʒy'gal, ˌ'go] conjugal.

conjuguer [kɔ̃ʒy'ge] (1m) *v/t. gramm.* conjugate; pair (*guns etc.*).

conjungo F [kɔ̃ʒɔ̃'go] *m* marriage (formula).

conjurateur [kɔ̃ʒyra'tœ:r] *m* magician; **conjuration** [ˌ'sjɔ̃] *f* conspiracy, plot; exorcism; F ~s *pl.* entreaties; **conjuré** *m, e f* [kɔ̃ʒy're] conspirator; **conjurer** [ˌ] (1a) *v/t.* conspire, plot; exorcise (*spirits*); entreat (s.o. to *inf., q. de inf.*); se ~ conspire (together).

connais [kɔ'nɛ] *1st p. sg. pres. of* connaître; **connaissable** [kɔnɛ'sabl] recognizable (by, à); *phls.* cognizable; **connaissance** [ˌ'sɑ̃:s] *f* knowledge, learning; acquaintance (*a. person*); ♫ cognizance; 🖈 consciousness; en ~ de *cause* on good grounds, advisedly; **connaissement** ⚓ [kɔnɛs'mɑ̃] *m* bill of lading; ~ direct through bill of lading; **connaisseur, -euse** [ˌnɛ-'sœ:r, ˌ'sø:z] **1.** *adj.* (of an) expert; **2.** *su.* connoisseur; expert; **connaissons** [ˌnɛ'sɔ̃] *1st p. pl. pres. of* connaître; **connaître** [ˌ'nɛ:tr] (4k) *v/t.* know (*a. bibl.*); understand; experience; s'y *or* se ~ en *qch.* know all about s.th., be an expert in s.th.; *v/i.:* ~ de take cognizance of; deal with; *faire* ~ q. à introduce s.o. to.

connard *m, e f sl.* [kɔ'na:r, ˌ'nard], **connasse** [ˌ'nas] *f* idiot, goddamn fool.

connecter [kɔnɛk'te] (1a) *v/t.* connect (to, with avec); **connectif, -ve** [ˌ'tif, ˌ'ti:v] **1.** *adj. anat.* connective; **2.** *su./m* ♀ connective.

connexe [kɔ'nɛks] connected; **connexion** [kɔnɛk'sjɔ̃] *f* connection (*a. ⚡*); ⚡ lead; Å connex; ⊕ ~ directe positive drive; **connexité** [ˌsi'te] *f* connexity, relationship.

connivence [kɔni'vɑ̃:s] *f* complicity, connivance.

conoïde Å [kɔnɔ'id] *adj., a. su./m* conoid.

connu, e [kɔ'ny] *p.p. of* connaître; **connus** [ˌ] *1st p. sg. p.s. of* connaître.

conque [kɔ̃:k] *f* conch; *anat.* external ear; ⚕ apse; ⊕ delivery space.

conquérant, e [kɔ̃ke'rɑ̃, ˌ'rɑ̃:t] **1.** *adj.* conquering; *fig.* swaggering; **2.** *su.* conqueror, victor; **conquérir** [ˌ'ri:r] (2l) *v/t.* conquer; *fig.* win;

conquête [kɔ̃'kɛːt] *f* conquest; **conquis, e** [~'ki, ~'kiːz] *p.p. of* conquérir.

consacrer [kɔ̃sa'kre] (1a) *v/t.* consecrate (*a. fig.*); devote (*energies*); hallow (*the memory etc.*); *expression f* consacrée stock phrase, cliché.

consanguin, e [kɔ̃sɑ̃'gɛ̃, ~'gin] consanguineous; half-(*brother etc.*); inbred (*horse etc.*); **consanguinité** [~gini'te] *f* 🏛 consanguinity; inbreeding.

conscience [kɔ̃'sjɑ̃ːs] *f* consciousness; conscience; ~ *de soi* self-awareness; *perdre (reprendre)* ~ lose (regain) consciousness; *avoir bonne (mauvaise)* ~ have a clear (bad) conscience; *avoir* ~ *de* be aware of; **consciencieux, -euse** [~sjɑ̃'sjø, ~'sjøːz] conscientious; **conscient, e** [~'sjɑ̃, ~'sjɑ̃ːt] conscious, aware (of, *de*).

conscription ✕ [kɔ̃skrip'sjɔ̃] *f* conscription, *Am.* draft; **conscrit** [~'kri] *m* ✕ conscript, *Am.* draftee; *fig.* novice. [secration.\

consécration [kɔ̃sekra'sjɔ̃] *f* con-⌐

consécutif, -ve [kɔ̃seky'tif, ~'tiːv] consecutive; ~ *à* following upon.

conseil [kɔ̃'sɛːj] *m* advice; committee, board; 🏛 counsel; ✝ ~ *d'administration* board of directors; ✕, ⚓ ~ *de guerre* council of war; court-martial; ~ *d'employés* works committee; ~ *d'entreprise* works council; *pol.* ~ *de sécurité* Security Council; *pol.* ~ *des ministres* Cabinet; ✝ ~ *de surveillance* board of trustees; *admin.* ~ *général* county council; 🏛 ~ *judiciaire* guardian; *ingénieur-*~ *m* consulting engineer; *président m du* ♀ Premier, Prime Minister; **conseiller** [~sɛ'je] **1.** (1a) *v/t.* advise; recommend; **2.** *su./m* adviser; *admin.* councillor; ~ *d'orientation professionnelle* careers adviser, vocational guidance counsellor; ~ *économique* economic adviser; ~ *général* county councillor; ~ *municipal* town *or* city councillor.

consensus [kɔ̃sɛ̃'sys] *m* consensus.

consentement [kɔ̃sɑ̃t'mɑ̃] *m* consent, assent; *du* ~ *de tous* by universal consent; *par* ~ *mutuel* by mutual consent; **consentir** [~sɑ̃'tiːr] (2b) *v/i.* consent (to, *à*), agree (with, *à*); ⊕ yield (*beam*); *v/t.* authorize; grant; accept (*an opinion*).

conséquence [kɔ̃se'kɑ̃ːs] *f* consequence, result; importance; *de* ~ of importance, important; *en* ~ consequently; *en* ~ *de* in consequence of; **conséquent, e** [~'kɑ̃, ~'kɑ̃ːt] **1.** *adj.* consistent; following; **2.** *su./m* Ⱥ, *gramm.*, *phls.* consequent; *par* ~ consequently.

conservable [kɔ̃sɛr'vabl] that will keep (*food*); **conservateur, -trice** [~va'tœːr, ~'tris] **1.** *adj.* preservative; *pol.* Conservative; **2.** *su.* keeper, curator, guardian; *pol.* Conservative; **conservation** [~va'sjɔ̃] *f* preservation; **conservatisme** [~va'tism] *m* conservatism; **conservatoire** [~va'twaːr] **1.** *adj.* preservative, of conservation; **2.** *su./m* school, academy (*of music etc.*); conservatoire, *Am.* conservatory.

conserve[1] ⚓ [kɔ̃'sɛrv] *f* convoy; *naviguer de* ~ sail in company.

conserve[2] [kɔ̃'sɛrv] *f* preserve; tinned food; **conserver** [~sɛr've] (1a) *v/t.* preserve, keep; *fig.* maintain; *se* ~ keep (*food*); *bien conservé* well-preserved.

considérable [kɔ̃side'rabl] considerable; extensive; *fig.* important; **considération** [~ra'sjɔ̃] *f* consideration; attention; motive; esteem; **considérer** [~'re] (1f) *v/t.* consider; contemplate; regard; *hautement considéré* highly respected; *bien considéré* well-thought-of.

consignataire [kɔ̃sina'tɛːr] *m* ✝ consignee; 🏛 trustee; depositary; **consignateur** *m*, **-trice** *f* [~'tœːr, ~'tris] consignor; shipper; **consignation** [~'sjɔ̃] *f* ✝ consignment; deposit; ✝ *Caisse f des dépôts et* ~s Deposit and Consignment Office; *stock m en* ~ goods *pl.* on consignment; **consigne** [kɔ̃'siɲ] *f* order, instructions *pl.*; ✕, ⚓ order-board; ✕ password; ✕, ⚓ confinement; *school:* detention; ✕ guardroom; 🚉 left-luggage office, *Am.* baggage room, checkroom; ✝ deposit (on *a bottle etc. sur*); **consigner** [~si'ɲe] (1a) *v/t.* deposit; ✝ consign; ✝ put a deposit on (*a bottle etc.*); ✕ confine to barracks; *school:* detain (*a pupil*); close, put out of bounds; 🚉 put in the left-luggage office, *Am.* check (*baggage*); ~ (*par écrit*) set down, record, register; ~ *sa porte à q.* not to be at home to s.o.

consistance [kõsis'tã:s] *f* consistency; firmness; *fig.* standing, credit; **consister** [~'te] (1a) *v/i.* consist (of *en, dans*).

consolant, e [kõsɔ'lã, ~'lã:t] *see* consolateur *1*; **consolateur, -trice** [~la'tœ:r, ~'tris] **1.** *adj.* consoling, comforting; **2.** *su.* consoler, comforter; **consolation** [~la'sjõ] *f* consolation, comfort.

console [kõ'sɔl] *f* ♪, ♣, *a.* table: console.

consoler [kõsɔ'le] (1a) *v/t.* console, comfort.

consolider [kõsɔli'de] (1a) *v/t.* consolidate (*a.* ✝); ♣ brace (*a wall*); fund (*a debt*); ✚ unite, heal (*a fracture etc.*); se ~ grow firm; ✚ unite, heal.

consommateur *m*, **-trice** *f* [kõsɔma'tœ:r, ~'tris] consumer; *café etc.*: customer; **consommation** [~ma-'sjõ] *f* consumption; ✕, ♣ expenditure; consummation (*a. of marriage*); *café:* drink; ✝ biens *m/pl.* de ~ consumer goods; *mot. concours m* de ~ economy run; *impôt m sur la* ~, taxe *f* de ~ purchase tax; ✝ société *f* coopérative de ~ co(-)operative stores *pl.*; **consommé, e** [~'me] **1.** *adj.* consummate (*skill*); **2.** *su./m cuis.* stock; clear soup, broth; **consommer** [~'me] (1a) *v/t.* consummate (*a. marriage*); accomplish; consume, use up.

consomption [kõsõp'sjõ] *f* consumption; destruction (*by fire*); ✚ decline.

consonance ♪, *gramm.* [kõsɔ'nã:s] *f* consonance; **consonant, e** ♪, *gramm.* [~'nã, ~'nã:t] consonant; **consonne** *gramm.* [kõ'sɔn] *f* consonant.

consort [kõ'sɔ:r] *m* consort; ~s *pl.* associates, confederates; *prince m* ~ prince consort; **consortium** [~sɔr-'sjɔm] *m* consortium.

conspirateur, -trice [kõspira'tœ:r, ~'tris] **1.** *adj.* conspiring; **2.** *su.* conspirator; **conspiration** [~ra'sjõ] *f* conspiracy, plot; **conspirer** [~'re] (1a) *v/i.* conspire (*a. fig.*), plot; *fig.* tend.

conspuer [kõs'pɥe] (1a) *v/t.* decry; *thea. etc.* boo; *sp.* barrack.

constamment [kõsta'mã] *adv.* steadfastly; continually, constantly; **constance** [~'tã:s] *f* constancy;

steadiness; perseverance; **constant, e** [~'tã, ~'tã:t] **1.** *adj.* constant; invariable (*a.* Å); steadfast; patent (*fact*); **2.** *su./f* ♪, *phys.* constant.

constat [kõs'ta] *m* certified *or* official report; established fact; ✝✝ ~ d'huissier affidavit made by processserver; **constatation** [kõstata'sjõ] *f* establishment, finding (*of facts*); certified statement; proof (*of identity*); **constater** [~'te] (1a) *v/t.* establish, ascertain; record, state; certify (*s.o.'s death*); note.

constellation [kõstɛlla'sjõ] *f* constellation; **constellé, e** [~'le] spangled; studded; **consteller** [~'le] (1a) *v/t.* constellate; stud (*with jewels*).

consternation [kõstɛrna'sjõ] *f* consternation, dismay; **consterner** [~'ne] (1a) *v/t.* (fill with) dismay.

constipation ✚ [kõstipa'sjõ] *f* constipation; **constiper** ✚ [~'pe] (1a) *v/t.* constipate.

constituant, e [kõsti'tɥã, ~'tɥã:t] **1.** *adj.* constituent (*a. pol.*); component; **2.** *su.* ✝✝ constituent; ✝✝ dowry, annuity: grantor; *pol.* elector; *su./m* constituent part; *pol.* member of the Constituent Assembly (*1789*); *su./f l'Ϩe* the Constituent Assembly (*1789*); **constituer** [~-'tɥe] (1n) *v/t.* constitute; establish; appoint; settle; ✝✝ empanel (*the jury*); set up, institute (*a committee*).

constitutif, -ve [~ty'tif, ~'ti:v] constituent; ✝✝ constitutive; **constitution** [~ty'sjõ] *f* ✚, *pol.* constitution; establishing; formation; composition (*a.* ⛰); ✝✝ briefing (*of a lawyer*); **constitutionnel, -le** [~tysjɔ'nɛl] constitutional.

constricteur *physiol., a. zo.* [kõs-trik'tœ:r] *adj., a. su./m* constrictor; **constrictif, -ve** [~'tif, ~'ti:v] constrictive.   [constringent.]

constringent, e ✚ [kõstrɛ̃'ʒã,~'ʒã:t]|

constructeur [kõstryk'tœ:r] *m* builder, constructor; engineer; ~ de maisons (master-)builder; ~ mécanicien manufacturing engineer; **construction** [~'sjõ] *f* construction (*a.* ♣, Å, *gramm.*); building; structure; de ~ française Frenchbuilt; en ~ on the stocks (*boat*); société *f* de ~ building society; **construire** [kõs'trɥi:r] (4h) *v/t.* construct (*a.* ♣, Å, *gramm., a. fig.*);

build; **construisis** [ˌtrɥi'zi] *1st p. sg. p.s. of construire;* **construisons** [ˌtrɥi'zɔ̃] *1st p. pl. pres. of construire;* **construit, e** [ˌ'trɥi, ˌ'trɥit] *p.p. of construire.*

consul [kɔ̃'syl] *m* consul; **consulaire** [kɔ̃sy'lɛːr] consular; **consulat** [ˌ'la] *m* consulate.

consultant, e [kɔ̃syl'tã, ˌ'tãːt] **1.** *adj.* consulting, consultant; *avocat m* ˌ chamber counsel; **2.** *su.* consulter; ⚘ consultant; **consultatif, -ve** [ˌta'tif, ˌ'tiːv] advisory, consulting; **consultation** [ˌta'sjɔ̃] *f* consultation, conference; ⚕ opinion; **consulter** [ˌ'te] (1a) *v/t.* consult; se ˌ consider; *v/i.*: ⚘ ˌ *avec* hold a consultation with.

consumer [kɔ̃sy'me] (1a) *v/t.* consume; devour; burn; *fig.* se ˌ waste away; **consumérisme** [ˌme'rism] *m* consumerism.

contact [kɔ̃'takt] *m* contact (*a. ⚡ etc.*); ⚡ˌ *à fiche* plug; ⚡ F ˌ *de terre* earth; *mot. clef f de* ˌ ignition key; *entrer en* ˌ *avec* get in touch with; **contacter** [ˌtak'te] (1a) *v/t.* contact; **contacteur** ⚡ [ˌtak'tœːr] *m* circuit-maker; contact-maker.

contage ⚕ [kɔ̃'taːʒ] *m* contagium; **contagieux, -euse** [kɔ̃ta'ʒjø, ˌ'ʒjøːz] ⚕ contagious; infectious; catching; **contagion** ⚕ [ˌ'ʒjɔ̃] *f* contagion; infection.

contaminer [kɔ̃tami'ne] (1a) *v/t.* ⚕ infect; contaminate.

conte [kɔ̃ːt] *m* story, tale.

contemplatif, -ve [kɔ̃tãpla'tif, ˌ'tiːv] **1.** *adj.* contemplative; **2.** *su.* dreamer; **contempler** [ˌ'ple] (1a) *v/t.* contemplate; *fig.* meditate upon; *v/i.* meditate.

contemporain, e [kɔ̃tãpɔ'rɛ̃, ˌ'rɛn] *adj., a. su.* contemporary.

contenance [kɔ̃t'nãːs] *f* capacity; content(s *pl.*); *fig.* bearing, countenance; **conteneur** ✝ [ˌ'nœːr] *m* container; **contenir** [ˌ'niːr] (2h) *v/t.* contain, hold (*a.* ✂); *fig.* control, restrain; se ˌ control o.s., keep one's temper.

content, e [kɔ̃'tã, ˌ'tãːt] **1.** *adj.* content(ed); pleased, happy; **2.** *su./m* F sufficiency; *tout son* ˌ to one's heart's content; **contentement** [ˌtãt'mã] *m* contentment, satisfaction; **contenter** [ˌtã'te] (1a) *v/t.* content,

satisfy; se ˌ make do, be content (with, *de*).

contentieux, -euse [kɔ̃tã'sjø, ˌ'sjøːz] **1.** *adj.* contentious; **2.** *su./m* ⚕ matters *pl.* in dispute; ✝, *admin.* legal department; **contention** [ˌ'sjɔ̃] *f* application; ⚘ holding; ✝ dispute.

contenu [kɔ̃t'ny] *m* content(s *pl.*).

conter [kɔ̃'te] (1a) *v/t.* tell, relate; *en* ˌ *à q.* pull s.o.'s leg; *en* ˌ *de belles* tell tall stories (about, *sur*).

contestable [kɔ̃tɛs'tabl] debatable, questionable; **contestataire** *pol.* [ˌta'tɛːr] **1.** *adj.* anti-establishment; **2.** *su.* protester; **contestation** [ˌta'sjɔ̃] *f* dispute; *pol.* anti-establishment movement; **contester** [ˌ'te] (1a) *vt/i.* dispute; *pol.* protest.

conteur *m*, **-euse** *f* [kɔ̃'tœːr, ˌ'tøːz] narrator; story-teller; *fig.* romancer, F bit of a liar.

contexte [kɔ̃'tɛkst] *m* context; ⚕ text (*of a deed etc.*); **contextuel, -le** [ˌtɛksty'ɛl] contextual.

contigu, -guë [kɔ̃ti'gy] adjoining; adjacent (*a.* Ⓐ); **contiguïté** [ˌgɥi'te] *f* contiguity, adjacency.

continence [kɔ̃ti'nãːs] *f* continence, continency; **continent, e** [ˌ'nã, ˌ'nãːt] **1.** *adj.* continent, chaste; ⚕ unintermitting (*fever*); **2.** *su./m geog.* continent; mainland; **continental, e**, *m/pl.* **-aux** [ˌnã'tal, ˌ'to] continental.

contingence [kɔ̃tɛ̃'ʒãs] *f phls.* contingency; *les* ˌs incidents; chance happenings.

contingent, e [kɔ̃tɛ̃'ʒã, ˌ'ʒãːt] **1.** *adj.* contingent; **2.** *su./m* quota; ration, allowance; **contingentement** [ˌʒãt'mã] *m* quota system; **contingenter** [ˌʒã'te] (1a) *v/t.* fix quotas for.

continu, e [kɔ̃ti'ny] **1.** *adj.* continuous (*a.* Ⓐ *function*), continual; uninterrupted, unbroken; ⚡ direct (*current*); Ⓐ continued (*fraction*); **2.** *su./m phys.* continuum; **continuation** [ˌnɥa'sjɔ̃] *f* continuation; *weather:* long spell; *war etc.*: carrying on; **continuel, -elle** [ˌ'nɥɛl] continual, unceasing; **continuer** [ˌ'nɥe] (1n) *v/t.* continue; carry on; extend; *v/i.*: ˌ *à* (*inf.*) continue (*ger.*), continue to (*inf.*); *v/t.* prolong; **continuité** [ˌnɥi'te] *f* continuity; uninterrupted connection; **conti-**

nûment [ˏny'mã] *adv.* continuously, without a break.

contorsion [kõtɔr'sjõ] *f* contortion; ✄ distortion; *faire des* ⁓s pull a wry face.

contour [kõ'tuːr] *m* contour, outline; *town:* circuit; **contourner** [ˏtur'ne] (1a) *v/t.* outline; go round; by-pass (*a town*); distort (*one's face*); F get round (*the law*).

contraceptif, -ive [kõtrasep'tif, ⁓'tiːv] *adj., a. su./m* contraceptive; **contraception** [ˏ'sjõ] *f* contraception.

contractant, e [kõtrak'tã, ⁓'tãːt] 1. *adj.* contracting; 2. *su.* contracting party; **contracter** [ˏ'te] (1a) *v/t.* contract (*debt, habit, illness, marriage, etc.*); incur (*debts*); catch (*cold*); **contractile** *physiol.* [ˏ'til] contractile; **contraction** [ˏ'sjõ] *f* contraction; *road:* narrowing.

contractuel, -elle [kõtrak'tɥɛl] 1. *adj.* contractual; 2. *su.* employee on contract; traffic warden, *f a.* F meter maid.

contradicteur [kõtradik'tœːr] *m* contradictor; opponent; **contradiction** [ˏ'sjõ] *f* contradiction; opposition; **contradictoire** [ˏ'twaːr] contradictory; inconsistent; conflicting (with, *à*); *jugement m* ⁓ judgment given after a full hearing.

contraindre [kõ'trɛ̃ːdr] (4m) *v/t.* compel, force; coerce; *fig.* restrain (*one's feelings etc.*); *se* ⁓ restrain o.s.; **contraint, e** [ˏ'trɛ̃, ⁓'trɛ̃ːt] 1. *adj.* cramped (*position, style*); forced (*smile*); stiff (*manner*); 2. *su./f* compulsion, constraint; embarrassment; *par* ⁓e under duress; *sans* ⁓e freely.

contraire [kõ'trɛːr] 1. *adj.* contrary, opposite (to, *à*); averse; *en sens* ⁓ in the opposite direction; 2. *su./m* contrary, opposite; *au* ⁓ on the contrary.

contralto ♩ [kõtral'to] *m* contralto.

contrariant, e [kõtra'rjã, ⁓'rjãːt] provoking, tiresome; vexatious; **contrarier** [ˏ'rje] (1o) *v/t.* thwart, oppose; annoy, vex; contrast; **contrariété** [ˏrie'te] *f* difficulty; annoyance, vexation; clash (*of colours, interests, etc.*).

contraste [kõ'trast] *m* contrast; **contraster** [ˏtras'te] (1a) *vt/i.* contrast.

contrat [kõ'tra] *m* contract; *marriage:* settlement; *passer un* ⁓ enter into an agreement.

contravention [kõtravã'sjõ] *f* ⚖ infringement; *mot.* parking ticket *or* fine.

contre [kõ:tr] 1. *prp.* against; contrary to; (in exchange) for; ⚖, *sp.* versus; ⁓ *son gré* against his will; *dix* ⁓ *un* ten to one; 2. *adv.* against; near; *tout* ⁓ close by; 3. *su./m box.* counter; *cards:* double; *le pour et le* ⁓ the pros *pl.* and the cons *pl.*; *règlement m par* ⁓ settlement per contra.

contre... [kõtr(ə)] counter...; anti...; contra...; back...; **⁓-accusation** ⚖ [kõtrakyza'sjõ] *f* counter-charge; **⁓-allée** [ˏa'le] *f* side-walk, side-lane; **⁓-amiral** ⚓ [ˏami'ral] *m* rear-admiral; **⁓-assurance** [ˏasy'rãːs] *f* reinsurance; **⁓-attaque** ✕ [ˏa'tak] *f* counter-attack; **⁓balancer** [kõtrə-balã'se] (1k) *v/t.* counterbalance; **⁓bande** [ˏ'bãːd] *f* contraband, smuggling; smuggled goods *pl.*; *faire la* ⁓ smuggle; **⁓ba-** 'dje] *m* smuggler; **⁓bas** [ˏ'ba] *adv.*: *en* ⁓ lower down (than, *de*); downwards; **⁓basse** ♩ [ˏ'bɑːs] *f* doublebass; **⁓-bouter** [ˏbu'te], **⁓-buter** [ˏby'te] (1a) *v/t.* buttress; **⁓carrer** [ˏkɑ're] (1a) *v/t.* thwart; counteract; **⁓cœur** [ˏ'kœːr] *adv.*: *à* ⁓ reluctantly; **⁓coup** [ˏ'ku] *m* rebound; recoil; repercussion; *fig.* side-effects *pl.*; *par* ⁓ as a result (*indirect*); **⁓dire** [ˏ'diːr] (4p) *v/t.* contradict; *se* ⁓ contradict o.s. *or* each other; **⁓dit** [ˏ'di] *adv.*: *sans* ⁓ unquestionably.

contrée [kõ'tre] *f* region.

contre... [kõtr...] : **⁓-écrou** ⊕ [kõtre'kru] *m* counter-nut; **⁓-épreuve** [ˏe-'prœːv] *f* countercheck, crosscheck; *typ.* counterproof; **⁓-espionnage** [ˏɛspjɔ'naːʒ] *m* counter-espionage; **⁓-expertise** [ˏɛkspɛr'tiːz] *f* counter-valuation; **⁓façon** [kõtrəfa'sõ] *f* forgery, counterfeit; counterfeiting; infringement of copyright; **⁓facteur** [ˏfak'tœːr] *m* forger, counterfeiter; **⁓faction** [ˏfak'sjõ] *f* forgery; counterfeiting; **⁓faire** [ˏ'fɛːr] (4r) *v/t.* imitate, mimic; forge; counterfeit (*money*); disguise (*one's voice etc.*); *fig.* deform; **⁓-fiche** △, ⊕ [ˏ'fiʃ] *f* brace, strut; **⁓ficher** *sl.* [ˏfi'ʃe] *v/t.*:

se ~ de care a damn about; ~-**fil** ⊕
[~'fil] *m*: à ~ against the grain; ~**fort**
[~'fɔːr] *m* ⚠ buttress; *geog.* spur;
boot: stiffening; ~*s pl.* foot-hills; ~-
haut [~'o] *adv.*: en ~ higher up; on a
higher level; ~-**jour** [~'ʒuːr] *m*
backlightning; à ~ against the light;
~-**lettre** ⚖ [~'lɛtr] *f* counter-deed;
defeasance; ~-**maître** [~'mɛːtr] *m*
foreman; ⚓ petty officer; first mate;
~-**mesure** [~mə'zyːr] *f* counter-
measure; ~**partie** [~par'ti] *f* opposite view; *fig.* compensation; en ~ in
compensation; in return; ~-**pied** *fig.*
[~'pje] *m* opposite view; ~-**plaqué**
[~pla'ke] *m* plywood; ~**poids**
[~'pwa] *m* counterweight; *clock*:
balanceweight; counterpoise; ~-
poil [~'pwal] *adv.*: à ~ the wrong
way; ~**point** ♪ [~'pwɛ̃] *m* counterpoint; ~-**pointe** ⊕ [~'pwɛ̃ːt] *f* tail-
stock; ~-**poison** [~pwa'zɔ̃] *m* antidote
(to, *de*); ~-**porte** [~'pɔrt] *f* ⚠ inner
door, *Am.* storm-door; ⊕ *furnace*:
shield.
contrer [kɔ̃'tre] (1a) *v/t.* box. counter; *cards*: double; *fig.* cross, thwart.
contre...: ~-**rail** 🚋 [kɔ̃trə'raːj] *m*
safety-rail; ~-**sceller** [~se'le] (1a)
v/t. counter-seal; ~**seing** [~'sɛ̃] *m*
counter-signature; ~**sens** [~'sɑ̃ːs] *m*
misinterpretation; nonsense; à ~ in
the wrong way; ~**signataire** [~sina-
'tɛːr] *m* one who countersigns;
~**temps** [~'tɑ̃] *m* mishap; inconvenience; disappointment; ♪ syncopation; à ~ at the wrong moment;
♪ out of time; ♪ contra tempo;
~-**terroriste** [~terɔ'rist] *adj., a. su.*
anti-terrorist; ~-**torpilleur** ⚓ [~-
tɔrpi'jœːr] *m* destroyer; light cruiser; ~-**valeur** ✝ [~va'lœːr] *f* exchange
value; ~-**vapeur** ⊕ [~va'pœːr]
f/inv. reversed steam; ~**venant** *m*,
e *f* ⚖ [~və'nɑ̃, ~'nɑ̃ːt] contravener;
offender; ~**venir** [~və'niːr] (2h) *v/i.*:
~ à contravene; ~**vent** [~'vɑ̃] *m* outside shutter; ⊕ wind-brace;
back-draught; ~**ventement** ⊕
[~vɑ̃t'mɑ̃] *m* wind-bracing; ~**vérité**
[~veri'te] *f* ironical statement; un-
truth; ~-**visite** ⚖ [~vi'zit] *f* check
inspection; ~-**voie** 🚋 [~'vwa] *f*
wrong side of the train.
contribuable [kɔ̃tri'bɥabl] **1.** *su.*
taxpayer; ratepayer; **2.** *adj.* tax-
paying; ratepaying; **contribuer**
[~'bɥe] (1n) *v/i.* contribute; **con-**

tribution [~by'sjɔ̃] *f* contribution;
admin. tax; rate; mettre à ~ make use
of, have recourse to, use.
contrit, e [kɔ̃'tri, ~'trit] penitent,
contrite; **contrition** [~tri'sjɔ̃] *f* penitence, contrition.
contrôle [kɔ̃'troːl] *m* check(ing), inspection; supervision; verification;
control; *thea.* box-office; ✝ audit-
ing; *gold, silver*: hallmark(ing); *gold,
silver*: assaying; assay office; ~ des
changes exchange control; ⚖ ~ des
naissances birth-control; coupon *m* de
~ ticket: stub; **contrôler** [kɔ̃tro'le]
(1a) *v/t.* check; verify; examine (*a
passport etc.*); stamp (*gold, silver*);
control (*s.o.*); **contrôleur** *m*, -**euse**
f [~'lœːr, ~'løːz] inspector; supervisor; ticket-collector; controller;
métro etc.: driver; ✈ ~ (aérien or de la
navigation aérienne) air traffic controller.
contrordre [kɔ̃'trɔrdr] *m* countermand; sauf ~ unless countermanded.
controuvé, e [kɔ̃tru've] forged,
spurious.
controverse [kɔ̃trɔ'vɛrs] *f* contro-
versy; **controverser** [~vɛr'se] (1a)
v/t. debate (*a topic*); controvert
(*an opinion*); *v/i.* hold a discussion.
contumace ⚖ [kɔ̃ty'mas] *f*: par ~ in
absentia.
contus, e ⚕ [kɔ̃'ty, ~'tyːz] contused,
bruised; **contusion** [kɔ̃ty'zjɔ̃] *f*
contusion, bruise; **contusionner**
[~zjɔ'ne] (1a) *v/t.* contuse, bruise.
conurbation [kɔnyrba'sjɔ̃] *f* conurbation; megalopolis.
convaincant, e [kɔ̃vɛ̃'kɑ̃, ~'kɑ̃ːt]
convincing; **convaincre** [~'vɛ̃ːkr]
(4gg) *v/t.* convince; *fig.* prove (*s.o.*)
guilty (of, *de*).
convalescence [kɔ̃valɛ'sɑ̃ːs] *f* convalescence; être en ~ convalesce;
convalescent, e [~'sɑ̃, ~'sɑ̃ːt] *adj.,
a. su.* convalescent.
convenable [kɔ̃v'nabl] suitable;
decent, seemly; **convenance**
[~'nɑ̃ːs] *f* fitness; propriety; decency; convenience; expediency; à
la ~ de q. to s.o.'s liking; to suit s.o.'s
convenience; mariage *m* de ~ marriage of convenience; par ~ for the
sake of decency; **convenir** [~'niːr]
(2h) *v/i.*: ~ à suit, fit; ~ de agree upon;
reach agreement about; admit, acknowledge (*s.th.*); c'est convenu!

agreed!; *il convient de* (*inf.*) it is advisable *or* fitting to (*inf.*).

convention [kɔ̃vãˈsjɔ̃] *f* convention; agreement; *pol.* assembly; ~*s pl.* clauses; ~ *collective* collective bargaining; **conventionné** [~sjɔˈne]: *médecin* ~ panel doctor; **conventionnel, -elle** [~sjɔˈnɛl] **1.** *adj.* conventional; **2.** *su./m hist.* member of the National Convention.

conventuel, -elle [kɔ̃vãˈtɥɛl] conventual.

convergence [kɔvɛrˈʒãːs] *f* convergence; ⚔, *a. fig.* concentration; **convergent, e** [~ˈʒã, ~ˈʒãːt] converging; ⚔ concentrated; **converger** [~ˈʒe] (1l) *v/i.* converge.

convers, e [kɔ̃ˈvɛːr, ~ˈvɛrs] lay ...

conversation [kɔ̃vɛrsaˈsjɔ̃] *f* conversation, talk; *teleph.* call; **converser** [~ˈse] (1a) *v/i.* converse, talk.

conversion [kɔ̃vɛrˈsjɔ̃] *f* conversion (*a.* ✝); ⚔ wheel(ing), change of front; **converti** *m, e f* [~ˈti] convert; **convertible** [~ˈtibl] convertible (into, en); **convertir** [~ˈtiːr] (2a) *v/t.* ✝, *eccl., phls., fig.* convert; **convertisseur** [~tiˈsœːr] *m* ⊕ converter; ✄ transformer.

convexe [kɔ̃ˈvɛks] convex.

conviction [kɔ̃vikˈsjɔ̃] *f* conviction.

convier [kɔ̃ˈvje] (1o) *v/t.* invite; urge.

convive [kɔ̃ˈviːv] *su.* guest; table companion.

convocation [kɔ̃vɔkaˈsjɔ̃] *f* convocation, summons *sg.*; notice of a meeting *or* an appointment; ⚔ calling-up papers *pl.*

convoi [kɔ̃ˈvwa] *m* convoy; ➏ train; (*a.* ~ *funèbre*) funeral procession; ~ *automobile* motor transport column.

convoiter [kɔ̃vwaˈte] (1a) *v/t.* covet, desire; **convoitise** [~ˈtiːz] *f* covetousness; lust.

convoler *iro.* [kɔ̃vɔˈle] (1a) *v/i.* (re)marry.

convoquer [kɔ̃vɔˈke] (1m) *v/t.* summon; ⚔ call up; *admin.* summon to an interview.

convoyer ⚔, ⚓ [kɔ̃vwaˈje] (1h) *v/t.* convoy; **convoyeur** [~ˈjœːr] *m* ⚓ convoy(-ship); ⚓ convoying officer; ⚔ officer in charge of a convoy; ⊕ conveyor, endless belt.

convulser [kɔ̃vylˈse] (1a) *v/t. physiol.* convulse; F frighten into fits; **con-**

vulsif, -ve [~ˈsif, ~ˈsiːv] convulsive; **convulsion** [~ˈsjɔ̃] *f* convulsion; spasm.

coopérateur *m,* **-trice** *f* [kɔɔperaˈtœːr, ~ˈtris] co(-)operator; **coopératif, -ve** [~ˈtif, ~ˈtiːv] **1.** *adj.* co(-)operative; **2.** *su./f* co(-)operative stores *pl.*; ~*ve immobilière* building society; **coopération** [~ˈsjɔ̃] *f* co(-)operation; **coopératisme** [~ˈtism] *m* co(-)operative system; **coopérer** [kɔɔpeˈre] (1f) *v/i.* co(-)operate.

cooptation [kɔɔptaˈsjɔ̃] *f* co-optation; **coopter** [~ˈte] (1a) *v/t.* co-opt.

coordinateur *m,* **-trice** *f* [kɔɔrdinaˈtœːr, ~ˈtris] coordinator; **coordination** [~ˈsjɔ̃] *f* coordination.

coordonnées ⚓ [kɔɔrdɔˈne] *f/pl.* co-ordinates; **coordonner** [~] (1a) *v/t.* coordinate (with, à); arrange.

copain F [kɔˈpɛ̃] *m* pal, chum, *Am.* buddy.

copeau [kɔˈpo] *m* wood shaving; ⊕ ~*x pl.* turnings.

copiage [kɔˈpjaːʒ] *m school:* copying; **copie** [~ˈpi] *f* (carbon) copy, transcript; *fig.* imitation; *phot.* print; *school:* exercise, paper; ~ *au net* fair copy; **copier** [~ˈpje] (1o) *v/t.* copy; *fig.* imitate; *school:* crib (from, *sur*).

copieux, -euse [kɔˈpjø, ~ˈpjøːz] copious, abundant.

copilote ⚔ [kopiˈlɔt] *m* second pilot, *Am.* co-pilot.

copinage F [kɔpiˈnaːʒ] *m* cronyism; **copine** F [kɔˈpin] *f girl:* pal, chum; **copiner** [kɔpiˈne] (1a) *v/i.* be pally; be pals; **copinerie** F [kɔpinˈri] *f* pallyness; *coll.* the pals *pl.*

copiste [kɔˈpist] *su.* copier, copyist; *fig.* imitator.

copra(h) [kɔˈpra] *m* copra.

copreneur ⚖ [kɔprəˈnœːr] *m* co-tenant, co-lessee.

coproduction [kɔprɔdykˈsjɔ̃] *n* joint production, coproduction.

copropriétaire [kɔprɔprijeˈtɛːr] *su.* joint owner, co-owner; **copropriété** [~ˈte] *f* joint ownership, co-ownership.

copule *gramm.* [kɔˈpyl] *f* copula.

coq[1] ⚓ [kɔk] *m* ship's cook.

coq[2] *orn.* [kɔk] *m* cock, *Am.* rooster; *box.* (*a. poids m* ~) bantam weight; ~ *de bruyère* (great) grouse; ~ *d'Inde* see *dindon; être comme un ~ en pâte* live like a fighting cock, be in clover; *être le ~ du village* be cock of the walk; **~-à-l'âne** [~ka'lɑ:n] *m/inv.* abrupt jump from one subject to another.

coque [kɔk] *f egg:* shell; ⚓ hull, bottom; ⊕ *boiler:* body; *œuf m à la ~* boiled egg.

coquelicot ♀ [kɔkli'ko] *m* red poppy.

coqueluche [kɔ'klyʃ] *f* 🌸 whooping-cough; *fig.* darling, favo(u)rite.

coqueriquer [kɔkri'ke] (1m) *v/i.* crow.

coquet, -ette [kɔ'kɛ, ~'kɛt] **1.** *adj.* coquettish; smart, stylish (*hat etc.*); trim (*garden*); F tidy (*sum*); **2.** *su./f* flirt; **coqueter** [kɔk'te] (1c) *v/i.* coquette; flirt (with, *avec*); *fig.* toy (with, *avec*).

coquetier [kɔk'tje] *m* egg-cup; egg-merchant.

coquetterie [kɔkɛ'tri] *f* coquetry; affectation; smartness, daintiness.

coquillage [kɔki'jaːʒ] *m* shell-fish; shell; **coquille** [~'kiːj] *f egg, nut, oyster, snail, a. fig.:* shell; *typ.* misprint, printer's error; *metall.* chill-mould; bank paper; *size:* small post; *fig. sortir de sa ~* come out of one's shell.

coquin, e [kɔ'kɛ̃, ~'kin] **1.** *adj.* roguish; **2.** *su.* rogue; rascal (*a. co.*); *su./f* hussy; **coquinerie** [~kin'ri] *f* roguery; rascality.

cor¹ [kɔ:r] *m hunt.* tine; ♪, *a. hunt.* horn; ♪ horn-player; ♪ *~ d'harmonie* French horn; *fig. à ~ et à cri* insistently; *sonner* (*or donner*) *du ~* sound the horn.

cor² 🌸 [~] *m* corn.

corail, *pl.* **-aux** [kɔ'raːj, ~'ro] *m* coral; **corailleur** [kɔra'jœːr] *m* coral fisher; coral worker; coral-fishing boat; **corallin, e** [~'lɛ̃, ~'lin] coral-red.

corbeau [kɔr'bo] *m orn.* crow; raven; △ corbel; F person of ill omen.

corbeille [kɔr'bɛːj] *f* basket; *thea.* dress-circle; ⊕ *valve:* cage; 🌸 (round) flower-bed; **corbeillée** [~bɛ'je] *f* basketful.

corbillard [kɔrbi'jaːr] *m* hearse.

cordage [kɔr'daːʒ] *m* rope; *racket:* stringing; cord of wood; ⚓ *~s pl.* gear *sg.*; **corde** [kɔrd] *f* rope, cord, line; ♪ string; ♪ chord; 🌸 lift wire; hangman's rope, *fig.* gallows

sg.; anat. ~s pl. vocales vocal c(h)ords.

cordé, e ♀ *etc.* [kɔr'de] cordate, heart-shaped.

cordeau [kɔr'do] *m* chalk-line, string; (measuring) tape; (⚓ tow-) rope; *tex.* selvedge; ✕, ✕ fuse; **cordée** [~'de] *f mount.* rope (*of climbers*); † cord (*of wood*); *racket:* stringing; **cordeler** [kɔrdə'le] (1c) *v/t.* twist (*hemp etc.*) into rope; **cordelette** [~'lɛt] *f* small cord *or* string; *en ~s* in small plaits; **cordelier** [~'lje] *m* Franciscan friar; **cordelière** [~'ljɛːr] *f* † Franciscan nun; girdle; *typ.* ornamental border; **corder** [kɔr'de] (1a) *v/t.* twist (*hemp etc.*) into rope; † measure (*wood*) by the cord; string (*a racket*); twist (*tobacco*); cord (*a trunk etc.*); **corderie** [~'dri] *f* rope-making; rope-trade.

cordial, e, *m/pl.* **-aux** [kɔr'djal, ~'djo] **1.** *adj.* cordial; 🌸 stimulating; **2.** *su./m* cordial; **cordialité** [~djali'te] *f* cordiality.

cordier [kɔr'dje] *m* rope-maker; dealer in ropes; ♪ *violin:* tail-piece; **cordon** [~'dɔ̃] *m* cord, string, tape; (shoe-)lace; door-pull, bell-pull; line (*of trees etc.*); *admin.* cordon, edge; *anat. ~ ombilical* navel string, umbilical cord; **cordon-bleu,** *pl.* **cordons-bleus** F *fig.* [~dɔ̃'blø] *m* first-rate cook; **cordonner** [~dɔ'ne] (1a) *v/t.* twist, cord (*hemp etc.*); edge-roll (*coins*).

cordonnerie [kɔrdɔn'ri] *f* shoe-making; shoemaker's shop.

cordonnet [kɔrdɔ'nɛ] *m* braid, cord.

cordonnier [kɔrdɔ'nje] *m* shoe-maker, F cobbler.

coréen, -enne [kɔre'ɛ̃, ~'ɛn] *adj., a. su.* ♀ Korean.

coriace [kɔ'rjas] tough (*a. fig.*).

coricide 🌸 [kɔri'sid] *m* corn cure.

corindon *min.* [kɔrɛ̃'dɔ̃] *m* corundum.

corinthien, -enne [kɔrɛ̃'tjɛ̃, ~'tjɛn] **1.** *adj.* Corinthian; **2.** *su.* ♀ Corinthian; *su./m* △ Corinthian.

cormier ♀ [kɔr'mje] *m* service (-tree, -wood).

cormoran *orn.* [kɔrmɔ'rɑ̃] *m* cormorant.

cornac [kɔr'nak] *m* mahout, elephant driver; F *fig.* guide, companion, chaperon; **cornaquer** F [~na'ke]

(1a) *v/t.* guide, show (*s.o.*) around, accompany, chaperon.

corne [kɔrn] *f* horn (*a. fig.*); dog's-ear (*in a book*); ~ *à chaussures* shoe-horn, shoe-lift; *de* ~ horn...; *bêtes f/pl. à* ~*s* horned cattle; **corné, e** [kɔr'ne] **1.** *adj.* horny; horn...; **2.** *su./f anat.* cornea; **cornéen, -enne** [~ne'ɛ̃, ~'ɛn] *adj.*: *opt. lentilles f/pl.* ~*ennes* contact lenses.

corneille *orn.* [kɔr'nɛːj] *f* crow, rook.

cornemuse ♪ [kɔrnə'myːz] *f* bagpipe(s *pl.*); **cornemuseur** [~my-'zœːr] *m* piper.

corner¹ *foot.* [kɔr'nɛːr] *m* corner.

corner² [kɔr'ne] (1a) *v/i.* hoot; *v/t. fig.* trumpet (*news etc.*); turn down the corner of (*a page etc.*); **cornet** [~'nɛ] *m pastry:* horn; *icecream:* cone; paper bag, screw of paper; ♪ (*à pistons*) cornet; F *se mettre qch. dans le* ~ have s.th. to eat; **cornette** [~'nɛt] *su./f nun:* coif; mob-cap.

corniche [kɔr'niʃ] *f rock:* ledge; coast road; △ cornice.

cornichon [kɔrni'ʃɔ̃] *m* gherkin; F nitwit.

cornière [kɔr'njɛːr] *f* ⊕ angle(-iron, -bar).

cornouille ♀ [kɔr'nuːj] *f* cornel-berry; **cornouiller** [~nu'je] *m* cornel(-tree); ♱ dogwood.

cornu, e [kɔr'ny] horned; spurred (*wheat*); *fig.* absurd.

cornue [~] *f* 🜛 *etc.* retort; *metall.* steel converter.

corollaire [kɔrɔl'lɛːr] *m* ♣ corollary; ♀ corollary tendril; **corolle** ♀ [~'rɔl] *f* corolla.

coron [kɔ'rɔ̃] *m* miners' quarters *pl.*

coronaire 🜛, *anat.* [kɔrɔ'nɛːr] coronary; **coronal, e** [~'nal, ~'no] coronal.

corporatif, -ve [kɔrpɔra'tif, ~'tiːv] corporat(iv)e; **corporation** [~'sjɔ̃] *f* corporation; ♱ *hist.* (trade-)guild.

corporel, -elle [kɔrpɔ'rɛl] corporeal; corporal (*punishment*); bodily.

corps [kɔːr] *m* body (*a.* 🜛); flesh; matter; ✕ (army) corps; ♣ (battle) fleet; F person, figure; *fig.* profession; ⚖ *corpus* (*of law*); ~ *à* ~ hand to hand; ~ *de bâtiment* main building; ~ *de logis* housing unit; ~ *de métier* g(u)ild; trade association; ♣ ~ *mort* (fixed) moorings *pl.*; *à* ~ *perdu* desperately; *en* ~ in a

body; *faire* ~ *avec* be an integral part of; *levée f du* ~ start of the funeral; ♣ *perdu* ~ *et biens* lost with all hands.

corpulence [kɔrpy'lãːs] *f* stoutness, corpulence; **corpulent, e** [~'lã, ~'lãːt] stout, corpulent; portly.

corpus [kɔr'pys] *m* corpus; **corpuscule** [kɔrpys'kyl] *m* corpuscle; particle.

correct, e [kɔ'rɛkt] correct, proper; accurate; **correcteur** *m*, **-trice** *f* [kɔrɛk'tœːr, ~'tris] corrector, proof-reader; **correctif, -ve** [~'tif, ~'tiːv] *adj., a. su./m* corrective; **correction** [~'sjɔ̃] *f* punishment; correction; *maison f de* ~ reformatory; *sauf* ~ subject to correction; **correctionnel, -elle** ⚖ [~sjɔ'nɛl] **1.** *adj.* correctional; *délit m* ~ minor offence; *tribunal m* ~ = **2.** *su./f* court of petty sessions, *Am.* police court.

corrélation [kɔrrela'sjɔ̃] *f* correlation.

correspondance [kɔrɛspɔ̃'dãːs] *f* correspondence; 🚌 *etc.* connection; 🚌 railway omnibus, transfer coach; *cours m par* ~ correspondence course; *par* ~ by letter, by post; *vote f par* ~ postal vote; *voter par* ~ vote by post; **correspondancier** *m*, **-ère** *f* ✝ [~dã'sje, ~'sjɛːr] correspondence clerk; **correspondant, e** [~'dã, ~'dãːt] **1.** *adj.* corresponding; 🚌 connecting; **2.** *su.* ✝, *journ.* correspondent; pen friend, *Am.* pen pal; *school:* parents' representative; **correspondre** [kɔrɛs'pɔ̃ːdr] (4a) *v/i.:* ~ *à* correspond to *or* with, suit; tally with; communicate with (*another room etc.*); ~ *avec q.* be in correspondence with s.o.   [passage.﹚

corridor [kɔri'dɔːr] *m* corridor,﹚

corrigé [kɔri'ʒe] *m* fair copy; key, crib; **corriger** [~'ʒe] (1l) *v/t.* correct; read (*proofs*); punish; rectify; cure; **corrigible** [~'ʒibl] corrigible.

corroborer [kɔrrɔbɔ're] (1a) *v/t.* corroborate, confirm.

corroder [kɔrrɔ'de] (1a) *v/t.* corrode, eat away.

corroi [kɔ'rwa] *m leather:* currying; **corroierie** [~rwa'ri] *f* currying; curriery.

corrompre [kɔ'rɔ̃ːpr] (4a) *v/t.* corrupt; spoil (*the taste*); taint (*meat*); ⚖ suborn; *se* ~ become corrupt(ed) *or* tainted.

corrosif, -ve [kɔrɔ'zif, ~'ziːv] *adj.,
a. su./m* corrosive; **corrosion** [~'zjɔ̃]
f corrosion; *soil:* erosion; ⊕ pitting.
corroyer [kɔrwa'je] (1h) *v/t.* curry
(*leather*); rough-plane (*wood*); weld
(*iron, steel*); puddle (*clay*); **corroyeur** [~'jœːr] *m* currier; *metall.*
blacksmith.
corrupteur, -trice [kɔryp'tœːr, ~-
'tris] **1.** *adj.* corrupting; **2.** *su.* cor-
rupter; briber; ⚖ suborner; **corruptible** [~'tibl] corruptible; open
to bribery; **corruption** [~'sjɔ̃] *f*
corruption; bribery; *Am.* graft; ⚖
subornation; *food:* tainting; *air,
water:* pollution.
corsage *cost.* [kɔr'saːʒ] *m* bodice; †
blouse.
corsaire [kɔr'sɛːr] *m* corsair, priva-
teer.
corse [kɔrs] *adj., a. su.* ♀ Corsican.
corsé, e [kɔr'se] strong; full-bodied
(*wine*); spicy (*story*); F substantial.
corselet *zo., a. hist.* [kɔrsə'lɛ] *m*
cors(e)let.
corser [kɔr'se] (1a) *v/t.* give body
or flavo(u)r to; strengthen; **se ~**
take a turn for the worse.
corset [kɔr'sɛ] *m* corset; **corsetière**
[~sə'tjɛːr] *f* corsetmaker.
cortège [kɔr'tɛːʒ] *m* procession; retinue, train; **~ funèbre** funeral procession.
cortisone ✻ [kɔrti'zɔn] *f* cortisone.
corvéable ✗ [kɔrve'abl] liable to fatigue duty; **corvée** [~'ve] *f* ✗ fatigue; ⚓ duty; ✗ fatigue party; *fig.*
drudgery, hard work, chore, drag;
thankless job.
corvette ⚓ *hist.* [kɔr'vɛt] *f* corvette.
coryphée [kɔri'fe] *m* leader of the
ballet, principal dancer; *fig.* party
leader, chief.
coryza ✻ [kɔri'za] *m* cold in the head.
cosmétique [kɔsme'tik] *adj., a. su./m*
cosmetic.
cosmique [kɔs'mik] cosmic.
cosmo... [kɔsmɔ] cosmo...; **~drome**
[~'droːm] *m* cosmodrome; **~graphie**
[~gra'fi] *f* cosmography; **~naute**
[~'noːt] *su.* cosmonaut; **~polite**
[~pɔ'lit] *adj., a. su.* cosmopolitan.
cosse [kɔs] *f* pod, husk; shell; ✁ eye *or*
spade terminal; *sl.* laziness; **cossu, e**
F [kɔ'sy] rich (*a. fig.*); well-to-do.
costal, e [kɔs'tal, ~'to] costal; **costaud, e** *sl.* [~'to,
~'toːd] strong, sturdy, hefty.

costume [kɔs'tym] *m* costume,
dress; suit; **~ de bain** bathing-
costume; **~ de golf** plus-fours *pl.*; **~
tailleur** tailor-made suit (*for women*);
coat and skirt; **costumer** [~ty'me]
(1a) *v/t.* dress up; **bal *m* costumé**
fancy-dress ball; **costumier** [~ty-
'mje] *m* costumier; ⚖, *univ.* out-
fitter; *thea.* wardrobe-keeper.
cotation † [kɔta'sjɔ̃] *f* quotation,
quoting; **cote** [kɔt] *f* quota; *admin.*
assessment; ⚖, †, *etc. document:*
identification *or* classification mark;
sp. odds *pl.*; ⚓ classification; †
prices etc.: quotation; *school:* mark
(*for an essay etc.*); *fig.* rating, standing; popularity; **~ d'alerte** danger
mark; F **avoir la ~** be (very) popular.
côte [koːt] *f* △, *anat., cuis.* rib; ♀
midrib; slope; hill; coast, shore; **~ à ~**
side by side.
côté [ko'te] *m* side; direction; **à ~ de**
beside; **de ~** sideways; **de mon ~** for
my part; **du ~ de** in the direction of;
d'un ~ on one side; **d'un ~ ..., de l'autre
~** on the one hand ..., on the other
hand; **la maison d'à ~** next door.
coteau [kɔ'to] *m* slope, hillside;
hillock.
côtelé, e *tex.* [kot'le] ribbed; **côtelette** [~'lɛt] *veal:* cutlet; *pork, mutton:*
chop; F **~s** *pl.* whiskers: mutton-
chops.
coter [kɔ'te] (1a) *v/t.* classify, number, letter (*a document*); ⚓ class (*a
ship*); quote (*prices*); *admin.* assess.
coterie [kɔt'ri] *f* set, circle, clique.
côtier, -ère [ko'tje, ~'tjɛːr] coast
(-ing); coastal; inshore (*fishing*).
cotillon [kɔti'jɔ̃] *m* † petticoat; **courir
le ~** flirt with the girls.
cotisation [kɔtiza'sjɔ̃] *f* subscription;
contribution; fee; *admin.* assessment; quota; **cotiser** [~'ze] (1a) *v/t.
admin.* assess; **se ~** subscribe; get up
a subscription.
coton [kɔ'tɔ̃] *m* cotton; *a.* **~ hydrophile**
cotton wool, *Am.* absorbent cotton;
élever dans du ~ coddle (*a baby*);
cotonnade [kɔtɔ'nad] *f* cotton
fabric; **~s** *pl.* cotton goods; **cotonner** [~'ne] (1a) *v/t.:* **se ~** become
covered with down; become woolly
(*fruit*); become fluffy (*cloth*); **coton-
nerie** [kɔtɔn'ri] *f* cotton growing;
cotton-plantation; cotton-mill; **cotonneux, -euse** [~tɔ'nø, ~'nøːz] cot-
tony; woolly (*fruit, style*); sleepy

(pear); fleecy *(cloud)*; **cotonnier, -ère** [ˌtɔ'nje, ˌ'njɛːr] **1.** *adj.* cotton-...; **2.** *su./m* ♀ cotton-plant; **coton-poudre,** *pl.* **cotons-poudre** [ˌtɔ̃'puːdr] *m* guncotton.

côtoyer [kotwa'je] (1h) *v/t.* hug *(the shore)*; keep close to; skirt *(the forest)*; border on *(a. fig.)*; *fig.* rub shoulders with *(s.o.)*; **se ~** rub shoulders.

cotte [kɔt] *f* workman's overalls *pl.*; petticoat; **~ de mailles** coat of mail.

cou [ku] *m* neck.

couac ♪ [kwak] *m* squawk.

couard, e [kwaːr, kward] **1.** *adj.* coward(ly); **2.** *su.* coward; **couardise** [kwar'diːz] *f* cowardice.

couchage [ku'ʃaːʒ] *m* night's lodging; *clothes:* bedding; **sac** *m* **de ~** sleeping-bag; **couchant, e** [ˌ'ʃɑ̃, ˌ'ʃɑ̃ːt] **1.** *su./m* sunset, setting of the sun; west; **2.** *adj.:* **chien** *m* **~** setter; *fig.* crawler, fawner; **soleil** *m* **~** setting sun; **couche** [kuʃ] *f* layer; *paint etc.:* coat; *geol. (a. social etc.)* stratum; napkin, nappy, *Am.* diaper *(for baby)*; ✂ seam; ♪ hotbed; *tree:* ring; † *pl.* childbirth *sg.*; **~ d'arrêt** barrier layer; ⊕ **~ de roulement** running surface; **fausse ~** miscarriage; *fig.* **il en a une ~!** what a fathead!; F **se donner une belle ~** drink o.s. blind; **coucher** [ku'ʃe] **1.** (1a) *v/t.* put to bed; lay down; beat down; put or write *(s.th.)* down (on, *sur*); mention *(s.o.)* (in one's will, *sur son testament)*; **~ qch.** en joue aim s.th.; **se ~** go to bed; lie down; set *(sun)*; *v/i.* sleep; **2.** *su./m* going to bed; *sun:* setting; **coucherie** *sl.* [kuʃ'ri] *f* oft. *pl.* love-making; **couchette** [ˌ'ʃɛt] *f* cot; ⚓ bunk; 🚂, ⚓ berth; **coucheur** [ˌ'ʃœːr] *m:* **mauvais ~** awkward customer, nasty fellow.

couci-couça [kusiku'sa], **couci-couci** [ˌ'si] *adv.* so-so.

coucou [ku'ku] *m* cuckoo(-clock); ♀ F cowslip.

coude [kud] *m* elbow *(a. river, road)*; ⊕ *shaft:* crank; **coup** *m* **de ~** nudge; **jouer des ~s** elbow one's way; **coudée** [ku'de] *f* cubit; F **avoir ses ~s franches** have elbow-room; *fig.* have a free hand.

cou-de-pied, *pl.* **cous-de-pied** [kud'pje] *m* instep.

couder ⊕ [ku'de] (1a) *v/t.* crank *(a shaft)*; bend *(a pipe)* into an elbow;

coudoyer [ˌdwa'je] (1h) *v/t.* elbow, jostle; rub shoulders with.

coudre[1] [kudr] (4l) *v/t.* sew; stitch; **machine** *f* **à ~** sewing-machine; **rester bouche cousue** remain silent.

coudre[2] ♀ [kudr] *m,* **coudrier** ♀ [ku'drje] *m* hazel-tree.

couenne [kwan] *f* bacon-rind; *roast pork:* crackling; 🐗 mole; **couenneux, -euse** 🐗 [kwa'nø, ˌ'nøːz] buffy *(blood)*; **angine** *f* **~euse** diphtheria.

couffe [kuf] *f,* **couffin** [ku'fɛ̃] *m* basket.

couillon *sl.* [ku'jɔ̃] *m* fool; **~!** bloody fool!

coulage [ku'laːʒ] *m* pouring *(a. metall.)*; *metall.* casting; *liquid:* leaking; ⚓ scuttling; *fig.* leakage; **coulant, e** [ˌ'lɑ̃, ˌ'lɑ̃ːt] **1.** *adj.* running; flowing *(a. style)*; *fig.* easy; F easy-going; F accommodating; **2.** *su./m* sliding ring *(a.* ⊕*)*; ♀ runner; 🔨 case-slide.

coule [kul] *adv.:* **être à la ~** be wise, know the ropes, know all the tricks of the trade, be with it.

coulé [ku'le] *m dancing:* slide; ♪ slur; *billiards:* follow-through; ⊕ cast (-ing); **coulée** [ˌ] *f writing:* running-hand; *lava, liquid:* flow; ⊕ casting; ⊕ tapping; *fig.* streak; **couler** [ˌ] (1a) *v/t.* pour; ⚓ sink *(a ship)*; ♪ slur; *fig.* slip; F ruin; **se ~** slide, slip; F *fig.* **se la ~ douce** have an easy time; *v/i.* flow, run; ⚓ founder, sink; ⊕ run; slip; leak *(pen, vat, etc.)*; *fig.* slip by *(time)*; pass over *(facts)*.

couleur [ku'lœːr] *f* colo(u)r *(a. fig.)*; complexion; *cards:* suit; *cin.* **en ~(s** *pl.)* technicolor-...; 🐗 **pâles ~s** *pl.* chlorosis *sg.*, green-sickness *sg.*; **sous ~ de** under the pretence of.

couleuvre [ku'lœːvr] *f* grass snake; F **avaler des ~s** pocket an insult.

coulis [ku'li] **1.** *adj./m:* **vent** *m* **~** insidious draught; **2.** *su./m* ⊕ *(liquid)* filling; *cuis.* purée.

coulisse [ku'lis] *f* ⊕ groove, slot; ⊕ slide; △ wooden shoot; *thea.* wing; backstage; *fig.* background; ✝ outside market; **dans les ~s** backstage *(a. fig.)*; **porte** *f* **à ~** sliding door; *fig.* **regard** *m* **en ~** sideglance; **coulisser** [kuli'se] (1a) *v/t.* fit with slides; *v/i.* slide; **coulissier** ✝ [ˌ'sje] *m* outside broker.

couloir [ku'lwa:r] *m* corridor (*a.* 🐎, *geog.*), passage; *parl.* lobby; ⊕ shoot; *cin. film*: track; *water, mountain*: gully; *tennis*: tram-lines *pl.*; ✈ ~ aérien air corridor.

coup [ku] *m* blow, knock; hit; thrust; *knife*: stab; wound; ⊕, *sp.* stroke; sound; beat; *gun etc.*: shot; *wind*: gust; turn; (evil) deed; *sl.* drink, glass (*of wine*); *fig.* influence; ⚕ ~ de chaleur heat-stroke; F ~ de fil (telephone) call, ring; ~ de filet haul; ~ de grâce finishing stroke, quietus; ⚒ ~ de grisou firedamp explosion; ~ de Jarnac treacherous attack; F low trick; ⚔ ~ de main surprise attack, raid; ~ de maître master stroke; *foot.* ~ d'envoi kick-off; place-kick; ~ de pied kick; ~ de poing blow (with the fist); ⚕ ~ de sang apoplectic fit, F stroke; ⚕ ~ de soleil sunburn; ~ d'essai trial shot; ~ d'État coup d'état; ~ de téléphone (telephone) call; ~ de tête butt; *fig.* impulsive act; *fig.* ~ de théâtre dramatic turn; ~ d'œil glance; view; ~ franc *foot.* free kick; *hockey*: free hit; à ~ sûr certainly; après ~ after the event; as an afterthought; *sp.* donner le ~ d'envoi kick off; donner un ~ de brosse give a brush (down); donner un ~ de main à help; give a helping hand to; d'un (seul) ~ at one go; du premier ~ at the first attempt; entrer en ~ de vent burst in, rush in; être aux cent ~s be desperate; F être dans le ~ be with it; F monter le ~ à q. deceive s.o.; pour le ~ this time; for the moment; saluer d'un ~ de chapeau raise one's hat to; tenir le ~ take it; keep a stiff upper lip; tout à ~ suddenly, all of a sudden; tout d'un ~ (all) at once; traduire qch. à ~s de dictionnaire translate s.th., looking up each word in the dictionary.

coupable [ku'pabl] **1.** *adj.* guilty; **2.** *su.* culprit; ⚖ delinquent.

coupage [ku'pa:ʒ] *m* cutting; *wine*: blending; diluting (*of wine with water*); **coupant** [~'pɑ̃] *m* (cutting) edge.

coup-de-poing, *pl.* **coups-de-poing** [kud'pwɛ̃] *m* (~ américain) knuckleduster.

coupe¹ [kup] *f* cutting; *trees*: felling; ⊕ wood etc., a. fig. cut; section; ~ des cheveux haircut; *fig. sous la* ~ *de q.* under s.o.'s control *or* thumb.

coupe² [~] *f* (drinking) cup; *sp.* cup; *sl.* dial, mug.

coupé [ku'pe] *m* brougham; 🚋 coupé (*a. mot.*), half-compartment; **coupée** ⚓ [~] *f* gangway.

coupe...: ~**-cigares** [kupsi'ga:r] *m/inv.* cigar-cutter; ~**-circuit** ⚡ [~sir'kɥi] *m/inv.* circuit-breaker; ~**-faim** [~'fɛ̃] *m/inv.* appetite suppressant; ~**-gorge** [~'gɔrʒ] *m/inv.* death-trap; ~**-jarret** [~ʒa'rɛ] *m* cut-throat; assassin; ~**-légumes** [~le'gym] *m/inv.* vegetable-cutter; ~**-papier** [~pa'pje] *m/inv.* paperknife; letter-opener.

couper [ku'pe] (1a) *v/t.* cut (*a. tennis*); cut off (*a.* ⚔); cut down (*trees*), chop (*wood*); intercept; intersect; interrupt; water down (*wine*); ⚡ switch off; *cards*: trump; *teleph.* ~ la communication ring off; *mot.* ~ l'allumage switch off the ignition; ~ ~ intersect; F *fig.* give o.s. away; *v/i.*: *sl.* ~ à dodge (*s.th.*); F ~ dans le vif resort to extreme measures; *teleph.* ne coupez pas! hold the line!

couperet [ku'prɛ] *m* chopper; *guillotine*: blade.

couperose [ku'pro:z] *f* ⚕ blotchiness; ⚗ ~ verte (bleue) green (blue) vitriol; **couperosé, e** [~pro'ze] blotchy (*skin*).

coupeur, -euse [ku'pœːr, ~'pø:z] *su. person*: cutter; *su./f* cutting machine; ⚒ header.

couplage [ku'pla:ʒ] *m* ⚡ *etc.* coupling, connection; **couple** [kupl] *m* pair, couple; ⊕ torque, turning moment; **coupler** [ku'ple] (1a) *v/t.* couple; ⚡ connect; **couplet** [~'plɛ] *m* verse; ⊕ hinge.

coupoir [ku'pwa:r] *m* instrument: cutter.

coupole [ku'pɔl] *f* cupola, dome; ⚔ revolving gun-turret.

coupon [ku'pɔ̃] *m* bread, dividend, etc.: coupon; 🐎, *thea.* ticket; *material*: remnant; ⊕ test-bar; ~-réponse postal *post*: international reply coupon; **coupure** [~'py:r] *f* cut, gash; (newspaper-)cutting, clipping; ⚡, *thea.* cut; paper money; *geol.* fault.

cour [ku:r] *f* court (*a.* ⚖); (court-)yard; ⚔ square; *Northern France*: lavatory; *thea.* côté ~ O.P.; ♀ inter-

nationale de justice International Court of Justice (*at the Hague*); *faire la ~ à* court, woo.

courage [ku'ra:ʒ] *m* courage, F pluck; valo(u)r; **courageux, -euse** [~ra'ʒø, ~'ʒø:z] brave, courageous, F plucky; zealous.

couramment [kura'mã] *adv.* fluently; in general use, usually; **courant, e** [~'rã, ~'rã:t] **1.** *adj.* running; current; ♱ floating (*debt*); ♱ standard (*make*); *chien m ~* hound; **2.** *su./m* ⚡, *water:* current; stream; *metall.* blast; present month, ♱ instant, *abbr.* inst.; *fig.* course; ⚡ *~ alternatif (continu)* alternating (direct) current; *~ d'air* draught, *Am.* draft; ⚡ *~ triphasé* three-phase current; *au ~ (de)* conversant (with), acquainted (with), well informed (of *or* about); *être au ~ de a.* know all about; *mettre q. au ~ (de)* inform s.o. (about *or* of); *se tenir au ~* keep up to date; *dans le ~ de* in the course of; *fin ~* at the end of this month; ⚡ *... pour tous ~s* A.C./D.C. ...

courbatu, e [kurba'ty] stiff, aching; **courbature** [~'ty:r] *f* stiffness, muscle soreness; *~s pl.* aches and pains.

courbe [kurb] **1.** *adj.* curved; **2.** *su./f* curve; sweep; graph; **courber** [kur'be] (1a) *vt/i.* bend, curve; *v/t.:* *se ~* bend, stoop; **courbette** [~'bɛt] *f:* *fig. faire des ~s à* knowtow to; **courbure** [~'by:r] *f* curve; *road:* camber; *earth, space:* curvature; ⊕ *beam:* sagging; ⊕ *double ~ pipe:* S-bend.

coureur, -euse [ku'rœ:r, ~'rø:z] *su.* runner (*a. sp.*); *fig.* frequenter (*of cafés etc.*); *fig.* hunter (*of prizes etc.*); *su./m: sp. ~ de fond* stayer; *~ de jupons* skirt-chaser; *su./f* streetwalker.

courge ♀ [kurʒ] *f* gourd; pumpkin; *Am.* squash.

courir [ku'ri:r] (2i) *v/i.* run; race; flow (*blood, river, etc.*); *fig.* be current; ⚓ sail; *v/t.* run after; pursue; hunt; overrun; *sp.* run (*a race*); frequent, haunt; F *~ le cachet* give private lessons; *~ le monde* travel widely; *être fort couru* be much sought after.

courlis *orn.* [kur'li] *m* curlew.

couronne [ku'rɔn] *f* crown; coronet; *flowers, laurel:* wreath; ⊕ *wheel:* rim; **couronnement** [~rɔn'mã] *m*

crowning; coronation; **couronner** [~rɔ'ne] (1a) *v/t.* crown (*a. fig.; a. ⚡ a tooth*); *fig.* award a prize to.

courrai [ku're] *1st p. sg. fut. of courir.*

courre [ku:r] *v/t.:* *chasse f à ~* hunt(ing); **courrier** [ku'rje] *m* courier; post, mail; letters *pl.*; *journ.* (*news, theatrical, etc.*) column; *faire son ~* deal with one's mail; **courriériste** *journ.* [~rje'rist] *su.* columnist.

courroie [ku'rwa] *f* strap; ⊕ belt; *mot. ~ de ventilateur* fan belt.

courroucer [kuru'se] (1k) *v/t.* anger; *se ~* get angry; **courroux** *poet.* [~'ru] *m* anger.

cours [ku:r] *m* course; △ *bricks:* course, layer; *money:* circulation; ♱ quotation; *univ.* course (of lectures); *school:* class(es *pl.*), lesson; *~ d'eau* stream, river; ♱ *~ des changes* rate of exchange; ♱ *~ du marché mondial* price on the world market; *au ~ de* during, in the course of; *en ~* in progress.

course [kurs] *f* run(ning); race; excursion, trip; ⚓ cruise; ⊕ stroke; errand; *~ à pied* (foot-)race; *~ aux armements* armaments race; *~ de chevaux* horse-race; *~ de côte* hill climb; ⊕ *~ d'essay* test run; F *fig. être dans la ~* be with it; *faire des ~s* go shopping, run errands; *garçon de ~s* errand boy. [charger; steed.]

coursier [kur'sje] *m* mill-race; *poet.*)

court¹ [ku:r] *m* (tennis-)court.

court², courte [ku:r, kurt] **1.** *adj.* short, brief; *à ~ (de)* short (of); *sl. avoir la peau ~e* be lazy; **2.** *court adv.* short; *couper ~* cut short; *tout ~* simply, only.

courtage ♱ [kur'ta:ʒ] *m* brokerage.

courtaud, e [kur'to, ~'to:d] **1.** *adj.* squat, dumpy; **2.** *su.* stocky person; **courtauder** [~to'de] (1a) *v/t.* dock the tail of; crop the ears of.

court...: *~-bouillon, pl. ~s-bouillons cuis.* [kurbu'jõ] *m wine-sauce in which fish or meat is cooked*; *~-circuit, pl. ~s-circuits* ⚡ [~sir'kɥi] *m* short-circuit; *~-circuiter* ⚡, *a. fig.* [~sirkɥi'te] (1a) *v/t.* short-circuit; *fig. a.* bypass.

courtepointe [kurtə'pwɛ:t] *f* counterpane.

courtier, -ère ♱ [kur'tje, ~'tjɛ:r] *su.* broker; (electoral) agent; *su./m: ~ marron* ♱ outside broker; F bucket shop swindler.

courtine [kur'tin] *f* † curtain; ✕ line of trenches; ⌂ façade.

courtisan [kurti'zɑ̃] *m* courtier; **courtisane** [ˏ'zan] *f* courtesan; **courtiser** [ˏ'ze] (1a) *v/t.* pay court to; woo; *fig.* toady to, F suck up to.

courtois, e [kur'twa, ˏ'twaːz] courteous, polite (to[wards], *envers*); **courtoisie** [ˏtwa'zi] *f* courtesy.

couru, e [ku'ry] **1.** *p.p. of courir*; **2.** *adj.* sought after; popular; † accrued (*interest*); **courus** [ˏ] *1st p. sg. p.s. of courir*.

couseuse [ku'zøːz] *f* seamstress; stitcher (*of books*); stitching machine; **cousis** [ˏ'zi] *1st p. sg. p.s. of coudre*[1]; **cousons** [ˏ'zɔ̃] *1st p. pl. pres. of coudre*[1].

cousin[1] [ku'zɛ̃] *m* midge, gnat.

cousin[2] *m*, *e f* [ku'zɛ̃, ˏ'zin] cousin; **cousinage** F [ˏzi'naːʒ] *m* cousinship; cousinry; (poor) relations *pl.*

coussin [ku'sɛ̃] *m* cushion; pad; bolster; pillow (*of lacemaker*); **coussinet** [ˏsi'nɛ] *m* small cushion; ⊕ bearing; ♣ F bilberry, huckleberry; ⊕ ˏ de billes ball-bearings *pl.*; ⚙ ˏ de rail (rail-)chair.

cousu, e [ku'zy] **1.** *p.p. of coudre*[1]; **2.** *adj.* sewn; *fig.* ˏ d'or rolling in money; ˏ (à la) main hand-sewn; F ˏ main solid; excellent, first-rate; F *rester bouche* ˏe keep one's mouth shut.

coût [ku] *m* cost; ˏs *pl.* expenses; ˏ de la vie cost of living; **coûtant, e** [ku'tɑ̃, ˏ'tɑ̃ːt] *adj.*: *prix m* ˏ cost price.

couteau [ku'to] *m* knife; ⚡ blade; *être à* ˏx *tirés* be at daggers drawn; **coutelas** [kut'lɑ] *m* ♣ cutlass; *cuis.* broad-bladed knife; *icht.* F swordfish; **coutelier** [kutə'lje] *m* cutler; **coutellerie** [ˏtɛl'ri] *f* cutlery; cutlery works *usu. sg.*; cutler's shop.

coûter [ku'te] (1a) *vt/i.* cost; *v/i.*: ˏ *cher (peu)* be (in)expensive; *coûte que coûte* at all costs; **coûteux, -euse** [ˏ'tø, ˏ'tøːz] expensive, costly.

coutil *tex.* [ku'ti] *m* twill.

coutre [kutr] *m* ↗ plough-share; (wood-)chopper.

coutume [ku'tym] *f* custom, habit; *avoir* ˏ *de* be accustomed to; *comme de* ˏ as usual; **coutumier, -ère** [ˏty'mje, ˏ'mjɛːr] customary; ⚖ unwritten (*law*).

couture [ku'tyːr] *f* sewing; dressmaking; seam (*a.* ⊕); F *fig.* angle, aspect; *battre q. à plate* ˏ beat s.o. hollow; *haute* ˏ high-class dressmaking; *maison f de haute* ˏ fashion house; **couturier, -ère** [ˏty'rje, ˏ'rjɛːr] *su.* dressmaker; *su./f: thea.* répétition *f des* ˏères dress rehearsal.

couvain [ku'vɛ̃] *m* nest of insect eggs; brood-comb (*for bees*); **couvaison** [ˏvɛ'zɔ̃] *f* brooding time; incubation; **couvée** [ˏ've] *f* eggs: clutch; *chicks:* brood.

couvent [ku'vɑ̃] *m* nuns: convent; *monks:* monastery.

couver [ku've] (1a) *v/t.* sit on (*eggs*); hatch (out) (*eggs*); ⚕ be sickening for; *fig.* hatch (*a plot*); *fig.* (molly-)coddle (*a child*); *fig.* ˏ *des yeux* not to take one's eyes off (*s.o., s.th.*); gloat over (*one's victim*); *v/i.* smoulder (*fire, a. fig.*); *fig.* be brewing; *fig., a.* ⚕ develop, be developing.

couvercle [ku'vɛrkl] *m* lid, cover; ⊕ *a.* cap.

couvert, e [ku'vɛːr, ˏ'vɛrt] **1.** *p.p. of couvrir*; **2.** *adj.* covered; hidden; obscure; wooded (*country*); overcast (*sky*); *rester* ˏ keep one's hat on; **3.** *su./m* table things *pl.*; *restaurant:* cover-charge; shelter, cover(ing); *être à* ˏ be sheltered, *a. fig.* be safe (*from de*); *le vivre et le* ˏ board and lodging; *mettre (ôter) le* ˏ lay (clear) the table; *sous le* ˏ *de* under the cover or pretext of; *su./f pottery:* glaze; **couverture** [ˏvɛr'tyːr] *f* covering; cover; coverage (*a. journ.*); ⌂ roofing; rug, blanket; † security; *fig. sous* ˏ *de* under cover or cloak of.

couveuse [ku'vøːz] *f* sitting hen; incubator.

couvi [ku'vi] *adj./m* addled (*egg*).

couvre [kuːvr] *1st p. sg. pres. of couvrir*; ˏ**-chef** F [kuvrə'ʃɛf] *m* headgear, hat; ˏ**-feu** [ˏ'fø] *m* curfew; ˏ**-joint** ⊕ [ˏ'ʒwɛ̃] *m wood:* covering bead; *metall.* flat coverplate; *butt-joint:* welt; ˏ**-lit** [ˏ'li] *m* bedspread; ˏ**-pied(s)**, *pl.* ˏ**-pieds** [ˏ'pje] *m* coverlet; bedspread.

couvreur [ku'vrœːr] *m* ⌂ roofer; *freemason:* tiler; **couvrir** [ˏ'vriːr] (2f) *v/t.* cover (*a. journ.*, †); ⌂ roof; *post:* refund; *se* ˏ cover o.s. (*a. with honour etc.*); put one's hat on; clothe o.s.; become overcast (*sky etc.*).

crabe [krɑ:b] *m* crab.

crac! [krak] *int.* crack!

crachat [kra'ʃa] *m* spit; *ᵴ* sputum; F star (*of an Order*); **craché, e** F [~'ʃe] *adj.*: ce garçon est son père tout ~ this boy is the dead spit of his father; **cracher** [~'ʃe] (1a) *vt/i.* spit; *v/t.* F cough up, fork out (*money*); *v/i.* splutter (*pen*); **cracheur** *m*, **-euse** *f* [~'ʃœːr, ~'ʃøːz] spitter; **crachoir** [~'ʃwaːr] *m* spittoon; F tenir le ~ do all the talking, hold the floor; **crachoter** [~ʃɔ'te] (1a) *v/i.* sputter.

crack *sp.* [krak] *m* crack (*horse*); champion; ace.

craie [krɛ] *f* chalk; (*a.* bâton *m* de ~) stick of chalk.

craindre [krɛ̃:dr] (4m) *v/t.* fear, be afraid of; ~ de (*inf.*) be afraid of (*ger.*); ✝ craint l'humidité *inscription*: keep dry *or* in a dry place; je crains qu'il (ne) vienne I am afraid he is coming *or* will come; je crains qu'il ne vienne pas I am afraid he will not come; **craignis** [krɛ'ni] *1st p. sg. p.s. of* craindre; **craignons** [~'nõ] *1st p. pl. pres. of* craindre; **crains** [krɛ̃] *1st p. sg. pres. of* craindre; **craint, e** [krɛ̃, krɛ̃:t] 1. *p.p. of* craindre; 2. *su./f* dread; de ~ que ... (ne) (*sbj.*) lest; **craintif, -ve** [krɛ̃'tif, ~'tiːv] timid, fearful.

cramoisi, e [kramwa'zi] *adj., a. su./m* crimson.

crampe *ᵴ* [krɑ̃:p] *f* cramp; **crampon** [krɑ̃'põ] *m* ⚓ cramp(-iron), staple; *boot sole*: stud; *horseshoe*: calk; 🌱 crampon; 🌱 tendril; F (clinging) bore; **cramponner** [~pɔ'ne] (1a) *v/t.* ⚓ clamp; calk (*a horseshoe*); F pester; buttonhole (*s.o.*); se ~ à cling to.

cran ⊕ [krɑ̃] *m* notch; *ratchet, rifle, etc.*: catch; *wheel*: cog; *geol., metall.* fault; F pluck, guts *pl.*; *hair*: wave; ~ d'arrêt stop; F être à ~ be on edge; be edgy.

crâne¹ [krɑ:n] *m* cranium, skull.

crâne² F [krɑ:n] plucky; jaunty; **crânement** F [krɑn'mɑ̃] *adv.* pluckily; jauntily; F jolly; **crânerie** [~'ri] *f* pluck; jauntiness, swagger; **crâneur, -euse** F [krɑ'nœːr, ~øːz] 1. *adj.* être ~ be a show-off; 2. *su.* show-off.

crapaud [kra'po] *m* toad (*a. fig. pej.*); *zo.* grease; tub easy-chair; *piano*: baby-grand; F *fig.* brat, urchin; **crapaudière** [~po'djɛːr] *f* toadhole; swampy place; **crapaudine** [~po-'din] *f* toadstone; 🌱 ironwort; ⊕ grating; *bath*: waste hole; *cuis.* à la ~ boned and broiled, spatchcocked.

crapule [kra'pyl] *f* debauchery; dissolute person; blackguard; *coll.* dissolute crowd; **crapuleux, -euse** [~py'lø, ~'løːz] dissolute; filthy, lewd, foul.

craque F [krak] *f* tall story; (whopping) lie.

craquelé, e [kra'kle] crackled (*china, glass*).

craquelin [kra'klɛ̃] *m* biscuit: cracknel; *stocking*: wrinkle; *fig.* shrimp of a man.

craquelure [kra'klyːr] *f* crack; fine cracks *pl.*

craquement [krak'mɑ̃] *m* crackling; creaking; *fingers*: crack; *snow*: crunching; **craquer** [kra'ke] (1m) *v/i.* crack; crackle; crunch (*snow*); squeak (*shoes etc.*); come apart at the seams (*clothes, a. fig.*); *fig.* give way; F *fig.* break down (*person, thing*); *v/t.* strike (*a match*); **craqueter** [krak-'te] (1c) *v/i.* crackle; chirp (*cricket*); clatter (*stork*); **craqueur** *m*, **-euse** *f* F [kra'kœːr, ~'køːz] teller of tall stories, fibber.

crash 🛩 [kraʃ] *m* crash-landing.

crasse [kras] 1. *adj./f* crass (*ignorance*); 2. *su./f* filth, dirt; *metall.* dross; meanness; F dirty trick; **crasseux, -euse** [kra'sø, ~'søːz] dirty, filthy; F mean; **crassier** [~'sje] *m* slag-heap, tip.

cratère [kra'tɛːr] *m* crater; ⚒ shellhole.

cravache [kra'vaʃ] *f* hunting-crop, riding-whip.

cravate [kra'vat] *f* (*neck*)tie; ⚓ sling; ⊕ collar; *orn.* ruff; **cravater** [~va'te] (1a) *v/t.* put a tie on; ⊕ wind round; se ~ put one's tie on; *sp. etc.* collar (*s.o.*); *sl.* take *s.o.* for a ride.

crawl *sp.* [kro:l] *m* crawl(-stroke).

crayeux, -euse [krɛ'jø, ~'jøːz] chalky; *geol.* cretaceous; **crayon** [~'jõ] *m* pencil; pencil sketch; ✎ carbon-pencil; ~ à bille ball-point pen; ~ à cils eyebrow pencil; ~ d'ardoise slate pencil; ~ de couleur colo(u)ring pencil; ~ feutre felt(-tip) pen; ~ (de rouge) à lèvres lipstick; ~ lèvres lip-pencil; ~ noir lead pencil; ~

pour les yeux eyeliner (pencil); **crayonnage** [~jɔ'na:ʒ] *m* pencil sketch; **crayonner** [~jɔ'ne] (1a) *v/t.* sketch; make a pencil note of, jot down.

créance [kre'ã:s] *f* belief, credence; confidence; ✝ credit; *pol. lettres f/pl.* de~ credentials; **créancier** *m*, **-ère** *f* [~ã'sje, ~'sjɛ:r] creditor.

créateur, -trice [krea'tœ:r, ~'tris] **1.** *adj.* creative; **2.** *su.* creator; inventor; ✝ issuer; **créatif, -ive** [~'tif, ~'ti:v] creative; **création** [~'sjɔ̃] *f* creation (*a. bibl., cost., thea., a. fig.*); establishment; **créativité** [~tivi'te] *f* creativeness, creativity; **créature** [~'ty:r] *f* creature; *fig.* tool; F person.

crécelle [kre'sɛl] *f* rattle; *fig.* chatterbox.

crèche [krɛʃ] *f* manger; crib (*a. eccl.*); crèche, day-nursery; *sl.* pad (= home, house room); **crécher** *sl.* [kre'ʃe] (1f) *v/i.* live, *sl.* hang out; stay.

crédence [kre'dã:s] *f* sideboard; *eccl.* credence-table.

crédibilité [kredibili'te] *f* credibility.

crédit [kre'di] *m* credit (*a. ✝, a. fig.*); *parl.* sum (voted); prestige; *admin.* ~ municipal pawn-office; *à* ~ on credit; on trust; gratuitously; *faire* ~ *à* give credit to; **créditer** [~di'te] (1a) *v/t.:* ~ *q. de* credit s.o.'s account with (*a sum*); give s.o. credit for; **créditeur, -trice** [~di'tœ:r, ~'tris] **1.** *su.* creditor; **2.** *adj.* credit-...

credo [kre'do] *m/inv.* creed (*a. fig.*).

crédule [kre'dyl] credulous; **crédulité** [~dyli'te] *f* credulity.

créer [kre'e] (1a) *v/t.* create (*a. fig.*); ✝ make out (*a cheque*), issue (*a bill*); *admin. etc.* appoint, make (*s.o. magistrate etc.*).

crémaillère [krema'jɛ:r] *f* pot-hook; ⊕ rack; ⚙ cog-rail; ⚙ (*a. chemin m de fer à* ~) rack-railway; *pendaison f de* ~ housewarming (party); *pendre la* ~ give a house-warming (party).

crémation [krema'sjɔ̃] *f* cremation; **crématoire** [~'twa:r] crematory; *four m* ~ crematorium.

crème [krɛm] *f* cream (*a. fig.*); *cuis. a.* custard; *fig. the* best; ~ *fouettée* whipped cream; ~ *glacée* ice-cream; **crémer** [kre'me] (1f) *v/i.* cream; **crémerie** [krɛm'ri] *f* creamery, dairy; small restaurant; **crémeux, -euse** [kre'mø, ~'mø:z] creamy; **cré-**

mier, -ère [~'mje, ~'mjɛ:r] *su.* keeper of a small restaurant; *su./m* dairyman; *su./f* dairymaid; cream-jug.

crémone △ [kre'mɔn] *f* casement bolt.

créneau [kre'no] *m* △ crenel; loophole; look-out slit; *fig., a.* ✝ *etc.* gap; slot; *mot.* parking space; *mot. faire un* ~ get into the *or* a parking space; **créneler** [krɛn'le] (1c) *v/t.* △ crenel(l)ate (*a wall*); cut loop-holes in (*a wall*); ⊕ tooth, notch; mill (*a coin*); **crénelure** [~'ly:r] *f* indentation; notches *pl.*; ⚓ crenel(l)ing.

crépage [kre'pa:ʒ] *m* crimping; F ~ *de chignon* fight, set-to (between women).

crêpe¹ [krɛp] *m tex.* crape; crêpe (-rubber).

crêpe² *cuis.* [~] *f* pancake.

crêper [kre'pe] (1a) *v/t.* frizz, crimp; F *se* ~ *le chignon* tear each other's hair, fight (*women*).

crépi △ [kre'pi] *m* rough-cast.

crépine [kre'pin] *f* fringe; ⊕ pump: rose, strainer; **crépins** [~'pɛ̃] *m/pl.* shoemaker: grindery *sg.*; **crépir** [~'pi:r] (2a) *v/t.* crimp; △ roughcast; pebble (*leather*); **crépissure** △ [~pi'sy:r] *f* rough-cast.

crépitation [krepita'sjɔ̃] *f* crackle; ✼ crepitation; **crépiter** [~'te] (1a) *v/i.* crackle; sputter (*butter, etc.*); ✼ crepitate.

crépon [kre'pɔ̃] *m tex.* crépon; hairpad; **crépu, e** [~'py] fuzzy (*hair*), crinkled; **crêpure** [kre'py:r] *f hair:* frizzing, crimping.

crépuscule [krepys'kyl] *m* twilight, dusk.

cresson [kre'sɔ̃] *m* (water)cress; *sl.* ne pas avoir de ~ sur la fontaine have lost one's thatch (= *hair*).

crétacé, e *geol.* [kreta'se] chalky, cretaceous.

crête [krɛt] *f* △, *geog., zo,. anat.,* helmet, wave: crest; *mountain:* ridge, summit; *cock:* comb; *fig.* head; **crêté, e** *zo.* [krɛ'te] tufted, crested.

crétin *m*, **e** *f* [kre'tɛ̃, ~'tin] ✼ cretin; F fool; **crétinisme** ✼ [~ti'nism] *m* cretinism.

cretonne *tex.* [krə'tɔn] *f* cretonne.

creuser [krø'ze] (1a) *v/t.* hollow out; excavate; dig; sink (*a well*); plough, *Am.* plow (*a furrow*); *fig.* wrinkle;

fig. hollow; se ~ *la tête* (*or la cervelle*) rack one's brains.

creuset ⊕ [krø'zɛ] *m* crucible; *a. fig.* test, trial.

creux, creuse [krø, krø:z] **1.** *adj.* hollow, empty; sunken (*cheeks*); ⊕, 🕮 slack (*period*); *fig.* futile; *assiette f creuse* soup-plate; *heures f/pl. creuses* off-peak hours; **2.** *su./m* hollow; *stomach*: pit; *wave, graph*: trough; F bass voice; ~ *de la main* hollow of the hand.

crevaison [krəvɛ'zɔ̃] *f* bursting (*a.* ⊕, *mot.*); *mot.* puncture; *sl.* death.

crevant, e F [krə'vɑ̃, ~'vɑ̃:t] boring; killing (*work*); very funny (*story*).

crevasse [krə'vas] *f* crack; *wall*: crevice; *glacier*: crevace; *skin*: chap; *metal etc.*: flaw; **crevasser** [~va'se] (1a) *v/t.* crack; chap (*the skin*); se ~ crack; chap (*skin*).

crève F [krɛ:v] *f* death; **~-cœur** [krɛv'kœ:r] *m/inv.* heart-ache, grief.

crever [krə've] (1d) *v/i.* burst, split; *v/i.* F die (*animal*); F ~ *de faim* starve; F ~ *de rire* split one's sides with laughter; *v/t.* work or ride (*a horse*) to death; ~ *le cœur à q.* break s.o.'s heart; F ~ *les yeux à q.* be staring s.o. in the face, be obvious; se ~ *de travail* work o.s. to death.

crevette *zo.* [krə'vɛt] *f* shrimp; prawn.

cri [kri] *m* cry; shriek (*of horror, pain, etc.*); F fashion, style; *hinge, spring*: creak; *bird*: chirp; *mouse*: squeak; ~ *de guerre* war-cry; F *pol. etc.* slogan; *à* ~ *public* by public proclamation; *... dernier* ~ the latest thing in ...; *pousser un* ~ (*or des* ~s) scream; **criailler** [~a'je] (1a) *v/i.* bawl; whine, F grouse; ~ *contre* scold, rail at; **criaillerie** [~aj'ri] *f* bawling; whining; scolding; **criant, e** [~'ã, ~'ã:t] glaring, crying; **criard, e** [~'a:r, ~'ard] **1.** *adj.* crying; shrill (*voice*); pressing (*debt*); loud (*colour*); **2.** *su.* bawler; *su./f* shrew.

crible [kribl] *m* sieve; ⊕, ⚒ screen; **cribler** [kri'ble] (1a) *v/t.* riddle; *fig.* overwhelm, cover (with, *de*); *être criblé de dettes* be over head and ears in debt; **cribleur** *m*, **-euse** *f* [~'blœ:r, ~'blø:z] riddler; ⊕, ⚒ screener; ⊕ screening machine; **criblure** [~'bly:r] *f* ⚒ screenings *pl.*; siftings *pl.*

cric ⊕ [krik] *m* jack.

cricri F [kri'kri] *m* cricket; chirping.

criée [kri'e] *f* auction; *vente f à la* ~ sale by auction; **crier** [~'e] (1a) *v/i.* cry, call out; scream; squeak (*door, hinge, mouse, shoes*); *v/t.* cry, proclaim; hawk (*wares*); shout (*abuses, orders*); **crieur, -euse** [~'œːr, ~'øːz] *su.* shouter; hawker; *su./m thea.* call-boy.

crime [krim] *m* crime; ⚖️ felony; ~ *d'État* treason; ~ *d'incendie* arson; **criminaliser** [kriminali'ze] (1a) *v/t.* refer (*a case*) to a criminal court; **criminaliste** [~'list] *su.* criminologist; **criminalité** [~li'te] *f* criminal nature (*of an act*); ⚖️ *juvénile* juvenile delinquency; **criminel, -elle** [krimi'nɛl] **1.** *adj.* criminal (*law, action*); guilty (*person*); **2.** *su.* criminal, felon; *su./m* criminal action.

crin [krɛ̃] *m* horsehair; coarse hair; ~ *végétal* vegetable horsehair; *fig.* ... *à tout* ~ (*or tous* ~s) out and out ...; F *être comme un* ~ be very touchy.

crincrin F [krɛ̃'krɛ̃] *m* fiddle; fiddler.

crinière [kri'njɛ:r] *f* mane; *helmet*: (horse-)tail; F crop of hair.

crinoline [krino'lin] *f* crinoline.

crique [krik] *f* creek, cove, small bay; ⊕ *metal*: flaw.

criquet [kri'kɛ] *m zo.* locust; *zo.* F cricket; F small pony; *sl. person*: shrimp.

crise 🩺, *pol., fig.* [kri:z] *f* crisis; 🩺 attack; shortage; 🩺 *cardiaque* heart attack; ~ *du logement* housing shortage; ~ *économique* (*mondiale*) (worldwide) slump; *une* ~ *se prépare* things are coming to a head.

crispation [krispa'sjɔ̃] *f* contraction; contortion; tensing (up); twitch(ing); puckering; **crispé, e** [~'pe] tense, strained; uptight; **crisper** [~'pe] (1a) *v/t.* contract; clench (*one's fists*); contort (*one's face*); tense (up); F irritate (s.o.); se ~ *a.* tighten; *a.* pucker up (*face*).

crisser [kri'se] (1a) *v/i.* grate, rasp; squeak (*brakes*); ~ *des dents* grind one's teeth.

cristal [kris'tal] *m* crystal; crystal-glass; **cristallin, e** [~ta'lɛ̃, ~'lin] **1.** *adj.* crystalline; clear as crystal; **2.**

su./m anat. crystalline lens; **cristalliser** [ˌtaliˈze] (1a) vt/i. crystallize.
critère [kriˈtɛːr] m criterion, test; **critérium** sp. [ˌteˈrjɔm] m selection match or race.
critique [kriˈtik] **1.** adj. critical; **2.** su./m critic; su./f criticism; **critiquer** [ˌtiˈke] (1m) vt. criticize, find fault with; review (a book); censure; **critiqueur** m, **-euse** f [ˌtiˈkœːr, ˈkøːz] fault-finder.
croasser [krɔaˈse] (1a) vi. croak (raven, a. fig.); caw (crow, rook).
croc [kro] m hook; ⊕ pawl; zo. fang.
croc-en-jambe, pl. **crocs-en-jambe** [krɔkãˈʒãːb] m trip (up); donner (or faire) un ~ à q. trip s.o. up.
croche [krɔʃ] f ♪ quaver; ⊕ ~s pl. crook-bit tongs.
crochet [krɔˈʃɛ] m hook; crochet-hook; skeleton key; typ. square bracket; zo. fang; faire un ~ swerve; make a detour; fig. vivre aux ~s de q. live off s.o.; **crocheter** [krɔʃˈte] (1d) vt. pick (a lock); hook s.th. out or up; **crocheteur** [ˌtœːr] m thief: picklock; **crochu, e** [krɔˈʃy] hooked; crooked (ideas); fig. avoir les doigts ~es be light-fingered (thief); be close-fisted.
crocodile [krɔkɔˈdil] m zo. crocodile; 🕪 audible warning system.
croire [krwaːr] (4n) vi. believe (in, à; in God, en Dieu); vt. believe; think; ~ q. intelligent believe s.o. to be intelligent; à l'en ~ according to him (her); faire ~ qch. à q. lead s.o. to believe s.th.; s'en ~ be conceited.
crois [krwa] 1st p. sg. pres. of croire.
croîs [~] 1st p. sg. pres. of croître.
croisade [krwaˈzad] f crusade; **croisé, e** [ˌze] **1.** adj. crossed; folded (arms); double-breasted (coat); tex. twilled; mots m/pl. ~s crossword puzzle; **2.** su./m crusader; tex. twill; su./f crossing; casement window; ⚔ church: transept; **croisement** [krwazˈmã] m crossing; intersection; animals: interbreeding; cross(-breed); **croiser** [krwaˈze] (1a) vt. cross (a. ♀, biol.); fold (one's arms); tex. twill; vi. ⚓ cruise; **croiseur** [ˌˈzœːr] m cruiser; **croisière** [ˌˈzjɛːr] f cruise; vitesse f de ~ cruising speed; fig. pace; **croisillon** [ˌziˈjɔ̃] m cross-piece; ⊕ star-handle.
croissance [krwaˈsãːs] f growth; ✝~ zéro zero growth; **croissant, e** [ˌsã,

~ˈsãːt] **1.** adj. waxing (moon); **2.** su./m moon: crescent; cuis. croissant; ⚑ lune; **croissons** [ˌsɔ̃] 1st p. pl. pres. of croître.
croisure [krwaˈzyːr] f tex. twill weave; cost. cross-over.
croître [krwaːtr] (4o) vi. grow; increase; wax (moon); lengthen (days, shadows).
croix [krwa] f cross (a. decoration; fig. = trial, affliction); typ. dagger, obelisk; ~ de Lorraine cross of Lorraine; ✚♀-Rouge Red Cross; en ~ crosswise; fig. avec la ~ et la bannière with great ceremony; F fig. il faut or c'est la ~ et la bannière pour ... it's the devil's job to ...
croquant[1], **e** [krɔˈkã, ~ˈkãːt] **1.** adj. crisp; **2.** su./m cuis. gristle.
croquant[2] [krɔˈkã] m F clodhopper; unimportant person.
croque au sel [krɔkoˈsɛl] adv.: manger à la ~ eat (s.th.) with salt only.
croque...: ~-**madame** cuis. [krɔkmaˈdam] m/inv. toasted ham and cheese sandwich with fried egg; ~-**mitaine** f [ˌmiˈtɛn] m bog(e)y man; ~-**monsieur** cuis. [ˌmɔˈsjø] m/inv. toasted ham and cheese sandwich; ~-**mort** F [ˌˈmɔːr] m undertaker's mute; ~-**note** F pej. [ˌˈnɔt] m third-rate musician.
croquer [krɔˈke] (1m) vt/i. crunch; vt. munch; sketch; fig. gobble up; ♣ leave out (notes); ⚓ hook; F ~ le marmot cool one's heels; F joli à ~ pretty enough to eat.
croquet[1] sp. [krɔˈkɛ] m croquet.
croquet[2] [krɔˈkɛ] m crisp almond-covered biscuit; F snappy person; **croquette** cuis. [ˌˈkɛt] f croquette; rissole.
croquis [krɔˈki] m sketch.
cross-country sp. [krɔskœnˈtri] m cross-country running.
crosse [krɔs] f crook (a. eccl.); eccl. crozier; gun: butt; ⊕ piston: cross-head; sp. golf: club; hockey: stick.
crotale [krɔˈtal] m antiquity: crotalum; zo. rattlesnake, Am. a. rattler.
crotte [krɔt] f droppings pl.; cuis. une ~ de chocolat a chocolate; **crotté, e** [krɔˈte] dirty; **crottin** [ˌˈtɛ̃] m horse dung.
croulant, e [kruˈlã, ~ˈlãːt] **1.** adj. tumble-down; ramshackle; **2.** su./m: vieux ~ old fossil; ~s pl. old people;

crouler [ˌ‿'le] (1a) *v/i.* totter, crumble; collapse.

croup ✳ [krup] *m* croup.

croupade [kru'pad] *f horsemanship:* croupade; **croupe** [krup] *f animal:* croup, rump; F *person:* rump, bottom, behind; *hill:* crest, brow; ⚕ hip; en ‿ behind (the rider *or* driver); on the pillion; *monter en* ‿ *a.* ride pillion; **croupetons** [ˌ‿'tɔ̃] *adv.:* à ‿ crouching, squatting; **croupi, e** [kru'pi] stagnant (*water*); *fig.* sunk (in, *dans*); **croupier** ✝ [ˌ‿'pje] *m* broker's backer; *casino:* croupier; **croupière** [ˌ‿'pjɛːr] *f* crupper; *fig.* † *tailler des* ‿*s à* make things difficult for; **croupion** [ˌ‿'pjɔ̃] *m bird:* rump; F *chicken etc.:* parson's nose; **croupir** [ˌ‿'piːr] (2a) *v/i.* stagnate; *fig.* ‿ *dans* wallow in.

croustade *cuis.* [krus'tad] *f* pie, pasty; **croustillant, e** [krusti'jɑ̃, ˌ‿'jɑ̃ːt] crisp; short (*pastry*); crusty (*bread etc.*); *fig.* spicy (*story*); attractive (*woman*); **croustiller** [ˌ‿'je] (1a) *v/i.* nibble crusts (*with wine*); crunch (*food*); **croûte** [krut] *f* crust (*a. ⚕*); *cheese:* rind; ✳ scab; F daub (= *poor picture*); *fig. pej.* old fossil; *pej.* dunce; F *casser la* ‿ have a snack; **croûter** F [kru'te] (1a) *v/i.* eat, feed; **croûteux, -euse** ✳ [ˌ‿tø, ˌ‿'tøːz] covered with scabs; **croûton** [ˌ‿'tɔ̃] *m* piece of crust; *sl.* dauber (= *poor painter*); *fig. pej.* old fossil.

croyable [krwa'jabl] believable; trustworthy (*person*); **croyance** [ˌ‿'jɑ̃ːs] *f* belief; faith; **croyant, e** [ˌ‿jɑ̃, ˌ‿'jɑ̃ːt] **1.** *adj.* believing; **2.** *su.* believer; *les* ‿*s m/pl.* the faithful; **croyons** [ˌ‿'jɔ̃] *1st p. pl. pres. of* croire.

cru¹, crue [kry] raw; uncooked; *fig.* broad; ‿ *à l'estomac* indigestible.

cru² [ˌ‿] *m* wine region; 🍇 vineyard; wine, vintage; *fig.* soil; F locality; *de mon* ‿ of my own (invention); *du* ‿ local (*wine,* F *a. person etc.*); *(vin de) grand* ‿ great wine.

cru³, crue [ˌ‿] *p.p. of* croire.

crû, crue, *m/pl.* **crus** [ˌ‿] *p.p. of* croître.

cruauté [kryo'te] *f* cruelty (to, *envers*).

cruche [kryʃ] *f* jug, pitcher; *sl.* dolt, duffer; **cruchon** [kry'ʃɔ̃] *m* small jug; *beer:* mug; *sl.* dolt, duffer.

crucial, e *m/pl.* **-aux** [kry'sjal, ˌ‿'sjo] crucial (*a. fig.*), cross-shaped; **crucifiement** [krysifi'mɑ̃] *m* crucifixion; *fig.* crucify; **crucifier** [ˌ‿'fje] (1o) *v/t.* crucify; **crucifix** [ˌ‿'fi] *m* crucifix; **crucifixion** [ˌ‿fik'sjɔ̃] *f* crucifixion; **cruciforme** [ˌ‿'fɔrm] cruciform, cross-shaped.

crudité [krydi'te] *f* crudity; coarseness (*of an expression*); indigestibility (*of food*); ‿*s pl.* offensive *or* gross passages *or* words; *cuis.* raw vegetables.

crue [kry] *f water:* swelling, rise; flood; *en* ‿ in spate, in flood (*river*).

cruel, -elle [kry'ɛl] cruel (to, *envers*).

crûment [kry'mɑ̃] *adv. of* cru¹.

crus [kry] *1st p. sg. p.s. of* croire.

crûs [ˌ‿] *1st p. sg. p.s. of* croître.

crusse¹ [krys] *1st p. sg. impf. sbj. of* croire.

crusse² [ˌ‿] *1st p. sg. impf. sbj. of* croître.

crustacé *zo.* [krysta'se] *m* crustacean, F shellfish.

crypte ⚕, ⚕, *anat.* [kript] *f* crypt.

crypto... [kriptɔ] crypto...

cubage [ky'baːʒ] *m* cubic content.

cubain, e [ky'bɛ̃, ˌ‿'bɛn] *adj., a. su.* ♀ Cuban.

cube [kyb] **1.** *su./m* cube; cubic space; ‿*s pl. toy:* building blocks, bricks; **2.** *adj.* cubic; **cuber** [ky'be] (1a) *v/t.* cube; find the cubic contents of; have a cubic content of.

cubilot *metall.* [kybi'lo] *m* smelting cupola.

cubique [ky'bik] **1.** *adj.* cubic; ⚕ *racine f* ‿ cube root; **2.** *su./f* ⚕ cubic (curve); **cubisme** *paint.* [ˌ‿'bism] *m* cubism; **cubiste** *paint.* [ˌ‿'bist] *su., a. adj.* cubist.

cubitus *anat.* [kybi'tys] *m* cubitus, ulna.

cueillaison [kœjɛ'zɔ̃] *f* picking, gathering; **cueille** [kœːj] *1st p. sg. pres. of* cueillir; **cueillerai** [kœj're] *1st p. sg. fut. of* cueillir; **cueillette** [kœ'jɛt] *f* picking, gathering; **cueillir** [ˌ‿'jiːr] (2c) *v/t.* gather, pick; *fig.* win; *fig.* snatch, steal (*a kiss*); F pick (*s.o.*) up; F catch, nab; ‿ *q. à froid* catch s.o. off (his *or* her) guard, take s.o. unawares; **cueilloir** [kœj'waːr] *m* fruit-basket; *tool:* fruit-picker.

cuiller, cuillère [kɥi'jɛːr] *f* spoon; ⊕ *tool:* spoon-drill; ⊕ scoop; *sl.* fin (=

cuillerée

hand); ~ *à bouche* table-spoon; ~ *à café* coffee-spoon; ~ *à dos d'âne* heaped spoon; ~ *à pot* ladle; **cuillerée** [kɥij're] *f* spoonful.

cuir [kɥiːr] *m* leather; *razor:* strop; *animal:* hide; F faulty liaison (*in speech*); ~ *chevelu* scalp; ~ *de Russie* Russia (leather); F *faire un* ~ drop a brick (= *make an incorrect liaison*); **cuirasse** [kɥi'ras] *f* breast-plate, cuirass; ⚓, *zo.* armo(u)r; **cuirassé, e** [kɥira'se] **1.** *adj.* armo(u)red, armo(u)r-plated; *fig.* hardened (against, *contre*); **2.** *su./m* battleship; **cuirasser** [~'se] (1a) *v/t.* put a cuirass on (*s.o.*); ⚓ armo(u)r; ⊕ protect; *fig.* harden (against, *contre*); **cuirassier** ✕ [~'sje] *m* cuirassier.

cuire [kɥiːr] (4h) *v/t.* cook; bake (*bread*); fire (*bricks, pottery*); boil (*sugar*); ~ *à l'eau* boil; ~ *au four* bake, roast; *v/i.* cook; be boiling (*a. fig.*); smart (*eyes etc.*); *il lui en cuira* he'll be sorry for it; *faire* ~ cook (*s.th.*); **cuisant, e** [kɥi'zɑ̃, ~'zɑ̃ːt] burning, stinging, smarting; *fig.* bitter (*cold, disappointment*); burning (*desire*); **cuiseur** ⊕ [~'zœːr] *m* burner.

cuisine [kɥi'zin] *f* kitchen; ✕ cook-house; ⚓ galley; cookery; cooking; ✕ ~ *roulante* field-kitchen; *faire la* ~ do the cooking; **cuisiner** [~zi'ne] (1a) *vt/i.* cook; *v/t. fig.* F grill (*s.o.*); F cook (*accounts etc.*); **cuisinier, -ère** [~zi'nje, ~'njeːr] *su.* cook; *su./f* (~ *à gas, électrique*) gas, electric) cooker, *Am.* range.

cuisis [kɥi'zi] *1st p. sg. p.s. of cuire;* **cuisons** [~'zɔ̃] *1st p. pl. pres. of cuire.*

cuissard [kɥi'saːr] *m armour:* cuisse; ⊕ (water-)leg; **cuisse** [kɥis] *f* thigh; *cuis. chicken:* leg; **cuisseau** *cuis.* [kɥi'so] *m veal:* fillet of leg.

cuisson [kɥi'sɔ̃] *f* cooking; baking; *sugar:* boiling; *bricks etc., a. fig.:* burning.

cuissot [kɥi'so] *m venison:* haunch.

cuistre [kɥistr] *m* (priggish) pedant; F cad.

cuit, e [kɥi, kɥit] **1.** *p.p. of cuire;* **2.** *su./f* ⊕ *bricks etc.:* baking, firing; *sugar:* boiling; batch (*of baked things*); F *prendre une* ~ get tight (= *drunk*); **cuiter** *sl.* [kɥi'te] (1a) *v/t.: se* ~ get drunk.

cuivre [kɥiːvr] *m* copper; ~ *jaune* brass; ♪ ~*s pl.* brass *sg.*; **cuivré, e** [kɥi'vre] coppery, copper-colo(u)red;

bronzed (*complexion*); *fig.* metallic (*voice*); brassy, blaring; **cuivrer** [~'vre] (1a) *v/t.* copper; **cuivreux, -euse** [~'vrø, ~'vrøːz] coppery; ⊕ cupreous (*ore*); 🜍 cuprous; *fig.* blaring.

cul ∨ [kyl] *m* backside, ∨ arse, *Am.* ass; *animal:* haunches *pl.*; F bottom (*of an object*); *cart:* tail; **culasse** [ky'las] *f* ✕ breech; ⚡ yoke, heel-piece; *mot.* detachable cylinderhead.

culbute [kyl'byt] *f* somersault; tumble, F purler; *sl.* failure; F *faire la* ~ ✝ fail; *pol.* fall; F make a scoop; **culbuter** [~by'te] (1a) *v/i.* turn a somersault; topple over; tumble; F ✝ fail; F *pol.* fall; *v/t.* throw over; overthrow (*a. pol.*); upset; knock head over heels; tip; **culbuteur** [~by'tœːr] *m* tipping device; *mot.* rocker-arm, valve-rocker; ⚡ tumbler.

cul...: ~-**de-jatte,** *pl.* ~**s-de-jatte** [kyd'ʒat] *m* legless cripple; ~-**de-lampe,** *pl.* ~**s-de-lampe** [~'lɑ̃ːp] *m* ⚡ pendant; ⚡ bracket, corbel; *typ.* tail-piece; ~-**de-sac,** *pl.* ~**s-de-sac** [~'sak] *m* blind alley (*a fig.*).

culée [ky'le] *f* ⚡ abutment; ⚓ stern-way; **culer** [~'le] (1a) *v/i.* go backwards, back; ⚓ veer astern (*wind*); ⚓ make stern-way; **culière** [~'ljeːr] *f* crupper.

culinaire [kyli'neːr] culinary.

culminant, e [kylmi'nɑ̃, ~'nɑ̃ːt] *astr.* culminant; *point m* ~ highest point; *glory, power:* height; *power:* zenith; **culmination** *astr.* [~na-'sjɔ̃] *f* culmination; **culminer** [~'ne] (1a) *v/i.* culminate, reach the highest point (*a. fig.*).

culot [ky'lo] *m* ⊕ bottom, base; *fig.* F baby of the family; F cheek, nerve, impudence; *tobacco pipe:* dottle; F *avoir du* ~ have a lot of cheek; **culotte** [~'lɔt] *f* breeches *pl.*; pants *pl.*; knickers *pl.*, panties *pl.* (*for women*); *beef:* rump; ⊕ breeches pipe, Y pipe; F *porter la* ~ wear the trousers; F *prendre une* ~ *cards etc.:* lose heavily; **culotté, e** [kylɔ'te] seasoned (*pipe*); F cheeky; **culotter** [kylɔ'te] (1a) *v/t.* put trousers on; season (*a pipe*).

culpabiliser [kylpabili'ze] (1a) *v/t.* make (*s.o.*) feel guilty; **culpabilité** [~'te] *f* guilt.

culte [kylt] *m* worship; creed, cult; religion; *protestant church:* (church) service; **cultivable** [kylti'vabl] arable; **cultivateur, -trice** [∼va-'tœːr,∼'tris] **1.** *su.* cultivator; farmer; *su./m* cultivator, light plough; **2.** *adj.* farming; **cultivé, e** [∼'ve] ✔ cultivated; *fig.* cultured; **cultiver** ✔ [∼'ve] (1a) *v/t.* cultivate (*a. fig.*); farm, till.

culture [kyl'tyːr] *f* ✔ cultivation (*a. fig.*), farming, growing; *fish etc.*: breeding; *fig.* culture (*a. of bacteria*); ✔ ∼s *pl.* crops, cultivated land *sg.*; *physique* physical culture; **culturel, -elle** [∼ty'rɛl] cultural; **culturisme** [∼ty'rism] *m* bodybuilding; **culturiste** [∼ty'rist] *su.* bodybuilder.

cumin ♀ [ky'mɛ̃] *m* cum(m)in.

cumul [ky'myl] *m* plurality (*of offices*); ♱♱ consecutiveness (*of sentences*); **cumulard** *pej.* [kymy'laːr] *m* pluralist; **cumuler** [∼'le] (1a) *v/t.* hold a plurality (*of offices*); draw (*salaries*) simultaneously.

cupide [ky'pid] greedy, covetous; **cupidité** [∼pidi'te] *f* greed, cupidity.   [ing.\
cuprifère [kypri'fɛːr] copper-bear-∫

curable [ky'rabl] curable; **curage** [∼'raːʒ] *m teeth:* picking; *drain etc.:* clearing (out); ∼s *pl.* dirt *sg.*; **curatelle** ♱♱ [kyra'tɛl] *f* trusteeship, guardianship; **curateur, -trice** [∼'tœːr, ∼'tris] *su.* ♱♱ trustee; guardian (*of a minor*); committee (*of a lunatic*); *su./m* administrator; *su./f* administratrix; **curatif, -ve** [∼'tif, ∼'tiːv] *adj., a. su./m* curative; **cure** [kyːr] *f* care; ✂, *eccl.* cure; *eccl.* living; ∼ *de rajeunissement* rejuvenation; ∼ *de repos* rest cure.

curé [ky're] *m* parish priest; (Anglican) vicar, rector.

cure-dent [kyr'dɑ̃] *m* toothpick.

curée [ky're] *f hunt.* deer's entrails *pl.* given to the hounds; *fig.* ∼ *des places* scramble for office.

cure...: ∼**-ongles** [ky'rɔ̃ːgl] *m/inv.* nail-cleaner; ∼**-oreille** [kyrɔ'rɛːj] *m* ear-pick; ∼**-pipe** [kyr'pip] *m* pipe-cleaner.

curer [ky're] (1a) *v/t.* clean (out); pick (*one's teeth etc.*); dredge (*a river*); **curetage** [kyr'taːʒ] *m* scraping; ✂ curetting; **cureur** [ky'rœːr] *m* cleaner.

curial, e, *m/pl.* **-aux** *eccl.* [ky'rjal, ∼'rjo] of the parish priest, curé's ...; **curie** *eccl.* [∼'ri] *f* curia.

curieux, -euse [ky'rjø,∼'rjøːz] **1.** *adj.* curious; interested (in, *de*); inquisitive; odd; strange; *curieusement a.* oddly enough; **2.** *su.* curious *or* interested person; *su./m the* odd thing (about, *de*); **curiosité** [∼rjozi'te] *f* curiosity; ∼s *pl.* sights (*of a town*).

curiste [ky'rist] *su.* patient taking a cure.

curseur ⊕ [kyr'sœːr] *m* slide; slider; runner (*a. ✍*).

cursif, -ve [kyr'sif, ∼'siːv] **1.** *adj.* cursive; cursory; **2.** *su./f writing:* cursive, running hand; *typ.* script.

cuscute ♀ [kys'kyt] *f* dodder.

cuspide ♀ [kys'pid] *f* cusp; **cuspidé, e** ♀ [∼pi'de] cuspidate.

custode [kys'tɔd] *f eccl.* altar-curtain; pyx-cloth; custodial (*for host*); *mot.* ∼ *arrière* rear-window.

cutané, e [kyta'ne] cutaneous; (*disease*) of the skin.

cuvage [ky'vaːʒ] *m,* **cuvaison** [∼vɛ-'zɔ̃] *f* fermenting in vats; vat room; **cuve** [kyːv] *f* vat; ⊕ tank; cistern; *mot.* float-chamber; **cuveau** [ky'vo] *m* small vat; small tank; **cuvée** [∼'ve] *f* vatful; *wine:* growth.

cuveler [ky'vle] (1c) *v/t.* line (*a shaft etc.*).

cuver [ky've] (1a) *vt/i.* ferment, work; **cuvette** [∼'vet] *f* wash-basin; bowl; *geol., geog.* basin; *phot.* dish; *W.C.:* pan, bowl; *barometer:* cup; *thermometer:* bulb; *watch:* cap; ⊕ *ball-bearing:* race; ball-socket; **cuvier** [∼'vje] *m* wash-tub.

cyanose [sja'noːz] *f* ✍ cyanosis; *min.* cyanose; **cyanuration** [∼nyra'sjɔ̃] *f* cyanidization; **cyanure** ⚗ [∼'nyːr] *m* cyanide.

cybernéticien [sibɛrneti'sjɛ̃] *m* cyberneticist; **cybernétique** [∼'tik] **1.** *su./f* cybernetics *sg.*; **2.** *adj.* cybernetic; **cybernétiser** [∼ti'ze] (1a) *v/t.* control cybernetically.

cyclable [si'klabl] for cyclists; *piste f* ∼ cycle path.

cyclamen ♀ [sikla'mɛn] *m* cyclamen.

cycle [sikl] *m* cycle (*a. fig.*); **cyclique** [si'klik] cyclic(al); **cyclisme** *sp.* [∼'klism] *m* cycling; **cycliste** [∼'klist] **1.** *su.* cyclist; **2.** *adj.* cycling.

cyclo... [siklɔ] cyclo...; **cycloïde** ⋔ [∼'id] *f* cycloid; **cyclomoteur** [∼mɔ'tœːr] *m* moped, auto-cycle; **cyclomotoriste** [∼mɔtɔ'rist] *su.* moped-rider.

cyclone *meteor.* [si'klɔn] *m* cyclone.
cyclotourisme [siklɔtu'rism] *m* cycle-touring, touring on (bi)cycles.
cyclotron *phys.* [siklɔ'trɔ̃] *m* cyclotron.
cygne *orn.* [siɲ] *m* swan.
cylindrage [silɛ̃'dra:ʒ] *m* rolling (*a.* ⊕); *tex.* calendering; **cylindre** ⊕ [~'lɛ̃:dr] *m* cylinder; roller.
cylindrée *mot.* [silɛ̃'dre] *f* (cubic) capacity; **cylindrer** [~'dre] (1a) *v/t.* ⊕ roll; *tex.* calender; **cylindrique** [~'drik] cylindrical.

cymbale ♪ [sɛ̃'bal] *f* cymbal; **cymbalier** [~ba'lje] *m* cymbalist.
cynique [si'nik] **1.** *adj.* cynical; *phls.* cynic; *fig.* shameless; **2.** *su./m phls.* cynic; *fig.* shameless person; **cynisme** [~'nism] *m phls.* cynicism; *fig.* effrontery.
cynocéphale *zo.* [sinɔse'fal] *m* cynocephalus, dog-faced baboon.
cyprès ♀ [si'prɛ] *m* cypress; **cyprière** [~pri'ɛ:r] *f* cypress-grove.
cyprin *icht.* [si'prɛ̃] *m* carp.
cystite ⚕ [sis'tit] *f* cystitis.

D

D, d [de] *m* D, d.

da [da]: *oui-da!* yes indeed!

d'ac *sl.* [dak] okay, Ok.

dactylo F [dakti'lo] *su. person:* typist; *su./f* typing; F typing pool; **~graphe** [daktilɔ'graf] *su.* typist; **~graphie** [~gra'fi] *f* typing, typewriting; **~graphier** [~gra'fje] (1o) *v/t.* type.

dada F [da'da] *m ch.sp.* gee-gee; *fig.* hobby(-horse), fad.

dadais F [da'dɛ] *m* simpleton.

dague [dag] *f* dagger; ⚓ dirk; ⊕ scraping-knife; *zo. deer:* first antler; *wild boar:* tusk.

daguet *hunt.* [da'gɛ] *m* brocket.

daigner [dɛ'ɲe] (1b) *v/t.* deign (to *inf.*), condescend (to *inf.*).

daim [dɛ̃] *m zo.* deer; buck; ✝ buckskin; en ~ suède (*gloves*); **daine** *zo.* [dɛn] *f* doe.

dais [dɛ] *m* canopy.

dallage [da'la:ʒ] *m* paving; flagging; tiled floor; **dalle** [dal] *f* paving-stone; flagstone; floor tile; *sl.* throat; **daller** [da'le] (1a) *v/t.* pave; tile (*the floor*).

daltonien, -enne 𝔰 [daltɔ'njɛ̃, ~'njɛn] 1. *adj.* colo(u)r-blind; 2. *su.* colo(u)r-blind person; **daltonisme** 𝔰 [~'nism] *m* colo(u)r-blindness.

dam [dɑ̃] *m* ✝ hurt, prejudice; *au* (*grand*) ~ *de* (much) to the detriment *or* displeasure of.

damas [da'mɑ] *m* Damascus blade; *tex.* damask; ♀ damson; **damasquiner** [~maski'ne] (1a) *v/t.* damascene; **damasser** [~mɑ'se] (1a) *v/t.* damask; *acier m damassé* Damascus steel.

dame [dam] 1. *su./f* lady (*a. chess*); *cards, chess:* queen; *draughts:* king; ⊕ (*paving*) beetle; rammer; ~ *de charité* lady visitor; ♀s *pl.* Ladies (= *toilet*); ~ *d'honneur* matron of hono(u)r; ~ *du vestiaire* cloakroom (*Am.* checkroom) attendant, *Am. a.* hatcheck girl; *jeu m de* ~s draughts, *Am.* checkers; 2. *int.* indeed!; *of course!*; **~-jeanne**, *pl.* **~s-jeannes** [~'ʒan] *f* demijohn; **damer** [da'me]

(1a) *v/t.* crown (*a piece at draughts*); ⊕ ram (*the earth etc.*); *fig.* ~ *le pion à* outdo *or* outwit (*s.o.*).

damier [da'mje] *m* draught-board, *Am.* checker-board; *tex. à* ~ chequered, checked.

damnable [dɑ'nabl] *fig.* detestable, damnable; *eccl.* deserving damnation; **damnation** [~na'sjɔ̃] *f* damnation; **damner** [~'ne] (1a) *v/t.* damn; F *faire* ~ *q.* drive s.o. crazy.

damoiseau [damwa'zo] *m* ✝ squire; F fop; **damoiselle** ✝ [~'zɛl] *f* damsel.

dancing [dɑ̃'siŋ] *m* public dancehall; supper-club.

dandin F [dɑ̃'dɛ̃] *m* simpleton; **dandiner** [~di'ne] (1a) *v/t.* dandle; *se* ~ waddle; strut.

danger [dɑ̃'ʒe] *m* danger; ~ *de mort!* danger of death!; *en* ~ *de mort* in danger of one's life; **dangereux, -euse** [dɑ̃ʒ'rø, ~'rø:z] dangerous (to, *pour*).

danois, e [da'nwa, ~'nwa:z] 1. *adj.* Danish; 2. *su./m ling.* Danish; *zo.* great Dane; *su.* ♀ Dane; *les* ♀ *m/pl.* the Danes.

dans [dɑ̃] *prp. usu.* in (*the street, the house, a moment, a month, the morning, the past*); *place:* within (*the limits*); among (*the crowd*); *direction:* into; *time:* within (*an hour*), during; *condition:* in; with; under (*these circumstances, the necessity*); *source, origin:* out of, from; ~ *la ville* (with)in the town; *entrer* ~ *une pièce* enter a room; ~ *Racine* in Racine; *mettre qch.* ~ *un tiroir* put s.th. in(to) a drawer; ~ *le temps* formerly; *périr* ~ *un accident* be killed in an accident; ~ *le commerce* in trade; ~ *l'embarras* embarrassed; ~ *l'intention de* (*inf.*) with the intention of (*ger.*); *faire qch.* ~ *la perfection* do s.th. to perfection; *avoir foi* ~ have confidence in; *consister* ~ consist of; *puiser* (*boire, manger*) ~ draw (drink, eat) from; *prendre* ~ take from *or* out of.

dansant, e [dã'sã, ~'sã:t] dancing; springy (*step*); lively (*tune*); thé *m* ~ tea-dance, thé dansant; **danse** [dã:s] *f* dance; dancing; *fig.* F battle; *sl.* thrashing; ⚔ ~ de Saint-Guy St. Vitus' dance; ~ macabre Dance of Death; salle *f* de ~ ballroom; **danser** [dã'se] (1a) *v/t.* dance; dandle (*a baby*); *v/i.* dance; prance (*horse*); faire ~ q. dance with s.o.; *fig.* F lead s.o. a dance; **danseur, -euse** [~'sœ:r, ~'sø:z] *su.* dancer; (dance-)partner; ballet-dancer; en~ de corde tight-rope dancer; *su./f* ballerina; **dansotter** [~sɔ'te] (1a) *v/i.* hop, skip.

danubien, -enne *geog.* [dany'bjẽ, ~'bjɛn] Danubian.

dard [da:r] *m* † javelin, dart; *zo.* bee etc.: sting (*a. fig.*); *sun*: piercing ray; *flame*: tongue; ⚔ pistil; *icht.* dace; **darder** [dar'de] (1a) *v/t.* hurl; shoot forth; *icht.* spear; *fig.* shoot (*a glance*) (at, sur).

dare-dare F [dar'da:r] *adv.* posthaste, at top speed.

darne *cuis.* [darn] *f fish*: slice, steak.

dartre [dartr] *f* ⚔ dartre; scurf; *metall.* scab; **dartreux, -euse** [dar'trø, ~'trø:z] ⚔, *metall.* scabby; ⚔ herpetic.

date [dat] *f* date; ~ limite deadline; target date; de longue~ of long standing; en~ de ... dated ...; être le premier en ~ come first; faire ~ mark an epoch; jusqu'à une ~ récente until recently; **dater** [da'te] (1a) *v/i.* date (from, de); à ~ de ce jour from today; from that day; cela date de loin it goes a long way back; *v/t.* date (*a letter*); **dateur** [~'tœ:r] *m*, **datographe** [~tɔ'graf] *m watch*: date indicator.

datte ⚔, ✝ [dat] *f* date; *sl.* des ~s! not on your life!, *Am.* no dice!; **dattier** ⚔ [da'tje] *m* date-palm.

daube *cuis.* [do:b] *f* stew; en ~ stewed, braised.

dauber[1] † [do'be] (1a) *v/t.* (or *v/i.* ~ sur) q. pull s.o. to pieces behind his back; jeer at s.o.

dauber[2] *cuis.* [do'be] (1a) *v/t.* stew, braise; **daubière** *cuis.* [~'bjɛ:r] *f* stew-pan, braising-pan.

dauphin [do'fẽ] *m zo.* dolphin; *hist.* Dauphin (= *eldest son of French king*); *fig.* successor; **dauphine** *hist.* [~'fin] *f* Dauphiness, wife of the

Dauphin; **dauphinelle** ⚔ [~fi'nɛl] *f* delphinium.

davantage [davã'ta:ʒ] *adv.* more (and more); longer (*space, time*).

davier [da'vje] *m* ⚔ (extraction) forceps; ⊕ cramp; ⚓ davit.

de [də] *prp. usu.* of; *material*: (made) of (*wood*), in (*velvet*); *cause*: of (*hunger*), from (*exhaustion*); with, for (*pain, joy*); *origin*: from (*France, the house*), out of; *distance*: of, from; *direction*: to (*the station*); *place*: at, in; *time*: by (*day, night*); in; for (*ten month*); *agent, instrument*: with (*a stick*); by (*name*); in (*a low voice*); on; *manner*: in (*this way*); *measure, comparison*: by; *price*: for; *partitive article*: du (some) bread; ~ la viande (some) meat; des légumes vegetables; un litre ~ vin a litre of wine; une douzaine ~ bouteilles a dozen bottles; la ville ~ Paris (the city of) Paris; le mois ~ janvier January; assez ~ enough; beaucoup ~ much (*money*), many (*things*); moins ~ less; pas ~ no; peu ~ few; plus ~ more; tant ~ so much, so many; trop ~ too much, too many; qch. ~ rouge s.th. red; *genitive, possession*: ~ mon père of my father, my father's; ~ la table of the table; le journal d'hier yesterday's paper; les œuvres ~ Molière Molière's works; matériaux ~ construction building materials; membre du Parlement Member of Parliament; habitant des villes city-dweller; le meilleur élève ~ la classe the best pupil in the class; souvenirs d'enfance childhood memories; amour (crainte) ~ love (fear) of; chapeau ~ paille straw hat; une robe ~ soie rouge a dress in red silk; mourir ~ cancer (fatigue) die of cancer (from fatigue); ~ haut en bas from top to bottom; tirer qch. ~ sa poche take s.th. out of or from one's pocket; saigner du nez bleed from the nose; à trois milles ~ distance at a distance of three miles; ~ ... à ... from ... to ...; between ... and ...; prendre la route (le train) ~ Bordeaux take the Bordeaux road (train); près ~ near, close to; d'un côté on one side; ~ ce côté on this side; ~ nos jours in our times; ~ ma vie in my lifetime; du temps ~ Henri IV in the days of Henry IV; à 2 heures ~ l'après-

midi at 2 p.m.; *avancer (retarder)* ~ *5 minutes* be 5 minutes fast (slow) *(watch)*; *vêtir (couvrir, orner)* ~ clothe (cover, decorate) with; *se nourrir (vivre)* ~ feed (live) on; *frapper (toucher)* ~ strike (touch) with; *montrer du doigt* point at; *fig.* scorn; *précédé* ~ preceded by; *trois mètres* ~ *long (haut)* three metres long (high); *âgé* ~ *5 ans* 5 years old *or* of age; *plus âgé* ~ *2 ans* older by 2 years; *plus* ~ *6* more than 6; *d'un œil curieux* with an inquiring look *or* eye; *un chèque (des marchandises)* ~ *20 F.* a cheque (goods) for 20 F.; ~ *beaucoup* by far; *content* ~ content *or* pleased with; *digne* ~ ...-worthy, worthy of; *fier* ~ proud of; *paralysé d'un bras* paralyzed in one arm; *un jour* ~ *libre* a free day; *un drôle* ~ *bonhomme* an odd chap.

dé¹ [de] *m gaming:* die; *domino:* piece; *golf:* tee; ~*s pl.* dice; *le* ~ *en est jeté* the die is cast.

dé² [~] *m (a.* ~ *à coudre)* thimble.

déambuler F [deãby'le] (1a) *v/i.* stroll about, saunter.

débâcle [de'bɑ:kl] *f ice:* breaking up; *fig.* disaster; downfall, collapse; F *pol.* landslide; ✝ crash; **débâcler** [~bɑ'kle] (1a) *v/t.* ✝ unfasten *(a door etc.)*; clear *(a harbour)*; *v/i.* break up *(ice).*

déballage [deba'la:ʒ] *m* unpacking; display *(a. fig.)*; F *fig.* effusion, outpouring; **déballer** [~'le] (1a) *v/t.* unpack; F *fig.* let out *(emotions, complaints, etc.)*, air, display *(knowledge etc.).*

débandade [debã'dad] *f* stampede, flight; rout; *à la* ~ in disorder; **débander** [~'de] (1a) *v/t.* unbend; remove the bandage from *(a wound, the eyes)*; ✕ disband; *se* ~ slacken, relax; scatter, disperse *(crowd)*; ✕ break into a rout.

débaptiser [debati'ze] (1a) *v/t.* rename.

débarbouiller [debarbu'je] (1a) *v/t.* wash *(s.o.'s)* face; *se* ~ wash one's face; *fig.* get out of difficulties as best one can.

débarcadère [debarka'dɛ:r] *m* ⚓ landing-stage, wharf; 🚋 arrival platform.

débardage ⚓ [debar'da:ʒ] *m* unloading; **debarder** [~'de] (1a) *v/t.* remove *(timber)* from the woods or

(stone) from the quarry; ⚓ unload, discharge; **débardeur** [~'dœ:r] *m* ⚓ stevedore, docker; *garment:* slipover, *Brit.* tank top.

débarquement [debarkə'mã] *m* ⚓ unloading, discharge; *passengers:* landing; 🚋 F detraining, arrival; **débarquer** [~'ke] (1m) *v/t.* ⚓ unship, unload; land, disembark *(passengers)*; *bus etc.:* set down; F dismiss *(s.o.)*; *v/i.* ⚓ land, disembark; 🚋 alight, ✕ detrain.

débarras [deba'rɑ] *m* lumber room, junk room; *bon* ~! good riddance!; **débarrasser** [~ra'se] (1a) *v/t.* clear; relieve (of, *de)*; *se* ~ *de* get rid of *(s.o., s.th.)*; get clear of *(s.th.)*; extricate o.s. from.

débat [de'ba] *m* discussion; debate *(a. pol.)*; dispute; ⚖ ~*s pl.* proceedings; court hearing *sg.*

débâter [debɑ'te] (1a) *v/t.* unsaddle.

débâtir [debɑ'ti:r] (2a) *v/t.* demolish; take the tacking threads out of *(a dress).*

débattre [de'batr] (4a) *v/t.* debate, discuss; *fig. se* ~ struggle; flounder about (in the water, *dans l'eau).*

débauchage [debo'ʃa:ʒ] *m* laying off, dismissal; **débauche** [de'bo:ʃ] *f* debauch(ery); *fig.* profusion; **débauché, e** [debo'ʃe] **1.** *adj.* debauched; **2.** *su.* debauchee; **débaucher** [~] (1a) *v/t.* ✝ lead *(s.o.)* astray; entice away *(a workman)*; F tempt away; lay off *(workmen).*

débile [de'bil] feeble, weak; F foolish, ridiculous; **débilitant, e** [debili'tã, ~'tã:t] debilitating, weakening; **débilité** [~'te] *f* weakness, debility; **débiliter** [~'te] (1a) *v/t.* weaken; debilitate; ✞ undermine *(the health).*

débinage *sl.* [debi'na:ʒ] *m* disparagement, running down; **débine** *sl.* [~'bin] *f* poverty; **débiner** *sl.* [~bi'ne] (1a) *v/t.* disparage, run *(s.o.)* down; *se* ~ come down in the world; slip quietly away, make o.s. scarce.

débit [de'bi] *m* retailshop; ✝ turnover; sales *pl.*; ⊕ output; ⊕, *a. speaker:* delivery; ✝ debit; *river:* flow; ~ *de boissons (de tabac)* pub (tobacconist's [shop]); *avoir un* ~ *facile* be glib, F have the gift of the gab; *portez ... au* ~ *de mon compte* debit me with ...; **débitant** *m*, **e** *f* [debi'tã, ~'tã:t] dealer; **débiter** [~'te] (1a) *v/t.* sell, retail *(a. fig. lies)*; cut up *(logs* *etc.*); ⊕ yield; reel off (*a poem*); *usu. pej.* utter (*threats*); *usu. pej.* deliver (*a speech*); ✝ debit (s.o. with s.th. *qch. à q.*, *q. de qch.*).

débiteur¹, -trice [debi'tœːr, ~'tris] **1.** *su.* debtor; **2.** *adj.* debit...

débiteur² *m*, **-euse** *f* [debi'tœːr, ~'tøːz] retailer; *usu. pej.* utterer, ...monger; ~ *de calomnies* scandalmonger.

déblai [de'blɛ] *m* cutting, excavation; excavated material; **déblaiement** [~blɛ'mɑ̃] *m* excavating, excavation, digging out; removal (*of excavated material*).

déblatérer [deblate're] (1f) *v/t.* talk, utter; *v/i.* rail (against, *contre*).

déblayer [deblɛ'je] (1h) *v/t.* clear away, remove; clear (*a. fig.*).

déblocage [deblɔ'kaːʒ] *m* clearing; ✝, ⊕ releasing; **débloquer** [~'ke] (1m) *v/t.* clear; unblock; ✝, ⊕ release; ✕ relieve (*a place*); unclamp (*an instrument*).

débobiner [debɔbi'ne] (1a) *v/t.* unwind, unreel.

déboire [de'bwaːr] *m* nasty aftertaste; disappointment.

déboiser [debwa'ze] (1a) *v/t.* clear of trees; ✕ untimber (*a mine*).

déboîter [debwa'te] (1a) *v/t.* ✕ dislocate; ⊕ disconnect; *v/i. mot.* filter; haul out of the line.

débonder [debɔ̃'de] (1a) *v/t.* unbung (*a cask*); open the sluice-gates of (*a reservoir*); *fig.* ~ *son cœur*, *se* ~ pour out one's heart; *v/i. a. se* ~ burst (out).

débonnaire [debɔ'nɛːr] good-natured, easy-going; **débonnaireté** [~nɛr'te] *f* good nature; good humo(u)r.

débordé, e [debɔr'de] overflowing; *fig.* overwhelmed (with work, *de travail*); dissipated (*life*, *man*); **débordement** [~də'mɑ̃] *m* overflowing, flood; *fig.* outburst (*of temper etc.*); ⚓, ✕ outflanking; ~s *pl.* dissipation *sg.*, excess(es *pl.*) *sg.*; **déborder** [~'de] *vt/i.* overflow, run over; *v/t.* project beyond, stick out beyond; ✕ outflank; ⚓ sheer off; ⊕ trim.

débotter [debɔ'te] (1a) *v/t.* take off (*s.o.'s*) boots; *v/i. a. se* ~ take off one's boots; *fig. au débotté* immediately on arrival.

débouché [debu'ʃe] *m* outlet; opening (*a. fig.*, *a.* ✝); ✝ *a.* market; ✝ *créer de nouveaux* ~s open up new markets; **déboucher** [~] (1a) *v/t.* clear; open, uncork (*a bottle*); *v/i.* emerge; open (on[to], *sur*); ~ *sur or dans a.* lead to; end up in.

déboucler [debu'kle] (1a) *v/t.* unbuckle (*one's belt*); uncurl (*one's hair*); F release.

débouler [debu'le] (1a) *vt/i.* roll down; tumble down; *hunt.* bolt.

déboulonner [debulɔ'ne] (1a) *v/t.* unrivet, unbolt; F debunk.

débourber [debur'be] (1a) *v/t.* clean (out); haul (*a carriage*) out of the mire; F get (*s.o.*) out of a mess.

débourrer [debu're] (1a) *v/t.* remove the stuffing from; break in (*a horse*); remove the wad from (*a gun*); clean out (*a pipe*); *fig.* smarten (*s.o.*) up.

débours [de'buːr] *m* (*usu. pl.*) disbursement; outlay; expenses *pl.*; *rentrer dans ses* ~ recover *or* recoup one's expenses; **débourser** [~bur'se] (1a) *v/t.* lay out, spend, disburse; *v/i.* F shell out, fork out.

déboussoler F *fig.* [debusɔ'le] (1a) *v/t.* disorient(ate); disconcert.

debout [də'bu] *adv.* upright; standing (up); on its hind legs (*animal*); ~! get up!; *être* ~ be up, be out of bed; *fig. ne pas tenir* ~ not to hold water, be fantastic (*theory*); *4 places* ~ 4 standing; *se tenir* ~ stand.

débouter [debu'te] (1a) *v/t.* nonsuit; dismiss.

déboutonner [debutɔ'ne] (1a) *v/t.* unbutton; *manger* (*rire*) *à ventre déboutonné* eat (laugh) immoderately; *fig. se* ~ unburden o.s.; F get s.th. off one's chest.

débraillé, e [debra'je] untidy; slovenly (*appearance*, *voice*); free, rather indecent (*conversation*); loose (*morals*, *life*).

débranchement [debrɑ̃ʃ'mɑ̃] *m* disconnecting; **débrancher** ⚡ [~brɑ̃'ʃe] (1a) *v/t.* disconnect.

débrayage [debrɛ'jaːʒ] *m mot.* declutching; F strike, *Am.* walkout; **débrayer** [~'je] (1i) *v/t.* ⊕ disconnect; *v/i. mot.* declutch; F knock off work.

débrider [debri'de] (1a) *v/t.* unbridle; halt; ✚ incise; F open (*s.o.'s eyes*); *sans* ~ at a stretch, on end.

débris [de'bri] *m/pl.* debris *sg.*; remains; wreckage *sg.*; fragments; rubble *sg.*; rubbish *sg.*; ⊕ *metal:* scraps.

débrouillard, e F [debru'ja:r,ᴠ'jard] 1. *adj.* resourceful; 2. *su.* resourceful *or* smart person; **débrouiller** [ᴠ'je] (1a) *v/t.* disentangle; *fig.* clear up; se ᴠ find a way out of difficulties; manage; cope.

débroussailler [debrusɑ'je] (1a) *v/t.* clear of undergrowth; *fig.* clear (up *or* out), unravel.

débucher *hunt.* [deby'ʃe] (1a) *v/t.* drive (*a stag*) from cover; *v/i.* break cover.

débusquer [debys'ke] (1m) drive (*an animal*) out (from cover); drive *or* chase (*s.o.*) out.

début [de'by] *m* beginning, start; first move *etc.*; *thea.* debut, first appearance; *salaire de* ᴠ starting salary; *faire ses* ᴠs make a first appearance; **débutant, e** [deby'tɑ̃, ᴠ'tɑ̃:t] *su.* beginner; novice; *su./m thea.* debutant; *su./f* debutante, F deb; **débuter** [ᴠ'te] (1a) *v/i.* begin, start; play first (*in a game*).

déc(a)... [dek(a)] dec(a)...

deçà [də'sa] *adv.* on this side; ᴠ *delà* here and there, on all sides; *en* ᴠ *de* on this side of.

décacheter [dekaʃ'te] (1c) *v/t.* unseal, open (*a letter*).

décade [de'kad] *f* decade; period of ten days *or* years.

décadence [deka'dɑ̃:s] *f* decadence, decline, decay; **décadent, e** [ᴠ'dɑ̃, ᴠ'dɑ̃:t] *adj., a. su.* decadent.

décaèdre ⚛ [deka'ɛ:dr] 1. *adj.* decahedral; 2. *su./m* decahedron.

décaféiné, e [dekafei'ne] caffeine-free, decaffeinated.

décagone ⚛ [deka'gɔn] *m* decagon.

décaisser [dekɛ'se] (1b) *v/t.* unpack, unbox; ✝ pay out; ⚘ plant out.

décalage [deka'la:ʒ] *m* shifting; *fig.* gap, discrepancy; lag; **décaler** [ᴠ'le] (1a) *v/t.* shift (forward *or* back); move forward; put back.

décalogue [deka'lɔg] *m* the Decalogue, *the* Ten Commandments *pl.*

décalquage [dekal'ka:ʒ] *m*, **décalque** [ᴠ'kalk] *m* transfer(ring); tracing (off); **décalquer** [ᴠkal'ke] (1m) *v/t.* transfer; trace off.

décamper [dekɑ̃'pe] (1a) *v/i. fig.* decamp; F clear out, *sl.* vamoose.

décanat [deka'na] *m* deanship.

décanter [dekɑ̃'te] (1a) *v/t.* decant, pour off.

décapage [deka'pa:ʒ] *m*, **décapement** [ᴠkap'mɑ̃] *m* scouring; *metal:* pickling; ᴠ *au jet de sable* sandblasting; **décapant** [ᴠ'pɑ̃] *m* scouring agent *or* solution; paint *or* varnish remover; **décaper** [ᴠka'pe] (1a) *v/t.* scour; cleanse.

décapiter [dekapi'te] (1a) *v/t.* behead, decapitate; cut the head off (*a.* ⚔).

décapotable *mot.* [dekapɔ'tabl] convertible; drop-head (*coupé*).

décapsulateur [dekapsyla'tœ:r] *m* (crown-cork) opener.

décarburer *metall.* [dekarby're] (1a) *v/t.* decarbonize.

décartellisation ✝ [dekartɛliza'sjɔ̃] *f* decartel(l)ization.

décatir [deka'ti:r] (2a) *v/t. tex.* sponge, take the gloss off; F se ᴠ lose one's beauty, age.

décavé, e F [deka've] 1. *adj.* ruined, F broke (*person*); worn out; haggard (*face*); 2. *su.* ruined person; **décaver** [ᴠ] (1a) *v/t.* win all (*s.o.'s*) money (*at cards etc.*), F clean (*s.o.*) out.

décéder *admin., eccl.* [dese'de] (1f) *v/i.* die, decease.

déceler [desə'le] (1d) *v/t.* reveal, disclose.

décélération [deselera'sjɔ̃] *f* deceleration.

décembre [de'sɑ̃:br] *m* December.

décemment [desa'mɑ̃] *adv. of* *décent;* **décence** [ᴠ'sɑ̃:s] *f* decency, decorum.

décennal, e [dese'nal, ᴠ'no] *m/pl.* -aux decennial.

décent, e [de'sɑ̃, ᴠ'sɑ̃:t] decent; modest; seemly; *peu* ᴠ unseemly.

décentraliser *admin.* [desɑ̃trali'ze] (1a) *v/t.* decentralize.

décentré, e [desɑ̃'tre] off-centre; **décentrer** [ᴠ] (1a) *v/t.* throw off centre; se ᴠ move off centre.

déception [desɛp'sjɔ̃] *f* disappointment.

décercler [desɛr'kle] (1a) *v/t.* unhoop.

décerner [desɛr'ne] (1a) *v/t.* award (*a price*) (to, *à*), confer (*an honour*) (on, *à*); ⚖ issue (*a writ etc.*).

décès [de'sɛ] *m admin. etc.* decease, death; ⚖ demise.

décevant, e [desə'vɑ̃, ᴠ'vɑ̃:t] deceptive; disappointing; **décevoir** [ˌ~'vwa:r] (3a) v/t. deceive; disappoint.

déchaînement [deʃɛn'mã] m unbridling; fig. outburst; **déchaîner** [ˌ~ʃe'ne] (1b) v/t. let loose (a. fig.); se ~ break loose; break (storm); se ~ contre storm at.

déchanter F [deʃã'te] (1a) v/i. F change one's tune; F sing small, come down a peg.

décharge [de'ʃarʒ] f ⚡, ✗, ♦️, ⊕ discharge; ⚡ output; ✗ volley; ♦️ acquittal; ✝ receipt (for delivery); ✝ credit; fig. relief, easing; lumberroom, F gloryhole; reservoir; ~ (publique or municipale) rubbish (Am. garbage) dump; ♦️ témoin m à ~ witness for the defence; ⊕ tuyau m de ~ outlet; à sa ~ in his defence; **déchargeoir** ⊕ [deʃar'ʒwa:r] m outlet; waste pipe; **décharger** [ˌ~'ʒe] (11) v/t. unload (a cart, a gun); ⚓ unlade; discharge (a. ⚡, ♦️, ♦️, a gun) (at sur, contre); empty (a boiler, a reservoir); admin. exempt (from, de); ♦️ acquit; fig. relieve, ease; fig. vent; se ~ go off (gun); ⚡ run down; fig. vent itself (anger); se ~ de pass off (a responsibility etc.) (onto, sur).

décharné, e [deʃar'ne] lean, emaciated, fleshless; gaunt.

déchaumer ✗ [deʃo'me] (1a) v/t. plough (Am. plow) up the stubble of (a field); break (the ground).

déchausser [deʃo'se] (1a) v/t. take off (s.o.'s) shoes and stockings; lay bare (a tooth, tree roots, etc.).

dèche sl. [dɛʃ] f poverty, distress; F dans la ~ hard up, broke.

déchéance [deʃe'ã:s] f downfall; (moral) decay; insurance: expiration; ♦️ forfeiture; lapse (of a right).

déchet [de'ʃɛ] m loss, decrease; ~s pl. waste sg. (a. phys.), refuse sg., scrap sg.; waste products; ~s pl. radioactifs radio-active waste sg.; ✝ ~ de route loss in transit.

déchiffrer [deʃi'fre] (1a) v/t. decipher; decode (a message); ♪ read at sight; **déchiffreur, -euse** [ˌ~'frœ:r, ˌ~'frø:z] su. decipherer; decoder; ♪ sight-reader; su./m: ~ de radar radar scanner.

déchiqueter [deʃik'te] (1c) v/t. hack, slash, tear to shreds (a. fig.), tear up.

déchirant, e [deʃi'rã, ˌ~'rã:t] heart-rending; agonizing (cry, pain, scene); racking (cough); **déchirement** [ˌ~ʃir'mã] m tearing (a. ✗); laceration; pang, wrench; ~ de cœur heartbreak; **déchirer** [deʃi're] (1a) v/t. tear (a. fig.); tear up; fig. rend; **déchirure** [ˌ~'ry:r] f tear, rent; ✗ laceration.

déchoir [de'ʃwa:r] (3d) v/i. decay, decline, fall off.

déchristianiser [dekristjani'ze] (1a) v/t. dechristianize.

déchu, e [de'ʃy] 1. p.p. of déchoir; 2. adj. fallen; expired (insurance policy); disqualified.

déci... [desi] deci...

décidé, e [desi'de] decided, determined; resolute, confident (manner, person); **décidément** [ˌ~de'mã] adv. certainly, positively, really; **décider** [ˌ~'de] (1a) v/t. decide, settle; decide on; ~ q. à (inf.) persuade s.o. to (inf.); v/i.: ~ de (inf.) decide to (inf.), make up one's mind to (inf.).

décimal, e, m/pl. -aux [desi'mal, ˌ~'mo] adj., a. su./f decimal; **décimer** [ˌ~'me] (1a) v/t. decimate (a. fig.); fig. deplete; **décimo** [ˌ~'mo] adv. tenthly.

décisif, -ve [desi'sif, ˌ~'si:v] decisive (battle etc.); conclusive (proof); positive (tones); F cock-sure (person); **décision** [ˌ~'sjõ] f decision (a. ♦️); fig. resolution.

déclamateur, -trice [deklama'tœ:r, ˌ~'tris] 1. su./m declaimer; stump orator, F tub-thumper; bombastic writer; 2. adj. see déclamatoire; **déclamation** [ˌ~ma'sjõ] f declamation; ranting; **déclamatoire** [ˌ~ma-'twa:r] declamatory; ranting (speech); turgid (style); **déclamer** [ˌ~'me] (1a) v/t. declaim; recite (a poem); v/i. rant; rail (against, contre).

déclaration [deklara'sjõ] f declaration; statement; admin. registration, notification; ~ de revenu income-tax return; **déclarer** [ˌ~'re] (1a) v/t. declare (a. ♦️); ♦️ ~ coupable find guilty; avez-vous qch. à ~? have you anything to declare?; se ~ declare (for, pour; against, contre); speak one's mind; declare one's love; break out (fire, war, epidemic, etc.).

déclasser [dekla'se] (1a) v/t. bring (s.o.) down in the world; ✗ etc. declare obsolete (a weapon etc.); ⚓

disrate (*a sailor*); ⚓ transfer from one class to another; *sp.* penalize (*a runner*).

déclencher [deklɑ̃'ʃe] (1a) *v/t.* launch (*an attack*); unlatch (*a door*); ⊕ release (*a. phot.*), disengage, disconnect (*a. ⨍*); F start; **déclencheur** [~'ʃœ:r] *m* release (*a. phot.*); *phot.* ~ automatique self-timer.

déclic ⊕ [de'klik] *m* catch, pawl, trip-dog, trip pin; nippers *pl.*; *montre f à* ~ stop-watch.

déclin [de'klɛ̃] *m* decline, decay; *moon, talent:* waning; *year:* fall; *au* ~ *du jour* at the close of day; *au* ~ *de sa vie* in his declining years, towards the end of his days; **déclinaison** [dekline'zɔ̃] *f astr.* declination; *⨍* variation; *gramm.* declension; **décliner** [~'ne] (1a) *v/i.* deviate; decline; *fig.* fade, fail, wane; *v/t.* decline (*a. gramm.*); refuse; state (*one's name*). [release.\
décliqueter ⊕ [deklik'te] (1c) *v/t.*⌡
déclive [de'kli:v] **1.** *adj.* sloping; **2.** *su./f* slope; **déclivité** [~klivi'te] *f* slope, gradient, incline.

décloisonner [deklwazo'ne] (1a) *v/t.* decompartmentalize.

déclouer [deklu'e] (1a) *v/t.* unnail; take down (*a picture*); *sl.* take out of pawn.

décocher [dekɔ'ʃe] (1a) *v/t.* shoot, let fly; let off (*an epigram*); discharge.

décoction [dekɔk'sjɔ̃] *f* decoction.

décoder [dekɔ'de] (1a) *v/t.* decode; decipher.

décoiffer [dekwa'fe] (1a) *v/t.* remove (*s.o.'s*) hat; take (*s.o.'s*) hair down; ruffle (*s.o.'s*) hair.

décollage [dekɔ'la:ʒ] *m* unsticking; ✈ takeoff; **décoller** [~'le] (1a) *v/t.* unstick; disengage; loosen; *se* ~ come loose; *v/i.* ✈ take off; F budge, depart.

décolleté, e [dekɔl'te] **1.** *adj.* low-necked (*dress*); wearing a low-necked dress (*woman*); **2.** *su./m* low neckline; bare neck and shoulders *pl.*; **décolleter** [~] (1c) *v/t.* cut out the neck of (*a dress*); ⊕ cut (*a screw*); *se* ~ wear a low-necked dress.

décolonisation [dekɔlɔniza'sjɔ̃] *f* decolonization; **décoloniser** [~'ze] (1a) *v/t.* decolonize.

décolorer [dekɔlɔ're] (1a) *v/t.* discolo(u)r; fade; bleach; *se* ~ fade; grow pale (*person*).

décombres [de'kɔ̃br] *m/pl.* rubbish *sg.*; debris *sg.*, *buildings:* rubble *sg.*

décommander [dekɔmɑ̃'de] (1a) *v/t.* cancel (*an invitation etc.*); ✝ countermand; *se* ~ excuse o.s. from an invitation; cancel an appointment.

décomposer [dekɔ̃po'ze] (1a) *v/t.* 🜍, *phys.* decompose; 🜍 analyse; ⚕ split up; distort (*the features*); *se* ~ decay; become convulsed (*features*); **décomposition** [~zi'sjɔ̃] *f* decomposition; rotting, decay; *features:* distortion; *gramm.* construing.

décompte [de'kɔ̃:t] *m* ✝ deduction; balance due; detailed account; *fig.* éprouver du ~ be disappointed (in, à); **décompter** [~kɔ̃'te] (1a) *v/t.* deduct; calculate (*the interest*); reckon off.

déconcerter [dekɔ̃sɛr'te] (1a) *v/t.* disconcert; upset (*plans*); ✝ ♪ put out of tune; *se* ~ lose one's assurance.

déconfit, e [dekɔ̃'fi, ~'fit] crestfallen, discomfited; **déconfiture** [~fi'ty:r] *f* ruin, failure; insolvency; collapse; defeat.

décongeler [dekɔ̃'ʒle] (1d) *v/t.* defreeze, thaw (out).

décongestionner [dekɔ̃ʒɛstjo'ne] (1a) *v/t.* relieve congestion in; clear.

déconnecter [dekɔnɛk'te] (1a) *v/t.* disconnect; *fig.* separate.

déconner *sl.* [dekɔ'ne] (1a) *v/i.* talk a load of bullshit; blunder; *sl.* boob.

déconseiller [dekɔ̃sɛ'je] (1a) *v/t.* advise (s.o. against s.th., *qch. à q.*; s.o. against *ger.*, *q. de inf.*).

déconsidérer [dekɔ̃side're] (1f) *v/t.* discredit.

décontenancer [dekɔ̃tnɑ̃'se] (1k) *v/t.* put out of countenance, abash; *se* ~ lose one's self-assurance.

décontracter [dekɔ̃trak'te] (1a) *v/t.* relax; **décontraction** [~'sjɔ̃] *f* relax, cool(ness).

déconvenue [dekɔ̃v'ny] *f* disappointment; discomfiture; *fig.* blow; set-back.

décor [de'kɔ:r] *m house:* decoration; *thea.* set(ting), scene; *thea.* ~s *pl.* scenery *sg.*; *mot. sl.* rentrer dans *le* ~ run into a wall *etc.*; **décorateur** *m,* -**trice** *f* [dekɔra'tœ:r, ~'tris] decorator; *thea.* stage-designer; **décoration** [~ra'sjɔ̃] *f* decoration (*a.* = *medal, insignia, ribbon of an order*); **décorer** [~'re] (1a) *v/t.* decorate; confer a decoration on.

décortiquer [dekɔrti'ke] (1m) *v/t.* husk (*rice*); shell (*nuts*); peel (*fruit*).

décorum [dekɔ'rɔm] *m* decorum, propriety.

découcher [deku'ʃe] (1a) *v/i.* sleep out; stay out all night.

découdre [de'kudr] (4l) *v/t.* unpick (*a garment*); rip open.

découler [deku'le] (1a) *v/i.*: ~ de follow *or* result from.

decoupage [deku'pa:ʒ] *m* cutting up *or* out; carving; cut-out (figure); **découper** [~'pe] (1a) *v/t.* carve (*a chicken*); cut up; cut out (*a newspaper article, a pattern*); ⊕ stamp out, punch; *fig.* se ~ stand out (against, *sur*).

découplé, e [deku'ple] well-built, strapping; **découpler** [~] (1a) *v/t.* uncouple (*a.* ♪), unleash; *radio:* decouple.

découpoir ⊕ [deku'pwa:r] *m* cutter; **découpure** [~'py:r] *f* cutting-out; pinking; *newspaper:* cutting; *geog.* indentation.

découragement [dekuraʒ'mã] *m* discouragement, despondency; **décourager** [~ra'ʒe] (11) *v/t.* discourage; dissuade (from, *de*); se ~ lose heart.

décousu, e [deku'zy] 1. *p.p. of* découdre; 2. *adj.* unstitched, unsewn; *fig.* disconnected; disjointed; rambling; 2. *su./m* disconnectedness; **décousure** [~'zy:r] *f* seam that has come unsewn; gash, rip (*from animal's horns etc.*).

découvert, e [deku've:r, ~'vert] 1. *p.p. of* découvrir; 2. *adj.* uncovered; ⚔ exposed; ✝ overdrawn (*account*); 3. *su./m* ✝ overdraft; ⚔ open ground; *admin.* deficit; à ~ openly; in the open; ✝ unsecure (*credit*), short (*sale*); *su./f* uncovering; discovery (*a. fig.*); *aller à la* ~e explore, ⚔ reconnoitre; **découvreur** [~'vrœ:r] *m* discoverer; **découvrir** [~'vri:r] (2f) *v/t.* uncover; lay bare, expose; discover; find out, detect; se ~ take off one's hat; come into sight; come to light (*secret, truth*); clear up (*sky*).

décrasser [dekra'se] (1a) *v/t.* clean, scrape; ⊕ scale (*a boiler*); draw (*a furnace*); decarbonize (*an engine*);

fig. rub the rough edges off (*s.o.*), polish (*s.o.*) up.

décrépir △ [dekre'pi:r] (2a) *v/t.* strip the plaster *or* rough-cast off; **décrépit, e** [~'pi, ~'pit] decrepit, senile; **décrépiter** ⚗ [~pi'te] (1a) *v/i.* decrepitate; **décrépitude** [~pi'tyd] *f* decrepitude; (senile) decay.

décret [de'krɛ] *m* decree; **décréter** [~kre'te] (1f) *v/t.* order; declare; decree; **décret-loi**, *pl.* **décrets-lois** [~kre'lwa] *m* order in council, *Am.* executive order.

décrire [de'kri:r] (4q) *v/t.* describe (*a.* ⚛).

décrocher [dekrɔ'ʃe] (1a) *v/t.* unhook; *teleph.* lift (*the receiver*); uncouple; F get, land (o.s.) (*s.th.*); *v/i.* *teleph.* lift the receiver; *fig.* switch off; *fig.* hang up one's boots; **décrochez-moi-ça** *sl.* [~ʃemwa'sa] *m/inv.* reach-me-down; second-hand clothes' shop.

décroissance [dekrwa'sã:s] *f*, **décroissement** [~krwas'mã] *m* decrease; decline; *moon:* wane; **décroître** [de'krwa:tr] (4o) *v/i.* decrease, diminish; wane (*moon*).

décrotter [dekrɔ'te] (1a) *v/t.* remove the mud from; clean; scrape; F *fig.* rub the rough edges off (*s.o.*); **décrotteur** [~'tœ:r] *m* shoe-black; *hotel:* boots; **décrottoir** [~'twa:r] *m* door-scraper; wire-mat.

décru, e [de'kry] 1. *p.p. of* décroître; 2. *su./f water:* fall, subsidence; decrease.

déçu, e [de'sy] *p.p. of* décevoir.

déculotter [dekylɔ'te] (1a) *v/t.* take off (*s.o.'s*) trousers; se~ take off one's trousers; *sl.* chicken out.

déculpabiliser [dekylpabili'ze] (1a) *v/t.* excuse; free from a sense of guilt.

décuple [de'kypl] 1. *adj.* tenfold; 2. *su./m* tenfold; le ~ de ten times as much as; **décupler** [~ky'ple] (1a) *vt/i.* increase tenfold.

décuver [deky've] (1a) *v/t.* rack off (*wine*).

dédaigner [dedɛ'ɲe] (1b) *v/t.* scorn, disdain; **dédaigneux, -euse** [~'ɲø, ~'ɲø:z] scornful, disdainful; **dédain** [de'dɛ̃] *m* disdain, scorn (of, *de*); disregard (of, *de*; for, *pour*); contempt (for, *de*).

dédale [de'dal] *m* labyrinth (*a. fig.*).

dedans [də'dã] 1. *adv.* in, inside, within; en ~ inside; en ~ de within;

F *mettre q.* ~ take s.o. in; **2.** *su./m* inside, interior.

dédicace [dedi'kas] *f* dedication (*a. fig.*); *church*: consecration; **dédier** [~'dje] (1o) *v/t.* dedicate (*a. fig.*); *fig.* inscribe (*a book*).

dédire [de'di:r] (4p) *v/t.*: se ~ de go back upon, retract, take back; break (*an engagement, a promise*); **dédit** [~'di] *m* renunciation; withdrawal; *promise etc.*: breaking; 🏛 forfeit, penalty.

dédommagement [dedɔmaʒ'mã] *m* indemnity; compensation, damages *pl.*; **dédommager** [~ma'ʒe] (1l) *v/t.* compensate (for, de).

dédouanement [dedwanmã] *m* customs clearance; **dédouaner** [~'ne] (1a) *v/t.* clear (*goods etc.*) through the customs; *fig.* clear the name of, rehabilitate.

dédoubler [dedu'ble] (1a) *v/t.* divide into two; undouble (*a cloth*); remove the lining of (*a coat etc.*); 🚂 run (*a train*) in two parts.

déductible [dedyk'tibl]:~ (de l'impôt tax-)deductible; **déduction** [~'sjɔ̃] *f* ✝, *phls.* deduction; ✝ allowance.

déduire [de'dɥi:r] (4h) *v/t. phls.* deduce, infer; ✝ deduct, allow.

déesse [de'ɛs] *f* goddess.

défaillance [defa'jã:s] *f* failure, failing; ⚕ faint, swoon; 🏛 *witness*: default; **défaillant, e** [~'jã, ~'jã:t] **1.** *adj.* failing; sinking (*heart*); faltering (*steps*); waning (*light*); ⊕, *fig.* at fault; faint (*person*); defaulting; **2.** *su.* 🏛, ✝ defaulter; **défaillir** [~'ji:r] (2t) *v/i.* fail, lose strength; falter (*courage*); *fig.* sink (*heart*); faint, swoon (*person*); 🏛 fail to appear.

défaire [de'fɛ:r] (4r) *v/t.* undo; ✗ defeat; annul (*a treaty*); unpack; unwrap; *fig.* distort (*the face*); *fig.* upset (*s.o.'s plans*); rid (s.o. of s.th., q. de qch.); se ~ come undone; *fig.* one's coat; get rid (of, de); **défaite** [~'fɛt] *f* defeat; *fig.* lame excuse, evasion; *fig.* failure; **défaitisme** [defɛ'tism] *m* defeatism, pessimism; **défaitiste** [~'tist] *adj., a. su.* defeatist, pessimist.

défalquer [defal'ke] (1m) *v/t.* deduct; write off (*a debt*).

défausser [defo'se] (1a) *v/t.* straighten; *cards*: se ~ discard.

défaut [de'fo] *m* defect; want, lack;

fault, shortcoming; ⊕ flaw; 🏛 default; ✝ ~ de provision no funds; à ~ de for want of, in place of; *hunt.* être en ~ be at fault (*a. fig.*); faire ~ be lacking; be missing; be in short supply; *il nous a fait* ~ we have missed him; *sans* ~ faultless, flawless.

défaveur [defa'vœ:r] *m* disfavo(u)r (with,, auprès de), discredit; **défavorable** [~vɔ'rabl] unfavo(u)rable.

défécation [defeka'sjɔ̃] *f* 🜲, *physiol.* defecation; clarification.

défectif, -ve [defɛk'tif, ~'ti:v] *gramm.* defective; 🜿 deficient; **défection** [~'sjɔ̃] *f* defection (from, de); *faire* ~ fall away; **défectueux, -euse** [~'tɥø, ~'tɥø:z] faulty, defective; **défectuosité** [~tɥozi'te] *f* defect, flaw; faultiness.

défendable [defã'dabl] defensible; tenable; **défendeur** *m*, **-eresse** *f* 🏛 [~'dœ:r, ~'drɛs] defendant; respondent; **défendre** [de'fã:dr] (4a) *v/t.* defend (*a.* 🏛, *a.* ✗); protect; support; forbid; à son corps défendant reluctantly; *fig.* se ~ de (*inf.*) refrain from (*ger.*), help (*ger.*); F *fig.* se ~ hold one's own; get along or by, manage, cope; F *fig.* se ~ bien en qch. be good at s.th.

défense [de'fã:s] *f* defence, *Am.* defense; protection; prohibition; *elephant*: tusk; 🏛 defence, plea; ⚓ fender; ~ de fumer no smoking; ~ légitime ~ self-defence; *psych.* ~s *pl.* defence mechanism *sg.*; **défenseur** [defã'sœ:r] *m* defender; *fig.* supporter; 🏛 counsel for the defence; **défensif, -ve** [~'sif, ~'si:v] *adj., a. su./f* defensive.

déférence [defe'rã:s] *f* deference, regard, respect; *par* ~ pour in deference to, out of regard for; **déférer** [~'re] (1f) *v/t.* 🏛 submit; remove (*to the Court of Appeal*); inform against (*a criminal*); administer (*an oath*); bestow, confer (*an honour*); *v/i.* defer (to, à); comply (with, à) (*an order*).

déferler [defɛr'le] (1a) *v/t.* unfurl (*a flag*); set (*sails*); *v/i.* break (*waves*); ✗ F break up (*attack*).

déferrer [defɛ're] (1a) *v/t.* remove the iron from; unshoe (*a horse*); *fig.* disconcert; ⚓ ~ un navire slip anchor.

défeuiller [defœ'je] (1a) *v/t.* strip

(*a tree*) of its leaves, defoliate; se ~ shed its leaves (*tree*).

défi [de'fi] *m* challenge; *lancer un ~ à* challenge; *mettre q. au ~* dare *or* defy s.o. (*to inf., de inf.*).

défiance [de'fjã:s] *f* suspicion, distrust; *~ de soi-même* lack of self-confidence; *pol.* vote *m de ~* vote of no confidence; **défiant, e** [~'fjã, ~'fjã:t] distrustful, suspicious, cautious.

déficeler [defis'le] (1c) *v/t.* untie (*a parcel etc.*).

déficient, e [defi'sjã, ~'sjã:t] *adj., a. su.* deficient.

déficit [defi'si] *m* deficit, shortage; deficiency; **déficitaire** [~si'tε:r] ✝ showing a deficit; ✿ short (*harvest*).

défier [de'fje] (1o) *v/t.* challenge; dare; *fig.* brave, defy; *se ~ de* distrust, be on one's guard against; *se ~ de soi-même* lack self-confidence.

défigurer [defigy're] (1a) *v/t.* disfigure; *fig.* distort (*the sense, the truth*).

défilade F [defi'lad] *f* procession; **défilé** [~'le] *m geog.* pass, gorge; march past *or* parade; **défiler** [~'le] (1a) *v/t.* unthread; ✕ defilade (*a fortress*); ✕ conceal (*guns, troops*); *~ son chapelet* speak one's mind; *se ~* come unstrung; ✕ take cover; *sl.* clear off, get out; *v/i.* ✕ file off; march past.

défini, e [defi'ni] definite (*a. gramm.*); defined; *bien ~ a.* clean-cut; **définir** [~'ni:r] (2a) *v/t.* define; *fig.* describe; *se ~* become clear; **définissable** [defini'sabl] definable; **définitif, -ve** [~'tif, ~'ti:v] **1.** *adj.* definitive, final; *à titre ~* permanently; **2.** *su./f:* en *~ve* in short; **définition** [~'sjõ] *f* definition; *crosswords:* clue; *telev.* picture: resolution.

déflagration [deflagra'sjõ] *f* combustion, deflagration.

déflation [defla'sjõ] *f* deflation.

défleuraison ✿ [deflœrε'zõ] *f* fall(ing) of blossom; **défleurir** [~'ri:r] (2a) *v/t.* strip (*a plant*) of its bloom; take the bloom off (*a fruit*); *v/i. a. se ~* lose its blossom.

déflorer [deflɔ're] (1a) *v/t.* ✿ strip (*a plant*) of its bloom; deflower (*a virgin*); *fig.* F take the freshness off.

défoncer [defõ'se] (1k) *v/t.* stave

in; break up (*the ground, a road*); smash in (*a door etc.*); *fig.* destroy, F knock the bottom out of (*an argument*); *se ~* break up; collapse (*roof*); *sl.* get high (*on drugs*); *sl.* défoncé high, stoned.

déformation [defɔrma'sjõ] *f* deformation (*a.* ⊕); ⊕ *wood:* warping; ⚡, *phot.* distortion; **déformer** [~'me] (1a) *v/t.* deform; ⊕, ⚡, *phot., phys., a. fig.* distort; ⊕ buckle, warp; *se ~* warp (*wood*); get out of shape.

défouler F [defu'le] (1a) *v/t.: se ~* release one's pent-up feelings, F let off steam.

défourner [defur'ne] (1a) *v/t.* draw from the oven *or* kiln.

défraîchi, e [defrε'ʃi] (shop)soiled, *Am.* shopworn; faded; **défraîchir** [~'ʃi:r] (2a) *v/t.* take away the freshness of; *se ~* lose its freshness; fade.

défrayer [defrε'je] (1i) *v/t.* defray (*s.o.'s*) expenses; *fig. ~ la conversation* be the (main) topic *or* subject of conversation; be the life of the conversation.

défricher [defri'ʃe] (1a) *v/t.* ✿ clear, reclaim (*land*); F *fig.* break new ground in (*a subject*).

défriser [defri'ze] (1a) *v/t.* uncurl; *fig.* disappoint.

defroisser [defrwa'se] (1a) *v/t.* smooth out.

défroncer [defrõ'se] (1k) *v/t.* take out the gathers in (*a cloth*); *~ les sourcils* cease to frown.

défroque *fig.* [de'frɔk] *f usu. ~s pl.* cast-off clothing *sg.*; **défroquer** [~frɔ'ke] (1m) *v/t.* unfrock (*a priest*).

défunt, e [de'fœ̃, ~'fœ̃:t] **1.** *adj.* deceased; late; **2.** *su.* deceased, *Am.* decedent.

dégagé, e [dega'ʒe] clear (*sky, road*); free, unconstrained; off-hand (*manner, tone*); **dégagement** [~gaʒ-'mã] *m* clearing; freeing; extrication; relief; emission; passage; *esca-lier m de ~* emergency stairs; ⊕ *tuyau m de ~* waste pipe; **dégager** [~ga'ʒe] (11) *v/t.* clear; free; extricate; relieve; release (from a promise, d'une promesse); give off, emit (*a smell etc.*); *fig.* bring out (*an idea etc.*); ⚡ *~ l'inconnue* isolate the unknown quantity; *se ~* free o.s.; clear; emanate, be given off; emerge, come out; *v/i.: dégagez!* clear the way!; *bus:* gangway!

dégaine F [de'gɛːn] f (awkward) way of carrying o.s.; gawkiness; **dégainer** [~gɛ'ne] (1b) v/t. unsheathe, draw (*one's sword*); v/i. draw.

déganter [degɑ̃'te] (1a) v/t. unglove (*one's hand*); se ~ take off one's gloves.

dégarnir [degar'niːr] (2a) v/t. strip; dismantle; unsaddle (*a horse*); ⚓ unrig; ✕ withdraw the troops from; 🌳 thin out (*a tree*); se ~ be stripped; empty (*room*); become bald (*head*); lose its leaves (*tree*).

dégât [de'gɑ] m food etc.: waste; ~s pl. damage sg.; havoc sg.

dégauchir ⊕ [dego'ʃiːr] (2a) v/t. rough-plane (*wood*); dress (*a stone*); straighten, true up (*the machinery*); fig. knock the corners off (*s.o.*).

dégel [de'ʒɛl] m thaw; **dégelée** F [deʒɔ'le] f shower of blows; **dégeler** [~] (1d) vt/i. thaw; unfreeze, defrost; v/t.: F se ~ thaw (*person*).

dégénérer [deʒene're] (1f) v/i. degenerate (from, de; into, en); **dégénérescence** ✝ [~rɛ'sɑ̃ːs] f degeneration.

dégingandé, e [deʒɛ̃gɑ̃'de] awkward, lanky, ungainly.

dégivrer [deʒi'vre] (1a) v/t. de-ice, defrost; **dégivreur** [~'vrœːr] m de-icer, defroster.

déglacer [degla'se] (1k) v/t. thaw; defrost (*the refrigerator*); unglaze (*paper*).

déglinguer F [deglɛ̃'ge] (1m) v/t. knock to pieces, F bust up.

dégluer [degly'e] (1a) v/t. remove the sticky substance from; remove the bird-lime from (*a bird*).

déglutition physiol. [deglyti'sjɔ̃] f swallowing.

dégobiller sl. [degɔbi'je] (1a) v/t. bring up (*food*); v/i. vomit, F spew, puke.

dégoiser F [degwa'ze] (1a) v/t. reel off, spout (*a speech etc.*).

dégommer [degɔ'me] (1a) v/t. ungum; ⊕ clean off old oil from; F dismiss (*s.o.*); F beat (*s.o.*) (*at a game*); F se faire ~ get the sack.

dégonflé sl. [degɔ̃'fle] m funk; **dégonfler** [~] (1a) v/t. deflate; reduce (✝ a swelling, ✝ prices, fig. s.o.'s importance etc.); fig. debunk (*s.o.*); se ~ mot. go flat (*tyre*); F back out, F chicken out.

dégorgeoir [degɔr'ʒwaːr] m outlet,

outflow; *pump*: spout; **dégorger** [~'ʒe] (11) v/t. cleanse; clear, unstop (*a pipe etc.*); disgorge (*a. fig.*); v/i. a. se ~ flow out; overflow; 🖢 discharge (*abscess*); become free (*pipe etc.*).

dégot(t)er sl. [degɔ'te] (1a) v/t. find, F unearth; v/i. ~ (*bien*) look great; ~ mal look awful.

dégouliner F [deguli'ne] (1a) v/i. roll (down); trickle.

dégourdi, e [degur'di] **1.** adj. lively, sharp, smart; **2.** su. brisk person, F live wire; **dégourdir** [~'diːr] (2a) v/t. warm (up), take the stiffness from (*one's legs etc.*); take the chill off (*a liquid*); fig. smarten (*s.o.*) up, F lick (*s.o.*) into shape; se ~ les jambes stretch one's legs; se ~ a. feel warmer; become more alert; F learn the ropes.

dégoût [de'gu] m disgust, loathing (for, pour); dislike, repugnance (for, pour); **dégoûtant, e** [degu'tɑ̃, ~'tɑ̃ːt] disgusting, loathsome, repulsive; **dégoûter** [~'te] (1a) v/t. disgust, repel; se ~ de take a dislike to, grow sick of.

dégoutter [degu'te] (1a) v/i. drip, trickle (from, with de).

dégradation [degrada'sjɔ̃] f degradation (a. phys.); rock: weathering; phys. energy: dissipation; colours etc.: shading off; ⚖ ~ civique loss of civil rights; **dégrader** [~'de] (1a) v/t. degrade; ✕ demote, reduce to the ranks; shade off (*colours*); damage, deface (*a building*); se ~ deteriorate.

dégrafer [degra'fe] (1a) v/t. unhook, unfasten.

dégraissage [degrɛ'saːʒ] m cuis. skimming; (dry-)cleaning; **dégraisser** [~'se] (1a) v/t. remove the fat from; cuis. skim; take the grease marks out of; **dégraisseur** [~'sœːr] m person: drycleaner.

degré [də'gre] m degree (a. ⚕ etc., a. of parentage); stage; step; rank; ~ centésimal degree centigrade; ~ de congélation freezing point; par ~s by degrees, progressively.

dégréer ⚓ [degre'e] (1a) v/t. unrig (*a mast, a ship*); dismantle (*a crane*).

dégrèvement [degrɛv'mɑ̃] m abatement of tax; derating; **dégrever** [~grə've] (1d) v/t. reduce (*a duty, a tax*); derate; reduce the assessment on; disencumber (*an estate*).

dégringolade F [degrɛ̃gɔ'lad] f

tumble, fall; *currency*: collapse;
dégringoler F [~'le] (1a) *vt/i.*
tumble down.

dégriser [degri'ze] (1a) *v/t.* sober
(*s.o.*); *fig.* bring (*s.o.*) to his senses;
se ~ sober up; *fig.* come to one's
senses. [draw down (*a wire*).]

dégrosser ⊕ [degro'se] (1a) *v/t.*)

dégrossir [degro'si:r] (2a) *v/t.*
rough-hew (*a stone*); rough-plane
(*wood*); rough out (*a plan*); F lick
(*s.o.*) into shape.

dégrouiller *sl.* [degru'je] (1a) *v/t.*:
se ~ hurry up, F get a move on.

déguenillé, e [degəni'je] **1.** *adj.*
ragged, tattered; **2.** *su.* ragamuffin.

déguerpir [deger'pi:r] (2a) *v/t.* 🏛
abandon (*one's property etc.*); *v/i.*
move out; clear out, *Am.* beat it;
faire ~ send (*s.o.*) packing.

déguisement [degiz'mã] disguise;
fig. concealment; fancy dress; *sans*
~ openly; **déguiser** [~gi'ze] (1a)
v/t. disguise; conceal; se ~ *a.* put
on fancy dress.

dégustateur *m*, **-trice** *f* [degysta-
'tœ:r, ~'tris] taster; **dégustation**
[~ta'sjõ] *f* tasting; **déguster** [~'te]
(1a) *v/t.* taste; F sip; relish, enjoy.

déhanché, e [deã'ʃe] *horse*: hip-
shot; *fig.* ungainly, slovenly; moving with a loose gait; **déhancher**
[~] (1a) *v/t.*: se ~ dislocate its hip
(*horse*); *fig.* move with a loose gait;
sway one's hips.

déharnacher [dearna'ʃe] (1a) *v/t.*
unharness.

dehors [də'ɔ:r] **1.** *adv.* outside, out;
dîner ~ dine out; *en* ~ outside; out-
wards; *en* ~ de outside; in addition
to; *en* ~ de moi without my knowledge or participation; *mettre* q. ~
turn s.o. out; F sack s.o., *Am.* lay
s.o. off; ⚓ *toutes voiles* ~ with
every sail set; **2.** *su./m* outside, exterior; ~ *pl.* appearances.

déifier [dei'fje] (1o) *v/t.* deify; *fig.*
make a god of; **déité** [~'te] *f* deity.

déjà [de'ʒa] *adv.* already, before.

déjection [deʒek'sjõ] *f* 🩺 evacuation; ~s *pl. a.* ejecta (*of a volcano*).

déjeter ⊕ [deʒə'te] (1c) *v/t. a.* se ~
warp (*wood*); buckle (*metal*).

déjeuner [deʒœ'ne] **1.** (1a) *v/i.* have
breakfast; F lunch; **2.** *su./m*
lunch; *petit* ~ breakfast; ~**-débat**, *pl.*
~**s-débats** [~nede'ba] *m* working
lunch.

déjouer [de'ʒwe] (1p) *v/t.* thwart;
foil; outwit; elude; baffle.

déjucher [deʒy'ʃe] (1a) *v/t.* unroost
(*hens*); F *fig.* make (*s.o.*) come off
his perch; *v/i.* come off the roost.

déjuger [deʒy'ʒe] (1l) *v/t.*: se ~
reverse one's opinion.

delà [də'la] *adv., a. prp.* beyond.

délabré, e [dela'bre] dilapidated;
ramshackle, tumble-down; impaired (*health*); **délabrer** [~] (1a)
v/t. dilapidate, wreck; ruin (*a. one's
health*); se ~ fall into decay (*house*);
become impaired (*health*).

délacer [dela'se] (1k) *v/t.* unlace;
undo (*one's shoes*).

délai [de'lɛ] *m* delay; respite; reprieve; *à bref* ~ at short notice;
dans un ~ de 2 mois at a two-months'
notice; ~**-congé**, *pl.* ~**s-congés**
[~lɛkõ'ʒe] *m* term of notice.

délaisser [delɛ'se] (1b) *v/t.* forsake,
desert; abandon (*a.* 🏛 *prosecution*); 🏛 relinquish. [(*butter*).)

délaiter [delɛ'te] (1b) *v/t.* work)

délarder [delar'de] (1a) *v/t.* remove
the fat from; ⊕ thin down (*wood*);
bevel, chamfer (*an edge*).

délassement [delas'mã] *m* rest, relaxation; recreation; **délasser** [~-
la'se] (1a) *v/t.* rest, refresh; se ~
relax.

délateur, -trice [dela'tœ:r, ~'tris]
su. informer, spy; *su./m* ⊕ detector
(*of a lock*); **délation** [~'sjõ] *f* in-
forming, denunciation; squealing.

délavé, e [dela've] washed out;
wishy-washy; weak.

délayer [delɛ'je] (1i) *v/t.* dilute; *fig.*
spin out (*a speech*).

délectable [delɛk'tabl] delectable;
delightful; **délecter** [~'te] (1a) *v/t.*:
se ~ *à* take delight in.

délégataire 🏛 [delega'tɛ:r] *su.* del-
egatee; **délégateur** *m*, **-trice** *f* 🏛
[~'tœ:r, ~'tris] delegator; **délégation** [~'sjõ] *f* delegation (*a. coll.*);
🏛 assignment; **délégué, e** [dele-
'ge] **1.** *adj.* deputy..., delegated; **2.**
su. delegate; deputy; *su./m*: ⊕ ~
syndical shop steward; ⊕ ~ *du personnel* union steward; **déléguer** [~]
(1s) *v/t.* delegate; 🏛 *a.* assign.

délester [delɛs'te] (1a) *v/t.* ⚓ *etc.*
unballast; unload; *fig.* relieve (of,
de); ⚡ shed the load.

délétère [dele'tɛ:r] deleterious;
noxious; poison(ous) (*gas, a. fig.*);

151   **démantèlement**

fig. pernicious (*doctrine*); offensive (*smell*).

délibératif, -ve [delibera'tif, ~'tiːv] deliberative; *avoir voix* ~ve be entitled to speak and vote; **délibération** [~ra'sjõ] *f* deliberation, debate, discussion (on, *sur*); reflection; resolution, vote; **délibéré, e** [~'re] **1.** *adj.* deliberate; determined; *de propos* ~ deliberately; **2.** *su./m* 🏛 private sitting, consultation; **délibérer** [~'re] (1f) *v/i.* deliberate; consult together; ponder, reflect (on *de, sur*).

délicat, e [deli'ka, ~'kat] delicate; fragile; dainty; nice, difficult, tricky (*situation, question*); fastidious (*eater*); sensitive (*skin*); scrupulous; *peu* ~ unscrupulous, dishonest; *su./m: faire le* ~ be squeamish; **délicatesse** [~ka'tɛs] *f* delicacy; fragility; fastidiousness; tact; difficulty; *avec* ~ tactfully.

délice [de'lis] *su./m* delight; *su./f:* ~*s pl.* delight *sg.*, pleasure *sg.*; *faire les* ~*s de* be the delight of; *faire ses* ~*s de* revel in; **délicieux, -euse** [~li'sjø, ~'sjøːz] delicious; delightful.

délictueux, -euse 🏛 [delik'tɥø, ~'tɥøːz] punishable, unlawful; felonious; *acte m* ~ misdemeano(u)r.

délié, e [de'lje] slim, thin, slender; glib (*tongue*); nimble (*fingers, wit*); **délier** [~] (1o) *v/t.* untie, undo; release; *eccl.* absolve; *sans bourse* ~ without spending a (half)penny.

délimiter [delimi'te] (1a) *v/t.* delimit; fix the boundaries of; demarcate; define (*powers*).

délinquance 🏛 [delɛ̃'kãːs] *f* delinquency; ~ *juvénile* juvenile delinquency; **délinquant, e** *f* 🏛 [~'kã, ~'kãːt] delinquent, offender; trespasser.

délirant, e [deli'rã, ~'rãːt] frantic, frenzied; rapturous; 🩺 delirious; raving; **délire** [~'liːr] *m* 🩺 delirium; *fig.* frenzy; **délirer** [~li're] (1a) *v/i.* be delirious; rave (*a. fig.*); **délirium tremens** 🩺 [~li'rjɔm tre'mɛ̃ːs] *m* delirium tremens, F d.t.'s.

délit 🏛 [de'li] *m* misdemeano(u)r, offence; *en flagrant* ~ in the act, redhanded.

délivrance [deli'vrãːs] *f* deliverance; release; rescue; 🩺 confinement; delivery; *certificate, ticket, etc.:* issue; **délivrer** [~'vre] (1a) *v/t.*

(set) free; deliver (*a.* 🩺, *a. a certificate, a ticket*); release; issue (*a certificate, a ticket*); se ~ *de* free o.s. from.

déloger [delɔ'ʒe] (11) *v/i.* remove, move house; go away; ✕ march off; *v/t.* oust, drive out; ✕ dislodge.

déloyal, e *m/pl.* -**aux** [delwa'jal, ~'jo] disloyal, false; 🏆 unfair (*competition*); *sp.* foul; **déloyauté** [~jo'te] *f* disloyalty, treachery.

déluge [de'lyːʒ] *m* deluge, flood (*a. fig.*); F *rain:* downpour.

déluré, e [dely're] smart, sharp, knowing; forward, cheeky.

délustrer [delys'tre] (1a) *v/t. tex.* take the gloss off (*a cloth*); *fig.* take the shine off; se ~ lose its gloss; grow shabby; *fig.* fade.

démagogue [dema'gɔg] *m* demagogue.

démailler [demɑ'je] (1a) *v/t.* unshackle (*a chain*); unpick (*a knitted object*); se ~ run, ladder (*stocking*); **démailloter** [~jɔ'te] (1a) *v/t.* unswaddle (*a baby*).

demain [də'mɛ̃] *adv., a. su./m* tomorrow; *à* ~*!* good-bye till tomorrow!, F see you to-morrow!; ~ *en huit* to-morrow week.

démancher [demã'ʃe] (1a) *v/t.* unhaft, remove the handle of (*a tool*); 🩺 F dislocate; *fig.* upset; *v/i.* ♪ shift.

demande [də'mãːd] *f* question; enquiry; request (for, *de*); 🏆 demand; 🏛 claim, action; ~ *d'emploi* application for a job; 🏛 ~ *en dommages-intérêts* claim for damages; ~ *en mariage* proposal (of marriage); *à la* ~ as required; *à la* ~ *générale* by general request; *sur* ~ on application *or* request; **demander** [~mã'de] (1a) *v/t.* ask (for); beg, request; wish, want; order; apply for; ~ *q.* ask for s.o.; ~ *qch. à q.* ask s.o. for s.th.; se ~ wonder.

demandeur[1] *m*, -**euse** [dəmã'dœːr, ~'døːz] petitioner; applicant (for, *de*); demander; *cards:* declarer; *teleph.* caller.

demandeur[2] *m*, -**eresse** *f* 🏛 [dəmã'dœːr, ~'drɛs] plaintiff.

démangeaison [demãʒɛ'zõ] *f* itching; *fig.* F itch, longing; **démanger** [~'ʒe] (11) *v/i.* itch (*arm, leg, etc.*); *fig. ça me démange de* (*inf.*) I'm dying to (*inf.*).

démantèlement [demãtɛl'mã] *m*

dismantling; **démanteler** [∼mɑ̃t'le] (1d) v/t. dismantle; demolish, raze; break up (a gang).

démantibuler [demɑ̃tiby'le] (1a) v/t. ruin, break up, smash up.

démaquillage [demaki'jaːʒ] m: crème m de ∼cleansing cream; **démaquillant** [∼'jɑ̃] m make-up remover, cleanser; **démaquiller** [∼'je] (1a) v/t.: se ∼ take off one's make-up.

démarcation [demarka'sjɔ̃] f demarcation, boundary.

démarche [de'marʃ] f step (a. fig.), walk, gait; fig. a. procedure(s pl.); faire des ∼s pour take steps to.

démarquer [demar'ke] (1m) v/t. remove the marks from; ✝ mark down (prices); fig. plagiarize.

démarrage [dema'raːʒ] m mot., ⚓, ✈ start; ⚓cleansing; **démarrer** [∼'re] (1a) vt/i. ⚓ cast off; mot., ⚓, ✈ start; v/i. fig. get moving, get off the ground; faire ∼ mot. start; ⊕ set in motion; **démarreur** ⊕, mot. [∼'rœːr] m starter.

démasquer [demas'ke] (1m) v/t. unmask (a. ⚔); ⚓ show (a light); fig. ∼ ses batteries show one's hand.

démêlé [demɛ'le] m dispute; contest; **démêler** [∼'le] (1a) v/t. unravel; comb out (one's hair); fig. make out; clear up; avoir qch. à ∼ avec q. have a bone to pick with s.o.; **démêloir** [∼'lwaːr] m large-toothed comb.

démembrer [demɑ̃'bre] (1a) v/t. dismember; break up.

déménagement [demena3'mɑ̃] m removal, moving (house); voiture f de ∼ furniture van; **déménager** [∼na'ʒe] (1l) v/t. (re)move; move the furniture out of (a house); v/i. move house; fig. go out of one's mind; F sa tête déménage he has taken leave of his senses; **déménageur** [∼na'ʒœːr] m furniture remover.

démence [de'mɑ̃ːs] f insanity, madness; ⚕ dementia; ⚖ lunacy.

démener [dema'ne] (1d) v/t.: se ∼ struggle; fling o.s. about; fig. strive hard.

dément, e [de'mɑ̃, ∼'mɑ̃ːt] 1. adj. mad; ⚖ lunatic; 2. su. mad person, lunatic.

démenti [demɑ̃'ti] m denial, contradiction; fig. failure; **démentir** [∼'tiːr] (2b) v/t. contradict; deny

(a fact); belie; se ∼ contradict o.s.; fail (to keep one's word).

démérite [deme'rit] m demerit; **démériter** [∼'rite] (1a) v/i. act in a blameworthy manner; ∼ auprès de q. forfeit s.o.'s esteem; ∼ de break faith with (s.o.); become unworthy of (s.th.).

démesuré, e [demazy're] inordinate, beyond measure; excessive; out of all proportion.

démettre [de'mɛtr] (4v) v/t. dislocate; ✝ deprive; ⚖ ∼ q. de son appel dismiss s.o.'s appeal; se ∼ l'épaule dislocate one's shoulder, put one's shoulder out (of joint); se ∼ de qch. give s.th. up, abandon s.th.; se ∼ (de ses fonctions) resign.

démeubler [demœ'ble] (1a) v/t. remove the furniture from.

demeurant [dəmœ'rɑ̃]: au ∼ after all; **demeure** [∼'mœːr] f dwelling, residence; ✝ delay; à ∼ permanent(ly); dernière ∼ last resting place; ✝ en ∼ in arrears; mettre q. en ∼ de (inf.) call upon s.o. to (inf.); mise f en ∼ summons; **demeuré, e** [∼mœ're] mentally retarded; half-witted; **demeurer** [∼mœ're] (1a) v/i. live, reside; stay, stop; en ∼ là stop, leave off.

demi, e [də'mi] 1. adj. (inv. before su.) half, demi-..., semi-...; une demi-heure half an hour, a half-hour; une heure et demie an hour and a half; dix heures et demie half past ten; 2. su./m half; sp. half-back; **∼-cercle** [dəmi'sɛrkl] m semicircle; surv. demi-circle; **∼-fond** sp. [∼'fɔ̃] m medium distance; **∼-frère** [∼'frɛːr] m half-brother, step-brother; **∼-gros** ✝ [∼'gro] m wholesale dealing in small quantities; **∼-jour** [∼'juːr] m/inv. half-light; **∼-journée** [∼jur'ne] f part-time work; half-day.

démilitariser [demilitari'ze] (1a) v/t. demilitarize.

demi...: ∼-monde [dəmi'mɔ̃ːd] m demi-monde; **∼-mot** [∼'mo] adv.: à ∼ without many words; **∼-pension** [∼pɑ̃'sjɔ̃] f part board; **∼-reliure** [rə'ljyːr] f quarter-binding; **∼-saison** [∼sɛ'zɔ̃] f between-season, mid-season; **∼-sec** [∼'sɛk] adj./m medium dry (wine); **∼-sœur** [∼'sœːr] f half-sister, step-sister; **∼-solde** ⚔ [∼'sɔld] f half pay; **∼-sommeil** [∼sɔ'mɛːj] m somnolence; **∼-soupir** ♪ [∼su'piːr] m quaver rest.

démission [demi'sjɔ̃] *f* resignation; abdication; *donner sa* ~ hand in one's resignation; **démissionnaire** [~sjɔ'nɛːr] **1.** *adj.* resigning; **2.** *su.* resigner; **démissionner** [~sjɔ'ne] (1a) *v/i.* resign, step down; *fig.* give up.

demi...: ~-**tarif** [dəmita'rif] *m*: (*à* ~ at) half-price *or* half-fare; ~-**teinte** *paint., phot.* [~'tɛ̃ːt] *f* half-tone, half-tint; ~-**ton** ♪ [~'tɔ̃] *m* semitone; ~-**tour** [~'tuːr] *m* half-turn; ⚔ about turn; *mot.* U-turn; *faire* ~ turn back; turn about; ⚔ about-turn; ⚓ turn a half-circle.

démobiliser ⚔ [demɔbili'ze] (1a) *v/t.* demobilize.

démocrate [demɔ'krat] **1.** *adj.* democratic; **2.** *su.* democrat; **démocratie** [~kra'si] *f* democracy; **démocratiser** [~krati'ze] (1a) *v/t.* democratize; *fig.* put in the reach of the average man.

démodé, e [demɔ'de] old-fashioned, out of date, dated, outmoded; **démoder** [~] (1a) *v/t.*: *se* ~ go out of fashion.

démographe [demɔ'graf] *m* demographer; **démographie** [~gra'fi] *f* demography.

demoiselle [dəmwa'zɛl] *f* young lady; spinster; ⊕ paving-beetle; *zo.* dragon-fly; ⚓ rowlock; ~ (*de magasin*) shop-girl; ~ *d'honneur* bridesmaid; maid of hono(u)r.

démolir [demɔ'liːr] (2a) *v/t.* demolish (*a. fig. an argument*), pull down; *fig.* overthrow; *fig.* ruin; F give a good thrashing to (*s.o.*); **démolisseur** [~li'sœːr] *m* demolition worker *or* contractor, wrecker; *fig.* demolisher; **démolition** [~li'sjɔ̃] *f* demolition; ~*s pl.* rubbish *sg.*; rubble *sg.* (*from demolished building*).

démon [de'mɔ̃] *m* demon, devil, fiend; *fig.* imp; *le* ~ *de midi* love in middle age.

démonétiser [demɔneti'ze] (1a) *v/t.* demonetize (*metal*); *fig.* discredit (*s.o.*).

démoniaque [demɔ'njak] *adj., a. su.* demoniac.

démonstrateur *m*, -**trice** *f* [demɔ̃stra'tœːr, ~'tris] ♱ demonstrator; **démonstratif, -ve** [~'tif, ~'tiːv] **1.** *adj.* demonstrative (*a. gramm.*); *peu* ~ undemonstrative, dour; **2.** *su./m gramm.* demonstrative; **démon-stration** [~'sjɔ̃] *f* demonstration; ⚔ show of force.

démontable ⊕ [demɔ̃'tabl] that can be taken to pieces; collapsible (*boat*); **démontage** [~'taːʒ] *m* dismantling; *tyre*: removal; **démonté, e** [~'te] stormy, wild (*sea*); flustered; **démonter** [~'te] (1a) *v/t.* unseat (*a rider*); ⊕ dismantle, take down; *fig.* upset, take aback, fluster; *se* ~ lose countenance; get flustered.

démontrer [demɔ̃'tre] (1a) *v/t.* demonstrate, show.

démoraliser [demɔrali'ze] (1a) *v/t.* demoralize; *fig.* dishearten; ⚔ destroy *or* undermine the morale of (*troops etc.*).

démordre [de'mɔrdr] (4a) *v/i.* let go; *fig.* give in; *fig. ne pas* ~ *de* stick to.

démouler [demu'le] (1a) *v/t.* withdraw from the mould; turn out (*a cake*).

démunir [demy'niːr] (2a) *v/t.* deprive (of, *de*); *se* ~ *de* part with; ♱ run short of.   [muzzle (*a dog*).↓]

démuseler [demyz'le] (1c) *v/t.* un-⌉

démystification [demistifika'sjɔ̃] *f* debunking; demystification; **démystifier** [~'fje] (1a) *v/t.* debunk; demystify.

démythifier [demiti'fje] (1a) demythologize; debunk; demystify.

dénatalité [denatali'te] *f* fall in the birth-rate.

dénationaliser [denasjɔnali'ze] (1a) *v/t.* denationalize; *se* ~ lose one's nationality.

dénaturaliser [denatyrali'ze] (1a) *v/t.* denaturalize.

dénaturé, e [denaty're] unnatural; ⚗ *alcool m* ~ methylated spirit; **dénaturer** [~] (1a) *v/t.* adulterate; *fig.* misrepresent, distort; pervert.

dénégation [denega'sjɔ̃] *f* denial; ⚖ traverse.

déni ⚖ [de'ni] denial, refusal.

déniaiser F [denjɛ'ze] (1a) *v/t.* educate (*s.o.*) in the ways of the world; smarten (*s.o.'s*) wits; *fig.* initiate (*s.o.*) sexually.

dénicher [deni'ʃe] (1a) *v/t.* take from the nest; ✗ dislodge; *fig.* unearth, rout out; discover; *v/i.* fly away; F *fig.* clear out, depart.

denier [də'nje] *m* small coin; penny; cent; money; *stockings*: denier; *les* ~*s pl. publics* public funds; *le* ~ *de Saint-Pierre* Peter's pence.

dénier [de'nje] (1o) v/t. deny; disclaim; refuse.

dénigrer [deni'gre] (1a) v/t. disparage, run (s.o.) down.

déniveler [deni'vle] (1c) v/t. make uneven (the surface); surv. determine differences in level.

dénombrement [denõbrə'mã] m counting; population: census; **dénombrer** [~'bre] (1a) v/t. count; take a census of (the population).

dénominateur [denomina'tœːr] m denominator; **dénominatif, -ve** [~'tif, ~'tiːv] denominative; **dénomination** [~sja'sjõ] f name, denomination; **dénommer** [denɔ'me] (1a) v/t. denominate, call, designate.

dénoncer [denõ'se] (1k) v/t. denounce (a. a treaty); betray; indicate; expose; ~ q. (à la police) inform against s.o.; **dénonciateur, -trice** [~sja'tœːr, ~'tris] 1. su. informer; F stoolpigeon; 2. adj. telltale, revealing; laying information (letter); **dénonciation** [~sja'sjõ] f denunciation; information (against, de); notice of termination (of treaty etc.).

dénoter [denɔ'te] (1a) v/t. denote, show, mark.

dénouement [denu'mã] m untying; result, outcome; difficulty: solution; thea. etc. dénouement; **dénouer** [~'nwe] (1p) v/t. untie, unravel, undo; fig. clear up; loosen (limbs, the tongue); se ~ come undone; end (story); loosen (tongue).

denrée [dã're] f usu. ~s pl. commodity sg.; produce sg.; ~s pl. alimentaires food-stuffs; ~s pl. coloniales colonial produce sg.

dense [dãːs] dense (a. phys.); thick; peu ~ thin; sparse; **densimètre** phys. [dãsi'metr] m densimeter, hydrometer; **densité** [~'te] f density (a. phys., a. of population); phys. specific weight.

dent [dã] f tooth (a. ⊕); elephant: tusk; geog. jagged peak; ⊕ cog; fork: prong; ~ de lait (de sagesse) milk tooth (wisdom tooth); ~s pl. artificielles denture sg.; sl. avoir la ~ be hungry; avoir une ~ contre have a grudge against; être sur les ~s be worn out; mal m aux ~s toothache; sans ~s toothless; **dentaire** anat. [dã'tɛːr] dental (art, pulp); **dental, e**, m/pl. **-aux** [~'tal, ~'to] 1. adj.

dental (nerve, consonant); 2. su./f gramm. dental (consonant); **dent-de-lion**, pl. **dents-de-lion** ♀ [dãd-'ljõ] f dandelion; **denté, e** [dã'te] toothed; ⊕ roue f ~e cogwheel; **dentelé, e** [dãt'le] jagged, notched; serrated (a. leaf); **denteler** [~] (1c) v/t. notch; indent (a. fig.); **dentelle** [dã'tɛl] f lace; wrought ironwork; **dentelure** [dãt'lyːr] f indentation; post: perforation (of stamps); **denter** [dã'te] (1a) v/t. ⊕ tooth, cog (a wheel); **denticulé, e** [~tiky'le] ♀ denticulate; △ denticular; **dentier** [~'tje] m denture, F plate; set of false teeth; **dentifrice** [~ti'fris] 1. su./m dentifrice, tooth-paste; 2. adj.: eau f ~ mouth-wash; **dentine** anat. [~'tin] f dentine; **dentiste** [~'tist] m dentist; **dentition** [~ti'sjõ] f dentition; baby: teething; **denture** [~'tyːr] f set of (natural) teeth; ⊕ teeth pl., cogs pl., gear teeth pl.

dénucléarisé, e [denykleari'ze] atom-free (zone).

dénuder [deny'de] (1a) v/t. lay bare; strip; **dénuement** [~ny'mã] m destitution; poverty (a. fig.); room: bareness; **dénuer** [~'nɥe] (1n) v/t. strip (of, de); dénué de devoid of, lacking, ...less.

dépannage [depa'naːʒ] m repairing; fixing; repairs pl.; fig. helping (out); help, relief, F troubleshooting; mot. (a. service m de ~) breakdown service; **dépanner** [~'ne] (1a) v/t. repair, fix; fig. help (out), tide over, relief; **dépanneur** mot. [~'nœːr] m breakdown mechanic; **dépanneuse** mot. [~'nøːz] f breakdown lorry, Am. wrecker.

dépaqueter [depak'te] (1c) v/t. unpack.

dépareillé, e [deparɛ'je] odd (= unpaired); ✝ articles m/pl. ~s job lot sg., oddments.

déparer [depa're] (1a) v/t. strip (of ornaments); divest (of medals etc.); fig. spoil, mar.

déparier [depa'rje] (1o) v/t. remove one of a pair of; separate (a pair); gant m déparié odd glove.

départ¹ [de'paːr] m departure (a. ⚞), start; ⚓ sailing; fig. start, beginning; sp. bloc m de ~ starting block; sp. ~ lancé flying start; point m de ~ starting point (a. fig.); fig. au ~ in the beginning; at the outset.

départ[2] [~] *m* division, separation.

départager [departa'ʒe] (11) *v/t.* decide between; ~ *les voix* give the casting vote.

département [depart'mã] *m* department (*a. pol. Am.*); *pol.* Ministry; *admin.* department; *fig.* province.

departir [depar'tiːr] (2b) *v/t.* distribute, deal out; *se ~ de* abandon, give up.

dépassement [depɑs'mã] *m* overstepping, going beyond; *credit etc.*: exceeding; **dépasser** [~pɑ'se] (1a) *v/t.* pass, go beyond; exceed (*a. a speed*); overtake (*a car, a person, etc.*); project beyond; *fig.* outshine; *fig.* be beyond (*s.o.'s means etc.*); F *cela me dépasse* it is beyond my comprehension, F it's beyond me; *sp.* ~ *à la course* outrun.

dépassionner [depasjɔ'ne] (1a) *v/t.* take the heat out of (*a discussion etc.*).

dépaver [depa've] (1a) *v/t.* take up the pavement of (*a street*).

dépayser [depei'ze] (1a) *v/t.* take (*s.o.*) out of his element; mislead; *fig.* bewilder.

dépecer [depə'se] (1d *a.* 1k) *v/t.* cut up; dismember; break up (*an estate, a ship*).

dépêche [de'pɛːʃ] *f* dispatch; telegram, F wire; **dépêcher** [depɛ'ʃe] (1a) *v/t.* hasten; expedite; dispatch; *se ~* hurry up, make haste (to *inf.*, *de inf.*).

dépeigner [depe'ɲe] (1a) *v/t.* ruffle.

dépeindre [de'pɛ̃ːdr] (4m) *v/t.* depict; describe.

dépenaillé, e [depənɑ'je] tattered, ragged.

dépendance [depã'dãːs] *f* dependence; dependency (*of a country*); *fig.* subjection, domination; ~*s pl.* outbuildings, annexes.

dépendre[1] [de'pãːdr] (4a) *v/i.* depend (on, *de*); *cela dépend* that depends; *il dépend de vous de* (*inf.*) it lies with you to (*inf.*).

dépendre[2] [~] (4a) *v/t.* take down, unhang.

dépens [de'pã] *m/pl.* cost *sg.*, expense *sg.*, ⚖ costs; *aux ~ de q.* at s.o.'s expense.

dépense [de'pãːs] *f* expenditure, spending, outlay, expense; *gas, steam, etc.*: consumption; **dépenser** [depã'se] (1a) *v/t.* spend; consume (*coal etc.*), use (up); *fig. se ~* exert

o.s.; **dépensier, -ère** [~'sje, ~'sjɛːr] 1. *su.* storekeeper; *hospital*: dispenser; spendthrift; 2. *adj.* extravagant, spendthrift.

déperdition [depɛrdi'sjɔ̃] *f* waste; loss; *gas*: escape.

dépérir [depe'riːr] (2a) *v/i.* decline, pine (away), dwindle; **dépérissement** [~ris'mã] *m* declining, pining, dwindling; decay(ing); deterioration.

dépersonnaliser [depɛrsɔnali'ze] (1o) *v/t.* depersonalize; *se ~* loose one's personality; become impersonal.

dépêtrer [depɛ'tre] (1a) *v/t.* extricate, free; *se ~ de* get o.s. out of (*s.th.*); F *se ~ de q.* shake s.o. off.

dépeupler [depœ'ple] (1a) *v/t.* depopulate; thin (*a forest*).

déphasage [defa'zaːʒ] *m phys.* phase difference; *fig.* discrepancy, gap; *fig.* lag; **déphasé, e** [~'ze] *phys.* out of phase; *fig.* disoriented; *fig.* lagging behind; F *fig.* no longer with it.

dépiauter F [depjo'te] (1a) *v/t.* skin; *fig.* dissect (*a book*).

dépilation [depila'sjɔ̃] *f* depilation; removal of hair; **dépilatoire** [~la-'twaːr] 1. *adj.* depilatory; *pâte f* ~ hair-removing cream; 2. *su./m* depilatory, hair-remover; **dépiler** [~'le] (1a) *v/t.* remove the hair from.

dépister [depis'te] (1a) *v/t. hunt.* run to earth (*a.* F *fig. s.o.*); *fig.* detect, discover; put off the scent; *fig.* baffle.

dépit [de'pi] vexation, frustration; *en ~ de* in spite of; **dépiter** [~pi'te] (1a) *v/t.* annoy; spite; *se ~* be annoyed *or* vexed (at, *de*).

déplacé, e [depla'se] out of place; displaced; *fig.* misplaced; improper; **déplacement** [~plas'mã] *m* moving, shifting; movement; displacement, relocation, transfer, removal; travel(ling); ⚓ displacement; ~ *disciplinaire* disciplinary transfer; *frais m/pl. de ~* travelling expenses; **déplacer** [~pla'se] (1k) *v/t.* displace, shift, move; dislodge; ⚓ have a displacement of; *fig.* transfer (*s.o.*); *se ~* move; move *or* get around *or* about; travel.

déplaire [de'plɛːr] (4z) *v/i.*: ~ *à* displease; *v/t.*: *se ~ à* dislike; **déplaisant, e** [deplɛ'zã, ~'zãːt] unpleasant, disagreeable; **déplaisir** [~'zi:r] *m* displeasure; annoyance.

déplanter ✔ [deplã'te] (1a) *v/t.* displant; take up (*a plant*); transplant.

dépliant [depli'ã] *m* folding album; folder; **déplier** [~'e] (1a) *v/t.* unfold.

déplisser [depli'se] (1a) *v/t.* unpleat, take the pleats out of; se ~ come out of pleats.

déploiement [deplwa'mã] *m* unfolding; *goods, courage, etc.*: display; ✕, ⚓, *troops, etc.*: deployment.

déplomber [deplɔ̃'be] (1a) *v/t.* unseal; ⚙ unstop, *Am.* remove the filling from (*a tooth*).

déplorable [deplɔ'rabl] deplorable, lamentable; wretched; **déplorer** [~'re] (1a) *v/t.* deplore; lament, mourn.

déployer [deplwa'je] (1h) *v/t.* unfold; display (*a flag, goods, patience, etc.*); ✕ deploy (*troops*) ⚓ unfurl (*the sail*).

déplumer [deply'me] (1a) *v/t.* pluck; se ~ moult; F grow bald.

dépolir ⊕ [depo'li:r] (2a) *v/t.* remove the polish from; grind, frost (*glass*); se ~ grow dull; *verre m* dépoli ground *or* frosted glass.

dépolluer [depɔl'lɥe] (1n) *v/t.* depollute; **dépollution** [depɔly'sjɔ̃] *f* depolluting.

dépopulation [depɔpyla'sjɔ̃] *f* depopulation; falling population.

déport ✝ [de'pɔ:r] *m* backwardation.

déportation [depɔrta'sjɔ̃] *f* ⚖ transportation; *pol.* deportation; **déportements** [depɔrta'mã] *m/pl.* misconduct *sg.*; dissolute life *sg.*; **déporter** [~'te] (1a) *v/t.* deport (*s.o.*); carry away; ⊕ off-set (*a part*); *v/i.* ✖ drift.

déposant *m*, **e** *f* [depo'zã, ~'zã:t] ✝ depositor; ⚖ bailor; ⚖ deponent, witness; **déposer** [~'ze] (1a) *v/t.* deposit (*s.th., money, required documents*, ⚙ *a sediment, etc.*); lay down; leave; depose (*a king etc.*); *parl.* introduce, table (*a bill*); ⚖ file (*a petition*), prefer (*a charge*), lodge (*a complaint*); ✝ register (*a trade-mark*); *v/i.* settle (*wine*); ⚖ give evidence (against, *contre*); depose (that, *que*); **dépositaire** [~zi'tɛ:r] *su.* trustee; ⚖ bailee; ✝

agent (for, *de*); **déposition** [~zi-'sjɔ̃] *f* ⚖, *a.* king: deposition; ⚖ evidence; ⚖ ~ *sous serment* affidavit.

déposséder [depose'de] (1f) *v/t.* (*de*) dispossess (from), deprive (of); **dépossession** [~sɛ'sjɔ̃] *f* dispossession.

dépôt [de'po] *m* deposit; ⚖ bailment; *telegram:* handing in; ✝ store; depot (*a.* ✕); ✝ warehouse; *Customs:* bond; sediment (*in liquid*); ⚙ depositing; 🚂 *engine:* shed; police station; ⚙ accumulation of matter; ✝ *trade-mark:* registration; ~ *de marchandises* goods depot; freight yard; ~ *de mendicité* workhouse; ~ *mortuaire* mortuary; *caisse f de* ~*s et consignations* Deposit and Consignment Office; en ~ on sale; in stock; on trust.

dépoter [depɔ'te] (1a) *v/t.* ✔ plant out (*seedlings*); unpot (*a plant*); decant (*wine etc.*).

dépotoir [depo'twa:r] *m* rubbish (*Am.* garbage) dump; junk room *or* yard.

dépouille [de'pu:j] *f animal:* skin; *serpent:* slough; ⊕ rake, clearance; *metall.* draw; ~*s pl.* spoils, booty *sg.*; effects; ~ *mortelle* mortal remains *pl.*; **dépouillement** [~puj'mã] *m* despoiling; scrutiny, examination; *votes:* count; **dépouiller** [~pu'je] (1a) *v/t.* skin; strip; plunder; rob; examine; open (*letters*); count (votes); *fig.* cast off *or* aside (*one's pride etc.*); se ~ shed its leaves (*tree*); cast its skin (*serpent*); divest o.s., get rid (of, *de*).

dépourvoir [depur'vwa:r] (3m) *v/t.* deprive (of s.th., de *qch.*); **dépourvu, e** [~'vy] 1. *adj.:* ~ *de* lacking, short of, devoid of; 2. *dépourvu adv.: au* ~ unawares.

dépoussiérage [depusje'ra:ʒ] *m* dusting; ⊕ dust extraction; *air:* filtering; **dépoussiérer** [~'re] (1a) *v/t.* remove (the) dust from; dust down; *fig.* dust off.

dépravation [deprava'sjɔ̃] *f taste etc.:* depravation; *morals:* depravity; **dépraver** [~'ve] (1a) *v/t.* deprave, corrupt.

dépréciation [depresja'sjɔ̃] *f* depreciation; wear and tear; **déprécier** [~'sje] (1o) *v/t.* depreciate (*a.* ✝), undervalue; belittle, F run

down; devalue (*coinage*); se ~ ♱
depreciate; *fig.* belittle o.s.

déprédateur, -trice [depreda'tœːr,
~'tris] **1.** *su.* depredator; embezzler;
2. *adj.* depredatory; **déprédation**
[~'sjɔ̃] *f* depredation, pillaging;
peculation.

déprendre [de'prɑ̃ːdr] (4q) *v/t.*: se ~
de break away from; free *or* rid o.s.
of; cast off.

dépressif, -ve [depre'sif, ~'siːv]
bearing down; *fig.* depressing; **dépression** [~'sjɔ̃] *f* depression (*a.* ♱,
a. meteor., *a.* *fig.*); fall (*in value*);
barometer: fall in pressure; ♂ (~
nerveuse nervous) breakdown; **dé-
prime** F [de'prim] *f* depression;
déprimer [depri'me] (1a) *v/t.*
depress; *fig.* lower; se ~ become
depressed.

depuis [də'pɥi] **1.** *prp.* since, for;
from; ~ *quand?* since when?; *je suis
ici* ~ *cinq jours* I have been here for
five days; ~ ... *jusqu'à* from ... (down)
to; **2.** *adv.* since (then); afterwards;
3. *cj.*: ~ *que* since.

dépuratif, -ve [depyra'tif, ~'tiːv]
adj., a. *su./m* depurative; **dépurer**
[~'re] (1a) *v/t.* depurate, cleanse (*the
blood*); purify (*water, metal*).

députation [depyta'sjɔ̃] *f* deputa-
tion; membership of Parliament; se
présenter à la ~ stand for Parliament,
Am. run for Congress; **député** [~'te]
m deputy, M.P., *Am.* Congressman;
députer [~'te] (1a) *v/t.* depute;
delegate (to *à, vers*).

déraciner [derasi'ne] (1a) *v/t.*
uproot; *fig.* eradicate.

déraidir [dere'diːr] (2a) *v/t.* take the
stiffness out of; *fig.* relax.

dérailler [derɑ'je] (1a) *v/i.* 🚂 etc. go
off the rails; be derailed, leave the
track; F talk wildly; F behave
weirdly; F be on the blink (*machinery*); **dérailleur** [~'jœːr] *m* 🚂
shifting track; *bicycle:* gearshift.

déraison [dere'zɔ̃] *f* unreasonable-
ness; unwisdom; **déraisonnable**
[~zɔ'nabl] unreasonable, irrational;
unwise; foolish; **déraisonner** [~zɔ-
'ne] (1a) *v/i.* talk nonsense; rave
(*sick man*).

dérangement [derɑ̃ʒ'mɑ̃] *m* derangement; disturbance, disorder;
trouble; upset; ⚡, ⊕ fault; **déranger** [~rɑ̃'ʒe] (11) *v/t.* derange; bother; disturb; upset (*a. fig.*); ⊕ put

out of order; se ~ move; take trouble
(to *inf., pour inf.*); lead a wild life;
⊕ get out of order; get upset.

dérapage [dera'paːʒ] *m* mot. skid
(-ding); ⚓ dragging; **déraper** [~'pe]
(1a) *v/t.* ⚓ trip, weigh (*the anchor*);
v/i. ⚓ drag; drag its anchor (*ship*);
mot. skid.

dératé, e F [dera'te] **1.** *adj.* scatterbrained, harum-scarum; **2.** *su./m:*
courir comme un ~ run like a hare.

derby *sp.* [dɛr'bi] *m* derby, horse-
race; contest. [more.]

derechef [dərə'ʃef] *adv.* again, once]

déréglé [dere'gle] ⊕ out of order;
fig. immoderate; dissolute (*life*);
dérèglement [~rɛglə'mɑ̃] *m* disorder; *pulse:* irregularity; profli-
gacy; dissolute life; **dérégler** [~re-
'gle] (1f) *v/t.* upset, disarrange;
unsettle; ⊕ put out of order; se ~
get out of order; *fig.* get into evil
ways.

dérider [deri'de] (1a) *v/t.* smooth;
unwrinkle; *fig.* cheer (*s.o.*) up.

dérision [deri'zjɔ̃] *f* derision, ridicule; *tourner en* ~ hold up to ridicule; **dérisoire** [~'zwaːr] ridiculous, laughable; *prix m* ~ ridicu-
lously low price.

dérivatif, -ve [deriva'tif, ~'tiːv] *adj.,
a. su./m* derivative; **dérivation**
[~'sjɔ̃] *f* ⚡, gramm. derivation;
watercourse: diversion; ⚡ loop-
(-line); ⚡ shunt(ing); teleph. branch-
circuit; ⚡ differentiation; ⚓ drift;
dérive [de'riːv] *f* ⚓ leeway; *aller
à la* ~ drift; **dérivé** [~m, gramm.
[deri've] *m* derivative; **dérivée** [~]
[~] *f* differential coefficient.

dériver¹ [deri've] (1a) *v/i.* drift.

dériver² [~] (1a) *v/t.* divert; ⚡,
shunt; ♱ free from the board; ⚡, ⚡,
gramm. derive; *v/i.* derive *or* be derived (from, *de*); spring (from, *de*).

dériver³ ⊕ [~] (1a) *v/t.* unrivet;
unhead (*a rivet*).

dermatologiste [dɛrmatɔlɔ'ʒist],
dermatologue [~'lɔg] *su.* dermato-
logist.

dernier, -ère [dɛr'nje, ~'njɛːr] **1.**
adj. last, latest; highest, utmost
(*importance etc.*); ♱ closing (*price*);
least (*trouble, worry*); vilest (*of
men*); *le jugement* ~ judgment-day,
the last judgment; *mettre la* ~ère
main à give the finishing touch to;
2. *su.* last, latest; **dernièrement**

[‿njɛr'mã] adv. lately, not long ago, recently.

dérobade [derɔ'bad] f escape; *horse*: balking; **dérobé, e** [‿'be] hidden, concealed; **dérobée** [‿'be] adv.: à la ‿ secretly, on the sly; **dérober** [‿'be] (1a) v/t. steal; hide; *cuis.* skin (*beans*), blanch (*almonds*); se ‿ steal away; hide; escape (from, à).

dérogation [derɔga'sjɔ̃] f derogation (of, à); faire ‿ à deviate from; **déroger** [‿'ʒe] (1l) v/i. derogate (from, à); deviate (from, à); *fig.* lower o.s., stoop (to *inf.*, jusqu'à *inf.*).

dérouiller [deru'je] (1a) v/t. remove the rust from; *fig.* polish up.

dérouler [deru'le] (1a) v/t. unroll; unreel (*a cable, a wire*); *fig.* unfold (*one's plan*); se ‿ unroll; come unwound; *fig.* unfold (*scene*); *fig.* occur, develop.

déroute [de'rut] f rout; *fig.* ruin; mettre en ‿ rout; **dérouter** [‿ru'te] (1a) v/t. re-route (*an aircraft etc.*); *fig.* confuse, disconcert (*s.o.*), baffle (*s.o., s.th.*).

derrick [dɛ'rik] m oil-well: derrick.

derrière [dɛ'rjɛːr] **1.** adv. behind, at the back, in the rear; ⚓ astern; ⚓ aft; par ‿ from the rear; **2.** prp. behind, at the back of, in the rear of, *Am.* back of; ⚓ astern of; ⚓ abaft; être ‿ q. back s.o. up; **3.** su./m back, rear; F backside, behind, bottom, rump; ✂ ‿s pl. rear sg.; de ‿ rear..., hind...

derviche [dɛr'viʃ] m, **dervis** [‿'vi] m dervish.

dès [de] prp. from, since; upon (*arrival, entry*); as early as; ‿ demain from tomorrow; ‿ lors from then on; ‿ que as soon as.

désabonner [dezabɔ'ne] (1a) v/t.: se ‿ cancel one's subscription (to, à).

désabuser [dezaby'ze] (1a) v/t. disabuse, disillusion; se ‿ have one's eyes opened.

désaccord [deza'kɔːr] m discord; disharmony; disagreement; discrepancy; *fig.* en ‿ at variance; **désaccorder** [‿kɔr'de] (1a) v/t. ♪ put out of tune; *radio:* detune; *fig.* set at variance; ♪ se ‿ get out of tune.

désaccoupler [dezaku'ple] (1a) v/t. unpair; unleash (*hounds*).

désaccoutumer [dezakuty'me] (1a)

v/t.: ‿ q. de (*inf.*) break s.o. of the habit of (*ger.*).

désaffecté, e [dezafɛk'te] disused; abandoned.

désaffection [dezafɛk'sjɔ̃] f loss of affection; disaffection.

désagréable [dezagre'abl] disagreeable, unpleasant, nasty.

désagréger [dezagre'ʒe] (1a) v/t. disaggregate, disintegrate; *geol.* weather (*rock*).

désagrément [dezagre'mã] m unpleasantness; nuisance, inconvenience; discomfort.

désajuster [dezaʒys'te] (1a) v/t. disarrange; ⊕ throw out of adjustment.

désaltérant, e [dezalte'rã, ‿'rãːt] thirst-quenching; **désaltérer** [‿'re] (1f) v/t. quench (*s.o.'s*) thirst; refresh, water (*a plant*).

désamarrer ⚓ [dezama're] (1a) v/t. unmoor.

désamorcer [dezamɔr'se] (1k) v/t. unprime; defuse (*a. fig.*); se ‿ run dry (*pump etc.*).

désappointement [dezapwɛ̃t'mã] m disappointment; **désappointer** [‿pwɛ̃'te] (1a) v/t. disappoint.

désapprendre [deza'prãːdr] (4aa) v/t. unlearn; forget (*a subject, a skill*).

désapprobateur, -trice [dezaprɔba'tœːr, ‿'tris] **1.** su. disapprover; **2.** adj. disapproving; **désapprouver** [‿pru've] (1a) v/t. disapprove (of), object to.

désarçonner [dezarsɔ'ne] (1a) v/t. unseat (*a rider*); *fig.* dumbfound.

désarmement [dezarmə'mã] m disarmament; **désarmer** [‿'me] (1a) v/t. disarm (*a. fig.*); ⚓ lay up (*a ship*); unship (*oars*); ✂ unload (*a gun*); uncock (*a rifle*); v/i. disarm; ⚓ be laid up (*ship*).

désarrimer ⚓ [dezari'me] (1a) v/t. unstow (*the cargo*); put (*a ship*) out of trim; se ‿ shift.

désarroi [deza'rwa] m confusion, disorder.

désarticuler [dezartiky'le] (1a) v/t. dislocate; ⚕ disarticulate.

désassembler [dezasã'ble] (1a) v/t. take (*s.th.*) to pieces; disassemble; disconnect (*joints, couplings*).

désastre [de'zastr] m disaster; **désastreux, -euse** [‿zas'trø, ‿'trøːz] disastrous, calamitous.

désavantage [dezavā'ta:ʒ] *m* disadvantage; drawback; **désavantager** [ˌta'ʒe] (1l) *v/t.* (put at a) disadvantage; handicap; **désavantageux, -euse** [ˌta'ʒø, ˌ'ʒø:z] unfavo(u)rable.

désaveu [deza'vø] *m* disavowal, denial; repudiation; disclaimer; **désavouer** [ˌ'vwe] (1p) *v/t.* disown; disavow; repudiate; disclaim.

désaxé, e [dezak'se] ⊕ out of true (*wheel*); off-centre; offset (*cylinder*); eccentric (*cam, a. fig.*); *fig.* F unbalanced.

desceller [desɛ'le] (1a) *v/t.* unseal, break the seal of; ⊕ loosen; force (*a safe*).

descendance [desā'dā:s] *f* descent; *coll.* descendants *pl.*; **descendant, e** [ˌ'dā, ˌ'dā:t] **1.** *adj.* descending, downward; ♪ decreasing (*series*); 🚂 up-... (*platform, train*); **2.** *su.* descendant; **descendre** [dɛ'sā:dr] (4a) *v/i.* descend (*a. fig.*), go *or* come down(stairs); fall (*temperature*); alight; get off (*a bus etc.*); dismount (*from a horse*); put up, stay (*at a hotel*); be descended (*from a family etc.*); ~ chez q. stay with s.o.; 🚓 ~ dans (*or* chez) raid; 🐎 ~ en piqué nose-dive; 🚓 ~ sur les lieux visit the scene (*of the accident, crime, etc.*); *v/t.* go *or* come down; bring (*s.th.*) down; take (*s.th.*) down (*from a shelf etc.*); lower (*by rope etc., a. ♪*); bring *or* shoot down; set (*s.o.*) down, F drop (*s.o.*) (*at an address*); **descente** [ˌ'sā:t] *f* descent; slope; *police:* raid; 🚂 alighting from (*a train*); ⚓ landing; ✗ prolapse; lowering (*by rope etc.*); taking down (*from the wall etc.*); ⊕ *piston:* downstroke; ⚡ downpipe; *radio:* down-lead; ✝ run (on a bank); ~ à pic ski: straight (down-hill) run; *paint. etc.* ~ de croix descent from the cross; ~ de lit (bed-side) rug; 🎿 ~ piquée nose-dive.

descriptif, -ve [dɛskrip'tif, ˌ'ti:v] descriptive; **description** [ˌ'sjõ] *f* description.

déséchouer ⚓ [deze'ʃwe] (1p) *v/t.* refloat.

déségrégation *pol.* [desegrega'sjõ] *f* desegregation.

désempar|é, e [dezāpa'ʀe] helpless, all at sea; crippled (*vehicle etc.*); **~er** [~] (1a) *v/i.:* sans ~ without stopping), on end; *v/t.* ♣ disable; undo.

désemplir [dezā'pli:r] (2a) *v/i.* half-empty; *v/i.: ne pas* ~ be always full.

désenchaîner [dezāʃɛ'ne] (1b) *v/t.* unchain, unfetter.

désenchanter [dezāʃā'te] (1a) *v/t.* disenchant; *fig.* disillusion.

désencombrer [dezākõ'bre] (1a) *v/t.* clear; disencumber.

désenfler [dezā'fle] (1a) *v/t.* reduce the swelling of (*the ankle*); deflate (*a tyre etc.*); *v/i. a.* se ~ go down, become less swollen.

désengager [dezāga'ʒe] (1l) *v/t.* free from an engagement *or* an obligation.

désengorger ⊕ [dezāgɔr'ʒe] (1l) *v/t.* unstop (*a pipe*).

désenivrer [dezāni'vre] (1a) *v/t.* sober (*s.o.*) (up).

désennuyer [dezānɥi'je] (1h) *v/t.* amuse (*s.o.*); divert (*s.o.*); se ~ seek diversion (in *ger.*, à *inf.*; from, de).

désenrayer ⊕ [dezāʀɛ'je] (1i) *v/t.* release (*a brake etc.*).

désensibiliser [desāsibili'ze] (1a) *v/t.* desensitize.

désenvenimer 🩹 [dezāvəni'me] (1a) *v/t.* cleanse (*a wound*).

déséquilibre [dezeki'libr] *m* lack of balance; unbalance; **déséquilibré, e** [dezekili'bre] unbalanced (*a. mind*); out of balance; **déséquilibrer** [ˌ] (1a) *v/t.* throw (*s.th.*) off balance; unbalance.

désert, e [de'zɛ:r, ˌ'zert] **1.** *adj.* deserted; desert (*island, country*); wild (*country*); lonely (*spot*); **2.** *su./m* desert, wilderness; **déserter** [dezɛr'te] (1a) *v/t.* desert (*a.* ✗), forsake, abandon; *v/i.* ✗ desert; **déserteur** [ˌ'tœ:r] *m* deserter; **désertion** [ˌ'sjõ] *f* desertion.　　　　[lation.]

désescalade [dezɛskalad] *f* de-esca-⟩

désespérant, e [dezɛspe'rā, ˌ'rā:t] heart-breaking; disheartening; **désespéré, e** [ˌ're] desperate; hopeless ; être dans un état ~ be past recovery; **désespérément** [ˌre-'mā] *adv.* desperately; **désespérer** [ˌ're] (1f) *v/i.* despair (of, de); lose hope; lose heart; *v/t.* drive (*s.o.*) to despair; **désespoir** [dezɛs'pwa:r] *m* despair; desperation; en ~ de cause as a last resource.

désétatiser [dezetati'ze] (1a) *v/t.* denationalize; ✝ etc. decontrol.

déshabillé [dezabi'je] *m* undress; **en ~** in dishabille; in undress; **déshabiller** [~] (1a) *v/t.* undress, disrobe; strip (*a.* ⚓).

déshabituer [dezabi'tɥe] (1n) *v/t.*: ~ **q. de** (*inf.*) break s.o. of the habit of (*ger.*); **se ~** grow unused (to, *de*); break o.s. of the habit (of *ger.*, *de inf.*).

déshériter [dezeri'te] (1a) *v/t.* disinherit; deprive; *les déshérités* the underprivileged.

déshonnête [dezɔ'nɛt] improper, immodest; **déshonneur** [~'nœːr] *m* dishono(u)r, disgrace; **déshonorant, e** [~nɔ'rɑ̃, ~'rɑ̃ːt] dishono(u)ring, dishono(u)rable; degrading; disgraceful; **déshonorer** [~nɔ're] (1a) *v/t.* dishono(u)r, disgrace; disfigure (*a picture etc.*).

déshumaniser [dezymani'ze] (1a) *v/t.* dehumanize.

déshydrater ⚕ [dezidra'te] (1a) *v/t.* dehydrate.

désignation [deziɲa'sjɔ̃] *f* designation; appointment (as, *au poste de*); **désigner** [~'ɲe] (1a) *v/t.* designate, indicate; appoint.

désillusionner [dezillyzjɔ'ne] (1a) *v/t.* disillusion, undeceive.

désinence *gramm.* [dezi'nɑ̃ːs] *f* ending.

désinfecter [dezɛ̃fɛk'te] (1a) *v/t.* disinfect; decontaminate.

désintégration [dezɛ̃tegra'sjɔ̃] *f* disintegration; *atom.*: splitting; *rock*: weathering.

désintéressé, e [dezɛ̃terɛ'se] unselfish; disinterested, unbiased; **désintéressement** [~res'mɑ̃] *m* impartiality; unselfishness; ✝ *partner*: buying out; ✝ *creditor*: paying off; **désintéresser** [~rɛ'se] (1a) *v/t.* ✝ buy out (*a partner*); ✝ pay off (*a creditor*); reimburse (*s.o.*); **se ~ de** lose interest in; take no part in; take no further interest in; **désintérêt** [~'rɛ] *m* disinterest, indifference.

désintoxiquer [dezɛ̃tɔksi'ke] (1a) *v/t.* ⚕ detoxicate; treat for alcoholism *or* drug addiction.

désinvolte [dezɛ̃'vɔlt] free, easy (*bearing, gait*); off-hand, airy (*manner*); rakish; F cheeky (*reply*); **désinvolture** [~vɔl'tyːr] *f* ease, freedom (*of bearing*); off-handedness; F cheek.

désir [de'ziːr] *m* desire, wish; **désirable** [dezi'rabl] desirable; *peu ~* undesirable; **désirer** [~'re] (1a) *v/t.* desire, wish, want; *laisser à ~* leave much to be desired; **désireux, -euse** [~'rø, ~'røːz] (*de*) desirous (of); eager (to).

désister [dezis'te] (1a) *v/t.*: **se ~ de** withdraw; desist from; renounce.

désobéir [dezɔbe'iːr] (2a) *v/i.*: **~ à** disobey; **désobéissance** [~i'sɑ̃ːs] *f* disobedience (to, *à*); **désobéissant, e** [~i'sɑ̃, ~'sɑ̃ːt] disobedient.

désobligeant, e [dezɔbli'ʒɑ̃, ~'ʒɑ̃ːt] disobliging, unfriendly; **désobliger** [~'ʒe] (1l) *v/t.* disoblige (*s.o.*); offend (*s.o.*).

désobstruer [dezɔpstry'e] (1a) *v/t.* free (*s.th.*) of obstructions; ⊕ clear (*a pipe*). [deodorant.]

désodorisant [dezɔdɔri'zɑ̃] *m*⟩

désœuvré, e [dezœ'vre] **1.** *adj.* idle, unoccupied; at a loose end; **2.** *su.* idler; **désœuvrement** [~vrə'mɑ̃] *m* idleness; leisure.

désolant, e [dezɔ'lɑ̃, ~'lɑ̃ːt] sad, distressing; troublesome; **désolation** [~la'sjɔ̃] *f* desolation; grief; **désolé, e** [~'le] desolate; very sorry; **désoler** [~'le] (1a) *v/t.* desolate; lay waste; distress, grieve (*s.o.*).

désolidariser [desɔlidari'ze] (1a) *v/t.*: **se ~** (*de*) dissociate o.s. (from).

désopilant, e F [dezɔpi'lɑ̃, ~'lɑ̃ːt] side-splitting, screaming; **désopiler** *fig.* [~'le] (1a) *v/t.*: **se ~** shake with laughter.

désordonné, e [dezɔrdɔ'ne] disorderly; untidy; excessive (*pride, appetite*); immoderate (*appetite*); dissolute (*life, man, etc.*); **désordre** [~'zɔrdr] *m* disorder (*a.* ✱), confusion; *fig.* dissoluteness; **~s** *pl.* disturbances, riots; *vivre dans le ~* lead a wild life.

désorganisation [dezɔrganiza'sjɔ̃] *f* disorganization.

désorienter [dezɔrjɑ̃'te] (1a) *v/t.* mislead; *fig.* bewilder, confuse, disconcert; puzzle; *fig. tout désorienté a.* at a loss, all at sea.

désormais [dezɔr'mɛ] *adv.* from now on, henceforth.

désossé, e [dezɔ'se] boned (*fish etc.*); F boneless, flabby (*person*); **désosser** [~] (1a) *v/t. cuis.* bone (*a fish etc.*); *fig.* take to pieces, dissect (*a book etc.*).

despote [dɛs'pɔt] *m* despot; **despotique** [~pɔ'tik] despotic; **despotisme** [~pɔ'tism] *m* despotism.

dessaisir [desɛ'ziːr] (2a) *v/t.* ⚼ dispossess; se ~ de part with, give up.

dessalé, e *fig.* [desa'le] knowing, sharp (*person*); **dessaler** [~] (1a) *v/t.* desalinate; *cuis.* soak (*fish*); *fig.* put (*s.o.*) up to a thing or two; *fig.* se ~ learn a thing or two.

dessécher [dese'ʃe] (1f) *v/t.* dry (up); wither (*a plant, a limb*); drain (*a swamp*); parch (*one's mouth*); sear (*the heart*); se ~ dry up; wither.

dessein [dɛ'sɛ̃] *m* design; scheme, plan; intention; *à* ~ intentionally, on purpose.

desseller [dese'le] (1a) *v/t.* unsaddle.

desserrer [dese're] (1a) *v/t.* loosen (*the belt, a screw*); unclamp; unscrew (*a nut*); release (*the brake*); unclench (*one's fist, one's teeth*).

dessert [de'sɛːr] *m* dessert; **desserte** [~'sɛrt] *f* sideboard; *public transport:* service, servicing.

desservir[1] [desɛr'viːr] (2b) *v/t.* clear (*the table*); clear (*s.th.*) away; (*a.* ~ *la table*) clear the table.

desservir[2] [~] (2b) *v/t. public transport:* serve; call at (*a port,* 🚂 *station*); *eccl.* minister to (*a parish*); lead (*in*)to (*road etc.*).

desservir[3] [~] (2b) *v/t.* put (*s.o.*) at a disadvantage; harm (*s.o.'s*) interests.

dessiccatif, -ve [desika'tif, ~'tiːv] drying.

dessiller [desi'je] *v/t.:* F ~ *les yeux à* (*or de*) *q.* open s.o.'s eyes (*to the truth*).

dessin [de'sɛ̃] *m* drawing, sketch; △ *etc.* plan; ⊕ draughtsmanship; pattern, design; ~ *à main levée* free-hand drawing; *cin.* ~ *animé* (animated) cartoon; **dessinateur, -trice** [desina'tœːr, ~'tris] *su.* drawer, sketcher; designer; cartoonist; *su./m* ⊕ draughtsman; *su./f* ⊕ draughtswoman; **dessiner** [~'ne] (1a) *v/t.* draw, sketch; design (*material etc.*); lay out (*a garden*); outline; se ~ stand out, be outlined; appear; *fig.* take shape.

dessouder ⊕ [desu'de] (1a) *v/t.* unsolder; reopen (*a welded seam etc.*).

dessouler [desu'le] (1a) *v/t.* sober (up); *v/i. a.* se ~ sober up.

dessous [dǝ'su] **1.** *adv.* under(neath),

beneath, below; *de* ~ underneath; *en* ~ underneath; *fig.* in an underhand way; **2.** *prp.:* *de* ~ from under; **3.** *su./m* underside, lower part; ~ *pl.* (*women's*) underclothing *sg.*, F undies; *fig.* seamy *or* shady side *sg.*; F *avoir le* ~ be defeated, get the worst of it; ~**-de-bras** *cost.* [dǝsudǝ'bra] *m/inv.* dress-shield.

dessus [dǝ'sy] **1.** *adv.* above, over; on (it, them, *etc.*); *en* ~ at the top, above; *sens* ~ *dessous* in confusion, topsy-turvy; ⚓ *avoir le vent* ~ be aback; *fig.* mettre le doigt ~ hit the nail on the head; **2.** *prp.* † on, upon; *de* ~ from, (from) off; **3.** *su./m* top, upper side; ♪ treble; *thea.* ~ *pl.* flies; *avoir* (*prendre*) *le* ~ have (get) the upper hand, have (get) the best of it; ~ *de cheminée* mantelpiece; *fig.* le ~ *du panier* the pick of the basket; ~**-de-lit** [dǝsyd'li] *m/inv.* bedspread, coverlet.

déstabiliser [destabili'ze] (1a) *v/t.* destabilize, make unstable.

destin [dɛs'tɛ̃] *m* fate, destiny; **destinataire** [dɛstina'tɛːr] *su.* addressee; ✝ *money order:* payee; *goods:* consignee; **destination** [~na'sjɔ̃] *f* destination; *à* ~ *de* for, to; ⚓ bound for; *post:* addressed to; **destinée** [~'ne] *f* destiny; **destiner** [~'ne] (1a) *v/t.* destine; intend (for, *à*); se ~ *à* intend to take up, enter (*a profession*).

destituer [desti'tɥe] (1n) *v/t.* dismiss, discharge; **destitution** [~ty-'sjɔ̃] *f* dismissal; removal.

destrier *poet.* [dɛstri'e] *m* charger, steed.

destroyer ⚓ [dɛstrwa'jœːr] *m* destroyer.

destructeur, -trice [dɛstryk'tœːr, ~'tris] **1.** *adj.* destructive; destroying; **2.** *su.* destroyer; **destructif, -ve** [~'tif, ~'tiːv] destructive (of, *de*); **destruction** [~'sjɔ̃] *f* destruction; demolition.

désuet, -ète [de'sɥɛ, ~'sɥɛt] obsolete (*a. gramm.*), out-of-date; **désuétude** [~sɥe'tyd] *f* disuse; *tomber en* ~ fall into disuse; ⚼ fall into abeyance (*law*), lapse (*right*).

désunion [dezy'njɔ̃] *f* disunion; *parts:* separation; *fig.* dissension; **désunir** [~'niːr] (2a) *v/t.* disunite, divide; take apart; *fig.* set at variance.

détachant [deta'ʃã] *m* stain remover.
détachement [detaʃ'mã] *m* loosening; detachment (*a.* ✕); *fig.* indifference (to, *de*), unconcern.
détacher[1] [deta'ʃe] (1a) *v/t.* detach (*a.* ♪); undo, unfasten; separate; ✕ detail (*a company*); 🚋 uncouple; *fig.* estrange; se ~ come loose; part; stand out (against, *sur*).
détacher[2] [~] (1a) *v/t.* clean, remove stains from.
détail [de'ta:j] *m* detail; particular; *fig.* trifle; ✝ retail; *marchand m en* ~ retailer; *vendre au* ~ retail; **détaillant** *m*, e *f* [deta'jã, ~'jã:t] retailer; **détailler** [~'je] (1a) *v/t.* enumerate; itemize (*an account*); relate in detail; cut up; ✝ (sell) retail.
détaler F [deta'le] (1a) *v/i.* decamp, clear out.
détaxation [detaksa'sjõ] *f* tax reduction *or* removal; **détaxe** [de'taks] *f* tax reduction *or* removal *or* refund; **détaxer** [detak'se] (1a) *v/t.* reduce *or* remove the tax on (*s.th.*).
détecteur ⚡ [detɛk'tœ:r] *m radio:* detector; ⚡ ~ *de fuites* fault-finder.
détective [detɛk'ti:v] *m* detective; *phot.* box-camera.
déteindre [de'tɛ̃:dr] (4m) *v/t.* remove the colo(u)r from; *v/i. a.* se ~ fade, lose colo(u)r; run, bleed (*colour*).
dételer [det'le] (1c) *v/t.* unharness; 🚋 uncouple; *v/i.* F stop (working); F knock off; *sans* ~ without a break.
détendre [de'tã:dr] (4a) *v/t.* loosen, slacken; *fig.* relax (*the mind*); steady (*one's nerves*); calm, reduce (*one's anger*); ⊕ expand (*steam*); se ~ slacken; relax.
détenir [det'ni:r] (2h) *v/t.* hold; detain (*goods, s.o., a.* ⚖).
détente [de'tã:t] *f* relaxation; slackening; *gun:* trigger; *pol.* détente; *fig.* improvement (*of relations*); ⊕ steam: expansion; *mot.* power stroke; *fig. dur à la* ~ close-fisted; *appuyer sur la* ~ press the trigger.
détenteur *m*, -trice *f* [detã'tœ:r, ~'tris] holder (*a. sp.*); detainer (*of goods, property*); **détention** [~'sjõ] *f* detention, imprisonment; ✝ holding; possession; withholding; ⚖ ~ *préventive* holding *or* remand in custody; ⚖ *maison f de* ~ remand home; house of detention; **détenu, e**

[det'ny] **1.** *p.p. of* détenir; **2.** *su.* prisoner.
détergent, e [detɛr'ʒã, ~'ʒã:t] **1.** *adj.* detergent; **2.** *su./m* detergent; cleanser; **déterger** [~'ʒe] (1l) *v/t.* cleanse.
détériorer [deterjɔ're] (1a) *v/t.* make worse; spoil; impair, damage; se ~ deteriorate; spoil.
déterminant [detɛrmi'nã] *m* ⅋ determinant; *gramm.* determiner; **détermination** [~na'sjõ] *f* determination; *fig. a.* resolution; **déterminé, e** [~'ne] determined; definite; specific; *fig.* resolute; **déterminer** [~'ne] (1a) *v/t.* determine, settle; ascertain; induce; bring about; ~ *q. à* lead *or* induce s.o. to; ~ *de* (*inf.*) resolve to (*inf.*); se ~ make up one's mind (to *inf.*, *à inf.*); resolve (upon s.th., *à qch.*).
déterrer [detɛ're] (1a) *v/t.* unearth (*a. fig.*); dig up; exhume (*a corpse*).
détersif, -ve [detɛr'sif, ~'si:v] *m* detergent; cleansing product.
détestable [detɛs'tabl] detestable, hateful; **détester** [~'te] (1a) *v/t.* hate; detest.
détonateur [detɔna'tœ:r] *m* detonator; *fig.* trigger; **détonation** [~na'sjõ] *f* detonation; *gun:* report; **détoner** [~'ne] (1a) *v/i.* detonate, explode; *faire* ~ detonate; *mélange m détonant* detonating mixture.
détonner [detɔ'ne] (1a) *v/i.* ♪ sing *or* play out of tune; *fig.* clash (*colours*).
détordre [de'tɔrdr] (4a) *v/t.* untwist, unravel; unlay (*a rope*); **détors, e** [~'tɔ:r, ~'tɔrs] untwisted; unlaid (*rope*); **détortiller** [~tɔrti'je] (1a) *v/t.* untwist; disentangle.
détour [de'tu:r] *m* detour, roundabout way; ~*s pl.* curves, turns; *sans* ~ straightforward(ly *adv.*); *tours et* ~*s* ins and outs (*a. fig.*), nooks and corners.
détourné, e [detur'ne] roundabout (*way*), *fig. a.* indirect; *sentier m* ~ by-path; **détournement** [~nə'mã] *m* diversion; *money:* embezzlement; *funds:* misappropriation; ⚖ abduction (*of a minor*); ~ *d'avion* highjacking; **détourner** [~'ne] (1a) *v/t.* turn away; divert (*a river, the traffic, etc.*, *fig. s.o.*); avert (*s.o.'s anger, a blow, one's eyes, etc.*); embezzle (*money*); misappropriate (*funds*); entice (*a wife from her husband, s.o. from his*

duty); abduct (*a minor*); highjack (*an airplane*); se ~ de turn aside from.

détracteur *m*, **-trice** *f* [detrak'tœːr, ~'tris] detractor, maligner; slanderer.

détraqué, e [detra'ke] out of order; deranged (*mind*); shattered (*health*); F *il est* ~ he is out of his mind; **détraquer** [~] (1m) *v/t.* put out of order; throw (*a machine*) out of gear; *fig.* upset; se ~ break down; F go all to pieces (*person*).

détrempe [de'trãːp] *f* distemper; *metall.* annealing; **détremper** [~trã'pe] (1a) *v/t.* soak; dilute; *metall.* anneal.

détresse [de'tres] *f* distress.

détriment [detri'mã] *m* detriment, injury; *au* ~ *de* to the prejudice of.

détritus [detri'tys] *m* detritus, debris; refuse, rubbish.

détroit *geog.* [de'trwa] *m* strait(s *pl.*).

détromper [detrõ'pe] (1a) *v/t.* undeceive, enlighten; F *détrompez-vous!* don't you believe it!; se ~ recognize one's error.

détrôner [detro'ne] (1a) *v/t.* dethrone; *fig.* replace, supersede.

détrousser [detru'se] (1a) *v/t.* rob (*s.o.*); **détrousseur** [~'sœːr] *m* highwayman, footpad.

détruire [de'trɥiːr] (4h) *v/t.* destroy (*a. fig.*); demolish (*buildings, a. arguments*).

dette [dɛt] *f* debt (*a. fig.*); ♀ *publique* National Debt; ~*s pl. actives* assets; ~*s pl. passives* liabilities.

deuil [dœːj] *m* mourning (*a. clothes, a. time*); bereavement; *fig. faire son* ~ *de qch.* give s.th. up as lost, F say goodbye to s.th.; *porter le* ~ *de q.* mourn for s.o.

deux [dø] *adj./num., a. su./m/inv.* two; *date, title:* second; ~ *fois* twice; ~ *p* double p (*in spelling*); *à nous* ~ between us; *de* ~ *jours l'un, tous les* ~ *jours* every other day, on alternate days; *diviser en* ~ halve; *en* ~ in two (*pieces*); *Georges* ♀ George the Second; *le* ~ *mai* the second of May; *nous* ~ the two of us; *tous (les)* ~ both; **deuxième** [dø'zjɛm] **1.** *adj./num.* second; **2.** *su.* second; *su./m* second, *Am.* third floor; *su./f secondary school:* (*approx.*) fifth form.

deux…: ~-**pièces** [dø'pjɛs] *m* (woman's) two-piece suit; ~-**points**

[~'pwɛ̃] *m/inv.* colon; ~-**roues** [~'ru] *m/inv.* two-wheeled vehicle.

dévaler [deva'le] (1a) *vt/i.* run *or* rush down.

dévaliser [devali'ze] (1a) *v/t.* rob; rifle, burgle (*a house*).

dévalorisation ✝ [devalɔriza'sjõ] *f currency:* devaluation; depreciation, fall in value; **dévaloriser** ✝ [~'ze] (1a) *v/t.* devaluate (*the currency*).

dévaluation ✝ [devalɥa'sjõ] *f* devaluation; **dévaluer** ✝ [~'lɥe] (1n) *v/t.* devaluate.

devancer [dəvã'se] (1k) *v/t.* precede; outstrip, leave (*s.o.*) behind; *fig.* forestall; **devancier** *m*, **-ère** *f* [~'sje, ~'sjɛːr] precursor; predecessor; **devant** [də'vã] **1.** *adv.* in front, ahead, before; **2.** *prp.* in front of, before; ahead of; in the presence of (*s.o.*); *fig.* in the eyes of (*the law*); **3.** *su./m* front, forepart; *gagner les* ~*s* take the lead; *zo. patte f de* ~ foreleg; *prendre les* ~*s* make the first move, forestall the others *etc.*; **devanture** [~vã'tyːr] *f* front; shop window.

dévastateur, -trice [devasta'tœːr, -'tris] devastating; destructive; **dévaster** [~'te] (1a) *v/t.* devastate, lay waste, ravage, wreck.

déveinard F [devɛ'naːr] *m* a man whose luck is out; **déveine** F [~'vɛn] *f* (run of) ill-luck, bad *or* hard luck.

développement [devlɔp'mã] *m* development (*a. phot., a.* ♪); ✗ *algebra:* expansion; *pays m en voie de* ~ developing country; **développer** [~lɔ'pe] (1a) *v/t.* develop; expand (*a.* ✗); spread out; *fig.* amplify, unfold (*a plan*); se ~ develop, expand; spread out.

devenir [dəv'niːr] (2h) *v/i.* become, grow (*tall, sad, etc.*).

dévergondé, e [devɛrgõ'de] **1.** *adj.* profligate; shameless; F extravagant (*style etc.*); **2.** *su.* profligate.

déverrouiller [devɛru'je] (1a) *v/t.* unbolt.

dévers [de'vɛːr] *m* slope, cant; *road:* banking; ♜ cant, vertical slant.

déversement [devɛrsə'mã] *m water etc.:* discharge; *cart:* tilting; *refuse:* dumping.

déverser [devɛr'se] (1a) *v/t.* pour (out) (*water etc.*); dump (*refuse etc.*); tip (out); unload; *fig.* discharge, empty; se ~ pour, empty; **déversoir**

dévêtir

[∼'swa:r] *m* overflow; overfall, waste-weir; *fig.* outlet.

dévêtir [devɛ'ti:r] (2g) *v/t.* undress; take off (*one's coat etc.*); *metall.* open up (*a mould*); se∼ *de qch.* divest o.s. of s.th.

déviation [devja'sjɔ̃] *f* road: deviation, diversion; *compass:* variation; ⊕ *tool:* deflection; *fig.* deviation; **deviationniste** [∼sjɔ'nist] *adj., a. su.* deviationist.

dévider [devi'de] (1a) *v/t. tex.* unwind; reel; *fig.* reel off; **dévideur** *m*, **-euse** *f tex.* [∼'dœ:r, ∼'dø:z] reeler; **dévidoir** [∼'dwa:r] *m tex.* winder; ⚡ (cable-)drum.

dévier [de'vje] (1o) *v/i.* deviate, swerve; *faire* ∼ deflect (*s.th.*); *fig.* divert (*the conversation*); *v/t.* deflect; turn aside (*a blow*); se ∼ become crooked; warp (*wood*).

devin [də'vɛ̃] *m* soothsayer; **deviner** [∼vi'ne] (1a) *v/t.* guess; foretell, foresee (*the future*); see through (*s.o.*); **devineresse** [∼vin'rɛs] *f* fortune teller; **devinette** [dəvi'nɛt] *f* riddle, conundrum; **devineur** *m*, **-euse** *f* [∼'nœ:r, ∼'nø:z] guesser.

devis [də'vis] *m* estimate; tender.

dévisager [deviza'ʒe] (11) *v/t.* stare at (*s.o.*).

devise [də'vi:z] *f* motto; ⊘ device; ⛿ currency; ⛿ ∼s *pl. étrangères* foreign currency *sg.*; **deviser** [∼vi'ze] (1a) *v/i.* chat.

dévisser ⊕ [devi'se] (1a) *v/t.* unscrew; *sl.* ∼ *son billard* die, *sl.* peg out.

dévoiler [devwa'le] (1a) *v/t.* unveil; reveal (*a. fig.*).

devoir [də'vwa:r] **1.** (3a) *v/t.* owe; *v/aux.* have to, must; should, ought to, be to; *j'aurais dû le faire* I should have done it; *je devrais le faire* I ought to do it; **2.** *su./m* duty; *school:* home-work; exercise; ⛿ debit; ∼*s pl.* respects; *faire ses* ∼*s* do one's homework; *rendre ses* ∼*s à* pay one's respects to (*s.o.*).

dévolu, e [devɔ'ly] **1.** *adj.* (*à*) devolved (upon); *eccl.* lapsing (to); **2.** *su./m: jeter son* ∼ *sur* have designs on; lay claim to; choose (*s.th.*).

dévorant, e [devɔ'rɑ̃, ∼'rɑ̃:t] ravenous (*animal, a. fig. hunger*); consuming (*fire, a. fig. passion*); **dévorer** [∼'re] (1a) *v/t.* devour; consume; squander (*a fortune*); F *mot.* ∼ *l'espace* eat up the miles.

dévot, e [de'vo, ∼'vɔt] **1.** *adj.* devout, pious; *pej.* sanctimonious; **2.** *su.* devout person; *pej.* sanctimonious person; *faux* ∼ hypocrite; **dévotion** [∼vo'sjɔ̃] *f* devotion; piety; **dévoué, e** [∼'vwe] devoted; *votre tout* ∼ yours faithfully *or* sincerely; **dévouement** [∼vu'mɑ̃] *m* devotion (to, *à*), self-abnegation; **dévouer** [∼'vwe] (1p) *v/t.* devote; dedicate.

devoyé, e [devwa'je] *adj., a. su.* delinquent; **dévoyer** [∼] (1h) *v/t.* lead (*s.o.*) astray; se ∼ go astray.

devrai [də'vre] *1st p. sg. fut. of devoir 1.*

dextérité [dɛksteri'te] *f* dexterity, ability, skill.

dextrose [dɛks'tro:z] *m* dextrose.

diabète ⚕ [dja'bɛt] *m* diabetes; **diabétique** ⚕ [∼be'tik] *adj., a. su.* diabetic.

diable [djɑ:bl] *m* devil; ⊕ (stone-) lorry; trolley; porter's barrow, *Am.* porter's dolly; *comment* (*où, pourquoi*) ∼ how (where, why) the devil; *au* ∼ *vauvert* at the back of beyond; *bon* ∼ not a bad fellow; *tirer le* ∼ *par la queue* be hard up; **diablement** F [djablə'mɑ̃] *adv.* devilish; **diablerie** [∼blə'ri] *f* devilry; F fun; mischievousness; **diablesse** F [∼'blɛs] *f* she-devil; virago, shrew; **diablotin** [∼blɔ'tɛ̃] *m imp* (*a.* F = *mischievous child*); cracker; **diabolique** [∼bɔ'lik] fiendish, diabolic(al), devilish.

diacre *eccl.* [djakr] *m* deacon.

diadème [dja'dɛm] *m* diadem.

diagnose [djag'no:z] *f* ⚕ diagnosis; ⚕ diagnostics *sg.*; **diagnostic** ⚕ [djagnɔs'tik] *m* diagnosis (*of disease*); *faire le* ∼ *de* diagnose; **diagnostique** ⚕ [∼'tik] diagnostic; **diagnostiquer** [∼ti'ke] (1m) *v/t.* diagnose.

diagonal, e [djagɔ'nal, ∼'no] *adj., a.* ⚔ *su./f* diagonal.

diagramme [dja'gram] *m* diagram.

dialecte [dja'lɛkt] *m* dialect.

dialectique [djalɛk'tik] *f* dialectics *pl.*

dialogue [dja'lɔg] *m* dialog(ue); **dialoguer** [∼lɔ'ge] (1m) *v/i.* converse, talk; *v/t.* write (*s.th.*) in dialog(ue) form.

diamant [dja'mɑ̃] *m* diamond; **diamanter** [∼mɑ̃'te] (1a) *v/t.* set with diamonds; ⊕ diamondize; **dia-**

mantin, e [ˌmãˈtɛ̃, ˌˈtin] diamond-like.

diamètre ⚕ [djaˈmɛtr] *m* diameter.

diane [djan] *f* ⚔ reveille; ⚓ morning watch.

diantre! † [djãːtr] *int.* deuce!; *sl.* hell!

diapason ♪ [djapaˈzɔ̃] *m* diapason, pitch; tuning-fork; *voice:* range; *fig. au* ~ (de) in harmony *or* tune (with).

diaphane [djaˈfan] diaphanous; transparent.

diaphragme [djaˈfragm] *m* ⊕, *anat.* diaphragm; *phot.* diaphragm stop; *gramophone:* sound-box; **diaphragmer** [ˌfragˈme] (1a) *v/t.* provide with a diaphragm; *phot.* stop down (*the lens*).

diapositive *phot.* [djapoziˈtiːv] *f* transparency.

diapré, e [djaˈpre] variegated, mottled.

diarrhée ⚕ [djaˈre] *f* diarrhoea.

diatomique ⚛ [diatoˈmik] diatomic.

diatribe [djaˈtrib] *f* diatribe; harangue.

dictaphone [diktaˈfɔn] *m* dictaphone.

dictateur [diktɑˈtœːr] *m* dictator; *de* ~ dictatorial (*tone, attitude, etc.*); **dictature** [ˌˈtyːr] *f* dictatorship; **dictée** [ˌˈte] *f* dictation; **dicter** [ˌˈte] (1a) *v/t.* dictate (*a. fig.*); **diction** [ˌˈsjɔ̃] *f* diction; delivery; style; **dictionnaire** [ˌsjɔˈnɛːr] *m* dictionary; lexicon; ~ *ambulant* walking dictionary; **dicton** [ˌˈtɔ̃] *m* saying; proverb.

dièse ♪ [djɛːz] *m* sharp.

diesel ⊕ [diˈzɛl] *m* diesel engine; *équiper de moteurs* ~*s* dieselize.

diéser ♪ [djeˈze] (1f) *v/t.* sharp(en) (*a note*).

diète ⚕ [djɛt] *f* diet (*a. pol.*), regimen; ~ *absolue* starvation diet; **diététique** [djeteˈtik] dietary.

dieu [djø] *m* god; ♀ God; ♀ *merci* thank God; F thank heaven; *à* ♀ *ne plaise* God forbid; *grâce à* ♀ thanks be to God; by God's grace; *mon* ♀! good heavens!; dear me!; *pour l'amour de* ♀ for Christ's sake.

diffamant, e ⚖ [difaˈmã, ˌˈmãːt] defamatory; libellous; slanderous; **diffamateur** *m*, **-trice** *f* ⚖ [difamaˈtœːr, ˌˈtris] defamer; libeller; slanderer; **diffamation** ⚖ [ˌˈsjɔ̃] *f* defamation; ~ *écrite* libel; ~ *orale*

slander; **diffamatoire** [ˌˈtwaːr] defamatory; libellous; slanderous; **diffamer** [difaˈme] (1a) *v/t.* defame; slander; libel.

différemment [diferaˈmã] *adv. of* **différent**; **différence** [ˌˈrãːs] *f* difference; *à la* ~ *de* unlike; **différencier** [ˌrãˈsje] (1o) *v/t.* differentiate (*a.* ⚕) (from *de, d'avec*); distinguish (between, *entre*); **différend** [ˌˈrã] *m* dispute; quarrel; difference; **différent, e** [ˌˈrã, ˌˈrãːt] different; distinct (from, *de*); **différentiel, -elle** [ˌrãˈsjɛl] *adj., a. mot.* su./*m,* ⚕ *su./f* differential; **différer** [ˌˈre] (1f) *v/t.* postpone, put off, defer; delay; *v/i.* differ (from, *de*).

difficile [difiˈsil] **1.** *adj.* difficult (*a. fig.*); *fig.* hard to please; **2.** *su./m:* *faire le* ~ be hard to please; be squeamish; **difficulté** [ˌkylˈte] *f* difficulty; *faire des* ~*s* create obstacles, make difficulties, raise objections; **difficultueux, -euse** [ˌkylˈtɥø, ˌˈtɥøːz] over-particular, fussy; squeamish; *fig.* thorny (*business, enterprise*).

difforme [diˈfɔrm] deformed; misshapen; **difformité** [ˌfɔrmiˈte] *f* deformity, malformation.

diffracter *opt.* [difrakˈte] (1a) *v/t.* diffract.

diffus, e [diˈfy, ˌˈfyːz] diffused (*light*); *fig.* diffuse (*style etc.*); *éclairs m/pl.* ~ sheet lightning *sg.*; **diffuser** [difyˈze] (1a) *v/t.* diffuse (*heat, light*); *radio, rumour:* broadcast; **diffuseur** [ˌˈzœːr] *m* ⊕ spray nozzle; *radio:* broadcaster (*person*); *radio:* cone loud-speaker; **diffusion** [ˌˈzjɔ̃] *f* heat, light, news, germs: diffusion; *news:* spreading; *radio:* broadcasting; *disease, germs:* spread; *fig. style:* prolixity, diffuseness.

digérer [diʒeˈre] (1f) *v/t.* digest (*food, news*); *fig.* swallow (*an insult*); **digestif, -ve** [diʒɛsˈtif, ˌˈtiːv] *adj., a. su./m* digestive; **digestion** [ˌˈtjɔ̃] *f* digestion.

digital, e, *m/pl.* **-aux** [diʒiˈtal, ˌˈto] **1.** *adj.* digital; *empreinte f* ~*e* fingerprint; **2.** *su./f* ⚕ digitalis, foxglove.

digne [diɲ] worthy, deserving; dignified (*air*); ~ *d'éloges* praiseworthy; **dignitaire** [diɲiˈtɛːr] *m* dignitary; **dignité** [ˌˈte] *f* dignity.

digression [digrɛ'sjɔ̃] f digression (a. astr.).

digue [dig] f dike, dam, embankment; jetty; sea-wall; breakwater; fig. barrier.

dilapider [dilapi'de] (1a) v/t. squander (a fortune, money); misappropriate (trust funds).

dilatation [dilata'sjɔ̃] f eye: dilation; expansion (a. △, ♎, ⊕ truck); stomach: distension; **dilater** [~'te] (1a) v/t. dilate, expand; distend (the stomach); fig. ~ le cœur gladden the heart; se ~ dilate, expand; become distended; **dilatoire** ⚖️, a. fig. [~'twa:r] dilatory.

dilection [dilɛk'sjɔ̃] f dilection; loving-kindness.

dilemme [di'lɛm] m dilemma.

dilettante [dilɛt'tã:t] su. dilettante, amateur; **dilettantisme** [dilɛtã-'tism] m dilettantism, amateurism; amateurishness.

diligence † [dili'ʒã:s] f diligence, industry; speed, haste; stage-coach; **diligent, e** [~'ʒã, ~'ʒã:t] diligent, industrious; speedy; prompt.

diluer [di'lɥe] (1n) v/t. dilute (with, de); water down; **dilution** [~ly'sjɔ̃] f dilution.

diluvien, -enne [dily'vjɛ̃, ~'vjɛn] diluvial (clay, deposit); diluvian (fossil); fig. torrential (rain).

dimanche [di'mã:ʃ] m Sunday.

dîme [dim] f tithe.

dimension [dimã'sjɔ̃] f dimension (a. fig.); size; fig. a. importance, weight; prendre les ~s de measure out; fig. understand, seize; fig. become, grow or develop into.

dîmer [di'me] (1a) v/i. levy tithes.

diminuer [dimi'nɥe] (1n) vt/i. lessen, diminish; reduce; v/i. ⚓ go down; abate (fever, flood); ⚓ ~ de toile shorten sail; **diminution** [~ny'sjɔ̃] f diminution; reduction (a. price); ⚓ rebate (on account); dress: shortening; abatement.

dinanderie [dinã'dri] f brass-ware, copper-ware.

dinde [dɛ̃:d] f turkey-hen; cuis. turkey; fig. stupid woman; **dindon** [dɛ̃'dɔ̃] m turkey-cock; fig. fool; **dindonneau** [dɛ̃dɔ'no] m young turkey; **dindonnier** m, **-ère** f [~'nje, ~'njɛ:r] turkey-keeper.

dîner [di'ne] 1. (1a) v/i. dine, have dinner; 2. su./m dinner(-party);

~-débat, pl. ~s-débats [~nede'ba] m working dinner; **dînette** [~'nɛt] f snack (meal); **dîneur, -euse** [~'nœ:r, ~'nø:z] su. diner; su./m: F un beau ~ a good trencherman.

dingo [dɛ̃'go] 1. su./m zo. dingo; 2. adj. sl. crazy, nuts.

dingue sl. [dɛ̃:g] 1. adj. crazy, nuts; 2. su. crackpot, loony.

dinguer sl. [dɛ̃'ge] (1m) v/i.: aller ~ drop; crash down (things), go sprawling (person); envoyer ~ send (s.o.) packing; send (s.th.) flying.

diocèse eccl. [djɔ'sɛ:z] m diocese.

dioptrie phys., opt. [djɔp'tri] f diopter.

diphtérie ⚕️ [difte'ri] f diphtheria.

diphtongue gramm. [dif'tɔ̃:g] f diphthong.

diplomate [diplɔ'mat] m diplomat (a. fig.); **diplomatie** [~ma'si] f diplomacy (a. fig.); diplomatic service; **diplomatique** [~ma'tik] 1. adj. diplomatic; 2. su./f diplomatics pl.; pal(a)eography.

diplôme [di'plo:m] m diploma; certificate; **diplômé, e** [~plo'me] 1. adj. certificated; ingénieur m ~ qualified engineer; 2. su. (approx.) graduate.

dire [di:r] 1. v/t. (4p) say; tell; recite (a poem); show, reveal; ~ à q. de (inf.) tell s.o. to (inf.); ~ du mal de speak ill of; ~ que oui (non) say yes (no); F à qui le dites-vous? don't I know it!; sl. you're telling me!; à vrai ~ to tell the truth; cela ne me dit rien that conveys nothing to me; it doesn't appeal to me; cela va sans ~ it goes without saying; c'est-à-~ that is to say, i.e.; in other words; c'est tout ~ I need say no more; dites donc! I say!; on dirait que one (you) would think that; on le dit riche he is said to be rich; on dit people say; it is said; pour tout ~ in a word; qu'en dites-vous? what is your opinion?; sans mot ~ without a word; se ~ claim to be; be used (word); vouloir ~ mean; vous l'avez dit exactly; Am. F you said it; 2. su./m statement; ⚖️ allegation; au ~ de according to.

direct, e [di'rɛkt] 1. adj. direct; straight; ⚙ through (train, ticket); 2. su./m ⚙ through or express train; radio, telev.: live broadcast; en ~ live (broadcast, a. fig.); box. ~ du droit straight right; **directement** [dirɛktəmɑ̃] directly; straight (away).

directeur, -trice [dirɛk'tœːr, ~'tris] **1.** *su./m* director, manager; *school*: headmaster; principal; *prison*: warden; *journ.* editor; *eccl.* ~ de conscience confessor; ⳁ ~ *gérant* managing director; *su./f* directress; manageress; *school*: headmistress; **2.** *adj.* directing, controlling; guiding (*principle*); ⊕ driving; *mot.* steering (*wheel*); **direction** [~'sjɔ̃] *f* direction; *enterprise, war*: conduct; ⳁ management; ⳁ manager's office; ⳁ board of directors; *school*: headship; ⊕ driving; ⊕ steering; course, route; en ~ de bound *or* heading for, ...bound; *train m* en ~ de train for; **directive** [~'tiːv] *f* directive; ~ *s pl. a.* guidelines; **directoire** [~'twaːr] *m* *eccl.* directory; *hist.* ♀ Directory; **directrice** [~'tris] *f see directeur.*

dirigeable [diri'ʒabl] **1.** *adj.* dirigible; *antenne f* ~ directional aerial; **2.** *su./m* airship; **dirigeant** [~'ʒɑ̃] *m* ruler, leader; **diriger** [~'ʒe] (1l) *v/t.* direct; ⳁ *etc.* manage, F run; *mot.* drive; ⚓, *mot.* steer; ⚓ sail; ♩ conduct; aim (*a gun, a. fig. remarks*); *journ.* edit; se ~ vers make one's way towards, make for; **dirigisme** *pol.* [~'ʒism] *m* planning, planned economy.

dis [di] *1st p. sg. pres. and p.s. of dire 1.*

discernement [disɛrnə'mɑ̃] *m* discernment; discrimination (between...and, de...et de); **discerner** [~'ne] (1a) *v/t.* discern, make out; distinguish, discriminate (between s.th. and s.th., qᵉh. de qch.).

disciple [di'sipl] *m* disciple, follower; **discipline** [disi'plin] *f* discipline; *eccl.* scourge; ⚔ *compagnie f de* ~ disciplinary company; **discipliner** [~pli'ne] (1a) *v/t.* discipline; school; bring under control. [lus.]

discobole *sp.* [disko'bɔl] *m* discobo-

discontinu, e [diskɔ̃ti'ny] discontinuous; **discontinuer** [~'nɥe] (1n) *vt/i.* discontinue, stop; *sans* ~ without stopping; at a stretch.

disconvenance [diskɔ̃v'nɑ̃ːs] *f* unsuitability; disparity; **disconvenir** [~'niːr] (2h) *v/i.:* ~ de deny; ~ que (*sbj.*) deny that (*ind.*).

discophile [disko'fil] *su.* (gramophone) record fan.

discordance [diskɔr'dɑ̃ːs] *f* sounds: discordance; *opinions etc.*: disagreement, conflict; **discordant, e** [~'dɑ̃, ~'dɑ̃ːt] discordant (*sounds*); conflicting (*opinions etc.*); ♩ out of tune (*instrument*); *geol.* unconformable; **discorde** [dis'kɔrd] *f* discord, dissension; **discorder** [~kɔr'de] (1a) *v/i.* ♩ be discordant; clash (*colours*); disagree (*persons*).

discothèque [disko'tɛk] *f* record library; record collection; disco(thèque).

discoureur *m,* **-euse** *f* [disku'rœːr, ~'røːz] speechifier; talkative person; **discourir** [~'riːr] (2i) *v/i.* discourse; **discours** [dis'kuːr] *m* speech (*a. gramm.*); discourse; talk; language; ~ *improvisé* extempore speech; ~ *inaugural* inaugural address, *Am.* inaugural; *faire un* ~ make a speech; *gramm. partie f du* ~ part of speech.

discourtois, e [diskur'twa, ~'twaːz] discourteous, rude, unmannerly.

discrédit [diskre'di] *m* discredit, disrepute; **discréditer** [~di'te] (1a) *v/t.* bring into discredit; disparage.

discret, -ète [dis'krɛ, ~'krɛt] discreet; 𝕩, ⅁ discrete; cautious; tactful; quiet (*dress, taste, village, etc.*); modest (*request*); *sous pli* ~ under plain cover; **discrétion** [diskre'sjɔ̃] *f* discretion; prudence; tact; *à* ~ at will; unlimited; ⚔ unconditional (*surrender*); *être à la* ~ de be at the disposal of; be at the mercy of; **discrétionnaire** ⚖ [~sjɔ'nɛːr] discretionary.

discrimination [diskrimina'sjɔ̃] *f* discrimination, differentiation; ~ *raciale* racial discrimination.

disculper [diskyl'pe] (1a) *v/t.* clear (s.o. of s.th., q. de qch.).

discussion [disky'sjɔ̃] *f* discussion, debate; argument; **discuter** [~'te] (1a) *v/t.* discuss, debate; question; ⚖ sell up (*a debtor*).

disert, e [di'zɛːr, ~'zɛrt] eloquent.

disette [di'zɛt] *f* scarcity, dearth; shortage (of, de).

diseur, -euse [di'zœːr, ~'zøːz] *su.* speaker, reciter; talker; *su./f thea.* diseuse; ~ *euse de bonne aventure* fortune-teller.

disgrâce [dis'grɑːs] *f* disgrace, disfavo(u)r; misfortune; **disgracié, e** [disgra'sje] out of favo(u)r; **disgra-**

cier [~'sje] (1o) *v/t.* dismiss from favo(u)r; disgrace; **disgracieux, -euse** [~'sjø, ~'sjø:z] uncouth, awkward; ungracious (*reply*).

disjoindre [dis'ʒwɛ̃:dr] (4m) *v/t.* sever, separate; **se ~** come apart; break up; **disjoncteur** *≠* [disʒɔ̃k-'tœ:r] *m* circuit-breaker; switch (-board); **disjonctif, -ve** *gramm.* [~'tif, ~'ti:v] disjunctive; **disjonction** [~'sjɔ̃] *f* sundering, separation; *⅛* severance.

dislocation [dislɔka'sjɔ̃] *f* ⊕ taking down; ✕ breaking up (*of troops*); *ℱ* dislocation; *fig.* dismemberment; *geol.* fault; **disloquer** [~'ke] (1m) *v/t.* ✕ break up; *ℱ* dislocate; *fig.* dismember; disperse; *geol.* fault.

disons [di'zɔ̃] *1st p. pl. pres. of dire 1.*

disparaître [dispa'rɛ:tr] (4k) *v/i.* disappear; vanish.

disparate [dispa'rat] **1.** *adj.* illassorted, ill-matched; dissimilar, **2.** *su./f* disparity; *colours*: clash; incongruity; **disparité** [~ri'te] *f* disparity.

disparition [dispari'sjɔ̃] *f* disappearance.

dispendieux, -euse [dispɑ̃'djø, ~'djø:z] expensive.

dispensaire *ℱ* [dispɑ̃'sɛ:r] *m* community clinic; *hospital*: surgery; outpatients' department; **dispensateur** *m*, **-trice** *f* [~pɑ̃sa'tœ:r, ~'tris] distributor; **dispense** [~'pɑ̃:s] *f* exemption; certificate of exemption; *eccl.* dispensation; **dispenser** [~pɑ̃'se] (1a) *v/t.* dispense; exempt, excuse (from, *de*); **se ~ de** avoid, get out of.

disperser [dispɛr'se] (1a) *v/t.* disperse, scatter; **dispersion** [~'sjɔ̃] *f* dispersion; breaking up; *≠* dissipation; ✕ rout; *phys. light*: scattering.

disponibilité [dispɔnibili'te] *f* availability; disposal; release; **~s** *pl.* available funds *or* means *or* time *sg.*; **en ~** unattached; **disponible** [~'nibl] *⅛* disposable; available; spare (*time*); ✕ unattached.

dispos, e [dis'po, ~'po:z] fit, in good form; all right; alert (*mind*).

disposer [dispo'ze] (1a) *v/t.* dispose, arrange, lay out; **se ~** (*à*) prepare (for *s.th.*; to *inf.*); *v/i.*: **~ de** dispose of; have at one's disposal; **~ pour** apply to; *vous pouvez ~* you may go;

dispositif [~zi'tif] *m* ⊕ device, appliance; system; plan; **disposition** [~zi'sjɔ̃] *f* disposition; arrangement; disposal; state (*of mind*), frame of mind; tendency (to, *à*); **~s** *pl.* talent *sg.*; *à la ~ de* q. at s.o.'s disposal; *à votre entière ~ a.* entirely at your service.

disproportion [disprɔpɔr'sjɔ̃] *f* disproportion; **disproportionné, e** [~sjɔ'ne] disproportionate.

dispute [dis'pyt] *f* dispute, quarrel; *chercher ~ à* pick a quarrel with; **disputer** [~py'te] (1a) *vt/i.* dispute; contend; *v/i.* argue, quarrel; *v/t. sp.* play (*a match*); fight for (*victory*); F tell (*s.o.*) off; **~ qch. à** q. contend with s.o. for s.th.; F **se ~** argue, quarrel, have an argument; **disputeur, -euse** [~py'tœ:r, ~'tø:z] **1.** *adj.* contentious, quarrelsome; **2.** *su.* arguer, wrangler.

disquaire [dis'kɛ:r] *m* record dealer *or* seller.

disqualifier *sp.* [diskali'fje] (1o) *v/t.* disqualify.

disque [disk] *m* disk; *sp.* discus; ✿ signal; ⊕ plate; (gramophone) record, album, disc, *Am.* disk; **~s** *pl. des auditeurs radio*: listener's requests; *teleph.* **~ d'appel** dial; **~ de longue durée, ~ microsillon** longplaying record, F long-player; *mot.* **~ de stationnement** parking disc; *changeur m de* **~s** record changer.

dissection [disɛk'sjɔ̃] *f* dissection.

dissemblable [disɑ̃'blabl] *adj.*: **~ à** (*or de*) dissimilar to (*s.th.*), unlike (*s.th.*); **dissemblance** [~'blɑ̃:s] *f* dissimilarity.

disséminer [disemi'ne] (1a) *v/t.* spread; scatter; disseminate.

dissension [disɑ̃'sjɔ̃] *f* discord, dissension; **dissentiment** [~ti'mɑ̃] *m* disagreement, dissent.

disséquer [dise'ke] (1s) *v/t.* dissect.

dissertation [disɛrta'sjɔ̃] *f* dissertation; essay; **disserter** [~'te] (1a) *v/i.* discourse (on, *sur*), F hold forth.

dissidence *eccl. etc.* [disi'dɑ̃:s] *f* dissidence, dissent; **dissident, e** *eccl.*, *pol.* [~'dɑ̃, ~'dɑ̃:t] **1.** *adj.* dissident; dissenting; **2.** *su.* dissentient; *eccl.* nonconformist, dissenter.

dissimilitude [disimili'tyd] *f* dissimilarity.

dissimulation [disimyla'sjɔ̃] *f* dis-

sembling, dissimulation; concealment, cover-up; **dissimulé, e** [∼'le]
fig. hidden; secretive, double-
dealing, dissembling; **dissimuler**
[∼'le] (1a) *v/t.* conceal, hide; cover
up; se ∼ hide; *vt/i.* dissemble.

dissipateur, -trice [disipa'tœːr,
∼'tris] **1.** *su.* spendthrift; **2.** *adj.*
wasteful; **dissipation** [∼pa'sjɔ̃] *f*
dissipation (*a. fig.*); waste; inattention; *school:* fooling; **dissiper**
[∼'pe] (1a) *v/t.* dissipate; waste
(*money, time*); disperse, dispel
(*clouds, fear, a suspicion*); clear up
(*a misunderstanding*); divert; se ∼
disappear; amuse o.s.; *fig.* become
dissipated; be inattentive (*pupil*).

dissocier [diso'sje] (1o) *v/t.* dissociate.

dissolu, e [diso'ly] dissolute; **dissoluble** [∼'lybl] 🜛 soluble; ⚖
dissolvable; **dissolution** [∼ly'sjɔ̃] *f*
🜛 dissolving; 🜛 solution; ⚖, *a.
parl.* dissolution; disintegration;
dissoluteness; **dissolvant, e** [disɔl-
'vã, ∼'vãːt] **1.** *adj.* solvent; **2.** *su./m*
solvent; ∼ de *vernis à ongles* nail-
varnish remover.

dissonance [diso'nãːs] *f* ♩, *a. fig.*
dissonance; *fig. a.* clash, discord;
dissonant, e [∼'nã, ∼'nãːt] dissonant; discordant, clashing, jarring.

dissoudre [di'sudr] (4bb) *v/t.* dissolve; ⚖ annul (*a marriage*); **dis-
sous, -te** [∼'su, ∼'sut] *p.p.* of *dissoudre.*

dissuader [disɥa'de] (1a) *v/t.* dissuade (from [doing] s.th., de [*faire*]
qch.); **dissuasion** [∼'zjɔ̃] *f* dissuasion; ✗ *arme f de* ∼ deterrent weapon.

distance [dis'tãːs] *f* distance; *time:*
interval; *mot.* ∼ *d'arrêt* braking distance; ✗ ∼ *de tir* range; *opt.* ∼ *focale*
focal length; ⊕ *commande f à* ∼
remote control; *tenir à* ∼ keep (*s.o.*)
at arm's length; **distancer** [∼tã'se]
(1k) *v/t.* outrun, outstrip; *fig.* se
laisser ∼ lag behind; **distant, e**
[∼'tã, ∼'tãːt] distant; *fig. a.* aloof.

distendre ✍ [dis'tãːdr] (4a) *v/t.*
distend; pull, strain (*a muscle*);
distension ✍ [∼tã'sjɔ̃] *f* distension;
muscle: straining.

distiller [disti'le] (1a) *v/t.* 🜛, ⊕
distil; ⊕ condense (*water*); *fig.* exude; **distillerie** [∼til'ri] *f* distillery;
trade: distilling.

distinct, e [dis'tɛ̃(ːkt), ∼'tɛ̃ːkt] distinct; separate; clear; **distinctif,
-ve** [∼tɛ̃k'tif, ∼'tiːv] distinctive,
characteristic; **distinction** [∼tɛ̃k-
'sjɔ̃] *f* distinction; difference; discrimination; refinement; polished
manner.

distingué, e [distɛ̃'ge] distinguished;
eminent; refined; smart (*appearance, dress*); *sentiments m/pl.* ∼s
yours truly; **distinguer** [∼] (1m) *v/t.*
distinguish; make out; single out;
hono(u)r; se ∼ distinguish o.s.; *fig.*
stand out; **distinguo** [∼'go] *m*
distinction.

distique [dis'tik] *m Greek or Latin:*
distich; *French verse:* couplet.

distordre [dis'tordr] (4a) *v/t.* distort; twist (*the ankle etc.*); **distors,
e** [∼'toːr, ∼'tors] distorted (*limb*);
distorsion [∼tor'sjɔ̃] *f* distortion.

distraction [distrak'sjɔ̃] *f* absent-
mindedness; inattention, distraction; amusement, recreation; ✝ appropriation; ⚖ misappropriation
(*of funds*).

distraire [dis'trɛːr] (4ff) *v/t.* separate; ✝ set aside, appropriate; ⚖
misappropriate (*funds etc.*); amuse,
entertain; distract (*s.o.'s attention*);
distrait, e [∼'trɛ, ∼'trɛt] inattentive; absent-minded; *piéton m* ∼
jay-walker.

distribuer [distri'bɥe] (1n) *v/t.* distribute; give out; hand out; deal out;
post: deliver (*letters*); deal (*cards*);
distributeur, -trice [∼by'tœːr,
∼'tris] *su.* distributor; *su./m* ⊕ distributor; booking-clerk, *Am.* ticket
agent, ticket clerk; ∼ (*automatique*)
(slot *or* vending) machine; **distribution** [∼by'sjɔ̃] *f* distribution;
giving *etc.* out; *post:* delivery; *thea.*
cast(ing).

district [dis'trik(t)] *m* district,
region; *fig.* province.

dit, dite [di, dit] **1.** *p.p.* of *dire* 1; **2.**
adj. so-called; *autrement* ∼ in other
words; **dites** [dit] *2nd p. pl. pres. of
dire* 1.

diurétique ✍ [diyre'tik] *adj., a.
su./m* diuretic.

diurne [diyrn] diurnal; day-(*bird*).

divagation [divaga'sjɔ̃] *f* wandering; *fig.* digression; **divaguer** [∼'ge]
(1m) *v/i.* wander; *fig.* digress; F
ramble, rave.   [couch.⟩

divan [di'vã] *m* divan; (studio)⟩

divergence [diver'ʒãːs] f divergence (a. Ⓐ, ⚕); fig. difference; **diverger** [~'ʒe] (1l) v/i. diverge, branch off; fig. differ.

divers, e [di'vɛːr, ~'vɛrs] diverse, miscellaneous; various; sundry; **diversifier** [diversi'fje] (1o) v/t. diversify, vary; **diversion** [~'sjɔ̃] f diversion (a. ✕); change; **diversité** [~si'te] f diversity; variety.

divertir [diver'tiːr] (2a) v/t. divert; amuse; entertain; ✝ misappropriate (funds); **divertissement** [~tis-'mã] m entertainment, amusement; pastime; ✝ funds: misappropriation; thea. divertissement.

divette [di'vɛt] f light opera, music hall: singer.

dividende ✝, Ⓐ [divi'dãːd] m dividend.

divin, e [di'vɛ̃, ~'vin] divine (a. fig.); holy; godlike; **divinateur, -trice** [divina'tœːr, ~'tris] 1. su. soothsayer; diviner; 2. adj. prophetic; **divination** [~'sjɔ̃] f divination (a. fig.), soothsaying; **divinatoire** [~'twaːr] divining-...; baguette f ~ dowsing-rod; **diviniser** [divini'ze] (1a) v/t. deify; fig. glorify; **divinité** [~'te] f divinity; deity.

diviser [divi'ze] (1a) v/t. divide (a. Ⓐ); separate (from, d'avec); **diviseur** [~'zœːr] m ⚡ etc. divider; Ⓐ divisor; Ⓐ commun ~ common factor; **divisible** [~'zibl] divisible; **division** [~'zjɔ̃] f division (a. Ⓐ, ✕, ⚓, school); section; admin. department; fig. dissension, discord; ♪ double bar; typ. hyphen; biol. ~ binaire (or cellulaire) binary fission; ~ du travail division of labo(u)r.

divorce [di'vɔrs] m divorce (a. fig.); fig. disagreement; ⚖ former une demande en ~ seek a divorce; **divorcer** ⚖ [~vɔr'se] (1k) v/i. divorce (s.o., [d']avec q.); fig. break (with, [d']avec).

divulgation [divylga'sjɔ̃] f divulgence, disclosure; **divulguer** [~'ge] (1m) v/t. divulge, disclose, reveal.

dix [dis; before consonant di; before vowel and h mute diz] adj./num., a. su./m/inv. ten; date, title: tenth; **~-huit** [di'zɥit; before consonant ~'zɥi] adj./num., a. su./m/inv. eighteen; date, title: eighteenth; **dix-huitième** [~zɥi'tjɛm] adj./num., a. su. eighteenth; **dixième** [~'zjɛm]

1. adj./num., a. su., a. su./m fraction: tenth; **dix-neuf** [diz'nœf; before vowel and h mute ~'nœv] adj./num., a. su./m/inv. nineteen; date, title: nineteenth; **dix-neuvième** [~nœ'vjɛm] adj./num., a. su. nineteenth; **dix-sept** [dis'sɛt] adj./num., a. su./m/inv. seventeen; date, title: seventeenth; **dix-septième** [~sɛ-'tjɛm] adj./num., a. su. seventeenth.

dizain [di'zɛ̃] m ten-line stanza; rosary: decade; **dizaine** [~'zɛn] f (about) ten, half a score; dans la ~ within ten days.

do ♪ [do] m/inv. do, note: C.

docile [dɔ'sil] docile; amenable; submissive; **docilité** [~sili'te] f docility; obedience; meekness.

dock [dɔk] m ⚓ dock(yard); ✝ warehouse; **docker** [dɔ'kɛːr] m docker.

docte [dɔkt] learned (a. iro.).

docteur [dɔk'tœːr] m doctor; physician; **doctoral, e** [dɔktɔ'ral, ~'ro] doctoral; fig. pedantic; **doctorat** [~'ra] m doctorate, Doctor's degree; **doctoresse** [~'rɛs] f (lady) doctor.

doctrine [dɔk'trin] f doctrine, tenet.

document [dɔky'mã] m document; **documentaire** [~mã'tɛːr] adj., a. su./m documentary; **documenter** [~mã'te] (1a) v/t. document.

dodeliner [dɔdli'ne] (1a) v/i. ~ de la tête wag one's head.

dodo ch.sp. [dɔ'do] m bye-byes, sleep; bed; faire ~ (go to) sleep.

dodu, e [dɔ'dy] plump, chubby.

dogme [dɔgm] m dogma, tenet.

dogue zo. [dɔg] m: ~ anglais mastiff; **doguin** [dɔ'gɛ̃] m zo. pug; ⊕ (lathe-)dog.

doigt [dwa] m finger; zo., anat. digit; ~ de pied toe; à deux ~s de on the verge of, within an ace of; fig. mettre le ~ sur put one's finger on, pinpoint (a problem etc.); montrer du ~ point at; **doigté** [dwa'te] m ♪ fingering; fig. skill; fig. tact; **doigter** ♪ [~'te] (1a) v/t. finger (a piece of music); **doigtier** [~'tje] m finger-stall.

dois [dwa] 1st p. sg. pres. of devoir 1; **doit** ✝ [~] m debit, liability; **doivent** [dwaːv] 3rd p. pl. pres. of devoir 1.

dol ⚖ [dɔl] m fraud.

doléances [dɔle'ãːs] f/pl. complaints; grievances; **dolent, e** [~'lã,

~'lɑ̃:t] painful (*limb*); plaintive, doleful (*person, voice, etc.*).

doler [dɔ'le] (1a) *v/t.* pare (*wood, skins*); shave (*wood*).

dollar [dɔ'la:r] *m coinage:* dollar.

dolomie [dɔlɔ'mi] *f*, **dolomite** [~-'mit] *f* dolomite.

domaine [dɔ'mɛn] *m* domain; realm; estate, property; *fig.* sphere, field; ~ *public* public property.

dôme [do:m] *m* dome; *fig.* canopy; vault (*of heaven*).

domesticité [dɔmɛstisi'te] *f* menial condition; domestic service; *animal:* domesticity; *coll.* staff (*of servants*); **domestique** [~'tik] **1.** *adj.* domestic; menial; **2.** *su.* servant; domestic; ~s *pl.* staff *sg.* (*of servants*), household *sg.;* **domestiquer** [~ti'ke] (1m) *v/t.* domesticate; tame; se ~ become domesticated.

domicile [dɔmi'sil] *m* residence; ⚖ domicile; *travail m à* ~ home-work; **domiciliaire** [~misi'ljɛːr] domiciliary; **domicilié, e** [~'lje] domiciled, resident; **domicilier** [~'lje] (1o) *v/t.* domicile at; se ~ *à* take up residence at.

dominant, e [dɔmi'nɑ̃, ~'nɑ̃:t] **1.** *adj.* dominant, ruling; prevailing, predominating; **2.** *su./f* ♪ dominant; *fig.* dominant feature; **dominateur, -trice** [~na'tœːr, ~'tris] **1.** *adj.* dominant, ruling; domineering (*attitude, person*); **2.** *su.* ruler; **domination** [~na'sjɔ̃] *f* domination, rule; **dominer** [~'ne] (1a) *v/t.* dominate; master, rule; overlook; *v/i.* rule; predominate; prevail (*opinion*); ~ *sur* rule over; domineer.

dominical, e, *m/pl.* **-aux** [dɔmini-'kal, ~'ko] dominical; Sunday-...; *oraison f* ~ Lord's Prayer.

domino [dɔmi'no] *m cost., game:* domino.

dommage [dɔ'ma:ʒ] *m* damage, injury; ~s *pl.* damage *sg.* (*to property*); ~s *pl. de guerre* war damage (compensation) *sg.*; ⚖ ~s *pl. et intérêts m/pl.* damages; *c'est* ~*!, quel* ~*!* what a pity!; *c'est* ~ *que* it's a pity (that); **dommageable** [dɔma'ʒabl] harmful, prejudicial; ⚖ *acte m* ~ tort.

domptable [dɔ̃'tabl] tamable; **dompter** [~'te] (1a) *v/t.* tame; break in (*a horse*); *fig.* subdue (*feelings*); *fig.* reduce (*s.o.*) to obedience;

dompteur *m*, **-euse** *f* [~'tœːr, ~-'tøːz] tamer (*of animals*); subduer, vanquisher.

don [dɔ̃] *m* gift (*a. fig.*) (for, *de*), present; ⚖ donation; *fig.* talent (for, *de*); *faire* ~ *à q. de qch.* make a present of s.th. to s.o.; **donataire** ⚖ [dɔna'tɛːr] *su.* donee, Sc. donatary; **donateur, -trice** [~-'tœːr, ~'tris] *su.* giver; *su./m* ⚖ donor; *su./f* ⚖ donatrix; **donation** [~'sjɔ̃] *f* donation, gift.

donc [dɔ̃k; dɔ̃] **1.** *adv.* then; just ...; *allons* ~! come along!; come, come!, nonsense!; *pourquoi* ~? (but) why?; *viens* ~! come along!; **2.** *cj.* therefore, so, consequently, then; hence.

donjon [dɔ̃'ʒɔ̃] *m castle:* keep.

donnant, e [dɔ'nɑ̃, ~'nɑ̃:t] generous; ~ ~ tit for tat; **donne** [dɔn] *f cards:* deal; *à qui la* ~? whose deal is it?; *fausse* ~ misdeal; **donnée** [dɔ'ne] *f* datum; theme; fundamental idea; ~s *pl.* admitted facts; **donner** [~'ne] (1a) *v/t.* give (*a. advice, orders, an example*), present, bestow; yield (*a. a profit, a harvest, fig. a result*); deal (*cards, a blow*); set (*a problem, a price*); ✚ donate (*blood*); *sl.* give away (*an accomplice*); ~ *à* assign to; confer (*a title*) upon; ✝ ~ *avis* (*quittance*) give notice (a receipt); ~ *de la peine* give trouble; ~ *en mariage* give in marriage; *teleph.* ~ *à q. la communication avec* put s.o. through to; ~ *le bonjour à q.* wish (*s.o.*) good day; ~ *lieu à* give rise to, cause; ~ *q. pour perdu* give s.o. up for lost; *elle lui donna un enfant* she bore him a child; se ~ *à abandon* o.s. to; se ~ *de la peine* take pains; se ~ *pour* give o.s. out as; *v/i.* give, sag; ⊕, ✂ engage; *cards:* deal; ~ *à entendre* give to understand; ~ *contre* run against; ~ *dans* run into; *sun:* shine into (*a room*); *fig.* have a taste for; ~ *sur* overlook, look out on; lead to; **donneur** *m*, **-euse** *f* [~'nœːr, ~'nøːz] giver, donor; *cards:* dealer; ✚ *seller;* ~ *de sang* blood donor; ✝ ~ *d'ordre* principal.

dont [dɔ̃] *pron.* whose, of whom (which); by *or* from *or* among *or* about whom (which).

donzelle F [dɔ̃'zɛl] *f* wench, hussy.

dopage [dɔ'pa:ʒ] *m* doping; **dopant**

[dɔ'pɑ̃] *m* dope; **doper** *sp.* [dɔ'pe] (1a) *v/t.* dope; **doping** *sp.* [dɔ'piŋ] *m* action: doping; *drug*: dope.

doré, e [dɔ're] gilt, gilded; golden (*hair etc.*); browned (*meat*); glazed (*cake*).

dorénavant [dɔrena'vɑ̃] *adv.* henceforth.

dorer [dɔ're] (1a) *v/t.* gild; brown (*meat*); glaze (*a cake*); F ~ *la pilule* gild the pill; **doreur** *m*, **-euse** *f* [dɔ'rœ:r, ~'rø:z] gilder.

dorloter [dɔrlɔ'te] (1a) *v/t.* fondle; pamper; make a fuss of.

dormant, e [dɔr'mɑ̃, ~'mɑ̃:t] 1. *adj.* sleeping; ♱, ♀, *geol.* dormant; stagnant, still (*water*); 2. *su./m* sleeper; ⊕ casing, frame; **dormeur, -euse** [~'mœ:r, ~'mø:z] *su.* sleeper; *fig.* sluggard; *su./f* stud earring; **dormir** [~'mi:r] (2b) *v/i.* sleep, be asleep; ♀ close (*flower*); ♱ lie idle; *fig.* be still or latent; ~ *comme une souche* (*or une marmotte or un loir*) sleep like a log; ~ *sur les deux oreilles* be absolutely confident; ~ *trop longtemps* oversleep; *histoire f à ~ debout* incredible story; **dormitif, -ve** ♣ [~mi'tif, ~'ti:v] 1. *adj.* soporific; 2. *su./m* sleeping-draught.

dorsal, e, *m/pl.* **-aux** [dɔr'sal, ~'so] dorsal.

dortoir [dɔr'twa:r] *m* dormitory; sleeping-quarters *usu. pl.*

dorure [dɔ'ry:r] *f* gilding; *gold-braid*; *meat*: browning; *cake*: glazing.

doryphore *zo.* [dɔri'fɔ:r] *m* Colorado beetle.

dos [do] *m* back (*a. of chair, page, etc.*); *nose*: bridge; *geog.* ridge; *en ~ d'âne* ridged, high-crowned (*road*); △ ogee; hump-back (*bridge*); *en avoir plein le ~* be fed up with it; *faire le gros ~* arch its back (*cat*); *voir au ~* turn over!; see overleaf.

dosage [do'za:ʒ] *m* ♣ dosage; ⚗ titration, quantity determination; **dose** [do:z] *f* ♣ dose; ⚗ amount, proportion; *fig.* share; ~ *excessive*, ~ *trop forte* overdosis; **doser** [do'ze] (1a) *v/t.* ♣ determine the dose of; ⚗ titrate; *fig.* measure out.

dossier [do'sje] *m* chair *etc.*: back; file, papers *pl.*, documents *pl.*; ⚖ record; ♣ case history.

dot [dɔt] *f* dowry; **dotal, e**, *m/pl.*

-aux [dɔ'tal, ~'to] dotal; ⚖ *régime m ~* marriage settlement; **dotation** [~ta'sjɔ̃] *f* endowment; ⊕ *etc.* equipment; **doter** [~'te] (1a) *v/t.* give a dowry to (*a bride*); endow (*a hospital etc., a. fig.*) (with, de).

douaire [dwɛ:r] *m* (*widow's*) dower; (*wife's*) jointure; **douairière** [dwe-'rjɛ:r] *su./f*, *a. adj.* dowager.

douane *admin.* [dwan] *f* customs *pl.*; **douanier, -ère** [dwa'nje, ~'njɛ:r] 1. *adj.* customs-...; 2. *su./m* customs officer.

doublage [du'bla:ʒ] *m* cost. lining; ⊕ plating; *cin.* dubbing; **double** [dubl] 1. *adj.* double, twofold; *à ~ face* two-faced (*person*); *à ~ sens* ambiguous; ♱ *en partie ~* by double-entry; *sp. partie f ~ golf*: foursome; 2. *su./m* double; duplicate; ♱ *en ~* in duplicate; *plier en ~* fold in half or in two; ~*s pl. messieurs tennis*: men's doubles; **doublé** [du'ble] *m billiards*: stroke off the cushion; rolled gold; plated ware; **doubler** [~'ble] (1a) *v/t.* double (*a.* ⚓ *a cape*); fold in half or in two; *cost.* line; ⊕ *metal*: plate; *cin.* dub; pass, overtake; *thea.* understudy (*a role*); *mot.* défense de ~ no overtaking!; *mot.* ~ *à gauche* overtake *or* pass on the left; ~ *une classe* repeat a class; *v/i.* double; **doublet** [~'blɛ] *m* doublet; **doublon** [~'blɔ̃] *m* double; doublet; **doublure** [~'bly:r] *f cost.* lining; *thea.* understudy; *mot.* overtaking.

douce-amère, *pl.* **douces-amères** ♀ [dusa'mɛ:r] *f* bitter-sweet, woody nightshade; **douceâtre** [~-'sɑ:tr] sweetish; sickly; **doucement** [dus'mɑ̃] gently; softly; carefully; smoothly; **doucereux, -euse** [dus'rø, ~'rø:z] sweetish, sickly, cloying; *fig.* smooth-tongued; sugary; **doucet, -ette** [du'sɛ, ~'sɛt] 1. *adj.* meek; mild; 2. *su./f* lamb's lettuce, corn-salad; **douceur** [~'sœ:r] *f* sweetness; softness; gentleness; *weather*: mildness; ~*s pl.* sweets, *Am.* candies; *fig. en ~* soft (*landing, transition, etc.*); gently, smoothly; carefully.

douche [duʃ] *f* shower(-bath); ♣ douche; **doucher** [du'ʃe] (1a) *v/t.* give (*s.o.*) a shower-bath; F dowse (*s.o.*); ♣ douche.

doucir [du'si:r] (2a) *v/t.* grind down (*glass or metal*).

douer [dwe] (1p) *v/t.* endow (with, de) (*a. fig.*); *être doué pour* have a natural gift for.

douille [du:j] *f* ⊕, ⚡ socket; ⚡ (bulb-)holder; cartridge case; ⊕ *wheel*: sleeve.

douillet, -ette [du'jɛ, ~'jɛt] soft (*cushion etc., a. person*); *pej.* effeminate, over-delicate.

douleur [du'lœ:r] *f* pain; suffering; grief; **douloureux, -euse** [~lu'rø, ~'rø:z] 1. *adj.* painful; aching; *fig.* sad; *fig.* sorrowful (*look*); *fig.* grievous (*cry, event, loss*); 2. *su./f* F bill, *Am.* check.

doute [dut] *m* doubt, misgiving; suspicion; *mettre* (*or révoquer*) *en* ~ (call in) question (whether, *que*); *sans* ~ no doubt; probably; *sans aucun* ~ without (a) doubt, assuredly; **douter** [du'te] (1a) *v/i.* (*a.* ~ *de*) doubt, question; mistrust; *v/t.*: *se* ~ *de* suspect, think; **douteur, -euse** [~'tœ:r, ~'tø:z] 1. *su.* doubter; 2. *adj.* doubting; **douteux, -euse** [~'tø, ~'tø:z] doubtful, dubious; questionable; uncertain.

douve [du:v] *f* ⚔ moat; ⚑ trench; *sp.* water-jump; *tub*: stave.

doux, douce [du, dus] 1. *adj.* soft (*a. fig.*; *a. iron.*; *a. drug etc.*); sweet; mild (*a. steel*); gentle; smooth; pleasant (*memories, news*); *billet m* ~ love-letter; *eau f douce* fresh *or* soft water; *vin m* ~ must; 2. *adv.*: F *filer doux* sing small; submit; *tout doux!* take it easy!; *sl.* *en douce* on the quiet.

douzaine [du'zɛn] *f* dozen; *à la* ~ by the dozen; *une* ~ *de fleurs* a dozen flowers; **douze** [du:z] *adj./num.*, *a. su./m/inv.* twelve; *date, title*: twelfth; **douzième** [du'zjɛm] *adj./num.*, *a. su.* twelfth.

doyen *m*, **-enne** *f* [dwa'jɛ̃, ~'jɛn] *eccl., univ.* dean; *diplomat*: doyen; *fig.* (*a.* ~ *d'âge*) senior; **doyenné** [~jɛ'ne] *m* deanery; ⚡ *pear*: doyenne.

draconien, -enne [drakɔ'njɛ̃, ~'njɛn] draconian; harsh.

dragage ⊕ [dra'ga:ʒ] *m* dredging; dragging (*for body*); (*mine-*)sweeping.

dragée [dra'ʒe] *f* sugared almond; sweet; ⚡ dragee; ⚔ *sl.* bullet; *fig.* pill; *hunt.* small shot; *tenir la* ~

haute à make (*s.o.*) pay dearly; **drageoir** [~'ʒwa:r] *m* watch-glass: bezel; comfit-box, comfit-dish.

dragon ⚡ [dra'ʒɔ̃] *m* sucker.

dragon [dra'gɔ̃] *m* myth. dragon (*a. fig.*); *zo.* flying lizard; ⚔, *orn.* dragoon; **dragonne** [~'gɔn] *f* sword-knot; *umbrella*: tassel.

drague [drag] *f* ⊕ dredger; grappling-hook; *fishing*: drag-net, dredge; **draguer** [dra'ge] (1m) *v/t.* ⊕ dredge; drag (*a pond*); dredge for (*oysters*); ⚓ sweep for (*mines*); *sl.* (try and) pick up (*a girl etc.*); **dragueur** [~'gœ:r] *m* ⊕ dredger-man; *fishing*: dragman; (*a. bateau m* ~) dredger; ⚓ ~ *de mines* mine sweeper.

drain [drɛ̃] *m* drain(ing); drain-pipe; ⚡ drainage tube; ⚔ watercourse; **drainage** ⚡, ⚔ [drɛ'na:ʒ] *m* drainage, draining; ⚑ drain; **drainer** ⚡, ⚔ [~'ne] (1a) *v/t.* drain.

dramatique [drama'tik] 1. *adj.* dramatic (*a. fig.*); *auteur m* ~ playwright; 2. *su./m* drama (*a. fig.*); **dramatiser** [~ti'ze] (1a) *v/t.* dramatize (*a. fig.*); adapt (*a novel*) for the stage; **dramaturge** [~'tyrʒ] *m* playwright; **drame** [dram] *m* drama (*a. fig.*); play.

drap [dra] *m* cloth; ~ (*de lit*) sheet; ~ *mortuaire* pall; F *être dans de beaux* ~*s* be in a pretty mess; **drapeau** [dra'po] *m* flag; *telev.* irregular synchronism; ⚔ colo(u)rs *pl.*; *sous les* ~*x* ⚔ in the services; F *fig.* on the side (of, *de*); **draper** [~'pe] (1a) *v/t.* drape; cover with cloth (*buttons etc.*); *se* ~ drape o.s. (in, *dans*) (*a. fig.*); **draperie** [~'pri] *f* drapery; curtains *pl.*; ⚔ bunting; **drapier** [~'pje] *m* draper; cloth merchant *or* manufacturer.

drastique ⚡ [dras'tik] *adj.*, *a. su./m* drastic.

drawback ⚑ [dro'bak] *m* drawback.

drèche [drɛʃ] *f* draff.

dressage [drɛ'sa:ʒ] *m* preparation; *monument*: erection; ⊕ *stone, wood*: dressing; ⊕ facing; training (*a.* ⚔); *horse*: breaking in; **dressement** [drɛs'mɑ̃] *m* preparation, drawing up; **dresser** [drɛ'se] (1a) *v/t.* erect (*a monument etc.*); fix up (*a bed*); raise (*one's head*); prick up (*one's ears*); lay, set (*an ambush, the table, a trap*); draw up (*a contract, an* inventory, a list, a report); pitch (a tent); ✕ lay out (a camp); ✕ establish (a battery); ⚏ lodge (a complaint); ✝ make out (a cheque); dish up (food); train (an animal, a person); break in (a horse); ✕ drill (recruits); ⊕ line up (an engine, a machine); trim (a hedge); dress (wood, a stone); ⊕ straighten out (a wire); ~ un procès-verbal contre (or à) q. take down the particulars of a minor offence, F take s.o.'s name and address; se ~ rise, get to one's feet; stand on end (hair); stand (monument etc.); rise on its hind legs (horse); **dresseur** m, **-euse** f [~'sœːr, ~'søːz] trainer (of animals); adjuster; **dressoir** [~-'swaːr] m dresser, sideboard.

dribbler sp. [dri'ble] (1a) vt/i. dribble.

drille[1] [driːj] m: F bon ~ grand chap; F pauvre ~ poor devil.

drille[2] ⊕ [~] f hand-drill, drill-brace.

drisse ⚓ [dris] f halyard, yard-rope.

drogue [drɔg] f drug; coll. drugs pl.; pej. patent medicine; **drogué, e** [drɔ'ge] 1. adj. high (on drugs), sl. stoned; 2. su. drug addict; dope fiend; **droguer** [drɔ'ge] (1m) v/t. drug (up); dose up; se ~ take drugs, be on drugs; **droguerie** [~'gri] f chemist's, Am. drugstore.

droit, droite [drwa, drwat] 1. adj. straight (a. line); right (angle, hand, side); upright (a. fig.); vertical; stand-up (collar); fig. honest; au ~ de at right angles with; ⅄ section f ~e cross-section; 2. droit adv. straight; tout ~ straight ahead or on; 3. su./m right; privilege; law; fee, charge; ~s pl. d'auteur royalties; ~s pl. civiques civil rights; ✝ ~s pl. de magasinage storage sg. (charges); warehouse dues; ~ de douane (customs) duty; ~ des gens law of nations; ~ du plus fort right of the strongest; à qui de ~ right person or quarter; avoir ~ à be entitled to; be eligible for; de (bon) ~ by right; être en ~ de (inf.) have a right to (inf.), be entitled to (inf.); faire son ~ study law; su./f right hand; straight line; à ~e on the right; direction: to the right; tenir la ~e keep to the right; pol. la ⅔e the Right, the Conservatives pl.; **droitier, -ère** [drwa'tje, ~'tjɛːr] 1. adj. right-

handed; pol. right-wing; 2. su. right-handed person; pol. Rightist, Conservative; **droitiste** pol. [~'tist] adj., a. su. Rightist; **droiture** [~'tyːr] f uprightness; integrity; honesty.

drolatique [drɔla'tik] comic, humorous; spicy; **drôle** [droːl] 1. adj. funny; odd, queer; F la ~ de guerre the phoney war; un(e) ~ de a funny, an odd; 2. su./m rascal, knave; **drôlerie** [drol'ri] f jesting, fun; joke, jest, Am. gag; **drôlesse** † [dro'lɛs] f hussy.

dromadaire zo. [drɔma'dɛːr] m dromedary.

drosser ⚓, ✖ [drɔ'se] (1a) v/t. drive, carry, drift (wind etc.).

dru, drue [dry] 1. adj. thick, strong; dense; vigorous; 2. dru adv. thickly; ~ et menu in a steady drizzle (rain); (walk) with quick, short steps; tomber ~ fall thick and fast.

druide [druid] m druid.

drupe ⚘ [dryp] f drupe, stone-fruit.

dû, due, m/pl. **dus** [dy] 1. p.p. of devoir 1; 2. adj. due; owing; 3. su./m due.

dubitatif, -ve [dybita'tif, ~'tiːv] dubitative.

duc [dyk] m duke; orn. horned owl; **ducal, e**, m/pl. **-aux** [dy'kal, ~'ko] ducal; ... of a or the duke.

ducat † [dy'ka] m ducat.

duché [dy'ʃe] m duchy, dukedom; **duchesse** [~'ʃes] f duchess; tex. duchesse lace or satin; ⚘ duchess pear.

ductile [dyk'til] ductile, malleable (a. fig.); fig. pliable; **ductilité** [~-tili'te] f malleability; fig. docility.

duel[1] gramm. [dyɛl] m dual.

duel[2] [dyɛl] m duel; **duelliste** [dyɛ-'list] m duellist.

dum-dum [dum'dum] f dum-dum (bullet).

dûment [dy'mã] adv. duly, in due form, properly.

dumping ✝ [dœm'piŋ] m dumping; faire du ~ dump.

dune [dyn] f dune; ~s pl. downs.

dunette ⚓ [dy'nɛt] f poop-deck.

duo ♪ [dɥo] m duet.

duodénum anat. [dɥɔde'nɔm] m duodenum.

dupe [dyp] f dupe; F gull; être ~ de be taken in by; prendre q. pour ~ make a cat's-paw of s.o.; **duper**

[dy'pe] (1a) v/t. dupe, fool; take (s.o.) in; **duperie** [ˌ'pri] f deception, trickery; take-in; **dupeur** [ˌ'pœːr] m cheat, swindler, Am. sharper; hoaxer.

duplex ⊕ [dy'plɛks] adj., a. su./m duplex; **duplicata** [dyplika'ta] m/ inv. copy: duplicate; **duplicateur** [ˌka'tœːr] m duplicator; ⚡ doubler; **duplicatif, -ve** [ˌka'tif, ˌ'tiːv] duplicative; **duplicité** [ˌsi'te] f duplicity, double-dealing.

dur, dure [dyːr] **1.** adj. hard (a. fig.); stiff; tough (meat, wood); fig. harsh; unfeeling; hardened; avoir le sommeil ˌ be a heavy sleeper; être ˌ avec (or pour) q. be hard on s.o., be rough with s.o.; avoir l'oreille ˌe, être ˌ d'oreille be hard of hearing; **2.** dur adv. hard; **3.** su./m F tough guy; hard-liner; F un ˌ à cuire a tough nut to crack; ⚠ en ˌ permanent (structure etc.); su./f: coucher sur la dure sleep on the bare ground or on bare boards.

durabilité [dyrabili'te] f durability; **durable** [ˌ'rabl] durable, lasting; solid.

durant [dy'rɑ̃] prp. during; ˌ des années for many years; sa vie ˌ his whole life long; des heures ˌ for hours (and hours).

durcir [dyr'siːr] (2a) v/t. harden; hard-boil (an egg); metall. chill; v/i. a. se ˌ harden; set (concrete); **durcissement** [ˌsis'mɑ̃] m hardening, toughening; stiffening; metall. chilling.

durée [dy're] f duration; machine, building, etc.: wear, life; de courte ˌ short-lived; **durer** [ˌ] (1a) v/i. last, endure; wear (well) (goods); hold out, bear, F stick (it) (person); le temps me dure time hangs heavily on my hands, I find life dull.

duret, -ette F [dy'rɛ, ˌ'rɛt] rather hard; rather tough (meat); **dureté** [dyr'te] f hardness (a. fig.); meat: toughness; fig. harshness; austerity; ˌ d'oreille hardness of hearing; **durillon** [dyri'jɔ̃] m foot: corn; hand: callosity.

durit mot. (TM) [dy'rit] f radiator hose.

dus [dy] 1st p. sg. p.s. of devoir 1.

duvet [dy'vɛ] m down; tex. fluff, nap; F down quilt; **duveté, e** [dyv'te], a. **duveteux, -euse** [ˌ'tø, ˌ'tøːz] downy, fluffy.

dynamique [dina'mik] **1.** adj. dynamic; **2.** su./f dynamics sg.; **dynamiser** [ˌmi'ze] (1a) v/t. make (more) dynamic; **dynamite** [ˌ'mit] f dynamite; **dynamiter** [ˌmi'te] (1a) v/t. dynamite; blow up; fig. a. F bust (up); **dynamo** ⚡, ⊕ [ˌ'mo] f dynamo; ˌ lumière (or d'éclairage) lighting generator; **dynamomètre** ⊕ [ˌmo'mɛtr] m dynamometer.

dynastie [dinas'ti] f dynasty.

dysenterie 🕮 [disɑ̃'tri] f dysentery.

dysfonctionnement 🕮 [disfɔ̃ks-jɔn'mɑ̃] f dysfunction.

dyspepsie 🕮 [dispɛp'si] f dyspepsia, indigestion; **dyspepsique** [ˌpɛp-'sik] adj., a. su. dyspeptic.

dytique zo. [di'tik] m water-beetle, dytiscus.

E

E, e [ə] *m* E, e.

eau [o] *f* water; rain; *fruit:* juice; perspiration; *eccl.* ~ **bénite** holy water; ~ **de toilette** lotion; ~ **du robinet** tap water; ~ₘ *lourde* heavy water; ~ **oxygénée** hydrogen peroxide; ~ **potable** drinking water; ~ **vive** spring water, running water; **aller aux** ~x go to a watering-place; ⚓ **faire** ~ (spring a) leak; **faire de l'** ~ ⚓, 🚢 (take in) water; ~ **make water; grandes** ~x *pl.,* jeux *m/pl.* **d'** ~x ornamental fountains; *river:* high water *sg.;* **nager entre deux** ~x swim under water; **prendre les** ~x take the waters (*at a* spa); **ville** *f* **d'** ~ watering-place, spa; ~-**de-vie,** *pl.* ~**x-de-vie** [od'vi] *f* brandy; spirits *pl.;* ~-**forte,** *pl.* ~**x-fortes** ⚗ [o'fɔrt] *f* nitric acid; etching; ~**x-vannes** [o'van] *f/pl.* liquid manure *sg.,* sewage *sg.*

ébahir [eba'iːr] (2a) *v/t.* amaze, astound; take (*s.o.'s*) breath away; **s'** ~ be astounded, wonder (*at, de*); **ébahissement** [~is'mã] *m* amazement, wonder.

ébarber [ebar'be] (1a) *v/t.* trim (*a.* ✂); ✂ clip; ⊕ dress.

ébats [e'ba] *m/pl.* frolics, gambols; **prendre ses** ~ frolic, gambol; **ébattre** [e'batr] (4a): *v/t.:* **s'** ~ frolic, gambol, frisk about.

ébaubi, e [ebo'bi] amazed, astounded.

ébauchage [ebo'ʃaːʒ] *m* roughing out (*of s.th.*); **ébauche** [e'boːʃ] *f* outline (*a. fig.*); sketch (*a. fig.*); rough draft; *fig.* ghost (*of a smile*); **ébaucher** [ebo'ʃe] (1a) *v/t.* rough out, sketch (out); roughhew (*a stone etc.*); *fig.* give a ghost *or* a hint of (*a smile etc.*); **s'** ~ take shape, form, develop.

ébène [e'bɛn] *f* ebony; *fig.* **d'** ~ jet-black; **ébénier** ♣ [ebe'nje] *m* ebony-tree; **ébéniste** [~'nist] *m* cabinet-maker; **ébénisterie** [~nis-'tri] *f* cabinet-work; cabinet-making.

éberlué, e [ebɛrlɥ'e] flabbergasted.

éblouir [eblu'iːr] (2a) *v/t.* dazzle (*a. fig.*); **éblouissement** [~is'mã] *m* dazzle; glare; dizziness.

ébonite [ebɔ'nit] *f* ebonite, vulcanite.

éborgner [ebɔr'ɲe] (1a) *v/t.* blind in one eye, put (*s.o.'s*) eye out; ✿ disbud.

ébouillanter [ebujã'te] (1a) *v/t.* scald.

éboulement [ebul'mã] *m* caving in, collapsing; fall of stone; landslide; **ébouler** [ebu'le] (1a) *v/t.* bring down; **s'** ~ cave in, collapse; slip (*cliff, land*); **éboulis** [~'li] *m* △ debris; fallen earth; scree.

ébouriffant, e F [eburi'fã, ~'fãːt] amazing, startling; fantastic (*story*); **ébouriffer** [~'fe] (1a) *v/t.* ruffle (*a. fig.*), dishevel (*s.o.'s hair*); *fig.* amaze.

ébrancher ✿ [ebrã'ʃe] (1a) *v/t.* lop off the branches of (*a tree*); prune, trim; **ébranchoir** ✿ [~'ʃwaːr] *m* (long-hafted) billhook.

ébranlement [ebrã'mã] *m* shaking, shock; *fig.* agitation, commotion; *fig.* disturbance (*a. of the mind*); **ébranler** [ebrã'le] (1a) *v/t.* shake (*a. fig.*); loosen (*a tooth*); set in motion; disturb; **s'** ~ shake; ring (*bells*); start, set off; ✗ move off.

ébrécher [ebre'ʃe] (1f) *v/t.* notch; chip (*a plate etc.*); jag (*a knife*); *fig.* make a hole in (*one's fortune*); *fig.* damage (*s.o.'s. reputation*).

ébriété [ebrie'te] *f* drunkenness, intoxication.

ébrouement [ebru'mã] *m* snort (-ing); **ébrouer** [~'e] (1a) *v/t.:* **s'** ~ snort; take (*a dust-*)bath (*bird*).

ébruiter [ebrɥi'te] (1a) *v/t.* noise abroad, make known; divulge (*a secret*); **s'** ~ become known.

ébullition [ebyli'sjõ] *f* boiling; effervescence; *fig.* turmoil; **point** *m* **d'** ~ boiling point.

éburné, e [ebyr'ne] eburnean, like ivory; *anat.* **substance** *f* ~**e** dentine.

écaille [e'kaːj] *f* ☙, ⚘, *metall., fig.,*

fish: scale; *paint*: flake; *wood*: splinter; *tortoise etc.*: shell; ✝ tortoise-shell.

écailler[1] [eka'je] (1a) *v/t.* scale (*fish, a. metall.*); open (*oysters*); s'~ scale or flake off, peel off.

écailler[2], **-ère** [eka'je, ~'jɛːr] *su.* oyster-seller; *su./f* oyster-knife.

écailleux, -euse [eka'jø, ~'jøːz] scaly; flaky (*paint*).

écale [e'kal] *f pea*: pod; *nut*: husk; **écaler** [eka'le] (1a) *v/t.* shell (*peas*); hull (*walnuts*); shuck (*chestnuts*).

écarlate [ekar'lat] *adj., a. su./f* scarlet; ~ (*wide (one's eyes*).)

écarquiller [ekarki'je] (1a) *v/t.* open

écart [e'kaːr] *m* gap; divergence; difference; separation; *cards*: discard (-ing); ✕ *range*: error (*a. fig.*); ✝ margin (*of prices*); ⊕ deviation; ⊕ variation; swerve; *fig.* digression; *fig.* fancy: flight; ~ (*de conduite*) misdemeano(u)r; *à l'~* on one side, apart; aloof; out of the way; *faire un ~* swerve; shy (*horse*); *gymn.* grand ~ splits *pl.*; se tenir *à l'~* stand aside or aloof; **écarté, e** [ekar'te] remote; isolated; out-of-the-way; lonely.

écarteler [ekartə'le] (1d) *v/t.* ⚔ *hist.* quarter; *fig.* tear apart; *écartelé entre* torn between.

écartement [ekartə'mã] gap, space (between, de); 🚊 *track*: gauge; *mot.* wheelbase; ⊕ deflection; **écarter** [~'te] (1a) *v/t.* separate; spread; remove; avert; push aside (*a. proposals*); divert (*suspicion etc.*); s'~ move aside; diverge; stray, deviate (from, de).

Ecclésiaste [ekle'zjast] *m*: *livre m de l'~* Ecclesiastes; **ecclésiastique** [~zjas'tik] **1.** *adj.* ecclesiastical; clerical (*hat etc.*); **2.** *su./m* clergyman, ecclesiastic; *l'⚭* Ecclesiasticus.

écervelé, e [esɛrvə'le] **1.** *adj.* scatterbrained, wild, flighty; **2.** *su.* scatterbrain, harum-scarum, madcap.

échafaud [eʃa'fo] *m* scaffolding; *sp. etc.* stand; ⚖ scaffold, gallows *pl.*; **échafaudage** [~fo'daːʒ] *m* ⚠ scaffolding; *fig.* structure; *fig.* fortune: piling up; **échafauder** [~fo'de] (1a) *v/i.* erect a scaffolding; *v/t.* pile up; *fig.* build up; construct.

échalas [eʃa'la] *m* 🌱 vine-prop; hop-pole; *fig.* spindle-shanks (= *lanky person*); **échalasser** [~la'se] (1a) *v/t.* prop (*the vine etc.*).

échalier [eʃa'lje] *m* stile; gate.

échalote ⚘ [eʃa'lɔt] *f* shallot.

échancrer [eʃã'kre] (1a) *v/t.* indent, notch; scallop (*a handkerchief*); cut out (the neck of) (*a dress*); **échancrure** [~'kryːr] *f* indentation; cut; *dress*: neckline; notch.

échange [e'ʃãːʒ] *m* exchange (*a.* ✝); ✝ barter; *libre* ~ free trade; *en* ~ *de* in exchange or return for; **échanger** [eʃã'ʒe] (1l) *v/t.* exchange (for *pour, contre*) (*a.* ✝); ✝ barter; **échangeur** [~'ʒœːr] *m mot.* interchange; ⊕ exchanger.

échanson [eʃã'sɔ̃] *m* ✝ cup-bearer; butler.

échantillon [eʃãti'jɔ̃] *m* sample (*a. fig.*); specimen; pattern; ⊕ template; ~ *représentatif* adequate sample; **échantillonnage** [~jɔ'naːʒ] *m* sampling; (collection of) samples *pl.*; **échantillonner** [~jɔ'ne] (1a) *v/t.* sample.

échappatoire [eʃapa'twaːr] *f* evasion, way out, loop-hole; **échappé, e** [~'pe] **1.** *adj.* fugitive, runaway; **2.** *su.* fugitive, runaway; *su./f* escape; (free) space; *sp.* spurt; ~ (*de vue*) vista; ~ *de lumière* burst of light; *par* ~s by fits and starts; **échappement** [eʃap'mã] *m* gas *etc.*: escape; ⊕, *mot.* exhaust; ⊕ outlet; *clock*: escapement; *mot.* *tuyau m* (*pot m*) *d'*~ exhaust-pipe (silencer); **échapper** [eʃa'pe] (1a) *v/i.* escape; avoid, dodge; defy; *laisser* ~ let slip; set free; *le mot m'a échappé* the word has slipped my memory; *v/t.: fig. l'*~ *belle* have a narrow escape or F a close shave; s'~ escape (from, de); slip out; disappear.

écharde [e'ʃard] *f* splinter.

écharner ⊕ [eʃar'ne] (1a) *v/t.* flesh (*hides*); **écharnoir** [~'nwaːr] *m* fleshing knife.

écharpe [e'ʃarp] *f* (shoulder) sash; *cost.* stole, scarf; ⚔ *arm*: sling; *en* ~ diagonally, slantwise; **écharper** [eʃar'pe] (1a) *v/t.* slash; cut to pieces (*a.* ✕); *tex.* card (*wool*).

échasse [e'ʃaːs] *f* stilt; *scaffold*: pole; *fig. monté sur des* ~s on one's high horse; **échassier** [eʃa'sje] *m orn.* wader; *fig.* spindle-shanks.

échaudé *cuis.* [eʃo'de] *m* canary-bread; **échauder** [~'de] (1a) *v/t.* scald; *tex.* scour; F fleece (*s.o.*);

fig. se faire ~ burn one's fingers;
échaudoir [~'dwa:r] *m* scalding-
room; scalding-tub; *tex.* scour-
ingvat; **échaudure** [~'dy:r] *f*
scald.

échauffant, e [eʃo'fɑ̃, ~'fɑ̃:t] ⚕
heating; ⚕ constipating; *fig.* exciting; **échauffement** [eʃof'mɑ̃] *m*
⊕ heating; ⚕ overheating; ⚕ constipation; *fig.* over-excitement;
échauffer [eʃo'fe] (1a) *v/t.* overheat (⚕, *a.* a room); ⚕ constipate;
⊕ heat; *fig.* warm; *fig.* inflame;
s'~ become overheated; warm up;
⊕ get or run hot.

échauffourée [eʃofu're] *f* brawl;
scuffle; clash; ⚔ skirmish, affray.

échéance ✝ [eʃe'ɑ̃:s] *f* bill: falling
due, term; maturity; date; *tenancy*: expiration; *à longue* ~ long-
dated; long-term; **échéant, e**
[~'ɑ̃, ~'ɑ̃:t] ✝ falling due; *le cas* ~ if
necessary; should the occasion
arise.

échec [e'ʃɛk] *m chess*: check (*a. fig.*);
⊕, *a. fig.* failure; ~s *pl.* chess *sg.*;
chessmen; chessboard *sg.*; *voué à l'*~
doomed to failure.

échelette [eʃ'lɛt] *f cart etc.*: rack;
échelle [e'ʃɛl] *f* ladder (*a. fig.*); *colours, drawing, map, prices, wages,
etc.*: scale; *stocking*: ladder, run; ~
double pair of steps; ~ *mobile* (*des
salaires*) sliding scale (of wages); ~
sociale social scale; *faire la courte* ~ *à
q.* give s.o. a helping hand; *sur une
grande* ~ on a large scale; **échelon**
[eʃ'lɔ̃] *m ladder*: rung; *admin.* grade;
fig. step; ⚔ echelon; ♪ degree; *pol.
etc. à l'*~ *le plus élevé* at the highest
level; ⊕ *en* ~ stepped (*gearing*);
échelonnement [eʃlɔn'mɑ̃] *m* ⚔
echeloning; ⊕ placing at intervals; ✝
spreading (*over a period*); ⚡ *brushes,
a. fig. holidays*: staggering; **échelonner** [eʃlɔ'ne] (1a) *v/t.* ⚔ (draw up
in) echelon; space out; place at intervals; ⊕ spread (*gears*); ✝ spread (*payments over a period*); stagger (*a. fig.
holidays*); grade.

écheniller [eʃni'je] (1a) *v/t.* ⚡ clear
of caterpillars; *fig.* clean up, free
from undesirable elements; **éche-
nilloir** ⚡ [~nij'wa:r] *m* tree-pruner;
branch-lopper.

écheveau [eʃ'vo] *m* skein, hank; *fig.*
maze, jumble; **échevelé, e** [eʃə'vle]
dishevelled; tousled; *fig.* wild;

écheveler [~] (1c) *v/t.* dishevel,
rumple (*s.o.'s hair*).

échine *anat.* [e'ʃin] *f* backbone,
spine; **échiner** [eʃi'ne] (1a) *v/t.*
break (*s.o.'s*) back; *fig.* tire (*s.o.*) out;
fig. thrash (*s.o.*) within an inch of his
life; *sl.* ruin; *fig.* s'~ tire o.s. out.

échiquier [eʃi'kje] *m* chess-board;
checker pattern; *pol. Br.* ♀ Exchequer; *en* ~ chequerwise.

écho [e'ko] *m* echo; *faire* ~ echo.

échoir [e'ʃwa:r] (3d) *v/i.* ✝ fall due;
expire (*tenancy*); fall (*to s.o.'s lot*);
fig. befall.

échoppe¹ [e'ʃɔp] *f* (*covered*) stall,
booth.

échoppe² ⊕ [~] *f* burin; graver.

échotier *journ.* [eko'tje] *m* gossip-
writer, paragraphist; columnist.

échouer [e'ʃwe] (1p) *v/i.* ⚓ run
aground; *fig.* fail, come to naught;
fall through; *fig.* land, end up (in,
dans); *faire* ~ foil; ruin; thwart; *v/t.*
⚓ run (*a ship*) aground; beach.

échu, e [e'ʃy] ✝ due; expired.

écimer ⚡ [esi'me] (1a) *v/t.* pollard,
top.

éclabousser [eklabu'se] (1a) *v/t.*
splash, bespatter (*with, de*); **éclaboussure** [~'sy:r] *f* splash.

éclair [e'klɛ:r] *m* flash of lightning;
flash (*a. fig.*); *cuis.* éclair; ~s *pl. de
chaleur* heat lightning *sg.*; ⚔ *guerre f*
~ blitzkrieg; *visite f* ~ lightning visit;
éclairage [ekle'ra:ʒ] *m* light(ing);
⚔, ⚓ scouting; ~ *par projecteurs*
flood-lighting; ⚡ *circuit m d'*~
light(ing) circuit; **éclairagiste** [~ra-
'ʒist] *m* lighting engineer; **éclaircie**
[eklɛr'si] *f* fair period; break (*of
clouds*); clearing (*in a forest*); *fig.*
bright period (*in life*); **éclaircir**
[~'si:r] (2a) *v/t.* clear (up); brighten;
thin (*a forest*); clarify (*a liquid*); thin
out (*a sauce*); *fig.* solve, explain,
elucidate; **éclairer** [ekle're] (1b) *v/t.*
light, illuminate; *fig.* enlighten; ⚔
reconnoitre; s'~ light up; become
clear(er); **éclaireur** [~'rœ:r] *m* ⚔,
⚓, *etc.* scout.

éclat [e'kla] *m* splinter, chip; burst (*of
laughter, of thunder*); explosion;
flash (*of gun, light*); brightness, radiance, brilliance (*a. fig.*); *fig.* splen-
do(u)r; *fig.* glamo(u)r; ~ *de rire* burst
of laughter; *faire* ~ create a stir; *faux*
~ tawdriness; *rire aux* ~s roar with
laughter; **éclatant, e** [ekla'tɑ̃, ~'tɑ̃:t]

brilliant; sparkling, glittering; magnificent; loud (*noise*); *fig.* obvious; **éclater** [~'te] (1a) *v/i.* burst, explode; shatter; break up, split (up); flash (*a. fig.*); shine out *or* forth; clap (*thunder*); break out (*fire, laughter, war*); ~ *de rire* burst out laughing; **éclateur** ⚡ [~'tœːr] *m* spark-gap; spark-arrester; ~ *à boule* discharger.

éclipse [e'klips] *f* eclipse; *fig.* disappearance; **éclipser** [eklip'se] (1a) *v/t.* eclipse (*a. fig.*); obscure (*a beam*); s'~ vanish.

éclisse [e'klis] *f* wedge; ⚕ splint; ⊕ butt-strap; 🚂 fish-plate; **éclisser** [ekli'se] (1a) *v/t.* ⚕ splint; 🚂 fish.

éclopé, e [eklɔ'pe] **1.** *adj.* lame, footsore; **2.** *su.* cripple; lame person.

éclore [e'klɔːr] (4f) *v/i.* hatch (*bird*); ⚘ open; ⚘ bloom; *fig.* develop, come to light; **éclosion** [eklɔ'zjɔ̃] *f eggs*: hatching; ⚘ opening; ⚘ blooming; *fig.* birth, dawning.

écluse [e'klyːz] *f* lock; sluice; floodgate; **éclusée** [ekly'ze] *f* lockful; sluicing-water; **écluser** [~'ze] (1a) *v/t.* provide (*a canal*) with locks; pass (*a barge*) through a lock; **éclusier, -ère** [~'zje, ~'zjɛːr] **1.** *su.* lock-keeper; **2.** *adj.* lock-...

écœurer [ekœ're] (1a) *v/t.* disgust, sicken, nauseate; *fig.* dishearten.

école [e'kɔl] *f* school (*a. fig.*); ⚔, ⚓ drill; ~ *confessionnelle* denominational school; ~ *de commerce* commercial school; ~ *des arts et métiers* industrial school; engineering college; technical school *or* institute; ~ *des hautes études commerciales* commercial college (*of university standing*); ~ *laïque* undenominational school; ~ *libre* private school; ~ *maternelle* infant school; kindergarten; ~ *mixte* mixed school, *Am.* co-educational school; ~ *moyenne* intermediate school; ~ *primaire supérieure* central school; ~ *professionnelle* training school; ~ *secondaire* secondary school; ~ *supérieure* college, academy; *faire* ~ get a following (*person*); become the accepted thing; attract followers; *faire l'*~ (*à*) teach; *faire l'*~ *buissonnière* play truant; **écolier, -ère** [ekɔ'lje, ~'ljɛːr] *su.* pupil; *su./m* schoolboy; *su./f* schoolgirl.

écologie [ekɔlɔ'ʒi] *f* ecology; **écologique** [~'ʒik] ecological; **écologisme** [~'ʒism] *m* ecology movement; **écologiste** [~'ʒist] *su.* ecologist.

éconduire [ekɔ̃'dɥiːr] (4h) *v/t.* show out; get rid of; reject (*a suitor*); *être éconduit* meet with a polite refusal.

économat [ekɔnɔ'ma] *m* † stewardship; *school, univ.*: bursarship; *society*: treasurership; steward's (*etc.*) office; **économe** [~'nɔm] **1.** *adj.* economical, thrifty; sparing; **2.** *su.* † steward, housekeeper; treasurer; bursar; **économie** [ekɔnɔ'mi] *f* economy, saving; thrift; management; ~*s pl.* savings; ~ *dirigée* controlled economy; ~ *domestique* domestic economy; housekeeping; ~ *politique* political economy; economics *sg.*; *faire des* ~*s* save (up); **économique** [~'mik] **1.** *adj.* economic (*doctrine, problem, system*); inexpensive, economical, cheap; **2.** *su./f* economics *sg.*; **économiser** [~mi'ze] (1a) *v/t.* economize, save (on, *sur*); **économiste** [~'mist] *m* (political) economist.

écope [e'kɔp] *f* ladle (*a. cuis.*); ⚓ scoop; **écoper** [ekɔ'pe] (1a) *v/t.* bail out; *v/i. sl.* be hit; cop it; get the blame.

écorce [e'kɔrs] *f tree*: bark; *fruit*: rind, peel; *fig.* outside, crust; **écorcer** [ekɔr'se] (1k) *v/t.* bark; peel (*a fruit*).

écorcher [ekɔr'ʃe] (1a) *v/t.* skin, flay; graze, chafe (*the skin*); scrape, scratch; *fig.* murder (*a language*); *fig.* grate on (*the ear*); *fig.* burn (*one's throat*); *fig.* fleece (*a client*); **écorcheur** [~'ʃœːr] *m* flayer; *fig.* fleecer; **écorchure** ⚕ [~'ʃyːr] *f* abrasion, F graze, scratch.

écorner [ekɔr'ne] (1a) *v/t.* break *or* chip the corner(s) off (*s.th.*); dog-ear (*a book*); *fig.* make a hole in (*one's fortune*); **écornifler** F [~ni'fle] (1a) *v/t.* scrounge; sponge; **écornifleur** *m*, **-euse** *f* F [~ni'flœːr, ~'fløːz] cadger, scrounger; sponger; **écornure** [~'nyːr] *f* chip (*off wood, stone, etc.*).

écossais, e [ekɔ'sɛ, ~'sɛːz] **1.** *adj.* Scottish; *étoffe f* ~*e* tartan, plaid; **2.** *su./m ling.* Scots; ♀ Scot, Scotsman; *les* ♀ *m/pl.* the Scots; *su./f* ♀ Scot, Scotswoman.

écosser [ekɔ'se] (1a) *v/t.* shell, hull.

écosystème [ekɔsi'stɛm] *m* ecosystem.

écot [e'ko] *m* share (of the bill); *payer chacun son ~* go Dutch treat, *Am.* go Dutch.

écoulement [ekul'mã] *m* outflow, flow (*a.* ⚕); (*nasal*) discharge; *bath etc.*: waste-pipe; *crowd*: dispersal; ✝ sale, disposal; ✝ *~ facile* ready sale; **écouler** [eku'le] (1a) *v/t.* ✝ sell off, dispose of; *s'~* flow out; pass, elapse (*time*); ✝ sell.

écourter [ekur'te] (1a) *v/t.* shorten, F cut short; dock (*a horse*); crop (*dog's ears*); *fig.* clip (*words*).

écoute¹ [e'kut] *f* listening(-in); *être aux ~s* listen (in); *fig.* keep one's ears open (for, *de*); *heures f/pl. de grande ~ radio, telev.*: peak listening (viewing) hours; *mettre q. sur ~(s)* tap s.o.'s telephone; *station f d'~* monitoring station.

écoute² ⚓ [~] *f* sail: sheet.

écouter [eku'te] (1a) *v/t.* listen to; pay attention to; *v/i.* listen (in); **écouteur, -euse** [~'tœːr, ~'tøːz] *su.* person, *a. radio*: listener; *su./m teleph.* receiver; *radio*: head-phone, ear-phone.

écoutille ⚓ [eku'tiːj] *f* hatchway.

écran [e'krã] *m* screen; *phot.* filter; *faire ~ à* screen; *fig.* be *or* get in the way of; *le petit ~* television; *porter à l'~* film (*a novel, a play*).

écraser [ekra'ze] (1a) *v/t.* crush; *mot.* run over; ✝ F glut (*the market*); *fig.* overwhelm; *fig.* ruin; *mot. ~ l'accélérateur* (*or* F *le champignon*) put one's foot hard down (on the accelerator); *mot. ~ le frein* slam on the brakes; *s'~* collapse; break; ✍, *mot.* crash (into, *contre*); *sl.* (*a. v/i.*) keep one's mouth shut, shut up.

écrémer [ekre'me] (1f) *v/t.* cream (*milk, a. fig.*); skim (*milk, molten glass*); *fig.* take the cream of (*s.th.*); *lait m non écrémé* whole milk; **écrémeuse** [~'møːz] *f* separator; creamer; *metall., a. glass-making*: skimmer; **écrémoir** [~'mwaːr] *m* skimmer.

écrêter [ekre'te] (1a) *v/t.* level off *or* down; *fig.* take the edge off.

écrevisse *zo.* [ekrə'vis] *f* crayfish, *Am.* crawfish.

écrier [ekri'e] (1a) *v/t.*: *s'~* cry (out), shout (out); exclaim.

écrin [e'krɛ̃] *m* (jewel-)case.

écrire [e'kriːr] (4q) *v/t.* write (down); spell (*a word*); **écrivis** [ekri'vi] *1st*

p. sg. p.s. of écrire; **écrivons** [~'vɔ̃] *1st p. pl. pres. of écrire*; **écrit, e** [e'kri, ~'krit] **1.** *p.p. of écrire*; **2.** *su./m* writing; document; *univ. etc.* written examination; *par ~* in writing; **écriteau** [ekri'to] *m* bill, poster, placard; notice; notice-board; **écritoire** [~'twaːr] *m* inkstand; *eccl.* scriptorium; **écriture** [~'tyːr] *f* (hand)writing; script; ✝ entry, item; ✝ *~ en partie double* double entry; ⚹, *sainte* Holy Scripture; ⚹, ✝ *~s pl.* paper *sg.*, documents; books; **écrivailler** F [~va'je] (1a) *v/i.* scribble; be a hack-writer of the poorest kind; **écrivain** [~'vɛ̃] *m* writer, author; *femme f ~* authoress; woman writer; **écrivassier** F [~va'sje] *m* hack-writer, penny-a-liner.

écrou¹ [e'kru] *m* ⊕ nut, female screw.

écrou² ⚖ [~] *m* entry (*on calendar*) of receipt of prisoner into custody; committal to jail; *levée f d'~* release from prison.

écrouelles ⚕ [ekru'ɛl] *f/pl.* scrofula *sg.*

écrouer ⚖ [ekru'e] (1a) *v/t.* imprison; send to prison.

écrouir *metall.* [ekru'iːr] (2a) *v/t.* cold-hammer; cold-draw; cold-harden; cold-roll.

écroulement [ekrul'mã] *m* collapse, falling-in; crumbling (*a. fig.*), *fig.* ruin; **écrouler** [ekru'le] (1a) *v/t.*: *s'~* collapse (*a. fig.*); fall (down); crumble; break up; give way; come to nothing.

écroûter [ekru'te] (1a) *v/t.* cut the crust off; ✍ scarify (*land*).

écru, e [e'kry] unbleached, ecru; *soie f ~e* raw silk; *toile f ~e* holland.

écu [e'ky] *m* shield; ▨ coat of arms; *~s pl.* plenty *sg.* of money.

écueil [e'kœːj] *m* reef; rock (*a. fig.*); shelf; *fig.* danger.

écuelle [e'kɥɛl] *f* bowl, basin; ✂ pan; **écuellée** [ekɥe'le] *f* bowlful.

éculer [eky'le] (1a) *v/t.* wear (*one's shoes*) down at the heel.

écume [e'kym] *f* froth; *waves*: foam; *jam, metal, a. fig.*: lather; scum; *~ de mer* meerschaum; **écumer** [eky'me] (1a) *v/t.* skim; *fig.* scour (*the sea[s], les mers*); *v/i.* foam, froth (*a. metal, a. fig.*); **écumeur** [~'mœːr] *m*: F *~ de marmites* sponger, parasite; ~ de mer pirate; **écumeux, -euse** [~'mø, ~'møːz] foamy, frothy; scummy; **écumoire** [~'mwaːr] f skimmer.

écurage [eky'raːʒ] m cleansing; cleaning (out); **écurer** [~'re] (1a) v/t. cleanse, scour; clean (out); pick (one's teeth).

écureuil zo. [eky'rœːj] m squirrel.

écureur m, **-euse** f [eky'rœːr, ~'røːz] cleanser, cleaner, scourer.

écurie [eky'ri] f stable; fig. team.

écusson [eky'sɔ̃] m Ⓩ shield, escutcheon; ⊕ key-plate; ✕ badge; ♀ shield-bud.

écuyer, -ère [ekɥi'je, ~'jeːr] su. rider; su./m horseman; riding-master; ▲ staircase: hand-rail; ✔ tree: prop; hist. (e)squire; † equerry; su./f horsewoman; bottes f/pl. à l'~ère riding-boots.

eczéma ✷ [ɛgze'ma] m eczema.

édénien, -enne [ede'njɛ̃, ~'njɛn] paradisaic.

édenté, e [edã'te] toothless; zo. edentate; **édenter** [~] (1a) v/t. break the teeth of; s'~ lose one's teeth.

édicter ⚗ etc. [edik'te] (1a) v/t. decree; enact (a law).

édifiant, e [edi'fjã, ~'fjãːt] edifying; **édificateur** [edifika'tœːr] m builder; **édification** [~'sjɔ̃] f erection, building; (moral) edification; fig. F information; **édifice** [edi'fis] m building, edifice; structure (a. fig.); **édifier** [~'fje] (1o) v/t. build, erect; edify (morally); fig. F enlighten.

édit [e'di] m edict.

éditer [edi'te] (1a) v/t. edit; publish (a book etc.); **éditeur** [~'tœːr] m text: editor; book etc.: publisher; **édition** [~'sjɔ̃] f edition; publishing (trade); **éditorial, e,** m/pl. **-aux** [~tɔ'rjal, ~'rjo] 1. adj. editorial; leading (article); 2. su./m leader; editorial.

édredon [edrə'dɔ̃] m eiderdown.

éducable [edy'kabl] educable; trainable (animal); **éducatif, -ve** [~ka'tif, ~'tiːv] educational; educative; **éducation** [~ka'sjɔ̃] f education, schooling; rearing; training (a. animals); ~ physique physical training.

édulcorant [edylkɔ'rã] m sweetener; **édulcorer** [~'re] (1a) v/t. sweeten; ♎ edulcorate.

éduquer [edy'ke] (1m) v/t. educate;

bring up (a child); train (an animal, a faculty); mal éduqué ill-bred.

éfaufiler [efofi'le] (1a) v/t. unravel.

effacé, e [efa'se] faded; unobtrusive, inconspicuous; retiring (manners, person, etc.), retired (life); receding (chin etc.); **effacer** [~] (1k) v/t. efface, blot out, erase; fig. outshine, throw into the shade; s'~ wear away; fade away; stand aside; keep in the background, F take a back seat.

effarement [efar'mã] m alarm; dismay; **effarer** [efa're] (1a) v/t. frighten, scare; startle; dismay; s'~ be scared (at, by de); take fright (at, de).

effaroucher [efaru'ʃe] (1a) v/t. startle; scare away; alarm; fig. shock (the modesty).

effectif, -ve [efɛk'tif, ~'tiːv] 1. adj. effective; ✔ active, real; 2. su./m manpower; ✕ total strength; ⚓ complement; ⊕ stock; **effectuer** [~'tɥe] (1n) v/t. effect, carry (out), execute; accomplish; go into (training).

efféminer [efemi'ne] (1a) v/t. render effeminate; mollycoddle (a child).

effervescence [efɛrve'sãːs] f effervescence; fig. agitation, exitement; restiveness; **effervescent, e** [~'sã, ~'sãːt] effervescent (liquid); fig. in a turmoil.

effet [e'fɛ] m effect, result; operation, action; impression; ✔ bill; ✔ commencement (of policy); ~ secondaire side effect; ~s pl. things, clothes; ✔ stocks; ✔ bonds; ✔ ~s pl. à payer (à recevoir) bills payable (receivable); ✔ ~s pl. publics government stock sg. or securities; ✔ ~ à court terme short-dated bill; à cet ~ with this end in view, for this purpose; en ~ indeed; mettre à l'~ put (s.th.) into operation; prendre ~ become operative; produire son ~ operate, act; sans ~ ineffective.

effeuiller [efœ'je] (1a) v/t. pluck the petals off (a flower); thin out the leaves of (a fruit-tree); fig. destroy bit by bit; s'~ lose its petals (flower) or leaves (tree); **effeuilleuse** F [~'jøːz] stripper.

efficace [efi'kas] effective; efficient (a. ⊕); **efficacité** [~kasi'te] f efficacy; efficiency (a. ⊕).

efficience [efi'sjãːs] f efficiency; **efficient, e** [~'sjã, ~'sjãːt] efficient.

effigie [efi'ʒi] f effigy.

effilé, e [efi'le] tapering; slender; *tex.* frayed, fringed; *mot.* streamlined; **effiler** [~'le] (1a) *v/t. tex.* fray, unravel; taper; *cuis.* string (*beans*); **effilocher** *tex.* [~lɔ'ʃe] (1a) *v/t.* ravel out; fray; break (*cotton waste etc.*).

efflanqué, e [eflɑ̃'ke] lean, F skinny, lanky; *fig.* inadequate (*style*).

effleurer [eflœ're] (1a) *v/t.* graze, touch lightly; brush; skim (*the water*); ✔ plough lightly; *fig.* touch lightly upon (*a subject*).

efflorescence [eflɔrɛ'sɑ̃:s] *f* ♀ flowering; ♒ efflorescence; ✚ rash, eruption.

effluent, e [efly'ɑ̃, ~'ɑ̃:t] *adj., a. su./m* effluent; **effluve** [e'fly:v] *m* effluvium; exhalation; *fig.* breath; ✚ ~ électrique glow discharge.

effondrement [efɔ̃drə'mɑ̃] *m* collapse (*a.* ✝, *a. fig.*); caving in; ✝ *prices:* slump; ✔ trenching; **effondrer** [~'dre] (1a) *v/t.:* s'~ collapse; cave in; break down.

efforcer [efɔr'se] (1k) *v/t.:* s'~ de *or* à (*inf.*) do one's best to (*inf.*); strive to (*inf.*).

effort [e'fɔːr] *m* effort, exertion; pressure; ⊕ stress; ⊕, ✚ strain; *sp. ball:* spin.

effraction ⚖ [efrak'sjɔ̃] *f* breaking open; *vol m avec* ~ house-breaking (*by day*), burglary (*by night*).

effrayant, e [efrɛ'jɑ̃, ~'jɑ̃:t] terrifying, dreadful, appalling; *fig.* awful; **effrayer** [~'je] (1i) *v/t.* frighten, scare, terrify; s'~ take fright, be frightened (at, de).

effréné, e [efre'ne] unbridled, unrestrained.

effriter [efri'te] (1a) *v/t.* crumble; cause to crumble; s'~ crumble.

effroi [e'frwa] *m* terror, fear, fright; dread.

effronté, e [efrɔ̃'te] brazen-faced, impudent; saucy (*child*); **effronterie** [~'tri] *f* effrontery, impudence, impertinence.

effroyable [efrwa'jabl] frightful (*a. fig.*).

effusion [efy'zjɔ̃] *f* effusion (*a. fig.*); outpouring; ~ *de sang* bloodshed; ✚ haemorrhage; *avec* ~ effusively.

égailler [ega'je] (1a) *v/t. a.* s'~ scatter (*birds*).

égal, e, *m/pl.* **-aux** [e'gal, ~'go] **1.** *adj.* equal; level, smooth; even (*a. fig.*), regular; steady (*pace*); *cela*

m'est ~ it is all the same to me, I don't mind; F *c'est* ~ all the same; **2.** *su.* equal, peer; *su./m: à l'*~ *de* as much as; **égaler** [ega'le] (1a) *v/t.* regard as equal; be equal to, equal; *fig.* compare with, F touch; **égaliser** [egali'ze] (1a) *v/t.* equalize (*a. sp.*); level; make even; Å equate; **égalitaire** [~'te:r] *adj., a. su.* egalitarian; **égalité** [~'te] *f* equality; evenness (*a. fig., a.* ♪); *sp. à* ~ equal on points.

égard [e'gaːr] *m* regard, consideration, respect; ~s *pl.* respect *sg.*; attentions (to, *pour*); *à cet* ~ in this respect; *à l'*~ *de* with respect to; as regards; *à mon* ~ concerning me; *à tous* ~s in every respect; *eu* ~ à considering; *manque m d'*~ lack of consideration; slight; *par* ~ *pour* out of respect for; *sans* ~ *pour* without regard for.

égarement [egar'mɑ̃] *m* mislaying; error; *fig.* (*mental*) aberration; *feelings:* frenzy; *conduct, expression:* wildness; bewilderment; **égarer** [ega're] (1a) *v/t.* mislay; lead astray; mislead; let (*one's eyes*) wander; bewilder; *fig. avoir l'air égaré* look distraught; s'~ lose one's way; go astray; become unhinged (*mind*).

égayer [egɛ'je] (1i) *v/t.* cheer up; enliven; s'~ amuse o.s.; cheer up; make merry (about, de).

églantier ♀ [eglɑ̃'tje] *m* wild rose (-bush); ~ *odorant* sweet briar; **églantine** ♀ [~'tin] *f flower:* wild rose; ~ *odorante flower:* sweet briar.

église [e'gliːz] *f* church.

églogue [e'glɔg] *f* eclogue.

égocentrique [egɔsɑ̃'trik] egocentric.

égoïne ⊕ [egɔ'in] *f* compass saw.

égoïsme [egɔ'ism] *m* egoism; selfishness; **égoïste** [~'ist] **1.** *su.* egoist; **2.** *adj.* egoistic; selfish.

égorger [egɔr'ʒe] (11) *v/t.* cut the throat of; F stick (*a pig*); slaughter, massacre (*people*); *fig.* fleece; **égorgeur** *m*, **-euse** *f* [~'ʒœːr, ~'ʒøːz] cut-throat; (*pig-*)sticker.

égosiller [egozi'je] (1a) *v/t.:* s'~ bawl; shout; make o.s. hoarse.

égout [e'gu] *m* sewer; **égoutter** [egu'te] (1a) *v/t.* drain (*a.* ✔); strain (*vegetables*); s'~ drain, drip; **égouttoir** [~'twaːr] *m* drainer; *cuis.* plate-rack.

égrapper [egra'pe] (1a) v/t. pick off (grapes etc.); ✗ clean (ore).

égratigner [egrati'ɲe] (1a) v/t. scratch (a. ✗); fig. gibe at, F have a dig at; **égratignure** [~'ɲy:r] f scratch; fig. gibe, F dig.

égrener [egrə'ne] (1d) v/t. pick off (grapes); shell (peas, corn); gin (cotton); ripple (flax); tree: shed (the leaves) one by one; fig. deal with one by one; s'~ drop (away), scatter.

égrillard, e [egri'ja:r, ~'jard] ribald, lewd, F dirty.

eh! [e] int. hey!; hi!; ~ bien! well!; now then!

éhonté, e [eɔ̃'te] shameless.

éjaculer [eʒaky'le] (1a) v/t. ejaculate.

éjection [eʒek'sjɔ̃] f ejection.

élaborer [elabɔ're] (1a) v/t. elaborate, work out (a. fig.).

élaguer [ela'ge] (1m) v/t. ✗ prune (a. fig.); fig. a. cut out or down.

élan¹ [e'lɑ̃] m spring, dash, bound; impetus; fig. impulse; fig. outburst (of temper etc.).

élan² zo. [~] m elk, moose.

élancé, e [elɑ̃'se] (tall and) slim, slender; **élancement** [elɑ̃s'mɑ̃] m spring; fig. yearning (towards, vers); 🖉 twinge, shooting pain; **élancer** [elɑ̃'se] (1k) v/i. twinge, throb; v/t.: s'~ shoot; rush; ♀ shoot up.

élargir [elar'ʒi:r] (2a) v/t. enlarge; widen; broaden (a. fig.); fig., a. 🕮 release; **élargissement** [~ʒis'mɑ̃] m enlarging; widening, broadening, fig., a. 🕮 release.

élasticité [elastisi'te] f elasticity; fig. springiness; **élastique** [~'tik] 1. adj. elastic; fig. flexible; gomme f ~ (india-)rubber; 2. su./m (india-)rubber; cost. elastic; rubber band.

électeur [elɛk'tœ:r] m pol. voter; elector (a. hist.); ~ par correspondance absent voter; **électif, -ve** [~'tif, ~'ti:v] elective; **élection** [~'sjɔ̃] f election (a. fig.); fig. choice; ~s pl. partielles by-election sg.; **électoral, e**, m/pl. **-aux** [~tɔ'ral, ~'ro] electoral, election ...; **électoralisme** pej. [~tɔra'lism] m electioneering; **électorat** [~tɔ'ra] m coll., a. hist. electorate; franchise; **électrice** [~'tris] f pol. electress (a. hist.), voter.

électricien [elɛktri'sjɛ̃] m electrician; **électricité** [~si'te] f electricity; **électrifier** [~'fje] (1o) v/t. elec-

trify; **électrique** [elɛk'trik] electric; electrical (unit); **électriser** [~tri'ze] (1a) v/t. electrify (a. fig.); fig. thrill; fil m électrisé live wire.

électro... [elɛktrɔ] electro...; **~aimant** [~ɛ'mɑ̃] m electro-magnet; **~cardiogramme** 🖉 [~kardjɔ'gram] m electrocardiogram; **~choc** 🖉 [~'ʃɔk] m treatment: electric shock.

électrode [elɛk'trɔd] f electrode.

électro...: **~magnétique** [elɛktrɔmaɲe'tik] electromagnetic; **~ménager** [~mena'ʒe] adj./m: appareils m/pl. ~s domestic electrical equipment sg.

électron phys. [elɛk'trɔ̃] m electron; **électronicien** [~trɔni'sjɛ̃] m electronics engineer; **électronique** [~trɔ'nik] 1. adj. electronic; 2. su./f electronics sg.

électrophone [elɛktrɔ'fɔn] m record player.

électuaire [elɛk'tɥɛ:r] m electuary.

élégamment [elega'mɑ̃] adv. elegantly; **élégance** [~'gɑ̃:s] f elegance; **élégant, e** [~'gɑ̃, ~'gɑ̃:t] 1. adj. elegant, stylish; smart; 2. su./m man of fashion; su./f woman of fashion.

élément [ele'mɑ̃] m element; ingredient; ⚡ cell; ~s pl. rudiments, first principles, basics; **élémentaire** [~mɑ̃'tɛ:r] elementary; rudimentary; fundamental, basic.

éléphant zo. [ele'fɑ̃] m elephant; ~ femelle cow-elephant.

élevage [el'va:ʒ] m breeding, rearing; ranch; **élévateur, -trice** [eleva'tœ:r, ~'tris] 1. adj. lifting; anat. elevator (muscle); 2. su./m elevator (a. anat.); lift; **élévation** [~'sjɔ̃] f elevation (a. ⚗, △); lifting; raising; rise, increase; height; altitude (a. astr.); **élévatoire** [~'twa:r] hoisting.

élève [e'lɛ:v] su. pupil; univ. student; apprentice; su./f young rearing animal; cattle etc.: breeding; ✗ seedling.

élevé, e [el've] high; fig. lofty; bred, brought-up; mal ~ ill-bred; **élever** [~'ve] (1d) v/t. raise (a. ⚗), lift; △ erect, set up; breed (cattle etc.); keep (bees, hens); bring up (a child); ⚗ ~ au carré (au cube) square (cube); s'~ rise; get up; amount (to, à); protest, take a stand (against, contre); **éleveur** [~'vœ:r] m breeder (of horses, cattle); ~ de élevure   184

chiens dog-fancier; **élevure** ⚕ [~-
'vy:r] *f* pimple, pustule.
élider *gramm.* [eli'de] (1a) *v/t.*
elide.
éligible [eli'ʒibl] eligible.
élimer [eli'me] (1a) *v/t. a. s'~* wear
threadbare.
éliminer [elimi'ne] (1a) *v/t.* elimi-
nate (*a.* ⚕); get rid of; ⚕ *s'~* cancel
out.
élire [e'li:r] (4t) *v/t.* elect, choose;
parl. return (*a member*).
élision *gramm.* [eli'zjɔ̃] *f* elision.
élitaire [eli'tɛ:r] elitist; **élite** [e'lit] *f*
elite, pick, choice, best; *d'~* picked;
crack (*team etc.*).
élixir [elik'si:r] *m* elixir.
elle [ɛl] *pron./pers./f subject:* she, it; ~s
pl. they; *object:* her, it; (to) her, (to)
it; ~s *pl.* them; (to) them; *à ~* to her,
to it; hers, its; *à ~s pl.* to them; theirs;
c'est~ it is she, F it's her; *ce sont~s pl.,*
F *c'est ~s pl.* it is they, F it's them.
ellébore ⚘ [elle'bɔ:r] *m* hellebore; ~
noir Christmas rose.
elle-même [ɛl'mɛ:m] *pron./rfl.* herself; *elles-mêmes pl.* themselves.
ellipse [e'lips] *f gramm.* ellipsis; ⚕
ellipse; **elliptique** [elip'tik] ellip-
tic(al).
élocution [elɔky'sjɔ̃] *f* elocution.
éloge [e'lɔ:ʒ] *m* praise; eulogy, panegyric.
éloigné, e [elwa'ɲe] remote; distant
(*a. relative*); far-off, faraway; far
(off *or* away); **éloignement** [elwaɲ-
'mã] *m* distance; remoteness; removal; *fig.* estrangement; **éloigner**
[elwa'ɲe] (1a) *v/t.* remove; move
(*s.th.*) away; dismiss (*a thought*);
avert (*a suspicion, a danger*); postpone; estrange (*s.o.*); *s'~* move away,
go away; digress (*s.o.*); *s'~ du sujet* wander
from the subject, divagate.
éloquence [elɔ'kã:s] *f* eloquence;
éloquent, e [~'kã, ~'kã:t] eloquent.
élucider [elysi'de] (1a) *v/t.* elucidate, clear up.
élucubrations [elykybra'sjɔ̃] *f/pl.
pej.* wild imaginings.
éluder [ely'de] (1a) *v/t. fig.* evade;
shirk (*work*).
Élysée [eli'ze] **1.** *su./m myth.* Ely-
sium; *pol.* Élysée (= *Paris residence of
the President of the French Republic*);
2. *adj. myth.* Elysian (*Fields*).
émacier [ema'sje] (1o) *v/t. s'~* waste
away, become emaciated.

émail, *pl.* -aux [e'ma:j, ~'mo] *m* enamel (*a. of teeth*); enamelling material; *phot.* glaze; **émailler** [ema-
'je] (1a) *v/t.* enamel; glaze (*porcelain, a. phot.*); *fig.* sprinkle, spangle
(with, *de*).
émanation [emana'sjɔ̃] *f* emanation;
efflux.
émancipation [emãsipa'sjɔ̃] *f* eman-
cipation; **émancipé, e** *fig.* [~'pe]
free, forward; **émanciper** [~'pe]
(1a) *v/t.* emancipate.
émaner [ema'ne] (1a) *v/i.* emanate,
issue, originate.
émarger [emar'ʒe] (1l) *v/t.* make
marginal notes in, write in the
margin of; *v/i.* † draw one's salary.
émasculation [emaskyla'sjɔ̃] *f*
emasculation (*a. fig.*).
embâcle [ã'ba:kl] *m* obstruction;
ice-jam (*in water-way*).
emballage [ãba'la:ʒ] *m* packing;
package; packaging; *sp.* burst of
speed; F blowing-up; ⚓ ~ *perdu*
(*consigné*) non-returnable (return-
able) packing (or can, bottle, *etc.*);
emballer [~'le] (1a) *v/t.* pack (up);
wrap up; *mot.* race (*the engine*); F
thrill, excite; F blow (*s.o.*) up; *sl.*
arrest; *sl.* get (*s.o.*) round; *s'~* bolt
(*horse*); race (*engine*); F get excited; F
fly into a temper; *v/i. sp.* spurt;
emballeur *m,* -euse *f* [~'lœ:r,
~'lø:z] packer; *sl.* cajoler.
embarbouiller F [ãbarbu'je] (1a)
v/t. dirty; *fig.* muddle (*s.o.*); *s'~* get
muddled.
embarcadère [ãbarka'dɛ:r] *m* ⚓
landing-stage; wharf, quay; ⚓ (departure) platform; **embarcation**
[~'sjɔ̃] *f* craft; ship's boat.
embardée [ãbar'de] *f* swerve.
embargo ⚓, *pol.* [ãbar'go] *m* embargo.
embarquement [ãbarkə'mã] *m* ⚓
embarkation; *goods:* shipment;
embarquer [~'ke] (1m) *v/t.* ⚓
embark; ship (*goods,* F *a. water*); take
on board; *v/i. a. s'~* embark (*a. fig.*
upon, *dans*), go aboard.
embarras [ãba'ra] *m* obstruction;
impediment (*of speech*); difficulty,
trouble; embarrassment; ~ *pl. d'argent* money difficulties; ~ *de voitures*
traffic jam; F *faire des* ~ make a fuss;
embarrasser [~ra'se] (1a) *v/t.* clutter (up); hinder; bother; put in an
awkward position; *fig.* perplex,

puzzle; ✵ clog *(the digestion)*; s'~ *de* burden o.s. with.

embasement △ [ābaz'mã] *m* base; ground-table.

embauchage [ābo'ʃaːʒ] *m*, **embauche** [ā'boːʃ] *f* taking on *(of workmen)*; hiring; *labour: pas d'embauche* no vacancies; **embaucher** [ābo'ʃe] (1a) *v/t.* take on, hire; **embauchoir** [~'ʃwaːr] *m* boot tree.

embaumé, e [ābo'me] balmy *(air)*; **embaumer** [~] (1a) *v/t.* embalm *(a corpse, a. the garden)*; scent, perfume; smell of; *v/i.* smell sweet.

embecquer [ābɛ'ke] (1m) *v/t.* feed *(a bird)*; bait *(the hook)*.

embéguiner [ābegi'ne] (1a) *v/t.* wrap up *(s.o.'s)* head (in, *de*); *fig.* infatuate; s'~ *de* become infatuated with *(s.o.)*.

embellie [ābɛ'li] *f* ✥ lull; fair period; **embellir** [~'liːr] (2a) *v/t.* make (look) more attractive; embellish *(a. fig.)*; beautify; *fig.* glamorize; *v/i.* become better-looking; **embellissement** [~lis'mã] *m* embellishment; improvement in looks.

emberlificoter *sl.* [ābɛrlifiko'te] (1a) *v/t.* entangle; get round, cajole; s'~ get tangled; get in a muddle.

embêtant, e F [ābɛ'tã, ~'tãːt] annoying, irritating, tiresome; **embêtement** F [ābɛt'mã] *m* nuisance; worry; annoyance; F bother; **embêter** F [ābɛ'te] (1a) *v/t.* annoy; bore; get on *(s.o.'s)* nerves.

emblave ⚴ [ā'blaːv] *f* land sown with corn; *corn:* sown seed; **emblaver** ⚴ [ābla've] (1a) *v/t.* sow with corn.

emblée [ā'ble] *adv.: d'~* right away, then and there, at the first attempt.

emblème [ā'blɛːm] *m* emblem; symbol; badge.

embob(el)iner F [ābɔb(l)i'ne] (1a) *v/t.* get round, coax.

emboîter [ābwa'te] (1a) *v/t.* encase; nest *(boats, boxes, tubes)*; pack in boxes; ⊕ joint; F hiss, hoot; ~ *le pas à q.* dog s.o.'s footsteps; ✕ fall into step with s.o.; *fig.* model o.s. on s.o.; **emboîture** [~'tyːr] *f* fit; ⊕ socket; ⊕ joint; ✵ juncture.

embolie ✵ [ābɔ'li] *f* embolism.

embonpoint [ābɔ̃'pwɛ̃] *m* stoutness; plumpness.

emboucher [ābu'ʃe] (1a) *v/t.* ♪ put to one's mouth; *fig. mal embouché*

foul-mouthed; **embouchure** [~'ʃyːr] *f river:* mouth; ♪ mouthpiece; opening.

embourber [ābur'be] (1a) *v/t.* bog; *fig.* implicate; s'~ get stuck in the mud *(etc.)*; *fig.* get tied up.

embourgeoiser [āburʒwa'ze] (1a) *v/t.:* s'~ become conventional.

embout [ā'bu] *m stick, umbrella:* ferrule.

embouteillage [ābutɛ'jaːʒ] *m* bottling; ✥ bottling up; *fig.* traffic jam; ✝ bottleneck; **embouteiller** [~'je] (1a) *v/t.* bottle; ✥ bottle up, block up; *fig.* hold up *(the traffic)*; block *(the road)*.

embouter [ābu'te] (1a) *v/t.* tip, put a ferrule on.

emboutir [ābu'tiːr] (2a) *v/t.* ⊕ stamp, press *(metal)*; emboss; tip, put a ferrule on; *mot.* hit, run *or* crash into.

embranchement [ābrãʃ'mã] *m* junction; branching (off); ⊕, *a. fig.* branch; 🚂 branch-line; 🚂 siding; fork *(of a road)*; branch-road; *geog.* spur; **embrancher** [ābrã'ʃe] (1a) *v/t.* join up; 🚂 form a junction *(roads)*; branch off (from, *sur*).

embrasement [ābraz'mã] *m* conflagration; *fig.* fire; *fig.* burning passion; *pol.*, *fig.* conflagration; **embraser** [ābra'ze] (1a) *v/t.* set on fire; *fig.* fire; *fig.* set aglow.

embrassade [ābra'sad] *f* embrace, hug; kissing; **embrasser** [~'se] (1a) *v/t.* embrace *(a. fig.)*; hug; *fig.* take up *(a career, a cause)*; *fig.* encircle; kiss; include, take in.

embrasure [ābra'zyːr] *f* embrasure; window-recess; ✥ gun-port.

embrayage [ābrɛ'jaːʒ] *m* ⊕ connecting, coupling; *mot.* clutch: engaging; putting *(the engine)* into gear; *mot.* clutch; *mot.* ~ *à* cône cone clutch; *mot.* ~ *à disques* multi-disc clutch; **embrayer** [~'je] (1i) *v/t.* ⊕ connect, couple; throw into gear; F *fig.* start, set *(s.th.)* rolling; *v/i. mot.* let in the clutch; F *fig.* start, begin.

embrigader [ābriga'de] (1a) *v/t.* ✕ recruit; *fig.* enrol; F organize.

embrocher [ābrɔ'ʃe] (1a) *v/t. cuis.* (put on the) spit; ⚡ wire on to a circuit; F run *(s.o.)* through.

embrouillage [ābru'jaːʒ] *m*, **embrouillement** [ābruj'mã] *m* confusion; tangle; **embrouillamini** F

embrouiller [ăbrujami'ni] *m* tangle, mess(-up); **embrouiller** [ăbru'je] (1a) *v/t.* tangle (up); muddle (up); *fig.* confuse (*an issue*); s'~ get into a tangle; *fig.* get into a muddle.

embroussaillé, e [ăbrusa'je] covered with bushes; *fig.* tousled; F complicated.

embruiné, e [ăbrɥi'ne] ✔ blighted with cold drizzle; lost in a haze of rain.

embrumer [ăbry'me] (1a) *v/t.* shroud with mist *or* haze *or* fog; *fig.* cloud.

embruns [ă'brœ̃] *m/pl.* sea spray *sg.*, spindrift *sg.*

embrunir [ăbry'ni:r] (2a) *v/t.* darken.

embryon [ăbri'jɔ̃] *m* embryo (*a. fig.*); F insignificant little man.

embûche [ă'by:ʃ] *f* trap, pitfall; † ambush.

embuer [ă'bɥe] (1n) *v/t.* steam up; dim (*a. fig.*).

embuscade [ăbys'kad] *f* ambush; **embusqué** [~'ke] *m* man in ambush; man under cover; F ⚔ shirker, dodger; **embusquer** ⚔ *etc.* [~'ke] (1m) *v/t.* place in ambush *or* in wait; s'~ lie in wait; take cover; F ⚔ shirk.

éméché, e e F [eme'ʃe] slightly the worse for drink *or* F for wear.

émeraude [em'ro:d] *su./f, a. adj./inv.* emerald.

émerger [emɛr'ʒe] (1l) *v/i.* emerge; come into view, appear.

émeri [em'ri] *m* emery(-powder).

émérite [eme'rit] emeritus (*professor*); experienced, practised.

émersion [emɛr'sjɔ̃] *f* emergence (*a. opt.*); *astr.* emersion.

émerveiller [emɛrvɛ'je] (1a) *v/t.* amaze, fill with wonder; s'~ marvel, be amazed (at, *de*).

émétique ✎ [eme'tik] *adj., a. su./m* emetic.

émetteur, -trice [emɛ'tœ:r, ~'tris] **1.** *adj.* issuing; *radio*: transmitting, broadcasting; **2.** *su./m* † issuer; *radio*: transmitter; ~ à modulation de fréquence V.H.F. transmitter; ~ à ondes courtes short wave transmitter; ~ de télévision television transmitter; ~-récepteur *radio*: transmitter-receiver, F walkie-talkie; **émettre** [e'mɛtr] (4v) *v/t.* emit, send out; † issue; utter (*a*

sound, *a.* counterfeit coins); express (*an opinion*); *radio*: transmit, broadcast; put forward (*a claim*).

émeute [e'mø:t] *f* riot, disturbance; **émeutier** [emø'tje] *m* rioter.

émietter [emjɛ'te] (1a) *v/t.* crumble; *fig.* waste.

émigration [emigra'sjɔ̃] *f* emigration; **émigré, e** [~'gre] *su.* expatriate; **émigrer** [~'gre] (1a) *v/i.* emigrate (*people*); *pol.* fly the country.

émincé *cuis.* [emɛ̃'se] *m* sliced meat; **émincer** [~] (1k) *v/t.* mince, slice (up) (*meat*).

éminemment [emina'mã] *adv.* to a high degree; **éminence** [~'nã:s] *f* eminence (*a. fig., a. title*); **éminent, e** [~'nã, ~'nã:t] eminent; high, elevated; *fig.* distinguished.

émissaire [emi'sɛ:r] **1.** *su./m* emissary (*a.* ⊕), messenger; ⊕ outlet; *anat.* emissary vein; **2.** *adj.*: bouc *m* ~ scapegoat; **émission** [~'sjɔ̃] *f* emission; † issue, issuing; uttering (*of sound, a.* of counterfeit coins); *heat*: radiation; *radio*: transmission, broadcast(ing); ~ de télévision television transmission.

emmagasiner [ămagazi'ne] (1a) *v/t.* † store, warehouse; ⚡, *phys., a. fig.* store up.

emmailloter [ămajɔ'te] (1a) *v/t.* swaddle (*a baby*); swathe (*one's leg etc.*).

emmancher [ămã'ʃe] (1a) *v/t.* fix a handle to, haft; ⊕ joint (*pipes*); *fig.* start (*an affair*).

emmanchure [ămã'ʃy:r] *f* armhole.

emmêler [ămɛ'le] (1a) *v/t.* tangle; *fig.* mix up, get in a tangle *or* muddle.

emménager [ămena'ʒe] (1l) *v/i.* move in; *v/t.* move (*s.o., s.th.*) in, install.

emmener [ăm'ne] (1d) *v/t.* take (*s.o.*) away, lead (*s.o.*) away *or* out.

emmerdant, e ∨ [ămɛr'dã, ~'dã:t] boring; annoying; **emmerder** ∨ [~'de] (1a) *v/t.* bore (*s.o.*) (stiff); get on (*s.o.'s*) nerves; bug, give (*s.o.*) a pain in the neck; s'~ be bored (stiff).

emmieller [ămjɛ'le] (1a) *v/t.* sweeten with honey; *fig.* sugar (*one's words*); ∨ irritate.

emmitoufler [ămitu'fle] (1a) *v/t.* muffle up (in *dans, de*).

émoi [e'mwa] *m* emotion, agitation; excitement; commotion; anxiety.

émollient, e ✻ [emɔ'ljã, ‿'ljãːt] *adj.*, *a. su./m* emollient, counter-irritant.

émoluments [emɔly'mã] *m/pl.* emoluments, pay *sg.*, salary *sg.*

émonder [emɔ̃'de] (1a) *v/t.* ✔ prune (*a. fig. a book*), trim; *fig.* clean.

émotion [emo'sjɔ̃] *f* emotion; *fig.* agitation, disturbance; ✻ quickening (*of pulse*); **émotionnable** [‿sjɔ'nabl] emotional; excitable; **émotionner** F [‿sjɔ'ne] (1a) *v/t.* affect; thrill.

émotivité [emɔtivi'te] *f* emotivity.

émoucher [emu'ʃe] (1a) *v/t.* drive the flies from *or* off; **émouchette** [‿'ʃɛt] *f* fly-net (*for horses*); **émouchoir** [‿'ʃwaːr] *m* fly-whisk; fly-net (*for horses*).

émoudre ⊕ [e'mudr] (4w) *v/t.* grind, sharpen, whet; **émoulu, e** [emu'ly] sharp(ened); *fig. frais ‿ de* fresh from (*school etc.*).

émousser [emu'se] (1a) *v/t.* ⊕ blunt, take the edge off (*a. fig.*); ✔ remove the moss from; ⊕ *s'‿* become blunt(ed) (*a. fig.*); lose its edge *or* point.

émoustiller F [emusti'je] (1a) *v/t.* exhilarate, F ginger up; put on one's mettle; *s'‿* get jolly; cheer up.

émouvant, e [emu'vã, ‿'vãːt] moving, touching; **émouvoir** [‿'vwaːr] (3f) *v/t.* move; affect, touch; stir up, rouse (*the audience, a crowd*).

empailler [ãpɑ'je] (1a) *v/t.* pack (*s.th.*) in straw; stuff (*a dead animal*); ✔ cover up with straw.

empaler [ãpɑ'le] (1a) *v/t.* impale.

empan [ã'pã] *m* span.

empaqueter [ãpak'te] (1c) *v/t.* pack up; wrap up; do up (*a parcel*).

emparer [ãpa're] (1a) *v/t.: s'‿ de* seize, lay hands on; take possession of.

empâté, e [ãpɑ'te] coated (*tongue*); *fig.* thick (*voice*); bloated (*face*); **empâter** [‿] (1a) *v/t.* make thick; *s'‿* put on flesh.

empattement [ãpat'mã] *m mot.* wheel base; ⌂ foundation; ⌂ *wall:* footing.

empaumer F [ãpo'me] (1a) *v/t.* trick (*s.o.*), take (*s.o.*) in.

empêchement [ãpɛʃ'mã] *m* obsta-cle, hindrance; prevention; impediment (*of speech*); *sans ‿* without let or hindrance; **empêcher** [ãpɛ'ʃe] (1a) *v/t.* prevent (from *ger.*, *de inf.*); stop; hinder; *s'‿ de* refrain from, stop o.s. (from) (*doing s.th.*); *on ne peut s'‿ de a.* one cannot help (*doing s.th.*).

empeigne [ã'pɛɲ] *f shoe:* vamp.

empennage ✈ [ãpɛ'naːʒ] *m* tail unit; stabilizer(s *pl.*); *bomb:* fin assembly.

empereur [ãp'prœːr] *m* emperor.

empesé, e F [ãpə'ze] stiff, starchy (*manner etc.*); **empeser** [‿] (1d) *v/t.* starch (*linen etc.*); stiffen.

empester [ãpɛs'te] (1a) *v/t.* stink out (*a room*); stink (of).

empêtrer [ẽpɛ'tre] (1a) *v/t.* hobble (*an animal*); entangle; *fig.* involve (in, *dans*); *fig.* embarrass (*s.o.*).

emphase [ã'faːz] *f* bombast, pomposity; *gramm.* emphasis; **emphatique** [ãfa'tik] bombastic, pompous; grandiloquent; *gramm.* emphatic.

empierrer [ãpjɛ're] (1a) *v/t.* metal (*a road*); pave; 🚊 ballast (*a track*).

empiéter [ãpje'te] (1f) *v/i.* trespass, encroach (upon, *sur*) (*a. fig.*); *v/t.* appropriate (from, *sur*).

empiffrer F [ãpi'frɛ] (1a) *v/t.: s'‿ de* stuff o.s. with.

empiler [ãpi'le] (1a) *v/t.* pile (up); F rob, cheat (out of, *de*); *fig.* F *s'‿ dans* pile into.

empire [ã'piːr] *m* empire; dominion; sway; control; influence; *‿ sur soi-même* self-control.

empirer [ãpi're] (1a) *v/t.* make (*s.th.*) worse; *v/i.* become *or* grow worse.

empirique [ãpi'rik] **1.** *adj.* empirical, rule-of-thumb; **2.** *su./m* empiricist; **empirisme** [‿'rism] *m* empiricism; *fig.* guess-work.

emplacement [ãplas'mã] *m building etc.:* site; place, spot; ⚓ berth (*of a ship*); ✕ *gun:* emplacement; ✕(dis)position (*of troops for battle*), station (*of peace-time troops*).

emplâtre [ã'plɑːtr] *m* ✻ plaster; *mot. etc.* patch.

emplette [ã'plɛt] *f* purchase, shopping.

emplir [ã'pliːr] (2a) *v/t. a. s'‿* fill (up).

emploi [ã'plwa] *m* employment; use; post, job, situation; *‿ du temps*

employé

188

schedule, timetable; *mode* m d'~ directions *pl.* for use; *plein* ~ full employment; *sans* ~ unemployed, jobless; **employé** m, e f [ăplwa'je] employee; clerk; *shop:* assistant; **employer** [~'je] (1h) *v/t.* employ; use; spend (*time*); s'~ be used; s'~ à apply *or* devote o.s. to ([*doing*] *s.th.*); **employeur** m, **-euse** f [~'jœːr, ~'jøːz] employer.

empocher [ăpɔ'ʃe] (1a) *v/t.* pocket (*a. fig.*); *fig.* receive, F get.

empoigner [ăpwa'ɲe] (1a) *v/t.* grip (*a. fig.*); grasp, seize; catch, arrest.

empois [ă'pwɑ] m starch; *tex.* dressing.

empoisonnant, e F [ăpwazɔ'nă, ~'nãːt] irritating, annoying; *fig.* poisonous; **empoisonner** [~'ne] (1a) *v/t.* poison; *fig.* corrupt; *fig.* bore (*s.o.*) to death; reek of; **empoisonneur, -euse** [~'nœːr, ~'nøːz] 1. *su.* poisoner; 2. *adj.* poisonous.

empoissonner [ăpwasɔ'ne] (1a) *v/t.* stock (*a lake etc.*) with fish.

emporté, e [ăpɔr'te] 1. *adj.* hotheaded, hasty; quick-tempered; 2. *su.* hot-headed *or* quick-tempered person; **emportement** [~tə'mã] m (fit of) anger; *avec* ~ angrily; **emporte-pièce** [~tə'pjɛs] m/inv. punch; *fig. à l'*~ cutting, sarcastic; **emporter** [~'te] (1a) *v/t.* carry away, take away; remove; ✂ *etc.* capture; *plats* m/pl. à ~ take-away meals, *Am.* meals to go; *l'*~ win, get the upper hand (of, *sur*); prevail (over, *sur*); *l'*~ *sur a.* get the better of; *fig.* surpass, triumph over; s'~ lose one's temper, flare up; bolt (*horse*).

empoté, e [ăpɔ'te] 1. *adj.* awkward, clumsy; 2. *su.* awkward *or* clumsy person; **empoter** [~] (1a) *v/t.* pot (*jam etc., a.* ✍).

empourprer [ăpur'pre] (1a) *v/t.* tinge with crimson *or* with purple (*grapes*); s'~ flush (*person*); turn red.

empreindre [ă'prɛ̃ːdr] (4m) *v/t.* imprint, stamp, impress; **empreinte** [ă'prɛ̃ːt] f impress, (im-)print, stamp, impression; ~ *digitale* finger-print.

empressé, e [ăprɛ'se] eager; earnest, fervent; willing; fussy; **empressement** [ăprɛs'mã] m eagerness, promptness, readiness; hurry; *avec* ~ readily; *peu d'*~ reluctance; **empresser** [ăprɛ'se] (1a) *v/t.:* s'~

à (*inf.*) be eager to (*inf.*), show zeal in (*ger.*); s'~ *de* (*inf.*) hasten to (*inf.*).

emprise [ă'priːz] f hold (on, *sur*); mastery.

emprisonner [ăprizɔ'ne] (1a) *v/t.* imprison; confine (*s.o. to his room*).

emprunt [ă'prœ̃] m loan; borrowing; *gramm.* loanword; *nom* m d'~ assumed name; ✝ *souscrire à un* ~ subscribe to a loan; **emprunté, e** [ăprœ̃'te] assumed; sham; borrowed; derived; stiff, awkward (*manner etc.*); **emprunter** [~'te] (1a) *v/t.* borrow (from, *of* à); assume (*a name*); take (*a road, a track*); **emprunteur** m, **-euse** f [~'tœːr, ~'tøːz] borrower; ✝ bailee.

empuantir [ăpɥă'tiːr] (2a) *v/t.* make (*s.th.*) stink; infect (*the air*); s'~ become foul.

ému, e [e'my] *p.p. of émouvoir.*

émulateur, -trice [emyla'tœːr, ~'tris] emulative, rival; **émulation** [~'sjɔ̃] f emulation, rivalry, competition; **émule** [e'myl] *su.* emulator, rival, competitor.

émulsion [emyl'sjɔ̃] f emulsion; **émulsionner** [~sjɔ'ne] (1a) *v/t.* emulsify.

en[1] [ă] *prp. place:* in (*France*); at; *direction:* into (*town*); to (*France, town*); *time:* in (*summer*); (with)in (*an hour, two days*); *state:* in (*good health, mourning, prayer, English*); on (*leave, strike, sale*); at (*war, peace*); as, like (*some character*); *change:* into (*decay, oblivion, English*); to (*dust, ashes, pieces*); *material:* of; *ger.:* ~ *dansant* (while) dancing; ~ *attendant* in the meantime; *partir* ~ *courant* run away; ~ *ne pas* (*ger.*) by not (*ger.*); ~ *ville* in town, *Am.* downtown; ~ *tête* at the head (of, *de*); *aller* ~ *ville* go to town; ~ *voiture* in a *or* by car; 🚋 ~ *voiture!* all aboard!; ~ *avion* by air; ~ *arrière* (de) behind; *direction:* ~ *arrière* backward; ~ *avant* in front; *direction:* forward, on; *de* ... ~ ... from ... to ...; ~ (*l'an*) *1789* in 1789; ~ *colère* in anger, angry; ~ *défaut* at fault; ~ *fait* in fact; ~ *hâte* in a hurry; ~ *honnête homme* (*ami*) as *or* like an honest man (a friend); *mettre* ~ *vente* put up for sale; ~ *vérité* really, actually; ~ *vie* alive, living; *changer* des *livres* ~ *francs* change pounds into francs; *briser* ~ *morceaux* break to pieces *or* into bits; ... ~ *bois* (or) wooden (gold) ...; *escalier m* ~ *spirale* spiral staircase; *fertile* (*riche*) ~ fertile (rich) in; ~ *l'honneur de* in hono(u)r of; ~ *punition de* as a punishment for; *docteur m* ~ *droit* Doctor of Laws; *admirer qch.* ~ *q.* admire s.th. about s.o.; *de mal* ~ *pis* from bad to worse; *de plus* ~ *plus* more and more.

en² [~] **1.** *adv.* from there; on that account, for it; ~ *être plus riche* be the richer for it; *j'*~ *viens* I have just come from here; **2.** *pron.* *genitive*: of *or* about *or* by *or* from *or* with him (her, it, them); *quantity or inanimate possessor*: of it *or* them; *partitive use*: some, any, *negative*: not any, none; *sometimes untranslated*: *qu'*~ *pensez-vous?* what do you think (about it)?, what is your opinion?; *qu'*~ *dira-t-on?* what will people say (about it)?; *il* ~ *mourut* he died of it; *il s'*~ *soucie* he worries about it; *j'*~ *ai cinq* I have five (of them); *je vous* ~ *offre la moitié* I offer you a half *or* half of it; *j'*~ *connais qui* ... I know some people who ...; *je connais cet auteur et j'*~ *ai lu tous les livres* I know this author and have read all his books; *j'*~ *ai besoin* I need it *or* some; *je n'*~ *ai pas* I have none, I haven't any; *prenez-*~ take some; *c'*~ *est fait* the worst has happened; *c'*~ *est fait de moi* I am done for; *je vous* ~ *félicite!* congratulations!; *s'*~ *aller* go away.

enamourer [ănamu're] (1a) *v/t.*: *s'*~ fall in love (with, de).

encablure ⚓ [ăka'bly:r] *f* cable('s-length).

encadrement [ăkadrə'mă] *m* framing; frame(work); setting; **encadrer** [~'dre] (1a) *v/t.* frame; enclose, surround; ✕ officer (*a battalion*); ✕ enrol (*recruits*); ✕ straddle (*an objective*).

encager [ăka'ʒe] (1l) *v/t.* put in a cage; ♘ cage.

encaisse [ă'kɛs] *f* ♱ cash (in hand); *box.* punishment; **encaissé, e** [ăke'se] encased; deep (*valley*); sunken (*road*); **encaisser** [~] (1b) *v/t.* ♱ box, encase; ✔ plant in tubs; ♱ collect, (en)cash (*a bill,*

money); ⊕ embank (*a river*); ballast (*a road*); *fig.* swallow (*an insult*); *fig.* stand, bear; F ~ *une gifle* get one's ears boxed.

encan [ăkă] *m* (public) auction; *mettre à l'*~ put (*s.th.*) up for auction.

encanailler [ăkana'je] (1a) *v/t.* degrade; fill (*the house*) with low company; *s'*~ lower o.s.; keep low company; *fig.* have one's fling.

encapuchonner [ăkapyʃɔ'ne] (1a) *v/t.* put a cowl on; ⊕ cover, hood; *s'*~ put a cowl *or* hood on; *fig.* become a monk.

encaquer [ăka'ke] (1m) *v/t.* ♱ barrel; *fig.* pack (*people*) like sardines.

encartage [ăkar'ta:ʒ] *m* insetting; inset; ♱ card(ing) (*of pins*); **encarter** [~'te] (1a) *v/t.* inset; insert (*a loose leaflet*); card (*pins*).

en-cas [ă'kɑ] *m/inv. cuis.* snack, light meal; stand-by, thing kept for emergencies; dumpy umbrella.

encastrement ⊕ [ăkastrə'mă] *m* fixing; embedding; bed, recess; casing, frame; rigid fixing; **encastrer** ⊕ [~'tre] (1a) *v/t.*: ~ *dans* fit or sink *or* embed into; *s'*~ *dans* fit into.

encaustique [ăkos'tik] *f* encaustic; *floor, furniture*: wax polish; **encaustiquer** [~ti'ke] (1m) *v/t.* wax, polish.

encaver [ăka've] (1a) *v/t.* cellar.

enceindre [ă'sɛ̃:dr] (4m) *v/t.* surround, gird, enclose.

enceinte¹ [ă'sɛ̃:t] *f* enclosure; precincts *pl.*; *box.* ring; surrounding wall(s *pl.*).

enceinte² [~] *adj./f* pregnant.

encens [ă'să] *m* incense; *fig.* flattery; **encenser** [ăsă'se] (1a) *v/t. eccl.* cense; burn incense to; *fig.* flatter; **encenseur** [~'sœ:r] *m eccl.* thurifer; *fig.* flatterer; **encensoir** [~'swa:r] *m* thurible, censer; *fig.* flattery, fulsome praise.

encéphale ✻ [ăse'fal] *m* encephalon, brain; **encéphalite** ✻ [~fa'lit] *f* encephalitis.

encerclement [ăserklə'mă] *m* encircling; **encercler** [~'kle] (1a) *v/t.* encircle, shut in.

enchaînement [ăʃɛn'mă] chain, series, linking; *dog etc.*: chaining (up); *fig.* sequence; **enchaîner** [ăʃɛ'ne] (1b) *v/t.* chain (*a dog, a* *prisoner*); connect, link up (*a. fig. ideas*); *fig.* captivate; *fig.* curb, enchain.

enchanté, e [ãʃã'te] enchanted; delightful (*place*); *fig.* delighted (at, with *de*; to *inf.*, *de inf.*); ~ de vous *voir* pleased to meet you; **enchantement** [ãʃãt'mã] *m* magic; spell; *fig.* charm; *fig.* delight; **enchanter** [ãʃã'te] (1a) *v/t.* bewitch; delight; **enchanteur, -eresse** [~'tœːr, ~'trɛs] **1.** *su. fig.* charmer; *su./m* enchanter; *su./f* enchantress; **2.** *adj.* entrancing; enchanting; delightful, charming.

enchâsser [ãʃã'se] (1a) *v/t.* mount, set (*jewels*, *a.* ⊕); ⊕, *a. fig.* frame, house; *eccl.* enshrine; **enchâssure** [~'syːr] *f* jewel *etc.*: setting; ⊕ *axle*: housing.

enchère [ã'ʃɛːr] *f* bidding, bid; *dernière (folle)* ~ highest (irresponsible) bid; *mettre (or vendre) aux* ~s put up for auction; *vente f aux* ~s auction sale.

enchérir [ãʃe'riːr] (2a) *v/t.* ✝ raise the price of; *v/i.* ✝ grow dearer, go up (*in price*); make a higher bid, go higher; ~ *sur* outbid (*s.o.*); *fig.* outdo (*s.o.*); *fig.* improve on (*s.th.*); **enchérissement** ✝ [~ris'mã] *m* rise (in price); **enchérisseur** [~ri-'sœːr] *m* bidder; *dernier* ~ highest bidder.

enchevêtrer [ãʃvɛ'tre] (1a) *v/t.* halter (*a horse*); *fig.* entangle, confuse; △ join (*joists*).

enclave *pol.* [ã'klaːv] *f* enclave; **enclaver** [ãkla've] (1a) *v/t. pol.* enclave (*a territory*); *fig.* hem in, enclose.

enclenche ⊕ [ã'klãːʃ] *f* gab; **enclencher** [ãklã'ʃe] (1a) *v/t.* ⊕ engage; throw into gear; ⚡ switch on; *fig.* set going. [prone (to, à).]

enclin, e [ã'klɛ̃, ~'klin] inclined,]

enclore [ã'klɔːr] (4f) *v/t.* enclose; wall in, fence in; **enclos** [ã'klo] *m* enclosure; paddock; sheep-fold; (enclosing) wall.

enclume [ã'klym] *f* anvil (*a. anat.*).

encoche [ã'kɔʃ] *f* notch, nick; slot; ⊕ gab; *avec* ~s thumb-indexed; **encocher** [ãkɔ'ʃe] (1a) *v/t.* notch, nick; slot; shove home (*a pin etc.*).

encoffrer [ãkɔ'fre] (1a) *v/t.* lock up (*a. fig.*); *fig.* hoard (*money*).

encoignure [ãkɔ'ɲyːr] *f* corner; corner-cupboard.

encoller [ãkɔ'le] (1a) *v/t.* glue; paste, gum (*paper*); size (*cloth*).

encolure [ãkɔ'lyːr] *f* neck (*a. of horse*); size in collars; neck-line.

encombrant, e [ãkɔ̃'brã, ~'brãːt] cumbersome; bulky (*goods, luggage*); **encombre** [ã'kɔ̃ːbr] *m: sans* ~ without difficulty; **encombrement** [ãkɔ̃brə'mã] *m* obstruction; litter; *traffic:* congestion; ✝ glut; *people:* overcrowding; *article:* bulk (-iness); **encombrer** [~'bre] (1a) *v/t.* encumber; obstruct, block up; clutter up; ✝ glut (*the market*); *fig.* saddle with.

encontre [ã'kɔ̃ːtr] *prp.: à l'*~ *de* against; *aller à l'*~ *de* run counter to.

encorbellement [ãkɔrbɛl'mã] *m* △, ⊕ cantilever; △ corbel-table.

encorder *mount.* [ãkɔr'de] (1a) *v/t.* rope (*climbers*) up; *s'*~ rope up.

encore [ã'kɔːr] **1.** *adv.* still; yet; too, besides; more; once again; ~ *un* another one; ~ *une fois* once again *or* more; *en voulez-vous* ~? do you want some more?; *non seulement* ... *mais* ~ not only ... but also; *pas* ~ not yet; *quoi* ~? what else?; **2.** *cj.*: ~ *que* (*sbj. or cond.*) although (*ind.*).

encorner [ãkɔr'ne] (1a) *v/t.* gore.

encourager [ãkura'ʒe] (1l) *v/t.* encourage; cheer up.

encourir [ãku'riːr] (2i) *v/t.* incur; take (*a risk*).

encrasser [ãkra'se] (1a) *v/t.* dirty, soil, grease; ⊕ clog, choke (*a machine*); *mot.* soot up (*a plug*); foul (*a gun*).

encre [ã:kr] *f* ink; ~ *de Chine* Indian ink; ~ *d'imprimerie* printer's ink; ~ *sympathique* invisible ink; **encrer** *typ.* [ã'kre] (1a) *v/t.* ink; **encrier** [ãkri'e] *m* ink-pot, ink-well; *typ.* ink-trough.

encroûter [ãkru'te] (1a) *v/t.* crust, encrust; cake with mud *etc.*; △ rough-cast; *fig. s'*~ get into a rut.

encuver [ãky've] (1a) *v/t.* vat.

encyclopédie [ãsiklɔpe'di] *f* encyclop(a)edia.

endauber *cuis.* [ãdo'be] (1a) *v/t.* stew; tin, can.

endémique ✱ [ãde'mik] endemic.

endenter [ãdã'te] (1a) *v/t.* tooth, cog (*a wheel*); mesh (*wheels*); indent (*timber*).

endetter [ãdɛ'te] (1a) *v/t. a. s'*~ get into debt.

enflure

endeuiller [ãdœ'je] (1a) v/t. plunge into mourning; fig. shroud in gloom.
endiablé, e [ãdja'ble] possessed; fig. wild; reckless; fig. mischievous.
endiguer [ãdi'ge] (1m) v/t. dam up (a river); dike (land); fig. stem.
endimanché, e [ãdimã'ʃe] in one's Sunday best.
endive ⚕ [ã'diːv] f endive.
endoctriner [ãdɔktri'ne] (1a) v/t. indoctrinate, instruct; F win over (to one's cause).
endolori, e [ãdɔlɔ'ri] sore; tender.
endommager [ãdɔma'ʒe] (1l) v/t. damage; injure.
endormeur m, **-euse** f [ãdɔr'mœːr, ~'møːz] fig. humbug, cajoler; swindler; bore; **endormi, e** [~'mi] 1. adj. asleep; sleepy, drowsy; numb (leg etc.); dormant (passion); 2. su. sleeper; fig. sleepyhead; **endormir** [~'miːr] (2b) v/t. send to sleep; make (s.o.) sleep; numb (the leg etc.); deaden (a pain); fig. bore; fig. lull (a suspicion); fig. hoodwink, beguile (s.o.); s'~ go to sleep (a. fig.); fall asleep; **endormissement** [~mis'mã] m going to sleep; ⚕ passing into inconsciousness; sleepiness, somnolence.
endos † [ã'do] m, **endossement** † [ãdos'mã] m endorsement; **endossataire** † [ãdosa'tɛːr] su. endorsee; **endosser** [~'se] (1a) v/t. † endorse; † back; put on (clothes); fig. assume; ~ qch. à q. saddle s.o. with s.th.; **endosseur** † [~'sœːr] m endorser.
endroit [ã'drwa] m place, spot; site; side; tex. right side; à l'~ de as regards; par ~s in places.
enduire [ã'dɥiːr] (4h) v/t. △ coat, plaster (with, de) (a. fig.); smear (with, de); **enduit** [ã'dɥi] m paint, tar, etc.: coat, coating; △ coat of plaster, plastering; tex. proofing.
endurance [ãdy'rãːs] f endurance; fig. patience; **endurant, e** [~'rã, ~'rãːt] patient, long-suffering.
endurcir [ãdyr'siːr] (2a) v/t. harden (a. fig. the heart); fig. inure (to, à); s'~ harden (a. fig.); become fit or tough.
endurer [ãdy're] (1a) v/t. endure, bear, tolerate.
énergétique [enɛrʒe'tik] ⚕ energizing; ⊕ of energy; **énergie** [~'ʒi] f energy; ⊕ fuel and power; ~ atomi-

que (or nucléaire) atomic or nuclear energy; ⊕ ~ consommée power consumption; **énergique** [~'ʒik] energetic; drastic (measures, steps, remedy); emphatic.
énergumène [enɛrgy'mɛn] su. person in a frenzied state of mind.
énervement [enɛrvə'mã] m exasperation; F state of nerves; **énerver** [~'ve] (1a) v/t. enervate (the body, the will); irritate, annoy; F get on (s.o.'s) nerves.
enfance [ã'fãːs] f childhood; fig. infancy; childishness; dotage; **enfant** [ã'fã] su. child; ~ de chœur eccl. altar boy; F fig. choir boy (= naïve person); ~ gâté spoilt child; fig. pet; fig. ~ terrible enfant terrible; ~ trouvé foundling; d'~ childlike; childish; mes ~s! boys (and girls)!; ⚔ men!; lads!; su./m boy; su./f girl; **enfanter** [ãfã'te] (1a) v/t. give birth to, bear; fig. beget; father (an idea); **enfantillage** [~ti'jaːʒ] m childishness; fig. ~s pl. baby tricks; **enfantin, e** [~'tɛ̃, ~'tin] childish; infantile.
enfariner [ãfari'ne] (1a) v/t. cuis. flour, cover with flour; fig. être enfariné de have a smattering of.
enfer [ã'fɛːr] m hell; ~s pl. the underworld sg.; aller un train d'~ go at top speed.
enfermer [ãfɛr'me] (1a) v/t. shut up; lock up; shut in, enclose.
enferrer [ãfe're] (1a) v/t. pierce; fig. F s'~ be hoist with one's own petard.
enfiévrer [ãfje'vre] (1f) v/t. make (s.o.) feverish; fig. excite, stir up; s'~ grow feverish; fig. get excited.
enfilade [ãfi'lad] f series; rooms: suite; houses: row; fig. string; **enfiler** [~'le] (1a) v/t. thread (a needle); string (pearls etc.); enter, take (a road etc.); slip on (clothes); F (a. s'~) eat, F get through; drink, F knock back.
enfin [ã'fɛ̃] 1. adv. at last, finally; in short, that is to say; 2. int. at last!; still!
enflammer [ãfla'me] (1a) v/t. inflame; set on fire; strike (a match); fig. stir up; s'~ catch fire; fig. flare up; ⚕ inflame.
enfler [ã'fle] (1a) v/t. swell (a. fig.); bloat; puff out (one's cheeks); fig. inflate (one's style); fig. puff (s.o.) up; v/i. a. s'~ swell; **enflure** [ã'flyːr] f ⚕ swelling; fig. style: turgidity.

enfoncement [ãfɔ̃s'mã] *m door*: breaking open; *nail*: driving in; sinking (*a.* ⊕ *of a pile*); *ground*: hollow; ⚠ recess; ⚓ bay; **enfoncer** [ãfɔ̃'se] (1k) *v/t.* break in *or* open; drive in; thrust; ✗ *etc.* break through; F get the better of; F down (*s.o.*); s'~ plunge; sink, go down; subside; go in; *v/i.* sink; **enfonçure** [~'sy:r] *f ground*: hollow; *rock*: cavity; *cask*: bottom. [hide.\

enfouir [ã'fwi:r] (2a) *v/t.* bury.]

enfourchement [ãfurʃə'mã] *m* ⊕ fork link; *wood*: open mortisejoint, slit-and-tongue joint; **enfourcher** [~'ʃe] (1a) *v/t.* get astride, mount (*a bicycle, a horse*); ~ son dada get on to one's pet subject.

enfourner [ãfur'ne] (1a) *v/t.* put in the oven; put in a kiln (*bricks, pottery*); *sl.* gobble (*one's food*).

enfreindre [ã'frɛ̃:dr] (4m) *v/t.* infringe, break, transgress (*the law*); violate (*a treaty*).

enfuir [ã'fɥi:r] (2d) *v/t.*: s'~ flee, run away; escape (from, de); leak (*liquid*).

enfumer [ãfy'me] (1a) *v/t.* fill with smoke; blacken with smoke; smoke out (*bees, animals*).

enfutailler [ãfyta'je] (1a) *v/t.* cask (*wine*).

engagé [ãga'ʒe] **1.** *adj.* ✗ enlisted; *fig.* committed (*literature*); **2.** *su./m* ✗ volunteer; *sp.* entry; **engagement** [ãgaʒ'mã] *m* engagement; promise; bond; pawning; appointment; ✗ enlistment; ✗ skirmish; *sp.* entry; ~s *pl.* liabilities; ✝ sans ~ without obligation; **engager** [ãga-'ʒe] (1l) *v/t.* engage (*a.* ⊕ *machinery*); employ; ✗ enlist; ⊕ take on (*hands*); pawn (*a watch etc.*); pledge (*one's word*); ⚖ institute (*proceedings*); ⊕ put in gear; *fig.* begin, open, ✗ join (*battle*); ⚓ foul (*the anchor etc.*); jam (*a machine*); s'~ undertake, promise (to *inf.*, à *inf.*); commit o.s. (to *inf.*, à *inf.*); take service (with, chez); ⚓ foul; jam (*machine*); ⚓ get out of control; *fig.* enter; *fig.* begin (*battle, discussion*); ✗ enlist; *v/i.* ⊕ (come into) gear.

engainer [ãgɛ'ne] (1b) *v/t.* sheathe, ✿ ensheathe.

engeance *pej.* [ã'ʒã:s] *f* brood, bunch, lot.

engelure ✿ [ãʒ'ly:r] *f* chilblain.

engendrer [ãʒã'dre] (1a) *v/t.* beget; *fig.* engender; produce; generate (*heat*); *fig.* breed (*a disease, contempt*).

engin [ã'ʒɛ̃] *m* machine; tool; device; F gadget, contraption; ✗ ballistic missile; ~s *pl. fishing*: tackle *sg.*

englober [ãglɔ'be] (1a) *v/t.* include, take in; unite, merge.

engloutir [ãglu'ti:r] (2a) *v/t.* swallow; gulp; *fig.* swallow up; *fig.* sink (*money in s.th.*).

engluer [ãgly'e] (1a) *v/t.* lime (*a bird, twigs*); *fig.* trap, ensnare (*s.o.*).

engorger [ãgɔr'ʒe] (1l) *v/t.* block, choke up; ⊕ obstruct; ✿ congest.

engouement [ãgu'mã] *m* ✿ obstruction; *fig.* infatuation (with, pour); **engouer** [~'e] (1a) *v/t.* ✿ obstruct; s'~ ✿ become obstructed; *fig.* become infatuated (with, de).

engouffrer [ãgu'fre] (1a) *v/t.* engulf; F devour (*food*); *fig.* swallow up; s'~ be swallowed up, rush (*wind*); F dive (into, dans).

engoulevent *orn.* [ãgul'vã] *m* nightjar, goatsucker.

engourdir [ãgur'di:r] (2a) *v/t.* (be)numb; *fig.* dull (*the mind*); s'~ grow numb, F go to sleep; *fig.* become sluggish; **engourdissement** [~dis'mã] *m* numbness; *fig.* dullness; ✝ *market*: slackness.

engrais ✿ [ã'grɛ] *m* manure; fattening pasture *or* food; ~ *pl.* azotés nitrate fertilizers, F nitrates; ~ vert manure crop; **engraisser** [ãgrɛ'se] (1a) *v/t.* fatten (*animals*), cram (*poultry*); make (*s.o.*) fat; ✿ manure, fertilize; *v/i.* grow fat; thrive (*cattle*); **engraisseur** [~'sœ:r] *m* fattener; *poultry*: crammer.

engranger ✿ [ãgrã'ʒe] (1l) *v/t.* garner, get in (*the corn*).

engraver [ãgra've] (1a) *v/t.* ⚓ strand (*a ship*); cover (*ground*) with sand *or* gravel; ⚓ s'~ ground; run on to the sand; silt up (*harbour*).

engrenage [ãgrə'na:ʒ] *m* ⊕ gearing; (toothed) gear; throwing *or* coming into gear; *fig.* network, mesh; **engrener** [~'ne] (1d) *v/t.* feed corn into (*a threshing-machine*); feed (*animals*) on corn; ⊕ (put into) gear, engage (*wheels*); *fig.* start (*s.th.*) off, set (*s.th.*) going; s'~ engage, cog, mesh with one another; *v/i.* be in mesh; **engrenure** ⊕ [~'ny:r] *f* gear ratio; engaging.

engrosser *sl.* [ãgrɔ'se] (1a) *v/t.* get (*s.o.*) pregnant, *sl.* knock (*s.o.*) up.

engrumeler [ãgrym'le] (1c) *v/t.*: s'~ clot, curdle.

engueulade *sl.* [ãgœ'lad] *f* telling-off, F dressing-down, blow-up; **engueuler** *sl.* [~'le] (1a) *v/t.* tell (*s.o.*) off, blow (*s.o.*) up, go for (*s.o.*).

enguirlander [ãgirlã'de] (1a) *v/t.* garland; wreathe (with, de); F tell (*s.o.*) off, go for (*s.o.*).

enhardir [ãar'di:r] (2a) *v/t.* embolden; *fig.* encourage (to *inf.*, *à inf.*); s'~ grow bold, take courage; make bold (to, *à*).

énigmatique [enigma'tik] enigmatic; **énigme** [e'nigm] *f* enigma; *parler par* ~s speak in riddles.

enivrement [ãnivrə'mã] *m* intoxication; *fig.* elation; **enivrer** [~'vre] (1a) *v/t.* intoxicate; make (*s.o.*) drunk; *fig.* elate, go to (*s.o.'s*) head; s'~ get drunk.

enjambée [ãʒã'be] *f* stride; **enjambement** [ãʒãb'mã] *m prosody:* run-on line; enjambment; **enjamber** [ãʒã'be] (1a) *v/t.* bestride (*a horse*, *a. fig.*); stride over (*an object*); *fig.* span, straddle; *v/i.* stride; *prosody:* run on (*line*).

enjeu [ã'ʒø] *m gambling*, *a. fig.*: stake.

enjoindre [ã'ʒwɛ̃:dr] (4m) *v/t.* enjoin, order, direct; call upon.

enjôler [ãʒo'le] (1a) *v/t.* wheedle, coax; cajole; **enjôleur, -euse** [~'lœ:r, ~'lø:z] **1.** *su.* coaxer, wheedler; cajoler; **2.** *adj.* wheedling, coaxing; cajoling; 🎵 smooth-tongued.

enjoliver [ãʒoli've] (1a) *v/t.* beautify, embellish; *fig.* embroider (*a story*); **enjoliveur** *mot.* [~'vœ:r] *m* hub cap.

enjoué, e [ã'ʒwe] jaunty, sprightly; playful, lively; **enjouement** [ãʒu'mã] *m* sprightliness; playfulness.

enlacer [ãla'se] (1k) *v/t.* entwine; interlace; embrace, clasp; ⊕ dowel.

enlaidir [ãlɛ'di:r] (2a) *v/t.* disfigure; make (*s.o.*) ugly; *v/i.* grow ugly.

enlevé, e [ãl've] *paint.* dashed off; ♪ (*played*) con brio; **enlèvement** [ãlɛv'mã] *m* removal; carrying off; kidnapping; abduction; ✕ storming; ✝ snapping up (*of goods*); **enlever** [ãl've] (1d) *v/t.* remove; take

away *or* off; lift up; carry off (*a. fig. a prize*); kidnap; abduct; deprive (s.o. of s.th., *qch. à q.*); *fig.* urge on; ✕ storm; *fig.* do (*s.th.*) brilliantly; ~ en arrachant (*grattant*) snatch (rub) away; s'~ take off (*balloon etc.*); peel off (*bark, paint, skin, etc.*); boil over (*milk*); *fig.* flare up (*person*); se faire ~ par elope with.

enliser [ãli'ze] (1a) *v/t.* get (*a car etc.*) stuck in the sand *etc.*; s'~ sink (*in a quicksand*); get bogged, get stuck; *fig.* get bogged down.

enluminer [ãlymi'ne] (1a) *v/t.* illuminate; colo(u)r (*a map etc.*); *fig.* flush, redden; **enluminure** [~'ny:r] *f* illumination; *maps etc.*: colo(u)ring; *fig.* redness, high colo(u)r.

enneigé, e [ãnɛ'ʒe] snow-covered, snow-clad; **enneigement** [ãnɛʒ-'mã] *m* condition of the snow; *bulletin m d'*~ snow report.

ennemi, e [ɛn'mi] **1.** *adj.* enemy ...; hostile (to, de); opposing; **2.** *su.* enemy; adversary.

ennoblir [ãnɔ'bli:r] (2a) *v/t.* ennoble (*a. fig.*).

ennui [ã'nɥi] *m* nuisance, annoyance; boredom, tediousness; *fig.* bore; trouble; ~s *pl.* worries; **ennuyer** [ãnɥi'je] (1h) *v/t.* bore, weary; worry, annoy; s'~ be bored (with, de); long (for, de); *fig.* s'~ mortellement be bored to death, *sl.* be bored stiff; **ennuyeux, -euse** [~'jø, ~'jø:z] boring, tedious, annoying, vexing.

énoncé [enɔ̃'se] *m* statement; wording; **énoncer** [~'se] (1k) *v/t.* state, set forth; express; **énonciation** [~sja'sjɔ̃] *f* stating, declaring; expressing.

enorgueillir [ãnɔrgœ'ji:r] (2a) *v/t.* make (*s.o.*) proud; s'~ de glory in; pride o.s. on.

énorme [e'nɔrm] enormous, tremendous, huge; *pej.* outrageous, shocking; **énormément** [enɔrme-'mã] *adv.* enormously; *fig.* extremely, very; ~ de a great many; **énormité** [~mi'te] *f* vastness, hugeness; *fig.* enormity; gross blunder; *fig.* shocking thing.

enquérir [ãke'ri:r] (2l) *v/t.*: s'~ de inquire *or* ask about; **enquête** [ã'kɛ:t] *f* inquiry; investigation; ~ par sondage sample survey; **enquêter** [ãkɛ'te] (1a) *v/i.* make an investigation; hold an inquiry; **enquêteur** *m*, **-euse** *f* [~'tœːr, ~'tøːz] investigator; pollster.

enquiquiner F [ãkiki'ne] (1a) *v/t.* get on (*s.o.'s*) nerves.

enracinement [ãrasin'mã] *m* taking root; *fig.* deep-rootedness; **enraciner** [~si'ne] (1a) *v/t.* ✔ root; ✔, ⚠ dig in; *fig.* implant; s'~ take root; *fig.* become rooted.

enragé, e [ãra'ʒe] **1.** *adj.* mad; rabid (*dog, a. fig. opinions*); *fig.* keen, enthusiastic; wild (*life*); **2.** *su.* enthusiast; **enrager** [~] (1l) *v/i.* be mad (*a. fig.*); fume; *faire* ~ *q.* tease s.o.; drive s.o. wild.

enrayer [ãrɛ'je] (1i) *v/t.* fit (*a wheel*) with spokes; *fig.* check, stem; ⊕ s'~ jam.

enrégimenter [ãreʒimã'te] (1a) *v/t.* enlist; enrol.

enregistrement [ãrəʒistrə'mã] *m* registration; record(ing); entry; registry (*a. admin.*); *cin., radio, gramophone:* recording; *admin.* register office; **enregistrer** [~'tre] (1a) *v/t.* register (*a.* 🌐); record (*a. cin., radio, music*); *sp.* score (*a goal*); **enregistreur, -euse** [~'trœːr, ~'trøːz] **1.** *adj.* recording; registering; **2.** *su./m* (*tape- etc.*)recorder; ✈ ~ *de vol* flight recorder.

enrhumer [ãry'me] (1a) *v/t.* give (*s.o.*) a cold; s'~ catch (a) cold.

enrichi, e [ãri'ʃi] ⊕ *etc.* enriched (*uranium etc.*), improved; *a. su.* newrich, parvenu, upstart; **enrichir** [~'ʃiːr] (2a) *v/t.* enrich (*a. fig.*); make (*s.o.*) wealthy; s'~ grow rich.

enrober [ãrɔ'be] (1a) *v/t.* coat (with, *de*); imbed (in, *de*).

enrôler [ãro'le] (1a) *v/t.* enrol(l), recruit; ✕ enlist; *l*s'~ enrol(l) (in, *dans*); ✕ enlist.

enroué, e [ã'rwe] hoarse, husky; **enrouement** [ãru'mã] *m* hoarseness, huskiness; **enrouer** [ã'rwe] (1p) *v/t.* make hoarse *or* husky; s'~ become hoarse.

enrouiller [ãru'je] (1a) *v/t.* cover with rust.

enroulement [ãrul'mã] *m* rolling up; ⊕, ✔, ✕, *etc.* winding; wrapping up (in, *dans*); **enrouler** [ãru'le] (1a) *v/t.* roll up; ⊕, ✔, ✕, *etc.* wind; wrap up (in, *dans*).

enrouté, e [ãruti'ne] routine-minded; stick-in-the-mud.

enrubanner [ãryba'ne] (1a) *v/t.* decorate with ribbons.

ensabler [ãsɑ'ble] (1a) *v/t.* ⚓ run (*a ship*) aground; strand; cover (*the soil*) with sand; silt up (*a harbour*); s'~ ⚓ settle in the sand; silt up.

ensacher [ãsa'ʃe] (1a) *v/t.* put into sacks; bag.

ensanglanter [ãsãglã'te] (1a) *v/t.* stain *or* cover with blood.

enseigne [ã'sɛɲ] *su./f* (shop) sign; signboard; *à telle(s)* ~*(s) que* so much so that; *fig. être logé à la même* ~ be in the same boat; *su./m* ✕ † standardbearer; ⚓ sublieutenant, *Am.* ensign.

enseignement [ãsɛɲ'mã] *m* teaching; tuition; education, instruction; *fig.* lesson; ~ *par correspondance* postal tuition; ~ *primaire (secondaire, supérieur)* primary (secondary, higher) education; **enseigner** [ãsɛ'ne] (1a) *v/t.* teach; *fig.* point out; ~ *qch. à q.* teach s.o. s.th.

ensemble [ã'sãːbl] **1.** *adv.* together; at the same time; **2.** *su./m* whole; unity; *cost.* ensemble, suit, outfit; ⊕ set (*of tools*); ⊕ assembly unit; ⚠ block (*of buildings*); ⚠ *grand* ~ housing scheme *or* development; *dans l'*~ on the whole; *d'*~ comprehensive; combined; ⅄ *théorie f des* ~*s* set theory; *vue f d'*~ general view; **ensemblier** [ãsãbli'e] *m* (interior) decorator.

ensemencer ✔ [ãsmã'se] (1k) *v/t.* sow (with, *en*).

enserrer [ãsɛ're] (1a) *v/t.* squeeze; be too tight for; hem in.

ensevelir [ãsə'vliːr] (2a) *v/t.* bury (*a. fig.*); shroud (*a corpse*).

ensiler ✔ [ãsi'le] (1a) *v/t.* silo, silage.

ensoleillé, e [ãsɔlɛ'je] sunny, sunlit.

ensommeillé, e [ãsɔmɛ'je] sleepy, drowsy.

ensorceler [ãsɔrsə'le] (1c) *v/t.* put a spell on; bewitch (*a. fig.*); **ensorceleur, -euse** [~sɔ'lœːr, ~'løːz] **1.** *su. fig.* charmer; *su./m* sorcerer; *su./f* sorceress; **2.** *adj.* bewitching (*a. fig.*); **ensorcellement** [~sɛl'mã] *m* sorcery, witchcraft; spell.

ensuite [ã'sɥit] *adv.* then, after (-wards); next; et ~? what then?

ensuivre [ã'sɥiːvr] (4ee) *v/t.:* s'~ follow, ensue, result (from, *de*).

entablement ⚠ [ãtablə'mã] *m* coping; entablature (*a.* ⊕).

entacher [ăta'ʃe] (1a) *v/t.* sully; taint (with, *de*); ⚖ vitiate; *entaché de nullité* void for want of form.

entaille [ăta:j] *f wood etc.*: notch, nick; groove; *chin etc.*: gash, cut; **entailler** [ˌtɑ'je] (1a) *v/t.* notch, nick (*wood*); groove; gash, cut (*s.o.'s chin etc.*).

entame [ă'tam] *f loaf, meat*: outside slice; **entamer** [ăta'me] (1a) *v/t.* cut into (*a loaf*); open (*a bottle, a jar of jam, etc., a. fig.*); *fig.* smear (*s.o.'s reputation*); begin, start (*a discussion, a quarrel, etc.*); broach (*a cask, a. fig. a subject*); ⚖ institute (*proceedings*); ✂ commence (*operations*).

entasser [ăta'se] (1a) *v/t. a. s'~* pile up; accumulate; crowd together (*people, animals*).

ente [ă:t] *f* ✔ graft, scion; ⊕ *paintbrush*: handle.

entendement [ătăd'mă] *m* understanding; **entendre** [ă'tă:dr] (4a) *v/t.* hear (*a.* ⚖); understand; intend, mean; attend (*a lecture*); *~ dire que* hear that; *~ parler de* hear of; *~ raison* listen to reason; *laisser ~ hint*; *s'~* agree; get on (with, *avec*); get on (together); be heard; *s'~ à* be good at, be an expert at; know all about; **entendu, e** [ătă'dy] **1.** *adj.* agreed; knowing (*smile, etc.*); **2.** *int.* all right; F O.K.; *bien ~!* of course!; **entente** [ă'tă:t] *f* understanding; agreement; meaning; ✝~ *industrielle* combine.

enter [ă'te] (1a) *v/t.* ✔ graft (*a.* ⊕); ⊕ scarf (*timbers*).

entériner ⚖ [ăteri'ne] (1a) *v/t.* ratify, confirm.

entérique *anat.* [ăte'rik] enteric; **entérite** ⚕ [ˌ'rit] *f* enteritis.

enterrement [ătɛr'mă] *m* burial, interment; funeral; **enterrer** [ătɛ-'re] (1a) *v/t.* bury, inter; *fig.* outlive; *fig.* shelve (*a question*).

en-tête [ă'tɛ:t] *m* letterhead; heading; *typ.* headline, *Am.* caption; **entêté, e** [ătɛ'te] obstinate, stubborn, F pig-headed; **entêtement** [ătɛt'mă] *m fig.* obstinacy, stubbornness, F pig-headedness; **entêter** [ătɛ'te] (1a) *v/t. odour*: make (*s.o.*) giddy; go to (*s.o.'s*) head; *s'~* be obstinate; *s'~ à* (*inf.*) persist in (*ger.*).

enthousiasme [ătu'zjasm] *m* enthusiasm; *avec* (*sans*) *~* (un)enthusiastically; **enthousiasmer** [ˌzjas'me] (1a) *v/t.* fill with enthusiasm; *fig.* carry (*s.o.*) away; *s'~* enthuse (over, *pour*); **enthousiaste** [ˌ'zjast] **1.** *adj.* enthusiastic; **2.** *su.* enthusiast (for, *de*).

entichement [ătiʃ'mă] *m* infatuation (for *de, pour*); keenness (on, *pour*); **enticher** [ăti'ʃe] (1a) *v/t.*: *s'~ de* become infatuated with.

entier, -ère [ă'tje, ˌ'tjɛ:r] **1.** *adj.* whole (*a. number*); entire, complete; total; full (*authority, control, fare, etc.*); *fig.* headstrong; *cheval m ~* stallion; **2.** *su./m* entirety; *en ~* in full; completely.

entité *phls.* [ăti'te] *f* entity.

entôler *sl.* [ăto'le] (1a) *v/t.* rob; fleece, *sl.* con.

entomologie [ătɔmɔlɔ'ʒi] *f* entomology.

entonner¹ [ătɔ'ne] (1a) *v/t.* barrel (*wine*).

entonner² ♪ [ˌ] (1a) *v/t.* begin to sing (*a song*); strike up (*a tune*); *eccl.* intone; *fig.* sing (*s.o.'s praises*).

entonnoir [ătɔ'nwa:r] *m* funnel; ✂ crater; *geog.* hollow; *geol.* sink-hole.

entorse ⚕ [ă'tɔrs] *f* sprain, wrench; *se donner une ~* sprain one's ankle.

entortiller [ătɔrti'je] (1a) *v/t.* twist, wind; wrap up; entangle; *fig.* wheedle, get (*s.o.*) round; F express (*views etc.*) in an obscure fashion; *s'~* twine; *fig.* get entangled.

entourage [ătu'ra:ʒ] *m* surroundings *pl.*; setting, frame(work) *pl.*; circle (*of associates, friends, etc.*); attendants *pl.*; ⊕ *machinery*: casing; **entourer** [ˌ're] (1a) *v/t.* surround (with, *de*); encircle (*a.* ✂).

entournure *cost.* [ătur'ny:r] *f* armhole.

entracte [ă'trakt] *m thea., cin.* interval, *Am.* intermission; ♪ interlude.

entraide [ă'trɛ:d] *f* mutual aid; **entraider** [ătrɛ'de] (1b) *v/t.*: *s'~* help one another.

entrailles [ă'trɑ:j] *f/pl.* intestines, entrails, bowels; *fig.* pity *sg.*; compassion *sg.*; *~ de la terre* bowels of the earth.

entrain [ă'trɛ̃] *m* liveliness; spirit, go, mettle.

entraînement [ătrɛn'mă] *m* impetus, force, impulse; *fig.* heat (*of*

discussion); ⊕ *machine*: drive; *sp. etc.*
training; **entraîner** [ãtrɛ'ne] (1a)
v/t. carry away; pull; drag along; *fig.*
lead (*s.o.*), incite (*s.o.*); ⊕ drive; *fig.*
involve; *fig.* give rise to, bring about;
sp. train; *sp.* coach (*a team*); **entraîneur** [ʌ'nœːr] *m sp.* trainer; *team*:
coach; pace-maker; ⊕ driving
device; **entraîneuse** [ʌ'nøːz] dance
hostess.

entrave [ã'traːv] *f* fetter; shackle;
fig. hindrance, obstacle; **entraver**
[ãtra've] (1a) *v/t.* fetter; shackle;
fig. impede, hinder.

entre [ãːtr] *prp.* between (*two points
in space or time*); in (*s.o.'s hands
etc.*); among (*others, other things,
my brothers*); out of (*a number*); ~
eux one another, each other; between themselves; *soit dit* ~ nous
between ourselves, between you
and me and the lamp-post; ~ *amis*
among friends; ~ *quatre yeux* in
private; ~ *deux ages* middle-aged
(*woman*); ~ *la vie et la mort* between
life and death; *moi* ~ *autres* I for
one; d'~ (out) of, (from) among;
l'un (ceux) d'~ eux one (these) of
them; *see* nager.

entre...: **~bâiller** [ãtrəba'je] (1a)
v/t. half-open; **~chats** *fig.* [ʌ'ʃa]
m/pl. capers; **~choquer** [ʌʃɔ'ke]
(1m) *v/t.* clink (*glasses*); s'~ collide;
clash (*a. fig.*); knock against one
another (*bottles etc.*); **~côte** *cuis.*
[ʌ'koːt] *f* entrecôte, rib of beef; **~
couper** [ʌku'pe] (1a) *v/t.* intersect;
fig. interrupt; s'~ *la corde* cut one
another's throats; **~croiser** [ʌ-
krwa'ze] (1a) *v/t. a.* s'~ intersect,
cross; interlock; **~deux** [ʌ'dø]
m/inv. space between, interspace;
⚔ partition; *basket-ball*: center
jump; *cost.* insertion; **~deux-
guerres** [ʌdø'gɛːr] *f or m/inv. the
inter-war years *pl.* (*between World
War I and II*).

entrée [ã'tre] *f* entry; entrance; admission (*a.* ⊕), access; price of entry;
import (duty); *cuis.* entrée; ⊕ inlet,
intake; *fig.* start, beginning; ✝ receipt; ⚓ arrival (*of ship*); *cave, harbour*: mouth; ~ *en vacances school*:
breaking up; ~ *gratuite* free admission; ~ *latérale* side entrance; d'~ (*de
jeu*) from the outset, right from the
beginning, from the very first.

entre...: **~faites** [ãtrə'fɛt] *f/pl.*: *sur*

ces ~ meanwhile, meantime; **~fer**
⚡ [ʌ'fɛr] *m* air-gap; **~filet** [ʌfi'lɛ] *m
newspaper*: paragraph; **~gent** [ʌ'ʒã]
m tact; worldly wisdom; **~lacer**
[ʌla'se] (1k) *v/t.* interlace; inter-
twine; **~lacs** [ʌ'lɑ] *m* ⚔ knotwork;
⚔ tracery; *fig.* tangle; **~lardé, e**
[ʌlar'de] streaky; **~larder** [ʌlar'de]
(1a) *v/t. cuis.* lard; *fig.* interlard (*a
speech*) (with, de); **~ligne** [ʌ'liɲ] *m*
space between lines; interlineation;
~mêler [ʌmɛ'le] (1a) *v/t.* inter-
mingle; intersperse; mix; blend;
fig. intersperse (*a speech*) (with, de);
s'~ mingle; *fig.* s'~ *dans* meddle
with; **~mets** *cuis.* [ʌ'mɛ] *m* sweet;
~metteur, -euse [ʌmɛ'tœːr, ʌ'tøːz]
su. go-between; *su./m* ✝ middleman; procurer; *su./f* procuress; **~
mettre** [ʌ'mɛtr] (4v) *v/t.*: s'~ intervene; act as go-between; **~mise**
[ʌ'miːz] *f* intervention; mediation;
~pont ⚓ [ʌ'põ] *m* between-decks;
d'~ steerage (*passenger*); **~poser** ✝
[ʌpo'ze] (1a) *v/t.* warehouse, store;
put in bond (*at the customs*); **~po-
seur** ✝ [ʌpo'zœːr] *m* warehouseman; *customs*: officer in charge of
a bonded store; **~positaire** ✝ [ʌ-
pozi'tɛːr] *m* warehouseman; *customs*: bonder; **~pôt** [ʌ'po] *m* ✝
warehouse, store, repository; *customs*: bonded warehouse; ⚔ *ammunition*: depot; ~ *frigorifique* cold
store; *en* ~ in bond; **~prenant, e**
[ʌprə'nã, ʌ'nãːt] enterprising; **~
prendre** [ʌ'prãːdr] (4aa) *v/t.* undertake, embark (up)on; contract
for (*work*); *fig.* worry; F *fig.* besiege
(*s.o.*); **~preneur** [ʌprə'nœːr] *m* contractor; ~ *de pompes funèbres*
undertaker, *Am.* mortician; **~prise**
[ʌ'priːz] *f* undertaking; concern; ✝
contract; attempt; ~ *de transport*
carriers *pl.*

entrer [ã'tre] (1a) *v/i.* enter, go *or*
come in; take part, be concerned;
be included; ~ *dans* enter; ~ *dans
une famille* marry into a family; ~
en enter upon (*s.th.*) *or* into (*competition*); *fig.* ~ *en jeu* come into
play; ~ *pour beaucoup dans*
play an important role *or* part in;
faire ~ show (*s.o.*) in(to the room);
drive (*s.th. into s.th.*); *v/t.* bring in,
introduce.

entre...: **~rail** 🚂 [ãtrə'raːj] *m
ga(u)ge; **~sol** ⚔ [ʌ'sɔl] *m floor*: mez-

zanine; **~-temps** [~'tɑ̃] **1.** *m/inv.* interval; *dans l'~* meanwhile; **2.** *adv.* meanwhile; **~teneur** [~tə'nœːr] *m* maintainer; **~tenir** [~tə'niːr] (2h) *v/t.* maintain; keep up; support; talk to (*s.o.*) (about, *de*); entertain (*suspicions, doubts*); s'~ support o.s.; converse, talk (with, *avec*); *sp.* keep o.s. fit; **~tien** [~'tjɛ̃] *m* maintenance; upkeep; conversation; **~toise** △ [~'twaːz] *f* strut, (cross-)brace, cross-piece, tie; **~toisement** △ [~twaz'mɑ̃] *m* (counter)bracing; strutting, staying; **~voir** [~'vwaːr] (3m) *v/t.* catch a glimpse of; *fig.* foresee, have an inkling of; *laisser* ~ disclose, give to understand; **~vue** [~'vy] *f* interview.

entrouvrir [ɑ̃tru'vriːr] (2f) *v/t.* half-open; open (*curtains*) a little; *fig.* s'~ yawn (*chasm*).

énumération [enymera'sjɔ̃] *f* enumeration; *votes:* counting; *facts:* recital; **énumérer** [~'re] (1f) *v/t.* enumerate; count (*votes*); recite (*facts*).

envahir [ɑ̃va'iːr] (2a) *v/t.* overrun; invade; encroach upon; *fig. feeling:* steal *or* come over (*s.o.*); **envahisseur** [~i'sœːr] *m* invader.

envaser [ɑ̃va'ze] (1a) *v/t.* silt up; choke with mud; ⚓ run on the mud; s'~ silt up; ⚓ stick in the mud.

enveloppe [ɑ̃'vlɔp] *f* post, *a.* ✿; envelope; *parcel:* wrapping; ⊕ casing, jacket, lagging; *mot. tyre:* outer cover, casing; *fig.* exterior; ⚡ *cable:* sheathing; ~ *à fenêtre* window envelope; **enveloppement** [ɑ̃vlɔp'mɑ̃] *m* wrapping; ✿ ~ *humide* wet pack; **envelopper** [ɑ̃vlɔ-'pe] (1a) *v/t.* envelop; wrap (up); cover; ✕ encircle (*the enemy*); ⊕ lag; *fig.* involve; *fig.* wrap, shroud (in, *de*).

envenimer [ɑ̃vəni'me] (1a) *v/t.* ✿ poison; aggravate (*a. fig.*); *fig.* embitter (*s.o.*); s'~ ✿ fester; *fig.* grow bitter.

enverguer ⚓ [ɑ̃vɛr'ge] (1m) *v/t.* bend (*the sail*); **envergure** [~'gyːr] *f* ⚓ spread of sail; ✈, *orn., etc.* (wing-)span; spread, breadth; *fig.* calibre; *fig.* scope, scale; *de grande* ~ *a.* large-scale. [*envoyer.*↑
enverrai [ɑ̃vɛ're] *1st p. sg. fut. of* ↓

envers[1] [ɑ̃'vɛːr] *prp.* to(wards).

envers[2] [~] *m tex.* reverse (*a. fig., a. of medal*), wrong side, back; *fig.* seamy side; *à l'~* inside out; *fig.* topsy-turvy.

envi [ɑ̃'vi] *adv.: à l'~* vying with each other; in emulation.

enviable [ɑ̃'vjabl] enviable; **envie** [ɑ̃'vi] *f* envy; longing, desire, fancy; ✿ agnail, F hangnail; ✿ birthmark; *avoir* ~ *de* be in the mood for, have a mind to; *faire* ~ *à q.* make s.o. envious; *porter* ~ *à q.* envy s.o.; **envier** [ɑ̃'vje] (1o) *v/t.* envy; long for; covet; begrudge (s.o. s.th., *qch. à q.*); **envieux, -euse** [ɑ̃'vjø, ~'vjøːz] envious.

environ [ɑ̃vi'rɔ̃] *adv.* about, approximately; **environs** [~'rɔ̃] *m/pl.* vicinity *sg.*; neighbo(u)rhood *sg.*, surroundings; *aux* ~ *de* about (*fifty*), towards (*Christmas*); **environnement** [~rɔn'mɑ̃] *m* surroundings *pl.*; environment; **environner** [~rɔ'ne] (1a) *v/t.* surround; encompass (*a. fig.*).

envisager [ɑ̃viza'ʒe] (11) *v/t.* envisage; consider, view, contemplate; ~ *de* (*inf.*) think of (*ger.*), consider (*ger.*), contemplate (*ger.*).

envoi [ɑ̃'vwa] *m* sending, dispatch (*a.* ✕); consignment, parcel; *post:* delivery; ~ *par bateau* shipment; *coup m d'~ foot.* kickoff; *fig.* (starting) signal; ✝ *lettre f d'~* letter of advice.

envol [ɑ̃'vɔl] *m orn.* (taking) flight; ✈ taking off, takeoff; **envoler** [ɑ̃vɔ'le] (1a) *v/t.:* s'~ fly away; ✈ take off; *fig.* fly (*time*); ✝ zoom (up) (*prices etc.*).

envoûter [ɑ̃vu'te] (1a) *v/t. fig.* put under a spell, bewitch.

envoyé, e [ɑ̃vwa'je] **1.** *p.p. of envoyer;* **2.** *su.* envoy, messenger; *su./m: journ.* ~ *spécial* special correspondent; **envoyer** [~] (1r) *v/t.* send; forward; fling, hurl; shoot, fire; ~ *chercher* send for; ~ *coucher* (*or promener*) send (*s.o.*) packing, send (*s.o.*) about his business; *sl.* s'~ get saddled with (*work*); gulp down (*wine*), get outside (*a meal*).

enzyme [ɑ̃'zim] *m* enzyme.

éolien, -enne [eɔ'ljɛ̃, ~'ljɛn] **1.** *adj.* Aeolien (*harp etc.*); **2.** *su./f* windmill (*for pumping*); air-motor.

épagneul *m,* **e** *f* [epa'nœl] spaniel.

épais, e [e'pɛ, ~'pɛːs] thick; dense (*a. fig. mind*); *fig.* dull (*person*); stout (*glass*); **épaisseur** [epɛ'sœːr] *f* thickness; depth; density; *fig.* denseness; **épaissir** [~'siːr] (2a) *v/t.* thicken; *v/i. a. s'~* thicken, become thick; *cuis.* jell; grow stout (*person*).

épanchement [epɑ̃'mɑ̃] *blood*: effusion (*a. fig.*); *fig.* outpouring; **épancher** [epɑ̃'ʃe] (1a) *v/t.* pour out; *s'~* pour (out); *fig.* open one's heart.

épandage ✔ [epɑ̃'daːʒ] *m* manuring; *champs m/pl. d'~* sewage farm *sg.*; **épandre** [e'pɑ̃dr] (4a) *v/t.* spread; shed (*light*); pour out (*a liquid*); *s'~* spread.

épanoui e [epa'nwi] ❦ in full bloom; *fig.* beaming; cheerful; **épanouir** [~'nwiːr] (2a) *v/t.* ❦ open (out); *s'~* bloom (*flower, a. fig.*); open up; *fig.* light up (*face*).

épargne [e'parɲ] *f* economy, thrift; saving; ✝ *caisse f d'~* savings bank; *la petite ~* small investors *pl.*; **épargner** [epar'ɲe] (1a) *v/t.* save (up), economize (on); be sparing with; *fig.* spare (*s.o.*).

éparpiller [eparpi'je] (1a) *v/t. a. s'~* scatter, disperse.

épars, e [e'paːr, ~'pars] scattered; sparse (*population*); dishevelled (*hair*).

épatant, e F [epa'tɑ̃, ~'tɑ̃ːt] stunning, wonderful, marvellous, first-rate, *Am.* swell, great; **épater** [~'te] (1a) *v/t.* break off the foot of (*a wineglass*); F amaze, flabbergast; *nez m épaté* flat *or* squat nose; F *~ le bourgeois* shock conventional people; **épateur** *m*, **-euse** *f* F [~'tœːr, ~'tøːz] swanker; bluffer.

épaule [e'poːl] *f anat., a. cuis.* shoulder; ⚓ *bows*: luff; *un coup d'~* a shove; *fig.* a leg-up; *par-dessus l'~* disdainfully; **épaulement** [epòl'mɑ̃] *m geog., a.* ⊕ shoulder; △ revetment wall; **épauler** [epo'le] (1a) *v/t.* support (*a.* △); help (*s.o.*), back (*s.o.*) up; bring (*a gun*) to the shoulder; *v/i.* take aim; **épaulette** [~'lɛt] *f* ✕ epaulette (*a. = commission*); *cost.* shoulder strap.

épave [e'paːv] *f* ⚖ unclaimed object; waif, stray; ⚓ wreck (*a. fig.*), flotsam.

épée [e'pe] *f* sword (*a. tex.*); rapier; swordsman; *coup m d'~ dans l'eau* wasted effort.

épeler [e'ple] (1c) *v/t.* spell (*a word*);

spell out (*a message*); **épellation** [epɛlla'sjɔ̃] *f* spelling.

éperdu, e [epɛr'dy] distrought; frantic; beside o.s., wild; desperate; *éperdument amoureux* head over heels in love; *je m'en moque éperdument* I couldn't care less.

éperlan *icht.* [epɛr'lɑ̃] *m* smelt.

éperon [e'prɔ̃] *m* spur (*on rider's heel, a. zo.*, ❦, *geog.*); ⚓ *warship*: ram; *bridge*: cutwater; △ *wall*: buttress; *fig. eyes*: crow's-foot; **éperonné, e** [epro'ne] spurred; ❦ calcarate; crow-footed (*eyes*); **éperonner** [~] (1a) *v/t.* spur (*a. fig.*); ⚓ ram.

épervier [epɛr'vje] *m orn.* sparrow-hawk; *fishing*: cast-net; *pol.* hawk.

éphémère [efe'mɛːr] **1.** *adj.* ephemeral; *fig.* transitory, fleeting; **2.** *su./ m zo.* day-fly.

éphéméride [efeme'rid] *f* tear-off calendar, block-calendar.

épi [e'pi] *m corn, grain*: ear; ❦ spike; *fig.* cluster; ⊕ wharf; 🚋 marshalling tracks *pl.*

épice [e'pis] *f* spice; *pain m d'~* gingerbread; *quatre ~s pl.* allspice *sg.*; **épicé, e** [epi'se] highly spiced; hot; *fig.* spicy (*story*); **épicer** [~] (1k) *v/t.* spice (*a. fig. a story*); **épicerie** ✝ [epis'ri] *f* groceries *pl.*; grocer's (shop), *Am.* grocery; **épicier** *m*, **-ère** *f* [epi'sje, ~'sjɛːr] grocer; *fig.* philistine.

épidémie ⚕ [epide'mi] *f* epidemic (*a. fig.*).

épiderme [epi'dɛrm] *m* epidermis.

épier [e'pje] (1o) *v/t.* watch (*s.o.*); spy on (*s.o.*); watch *or* look out for.

épierrer ✔ [epjɛ're] (1a) *v/t.* clear of stones.

épieu [e'pjø] *m* boar-spear; pike.

épigastre *anat.* [epi'gastr] *m* pit of the stomach, epigastrium.

épigone [epi'gɔn] *m* epigone, follower.

épigraphe [epi'graf] *f* epigraph; motto.

épilation [epila'sjɔ̃] *f* depilation; removal of superfluous hairs; *eyebrows*: plucking; **épilatoire** [~'twaːr] *adj., a. su./m* depilatory.

épilepsie ⚕ [epilɛp'si] *f* epilepsy.

épiler [epi'le] (1a) *v/t.* depilate; remove hairs; pluck (*one's eyebrows*).

épilogue [epi'lɔg] *m* epilogue; **épi-**

loguer [ᴧlɔˈge] (1m) (*sur*) carp (at), find fault (with).

épiloir [epiˈlwaːr] *m eyebrow etc.*: tweezers *pl.*

épinaie [epiˈnɛ] *f* thicket.

épinard ♀ [epiˈnaːr] *m* (*a. cuis.* ~s *pl.*) spinach.

épine [eˈpin] *f* ♀ thorn (*a. fig.*), prickle; ♀ thorn-bush; *anat.* ~ *dorsale* backbone, spine.

épinette [epiˈnɛt] *f* ♪ spinet; ✗ (hen-)coop; ♀ spruce.

épineux, -euse [epiˈnø, ~ˈnøːz] thorny (*a. fig.*); prickly (*a. fig. person*); *fig.* knotty (*problem*).

épingle [eˈpɛ̃ːgl] *f* pin; † ~s *pl.* pin-money *sg.*; ~ *à chapeau* hatpin; ~ *à cheveux* hairpin; ~ *à linge* clothes-peg; ~ *de cravate* tie-pin, *Am.* stick-pin; ~ *de nourrice* safety-pin; *fig. coup m d'*~ pin-prick; *tiré à quatre* ~s dapper, spruce, spick and span; *mot. virage m en* ~ *à cheveux* hairpin bend; **épinglé** [epɛ̃ˈgle] *m* (*a. velours m* ~) uncut velvet; **épingler** [~ˈgle] (1a) *v/t.* pin; pin up; *metall.* pierce (*a mould etc.*); F pin (*s.o.*) down; **épinglerie** ⊕ [~glɔˈri] *f* pin-factory; **épinglette** [~ˈglɛt] *f* ✗ priming-needle; ⚒ boring-tool; **épinglier** [~gliˈe] *m* pin-tray.

épinière [epiˈnjɛːr] *adj./f: moelle f* ~ spinal cord.

épinoche *icht.* [epiˈnɔʃ] *f* stickle-back.

épique [eˈpik] epic.

épiscopal, e, *m/pl.* **-aux** [episkɔˈpal, ~ˈpo] episcopal; cathedral (*city*); **épiscopat** [~ˈpa] *m* episcopate; *coll. the* bishops *pl.*

épisode [epiˈzɔd] *m* episode; *cin. film m à* ~s serial film.

épistolaire [epistɔˈlɛːr] epistolary; *être en relations* ~s *avec q.* correspond with s.o.

épitaphe [epiˈtaf] *f* epitaph.

épithète [epiˈtɛt] *f* epithet; *gramm.* attributive adjective.

épître [eˈpiːtr] *f* epistle; *fig.* (long) letter.

éploré, e [eplɔˈre] tearful, in tears.

éployée ▨ [eplwaˈje] *adj./f* spread (*eagle*).

éplucher [eplyˈʃe] (1a) *v/t.* pick (*a. tex. wool, a. salad*); pare, peel (*a fruit*); prune (*a fruit-tree*); clean (*a. plumage, salad*); preen (*feath-*

ers); ✗ weed (*a field*); *fig.* pick holes in; **éplucheur** *m,* **-euse** *f* [~ˈʃœːr, ~ˈʃøːz] cleaner; (*wool-*)picker; (*potato-*)peeler; ✗ weeder; F *fig.* faultfinder; **épluchoir** [~-ˈʃwaːr] *m* paring-knife; *cuis.* potato-knife; **épluchures** [~ˈʃyːr] *f/pl. potatoes etc.*: peelings; *fig.* refuse *sg.*; waste *sg.*

épointé, e [epwɛ̃ˈte] blunt (*pencil etc.*); hipshot (*horse*); **épointer** [~] (1a) *v/t.* break the point of; blunt (*s.th.*); *s'*~ lose its point (*pencil etc.*).

éponge [eˈpɔ̃ːʒ] *f* sponge; F *fig. jeter l'*~ throw in the towel or sponge; *fig. passer l'*~ *sur* say no more about (*s.th.*); **éponger** [epɔ̃ˈʒe] (11) *v/t.* sponge; mop (*the surface, one's brow*); mop up (*a liquid*); sponge down (*a horse*); dab (*one's eyes*); *a. fig.* absorb; *fig.* compensate.

épopée [epɔˈpe] *f* epic (poem).

époque [eˈpɔk] *f* epoch, age, era; period; time; *à l'*~ at the time (of, *de*); at that time, then; *la Belle* ♀ *that up to 1914*; *faire* ~ mark an epoch; *qui fait* ~ epoch-making.

épouiller [epuˈje] (1a) *v/t.* delouse.

époumoner [epumɔˈne] (1a) *v/t.* put (*s.o.*) out of breath; *s'*~ shout o.s. out of breath.

épousailles [epuˈzaːj] *f/pl.* nuptials, wedding *sg.*; **épouse** [eˈpuːz] *f* wife, spouse; **épousée** [epuˈze] *f* bride; **épouser** [~ˈze] (1a) *v/t.* marry, wed; *fig.* take up, espouse (*a cause*); *fig.* embrace (*an idea*); *fig.* fit (*dress etc.*); *fig.* accept, make (*s.th.*) one's own; ~ *son temps* move with the times; **épouseur** † [~ˈzœːr] *m* suitor, eligible man.

épousseter [epusˈte] (1c) *v/t.* dust; beat (*a carpet etc.*); rub down (*a horse*); **époussette** [epuˈsɛt] *f* feather-duster; rag (*for rubbing down a horse*).

époustouflant, e F [epustuˈflɑ̃, ~ˈflɑ̃ːt] extraordinary, amazing.

épouvantable [epuvɑ̃ˈtabl] horrible, dreadful, terrible; appalling; **épouvantail** [~vɑ̃ˈtaːj] *m* scarecrow; *fig.* bogy, bugbear; *fig. person:* fright; **épouvante** [~ˈvɑ̃ːt] *f* terror, fright; **épouvanter** [~vɑ̃ˈte] (1a) *v/t.* scare; appal.

époux [eˈpu] *m* husband; ⚏ *a.* spouse; *les* ~ *pl. ...* the *...* couple *sg.*

éprendre [eˈprɑ̃ːdr] (4aa) *v/t.*: *s'*~

de become enamo(u)red of; fall in love with (*s.o.*); take a fancy to (*s.th.*).

épreuve [e'prœːv] *f* test (*a.* ⊕, *a. school examination*); proof (*a. typ.*); *phot.* print; *fig.* ordeal, trial; *sp.* event; *à l'~ de* proof against (*s.th.*); *à toute* ~ never-failing; ⊕ foolproof; *mettre à l'~* put to the test.

épris, e [e'pri, ~'priːz] **1.** *p.p. of* éprendre; **2.** *adj.* in love (with, *de*).

éprouver [epru've] (1a) *v/t.* try (*a. fig.*); test; put (*s.o.*) to the test; *fig.* feel (*sympathy etc.*), experience (*pain etc., a. fig. a difficulty*); **éprouvette** [~'vɛt] *f* ⚗ test-tube; probe; *metall.* test-piece.

épucer [epy'se] (1k) *v/t.* clean (*a dog etc.*) of fleas.

épuisé, e [epɥi'ze] exhausted; run down; spent (*energy etc.*); ✝ sold out; *typ.* out of print; **épuisement** [epɥiz'mã] *m* exhaustion (⊕, ⚕, *a. fig.*); *cistern, a. fig. finances*: draining; *resources*: depletion; **épuiser** [epɥi'ze] (1a) *v/t.* exhaust; use up; *fig.* wear (*s.o.*) out; *s'~* run out (*provisions etc.*); run dry, dry up (*source*); wear o.s. out; **épuisette** [~'zɛt] *f* ⚓ scoop, bailer; *fisherman*: landing-net.

épuration [epyra'sjõ] *f* purifying; *oil, metal*: refining; *gas*: filtering; *pol.* purge; *morals*: purging; **épuratoire** ⊕ [~'twaːr] purifying.

épure [e'pyːr] *f* working drawing; diagram (*a.* ⚕).

épurer [epy're] (1a) *v/t.* purify; refine; filter; *pol.* purge; *fig.* expurgate (*a novel*).

équarrir [eka'riːr] (2a) *v/t.* ⊕ square; cut up *or* quarter the carcass of (*a horse*); △ *bois m équarri* squared timber; **équarrisseur** [~ri'sœːr] *m* knacker.

équateur [ekwa'tœːr] *m* equator.

équation ⚕, ⚕, *astr., fig.* [ekwa'sjõ] *f* equation.

équerre [e'kɛːr] *f* square; △ right angle; ⊕ angle-iron; ~ *à coulisses* sliding callipers *pl.*; ~ *à dessin*, ~ *de dessinateur* set square; ~ *en T* T-square; *d'*~ square; *en* ~ square.

équestre [e'kɛstr] equestrian.

équilibrage [ekili'braːʒ] *m* balancing (*a. mot.*); **équilibre** [eki'libr] *m* balance (*a. fig.*); equilibrium; *fig.*

poise; *pol.* ~ *politique* balance of power; **équilibrer** [ekili'bre] (1a) *v/t.* balance; counterbalance; **équilibreur** [~'brœːr] *m see stabilisateur*; **équilibriste** [~'brist] *su.* equilibrist.

équinoxe [eki'nɔks] *m* equinox.

équipage [eki'paːʒ] *m* retinue, suite; ⚓, ✈ crew; ✗ train, equipment; *cost.* attire, F get-up; *fig.* state, plight; ⊕ gear, outfit; ⊕ *factory*: plant; *hunt.* pack of hounds; carriage and horses; **équipe** [e'kip] *f* ⊕ workmen: gang; ⊕ shift; ✗ working party; *sp.* team; ⚓ crew; ~ *de nuit* night shift; *esprit m d'*~ team spirit; ⚙ *homme m d'*~ yardman.

équipée [eki'pe] *f* escapade; sally.

équipement [ekip'mã] *m* ✗, ⚓, *sp., etc.* equipment; gear; outfit (*a.* ⊕); **équiper** [eki'pe] (1a) *v/t.* equip (*a.* ✗); fit out; ⚓ man (*a vessel*).

équitable [eki'tabl] equitable, fair, just.

équitation [ekita'sjõ] *f* horsemanship; *école f d'*~ riding-school.

équité [eki'te] *f* equity (*a.* ⚖); fairness, fair dealing.

équivalent, e [ekiva'lã, ~'lãːt] *adj., a. su./m* equivalent; **équivaloir** [~'lwaːr] (3l) *v/i.* be equivalent *or* tantamount (to, *à*).

équivoque [eki'vɔk] **1.** *adj.* equivocal; *fig.* dubious; **2.** *su./f* ambiguity; quibble; **équivoquer** [~vɔ'ke] (1m) *v/i.* quibble, equivocate.

érable ♀ [e'rabl] *m tree, a. wood*: maple.

érafler [erɑ'fle] (1a) *v/t.* graze, scratch; **éraflure** [~'flyːr] *f* graze, abrasion, scratch.

érailler [erɑ'je] (1a) *v/t. tex.* unravel, fray; fret (*a rope*); roughen (*the voice*); graze, chafe (*the skin*); *s'*~ become unravelled; fray (*cloth*).

ère [ɛːr] *f* era, epoch.

érection [erɛk'sjõ] *f statue etc.*: erection (*a. biol.*); *position*: establishment.

éreintement F [erɛ̃t'mã] *m* exhaustion; slating (= *harsh criticism*); **éreinter** [erɛ̃'te] (1a) *v/t.* break the back of (*a horse*); F exhaust; *fig.* slash, cut to pieces; F *être éreinté a.* be all in, be worn out.

erg *phys.* [ɛrg] *m* erg.

ergot [ɛr'go] *m cock*: spur; ✿ stub; ♀, ⚘ ergot; ⊕ catch, lug; *electric bulb*: pin; **ergotage** F [ɛrgɔ'taːʒ] *m* quibbling; **ergoté, e** [~'te] spurred (*cock, rye*); ergoted (*corn*); **ergoter** F [~'te] (1a) *v/i.* quibble (about, *sur*); split hairs; **ergoteur, -euse** [~'tœːr, ~'tøːz] **1.** *adj.* quibbling, pettifogging; **2.** *su.* quibbler, pettifogger.

ergothérapie [ɛrgɔtera'pi] *f* occupational therapy; work therapy.

ériger [eri'ʒe] (1l) *v/t.* erect (*a statue etc.*); establish, found (*an office, a position*); *fig.* exalt, raise (to, *en*); ~ qch. en principe lay s.th. down as a principle; *s'~ en* set o.s. up as, pose as.

ermitage [ɛrmi'taːʒ] *m* hermitage; **ermite** [~'mit] *m* hermit; recluse.

éroder [erɔ'de] (1a) *v/t.* erode; wear away; **érosif, -ve** [~'zif, ~'ziːv] erosive; **érosion** [~'zjɔ̃] *f* erosion; eating away (*of metal, rock*).

érogène [erɔ'ʒɛn] erogenous.

érotique [erɔ'tik] erotic; **érotisme** [~'tism] *m* eroticism; *🡒* erotism.

errant, e [ɛ'rɑ̃, ~'rɑ̃ːt] rambling, roving, wandering; *chevalier m* ~ knight-errant.

errate *typ.* [ɛra'ta] *m/inv.* errata slip; **erratum,** *pl.* **-ta** [ɛra'tɔm, ~'ta] *m* erratum.

errements [ɛr'mɑ̃] *m/pl.* ways, methods; *pej.* bad habits; *anciens* ~ bad old ways; **errer** [ɛ're] (1b) *v/i.* ramble, roam, wander; stroll ~(about); *fig.* err, make a mistake; **erreur** [ɛ'rœːr] *f* error; mistake, slip; ~ de traduction mistranslation; *faire*~ be mistaken, be wrong; *revenir de ses* ~s turn over a new leaf.

erroné, e [ɛrɔ'ne] erroneous, mistaken, wrong.

ersatz [ɛr'sats] *m* ersatz, substitute.

éructation [erykta'sjɔ̃] *f* eructation, F belch(ing).

érudit, e [ery'di, ~'dit] **1.** *adj.* erudite, scholarly, learned; **2.** *su.* scholar; **érudition** [~di'sjɔ̃] *f* erudition, learning, scholarship.

éruptif, -ve [eryp'tif, ~'tiːv] *geol.* eruptive; **éruption** [~'sjɔ̃] *f* eruption, *🡒 a.* rash; cutting (*of teeth*).

érysipèle *🡒* [erizi'pɛl] *m* erysipelas.

es [ɛ] *2nd p. sg. pres. of être 1.*

ès [ɛs] *prp.*: *docteur m* ~ *sciences* doctor of science.

esbroufe [ɛs'bruf] *f*: F *faire de l'*~ swank, show off; *🡒 à l'*~ snatch-and-grab (*theft*); **esbroufeur** *m*, **-euse** *f*

[~bru'fœːr, ~'føːz] swanker; hustler; *🡒* snatch-and-grab thief.

escabeau [ɛska'bo] *m* stool; pair of steps, step-ladder; **escabelle** [~'bɛl] *f* stool.

escadre [ɛs'kadr] *f* ⚓ squadron; 🡒 wing; **escadrille** [ɛska'driːj] *f* ⚓ flotilla; 🡒 squadron; **escadron** ✗ [~'drɔ̃] *m* squadron; *chef m d'*~ major.

escalade [ɛska'lad] *f* cliff, wall: climbing, scaling; climb; *pol., fig.* escalation; **escalader** [~la'de] (1a) *v/t.* scale, climb.

escalator [ɛskala'tɔːr] *m* escalator.

escale [ɛs'kal] *f* ⚓ port of call; 🡒 stop; call; *faire* ~ *à* call at; 🡒 *sans* ~ non-stop (*flight*).

escalier [ɛska'lje] *m* staircase; stairs *pl.*; ~ *roulant* escalator; ~ *tournant* (*or en colimaçon or à vis*) spiral staircase.

escalope *cuis.* [ɛska'lɔp] *f meat*: scallop; *fish*: steak; escalope.

escamotable [ɛskamɔ'tabl] disappearing, F pull-down (*arm-rest*); 🡒 retractable (*undercarriage*); **escamoter** [~'te] (1a) *v/t.* conjure away; 🡒 retract (*the undercarriage*); *fig.* dodge, evade, get round; filch, pinch; **escamoteur** [~'tœːr] *m* conjuror.

escampette F [ɛskɑ̃'pɛt] *f*: *prendre la poudre d'*~ skedaddle, vamoose, *Am. sl.* take a powder.

escapade [ɛska'pad] *f* escapade; prank.

escarbille [ɛskar'biːj] *f* cinder; ~s *pl.* clinkers.

escarbot *zo.* [ɛskar'bo] *m* beetle.

escarboucle [ɛskar'bukl] *f* carbuncle.

escargot [ɛskar'go] *m* snail.

escarmouche ✗ [ɛskar'muʃ] *f* skirmish, brush.

escarole 🡒 [ɛska'rɔl] *f* endive.

escarpe [ɛs'karp] *m* cut-throat.

escarpé, e [ɛskar'pe] sheer (*rock*), steep; **escarpement** [~pə'mɑ̃] *m* steepness; ✗, *geol.* escarpment; abrupt descent; *mountain*: slope.

escarpin [ɛskar'pɛ̃] *m* light shoe.

escarpolette [ɛskarpɔ'lɛt] *f* swing.

escarre *🡒* [ɛs'kaːr] *f* scab; bed-sore.

escient [ɛ'sjɑ̃] *m*: *à bon* ~ advisedly.

esclaffer [ɛskla'fe] (1a) *v/t.*: *s'*~ burst out laughing, guffaw.

esclandre [ɛs'klɑ̃ːdr] *m* scandal; scene.

esclavage [ɛskla'vaːʒ] *m* slavery; *fig.*

drudgery; **esclave** [~'kla:v] *su.* slave; *fig.* drudge; *être* ~ *de sa parole* stick to one's promise.

escoffier *sl.* [ɛskɔ'fje] (1o) *v/t.* kill.

escogriffe F [ɛskɔ'grif] *m* lanky fellow, F beanpole.

escompte ✝ [ɛs'kɔ̃:t] *m* discount, rebate; *à* ~ at a discount; **escompter** [~kɔ̃'te] (1a) *v/t.* ✝ discount; *fig.* anticipate; *fig.* reckon on, bank on.

escorte [ɛs'kɔrt] *f* ✗ *etc.* escort; ⚓ convoy; **escorter** [~kɔr'te] (1a) *v/t.* escort; ⚓ *a.* convoy.

escouade ✗ [ɛs'kwad] *f* gang, squad.

escrime [ɛs'krim] *f* fencing; *faire de l'*~ fence; **escrimer** F [ɛskri'me] (1a) *v/t.:* *s'*~ fight (with, *contre*); *s'*~ *à* work hard at; try hard to (*inf.*); **escrimeur** [~'mœ:r] *m* fencer, swordsman.

escroc [ɛs'kro] *m* crook; swindler; **escroquer** [~krɔ'ke] (1m) *v/t.* swindle (*s.o.*); ~ *qch. à q.* cheat s.o. out of s.th.; **escroquerie** [~krɔ'kri] *f* fraud; swindling; false pretences *pl.*

ésotérique [ezɔte'rik] esoteric.

espace [ɛs'pa:s] *su./m* space; *space, a. time:* interval; room; ⊕ clearance; ~ *vert* green space *or* area; ~ *vital* living space; *dans* (*or en*) *l'*~ *de* within (*a certain time*); *su./f typ.* space; **espacement** [~pas'mɑ̃] *m* objects, *typ.:* spacing; **espacer** [~pa'se] (1k) *v/t.* space; leave a space between; *typ., a. fig.* space out; *s'*~ become less frequent (*space, a. time*).

espadon [ɛspa'dɔ̃] *m* † two-handled sword; *icht.* sword-fish.

espadrille [ɛspa'dri:j] *f* rope-soled canvas shoe.

espagnol, e [ɛspa'ɲɔl] **1.** *adj.* Spanish; **2.** *su./m ling.* Spanish; *su.* ♀ Spaniard; **espagnolette** [~ɲɔ'lɛt] *f* espagnolette.

espalier ✔ [ɛspa'lje] *m* espalier.

espèce [ɛs'pɛs] *f* kind, sort; ✝ case (in question); ♀, *zo., eccl.* species; ~*s pl.* cash *sg.*, specie *sg.*; ~ *de* ...! silly ...!; ~ *humaine* mankind; *en* ~*s* in hard cash; *en l'*~ in the present case (*a.* ✝).

espérance [ɛspe'rɑ̃:s] *f* hope; expectation; *fig.* promise; ✝ ~*s pl.* expectations; ~ *de vie* life expectancy; **espérer** [~'re] (1f) *v/t.* hope for; ~ *que* hope that; *je l'espère, j'espère* I hope so; ~ *quand même* hope against hope; *v/i.* hope, trust (in, *en*).

espiègle [ɛs'pjɛgl] **1.** *adj.* mischie-

vous, roguish; **2.** *su.* imp; **espièglerie** [~pjɛglə'ri] *f* mischief; prank; *par* ~ out of mischief.

espion, -onne [ɛs'pjɔ̃, ~'pjɔn] *su.* spy; secret agent; *micro.*/*m* concealed microphone; window-mirror; **espionnage** [ɛspjɔ'na:ʒ] *m* espionage, spying; ✝ ~ *industriel* industrial espionage; **espionner** [~'ne] (1a) *v/t.* spy (upon).

esplanade [ɛspla'nad] *f* esplanade, promenade.

espoir [ɛs'pwa:r] *m* hope; expectation.

esprit [ɛs'pri] *m* spirit; mind, intellect; sense; wit; disposition; talent; meaning; soul; ~*-de-vin* spirit(s *pl.*) of wine; ~*fort* free-thinker; *le Saint-*♀ the Holy Ghost *or* Spirit; *plein d'*~ witty; *présence f d'*~ presence of mind; *rendre l'*~ give up the ghost; *venir à* (*sortir de*) *l'*~ *de q.* cross (slip) s.o.'s mind.

esquif ⚓ *poet.* [ɛs'kif] *m* small boat, skiff.

esquille ✗ [ɛs'ki:j] *f bone:* splinter.

esquimau [ɛski'mo] **1.** *adj.* Esquimo; **2.** *su.* ♀ Esquimo; *su./m cuis.* chocice; *cost.* child's rompers *pl.*

esquinter F [ɛskɛ̃'te] (1a) *v/t.* exhaust; tire (*s.o.*) out; *fig.* ruin; run (*s.o.*) down.

esquisse [ɛs'kis] *f* sketch; outline, draft; **esquisser** [~ki'se] (1a) *v/t.* sketch, outline.

esquiver [ɛski've] (1a) *v/t.* avoid, evade; dodge; *fig. s'*~ slip *or* steal away, F make o.s. scarce.

essai [e'sɛ] *m* ⊕, ᵱ trial, essay; test; *sp.* try; trial (to, *pour*); ~ *nucléaire* atomic test; *mot.* ~ *sur route* trial run; *à l'*~ on trial; *coup m d'*~ first attempt; *faire l'*~ *de* try (*s.th.*); ᵷ *pilote m d'*~ test pilot.

essaim [e'sɛ̃] *m* swarm (*a. fig.*); **essaimage** [esɛ'ma:ʒ] *m* hiving off (*a. fig.*); *fig.* excessive growth; **essaimer** [esɛ'me] (1a) *v/i.* swarm.

essarter ✔ [esar'te] (1a) *v/t.* clear (*the ground*); grub up (*roots etc.*).

essayage [esɛ'ja:ʒ] *m* testing; *cost.* trying on, fitting; **essayer** [~'je] (1i) *v/i.* try (to *inf.*, *de inf.*), attempt; ᵱ test; *metall.* assay; *cost.* try on; taste; *s'*~ *à* try one's hand at; **essayeur** *m*, **-euse** *f* [~'jœ:r, ~'jø:z] ⊕ tester; analyst; *metall.* assayer; *cost.* fitter; **essayiste** [~'jist] *su.* essayist.

esse [ɛs] *f* ⊕ S-hook; S-shaped link *or* hook *etc.*; ♪ *violin*: sound-hole.

essence [e'sɑ̃:s] *f* essence; *trees*: species; ♣, ♠, *etc.* oil; petrol, *Am.* gasoline; extract *(of beef etc.)*; *fig.* pith; *poste m d'~* filling-station, *Am.* service station; **essentiel, -elle** [esɑ̃'sjɛl] **1.** *adj.* essential; **2.** *su./m* main thing.

essieu [e'sjø] *m* axle.

essor [e'sɔ:r] *m* flight, soaring; *fig.* scope; *fig.* progress; **essorrer** [esɔ-'re] (1a) *v/t.* dry; wring *(linen)*; *~ à la machine* spin-dry *(linen)*; **essoreuse** [~'rø:z] *f* ⊕ drainer; *laundry*: wringer, mangle.

essouflé, e [esu'fle] out of breath; breathless; **essoufler** [~] (1a) *v/t.* wind, make *(s.o.)* breathless; *s'~* get out of breath; *fig.* exhaust o.s.

essuie...: *~-glace mot.* [esɥi'glas] *m* windscreen wiper, *Am.* windshield wiper; *~-mains* [~'mɛ̃] *m/inv.* (hand-)towel; *~-pieds* [~'pje] *m/inv.* door-mat; *~-verres* [~'vɛr] *m/inv.* glass cloth.

essuyer [esɥi'je] (1h) *v/t.* wipe; dry; mop up; dust; *fig.* suffer *(defeat etc.)*; *fig.* meet with *(a refusal)*; F *~ les plâtres* be the first occupant of a new house; *fig.* be first to do the disagreeable job.

est¹ [ɛst] **1.** *su./m* east; *de l'~* east (-ern); *d'~* easterly *(wind)*; *l'♌* the east *(of a country)*; *vers l'~* eastward(s), to the east; **2.** *adj./inv.* east(ern); easterly *(wind)*.

est² [ɛ] *3rd p. sg. pres. of* être 1.

estacade [ɛsta'kad] *f* ⚔ stockade; ⚓ breakwater; pier; 🛢 coalpit.

estafette [ɛsta'fɛt] *f* courier; ⚔ dispatch-rider.

estafilade [ɛstafi'lad] *f* gash; slash.

estagnon [ɛsta'ɲɔ̃] *m* oil-can; (oil-)drum.

estaminet † [ɛstami'nɛ] *m* tavern; pub; bar.

estampe [ɛs'tɑ̃:p] *f* print, engraving; ⊕ stamp, punch, die; **estamper** [ɛstɑ̃'pe] (1a) *v/t.* stamp, emboss; ⊕ punch; *fig.* fleece *(s.o.)*, swindle *(s.o.)*; **estampille** [~'pi:j] *f* stamp; brand; ♦ trade-mark; **estampiller** [~pi'je] (1a) *v/t.* stamp; brand; ♦ mark *(goods)*.

esthète [ɛs'tɛt] *su.* (a)esthete; **esthéticien** *m*, **-enne** *f* [ɛsteti'sjɛ̃, ~'sjɛn] (a)esthetician; beautician; **esthéti-que** [~'tik] **1.** *adj.* (a)esthetic; **2.** *su./f* (a)esthetics *pl.*

estimable [ɛsti'mabl] estimable; quite good; assessable; **estimateur** [ɛstima'tœ:r] *m* estimator; ♦ valuer, appraiser; **estimatif, -ve** [~'tif, ~'ti:v] estimated *(cost etc.)*; estimative *(faculty)*; *devis m ~* estimate; **estimation** [~'sjɔ̃] *f* estimation; valuation; assessment, appraisal; **estime** [ɛs'tim] *f* esteem, respect; *à l'~* by guesswork; *tenir q. en haute (petite) ~* hold s.o. in high (low) esteem; **estimer** [~ti'me] (1a) *v/t.* estimate; value, appraise, assess; *fig.* (hold in) esteem; consider, think.

estival, e, *m/pl.* **-aux** [ɛsti'val, ~'vo] summer...; ♣ *etc.* estival; **estivant** *m*, **e** *f* [~'vɑ̃, ~'vɑ̃:t] summer visitor; **estivation** ♣, *zo.* [~va'sjɔ̃] *f* estivation.

estoc [ɛs'tɔk] *m* coup *m d'~ fencing*: thrust; *frapper d'~ et de taille* cut and thrust; **estocade** [ɛstɔ'kad] *f* † *fencing*: thrust; *fig.* sudden onset; *a. fig.* death-blow, finishing blow.

estomac [ɛstɔ'ma] *m* stomach; *~ dérangé* upset stomach; *avoir l'~ dans les talons* be faint with hunger; *mal m d'~* stomach-ache; **estomaquer** F [~ma'ke] (1m) *v/t.* take *(s.o.'s)* breath away, stagger *(s.o.)*.

estompe [ɛs'tɔ̃:p] *f* stump; stump drawing; **estomper** [~tɔ̃'pe] (1a) *v/t.* stump, shade off; *fig.* blur; *fig.* tone down *(crudities)*; *fig. s'~* grow blurred; loom up.

estrade [ɛs'trad] *f* platform, stage.

estragon ♣, *cuis.* [ɛstra'gɔ̃] *m* tarragon.

estrapade ⚙ † [ɛstra'pad] *f* strappado.

estropié, e [ɛstrɔ'pje] **1.** *adj.* crippled; ⚔ disabled; lame; **2.** *su.* cripple; **estropier** [~] (1o) *v/t.* cripple, lame, maim; ⚔ disable; *fig.* mangle *(a quotation, a word)*, murder *(music, a language)*.

estuaire [ɛs'tɥɛ:r] *m* estuary, *Sc.* firth.

estudiantin, e [ɛstydjɑ̃'tɛ̃, ~'tin] student... [geon.〕

esturgeon *icht.* [ɛstyr'ʒɔ̃] *m* sturⁿ〕

et [e] and; *et ... et* and both ... and.

étable [e'tabl] *f* cattle-shed, cowshed; pigsty *(a. fig.)*; **établer** [eta-'ble] (1a) *v/t.* stall *(cattle)*; stable *(horses)*.

établi 204

établi¹ [eta'bli] *m* work-bench.

établi², e [eta'bli] established (*fact*); determined (*limit*); **établir** [~'bli:r] (2a) *v/t*. establish (*a.* ⚖); set up (*a business, a statue, sp. a record*); construct, erect; ascertain (*facts*); prove (*a charge*); draw up (*an account, a budget, a plan*); institute (*a rule, a tax, a post*); ⚡ ~ *le contact* make contact; *s'~* become established; establish (o.s.); settle (*in a place*); **établissement** [~blis'mã] *m* establishment; institution; settlement; ✝ concern, business, firm; ⊕ factory, plant; ✝ *accounts:* drawing up; ✝ *balance:* striking.

étage [e'ta:ʒ] *m* stor(e)y, floor; *fig.* degree, rank; ⊕, *geol.* stage (*a. of rocket*); *geol.* stratum, layer; ⚒ level; *fig. de bas* ~ of the lower classes (*people*); low; *deuxième* ~ second floor, *Am.* third floor; **étager** [eta'ʒe] (11) *v/t*. range in tiers; terrace (*the ground*); perform (*an operation*) in stages; **étagère** [~'ʒɛ:r] *f* whatnot; shelves *pl.*; shelf.

étai [e'te] *m* ⚓ stay (*a.* ⚓), prop (*a. fig.*), strut; ⚒ pit-prop; **étaiement** ⚓, ⊕ [ete'mã] *m see étayage.*

étain [e'tɛ̃] *m* tin; pewter; *papier m d'~* tinfoil; ~ *de soudure* plumber's solder.

étal, *pl. a.* **étals** [e'tal] *m market:* stall; **étalage** [eta'la:ʒ] *m* ✝ display, show (*a. fig.*); shop window; *fig. a.* parade; **étalagiste** ✝ [~la'ʒist] window dresser; **étalement** [etal'mã] *m* displaying; spreading(-out); *holidays etc.:* staggering; **étaler** [eta'le] (1a) *v/t*. ✝ display (*a. fig.*), expose for sale; *fig.* show, disclose; stagger (*holidays*); spread (out); *s'~* sprawl; spread *or* stretch out.

étalon¹ [eta'lɔ̃] *m* stallion.

étalon² [eta'lɔ̃] *m* standard; ~*-or* gold standard; *poids-*~ troy weight; **étalonnage** [~lɔ'na:ʒ] *m* standardization; *tubes etc.:* calibration; ga(u)ging; *radio:* logging; *phot.* grading; **étalonner** [~lɔ'ne] (1a) *v/t*. standardize; calibrate; ga(u)ge; *radio:* log (*stations*); *phot.* grade; stamp (*weights*).

étamer ⊕ [eta'me] (1a) *v/t*. tin; galvanize; silver (*a mirror*); **étameur** [~'mœ:r] *m* tinsmith; *mirrors:* silverer.

étamine¹ [eta'min] *f* butter-muslin;

bolting-cloth; *passer qch. par l'~* sift s.th. (*a. fig.*).

étamine² ⚘ [~] *f* stamen.

étampe ⊕ [e'tã:p] *f* stamp, die; punch; swage.

étanche [e'tã:ʃ] (*water-, air*)tight; impervious; ⚡ insulated; ~ *à l'eau* watertight; **étanchéité** [etãʃei'te] *f* watertightness; airtightness; ⚡ *d'~* insulating; **étancher** [~'ʃe] (1a) *v/t*. sta(u)nch (*blood*); stem (*a liquid*); quench (*one's thirst*); stop (*a leak*); make watertight *or* airtight.

étang [e'tã] *m* pond, pool; ~ *à poissons* fish pond.

étant [e'tã] *p. pr. of être* 1.

étape [e'tap] *f* ⚔, *a. fig.* stage; halting-place; *fig.* step (towards, *vers*); *par petites* ~s by easy stages; *faire* ~ stop off, stop over.

état [e'ta] *m* state (*a. pol., a. fig.*), condition; *fig.* position; ⚖ status; profession, trade; *hist.* ~s *pl. the* estates; ~ *civil* civil status; *bureau m de l'*~ *civil* register office; ⚖ *en* ~ *de légitime défense* able to plead self-defence; ~ *d'esprit* frame of mind; *en tout* ~ *de cause* in any case; ~ *transitoire* transition stage; *réduit à l'*~ *de* reduced to; *coup m d'*⚡ coup d'état; F *dans tous ses* ~s all of a dither; *en* ~ *de vol* in flying condition (*airplane*); *être en* ~ *de* (*inf.*) be in a position to (*inf.*); *faire* ~ *de* put forward; *homme m d'*⚡ statesman; *hors d'*~ useless; *remettre en* ~ put in order; **étatique** *pol.* [eta'tik] state ...; (of) state control; **étatisation** [etatiza'sjɔ̃] *f* nationalisation (*of industries*); **étatisme** [~'tism] *m* state control; **état-major**, *pl.* **états-majors** [~ma'ʒɔ:r] *m* ⚔ (general) staff; headquarters *pl.*; *fig.* management.

étau ⊕ [e'to] *m* vice, *Am.* vise; ~ *à main* hand-vice; ~*-limeur* shaping-machine.

étayage ⚓, ⊕ [etɛ'ja:ʒ] *m* shoring, staying, propping (up); buttressing; **étayer** [~'je] (1i) *v/t*. prop (up), shore, stay; support (*a. fig.*).

été¹ [e'te] *p.p. of être* 1.

été² [~] *m* summer; F ~ *de la Saint-Martin* Indian summer.

éteignoir [ete'ɲwa:r] *m candle:* extinguisher; **éteindre** [e'tɛ̃:dr] (4m) *v/t*. extinguish (*the light, a race, etc.*); put out; ⚡ switch off (*the light*); quench (*one's thirst, a.* ⊕ *red-hot* *iron*); pay off (*a debt*); abolish (*a right*); *fig.* put an end to (*s.o.'s ambition, hope*); *fig.* soften, dim (*the colour, the light*); deaden (*a sound*); allay (*passions*); slake (*lime*); s'~ die out; go out (*light etc.*); fade, grow dim; die down (*passions*); die, pass away (*person*).

étendage [etɑ̃'da:ʒ] *m* clothes lines *pl.*; drying-yard; **étendard** [~'da:r] *m* standard, flag; **étendoir** [~-'dwa:r] *m* clothes line; **étendre** [e'tɑ̃:dr] (4a) *v/t.* extend; stretch; spread (out); lay (*a tablecloth*); expand (*the wings*); dilute (with, de); lay (*s.o.*) down; hang (*linen*) out; *cuis.* roll out (*pastry*); *fig.* widen, enlarge; s'~ spread; stretch (out), extend; stretch out, lie down; **étendu, e** [etɑ̃'dy] 1. *adj.* extensive; outspread (*wings*); outstretched (*hands*); widespread (*influence*); 2. *su./f* extent; expanse; *voice, knowledge:* range; capacity; *speech etc.:* length.

éternel, -elle [eter'nɛl] eternal; everlasting, unending; **éterniser** [eterni'ze] (1a) *v/t.* perpetuate; eternalize; s'~ last for ever; **éternité** [~'te] *f* eternity; *fig.* ages *pl.*

éternuer [eter'nɥe] (1n) *v/i.* sneeze.

êtes [ɛt] *2nd p. pl. pres.* of être 1.

éteule [e'tœl] *f* stubble.

éther [e'tɛːr] *m* ether; **éthéré, e** [ete're] etherial (*a.* 🜃); **éthériser** [~ri'ze] (1a) *v/t.* etherize.

éthique [e'tik] 1. *adj.* ethical; 2. *su./f* ethics *pl.*; moral philosophy.

ethnique [ɛt'nik] ethnic(al).

ethno... [ɛtnɔ] ethno...

éthylène 🜃 [eti'lɛːn] *m* ethylene.

étiage [e'tja:ʒ] *m* low water mark; *fig.* level.

étinceler [etɛ̃s'le] (1c) *v/i.* sparkle (*a. fig. conversation*); gleam (*anger*); twinkle (*star*); **étincelle** [etɛ̃'sɛl] *f* spark; *mot.* ~ d'allumage ignition spark; **étincellement** [~sɛl'mɑ̃] *m* sparkling; twinkling (*of the stars*).

étioler [etjɔ'le] (1a) *v/t.*: s'~ droop, wilt (*plant*); waste away.

étique [e'tik] emaciated.

étiqueter [etik'te] (1c) *v/t.* label; **étiquette** [eti'kɛt] *f* label, ticket, tag; etiquette, ceremony.

étirer [eti're] (1a) *v/t.* stretch; pull out, draw out; ⊕ draw (*metals*).

étoffe [e'tɔf] *f* material, cloth; *fig.* stuff; *avoir l'*~ *de* have the makings

of; **étoffé, e** [etɔ'fe] plump (*person*); meaty (*style etc.*); rich (*voice*); **étoffer** [~] (1a) *v/t.* stuff; *fig.* fill out; *cost.* give fulness to; *fig.* s'~ fill out (*person*).

étoile [e'twal] *f* star (*a. film*); *typ.* asterisk; blaze (*on horse*); ~ *du berger* evening star; *zo.* ~ *de mer* starfish; ~ *filante* shooting *or* falling star; *à la belle* ~ out of doors, in the open; **étoiler** [etwa'le] (1a) *v/t.* stud with stars; star (*glass etc.*); s'~ star (*glass etc.*); glow with stars (*sky*).

étole *cost., eccl.* [e'tɔl] *f* stole.

étonnant, e [etɔ'nɑ̃, ~'nɑ̃:t] astonishing, surprising; **étonnement** [etɔn'mɑ̃] *m* astonishment, surprise, amazement; **étonner** [etɔ'ne] (1a) *v/t.* astonish, amaze; s'~ be surprised (at s.th., *de qch*; at *ger.*, *de inf.*).

étouffant, e *fig.* [etu'fɑ̃, ~'fɑ̃:t] stifling; **étouffée** *cuis.* [~'fe] *f: cuire à l'*~ braise; **étouffement** [etuf'mɑ̃] *m* stifling; suffocation; *scandal:* hushing up; choking sensation; **étouffer** [etu'fe] (1a) *vt/i. a.* s'~ suffocate, choke; stifle; *v/t. a.* damp (*a sound*); 🜇 quench (*a spark*); hush up (*an affair*); **étouffoir** [~'fwa:r] *m* charcoal extinguisher; ♪ damper; *fig.* stuffy room.

étoupe [e'tup] *f* tow; oakum; ⊕ packing; **étouper** [etu'pe] (1a) *v/t.* stop; ⊕ pack; ⚓ caulk; **étoupille** [~'pi:j] *f* 🗲 friction-tube; ⚔ fuse.

étourderie [eturdə'ri] *f* inadvertence; blunder, careless mistake; oversight; **étourdi, e** [~'di] 1. *adj.* thoughtless, scatter-brained; foolish (*reply etc.*); 2. *su.* scatter-brain (*reply etc.*); **étourdir** [~'di:r] (2a) *v/t.* stun, daze; make dizzy; soothe (*a pain etc.*); appease (*one's hunger*); **étourdissement** [~dis'mɑ̃] *m* dizziness, giddiness; dizzy spell; *mind:* dazing; *pain etc.:* deadening; *fig.* shock, bewilderment.

étourneau [etur'no] *m orn.* starling; F feather-brain.

étrange [e'trɑ̃:ʒ] strange, odd, peculiar; **étranger, -ère** [etrɑ̃'ʒe, ~'ʒɛ:r] 1. *adj. pol.* foreign (*a. fig.*); *pej.* alien; strange, unknown; irrelevant (to, *à*); ~ *à* unacquainted with (*an affair*); a stranger in (*a place*); 2. *su.* foreigner; stranger; *su./m* foreign parts *pl.*; *à l'*~ abroad;

étrangeté [etrãʒ'te] *f* strangeness, oddness.

étranglement [etrãglə'mã] *m* strangulation; *pipe, tube*: neck; *fig.* narrow passage; *fig.* goulet *m* (*or* goulot *m*) d'~ bottleneck; **étrangler** [~'gle] (1a) *v/t.* strangle, choke, throttle (*a.* ⊕), stifle; ✆ strangulate; *fig.* constrict; ⊕ throttle down (*the engine*); *v/i.*: ~ de colère choke with rage; ~ de soif be parched.

étrave ⚓ [e'tra:v] *f* stem(-post).

être [ɛ:tr] **1.** (1) *v/i.* be, exist; belong (to, à); lie, stand; F go; *passive voice*: be (*seen*); ~ malade be *or* feel sick; *si cela est* if so; *ça y est* it is done; *ç'est ça* that's it; *c'est moi* it is me; *c'en est assez!* enough (of it)!; *lequel sommes-nous?* what is the date today?; *à qui est cela?* whose is it?; *c'est à lui de* (*inf.*) it is his turn to (*inf.*); it rests with him to (*inf.*); ~ de come *or* be from (*a town*); ~ assis sit; ~ debout stand; *j'ai été voir ce film* I have seen this film; *elle s'est blessée* she has hurt herself; *elle s'est blessé le doigt* she has hurt her finger; *en* ~ *à* (*inf.*) be reduced to (*ger.*); *en êtes-vous?* will you join us?; *où en sommes-nous?* how far have we got?; *quoi qu'il en soit* however that may be; *en* ~ *pour* have spent (*s.th.*) to no purpose; *vous y êtes?* do you follow *or* F get it?; *il est* it is (2 o'clock); *il était une fois* once upon a time there was; *est-ce qu'il travaille?* does he work?, is he working?; *elle est venue, n'est-ce pas?* she has come, hasn't she?; *n'était* but for; **2.** *su./m* being, creature; existence.

étreindre [e'trɛ̃:dr] (4m) *v/t.* clasp; grasp; embrace, hug; *fig.* grip; **étreinte** [e'trɛ̃:t] *f* embrace; grasp; grip.

étrenne [e'trɛn] *f*: ~s *pl.* New Year's gift *sg.*; Christmas box *sg.*; *avoir l'~ de* = **étrenner** [etrɛ'ne] (1a) *v/t.* wear (*a garment*) *or* use (*s.th.*) for the first time.

êtres [ɛ:tr] *m/pl.*: *les* ~ *d'une maison* the ins and outs of a house.

étrier [etri'e] *m* stirrup (*a. anat.*); *fig. mettre le pied à l'*~ *à q.* help s.o.

étrille [e'tri:j] *f* curry-comb; **étriller** [etri'je] (1a) *v/t.* curry (*a horse*); F † thrash, trounce.

étriper [etri'pe] (1a) *v/t.* disembowel (*a horse*); draw (*a chicken*); gut (*a fish*).

étriquer [etri'ke] (1m) *v/t.* make too narrow *or* tight; *fig.* curtail (*a speech*); *habit m étriqué* skimped coat.

étroit, e [e'trwa, ~'trwat] narrow (*a. fig. mind*); tight; confined; limited; *fig.* strict (*sense of a word*); *à l'*~ cramped for room; (*live*) economically; **étroitesse** [etrwa'tɛs] *f* narrowness; tightness; ~ *d'esprit* narrow-mindedness.

étron [e'trɔ̃] *m* turd.

étude [e'tyd] *f* study (*a.* ♪); office; (*barrister's*) chambers *pl.*; prep-room; research; preparation; (*law-yer's*) practice; ✝ ~ *du marché* (*de motivation*) marketing (motivation) research; *à l'*~ under consideration; *thea.* under rehearsal; *faire ses* ~s study; **étudiant** *m*, **e** *f* [ety'djã, ~'djã:t] student; undergraduate; **étudier** [~'dje] (1o) *v/t.* study; prepare (*a lesson*); examine, go into, investigate; design; † *s'*~ *à* (*inf.*) make a point of (*ger.*); be very careful to (*inf.*).

étui [e'tɥi] *m* case, cover; *book, hat*: box; ✕ ~ *de cartouche* cartridge case.

étuve [e'ty:v] *f* ⚗, ⊕, *baths*: sweating-room; sterilizer; drying cupboard; F oven; **étuvée** *cuis.* [ety've] *f*: *cuire à l'*~ steam; **étuver** [~] (1a) *v/t. cuis.* stew (*meat*); steam (*vegetables*); ⊕ dry; sterilize.

étymologie [etimɔlɔ'ʒi] *f* etymology.

eu, e [y] *p.p. of avoir 1.*

eucalyptus ♀, *a.* ✆ [økalip'tys] *m* eucalyptus.

eucharistie *eccl.* [økaris'ti] *f* Eucharist; Lord's Supper.

eunuque [ø'nyk] *m* eunuch.

euphémique [øfe'mik] euphemistic; **euphémisme** [~'mism] *m* euphemism.

euphonie [øfɔ'ni] *f* euphony.

euphorie [øfɔ'ri] *f* euphoria; **euphorique** [~'rik] euphoric; **euphorisant, e** [~ri'zã, ~'zã:t] *adj., a. su.* euphoriant; **euphoriser** [~ri'ze] (1a) *v/t.* put into a euphoric mood.

européen, -enne [ørɔpe'ɛ̃, ~'ɛn] *adj., a. su.* ♀ European.

eus [y] *1st p. sg. p.s. of avoir 1.*

euthanasie [øtana'zi] *f* euthanasia, F mercy-killing.

eux [ø] *pron./pers. m/pl. subject:* they; *object:* them; *à ~* to them; theirs; *ce sont ~,* F *c'est ~* it is they, F it's them; *~-mêmes* [~'mɛːm] *pron./rfl.* themselves.

évacuation [evakɥa'sjɔ̃] *f* evacuation (*a.* ✽, ✕); *water:* drainage; **évacué** *m,* **e** *f* [eva'kɥe] evacuee; **évacuer** [~] (1n) *v/t.* ✕, ✽ evacuate; ⊕ exhaust (*steam*); drain (*water*).

évadé, e [eva'de] *adj., a. su.* fugitive; **évader** [~] (1a) *v/t.: s'~* escape, run away.

évaluation [evalɥa'sjɔ̃] *f* valuation; estimate; assessment; **évaluer** [~-'lɥe] (1n) *v/t.* value; estimate; assess.

évangélique [evɑ̃ʒe'lik] evangelical; **Évangile** [~'ʒil] *m* Gospel.

évanouir [eva'nwiːr] (2a) *v/t.: s'~* ✽ faint, swoon; *fig.* vanish, fade away; *radio:* fade; **évanouissement** [~nwis'mɑ̃] *m* ✽ faint, swoon; *fig.* disappearance; *radio:* fading; ✽ *revenir de son ~* come to.

évaporation [evapɔra'sjɔ̃] *f* evaporation; **évaporé, e** [~'re] **1.** *adj.* scatterbrained; flighty; irresponsible; **2.** *su.* flighty person; **évaporer** [~'re] (1a) *v/t.: s'~* evaporate.

évasé, e [eva'ze] bell-mouthed; flared (*skirt*); △ splayed; **évaser** [~'ze] (1a) *v/t.* widen the opening of; open out; flare (*a skirt*); △ splay; *s'~* widen at the mouth; flare (*skirt*); **évasif, -ve** [~'zif, ~'ziːv] evasive; **évasion** [~'zjɔ̃] *f* escape, flight; evasion, quibble; *literature:* escapism; *~ de prison* jailbreak; *d'~* escapist (*novel etc.*); ✚ *~ des capitaux* exodus of capital.

évêché [eve'ʃe] *m* bishopric, see; diocese; bishop's palace.

éveil [e'vɛːj] *m* awakening; alertness; *fig.* dawn; *en ~* on the alert; **éveillé, e** [eve'je] awake; wide-awake; alert, bright; **éveiller** [~] (1a) *v/t.* awaken; *fig.* arouse; *s'~* wake up; *fig.* awaken.

événement [even'mɑ̃] *m* event; occurrence; incident; emergency.

évent [e'vɑ̃] *m* open air; ⊕ vent (-hole); *zo. whale:* blowhole; *beverage:* flatness; *sentir l'~* smell musty; F *tête f à l'~* feather-brain.

éventail [evɑ̃'taːj] *m* fan; *fig. salaries:* range; *en ~* fan-wise.

éventaire [evɑ̃'tɛːr] *m* (hawker's) tray; street stall.

éventé, e [evɑ̃'te] stale, musty; flat (*beer etc.*); *fig.* hare-brained; divulged (*secret*); **éventer** [~] (1a) *v/t.* air; fan; *hunt.* scent, *fig.* get wind of; *fig.* divulge; let (*beer etc.*) grow flat; F *fig. ~ la mèche* uncover a plot; *s'~* go flat or stale; spoil.

éventrer [evɑ̃'tre] (1a) *v/t.* disembowel; *fig.* break *or* rip open; gut (*a fish*); *mot.* rip (*a tyre*).

éventualité [evɑ̃tɥali'te] *f* possibility, contingency; **éventuel, -elle** [~'tɥɛl] possible, contingent; eventual.

évêque [e'vɛːk] *m* bishop.

évertuer [ever'tɥe] (1n) *v/t.: s'~* strive, do one's utmost (to *inf., à inf.*).

évidemment [evida'mɑ̃] *adv.* of course, certainly; obviously; **évidence** [~'dɑ̃ːs] *f* obviousness, evidence; obvious fact; *à l'~, de toute ~* (quite) obviously; *en ~* in a prominent *or* conspicuous position; *se mettre en ~* push o.s. forward; **évident, e** [~'dɑ̃, ~'dɑ̃ːt] evident, obvious.

évider [evi'de] (1a) *v/t.* hollow out; groove; pink (*cloth, leather*); cut away.

évier [e'vje] *m scullery:* sink.

évincer [evɛ̃'se] (1k) *v/t.* ✚ evict, eject, dispossess; *fig.* oust (*s.o.*), supplant (*s.o.*).

évitable [evi'tabl] avoidable; **évitement** [evit'mɑ̃] *m* avoidance, shunning; *route f d'~* bypass (road); *voie f d'~* siding; **éviter** [evi'te] (1a) *v/t.* avoid; *fig.* spare (*trouble*); *v/i.: ~ de* (*inf.*) avoid (*ger.*).

évocateur, -trice [evɔka'tœːr, ~-'tris] evocative (of, *de*); **évocation** [~'sjɔ̃] *f* evocation (✚, *a.* spirits, *a.* past); *past, spirits:* conjuring up.

évoluer [evɔ'lɥe] (1n) *v/i.* develop, evolve; ✕, ⚓ manœuvre; move; **évolution** [~ly'sjɔ̃] *f* ✕, ⚓ manœuvre; *biol. etc.* evolution; *fig.* development.

évoquer [evɔ'ke] (1m) *v/t.* evoke (*a.* ✚), bring to mind; conjure up (*a.* spirits).

ex... [eks] former; ex-...; late; *~-ministre* former minister.

exact, e [ɛg'zakt] exact (*a. science*);

correct, right; true; punctual (*time*).

exacteur [ɛgzak'tœːr] *m* exactor; extortioner; **exaction** [ˏ'sjɔ̃] *f* extortion; *tax*: exaction.

exactitude [ɛgzakti'tyd] *f* exactitude, exactness; accuracy; *time*: punctuality.

exagération [ɛgzaʒera'sjɔ̃] *f* exaggeration; overstatement; **exagérer** [ˏʒe're] (1f) *v/t.* exaggerate; overstate; overestimate; *v/i.* *fig.* go too far.

exaltation [ɛgzalta'sjɔ̃] *f* eccl., a. emotion: exaltation; excitement; over-excitement; **exalté, e** [ˏ'te] **1.** adj. heated; excited; overstrung (*person*); **2.** su. hot-head; fanatic; **exalter** [ˏ'te] (1a) *v/t.* exalt, praise; excite, rouse (*emotions*); s'ˏ grow excited; enthuse.

examen [ɛgza'mɛ̃] *m* examination; ⊕ test; ⊕ *machine*: overhaul; survey; investigation; ✝ *accounts*: inspection; à l'ˏ under consideration (*question*); ˏ d'entrée entrance examination; ˏ de passage end-of-year examination; *mot.* ˏ pour le permis de conduire driving test; **examinateur** *m*, **-trice** *f* [ˏmina'tœːr, ˏ'tris] examiner; ⊕ inspector; **examiner** [ˏmi'ne] (1a) *v/t.* examine (a. ✿); scrutinize; look into, investigate; ⊕ overhaul (a *machine*); *fig.* scan; ✝ inspect (*accounts*).

exaspération [ɛgzaspera'sjɔ̃] *f* disease, pain, a. F *fig.*: aggravation; *fig.* exasperation, irritation; **exaspérer** [ˏ're] (1f) *v/t.* exasperate, irritate, aggravate.

exaucer [ɛgzo'se] (1k) *v/t.* grant, fulfill (a *wish*); hear (a *prayer*).

excavateur *m*, **-trice** *f* ⊕ [ɛkskava'tœːr, ˏ'tris] excavator, grub; **excavation** [ˏ'sjɔ̃] *f* excavation; hole.

excédant, e [ɛkse'dɑ̃, ˏ'dɑ̃ːt] surplus; excess (*luggage*); F tiresome (*person*); **excédent** [ˏ'dɑ̃] *m* excess, surplus; ˏ de poids excess weight; **excéder** [ˏ'de] (1f) *v/t.* exceed; *fig.* tire, weary (*s.o.*); irritate.

excellence [ɛkse'lɑ̃ːs] *f* excellence; ♀ *title*: Excellency; par ˏ particularly; pre-eminently; **excellent, e** [ˏ'lɑ̃, ˏ'lɑ̃ːt] excellent, F first-rate, capital; delicious (*meal etc.*); **exceller** [ˏ'le] (1a) *v/i.* excel (in, en; in ger., à inf.).

excentrer ⊕ [ɛksɑ̃'tre] (2a) *v/t.* throw off centre; **excentrique** [ˏ'trik] **1.** adj. ⊕ eccentric (a. *person*); *fig.* odd (*person*); remote (*quarter of a town*); **2.** su./m ⊕ eccentric; cam; *lathe*: eccentric chuck; su. eccentric, crank.

excepté [ɛksɛp'te] prp. except(ing), save; **excepter** [ˏ'te] (1a) *v/t.* except, exclude (from, de); **exception** [ˏ'sjɔ̃] *f* exception (a. ⚖); ˏ faite de, à l'ˏ de with the exception of; *pol.* état *m* d'ˏ state of emergency; sauf ˏ with certain exceptions; **exceptionnel, -elle** [ˏsjɔ'nɛl] exceptional, uncommon; ✝ prix *m* ˏ bargain.

excès [ɛk'sɛ] *m* excess; *powers, mot. speed limit*: exceeding; à l'ˏ, avec ˏ excessively, to excess; **excessif, -ve** [ˏsɛ'sif, ˏ'siːv] excessive, extreme; unreasonable; exorbitant (*price*).

exciser ✂ [ɛksi'ze] (1a) *v/t.* excise.

excitable [ɛksi'tabl] excitable; **excitant** [ˏ'tɑ̃] **1.** su./m stimulant; **2.** adj. exciting; **exciter** [ˏ'te] (1a) *v/t.* excite (a. *fig.*); arouse (*emotions*); incite (*s.o.*, a rebellion, etc.); cause; s'ˏ get excited; get worked up.

exclamation [ɛksklama'sjɔ̃] *f* exclamation; point *m* d'ˏ exclamation mark; **exclamer** [ˏ'me] (1a) *v/t.*: s'ˏ exclaim; protest; make an outcry.

exclure [ɛks'klyːr] (4g) *v/t.* exclude (from, de); *fig.* preclude, prevent; s'ˏ mutuellement be mutually exclusive; **exclusif, -ve** [ɛkskly'zif, ˏ'ziːv] exclusive; sole (*agent, right*); **exclusion** [ˏ'zjɔ̃] *f* exclusion; *pupil*: expulsion; à l'ˏ de excluding; **exclusivité** [ˏzivi'te] *f* exclusiveness; sole right (in, de); ... en ˏ exclusive ...

excommunier eccl. [ɛkskɔmy'nje] (1o) *v/t.* excommunicate.

excorier [ɛkskɔ'rje] (1o) *v/t.* a. s'ˏ excoriate; peel off.

excrément [ɛkskre'mɑ̃] *m* physiol. excrement; *fig.* scum; **excréter** physiol. [ˏ'te] (1f) *v/t.* excrete.

excroissance [ɛkskrwa'sɑ̃ːs] *f* excrescence.

excursion [ɛkskyr'sjɔ̃] *f* excursion, tour, trip; hike; **excursionniste** [ˏsjɔ'nist] su. tourist, tripper; hiker.

excuse [ɛks'kyːz] *f* excuse; ˏs pl. apology sg., apologies; **excuser** [ˏky'ze] (1a) *v/t.* excuse; s'ˏ apol-

ogize (for, *de*); excuse o.s.; † decline
an invitation.

exécrable [εgze'krabl] abominable;
horrible; disgraceful; **exécration**
[⌣kra'sjɔ̃] *f* detestation, execration;
fig. disgrace; **exécrer** [⌣'kre] (1f)
v/t. loathe, detest.

exécutant *m*, e *f* ♪ [εgzeky'tã, ⌣-
'tã:t] performer; executant; **exécuter** [⌣'te] (1a) *v/t.* execute (*a.* ⚔,
a. ⚖ *a murderer, etc.*), perform (*a.*
♪), carry out (*a. a plan, an order,
etc.*); ⚖ distrain on (*a debtor*); †
hammer (*a defaulter*); *fig.* slash
(*s.o.*); s'⌣ comply; yield; *fig.* pay
up; **exécuteur-trice** [⌣'tœ:r, ⌣'tris]
su. promise etc.: performer; ⚖ ⌣
testamentaire executor; *su./m* †
executioner; **exécutif, -ve** [⌣'tif,
⌣'ti:v] *adj.*, *a. su./m* executive;
exécution [⌣'sjɔ̃] *f* execution (*a.*
⚔, *a.* ⚖ *of a murderer*), performance (*a.* ♪); *promise*: fulfilment;
⌣ *forcée* ⚖ *debtor*: distraint;
† *defaulter*: hammering; ⚖ *law*:
enforcement; *mettre à* ⌣ carry
out.

exemplaire [εgzã'plε:r] **1.** *adj.*
exemplary; **2.** *su./m* sample, specimen; model, pattern; *book*: copy;
en double ⌣ in duplicate; **exemple**
[⌣'zã:pl] *m* example; *par* ⌣ for
instance; *par* ⌣! well I never!; *ah
ça par* ⌣! well really!; *ah non, par* ⌣!
no indeed!

exempt, e [εg'zã, ⌣'zã:t] *adj.* exempt (from, *de*); free; immune; †
⌣ *de défauts* perfect; ⌣ *d'impôts* tax-
free.

exempter [εgzã'te] (1a) *v/t.* exempt; exonerate; **exemption** [⌣'sjɔ̃]
f exemption; *fig.* freedom.

exercer [εgzεr'se] (1k) *v/t.* exercise;
✕ *etc.* train, drill; use, exert (*one's
influence, one's power*); practise (*a
profession, a trade*); s'⌣ practise
(s.th., *à qch.*); drill; be exerted; *fig.*
operate; **exercice** [⌣'sis] *m* exercise; ✕ drill, training; *influence,
power*: use; practice; † ⌣ *fiscal*
financial year; (*month's, year's*)
trading; *sp.* ⌣s *pl. aux agrès* apparatus work; *sp.* ⌣s *pl. libres* light
gymnastics *sg.*

exhalaison [εgzalε'zɔ̃] *f* exhalation;
⌣s *pl.* fumes; **exhalation** [⌣la'sjɔ̃] *f*
exhaling, exhalation; **exhaler** [⌣'le]
(1a) *v/t.* exhale, give out, emit; *fig.*

express, utter; *fig.* give vent to (*one's
anger*); *fig.* breathe (*a sigh*).

exhausser [εgzo'se] (1a) *v/t.* raise
(by, *de*), heighten.

exhausteur *mot.* [εgzos'tœ:r] *m*
suction-pipe; vacuum-feed tank.

exhérédation ⚖ [εgzereda'sjɔ̃] *f*
disinheritance; **exhéréder** ⚖ [⌣'de]
(1f) *v/t.* disinherit.

exhiber [εgzi'be] (1a) *v/t.* ⚖ produce; show (*animals, the ticket,
etc.*); *pej.* flaunt, show off; *pej.* s'⌣
make an exhibition of o.s.; **exhibition** [⌣bi'sjɔ̃] *f* ⚖ production;
showing, display, exhibition; (*cattle-
etc.*) show.

exhorter [εgzɔr'te] (1a) *v/t.* exhort,
urge, encourage.

exhumer [εgzy'me] (1a) *v/t.* exhume, disinter; *fig.* unearth, bring
to light.

exigeant, e [εgzi'ʒã, ⌣'ʒã:t] exacting, hard to please; **exigence**
[⌣'ʒã:s] *f* demand; requirement; *fig.*
exactingness; † ⌣s *pl.* conditions;
exiger [⌣'ʒe] (1l) *v/t.* demand; require; **exigible** [⌣'ʒibl] due (*payment*).

exigu, -guë [εgzi'gy] exiguous;
scanty; slender (*income, means*);
exiguïté [⌣gµi'te] *f* tininess, smallness; slenderness.

exil [εg'zil] *m* exile, banishment;
exilé *m*, e *f* [εgzi'le] exile; **exiler**
[⌣] (1a) *v/t.* exile, banish.

existence [εgzis'tã:s] *f* existence;
life; † ⌣s *pl.* stock *sg.*; *moyens m/pl.
d'*⌣ means of subsistence; **existen-
tialisme** *phls.* [⌣tãsja'lism] *m* ex-
istentialism; **existentialiste** *phls.*
[⌣tãsja'list] *adj.*, *a. su.* existential-
ist; **exister** [⌣'te] (1a) *v/i.* exist,
be; be extant.

exode [εg'zɔd] *m* exodus (*a. fig.*);
bibl. ⚥ Exodus; ⌣ *rural sociology*:
drift to the towns, urban drift.

exonérer [εgzɔne're] (1f) *v/t.* exempt; free; exonerate; remit (*s.o.'s*)
fees.

exorbitant, e [εgzɔrbi'tã, ⌣'tã:t]
exorbitant, excessive.

exorciser *eccl.* [εgzɔrsi'ze] (1a) *v/t.*
exorcize; lay (*a ghost*).

exotique [εgzɔ'tik] exotic; *fig.* foreign.

expansibilité [εkspãsibili'te] *f phys.*
expansibility; *fig.* expansiveness;
expansible *phys.* [⌣'sibl] expan-

sible; **expansif, -ve** [ˌʌˈsif, ˌʌˈsiːv] *phys.*, *a. fig.* expansive; *fig.* effusive; **expansion** [ˌʌˈsjɔ̃] *f phys.*, *a.* ⊕ expansion; *fig.* expansiveness; *culture*: spread; **expansionnisme** [ˌʌsjɔˈnism] *m* expansionism.

expatrié, e [ɛkspatriˈe] exile, expatriate; **expatrier** [ˌʌ] (1a) *v/t.* expatriate; exile, banish; s'ˌʌ leave one's own country.

expectant, e [ɛkspɛkˈtɑ̃, ˌʌˈtɑ̃ːt] expectant; **expectative** [ˌʌtaˈtiːv] *f* expectancy; *dans l'*ˌʌ de waiting for.

expectoration ✧ *etc.* [ɛkspɛktɔraˈsjɔ̃] *f* expectoration; sputum; **expectorer** [ˌʌˈre] (1a) *v/t.* expectorate.

expédient, e [ɛkspeˈdjɑ̃, ˌʌˈdjɑ̃ːt] **1.** *adj.* expedient, advisable, proper (to, de); **2.** *su./m* expedient, shift; *vivre d'*ˌʌs live by one's wits.

expédier [ɛkspeˈdje] (1o) *v/t.* dispatch; get rid of; dispose of (*s.th.*) quickly, hurry through; send (off), forward (*mail etc.*), clear (*the customs*); ⚖ draw up (*a contract*); ˌʌ qch. par bateau ship s.th.; **expéditeur** *m*, **-trice** *f* [ɛkspediˈtœːr, ˌʌˈtris] sender; ✝ consigner, shipper; forwarding agent; **expéditif, -ve** [ˌʌˈtif, ˌʌˈtiːv] expeditious, prompt; **expédition** [ˌʌˈsjɔ̃] *f* expedition (*a. geog.*), dispatch (*a.* ✝); ✝ sending; ✝ consignment; ✝ shipping; copy; **expéditionnaire** [ˌʌsjɔˈnɛːr] *m* ✝ sender; ✝ forwarding agent; shipper, consigner.

expérience [ɛkspeˈrjɑ̃ːs] *f* experience; ⚗ *etc.* experiment, test; *par* ˌʌ from experience.

expérimenté, e [ɛksperimɑ̃ˈte] experienced; skilled (*workman*); **expérimenter** [ˌʌ] (1a) *v/t.* test, try; *v/i.* experiment (on, *sur*).

expert, e [ɛksˈpɛːr, ˌʌˈpɛrt] **1.** *adj.* expert, skilled (in en, *dans*); able; **2.** *su./m* expert (in, at en) (*a.* ⚖); ✝ valuer; *fig.* connoisseur; ✝ ˌʌ comptable chartered accountant; **expertise** [ɛkspɛrˈtiːz] *f* ✝ expert appraisal *or* valuation; ⚓ survey; expert evidence; expert opinion; **expertiser** [ˌʌtiˈze] (1a) *v/t.* ✝ value, appraise; ⚓ survey.

expiable [ɛksˈpjabl] expiable; **expiation** [ˌʌpjaˈsjɔ̃] *f* expiation; *eccl.* atonement (for, *de*); **expiatoire** [ˌʌpjaˈtwaːr] expiatory; **expier**

[ˌʌˈpje] (1o) *v/t.* expiate, atone for, F pay for.

expiration [ɛkspiraˈsjɔ̃] *f* expiration, breathing out; termination, expiry; ⊕ *steam*: discharge; **expirer** [ˌʌˈre] (1a) *v/t.* breathe out; *v/i.* expire (*a.* ⚖), die.

explétif, -ve [ɛkspleˈtif, ˌʌˈtiːv] *adj.*, *a. su./m* expletive.

explicable [ɛkspliˈkabl] explicable, explainable; **explicatif, -ve** [ˌʌkaˈtif, ˌʌˈtiːv] explanatory; **explication** [ˌʌkaˈsjɔ̃] *f* explanation; ˌʌ de texte textual commentary.

explicite [ɛkspliˈsit] explicit, plain.

expliquer [ɛkspliˈke] (1m) *v/t.* explain; comment upon (*a text*); account for; s'ˌʌ explain o.s.; be explained; s'ˌʌ avec have it out with; je m'explique what I mean is this.

exploit [ɛksˈplwa] *m* exploit, deed, feat; ⚖ writ, summons *sg.*; ⚖ signifier un ˌʌ à serve a writ on; **exploitable** [ɛksplwaˈtabl] workable (*quarry*); ⚒ gettable (*coal*); exploitable (*person*); ⚖ distrainable; **exploitation** [ˌʌtaˈsjɔ̃] *f* exploitation (*a. fig.*); ✝ management; ⚒, ⚱, quarry: working; farming; trees: felling; *fig.* swindling; mine, workings *pl.*; **exploiter** [ˌʌˈte] (1a) *v/t.* exploit (*a. fig.*); ⚒ work; ✚ cultivate; ✝ manage; fig. take advantage of; *fig.* swindle; *v/i.* ⚖ serve a writ.

explorateur, -trice [ɛksplɔraˈtœːr, ˌʌˈtris] **1.** *adj.* exploratory; **2.** *su.* explorer; **exploration** [ˌʌraˈsjɔ̃] *f* exploration; ⚔ reconnaissance; *telev.* scanning; **explorer** [ˌʌˈre] (1a) *v/t.* explore; ✧ probe; ⚔ reconnoitre; *telev.*, *cin.* scan.

exploser [ɛksplɔˈze] (1a) *v/i.* ⊕, ⚔, *a. fig.* explode; *faire* ˌʌ blow up; **explosible** [ˌʌˈzibl] explosive; detonable; **explosif, -ve** [ˌʌˈzif, ˌʌˈziːv] *adj.*, *a. su./m* explosive; **explosion** [ˌʌˈzjɔ̃] *f* explosion; ⊕ bursting; ˌʌ démographique population explosion; *moteur m à* ˌʌ internal combustion engine.

exportation ✝ [ɛkspɔrtaˈsjɔ̃] *f* exportation; export trade; ˌʌs *pl.* exports.

exposant, e [ɛkspoˈzɑ̃, ˌʌˈzɑ̃ːt] *su.* ⚖ petitioner; *paint. etc.* exhibitor; *su./m* ⅄ exponent; index; **exposé** [ˌʌˈze] *m* report; outline; account;

statement; **exposer** [~'ze] (1a) *v/t.* expose; disclose (*plans*); set forth; state; *paint.* exhibit; jeopardize; s'~ take risks; **exposition** [~zi'sjɔ̃] *f* exhibition; *eccl.* exposition; exposure (*to cold, to danger*); *of a baby*; *of a house*); *facts etc.:* statement, exposition.

exprès, expresse [ɛks'prɛ, ~'prɛs] **1.** *adj.* explicit, express, definite; **2.** *exprès adv.* deliberately, on purpose; **3.** *su./m* express messenger; *lettre f exprès* express letter.

express 🚂 [ɛks'prɛs] *m* express.

expressément [ɛksprɛse'mɑ̃] expressly.

expressif, -ve [ɛksprɛ'sif, ~'siːv] expressive; **expression** [~'sjɔ̃] *f* expression; Å, *fig. réduire à la plus simple* ~ reduce to the simplest terms.

exprimer [ɛkspri'me] (1a) *v/t.* express; put into words, voice; show (*an emotion*); squeeze out (*juice*); *si l'on peut s'~ ainsi* if one may put it that way.

expropriation 🏛 [ɛksprɔpria'sjɔ̃] *f* expropriation; compulsory purchase; **exproprier** 🏛 [~'e] (1a) *v/t.* expropriate.

expulser [ɛkspyl'se] (1a) *v/t.* expel (*a. an electron, a. a pupil*); eject (*s.o.*); 🏛 evict (*a tenant*); *univ.* send (*a student*) down; ⊕ discharge.

expurger [ɛkspyr'ʒe] (11) *v/t.* expurgate, bowdlerize (*a book*).

exquis, e [ɛks'ki, ~'kiːz] exquisite; **exquisément** [~kize'mɑ̃] *adv. of exquis.*

exsangue [ɛk'sɑ̃ːg] an(a)emic, bloodless.

exsuder [ɛksy'de] (1a) *vt/i.* exude.

extase [ɛks'taːz] *f* ecstasy; *fig.* rapture; 🌟 trance; **extasié, e** [~tɑ'zje] enraptured; **extasier** [~tɑ'zje] (1o) *v/t.:* s'~ go into ecstasies (over *devant, sur*).

extenseur [ɛkstɑ̃'sœːr] **1.** *adj./m anat.* extensor; **2.** *su./m anat. muscle:* extensor; *sp.* chest-expander; *trousers:* stretcher; 🚗 shock-absorber; **extensible** [~'sibl] extensible; *metall.* tensile; **extension** [~'sjɔ̃] *f* extent; extension (*a.* ✝); spreading; stretching; ⊕ *etc.* tension; *gramm. par* ~ in a wider sense.

exténuer [ɛkste'nɥe] (1n) *v/t.* exhaust, tire out; † extenuate.

extérieur, e [ɛkste'rjœːr] **1.** *adj.* exterior, external, outer; *pol.* foreign; *affaires f/pl.* ~es foreign affairs; **2.** *su./m* exterior (*a. cin.*); outside; *fig.* appearance; *pol.* foreign countries *pl.*

exterminateur, -trice [ɛkstɛrmina'tœːr, ~'tris] **1.** *adj.* exterminating, destroying; **2.** *su.* exterminator, destroyer; **exterminer** [~'ne] (1a) *v/t.* exterminate, destroy, wipe out.

externat [ɛkstɛr'na] *m* day-school; 🩺 non-resident studentship; **externe** [~'tɛrn] **1.** *adj.* external, outer, 🩺 out-(*patient*); 🩺 *usage m* ~ external application; **2.** *su.* daypupil; 🩺 non-resident medical student.

extincteur, -trice [ɛkstɛ̃k'tœːr, ~'tris] **1.** *adj.* extinguishing; **2.** *su./m* fire-extinguisher; ~ *à mousse* foam extinguisher; **extinction** [~'sjɔ̃] *f* extinction; *fire, light:* extinguishing; suppression; termination; *race etc.:* dying out; *voice:* loss; 🚂 ~ *des feux* lights out, *Am.* taps.

extirper [ɛkstir'pe] (1a) *v/t.* eradicate (*a. fig.*).

extorquer [ɛkstɔr'ke] (1m) *v/t.* extort (from, out of *à*); **extorsion** [~tɔr'sjɔ̃] *f* extortion; blackmail.

extra [ɛks'tra] **1.** *su./m/inv.* extra; hired waiter; temporary job; **2.** *adj./inv.* extra-special; **3.** *adv.* extra-...

extraction [ɛkstrak'sjɔ̃] *f* extraction (*a.* Å, 🩺, *a. fig.*); *stone:* quarrying; *gold:* winning; *fig.* origin, descent.

extradition 🏛 [ɛkstradi'sjɔ̃] *f* extradition.

extraire [ɛks'trɛːr] (4ff) *v/t.* extract (*a.* 🏛); pull (*a tooth*); quarry (*stone*); win (*gold*); copy out (*a passage*); *fig.* rescue; **extrait** [~'trɛ] *m* extract; *admin.* (*birth- etc.*) certificate; abstract; ✝ ~ *de compte* statement of account.

extraordinaire [ɛkstraɔrdi'nɛːr] **1.** *adj.* extraordinary; uncommon; special; wonderful; queer; **2.** *su./m* extraordinary thing; *the* unusual.

extrapoler [ɛkstrapɔ'le] (1a) *v/t.* extrapolate.

extravagance [ɛkstrava'gɑ̃ːs] *f* extravagance; absurdity; *fig.* ~s *pl.* nonsense *sg.*; **extravagant, e** [~'gɑ̃, ~'gɑ̃ːt] extravagant; absurd; exorbitant, prohibitive (*price*); **ex-**

travaguer [ˌ‿'ge] (1m) *v/i*. ⚕ rave; *fig*. talk nonsense; act wildly.

extrême [eks'trɛːm] **1.** *adj*. extreme; utmost, furthest; drastic (*measures*); intense (*cold*, *emotions*, *etc*.); **2.** *su./m* extreme; *à l'*‿ in the extreme; ‿**-onction** *eccl*. [ekstremɔ̃k'sjɔ̃] *f* extreme unction; ♀**-Orient** *geog*. [ˌ‿mɔ'rjɑ̃] *m* the Far East; **extrémiste** *pol. etc*. [ekstre'mist] *adj*., *a. su*. extremist; **extrémité** [ˌ‿mi'te] *f* extremity; very end, tip; extreme; plight, straits *pl*.; last moment; point

of death; ‿*s pl*. extremities; extreme measures.

extrinsèque [ekstrɛ̃'sɛk] extrinsic.

exubérance [egzybe'rɑ̃ːs] *f* exuberance, luxuriance, superabundance; **exubérant, e** [ˌ‿'rɑ̃, ˌ‿'rɑ̃ːt] exuberant, luxuriant, superabundant; immoderate (*laughter*).

exultation [egzylta'sjɔ̃] *f* exultation, rejoicing; *avec* ‿ exultantly; **exulter** [ˌ‿'te] (1a) *v/i*. exult, rejoice.

ex-voto [eksvɔ'to] *m/inv*. votive offering; ex-voto.

F

F, f [ɛf] *m* F, f.

fa ♪ [fa] *m/inv.* fa, *note*: F; ~ *dièse* F sharp; *clef f de* ~ F-clef.

fable [faːbl] *f* fable; story; *fig.* falsehood; *fig.* talk, laughing-stock (*of the town*); **fabliau** [fabli'o] *m* Old French *literature*: fabliau; **fablier** [~'e] *m* book of fables.

fabricant [fabri'kɑ̃] *m* manufacturer; mill-owner; maker; **fabrication** [~ka'sjɔ̃] *f* manufacture; production; *document*: forging; *fig.* fabrication; ~ *en série* mass production; **fabrique** [fa'brik] *f* manufacture; factory, works *usu. sg.*; *paper, cloth*: mill; make; *eccl.* fabric (*of a church*); *eccl.* church council; **fabriquer** [~bri'ke] (1m) *v/t.* ⊕ manufacture; *fig.* make, do; *fig.* fabricate (*a charge, lies, a document*); coin (*a word*); *sl.* cheat, pinch.

fabulation [fabyla'sjɔ̃] *f* fantasizing; fabrication; **fabuler** (1a) *v/i.* fantasize; make up stories (*a. fig.*); **fabuleux, -euse** [faby'lø, ~'løːz] fabulous (*a. fig.*).

façade [fa'sad] *f* façade; frontage; front; F window-dressing.

face [fas] *f* face; countenance; aspect; front; ♣, *a.* ♪ *record*: side; surface; *de*~ full-face (*photo*); *d'en*~ opposite; *en* ~ *de* in front of; in the presence of; opposite; *faire* ~ *à* face; *fig.* meet; cope with; *pile ou* ~ heads or tails; ~ *à* **face** *telev.* [~a'fas] *m/inv.* encounter; ~-**à-main,** *pl.* ~**s-à-main** [~a'mɛ̃] *m* lorgnette.

facétie [fase'si] *f* facetious remark; joke; **facétieux, -euse** [~'sjø,~'sjøːz] facetious, waggish.

facette [fa'sɛt] *f* facet (*a. zo.*).

fâché, e [fa'ʃe] sorry; angry, cross (about, *de*; with s.o., *avec*); annoyed; offended; **fâcher** [~] (1a) *v/t.* anger, make angry; offend; grieve, pain; *se* ~ get angry; get angry *or* annoyed (with, *contre*; over, *pour*); fall out (with, *avec*); F *se* ~ *tout rouge* blow one's top, *Br. a.* go spare; **fâcherie** [faʃ'ri] *f* tiff, quarrel; bad

feeling; **fâcheux, -euse** [fa'ʃø, ~'ʃøːz] annoying; deplorable, regrettable; awkward (*situation*).

facial, e, *m/pl.* **-aux** [fa'sjal, ~'sjo] facial, face-...

facile [fa'sil] easy; simple; facile; *fig.* pliable; fluent (*tongue*); **facilité** [fasili'te] *f* easiness; ease; readiness; facility (*a.* ♣), aptitude; complaisance; ♣ ~*s pl. de* **paiement** easy terms; **faciliter** [~] (1a) *v/t.* facilitate, make easy *or* easier (for s.o., *à* q.).

façon [fa'sɔ̃] *f* make; fashioning; way, manner; ~*s pl.* manners, behavio(u)r *sg.*; ceremony *sg.*, fuss *sg.*; affectation *sg.*; *de* ~ *à* so as to; *de* ~ *que* so that; *de la bonne* ~ properly; in fine style; *de ma* ~ of my own composition; *de toute* ~ in any case; *faire des* ~*s* stand on ceremony; *cost. on travaille à* ~ customers' own materials made up; *sans* ~(*s*) simple; offhanded(ly *adv.*); unceremonious(ly *adv.*); without further ado.

faconde [fa'kɔ̃d] *f* loquaciousness.

façonner [fasɔ'ne] (1a) *v/t.* shape; form, fashion; make (*a dress etc.*); train; ✔ dress (*the soil*); *fig.* mould (*s.o.*); **façonnier, -ère** [~'nje, ~'njɛːr] **1.** *adj.* fussy; bespoke (*worker*); **2.** *su.* home-worker.

fac-similé [faksimi'le] *m* facsimile, exact copy.

facteur [fak'tœːr] *m* postman, *Am.* mailman; maker; ♪ instrument maker; ♣, *a. fig.* factor.

factice [fak'tis] artificial, factitious.

factieux, -euse [fak'sjø, ~'sjøːz] **1.** *adj.* factious, seditious; **2.** *su.* sedition-monger; **faction** [~'sjɔ̃] *f* ⚔ sentry-duty, guard, watch; *fig.* faction; *être de* ~ be on sentry-go *or* on guard; **factionnaire** [~sjɔ'nɛːr] *m* sentry; sentinel.

factotum [faktɔ'tɔm] *m* factotum; man-of-all-work.

factuel, -elle [fakty'ɛl] factual, objective.

facture [fak'tyːr] *f* ♣ workmanship,

make (*of an article*); ⚕ bill, invoice;
♪ *instruments*: manufacturing; ♪
organ pipes: scale; **facturer** ⚕
[⌣ty're] (1a) *v/t.* invoice; **facturier**
⚕ [⌣ty'rje] *m* invoice clerk; sales-
book.

facultatif, -ve [fakylta'tif, ⌣'ti:v]
optional; ⚖ permissive; *arrêt m* ⌣
request stop; **faculté** [⌣'te] *f* faculty (*a. univ., a. fig.*); option; power,
ability; ⌣s *pl.* means, resources.

fada F [fa'da] *m* fool; **fadaise**
[fa'dɛ:z] *f* nonsense, *Am. sl.* baloney.

fadasse [fa'das] sickly (*taste*); pale
(*colour*).

fade [fad] insipid, tasteless; washed-
out (*colour*); **fadeur** [fa'dœ:r] *f*
insipidity; *smell*: sickliness; *fig.*
pointlessness; *fig.* ⌣s *pl.* insipid talk
sg. or compliments.

fading [fɛ'diŋ] *m radio*: fading.

fafiot † *sl.* [fa'fjo] *m* bank-note.

fagot [fa'go] *m* bundle of firewood;
fig. sentir le ⌣ smack of heresy; **fago-
ter** [⌣'te] (1a) *v/t.* † bundle (*firewood*); F dress (*s.o.*) badly.

faible [fɛbl] **1.** *adj.* weak; feeble (*a.
fig.*); faint (*smell, sound, voice*); slight
(*difference, hope, pain*); gentle
(*slope*); slender (*means*); poor (*performance*); lame (*excuse*). **2.** *su.*
weakness, foible; *person*: weakling;
les économiquement ⌣s *pl.* the lower
income groups; **faiblesse** [fɛ'blɛs] *f*
weakness, feebleness; frailty; ⚕
fainting fit; *fig.* weak point; *amount,
number*: smallness; **faiblir** [⌣'bli:r]
(2a) *v/i.* weaken; ⊕ lose power.

faïence [fa'jã:s] *f* earthenware,
crockery; **faïencerie** [⌣jãs'ri] *f*
trade, *a. works*: pottery; crockery
shop; earthenware, crockery; **faïen-
cier** *m*, **-ère** *f* [⌣jã'sje, ⌣'sjɛ:r]
crockery- or earthenware-maker or
dealer. [*falloir.*⟩

faille¹ [faj] *3rd p. sg. pres. sbj. of*⟩

faille² [fa:j] *f* ⚒, *geol.* fault; *fig.* flaw,
weakness.

failli *m*, **e** *f* ⚖ [fa'ji] bankrupt,
faillible [⌣'jibl] fallible; **faillir**
[⌣'ji:r] (2n) *v/i.*: ⌣ *faire qch.* almost or
nearly do s.th., all but do s.th.; *j'ai
failli tomber* I nearly fell; ⌣ *à un devoir*
fail in a duty; **faillite** [⌣'jit] *f* bankruptcy; *fig.* failure; *faire* ⌣ go bankrupt; *mettre q. en* ⌣ declare s.o.
bankrupt.

faim [fɛ̃] *f* hunger; *fig.* thirst (for
glory, *de gloire*); *avoir (très)* ⌣ be
(very) hungry; *avoir une* ⌣ *canine* (*or
de loup*) be ravenous; *mourir de* ⌣ die
of starvation; F be famished.

faine ⚘ [fɛ:n] *f* beechnut.

fainéant, e [fɛne'ã, ⌣'ã:t] **1.** *adj.*
idle, lazy; slothful; **2.** *su.* idler;
sluggard; **fainéanter** [⌣ã'te] (1a)
v/i. idle, loaf; **fainéantise** [⌣ã'ti:z]
f idleness, laziness.

faire [fɛ:r] (4r) **1.** *v/t.* make (*bread,
a voyage, a declaration, one's bed, a
profit*), do; create; form; beget (*a
child*); make out (*a list*, ⚕ *a cheque*);
pay (*attention, a visit*); clean (*one's
shoes*), do (*a room*); pack (*a trunk*);
cover (*a distance*), travel; carry out,
perform (*a.* ⚕ *an operation*); work
(*miracles*); play (*a.* ♪), feign; see to
it (that *ind.*, *que sbj.*); deal (*cards*);
matter; ⚕ run (*a temperature*); ⚕
place (*an order*); *thea.* act (*a part*),
F look; *followed by an inf.:* make,
cause, have; ⌣ *attention* take care;
⌣ *de la peine à hurt* (*s.o.'s*) feelings;
⌣ *de la peinture* paint; ⌣ *de q. son
héritier* make s.o. one's heir; ⌣ *du
bien à* do (*s.o.*) good; *mot.* ⌣ *du 150
kilomètres à l'heure* do 150 kilometres per hour; ⌣ *du ski* ski;
⌣ *du sport* go in for sports; *thea.* ⌣
du théâtre be on the stage (*professional*); ⌣ *école* set a fashion; ⌣
entrer show (*s.o.*) in; ⌣ *faire* have
(*s.th.*) done or made (*by s.o., à q.*);
⌣ *fortune* make a fortune; ⌣ *la
cuisine* do the cooking; ⌣ *la vaisselle* wash up the dishes; ✧ ⌣ *le
commerce de* deal in; *mot.* ⌣ *le plein*
fill up (with, *de*); ⌣ *mention de*
mention; ⌣ *partie de* form part of;
⌣ *pendre* get (*s.o.*) hanged; ⌣ *sa
philosophie* read philosophy; ⌣
savoir inform (*s.o. of s.th., qch. à
q.*); ⌣ *un sourire à* give (*s.o.*) a
smile; ⌣ *venir* send for; *ça ne fait
rien* it does not matter; *en* ⌣ *trop*
overdo; *faites-lui mes amitiés* give
him my kindest regards; *ne* ⌣ *que
(inf.)* do nothing but (*inf.*); *qu'est-
ce que ça peut nous* ⌣? what is that
to us!; *trois et six font neuf* three
and six are or make nine; *se* ⌣ be
done; become; happen; get used
to; *cela ne se fait pas* that is not
done; *comment se fait-il que?* how
does it happen that?, how is it

that?; *il peut se ~ que* it may happen that; *ne vous en faites pas!* don't worry!; don't bother!; *se ~ entendre* make o.s. heard; be heard; **2.** *v/i.* do, act; manage; make (with, de); look; last; *cards:* deal; fit; say, remark; *~ bien de* (*inf.*) do well *or* right to (*inf.*); *~ bien sur dress:* look well on (*s.o.*); *~ de son mieux* do one's best (to *inf.*, *pour inf.*); *elle fait très jeune* she looks quite young; *fit-il* he said, said he; *je ne peux ~ autrement que de* (*inf.*) I cannot but (*inf.*); *laisser ~ q.* let s.o. alone; *qu'y ~?* what can be done about it?; **3.** *v/impers.* be; *il fait chaud* (*beau, nuit*) it is hot (fine, dark); *il fait bon* (*inf.*) it is nice to (*inf.*); **~-part** [fɛr-'pa:r] *m/inv.* notice, announcement; **~-valoir** *thea., fig.* [~va'lwa:r] *m/inv.* foil.

faisable [fə'zabl] feasible, practicable.

faisan [fə'zɑ̃] *m* pheasant; **faisan(d)e** [~'zan, ~'zɑ̃:d] *f* (*a. poule f ~*) hen-pheasant; **faisandé, e** [fəzɑ̃-'de] high; gamy; *fig.* spicy (*story*); **faisandeau** [~'do] *m* young pheasant; **faisander** *cuis.* [~'de] (1a) *v/t.* hang (*game etc.*); *se ~* get high; **faisanderie** [~'dri] *f* pheasantry; **faisandier** [~'dje] *m* pheasant breeder.

faisceau [fɛ'so] *m* bundle; cluster; *rays:* pencil; beam; 🚂 sidings; group; *~x pl.* fasces; ✗ *~ d'armes* pile *or* stack of arms; former (*rompre*) *les ~x* (un)pile arms.

faiseur *m*, **-euse** *f* [fə'zœːr, ~'zøːz] maker, doer; *fig.* bluffer; *faiseuse d'anges* back-street abortionist; *~ de mariages* matchmaker; *~ d'intrigues* schemer; *~ de vers* versifier; **faisons** [fə'zɔ̃] *1st p. pl. pres. of faire*; **fait, e** [fɛ, fɛt] **1.** *p.p. of faire*; *c'en est ~ de it's* all up with; **2.** *su./m* fact; deed; act; feat, achievement; happening; development; case; matter, point; *au ~* after all; *de* (*or en*) *~* as a matter of fact; actually; *~s pl. divers* news items; news in brief; *du ~ de on* account of; *en ~ de* as regards; *en venir au ~* come to the point, get down to business; *être au ~ de qch.* be informed of s.th., know how s.th. stands; *il est de ~ que* it is a fact that; *mettre q. au ~ de qch.* acquaint s.o.

with s.th.; give s.o. full information about s.th.

faîtage 🏠 [fɛ'ta:ʒ] *m* ridge-piece; roof-tree; ridge tiling; roof timbers *pl.*; **faîte** [fɛ:t] *m* top, summit; 🏠 ridge; *geog.* crest.

faites [fɛt] *2nd p. pl. pres. of faire*.

faix [fɛ] *m* burden, load.

fakir [fa'ki:r] *m* fakir.

falaise [fa'lɛ:z] *f* cliff.

fallacieux, -euse [fala'sjø, ~'sjø:z] fallacious, misleading.

falloir [fa'lwa:r] (3e) *v/impers.* be necessary, be lacking; *il faut que je* (*sbj.*) I must (*inf.*); *il me faut* (*inf.*) I must (*inf.*); *il me faut qch.* I want s.th.; I need s.th.; *comme il faut* proper(ly *adv.*); *il s'en faut de beaucoup* far from it; *peu s'en faut* very nearly; *tant s'en faut* not by a long way; **fallu** [~'ly] *p.p. of falloir*; **fallut** [~'ly] *3rd p. sg. p.s. of falloir*.   [(stable) lamp.]

falot¹ [fa'lo] *m* (hand) lantern; **falot², e** [fa'lo, ~'lɔt] wan (*light*); *fig.* dull, dreary (*person*); † odd, quaint.

falsificateur *m*, **-trice** *f* [falsifika-'tœːr, ~'tris] forger (*of papers*); adulterator (*of food, milk, etc.*); **falsification** [~'sjɔ̃] *f* forgery, forging; adulteration; **falsifier** [falsi'fje] (1o) *v/t.* falsify; forge; adulterate (*food etc.*).

famé, e [fa'me] *adj.:* *bien* (*mal*) *~* of good (evil) repute.

famélique [fame'lik] **1.** *adj.* starving, famished; **2.** *su.* starveling.

fameux, -euse [fa'mø, ~'møːz] famous, renowned, celebrated; F first-class, magnificent, capital, *Am.* swell.

familial, e, *m/pl.* **-aux** [fami'ljal, ~'ljo] family...; domestic; **familiariser** [familjari'ze] (1a) *v/t.* familiarize; *se ~ avec* make o.s. familiar with; **familiarité** [~'te] *f* familiarity; *fig. ~s pl.* liberties; **familier, -ère** [fami'lje, ~'lje:r] **1.** *adj.* family..., domestic; familiar, well-known; intimate; colloquial; *expression f ~ère* colloquialism; **2.** *su.* intimate; regular visitor; **famille** [~'mi:j] *f* family; household.

famine [fa'min] *f* famine, starvation.

fana F [fa'na] **1.** *adj.* enthusiastic, fanatic; **2.** *su.* enthusiast, fan(atic).

fanal [fa'nal] *m* lantern; beacon; ⚓ navigation light; 🚂 headlight.

fanatique [fana'tik] 1. *adj.* fanatical; enthusiastic; 2. *su.* fanatic; enthusiast; **fanatisme** [~'tism] *m* fanaticism.

fane [fan] *f potatoes*: haulm; *carrots*: top; *dead leaves pl.*; **faner** [fa'ne] (1a) *v/t.* ted, toss (*the hay*); *fig.* cause (*colour etc.*) to fade; **se ~** fade (*colour*); wither, droop (*flower*); *v/i.* make hay; **faneur, -euse** [~'nœ:r, ~'nø:z] *su.* haymaker; *su./f* tedder, tedding machine.

fanfare [fɑ̃'fa:r] *f trumpets*: flourish; *hunt. etc.* fanfare; brass band; ✕ bugle band; **fanfaron, -onne** [fɑ̃fa'rɔ̃, ~'rɔn] 1. *adj.* boastful, bragging, swaggering; 2. *su.* swaggerer, braggart, boaster; *su./m: faire le ~* bluster; brag; **fanfaronnade** [~rɔ'nad] *f* swagger, boasting; bluster.

fanfreluche [fɑ̃frə'lyʃ] *f* bauble; *cost.* **~s** *pl.* fal-lals.

fange [fɑ̃:ʒ] *f* mud; filth, F muck; **fangeux, -euse** [fɑ̃'ʒø, ~'ʒø:z] muddy; dirty, filthy.

fanion ✕ [fa'njɔ̃] *m* flag; pennon.

fanon [fa'nɔ̃] *m eccl.* maniple; *ox*: dewlap; *horse*: fetlock; whalebone.

fantaisie [fɑ̃te'zi] *f* imagination; fancy (*a. fig.*); *fig.* whim; ♪ fantasia; *à ma ~* as the fancy takes (took) me; ✝ *articles m/pl. de ~* fancy goods; *de ~* imaginary; ✝ fancy-...; **fantaisiste** [~'zist] 1. *adj.* fantastic, freakish; 2. *su.* fanciful person.

fantasmagorie [fɑ̃tasmagɔ'ri] *f* phantasmagoria; *fig.* weird spectacle.

fantasque [fɑ̃'task] odd; whimsical, queer (*person*).

fantassin [fɑ̃ta'sɛ̃] *m* infantryman, foot-soldier.

fantastique [fɑ̃tas'tik] fantastic; weird; *fig.* incredible.

fantoche [fɑ̃'tɔʃ] *m* puppet (*a. fig.*), marionette; *gouvernement ~* puppet government.

fantôme [fɑ̃'to:m] *m* phantom, ghost, spectre; illusion; *le vaisseau ~* the Flying Dutchman.

faon [fɑ̃] *m* fawn; roe calf.

faquin [fa'kɛ̃] *m* cad, scoundrel; low fellow.

faraud, e [fa'ro, ~'ro:d] 1. *adj.* full of o.s.; affected; 2. *su.* swanker.

farce [fars] 1. *su./f* practical joke, trick; *thea., a. fig.* farce; *cuis.* stuffing, forcemeat; 2. *adj. sl.* funny, comical; **farceur** *m*, **-euse** *f* [far-'sœ:r, ~'sø:z] practical joker; wag, humorist.

farcir *cuis., a. fig.* [far'si:r] (2a) *v/t.* stuff.

fard [fa:r] *m* make-up; rouge; *fig.* artifice, camouflage; *parler sans ~* speak plainly *or* candidly; *sl.* piquer *un ~* blush.

fardeu [far'do] *m* burden (*a.* ♫), load.

farder [far'de] (1a) *v/t.* make (*s.o.*) up; paint; *fig.* disguise, camouflage; **se ~** make up. [lorry.\ ]

fardier [far'dje] *m* trolley; truck,∫

farfadet [farfa'dɛ] *m* goblin; elf.

farfelu, e F [farfə'ly] 1. *adj.* excentric, crazy, F cranky, F far-out; 2. *su.* eccentric, F nutcase, F srewball.

farfouiller [farfu'je] (1a) *v/i.* rummage (in, among *dans*); *v/t.* explore.

faribole [fari'bɔl] *f* (stuff and) nonsense.

farinacé, e [farina'se] farinaceous; **farine** [fa'rin] *f* flour, meal; *fig.* type, sort; **~** *de riz* ground rice; **fariner** *cuis.* [fari'ne] (1a) *v/t.* dust with flour; **farineux, -euse** [~'nø, ~'nø:z] 1. *adj.* farinaceous; floury; flour-covered; 2. *su./m* farinaceous food.

farouche [fa'ruʃ] wild, fierce; cruel; timid, shy; unsociable, unapproachable.

fart [fa:r] *m* ski wax; **farter** [far'te] (1a) *v/t.* wax (*one's skis*).

fascicule [fasi'kyl] *m encyclopaedia etc.*: part, section; ✿ zo. bunch; ✿, zo. fascic(u)le.

fascinateur, -trice [fasina'tœ:r, ~'tris] fascinating; **fascination** [~-'sjɔ̃] *f* fascination, charm.

fasciner [fasi'ne] (1a) *v/t.* fascinate; *fig.* entrance.

fascisme *pol.* [fa'ʃism] *m* fascism; **fasciste** *pol.* [~'ʃist] *su., a. adj.* fascist.

fasse [fas] *1st p. sg. pres. sbj. of* faire.

faste [fast] *m* pomp, display.

fastes [~] *m/pl. hist.* fasti; F records.

fastidieux, -euse [fasti'djø, ~'djø:z] tedious, dull; irksome, tiresome.

fastueux, -euse [fas'tɥø, ~'tɥø:z] ostentatious, showy; sumptuous.

fat [fat] 1. *adj./m* foppish; conceited; 2. *su./m* fop; conceited idiot.

fatal, e, *m/pl.* **-als** [fa'tal] fatal; *fig.*
inevitable; *femme f* ~e vamp; **fata-lisme** [fata'lism] *m* fatalism; **fata-liste** [~'list] **1.** *adj.* fatalistic; **2.** *su.*
fatalist; **fatalité** [~li'te] *f* fatality.
fatidique [fati'dik] prophetic (*utter-ance*); fateful.
fatigant, e [fati'gã, ~'gã:t] tiring;
tiresome, tedious; **fatigue** [fa'tig]
f fatigue (*a.* ⊕, *metall.*); tiredness,
weariness; hard work; *fig.* wear
(and tear); *brisé (or mort) de* ~ dog-tired; *de* ~ strong (*shoes*); working
(*clothes*); F *tomber de* ~ be worn
out; **fatigué, e** [fati'ge] tired,
weary; **fatiguer** [~] (1m) *v/t.* tire,
make (*s.o.*) tired; overwork; over-strain; *fig.* bore (*s.o.*); *v/i.* ⊕ labo(u)r,
strain (*engine etc.*); se ~ get tired; tire
o.s.
fatras [fa'trɑ] *m* hotchpotch, jum-ble; lumber.
fatuité [fatɥi'te] *f* conceit, self-satisfaction.
faubourg [fo'bu:r] *m* suburb; out-skirts *pl.*; *fig.* ~s *pl.* working classes;
faubourien, -enne [~bu'rjɛ̃, ~-'rjɛn] **1.** *adj.* suburban; *fig.* common
(*accent*); **2.** *su.* suburbanite; *fig.*
common person.
fauchage [fo'ʃa:ʒ] *m*, **fauchaison**
[~ɛ'zõ] *f*, **fauche** [fo:ʃ] *f* mowing,
cutting; reaping (time); **fauché, e**
[fo'ʃe] **1.** *adj.* F broke; **2.** *su./f* (one)
day's mowing *or* cutting; swath;
faucher [~'ʃe] (1a) *v/t.* mow, cut;
reap (*corn*); ✕ mow down (*troops*);
✕ sweep by fire; *sl.* pinch,
steal; **fauchet** ✔ [~'ʃɛ] *m* hay-rake;
bill-hook; **fauchette** ✔ [~'ʃɛt] *f*
bill-hook; **faucheur, -euse** [~-'ʃœ:r, ~'ʃø:z] *su. person*: reaper;
su./m zo. harvest-spider, *Am.*
daddy-longlegs; *su./f machine*:
reaper; **faucheux** *zo.* [~'ʃø] *m*
harvest-spider, *Am.* daddy-long-legs.
faucille ✔ [fo'si:j] *f* sickle.
faucon *orn.* [fo'kõ] *m* falcon, hawk (*a.
pol.*).   [*falloir.*}
faudra [fo'dra] *3rd p. sg. fut. of*}
faufil [fo'fil] *m* tacking *or* basting
thread; **faufiler** [fofi'le] (1a) *v/t.*
tack, baste; † slip (*s.th., s.o.*) in; se ~
creep in, slip in; thread *or* worm
one's way (into, *dans*); **faufilure**
[~'ly:r] *f* tacked seam; tacking, bast-ing.

faune [fo:n] *su./m myth.* faun; *su./f
zo.* fauna.
faussaire [fo'sɛ:r] forger; *fig.* falsi-fier; **fausser** [~'se] (1a) *v/t.* falsify;
distort (*facts, ideas, words*); ⊕ force
(*a lock etc.*); ⊕ warp, strain; ⊕ put
(*s.th.*) out of true; ♪ put (*s.th.*) out
of tune; F ~ *compagnie à q.* give s.o.
the slip; ~ *parole à q.* break one's
promise to s.o.
fausset[1] ♪ [fo'sɛ] *m* falsetto.
fausset[2] ⚹ [~] *m* spigot, vent-plug.
fausseté [fos'te] *f* falseness, falsity;
falsehood; *fig.* treachery, duplicity.
faut [fo] *3rd p. sg. pres. of falloir.*
faute [fo:t] *f* fault (*a. tennis*); error,
mistake; *foot. etc.* foul; ~ *de* for want
of, lacking; ~ *de mieux* for want of
anything better; *faire* ~ be lacking;
sans ~ without fail; **fauter** F † [fo'te]
(1a) *v/i.* go wrong.
fauteuil [fo'tœ:j] *m* arm-chair, easy
chair; *meeting*: chair; *thea.* stall;
Académie française: seat; ~ *à bascule*
see rocking-chair; ~ *club* club chair; ~
⚹⚹ *électrique* electric chair; ~
roulant wheel chair; Bath chair.
fauteur *m,* **-trice** *f* [fo'tœ:r, ~'tris]
instigator; ⚹⚹ abettor.
fautif, -ve [fo'tif, ~'ti:v] faulty,
wrong, incorrect; offending.
fauve [fo:v] **1.** *adj.* tawny; musky
(*smell*); lurid (*sky*); **2.** *su./m* fawn;
coll. deer *pl.*; ~s *pl.* wild beasts;
deer *pl.*; **fauvette** *orn.* [fo'vɛt] *f*
warbler.
faux[1] ✔ [fo] *f* scythe.
faux[2], **fausse** [fo, fo:s] **1.** *adj.* false;
untrue, wrong; imitation...; fraudu-lent; forged (*document*); ♪ out of
tune; ~ *col m* detachable *or* loose
collar; ~ *frais m/pl.* incidental ex-penses; *teleph.* ~ *numéro m* wrong
number; *fig.* ~ *pas m* blunder;
fausse clef f skeleton key; ⚹ *fausse
couche f* miscarriage; *fausse mon-naie f* counterfeit coin(s *pl.*); *faire
fausse route* take the wrong road;
2. *faux adv.* falsely; ♪ out of tune;
3. *su./m* falsehood; *the* untrue; ⚹⚹
forgery; ⚹⚹ *s'inscrire en* ~ *contre*
deny (*s.th.*); ~**-bourdon** ♪ [fobur-'dõ] *m* faux-bourdon; ~**-fuyant** *fig.*
[~fɥi'jã] *m* subterfuge, evasion;
~**-monnayeur** [~mɔnɛ'jœ:r] *m*
counterfeiter.
faveur [fa'vœ:r] *f* favo(u)r; *à la* ~ *de*
by the help of; under cover of

favorable

(*darkness etc.*); de ~ complimentary (*ticket*); preferential, special (*treatment, price*); en ~ in favo(u)r (of, de); mois *m* de ~ month's grace; **favorable** [favɔ'rabl] favo(u)rable; advantageous (*price etc.*); propitious; **favori, -te** [~'ri, ~'rit] **1.** *adj.* favo(u)rite; **2.** *su.* favo(u)rite; *su./m:* ~s *pl.* (side-)whiskers; **favoriser** [~ri'ze] (1a) *v/t.* favo(u)r; promote; **favoritisme** [~ri'tism] *m* favo(u)ritism.

fayot *sl.* [fa'jo] *m* ⚕ kidney-bean; *person:* eager beaver, *pej.* bootlicker.

fébrifuge ✻ [febri'fyːʒ] *adj., a. su./m* febrifuge; **fébrile** [~'bril] feverish (*a. fig.*).

fécal, e, *m/pl.* **-aux** ⚕ *physiol.* [fe'kal, ~'ko] f(a)ecal; *matières f/pl.* ~es = **fèces** [fɛs] *f/pl. physiol., a.* ⚕ f(a)eces; ⚕ precipitate *sg.*; ✻ stool *sg.*

fécond, e [fe'kɔ̃, ~'kɔ̃ːd] fruitful, fertile; productive (of, en); prolific; **fécondation** [fekɔ̃da'sjɔ̃] *f* fertilisation; impregnation; ~ *artificielle* artificial insemination; ~ *croisée, a. fig.* ~ *mutuelle* cross-fertilization; **féconder** [fekɔ̃'de] (1a) *v/t.* fecundate; fertilize; **fécondité** [~di'te] *f* fertility; fecundity; fruitfulness.

fécule [fe'kyl] *f* starch, fecula; **féculent, e** [~ky'lɑ̃, ~'lɑ̃ːt] **1.** *adj.* starchy; ⚕ thick; **2.** *su./m* starchy food.

fédéral, e, *m/pl.* **-aux** [fede'ral, ~'ro] *adj., a. su./m* federal; **fédéraliser** [~rali'ze] (1a) *v/t.* federalize; **fédératif, -ve** [~ra'tif, ~'tiːv] federative; **fédération** [~ra'sjɔ̃] *f* federation; ~ *syndicale ouvrière* trade union; **fédéré, e** [~'re] *adj., a. su./m* federate; **fédérer** [~'re] (1f) *v/t. a. se* ~ federate.

fée [fe] *f* fairy; *conte m* de ~s fairytale; *pays m* des ~s fairyland; F *vieille* ~ old hag; **féerie** [~'ri] *f* fairyland; fairy scene; *fig.* enchantment; *thea.* pantomime; fairy-play; **féerique** [~'rik] fairy, magic; *fig.* enchanting.

feindre [fɛ̃ːdr] (4m) *v/t.* feign, sham, pretend (to *inf.*, de *inf.*); *v/i.* limp slightly (*horse*); **feinte** [fɛ̃ːt] *f* pretence, sham; make-believe; bluff; *box. etc.* feint; *horse:* slight limp.

fêlé, e [fɛ'le] cracked (*a. sl. fig.*);

fêler [~] (1a) *v/t.* crack (*a glass etc.*); se ~ crack (*glass*).

félicitation [felisita'sjɔ̃] *f* congratulation; *faire des* ~s *à q.* congratulate s.o.; **félicité** [~'te] *f* bliss, joy; **féliciter** [~'te] (1a) *v/t.:* ~ *q.* de congratulate s.o. on; se ~ de be pleased with; be thankful for.

félin, e [fe'lɛ̃, ~'lin] **1.** *adj. zo.* feline, cat-...; *fig.* cat-like; **2.** *su./m zo.* feline, cat.

félon, -onne *hist.* [fe'lɔ̃, ~'lɔn] **1.** *adj.* disloyal, felon; **2.** *su./m* felon, caitiff; **félonie** *hist.* [~lɔ'ni] *f* disloyalty; *feudality:* felony.

fêlure [fɛ'lyːr] *f* crack; split; ✻ *skull:* fracture; F *avoir une* ~ be a bit cracked (= *crazy*).

femelle *zo.* [fə'mɛl] *adj., a. su./f* female.

féminin, e [femi'nɛ̃, ~'nin] **1.** *adj.* feminine; female (*sex*); woman's ...; womanly; **2.** *su./m gramm.* feminine (gender); **féminiser** [~ni'ze] (1a) *v/t.* make feminine (*a. gramm.*); give a feminine appearance to; **féminisme** [~'nism] *m* feminism; **féministe** [~'nist] *su., a. adj.* feminist.

femme [fam] **1.** *su./f* woman; wife; woman ...; ~ de chambre housemaid; ~ de charge housekeeper; ~ de ménage charwoman, cleaner; housekeeper; **2.** *adj.* female, woman ...; lady ...; **femmelette** F [~'lɛt] *f* little *or* weak woman; *man:* weakling.

fémur *anat.* [fe'myːr] *m* femur, thigh-bone.

fenaison ✟ [fənɛ'zɔ̃] *f* haymaking.

fenderie ⊕ [fɑ̃'dri] *f* metal, wood: splitting into rods; splitting-mill; splitting-machine; cutting shop; **fendeur** [~'dœːr] *m* splitter; cleaver; F woodcutter; **fendiller** [~di'je] (1a) *v/t. a. se* ~ crack (*wood, a. paint.*); crackle (*china, glaze*); craze (*china, concrete, glaze*); **fendre** [fɑ̃ːdr] (4a) *v/t.* split, cleave; slit; crack; rend (*the air*); break through (*a crowd*); se ~ split, crack; F se ~ la gueule (*or la pomme*) split one's sides; F se ~ de fork out (*a sum*); buy, stand (*a round etc.*); F il ne s'est pas fendu he didn't overspend himself.

fenêtrage [fənɛ'traːʒ] *m* windows *pl.*; **fenêtre** [~'nɛːtr] *f* window; ~ *à bascule* balance *or* pivoted window; ~ *à coulisse* (*or guillotine*) sash-window; *jeter l'argent par la* ~ throw money down the drain; **fenêtrer** △ [~nɛ'tre] (1a) *v/t.* put windows in.

fenil [fə'ni] *m* hayloft.

fenouil ♀ [fə'nu:j] *m* fennel.

fente [fɑ̃:t] *f* crack, fissure, split; slit; chink; gap; crevice; opening; ⊕ slot.

féodal, e, *m/pl.* -aux [feɔ'dal, ~'do] feudal; **féodalité** [~dali'te] *f* feudality; feudal system.

fer [fɛ:r] *m* iron; *fig.* sword; (horse-) shoe; ~s *pl.* fetters, chains; ~ à *repasser* (flat-)iron; ⊕ ~ à *souder* soldering-iron; ~ à T T-iron; *fig.* ~ *de lance* spearhead; most important factor; ~ *électrique* electric iron; ~ *en barres* bar *or* strip iron; △ *construction f en* ~ ironwork; *de* ~ iron; *donner un coup de* ~ à press, iron; *fil m de* ~ wire.

ferai [fə're] *1st p. sg. fut. of faire.*

fer-blanc, *pl.* **fers-blancs** [fɛr'blɑ̃] *m* tin(-plate); **ferblanterie** [fɛrblɑ̃'tri] *f* tin-plate; tin goods *pl.,* tinware; ⊕ tin-shop; **ferblantier** [~'tje] *m* tinsmith.

férié [fe'rje] *adj./m:* jour *m* ~ public holiday; *eccl.* holy day.

férir † [fe'ri:r] (2u) *v/t.* strike; *sans coup* ~ without striking a blow.

fermage ✍ [fɛr'ma:ʒ] *m* (farm-) rent; tenant farming.

ferme[1] [fɛrm] **1.** *adj.* firm, steady (*a.* ✝); rigid; fixed, fast; resolute; *vente f* ~ definite sale; **2.** *adv.* firmly; ~! steady!; *frapper* ~ hit hard; *tenir* ~ stand firm.   [à ~ on lease.]

ferme[2] [~] *f* farm; farming lease;)

ferme[3] △ [~] *f* truss(ed girder).

fermé [fɛr'me] **1.** *p.p. of fermer;* **2.** *adj.* shut; locked; closed (*road, shop, etc.*); closed-in (*area, site, etc.*); ⊕ *etc.* off (*faucet, tap, radio, switch, etc.*); *fig.* impenetrable, inscrutable (*face, expression, etc.*); *fig.* exclusive (*circle, club, society, etc.*); *être* ~ à *qch.* be impervious to s.th.; have no appreciation of s.th.; *être* ~ à q. be closed to s.o. (*career, circle, etc.*).

ferment [fɛr'mɑ̃] *m* ferment (*a. fig.*); *bread:* leaven; **fermentation** [~mɑ̃ta'sjɔ̃] *f* fermentation; *dough:* rising; *fig.* unrest, ferment; **fermenter** [~'te] (1a) *v/i.* ferment; rise (*dough*); *fig.* be in a ferment.

fermer [fɛr'me] (1a) *vt/i.* close,

shut; *v/t.* fasten; turn off (*the electricity, the gas, the light*); clench (*one's fist*); block (*a game, a.* 🎮); ~ à *clef* lock; ~ *au verrou* bolt; ~ à *vis* screw (*s.th.*) down; *sl.* *ferme ça!, la ferme!* shut up!; *v/i.* close (down) (*firm etc.*); wrap round (*clothes*).

fermeté [fɛrmə'te] *f* firmness; steadiness (*a. of purpose*); constancy; *fig.* strength (*of mind*).

fermette [fɛr'met] *f* (*small*) farmhouse; (*small*) rural residence.

fermeture [fɛrmə'ty:r] *f* shutting, closing; fastening; ~ *éclair* (*or* à *glissière*) zip fastener, F zip, *Am.* zipper.

fermier, -ère [~'mje, ~'mjɛːr] *su.* farmer; tenant farmer; *su./f a.* farmer's wife.

fermoir [fɛr'mwa:r] *m* snap; clasp, fastener, catch; ⊕ firmer (= *sort of chisel*).

féroce [fe'rɔs] ferocious (*a. fig.*), fierce, savage, wild; **férocité** [~rɔsi'te] *f* fierceness; ferocity.

ferraille [fɛ'raːj] *f* old iron, scrap iron; scrap-heap; *mettre à la* ~ scrap; **ferrailleur** [~ra'jœːr] *m* scrap-iron dealer; junkdealer; † F swashbuckler; **ferrant** [~'rɑ̃] *adj./m:* maréchal-~ *m* farrier; **ferré, e** [~'re] fitted with iron; iron-tipped; studded (*boots, tyres*); F well up (in, en); **ferrer** [~'re] *v/t.* (1a) shoe (*a horse*); **ferret** [~'rɛ] *m* tag, tab; *min. stone:* core; **ferronnerie** [~rɔn'ri] *f* ironworks; ironmongery; **ferronnier** [~rɔ'nje] *m* ironworker; ironmonger; **ferronnière** [~rɔ'njɛːr] *f* frontlet.

ferroutage [fɛru'ta:ʒ] *m transport:* piggyback (system).

ferroviaire [fɛrɔ'vjɛːr] railway-...

ferrugineux, -euse ♫ [fɛryʒi'nø, ~'nøːz] ferruginous, iron-...

ferrure [fɛ'ry:r] *f* iron-fitting; ironwork.

ferry-boat [fɛri'bo:t] *m* train ferry.

fertile [fɛr'til] fertile, fruitful, rich (in, en); **fertiliser** [fɛrtili'ze] (1a) *v/t.* fertilize; *se* ~ become fertile; **fertilité** [~'te] *f* fertility; richness; abundance.

féru, e [fe'ry] **1.** *p.p. of férir;* **2.** *adj.:* ~ *de* smitten with; set on (*an idea*).

férule [fe'ryl] *f* ♀ giant fennel; *school:* cane; *fig. être sous la* ~ *de q.* be under s.o.'s (iron) rule.

fervent, e [fɛr'vɑ̃, ~'vɑ̃:t] **1.** *adj.*

fervent, earnest, ardent; **2.** *su.* enthusiast; devotee, ... fan; **ferveur** [ᴧˈvœːr] *f* fervo(u)r, earnestness.

fesse [fɛs] *f* buttock; ~s *pl.* buttocks, bottom *sg.*; **fessée** [fɛˈse] *f* spanking; **fesse-mathieu** [fɛsmaˈtjø] *m* skinflint; **fesser** [fɛˈse] (1a) *v/t.* spank.

festin [fɛsˈtɛ̃] *m* feast, banquet; **festiner** [ᴧtiˈne] (1a) *v/i.* feast.

festival, *pl.* **-als** [fɛstiˈval] *m* festival; **festivité** [ᴧviˈte] *f* festivity.

feston [fɛsˈtɔ̃] *m* festoon; *needlework*: scallop; *point m de* ~ buttonhole stitch; **festonner** [ᴧtɔˈne] (1a) *v/t.* festoon; scallop (*a hem*); *v/i. sl.* stagger about.

festoyer [fɛstwaˈje] (1h) *vt/i.* feast.

fêtard *m*, **e** *f* F [fɛˈtaːr, ᴧˈtard] reveller, roisterer; **fête** [fɛːt] *f* feast, festival; holiday; name *or* Saint's day; festivity; fête; party; ~ foraine fun fair; ~ des Mères Mother's Day; ~ du travail Labo(u)r Day; *faire* ~ *à* welcome; *sl. faire sa* ~ *à q.* beat s.o. up; make things hot for s.o.; **fête-Dieu,** *pl.* **fêtes-Dieu** *eccl.* [fɛtˈdjø] *f* Corpus Christi; **fêter** [fɛˈte] (1a) *v/t.* keep (*a feast, a holiday*); feast, entertain (*s.o.*); celebrate (*a birthday, an event*).

fétiche [feˈtiʃ] *m* fetish; *mot.* mascot.

fétide [feˈtid] fetid, stinking, rank; **fétidité** [ᴧtidiˈte] *f* fetidness, foulness.

fétu [feˈty] *m* straw; F *fig.* rap.

feu¹ [fø] *m* fire (*a. of a gun or rifle*); flame; fireplace; *fig.* ardo(u)r; heat; *stove:* burner; *mot. etc.* light; *mot.* ~ *arrière* rearlight; ~ *d'artifice* firework(s *pl.*); ~ *de joie* bonfire; *mot.* ~x *pl. de signalisation* (*routière*), F ~ *rouge* traffic lights *pl.*; ~ *follet* will-o'-the-wisp; *mot.* ~ *vert* (*rouge*) green (red) light (*a. fig.*); ᴕᴕ *aller au* ~ go into action; *à petit* ~ on *or* over a slow fire; *fig.* by inches; *arme f à* ~ fire-arm; *coup m de* ~ shot; *donner du* ~ *à q.* give s.o. a light; *fig. donner le* ~ *vert* (*à q.*) give (s.o.) the green light; *fig. entrer dans le* ~ *pour q.* go through fire and water for s.o.; *faire* ~ fire (at, *sur*); *fig. faire long* ~ fail; *fig. ne pas faire long* ~ be short-lived; *mettre le* ~ *à qch.* set fire to s.th., set s.th. on fire; *par le fer et le* ~ by fire and sword; *prendre* ~ catch fire; *fig.* flare up, fly into a temper.

feu², **feue** [fø] *adj.* (*inv. before article and poss. adj.*) late, deceased; *la feue reine, feu la reine* the late queen.

feuillage [fœˈjaːʒ] *m* leaves *pl.*, foliage; **feuillaison** ᴕ [ᴧjɛˈzɔ̃] *f* foliation; springtime; **feuillard** [ᴧˈjaːr] *m* hoop-wood; hoop-iron; ⊕ metallic ribbon; **feuille** [fœːj] *f* ᴕ leaf; *paper:* sheet; *admin.* form; ⚹ chart; ⚏ list; F *journ.* ~ *de chou* rag; ~ *de paie* wage-sheet; ~ *de présence* attendance list; ⊕ time-sheet; ~ *de route* ⚼ way-bill; ᴕᴕ marching orders *pl.*; ᴕᴕ travel warrant; ~ *volante* fly-sheet; **feuillée** [fœˈje] *f* arbo(u)r; foliage; ᴕᴕ ~s *pl.* latrines; **feuille-morte** [fœːjˈmɔrt] *adj./inv.* dead-leaf (*colour*); oak-leaf brown; russet; **feuillet** [fœˈje] *m book:* leaf; *admin.* form; sheet; ⊕ thin sheet, plate; **feuilletage** *cuis.* [fœjˈtaːʒ] *m*, **feuilletée** *cuis.* [ᴧˈte] *m* puff paste; **feuilleter** [ᴧˈte] (1c) *v/t.* skim through, thumb through, turn over the pages of (*a book*); *cuis.* roll and fold; ⊕ divide into sheets; **feuilleton** [ᴧˈtɔ̃] *m journ.* feuilleton; serial (story).

feuillette [fœˈjɛt] *f* (*approx.*) half-hogshead.

feuillu, e [fœˈjy] leafy; deciduous (*forest*).

feutre [føːtr] *m* felt; felt hat; *saddle:* stuffing; **feutrer** [føˈtre] (1a) *v/t.* felt; stuff, pad (*a saddle etc.*); *à pas feutrés* noiselessly; **feutrier** [ᴧtriˈe] *m* felt-maker.

fève [fɛːv] *f* bean; **fèverole** ᴕ [fɛˈvrɔl] *f* field-bean.

février [fevriˈe] *m* February.

fi! [fi] *int.* fie!; for shame!; ~ *de* ...! a fig for ...!; *faire* ~ *de* scorn, turn up one's nose at.

fiabilité [fjabiliˈte] *f* reliability; **fiable** [fjabl] reliable.

fiacre [fjakr] *m* cab, hackney carriage.

fiançailles [fjãˈsaːj] *f/pl.* engagement *sg.*, betrothal *sg.* (to, *avec*); **fiancé** [ᴧˈse] *m* fiancé; **fiancée** [ᴧˈse] *f* fiancée; **fiancer** [ᴧˈse] (1k) *v/t.* betroth; *se* ~ become engaged (to, *à*).

fiasco [fjasˈko] *m* fiasco; *faire* ~ turn out *or* be a fiasco.

fibranne *tex.* [fiˈbran] *f* staple fibre. **fibre** [fibr] *f* fibre; *wood:* grain; *fig.* feeling; ~ *de bois packing:* wood-

wool, *Am.* excelsior; ~ *de verre*
glass-wool; *(la)* ~ *de la poésie* (a)
soul for poetry; *avoir la* ~ *sensible*
be impressionable; **fibreux, -euse**
[fi'brø, ~'brøːz] fibrous, stringy;
fibrille *physiol.* [~'briːj] *f* fibril.

ficeler [fis'le] (1c) *v/t.* tie up, do up;
sl. dress *(s.o.)* badly; **ficelle** [fi'sɛl]
1. *su./f* string (*a. fig.*); twine;
tricks *pl.*; *sl.* *connaître toutes les* ~s
know the ropes; **2.** *adj.* wily,
cunning.

fiche [fiʃ] *f iron, wood:* peg, pin;
paper: form, voucher; sheet, slip (*of
paper*); label; index card; *games:*
counter; ⚡ plug; *fig.* scrap; ~ *de paye*
wages slip; ⚡ ~ *femelle* jack; *mettre
qch. sur* ~s card(-index) *s.th.*; **ficher**
[fi'ʃe] (1a) *v/t.* stick in, drive in; ⚠
point (*a wall*); *sl.* do; *sl.* put; *sl.* give;
sl. ~ *q. à la porte* throw *s.o.* out; *sl.*
fichez-moi la paix! leave me alone!;
sl. *fichez(-moi) le camp!* clear off!;
clear out!; *sl.* *se* ~ *de* make fun of; not
to care (a hang) about; **fichier**
[~'fje] *m* card index; file (*case*); ~ *de
données* data file.

fichoir [fi'ʃwaːr] *m* clothes-peg.

fichtre! *sl.* [fiʃtr] *int.* my word!;
indeed!; hang it!

fichu¹ [fi'ʃy] *m* neck scarf; small
shawl.

fichu², e *sl.* [~] **1.** *p.p.* of *ficher;*
2. *adj.* lost, done for, *sl.* bust; rotten,
sl. lousy; *mal* ~ wretched; out of
sorts.

fictif, -ve [fik'tif, ~'tiːv] fictitious;
sham; ✝ *facture f fictive* pro forma
invoice; **fiction** [~'sjø] *f* fiction, invention, fabrication.

fidèle [fi'dɛl] **1.** *adj.* faithful, true,
staunch; exact (*copy*); **2.** *su. eccl. les*
~s *pl.* the congregation *sg.*; the faithful; **fidélité** [~deli'te] *f* fidelity;
integrity; *de haute* ~ high fidelity, F
hi-fi (*record etc.*).

fiduciaire [fidy'sjɛːr] fiduciary;
trust ...; *monnaie f* ~ paper money.

fief [fjɛf] *m hist.* fief; *fig.* preserve,
(private) kingdom; **fieffé, e** [fjɛ'fe]
hist. enfeoffed; given in fee (*land*); F
pej. out and out, arrant, thorough-
paced; **fieffer** *hist.* [~] (1a) *v/t.* en-
feoff (*s.o.*); give (*land*) in feoff.

fiel [fjɛl] *m animal:* gall; *person:*
bile; *fig.* spleen; *fig.* bitterness; *sans*
~ without malice.

fiente [fjɑ̃ːt] *f* dung; *birds:* drop-

pings *pl.*; **fienter** [fjɑ̃'te] (1a) *v/i.*
dung; mute (*birds*).

fier¹ [fje] (1o) *v/t.*: *se* ~ *à* trust
(*s.o.*), rely on; *fiez-vous à moi!* leave
it to me!; *ne vous y fiez pas!* don't
count on it!

fier², fière [fjeːr] proud; haughty;
fig. magnificent.

fier-à-bras, *pl.* **fier(s)-à-bras**
[fjera'bra] *m* swaggerer, bully.

fierté [fjɛr'te] *f* pride; haughtiness;
vanity.

fièvre ⚕ [fjeːvr] *f* fever; **fiévreux,
-euse** [fje'vrø, ~'vrøːz] **1.** *adj.* feverish; fever-ridden; *fig.* excited;
2. *su.* fever patient.

fifre ♪ [fifr] *m* fife (*a. player*).

figer [fi'ʒe] (11) *v/t. a. se* ~ congeal,
coagulate; *se* ~ *a.* set (*face*); *fig.*
freeze (*smile*).

fignoler F [fiɲɔ'le] (1a) *v/i.* finick,
be finicky; *v/t.* fiddle over (*s.th.*)
with extreme care; *se* ~ titivate *o.s.*

figue ♀ [fig] *f* fig; F *mi-*~, *mi-raisin*
wavering; so-so; middling; **figuier**
♀ [fi'gje] *m* fig-tree.

figurant *m*, **e** *f* [figy'rɑ̃, ~'rɑ̃ːt]
thea. supernumerary; F super;
extra; walker-on; **figuratif, -ve**
[~ra'tif, ~'tiːv] figurative; **figuration** [~ra'sjø] *f* figuration, representation; *thea.* extras *pl.*; **figure**
[fi'gyːr] *f* ♀, *person:* figure; shape,
form; face; appearance; court-
card; **figuré, e** [figy're] **1.** *adj.*
figured (*cloth etc.*); *fig.* figurative;
2. *su./m: au* ~ figuratively; **figurer**
[~'re] (1a) *v/t.* represent; *thea.* act,
play the part of; *se* ~ imagine,
fancy; *v/i.* figure, appear; *thea.* ~ *sur
la scène* walk on; **figurine** [~'rin] *f*
statuette; ✝ (wax-)model.

fil [fil] *m* thread (*a. fig.*); wire; ⚡
filament; *blade:* edge; *meat, wood:*
grain; *wool:* ply; ⚠ ~ *à plomb*
plumb-line; ~ *d'archal* brass wire;
binding wire; ~ *de fer barbelé*
barbed wire; ~ *de la Vierge* gossamer; *au bout du* ~ on the phone;
coup m de ~ ring, call; *donner du* ~
à retordre à give a lot of trouble to;
⚡ *sans* ~ wireless; **filage** [fi'laːʒ] *m*
spinning; yarn; *metall.* drawing;
filament [~la'mɑ̃] *m* ♀, ⚡ filament;
silk: thread; **filamenteux, -euse** [~
lamɑ̃'tø, ~'tøːz] fibrous; *fig.* stringy;
filandière ✝ [~lɑ̃'djɛːr] *f* spinner;
les sœurs ~s *pl.* the Fates; **filandre**

[ˌ~ˈlãːdr] f fibre; ~s pl. meat etc.: stringy parts; gossamer sg.; **filandreux, -euse** [ˌlã'drø, ˌ~'drøːz] stringy, tough (meat); streaked (marble etc.); fig. involved, complicated; **filant, e** [ˌ~ˈlã, ~ˈlãːt] flowing; shooting (star); ropy (wine); **filasse** [ˌ~ˈlas] f tow; oakum; sl. stringy meat; **filateur** m, **-trice** f [ˌ~la'tœːr, ~ˈtris] tex. spinner; (spinning-)mill owner; informer, shadower; **filature** [ˌ~la'tyːr] f spinning-mill, cotton-mill; spinning; shadowing.

file [fil] f line, file; (~ d'attente) queue, Am. line; à la ~ in file; fig. on end, without a break; chef m de ~ leader; en ~ indienne in single file; ✿ en ligne de ~ (single) line ahead; **filer** [fi'le] (1a) v/t. tex. spin; draw (metal); play out (cards); ✿ run out (a cable); ✿ slip (the moorings); shadow (s.o.); v/i. flow smoothly; run (oil); rope (wine); smoke (lamp); fig. slip by, go by; go, travel; F clear out; ~ doux sing small; filez! clear out!; go away!; **filerie** [fil'ri] f spinning mill; metall. wire drawing.

filet [fi'lɛ] m net; ⊕ screw: thread; cuis. fillet; water: trickle; dash (of lemon); ✿ etc. luggage rack; ~ à provisions string bag; ~ de voix thin voice; coup m de ~ fish: catch, haul; **filetage** [fil'taːʒ] m ⊕ metal, wire: drawing; screw-cutting; screw: thread(ing); **fileter** [ˌ~ˈte] (1d) v/t. ⊕ draw (metal, a. wire); thread, screw (a bolt); poach (fish with nets); **fileur** m, **-euse** f tex. [fi'lœːr, ~'løːz] spinner.

filial, e, m/pl. **-aux** [fi'ljal, ~ˈljo] **1.** adj. filial; **2.** su./f ✝ subsidiary company; ✝, a. association: branch; **filiation** [ˌ~lja'sjõ] f filiation; descendants pl.; fig. relationship; en ~ directe in direct line.

filière [fi'ljɛːr] f ⊕ die; ⊕ drawplate; ✿ man-rope; fig. usual channels pl.; fig. passer par la ~ work one's way up from the bottom; **filiforme** [fili'fɔrm] threadlike.

filigrane [fili'gran] m filigree (work); paper, banknotes: watermark.

fille [fiːj] f daughter; girl; maid; spinster; ~ publique prostitute; ~ à papa rich man's daughter; ~ de salle hotel etc.: waitress; jeune ~ girl, young woman; vieille ~ old maid; ~-mère, pl. ~s-mères [fij'mɛːr] f unmarried mother; **fillette** [fi'jɛt] f little girl; F lass; **filleul, e** [ˌ~ˈjœl] su. godchild; su./m godson; su./f goddaughter.

film [film] m film (a. cin.); cin. F picture; Am. movie; ~ documentaire documentary (film); ~ en couleurs colo(u)r film; ~ muet silent film; ~ parlant talking picture, F talkie; ~ policier detective film; ~ sonore sound-film; ~ truqué trick film; tourner un ~ make a film; F act in a film (person); **filmer** [fil'me] (1a) v/t. film; **filmothèque** [ˌ~mɔ'tɛk] f film library or collection.

filon [fi'lõ] m ✕ vein, seam, lode; sl. good fortune; sl. cushy job.

filou [fi'lu] m pickpocket, thief; (card-)sharper; F swindler; **filouter** [filu'te] (1a) v/t. swindle (s.o. out of s.th., q. de qch.); rob (s.o. of s.th., qch. à q.); **filouterie** [ˌ~'tri] f swindle, fraud; picking pockets, stealing; cheating.

fils [fis] m son; F lad, boy; ~ à papa rich man's son; fig. ~ de ses œuvres self-made man.

filtrage [fil'traːʒ] m liquid: filtering; ~ à interférences radio: interference elimination; **filtre** [filtr] m filter; coffee: percolator; radio: by-pass, filter; bout m ~ cigarette: filter-tip; **filtrer** [fil'tre] (1a) v/i. a. se ~ filter; v/t. filter; by-pass (a radio-station).

fin¹ [fɛ̃] f end, termination, close, conclusion; aim, object; ~ d'alerte all clear; ✝ ~ de mois monthly statement; à la ~ in the long run; at last; à toutes ~s for all purposes; en ~ de compte, F à la ~ des ~s when all is said and done; mettre ~ à put an end to; prendre ~ come to an end; tirer à sa ~ be drawing to a close.

fin², fine [fɛ̃, fin] fine; pure; choice; slender (waist etc.); artful, sly; small; subtle; keen (ear).

final, e, m/pl. **-als** [fi'nal] **1.** adj. final (a. gramm.); last; eventual; **2.** su./f gramm. end syllable; ♪ keynote; ♪ plainsong: final; sp. finals pl.

final(e) ♪ [ˌ~] m finale.

finance [fi'nãːs] f finance; finan-

cial world; ready money; ~s *pl.*
resources; *ministère m des* ⚥s Exchequer, Treasury (*a. Am.*); **financer** [finã'se] (1k) *v/t.* finance;
financier, -ère [~'sje, ~'sjɛːr] (1a)
1. *adj.* financial; stock (*market*);
2. *su./m* financier.

finasser F [fina'se] (1a) *v/i.* finesse;
use subterfuges; **finasserie** [~-
nas'ri] *f* trickery; (piece of) cunning; ~s *pl.* wiles; **finasseur, -euse**
[~fina'sœːr, ~'søːz], **finassier, -ère**
[~'sje, ~'sjɛːr] **1.** *adj.* cunning,
wily; **2.** *su.* wily person.

finaud, e [fi'no, ~'noːd] **1.** *adj.* cunning, wily; **2.** *su.* wily person.

fine [fin] *f* liqueur brandy.

finesse [fi'nɛs] *f* fineness; *waist:*
slenderness; cunning; shrewdness;
opt., radio, telev.: sharpness; **finette**
tex. [~'nɛt] *f* flannelette.

fini, e [fi'ni] **1.** *adj.* finished (*a. fig.*),
ended, over; Ⱥ, *gramm., etc.* finite;
fig. pej. absolute, complete; **2.** *su./m*
finish; *phls. etc.* finite; **finir** [~'niːr]
(2a) *vt/i.* finish; end; end up; ~ *de
faire qch.* stop doing s.th.; ~ *par faire
qch.* finally or eventually do s.th.; *en
~ avec* get over (and done) with; put
an end to; *à n'en plus ~* endless(ly);
finition ⊕ [~ni'sjɔ̃] *f* finishing.

finlandais, e [fɛ̃lɑ̃'dɛ, ~'dɛːz] **1.** *adj.*
Finnish; **2.** *su.* ♀ Finn, Finlander;
finnois, e [fi'nwa, ~'nwaːz] **1.** *adj.*
Finnish; **2.** *su./m ling.* Finnish; *su.*
♀ Finn.

fiole [fjɔl] *f* small bottle; flask; *sl.*
head.

fioritures [fjɔri'tyːr] *f/pl.* hand-
writing, style: flourishes; ♩ grace-
notes.

firmament [firma'mɑ̃] *m* firmament, sky, heavens *pl.*

firme ⚔ [firm] *f* firm; *book:* imprint.

fis [fi] *1st p. sg. p.s. of faire.*

fisc [fisk] *m* Exchequer, Treasury;
Inland (*Am.* Internal) Revenue,
taxes *pl.*; **fiscal, e,** *m/pl.* **-aux**
[fis'kal, ~'ko] fiscal, tax ...

fissile [fi'sil] fissile; **fission** [~'sjɔ̃]
f (*esp. phys.* nuclear) fission; **fissure** [~'syːr] *f* fissure (*a.* ⚕), crack,
split, crevice; **fissurer** [~sy're] (1a)
v/t. a. se ~ crack, fissure.

fiston *sl.* [fis'tɔ̃] *m* son, youngster.

fistule ⚕ [fis'tyl] *f* fistula.

fixage [fik'saːʒ] *m* fixing; **fixateur**

[~sa'tœːr] *m* fixer; **fixation** [~sa-
'sjɔ̃] *f* fixing; *admin.* assessment;
🧠 fixation; attachment; **fixe** [fiks]
1. *adj.* fixed; steady; firm, fast;
stationary; regular (*price*); *arrêt m*
~ regular stop; *traffic sign:* all
buses *etc.* stop here; *étoile f* ~ fixed
star; **2.** *su./m* fixed salary; **fixe-
chaussettes** [~ʃo'sɛt] *m* suspender, *Am.* sock-suspender, gar-
ter; **fixer** [fik'se] (1a) *v/t.* fix (*a.
phot.,* 🧠, ✝, *value, time*), fasten;
settle, appoint; hold (*s.o.'s attention*);
decide, determine; keep one's eye
on (*s.th.*), stare at; ⚔ fix, hold; ✝
assess (*damages*); ~ *les yeux sur*
stare at, look hard at; *se* ~ settle
(down); **fixité** [~si'te] *f* fixity.

flac! [flak] *int.* slap!; crack!; plop!
(*into water*); *faire* ~ plop.

flacon [fla'kɔ̃] *m* bottle; flask; ~ *plat*
hip flask.

flageller [flaʒɛl'le] (1a) *v/t.* scourge,
lash.

flageoler [flaʒɔ'le] (1o) *v/i.* tremble,
shake.

flageolet[1] ♩ [flaʒɔ'lɛ] *m* flageolet.

flageolet[2] *cuis.* [~] *m* (small) kidney
bean, flageolet.

flagorner [flagɔr'ne] (1a) *v/t.* flatter;
toady to; fawn upon; **flagornerie**
[~nə'ri] *f* flattery, F soft soap;
toadying.

flagrant, e [fla'grɑ̃, ~'grɑ̃ːt] flagrant;
striking; *en* ~ *délit* red-handed, in
the very act.

flair [flɛːr] *m dog:* scent; *fig.* nose;
fig. person: flair; *avoir du* ~ *pour*
have a flair for; **flairer** [flɛ're] (1b)
v/t. scent (*a. fig.*); smell; *fig.* suspect; *sl.* smell of.

flamand, e [fla'mɑ̃, ~'mɑ̃ːd] **1.** *adj.*
Flemish; **2.** *su./m ling.* Flemish; *su.*
♀ Fleming.

flamant *orn.* [fla'mɑ̃] *m* flamingo.

flambant, e [flɑ̃'bɑ̃, ~'bɑ̃ːt] **1.** *adj.*
blazing; *fig.* brilliant; **2.** *flambant
adv.:* tout ~ neuf brandnew; **flambeau** [~'bo] *m* torch; candlestick; candelabra; **flambée** [~'be]
f blaze, blazing fire; *fig.* surge, outburst; ✝ *prices etc.:* zooming *or*
shooting up; **flamber** [~'be] (1a)
v/i. flame, blaze; burn; ⊕ buckle
(*metal rod*); *v/t.* singe; ⚕ sterilize (*a
needle in a flame*); *fig. sl. être flambé*
be done for; **flamboyer** [~bwa'je]
(1h) *v/i.* blaze (*fire, a. fig.*).

flamme [flɑ:m] *f* flame; *fig.* love, passion;⚔, ⚓ pennon, pennant; *être en ~s* be on fire.

flammèche [flaˈmɛʃ] *f* spark.

flan [flɑ̃] *m cuis.* baked-custard tart; ⊕ *etc.* blank; *sl. c'est du ~!* that's a load of hooey!

flanc [flɑ̃] *m* flank, side; *~ de coteau* hillside; F *sur le ~* (a*id up;* exhausted; *sl. tirer au ~* malinger, F swing the lead.

flancher F [flɑ̃ʃe] (1a) *v/i.* flinch; give in; F quit, chicken out; ⊕ break down.

flandrin † F [flɑ̃ˈdrɛ̃] *m* lanky fellow.

flanelle *tex.* [flaˈnɛl] *f* flannel.

flâner [flɑne] (1a) *v/i.* stroll; lounge about; loaf; saunter; **flâneur** *m*, **-euse** *f* [~ˈnœːr, ~ˈnøːz] stroller; lounger, loafer.

flanquer¹ F [flɑ̃ˈke] (1m) *v/t.* throw, chuck; deal; land (*a blow*); *~ q. à la porte* chuck s.o. out; give s.o. the sack.

flanquer² [flɑ̃ˈke] (1m) *v/t.* ⚔, ⚖, *etc.* flank; **flanqueur** ⚔ [~ˈkœːr] *m* flanker.

flapi, e F [flaˈpi] tired out, fagged out.

flaque [flak] *f* puddle, pool.

flash, *pl.* **flashes** [flaʃ] *m phot.* flash-light; *radio, telev.:* newsflash.

flasque¹ [flask] flabby, limp.

flasque² [~] *f* ✝ flask; † powder-horn.

flasque³ [~] *m* ⊕ *lathe etc.:* cheek; support (*of dynamo*); *mot.* wheel-disk.

flatter [flaˈte] (1a) *v/t.* flatter (s.o. on s.th., *q. sur qch.*; s.o. by *or* in *ger., q. de inf.*); humo(u)r (*s.o.*); caress, stroke; **flatterie** [~ˈtri] *f* flattery; **flatteur, -euse** [~ˈtœːr, ~ˈtøːz] **1.** *adj.* flattering; pleasing; **2.** *su.* flatterer; sycophant.

flatulence ⚕ [flatyˈlɑ̃:s] *f* flatulence, F wind; **flatulent, e** [~tyˈlɑ̃, ~ˈlɑ̃:t] flatulent, caused by flatulence; **flatuosité** ⚕ [~tɥoziˈte] *f* flatus, F wind.

fléau [fleˈo] *m* flail; *balance:* beam; *fig.* scourge; pest, curse.

flèche¹ [flɛːʃ] *f* arrow; *balance etc.:* pointer; *church:* spire; ⚓ pole; ⊕ *crane:* jib; *en ~* swept-back (*wings*); very rapidly, like an arrow; *fig. flèche ~ de tout bois* use all means; *fig. monter en ~* rocket *or* zoom up.

flèche² [~] *f bacon:* flitch.

flécher [fleˈʃe] (1f) *v/t.* mark with arrows, arrow (*a course etc.*).

fléchir [fleˈʃiːr] (2a) *v/t.* bend; *fig.* move, touch (*s.o.*); *anat.* flex; *v/i.* bend; give way (a. ⚔); sag (*cable, wire, a.* ✝); weaken; *fig.* flag, fall off; ✝ go down (*prices*); **fléchissement** [~ʃisˈmɑ̃] *m* bending *etc.*; *see* fléchir; **fléchisseur** *anat.* [~ʃiˈsœːr] *adj./m, a. su./m* flexor.

flegmatique [flɛgmaˈtik] phlegmatic; **flegme** [flɛgm] *m* phlegm; imperturbability, coolness.

flemmard, e *sl.* [flɛˈmaːr, ~ˈmard] **1.** *adj.* lazy; **2.** *su.* slacker; **flemme** *sl.* [flɛm] *f* laziness; *avoir la ~* not to feel like work, feel lazy; *tirer sa ~* idle one's time away.

flet *icht.* [flɛ] *m* flounder.

flétrir¹ [fleˈtriːr] (2a) *v/t.* fade; wilt; wither; *fig.* blight (*s.o.'s hopes*); *se ~* fade; wilt, wither (*flowers*).

flétrir² [~] (2a) *v/t.* condemn; stain, blemish; *hist.* brand.

flétrissure¹ [fletriˈsyːr] *f* fading; withering.

flétrissure² [~] *f* stain, blemish; *hist.* brand.

fleur [flœːr] *f* flower (*a. fig.*); blossom; bloom (*a. on fruit*); *fig.* prime; *~ de farine* pure wheaten flour; *à ~ de* level with; *à ~ de peau* skin-deep; *en ~* in bloom; F *faire une ~ à q.* do s.o. a good turn; **fleuraison** [flœrɛˈzɔ̃] *f* flowering, blooming.

fleurer [flœˈre] (1a) *v/t.* smell of; *v/i.* smell.

fleuret [flœˈrɛ] *m fencing:* foil; *tex.* floss silk; ⚒ drill, borer; *tex. ~ de ...* first-quality ...; **fleurette** [~ˈrɛt] *f* small flower; *conter ~ à* say sweet nothings to; **fleurir** [~ˈriːr] (2o) *v/i.* flower, bloom; *fig.* flourish, thrive; *v/t.* decorate with flowers; *fig.* make florid; **fleuriste** [~ˈrist] *adj., a. su.* florist; (*boutique de*) ~ flower shop; **fleuron** [~ˈrɔ̃] *m* ✿ floret; rosette; ⚓ finial; *typ.* fleuron; *fig. un ~ à sa couronne* a feather in one's cap.

fleuve [flœːv] *m* river.

flexible [flɛkˈsibl] **1.** *adj.* flexible; **2.** *su./m* ⚡ flex; **flexion** [~ˈsjɔ̃] *f* ⊕, *a. sp.* bending; ⊕ flexion, sagging; *gramm.* inflexion; **flexueux, -euse** [~ˈsɥø, ~ˈsɥøːz] winding; ✿ flexuose.

flibuster [flibysˈte] (1a) *v/i.* buccaneer; *v/t. sl.* steal, pinch.

flic *sl.* [flik] *m* policeman, copper,

Am. cop; detective; **flicaille** *sl.* [fli'kaj] *f: la ~* the police, *sl.* the fuzz.

flic flac [flik'flak] *int.* crack.

flingot *sl.* [flɛ̃'go] *m* rifle, gun; **flinguer** F [~'ge] (1m) *v/t.* shoot (s.o.), F gun (*s.o.*) down.

flipper[1] [fli'pœːr] *m* pin-ball machine.

flipper[2] F [fli'pe] (1a) *v/i.* flip.

flirt [flœrt] *m* flirt(ation); **flirter** [flœr'te] (1a) *v/i.* flirt.

floche [flɔʃ] soft, flabby; floss (*silk*).

flocon [flɔ'kɔ̃] *m snow:* flake; *wool:* flock; **floconneux, -euse** [~kɔ'nø, ~'nøːz] fleecy; ⚛ flocculent.

flonflons [flɔ̃'flɔ̃] *m/pl.* blare *sg.*

floraison [flɔrɛ'zɔ̃] *f* flowering, blooming; **floral, e,** *m/pl.* **-aux** [~'ral, ~'ro] floral.

flore [flɔːr] *f* ♀ flora; *myth.* ♀ Flora.

florès [flɔ'rɛːs] *m: faire ~* be in vogue; be a success.

floriculture [flɔrikyl'tyːr] *f* flower growing; **florilège** [~'lɛːʒ] *m* (verse) anthology.

florissant, e *fig.* [flɔri'sɑ̃, ~'sɑ̃ːt] flourishing.

flot [flo] *m* wave; stream; crowd; *fig.* flood; *à ~* afloat; ⚓ *mettre qch. à ~* (re)float s.th.; launch s.th.; **flottaison** ⚓ [flɔtɛ'zɔ̃] *f* floating; *ligne f de ~ ship:* water-line; **flottant, e** [~'tɑ̃, ~'tɑ̃ːt] (*a.* ✦) flowing (*hair*); loose (*garment*); *fig.* irresolute; *fig.* elusive (*personality*); *pol.* électeur ~ floating voter.

flotte[1] [flɔt] *f* ⚓ fleet; F *the* navy; F water, rain.

flotte[2] [~] *f fishing:* float.

flotter [flɔ'te] (1a) *v/i.* float; flow (*hair*); *fig.* waver (*a.* ✕), be irresolute; **flotteur** [~'tœːr] *m* raftsman; ⊕, *a. fishing:* float; ⚓ anchor buoy.

flottille ⚓ [flɔ'tiːj] *f* flotilla; *~ de pêche* fishing fleet.

flou, floue [flu] **1.** *adj.* blurred; soft (*hair*); loose-fitting (*garment*); **2.** *su./ m* haziness; *phot.* blurring.

flouer *sl.* [flu'e] (1a) *v/t.* swindle; do (*s.o.*).

fluctuation [flyktɥa'sjɔ̃] *f* fluctuation (*a.* ✦); ⊕ *~ de charge* variation of load; **fluctuer** [~'tɥe] (1n) *v/i.* fluctuate. (*voice*), slender.)

fluet, -ette [fly'ɛ, ~'ɛt] thin (*a.*)

fluide [flɥid] **1.** *adj.* fluid; *fig. a.* (smoothly) flowing; **2.** *su./m* fluid;

fluidifier [flɥidi'fje] (1o) *v/t.* fluidify; **fluidité** [~'te] *f* fluidity.

flûte [flyt] *f* ♪ flute; tall champagne (*etc.*) glass; long thin roll (*of bread*); *tex.* shuttle; F *~s pl.* (long, thin) legs; *sl. ~!* dash it!; bother!; *sl. jouer des ~s* take to one's heels; **flûter** [fly'te] (1a) *v/i.* ♪ play the flute; *sl.* drink; F *envoyer ~ q.* tell s.o. to go to blazes; *voix f flûtée* melodious voice; piping voice; **flûtiste** ♪ [~'tist] *m* fl(a)utist.

fluvial, e, *m/pl.* **-aux** [fly'vjal, ~'vjo] river...; water...

flux [fly] *m* flow; *cards, face:* flush; ⚡, ⚛, ⚗ *metall.* flux; *le ~ et le reflux* the ebb and flow; **fluxion** ⚡, *a.* † ⚛ [flyk'sjɔ̃] *f* fluxion, ⚡ *a.* inflammation, swelling; *~ à la joue* gumboil; *~ de poitrine* pneumonia.

foc ⚓ [fɔk] *m* jib; *grand (petit) ~* outer (inner) jib.

focal, e, *m/pl.* **-aux** *phot., opt.,* ⚛ [fɔ'kal, ~'ko] focal; **focalisation** [~kaliza'sjɔ̃] *f* focussing; **focaliser** [~kali'ze] (1a) *v/t.* focus.

foëne [fwɛn] *f* pronged harpoon.

foi [fwa] *f* faith; belief; trust, confidence; *ajouter ~ à* believe (in); *de bonne (mauvaise) ~ adv.* in good (bad) faith; *adj.* honest (dishonest); *digne de ~* reliable; *faire ~* be a proof; be authentic (of, de); attest (that, que); *ma ~!* upon my word!; *mauvaise ~* insincerity; unfairness; *sous la ~ du serment* on oath.

foie [~] *m* liver; *sl. avoir les ~s* be in a funk.

foin[1] [fwɛ̃] **1.** *su./m* hay; *sl.* row; F *avoir du ~ dans ses bottes* have feathered one's nest; *faire du ~* kick⎫
foin[2]! [~] *int.* bah! [up a row.⎭

foire[1] [fwaːr] *f* fair; F *fig.* madhouse; F *fig. ~ d'empoigne* free-for-all; rat race; *sl. faire la ~* whoop it up.

foire[2] *sl.* † [~] *f* diarrhoea.

fois [fwa] *f* time, occasion; *une ~* once; *deux ~* twice; *trois ~* three times; *à la ~* at once; at the same time; *encore une ~* once more; *une ~ que* when.

foison [fwa'zɔ̃] *f* abundance, plenty; *à ~* in abundance; galore; **foisonner** [~zɔ'ne] (1a) *v/i.* abound (in, with de), teem (with, de); swell (*earth, lime*); ⊕ buckle (*metal*).

fol [fɔl] *see* fou.

folâtre [fɔ'laːtr] playful, frisky; **folâtrer** [~la'tre] (1a) *v/i.* frolic, frisk; gambol; F act the fool; **folâtrerie** [ˌʃlɑtraˈri] f playfulness; sportiveness; frolic; **folichon, -onne** F [ˌʃliˈʃɔ̃, ˌʃˈʃɔn] playful, frolicsome; wanton; **folie** [ˌʃˈli] f madness; folly; mania; ˷ des grandeurs megalomania; aimer q. à la ˷ love s.o. to distraction.

folié, e ♀ [fɔˈlje] foliate(d); **folio** typ. etc. [ˌʃˈljo] m folio; **folioter** [ˌʃljoˈte] (1a) v/t. folio, paginate.

folklore [fɔlˈklɔːr] m folklore.

folle [fɔl] see fou; ˷ farine flour dust; **follet, -ette** [fɔˈlɛ, ˌʃˈlɛt] (slightly) mad; scatterbrained; esprit m ˷ goblin; poil m ˷ down; see feu.

folliculaire F [fɔlikyˈlɛːr] m hack writer; **follicule** ♀, anat. [ˌʃˈkyl] m follic(u)le.

fomentateur m, **-trice** f [fɔmɑ̃taˈtœːr, ˌʃˈtris] fomenter; **fomentation** ♂, a. fig. [ˌʃtaˈsjɔ̃] f fomentation; **fomenter** [ˌʃˈte] (1a) v/t. foment (a. fig.); fig. stir up.

foncé, e [fɔ̃ˈse] dark, deep (colour); bleu ˷ dark blue; **foncer** [ˌʃˈse] (1k) v/t. make darker, darken, deepen (a colour); bottom (a cask); v/i. darken, grow darker; F rush, dash (at, sur).

foncier, -ère [fɔ̃ˈsje, ˌʃˈsjɛːr] landed, real (property); ground (landlord, rent); fig. thorough, fundamental.

fonction [fɔ̃kˈsjɔ̃] f function (a. ♀, a. ♂); fig. en ˷ de in step with, hand in hand with; faire ˷ de act as; **fonctionnaire** [jɔ̃ksɔˈnɛːr] m official; civil servant; office bearer; **fonctionnel, -elle** [ˌʃˈnɛl] functional; **fonctionner** [ˌʃˈne] (1a) v/i. function (a. ♂); ⊕ work (brake, machine, etc.).

fond [fɔ̃] m bottom; sea: bed; △, a. fig. foundation, fig. basis; paint. background; back, far end; fig. gist, essence; à ˷ thoroughly; à ˷ de train at top speed; article m de ˷ leading article, leader; au ˷ after all; at bottom; de ˷ en comble from top to bottom; **fondamental, e** m/pl. **-aux** [fɔ̃damɑ̃ˈtal, ˌʃˈto] fundamental; radical; essential.

fondant, e [fɔ̃ˈdɑ̃, ˌʃˈdɑ̃t] **1.** adj. melting; juicy (fruit); **2.** su./m fondant; metall. flux.

fondateur m, **-trice** f [fɔ̃daˈtœːr, ˌʃˈtris] founder; **fondation** [ˌʃˈsjɔ̃] f founding; foundation (a. △); institution; **fondé, e** [fɔ̃ˈde] **1.** adj.

founded, justified; authorized; ✝ funded (debt); être ˷ à (inf.) be entitled to (inf.), have reason to (inf.); **2.** su./m: ˷ de pouvoir ✝ proxy, holder of a power of attorney; ✝ managing director; ✝ chief clerk; **fondement** [fɔ̃dˈmɑ̃] m base, foundation; F behind, bottom; sans ˷ groundless, unfounded; **fonder** [fɔ̃ˈde] (1a) v/t. found (a. ✝, a. fig.); ✝ start (a firm, a paper); ✝ fund (a debt); fig. base, justify.

fonderie ⊕, metall. [fɔ̃ˈdri] f foundry; smelting works usu. sg.; founding; **fondeur** [ˌʃˈdœːr] m founder; smelter; typ. ˷ en caractères type-founder; **fondre** [fɔ̃ːdr] (4a) v/t. metall. smelt; metall. cast (a bell, a statue); melt; dissolve; thaw (snow); blend (colours); ✝ amalgamate; v/i. melt (a. fig.); fig. grow thinner; dissolve (fig. in, en); ⟨ blow (fuse); ˷ sur swoop upon, pounce upon; fig. bear down upon (s.o.).

fondrière [fɔ̃driˈɛːr] f bog, quagmire; hollow (in the ground).

fonds [fɔ̃] m land, estate; ✝ stock-in-trade; fund; ˷ pl. cash sg., capital sg., means; ✝ public funds; ✝ ˷ de commerce business, goodwill; ✝ ˷ pl. de roulement working capital sg., cash reserve sg.; ˷ perdu life annuity; F à ˷ perdu without security. [melted cheese.]

fondue cuis. [fɔ̃ˈdy] f fondue.

font [fɔ̃] 3rd p. pl. pres. of faire.

fontaine [fɔ̃ˈtɛn] f fountain; spring; eau f de ˷ spring water; F ouvrir la ˷ turn on the waterworks (= start to cry); **fontainier** [ˌʃtɛˈnje] m fountain-maker; filter-maker; wellsinker; admin. turncock.

fonte [fɔ̃ːt] f melting; ore: smelting; metal: casting; snow: thawing; typ. fount; cast iron.

fonts eccl. [fɔ̃] m/pl. (a. ˷ baptismaux) font sg.; tenir (or porter) sur les ˷ baptismaux stand sponsor to (a child); fig. (help to) launch (s.th.).

foot F [fut] m, **football** sp. [futˈbɔl] m (Association) football, F soccer; **footballeur** [ˌʃbɔlˈlœːr] m footballer.

for [fɔːr] m: ˷ intérieur conscience; dans (or en) mon ˷ intérieur in my heart of hearts.

forage ⊕, ⚒ [fɔˈraːʒ] m boring, drilling; bore-hole.

forain, e [fɔ'rɛ̃, ~'rɛn] **1.** *adj.* † alien, foreign; itinerant; *fête f* ~e fun fair; **2.** *su.* strolling player; hawker.

forban [fɔr'bã] *m hist.* buccaneer, pirate; crook, shark.

forçat [fɔr'sa] *m* convict; † galley-slave.

force [fɔrs] **1.** *su./f* strength; might; force (*a.* ✕, *a.* ⊕); power (*a.* ⊕); authority; ~ *aérienne* (*tactique*) (tactical) air force; ~ *de frappe* ✕ strike force; *fig.* force(fulness); ⚡ ~ *majeure* overpowering circumstances *pl.*; ~ *motrice* ⊕ horsepower; *fig.* motive power; *phys.* ~ *vive* kinetic energy; momentum; *à* ~ *de* by dint of, by means of; *à toute* ~ despite opposition, at all costs; *de première* ~ first-class ...; *de vive* ~ by sheer force; *un cas de* ~ *majeure* an act of God; **2.** *adv.* † many, plenty of; **forcément** [fɔrse'mã] *adv.* necessarily, inevitably.

forcené, e [fɔrsə'ne] **1.** *adj.* mad, frantic, frenzied; **2.** *su./m* madman; *su./f* madwoman.

forcer [fɔr'se] (1k) *v/t.* force; compel, oblige; ✕ take by storm; run (*a blockade*); break open; pick (*a lock*); ⚡, ⊕ strain; ⊕ buckle (*a plate*); increase (*one's pace, speed*); être forcé de (*inf.*) be obliged to (*inf.*); **forcerie** ⚡ [~sə'ri] *f* forcing house; forcing bed.

forer ⊕ [fɔ're] (1a) *v/t.* bore, drill.

forestier, -ère [fɔrɛs'tje, ~'tjɛ:r] **1.** *adj.* forest-...; forest-clad; forester's ...; **2.** *su./m* forester.

foret ⊕ [fɔ'rɛ] *m* drill; bit; gimlet.

forêt [~] *f* forest (*a. fig.*); *fig.* hair: shock; ~ *vierge* virgin forest.

foreur ⊕ [fɔ'rœːr] *m* borer, driller; **foreuse** [~'røːz] *f* ⊕ *machine:* drill; ✕ rock-drill.

forfaire [fɔr'fɛːr] (4r) *v/i.* be false (to, *à*); ~ *à* fail in (*one's duty*).

forfait[1] [fɔr'fɛ] *m* heinous crime.

forfait[2] *sp.* [~] *m* forfeit, fine; withdrawal; *déclarer* ~ *sp.* scratch (a horse); withdraw from the competition (*a. fig.*); *fig.* give up.

forfait[3] [fɔr'fɛ] *m* contract; *à* ~ for a fixed sum; by contract; job-(*work*); (*buy, sell*) as a job lot; *travail m à* ~ contract work; **forfaitaire** [~fɛ'tɛːr] lump (*sum*); **forfaiture** [~fɛ'tyːr] *f* abuse (*of authority*); breach (*of duty, honour, etc.*).

15*

forfanterie [fɔrfã'tri] *f* bragging, boasting.

forge [fɔrʒ] *f* forge, smithy; ~s *pl.* ironworks *usu. sg.*; **forgeable** [fɔr-'ʒabl] forgeable; **forger** [~'ʒe] (11) *v/t.* forge; *fig.* invent; **forgeron** [~ʒə'rɔ̃] *m* (black)smith; ironsmith; **forgeur** [~'ʒœːr] *m* forger.

formaliser [fɔrmali'ze] (1a) *v/t.:* se ~ take offence (at, *de*); **formaliste** [~'list] **1.** *adj.* formal, stiff; **2.** *su.* formalist (*a. phls.*); stickler for formalities; **formalité** [~li'te] *f* form(ality); ceremony; *une simple* ~ a pure formality; **format** [fɔr'ma] *m* size (*a. phot.*); *book:* format; **formateur, -trice** [~ma'tœːr, ~'tris] **1.** *adj.* formative; **2.** *su.* former, maker; **formation** [~ma'sjɔ̃] *f* formation (*a.* ✕, ✈); education; ~ (*professionnelle* vocational) training; **forme** [fɔrm] *f* form (*a.* ⚡, *sp., fig., typ., a. = hare's lair*); shape; pattern; mo(u)ld; formality; ♣ dock; ~s *pl.* manners; *en* ~ fit, up to the mark or to scratch; *par* ~ *d'avertissement* by way of warning; *pour la* ~ for the sake of appearances; *sous* (*la*) ~ *de* in the form of; *prendre* ~ take shape; *prendre la* ~ *de* take the form or shape of; **formel, -elle** [fɔr'mɛl] formal; strict; categorical; **former** [~'me] (1a) *v/t.* form; fashion, shape; *fig.* constitute; mo(u)ld; *fig.* train (*s.o.*).

formidable [fɔrmi'dabl] formidable, dreadful; F terrific, *sl.* smashing, *Am.* swell.

formique ⚗ [fɔr'mik] formic (*acid etc.*).

formulaire [fɔrmy'lɛːr] *m* formulary; pharmacopoeia; *admin.* form; **formule** [~'myl] *f* ⚗, ⚗; *a. fig.* formula; ⚡ recipe; *admin.,* †, *post:* form; **formuler** [~my'le] (1a) *v/t.* formulate, draw up; lodge (*a complaint*); state precisely; *fig.* put into words; ⚡ ~ *une ordonnance* write out a prescription.

fornication [fɔrnika'sjɔ̃] *f* fornication.

fors † [fɔːr] *prp.* except.

fort, forte [fɔːr, fɔrt] **1.** *adj.* strong; robust; clever (at, *en*); good (at, *en*); large (*sum*); *fig.* big; ample (*resources*); thick; stout (*person*); heavy (*beard, rain, sea, soil*); steep (*slope*); high (*fever, wind*); *fig.* difficult; *fig.* severe; *à plus* ~e *rai-*

son all the more; *esprit m* ~
free-thinker; *se faire* ~ *de* undertake to; **2. fort** *adv.* very; strongly;
loud(ly); **3.** *su./m* strong part;
strong man; *fig.* strong point; *fig.*
height (*of debate, fever, season*); ⚔
fort, stronghold; ~ *de la Halle*
market porter.

forteresse ⚔ [fɔrtə'rɛs] *f* fortress;
stronghold (*a. fig.*).

fortifiant, e [fɔrti'fjɑ̃, ~'fjɑ̃:t] **1.** *adj.*
strengthening; invigorating; **2.** *su./m*
tonic; **fortification** [~fika'sjɔ̃] *f*
fortification; **fortifier** [~'fje] (1o)
v/t. ⚔, *fig.* fortify; strengthen (*a.
fig.*); invigorate; *se* ~ grow stronger.

fortin ⚔ [fɔr'tɛ̃] *m* small fort.

fortuit, e [fɔr'tɥi, ~'tɥit] chance...,
accidental.

fortune [fɔr'tyn] *f* fortune, luck;
chance; wealth; *bonne (mauvaise)* ~
good (bad) luck; *dîner à la* ~ *du pot*
take pot-luck; ⚓ *mât m de* ~ jury-
mast; *sans* ~ poor; *tenter* ~ try
one's luck; **fortuné, e** [fɔrty'ne]
fortunate; well-off, rich.

forure ⊕ [fɔ'ry:r] *f* bore(-hole).

fosse [fo:s] *f* pit, hole; trench;
grave; *lions*: den; *mot.* inspection
pit; **fossé** [fo'se] *m* ditch, trench;
castle: moat; **fossette** [~'sɛt] *f*
dimple.

fossile [fɔ'sil] **1.** *adj.* fossilized (*a.
fig.*); **2.** *su./m* fossil (*a. fig.*).

fossoyer ↗ [foswa'je] (1h) *v/t.*
trench, drain; **fossoyeur** [~'jœ:r]
m grave-digger.

fou (*adj. before vowel or h mute* fol)
m, **folle** *f*, *m/pl.* **fous** [fu, fɔl, fu]
1. *adj.* mad, insane, crazy; *fig.*
enormous, tremendous; silly, foolish; *devenir (rendre q.)* ~ go (drive
s.o.) mad; **2.** *su.* lunatic; *su./m* fool;
madman; *chess*: bishop; ~*s pl. du
volant* reckless drivers; *su./f* madwoman.

fouailler † [fwɑ'je] (1a) *v/t.* flog;
beat.

foudre¹ [fudr] *m* tun.

foudre² [fudr] *f* thunderbolt; lightning; *coup m de* ~ thunderbolt (*a.
fig.*); *fig.* love at first sight; *fig.* bolt
from the blue; *la* ~ *est tombée* lightning struck (at, *à*); **foudroyer**
[fudrwa'je] (1h) *v/t.* strike (by lightning); *fig.* strike down; *fig.* dumbfound, crush; ~ *du regard* look daggers at.

fouëne [fwɛn] *f see* foëne.

fouet [fwɛ] *m* whip; ~ (*à œufs*) (egg)
whisk; **fouetter** [fwɛ'te] (1a) *v/t.*
whip; birch; flog (*a child*); whisk
(*eggs*); *rain*: lash against (*a window*);
v/i. lash (*rain*).

fougère ♣ [fu'ʒɛ:r] *f* fern.

fougue [fug] *f* fire, spirit, dash;
(*youthful*) enthusiasm; **fougueux,
-euse** [fu'gø, ~'gø:z] fiery, mettle-
some, spirited (*horse*); impetuous.

fouille [fu:j] *f* excavation; *fig.* search;
fouillé, e [fu'je] detailed; elaborate;
fouiller [~] (1a) *v/t.* dig, excavate;
search (*s.o.*); *v/i.* rummage; **fouillis**
[~'ji] *m* jumble, mess.

fouinard, e F [fwi'na:r, ~'nard] inquisitive; sneaking; **fouine** *zo.*
[fwin] *f* stone marten; **fouiner** F
[fwi'ne] (1a) *v/i.* nose *or* ferret about.

fouir [fwi:r] (2a) *v/t.* dig; **fouisseur,
-euse** [fwi'sœ:r, ~'sø:z] **1.** *adj.*
burrowing (*animal*); **2.** *su./m* bur-
rower, burrowing animal.

foulage [fu'la:ʒ] *m* pressing; ⊕
cloth, *leather*: fulling; *metall.* ramming; *typ.* impression.

foulard [fu'la:r] *m* silk neckerchief
or handkerchief; *tex.* foulard.

foule [ful] *f* crowd, multitude,
throng; mob; heaps *pl.*; *tex., cloth,
leather*: fulling; **fouler** [fu'le] (1a)
v/t. tread; trample down; press,
crush; ⚕ strain, wrench; *tex.* full;
metall. ram; *fig.* ~ *aux pieds* ride
rough-shod over; **foulerie** [ful'ri] *f*
fulling-mill; **fouleur** *tex.* [fu'lœ:r]
m fuller; **fouloir** [~'lwa:r] *m tex.*
fulling-stock; fulling-mill; *metall.*
rammer; **foulon** *tex.* [~'lɔ̃] *m person*: fuller; *terre f à* ~ fuller's earth;
foulure ⚕ [~'ly:r] *f* sprain, wrench.

four [fu:r] *m* oven; cooker; ⊕ furnace, kiln; *thea., a.* F failure, F
flop; ~ *à chaux* lime-kiln; *faire* ~
be a failure *or* F a flop; *petits* ~*s
pl.* small fancy cakes.

fourbe [furb] **1.** *adj.* rascally;
double-dealing; **2.** *su.* cheat; **fourberie** [furbə'ri] *f* swindle; deceit,
trickery; *Am.* skulduggery.

fourbi F [fur'bi] *m* equipment, ⚔
kit; thingumajig; **fourbir** [~'bi:r]
(2a) *v/t.* furbish, polish up.

fourbu, e [fur'by] tired out, exhausted.

fourche [furʃ] *f* fork; *en* ~ forked;
fourcher [fur'ʃe] (1a) *v/i.* fork,

branch; *fig. la langue m'a fourché* I made a slip of the tongue; **fourchet** [~'ʃɛ] *m* fork; *vet.* foot-rot; **fourchette** [~'ʃɛt] *f* (table)fork; wishbone; *statistics etc.*: bracket; *prices etc.*: range; *avoir un bon coup de ~* be a hearty eater; **fourchon** [~'ʃɔ̃] *m* fork: prong; *bough*: fork; **fourchu, e** [~'ʃy] forked; cloven (*hoof*).

fourgon[1] [fur'gɔ̃] *m* van, waggon; 🚋 luggage van, *Am.* baggage *or* freight car.

fourgon[2] [fur'gɔ̃] *m* poker, firerake; **fourgonner** [~gɔ'ne] (1a) *v/t.* poke (*the fire*); *v/i.* poke (*the fire*); *fig.* poke about (in, *dans*).

fourgonnette *mot.* [furgɔ'nɛt] *f* light van.

fourmi *zo.* [fur'mi] *f* ant; *~ blanche* termite; *fig. avoir des ~s* have pins and needles; **fourmilier** *zo.* [furmi'lje] *m* ant-eater; **fourmilière** [~'ljɛːr] *f* ant-hill, ants' nest; *fig.* swarm, nest; **fourmi(-)lion**, *pl.* **fourmis(-)lions** *zo.* [~'ljɔ̃] *m* ant-lion; **fourmiller** [~'je] (1a) *v/i.* swarm, teem (with, *de*); *fig.* tingle.

fournaise *poet., a. fig.* [fur'nɛːz] *f* furnace; **fourneau** [~'no] *m* ⊕ furnace; cooker, stove; 🔥, ⚒ *mine*: chamber; *pipe*: bowl; *sl.* fool, idiot; *metall. haut ~* blast-furnace; **fournée** [~'ne] *f* ovenful; ⊕, *metall.* charge; ⊕ *bricks*: baking; *loaves, a. fig.*: batch.

fourni, e [fur'ni] supplied; thick, abundant; bushy (*beard*).

fournier [fur'nje] *m* baker; ovenman; **fournil** [~'ni] *m* bakehouse.

fourniment ⚒ [furni'mɑ̃] *m* kit, equipment; **fournir** [~'niːr] (2a) *v/t.* furnish, supply, equip (with, *de*); provide; ♱ stock (*a shop*); **fournisseur** ♱ [~ni'sœːr] *m* supplier, caterer; tradesman; **fourniture** [~'tyːr] *f* supplying; *~s pl.* supplies; equipment *sg.*

fourrage [fu'raːʒ] *m* forage, fodder; ⚒ foraging; **fourrager** [fura'ʒe] (11) *v/i.* forage; *fig.* rummage, search; *v/t. fig.* ravage; **fourragère** ⚒ [~'ʒɛːr] **1.** *su./f* forage waggon; lanyard; shoulder-braid; **2.** *adj./f: plante f ~* fodder plant.

fourré, e [fu're] fur-lined; furry; lined; filled (with, *de*); *fig. coup m ~* backhanded blow; *paix f ~e* sham peace.

fourreau [fu'ro] *m* ✂ sheath (*a. cost., a. fig.*); case; ⊕ sleeve; ⊕ *cylinder*: liner.

fourrer [fu're] (1a) *v/t.* line with fur; stuff, thrust; cram; F stick, poke; ⊕ pack (*a joint*); *se ~* wrap o.s. up; hide o.s.; thrust o.s.; **fourreur** [~'rœːr] *m* furrier.

fourrier [fu'rje] *m* ✂ quartermaster-sergeant; *fig.* forerunner; **fourrière** [~'rjɛːr] *f* pound; *emmener une voiture à la ~, mettre une voiture en ~* tow a car away.

fourrure [fu'ryːr] *f* fur; skin; lining (*a. mot. brake*); ⊕ *joint*: packing; ⚙ filler-block.

fourvoyer [furvwa'je] (1h) *v/t.* lead astray, mislead; *se ~* go astray; be mistaken.

foutaise F [fu'tɛːz] *f* rubbish, rot.

foutre ∨ [futr] **1.** (4a) *v/t.* throw; give; do; *~ la paix à q.* leave s.o. alone; shut up; *~ le camp* clear out, go; *~ q. dedans* do *or* cheat s.o.; *je m'en fous* I don't care, I don't give a damn; *se ~ de* not to care a hang *or sl.* a damn about; **2.** *int.* gosh!; damn it!; **foutu, e** F [fu'ty] damned, *Br. sl.* bloody; done for, finished, *sl.* bust(ed).

fox *zo.* [fɔks] *m* (*a. fox-terrier*) fox terrier; *~-trot* [~'trɔt] *m/inv.* foxtrot.

foyer [fwa'je] *m* hearth, fire-place; *fig.* home; ⊕ fire-box, combustion chamber; *boiler*: furnace; ⚡, 🔥, *phot., phys.* focus; *hotel*: lounge; *fig.* seat, centre; *thea. ~ des artistes* green-room; *~ des étudiants* (university) hall of residence; *building*: Students' Union.

frac [frak] *m* dress-coat.

fracas [fra'ka] *m* crash; din, shindy; **fracassant, e** [~ka'sɑ̃, ~'sɑ̃t] deafening (*noise*); *fig.* sensational, F shattering, F thundering; **fracasser** [~ka'se] (1a) *v/t.* shatter; smash to pieces.

fraction [frak'sjɔ̃] *f* fraction (*a.* ⚡), portion; *pol.* group; ⚡ *~ continue* continued fraction; **fractionnaire** [fraksjɔ'nɛːr] fractional; *nombre m ~* mixed number; improper fraction; **fractionner** [~'ne] (1a) *v/t.* split up; ⊕, 🔥 fractionate; crack (*mineral oils*); ⚡ fractionize.

fracture [frak'tyːr] *f* breaking open; *lock*: forcing; 🔥, *geol.* fracture; **fracturer** [~ty're] (1a) *v/t.* break open; force (*a lock*); ⚡ fracture, break; ⚡ se ~ *un bras* fracture *or* break one's arm.

fragile [fra'ʒil] fragile; brittle; *fig.* weak; ✝ *inscription*: with care; **fragilité** [~ʒili'te] *f* fragility; brittleness; *fig.* weakness, frailty.

fragment [frag'mɑ̃] *m* fragment, bit; snatch (*of a song*); **fragmentaire** [~mɑ̃'tɛːr] fragmentary; in fragments.

frai [frɛ] *m* spawning (season); spawn; fry.

fraîcheur [frɛ'ʃœːr] *f* freshness (*a. fig.*); coolness; *fig.* bloom (*a. of flowers*); **fraîchir** [~'ʃiːr] (2a) *v/i.* grow colder; freshen (*wind*).

frais¹, fraîche [frɛ, frɛʃ] **1.** *adj.* fresh; cool; recent; new (*bread*); wet (*paint*); new-laid (*egg*); **2.** *adv.*: *frais arrivé* just arrived; *fleur f fraîche cueillie* freshly gathered *or* picked flower; **3.** *su./m* cool; coolness; *au* ~ in a cool place; *de* ~ freshly.

frais² [frɛ] *m/pl.* cost *sg.*, expenses; outlay *sg.*; fees; ⚖ costs; charges; ~ *de livraison* delivery charges; ~ *d'entretien* maintenance costs, upkeep *sg.*; ✝ ~ *de port en plus* carriage *sg.* extra; ~ *de transport* freight charges; carriage *sg.*; *aux* ~ *de* at the expense of; *faire les* ~ *de* bear the cost of; *fig.* provide the topic(s) of (*a conversation*); *peu de* ~ small cost *sg.*; ... *pour* ~ *d'envoi* postage and packing ...

fraise¹ [frɛːz] *f* ♀ strawberry; ⚡ strawberry mark, n(a)evus.

fraise² [~] *f cuis.* calf, lamb: crow; *turkey*: wattle; *collar*: ruff.

fraise³ ⊕ [frɛːz] *f* countersink (bit); mill; ⊕ ~ *champignon (or conique)* rose bit.

fraiser ⊕ [frɛ'ze] (1a) *v/t.* mill; countersink.

fraiseuse ⊕ [frɛ'zøːz] *f* milling machine. [plant.]

fraisier ♀ [frɛ'zje] *m* strawberry]

framboise [frɑ̃'bwaːz] *f* raspberry; **framboiser** [frɑ̃bwa'ze] (1a) *v/t.* flavo(u)r with raspberry; **framboisier** ♀ [~'zje] *m* raspberry-bush.

franc¹, franche [frɑ̃, frɑ̃ːʃ] **1.** *adj.* frank; free; open, candid; straightforward; fair (*play*); *fig.* real, pure; ~ *de port* carriage paid; post-free; *foot. coup m* ~ free kick; **2.** *franc adv.* frankly; candidly; *pour parler* ~ to be frank.

franc² [frɑ̃] *m coin*: franc; *pour un* ~ *de* a franc's worth of.

franc³, franque [frɑ̃, frɑ̃ːk] **1.** *adj.* Frankish; **2.** *su.* ♀ Frank; *in Levant*: European.

français, e [frɑ̃'sɛ, ~'sɛːz] **1.** *adj.* French; **2.** *su./m ling.* French; ♀ Frenchman; *les* ♀ *m/pl.* the French; *su./f* ♀ Frenchwoman.

franchement [frɑ̃ʃ'mɑ̃] *adv.* frankly; openly; straight (out); F really.

franchir [frɑ̃'ʃiːr] (2a) *v/t.* jump over, clear; cross; pass through; ♣ weather (*a headland*); *fig.* overcome; **franchise** [~'ʃiːz] *f* frankness; openness; *city*: freedom; *admin.* exemption; ~ *de bagages* baggage (*Am.* luggage) allowance; *en* ~ duty-free; **franchissable** [~ʃi'sabl] passable (*river*); negotiable (*hill*).

franciser [frɑ̃si'ze] (1a) *v/t.* gallicize; **franciste** [~'sist] *su.* French scholar *or* specialist.

franc-maçon, *pl.* **francs-maçons** [frɑ̃ma'sɔ̃] *m* freemason; **franc-maçonnerie** [~sɔn'ri] *f* freemasonry.

franco ✝ [frɑ̃'ko] *adv.* free (of charge).

francophone [frɑ̃ko'fɔn] **1.** *adj.* French-speaking; **2.** *su.* French-speaking person.

franc-tireur, *pl.* **francs-tireurs** [frɑ̃ti'rœːr] *m* ✕ sniper; *fig.* free lance.

frange [frɑ̃ːʒ] *f* fringe; fringe group; **franger** [frɑ̃'ʒe] (11) *v/t.* fringe.

frangin *sl.* [frɑ̃'ʒɛ̃] *m* brother; **frangine** *sl.* [~'ʒin] *f* sister.

franquette F [frɑ̃'kɛt] *adv.*: *à la bonne* ~ without ceremony.

frappage ⊕ [fra'paːʒ] *m* stamping; striking; *coins*: minting; **frappe** [frap] *f* minting; striking; stamp; **frappé, e** [fra'pe] iced; **frapper** [~'pe] (1a) *v/t.* strike (*a. fig.*), hit; mint (*money*); ice (*a drink*); type (*a letter*); punch (out) (*a design*); F se ~ get alarmed; *v/i.* strike; knock (at the door, *à la porte*); ~ *du pied* stamp one's foot; ~ *juste* strike home; **frappeur** [~'pœːr] **1.** *su./m* ⊕ *etc.* striker; *tel.* tapper; ⊕ stamper; puncher; **2.** *adj./m*: *esprit m* ~ rapping spirit.

frasque [frask] *f* escapade.

fraternel, -elle [frater'nɛl] fraternal, brotherly; **fraterniser** [~ni'ze]

(1a) v/i. fraternize (with, avec);
fraternité [ˌni'te] f fraternity,
brotherhood.
fratricide [fratri'sid] **1.** su. person:
fratricide; su./m crime: fratricide;
2. adj. fratricidal.
fraude [fro:d] f fraud, deception;
~ fiscale tax evasion; faire entrer en ~
smuggle in; **frauder** [fro'de] (1a)
v/i. cheat; v/t. defraud, cheat,
swindle; **fraudeur, -euse** [ˌ'dœːr,
ˌ'døːz] **1.** adj. fraudulent; **2.** su. de-
frauder; cheat; ~ fiscal(e) tax evader.
frayer [frɛ'je] (1i) v/t. rub; clear
(a path, a way); se ~ un chemin make a
way for o.s.; v/i. spawn (fish); ~ avec
associate with.
frayeur [frɛ'jœːr] fright, terror.
fredaine [frə'dɛn] f escapade; faire
des ~s sow one's wild oats.
fredonner [frədɔ'ne] (1a) v/t. hum
(a tune).
frégate [fre'gat] f ⚓ frigate; orn.
frigate-bird.
frein [frɛ̃] m mot. etc., a. fig. brake;
fig. a. curb, restraint; horse: bit; ~ à
air comprimé air-brake; ~ à rétropéda-
lage back-pedalling brake; ⚙ ~ de
secours emergency-brake; ~s pl. à
disque disc brakes; ~ sur jante rim-
brake; mettre un ~ à curb, bridle;
ronger son ~ champ the bit; **freinage**
[frɛ'naːʒ] m braking; puissance de ~
braking power; mot. traces f/pl. de ~
skid marks; **freiner** [frɛ'ne] (1a)
vt/i. mot. brake; v/i. mot. apply the
brakes; v/t. mot. apply the brakes to;
fig. restrain, curb; fig. put a brake
on, check.
frelater [frəla'te] (1a) v/t. adulterate (food, wine).
frêle [frɛl] frail, weak.
frelon zo. [frə'lɔ̃] m hornet.
freluquet F [frəly'kɛ] m whipper-
snapper.
frémir [fre'miːr] (2a) v/i. tremble,
shudder; rustle (leaves); quiver (a.
fig. with, de); **frémissement** [ˌmis-
'mã] m quiver(ing); shudder(ing);
leaves: rustle; wind: sighing.
frêne ♀ [frɛːn] m ash(-tree).
frénésie [frene'zi] f frenzy, madness; **frénétique** [ˌ'tik] frantic;
frenzied (a. fig.).
fréquemment [freka'mã] adv. of
fréquent; **fréquence** [fre'kãːs] f ⚡,
♪, etc. frequency; **fréquent, e**
[ˌ'kã, ˌ'kãːt] frequent; ♪ rapid

(pulse); **fréquentation** [ˌkãta'sjɔ̃]
f frequenting; association (with,
de); regular attendance (at, de); (a. ~s
pl.) company (sg.); **fréquenté, e**
[ˌkã'te]: (très ~ very) busy (place);
bien (mal) ~ of good (ill) repute;
fréquenter [ˌkã'te] (1a) v/t. frequent; visit; see (s.o.) frequently);
attend (s.th.) frequently.
frère [frɛːr] m brother; eccl. monk;
friar; faux ~ traitor, double-crosser.
frérot F [fre'ro] m little brother.
fresque [frɛsk] f fresco.
fret ⚓ [frɛ] m freight; cargo; prendre à ~ charter; **frètement** ⚓
[frɛt'mã] m chartering; **fréter**
[fre'te] (1f) v/t. freight; charter;
fit out (a ship); F hire (a car etc.);
fréteur [ˌ'tœːr] m shipowner;
charterer.
frétiller [freti'je] (1a) v/i. wriggle;
wag (tail); fig. fidget.
fretin [frə'tɛ̃] m: (le menu ~ the small)
fry.
freudien, -enne [frø'djɛ̃, ˌ'djɛn]
Freudian.
friable [fri'abl] crumbly.
friand, e [fri'ã, ˌ'ãːd] dainty; ~ de
partial to; **friandise** [ˌã'diːz] f
titbit, delicacy; epicurism.
fric sl. [frik] m dough (= money).
fricandeau cuis. [frikã'do] m stewed
larded veal; **fricassée** cuis. [frika-
'se] f fricassee, hash; **fricasser**
[ˌ'se] (1a) v/t. cuis. fricassee; fig.
squander; **fricasseur** m, -euse f F
[ˌ'sœːr, ˌ'søːz] poor cook; fig.
squanderer; journ. ~ d'articles pot-
boiler.   [glary.\
fric-frac sl. [frik'frak] m/inv. bur-\
friche ✒ [friʃ] f fallow land; waste
land; en ~ fallow; fig. undeveloped.
fricoter F [friko'te] (1a) vt/i. stew;
cook (up) (a. fig.); F fig. a. be up to
(s.th.); **fricoteur** m, -euse f F
[ˌ'tœːr, ˌ'tøːz] schemer; wangler;
trafficker.
friction [frik'sjɔ̃] f ⊕ friction; scalp:
massage; ⚕ rubbing; sp. rub-down;
frictionner [ˌsjɔ'ne] (1a) v/t. rub;
give (s.o.) a rub-down; massage
(s.o.'s scalp); give (s.o.) a dry
shampoo.
frigidaire (TM) [friʒi'dɛːr] m refrigerator; F fig. mettre qch. au ~ put
s.th. on ice or into cold storage.
frigidité ⚕ [friʒidi'te] f frigidity.
frigo F [fri'go] m refrigerator, Br. F

fridge; **frigorifier** [frigɔri'fje] (1o) *v/t.* refrigerate; *viande f frigorifiée* frozen meat; **frigorifique** [~'fik] refrigerating, chilling.

frileux, -euse [fri'lø, ~'løːz] chilly.

frimas [fri'mɑ] *m* hoar-frost.

frime F [frim] *f* sham; *pour la ~* for the sake of appearances.

frimousse F [fri'mus] *f* little face.

fringale F [frɛ̃'gal] *f* keen appetite.

fringant, e [frɛ̃'gɑ̃, ~'gɑ̃ːt] frisky, lively; *fig.* dashing (*person*).

fringues F [frɛ̃ːg] *f/pl.* togs.

friper [fri'pe] (1a) *v/t.* crease; crumple; *se ~* get crumpled; **friperie** [~'pri] *f* old clothes *pl.*; second-hand goods *pl. or* business; old-clothes shop *or* business; *fig.* rubbish; **fripier** *m*, **-ère** *f* [~'pje, ~'pjeːr] dealer in old clothes; second-hand dealer.

fripon, -onne [fri'pɔ̃, ~'pɔn] **1.** *adj.* roguish; **2.** *su.* rascal; **friponnerie** [~pɔn'ri] *f* (piece of) mischief, prank(s *pl.*).

fripouille F [fri'puːj] *f* bad lot, cad.

frire [friːr] (4s) *vt/i.* (*a. faire ~*) fry.

frise¹ [friːz] *f* △ frieze; *thea.* ~s *pl.* borders.

frise² *tex.* [~] *f* frieze; *see cheval.*

friselis [friz'li] *m* rustle.

friser [fri'ze] (1a) *v/t.* curl; wave; crimp (*cloth*); skim, graze; *fig.* verge on, border on; *v/i.* curl (*hair*); **frisoir** [~'zwaːr] *m* (hair-)curler; curling-tongs *pl.*

frison¹ [fri'zɔ̃] *m* curl, ringlet.

frison², -onne [fri'zɔ̃, ~'zɔn] *adj., a. su.* ♀ Frisian.

frisquet, -ette F [fris'kɛ, ~'kɛt] chilly, *sl.* parky.

frisson [fri'sɔ̃] *m* shiver, shudder; *pleasure:* thrill; **frissonner** [~sɔ'ne] (1a) *v/i.* (with, de) shiver, shudder; quiver; be thrilled.

frit, e [fri, frit] *p.p. of frire;* **friterie** [fri'tri] *f* fried-fish shop *or* stall; **frites** F [frit] *f/pl.* chipped potatoes, F chips, *Am.* French fries, French fried potatoes; **friteuse** [fri'tøːz] *f* deep-frying pan; **frittage** ⊕ [fri-'taːʒ] *m* sintering; roasting; **fritter** ⊕ [~'te] (1a) *v/t.* roast; sinter; **friture** [~'tyːr] *f* frying; frying fat; fried fish; *radio, teleph.:* crackling.

frivole [fri'vɔl] frivolous; *fig.* trifling; **frivolité** [~vɔli'te] *f* frivolity; *fig.* trifle; *lace:* tatting.

froc *eccl.* [frɔk] *m* cowl; frock; **frocard** *sl.* [frɔ'kaːr] *m* monk.

froid, froide [frwa, frwad] **1.** *adj.* cold (*a. fig. smile, reception*); chilly (*a. fig. manner*); frigid (*style*); *à ~* in the cold state; when cold (*a. cuis.*); *avoir ~* be cold (*person*); *battre ~ à* cold-shoulder (*s.o.*); *en ~ avec* on chilly terms with, cool towards; *faire ~* be cold (*weather*); *prendre ~* catch a chill; **2.** *su./m* cold; *fig.* coldness; ♱ *industrie f du ~* refrigeration industry; **froideur** [frwa'dœːr] *f* coldness; chilliness; indifference; *fig.* chill; ⚙ frigidity.

froissement [frwas'mɑ̃] *m* crumpling; rustle; bruising; *fig.* conflict; giving *or* taking offence; **froisser** [frwa'se] (1a) *v/t.* crumple, crease; *fig.* offend, hurt, ruffle (*s.o.*); *se ~* take offence (at, de); **froissure** [~'syːr] *f* cloth, paper: crumple.

frôlement [frol'mɑ̃] *m* light brushing; light touch; **frôler** [fro'le] (1a) *v/t.* graze; brush against *or* past; *fig.* come near to.

fromage [frɔ'maːʒ] *m* cheese; *fig.* F cushy job; *~ de tête* pork brawn; **fromager, -ère** [~ma'ʒe, ~'ʒɛːr] **1.** *adj.* cheese...; **2.** *su.* cheesemonger; cheesemaker; **fromagerie** [~maʒ-'ri] *f* cheesemonger's (shop); cheese dairy.

froment ✔ [frɔ'mɑ̃] *m* wheat.

fronce [frɔ̃ːs] *f* crease; *dress etc.:* gather; **froncement** [frɔ̃s'mɑ̃] *m* puckering; *~ des sourcils* frown; **froncer** [frɔ̃'se] (1k) *v/t.* pucker, wrinkle; gather (*one's skirt etc.*); *~ les sourcils* frown; scowl; **froncis** [~'si] *m* skirt, dress: gathering.

frondaison [frɔ̃de'zɔ̃] *f* foliage, leaves *pl.*; foliation.

fronde [frɔːd] *f* sling; (toy) catapult; *hist. la ♀* the Fronde (*1648 - 1653*); **fronder** [frɔ̃'de] (1a) *v/t.* sling, catapult (*a stone*); hit with a sling; (*a. contre*) scoff at; **frondeur** *m*, **-euse** *f* [~'dœːr, ~'døːz] **1.** *su.* slinger; *hist.* member of the Fronde; *fig.* scoffer; F grouser; **2.** *adj.* bantering; irreverent.

front [frɔ̃] *m* front (*a.* ✕); forehead, brow; face; *fig.* impudence, cheek; *pol. ♀ populaire* Popular Front; *de ~* abreast; front-...; head-on (*collision*); at once; *faire ~ à* face (*s.th.*); **frontal, e,** *m/pl.* **-aux** [frɔ̃'tal, ~'to]

1. *adj.* frontal, front-...; *mot. collision*
~e head-on collision; **2.** *su./m horse*:
headband; *anat.* frontal (bone);
fronteau [~'to] *m horse*: headband;
△ frontal; *eccl.* frontlet; **frontière**
[~'tjɛːr] **1.** *su./f* frontier; border;
boundary; **2.** *adj./f*: *ville f* ~ frontier
town; **frontispice** [~tis'pis] *m*
frontispiece (*a.* △); titlepage.
fronton [frɔ̃'tɔ̃] *m* △ fronton,
pediment; *pelota*: front wall.
frottage [frɔ'taːʒ] *m* polishing; rubbing; *flesh*: chafing; *metal*: scouring; **frottée** F [~'te] *f* thrashing;
frottement [frɔt'mɑ̃] *m* rubbing;
chafing; ⊕ friction; **frotter** [frɔ'te]
(1a) *v/t.* rub; chafe (*one's leg*);
polish; scour (*metal*); strike (*a
match*); F thrash; *paint.* scumble;
fig. se ~ *à q.* associate with s.o.; come
up against s.o.; *v/i.* rub; **frottoir**
[~'twaːr] *m* polishing cloth, polisher;
⊕ friction-plate; ⚡ brush.
frou(-)frou [fru'fru] *m gown*: rustle,
swish; **froufrouter** [~fru'te] (1a)
v/i. rustle, swish.
froussard, e *sl.* [fru'saːr, ~'sard] **1.**
adj. cowardly, *sl.* chicken; **2.** *su.*
coward; **frousse** *sl.* [frus] *f* fear, F
funk; *avoir la* ~ be scared.
fructifier [frykti'fje] (1o) *v/i.*
bear fruit; **fructueux, -euse** [~-
'tɥø, ~'tɥøːz] fruitful, profitable.
frugal, e, *m/pl.* **-aux** [fry'gal, ~'go]
frugal; **frugalité** [~gali'te] *f* fru-
gality.
fruit [frɥi] *m* fruit; *fig.* advantage,
profit; *fig.* result; ⚡ profit, revenue;
zo. ~*s pl.* de mer fish and shellfish;
Am. sea-food *sg.*; ~ *sec* dried fruit;
fig. person: failure; **fruité, e** [frɥi-
'te] fruity (*wine, olives*); **fruiterie**
[~'tri] *f* store-room for fruit; fruiterer's (shop); greengrocery; **fruitier, -ère** [~'tje, ~'tjɛːr] **1.** *adj.*
fruit-bearing; fruit(-*tree*); **2.** *su.*
fruiterer, greengrocer; *su./m* store-
room for fruit.
frusques *sl.* [frysk] *f/pl.* togs (=
clothes).
fruste [fryst] rough (*a. fig.*).
frustration [frystra'sjɔ̃] *f* frustration; **frustrer** [frys'tre] (1a) *v/t.*
frustrate; ~ *q. de qch.* deprive s.o. of
s.th.; cheat s.o. out of s.th.
fuel(-oil) [fjul, fju'lɔjl] *m* fuel-oil.
fugace [fy'gas] fleeting, passing,
transient.

fugitif, -ve [fyʒi'tif, ~'tiːv] **1.** *adj.*
fugitive; *fig.* fleeting, passing, transient; **2.** *su.* fugitive.
fugue [fyg] *f* ♪ fugue; running away;
faire une ~ run away.
fuir [fɥiːr] (2d) *v/i.* flee, run away;
leak (*barrel*); recede (*forehead, landscape*); *v/t.* avoid, shun; **fuis** [fɥi]
1st p. sg. pres. and p.s. of fuir; **fuite**
[fɥit] *f* flight; escape; *gas, liquid,
a. fig. secrets*: leak, leakage; shunning; *mettre en* ~ put to flight;
prendre la ~ take to flight, F take
to one's heels.
fulgurant, e [fylgy'rɑ̃, ~'rɑ̃ːt] flashing; fulgurating (*pain*); **fulgura-
tion** [~ra'sjɔ̃] *f* flashing; ⚡ fulgura-
tion; **fulgurer** [~'re] (1a) *v/i.* flash,
fulgurate. [smoky, sooty; murky.\
fuligineux, -euse [fyliʒi'nø, ~'nøːz]\
fulmicoton [fylmikɔ'tɔ̃] *m see coton-
poudre;* **fulmination** *eccl.,* ⚑ [~na-
'sjɔ̃] *f* fulmination; **fulminer** [~'ne]
(1a) *vt/i.* fulminate; *v/i.: fig.* ~
contre fulminate against.
fumage¹ ⚹ [fy'maːʒ] *m* dunging,
dressing; manure.
fumage² [~] *fish, meat*: smoking.
fume-cigare(tte) [fymsi'gaːr, ~ga-
'rɛt] *m/inv.* cigar(ette)-holder.
fumée [fy'me] *f* smoke; *soup*:
steam; fumes *pl.*; *fig.* vanity.
fumer¹ [~] (1a) *v/t.* smoke (*cigars,
fish, meat*); *v/i.* smoke; steam; *fig.* ~
de colère fume.
fumer² ⚹ [~] (1a) *v/t.* manure,
dung (*the soil*).
fumerie [fym'ri] *f* † tobacco *etc.*:
smoking; *opium*: den; **fumeron**
[~'rɔ̃] *m* smoky charcoal; **fumet**
[fy'mɛ] *m cooking*: aroma; *wine*:
bouquet; *cuis.* concentrate; *hunt.*
scent; **fumeur** *m*, **-euse** *f* [~'mœːr,
~'møːz] smoker; *su./m* 🚂 F smoker,
smoking compartment; **fumeux,
-euse** [~'mø, ~'møːz] smoky; heady
(*wine*); *fig.* hazy.
fumier [fy'mje] *m* manure, dung;
dunghill; *fig. mourir sur le* ~ die
in squalor.
fumiste [fy'mist] *m* stove-setter; F
humbug; F practical joker; **fumisterie** [~mis'tri] *f* stove-setting;
F practical joke; *sl.* monkey business; **fumivore** ⊕ [~mi'vɔːr] *m*
smoke-consumer; **fumoir** [~-
'mwaːr] *m* smoking-room; smoke-
house (*for curing of fish, meat*).

funèbre [fy'nɛbr] funeral; gloomy, funereal; **funérailles** [fyne'rɑːj] f/pl. funeral sg.; obsequies; **funéraire** [~'rɛːr] funeral; tomb(stone).

funeste [fy'nɛst] fatal, deadly.

funiculaire [fyniky'lɛːr] **1.** adj. funicular; **2.** su./m funicular railway.

fur [fyːr] m: au ~ et à mesure progressively, gradually; au ~ et à mesure que (as soon) as; (in proportion) as; au ~ et à mesure de according to.

furet [fy'rɛ] m zo. ferret; fig. Nosey Parker, Paul Pry; **fureter** [fyr-'te] (1d) v/i. ferret (a. fig.); fig. rummage, nose about; **fureteur, -euse** [~'tœːr, ~'tøːz] **1.** adj. prying; **2.** su. ferreter; fig. rummager; Nosey Parker.

fureur [fy'rœːr] f fury, rage; passion; aimer avec (or à la) ~ be passionately fond of; fig. faire ~ be all the rage; **furibond, e** [~ri'bɔ̃, ~-'bɔ̃d] **1.** adj. furious; **2.** su. furious person; **furie** [~'ri] f fury, rage; fig. avec ~ frantically, wildly; entrer en ~ become furious; **furieux, -euse** [~'rjø, ~'rjøːz] furious, mad, raging.

furole [fy'rɔl] f will-o'-the-wisp.

furoncle [fy'rɔ̃ːkl] m furuncle, boil. [stealthy.]

furtif, -ve [fyr'tif, ~'tiːv] furtive,]

fus [fy] 1st p. sg. p.s. of être 1.

fusain [fy'zɛ̃] m spindle-tree; (drawing-)charcoal; charcoal sketch;

fuseau [~'zo] m tex. spindle; spherical lune; ⊕ roller-chain: link-pin; ⊕ trundle: stave; biol. nucleus spindle; cost. pantalon m ~ tapering or peg-top trousers pl.; ~ horaire time zone; en ~ tapering (at both ends); F fig. jambes f/pl. en ~ spindle-shanks.

fusée[1] [fy'ze] f tex. spindleful; ⊕ spindle.

fusée[2] [~] f ✕ bomb etc.: fuse; ✕, phys. rocket; ~ éclairante flare; ~ engin booster, carrier vehicle; avion m ~ rocket-propelled aircraft; lancer une ~ send up a flare.

fuselage ✈ [fyz'laːʒ] m fuselage; **fuselé, e** [~'le] spindle-shaped; tapering; mot. stream-lined; **fuseler** [~'le] (1c) v/t. taper; mot. streamline.

fuser [fy'ze] (1a) v/i. run, spread (colours); fuse, melt; fig. burst out (laughter); ⌢ crackle, F fizz; slake (lime); burn slowly (fuse); **fusible** [~'zibl] **1.** adj. fusible; **2.** su./m ⚡ fuse(-wire).

fusil [fy'zi] m rifle, gun; ~ de chasse shotgun; à portée de ~ within gunshot; coup m de ~ shot; **fusilier** ✕ [fyzi'lje] m fusilier; **fusillade** [~'jad] f rifle-fire, fusillade; (execution by) shooting; **fusiller** [~'je] (1a) v/t. shoot; sl. smash (up), mess up.

fusion [fy'zjɔ̃] f fusion (a. fig.), melting; † merger; **fusionner** [~zjɔ'ne] (1a) vt/i. a. se ~ amalgamate, merge.

fustiger [fysti'ʒe] (11) v/t. censure, denounce; fig. flay; † thrash.

fût [fy] m gun: stock; tools etc.: handle; △ chimney, column, etc.: shaft; barrel, cask; box, drum: body; beer: wood; ♀ tree: bole.

futaie [fy'tɛ] f forest; arbre m de haute ~ full-grown tree, timber tree; **futaille** [~'taːj] f cask, tun.

futaine tex. [fy'tɛn] f fustian.

futé, e F [fy'te] sharp, cunning.

futile [fy'til] futile; trifling; **futilité** [~tili'te] f futility; ~s pl. trifles.

futur, e [fy'tyːr] **1.** adj. future; **2.** su./m intended (husband); gramm. future; su./f intended (wife); **futurisme** paint. [~ty'rism] m futurism; **futuriste** [~ty'rist] **1.** su. futurist; **2.** adj. futuristic; **futurologie** [~tyrɔlɔ'ʒi] f futurology; **futurologue** [~tyrɔ'lɔg] su. futurologist.

fuyant, e [fɥi'jɑ̃, ~'jɑ̃ːt] fleeing; fleeting (moment); shifty (eyes); fig. receding (forehead, a. paint. etc. line); **fuyard, e** [~'jaːr, ~'jard] **1.** su. fugitive; **2.** adj. timid; **fuyons** [~'jɔ̃] 1st p. pl. pres. of fuir.

G

G, g [ʒe] *m* G, g.

gabare ⚓ [gaˈbaːr] *f* lighter; transport-vessel; drag-net; **gabarier** [∼baˈrje] *m* barge: skipper; bargee, lighterman.

gabarit [gabaˈri] *m* size; *fig.* calibre; *ships*: model; ⊕ template; ⊕ clearance; 🚗, ⊕ ga(u)ge; *fig.* sort, kind; *fig. du même* ∼ of the same sort.

gabelle† [gaˈbɛl] *f* salt-tax; **gabelou** *pej.* [∼ˈblu] *m* customs officer.

gabier ⚓ [gaˈbje] *m* topman.

gâche¹ ⊕ [gɑːʃ] *f* staple; wall-hook; catch; *pawl*: notch.

gâche² [gɑːʃ] *f* ⊕ trowel; *cuis.* spatula; **gâcher** [gɑˈʃe] (1a) *v/t.* mix (*mortar*); slack, slake (*lime*); *fig.* waste; spoil; bungle (*work*).

gâchette [gɑˈʃɛt] *f* lock: springcatch; ⊕ pawl; *gun-lock*: tumbler; F *gun*: trigger.

gâcheur, -euse [gɑˈʃœːr, ∼ˈʃøːz] *su.* bungler; *su./m* ▲ builder's labo(u)rer; **gâchis** [∼ˈʃi] *m* ▲ wet mortar; mud; F *fig.* mess.

gadget [gaˈdʒɛ(t)] *m* gadget; **gadgetiser** [∼dʒɛtiˈze] (1a) *v/t.* make a gadget out of; fit up with gadgets; customize (*a car etc.*). [Gaelic.)

gaélique [gaeˈlik] *adj., a. su./m ling.∫*

gaffe [gaf] *f* boat-hook; *fishing*: gaff; F *fig.* blunder, bloomer; F *faire une* ∼ put one's foot in it, drop a brick; *sl. faire* ∼ be careful; **gaffer** [gaˈfe] (1a) *v/t.* hook; gaff (*a fish*); *v/i.* F blunder, drop a brick; **gaffeur** *m*, **-euse** *f* F [∼ˈfœːr, ∼ˈføːz] *m* blunderer.

gaga *sl.* [gaˈga] **1.** *su./m* dodderer; **2.** *adj.* doddering, senile.

gage [gaːʒ] *m* ✝ pledge, pawn; *gambling*: stake; *fig.* token; forfeit; ∼s *pl.* wages, pay *sg.*; *mettre en* ∼ pawn; **gager** [gaˈʒe] (1l) *v/t.* ✝ guarantee; ✝ bet; **gageur** *m*, **-euse** *f* [∼ˈʒœːr, ∼ˈʒøːz] better, wagerer; **gageure** [∼ˈʒyːr] *f* hopeless *or* (almost) impossible undertaking; † wager, bet.

gagne-pain [gaɲˈpɛ̃] *m/inv.* livelihood; bread-winner; **gagne-petit** [∼pəˈti] *m/inv.* (itinerant) knife-grinder; cheap-jack; **gagner** [gaˈɲe] (1a) *v/t.* win (*a. fig.*); gain; earn (*a salary etc.*); reach, arrive at; overtake; *v/i.* gain profit (by, *à*); spread (*disease, fire*); **gagneur** *m*, **-euse** *f* [∼ˈɲœːr, ∼ˈɲøːz] earner; gainer; winner.

gai, gaie [ge] gay, merry, jolly, cheerful; lively, bright; ⊕ easy (*bolt, tenon*); F *un peu* ∼ a bit merry (= *tipsy*); **gaieté** [∼ˈte] *f* cheerfulness; mirth; ∼s *pl.* frolics; escapades; broad jokes; *de* ∼ *de cœur* out of sheer wantonness.

gaillard, e [gaˈjaːr, ∼ˈjard] **1.** *adj.* jolly, merry; strong, well (*health etc.*); broad, spicy, risky (*song, story*); **2.** *su./m* fellow, chap; *su./f* wench; bold young woman; **gaillardise** [∼jarˈdiːz] *f* jollity; ∼s *pl.* broad jokes, risky stories.

gain [gɛ̃] *m* gain, profit; earning; *cards etc.*: winnings *pl.*

gaine [gɛːn] *f* 💧, *anat., a. knife*: sheath; case, casing; corset, girdle; ▲, ⚒ shaft; *geol.* matrix; **gainer** [gɛˈne] (1b) *v/t.* sheathe.

gala [gaˈla] *m* gala, fête; *en grand* ∼ in state; *habits m/pl. de* ∼ full dress *sg.*; *fig.* one's Sunday best.

galamment [galaˈmɑ̃] *adv. of galant* 1; **galant, e** [∼ˈlɑ̃, ∼ˈlɑ̃ːt] **1.** *adj.* courteous, gallant; † gay, elegant; *aventure f* ∼*e* (love) affair; *pej. femme* ∼*e* woman of easy virtue; *en* ∼*e compagnie* with a lady friend (*man*); with a gentleman friend (*woman*); **2.** *su./m* ladies' man; lover; **galanterie** [∼lɑ̃ˈtri] *f* politeness, attentiveness; love-affair; pretty speech; ∼s *pl.* compliments (*to a woman*); **galantin** [∼lɑ̃ˈtɛ̃] *m* dandy.

galaxie *astr.* [galakˈsi] *f* galaxy; *the* Milky Way.

galbe [galb] *m* curve; contour; line(s *pl.*) (*of a car*); shapeliness; **galber** ⊕ [galˈbe] (1a) *v/t.* shape.

gale [gal] *f* 🐛 scabies, *the* itch; *hunt.* mange; *fig.* defect (*in material*); *fig. sl. woman*: shrew.

galène min. [ga'lɛn] f galena; ~ de fer wolfram.

galère [ga'lɛːr] f galley; ⊕ barrow; qu'allait-il faire dans cette ~? what was he doing there?; F vogue la ~! let's risk it!

galerie [gal'ri] f ⚔, ✕, thea., museum: gallery; ✕ drift, level; arcade; mot. roof rack; ✕ ~ de roulage drawing-road.

galérien [gale'rjɛ̃] m † galley-slave; † convict; fig. drudge.

galet [ga'lɛ] m pebble; ⊕ roller; ⊕ pulley; ~s pl. shingle sg.

galetas [gal'ta] m garret; hovel.

galette [ga'lɛt] f flat cake; sl. money.

galeux, -euse [ga'lø, ~'løːz] mangy (dog); ✿ scurfy (tree); with the itch (person); F fig. brebis f ~euse black sheep.

galimatias [galima'tja] m farrago; gibberish.

galle ✿ [gal] f gall(-nut); noix f de ~ nut-gall.

gallicanisme eccl. [galika'nism] m Gallicanism.

gallicisme [gali'sism] m gallicism, French turn of phrase.

gallois, e [ga'lwa, ~'lwaːz] 1. adj. Welsh; 2. su./m ling. Welsh; ♀ Welshman; les ♀ m/pl. the Welsh; su./f ♀ Welshwoman.

galoche [ga'lɔʃ] f clog; galosh; Am. rubber.

galon [ga'lɔ̃] m braid; ✕, ⚓ stripe; **galonner** [~lɔ'ne] (1a) v/t. trim with braid or lace; braid.

galop [ga'lo] m gallop; fig. ~ d'essai trial run; fig. au ~ (very) quickly; au grand ~ at full gallop; au petit ~ at a canter; **galoper** [galɔ'pe] (1a) v/i. gallop; **galopin** [~'pɛ̃] m errand-boy; urchin; ⊕ loose pulley.

galure, galurin sl. [ga'lyːr, galy'rɛ̃] m hat.

galvaniser [galvani'ze] (1a) v/t. ⊕ galvanize; (electro)plate; fig. stimulate; **galvanoplastie** ⊕ [~nɔplas-'ti] f electroplating.

galvauder [galvo'de] (1a) v/t. tarnish, sully; se ~ sully one's reputation; lower o.s.

gambade [gɑ̃'bad] f gambol, caper; **gambader** [~ba'de] (1a) v/i. gambol, caper; frisk.

gamberge sl. [gɑ̃'bɛrʒ] f thinking, co. cerebration; **gamberger** sl. [~bɛr'ʒe] (1l) v/i. think.

gambiller † F [gɑ̃bi'je] (1a) v/i. dance; fidget.

gamelle [ga'mɛl] f ✕ mess tin; billy (can).

gamin, e [ga'mɛ̃, ~'min] su. urchin; street-arab; su./m little boy; su./f little girl; **gaminerie** [~min'ri] f child's trick.

gamma phys. [ga'ma] m: rayons m/pl. ~ gamma rays.

gamme [gam] f ♪ scale (a. paint.); gamut; range; fig. changer de ~ change one's tune; ♦ haut (bas) de ~ high-(low-)grade; (un)expensive.

gammé, e [ga'me] adj.: croix f ~e swastika.

gang [gɑ̃ːg] m gang.

ganglion anat. [gɑ̃gli'ɔ̃] m ganglion.

gangrène [gɑ̃'grɛn] f ✿ gangrene; ✿, a. fig. canker; fig. corruption; **gangrener** [gɑ̃grə'ne] (1d) v/t. ✿ gangrene, cause mortification in; fig. corrupt; **gangreneux, -euse** [~'nø, ~'nøːz] ✿ gangrenous; ✿ cankerous. [hooligan.]

gangster [gɑ̃gs'tɛːr] m gangster,]

ganse [gɑ̃ːs] f braid; piping; loop.

gant [gɑ̃] m glove; ~ de boxe boxing-glove; ~ de toilette washing-glove; jeter (relever) le ~ throw down (take up) the gauntlet; **gantelet** [gɑ̃t'lɛ] m gauntlet; **ganter** [gɑ̃'te] (1a) v/t. glove; fig. suit (s.o.); se ~ put one's gloves on; buy gloves; **ganterie** [~'tri] f glove-making, glove-trade; glove-shop, glove-counter; glove-factory; ♦ coll. gloves pl.; **gantier** m, **-ère** f [~'tje, ~'tjɛːr] glover.

garage [ga'raːʒ] m mot. garage; hangar; shed; 🚂 shunting; ⚓ dock(ing); 🚂 voie f de ~ siding; fig. mettre q. sur une voie de ~ put s.o. out in the cold; push s.o. aside; **garagiste** mot. [~ra'ʒist] m garage owner; garage mechanic.

garance [ga'rɑ̃ːs] f 1. su./f ✿ madder(-wort); dye: madder; (madder-)red; 2. adj./inv. (madder-)red.

garant, e [ga'rɑ̃, ~'rɑ̃ːt] su. surety, bail; security; se porter ~ vouch (for, de); su./m guarantee, authority; **garantie** [garɑ̃'ti] f safeguard; guarantee (a. ✝); ✝ warranty; pledge; **garantir** [~'tiːr] (2a) v/t. guarantee (a. ✝); ✝ underwrite; vouch for; fig. protect.

garce sl. [gars] f bitch, strumpet.

garçon [gar'sɔ̃] *m* boy, lad; young man; (*a. vieux* ∼) bachelor; *café etc.*: waiter; ∼ *de bureau* office-messenger; ∼ *d'honneur* best man; F *brave* ∼ nice fellow; **garçonne** [∼'sɔn] *f* bachelor girl; *cheveux m/pl.* (*or coiffure f*) *à la* ∼ Eton crop *sg.*; **garçonnet** [∼sɔ'nɛ] *m* little boy; **garçonnière** [∼sɔ'njɛːr] *f* bachelor apartment *or* rooms *pl.*

garde [gard] *su./f* watch, guard; care, protection; custody, keeping; nurse; *book:* fly-leaf; *book:* end-paper; ∼ *à vous!* look out!; ✕ attention!, 'shun!; ✕ *de* ∼ on guard, on duty; *faire la* ∼ keep watch; ✕ *monter la* ∼ mount guard; *prendre* ∼ beware, be careful; *être sur ses* ∼*s* be on one's guard; *su./m* guardian, watchman; keeper; warden; ∼ *champêtre* rural constable; ♀ *des Sceaux* (French) Minister of Justice; ∼-**barrière**, *pl.* ∼**s-barrière(s)** 🚂 [gardəba'rjɛːr] gate-keeper; ∼-**boue** *mot.* [∼'bu] *m/inv.* mud-guard, *Am.* fender; ∼-**chasse**, *pl.* ∼**s-chasse(s)** [∼'ʃas] *m* gamekeeper; ∼-**corps** [∼'kɔːr] *m/inv.* life-line; ∼-**côte** [∼'koːt] *m* coastguard vessel; ∼-**feu** [∼'fø] *m/inv.* fender; ∼-**fou** [∼'fu] *m* parapet; railing, handrail; ∼-**frein**, *pl.* ∼**s-frein(s)** 🚂 [∼'frɛ̃] *m* brakesman; ∼-**malade**, *pl.* ∼**s-malades** [∼ma'lad] *su./m* male nurse; *su./f* nurse; ∼-**manger** [∼mɑ̃'ʒe] *m/inv.* larder, pantry; meat-safe; ∼-**nappe**, *pl.* ∼**s-nappe(s)** [∼'nap] *m* table-mat.

garder [gar'de] (1a) *v/t.* keep; preserve; retain; look after; mind; guard; *se* ∼ protect o.s.; refrain (from *ger.*, *de inf.*); take care (not to *inf.*, *de inf.*); baware (of, *de*); **garderie** [∼'dri] *f* day nursery; **garde-robe** [∼də'rɔb] *f* furniture, clothes: wardrobe; toilet, watercloset; **gardeur** *m*, -**euse** *f* [∼'dœːr, ∼'døːz] keeper, minder; preserver; **garde-voie**, *pl.* ∼**s-voie(s)** 🚂 [∼də'vwa] *m* track-watchman; **garde-vue** [∼də'vy] *m/inv.* eye-shade; lampshade; **gardien, -enne** [∼'djɛ̃, ∼'djɛn] **1.** *su.* guardian; keeper; attendant; *prison:* warder, guard; *foot.* ∼ *de but* goal-keeper; ∼ *de la paix* policeman; **2.** *adj.:* *ange m* ∼ guardian angel.

gare[1] [gaːr] siding (✕, *a. canal, river, a.* 🚂); 🚂 (railway) station; 🐟 ∼

aérienne airport; 🚂 ∼ *de triage* marshalling yard; ⚓ ∼ *maritime* harbo(u)r-station; ∼ *routière* bus station; 🚂 *chef m de* ∼ stationmaster.

gare[2]! [∼] *int.* look out!; ∼ *à* ... beware of ...; ∼ *à toi!* just watch it!; *sans crier* ∼ without warning.

garenne [ga'rɛn] *su./f* (rabbit-)warren; fishing preserve; *su./m* wild rabbit.

garer [ga're] (1a) *v/t. mot.* park; dock (*a vessel*); *se* ∼ *mot. etc.* pull to one side; move out of the way; F *mot.* park (one's car); take cover (from, *de*).

gargariser [gargari'ze] (1a) *v/t.:* *se* ∼ gargle; F revel (in, *de*); **gargarisme** [∼'rism] *m* gargle; gargling.

gargote [gar'gɔt] *f* (third-rate) eating house; cook-shop; **gargotier** *m*, -**ère** *f* [∼gɔ'tje, ∼'tjɛːr] cook-shop owner.

gargouille ⚠ [gar'guːj] *f* gargoyle; water-spout; culvert; **gargouiller** [∼gu'je] (1a) *v/i.* gurgle; rumble (*bowels*); F paddle (in the gutter); **gargouillis** [∼gu'ji] *m* gurgling.

garnement F [garnə'mɑ̃] *m* good-for-nothing, rogue.

garni [gar'ni] *m* furnished room(s *pl.*), F digs *pl.*; **garnir** [∼'niːr] (2a) *v/t.* furnish, provide, fit up (with, *de*); ✕ occupy, garrison, line (with, *de*); trim; ⊕ lag (*pipes*); 🌱 stock (*a shop*); **garnison** ✕ [∼ni'zɔ̃] *f* garrison; **garniture** [∼ni'tyːr] *f* fittings *pl.*; *cost.*, *cuis.* trimming(s *pl.*); ⊕ lagging; ⊕ packing; *mot.* brakes, clutch: lining; buttons, ⊕ pulleys, toilet, etc.: set.

garrot [ga'ro] *m* ⊕ tongue (*of saw*); 🩺 tourniquet; **garrotter** [∼rɔ'te] (1a) *v/t.* pinion; bind down; † gar(r)otte.

gars F [gɑ] *m* lad, young fellow, boy.

gascon *m*, -**onne** *f* [gas'kɔ̃, ∼'kɔn] **1.** *adj.* Gascon; **2.** *su./m ling.* Gascon; F *faire le* ∼ brag, boast; *su.* ♀ Gascon; **gasconnade** [∼kɔ'nad] *f* boast(ing), bragging; tall story; **gasconner** [∼kɔ'ne] (1a) *v/i.* speak with a Gascon accent; F brag, boast.

gas(-)oil [ga'zɔjl] *m* fuel *or* diesel oil.

gaspiller [gaspi'je] (1a) *v/t.* waste, squander; dissipate; *se* ∼ be wasted.

gastrite 🩺 [gas'trit] *f* gastritis.

gastro... [gastrɔ] gastro...; **gas-**

tronome [~'nɔm] *m* gastronome(r).
gâteau [gɑ'to] *m* cake; (open) tart; pudding (*usu. cold*); *fig.* profit; ~ *des Rois* Twelfth-night cake; *fig. partager le* ~ go shares, split the profit.

gâter [gɑ'te] (1a) *v/t.* spoil (*a. fig.*); *fig.* pamper (*a child*); damage; taint (*the meat*); se ~ deteriorate; **gâterie** [~'tri] *f* spoiling (*of a child*); over-indulgence; ~s *pl.* goodies; **gâteux, -euse** [~'tø, ~'tø:z] **1.** *su.* old dotard; **2.** *adj.* senile, doddering; **gâtisme** [~'tism] *m* senile decay.

gauche [go:ʃ] **1.** *adj.* left; crooked; awkward, clumsy; *à* ~ on *or* to the left; *tourner à* ~ turn left; **2.** *su.* left hand; left-hand side; *tenir sa* ~ keep to the left; **gaucher, -ère** [go'ʃe, ~'ʃɛːr] **1.** *adj.* left-handed; **2.** *su.* left-hander; **gaucherie** [goʃ'ri] *f* awkwardness, clumsiness; **gauchir** [go'ʃiːr] (2a) *v/i. a.* se ~ warp (*wood*); buckle (*metal*); *v/t.* warp; buckle; *fig.* distort; **gauchisme** *pol.* [~'ʃism] left-ism; **gauchissement** [~ʃis'mɑ̃] *m* warping; buckling; *fig.* distortion; **gauchiste** *pol.* [~'ʃist] *adj., a. su.* leftist.

gaudriole F [godri'ɔl] *f* broad joke(s *pl.*).

gaufre *cuis.* [go:fr] *f* waffle; ~ *de miel* honeycomb; **gaufrer** [go'fre] (1a) *v/t.* ⊕ emboss (*leather etc.*); crimp (*linen*); corrugate (*iron, paper*); *tex.* diaper; **gaufrette** *cuis.* [~'frɛt] *f* wafer biscuit; **gaufrier** *cuis.* [~fri'e] *m* waffle-iron.

gaule [go:l] *f* long pole; (one-piece) fishing rod; **gauler** [go'le] (1a) *v/t.* knock down (*fruit etc. from a tree*); beat (*with a pole*).

gaulois, e [go'lwa, ~'lwaːz] **1.** *adj.* of Gaul; Gallic; *fig.* spicy, broad; **2.** *su./m ling.* Gaulish; *su.* ♀ Gaul; **gauloiserie** [~lwaz'ri] *f* broad joke *or* story.

gausser [go'se] (1a) *v/t.*: se ~ *de* make fun of.

gave [ga:v] *m* mountain-torrent (*in the Pyrenees*).

gaver [ga've] (1a) *v/t.* cram (*a. fig. a pupil*); ✍ feed forcibly; se ~ stuff o.s. (with, *de*); gorge.

gavroche [ga'vrɔʃ] *su.* Paris: street arab, ragamuffin.

gaz [gɑːz] *m* gas; gas works *usu. sg.*; ✍

wind; ~ *d'échappement* exhaust gas; ~ *d'éclairage* (*or de ville*) illuminating gas; 🜨 ~ *hilarant* laughing-gas; 🜨 ~ *pl. rares* rare gases; *mot. couper les* ~ throttle back; *mot. ouvrir les* ~ open the throttle; F *mot. mettre les* ~ step on the gas; *mot. pédale f de* ~ accelerator.

gaze [~] *f* gauze.

gazéifier [gɑzei'fje] (1o) *v/t.* gasify; aerate (*mineral waters etc.*); **gezéiforme** 🜨 [~'fɔrm] gasiform.

gazer[1] [gɑ'ze] (1a) *v/t.* ✗, *tex.* gas; *v/i.* F *mot.* move at top speed, tear *or* speed along; *fig.* go smoothly; F *ça gaze?* things O.K.?

gazer[2] [~] (1a) *v/t.* cover with gauze; *fig.* draw a veil (*of reticence*) over.

gazetier † [gazə'tje] *m* journalist; *fig.* newsmonger; **gazette** [~'zɛt] *f* gazette; *person:* gossip(er).

gazeux, -euse [gɑ'zø, ~'zø:z] gaseous; ♥ aerated, fizzy; **gazier** [~'zje] *m* gas-worker; gas-fitter; **gazoduc** [~zɔ'dyk] *m* gas pipeline; **gazogène** [~zɔ'ʒɛn] *m* gas-producer, generator; gasogene; **gazomètre** [~zɔ'mɛtr] *m* gasometer, gas-holder.

gazon [gɑ'zɔ̃] *m* grass; turf; lawn; **gazonner** [~zɔ'ne] (1a) *v/t.* turf; *v/i.* sward.

gazouillement [gazuj mɑ̃] *m* warbling, chirping, *birds:* twittering, *brook etc.:* babbling; *fig.* prattle; **gazouiller** [gazu'je] (1a) *v/i.* warble, chirp, twitter (*birds*); babble (*brook*); *fig.* prattle; *sl.* stink; **gazouillis** [~'ji] *m see gazouillement*.

geai *orn.* [ʒɛ] *m* jay.

géant, e [ʒe'ɑ̃, ~'ɑ̃:t] **1.** *su./m* giant; *su./f* giantess; **2.** *adj.* gigantic.

géhenne [ʒe'ɛn] *f* gehenna, hell (*a. fig.*).

geignard, e F [ʒɛ'ɲaːr, ~'ɲard] whining; moaning; **geindre** [ʒɛ̃:dr] (4m) *v/i.* whine; moan; whimper; complain.

gel [ʒɛl] *m* frost; freezing (*a.* ♥, *a. fig.*); 🜨 gel.

gélatine [ʒela'tin] *f* gelatine; **gélatineux, -euse** [~ti'nø, ~'nø:z] gelatinous.

gelée [ʒə'le] *f* frost; *cuis.* jelly; ~ *blanche* hoar-frost; ground frost; ~ *nocturne* night frost; **geler** [~] (1d) *v/t.* freeze (*a.* ♥ *credits*); ✍, ✍ frostbite; *v/i.* freeze, become frozen;

avoir gelé be frozen (*river*); *il gèle blanc* there is a white frost; *on gèle ici* it is freezing (in) here.

gelinotte *orn.* [ʒəliˈnɔt] *f* hazel-grouse; fat(tened) pullet.

gélivure [ʒeliˈvyːr] *f* frost-crack.

Gémeaux *astr.* [ʒeˈmo] *m/pl.*: *les* ~ Gemini; the Twins; **géminé, e** [~miˈne] △, *biol.* twin; *biol.* geminate; mixed, co-educational (*school*).

gémir [ʒeˈmiːr] (2a) *v/i.* groan, moan; lament, bewail; **gémissement** [~misˈmɑ̃] *m* groan(ing), moan(ing).

gemme [ʒɛm] *f min.* gem; precious stone; ⚕ (leaf-)bud; resin; *biol.* gemma; *sel m* ~ rock-salt.

gênant, e [ʒɛˈnɑ̃, ~ˈnɑ̃ːt] inconvenient, in the way; *fig.* awkward (*silence etc.*).

gencive *anat.* [ʒɑ̃ˈsiːv] *f* gum.

gendarme [ʒɑ̃ˈdarm] *m police militia*: gendarme, constable; F virago; *sl.* red herring; **gendarmer** [ʒɑ̃darˈme] (1a) *v/t.*: *se* ~ flare up, be up in arms; **gendarmerie** [~məˈri] *f* constabulary; barracks *pl.* or headquarters *pl.* of the gendarmes.

gendre [ʒɑ̃ːdr] *m* son-in-law.

gène *biol.* [ʒɛn] *m* gene.

gêne [ʒɛn] *f* embarrassment, uneasiness; difficulty; trouble; bother; discomfort; want, financial straits *pl.*; *sans* ~ free and easy; familiar; **gêner** [ʒɛˈne] (1a) *v/t.* cramp *s.o.'s* style; *fig.* embarrass; inconvenience; hamper, hinder; trouble; *cela vous gêne-t-il?* is that in your way?; *la robe me gêne* the dress is too tight for me; *fig. se* ~ put o.s. out (to, *pour*); be embarrassed, be shy; squeeze up; *sourire m gêné* embarrassed smile.

général, e *m/pl.* **-aux** [ʒeneˈral, ~ˈro] **1.** *adj.* general; *d'une façon* ~*e* broadly speaking; *en* ~ generally; **2.** *su./m* ✕ general (*a. eccl. of an order*); ~ *de brigade* ✕ brigadier, *Am.* brigadier general (*a.* ✈); ✈ *Br.* Air Commodore; *su./f* ✕ general's wife; ✕ alarm; *eccl.* general (*of order of nuns*); *thea.* dress-rehearsal; **généraliser** [~raliˈze] (1a) *v/t.* generalize; **généraliste** ✚ [~raˈlist] *m* (*a. médecin* ~) general practitioner, G.P.; **généralité** [~raliˈte] *f* generality.

générateur, -trice [ʒeneraˈtœːr, ~-ˈtris] **1.** *adj.* generating; productive; **2.** *su./f* generator; dynamo; *su./m* ⊕ boiler; ~ *à gaz* gas-producer; **génération** [~ˈsjɔ̃] *f* generation.

généreux, -euse [ʒeneˈrø, ~ˈrøːz] generous (*person*, *fig.* heart, help, wine); liberal; abundant; ✎ fertile (*soil*); **générosité** [~roziˈte] *f* generosity; liberality; *wine*: body.

genèse [ʒəˈnɛːz] *f* genesis; *bibl. la* ♀ Genesis.

genêt ♣ [ʒəˈnɛ] *m* broom; ~ *épineux* gorse, furze.

génétique [ʒeneˈtik] **1.** *adj.* genetic; **2.** *su./f* genetics *pl.*

gêneur *m*, **-euse** *f* [ʒɛˈnœːr, ~ˈnøːz] intruder; nuisance; spoil-sport.

genevois, e [ʒənˈvwa, ~ˈvwaːz] *adj.*, *a. su.* ♀ Genevese.

genévrier ♣ [ʒənevriˈe] *m* juniper (-tree).

génial, e, *m/pl.* **-aux** [ʒeˈnjal, ~ˈnjo] inspired, of genius; **génie** [~ˈni] *m* spirit, *a. person*: genius; spirit, characteristic; ✕ engineers *pl.*; ~ *civil* civil engineering; *coll.* civil engineers *pl.*; *mauvais* (*bon*) ~ bad (good) genius.

genièvre [ʒəˈnjɛːvr] *m* ♣ juniper-berry; juniper(-tree); gin.

génisse [ʒeˈnis] *f* heifer.

génital, e, *m/pl.* **-aux** [ʒeniˈtal, ~ˈto] genital; *anat. organes m/pl.* ~*aux* genitals.

génocide [ʒenɔˈsid] *m* genocide.

génois, e [ʒeˈnwa, ~ˈnwaːz] *adj.*, *a. su.* ♀ Genoese.

genou, *pl.* **-x** [ʒəˈnu] *m* knee; ⊕ *pipe*: elbow-joint; ⊕ (*a. joint m à* ~) ball-and-socket joint; *se mettre à* ~*x* kneel down; **genouillère** [~nuˈjɛːr] *f* knee-pad; *armour, a. horse*: knee-cap; ⊕ *articulation f à* ~ ball-and-socket joint.

genre [ʒɑ̃ːr] *m* kind, type, sort; *gramm.* gender; *art*: genre; *zo. etc.* genus; *se donner du* ~ put on airs; *le* ~ *humain* mankind.

gens [ʒɑ̃] *m/pl.* (*an adj. or participle immediately preceding it is made feminine; if, however, both masculine and feminine forms end in a mute e, the adj. is made masculine*) people, folk *sg.*; servants; nations; *les jeunes* ~ the young folks; *tous les* ~ *intéressés* all people interested; *petites* ~ small fry; *vieilles* ~ old folks; ~ *d'église* clergy *pl.*; church people; ~ *de lettres* men of letters; ~ *de mer* sailors; ~ *de robe* lawyers; ⚖ *droit* m *des* ~ law of nations.

gent †, *a. co.* [~] *f* race, tribe.

gentiane [ʒãˈsjan] *f* ♀ gentian; gentian-bitters *pl.*

gentil¹ *hist.* [ʒãˈti] *m* Gentile.

gentil², **-ille** [ʒãˈti, ~ˈtiːj] nice; kind; pretty, pleasing; *sois* ~! be good!; **gentilhomme**, *pl.* **gentils-hommes** [ʒãtiˈjɔm, ~tiˈzɔm] *m* nobleman; gentleman (= *man of gentle birth*); **gentillesse** [~ˈjɛs] *f* graciousness; politeness; *avoir la* ~ *de* (*inf.*) be so kind as to (*inf.*); **gentiment** [~ˈmã] *adv. of gentil².*

génuflexion *eccl.* [ʒenyflɛkˈsjɔ̃] *f* genuflexion; *faire une* ~ genuflect.

géodésie [ʒeɔdeˈzi] *f* surveying, geodesy; **géodésique** [~ˈzik] geodetic, geodesic; *surv. point* m ~ triangulation point.

géographe [ʒeɔˈgraf] *m* geographer; **géographie** [~graˈfi] *f* geography; **géographique** [~graˈfik] geographic(al).

geôle [ʒoːl] *f* gaoler's lodge; † gaol, prison; **geôlier** [ʒoˈlje] *m* jailer.

géologie [ʒeɔlɔˈʒi] geology. [etry.} **géométrie** ⚖ [ʒeɔmeˈtri] *f* geom-}

géopolitique [~ʒeɔpoliˈtik] **1.** *adj.* geopolitical; **2.** *su./f* geopolitics *sg.*

gérance [ʒeˈrãːs] *f* direction, management; managership; board of directors *or* governors; **gérant, e** [~ˈrã, ~ˈrãːt] *su./m* director; *company:* managing director; manager; *journ. rédacteur-*~ managing editor; *su./f* manageress.

gerbage [ʒɛrˈbaːʒ] *m sheaves:* binding; *bales etc.:* stacking; **gerbe** [ʒɛrb] *f corn:* sheaf; *flowers, water:* spray; *sparks:* shower, flurry; *fig.* bundle, collection; ✕ cone of fire; **gerber** [ʒɛrˈbe] (1a) *v/t.* bind (*corn-sheaves*); stack, pile; ✕ bombard; **gerbier** [~ˈbje] *m corn:* stack; barn; **gerbière** [~ˈbjɛːr] *f* harvest wain.

gercer [ʒɛrˈse] (1k) *vt./i. a. se* ~ crack (*wood, skin, soil*); chap (*hands*); **gerçure** [~ˈsyːr] *f* crack, fissure; *hands:* chap; ⊕ flaw (*in wood*), hair-crack (*in metal*).

gérer [ʒeˈre] (1f) *v/t.* manage, administer; *mal* ~ mismanage.

gériatrie ⚕ [ʒerjaˈtri] *f* geriatrics *sg.*

germain¹, e [ʒɛrˈmɛ̃, ~ˈmɛn] full, own (*brother, sister*); first (*cousin*).

germain², **e** *hist.* [ʒɛrˈmɛ̃, ~ˈmɛn] **1.** *adj.* Germanic, Teutonic; **2.** *su.* ♀ German, Teuton; **germanique** [~maˈnik] *adj.*, *a. su./m ling.* Germanic; **germanisme** [~maˈnism] *m* Germanism; German turn of phrase.

germe [ʒɛrm] *m biol.* germ (*a. fig.*); *potato:* eye; *fig.* seed, origin; **germer** [ʒɛrˈme] (1a) *v/i.* germinate; sprout, shoot; *fig.* develop; **germination** *biol.* [~minaˈsjɔ̃] *f* germination; **germoir** [~ˈmwaːr] *m ✱* seed-bed, hot-bed; *brewing:* malt-house.

gérondif *gramm.* [ʒerɔ̃ˈdif] *m* gerund.

gerzeau ♀ [ʒɛrˈzo] *m* corn-cockle.

gésier *zo.* [ʒeˈzje] *m* gizzard.

gésir [ʒeˈziːr] (2q) *v/i.* lie; *ci-gît* here lies.

gestation *physiol.* [ʒɛstaˈsjɔ̃] *f* (period of) gestation, pregnancy.

geste¹ [ʒɛst] *f* (*a. chanson f de* ~) medieval verse chronicle; *faits m/pl. et* ~*s pl.* doings.

geste² [ʒɛst] *m* gesture, motion, sign; **gesticulation** [ʒɛstikylaˈsjɔ̃] *f* gesticulation; **gestion** [ʒɛsˈtjɔ̃] *f* administration, management.

gestique [ʒɛsˈtik] *f* gestures *pl.*

ghetto [gɛˈto] *m* ghetto (*a. fig.*).

gibbeux, -euse [ʒiˈbø, ~ˈbøːz] gibbous; humped; **gibbosité** [~boziˈte] *f* gibbosity; hump.

gibecière [ʒibˈsjɛːr] *f* game-bag; *school:* satchel.

gibelotte *cuis.* [ʒiˈblɔt] *f* fricassee of rabbit *or* hare in white wine.

giberne [ʒiˈbɛrn] *f* cartridge-pouch.

gibet [ʒiˈbɛ] *m* gibbet, gallows *usu.*} **gibier** [ʒiˈbje] *m* game.   [*sg.*}

giboulée [ʒibuˈle] *f* sudden shower; F *fig.* shower of blows.

giboyer [ʒibwaˈje] (1h) *v/i.* go shooting; **giboyeux, -euse** [~ˈjø, ~ˈjøːz] abounding in game; *pays m* ~ good game country.

gicler [ʒiˈkle] (1a) *v/i.* squirt, spurt; splash; **gicleur** *mot.* [~ˈklœːr] *m* jet; (spray) nozzle.

gifle [ʒifl] *f* slap in the face; box on the ear; **gifler** [ʒiˈfle] (1a) *v/t.:* ~ *q.* slap s.o.'s face; box s.o.'s ears.

gigantesque [ʒigãˈtɛsk] gigantic; **gigantisme** [~ˈtism] *m ✱* gigantism; *fig.* gigantic proportions *pl.*; *fig.* overexpansion.

241   **glapissement**

gigogne [ʒi'gɔɲ] **1.** *su./f: la mère* ♀
(*approx.*) the Old Woman who lived
in a shoe; **2.** *adj.: fusée f* ⁓ multi-stage
rocket; *lit m* ⁓ stowaway bed; *poupée f*
⁓ nest of dolls; *table f* ⁓ nest of tables;
⚓ *vaisseau m* ⁓ mother ship.
gigot [ʒi'go] *m cuis.* leg of mutton;
cost. manches f/pl. à ⁓ leg-of-mutton
sleeves; **gigoter** F [⁓gɔ'te] (1a) *v/i.*
kick; jig.
gigue¹ [ʒig] *f* haunch of venison;
gawky girl; F ⁓s *pl.* legs.
gigue² ♪ [⁓] *f* jig.
gilet [ʒi'lɛ] *m* waistcoat, vest; *knitwear:* cardigan; ⁓ *de sauvetage* life-
jacket.
gin [dʒin] *m* gin.
gingembre ♀ [ʒɛ̃'ʒɑ̃:br] *m* ginger.
gingivite ⚕ [ʒɛ̃ʒi'vit] *f* gingivitis.
girafe *zo.* [ʒi'raf] *f* giraffe.
girandole [ʒirɑ̃'dɔl] *f chandelier,
jewels:* girandole; *flowers:* cluster.
giratoire [ʒira'twa:r] *gyratory (traffic);* sens m ⁓ roundabout.
girofle ♀ [ʒi'rɔfl] *m* clove; *cuis.
clou m de* ⁓ clove; **giroflée** [ʒirɔ-
'fle] *f* stock; wallflower; **giroflier**
♀ [⁓fli'e] *m* clove-tree.
girolle ♀ [ʒi'rɔl] *f* mushroom, *usu.*
chanterelle.
giron [ʒi'rɔ̃] *m* lap; ⊕ loose handle;
⚓ tread; *fig.* bosom (*of the Church*).
girouette [ʒi'rwɛt] *f* weathercock
(*a. fig.*), vane.
gisant [ʒi'zɑ̃] *m arts:* recumbent
effigy; **gisement** [ʒiz'mɑ̃] *m geol.*
bed, layer, stratum; ⚓ bearing; ⚒
lode, vein; ⁓s *pl.* houillers coal
measures; **gisons** [ʒi'zɔ̃] *1st p. pl.
pres. of gésir;* **gît** [ʒi] *3rd p. sg. pres.
of gésir.*
gitan *m,* e *f* [ʒi'tɑ̃, ⁓'tan] gipsy.
gîte [ʒit] *su./m* resting-place, lodging; *hare:* form; *animal:* lair; *geol.*
bed, stratum; ⚒ vein; ⚓ joist;
su./f ⚓ list; **gîter** [ʒi'te] (1a) *v/i.*
lodge; lie; sleep; ⚓ list; ⚓ run
aground.
givrage ✈ [ʒi'vra:ʒ] *m* icing; **givre**
[ʒi:vr] *m* hoar-frost; **givré, e** [ʒi-
'vre] rimy; frosted; ✈ iced-up;
givrer [⁓] (1a) *v/t.* cover with
hoarfrost, frost (*s.th.*) over; frost
(*a cake*); ✈ ice up.
glabre [glɑ:br] smooth, hairless;
fig. clean-shaven (*face*).
glaçage [gla'sa:ʒ] *m* glazing; *cuis.*
icing, frosting; **glace** [glas] *f* ice;

ice-cream; *cuis.* icing; *fig.* chill;
mirror; (plate-)glass; *mot. etc.* window; ⊕ flaw; ⚓ *pris dans les* ⁓s
ice-bound; **glacé, e** [gla'se] **1.** *adj.*
icy (*a. fig. stare, politeness*), freezing; iced (*drink*); chilled (*wine*);
frozen; glazed (*paper etc.*); glacé,
kid ...; **2.** *su./m* glaze; **glacer** [⁓] (1k)
v/t. freeze; glaze; *fig.* chill (*the
wine*); surface (*paper etc.*); *cuis.*
frost, ice (*a cake*); ✝ polish (*the
rice*); se ⁓ freeze; *fig.* run cold;
glacerie [glas'ri] *f* ice-cream trade;
glass-works *usu sg.*; **glaceur** ⊕ [gla-
'sœ:r] *m paper, material:* glazer; roll-
ing-machine; glazing-pad; **glaciaire** *geol.* [⁓'sjɛ:r] glacial; ice-(age)
...; **glacial, e,** *m/pl.* **-als** [⁓'sjal] icy
(*temperature, a. fig.*); frosty (*air*);
ice-...; frigid (*style, manner, politeness, zone*); **glacier** [⁓'sje] *m geol.*
glacier; ice-cream man; maker of
mirrors *or* plate-glass; **glacière**
[⁓'sjɛ:r] *f* ice-house; ice-box; refrigerator; 🔌 refrigerator van; **glacis** [⁓'si] *m* slope; ⚔ ramp; ⚔ *hist.*
glacis; *paint.* glaze, scumble; **glaçon** [⁓'sɔ̃] *m* icicle (*a. fig. person*);
ice cube; block of ice; **glaçure**
[⁓'sy:r] *f pottery etc.:* glaze, glazing.
glaïeul ♀ [gla'jœl] *m* gladiolus.
glaire [glɛ:r] *f* white of egg; mucus;
phlegm; flaw (*in precious stone*);
glaireux, -euse [glɛ'rø, ⁓'rø:z]
glaireous; full of phlegm (*throat*).
glaise [glɛ:z] *f* clay, loam; **glaiser**
[glɛ'ze] (1b) *v/t.* line with clay; ⚒
coffer; ✎ dress (*the soil*) with clay;
⊕ puddle (*a reservoir*); **glaisière**
[⁓'zjɛ:r] *f* clay-pit.
glaive [glɛ:v] *m* sword.
glanage ✎ [gla'na:ʒ] *m* gleaning.
gland [glɑ̃] *m* ♀ acorn; *curtain:*
tassel; **glandage** [glɑ̃'da:ʒ] *m* pan-
nage.
glande ♀, *anat.* [glɑ̃:d] *f* gland.
glander *sl.* [glɑ̃'de], **glandouiller**
sl. [⁓du'je] (1a) *v/i.* hang around;
footle around.
glane [glan] *f* gleaning; *pears:* cluster; *onions:* rope; F ⁓s *pl.* pickings;
glaner [gla'ne] (1a) *v/t.* glean (*a.
fig.*); **glaneur** *m,* **-euse** [⁓'nœ:r,
⁓'nø:z] gleaner; **glanure** [⁓'ny:r] *f*
gleanings *pl.* (*a. fig.*).
glapir [gla'pi:r] (2a) *v/i.* yelp; bark
(*fox*); **glapissement** [⁓pis'mɑ̃] *m*
yelping, yapping; *fox:* barking.

16 GTW Fr-E

glas [glɑ] *m* knell; ✗ *etc.* salvo of guns (*at funeral*).

glauque [gloːk] sea-green; bluish green.

glèbe [glɛb] *f earth*: sod; † land; *hist.* feudal land; *attaché à la ~* bound to the soil.

glissade [gliˈsad] *f* slip; sliding; slide (*on snow etc.*); *dancing*: glide; *geol. ~ de terre* landslide; ✗ *~ sur l'aile* side-slip; ✗ *~ sur la queue* tail-dive; *mount. faire une descente en ~* glissade; **glissant, e** [ˌsɑ̃, ˌsɑ̃ːt] sliding (*a.* ⊕ *joint*); slippery (*a. fig.*); **glissement** [glisˈmɑ̃] *m* sliding; slipping; gliding; *geol.* landslide; ⊕ *belt*: creeping; **glisser** [gliˈse] (1a) *v/i.* slip; slide (*on ice etc.*); glide; *mot.* skid (*wheel*); ⊕ creep (*belt*); *~ sur* glance off (*s.th., s.o.*); *fig.* not to dwell upon, let pass; *v/t.* slip (*s.th. into s.th., a stitch, etc.*); *se ~* slip; creep (*a. fig.*); **glissière** [ˌsjɛːr] *f* slide; (*coal-*)shoot; ⊕ slide-bar; *mot. ~ de sécurité* crash barrier; **glissoir** [gliˈswaːr] *m* ⊕ slide; chute; **glissoire** [ˌ] *f* slide (*on ice etc.*).

global, e, *m/pl.* **-aux** [glɔˈbal, ˌbo] total; overall; global; **globe** [glɔb] *m* globe (*a.* ♂), sphere; *sun*: orb; *anat.* (*eye*)ball; *~ terrestre* terrestrial globe; **globulaire** [glɔbyˈlɛːr] **1.** *adj.* globular; **2.** *su./f* ♀ globularia; **globule** [ˌˈbyl] *m* globule (*a.* ♂); *water*: drop; ⊕ *metals*: airhole; ♂ small pill; *blood*: corpuscle; **globuleux, -euse** [ˌbyˈlø, ˌløːz] globular.

gloire [glwaːr] *f* glory; fame; pride; halo; *se faire ~ de* glory in; **gloria** [glɔˈrja] *m eccl.* gloria; F coffee with brandy; **gloriette** [ˌˈrjɛt] *f* summer-house, arbo(u)r; **glorieux, -euse** [ˌˈrjø, ˌˈrjøːz] **1.** *adj.* glorious; vain, conceited (*about, de*); *eccl.* glorified; **2.** *su./m* braggart; **glorification** [ˌrifikaˈsjɔ̃] *f* glorification; **glorifier** [ˌriˈfje] (1o) *v/t.* glorify; praise; *se ~* boast (*of, de*); glory (*in ger., de inf.*); **gloriole** [ˌˈrjɔl] *f* vainglory, vanity.

glose [gloːz] *f* gloss, commentary; *fig.* criticism; **gloser** [gloˈze] (1a) *v/t.* gloss; *v/i.: ~ sur* find fault with; criticize; gossip about.

glossaire [glɔˈsɛːr] *m* glossary; vocabulary.

glotte *anat.* [glɔt] *f* glottis.

glouglou [gluˈglu] *m* gurgle; *turkey*: gobble; **glouglouter** [ˌgluˈte] (1a) *v/i.* cluck (*hen*); gobble (*turkey*); chuckle (*person*).

glouteron ♀ [gluˈtrɔ̃] *m* burdock.

glouton, -onne [gluˈtɔ̃, ˌˈtɔn] **1.** *adj.* greedy; **2.** *su.* glutton; *su./m zo.* wolverine; **gloutonnerie** [ˌtɔnˈri] *f* gluttony.

glu [gly] *f* bird-lime; glue; **gluant, e** [ˌˈɑ̃, ˌˈɑ̃ːt] sticky, gluey; *sl. il est ~* he's a sticker; **gluau** [ˌˈo] *m* lime-twig; snare.

glucose ♫ [glyˈkoːz] *m* glucose.

gluer [glyˈe] (1a) *v/t.* lime (*twigs*); *fig.* make sticky.

glume [glym] *f* chaff; ♀ glume.

glutineux, -euse [glytiˈnø, ˌˈnøːz] glutinous.

glycérine [gliseˈrin] *f* glycerine.

glycine [gliˈsin] *f* ♀ wistaria, wisteria; *phot.* glycin(e).

gnangnan [ɲɑ̃ˈɲɑ̃] **1.** *adj./inv.* peevish; **2.** *su.* peevish person.

gn(i)ole, gnôle, *a.* **gnaule** *sl.* [ɲɔl] *f* brandy.

gnome [gnoːm] *m* gnome.

go F [go] *adv.: tout de ~* immediately, straight away.

goal *sp.* [gol] *m* goal; goalkeeper.

gobelet [gɔˈblɛ] *m* goblet; cup; mug; **gobeleterie** [gɔbleˈtri] *f* hollow-glass factory *or* trade *or* ware; **gobeletier** [ˌˈtje] *m* manu-facturer *or* dealer in glass-ware.

gobe-mouches [gɔbˈmuʃ] *m/inv. orn.* fly-catcher; ♀ fly-trap; F simpleton.

gober [gɔˈbe] (1a) *v/t.* swallow (*a.* F *fig. = believe blindly*); F *fig.* like (*s.o.*) very much; *sl.* catch; F *se ~* be conceited, think no end of o.s.

goberger [gɔbɛrˈʒe] (11) *v/t.: se ~* feed well, F have a good tuck-in.

gobeur *m*, **-euse** *f* [gɔˈbœːr, ˌˈbøːz] F simpleton, credulous person.

godaille *sl.* [gɔˈdaːj] *f* feast, guzzle; **godailler** F [ˌdaˈje] (1a) *v/i.* feast, guzzle; pub-crawl.

godasses *sl.* [gɔˈdas] *f/pl.* boots.

godelureau [gɔdlyˈro] *m* (*young*) dandy.

goder [gɔˈde] (1a) *v/i.* crease, pucker; bag (*trousers*); **godet** [ˌˈdɛ] *m* mug; cup (*a.* ♀); bowl (*a. of pipe*); ⊕ *dredger*: bucket; *cost.* flare; pucker (*in cloth*).

godiche F [gɔˈdiʃ], **godichon, -onne** [ˌdiˈʃɔ̃, ˌˈʃɔn] **1.** *adj.* awkward, stupid; **2.** *su.* simpleton; gawk; lout.

godille ⚓ [gɔˈdiːj] *f* stern-oar.

godillot *sl.* [gɔdiˈjo] *m* (military) boot.

goéland *orn.* [gɔeˈlɑ̃] *m* (sea-)gull; **goélette** [~ˈlɛt] *f* ⚓ schooner; ⚓ trysail; *orn.* sea-swallow.

goémon [gɔeˈmɔ̃] *m* seaweed; wrack.

gogo F [goˈgo] *m* dupe, *sl.* mug; *fig. à* ~ in abundance; galore; (*money*) to burn.

goguenard, e [gɔgˈnaːr, ~ˈnard] 1. *adj.* bantering; 2. *su.* mocker, chaffer; **goguette** F [gɔˈgɛt] *f: en* ~ on the spree.

goinfre [gwɛ̃ˈfr] *m* glutton, guzzler; **goinfrer** [gwɛ̃ˈfre] (1a) *v/t.: se* ~ guzzle (s.th., *de qch.*); **goinfrerie** [~frəˈri] *f* gluttony.

goitre ✱ [gwaːtr] *m* goitre; **goitreux, -euse** [gwaˈtrø, ~ˈtrøːz] 1. *adj.* goitrous; 2. *su.* goitrous person.

golf *sp.* [gɔlf] *m* golf; F golf-links; *joueur m de* ~ golfer.

golfe *geog.* [~] *m* gulf, bay; *anat.* sinus.

gomme [gɔm] *f* gum; india-rubber; **gommer** [gɔˈme] (1a) *v/t.* gum; mix with gum; rub ⊕ out, erase; *fig.* suppress; *fig.* blur; *v/i.* ⊕ jam, stick; **gommeux, -euse** [~ˈmø, ~ˈmøːz] 1. *adj.* gummy, sticky; 2. *su./m* F toff, swell, *Am.* dude.

gond [gɔ̃] *m* (door-)hinge; F *sortir de ses* ~s fly into a rage *or* off the handle; F *hors de ses* ~s beside oneself.

gondole [gɔ̃ˈdɔl] *f* gondola; ✈ *dirigible balloon*: nacelle; ✱ eyebath; **gondoler** [~dɔˈle] (1a) *v/i. a.* se ~ warp (*wood*); buckle (*metal*); blister (*paint*); *v/t.: sl.* se ~ split one's sides with laughter.

gonflage [gɔ̃ˈflaːʒ] *m* inflation; *mot.* blowing-up; **gonflé, e** [~ˈfle] swollen; puffy; bloated; ✱ distended; *pej.* puffed-up; F *il est vraiment* ~ he's got some nerve *or* cheek; F ~ *à bloc* keyed-up; completely sure of oneself, *pej.* cocksure; **gonflement** [~flɔˈmɑ̃] *m* inflation, inflating; swelling; bulging; ✱ distension; **gonfler** [~ˈfle] (1a) *v/t.* swell; inflate; blow up; puff out; fill (*the tyres*); ✱ distend (*the stomach*); F *mot., a. fig.* soup up; *v/i. a.* se ~ swell (up); become inflated *or* ✱ distended; *pej.* se ~ puff o.s. up; **gonfleur** *mot.* [~ˈflœːr] *m* air-pump.

gonio ⚓, ✈ [gɔˈnjo] *m* direction-

16*

finder; ~**mètre** [~njɔˈmɛtr] *m* goniometer.

gordien [gɔrˈdjɛ̃] *adj./m: nœud m* ~ Gordian knot.

goret [gɔˈrɛ] *m* little pig, piglet; F *fig.* dirty pig.

gorge [gɔrʒ] *f* throat, neck; *woman:* breast, bosom; *geog., a. hunt.* gorge; *geog.* pass, defile; ⊕ *etc.* groove; *axle:* neck; *lock:* tumbler; *à pleine* ~ at the top of one's voice; *mal m à la* ~ sore throat; F *fig. rendre* ~ make restitution; **gorgée** [gɔrˈʒe] *f* draught; gulp; *petite* ~ sip; **gorger** [~ˈʒe] (1l) *v/t.* gorge; cram (*fowls, a. fig.*); **gorgerette** [~ʒə-ˈrɛt] *f orn.* blackcap; *cost.* gorget; **gorget** ⊕ [~ˈʒe] *m* mo(u)lding plane.

gorille [gɔˈriːj] *m zo.* gorilla; F *fig.* bodyguard.

gosier [goˈzje] *m* throat; gullet; *à plein* ~ loudly; *avoir le* ~ *pavé* have a cast-iron throat.

gosse F [gɔs] *su.* kid, youngster.

gothique [gɔˈtik] 1. *adj.* Gothic; 2. *su./m* △, *ling., art:* Gothic; *su./f typ.* Old English.

gouache *paint.* [gwaʃ] *f* gouache.

gouailler [gwaˈje] (1a) *vt/i.* chaff; **gouaillerie** [gwajˈri] *f* banter, chaff; **gouailleur, -euse** [gwa-ˈjœːr, ~ˈjøːz] 1. *adj.* mocking (*tone*); waggish (*humour*); 2. *su.* banterer.

gouape F [gwap] *f* blackguard, hooligan.

goudron [guˈdrɔ̃] *m* tar; ⚓ *a.* pitch; **goudronnage** [~drɔˈnaːʒ] *m* tarring; **goudronner** [~drɔˈne] (1a) *v/t.* tar; **goudronnerie** [~drɔnˈri] *f* tar-works *usu. sg.*; tar-shed; **goudronneux, -euse** [~drɔˈnø, ~ˈnøːz] tarry; gummy (*oil*).

gouffre [gufr] *m* gulf, pit, abyss.

gouge [guːʒ] *f* ⊕ gouge, hollow chisel; ⊕ barrel plane.

gouine *sl.* [gwin] *f* dike, dyke (= *lesbian*).

goujat [guˈʒa] *m* △ hodman; farmhand; *fig.* boor, cad.

goujon[1] *icht.* [guˈʒɔ̃] *m* gudgeon.

goujon[2] [guˈʒɔ̃] *m* △ gudgeon (*a.* ⊕ *of a shaft*); △ stud; ⊕ tenon; bolt; ⊕ coak; ⊕ *hinge:* pin(tle); **goujonner** [~ʒɔˈne] (1a) *v/t.* ⊕ coak, dowel; pin, bolt; ⊕ joggle.

goulée [guˈle] *f metall.* channel; F mouthful; **goulet** [~ˈlɛ] *m* neck; ⚓ narrows *pl.*; △ neck-gutter; **goulot**

[~'lo] *m* bottle: neck; spout; *sl.* mouth; **goulotte** [~'lɔt], **goulette** [~'lɛt] *f* shoot; water-channel; **goulu, e** [~'ly] greedy, gluttonous.

goupille ⊕ [gu'piːj] *f* pin; (stop-) bolt; gudgeon; cotter; **goupiller** [~pi'je] (1a) *v/t.* ⊕ pin, key; *sl.* wangle, arrange.

goupillon [gupi'jõ] *m eccl.* aspergillum; *bottle, gun, lamp*: brush.

gourbi [gur'bi] *m* (Arab) hut; shack; F funk-hole.

gourd, gourde [guːr, gurd] benumbed; stiff.

gourde [gurd] **1.** *su./f* ♀ gourd, calabash; (brandy-)flask; *sl.* blockhead; **2.** *adj. sl.* blockheaded, thick.

gourdin [gur'dɛ̃] *m* cudgel, club, bludgeon.

gourgandine † F [gurgã'din] *f* hussy.

gourmand, e [gur'mã, ~'mãːd] **1.** *adj.* greedy, gluttonous; F *fig.* sweet-toothed; **2.** *su.* gourmand, glutton; epicure; **gourmander** [~mã'de] (1a) *v/t.* scold, rebuke; *fig.* treat roughly; **gourmandise** [~mã'diːz] *f* greediness, gluttony; ~s *pl.* sweetmeats.

gourme [gurm] *f hunt.* strangles *pl.*; ✻ impetigo; ✻ teething rash; *jeter sa ~* run at the nose (horse); F *fig.* blow off steam; F sow one's wild oats; **gourmé, e** [gur'me] stiff, formal (manners); aloof (person).

gourmet [gur'mɛ] *m* gourmet, epicure.

gourmette [gur'mɛt] *f horse*: curb; curb-bracelet; curb watch-chain; ⊕ polishing-chain.

gousse [gus] *f* pod, shell; *garlic*: clove; **gousset** [gu'sɛ] *m cost., a.* ⊕ gusset; *cost.* fob, waistcoat pocket; ⊕ bracket; ⊕ stayplate.

goût [gu] *m* taste (a. fig.); flavo(u)r; smell; liking, fancy; style, manner; *avoir bon ~ (mauvais)* ~ taste nice (nasty); *mauvais ~* bad taste; **goûter** [gu'te] **1.** (1a) *v/t.* taste; *fig.* enjoy, appreciate; *v/i.* take a snack; picnic; ~ *à* try, sample (s.th.); ~ *de* taste (s.th.) (for the first time); **2.** *su./m* snack; *Am.* lunch; *meal*: tea.

goutte¹ ✻ [gut] *f* gout.

goutte² [gut] *f* drop; speck, *colour*: spot; F sip, drop; *sl.* spot of brandy *etc.*; ~ *à* ~ drop by drop; *ne ... ~* not ...

in the least, not ... at all; **goutte-à-goutte** ✻ [~a'gut] *m/inv.* drip; *alimenter au* ~ drip-feed; **gouttelette** [~'lɛt] *f* droplet; **goutter** [gu'te] (1a) *v/i.* drip.

goutteux, -euse ✻ [gu'tø, ~'tøːz] **1.** *adj.* gouty; **2.** *su.* sufferer from gout.

gouttière [gu'tjɛːr] *f* ⚠ gutter(ing); drainpipe; spout; shoot; ✻ cradle; ⚠ ~s *pl.* eaves.

gouvernail [guvɛr'naːj] *m* ⚓ rudder (a. ✈), helm; ✈ ~ *de direction* vertical rudder; ✈ ~ *de profondeur* elevator; **gouvernant, e** [~'nã, ~'nãːt] **1.** *adj.* governing, ruling; **2.** *su./f* housekeeper; governess; regent; **gouverne** [gu'vɛrn] *f* guidance; ⊕ control; ⚓ steering; ✈ ~s *pl.* control surfaces; rudders and ailerons; *fig. pour ta* ~ for your guidance; **gouvernement** [guvɛrnə'mã] *m* government; management; governorship; ⚓ steering; **gouvernemental, e** *m/pl.* -aux [~nəmã'tal, ~'to] governmental; Government-...; **gouverner** [~'ne] (1a) *v/t.* govern (a. ⊕, a. gramm.), rule, control; ⚓ steer; **gouverneur** [~'nœːr] *m* governor.

grabat [gra'ba] *m* pallet; wretched bed; *fig. sur un* ~ in abject poverty.

grabuge F [gra'byːʒ] *m* row, ructions *pl.*

grâce [grɑːs] *f* grace (a. eccl., a. ✝), gracefulness, charm; favo(u)r; mercy; ⚖ pardon; ~! for pity's sake; ~s *pl.* thanks; ~ *à* thanks to; *action f de* ~s thanksgiving; *coup m de* ~ finishing stroke, quietus; *de mauvaise* ~ unwillingly, ungraciously; *dire ses* ~s say grace after a meal; *faire* ~ *de qch. à q.* spare s.o. s.th.; *rendre* ~(s) give thanks (to s.o. for s.th., *à q. de qch.*); **gracier** [gra'sje] (1o) *v/t.* pardon, reprieve.

gracieuseté [grasjøz'te] *f* graciousness; kindness; affability; **gracieux, -euse** [~'sjø, ~'sjøːz] graceful, pleasing; gracious; courteous; *à titre* ~ free (of charge), complimentary.

gracile [gra'sil] slender, slim; thin (voice).

gradation [grada'sjõ] *f* gradual process; *gramm.* ~ *inverse* anti-climax; *par* ~ gradually; **grade** [grad] *m* rank (a. ✕), grade (a. ✻); *univ.*

degree; ⚓ rating; **gradé** [gra'de] *m* ✗ non-commissioned officer, N.C.O.; ⚓ rated man; **gradin** [ʌ'dɛ̃] *m* step; en ʌs in tiers, tier upon tier; **graduation** *phys.* [ʌdɥa'sjɔ̃] *f* graduating; scale; **graduel, -elle** [ʌ'dɥel] *adj., a. su./m eccl.* gradual; **graduer** [ʌ'dɥe] (1n) *v/t.* graduate; increase gradually; *univ.* confer a degree on.

grailler [gra'je] (1a) *v/i.* speak in a husky voice.

graillon [gra'jɔ̃] *m* smell of burnt fat; F clot of phlegm; **graillonner** [ʌjɔ'ne] (1a) *v/i. cuis.* catch; taste of burnt fat; F bring up phlegm, hawk.

grain [grɛ̃] *m* grain (*a. of sand, powder, salt*); seed; *coffee:* bean; berry; *rosary etc.:* bead; texture, grain; particle, speck (*a. fig.*); ⚓ squall; ⊕ lining; ⚙ cam-roller; F bee in the bonnet, quirk; ʌ *de beauté* beauty spot; mole; ʌ *de raisin* grape; *à gros* ʌs coarse-grained; F *avoir son* ʌ be a bit fuddled (= *drunk*).

graine [grɛn] *f* seed; *silkworm:* eggs *pl.*; *monter en* ʌ run to seed; *fig.* grow into an old maid; F *de la mauvaise* ʌ a bad lot; **graineterie** [ʌ'tri] *f* seed-trade; seed-shop; **grainetier** [ʌ'tje] *m* corn-chandler.

graissage [grɛ'sa:ʒ] *m* greasing, lubrication; oiling; **graisse** [grɛs] *f* grease (*a.* ⊕); fat; *wine:* ropiness; *sl.* money; **graisser** [grɛ'se] (1a) *v/t.* grease, lubricate, oil; get grease on (*clothes*); F ʌ *la patte à q.* grease s.o.'s palm (= *bribe s.o.*); *v/i.* become ropy (*wine*); **graisseur** [ʌ'sœ:r] *m person:* greaser; ⊕ lubricator, grease-cup; **graisseux, -euse** [ʌ'sø, ʌ'sø:z] greasy, oily; fatty; ropy (*wine*).

grammaire [gram'mɛ:r] *f* grammar; **grammairien** *m*, **-enne** [ʌme'rjɛ̃, ʌ'rjɛn] grammarian; **grammatical, e,** *m/pl.* **-aux** [ʌmati'kal, ʌ'ko] grammatical.

gramme [gram] *m measure:* gram (-me). [ophone.\
gramophone [gramɔ'fɔn] *m* gram-\
grand, grande [grɑ̃, grɑ̃:d] **1.** *adj.* great, big; large; tall; high (*building, explosives, wind*); wide, extensive; grown-up; noble; high-class (*wines*); chief; main (*road*); ʌ *public m* general public; *au* ʌ *jour* in broad daylight; *de* ʌ *cœur* with a will,

heartily, willingly; *de* ʌ *matin* early in the morning; en ʌ on a large scale; *un* ʌ *homme* a great man; *un homme* ʌ a tall man; **2.** *su./m* (Spanish) grandee; great man; adult, grown-up; *school:* senior pupil.

grand...: ʌ**-chose** [grɑ̃'ʃo:z] *su./inv.:* *ne ... pas* ʌ not much; **grandeur** [ʌ'dœ:r] *f* size; height; greatness; magnitude; splendo(u)r; **grandir** [ʌ'di:r] (2a) *v/i.* grow tall; grow up (*child*); increase, grow; *v/t.* make look taller *or* bigger; magnify (*a. fig.*); enlarge.

grand...: ʌ**-livre**, *pl.* ʌ**s-livres** [grɑ̃'li:vr] *m* ledger; ʌ**-mère**, *pl.* ʌ**(s)-mères** [ʌ'mɛ:r] *f* grandmother; ʌ**-messe** *eccl.* [ʌ'mɛs] *f* high mass; ʌ**-oncle**, *pl.* ʌ**s-oncles** [ʌ'tɔ̃:kl] *m* great-uncle; ʌ**-peine** [ʌ'pɛn] *adv.:* *à* ʌ with great difficulty *or* much trouble; ʌ**-père**, *pl.* ʌ**s-pères** [ʌ'pɛ:r] *m* grandfather; ʌ**-route** [ʌ'rut] *f* highway, high road; ʌ**-rue** [ʌ'ry] *f* high *or* main street; ʌ**s-parents** [ʌpa'rɑ̃] *m/pl.* grandparents.

grange [grɑ̃:ʒ] *f* barn; *mettre en* ʌ garner.

granit [gra'ni] *m* granite; **graniteux, -euse** [ʌni'tø, ʌ'tø:z] granit-ic.

granivore [grani'vɔ:r] granivorous **granulaire** [grany'lɛ:r] granular; **granulation** [ʌla'sjɔ̃] *f* granulation (*a.* ✵); *gunpowder:* corning; **granule** [gra'nyl] *m*, **granulé** [grany'le] *m* granule; **granuler** [ʌ'le] (1a) *v/t.* granulate; corn (*gunpowder*); stipple (*an engraving*); **granuleux, -euse** [ʌ'lø, ʌ'lø:z] granular.

graphique [gra'fik] **1.** *adj.* graphic; **2.** *su./m* graph; (*a. dessin m* ʌ) diagram.

grappe [grap] *f fruit:* bunch; cluster; ✝ *onions:* string; *vet.* ʌs *pl.* grapes; **grappiller** [grapi'je] (1a) *v/t.* glean (*vineyards*); F pilfer, scrounge; *v/i.* F make petty profits; **grappilleur** *m*, **-euse** *f* [ʌ'jœ:r, ʌ'jø:z] gleaner; F pilferer, scrounger; **grappillon** [ʌ'jɔ̃] *m* small bunch *or* cluster.

grappin [gra'pɛ̃] *m* ⚓ grapnel, grappling-iron; ⊕ grab; ⚓ anchor-iron; ʌs *pl.* climbing-irons; F *mettre le* ʌ *sur* lay hands on, get hold of.

gras, grasse [grɑ, grɑ:s] **1.** *adj.*
fat(ted) (*animal*); fatty (*acid, tissue*);
greasy, oily (*rag, voice*); stout; thick
(*beam, mud, speech, weather*); heavy
(*soil*); rich (*food, coal*); soft (*outline, stone*); ⌒ aliphatic; *typ.* heavy,
bold(-faced); *fig.* broad, smutty;
fromage m ~ cream cheese; *eccl.*
jour m ~ meat day; **2.** *su./m* fat; ⊕
beam: thickness; thick (*of thumb*);
~ *de la jambe* calf (of the leg); *faire*
~ eat meat; **gras-double** *cuis.*
[grɑˈdubl] *m* tripe.
grasseyer [grɑsɛˈje] (1a) *v/i.* speak
with a strong guttural r.
grassouillet, -ette F [grɑsuˈjɛ, ~ˈjɛt]
plump, chubby; buxom (*woman*).
gratifiant, e [gratiˈfjɑ̃, ~ˈfjɑ̃:t] grati-
fying; satisfying; **gratification**
[~fikaˈsjɔ̃] *f* tip, gratuity; bonus;
gratifier [~ˈfje] (1o) *v/t.* ~ *q. de qch.*
bestow s.th. upon s.o.; present *or*
favo(u)r *or* hono(u)r s.o. with s.th.;
fig. attribute s.th. to s.o.
gratin [graˈtɛ̃] *m cuis.* cheese topping; cheese-topped dish; F *fig. the*
upper crust; *cuis. au* ~ with cheese
topping; **gratiné, e** *cuis.* with cheese
topping; F hellish, *a* hell of a ...
gratis [graˈtis] *adv.* free (of charge),
gratis.
gratitude [gratiˈtyd] *f* gratitude;
thankfulness.
gratte [grat] *f* ⊕ scraper; pickings
pl., F perks *pl.*, graft; ✝ fringe benefits *pl.*; **~-ciel** [~ˈsjɛl] *m/inv.* sky-
scraper; **~-cul** [~ˈky] *m/inv.* dog-rose:
hip; **~-papier** F [~paˈpje] *m/inv.*
penpusher; **~-pieds** [~ˈpje] *m/inv.*
shoe-scraper; **gratter** [graˈte] (1a)
v/t. scrape; scratch; scrape off; *sp.*
overtake (*a rival*); *sl.* make (*s.th.*) on
the side; *se* ~ scratch (o.s.); *v/i.:* ~ *du
pied* paw the ground (*horse*); **grattoir** [~ˈtwaːr] *m* scraper; **grattures**
[~ˈtyːr] *f/pl. metal:* scrapings.
gratuit, e [graˈtɥi, ~ˈtɥit] free; gratuitous; unmotivated; unfounded; un-
provoked (*abuse, insult*); *à titre* ~ free
of charge, gratis; **gratuité** [~tɥiˈte] *f*
gratuitousness.
gravatier [gravaˈtje] *m* rubbish-
carter; **gravats** [~ˈva] *m/pl.* (plaster)
screenings; *buildings:* rubbish *sg.*
grave [graːv] **1.** *adj.* grave; solemn;
serious, bad; important; ♪ deep,
low; **2.** *su./m* ♪ low register.
graveler [gravˈle] (1c) *v/t.* gravel;

graveleux, -euse [~ˈlø, ~ˈløːz]
gravelly (*soil*); gritty; ✳ suffering
from gravel; ✳ showing traces of
gravel (*urine*); *fig.* smutty (*song etc.*);
gravelle ✳ [graˈvɛl] *f* gravel; **gra-
velure** [gravˈlyːr] *f* smutty story.
graver [graˈve] (1a) *v/t.* engrave,
carve; *fig.* ~ *qch. dans sa mémoire*
engrave s.th. on one's memory;
graveur [~ˈvœːr] *m* engraver;
stone: carver; ~ *sur bois* wood-
engraver.
gravier [graˈvje] *m* gravel, grit; ✳
~*s pl.* gravel *sg.*
gravir [graˈviːr] (2a) *v/t.* climb,
ascend; mount.
gravitation [gravitaˈsjɔ̃] *f* gravita-
tion(al pull); **gravité** [~ˈte] *f phys.*,
a. fig. gravity; *fig.* seriousness; ♪
deepness; **graviter** [~ˈte] (1a) *v/i.*
revolve (round, *autour de*); move;
gravitate (to, towards *à, vers*).
gravure [graˈvyːr] *f* engraving;
etching; print; ~ *en taille-douce*, ~ *sur
cuivre* copper-plate engraving; ~ *sur
acier* steel engraving.
gré [gre] *m* will, wish, pleasure;
liking, taste; consent; *à mon* ~ as I
please, to suit myself; *au* ~ *de* at the
mercy of (*the winds etc.*); *bon* ~, *mal* ~
willy-nilly; *contre mon* ~ against my
will, unwillingly; *de bon* ~ willingly;
de mon plein ~ of my own accord;
savoir ~ *à q. de qch.* be grateful to s.o.
for s.th.
grec, grecque [grɛk] **1.** *adj.* Greek;
2. *su./m ling.* Greek; *su.* ♀ Greek;
gréco-latin, e [grekɔlaˈtɛ̃, ~ˈtin]
Gr(a)eco-Latin.
gredin *m, e f* † [grəˈdɛ̃, ~ˈdin] scoundrel, rogue.
gréement ⚓, ✂ [greˈmɑ̃] *m* rig-
ging; gear; **gréer** ⚓, ✂ [~ˈe] (1a)
v/t. rig.
greffage ⚹ [grɛˈfaːʒ] *m* grafting;
greffe [grɛf] *su./m* ⚖ office of the
clerk of the court; ⚖ registry (*a.* ✝),
record-office; *su./f* ⚹, ✳ graft,
grafting; ✳ ~ *de cœur* heart transplant; **greffer** ⚹, ✳ [grɛˈfe] (1a)
v/t. graft; **greffier** [~ˈfje] *m* ⚖
clerk of the court; ⚖, ✝, *admin.*
registrar; **greffoir** ⚹ [~ˈfwaːr] *m*
grafting-knife; **greffon** ⚹ [~ˈfɔ̃] *m*
graft, slip, scion.
grégaire [greˈgɛːr] gregarious; **gré-
garisme** [~gaˈrism] *m* gregarious-
ness.

grège [grɛːʒ] *adj./f* raw (*silk*).

grégeois [greˈʒwa] *adj./m:* feu *m* ∼ Greek fire.

grêle[1] [grɛːl] slender; thin (*a. fig. voice*); *anat.* small (*intestine*).

grêle[2] [grɛːl] *f* hail; *fig.* hail, shower; **grêlé, e** ✱ [greˈle] pock-marked; **grêler** [∼ˈle] (1a) *v/impers.* hail; *v/t.* damage by hail; ✱ pock-mark; **grêlon** [∼ˈlɔ̃] *m* hail-stone.

grelot [grəˈlo] *m* small bell; sleigh-bell; F *attacher le* ∼ bell the cat; **grelotter** [∼lɔˈte] (1a) *v/i.* shiver, tremble, shake (with, *de*); tinkle.

grenade [grəˈnad] *f* ♀ pomegranate; ✕ grenade; **grenadier** [grənaˈdje] *m* ♀ pomegranate(-tree); ✕ grenadier; ✕ bomber; F *woman:* amazon; **grenadille** [∼ˈdiːj] *f* ♀ granadilla; ✝ red ebony; **grenadin, e** [∼ˈdɛ̃, ∼ˈdin] **1.** *adj.* of Granada; of Grenada; **2.** *su./m cuis.* fricassee of chicken; ♀ grenadin; *orn.* African finch; *su./f tex.* grenadine.

grenaille [grəˈnaːj] *f* small grain; (small) shot; *en* ∼ granulated.

grenat [grəˈna] **1.** *su./m* garnet; **2.** *adj./inv.* garnet(-red).

greneler [grənˈle] (1c) *v/t.* grain (*leather etc.*).

grener [grəˈne] (1d) *v/i.* corn, seed (*cereals etc.*); *v/t.* corn (*gunpowder*); grain (*salt, a. leather, paper*); stipple (*an engraving*).

grènetis [grɛnˈti] *m* milled edge (*of a coin*).

grenier [grəˈnje] *m* granary; (*hay-, corn-*) loft; ⌂ attic, garret.

grenouillage [grənuˈjaːʒ] *m* (shady) dealings *pl.*, wangling; **grenouille** [grəˈnuːj] *f* frog; F kitty, club-money, funds *pl.*, ✕ mess-funds *pl.*; F *manger la* ∼ run off with the funds; **grenouillère** [∼nuˈjɛːr] *f* marsh; froggery; **grenouillette** [∼nuˈjɛt] *f* ♀ water-crowfoot; ✱ ranula.

grès [grɛ] *m* sandstone; (*a.* ∼ *cérame*) stoneware; earthenware; **gréseux, -euse** [greˈzø, ∼ˈzøːz] sandy, gritty; *geol.* sandstone (*rocks*); **grésière** [∼ˈzjɛːr] *f* sandstone quarry; **grésil** [greˈzi(l)] *m* (fine) hail.

grésiller[1] [greziˈje] (1a) *v/impers.* patter (*hail*).

grésiller[2] [∼] (1a) *v/i.* crackle (*fire*); sizzle; sputter (*candle*).

grève [grɛːv] *f* seashore; (*sandy*) beach; ⊕ strike, walkout; ∼ *bouchon*

disruptive action, selective action; ∼ *de la faim* hunger-strike; ∼ *perlée* go-slow strike, *Am.* slow-down strike; ∼ *sauvage* wildcat strike; ∼ *sur le tas* sit-down strike; *faire* ∼ be on strike; *faire la* ∼ *du zèle* work to rule; *faire une* ∼ *de sympathie* come out in sympathy; *se mettre en* ∼ walk out.

grever [grəˈve] (1d) *v/t.* burden (*an estate*) (with, *de*); ⚖ entail (*an estate*); ⚖ mortgage (*land*); *admin.* rate (*a building*).

gréviste [greˈvist] *su.* striker.

gribouiller [gribuˈje] (1a) *vt/i.* daub; scribble; **gribouillis** [∼ˈji] *m* scrawl, scribble.

grief [griˈɛf] *m* grievance, ground for complaint; *faire* ∼ *à q. de qch.* hold s.th. against s.o.

grièvement [griɛvˈmɑ̃]: ∼ *blessé(e)* seriously injured.

griffade [griˈfad] *f* scratch (*of claw*); **griffe** [grif] *f* claw (*a.* ⊕); *fig. a.* clutches *pl.*; maker's label; signature (*stamp*); *a. fig.* stamp; **griffé, e** ✝ [∼ˈfe] with a famous label; **griffer** [∼ˈfe] (1a) *v/t.* scratch, claw; fasten with a clamp; stamp (a signature on).

griffon [griˈfɔ̃] *m myth.* griffin; *orn.* tawny vulture; *dog:* griffon.

griffonnage [grifɔˈnaːʒ] *m* scrawl, scribble; **griffonner** [∼ˈne] (1a) *v/t.* scrawl, scribble; do a rough sketch of; **griffonneur** *m*, **-euse** *f* [∼ˈnœːr, ∼ˈnøːz] scribbler.

grignoter [griɲɔˈte] (1a) *v/t.* nibble (at); pick at (*one's food*); gnaw (away) (at); *fig.* eat away (at); *fig.* wear down or out; *fig.* win, get; *v/i.* nibble (at one's food).

grigou F [griˈgu] *m* miser, skinflint.

gril [gril] *m cuis.* grill, gridiron (*a.* ⚓, *a.* ♣); ⊕ *sluice-gate:* grating; *fig. être sur le* ∼ be on tenterhooks.

grillade *cuis.* [griˈjad] *f* grill, grilled steak; grilling.

grillage[1] [griˈjaːʒ] *m cuis.* grilling; roasting (*a. metall.*); ✂ F *bulb:* burn-ing-out.

grillage[2] [griˈjaːʒ] *m* lattice; (wire) netting *or* fencing; **grillager** [∼jaˈʒe] (1l) *v/t.* surround with wire fencing *or* netting; **grille** [griːj] *f* grate (*a.* ⊕); grating; iron gate, rail-ing; ⚡, *radio, fig.* grid; *mot.* grille; *fig.* schedule.

griller[1] [griˈje] (1a) *v/t. cuis.* grill; toast (*bread*); roast (*beans, a.* ⊕ *ore*);

singe (*cloth*); 🔥 calcine; scorch, burn; ⚡ burn out, blow (*a bulb, etc.*); *mot.* F race past; F jump (*the traffic lights*), jump, cut out (*a stop etc.*); F smoke (*a cigarette*); F *sp.* outrun (*an opponent*); *v/i.* F *fig.* be roasting (*in the heat*); *fig.* be burning (with s.th., de qch.; to *inf.*, de *inf.*).

griller[2] [~] (1a) *v/t.* rail in; bar (*a window*).

grillon *zo.* [gri'jɔ̃] *m* cricket.

grill-room [gril'rum] *m* grill-room.

grimace [gri'mas] *f* grimace, wry face; **grimacer** [~ma'se] (1k) *v/i.* make faces, screw one's face up, grimace; simper; *v/t.:* ~ un sourire force a smile; **grimacier, -ère** [~ma'sje, ~'sjɛːr] 1. *adj.* grimacing; grinning; affected; 2. *su.* affected person; hypocrite.

grimer *thea.* [gri'me] (1a) *v/t. a.* se ~ make up.

grimoire [gri'mwaːr] *m* book of spells, gibberish; scribble, scrawl.

grimpant, e [grɛ̃'pɑ̃, ~'pɑ̃ːt] climbing; ♣ *a.* creeping, trailing; **grimper** [~'pe] (1a) *vt/i.* climb; *v/i.* climb up; ♣ climb, creep, trail; **grimpereau** *orn.* [~'pro] *m* tree-creeper; **grimpette** [~'pɛt] *f* steep slope *or* climb; **grimpeur, -euse** [~'pœːr, ~'pøːz] 1. *adj.* climbing; 2. *su./m orn.* climber; *cyclism:* good hill-climber.

grincement [grɛ̃s'mɑ̃] *m door, teeth, wheel:* grinding, grating; *door, gate:* creaking; *pen:* scratch; **grincer** [grɛ̃'se] (1a) *v/i.* grate, grind; gnash (*teeth*); creak (*door*); scratch (*pen*).

grincheux, -euse [grɛ̃'ʃø, ~'ʃøːz] 1. *adj.* grumpy; testy; touchy; crabbed; 2. *su.* grumbler, F grouser.

gringalet F [grɛ̃ga'le] *m* shrimp (= seedy boy); whipper-snapper.

griot [gri'o] *m* ✦ flour etc.: seconds *pl.*

griotte [gri'ɔt] *f* ♣ morello cherry; *min.* griotte (= sort of marble flecked with red and brown).

grippage ⊕ [gri'paːʒ] *m* rubbing, friction; jamming; abrasion.

grippe [grip] *f* dislike; ✦ influenza, F 'flu; *prendre q. en* ~ take a dislike to s.o.; **grippé, e** ✦ [gri'pe] *adj.:* être~ have influenza, F have the 'flu; **gripper** [~] (1a) *v/i. a.* se ~ ⊕ seize up, jam; run hot; become abraded; *tex.* pucker; *v/t.* seize,

snatch; **grippe-sou,** *pl.* **grippe-sou(s)** F [grip'su] *m* skinflint, miser.

gris, grise [gri, griːz] grey; dull (*weather, a. fig.*); F tipsy, fuddled; *faire grise mine à* give a cold welcome to; **grisaille** [gri'zɑːj] *f paint.* grisaille; greyness; *fig.* dullness; **grisailler** [~zɑ'je] (1a) *v/t.* paint grey; paint (*s.th.*) in grisaille; *v/i.* turn grey (*hair*); **grisâtre** [~'zɑːtr] greyish.

grisbi *sl.* [gris'bi] *m* dough (= money).

griser [gri'ze] (1a) *v/t.* intoxicate, make drunk; se ~ get drunk; **grisette** [~'zɛt] *f* grisette (*a. tex.*).

grisoller [grizɔ'le] (1a) *v/i.* sing (*lark*).

grison[1], **-onne** [gri'zɔ̃, ~'zɔn] 1. *adj.* of the canton of Grisons; 2. *su.* inhabitant of the canton of Grisons.

grison[2], **-onne** † [gri'zɔ̃, ~'zɔn] 1. *adj.* grey(-haired), grizzled; 2. *su./m* grey-beard; donkey; **grisonner** [~zɔ'ne] (1a) *v/i.* turn grey (*hair*).

grisou 🔥 [gri'zu] *m* fire-damp; gas; *coup m de* ~ fire-damp explosion.

grive *orn.* [griːv] *f* thrush; **grivelé, e** [griv'le] speckled; **griveler** [~] (1d) *v/t.* obtain (*a meal etc.*) without being able to pay; **grivèlerie** [grivɛl'ri] *f* sponging; graft; pilfering; **grivois, e** [gri'vwa, ~'vwaːz] broad, spicy (*joke, story, etc.*); **grivoiserie** [~vwaz'ri] *f* broad *or* smutty joke *or* story *etc.*; licentious gesture.

grog [grɔg] *m* grog, toddy.

grognard *hist.* [grɔ'naːr] *m* soldier of Napoleon's Old Guard; **grognement** [grɔɲ'mɑ̃] *m* grunt; growl; snarl; grumbling; **grogner** [grɔ'ɲe] (1a) *v/i.* grunt; growl; grumble; *v/t.* growl out (*s.th.*); **grogneur, -euse** [~'ɲœːr, ~'ɲøːz] 1. *adj.* grumbling; 2. *su./m* grumbler, F grouser; **grognon, -onne** [~'ɲɔ̃, ~'ɲɔn] 1. *adj.* grumbling; peevish; 2. *su./m* grumbler; cross-patch; **grognonner** F [~ɲɔ'ne] (1a) *v/i.* grunt; grumble, grouse; be peevish.

groin [grwɛ̃] *m pig:* snout.

grol(l)e *sl.* [grɔl] *f* shoe.

grommeler [grɔm'le] (1c) *vt/i.* mutter; growl; grumble.

grondement [grɔ̃d'mɑ̃] *m thunder:* rumble, rumbling; *storm:* roar(ing); *sea:* boom; *dog:* growl; **gronder** [grɔ̃'de] (1a) *v/i.* growl (*dog*);

grumble (at, *contre*); rumble (*thunder*); roar (*sea, storm*); *v/t.* scold; **gronderie** [~'dri] *f* scolding; **grondeur, -euse** [~'dœːr, ~'døːz] **1.** *adj.* grumbling, scolding; **2.** *su.* grumbler; *su./f* shrew.

groom [grum] *m* page-boy, *Am.* bell-hop.

gros, grosse [gro, groːs] **1.** *adj.* big, large, stout, fat; thick; broad (*humour etc.*); foul (*weather, word*); heavy (*rain, sea*); swollen (*river*); † *⚥* pregnant; *fig.* teeming (with, de); *fig.* fraught (with, de); ~ *bétail m* cattle; ~ *doigt m du pied* big toe; F *grosse légume f* big shot; △ ~ *œuvre m* foundations *pl.*; main walls *pl.*; *avoir le cœur* ~ be heavy-hearted; **2.** *gros adv.* a great deal, a lot; *gagner* ~ earn a lot, make big money; *écrire* ~ write in large letters; **3.** *su./m* bulk, main part; ⚔ main body (*of an army*); thickest part; essential (part); *winter etc.*: heart; † *de* ~ wholesale (*price, firm, business, etc.*); *en* ~ rough, broad (*estimate etc.*); (*describe etc.*) roughly, broadly; all told, altogether; (*write*) in large letters; † wholesale (*a. fig.*); † *marchand m en* ~ wholesaler; † *faire le* ~ deal in wholesale; *su./f* gross, twelve dozen.

groseille ⚭ [gro'zɛːj] *f* (red *etc.*) currant; ~ *à maquereau* gooseberry; **groseillier** ⚭ [~zɛ'je] *m* currant bush.

gros-grain *tex.* [gro'grɛ̃] *m* grogram.

grossesse *⚥* [gro'sɛs] *f* pregnancy; **grosseur** [~'sœːr] *f* size, bulk; *lips*: thickness; *⚥* swelling; **grossier, -ère** [~'sje, ~'sjɛːr] coarse; gross, crude; rude, unmannerly; rough; boorish; crass (*ignorance, stupidity, etc.*); **grossièreté** [~sjɛr'te] *f* coarseness, roughness; rudeness; grossness; coarse language; *dire des* ~s be offensive; **grossir** [~'siːr] (2a) *v/t.* enlarge, magnify (*a. opt., a. fig.*); swell; *v/i.* grow bigger, increase; put on weight (*person*); **grossissement** [~sis'mã] *m* magnification; enlargement; increase, swelling; **grossiste** † [~'sist] *m* wholesaler; **grossoyer** [~swa'je] (1h) *v/t.* engross (*a document*).

grotesque [gro'tɛsk] **1.** *adj.* grotesque; **2.** *su./m* grotesque person; freak.

grotte [grɔt] *f* grotto; cave.

grouiller [gru'je] (1a) *v/i.* swarm, crawl, teem, be alive (with, de); rumble (*belly*); † stir; *v/t.*: *sl. se* ~ hurry up, F get a move on.

groupe [grup] *m persons, objects, a. ♪*: group; *stars*: cluster; *trees*: clump; *biol.* division; ~ *de pression* pressure group; *⚕* ~ *sanguin* blood-group; **groupement** [~'mã] *m* grouping; group; **grouper** [gru'pe] (1a) *v/t.* group; *se* ~ form a group or groups; gather, cluster (round, autour de).

gruau [gry'o] *m* flour of wheat; ~ *d'avoine* groats *pl.*; *cuis.* gruel.

grue [gry] *f orn., a.* ⊕ crane; F street-walker, prostitute; ⊕ ~ *à bras* (or *à flèche*) jib-crane; *🚂* ~ *d'alimentation* water-pillar; F *faire le pied de* ~ cool one's heels, hang about (*ger., à inf.*).

gruger [gry'ʒe] (1l) *v/t.* crunch; F eat; *fig.* sponge on (*s.o.*), fleece (*s.o.*).

grume [grym] *f* log; *bois m de* (or en) ~ undressed timber.

grumeau [gry'mo] *m* clot; *salt*: speck; **grumeler** [grym'le] (1c) *v/t.*: *se* ~ clot, curdle; **grumeleux, -euse** [~'lø, ~'løːz] curdled; gritty (*pear*).

grutier ⊕ [gry'tje] *m* crane-driver.

gruyère [gry'jɛːr] *m* gruyère.

gué [ge] *m* ford; **guéable** [~'abl] fordable; **guéer** [~'e] (1a) *v/t.* ford (*a river, a stream*); water (*a horse*).

guenille [gə'niːj] *f* rag; F trollop; *en* ~s in rags.

guenon [gə'nõ] *f zo.* long-tailed monkey; F ugly woman.

guêpe *zo.* [gɛːp] *f* wasp; **guêpier** [gɛ'pje] *m* wasps' nest; *orn.* bee-eater.

guère [gɛːr] *adv.*: *ne ...* ~ hardly, little, scarcely, not much *or* many.

guéret [ge'rɛ] *m* ploughed land; fallow land.

guéridon [geri'dõ] *m* pedestal table.

guérilla ⚔ [geri'ja] *f* guerilla (warfare); **guérillero** ⚔ [~je'ro] *m person*: guerilla.

guérir [ge'riːr] (2a) *v/t.* cure; heal (*a wound etc.*); *v/i.* get better, be cured; heal (*wound*); **guérison** [geri'zõ] *f* cure; *wound*: healing; recovery; **guérissable** [~'sabl] curable; healable; **guérisseur, -euse** [~'sœːr, ~'søːz] *su.* healer; quack-doctor.

guérite [ge'rit] *f* ⚔ sentry box; workman's hut; (*watchman's*) shelter.

guerre [gɛːr] *f* war(fare); *fig.* quarrel; *Grande* ⚔ Great War, World War I; *faire la* ~ make war (on, *à*); *faire la* ~ *à qch. a.* fight s.th.; *fig. de bonne* ~ fair; **guerrier, -ère** [gɛˈrje,~ˈrjɛːr] **1.** *adj.* warlike; **2.** *su./m* warrior; **guerroyer** [~rwaˈje] (1h) *v/i.* wage war.

guet [gɛ] *m* watch; look-out; patrol; *faire le* ~ be on the look-out; ~**apens**, *pl.* ~**s-apens** [gɛtaˈpɑ̃] *m* ambush, trap.

guêtre [gɛːtr] *f* gaiter; *mot.* patch, sleeve.

guetter [gɛˈte] (1a) *v/t.* lie in wait for, watch for; *fig.* wait (*one's opportunity*); **guetteur** ⚔, ⚓ [~ˈtœːr] *m person:* look-out.

gueulard, e F [gœˈlaːr, ~ˈlard] **1.** *adj.* loud-mouthed (*person*); noisy; **2.** *su.* loudmouth, bigmouth; **gueule** [gœl] *f animal, a. sl. person:* mouth; *sl.* face; F look, appearance; *gun:* muzzle; opening; *sl. casser la* ~ *à* q. break s.o.'s jaw, F sock s.o.; *sl. ta* ~! shut up!; F *avoir une drôle de* ~ look funny; F *avoir de la* ~ look *or* be great; **gueule-de-loup**, *pl.* **gueules-de-loup** ⚘ [~dəˈlu] snapdragon, antirrhinum; **gueuler** *sl.* [gœˈle] (1a) *vt/i.* bawl; **gueuleton** F [gœlˈtɔ̃] *m* blow-out, spread; **gueuletonner** F [~tɔˈne] (1a) *v/i.* have a blow-out.

gueusaille F [gøˈzaːj] *f* rabble; **gueusard** [~ˈzaːr] *m* beggar; rascal, rogue.

gueuse *metall.* [gøːz] *f* pig-mo(u)ld; **gueuserie** [gøzˈri] *f* beggary; begging; *fig.* poor show, poor affair.

gueux, gueuse [gø, gøːz] **1.** *adj.* poverty-stricken, poor; **2.** *su.* beggar; tramp, vagabond; *su./f* wench; *courir la* ~ lead a wild life.

gui¹ ⚘ [gi] *m* mistletoe.

gui² ⚓ [gi] *m* boom; guy(-rope).

guibolle *sl.* [giˈbɔl] *f* leg.

guichet [giˈʃɛ] *m post office, bank etc.:* counter, window; wicket, hatch; 🎫 booking office (window); *thea.* box office; *sp. cricket:* wicket; **guichetier** [giʃˈtje] *m prison:* turnkey.

guide¹ [gid] *m* guide (*a.* ⚔, *a.* ⊕); guide-book.

guide² [~] *f* rein; girl guide.

guide-âne [giˈdaːn] *m* (handbook of) elementary instructions *pl.*; *writing pad:* black lines *pl.*, ruled guide; **guider** [~ˈde] (1a) *v/t.* guide; direct, steer; lead; ⊕ control; *se* ~ *sur* use as

a guide; ⊕ *guidé par ordinateur* computer-controlled.

guidon [giˈdɔ̃] *m* ⚓ pennant; *cycle:* handle-bar; ✕ *gun:* foresight.

guigne [giɲ] *f* heart-cherry; F *fig.* bad luck; F *avoir la* ~ be out of luck.

guigner F [giˈɲe] (1a) *v/t.* steal a glance at; have an eye to; ogle (*s.o.*). [(tree).\ ]

guignier ⚘ [giˈnje] *m* heart-cherry ⌉

guignol [giˈɲɔl] *m* Punch and Judy show; puppet (show).

guignolet [giɲɔˈlɛ] *m* cherry-brandy.

guignon [giˈɲɔ̃] *m* bad luck; *avoir du* ~ have a run of bad luck.

guillaume ⊕ [giˈjoːm] *m plane:* rabbet.

guillemets [gijˈmɛ] *m/pl.* inverted commas, quotation marks.

guilleret, -ette [gijˈrɛ, ~ˈrɛt] gay; broad (*joke*).

guillocher ⊕ [gijɔˈʃe] (1a) *v/t.* chequer.

guillotine [gijɔˈtin] *f* guillotine (*a.* for cutting paper); *fenêtre f à* ~ sash-window.

guimauve ⚘ [giˈmoːv] *f* marshmallow.

guimbarde [gɛ̃ˈbard] *f* ♪ Jew's-harp; ⊕ grooving-plane; *sl.* rattle-trap, *Am.* jalopy.

guimpe [gɛ̃ːp] *f* (*nun's*) wimple; chemisette.

guindage [gɛ̃ˈdaːʒ] *m* ⊕ hoisting; ⊕ *tackle:* hoist; **guindé, e** [~ˈde] stiff, starchy; strained; stilted (*style*); **guinder** [~ˈde] (1a) *v/t.* hoist; *fig.* strain; *fig.* make look stiff; *fig. se* ~ become stilted *or* strained (*story, etc.*); adopt a stiff manner (*person*).

guinguette [gɛ̃ˈgɛt] *f* suburban tavern; out-of-town inn.

guiper [giˈpe] (1a) *v/t.* wind; wrap; lap (*a.* ⚡); **guipure** [~ˈpyːr] *f* pillow-lace; ⚡ lapping.

guirlande [girˈlɑ̃ːd] *f* garland, wreath, festoon; *pearls:* rope.

guise [giːz] *f* manner, way; *à votre* ~! as you like!; please yourself!; *en* ~ *de* by way of, as.

guitare ♪ [giˈtaːr] *f* guitar.

gustatif, -ve [gystaˈtif, ~ˈtiːv] gustative; gustatory (*nerve*); **gustation** [~taˈsjɔ̃] *f* tasting.

gutta-percha [gytapɛrˈka] *f* gutta-percha.

guttural, e, *m/pl.* **-aux** [gytyˈral, ~ˈro] **1.** *adj.* guttural; throaty

(voice); **2.** *su./f gramm.* guttural.
gymnase [ʒim'nɑːz] *m* gymnasium,
F gym; **gymnaste** [ˌ'nast] *su.*
gymnast; **gymnastique** [ˌnas'tik]
1. *adj.* gymnastic; **2.** *su./f* gymnastics *sg.*, F gym; ~ *rythmique*
eurhythmics *sg.*; *faire de la* ~ do
gymnastics.
gymnote *icht.* [ʒim'nɔt] *m* electric
eel.
gynécologiste ⚕ [ʒinekɔlɔ'ʒist], **gy-**

nécologue ⚕ [ˌ'lɔg] *su.* gyn(a)ecol-
ogist.
gypaète *orn.* [ʒipa'ɛt] *m* lammer-
geyer.   [plaster of Paris.)
gypse [ʒips] *m min.* gypsum; ✝)
gyrophare [ʒirɔ'faːr] *m* flashing
light; **gyroscope** [ˌ'skɔp] *m* gyroscope; **gyroscopique** [ˌskɔ'pik] gy-
roscopic; ✈ *appareil m* ~ *de pilotage*
gyro-pilot; ⚓ *compas m* ~ gyro-compass.

H

(Before the so-called aspirate *h*, marked ***h**, there is neither elision nor liaison.)

H, h [aʃ] *m* H, h.

habile [a'bil] clever; skilful; ⚖ competent (to, *à*); **habileté** [abil'te] *f* skill, ability; cleverness; (clever) trick; **habilité** ⚖ [∼'te] *f* competency; **habiliter** ⚖ [∼'te] (la) *v/t*. entitle (s.o. to *inf.*, *q. à inf.*).

habillage [abi'ja:ʒ] *m* dressing; ⊕ assembling; ⚙ get-up; **habillement** [abij'mɑ̃] *m* clothing; clothes *pl.*; dress; **habiller** [abi'je] (la) *v/t*. dress; clothe; ⚙ get up; cover; *dress*: suit (*s.o.*); s'∼ dress (o.s.), get dressed; dress up (as, *en*); **habilleur** *m*, **-euse** *f* [∼'jœːr, ∼'jøːz] *thea. etc.* dresser.

habit [a'bi] *m* (*a.* ∼ *de soirée*) dress coat; dress; coat; *eccl.* habit; *eccl.* frock; ∼ **vert** green coat (*of the Members of the Académie française*).

habitable [abi'tabl] habitable; **habitacle** [∼'takl] *m* ♎ binnacle; ✈ cockpit; *poet.* dwelling; **habitant** *m*, **e** *f* [∼'tɑ̃, ∼'tɑ̃:t] inhabitant; occupier (*of a house*); resident; **habitat** ♀, *zo., etc.* [∼'ta] *m* habitat; **habitation** [∼ta'sjɔ̃] *f* habitation; dwelling, residence; **habiter** [∼'te] (la) *v/t*. inhabit, live in; *v/i.* dwell, live, reside.

habitude [abi'tyd] *f* habit, custom, practice, use; *avoir l'* ∼ *de* be used to (*s.th., doing s.th.*); *avoir l'*∼ *de* (*inf.*) *a.* be in the habit of (*ger.*); *j'ai l'*∼, *j'en ai l'*∼ I am used to it; *d'*∼ usually; *par* ∼ from sheer force of habit; **habitué** *m*, **e** *f* [∼'tɥe] frequenter, regular attendant *or* customer; **habituel, -elle** [∼'tɥɛl] usual; customary; **habituer** [∼'tɥe] (1n) *v/t.*: ∼ *q. à* accustom s.o. to *or* get s.o. used to (*s.th., doing s.th.*); s'∼ *à* get used to.

***hâblerie** [ɑblə'ri] *f* boasting; ***hâbleur** *m*, **-euse** *f* [ɑ'blœːr, ∼'bløːz] boaster.

***hache** [aʃ] *f* axe; ∼-**légumes** [∼le'gym] *m/inv.* vegetable-cutter; ∼-**paille** [∼'pɑːj] *m/inv.* chaff-cutter.

***hacher** [a'ʃe] (la) *v/t.* chop (up); hash (*meat*); hack up; *fig.* score (*s.o.'s face*); hatch (*a drawing etc.*); ***hachereau** [aʃ'ro] *m* small axe, hatchet; ***hachette** [a'ʃɛt] *f* hatchet; ***hachis** *cuis.* [a'ʃi] *m* hash (*a. fig.*), mince.

***hachisch** [a'ʃiʃ] *m* hashish.

***hachoir** [a'ʃwaːr] *m* chopper; chopping-knife; chopping-board; ***hachure** [a'ʃyːr] *f* hachure, hatching; *en* ∼s hachured.

***hagard, e** [a'gaːr, ∼'gard] wild, wild-looking; distraught.

***haï, e** [a'i] *p.p. of haïr.*

***haie** [ɛ] *f* hedge(row); *people*: line; *sp.* hurdle; ∼ *d'honneur* guard of hono(u)r; *sp. course f de* ∼*s* hurdle-race; *faire la* ∼ be lined up.

***haillon** [a'jɔ̃] *m* rag, tatter.

***haine** [ɛːn] *f* hate, hatred; ***haineux, -euse** [ɛ'nø, ∼'nøːz] full of hatred.

***haïr** [a'iːr] (2m) *v/t.* hate, detest, loathe.

***haire** [ɛːr] *f* hair-shirt; *tex.* hair-cloth.

***hais** [ɛ] *1st p. sg. pres. of haïr*; ***haïs** [a'i] *1st p. sg. p.s. of haïr*; ***haïssable** [ai'sabl] hateful, odious; ***haïssent** [a'is] *3rd p. pl. pres. of haïr.*

***halage** [a'laːʒ] *m* ♎ *ship*: hauling; towing; *chemin m de* ∼ tow(ing)-path.

***hâle** [ɑːl] *m* tan(ning); sunburn; ***hâlé, e** [ɑ'le] (sun)tanned, sunburnt.

haleine [a'lɛn] *f* breath; *fig.* wind; *à perte d'*∼ until out of breath; *avoir l'*∼ *courte* be short-winded; *de longue* ∼ long and exacting, of long duration; long-term (*plans*); *hors d'*∼ out of breath; *tenir en* ∼ keep (*s.o.*) breathless.

***haler** [a'le] (la) *v/t.* ♎ haul (in); tow.

***halètement** [alɛt'mɑ̃] *m* panting, gasping; ***haleter** [al'te] (1d) *v/i.* pant; gasp (for breath); puff.

***haleur** ♎ [a'lœːr] *m* hauler; tower.

***hall** [ɔl] *m* entrance hall; *hotel*:

lounge; *mot.* open garage; ⊕ shop, room; ***hallage** ⚓ [a'la:ʒ] *m* market dues *pl.*; ***halle** [al] *f* (covered) market.

*hallebarde *hist.* [al'bard] *f* halberd.

*hallier [a'lje] *m* thicket, copse; ~*s pl.* brushwood *sg.*

hallucinant, e [alysi'nɑ̃, ~'nɑ̃t] hallucinating; *fig.* incredible, staggering; **hallucination** [~na'sjɔ̃] *f* hallucination; **hallucinogène** [~nɔ-'ʒɛn] **1.** *adj.* hallucinogenic; **2.** *su./m* hallucinogen.

*halo [a'lo] *m meteor.* halo; *phot.* halation; *opt.* blurring.

halogène ⚗ [alɔ'ʒɛn] **1.** *adj.* halogenous; **2.** *su./m* halogen.

*halte [alt] *f* halt (*a.* 🚂), stop; stopping-place; *faire* ~ stop, ✕ halt; ~(*-là*)! stop!, ✕ halt!

haltère [al'tɛːr] *m* dumbbell.

*hamac ⚓ *etc.* [a'mak] *m* hammock.

*hameau [a'mo] *m* hamlet.

hameçon [am'sɔ̃] *m* (fish) hook; *fig.* bait; *fig. mordre à l'*~ take the bait.

*hampe¹ [ɑ̃:p] *f flag:* pole; *spear:* shaft; handle; ♀ stem.

*hampe² *cuis.* [~] *f* (thin) flank of beef.

*hamster [ams'tɛːr] *m zo.* hamster; F hoarder (*of food*).

hanap † [a'nap] *m* hanap, goblet.

*hanche [ɑ̃:ʃ] *f* hip; *horse:* haunch; ⚓ *ship:* quarter.

*handicap [ɑ̃di'kap] *m sp.* handicap (*a. fig.*); *fig.* disadvantage; ***handicaper** *sp.* [~ka'pe] (1a) *v/t.* handicap (*a. fig.*); *les handicapés* (*mentaux or physiques*) the (mentally *or* physically) handicapped.

*hangar [ɑ̃'ga:r] *m* shed; lean-to; ✈ hangar.

*hanneton [an'tɔ̃] *m zo.* cockchafer; F *fig.* harum-scarum, scatterbrain.

*hanter [ɑ̃'te] (1a) *v/t.* haunt; *maison f hanté*e haunted house; ***hantise** [ɑ̃'ti:z] *f* obsession; haunting memory.

*happement [ap'mɑ̃] *m* snatching up, seizing; ***happer** [a'pe] (1a) *v/t.* catch, snatch; *v/i.* cling, stick.

*haquenée [ak'ne] *f* hack; ambling mare; *aller à la* ~ amble along.

*haquet [a'kɛ] *m* dray, waggon (*a.* ✕); ***haquetier** [ak'tje] *m* drayman.

*hara-kiri [araki'ri] *m* harakiri, happy dispatch.

*harangue [a'rɑ̃:g] *f* harangue; ***haranguer** [arɑ̃'ge] (1m) *v/t.* harangue; F *fig.* lecture (*s.o.*); F hold forth to; ***harangueur** [~'gœːr] *m* orator; F tub-thumper.

*haras [a'rɑ] *m* stud-farm; stud.

*harasser [ara'se] (1a) *v/t.* wear out, exhaust.

*harcèlement [arsɛl'mɑ̃] *m* harassing, harrying (*a.* ✕); ***harceler** [~sə'le] (1d) *v/t.* harass, harry (*a.* ✕); badger; nag at, be on at.

*harde¹ [ard] *f* herd; *orn.* flock.

*harde² *hunt.* [ard] *f* leash; ***harder** *hunt.* [ar'de] (1a) *v/t.* leash (*the hounds in couples*).

*hardes [ard] *f/pl.* old clothes.

*hardi, e [ar'di] bold; daring; rash; impudent; ***hardiesse** [~'djɛs] *f* boldness; temerity, daring; rashness; effrontery.

*hareng [a'rɑ̃] *m* herring; ~ *fumé* kipper; ~ *saur* red herring; ***harengaison** [arɑ̃gɛ'zɔ̃] *f* herring-season; herring-fishing; **'harengère** [~'ʒɛːr] *f* fishwife.

*hargne [arɲ] *f* ill-temper; aggressiveness; ***hargneux, -euse** [ar'nø, ~'nøːz] surly; peevish; bad-tempered; aggressive; nagging (*wife*).

*haricot¹ ♀ [ari'ko] *m* bean; ~ *blanc* haricot bean; ~ *rouge* kidney bean; ~ *vert* French bean; *sl. courir sur le* ~ *à q.* get on s.o.'s nerves.

*haricot² [~] *m* stew, haricot; ~ *de mouton* haricot mutton, *Am.* lamb stew.

*haridelle F [ari'dɛl] *f* jade, nag.

harmonica ♪ [armɔni'ka] *m* harmonica; mouth-organ.

harmonie [armɔ'ni] *f* ♪ harmony (*a. fig.*); *fig.* agreement; ♪ brass and reed band; **harmonieux, -euse** [~'njø, ~'njøːz] harmonious; **harmonique** [~'nik] harmonic; **harmoniser** [~ni'ze] (1a) *v/t. a. s'*~ harmonize; match (*colours*); **harmonium** ♪ [~'njɔm] *m* harmonium.

*harnacher [arna'ʃe] (1a) *v/t.* harness; rig (*s.o.*) out; ***harnacheur** [~'ʃœːr] *m* harness-maker; saddler; groom.

*harnais [ar'nɛ] *m*, † ***harnois** [~'nwa] *m horse, a. tex.:* harness.

*haro [a'ro] *m* hue and cry; *crier* ~ *sur* denounce.

harpagon [arpa'gɔ̃] *m* skinflint.

*harpe¹ ♪ [arp] *f* harp.

*harpe² △ [~] *f* toothing-stone.
*harpie [ar'pi] *f myth.*, *a. fig.* harpy;
fig. hell-cat.
*harpin ⚓ [ar'pɛ̃] *m* boat-hook.
*harpiste ♪ [ar'pist] *su.* harpist.
*harpon [ar'pɔ̃] *m* harpoon; △
wall-staple; ***harponner** [~pɔ'ne]
(1a) *v/t.* harpoon; *fig.* buttonhole
(*s.o.*).
*hasard [a'za:r] *m* chance, luck;
risk; hazard (*a. golf*); *à tout* ~ at
all hazards *or* events; *au* ~ at random; ... *de* ~ chance ...; *par* ~ by
chance; ***hasardé, e** [azar'de]
risky, foolhardy; bold; hazardous;
*hasarder [~'de] (1a) *v/t.* risk,
venture; ***hasardeux, -euse** [~'dø,
~'dø:z] perilous, risky; daring, foolhardy.
*hase *zo.* [ɑ:z] *f* doe-hare; doe-rab-
bit.
*hâte [ɑ:t] *f* haste, hurry; *à la* ~ in a
hurry; hurriedly; *avoir* ~ *de* (*inf.*) be
in a hurry to (*inf.*); long to (*inf.*); *en
(toute)* ~ with all possible speed;
*hâter [ɑ'te] (1a) *v/t. a.* se ~ hasten,
hurry; ***hâtif, -ve** [ɑ'tif, ~'ti:v]
hasty; premature; early (*fruit etc.*);
*hâtiveau ✔ [ɑti'vo] *m* early fruit
(*esp. pear*); early vegetable.
*hauban [o'bɑ̃] *m* ⚓ shroud; △, ⊕
stay; ✗ (*bracing-*)wire; ***haubaner**
[oba'ne] (1a) *v/t.* stay, guy.
*haubert *hist.* [o'bɛːr] *m* hauberk,
coat of mail.
*hausse [o:s] *f* rise (*a.* ✝), *Am.* raise;
rifle: back-sight, rear-sight; ⊕
block, prop; *à la* ~ on the rise;
*haussement [os'mɑ̃] *m* raising; ~
d'épaules shrug; ***hausser** [o'se] (1a)
v/t. raise (*a.* ♪; *a. a house, the price,
one's voice*); lift; increase; shrug
(*one's shoulders*); *v/i.* rise, go up; ⚓
heave in sight; ***haussier** ✝ [o'sje]
m bull.
*haussière ⚓ [o'sjɛːr] *f* hawser.
*haut, haute [o, o:t] **1.** *adj.* high;
elevated; eminent, important; loud
(*voice*); erect (*head*); upper (*floor
etc.*); *la haute mer* the open sea; *la
mer haute* high tide; **2.** *haut adv.*
high (up); aloud; haughtily; further
back (*in time*); *fig.* ~ *la main* easily;
~ *les mains*! hands up!; *d'en* ~ from
upstairs; upper; *en* ~ *adv.* above;
upstairs; **3.** *su./m* height; top;
summit; *tomber de son* ~ fall flat;
fig. fall; *fig.* be dumbfounded;

vingt pieds de ~ 20 feet *or* foot
high; *su./f: la haute* the smart
set, the upper crust.
*hautain, e [o'tɛ̃, ~'tɛn] proud;
haughty.
*haut...: ***~bois** ♪ [o'bwa] *m* oboe;
(*a.* ***~boïste** [obɔ'ist] *m*) oboist;
*~-de-chausses, *pl.* ***~s-de-chaus-
ses** [od'ʃo:s] *m* breeches *pl.*; ***~-de-
forme**, *pl.* ***~s-de-forme** [~'fɔrm]
m top hat.
*haute-contre, *pl.* ***hautes-contre**
♪ [ot'kɔ̃:tr] *f voice:* alto.
*hautement [ot'mɑ̃] *adv.* highly;
loudly; loftily; frankly.
*Hautesse [o'tɛs] *f title of sultan:*
Highness.
*hauteur [o'tœːr] *f* height; eminence, high place; hill(-top); level;
depth; ⚓, *astr.* altitude; ♪ pitch;
fig. arrogance; *fig.* principles *etc.*:
loftiness; *être à la* ~ *de* be equal to; be
a match for; *fig.* be abreast of (*developments, news*); ⚓ be off (*Calais*);
✗ *prendre de la* ~ gain height; *tomber
de sa* ~ fall flat; ⼧ *fig.* be dumbfounded; *sp. saut en* ~ high jump.
*haut...: ***~-fond**, *pl.* ***~s-fonds**
[o'fɔ̃] *m sea:* shoal, shallows *pl.*; ***~
le-cœur** [ol'kœːr] *m/inv.* heave;
nausea; *avoir des* ~ retch; ***~-le-
corps** [~'kɔːr] *m/inv.* sudden start;
*~-lieu, *pl.* ***~s-lieux** [o'ljø] centre,
Mecca (*of art etc.*); ***~-parleur**
[opar'lœːr] *m radio etc.*: loudspeaker;
amplifier; ***~-relief**, *pl.* ***~s-reliefs**
[orə'ljɛf] *m arts:* alto-relievo.
*havanais, e [ava'nɛ, ~'nɛːz] *adj.*, *a.
su.* ♀ Havanese; ***havane** [a'van] **1.**
su./m Havana (cigar); **2.** *adj./inv.*
tobacco-colo(u)red; brown.
*hâve [ɑ:v] haggard, gaunt; wan.
*havre ⚓ [ɑ:vr] *m* harbo(u)r, haven.
*havresac [ɑvrə'sak] *m* ✗ knapsack;
tool-bag; *camping:* haversack.
*hayon *mot.* [ɛ'jɔ̃] *m* rear door, tail-
gate; *a. voiture à* ~ *arrière* hatchback.
hé [e] *int.* hi!; I say!; what!
*heaume *hist.* [o:m] *m* helm(et).
hebdomadaire [ɛbdɔma'dɛːr] **1.**
adj. weekly; **2.** *su./m* weekly (paper *or*
publication).
héberger [ebɛr'ʒe] (1l) *v/t.* accommodate, put up, take in, lodge.
hébéter [ebe'te] (1f) *v/t.* stupefy;
daze; *fig.* stun; **hébétude** [~'tyd] *f
fig.* daze, dazed condition; ✗
hebetude.

hébraïque [ebra'ik] Hebrew, Hebraic; **hébraïsant** *m*, e *f* [~i'zã, ~'zã:t] Hebraist; **hébreu** [e'brø] *adj./m, a. su./m* ling. Hebrew.

hécatombe [eka'tõ:b] *f* hecatomb; F *fig. persons:* (great) slaughter.

hectare [ɛk'ta:r] *m* hectare (2.47 *acres*).

hectique ✍ [ɛk'tik] hectic.

hecto... [ɛktɔ] hecto...; **~gramme** [~'gram] *m* hectogram(me); **~litre** [~'litr] *m* hectolitre (2.75 *bushels*); **~mètre** [~'mɛtr] *m* hectometre.

*hein! F [ɛ̃] *int.* what?; isn't it?; did I not?, *etc.*

hélas! [e'lɑ:s] *int.* alas!

*héler [e'le] (1f) *v/t.* hail (*a ship, a taxi*).   [helianthus.\

hélianthe ✿ [e'ljã:t] *m* sunflower.\

hélice [e'lis] *f* ⚓, *anat.* helix (*a.* = *snail*); ⚓ screw; ⚓, ✈ propeller; Archimedean screw; *escalier m en* ~ spiral staircase; *en* ~ helical(ly *adv.*); ⚓ *vaisseau m à* ~ screw-steamer.

hélicoptère ✈ [elikɔp'tɛ:r] *m* helicopter.

hélio... [eljɔ] helio...; **~graphe** *astr.* [~'graf] *m* heliograph; **~gravure** [~gra'vy:r] *f* photogravure; heliogravure; **~scope** *astr.* [~s'kɔp] *m* solar prism; **~thérapie** ✍ [~tera-'pi] *f* sunlight or sun ray treatment; **~trope** ✿ [~'trɔp] *m* heliotrope.

héliport ✈ [eli'pɔ:r] *m* heliport.

hélium 🜍 [e'ljom] *m* helium.

helvétien, -enne [ɛlve'sjɛ̃, ~'sjɛn] *adj., a. su.* ♀ Swiss; **helvétique** [~'tik] Helvetic (*confederation*), Swiss.

*hem! [ɛm] *int.* ahem!; hm!

héma... [ema], **hémat(o)...** [emat(o)] h(a)ema..., h(a)emat(o)...; *blood...;* **hématite** *min.* [ema'tit] *f* h(a)ematite; ~ *rouge* red iron.

hémi... [emi] hemi...; **~cycle** △ [~'sikl] *m* hemicycle; **~sphère** [emis'fɛ:r] *m* hemisphere.

hémo... [emo] h(a)em(o)... **~globine** *physiol.* [~glɔ'bin] *f* h(a)emoglobin; **~philie** ✍ [~fi'li] *f* h(a)emophilia; **~rragie** ✍ [~ra'ʒi] *f* h(a)emorrhage; **~rroïdes** ✍ [~rɔ'id] *f/pl.* h(a)emorrhoids, piles.

*henné ✿ [ɛn'ne] *m* henna (*a.* for *hair*); *teindre au* ~ henna.

*hennir [ɛ'ni:r] (2a) *v/i.* whinny, neigh; ***hennissement** [enis'mã] *m* whinny(ing), neigh(ing).

hépatique [epa'tik] **1.** *adj.* hepatic; **2.** *su.* ✍ hepatic; *su./f* ♀ hepatica, liverwort; **hépatite** [~'tit] *f* ✍ hepatitis; *min.* hepatite.

hepta... [ɛpta] hepta...

héraldique [eral'dik] heraldic, armorial.

*héraut [e'ro] *m* herald (*a. fig.*).

herbacé, e ♀ [ɛrba'se] herbaceous; **herbage** [~'ba:ʒ] *m* grass-land; pasture; grass; *cuis.* green stuff; **herbager** [~ba'ʒe] *m* grazier; **herbe** [ɛrb] *f* grass; herb; weed; ~s *pl. potagères* pot herbs; *en* ~ unripe; *fig.* budding; *fines* ~s *pl.* herbs for seasoning; *mauvaise* ~ weed; *fig.* bad lot; *couper l'*~ *sous le pied de q.* cut the ground from under s.o.'s feet; *déjeuner sur l'*~ (have a) picknick; *manger son blé en* ~ spend one's money before getting it; **herbeux, -euse** [~'bø, ~'bø:z] grassy; **herbicide** [~bi'sid] *m* weed-killer; **herbivore** *zo.* [~bi'vɔ:r] **1.** *adj.* herbivorous; **2.** *su./m* herbivore; **herboriser** [~bɔri'ze] (1a) *v/i.* go botanizing; gather plants *or* herbs; **herboriste** [~bɔ'rist] *su.* herbalist; **herbu, e** [~'by] **1.** *adj.* grassy; **2.** *su./f* light grazing-land.

*here [ɛːr] *m: pauvre* ~ poor devil.

héréditaire [eredi'tɛ:r] hereditary; **hérédité** [~'te] *f* heredity; 🜍 (right of) inheritance.

hérésie [ere'zi] *f* heresy; **hérétique** [~'tik] **1.** *adj.* heretical; **2.** *su.* heretic.

*hérissé, e [eri'se] bristling (with, de); spiked (with, de); prickly; bristly (*moustache*); ***hérisser** [~'se] (1a) *v/t.* bristle up; cover with spikes; ruffle (*its feathers*); *se* ~ stand on end (*hair*); bristle (up) (*a. fig.*); ***hérisson** [~'sɔ̃] *m zo.* hedgehog; ⊕ brush.

héritage [eri'ta:ʒ] *m* inheritance, heritage; **hériter** [~'te] (1a) *vt/i.* inherit; ~ (*de*) *qch.* inherit s.th. (from s.o., de "q.); **héritier, -ère** [~'tje, ~'tjɛ:r] *su.* heir; *su./f* heiress.

hermétique [ɛrme'tik] hermetic; (air-, water)tight; light-proof; impenetrable.

hermine *zo.* [ɛr'min] *f* ermine (*a.* ✦ *fur*), stoat.

*herniaire ✍ [ɛr'njɛ:r] hernial; *bandage m* ~ truss; ***hernie** ✍ [~'ni] *f* hernia, rupture.

héroïne [erɔ'in] *f* heroine; 🜍 heroin; **héroïque** [~'ik] heroic (a. ✗); **héroïsme** [~'ism] m heroism.

*héron orn. [e'rɔ̃] m heron.

*héros [e'ro] m hero.

herpès ✗ [ɛr'pɛs] m herpes.

*herse [ɛrs] f ✗ harrow; ⚠ portcullis; thea. ~s pl. battens; ***herser** ✗ [ɛr'se] (1a) v/t. harrow.

hésitation [ezita'sjɔ̃] f hesitation; hesitancy; faltering; misgiving; **hésiter** [~'te] (1a) v/i. hesitate, waver; falter (in speaking).

hétéro... [eterɔ] hetero...; **~clite** [~'klit] heteroclite, irregular; fig. odd, strange; **~doxe** [~'dɔks] heterodox, unorthodox; **~gène** [~'ʒɛn] heterogeneous; fig. incongruous; mixed (society).

*hêtre ♦ [ɛ:tr] m beech.

heure [œːr] f hour; time; moment; period; ... o'clock; six~s pl. 6 o'clock; ~ d'été summer time; ✗ ~ H zero hour; ~ légale standard time; ~s pl. supplémentaires overtime sg.; à l'~ on time, punctual(ly adv.); à l'~ (de) ... in the ... age; in the ... fashion; à la bonne ~! well done!; fine!; tout à l'~ a few minutes ago; in a few minutes; presently; à tout à l'~! so long!; see you later!; F c'est l'~ time's up!; de bonne ~ early; quelle ~ est-il? what time is it?; livre m d'~s book of hours; prayer-book.

heureux, -euse [œ'rø, ~'røːz] happy, glad, pleased, delighted; lucky, successful; fortunate (accident, position, etc.); apt (expression, phrase, word).

*heurt [œːr] m blow, knock, shock; fig. sans ~ smoothly; ***heurté, e** [œr'te] clashing (colours); ***heurter** [~'te] (1a) vt/i. knock, hit, strike; jostle; v/t. run into; collide with; fig. offend (s.o.'s feelings); ⚓ ram, strike; v/i. a. se ~ collide; clash (colours); ***heurtoir** [~'twaːr] m knocker; ⊕ stop; ⊕ tappet; ⛏ buffer.

hexagonal, e, m/pl. -aux ⚛ [ɛgzagɔ'nal, ~'no] hexagonal; **hexagone** [~'gɔn] m ⚛ hexagon; fig. l'~ France.

hiatus [ja'tys] m ling. hiatus; fig. gap; fig. break.

hibernal, e, m/pl. -aux [ibɛr'nal, ~'no] winter-...; hibernal; wintry; **hibernant, e** [~'nɑ̃, ~'nɑ̃:t] hibernating; **hiberner** [~'ne] (1a) v/i. hibernate.

*hibou orn. [i'bu] m owl; jeune~ owlet.

*hic [ik] m: voilà le ~! there's the snag!

*hideux, -euse [i'dø, i'døːz] hideous.

hiémal, e, m/pl. -aux [je'mal, ~'mo] winter-...

hier [jɛːr] adv. yesterday; ~ soir yesterday evening, last night; d'~ very recent; F fig. né d'~ green.

*hiérarchie [jerar'ʃi] f hierarchy; ***hiérarchique** [~'ʃik] hierarchical; voie f ~ official channels pl.

hiéroglyphe [jerɔ'glif] m hieroglyph; fig. scrawl.

hilarant, e [ila'rɑ̃, ~'rɑ̃:t] mirthprovoking; **hilarité** [~ri'te] f hilarity, laughter, mirth.

hippique [ip'pik] equine, horse-...; concours m ~ horse-show; racemeeting, Am. race-meet; **hippisme** [~'pism] m horse-racing.

hippo... [ipɔ] hippo...; horse...; **~campe** zo. [~'kɑ̃:p] m sea-horse, hippocampus; **~drome** [~'droːm] m hippodrome, circus, race-course, race-track; **~mobile** [~mɔ'bil] horsedrawn; **~potame** zo. [~pɔ'tam] m hippopotamus.

hirondelle [irɔ̃'dɛl] f orn. swallow.

hirsute [ir'syt] hirsute, hairy; fig. boorish, rough.

hispanique [ispa'nik] Hispanic, Spanish.

hispide ♦ [is'pid] hispid; hairy.

*hisser [i'se] (1a) v/t. hoist (a. ⚓); se ~ a. pull o.s. up.

histoire [is'twaːr] f history; story; F fib, invention; faire des ~s make a to-do; F ~ de (faire qch.) just to (do s.th.); **historien** [~tɔ'rjɛ̃] m historian; chronicler; narrator; **historier** [~'rje] (1o) v/t. illustrate; embellish (a. fig.); **historiette** [~'rjɛt] f anecdote; short story; **historique** [~'rik] 1. adj. historic(al); 2. su./m historical record or account.

histrion [istri'ɔ̃] ham (actor).

hiver [i'vɛːr] m winter; **hivernage** [ivɛr'naːʒ] m ⚓ laying up for the winter; winter season; winter quarters pl., ⚓ winter harbo(u)r; tropics: rainy season, wintering (of cattle); **hivernal, e,** m/pl. -aux [~'nal, ~'no] winter-...; wintry (weather); **hivernant m, e** f [~'nɑ̃, ~'nɑ̃:t] winter visitor; **hiverner** [~'ne] (1a) v/i.

winter; hibernate (*animal*); v/t.
🖅 plough before winter.
*hobereau [ɔ'bro] *m* orn. hobby; F
small country squire, squireen.
*hochement [ɔʃ'mɑ̃] *m* shake or nod
(*of the head*); ***hochequeue** orn.
[~'kø] *m* wagtail; ***hocher** [ɔ'ʃe] (1a)
v/t.: ~ *la tête* shake or nod one's head;
*hochet [ɔ'ʃɛ] *m* rattle (*for babies*);
toy, bauble.
*hockey sp. [ɔ'kɛ] *m* hockey; ~ *sur
glace* ice-hockey; ***hockeyeur** sp.
[ɔkɛ'jœːr] *m* hockey-player.
hoir 🖅 [wa:r] *m* heir; **hoirie** 🖅
[wa'ri] *f* inheritance, succession.
*holà [ɔ'la] 1. *int.* hallo!; stop!; 2.
m/inv.: *mettre le* ~ *à qch.* put a stop to
s.th.
*holding 🕂 [ɔl'diŋ] *m* holding
company.
*hold-up [ɔl'dœp] *m/inv.* hold-up.
*hollandais, e [ɔlɑ̃'dɛ, ~'dɛːz] 1. *adj.*
Dutch; 2. *su./m ling.* Dutch; ♀
Dutchman; *les* ♀ *m/pl.* the Dutch;
su./f ♀ Dutchwoman.
*Hollande [ɔ'lɑ̃:d] *su./m* Dutch
cheese; *su./f tex.* Holland.
holocauste [ɔlɔ'ko:st] *m* holocaust;
fig. sacrifice.
*homard zo. [ɔ'ma:r] *m* lobster.
homélie [ɔme'li] *f eccl.* homily; F
*fig.*sermon, lecture.
homicide [ɔmi'sid] 1. *su. person*:
homicide; *su./m crime*: homicide;
~ *par imprudence* (*or involontaire*)
manslaughter; ~ *volontaire* (*or prémédité*) murder; 2. *adj.* homicidal.
hommage [ɔ'ma:ʒ] *m* homage; token
of esteem; ~*s pl.* compliments; ~*s
de l'auteur* with the author's compliments; *rendre* ~ do homage,
pay tribute (to, *à*); **hommasse**
F [ɔ'mas] mannish, masculine
(*woman*); **homme** [ɔm] *m* man;
mankind; ~ *d'affaires* businessman;
~ *d'État* statesman; ⊕ ~ *de métier*
craftsman; ~**-grenouille**, *pl.* ~**s-
grenouilles** [~grə'nu:j] *m* frogman;
~**-sandwich**, *pl.* ~**s-sandwichs**
[~sɑ̃'dwitʃ] *m* sandwich-man.
homo... [ɔmɔ] homo...; ~**gène**
[~'ʒɛn] homogeneous; ~**généiser**
[~ʒenei'ze] (1a) v/t. homogenize;
~**logue** [~'lɔg] 1. *adj.* homologous; 2.
su./m homologue; *person*: counterpart, opposite number; ~**loguer** 🖅
[~lɔ'ge] (1m) v/t. confirm, endorse;
ratify (*a decision*); prove (*a will*);

~**nyme** *gramm.* [~'nim] 1. *adj.*
homonymous; 2. *su./m* homonym;
~**sexuel, -elle** [~sɛk'sɥɛl] *adj. a. su.*
homosexual.
*hongre [ɔ̃:gr] 1. *adj./m* gelded; 2.
su./m gelding; ***hongrois, e** [ɔ̃'grwa,
~'grwa:z] 1. *adj.* Hungarian; 2. *su./m
ling.* Hungarian; *su.* ♀ Hungarian.
honnête [ɔ'nɛːt] honest; upright,
decent; respectable; courteous,
well-bred; seemly (*behaviour*); reasonable (*price*); virtuous (*woman*); ~*s
gens m/pl.* decent people; **honnêteté** [ɔnɛt'te] *f* honesty; integrity; politeness; respectability (*of
behaviour*); 🕂 fairness; *price etc.*:
reasonableness; (*feminine*) modesty.
honneur [ɔ'nœːr] *m* hono(u)r; ~*s pl.*
hono(u)rs, preferments; regalia;
avoir l'~ have the hono(u)r (of *ger.*,
de inf.); 🕂 beg (to *inf.*, *de inf.*); 🕂
faire ~ *à* hono(u)r, meet (*a bill, an
obligation*); ⚔ *rendre les* ~*s* present
arms (to, *à*).
*honnir † [ɔ'ni:r] (2a) v/t. disgrace;
spurn; revile; *honni soit qui mal
y pense* evil be to him who evil
thinks.
honorabilité [ɔnɔrabili'te] *f* respectability; **honorable** [~'rabl]
hono(u)rable; respectable, credit-
able, 🕂 reputable; **honoraire**
[~'rɛːr] 1. *adj.* honorary; 2. *su./m*: ~*s
pl.* fee(s *pl.*) *sg.*, honorarium *sg.*; 🖅
retainer *sg.*; **honorer** [~'re] (1a) v/t.
hono(u)r (*a.* 🕂); respect; do hono(u)r
to; 🕂 meet; *s'*~ *de* pride o.s. on;
honorifique [~ri'fik] honorary
(*title*).
*honte [ɔ̃:t] *f* (sense of) shame; dis-
hono(u)r, disgrace; *fig.* reproach;
avoir ~ be ashamed (of, *de*); *faire* ~
à put to shame; **honteux, -euse**
[ɔ̃'tø, ~'tø:z] ashamed; disgraceful,
shameful, scandalous; bashful.
hôpital [ɔpi'tal] *m* 🎗 hospital; poor-
house, (*orphan's*) home; ⚔ ~ *militaire* (*de campagne*) station (field)
hospital.
*hoquet [ɔ'kɛ] *m* hiccough, hiccup;
emotion: gasp (*of surprise etc.*); ***hoqueter** [ɔk'te] (1c) v/i. hiccup;
have the hiccups.
horaire [ɔ'rɛːr] 1. *adj.* time...;
hour-...; ⊕ per hour, hourly;
2. *su./m* time-table; ~ *souple* flexible
working hours *pl.*
*horde [ɔrd] *f* horde.

horizon [ɔri'zɔ̃] *m* horizon (*a. fig.*); panorama, view; *fig. à l'~ 2000 etc.* in *or* for the year 2000 *etc.*; **horizontal, e,** *m/pl.* **-aux** [~zɔ̃'tal, ~'to] horizontal.

horloge [ɔr'lɔːʒ] *f* clock; ⊕~ *centrale* master clock; ~ *normande* grandfather('s) clock; *teleph.* ~ *parlante* speaking clock, Tim; **horloger** [~lɔ'ʒe] *m* watch-maker, clock-maker; **horlogerie** [~lɔʒ'ri] *f* watch-making, clock-making; watch-maker's (shop).

hormis [ɔr'mi] *prp.* except.

hormone *physiol.* [ɔr'mɔn] *f* hormone.

horoscope [ɔrɔs'kɔp] *m* horoscope; *faire (or tirer) un ~* cast a horoscope.

horreur [ɔ'rœːr] *f* horror; *avoir ~ de* loathe; abhor; hate; *avoir en ~* detest, hold in abhorrence; *faire ~ à* disgust; horrify; **horrible** [ɔ'ribl] horrible, dreadful; appalling; **horripiler** [ɔripi'le] (1a) *v/t.* give (*s.o.*) gooseflesh; F make (*s.o.'s*) flesh creep; F *fig.* exasperate.

***hors** [ɔːr] *prp.* out of; outside (*the town*); beyond, but, save (*two, this*); *≠ ~ circuit* cut off; ~ *concours* hors concours; *sp.* ~ *jeu* offside; ~ *ligne* (*or classe*) outstanding; *↑ ~ vente* no longer on sale; *mettre ~ la loi* outlaw (*s.o.*); ~ (*de*) *pair* peerless; ~ *de* outside; out of (*breath, danger, fashion, hearing, reach, sight, use*); beyond (*dispute, doubt*); ~ *d'affaire* out of the wood; ~ *de combat* disabled; out of action; ~ *de propos* illtimed; irrelevant (*remark*); ~ *de saison* unseasonable; ~ *de sens* out of one's senses; ~ *de soi* beside o.s. (with rage); ~ *d'ici!* get out!; *qch. est ~ de prix* the price of s.th. is prohibitive.

***hors...: *~-bord** [ɔr'bɔːr] *m/inv.* outboard motor boat, F speed-boat; ***~-d'œuvre** [~'dœːvr] *m/inv.* *art etc.*: irrelevant matter; *cuis.* horsd'œuvre, side dish; ***~-jeu** *sp.* [~'ʒø] *m/inv.* off side; ***~-la-loi** [~la'lwa] *m/inv.* outlaw; ***~-saison** [~sɛ'zɔ̃] *adj./inv.* off-season (*tariff etc.*); ***~-texte** [~'tɛkst] *m/inv.* (full page) plate (*in a book*).

hortensia ♀ [ɔrtɑ̃'sja] *m* hydrangea.

horticole [ɔrti'kɔl] horticultural; **horticulture** [~kyl'tyːr] *f* horticulture, gardening.

hosanna [ɔzan'na] *int., a. su./m* hosanna.

hospice [ɔs'pis] *m* hospice; almshouse; (*orphan's*) home; **hospitalier, -ère** [ɔspita'lje, ~'ljɛːr] **1.** *adj.* hospitable; hospital-...; **2.** *su./m eccl.* hospitaller; *su./f eccl.* Sister of Mercy; **hospitaliser** [~li'ze] (1a) *v/t.* send *or* admit to a hospital *or* home, hospitalize; **hospitalité** [~li'te] *f* hospitality; *donner l'~ à q.* give s.o. hospitality, F put s.o. up.

hostie [ɔs'ti] *f bibl.* (sacrificial) victim; *eccl.* host.

hostile [ɔs'til] hostile; **hostilité** [~tili'te] *f* hostility (against, *contre*); enmity; ✗ ~*s pl.* hostilities.

hôte, hôtesse [oːt, o'tɛs] *su.* guest, visitor, lodger; *su./m* host; landlord; *su./f* hostess; landlady; ✈ *hôtesse de l'air* air hostess.

hôtel [o'tɛl] *m* hotel; ~ (*particulier*) (private) mansion; ~ *de ville* town hall, city hall; ~ *garni* residential hotel; *pej.* lodgings *pl.*, lodging-house; *maître m d'~* head waiter; *private house*: butler; *~-Dieu, pl.* *~s-Dieu* [otɛl'djø] *m* principal hospital; **hôtelier, -ère** [otə'lje, ~'ljɛːr] *su.* innkeeper; hotel-keeper; *su./m* landlord; *su./f* landlady; **hôtellerie** [otɛl'ri] *f* hostelry, inn; hotel trade.

***hotte** [ɔt] *f* basket; pannier; (*bricklayer's*) hod; ⊕ hopper; △ hood.

***houblon** ♀ *etc.* [u'blɔ̃] *m* hop(s *pl.*); ***houblonner** [ublɔ'ne] (1a) *v/t.* hop (*beer*); ***houblonnier, -ère** [~'nje, ~'njɛːr] **1.** *adj.* hop-(growing); **2.** *su./f* hop-field.

***houe** ✔ [u] *f* hoe; ***houer** [u'e] (1a) *v/t.* hoe.

***houille** ✗ [u:j] *f* coal; *fig.* ~ *blanche* water-power; ***houiller, -ère** ✗ [u'je, ~'jɛːr] **1.** *adj.* coal-...; carboniferous; *production f ~ère* output of coal; **2.** *su./f* coal-mine, pit, colliery; ***houilleux, -euse** [u'jø, ~'jøːz] carboniferous, coal-bearing.

***houle** [ul] *f* swell, surge, billows *pl.*

***houlette** [u'lɛt] *f* (shepherd's *etc.*) crook; ✔ trowel; *metall.* handladle.

***houleux, -euse** [u'lø, ~'løːz] swelling, surging (*a. fig.*), billowing; ⚓ rather rough (*sea*); *fig.* stormy (*meeting*).

***houp!** [up] *int.* up!; off you go!

***houppe** [up] *f orn., a. feathers,*

hair, wool: tuft; tassel, bob; pompom; *orn., a. hair, tree*: crest; (powder-)puff; *hair*: topknot; ***houpper** [u'pe] (1a) *v/t.* tuft; trim with tufts *or* pompoms; *tex.* comb (*wool*); ***houppette** [u'pɛt] *f* small tuft; powder-puff.

*hourra [u'ra] **1.** *int.* hurrah!; **2.** *su./m*: pousser des ⁓s cheer.

*houspiller [uspi'je] (1a) *v/t.* scold, tell (*s.o.*) off; rag (*s.o.*) (*audience etc.*); handle (*s.o.*) roughly.

*houssaie [u'sɛ] *f* holly-grove.

*housse [us] *f* furniture cover, *Am.* slip-cover; dust-sheet; horse-cloth; *cost.* (protective) bag; ***housser** [u'se] (1a) *v/t.* dust (*furniture*).

*houssine [u'sin] *f furniture, riding*: switch; ***houssiner** [usi'ne] (1a) *v/t.* switch.

*houssoir [u'swa:r] *m* feather-duster; whisk.

*houx ⚘ [u] *m* holly.

*hoyau ⚒ [wa'jo] *m* grubbing-hoe, mattock.

*hublot ⚓ [y'blo] *m* port-hole, scuttle; air-port; *faux* ⁓ dead-light.

*huche [yʃ] *f* kneading-trough; bin; ⊕ hopper.

*hue! [y] *int.* gee up!; *a. to a horse*: to the right!; *fig. tirer à* ⁓ *et à dia* pull in opposite directions.

*huée [y'e] *f hunt. etc.* hallooing; *fig.* boo, hoot; ⁓s *pl.* booing *sg.*, jeers; ***huer** [y'e] (1a) *v/t.* boo *or* jeer (*s.o.*); *v/i.* hoot (*owl*).

*huguenot, e [yg'no, ⁓'nɔt] **1.** *adj. eccl.* Huguenot; **2.** *su. eccl.* Huguenot; *su./f cuis.* pipkin.

huilage [ɥi'la:ʒ] *m* oiling, lubrication; *metall.* oil-tempering; **huile** [ɥil] *f* oil; 🍔, ⚒ ⁓ *de foie de morue* cod-liver oil; ⁓ *de graissage* (*de machine*) lubricating (engine) oil; ⁓ *minérale* mineral oil, petroleum; ⁓ *végétale* vegetable oil; F *les* ⁓s *pl.* the big pots (= *important people*); *eccl. les saintes* ⁓s *pl. extreme unction*: the holy oil *sg.*; **huiler** [ɥi'le] (1a) *v/t.* oil, lubricate; *fig. huilé* working *or* running smoothly; **huilerie** [ɥil'ri] *f* oil-works *usu. sg.*; oil-store; **huileux, -euse** [ɥi'lø, ⁓'lø:z] oily, greasy; **huilier** [⁓'lje] *m* ⊕ oil-can; oil-merchant; *cuis.* oil-cruet; cruet-stand.

huis [ɥi] *m* † door; ⚖ à **⁓ clos* in camera; F *à* ⁓ *clos* in private; ⚖

ordonner le **⁓ clos* clear the court; **huisserie** △ [ɥis'ri] *f* door-frame; **huissier** [ɥi'sje] *m* usher; ⚖ bailiff, process-server.

*huit [ɥit; *before consonant* ɥi] *adj./ num., a. su./m/inv.* eight; *date, title*: eighth; *d'aujourd'hui en* ⁓ today week; *tous les* ⁓ *jours* once a week; every week; ***huitain** [ɥi'tɛ̃] *m* octet; ***huitaine** [⁓'tɛn] *f* (about) eight; week; ***huitième** [⁓'tjɛm] **1.** *adj./ num.* eighth; **2.** *su.* eighth; *su./m fraction*: eighth; *su./f secondary school*: (*approx.*) second form.

huître [ɥi:tr] *f* oyster; F *fig.* ninny; **huîtrier, -ère** [ɥitri'e, ⁓'ɛ:r] **1.** *adj.* oyster-...; **2.** *su./f* oyster-bed.

*hulotte *orn.* [y'lɔt] *f* brown owl, common wood-owl.

humain, e [y'mɛ̃, ⁓'mɛn] **1.** *adj.* human; humane; **2.** *su./m: les* ⁓s *pl.* mankind *sg.*; human beings; **humaniser** [ymani'ze] (1a) *v/t.* humanize; *s'*⁓ become (more) human; *fig.* become more sociable; **humanitaire** [⁓'tɛ:r] *adj., a. su.* humanitarian; **humanité** [⁓'te] *f* humanity; kindness; mankind; ⁓s *pl.* classical studies, *the* humanities.

humble [œ̃:bl] humble; lowly; meek; ⁓ *serviteur* humble servant.

humecter [ymɛk'te] (1a) *v/t.* moisten, damp, wet; *s'*⁓ become moist.

*humer [y'me] (1a) *v/t.* breathe in (*the air, a perfume*); sip (*tea, coffee*); swallow (*a raw egg*).

humeur [y'mœ:r] *f* mood; disposition, temperament; temper; bad temper; ill humo(ur); ⚕ †⁓s *pl.* body fluids; *avec* ⁓ crossly; peevishly; *de bonne* (*mauvaise*) ⁓ in a good (bad) mood; *être or se sentir d'*⁓ *à faire qch.* be in the mood to do *or* for doing s.th.; feel like doing s.th.

humide [y'mid] damp; humid; **humidité** [ymidi'te] *f* dampness; moisture; humidity.

humilier [ymi'lje] (1o) *v/t.* humiliate, humble; **humilité** [⁓li'te] *f* humility.

humoriste [ymɔ'rist] **1.** *adj.* humorous (*writer*); **2.** *su.* humorist; **humoristique** [⁓ris'tik] humorous.

humour [y'mu:r] *m* (sense of) humo(u)r. [mo(u)ld.\
humus ⚒ [y'mys] *m* humus, leaf\
*hune ⚓ [yn] *f* top; ***hunier** ⚓ [y'nje] *m* topsail.

*huppe [yp] *f orn.* hoopoe; *bird*: crest, tuft; ***huppé, e** [y'pe] *orn.* tufted, crested; F *fig.* smart; F *les gens m/pl.* ⁓s the swells.

*hure [y:r] *f* head (*usu. of boar*); *salmon*: jowl; *cuis.* brawn, *Am.* headcheese; *sl.* (ugly) head.

*hurlement [yrlə'mã] *m animal*: howl(ing); roar; bellow; ***hurler** [⁓'le] (1a) *v/i.* howl; roar; *v/t.* bawl out; ***hurleur, -euse** [⁓'lœːr, ⁓'løːz] **1.** *adj.* howling; **2.** *su./m zo.* monkey: howler.

hurluberlu [yrlybɛr'ly] *m* scatter-brain; harum-scarum.

*hussard ⚔ [y'saːr] *m* hussar; ***hussarde** [y'sard] *f dance*: hussarde; *à la* ⁓ cavalierly.

*hutte [yt] *f* hut, cabin, shanty.

hybride [i'brid] *adj., a. su./m* hybrid; **hybridité** [ibridi'te] *f* hybrid character, hybridity.

hydratation 🜋 [idrata'sjõ] *f* hydration; **hydrater** [⁓'te] (1a) *v/t.* hydrate, moisturize.

hydraulique [idro'lik] **1.** *adj.* hydraulic; water-...; **2.** *su./f* hydraulics *sg.*

hydravion [idra'vjõ] *m* seaplane; ⁓ *à coque* flying boat.

hydro... [idrɔ] hydro...; water-...; **⁓carbure** 🜋 [⁓kar'byːr] *m* hydrocarbon; **⁓céphalie** 🜋 [⁓sefa'li] *f* hydrocephaly, F water on the brain; **⁓fuge** [⁓'fyːʒ] waterproof; **⁓gène** 🜋 [⁓'ʒɛn] *m* hydrogen; **⁓glisseur** [⁓gli'sœːr] *m* hovercraft; **⁓mel** [⁓'mɛl] *m* hydromel; **⁓phile** [⁓'fil] absorbent (*cotton*); **⁓phobie** [⁓fɔ'bi] *f* rabies; **⁓pisie** 🜋 [⁓pi'zi] *f* dropsy; **⁓thérapie** 🜋 [⁓tera'pi] *f* hydrotherapy; water-cure.

hyène *zo.* [jɛn] *f* hyena.

hygiène [i'ʒjɛn] *f* hygiene; *admin.* health; **hygiénique** [iʒje'nik] hygienic, sanitary; healthy; *papier m* ⁓ toilet paper; **hygiéniste** [⁓'nist] *su.* hygienist, authority on public health.

hygromètre *phys.* [igrɔ'mɛtr] *m* hygrometer; **hygrométricité** *phys.* [⁓metrisi'te] *f* humidity; humidity-absorption index.

hymen [i'mɛn] *m anat.* hymen; *poet.* = **hyménée** *poet.* [ime'ne] *m* marriage.

hymne [imn] *su./m* patriotic song; national anthem; *su./f eccl.* hymn.

hyper... [ipɛr] hyper...; **⁓bole** [⁓'bɔl] *f* Å hyperbola; *gramm.* hyperbole; **⁓critique** [⁓kri'tik] hypercritical; **⁓métrope** 𝓼 [⁓me'trɔp] hypermetropic; long-sighted; **⁓tension** 𝓼 [⁓tã'sjõ] *f* hypertension; *a.* ⁓ *artérielle* high blood pressure; **⁓trophie** 𝓼 [⁓trɔ'fi] *f* hypertrophy.

hypnose [ip'noːz] *f* hypnosis; trance; **hypnotiser** [ipnɔti'ze] (1a) *v/t.* hypnotize; **hypnotiseur** [⁓ti'zœːr] *m* hypnotist; **hypnotisme** [⁓'tism] *m* hypnotism.

hypo... [ipɔ] hypo...; **⁓crisie** [⁓kri'zi] *f* hypocrisy; cant; **⁓crite** [⁓'krit] **1.** *adj.* hypocritical; **2.** *su.* hypocrite; **⁓thécaire** [⁓te'kɛːr] ... on mortgage; mortgage-...; *créancier m* ⁓ mortgagee; **⁓thèque** [⁓'tɛk] *f* mortgage; *prendre* (*purger*) *une* ⁓ raise (pay off *or* redeem) a mortgage; **⁓théquer** [⁓te'ke] (1f) *v/t.* mortgage; secure (*a debt*) by mortgage; **⁓thèse** [⁓'tɛːz] *f* hypothesis; F theory.

hystérie 𝓼 [iste'ri] *f* hysteria; **hystérique** 𝓼 [⁓'rik] hysteric(al).

I

I, i [i] *m* I, i; *i grec* y.
ïambe [jãːb] *m* iambus; iambic; ~*s pl.*
satirical poem *sg.*; **ïambique** [jã-
ˈbik] iambic.
ibérique *geog.* [ibeˈrik] Iberian,
Spanish.
iceberg [isˈbɛrg] *m* iceberg.
ichtyo... [iktjɔ] ichthyo..., fish-...;
~**colle** [~ˈkɔl] *f* fish-glue, isinglass;
~**phage** [~ˈfaːʒ] 1. *adj.* fish-eating; 2.
su. ichthyophagist; ~**saure** [~ˈsɔːr] *m*
ichthyosaurus.
ici [iˈsi] *adv.* here; now, at this point;
teleph. ~ *Jean* John speaking; ~ *Londres radio:* London calling; this is
London; *d'*~ (*à*) *lundi* by Monday;
d'~ (*à*) *trois jours* within the next
three days; *d'*~ *demain* by tomorrow;
d'~ *là* by that time, by then; in the
meantime; *d'*~ *peu* before long; *jusqu'*
~ *place:* as far as here; *time:* up to
now; *par* ~ here(abouts); this way;
près d'~ nearby; ~**-bas** [isiˈbɑ] *adv.*
on earth, here below.
iconoclaste [ikɔnɔˈklast] 1. *adj.*
iconoclastic; 2. *su.* iconoclast; **ico-
nolâtrie** [~laˈtri] *f* image-worship.
icosaèdre ⚛ [ikozaˈɛːdr] *m* icosa-
hedron.
ictère ⚕ [ikˈtɛːr] *m* jaundice; **ictérique** [~teˈrik] 1. *adj.* jaundiced
(*eyes, person*); icteric (*disorder*);
2. *su.* sufferer from jaundice.
idéal, e, *m/pl.* **-als, -aux** [ideˈal, ~ˈo]
1. *adj.* ideal; 2. *su./m* ideal.
idée [iˈde] *f* idea; notion; intention,
purpose; mind, head; suggestion,
hint; ~ *fixe* fixed idea, obsession.
idem [iˈdɛm] *adv.* idem; ditto.
identifier [idãtiˈfje] (1o) *v/t.* identify; *s'*~ *à* identify o.s. with; **identique** [~ˈtik] identical (with, *à*);
identité [~tiˈte] *f* identity; *carte f*
d'~ identity card.
idéologie [ideɔlɔˈʒi] *f* ideology (*a.*
pol.).
idiomatique [idjɔmaˈtik] idiomatic;
idiome [iˈdjoːm] *m* idiom; language.
idiot, e [iˈdjo, ~ˈdjɔt] 1. *adj.* ⚕ idiot;

fig. idiotic, absurd; 2. *su.* ⚕ idiot (*a.*
fig.), imbecile; *fig.* fool; **idiotie**
[idjɔˈsi] *f* ⚕ idiocy; *fig.* piece of
nonsense; **idiotisme** [~ˈtism] *m*
idiom(atic expression).
idoine [iˈdwan] appropriate.
idolâtre [idɔˈlɑːtr] 1. *adj.* idolatrous;
fig. être ~ *de* be passionately fond of,
worship; 2. *su./m* idolater; *su./f* ido-
latress; **idolâtrer** [~lɑˈtre] (1a) *v/i.*
worship idols; *v/t. fig.* be passionately fond of, worship; **idolâtrie**
[~lɑˈtri] *f* idolatry; **idole** [iˈdɔl] *f* idol,
image.
if ♣ [if] *m* yew (tree).
ignare [iˈɲaːr] 1. *adj.* illiterate, ignorant; 2. *su.* ignoramus.
igné, e [igˈne] igneous; **ignicole**
[igniˈkɔl] 1. *adj.* fire-worshipping;
2. *su.* fire-worshipper; **ignifuge**
[~ˈfyːʒ] 1. *adj.* fireproof; non-inflammable; 2. *su./m* fireproof(ing)
material; **ignifuger** [~fyˈʒe] (11)
v/t. fireproof; **ignition** [~ˈsjõ] *f*
ignition. [wretched.)
ignoble [iˈɲɔbl] ignoble, base; vile;)
ignominie [iɲɔmiˈni] *f* ignomiy,
shame, disgrace; **ignominieux,
-euse** [~ˈnjø, ~ˈnjøːz] ignominious,
shameful, disgraceful.
ignorance [iɲɔˈrãːs] *f* ignorance;
ignorant, e [~ˈrã, ~ˈrãːt] 1. *adj.*
ignorant (of, *de*), uneducated; 2.
su. ignoramus; **ignorer** [~ˈre] (1a)
v/t. be unaware of, not to know
(about); *ne pas* ~ *que* not to be
unaware that (*ind.*), know quite well
that (*ind.*).
il [il] 1. *pron./pers./m* he, it, she
(*ship etc.*); ~*s pl.* they; 2. *pron./im-
pers.* it; there; *il est dix heures* it is
10 o'clock; *il vint deux hommes*
two men came.
île [iːl] *f* island; isle.
illégal, e, *m/pl.* **-aux** [illeˈgal, ~ˈgo]
illegal, unlawful.
illégitime [illeʒiˈtim] illegitimate
(*child*); unlawful (*marriage*); *fig.*
spurious; *fig.* unwarranted; **illégitimité** [~timiˈte] *f* illegitimacy.

illettré, e [illɛ'tre] illiterate, uneducated.

illicite [illi'sit] illicit; *sp.* foul.

illico F [illi'ko] *adv.* at once, straightaway.

illimité, e [illimi'te] unlimited.

illisible [illi'zibl] illegible; unreadable (*book*).

illogique [illɔ'ʒik] illogical.

illuminant, e [illymi'nã, ~'nãːt] illuminating; **illuminer** [~'ne] (1a) *v/t.* illuminate, flood-light (*buildings*); light up (*a. fig.*); *fig.* enlighten (*s.o.*).

illusion [illy'zjɔ̃] *f* illusion; delusion; **illusionner** [~zjɔ'ne] (1a) *v/t.* delude; deceive; *s'~* delude o.s.; labo(u)r under a delusion; **illusoire** [~'zwaːr] illusory.

illustration [illystra'sjɔ̃] *f* illustration; illustrating; † renown, illustriousness; **illustre** [~'lystr] illustrious, renowned, famous; **illustré** [illys'tre] *m* pictorial (paper), F magazine; **illustrer** [~] (1a) *v/t.* illustrate; † elucidate; *s'~* win fame.

îlot [i'lo] *m* islet, small island; *houses:* block.

ilote *hist.* [i'lɔt] *m* helot.

image [i'maːʒ] *f* image; picture; **imagé, e** [ima'ʒe] colo(u)rful (*style*); **imagerie** [imaʒ'ri] *f* imagery; **imaginable** [imaʒi'nabl] imaginable; **imaginaire** [~'nɛːr] imaginary (*a. Ⓐ*); fictitious; **imaginatif, -ve** [~na'tif, ~'tiːv] imaginative; **imagination** [~na'sjɔ̃] *f* imagination; fancy; **imaginer** [~'ne] (1a) *v/t.* imagine, picture; think up; *s'~* imagine; imagine *or* picture o.s.

imbécile [ɛ̃be'sil] **1.** *adj.* imbecile, half-witted; *fig.* idiotic; **2.** *su.* imbecile; *fig.* idiot, F fat-head, *Am. sl.* nut; **imbécilité** [~sili'te] *f* imbecility; *fig.* stupidity; *~s pl.* nonsense *sg.*

imberbe [ɛ̃'bɛrb] beardless; F callow.

imbiber [ɛ̃bi'be] (1a) *v/t.* impregnate (with, *de*); *s'~ de* soak up; become saturated with (*de*).

imbu, e [ɛ̃'by] *~ de* full of; steeped in.

imbuvable [ɛ̃by'vabl] undrinkable.

imitable [imi'tabl] imitable; worthy of imitation; **imitateur, -trice** [imita'tœːr, ~'tris] **1.** *adj.* imitative; **2.** *su.* imitator; **imitatif, -ve** [~'tif,

~'tiːv] imitative; **imitation** [~'sjɔ̃] *f* imitation; *money:* counterfeiting; *signature:* forgery; *à l'~ de* in imitation of; **imiter** [imi'te] (1a) *v/t.* imitate; copy.

immaculé, e [immaky'le] immaculate; unstained.

immanent, e *phls.* [imma'nã, ~'nãːt] immanent.

immangeable [ɛ̃mã'ʒabl] uneatable.

immanquable [ɛ̃mã'kabl] infallible, inevitable; which cannot be missed (*target etc.*).

immatériel, -elle [immate'rjɛl] immaterial; ✝ intangible.

immatriculation [immatrikyla'sjɔ̃] *f* registration; *univ. etc.* enrolment, matriculation; *mot.* numéro m d'~ registration (*Am.* license) number.

immaturité [immatyri'te] *f* immaturity.

immédiat, e [imme'dja, ~'djat] immediate; *dans l'~* for the moment.

immémorial, e, *m/pl.* **-aux** [immemɔ'rjal, ~'rjo] immemorial.

immense [im'mãːs] immense, huge, vast; *sl.* terrific (= *wonderful*); **immensité** [~mãsi'te] *f* immensity; vastness.

immerger [immɛr'ʒe] (1l) *v/t.* immerse.

immérité, e [immeri'te] unmerited, undeserved.

immersion [immɛr'sjɔ̃] *f* immersion; ⚓ *submarine:* submergence; *astr.* occultation.

immeuble [im'mœbl] **1.** *adj.* 🏛 real; **2.** *su./m* 🏛 real estate, realty; ✝ building, house; *~ tour* tower block.

immigrant, e [immi'grã, ~'grãːt] *adj., a. su.* immigrant; **immigration** [~gra'sjɔ̃] *f* immigration; **immigré, e** *m, e f* [~'gre] immigrant; **immigrer** [~'gre] (1a) *v/i.* immigrate.

imminence [immi'nãːs] *f* imminence; **imminent, e** [~'nã, ~'nãːt] imminent, impending.

immiscer [immi'se] (1k) *v/t.: s'~ dans* interfere with; **immixtion** [immik'sjɔ̃] *f* interference.

immobile [immɔ'bil] motionless, unmoving, *fig.* steadfast, unshaken; **immobilier, -ère** 🏛 [immɔbi'lje, ~'ljɛːr] (real) estate (*agency, agent*); **immobiliser** [~li'ze] (1a) *v/t.* immobilize; fix in position; ✝ tie up (*capital*); s'~ stop; come to a stand-still; **immobilisme** [~'lism] *m* ultra-conservatism; **immobilité** [~li'te] *f* immobility.

immodéré, e [immɔde're] immoderate, excessive.

immodeste [immɔ'dɛst] immodest; shameless.

immoler [immɔ'le] (1a) *v/t.* sacrifice, immolate.

immonde [im'mɔ̃:d] filthy, foul; unclean (*animal, eccl. spirit*); **immondices** [~mɔ̃'dis] *f/pl.* rubbish *sg.*, refuse *sg.*, dirt *sg.*

immoral, e, *m/pl.* **-aux** [immɔ'ral, ~'ro] immoral; **immoralité** [~rali-'te] *f* immorality; immoral act.

immortaliser [immɔrtali'ze] (1a) *v/t.* immortalize; **immortalité** [~tali'te] *f* immortality; **immortel, -elle** [~'tɛl] **1.** *adj.* immortal; everlasting, imperishable; **2.** *su./f* ♀ everlasting flower; *su./m:* ♀s *pl.* immortals, F members of the *Académie française.* [vated.)

immotivé, e [immɔti've] unmoti-)

immuable [im'mɥabl] unalterable; unchanging.

immuniser ✞ [immyni'ze] (1a) *v/t.* immunize; **immunité** [~'te] *f* immunity (from, *contre*); *admin.* exemption from tax.

immuno-dépresseur ✞ [immyno-depre'sœːr] *m* immuno-suppressive drug.

immu(t)abilité [immɥabili'te, ~mytabili'te] *f* immutability, fixity.

impact [ɛ̃'pakt] *m* impact; effect.

impair, e [ɛ̃'pɛːr] **1.** *adj.* ♀ odd; *anat.* unpaired (*organ*), single (*bone*); 🎱 down (*line*); **2.** *su./m* F bloomer, blunder.

impalpable [ɛ̃pal'pabl] impalpable, intangible.

impardonnable [ɛ̃pardɔ'nabl] unpardonable; unforgivable.

imparfait, e [ɛ̃par'fɛ, ~'fɛt] **1.** *adj.* imperfect; unfinished; **2.** *su./m gramm.* imperfect (tense).

imparité [ɛ̃pari'te] *f* inequality; ♀ oddness.

impartial, e, *m/pl.* **-aux** [ɛ̃par'sjal, ~'sjo] impartial, unprejudiced, unbiassed.

impasse [ɛ̃'pɑːs] *f* dead end, blind alley; 'no through road'; *fig.* impasse, deadlock; ✞ (*a.* ~ *budgetaire*) budget deficit; *faire une* ~ *cards:*

finesse; *fig. faire l'*~ *sur qch.* neglect s.th. consciously.

impassibilité [ɛ̃pasibili'te] *f* impassiveness, impassibility; **impassible** [~'sibl] impassive, unmoved; unimpressionable.

impatience [ɛ̃pa'sjɑ̃:s] *f* impatience; **impatient, e** [~'sjɑ̃, ~'sjɑ̃:t] impatient; *eager* (to *inf., de inf.*); **impatienter** [~sjɑ̃'te] (1a) *v/t.* irritate, annoy; s'~ lose patience; grow impatient.

impayable [ɛ̃pɛ'jabl] ✝ invaluable; F *fig.* screamingly funny; **impayé, e** ✝ [~'je] unpaid (*debt*); dishono(u)red (*bill*).   [infallible.)

impeccable [ɛ̃pɛ'kabl] impeccable;)

impénétrable [ɛ̃pene'trabl] impenetrable (by, *à*); impervious (to, *à*); *fig.* inscrutable; close (*secret*).

impénitence [ɛ̃peni'tɑ̃:s] *f* impenitence; **impénitent, e** [~'tɑ̃, ~'tɑ̃:t] impenitent, unrepentant.

imper F [ɛ̃'pɛr] *m* (*abbr. of imperméable*) raincoat.

impératif, -ve [ɛ̃pera'tif, ~'tiːv] *adj., a. su./m* imperative.

impératrice [ɛ̃pera'tris] *f* empress.

imperceptible [ɛ̃pɛrsɛp'tibl] imperceptible, undiscernible.

imperfection [ɛ̃pɛrfɛk'sjɔ̃] *f* imperfection; incompleteness; defect, flaw, fault; faultiness.

impérial, e, *m/pl.* **-aux** [ɛ̃pe'rjal, ~'rjo] **1.** *adj.* imperial; **2.** *su./f* top; *bus, tram:* top-deck, outside; *beard:* imperial; **impérialisme** [~rja-'lism] *m* imperialism; **impérieux, -euse** [~'rjø, ~'rjøːz] imperious; domineering; peremptory; urgent, pressing.   [able, undying.)

impérissable [ɛ̃peri'sabl] imperish-)

imperméable [ɛ̃pɛrme'abl] **1.** *adj.* impermeable; watertight, waterproof; impervious (to, *à*); **2.** *su./m* rain-coat; waterproof.

impersonnel, -elle [ɛ̃pɛrsɔ'nɛl] impersonal.

impertinence [ɛ̃pɛrti'nɑ̃:s] *f* impertinence; rudeness, cheek; ✷✷ irrelevance; **impertinent, e** [~'nɑ̃, ~'nɑ̃:t] **1.** *adj.* impertinent; cheeky, pert; ✷✷ irrelevant; **2.** *su./m* impertinent fellow; *su./f* saucy girl.

imperturbable [ɛ̃pɛrtyr'babl] unruffled; imperturbable, phlegmatic.

impétrant, e e ✷✷ [ɛ̃pe'trɑ̃, ~'trɑ̃:t] *su.* grantee.

impétueux, -euse [ɛ̃pe'tɥø, ~'tɥøːz] impetuous; hot-headed, precipitate, impulsive; **impétuosité** [~tɥozi'te] f impetuosity; impulsiveness.

impitoyable [ɛ̃pitwa'jabl] pitiless (to[wards] à, envers); merciless; relentless.

implacable [ɛ̃pla'kabl] implacable, unrelenting (towards à, à l'égard de, pour).

implanter [ɛ̃plɑ̃'te] (1a) v/t. plant; fig. implant; ⚕ graft; s'~ take root.

implication [ɛ̃plika'sjɔ̃] f implication; phls. contradiction; ~s pl. consequences; **implicite** [~'sit] implicit; implied, tacit; **impliquer** [~'ke] (1m) v/t. involve; imply; implicate.

implorer [ɛ̃plɔ're] (1a) v/t. implore, beseech.

imploser [ɛ̃plɔ'ze] (1a) v/i. implode; **implosion** [~'zjɔ̃] f implosion.

impoli, e [ɛ̃pɔ'li] impolite, discourteous; rude (to envers, avec); **impolitesse** [~li'tɛs] f impoliteness, discourtesy; rudeness.

impolitique [ɛ̃pɔli'tik] impolitic; ill-advised.

impondérable [ɛ̃pɔ̃de'rabl] adj., a. su./m imponderable.

impopulaire [ɛ̃pɔpy'lɛːr] unpopular; **impopularité** [~lari'te] f unpopularity.

importance [ɛ̃pɔr'tɑ̃ːs] f importance; size, extent; **important, e** [~'tɑ̃, ~'tɑ̃ːt] 1. adj. important; considerable; weighty; fig. pej. self-important, F bumptious; 2. su.: F faire l'~ give o.s. airs; su./m main thing, essential point.

importateur, -trice † [ɛ̃pɔrta'tœːr, ~'tris] 1. su. importer; 2. adj. importing; **importation** † [~'sjɔ̃] f importation; ~s pl. goods: imports.

importer[1] [ɛ̃pɔr'te] (1a) v/t. † import; fig. introduce.

importer[2] [~] (1a) v/i. matter; be important; n'importe! it doesn't matter!; never mind!; n'importe quoi no matter what, anything; qu'importe? what does it matter?

importun, e [ɛ̃pɔr'tœ̃, ~'tyn] 1. adj. importunate; tiresome; unwelcome; untimely (request); 2. su. person: nuisance; bore; **importunément** [ɛ̃pɔrtyne'mɑ̃] adv. of importun 1; **importuner** [~'ne] (1a) v/t. importune; bother, pester (with,

de); inconvenience; **importunité** [~ni'te] f importunity.

imposable [ɛ̃pɔ'zabl] taxable; **imposant, e** [~'zɑ̃, ~'zɑ̃ːt] imposing; commanding; **imposer** [~'ze] (1a) v/t. prescribe, impose; force (an opinion, one's viewpoint) (upon, à); admin. tax, rate; eccl. lay on (hands); ~ du respect à q. fill s.o. with respect; ~ silence à q. enjoin silence on s.o.; s'~ assert o.s.; be essential; v/i.: en ~ à q. impress s.o.; en ~ be imposing; **imposition** [~zi'sjɔ̃] f taxation; rating.

impossibilité [ɛ̃pɔsibili'te] f impossibility (a. = impossible thing); **impossible** [~'sibl] impossible; F fantastic.

imposteur [ɛ̃pɔs'tœːr] m impostor; F sham; **imposture** [~'tyːr] f imposture; deception.

impôt [ɛ̃'po] m tax, duty; taxation.

impotence [ɛ̃pɔ'tɑ̃ːs] f impotence; helplessness; **impotent, e** [~'tɑ̃, ~'tɑ̃ːt] 1. adj. impotent; crippled, helpless; 2. su. cripple, invalid.

impraticable [ɛ̃prati'kabl] impracticable; impassable (road); sp. unplayable (tennis court etc.).

imprécation [ɛ̃preka'sjɔ̃] f curse.

imprécis, e [ɛ̃pre'si, ~'siːz] vague; unprecise.

imprégner [ɛ̃pre'ɲe] (1f) v/t. impregnate (a. fig.) (with, de).

imprenable ⚔ [ɛ̃prə'nabl] impregnable.

imprésario [ɛ̃presar'jo] su. impresario.

imprescriptible ⚖ [ɛ̃preskrip'tibl] indefeasible.

impression [ɛ̃prɛ'sjɔ̃] f fig., a. book, seal: impression; tex., typ. book: printing; wind: pressure; footsteps: imprint; coins: stamping; (colour-) print; paint. priming; envoyer à l'~ send to press; **impressionnable** [ɛ̃presjɔ'nabl] impressionable; **impressionnant, e** [~'nɑ̃, ~'nɑ̃ːt] impressive; moving (sight, voice); stirring (news); **impressionner** [~'ne] (1a) v/t. impress, affect, move; make an impression on; **impressionnisme** [~'nism] m impressionism; **impressionniste** [~'nist] su. impressionist.

imprévisible [ɛ̃previ'zibl] unforeseeable, unpredictable; **imprévision** [~'zjɔ̃] f lack of foresight.

imprévoyance [ɛ̃prevwa'jɑ̃ːs] f

inanimé

lack of foresight; improvidence; **imprévu, e** [~'vy] unforeseen, unexpected.

imprimé [ɛ̃pri'me] *m* printed paper or book; ~s *pl. post*: printed matter *sg.*; **imprimer** [~'me] (1a) *v/t. typ., tex.* print; impress (*a seal*); communicate, impart (*a movement*); *paint.* prime; **imprimerie** [ɛ̃prim-'ri] *f* printing; printing-house; printing-press; **imprimeur** [ɛ̃pri-'mœːr] *m* printer; **imprimeuse** [~'møːz] *f* (small) printing-machine.

improbable [ɛ̃prɔ'babl] improbable, unlikely; **improbateur, -trice** [~ba'tœːr, ~'tris] disapproving; **improbation** [~ba'sjɔ̃] *f* strong disapproval.

improbité [ɛ̃prɔbi'te] *f* dishonesty.

improductif, -ve [ɛ̃prɔdyk'tif, ~'tiːv] unproductive; ✝ idle (*assets, money*).

impromptu [ɛ̃prɔp'ty] 1. *adj./inv.* extempore (*speech*); impromptu, scratch (*meal*); 2. *adv.* without preparation, off the cuff; out of the blue; 3. *su./m* ♪ impromptu.

impropre [ɛ̃'prɔpr] wrong, unfit, unsuitable (for, *à*); **impropriété** [ɛ̃prɔprie'te] *f* impropriety; incorrectness.

improuvable [ɛ̃pru'vabl] unprovable.

improviser [ɛ̃prɔvi'ze] (1a) *vt/i.* improvise; *v/i.* speak extempore; F ad-lib; **improviste** [~'vist] *adv.*: à l'~ unexpectedly, by surprise; without warning.

imprudence [ɛ̃pry'dãːs] *f* imprudence; rashness; imprudent act; **imprudent, e** [~'dã, ~'dãːt] imprudent, rash; unwise.

impudence [ɛ̃py'dãːs] *f* impudence; effrontery; impudent act; **impudent, e** [~'dã, ~'dãːt] 1. *adj.* impudent; 2. *su.* impudent person; **impudeur** [~'dœːr] *f* shamelessness; lewdness; effrontery; **impudicité** [~disi'te] *f* indecency; **impudique** [~'dik] indecent; shameless.

impuissance [ɛ̃pɥi'sãːs] *f* powerlessness, helplessness; impotence (*a.* ✍); *dans l'~ de* (*inf.*) powerless to (*inf.*); **impuissant, e** [~'sã, ~'sãːt] powerless, helpless; vain (*effort*); ✍ impotent.

impulsif, -ve [ɛ̃pyl'sif, ~'siːv] impulsive; **impulsion** [~'sjɔ̃] *f* ✎, ⊕,

a. fig. impulse; F stimulus; *fig.* prompting; *force f d'~* impulsive force.

impunément [ɛ̃pyne'mã] *adv.* with impunity; *fig.* harmlessly; **impuni, e** [~'ni] unpunished; **impunité** [~ni'te] *f* impunity.

impur, e [ɛ̃'pyːr] impure, tainted; unclean; **impureté** [ɛ̃pyr'te] *f* impurity, unchastity.

imputable [ɛ̃py'tabl] imputable, ascribable (to, *à*); ✝ chargeable (to, *sur*); **imputer** [~'te] (1a) *v/t.* impute, ascribe (to, *à*); ✝ ~ *une somme à* (*or sur*) *un compte* charge a sum to an account.

imputrescible [ɛ̃pytrɛ'sibl] incorruptible; rot-proof.

inabordable [inabɔr'dabl] unapproachable, inaccessible; prohibitive (*price*).

inacceptable [inaksɛp'tabl] unacceptable.

inaccessible [inaksɛ'sibl] inaccessible; impervious (to, *à*) (*flattery, light, rain*).

inaccompli, e [inakɔ̃'pli] unaccomplished, unfulfilled.

inaccordable [inakɔr'dabl] ungrantable (*favour*).

inaccoutumé, e [inakuty'me] unaccustomed (to, *à*); unusual.

inachevé, e [inaʃ've] incomplete, unfinished.

inactif, -ve [inak'tif, ~'tiːv] inactive; idle (*a.* ✝ *capital*); ✝ dull (*market*); 🜍 inert; **inaction** [~'sjɔ̃] *f* inaction, idleness; ✝ dullness; **inactivité** [~tivi'te] *f* inactivity; ✝ dullness; 🜍 inertness.

inadapté, e [inadap'te] 1. *adj.* not adapted (to, *à*); maladjusted; 2. *su.* maladjusted person; misfit.

inadmissible [inadmi'sibl] inadmissible.

inadvertance [inadvɛr'tãːs] *f* inadvertence, oversight; *par ~* inadvertently; ~[able.]

inaliénable [inalje'nabl] inalien-⌡

inaltérable [inalte'rabl] unchanging, unvarying; which does not deteriorate.

inamovible [inamɔ'vibl] irremovable; for life (*post*); built in (*furniture etc.*); *agencements m/pl.* ~s fixtures.

inanimé, e [inani'me] inanimate, lifeless; unconscious.

inanité [inani'te] *f* futility; inane remark.

inanition [inani'sjõ] *f* starvation.

inaperçu, e [inaper'sy] unnoticed.

inappréciable [inapre'sjabl] inappreciable (*quantity*); *fig.* invaluable.

inapte [i'napt] unfit (for, *à*); unsuited (to, *à*); incapable (of *ger.*, *à inf.*); **inaptitude** [inapti'tyd] *f* inaptitude; unfitness (for, *à*).

inassouvi, e [inasu'vi] unappeased (*hunger*); unslaked, unquenched (*thirst*); *fig.* unsatisfied.

inattaquable [inata'kabl] unattackable; unassailable; irrefutable; irreproachable.

inattendu, e [inatã'dy] unexpected. **inattentif, -ve** [inatã'tif, ‿'ti:v] inattentive (to, *à*); heedless (of, *à*).

inaugurer [inogy're] (1a) *v/t.* inaugurate, open; unveil (*a monument*); *fig.* usher in (*an epoch*).

inavoué, e [ina'vwe] unacknowledged.

incalculable [ẽkalky'labl] countless, incalculable.

incandescence [ẽkãdɛ'sã:s] *f* incandescence, glow; *⚡ lampe f à ‿* glow-lamp.

incapable [ẽka'pabl] incapable (of *ger.*, *de inf.*); unfit (to *inf.*, *de inf.*); **incapacité** [‿pasi'te] *f* incapacity (*a. ⚖*); unfitness; incompetency.

incarcération [ẽkarsera'sjõ] *f* incarceration, imprisonment; **incarcérer** [‿'re] (1f) *v/t.* incarcerate, imprison.

incarnadin, e [ẽkarna'dẽ, ‿'din] incarnadine, flesh-pink; **incarnat, e** [‿'na, ‿'nat] fleshcolo(u)red, rosy; **incarnation** [‿na'sjõ] *f* incarnation; *fig.* personification; *🌱* nail: ingrowing; **incarné, e** [‿'ne] incarnate; *fig.* personified; *🌱* ingrowing (*nail*); **incarner** [‿'ne] (1a) *v/t.* incarnate; *fig.* personify; *🌱* s'‿ grow in (*nail*).

incartade [ẽkar'tad] *f* prank; freak; (*verbal*) outburst.

incassable [ẽka'sabl] unbreakable.

incendiaire [ẽsã'djɛ:r] 1. *adj.* incendiary (*bomb*); *fig.* inflammatory; 2. *su.* incendiary; fire-brand; **incendie** [‿'di] *m* fire; *⚖ ‿ volontaire* arson; **incendié m, e** *f* [‿'dje] person rendered homeless by fire; **incendier** [‿'dje] (1o) *v/t.* set (*s.th.*) on fire, burn (*s.th.*) down.

incertain, e [ẽsɛr'tẽ, ‿'tɛn] uncertain, doubtful; unreliable; undecided (about, *de*) (*person*); unsettled (*weather*); **incertitude** [‿ti'tyd] *f* uncertainty, doubt; *result:* inaccuracy; *fig.* indecision; unsettled state (*of the weather*).

incessamment [ẽsesa'mã] *adv.* incessantly; at any moment; without delay, at once; **incessant, e** [‿'sã, ‿'sã:t] ceaseless, unceasing, incessant.

inceste [ẽ'sɛst] 1. *adj.* incestuous; 2. *su./m* incest; *su. see incestueux* 2; **incestueux, -euse** [ẽsɛs'tɥø, ‿'tɥø:z] 1. *adj.* incestuous; 2. *su.* incestuous person.

inchiffrable [ẽʃi'frabl] immeasurable (*wealth etc.*); *fig.* invaluable.

incidemment [ẽsida'mã] *adv. of incident 1*; **incidence** [‿'dã:s] *f* incidence; consequence, effect; **incident, e** [‿'dã, ‿'dã:t] 1. *adj.* incidental; *opt.* incident; 2. *su./m* incident; occurrence; *⚖* point of law; *fig.* difficulty, hitch; *‿ de parcours* mishap, (minor) setback; *‿ technique* technical hitch.

incinération [ẽsinera'sjõ] *f* incineration; cremation; **incinérer** [‿'re] (1f) *v/t.* incinerate; cremate.

inciser [ẽsi'ze] (1a) *v/t.* make an incision in; *𝅘* lance (*an abscess*); **incisif, -ve** [‿'zif, ‿'zi:v] 1. *adj.* incisive, cutting; *dent f ‿ve =* 2. *su./f tooth:* incisor; **incision** [‿'zjõ] *f* incision; *𝅘* abscess: lancing.
[instigate, urge (on).]

inciter [ẽsi'te] (1a) *v/t.* incite;

incivil, e [ẽsi'vil] uncivil, rude; **incivilité** [‿vili'te] *f* incivility, rudeness; rude remark.

inclinaison [ẽklinɛ'zõ] *f* incline, slope; *⚓ ship:* list; *‿ magnétique* magnetic dip; **inclination** [‿na'sjõ] *f* inclination (*a. fig.*); *body:* bending; *head:* nod; *fig.* bent; **incliner** [‿'ne] (1a) *v/t.* incline (*a. fig.*), slope; bend; nod (*one's head*); s'‿ slant; bow; *fig.* yield (to, *devant*); *⚓* heel; *⚖* bank; *v/i.* incline (*a. fig.*); lean; *⚓* list.

inclure [ẽ'kly:r] (4g) *v/t.* include; *letter:* enclose; **inclus, e** [ẽ'kly, ‿'kly:z] 1. *adj.* enclosed; *la lettre ci-‿e* enclosed letter; **inclusif, -ve** [ẽkly'zif, ‿'zi:v] inclusive.

incognito [ẽkɔɲi'to] *adv.*, *a. su./m* incognito.

incohérent, e [ɛkɔeˈrɑ̃, ˌˈrɑ̃ːt] incoherent (*a. phys.*), rambling.

incolore [ɛkɔˈlɔːr] colo(u)rless (*a. fig.*); *fig.* insipid.

incomber [ɛkɔ̃ˈbe] (1a) *v/i.*: ˌ *à* be incumbent upon; devolve upon.

incombustible [ɛkɔ̃bysˈtibl] incombustible, fireproof.

incommensurable [ɛkɔmɑ̃syˈrabl] *Å* incommensurable; irrational (*root*); incommensurate; *fig.* enormous, huge.

incommode [ɛkɔˈmɔd] inconvenient; uncomfortable; troublesome; unwieldy (*object*); **incommodément** [ɛkɔmɔdeˈmɑ̃] *adv.* inconveniently, uncomfortably; **incommoder** [ˌˈde] (1a) *v/t.* inconvenience, hinder; disturb, trouble; *food etc.*: disagree with (*s.o.*); **incommodité** [ˌdiˈte] *f* inconvenience; discomfort; awkwardness.

incomparable [ɛkɔ̃paˈrabl] incomparable, unrivalled.

incompatible [ɛkɔ̃paˈtibl] incompatible.

incomplet, -ète [ɛkɔ̃ˈplɛ, ˌˈplɛt] incomplete, unfinished.

incompréhensible [ɛkɔ̃preɑ̃ˈsibl] incomprehensible; **incompréhensif, -ve** [ˌˈsif, ˌˈsiːv] uncomprehending; unwilling *or* unable to understand; **incompréhension** [ˌˈsjɔ̃] *f* incomprehension; unwillingness *or* inability to understand.

incompris, e [ɛkɔ̃ˈpri, ˌˈpriːz] misunderstood; unappreciated.

inconcevable [ɛkɔ̃səˈvabl] unimaginable, unthinkable.

inconciliable [ɛkɔ̃siˈljabl] irreconcilable.

inconditionnel, -le [ɛkɔ̃disjɔˈnɛl] unconditional, unreserved; unquestioning.

inconduite [ɛkɔ̃ˈdɥit] *f* misbehavio(u)r; loose living; ⚖ misconduct.

incongelable [ɛkɔ̃ʒˈlabl] unfreezable; non-freezing.

incongru, e [ɛkɔ̃ˈgry] incongruous; improper, unseemly; **incongruité** [ˌgrɥiˈte] *f* incongruity; unseemliness; **incongrûment** [ˌgryˈmɑ̃] *adv. of* incongru.

inconnu, e [ɛkɔˈny] **1.** *adj.* unknown (to *à*, *de*); **2.** *su.* unknown, stranger; *su./f* *Å* unknown (quantity).

inconscience [ɛkɔ̃ˈsjɑ̃ːs] *f* unconsciousness; ignorance (of, *de*); **inconscient, e** [ˌˈsjɑ̃, ˌˈsjɑ̃ːt] **1.** *adj.* unconscious; **2.** *su.* unconscious person; *su./m* *psych.* the unconscious.

inconséquence [ɛkɔ̃seˈkɑ̃ːs] *f* inconsequence, inconsistency; thoughtlessness.

inconsidéré, e [ɛkɔ̃sideˈre] inconsiderate (*person*); rash, ill-considered.

inconsistant, e [ɛkɔ̃sisˈtɑ̃, ˌˈtɑ̃ːt] unsubstantial; loose (*ground*); soft (*mud*); *fig.* inconsistent.

inconsolable [ɛkɔ̃sɔˈlabl] unconsolable; disconsolate (*person*).

inconstance [ɛkɔ̃sˈtɑ̃ːs] *f* inconstancy, fickleness; changeableness (*of weather*); *biol.* variability; **inconstant, e** [ˌˈtɑ̃, ˌˈtɑ̃ːt] inconstant, fickle; changeable (*weather*); *biol.* variable.

inconstitutionnel, -elle [ɛkɔ̃stitysjɔˈnɛl] unconstitutional.

incontestable [ɛkɔ̃tɛsˈtabl] indisputable, unquestionable, beyond (all) question; **incontesté, e** [ˌˈte] undisputed.

incontinence [ɛkɔ̃tiˈnɑ̃ːs] *f* incontinence (*a.* ⚕); **incontinent, e** [ˌˈnɑ̃, ˌˈnɑ̃ːt] **1.** *adj.* incontinent; unchaste; **2.** *incontinent adv.* † forthwith.

inconvenance [ɛkɔ̃vˈnɑ̃ːs] *f* unsuitableness; impropriety; indecency.

inconvénient [ɛkɔ̃veˈnjɑ̃] *m* disadvantage, drawback; inconvenience; *fig.* objection; *si vous n'y voyez pas d'*ˌ if you dont mind, if you have no objections.

inconvertible [ɛkɔ̃vɛrˈtibl] inconvertible (*a.* ⭰); **inconvertissable** [ˌtiˈsabl] *fig.* incorrigible; past praying for; ⭰ inconvertible.

incorporation [ɛkɔrpɔraˈsjɔ̃] *f* incorporation; ⚔ enrolment; **incorporel, -elle** [ˌˈrɛl] incorporeal; ⚖ intangible (*property*); **incorporer** [ˌˈre] (1a) *v/t.* incorporate; mix (with *à*, *avec*, *dans*); ⚔ draft (*men*).

incorrect, e [ɛkɔˈrɛkt] incorrect; wrong; inaccurate; indecorous; **incorrection** [ˌrɛkˈsjɔ̃] *f* incorrectness; error; wrong act; indecorousness.

incorrigible [ɛkɔriˈʒibl] incorrigible; *fig.* F hopeless.

incorruptible [ɛkɔrypˈtibl] incor-

[ruptible.\
[ruptible.⟩

incrédibilité [ɛ̃kredibili'te] *f* incredibility; **incrédule** [~'dyl] **1.** *adj.* incredulous; sceptical (about, of *à l'égard de*); *eccl.* unbelieving; **2.** *su. eccl.* unbeliever; **incrédulité** [~dyli'te] *f* incredulity; *eccl.* unbelief.
incrimination [ɛ̃krimina'sjɔ̃] *f* (in-)crimination; indictment; charge; **incriminer** [~'ne] (1a) *v/t.* accuse, charge; *fig.* impeach (*s.o.'s conduct*).
incrochetable [ɛ̃krɔʃ'tabl] burglar-proof.
incroyable [ɛ̃krwa'jabl] **1.** *adj.* incredible; **2.** *su./m hist.* beau; **incroyance** [~'jɑ̃:s] *f* unbelief; **incroyant, e** [~'jɑ̃, ~'jɑ̃:t] **1.** *adj.* unbelieving; **2.** *su.* unbeliever.
incrustation [ɛ̃krysta'sjɔ̃] *f* incrustation; ⊕ inlaid work; ⊕ *boiler*: fur(ring); **incruster** [~'te] (1a) *v/t.* incrust; ⊕ inlay (with, *de*); ⚠ line; form a crust on; *fig.* *s'*~ become ingrained (*in the mind*); outstay one's welcome.
incubateur [ɛ̃kyba'tœ:r] *m* incubator; **incubation** [~'sjɔ̃] *f eggs, a.* ⚕: incubation; *hens*: sitting.
incube [ɛ̃'kyb] *m* incubus, nightmare.
inculper [ɛ̃kyl'pe] (1a) *v/t.* charge, indict.
inculquer [ɛ̃kyl'ke] (1m) *v/t.* inculcate, instil (into, *à*).
inculte [ɛ̃'kylt] uncultivated, wild; waste (*land*); *fig.* rough; *fig.* unkempt (*hair*).
incunable [ɛ̃ky'nabl] *m* early printed book; ~*s pl.* incunabula.
incurable [ɛ̃ky'rabl] *adj., a. su.* incurable; **incurie** [~'ri] *f* carelessness, negligence.
incursion [ɛ̃kyr'sjɔ̃] *f* inroad, foray, raid; *fig.* excursion (into, *dans*).
indébrouillable [ɛ̃debru'jabl] impossible to disentangle; *fig.* inextricable.
indécence [ɛ̃de'sɑ̃:s] *f* indecency; **indécent, e** [~'sɑ̃, ~'sɑ̃:t] indecent; improper.
indéchiffrable [ɛ̃deʃi'frabl] undecipherable; *fig.* illegible; *fig.* unintelligible.
indécis, e [ɛ̃de'si, ~'si:z] undecided; irresolute; blurred, vague (*outline etc.*); indecisive (*battle, victory*); **indécision** [~si'zjɔ̃] *f* indecision; uncertainty.
indéfini, e [ɛ̃defi'ni] indefinite; undefined; **indéfinissable** [~ni'sabl] indefinable; nondescript.
indéfrisable [ɛ̃defri'zabl] *f* permanent wave.
indélébile [ɛ̃dele'bil] indelible; kiss-proof (*lipstick*).
indélibéré, e [ɛ̃delibe're] unconsidered.
indélicat, e [ɛ̃deli'ka, ~'kat] indelicate, coarse; tactless (*act*); dishonest.
indémaillable [ɛ̃dema'jabl] ladder-proof, non-run (*stocking*).
indemne [ɛ̃'dɛmn] undamaged; uninjured; without loss; free (from, *de*); **indemnisation** [ɛ̃demniza'sjɔ̃] *f* indemnification; **indemniser** [~'ze] (1a) *v/t.* indemnify, compensate (for, *de*); **indemnité** [~'te] *f* indemnity; compensation; allowance; ~ *de déplacement* travel allowance; ~ *de maladie* sick pay; ~ *journalière* daily allowance.
indéniable [ɛ̃de'njabl] undeniable.
indépendamment [ɛ̃depɑ̃da'mɑ̃] *adv. of indépendant*; **indépendance** [~'dɑ̃:s] *f* independence (of *de, à l'égard de*); **indépendant, e** [~'dɑ̃, ~'dɑ̃:t] independent (of, *de*); free (from, *de*); self-contained (*flat etc.*).
indéracinable *fig.* [ɛ̃derasi'nabl] ineradicable.
indéréglable [ɛ̃dere'glabl] foolproof (*machine etc.*).
indescriptible [ɛ̃dɛskrip'tibl] indescribable (F *a. fig.*).
indestructible [ɛ̃dɛstryk'tibl] indestructible.
indéterminé, e [ɛ̃detɛrmi'ne] undetermined; indeterminate (⚗, *a. fig.*).
index [ɛ̃'dɛks] *m* forefinger, index (finger); *book*: index; pointer; *eccl. the* Index; *fig.* black list; *mettre à l'*~ blacklist.
indicateur, -trice [ɛ̃dika'tœ:r, ~'tris] **1.** *adj.* indicatory; ~ *de* indicating (*s.th.*); **2.** *su./m* ⊕ indicator, ga(u)ge, pointer; 🚂 guide, time-table; directory (*of streets etc.*); informer, police spy; ~ *de pression* pressure-ga(u)ge; *mot.* ~ *de vitesse* speedometer; **indicatif, -ve** [~'tif, ~'ti:v] **1.** *adj.* indicative; **2.** *su./m radio etc.*: station-signal; signature-tune; ⚡ call sign; *gramm.* indicative; **indication** [~'sjɔ̃] *f* indication; information; sign, token; mark; ⚖

declaration; ⁓s *pl.* ✻ *etc.* instructions; ⊕ particulars; *thea.* ⁓s *pl.* *scéniques* stage-directions.

indice [ɛ̃'dis] *m* indication, sign; *opt.*, ♃ index; *fig.* clue; rating, grading; ⁓ *de popularité* popularity rating.

indicible [ɛ̃di'sibl] unspeakable; unutterable; *fig.* indescribable.

indien, -enne [ɛ̃'djɛ̃, ⁓'djɛn] **1.** *adj.* Indian; **2.** *su.* ♀ Indian; *su./f tex.* printed calico; *tex.* chintz.

indifférence [ɛ̃dife'rɑ̃:s] *f* indifference, apathy (towards, *pour*); **indifférent, e** [⁓'rɑ̃, ⁓'rɑ̃:t] indifferent (*a.* ♀) (to, *à*); unaffected (by, *à*); unconcerned; ♀ neutral (*salt etc.*); unimportant.   [*fig.*)|

indigence [ɛ̃di'ʒɑ̃:s] *f* poverty (*a.*)

indigène [ɛ̃di'ʒɛn] **1.** *adj.* indigenous (to, *à*); native; ♣ homegrown; **2.** *su.* native.

indigent, e [ɛ̃di'ʒɑ̃, ⁓'ʒɑ̃:t] **1.** *adj.* poor, needy; **2.** *su.* pauper; *su./m: les* ⁓*s pl.* the poor.

indigeste [ɛ̃di'ʒɛst] indigestible; stodgy (*a. fig.*); **indigestion** ✻ [⁓ʒɛs'tjɔ̃] *f* indigestion; F *fig. avoir une* ⁓ *de* be fed up with.

indignation [ɛ̃diɲa'sjɔ̃] *f* indignation.

indigne [ɛ̃'diɲ] unworthy (of, *de*; to *inf.*, *de inf.*).

indigner [ɛ̃di'ɲe] (1a) *v/t.* make (*s.o.*) indignant; *s'*⁓ be indignant (with, at *contre*, *de*).

indignité [ɛ̃diɲi'te] *f* unworthiness; vileness; indignity.

indigo [ɛ̃di'go] *m* indigo.

indiquer [ɛ̃di'ke] (1m) *v/t.* indicate; point out; recommend; *fig.* show; fix.

indirect, e [ɛ̃di'rɛkt] indirect; *pej.* underhand; ⚖ circumstantial; ⚡ *éclairage m* ⁓ concealed lighting.

indiscipliné, e [ɛ̃disipli'ne] undisciplined; unmanageable; unruly; out of hand.

indiscret, -ète [ɛ̃dis'krɛ, ⁓'krɛt] indiscreet; tactless; *fig.* prying (*look*).

indiscutable [ɛ̃disky'tabl] indisputable, unquestionable.

indispensable [ɛ̃dispɑ̃'sabl] **1.** *adj.* indispensable (to, for *à*); essential; unavoidable; **2.** *su./m the* necessary.

indisponible [ɛ̃dispɔ'nibl] unavailable; ⚖ inalienable.

indisposé, e [ɛ̃dispo'ze] unwell, indisposed; **indisposer** [⁓'ze] (1a) *v/t.*

make (*s.o.*) unwell; *fig.* antagonize, irritate, annoy; *fig.* ⁓ *q. contre* make s.o. hostile to; **indisposition** [⁓zi-'sjɔ̃] *f* indisposition; upset.

indisputable [ɛ̃dispy'tabl] unquestionable.

indissociable [ɛ̃disɔ'sjabl] inseparable.

indissoluble [ɛ̃disɔ'lybl] ♀ insoluble; *fig.* indissoluble.

indistinct, e [ɛ̃dis'tɛ̃(:kt), ⁓'tɛ̃:kt] indistinct; faint; dim, hazy.

individu [ɛ̃divi'dy] *m* individual (*a. pej.*); **individualiser** [⁓dɥali'ze] (1a) *v/t.* particularize; individualize; **individualiste** [⁓dɥa'list] **1.** *adj.* individualistic; **2.** *su.* individualist; **invididualité** [⁓dɥali-'te] *f* individuality; **individuel, -elle** [⁓'dɥɛl] individual, personal; private; separate.

indivis, e ⚖ [ɛ̃di'vi, ⁓'vi:z] joint; *par* ⁓ jointly; **indivisible** [⁓vi'zibl] indivisible; ⚖ joint.

indocile [ɛ̃dɔ'sil] unmanageable, intractable; **indocilité** [⁓sili'te] *f* intractability.

indolence [ɛ̃dɔ'lɑ̃:s] *f* ✻, *a. fig.* indolence; sloth; **indolent, e** [⁓'lɑ̃, ⁓'lɑ̃:t] **1.** ✻, *a. fig.* indolent; *fig.* apathetic; *fig.* sluggish; **2.** *su.* idler.

indolore ✻ [ɛ̃dɔ'lɔ:r] painless.

indomptable [ɛ̃dɔ̃'tabl] unconquerable; *fig.* indomitable; uncontrollable.

indu, e [ɛ̃'dy] undue (*haste*); unseasonable (*remark*); *à une heure* ⁓e at some ungodly hour.

indubitable [ɛ̃dybi'tabl] unquestionable, undeniable.

inductance ⚡ [ɛ̃dyk'tɑ̃:s] *f* inductance; **inducteur, -trice** ⚡ [⁓'tœ:r, ⁓'tris] **1.** *adj.* inducing (*current*); inductive (*capacity*); **2.** *su./m* inductor; field-magnet; **induction** ⚡, *phls.* [⁓'sjɔ̃] *f* induction.

induire [ɛ̃'dɥi:r] (4h) *v/t.* infer, induce; *fig.* lead (into, *à*); ⁓ *q. en erreur* mislead s.o.; **induit** [ɛ̃'dɥi] **1.** *adj./m* induced; **2.** *su./m* ⚡ induced circuit; armature.

indulgence [ɛ̃dyl'ʒɑ̃:s] *f* indulgence (*a. eccl.*); forbearance; **indulgent, e** [⁓'ʒɑ̃, ⁓'ʒɑ̃:t] *adj.:* ⁓ *pour* indulgent to, lenient with.

indûment [ɛ̃dy'mɑ̃] *adv.* unduly; improperly.

industrialiser [ɛ̃dystriali'ze] (1a)

industrie

v/t. industrialize; **industrie** [~'tri] *f* industry; trade, manufacture; *fig.* activity; † *fig.* skill, ingenuity; ~-clef key-industry; ~ minière mining industry; *co.* exercer sa coupable~ practise one's disreputable trade; **industriel, -elle** [~tri'ɛl] 1. *adj.* industrial; 2. *su./m* manufacturer; industrialist; **industrieux, -euse** [~tri'ø, ~'ø:z] industrious, busy; skil(l)ful.

inébranlable [inebrɑ̃'labl] unshakable.

inédit, e [ine'di, ~'dit] unpublished; novel, new; original.

ineffable [ine'fabl] ineffable, beyond expression.

inefficace [inefi'kas] ineffective; unavailing; **inefficacité** [~kasi'te] *f* inefficacy; ineffectiveness.

inégal, e, *m/pl.* -aux [ine'gal, ~'go] unequal; irregular (*pulse etc.*); uneven (*ground, temper*); changeable (*moods, wind*); **inégalité** [~gali'te] *f* inequality (*a. Ⱥ*); irregularity; unevenness.

inéligible [ineli'ʒibl] ineligible.

inéluctable [inelyk'tabl] inescapable.

inemployé, e [inɑ̃plwa'je] unemployed; not made use of.

inepte [i'nɛpt] inept, fatuous, stupid; **ineptie** [inɛp'si] *f* ineptitude; stupidity, ineptness.

inépuisable [inepɥi'zabl] inexhaustible.

inerte [i'nɛrt] inert (*mass, a. Ⱥ*); inactive (Ⱥ, *a. mind*); *fig.* sluggish; *fig.* passive (*resistance*); **inertie** [inɛr'si] *f phys.* inertia; *a. fig.* inertia; *fig.* listlessness; *fig.* passive resistance; force *f* d'~ inertia, vis inertiae.

inespéré, e [inɛspe're] unhoped-for, unexpected.

inestimable [inɛsti'mabl] invaluable; without price.

inévitable [inevi'tabl] inevitable; unavoidable.

inexact, e [inɛg'zakt] inexact; inaccurate; unpunctual; **inexactitude** [~zakti'tyd] *f* inexactitude; inaccuracy; unpunctuality.

inexcusable [inɛksky'zabl] inexcusable.

inexistant, e [inɛgzis'tɑ̃, ~'tɑ̃:t] nonexistent.

inexorable [inɛgzɔ'rabl] inexorable, unrelenting.

inexpérience [inɛkspe'rjɑ̃:s] *f* lack of experience; **inexpérimenté, e** [~rimɑ̃'te] unskilled (*worker*); untested, untried; inexperienced (*person*).

inexplicable [inɛkspli'kabl] inexplicable.

inexploré, e [inɛksplɔ're] unexplored.

inexprimable [inɛkspri'mabl] inexpressible; unspeakable (*pleasure etc.*).

inexpugnable [inɛkspyg'nabl] impregnable.

inextinguible [inɛkstɛ̃'gɥibl] inextinguishable (*fire*); unquenchable; *fig.* uncontrollable.

inextirpable [inɛkstir'pabl] ineradicable.

inextricable [inɛkstri'kabl] inextricable.

infaillible [ɛ̃fa'jibl] infallible.

infaisable [ɛ̃fə'zabl] unfeasible; impracticable.

infamant, e [ɛ̃fa'mɑ̃, ~'mɑ̃:t] defamatory; ignominious; **infâme** [ɛ̃'fɑ:m] infamous; vile (*deed, quarter, slum*); foul (*behaviour, deed*); **infamie** [ɛ̃fa'mi] *f* infamy, dishono(u)r; vile deed *or* thing; ~s *pl.* abuse *sg.*, infamous accusations.

infant [ɛ̃'fɑ̃] *m* infante; **infante** [ɛ̃'fɑ̃:t] *f* infanta; **infanterie** ⚔ [ɛ̃fɑ̃'tri] *f* infantry; **infanticide** [~ti'sid] 1. *adj.* infanticidal; 2. *su. person:* infanticide; *su./m crime:* infanticide; **infantile** [~'til] infantile (*disease, mortality*); *fig.* childish; **infantiliser** *psych.* [~tili'ze] (1a) *v/t.* make infantile.

infarctus 𝕁 [ɛ̃fark'tys] *m* infarct(ion); ~ du myocarde coronary (thrombosis).

infatigable [ɛ̃fati'gabl] indefatigable, untiring.

infatuer [ɛ̃fa'tɥe] (1n) *v/t.* infatuate; s'~ de become infatuated with.

infécond, e [ɛ̃fe'kɔ̃, ~'kɔ̃:d] barren; *fig.* unfruitful.

infect, e [ɛ̃'fɛkt] stinking; noisome (*smell*); filthy (*book, a. fig. lie, weather*); **infecter** [ɛ̃fɛk'te] (1a) *v/t.* infect; pollute; stink of; **infection** [~'sjɔ̃] *f* infection; stench.

inférer [ɛ̃fe're] (1f) *v/t.* infer (from, de).

inférieur, e [ɛ̃fe'rjœ:r] 1. *adj.* inferior; lower; ~ à below; 2. *su.* inferior; subordinate; **inférioriser** [~rjɔri'ze] (1a) v/t. regard as inferior; **infériorité** [~rjɔri'te] f inferiority; *complexe m d'~* inferiority complex.

infernal, e, m/pl. **-aux** [ɛ̃fɛr'nal, ~'no] infernal (a. fig.); fig. devilish; ℞ pierre f ~e lunar caustic.

infertile [ɛ̃fɛr'til] infertile, barren.

infestation [ɛ̃fɛsta'sjɔ̃] f infestation; **infester** [~'te] (1a) v/t. infest (with, de) (a. fig.).

infidèle [ɛ̃fi'dɛl] **1.** adj. unfaithful; inaccurate; infidel; unbelieving; **2.** su. unbeliever; infidel; **infidélité** [~deli'te] f infidelity (to, envers); unfaithfulness; inaccuracy; unbelief.

infiltration [ɛ̃filtra'sjɔ̃] f infiltration (a. ℞); **infiltrer** [~'tre] (1a) v/t.: s'~ infiltrate (a. ✕, a. ℞); filter in, seep in (a. fig.).

infime [ɛ̃'fim] lowly; lowest, least; minute, tiny.

infini, e [ɛ̃fi'ni] **1.** adj. infinite; endless; **2.** su./m infinity; the infinite; à l'~ endless(ly); **infiniment** [~ni'mã] adv. infinitely; F extremely; **infinité** [~ni'te] f Å etc. infinity; fig. host.

infirme [ɛ̃'firm] **1.** adj. infirm; disabled, crippled; fig. weak; **2.** su. invalid; cripple; **infirmer** [ɛ̃fir'me] (1a) v/t. fig. weaken; disprove; ℔ quash; **infirmerie** [~mə'ri] f infirmary; sick-room; ⚓ sick-bay; **infirmier** [~'mje] m (hospital-)attendant; male nurse; ✕ medical orderly; ambulance man; **infirmière** [~'mjɛ:r] f nurse; **infirmité** [~mi'te] f infirmity; disability; fig. weakness.

inflammable [ɛ̃fla'mabl] inflammable, Am. a. flammable; easily set on fire (a. fig.); **inflammation** [~ma-'sjɔ̃] f inflammation (a. ℞); ignition; **inflammatoire** [~ma'twa:r] inflammatory.

inflation ✝ etc. [ɛ̃fla'sjɔ̃] inflation.

infléchir [ɛ̃fle'ʃi:r] (2a) v/t. bend, inflect; **infléchissement** [~ʃis'mã] m modification.

inflexible [ɛ̃flɛk'sibl] inflexible; **inflexion** [~'sjɔ̃] f inflection, inflexion (a. Å, opt., gramm.); voice: modulation; body: bow.

infliger [ɛ̃fli'ʒe] (1l) v/t. inflict.

inflorescence ♀ [ɛ̃flɔrɛ'sɑ̃:s] f inflorescence.

influence [ɛ̃fly'ɑ̃:s] f influence; **influencer** [~ɑ̃'se] (1k) v/t. influence; **influent, e** [~'ɑ̃, ~'ɑ̃:t] influential; **influer** [~'e] (1a) v/i.: ~ sur influence.   [inv. folio.]

in-folio typ. [ɛ̃fɔ'ljo] m/inv., a. adj.

informaticien [ɛ̃fɔrmati'sjɛ̃] m computer scientist.

information [ɛ̃fɔrma'sjɔ̃] f information; inquiry; ~s pl. radio: news (-bulletin) sg.; newscast sg.

informatique [ɛ̃fɔrma'tik] f computer science; data processing; **informatisation** [~tiza'sjɔ̃] f computerization; **informatiser** [~ti'ze] (1a) v/t. computerize.

informe [ɛ̃'fɔrm] unformed; shapeless, unshapely; ℔ irregular, informal.

informel, -le [ɛ̃fɔr'mɛl] informal; casual.

informer [ɛ̃fɔr'me] (1a) v/t. inform, notify; s'~ inquire (about, de; of, from auprès de); v/i.: ℔ ~ contre inform against; ~ de, ~ sur investigate, inquire into.

infortune [ɛ̃fɔr'tyn] f misfortune; adversity; **infortuné, e** [~ty'ne] unfortunate, unlucky.

infraction [ɛ̃frak'sjɔ̃] f infraction; right, treaty, etc.: infringement; ℔ offence; duty, peace: breach (of, à).

infranchissable [ɛ̃frɑ̃ʃi'sabl] impassable; fig. insuperable (difficulty).

infrarouge [ɛ̃fra'ru:ʒ] infra-red.

infrastructure [ɛ̃frastryk'ty:r] f infrastructure; ✈ ground organization; ⊕ etc. substructure.

infroissabilité tex. [ɛ̃frwasabili'te] f crease-resistance; **infroissable** tex. [~'sabl] uncreasable.

infructueux, -euse [ɛ̃fryk'tɥø, ~'tɥø:z] unfruitful, barren; fig. unavailing, fruitless.

infus, e [ɛ̃'fy, ~'fy:z] fig. innate, intuitive; avoir la science ~e know things by intuition; **infuser** [ɛ̃fy'ze] (1a) v/t. infuse (a. fig. life), brew (tea); v/i. infuse; draw (tea); **infusible** [~'zibl] non-fusible; **infusion** [~'zjɔ̃] f infusion; herb tea; **infusoires** [~'zwa:r] m/pl. infusoria.

ingambe [ɛ̃'gɑ̃:b] active, nimble.

ingénier [ɛ̃ʒe'nje] (1o) v/t.: s'~ à tax one's ingenuity to, F go all out to; **ingénieur** [~'njœ:r] m engineer; ~ de l'État Government civil engineer; ～ *du son radio*: sound engineer, *Am.* sound man; ～ *mécanicien* mechanical engineer; **ingénieux, -euse** [～'njø, ～'njø:z] ingenious; clever; **ingéniosité** [～njozi'te] *f* ingenuity; cleverness.

ingénu, e [ɛ̃ʒe'ny] **1.** *adj.* ingenuous, artless, unsophisticated; **2.** *su.* artless person; *su./f thea.* ingénue; **ingénuité** [～nɥi'te] *f* artlessness, ingenuousness.

ingérence [ɛ̃ʒe'rɑ̃:s] *f* interference; **ingérer** [～'re] (1f) *v/t.* ingest; F consume (*a meal*); *s'～ dans* interfere in, meddle in.

ingrat, e [ɛ̃'gra, ～'grat] ungrateful (to[wards], *envers*; for, *à*); thankless (*task*); unpleasant (*work*); unpromising; ✗, *fig.* unproductive; *âge m* ～ awkward age; **ingratitude** [ɛ̃grati'tyd] *f* ingratitude; thanklessness; ✗, *fig.* unproductiveness.

ingrédient [ɛ̃gre'djɑ̃] *m* ingredient.

inguérissable [ɛ̃geri'sabl] incurable.

ingurgiter [ɛ̃gyrʒi'te] (1a) *v/t.* ✗ ingurgitate; F swallow.

inhabile [ina'bil] unskilful, inexpert; ✗✗ incompetent; **inhabileté** [～bil'te] *f* lack of skill (in, *à*); clumsiness; **inhabilité** ✗✗ [～bili'te] *f* incapacity, disability; incompetency.

inhabitable [inabi'tabl] uninhabitable; **inhabité, e** [～'te] uninhabited; untenanted (*house*).

inhalateur ✗ [inala'tœ:r] *m* inhaler; (*oxygen-*)breathing apparatus; **inhaler** ✗ [～'le] (1a) *v/t.* inhale.

inhérence [ine'rɑ̃:s] *f* inherence (in, *à*); **inhérent, e** [～'rɑ̃, ～'rɑ̃:t] inherent (in, *à*); intrinsic.

inhiber [ini'be] (1a) *v/t.* physiol., psych. inhibit; ✗✗ prohibit; **inhibition** [～bi'sjɔ̃] *f* ✗✗ prohibition; physiol., psych. inhibition.

inhospitalier, -ère [inɔspita'lje, ～-'ljɛ:r] inhospitable.

inhumain, e [iny'mɛ̃, ～'mɛn] inhuman; cruel. [inter.]

inhumer [iny'me] (1a) *v/t.* bury.

inimaginable [inimaʒi'nabl] unimaginable.

inimitable [inimi'tabl] inimitable.

inimitié [inimi'tje] *f* hostility (*a. fig.*); enmity.

ininflammable [inɛ̃fla'mabl] non-inflammable, uninflammable.

inintelligence [inɛ̃tɛli'ʒɑ̃:s] *f* lack of intelligence; **inintelligent, e** [～'ʒɑ̃, ～'ʒɑ̃:t] unintelligent; obtuse; **inintelligible** [～'ʒibl] unintelligible.

inique [i'nik] iniquitous; **iniquité** [iniki'te] *f* iniquity (*a. eccl., a. fig.*).

initial, e, *m*/*pl.* **-aux** [ini'sjal, ～'sjo] *adj., a. su./f* initial; *adj. a.* starting...; first; **initiateur, -trice** [～sja'tœ:r, ～'tris] **1.** *adj.* initiatory; initiation...; **2.** *su.* initiator; originator; **initiatique** [～sja'tik] initiatory (*rite etc.*); **initiative** [～sja'ti:v] *f* initiative; **initier** [～'sje] (1o) *v/t.* initiate (*a. fig.*).

injecter [ɛ̃ʒɛk'te] (1a) *v/t.* inject (with *de, avec*); impregnate (*wood*); *injecté de sang* bloodshot (*eye*); *s'～* become bloodshot (*eye*); **injection** [～'sjɔ̃] *f* ✗, ⊕ injection; *wood*: impregnation.

injonction ✗✗ [ɛ̃ʒɔ̃k'sjɔ̃] *f* injunction; order.

injure [ɛ̃'ʒy:r] *f* insult; ravages *pl.* (*of time*); † wrong, injury, ✗✗ tort; ～*s pl.* abuse *sg.*; **injurier** [ɛ̃ʒy'rje] (1o) *v/t.* insult, abuse; call (*s.o.*) names; **injurieux, -euse** [～'rjø, ～'rjø:z] insulting, abusive (towards, *pour*); † ✗✗ tortious.

injuste [ɛ̃'ʒyst] **1.** *adj.* unjust, unfair (to, *envers*); unrighteous (*person*); **2.** *su./m* wrong; **injustice** [ɛ̃ʒys'tis] *f* injustice, unfairness; **injustifiable** [～ti'fjabl] unwarrantable, unjustifiable.

inlassable [ɛ̃la'sabl] tireless; *fig.* untiring.

inné, e [in'ne] innate.

innocemment [inɔsa'mã] *adv.* of *innocent 1*; **innocence** [～'sã:s] *f* innocence; **innocent, e** [～'sã, ～'sã:t] **1.** *adj.* innocent; simple; artless; **2.** *su.* simple *or* artless person; **innocenter** [～sã'te] (1a) *v/t.* clear (*s.o.*) (of, *de*), prove (*s.o.*) innocent; justify. [ness.]

innocuité [innɔkɥi'te] *f* harmlessness.

innombrable [innɔ̃'brabl] innumerable, countless.

innovation [innɔva'sjɔ̃] *f* innovation; **innover** [～'ve] (1a) *vt/i.* innovate; *v/i.* introduce innovations (in, *en*); break new ground.

inoccupé, e [inɔky'pe] unoccupied; vacant; unemployed; idle (*person*).

in-octavo *typ.* [inɔkta'vo] *m*/*inv., a. adj./inv.* octavo.

insolence

inoculer [inɔky'le] (1a) v/t. 💉, a. fig. inoculate, infect (s.o. with s.th., qch. à q.).

inodore [inɔ'dɔ:r] odo(u)rless; 🌿 scentless.

inoffensif, -ve [inɔfã'sif, ~'si:v] inoffensive; harmless.

inondation [inõda'sjõ] f inundation; flood; fig. deluge; **inonder** [~'de] (1a) v/t. inundate; flood (a. ✝); fig. deluge (with, de); F soak.

inopérant, e 🜲 [inɔpe'rã, ~'rã:t] inoperative.

inopiné, e [inɔpi'ne] unforeseen, sudden.

inopportun, e [inɔpɔr'tœ̃, ~'tyn] inopportune; untimely; **inopportunément** [~tyne'mã] adv. of inopportun.

inorganisation [inɔrganiza'sjõ] f disorganization, lack of organization.

inoubliable [inubli'abl] unforgettable.

inouï, e [i'nwi] unheard of; extraordinary.

inoxydable [inɔksi'dabl] rust-proof; rustless; stainless (steel).

inqualifiable [ɛ̃kali'fjabl] beyond words; fig. indescribable; fig. scandalous.

in-quarto typ. [ɛ̃kwar'to] m/inv., a. adj./inv. quarto.

inquiet, -ète [ɛ̃'kjɛ, ~'kjɛt] restless; uneasy; anxious; **inquiétant, e** [ɛ̃kje'tã, ~'tã:t] alarming, disturbing; fig. disquieting; **inquiéter** [~'te] (1f) v/t. alarm, disturb; make (s.o.) uneasy; s'~ worry (about, de); **inquiétude** [~'tyd] f disquiet; uneasiness, anxiety; restlessness.

insaisissable [ɛ̃sɛzi'sabl] unseizable; elusive; imperceptible (difference, sound, etc.); 🜲 not attachable.

insalissable [ɛ̃sali'sabl] dirt-proof.

insalubre [ɛ̃sa'lybr] unhealthy; insanitary; **insalubrité** [~lybri'te] f unhealthiness; insanitary condition.

insanité [ɛ̃sani'te] f insanity; fig. nonsense.

insatiable [ɛ̃sa'sjabl] insatiable.

insciemment [ɛ̃sja'mã] adv. unconsciously.

inscription [ɛ̃skrip'sjõ] f inscription; registration, enrolment; univ. matriculation; ✝ scrip; ⚓ ~ maritime seaboard conscription; **inscrire** [~'kri:r] (4q) v/t. inscribe,

write down; register; enroll; s'~ register.

inscrutable [ɛ̃skry'tabl] inscrutable.

insecte [ɛ̃'sɛkt] m insect, Am. F bug; **insecticide** [ɛ̃sɛkti'sid] **1.** adj. insecticidal; poudre f ~ insect-powder; **2.** su./m insecticide; pesticide; **insectivore** zo. [~'vɔ:r] **1.** su./m insectivore; **2.** adj. insectivorous.

insécuriser [ɛ̃sekyri'ze] (1a) v/t. make (s.o.) feel unsure or uncertain, give (s.o.) a feeling of insecurity.

insensé, e [ɛ̃sã'se] **1.** adj. mad (a. fig.); fig. senseless; fig. crazy (idea, plan); **2.** su./m madman; su./f madwoman.

insensibilisation 💉 [ɛ̃sãsibiliza'sjõ] f an(a)esthetization; **insensibiliser** 💉 [~'ze] (1a) v/t. an(a)esthetize; **insensibilité** [~'te] f insensibility (a. fig.); insensitiveness; callousness, indifference; **insensible** [ɛ̃sã'sibl] insensible; insensitive; indifferent; imperceptible (difference).

inséparable [ɛ̃sepa'rabl] **1.** adj. inseparable; **2.** su. inseparable companion; su./m: orn. ~s pl. love-birds.

insérer [ɛ̃se're] (1f) v/t. insert; **insertion** [ɛ̃ser'sjõ] f insertion.

insidieux, -euse [ɛ̃si'djø, ~'djø:z] insidious (a. 💉 disease); crafty (person).

insigne[1] [ɛ̃'siɲ] distinguished (by, for par); signal (favour); pej. notorious; glaring.

insigne[2] [~] m ✖, sp., etc. badge; ~s pl. insignia; ~s pl. de la royauté royal insignia.

insignifiant, e [ɛ̃siɲi'fjã, ~'fjã:t] insignificant; trifling; trivial.

insinuer [ɛ̃si'nɥe] (1n) v/t. insinuate (a. fig.); 💉 insert (a probe etc.); s'~ insinuate o.s.; worm one's way (into, dans).

insipide [ɛ̃si'pid] insipid; tasteless (food); fig. dull, uninteresting; **insipidité** [~pidi'te] f food: tastelessness, lack of taste; fig. insipidity, dullness; tameness.

insistance [ɛ̃sis'tã:s] f insistence (on ger., à inf.); avec ~ insistently; **insister** [~'te] (1a) v/i. insist (on ger. à, pour inf.); ~ sur stress; persist in.

insociable [ɛ̃sɔ'sjabl] unsociable.

insolation [ɛ̃sɔla'sjõ] f 💉 sunstroke; sun-bathing; phot. daylight printing.

insolence [ɛ̃sɔ'lã:s] f insolence; im-

pertinence; impudence; **insolent, e**
[‿'lɑ̃, ‿'lɑ̃:t] insolent, impertinent;
overbearing.
insoler [ɛ̃sɔ'le] (1a) v/t. expose (s.th.)
to the sun; *phot.* print by daylight.
insolite [ɛ̃sɔ'lit] unusual; strange.
insoluble [ɛ̃sɔ'lybl] insoluble (a.
fig.).
insolvable † [ɛ̃sɔl'vabl] insolvent.
insomnie [ɛ̃sɔm'ni] f insomnia,
sleeplessness.
insondable [ɛ̃sɔ̃'dabl] unsoundable
(*sea*); *fig.* unfathomable.
insonorisé, e [ɛ̃sɔnɔri'ze] sound-
proof(ed); **insonoriser** [‿] (1a) v/t.
soundproof.
insouciance [ɛ̃su'sjɑ̃:s] f unconcern;
jauntiness; carelessness; **insouciant, e** [‿'sjɑ̃, ‿'sjɑ̃:t] unconcerned,
carefree, jaunty; thoughtless; **insoucieux, -euse** [‿'sjø, ‿'sjø:z]
carefree; unconcerned (about, de).
insoumis, e [ɛ̃su'mi, ‿'mi:z] 1. adj.
unsubdued; unruly, refractory; insubordinate; ✕ absent; 2. su./m ✕
absentee.
insoutenable [ɛ̃sut'nabl] untenable,
indefensible; unbearable (*pain*).
inspecter [ɛ̃spɛk'te] (1a) v/t. ✕ etc.
inspect; † examine (*accounts*); **inspecteur** [‿'tœ:r] m factory, mines,
police, school, sanitary, taxes: inspector; *works*: overseer; † examiner; shop-walker, *Am.* floorwalker; **inspection** [‿'sjɔ̃] f inspection; examination; inspectorate; ✕
muster parade.
inspiration [ɛ̃spira'sjɔ̃] f inspiration
(a. *fig.*); **inspirer** [‿'re] (1a) v/t.
inspire (s.o. with s.th., qch. à q.)
(a. *fig.*); *fig.* prompt (to inf., de
inf.).
instabilité [ɛ̃stabili'te] f instability
(a. *fig.*); **instable** [‿'tabl] unstable;
fig. unreliable.
installation [ɛ̃stala'sjɔ̃] f installation; setting (in); moving in, setting
up house *or* shop; putting in; ⊕
equipment; ⊕ plant; ⊕ ‿ d'aérage
ventilation plant; **installer** [‿'le]
(1a) v/t. install; put in *or* up; ⊕ etc. fit
up; fit out; furnish (a *house*); *fig.*
establish, settle; s'‿ settle down;
settle in; set up house *or* shop.
instamment [ɛ̃sta'mɑ̃] adv. ear-
nestly; urgently.
instance [ɛ̃s'tɑ̃:s] f admin., ✝ authority; ✝ (legal) proceedings pl.; ‿s

pl. entreaties; en ‿ de on the point of;
instant, e [‿'tɑ̃, ‿'tɑ̃:t] 1. adj. pressing; imminent; 2. su./m moment,
instant; à l'‿ just now; immediately;
instantané, e [‿tɑ̃ta'ne] 1. adj.
instantaneous; instant (*coffee etc.*); 2.
su./m phot. snapshot; **instantanéi-
té** [‿tɑ̃tanei'te] f instantaneousness.
instar [ɛ̃s'ta:r] m: à l'‿ de after the
manner of, like.
instauration [ɛ̃stɔra'sjɔ̃] f founding; establishment; **instaurer** [‿-
're] (1a) v/t. found; establish.
instigateur m, **-trice** f [ɛ̃stiga'tœ:r,
‿'tris] instigator (of, de); inciter (to,
de); **instigation** [‿'sjɔ̃] f instigation.
instiller ✝ [ɛ̃sti'le] (1a) v/t. instil (a.
fig.), drop (*liquid in the eye*).
instinct [ɛ̃s'tɛ̃] m instinct; d'‿, par ‿
instinctively; **instinctif, -ve** [‿tɛ̃k-
'tif, ‿'ti:v] instinctive.
instituer [ɛ̃sti'tɥe] (1n) v/t. institute;
establish; admin., a. ✝ appoint (an
heir etc.); **institut** [‿'ty] m institute;
eccl. order; eccl. rule; **instituteur,
-trice** [‿ty'tœ:r, ‿'tris] su. school-
teacher; **institution** [‿ty'sjɔ̃] f institution; **institutionnaliser** [‿tysjɔ-
nali'ze] (1a) v/t. institutionalize.
instructeur [ɛ̃stryk'tœ:r] 1. su./m
instructor (a. ✕), teacher; 2. adj./m:
✝ juge m ‿ examining magistrate;
instructif, -ve [‿'tif, ‿'ti:v] in-
structive; **instruction** [‿'sjɔ̃] f instruction; education; ✕ training (of
troops); ✝ preliminary investigation,
judicial inquiry; ‿s pl. instructions,
directions; ‿ civique civics sg.; ‿
publique state education; avoir de l'‿
be well educated; **instruire** [ɛ̃s-
'trɥi:r] (4h) v/t. inform; educate,
teach; ✕ train (*troops etc.*); ✕ drill
(*troops*); ✝ investigate; **instruit, e**
[ɛ̃s'trɥi, ‿'trɥit] educated, learned.
instrument [ɛ̃stry'mɑ̃] m instrument (a. ♪, a. ✝), tool (a. *fig.*); ✝
deed; **instrumenter** [‿mɑ̃'te] (1a)
v/t. ♪ score; v/i. ✝ draw up a document; ‿ contre order proceedings
to be taken against.
insu [ɛ̃'sy] m: à l'‿ de without the
knowledge of, unknown to.
insubmersible [ɛ̃sybmɛr'sibl] un-
sinkable.
insubordination [ɛ̃sybɔrdina'sjɔ̃] f
insubordination; **insubordonné, e**
[‿dɔ'ne] insubordinate.

insuccès [ɛ̃syk'sɛ] *m* failure.

insuffisance [ɛ̃syfi'zɑ̃:s] *f* insufficiency; *fig.* unsatisfactoriness; **insuffisant, e** [~'zɑ̃, ~'zɑ̃:t] insufficient; inadequate; *fig.* incompetent.

insuffler [ɛ̃sy'fle] (1a) *v/t.* inflate (*a balloon etc.*); ⚕ spray (*one's throat*); *fig.* inspire (s.o. with s.th., *qch. à q.*).

insulaire [ɛ̃sy'lɛ:r] **1.** *adj.* insular; **2.** *su.* islander.

insuline ⚕ [ɛ̃sy'lin] *f* insulin.

insulte [ɛ̃'sylt] *f* insult; **insulter** [ɛ̃syl'te] (1a) *v/t.* insult; *v/i.:* † ~ à abuse, revile; be an insult to.

insupportable [ɛ̃sypɔr'tabl] unbearable; insufferable (*person*); intolerable; F aggravating.

insurgé, e [ɛ̃syr'ʒe] *adj., a. su.* insurgent, rebel; **insurger** [~] (1l) *v/t.:* s'~ revolt, rebel (against, *contre*).

insurmontable [ɛ̃syrmɔ̃'tabl] insurmountable, insuperable.

insurrection [ɛ̃syrɛk'sjɔ̃] *f* insurrection, rebellion, rising.

intact, e [ɛ̃'takt] intact; undamaged; untouched; *fig.* unblemished (*reputation*).

intarissable [ɛ̃tari'sabl] inexhaustible; never-failing; long-winded (*talker*).

intégral, e, *m/pl.* **-aux** [ɛ̃te'gral, ~'gro] **1.** *adj.* integral (*a.* Å), full, complete; **2.** *su./f* Å integral; *music etc.*: complete works *pl.* or series; **3.** *su./m* crash helmet; **intégralement** [~gral'mɑ̃] fully, in full; **intégrant, e** [~grɑ̃, ~'grɑ̃:t] integral (*part etc.*); **intégration** [~gra'sjɔ̃] *f* integration; **intègre** [ɛ̃'tɛgr] upright, honest; incorruptible; **intégrer** [ɛ̃te'gre] (1f) *v/t.* integrate; **intégrité** [ɛ̃tegri'te] *f* integrity.

intellect [ɛ̃tɛl'lɛkt] *m* intellect; **intellectuel, -elle** [~lɛk'tɥɛl] *adj., a. su.* intellectual.

intelligence [ɛ̃tɛli'ʒɑ̃:s] *f* intelligence; understanding; d'~ avec in agreement *or* collusion with; en bonne (*mauvaise*) ~ on good (bad) terms; **intelligent, e** [~'ʒɑ̃, ~'ʒɑ̃:t] intelligent; clever; **intelligible** [~'ʒibl] intelligible; *fig.* distinct.

intempérance [ɛ̃tɑ̃pe'rɑ̃:s] *f* intemperance; **intempérant, e** [~'rɑ̃, ~'rɑ̃:t] intemperate; **intempérie** [~'ri] *f weather:* inclemency; ~s *pl.* bad weather *sg.*

intempestif, -ve [ɛ̃tɑ̃pɛs'tif, ~'ti:v] untimely, unseasonable.

intendance [ɛ̃tɑ̃'dɑ̃:s] *f* intendance; stewardship; ✕ Commissariat; *pol.* (*approx.*) domestic affairs *pl.*; **intendant** [~'dɑ̃] *m* intendant; steward; ✕ Commissariat officer; ⚓ paymaster; *school:* bursar.

intense [ɛ̃'tɑ̃:s] intense; severe (*cold, pain*); powerful; deep (*colour*); ⚡ strong (*current*); heavy (*flow*); high (*fever*); bitter (*cold*); **intensif, -ive** [ɛ̃tɑ̃'sif, ~'i:v] intensive; **intensifier** [ɛ̃tɑ̃si'fje] (1a) *v/t.* (*a.* s'~) intensify; **intensité** [ɛ̃tɑ̃si'te] *f* intensity; severity; strength; *light:* brilliance; *colour:* depth, richness; *cold:* bitterness; *wind:* force.

intenter ⚖ [ɛ̃tɑ̃'te] (1a) *v/t.* bring (*an action*); institute (*proceedings*).

intention [ɛ̃tɑ̃'sjɔ̃] *f* intention; aim, purpose; à ton ~ for you; **intentionné, e** [~sjɔ'ne] ...-disposed, ...-intentioned; bien ~ well-intentioned, well-meaning; **intentionnel, -elle** [~sjɔ'nɛl] intentional, wilful.

inter... [ɛ̃tɛr] inter...; **~agir** [~a'ʒi:r] (2a) *v/i.* interact; **~allié, e** *pol.* [~a'lje] interallied; **~calaire** [~ka-'lɛ:r] intercalated; intercalary (*day etc.*); **~caler** [~ka'le] (1a) *v/t.* intercalate; insert; ⚡ cut in; **~céder** [~se-'de] (1f) *v/t.* intercede (on s.o.'s behalf, *pour* q.; with s.o., *auprès de* q.); **~cepter** [~sɛp'te] (1a) *v/t.* intercept; ⊕ shut off (*steam*); **~ception** [~sɛp'sjɔ̃] *f* interception; ⊕ *steam:* shutting off; **~cesseur** [~sɛ'sœ:r] *m* intercessor; **~cession** [~sɛ'sjɔ̃] *f* intercession; **~changeable** [~ʃɑ̃'ʒabl] interchangeable; **~continental, e** *m/pl.* **-aux** [~kɔ̃tinɑ̃'tal, ~'to] intercontinental (*a.* ✕ *missile*); **~dépendance** [~depɑ̃'dɑ̃:s] *f* interdependence; **~diction** [~dik'sjɔ̃] *f* interdiction; **~dire** [~'di:r] (4p) *v/t.* prohibit, forbid; *fig.* bewilder, dumbfound; *eccl.* (lay under an) interdict; *admin.* suspend; **~disciplinaire** [~disipli'nɛ:r] interdisciplinary; **~dit, e** [~'di, ~'dit] **1.** *adj.* forbidden; bewildered, perplexed, taken aback; **2.** *su./m eccl.* interdict.

intéressé, e [ɛ̃tere'se] **1.** *adj.* interested; selfish; **2.** *su.* interested party; **interessement** † [~rɛs'mɑ̃] *m* (*workers'*) profit-sharing (scheme); **intéresser** [~rɛ'se] (1b) *v/t.* inter-

interêt

est; concern; s'~ take an interest (in, à); **intérêt** [~'rɛ] *m* interest (*a.* ✝); advantage; *par* ~ out of selfishness; ✝ *à* ~ *fixe* fixed-interest; *sans* ~ uninteresting; ✝ interest-free. **interférence** *phys., fig.* [ɛ̃tɛrfe'rɑ̃:s] *f* interference (*a. radio*).

interfolier [ɛ̃tɛrfɔ'lje] (1o) *v/t.* interleave (*a book*).

intérieur, e [ɛ̃te'rjœ:r] **1.** *adj.* interior, inner; inward; *geog., a.* ⚓ inland...; *admin., pol.* domestic, home...; **2.** *su./m* interior, inside; home; *sp.* inside; *d'*~ domestic; domesticated (*person*).

intérim [ɛ̃te'rim] *m/inv.* interim; *par* ~ *adj.* interim; *adv.* temporarily; **intérimaire** [~ri'mɛ:r] **1.** *adj.* temporary, acting; **2.** *su.* locum tenens; deputy; F temp.

inter...: ~**jection** [ɛ̃tɛrʒɛk'sjɔ̃] *f* interjection; ⚖ ~ *d'appel* lodging of an appeal; ~**jeter** [~ʒə'te] (1c) *v/t.* interject; ⚖ ~ *appel* appeal; ~**ligne** [~'liɲ] *su./m* space (between two lines); *su./f typ.* lead; ~**ligner** [~li'ɲe] (1a) *v/t.* interline; *typ.* lead out; ~**linéaire** [~line'ɛ:r] interlinear; ~**locuteur** *m*, -**trice** *f* [~lɔky'tœ:r, ~'tris] interlocutor; *conversation:* speaker; questioner; ~ *valable* pol. etc. valid representative; *fig.* worthy opponent; ~**lope** [~'lɔp] **1.** *adj.* ✝ illegal, dishonest; *fig.* shady, dubious; **2.** *su./m* smuggler; blockade-runner; ~**loquer** *fig.* [~lɔ'ke] (1m) *v/t.* disconcert, nonplus; ~**mède** [~'mɛd] *m* medium; *thea.* interlude; ~**médiaire** [~me'djɛ:r] **1.** *adj.* intermediate; ✝ middleman's ...; ⊕ *arbre m* ~ countershaft; **2.** *su./m* intermediary, go-between; medium; ✝ middleman; agent; *par l'*~ *de* through (the medium of).

interminable [ɛ̃tɛrmi'nabl] never-ending, interminable.

intermittence [ɛ̃tɛrmi'tɑ̃:s] *f* intermittence; *par* ~ intermittently; **intermittent, e** [~'tɑ̃, ~'tɑ̃:t] intermittent (*a.* 🩺 *fever*); 🩺 irregular (*pulse*); ⚡ make-and-break (*current*).

internat [ɛ̃tɛr'na] *m* living-in; boarding-school; 🩺 post of assistant house-physician *or* house-surgeon, *Am.* internship; *coll.* boarders *pl.*

international, e, *m/pl.* -**aux** [ɛ̃tɛrnasjɔ'nal, ~'no] **1.** *adj.* international; **2.** *su. sp.* international; *su./f* Inter-

national (Working Men's Association); *song:* Internationale.

interne [ɛ̃'tɛrn] **1.** *adj.* internal; inner; municipal (*law*); ⚕ interior (*angle*); inner; **2.** *su. school:* boarder; 🩺 resident medical student in a hospital; **internement** [ɛ̃tɛrnə'mɑ̃] *m admin.* internment; *lunatic:* confinement; **interner** [~'ne] (1a) *v/t. admin.* intern; shut up, confine (*a lunatic*).

inter...: ~**pellateur** *m*, -**trice** *f* [ɛ̃tɛrpɛla'tœ:r, ~'tris] interpellator; ~**pellation** [~pɛla'sjɔ̃] *f* peremptory question(ing); interruption; ⚖ challenge; *parl.* interpellation; ~**peller** [~pɛ'le] (1a) *v/t.* interpellate; ⚖ *etc.* challenge; ⚖ *etc.* call upon (*s.o.*) to answer; ~**phone** [~'fɔn] *m* intercom; ~**planétaire** [~plane'tɛ:r] interplanetary; ~**polateur** *m*, -**trice** *f* [~pɔla'tœ:r, ~'tris] interpolator; ~**polation** [~pɔla'sjɔ̃] *f* interpolation; ~**poler** [~pɔ'le] (1a) *v/t.* interpolate; ~**poser** [~pɔ'ze] (1a) *v/t.* interpose; ⚖ *personne f interposée* intermediary; third party fraudulently hold out as a principal; *par ... interposé* through ..., by ..., with the help of ...; s'~ interpose *or* place o.s. (between, *entre*); ~**position** [~pozi'sjɔ̃] *f* interposition; *fig.* intervention; ⚖ *de personnes* fraudulent holding out of a third party as principal; ~**prétation** [~preta'sjɔ̃] *f* interpreting; interpretation (*a. thea.*, ♪, *etc.*); explanation; ~**prète** [~'prɛt] *su.* interpreter; *fig.* exponent; ~**préter** [~pre'te] (1f) *v/t.* interpret; expound; read (*a signal*); *mal* ~ misconstrue; ~**professionnel, -elle** [~prɔfɛsjɔ'nɛl] (*salaries*) in comparable professions; ~**rogateur, -trice** [ɛ̃tɛrɔga'tœ:r, ~'tris] **1.** *adj.* interrogative; questioning; **2.** *su.* questioner; interrogator; *school:* examiner; ~**rogatif, -ive** *gramm.* [~rɔga'tif, ~'ti:v] *adj., a. su./m* interrogative; ~**rogation** [~rɔga'sjɔ̃] *f* interrogation; question; questioning; *point m d'*~ question-mark; ~**rogatoire** [~rɔga'twa:r] *m* ⚖ interrogatory, examination (*of an accused*); ⚖ questioning; ~**roger** [~rɔ'ʒe] (1l) *v/t.* interrogate, question; examine; *fig.* consult; ~**rompre** [~'rɔ̃:pr] (4a) *v/t.* interrupt; break (*a. journey, a.* ⚡); suspend, stop, cut short; ⊕ shut off (*steam*); ~**rupteur, -trice** [~ryp-

'tœːr, ~'tris] **1.** *adj.* interrupting; **2.** *su.* interrupter; *su./m* ⚡ switch, circuit breaker; **~ruption** [~ryp'sjɔ̃] *f* interruption; stopping; *communications*: severing; *work*: stopping; ⚡ *current*: breaking; ⊕ *steam*: shutting off; *sans* ~ without a break; **~section** [~sɛk'sjɔ̃] *f* Å *etc.* intersection; *track, road*: crossing; **~stellaire** [~ste'lɛːr] interstellar; **~stice** [ɛ̃tɛrs'tis] *m* interstice; chink; **~urbain, e** [ɛ̃tɛryr-'bɛ̃, ~'bɛn] interurban; *teleph.* trunk(-*call, -line, etc.*); **~valle** [~'val] *m* interval (*a.* ♪); space, gap; *time*: period; ⚡ clearance; *dans l'* ~ in the meantime; *par* ~s off and on, at intervals; **~venir** [~və'niːr] (2h) *v/i.* intervene, interfere; *fig.* occur, happen; **~vention** [~vɑ̃'sjɔ̃] *f* intervention (*a.* ⚕⚕); interference; ⚕ operation; ⚕ ~ *chirurgicale* surgical intervention; **~vertir** [~vɛr'tiːr] (2a) *v/t.* invert (*an order, a.* ♫); **~view** [~'vju] *f* interview(ing); **~viewer 1.** (1a) *v/t.* [~vju've] interview; *interviewé*(e) interviewee; **2.** *su./m* [~vju'vœːr] interviewer.

intestin, e [ɛ̃tɛs'tɛ̃, ~'tin] **1.** *adj.* internal; civil (*war*); **2.** *su./m* *anat.* intestine, bowel, gut; ~ *grêle* small intestine; *gros* ~ large intestine; **intestinal, e,** *m/pl.* **-aux** [~ti'nal, ~'no] intestinal.

intimation [ɛ̃tima'sjɔ̃] *f* intimation; *admin.* notice; ⚖ notice of appeal; **intime** [ɛ̃'tim] intimate, close, inner; private; **intimer** [ɛ̃ti'me] (1a) *v/t.* intimate; notify; ⚖ summons (*s.o.*) to appear before the Court of Appeal.

intimider [ɛ̃timi'de] (1a) *v/t.* intimidate; frighten; threaten; F bully.

intimité [ɛ̃timi'te] *f* intimacy; privacy; *fig.* depths *pl.*; *dans l'* ~ privately, in private life; in privacy.

intitulé [ɛ̃tity'le] *m* *book etc.*: title; *chapter*: heading; *deed*: premises *pl.*; **intituler** [~] (1a) *v/t.* entitle, call.

intolérable [ɛ̃tɔle'rabl] intolerable, unbearable; **intolérance** [~'rɑ̃ːs] *f* intolerance; **intolérant, e** [~'rɑ̃, ~'rɑ̃ːt] intolerant.

intonation [ɛ̃tɔna'sjɔ̃] *f* *speech*: intonation; *voice*: modulation, pitch.

intoxication ⚕ [ɛ̃tɔksika'sjɔ̃] *f* poisoning; ~ *alimentaire* food poi-

soning; **intoxiquer** ⚕ [~'ke] (1m) *v/t.* poison.

intraitable [ɛ̃trɛ'tabl] unmanageable; obstinate, inflexible; ⚕ beyond treatment.

intramusculaire [ɛ̃tramysky'lɛːr] **1.** *adj.* intramuscular; **2.** *su./f* intramuscular injection.

intransigeant, e [ɛ̃trɑ̃zi'ʒɑ̃, ~'ʒɑ̃ːt] **1.** *adj.* uncompromising; peremptory (*tone*); *pol.* intransigent; **2.** *su. pol.* die-hard.

intransitif, -ve *gramm.* [ɛ̃trɑ̃zi'tif, ~'tiːv] intransitive.

intraveineux, -euse ⚕ [ɛ̃travɛ'nø, ~'nøːz] **1.** *adj.* intravenous; **2.** *su./f* intravenous injection.

intrépide [ɛ̃tre'pid] intrepid, fearless; *pej.* brazen; **intrépidité** [~pidi'te] *f* intrepidity, fearlessness.

intrigant, e [ɛ̃tri'gɑ̃, ~'gɑ̃ːt] **1.** *adj.* scheming; **2.** *su.* intriguer, schemer; **intrigue** [ɛ̃'trig] *f* intrigue; machination; plot (*a.* *thea., novel, etc.*); love-affair; **intriguer** [ɛ̃tri'ge] (1m) *v/i.* plot, intrigue; *v/t.* puzzle, intrigue (*s.o.*).

intrinsèque [ɛ̃trɛ̃'sɛk] intrinsic; specific (*value*).

introducteur *m*, **-trice** *f* [ɛ̃trɔdyk-'tœːr, ~'tris] introducer; **introduction** [~dyk'sjɔ̃] *f* introduction; ushering in; ⊕ *steam*: admission; *book*: preface; **introduire** [~'dɥiːr] (4h) *v/t.* introduce; usher in, show in; ⊕ admit (*steam*); s' ~ get in, enter.

introniser [ɛ̃trɔni'ze] (1a) *v/t.* enthrone; *fig.* establish (*a fashion*); s' ~ establish o.s.; become established (*fashion*).

introuvable [ɛ̃tru'vabl] undiscoverable.

intrus, e [ɛ̃'try, ~'tryːz] **1.** *adj.* intruding; **2.** *su.* intruder; ⚖ trespasser; F *reception etc.*: gate-crasher; **intrusion** [ɛ̃try'zjɔ̃] *f* intrusion.

intuitif, -ve [ɛ̃tɥi'tif, ~'tiːv] intuitive; **intuition** [~'sjɔ̃] *f* intuition, insight.

inusable [iny'zabl] everlasting; proof against wear.

inusité, e [inyzi'te] unusual; not in use (*word*).

inutile [iny'til] useless; pointless; needless; unnecessary; superfluous; **inutilisable** [inytili'zabl] unserviceable, unemployable (*person*);

worthless; **inutilisé, e** [~'ze] unused; **inutilité** [~'te] *f* uselessness; futility; useless thing.

invaincu, e [ɛ̃vɛ̃'ky] unbeaten; unvanquished; unconquered.

invalide [ɛ̃va'lid] **1.** *adj.* invalid (*a.* ⚖), infirm; ⚔ disabled; rickety (*chair etc.*); **2.** *su.* invalid; *su./m* disabled soldier, pensioner; **invalider** [ɛ̃vali'de] (1a) *v/t.* ⚖ invalidate; quash (*elections*); *pol.* unseat (*a member of Parliament etc.*); **invalidité** [~di'te] *f* infirmity; disablement; ⚕ invalidism; ⚖ invalidity.

invariable [ɛ̃va'rjabl] invariable, unchanging.

invariance ⚗ [ɛ̃va'rjɑ̃:s] *f* invariance.

invasion [ɛ̃va'zjɔ̃] *f* invasion.

invective [ɛ̃vɛk'ti:v] *f* invective; ~s *pl.* abuse *sg.*; **invectiver** [~ti've] (1a) *v/t.* rail at, abuse (*s.o.*); *v/i.*: ~ *contre* rail at, revile, inveigh against.

invendable † [ɛ̃vɑ̃'dabl] unsaleable, unmerchantable.

inventaire [ɛ̃vɑ̃'tɛ:r] *m* inventory; † stock-list; *faire son* ~ take stock; **inventer** [~'te] (1a) *v/t.* invent; **inventeur, -trice** [~'tœ:r, ~'tris] **1.** *adj.* inventive; **2.** *su.* inventor; discoverer; ⚖ finder; **inventif, -ve** [~'tif, ~'ti:v] inventive; **invention** [~'sjɔ̃] *f* invention; imaginative capacity; **inventorier** † [~tɔ'rje] (1o) *v/t.* inventory, list; value (*bills etc.*); take stock of.

inverse [ɛ̃'vɛrs] *adj., su./m* opposite; inverse; reverse; **inverser** [ɛ̃vɛr'se] (1a) *vt/i.* reverse (*a.* ⚡); **inverseur** [~'sœ:r] *m* ⚡ reverser; ⊕ reversing device *or* handle; **inversible** [~'sibl] reversible; **inversion** [~'sjɔ̃] *f* ⚗, *gramm.* inversion; ⚡ *current*: reversal; **invertir** [~'ti:r] (2a) *v/t.* reverse (*a.* ⚡ *the current*); invert.

investigateur, -trice [ɛ̃vɛstiga'tœ:r, ~'tris] **1.** *adj.* investigating; searching (*a. glance*); **2.** *su.* investigator, inquirer; **investigation** [~'sjɔ̃] *f* investigation, inquiry.

investir [ɛ̃vɛs'ti:r] (2a) *v/t.* invest; ⚔ *a.* blockade; **investissement** [~tis'mɑ̃] *m* investment; **investisseur** [~ti'sœ:r] investor.

invétérer [ɛ̃vete're] (1f) *v/t.*: *s'*~ become inveterate, become deep-rooted.

invincible [ɛ̃vɛ̃'sibl] invincible; *fig.* insuperable (*difficulty*).

inviolable [ɛ̃vjɔ'labl] inviolable; burglar-proof (*lock*); immune (*diplomat, etc.*).

invisible [ɛ̃vi'zibl] invisible.

invitation [ɛ̃vita'sjɔ̃] *f* invitation; *sans* ~ uninvited(ly *adv.*); *sur l'*~ *de* at the invitation of; **invite** [ɛ̃'vit] *f* invitation, inducement; *cards*: lead; **invité** *m*, **e** *f* [ɛ̃vi'te] guest; **inviter** [~] (1a) *v/t.* invite (to *inf.*, *à inf.*); ask, request; *fig.* tempt; *cards*: call for.

invivable F [ɛ̃vi'vabl] unlivable-with, unbearable (*person*); impossible to live in (*building etc.*).

invocation [ɛ̃vɔka'sjɔ̃] *f* invocation.

involontaire [ɛ̃vɔlɔ̃'tɛ:r] involuntary.

invoquer [ɛ̃vɔ'ke] (1m) *v/t.* invoke; call upon; put forward (*an excuse, a reason, etc.*).

invraisemblable [ɛ̃vrɛsɑ̃'blabl] unlikely, improbable; **invraisemblance** [~'blɑ̃:s] *f* unlikelihood, improbability.

invulnérable [ɛ̃vylne'rabl] invulnerable.

iode ⚗, ⚕ [jɔd] *m* iodine; **ioder** [jɔ'de] iodize; **iodique** [~'dik] iodic.

ion ⚗, ⚡, *phys.* [jɔ̃] *m* ion.

ionique[1] △ [jɔ'nik] Ionic.

ionique[2] [jɔ'nik] *phys.* ionic; *radio*: thermionic (*tube, valve*); **ionisation** ⚗, *phys.* [~niza'sjɔ̃] *f* ionization.

iouler ♪ [ju'le] (1a) *v/i.* yodel.

irai [i're] *1st p. sg. fut. of aller 1.*

irascible [ira'sibl] irritable, testy; quick-tempered.

iris [i'ris] *m* ⚘, *anat., phot.* iris; *poet.* rainbow; ⚘ *a.* flag; **irisation** [iriza'sjɔ̃] *f* iridescence; **irisé, e** [~'ze] iridescent; **iriser** [~'ze] (1a) *v/t.* make iridescent.

irlandais, e [irlɑ̃'dɛ, ~'dɛ:z] **1.** *adj.* Irish; **2.** *su./m ling.* Irish; ♀ Irishman; *les* ♀ *pl.* the Irish; *su./f* ♀ Irishwoman.

ironie [irɔ'ni] *f* irony; **ironique** [~'nik] ironic(al); **ironiser** [~ni'ze] (1a) *v/i.* speak ironically.

irradiation [irradja'sjɔ̃] *f* ⚕, *phys.* irradiation; *phot.* halation; **irradier** [~'dje] (1o) *v/i.* radiate, spread (*pain, etc.*); *v/t.* irradiate.

irraisonnable [irrɛzɔ'nabl] irrational.

irréalisable [irreali'zabl] unrealizable (a. ✝); impracticable; **irréalité** [~'te] f unreality.

irrécusable [irreky'zabl] unimpeachable; unchallengeable.

irréductible [irredyk'tibl] ♣, ⚙ irreducible; fig. unshakable.

irréel, -elle [irre'ɛl] unreal.

irréfléchi, e [irrefle'ʃi] thoughtless; unthinking, rash (person).

irrégularité [irregylari'te] f irregularity; unevenness; **irrégulier, -ère** [~'lje, ~'ljɛːr] irregular; uneven; erratic.

irrémédiable [irreme'djabl] incurable; fig. irreparable; irremediable, past remedy.

irréparable [irrepa'rabl] irreparable; fig. irretrievable.

irrépréhensible [irrepreã'sibl] blameless.

irrépressible [irrepre'sibl] uncontrollable, irrepressible.

irréprochable [irreprɔ'ʃabl] irreproachable; ⚖ unimpeachable.

irrésistible [irrezis'tibl] irresistible.

irrésolu, e [irrezɔ'ly] irresolute; unsolved (problem); **irrésolution** [~ly'sjɔ̃] f indecision, irresolution.

irrespectueux, -euse [irrɛspɛk-'tɥø, ~'tɥøːz] disrespectful (to [-wards] pour, envers).

irresponsabilité [irrɛspɔ̃sabili'te] f irresponsibility; **irresponsable** [~'sabl] irresponsible.

irrétrécissable tex. [irretresi'sabl] unshrinkable; rendre ~ sanforize.

irréversible [irevɛr'sibl] irreversible.

irrévocable [irrevɔ'kabl] irrevocable; absolute (decree).

irrigateur [irriga'tœːr] m 🪝 hose (-pipe); water-cart; ⚕ wounds: irrigator; ⚕ douche, enema; **irrigation** [~ga'sjɔ̃] f 🪝, ⚕ irrigation; 🪝 flooding; ⚕ douching; **irriguer** [~'ge] (1m) v/t. 🪝, ⚕ irrigate; 🪝 water; ⚕ douche.

irritable [irri'tabl] irritable; touchy (person); sensitive (skin); **irritant, e** [~'tã, ~'tãːt] irritating; ⚕ irritant; **irriter** [~'te] (1a) v/t. irritate; ⚕ inflame; s'~ become angry (at, with s.o. contre q.; at s.th., de qch.); ⚕ become inflamed.

irruption [irryp'sjɔ̃] f irruption; invasion; inrush; river: overflow, flood; faire ~ burst or barge in (on s.o., chez q.).

isard zo. [i'zaːr] m izard, (Pyrenean) wild goat.

islamique [isla'mik] Islamic; **islamisme** [~'mism] m Islam(ism).

islandais, e [islɑ̃dɛ, ~'dɛːz] **1.** adj. Icelandic; **2.** su./m ling. Icelandic; su. ♀ Icelander.

isobare meteor. [izɔ'baːr] f isobar; **isocèle** ♣ [~'sɛl] isosceles; **isochrone** ⊕ [~'krɔn], **isochronique** ⊕ [~krɔ'nik] isochronous.

isolant, e [izɔ'lɑ̃, ~'lɑ̃ːt] **1.** adj. isolating; ⚡ insulating; bouteille f ~e vacuum or thermos flask; **2.** su./m insulator; insulating material; **isolateur** ⚡ [~la'tœːr] m insulator; **isolé, e** [~'le] isolated; lonely; lone; remote, out-of-the way; **isolement** [izɔl'mɑ̃] m ♣, ⊕, a. fig. isolation; ⚡ insulation; **isolément** [izɔle'mɑ̃] adv. separately; **isoler** [~'le] (1a) v/t. isolate (a. 🐟) (from d'avec, de); ⚡ insulate; **isoloir** [~'lwaːr] m polling booth.

isomère [izɔ'mɛːr] **1.** adj. 🐟, ♀ isomerous, isomeric; **2.** su./m 🐟 isomer.

isotope 🐟, phys. [izɔ'tɔp] m isotope.

israélien, -enne [israe'ljɛ̃, ~'ljɛn] adj., a. su. ♀ Israeli; **israélite** [~'lit] **1.** adj. Jewish, of the Israelites; **2.** su. ♀ Israelite, Jew.

issu, e [i'sy] **1.** adj.: ~ de descended from; born of; **2.** su./f issue, end; upshot, result; outlet; ⊕ ~es pl. by-products; à l'~e de at the end of; after; sans ~e blind (alley).

isthme geog., anat. [ism] m isthmus.

italien, -enne [ita'ljɛ̃, ~'ljɛn] **1.** adj. Italian; **2.** su./m ling. Italian; su. ♀ Italian; **italique** typ. [~'lik] adj., a. su./m italic.

item [i'tɛm] adv. item, also.

itératif, ve [itera'tif, ~'tiːv] gramm. iterative; ⚖ repeated.

itinéraire [itine'rɛːr] **1.** adj. road-..., direction-...; **2.** su./m itinerary; route; guide-book; **itinérant, e** [~'rɑ̃, ~'rɑ̃ːt] itinerant; ⚔ mobile.

ivoire [i'vwaːr] m ivory; **ivoirerie** [ivwarə'ri] f ivory work or trade.

ivraie ♀ [i'vrɛ] f cockle, darnel; bibl. tares pl.

ivre [i:vr] drunk (with, de); intoxicated; fig. mad (with, de); **ivresse** [i'vrɛs] f drunkenness, intoxication; *fig*. ecstasy; **ivrogne, -esse** [i'vrɔɲ, ivrɔ'ɲes] **1.** *adj*. addicted to drink; drunken; **2.** *su*. drunkard, toper, *sl*. boozer; **ivrognerie** [ivrɔɲ'ri] *f* (habitual) drunkenness.

J

J, j [ʒi] *m* J, j.
jabot [ʒa'bo] *m bird*: crop; *cost.
blouse, shirt*: frill; ruffle, jabot; **jaboter** F † [∼bɔ'te] (1a) *v/i.* jabber,
chatter.
jacasse [ʒa'kas] *f zo.* magpie; F †
chatterbox; **jacasser** [∼ka'se] (1a)
v/i. chatter, gossip; **jacasserie**
[∼kas'ri] *f* gossip.
jachère ✔ [ʒa'ʃɛːr] *f* fallow; **jachérer** ✔ [∼ʃe're] (1f) *v/t.* plough up
(*fallow land*); fallow (*land*).
jacinthe [ʒa'sɛ̃ːt] *f* ♀ hyacinth; *min.*
jacinth; ♀ ∼ des bois bluebell.
jack ⚡ [ʒak] *m* jack.
jacobin, e [ʒakɔ'bɛ̃, ∼'bin] *su. hist.*
Jacobin; *fig.* sympathizer with radical democracy.
Jacques [ʒɑ:k] *npr./m* James; *sl.* faire
le ♀ play the fool.
ja(c)quot *orn.* [ʒa'ko] *m parrot*:
Poll(y).
jactance [ʒak'tɑ̃ːs] *f* boast(ing); **jac-
ter** *sl.* [∼'te] (1a) *v/i.* boast; brag.
jade *min.* [ʒad] *m* jade.
jadis [ʒa'dis] *adv.* formerly, long ago;
de ∼ *a.* of old.
jaillir [ʒa'jiːr] (2a) *v/i.* gush, spurt
out; shoot or burst forth; fly (*sparks*);
flash (*light*); **jaillissement** [∼jis-
'mɑ̃] *m* gushing *etc.* [jet-black.⟩
jais *min.* [ʒɛ] *m* jet; *noir comme du* ∼⟩
jalon [ʒa'lɔ̃] *m* surveying staff;
(range-)pole; ✂ aiming-post; *fig.*
planter (or *poser*) *des* ∼s (or *les premiers* ∼s) pave the way *or* prepare the
ground *for de, pour*); **jalonner**
[∼lɔ'ne] (1a) *v/t.* stake out; *fig.* mark;
fig. be a landmark in (*a period*).
jalouser [ʒalu'ze] (1a) *v/t.* be jealous
of (*s.o.*); **jalousie** [∼'zi] *f* jealousy;
Venetian blind; screen; ♀ sweet-
william; ∼ *du métier* professional
jealousy; **jaloux, -ouse** [ʒa'lu,
∼'luːz] jealous; envious; *fig.* eager
(*for, de*).
jamais [ʒa'mɛ] *adv.* ever; never;
∼ *de la vie!* out of the question!;
∼ *plus* never again; *à* (or *pour*) ∼
for ever; *ne … ∼* never.

jambage [ʒɑ̃'baːʒ] *m* △ *door*: jamb;
door, window: post; *fireplace*:
cheek, jamb; foundation-wall; *writing*: down-stroke; **jambe** [ʒɑ̃:b] *f
leg*; *glass*: stem; △ *brickwork*: stone
pier; △ ∼ *de force* strut, prop; *mot.*
stay-rod; *à toutes* ∼s at top speed;
cela me fait une belle ∼! a fat lot
of good that does me; *sp.* jeu *m de*
∼s foot-work; *prendre ses* ∼s *à son
cou* take to one's heels; **jambé, e**
[ʒɑ̃'be] *adj.*: *bien* ∼ with shapely
legs; **jambette** [∼'bɛt] *f* small leg;
△ stanchion; **jambier, -ère**
[∼'bje, ∼'bjeːr] **1.** *adj. anat.* tibial;
2. *su./f* elastic stocking; legging;
sp. shinguard; **jambon** [∼'bɔ̃] *m*
ham; *œufs m/pl. au* ∼ ham and eggs;
jambonneau [∼bɔ'no] *m* knuckle
of ham; small ham.
jamboree [ʒɑ̃bɔ're] *m* jamboree.
jansénisme *eccl.* [ʒɑ̃se'nism] *m*
Jansenism.
jante [ʒɑ̃:t] *f wheel*: felloe; rim.
janvier [ʒɑ̃'vje] *m* January.
japon [ʒa'pɔ̃] *m* Japan porcelain;
japonais, e [∼pɔ'nɛ, ∼'nɛːz] **1.** *adj.*
Japanese; **2.** *su./m ling.* Japanese;
su. ♀ Japanese; *les* ♀ *m/pl.* the Japanese.
japper [ʒa'pe] (1a) *v/i.* yelp.
jaquette [ʒa'kɛt] *f* morning coat;
(*lady's*) jacket; *book etc.*: (dust)
cover.
jardin [ʒar'dɛ̃] *m* garden; ∼ *alpin*
rock-garden; ∼ *anglais* landscape
garden; ∼ *d'enfants* kindergarten;
thea. côté *m* ∼ prompt-side; **jardinage** [ʒardi'naːʒ] *m* gardening; *diamond*: flaw; ∼ *paysagiste* landscape
gardening; **jardiner** [∼'ne] (1a) *v/i.*
garden; **jardinet** [∼'nɛ] *m* small
garden; **jardinier, -ère** [∼'nje,
∼'njeːr] **1.** *adj.* garden…; **2.** *su.*
gardener; ∼ *paysagiste* landscape
gardener; *su./f* flower stand; win-
dow-box; spring cart; *orn.* ortolan;
∼ère *d'enfants* kindergarten teacher;
cuis. à la ∼ère garnished with
vegetables.

jargon [ʒarˈɡɔ̃] *m* jargon; slang; *fig.* gibberish; **jargonner** [~ɡɔˈne] (1a) *v/i.* talk jargon.

jarre [ʒaːr] *f* (earthenware) jar; ⚡ ~ électrique Leyden jar.

jarret [ʒaˈrɛ] *m anat. man:* back of the knee; *horse:* hock; *cuis. beef:* shin; *veal:* knuckle; ⊕ *pipe:* elbow; △ bulge; **jarretelle** [ʒarˈtɛl] *f* suspender, *Am. a.* garter; **jarretière** [~ˈtjɛːr] *f* garter.

jars *orn.* [ʒaːr] *m* gander.

jaser [ʒaˈze] (1a) *v/i.* chatter, talk; gossip; **jaseur, -euse** [~ˈzœːr, ~ˈzøːz] **1.** *adj.* talkative; **2.** *su.* chatterbox; gossip; tale-bearer.

jasmin ♀ [ʒazˈmɛ̃] *m* jasmine.

jaspe *min.* [ʒasp] *m* jasper; ~ sanguin bloodstone; **jaspé, e** [ʒasˈpe] marbled, veined.

jatte [ʒat] *f* bowl; *milk:* pan, basin; **jattée** [ʒaˈte] *f* bowlful; *milk:* panful.

jauge [ʒoːʒ] *f* ga(u)ge (*a.* ⊕); ga(u)ging-rod; *mot.* (~ *d'huile*) dipstick; (~ *d'essence*) petrol ga(u)ge, *Am.* gasoline ga(u)ge; ⚓ tonnage; ⊕); measure; *fig.* size up. **jauger** [ʒoˈʒe] (1l) *v/t.* ga(u)ge (*a.* ⊕); measure; *fig.* size up.

jaunâtre [ʒoˈnɑːtr] yellowish; sallow (*face*); **jaune** [ʒoːn] **1.** *adj.* yellow; **2.** *adv.*: *rire ~* give a sickly smile; **3.** *su./m* yellow; *egg.:* yolk; F blackleg, scab, *Am.* strike-braker; **jaunet, -ette** [ʒoˈnɛ, ~ˈnɛt] yellowish; **jaunir** [~ˈniːr] (2a) *vt/i.* yellow; **jaunisse** ♂ [~ˈnis] *f* jaundice.

Javel [ʒaˈvɛl] *m*: *eau f de* ~ liquid bleach (and disinfectant).

javeler [ʒavˈle] (1c) *v/t.* ✦ lay (*corn*) in swaths; *v/i.* turn yellow; **javelle** ✦ [ʒaˈvɛl] *f corn:* swath; bundle.

javelot [ʒavˈlo] *m* javelin.

jazz [dʒaːz] *m* jazz.

je [ʒə] *pron./pers.* I.

jeannette F [ʒaˈnɛt] *f* sleeve-board.

je-m'en-fichisme F [ʒəmɑ̃fiˈʃism], **je-m'en-foutisme** F [~fuˈtism] *m/inv.* couldn't-care-less attitude.

je(-)ne(-)sais(-)quoi [ʒənseˈkwa] *m/inv.* indefinable something.

jerrycan *mot.* [dʒɛriˈkan] *m* petrolcan.

jet [ʒɛ] *m* throw, cast(ing); jet (*a. gas, nozzle, etc.*); *liquid:* gush, spurt; *light:* flash; ⚓, ♒ jetsam; ♀ shoot, sprout; *metall.* casting; ✈ jet (aeroplane); ~ *de sable* sandblast; ✕ *armes*

f/pl. de ~ projectile *or* missile weapons; *du premier ~* at the first try; **jetable** [ʒəˈtabl] disposable, throwaway; **jetée** [ʒəˈte] *f* jetty; breakwater; **jeter** [~ˈte] (1c) *v/t.* throw, fling, hurl; throw away; ⚓ drop (*anchor*), jettison (*goods*); △ lay (*the foundations*); ✍ discharge; utter (*a cry, a threat*); give off (*sparks*); *se ~ river:* flow (into, *dans*); *se ~ sur* pounce on; *se ~ vers* rush towards; **jeton** [~ˈtɔ̃] *m* counter; token; *teleph.* ~ *de téléphone* telephone token.

jeu [ʒø] *m* game; play (*a.* ⊕); gambling; fun; *thea.* acting; *tools etc.:* set; *machine etc., a. fig.* working; ⊕ clearance; *fig.* action; *fig.* interaction; ♪ *organ:* stop; *cards:* pack, *Am.* deck; *thea.* ~*x pl. de scène* stage business *sg.*; ~ *de mots* pun, play on words; ~ *d'esprit* witticism; *cacher son* ~ hide one's cards; *être en* ~ be at stake; *entrer en* ~ come into play; *mettre en* ~ stake; *il a beau ~ de* (*or pour*) (*inf.*) it's easy for him to (*inf.*).

jeudi [ʒøˈdi] *m* Thursday; ~ *saint* Maundy Thursday.

jeun [ʒœ̃] *adv.*: *à* ~ on an empty stomach, fasting.

jeune [ʒœn] **1.** *adj.* young; youthful; younger, junior; *fig.* new; recent; unripe, early (*fruit*); ~ *fille* girl; ~ *homme* youth, lad; **2.** *su.* young person *or* animal; *su./m*: *les* ~*s pl.* the young *pl.*; youth (*coll.*) *sg.*

jeûne [ʒøːn] *m* fast(ing), abstinence; **jeûner** [ʒøˈne] (1a) *v/i.* fast (from, *de*).

jeunesse [ʒœˈnɛs] *f* youth; boyhood; girlhood; *fig.* youthfulness, freshness; F girl; ~ *scolaire* schoolchildren *pl.*; **jeunet, -ette** F [~ˈnɛ, ~ˈnɛt] very young.

jiu-jitsu [dʒydʒitˈsy] *m* ju-jutsu.

joaillerie [ʒɔajˈri] *f* jewellery; jeweller's business; **joaillier** *m*, **-ère** [ʒɔaˈje, ~ˈjɛːr] jeweller.

job F [ʒɔb] *m* job, employment.

jobard F [ʒɔˈbaːr] *m* dupe, F mug; **jobarder** [ʒɔbarˈde] (1a) *v/t.* fool, dupe; **jobarderie** F [~ˈdri] *f* gullibility.

jociste [ʒɔˈsist] *su.* member of the *Jeunesse ouvrière chrétienne.*

jocrisse [ʒɔˈkris] *m* fool; clown; F mug.

joie [ʒwa] *f* joy; delight; pleasure; ~

de vivre joy in life; *fille de* ~ prostitute.

joignis [ʒwaˈɲi] *1st p. sg. p.s. of* joindre; **joignons** [~ˈɲɔ̃] *1st p. pl. pres. of* joindre; **joindre** [ʒwɛ̃ːdr] (4m) *v/t.* join (*a.* ⊕); unite, combine; bring together; clasp (*one's hands*); ✝ attach (*to a letter*); adjoin (*a house etc.*); ✝ *etc.* pièces *f/pl. jointes* enclosures; *se* ~ *à* join (in); *v/i.* meet; **joins** [ʒwɛ̃] *1st p. sg. pres. of* joindre; **joint, e** [ʒwɛ̃, ʒwɛ̃ːt] 1. *p.p. of* joindre; 2. *su./m* △, ⊕, ♪, *anat., geol.* joint; join; *metall.* seam; ⊕ *piston*: packing; ⊕ ~ *à rotule* ball-and-socket joint; *mot.* ~ *de culasse* gasket; *sans* ~ seamless; F *trouver le* ~ find a way (to, *inf., pour inf.*; *of ger., de inf.*); **jointé, e** [ʒwɛ̃ˈte] jointed; pasterned (*horse*); **jointif, -ve** △ [~ˈtif, ~ˈtiːv] placed edge to edge; joined; **jointoyer** △ [~twaˈje] (1h) *v/t.* point; grout; **jointure** [~ˈtyːr] *f* ⊕, *anat.* joint; *fingers*: knuckle.

joli, e [ʒɔˈli] pretty; nice; **joliet, -ette** [~ˈljɛ, ~ˈljɛt] rather pretty; **joliment** [~liˈmɑ̃] *adv.* prettily; *fig.* well; F awfully; F pretty.

jonc ♀ [ʒɔ̃] *m* rush; Malacca cane; *droit comme un* ~ straight as a die; **jonchaie** ♀ [ʒɔ̃ˈʃɛ] *f* rush bed; caneplantation; **joncher** [~ˈʃe] (1a) *v/t.* strew (with, de); *fig.* litter; **jonchère** [~ˈʃɛːr] *f see* jonchaie.

jonction [ʒɔ̃kˈsjɔ̃] *f* junction (*a.* ⊕, *a.* 🚗); ✂ connector; joining, meeting; 🚉 joinder.

jongler [ʒɔ̃ˈgle] (1a) *v/i.* juggle (*a. fig.*); **jonglerie** [~gləˈri] *f* juggling; *fig.* trick(ery); **jongleur** [~ˈglœːr] *m* juggler; cheat, charlatan; ✝ jongleur.

jonque ⚓ [ʒɔ̃ːk] *f* junk.

jouable ♪, *thea., etc.* [ʒwabl] playable; **jouailler** F [ʒwaˈje] (1a) *v/i. cards*: play for love; ♪ *piano*: strum, *violin*: scrape.

joue [ʒu] *f* cheek; ~ *contre* ~ cheek by jowl; *mettre en* ~ take aim at.

jouer [ʒwe] (1p) *v/t.* play (*a.* ♪, *thea., a game, cards*); back (*a horse*); stake, bet (*money*); pretend to be; imitate (*s.o.*); look like (*wool*); F fool (*s.o.*); *se* ~ *de* take (*s.th.*) in one's stride; make light of; *v/i.* play; gamble (on the Stock Exchange), speculate; ⊕ work, run well (*ma-*

chine); ⊕ have too much play; ~ *à* play (*a play, cards, football, at soldiers, etc.*); ~ *de* ♪ play (*an instrument*); *fig.* use, make use of; *à qui de* ~? *cards*: whose turn is it?; *faire* ~ set in motion, release; **jouet** [ʒwɛ] *m* toy; plaything (*a. fig.*); **joueur, -euse** [ʒwœːr, ʒwøːz] 1. *su.* player; gambler; ✝ speculator, operator; ✝ ~ *à la hausse* (*à la baisse*) bull (bear); 2. *adj.* fond of playing *or* gambling.

joufflu, e [ʒuˈfly] chubby. [beam.\
joug [ʒu] *m* yoke (*a.* ⊕); *balance*:\
jouir [ʒwiːr] (2a) *v/i.* enjoy o.s.; ~ *de* enjoy (*s.th.*); **jouissance** [ʒwiˈsɑ̃ːs] *f* enjoyment; ✝ fruition, right to interest *etc.*

joujou, *pl.* -x F [ʒuˈʒu] *m* toy, plaything; *faire* ~ avec play with.

jour [ʒuːr] *m* day(light); daytime; light (*a. fig.*); dawn, daybreak; opening, gap; *sewing*: open-work; *fig.* aspect; ~ *de fête* holiday; ~ *de l'an* New Year's Day; ~ *ouvrable* working-day; *à* ~ *sewing*: openwork ...; ✝ posted, up to date; *au grand* ~ in broad daylight; *fig.* publicly; *au* ~ *le* ~ from day to day; *au point* (*or lever*) *du* ~ at daybreak; *de* ~ by day; *de nos* ~s nowadays; *donner le* ~ *à* give birth to; *du* ~ *au lendemain* overnight; at a moment's notice; ✕ *être de* ~ be on duty for the day; *l'autre* ~ the other day; *fig. mettre au* ~ reveal, disclose; *par* ~ per *or* a *or* each day; *cuis. plat m du* ~ today's special dish; *petit* ~ morning twilight; *sous un nouveau* ~ in a new light; *tous les* (*deux*) ~s every (other) day; *un* ~ one day (*in the past*), some day (*in the future*); *un* ~ *ou l'autre* sooner or later; *vivre au* ~ *le* ~ live from hand to mouth; *see* voir.

journal [ʒurˈnal] *m* record, diary; journal (*a.* ✝); ✝ day-book; ⚓, ⊕ log-book; newspaper; ~ *financier* (*officiel*) financial (official) gazette; ~ *parlé radio*: news(-bulletin), *Am.* newscast; *le* ~ *du jour* today's paper; **journalier, -ère** [ʒurnaˈlje, ~ˈljɛːr] 1. *adj.* daily; variable (*character*); 2. *su./m* day-labo(u)rer, journeyman; **journalisme** [~ˈlism] *m* journalism; **journaliste** [~ˈlist] *su.* journalist; reporter; ✝ journalizer.

journée [ʒurˈne] *f* day; daytime; day's work *or* journey; *à la* ~ by

the day; *femme f de* ~ charwoman,
F daily; **journellement** [~nɛl'mã]
adv. daily, every day.

joute [ʒut] *f* contest; † joust, tilt;
jouter [ʒu'te] (1a) *v/i.* fight; † joust,
tilt.

jovial, e, *m/pl.* -als, -aux [ʒɔ'vjal,
~'vjo] jolly, jovial; good-natured;
jovialité [~vjali'te] *f* joviality, jollity.

joyau [ʒwa'jo] *m* jewel (*a. fig.*).

joyeux, -euse [ʒwa'jø, ~'jøːz] merry,
joyful, cheerful.

jubé ⚠, *eccl.* [ʒy'be] *m* rood-screen,
rood-loft.

jubilaire [ʒybi'lɛːr] jubilee-...; **jubilation** F [~la'sjõ] *f* jubilation; **jubilé** [~'le] *m* jubilee; fiftieth anniversary; golden wedding; **jubiler** F
[~'le] (1a) *v/i.* be delighted, rejoice;
F gloat.

jucher [ʒy'ʃe] (1a) *vt/i.* perch (*bird,
a. fig. person*); roost; **juchoir** [~-
'ʃwaːr] *m* perch, hen-roost.

judaïque [ʒyda'ik] Judaic (*law*);
Jewish (*history*); **judaïser** [~i'ze]
(1a) *v/i.* Judaize; **judaïsme** [~'ism]
m Judaism.

Judas [ʒy'dɑ] *m* Judas (*a. fig.*); F
traitor; ♀ spy-hole, Judas(-hole) (*in
a door*).

judicature [ʒydika'tyːr] *f* judicature; judgeship; **judiciaire** [~'sjɛːr]
judicial, legal; *poursuites f/pl.*
~s legal proceedings; **judicieux,
-euse** [~'sjø, ~'sjøːz] judicious, sensible; discerning; *peu* ~ injudicious;
ill-advised.

judo *sp.* [ʒy'do] *m* judo.

juge [ʒy:ʒ] *m* judge (*a. fig.*); *sp.*
umpire; ~ *d'instruction* examining
magistrate; **jugement** [ʒyʒ'mã] *m*
judgment; ⚖ *case*: trial; sentence (*on
criminal*), civil *case*: award; *fig.*
opinion; *fig.* discrimination, good
sense; *eccl.* ~ *dernier* Last Judgment,
doomsday (*a. fig.*); ⚖ ~ *par défaut*
judgment by default; ⚖ *passer en* ~
stand trial; **jugeote** F [ʒy'ʒɔt] *f* common sense; **juger** [~'ʒe] (1l) *v/t.*
judge; ⚖ *a.* pass sentence on; ⚖ *try*
(*for, pour*); *fig.* think; ~ *à propos de*
think it proper to; *mal* ~ misjudge
(*s.o.*).

jugulaire [ʒygy'lɛːr] **1.** *adj.* jugular;
2. *su./f anat.* jugular (vein); *helmet
etc.*: chin strap; **juguler** [~'le] (1a)
v/t. † strangle; *fig.* nip (*s.th.*) in the

bud; *fig.* check, stop; *fig.* stifle, put
down; ⚕ jugulate.

juif, juive [ʒɥif, ʒɥiːv] **1.** *adj.* Jewish;
2. *su./m eccl.* (*practising*) Jew; ♀ Jew;
petit ~ funny bone; *su./f* ♀ Jewess.

juillet [ʒɥi'jɛ] *m* July.

juin [ʒɥɛ̃] *m* June.

juiverie [ʒɥi'vri] *f* Jewry; *coll. the
Jews pl.*

Jules [ʒyl] *m sl.* man, guy; F boy-
friend.

julienne [ʒy'ljɛn] *f cuis.* vegetable
soup; ♀ rocket.

jumeau, -elle, *m/pl.* -aux [ʒy'mo,
~'mɛl, ~'mo] **1.** *adj.* twin; **2.** *su.* twin;
su./f: ~*elles pl. opt.* binoculars;
opera-glasses; ⊕ cheeks; *lathe-bed*:
slide-bars; **jumelage** [ʒym'la:ʒ] *m*
twinning (*of towns*); **jumelé, e** [~'le]
twin; coupled.

jument [ʒy'mã] *f* mare.

jumping *sp.* [dʒœm'piŋ] *m* jumping.

jungle [ʒõ:gl] *f* jungle.

jupe [ʒyp] *f* skirt; **jupe-culotte,** *pl.*
jupes-culottes [~ky'lɔt] *f* culotte,
divided skirt; **jupon** [ʒy'põ] *m* petticoat; slip, *Am.* half-slip; *Sc.* kilt;
fig. women *pl.*; *courir le* ~ be a skirt-
chaser, run after women.

juré, e [ʒy're] **1.** *adj.* sworn; **2.** *su./m*
juror, juryman; ~s *pl.* jury; **jure-
ment** [ʒyr'mã] *m* swearing, oath;
jurer [ʒy're] (1a) *v/t.* swear; vow;
v/i. curse; *fig.* clash (*colours*); **jureur**
[~'rœːr] *m* swearer.

juridiction [ʒyridik'sjõ] *f* ⚖ jurisdiction; venue; *fig.* province; **juridique** [~'dik] judicial; legal.

jurisconsulte ⚖ [ʒyriskõ'sylt] *m*
jurist; legal expert; **jurisprudence**
⚖ [~pry'dã:s] *f* jurisprudence;
statute law; case-law; (*legal*) prece-
dents *pl.*

juriste ⚖ [ʒy'rist] *m* jurist; legal
writer.

juron [ʒy'rõ] *m* oath, swear-word.

jury [ʒy'ri] *m* ⚖ jury; *univ. etc.*
board of examiners; selection committee.

jus [ʒy] *m* juice; *cuis.* gravy; *sl.* coffee; ⚡ *sl.* juice (= *current*); *sl.*
petrol, *Am.* gas; *sl.* elegance; *cuis.
arroser de* ~ baste (*meat*); *mot. sl.
donner du* ~ step on the gas.

jusant ⚓ [ʒy'zã] *m* ebb(-tide).

jusqu'au-boutisme *pol. etc.* [ʒysko-
bu'tism] *m* extremism; **jusqu'au-
boutiste** *pol. etc.* [~'tist] *su.* whole-

hogger; die-hard; **jusque** [ʒysk(ə)] *prp.* (*usu. jusqu'à*) until, till; as far as (to), up *or* down to; *jusqu'à ce que* (*sbj.*) until; *jusqu'au bout* to the (bitter) end; *jusqu'ici* thus *or* so far.
juste [ʒyst] **1.** *adj.* just, legitimate, fair; proper, fit; accurate; exact (*word*); tight (*fit*); right (*time, watch, word*); ~-*milieu m* happy *or* golden mean; *au* ~ exactly; **2.** *adv.* rightly; just; precisely; ♩ true; scarcely; *à 10 heures* ~ at ten (o'clock) sharp; **juste-ment** [ʒystə'mɑ̃] rightly; just, precisely; **justesse** [~'tɛs] *f* exactness; accuracy; *de* ~ just, barely, by a hair's breadth; **justice** [~'tis] *f* justice; equity; legal proceedings *pl.*; *aller en* ~ go to law; *poursuivre en* ~ take legal action against; *se faire* ~ revenge o.s.; commit suicide; **justiciable** [~ti-

'sjabl] *adj.*: ~ *de* amenable to (*a. fig.*); open to (*criticism*); **justicier,** **-ère** [~ti'sje, ~'sjɛːr] *adj., a. su.* justiciary.
justificatif, -ve [ʒystifika'tif, ~'tiːv] **1.** *adj.* justificatory; *pièce f* ~*ve* = **2.** *su./m* supporting document; ✝ voucher; **justification** [~fika'sjɔ̃] *f* justification; **justifier** [~'fje] (1o) *v/t.* justify, vindicate; *se* ~ clear o.s.; *v/i.*: ~ *de* give proof of.
jute *tex.* [ʒyt] *m* jute.
juteux, -euse [ʒy'tø, ~'tøːz] **1.** *adj.* juicy; F *fig.* lucrative; **2.** *su./m* ✕ *sl.* company sergeant-major.
juvénile [ʒyve'nil] juvenile; youthful; **juvénilité** [~nili'te] *f* youthfulness.
juxtaposer [ʒykstapo'ze] (1a) *v/t.* juxtapose, place side by side.

K

K, k [ka] *m* K, k.
kakatoès *orn.* [kakatɔ'ɛs] *m* cockatoo.
kaki *tex.* [ka'ki] *su./m, a. adj./inv.*
khaki.
kangourou *zo.* [kãgu'ru] *m* kanga-
roo.
kaolin [kaɔ'lɛ̃] *m* china clay, kaolin.
karaté [kara'te] *m* karate.
képi [ke'pi] *m* peaked cap, kepi.
kermesse [~] *f* village fair; church
bazaar.
kérosène [kerɔ'zɛn] *m* paraffin(-oil),
Am. kerosene.
khâgne [kaɲ] *f see* cagne.
kibboutz [ki'buts] *m* kibbutz.
kidnapper [kidna'pe] (1a) *v/t.* kidnap; **kidnappeur** *m*, **-euse** *f*
[~'pœːr, ~'pøːz] kidnapper.
kif kif *sl.* [kif'kif] *adj./inv.* same; the
same thing, much of a muchness.
kiki *sl.* [ki'ki] *m* throat, neck.
kilo... [kilɔ] kilo...; **~cycle** ⚡ [~'sikl] *m*
kilocycle; **~(gramme)** [~('gram)] *m*
measure: kilogram(me); **~métrage**
[~me'traːʒ] *m* measuring *or* length
in kilometres, mileage; **~mètre**
[~'mɛtr] *m measure*: kilometre, *Am.*
kilometer; **~métrer** [~me'tre] (1f)

v/t. measure in kilometres; mark (*a
road*) with kilometre stones; **~watt**
⚡ [~'wat] *m* kilowatt; **~-heure** kilowatt-hour.
kimono *cost.* [kimɔ'no] *m* kimono;
manche *f* ~ Magyar sleeve.
kinésithérapeute [kinezitera'pøːt]
su. physiotherapist; **kinésithérapie** [~'pi] *f* physiotherapy.
kiosque [kjɔsk] *m* kiosk; *band*: stand;
flower, newspaper: stall; ⚓ house; ⚓
submarine: conning tower.
kirsch [kirʃ] *m* kirsch(wasser).
kitchenette [kitʃə'nɛt] *f* kitchenette.
klaxon *mot. etc.* [klak'sɔ̃] *m* horn,
hooter, klaxon; **klaxonner** [~sɔ'ne]
(1a) *v/i.* hoot, sound the horn; *v/t.*
hoot at.
kleptomane [klɛptɔ'man] *adj., a. su.*
kleptomaniac; **kleptomanie** [~ma-
'ni] *f* kleptomania.
knock-out *box.* [nɔ'kaut] **1.**
su./m/inv. knock-out; **2.** *adj./inv.*:
mettre q. ~ knock s.o. out.
krach ✝ [krak] *m* crash.
kyrielle F [ki'rjɛl] *f* rigmarole; long
list (of, de).
kyste 🎗 [kist] *m* cyst.

L

L, l [ɛl] *m* L, l.
la¹ [la] *see* le.
la² ♪ [~] *m*|*inv.* la, *note*: A; *donner le* ~ give the pitch.
là [la] *adv. place*: there; *time*: then; ~ *où* where; *ce livre-*~ that book; *c'est* ~ *que* that is where; *de* ~ hence; ~-**bas** [~ˈba] *adv.* over there.
labeur [laˈbœːr] *m* labo(u)r, toil; *typ.* bookwork.
labial, e *m*|*pl.* -**aux** [laˈbjal, ~ˈbjo] *adj., a. su.*|*f* labial (*a. gramm.*).
labile [laˈbil] ♀, ♫ labile; *fig.* unstable; *fig.* untrustworthy (*memory*).
laborantine [laborɑ̃ˈtin] *f* female laboratory assistant; **laboratoire** [~raˈtwaːr] *m* ♫ laboratory; *metall. furnace*: hearth; ~ *de langues* language laboratory; ~ *spatial* space lab; **laborieux, -euse** [~ˈrjø, ~ˈrjøːz] laborious, hardworking; working (*classes*).
labour [laˈbuːr] *m* ploughing, tillage; ~*s pl.* ploughed land *sg.*; *cheval m de* ~ plough-horse; **labourable** [labuˈrabl] arable; plough-...; **labourage** [~raˈʒ] *m* ploughing, tilling; **labourer** [~ˈre] (1a) *v/t.* plough, till; *fig.* furrow, gash, slash (into), dig into; *fig.* lacerate; **laboureur** [~ˈrœːr] *m* ploughman; farm-hand.
labyrinthe [labiˈrɛ̃ːt] *m* labyrinth (*a. anat.*); maze.
lac [lak] *m* lake; F *dans le* ~ in a fix, in the soup.
laçage [laˈsaːʒ] *m* lacing (up); **lacer** [~ˈse] (1k) *v/t.* lace (up); ♪ belay (*a rope*).
lacérer [laseˈre] (1f) lacerate; tear; slash.
lacet [laˈse] *m* (*shoe- etc.*) lace; *hunt.* noose, snare (*a. fig.*); *road*: hairpin bend; *en* ~*s* winding (*road*).
lâchage [lɑˈʃaːʒ] *m* release; F *friends*: dropping; **lâche** [lɑːʃ] 1. *adj.* loose, slack; lax (*discipline, style*); cowardly; 2. *su.*|*m* coward; **lâcher** [lɑˈʃe] (1a) *v/t.* release (*a. mot.*), loosen, slacken; let go of; *fig.* give up, *a. friend*: drop; let out (*a curse, an*

oath, a secret); ⊕ blow off (*steam*); *fig.* ~ *pied* give way; *v/i.* become loose; give way; snap (*rope etc.*); *sp.* F give up; **lâcheté** [lɑʃˈte] *f* cowardice; **lâcheur** *m*, -**euse** *f* F [lɑˈʃœːr, ~ˈʃøːz] fickle person; quitter.
lacis ✗, *anat., etc.* [laˈsi] *m* network.
laconique [lakoˈnik] laconic.
lacrymal, e *m*|*pl.* -**aux** [lakriˈmal, ~ˈmo] tear-...; **lacrymogène** [~ˈʒɛn] tear-exciting; *gaz m* ~ tear-gas.
lacs [lɑ] *m* noose, snare; *fig.* trap.
lacté, e [lakˈte] milky; milk-(*diet, fever*); *anat.* lacteal; *voie f* ~*e* Milky Way, Galaxy; **lactose** ♫ [~ˈtoːz] *f* lactose, milk-sugar.
lacune [laˈkyn] *f* gap, blank.
lacustre [laˈkystr] lacustrine (*a. zo.*); *cité f* ~ lake-dwelling.
lad *sp.* [lad] *m* stable-boy.
là-dessous [latˈsu] *adv.* underneath, under there; **là-dessus** [~ˈsy] *adv.* thereupon (*place, a. time*); on that.
ladite [laˈdit] *see* ledit.
ladre [lɑːdr] 1. *adj.* stingy, mean; 2. *su.*|*m* skinflint, miser; **ladrerie** [lɑdrəˈri] *f* stinginess, meanness.
lai, e [le] 1. *adj. eccl.* lay-...; 2. *su.*|*m eccl.* layman; lay; **laïc, -ïque** [laˈik] *adj., a. su. see* laïque; **laïcisation** [laisizaˈsjɔ̃] *f* secularisation; **laïciser** [~ˈze] (1a) *v/t.* secularize; **laïcité** [~ˈte] *f* secularity, undenominationalism.
laid, e [lɛ, lɛːd] ugly; plain (*face*); *Am.* homely; mean (*deed*); **laideron** F [lɛˈdrɔ̃] *mf* plain woman *or* girl; **laideur** [~ˈdœːr] *f* ugliness; *face*: plainness, *Am.* homeliness.
laie¹ [lɛ] *f* wild sow.
laie² [~] *f* ride; forest-path.
lainage [lɛˈnaːʒ] *m* fleece; woollen article; *tex.* teaseling; ✝ ~*s pl.* woollens, woollen goods; **laine** [lɛn] *f* wool; *carpet*: pile; ~ *artificielle* àrtificial wool; ~ *peignée* worsted; **lainer** *tex.* [lɛˈne] (1b) *v/t.* teasle, nap; **laineux, -euse** [~ˈnø, ~ˈnøːz] fleecy; woolly (*hair, sheep, a.* ♀); **lainier, -ère** [~ˈnje, ~ˈnjɛːr]

1. *adj.* wool(len); **2.** *su.* manufacturer of woollens.
laïque [la'ik] **1.** *adj.* secular; undenominational (*school*); **2.** *su./m* layman; ~s *pl.* laity; *su./f* laywoman.
laisse [lɛs] *f* leash, lead; *fig.* tenir q. en ~ keep s.o. in leading-strings.
laissé(e)-pour-compte, *pl.* **laissé(e)s-pour-compte 1.** *adj.* † returned; unsold; *a. fig.* rejected; **2.** *su.* † returned *or* unsold article; *a. fig.* reject.
laisser [lɛ'se] (1b) *v/t.* leave; let, allow, permit; abandon, quit; ~ là q. leave s.o. in the lurch; ~ là qch. give s.th. up; *v/i.:* ~ à désirer leave much to be desired; ~ à penser give food for thought; **~-aller** [lɛsea'le] *m/inv.* unconstraint; carelessness; **~-faire** *pol. etc.* [~'fɛːr] *m* inaction, non-interference; **laissez-passer** [~pɑ'se] *m/inv.* pass, permit.
lait [lɛ] *m* milk; ~ de chaux whitewash; ~ en poudre powdered milk; cochon m de ~ sucking-pig; **laitage** [lɛ'taːʒ] *m* dairy products *pl.*; **laitance** [~'tãːs] *f*, **laite** [lɛt] *f* milt; soft roe; **laité, e** [lɛ'te] soft-roed; **laiterie** [~'tri] *f* dairy; dairy-farming; **laiteux, -euse** [~'tø, ~'tøːz] milky; **&** lacteal, milk-...; **laitier, -ère** [~'tje, ~'tjɛːr] **1.** *adj.* milk-...; dairy-...; **2.** *su./m* milk-man; ⊕ slag; *su./f* milk-woman; milkmaid; dairymaid; milk-cart.
laiton [lɛ'tɔ̃] *m* (yellow) brass.
laitue ♀ [lɛ'ty] *f* lettuce; ~ pommée cabbage-lettuce.
laïus F [la'jys] *m* speech.
lama[1] [la'ma] *m* Buddhism: lama.
lama[2] *zo.* [~] *m* llama.
lambeau [lã'bo] *m* shred, bit, scrap; rag.
lambin, e F [lã'bɛ̃, ~'bin] **1.** *adj.* dawdling, slow; **2.** *su.* dawdler; **lambiner** F [~bi'ne] (1a) *v/i.* dawdle.
lambrequin [lãbrə'kɛ̃] *m* valance, pelmet.
lambris ⚠ [lã'bri] *m* wood: wainscoting, panelling; marble, stone: wall-lining; **lambrissage** ⚠ [lãbri'saːʒ] *m* wainscoting, panelling; room: lining; **lambrisser** ⚠ [~'se] (1a) *v/t.* wainscot, panel; line (*a room*); plaster (*attic walls*).
lame [lam] *f* metal: thin plate, strip; sword, razor, ♀ leaf, etc.: blade; ⚡ accumulator etc.: plate; ⚓ wave;

feather: vane; blind: slat; (*metallic*) foil; **lamelle** [la'mɛl] *f* lamella; scale, flake; metal: thin sheet; blind: slat; ~s *pl.* à parquet steel shavings; **lamelleux, -euse** [~mɛ'lø, ~'løːz] fissile, F flaky; lamellate(d) (*fungus etc.*).
lamentable [lamã'tabl] deplorable, lamentable; grievous (*error*); pitiful; full of woe (*voice*); **lamentation** [~ta'sjɔ̃] *f* lamentation; **lamenter** [~'te] (1a) *v/t.:* se ~ lament, deplore (s.th., de qch.).
lamette [la'mɛt] *f* metal: small plate; small blade.
laminer [lami'ne] (1a) *v/t.* ⊕ laminate, roll (*metal*); calender (*paper*); throttle (*steam*); *fig.* reduce, cut down, curtail; **laminoir** ⊕ [~'nwaːr] *m* rolling mill; *fig.* passer au ~ put (*s.o.*) *or* go through the mill.
lampadaire [lãpa'dɛːr] *m* street: street lamp *or* light; room: standard lamp, *Am.* floor lamp; lamp post.
lampe [lãːp] *f* lamp; radio: valve; telev. tube; ~ à arc arc-light; ~ amplificatrice radio: amplifying valve; ⊕ ~ à souder blowlamp, blowtorch; ~ de chevet bedside lamp; ⚒ ~ de mineur safety-lamp; ~ de poche flashlamp, electric torch; ~ témoin pilot-lamp; ~ triode three-electrode lamp.
lampée [lã'pe] *f* water etc.: draught, *Am.* draft; d'une seule ~ at one gulp; **lamper** [~] (1a) *v/t.* gulp down, F swig (*a drink*).
lampion [lã'pjɔ̃] *m* decorations: fairy-light; Chinese lantern; **lampiste** [~'pist] *m* lamp-maker; lamplighter; F underling.
lamproie icht. [lã'prwa] *f* lamprey.
lampyre zo. [lã'piːr] *m* fire-fly, glow-worm.
lance [lãːs] *f* spear; lance; waterhose: nozzle; railing: spike; ~ d'incendie fire hose; ⊕ ~ hydraulique monitor; *fig.* rompre une ~ (or des ~s) avec cross swords with (*s.o.*); **lancée** [lã'se] *f* momentum; continuer sur sa ~ keep up the momentum (*a. fig.*); keep up, be (still) going strong.
lance...: **~-eau** [lã'so] *m/inv.* water cannon; **~-flammes** ⚔ [lãs'flaːm] *m/inv.* flame-thrower; **~-grenades** ⚔ [~grə'nad] *m/inv.* grenade-thrower; **lancement** [~'mã] *m* throwing; *Am.* baseball: pitch; ⚓ launching (*a. rocket, a. fig.*); bomb:

releasing; *propeller*: swinging; ✝ floating; **lancer** [lɑ̃'se] **1.** (1k) *v/t.* throw, fling, hurl; *Am. baseball*: pitch (*a ball*); launch (⚓, ✝ *an article, a rocket, fig. an attack, a. fig. a person*); ⚓ fire (*a torpedo*); utter (*an oath*); emit (*smoke, steam*); set (*a dog on s.o.*); ⚡ switch on; *mot.* start; ⚡ swing (*the propeller*); ✝ float (*a company*); *fig.* crack (*a joke*); se ~ rush, dash, dart; *fig.* se ~ *dans* go or launch (out) into; **2.** *su./m sp.* throw; **lance-torpilles** ⚓ [lɑ̃stɔr'pi:j] *m/inv.* torpedo tube.

lancette ✻, ⚕ [lɑ̃'sɛt] *f* lancet.

lanceur *m*, **-euse** *f* [lɑ̃'sœːr, ~'søːz] thrower; *cricket*: bowler; *Am. sp. baseball*: pitcher; ✝ promoter, floater; *fig.* initiator; **lancier** ✗ [~'sje] *m* lancer.

lancinant, e [lɑ̃si'nɑ̃, ~'nɑ̃:t] shooting, throbbing (*pain*).

landau, *pl.* **-s** [lɑ̃'do] *m* pram, *Am.* baby carriage; landau.

lande [lɑ̃:d] *f* heath, moor.

langage [lɑ̃'ga:ʒ] *m* language; speech; ~ *chiffré* coded text.

lange [lɑ̃:ʒ] *m* baby's napkin; ~s *pl.* swaddling-clothes (*a. fig.*).

langoureux, -euse [lɑ̃gu'rø, ~'røːz] languid, languishing.

langouste *zo.* [lɑ̃'gust] *f* lobster; F crayfish.

langue [lɑ̃:g] *f* tongue; language; ~ *d'arrivée* target language; ~ *de départ* source language; ~ *maternelle* native language, mother tongue; ~ *verte* slang; *avoir la ~ bien pendue* have a glib tongue; *de ~ anglaise* English-speaking (*country*); *donner sa ~ aux chats* give up (*a riddle etc.*); *ne pas avoir sa ~ dans sa poche* have a quick or ready tongue; **languette** [lɑ̃'gɛt] *f metal, wood*: small tongue; strip; *shoe,* ⊕*joint, a.* ♪: tongue; ⊕*feather*; *balance*: pointer.

langueur [lɑ̃'gœːr] *f* languor; listlessness.

languir [lɑ̃'giːr] (2a) *v/i.* languish, pine; *thea.* drag; *fig.*, ✝ be dull; **languissant, e** [~gi'sɑ̃, ~'sɑ̃:t] languid, listless; languishing (*look etc.*); ✝ dull.

lanière [la'njɛːr] *f* thong, lash.

lansquenet [lɑ̃skə'nɛ] *m* lansquenet (*a. card game*).

lanterne [lɑ̃'tɛrn] *f* lantern; *opt.* ~ *à projections* slide projector; ~ *rouge*

rear light; *fig.* tail-ender; ~ *vénitienne* Chinese lantern; **lanterneau** [lɑ̃tɛr'no] *m* ⚠ staircase: skylight; 🚋 *Am.* monitor roof; **lanterner** F [~'ne] (1a) *v/i.* dawdle; *v/t.* put (*s.o.*) off; pester (*s.o.*); **lanternier** [~'nje] *m* lantern-maker; lamp-lighter.

lanugineux, -euse ♀ [lany3i'nø, ~'nøːz] downy.

lapalissade [lapali'sad] *f* truism, glimpse of the obvious.

laper [la'pe] (1a) *v/t.* lap.

lapereau [la'pro] *m* young rabbit.

lapidaire [lapi'dɛːr] *adj., a. su./m* lapidary; **lapidation** [~da'sjɔ̃] *f* stoning; **lapider** [~'de] (1a) *v/t.* stone to death; F throw stones at; *fig.* hurl (*abuse etc.*); **lapidifier** [~di'fje] (1o) *v/t.* petrify.

lapin, e [la'pɛ̃, ~'pin] *su./m* rabbit; F chap; ~ *de choux* (or *domestique*) tame rabbit; ~ *de garenne* wild rabbit; ~ *mâle* buck rabbit; ✝ *peau f de ~* cony; F *poser un ~ à q.* fail to turn up; *su./f* doe; **lapinière** [~pi'njɛːr] *f* rabbit-hutch; rabbit-warren.

lapis(-lazuli) [la'pis, ~pislazy'li] *m min.* lapis lazuli; *colour*: bright blue.

lapon, -onne [la'pɔ̃, ~'pɔn] **1.** *adj.* Lapp(ish); **2.** *su./m ling.* Lapp(ish); *su.* ♀ Laplander, Lapp.

laps [laps] *m*: ~ *de temps* lapse or space of time; **lapsus** [la'psys] *m pen, tongue*: slip; *memory*: lapse.

laque [lak] *su./f* lac; *paint.* lake; hair spray; *su./m* lacquer; **laquer** [la'ke] (1m) *v/t.* lacquer, japan.

laquelle [la'kɛl] *see lequel.*

larbin F [lar'bɛ̃] *m* flunkey.

larcin 🕎 [lar'sɛ̃] *m* larceny; pilfering.

lard [laːr] *m* bacon; back-fat; F *faire du ~* grow stout; **larder** [lar'de] (1a) *v/t. cuis.* (inter)lard (*a. fig.*); *fig.* assail (with, *de*); **lardoire** [~'dwaːr] *f cuis.* larding-pin; ⚠ *pile*: shoe; **lardon** [~'dɔ̃] *m cuis.* piece of larding bacon; *fig.* cutting remark, jibe; F kid, baby; **lardonner** [~dɔ'ne] (1a) *v/t. cuis.* cut (*bacon*) into strips; *fig.* taunt.

large [larʒ] **1.** *adj.* broad; wide; big, ample; loose-fitting (*suit etc.*); **2.** *adv.* broadly; **3.** *su./m* breadth, width; room, space; ⚓ open sea; offing; *au ~!* keep away!; **largesse** [lar'ʒɛs] *f* liberality; bounty, largesse; **largeur** [~'ʒœ:r] *f* breadth, width; △ *arch:* span; ~ *d'esprit* broadness of mind.

largue ⚓ [larg] slack (*rope*); free, large (*wind*); **larguer** [lar'ge] (1m) *v/t.* ⚓ let go *or* cast off (*a rope*); unfurl (*a sail*); ✈ release (*bombs*); drop (*a. fig.*); F *fig.* chuck up (*one's job etc.*), chuck (out) (*principles etc.*).

larme [larm] *f* tear; teardrop; *fig.* drop; *fig.* ~*s pl.* de crocodile crocodile tears; **larmier** [lar'mje] *m* △ dripstone; *anat. eye:* corner; **larmoyant, e** [larmwa'jã, ~'jã:t] weeping; tearful; *pej.* maudlin; **larmoyer** [~'je] (1h) *v/i. fig. pej.* weep.

larron [la'rɔ̃] *m* † thief; *s'entendre comme ~s en foire* be as thick as thieves.

larve *biol.* [larv] *f* larva, grub.

laryngite ✻ [larɛ̃'ʒit] *f* laryngitis; **laryngoscope** ✻ [~gɔs'kɔp] *m* laryngoscope; **laryngotomie** ✻ [~gɔtɔ'mi] *f* laryngotomy; **larynx** *anat.* [la'rɛ̃:ks] *m* larynx.

las, lasse [lɑ, lɑ:s] tired, weary.

lascar [las'ka:r] *m* lascar; F (smart) fellow.

lascif, -ve [la'sif, ~'si:v] lascivious, lewd; **lasciveté** [~siv'te] *f* lasciviousness, lewdness.

lasser [lɑ'se] (1a) *v/t.* tire; *fig.* exhaust; *se* ~ grow weary (of, *de*); **lassitude** [~si'tyd] *f* weariness, lassitude.

latent, e [la'tã, ~'tã:t] ✻, *phys., phot., etc.* latent; *fig.* concealed.

latéral, e, *m/pl.* **-aux** [late'ral, ~'ro] lateral; side-...

latin, e [la'tɛ̃, ~'tin] **1.** *adj.* Latin; ⚓ lateen (*sail*); *les nations f/pl.* ~*es* the Latin peoples; **2.** *su./m ling.* Latin.

latitude [lati'tyd] *f geog., fig.* latitude; *fig.* freedom; *geog. par 10° de* ~ *Sud* in latitude 10° South.

latrines [la'trin] *f/pl.* latrines.

latte [lat] *f* lath; *floor:* board; **latter** [la'te] (1a) *v/t.* lath; ⊕ lag; **lattis** [~'ti] *m* lathwork.

laudanum [loda'nɔm] *m* laudanum.

laudatif, -ve [loda'tif, ~'ti:v] laudatory.

lauréat, e [lɔre'a, ~'at] **1.** *adj.* laureate; **2.** *su.* laureate, prize-winner.

laurier ♀, *a. fig.* [lɔ'rje] *m* laurel; ~**rose** *pl.* ~**s-roses** ♀ [~rje'ro:z] *m* common oleander.

lavable [la'vabl] washable; ~ *en ma-*

chine machine-washable; **lavabo** [~va'bo] *m* wash-stand; lavatory; ⚔ baths *pl.*; **lavage** [~'va:ʒ] *m* washing; *pol.* ~ *de cerveau* brain-washing; *terre f de* ~ alluvium; *faire (subir) un* ~ *de cerveau à q.* brainwash s.o.

lavande ♀ [la'vã:d] *f* lavender.

lavandière [lavã'dje:r] *f* washerwoman; laundress; **lavasse** F [~'vas] *f* watery soup; slops *pl.*, dishwater, hog-wash.

lave *geol.* [la:v] *f* lava.

lave-glace, *pl.* **lave-glaces** [lav'glas] *m* windscreen (*Am.* windshield) washer; **lave-mains** [~'mɛ̃] *m/inv.* hand-basin; **lavement** [~'mã] *m eccl.* washing; ✻ enema; **laver** [la've] (1a) *v/t.* wash; scrub (⚔ ⊕); bathe (*a wound*); *fig.* clear; F ~ *la tête à* tell (*s.o.*) off, *Am.* call (*s.o.*) down; **laverie** [lav'ri] *f* launderette; **lavette** [~'vɛt] *f* dish-mop; dishcloth; **laveur, -euse** [~'vœ:r, ~'vø:z] *su. person:* washer; ⊕, ⚔ *gas:* scrubber; *su./m* ⊕ scrubber; *su./f* washing-machine; **lave-vaisselle** [lavvɛ'sɛl] *m/inv.* dish washer; **lavis** *paint.* [la'vi] *m* washing; wash-tint; wash-drawing; **lavoir** [~'vwa:r] *m* wash-house, ⚔ washing-plant; ~ *de cuisine* scullery; **lavure** [~'vy:r] *f* (*a.* ~ *de vaisselle*) dishwater.

laxatif, -ve ✻ [laksa'tif, ~'ti:v] *adj., a. su./m* laxative, aperient; **laxisme** [la'ksism] *m* laxity, laxness; **laxité** [laksi'te] *f* laxity.

layette [lɛ'jɛt] *f* packing-case; (*baby's*) layette, baby-linen.

lazaret ⚓ [laza're] *m* lazaret(to) (*a.* = *quarantine station*).

lazulite *min.* [lazy'lit] *f see* lapis (-*lazuli*).

le *m,* **la** *f,* **les** *pl.* [lə, la, le] **1.** *art./def.* the; **2.** *pron./pers.* him, her, it; *pl.* them.

lé [le] *m tex.* width, breadth; ⚓ tow-path.

leader *pol., journ., sp.* [li'dœ:r] *m* leader.

lèche [lɛʃ] *f* F *bread etc.:* thin slice; *sl. faire de la* ~ *à* suck up to; ~**cul** V [~'ky] *m/inv.* arse-crawler; ~**frite** [~'frit] *f* dripping-pan.

lécher [le'ʃe] (1f) *v/t.* lick; *fig.* over-polish, elaborate (*one's style*); **lécheur** *m,* **-euse** *f* [~'ʃœ:r, ~'ʃø:z] † gourmand; *pej.* toady; **lèche-vitrines** F [lɛʃvi'trin] *m/inv.* window-shopping; *faire du* ~ go window-shopping, window-shop.

leçon [lə'sɔ̃] *f* reading; *school, a. fig.*: lesson; *univ.* lecture; ~ *particulière* private lesson.

lecteur *m*, **-trice** [lɛk'tœːr, ~'tris] reader; *univ.* foreign assistant; *typ.* proof-reader; **lecture** [~'tyːr] *f* reading (*a. parl., a.* ⊕); reading matter; *avoir de la* ~ be well read; *faire la* ~ *à q.* read to s.o.

ledit *m*, **ladite** *f*, **lesdits** *m/pl.*, **lesdites** *f/pl.* [lə'di, la'dit, le'di, le'dit] *adj.* the aforesaid, the above-mentioned, the said ...

légal, e *m/pl.* **-aux** [le'gal, ~'go] legal; forensic (*medicine*); *monnaie f* ~e legal tender; **légaliser** [legali'ze] (1a) *v/t.* legalize; attest, certify (*a declaration, a signature*); **légalité** [~'te] *f* legality, lawfulness.

légat *hist., a. eccl.* [le'ga] *m* legate; **légataire** ⚖ [lega'tɛːr] *su.* legatee; heir; ~ *universel* residuary legatee; **légation** *eccl., pol.* [~'sjɔ̃] *f* legation.

légendaire [leʒɑ̃'dɛːr] 1. *adj.* legendary; F epic (*struggle, fight*); 2. *su./m* legendary; **légende** [~'ʒɑ̃ːd] *f* legend (*a. coins, illustrations, etc.*); *typ.* caption; *diagram, map, etc.*: key.

léger, -ère [le'ʒe, ~'ʒɛːr] light (*a. wine*); slight (*error, pain*); weak (*tea, coffee*); mild (*beer, tobacco*); *fig.* flighty (*conduct, woman*); *fig.* frivolous; free (*talk*); *à la légère* lightly; unthinkingly, too hastily; *prendre à la légère a.* make light of; **légèreté** [leʒɛr'te] *f* lightness *etc., see léger.*

légion [le'ʒjɔ̃] *f* ⚔ *etc.* legion; *fig.* host; ~ *d'Honneur* Legion of Hono(u)r; ⚔ ~ *étrangère* Foreign Legion; **légionnaire** [~ʒjɔ'nɛːr] *m hist.* legionary; ⚔ soldier of the Foreign Legion; member of the Legion of Hono(u)r.

législateur *m*, **-trice** *f* [leʒisla'tœːr, ~'tris] legislator; **législatif, -ve** [~'tif, ~'tiːv] legislative; **législation** [~'sjɔ̃] *f* legislation; law; **législature** [~'tyːr] *f* legislature; period of office of a legislative body; **légiste** [le'ʒist] 1. *su./m* legist, jurist; 2. *adj.*: *médecin m* ~ medical expert.

légitimation [leʒitima'sjɔ̃] *f child*: legitimation; official recognition;

légitime [~'tim] 1. *adj.* legitimate, lawful; *fig.* justifiable; sound (*inference*); ~ *défense f* self-defence; 2. *su./f* ⚖ child's portion; *sl.* wife; **légitimer** [~ti'me] (1a) *v/t.* legitimate; *fig.* justify; *admin. etc.* recognize; **légitimité** [~timi'te] *f* legitimacy; lawfulness.

legs [lɛ] *m* legacy; bequest; **léguer** [le'ge] (1s) *v/t.* bequeath (*a. fig.*), leave.

légume [le'gym] *m* vegetable; ⚘ pod; **légumier, -ère** [legy'mje, ~'mjɛːr] 1. *adj.* vegetable...; 2.*su./m* vegetable dish; **légumineux, -euse** ⚘ [~mi'nø, ~'nøːz] 1. *adj.* leguminous; 2. *su./f* leguminous plant.

lendemain [lɑ̃d'mɛ̃] *m* next day, day after; *fig.* morrow; *fig.* future; *fig.* consequences; *le* ~ *matin* the next morning; *fig. sans* ~ short-lived.

lénifier ⚕ [leni'fje] (1o) *v/t.* soothe, assuage, alleviate; **lénitif, -ve** ⚕ [~'tif, ~'tiːv] 1. *adj.* lenitive; soothing; 2. *su./m* lenitive.

lent, lente [lɑ̃, lɑ̃ːt] slow; slow-burning (*powder*).

lente [lɑ̃ːt] *f louse*: nit.

lenteur [lɑ̃'tœːr] *f* slowness; ~s *pl.* slowness *sg.*; dilatoriness *sg.*

lentille [lɑ̃'tiːj] *f* ⚘ lentil; *opt.* lens; ⊕, *clock pendulum*: bob, ball; ~s *pl. face*: freckles, spots; *opt.* ~s *pl. cornéennes* contact lenses.

léonin, e [leɔ'nɛ̃, ~'nin] leonine; *fig. part f* ~e lion's share; **léopard** *zo.* [~'paːr] *m* leopard.

lépidoptères [lepidɔp'tɛːr] *m/pl.* lepidoptera.

lèpre ⚕ [lɛpr] *f* leprosy (*a. fig.*); **lépreux, -euse** ⚕ [le'prø, ~'prøːz] 1. *adj.* leprous; 2. *su.* leper; **léproserie** ⚕ [~prɔz'ri] *f* leper-hospital.

lequel *m*, **laquelle** *f*, **lesquels** *m/pl.*, **lesquelles** *f/pl.* [lə'kɛl, la-'kɛl, le'kɛl] 1. *pron./rel.* who, whom, which; 2. *pron./interr.* which (one)?; 3. *adj.* which.

lérot *zo.* [le'ro] *m* garden dormouse, leriot.

les [le] *see le.*

lès [le] *prp.* near ... (*only in place names*).

lesbienne [lɛs'bjɛn] *f* lesbian.

lèse-majesté ⚖ [lɛzmaʒɛs'te] *f* high treason, lese-majesty; **léser** [le'ze] (1f) *v/t.* wrong (*s.o.*); injure (*a. fig. s.o.'s pride*); *fig.* damage.

lésine [le'zin] *f* stinginess; **lésiner** [~zi'ne] (1a) *v/i.* be stingy; ~ *sur* haggle over; **lésinerie** [~zin'ri] *f* stinginess.

lésion [le'zjɔ̃] *f* injury (*a.* 🏥); 🩹 lesion.

lessivage [lɛsi'va:ʒ] *m* washing; ⊕ *boiler*: cleaning; ⊕, ⚒ leaching; **lessive** [~'si:v] *f* wash(ing); ✝ washing powder; *faire la* ~ do the laundry; *jour m de* ~ washing-day; **lessivé, e** F [lesi've] washed out, all in; **lessiver** [~] (1a) *v/t.* wash, scrub (*the floor*); ⊕ clean (*a boiler*); ⊕, ⚒ leach; *sl.* clean (*s.o.*) out.

lest ⚓ [lɛst] *m* ballast.

leste [~] light, nimble, agile; *fig.* unscrupulous; *fig.* broad (*humour*).

lester [lɛs'te] (1a) *v/t.* ballast; weight (*a net*).

léthargie [letar'ʒi] *f* lethargy; **léthargique** [~'ʒik] lethargic.

letton, -onne [lɛ'tɔ̃, ~'tɔn] **1.** *adj.* Lettonian; *geog.* Latvian; **2.** *su./m ling.* Lettish; *su.* ♀ Lett.

lettre [lɛtr] *f* letter; ~*s pl.* literature *sg.*, letters; ⚖ ~*s pl. de procuration* letters of procuratory; ~*s pl. patentes* letters patent; ~ *chargée* (*or recommandée*) *post*: registered letter; *hist.* ~ *de cachet* order under the king's private seal; ✝ ~ *de change* bill of exchange; ~ *de commerce* business letter; *pol.* ~ *de créance* credentials *pl.*; ~ *de crédit* letter of credit; ~ *de faire-part* notice (*of wedding etc.*); ~ *de voiture* way-bill, consignment note; *à la* ~ literally; *en toutes* ~*s* in full; *homme m* (*femme m*) *de* ~*s* man (woman) of letters; *lever les* ~*s post*: collect the post; F *passer comme une* ~ *à la poste* go off smoothly; go through easily; **lettré, e** [lɛ'tre] well-read, literate.

leu [lø] *m*: *à la queue* ~ in single file.

leur [lœ:r] **1.** *adj./poss.* their; **2.** *pron./pers.* them; (to) them; **3.** *pron./poss.*: *le* (*la*) ~, *les* ~*s pl.* theirs, their own; **4.** *su./m* theirs, their own; *les* ~*s pl.* their (own) people.

leurre [lœ:r] *m fish, a. fig.*: bait; *fig.* illusion, deception; **leurrer** [lœ're] (1a) *v/t.* bait (*a fish*); decoy; allure; *fig.* deceive, delude, take in; *se* ~ delude o.s.

levage [lə'va:ʒ] *m* hoisting, raising; *dough*: rising; *appareil m de* ~ hoist.

levain [lə'vɛ̃] *m* yeast; leaven (*a.fig.*).

levant [lə'vɑ̃] *m* east; **levantin, e** [~vɑ̃'tɛ̃, ~'tin] *adj., a. su.* ♀ Levantine.

levé [lə've] *m ♩* up beat; *surv.* survey; **levée** [~'ve] *f thing, ⚔ siege*: raising; *thing, ban, embargo*: lifting; *meeting*: closing; ⚖ *court*: rising; ⚔ levy(ing); embankment, causeway; *post*: collection; ⚔ *camp*: striking; ⚓ *anchor*: weighing, *sea*: swell; *removal*; ⊕ *piston*: travel, cam, *valve*: lift, cam, cog; *cards*: trick; **lever** [~'ve] **1.** (1d) *v/t.* lift; raise (*a.* ⚔); adjourn, close (*a meeting*); levy (⚔, *a. taxes*); shrug (*one's shoulders*); *post*: collect; *post*: clear (*a letter-box*); ⚔ *etc.* strike (*a. camp*); ⚓ weigh (*anchor*); remove (*a bandage, a difficulty, a doubt*); *cards*: pick up (*a trick*); *se* ~ rise, stand up; clear (*weather*); *v/i.* ⚑ shoot; rise (*dough*); **2.** *su./m person, thing, sum*: rising; *thea. curtain*: rise; (*royal*) levee; *surv.* surveying; **lève-tard** [lɛv'ta:r] *su./inv.* late riser; **lève-tôt** [lɛv'to] *su./inv.* early riser.

levier [lə'vje] *m* lever; *mot.* ~ *du changement de vitesse* gear lever.

levraut [lə'vro] *m* leveret, young hare.

lèvre [lɛ:vr] *f* lip (*a.* ♀); *crater*: rim; *geol. fault*: wall; ~*s pl. wound*: lips; *se mordre les* ~*s d'avoir parlé* regret having spoken.

levrette [lə'vrɛt] *f* greyhound bitch; **lévrier** [le'vrje] *m* greyhound.

levure [lə'vy:r] *f* yeast; ~ *artificielle* baking-powder.

lexicographe [lɛksikɔ'graf] *m* lexicographer; **lexicographie** [~gra'fi] *f* lexicography.

lez [le] *see* **lès**. [*f* lexicography.]

lézard [le'za:r] *m zo.* lizard; *fig.* idler, lounger; *faire le* ~ bask in the sun; **lézarde** [~'zard] *f* chink, crevice, crack; **lézarder** [~zar'de] (1a) *v/t.* crack, split; *v/i.* F bask in the sun; F lounge.

liage [lja:ʒ] *m* binding, tying, fastening; **liaison** [ljɛ'zɔ̃] *f* † joining; connection (*a.* ✝); relationship; contact; dealings *pl.*; *fig.* link; ⚗ mortar, cement; ⚔, *gramm.* liaison (*a.* = *intimacy*); ♩ slur; **liant, liante** [ljɑ̃, ljɑ̃:t] **1.** *adj.* elastic; good-natured, sociable; **2.** *su./m* sociability; flexibility, springiness; ⚗ binding agent.

liarder † [ljar'de] (1a) *v/i.* pinch and scrape; count every halfpenny.

liasse [ljas] *f* bundle, packet; wad.

libation [liba'sjɔ̃] *f* libation; F *faire d'amples* ⁓s drink deeply.

libelle [li'bɛl] *m* lampoon; ᵼᵗ₂ libel; **libeller** [libɛl'le] (1a) *v/t.* draw up (*a cheque, a document*); make out (*a cheque*); **libelliste** [⁓'list] *m* lampoonist.

libellule *zo.* [libɛl'lyl] *f* dragon-fly, (devil's) darning-needle.

liber ⚘ [li'bɛːr] *m* bast, inner bark.

libéral, e, *m/pl.* **-aux** [libe'ral, ⁓'ro] **1.** *adj.* liberal; broad; generous; **2.** *su./m* liberal; **libéralisme** *pol.* [libera'lism] *m* liberalism; **libéralité** [⁓li'te] *f* liberality; *fig.* generosity; **libérateur, -trice** [⁓'tœːr, ⁓'tris] **1.** *adj.* liberating; **2.** *su.* liberator, deliverer; rescuer; **libération** [⁓'sjɔ̃] *f* liberation; ᵼᵗ₂ discharge (*a.* ✕), release; ✝ payment in full; **libérer** [libe're] (1f) *v/t.* liberate; set free; ᵼᵗ₂, ✕ discharge; ✕ exempt from military service; ✝ free (*s.o. of a debt*); se ⁓ de free o.s. from; ✝ liquidate (*a debt*); **libertaire** [libɛr'tɛːr] *su. a. adj.* libertarian; **liberté** [⁓'te] *f* liberty, freedom; ⊕ *piston:* clearance; ⁓ *de la presse* freedom of the press; ⁓ *religieuse* freedom of worship; *prendre des* ⁓s *avec* take liberties with; *prendre la* ⁓ *de* (*inf.*) take the liberty of (*ger.*); **libertin, e** [⁓'tɛ̃, ⁓'tin] **1.** *adj.* dissolute; licentious; **2.** *su.* libertine; **libertinage** [⁓ti'naːʒ] *m* dissolute behavio(u)r *or* ways *pl.*; licentiousness.

libidineux, -euse [libidi'nø, ⁓'nøːz] lewd, lustful; **libido** *psych.* [⁓'do] *f* libido.

libraire [li'brɛːr] *su.* bookseller; **⁓-éditeur,** *pl.* **⁓s-éditeurs** [⁓brɛredi'tœːr] *m* publisher; **librairie** [⁓brɛ'ri] *f* bookshop; book-trade; publishing house.

libre [libr] free; clear (*passage etc.*); independent (*school*); *temps m* ⁓ spare time; ⁓ *à vous de* (*inf.*) you are welcome *or* at liberty to (*inf.*); *teleph.* *pas* ⁓ line engaged, *Am.* line busy; **⁓-échange** [libre'ʃãːʒ] *m* free(-)trade; **⁓-échangiste** [⁓ʃã'ʒist] *m* free-trader; **⁓-service,** *pl.* **⁓s-services** [librəsɛr'vis] *m* self-service; self-service store *or* restaurant, *etc.*

librettiste *thea.* [librɛ'tist] *m* librettist; **libretto** *thea.* [⁓'to] *m* libretto.

lice [lis] *f* † lists *pl.*; *fig.* entrer en ⁓ contre enter the lists against, have a tilt at.

licence [li'sãːs] *f fig., a. admin.* licence; *univ.* degree of licentiate; *fig.* licentiousness; ⁓ *poétique* poetic licence; *prendre des* ⁓s *avec* take liberties with; **licencié** *m,* **e** *f* [lisã'sje] licentiate; *univ.* bachelor (*of arts etc.*); ✝ licensee; **licenciement** ✕ *etc.* [⁓si'mã] *m* disbanding; **licencier** [⁓'sje] (1o) *v/t.* disband; ⊕ lay off (*workmen*); **licencieux, -euse** [⁓'sjø, ⁓'sjøːz] licentious.

lichen ⚘ [li'kɛn] *m* lichen.

licher *sl.* [li'ʃe] (1a) *v/t.* lick; drink (up).

licite [li'sit] licit, lawful.

licol [li'kɔl] *m* halter.

licorne [li'kɔrn] *f* ⌀, *myth.* unicorn; *icht.* ⁓ *de mer* narwhal.

licou [li'ku] *m see* licol.

lie [li] *f* lees *pl.*; dregs *pl.* (*a. fig.*).

liège [ljɛːʒ] *m* ⚘ cork oak; cork; float; **liégeux, -euse** [lje'ʒø, ⁓'ʒøːz] cork-like.

lien [ljɛ̃] *m* tie (*a.* ⊕), bond, link; ⊕ *metal:* strap, band; ⁓s *pl.* chains; **lier** [lje] (1o) *v/t.* bind (*a.* ᵼᵗ₂), fasten, tie; connect, link (*ideas, questions, topics*); *cuis.* thicken (*a sauce*); ⁓ *connaisance avec* strike up an acquaintance with; se ⁓ *avec* make friends with.

lierre ⚘ [ljɛːr] *m* ivy.

liesse [ljɛs] *f* rejoicing, jollity.

lieu [ljø] *m* place; locality, spot; *fig.* grounds *pl.*, reason, cause; ✝ locus; site; ⁓x *pl.* premises; ⁓x *pl.* (*d'aisance*) privy *sg.*, toilet *sg.*; *gramm.* ⁓x *pl.* communs commonplaces; *au* ⁓ *de* instead of; *au* ⁓ *que* whereas; *avoir* ⁓ take place, occur; *donner* ⁓ *à* give rise to; *en haut* ⁓ in high places; *en premier* ⁓ in the first place, first of all; *il y a* (*tout*) ⁓ *de* (*inf.*) there is (every) reason for (*ger.*); *sur les* ⁓x on the premises; F on the spot.

lieue [ljø] *f measure:* league.

lieur, -euse [ljœːr, ljøːz] *su. person:* binder; *su./f* (*mechanical*) binder.

lieutenance [ljøt'nãːs] *f* lieutenancy; **lieutenant** [⁓'nã] *m* ✕ lieutenant; ⚓ ⁓ *de vaisseau* lieutenant; **⁓-colonel** ✕ lieutenant-colonel; ✈ wing-commander.

lièvre zo. [ljɛːvr] m hare.
liftier [lif'tje] m lift boy, Am. elevator operator.
ligament anat. [liga'mã] m ligament; **ligamenteux, -euse** [ˌmã-'tø, ˌ'tøːz] ligamentous; **ligature** [ˌ'tyːr] f binding, tying; ♪, typ. ligature; ⚓, ♪ splice; ♪ tie; **ligaturer** [ˌty're] (1a) v/t. bind; ♪ ligature; ♪ tie.
lignage [li'ɲaːʒ] m lineage; **lignard** ✕ F [ˌ'ɲaːr] m soldier of the line, infantryman; **ligne** [liɲ] f line, row; ✈ flight; geog. the equator; (∼ de pêche) fishing (Am. fish) line; ∼ aérienne ✈ overhead line; airline; à la ∼! new paragraph!, indent!; F elle a de la ∼ she has a good figure; sp. dernière ∼ droite home straight or stretch; 🚂 grande ∼ main line; hors ∼ incomparable; lire entre les ∼s read between the lines; pêcher à la ∼ angle; **lignée** [li'ɲe] f line(age); stock; descendants pl.
ligneux, -euse [li'ɲø, ˌ'ɲøːz] ligneous, woody; **lignifier** [ˌɲi'fje] (1o) v/t. a. se ∼ turn into wood; **lignite** min. [ˌ'ɲit] m lignite, brown coal.
ligoter [ligɔ'te] (1a) v/t. tie up.
ligue [lig] f league; **liguer** [li'ge] (1m) v/t. league; **ligueur** hist. [ˌ'gœːr] m leaguer.
lilas ♀ [li'la] su./m, a. adj./inv. lilac.
limace [li'mas] f zo. slug; ⊕ Archimedean screw; **limaçon** [ˌma'sɔ̃] m zo. snail; anat. cochlea; ∼ de mer periwinkle; escalier m en ∼ spiral staircase.
limaille ⊕ [li'maːj] f filings pl.
limande [li'mãːd] f icht. dab; ⊕ graving piece.
limbe [lɛːb] m astr. rim; ♓, ♀ limb; ♀ leaf: lamina; eccl. ∼s pl. limbo sg.; fig. dans les ∼s rather vague, in the air.
lime ⊕ [lim] f file; ∼ à ongles nailfile; ∼ d'émeri emery board; enlever à la ∼ file (s.th.) off; **limer** [li'me] (1a) v/t. file; fig. polish; **limeuse** ⊕ [ˌ'møːz] f filing-machine.
limier [li'mje] m zo. bloodhound; F sleuth.
limitatif, -ve [limita'tif, ˌ'tiːv] limiting, restrictive; **limitation** [ˌ'sjɔ̃] f limitation, restriction; ∼ des naissances birth-control; **limite** [li'mit] 1. su./f limit; boundary (a. sp.); ∼ d'élasticité elastic limit, tensile

strength; sans ∼ de durée a. open-end(ed); **limite** ∼ f border-line case; vitesse f ∼ maximum speed, speed limit; **limiter** [limi'te] (1a) v/t. limit; restrict; **limitrophe** [ˌ'trɔf] (de) adjacent (to); bordering (on); pays m ∼ borderland.
limoger [limɔ'ʒe] (1l) v/t. supersede (a general etc.); dismiss.
limon¹ [li'mɔ̃] m mud, slime, alluvium.
limon² [ˌ] m cart etc.: shaft; △ string-board.
limon³ ♀ [li'mɔ̃] m sour lime; **limonade** [limɔ'nad] f lemonade; **limonadier** m, **-ère** [ˌna'dje, ˌ'djɛːr] bar-keeper; dealer in soft drinks, Am. soda-fountain keeper.
limoneux, -euse [limɔ'nø, ˌ'nøːz] muddy (water); geol. alluvial; ♀ growing in mud; bog-...
limousine [limu'zin] f rough woollen coat or cloak; mot. † limousine; **limousiner** △ [ˌzi'ne] (1a) v/t. build in rubble work.
limpide [lɛ̃'pid] clear, transparent, limpid; **limpidité** [ˌpidi'te] f limpidity; clarity.
lin [lɛ̃] m ♀ flax; tex. linen; **linaire** ♀ [li'nɛːr] f linaria, F toad-flax; **linceul** [lɛ̃'sœl] m shroud.
linéaire [line'ɛːr] linear; ⊕ dessin m ∼ geometrical drawing; mesure f ∼ measure of length; **linéament** [ˌa'mã] m feature (a. fig.).
linette ♀ [li'net] f linseed.
linge [lɛ̃ːʒ] m linen, calico; ∼ de corps underwear; ∼ de table table linen; ∼ sale dirty linen (a. fig.); **linger** m, **-ère** [lɛ̃'ʒe, ˌ'ʒɛːr] su. linen-draper; su./f wardrobe keeper; seamstress; **lingerie** [lɛ̃ʒ'ri] f underwear; ✝ linen-drapery; ✝ linen-trade; linen-room.
lingot metall. [lɛ̃'go] m ingot; **lingotière** metall. [ˌgɔ'tjɛːr] f ingot-mo(u)ld.
lingual, e, m/pl. **-aux** [lɛ̃'gwal, ˌ'gwo] lingual; **linguiste** [ˌ'gɥist] su. linguist; **linguistique** [ˌgɥis-'tik] 1. adj. linguistic; 2. su./f linguistics sg.
linier, -ère [li'nje, ˌ'njɛːr] 1. adj. linen...; flax...; 2. su./f flax-field.
liniment ✚ [lini'mã] m liniment.
linoléum [linɔle'ɔm] m linoleum; oilcloth.
linon tex. [li'nɔ̃] m lawn; buckram.

linotte *orn.* [li'nɔt] *f* linnet; red poll; F *tête f de ~* feather-brain.

linteau ⚠ [lɛ̃'to] *m* lintel.

lion [ljɔ̃] *m* lion (*a.* F); F celebrity; *astr.* le ♀ Leo, the Lion; *fig.* part *f du ~* lion's share; **lionceau** [ljɔ̃-'so] *m* lion cub; **lionne** [ljɔn] *f* lioness.

lippe [lip] *f* thick lower lip; F *faire la ~* pout; **lippée** † [li'pe] *f* feast; **lippu, e** [~'py] thick-lipped.

liquéfaction ♎ *etc.* [likefak'sjɔ̃] *f* liquefaction; **liquéfier** ♎ *etc.* [~'fje] (1o) *v/t.* liquefy; reduce to the liquid state; *se ~* liquefy.

liquette F [li'kɛt] *f* shirt.

liqueur [li'kœːr] *f* liquor, drink; liqueur; ♎ solution, liquid.

liquidateur ⚖ [likida'tœːr] *m* liquidator; **liquidation** [~'sjɔ̃] *f* liquidation; ✝ *Stock Exchange:* settlement; ✝ clearance sale; ⚖ † *judiciaire* winding up.

liquide [li'kid] **1.** *adj.* liquid (*a. gramm., a.* ✝ *debt*); ready (*money*); *actif m ~* liquid assets *pl.*; **2.** *su./m* liquid; drink; *su./f gramm.* liquid consonant; **liquider** [~ki'de] (1a) *v/t.* liquidate (*a. fig.*); ✝ settle (*an account, a. fig. a question*); ✝ sell off (*goods*); *fig.* get rid of; *se ~ avec* clear off one's debt to.

liquoreux, -euse [likɔ'rø, ~'røːz] liqueur-like; sweet (*wine*); **liquoriste** [~'rist] *m* wine and spirit merchant.

lire¹ [liːr] (4t) *v/i.* read (*about, sur*); *v/t.* read; *cela se lit sur votre visage* it shows in your face; *je vous lis difficilement* I have difficulty with your handwriting.

lire² [~] *f Italian currency:* lira.

lis ♀ [lis] *m* lily; ⌸ *fleur f de ~* fleur-de-lis.

liséré [lize're] *m* border, edging; piping, binding; **lisérer** [~] (1d) *v/t.* border, edge; pipe.

liseron ♀ [liz'rɔ̃] *m* bindweed, convolvulus.

liseur, -euse [li'zœːr, ~'zøːz] *su.* great reader; *su./f* reading stand; *book:* dust jacket; reading-lamp; *cost.* bed jacket; **lisibilité** [~zibili'te] *f* legibility; **lisible** [~'zibl] legible; *fig.* readable (*book*).

lisière [li'zjɛːr] *f tex.* selvedge, list; *field, forest:* edge; *country, field:* border; *fig.* leading-strings *pl.*

lisons [li'zɔ̃] *1st p. pl. pres. of lire¹.*

lissage [li'saːʒ] *m* ⊕ polishing; *metal:* burnishing.

lisse¹ [lis] smooth, polished; glossy.

lisse² ⚓ [~] *f* rail; *hull:* ribband.

lisser [li'se] (1a) *v/t.* smooth, polish; burnish (*metal*); glaze (*paper*); *bird:* preen (*its feathers*); *se ~* become smooth; **lissoir** ⊕ [~'swaːr] *m* smoother; polishing-iron.

liste [list] *f* list; roll; register; ✗ roster; ⚖ *jury:* panel; *~ civile* civil list; *~ électorale* register of voters; *~ noire* blacklist; *mettre sur la ~ noire a.* blacklist.

listeau [lis'to] *m*, **listel** [~'tɛl] *m* ⚠ listel, fillet; *coin:* rim; ⚓ sheer rail.

lit [li] bed (*a.* ⚠, ⊕, *river, etc.*); *river:* bottom; *geol.* layer, stratum; *~ de camp* camp-bed; *hist. ~ de justice king's throne in old French parliament*; *~ de mort* death-bed; *~ d'enfant* cot; *~ de plume* feather bed; *fig.* comfortable job; ⚓ *~ du vent* wind's eye; *~ escamotable* folding-bed; *chambre f à deux ~s* twin-bedded room; *enfant mf du second ~* child of the second marriage; *faire ~ à part* sleep apart; *garder le ~* be confined to one's bed.

litanie [lita'ni] *f* F litany; *eccl. ~s pl.* litany *sg.*; F *la même ~* the old, old story; the same refrain.

liteau [li'to] *m* ⚠ batten, rail; *tex.* stripe.

literie [li'tri] *f* bedding.

litho... [litɔ] litho...; **~graphe** [~'graf] *m* lithographer; **~graphie** [~gra'fi] *f* lithography; lithograph.

litière [li'tjɛːr] *f* litter; *fig.* faire *~ de* trample underfoot.

litigant, e ⚖ [liti'gã, ~'gãːt] litigant; **litige** [~'tiːʒ] *m* dispute; ⚖ (law-) suit; *en ~* under dispute, at issue; **litigieux, -euse** [~ti'ʒjø, ~'ʒjøːz] litigious.

litre [litr] *m measure:* litre, *Am.* liter.

littéraire [lite'rɛːr] literary; **littéral, e**, *m/pl.* **-aux** [~'ral, ~'ro] literal (*a.* Ⓐ); ⚖ documentary (*evidence*); **littérateur** [~ra'tœːr] *m* man of letters; **littérature** [~ra-'tyːr] *f* literature; *~ professionnelle* technical literature.

littoral, e *m/pl.* **-aux** [litɔ'ral, ~'ro] **1.** *adj.* coastal, littoral; **2.** *su./m* coast-line; shore.

liturgie *eccl.* [lityr'ʒi] *f* liturgy;
liturgique *eccl.* [~'ʒik] liturgical.

liure [ljy:r] *f* cart-load etc.: lashing.

livide [li'vid] livid; ghastly; **lividité** [~vidi'te] *f* lividness; ghastliness.

livrable ✝ [li'vrabl] deliverable; ready for delivery; **livraison** [~vrɛ-'zɔ̃] *f* ✝ delivery; *book*: instalment; ✝ ~ à domicile home delivery.

livre[1] [li:vr] *m* book; ⚓ ~ de bord logbook; ~ de cuisine cookery book, *Am.* cookbook; ~ de raison register; record; *pol.* ~ jaune (approx.) blue book; à ~ ouvert at sight; tenir les ~s keep the accounts; ✝ tenue *f* des ~s book-keeping; *see* grand-livre.

livre[2] [~] *f money, weight*: pound.

livrée [li'vre] *f* livery; *coll.* servants *pl.*

livrer [~] (1a) *v/t.* deliver; give away (*a secret etc.*); ~ à give *or* hand over to, deliver up to; se ~ à give o.s. up to; confide in; indulge in; engage in; carry out; ✕ ~ bataille give battle.

livret [li'vrɛ] *m* booklet; ♪ libretto; (*bank*-)book; *school*: record-book; (*student's*) handbook.

livreur ✝ [li'vrœ:r] *m* delivery-man, delivery-boy; **livreuse** [li'vrø:z] *f* delivery-girl; delivery-van.

lobe [lɔb] *m* ♀, *anat.* lobe; ~ de l'oreille earlobe; **lobé, e** ♀ [lɔ'be] lobed, lobate; **lobule** ♀, *anat.* [~'byl] *m* lobule.

local, e, *m/pl.* **-aux** [lɔ'kal, ~'ko] **1.** *adj.* local; **2.** *su./m* premises *pl.*; site; room; **localiser** [lɔkali'ze] (1a) *v/t.* locate; localize; **localité** [~li'te] *f* locality, place; **locataire** [~'tɛ:r] *su.* tenant, occupier; ⚌ lessee; lodger; hirer; **locatif, -ve** [~'tif, ~'ti:v] rental; tenant's ...; réparations *f/pl.* ~ves repairs for which the tenant is liable; **location** [~'sjɔ̃] *f* hiring, letting, renting; tenancy; *thea. etc.* booking; ~ de livres lending-library; *bureau m* de ~ box-office; booking-office (*a.* 📞); **location-vente,** *pl.* **locations-ventes** [~sjɔ̃'vɑ̃:t] *f* hire-purchase system.

loch ⚓ [lɔk] *m* log.

lock-out ⊕ [lɔ'kaut] *m/inv.* lock-out.

locomobile [lɔkɔmɔ'bil] **1.** *adj.* travelling; locomotive; **2.** *su./f* transportable steam-engine, locomobile; **locomotif, -ve** [~'tif, ~-'ti:v] **1.** *adj.* ⊕, *a. physiol.* locomotive; transportable; **2.** *su./f* locomotive, engine; *fig.* pacemaker; *fig.* dynamic element; **locomotion** [~'sjɔ̃] *f* locomotion.

locuste *zo.* [lɔ'kyst] *f* locust.

locution [lɔky'sjɔ̃] *f* expression, phrase.

lof ⚓ [lɔf] *m* windward side; *sail*: luff; **lofer** ⚓ [lɔ'fe] (1a) *v/i.* luff.

loge [lɔ:ʒ] *f* hut; cabin; *freemason, gardener, porter*: lodge; *dog*: kennel; *thea.* box; *thea.* (*artist's*) dressing-room; ♀ cell, loculus; **logeable** [lɔ'ʒabl] fit for occupation (*house*); *mot.* comfortable; **logement** [lɔʒ-'mɑ̃] *m* lodging, housing; accommodation; ✕ billeting; ✕ quarters *pl.*; ⊕ bed, seating; ✝ container; **loger** [lɔ'ʒe] (1l) *v/t.* lodge, house; ✕ billet, quarter; put; ⊕ fix, fit, set; *v/i.* lodge, live; ✕ be quartered; ~ en garni live in lodgings; **logette** [~'ʒɛt] *f* small lodge; *thea.* small box; **logeur** [~'ʒœ:r] *m* landlord, lodging-house keeper; ✕ householder (*on whom a soldier is billeted*); **logeuse** [~'ʒø:z] *f* landlady.

logiciel [lɔʒi'sjɛl] *m computer*: software.

logicien *m,* **-enne** *f* [lɔʒi'sjɛ̃, ~'sjɛn] logician; **logique** [~'ʒik] **1.** *adj.* logical; **2.** *su./f* logic.

logis [lɔ'ʒi] *m* abode, home, dwelling; hostelry; *fig.* la folle du ~ imagination. [tics *sg.*)

logistique(s) [lɔʒis'tik] *f/(pl.)* logis-∫

loi [lwa] *f* law; rule; mettre hors la ~ outlaw; *parl.* projet *m* de ~ bill; se faire une ~ de (*inf.*) make a point of (*ger.*); **~-cadre,** *pl.* **~s-cadres** [~'kɑ:dr] *f* skeleton law.

loin [lwɛ̃] *adv.* far, distant (from, de); ~ de (*inf.*) far from (*ger.*); aller trop ~ overdo it, go too far; au ~ far away; bien ~ very far; far back (*in the past*); further on (*in the book etc.*); de ~ at a distance; from afar; de ~ en ~ at long intervals, now and then; **lointain, e** [~'tɛ̃, ~'tɛn] **1.** *adj.* far (off), distant, remote; **2.** *su./m* distance; dans le ~ in the distance.

loir *zo.* [lwa:r] *m* dormouse.

loisible [lwa'zibl] permissible; *il lui* est ~ de (*inf.*) he is at liberty to (*inf.*); **loisir** [~'zi:r] *m* leisure; spare time; ~s *pl.* leisure activities; à ~ at leisure, leisurely.

lombaire *anat.* [lɔ̃'bɛːr] lumbar; **lombes** [lɔ̃:b] *m/pl.* lumbar region *sg.*; loins.

londonien, -enne [lɔ̃dɔ'njɛ̃, ~'njɛn] **1.** *adj.* London...; **2.** *su.* ♀ Londoner.

long, longue [lɔ̃, lɔ̃:g] **1.** *adj.* long; thin (*sauce*); ~ *à croître* slow-growing; ✝ *à ~ terme* long-dated (*bill*); de *longue main* well in advance; *être ~ à* (*inf.*) be long in (*ger.*); **2.** *long adv.*: *fig.* en dire ~ speak volumes; *en savoir* ~ know a lot (about, *sur*); **3.** *su./m* length; de ~ *en large* to and fro; *deux pieds de* ~ two feet long; *le* (*or au*) ~ *de* (all) along; *tomber de tout son* ~ fall full length; *su./f gramm.* long syllable; *cards:* long suit; *à la longue* in the long run; at length.

longanimité [lɔ̃ganimi'te] *f* forbearance; long-suffering.

long-courrier ✈ [lɔ̃ku'rje] *m* long-distance plane.

longe [lɔ̃:ʒ] *f* tether; *whip:* thong; longe; *cuis. veal, venison:* loin.

longer [lɔ̃'ʒe] (1l) *v/t.* pass *or* go along; skirt (*the coast, a wall*); **longeron** [lɔ̃ʒ'rɔ̃] *m* △ stringer; longitudinal girder; ✈ *fuselage:* longeron, *wing:* spar.

longévité [lɔ̃ʒevi'te] *f* longevity, long life.

longitude *geog.* [lɔ̃ʒi'tyd] *f* longitude; **longitudinal, e,** *m/pl.* **-aux** [~tydi'nal, ~'no] longitudinal, lengthwise; ⚓ fore-and-aft.

longtemps [lɔ̃'tɑ̃] *adv.* long, a long time; *il y a* ~ long ago.

longueur [lɔ̃'gœːr] *f* length (*a. sp.*); *fig. film, novel, etc.:* tedious passage; *à ~ de* all (*day, year, etc.*) long, throughout the (*day, year, etc.*); for (*days, years, etc.*); *phys.* ~ *d'onde radio:* wavelength; *a. fig.* être sur la même ~ d'onde(s) be on the same wavelength.

longue-vue, *pl.* **longues-vues** [lɔ̃g-'vy] *f* telescope, field-glass.

looping ✈ [lu'piŋ] *m* loop(ing); *faire un* ~ loop (the loop).

lopin [lɔ'pɛ̃] *m ground:* patch, plot.

loquace [lɔ'kwas] talkative; garrulous; **loquacité** [~kwasi'te] *f* loquacity, talkativeness.

loque [lɔk] *f* rag.

loquet [lɔ'kɛ] *m* latch; *knife:* clasp; **loqueteau** [lɔk'to] *m* catch, small latch.

loqueteux, -euse [lɔk'tø, ~'tøːz]

1. *adj.* ragged, in tatters; **2.** *su.* tatterdemalion.

lorgner [lɔr'ɲe] (1a) *v/t.* ogle, leer at; *fig.* have one's eye on; stare at; **lorgnette** [~'ɲet] *f* opera-glasses *pl.*; **lorgnon** [~'ɲɔ̃] *m* eye-glasses *pl.*; pince-nez.

loriot *orn.* [lɔ'rjo] *m* oriole.

lorrain, e [lɔ'rɛ̃, ~'rɛn] **1.** *adj.* of *or* from Lorraine; **2.** *su.* ♀ Lorrainer.

lors [lɔːr] *adv.*: ~ *de* at the time of; ~ *même que* even when; *dès* ~ since that time; consequently; *pour* ~ so ...; **lorsque** [lɔrsk(ə)] *cj.* when.

losange ⧫ [lɔ'zɑ̃:ʒ] *m* rhomb(us); *en* ~ diamond-shaped.

lot [lo] *m* portion, share, lot (*a. fig.*); prize; *gros* ~ first prize, jackpot; **loterie** [lɔ'tri] *f* lottery (*a. fig.*); draw, raffle.

lotier ♀ [lɔ'tje] *m* lotus.

lotion [lɔ'sjɔ̃] *f* ⚕, ⊕ washing; ⚕ lotion; ~ *capillaire* hairwash; **lotionner** [~sjɔ'ne] (1a) *v/t.* wash, bathe; sponge.

lotir [lɔ'tiːr] (2a) *v/t.* parcel out (✝, *a. an estate*); divide up (into lots *or* plots); ~ *q. de qch.* allot s.th. to s.o.; **lotissement** [~tis'mɑ̃] *m* lot, plot; (*housing*) development; ✝ parcelling out; dividing into lots; *estate:* apportionment.

loto [lɔ'to] *m* lotto; lotto set.

louable [lwabl] laudable, praiseworthy (for, *de*).

louage [lwa:ʒ] *m* hiring out; hire; ✆ chartering; *de* ~ hired; ✆ charter...

louange [lwɑ̃:ʒ] *f* praise; **louanger** [lwɑ̃'ʒe] (1l) *v/t.* praise, extol; **louangeur, -euse** [~'ʒœːr, ~'ʒøːz] **1.** *adj.* adulatory; **2.** *su.* adulator, lauder. [ligan.\]

loubar(d) [lu'baːr] *m* young hoo-∫

louche¹ [luʃ] ✝ squinting; cross-eyed; *fig.* dubious, shady, F fishy, funny.

louche² [~] *f* (soup-)ladle; ⊕ reamer.

loucher [lu'ʃe] (1a) *v/i.* squint; **loucherie** [luʃ'ri] *f* squint.

louchet [lu'ʃɛ] *m* draining-spade.

louer¹ [lwe] (1p) *v/t.* rent, hire; book, reserve (*a place, seats*).

louer² [~] (1p) *v/t.* praise; commend (*s.o.* for s.th., *q. de qch.*); *se* ~ *de* be very pleased with (*s.o., s.th.*); congratulate o.s. on (*ger., de inf.*).

loueur¹ *m*, **-euse** *f* [lwœːr, lwøːz] hirer out.

loueur², **-euse** [~] 1. *adj.* flattering; 2. *su.* flatterer.
loufoque F [lu'fɔk] loony, daft, F dippy.
loulou *zo.* [lu'lu] *m* Pomeranian.
loup [lu] *m zo.* wolf; *fig.* (black velvet) mask; ✗ *gas-mask:* face-piece; ~ *de mer icht.* sea-perch; F old salt; *à pas de* ~ stealthily; *entre chien et* ~ in the twilight; *hurler avec les* ~*s* do in Rome as the Romans do; *jeune* ~ ambitious young manager; ~-**cervier**, *pl.* ~-**s-cerviers** [~sɛr'vje] *m zo.* lynx; *fig.* profiteer.
loupe [lup] *f* ✗ wen; ♀ excrescence; *opt.* lens, magnifying-glass.
loupé ⊕ [lu'pe] defective (*piece*);
louper F [~'pe] (1a) *v/t.* mess up; bungle, botch; miss (*one's train, an occasion, etc.*).
loup-garou, *pl.* **loups-garous** [luga'ru] *m myth.* werewolf; F *fig.* bear; F bogy.
lourd, lourde [lu:r, lurd] heavy; clumsy; *fig.* dull (*mind etc.*); sultry, close (*weather*); **lourdaud, e** [lur'do, ~'do:d] 1. *adj.* clumsy, awkward; dull-witted; 2. *su.* lout; clod; blockhead; **lourdeur** [~'dœ:r] *f* heaviness; clumsiness.
loustic F [lus'tik] *m* wag.
loutre [lutr] *f zo.* otter; ✝ sealskin.
louve *zo.* [lu:v] *f* she-wolf; **louveteau** [luv'to] *m* wolf-cub (*a. Boy Scouts*).
louvoyer [luvwa'je] (1h) *v/i.* ⚓ tack; *fig.* manœuvre; *fig.* hedge.
loyal, e, *m/pl.* **-aux** [lwa'jal, ~'jo] fair, straightforward, sincere; faithful; ⚖ true; **loyauté** [~jo'te] *f* fairness; honesty; loyalty (to, *en-vers*).
loyer [lwa'je] *m* rent; ✝ *money:* price.
lu, e [ly] *p.p. of* lire¹.
lubie [ly'bi] *f* whim, fad.
lubricité [lybrisi'te] *f* lubricity, lust; **lubrifiant, e** ⊕ [~'fjã, ~'fjã:t] 1. *adj.* lubricating; 2. *su./m* lubricant; **lubrification** [~fika'sjɔ̃] *f* lubrication; greasing; **lubrifier** [~'fje] (1o) *v/t.* lubricate; grease, oil; **lubrique** [ly'brik] lustful, lewd; wanton.
lucane [ly'kan] *m* lucanus; stag beetle.
lucarne [ly'karn] *f* dormer *or* attic window; gable-window.

lucide [ly'sid] lucid (*a.* ✱), clear;
lucidité [~sidi'te] *f* lucidity (*a.* ✱); ✱ sanity; clearness.
luciole *zo.* [ly'sjɔl] *f* firefly, glowworm.
lucratif, -ve [lykra'tif, ~'ti:v] lucrative; **lucre** [lykr] *m* lucre, profit.
ludique [ly'dik] play ...
luette *anat.* [lɥɛt] *f* uvula.
lueur [lɥœ:r] *f* gleam, glimmer (*a. fig.*); flash.
luge [ly:ʒ] *f* toboggan, sledge, *Am.* sled; **luger** [ly'ʒe] (1l) *v/i.* toboggan, sledge, *Am.* sled; **lugeur** *m*, **-euse** *f* [~'ʒœ:r, ~'ʒø:z] tobogganer.
lugubre [ly'gybr] dismal, gloomy; ominous.
lui¹ [lɥi] *p.p. of* luire.
lui² [~] *pron./pers. subject:* he; *object:* him, her, it; (to) him, (to) her, (to) it; *à* ~ to him, to her, to it; his, hers, its; *c'est* ~ it is he, F it's him; ~-**même** [~'mɛːm] *pron./rfl./m* himself, itself.
luire [lɥi:r] (4u) *v/i.* shine, gleam; *fig.* dawn (*hope*); **luisant, e** [lɥi'zɑ̃, ~'zɑ̃:t] 1. *adj.* shining; gleaming; glossy (*surface*); 2. *su./m* gloss, shine; **luisis** [~'zi] *1st p. sg. p.s. of* luire; **luisons** [~'zɔ̃] *1st p. pl. pres. of* luire.
lumière [ly'mjɛ:r] *f* light; ⊕ port; *fig.* (*a.* ~*s*) knowledge; *à la* ~ *de* by (*fig.* in) the light of; **lumignon** [lymi'ɲɔ̃] *m* candle-end; poor light; **luminaire** [~'nɛ:r] *m coll.* lighting; **luminescence** [~nɛ'sã:s] *f* luminescence; *éclairage m par* ~ fluorescent lighting; **luminescent, e** [~nɛ'sã, ~'sã:t] luminescent; **lumineux, -euse** [~'nø, ~'nø:z] luminous; *phys.* light (-*wave*); bright, brilliant (*a. fig. idea*); illuminated (*advertisement*); **luminosité** [~nozi'te] *f* luminosity; brightness; radiance.
lunaire [ly'nɛ:r] 1. *adj.* lunar; 2. *su./f* ♀ lunaria; **lunaison** *astr.* [~nɛ'zɔ̃] *f* lunation; **lunatique** [~na'tik] ✝ moonstruck; *fig.* capricious, whimsical.
lunch [lœ̃:ʃ] *m* lunch(eon); snack; **luncher** [lœ̃'ʃe] (1a) *v/i.* lunch; have a snack.
lundi [lœ̃'di] *m* Monday; F *faire le* ~ take Monday off.
lune [lyn] *f* moon; *poet.* month; ~ *de miel* honeymoon; *clair m de* ~ moonlight; *être dans la* ~ be in the clouds; *promettre la* ~ promise the moon and stars; **luné, e** [ly'ne]: *bien (mal)* ~

well- (ill-)disposed; in a good (bad) mood.

lunetier [lyn'tje] *m* spectacle-maker; optician; **lunette** [ly'nɛt] *f* telescope; ~s *pl.* spectacles, glasses; *mot. etc.* goggles; 🚋 cab-window; ⊕ die; ⊕ *lathe:* back-rest; ~s *pl. de soleil* sunglasses; **lunetterie** [lynɛ'tri] *f* spectacle-making; making of optical instruments.

lunule [ly'nyl] *f anat., a.* ♃ lunule, lunula; *finger-nail:* half-moon.

lupanar [lypa'na:r] *m* brothel.

lupin ♀ [ly'pɛ̃] *m* lupin.

lurette F [ly'rɛt] *f: il y a belle* ~ a long time ago.

luron [ly'rɔ̃] *m* (jolly) fellow; **luronne** [~'rɔn] *f* (lively) lass.

lus [ly] *1st p. sg. p.s. of* lire[1].

lustre[1] *poet.* [lystr] *m* lustre, period of five years.

lustre[2] [lystr] *m* lustre (*a. fig.*), gloss; chandelier; **lustrer** [lys'tre] (1a) *v/t.* glaze, gloss; F make shiny (*with wear*); **lustrine** *tex.* [~'trin] *f* (silk) lustrine; cotton lustre; *manches f/pl. de* ~ oversleeves.

lut ⊕ [lyt] *m* luting; **luter** ⊕ [ly'te] (1a) *v/t.* lute, seal with luting.

luth ♪ [lyt] *m* lute; **lutherie** [ly'tri] *f* stringed-instrument trade *or* industry.

luthérien, -enne *eccl.* [lyte'rjɛ̃, ~'rjɛn] *adj., a. su.* Lutheran.

luthier [ly'tje] *m* lute-maker; stringed-instrument maker *or* seller.

lutin, e [ly'tɛ̃, ~'tin] **1.** *adj.* mischievous, impish; **2.** *su./m* imp (*a. fig. child*), elf, goblin; **lutiner** [~ti'ne] (1a) *v/t.* tease; pester.

lutrin *eccl.* [ly'trɛ̃] *m* lectern; *coll.* succentors *pl.*

lutte [lyt] *f* fight; struggle; conflict; *sp.* wrestling; *sp.* ~ *à la corde* tug-of-war; *pol.* ~ *des classes* class war *or* struggle; **lutter** [ly'te] (1a) *v/i.* fight, struggle; *sp., a. fig.* wrestle; **lutteur** *m*, **-euse** *f* [~'tœ:r, ~'tø:z] wrestler; *fig.* fighter.

luxation ✝ [lyksa'sjɔ̃] *f* luxation, dislocation.

luxe [lyks] *m* luxury; wealth; *fig.* profusion; *de* ~ luxury, de luxe.

luxer ✝ [lyk'se] (1a) *v/t.* luxate, dislocate.

luxueux, -euse [lyk'sɥø, ~'sɥø:z] luxurious; sumptuous (*feast*).

luxure [lyk'sy:r] *f* lewdness, lechery; **luxuriant, e** [~sy'rjɑ̃, ~'rjɑ̃:t] luxuriant; **luxurieux, -euse** [~sy'rjø, ~'rjø:z] lecherous, lewd.

luzerne ♀ [ly'zɛrn] *f* lucern(e), *Am.* alfalfa; **luzernière** ✿ [~zɛr'njɛ:r] *f* lucern(e)-field.

lycée [li'se] *m* (state) grammar-school; **lycéen, -enne** [~se'ɛ̃, ~se-'ɛn] *su.* pupil at a *lycée; su./m* grammar-schoolboy; *su./f* grammar-schoolgirl.

lymphe ✝ [lɛ̃:f] *f* lymph.

lynchage [lɛ̃'ʃa:ʒ] *m* lynching; **lyncher** [~'ʃe] (1a) *v/t.* lynch.

lynx *zo.* [lɛ̃:ks] *m* lynx; *aux yeux de* ~ lynx-eyed.

lyre [li:r] *f* ♪ lyre; ⊕ quadrant; ⚓ *rowlock:* stirrup; *orn. oiseau-*~ lyrebird; **lyrique** [li'rik] **1.** *adj.* lyric (-al); **2.** *su./m* lyric poet; **lyrisme** [~'rism] *m* lyricism.

lys ♀ [lis] *m* lily.

M

M, m [ɛm] *m* M, m.

ma [ma] *see* mon.

maboul, e F [ma'bul] **1.** *adj.* cracked, dippy; **2.** *su.* loony.

macabre [ma'kɑːbr] gruesome; ghastly; *danse f ∼* dance of Death.

macadamiser [makadami'ze] (1a) *v/t.* macadamize (*a road*).

macaque *zo.* [ma'kak] *m* macaque.

macaron *cuis.* [maka'rɔ̃] *m* macaroon; **macaroni** [∼rɔ'ni] *m/inv. cuis.* macaroni; F dago (= *Italian*).

macédoine [mase'dwan] *f* (∼ *de fruits*) fruit salad; *fig.* miscellany, *pej.* hotchpotch; ∼ *de légumes* mixed (diced) vegetables *pl.*

macérer [mase're] (1f) *v/t.* soak, steep; *fig.* mortify (*the flesh*).

Mach *phys.* [mak] *npr.*: *nombre m de ∼* mach (number).

mâche [mɑːʃ] *f horses*: mash; ♀ corn-salad.

mâchefer ⊕ [maʃ'fɛːr] *m* clinker, slag; *lead*: dross.

mâcher [mɑ'ʃe] (1a) *v/t.* chew; munch; ∼ *à q. la besogne* half-do s.o.'s work for him; *ne pas ∼ ses mots* not to mince matters.

machin F [ma'ʃɛ̃] *m* thing, gadget; what's-his-name.

machinal, e, *m/pl.* -aux [maʃi'nal, ∼'no] mechanical, unconscious; **machinateur** [∼na'tœːr] *m* plotter, schemer; **machination** [∼na'sjɔ̃] *f* machination, plot; **machine** [ma-'ʃin] *f* machine; engine (a. 🚗); ⚡ dynamo; F thing, gadget; ∼*s pl.* machinery *sg.*; ∼ *à calculer* calculating machine, calculator; ∼ *à écrire* typewriter; ∼ *à photocopier* photocopier; ∼ *à sous* slot-machine; **machine-outil**, *pl.* **machines-outils** [∼ʃinu-'ti] *f* machine-tool; **machiner** [∼ʃi-'ne] (1a) *v/t.* scheme, plot; hatch; *machiné à l'avance* put-up (*affair*); **machinery** [∼ʃin'ri] *f* machinery; ⚓ engine-room; **machiniste** [∼ʃi-'nist] *m* bus driver; *thea.* scene shifter.

mâchoire [mɑ'ʃwaːr] *f* jaw (a. ⊕); ⊕

vice; ⊕ flange; *mot.* ∼*s pl.* (brake-)shoes; **mâchonner** [∼ʃɔ'ne] (1a) *v/t.* mumble; mutter; chew; *animal*; champ (*fodder*); **mâchure** [∼'ʃyːr] *f tex.* flaw; *fruit*, *flesh*: bruise; **mâchurer** [∼ʃy're] (1a) *v/t.* soil, stain; *typ.* smudge; chew, munch.

macis ♀, *cuis.* [ma'si] *m* mace.

maçon [ma'sɔ̃] *m* ⚒ mason; F freemason.

mâcon [mɑ'kɔ̃] *m* Mâcon (= *wine of Burgundy*).

maçonner [masɔ'ne] (1a) *v/t.* ⚒ build; face (*with stone*); wall up (*a door*, *a window*); **maçonnerie** [∼sɔn'ri] *f* ⚒ masonry; ⚒ stonework; F freemasonry; **maçonnique** [∼sɔ-'nik] masonic.

macro... [makrɔ] macro...; ∼**biotique** [∼bjɔ'tik] macrobiotic; ∼**biotisme** [∼bjɔ'tism] *m* macrobiotics *sg.*; ∼**céphale** *zo.*, ♀ [∼se'fal] macrocephalic, large-headed; ∼**cosme** [∼'kɔsm] *m* macrocosm.

macule [ma'kyl] *f* spot, blemish, stain; *astr.* sun-spot; **maculer** [∼-ky'le] (1a) *v/t.* maculate; stain; *typ.* mackle; *v/i. a.* se ∼ mackle, blur.

madame, *pl.* **mesdames** [ma'dam, me'dam] *f* Mrs.; madam; F lady.

madeleine [mad'lɛn] *f* ♀ (*sort of*) pear; *cuis.* sponge-cake.

mademoiselle, *pl.* **mesdemoiselles** [madmwa'zɛl, medmwa'zɛl] *f* Miss; young lady.

madère [ma'dɛːr] *m* Madeira (wine).

Madone [ma'dɔn] *f* Madonna.

madras ✝, *tex.* [ma'drɑːs] *m* Madras (handkerchief).

madré, e [ma'dre] **1.** *adj.* mottled; spotted; *fig.* sly, wily; **2.** *su. fig.* sly fox.

madrier ⚒ [madri'e] *m* timber; plank.

madrilène [madri'lɛn] **1.** Madrilenian; of Madrid; **2.** *su.* ♀ inhabitant of Madrid.

maestria [maestri'ja] *f* skill.

mafflu, e F [ma'fly] heavy-jowled.

magasin [maga'zɛ̃] *m* shop, *Am.*

store; warehouse, store; *camera,*
rifle: magazine; ⚔ armo(u)ry; ~ *à*
succursales multiples chain stores *pl.*;
† *grand* ~ department store; † *en* ~
in stock; **magasinage** [~ziˈnaːʒ]
m warehousing, storing; storage
(charges *pl.*); **magasinier** [~ziˈnje]
m warehouseman, store-keeper.

magazine [magaˈzin] *m* (illustrated)
magazine.

mage [maːʒ] **1.** *su./m* magus; seer;
2. *adj.: bibl. les Rois m/pl.* ~s the
Three Wise Men, the (Three)
Magi; **magicien** *m*, **-enne** *f* [maʒi-
ˈsjɛ̃, ~ˈsjɛn] magician; wizard;
magie [~ˈʒi] *f* magic (*a. fig.*);
magique [~ˈʒik] magic(al) (*a. fig.*).

magistral, e, *m/pl.* **-aux** [maʒisˈtral,
~ˈtro] magisterial; *fig.* pompous;
fig. masterly (*work*); F first-rate; ⚔
magistral; **magistrat** [~ˈtra] *m*
magistrate, judge; **magistrature**
[~traˈtyːr] *f* magistrature; magis-
tracy; ~ *assise* Bench, judges *pl.*;
~ *debout* public prosecutors *pl.*

magma [magˈma] *m geol.* magma;
fig. muddle.

magnanime [manaˈnim] magnan-
imous; **magnanimité** [~nimiˈte] *f*
magnanimity.

magnat [magˈna] *m* magnate.

magnésie ⚗ [maneˈzi] *f* magnesia,
magnesium oxide; *sulfate m de* ~
Epson salts *pl.*

magnésite [maneˈzit] *f* magnesite,
meerschaum.

magnésium [maneˈzjɔm] *m* ⚗ magnesium; *phot.* flash-light.

magnétique [maneˈtik] magnetic;
magnétisme [~ˈtism] *m* magnet-
ism; **magnétite** *min.* [~ˈtit] *f* lode-
stone, magnetite; **magnéto** [~ˈto] *f*
magneto; **magnétophone** [~toˈfɔn]
m tape recorder; ~ *à cassettes* cassette
recorder; **magnétoscope** [~to-
ˈskɔp] *m* video(-tape) recorder;
magnétoscoper (1a) *v/t.* video-ta-
pe.

magnificence [maɲifiˈsãːs] *f* magnificence, splendo(u)r; ~s *pl.* lavishness *sg.*; **magnifier** [~ˈfje] (1a) *v/t.*
magnify, glorify, glamorize; **magnifique** [~ˈfik] magnificent, splendid; *fig.* marvellous.

magnolia ⚘ [manɔˈlja] *m*, **magno-
lier** ⚘ [~ˈlje] *m* magnolia(-tree).

magot¹ [maˈgo] *m zo.* barbary ape;
macaque; *fig.* ugly man.

magot² F [~] *m* savings *pl.*, hoard.
magouille *sl.* [maˈguj] *f* dealings *pl.*,
tricks *pl.*; wangle; graft.

mahométan, e [maɔmeˈtã, ~ˈtan]
adj., a. su. Mohammedan, Moslem;
mahométisme [~ˈtism] *m* Mo-
hammedanism.

mai [mɛ] *m* May; may-pole.

maie [~] *f* kneading-trough.

maigre [mɛːgr] **1.** *adj.* thin, lean;
meagre, scanty (*meal, a. fig.*);
2. *su./m meat:* lean; *icht.* meagre;
faire ~ fast, abstain from meat;
maigrelet, -ette [mɛgrəˈlɛ, ~ˈlɛt]
rather thin, slight; **maigreur** [~-
ˈgrœːr] *f* thinness; emaciation; *fig.*
meagreness, poorness; **maigrir**
[~ˈgriːr] (2a) *v/i.* grow thin; lose
weight; *v/t.* make thinner; ⊕ thin
(*wood*).

mail [maːj] *m* ⊕ sledge-hammer;
avenue; † *club, game:* mall.

maille¹ [maːj] *f* stitch; *chain:* link;
(chain-)mail; *net:* mesh; *feather:*
speckle; *vine etc.:* bud; ⊕ two-
handed mallet; *à larges (petites)* ~s
wide-(close-)meshed.

maille² [~] *f: avoir* ~ *à partir avec q.*
have a bone to pick with s.o.

maillechort [majˈʃɔːr] *m* nickel *or*
German silver.

mailler [maˈje] (1a) *v/t.* net; ⚓
lace; ⊕ shackle (*chains*); ⊕ make
(*s.th.*) in lattice-work; *v/i.* ⚘ bud;
a. se ~ become speckled (*partridge
etc.*).

maillet [maˈjɛ] *m* mallet, maul; *sp.*
polo-stick; croquet mallet.

maillon [maˈjõ] *m chain:* link; *tex.*
mail; ⚓ shackle; **maillot** [maˈjo]
m swaddling-clothes *pl.*; *sp. football:*
jersey; *rowing, running:* vest; ~ *de
bain woman:* swimsuit; *man:* bathing
trunks *pl.*

main [mɛ̃] *f* hand (*a cards; a.* =
handwriting); † *paper:* quire; *cards:*
deal; ~ *courante* handrail; *à la* ~ in the
or one's hand; (*do s.th.*) by hand; *à* ~
levée freehanded; *à pleines* ~s lavishly; *avoir la* ~ *cards:* have the lead *or*
deal; *bas (haut) les* ~s! hands off
(up)!; *battre des* ~s clap (one's
hands); *fig. de bonnes* ~s on good
authority; *en* ~ under control; in
hand; *en un tour de* ~ straight off, F in
a jiffy; *en venir aux* ~s come to blows
or grips; *fait à la* ~ handmade; *la* ~
dans la ~ hand in hand; *payer de la* ~ *à*

la ~ pay direct without formalities; *mettre la ~ sur* lay hands on; *prêter la ~* lend a hand; *savoir de longue ~* have known for a long time; *serrer la ~ à q.* shake hands with s.o.; *sous la ~* to hand, at hand, handy; *sous ~* underhanded(ly *adv.*); **~-d'œuvre**, *pl.* **~s-d'œuvres** ⊕ [~'dœːvr] *f* labo(u)r; manpower; **~forte** [~'fɔrt] *f*: *prêter ~* give assistance (*to the police etc.*); **~levée** ⚖ [~lə've] *f* withdrawal; **~mise** [~'miːz] *f* seizure (of, *sur*); ⚖ distraint; **~morte** ⚖ [~'mɔrt] *f* mortmain.

maint, mainte *poet.* [mɛ̃, mɛ̃ːt] many a; *maintes fois* many a time.

maintenance [mɛ̃t'nɑ̃s] *f* maintenance.

maintenant [mɛ̃t'nɑ̃] *adv.* now; *dès ~* from now on, henceforth.

maintenir [mɛ̃t'niːr] (2h) *v/t.* maintain (*a. fig.*); keep; support; uphold; *se ~* continue; remain; hold one's own; **maintien** [mɛ̃'tjɛ̃] *m* maintenance; bearing, carriage; *perdre son~* lose countenance.

maire [mɛːr] *m* mayor; **mairie** [mɛ'ri] *f* town hall; mayoralty.

mais [mɛ] **1.** *cj.* but; *~ non!* no indeed!; not at all!; *~ oui!* sure!, of course!; **2.** *adv.*: *je n'en puis ~* I am completely exhausted; I don't know what to say.

maïs ♀ [ma'is] *m* maize, Indian corn, *Am.* corn.

maison [mɛ'zɔ̃] *f* house; home; household; family; ♥ (*a. ~ de commerce*) firm; *~ close* brothel; *~ d'arrêt* gaol, lock-up; *~ de commission* commission agency; *~ de rapport* apartment house; *~ de santé* nursing home; mental hospital; *~ du Roi* Royal Household; *~ jumelle* semi-detached house; ♥ *~ mère* head office; *de bonne ~* of a good family; *la ~ des Bonaparte* the House of Bonaparte; *tenir ~ ouverte* keep open house; **maisonnée** [mɛzɔ'ne] *f* household, family; **maisonnette** [~'nɛt] *f* cottage, small house.

maître, -esse [mɛːtr, mɛ'trɛs] **1.** *su./m* master (*a. fig.*); *fig.* ruler; owner; *school:* teacher; ⚓ petty officer; ⚖ *title given to lawyers:* maître; *~ d'armes* fencing-master; *univ. ~ de conférences* lecturer; *~ d'hôtel* headwaiter; ⚓ chief steward; *~ d'œuvre* foreman; *être ~ de* be in control of;

have at one's disposal; *être passé ~ en* be a past master of *or* in; *su./f* mistress; **2.** *adj.* ⚔, ⊕, *etc.*, *a. fig.* principal, main; **~-autel**, *pl.* **~s-autels** *eccl.* [mɛtro'tɛl] *m* high altar; **maîtrisable** [~tri'zabl] controllable; **maîtrise** [~'triːz] *f* mastership; *fig.* feeling, profession, *etc.*: mastery; command, control; **maîtriser** [~tri-'ze] (1a) *v/t.* master, overcome; *se ~* control o.s.

majesté [maʒɛs'te] *f* majesty; **majestueux, -euse** [~'tɥø, ~'tɥøːz] majestic, stately.

majeur, e [ma'ʒœːr] **1.** *adj.* major (*a.* ⚖, ♪, *phls.*), greater; *fig.* main, chief; *devenir ~* reach one's majority; **2.** *su./m* ⚖ major; middle finger; **major** ⚔ [ma'ʒɔːr] *m* regimental adjutant; *~ de place* town major; *~ général* chief of staff; **majoration** [~ʒɔra'sjɔ̃] *f* over-estimation; increase; *admin.* advancement; **majordome** [~ʒɔr'dɔm] *m* major-domo, steward; **majorer** [maʒɔ're] (1a) *v/t.* over-estimate; ♥ add to (*a bill*); increase; **majorité** [~ri'te] *f* majority (*a.* ⚖); ⚖ coming of age; ⚔ adjutancy.

majuscule [maʒys'kyl] **1.** *adj.* capital (*letter*); **2.** *su./f* capital letter.

mal [mal] **1.** *su./m* evil; hurt, harm, pain; ♣ disease; wrong; *~ à l'estomach* stomachache; *~ aux reins* backache; *~ de cœur* nausea, sickness; *~ de l'air* air sickness; *~ de mer* seasickness; *~ de tête* headache; *~ du pays* homesickness; *avoir ~ au ventre* have a stomachache; *avoir du ~ à faire qch.* have difficulty (in) doing s.th.; *donner du ~ à q.* give s.o. some trouble; *faire ~ (à q.)* hurt (s.o.); *faire du ~ à q.* harm s.o.; ♣ *haut ~* epilepsy; *prendre ~* be taken ill; *se donner du ~* take pains *or* trouble; **2.** *adv.* badly; ill; uncomfortable; *~ à l'aise* ill at ease; *~ à propos* inopportunely, at the wrong time; *~ fait* badly made; botched (*work*); *être ~* be uncomfortable; be wrong; *pas ~* good-looking, presentable (*person*); quite good; F *pas ~ de* a good many, a lot of; *prendre ~ qch.* take offence at s.th.; *se sentir ~* feel ill; *se trouver ~* faint.

malade [ma'lad] **1.** *adj.* ill, sick; diseased; **2.** *su.* patient; sick person; **maladie** [mala'di] *f* disease; illness, sickness; ailment; *~ de carence* deficiency disease, vitamin deficiency; ~ *infantile* childhood disease; *fig.* teething troubles *pl.*; **maladif, -ve** [~'dif, ~'di:v] sickly, ailing.

maladresse [mala'drɛs] *f* clumsiness; blunder; **maladroit, e** [~'drwa, ~'drwat] 1. *adj.* clumsy, awkward; 2. *su.* duffer; blunderer; awkward person.

malais, e [ma'lɛ, ~'lɛːz] 1. *adj.* Malay(an); 2. *su./m ling.* Malay(an); *su.* ♀ Malay(an).

malaise [ma'lɛːz] *f* uneasiness; discomfort; *fig.* unrest; **malaisé, e** [~lɛ'ze] difficult.

malappris, e [mala'pri, ~'priːz] 1. *adj.* ill-mannered; 2. *su.* ill-mannered person.

malavisé, e [malavi'ze] 1. *adj.* ill-advised; injudicious (*person*); 2. *su.* blunderer.

malaxage [malak'saːʒ] *m* mixing; *dough:* kneading; **malaxer** [~'se] (1a) *v/t.* mix; knead (*dough*); **malaxeur** ⊕ [~'sœːr] *m* (cement) mixer; mixing machine. [uncouth.] **malbâti, e** [malbɑ'ti] misshapen;

malchance [mal'ʃɑ̃ːs] *f* bad luck; mishap; **malchanceux, -euse** [~ʃɑ̃sø, ~'søːz] 1. *adj.* unlucky, luckless; 2. *su.* unlucky person.

maldonne [mal'dɔn] *f cards:* misdeal; error, mistake; misunderstanding.

mâle [mɑːl] 1. *adj.* male (♀, ⊕ *screw*, *person*); *zo.* buck (*rabbit*), dog (*fox*, *wolf*), bull (*elephant*); *orn.* cock; *fig.* virile; manly; 2. *su./m* male.

malédiction [maledik'sjɔ̃] *f* curse.

maléfice [male'fis] *m* evil spell; **maléfique** [~'fik] evil; maleficent.

malencontre † [malɑ̃'kɔ̃ːtr] *f* mishap; **malencontreux, -euse** [malɑ̃kɔ̃'trø, ~'trøːz] unfortunate, awkward.

malentendu [malɑ̃tɑ̃'dy] *m* misunderstanding.

mal-être [mal'ɛːtr] *m* (feeling of) discomfort; uneasiness.

malfaçon [malfa'sɔ̃] *f* bad workmanship; defect; **malfaire** [mal'fɛːr] (4r) *v/i.* do evil; **malfaisant, e** [~fə'zɑ̃, ~'zɑ̃ːt] harmful; mischievous; evil-minded (*person*); **malfaiteur** *m*, **-trice** *f* [~fɛ'tœːr, ~'tris] malefactor; offender.

malfamé, e [malfa'me] ill-famed; notorious.

malformation [malfɔrma'sjɔ̃] *f* malformation (*a.* ♀).

malgré [mal'gre] *prp.* despite, in spite of; ~ *moi* against my will; ~ *tout* still.

malhabile [mala'bil] clumsy; inexperienced (in *ger.*, *à inf.*).

malheur [ma'lœːr] *m* bad luck; misfortune; unhappiness; ~ *à lui!* woe betide him!; *quel* ~*!* what a pity!; **malheureux, -euse** [~lœ'rø, ~'røːz] 1. *adj.* unlucky, unhappy; unfortunate; *fig.* poor; *fig.* paltry; 2. *su.* unfortunate person; *pauvre* ~*!* poor soul!

malhonnête [malɔ'nɛt] dishonest; *fig.* impolite; indecent (*gesture*); **malhonnêteté** [~nɛt'te] *f* dishonesty; *fig.* rudeness; *gesture:* indecency.

malice [ma'lis] *f* malice; *fig.* trick; *ne pas voir* ~ *à* not to see any harm in; **malicieux, -euse** [~li'sjø, ~'sjøːz] mischievous; waggish, sly (*remark etc.*).

malignité [maliɲi'te] *f* malignity (*a.* ♀); piece of spite; **malin, -igne** [~'lɛ̃, ~'liɲ] 1. *adj.* malignant (*a.* ♀); wicked; *fig.* cunning, sharp, sly; *fig.* clever, smart; *fig.* difficult; 2. *su. fig.* shrewd person; *su./m:* le ♀ the Devil.

malingre [ma'lɛ̃ːgr] sickly, weakly.

malintentionné, e [malɛ̃tɑ̃sjɔ'ne] 1. *adj.* evil-minded, ill-intentioned; 2. *su.* evil-minded person.

malique ♪ [ma'lik] malic (*acid*).

mal-jugé ⚖ [malʒy'ʒe] *m* miscarriage of justice.

malle [mal] *f* trunk; ♣ mail-boat; *(dé)faire sa* ~ (un)pack.

malléable [malle'abl] malleable (*a. fig.*); *fig.* pliant.

malle-poste, *pl.* **malles-poste** [mal'pɔst] *f* mail-coach; **malletier** [mal'tje] *m* trunk-maker; **mallette** [ma'lɛt] *f* suitcase; attaché case; small case.

malmener [malmə'ne] (1d) *v/t.* ill-treat, maltreat, handle roughly.

malotru, e [malɔ'try] 1. *adj.* uncouth; vulgar; 2. *su.* boor, churl.

malpeigné, e [malpɛ'ɲe] unkempt, untidy (*person*).

malpropre [mal'prɔpr] dirty (*a. fig.*); slovenly (*appearance*); **malpropreté** [~prɔprə'te] *f* dirtiness (*a. fig.*); dirt; slovenliness; ~*s pl.* dirty stories, F smut *sg.*

malsain, e [mal'sɛ̃, ~'sɛn] unhealthy; unwholesome (*a. fig.*); dangerous (*coast*); *fig.* unsound.

malséant, e [malse'ã, ~'ãːt] unbecoming, unseemly.

malsonnant, e [malsɔ'nã, ~'nãːt] offensive.

malt [malt] *m* malt; **malter** [mal'te] (1a) *v/t.* malt; **malterie** [~'tri] *f* malting; malt-house; **malteur** [~'tœːr] *m* maltster; **maltose** ⚗, ⊕ [~'toːz] *m* maltose.

maltraiter [maltrɛ'te] (1a) *v/t.* ill-treat, maltreat; handle roughly; batter.

malveillance [malvɛ'jãːs] *f* malevolence, ill will, spite (to[wards] *pour, envers*); **malveillant, e** [~'jã, ~'jãːt] ill-willed; malicious; spiteful.

malversation ⚖ [malvɛrsa'sjɔ̃] *f* embezzlement; breach of trust.

malvoisie [malvwa'zi] *mf wine*: malmsey.

maman [ma'mã] *f* mam(m)a, mummy, *Am. a.* mom.

mamelle [ma'mɛl] *f* breast; *cow etc.*: udder; teat; **mamelon** [mam-'lɔ̃] *m* nipple (*a.* ⊕ *for oiling*); *person, a. animal*: teat; ⊕ boss; *geog.* rounded hillock; **mamelonné, e** [~lɔ'ne] mamillate; hilly.

mamel(o)uk [mam'luk] *m* mameluke.

m'amie †, ma mie [ma'mi] *f* my dear.

mamillaire [mamil'lɛːr] mamillary; **mammaire** *anat.* [~'mɛːr] mammary; **mammifère** *zo.* [~mi'fɛːr] **1.** *adj.* mammalian; **2.** *su./m* mammal.

mamours [ma'muːr] *m/pl.* billing *sg.* and cooing *sg.*, caresses.

mammouth *zo.* [ma'mut] *m* mammoth.

manant [ma'nã] *m* boor; yokel; † villager.

manche¹ [mã:ʃ] *m* handle; haft; (*broom-*)stick; *whip*: stock; ♪ *violin*: neck; ⚡ ~ à balai joy-stick; jeter le ~ après la cognée give up.

manche² [~] *f* sleeve; *water*: hose; (*air-*)shaft; *geog.* strait; *sp.* heat; *tennis*: set; *cards*: hand; ⚡ ~ à air wind sock; la ⚓ the (English) Channel; F faire la ~ beg (for alms).

mancheron [mãʃ'rɔ̃] *m plough*: handle; *cost.* cuff; short sleeve; **manchette** [mã'ʃɛt] *f* cuff; wrist-

band; *journ.* headline; *sl.* ~s *pl.* handcuffs; **manchon** [~'ʃɔ̃] *m* muff; ⊕ casing, sleeve; gas-mantle.

manchot, e [mã'ʃo, ~'ʃɔt] **1.** *adj.* one-armed; *fig.* awkward with one's hands, F ham-fisted; **2.** *su.* one-armed person; *su./m orn.* penguin.

mandant [mã'dã] *m* ⚖ principal; employer; *pol.* constituent.

mandarin [mãda'rɛ̃] mandarin (*a. fig., pej.*); **mandarinat** [mãdari'na] *m* mandarinate.

mandarine ♀ [mãda'rin] *f* mandarin(e), tangerine.

mandat [mã'da] *m* mandate; commission; ⚖ power of attorney; ⚖ warrant; ✝ draft, order; *sous* ~ mandated (*territory*); **mandataire** [mãda'tɛːr] *su.* agent; ⚖ attorney; trustee; *pol.* mandatory; **mandat-carte**, *pl.* **mandats-cartes** [~'kart] *m post*: money order (*in post-card form*); **mandater** [~'te] (1a) *v/t.* give a mandate to; write a money order for (*a sum*); **mandat-poste**, *pl.* **mandats-poste** [~'pɔst] *m* postal money order.

mandement [mãd'mã] *m eccl.* pastoral letter; instructions *pl.*; **mander** [mã'de] (1a) *v/t.* instruct (*s.o.*); summon (*s.o.*); *journ. on mande* ... it is reported ...

mandibule *anat.* [mãdi'byl] *f* mandible.

mandoline ♪ [mãdɔ'lin] *f* mandolin(e).

mandragore ♀ [mãdra'gɔːr] *f* mandragora, F mandrake.

mandrin ⊕ [mã'drɛ̃] *m* mandrel; chuck; punch.

manducation [mãdyka'sjɔ̃] *f* mastication; *eccl.* manducation.

manège [ma'nɛːʒ] *m* riding school; *fig.* trick, stratagem; (*a.* ~ *de chevaux de bois*) roundabout, merry-go-round.

mânes [mɑːn] *m/pl.* manes, spirits (*of the departed*).

manette ⊕ [ma'nɛt] *f* lever (*a. mot.*); *Morse*: key.

manganèse ⚗, *min., metall.* [mãga-'nɛːz] *m* manganese.

mangeable [mã'ʒabl] edible, eatable; **mangeaille** [~'ʒaːj] *f* † feed (*for animals*); F food, F grub; **mangeoire** [~'ʒwaːr] *f* manger; feeding-trough; **manger** [mã'ʒe] **1.** (1l) *vt/i.* eat; *v/t.* corrode (*metal*); squander *(money)*; mumble *(words)*; *fig.* use up, consume *(coal, gas, petrol, etc.)*; **2.** *su./m* food; **mangetout** [mãʒ'tu] *m/inv.* † spendthrift; ❦ French bean; **mangeur** *m*, **-euse** *f* [mã'ʒœːr, ~'ʒøːz] eater; *fig.* devourer; **mangeure** † [~'ʒyːr] *f* place eaten *(by mice, moths, etc.)*.

maniabilité [manjabili'te] *f* handiness; manageableness; ✍, *mot.* manœuvrability; **maniable** [~'njabl] manageable, manœuvrable; handy *(tool)*; *fig.* tractable.

maniaque [ma'njak] **1.** *adj.* finnicky, fussy; fanatic; suffering from a mania; **2.** *su.* ✍ maniac; **manie** [~'ni] *f* mania; funny habit.

maniement [mani'mã] *m* management; handling; **manier** [~'nje] (1o) *v/t.* manage; handle.

manière [ma'njɛːr] *f* manner *(a. paint. etc.)*, way; *fig.* mannerisms *pl.*; ~s *pl.* manners; *à la* ~ *de* after the manner of; *de* ~ *à* so as to; *de* ~ *que* so that; *d'une* ~ *ou d'une autre* somehow or other; *en aucune* ~ in no way; *en* ~ *de* by way of; *faire des* ~s be affected; affect reluctance; **maniéré, e** [manje're] affected; *paint. etc.* mannered; *fig.* genteel *(voice etc.)*; **maniérisme** [~'rism] *m* mannerism.

manieur [ma'njœːr] *m* controller; *pej.* ~ *d'argent* financier; financial adventurer.

manif F [ma'nif] *f (abbr. of manifestation)* demo; **manifestant, e** *pol.* [manifɛs'tã, ~'tãt] **1.** *adj.* demonstrating; **2.** *su.* demonstrator; **manifestation** [~ta'sjɔ̃] *f* manifestation; *pol.* demonstration; *eccl.* revelation; **manifeste** [~'fɛst] **1.** *adj.* manifest, obvious; ✝ overt; **2.** *su./m* manifesto; ⚓ manifest; **manifester** [~fɛs'te] (1a) *v/t.* show, manifest; reveal; *se* ~ appear; show o.s.; *v/i.* *pol.* demonstrate.

manigance F [mani'gãːs] trick, scheme; F monkey business; dealings *pl.*; **manigancer** F [~gã'se] (1k) *v/t.* plot, scheme.

manipulateur [manipyla'tœːr] *m* handler; *tel.* sending key; *radio:* sender; **manipulation** [~la'sjɔ̃] *f* manipulation; handling; **manipuler** [~'le] (1a) *v/t.* manipulate *(a. fig.)*, handle; *🕯, tel.* operate *(a key etc.)*.

manitou F [mani'tu] *m* boss, tycoon.

manivelle ⊕ [mani'vɛl] *f* crank (-handle).

manne¹ [man] *f* basket; *(baby's)* bassinet.

manne² [~] *f bibl.* manna; *fig.* godsend.

mannequin¹ [man'kɛ̃] *m* small hamper.

mannequin² [man'kɛ̃] *m* 🦋, *paint.* manikin; *paint.* lay figure; *cost.* dummy; mannequin; *fig.* puppet; **mannequiner** *paint.* [~ki'ne] (1a) *v/t.* pose *(s.o.)* unnaturally.

manœuvrabilité [manœvrabili'te] *f* manœuvrability; **manœuvrable** [~'vrabl] manageable; workable; **manœuvre** [ma'nœːvr] *su./f* working; operation; 🚂 shunting, *Am.* switching; ✕, ⚓ manœuvre *(a. fig.)*; exercise; ✕, ⚓ movement; *fig.* intrigue; *su./m* (manual) labo(u)rer; unskilled worker; *fig.* hack; **manœuvrer** [manœ'vre] (1a) *v/t.* work *(a machine etc.)*; 🚂 shunt, marshal; *vt/i.* manœuvre *(a. ✕, ⚓, fig.)*; **manœuvrier, -ère** [~vri'e, ~'ɛːr] skilful; capable.

manoir [ma'nwaːr] *m* country-house; *hist.* manor.

manomètre ⊕ [manɔ'mɛtr] *m* manometer.

manouvrier [manuvri'e] *m* day-labo(u)rer.

manque [mãːk] *m* lack, want; deficiency, shortage; *fig.* emptiness; *drugs etc.*, *a. fig.* (*symptôme m de*) ~ withdrawal (symptom); ~ *de* lack of; ~ *de foi* breach of faith; ~ *de parole* breaking of one's promise; F *à la* ~ poor, fifth-rate; **manqué, e** [mã'ke] unsuccessful; **manquement** [mãk'mã] *m* failure, lapse; ~ *à* breach of; **manquer** [mã'ke] (1m) *v/t.* miss *(a. fig.)*; spoil *(one's life, a picture)*; *se* ~ miss one another; *v/i.* lack; be absent; be missing; fail; ~ *à q.* be missed by s.o.; ~ *à qch.* fail in s.th.; commit a breach of s.th.; ~ *de qch.* lack s.th., not to have s.th.; *ne pas* ~ *de rien* lack for nothing; ~ *(de) faire qch.* nearly do s.th.; *j'ai manqué (de) tomber* I nearly fell; *ne pas* ~ *de (inf.)* not to fail to *(inf.)*.

mansarde △ [mã'sard] *f* attic, garret(-window); *roof:* mansard.

mansuétude [mãsɥe'tyd] *f* gentleness, meekness.

mante [mãːt] *f (woman's)* sleeveless

manteau

cloak; *zo.* ~ *religieuse* (*or prie-Dieu*) praying mantis.

manteau [mã'to] *m* coat; cloak (*a. fig.*); mantle (*a. zo.*); ⊕ casing; ⚕ mantelpiece; *sous le* ~ on the quiet, secretly; **mantelet** [mãt'lɛ] *m cost.* tippet, mantlet; ⚓ port-lid; **mantille** *cost.* [mã'ti:j] *f* mantilla.

manucure [many'ky:r] *su.* manicurist; **manucurer** [~ky're] (1a) *v/t.* manicure.

manuel, -elle [ma'nɥɛl] 1. *adj.* manual; 2. *su./m* handbook, manual; text-book; ~ *d'entretien* instruction handbook.

manufacture [manyfak'ty:r] *f* (manu)factory; ⊕ plant; **manufacturer** [~ty're] (1a) *v/t.* manufacture; **manufacturier, -ère** [~ty'rje, ~'rjɛ:r] 1. *adj.* manufacturing; 2. *su./m* manufacturer; mill-owner.

manuscrit, e [manys'kri, ~'krit] 1. *adj.* manuscript; hand-written; 2. *su./m* manuscript.

manutention [manytã'sjõ] *f* control; handling; ✕, ⚓ store-keeping; stores *pl.*; bakery; **manutentionner** [~sjɔ'ne] (1a) *v/t.* handle; ✕, ⚓ store; bake.

mappemonde [map'mõ:d] *f* map of the world.

maquereau [ma'kro] *m icht.* mackerel; V pimp.

maquette [ma'kɛt] *f* model (*a. thea.*); ⊕ mock-up; *book:* dummy; *metall.* bloom.

maquignon [maki'ɲõ] *m* horse-dealer; *pej.* shady dealer *or* go-between; **maquignonnage** [~ɲɔ'na:ʒ] *m* horse-dealing; *pej.* sharp practice; **maquignonner** [~ɲɔ'ne] (1a) *v/t.* fake up (*a horse*); arrange (*s.th.*) by sharp practices, F work, *sl.* cook.

maquillage [maki'ja:ʒ] *m* make-up; **maquiller** [~'je] (1a) *v/t.* make up; *phot.* work up; *fig.* disguise; *se* ~ make up; **-euse** *f* [~'jœ:r, ~'jø:z] *thea.* make-up artist; *fig.* faker.

maquis [ma'ki] *m* scrub; *fig.* maze; jungle; ✕ underground forces *pl.*, maquis; *prendre le* ~ go underground.

maraîcher, -ère [marɛ'ʃe, ~'ʃɛ:r] 1. *adj.* market-(gardening)...; *culture f mâraichère* market gardening, *Am.* truck farming; 2. *su./m* market-gardener, *Am.* truck farmer.

marais [ma'rɛ] *m* marsh; bog; swamp.

marasme [ma'rasm] *m* ✱ marasmus, wasting; *fig.* depression (*a.* ♱).

marathon *sp.* [mara'tõ] *m* marathon (*a. fig.*).

marâtre [ma'rɑ:tr] *f* step-mother; cruel *or* unnatural mother.

maraude [ma'ro:d] *f* plundering, looting; filching; F *en* ~ cruising, crawling (*taxi*); **marauder** [~ro'de] (1a) *v/i.* plunder; filch; F cruise (*taxi*).

marbre [marbr] *m* marble; *typ.* press-stone; ⊕ (sur)face-plate; *sur le* ~ in type; **marbrer** [mar'bre] (1a) *v/t.* marble; *fig.* mottle; **marbrerie** [~brə'ri] *f* marble-cutting, marble-work; marble-mason's yard; **marbrier, -ère** [~bri'e, ~'ɛ:r] 1. *adj.* marble...; 2. *su./m* marble-cutter; monumental mason; *su./f* marble-quarry; **marbrure** [~'bry:r] *f* marbling; *fig.* mottling.

marc [ma:r] *m* grapes *etc.*: marc; (*tea-*)leaves *pl.*, (*coffee-*)grounds *pl.*

marcassin *zo.* [marka'sɛ̃] *m* young wild boar.

marchand, e [mar'ʃɑ̃, ~'ʃɑ̃:d] 1. *adj.* saleable, marketable; trade (*name, price*); shopping (*centre*); commercial (*town*); ⚓ merchant (*navy, ship*); 2. *su.* dealer, shopkeeper; (*coster-, fish-, iron-*)monger; ~ *d'antiquités* antique dealer; ~ *des quatre-saisons* costermonger; ~ *de tabac* tobacconist; ~ *en* (*or au*) *détail* retailer; ~ *en gros* wholesaler; **marchandage** [marʃɑ̃'da:ʒ] *m* bargaining; **marchander** [~'de] (1a) *v/t.* haggle with (*s.o., q.*); bargain for (*s.th., qch.*); beat (*s.o.*) down; ⊕ subcontract (*a job*); *ne pas* ~ not to spare; **marchandeur** *m*, **-euse** *f* [~'dœ:r, ~'dø:z] bargainer; ⊕ subcontractor of labo(u)r; **marchandise** [~'di:z] *f* merchandise, wares *pl.*, goods *pl.*; ⬛ *train m de* ~*s* goods train, *Am.* freight train.

marche¹ [marʃ] *f* walk; ✕, ♪ march; tread; step, stair; ⊕, ⬛ *machine, train:* running; *fig.* events, stars, time, *etc.:* course; *fig.* (rate of) progress; ~ *arrière mot.* reversing; ⬛ backing; *en* ~ ⬛ *etc.* moving...; ⊕ running; *en état de* ~ in working order; ⊕, *a. fig. mettre en* ~ start, set going, set in motion.

marche² *geog.* [~] *f* border(land); march(-land).

marché [mar'ʃe] *m* market (*a. financial*); deal, bargain; ✝ ~ *à terme* time-bargain; ~ *au comptant* cash transaction; ✝, *pol.* ♀ *commun* Common Market; ~ *des changes* exchange market; ~ *du travail* labo(u)r market; ~ *intérieur (étranger)* home (foreign) market; ~ *noir* black market; (*à*) *bon* ~ cheap(ly); (*à*) *meilleur* ~ more cheaply; cheaper; *le bon* ~ the cheapness (of, de); (*aller*) *faire son* ~ go shopping; *fig. par-dessus le* ~ into the bargain.

marchepied [marʃə'pje] *m vehicle:* footboard; *mot.* running-board; *wagon:* tail-board; step-ladder; *fig.* stepping-stone.

marcher [mar'ʃe] (1a) *v/i.* walk, go (*a.* 🚂 *engine*); ✗ *etc.* march; ⊕ run (*a.* 🚂 *train*), work; *fig.* ✝ swallow; ⚓ sail, head (for, *vers*); ⊕ ~ *à vide* run idle; ~ *sur les pas de q.* follow in s.o.'s footsteps; ~ *sur les pieds de q.* tread on s.o.'s feet; *faire* ~ run (*a house, a business*); F *faire* ~ *q.* pull s.o.'s leg; F (*je ne*) *marche pas!* nothing doing!; F *ne pas se laisser* ~ *sur les pieds* not to let o.s. be put upon; *ma montre ne marche plus* my watch is broken; **marcheur, -euse** [~'ʃœːr, ~'ʃøːz] **1.** *adj.* walking; ⚓ *bon* ~ fast-sailing; **2.** *su. walker; su./m:* F *vieux* ~ old rake.

marcotte ⚹ [mar'kɔt] *f* layer; runner; **marcotter** ⚹ [~kɔ'te] (1a) *v/t.* layer.

mardi [mar'di] *m* Tuesday; ~ *gras* Shrove Tuesday.

mare [maːr] *f* pond; pool (*a. fig.*).

marécage [mare'kaːʒ] *m* bog, swamp, fen, marshland; **marécageux, -euse** [~ka'ʒø, ~'ʒøːz] boggy, swampy, marshy.

maréchal ✗ [mare'ʃal] *m* marshal; (*a.* ~*-ferrant*) farrier; ~ *des logis cavalry:* sergeant; ~ *des logis-chef* battery *or* squadron sergeant-major; **maréchalat** [~ʃa'la] *m* marshalship; **maréchalerie** [~ʃal-'ri] *f* horse-shoeing; smithy.

marée [ma're] *f* tide; ✝ fresh fish; *fig.* flood, wave, surge; ~ *basse* (*haute*) low (high) tide, low (high) water; *grande* ~ springtide; *la* ~ *descend* (*monte*) the tide is going out (coming in).

marelle [ma'rɛl] *f game:* hopscotch.

marémoteur, -trice [maremɔ'tœːr, ~'tris] tidal (*energy*); *usine* ~*trice* tidal power station.

mareyeur *m*, **-euse** *f* [marɛ'jœːr, ~'jøːz] fishmonger.

margarine ✝ [marga'rin] *f* margarine.

marge [marʒ] *f* border, edge; margin (*a. fig., a.* ✝); *fig.* scope; ~ *bénéficiaire* profit margin; ~ *de sécurité* safety margin; *fig. en* ~ (*de*) on the fringe (of); **margelle** [mar'ʒɛl] *f well:* curb(-stone); **margeur** [~'ʒœːr] *m typ.* layer-on; *typewriter:* margin stop; **marginal, e** *m/pl.* **-aux** [~ʒi'nal, ~'no] marginal.

margotin [margɔ'tɛ] *m* bundle of firewood.

margouillis F [margu'ji] *m* mud, slush; mess.

margoulin F [margu'lɛ] *m* petty tradesman; swindler; (small-time) crook.

marguerite ⚹ [margə'rit] *f* daisy; *grande* ~ marguerite, ox-eye daisy; *petite* ~ daisy.

mari [ma'ri] *m* husband; **mariable** [~'rjabl] marriageable, F in the marriage market; **mariage** [~'rjaːʒ] *m* marriage; wedding; matrimony; ~ *d'amour* love match; **marié, e** [~'rje] **1.** *adj.* married; **2.** *su./m* bridegroom; *su./f* bride; **marier** [~'rje] (1o) *v/t.* marry (*a. fig.*), give *or* join in marriage; *fig.* join; *fig.* blend (*colours*); *se* ~ marry, get married; *fig.* harmonize (with, *à*); **marieur** *m*, **-euse** *f* [~'rjœːr, ~'rjøːz] matchmaker.

marihuana [mariɥa'na], **marijuana** [mariʒɥa'na] *f* marijuana.

marin, e [ma'rɛ̃, ~'rin] **1.** *adj.* marine (*plant*); sea...; nautical; **2.** *su./m* sailor; moist wind (*in South-Eastern France*); F ~ *d'eau douce* land-lubber.

marinade [mari'nad] *f* pickle; brine; *cuis.* marinade.

marine [ma'rin] **1.** *adj./inv.* navy (-blue); **2.** *su./f* ⚓ navy; ⚓ seamanship; *paint.* seascape; ~ *de guerre* Navy; ~ *marchande* merchant service *or* navy, *Am.* merchant marine.

mariner *cuis.* [mari'ne] (1a) *v/t.* marinade; pickle.

marinier, -ère [mari'nje, ~'njɛːr] **1.** *adj.* naval; **2.** *su./m* waterman, bargee; *su./f swimming:* side-stroke.

marionnette [marjɔ'nɛt] *f* puppet

marital 308

(a. fig.); théâtre m de ~s puppet-show.

marital, e, m/pl. -aux [mari'tal, ~'to] marital; **maritalement** [~tal-'mã] adv. maritally; vivre ~ live together as husband and wife.

maritime [mari'tim] maritime (⚓, law, power, province); shipping (agent, intelligence); naval (dock-yard); marine (insurance); seaborne (trade); seaside (town). [tern.\

maritorne [mari'tɔrn] f slut, slat-\

marivaudage [marivo'da:ʒ] m preciosity in writing; mild flirting.

marjolaine ♀ [marʒɔ'lɛn] f marjoram.

marmaille F coll. [mar'ma:j] f children pl., F kids pl.

marmelade [marmə'lad] f compote (of fruit); (orange) marmalade; F mess; fig. en ~ pounded to a jelly.

marmite [mar'mit] f pan; (cooking-)pot; ✖ F heavy shell; ~ à pression (or de Papin) pressure-cooker; ~ norvégienne hay-box; F faire bouillir la ~ keep the pot boiling; **marmiton** [~mi'tõ] m cook's boy; (pastry-cook's) errand-boy.

marmonner [marmɔ'ne] (1a) v/t. mumble, mutter.

marmoréen, -enne [marmɔre'ɛ̃, ~'ɛn] marmoreal, marble...; **marmoriser** ⚙ [~ri'ze] (1a) v/t. marmarize.

marmot [mar'mo] m F brat; F croquer le ~ cool one's heels; wait.

marmotte [mar'mɔt] f zo. marmot, Am. ✖ woodchuck; ✝ case of samples; head-scarf.

marmotter [marmɔ'te] (1a) v/t. mumble, mutter.

marmouset [marmu'zɛ] m fig. F whipper-snapper, little chap; ⊕ fire-dog.

marne ✎, geol. [marn] f marl; **marner** [mar'ne] (1a) v/t. ✎ marl; v/i. ⚓ rise (tide).

marocain, e [marɔ'kɛ̃, ~'kɛn] adj., a. su. ♀ Moroccan.

maronner [marɔ'ne] (1a) vt/i. growl, mutter.

maroquin [marɔ'kɛ̃] m morocco (-leather); pol. F ministerial portfolio; **maroquiner** [~ki'ne] (1a) v/t. give a morocco finish to; make (skin) into morocco-leather; **maroquinerie** [~kin'ri] f fancy leather goods pl.

marotte [ma'rɔt] f (fool's) cap and bells pl.; hairdresser etc.: dummy head; F fad, F bee in the bonnet.

maroufle¹ ✝ [ma'rufl] m lout, hooligan.

maroufle² [ma'rufl] f strong paste; **maroufler** [~ru'fle] (1a) v/t. remount (a picture); prime, size (canvas); ✂ tape (a seam).

marquant, e [mar'kã, ~'kã:t] outstanding, prominent; **marque** [mark] f mark (a. ✝, a. fig.); ✝ brand, make (a. mot.); ✝ tally; sp. score; fig. token; fig. highest quality; ~ au crayon pencil mark; ~ de fabrique, ~ de fabrication trade mark; brand (name); ~ déposée registered trademark; de ~ distinguished (person); ✝ F choice, best quality; **marquer** [mar'ke] (1m) v/t. mark; stamp; brand; sp. score (goals, points); fig. denote, indicate; fig. show (one's age, one's feelings); fig. emphasize; ascertain (facts); fig. watch, keep a watch on (one's opponent etc.); ♪ ~ la mesure beat time; v/i. be outstanding; F ~ mal make a bad impression; **marqueter** [~kə'te] (1c) v/t. speckle; inlay (wood); **marqueterie** [~kə'tri] f inlaid work, marquetry; fig. patchwork.

marqueur, -euse [mar'kœ:r, ~'kø:z] su. marker; sp. scorer.

marquis [mar'ki] m marquis, marquess; **marquise** [~'ki:z] f title: marchioness; marquee; awning, canopy.

marraine [ma'rɛn] f godmother; eccl., a. fig. sponsor.

marrant, e sl. [ma'rã, ~'rã:t] screamingly funny; odd.

marre sl. [ma:r] f: en avoir ~ be fed up (with, de); **marrer** sl. [ma're] (1a) v/t.: se ~ (have a good) laugh, F split one's sides.

marri, e ✝ [ma'ri] grieved.

marron¹ [ma'rõ] 1. su./m ♀ (edible) chestnut; F blow; ♀ ~ d'Inde horse-chestnut; 2. adj./inv. brown; chestnut(-coloured).

marron², -onne [ma'rõ, ~'rɔn] unqualified; unlicensed (taxi-driver, trader, etc.).

maronnier ♀ [marɔ'nje] m chestnut (-tree).

mars [mars] m March; astr. Mars; ✎ ~ pl. spring wheat sg.

marsouin [mar'swɛ̃] m zo. porpoise;

                             mat

⚓ forecastle awning; ⚔ F colonial infantry soldier.

marsupial *m*, **-e** *f*, *m/pl.* **-aux** *zo.* [marsy'pjal, ~'pjo] *adj.*, *a.* *su./m* marsupial.

marteau [mar'to] *m* hammer (*a.* ♪, *a. anat.*); (*door-*)knocker; *clock*: striker; *icht.* hammerhead; ~ *pneumatique* pneumatic drill; **~-pilon**, *pl.* **~x-pilons** *metall.* [~topi'lɔ̃] *m* power-hammer; forging-press.

martel [mar'tɛl] *m* † hammer; *fig.* se *mettre* ~ *en tête* worry; **marteler** [~tə'le] (1d) *v/t.* hammer; pound; *fig.* ~ *ses mots* speak each word with emphasis.

martial, e, *m/pl.* **-aux** [mar'sjal, ~'sjo] martial (*a. law*); soldierly; **martien, -enne** [~'sjɛ̃, ~'sjɛn] *adj.*, *a. su.* ♀ Martian.

martinet[1] [marti'nɛ] *m* ⊕ tilt-hammer; (small) whip.

martinet[2] *orn.* [~] *m* swift, martlet.

martin-pêcheur, *pl.* **martins-pê-cheurs** *orn.* [martɛ̃pɛ'ʃœːr] *m* king-fisher.

martre *zo.* [martr] *f* marten.

martyr, e *m*, **e** *f* [mar'tiːr] martyr; *enfant m* ~ battered child; **martyre** [~'tiːr] *m* martyrdom; *fig.* agonies *pl.*; **martyriser** [~tiri'ze] (1a) *v/t. eccl.* martyr; *fig.* torment; *fig.* make a martyr of.

marxiser [marksi'ze] (1a) *v/t.* make Marxist; se ~ become Marxist; **marxisme** *pol.* [mark'sism] *m* Marxism; **marxiste** *pol.* [~'sist] *adj.*, *a. su.* Marxist.

mas [mɑs] *m* small farmhouse.

mascarade [maska'rad] *f* masquer-ade (*a. fig.*).

mascaret [maska'rɛ] *m* bore, tidal wave.

mascotte [mas'kɔt] *f* mascot, charm.

masculin, e [masky'lɛ̃, ~'lin] **1.** *adj.* masculine; male; **2.** *su./m gramm.* masculine.

masochiste [mazo'ʃist] *su.* mas-ochist.

masque [mask] *m* mask (*a. fig.*); *fig.* cloak, cover; *thea.* masque; mas-querader; ~ *à gaz* gas-mask, respi-rator; **masquer** [mas'ke] (1m) *v/t.* mask; *fig.* conceal; ⚓ back (*a sail*).

massacrant, e [masa'krɑ̃, ~'krɑ̃t] *adj.*: *humeur f* ~*e* bad *or* F foul temper; **massacre** [~'sakr] *m* mas-

sacre; slaughter (*a. fig.*); **massa-crer** [masa'kre] (1a) *v/t.* massacre, slaughter; *fig.* make a hash of, ruin; murder (*music*); *tennis*: kill (*a ball*); **massacreur** *m*, **-euse** *f* [~'krœːr, ~'krøːz] slaughterer; *fig.* bungler; *fig. music*: murderer.

massage ✍ [ma'saːʒ] *m* massage.

masse[1] [mas] *f* ⊕ sledge-hammer; (*ceremonial*) mace.

masse[2] [~] *f* ⚔, *phys.*, *fig.* mass; ⚑ bulk; ⚑ fund; ⚡ earth; *persons*, *water*: body; *fig.* crowd, heap; *en* ~ in a body; *as a whole*; *fig.* mass..., a great number of.

massé [ma'se] *m billiards*: massé (shot).

massepain [mas'pɛ̃] *m* marzipan.

masser[1] [ma'se] (1a) *v/t.* mass (*people*); se ~ form a crowd.

masser[2] [ma'se] (1a) *v/t.* ✍ mas-sage; rub down (*a horse*); **masseur** [~'sœːr] *m* (*a.* ~ *kinésithérapeute*) masseur; **masseuse** [~'søːz] *f* mas-seuse.

massicot[1] ⚗, ⊕ [masi'ko] *m* yellow lead.

massicot[2] [~] *m books*: guillotine, trimmer.

massier [ma'sje] *m* mace-bearer.

massif, -ve [ma'sif, ~'siːv] **1.** *adj.* massive, bulky; heavy; solid (*gold*); **2.** *su./m* clump, cluster; △ block, solid mass; *geog.* mountain mass.

massue [ma'sy] *f* club (*a. zo.*, ⚡); *fig. en coup de* ~ sledge-hammer (*arguments*).

mastic [mas'tik] *m iron etc.*: mastic; *glazier*: cement; putty; *tooth*: fill-ing, stopping.

masticateur [mastika'tœːr] **1.** *adj./ m* masticatory; **2.** *su./m* masticator; **masticatoire** [~'twaːr] **1.** *adj.* mas-ticatory; **2.** *su./m* ✍ masticatory; chewing-gum.

mastiquer[1] [masti'ke] (1m) *v/t.* masticate; chew.

mastiquer[2] [~] (1m) *v/t.* ⊕ cement; stop (*a hole*, *a. a tooth*); putty (*a window*).

mastroquet F [mastro'kɛ] *m* public-house keeper, F pub-keeper.

masure [ma'zyːr] *f* hovel, shack.

mat[1], **mate** [mat] dull, flat, lustre-less (*colour*); heavy (*bread*, *dough*).

mat[2] [~] *adj./inv.* checkmated; *être* ~ be checkmate; *faire* ~ checkmate (*s.o.*).

mât [mɑ] *m* ⚓ mast; (*tent*-)pole; ⚔️ strut; ~ *de pavillon* flagstaff, flagpole; ⛴~ *de signaux* signalpost; ⚓ *navire m à trois* ~*s* threemaster.

matador [mata'dɔːr] *m* matador; *fig.* magnate; *fig.* bigwig.

matamore [mata'mɔːr] *m* swash-buckler.

match, *pl. a.* **matches** *sp.* [matʃ] *m* match; ~ *de championnat* league match; ~ *de retard* match in hand; ~ *retour* return match.

matelas [mat'la] *m* mattress; ⊕ ~ *d'air* air-cushion; ~ *pneumatique* air-bed, air-mattress; **matelasser** [matla'se] (1a) *v/t.* pad; stuff; *porte f matelassée* baize door; **matelassier** *m*, **-ère** *f* [⌣'sje, ⌣'sjɛːr] mattress-maker; mattress-cleaner; **matelassure** [⌣'syːr] *f* padding, stuffing.

matelot [mat'lo] *m* sailor; **matelote** [⌣'lɔt] *f cuis.* matelote; † (*approx.*) hornpipe; *à la* ~ sailor-fashion.

mater[1] [ma'te] (1a) *v/t.* mat, dull; ⊕ hammer; work (*the dough*).

mater[2] [⌣] (1a) *v/t.* (check)mate (*at chess*); *fig.* subdue, humble.

mâter ⚓ [mɑ'te] (1a) *v/t.* mast; rig (*booms*); up-end (*a boat*).

matérialiser [materjali'ze] (1a) *v/t. a. se* ~ materialize; **matérialisme** [⌣'lism] *m* (~ *dialectique* dialectic) materialism; **matérialiste** 1. *adj.* materialistic; 2. *su.* materialist; **matériau** △ [⌣'rjo] *m* material; **matériaux** ⊕, △, *fig.* [⌣'rjo] *m/pl.* materials; **matériel, -elle** [⌣'rjɛl] 1. *adj.* material; physical; *fig.* sensual; ⚖️ *dommages m/pl.* ~*s* damage *sg.* to property; *vie f* ~*elle* necessities *pl.* of life; 2. *su./m* ⊕ plant; apparatus; *school, a.* ⚔️: furniture; *war*: material; *computer*: hardware; ~ *humain* manpower; men *pl.*; ⛴ ~ *roulant* rolling stock.

maternel, -elle [matɛr'nɛl] maternal; mother (*tongue*); *école f* ~*elle* infant school; **maternité** [⌣ni'te] *f* maternity, motherhood; maternity hospital.

mathématicien *m*, **-enne** *f* [matemati'sjɛ̃, ⌣'sjɛn] mathematician; **mathématique** [⌣'tik] 1. *adj.* mathematical; 2. *su./f:* ~*s pl.* mathematics; ~*s pl. spéciales* higher mathematics.

matière [ma'tjɛːr] *f* material; matter, substance; *fig.* subject; *fig.* grounds *pl.* (*oft.* ⚖️); *anat.*, *fig.* ~ *grise* grey matter; ~*s pl. premières* raw material *sg.*; ⊕~*s plastiques* plastics; *en* ~ *de* as regards; in matters of; *en la* ~ on the subject; *entrer en* ~ broach the subject; *table f des* ~*s* table of contents.

matin [ma'tɛ̃] 1. *su./m* morning; *au* ~ in the morning; *de bon* (*or grand*) ~, *au petit* ~ early in the morning; 2. *adv.* early.

mâtin [mɑ'tɛ̃] *su./m* mastiff hound.

matinal, e, *m/pl.* **-aux** [mati'nal, ⌣'no] morning...; early; *être* ~ be an early riser (*person*); **matinée** [⌣'ne] *f* morning, forenoon; morning's work; *cost.* wrapper; *thea.* matinee, afternoon performance; *faire la grasse* ~ sleep late, F have a lie in; **matines** *eccl.* [ma'tin] *f/pl.* mat(t)ins; **matineux, -euse** [mati'nø, ⌣'nøːz] 1. *adj.* early rising; 2. *su.* early riser; **matinier, -ère** [⌣'nje, ⌣'njɛːr] *adj.*: *l'étoile f* ~*ère* the morning star. [⊕ hammer.)

matir [ma'tiːr] (2a) *v/t.* mat, dull;)

matois, e [ma'twa, ⌣'twaːz] 1. *adj.* sly, foxy, cunning; 2. *su.* crafty person.

matou *zo.* [ma'tu] *m* tom-cat.

matraquage [matra'kaːʒ] *m* bludgeoning, *etc.*; *see matraquer*; **matraque** [ma'trak] *f* bludgeon; rubber truncheon; **matraquer** [matra'ke] (1a) *v/t.* bludgeon, beat (*s.o.*) up; *fig.* overcharge (*customer, etc.*), overburden (*tax-payer etc.*); *fig.* bombard (*the public*); *fig.* plug (*a song, etc.*).

matriarcat [matriar'ka] *m* matriarchy; **matrice** [⌣'tris] 1. *su./f* matrix; ⊕ die; ⊕ master record; *typ.* type mo(u)ld; *anat.* womb, uterus; 2. *adj.* primary (*colour*); mother (*church, tongue*); **matricer** ⊕ [matri'se] (1k) *v/t.* stamp (out); swage; **matricide** [⌣'sid] 1. *su. person*: matricide; *su./m crime*: matricide; 2. *adj.* matricidal.

matricule [matri'kyl] *su./f* roll, register; registration; *su./m* registration or reference number; ✗ regimental number; *sl.* *ça devient mauvais pour son* ~ his number is up, things are going to be hot for him.

matrimonial, e, *m/pl.* **-aux** [matrimɔ'njal, ⌣'njo] matrimonial.

matrone [ma'trɔn] *f* matron.

maturation [matyra'sjɔ̃] *f* ripening; *tobacco*: maturing.

mâture ⚓ [mɑ'tyːr] *f* masting; *coll.* masts *pl.*; sheer-legs *pl.*

maturité [matyri'te] *f* maturity; ripeness; *avec* ~ after mature consideration.

matutinal, e, *m/pl.* **-aux** [matyti-'nal, ~'no] matutinal.

maudire [mo'diːr] (4p) *v/t.* curse; *fig.* grumble about; **maudit, e** [~'di, ~'dit] **1.** *p.p. of* maudire; **2.** *adj.* (ac)cursed; *fig.* execrable, damnable.

maugréer [mogre'e] (1a) *v/i.* curse; *fig.* grumble (about, at *contre*).

maure [moːr] **1.** *adj./m* Moorish; **2.** *su./m* ♀ Moor; **mauresque** [mɔ-'resk] **1.** *adj.* Moorish; △ Moresque; **2.** *su./f* ♀ Moorish woman.

mausolée [mozo'le] *m* mausoleum.

maussade [mo'sad] surly, sullen; *fig.* depressing, dull (*weather*); irritable (*person, tone*); **maussaderie** [~sa'dri] *f* sullenness; irritability, peevishness.

mauvais, e [mɔ've, ~'veːz] **1.** *adj.* bad (*a. influence, news,* † *season*); evil, wicked; wrong; ill; nasty, unpleasant; offensive (*smell*); 🞰 severe (*illness*); ~e excuse lame excuse; ~e foi dishonesty; unfairness; ~e tête unruly *or* obstinate 'person; de ~e humeur in a bad temper; **2.** *mauvais adv.*: il fait ~ the weather is bad; sentir ~ smell bad, stink.

mauve [moːv] *su./f* ♀ mallow; *su./m, a. adj.* mauve, purple.

mauviette [mo'vjet] *f orn.* skylark; *fig.* frail person; **mauvis** *orn.* [~'vi] *m* redwing.

maxillaire *anat.* [maksil'leːr] *m* jaw-bone; ~ supérieur maxilla.

maximal, e, *m/pl.* **-aux** [maksi'mal, ~'mo] maximal; **maxime** [mak'sim] *f* maxim; **maximiser** [~simi'ze] (1a) *v/t.* maximize; **maximum,** *pl.* *a.* **maxima** [~si'mɔm, ~'ma] *su./m, a. adj.* maximum; *porter au* ~ maximize.

mayonnaise *cuis.* [majɔ'neːz] *f* mayonnaise.

mazout [ma'zut] *m* fuel oil; crude oil.

me [mə] **1.** *pron./pers.* me; to me; ~ voici! here I am!; **2.** *pron./rfl.* myself, to myself.

méandre [me'ɑ̃ːdr] *m* wind(ing), bend; *faire des* ~s meander, wind (*river*).

mec F [mɛk] *m* gay, fellow.

mécanicien [mekani'sjɛ̃] *m* mechanic; engineer; 🚂 engine driver, *Am.* engineer; **mécanique** [~'nik] **1.** *adj.* mechanical; **2.** *su./f* mechanics *sg.*; mechanism, (piece of) machinery; engineering; *phys.* ~ ondulatoire wave-mechanics *sg.*; **mécaniser** [~ni'ze] *v/t.* mechanize; turn (*s.o.*) into a machine; **mécanisme** [~'nism] *m* mechanism; machinery.

mécano ⊕ F [meka'no] *m* mechanic.

méchamment [meʃa'mɑ̃] *adv. of* méchant; **méchanceté** [~ʃɑ̃s'te] *f* nastyness; meanness; malice, spite; spiteful remark *or* action; **méchant, e** [~'ʃɑ̃, ~'ʃɑ̃ːt] **1.** *adj.* nasty; mean; bad; spiteful; *fig.* † poor, sorry, paltry; il n'est pas ~ he's all right; he's harmless; **2.** *su./m* naughty boy; *su./f* naughty girl.

mèche[1] [mɛʃ] *f candle, lamp*: wick; ⚔ match fuse; *whip*: cracker, *Am.* snapper; *hair*: lock; ⊕ bit, drill; *éventer la* ~ discover a secret; *vendre la* ~ let the cat out of the bag, *sl.* blow the gaff.

mèche[2] F [~] *f: de* ~ *avec* in collusion with; hand in glove with; il n'y a pas ~! it can't be done!

mécompte [me'kɔ̃ːt] *m* miscalculation, mistake in reckoning, error; *fig.* disappointment.

méconnaissable [mekɔne'sabl] unrecognizable; hardly recognizable; **méconnaissance** [~ne'sɑ̃ːs] *f* failure to recognize; **méconnaître** [~'neːtr] (4k) *v/t.* refuse to recognize, cut; *fig.* not to appreciate; *fig.* underrate; *fig.* disown.

mécontent, e [mekɔ̃'tɑ̃, ~'tɑ̃ːt] dissatisfied, discontented (with, *de*); annoyed (at, *de*; that, *que*); **mécontentement** [~tɑ̃t'mɑ̃] *m* dissatisfaction (with, *de*); displeasure, annoyance (at, *de*); *pol.* disaffection; **mécontenter** [~tɑ̃'te] (1a) *v/t.* dissatisfy; displease, annoy.

mécréant, e [mekre'ɑ̃, ~'ɑ̃ːt] **1.** *adj.* unbelieving; heterodox; **2.** *su.* unbeliever; misbeliever; miscreant.

médaille [me'daːj] *f* medal; badge; △ medallion; **médaillé, e** [meda-'je] **1.** *adj.* decorated; holding a medal; **2.** *su.* medallist; medalwinner, prize-winner; **médaillier** [~'je] *m* medal cabinet; collection of medals; **médailliste** [~'jist] *m* collector of medals; medal-maker; **médaillon** [∼'jɔ̃] *m* medallion; locket; *journ.* inset; *cuis. butter*: pat; *cuis.* medaillon.

médecin [met'sɛ̃] *m* doctor, physician; ⚓ ∼ *du bord* ship's doctor; ∼ *légiste* medical expert; ∼ *traitant* doctor in charge of the case; *femme f* ∼ lady doctor; **médecine** [∼'sin] *f* medicine; ∼ *légale* forensic medicine.

media, média [me'dja] *m/pl.* (mass) media.

médian, e [me'djɑ̃, ∼'djan] median; middle...; *foot.* half-way (*line*); **médiat, e** [∼'dja, ∼'djat] mediate; **médiateur, -trice** [medja'tœːr, ∼'tris] 1. *adj.* mediatory; 2. *su.* mediator; intermediary; *pol.* ombudsman; **médiation** [∼'sjɔ̃] *f* mediation.

médical, e, *m/pl.* **-aux** [medi'kal, ∼'ko] medical; **médicalisation** [∼kaliza'sjɔ̃] *f* medical care; **medicaliser** [∼kali'ze] (1a) *v/t.* provide medical care for; **médicament** [medika'mɑ̃] *m* medicament, F medicine; **médicamenter** [∼mɑ̃'te] (1a) *v/t.* doctor, dose (*s.o.*); **médicamenteux, -euse** [∼mɑ̃'tø, ∼'tøːz] medicinal; **médicastre** [medi'kastr] *m* quack (doctor); **médication** [∼ka'sjɔ̃] *f* medical treatment, medication; **médicinal, e**, *m/pl.* **-aux** [∼si'nal, ∼'no] medicinal; **médico-legal, e**, *m/pl.* **-aux** [∼kɔle'gal, ∼'go] medico-legal.

médiéval, e, *m/pl.* **-aux** [medje'val, ∼'vo] medi(a)eval; **médiéviste** [∼'vist] *su.* medi(a)evalist.

médiocre [me'djɔkr] mediocre; poor, second-rate; indifferent; **médiocrité** [∼djɔkri'te] *f* mediocrity; F *person*: second-rater.

médire [me'diːr] (4p) *v/i.*: ∼ *de q.* slander s.o., speak ill of s.o., F run s.o. down; **médisance** [medi'zɑ̃ːs] *f* slander; scandal-mongering; **médisant, e** [∼'zɑ̃, ∼'zɑ̃ːt] 1. *adj.* slanderous, backbiting; 2. *su.* slanderer; scandal-monger.

méditatif, -ve [medita'tif, ∼'tiːv] meditative; contemplative, pensive; **méditation** [∼ta'sjɔ̃] *f* meditation (*a. eccl.*); cogitation, thought; **méditer** [∼'te] (1a) *v/i.* meditate; *v/t.* contemplate (*s.th.*).

méditerrané, e *geog.* [meditera'ne] mediterranean.

médium [me'djɔm] *m psychics*: medium; ♩ middle register.

médius *anat.* [me'djys] *m* middle finger.

médullaire ♀, *anat.* [medyl'lɛːr] medullary.

méduse [me'dyːz] *f* jelly-fish; **méduser** [∼dy'ze] (1a) *v/t.* dumbfound; petrify.

meeting *sp., pol.* [mi'tiŋ] *m* meeting.

méfaire † [me'fɛːr] *v/i.* occurs only in *inf.* do wrong; **méfait** [∼'fɛ] *m* misdeed; *fig.* ill *or* damaging effect, ravages *pl.*

méfiance [me'fjɑ̃ːs] *f* distrust; **méfiant, e** [∼'fjɑ̃, ∼'fjɑ̃ːt] suspicious, distrustful; **méfier** [∼'fje] (1o) *v/t.*: se ∼ be on one's guard; se ∼ *de* be suspicious of, distrust; look out for, watch.

mégalo... [megalɔ] megalo...; **∼mane** [∼'man] *su.* megalomaniac; **∼manie** [∼ma'ni] *f* megalomania; **∼pole** [∼'pɔl] *f* megalopolis.

mégaphone [mega'fɔn] *m* megaphone.

mégarde [me'gard] *f*: *par* ∼ inadvertently; accidentally.

mégatonne [mega'tɔn] *f* megaton.

mégère [me'ʒɛːr] *f* shrew, termagant.

mégot F [me'go] *m cigarette*: fag end, *Am.* butt; *cigar*: stump; (poor) cigar; **mégoter** F [∼gɔ'te] (1a) *v/i.* skimp (on, *sur*).

meilleur, e [mɛ'jœːr] 1. *adj.* better; *le* ∼ the better (*of two*), the best (*of several*); 2. *su./m* best (thing).

mélancolie [melɑ̃kɔ'li] *f* melancholy, gloom; ⚕ melancholia; **mélancolique** [∼'lik] mournful, gloomy, melancholy; ⚕ melancholic.

mélange [me'lɑ̃ːʒ] *m* mixture, blend; *cards*: shuffling; ∼*s pl.* miscellany *sg.*; ∼ *réfrigérant* freezing-mixture; **mélanger** [melɑ̃'ʒe] (11) *v/t. a.* se ∼ mix; blend; **mélangeur** [∼'ʒœːr] *m* mixing-machine, mixer.

mélasse [me'las] *f* molasses *pl.*, treacle; *sl. dans la* ∼ in the soup.

mêlée [mɛ'le] *f* ✕ mêlée, fray; scuffle; scramble; *sp. rugby*: scrum; **mêler** [∼] (1a) *v/t.* mix; mingle, blend; ∼ *q. à* (*or dans*) involve s.o. in; se ∼ *à* join; mix with; se ∼ *de* meddle in, interfere in *or* with; dabble in (*politics*).

mélèze ♀ [me'lɛ:z] *m* larch.
mélilot ♀ [meli'lo] *m* sweet clover, melilot.
méli-mélo, pl. mélis-mélos F [me-lime'lo] *m* jumble; clutter; hotch-potch.
mellifère [mɛlli'fɛ:r] honey-bearing; **mellifique** [ˌˊfik] mellific, honey-making; **melliflue** *fig.* [ˌˊfly] mellifluous, honeyed.
mélodie [melɔ'di] *f* ♪ melody, tune; melodiousness; **mélodieux, -euse** [ˌˊdjø, ˌˊdjø:z] melodious, tuneful; **mélodique** ♪ [ˌˊdik] melodic; **mélodrame** [ˌˊdram] *m* melodrama; **mélomane** [ˌˊman] **1.** *adj.* mad on music; **2.** *su.* melomaniac.
melon [mə'lɔ̃] *m* ♀ melon; bowler (hat).
membrane [mã'bran] *f* ♀, *anat.*, ⊕ membrane; *zo.* duck, goose, *etc.*: web; **membraneux, -euse** [ˌˊbra-'nø, ˌˊnø:z] membranous.
membre [mã:br] *m* member; *body*: limb; ⚓ rib; **membré, e** [mã'bre] *adj.*: **bien ~** well-limbed; **membru, e** [ˌˊbry] strong-limbed; big-limbed; **membrure** [ˌˊbry:r] *f coll.* limbs *pl.*, ⚓ ribs *pl.*; ⚓ frame.
même [mɛ:m] **1.** *adj.* same; *after noun*: self, very; *ce ~ soir* the same evening; *ce soir ~* this very evening; *en ~ temps* at the same time; *la bonté ~* kindness itself; *les ~s personnes* the same persons; *see vous-même*; **2.** *adv.* even; *à ~ de (inf.)* able to (*inf.*), in a position to (*inf.*); *boire à ~ la bouteille* drink out of the bottle; *de ~* in the same way, likewise; *de ~ que* like, (just) as; *pas ~* not even; *quand ~* even if; all the same; *tout de ~* all the same; *voire ~ ... indeed ...*
mémère F [me'mɛ:r] *f* mother; mum(my); grandmother, F granny.
mémoire¹ [me'mwa:r] *f* memory; *de ~* by heart, from memory; *de ~ d'homme* within living memory; *en ~ de* in memory of.
mémoire² [ˌˊ] *m* memorandum; memorial; memoir, dissertation; abstract; **~s** *pl.* transactions; **♀s** *pl.* (*historical*) memoirs.
mémorable [memɔ'rabl] memorable, noteworthy; **mémorial** [ˌˊrjal] *m* Gazette; ♀ memoirs *pl.*; **mémorialiste** [ˌˊrja'list] *m* memorialist.

menace [mə'nas] *f* threat, menace; **menacer** [ˌˊna'se] (1k) *v/t.* threaten (with, *de*).
ménage [me'na:ʒ] *m* housekeeping; housework; † set of furniture; *fig.* household, family; *fig.* married couple; *faire bon ~ (avec)* get on well (with); *faire le ~* do the housework; *faux ~* unmarried couple living together; *femme f de ~* charwoman, cleaner; *être heureux en ~* be happily married; *jeune ~* newly married couple; *monter son ~* set up house; *tenir le ~ de* keep house for; **ménagement** [ˌˊnaʒ'mã] *m* care; consideration, caution.
ménager¹ [mena'ʒe] (1l) *v/t.* save; use economically, make the most of; arrange; provide.
ménager², -ère [mena'ʒe, ˌˊʒɛ:r] **1.** *adj.* domestic; *fig.* thrifty, sparing (of, *de*); *enseignement m ~* domestic science; **2.** *su./f* housewife; housekeeper; canteen of cutlery; cruet-stand; **ménagerie** [ˌˊnaʒ'ri] *f* menagerie.
mendiant, e [mã'djã, ˌˊdjã:t] **1.** *adj.* mendicant; *su.* beggar; *su./m* F *les quatre ~s pl.* figs, raisins, almonds and hazel-nuts as dessert; **mendicité** [ˌˊdisi'te] *f* begging; beggary; beggardom; **mendier** [ˌˊdje] (1o) *v/i.* beg; *v/t.* beg for; *~ des compliments* fish for compliments; **mendigot** F [ˌˊdi'go] *m* beggar.
meneau ⌂ [mə'no] *m* mullion; *à ~x* mullioned.
menée [mə'ne] *f hunt.* track; *fig.* manœuvre, intrigue.
mener [ˌˊ] (1d) *v/t.* lead; take, get (s.o. to, *q. à*); ⚡ draw (*a line*); *fig.* run, control, manage; steer (*a boat*); *~ qch. à bien* (or *à bonne fin*) see s.th. through; *~ par le bout du nez* lead by the nose; *cela peut le ~ loin* that may take him a long way; *v/i.* lead (to, *à*).
ménestrel *hist.* [menɛs'trɛl] *m* minstrel; **ménétrier** [ˌˊne'trje] *m* village musician, fiddler.
meneur [mə'nœ:r] *m* leader; ring-leader; driver; *pej.* agitator, fomenter; *~ de jeu* emcee, Br. *a.* compère; quizmaster.
menhir *geol.* [me'ni:r] *m* menhir.
méninge [me'nɛ̃ʒ] *m anat.* meninx; F **~s** *pl.* brains; F *se creuser les ~s* rack one's brains; F *se fatiguer les ~s*

overtax one's brains; **méningite** ⚕
[menɛ̃'ʒit] f meningitis.
ménisque anat. [me'nisk] m menis-
cus.
ménopause ⚕ [menɔ'poːz] f meno-
pause.
menotte [mə'nɔt] f ⊕ handle; mot.
etc. link; F little hand; ~s pl. handcuffs.
mensonge [mã'sɔ̃ːʒ] m lie, falsehood; fig. delusion; ~ officieux (or
pieux) white lie; **mensonger, -ère**
[~sɔ̃'ʒe, ~'ʒɛːr] untrue; false; fig.
illusory.
mensualité [mãsɥali'te] f monthly
payment or instalment; monthly
salary; **mensuel, -elle** [~'sɥɛl] 1.
adj. monthly; 2. su. employee paid
by the month.
mensurations [mãsyra'sjɔ̃] f/pl.
measurements.
mental, e, m/pl. **-aux** [mã'tal, ~'to]
mental; restriction f ~e mental reservation; **mentalité** [~tali'te] f men-
tality.
menterie F [mã'tri] f lie, F fib;
menteur, -euse [~'tœːr, ~'tøːz] 1.
adj. lying; deceptive, false; 2. su. liar,
F fibber.
menthe ♧ [mãːt] f mint.
mention [mã'sjɔ̃] f mention; faire ~
de = **mentionner** [~sjɔ'ne] (1a) v/t.
mention; name.
mentir [mã'tiːr] (2b) v/i. lie (to, à).
menton [mã'tɔ̃] m chin; **menton-**
net [mãtɔ'nɛ] m ⊕ catch; ⊕ lug;
🚋 flange; **mentonnière** [~'njɛːr] f
(bonnet-)string; ⚕ chin-bandage; ✕
check-strap; ♪ violin: chin-rest.
mentor [mɛ̃'tɔːr] m mentor.
menu, e [mə'ny] 1. adj. small; fine;
minute (details, fragments); slim,
slender (figure); petty, trifling;
2. menu adv. small, fine; hacher ~
mince; chop (s.th.) up small; 3. su./m
detail; meal: menu; ~ à prix fixe
table d'hôte; par le ~ in detail.
menuiser [mənɥi'ze] (1a) v/t. cut
(wood) down; v/i. do woodwork;
menuiserie [~nɥiz'ri] f woodwork,
carpentry; joiner's shop; **menui-**
sier [~nɥi'zje] m joiner; carpenter.
méphitique [mefi'tik] noxious,
foul; gaz m ~ choke-damp.
méplat, e [me'pla, ~'plat] 1. adj.
flat; △ flat-laid; in planks (wood);
2. su./m flat part; geol. rock: ledge.
méprendre [me'prãːdr] (4aa) v/t.:

se ~ sur be mistaken about, misjudge; fig. à s'y ~ to the life; il n'y
a pas à s'y ~ there can be no mistake.
mépris [me'pri] m contempt, scorn;
au ~ de in defiance of, contrary to;
méprisable [mepri'zabl] contemptible; **méprisant, e** [~'zã,
~'zãːt] scornful, contemptuous.
méprise [me'priːz] f mistake.
mépriser [mepri'ze] (1a) v/t. de-
spise; scorn.
mer [mɛːr] f sea; tide; ~ haute high
tide; haute ~ open sea; porter de
l'eau à la ~ carry coals to Newcastle.
mercanti F [mɛrkã'ti] m profiteer;
mercantile [~'til] profit-minded,
mercenary; esprit m ~ (absolute)
profit-mindedness.
mercenaire [mɛrsə'nɛːr] 1. adj.
mercenary (a. ✕); 2. su./m hireling;
✕ mercenary.
mercerie [mɛrsə'ri] f haberdashery;
haberdasher's (shop), Am. notions
shop.
merci [mɛr'si] 1. adv. thank you,
thanks (for, de); ~ bien, ~ beaucoup
many thanks, thank you very much;
2. su./m thanks pl.; su./f mercy; à la ~
de at the mercy of; crier ~ cry mercy,
beg for mercy; sans ~ pitiless(ly
adv.), merciless(ly adv.).
mercier m, **-ère** f [mɛr'sje, ~'sjɛːr]
haberdasher; small-ware dealer.
mercredi [mɛrkrə'di] m Wednesday.
mercure ♆ [mɛr'kyːr] m mercury,
quicksilver; **mercureux** ♆[~ky'rø]
adj./m mercurous.
mercuriale [mɛrky'rjal] f ♣ market-
prices pl.; F fig. reprimand.
mercuriel, -elle [mɛrky'rjɛl] mer-
curial.
merde V [mɛrd] 1. su./f shit; 2. int.
hell!; **merdier** sl. [mɛr'dje] m (hell
of a) mess.
mère [mɛːr] f mother (a. fig.); ⊕ die;
mo(u)ld; fig. source, root; ~(-)céliba-
taire unmarried mother; ~ patrie
mother country; ♣ maison f ~ head
office.
méridien, -enne [meri'djɛ̃, ~'djɛn]
1. adj. geog. meridian; midday;
astr. transit; 2. su./m meridian; su./f
meridian line; midday nap; sofa;
méridional, e, m/pl. **-aux** [~djɔ-
'nal, ~'no] 1. adj. south(ern); me-

ridional; **2.** *su.* southerner; merid-
ional.

meringue *cuis.* [məˈrɛ̃ːg] *f* meringue.

mérinos ✝, *zo.* [meriˈnos] *m* me-
rino.

merise ⚘ [məˈriːz] *f* wild cherry;
merisier [ˌriˈzje] *m* wild cherry
(-tree).

mérite [meˈrit] *m* merit; quality;
ability; *sans* ～ undeserving; **mériter** [meriˈte] (1a) *vt/i.* deserve,
merit; **méritoire** [ˌˈtwaːr] merito-
rious, praiseworthy, commendable.

merlan [mɛrˈlɑ̃] *m icht.* whiting; *sl.*
hairdresser; **merle** [mɛrl] *m orn.*
blackbird; F *fig.* ～ *blanc* rara avis;
F *fig. fin* ～ sly fellow.

merluche [mɛrˈlyʃ] *f icht.* hake;
✝ dried cod.

merrain [mɛˈrɛ̃] *m* ⊕ stave-wood;
wood for cooperage; *deer's antlers:*
beam.

merveille [mɛrˈvɛːj] *f* marvel, wonder; *à* ～ magnificently, F fine; **merveilleux, -euse** [ˌvɛˈjø, ˌˈjøːz]
marvellous, wonderful; supernatural.

mes [me] *see* mon.

més... [mez] mis...; ～**alliance** [me-
zaˈljɑ̃ːs] *f* misalliance.

mésange *orn.* [meˈzɑ̃ːʒ] *f* tit(mouse);
mésangette [ˌzɑ̃ˈʒɛt] *f* bird-trap.

mésaventure [mezavɑ̃ˈtyːr] *f* mis-
adventure, mishap, mischance.

mesdames [meˈdam] *pl. of madame;* **mesdemoiselles** [medmwa-
ˈzɛl] *pl. of mademoiselle.*

mésentente [mezɑ̃ˈtɑ̃ːt] *f* misunderstanding, disagreement.

mésentère *anat.* [mezɑ̃ˈtɛːr] *m*
mesentery.

mésestimer [mezɛstiˈme] (1a) *vt/i.*
underestimate; hold (*s.o.*) in low
esteem.

mésintelligence [mezɛ̃teliˈʒɑ̃ːs] *f*
disagreement; *en* ～ *avec* at loggerheads with.

mesquin, e [mɛsˈkɛ̃, ～ˈkin] mean,
stingy; **mesquinerie** [ˌkinˈri] *f*
meanness; pettiness.

mess ✕ [mɛs] *m* mess.

message [mɛˈsaːʒ] *m* message (*a.
fig.*); **messager** *m,* **-ère** *f* [ˌsaˈʒe,
～ˈʒɛːr] messenger, *fig.* harbinger;
messageries [ˌsaʒˈri] *f/pl.* delivery
or distribution service *sg.*; shipping
(company) *sg.*

messe *eccl., a.* ♪ [mɛs] *f* mass.

messeoir [mɛˈswaːr] (3k) *v/i.* be
unbecoming (to, *à*).

Messie *bibl.* [mɛˈsi] *m* Messiah.

messieurs [mɛˈsjø] *pl. of monsieur.*

mesurable [məzyˈrabl] measurable;
mesurage [ˌˈraːʒ] *m* measurement;
mesure [məˈzyːr] *f* measure; measurement; extent, degree; step; *fig.*
moderation; *verse:* metre; ♪ time;
♪ bar; *à* ～ one by one; in proportion; *à* ～ *que* (in proportion) as;
donner sa ～ show what one is capable of; *en* ～ *de* in a position to;
outre ～ excessively, beyond measure; *poids m/pl. et* ～*s pl.* weights
and measures; *prendre des* ～*s contre*
take steps *or* measures against; *fig.
prendre la* ～ *de q.* size s.o. up;
prendre les ～*s de q.* take s.o.'s measurements; *fig. sans* ～ boundless; *sur* ～
to measure; to order; **mesurer**
[məzyˈre] (1a) *v/t.* measure; calculate; *fig.* estimate; *se* ～ *avec* pit o.s.
against; **mesureur** [ˌˈrœːr] *m person, machine:* measurer; ga(u)ge; ⚡
metre.

méta... [meta] meta...

métairie [meteˈri] *f* small farm.

métal [meˈtal] *m* metal; ～ *brut* (com-
mun) raw (base) metal; **métallifère** [metalliˈfɛːr] metalliferous;
métallique [ˌˈlik] metallic; wire
(*rope*); ✝ *encaisse f* ～ gold reserve;
métalliser ⊕ [ˌliˈze] (1a) *v/t.*
cover with metal, plate; metallize;
métallo F [ˌˈlo] *m* metal-worker;
métallurgie ⊕ [ˌlyrˈʒi] *f* metallurgy; smelting; **métallurgiste** ⊕
[ˌlyrˈʒist] *m* metallurgist; metal-
worker.

méta...: ～**morphose** [metamɔrˈfoːz]
f metamorphosis, transformation;
～**morphoser** [ˌmɔrfoˈze] (1a) *v/t.*
metamorphose; *se* ～ change; ～
phore [ˌˈfɔːr] *f* metaphor; image;
～**phorique** [ˌfɔˈrik] metaphorical;
～**physique** [ˌfiˈzik] *f* metaphysics
sg.; ～**psychique** [ˌpsiˈʃik] *f* para-
psychology; ～**stase** ⚕ [ˌˈstaːz] *f*
metastasis.

métayer [meteˈje] *m* metayer, tenant
farmer; *Am.* share-cropper.

métempsycose [metɑ̃psiˈkoːz] *f*
metempsychosis.

météo [meteˈo] *su./f* weather report;
meteorological office; *su./m* meteor-
ologist; weather man; **météore**
[ˌˈɔːr] *m* meteor; **météorisme** [ˌˈɔ-

'rism] *m* 🐝 meteorism; flatulence; *vet.* hoove; **météorologie** [∼ɔrɔlɔ-'ʒi] *f* meteorology.

métèque *pej.* [me'tɛk] *m sl.* wop, *Br. sl.* wog.

méthode [me'tɔd] *f* method, system; way; **méthodique** [∼tɔ'dik] methodical, systematic.

méticuleux, -euse [metiky'lø, ∼'lø:z] meticulous, punctilious, F fussy.

métier [me'tje] *m* job; trade; craft; profession; (∼ à tisser weaving) loom.

métis, -isse [me'tis] 1. *su.* half-breed; *dog:* mongrel; 2. *adj.* half-bred; cross-bred; mongrel (*dog*).

métrage [me'tra:ʒ] *m* measurement; metric length; *cin. court (long)*∼ short (full-length) film; **mètre** [mɛtr] *m* metre, *Am.* meter; rule, yardstick; ∼ à ruban tape measure; ∼ carré square metre; ∼ cube cubic metre; ∼ pliant folding rule; **métrique** [∼'trik] 1. *adj.* metric; 2. *su./f* metrics *sg.*

métro F [me'tro] *m* underground railway, tube, *Am.* subway.

métro...: ∼**logie** [metrɔlɔ'ʒi] *f* metrology; ∼**manie** [∼ma'ni] *f* metromania; ∼**nome** ♪ [∼'nɔm] *m* metronome.

métropole [metrɔ'pɔl] *f* metropolis; capital; mother country; **métropolitain, e** [∼pɔli'tɛ̃, ∼'tɛn] 1. *adj.* metropolitan; 2. *su./m* metropolitan; *eccl.* archbishop; underground railway.

mets¹ [mɛ] *m* food; dish; ∼ tout préparé ready-to-serve meal.

mets² [∼] *1st p. sg. pres. of* mettre.

mettable [mɛ'tabl] wearable (*clothes*); **metteur** [∼'tœ:r] *m* ⊕ setter; 📷 (*plate-*)layer; ∼ en scène *thea.* producer; *cin.* director.

mettre [mɛtr] (4v) *v/t.* put; place, set; lay (*a. the table*); put on (*clothes*); translate (into, en); bet (on, sur); *fig.* suppose, assume; ∼ à l'aise put (*s.o.*) at his ease; ⚡ ∼ à la terre earth; ∼ au point adjust; *opt.* focus (*a lens*); *fig.* clarify (*an affair*); ∼ bas lamb (*sheep*), litter, whelp (*bitch*), foal (*mare*), farrow (*pig*), calve (*cow*); ∼ de côté save; ∼ deux heures à (*inf.*) take two hours to (*inf.*); ∼ en colère make angry; ∼ en jeu bring into play *or* discussion; ⊕ ∼ en marche start (*a. fig.*); *typ.* ∼ en pages make up; *thea.* ∼ en

scène stage; *mettons que ce soit vrai* let us suppose this to be true *or* that this is true; se ∼ place o.s., stand; se ∼ à (*inf.*) begin (*ger.*, to *inf.*); start (*ger.*), take to; se ∼ à l'œuvre set to work; se ∼ en colère get angry; se ∼ en gala put on formal dress; se ∼ en route start out; se ∼ ensemble live together (*unmarried couple*); se ∼ en tête de (*inf.*) take it into one's head to (*inf.*); s'y ∼ set about it.

meublant, e [mœ'blɑ̃, ∼'blɑ̃:t] decorative, effective, nice; **meuble** [mœbl] 1. *adj.* movable; loose (*ground*); ⚖ biens *m/pl.* ∼s movables; 2. *su./m* piece of furniture; ∼s *pl.* furniture; **meublé, e** [mœ'ble] 1. *adj.*: (non) ∼ (un)furnished; 2. *su./m* furnished room; **meubler** [∼] (1a) *v/t.* furnish; *fig.* fill (with, de).

meule¹ [mœ:l] *f* hay: stack, rick; charcoal: pile; bricks: clamp; ✦ mushrooms: bed.

meule² [mœ:l] *f* ⊕ millstone; grindstone; ∼ de fromage large round cheese; **meuler** ⊕ [mœ'le] (1a) *v/t.* grind; **meulerie** [mœl-'ri] *f* millstone-factory, grindstone-factory; **meulier** ⊕ [mø'lje] *m* millstone-maker, grindstone-maker; **meulière** ⊕ [∼'ljɛ:r] *f* millstone grit; millstone quarry.

meulon [mø'lɔ̃] *m* small haystack; corn: stook; (hay)cock.

meunerie [møn'ri] *f* flour: milling; **meunier** [mø'nje] miller; **meunière** [∼'njɛ:r] *f* woman mill-owner, *a.* miller's wife.

meurent [mœ:r] *3rd p. pl. pres. of* mourir; **meurs** [∼] *1st p. sg. pres. of* mourir; **meurt-de-faim** F [mœrdə'fɛ̃] *m/inv.* starveling; de ∼ starvation (*wage*).

meurtre [mœrtr] *m* murder; ⚖ non-capital murder, *Am.* murder in the second degree; au ∼! murder!; *fig.* c'est un ∼ it is a downright shame; **meurtrier, -ère** [mœrtri'e, ∼'ɛ:r] 1. *adj.* murderous; guilty of murder (*person*); 2. *su./m* murderer; *su./f* murderess; ⚔ loophole.

meurtrir [mœr'tri:r] (2a) *v/t.* bruise; **meurtrissure** [∼tri'sy:r] *f* bruise. [voir.]

meus [mø] *1st p. sg. pres. of* mou-|

meute [mø:t] *f* pack; *fig.* mob.

meuvent [mœːv] *3rd p. pl. pres. of* **mouvoir.**

mévendre ✝ † [meˈvãːdr] (4a) *v/t.* sell at a loss; **mévente** ✝ [ˌˈvãːt] *f* goods: sale at a loss; slump.

mezzanine [mɛdzaˈnin] *f* mezzanine (floor).

mi ♪ [mi] *m/inv.* mi, note: E.

mi... [mi] *adv.* half, mid, semi-; ﹏-clos half open; à ﹏-chemin half-way; la ﹏-janvier mid-January; *sp. poids m* ﹏-lourd light-heavy weight.

miaou [mjau] *m* miaow, mew.

miasme [mjasm] *m* miasma.

miauler [mjoˈle] (1a) *v/i.* mew, miaow.

mica *min.* [miˈka] *m* mica; **micelle** *biol.* [miˈsɛl] *m* micella.

miche [miʃ] *f* round loaf.

micheline 🚆 [miʃˈlin] *f* rail-car.

micmac F [mikˈmak] *m* intrigue; underhand work.

micro F [miˈkro] *m radio*: microphone, F mike; *au* ﹏ on the air.

micro... [mikro] micro...

microbe [miˈkrɔb] *m* microbe, F germ.

microcéphale [mikrɔseˈfal] *adj.*, *a. su.* microcephalic.

micron [miˈkrɔ̃] *m measure*: micron (1/1000 mm).

micro...: ﹏**cosme** [ˌkrɔˈkɔsm] *m* microcosm; ﹏**phone** [mikroˈfɔn] *m* microphone; ﹏**processeur** [ˌkrɔprɔsɛˈsœːr] *m* microprocessor; ﹏**scope** [ˌkrɔsˈkɔp] *m* microscope; ﹏**sillon** [ˌkrɔsiˈjɔ̃] *m* microgroove; long-playing record.

midi [miˈdi] *m* midday, noon, twelve o'clock; *fig.* heyday (*of life*); ﹏ *et demi* half past twelve; *plein* ﹏ high noon; *geog.* le ♀ the South of France; **midinette** F [ˌdiˈnɛt] *f* dressmaker's assistant, midinette.

mie [mi] *f bread*: soft part, cumb.

miel [mjɛl] *m* honey; **miellé, e** [mjɛˈle]honeyed; honey-colo(u)red; **mielleux, -euse** [ˌˈlø, ˌˈløːz] like honey; *fig.* honeyed (*words*); bland (*smile*); smooth-tongued (*person*).

mien, mienne [mjɛ̃, mjɛn] **1.** *pron./ poss.*: le ﹏, la ﹏ne, les ﹏s *m/pl.*, les ﹏nes *f/pl.* mine; **2.** *adj./poss.* † of mine; *un* ﹏ *ami* a friend of mine; **3.** *su./m* mine, my own; *les* ﹏s *pl.* my (own) people.

miette [mjɛt] *f* crumb; *fig.* piece, bit.

mieux [mjø] **1.** *adv.* better; rather; *aimer* ﹏ prefer; ✿ *aller* ﹏ feel *or* be better; *à qui* ﹏ ﹏ one trying to outdo the other; *de* ﹏ *en* ﹏ better and better; *je ne demande pas* ﹏ *que de* (*inf.*) I shall be delighted to (*inf.*); *le* ﹏ (the) best; *tant* ﹏ all the better; *valoir* ﹏ be better; *vous feriez* ﹏ *de* (*inf.*) you had better (*inf.*); **2.** *su./m* best; ✿ change for the better; *au* ﹏ as well as possible, ✝ at best; *faire de son* ﹏ do one's best.

mièvre [mjɛːvr] delicate; *fig.* affected (*style*); **mièvrerie** [mjɛvrəˈri] *f* delicateness; *fig. style etc.*: affectation.

mignard, e [miˈɲaːr, ˌˈɲard] affected, mincing; dainty; **mignardise** [ˌɲarˈdiːz] *f* affectation; *style*: finicalness; ♀ (garden) pink; **mignon, -onne** [ˌˈɲɔ̃, ˌˈɲɔn] **1.** *adj.* dainty, sweet, nice, cute; *péché m* ﹏ besetting sin; **2.** *su.* darling, pet; **mignoter** † [ˌɲɔˈte] (1a) *v/t.* caress; pet.

migraine [miˈgrɛn] *f* migraine, sick headache.

migrant, e [miˈgrã, ˌˈgrãːt] **1.** *adj.* migrant; **2.** *su.* migrant (worker); **migrateur, -trice** [migraˈtœːr, ˌˈtris] *orn.* migratory; migrant (*person*); **migration** [ˌˈsjɔ̃] *f* migration; **migratoire** [ˌˈtwaːr] migratory.

mijaurée [miʒoˈre] *f* affected woman.

mijoter [miʒɔˈte] (1a) *v/t.* let (*s.th.*) simmer (*a. fig. an idea*); hatch (*a plot*); *fig. se* ﹏ be brewing; *v/i.* simmer.

mil [mil] *adj./inv.* thousand (*only in dates*).

milan *orn.* [miˈlã] *m* kite.

mildiou ♀, ✍ [milˈdju] *m* mildew.

miliaire ✚ [miˈljɛːr] miliary (*fever*).

milice ⚔ [miˈlis] *f* militia; **milicien** ⚔ [ˌliˈsjɛ̃] *m* militiaman.

milieu [miˈljø] *m* middle; *phys.* medium; *fig.* circle, sphere; *fig.* environment; *fig.* (social) background; *fig.* middle course; *the* underworld; *au* ﹏ *de* in the middle of.

militaire [miliˈtɛːr] **1.** *adj.* military; ♪ martial; **2.** *su./m* military man; soldier; **militant, e** [ˌˈtã, ˌˈtãːt] **1.** *adj.* militant; **2.** *su.* fighter (for, de); militant; **militariser** [ˌtariˈze] (1a) *v/t.* militarize; **militarisme** [ˌtaˈrism] *m* militarism; **militer** [ˌˈte]

(1a) *v/i.* militate (against, *contre*; in favo[u]r of *pour, en faveur de*); be a militant.

mille [mil] **1.** *adj./num./inv.* (a *or* one) thousand; **2.** *su./m/inv.* thousand; *sp.* bull's eye; *mettre dans le* ~ hit the bull's eye; F *fig.* be bang on target; *su./m* mile.

mille-feuille [mil'fœ:j] *f* ♀ yarrow; *cuis.* mille-feuille (*sort of puff pastry*); **millénaire** [mille'nɛ:r] **1.** *adj.* millennial; **2.** *su./m* one thousand; thousand years, millennium.

mille...: ~**-pattes** *zo.* [mil'pat] *m/inv.* centipede, millepede; ~**(-)pertuis** ♀ [~pɛr'tɥi] *m* St. John's wort.

millésime [mille'zim] *m* date (*on coin*); ⊕ year of manufacture.

millet ♀ [mi'jɛ] *m* (wood) millet-grass; *grains m/pl.* de ~ bird-seed, canary-seed.

milliaire [mi'ljɛ:r] milliary; *borne f* ~ milestone; **milliard** [~'lja:r] *m* milliard, one thousand million(s *pl.*), *Am.* billion; **millième** [~'ljɛm] *adj., a. su., a. su./m fraction:* thousandth; **millier** [~'lje] *m* (about) a thousand; **million** [~'ljõ] *m* million.

mime [mim] *m* mimic; *thea. hist.* mime; **mimer** [mi'me] (1a) *v/t.* mime (*a scene*); mimic (*s.o.*).

mimétisme *zo.* [mime'tism] *m* mimicry. [ling.

mimi [mi'mi] *m* pussy; F pet, dar-]

mimique [mi'mik] mimic.

mimosa ♀ [mimo'za] *m* mimosa.

minable *fig.* [mi'nabl] seedy, shabby.

minauder [mino'de] (1a) *v/i.* simper, smirk; **minauderie** [~'dri] *f* simpering, smirking.

mince [mɛ̃:s] thin; slender, slight, slim; F ~ *alors!* hell!

mine¹ [min] *f* appearance, look; ~*s pl.* simperings; *avoir bonne (mauvaise)* ~ look well (ill); look good (bad); *faire* ~ *de (inf.)* make as if to (*inf.*); make a show of (*s.th.; doing s.th.*).

mine² [min] *f* ✕, ✕, ⚓, *fig.* mine; *pencil:* lead; *fig.* store; ~ *de houille* colliery, coal-mine; ~ *de plomb* graphite; *faire sauter une* ~ spring a mine; **miner** [mi'ne] (1a) *v/t.* ✕ mine; *fig.* undermine, consume;

minerai ✕ [min'rɛ] *m* ore.

minéral, e, *m/pl.* -**aux** [mine'ral, ~'ro] **1.** *adj.* mineral; inorganic (*chemistry*); *eau f* ~*e* mineral water; spa water; **2.** *su./m* mineral; **minéraliser** [~rali'ze] (1a) *v/t.* mineralize; **minéralogie** [~ralɔ'ʒi] *m* mineralogy; **minéralogique** [~ralɔ'ʒik] mineralogical; *mot.* numéro *m* ~ registration (*Am.* license) number; *mot. plaque f* ~ number plate.

minet *m,* -**ette** *f* [mi'nɛ, ~'nɛt] puss(ycat); F pet, darling; young trendy.

mineur¹, e [mi'nœ:r] **1.** *adj.* minor, (*a.* ⚛, *a.* ♪); **2.** *su.* ⚛, ♪ minor; *su./f* minor premise; assumption.

mineur² [~] *m* ✕ miner; ✕ sapper.

miniature [minja'ty:r] *f* miniature; **miniaturiser** [~tyri'ze] (1a) *v/t.* miniaturize; **miniaturiste** [~ty-'rist] *adj., a. su.* miniaturist.

minier, -ère [mi'nje, ~'njɛ:r] **1.** *adj.* mining; **2.** *su./f* open-cast mine.

mini-jupe [mini'ʒyp] *f* miniskirt.

minimal, e, *m/pl.* -**aux** [mini'mal, ~'mo] minimal; **minime** [~'nim] tiny; *fig.* trivial; **minimiser** [~ni-mi'ze] (1a) *v/t.* minimize, play down; **minimum,** *pl. a.* **minima** [~ni-'mɔm, ~'ma] **1.** *su./m* minimum; ~ *vital* minimum living wage; **2.** *adj.* minimum.

ministère [minis'tɛ:r] *m* agency; *pol., a. eccl.* ministry; *pol.* office, government department; service; *pol.* ♀ Office; Ministry; ♀ *de la Défense nationale* Ministry of Defence, *Am.* Department of Defense; ♀ *des Affaires étrangères* Foreign Office, *Am.* State Department; ⚖♀ *public* Public Prosecutor; **ministre** [~'nistr] *m pol., a. protestantism:* minister; ♀ *de la Défense nationale* Minister of Defence, *Am.* Secretary of Defense; ♀ *des Affaires étrangères* Foreign Secretary, *Am.* Secretary of State; ♀ *des Finances France:* Minister of Finance, *Britain:* Chancellor of the Exchequer, *Am.* Secretary of the Treasury.

minium ⚗ [mi'njɔm] *m* minium; red lead.

minois F [mi'nwa] *m* pretty face.

minorité [minɔri'te] *f* minority; ⚖ infancy; *pol. mettre en* ~ defeat (*the government*).

minoterie [minɔ'tri] *f* flour-mill;

flour-milling; **minotier** [ʌˈtje] *m* (flour-)miller.

minuit [miˈnɥi] *m* midnight; ~ *et demi* half past twelve (at night).

minuscule [minysˈkyl] **1.** *adj.* tiny; small (*letter*); **2.** *su./f* small letter, *typ.* lower-case letter.

minute [miˈnyt] **1.** *su./f* minute; *deed, judgment*: draft; record; *à la* ~ this instant; to the minute; while you wait; **2.** *int.* wait a bit!; **minuter** *admin.* [minyˈte] (1a) *v/t.* time; **minuterie** [ʌˈtri] *f clocks etc.*: motion work; ⚡ time switch.

minutie [minyˈsi] *f* (attention to) minute detail; **minutieux, -euse** [ʌˈsjø, ʌˈsjøːz] detailed, painstaking, thorough.

mioche F [mjɔʃ] *su.* urchin; kid(die), tot.

mi-parti, e [miparˈti] equally divided; halved.

miracle [miraːkl] *m* miracle (*a.fig.*); **miraculeux, -euse** [ʌrakyˈlø, ʌˈløːz] miraculous; F marvellous.

mirage [miraːʒ] *m* mirage; *fig.* illusion; **mire** [miːr] *f* ✕ aiming; *gun*: bead; *surv.* pole, levelling-rod; *telev.* test-card, test-pattern; *point m de* ~ ✕ aim; *fig.* cynosure; **mirer** [miˈre] (1a) *v/t.* aim at; *surv.* take a sight on; 🕯 candle (*an egg*); hold (*cloth*) against the light; *se* ~ look at o.s.; be reflected.

mirifique F [miriˈfik] wonderful.

mirliton [mirliˈtɔ̃] *m* 🎵 toy flute; *cuis.* cream puff; *vers m/pl. de* ~ doggerel.

mirobolant, e F [mirɔbɔˈlɑ̃, ʌˈlɑ̃ːt] marvellous; staggering.

miroir [miˈrwaːr] *m* mirror, looking-glass; *mot.* ~ *rétroviseur* driving mirror; **miroitement** [ʌrwatˈmɑ̃] *m* flash; gleam; *water*: shimmer; **miroiter** [mirwaˈte] (1a) *v/i.* flash; glitter; sparkle; *fig. faire* ~ *qch. à q.* paint s.th. in glowing colo(u)rs for s.o.

miroton *cuis.* [mirɔˈtɔ̃] *m* re-heated beef in onion sauce.

mis¹ [mi] *1st p. sg. p.s. of* mettre.

mis², e [mi, miːz] *p.p. of* mettre.

misaine ⚓ [miˈzɛn] *f* foresail; *mât m de* ~ foremast.

misanthrope [mizɑ̃ˈtrɔp] **1.** *su./m* misanthropist; **2.** *adj.* misanthropic.

miscible [miˈsibl] miscible.

mise [miːz] *f* placing, putting; *auc-*

tion: bid; *gamble*: stake; dress, attire; ✝ outlay; ~ *à la retraite* retirement; ⚡ ~ *à la terre* earthing; ⚓ ~ *à l'eau* launching; ~ *à mort bullfight*: kill (of the bull); ~ *à pied* sacking; ~ *au point* adjustment; *phot.* focussing; ~*-bas* dropping (*of young animals*); ✝ ~ *de fonds* putting up of money; ⊕ ~ *en fabrication* putting into production; ~ *en liberté* release; ⊕ ~ *en marche* starting; ~ *en ondes* radio adaptation; *typ.* ~ *en pages* making up; ~ *en plis hair*: setting; *mot.* ~ *en route* starting up; *thea.* ~ *en scène* staging, production; ~ *en service* commencement of service; ~ *en train* start(ing); ✝ ~ *en vente* putting up for sale; *ne pas être de* ~ be out of place *or* season; **miser** [miˈze] (1a) *v/t.* bid; stake; *v/i.* count (on, *sur*).

misérable [mizeˈrabl] **1.** *adj.* miserable; *fig.* wretched; *fig.* mean (*action*); **2.** *su.* (poor) wretch; **misère** [ʌˈzɛːr] *f* misery; poverty; *fig.* trifle.

miséricorde [mizeriˈkɔrd] **1.** *su./f* mercy, forgiveness; **2.** *int.* mercy!; **miséricordieux, -euse** [ʌkɔrˈdjø, ʌˈdjøːz] merciful (to, *envers*).

missel *eccl.* [miˈsɛl] *m* missal.

missile ✕ [miˈsil] *m* (guided) missile; ~ *de croisière* cruise missile.

mission [miˈsjɔ̃] *f* mission; **missionnaire** [ʌsjɔˈnɛːr] *m* missionary; **missive** [ʌˈsiːv] *f* missive, letter.

mistigri F [mistiˈgri] *m* puss.

mistral [misˈtral] *m* mistral (*cold north-east wind in Provence*).

mitage [miˈtaːʒ] *m* spoiling (of the countryside) through architectural development.

mitaine [miˈtɛn] *f* mitten.

mite [mit] *f* moth; *cheese*: mite; **mité, e** [miˈte] moth-eaten; **miter** [ʌ] (1a) *v/t.* spoil (*the countryside*) through architectural development.

mi-temps [miˈtɑ̃] *f sp.* half-time; interval; ✝ *à* ~ half-time (*work*).

miteux, -euse F [miˈtø, ʌˈtøːz] shabby; seedy (*person*).

mitiger [mitiˈʒe] (1l) *v/t.* mitigate; relax (*a law etc.*).

miton 🖤 F [miˈtɔ̃] *m*: *onguent m* ~ *mitaine* harmless but useless ointment.

mitonner [mitɔˈne] (1a) *v/i.* simmer; *v/t.* let (*s.th.*) simmer; *fig.* hatch.

mitoyen, -enne [mitwa'jɛ̃, ~'jɛn] common (*to two things*), △ party (*wall*).

mitraille ✕ [mi'traːj] *f* grape-shot; F coppers *pl.* (= *small change*); **mi-trailler** ✕ [mitra'je] (1a) *v/t.* machine-gun, strafe, rake with fire; **mitraillette** ✕ [~'jɛt] *f* submachine-gun; **mitrailleur** ✕ [~'jœːr] 1. *su./m* machine-gunner; 2. *adj./m*: **fusil** *m* ~ Bren gun; **mitrailleuse** ✕ [~'jøːz] *f* machine-gun.

mitre [mitr] *f* (*bishop's*) mitre; △ chimney-cowl; **mitron** [mi'trɔ̃] *m* journeyman baker; △ chimney-pot.

mixage [mik'saːʒ] *m* (sound) mixing; **mixer[1]** [~'se] (1a) *v/t.* mix (*sounds*); **mixer[2]** [~'sœːr] *m* (food) mixer; **mixte** [mikst] mixed; ⚫ combined; ~ *double m* tennis: mixed doubles *pl.*; *enseignement m* ~ co-education; **mixtion** ⚗ [miks'tjɔ̃] *f* mixture; *drugs*: compounding; **mixtionner** ⚗ [~tjɔ'ne] (1a) *v/t.* compound (*drugs*); **mixture** ⚗, ⚕ [~'tyːr] *f* mixture.

mobile [mɔ'bil] 1. *adj.* mobile; movable (*a. feast*); moving (*object, target, etc.*); detachable; *fig.* inconstant; ✕ *colonne f* ~ flying column; 2. *su./m* moving body; ⚫ moving part; *fig.* motive; *fig.* mainspring; *premier* ~ *person*: prime mover; **mobilier, -ère** [~bi'lje, ~'ljɛːr] 1. *adj.* ⚖ movable; ⚖ personal (*action, estate*); ⚕ transferable; 2. *su./m* furniture; suite.

mobilisation [mɔbiliza'sjɔ̃] *f* ✕, ⚖ mobilization; ⚕ realization; ⚕ liquidation; **mobiliser** [~'ze] (1a) *v/t.* ✕, ⚖ mobilize; ✕ call up; ⚕ realize (*an indemnity*); ⚕ liquidate (*capital*).

mobilité [mɔbili'te] *f* mobility; *fig. temperament etc.*: fickleness.

mobylette (*TM*) [mɔbi'lɛt] *f* moped.

moche F [mɔʃ] ugly; F lousy; rotten; poor, shoddy; F awful.

modal, e, *m/pl.* **-aux** [mɔ'dal, ~'do] modal; **modalité** [~dali'te] *f* phls. modality; ♪ form of scale; ~s *pl.* ⚕ terms and conditions; ⚖ restrictive clauses.

mode [mɔd] *su./m* ♪, *phls.* mood (*a. gramm.*); mode, method; ⚙ ~ *d'em-ploi* directions *pl.* for use; ⚕ ~ *de paiement* method of payment; *su./f* fashion; *à la* ~ fashionable, stylish, F

in; *à la* ~ *de* in the style of; *cuis.* ... fashion; *à la dernière* ~ in the latest fashion.

modèle [mɔ'dɛl] 1. *su./m* model (*a. fig.*), pattern; *prendre q. pour* ~ model o.s. on s.o.; 2. *adj.* model ...

modelé [mɔd'le] *m* relief; contours *pl.*; **modeler** [~'le] (1d) *v/t.* model (on, sur); mo(u)ld; shape; **mode-leur** ⚫ [~'lœːr] *m* pattern-maker.

modérateur, -trice [mɔdera'tœːr, ~'tris] 1. *su.* moderator, restrainer; *su./m* ⚫ regulator; ⚡, *phys.* moderator; (*volume-*)control; 2. *adj.* moderating, restraining; **modération** [~ra'sjɔ̃] *f* moderation, restraint; *price, tax*, ⚖ *sentence*: reduction; **modéré, e** [~'re] *adj.* moderate; sober; conservative (*estimate*); **modérer** [~'re] (1f) *v/t.* moderate, restrain; check; reduce (*the price etc.*); *se* ~ abate (*weather*).

moderne [mɔ'dɛrn] modern; **moderniser** [mɔdɛrni'ze] (1a) *v/t.* modernize; **moderniste** [~'nist] modernist; **modernité** [~ni'te] *f* modernity; modern times *pl.*

modeste [mɔ'dɛst] modest; unpretentious; quiet; moderate (*price*); **modestie** [~dɛs'ti] *f* modesty; unpretentiousness.

modicité [mɔdisi'te] *f means*: modesty; *prices*: reasonableness.

modifiable [mɔdi'fjabl] modifiable; **modificateur, -trice** [~fika'tœːr, ~'tris] modifying; **modification** [~fika'sjɔ̃] *f* modification, alteration; **modifier** [~'fje] (1o) *v/t.* modify (*a. gramm.*); alter; ⚕ rectify (*an entry*).

modique [mɔ'dik] reasonable, moderate (*price*); slender, modest (*means*).

modiste [mɔ'dist] *f* milliner, modiste.

modulateur ⚡ [mɔdyla'tœːr] *m* modulator; **modulation** [~'sjɔ̃] *f* modulation (♪, *a. voice*); *voice*: inflexion; **module** [mɔ'dyl] *m* ⚙ modulus; △ module; unit; size; **moduler** [~dy'le] (1a) *vt/i.* modulate.

moelle [mwal] *f* marrow; ⚘ pith (*a. fig.*); *anat.* medulla; ~ *épinière* spinal cord; **moelleux, -euse** [mwa'lø, ~'løːz] marrowy (*bone*); ⚘ pithy; *fig.* soft; *fig.* mellow (*light, voice*).

moellon [mwa'lɔ̃] *m* quarry-stone; ~ de roche rock rubble.

mœurs [mœrs] *f/pl.* morals; manners, ways, customs; *animals*: habits.

mohair [mɔ'ɛːr] *m* mohair.

moi [mwa] **1.** *pron./pers. subject*: I; *object*: me; (to) me; à ~ to me; mine; *c'est* ~ it is I, F it's me; *de vous à* ~ between you and me; *il a vu mon frère et* ~ he has seen my brother and me; **2.** *su./m* ego, self.

moignon ✱ [mwa'ɲɔ̃] *m* stump (*of amputated limb*).

moi-même [mwa'mɛːm] *pron./rfl.* myself.

moindre [mwɛ̃ːdr] less(er); *le* (*la*) ~ the least; the slightest; **moindrement** [mwɛ̃drə'mɑ̃] *adv.*: *pas le* ~ not in the least.

moine [mwan] *m* monk; *fig.* F bedwarmer, hot-water bottle; *metall.* blister; **moineau** *orn.* [mwa'no] *m* sparrow; *sl.* fellow; **moinerie** *usu. pej.* [mwan'ri] *f* friary; monkery; **moinillon** F [mwani'jɔ̃] *m* young monk.

moins [mwɛ̃] **1.** *adv.* less (than, que); fewer; ~ de *deux* less than two; à ~ de (*inf.*), à ~ que ... (ne) (*sbj.*) unless; au ~ at least; de ~ en ~ less and less; *du* ~ at least (= *at all events*); *le* ~ (the) least; **2.** *prp.* minus, less; *cinq heures* ~ *dix* ten minutes to five; **3.** *su./m* ⚹ minus (sign); **~-value** ✝ [~va'ly] *f* depreciation.

moire *tex.* [mwaːr] *f* moire; watered silk; **moirer** *tex.*, *a.* ⊕ [mwa're] (1a) *v/t.* moiré.

mois [mwa] *m* month; month's pay; ✝ à un ~ de date one month after date; *par* ~, *tous les* ~ monthly; *tous les* ~ every month.

moisi, e [mwa'zi] **1.** *adj.* mo(u)ldy; musty (*smell*, *taste*); **2.** *su./m* mo(u)ld, mildew; *sentir le* ~ smell musty; **moisir** [~'ziːr] (2a) *vt/i.* mildew; *v/i. a. se* ~ go mo(u)ldy; F vegetate; **moisissure** [~zi'syːr] *f* ✿ mildew, mo(u)ld; mustiness.

moisson [mwa'sɔ̃] *f* harvest, crop (*a. fig.*); harvest-time; **moissonner** [mwaso'ne] (1a) *v/t.* harvest, reap (*a. fig.*), gather; **moissonneur** [~'nœːr] *m* harvester, reaper; **moissonneuse** [~'nøːz] *f* harvester, reaper (*a. machine*); **~-batteuse** com-

bine-harvester; **~-lieuse** *machine*: self-binder.

moite [mwat] moist, damp; clammy; ✝ limp; **moiteur** [mwa'tœːr] *f* moistness; ✿ perspiration.

moitié [mwa'tje] **1.** *su./f* half; F better half (= *wife*); à ~ *chemin* half-way; à ~ *prix* (at) half-price; *se mettre de* ~ *avec q.* go halves with s.o.; **2.** *adv.* half.

mol [mɔl] *see* mou 1.

molaire [mɔ'lɛːr] *adj.*, *a. su./f* molar.

môle [moːl] *m* mole, breakwater; pier.

moléculaire [mɔleky'lɛːr] molecular; **molécule** [~'kyl] *f* molecule; ✿ **~-gramme** gram(me-)molecule.

molester [mɔlɛs'te] (1a) *v/t.* molest.

molette [mɔ'lɛt] *f* spur: rowel; ⊕ cutting-wheel; *paint.* small pestle; ⚒ winding-pulley; *lighter*: wheel; *clef f* à ~ adjustable spanner.

mollasse F [mɔ'las] soft, flabby; slow (*person*); **molle** [mɔl] *see* mou 1; **mollesse** [mɔ'lɛs] *f* softness, flabbiness; slackness; indolence; **mollet, -ette** [~'lɛ, ~'lɛt] **1.** *adj.* softish; soft-boiled (*egg*); tender (*feet*); *pain m* ~ roll; **2.** *su./m leg*: calf; **molletière** [mɔl'tjɛːr] *f* puttee; **mollir** [mɔ'liːr] (2a) *v/i.* soften; slacken; *fig.* get weak; ⚒ give ground; ✝ get easier (*price of commodity*). [F slowcoach.\
mollusque *zo.* [mɔ'lysk] *m* mollusc;\
mollo! [mɔ'lo] *int.* easy!; gently!; *vas-y* ~! easy does it!

molosse [mɔ'lɔs] *m* watch-dog; mastiff.

môme *sl.* [moːm] *su. child*: kid, brat.

moment [mɔ'mɑ̃] *m* moment (*a. phys.*); *au* ~ *où* (*or que*) since; *par* ~s now and again; *pour le* ~ for the time being; **momentané, e** [~mɑ̃ta'ne] momentary; temporary (*absence*).

momerie [mɔm'ri] *f* mummery; *fig.* affectations *pl.*

momie [mɔ'mi] *f* mummy; F old fogy; F bag of bones; **momifier** [~mi'fje] (1o) *v/t.* mummify.

mon *m*, **ma** *f*, *pl.* **mes** [mɔ̃, ma, me] *adj./poss.* my.

monacal, e, *m/pl.* **-aux** *eccl.* [mɔna'kal, ~'ko] monac(h)al; **monachisme** *eccl.* [~'kism] *m* monasticism.

monarchie [mɔnar'ʃi] f monarchy;
monarchiste [ʌ'ʃist] adj., a. su.
monarchist; **monarque** [mɔ'nark]
m monarch.

monastère [mɔnas'tɛːr] m monastery; nuns: convent; **monastique**
[ʌ'tik] monastic.

monceau [mɔ̃'so] m heap, pile.

mondain, e [mɔ̃'dɛ̃, ʌ'dɛn] **1.** adj.
mundane, worldly; fashionable;
2. su. worldly-minded person; su./m
man-about-town; su./f society
woman; police: la ♀ the vice squad;
mondanité [ʌdani'te] f worldliness; love of social functions; **monde** [mɔ:d] m world (a. fig.); people;
fig. society; au bout du ʌ at the back of
beyond; dans le ʌ entier all over the
world; homme m du ʌ man of good
breeding; il y a du ʌ there is a crowd;
recevoir du ʌ entertain (guests); tout le
ʌ everyone; fig. un ʌ de lots pl. of;
vieux comme le ʌ as old as the hills;
mondial, e, m/pl. **-aux** [mɔ̃'djal,
ʌ'djo] worldwide; world (war);
mondialisation [mɔ̃djaliza'sjɔ̃] f
establishing or application on a
worldwide basis; spread(ing)
throughout the world; **mondialiser** [ʌ'ze] (1a) v/t. establish or apply
on a worldwide basis; (a. se ʌ) spread
throughout the world.

monégasque [mɔne'gask] of
Monaco.

monétaire [mɔne'tɛːr] monetary;
monétisation [ʌtiza'sjɔ̃] f minting.

moniteur [mɔni'tœːr] m school, telev.
monitor; sp. coach; ✈ plane: instructor; **monition** eccl. [ʌ'sjɔ̃] f
monition; **monitoire** eccl. [ʌ'twa:r]
m (a. lettre f ʌ) monitory (letter).

monnaie [mɔ'nɛ] f money; (small)
change; currency; ✝ ʌ forte hard
currency; donner la ʌ de give change
for, change (a note etc.); **monnayer**
[ʌnɛ'je] (1i) v/t. mint, coin; **monnayeur** [ʌnɛ'jœːr] m minter, coiner.

mono [mɔ'no] f, a. adj. short for
monophonie, monophonique: mono;
en ʌ (in) mono.

mon(o)... [mɔn(ɔ)] mon(o)...; **monobloc** [mɔnɔ'blɔk] cast or made in
one piece.

monocle [mɔ'nɔkl] m monocle.

mono...: **~game** [mɔnɔ'gam] monogamous; **~gamie** [ʌga'mi] f monogamy; **~gramme** [ʌ'gram] m monogram; initials pl.; **~logue** [ʌ'lɔg] m

monologue; **~loguer** [ʌlɔ'ge] (1m)
v/i. soliloquize.

monôme ♣ [mɔ'no:m] m monomial.

mono...: **~phasé, e** ♂ [mɔnɔfa'ze]
single-phase; **~phonie** [ʌfɔ'ni] f
monaural reproduction; en ʌ (in)
mono; **~phonique** [ʌfɔ'nik] monaural, mono(phonic); **~place** ✈,
mot. [ʌ'plas] m single-seater; **~plan**
✈ [ʌ'plɑ̃] m monoplane; **~pole**
[ʌ'pɔl] m monopoly; **~poliser** [ʌpɔli-
'ze] (1a) v/t. monopolize; **~rail** 🚋
[ʌ'rɑːj] adj., a. su./m monorail; **~syllabe** [ʌsi'lab] m monosyllable; **~théisme** [ʌte'ism] m monotheism;
~tone [ʌ'tɔn] monotonous; **~tonie**
[ʌtɔ'ni] f monotony.

monseigneur, pl. **messeigneurs**
[mɔ̃sɛ'ɲœːr, mɛsɛ'ɲœːr] m My Lord;
archbishop, duke: Your Grace; prince:
Your Royal Highness; His Lordship;
His Grace; His Royal Highness;
monsieur, pl. **messieurs** [mə'sjø,
mɛ'sjø] m Mr.; sir; gentleman; man;
in letters: Dear Sir; ʌ le Président Mr.
President.

monstre [mɔ̃:str] **1.** su./m monster
(a. fig.); freak of nature; ʌ sacré
(super)star; **2.** adj. colossal, huge;
monstrueux, -euse [mɔ̃stry'ø,
ʌ'øːz] monstrous; huge; frightful;
monstruosité [ʌozi'te] f monstrosity; fig. enormity. [the Alps.)

mont [mɔ̃] m mount(ain); les ʌs pl.)

montage [mɔ̃'ta:ʒ] m putting up,
loads, materials: hoisting; ⊕ machine: assembling; gun, phot., etc.:
mounting; ♂ wiring, connecting up;
gems, scene, etc.: setting; mot. tyre:
fitting (on); cin. film: editing; ⊕
chaîne f de ʌ assembly line.

montagnard, e [mɔ̃ta'ɲaːr, ʌ'ɲard]
1. adj. mountain..., highland...; **2.** su.
mountaineer, highlander; **montagne** [ʌ'taɲ] f mountain; la ʌ the
mountains pl.; ʌs pl. russes switchback sg.; **montagneux, -euse**
[ʌta'ɲø, ʌ'ɲøːz] mountainous, hilly.

montaison [mɔ̃tɛ'zɔ̃] f salmon: runup; **montant, e** [ʌ'tɑ̃, ʌ'tɑ̃:t] **1.** adj.
rising; uphill; ⊕ up (train, platform); cost. high-necked; **2.** su./m
reckoning, account: total; tide: flow,
rising; ladder: upright; (tent-)pole;
stair: riser; (gate-)post; leg; (lamp-)
post.

mont-de-piété, pl. **monts-de-piété**
[mɔ̃dəpje'te] m pawn-shop.

monte...: **~-charge** [mɔ̃t'ʃarʒ] *m/ inv.* hoist; goods-lift; **~-pente** [~-'pɑ̃ːt] *m* ski-lift; **~-plats** [~'pla] *m/ inv.* service-lift, *Am.* dumb-waiter.

monté, e [mɔ̃'te] **1.** *adj.* mounted (*a. police*); equipped; F *fig.* coup *m* ~ plot, put-up job; *fig.* être ~ have a grudge (against, *contre*); **2.** *su./f* rising; rise; ascent; climb, gradient; ⚒, *mot.* climbing; **monter** [~'te] (1a) *v/i.* climb (up), ascend, mount; go upstairs; rise (*anger, price, sun, barometer, tide*); amount (to, *à*) (*cost, total*); boil up (*milk*); ~ à (or *sur*) un arbre climb a tree; ~ dans un train get on a train, *Am.* board a train; ~ en avion get into a plane; ~ sur un navire go aboard a ship; faire ~ raise (*prices*); *v/t.* mount (*a. phot., a.* ⚔ *guard*), climb, go up (*the stairs, a hill*); ride (*a horse*); ⚓ set up (*a factory*); take up, carry up; turn up (*a lamp, etc.*); equip; wind up (*a watch*); assemble (*a machine*); *thea.* stage (*a play*); *fig.* plan, plot; F ~ la tête à q. work s.o. up (against, *contre*); ~ son ménage set up house; se ~ amount (to, *à*); **monteur** *m,* **-euse** *f* [~'tœːr, ~'tøːz] ⊕ setter; *cin.* cutter; *thea.* producer; ⊕, ⚡ fitter; **monticule** [~ti'kyl] *m* hillock; *ice:* hummock.

montre [mɔ̃ːtr] *f* show, display; shop-window; show-case; watch, *mot.* clock; *mot. etc. course f contre la ~* race against the clock; *faire ~ de* display; **~-bracelet**, *pl.* **~s-bracelets** [mɔ̃trəbras'lɛ] *f* wrist-watch; **montrer** [mɔ̃'tre] (1a) *v/t.* show; display; indicate, point out; se ~ show o.s., *fig.* prove (o.s.); turn out; appear.

montueux, -euse [mɔ̃'tɥø, ~'tɥøːz] hilly, mountainous; **monture** [~-'tyːr] *f horse, picture:* mount; ⊕ mounting, assembling; *gem:* setting; *spectacles:* frame; *gun etc.:* handle, stock; *sans ~* rimless (*spectacles*).

monument [mɔny'mɑ̃] *m* monument (*a. fig.*), memorial; public building; **~s** *pl. town:* sights; ~ funéraire monument (*over tomb*); **monumental, e**, *m/pl.* **-aux** [~mɑ̃-'tal, ~'to] monumental; F huge, enormous.

moquer [mɔ'ke] (1m) *v/t.*: se ~ de make fun of; F s'en ~ not to care (a

damn); **moquerie** [mɔk'ri] *f* mockery; ridicule; jeer.

moquette¹ [mɔ'kɛt] *f* decoy(-bird).

moquette² [~] *f* fitted carpet, wall-to-wall carpet(ing); *tex.* moquette.

moqueur, -euse [mɔ'kœːr, ~'køːz] **1.** *adj.* mocking; derisive; **2.** *su.* mocker; *su./m orn.* mocking-bird.

moraine *geol.* [mɔ'rɛn] *f* moraine.

moral, e, *m/pl.* **-aux** [mɔ'ral, ~'ro] **1.** *adj.* moral; *fig.* mental; **2.** *su./m* morale; (moral) nature; *su./f* morals *pl.*; ethics; *fables etc.:* moral; **moralisateur, -trice** [mɔraliza-'tœːr, ~'tris] moralizing (*person*); edifying; **moraliser** [~li'ze] *vt/i.* moralize; *v/t.* F lecture, preach at (*s.o.*); **moraliste** [~'list] *su.* moralist; **moralité** [~li'te] *f* good (moral) conduct, morality; morals *pl.*; *story:* moral; *thea.* morality(-play).

moratoire [mɔra'twaːr] ⚖ moratory; ⚖ *intérêts m/pl.* ~s interest *sg.* on over-due payments.

morbide [mɔr'bid] morbid, sickly; *paint.* delicate (*flesh-tints*); **morbidesse** *paint.* [~bi'des] *f* delicacy of flesh-tints, morbidezza; **morbidité** [~bidi'te] *f* morbidity.

morceau [mɔr'so] *m* piece, morsel; bit, scrap; *avoir qch. pour un ~ de pain* get s.th. for a song; **morceler** [~sə'le] (1c) *v/t.* cut up (into pieces); divide (*land, an estate*); **morcellement** [~sɛl'mɑ̃] *m* cutting up; *land, estate:* parcelling out.

mordache ⊕ [mɔr'daʃ] *f* clamp; *chuck:* jaw, grip.

mordacité [mɔrdasi'te] *f* ⚗ corrosiveness; *fig.* causticity, mordancy; **mordant, e** [mɔr'dɑ̃, ~'dɑ̃t] biting, scathing, caustic; **mordicus** F [mɔrdi'kys] *adv.* stoutly, doggedly.

mordiller [mɔrdi'je] (1a) *v/t.* nibble; *puppy etc.:* bite playfully.

mordoré, e [mɔrdɔ're] *adj., a. su./m* bronze, reddish brown.

mordre [mɔrdr] (4a) *v/t.* bite; ⊕ catch; *acid:* corrode (*metal*); se ~ les lèvres bite one's lips; *v/i.* bite (*a. fig.*); ⊕ catch, engage (*wheel*); *fig.* ~ à get one's teeth into; take to (*a subject*); **mordu, e** F [mɔr'dy] **1.** *adj.* madly in love (with, *de*); mad or crazy or wild (about, *de*); **2.** *su.* fan, freak, buff; *un ~ du film* a film freak.

more [mɔːr] *adj./m, a. su./m* ♀ *see* maure; **moreau, -elle**, *m/pl.* **-eaux**

[mɔ'ro, ~'rɛl, ~'ro] 1. *adj.* black (*horse*); 2. *su./f* ✿ morel, black nightshade; **moresque** [~'rɛsk] *adj., a. su./f see* **mauresque**.

morfondre [mɔr'fɔ̃:dr] (4a) *v/t.* freeze; se ~ wait, F cool one's heels; *fig.* be bored.

morgue¹ [mɔrg] *f* haughtiness, arrogance.

morgue² [~] *f* mortuary, morgue.

moribond, e [mɔri'bɔ̃, ~'bɔ̃:d] 1. *adj.* moribund, dying; 2. *su.* dying person; *su./m*: les ~s *pl.* the dying.

moricaud, e [mɔri'ko, ~'ko:d] 1. *adj.* dark-skinned, dusky; 2. *su.* blackamoor; F darky.

morigéner [mɔriʒe'ne] (1f) *v/t.* lecture (*s.o.*); tell (*s.o.*) off.

morille ✿ [mɔ'ri:j] *f fungus*: morel.

morillon [mɔri'jɔ̃] *m* ✿ black grape; *orn.* tufted duck; ✕ rough emerald.

mormon, -onne [mɔr'mɔ̃, ~'mɔn] *adj., a. su.* Mormon.

morne [mɔrn] gloomy; dismal (*scene, existence*); bleak (*scenery*).

morose [mɔ'ro:z] morose; surly; forbidding (*aspect*); **morosité** [~rozi'te] *f* moroseness, surliness; gloominess.

morphine ✿ [mɔr'fin] *f* morphia, morphine; **morphinisme** ✿ [~fi-'nism] *m* morphinism; **morphinomane** [~fino'man] *adj., a. su.* morphia addict, F drug-fiend, *Am.* dope-fiend.

morphologie [mɔrfɔlɔ'ʒi] *f* morphology; **morphologique** [~'ʒik] morphological.

mors [mɔ:r] *m harness*: bit; ⊕ *vice*: jaw; *fig.* prendre le ~ aux dents lose one's temper, get mad.

morse *zo.* [mɔrs] *m* walrus.

morsure [mɔr'sy:r] *f* bite; *fig.* sting.

mort¹ [mɔ:r] *f* death; à ~ deadly; *attraper la* ~ catch one's death; *avoir la* ~ dans l'âme be sick at heart; *mourir de sa belle* ~ die in bed.

mort², **e** [mɔ:r, mɔrt] 1. *p.p. of* mourir; 2. *adj.* dead; stagnant (*water*); *paint.* nature *f* ~e still life; *poids m* ~ dead weight; *point m* ~ *mot.* neutral (*gear*); *fig.* dead-lock; 3. *su.* dead person; *su./m* dummy (*at cards*); *faire le* ~ be dummy; *fig.* sham dead; *jour m des* ♀s All Souls' Day; ~s *pl. et blessés m/pl.* casualties.

mortadelle [mɔrta'dɛl] *f* Bologna sausage.

mortaise ⊕ [mɔr'tɛ:z] *f* mortise.

mortalité [mɔrtali'te] *f* mortality; **mort-aux-rats** [mɔro'ra] *f* ratsbane; **mortel, -elle** [mɔr'tɛl] 1. *adj.* mortal; fatal (*accident, wound*); *fig.* deadly, boring; 2. *su.* mortal; **morte-saison**, *pl.* **mortes-saisons** ✝ [mɔrtsɛ'zɔ̃] *f* slack season, off-season.

mortier △, ✕ [mɔr'tje] *m* mortar.

mortification [mɔrtifika'sjɔ̃] *f* ✿, *eccl., fig.* mortification; ✿ gangrene; *cuis. game*: hanging; *fig.* humiliation; **mortifier** [~'fje] (1o) *v/t.* mortify (*the body, one's passions, fig. s.o.*); ✿ gangrene; *cuis.* hang (*game*); ✿ se ~ mortify, gangrene; **mortné, e** [mɔr'ne] 1. *adj.* still-born (*child, a. fig. project*); 2. *su.* stillborn baby; **mortuaire** [mɔr'tɥɛ:r] mortuary; death...; *drap m* ~ pall; *extrait m* ~ death certificate; *maison f* ~ house of the deceased.

morue *icht.* [mɔ'ry] *f* cod; ~ **sèche** salt cod; *huile f de foie de* ~ cod-liver oil.

morve [mɔrv] *f vet.* glanders *pl.*; (nasal) mucus, V snot; **morveux, -euse** [mɔr'vø, ~'vø:z] 1. *adj. vet.* glandered; F snotty; 2. *su.* F greenhorn.

mosaïque¹ *bibl.* [mɔza'ik] Mosaic.

mosaïque² [mɔza'ik] *f flooring, a. telev.*: mosaic; **mosaïste** [~'ist] *su.* worker in mosaic.

moscoutaire *pej.* [mɔsku'tɛ:r] 1. *adj.* Communist; 2. *su.* F Bolshie.

mosquée [mɔs'ke] *f* mosque.

mot [mo] *m* word; note, line (= *short letter*); saying; ✕ password; ~s *pl.* croisés crossword (puzzle) *sg.*; ~ à ~ word for word; ✕, *fig.* ~ d'ordre keyword, watchword; à ~s couverts by hints; *au bas* ~ at the lowest estimate; *avoir des* ~s *avec q.* fall out with s.o.; *bon* ~ witticism; *en un* ~ in a word, in a nutshell; *jouer sur les* ~s play upon words; *ne pas souffler* ~ keep one's mouth shut; *prendre q. au* ~ take s.o. at his word; *sans* ~ dire without a word.

motard F [mɔ'ta:r] *m* motor cyclist; courtesy cop.

motel [mɔ'tɛl] *m* motel.

moteur, -trice [mɔ'tœ:r, ~'tris] 1. *adj.* motive, driving; *anat.* motory; 2. *su./m* ⊕ motor; engine; *fig.*

(prime) mover, driving force; ~ *à combustion interne*, ~ *à explosion* internal combustion engine; ~ *à deux temps* two-stroke engine; ~ *à injection* injection engine; ~ *à réaction* jet engine; ~ *fixe* stationary engine.

motif, -ve [mɔ'tif, ~'tiːv] **1.** *adj.* motive; **2.** *su./m* motive; *fig.* grounds *pl.*; ♪ theme; *needlework*: pattern.

motion [mɔ'sjɔ̃] *f* motion; *parl.* ~ *de confiance* (censure) motion of confidence (no-confidence).

motivation [mɔtiva'sjɔ̃] *f* motivation; **motiver** [~'ve] (1a) *v/t.* motivate; cause; ⚙ give the reasons for.

moto F [mɔ'to] *f* motor cycle, F motor bike.

moto... motor...; power-driven...; **~culteur** [mɔtɔkyl'tœːr] *m* power-driven cultivator; **~culture** [~kyl'tyːr] *f* mechanized farming; **~cyclette** [~si'klɛt] *f* motor cycle; ~ *à sidecar* motor cycle combination; *faire de la* ~ motor-cycle; **~cycliste** [~si'klist] *su.* motor cyclist; **~glisseur** ⚓ [~gli'sœːr] *m* speed-boat; **~godille** ⚓ [~gɔ'diːj] *f* out-board slung motor; **motoriser** [mɔtɔri'ze] (1a) *v/t.* motorize.

mot-souche, *pl.* **mots-souches** *typ.* [mo'suʃ] *m* catchword.

motte [mɔt] *f* mound; *earth*: clod; *lawn, peat*: sod; *butter*: pad.

motus! [mɔ'tys] *int.* keep it quiet!

mou (*adj. before vowel or h mute* **mol**) *m*, **molle** *f*, *m/pl.* **mous** [mu, mɔl, mu] **1.** *adj.* soft; *fig.* weak; flabby (*flesh*); slack (*rope*); close (*weather*); calm, smooth (*sea*); **2.** *su./m* belt, rope, *etc.*: slack; *cuis.* lights *pl.*

mouchard *pej.* [mu'ʃaːr] *m* (police) informer, F stool-pigeon; F *school*: sneak; **moucharder** [~ʃar'de] (1a) *v/t.* spy on (*s.o.*); *school*: sneak on; *v/i.* spy; sneak (*at school*); **mouche** [muʃ] *f* fly; *foil*: button; *target*: bull's-eye; spot, speck, patch (*on face*); beauty-spot; *faire* ~ hit the bull's-eye; *faire d'une* ~ *un éléphant* make a mountain out of a molehill; *fig. pattes f/pl. de* ~ *handwriting*: scrwal; *prendre la* ~ get angry; F *quelle* ~ *le pique?* what is biting him?

moucher [mu'ʃe] (1a) *v/t.* wipe (*s.o.'s*) nose; snuff (*a candle*); ⚙

trim; *fig.* snub (*s.o.*); *se* ~ blow *or* wipe one's nose.

moucherolle *orn.* [muʃ'rɔl] *f* fly-catcher.

moucheron¹ [muʃ'rɔ̃] *m* gnat, midge; F kid.

moucheron² [~] *m candle*: snuff.

moucheter [muʃ'te] (1c) *v/t.* spot, fleck; button (*a foil*); **mouchette** [mu'ʃet] *f* ⚙ mo(u)lding-plane; ~*s pl.* snuffers; **moucheture** [muʃ'ty:r] *f* spot, speckle, fleck; *zo.* ermine: tail.

mouchoir [mu'ʃwaːr] *m* handkerchief; ⚙ triangular wooden bracket; ~ *de tête* head square; **mouchure** [~'ʃy:r] *f* (nasal) mucus; *candle*: snuff; *rope*: frayed end.

moudre [mudr] (4w) *v/t.* grind.

moue [mu] *f* pout; *faire la* ~ pout, look sulky.

mouette *orn.* [mwɛt] *f* gull.

moufle [mufl] *f* ⚙ set of pulleys; (block and) tackle; ⚙ tie, clamp; ~*s pl.* mitts; ⚡ wiring gloves.

mouflon *zo.* [mu'flɔ̃] *m* moufflon, wild sheep.

mouillage [mu'ja:ʒ] *m* moistening, dampening; *wine*: watering; ⚓ anchoring; **mouiller** [~'je] (1a) *v/t.* wet, damp, moisten; water (*wine etc.*); ⚓ moor (*a ship*); ⚓ drop (*the anchor*); *gramm.* palatalize (*a consonant*); *se* ~ get wet; grow moist (*with tears*); **mouillure** [~'jy:r] *f* wetting; damp-mark; *gramm.* palatalization.

moulage [~] *m* ⚙ cast(ing); *metall.* founding; ⚙ plaster mo(u)lding.

moulant, e [mu'lɑ̃, ~'lɑ̃:t] skintight (*dress*).

moule¹ [mul] *m* ⚙ mo(u)ld; matrix; *jeter en* ~ cast.

moule² [mul] *f* mussel; F fat-head; F lazy-bones *sg.*

moulé, e [mu'le] mo(u)lded, cast; *écriture moulée* block letters *pl.*

mouler [mu'le] (1a) *v/t.* cast; mo(u)ld; *metall.* found; *fig.* fit tightly; ~ *sur* model (*s.th.*) on; **mouleur** [~'lœːr] *m* mo(u)lder, caster.

moulière [mu'ljɛːr] *f* mussel-bed.

moulin [mu'lɛ̃] *m* mill (*a.* ⚙); ~ *à café* coffee-mill; **mouliner** [muli-'ne] (1a) *v/t. tex.* throw (*silk*); *insects*: eat into (*wood*); **moulinet** [~'ne] *m* winch; *fishing-rod*: reel; turnstile; *fencing, a. stick*: twirl; ~ *à musique* toy musical box; **mou-**

lineur *tex.* [∼'nœːr] *m*, **moulinier** *tex.* [∼'nje] *m* silk-thrower.

moulons [mu'lɔ̃] *1st p. pl. pres. of moudre*; **moulu, e** [∼'ly] **1.** *adj. fig.* F tired out; aching all over; **2.** *p.p. of moudre.*

moulure △, ⊕ [mu'lyːr] *f* mo(u)lding; profiling.

moulus [mu'ly] *1st p. sg. p.s. of moudre.*

mourant, e [mu'rɑ̃, ∼'rɑ̃ːt] **1.** *adj.* dying; faint (*voice*); languishing (*voice*); F screamingly funny; **2.** *su.* dying person; **mourir** [∼'riːr] (2k) *v/i.* die; die out (*fire*); die away (*sound*); fall (*hope*); ∼ *avant l'âge* come to an untimely end; *être à ∼ de rire* be screamingly funny; *ennuyer q. à ∼* bore s.o. to death; *v/t.:* se ∼ be dying; die away.

mouron [mu'rɔ̃] *m* ♀ (∼ *rouge*) scarlet pimpernel; ♀ ∼ *blanc* (*or des oiseaux*) chickweed; *sl.* hair; *sl.* se faire du ∼ worry (o.s. sick).

mourrai [mur're] *1st p. sg. fut. of mourir*; **mourus** [mu'ry] *1st p. sg. p.s. of mourir.*

mousquet ✗ [mus'kɛ] *m* musket; **mousquetade** [muskə'tad] *f* musket-shot; *musket-shots:* volley; **mousquetaire** ✗ [∼'tɛːr] *m* musketeer; **mousqueton** [∼'tɔ̃] *m* snaphook; ✗ † artillery carbine.

mousse[1] [mus] *m* ship's boy; cabinboy.

mousse[2] [∼] *f* ♀ moss; *beer:* froth; *sea:* foam; *soap:* lather; *cuis.* mousse.

mousse[3] [∼] blunt.

mousseline [mus'lin] **1.** *su./f tex.* muslin; **2.** *adj./inv.: cuis.* pommes *f/pl.* ∼ mashed potatoes; *verre m* ∼ muslin-glass.

mousser [mu'se] (1a) *v/i.* froth; lather (*soap*); effervesce, fizz (*champagne*); F faire ∼ *q.* crack s.o. up; **mousseux, -euse** [∼'sø, ∼'søːz] **1.** *adj.* mossy; foaming; sparkling (*wine*); **2.** *su./m* sparkling wine.

mousson [mu'sɔ̃] *f* monsoon.

moussu, e [mu'sy] mossy; ♀ *rose f* ∼e moss-rose.

moustache [mus'taʃ] *f* moustache; *cat:* whiskers *pl.*; **moustachu, e** [∼ta'ʃy] moustached.

moustiquaire [musti'kɛːr] *f* mosquito-net; **moustique** *zo.* [∼'tik] *m* mosquito; gnat.

moût [mu] *m grapes:* must; unfermented wine.

moutarde ♀, *a. cuis.* [mu'tard] *f* mustard; **moutardier** [∼tar'dje] *m* mustard-pot; mustard-maker; F se *croire le premier* ∼ *du pape* think no end of o.s.

mouton [mu'tɔ̃] *m* sheep; *cuis.* mutton; ∼s *pl.* fleecy clouds; *sea:* white horses; *revenons à nos* ∼s let us get back to the subject; **moutonner** [∼tɔ'ne] (1a) *v/i.* foam, break into white horses (*sea*); *ciel m* moutonné mackerel sky; **moutonnerie** [∼tɔn-'ri] *f* stupidity; **moutonneux, -euse** [mutɔ'nø, ∼'nøːz] fleecy (*sky*); frothy, covered with white horses (*sea*); **moutonnier, -ère** [∼'nje, ∼'njɛːr] ovine; *fig.* sheep-like, easily led.

mouture [mu'tyːr] *f* grinding, milling; milling dues *pl.*

mouvance [mu'vɑ̃ːs] *f* domain, sphere (of influence); mobility; instability; **mouvant, e** [mu'vɑ̃, ∼'vɑ̃ːt] moving; shifting (*sands*); loose (*ground*); *fig.* changeable; *sables m/pl.* ∼s quicksand *sg.*; **mouvement** [muv'mɑ̃] *m* movement (*a.* ♪); motion (*a. phys.*); ⬧, *a. fig.* change; ✝ *market:* fluctuation; *roads etc.:* traffic; ⊕ *machine:* action, works *pl.*; *fig.* impulse; *fig.* outburst; ∼ *clandestin* underground movement; ⊕ ∼ *perdu* idle motion; ∼ *perpétuel* perpetual motion; ∼ *populaire* popular uprising; ∼ *syndical* trade-unionism; ⚑ *faire un faux* ∼ strain o.s. *or* a muscle; **mouvementé, e** [∼mɑ̃'te] lively; busy; eventful (*life*); undulating (*ground*).

mouvoir [mu'vwaːr] (3f) *v/t.* ⊕ drive; ⚓ propel (*a ship*); *fig.* move; *fig.* urge, drive, prompt; se ∼ move; **mouvrai** [∼'vre] *1st p. sg. fut. of mouvoir.*

moyen, -enne [mwa'jɛ̃, ∼'jɛn] **1.** *adj.* middle; mean, average; medium (*size, quality*); ♀ Age Middle Ages *pl.*; *classe f* ∼enne middle class; *du* ♀ Age medi(a)eval; **2.** *su./m* means *sg.*, way, manner; medium; ⚖ mean; ⚖ grounds *pl.* of a claim; ∼s *pl.* resources; *au* ∼ *de* by means of; *il (n')y a (pas)* ∼ *de (inf.)* it is (im)possible to (*inf.*); *pas* ∼! nothing doing!; *le* ∼ *de (inf.)* how could one (*inf.*); *su./f* average, mean; *examination:* passmark; en ‿enne on an average; **moyenâgeux, -euse** F [‿jɛnaˈʒø, ‿ˈʒøːz] (pej. sham-)medi(a)eval, historic; fig. antiquated; **moyennant** [‿jɛˈnɑ̃] prp. for (money etc.); ‿ quoi in return for which.

moyeu¹ [mwaˈjø] m wheel: hub, nave.

moyeu² [‿] m preserved plum.

mû, mue, m/pl. **mus** [my] p.p. of mouvoir.

muance [mɥɑ̃ːs] f voice: breaking.

mucilage ⚘ [mysiˈlaːʒ] m gum, mucilage; **mucilagineux, -euse** [‿laʒiˈnø, ‿ˈnøːz] mucilaginous, viscous.

mucosité [mykoziˈte] f mucus.

mue [my] f birds: mo(u)lt(ing); snakes: sloughing; animals: shedding of coat etc.; mo(u)lting-season; hens: coop; voice: breaking; **muer** [mɥe] (1n) v/i. mo(u)lt (birds); slough (snake); shed its coat etc. (animal); break (voice); cast its antlers (stag).

muet, -ette [mɥɛ, mɥɛt] 1. adj. dumb; mute; 2. su. dumb or mute person.

mufle [myfl] m animal: muzzle, nose; fig. F boor, lout; F mug (= face); **muflerie** F [myfləˈri] f boorishness; **muflier** ⚘ [‿fliˈe] m snapdragon.

mugir [myˈʒiːr] (2a) v/i. bellow (bull, a. F person with rage); low (cow); howl (wind); roar (sea, a. fig.); **mugissement** [‿ʒisˈmɑ̃] m bellowing etc.

muguet [myˈgɛ] m ⚘ lily of the valley; ⚘ thrush.

mulâtre m, **-tresse** f [myˈlɑːtr, ‿ˈlɑːtres] mulatto.

mule¹ [myl] f mule, slipper; ⚘ kibe.

mule² zo. [‿] f (she-)mule.

mulet¹ zo. [myˈlɛ] m mule.

mulet² icht. [‿] m grey mullet.

muletier [mylˈtje] m muleteer.

mulot zo. [myˈlo] m field-mouse.

mulsion [mylˈsjɔ̃] f milking.

multi... [mylti] multi(-)...; many-...; **‿colore** [‿kɔˈlɔːr] many-colo(u)red, multi-colo(u)red; **‿latéral, e,** m/pl. **-aux** [‿lateˈral, ‿ˈro] multilateral.

multiple [mylˈtipl] 1. adj. multiple; multifarious; 2. su./m multiple; **multiplication** [‿tiplikaˈsjɔ̃] f multiplication; ⊕, mot. gear(-ratio); fig. increase; **multiplier** [‿tipliˈe]

(1a) vt/i. multiply; v/t.: ⊕ ‿ la vitesse gear up.

multitude [myltiˈtyd] f multitude; crowd.

municipal, e, m/pl. **-aux** [mynisiˈpal, ‿ˈpo] municipal; bye-(law); local, town...; conseil m ‿ town council; **municipalité** [‿paliˈte] f municipality, township.

munificence [mynifiˈsɑ̃ːs] f munificence; bounty; **munificent, e** [‿ˈsɑ̃, ‿ˈsɑ̃ːt] munificent; bounteous.

munir [myˈniːr] (2a) v/t. equip, provide (with, de); **munitions** [myniˈsjɔ̃] f/pl. ✕ ammunition sg.; ‿ de bouche provisions.

muqueux, -euse [myˈkø, ‿ˈkøːz] mucous.

mûr, mûre, m/pl. [myːr] ripe; mature (age, mind, wine).

mur [myːr] m wall; ✕ ‿ du son sound barrier; **murage** [myˈraːʒ] m walling (in); bricking up; **muraille** [‿ˈrɑːj] f high or thick wall; ⚓ ship: side; **mural, e,** m/pl. **-aux** [‿ˈral, ‿ˈro] mural; carte f ‿e wall-map.

mûre ⚘ [myːr] f mulberry; blackberry.

murer [myˈre] (1a) v/t. wall in; wall or block up.

mûrier ⚘ [myˈrje] m mulberry (-bush or -tree); ‿ sauvage bramble.

mûrir [myˈriːr] (2a) vt/i. ripen, mature (a. fig.); v/t. fig. meditate, think out thoroughly.

murmure [myrˈmyːr] m murmur (-ing); whisper; **murmurer** [‿myˈre] (1a) vt/i. murmur; whisper; babble (child, stream); fig. complain.

mûron ⚘ [myˈrɔ̃] m blackberry; wild raspberry.

mus [my] 1st p. sg. p.s. of mouvoir.

musaraigne zo. [myzaˈrɛɲ] f shrew-mouse.

musard, e [myˈzaːr, ‿ˈzard] 1. adj. idling; 2. su. idler; **musarder** F [‿zarˈde] (1a) v/i. idle; fritter away one's time.

musc [mysk] m musk; zo. musk-deer.

muscade ⚘ [mysˈkad] f nutmeg.

muscadet [myskaˈdɛ] m (sort of) muscatel (wine).

muscardin zo. [myskarˈdɛ̃] m dormouse.

muscat [mysˈka] m muscat (grape or wine); musk-pear.

muscle [myskl] *m* muscle; *fig.*
brawn; **musclé, e** [mys'kle] muscular; brawny; athletic; sinewy (*a.*
fig.); *fig.* powerful, strong; *fig.*
strong-arm (*politics etc.*); **muscler**
[~] (1a) *v/t.* develop the muscles of;
fig. strengthen; **musculaire** [~ky-
'lɛːr] muscular; **musculeux, -euse**
[~ky'lø, ~'løːz] muscular; *cuis.* sinewy (*meat*). [mug (= *face*).⟩
museau [my'zo] *m* muzzle; snout; F⟩
musée [my'ze] *m* museum.
museler [myz'le] (1c) *v/t.* muzzle (*a.*
fig.); **muselière** [~zə'ljɛːr] *f* muzzle.
muser [my'ze] (1a) *v/i.* dawdle; fritter away one's time.

musette [my'zɛt] *f horse*: nose-bag;
✕ haversack; ♪ country bagpipe;
bal m ~ popular dance-hall.
musical, e, *m/pl.* **-aux** [myzi'kal,
~'ko] musical; **music-hall** [myzi-
'koːl] *m* music-hall; variety; **musicien, -enne** [myzi'sjɛ̃, ~'sjɛn]
1. *adj.* musical; **2.** *su.* musician;
performer, player; **musique** [my-
'zik] *f* music; ✕ *etc.* band; ~ *enregistrée* recorded music.

musqué, e [mys'ke] musky, musk;
fig. paroles f/pl. ~es honeyed words;
poire f ~e musk-pear; *rose f* ~e
musk-rose.
musulman, e [myzyl'mã, ~'man]
adj., a. su. ♀ Moslem, Mohammedan.
mutabilité [mytabili'te] *f* instability; ⚖ alienability; **mutation**
[~ta'sjɔ̃] *f* change, alteration; ♪, *biol.*
mutation; ♪ *violin-playing*: shift;
personnel, property: transfer; **muter**
[~'te] (1a) *v/t.* transfer (*an official
etc.*).
mutilation [mytila'sjɔ̃] *f person,
book, statue, etc.*: mutilation; *person*: maiming; *book, statue, etc.*:
defacement; **mutilé** [~'le] *m*: ~ *de
guerre* disabled ex-serviceman; ~
du travail disabled workman; **muti-**

ler [~'le] (1a) *v/t.* mutilate; maim;
deface.
mutin, e [my'tɛ̃, ~'tin] **1.** *adj.* mischievous; † insubordinate; **2.** *su./m*
mutineer; **mutiner** [~ti'ne] (1a)
v/t.: *se* ~ rise in revolt, rebel; be
unruly; ✕ mutiny; **mutinerie**
[~tin'ri] *f* rebellion; ✕ mutiny; unruliness; pertness.
mutisme [my'tism] *m* silence.
mutualité [mytɥali'te] *f* mutuality,
reciprocity; **mutuel, -elle** [my-
'tɥɛl] **1.** *adj.* mutual; *pari m* ~
totalizator, F tote; *secours m/pl.* ~s
mutual benefit; *société f* de
secours ~ friendly society; **2.** *su./f*
mutual insurance company.
myocarde *anat.* [mjɔ'kard] *m* my-
ocardium; **myocardite** ✚ [~kar-
'dit] *f* myocarditis.
myope ✚ [mjɔp] **1.** *adj.* myopic,
near-sighted, short-sighted; **2.** *su.*
near-sighted *or* short-sighted person; **myopie** ✚ [mjɔ'pi] *f* myopia,
near-sightedness, short-sighted-
ness. [forget-me-not.⟩
myosotis ✿ [mjɔzɔ'tis] *m* myosotis,⟩
myrte ✿ [mirt] *m* myrtle; **myrtille**
✿ [mir'til] *f* whortleberry, bilberry,
Am. blueberry, huckleberry.
mystère [mis'tɛːr] *m* mystery (*a.
thea.*), secret; secrecy; **mystérieux,
-euse** [~te'rjø, ~'rjøːz] mysterious;
enigmatic; **mysticisme** [~ti'sism]
m mysticism; **mystification** [~tifi-
ka'sjɔ̃] *f* hoax; mystification; **mystifier** [~ti'fje] (1o) *v/t.* hoax, fool;
mystify; **mystique** [~'tik] **1.** *adj.*
mystic; **2.** *su.* mystic; *su./f* mystical
theology *or* doctrine.
mythe [mit] *m* myth (*a. fig.*); legend;
mythique [mi'tik] mythical; **mythologie** [mitɔlɔ'ʒi] *f* mythology;
mythologique [~lɔ'ʒik] mytholog-
ical; **mythologue** [~'lɔg] *m* mythol-
ogist; **mythomane** *psych.* [~'man]
adj., a. su. mythomaniac.

N

N, n [ɛn] *m* N, n.
nabab [na'bab] *m* nabob.
nabot, e [na'bo, ~'bɔt] **1.** *su.* dwarf, midget; **2.** *adj.* dwarfish.
nacelle [na'sɛl] *f* ⚓ skiff, wherry; ✈ cockpit; *airship:* gondola; *balloon:* basket.
nacre [nakr] *f* mother of pearl; **na-cré, e** [na'kre] pearly; **nacrer** [~] (1a) *v/t.* give a pearly sheen to.
nage [na:ʒ] *f* swimming; rowing; stroke; ~ *à la brasse* breast-stroke; ~ *libre* free style; ~ *sur le dos* back-stroke; *à la* ~ by swimming; *donner la* ~ *rowing:* set the stroke; F *(tout) en* ~ bathed in perspiration; **nageoire** [naʒwa:r] *f icht.* fin; *whale:* paddle; float; *sl.* arm; **nager** [~'ʒe] (11) *v/i.* swim; row; float; ~ *dans l'opulence* be rolling in money; *v/t.:* ~ *le crawl* swim the crawl; **nageur** *m*, **-euse** *f* [~'ʒœ:r, ~'ʒø:z] swimmer; rower.
naguère [na'gɛːr] *adv.* lately, a short time ago.
naïf, -ve [na'if, ~'iːv] naïve, artless, unaffected; unsophisticated, simple.
nain, naine [nɛ̃, nɛn] **1.** *su.* dwarf, midget; **2.** *adj.* dwarf(ish); stunted.
nais [nɛ] *1st p. sg. pres. of* naître.
naissance [nɛ'sɑ̃:s] *f* birth; *fig.* origin; *fig.* beginning; *acte m de* ~ birth-certificate; *Français de* ~ French-born; ~ *des cheveux* hair line; *fig. prendre* ~ originate; **naissant, e** [~'sɑ̃, ~'sɑ̃:t] dawning; *fig. a.* incipient; **naissent** [nɛs] *3rd p. pl. pres. of* naître; **naître** [nɛːtr] (4x) *v/i.* be born; dawn; *fig.* originate, begin; *faire* ~ give rise to, cause.
naïveté [naiv'te] *f* naïvety, ingenuousness; simpleness; ingenuous remark.
naja *zo.* [na'ʒa] *m* cobra. [woman).\
nana *sl.* [na'na] *f* chick (= *girl,*/
nantir [nɑ̃'tiːr] (2a) *v/t.* ⚖ *creditor:* secure; *fig.* provide (with, *de*); *bien nanti* well-off (for money); *les nantis* the well-to-do; **nantissement** [~tis'mɑ̃] *m* security; lien, hypothecation.

napalm ⚗, ✗ [na'palm] *m* napalm.
naphte ⚗ [naft] *m* naphtha.
nappe [nap] *f* (table)cloth; cover; *ice, water, etc.:* sheet; ~ *de pétrole* oil slick; **napperon** [na'prɔ̃] *m* (table)mat; ~ *individuel* place mat.
naquis [na'ki] *1st p. sg. p.s. of* naître.
narcisse ♀ [nar'sis] *m* narcissus; ~ *des bois* daffodil; **narcissique** [~si'sik] narcissistic; **narcissisme** [~si'sism] *m* narcissism.
narcose ⚕ [nar'ko:z] *f* narcosis; **nar-cotique** [~kɔ'tik] *adj., a. su./m* narcotic.
nard ♀ [na:r] *m* (spike)nard.
narguer [nar'ge] (1m) *v/t.* flout; jeer at (*s.o.*).
narine [na'rin] *f anat.* nostril.
narquois, e [nar'kwa, ~'kwa:z] mocking.
narrateur *m*, **-trice** *f* [nara'tœ:r, ~'tris] narrator, teller, relater; **nar-ratif, -ve** [~'tif, ~'ti:v] narrative; **narration** [~'sjɔ̃] *f* narration, narrative; **narrer** [na're] (1a) *v/t.* narrate, relate.
narval, *pl.* **-als** *zo.* [nar'val] *m* narwhal.
nasal, e, *m/pl.* **-aux** [na'zal, ~'zo] *adj., a. su./f gramm.* nasal; **nasaliser** *gramm.* [~zali'ze] (1a) *v/t.* nasalize; **naseau** [~'zo] *m* nostril; **nasillard, e** [nazi'jaːr, ~'jard] nasal, twanging; **nasiller** [~'je] (1a) *v/i.* speak through one's nose *or* with a twang; *v/t.* twang (*s.th.*) (out).
nasse [nas] *f* eel-pot; trap (*a. fig.*).
natal, e, *m/pl.* **-als** [na'tal] native; birth...; **natalité** [~tali'te] *f* birth-rate, natality.
natation [nata'sjɔ̃] *f* swimming; **natatoire** [~'twa:r] *zo.* natatory; *icht. vessie f* ~ air-bladder, swimming-bladder.
natif, -ve [na'tif, ~'ti:v] **1.** *adj.* native (*a.* ⚒); natural, innate; **2.** *su.* native.
nation [na'sjɔ̃] *f* nation; *bibl. les* ~*s pl.* the Gentiles; **national, e,** *m/pl.* **-aux** [~sjɔ'nal, ~'no] **1.** *adj.*

nationalisation 330

national; **2.** *su./m:* ~s *pl.* nationals; *su./f (a.* route *f* ~e) highway; main road; **nationalisation** [nasjɔnaliza-ˈsjɔ̃] *f* nationalization; **nationalisme** *pol.* [~ˈlism] *m* nationalism; **nationaliste** *pol.* [~ˈlist] **1.** *su.* nationalist; **2.** *adj.* nationalistic; **nationalité** [~liˈte] *f* nationality; nation.

nativité *eccl., astr.* [nativiˈte] *f* nativity.

natte [nat] *f (straw- etc.)* mat(ting); *hair:* plait, braid; F pigtail; **natter** [naˈte] (1a) *v/t.* cover (*s.th.*) with mats; plait (*one's hair, straw*).

naturalisation [natyraliza'sjɔ̃] *f* pol. naturalization; ♧, *zo.* acclimatizing; **naturaliser** [~liˈze] (1a) *v/t.* naturalize; ♧, *zo.* acclimatize; stuff, mount (*an animal*); se ~ become naturalized; **naturalisme** *paint. etc.* [~ˈlism] *m* naturalism; **naturaliste** [~ˈlist] **1.** *su.* naturalist; taxidermist; **2.** *adj.* naturalistic; **naturalité** [~liˈte] *f* naturalness.

nature [naˈtyːr] **1.** *su./f* nature; kind; type; disposition, temperament; *paint.* d'après ~ from nature; de ~ à (*inf.*) likely to (*inf.*), such as to (*inf.*); lois *f/pl.* de la ~ laws of nature; de ~, par ~ by nature, naturally; payer en ~ pay in kind; **2.** *adj./inv.* plain; café *m* ~ black coffee; **naturel, -elle** [natyˈrɛl] **1.** *adj.* natural; **2.** *su./m* disposition, nature; naturalness; native; au ~ realistically, true to life; *cuis.* plain; **naturiste** [~ˈrist] **1.** *su.* naturist; **2.** *adj.* naturistic.

naufrage [noˈfraːʒ] *m* shipwreck (*a. fig.*); faire ~ be shipwrecked; **naufragé, e** [nofraˈʒe] **1.** *adj.* shipwrecked; castaway; **2.** *su.* shipwrecked person; castaway; **naufrageur** [~ˈʒœːr] *m* wrecker.

nauséabond, e [nozeaˈbɔ̃, ~ˈbɔ̃ːd] nauseous, foul; evil-smelling; **nausée** [~ˈze] *f* nausea; seasickness; *fig.* loathing; **nauséeux, -euse** [~zeˈø, ~ˈøːz] nauseous; loathsome.

nautique [noˈtik] ♧ nautical; sea-...; aquatic (*sports*); **nautonier** [~tɔ-ˈnje] *m* ferryman, pilot.

naval, e [naˈval] naval, nautical; constructions *f/pl.* ~es ship-building *sg.*

navarin *cuis.* [navaˈrɛ̃] *m* mutton stew with turnips.

navet [naˈvɛ] *m* turnip; F paint. daub; F rubbish, tripe.

navette¹ [naˈvɛt] *f eccl.* incense boat; ⊕ shuttle; 🚌 *etc.* shuttle service; ~ spatiale space shuttle; *fig.* faire la ~ shuttle; come and go; ply.

navette² ♧ [~] *f* rape.

navigabilité [navigabiliˈte] *f* navigability; *ship:* seaworthiness; ✈ airworthiness; **navigable** [~ˈgabl] navigable; seaworthy (*ship*); ✈ airworthy; **navigateur** [~gaˈtœːr] **1.** *adj./m* seafaring; **2.** *su./m* navigator; sailor; **navigation** [~gaˈsjɔ̃] *f* navigation, sailing; ~ intérieure inland navigation; **naviguer** [~ˈge] (1m) *vt/i.* ♧, ✈ navigate; ♧ steer.

naviplane ♧ [naviˈplan] *m* hovercraft.

navire ♧ [naˈviːr] *m* ship, vessel; ♧ ~ de commerce merchantman; ~-citerne, *pl.* ~s-citernes ♧ [~virsiˈtɛrn] *m* tanker; ~-école, *pl.* ~s-écoles ♧ [~vireˈkɔl] *m* training ship; ~-hôpital, *pl.* ~s-hôpitaux ♧ [~virɔpiˈtal, ~ˈto] *m* hospitalship.

navrant, e [naˈvrɑ̃, ~ˈvrɑ̃ːt] heart-rending, heart-breaking; **navré, e** [~ˈvre] deeply grieved; heart-broken; **navrer** [~ˈvre] (1a) *v/t.* grieve (*s.o.*) deeply; j'en suis navré! I am awfully *or* F terribly sorry!

ne [nə] *adv.:* ne ... guère not ... much, scarcely; ne ... jamais never; ne ... pas not; ne ... plus no more, no longer; ne ... plus jamais never again; ne ... point not (at all); ne ... que only.

né, née [ne] **1.** *p.p. of* naître; **2.** *adj.* born; *fig.* cut out (for, pour); bien ~ of a good family; *fig.* être ~ coiffé be born with a silver spoon in one's mouth.

néanmoins [neɑ̃ˈmwɛ̃] *adv.* nevertheless, however; yet.

néant [neˈɑ̃] *m* nothing(ness), naught; *admin.* nil; ⚖ mettre à ~ dismiss; réduire à ~ reduce to naught; **néantiser** [~ɑ̃tiˈze] (1a) *v/t.* destroy; reduce to nothing.

nébuleux, -euse [nebyˈlø, ~ˈløːz] **1.** *adj.* nebulous; cloudy (*a. liquid*), misty (*sky, view*); *fig.* gloomy (*face*); F *fig.* obscure; **2.** *su./f astr.* nebula; **nébulosité** [~loziˈte] *f* haziness (*a. fig.*); patch of haze *or* mist.

nécessaire [neseˈsɛːr] **1.** *adj.* necessary (to, for *à*); requisite; 2. *su./m* necessaries *pl.*; outfit, kit, set; ~ de *toilette* toilet bag; **nécessité** [~si'te] *f* necessity, need; indigence; **nécessiter** [~si'te] (1a) *v/t.* necessitate, entail, require; **nécessiteux, -euse** [~si'tø, ~'tø:z] 1. *adj.* needy; 2. *su./m*: *les* ~ *pl.* the needy.

nécro... [nekrɔ] necro...; ~**loge** [~'lɔːʒ] *m* obituary list; death-roll; ~**logie** [~lɔ'ʒi] *f* obituary; ~**logue** [~'lɔg] *m* necrologist; ~**mancie** [~mã'si] *f* necromancy; ~**pole** [~'pɔl] *f* necropolis, city of the dead.

nécrose [ne'kroːz] *f* ✳ necrosis; ♀ canker.

nectar ♀, *a. myth.* [nɛk'taːr] *m* nectar.

néerlandais, e [neɛrlã'dɛ, ~'dɛːz] 1. *adj.* Dutch, Netherlandish; 2. *su.* ♀ Netherlander; *su./m* ♂ Dutchman; *su./f* ♀ Dutchwoman.

nef [nɛf] *f church:* nave; *poet.* ship.

néfaste [ne'fast] ill-omened; ill-starred; ill-fated; disastrous.

nèfle ♀ [nɛfl] *f* medlar; *sl. des* ~*s!* not likely!

négatif, -ve [nega'tif, ~'tiːv] 1. *adj.* negative (*a.* ⚡); *phot.* épreuve *f* ~ve = 2. *su./m phot.* negative; *su./f* negative; *dans la* ~ve in the negative; *if not; répondre par la* ~ve say no; *se tenir sur la* ~ve maintain a negative attitude; **négation** [~'sjõ] *f* negation, denial; *gramm.* negative.

négligé, e [negli'ʒe] 1. *adj.* neglected; slovenly (*dress, style*); careless (*appearance, dress*); 2. *su./m* undress; informal dress; dishabille; négligé; **négligeable** [~'ʒabl] negligible (*a.* ⚡); trifling; **négligence** [~'ʒãːs] *f* negligence, neglect; oversight; **négligent, e** [~'ʒã, ~'ʒãːt] negligent, careless; **négliger** [~'ʒe] (1l) *v/t.* neglect; overlook; disregard; slight (*s.o.*); *se* ~ become careless or slovenly.

négoce [ne'gɔs] *m* trade, business; **négociable** ♰ [negɔ'sjabl] negotiable; market (*value*); **négociant** [~'sjã] *m* (wholesale) merchant; trader; **négociateur, *m* -trice** [~sja'tœːr, ~'tris] negotiator; **négociation** [~sja'sjõ] *f* negotiation (*a.* ✕); ♰ transaction; ✕ parley; **négocier** [~'sje] (1o) *vt/i.* negotiate; *mot.* ~ *un virage* negotiate a bend.

nègre [nɛːgr] *m* negro; F ghost

(writer); (*barrister's*) devil; *fig. travailler comme un* ~ work like a slave; **négresse** [ne'grɛs] *f* negress; **négrier** [negri'e] *m* slave trader; ♣ (*a. bateau m* ~) slave ship; *fig.* slave driver; **négrillon** F [~'jõ] *m* negro boy; F piccaninny; **négrillonne** F [~'jɔn] *f* negro girl.

neige [nɛːʒ] *f* snow (*a. sl.* = *cocaine*); ~*s pl.* éternelles perpetual snow *sg.*; 🜋 ~ *carbonique* dry ice; ~ *croûteuse* (*poudreuse*) crusted (powdery) snow; *boule f de* ~ snowball; 🚆 *train m de* ~ winter sports train; **neiger** [nɛ'ʒe] (1l) *v/impers.* snow; **neigeux, -euse** [~'ʒø, ~'ʒøːz] snowy; snow-covered; snow-white.

nénuphar ♀ [neny'faːr] *m* water-lily.

néo... [neɔ] neo-...; ~**logisme** [~lɔ-'ʒism] *m* neologism.

néon 🜋 [ne'õ] *m* neon; *éclairage m au* ~ neon lighting.

néphrétique ✳ [nefre'tik] 1. *adj.* nephritic; 2. *su.* sufferer from nephritis; **néphrite** [~'frit] *f* ✳ nephritis; *min.* jade; ✳ ~ *chronique* Bright's disease.

népotisme [nepɔ'tism] *m* nepotism.

nerf [nɛːr] *m anat.* nerve; *fig.* vigo(u)r, F guts *pl.*; *fig.* ~ *de bœuf* cosh; life-preserver; *fig. avoir du* ~ be vigorous; *avoir ses* ~*s*, F *avoir les* ~*s en pelote or en boule* be on edge; *le* ~ *de la guerre* the sinews *pl.* of war; *porter (or donner or* F *taper) sur les* ~*s à q.* get on s.o.'s nerves.

nerprun ♀ [nɛr'prœ] *m* buckthorn.

nerveux, -euse [nɛr'vø, ~'vøːz] nervous; sinewy; *anat.* nerve...; excitable, highly-strung (*person*); *fig.* virile (*style etc.*); **nervin** ✳ [~'vɛ] *adj./m, a. su./m* nervine; **nervosisme** ✳ [~vo'zism] *m* nervous predisposition; **nervosité** [~vozi'te] *f* nervousness; irritability; irritation; **nervure** [~'vyːr] *f leaf etc.:* vein; △, ⊕ rib.

net, nette [nɛt] 1. *adj.* clean; neat; clear; clear-cut, distinct; ♰ net; 2. *net adv.* plainly, flatly; clearly; *refuser* ~ refuse point-blank; 3. *su./m*: *copie f au* ~ fair copy; *mettre qch. au* ~ make a fair copy of s.th.; **netteté** [nɛtə'te] *f* cleanness; (*bodily*) cleanliness; *fig. image, sound:* clarity; distinctness; *fig.* decidedness; **nettoiement** [nɛtwa'mã] *m* cleaning; clearing; **nettoyage** [~'ja:ʒ] *m* ⊕ scaling; ✂ mopping-up; ~ *à sec* dry-cleaning; **nettoyer** [~'je] (1h) *v/t.* clean; clear; ⊕ scale; ✂ mop up; F rifle (*a house, s.o.*); F clean out; ~ *à sec* dry-clean; **nettoyeur** *m*, **-euse** *f* [~'jœ:r, ~'jø:z] cleaner.

neuf¹ [nœf; *before vowel or h mute* nœv] *adj./num.*, *a. su./m/inv.* nine; *date, title*: ninth.

neuf², neuve [nœf, nœ:v] **1.** *adj.* new; *fig.* inexperienced; **2.** *su./m* new; *quoi de ~? what's new?*; *remettre à ~* do up (like new); *repeindre à ~* redecorate.

neurasthénie [nøraste'ni] *f* neurasthenia; **neurasthénique** [~'nik] *adj.*, *a. su.* neurasthenic; **neurologue** [nørɔ'lɔg] *m* neurologist, nerve specialist; **neurone** [nø'rɔn] *m* neuron.

neutraliser [nøtrali'ze] (1a) *v/t.* neutralize; **neutraliste** *pol.* [~'list] *adj.*, *a. su.* neutralist; **neutralité** [~li'te] *f* neutrality; ♞ neutral state; **neutre** [nø:tr] **1.** *adj.* neuter (*a. gramm.*); ♞, ⚥, *pol.*, *a. colour*: neutral; **2.** *su. pol.* neutral; *su./m gramm.* neuter.

neutron *phys.* [nø'trɔ̃] *m* neutron.

neuvaine *eccl.* [nœ'ven] *f* novena; **neuvième** [~'vjɛm] *adj./num.*, *a. su.*, *a. su./m fraction*: ninth.

névé *geol.* [ne've] *m* névé, firn.

neveu [nə'vø] *m* nephew; ~*x pl.* descendants.

névralgie [nevral'ʒi] *f* neuralgia; **névralgique** [~'ʒik] *adj.* neuralgic; *fig. point m* ~ sore spot.

névr(o)... [nevr(ɔ)] neur(o)...

névrose [ne'vro:z] *f* neurosis; **névrosé, e** [nevrɔ'ze] *adj.*, *a. su.* neurotic; **névrotique** [~'tik] neurotic.

nez [ne] *m* nose; *animal*: snout; ⚓, ✈ bow, nose; scent; F ~ *à ~* face to face; *au ~ de* q. under s.o.'s nose; *fig. avoir le ~ fin* be shrewd; F *avoir q. dans le ~* bear s.o. a grudge; *mener par le bout du ~* twist (*s.o.*) round one's little finger; *mettre le ~ dans* poke one's nose into.

ni [ni] *cj.* nor, or; *ni ... ni* neither ... nor; *ni moi non plus* nor I (either).

niable [njabl] deniable; ⚖ traversable.

niais, e [njɛ, njɛ:z] **1.** *adj.* simple, silly; *Am.* dumb; **2.** *su.* fool; simpleton; *Am.* dumbbell; **niaiserie** [njɛz'ri] *f* foolishness, silliness.

niche¹ [niʃ] *f* trick, practical joke.

niche² [niʃ] *f* niche, recess; ~ *à chien* kennel; **nichée** [ni'ʃe] *f* nestful; brood; **nicher** [~] (1a) *v/i.* nest; F *fig.* live, hang out; *v/t.*: se ~ (build it's) nest; *fig.* nestle; *fig.* lodge o.s. (*thing*), put o.s. (*person*).

nichrome *metall.* [ni'krɔm] *m* chrome-nickel steel.

nickel ♞ [ni'kɛl] *m* nickel; **nickelage** ⊕ [ni'kla:ʒ] *m* nickel-plating; **nickeler** ⊕ [~'kle] (1c) *v/t.* nickel (-plate).

nicotine ♞ [nikɔ'tin] *f* nicotine.

nid [ni] *m* nest; *fig. thieves*: den; *tex.* ~ *d'abeilles* honeycomb, *Am.* waffle weave; *mot.* ~-*de-poule* pothole (*on a road*); **nidification** [nidifika'sjɔ̃] *f* nest-building.

nièce [njɛs] *f* niece.

nielle [njɛl] *su./f* ✿ *wheat*: earcockle; ♣ nigella; *su./m* ⊕ niello, inlaid enamel-work; **nieller** [njɛ'le] (1a) *v/t.* ✿ blight, smut; ⊕ (inlay with) niello; ✿ se ~ smut; **niellure** [~'ly:r] *f* ✿ blighting; ⊕ niello-work.

nier [nje] (1o) *v/t.* deny; repudiate (*a debt*); *on ne saurait ~ que* there can be no denying that.

nigaud, e [ni'go, ~'go:d] **1.** *adj.* simple, silly; **2.** *su.* simpleton, booby, ass; **nigauderie** F [~go'dri] *f* stupidity; simplicity.

nimbe [nɛ̃:b] *m* nimbus, halo; **nimbé, e** [nɛ̃'be] haloed.

nipper F [ni'pe] (1a) *v/t.* rig (*s.o.*) out; **nippes** F [nip] *f/pl.* old clothes; togs.

nippon, e [ni'pɔ̃, ~'pɔn] *adj.*, *a. su.* ♀ Japanese, Nipponese.

nique F [nik] *f: faire la ~ à* cook a snook at (*s.o.*); treat (*s.th.*) with contempt.

nitouche [ni'tuʃ] *f: sainte ~* (little) hypocrite; F goody-goody.

nitrate ♞ [ni'trat] *m* nitrate; ~ *de ... ... nitrate; **nitre** ♞ [nitr] *m* nitre, saltpetre; **nitré, e** [ni'tre] nitrated; **nitro-...**; **nitreux, -euse** [~'trø, ~'trø:z] nitrous; **nitrière** [nitri'ɛ:r] *f* saltpetre-bed; nitreworks *usu. sg.*; **nitrification** [~fika'sjɔ̃] *f* nitrification; **nitrifier** [~'fje] (1o) *v/t. a.* se ~ nitrify; **nitrique** [ni'trik] nitric (*acid*).

nitro... [nitrɔ] nitro(-)...; ~**gène** ♞ [~'ʒɛn] *m* nitrogen.

nitruration ⌒ₘ [nitryra'sjɔ̃] *f* nitriding.   [nival.\

nivéal, e, *m/pl.* **-aux** ♀ [nive'al,ₓ'o]\
niveau [ni'vo] *m* level (*a.* ⊕); *fig.*
standard; ⊕ ga(u)ge; ~ *d'eau* water-level; ~ *de maçon* plumb-level;
mot. ~ *d'essence* petrol gauge, *Am.*
gasoline level gage; ~ *de vie* standard of living; *pol.* ~ *le plus élevé*
highest level; *fig. au* ~ *de* on a par
with; *de* ~ level (with, *avec*); 🚂
passage m à ~ level crossing, *Am.*
grade crossing; **niveler** [niv'le] (1c)
v/t. level, even up; ⊕ true up; survey (*the ground*); **niveleur** [ₓ'lœːr]
m leveller (*a. fig.*); **nivellement**
[nivel'mɑ̃] *m land:* surveying;
ground, a. fig.: levelling.

nobiliaire [nɔbi'ljɛːr] **1.** *adj.* nobiliary; **2.** *su./m* peerage-list; **noble**
[nɔbl] **1.** *adj.* noble; lofty (*style*);
2. *su./m* nobleman; *su./f* noble-woman; **noblesse** [nɔ'blɛs] *f* nobility (*a. fig.*).

noce [nɔs] *f* wedding; wedding-party; ~*s pl. d'argent* (*d'or*) silver
(golden) wedding *sg.*; F *faire la* ~ go
on the spree *or sl.* the binge; *voyage m
de* ~*s* honeymoon (trip); **noceur** *m,*
-euse *f* F [nɔ'sœːr, ~'søːz] reveller;
fast liver.

nocif, -ve [nɔ'sif, ~'siːv] harmful,
noxious; **nocivité** [ₓsivi'te] *f* harmfulness.

noctambule [nɔktɑ̃'byl] *su.* late-nighter, night bird; † sleepwalker;
nocturne [ₓ'tyrn] **1.** *adj.* nocturnal;
by night; **2.** *su./m orn.* nocturnal
(bird of prey); ♩ nocturne.

Noël [nɔ'ɛl] *m* (*oft. la* [fête *de*]~)
Christmas; yule-tide; Christmas
present; ♩♫ (Christmas) carol; *arbre
m de* ~ Christmas tree; *le Père* ~, *le Bon
homme* ~ Father Christmas, Santa
Claus; *joyeux* ~! merry Christmas!

nœud [nø] *m* knot (*a.* ⚓); *band:* bow;
fig. tie, bond; *fig. matter, play, question, etc.:* crux; ♀, ♣, ♂, *astr.*, *phys.*
node; ⚡ junction; ~ *de tisserand*
weaver's knot; ~ *papillon* bow tie.

noir, noire [nwaːr] **1.** *adj.* black;
dark; *fig.* gloomy (*thoughts*); *fig.* illegal, illicit; *sl.* dead drunk; *avoir des
idées noires* have the blues; *cuis. beurre m* ~ browned butter sauce; *blé m* ~
buckwheat; **2.** *su./m* black (man);
negro; *colour:* black; dark(ness); ~ *de
fumée* lampblack; *fig.* ~ *sur blanc* in

black and white; *au* ~ illegally, illicitly; *broyer du* ~ be in the dumps;
mettre dans le ~ hit the mark; *prendre
le* ~ go into mourning; *travailler au* ~
moonlight; *voir tout en* ~ look on the
black side of things; *su./f* black
woman; negress; ♩ crotchet; **noirâtre** [nwa'rɑːtr] blackish, darkish;
noiraud, e [ₓ'ro, ~'roːd] **1.** *adj.*
swarthy; **2.** *su.* swarthy person;
noirceur [nwar'sœːr] *f* blackness;
darkness; *fig.* gloominess; *fig.* foulness; *crime:* heinousness; **noircir**
[ₓ'siːr] (2a) *v/t.* blacken (*a. fig.*);
make gloomy (*a picture, one's
thoughts*); se ~ darken; *v/i.* turn black
or dark; **noircissure** [ₓsi'syːr] *f*
smudge.

noise [nwaːz] *f:* *chercher* ~ *à* (try to)
pick a quarrel with.

noisetier ♀ [nwaz'tje] *m* hazel(-tree,
-bush); **noisette** [nwa'zɛt] **1.** *su./f*
♀ hazel-nut; **2.** *adj./inv.* (*a. couleur
f* ~) (nut-)brown; hazel (*eyes*);
noix [nwɑ] *f* ♀ walnut; ♀, *a.* 🌰
nut; ⊕ half-round groove; *sl.* head;
sl. fellow; ~ *de terre* peanut;
cuis. ~ *de veau* round shoulder of
veal.

nom [nɔ̃] *m* name; *gramm.* noun;
fig. reputation; ~ *de baptême* Christian *or* baptismal name, *Am.* given
name; ~ *de famille* family name;
surname; ~ *de guerre* assumed
name; ~ *de jeune fille* maiden name; ~
de plume pen-name; ♦ ~ *déposé*
registered trade name; ♦ ~ *social*
name of (the) firm *or* company; *de* ~
by name; *décliner ses* ~ *et prénoms*
give one's full name; *du* ~ *de* called,
by the name of; *petit* ~ Christian
name, *Am.* given name.

nomade [nɔ'mad] **1.** *adj.* wandering;
nomadic; **2.** *su.* nomad.

nombrable [nɔ̃'brabl] countable;
nombre [nɔ̃:br] *m* number (*a.
gramm.*); ~ *cardinal* cardinal number; ~ *entier* integer; whole number; ~ *impair* (*pair, premier*) odd
(even, prime) number; *bon* ~ *de* a
good many ...; *du* ~ *de* one of; *bibl.
les* ~*s pl.* Numbers; *sans* ~ countless; **nombrer** [nɔ̃'bre] (1a) *v/t.*
count, number; **nombreux, -euse**
[ₓ'brø, ~'brøːz] numerous; manifold; rhythmic, harmonious.

nombril [nɔ̃'bri] *m anat.* navel; ♀
fruit: eye.

nomenclature [nɔmãkla'tyːr] *f* nomenclature; list.

nominal, e, *m/pl.* -**aux** [nɔmi'nal, ∼'no] nominal; of names; *appel m* ∼ roll-call; ✝ *valeur f* ∼*e* face-value; **nominatif, -ve** [∼na'tif, ∼'tiːv] **1.** *adj.* nominal; of names; ✝ registered (*securities*); **2.** *su./m gramm.* nominative; **nomination** [∼na'sjɔ̃] *f* nomination; appointment.

nommé, e [nɔ'me] **1.** *adj.* appointed (*day*); *à point* ∼ in the nick of time; **2.** *su.: le* ∼ *X, la* ∼*e X* the person named X; *su./m: un* ∼ *Jean* one John; **nommément** [∼me'mã] *adv.* by name; especially; **nommer** [∼'me] (1a) *v/t.* name; mention; appoint (*to a post*); se ∼ be called; give one's name.

non [nɔ̃] *adv.* no; not; ∼ *pas!* not at all!; ∼ (*pas*) *que* (*sbj.*) not that (*ind.*); *dire que* ∼ say no; *ne ... pas* ∼ *plus* not ... either.

non... [nɔ̃; *before vowel* nɔn] non-...; ∼**activité** [nɔnaktivi'te] *f* non-activity; *mettre en* ∼ suspend.

nonagénaire [nɔnaʒe'nɛːr] *adj., a. su.* nonagenarian.

non-agression *pol.* [nɔnagrɛ'sjɔ̃] *f* non-aggression; *pacte m de* ∼ non-aggression pact. [papal nuncio.)

nonce [nɔ̃ːs] *m* nuncio; ∼ *apostolique*)

nonchalance [nɔ̃ʃa'lɑ̃ːs] *f* nonchalance; languidness; **nonchalant, e** [∼'lɑ̃, ∼'lɑ̃ːt] nonchalant, unconcerned, languid.

non...: ∼**combattant** ⚔ [nɔ̃kɔ̃ba-'tɑ̃] *m* non-combattant; ∼**conducteur, -trice** [∼kɔ̃dyk'tœːr, ∼'tris] **1.** *adj.* non-conducting; **2.** *su./m* non-conductor; ∼**conformisme** *eccl.* [∼kɔ̃fɔr'mism] *m* nonconformity, dissent; ∼**conformiste** [∼kɔ̃-fɔr'mist] *m* non-conformist (*a. fig.*); ∼**engagé, e** *pol.* [∼ɑ̃ga'ʒe] **1.** non-aligned; **2.** *su./m* non-aligned country; ∼**ingérence** [nɔnɛ̃ʒe'rɑ̃ːs] *f*, ∼**intervention** [nɔnɛ̃tɛrvɑ̃'sjɔ̃] *f* non-intervention, non-interference; ∼**lieu** ⚖ [nɔ̃'ljø] *m* no true bill; *rendre une ordonnance de* ∼ dismiss the charge.

nonne ✝, *co.* [nɔn] *f* nun.

nonobstant [nɔnɔp'stɑ̃] **1.** *prp.* notwithstanding; **2.** *adv.* ✝ for all that.

nonpareil, -eille [nɔ̃pa'rɛːj] **1.** *adj.* matchless, unparalleled; **2.** *su./f apple, a. typ.:* nonpareil.

non...: ∼**retour** [nɔ̃rə'tuːr] *m:* point *m de* ∼ point of no return; ∼**réussite** [∼rey'sit] *f* failure; *plan:* miscarriage; ∼**sens** [∼'sɑ̃ːs] *m* meaningless or expression; ∼**valeur** [∼va'lœːr] *f* worthless object; unproductive land; F passenger (= *incompetent employee etc.*); *admin.* possible deficit; ∼**violence** [∼vjɔ'lɑ̃s] *f* non-violence.

nord [nɔːr] **1.** *su./m* north; ⚓ north wind; *du* ∼ north(ern); northerly (*wind*); *le* ⚲ the north (*of a country*); *fig. perdre le* ∼ lose one's bearings; *vers le* ∼ northward(s), to the north; **2.** *adj./inv.* northern (*latitudes etc.*); northerly (*wind*); ∼**est** [nɔ'rɛst] **1.** *su./m* north-east; **2.** *adj./inv.* north-east; north-eastern (*region*); north-easterly (*wind*); ∼**ouest** [nɔ'rwɛst] **1.** *su./m* north-west; **2.** *adj./inv.* north-west; north-western (*region*); north-westerly (*wind*).

noria [nɔ'rja] *f* ⊕ chain-pump; bucket-conveyor; *fig.* line, chain, string.

normal, e, *m/pl.* -**aux** [nɔr'mal, ∼'mo] **1.** *adj.* normal; usual; standard (*measures etc.*); natural; *École f* ∼*e* (teachers') training college; **2.** *su./f* norm; normal (*a.* ⚗); *au-dessous de la* ∼ above average; *revenir à la* ∼ get back to normal; **normalien** *m*, -**enne** *f* [nɔrma'ljɛ̃, ∼'ljɛn] student at an *École normale*; **normalisation** [∼liza'sjɔ̃] *f* standardization; **normaliser** [∼li'ze] (1a) *v/t.* standardize; normalize.

normand, e [nɔr'mɑ̃, ∼'mɑ̃ːd] **1.** *adj.* Norman; F *réponse f* ∼*e* non-committal answer; **2.** *su.* ⚲ Norman.

norme [nɔrm] *f* norm, standard.

norvégien, -enne [nɔrve'ʒjɛ̃, ∼'ʒjɛn] *adj., a. su.* ⚲ Norwegian.

nos [no] *pl. of* notre.

nostalgie [nɔstal'ʒi] *f* 𝓼 nostalgia; *fig.* homesickness; *fig.* yearning; **nostalgique** [∼'ʒik] nostalgic; *fig.* homesick.

notabilité [nɔtabili'te] *f* notability (*a. person*); prominent person; **notable** [nɔ'tabl] **1.** *adj.* notable; considerable; distinguished; **2.** *su./ m* person of distinction *or* note; *hist.* Notable.

notaire [nɔ'tɛːr] *m* notary (public).

notamment [nɔta'mã] *adv.* particularly, especially.

notarial, e, *m/pl.* **-aux** [nɔta'rjal, ~'rjo] notarial; **notarié, e** [~'rje] *adj.*: acte *m* ~ deed executed and authenticated by a notary.

notation ♪, ♪̸ [nɔta'sjɔ̃] *f* notation.

note [nɔt] *f* note (*a.* ♪, *pol.*, *fig.*), memo(randum); minute; annotation; *school:* mark; *journ.* notice; ♣ account, bill; *prendre* ~ *de* note, make a note of; *prendre des* ~s jot down notes; **noter** [nɔ'te] (1a) *v/t.* note, make a note of; jot down; take notice of; ♪ write down.

notice [nɔ'tis] *f* note, notice.

notification [nɔtifika'sjɔ̃] *f* notification, notice; **notifier** [~'fje] (1o) *v/t.* intimate (s.th. to s.o., *qch. à q.*); notify (s.o. of s.th., *qch. à q.*).

notion [nɔ'sjɔ̃] *f* notion, idea; ~s *pl.* smattering *sg.*; **notoire** [~'twa:r] well-known; manifest; *pej.* notorious; **notoriété** [~tɔrje'te] *f* notoriety; *person:* repute.

notre, *pl.* **nos** [nɔtr, no] *adj./poss.* our.

nôtre [no:tr] **1.** *pron./poss.:* le (la) ~, les ~s *pl.* ours; **2.** *su./m* ours, our own; les ~s *pl.* our (own) people.

nouage [nwa:ʒ] *m* tying; *bone:* knitting.

nouba *sl.* [nu'ba] *f: faire la* ~ go on a binge, live it up.

noué, e [nwe] knotty (*joint*); *fig.* stunted (*mind etc.*); **nouer** [nwe] (1p) *v/t.* tie (up); knot; *fig.* enter into (*conversation, relations*); se ~ become knotted; *fig.* be formed; build up; *v/i.* set (*fruit*); **nouet** *cuis.* [nwɛ] *m* bag of herbs; **noueux, -euse** [nwø, nwø:z] knotty; ✻ arthritic (*rheumatism*); gnarled (*hands, stem*).

nougat *cuis.* [nu'ga] *m* nougat.

nouille [nu:j] *f cuis.* noodle; F gutless individual, drip, idiot.

nourrain [nu'rɛ̃] *m* fry, young fish; **nourrice** [~'ris] *f* (wet-)nurse; ⊕, ✻ service-tank; *mot.* feed-tank; *mettre un enfant en* ~ put a child out to nurse; **nourricerie** [~ris'ri] *f* stock-farm; silkworm nursery; baby-farm; **nourricier, -ère** [~ri'sje, ~'sjɛ:r] nutritious, nutritive; foster-(*father, mother*); **nourrir** [~'ri:r] (2a) *v/t.* feed, nourish; suckle, nurse (*a baby*); *fig.* harbo(u)r (*hope, thoughts*); foster (*hatred*); cherish (*hope, a grudge*); strengthen; maintain (*a fire*); se ~ de live on;

v/i. be nourishing; **nourrissage** [nuri'sa:ʒ] *m cattle:* rearing; **nourrissant, e** [~'sɑ̃, ~'sɑ̃:t] nourishing; nutritious; rich (*food*); **nourrisseur** [~'sœ:r] *m* dairyman; ⊕ feed-roll; **nourrisson** [~'sɔ̃] *m* suckling, nursling; foster-child; **nourriture** [~'ty:r] *f* feeding; food; board, keep; *la* ~ *et le logement* board and lodging.

nous [nu] **1.** *pron./pers. subject:* we; *object:* us; (to) us; *à* ~ to us; ours; *ce sont* ~, F *c'est* ~ it is we, F it's us; **2.** *pron./rfl.* ourselves; **3.** *pron./ recip.* each other; one another; ~**-mêmes** [~'mɛ:m] *pron./rfl.* ourselves.

nouveau (*adj. before vowel or h mute* **-el**) *m*, **-elle**, *m/pl.* **-aux** [nu'vo, ~'vɛl, ~'vo] **1.** *adj.* new; recent, fresh; new-style; another, further; novel; ~*eaux riches m/pl.* nouveaux riches, newly rich; *le plus* ~ latest; *qch. (rien) de* ~ s.th. (nothing) new; *quoi de* ~? what's the news?; **2.** *nouveau adv.:* *à* ~ anew, afresh; *de* ~ again; **nouveau-né, e** [nuvo'ne] **1.** *adj.* new-born; **2.** *su./m* new-born child; **nouveauté** [~'te] *f* newness, novelty; latest model; innovation; ✝ ~s *pl.* fancy goods; linen-drapery *sg.*; **nouvel** [nu'vɛl] **1.** *adj. see* nouveau 1; ~ *an m* New Year; **nouvelle** [nu-'vɛl] **1.** *adj. see* nouveau 1; **2.** *su./f* news *sg.*, tidings *pl.*; short story; *avoir des* ~s *de q.* hear from *or* of s.o.; **nouvelliste** [~vɛ'list] *su.* short-story writer; *journ.* F par writer.

novateur, -trice [nɔva'tœ:r, ~'tris] **1.** *adj.* innovating; **2.** *su.* innovator.

novembre [nɔ'vã:br] *m* November.

novice [nɔ'vis] **1.** *adj.* inexperienced (in *à, dans*), new (to *à, dans*); **2.** *su.* novice (*a. eccl., a. fig.*); *fig.* tyro, beginner; *profession:* probationer; **noviciat** [~vi'sja] *m* noviciate; F apprenticeship.

noyade [nwa'jad] *f* drowning.

noyau [nwa'jo] *m fruit:* stone, kernel; *phys., biol., fig.* nucleus (*a. atom etc.*); ⊕ *wheel:* hub; *metall., a.* ⚡ core; △ newel; *fig.* group; *pol.* cell; *fig.* ~ *dur* hard core; ✔ *fruit m à* ~ stone-fruit; **noyautage** [~jo'ta:ʒ] *m pol.* infiltration (into, de); *metall.* coring.

noyer[1] [nwa'je] (1h) *v/t.* drown

(*a.* F *fig.*); flood (*a. mot.*), inundate, immerse); ⊕ countersink (*a screw*); ⊕ bed (*s.th.*) in cement; se ~ *suicide*: drown o.s.; *accident*: be drowned; *fig.* be steeped (in, *dans*); ⊕ *vis f* noyée countersunk screw.

noyer² ⚘ [~] *m* walnut(-tree).

nu, nue [ny] **1.** *adj.* naked, nude, bare; *fig.* unadorned; ~-pieds, pieds ~s barefoot(ed); **2.** *su./m* nude; nudity; △ bare part; **3.** *adv.*: à nu bare; mettre à nu expose, lay bare; denude; *monter à nu* ride (*a horse*) bareback.

nuage [nɥɑːʒ] *m* cloud; sans ~s cloudless (*sky*), *fig.* perfect (*bliss*); **nuageux, -euse** [nɥɑˈʒø, ~ˈʒøːz] cloudy, overcast; *fig.* hazy (*idea*).

nuance [nɥɑ̃ːs] *f* shade (*a. fig.*), hue; *fig.* tinge; *fig.* nuance, shade of meaning; **nuancer** [nɥɑ̃ˈse] (1k) *v/t.* shade (with, *de*); vary (*the tone*); express slight differences in.

nubile [nyˈbil] nubile, marriageable.

nucléaire *phys.* [nykleˈɛːr] nuclear (*a. armament*); **nucléon** *phys.* [~ˈ5] *m* nucleon.

nudisme [nyˈdism] *m* nudism; **nudiste** [~ˈdist] *su.* nudist; **nudité** [~diˈte] *f* nudity, nakedness; *paint.* nude; △ bareness.

nue [ny] *f* high cloud; ~s *pl.* skies (*a. fig.*); porter aux ~s praise to the skies; *fig.* tomber des ~s be thunderstruck; **nuée** [nɥe] *f* storm-cloud; *fig.* cloud; swarm, host.

nuire [nɥiːr] (4u *a.* h) *v/i.*: ~ à harm, hurt; be injurious to; **nuisance** [nɥiˈzɑːs] *f environment etc.*: nuisance; **nuisant, e** [nɥiˈzɑ̃, ~ˈzɑ̃ːt] harmful, polluting; **nuisibilité** [nɥizibiliˈte] *f* harmfulness; **nuisible** [~ˈzibl] harmful, injurious.

nuit [nɥi] *f* night; de ~ by night; passer la ~ stay overnight (with, *chez*); **nuitée** [nɥiˈte] *f* night's work; *hotel etc.*: overnight stay; **nuiteux**

m, **-euse** *f* [nɥiˈtø, ~ˈtøːz] person working by night.

nul, nulle [nyl] **1.** *adj.* no, not one; void, null; *sp.* drawn (*game*); nonexistent; ⚕ invalid (*marriage*); **2.** *pron./indef.* no(t) one, nobody; **nullement** [nylˈmɑ̃] *adv.* not at all; **nullité** [nyliˈte] *f* ⚕ nullity, invalidity; *fig.* nothingness; non-existence; *person*: nonentity; *fig.* incapacity.

numéraire [nymeˈrɛːr] **1.** *adj.* legal (*tender*); numerary (*value*); **2.** *su./m* specie; cash; currency; **numéral, e**, *m/pl.* **-aux** [~ˈral, ~ˈro] numeral; **numérateur** ⚘ [~raˈtœːr] *m* numerator; **numération** ⚘ [~raˈsjɔ̃] *f* numeration; number system; **numérique** [~ˈrik] numerical; digital; **numéro** [~ˈro] *m* number; *periodical*: issue, copy; ⚘ size; F person, fellow; (~ de téléphone) telephone number; F ~ deux second-best; ~ de vestiaire cloak-room ticket; F ~ un first-class; **numérotage** [~rɔˈtaːʒ] *m* numbering; *book*: paging; **numéroter** [~rɔˈte] (1a) *v/t.* number; paginate (*a book*); **numéroteur** [~rɔˈtœːr] *m* numbering machine *or* stamp.

numismate [nymisˈmat] *m* numismatist; **numismatique** [~maˈtik] *f* numismatics *sg.*

nuptial, e, *m/pl.* **-aux** [nypˈsjal, ~ˈsjo] bridal; wedding...

nuque [nyk] *f* nape *or* F scruff of the neck.   [nanny.]

nurse [nœrs] *f* children's nurse, F/

nutritif, -ve [nytriˈtif, ~ˈtiːv] nourishing, nutritive; nutritional, food...; **nutrition** [~ˈsjɔ̃] *f* nutrition; **nutritionel, -le** [~sjɔˈnɛl] nutritional.

nylon *tex.* [niˈlɔ̃] *m* nylon.

nymphe [nɛ̃ːf] *f myth.* nymph (*a. fig.*); *zo.* pupa, chrysalis; **nymphéa** ⚘ [nɛ̃feˈa] *m* water-lily; nymphea; **nymphette** [nɛ̃ˈfɛt] *f* nymph.

O

O, o [o] *m* O, o.
ô! [o] *int.* oh!
oasis [oaˈzis] *f* oasis (*a. fig.*).
obédience [ɔbeˈdjãːs] *f eccl.* dutiful submission, obedience; F submission; *de même* ∼ of the same (*religious etc.*) persuasion; *d'*∼ *communiste* of Communist allegiance.
obéir [ɔbeˈiːr] (2a) *v/i.:* ∼ *à* obey; comply with (*s.th.*); yield to; ⚔, *mot.* respond to; ⚓ answer; *se faire* ∼ compel obedience (from, *par*); **obéissance** [ˌi'sãːs] *f* obedience; submission (*to authority*); *fig.* pliancy; **obéissant, e** [ˌi'sã, ˌi'sãːt] obedient; submissive; *fig.* pliant.   [lisk.\
obélisque *archeol.* [ɔbeˈlisk] *m* obe-)
obérer [ɔbeˈre] (1f) *v/t.* burden with debt; *s'*∼ run deep into debt.
obèse [ɔˈbɛːz] **1.** *adj.* obese, stout; **2.** *su.* obese *or* stout person; **obésité** [ɔbeziˈte] *f* obesity, corpulence.
obit *eccl.* [ɔˈbit] *m* obit; **obituaire** [ɔbiˈtɥɛːr] *m* obituary list.
objecter [ɔbʒɛkˈte] (1a) *v/t.* raise as an objection (to, *à*); ∼ *qch. à q.* allege *or* hold s.th. against s.o.; **objecteur** [ˌtœːr] *m:* ✕ ∼ *de conscience* conscientious objector; **objectif, -ve** [ˌ'tif, ˌ'tiːv] **1.** *adj.* objective; **2.** *su./ m opt.* objective; *phot.* lens; ✕, ⚓ target; *fig.* aim, object; **objection** [ˌ'sjõ] *f* objection; **objectiver** *phls.* [ˌtiˈve] (1a) *v/t.* objectify; **objectivité** [ˌtiviˈte] *f* objectivity.
objet [ɔbˈʒɛ] *m* object (*a. gramm., phls., a. fig.*); thing; subject(-matter); *fig.* purpose, aim; *gramm.* complement; ✝ article; ∼*s pl. trouvés* lost property *sg.*; *remplir son* ∼ reach one's goal.
obligataire ✝ [ɔbligaˈtɛːr] *m* bond-holder, debenture-holder; **obligation** [ˌ'sjõ] *f* obligation, duty; ✝ bond, debenture; favo(u)r; gratefulness; **obligatoire** [ˌ'twaːr] obligatory; compulsory; binding (*agreement, decision*); *enseignement m* ∼ compulsory education; ✕ *service m*

militaire ∼ compulsory military service.
obligé, e [ɔbliˈʒe] **1.** *adj.* obliged, compelled (to *inf.*, *de inf.*); necessary, indispensable; inevitable; *fig.* grateful; **2.** *su.* person under an obligation; ✝ obligor; **obligeamment** [ˌʒaˈmã] *adv. of obligeant;* **obligeance** [ˌ'ʒãːs] *f* kindness; *avoir l'*∼ *de* (*inf.*) be so kind as to (*inf.*); **obligeant, e** [ˌ'ʒã, ˌ'ʒãːt] obliging; kind; **obliger** [ˌ'ʒe] (1l) *v/t.* oblige, bind (to, *à*); compel (to, *de*); do (*s.o.*) a favo(u)r; *s'*∼ *à* bind o.s. to.
oblique [ɔˈblik] **1.** *adj.* oblique; slanting; *fig. regard m* ∼ sidelong glance; **2.** *su./f* oblique line; **obliquer** [ɔbliˈke] (1m) *v/i.* turn off (to[wards] *à, vers*); **obliquité** [ˌkiˈte] *f* obliqueness.
oblitération [ɔbliteraˈsjõ] *f* obliteration; *stamp:* cancellation; ⚙ obstruction; **oblitérer** [ˌ're] (1f) *v/t.* obliterate; cancel (*a stamp*); ⚙ obstruct (*a vein*).
oblong, -gue [ɔˈblõ, ˌ'blõːg] oblong.
obnubiler [ɔbnybiˈle] (1a) *v/t.* cloud, obnubilate (*the mind*); obsess (*idea etc.*).
obole [ɔˈbɔl] *f* ✝ obol(us); F farthing; (*widow's*) mite; *apporter son* ∼ *à* contribute one's mite to.
obombrer [ɔbõˈbre] (1a) *v/t.* cloud over.
obscène [ɔpˈsɛn] obscene; smutty; **obscénité** [ˌseniˈte] *f* obscenity; smuttiness.
obscur, e [ɔpsˈkyːr] dark; gloomy (*weather*); obscure (*a. fig.*); abstruse (*argument etc.*); dim (*horizon, light*); humble (*person*); **obscurantisme** [ˌkyrãˈtism] *m* obscurantism; **obscuration** *astr.* [ˌkyraˈsjõ] *f* occultation; **obscurcir** [ˌkyrˈsiːr] (2a) *v/t.* obscure; darken; dim (*the view*); **obscurcissement** [ˌkyrsisˈmã] *m* darkening; dimming; obscuring; **obscurément** [ˌkyreˈmã] *adv. of obscur;* **obscurité** [ˌkyriˈte]

f obscurity (*a. fig.*); darkness; *fig.* vagueness.   [importune, pester.]
obséder [ɔpse'de] (1f) *v/t.* obsess;
obsèques [ɔp'sɛk] *f/pl.* funeral *sg.*, obsequies; **obséquieux, -euse** [ɔpse'kjø, ~'kjø:z] obsequious, fawning; **obséquiosité** [~kjozi'te] *f* obsequiousness.
observable [ɔpsɛr'vabl] observable; **observance** [~'vɑ̃:s] *f* observance (*a. eccl.*); **observateur, -trice** [~va'tœ:r, ~'tris] 1. *adj.* observant; 2. *su.* observer; ✗, ✍ spotter; **observation** [~va'sjɔ̃] *f* observation; *eccl., law, rule:* observance; reprimand; **observatoire** [~va'twa:r] *m* *astr.* observatory; ✗ observation post; **observer** [~'ve] (1a) *v/t.* observe, keep (*feast, law, rule, sabbath*); watch; notice; *faire* ~ *qch. à q.* draw s.o.'s attention to s.th.; *s'*~ be careful *or* cautious.
obsessif, -ve [ɔpsɛ'sif, ~'si:v] obsessive; **obsession** [~'sjɔ̃] *f* obsession.
obstacle [ɔps'takl] *m* obstacle; *sp.* hurdle; *sp. course f d'*~*s* obstacle *or* hurdle race; *faire* ~ *à* stand in the way of; hinder; obstruct.
obstétrique ✍ [ɔpste'trik] 1. *adj.* obstetric(al); 2. *su./f* obstetrics *sg.*
obstination [ɔpstina'sjɔ̃] *f* obstinacy; perversity; pig-headedness; **obstiné, e** [~'ne] obstinate, stubborn; persistent; pig-headed; **obstiner** [~'ne] (1a) *v/t.*: *s'*~ show obstinacy; *s'*~ *à* (*inf.*) persist in (*ger.*).
obstructif, -ve [ɔpstryk'tif, ~'ti:v] *pol.* obstructive; ✍ obstruent; **obstruction** [~'sjɔ̃] *f* ✍, *pol.* obstruction; *pol.* filibustering; ✍ stoppage; **obstructionnisme** *pol.* [~sjɔ'nism] *m* obstructionism, filibustering; **obstruer** [ɔpstry'e] (1a) *v/t.* obstruct, block; ⊕ choke.
obtempérer [ɔptɑ̃pe're] (1f) *v/i.*: ~ *à* comply with, obey.
obtenir [ɔptə'ni:r] (2h) *v/t.* obtain, get; **obtention** [~tɑ̃'sjɔ̃] *f* obtaining.
obturateur, -trice [ɔptyra'tœ:r, ~'tris] 1. *adj.* obturating, closing; 2. *su./m* ⌂, ✗, *anat.* obturator; *phot.* shutter; ⊕ stop-valve; *mot.* throttle; **obturation** [~ra'sjɔ̃] *f* obturation; closing; sealing; *tooth:* filling; **obturer** [~'re] (1a) *v/t.* stop, seal, obturate; fill (*a tooth*).

obtus, e [ɔp'ty, ~'ty:z] ⚭, *a. fig.* obtuse; blunt; *fig.* dull; **obtusangle** ⚭ [~ty'zɑ̃:gl] obtuse-angled.
obus [ɔ'by] *m* ✗ shell; *mot.* valveplug; ~ *à balles* shrapnel; ~ *non éclaté* unexploded shell, dud; ~ *perforant* armo(u)r-piercing shell; **obusier** ✗ [ɔby'zje] *m* howitzer.
obvier [ɔb'vje] (1o) *v/i.*: ~ *à* prevent.
oc [ɔk] *adv.*: *langue f d'*~ Langue d'oc, Old Provençal.
occasion [ɔka'zjɔ̃] *f* opportunity, chance; occasion; *fig.* reason (for, de); ✝ bargain; *à l'*~ when the chance occurs; *à l'*~ *de* on the occasion of; *d'*~ second-hand; cheap; *par* ~ occasionally; **occasionner** [~zjɔ'ne] (1a) *v/t.* cause, give rise to.
occident [ɔksi'dɑ̃] *m* west, occident; **occidental, e**, *m/pl.* -aux [~dɑ̃'tal, ~'to] 1. *adj.* west(ern); occidental; 2. *su.* occidental; westerner.
occiput *anat.* [ɔksi'pyt] *m* occiput, back of the head.
occire ✝ [ɔk'si:r] (4y) *v/t.* kill, slay; **occis, e** [~'si, ~'si:z] *p.p. of occire.*
occlusion [ɔkly'zjɔ̃] *f* ✍ stoppage, obstruction; ⊕ *valve:* closure; ✍, ✍ occlusion.
occultation *astr.* [ɔkylta'sjɔ̃] *f* occultation; **occulte** [ɔ'kylt] occult; secret; hidden; **occultisme** [ɔkyl'tism] *m* occultism.
occupant, e [ɔky'pɑ̃, ~'pɑ̃:t] 1. *adj.* occupying, in occupation; *fig.* engrossing (*work*); 2. *su./m* occupant; ⚖, ✗ occupier; **occupation** [~pa'sjɔ̃] *f* occupation; profession; employment, work; ✗ *forces f/pl. d'*~ occupying forces; *sans* ~ unemployed; **occuper** [~'pe] (1a) *v/t.* occupy (*a.* ✗); employ (*workers etc.*); *s'*~ keep (o.s.) busy; *s'*~ *à* be engaged in; *s'*~ *de* see to (*s.th.*); take care of; deal with; be in charge of; look after; attend to (*customer*); be interested in.
occurrence [ɔky'rɑ̃:s] *f* occurrence, happening; emergency; juncture; *en l'*~ at this juncture; in *or* F under the circumstances; in the present case.
océan [ɔse'ɑ̃] *m* ocean, sea (*a. fig.*); F *l'*~ the Atlantic; **océanien, -enne** [~a'njɛ̃, ~'njɛn] 1. *adj.* Oceanian, Oceanic; 2. *su.* ♀ South Sea Islander; **océanique** [~a'nik] oceanic, ocean...
ocelot *zo.* [ɔs'lo] *m* ocelot.

ocre [ɔkr] *f* ochre; ocrer [ɔ'kre] (1a) *v/t.* ochre; ocreux, -euse [ɔ'krø, ~'krø:z] ochrous.

oct... [ɔkt], octa... [ɔkta], octo... [ɔkto] oct..., octa..., octo...; octaèdre [ɔkta'ɛ:dr] 1. *adj.* octahedral; 2. *su./m* ⚛ octahedron.

octane ⚛ [ɔk'tan] *m* octane.

octant ⚓, *astr.*, *surv.* [ɔk'tɑ̃] *m* octant.

octobre [ɔk'tɔbr] *m* October.

octogénaire [ɔktɔʒe'nɛ:r] *adj., a. su.* octogenarian.

octogone ⚛ [ɔktɔ'gɔn] *m* octagon.

octroi [ɔk'trwa] *m* concession, grant; city toll; toll-house; octroyer [~trwa'je] (1h) *v/t.* grant; bestow (on, *à*).

octuple [ɔk'typl] eightfold; octuple.

oculaire [ɔky'lɛ:r] 1. *adj.* ocular; eye(-*witness*); 2. *su./m* opt. eye-piece; oculiste ⚕ [~'list] *m* oculist.

odeur [ɔ'dœ:r] *f* odo(u)r (*a. fig.*), smell, scent.

odieux, -euse [ɔ'djø, ~'djø:z] 1. *adj.* odious; hateful; heinous (*crime*); 2. *su./m* odiousness; odium.

odontalgie ⚕ [ɔdɔ̃tal'ʒi] *f* tooth-ache, odontalgia.

odorant, e [ɔdɔ'rɑ̃, ~'rɑ̃:t] fragrant, sweet-smelling; scented; odorat [~'ra] *m* (sense of) smell; odoriférant, e [~rife'rɑ̃, ~'rɑ̃:t] fragrant, odoriferous.

œcuménique [ekyme'nik] (o)ecu-menical.

œil, *pl.* yeux [œ:j, jø] *m* eye; bread, cheese: hole; notice, attention; *à l'~ by the eye; sl.* on credit *or* tick; *à l'~ nu* with the naked eye; *à mes yeux* in my opinion; *avoir l'~ à qch.* see to s.th.; *avoir l'~ sur* keep an eye on; *coup m d'~* glance; *entre quatre yeux* in confidence; *être tout yeux* be all eyes; F *faire de l'~* ogle; tip s.o. the wink; *fermer les yeux sur* shut one's eyes to; *perdre des yeux* lose sight of; F *pour vos beaux yeux* for love, for your pretty face; *sauter aux yeux* be obvious; *sous mes yeux* before my face; ~-de-bœuf, *pl.* ~s-de-bœuf [œjdə'bœf] *m* bull's-eye window; ~-de-perdrix, *pl.* ~s-de-perdrix ⚕ [~pɛr'dri] *m* soft corn; œillade [œ'jad] *f* wink, glance.

œillère [œ'jɛ:r] *f* blinker (*a. fig.*), *Am.*

blind; ⚕ eye-bath; œillet [œ'jɛ] *m* eyelet(-hole); ⚘ pink, carnation; œilleton [œj'tɔ̃] *m* ⚘ eyebud; *phot.* eye; ✕ *rifle sight:* peephole; œillette ⚘ [œ'jɛt] *f* oil-poppy.

œsophage *anat.* [ezɔ'fa:ʒ] *m* (o)esophagus, gullet.

œstre *zo.* [ɛstr] *m* oestrus; bot-fly.

œstrogène [østrɔ'ʒɛn] *m* (o)estrogen.

œuf [œf, *pl.* ø] *m* egg; *biol.* ovum; *icht.* spawn, roe; ~*s pl.* brouillés scrambled eggs; ~*s pl.* sur le plat fried eggs; ~ *à la coque* (soft-)boiled egg; ~ *dur* hard-boiled egg; *blanc m d'~* white of egg; *fig. dans l'~* in the bud; *jaune m d'~* egg-yolk.

œuvre [œ:vr] *su./f* work; effect; product(ion); (*welfare*) society; occupation; ~*s pl.* works (*a. eccl.*); *bois m d'~* timber; *se mettre à l'~* start working; *su./m* ⚛ main work; *writer:* complete works *pl.*; ♪ opus; *grand ~* philosopher's stone; ⚛ *gros ~* foundations *pl.* and walls *pl.*; œuvrer [œ'vre] (1a) *v/i.* work.

offense [ɔ'fɑ̃:s] *f* insult; ⚖ contempt (of Court, *à la Cour*); *eccl.* sin; offenser [ɔfɑ̃'se] (1a) *v/t.* offend; injure; *s'~* take offence (at, *de*); offenseur [~'sœ:r] *m* offender; offensif, -ve [~'sif, ~'si:v] *adj., a.* ✕ *su./f* offensive.

offert, e [ɔ'fɛ:r, ~'fɛrt] *p.p. of offrir;* offertoire *eccl.* [ɔfɛr'twa:r] *m* offer-tory.

office [ɔ'fis] *su./m* office (*a. fig.*); agency, bureau; service (*a. eccl., a. fig. = turn*); *d'~* officially; automatically; *faire ~ de* act as; *su./f* butler's pantry; servants' hall; officiant *eccl.* [ɔfi'sjɑ̃] *m* officiating priest; officiant; officiel, -elle [~'sjɛl] official; formal (*call*).

officier [ɔfi'sje] 1. (1o) *v/i.* officiate; 2. *su./m* officer; officière [~'sjɛ:r] *f* woman officer (*in the Salvation Army*); officieux, -euse [~'sjø, ~'sjø:z] unofficial; *à titre ~* unofficially.

officinal, e, *m/pl.* -aux ⚕ [ɔfisi'nal, ~'no] medicinal; officine [~'sin] *f* ⚕ dispensary; chemist's shop, *Am.* drugstore; F *fig.* den.

offrande *usu. eccl.* [ɔ'frɑ̃:d] *f* offering; offrant [ɔ'frɑ̃] *m: au plus ~* to the highest bidder; offre [ɔfr] 1. *1st p. sg. pres. of offrir;* 2. *su./f* offer; ⚖ tender; *auction:* bid; *journ.* ~*s pl. d'emploi* situations vacant; *l'~ et la demande* supply and demand; **offrir** [ɔ'friːr] (2f) *v/t.* offer; give (to, *à*); expose (to, *à*); hold out (*one's hand etc.*); bid (*at an auction*); ~ *le mariage à* propose to; s'~ *a.* present itself (*occasion etc.*); s'~ *qch.* treat o.s. to s.th.; buy o.s. s.th.; s'~ *à faire qch.* offer *or* volunteer to do s.th.

offset *typ.* [ɔf'sɛt] *m/inv.* offset.

offusquer [ɔfys'ke] (1m) *v/t.* obscure (*the view, a. fig.*); offend; s'~ take offence (at, *de*).

ogival, e, *m/pl.* -**aux** △ [ɔʒi'val, ~'vo] ogival, pointed, Gothic; **ogive** [ɔ'ʒiːv] *f* △ ogee, ogive; Gothic *or* pointed arch; △ *vault:* rib; ✕ war-head.

ogre [ɔgr] *m* ogre; *manger comme un* ~ eat like a horse; **ogresse** [ɔ'grɛs] *f* ogress.

oh! [o] *int.* oh!

ohé! [o'e] *int.* hi!; hullo!; ⚓ ahoy!

oie *zo.* [wa] *f* goose.

oignon [ɔ'ɲɔ̃] *m* onion; ♀ bulb; ✼ bunion; F turnip (= *watch*); *en rang d'~s* in a row; **oignonade** *cuis.* [ɔɲɔ'nad] *f* onion-stew; **oignonière** [~'njɛːr] *f* onion-bed.

oindre [wɛ̃ːdr] (4m) *v/t.* oil; *eccl.* anoint; **oint, ointe** *bibl., a. eccl.* [wɛ̃, wɛ̃ːt] *adj., a. su./m* anointed.

oiseau [wa'zo] *m* bird; △ (*bricklayer's*) hod; F fellow, *Am.* guy; ~ *de passage* bird of passage; ~ *de proie* bird of prey; *à vol d'*~ as the crow flies; *vue f à vol d'*~ bird's-eye view; ~-**mouche,** *pl.* ~**x-mouches** *orn.* [~zo'muʃ] *m* humming-bird; **oiseler** [waz'le] (1c) *v/i.* go birdcatching; **oiselet** [~'lɛ] *m* small bird; **oiseleur** [~'lœːr] *m* fowler, birdcatcher; **oiselier** [wazə'lje] *m* birdfancier; bird-seller; **oisellerie** [~zɛl'ri] *f* bird-catching; birdbreeding; bird-shop.

oiseux, -euse [wa'zø, ~'zøːz] idle (*a. fig.*); *fig.* useless; **oisif, -ve** [~'zif, ~'ziːv] idle (*a.* ✝); unemployed; unoccupied; **oisiveté** [~ziv'te] *f* idleness; sloth.

oison [wa'zɔ̃] *m* gosling.

oléagineux, -euse [ɔleaʒi'nø, ~'nøːz] oily, oleaginous; ♀ oilyielding; **oléoduc** [ɔleɔ'dyk] *m* pipeline.

olfactif, -ve [ɔlfak'tif, ~'tiːv] olfactory; **olfaction** *physiol.* [~'sjɔ̃] *f* olfaction.

oligarchie [ɔligar'ʃi] *f* oligarchy.

olivacé, e [ɔliva'se] olive-green; **olivaie** [~'vɛ] *f* olive-grove; **olivaire** [~'vɛːr] olive-shaped; **olivaison** [~ve'zɔ̃] *f* olive-harvest; **olivâtre** [~'vɑːtr] olive (*colour*); sallow (*complexion*); **olive** [ɔ'liːv] **1.** *su./f* ♀ olive; **2.** *adj./inv.* olive-green; **oliverie** [ɔli'vri] *f* olive-oil factory; **olivier** ♀ [~'vje] *m* olive-tree; olive-wood; *bibl.* Mont *m* des ~s Mount of Olives.

olympien, -enne [ɔlɛ̃'pjɛ̃, ~'pjɛn] Olympian; *fig.* godlike; **olympique** [~'pik] Olympic; Jeux *m/pl.* ~s Olympic games.

ombelle ♀ [ɔ̃'bɛl] *f* umbel; *en* ~ = **ombellé, e** ♀ [ɔ̃bɛl'le] umbellate.

ombilical, e, *m/pl.* -**aux** [ɔ̃bili'kal, ~'ko] umbilical.

ombrage [ɔ̃'braːʒ] *m* shade; *fig.* offence, umbrage; *porter* ~ *à q.* offend s.o.; *prendre* ~ *de qch.* take umbrage *or* offence at s.th.; **ombrager** [ɔ̃bra'ʒe] (1l) *v/t.* (give) shade; **ombrageux, -euse** [~'ʒø, ~'ʒøːz] shy (*horse*); touchy, sensitive (*person*); **ombre** [ɔ̃:br] *f* shadow (*a. fig.*); shade (*a. myth., a. paint.*); *fig.* dark; *fig.* obscurity; *fig. a.* hint, suspicion; ~s *pl.* chinoises shadow-show *sg.*; *fig.* ~ *d'une chance* the ghost of a chance; *à l'*~ in the shade; *à l'*~ *de* in the shade of; *fig.* under cover of; *rester dans l'*~ stay in the background; *sl. à l'*~ in jail; **ombrelle** [ɔ̃'brɛl] *f* sunshade, parasol; **ombrer** [ɔ̃'bre] (1a) *v/t.* shade; darken (*the eyelids*); **ombreux, -euse** [ɔ̃'brø, ~'brøːz] shady.

omelette *cuis.* [ɔm'lɛt] *f* omelet(te).

omettre [ɔ'mɛtr] (4v) *v/t.* omit, leave out; ~ *de* (*inf.*) fail to (*inf.*); **omission** [ɔmi'sjɔ̃] *f* omission; oversight.

omni... [ɔmni] omni...; ~**bus** [~'bys] *m* (omni)bus; 🚋 *train m* ~ stopping *or* local train, *Am.* accommodation train; ~**potence** [~pɔ'tãːs] *f* omnipotence; ~**potent, e** [~pɔ'tã, ~'tãːt] omnipotent; ~**présent, e** [~pre'zã, ~'zãt] omnipresent. [der-blade.\]

omoplate *anat.* [ɔmɔ'plat] *f* shoul-\]

on [ɔ̃] *pron.* one, people *pl.*; you; somebody; ~ *dit que* it is said that.

once[1] [ɔ̃ːs] *f measure:* ounce; F *fig.* scrap, bit.

once[2] *zo.* [~] *f* snow-leopard, ounce.

oncial, e, *m/pl.* -**aux** [ɔ̃'sjal, ~'sjo] *adj., a. su./f* uncial.

oncle [ɔ̃:kl] *m* uncle.

onction [ɔ̃k'sjɔ̃] *eccl.*, *a. fig. pej.* unction; **onctueux, -euse** [ˏˑ'tɥø, ˏˑ'tɥøːz] creamy, rich; smooth; oily (*surface, a. pej. manner*); *fig.* unctuous (*speech*).

onde [ɔ̃:d] *f* wave (*a. hair, a. radio*); undulation; ˏˑs *pl. moyennes radio*: medium waves; *phys.* ˏˑ *sonore* sound wave; ˏˑ *ultra-courte* ultrashort wave; *grandes* ˏˑs *pl. radio*: long waves; *longueur f d'*ˏˑ wavelength; *mettre en* ˏˑs *radio*: put on the air; **ondé, e** [ɔ̃'de] **1.** *adj.* wavy (*hair, surface*); undulating; watered (*silk*); **2.** *su./f* heavy shower; **ondin** *m*, **e** *f* [ɔ̃'dɛ̃, ˏˑ'din] water-sprite.

on-dit [ɔ̃'di] *m/inv.* rumo(u)r, hearsay.

ondoiement [ɔ̃dwa'mɑ̃] *m* undulation; *eccl.* emergency *or* private baptism; **ondoyant, e** [ˏˑ'jɑ̃, ˏˑ'jɑ̃:t] undulating, wavy; swaying (*crowd*); *fig.* changeable; **ondoyer** [ˏˑ'je] (1h) *v/i.* undulate, wave; sway (*crowd*); fall in waves (*hair*); *v/t. eccl.* baptize privately (*a child*); **ondulation** [ɔ̃dyla'sjɔ̃] *f ground, water*: undulation; *hair*: wave; ⊕ *metal etc.*: corrugation; **ondulatoire** *phys.* [ˏˑla'twa:r] undulatory; wave-(*motion*); **ondulé, e** [ˏˑ'le] undulating (*ground*); corrugated (*metal etc.*); wavy, waved (*hair*); *tôle f* ˏˑe corrugated iron; **onduler** [ˏˑ'le] (1a) *v/i.* undulate, ripple; *v/t.* wave (*one's hair*); ⊕ corrugate; **onduleux, -euse** [ˏˑ'lø, ˏˑ'løːz] wavy, sinuous.

onéreux, -euse [ɔne'rø, ˏˑ'røːz] onerous; troublesome; *fig.* heavy; *à titre* ˏˑ subject to liabilities; ⚖ for valuable consideration.

ongle [ɔ̃:gl] *m* (finger)nail; *zo.* claw; *eagle, falcon, etc.*: talon; ˏˑ *des pieds* toenail; *jusqu'au bout des* ˏˑs to the fingertips; **onglée** [ɔ̃'gle] *f* numbness of the fingertips; **onglet** [ɔ̃'glɛ] *m* thimble; *book*: tab, thumb-index; ⚖ ungula; ⊕ mitre; **onglier** [ɔ̃gli'e] *m* manicure-set; ˏˑs *pl.* nail-scissors.

onguent [ɔ̃'gɑ̃] *m* ointment, salve.

ongulé, e *zo.* [ɔ̃gy'le] **1.** *adj.* ungulate, hoofed; **2.** *su./m*: ˏˑs *pl.* ungulates, ungulata.

ont [ɔ̃] *3rd. p. pl. pres. of avoir* 1.

onze [ɔ̃:z] **1.** *adj./num.*, *a. su./m/inv.* eleven; *date, title*: eleventh; **2.** *su./ m/inv. foot.* team; **onzième** [ɔ̃-'zjɛm] *adj./num.*, *a. su.* eleventh.

opacité [ɔpasi'te] *f* opacity; *fig.* denseness.

opale [ɔ'pal] **1.** *su./f* opal; **2.** *adj./inv.* opalescent; opal (*glass*); **opalin, e** [ɔpa'lɛ̃, ˏˑ'lin] *adj.*, *a. su./f* opaline.

opaque [ɔ'pak] opaque.

opéra [ɔpe'ra] *m* opera; *building*: opera-house.

opérable ⚕ [ɔpe'rabl] operable.

opéra-comique, *pl.* **opéras-comiques** ♪, *thea.* [ɔperakɔ'mik] *m* light opera.

opérateur, -trice [ɔpera'tœːr, ˏˑ'tris] *su.* operator; *su./m cin.* cameraman; ⚕ operating surgeon; **opération** [ˏˑ'sjɔ̃] *f* ⚕, ⚖, ✕, *a. fig.* operation; ✝ transaction; ⚕ *salle f d'*ˏˑ operating theatre; **opérationnel, -le** [ˏˑsjɔ'nɛl] operational; **opératoire** ⚕ [ˏˑ'twa:r] operating; postoperative; *médicine f* ˏˑ *subject*: surgery.

opercule [ɔpɛr'kyl] *m* cover; lid (*a.* ⚕); *icht.* gill-cover.

opérer [ɔpe're] (1f) *v/t.* operate, effect; ⚖, ✕ carry out; ⚕ operate on (*s.o.*) (for, *de*); *s'*ˏˑ take place; *v/i.* act; work.

opérette ♪ [ɔpe'rɛt] *f* operetta; musical comedy.

ophtalmie ⚕ [ɔftal'mi] *f* ophthalmia.

ophtalmo... ⚕ [ɔftalmɔ] ophthalmo...; ˏˑscope [ˏˑmɔs'kɔp] *m* ophthalmoscope.

opiacé, e [ɔpja'se] opiated.

opiner [ɔpi'ne] (1a) *v/i.* be of (the) opinion (that, *que*); decide, vote; ˏˑ *du bonnet* nod assent; **opiniâtre** [ˏˑ'njɑ:tr] obstinate, stubborn; **opiniâtrer** [ˏˑnjɑ'tre] (1a) *v/t.*: *s'*ˏˑ remain stubborn; persist (in, *dans*; in *ger.*, *à inf.*); **opiniâtreté** [ˏˑnjɑtrə'te] *f* obstinacy, stubbornness; **opinion** [ˏˑ'njɔ̃] *f* opinion; *à mon* ˏˑ in my opinion; *avoir bonne (mauvaise)* ˏˑ *de* think highly (poorly) of.

opiomane [ɔpjɔ'man] *su.* opiumeater; opium addict; **opium** [ɔ-'pjɔm] *m* opium.

opportun, e [ɔpɔr'tœ̃, ˏˑ'tyn] opportune, timely; advisable; **opportunément** [ɔpɔrtyne'mɑ̃] *adv. of opportun*; **opportunisme** [ˏˑ'nism] *m* opportunism; **opportuniste** *pol.*

[~'nist] **1.** adj. time-serving; **2.** su. opportunist; time-server; **opportunité** [~ni'te] f timeliness; opportuneness; advisability.

opposant, e [ɔpo'zɑ̃, ~'zɑ̃:t] **1.** adj. opposing, adverse; **2.** su. opponent; **opposé, e** [~'ze] **1.** adj. opposed; opposite (a. Å); fig. contrary; **2.** su./m opposite (of, de); à l'~ de contrary to, unlike; **opposer** [~'ze] (1a) v/t. oppose; contrast (with, à); s'~ à be opposed to; resist (s.th.); **opposition** [~zi'sjɔ̃] f opposition (a. parl., astr.); contrast; être en ~ avec clash with; **oppositionnel, -le** [~zisjɔ'nɛl] **1.** adj. oppositional; **2.** su. oppositionist.

oppresser [ɔprɛ'se] (1a) v/t. oppress (a. ✻); fig. depress; **oppresseur** [~'sœ:r] m oppressor; **oppressif, -ve** [~'sif, ~'si:v] oppressive; **oppression** ✻ [~'sjɔ̃] f oppression (a. fig.); difficulty in breathing.

opprimer [ɔpri'me] (1a) v/t. oppress, crush.

opprobre [ɔ'prɔbr] m opprobrium, shame, disgrace.

optatif, -ve [ɔpta'tif, ~'ti:v] adj., a. su./m gramm. optative.

opter [ɔp'te] (1a) v/i. opt; choose; ~ pour decide in favo(u)r of.

opticien [ɔpti'sjɛ̃] m optician.

optimal, e m/pl. **-aux** [ɔpti'mal, ~'mo] optimal; **optimiser** [ɔptimi'ze] (1a) v/t. optimize; **optimisme** [ɔpti'mism] m optimism; **optimiste** [~'mist] **1.** adj. optimistic; sanguine (disposition); **2.** su. optimist.

option [ɔp'sjɔ̃] f option (on, sur) (a. ✝); choice (between de, entre); **optionnel, -le** [ɔpsjɔ'nɛl] optional.

optique [ɔp'tik] **1.** adj. optic; optical; **2.** su./f optics sg.; optical device; illusion f d'~ optical illusion.

opulence [ɔpy'lɑ̃s] f affluence, wealth (a. fig.); **opulent, e** [~'lɑ̃, ~'lɑ̃:t] opulent, wealthy; abundant; F buxom (figure).

opuscule [ɔpys'kyl] m pamphlet; short treatise.

or¹ [ɔ:r] **1.** su./m gold; de l'~ en barres as good as ready money; d'~ gold(en); rouler sur l'~ be rolling in money.

or² [~] cj. now, well (now).

oracle [ɔ'ra:kl] m oracle.

orage [ɔ'ra:ʒ] m storm (a. fig.);

orageux, -euse [ɔra'ʒø, ~'ʒø:z] stormy (a. fig. debate); thundery (weather); threatening (sky etc.).

oraison [ɔrɛ'zɔ̃] f prayer; oration; ~ dominicale Lord's Prayer; ~ funèbre funeral oration.

oral, e, m/pl. **-aux** [ɔ'ral, ~'ro] **1.** adj. oral; **2.** su./m oral examination.

orange [ɔ'rɑ̃:ʒ] **1.** su./f ♀ orange; su./m colour: orange; **2.** adj./inv. orange (colour); **orangé, e** [ɔrɑ̃'ʒe] adj., a. su./m orange; **orangeade** [~'ʒad] f orangeade, orange squash; **orangeat** [~'ʒa] m candied orangepeel; **oranger** [~'ʒe] m ♀ orangetree; orange-seller; **orangerie** [ɔrɑ̃ʒ'ri] f orangery; orange-grove.

orang-outan(g) zo. [ɔrɑ̃u'tɑ̃] m orang-(o)utang.

orateur [ɔra'tœ:r] m orator, speaker; spokesman; bandmaster; **oratoire** [~'twa:r] **1.** adj. oratorical; **2.** su./m eccl. oratory; (private) chapel; **oratorio** ♪ [~tɔ'rjo] m oratorio.

orbe¹ ▲ [ɔrb] adj.: mur m ~ blind wall.

orbe² [ɔrb] **1.** su./m orb; globe, sphere; **orbite** [ɔr'bit] f orbit; anat. eye: socket; mettre (or placer) en (or sur) ~ put into orbit; **orbiter** [ɔrbi'te] (1a) v/i. orbit.

orchestre ♪ [ɔr'kɛstr] m orchestra; ~ à cordes string orchestra; chef m d'~ conductor; bandmaster; **orchestrer** [~kɛs'tre] (1a) v/t. ♪ orchestrate; score; fig. organize; fig. mastermind.

orchidée ♀ [ɔrki'de] f orchid.

ordalie † [ɔrda'li] f ordeal.

ordinaire [ɔrdi'nɛ:r] **1.** adj. ordinary, usual, customary; Å vulgar (fractions); average; peu ~ uncommon, unusual; mot. essence f ~ regular petrol (Am. gas); ⚖ tribunal m ~ civil court; vin m ~ table wine; **2.** su./m daily fare; ✕ mess; eccl. Ordinary; à l'~, d'~ as a rule, usually; sortir de l'~ be out of the ordinary.

ordinateur [ɔrdina'tœ:r] m computer.

ordination eccl. [ɔrdina'sjɔ̃] f ordination.

ordonnance [ɔrdɔ'nɑ̃:s] f order (a. ⚖); arrangement; ✻ prescription; pol., admin. statute; ✕ † orderly; ✝ ~ (de paiement) order to pay; **ordonnateur, -trice** [~na'tœ:r, ~'tris] **1.** su. director; organizer; **2.** adj.

managing; **ordonnée** ♣ [ˌˈne] *f*
ordinate; **ordonner** [ˌˈne] (1a) *v/t.*
order, command; arrange; direct;
✻ prescribe; tidy; *eccl., a. admin.*
ordain; *v/i.* dispose (of, de).

ordre [ɔrdr] *m* order; sequence;
orderliness; *(social)* estate; class,
sort; command; *eccl.* ˌs *pl.* Holy
Orders; ✞ ˌ *d'achat* purchase permit; ˌ *du jour* agenda; *admin.* ˌ
public law and order; *fig. de l'ˌ de*
in the region of *(2000)*; *fig. de premier* ˌ first-class, outstanding;
jusqu'à nouvel ˌ until further notice; ✻ *mot m d'ˌ* password; *numéro m d'ˌ* serial number; ✻ *porté
(or cité) à l'ˌ du jour* mentioned in
dispatches.

ordure [ɔrˈdyːr] *f* dirt, filth; ˌs *pl.*
refuse *sg.*, rubbish, *Am.* garbage;
ordurier, -ère [ˌdyˈrje, ˌˈrjɛr]
filthy; scurrilous; obscene *(book)*;
lewd.

oreillard, e *zo.* [ɔrɛˈjaːr, ˌˈjard] 1.
adj. lop-eared; 2. *su./m* longeared
bat; **oreille** [ɔˈrɛːj] *f* ear; *metall.* lug,
flange; *vase:* handle; *book:* dog's ear;
fig. hearing; *fig.* heed; *avoir de l'ˌ*
have a good ear (for music); ♪ *avoir
l'ˌ absolue* have perfect pitch; *avoir
l'ˌ dure* be hard of hearing; *être tout
ˌs* be all ears; *faire la sourde* ˌ turn a
deaf ear; F *se faire tirer l'ˌ* need a lot
of persuading; *tirer les ˌs à (or de)*
pull *(s.o.'s)* ears; **oreille-d'ours,** *pl.*
oreilles-d'ours ♣ [ɔrɛjˈdurs] *f*
bear's ear; **oreiller** [ɔrɛˈje] *m* pillow;
oreillette [ˌˈjɛt] *f anat.* auricle; *cap:*
ear-flap; **oreillons** ✻ [ˌˈjɔ̃] *m/pl.*
mumps *sg.*

ores [ɔːr] *adv.:* d'ˌ *et déjà* from now
on.

orfèvre [ɔrˈfɛːvr] *m* goldsmith; **orfè-
vrerie** [ˌfɛvrəˈri] *f* goldsmith's trade
or shop; gold plate.

orfraie *orn.* [ɔrˈfrɛ] *f* osprey.

organe [ɔrˈgan] *m anat., a. fig.* organ;
fig. voice; ⊕ ˌs *pl.* de commande
controls; **organigramme** [ɔrganiˈgram] *m* organization chart; flow
chart *or* diagram(me); **organique**
[ɔrgaˈnik] organic; **organisateur,
-trice** [ˌnizaˈtœːr, ˌˈtris] 1. *su.* organizer; 2. *adj.* organizing; **organisation** [ˌnizaˈsjɔ̃] *f* organization;
setting up; setup; **organisation-
nel, -le** [ˌnizasjɔˈnɛl] organization-
al; **organiser** [ˌniˈze] (1a) *v/t.*

organize; arrange; set up; *s'ˌ* settle
down, get into working order; **organisme** [ˌˈnism] *m* organism; **organiste** ♪ [ˌˈnist] *su.* organist.

orgasme *physiol.* [ɔrˈgasm] *m* or-
gasm.

orge ♣ [ɔrʒ] *su./f* barley; *su./m:* ˌ
mondé hulled barley; ˌ *perlé* pearl-
barley; **orgeat** [ɔrˈʒa] *m* orgeat
(sort of syrup); **orgelet** ✻ [ˌʒəˈlɛ]
m eyelid: stye.

orgie [ɔrˈʒi] *f* orgy; *colours etc., fig.:*
riot; *fig.* profusion.

orgue ♪ [ɔrg] *su./m* organ; ˌ *de
Barbarie* barrel-organ; *su./f: eccl.*
ˌs *pl.* organ *sg.*; *les grandes* ˌs *pl.*
the grand organ *sg.*

orgueil [ɔrˈgœːj] *m* pride; dignity;
pej. arrogance; **orgueilleux, -euse**
[ˌgœˈjø, ˌˈjøːz] proud; *pej.* arrogant.

orient [ɔˈrjɑ̃] *m* Orient, East; *pearl:*
water; **oriental, e,** *m/pl.* **-aux** [ɔrjɑ̃ˈtal, ˌˈto] 1. *adj.* oriental, east(ern);
orient *(jewel)*; 2. *su.* oriental; **orien-
tation** [ˌtaˈsjɔ̃] *f* orientation; bearings *pl.*; *ground·* lie, lay; aspect;
pol. trend; ˌ *professionnelle* vocational guidance; **orienter** [ˌˈte]
(1a) *v/t.* orient *(a house etc.)*; train,
point *(a gun, an instrument)*; direct
(a. radio), guide; *antenne f orientée
radio:* directional aerial; *s'ˌ* find
one's bearings; *fig. s'ˌ vers* turn
towards.

orifice [ɔriˈfis] *m* hole, opening; ⊕
port.

origan ♣ [ɔriˈgɑ̃] *m* origanum.

originaire [ɔriʒiˈnɛːr] originating
(in, from de); native; innate; **original, e,** *m/pl.* **-aux** [ˌˈnal, ˌˈno] 1. *adj.*
original; novel *(idea)*; inventive
(mind); *fig.* queer; 2. *su.* eccentric;
su./m text etc.: original; **originalité**
[ˌnaliˈte] *f* originality; *fig.* eccentricity; **origine** [ɔriˈʒin] *f* origin;
birth; *fig.* source; *dès l'ˌ* from the
outset; **originel, -elle** [ˌʒiˈnɛl] *eccl.
etc.* original *(sin, grace)*; primordial;
fundamental.

oripeaux [ɔriˈpo] *m/pl.* rags.

ormaie [ɔrˈmɛ] *f* elm-grove; **orme** ♣
[ɔrm] *m* tree, *a. wood:* elm; *fig.
attendez-moi sous l'ˌ!* you can wait
for me till the cows come home!

ornement [ɔrnəˈmɑ̃] *m* ornament,
adornment; trimming; ♪ grace
(-note); ✻ badge; *eccl.* ˌs *pl.* vest-

ments; *sans* ~s plain (*style*); **orne-mental, e** *m/pl.* **-aux** [~mã'tal,~'to] ornamental, decorative; **ornemen-ter** [~mã'te] (1a) *v/t.* ornament; **orner** [ɔr'ne] (1a) *v/t.* decorate, adorn; ornament; adorn (*a. fig.*).

ornière [ɔr'njɛːr] *f* rut (*a. fig.*); ⊕ groove.

ornitho... [ɔrnito] ornitho...; **~logie** [~lɔ'ʒi] *f* ornithology.

orphelin, e [ɔrfə'lɛ̃, ~'lin] **1.** *adj.* orphan(ed); ~ *de père* (*mère*) fatherless (motherless); **2.** *su.* orphan; **or-phelinat** [~li'na] *m* orphanage.

orteil *anat.* [ɔr'tɛːj] *m* (big) toe.

ortho... [ɔrto] orth(o)...; **~doxe** [~'dɔks] **1.** *adj.* orthodox; conventional; correct; **2.** *su.* orthodox; **~graphe** [~'graf] *f* spelling, orthography; **~graphier** [~gra'fje] (1o) *v/t.* spell (*a word*) correctly; *mal* ~ mis-spell; **~pédie** [~pe'di] *f* orthop(a)edy; **~phonie** [~fɔ'ni] *f* correct pronunciation; ✦ speech therapy.

ortie ✦ [ɔr'ti] *f* nettle; **ortier** ✦ [~'tje] (1o) *v/t.* urticate.

ortolan *orn.* [ɔrtɔ'lɑ̃] *m* ortolan.

orvet *zo.* [ɔr'vɛ] *m* slow-worm.

os [ɔs, *pl.* o] *m* bone; *fig. trempé jusqu'aux* ~ soaked to the skin.

oscillation [ɔsilla'sjɔ̃] *f* oscillation; *machine*: vibration; *pendulum*: swing; *fig.* fluctuation, change; **os-ciller** [~'le] (1a) *v/i.* oscillate, sway; swing (*pendulum*); ✦ fluctuate; *fig.* waver.

osé, e [o'ze] bold, daring.

oseille ✦ [ɔ'zɛːj] *f* sorrel.

oser [o'ze] (1a) *v/t.* dare.

oseraie ✦ [oz're] *f* osier-bed; **osier** ✦ [o'zje] *m* osier, willow; wicker.

osmose [ɔs'moːz] *f* osmosis.

ossature *anat.*, ⊕, *fig.* [ɔsa'tyːr] *f* skeleton, frame; **osselet** [ɔs'lɛ] *m* knucklebone; *anat.* ossicle; **osse-ments** [~'mã] *m/pl.* bones, remains; **osseux, -euse** [ɔ'sø, ~'søːz] bony; **ossification** ✦ [ɔsifika'sjɔ̃] *f* ossification; **ossifier** [~'fje] (1o) *v/t. a.* s'~ ossify; **ossuaire** [ɔ'sɥɛːr] *m* ossuary, charnel-house.

ostensible [ɔstã'sibl] open, patent; **ostensoir** *eccl.* [~'swaːr] *m* monstrance; **ostentation** [~ta'sjɔ̃] *f* ostentation, show.

ostéo... [ɔsteɔ] osteo...

ostracisme [ɔstra'sism] *m* ostra-cism; *frapper q. d'*~ ostracize s.o.

ostréicole [ɔstrei'kɔl] oyster-...; **ostréiculteur** [~kyl'tœːr] *m* oyster-breeder; **ostréiculture** [~kyl'tyːr] *f* oyster-breeding.

ostrogot(h), e [ɔstrɔ'go,~'gɔt] **1.** *adj.* Ostrogothic; *fig.* barbarous; **2.** *su.* ♀ Ostrogoth; *fig.* barbarian, vandal.

otage [ɔ'taːʒ] *m* hostage (for, de); *fig.* guarantee.

otalgie ✦ [ɔtal'ʒi] *f* ear-ache.

otarie *zo.* [ɔta'ri] *f* sea-lion.

ôter [o'te] (1a) *v/t.* remove, take away; take off (*one's gloves etc.*); Å deduct, subtract (*a number*).

otite ✦ [ɔ'tit] *f* otitis; ~ *moyenne* tympanitis.

oto-rhino ✦ [ɔtɔri'no], **oto-rhino-laryngologiste** [ɔtɔrinɔlarɛ̃gɔlɔ-'ʒist] *su.* ear, nose and throat specialist.

ottoman, e [ɔtɔ'mã, ~'man] **1.** *adj.* Ottoman; **2.** *su.* ♀ Ottoman; *su./m tex.* grogram; *su./f* divan, ottoman.

ou [u] *cj.* or; ou ... ou either ... or; *ou bien* or else; *si* ... *ou* whether ... or.

où [u] **1.** *adv.* place, direction: where; *time:* when; **2.** *pron./rel.* place, direction: where; *time:* when, on which; *fig.* at or in which; *d'où* whence, where ... from; hence, therefore; *par où?* which way?

ouaille [wa:j] *f* †, *a. dial.* sheep; *fig.*, *eccl.* ~s *pl.* flock sg.

ouate [wat] *f* wadding; cotton-wool; ~ *hydrophile* absorbent cotton-wool; **ouater** [wa'te] (1a) *v/t.* wad, pad; *fig.* soften (*a sound*); *cost.* quilt.

oubli [u'bli] *m* forgetfulness; forgetting; oblivion; oversight, omission.

oublie [~] *f wafer:* cornet.

oublier [ubli'e] (1a) *v/t.* forget; overlook; miss (*an occasion*); neglect; *faire* ~ live down; *n'oubliez pas* remember; s'~ forget o.s.; indulge (in, à); **oubliettes** [~'ɛt] *f/pl.* secret dungeon *sg.*, oubliette *sg.*; **oublieux, -euse** [~'ø, ~'øːz] forgetful, unmindful (of, de).

oued [wɛd] *m* wadi, watercourse.

ouest [wɛst] **1.** *su./m* west; *de l'*~ west(ern); *d'*~ westerly (*wind*); *vers l'*~ westward(s), to the west; **2.** *adj./inv.* west(ern); westerly

ouf! [uf] *int.* phew! [(*wind*).⌡

oui [wi] **1.** *adv.* yes; *dire que* ~ say

yes; *mais* ~! certainly!; yes indeed!;
2. *su./m/inv.* yes.
ouiche! *sl.* [wiʃ] *int.* not on your
life!
ouï-dire [wi'diːr] *m/inv.* hearsay;
par ~ by hearsay; **ouïe** [wi] *f* (sense
of) hearing; ⊕ ear; ~s *pl.* ♪ sound-
holes; *icht.* gills (*of a fish*); **ouïr**
[wiːr] (2r) *v/t.* hear.
ouragan [ura'gɑ̃] *m* hurricane.
ourdir [ur'diːr] (2a) *v/t.* *tex.* warp;
fig. weave (*an intrigue*), hatch (*a
plot*).
ourler [ur'le] (1a) *v/t.* hem; ⊕ lap-
joint; **ourlet** [~'lɛ] *m* hem; *fig.*
edge; ⊕ lap-joint.
ours [urs] *m* *zo.* bear (*a. fig.*); ~ *blanc*
polar bear; ~ *en peluche* Teddy
bear; **ourse** [~] *f* *zo.* she-bear;
astr. la Grande ♀ the Great Bear,
Charles's Wain; *astr. la Petite* ♀
the Little Bear; **oursin** *zo.* [ur'sɛ̃]
m sea-urchin; **ourson** *zo.* [~'sɔ̃] *m*
bear cub.
oust(e)! F [ust] *int.* get a move on!;
out you go!
outarde *orn.* [u'tard] *f* bustard;
Canada goose.
outil [u'ti] *m* tool; **outillage** [uti-
'jaːʒ] *m* tool set *or* kit; ⊕ equipment, plant, machinery; **outiller**
[~'je] (1a) *v/t.* equip with tools;
⊕ fit out (*a factory*); **outilleur**
[~'jœːr] *m* tool-maker.
outrage [u'traːʒ] *m* outrage; ⚖ ~ *à
magistrat* contempt of court; **outrager** [utra'ʒe] (1l) *v/t.* outrage; insult; violate (*a woman*); **outrageux, -euse** [~'ʒø, ~'ʒøːz] insulting,
scurrilous.
outrance [u'trɑ̃ːs] *f* excess; *à* ~ to
the bitter end; to the death (*war*);
outrancier, -ère [utrɑ̃'sje, ~'sjɛːr]
1. *adj.* extreme; **2.** *su.* extremist.
outre[1] [uːtr] *f* water-skin.
outre[2] [uːtr] **1.** *prp.* beyond; in addition to; **2.** *adv.:* en ~ moreover,
furthermore; *passer* ~ not to take
notice (of, *à*); *passer* ~ *à a.* disregard,
ignore; *percer q. d'*~ en ~ run s.o.
through; ~**cuidance** [utrəkɥi'dɑ̃ːs] *f*
bumptiousness, overweening conceit; ~**cuidant, e** [~'dɑ̃, ~'dɑ̃ːt]
bumptious, overweening; ~**mer**
[~'mɛːr] *m* lapis lazuli; *colour:* ultramarine; ~**-mer** [~'mɛːr] *adv.* overseas...; ~**passer** [~pɑ'se] (1a) *v/t.*
exceed; go beyond.

outrer [u'tre] (1a) *v/t.* exaggerate;
tire out; *outré de colère* provoked
to anger, infuriated.
ouvert, e [u'vɛːr, ~'vɛrt] **1.** *p.p.* of
ouvrir; **2.** *adj.* open (*a. fig.*, *a.* ✖
war, city); quick (*mind*); *fig. à bras*
~s with open arms; ✝ *compte m* ~
open account, open credit; **ouverture** [uvɛr'tyːr] *f* opening; aper-
ture; ♪ overture; ⊕ ~s *pl.* ports.
ouvrable [u'vrabl] workable; *jour
m* ~ working day; **ouvrage** [u'vraːʒ]
m work; *fig.* workmanship; product; **ouvrager** [uvra'ʒe] (1l) *v/t.*
⊕ work; *tex.* embroider.
ouvre [uːvr] *1st p. sg. pres.* of *ouvrir*.
ouvré, e [u'vre] wrought (*iron*);
worked (*timber*); *tex.* figured.
ouvre-boîtes [uvrə'bwat] *m/inv.*
tin-opener,   *Am.*   can-opener;
ouvre-bouteilles [~bu'tɛːj] *m/inv.*
bottle-opener; **ouvre-lettres** [~-
'lɛtr] *m/inv.* letter-opener.
ouvrer [u'vre] (1a) *v/t.* work; *tex.*
diaper, figure.
ouvreur, -euse [u'vrœːr, ~'vrøːz] *su.*
opener; *su./f thea.* usherette (*a. cin.*);
box-attendant; *tex. machine:* cotton-
opener.
ouvrier, -ère [uvri'e, ~'ɛːr] **1.** *su.*
worker; operator; factory-worker; ~
agricole farm-hand; ✂ ~ *au jour* surface hand; ~ *aux pièces* piece-worker;
su./m: ~ *qualifié* skilled workman; ~
simple unskilled worker; *su./f*
factory-girl; *zo.* worker (bee *or* ant);
2. *adj.* working (*class*); workmen's
...; labo(u)r...; worker (*ant, bee*);
ouvriérisme [~e'rism] *m* worker
control.
ouvrir [u'vriːr] (2f) *v/t.* open (*a. fig.*);
unfasten; turn on (*the gas, a tap*); *fig.*
begin; open (*s.th.*) up; ⚡ break (*the
circuit*); ⚔ lance (*a boil*); *fig.* ~ *à q.*
confide in s.o.; talk freely to s.o.; *v/i.
a.* s'~ open.   [charity workshop.⟩
ouvroir [u'vrwaːr] *m* workroom;⟩
ovaire ♀, *anat.* [ɔ'vɛːr] *m* ovary.
ovale [ɔ'val] *adj.*, *a. su./m* oval.
ovation [ɔva'sjɔ̃] *f* ovation; *faire
une* ~ *à q.* give s.o. an ovation.
ove [ɔːv] *m* △ ovolo; egg-shaped
section; **ové, e** [ɔ've] egg-shaped.
ovi... [ɔvi] ovi..., ovo...
ovin, e [ɔ'vɛ̃, ~'vin] ovine.
ovipare *zo.* [ɔvi'paːr] oviparous.
ovni [ɔv'ni] *m* (= *objet volant non identifié*) Ufo.

ovule *biol.* [ɔ'vyl] *m* ovum; ♀ ovule.
ox(y)... [ɔks(i)] ox(y)...
oxycoupeur [ɔksiku'pœːr] *m* oxyacetylene burner.
oxydable ♒ [ɔksi'dabl] oxidizable; **oxydation** ♒ [~da'sjɔ̃] *f* oxidization; **oxyde** ♒ [ɔk'sid] *m* oxide; ~ de *carbone* carbon monoxide; **oxyder** ♒ [~si'de] (1a) *v/t. a. s'*~ oxidize.
oxygène ♒ [ɔksi'ʒɛn] *m* oxygen; **oxygéné, e** [~ʒe'ne] ♒ oxygenated; F *cheveux m/pl.* ~s peroxided hair; *eau f* ~e hydrogen peroxide.
ozone ♒ [ɔ'noz] *m* ozone.

P

P, p [pe] *m* P, p.

pacage [pa'ka:ʒ] *m* pasturage; grazing; **pacager** [~ka'ʒe] (1l) *v/t.* pasture, graze.

pachyderme *zo.* [paʃi'dɛrm] **1.** *adj.* thick-skinned; **2.** *su./m* pachyderm.

pacificateur, -trice [pasifika'tœːr, ~'tris] **1.** *adj.* pacifying; **2.** *su.* peacemaker; **pacification** [~'sjɔ̃] *f* pacification, pacifying; **pacifier** [pasi-'fje] (1o) *v/t.* pacify (*a country*); calm (*the crowd, s.o.'s mind*); **pacifique** [~'fik] **1.** *adj.* pacific; peaceful, quiet; *l'océan m* ♀ = **2.** *su./m*: *le* ♀ the Pacific (Ocean).

pacotille [pako'tiːj] *f* ⚓ shoddy goods *pl.*; *fig.* cheap stuff, rubbish, junk; *de ~* cheap; jerry-built (*house*).

pacte [pakt] *m* pact, agreement; **pactiser** [pakti'ze] (1a) *v/i.* come to terms; compromise (with, *avec*).

paf F [paf] **1.** *int.* slap!; **2.** *adj.* F tight (= *drunk*).

pagaie [pa'gɛ] *f* paddle.

pagaïe F, **pagaille** F [pa'ga:j] *f* disorder, mess; *fig.* chaos.

paganiser [pagani'ze] (1a) *vt/i.* paganize; **paganisme** [~'nism] *m* paganism; heathendom.

pagayer [page'je] (1i) *vt/i.* paddle.

page[1] [pa:ʒ] *m* page(-boy).

page[2] [pa:ʒ] *f book*: page, leaf; *à la ~* in the know, up to date; **paginer** [paʒi'ne] (1a) *v/t.* paginate.

pagne [paɲ] *m* loin-cloth.

paie [pɛ] *f* pay(ment), wages *pl.*; *enveloppe f de ~* pay envelope; *jour m de ~* pay-day; **paiement** [~'mã] *m* payment; *~ anticipé* advance payment *or* instalment; *~ au comptant* cash payment; *~ contre livraison* cash on delivery; *~ partiel* part-payment; *suspendre ses ~s* suspend payment.

païen, -enne [pa'jɛ̃, ~'jɛn] *adj., a. su.* pagan, heathen.

paillage ⚹ [pɑ'ja:ʒ] *m* mulching.

paillard, e *sl.* [pɑ'ja:r, ~'jard] **1.** *adj.* ribald, lewd; **2.** *su./m* rake; *su./f* wanton; **paillardise** [~jar'di:z] *f* lechery; lewd talk.

paillasse[1] [pa'jas] *m* buffoon, clown.

paillasse[2] [pɑ'jas] *f* straw mattress, palliasse; 🔬 bench; **paillasson** [~ja'sɔ̃] *m* mat; matting; **paille** [pɑːj] **1.** *su./f* straw; ⊕ *iron*: shavings *pl.*; ⊕, *gem, glass, metal, a. fig.*: flaw; *fig.* poverty; *~ de fer* steel wool; *fig.* homme *m de ~* man of straw, tool, *Am.* front; *tirer à la courte ~* draw lots; **2.** *adj./inv.* straw-colo(u)red; **paillé, e** [pɑ'je] flawed, flawy; scaly (*metal*); straw-colo(u)red; **pailler** [~'je] **1.** (1a) *v/t.* mulch; (cover with) straw; **2.** *su./m* farm-yard; straw-yard; straw-stack; **paillet** [~'je] *m* pale red wine; **pailleter** [paj'te] (1c) *v/t.* spangle (with, *de*); **paillette** [pa'jɛt] *f* sequin, spangle; *mica, soap*: flake; *metall.* scale; *jewel*: flaw; grain of golddust; **pailleux, -euse** [pɑ'jø, ~'jøːz] strawy; ⊕ flawy; **paillis** [~'ji] *m* mulch; **paillotte** [~'jɔt] *f* straw hut.

pain [pɛ̃] *m* bread; loaf; *soap*: cake, tablet; *butter*: pat; *sugar*: lump; *fig.* livelihood; *sl.* punch, blow; *~ à cacheter* wafer, seal; *~ bis* brown bread; *~ complet* whole-meal bread; *~ d'épice* gingerbread; *petit ~* roll.

pair, paire [pɛːr] **1.** *adj.* equal; A even (*number*); **2.** *su./m* equality; ✝ par; *parl.* peer; *person*: equal; *au ~* in return for board and lodging, au pair; *de ~* together, hand in hand (with, *avec*); *hors (de) ~* peerless, unrivalled; *fig.* être au ~ de be up to date *or* schedule with; *parl.* la Chambre des ♀s the (House of) Lords *pl.*

paire [pɛːr] *f* pair; *birds etc.*: brace; *fig.* faire la ~ be two of a kind.

pairesse [pɛ'rɛs] *f* peeress; **pairie** [~'ri] *f* peerage.

paisible [pe'zibl] peaceful, quiet.

paître [pɛːtr] (4k) *v/t.* graze (*cattle*); drive to pasture; feed on (*grass*); *v/i.* feed, graze; pasture, browse; F *envoyer q. ~* send s.o. packing.

paix [pɛ] *f* peace; quiet; *fig.* recon-

pal

ciliation; ～ *donc!* keep quiet!; ～ *séparée* separate peace; *faire la* ～
make peace; F *ficher la* ～ *à q.* leave
s.o. alone, let s.o. be.

pal, *pl.* **pals** [pal] *m* pale (*a.* ▨),
stake.

palabre [pa'labr] *f* or *m* palaver; F
speech.

paladin [pala'dɛ̃] *m* paladin, knight;
knight-errant.

palais[1] [pa'lɛ] *m* (*royal or bishop's*)
palace; *coll.* lawyers *pl.*; ～ *de justice*
law-courts *pl.*

palais[2] ⚕, anat., fig. [～] *m* palate;
anat. *voile m du* ～ soft palate.

palan ⚓, ⊕ [pa'lɑ̃] *m* pulley-block,
tackle; set of pulleys.

palanche [pa'lɑ̃:ʃ] *f* yoke (*for carrying buckets etc.*).

palangre [pa'lɑ̃:gr] *f* trawl-line,
Am. trawl.

palanque [pa'lɑ̃:k] *f* stockade.

palanquin [palɑ̃kɛ̃] *m* palanquin.

palatal, e, *m/pl.* **-aux** [pala'tal, ～'to]
adj., a. su./f palatal; **palatin, e** anat.
[pala'tɛ̃, ～'tin] palatine.

pale[1] eccl. [pal] *f* chalice-cover, pall.

pale[2] [～] *f* ⚓, cin. blade (*a. fan*);
fan: vane; ⊕ arm.

pâle [pɑːl] pale, pallid; wan; ashen
(*complexion*); *fig.* colo(u)rless (*style*);
⚔ *sl.* sick; *fig.* sickly (*smile*).

palefrenier [palfrə'nje] *m* groom;
stable-boy; ostler; **palefroi** †
[～'frwa] *m* palfrey.

paléo... [paleɔ] pal(a)eo...; **paléon-
tologie** [～ɔ̃tɔlɔ'ʒi] *f* pal(a)eontology.

paleron [pal'rɔ̃] *m* ox etc.: shoulder-
blade; *cuis.* chuck.

palet [pa'lɛ] *m* game: quoit.

paletot [pal'to] *m* overcoat; *sl.* tomber
sur le ～ *à q.* jump on s.o., pitch into
s.o.

palette [pa'lɛt] *f paint., a. fig.* palette;
cuis. shoulder; ⊕ *wheel etc.:* paddle;
† pallet.

pâleur [pɑ'lœːr] *f* pallor, paleness;
moon: wanness.

palier [pa'lje] *m* ⚙ stairs: landing;
⊕ bearing; ⊕ pillow-block; ⚙,
⚙, *mot.* level; *sur le même* ～ on
the same floor; **palière** ⚙ [～'ljɛːr]
adj./f top (*step*).

palinodie [palinɔ'di] *f* recantation.

pâlir [pɑ'liːr] (2a) *v/i.* (grow) pale;
fig. fade; *v/t.* make pale; bleach
(*colours*).

palissade [pali'sad] *f* palisade,

fence; ⚔ stockade; **palissader** [～-
sa'de] *v/t.* fence in, enclose; ⚔
stockade; ⚓ hedge in (*a field*).

palissandre [pali'sɑ̃:dr] *m* rosewood.

palisser ⚓ [pali'se] (1a) *v/t.* train
(*vine etc.*).

palliatif, -ve [pallja'tif, ～'tiːv] *adj.,
a. su./m* palliative.

pallier [pal'lje] (1o) *v/t.* palliate.

palmarès [palma'rɛːs] *m* prize-list,
hono(u)rs list.

palme[1] [palm] *f* ⚕ palm(-branch);
fig. palm; *skin diving etc.:* flipper.

palme[2] † [～] *m measure:* hand('s-
breadth).

palmé, e [pal'me] ⚕ palmate; *orn.*
web-footed.

palmer ⊕ [pal'mɛːr] *m* micrometer
ga(u)ge.

palmeraie [palmə'rɛ] *f* palm-grove;
palmette [～'mɛt] *f* ⚓ palm-leaf,
palmette; ⚓ fan-shaped espalier;
palmier ⚕ [～'mje] *m* palm-tree;
palmipède zo. [～mi'pɛd] *adj., a.
su./m* palmipede; **palmite** [～'mit]
m palm-marrow; **palmure** *orn.*
[～'myːr] *f* web.

palombe *orn.* [pa'lɔ̃:b] *f* ring-dove,
wood-pigeon.

palonnier [palɔ'nje] *m* ⊕ *carriage
etc.:* swingle-bar; *mot.* compensation bar; ⚓ rudder-bar.

pâlot, -otte [pɑ'lo, ～'lɔt] palish;
peaky.

palpable [pal'pabl] palpable (*a. fig.*);
tangible; *fig.* obvious; **palpe** [palp]
m zo. feeler; *icht.* barbel; **palper**
[pal'pe] (1a) *v/t.* feel; ⚕ palpate; F
pocket (*money*).

palpitant, e [palpi'tɑ̃, ～'tɑ̃:t] **1.** *adj.*
fluttering (*heart*); throbbing; *fig.*
thrilling; **2.** *su./m sl.* ticker (= *heart*).

palpitation [～ta'sjɔ̃] *f* throb(bing),
⚕ palpitation; fluttering; **palpiter**
[～'te] (1a) *v/i.* palpitate; throb, beat
(*heart*); flutter; *fig.* thrill (with, *de*).

paltoquet F † [paltɔ'ke] *m* lout;
whipper-snapper.

paludéen, -enne [palyde'ɛ̃, ～'ɛn]
marsh...; ⚕ malarial (*fever*); **paludisme** ⚕ [～'dism] *m* malaria, marsh
fever; **palustre** [pa'lystr] paludous;
swampy (*ground*).

pâmer [pɑ'me] (1a) *v/t.:* † se ～ faint;
se ～ *de qch.* be overcome with s.th.; *se*
～ *de joie a.* be in raptures; se ～ *de rire*
split one's sides with laughter; **pâ-
moison** †, *co.* [～mwa'zɔ̃] *f* swoon.

pampa [pɑ̃'pa] *f* pampas *pl.*

pamphlet [pɑ̃'flɛ] *m* lampoon;
pamphlétaire [ˌflɛ'tɛːr] *m* pamphleteer, lampoonist.

pamplemousse ♀ [pɑ̃plə'mus] *m* grapefruit; shaddock.

pampre ♀ [pɑ̃:pr] *m* vine-branch, vine-shoot.

pan¹ [pɑ̃] *m cost.* flap; coat-tail; △ *wall:* piece, section; (*wooden*) partition, framing; *building, prism, nut:* side; *sky:* patch.

pan²! [ˌ] *int.* bang!; slap!

pan... [pɑ̃; *before vowel* pan] pan...

panacée [pana'se] *f* panacea, cure-all.

panachage [pana'ʃaːʒ] *m election:* splitting one's vote; **panache** [ˌ'naʃ] *m* plume, tuft (*on a helmet etc.*); *smoke:* wreath; *fig.* gallantry; *mot. etc.* faire ~ turn over; **panaché, e** [pana'ʃe] **1.** *adj.* mixed (*salad, ice*); **2.** *su./m* shandy(gaff); **panacher** [ˌ] (1a) *v/t.* variegate; *election:* split (*one's votes*).

panade [pa'nad] *f cuis.* panada; F *dans la* ~ in need; in the soup.

panais ♀ [pa'nɛ] *m* parsnip.

panama [pana'ma] *m* panama hat, F (*fine-*)straw hat.

panaris ♀ [pana'ri] *m* whitlow.

pancarte [pɑ̃'kart] *f* placard, bill; sign; notice.

pancréas *anat.* [pɑ̃kre'ɑ:s] *m* pancreas.

panda *zo.* [pɑ̃'da] *m* panda.

panégyrique [paneʒi'rik] *m* panegyric; faire le ~ de panegyrize (*s.o.*).

paner *cuis.* [pa'ne] (1a) *v/t.* cover with bread-crumbs; **paneterie** [pan'tri] *f* bread-pantry; ✕, *school, etc.:* bread-store; **panetier** [ˌ'tje] *m* bread-store keeper; **panetière** [ˌ'tjeːr] *f* bread-cupboard; sideboard.

panier [pa'nje] *m* basket (*a. sp.*); ~ à *salade* salad washer; *sl.* Black Maria, prison van; *fig.* ~ percé spendthrift; F le dessus du ~ the pick of the bunch; **panier-repas**, *pl.* **paniers-repas** [ˌrə'pa] *m* packed lunch, lunchpack.

panifiable [pani'fjabl] bread-...; *farine f* ~ bread-flour; **panification** [ˌfika'sjɔ̃] *f* panification; **panifier** [ˌ'fje] (1o) *v/t.* turn (*flour*) into bread.

panique [pa'nik] *adj., a. su./f* panic; **paniquer** [ˌni'ke] (1a) *v/t.* (throw

into a) panic; *se* ~ = *v/i.* (get into a) panic.

panne¹ *tex.* [pan] *f* plush.

panne² [ˌ] *f* lard, hog's fat.

panne³ [ˌ] *f mot. etc.* breakdown; ⚡ *etc.* current, *engine:* failure; être en ~ be stuck; être en ~ de ... have run out of ...; *laisser en* ~ leave (*s.o.*) in the lurch; *tomber en* ~ break down.

panne⁴ △ [ˌ] *f* pantile; *roof:* purlin.

panneau [pa'no] *m* wood, a. paint.: panel; (board); ✖ ground-signal; ⚓ hatch; ✎ glass frame; F snare, trap.

panneton ⊕ [pan'tɔ̃] *m* key: web; (*window-*)catch.

panoplie [panɔ'pli] *f* set (*of tools, toys, etc.*); outfit; ✕ armoury; *fig.* package, (whole) set, variety.

panorama [panɔra'ma] *m* panorama.

panse [pɑ̃:s] *f* F belly (*a.* ⚗ retort *etc.*); *zo.* first stomach, paunch.

pansement ✚ [pɑ̃s'mɑ̃] *m wound:* dressing; **panser** [pɑ̃'se] (1a) *v/t.* groom, rub down (*a horse*); ✚ dress (*a wound*), tend (*a wounded man*).

pansu, e [pɑ̃'sy] pot-bellied.

pantalon [pɑ̃ta'lɔ̃] *m* trousers *pl.*, *Am.* pants *pl.*; (*woman's*) knickers *pl.*; slacks *pl.*

panteler [pɑ̃'tle] (1c) *v/i.* pant.

panthère *zo.* [pɑ̃'tɛːr] *f* panther.

pantin [pɑ̃'tɛ̃] *m toy:* jumping-jack; *fig.* puppet.

panto... [pɑ̃tɔ] panto...; **~graphe** [ˌ'graf] *m drawing, a.* ✎: pantograph; lazy-tongs *pl.*

pantois [pɑ̃'twa] *adj./m* flabbergasted.

pantomime [pɑ̃tɔ'mim] *f* dumb show; pantomime.

pantouflard [pɑ̃tu'flaːr] *m* stay-at-home type; **pantoufle** [ˌ'tufl] *f* slipper; *fig.* en ~s in a slipshod way; **pantouflerie** ⊕ [ˌtuflə'ri] *f* slipper-making.

paon *orn.* [pɑ̃] *m* peacock (*a. fig.*); **paonne** *orn.* [pan] *f* peahen; **paonneau** [pa'no] *m* pea-chick.

papa F [pa'pa] *m* papa, dad(dy); *fig.* à *la* ~ in leisurely fashion; *fig.* de ~ old, antiquated, old-fashioned; (*good*) old; grandfather's ...

papal, e, *m/pl.* **-aux** [pa'pal, ~'po] papal; **papauté** [ˌpo'te] *f* papacy; **pape** *eccl., a. fig.* [pap] *m* pope.

papelard, e F [pa'plaːr, ~'plard] **1.** *adj.* sanctimonious; **2.** *su./m*

sanctimonious person; **papelardise**
F [⌣plar'diːz] f cant, sanctimoniousness.

paperasse [pa'pras] f red tape; useless paper(s pl.); **paperasserie** [⌣
pras'ri] f accumulation of old papers; F red tape, red-tapism; **paperassier** [⌣pra'sje] m bureaucrat.

papeterie [pap'tri] f paper-mill;
paper trade; stationery; stationer's
(shop); **papetier, -ère** [⌣'tje, ⌣
'tjɛːr] **1.** su. stationer; paper-manufacturer; **2.** adj. paper(-making);
papier [pa'pje] m paper; document; ✝ bill(s pl.); ⌣ à calquer tracing-paper; ⌣ à la cuve hand-made
paper;⌣à lettres letter-paper;⌣à musique music-paper; ⌣ bible (or indien)
India paper; ⌣ buvard blotting paper; ⌣ carbone carbon paper; ⌣ couché art paper; ⌣ d'emballage brown
paper; ⌣ de verre sand-paper, glass-
paper; ⌣-émeri emery-paper; ⌣-
filtre filter-paper; ⌣ hygiénique toilet-paper; ⌣ peint, ⌣-tenture wallpaper; ⌣ pelure tissue-paper; ⌣-
monnaie [⌣pjemɔ'nɛ] m paper
money.

papille ✿, anat. [pa'piːj] f papilla.

papillon [papi'jɔ̃] m zo. butterfly;
cost. butterfly bow, bow-tie; leaflet;
(parking) ticket; poster: fly-bill;
inset map; document: rider; ✝ label,
tag; ⊕ butterfly-valve; ⊕ wing-nut;
mot. throttle; F fig. ⌣s pl. noirs gloomy
thoughts; **papillonner** [⌣jɔ'ne] (1a)
v/i. flutter; F flit from subject to
subject; **papillotte** [⌣'jɔt] f curlpaper; frill (round ham etc.); twist of
paper; **papilloter** [⌣jɔ'te] (1a) v/i.
blink (eyes, light); cin. flicker; fig.
glitter.

paprika ✿, cuis. [papri'ka] m red
pepper.

papule ✿, ✿ [pa'pyl] f papula, papule; **papuleux, -euse** [⌣py'lø, ⌣
'løːz] papulose, F pimply.

papyrus [papi'rys] m papyrus.

pâque [pɑːk] f (Jewish) Passover.

paquebot ⚓ [pak'bo] m (passenger-)liner; packet-boat.

pâquerette ✿ [pɑ'krɛt] f daisy.

Pâques [pɑːk] su./m Easter; su./f:
⌣ pl. closes Low Sunday sg.; ⌣ pl.
fleuries Palm Sunday sg.; faire ses
♀ make one's Easter communion.

paquet [pa'kɛ] m parcel, package;
pack; bundle; ⚓ ⌣ de mer heavy sea;

faire son ⌣ or ses ⌣s pack one's bags;
lâcher son ⌣ à q. give s.o. a piece of
one's mind; (y) mettre le ⌣ give all one
has got; risquer le ⌣ chance the lot;
paqueter [pak'te] (1c) v/t. make up
into a parcel; **paqueteur** m, -euse f
✝, ⊕ [⌣'tœːr, ⌣'tøːz] packer.

par [par] prp. place: by (sea),
through (the door, the street); via
(Calais); over; to; time: on (a fine
evening, a summer's day); in (the
rain); motive: from, through; out
of (friendship, curiosity); agent: by;
instrument: by (mail, telephone,
train, boat, etc.); distribution: per
(annum, capita), each; a (day, week,
etc.); in (hundreds, numerical order);
⌣ eau et ⌣ terre by land and sea;
⌣ monts et ⌣ vaux over hill and
dale; ⌣ où? which way?; ⌣ toute la
terre (ville) all over the world
(town); regarder (jeter) ⌣ la fenêtre
look (throw) out of the window;
tomber ⌣ terre fall to the ground;
⌣ un beau temps in fine weather; ⌣
bonheur (malheur) by good (ill) fortune, (un)fortunately; ⌣ hasard by
chance; ⌣ pitié! for pity's sake!;
vaincu ⌣ César conquered by Caesar; Phèdre ⌣ Racine Phèdre by
Racine; ⌣ soi-même (by or for) oneself; célèbre ⌣ famous for; ⌣ conséquent consequently; ⌣ droit et raison by rights; ⌣ avion post: via airmail; venir ⌣ air à fly to; prendre ⌣
la main take by the hand; jour ⌣
jour day by day; deux ⌣ deux two
by two; commencer (finir etc.) ⌣
(inf.) begin (end) by (ger.); F ⌣
trop court (much or far) too short;
de ⌣ by, in conformity with (the
conditions, nature, etc.); de ⌣ le roi
by order of the King; in the King's
name; ⌣-ci here; ⌣-là there; ⌣-ci
⌣-là hither and thither; now and
then; ⌣ derrière from behind; ⌣-
dessous under, beneath; ⌣-dessus
over (s.th.); ⚖ ⌣-devant before, in
presence of.

para ⚔ F [pa'ra] m paratrooper.

para...: ⌣**bole** [para'bɔl] f parable;
Å parabola.

parachever [paraʃ've] (1d) v/t. perfect.

para...: ⌣**chute** [para'ʃyt] m ✈ parachute; ⚒ cage: safety device; ⌣-
chuter [⌣ʃy'te] (1a) v/t. (drop by)
parachute; fig. pitchfork (s.o. into, q.

dans); **~chutiste** [~ʃyˈtist] *m* parachutist; paratrooper.

parade [paˈrad] *f* box., *a. fencing*: parry; *horse*: checking; reply, repartee; ✗ parade (*a. fig.*); *fig.* show; *faire* ~ de show off, display; *lit m de* ~ lying-in-state bed; **parader** [~raˈde] (1a) *v/i.* strut (about).

paradigme *gramm.* [paraˈdigm] *m* paradigm.

paradis [paraˈdi] *m* paradise; *thea.* gallery, F the gods *pl.*; ✝ ~ *fiscal* tax haven; **paradisiaque** [~diˈzjak] paradisiac; of paradise; **paradisier** *orn.* [~diˈzje] *m* bird of paradise.

paradoxal, e, *m/pl.* **-aux** [paradɔkˈsal, ~ˈso] paradoxical; **paradoxe** [~ˈdɔks] *m* paradox.

parafe [paˈraf] *m see paraphe*; **parafer** [~raˈfe] *see parapher*.

paraffine ⚗ [paraˈfin] *f* paraffin.

parafoudre ⚡ [paraˈfudr] *m* lightning-arrester; *magneto*: safety-gap.

parage¹ ✝ [paˈra:ʒ] *m* birth, descent; *de haut* ~ of high lineage.

parage² [~] *m*: ~*s pl.* ⚓ latitudes; regions; vicinity *sg.*, quarters; *dans les* ~*s de ... a.* in the ... area, near ...; *dans les* ~ (around) here.

paragraphe [paraˈgraf] *m* paragraph.

parais [paˈrɛ] *1st p. sg. pres. of paraître*; **paraissons** [~rɛˈsɔ̃] *1st p. pl. pres. of paraître*; **paraître** [~ˈrɛːtr] (4k) *v/i.* appear; seem, look; be visible; come out (*book etc.*); *vient de* ~ just out (*book*); *v/impers.*: *à ce qu'il paraît* apparently; *il paraît que* (*ind.*) it seems that; *il paraît que oui* (*non*) it appears so (not).

parallèle [paralˈlɛl] **1.** *adj.* parallel; *fig.* unofficial (*institution etc.*); second, side (*job etc.*); alternative (*medicine etc.*); **2.** *su./f* Å, ✗ parallel; *su./m geog.*, ✗, *a. fig.* parallel; **parallélépipède** Å [~lelepiˈpɛd] *m* parallelepiped; **parallélisme** [~leˈlism] *m* parallelism (between ... and *de ... à, entre* ... *et*); **parallélogramme** Å [~lelɔˈgram] *m* parallelogram.

para...: **~lyser** [paraliˈze] (1a) *v/t.* paralyse (*a. fig.*); *fig.* cripple; **~lysie** ✗ [~ˈzi] *f* paralysis; ✝ palsy; ~ *agitante* Parkinson's disease; **~lytique** [~ˈtik] *adj., a. su.* paralytic; **~mètre** Å, *a. fig.* [paraˈmɛtr] *m* parameter; **~militaire** [paramiliˈtɛːr] semi-military.

parangon [parɑ̃ˈgɔ̃] *m* paragon, model; flawless gem; *typ. gros* ~ double pica.

parapet [paraˈpɛ] *m* △, ✗ parapet; ✗ breastwork.

paraphe [paˈraf] *m signature*: flourish; initials *pl.*; **parapher** [~raˈfe] (1a) *v/t.* initial.

para...: **~phrase** [paraˈfrɑːz] *f* paraphrase; *fig.* circumlocution; **~phraser** [~frɑˈze] (1a) *v/t.* paraphrase; *fig.* add to (*a story etc.*); **~plégie** ✗ [~pleˈʒi] *f* paraplegia; **~pluie** [~ˈplɥi] *m* umbrella (*a.* ✗, ✗); **~site** [~ˈzit] **1.** *adj.* ✗, ✗ parasitic; **2.** *su./m* ✗, *biol., zo., fig.* parasite; *fig.* sponger; ~*s pl. radio*: atmospherics; **~sol** [~ˈsɔl] *m* parasol, sunshade; *mot.* visor; **~tonnerre** [~tɔˈnɛːr] *m* lightning-conductor; lightning-rod; **~typhoïde** ✗ [~tifɔˈid] *f* paratyphoid fever; **~vent** [~ˈvɑ̃] *m* folding screen.

parbleu! [parˈblø] *int.* rather!; of course!

parc [park] *m* park; enclose; *horses*: paddock; *cattle*: pen; *sheep*: fold; *oysters*: bed; ⊕ *coal*: yard; 🚗, ✗ depot; *child*: playpen; ✝, *a. fig.* stock; *mot.* ~ *de stationnement* car park, *Am.* parking lot; **parcage** [parˈka:ʒ] *m mot.* parking; *cattle*: penning; *sheep*: folding; *oysters*: laying down; *mot.* ~ *interdit* no parking.

parcellaire [parsɛlˈlɛːr] divided into small portions; **parcelle** [~ˈsɛl] *f land*: lot, plot; small fragment; *fig.* grain; **parceller** [~sɛˈle] *v/t.* divide into lots; portion out; **parcelliser** [~sɛliˈze] (1a) *v/t.* divide *or* split up.

parce [pars] *cj.*: ~ *que* because.

parchemin [parʃəˈmɛ̃] *m* parchment; *bookbinding*: vellum; F ~*s pl. univ.* diplomas; ✍ title-deeds; **parcheminé, e** [parʃomiˈne] *fig.* parchment-like, dried; wizened (*skin*); **parcheminer** [~ˈne] (1a) *v/t.* give a parchment finish to; *se* ~ shrivel up; become parchment-like; **parchemineux, -euse** [~ˈnø, ~ˈnøːz] parchment-like.

parcimonie [parsimɔˈni] *f* parsimony, stinginess; **parcimonieux, -euse** [~ˈnjø, ~ˈnjøːz] parsimonious, stingy.

parc(o)mètre [park(ɔ)ˈmɛtr] *m* parking meter.

parcourir [parku'riːr] (2l) v/t. travel through; traverse (a. ⚡); cover (a distance); skim, look through (a book, papers, etc.); eye: survey; **parcours** [~'kuːr] m distance covered; sp., golf, river: course; ⊕ path; trip, journey.

pardessus [pardə'sy] m overcoat, top-coat.

par-devers [pardə'vɛːr] in the presence of, before; in one's possession; garder qch. ~ soi keep s.th. to o.s.

pardi! † [par'di] int. of course!; rather!

pardon [par'dɔ̃] 1. su./m pardon (a. eccl.); forgiveness; eccl. pilgrimage (in Brittany); 2. int.: ~! excuse me!; ~? I beg your pardon?; **pardonnable** [~dɔ'nabl] forgivable, excusable; **pardonner** [~dɔ'ne] (1a) v/t. pardon, forgive; excuse; je ne pardonne pas que vous l'ayez visité I cannot forgive your having visited him.

pare...: ~**balles** [par'bal] adj./inv. bullet-proof; ~**boue** [~'bu] m/inv. see garde-boue; ~**brise** mot. [~'briːz] m/inv. windscreen, Am. windshield; ~**chocs** mot. [~'ʃɔk] m/inv. bumper; ~**étincelles** [~etɛ̃'sɛl] m/inv. fire-guard; 🔥 spark-catcher; ~**feu** [~'fø] m/inv. forest: fire-break.

pareil, -eille [pa'rɛːj] 1. adj. like, similar; such (a); sans ~ unrivalled, unequalled; 2. su. equal, like; peer; match; su./f rendre la ~eille à pay (s.o.) back in his own coin.

parement [par'mã] m adorning or ornament; cost., a. ⬗ facing; ⬗ stone: face; ⊕, cuis. dressing; kerb-stone; curb-stone.

parent, e [pa'rã, ~'rãːt] su. relative; relation; su./m: ~s pl. parents, father and mother; **parental, e,** m/pl. -aux [parã'tal, ~'to] parental; **parenté** [~rã'te] f relationship, kinship.

parenthèse [parã'tɛːz] f parenthesis, digression; typ. bracket; entre ~s in brackets; fig. incidentally.

parer [pa're] (1a) v/t. ornament, adorn; dress (meat, vegetables); ⚓ clear (the anchor); ⚓ steer clear of, clear; ward off, parry; avoid; pull up (a horse); se ~ deck o.s. out (in, de); fig. show off; v/i.: ~ à provide against or for; obviate (a difficulty); avert (an accident).

pare-soleil [parsɔ'lɛːj] m/inv. sun-visor (a. mot.).

paresse [pa'rɛs] f laziness, idleness; mind, a. 💊 bowels, etc.: sluggishness; **paresseux, -euse** [~rɛ'sø, ~'søːz] 1. adj. sluggish; lazy, idle; 2. su. lazy or idle person; su./m zo. sloth.

pareur m, -euse f ⊕ [pa'rœːr, ~'røːz] finisher, trimmer.

parfaire [par'fɛːr] (4r) v/t. complete, finish; make up (a total of money); **parfait, e** [~'fɛ̃, ~'fɛt] 1. adj. perfect; fig. thorough, utter; ✝ full (payment); F capital; (c'est) ~! splendid!; 2. su./m gramm. perfect; cuis. ice-cream; **parfaitement** [~fɛt'mã] adv. perfectly; thoroughly; ~! precisely!; exactly!

parfois [par'fwa] adv. sometimes, now and then.

parfum [par'fœ̃] m perfume, scent; fragrance; sl. être au ~ be in the know; sl. mettre q. au ~ put s.o. in the picture, wise s.o. on, sur); **parfumer** [~fy'me] (1a) v/t. perfume, scent; se ~ use scent; **parfumerie** [~fym'ri] f perfumery; **parfumeur** m, -euse f ✝ [~fy'mœːr, ~'møːz] perfumer.

pari [pa'ri] m bet, wager; sp. betting; ~ mutuel totalizator system, F tote; **pariade** orn. [~'rjad] f pairing; pairing season; pair; **parier** [~'rje] (1o) vt/i. bet (on, sur); wager.

pariétaire ♀ [parje'tɛːr] f wall-pellitory; **pariétal, e,** m/pl. -aux [~'tal, ~'to] 1. ♀, anat. parietal; paint. mural; 2. su./m anat. parietal bone.

parieur m, -euse f [pa'rjœːr, ~'rjøːz] better, punter.

Parigot m, e f F [pari'go, ~'gɔt] Parisian; **parisien, -enne** [~'zjɛ̃, ~'zjɛn] adj., a. su. ♀ Parisian.

paritaire [pari'tɛːr] adj.: réunion f ~ round-table conference; **parité** [~'te] f parity; equality; ♂ evenness.

parjure [par'ʒyːr] 1. adj. perjured; 2. su. person: perjurer; su./m perjury; **parjurer** [~ʒy're] (1a) v/t.: se ~ perjure o.s.

parking mot. [par'kiŋ] m parking; car park, Am. parking lot.

parlant, e [par'lã, ~'lãːt] speaking (a. fig.); fig. talkative; cin. sound (film); fig. expressive; fig. eloquent, that speaks for itself; **parlé, e** [~'le] spoken (language).

parlement [parlə'mã] m parliament; **parlementaire** ⌊parləmã-'tɛ:r⌋ **1.** *adj.* parliamentary, *Am.* Congressional; *drapeau m* ~ flag of truce; **2.** *su./m* member of parliament, *Am.* Congressman; negotiator; **parlementarisme** *pol.* [~ta'rism] *m* parliamentary government; **parlementer** [~'te] (1a) *v/i.* parley.

parler [par'le] **1.** (1a) *v/i.* speak, talk (to, *à*; of, about de); be on speaking terms (with, *à*); *les faits parlent* the facts speak for themselves; *on m'a parlé de* I was told about; *sans* ~ *de* let alone ...; *v/t.* speak (*a language*); ~ *affaires* (F *boutique, politique, raison*) talk business (F shop, about politics, sense); *se* ~ be spoken (*language*); **2.** *su./m* speech; dialect; way of speaking; **parleur, -euse** [~'lœ:r, ~'lø:z] *su.* talker; **parloir** [~'lwa:r] *m* parlo(u)r; **parlote** F [~'lɔt] *f* chitchat.

parmesan [parmə'zã] *m* Parmesan (cheese).

parmi [par'mi] *prp.* among; amid.

parodie [parɔ'di] *f* parody; skit ([up]on, de); **parodier** [~'dje] (1o) *v/t.* parody, burlesque.

paroi [pa'rwa] *f biol.,* ⊕ *boiler, cylinder, a. rock, tent:* wall; △ partition-wall; *case, stomach, tunnel:* lining; *thea.* flat.

paroisse [pa'rwas] *f* parish; parish church; **paroissial, e,** *m/pl.* **-aux** [parwa'sjal, ~'sjo] parochial; parish-...; **paroissien, -enne** [~'sjɛ̃, ~'sjɛn] *su.* parishioner; *su./m* prayerbook; F *drôle de* ~ queer stick.

parole [pa'rɔl] *f* word; remark; promise, ✕ parole; *fig.* speech; eloquence; saying; *avoir la* ~ have the floor; *donner la* ~ *à q.* call upon s.o. to speak.

parpaing △ [par'pɛ̃] *m* parpen; breeze-block.

Parque *myth.* [park] *f* one of the Fates; *les* ~ the Fates, the Parcae.

parquer [par'ke] (1m) *v/t.* enclose; pen (*cattle*); fold (*sheep*); put (*a horse*) in paddock; *mot.,* ✕ park; *v/i. a. se* ~ park; **parquet** [~'kɛ] *m* △ floor(ing); *mirror:* backing; ⚖ public prosecutor's department; ⚖ well; ✝ official market; *bourse:* Ring; **parqueter** ⊕ [parkə'te] (1c) *v/t.* lay a floor in (*a room*); parquet; **parqueterie** ⊕ [~'tri] *f* laying of

floors; ~ *en mosaïque* inlaid floor; inlaying; **parqueteur** ⊕ [~'tœ:r] *m* parquet-layer.

parrain [pa'rɛ̃] *m* godfather; sponsor (*a. fig.*).

parricide [pari'sid] **1.** *adj.* parricidal; **2.** *su. person:* parricide; *su./m crime:* parricide.

parsemer [parsə'me] (1d) *v/t.* strew, sprinkle (with, de); *fig.* stud, spangle.

part [pa:r] *f* share (*a.* ✝); part; portion (*a.* ⚖); place; *food:* helping, *cake:* piece; *à* ~ apart, separately; *à* ~ *cela* apart from that; except for that; *à* ~ *entière* full (*member etc.*); entirely, fully; *à* ~ *soi* in one's own heart, to o.s.; *autre* ~ elsewhere; *d'autre* ~ besides; *de la* ~ *de* on behalf of; from; *de ma* ~ from me; on my part; *de* ~ *en* ~ through and through; *de* ~ *et d'autre* on both sides (of, de), on either side; *d'une ... d'autre* ~ on the one hand ... on the other hand; *faire* ~ *de qch. à q.* inform s.o. of s.th.; *faire la* ~ *de* take into account; *nulle* ~ nowhere; *pour ma* ~ as to me, I for one; *prendre* ~ *à* take part in, join in; *quelque* ~ somewhere; **partage** [par'ta:ʒ] *m* division, sharing; ⚖ *a. pol.* partition; share, portion, lot (*a. fig.*); *geog. ligne f de* ~ *des eaux* watershed, *Am.* divide; *échoir en* ~ *à q.* fall to s.o.'s lot; **partager** [~ta'ʒe] (11) *v/t.* divide (up); share (*a. fig. an opinion*); *se* ~ be divided; differ; *être bien (mal) partagé* be well (ill) provided for *or* endowed.

partance ⚓, ✈ [par'tã:s] *f* departure; *en* ~ *pour* (bound) for.

partant¹ [par'tã] *cj.* therefore, hence.

partant² [par'tã] *m* departing traveller; *party leaving; sp.* starter, runner.

partenaire [partə'nɛ:r] *m* partner (*a. sp., cin., etc.*).

parterre [par'tɛ:r] *m* ✿ flower-bed; *thea.* pit.

parti¹, e [par'ti] away; gone; F tipsy; ... *est bien (mal)* ~ ... had a good (bad) start.

parti² [par'ti] *m pol., fig.* party; *fig.* side; *marriage:* match; *fig.* choice, decision, option; *fig.* course of action, solution; ~ *pris* bias, set purpose; *prendre* ~ (*pour*) take sides (with); *prendre un* ~ come to a decision; *prendre le* ~ *de* (*inf.*) decide to (*inf.*); *prendre son* ~ *de* resign o.s. to; *tirer* ~ *de* turn (*s.th.*) to account; utilize; use; **partial, e**, *m/pl.* -**aux** [~'sjal, ~'sjo] biased; partial (to, *envers*); **partialité** [~sjali'te] *f* partiality (for, to *envers*); bias.

participation [partisipa'sjõ] *f* participation; ✝, *a. fig.* share (in, *à*); ✝ ~ *majoritaire* controlling interest; **participe** *gramm.* [~'sip] *m* participle; **participer** [~si'pe] (1a) *v/i.* ~ *à* participate, (have a) share (in, *à*); take part (in, *à*); ~ *de* partake of; resemble.

particulariser [partikylari'ze] (1a) *v/t.* particularize; specify; *se* ~ (*par*) be distinguished (by); **particularité** [~'te] *f* particularity; (distinctive) feature; characteristic.

particule [parti'kyl] *f* particle (*a. phys., a. gramm.*).

particulier, -ère [partiky'lje,~'ljɛːr] **1.** *adj.* particular, special; unusual; private (*collection, room, etc.*); **2.** *su.* private individual; *su./m* private life; *en* ~ privately; particularly.

partie [par'ti] *f* part (*a. ♪*); *pleasure, hunt., a.* ♟: party; *cricket, foot., tennis:* match; ✝ line of business; ♟ ~ *civile* plaintiff; ✝ ~ *simple* (*double*) single (double) entry; *en grande* ~ largely; *en* ~ in part, partly; *faire* ~ *de* be one of, belong to; **partiel, -elle** [~'sjɛl] partial, incomplete.

partir [par'tiːr] (2b) *v/i.* go (away); start; leave (for, *pour*); set out; go off (*a. gun etc.*); *hunt.* rise; come off (*button etc.*); ~ *en voyage* go on a journey; *à* ~ *de* (starting) from.

partisan, e [parti'zã, ~'zan] **1.** *su.* partisan, follower; supporter, advocate; *j'en suis* ~ I am (all) for it; *su./m* ✗ soldier: guerilla; *guerre f de* ~*s* guerilla warfare; **2.** *adj.* party ...

partitif, -ve *gramm.* [parti'tif,~'tiːv] partitive (*article*).   [quarter.]

partition [parti'sjõ] *f* ♪ score; ▨]

partout [par'tu] *adv.* everywhere; ~ *où* wherever; *rien* ~ *tennis:* love all.

partouze *sl.* [par'tuːz] *f* orgy.

paru, e [pa'ry] *p.p. of paraître.*

parure [pa'ryːr] *f* adornment; ornament; *jewels etc.:* set; ⊕ parings *pl.*

parus [pa'ry] *1st p. sg. p.s. of paraître.*

parution [pary'sjõ] *f* book: publication.

parvenir [parvə'niːr] (2h) *v/i.:* ~ *à* arrive; reach; succeed in (doing s.th., *faire qch.*); **parvenu** *m*, **e** *f* [~'ny] upstart.

parvis [par'vi] *m* ⚔ square (*in front of church*); *bibl., a. fig.* court.

pas [pɑ] **1.** *su./m* step (*a. dancing, a. of staircase*), pace, gait, walk; footprint; *door:* threshold; *geog.* pass(age); ⚓, *fig.* straits *pl.*; ⊕ screw: thread; *fig.* move; distance (*between seats, rows, etc.*); *fig.* precedence; *fig.* difficulty, obstacle; ~ *à* ~ step by step; ~ *cadencé* measured step; ✗, *sp.* ~ *gymnastique* double; *à grands* ~ apace, quickly; *mot. aller au* ~ go dead slow; *à* ~ *de loup* stealthily; *au* ~ at a walking pace; *faux* ~ slip (*a. fig.*); *fig.* (social) blunder; *geog. le* ~ *de Calais* the Straits *pl.* of Dover; ~ *de porte* key money; *ceder le* ~ *à* give way to; *être dans un mauvais* ~ be in a bad patch; *prendre le* ~ *sur* take the lead from, outstrip; ✗, *sp. marquer le* ~ mark time; **2.** *adv.* not; *ne* ... *pas* not; *ne* ... *pas de* no; *ne* ... *pas un* not (a single) one; *ne* ... *pas non plus* nor or not ... either.

pascal, e, *m/pl.* -**als**, -**aux** [pas'kal, ~'ko] paschal; Easter (*vacation*).

pas-d'âne ♀ [pɑ'dɑːn] *m/inv.* coltsfoot.

pasquinade † [paski'nad] *f* lampoon.

passable [pɑ'sabl] passable, acceptable; middling; *mention f* ~ *examination:* pass; **passade** F [~'sad] *f* passing fancy; F brief love affair; **passage** [~'saːʒ] *m* passage (*a. in a book*); ⚔, *mountains, river, etc.*: crossing; way; *mountain:* pass; ⚔ arcade; ✍ flow; *fig.* transition; ⚔ ~ *à niveau* level crossing, *Am.* grade crossing; *psych.* ~ *à vide* blank; ~ *clouté* pedestrian crossing, *Am.* crosswalk; ~ *souterrain* subway; ~ *supérieur* railway bridge; *de* ~ migratory (*bird*); *fig.* passing, casual; *être de* ~ *à* be passing through (*a town etc.*), be in (*a town etc.*) at the moment; **passager, -ère** [~sa'ʒe, ~'ʒɛːr] **1.** *adj.* of passage (*bird*); passing (*a. fig.*); **2.** *su.* ⚓, ✈ passenger; **passant, e** [~'sã, ~'sãːt] **1.** *su.* passer-by; **2.** *adj.* busy, frequented (*road*); **passavant** [~sa'vã] *m* ⚓ gangway; *admin.* permit; *customs:* transire.

passe [pɑːs] *f* ⚓, ⚔, *fencing, foot:*

pass; *bonne* (*mauvaise*) ~ good (bad) position; *en* ~ *de* (*inf.*) in a fair way to (*inf.*), on the point of (*ger.*); *mot m de* ~ password.

passé, e [pɑ'se] **1.** *su.*/*m* past; ⚖ record; *gramm.* past (tense); **2.** *adj.* past; over; faded (*colour*); last (*week etc.*); **3.** *prp.* after, beyond.

passe...: ~-**bouillon** *cuis.* [pɑsbu-'jɔ̃] *m*/*inv.* soup-strainer; ~**carreau** [~ka'ro] *m* sleeve-board; ~-**debout** *hist.* [~də'bu] *m*/*inv.* transire; ~-**droit** [~'drwa] undeserved privilege; unfair promotion.

passéisme [pase'ism] *m* clinging to the past; **passéiste** [~'ist] *adj.* (*a. su.* person) clinging to the past.

passe...: ~-**lacet** [~la'sɛ] *m* bodkin; ~-**lait** *cuis.* [~'lɛ] *m*/*inv.* milk strainer.

passement [pas'mɑ̃] *m cost.* lace; *chair etc.*; braid; **passementer** [~mɑ̃'te] (1a) *v/t.* trim with lace; braid (*furniture*); **passementier** *m*, **-ère** *f* [~mɑ̃'tje, ~'tjɛːr] dealer in trimmings.

passe...: ~-**montagne** [pɑsmɔ̃'taɲ] *m* Balaclava helmet; ~-**partout** [~par'tu] **1.** *su.*/*m*/*inv.* passkey, master key; *phot.* slip-in mount; ⊕ crosscut saw; compass-saw; **2.** *adj.*/*inv.* all-purpose; general-purpose; *pej.* nondescript; ~-**passe** [~'pas] *m*/*inv.* legerdemain, sleight-of-hand; *tour m de* ~ conjuring trick; ~-**plats** [~'pla] *m*/*inv.* service-hatch; ~**poil** *cost.* [~'pwal] *m* piping, braid; ~**port** [~'pɔːr] *m admin.* passport; ⚓ sea-letter; ~-**purée** *cuis.* [~py're] *m*/*inv.* potato masher.

passer [pɑ'se] (1a) **1.** *v/i.* pass (*a. time*); go (to, *à*); be moved (*pupil*); become, ✕ be promoted; fade (*colour*), vanish; pass away, die; *fig.* wear off (*success etc.*); go by, elapse (*time*); be transmitted *or* handed down (*heritage, tradition*); ⚖ fly (over, *sur*); ⚖ ~ *à la douane* go through the customs; ~ *chez q.* call at s.o.'s *or* on s.o.; ~ *en proverbe* become proverbial; *mot.* ~ *en seconde* change into second gear; ~ *par* go through; *road:* go over (*a mountain*); ~ *pour* be thought to be, be considered (*s.th.*), seem; ~ *sur* overlook (*a fault*); *faire* ~ pass (*s.th.*) on (to, *à*); while away (*the time*); get rid of; *j'en passe I*

am skipping over many items; *laisser* ~ let (*s.o.*) pass; miss (*an opportunity*); *passons!* no more about it!; *se faire* ~ *pour* pose as; **2.** *v/t.* pass; cross; go past; hand (over) (to, *à*); slip (*s.th. into a pocket*); slip on, put on (*a garment*); omit, leave out; overlook, excuse (*a mistake*); spend (*time*); sit for (*an examination*); vent (*one's anger*) (on, *sur*); *cuis.* strain (*a liquid*), sift (*flour*); ✝ place (*an order*); *parl.* pass (*a bill*); ~ *en fraude* smuggle in; *elle ne passera pas le jour* she will not live out the day; *se* ~ pass, go by (*time*); happen, take place; pass away, cease; abate (*anger*); fade (*colour*); *se* ~ *de* do without (*s.th., qch.; ger., inf.*).

passereau *orn.* [pas'ro] *m* sparrow.
passerelle [pas'rɛl] *f* footbridge; ✕ gangway; catwalk; ⊕ crane: platform; ⚓ bridge; *fig.* (inter)link.
passe...: ~-**temps** [pas'tɑ̃] *m*/*inv.* pastime; hobby; ~-**thé** [~'te] *m*/*inv.* tea-strainer.
passeur [pɑ'sœːr] *m* ferryman; smuggler.
passible ⚖ [pa'sibl] liable (to, *de*).
passif, -ve [pa'sif, ~'siːv] **1.** *adj.* passive (*a. gramm.*); *fig.* blind (*obedience*); *défense f* ~*ve* Civil Defence; Air Raid Precautions *pl.*; ✝ *dettes f*/*pl.* ~*ves* liabilities; **2.** *su.*/*m gramm.* passive (voice); ✝ liabilities *pl.*
passion [pɑ'sjɔ̃] *f* passion (for, *de*) (*a.* ✞, *eccl., a. fig.*); **passionnant, e** [pasjɔ'nɑ̃, ~'nɑ̃ːt] thrilling; fascinating; **passionné, e** [~'ne] **1.** *adj.* passionate, impassioned (for, *pour*); enthusiastic (about, *de*); **2.** *su.* enthusiast, F fan; **passionnel, -elle** [~'nɛl] *adj.*: ⚖ *crime m* ~ crime due to sexual passion; **passionner** [~'ne] (1a) *v/t.* rouse, excite; *fig.* fascinate; *se* ~ become passionately fond (of, *pour*); get excited.
passivité [pasivi'te] *f* passivity.
passoire *cuis.* [pɑ'swaːr] *f* strainer.
pastel [pas'tɛl] *m* crayon; pastel drawing; *bleu m* ~ pastel blue.
pasteur [pas'tœːr] *m* shepherd; *eccl.* pastor.
pasteuriser [pastœri'ze] (1a) *v/t.* pasteurize (*milk*).
pastiche [pas'tiʃ] *m* pastiche; par-

ody; **pasticher** [ˌti'ʃe] (1a) v/t. copy the style of; parody.

pastille [pas'ti:j] f pastille, lozenge.

pastis [pas'tis] m aniseed aperitif; F muddle.

pastoral, e, m/pl. **-aux** [pastɔ'ral, ˌ'ro] **1.** adj. pastoral; episcopal (ring); **2.** su./f pastoral; **pastorat** [ˌ'ra] m pastorate.

pastourelle [pastu'rɛl] f poem: pastoral.

pat [pat] su./m, a. adj./m stalemate.

pataquès [pata'kɛːs] m faulty liaison (in speech).

patate [pa'tat] f ♥ sweet potato; F spud (= potato); sl. idiot, fathead.

patati* [pata'ti] int.: et ~ et patata and so forth and so on.

patatras* [pata'tra] int. crash!

pataud, e [pa'to, ˌ'to:d] **1.** su. clumsy puppy; F lout; **2.** adj. clumsy, loutish.

patauger [pato'ʒe] (1l) v/i. flounder (a. fig.); paddle, wade (in sea); **pataugeoire** [ˌ'ʒwaːr] f paddling pool.

pâte [pɑ:t] f paste; dough; paper: pulp; fig. stuff; fig. type; ~s pl. alimentaires Italian pastes; ~ dentifrice tooth-paste; F une bonne ~ a good sort; F une ~ molle a softy, a spineless individual; vivre comme un coq en ~ live like a fighting cock; **pâté** [pɑ'te] m cuis. pie; liver: paste; fig. trees etc.: clump, cluster; ink: blot; ~ de maisons block (of houses); ~ (de sable) sandcastle; **pâtée** [ˌ] f hens: mash; dog food; fig. coarse food; F hiding, threshing.

patelin F [pat'lɛ̃] m native village; small place.

patelinage [patli'na:ʒ] m smooth words pl., F blarney; **pateliner** F [ˌli'ne] (1a) v/t. cajole (s.o.); wheedle; v/i. blarney; **patelinerie** [ˌlin'ri] f see patelinage.

patelle [pa'tɛl] f zo., anat., archeol. patella; zo. limpet, barnacle.

patène eccl. [pa'tɛn] f paten.

patenôtre [pat'noːtr] f Lord's prayer; ⚒ bucket elevator; ~s pl. rosary sg., F beads.

patent, e [pa'tɑ̃, ˌ'tɑ̃:t] **1.** adj. patent; obvious; hist. Lettres f/pl. ~es Letters patent; **2.** su./f licence; ♣ etc. tax; ⚓ (a. ~e de santé) bill of health; **patenté, e** [ˌtɑ̃'te] **1.** adj. licensed; **2.** su. licensee.

pater eccl. [pa'tɛːr] m/inv. Lord's prayer; paternoster.

patère [ˌ] f hat-peg, coat-peg; curtain-hook.

paterne [pa'tɛrn] benevolent; **paternel, -elle** [patɛr'nɛl] paternal; fatherly; **paternité** [ˌni'te] f paternity, fatherhood.

pâteux, -euse [pɑ'tø, ˌ'tø:z] pasty; cloudy (jewel); thick (voice etc.); coated (tongue).

pathétique [pate'tik] **1.** adj. pathetic (a. anat.), moving, touching; **2.** su./m pathos, the pathetic.

pathogène ⚕ [patɔ'ʒɛn] pathogenic; **pathologie** ⚕ [ˌlɔ'ʒi] f pathology; **pathologique** ⚕ [ˌlɔ'ʒik] pathological.

pathos [pa'tɔs] m pathos; emotionalism.

patibulaire [patiby'lɛːr] gallows...; fig. hang-dog (look).

patience [pa'sjɑ̃:s] f patience; forbearance; (jig-saw) puzzle; prendre ~ be patient; **patient, e** [ˌ'sjɑ̃, ˌ'sjɑ̃:t] adj., a. su. patient; **patienter** [ˌsjɑ̃'te] (1a) v/i. be patient; wait patiently.

patin [pa'tɛ̃] m skate; sledge: runner; ⊕ brake, wheel: shoe; brake-block; ⊕ rail: flange; staircase: sleeper; ~ à roulettes roller-skate; **patinage** [ˌti'na:ʒ] m skating; wheel, belt: slipping.

patine [pa'tin] f bronze: patina.

patiner¹ [pati'ne] (1a) v/t. give a patina to.

patiner² [pati'ne] (1a) v/i. skate; slip (wheel, belt); skid (wheel); fig. get nowhere (fast), make no progress; **patinette** [ˌ'nɛt] f scooter; **patineur** m, **-euse** f [ˌ'nœːr, ˌ'nøːz] skater; **patinoire** [ˌ'nwaːr] f skating-rink.

pâtir [pɑ'tiːr] (2a) v/i. suffer (from, de); vous en pâtirez you will rue it.

pâtisser [pɑti'se] (1a) v/i. make pastry; **pâtisserie** [ˌtis'ri] f pastry; pastry shop; pastry-making; cakes pl.; **pâtissier** m, **-ère** f [ˌti'sje, ˌ'sjɛːr] pastry-cook.

patois [pa'twa] m dialect, patois; F jargon.

patouiller F [patu'je] (1a) v/i. flounder, splash (in the mud).

patraque F [pa'trak] **1.** su./f worn-out machine; person: old crock;

2. *adj.* seedy (*person*); worn-out (*machine*).

pâtre [pɑ:tr] *m* shepherd; herdsman.

patriarcal, e, *m/pl.* -aux [patriar-'kal, ‿'ko] patriarchal; **patriarche** [‿'arʃ] *m* patriarch (*a. eccl.*).

patricien, -enne [patri'sjɛ̃, ‿'sjɛn] *adj., a. su.* patrician.

patrie [pa'tri] *f* fatherland; native or mother country; *fig.* home.

patrimoine [patri'mwan] *m* patrimony, inheritance; **patrimonial, e,** *m/pl.* -aux [‿mɔ'njal, ‿'njo] patrimonial.

patriote [patri'ɔt] **1.** *adj.* patriotic (*person*); **2.** *su.* patriot; **patriotique** [‿ɔ'tik] patriotic (*sentiments, song, etc.*); **patriotisme** [‿ɔ'tism] *m* patriotism.

patron [pa'trɔ̃] *m* master, F boss; head (*of a firm*); *hotel*: proprietor; protector; *eccl.* patron (saint); *cost.* pattern; ⊕ template; ✝ model; **patronage** [patrɔ'na:ʒ] *m* patronage (*a.* ✝); support; *eccl.* young people's club; **patronal, e,** *m/pl.* -aux [‿'nal, ‿'no] *eccl.* patronal (*festival*); patron (saint); ⊕ employers' ...; **patronat** [‿'na] *m* protection; ✝ *coll.* employers *pl.*; **patronne** [pa'trɔn] *f* mistress; protectress; *eccl.* patroness; **patronner** [patrɔ'ne] (1a) *v/t.* patronize, sponsor, support; **patronnesse** [‿'nɛs] *adj./f* patroness.

patrouille ⚔ [pa'tru:j] *f* patrol; **patrouiller** ⚔ [patru'je] (1a) *v/i.* (go on) patrol; **patrouilleur** [‿'jœːr] *m* ⚓ patrol-boat; ⚔ scout; ⚔ member of a patrol.

patte [pat] *f zo.* paw (*a.* F = *hand*); *orn.* foot; *insect*: leg; ⊕ cramp, hook; ⊕ flange; clamp; ⚓ anchor: fluke; *cost.* strap; *envelope, a. pocket*: flap; F authority, power; F ‿s *pl. de mouche writing*: scrawl; **faire ~ de velours** draw in its claws (*cat*); *fig.* speak s.o. fair; F **tomber sous la ~ de q.** fall into s.o.'s clutches; **‿d'oie,** *pl.* **‿s-d'oie** [‿'dwa] *f* crossroads *pl.*; *wrinkle*: crow's-foot.

pâturage [pɑty'ra:ʒ] *m* grazing; pasture(-land); pasturage; **pâture** [‿'ty:r] *f* fodder; food (*a. fig.*); pasture; **pâturer** [‿ty're] (1a) *vt/i.* graze.

pâturin ♀ [pɑty'rɛ̃] *m* meadow-grass, *Am.* spear-grass.

paturon [paty'rɔ̃] *m horse*: pastern.

paume [po:m] *f* palm of hand.

paumé, e F [po'me] miserable, wretched; *fig.* lost, at a loss; *a. su.* down(-)and(-)out; derelict.

paupérisme [pope'rism] *m* pauperism.

paupière [po'pjɛːr] *f* eyelid.

paupiette *cuis.* [po'pjɛt] *f* (beef- or veal-)olive.

pause [po:z] *f* pause, break; *foot.* half time; ♩ rest; (*lunch- etc.*)interval; ~-café coffee break; **pauser** [po'ze] (1a) *v/i.* pause; ♩ dwell (*on a note*).

pauvre [po:vr] **1.** *adj.* poor; needy; scanty (*vegetation*); *fig.* slight (*chance*); unfortunate; **2.** *su./m* poor man; *admin.* pauper; **pauvresse** [po'vrɛs] *f* poor woman; *admin.* pauper; **pauvret** *m*, **-ette** *f fig.* [‿'vrɛ, ‿'vrɛt] *person*: poor little thing; **pauvreté** [‿vrə'te] *f* poverty (*a. fig.*), destitution.

pavage [pa'va:ʒ] *m* paving; pavement.

pavaner [pava'ne] (1a) *v/t.*: **se ~** strut; F show off.

pavé [pa've] *m* paving-stone, paving-block; pavement; highway; *fig. the streets pl.*; F thick (boring) book; heavy tome; **pavement** [pav'mã] *m* see *pavage*; **paver** [pa've] (1a) *v/t.* pave; **paveur** [‿'vœ:r] *m* paver.

pavillon [pavi'jɔ̃] *m* pavilion; lodge, house; ✝ *bed*: canopy; *gramophone, loud-speaker*: horn; *funnel*: mouth; *teleph.* mouthpiece; ⚓ flag, colo(u)rs *pl.*; ♩ *trumpet*: bell; *anat.* auricle, external ear.

pavois [pa'vwa] *m hist.* (body-)shield; ⚓ bulwark; *coll.* flags *pl.*; **élever sur le ~** *hist.* raise to the throne; *fig.* extol; **pavoiser** [‿vwa'ze] (1a) *v/t.* deck with flags; *v/i.* put out (the) flags; *a. fig.* wave the banners.

pavot ♀ [pa'vo] *m* poppy.

payable [pɛ'jabl] payable; **payant, e** [‿'jã, ‿'jã:t] **1.** *adj* paying; charged for; with a charge for admission; *fig.* profitable; **2.** *su.* payer; ✝ drawee; **paye** [pɛ:j] *f see paie;* **payement** [pɛj'mã] *m see paiement;* **payer** [pɛ'je] (1i) *v/t.* pay; pay for (*an article, a. fig.*); ✝ defray (*expenses*); settle (*a debt*); *fig.* reward (for, de); ~ **cher** pay dear, *fig.* be sorry for; **~ de retour** reciprocate (*an affection etc.*); **trop payé** overpaid; **trop peu payé** underpaid; **se ~** be paid *or* recompensed; se ~ de paroles be satisfied by mere words; **payeur, -euse** [~'jœːr, ~'jøːz] su. payer; su./m✕, ♣ paymaster; bank: teller.

pays [pe'i] m country; land; region; home, native land; F fellow-countryman; mal m du ~ homesickness; vin m du ~ local wine; **paysage** [pei'zaːʒ] m landscape, scenery; fig. scene; **paysagiste** [~za'ʒist] m landscape painter; landscape gardener; **paysan, -anne** [~'zɑ̃, ~'zan] adj., a. su. peasant, rustic; **paysannat** [~za'na] m, **paysannerie** [~zan'ri] f peasantry; farmers pl.; **payse** [pe'iz] f fellow-countrywoman.

péage [pe'aːʒ] m toll; tollgate; autoroute f à ~ toll motorway, Am. turnpike (road); **péagiste** [pea'ʒist] su. toll collector.

peau [po] f ✝, anat., a. fruit, sausage, milk: skin; ✝ pelt, hide; ✝ leather; fruit: peel; faire ~ neuve change clothes; fig. turn over a new leaf; ♀-**Rouge**, pl. ♀x-**Rouges** [~'ruːʒ] m Red Indian, redskin.

peccable [pɛk'kabl] liable to sin.

peccadille [pɛka'diːj] f peccadillo.

pechblende ⚒, phys. [pɛʃ'blɛ̃ːd] f pitchblende.

pêche[1] ♀ [pɛːʃ] f peach.

pêche[2] [~] f fishing; fishery; catch; ~ à la ligne angling; aller à la ~ go fishing.

péché [pe'ʃe] m sin; fig. indiscretion, error; ~ mignon little weakness; **pécher** [~] (1f) v/i. sin; fig. offend (against, contre); fig. err.

pêcher[1] [pɛ'ʃe] m peach-tree.

pêcher[2] [pɛ'ʃe] (1a) v/t. fish for; drag up (a corpse); fig. find, pick up; v/i.: ~ à la ligne angle; **pêcherie** [pɛʃ'ri] f fishing-ground.

pécheur, -eresse [pe'ʃœːr, peʃ'rɛs] 1. adj. sinning; sinful; 2. su. sinner.

pêcheur, -euse [pɛ'ʃœːr, ~'ʃøːz] 1. adj. fishing; 2. su./m fisherman; su./f fisherwoman.

pectoral, e, m/pl. -**aux** [pɛkto'ral, ~'ro] pectoral; cough-(lozenge, syrup).

péculat [peky'la] m embezzlement, peculation; **péculateur** [~la'tœːr] m embezzler, peculator.

pécule [pe'kyl] m savings pl., F nest-egg;✕, ♣ gratuity.

pécuniaire [peky'njɛːr] pecuniary, financial.

pédagogie [pedagɔ'ʒi] f pedagogy; **pédagogique** [~gɔ'ʒik] pedagogic; **pédagogue** [~'gɔg] su. pedagogue.

pédale [pedal] f cycle, a. ♪: pedal; ⊕ treadle; sl. queer, gay; mot. ~ d'embrayage clutch (pedal); sl. perdre les ~s get all mixed up; **pedaler** [peda'le] (1a) v/i. pedal; F cycle; **pédaleur, m, -euse** f F [~'lœːr, ~'løːz] pedalist; cyclist; **pédalier** [~'lje] m cycle: crank gear; ♪ pedal-board; **pédalo** F [~'lo] m pedal-craft.

pédant, e [pe'dɑ̃, ~'dɑ̃ːt] 1. adj. pedantic, priggish; 2. su. pedant, prig; **pédanterie** [pedɑ̃'tri] f pedantry; priggishness; **pédantesque** [~'tɛsk] pedantic; **pédantisme** [~'tism] m see pédanterie.

pédé sl. [pe'de] m gay, queer.

pédestre [pe'dɛstr] pedestrian; **pédestrement** [~dɛstrə'mɑ̃] adv. on foot.

pédiatre ⚕ [pe'djaːtr] m p(a)ediatrist; **pédiatrie** ⚕ [~dja'tri] f p(a)ediatrics pl.

pédiculaire [pediky'lɛːr] pediculous, lousy; ⚕ maladie f ~ phthiriasis; **pédicule** biol. [~'kyl] m pedicle; **pédiculé, e** [~ky'le] pediculate.

pédicure [pedi'kyːr] su. chiropodist.

pédologie [pedɔlɔ'ʒi] f subject: child psychology.

pègre [pɛːgr] f coll. thieves pl., underworld, gangsterdom.

peignage tex. [pɛ'ɲaːʒ] m combing, carding; **peigne** [pɛɲ] m comb (a. ⊕); shell-fish: scallop, clam; tex. wool: card; hemp: hackle; ~ de chignon back-comb; se donner un coup de ~ run a comb through one's hair; fig. passer qch. au ~ fin go through or over s.th. with a fine-tooth comb; **peigné, e** [pɛ'ɲe] 1. adj. combed; fig. affected (style); bien ~ trim; mal ~ unkempt; 2. su./m tex. worsted; su./f tex. cardful (of wool etc.); F fig. thrashing; **peigner** [~'ɲe] (1a) v/t. comb (a. tex.); tex. card (wool), hackle (hemp); polish (one's style); **peigneur, -euse** tex. [~'ɲœːr, ~'ɲøːz] su. wool-comber; su./f wool-combing machine; hackling-machine; **peignier** [~'ɲje] m comb-maker; ✝ comb-seller; **peignoir** [~'ɲwaːr] m (lady's) dressing gown; morning wrapper; ~ de bain bath-wrap; **peignures** [ˌⁿˈɲyːr] f/pl. combings.

peinard, e F [pɛˈnaːr, ˌˈnard] adj. quiet; cushy (job etc.); se tenir (or rester) ˌ keep quiet or out of trouble.

peindre [pɛ̃ːdr] (4m) v/t. paint; ˌ au pistolet spray (with paint); fig. ˌ en beau paint (things) in rosy colo(u)rs; F se ˌ make up.

peine [pɛn] f sorrow; trouble, difficulty; effort; punishment; pain; à ˌ hardly, scarcely; à grand-ˌ with difficulty; en valoir la ˌ be worth while; être en ˌ de be at a loss to; faire de la ˌ à hurt (s.o.); sous ˌ de under pain of; **peiner** [pɛˈne] (1a) v/t. pain, hurt, grieve; fig. tire; v/i. toil; labo(u)r (a. mot. engine).

peintre [pɛ̃ːtr] m painter; artist; ˌ en bâtiments house: painter and decorator, house-painter; femme f ˌ woman artist; **peinture** [pɛ̃ˈtyːr] f painting; paint(work); ˌ au pistolet spray-painting; prenez garde à la ˌ! wet paint!; **peinturer** [ˌtyˈre] (1a) v/t. paint; daub; **peinturlurer** F [ˌtyrlyˈre] (1a) v/t. daub (with colo[u]r); paint in all the colo(u)rs of the rainbow.

péjoratif, -ve [peʒɔraˈtif, ˌˈtiːv] pejorative; disparaging; au sens ˌ in a disparaging sense.

pékin [peˈkɛ̃] m F ✕ civilian; F ✕ en ˌ in civvies.

pékiné, e tex. [pekiˈne] candy-striped.

pelade ✤ [pəˈlad] f alopecia.

pelage [pəˈlaːʒ] m pelt, coat, fur; **pelé, e** [pəˈle] 1. adj. peeled (fruit, tree-bark); bald (person); 2. su. F bald-pate, bald person.

pêle-mêle [pɛlˈmɛl] 1. adv. higgledy-piggledy, in confusion; 2. su./m/inv. disorder, jumble.

peler [pəˈle] (1d) vt/i. peel.

pèlerin, e [pɛlˈrɛ̃, ˌˈrin] su. pilgrim; su./m orn. peregrine falcon; icht. basking shark; su./f cost. cape; **pèlerinage** [ˌriˈnaːʒ] m (place of) pilgrimage; aller en ˌ go on a pilgrimage.

pélican [peliˈkɑ̃] m orn. pelican; ⊕ bench: holdfast. [coat.\

pelisse [pəˈlis] f pelisse, fur-lined]

pellagre ✤ [pelˈlaːgr] f pellagra.

pelle [pɛl] f ⊕ shovel, scoop; oar: blade; (child's) spade; ˌ à poussière dust-pan; ⊕ ˌ mécanique grab;

shovel-dredger; F fig. ramasser une ˌ come a cropper (off a horse, a. fig.); have a spill (off a cycle); **pelletée** [ˌˈte] f shovelful, spadeful; **pelleter** [ˌˈte] (1c) v/t. shovel; turn with a shovel.

pelleterie [pɛlˈtri] f ⊕ fur-making; ✝ fur-trade; coll. peltry.

pelleteur m, **-euse** f [pɛlˈtœːr, ˌˈtøːz] shovel excavator.

pelletier m, **-ère** f [pɛlˈtje, ˌˈtjɛːr] furrier.

pelliculaire [pellikyˈlɛːr] pellicular (metal); **pellicule** [ˌˈkyl] f (thin) skin; phot., a. ice, oil: film; scalp: dandruff, scurf.

pelotage [pəlɔˈtaːʒ] m string, wool, etc.: winding into balls; billiards: knocking the balls about; F petting; **pelote** [ˌˈlɔt] f string, wool: ball; cotton-wool: wad; (pin) cushion; game: pelota; fig. faire sa ˌ feather one's nest; make one's pile; **peloter** [pəlɔˈte] (1a) v/t. ✝ wind (s.th.) into a ball; F handle (s.o.) roughly; F pet (a girl); F paw (a woman); F flatter (s.o.); F se ˌ pet, neck; **peloton** [ˌˈtɔ̃] m string, wool: ball; ✕ squad, platoon; fig. group; sp. runners: bunch, field, main body; ˌ de tête sp. leaders pl. (a. fig.), fig. front-runners pl.; ˌ d'exécution firing squad or party; **pelotonner** [ˌtɔˈne] (1a) v/t. wind (s.th.) into a ball; se ˌ curl up, roll o.s. up; huddle together.

pelouse [pəˈluːz] f lawn; grass-plot; turf, a. golf: green.

peluche tex. [pəˈlyʃ] f plush; ours m en ˌ teddy bear; **pelucher** [pəlyˈʃe] (1a) v/i. become fluffy; shed fluff; **pelucheux, -euse** [ˌˈʃø, ˌˈʃøːz] shaggy; fluffy.

pelure [pəˈlyːr] f fruit: peel; vegetable: paring, peeling; cheese: rind; F overcoat, outer garment(s pl.).

pénal, e, m/pl. **-aux** [peˈnal, ˌˈno] penal; penalty (clause); **pénalisation** sp. [penalizaˈsjɔ̃] f penalizing; area: penalty; **pénalité** sp., a. ⚖ [ˌˈte] f penalty; **penalty** foot. [peˈnalˈti] m penalty (kick).

pénates [peˈnat] m/pl. penates, household gods; fig. home sg.

penaud, e [pəˈno, ˌˈnoːd] shame-faced, abashed, crestfallen.

penchant, e [pɑ̃ˈʃɑ̃, ˌˈʃɑ̃ːt] 1. adj. sloping, leaning; fig. declining; 2. su./m slope; (hill)side; fig. inclination, propensity (to, for *à*), tendency; *fig.* fondness (for s.o., *pour q.*); **pencher** [˷ˈʃe] (1a) *v/t.* tip, tilt (*s.th.*); bend (*one's head*); se ˷ lean (over); bend (down); *v/i.* tilt, lean (over); be slanting; *fig.* se ˷ *sur* study, look into; *fig.* incline, be inclined (to, *vers*).

pendable [pãˈdabl] † meriting the gallows; *fig.* outrageous; **pendaison** [dɛˈzɔ̃] *f death:* hanging; **pendant, e** [˷ˈdã, ˷ˈdã:t] 1. *adj.* hanging; lop-(*ears*); flabby (*cheeks*); ⚖ pending; 2. *su./m* pendant; *fig.* fellow, counterpart; 3. *pendant prp.* during; for (*2 days, 3 miles*); ˷ *que* while, whilst; **pendard, e** F [˷ˈda:r, ˷ˈdard] *su.* gallows-bird; rogue; *su./f* hussy.

pendeloque [pãdˈlɔk] *f* ear-drop; F *cloth:* shred; ˷s *pl.* pendants; *chandelier:* drops; **pendentif** [pãdãˈtif] *m necklace, a.* ⚙: pendant; △ pendentive; en ˷ hanging; **penderie** [˷ˈdri] *f* hanging-wardrobe; hanging cupboard.

pendiller [pãdiˈje] (1a) *v/i.* dangle.

pendre [pã:dr] (4a) *v/t/i.* hang (on, from *à*); *dire pire* (*or pis*) *que* ˷ *de q.* sling mud at s.o.; run s.o. down; **pendu, e** [pãˈdy] 1. *p.p. of pendre;* 2. *adj.* hanged; hanging (on, from *à*) 3. *su.* person who has been hanged *or* who has hanged himself.

pendulaire [pãdyˈlɛ:r] swinging, pendular (*motion*); **pendule** [˷ˈdyl] *su./m phys. etc.* pendulum; *su./f* clock; **pendulette** [˷dyˈlɛt] *f* small clock.

pêne [pɛːn] *m lock:* bolt; latch.

pénétrable [peneˈtrabl] penetrable; **pénétrant, e** [˷ˈtrã, ˷ˈtrã:t] penetrating; keen (*glance, intelligence, wind*); pervasive (*smell*); acute (*person*); **pénétration** [˷traˈsjɔ̃] *f* penetration (*a. fig.*); *fig.* insight, shrewdness; **pénétrer** [˷ˈtre] (1f) *v/t.* penetrate; *fig.* fathom (*a secret*); permeate (with, *de*); *v/i.* penetrate; enter; force one's way.

pénible [peˈnibl] painful; hard, laborious.

péniche ⚓ [peˈniʃ] *f* barge; lighter; ✕ ˷ *de débarquement* landing-craft.

pénicillé, e [penisilˈle] penicillate; **pénicilline** ⚕ [˷ˈlin] *f* penicillin.

péninsulaire [penɛ̃syˈlɛ:r] peninsu-

lar; **péninsule** *geog.* [˷ˈsyl] *f* peninsula.

pénis *anat.* [peˈnis] *m* penis.

pénitence [peniˈtã:s] *f* penitence, repentance; *eccl.* penance; *mettre q. en* ˷ *school:* make s.o. stand in the corner; **pénitencerie** *eccl.* [˷tãsˈri] *f* penitentiary(ship); **pénitencier** [˷tãˈsje] *m eccl.,* ⚖ penitentiary; ⚖ reformatory; **pénitent, e** [˷ˈtã, ˷ˈtã:t] *adj., a. su.* penitent; **pénitentiaux** [˷tãˈsjo] *adj./m/pl.* penitential (*psalms*); **pénitentiel, -elle** [˷tãˈsjɛl] penitential, (*works*) of penance.

pennage [pɛnˈna:ʒ] *m* plumage.

penne¹ ⚓ [pɛn] *f* peak.

penne² [pɛn] *f* quill-feather; wing-feather; tail-feather; *arrow:* feather; *tex.* warp end; **penné, e** ♀ [pɛˈne] pennate, pinnate; **pennon** [˷ˈnɔ̃] *m* pennon; *arrow:* feather.

pénombre [peˈnɔ̃:br] *f* half-light; penumbra; obscurity (*a. fig.*).

pensant, e [pãˈsã, ˷ˈsã:t] thinking; *mal* ˷ heretical; *see bien-pensant.*

pensée¹ ♀ [pãˈse] *f* pansy.

pensée² [pãˈse] *f* thought; idea; *fig.* mind; intention; **penser** [˷ˈse] (1a) *v/i.* think (of, *à*); remember; intend; *fig.* expect; *faire* ˷ remind (s.o. of s.th., *q. à qch.*); *pensez à faire cela* don't forget to do this; *sans y* ˷ thoughtlessly; *v/t.* think, believe; consider; think out; *elle pense venir* she means to come; *qu'en pensez-vous?* what do you think of it?; **penseur** [˷ˈsœ:r] *m* thinker; *libre* ˷ freethinker; **pensif, -ve** [˷ˈsif, ˷ˈsi:v] pensive, thoughtful.

pension [pãˈsjɔ̃] *f* pension, allowance; boarding house; boarding school; (charge for) board and lodging; ˷ *alimentaire* maintenance allowance; **pensionnaire** [pãsjɔˈnɛ:r] *su. boarding house, school:* boarder; *hotel:* resident; ✱ inmate; **pensionnat** [˷ˈna] *m* boarding school; *school:* hostel; *coll.* boarders *pl.*; **pensionner** [˷ˈne] (1a) *v/t.* pension off. [tion.\

pensum [pɛ̃ˈsɔm] *m school:* imposi-\

pent(a)... [pɛ̃t(a)] pent(a)...; five...; **pentathlon** *sp.* [pɛ̃taˈtlɔ̃] *m* pentathlon.

pente [pã:t] *f* slope, incline; gradient; *river:* fall; △ *roof:* pitch; *fig.* bent, propensity.

perdu

Pentecôte [pãt'koːt] *f* Whitsun (-tide); Pentecost; *dimanche m de la* ~ Whit Sunday.

pénultième [penyl'tjɛm] **1.** *adj.* penultimate; **2.** *su./f gramm.* penult, last syllable but one.

pénurie [peny'ri] *f* shortage, scarcity; *fig.* poverty, need.

pépère F [pe'pɛːr] **1.** *su./m* granddad; *gros* ~ big, quiet fellow; chubby child; **2.** *adj.* F quiet; cosy; cushy.

pépie [pe'pi] *f disease of birds:* pip; F *fig.* avoir la ~ have a terrible thirst.

pépiement [pepi'mã] *m* chirp(ing), cheep(ing); **pépier** [~'pje] (1o) *v/i.* chirp, cheep.

pépin [pe'pɛ̃] *m fruit:* pip; F snag; F umbrella, F brolly; *sl.* avoir un ~ *pour* be in love with, F be smitten by; **pépinière** [pepi'njɛːr] *f* ✍ seed-bed; ✍, *a. fig.* nursery; **pépiniériste** [~nje'rist] *m* nurseryman.

pépite [pe'pit] *f gold:* nugget.

pepsine ⚕ [pɛp'sin] *f* pepsin.

péquin F ⚔ [pe'kɛ̃] *m see* pékin.

perçage [pɛr'saːʒ] *m* piercing, boring; *cask:* tapping.

percale *tex.* [pɛr'kal] *f* cambric; percale; **percaline** [~ka'lin] *f tex.* percaline; calico; *bookbinding:* cloth.

perçant, e [pɛr'sã, ~'sãːt] piercing; penetrating, keen (*cold, mind, etc.*); **perce** [pɛrs] *f* ⊕ borer, drill; ♩ *flute:* hole; *en* ~ broached (*cask*); *mettre en* ~ broach; **perce-bois** *zo.* [~'bwa] *m/inv.* wood-borer; **percée** [pɛr'se] *f* opening; ⚔, *a. fig.* break-through; *metall.* tap-hole; *furnace:* tapping; **percement** [~sə'mã] *m* piercing, boring; perforation; opening; **perce-neige** ⚘ [pɛrs'nɛːʒ] *f/inv.* snowdrop; **perce-oreille** *zo.* [pɛrsɔ'rɛːj] *m* earwig.

percepteur, -trice [pɛrsɛp'tœːr, ~'tris] **1.** *adj.* perceiving; **2.** *su./m* collector of taxes; **perceptibilité** [~tibili'te] *f* perceptibility; *sound:* audibility; *tax:* liability to collection; **perceptible** [~'tibl] perceptible; audible (*sound*); collectable, collectible (*tax*); **perceptif, -ve** [~'tif, ~'tiːv] perceptive; **perception** [~'sjɔ̃] *f* perception; *admin.* taxes, *etc.*: collection; collectorship (of taxes).

percer [pɛr'se] (1k) *v/t.* pierce; *fig.* penetrate; break through; perforate; make a hole in (*a wall etc.*);

broach (*a cask*); sink (*a well*); ⊕ drill, punch; ⚕ lance (*an abscess*); *v/i.* pierce; come through; **perceur, -euse** [~'sœːr, ~'søːz] *su.* borer; driller; puncher; *su./f* drill (-ing-machine).

percevable [pɛrsə'vabl] perceivable; leviable (*tax*); **percevoir** [~'vwaːr] (3a) *v/t.* perceive; hear (*a sound*); collect (*taxes, fares, etc.*).

perche¹ *icht.* [pɛrʃ] *f* perch.

perche² [pɛrʃ] *f* pole; F lanky individual; *fig.* tendre la ~ à q. give s.o. a helping hand; *sp.* saut *m* à la ~ pole vault; **percher** [pɛr'ʃe] (1a) *v/i. a.* se ~ perch, roost; F *fig.* live, F hang out; *v/t.* F put, stick (*somewhere*); **percheur, -euse** [~'ʃœːr, ~'ʃøːz] perching, roosting; *oiseau m* ~ percher; **perchoir** [~'ʃwaːr] *m* perch, roost.

perclus, e [pɛr'kly, ~'klyːz] anchylosed; stiff; lame; paralyzed (*a. fig.*).

perçoir ⊕ [pɛr'swaːr] *m* punch, drill; gimlet.

percolateur [pɛrkɔla'tœːr] *m coffee:* percolator.

percussion [pɛrky'sjɔ̃] *f* ⚔, ♩, *a.* gun: percussion; **percutant, e** [~'tã, ~'tãːt] percussive; *fig.* that strikes home; *fig.* trenchant; **percuter** [~'te] (1a) *v/t.* strike; hit; ⚔ percuss; *v/i.:* ~ *contre* crash into, hit; **percuteur** [~'tœːr] *m fuse,* gun: hammer; *fuse:* plunger.

perdable [pɛr'dabl] losable; **perdant, e** [~'dã, ~'dãːt] **1.** *adj.* losing; *billet m* ~ ticket: blank; **2.** *su.* loser; **perdition** [~di'sjɔ̃] *f eccl.* perdition; ⚓ *en* ~ sinking; in distress; **perdre** [pɛrdr] (4a) *v/t.* lose; waste (*time, pains*); get rid of; be the ruin of; ~ *la pratique* get out of practice; ~ *q. de vue* lose sight of s.o.; *je m'y perds* I can't make head or tail of it; se ~ be lost; disappear; lose one's way; be wasted; go bad; be wrecked; *v/i.* lose; ⊕ *etc.* leak.

perdreau [pɛr'dro] *m orn.* young partridge; *cuis.* partridge; **perdrix** *orn.* [~'dri] *f* partridge.

perdu, e [pɛr'dy] **1.** *p.p. of* perdre; **2.** *adj.* lost; waisted; *fig.* ruined; ⊕, ⚓ sunk; *phys.* idle (*motion*); ⚔ stray (*bullet*); loose (*woman*); spare (*time*); out-of-the-way, god-forsaken (*place*); à *corps* ~ desperately; recklessly; *crier comme un* ~ shout like a madman; *reprise f* ~e invisible darn.

père [pɛːr] *m* father (*a. fig.*); *eccl.* ♀ Father; ~*s pl.* forefathers; ~ *de famille* paterfamilias; ~ *spirituel* father confessor; F *le* ~ ... old ...; *Dumas* ~ Dumas Senior; *ses* ~ *et mère* his parents.

pérégrination [peregrina'sjɔ̃] *f* peregrination.

péremption ⚖ [perɑ̃p'sjɔ̃] *f* striking out of an action by reason of failure to comply with a time-limitation; **péremptoire** [~'twaːr] peremptory (*tone, a.* ⚖ *exception*); decisive (*argument*); ⚖ strict (*time-limit*).

perenniser [perɛni'ze] (1a) *v/t.* perpetuate; **pérennité** [~'te] *f* everlastingness.

péréquation *admin.* [perekwa'sjɔ̃] *f* equalization; standardizing; adjustment; balancing (out).

perfectibilité [pɛrfɛktibili'te] *f* perfectibility; **perfectible** [~'tibl] perfectible; **perfection** [~'sjɔ̃] *f* perfection; *à (or dans) la* ~ to perfection; **perfectionnement** [~sjɔn'mɑ̃] *m* improvement; perfecting; **perfectionner** [~sjɔ'ne] (1a) *v/t.* improve; perfect.

perfide [pɛr'fid] false; treacherous (to, *envers*); perfidious; **perfidie** [~fi'di] *f* perfidy, (act of) treachery.

perforage ⊕ [pɛrfɔ'raːʒ] *m see perforation;* **perforateur, -trice** [~ra'tœːr, ~'tris] **1.** *adj.* perforating; **2.** *su./m* perforator; *su./f* ⊕ boring *or* drilling machine; card punch; **perforation** [~ra'sjɔ̃] *f* perforation (*a.* ⚕); drilling; *mot. etc.* puncture, puncturing; **perforer** [~'re] (1a) *v/t.* perforate; ⊕ drill, bore through; punch (*leather, paper*); *mot.* puncture; **perforeuse** [~'røːz] *f see perforatrice.*

performance [pɛrfɔr'mɑ̃ːs] *f* performance.

pergola [pɛrgɔ'la] *f* pergola.

péri... [peri] peri...; ~**carde** *anat.* [~'kard] *m* pericardium; ~**cardique** ⚕ [~kar'dik] pericardial; ~**cardite** ⚕ [~kar'dit] *f* pericarditis; ~**carpe** ♀ [~'karp] *m* pericarp, seed-vessel.

péricliter [perikli'te] (1a) *v/i.* be in jeopardy *or* F in a bad way.

péril [pe'ril] *m* peril, danger; risk; *au* ~ *de* at the risk of; **périlleux,**

-**euse** [~ri'jø, ~'jøːz] perilous, dangerous.

périmé, e [peri'me] out-of-date; expired (*ticket etc.*); ⚖ barred by limitation.

périmètre [peri'mɛtr] *m* Å perimeter; *fig.* sphere.

périnée *anat.* [peri'ne] *m* perineum.

période [pe'rjɔd] *su./f* time, *a. astr., geol., gramm.,* ⚕, *a. phys.* wave: period; ⚕ phase; ♪ phrase; age, era, epoch; *su./m poet.* point; zenith; **périodicité** [perjɔdisi'te] *f* periodicity; **périodique** [~'dik] **1.** *adj.* periodic(al); intermittent; ⚕ recurrent (*fever*); **2.** *su./m* periodical.

péri...: ~**oste** *anat.* [pe'rjɔst] *m* periosteum; ~**ostite** ⚕ [~rjɔs'tit] *f* periostitis; ~**pétie** [peripe'si] *f* sudden change; ~*s pl.* vicissitudes; ~**phérie** [~fe'ri] *f* Å periphery, circumference; *town:* outskirts *pl.*; ~**phérique** [~fe'rik] **1.** *adj.* peripheral; outlying (*district etc.*); *mot. boulevard m* ~ = **2.** *su./m* ring road, circular route; ~**phrase** *gramm.* [~'fraːz] *f* periphrasis; circumlocution; *par* ~ periphrastically; ~**phrastique** *gramm.* [~fras'tik] periphrastic.

périr [pe'riːr] (2a) *v/i.* perish, die; ⚓ be wrecked, be lost.

périscope [peris'kɔp] *m* periscope; **périscopique** [~kɔ'pik] periscopic.

périssable [peri'sabl] perishable; **périssoire** [~'swaːr] *f* canoe.

péri...: ~**style** △ [peris'til] *m* peristyle; *eccl.* cloisters *pl.*; ~**toine** *anat.* [peri'twan] *m* periton(a)eum; ~**tonite** ⚕ [~tɔ'nit] *f* peritonitis; ~**urbain, e** [~yr'bɛ̃, ~'bɛn] suburban, suburb ...

perle [pɛrl] *f* pearl (*a. typ.*); bead (*a. fig. of dew*); *fig.* maid, wife, *etc.*: jewel; F *school:* howler; **perlé, e** [pɛr'le] set with pearls; *fig.* pearly; ♪ *etc.* exquisitely executed; **perler** [~'le] (1a) *v/t.* pearl (*an article, a. barley*); set with pearls; ♪ *etc.* execute perfectly; *v/i.* stand in beads (*sweat*); bead (*sugar*); **perlier, -ère** [~'lje, ~'ljɛːr] pearl-bearing; pearl-...

perlimpinpin [pɛrlɛ̃pɛ̃'pɛ̃] *m*: *poudre f de* ~ quack powder; *fig.* magic cure-all.

permanence [pɛrma'nɑ̃ːs] *f* permanence; office *etc.* always open to the public; *en* ~ permanently; **perma-**

nent, e [ˌ'nɑ̃, ˌ'nɑ̃ːt] **1.** *adj.* permanent; *fig.* lasting; *admin.* standing (*committee, order*); *cin.* non-stop (*performance*); **2.** *su./f* permanent wave, perm; **permanenter** [ˌmanɑ̃'te] (1a) *v/t.* perm.

perméable [pɛrme'abl] permeable, pervious.

permettre [pɛr'mɛtr] (4v) *v/t.* permit, allow; authorize; se ~ de (*inf.*) venture to (*inf.*), take the liberty of (*ger.*); **permis, e** [ˌ'mi, ˌ'miːz] **1.** *p.p.* of permettre; **2.** *adj.* permitted, allowed; lawful; **3.** *su./m* permit; licence; *mot.* ~ de conduire driving licence, *Am.* driver's license; ~ de séjour residence permit; **permissif, -ve** [ˌmi'sif, ˌ'siːv] permissive; **permission** [ˌmi'sjɔ̃] *f* permission; ✕, ⚓ leave (of absence); ✕ ~ de détente furlough after strenuous service; **permissionnaire** [ˌmisjɔ'nɛːr] *m* permit holder; ✕ soldier on leave; ⚓ liberty man.

permutable [pɛrmy'tabl] interchangeable; **permutation** [ˌta'sjɔ̃] *f* exchange of posts; ♉ etc. permutation; **permuter** [ˌ'te] (1a) *v/t.* exchange (*posts etc.*); ⚡ change over; ♉ etc. permute; *v/i.* exchange posts (with, *avec*).

pernicieux, -euse [pɛrni'sjø, ˌ'sjøːz] pernicious, injurious.

péronnelle F *pej.* [perɔ'nɛl] *f* silly goose.

péroraison [perɔrɛ'zɔ̃] *f* peroration; **pérorer** [ˌ're] (1a) *v/i.* hold forth; F speechify.

peroxyde ⚗ [pɛrɔk'sid] *m* peroxide.

perpendiculaire [pɛrpɑ̃diky'lɛːr] upright; ♉ perpendicular (to, *à*) (*a.* △ *style*).

perpétration [pɛrpetra'sjɔ̃] *f* perpetration; **perpétrer** [ˌ'tre] (1f) *v/t.* perpetrate, commit.

perpétuel, -elle [pɛrpe'tɥɛl] perpetual, everlasting; for life; **perpétuer** [ˌ'tɥe] (1n) *v/t.* perpetuate; **perpétuité** [ˌtɥi'te] *f* perpetuity; à ~ in perpetuity; for life (⚖ *sentence*).

perplexe [pɛr'plɛks] perplexed (*person*); perplexing (*situation*); **perplexité** [ˌplɛksi'te] *f* perplexity.

perquisition ⚖ [pɛrkizi'sjɔ̃] *f* search; ~ *domiciliaire* search of a house; **perquisitionner** ⚖ [ˌsjɔ-'ne] (1a) *v/i.* (carry out a) search.

perron △ [pɛ'rɔ̃] *m* front steps *pl.*
perroquet [pɛrɔ'kɛ] *m orn.* parrot; ⚓ sail: topgallant; **perruche** [ˌ'ryʃ] *f orn.* parakeet; hen-parrot; (~ *ondulée*) budgerigar; ⚓ mizzen topgallant sail.

perruque [pɛ'ryk] *f* wig; F *fig. vieille* ~ fogey; **perruquier** † [ˌry-'kje] *m* wig-maker; barber.

persan, e [pɛr'sɑ̃, ˌ'san] **1.** *adj.* Persian; **2.** *su./m ling.* Persian; *su.* ♀ Persian; **perse** *tex.* [pɛrs] *f* chintz.

persécuter [pɛrseky'te] (1a) *v/t.* persecute; F *fig.* harass; **persécuteur, -trice** [ˌ'tœːr, ˌ'tris] **1.** *adj.* persecuting; *fig.* troublesome; **2.** *su.* persecutor; **persécution** [ˌ'sjɔ̃] *f* persecution; *fig.* importunity.

persévérance [pɛrseve'rɑ̃ːs] *f* perseverance (in *ger.*, à *inf.*); **persévérant, e** [ˌ'rɑ̃, ˌ'rɑ̃ːt] persevering (in *ger.*, à *inf.*); dogged (*work*); **persévérer** [ˌ're] (1f) *v/i.* persevere.

persienne [pɛr'sjɛn] *f* Venetian blind; slatted shutter.

persiflage [pɛrsi'flaːʒ] *m* mockery; **persifler** [ˌ'fle] (1a) *v/t.* make fun of, mock; **persifleur, -euse** [ˌ'flœːr, ˌ'fløːz] **1.** *adj.* mocking; **2.** *su.* mocker.

persil ♀ [pɛr'si] *m* parsley; **persillade** *cuis.* [ˌsi'jad] *f* beef salad with parsley-sauce; **persillé, e** [ˌsi'je] blue(-moulded) (*cheese*); spotted with green; marbled (*meat*).

persistance [pɛrsis'tɑ̃ːs] *f* persistence (in *ger.*, à *inf.*); ⚕, *a. fig.* continuance; **persistant, e** [ˌ'tɑ̃, ~-'tɑ̃ːt] persistent (*a.* ♀ *leaves*); dogged (*effort*); *fig.* lasting; steady (*rain*); **persister** [ˌ'te] (1a) *v/i.* persist (in s.th., *dans qch.*; in *ger.*, à *inf.*); *la pluie persiste* it keeps on raining.

personnage [pɛrsɔ'naːʒ] *m* personage; person of distinction; *thea. etc.* character; *pej.* individual, person; **personnaliser** [ˌnali'ze] (1a) *v/t.* personalize; give a personal touch to; **personnalité** [ˌnali'te] *f* personality; person of distinction; *fig.* ~s *pl.* personal remarks, personalities; **personne** [pɛr'sɔn] **1.** *su./f* person (*a. gramm.*); one's self; body, appearance; ⚖ ~ *morale* corporate body, artificial person; *jeune* ~ young lady; **2.** *pron./indef./m/inv.* anybody, anyone; (*with negative*) not anyone, nobody; *qui l'a vu?* ~! who saw him? no one!; **personnel, -elle** [pɛrsɔ-'nɛl] **1.** *adj.* personal (*a.* 🕮, *gramm.*); selfish, self-(*interest etc.*); not transferable (*ticket*); **2.** *su./m* staff, personnel; ♣ complement; ✕ ~ *à terre* (*or rampant*) ground staff *or* crew; ~ *enseignant school*: staff, *univ.* academic staff, *Am.* faculty; **personnification** [~nifika'sjɔ̃] *f* personification; impersonation; **personnifier** [~ni'fje] (1o) *v/t.* personify; impersonate.

perspectif, -ve [pɛrspɛk'tif, ~'tiːv] **1.** *adj.* perspective; **2.** *su./f* perspective; *fig.* outlook; prospect; vista; *en* ~ in view.

perspicace [pɛrspi'kas] shrewd, perspicacious; **perspicacité** [~kasi'te] *f* perspicacity, shrewdness, insight.

persuader [pɛrsɥa'de] (1a) *v/t.* persuade; (of, *de*; to *inf.*, *de inf.*); convince; **persuasif, -ve** [~'zif, ~'ziːv] persuasive; **persuasion** [~'zjɔ̃] *f* persuasion; conviction.

perte [pɛrt] *f* loss, ruin; waste; leakage; ✕ ~*s pl.* casualties; ~ *sèche* dead loss; ✝ *à* ~ at a loss; *à* ~ *de vue* as far as the eye can see; F *fig.* endlessly; *en pure* ~ to no purpose; *être en* ~ *de 10 F* be 10 francs down *or* out of pocket; *être en* ~ *de vitesse* ✕ lose lift, *fig.* lose momentum.

pertinence [pɛrti'nɑ̃ːs] *f* pertinence; **pertinent, e** [~'nɑ̃, ~'nɑ̃ːt] pertinent, relevant; judicious.

pertuis [pɛr'tɥi] *m* sluice; *metall.* tap-hole; *geog.* channel; *river*: narrows *pl.*; *geog.* pass.

perturbateur, -trice [pɛrtyrba-'tœːr, ~'tris] **1.** *adj.* disturbing; **2.** *su.* disturber; interferer; **perturbation** [~'sjɔ̃] *f* perturbation, agitation; ~*s pl.* atmosphériques *radio*: atmospherics.

péruvien, -enne [pery'vjɛ̃, ~'vjɛn] *adj., a. su.* ♀ Peruvian.

pervenche ♀ [pɛr'vɑ̃ːʃ] *f* periwinkle.

pervers, e [pɛr'vɛːr, ~'vɛrs] **1.** *adj.* perverse; perverted; **2.** *su.* ♂ pervert; **perversion** [~vɛr'sjɔ̃] *f* perversion; **perversité** [~vɛrsi'te] *f* perversity; **pervertir** [~vɛr'tiːr] (2a) *v/t.* corrupt; pervert.

pesage [pə'zaːʒ] *m* weighing; *turf*: weighing-in; weighing-in room; paddock; **pesamment** [~za'mɑ̃] *adv. of* **pesant** 1; **pesant, e** [~'zɑ̃,

~'zɑ̃ːt] **1.** *adj.* heavy; *fig.* ponderous (*style*); *fig.* dull (*mind*); **2.** *su./m* weight; **pesanteur** [~zɑ̃'tœːr] *f* weight; *phys.* gravity; heaviness; *fig.* clumsiness; *fig.* dullness.

pèse... [pɛz] ...ometer; ...-scales *pl.*; ~-**bébé** [~be'be] *m* baby-scales *pl.*

pesée [pə'ze] *f* weighing; *faire la* ~ *de* weigh (*s.th.*); **pèse-lettre** [~'lɛtr] *m* letter scales *pl.*; **pèse-personnes** [~pɛr'sɔn] *m* (bathroom) scales *pl.*; **peser** [pə'ze] (1d) *v/t.* weigh; consider; *v/i. fig.* lie *or* weigh heavy (on *sur, à*); ~ *à q. a.* weigh s.o. down; ~ *sur a.* press hard on (*a lever*); **pesette** [~'zɛt] *f* assay scales *pl.*; **peseur** *m*, **-euse** *f* [~'zœːr, ~'zøːz] weigher; **peson** [~'zɔ̃] *m* balance.

pessimisme [pɛsi'mism] *m* pessimism; **pessimiste** [~'mist] **1.** *adj.* pessimistic; **2.** *su.* pessimist.

peste [pɛst] *f* plague (*a. fig.*), pestilence; F *fig.* pest, nuisance; F ~! confound it!; *vet.* ~ *bovine* cattleplague; ✿ ~ *bubonique* bubonic plague, *hist.* Black Death; ~ *soit de lui* a plague on him!; **pester** [pɛs-'te] (1a) *v/i.* rave, storm (at, *contre*); **pestiféré, e** [pɛstife're] **1.** *adj.* plague-stricken; **2.** *su.* plague-stricken person; **pestilence** ✿ ✝ [~'lɑ̃ːs] *f* pestilence; **pestilentiel, -elle** [~lɑ̃'sjɛl] pestilential.

pet [pe] *m* ∨ fart; *cuis.* ~-*de-nonne* doughnut, fritter.

pétale ♀ [pe'tal] *m* petal.

pétarade [peta'rad] *f* fireworks: crackle; *mot.* back-fire; ✕ random firing; **pétard** [~'taːr] *m* ✕ shot; ✿ detonator; *firework*: cracker; F sensational news; *sl.* backside, bum; F *faire du* ~ kick up a row; **péter** [~'te] (1f) *v/i.* crack (*fire, gun*); pop (*cork*); ∨ fart; **pétillant, e** [~ti'jɑ̃, ~'jɑ̃t] sparkling; fizzy, bubbly (*liquid*); **pétiller** [~ti'je] (1a) *v/i.* crackle (*fire etc.*); sparkle (*champagne, eyes*); *fig.* scintillate (with wit, *d'esprit*).

petiot, e F [pə'tjo, ~'tjɔt] **1.** *adj.* tiny, little; **2.** *su./m* little boy; *su./f* little girl.

petit, e [pə'ti, ~'tit] **1.** *adj.* small, little; slight (*sound*); minor (*nobility, subject*); *school*: lower (*forms*); tight (*shoes*); short; young (*a. zo.*); petty, trifling; *pej.* mean; ~ *à* ~ little by little; ~*e industrie* smaller industries

phase

pl.; *~es gens pl.* humble people; **2.** *su.* child, kid; *zo.* cub, young; **petit-déjeuner** F [ˌtideʒøˈne] (1a) *v/i.* (have) breakfast; **petite-fille,** *pl.* **petites-filles** [ˌtitˈfiːj] *f* granddaughter; **petitement** [ˌtitˈmɑ̃] poorly; pettily; meanly; **petitesse** [ˌtiˈtɛs] *f* smallness, littleness; *pej.* meanness, pettiness; mean trick; **petit-fils,** *pl.* **petits-fils** [ˌtiˈfis] *m* grandson; **petit-gris,** *pl.* **petits-gris** [ˌtiˈgri] *m zo.* miniver; ✝ *fur:* squirrel.

pétition [petiˈsjɔ̃] *f* petition; **pétitionnaire** [ˌsjɔˈnɛːr] *su.* petitioner; **pétitionner** [ˌsjɔˈne] (1a) *v/i.* petition.

petit...: **~-lait,** *pl.* **~s-laits** [pətiˈlɛ] *m* whey; **~-maître,** *pl.* **~s-maîtres** [ˌˈmɛːtr] *m* fop; **~-nègre** F [ˌˈnɛːgr] *m: parler ~* talk pidgin; **~-neveu,** *pl.* **~s-neveux** [ˌnəˈvø] *m* grandnephew; **~s-enfants** [ˌzɑ̃ˈfɑ̃] *m/pl.* grandchildren; **~-suisse,** *pl.* **~s-suisses** *cuis.* [ˌˈsɥis] *m* small cream cheese.

peton F [pəˈtɔ̃] *m* tiny foot, F tootsy.

pétrel *orn.* [peˈtrɛl] *m* petrel.

pétrification [petrifikaˈsjɔ̃] *f* petrifaction; **pétrifier** [ˌˈfje] (1o) *v/t.* petrify; *se ~* petrify.

pétrin [peˈtrɛ̃] *m* kneading-trough; F *fig.* mess; F *dans le ~* in a mess *or* fix; **pétrir** [ˌˈtriːr] (2a) *v/t.* knead; mo(u)ld (*clay, a. s.o.'s mind*); **pétrissage** [petriˈsaːʒ] *m* kneading; *clay, a. fig. mind:* mo(u)lding; **pétrisseur, -euse** [ˌˈsœːr, ˌˈsøːz] *su.* kneader; *su./f* kneading-machine.

pétrochimie [petrɔʃiˈmi] *f* petrochemistry; **pétrochimique** [ˌˈmik] petrochemical; **petrochimiste** [ˌˈmist] *su.* petrochemist.

pétrole [peˈtrɔl] *m* petroleum; mineral oil; paraffin, *Am.* kerosene; ~ *brut* crude oil; *puits m de ~* oil-well; **pétrolier, -ère** [petrɔˈlje, ˌˈljɛːr] **1.** *adj.* oil-...; **2.** *su./m* (*a. navire m ~*) tanker; **pétrolifère** [ˌliˈfɛːr] oil-bearing; oil-(*belt, field, well*).

pétulance [petyˈlɑ̃ːs] *f* liveliness; *horse:* friskiness; **pétulant, e** [ˌˈlɑ̃, ˌˈlɑ̃ːt] lively; frisky (*horse*).

peu [pø] **1.** *adv.* little; few; *before adj.:* un-..., not very; ~ *à* ~ bit by bit, little by little; ~ *de* little (*bread etc.*), few (*people, things, etc.*); ~ *de chose* nothing much; ~ *d'entre eux*

few of them; *à* ~ *près* approximately, nearly; *depuis* ~ of late; *pour* ~ *que* (*sbj.*) however little (*ind.*), if ever (*ind.*); *quelque* ~ rather, slightly; *sous* (*or dans*) ~ before long; *tant soit* ~ ever so little, a little bit; *viens un* ~! come here!; **2.** *su./m* little, bit; want, lack; *le* ~ *de* ... the little ..., the lack of ...; *un* ~ *de* a bit of.

peuplade [pœˈplad] *f* small tribe, people; **peuple** [pœpl] *m* people; nation; **peupler** [pœˈple] (1a) *v/t.* populate (with, *de*); stock (*with animals etc.*); *fig.* fill; *se* ~ become populated; fill up with people; *v/i.* multiply, breed.

peuplier ♀ [pœpliˈe] *m* poplar.

peur [pœːr] *f* fear, dread; *avoir* ~ be afraid (of, *de*), be scared (of, *de*); *de* ~ *de* (*faire*) *qch.* for fear of (doing) s.th.; *de* ~ *que* ... (*ne*) (*sbj.*) for fear of (*ger.*); *faire* ~ *à* frighten (*s.o.*); **peureux, -euse** [pœˈrø, ˌˈrøːz] fearful; timid.

peut-être [pøˈtɛːtr] *adv.* perhaps, maybe; **peuvent** [pœːv] *3rd p. pl. pres. of pouvoir 1*; **peux** [pø] *1st p. sg. pres. of pouvoir 1*.

phagocyter [fagɔsiˈte] (1a) *v/t. biol.* phagocytose; *fig.* absorb.

phalange [faˈlɑ̃ːʒ] *f anat., a.* ♀ phalanx; *fig.* host.

phalène *zo.* [faˈlɛn] *f* moth.

phallocrate [falɔˈkrat] *m* male chauvinist; **phallocratie** [ˌkraˈsi] *f* male chauvinism.

phare [faːr] *m* lighthouse; ⚓, ⚔ beacon; ⛟, *mot.* headlight, headlamp; *mot.* ~s *pl.* code dipped *or* dimmed headlights, *Am. a.* dimmers; *mot. baisser les* ~s dim or dip the headlights.

pharisaïque [farizaˈik] pharisaic(al); **pharisaïsme** [ˌzaˈism] *m* pharisaism (*a. fig.*); **pharisien** [ˌˈzjɛ̃] *m* pharisee (*a. fig.*); *fig.* self-righteous person; *fig.* hypocrite.

pharmaceutique [farmasøˈtik] **1.** *adj.* pharmaceutic(al); **2.** *su./f* pharmaceutics *sg.*; **pharmacie** [ˌˈsi] *f* pharmacy; chemist's (shop), *Am.* drugstore; medicine-chest; **pharmacien** *m*, **-enne** *f* [ˌˈsjɛ̃, ˌˈsjɛn] chemist, *Am.* druggist; **pharmacologie** [ˌkɔlɔˈʒi] *f* pharmacology; **pharmacopée** [ˌkɔˈpe] *f* pharmacopoeia.

phase [fɑːz] *f* phase (*a.* ⚡, ⚔, *fig.*).

phénicien, -enne [feni'sjɛ̃, ‿'sjɛn] **1.** *adj.* Phoenician; **2.** *su./m ling.* Phoenician; *su.* ♀ Phoenician.

phénique ⚗ [fe'nik] *adj.*: *acide m* ‿ = **phénol** ⚗ [‿'nɔl] *m* phenol, carbolic acid.

phénomène [fenɔ'mɛn] *m* phenomenon; *fig.* wonder; freak.

philanthrope [filɑ̃'trɔp] *su.* philanthropist.

philatélie [filate'li] *f* stamp-collecting, philately; **philatéliste** [‿'list] *su.* stamp-collector, philatelist.

philippique [fili'pik] *f* philippic.

Philistin [filis'tɛ̃] *m* Philistine (*a. fig.*).

phil(o)... [fil(ɔ)] phil(o)...

philo...: ‿**logie** [filɔlɔ'ʒi] *f* philology; ‿**logue** [‿'lɔg] *su.* philologist; ‿**sophe** [‿'zɔf] **1.** *su.* philosopher; **2.** *adj.* philosophical; ‿**sophie** [‿zɔ'fi] *f* philosophy; *faire sa* ‿ be in the philosophy class (= [*approx.*] *lower 6th form*); ‿**sophique** [‿zɔ-'fik] philosophic(al).

philtre [filtr] *m* philtre.

phlébite ⚕ [fle'bit] *f* phlebitis.

phobie *psych.* [fɔ'bi] *f* phobia.

phonétique [fɔne'tik] **1.** *adj.* phonetic; **2.** *su./f* phonetics *pl.*; **phonique** [‿'nik] phonic; sound (*signal*).

phonographe [fɔnɔ'graf] *m*, F **phono** [‿'no] *m* gramophone, record-player, *Am. a.* phonograph.

phoque [fɔk] *m zo.* seal; ✝ sealskin.

phosphate ⚗, ✎ [fɔs'fat] *m* phosphate; **phosphore** ⚗ [‿'fɔ:r] *m* phosphorus; **phosphoré, e** [fɔsfɔ-'re] containing phosphorus, phosphorated, phosphuretted (*hydrogen*); **phosphorescence** [‿re'sɑ̃:s] *f* phosphorescence; **phosphorescent, e** [‿re'sɑ̃, ‿'sɑ̃:t] phosphorescent; **phosphoreux, -euse** ⚗ [‿-'rø, ‿'rø:z] phosphorous; **phosphorique** ⚗ [‿'rik] *adj./m* phosphoric; **phosphorite** *min.* [‿'rit] *f* phosphorite; **phosphure** ⚗ [fɔs-'fy:r] *m* phosphide; **phosphuré, e** ⚗ [‿fy're] phosphuretted.

photo F [fɔ'to] *f* photograph, F photo; *faire de la* ‿ go in for photography.

photo... [fɔtɔ] photo...; ‿**calque** ⊕ [‿'kalk] *m* blue print; ‿**chimie** [‿ʃi'mi] *f* photochemistry; ‿**chromie** [‿krɔ'mi] *f* colo(u)r photography; photochromy; ‿**copie** [‿kɔ'pi]

f photocopy; ‿**copier** [‿kɔ'pje] (1o) *v/t.* photocopy; ‿**copieur** [‿kɔ'pjœ:r] *m* photocopier; ‿**-électrique** *phys.* [‿elɛk'trik] photoelectric; ‿**gène** *phys.* [‿'ʒɛn] photogenic; ‿**génique** [‿ʒe'nik] actinic; *cin.*, *phot.* photogenic; ‿**graphe** [‿'graf] *m* photographer; ‿**graphie** [‿gra'fi] *f* photograph, F photo; photography; ‿ *aérienne* aerial photography; ‿**graphier** [‿gra'fje] (1o) *v/t.* photograph, take a photo(graph) of; *se faire* ‿ have one's photo(graph) taken; ‿**graphique** [‿gra'fik] photographic; *appareil m* ‿ camera; 🎦 *reconnaissance f* ‿ photoreconnaissance; ‿**gravure** [‿gra'vy:r] *f process*, *a. print:* photogravure; ‿**lithographie** [‿litɔgra'fi] *f* photolithography; photolithograph; ‿**mètre** [‿'mɛtr] *m* photometer, light meter; ‿**pile** [‿'pil] *f* solar battery; ‿**sensible** [‿sɑ̃'sibl] photosensitive; ‿**stoppeur** [‿stɔ'pœ:r] *m* street photographer; ‿**thérapie** [‿tera-'pi] *f* phototherapy; light-cure; ‿**tropisme** ♀ [‿trɔ'pism] *m* phototropism; ‿**type** [‿'tip] *m* phototype; collotype; ‿**typie** ⊕ [‿ti'pi] *f process:* collotype.

phrase [frɑ:z] *f* sentence; ♪ phrase; **phraséologie** [frazeɔlɔ'ʒi] *f* phraseology; **phraséologique** [‿'ʒik] phraseological; **phraser** [frɑ'ze] (1a) *vt/i.* phrase (*a.* ♪); **phraseur** *m*, **-euse** *f* F [‿'zœ:r, ‿'zø:z] phrasemonger, speechifier.

phrénologie [frenɔlɔ'ʒi] *f* phrenology; **phrénologique** [‿'ʒik] phrenological; **phrénologiste** [‿'ʒist] *m* phrenologist.

phtisie ⚕ [fti'zi] *f* phthisis; consumption.

phyllo... *zo.* [filɔ] phyllo...; ‿**xéra** [‿ɔkse'ra] *m* phylloxera.

physicien *m*, **-enne** *f* [fizi'sjɛ̃, ‿'sjɛn] physicist.

physico... [fizikɔ] physico...; physical (*chemistry*).

physio... [fizjɔ] physio...; ‿**logie** [‿lɔ'ʒi] *f* physiology; ‿**logique** [‿lɔ'ʒik] physiological; ‿**logiste** [‿lɔ-'ʒist] *su.* physiologist; ‿**nomie** [‿nɔ-'mi] *f* physiognomy; appearance; countenance; *fig.* aspect, character.

physique [fi'zik] **1.** *adj.* physical; bodily; **2.** *su./f* physics *sg.*; ‿ *nucléaire* nuclear physics *sg.*; *su./m*

physique; constitution; appearance.
phyto... [fitɔ] phyto...; **phytopte** *zo.* [~'tɔpt] *m* rust-mite.
piaffement [pjaf'mɑ̃] *m horse*: pawing, piaffer; **piaffer** [pja'fe] (1a) *v/i.* paw the ground (*horse*); prance (*horse*); *fig.* ~ *d'impatience* fidget; **piaffeur, -euse** [~'fœ:r, ~'fø:z] prancing, high-stepping (*horse*); *fig.* fidgety; swaggering.
piaillard, e F [pjɑ'ja:r, ~'jard] **1.** *adj.* cheeping (*bird*); squalling (*child*); **2.** *su.* squalling child; **piailler** [~'je] (1a) *v/i.* cheep (*bird*); squeal, screech (*child, animal*); **piaillerie** [pjɑj'ri] *f birds*: (continuous) cheeping; *children etc.*: squealing, screeching; **piailleur** *m*, **-euse** *f* [pjɑ'jœ:r, ~'jø:z] *bird*: cheeper; *child etc.*: squealer, squaller.
pianino ♪ [pjani'no] *m* pianino; **pianiste** ♪ [~'nist] *su.* pianist; **piano** [~'no] **1.** *adv.* ♪ piano; F *fig.* gently, easy; **2.** *su./m* piano(forte); ~ *à queue* grand piano; ~ *droit* upright piano; *jouer du* ~ play the piano; **pianoter** F [~nɔ'te] (1a) *v/i.* ♪ tinkle (on the piano); *fig.* drum one's fingers (on, *sur*).
piaule *sl.* [pjol] *f* digs *pl.* (= *lodgings*); **piauler** [pjo'le] (1a) *v/i.* cheep (*chicks*); whine, pule (*children*).
pic¹ [pik] *m* ⚒ *etc.* pick(axe); *geog., a.* ⚓ peak; *cards*: pique (*at piquet*); ~ *pneumatique* pneumatic drill; *à* ~ perpendicular(ly *adv.*), sheer; just at the right moment *or* time.
pic² *orn.* [~] *m* woodpecker.
picaillons *sl.* [pika'jɔ̃] *m/pl.* dough *sg.* (= *money*).
picaresque [pika'rɛsk] picaresque (*novel*).
pichet [pi'ʃɛ] *m* pitcher, jug.
pickpocket [pikpɔ'kɛt] *m* pickpocket.
pick-up [pi'kœp] *m/inv. radio*: pickup, record-player.
picorer [pikɔ're] (1a) *vt/i.* peck (at).
picoté, e [pikɔ'te] pitted (*face etc.*); **picotement** [~'mɑ̃] *m* smarting (sensation); prickling; **picoter** [~te] (1a) *v/t.* make smart; prickle; peck (at) (*bird*).
picotin [pikɔ'tɛ̃] *m measure*: peck.
pie¹ [pi] **1.** *su./f orn.* magpie; **2.** *adj./inv.* piebald (*horse*).
pie² [~] *adj./f*: *œuvre f* ~ charitable deed, good work.
pièce [pjɛs] *f* piece; bit, fragment; *cost.* patch; *wine*: cask, barrel; *tex.* roll; *money*: coin, piece; ⊕ *machine*: part; *thea.* play; room (*in a house*); *fig.* mo(u)ld; ⚖ document (*in a case*); ⊕, *mot., etc.* ~*s pl. de rechange* spare parts; ⊕ ~*s pl. détachées* attendant parts; ~ *d'eau* ornamental lake; ~ *de résistance cuis.* principal dish; *fig.* principal feature; *à la* ~ in ones, separately; *5 F (la)* ~ 5 F each; *mettre en* ~*s* break *or* tear (*s.th.*) to pieces; *tout d'une* ~ all of a piece.
pied [pje] *m* ♘, *anat., column, glass, measure, mountain, stocking, tree, verse, wall*: foot; foothold; footing (*a.* ⚔); *furniture*: leg; ⚘ stalk; *wine-glass*: stem; *camera etc.*: stand, rest; *asparagus, lettuce, etc.*: head; *hunt.* track; ~ *à coulisse* slide ga(u)ge, sliding cal(l)ipers *pl.*; ~ *plat* flat-foot; *à* ~ on foot; walking; *au* ~ *de la lettre* literal(ly *adv.*); *au* ~ *levé* off the cuff; at a moment's notice; *avoir* ~ have a footing; *sl. c'est le* ~*!* that's great!; *coup m de* ~ kick; *en* ~ full-length (*portrait*); F *faire du* ~ play footsie (with *à, avec*); F *lever le* ~ make o.s. scarce; get out; F *mettre q. à* ~ dismiss *or* F sack s.o.; *mettre sur* ~ establish, set up; *prendre (perdre)* ~ gain a (lose one's) foothold; **~-à-terre** [~ta'tɛ:r] *m/inv.* temporary lodging; town apartment; **~-bot,** *pl.* **~s-bots** [~'bo] *m* club-footed person; **~-d'alouette,** *pl.* **~s-d'alouette** [~da'lwɛt] *m* larkspur, delphinium; **~de-biche,** *pl.* **~s-de-biche** [~də'biʃ] *m* bell-pull; ⊕ nail-claw; *sewing-machine*: presser-foot; ⚕ molar forceps; **~-de-chèvre,** *pl.* **~s-de-chèvre** ⊕ [~də'ʃɛ:vr] *m* footing; **~-de-poule** *tex.* [~də'pul] *m* broken-check; **~-droit,** *pl.* **~s-droits** [~'drwa] ⚠ *arch, bridge*: pier; side-wall; *window*: jamb.
piédestal [pjedɛs'tal] *m* pedestal.
pied-noir, *pl.* **pieds-noirs** F [pje'nwa:r] *m* European settler in Algeria.
piège [pjɛ:ʒ] *m* trap (*a. fig.*); *prendre au* ~ trap; *tendre un* ~ *à* set a trap for; **piéger** [pje'ʒe] (1g) *v/t.* trap (*a. fig. s.o.*); booby-trap (*s.th.*).
pie-grièche, *pl.* **pies-grièches** [pi-gri'ɛʃ] *f orn.* shrike; F *fig. woman*: shrew.

pierraille [pjɛ'rɑ:j] f rubble; road metal; **pierre** [pjɛ:r] f stone (a. 🎯); ~ à briquet flint; 🔺 ~ de taille freestone; ashlar; ~ fine semi-precious stone; ~ précieuse precious stone, gem; **pierreries** [pjɛrə'ri] f/pl. precious stones, gems, jewels; **pierrette** [~'rɛt] f small stone; thea. pierrette; **pierreux, -euse** [~'rø, ~'rø:z] stony; gravelly (river-bed); gritty (pear); 🎯 calculous; 🎯 suffering from calculus.

pierrot [pjɛ'ro] m thea. pierrot, clown; F orn. cock-sparrow; F fellow.

piété [pje'te] f piety; devotion.

piétiner [pjeti'ne] (1a) v/t. trample (s.th.) underfoot; ✓, ⊕ tread; v/i. stamp; (a. ~ sur place) mark time.

piétisme [pje'tism] m pietism; **piétiste** [~'tist] 1. su. pietist; 2. adj. pietistic.

piéton, -onne [pje'tɔ̃, ~'tɔn] 1. su. pedestrian; 2. adj. = **piétonnier, -ère** [~tɔ'nje, ~njɛ:r] pedestrian, for pedestrians; rue f (or aire f or zone f) piétonne (or piétonnière) pedestrian precinct.

piètre [pjɛtr] wretched, poor (a. fig.); fig. lame (excuse).

pieu [pjø] m stake, pile, post; sl. bed; **pieuter** sl. [~'te] (1a) v/rfl.: se ~ hit the sack.

pieuvre zo. [pjœ:vr] f octopus, squid, devil-fish.

pieux, -euse [pjø, pjø:z] pious, devout; dutiful (child); ⚖ charitable (bequest).

pif¹ F [pif] m nose.

pif²! [~] int.: ~ ~!, ~ paf! bang, bang!

pif(f)er sl. [pi'fe]: je ne peux pas le ~ I can't stand him; **pifomètre** F [pifɔ'mɛːtr] m instinct, intuition; au ~ by guesswork; by chance.

pige [pi:ʒ] f measuring rod; journ. etc. à la ~ (paid) by the line; sl. faire la ~ à do better than, outdo.

pigeon [pi'ʒɔ̃] m orn. pigeon (a. F fig.); 🔺 builder's plaster; ~ voyageur carrier-pigeon; **pigeonne** orn. [~'ʒɔn] f hen-pigeon; **pigeonneau** [piʒɔ'no] m young pigeon; F fig. dupe; **pigeonnier** [~'nje] m pigeon-house, dovecot(e).

piger sl. [pi'ʒe] (1l) vt/i. cotton on (to, à), get (it), get the message (= understand); look (at).

pigment [pig'mɑ̃] m skin etc.: pigment.

pigne 🌿 [piɲ] f fir-cone, pine-cone.

pignocher F [piɲɔ'ʃe] (1a) v/i. pick (at one's food).

pignon [pi'ɲɔ̃] m 🔺 gable; ⊕ pinion; ⊕ cogwheel; 🌿 pine seed; fig. avoir ~ sur rue be well set up.

pignouf F [pi'ɲuf] m rotten cad; miser.

pilage [pi'la:ʒ] m pounding, crushing.

pilastre 🔺 [pi'lastr] m pilaster; newel.

pile¹ [pil] f pile, heap; 🔺 bridge: pier; phys. (atomic, nuclear) pile; 🎯 battery; ⊕ beating-trough; sl. thrashing; 🎯 ~ sèche dry cell.

pile² [~] f reverse (of a coin); ~ ou face heads pl. or tails pl.; jouer à ~ ou face toss up; F exactly, just, right; F s'arrêter ~ stop short or dead.

piler [pi'le] (1a) v/t. pound, crush, grind (almonds, pepper).

pileux, -euse zo., a. 🌿 [pi'lø, ~'lø:z] pilose, hairy.

pilier [pi'lje] m 🔺 pillar (a. fig.), column; bridge: pier; fig. frequenter (of a place).

pillage [pi'ja:ʒ] m looting, pillaging; mettre au ~ plunder; **pillard, e** [~'ja:r, ~'jard] 1. adj. pillaging; pilfering; 2. su. looter, plunderer; **piller** [~'je] (1a) v/t. pillage, loot, plunder; fig. steal from (an author); fig. ransack (a book, a work); **pilleur, -euse** [~'jœ:r, ~'jø:z] 1. adj. looting; pilfering; 2. su. looter; plunderer; ⚓ ~ d'épaves wrecker.

pilon [pi'lɔ̃] m ⊕ rammer; metall. stamper; pestle; F wooden leg; cuis. fowl: drumstick; mettre au ~ pulp (a book); **pilonner** [~lɔ'ne] (1a) v/t. pound; ⊕ ram; metall. stamp (ore); ✕ shell, 🎯 bomb, a. fig. bombard.

pilori [pilɔ'ri] m pillory.

pilot [pi'lo] m 🔺 pile; salt-pans: heap of salt.

pilotage [pilɔ'ta:ʒ] m ⚓ pilotage (a. 🎯); 🎯 flying; ~ sans visibilité blind flying, flying on instruments; **pilote** [~'lɔt] 1. su./m ⚓, 🎯, etc., a. fig. pilot; fig. leader, guide; 🎯 ~ automatique automatic pilot, gyro-pilot; ~ d'essai test-pilot; 2. adj. pilot (project etc.), experimental; ✝ low-priced (drink etc.).

piloter [pilɔ'te] (1a) v/t. ⚓, 🎯 pilot;

⚹ fly (*a plane*); *fig.* guide, show (round Paris, *dans Paris*).

pilotis [pilɔ'ti] *m* pile-work; piling.

pilule ⚕, *a. fig.* [pi'lyl] *f* pill.

pimbêche F [pɛ̃'bɛʃ] *f* stuck-up woman *or* girl.

piment [pi'mɑ̃] *m* ⚕, *a. cuis.* pimento, Jamaica pepper; *cuis.* red pepper; *fig.* spice; **pimenter** [∼mɑ̃'te] (1a) *v/t. cuis.* season with pimento; *fig.* give spice to (*a story*).

pimpant, e [pɛ̃'pɑ̃, ∼'pɑ̃:t] smart; fresh and trim; spruce.

pin ⚕ [pɛ̃] *m* pine(-tree), fir(-tree); ∼ sylvestre Scotch fir; *pomme f de* ∼ fir-cone, pine-cone.

pinacle [pi'nakl] *m* pinnacle; *fig.* height of power *or* fame; F *porter au* ∼ praise (*s.o.*) to the skies.

pinailler *sl.* [pina'je] (1a) *v/i.* quibble.

pinard F [pi'na:r] *m* wine.

pinasse ⚓ [pi'nas] *f* pinnace.

pince [pɛ̃:s] *f* ⊕ pincers *pl.*, pliers *pl.*; *riveting, sugar, etc.*: tongs *pl.*; ⚡ clip (*a. bicycle, paper, etc.*); ⊕ crowbar; *zo.* crab, lobster: claw; *sl. fig.* paw, hand; *cost.* dart, pleat; *zo.* ∼s *pl. herbivora:* incisors; ∼ à épiler tweezers *pl.*; ∼ à linge clothes peg (*Am.* pin); ∼ à ongles nail clippers *pl.*

pincé, e [pɛ̃'se] **1.** *adj.* prim, affected; stiff (*voice*); tight-lipped (*smile*); **2.** *su./f* pinch (*of salt etc.*).

pinceau [pɛ̃'so] *m* (paint-)brush; *opt. light:* pencil; *fig.* touch.

pincement [pɛ̃s'mɑ̃] *m* pinch(ing); plucking; twinge; *j'ai eu un* ∼ *au cœur* my heart missed a beat; **pince-monseigneur**, *pl.* **pinces-monseigneur** [pɛ̃smɔ̃sɛ'ɲœːr] *m* crowbar, jemmy; **pince-nez** [∼'ne] *m/inv.* pince-nez, eye-glasses *pl.*; **pincer** [pɛ̃'se] (1k) *v/t.* pinch; nip; grip; purse (*one's lips*); F arrest; ♪ pluck (*the strings*); en ∼ *pour* have a crush on (*s.o.*); **pince-sans-rire** [pɛ̃ssɑ̃'ri:r] *m/inv.* man of dry and sly humo(u)r; **pincettes** [pɛ̃'sɛt] *f/pl.* tweezers; (fire) tongs; **pinçon** [∼'sɔ̃] *m* pinch mark.

pineraie [pin'rɛ] *f*, **pinède** ⚕ [pi'nɛd] *f see* pinière.

pingouin *orn.* [pɛ̃'gwɛ̃] *m* auk, razorbill.

pingre F [pɛ̃:gr] **1.** *adj.* miserly, stingy, near; **2.** *su.* skinflint; **pingrerie** F [pɛ̃grə'ri] *f* stinginess.

pinière ⚕ [pi'njɛ:r] *f* pine-wood, fir-grove.

pinson *orn.* [pɛ̃'sɔ̃] *m* finch.

pintade [pɛ̃'tad] *f orn.* guinea-fowl; F stuck-up woman.

pinte [pɛ̃:t] *f measure:* (French) pint, (*approx.*) English quart; **pinter** *sl.* [pɛ̃'te] (1a) *v/i.* tipple, booze; *v/t.* swill (*beer etc.*).

piochage [pjɔ'ʃa:ʒ] *m* swotting; **pioche** ⊕ [pjɔʃ] *f* pick(axe); **piocher** [pjɔ'ʃe] (1a) *vt/i.* dig (*with a pick*); F *fig.* grind; *v/t.* F *fig.* swot at; *v/i.* F *fig.* swot; **piocheur, -euse** [∼'ʃœ:r, ∼'ʃø:z] *su.* F *person:* swot, *Am.* grind; *su./m* navvy, digger; *su./f* ⊕ steam-digger.

piolet *mount.* [pjɔ'lɛ] *m* ice-axe.

pion [pjɔ̃] *m chess:* pawn; *draughts:* man; F *school:* usher, supervisor (*of preparation*).

pioncer *sl.* [pjɔ̃'se] (1k) *v/i.* sleep.

pionnier ⚒ [pjɔ'nje] *m* pioneer (*a. fig.*).

pipe [pip] *f* pipe (*a. measure for wine*); ⚡, *gas, liquid:* pipe; **pipeau** [pi'po] *m* ♪ (reed-)pipe; bird-call; *birds:* limed-twig, snare; **pipée** [∼'pe] *f* bird-snaring (*with bird-calls*).

pipe-line [pajp'lajn] *m oil:* pipe-line.

piper [pi'pe] (1a) *v/t.* lure (*with bird-calls*); *fig.* † trick, dupe (*s.o.*); load (*a dice*); mark (*a card*).

pipette ⚗ [pi'pɛt] *f* pipette.

pipeur [pi'pœ:r] *m* bird-lurer; F sharper, cheat.

pipi *ch.sp.* [pi'pi] *m: faire* ∼ wee.

piquant, e [pi'kɑ̃, ∼'kɑ̃:t] **1.** *adj.* pricking; stinging (*nettle, a. remark*); biting (*remark, wind*); tart (*wine*); pungent (*smell, taste*); *fig.* piquant (*a. sauce*), stimulating; *cuis.* hot (*spice*); mot *m* ∼ witty remark, quip; **2.** *su./m plant:* sting; *porcupine:* quill; *sauce etc.:* bite; *fig.* piquancy; *fig.* point; **pique** [pik] *su./f* † ✕ pike; pointed tip; pique, ill feeling; *su./m cards:* spade(s *pl.*); **piqué, e** [pi'ke] **1.** *adj.* quilted (*garment*); sour (*wine*); ♪ staccato (*note*); ✈ nose-(dive); *cuis.* larded (*meat*); F cracked, dotty, moth-eaten; **2.** *su./m* quilting; piqué; ✈ nose-dive, vertical dive; **pique-assiette** F [pika'sjɛt] *m* sponger; **pique-**

feu [pik'fø] *m/inv.* fire-rake, poker; **pique-nique** [ˌ~'nik] *m* picnic; **pique-notes** [ˌ~'nɔt] *m/inv.* spike-file; **piquer** [pi'ke] (1m) *vt/i.* prick; sting; *v/t.* nettle, wasp, *fig. remark:* sting (*s.o.*); make (*eyes, tongue*) smart; *moths, worms:* eat into; *tex.* quilt; pink (*silk*); *fig.* offend; arouse (*s.o.'s curiosity*); *cuis.* lard; *fig.* interlard (*an account, a story*); ✗ ~ *q. à qch.* give an injection of s.th. to s.o.; ✗ ~ *un animal* put an animal to sleep; ~ *une tête* dive, take a header; F ~ *un soleil* blush; *se* ~ get mildewy; turn sour; *fig.* get offended; *se* ~ *de* pride o.s. on; have pretensions to; *v/i.:* ~ *des deux* spur one's horse; ~ *sur* head for; ✗ etc. dive down on.

piquet[1] [pi'kɛ] *m* peg, stake, post; ✗ picket; ~ *de grève* strike picket.

piquet[2] [ˌ~] *m cards:* piquet; pack of piquet cards.

piqueter [pik'te] (1c) *v/t.* stake out (*a camp, a. surv., a.* ⚔); peg out; spot, dot; ⊕ picket (*a factory etc.*).

piquette [pi'kɛt] *f* second wine; poor wine; **piqueur, -euse** [ˌ~'kœːr, ~'køːz] *su.* stitcher, sewer; *su./m hunt.* whip(per-in); groom; outrider; ✗ hewer; ⊕ plate-layer; **piqûre** [ˌ~'kyːr] *f* sting, prick; (*flea-*)bite; ✗ injection; puncture; spot; *books, leather, etc.:* stitching, sewing.

pirate [pi'rat] *m* pirate; ~ *de l'air* highjacker; **pirater** [pi'ra'te] (1a) *v/i.* practise piracy; pirate; **piraterie** [ˌ~'tri] *f* piracy (*a. fig.*); ~ *aérienne* highjacking.

pire [piːr] worse; *au* ~ if the worst comes to the worst; *le* ~ (the) worst.

piriforme [piri'fɔrm] pear-shaped.

pirogue [pi'rɔg] *f* (dug-out) canoe.

pirouette [pi'rwɛt] *f toy:* whirligig; *horsemanship, a. dancing:* pirouette; **pirouetter** [ˌ~rwɛ'te] (1a) *v/i.* pirouette; twirl.

pis[1] *zo.* [pi] *m* udder.

pis[2] [pi] *adv.* worse; *le* ~ (the) worst; **~-aller** [piza'le] *m/inv.* stopgap, last resource.

piscicole [pisi'kɔl] piscicultural; **pisciculteur** [ˌ~kyl'tœːr] *m* pisciculturist; **pisciculture** [ˌ~kyl'tyːr] *f* pisciculture, fish-breeding; **pisciforme** [ˌ~'fɔrm] pisciform, fish-shaped.

piscine [pi'sin] *f* swimming-pool; public baths *pl.*; † fish-pond.

piscivore [pisi'vɔːr] piscivorous.

pisé ⚠ [pi'ze] *m* puddled clay.

pissat [pi'sa] *m* (*animal*) urine; **pissenlit** ⚘ [ˌ~sã'li] *m* dandelion; F *fig. manger les* ~*s par la racine* be pushing up the daisies (= *be dead*); **pisser** V [ˌ~'se] (1a) *v/i.* piss, pee; **pissoir** [ˌ~'swaːr] *m* urinal; **pissotière** V [ˌ~sɔ'tjɛːr] *f* urinal.

pistache ⚘ [pis'taʃ] *f* pistachio-nut; **pistachier** ⚘ [ˌ~ta'ʃje] *m* pistachio tree.

piste [pist] *f* track; race-track; race-course; *circus:* ring; *hunt., a. fig.* trail, scent; clue, lead; ✈ tarmac; ✈ ~ *d'atterrissage* landing-strip; ✈ ~ *d'envol* runway; *cin.* ~ *sonore* soundtrack; **pister** [pis'te] *v/t. hunt.* track; tail (*s.o.*).

pistil ⚘ [pis'til] *m* pistil.

pistolet [pistɔ'le] *m* pistol; gun; *a.* ~-*pulvérisateur* spray gun.

piston [pis'tɔ̃] *m* ⊕ piston; ♪ valve; ♪ cornet; *fig.* influence, F pull; ⊕ *course f du* ~ piston-stroke; **pistonner** F [ˌ~tɔ'ne] (1a) *v/t.* pull strings for (*s.o.*).

pitance [pi'tãːs] *f* (allowance of) food; **piteux, -euse** [ˌ~'tø, ~'tøːz] piteous, sorry, woeful.

pithécanthrope [pitekã'trɔp] ~*m* pithecanthrope, ape-man.

pitié [pi'tje] *f* pity (on, *de*).

piton [pi'tɔ̃] *m* ⊕ eye-bolt, ring-bolt; F large nose; *geog.* peak; *mount.* piton, peg; ~ *à vis* screweye.

pitoyable [pitwa'jabl] pitiful; pitiable; poor.

pitre [pitr] *m* clown (*a. pej. fig.*); **pitrerie** [pitrə'ri] *f* buffoonery.

pittoresque [pitɔ'resk] **1.** *adj.* picturesque; graphic (*description, style*); **2.** *su./m* picturesqueness; vividness.

pivert *orn.* [pi'vɛːr] *m* green woodpecker.

pivoine ⚘ [pi'vwan] *f* peony.

pivot [pi'vo] *m* ⊕ pivot (*a.* ✗ *sl.*), pin, axis; *lever:* fulcrum; *fig.* central figure *etc.*; ⚘ tap-root; F ~*s pl.* legs; **pivoter** [ˌ~vɔ'te] (1a) *v/i.* pivot; turn, swivel; ✗ wheel; ⚘ form tap-roots; F *faire* ~ drill, put (*s.o.*) through it.

placage [pla'kaːʒ] *m* ⊕ veneer(ing); *metal:* plating; ♪ patchwork; **placard** [ˌ~'kaːr] *m* cupboard; ⚠ *door:*

panel; poster, bill; *typ. proof*: galley; **placarder** [⌣kar'de] (1a) *v/t.* post (*a bill*); stick (*a poster*) on a wall.

place [plas] *f* place, position; space, room; seat (*a. 🌊, thea., etc.*); square; (*taxi-*)stand; job, employment; rank; ⚔ ~ *d'armes* parade-ground; ⚔ ~ *forte* fortified town; fortress; *à la* ~ *de* instead of; *à votre* ~ if I were you; ✝ *faire la* ~ canvass for orders; *par* ~*s* here and there; *sur* ~ on the spot; **placement** [plas'mã] *m* placing; ✝ sale, disposal; ✝ *money*: investing, investment.

placer [pla'se] (1k) *v/t.* place; put; find employment for; ✝ sell, dispose of; ✝ invest (*money*); seat (*s.o.*); show (*s.o.*) to a seat; F *il n'a pu* ~ *un mot* he couldn't get a word in; *se* ~ find a job; sell (*article*).

placet ⚏ [pla'sɛ] *m* claim; petition.

placeur, -euse [pla'sœːr, ~'søːz] *su.* manager of an employment agency; steward (*at meetings*); ✝ placer, seller; *su./f thea.* usherette, attendant.

placide [pla'sid] placid, calm; **placidité** [⌣sidi'te] *f* calmness, serenity, placidity.

placier *m*, **-ère** *f* [pla'sje, ~'sjɛːr] agent, canvasser; *admin.* clerk in charge of letting market pitches.

plafond [pla'fɔ̃] **1.** *su./m* ceiling (*a. fig., a.* ⚞); *mot.* maximum speed; ⚒ roof; ⚓ *hold*: floor; ⊕ *canal*: bottom; **2.** *adj.* maximum, ceiling; **plafonner** [⌣fɔ'ne] (1a) *v/t.* ⚛ ceil; *v/i.* reach a maximum; *mot.* reach one's top speed; ⚞ fly at the ceiling; ✝ reach the ceiling (of, *à*) (*prices*); **plafonnier** [⌣fɔ'nje] *m* ceiling-light; *mot.* roof-light.

plage [plaːʒ] *f* beach, shore; seaside resort; surface; place; area, zone; period (of time); section, portion; range; ~ *arrière* ⚓ quarter-deck; *mot.* back shelf.

plagiaire [pla'ʒjɛːr] *m* plagiarist (from, *de*); **plagiat** [~'ʒja] *m* plagiarism, plagiary; **plagier** [~'ʒje] (1o) *v/t.* plagiarize, F crib from.

plaid [plɛd] *m tex., cost.* plaid; travelling-rug.

plaider [plɛ'de] (1a) *v/i.* plead; litigate, go to court; *v/t.* plead; **plaideur** *m*, **-euse** *f* ⚏ [~'dœːr, ~'døːz]

litigious person; **plaidoirie** ⚏ [⌣dwa'ri] *f* counsel's speech; **plaidoyer** [⌣dwa'je] *m* ⚏ defence speech; *fig.* plea, argument (for, *en faveur de*).

plaie [plɛ] *f* wound; sore (*a. fig.*); scourge; *bibl., fig.* plague.

plaignant, e ⚏ [plɛ'nã, ~'nãːt] *adj., a. su.* plaintiff; complainant.

plain, plaine [plɛ̃, plɛn] *adj.*: *de* ~*-pied* on a level (with, *avec*), on the same floor; *fig.* straight; ~*-chant, pl.* ~*s-chants* ♪ [plɛ̃'ʃã] *m* plainsong.

plaindre [plɛ̃ːdr] (4m) *v/t.* pity, be sorry for; ✝ grudge; *se* ~ complain; grumble.[]
plaine [plɛn] *f* plain.
plainte [plɛ̃t] *f* complaint (*a.* ⚏); reproach; lamentation; **plaintif, -ve** [plɛ̃'tif, ~'tiːv] plaintive; querulous (*person, voice*).

plaire [plɛːr] (4z) *v/i.*: ~ *à* please; *à Dieu ne plaise* God forbid (that, *que*); *v/impers.*: *cela lui plaît* he likes that; *plaît-il?* I beg your pardon?; *qu'il vous plaise ou non* if you like it or not; *s'il vous plaît, s'il te plaît* please; *v/t.*: *se* ~ delight (in, *à*); enjoy o.s.; be happy; please one another.

plaisamment [plɛza'mã] *adv. of plaisant* 1; **plaisance** [~'zãːs] *f*: *de* ~ pleasure-(*boat, ground*); country (*seat*), in the country (*house*); **plaisant, e** [~'zã, ~'zãːt] **1.** *adj.* pleasant; amusing; ✝ ridiculous; **2.** *su./m the* amusing part (*of s.th.*); *mauvais* ~ practical joker; **plaisanter** [plɛzã'te] (1a) *v/i.* joke; *pour* ~ for fun, for a joke; *v/t.* chaff (*s.o.*); **plaisanterie** [~'tri] *f* joke; *mauvaise* ~ silly joke; *par* ~ for fun; **plaisantin** [~'tɛ̃] *m* joker.

plaisir [plɛ'ziːr] *m* pleasure (*a. fig.*); delight; amusement; favo(u)r; *à* ~ at will; without cause; *avec* ~ willingly; *de* ~ pleasure-...; *faire* ~ *à* please; *les* ~*s de la table* the pleasures of the palate; *menus* ~*s pl.* little luxuries; *par* ~ for pleasure.

plaisons [plɛ'zɔ̃] *1st p. pl. pres. of plaire*; **plaisant** [~'zɑ̃] ...; **plaît** [plɛ] *3rd p. sg. pres. of plaire*.

plan, plane [plã, plan] **1.** *adj.* plane (*a.* Å), level, flat; **2.** *su./m* Å, Δ, ♂, *opt.* plane; ⊕ *plane*: sole; ⚔ *fire*: line; ⚞ wing; *fig.* level, sphere; *fig.* rank, importance; Δ *etc., fig.* plan; draft, drawing; *cin. gros* ~ close-up; F

24*

laisser q. en ~ leave s.o. in the lurch; *premier* ~ *thea.* down-stage; *paint.* foreground; *fig.* first importance; *second* ~ *paint.* middle ground; *fig.* background, *fig.* second rank.

planche [plɑ̃:ʃ] *f* board; plank; (*book-*)shelf; ⊕ plate, block; ✔ land; ✔ (*flower-* etc.)bed; *thea.* ~s *pl.* boards, stage *sg.*; ⚓ ~ *de débarquement* gang-plank; *faire la* ~ *swimming*: float (on one's back); ⚓, ✝ *jours* m/*pl. de* ~s lay days; **planchéier** [plɑ̃ʃe'je] (1a) *v/t.* board (over); floor (*a room*); **plancher** [~'ʃe] **1.** *su./m* (*boarded*) floor; ⚓ planking, ✔, *mot.* floor-board; F *des vaches* terra firma; F *débarrasser le* ~ clear out (= *go away*); F *mot.* *mettre le pied au* ~ step on it; **2.** *adj.* bottom, minimum (*price etc.*); **planchette** [~'ʃɛt] *f* small board *or* plank.

plan-concave *opt.* [plɑ̃kɔ̃'ka:v] planoconcave; **plan-convexe** *opt.* [~'vɛks] planoconvex.

plane ⊕ [plan] *f* drawing-knife; turning-chisel.

plané, e ✈ [pla'ne] gliding; *vol m* ~ glide, volplane; *birds:* soaring.

planer¹ [pla'ne] (1a) *v/t.* ⊕ make even; plane (*wood*).

planer² [~] (1a) *v/i.* ✈ glide; soar (*bird*); hover (*bird, mist, a. fig.*).

planétaire [plane'tɛːr] **1.** *adj.* planetary; **2.** *su./m* planetarium; **planète** *astr.* [~'nɛt] *f* planet.

planeur [pla'nœːr] *m* ✈ glider; ⊕ *metals:* planisher; **planeuse** ⊕ [~'nøːz] *f* planing-machine; planishing-machine.

planification *pol.* [planifika'sjɔ̃] *f* planning; **planifier** [~'fje] (1a) *v/t.* plan; *économie f planifiée* planned economy.

planimétrie ⚕ [planime'tri] *f* planimetry; **planimétrique** [~'trik] planimetric(al).

planning [pla'niŋ] *m* planning (*a. pol.*); ~ *familial* family planning.

planque *sl.* [plɑ̃k] *f* hideaway; cushy job; **planquer** *sl.* [plɑ̃'ke] (1m) *v/t.* hide; *se* ~ take cover; hide; lie flat.

plant ✔ [plɑ̃] *m* sapling; slip; (nursery) plantation; **plantage** ✔ [plɑ̃-'ta:ʒ] *m* planting; plantation.

plantain ⚘ [plɑ̃'tɛ̃] *m* plantain.

plantation [plɑ̃ta'sjɔ̃] *f* planting; plantation; *fig.* setting up, erection; **plante** [plɑ̃:t] *f* ⚘ plant; *anat. foot:*

sole; ~ *d'appartement* indoor plant; ~ *marine* seaweed; *jardin m des* ~s botanical gardens *pl.*, F zoo; **planter** [plɑ̃'te] (1a) *v/t.* plant; fix, set up; F *fig.* ~ *là* run out on (*s.o.*); jilt (*s.o.*); chuck (up); *se* ~ take (up) a stand; **planteur** [~'tœːr] *m* planter; **planteuse** [~'tøːz] *f* planting-machine.

plantigrade *zo.* [plɑ̃ti'grad] *adj., a. su./m* plantigrade.

plantoir ✔ [plɑ̃'twaːr] *m* dibble.

planton ⚔ [plɑ̃'tɔ̃] *m* orderly.

plantule ⚘ [plɑ̃'tyl] *f* plantlet, plantling.

plantureux, -euse [plɑ̃ty'rø, ~'røːz] plentiful, copious; fertile, rich (*country*); *fig.* buxom (*woman*).

plaque [plak] *f* sheet; *metal, a. phot.*: plate; *marble:* slab; *engine, a.* 🚂: bed-plate; (*ornamental*) plaque; badge; ~ *commémorative* (votive) tablet; *mot.* ~ *de police,* ~ *minéralogique* number plate; ~ *de porte* (*rue*) name plate (street plate); ~ *d'identité* identification plate, ⚔ identity disc; ~ *tournante* 🚂 turntable; *fig.* centre; **plaqué** ⊕ [pla'ke] *m* plated metal; electroplate; veneered wood; **plaquer** [~'ke] (1m) *v/t.* ⊕ plate (*metal*); ⊕ veneer (*wood*); ✔ lay down (*turf*); *foot.* tackle; ♪ strike (*a chord*); F run out on (*s.o.*); jilt (*s.o.*); chuck (up); **plaquette** [~'kɛt] *f metal, wood:* small plate; *stone, marble:* thin slab; brochure; **plaqueur** [~'kœːr] *m* ⊕ *metal:* plater; *wood:* veneerer; *foot.* tackler.

plastic 🎇 [plas'tik] *m* explosive gelatine; **plasticité** [~tisi'te] *f* plasticity; **plastique** [~'tik] **1.** *adj.* plastic; **2.** *su./f* plastic art; *fig.* figure; *su./m* ⊕ plastic goods *pl.*

plastron [plas'trɔ̃] *m* ⚔ breast-plate; ⊕ drill-plate; fencing-jacket; *fig.* butt; *cost.* woman's modesty-front; *cost.* man's shirt-front; **plastronner** [~trɔ'ne] (1a) *v/i.* F strut, put on side.

plat, plate [pla, plat] **1.** *adj.* flat (*a. fig.*); level; smooth (*sea*); straight (*hair*); low-heeled (*shoes*); empty (*purse*); plain (*water*); *fig.* dull; *fig.* poor, paltry; *calme m* ~ dead calm; **2.** *su./m* flat part (*of s.th.*); *oar, tongue:* blade; *book:* board; *cuis.* dish; *cuis.* course; *à* ~ flat; F *fig.* washed out, all in; F *mettre les pieds dans le* ~ put one's foot in it; *tomber à ~* fall flat on one's face, *thea.* fall flat (*play*).

platane ♀ [pla'tan] *m* plane-tree; *faux ~* sycamore, great maple.

plateau [pla'to] *m* tray; platform; *thea.* stage; *geog.* plateau; *balance*: scale; ⊕ (bed-)plate; ⊕ table.

plate-bande, *pl.* **plates-bandes** [plat'bɑ̃:d] *f* ✿ flower-bed; (grass) border; △ plat band; F *plates-bandes pl.* preserves, private ground *sg.*

platée [pla'te] *f* △ *concrete*: foundation; F dishful.

plate-forme, *pl.* **plates-formes** [plat'fɔrm] *f bus, a. fig.*: platform; 🚂 *engine*: foot-plate.

platine [pla'tin] *su./f lock, watch*: plate; *typewriter, printing press*: platen; *record player*: turntable; deck; *su./m* ⚗ min. platinum; **platiné, e** [~ti'ne] platinized; *une blonde ~e* a platinum blonde.

platitude [plati'tyd] *f* platitude, commonplace remark; *fig.* servility; *style*: flatness.

plâtrage [plɑ'tra:ʒ] *m* ⊕ plastering; △ plaster-work; F rubbish; **plâtras** [~'trɑ] *m* debris (of building materials); **plâtre** [plɑ:tr] *m* plaster; plaster cast; plaster-work; *battre comme ~* beat (*s.o.*) to a jelly; ✿ *mettre en ~* (put into) plaster; **plâtrer** [plɑ'tre] (1a) *v/t.* plaster; *fig.* patch up; ✿ (put into) plaster; **plâtreux, -euse** [~'trø, ~'trø:z] plastery; chalky (*soil, water*); gypseous; **plâtrier** [~tri'e] *m* plasterer; calciner of gypsum; **plâtrière** [~tri-'ɛ:r] *f* gypsum-quarry, gypsum-kiln; chalk-pit.

plausible [plo'zibl] plausible; specious.

plèbe [plɛb] *f the* plebs; *the* common people *pl.*; **plébéien, -enne** [plebe'jɛ̃, ~'jɛn] *adj., a. su.* plebeian; **plébiscite** [plebi'sit] *m* plebiscite; **plébisciter** [~si'te] (1a) *v/t.* vote for by plebiscite; vote for *or* elect *or* approve (of) by an overwhelming majority; F measure (*s.o.'s*) popularity.

plein, pleine [plɛ̃, plɛn] **1.** *adj.* full (of, de); filled (with, de); high (*sea, tide*); open (*country, street*); big with young (*animal*); solid (*brick, wood, tyre, wire*); *~ emploi see plein-emploi; fig. pleine saison the*

height of the season; *de son ~ gré* of one's own free will; *en ~ air* in the open; *en ~ jour* in broad daylight; *fig.* publicly, openly; ⚓ *en pleine mer* on the open sea; *en pleine rue* in the open street; openly; **2.** *su./m* full part; *building*: solid part; ⚔ *etc.* bull's-eye; fill(ing); *battre son ~* be at the full (*tide*); *fig.* be in full swing (*party, season, etc.*); *mot. faire le ~* fill up with petrol *or Am.* gas, fill up the tank; **plein-emploi** [plɛ̃ɑ̃'plwa] *m* full employment; **plein-temps** [plɛ̃'tɑ̃] **1.** *adj./inv.* full-time; **2.** *m/inv.* full-time job.

plénier, -ère [ple'nje, ~'njɛ:r] complete, absolute; ✝, *eccl.* plenary; **plénipotentiaire** [plenipotɑ̃'sjɛ:r] *adj., a. su./m* plenipotentiary; **plénitude** [~'tyd] *f* fullness; completeness.

plénum, plenum [ple'nɔm] *m* plenum.

pléonasme [pleɔ'nasm] *m* pleonasm.

pléthore [ple'tɔ:r] *f* ⚕, *a. fig.* plethora; *fig.* (super)abundance; **pléthorique** [~tɔ'rik] ⚕ plethoric, full-blooded; *fig.* superabundant.

pleur [plœ:r] *f* tear; **pleurard, e** [plœ'ra:r, ~'rard] **1.** *adj.* whimpering; whining (*voice*); tearful; **2.** *su.* whiner; F cry-baby; **pleure-misère** [plœrmi'zɛ:r] *su./inv.* person who is always pleading poverty; **pleurer** [plœ're] (1a) *v/t.* weep for, mourn for; *v/i.* weep; cry (for, de; over, sur) (*a. fig.*); water, run (*eyes*); ⊕ *etc.* drip; 🩸 bleed.

pleurésie ⚕ [plœre'zi] *f* pleurisy.

pleureur, -euse [plœ'rœ:r, ~'rø:z] **1.** *adj.* tearful, lachrymose; weeping (*person, rock, ♀ willow*); **2.** *su.* weeper; whimperer; *su./f* hired mourner; **pleurnicher** F [plœrni-'ʃe] (1a) *v/i.* whimper, whine, snivel; **pleurnicherie** [~niʃ'ri] *f* whining; **pleurnicheur, -euse** [~ni'ʃœ:r, ~'ʃø:z] **1.** *adj.* whining, whimpering, peevish; **2.** *su.* whiner, whimperer; F cry-baby.

pleut [plø] *3rd p. sg. pres. of pleuvoir.*

pleutre [plø:tr] *m* cad; coward.

pleuvoir [plœ'vwa:r] (3g) *v/impers.* rain; *il pleut à verse* it is pouring (with rain), it is raining hard; *v/i. fig.* pour in; **pleuvra** [~'vra] *3rd p. sg. fut. of pleuvoir.*

plèvre *anat.* [plɛ:vr] *f* pleura.

plexus *anat.* [plɛk'sys] *m*: ~ solaire solar plexus.

pli [pli] *m* fold, pleat; wrinkle; (*a. faux* ~) crease; ✝ cover, envelope; *bridge*, *whist*: trick; *arm*, *leg*: bend; *fig.* habit; *ground*: undulation; ~s *pl. non repassés* unpressed pleats; *faire des* ~s crease (*v/i*); *faire des* ~s *à pleat* (*s.th.*); F *cela ne fait pas un* ~ that's for sure; *fig. prendre un* ~ acquire a habit; ✝ *sous ce* ~ enclosed, herewith; ✝ *sous* ~ *séparé* under separate cover; **pliable** [~'abl] foldable, folding; pliable, flexible (*a. fig.*); **pliant, e** [~'ɑ̃, ~'ɑ̃:t] **1.** *adj.* pliant, flexible; folding; *fig.* docile; *mot. capote f* ~e collapsible hood; **2.** *su./m* folding-stool, camp-stool.

plie *icht.* [pli] *f* plaice.

plier [pli'e] (1a) *v/t.* fold (up); bend; bow (*one's head*); se ~ *à* submit to; *fig.* give o.s. up to; *v/i.* bend; yield (*a.* ✕); **plieur, -euse** [~'œːr, ~'øːz] *su.* folder; *su./f* folding-machine.

plinthe ⌂ *etc.* [plɛ̃ːt] *f* plinth.

plioir [pli'waːr] *m* *bookbinding*: folder; paper-knife; *fishing-line*: winder.

plisser [pli'se] (1a) *v/t.* pleat; crumple; crease; corrugate (*metal*, *paper*); pucker up (*one's face etc.*); *v/i.* crease, pucker; hang in *or* have folds; **plissure** [~'syːr] *f* pleating; pleats *pl.*

pliure [pli'yːr] *f* fold; bend; *book-binding*: folding.

plomb [plɔ̃] *m* lead; ⌂ lead sink; ⚡ fuse; ✝ lead seal; ⚓ plummet; *hunt. etc.* shot; *typ.* metal, type; *fig.* weight; *à* ~ vertically; upright; straight down; *mine f de* ~ black-lead, graphite; *sommeil m de* ~ heavy sleep; *tomber à* ~ fall plumb *or* vertically; **plombage** [plɔ̃'baːʒ] *m* leading, plumbing; ✝ sealing; *teeth*: stopping, filling; **plombagine** [~ba'ʒin] *f* graphite, plumbago; **plombé, e** [~'be] leaded (*a. cane*); leaden (*sky*); livid (*complexion*); **plomber** [~'be] (1a) *v/t.* cover *or* weight with lead; glaze (*pottery*); stop, fill (*a tooth*); ⌂ plumb; ✝ seal; *fig.* give a livid hue to; **plomberie** [~'bri] *f* plumbing; lead industry; lead-works *usu. sg.*; plumber's (shop); **plombier** [~'bje] *m* lead-worker; plumber;

plombifère [~bi'fɛːr] lead-bearing; lead (*glaze*).

plongeant, e [plɔ̃'ʒɑ̃, ~'ʒɑ̃:t] plunging; from above (*view*); **plongée** [~'ʒe] *f* plunge, dive; diving; slope; *ground*: dip; ~ *sous-marine* (skin) diving; **plongeoir** [~'ʒwaːr] *m* diving-board; **plongeon** [~'ʒɔ̃] *m* dive; *orn.* diver; *faire le* ~ dive; *fig.* make up one's mind, F take the plunge; **plonger** [~'ʒe] (1l) *vt/i.* plunge; *v/t.* dip (into, *dans*); se ~ immerse o.s.; *fig. être plongé dans* be absorbed in; *v/i.* dive; ⚓ submerge (*submarine*); dip (*ground*, *a.* ✕ *seam*); ⚓ ~ *du nez* pitch; **plongeur, -euse** [~'ʒœːr, ~'ʒøːz] **1.** *adj.* diving; **2.** *su. person*: diver; dish-washer, washer-up (*in a restaurant*); *su./m orn.* diver; ⊕ plunger.

plot ⚡ [plo] *m* stud, terminal; plug.

plouc, plouk, plouque *pej.* [pluk] **1.** *su./m* rustic, country bumpkin; provinciality, provincialism; **2.** *adj./inv.* rustic, provincial.

ploutocratie [plutɔkra'si] *f* plutocracy.

ployable [plwa'jabl] pliable; **ployer** [~'je] † (1h) *vt/i.* bend; *v/i.* give way.

plu[1] [ply] *p.p. of* plaire.

plu[2] [~] *p.p. of* pleuvoir.

pluie [plʉi] *f* rain (*a. fig.*); *fig.* shower; ~s (*pl.*) *acide(s)* acid rain; *craint la* ~! keep dry!; F *fig. faire la* ~ *et le beau temps* rule the roost.

plumage [ply'maːʒ] *m* plumage; **plumard** *sl.* [~'maːr] *m* bed; **plume** [plym] *f* feather; pen; pen-nib; *homme m de* ~ man of letters; **plumeau** [ply'mo] *m* feather duster; **plumée** [~'me] *f poultry*: plucking; **plumer** [~'me] (1a) *v/t.* pluck (*poultry*); F fleece (*s.o.*); **plumet** [~'mɛ] *m* ✕ *helmet*: plume; **plumier** [~'mje] *m* pen(cil) box; pen tray; **plumitif** *pej.* [~mi'tif] *m* penpusher; scribbler.

plupart [ply'paːr] *f*: *la* ~ most, the majority, the greater part; *la* ~ *des gens*, *la* ~ *du monde* most people; *la* ~ *du temps* most of the time; generally; *pour la* ~ mostly.

pluralité [plyrali'te] *f* plurality; *votes*: majority.

pluri... [plyri] pluri..., multi...

pluriel, -elle *gramm.* [ply'rjɛl] **1.** *adj.* plural; **2.** *su./m* plural; *au* ~ in the plural.

plus[1] [ply; *oft.* plys *at end of word-group*; *before vowel* plyz] **1.** *adv.* more; ⋏ plus; ~ ... ~ ... the more ... the more ...; ~ *confortable* more comfortable; ~ *de* more than (*2 days*); ~ *de soucis!* no more worries!; ~ *grand* bigger; ~ *haut!* speak up!; ~ *que* more than (*he*); ~ *rien* nothing more; *de* ~ further(more); *de* ~ *en* ~ more and more; *en* ~ in addition (to, de); extra; *le* ~ *confortable* most comfortable; *le* ~ *grand* biggest; *moi non* ~ nor I, F me neither; *ne* ... ~ no more, no longer; *non* ~ not again; *non* ~ (not) either; *rien de* ~ nothing else *or* more; *sans* ~ simply, only, nothing more; *tant et* ~ any amount, plenty; **2.** *su./m: le* ~ the most, the best; *au* ~ at the best, at most; *tout au* ~ at the best, at the very most.

plus[2] [ply] *1st p. sg. p.s. of* plaire.

plusieurs [ply'zjœːr] *adj./pl., a. pron./indef./pl.* several; some.

plus-que-parfait *gramm.* [plyskə-par'fɛ] *m* pluperfect.

plus-value ⋏, *pol.* [plyva'ly] *f* appreciation, increment value; betterment; extra-payment; *impôt m sur la* ~ (*approx.*) capital gains tax.

plut [ply] *3rd p. sg. p.s. of* pleuvoir.

plutonium ♄ [plytɔ'njɔm] *m* plutonium.

plutôt [ply'to] *adv.* rather, sooner (than, *que*); on the whole.

pluvial, e, *m/pl.* -aux [ply'vjal, ~-'vjo] rain-...; rainy (*season*); **pluvier** *orn.* [~'vje] *m* plover; **pluvieux, -euse** [~'vjø, ~'vjøːz] rainy; wet; of rain; **pluviomètre** *meteor.* [~vjɔ'mɛtr] *m* rain-ga(u)ge, udometer.

pneu, *pl.* **pneus** [pnø] *m mot.* tyre, *Am.* tire; express letter; ~ *antidérapant* non-skid tyre; **pneumatique** [~ma'tik] **1.** *adj.* air-..., pneumatic; **2.** *su./m* (pneumatic) tyre; (*a. carte f* ~) express letter.

pneumonie ⚕ [pnømɔ'ni] *f* pneumonia; **pneumonique** ⚕ [~'nik] pneumonic.

pochade [pɔ'ʃad] *f* rapid *or* rough sketch.   [drunk.⟩

pochard, e [pɔ'ʃaːr, ~'ʃard] *adj., su.⟩*

poche [pɔʃ] *f* pocket; sack; case; pouch; *geol.* pot-hole; *geol.* washout; *cost.* pucker, F bag; *fig.* isolated case(s *pl.*); ~ *d'air* ✈ air-pocket; ⊕

airlock; *argent m de* ~ pocket-money; **pochée** [pɔ'ʃe] *f* pocketful; **pocher** [~'ʃe] (1a) *v/t. cuis.* poach; *fig.* black (*s.o.'s eye*); dash off (*an essay, a sketch, etc.*); *cost.* make baggy at the knees; **pochetée** [pɔʃ'te] *f* pocketful; *sl.* stupid (person); **pochette** [pɔ'ʃɛt] *f* small pocket; handbag, sachet; *matches*: book; fancy handkerchief; ⋏ pocket-set (*of mathematical instruments*).

podagre ⚕ [pɔ'dagr] **1.** *su.* gouty person; *su./f* podagra; **2.** *adj.* gouty.

podomètre [pɔdɔ'mɛtr] *m* pedometer.

poêle[1] [pwaːl] *m* (funeral-)pall.

poêle[2] [pwaːl] *m* stove, cooker.

poêle[3] [pwaːl] *f* frying-pan; F *fig. tenir la queue de la* ~ be in charge *or* control; **poêlée** [pwa'le] *f* panful.

poêlier [pwa'lje] *m* dealer in stoves and cookers; stove-setter.

poêlon [pwa'lɔ̃] *m* small saucepan; casserole.

poème [pɔ'ɛm] *m* poem; **poésie** [~e'zi] *f* (piece of) poetry; **poète** [~'ɛt] *m* poet; *femme f* ~ woman poet, poetess; **poétereau** [pɔe'tro] *m* poetaster; **poétesse** [~'tɛs] *f* poetess; **poétique** [~'tik] **1.** *adj.* poetic(al); **2.** *su./f* poetics *sg.*; **poétiser** [~ti'ze] (1a) *v/i.* write poetry; *v/t.* poet(ic)ize.

poids [pwa] *m* weight; heaviness; *fig.* importance; load; *fig.* burden; ⋏ ~ *brut* gross weight; *box.* ~ *coq* bantam weight; *box.* ~ *léger* lightweight; ~ *lourd* box. heavy-weight; *mot.* heavy lorry *or* truck; *box.* ~ *mi-lourd* light heavy-weight; ~ *mort* dead weight; *box.* ~ *mouche* fly-weight; *box.* ~ *moyen* middle-weight; ⋏ ~ *net* net weight; *box.* ~ *plume* feather-weight; ♒ ~ *spécifique* specific gravity; ⚖ ~ *utile* payload; ~ *vif* live weight; *sp. lancer m* (*or* lancement *m*) *du* ~ shot put; *fig. ne pas faire le* ~ not to measure up.

poignant, e [pwa'nɑ̃, ~'nɑ̃ːt] poignant; keen; *fig.* heart-breaking.

poignard [pwa'naːr] *m* dagger; **poignarder** [~nar'de] (1a) *v/t.* stab; *fig.* wound (*s.o.*) deeply; **poigne** F [pwaɲ] *f* grip, grasp; **poignée** [pwa'ɲe] *f* handful (*a. fig.*); *door etc.*: handle; *sword*: hilt; ⊕ *tool*: haft; ~ *de main* handshake; **poignet** [~'ɲɛ] *m* wrist; *cost.* cuff; *shirt*: wristband.

poil [pwal] *m* hair; fur, coat (*of animal*); *tex. cloth*: nap; *velvet*: pile; ♥ down; *brush*: bristle; F *à* ~ naked; F *au* ~ great, fantastic; perfectly, fine; F *de bon* (*mauvais*) ~ in a good (bad) mood; **poilu, e** [pwaˡly] **1.** *adj.* hairy, shaggy; **2.** *su./m* ✕ F French soldier.

poinçon ⊕ [pwɛ̃ˡsɔ̃] *m* (brad)awl; punch; stamp; *silver etc.*: (hall-)mark; *embroidery*: pricker; **poinçonner** [pwɛ̃soˡne] (1a) *v/t.* prick; punch (*a. tickets*); stamp; hallmark (*silver etc.*); **poinçonneur** [~ˡnœːr] *m* puncher; **poinçonneuse** [~ˡnøːz] *f* ⊕ stamping-machine; ▭ ticket-punch.

poindre [pwɛ̃ːdr] (4m) *v/t.* † sting; *v/i.* dawn (*day*[*light*]); *fig.* come up, appear; ♥ sprout.

poing [pwɛ̃] *m* fist.

point¹ [pwɛ̃] *m* ♫, ♪, *phys.*, *typ.*, *sp.*, *fig.*, *time*, *place*: point; *gramm.* full stop, *Am.* period; ✂, needlework: stitch; *opt.* focus; *sp.* score; *school*: mark; speck; dot (*a. on letter i*); *cards*, *dice*: pip; *fig.* extent, degree; *fig.* state, condition; *cost.* lace; *fig.* ~ *chaud* hot spot, trouble spot; ~ *d'arrêt* stopping place; ✂ ~ *de côté* stitch in one's side; ✂ ~ *de suture* stitch (*in a wound*); ~ *de vue* point of view, viewpoint; ~ *d'exclamation* exclamation mark; ~ *d'interrogation* question mark; ~ *du jour* daybreak; *fig.* ~ *faible* weak point; *fig.* ~ *noir* problem; difficulty; weak spot *or* link; ~-*virgule* semicolon; *à ce* ~ *que* so much so that; *à* ~ in the right condition; in the nick of time; medium-cooked (*meat*); *au* ~ *mort* mot. in neutral; *fig.* at a standstill; *sp.* battre aux ~s beat (*s.o.*) on points; *de* ~ *en* ~ in every particular; *deux* ~s colon; *en tout* ~ in every way, on all points; être sur le ~ de (*inf.*) be about to (*inf.*); ⚓ faire le ~ take the ship's position; *mauvais* ~ *school*: bad *or* poor mark; *mettre au* ~ *opt.* focus; *mot. etc.* tune (*the engine*); restate (*a question*); clarify (*an affair*); *sur ce* ~ on that score *or* head.

point² [~] *adv.*: *ne ... ~* not ... at all; ~ *du tout!* not at all.

pointe [pwɛ̃ːt] *f* point; *arrow etc.*: tip; *bullet*: nose; *spire*, *tree*: top; touch (*of bronchitis etc.*, *a. fig.*); *geog.* headland, *land*: tongue; *day*: break; witticism; *fig.* peak, maximum; ~ *des*

pieds tiptoe; ⊕ ~ *sèche* etching-needle; dry-point engraving; F *avoir une* ~ *de vin* be slightly excited with drink; *fig. de* ~ top, leading; top, maximum; latest (*developments etc.*); décolleté *m en* ~ V-neck; *en* ~ pointed (*beard*); tapering; *fig.* top, leading; heures *f/pl. de* ~ peak hours.

pointer¹ [pwɛ̃ˡte] (1a) *v/t.* prick up (*one's ears*); sharpen (*a pencil*); ♪ dot (*a note*); *v/i.* ♥ sprout, come up; rear (*horse*); rise, soar (*bird*, *spire*).

pointer² [pwɛ̃ˡte] (1a) *v/t.* aim (*a gun etc.*); check (off) (*items*, *names*); prick; F *se* ~ turn up, show up; *v/i.* clock in *or* out (*worker*); **pointillé, e** [pwɛ̃tiˡje] *su./m* dotted line; stippling; **pointiller** [~ˡje] (1a) *v/t.* dot; stipple; **pointilleux, -euse** [~ˡjø, ~ˡjøːz] particular (about, *sur*); finicky; touchy.

pointu, e [pwɛ̃ˡty] pointed, sharp; *fig.* shrill (*voice*); *fig.* touchy (*disposition*); **pointure** [~ˡtyːr] *f collars*, *shoes*, *etc.*: size.

poire [pwaːr] *f* ♥ pear; ⚡ bulb; ⚡ pear-switch; *sl.* mug, sucker, F head; ~ *à poudre* powder-flask; F *garder une* ~ *pour la soif* put s.th. by for a rainy day; **poiré** [pwaˡre] *m* perry.

poireau [pwaˡro] *m* ♥ leek; F waiting person; F *faire le* ~ = **poireauter** F [~rɔˡte] (1a) *v/i.* be kept waiting, F cool *or* kick one's heels; **poirée** ♥ [~ˡre] *f* white beet.

poirier ♥ [pwaˡrje] *m* pear-tree.

pois [pwa] *m* ♥ pea; *tex.* polka dot; ~ *pl. cassés* split peas; ~ *chiche* chickpea; *tex. à* ~ spotted, dotted; *cuis.* petits ~ *pl.* green peas.

poison [pwaˡzɔ̃] *m* poison.

poissant, e F [pwaˡsɑ̃, ~ˡsɑ̃ːt] importunate, a pest.

poissard, e [pwaˡsaːr, ~ˡsard] **1.** *adj.* vulgar; **2.** *su./f* fishwife; foul-mouthed woman; *langue f de* ~ *e* F Billingsgate.

poisse F [pwas] *f* bad luck; **poisser** [pwaˡse] (1a) *v/t.* make sticky; ⊕ pitch; F nab (*s.o.*); **poisseux, -euse** [~ˡsø, ~ˡsøːz] sticky.

poisson [pwaˡsɔ̃] *m* fish; ~ *d'avril* April Fool trick *or* joke; ~ *rouge* goldfish; *faire un* ~ *d'avril à* make an April Fool of (*s.o.*); *astr.* les 2s *pl.* Pisces, the Fishes; ~-**chat**, *pl.* ~s-**chats** *icht.* [~sɔ̃ˡʃa] *m* cat-fish; **poissonnerie** [~sɔnˡri] *f* fish-market;

fish-shop; **poissonneux, -euse**
[͜sɔ'nø, ͜'nøːz] teeming with fish;
poissonnier, -ère [͜sɔ'nje, ͜'njɛːr]
su. fishmonger; su./f fishkettle.

poitrail [pwa'traːj] m zo. breast; co.
(human) chest; **poitrinaire** ⚥
[͜tri'nɛːr] adj., a. su. consumptive;
poitrine [͜'trin] f breast, chest;
woman: bust.

poivrade cuis. [pwa'vrad] f dressing
of oil, vinegar and pepper; **poivre**
[pwaːvr] m pepper; F ~ et sel grey-
haired (person); grain m de ~ pep-
percorn; **poivré, e** [pwa'vre] pep-
pery, hot (food); pungent (smell);
stiff (price); fig. spicy (story); **poivrer** [͜'vre] (1a) v/t. pepper; F
spice (a story etc.); **poivrier** [͜vri'e]
m pepper-box; ♀ pepper-plant;
poivrière [͜vri'ɛːr] f pepper-pot;
pepper-box (a. ⚠); pepper-plan-
tation; **poivron** [͜'vrɔ̃] m pimento,
allspice; **poivrot** F [͜'vro] m
drunkard.

poix [pwa] f pitch; cobbler's wax.

polaire ⚥, ⚦, geog. [pɔ'lɛːr] polar;
polarisation phys. [pɔlariza'sjɔ̃] f
polarization; **polariser** [͜'ze] (1a)
v/t. phys. polarize; fig. focus, centre;
polarité phys. [͜'te] f polarity.

pôle [poːl] m pole; geog. ~ Nord (Sud)
North (South) Pole.

polémique [pole'mik] 1. adj. polemic; 2. su./f polemic; eccl. po-
lemics pl.; **polémiquer** [͜mi'ke]
(1m) v/i. polemize.

poli, e [pɔ'li] 1. adj. polished (a. fig.);
burnished (metal); glossy; fig. polite; fig. urbane, elegant; 2. su./m
polish, gloss.

police¹ [pɔ'lis] f police, constabulary; policing; regulations pl.; ~ de
la circulation traffic police; ~ fluviale river police; ~ judiciaire (approx.) Criminal Investigation Department, C.I.D.; agent m de ~
policeman; appeler ͜(-)secours dial
999; ⚔ bonnet m de ~ forage cap;
fiche f de ~ registration form (at a
hotel); ⚔ salle f de ~ guard-room.

police² [͜] f insurance policy; †
~ de chargement bill of lading; ~
flottante floating policy.

policer † [pɔli'se] (1k) v/t. bring
law and order to; organize; civilize.
polichinelle [pɔliʃi'nɛl] m Punch;
F buffoon; secret m de ~ open secret.
policier, -ère [pɔli'sje, ͜'sjɛːr] 1. adj.

police...; detective (film, novel);
2. su./m policeman; detective; detective novel.
poliment [pɔli'mɑ̃] adv. of poli 1.
poliomyélite ⚕ [pɔljɔmje'lit] f
poliomyelitis, F polio; infantile
paralysis.
polir [pɔ'liːr] (2a) v/t. polish (a. fig.);
make glossy; burnish (metal); fig.
refine; **polisseur, -euse** [pɔli'sœːr,
͜'søːz] su. polisher; su./f polishing
machine; **polissoir** [͜'swaːr] m ⊕
tool: polisher; polishing machine;
buff-stick; nail-polisher.
polisson, -onne [pɔli'sɔ̃, ͜'sɔn] 1.
adj. naughty; pej. indecent; saucy; 2.
su. naughty child, scamp; dissolute
person; **polissonner** [͜sɔ'ne] (1a)
v/i. run the streets (child); behave or
talk lewdly; **polissonnerie** [͜sɔn'ri]
f child: mischievousness; indecent
act; smutty story; depravity.
polissure [pɔli'syːr] f polish(ing).
politesse [pɔli'tɛs] f politeness, courtesy; ~s pl. civilities.
politicien m, **-enne** f usu. pej [pɔ-
liti'sjɛ̃, ͜'sjɛn] politician; **politique**
[͜'tik] 1. adj. political; fig. prudent,
wary; fig. diplomatic; homme m ~
politician; 2. su./m politician; su./f
politics; policy; ~ de clocher par-
ish-pump politics; ~ de la porte
ouverte open-door policy; ~ extérieure (intérieure) foreign (home)
policy; **politiquer** F [͜ti'ke] (1m)
v/i. dabble in politics; talk politics;
politologie [pɔlitɔlɔ'ʒi] f political
science; **politologue** [͜'lɔg] su.
political scientist.
polka [pɔl'ka] f ♪ dance: polka; ⊕
quarryman's hammer.
pollen ♀ [pɔl'lɛn] m pollen; **polli-
nique** ♀ [͜li'nik] pollinic; pollen-
(sac, tube); **pollinisation** ♀ [͜-
liniza'sjɔ̃] f fertilisation, polliniza-
tion.
polluant, e [pɔ'lɥɑ̃, ͜'lɥɑ̃t] 1. adj.
polluting; 2. su./m pollutant, polluting agent; **polluer** [͜'lɥe] (1n) v/t.
pollute; defile; eccl. profane; **pollution** [͜ly'sjɔ̃] f pollution (a. ⚥); eccl.
profanation.
polochon sl. [pɔlɔ'ʃɔ̃] m bolster.
polonais, e [pɔlɔ'nɛ, ͜'nɛːz] 1. adj.
Polish; 2. su./m ling. Polish; su. ♀
Pole; su./f ♪ dance: polonaise.
poltron, -onne [pɔltrɔ̃, ͜'trɔn] 1. adj.
timid; cowardly; craven; 2. su.

coward, craven, *sl.* funk; **poltron-nerie** [∼trɔn'ri] *f* timidity; coward-ice.

poly... [pɔli] poly...; **∼clinique** [∼kli'nik] *f* polyclinic; **∼copier** [∼kɔ-'pje] (1o) *v/t.* duplicate, *Am.* mimeograph; **∼èdre** ₳ [∼'ɛ:dr] **1.** *adj.* polyhedral; **2.** *su./m* polyhedron; **∼game** [∼'gam] **1.** *adj.* polygamous; ♀ polygamic; **2.** *su.* polygamist; **∼gamie** [∼ga'mi] *f* polygamy; **∼glotte** [∼'glɔt] *adj., a. su.* polyglot; **∼gone** [∼'gɔn] **1.** *adj.* polygonal; **2.** *su./m* polygon; ✕ artillery: shooting-range; **∼mère** ⚘ [∼'mɛːr] polymeric; **∼nôme** ₳ [∼'no:m] *m* polynomial.

polype [pɔ'lip] *m zo.* polyp; ✚ polypus; **polypeux, -euse** [∼li'pø, ∼-'pø:z] polypous.

poly...: **∼phonie** ♪ [pɔlifɔ'ni] *f* polyphony; **∼phonique** ♪ [∼fɔ'nik] polyphonic; **∼technicien** [∼tɛkni-'sjɛ̃] *m* student at the *École polytechnique*; **∼technique** [∼tɛk'nik]: ♀ *f* or *École f* ∼ Academy of Engineering; **∼valance** [∼va'lã:s] *f* ⚗ polyvalency; ⊕ *etc., a. fig.* versatility, flexibility; **∼valant, e** [∼va'lã, ∼'lã:t] ⚗ polyvalent; ⊕ *etc., a. fig.* versatile, flexible, multi-purpose.

pomiculteur [pɔmikyl'tœːr] *m* fruit grower.

pommade [pɔ'mad] *f* pomade, pomatum, *(hair-)*cream; F *passer de la* ∼ *à* soft-soap *(s.o.)*; **pommader** [∼ma'de] (1a) *v/t.* pomade, put cream on *(one's hair)*.

pommard [pɔ'ma:r] *m* Pommard *(a red burgundy)*.

pomme [pɔm] *f* apple; ♀ pome; *lettuce etc.:* head; *bedstead, stick:* knob; *sprinkler etc.:* rose; F head; ∼ *de discorde* bone of contention; ∼ *de terre* potato; ∼*s pl. chips* potato crisps, *Am.* chips; ∼*s pl. frites* Br. chips, *Am.* French fries, French fried potatoes; ∼*s pl. mousseline* mashed potatoes; F *tomber dans les* ∼*s* pass out (= *faint*); **pommé, e** [pɔ'me] **1.** *adj.* rounded; F downright *(fool)*; first-rate; *chou m* ∼ white-heart cabbage; *laitue f* ∼*e* cabbage lettuce; **2.** *su./m* cider.

pommeau [pɔ'mo] *m* pommel; *fishing-rod:* butt.

pommelé, e [pɔm'le] dappled; *ciel m* ∼ mackerel sky; *gris* ∼ dapple-grey; **pommelle** ⊕ [pɔ'mɛl] *f*

grating *(over pipe)*; **pommer** [∼-'me] (1a) *v/i. a. se* ∼ form a head *(cabbage, lettuce, etc.)*; **pomme-raie** ✔ [pɔm'rɛ] *f* apple-orchard; **pommette** [pɔ'mɛt] *f* knob; *anat.* cheek-bone; **pommier** [∼'mje] *m* apple-tree; **pomologie** [∼mɔlɔ'ʒi] *f* pomology.

pompe¹ [pɔ̃:p] *f* pomp, ceremony; *entrepreneur m de* ∼*s funèbres* funeral director, undertaker, *Am.* mortician.

pompe² [pɔ̃:p] *f* ⊕ pump; *mot.* ∼ *à essence* petrol-pump, *Am.* gas-pump; *sl.* shoe, boot; ∼ *à graisse* grease-gun; ∼ *à incendie* fire-engine; ∼ *à pneumatique* tyre-pump; tyre-inflator; ∼ *aspirante* suction-pump; ∼ *aspirante-foulante* lift-and-force pump; F *à toute* ∼ at top speed, at full tilt; F *sp. faire des* ∼*s* do push-ups; **pomper** [pɔ̃'pe] (1a) *v/t.* pump *(a. fig.)*; suck up *or* in; F tire out; **pompette** F [∼'pɛt] tipsy.

pompeux, -euse [pɔ̃'pø, ∼'pø:z] pompous; stately; high-flown *(style)*.

pompier [pɔ̃'pje] **1.** *su./m* fireman; *les* ∼*s pl.* the fire brigade *sg.*; **2.** *adj.* F corny; high-falutin' *(style)*; **pompiste** *mot.* [∼'pist] *m* pump attendant.

pompon [pɔ̃'pɔ̃] *m* pompon, tuft; powder-puff; F *iro. avoir (or tenir) le* ∼ surpass everyone; **pomponner** [∼pɔ'ne] (1a) *v/t.* dress up, F doll up.

ponant *hist.* [pɔ'nã] *m* West; Occident.

ponce [pɔ̃:s] *f (a. pierre f* ∼) pumice-stone; *drawing:* pounce.

ponceau¹ ⚠ [pɔ̃'so] *m* culvert.

ponceau² [∼] **1.** *su./m* corn-poppy; poppy-red; **2.** *adj./inv.* poppy-red.

poncer ⊕ [pɔ̃'se] (1k) *v/t.* pumice; *floor etc.:* sand-paper; rub down *(paint)*; pounce *(a drawing)*; **ponceux, -euse** [∼'sø, ∼'sø:z] **1.** *adj.* pumiceous; **2.** *su./f* ⊕ sand-papering machine; **poncif, -ve** [∼'sif, ∼'si:v] **1.** *adj.* conventional; trite; stereotyped *(effect, plot)*; **2.** *su./m* conventionalism; *fig.* conventional piece of writing.

ponction ✚ [pɔ̃k'sjɔ̃] *f* puncture; *blister:* pricking; **ponctionner** [∼-sjɔ'ne] (1a) *v/t.* puncture; tap; prick *(a blister)*.

ponctualité [pɔ̃ktɥali'te] *f* punctuality; **ponctuation** *gramm.* [∼'sjɔ̃] *f* punctuation; **ponctuel, -elle** [pɔ̃k'tɥɛl] punctual; *phys.* pinpoint (*a. fig.*); *fig.* isolated, selective, individual; **ponctuer** [~'tɥe] (1n) *v/t.* punctuate; emphasize (*a spoken word*).

pondaison [pɔ̃dɛ'zɔ̃] *f eggs:* laying.

pondérable [pɔ̃de'rabl] ponderable; **pondérateur, -trice** [~ra'tœːr, ~'tris] stabilizing, balancing; **pondération** [~ra'sjɔ̃] *f* balance (*a. fig.*); *fig.* level-headedness; **pondéré, e** [~'re] level-headed.

pondeur, -euse [pɔ̃'dœːr, ~'døːz] **1.** *adj.* (egg-)laying; **2.** *su. fig.* prolific producer (*of novels etc.*); *su./f* hen: layer; **pondoir** [~'dwaːr] *m* nest-box; *hens:* laying-place; **pondre** [pɔ̃ːdr] (4a) *v/t.* lay (*an egg*); *F fig.* produce, bring forth.

poney *zo.* [pɔ'nɛ] *m* pony.

pongiste [pɔ̃'ʒist] *su.* table tennis player.

pont [pɔ̃] *m* △, ⊕, *fig.* bridge; ⊕, *mot.* axle; ⚓ deck; ~s *pl. et chaussées f/pl.* Highways Department *sg.* (*in France*); ⊕~ *à bascule* weigh-bridge; ~ *aérien* air-lift; *mot.* ~ *arrière* rear-axle; *mot.* ~ *élévateur garage:* repair or car ramp; ~ *roulant* ⊕ travelling crane; 🚋 traverser; △ ~ *suspendu* suspension-bridge; △ ~ *tournant* swing-bridge; *fig. couper les* ~s burn one's boats; **pontage** [pɔ̃'taːʒ] *m* bridge-building; bridging; 🐝 by-pass.

ponte[1] [pɔ̃ːt] *f eggs:* laying; eggs *pl.*

ponte[2] [~] *m cards:* punter; *F* top brass, V.I.P.

ponter [pɔ̃'te] (1a) *v/i. cards:* punt.

pontife [pɔ̃'tif] *m pontiff; fig.* pundit; *souverain m* ~ pope, sovereign pontiff; **pontifical, e,** *m/pl.* **-aux** [pɔ̃tifi'kal, ~'ko] *adj. a. su./m* pontifical; **pontificat** [~fi'ka] *m* pontificate; **pontifier** [~'fje] (1o) *v/i.* pontificate (*a. fig.*).

pont-levis, *pl.* **ponts-levis** [pɔ̃le'vi] *m* drawbridge.

ponton [pɔ̃'tɔ̃] *m* ⚔ pontoon; ⚓ lighter; *in river etc.:* floating landing stage; † hulk; **pontonnier** ⚔ [~tɔ'nje] *m* pontoneer.

popeline *tex.* [pɔ'plin] *f* poplin.

popote *F* [pɔ'pɔt] **1.** *su./f* cooking; ⚔ cook-shop; ⚔ (*field-*)mess; *faire la* ~ do the cooking; **2.** *adj.* stay-at-home, quiet.

populace *pej.* [pɔpy'las] *f* populace, rabble; **populacier, -ère** F [~la-'sje, ~'sjeːr] vulgar, common.

populage ♣ [pɔpy'laːʒ] *m* marsh marigold.

populaire [pɔpy'lɛːr] **1.** *adj.* popular (with, *auprès de*); **2.** *su./m* common people; herd; **populariser** [pɔpy-lari'ze] (1a) *v/t.* popularize; make (*s.o.*) popular; **popularité** [~'te] *f* popularity; **population** [pɔpyla-'sjɔ̃] *f* population; ~ *active* working population; **populeux, -euse** [~'lø, ~'løːz] populous; crowded (*city etc.*); **populo** F [~'lo] *m* common people, riff-raff.

porc [pɔːr] *m* pig, hog; *cuis.* pork; *fig.* (dirty) swine.

porcelaine [pɔrsə'lɛn] *f* china (-ware); porcelain; ~ *de Limoges* Limoges ware; **porcelainier, -ère** [~lɛ'nje, ~'njeːr] **1.** *adj.* china...; porcelain...; **2.** *su./m* porcelain manufacturer.

porcelet [pɔrsə'lɛ] *m* piglet, *ch.sp.* piggy.

porc-épic, *pl.* **porcs-épics** *zo.* [pɔr-ke'pik] *m* porcupine, *Am.* hedgehog.

porche △ [pɔrʃ] *m* porch, portal.

porcher [pɔr'ʃe] *m* swine-herd; **porchère** [~'ʃeːr] *f* swine-maiden; **porcherie** [~ʃə'ri] *f* pig-farm; pigsty (*a. fig.*).

pore [pɔːr] *m* pore; **poreux, -euse** [pɔ'rø, ~'røːz] porous; unglazed (*pottery etc.*).

porion ⚒ [pɔ'rjɔ̃] *m* overman.

pornographie [pɔrnɔgra'fi] *f* pornography.

porosité [pɔrozi'te] *f* porosity.

porphyre [pɔr'fiːr] *m min.* porphyry; 🐝 slab; **porphyrique** *min.* [~fi'rik] porphyritic.

porreau [pɔ'ro] *m see* poireau.

port[1] [pɔːr] *m* ⚓, ⚓ port; harbo(u)r; haven (*a. fig.*); ~ *d'attache* port of registry; ~ *de* (or *à*) *marée* tidal harbo(u)r; ~ *de mer* seaport; ~ *franc* free port; *arriver à bon* ~ ⚓ come safe into port; *fig.* arrive safely; *capitaine m de* ~ harbo(u)r-master; *entrer au* ~ come into port.

port[2] [pɔːr] *m* carrying; *goods etc.:* carriage; *letter, parcel:* postage; ⚓ *ship:* tonnage; *transport, telegram, etc.:* charge; *decorations, uniform:* wearing; *person:* bearing, carriage; ~ *dû* carriage forward; ~

payé carriage *or* postage paid; **portable** [pɔrˈtabl] portable; *cost.* wearable; **portage** [ˌ.ˈtaːʒ] *m* ✝ conveyance, transport; ⚓ portage; ⊕ bearing.   [door.⟩

portail ⚠ [pɔrˈtaːj] *m* portal; main⟩

portant, e [pɔrˈtɑ̃, ˌ.ˈtɑ̃ːt] **1.** *adj.* ⊕ bearing, carrying; *fig.* bien (mal) ~ in good (bad) health; **2.** *su./m* ⊕ stay, strut; *box, trunk:* handle; *thea.* framework (*of a flat*); **portatif, -ve** [ˌta'tif, ˌ'tiːv] portable.

porte [pɔrt] **1.** *su./f* ⚠, *a.* ⊕ door (*a. fig.*); gate (*a.* ⚓); doorway, entrance; *geog.* pass, gorge; ~ à deux battants folding-door; ~ *cochère* carriage entrance, gateway; ⚔ ~ d'aérage trap, air-gate; ~ *vitrée* glass door; *écouter aux* ~s eavesdrop; *mettre* (*or* F *flanquer*) *q. à la* ~ turn s.o. out; give s.o. the sack; *nous habitons* ~ *à* ~ we are next-door neighbo(u)rs; **2.** *adj.* *anat.* veine *f* ~ portal vein.

porte...: ~(-)à(-)**faux** [pɔrtaˈfo] *m:* en ~ in an unstable position; ~-**aiguilles** [ˌ.eˈɡɥiːj] *m/inv.* needle case; ~-**avions** ⚓ [ˌaˈvjɔ̃] *m/inv.* aircraft carrier; ~-**bagages** [ˌbaˈɡaːʒ] *m/inv.* luggage (*Am.* baggage) rack; ~-**billets** [ˌbiˈjɛ] *m/inv.* note case, *Am.* billfold; ~-**bonheur** [ˌbɔˈnœːr] *m/inv.* talisman, lucky charm; mascot; ~-**bouteilles** [ˌbuˈtɛːj] *m/inv.* bottle rack; ~-**cigarettes** [ˌsiɡaˈrɛt] *m/inv.* cigarette case; ~-**clefs** [ˌ.ˈkle] *m/inv.* key ring; *hotel:* key rack; ~-**drapeau** ⚔ [ˌ.draˈpo] *m/inv.* colo(u)r bearer.

portée [pɔrˈte] *f* bearing; ⚠ span; *gun:* range; *voice:* compass; *arm:* reach; ♪ stave; *animals:* litter; *fig.* comprehension; *fig.* meaning, consequences *pl.*, implications *pl.*; *à* (*la*) ~ (*de*) within reach (of); *hors de* (*la*) ~ (*de*) without reach (of); *à* (*hors de*) *de voix* within (out of) earshot; *être à la* ~ *de a.* be within the understanding of (*s.o.*); *vues f/pl. à longue* ~ farsighted policy *sg.*

porte...: ~-**enseigne** [pɔrtɑ̃ˈsɛɲ] *m/inv.* colo(u)r-bearer; ~-**faix** [ˌ.ˈfɛ] *m* (street-)porter; *docks:* stevedore.

porte-fenêtre, *pl.* **portes-fenêtres** ⚠ [pɔrtəˈfnɛːtr] *f* French window.

porte...: ~-**feuille** [pɔrtəˈfœːj] *m documents, a. pol.:* portfolio; wallet, note-case, *Am.* bill-fold; ✝ ~ *titres*

investments *pl.*, securities *pl.*; ~-**habits** [pɔrtaˈbi] *m/inv.* hall-stand; ~-**malheur** [ˌmaˈlœːr] *m/inv.* bringer of bad luck, F Jonah; ~-**manteau** [ˌmɑ̃ˈto] *m* coat-rack, hatstand; ~-**mine** [ˌ.ˈmin] *m/inv.* pencil-case; propelling pencil; ~-**monnaie** [ˌmɔˈnɛ] *m/inv.* purse; ~-**parapluies** [ˌparaˈplɥi] *m/inv.* umbrella-stand; ~-**parole** [ˌ.paˈrɔl] *m/inv.* spokesman, F mouthpiece; ~-**plume** [pɔrtəˈplym] *m/inv.* penholder.

porter [pɔrˈte] (1a) *v/t.* carry; bear; wear (*clothing*); take; strike, deal (*a blow*); ⚖ bring (*a charge, a complaint*); ✝ charge; ✝ place (*to s.o.'s credit*); ✝ post (*in ledger*); produce (*fruit etc.*); ⚔ shoulder (*arms*); *fig.* lead (*s.o.*) (to, *à*); *fig.* increase (*the number, the price, the temperature*); *fig.* have (*an affection, an interest*), bear (*the responsibility, witness*); *se* ~ proceed (to, *à*); feel, be (*well, unwell etc.*); *se* ~ *bien* (*mal*) *a.* be in good (bad) health; *se* ~ *comme un charme* be as fit as a fiddle; *se* ~ *candidat* stand as candidate; *pol.* run (for, *à*); *se* ~ *garant de* vouch for; *v/i.* bear (*a. fig.*), rest (on, *sur*); deal (with, *sur*); carry (*sound etc.*); hit the mark, strike home (*shot, a. fig. insult, etc.*); ⚕ be pregnant; be with young (*animal*); *fig.* ~ *à la tête* go to the head (*wine*); ~ *sur les nerfs* get on one's nerves.

porte...: ~-**respect** [pɔrtrɛsˈpɛ] *m/inv.* defensive weapon; ~-**savon** [ˌsaˈvɔ̃] *m or m/inv.* soap-dish, soapholder; ~-**serviettes** [ˌsɛrˈvjɛt] *m/inv.* towel-rack.

porteur, -euse [pɔrˈtœːr, ˌ.ˈtøːz] **1.** *su.* porter; *letter, message, news, etc.:* bearer; ⚕ (germ-)carrier; *su./m* ✝ bearer, payee (*of cheque*) (*stock-, share*)holder; *au* ~ (*payable*) to bearer (*cheque*); **2.** *adj.* pack-(*animal*); ⊕ bearing; suspension-...; carrier (*wave, rocket*).

porte-voix [pɔrtəˈvwa] *m/inv.* speaking-tube; megaphone.

portier, -ère [pɔrˈtje, ˌ.ˈtjɛːr] *su.* doorman; gatekeeper; porter; *su./f mot., a.* 🚗 door; door-curtain; **portillon** [ˌtiˈjɔ̃] *m* wicket(-gate); small gate.

portion [pɔrˈsjɔ̃] *f* portion, share, part; *meal:* helping; F ~ *congrue* bare living.

portique [pɔr'tik] *m* portico, porch; ⊕ gantry; *sp.* crossbar.

porto [pɔr'to] *m wine*: port.

portrait [pɔr'trɛ] *m paint.* portrait; face; *fig.* likeness; *fig.* description; character-sketch, profile; ~ *robot* identikit (picture); **portraitiste** [pɔrtrɛ'tist] *su.* portrait-painter; **portraiturer** [~ty're] (1a) *v/t.* portray.

portugais, e [pɔrty'gɛ, ~'gɛ:z] **1.** *adj.* Portuguese; **2.** *su./m ling.* Portuguese; *su.* ♀ Portuguese; *les* ♀ *m/pl.* the Portuguese.

posage ⊕ [po'za:ʒ] *m* placing; fixing; *bricks, pipes*: laying; **pose** [po:z] *f* ⊕ placing; fixing; *bricks, pipes*: laying; ✕ posting; *phot.* time-exposure; *fig.* posture; pose; *fig.* affectation; *prendre une* ~ adopt *or* strike an attitude; **posé, e** [po'ze] *fig.* sedate, staid, grave; steady (*bearing, person, voice*); sitting (*bird*); **posemètre** *phot.* [poz'mɛtr] *m* exposure meter; **poser** [po'ze] (1a) *v/t.* place, put (*a.* a question, a motion), lay (*a.* ⚠ bricks, pipes, carpet, ⚒ rails, *etc.*); lay down (*a book, a. fig.* a principle); hang (*curtains*); set (*a problem*); ⊕ fix, fit; ✕ ~ *les armes* lay down one's arms; ~ *q.* establish s.o.'s reputation; *posons le cas que* let us suppose that; *se* ~ *fig.* achieve a certain standing; 🛬 land (*plane*); *se* ~ *comme* pass o.s. off as, claim to be; *v/i.* rest, lie; *paint.* pose (*a. fig.*), sit; F *fig.* put it on, *Am.* put on dog; *fig.* ~ *pour* claim to be; **poseur, -euse** [~'zœ:r, ~'zø:z] *su.* affected person; attitudinizer; *su./m pipes, a. mines*: layer; (*bill-*) sticker.

positif, -ve [pozi'tif, ~'ti:v] **1.** *adj.* ♣, ♂, *gramm., phys., phot.* positive; real, actual; matter-of-fact, practical (*person*); **2.** *su./m phot., gramm., phot.* positive; ♪ choir-organ.

position [pozi'sjɔ̃] *f* position; situation (*a. fig.*); job; (*physical*) posture, attitude; (*social*) standing; ~ *clé* key position; *feux m/pl. de* ~ ⛵ navigation lights; ⚓ riding lights; *mot.* parking lights; *prendre* ~ *sur* take up a definite stand about.

posologie ⚕ [pozɔlɔ'ʒi] *f* dosage, directions *pl.* for use.

possédé, e [pose'de] **1.** *adj.* possessed (by, *de; fig. a.* with, *pour*); **2.** *su./m* madman, maniac; *su./f* madwoman.

posséder [~] (1f) *v/t.* possess (*a. fig.*); own; have; *fig. passion, influence*: dominate; have a thorough knowledge of; *fig. se* ~ contain o.s., control o.s.

possesseur [pose'sœ:r] *m* owner, possessor; **possessif, -ve** *gramm.* [~'sif, ~'si:v] *adj., a. su./m* possessive; **possession** [~'sjɔ̃] *f* possession (*a. by* a demon); *fig.* thorough knowledge (*of a subject*); ~ *de soi* self-control.

possibilité [posibili'te] *f* possibility; **possible** [~'sibl] **1.** *adj.* possible; *le plus* ~ as far as possible; as many *or* much as possible; *le plus vite* ~ as quickly as possible; **2.** *su./m* what is possible; *faire tout son* ~ do all one can (to *inf., pour inf.*).

post... [pɔst] post...

postal, e *m/pl.* **-aux** [pɔs'tal, ~'to] postal; *sac m* ~ mail-bag.

postdater [pɔstda'te] (1a) *v/t.* postdate.

poste[1] [pɔst] *f* post; mail; postal service; post office; ~ *aérienne* airmail; ~ *restante* to be called for, *Am.* general delivery; *mettre à la* ~ post, *Am.* mail (*a letter*); *par la* ~ by post.

poste[2] [~] *m* post (*a.* ✕); job; position; *pilot:* cockpit; ✕, ⊕, ♂, *police, fire, radio, tel., etc.*: station; *radio, teleph.*: set; *teleph.* extension; ♦ entry; ♦ item; *mot.* (*filling*) station, (*petrol*) pump; ✕ ~ *avancé* advanced post, outpost; ~ *d'aiguillage* signal-box; ⚒ ~ *de contrôle* control tower; ~ *de secours* first-aid post; ✕ regimental aid post; ~ *de télévision* television set; ~ *de T.S.F.* radio; ~ *téléphonique* telephone-station; *conduire q. au* ~ take s.o. to the police station.

poster [pɔs'te] (1a) *v/t.* post, *Am.* mail (*a letter*); post, station (*a sentry*).

postérieur, e [pɔste'rjœ:r] **1.** *adj.* posterior; subsequent (*time*); hind (*-er*) (*place*); back (*vowel*); **2.** F *su./m* posterior, F backside.

postérité [pɔsteri'te] *f* posterity; descendants *pl.; la* ~ generations *pl.* to come.

postface [pɔst'fas] *f book:* postscript.

posthume [pɔs'tym] posthumous.

postiche [pɔs'tiʃ] **1.** *adj.* false (*hair*

etc.); imitation (*pearl*); **2.** *su./m* hair-piece; postiche.

postier *m*, **-ère** *f* [pɔsˈtje, ~ˈtjɛːr] post-office employee; **postillon** [~tiˈjɔ̃] *m* postilion; F *speech*: splutter(ing).

post…: ~position [pɔstpoziˈsjɔ̃] *f* postposition; **~scolaire** [~skɔˈlɛːr] after-school; *class*, *school*: continuation …; **~scriptum** [~skripˈtɔm] *m/inv.* postscript, P.S.

postulant *m*, **e** *f* [pɔstyˈlɑ̃, ~ˈlɑ̃ːt] *post*: applicant, candidate; *eccl.* postulant; **postulat** [~ˈla] *m* postulate, assumption; **postulation** [~laˈsjɔ̃] *f* postulation; **postuler** [~ˈle] (1a) *v/t.* apply for (*a post*); postulate; *v/i.* ⅍ conduct a (law)suit.

posture [pɔsˈtyːr] *f* posture, attitude; *fig.* position.

pot [po] *m* pot; jar, jug, can; ⚗ crucible; ~ **à eau** water jug, ewer; ~ **à fleurs** flower-pot; ~ **à lait** milk-can, milk-jug; ~ **de chambre** chamber(-pot); ~ **de fleurs** pot of flowers; *fig. découvrir le ~ aux roses* smell out the secret; *manger à la fortune du ~* take pot luck; F *fig. tourner autour du ~* beat about the bush.

potable [pɔˈtabl] drinkable, fit to drink; F fair, acceptable; *eau f ~* drinking water.

potache F [pɔˈtaʃ] *m* secondary-school boy, grammar-school boy.

potage [pɔˈtaːʒ] *m* soup; *fig. pej. pour tout ~* in all; **potager, -ère** [~taˈʒe, ~ˈʒɛːr] **1.** *adj.* pot-(*herbs*); kitchen (*garden*); **2.** *su./m* (*a. jardin m ~*) kitchen *or* vegetable garden.

potasse [pɔˈtas] *f* ⚗ potash; ⚗ (impure) potassium carbonate; **potasser** F [pɔtaˈse] (1a) *v/t.* swot at *or* for; **potassique** ⚗ [~ˈsik] potassium…; potassic (*salt*); **potassium** ⚗ [~ˈsjɔm] *m* potassium.

pot-au-feu [pɔtoˈfø] **1.** *su./m/inv.* stock-pot; beef-broth; boiled beef and vegetables; **2.** *adj.* stay-at-home; **pot-bouille †** *sl.* [~ˈbuːj] *f: faire ~ ensemble* live together; **pot-de-vin,** *pl.* **pots-de-vin** F [pod'vɛ̃] *m* tip, gratuity; *pej.* bribe; *pej.* hush-money, *Am. sl.* rake-off.

pote *sl.* [pɔt] *m* pal, *Am.* buddy.

poteau [pɔˈto] *m* post (*a. sp.*), stake; pole; ⚒ pit-prop; *sl.* pal, *Am.*

buddy; ~ *indicateur* sign-post; ~ *télégraphique* telegraph pole.

potée [pɔˈte] *f* potful, jugful; *beer*: mugful; ⊕ emery, putty, etc.: powder.

potelé, e [pɔtˈle] plump, chubby; dimpled.

potence [pɔˈtɑ̃ːs] *f* gallows *usu. sg.*, gibbet; △, ⊕ arm, cross-piece; ⊕ *crane*: jib; *mériter la ~* deserve hanging.

potentat [pɔtɑ̃ˈta] *m* potentate; † F magnate.

potentialiser ⚗ *etc.* [pɔtɑ̃sjaliˈze] (1a) *v/t.* potentiate, increase the effect of; **potentiel, -elle** [~ˈsjɛl] *adj., a. su./m* potential (*a. gramm.*).

poterie [pɔˈtri] *f* pottery (*a. works*); earthenware; ~ **d'étain** pewter; **potiche** [~ˈtiʃ] *f* vase of Chinese *or* Japanese porcelain; F *fig.* figure-head; **potier** [~ˈtje] *m* potter; ~ **d'étain** pewterer.

potin [pɔˈtɛ̃] *m* pewter; pinchbeck; F gossip; F din, rumpus; ~ *jaune* brass; **potiner** F [pɔtiˈne] (1a) *v/i.* gossip; **potinier, -ère** [~ˈnje, ~ˈnjɛːr] **1.** *adj.* gossipy; **2.** *su.* scandalmonger, gossip; *su./f* gossip-shop.

potion ⚗ [poˈsjɔ̃] *f* potion, draught.

potiron ♀ [pɔtiˈrɔ̃] *m* pumpkin.

pot-pourri, *pl.* **pots-pourris** [popuˈri] *m cuis.* meat-stew; ♪ pot-pourri (*a. perfume*), medley.

pou, *pl.* **poux** [pu] *m* louse; (*bird-*)mite; (*sheep-*)tick.

pouah! [pwa] *int.* ugh!

poubelle [puˈbɛl] *f* refuse-bin, *Am.* garbage-can; dustbin.

pouce [puːs] *m* thumb; † *measure*: inch (*a. fig.*); big toe; *manger sur le ~* have a snack; *mettre les ~s* knuckle under, give in; *s'en mordre les ~s* regret it bitterly; *se tourner les ~s* twiddle one's thumbs; **poucettes** [puˈsɛt] *f/pl.* thumb-cuffs; † *torture*: thumb-screw *sg.*; **poucier** [~ˈsje] *m* ⚒ thumb-stall; ⊕ *latch*: thumb-piece.

pouding *cuis.* [puˈdiŋ] *m* pudding.

poudre [puːdr] *f* powder; dust (*a. fig.*); ⚔ (gun)powder; ⚔ ~ *de mine* blasting powder; *café m en ~* instant coffee; *il n'a pas inventé la ~* he won't set the Thames on fire; *fig. jeter de la ~ aux yeux de q.* throw dust in s.o.'s eyes; bluff s.o.;

réduire en ~ pulverize; *sucre m en* ~ castor sugar; **poudrer** [pu'dre] (1a) *v/t.* (sprinkle [*s.th.*] with) powder; **poudrerie** [~drə'ri] *f* (gun)powder-factory; **poudreux, -euse** [~'drø, ~'drø:z] **1.** *adj.* dusty; powdery; *neige f* ~*euse* = **2.** *su/f* powder snow; **poudrier** [~dri'e] *m* powder-case, powder-box; compact; **poudrière** [~dri'jɛ:r] *f esp. fig.* powder keg; **poudrin** [~'drɛ̃] *m see* embrun; **poudroyer** [~drwa'je] (1h) *v/i.* form *or* send up clouds of dust.

pouf [puf] **1.** *int.* sound of falling: plop!; plump!; *feelings:* phew!; **2.** *su./m* cushion: pouf; puff (= *exaggerated advertisement*); **pouffant, e** F [pu'fɑ̃, ~'fɑ̃:t] screamingly funny; **pouffer** [~'fe] (1a) *v/i.* (*a.* ~ *de rire*) burst out laughing.

pouffiasse *sl.* [puf'jas] *f* whore, tart; slattern, slut; fat woman.

pouillerie *sl.* [puj'ri] *f* abject poverty; filthy hole.

pouilles [pu:j] *f/pl.:* *chanter* ~ *à* jeer at.

pouilleux, -euse [pu'jø, ~'jø:z] lousy, lice-infested; F wretched.

poulailler [pula'je] *m* hen-house, hen-roost; F *thea.* gallery, gods *pl.*; **poulaillerie** [~laj'ri] *f* poultry-market.

poulain [pu'lɛ̃] *m zo.* foal, colt; ⊕ skid; slide-way.

poulaine [pu'lɛn] *f* ⚓ head; *hist. souliers m/pl. à la* ~ shoes with long pointed toes.

poularde *cuis.* [pu'lard] *f* fowl; fat (-tened) pullet; **poule** [pul] *f* hen; *cuis.* fowl; *games, a.* F *fencing:* pool; *races:* sweepstake; F girl; F tart, prostitute; ~ *d'Inde* turkey-hen; F ~ *mouillée* milksop; *fig. chair f de* ~ goose-flesh; **poulet** [pu'lɛ] *m* chicken; F love-letter; *sl.* copper (~ *policeman*); **poulette** [pu'lɛt] **1.** *su./f zo.* pullet; F girl; **2.** *adj.: cuis. sauce f* ~ sauce of butter, yolk of egg and vinegar.

pouliche *zo.* [pu'lif] *f* filly.

poulie ⊕ [pu'li] *f* pulley; block; driving wheel.

pouliner [puli'ne] (1a) *v/i.* foal.

poulot *m*, **-otte** *f* F [pu'lo, ~'lɔt] darling, pet (*addressing children*).

poulpe *zo.* [pulp] *m see* pieuvre.

pouls ✱ [pu] *m* pulse; *prendre le* ~ *à q.* feel s.o.'s pulse; F *fig. tâter le* ~ *à q.*

sound s.o.; F *se tâter le* ~ reflect, hesitate.

poumon [pu'mɔ̃] *m anat.* lung; ✱ ~ *d'acier* iron lung.

poupard [pu'pa:r] *m* baby in long clothes; baby-doll.

poupe ⚓ [pup] *f* stern, poop; *avoir le vent en* ~ ⚓ have the wind astern; *fig.* have the wind in one's sails, be on the road to success.

poupée [pu'pe] *f* doll; puppet; F chick (= *girl*); bandaged finger.

poupin, e [pu'pɛ̃, ~'pin] chubby; *visage* ~ baby face.

poupon *m*, **-onne** *f* F [pu'pɔ̃, ~'pɔn] baby; **pouponner** F [pupɔ'ne] (1a) *v/t.* coddle (*a child etc.*); **pouponnière** [~'njɛ:r] *f* babies' room (*in day-nursery*); day-nursery; infants' nursery.

pour [pu:r] **1.** *prp.* for (*s.o., this reason, negligence, ten dollars, the moment, Christmas, ever*); on account of, because of, for the sake of; instead of; in favo(u)r of; considering; as; (al)though, in spite of, for; calculated *or* of a nature to (*inf.*); about to (*inf.*); ✝ per (*cent*); *du respect* ~ consideration for; *prendre* ~ take for; *passer* ~ be looked upon as; *see partir*; ~ *le plaisir* (*la vie*) for fun (life); ~ *ma part* as for me; ~ *moi* in my opinion; ~ (*ce qui est de*) *cela* as far as that goes; *see amour*; *il fut puni* ~ *avoir menti* he was punished for lying *or* because he had lied; ~ *être riche il ... though he is rich he ...*; in spite of being rich he ...; *être* ~ (*inf.*) be on the point of (*ger.*); ~ *affaires* on business; ~ *de bon* seriously, in earnest; ~ *le moins* at least; ~ *ainsi dire* so to speak, as it were; ~ *important qu'il soit* however important it may be; ~ *peu que* (*sbj.*) if ever (*ind.*); however little (*ind.*); ~ *que* (*sbj.*) so *or* in order that; *être* ~ *beaucoup* (*peu*) *dans qch.* play a big (small) part in s.th.; *être* ~ be in favo(u)r of; ~ *sévère* ~ hard on, strict with; **2.** *su./m:* *le* ~ *et le contre* the pros *pl.* and cons *pl.*

pourboire [pur'bwa:r] *m* tip, gratuity.

pourceau [pur'so] *m* pig, hog, swine.

pour-cent ✝ [pur'sɑ̃] *m/inv.* percentage, rate per cent; **pourcen-**

tage † [~sã'tɑ:ʒ] *m* percentage; rate.
pourchasser [purʃa'se] (1a) *v/t.*
pursue; *fig.* chase; hound (*a debtor
etc.*).
pourfendeur *iro.* [purfã'dœ:r] *m* destroyer; **pourfendre** *iro.* [~'fã:dr]
(4a) *v/t.* attack, fight (against).
pourlécher F [purle'ʃe] (1f) *v/t.*: se
~ lick; se ~ les babines lick one's
chops.
pourparlers [purpar'le] *m/pl.* (diplomatic) talks, negotiations; ✕
parley *sg.*
pourpoint *cost.* † [pur'pwɛ̃] *m*
doublet.
pourpre [purpr] 1. *su./f* dye, robe,
a. fig.: purple; *su./m* dark red,
crimson; ♂ purpura; 2. *adj.* dark
red, crimson, purple; **pourpré, e**
[pur'pre] crimson; purple.
pourquoi [pur'kwa] 1. *adv.*, *cj.*
why; c'est ~ therefore; that's why;
2. *su./m/inv.*: le ~ the reason (for,
de).
pourrai [pu're] *1st p. sg. fut. of*
pouvoir 1.
pourri, e [pu'ri] 1. *adj.* rotten
(with, de) (*fruit, wood, a. fig.*);
bad (*egg, meat*); addled (*egg*); dank
(*air*); damp (*weather*); putrid (*flesh*);
2. *su./m* rotten part, bad patch (*of
fruit etc.*); **pourrir** [~'ri:r] (2a) *vt/i.*
rot; *v/i.* go bad *or* rotten; rot (away)
(*wood etc.*); addle (*egg*); *fig.* ~ en
prison rot in goal; **pourriture**
[~ri'ty:r] *f* decay, rot(ting); putrefaction; *fig.* rottenness, corruption.
poursuite [pur'sɥit] *f* pursuit (*a.
fig.*); chase; ~s *pl.* legal action *sg.*;
prosecution *sg.*; **poursuivant, e**
[~sɥi'vã, ~'vã:t] 1. *su.* pursuer; ⚖
plaintiff; prosecutor; 2. *adj.* pros-
ecuting; **poursuivre** [~'sɥi:vr]
(4ee) *v/t.* pursue (*a. ✕, a. fig.*); *fig.*
continue, go on with; ⚖ sue (*s.o.*);
prosecute (*s.o.*).
pourtant [pur'tã] *cj.* nevertheless,
(and) yet.
pourtour [pur'tu:r] *m* periphery;
precincts *pl.*; *thea.* gangway round
the stalls; avoir cent mètres de ~
be 100 metres round.
pourvoi ⚖ [pur'vwa] *m* appeal;
petition (for mercy, en grâce);
pourvoir [~'vwa:r] (3m) *v/t.* provide, supply, furnish (with, de); ⚖
se ~ appeal (to the Supreme Court,
en cassation); se ~ en grâce petition

for mercy; *v/i.*: ~ à provide for;
~ à un emploi fill a post; **pourvoyeur** *m*, **-euse** *f* [~vwa'jœ:r,
~'jø:z] provider; caterer; contractor.
(that).⟩
pourvu [pur'vy] *cj.*: ~ que provided⟨
poussah [pu'sa] *m toy*: tumbler;
fig. pot-bellied man.
pousse [pus] *f leaves, hair, etc.*:
growth; *teeth*: cutting; ♪ (young)
shoot; *wine*: ropiness; **~-café** F
[~ka'fe] *m/inv.* liqueur (after coffee), F chaser; **~-cailloux** ✕ *sl.*
[~ka'ju] *m/inv.* foot-slogger (= in-
fantrymen); **poussé, e** [pu'se] advanced; extensive, thorough (*studies
etc.*); highly developped; elaborate;
exaggerated; **poussée** [~] *f* ⊕, ✕
thrust; *phys.* pressure (*a. business*);
fig. push, shove; *fig.* upsurge; ♪
upward tendency; ♂ outbreak; ♪
growth; **pousse-pousse** [pus'pus]
m/inv. rickshaw (*in the East*); push-
chair; **pousser** [pu'se] (1a) *v/t.*
push, shove; push (*the door*) to, push
(*a bolt*) across; drive (*a tunnel*); jostle
(*s.o.*); *fig.* carry (to, jusqu'à); *fig.* urge
on (*a crowd, a horse*); incite (*a crowd,
s.o.*); *fig.* utter (*a cry*), heave (*a sigh*);
extend (*one's studies*); push (*s.o.*) on;
♀ put forth (*roots, leaves*); se ~ push
o.s. forward; push one's way to the
front; *v/i.* push, apply pressure; ♀
grow (*a. hair etc.*); *fig.* make one's
way, push on; **poussette** [~'sɛt] *f*
game: push-pin; baby-carriage;
push-chair.
poussier [pu'sje] *m* coal-dust; **poussière** [~'sjɛ:r] *f* dust; speck of dust;
water: spray, spindrift; ♀ ~ fécon-
dante pollen; mordre la ~ bite the
dust; F *fig.* 300 F et des ~s three-
hundred odd francs; **poussiéreux,
-euse** [~'sje'rø, ~'rø:z] dusty; dust-
colo(u)red.
poussif, -ve [pu'sif, ~'si:v] broken-
winded (*horse etc.*); F shortwinded
(*person*).
poussin [pu'sɛ̃] *m* chick; *cuis.* spring
chicken; **poussinière** [~si'nje:r] *f*
chicken-coop; incubator.
poussoir [pu'swa:r] *m electric bell,
clock, etc.*: push; ⊕, *mot.* push-rod;
✕ *machine-gun*: button.
poutrage ⚠ [pu'tra:ʒ] *m* framework,
beams *pl.*; **poutre** ⚠ [pu:tr] *f* beam;
joist; *metal*: girder; **poutrelle** ⚠
[pu'trɛl] *f* small beam; girder.

pouvoir [pu'vwa:r] 1. (3h) v/t. be able; can; be possible; *cela se peut bien* it is quite possible; *il se peut que* (sbj.) it is possible that (ind.); *puis-je?* may I?; *n'en~plus* be worn out; be at the end of one's resources; 2. su./m power; *en mon* (son etc.)~ (with)in my (his etc.) power.

pragmatique [pragma'tik] 1. adj. pragmatic; 2. su./f hist. Pragmatic Sanction; **pragmatisme** [~'tism] m pragmatism.

prairie [prɛ'ri] f meadow; grassland, Am. prairie.

praline cuis. [pra'lin] f burnt almond; praline; **praliner** cuis. [~li'ne] (1a) v/t. brown, crisp (almonds).

praticable [prati'kabl] practicable; feasible (idea, plan); negotiable, passable (road etc.); **praticien** m, -enne f [~sjɛ̃, ~'sjɛn] ⚕, ⚖ practitioner; practician; **pratiquant, e** eccl. [~'kɑ̃, ~'kɑ̃:t] practising (Catholic etc.), churchgoing; **pratique** [pra'tik] 1. adj. practical; convenient; useful; 2. su./f practice (a. eccl.); habit, use; experience; *mettre en ~* put into practice; **pratiquer** [~ti'ke] (1m) v/t. practise (⚕, ⚖, a. religion, etc.); exercise (a profession); put into practice (a rule, virtues, etc.); carry out; △ make, cut (a hole, a path, etc.); *se ~* be the practice.

pré [pre] m (small) meadow.

pré... [~] pre...; prae..., ante..., fore...

préalable [prea'labl] 1. adj. previous; preliminary; 2. su./m prerequisite, (pre)condition; † preliminary; *au ~* = **préalablement** [~lablə'mɑ̃] first, beforehand.

préambule [preɑ̃'byl] m preamble (to, de).

préau [pre'o] m yard; school: covered playground.

préavis [prea'vi] m previous (or advance) notice; warning; *donner son ~* give (one's) notice.

prébende eccl. [pre'bɑ̃:d] f prebend.

précaire [pre'kɛ:r] precarious; delicate (health); **précarité** [~kari'te] f precariousness.

précaution [preko'sjɔ̃] f precaution; caution, care; *avec ~* cautiously; warily; **précautionner** [~-'sjɔ'ne] (1a) v/t. warn, caution; *se ~ contre* take precautions against.

précédemment [preseda'mɑ̃] adv.

25 GTW Fr-E

previously, before; **précédent, e** [~'dɑ̃, ~'dɑ̃:t] 1. adj. preceding, previous, prior; former; 2. su./m precedent; ⚖ ~s pl. case-law sg.; *sans ~* unprecedented; **précéder** [~'de] (1f) v/t. precede; go before; fig. take precedence over, have precedence of.

précepte [pre'sɛpt] m precept; **précepteur** m, -trice f [presɛp'tœ:r, ~'tris] tutor; teacher; **préceptoral, e**, m/pl. -aux [~tɔ'ral, ~'ro] tutorial; **préceptorat** [~tɔ'ra] m tutorship.

prêche [prɛ:ʃ] m protestantism: sermon; fig. protestantism; **prêcher** [prɛ'ʃe] (1a) v/t. preach (a. fig.); preach to (s.o.); v/i. preach; fig. ~ à q. de (inf.) exhort s.o. to (inf.); ~ d'exemple (or par l'exemple) set an example; **prêcheur** m, -euse f fig. [~'ʃœ:r, ~'ʃø:z] sermonizer; **prêchi-prêcha** F [~ʃipre'ʃa] m preachifying.

précieux, -euse [pre'sjø, ~'sjø:z] 1. adj. precious; valuable; fig. affected (style etc.); 2. su. affected person; **préciosité** [~sjozi'te] f preciosity, affectation.

précipice [presi'pis] m precipice.

précipitamment [presipita'mɑ̃] adv. in a hurry, headlong; **précipitation** [~ta'sjɔ̃] f (violent) haste, hurry, precipitancy; 🜄, phys., meteor. precipitation; **précipité, e** [~'te] 1. adj. precipitate; hasty; 🜄 racing (pulse); headlong (flight); 2. su./m 🜄 etc. precipitate; **précipiter** [~'te] (1a) v/t. throw (down); hurl (down); fig. plunge (into war, despair, etc.); quicken, hasten; precipitate (events, a. 🜄); *se ~* rush (at, upon sur).

précis, e [pre'si, ~'si:z] 1. adj. precise, accurate, exact; definite (explanation, reason, time); *à dix heures ~es* at ten o'clock precisely or F sharp; 2. su./m summary, précis, abstract; **précisément** [presize'mɑ̃] adv. of précis 1; **préciser** [~'ze] (1a) v/t. state precisely; define; specify; make clear; *se ~* become clear(er); **précision** [~'zjɔ̃] f precision, accuracy, exactness; ~s pl. detailed information sg., particulars.

précité, e [presi'te] above(-mentioned), aforesaid.

précoce [pre'kɔs] precocious (child, talent, a. ⚘); early (⚘, a. season); fig.

premature; **précocité** [ₓkɔsi'te] f
precocity; earliness.

précompte ✝ [pre'kɔ̃:t] m previous
deduction; **précompter** [ₓkɔ̃'te]
(1a) v/t. deduct beforehand.

préconçu, e [prekɔ̃'sy] precon-
ceived; idée f ₓe preconception.

préconiser [prekɔni'ze] (1a) v/t.
recommend; advocate.

préconstruction ⚠ [prekɔ̃stryk-
'sjɔ̃] f prefabrication.

précontraint [prekɔ̃'trɛ̃, ₓ'trɛ̃:t]
prestressed (concrete).

précurseur [prekyr'sœ:r] **1.** su./m
forerunner, precursor; harbinger
(of spring); **2.** adj./m premonitory.

prédécesseur [predesε'sœ:r] m predecessor.

prédestination [predestina'sjɔ̃] f
predestination; **prédestiné, e**
[ₓ'ne] foredoomed; fig. fated (to,
à); **prédestiner** [ₓ'ne] (1a) v/t.
predestine (to, à) (a. fig.).

prédicateur m, **-trice** f [predika-
'tœ:r, ₓ'tris] preacher; **prédication**
[ₓ'sjɔ̃] f preaching; sermon.

prédiction [predik'sjɔ̃] f predic-
tion; forecast; **prédire** [ₓ'di:r] (4p)
v/t. predict, prophesy, foretell;
forecast.

prédisposer ✻, a. fig. [predispo'ze]
(1a) v/t. predispose; ₓ contre prejudice (s.o.) against (s.o.); **prédisposition** ✻, a. fig. [ₓzi'sjɔ̃] f predisposition.

prédominance [predɔmi'nã:s] f
predominance, prevalence; **prédominant, e** [ₓ'nã, ₓ'nã:t] pre-
dominant, prevalent, prevailing;
prédominer [ₓ'ne] (1a) v/i. predominate, prevail (over, sur); v/t.
take pride of place over.

prééminence [preemi'nã:s] f pre-
eminence (over, sur); **prééminent,
e** [ₓ'nã, ₓ'nã:t] pre-eminent.

préemption [preãmp'sjɔ̃] f pre-
emption; droit m de ₓ preemptive
right.

préexistant, e [preεksis'tã, ₓ'tã:t]
pre-existent, pre-existing.

préfabriqué, e [prefabri'ke] pre-
fabricated; maison f ₓe prefab
(-ricated house); **préfabriquer** [ₓ]
(1m) v/t. prefabricate.

préface [pre'fas] f preface (a. eccl.);
foreword, introduction (to à, de);
préfacer [ₓfa'se] (1k) v/t. write a
preface to.

préfectoral, e, m/pl. **-aux** [prefεk-
tɔ'ral, ₓ'ro] prefectorial; of the or a
prefect; **préfecture** [ₓ'ty:r] f hist.
prefectship; hist, a. admin. prefec-
ture; admin. Paris police headquarters pl.

préférable [prefe'rabl] preferable
(to, à), better (than, à); **préférence**
[ₓ'rãs] f preference (a. ✝); ₓ₸
priority; de ₓ in preference (to, à),
preferential (tariff), ✝ preference
(shares); **préférer** [ₓ're] (1f) v/t.
prefer.

préfet [pre'fε] m hist., a. admin.
prefect; civil administrator; ₓ de
police chief commissioner of the
Paris police; ₓ des études school:
master in charge of discipline; ⚓
ₓ maritime port-admiral; **préfète**
F [ₓ'fεt] f prefect's wife.

préfixe gramm. [pre'fiks] m prefix;
préfixer [ₓfik'se] (1a) v/t. fix
(a date etc.) in advance; gramm.
prefix.

préhistoire [preis'twa:r] f prehis-
tory; **préhistorique** [ₓtɔ'rik] pre-
historic.

préjudice [preʒy'dis] m prejudice,
harm; wrong, damage; ₓ₸ tort; au ₓ
de to the detriment of; sans ₓ de
without prejudice to; **préjudiciable** [preʒydi'sjabl] prejudicial,
detrimental (to, à); ₓ₸ tortious;
préjudiciaux ₓ₸ [ₓ'sjo] adj./m/pl.:
frais m/pl. ₓ security sg. for costs;
préjudiciel, -elle ₓ₸ [ₓ'sjεl] inter-
locutory; **préjudicier** [ₓ'sje] (1o)
v/i. be prejudicial or detrimental
(to, à); ₓ à injure.

préjugé [preʒy'ʒe] m prejudice;
bias; presumption; ₓ₸ (legal) precedent; sans ₓs unprejudiced; **préjuger** [ₓ] (1l) v/t. (or v/i.: ₓ de)
prejudge, judge in advance.

prélasser F [prela'se] (1a) v/t.: se ₓ
lounge, loll (in a chair etc.); strut.

prélat eccl. [pre'la] m prelate.

prélèvement [prelεv'mã] m previous deduction; deduction, amount
deducted; blood, gas, ore, etc.:
sample; **prélever** [prel've] (1d) v/t.
deduct in advance; levy; take (a
sample [a. ✻ of blood]) (from, à).

préliminaire [prelimi'nε:r] **1.** adj.
preliminary (to, de); **2.** su./m preliminary; ₓs pl. document: preamble sg.

prélude ♪, a. fig. [pre'lyd] m prel-

ude; **préluder** [~ly'de] (1a) v/i. ♪
(play a) prelude; fig. ~ à lead up to,
serve as prelude to.

prématuré, e [prematy're] premature, untimely; **prématurément**
[~re'mã] adv. of prématuré.

préméditation [premedita'sjɔ̃] f
premeditation; avec ~ wilfully; ⚖
with malice aforethought; **prémédité, e** [~'te] deliberate; **préméditer** [~'te] (1a) v/t. premeditate.

prémices [pre'mis] f/pl. first fruits;
cattle: firstlings; † fig. beginnings.

premier, -ère [prə'mje, ~'mjɛːr]
1. adj. first (time, place, position,
rank); fig. leading, best; title: the
first; ♪ prime (number); admin.
etc. principal, head (clerk); former
(of two); mot. ~ère vitesse f first or
low gear; ~ livre m school: primer;
pol. ~ ministre m Prime Minister;
au ~ coup at the first attempt; ce
n'est pas le ~ venu he isn't just anybody; le ~ venu the first comer; les
cinq ~s pl. the first five; Napoléon
Iᵉʳ Napoleon I, Napoleon the
First; partir le ~ be the first to
leave; **2.** su./m first; first, Am. second floor; en ~ in the first place;
thea. jeune ~ leading man; le ~ du
mois the first of the month; su./f
secondary school: (approx.) sixth
form; thea. first night or performance; cin., a. fig. première; mot. first
(gear); 🚂 first class (carriage); thea.
jeune ~ère leading woman; 🚂 voyager
en ~ère travel first (class); **premièrement** [~mjɛr'mã] adv. first; in the
first place; **premier-né, premier-
née** or **première-née,** m/pl.
premiers-nés [~mje'ne, ~mjɛr'ne]
adj., a. su./m first-born.

prémilitaire [premilitɛːr] premil-
itary (training).

prémisse [pre'mis] f logic: premise,
premiss.

prémonition [premɔni'sjɔ̃] f pre-
monition; **prémonitoire** ♪
[~'twaːr] premonitory.

prémunir [premy'niːr] (2a) v/t. put
(s.o.) on his guard, forewarn (s.o.)
(against, contre); se ~ take precautions (against, contre).

prenable [prə'nabl] pregnable; **prenant, e** [~'nã, ~'nãːt] captivating;
absorbing; † partie f ~e payee;
recipient.

prénatal, e, m/pl. **-als** or **-aux**
25*

[prena'tal, ~'to] prenatal, antenatal.

prendre [prãːdr] (4aa) **1.** v/t. take
(a. lessons, a degree, a road, ✗ a
town), grasp; catch (fire, a cold,
the train), trap (a rat); steal; seize;
accept; eat (a meal), have (tea, a
meal); pick up; engage (a servant);
take (up) (time); handle, treat; ✝
choose; buy (a ticket); ✗ conquer;
✗ etc. capture; ~ à mentir catch
(s.o.) in a lie; ~ corps put on weight;
~ en amitié take to (s.o.); ⚓ ~ le
large put to sea; ~ mal misunder-
stand; take (s.th.) badly; ~ plaisir à
take pleasure in; ~ pour take (s.o.)
for; ~ q. dans sa voiture give s.o. a
lift; ~ rendez-vous avec make an
appointment with; ~ sur soi take
(s.th.) upon o.s.; pour qui me pre-
nez-vous? what do you take me
for?; se laisser ~ let o.s. be taken
in; se ~ be caught; cling (to, à);
set (liquid); curdle (milk); se ~ à
undertake (a task), begin; fig. s'en
~ à find fault with (s.o.); fig. s'y ~
manage, go about things; **2.** v/i.
set (plaster etc.); congeal, freeze;
curdle (milk); cuis. thicken; cuis.
catch (milk in pan); take root (tree);
take (fire); fig. be successful; ça ne
prend pas that cock won't fight;
preneur m, **-euse** f [prə'nœːr,
~'nøːz] taker; ⚖ lessee; ✝ buyer,
purchaser; cheque: payee; **prennent** [prɛn] 3rd p. pl. pres. of prendre.

prénom [pre'nɔ̃] m first or Christian
name, Am. given name; **prénom-
mé, e** [prenɔ'me] above-named;
prénommer [~] (1a) v/t.: se ~ be
called.

prenons [prə'nɔ̃] 1st p. pl. pres. of
prendre.

préoccupation [preɔkypa'sjɔ̃] f pre-
occupation; anxiety, concern; **préoccuper** [~'pe] (1a) v/t. preoccupy;
worry, trouble; se ~ de concern o.s.
with; be concerned about, worry or
care about.

préparateur m, **-trice** f [prepara-
'tœːr, ~'tris] preparer; experiments:
demonstrator; assistant; **préparatifs** [~'tif] m/pl. preparations; **préparation** [~'sjɔ̃] f preparation (a.
♪ etc.) (for, à); preparing; ⊕ dressing; typ. ouvrage m en ~ work to
appear shortly; **préparatoire** [~-
'twaːr] preparatory (a. school); preliminary; **préparer** [prepa're] (1a)

v/t. prepare (for, *à*); train (*for a career*); coach (*a pupil*); prepare for (*an examination*); draw up (*a speech*); ⊕ dress; make (*tea etc.*); se ~ prepare (o.s.) (for, *à*); get ready; *fig.* be in the wind, be brewing (*event*).

prépondérance [prepɔ̃deˈrɑ̃ːs] *f* preponderance (over, *sur*); *avoir la* ~ preponderate; **prépondérant, e** [~ˈrɑ̃, ~ˈrɑ̃ːt] preponderant; leading (*part, role*); casting (*vote*).

préposé *m, e f* [prepoˈze] official in charge; employee, attendant; postman, *Am.* mailman; **préposer** [~] (1a) *v/t.* appoint (as *comme*, *pour*; to, *à*).

préposition *gramm.* [prepoziˈsjɔ̃] *f* preposition; **prépositionnel, -elle** *gramm.* [~sjɔˈnɛl] prepositional.

pré(-)retraite [preraˈtrɛt] *f* early retirement.

prérogative [prerɔgaˈtiːv] *f* prerogative; *parl.* privilege.

près [prɛ] **1.** *adv.* near, close (at hand); *à beaucoup* ~ by far; *à cela* ~ except for that; *à cela* ~ *que* except that; *à peu de chose* ~ little short of; *à peu* ~ nearly; about; *fig. au plus* ~ to the nearest point; *de* ~ closely; from close to; (*fire*) at close range; *ici* ~ near by, quite near, close at hand; *regarder de plus* ~ take a closer look, examine more closely; *tout* ~ very near, quite close; **2.** *prp.* near; to; *ambassadeur m* ~ *le Saint-Siège* ambassador to the Holy See; ~ *de* near, close to (*Paris, the station*), by; nearly (*two hours, two o'clock, ten pounds, three miles*), almost; ♣ *courir* ~ *du vent* sail close to the wind; *il était* ~ *de tomber* he was on the point of falling.

présage [preˈzaːʒ] *m* portent, foreboding; omen; **présager** [~zaˈʒe] (11) *v/t.* portend, bode; foresee.

pré-salé, *pl.* **prés-salés** [presaˈle] *m* salt-marsh sheep; *cuis.* salt-marsh mutton.

presbyte ✻ [prɛzˈbit] *adj., a. su.* long-sighted; **presbytéral, e,** *m/pl.* **-aux** [prɛzbiteˈral, ~ˈro] priestly; **presbytère** *eccl.* [~ˈtɛːr] *m* presbytery; *protestantism:* vicarage, rectory, *Sc.* manse; **presbytie** ✻ [~ˈsi] *f* long-sightedness.

prescience [preˈsjɑ̃ːs] *f* foreknowledge.

préscolaire [preskɔˈlɛːr] preschool.

prescriptible ⚖ [prɛskripˈtibl] prescriptible; **prescription** [~ˈsjɔ̃] *f* ⊕, *admin.* regulation(s *pl.*); ⚖, ✻ prescription; ⊕~s *pl.* specifications; **prescrire** [prɛsˈkriːr] (4q) *v/t.* prescribe (*s.o.'s conduct, a rule, a.* ✻), lay down (*the law, a time, s.o.'s conduct, etc.*); ⚖ bar (*by statute of limitations etc.*); ⚖ se ~ *par* be barred at the end of (*5 years*).

préséance [preseˈɑ̃ːs] *f* precedence (of, over *sur*).

présélection [preselɛkˈsjɔ̃] *f* preselection.

présence [preˈzɑ̃ːs] *f* presence (at, *à*); ~ *d'esprit* presence of mind; *en* ~ face to face (with, *de*); *faire acte de* ~ put in *or* enter an appearance.

présent¹, e [preˈzɑ̃, ~ˈzɑ̃ːt] **1.** *adj.* present (at, *à*); current; ~! present!; *esprit m* ~ ready wit; *gramm. temps m* ~ present (tense); **2.** *su./m* present (time *or gramm.* tense); *à* ~ just now, at present; *les* ~*s pl.* exceptés present company *sg.* excepted; *pour le* ~ for the time being, for the present; *quant à* ~ as for now; *su./f: la* ~*e* this letter.

présent² [preˈzɑ̃] *m* present, gift; *faire* ~ *de* make a present of; **présentable** F [prezɑ̃ˈtabl] presentable; **présentateur** *m,* **-trice** *f* [~taˈtœːr, ~ˈtris] presenter; show, *etc.*: host, emcee; **présentation** [~taˈsjɔ̃] *f* ✝, ✻, *eccl., thea., court:* presentation; introduction (to s.o., *à q.*); ⚔ trooping (*the* colo[u]r, *du drapeau*); ✝ *à* ~ on demand, at sight.

présentement † [prezɑ̃tˈmɑ̃] *adv.* now, this minute; at present.

présenter [prezɑ̃ˈte] (1a) *v/t.* present (*a.* ⚔, ✝, *a.* difficulties, ⚔ arms), offer; show; introduce (*formally*); nominate (*a candidate*) (for, *pour*); produce (*one's passport*); *parl.* table (*a bill*); submit (*a conclusion*); *cin. etc.* ~ *q.* (*en vedette*) star s.o.; *je vous présente ma femme* may I introduce my wife?; se ~ appear; arise (*problem, question*); occur; present o.s.; ⚔ report (o.s.); introduce o.s.; se ~ *chez q.* call on s.o.; se ~ *bien* (*mal*) look good (not too good); *v/i.:* ~ *bien* (*mal*) have a pleasant (an unattractive) appearance; **présentoir** [~ˈtwaːr] *m* display stand *or* shelf.

préservateur, -trice [prezɛrva-ˈtœːr, ‿ˈtris] preserving (from, de); **préservatif, -ve** [‿vaˈtif, ‿ˈtiːv] **1.** adj. preservative; **2.** su./m preservative; ✻ condom; **préservation** [‿vaˈsjɔ̃] f preservation, protection; **préserver** [‿ˈve] (1a) v/t. preserve, protect (from, de).

présidence [preziˈdɑ̃ːs] f presidency; President's house; ✝ board; ✝, a. admin. chairmanship; **président** m, e f [‿ˈdɑ̃, ‿ˈdɑ̃ːt] president; admin. chairman; ⚖ presiding judge; **présidentiel, -elle** [‿dɑ̃-ˈsjɛl] **1.** adj. presidential; **2.** su./f pol. ‿les pl. presidential elections; **présider** [‿ˈde] (1a) v/t. preside over or at (s.th.); fig. direct; v/i.: ‿ à preside at or over.

présomptif, -ve [prezɔ̃pˈtif, ‿ˈtiːv] presumptive; ⚖ héritier m ‿ heir apparent; **présomption** [‿ˈsjɔ̃] f presumption (a. ⚖, a. fig. pej.); **présomptueux, -euse** [‿ˈtɥø, ‿ˈtɥøːz] presumptuous; self-conceited, self-important.

presque [prɛsk(ə)] adv. almost, nearly; **presqu'île** geog. [prɛsˈkil] f peninsula.

pressage ⊕ [prɛˈsaːʒ] m pressing; **pressant, e** [‿ˈsɑ̃, ‿ˈsɑ̃ːt] pressing, urgent; earnest (request); **presse** [prɛs] f ⊕, journ., typ. press; pressing-machine; crowd, throng; haste; business: pressure; exemplaire m du service de ‿ review copy; heures f/pl. de ‿ rush hours; sous ‿ in the press (book); **pressé, e** [prɛˈse] hurried (style, words); in a hurry (person); crowded, close; ⊕ pressed; urgent (letter, task); citron m‿ (fresh) lemon squash; **presse-bouton** [prɛsbuˈtɔ̃] adj./inv. push-button; automatic; **presse-citron** [prɛsi-ˈtrɔ̃] m/inv. lemon-squeezer; **presse-étoffe** [‿eˈtɔf] m/inv. sewing-machine: presser-foot; **presse-étoupe** ⊕ [‿eˈtup] m/inv. stuffing box.

pressentiment [prɛsɑ̃tiˈmɑ̃] m presentiment, foreboding; F feeling, Am. hunch; **pressentir** [‿ˈtiːr] (2b) v/t. have a presentiment of; sound (s.o.) (out) (on, sur); faire ‿ foreshadow (s.th.).

presse...: ‿-**pantalon** [prɛspɑ̃taˈlɔ̃] m/inv. trouser-press; ‿-**papiers** [‿paˈpje] m/inv. paper-weight;

‿-**purée** [‿pyˈre] m/inv. potato-masher.

presser [prɛˈse] (1a) v/t. press (a. ⊕, a. fig.), squeeze; hasten (one's steps, le pas); hurry (s.o.); push on, urge on (a horse etc.); cuis. squeeze; se ‿ crowd, press, throng, hurry, hasten; v/i. press; be urgent; rien ne presse there is no hurry.

pressing [prɛˈsiŋ] m (steam) pressing.

pression [prɛˈsjɔ̃] f pressure (a. ⊕, meteor., mot., a. fig.); cost. snap fastener; ✻ ‿ artérielle blood pressure; bière f à la ‿ draught (Am. draft) beer; faire ‿ sur press (s.th.) down, press (down) on (s.th.); fig. a. exercer une ‿ sur put pressure on (s.o.), pressurize (s.o.); **pressoir** [‿ˈswaːr] m (wine- etc.)press; **pressurage** [prɛsyˈraːʒ] m pressing; F fig. extortion; **pressurer** [‿ˈre] (1a) v/t. press (grapes); press out (juice); F fig. extort money from; **pressureur** [‿ˈrœːr] m pressman; **pressuriser** [‿riˈze] (1a) v/t. pressurize.

prestance [prɛsˈtɑ̃ːs] f fine presence, commanding appearance; **prestataire** [‿taˈtɛːr] su. person receiving benefits or allowances; ‿ de services service(s) (trade etc.); **prestation** [‿taˈsjɔ̃] f dues: prestation; money: lending; (insurance-)benefit; service; sp., thea. etc., a. fig. performance; ⚖ ‿ de serment taking (of) the oath; ‿s pl. en nature allowances in kind.

preste [prɛst] nimble, quick; F ‿! quick!; **prestesse** [prɛsˈtɛs] f quickness, nimbleness; alertness.

prestidigitateur [prɛstidiʒitaˈtœːr] m conjurer; juggler; **prestidigitation** [‿ˈsjɔ̃] f conjuring, sleight of hand; juggling.

prestige [prɛsˈtiːʒ] m prestige; fig. influence; **prestigieux, -euse** [‿ti-ˈʒjø, ‿ˈʒjøːz] prestigious.

présumable [prezyˈmabl] presumable; **présumer** [‿ˈme] (1a) v/t. presume; assume; il est à ‿ que the presumption is that; trop ‿ de overestimate (s.th.); trop ‿ de soi be too presuming.

présure [preˈzyːr] f rennet.

prêt[1] m loan; wages: advance; ✖ pay; ‿ à intérêt loan at interest; ‿ sur gage loan against security.

prêt[2]**, prête** [prɛ, prɛt] ready (for

s.th., à qch.; to inf., à inf.); pre-
pared; ~ à on the verge of.
pretantaine F [pretã'tɛn] f: courir
la ~ gad about.
prêt-à-porter [prɛtapɔr'te] m
coll. ready-to-wear or ready-made
clothes pl. or clothing.
prêt-bail, pl. **prêts-baux** pol. [prɛ-
'ba:j, ~'bo] m lease-lend, lend-lease.
prétendant, e [pretã'dã, ~'dã:t] su.
candidate (for, à); su./m pretender
(to throne); suitor; **prétendre**
[~'tã:dr] (4a) v/t. claim; assert,
affirm, maintain; intend; v/i. lay
claim (to, à); aspire (to, à); **prétendu, e** [~tã'dy] 1. adj. alleged; pej. so-
called; 2. su. F (my) intended.
prête-nom usu. pej. [prɛt'nõ] m man
of straw, figure-head, F front.
pretentaine [pretã'tɛn] f see pretantaine.
prétentieux, -euse [pretã'sjø,
~'sjø:z] pretentious; conceited; **prétention** [~'sjõ] f pretension (a. fig.),
claim; fig. conceit.
prêter [prɛ'te] (1a) v/t. lend, Am.
loan; take (an oath); attribute; fig.
credit (s.o. with s.th., qch. à q.); ~ à
impart to; se ~ à lend o.s. to; be a
party to; v/i. give (gloves etc.); ~ à
give rise to.
prétérit gramm. [prete'rit] m (English) preterite.
prêteur m, **-euse** f [prɛ'tœ:r, ~'tø:z]
lender; ~ sur gages pawnbroker; ⚖
pledgee.
prétexte [pre'tɛkst] m pretext, excuse; prendre ~ que put forward as
a pretext that; sous ~ que on the plea
or under the pretext that; **prétexter**
[~tɛks'te] (1a) v/t. plead; allege; give
(s.th.) as a pretext.
prétoire [pre'twa:r] m hist. praeto-
rium; ⚖ court.
prêtraille † pej. [prɛ'tra:j] f priests
pl.; shavelings pl.; **prêtre** [prɛ:tr] m
priest; ~-ouvrier worker priest; **prêtresse** [prɛ'trɛs] f priestess; **prê-
trise** [~'tri:z] f priesthood.
preuve [prœ:v] f proof (a. ⚗, ⚖,
fig.); ⚖, a. fig. evidence; signs pl.;
faire ~ de show, display; faire la ~ de
prove; faire ses ~s prove o.s. or itself.
preux † [prø] 1. adj. valiant, gallant;
2. su./m/inv. valiant knight.
prévaloir [preva'lwa:r] (3l) v/i. prevail (against, sur); faire ~ make good
(a claim, one's right), win people over

to (an idea, an opinion); v/t.: se ~ de
take advantage of; exercise (a right);
pride o.s. on.
prévaricateur, -trice [prevarika-
'tœ:r, ~'tris] 1. adj. unjust; 2. su.
unjust judge; person guilty of a
breach of trust; **prévarication** [~-
ka'sjõ] f maladministration of justice; breach or abuse of trust; **pré-
variquer** [~'ke] (1m) v/i. be unjust (judge); betray one's trust.
prévenance [prev'nã:s] f kindness,
(kind) attention; **prévenant, e**
[~'nã, ~'nã:t] kind, attentive, con-
siderate (to, envers); prepossessing
(manners etc.); **prévenir** [~'ni:r]
(2h) v/t. forestall, prevent (an
accident, danger, illness); anticipate (a wish); warn; admin. inform,
give notice; prepossess; pej. prejudice; **préventif, -ve** [prevã'tif,
~'ti:v] ⚖, a. ⚖ preventive; deterrent (effect); ⚖ détention f ~ve remand in custody, detention await-
ing trial; **prévention** [~'sjõ] f prevention; prepossession, pej. prejudice; ⚖ custody; ~ routière road
safety; **préventionnaire** ⚖ [~sjɔ-
'nɛ:r] su. prisoner on remand; **pré-
ventorium** ⚕ [~tɔ'rjɔm] m observation sanatorium; **prévenu, e** [prev-
'ny] 1. p.p. of prévenir; 2. adj. prepos-
sessed; prejudiced; 3. su. accused;
prisoner.
prévisible [previ'zibl] foreseeable;
prévision [~'zjõ] f forecast (a.
meteor.); anticipation; expectation;
previsionnel, -elle [~zjɔ'nɛl] forward-looking; **previsionniste** †
[~zjɔ'nist] su. forecaster.
prévoir [pre'vwa:r] (3m) v/t. forecast (a. the weather), foresee, anticipate; plan, provide for; lay down
(s.th.) (in advance).
prévôt [pre'vo] m ⚖, a. hist. provost; ⚔ assistant provost marshal;
~ de salle fencing: assistant fencing-
master; **prévôté** [~vo'te] f hist.
provostship; hist. provostry; ⚔
military police (establishment or
service).
prévoyance [prevwa'jã:s] f foresight; precaution; ~ sociale national
insurance; mesures f/pl. de ~ pre-
cautionary measures; société f de ~
provident society; **prévoyant, e**
[~'jã, ~'jã:t] provident; careful,
cautious; far-sighted.

prie-Dieu [pri'djø] *m/inv.* prayer stool, prie-Dieu, praying-desk; **prier** [~'e] (1a) *v/t.* pray; ask, entreat, beg, beseech; invite (*to dinner etc.*); *je vous (en) prie!* please (do)!; don't mention it!; *les priés m/pl.* the guests; *sans se faire ~* willingly, readily; *se faire ~* require pressing, need persuading; **prière** [~'ɛ:r] *f* prayer; request, entreaty; *~ de (ne pas) (inf.)* please (do not) (*inf.*).

prieur *eccl.* [pri'œ:r] *m* prior; **prieure** *eccl.* [~'œ:r] *f* prioress; **prieuré** [~œ're] *m* priory; priorship.

primaire [pri'mɛ:r] primary; simplistic; simple-minded (*person*).

primat [pri'ma] *m eccl.* primate; *fig.* pre-eminence; **primates** *zo.* [~'mat] *m/pl.* primates; **primatie** *eccl.* [~ma'si] *f* primacy; **primauté** [~mo'te] *f* primacy (*a. eccl.*); priority.

prime¹ [prim] *f* ✝ premium; ✝ subsidy; ✝, ⊕ bonus; ✝ free gift; *fig. faire ~* be highly appreciated.

prime² [prim] **1.** *adj.* ⅄ prime; *fig.* first; *~ jeunesse* earliest youth; *de ~ abord* at first; *de ~ saut* at the first attempt; **2.** *su./f eccl., a. fencing:* prime.

primer¹ [pri'me] (1a) *v/i.* prevail; have priority; ⊕, *a. astr.* prime; *v/t.* surpass; take precedence of; have *or* take priority over; *la force prime le droit* might is right.

primer² [~] (1a) *v/t.* award a prize to; ✝ give a bonus to.

primerose ♀ [prim'ro:z] *f* hollyhock.

primesautier, -ère [primso'tje, ~'tjɛ:r] impulsive; ready.

primeur [pri'mœ:r] *f* ✝ freshness, newness; *~s pl.* ✔ early vegetables *or* fruit; *avoir la ~ d'une nouvelle* be the first to hear a piece of news; **primeuriste** ✔ [~mœ'rist] *m* grower of early vegetables *or* fruit.

primevère ♀ [prim'vɛ:r] *f* primula; primrose.

primitif, -ve [primi'tif, ~'ti:v] primitive; first, early; original, pristine; *gramm.* primary (*tense*).

primo [pri'mo] *adv.* first, in the first place; **primogéniture** [~mɔ-ʒeni'ty:r] *f* primogeniture.

primordial, e, *m/pl.* **-aux** [primɔr-'djal, ~'djo] primordial; *fig.* of primary importance.

prince [prɛ̃:s] *m* prince.

princeps [prɛ̃'sɛps] *adj.:* édition *f* ~ first edition.

princesse [prɛ̃'sɛs] *f* princess; **princier, -ère** [~'sje, ~'sjɛ:r] princely.

principal, e, *m/pl.* **-aux** [prɛ̃si'pal, ~'po] **1.** *adj.* principal (*fig., a.* ⅄, ⅃, ♪, *gramm.*), chief, main; **2.** *su./m school:* head(master); *admin.* chief clerk; ✝ principal; *fig.* main thing; **principalat** [~pa'la] *m school:* headship; **principat** *hist.* [~'pa] *m* principate; **principauté** [~po'te] *f* principality.

principe [prɛ̃'sip] *m* principle; *en ~* in principle; *par ~* on principle; *sans ~s* unprincipled (*person*).

printanier, -ère [prɛ̃ta'nje, ~'njɛ:r] spring...; **printemps** [~'tɑ̃] *m* spring; springtime (*a. fig.*); *fig.* heyday.

priorat [priɔ'ra] *m* priorate, priorship.

prioritaire [priɔri'tɛ:r] **1.** *adj.* having priority, priority...; **2.** *su.* priority-holder; **priorité** [~'te] *f* priority; *mot. a.* right of way; *de ~ mot.* major (*road*); ✝ preference (*shares*).

pris¹ [pri] *1st p. sg. p.s. of* prendre.

pris², e [pri, pri:z] **1.** *p.p. of* prendre; **2.** *adj.:* bien *~* well-proportioned (*figure*), well-built (*man*); *~ de sommeil* drowsy.

prise [pri:z] *f* hold, grip (*a. fig.*), grasp; ⚔ taking (*a. phot.*); ⚔ *town:* capture; ⚓ prize; ⊕ *machine:* mesh, engagement; ✝ *parcels:* collection; *cement etc.:* setting; *snuff:* pinch; *fish:* catch; ⊕ *ore:* sample; *analysis:* specimen, sample; ⊕ *air, steam, etc.:* intake; *~ d'air* ⊕ air-inlet; ⚔ air scoop; *~ d'eau* intake of water; tap, cock; hydrant; 🚒 water-crane; F *~ de bec* squabble; ⚖ *~ de corps* arrest; ⚡ *~ de courant* wall-plug, socket, power point; *trolley:* current collector; *~ de sang* blood specimen; ⚡ *~ de terre* earth-connection; *~ de vues* taking of photographs, photography; *cin.* shooting; *avoir ~ sur* have a hold over *or* on; *fig. donner ~ à* lay o.s. open to; *en ~* ⊕ engaged, in gear; ⚓ holding (*anchor*); *fig. en ~ directe avec* in close

prisée

contact with, in touch with; *être aux* ~*s avec* be at grips with; *faire* ~ set (*cement*); *faire une* ~ *à* (*or sur*) tap (*river, ⚓ coil, cable*); *lâcher* ~ let go; F *fig.* give in.

prisée 🕏 [pri'ze] *f* valuation; appraisal.

priser¹ [pri'ze] (1a) *v/t.* inhale, snuff, take; *v/i.* take snuff.

priser² [~] (1a) *v/t.* value, appreciate, prize.

priseur¹ *m*, **-euse** *f* [pri'zœ:r, ~'zø:z] snuff-taker.

priseur² 🕏 [pri'zœ:r] *m goods*: appraiser; valuer.

prismatique [prisma'tik] prismatic; **prisme** [prism] *m* prism.

prison [pri'zɔ̃] *f* prison; gaol, *Am.* jail; ✕, ⚓ cell(s *pl.*); imprisonment, ✕ F cells *pl.*; **prisonnier, -ère** [~zɔ'nje, ~'njɛ:r] **1.** *su.* prisoner; *se constituer* ~ give o.s. up (to the police); **2.** *adj.* ✕ captive; 🕏 imprisoned.

privatif, -ve *gramm.* [priva'tif, ~-'ti:v] *adj.*, *a. su./m* privative; **privation** [~'sjɔ̃] *f* 🕏, ✕, *fig.* deprivation, loss; *fig.* privation; 🕏 forfeiture.

privautés *pej.* [privo'te] *f/pl.* familiarity *sg.*, liberties.

privé, e [pri've] **1.** *adj.* private; **2.** *su./m* private life; private sector; *en* ~ privately; in private life.

priver [pri've] (1a) *v/t.* deprive; *se* ~ *de* do without; stint o.s. of.

privilège [privi'lɛ:ʒ] *m* privilege; **privilégier** [~le'ʒje] (1o) *v/t.* privilege; favo(u)r, prefer, give preference to.

prix [pri] *m* price, cost; value (*a. fig.*); prize; reward; *sp.* challenge-cup race, prize race, stakes *pl.*; ✝ *exchange*: rate; ~ *courant* market *or* current price; price-list; ~ *de revient* cost price; ~ *de vente* selling price; ~ *fait* (*or fixe*) fixed price; ~ *fort* list price; ~ *homologué* established price; ~ *régulateur* standard of value; ~ *unique* one-price store; ~ *unitaire* unit-price; *à* ~ *d'ami* cheap; *à aucun* ~ not at any price, on no account; *à tout* ~ at all costs; *à vil* ~ at a low price, F dirt cheap; *dernier* ~ lowest price, F rock-bottom price; *faire un* ~ quote a price (to, *à*); *hors de* ~ at ransom prices; ~ **fixe** F [~'fiks] *m* restaurant with a fixed-price meal.

pro F [pro] *m* pro(fessional).

probabilité [prɔbabili'te] *f* probability (*a. Ⱥ*); *selon toute* ~ in all probability; **probable** [~'babl] probable, likely.

probant, e 🕏 *etc.* [prɔ'bɑ̃, ~'bɑ̃:t] probative; conclusive; **probation** [~ba'sjɔ̃] *f* probation; **probatoire** [~ba'twa:r] probative; **probe** [prɔb] honest; of integrity (*man*); **probité** [prɔbi'te] *f* probity, integrity.

problématique [prɔblema'tik] **1.** *adj.* problematical; questionable; **2.** *su./f* problem(s *pl.*); **problème** [~'blɛm] *m* problem (*a. Ⱥ, a. fig.*); puzzle.

procédé [prɔse'de] *m fig.* proceeding; conduct; *billiard cue*: tip; ⊕ process; ~*s pl.* behaviour *sg.*; *bons* ~*s pl.* civilities; *manquer aux* ~*s* be ill-mannered; **procéder** [~'de] (1f) *v/i.* proceed (from, *de*; 🕏 against, *contre*; to, *à*); arise (from, *de*); act; **procédure** [~'dy:r] *f* procedure (*a. 🕏*); 🕏 proceedings *pl.*

procès [prɔ'sɛ] *m* 🕏 (legal) proceedings *pl.*; legal action; trial; ~ *civil* (law)suit; ~ *criminel* (criminal) trial; **processif, -ve** [~sɛ'sif, ~'si:v] litigious; procedural (*form*).

procession [prɔse'sjɔ̃] *f eccl. etc.* procession; parade; *fig.* cars, visitors: string; **processionnaire** *zo.* [prɔsesjɔ'nɛ:r] **1.** *adj.* processionary; **2.** *su./f zo.* processionary caterpillar; **processional** *eccl.* [~'nal] *m* processional; **processionnel, -elle** [~'nɛl] processional (*hymn etc.*); **processionnellement** [~nɛl'mɑ̃] *adv.* in procession.

processus [prɔse'sys] *m anat.*, *a. fig.* process; progress; method.

procès-verbal 🕏 [prɔsɛvɛr'bal] *m* official report, statement; *mot.* parking ticket; *meeting*: proceedings *pl.*; *dresser* (*un*) ~ *contre* q. make a report on s.o., take s.o.'s name and address; *mot.* book (*a motorist*).

prochain, e [prɔ'ʃɛ̃, ~'ʃɛn] **1.** *adj.* next (*in a series*); nearest; near; impending (*departure, storm, etc.*); **2.** *su./m* neighbo(u)r, fellow-creature; **prochainement** [~ʃɛn'mɑ̃] *adv.* soon, shortly; **proche** [prɔʃ] **1.** *adj.* near, close; **2.** *adv.*: *de* ~ *en* ~ by degrees; **3.** *su./m*: ~*s pl.* relatives.

proclamation [prɔklama'sjɔ̃] *f* proc-

lamation; *faire une* ~ issue a proclamation; **proclamer** [~'me] (1a)
v/t. proclaim (*a. fig.*); declare, announce.   [create.\
procréer [prɔkre'e] (1a) *v/t.* pro-\
procuration [prɔkyra'sjɔ̃] *f* ✝, *a.* 🕂
procuration, power of attorney; *par*
~ by proxy *or* procuration; **procurer** [~'re] (1a) *v/t. a. se* ~ obtain, get, procure; **procureur**
[~'rœ:r] *m* 🕂 procurator, proxy;
eccl. bursar; 🕂 attorney; ♀ *de la
République* (*approx.*) Public Prosecutor, *Am.* district attorney; ~ *général* (*approx.*) Attorney General.
prodigalité [prɔdigali'te] *f* prodi-
gality; extravagance, lavishness.
prodige [prɔ'di:ʒ] **1.** *su./m* prodigy;
marvel (*a. fig.*); **2.** *adj.*: *enfant mf* ~
infant prodigy; **prodigieux, -euse**
[~di'ʒjø, ~'ʒjø:z] prodigious, stupen-
dous.
prodigue [prɔ'dig] **1.** *adj.* prodigal
(*a. pej.*); lavish (of, with de), profuse (in, de); spendthrift; *bibl.
l'enfant m* ~ the Prodigal Son; **2.** *su.*
spendthrift, prodigal; **prodiguer**
[~di'ge] (1m) *v/t.* lavish; be un-
sparing of; squander; *se* ~ set out
to please.
prodrome [prɔ'dro:m] *m* prodrome
(to, de); 🌡 premonitory symptom;
fig. preamble (to, de).
producteur, -trice [prɔdyk'tœ:r,
~'tris] **1.** *adj.* productive (of, de);
⊕ generating (*appara-
tus*); **2.** *su.* producer; ✔ *a.* grower;
productible [~'tibl] producible;
productif, -ve [~'tif, ~'ti:v] productive, fruitful; **production** [~-
'sjɔ̃] *f* production (*a.* 🕂, ♪, ⊕, *cin.*);
⚡, *gas, steam:* generation; ⊕ output; product; 🎢 growth; **productivité** [~tivi'te] *f* productivity; **produire** [prɔ'dɥi:r] (4h) *v/t.* produce
(*a.* 🕂 *evidence, a. cin.*); ✝, ✔ yield;
⊕ turn out (*products*); generate (⚡,
gas, steam); *fig.* give rise to; *fig.*
bring about; *se* ~ take place, happen, occur; **produit** [~'dɥi] *m* Å,
⊕, 🎢 product; ✔ produce; pro-
ceeds *pl.* (*of sale*), receipts *pl.*; ✝
yield; ~ *accessoire* (*or secondaire*)
by-product; ~ *d'un capital* yield of
a capital sum; ✝ ~ *manufacturé*
manufacture(d product); ✝ ~ *national brut* gross national product;
✝ ~ *ouvré* finished article.

proéminence [prɔemi'nɑ̃:s] *f* prominence; protuberance; **proémi-
nent, e** [~'nɑ̃, ~'nɑ̃:t] prominent;
projecting.
profanateur *m*, **-trice** *f* [prɔfana-
'tœ:r, ~'tris] desecrator; **profanation** [~'sjɔ̃] *f* desecration; **profane**
[prɔ'fan] **1.** *adj.* profane; secular
(*history, art, theatre, etc.*); sacrilegious; impious; **2.** *su.* layman (*a.
fig.*); F *fig.* outsider; **profaner** [~-
fa'ne] (1a) *v/t.* profane; desecrate
(*a church, a tomb*); *fig.* degrade (*one's
talent etc.*).
proférer [prɔfe're] (1f) *v/t.* utter;
pour forth (*insults*).
professer [prɔfe'se] (1a) *v/t.* pro-
fess; be a professor of (*a subject*);
practise (*law, medicine, etc.*); **professeur** [~'sœ:r] *m* teacher, master;
(*a. femme f* ~) *secondary school:* mistress; *univ.* professor, lecturer; ~
d'athéisme avowed *or* open atheist;
profession [~'sjɔ̃] *f eccl.*, *a. fig.*
profession; occupation; trade; *de* ~
by profession; *fig.* habitual (*drunkard*); *sans* ~ of private means (*person*); **professionnaliser** [~sjɔna-
lize] (1a) *v/t.*: ~ become *or* go
professional; acquire (a) professional character; **professionnel, -elle**
[~sjɔ'nɛl] **1.** *adj.* professional; vocational; 🎢 occupational (*disease*);
enseignement m ~ vocational training;
2. *su. usu. sp.* professional; **professorat** [~sɔ'ra] *m secondary school:*
post of teacher; *univ.* professorship;
coll. teaching profession, teachers
pl.; *univ.* professoriate.
profil [prɔ'fil] *m* profile; outline;
🔺 *etc.* section; *geog.* contour; **profilé, e** [prɔfi'le] **1.** *adj.* 🖅, ⚓, *mot.*
streamlined; **2.** *su./m* ⚓, *mot., etc.*
section; **profiler** [~] (1a) *v/t.* ⊕
shape; draw (*s.th.*) in section; profile; *mot.* streamline; *se* ~ be sil-
houetted (against contre, sur, à).
profit [prɔ'fi] *m* ✝ profit (*a. fig.*);
fig. advantage, benefit; ✝ ~*s pl. et
pertes f/pl.* profit *sg.* and loss *sg.*;
mettre qch. à ~ turn s.th. to account,
take advantage of s.th.; **profitable**
[prɔfi'tabl] profitable, advantageous; **profiter** [~'te] (1a) *v/i.* profit
(by, de); *fig.* grow, thrive; *fig.* wear
well (*material etc.*), be economical; ~
à q. benefit s.o.; be profitable to s.o.;
~ *de* take advantage of, make the

most of; **profiteur** *pej.* [ₐ'tœːr] *m*
profit-taker; F profiteer; F ₐ *de guerre*
war profiteer.

profond, e [prɔ'fɔ̃, ₐ'fɔ̃:d] **1.** *adj.* deep
(*a. fig. sigh, sleep*); *fig.* profound; **2.**
profond adv. deep; **3.** *su./m* depth(s
pl.); *au* ₐ *de la nuit* in the dead of
night; **profondément** [ₐfɔ̃de'mɑ̃]
adv. of profond 1; **profondeur** [ₐfɔ̃-
'dœːr] *f* depth (*a. fig.*); *en* ₐ in depth;
thorough(going); in-depth.

profus, e [prɔ'fy, ₐ'fyːz] profuse;
profusément [prɔfyze'mɑ̃] *adv. of
profus;* **profusion** [ₐ'zjɔ̃] *f* profusion; abundance; *fig.* lavishness;
fig. à ₐ lavishly.

progéniture [prɔʒeni'tyːr] *f* prog-
eny, offspring.

prognose [prɔg'noːz] *f* prognosis.

programme [prɔ'gram] *m* programme, *Am.* program (*a. pol.,
radio, data processing*); *pol.* platform; *univ. etc.* examination: syllabus; ₐ *des auditeurs radio:* request
program(me); ₐ *d'études* curricu-
lum; **programmateur, -trice**
[prɔgrama'tœːr, ₐ'tris] *su. radio(person),* *su./m data processing (machine):*
programmer; **programmation**
[ₐma'sjɔ̃] *f* radio, *data processing:*
programming; **programmer** [ₐ'me]
vt/i. (1a) *data processing, etc.:* program; *fig. a.* plan; **programmeur**
m, **-euse** *f* [ₐ'mœːr, ₐ'møːz] *data
processing (person):* programmer.

progrès [prɔ'grɛ] *m* progress; advancement; *faire des* ₐ progress,
make headway; **progresser** [prɔ-
grɛ'se] (1a) *v/i.* progress, make
headway, advance; *fig.* improve;
progressif, -ve [ₐ'sif, ₐ'siːv] pro-
gressive; forward; gradual; gradu-
ated (*tax*); **progression** [ₐ'sjɔ̃] *f*
progress; progression (*a.* ♪); ad-
vance(ment); increase; **progressiste** *pol.* [ₐ'sist] *adj., a. su.* pro-
gressive.

prohiber [prɔi'be] (1a) *v/t.* forbid,
prohibit; *hunt. temps m prohibé*
close season; **prohibitif, -ve** [prɔi-
bi'tif, ₐ'tiːv] prohibitive (*price etc.*);
prohibitory (*law etc.*); **prohibition**
[ₐ'sjɔ̃] *f* prohibition; ₐ*s pl. de sortie*
ban *sg.* on exports; **prohibitionniste** [ₐsjɔ'nist] *adj., a. su./m* pro-
hibitionist.

proie [prwa] *f* prey (*a. fig.*); *être en* ₐ *à*
be a prey to, be consumed by (*hatred*

etc.), be tortured by (*pains, remorse,
etc.*).

projecteur [prɔʒɛk'tœːr] *m* projector; floodlight; spot(light); searchlight; **projectif, -ve** [ₐ'tif, ₐ'tiːv]
projective; **projectile** [ₐ'til] *adj., a.
su./m* projectile; missile; **projection** [ₐ'sjɔ̃] *f* projection (*a.* △, ♣); △
plan; (lantern) slide; **projecture** △
[ₐ'tyːr] *f* projection.

projet [prɔ'ʒɛ] *m* project, plan; draft;
scheme; *parl.* ₐ *de loi* government
bill; *état m de* ₐ planning stage;
projeter [prɔʒ'te] (1c) *v/t.* project;
throw; cast (*a shadow*); *fig.* plan,
contemplate, intend; *se* ₐ stand out;
be cast (*shadow*); jut out (*cliff etc.*).

prolétaire *pol.* [prɔle'tɛːr] *m* proletarian; **prolétariat** [ₐta'rja] *m coll.*
proletariate; **prolétarien, -enne**
[ₐta'rjɛ̃, ₐ'rjɛn] proletarian.

prolifération [prɔlifera'sjɔ̃] *f* pro-
liferation; **proliférer** [ₐfe're] (1f)
v/i. proliferate; **prolifique** [ₐ'fik]
prolific.

prolixe [prɔ'liks] prolix, diffuse; F
fig. long-winded; **prolixité** [ₐliksi-
'te] *f* prolixity; F *fig.* verbosity.

prologue [prɔ'lɔg] *m* prolog(ue) (*to,
de*).

prolongation [prɔlɔ̃ga'sjɔ̃] *f time:*
prolongation; *leave, stay, ticket:*
extension; *sp.* extra time; **prolonge**
✕ [prɔ'lɔ̃:ʒ] *f* ammunition waggon;
lashing-rope; **prolongement** [ₐ-
lɔ̃ʒ'mɑ̃] *m space:* prolongation; extension; **prolonger** [ₐlɔ̃'ʒe] (1l)
v/t. prolong, extend (*in time or
space*); ♪ protract (*a disease*); ⚕
produce (*a line*); ⚓ coast (along);
se ₐ continue; extend; be pro-
tracted.

promenade [prɔm'nad] *f* walk(ing);
stroll (*on foot*), drive (*in a car*), sail
(*in a boat*), ride (*on a bicycle*); trip,
excursion; *place:* promenade, avenue; ✕ ₐ (*militaire*) route march;
faire une ₐ go for *or* take a walk;
promener [ₐ'ne] (1d) *v/t.* take
(*s.o.*) for a walk *or* a drive *etc.*;
exercise (*an animal*); take, conduct;
fig. run (*one's hand, one's eyes*) (*over,
sur*); cast (*one's mind, one's thoughts*)
(*over, sur*); *envoyer* ₐ *q.* send s.o.
about his business; *se* ₐ walk, go
for a walk *or* ride *etc.*; *fig.* rove,
wander (*eyes, gaze*); *va te* ₐ*!* get
away with you!; **promeneur** *m,*

-euse *f* [∿'nœːr, ∿'nøːz] walker, stroller; tripper; *thea.* promenader; **promenoir** [∿'nwaːr] *m* promenade, covered walk; ⚓ promenade deck; 🚊 lobby.

promesse [prɔ'mɛs] *f* promise; assurance; ✝ promissory note; *manquer à sa* ∿ break one's promise; **prometteur, -euse** [∿mɛ'tœːr, ∿'tøːz] **1.** *adj.* free with his (her, *etc.*) promises; *fig.* promising, full of promise, attractive; **2.** *su.* person free with his (her) promises, ready promiser; **promettre** [∿'mɛtr] (4v) *v/t.* promise (*a. fig.*); *fig.* bid fair to (*inf.*); se ∿ *qch.* promise o.s. s.th.; look forward to s.th.; *v/i.* look *or* be promising; **promis, e** [∿'mi, ∿'miːz] **1.** *p.p. of* promettre; **2.** *adj.* promised; engaged (*to be married*); *la terre* ∿e the Promised Land (*a. fig.*); **3.** *su.* betrothed, F intended.

promiscuité [prɔmiskɥi'te] *f* promiscuity; *en* ∿ promiscuously.

promission *bibl., a. fig.* [prɔmi'sjɔ̃] *f*: *la terre de* ∿ the Promised Land.

promontoire *geog.* [prɔmɔ̃'twaːr] *m* promontory; headland.

promoteur, -trice [prɔmɔ'tœːr, ∿'tris] **1.** *adj.* promoting; **2.** *su.* promoter; (*a.* ∿-constructeur, ∿ de construction) property developer; ✝ ∿ de ventes sales promoter; **promotion** [∿mɔ'sjɔ̃] *f* promotion; *school:* class (= *year*); *coll.* persons *pl.* promoted; ✝ special offer; ✝ ∿ des ventes sales promotion *or* en ∿ on special offer; ∿ ouvrière *or* sociale rise in the social scale, social advancement; **promotionnel, -elle** ✝ [∿mɔsjɔ'nɛl] promotion(al); **promouvoir** [∿mu-'vwaːr] (3f) *v/t.* promote.

prompt, prompte [prɔ̃, prɔ̃ːt] prompt, quick, speedy, ready; ∿ à se décider quick to make up one's mind; **promptitude** [prɔ̃ti'tyd] *f* promptness, promptitude, quickness; readiness.

promu, e [prɔ'my] *p.p. of* promouvoir.

promulgation [prɔmylga'sjɔ̃] *f law:* promulgation; *decree:* publication; **promulguer** [∿'ge] (1m) *v/t.* promulgate (*a law*); publish, issue (*a decree*).

prône *eccl.* [proːn] *m* sermon; **prôner** [pro'ne] (1a) *v/t. eccl.* preach to; *fig.* extol, crack (*s.th., s.o.*) up;

read (*s.o.*) a lecture, scold; **prôneur** *m*, **-euse** *f* [∿'nœːr, ∿'nøːz] extoller, *sl.* booster.

pronom *gramm.* [prɔ'nɔ̃] *m* pronoun; **pronominal, e**, *m/pl.* **-aux** *gramm.* [∿nɔmi'nal, ∿'no] pronominal.

prononçable [prɔnɔ̃'sabl] pronounceable; **prononcé, e** [∿'se] **1.** *adj.* pronounced (*a. fig.*); *fig.* marked; **2.** *su./m* 🚊 decision; **prononcer** [∿'se] (1k) *v/t.* pronounce; 🚊 pass (*sentence*); make (*a. a speech*); *fig.* mention (*a name*); *mal* ∿ mispronounce (*a word etc.*); se ∿ give one's opinion *or* decision; come to a decision (on, about *sur*); be pronounced (*word*); 🚊 pronounce; ∿ *sur* rule upon, adjudicate upon (*a question*); 🚊 give one's verdict on; **prononciation** [∿sja-'sjɔ̃] *f gramm.* pronunciation; 🚊 *sentence:* passing; *verdict:* bringing in; *speech:* delivery.

pronostic [prɔnɔs'tik] *m* prognostic(ation); forecast; *turf:* (*tipster's*) selection; 🞧 prognosis; **pronostiquer** [∿ti'ke] (1m) *v/t.* foretell; prognose, give a prognosis; forecast (*the weather*); **pronostiqueur** *m*, **-euse** *f* [∿ti'kœːr, ∿'køːz] prognosticator.

propagande [prɔpa'gɑ̃ːd] *f* propaganda; publicity; advertising; *de* ∿ propaganda ...; **propagandisme** [∿gɑ̃'dism] *m* propagandism; **propagandiste** [∿gɑ̃'dist] *su.* propagandist.

propagateur, -trice [prɔpaga'tœːr, ∿'tris] **1.** *adj.* propagating; **2.** *su.* propagator; *news, germs, etc.:* spreader; **propagation** [∿ga'sjɔ̃] *f* propagation, spread(ing); *phys.* ∿ des ondes wave propagation; **propager** [∿'ʒe] (1l) *v/t.* propagate (*biol., phys., a. fig.*); spread (*news, germs*); *fig.* popularize; se ∿ propagate; spread; *phys.* be propagated.

propane ⚗ [prɔ'pan] *m* propane.

propension [prɔpɑ̃'sjɔ̃] *f* propensity, tendency.

prophète [prɔ'fɛt] *m* prophet, seer; *fig.* prophesier; **prophétesse** [∿fe'tes] *f* prophetess; **prophétie** [∿'si] *f* prophecy; **prophétique** [∿'tik] prophetic; **prophétiser** [∿ti'ze] (1a) *v/t.* prophesy, foretell.

prophylactique ⚕ [prɔfilak'tik] prophylactic; **prophylaxie** ⚕ [ʌ'si] f prophylaxis; prevention of disease.

propice [prɔ'pis] propitious (to, à; for s.th., à qch.); favo(u)rable (to, à); **propitiation** [prɔpisja'sjɔ̃] f propitiation; **propitiatoire** [ʌ'twaːr] propitiatory; F don m ~ sop (to Cerberus).

proportion [prɔpɔr'sjɔ̃] f proportion (with, avec); ratio; fig. ~s pl. size sg., dimensions; à ~ que in proportion as; en ~ de in proportion or relation to; **proportionnel, -elle** [ʌsjɔ'nɛl] 1. adj. proportional; ⅍ moyenne f ~elle mean proportional; 2. su./f ⅍ proportional; **proportionner** [ʌsjɔ'ne] (1a) v/t. proportion or adjust or adapt (to, à); bien proportionné well-proportioned.

propos [prɔ'po] m purpose; topic; remark; convenience; ~ pl. talk sg.; à ~ relevant, pertinent, timely; à ~! by the way!; à ~ de about; regarding, concerning, in connection with; à ~ de rien for no reason at all; à ce ~ in this connection; à tout ~ at every (end and) turn; changer de ~ change the subject; hors de ~ irrelevant (comment); ill-timed; juger à ~ think fit; mal à ~ inopportunely, at the wrong moment; **proposable** [prɔpo'zabl] worthy of consideration; **proposer** [ʌ'ze] (1a) v/t. propose; suggest; offer (a solution, money); put forward (a candidate, s.o. as a model); se ~ propose or offer o.s. (as, comme); se ~ de (inf.) propose or intend to (inf.); se ~ pour (inf.) offer to (inf.); **proposition** [ʌzi'sjɔ̃] f offer, proposal; ⅍, phls., ♪ proposition; gramm. clause; motion (to be voted upon).

propre [prɔpr] 1. adj. proper, correct; peculiar (to, à); characteristic (of, à); own; fit, able (to, à) calculated (to, à); clean; neat; house-trained, Am. housebroken (animal); toilet-trained, clean (child); ~ à rien good for nothing; ~ maison f own house; maison f ~ clean house; en ~s termes in so many words; 2. su./m nature, characteristic, peculiarity; gramm. literal sense; ~ à rien good-for-nothing; iro. c'est du ~! that's a fine thing!; **propret, -ette** † [prɔ'prɛ, ʌ'prɛt] neat, tidy; **propreté**

[ʌprə'te] f cleanness; neatness; cleanliness.

propriétaire [prɔprie'tɛːr] su./m proprietor, owner; landlord; su./f landlady; proprietress; **propriété** [ʌ'te] f property (a. phys.); estate; ownership; fig. characteristic, property; language, words, etc.: correctness; ~ immobilière real estate; ~ littéraire copyright.

proprio F [prɔpri'o] m proprietor; owner; landlord.

propulser [prɔpyl'se] (1a) v/t. propel; ✈ propulsé par réaction rocket-powered; **propulseur** [ʌ'sœːr] 1. adj./m propulsive, propelling, propellent; 2. su./m propeller; **propulsif, -ve** [ʌ'sif, ʌ'siːv] propulsive, propelling; **propulsion** [ʌ'sjɔ̃] f propulsion; ~ par réaction rocket-propulsion.

prorata [prɔra'ta] m/inv. proportion; au ~ pro rata (payment); au ~ de in proportion to, proportionately to.

prorogation [prɔrɔga'sjɔ̃] f parl. prorogation; ⅍ etc. extension of time; fig. prolongation; **proroger** [ʌ'ʒe] (1l) v/t. parl. adjourn, prorogue; ⅍, ✝ extend (a time-limit), prolong.

prosaïque [prɔza'ik] prosaic; fig. unimaginative, dull; **prosaïsme** [ʌ'ism] m prosaic style; fig. dullness; **prosateur** [ʌ'tœːr] m prose-writer.

proscription [prɔskrip'sjɔ̃] f proscription; banishment; fig. abolition; **proscrire** [ʌ'kriːr] (4q) v/t. proscribe; fig. abolish; fig. forbid; **proscrit** m, e f [ʌ'kri, ʌ'krit] proscript, outlaw, exile.

prose [proːz] f prose; eccl. sequence.
prosélyte [prɔze'lit] m proselyte.
prospecter [prɔspɛk'te] (1a) v/t. ⚒ prospect; ✝ canvass; **prospecteur** ⚒ etc. [ʌ'tœːr] m prospector; **prospectif, -ve** [ʌ'tif, ʌ'tiːv] 1. adj. prospective; forward-looking; 2. su./f forecasting (the future); research into the future development; **prospection** [ʌ'sjɔ̃] f ⚒ etc. prospecting; prospection; ✝ canvassing; **prospectus** [ʌ'tys] m prospectus; leaflet; brochure; handbill.

prospère [prɔs'pɛːr] prosperous, thriving; favo(u)rable (circumstances etc.); well-to-do (person); **prospé-**

rer [ˌ~pe're] (1f) v/i. prosper, thrive; succeed; **prospérité** [ˌ~peri'te] f prosperity; ✝ vague f de ~ boom.

prostate anat. [prɔ'stat] f prostate (gland).

prosterner [prɔster'ne] (1a) v/t.: se ~ prostrate o.s.; bow down (before, to devant); F kowtow (to, devant).

prostituée [prɔsti'tɥe] f prostitute, whore; **prostituer** [ˌ~'tɥe] (1a) v/t. prostitute (a. fig.); **prostitution** [ˌ~ty'sjɔ̃] f prostitution (a. fig.).

prostration [prɔstra'sjɔ̃] f prostration (a. 🖉); 🖉 exhaustion; **prostré, e** [ˌ~'tre] prostrate; 🖉 exhausted.

protagoniste thea., a. fig. [prɔtagɔ-'nist] m protagonist.

protecteur, -trice [prɔtek'tœːr, ˌ~'tris] 1. adj. ⊕, a. pol. protective; protecting; fig. pej. patronizing; 2. su. protector; patron; ~ de l'environnement environmentalist; **protection** [ˌ~'sjɔ̃] protection (against, from contre); patronage, influence; wire-pulling; ~ civile civil defence; F air m de ~ patronizing air; **protectionnisme** pol. [ˌ~sjɔ'nism] m protectionism; **protectionniste** pol. [ˌ~sjɔ'nist] adj., a. su. protectionist; **protectorat** [ˌ~tɔ'ra] m protectorate.

protégé [prɔte'ʒe] m favo(u)rite; protégé; **protégée** [ˌ~te'ʒe] f protégée; **protège-oreilles** [ˌ~tɛʒɔ're:j] m/inv. ear-protector; **protéger** [ˌ~te'ʒe] (1g) v/t. protect (from, contre); fig. be a patron of; patronize.

protéine [prɔte'iːn] f protein; **protéique** [ˌ~'ik] protein..., proteinic.

protestant, e [prɔtes'tɑ̃, ˌ~'tɑ̃:t] adj., a. su. Protestant; **protestantisme** [ˌ~tɑ̃'tism] m Protestantism; **protestataire** pol. [ˌ~ta'tɛːr] su. objector; **protestation** [ˌ~ta'sjɔ̃] f protest (against, contre); protestation (of friendship, innocence, etc.); **protester** [ˌ~'te] (1a) v/t. protest (a. ✝ a bill); v/i.: ~ contre challenge; protest against; ~ de qch. protest s.th.; **protêt** [prɔ'tɛ] m protest.

prothèse 🖉 [prɔ'tɛːz] f prosthesis; artificial limb; (a. ~ dentaire) false teeth pl., denture.

prot(o)... [prɔt(ɔ)] prot(o)...

protocolaire [prɔtɔkɔ'lɛːr] formal; of etiquette; **protocole** [ˌ~'kɔl] m protocol; ceremonial; F etiquette; pol. chef m du ~ Chief of Protocol.

prototype [prɔtɔ'tip] m prototype.

protubérance [prɔtybe'rɑ̃ːs] f protuberance; (solar) prominence; knob.

protuteur m, **-trice** f 👥 [prɔty-'tœːr, ˌ~'tris] acting guardian.

prou [pru] adv.: ni peu ni ~ none or not at all; peu ou ~ more or less.

proue ⚓ [ˌ~] f prow, bows pl.

prouesse [pru'ɛs] f prowess; ~s pl. exploits.

prouvable [pru'vabl] provable; **prouver** [ˌ~'ve] (1a) v/t. prove.

provenance [prɔv'nɑ̃ːs] f source, origin; ✝ product; produce; 🖉 en ~ de from; **provenir** [ˌ~'niːr] (2h) v/i.: ~ de arise from, come from; originate in.

proverbe [prɔ'vɛrb] m proverb; **proverbial, e** m/pl. -aux [ˌ~ver-'bjal, ˌ~'bjo] proverbial.

providence [prɔvi'dɑ̃ːs] f providence; F fig. guardian angel; **providentiel, -elle** [ˌ~dɑ̃'sjɛl] providential; fig. opportune, heaven-sent.

province [prɔ'vɛ̃ːs] f provinces pl.; fig. de ~ provincial; pej. countrified; **provincial, e** m/pl. -aux [ˌ~vɛ̃'sjal, ˌ~'sjo] 1. adj. provincial; fig. pej. countrified; 2. su., a. su./m eccl. provincial.

proviseur [prɔvi'zœːr] m lycee: headmaster; **provision** [ˌ~'zjɔ̃] f provision, stock, supply; finance: funds pl., cover; 👥 sum paid into court; faire ses ~s go shopping; par ~ provisional; sac m à ~s shopping-bag; **provisoire** [ˌ~'zwaːr] provisional; temporary; acting (official etc.); **provisorat** [ˌ~zɔ'ra] m lycee: headmastership.

provocant, e [prɔvɔ'kɑ̃, ˌ~'kɑ̃:t] provocative (a. fig.); fig. enticing; **provocateur, -trice** [ˌ~ka'tœːr, ˌ~'tris] 1. adj. provocative; 2. su. aggressor; instigator; provoker; **provocation** [ˌ~ka'sjɔ̃] f provocation; instigation; crime: incitement; challenge; 🖉 sleep etc.: inducement; **provoquer** [ˌ~'ke] (1m) v/t. provoke; incite (to, à); 🖉 induce (sleep etc.); fig. cause, bring about; fig. arouse (suspicion etc.).

proxénète [prɔkse'nɛt] su./m procurer; su./f procuress.

proximité [prɔksimi'te] f proximity; nearness; ~ de parenté near relationship; *à ~* near at hand; *à ~ de* close to.

prude [pryd] **1.** *adj.* prudish; **2.** *su./f* prude.

prudemment [pryda'mã] *adv.* of *prudent;* **prudence** [~'dãːs] *f* care-(fulness), cautiousness; prudence; discretion; wisdom; **prudent, e** [~'dã, ~'dãːt] careful, cautious; prudent; discreet; *fig.* wise, advisable (to *inf., de inf.*).

pruderie [pry'dri] *f* prudery, prudishness; **prud'homme** [~'dɔm] *m* man of integrity, *fig.* wise man; *conseil m des ~s* conciliation board.

prudhommerie [prydɔm'ri] *f* pomposity.

pruine [prɥin] *f* bloom (*on fruit*).

prune [pryn] **1.** *su./f* plum; F *fig. pour des ~s* for nothing; **2.** *adj./inv.* plum-colo(u)red; **pruneau** [pry'no] *m* prune; F ✕ (*rifle-*)bullet; *sl.* black eye; **prunelaie** ✔ [pryn'lɛ] *f* plum orchard; **prunelée** [~'le] *f* plum jam; **prunelle** [pry'nɛl] *f* ✔ sloe; ♀, *a. tex.* prunella; *anat. eye:* pupil; *fig.* apple (*of the eye*); **prunellier** ♀ [~ne'lje] *m* blackthorn, sloetree; **prunier** ♀ [~'nje] *m* plum-tree.

prurigineux, -euse ♀ [pryriʒi'nø, ~'nøːz] pruriginous; **prurit** ♀ [~'ri(t)] *m* pruritus, itching.

Prusse [prys] *f: bleu m de ~* Prussian blue; **prussien, -enne** [pry'sjɛ̃, ~'sjɛn] *adj., a. su.* ♀ Prussian; **prussique** ♫ [~'sik] *adj.: acide m ~* prussic acid.

psalmiste [psal'mist] *m* psalmist; *bibl. le* ♩ the Psalmist (= *king David*); **psalmodie** [~mɔ'di] *f eccl.* psalmody; intoned psalm; F *voice:* singsong; **psalmodier** [~mɔ'dje] (1o) *vt/i.* intone, chant; *v/t.* F *fig.* drone (*s.th.*) out; **psaume** [pso:m] *m* psalm; **psautier** [pso'tje] *m* psalter.

pseud(o)... [psød(ɔ)] pseud(o)...

pseudonyme [psødɔ'nim] *m* assumed name; pseudonym; nom de plume; stage name.

ps(it)t! [ps(i)t] *int.* psst!; I say!

psittacisme ♀ [psita'sism] *m* psittacism, parrotry; **psittacose** ♀ [~'ko:z] *f* psittacosis; parrot disease.

psych... [psik] psych(o)...; **~analyse** ♀ [psikana'liːz] *f* psychoanalysis;

psychanalyser [~li'ze] (1a) *v/t.* psychoanalyze; **~analyste** ♀ [~'list] *m* psychoanalyst; **~analytique** ♀ [~li'tik] psychoanalytic(al).

psyché [psi'ʃe] *f* cheval-glass.

psych...: **~iatre** [psi'kja:tr] *m* psychiatrist; **~iatrie** [psikja'tri] *f* psychiatry; **~iatrique** [~'trik] psychiatric; *hôpital m ~ a.* mental hospital.

psychique [psi'ʃik] psychic; **psychisme** [~'ʃism] *m* psychism.

psycho... [psikɔ] psycho...; **~logie** [~lɔ'ʒi] *f* psychology; *~ des enfants* (*foules*) child (mass) psychology; **~logique** [~lɔ'ʒik] psychological (*a.* F *fig. moment*); **~logue** [~'lɔg] *su.* psychologist; **~pathe** ♀ [~'pat] *su.* psychopath.

psychose [psi'ko:z] *f* ♀ psychosis; obsessive fear; *~ de guerre* war scare.

psycho...: **~somatique** [psikɔsɔma-'tik] **1.** *adj.* psychosomatic; **2.** *su./f* psychosomatics *sg.*; **~thérapeute** [~tera'pø:t] *su.* psychotherapist; **~thérapie** [~tera'pi] *f* psychotherapy; **~trope** [~'trɔp] **1.** *adj.* psychotropic; **2.** *su./m* psychotropic (substance).

ptomaïne ♀, 🍄 [ptɔma'in] *f* ptomaine.

pu [py] *p.p. of pouvoir* 1.

puant, e [pɥɑ̃, pɥɑ̃ːt] stinking; foul (*a. fig.*); F conceited; **puanteur** [pɥɑ̃'tœːr] *f* stench, stink.

pubère [py'bɛːr] pubescent; **pubertaire** [~bɛr'tɛːr] (of) puberty; adolescent; *l'âge m ~* puberty; **puberté** [~bɛr'te] *f* puberty.

pubescent, e ♀ [pybɛ'sɑ̃, ~'sɑ̃:t] pubescent, downy.

pubien, -enne *anat.* [py'bjɛ̃, ~'bjɛn] pubic; **pubis** *anat.* [~'bis] *m* pubis.

publiable [pybli'able] publishable; **public, -que** [~'blik] **1.** *adj.* public; *la chose ~que* the state, the government; *la vie ~que* public life, politics *pl.*; *maison f ~que* brothel; **2.** *su./m* public; *thea. etc.* audience; *en ~* in public; *le grand ~* the general public; F the man in the street; **publication** [pyblika'sjɔ̃] *f* publication; publishing; *en cours de ~* printing (*book*); **publiciste** [~'sist] *su.* publicist; public relations officer; **publicitaire** [~si'tɛːr] **1.** *adj.* publicity-..., advertising...; promotion...; **2.** *su./m* publicity man;

publicité [⁓si'te] f publicity; public relations pl.; advertising; ⁓ aérienne sky-writing; ⁓ lumineuse illuminated advertising; bureau m de ⁓ advertising agency; exemplaires m/pl. de ⁓ press copies; **publier** [⁓'e] (1a) v/t. publish; make public; release (news); proclaim.

puce [pys] 1. su./f flea; F marché m aux ⁓s flea market; F secouer les ⁓s à give (s.o.) a good hiding; 2. adj./inv. puce.

pucelle [py'sɛl] f maiden, virgin; la ⁓ (d'Orléans) the Maid of Orleans, Joan of Arc.

puceron ✒ [pys'rɔ̃] m plant-louse; aphis.

pucier sl. [py'sje] m bed.

pudeur [py'dœːr] f modesty; decency; reserve; sans ⁓ shameless(ly adv.); **pudibond, e** [⁓di'bɔ̃, ⁓'bɔ̃:d] prudish; **pudicité** [⁓disi'te] f modesty; bashfulness; chastity; **pudique** [⁓'dik] modest, bashful; chaste.

puer [pɥe] (1n) v/i. stink, reek, smell; v/t. smell of; stink of.

puériculture [pɥerikyl'ty:r] f rearing of children; infant care; **puéril, e** [⁓'ril] puerile, childish (a. argument etc.); âge m ⁓ childhood; **puérilité** [⁓rili'te] f childishness; puerility (a. fig.).

pugilat [pyʒi'la] m pugilism; F setto, fistfight; **pugiliste** [⁓'list] m pugilist, boxer, F pug.

puîné, e [pɥi'ne] 1. adj. younger; 2. su./m younger brother; su./f younger sister.

puis¹ [pɥi] adv. then, afterwards, next; et ⁓ and then; moreover; et ⁓ après? what then?; what about it?, so what?

puis² [⁓] 1st p. sg. pres. of pouvoir 1.

puisage ⊕ [pɥi'za:ʒ] m pumping up; **puisard** [⁓'za:r] m ⊕ sump; **puisatier** [⁓za'tje] m well digger; **puiser** [⁓'ze] (1a) v/t. draw (from à, dans) (a. fig.); dip (into, dans).

puisque [pɥisk(ə)] cj. since, as; seeing that.

puissamment [pɥisa'mã] adv. powerfully; fig. extremely; **puissance** [⁓'sã:s] f fig.; a. ⊕, ⚡, ⚛, eccl., pol., radio: power; force; fig. influence; ⚖, fig. authority; phys. ⁓ en bougies candle-power; ⁓ lumineuse searchlight: candle-power; pol. ⁓ mondiale world(-)power; **puissant, e** [⁓'sã, ⁓'sã:t] powerful; strong; weighty (argument); thick (coal-seams).

puisse [pɥis] 1st p. sg. pres. sbj. of pouvoir 1.

puits [pɥi] m well; ⚒ shaft; ⊕, ⚒ pit; ⁓ d'aérage air-shaft; cuis. ⁓ d'amour cream-puff; jam-puff; fig. ⁓ de science person: mine of information.

pull-over [pyl0'vœːr] m pullover;∫

pulluler [pyly'le] (1a) v/i. swarm, teem; multiply rapidly.

pulmonaire [pylmɔ'nɛːr] 1. adj. pulmonary; 2. su./f ♀ lungwort.

pulpe [pylp] f pulp; finger etc.: pad; **pulpeux, -euse** [pyl'pø, ⁓'pø:z] pulpy, pulpous.

pulsatif, -ve [pylsa'tif, ⁓'ti:v] pulsatory; throbbing (pain); **pulsation** [⁓'sjɔ̃] f pulsation (a. ⚡, a. phys.); heart: throb(bing), beat (-ing); **pulsatoire** ⚕ [⁓'twa:r] pulsatory.

pulsion psych. [pyl'sjɔ̃] f urge, drive; ⁓ sexuelle sexual urge.

pulsoréacteur ✈ [pylsɔreak'tœːr] m intermittent jet; pulsojet.

pulvérisateur [pylveriza'tœːr] m pulverizer; spray, atomizer; liquids: vaporizer; **pulvériser** [⁓'ze] (1a) v/t. pulverize (a. fig. s.o.); F sp. smash (a record); mot. etc., a. fig. atomize (petrol, liquids); **pulvérulence** [pylvery'lã:s] f powderiness; dustiness; **pulvérulent, e** [⁓'lã, ⁓'lã:t] powdery; dusty.

puma zo. [py'ma] m puma, cougar.

punais, e [py'nɛ, ⁓'nɛ:z] 1. adj. foul-smelling; 2. su./f zo. bug; drawing-pin, Am. thumbtack.

punch [pɔ̃:ʃ] m punch.

punique hist. [py'nik] Punic; fig. foi f ⁓ treachery.

punir [py'ni:r] (2a) v/t. punish (with, de); **punissable** [pyni'sabl] punishable; **punition** [⁓'sjɔ̃] f punishment; games: forfeit.

pupillaire anat., ⚖ [pypil'lɛ:r] pupil(l)ary; **pupillarité** ⚖ [⁓lari'te] f wardship.

pupille¹ [py'pil] su. ⚖ ward; orphanage-child; ⁓ de la nation war orphan (in France).

pupille² anat. [⁓] f eye: pupil.

pupitre [py'pitr] m desk; ∫ (music-) stand; eccl. lectern; ⊕⁓ de commande control desk; ⚡, thea. ⁓ de distribution (or commutation) switch-desk.

pur, pure [py:r] pure (*a. fig.*), spotless; *fig.* clear (*conscience etc.*); *fig.* innocent, chaste (*girl*); *fig.* sheer, downright; *zo.* ~ *sang* thoroughbred; *folie f pure* utter folly.

purée [py're] *f cuis. vegetables*: mash; mashed potatoes *pl.*; thick soup; *sl.* être *dans la* ~ be in the soup, be hard up.

pureté [pyr'te] *f* purity (*a. fig.*); chastity; *fig.* clearness.

purgatif, -ve [pyrga'tif, ~'ti:v] *adj.*, *a. su.*/*m* purgative; **purgation** [~'sjɔ̃] *f* ⚕, *eccl.* purgation; ⚕ purging; ⚕ purge; **purgatoire** *eccl.* [~'twa:r] *m* purgatory (*a. fig.*); **purge** [pyrʒ] *f* ⚕ purge (*a. pol.*), purgative; ⚖ *mortgage*: redemption; ⊕ blow-off; *tex.* cleaning; **purgeoir** ⊕ [pyr'ʒwa:r] *m* filtering-tank; **purger** [~'ʒe] (1l) *v/t.* purge (*fig.*, *a.* ⚕), cleanse; ⚖ serve (*a sentence*); ⊕, *a. fig.* clear; se ~ take a purgative; *fig.* clear o.s.

purification [pyrifika'sjɔ̃] *f* purification (*a. eccl.*); cleansing; **purifier** [~'fje] (1o) *v/t.* purify, cleanse; refine (*metal*); ⊕ disinfect (*the air etc.*).

purin ✍ [py'rɛ̃] *m* liquid manure.

purisme [py'rism] *m* purism; **puriste** [~'rist] **1.** *su.* purist; **2.** *adj.* puristic.

puritain, e [pyri'tɛ̃, ~'ten] **1.** *su.* Puritan; **2.** *adj.* puritan(ical) (*a. fig.*); **puritanisme** [~ta'nism] *m* puritanism (*a. fig.*).

purpurin, e [pyrpy'rɛ̃, ~'rin] purplish; crimson.   [thoroughbred.\

pur-sang {[pyr'sɑ̃] *m*/*inv.* horse:}

purulence ⚕ [pyry'lɑ̃:s] *f* purulence; **purulent, e** ⚕ [~'lɑ̃, ~'lɑ̃:t] purulent; *foyer m* ~ abscess.

pus[1] ⚕ [py] *m* pus, matter.

pus[2] [~] *1st p. sg. p.s. of pouvoir 1.*

pusillanime [pyzilla'nim] pusillanimous; faint-hearted; **pusillanimité** [~nimi'te] *f* faint-heartedness.

pustule ⚕ [pys'tyl] *f* pustule; **pustulé, e** ⚕ [~ty'le], **pustuleux, -euse** ⚕ [~ty'lø, ~'lø:z] pustulous.

putain V [py'tɛ̃] *f* whore; ~! goddamn it!

putatif, -ve [pyta'tif, ~'ti:v] putative; reputed.

putois *zo.* [py'twa] *m* polecat.

putréfaction [pytrefak'sjɔ̃] *f* putrefaction, decay; **putréfier** [~'fje] (1o) *v/t.* putrefy, rot, decompose; se ~ putrefy; **putrescence** [pytre'sɑ̃:s] *f* putrescence; ⚕ sepsis; **putrescent, e** [~'sɑ̃, ~'sɑ̃:t] putrescent; **putrescible** [~'sibl] liable to putrefaction; **putride** [py'trid] putrid; tainted.   [*Auvergne*).\

puy *geog.* [pɥi] *m* peak (*in the*

puzzle [pœzl] *m* jig-saw puzzle.

pygmée [pig'me] *m* pygmy.

pyjama [piʒa'ma] *m* (pair of) pyjamas *pl.*, *Am.* pajamas *pl.*

pylône [pi'lo:n] *m* ⚡ pylon (*a.* ⚠), mast; ⛴, ⚔ post.

pyramidal, e, *m*/*pl.* -aux [pirami'dal, ~'do] pyramidal; **pyramide** ⚠, ⚛ [~'mid] *f* pyramid; ~ *des âges statistics*: age pyramid.

pyrite *min.* [pi'rit] *f* pyrites.

pyro... [pirɔ] pyro...; **~gravure** [~gra'vy:r] *f* poker-work; **~ligneux** ⚗ [~li'nø] *adj.*: *acide m* ~ pyroligneous acid; **~mane** [~'man] *su.* pyromaniac; **~phore** ⚗, *zo.* [~'fɔ:r] *m* pyrophorus.

pyrosis ⚕ [pirɔ'zis] *m* pyrosis, heartburn.

pyro...: **~technicien** [pirɔtekni'sjɛ̃] *m* pyrotechnist; **~technie** [~tek'ni] *f* pyrotechnics *pl.*

pyroxyle ⚗ [pirɔk'sil] *m* pyroxyline; gun-cotton.

Pyrrhus [pi'rys] *npr.*/*m*: *victoire f à la* ~ Pyrrhic victory.

python *zo. etc.* [pi'tɔ̃] *m* python; **pythonisse** [~tɔ'nis] *f* prophetess; clairvoyante.

Q

Q, q [ky] *m* Q, q.
quadragénaire [kwadraʒe'nɛːr]· *adj., a. su.* quadragenarian.
quadrangulaire [kwadrãgy'lɛːr] Ⱥ *etc.* quadrangular; △ four-cornered.
quadrant Ⱥ [ka'drã] *m* quadrant; **quadrature** [kwadra'tyːr] *f* Ⱥ, *astr.* quadrature; Ⱥ *circle*: squaring (*a. fig.*).
quadri... [kwadri] quadri...; **~folié, e ♀** [~fɔ'lje] quadrifoliate.
quadrilatère Ⱥ *etc.* [kwadrila'tɛːr] *su./m, a. adj.* quadrilateral.
quadrillage [kadri'ja:ʒ] *m* cross-ruling; cross-gridding; chequerwork; squares *pl.*; *fig.* cover(ing), control(ling); **quadrille** [~'driːj] *m* ♪ *dance, a. cards*: quadrille; **quadriller** [~dri'je] (1a) *v/t.* square (*paper etc.*); grid (*map*); chequer; *fig.* cover (*an area etc.*); (bring under) control.
quadri...: **~moteur** ✈ [kwadrimɔ'tœːr] 1. *adj./m* four-engined; 2. *su./m* four-engined plane; **~phonie** [~fɔ'ni] *f* quadrophony; **en ~** in quadrophonic sound; **~réacteur** ✈ [~reak'tœːr] *m* four-engined jet plane.
quadrupède [kwadry'pɛd] 1. *adj.* four-footed, quadruped; 2. *su./m* quadruped.
quadruple [kwa'drypl] *adj., a. su./m* quadruple, fourfold; **quadruplé(e)s** [~dry'ple] *su./pl.* quadruplets; **quadrupler** [~] (1a) *vt/i.* quadruple; increase fourfold.
quai [ke] *m* quay, wharf; 🚋 platform; embankment (*along a river*); *droits m/pl. de ~* quayage (dues) *sg.*
qualifiable [kali'fjabl] subject to qualification; describable (as, de); **qualificatif, -ve** *gramm.* [~fika'tif, ~'tiːv] 1. *adj.* qualifying; 2. *su./m* qualifier; **qualification** [~fika'sjɔ̃] *f* qualification (*a. sp.*); calling; *gramm.*, ✝ qualifying; description, designation; **qualifié, e** [~'fje] qualified (to, pour); ⊕ skilled (*workman*); ⚖

aggravated (*larceny*); **qualifier** [~'fje] (1o) *v/t.* call, style (by, de; s.o. s.th., q. de qch.); qualify (*a. gramm.*); **se ~** call o.s.; qualify (for, pour); **qualitatif, -ve** [~ta'tif, ~'tiːv] qualitative; **qualité** [~'te] *f* quality, property; nature; qualification; *fig.* capacity (as, de); title; *avoir ~ pour* be qualified to; *de première ~* first-rate; *en (sa) ~ de* in his capacity as; ✝ *gens m/pl. de ~* gentlefolk.
quand [kã] 1. *adv.* when; *depuis ~?* how long?, since when?; *pour ~ est ...?* when is ...?; 2. *cj.* when; **~ même** none the less, nevertheless; even though.
quant à [kã'ta] *prp.* as for; as regards; in relation to.
quantième [kã'tjɛm] *m* day of the month, date.
quantifier [kãti'fje] (1o) *v/t.* quantify.
quantique *phys.* [kwã'tik] *adj.*: *mécanique f ~* quantum mechanics.
quantitatif, -ve [kãtita'tif, ~'tiːv] 🞐 *etc.* quantitative; *gramm.* (*adjective*) of quantity, (*adverb*) of degree; **quantité** [~'te] *f* quantity.
quantum, *pl.* **-ta** [kwã'tɔm, ~'ta] *m* Ⱥ, 🞐, *phys.* quantum; *phys. théorie f des quanta* quantum theory.
quarantaine [karã'ten] *f* (about) forty; ⚓ quarantine; *la ~* the age of forty, the forties *pl.*; *mettre q. en ~* ✱, ⚓ quarantine s.o.; *fig.* send s.o. to Coventry; **quarante** [~'rãːt] 1. *adj./num.,* forty; 2. *su./m/inv.* forty; *les ♀* the Forty (members of the *Académie française*); **~cinq tours** *m* record: single; **quarantième** [~'tjɛm] *adj./num., a. su.* fortieth.
quart [kaːr] *m* Ⱥ *etc.* quarter; ⚓ point (of the compass); ⚓ watch; ♪ *~ de soupir* semiquaver rest; *~ d'heure* quarter of an hour; *fig. passer un mauvais ~ d'heure* have a hard time (of it); *faire passer un mauvais ~ d'heure à q.* give s.o. a hard time; *deux heures moins le ~* a quarter to two; *le ~ a sonné* it has struck quarter past; *un*

~ (de livre) a quarter (of a pound); fig.
aux trois ~s almost (completely); fig.
les trois ~s de most (of); fig. au ~ de
tour immediately, straight off; fig. un
petit ~ d'heure a few minutes; **quarte** [kart] **1.** adj./f 🐎 quartan (fever);
2. su./f ♪ fourth; fencing: carte,
quart(e).

quartier [kar'tje] m quarter; (fourth)
part; piece, portion; venison:
haunch; bacon: gammon; stone:
block; district, neighbo(u)rhood;
fig. mercy, clemency; ⚔ quarters
pl.; ~ chic residential quarter; ⚔
~ général headquarters pl.; ~ ouvrier
working-class district; ⚔ demander
~ ask for or cry quarter; ⚔ faire ~
give quarter; **~-maître,** pl. **~-s-
maîtres** [ˌtje'mɛːtr] m ⚓ leading
seaman; ⚔ † quartermaster.

quarto [kwar'to] adv. fourthly.
quartz min. [kwarts] m quartz;
quartzeux, -euse min. [kwart'sø,
ˌ'søːz] quartzose; quartz (sand).
quasi [ka'zi] adv. almost, practically;
quasi; **~-délit** 🌐 [ˌzide'li] m technical offence; **quasiment** F [ˌzi-
'mã] adv. almost, practically.
Quasimodo eccl. [kazimɔ'dɔ] f Low
Sunday.
quaternaire ⚕, 🜍, geol., etc.
[kwatɛr'nɛːr] quaternary.
quatorze [ka'tɔrz] adj./num., a.
su./m/inv. fourteen; date, title:
fourteenth; **quatorzième** [ˌtɔr-
'zjɛm] adj./num., a. su. fourteenth.
quatrain [ka'trɛ̃] m quatrain.
quatre [katr] adj./num., a. su./m/inv.
four; date, title: fourth; à ~ pas
d'ici close by; à ~ pattes on all
fours; entre ~ yeux between you
and me; pol. les ♀ Grands the Big
Four; **~-mâts** ⚓ [katrə'ma] m/inv.
four-master; **~-saisons** [ˌsɛ'zɔ̃]
f/inv. (sort of) strawberry; see marchand 2; **~-temps** eccl. [ˌ'tã] m/pl.
ember days; **~-vingt-dix** [ˌvɛ̃'dis,
before consonant ˌ'di; before vowel or
h mute ˌ'diz] adj./num., a. su./m/inv.
ninety; **~-vingt-dixième** [ˌvɛ̃di-
'zjɛm] adj./num., a. su. ninetieth;
~-vingtième [ˌvɛ̃'tjɛm] adj./num.,
a. su. eightieth; **~-vingts** [ˌ'vɛ̃]
adj./num., a. su./m (loses its -s
when followed by another number)
eighty; quatre-vingt-un eighty-one;
quatrième [katri'em] **1.** adj./num.
fourth; **2.** su. fourth; su./m fraction:

fourth, quarter; fourth, Am.
fifth floor; su./f secondary school:
(approx.) third form.
quatuor ♪ [kwa'tɥɔːr] m quartet;
~ à cordes string quartet.
que [kə] **1.** pron./interr. what?; how
(many)!; ~ cherchez-vous?, qu'est-
ce que vous cherchez? what are you
looking for?; ~ c'est beau! how
beautiful it is!; ~ de monde! what
a lot of people!; ~ faire? what can
(could) be done?; qu'est-ce ~ c'est
~ cela? what's that?; qu'est-ce ~ la
littérature? what is literature?;
2. pron./rel. whom, that; which;
what; (autant) ~ je sache so far as I
know; je ne sais ~ dire I don't know
what to say; je sais ce qu'il veut I
know what he wants; le jour qu'il vint
the day (when) he came; l'homme ~
j'aime the man (whom or that) I
love; misérable ~ tu es! wretch that
you are!; you wretch!; **3.** cj. that;
so that; when; whether; replacing
another cj. to avoid its repetition:
puisque vous le dites et ~ nous le
croyons since you say so and we
believe it; ~ (sbj.) ... ~ (sbj.) whether
(ind.) ... or (ind.); ~ la lumière soit!
let there be light!; ~ le diable l'emporte! to hell with him!; approchez
~ je vous regarde come closer and
let me look at you; aussi ... ~ as ...
as; d'autant plus ... ~ all the more
... as or because; il ne partira pas
sans ~ cela ne soit fait he will not
leave before it is done; il y a ... ~
since ...; je crois ~ oui I think so;
ne ... ~ only, but; non (pas) ~ (sbj.)
not that (ind.); plus ~ more than;
tel ~ such as; tel ~ je suis as I am;
un tel vacarme ~ such a row that.
quel m, **quelle** f, **quels** m/pl.,
quelles f/pl. [kɛl] **1.** adj./interr.
what; who; which; what (a)!; quelle
bonté! how kind!; quelle heure est-
il? what time is it?; ~ que (sbj.)
whatever (ind.); quelle que soit son
influence whatever his influence
(may be); ~s que soient ces messieurs whoever these gentlemen
may be; **2.** adj./indef. whatever;
whoever; whichever.
quelconque [kɛl'kɔːk] adj./indef. any
whatever; some ... or other; ordinary, commonplace; indifferent,
poor.
quelque [kɛlk(ə)] **1.** adj. some, any;

~s *pl.* some, (a) few; ~ *chose* something, anything; ~ *peu* something; ~ ... *qui (or que)) (sbj.)* whatever *(ind.)*; ne ...~ *chose* not ... anything; **2.** *adv.* some, about; ~ *peu* somewhat, a little; ~ ... *que (sbj.)* however *(adj.)*; **~fois** [kɛlkə'fwa] *adv.* sometimes, now and then.

quelqu'un *m, e f, m/pl.* **quelques-uns** [kɛl'kœ̃, ~'kyn, ~kə'zœ̃] *pron./ indef.* someone, anyone; somebody, anybody; *pl.* some, any; ~! ✝ shop!; F *W.C.*: engaged!; ~ *des* ... one (or other) of the ...; *être* ~ be s.o. (important).

quémander [kemã'de] (1a) *v/i.* beg (from, *à*); *v/t.* beg for; **quémandeur,** *m* **-euse** *f* [~'dœːr, ~'døːz] importunate beggar; *(place-)*hunter.

qu'en-dira-t-on [kɑ̃dira'tɔ̃] *m/inv.* what people will say; public opinion.

quenelle *cuis.* [kə'nɛl] *f (fish-, meat-)*ball.

quenotte F [kə'nɔt] *f* tooth.

quenouille [kə'nuːj] *f* distaff; ♀ cat's-tail; *fig.* *tomber en* ~ fall to the distaff side.

querelle [kə'rɛl] *f* quarrel; dispute; ~ *d'Allemand* groundless quarrel; **quereller** [kərɛ'le] (1a) *v/t.* quarrel with *(s.o.)*, nag *(s.o.)*; *se* ~ quarrel; fall out (with, *avec*); **querelleur, -euse** [~'lœːr, ~'løːz] **1.** *adj.* quarrelsome; nagging *(wife)*; **2.** *su.* quarrelsome person.

quérir [ke'riːr] (2v) *v/t.: aller* ~ go and fetch, go for; *envoyer* ~ send for; *venir* ~ come and fetch, come for.

question [kɛs'tjɔ̃] *f* question; matter; ⚖ issue; ⚖ *hist.* torture; ⚖ *d'actualité* topic of the moment *or* day; ~ *en suspens* outstanding question, question still unresolved; ~*-piège* trick question, loaded question; *ce n'est pas la* ~ that is not the point; *il est* ~ *de* it is a question of; there is talk of; *mettre qch. en* ~ challenge s.th.; *question s.th.*; ... *ne fait pas* ~ there is no doubt about ...; **questionnaire** [kɛstjɔ'nɛːr] *m* list of questions; quiz; questionnaire; **questionner** [~'ne] (1a) *v/t.* question *(s.o.)*; **questionneur, -euse** [~'nœːr, ~'nøːz] **1.** *adj.* inquisitive; **2.** *su.* inquisitive person; *su./m: c'est un éternel* ~ he never stops asking questions.

quête [kɛːt] *f* quest, search; *hunt.*

tracking *(by dogs)*; *eccl. etc.* collection; *en* ~ *de* in search of; *fig.* looking for *(information)*; **quêter** [kɛ'te] (1a) *v/t.* collect; F *fig.* seek (for); *hunt.* seek *(game)*; *v/i.* take up a collection; **quêteur** *m,* **-euse** *f* [~'tœːr, ~'tøːz] collector *(of alms)*; *eccl.* taker-up of the collection.

quetsche [kwɛtʃ] *f* damson.

queue [kø] *f* ✂, *zo., astr., etc.* tail; *pan:* handle; *cost.* dress: train; *(billiard-)*cue; *fig.* bottom, (tail) end; *people:* queue, *Am.* line; rear; ♀ stalk; *tool, button:* shank; *en* ~ in the rear; *fig.* at the bottom *or* tail-end; *faire (la)* ~ queue up, form a queue, *Am.* line up, stand in line; *mot. faire une* ~ *de poisson* cut in (on, *à*); *fig. finir en* ~ *de poisson* fizzle out; *n'avoir ni* ~ *ni tête* be disconnected *(story)*; ♪ *piano m à* ~ grand piano; ~ **d'aronde,** *pl.* ~*s-d'aronde* ⊕ [~da'rɔːd] *f* dovetail; ~**-de-cochon,** *pl.* ~*s-de-cochon* ⊕ [~dkɔ'ʃɔ̃] *f* auger-bit, gimlet; ~**-de-morue,** *pl.* ~*s-de-morue* [~dmɔ'ry] *f (painter's)* flat brush; F evening dress, tails *pl.*; ~**-de-pie,** *pl.* ~*s-de-pie* [~d'pi] *f* swallow-tail coat; ~**-de-rat,** *pl.* ~*s-de-rat* [~d'ra] *f* ⊕ rattail(ed file); reamer; *(sort of)* snuffbox.

qui [ki] **1.** *pron./interr.* *subject: persons:* who, *two persons:* which; *things:* which; what; *object: persons:* whom; *things:* which; ~ *des deux?* which of the two?; ~ *est-ce* ~ *chante?* who sings?, who is singing?; ~ *est-ce que tu as vu?* who(m) did you see?; *à* ~ to whom? *à* ~ *est ce livre?* whose book is this?; *whom does this book belong to?; de* ~ whose?; of *or* from whom?; **2.** *pron./rel.* *subject: persons:* who, that; *(he or anyone) who; things:* which, that; what; *after prp.: persons:* whom; *things:* which; ~ *pis est* what is worse; ~ *que ce soit* whoever it is; anyone; *à* ~ *mieux mieux* vying with one another; *ce* ~ what; which; *n'avoir* ~ *tromper* have no one to deceive; **3.** *pron./indef.* some; ~ ..., ~ ... some ..., some *or* others ...

quia ✝ [kɥi'a] *adv.:* *être à* ~ be nonplussed; *mettre (or réduire) à* ~ nonplus.

quiconque [ki'kɔ̃k] *pron./indef.* whoever, anyone who; anybody.

quidam [ki'dam] *m*: un ⏝ an individual, someone.

quiétude [kᴜie'tyd] *f* quietude.

quignon [ki'ɲɔ̃] *m* bread: chunk, hunk.

quille[1] ⚓ [ki:j] *f* keel.

quille[2] [ki:j] *f sp.* skittle, ninepin; *sl.* leg; *fig. recevoir q. comme un chien dans un jeu de* ⏝s give s.o. a cold welcome; **quillier** *sp.* [ki'je] *m* skittle-alley.

quinaire [kᴜi'nɛ:r] Ⱥ quinary; ⚕, *zo.* pentamerous.

quincaille [kɛ̃'ka:j] *f* ✝ (piece of) hardware, ironmongery; F *coins:* coppers *pl.*; **quincaillerie** ✝ [⏝ka-'ri] *f* hardware, ironmongery; hardware shop; **quincaillier** ✝ [⏝ka'je] *m* hardware merchant, ironmonger.

quinconce [kɛ̃'kɔ̃s] *m*: en ⏝ staggered; zigzag.

quinine ⚗, ⚕ [ki'nin] *f* quinine.

quinquagénaire [kᴜɛ̃kwaʒe'nɛ:r] *adj.*, *a. su.* quinquagenarian.

quinquennal, e [kᴜɛ̃kᴜɛn'nal, ⏝'no] *m/pl.* -**aux** five-year (*plan*).

quinquina ⚕ [kɛ̃ki'na] *m* cinchona, quinquina.

quint ✝ [kɛ̃] *adj./m* fifth; *Charles* ♀ Charles V.

quinte [kɛ̃:t] *f cards:* quint; *fencing:* quinte; ♪ fifth; F *fig.* whim; *coughing:* fit.

quintessence [kɛ̃te'sɑ̃:s] *f* quintessence; **quintessencier** [⏝sɑ̃'sje] (1o) *v/t.* refine.

quintette ♪ [kɛ̃'tet] *f* quintet(te).

quinteux, -euse [kɛ̃'tø, ⏝'tø:z] crotchety, cantankerous (*person*); restive (*horse*); ⚕ fitful.

quintuple [kɛ̃'typl] *adj., a. su./m* quintuple, fivefold; **quintupler** [⏝ty'ple] (1a) *vt/i.* increase fivefold, quintuple.

quinzaine [kɛ̃'zɛn] *f* (about) fifteen; fortnight; fortnight's pay; **quinze** [kɛ̃:z] *adj./num., a. su./m/inv.* fifteen; *date, title:* fifteenth; ⏝ *jours*

a fortnight; **quinzième** [kɛ̃'zjɛm] *adj./num., a. su.* fifteenth.

quiproquo [kiprɔ'ko] *m* misunderstanding; mistake.

quittance ✝ [ki'tɑ̃:s] *f* receipt; *donner* ⏝ *à* give (*s.o.*) a receipt in full; *fig.* forgive (*s.o.*); **quittancer** ✝ [⏝tɑ̃'se] (1k) *v/t.* receipt.

quitte [kit] *adj.* free, clear (of, *de*); discharged (from, *de*); *être* ⏝ be quits, be even; *en être* ⏝ *pour qch.* get or come off with s.th.; *adj./inv.:* ⏝ *à* (*inf.*) even if (*ind.*); *il le fera* ⏝ *à perdre son argent* he will do it even if he loses his money.

quitter [ki'te] (1a) *v/t.* leave (*a person, a place*); resign (*a post*); give up (*a post, business, a. fig.*); take off (*one's coat, hat, etc.*); *teleph.* ne quittez pas! hold the line, please!

quitus ✝, ⚖ [ki'tys] *m* full discharge; receipt in full.

qui-vive [ki'vi:v] *m/inv.* ⚔ (*sentry's*) challenge; *fig. être sur le* ⏝ be on the qui vive *or* on the alert.

quoi [kwa] **1.** *pron./interr. things:* what; ⏝ *de neuf?* what's the news?; ⏝ *donc!* what!; **2.** *pron./rel.* what; ⏝ *que* (*sbj.*) whatever (*ind.*); ⏝ *qu'il en soit* be that as it may; *avoir de* ⏝ have the wherewithal; *avoir de* ⏝ *vivre* have enough to live on; (*il n'y a*) *pas de* ⏝! don't mention it!; you're welcome!; *sans* ⏝ ... otherwise, or else; *un je-ne-sais-*⏝ (*or je ne sais* ⏝) a(n indescribable) something, just something.

quoique [kwak(ə)] *cj.* (al)though.

quolibet [kɔli'bɛ] *m* gibe.

quote-part [kɔt'pa:r] *f* quota, share.

quotidien, -enne [kɔti'djɛ̃, ⏝'djɛn] **1.** *adj.* daily, everyday; ⚕ quotidian; **2.** *su./m* daily (paper); **quotidienneté** [⏝djɛn'te] *f* everyday life.

quotient [kɔ'sjɑ̃] *m* Ⱥ quotient; *pol., admin.* quota; *psych.* ⏝ *intellectuel* intelligence quotient, *abbr.* I. Q.

quotité [kɔti'te] *f* share, portion, amount.

R

R, r [ɛːr] *m* R, r.

rabâchage [rabɑˈʃaːʒ] *m* tiresome repetition; rigmarole; **rabâcher** [ˌ↗ˈʃe] (1a) *v/i.* repeat the same thing over and over again; *v/t.* repeat (*s.th.*) over and over again; **rabâcheur, -euse** [ˌ↗ˈʃœːr, ˌ↗ˈʃøːz] *su.* person who repeats the same thing over and over again.

rabais [raˈbɛ] *m ✝ price:* reduction, discount; *au* ⁓ at a discount *or* reduced price; **rabaisser** [ˌ↗bɛˈse] (1a) *v/t.* lower; ✝ depreciate (*the coinage*); *fig.* belittle; humble (*s.o., s.o.'s pride*).

rabat [raˈba] *m cost.* bands *pl.*; *handbag etc.:* flap; ⊕ rabbet; **⁓-joie** [ˌ↗baˈʒwa] *m/inv.* spoil-sport, wet blanket; **rabattage** [ˌ↗baˈtaːʒ] *m ✝ prices:* lowering; *hunt.* beating (*for game*); heading back (*of game*); *fig.* heading off (*of people*); ⚞ cutting back; **rabatteur** [ˌ↗baˈtœːr] *m ✝* tout; *hunt.* beater; **rabattre** [↗ˈbatr] (4a) *v/t.* fold back *or* down; lower (*a. fig.*); *fig.* reduce; ⚞ cut back; *hunt.* beat up (*game*); head (*game*) back; *fig.* head off (*people*); tone down (*a colour*); lower (*the price, s.o.'s pride, one's claims*); ⁓ qch. de take *s.th.* off (*the price etc.*); *fig.* en ⁓ climb down; *mot. etc.* se ⁓ get back into the inside lane; se⁓ *sur* fall down upon; *fig.* fall back on.

rabbin [raˈbɛ̃] *m* rabbi.

rabibocher F [rabiboˈʃe] (1a) *v/t.* patch up; *fig.* reconcile (*two adversaries*); se ⁓ make it up.

rabiot *sl.* [raˈbjo] *m food:* extra; overtime; extra time.

rabique ⚕ [raˈbik] rabic.

râble [rɑːbl] *m zo.* hare *etc.*: back; *cuis. hare:* saddle; **râblé, e** [rɑˈble] thick-backed (*hare*); broad-backed, strapping, strong (*person*).

rabonnir [raboˈniːr] (2a) *vt/i.* improve.

rabot ⊕ [raˈbo] *m* plane; ⁓ *en caout-chouc* squeegee; **raboter** [raboˈte] (1a) *v/t.* ⊕ plane (*wood*); *fig.* polish;

sl. filch, *Am.* lift (*s.o.'s money*); **raboteur** ⊕ [ˌ↗ˈtœːr] *m* planer; **raboteuse** ⊕ [ˌ↗ˈtøːz] *f* planing-machine; **raboteux, -euse** [ˌ↗ˈtø, ↗ˈtøːz] rough; knotty (*wood*); uneven (*road*); rugged (*country, a. fig. style*).

rabougri, e [rabuˈgri] stunted, dwarfed (*person, a. plant*); scraggy (*vegetation*); **rabougrir** [ˌ↗ˈgriːr] (2a) *v/t.* stunt the growth of; *v/i. a.* se ⁓ become stunted.

rabouter [rabuˈte] (1a), **raboutir** [ˌ↗ˈtiːr] (2a) *v/t.* join end to end.

rabrouer F [rabruˈe] (1a) *v/t.* scold, F dress down; snub.

racaille [raˈkɑːj] *f people:* riff-raff, scum; *things:* trash.

raccommodage [rakɔmɔˈdaːʒ] *m* mending, repairing; *socks etc.:* darning; repair; darn; **raccommodement** [ˌ↗mɔdˈmɑ̃] *m* reconciliation; *quarrel:* mending; **raccommoder** [ˌ↗mɔˈde] (1a) *v/t.* mend, repair; darn (*socks etc.*); *fig.* reconcile; se ⁓ *avec* make it up with (*s.o.*); **raccommodeur, m -euse** *f* [ˌ↗mɔˈdœːr, ↗ˈdøːz] repairer, mender.

raccord [raˈkɔːr] *m* ⊕ joint, connection; link; △ join (*a. picture etc.*); linking up; touch-up; **raccordement** [rakɔrdəˈmɑ̃] *m* ⊕, △ joining, linking, connection; ⚞ *voie f de* ⁓ slip line; **raccorder** [↗ˈde] (1a) *v/t.* join, connect, link (up).

raccourci, e [rakurˈsi] **1.** *adj.* shortened; abridged (*account*); ⚹ oblate; bobbed (*hair*); short (*stature*); *fig. à bras* ⁓(*s*) with might and main; **2.** *su./m* abridgement; short cut (*to somewhere*); *en* ⁓ in a few words, briefly; **raccourcir** [↗ˈsiːr] (2a) *v/t.* shorten; cut short (*a speech*); curtail; abridge (*an account, a story*); *v/i.* grow shorter; *tex.* shrink; **raccourcissement** [ˌ↗sisˈmɑ̃] *m* shortening; abridgement; *tex.* shrinking.

raccroc [raˈkro] *m billiards:* fluke;

fig. par ~ by chance; **raccrocher**
[rakrɔˈʃe] (1a) *v/t.* hang up again; F
get hold of (*s.o., s.th.*); F solicit,
accost (*s.o.*); se ~ clutch (at, *à*); *fig.*
link (with); F recoup one's losses; *v/i.*
teleph. hang up, ring off.

race [ras] *f* race; *zo.* species, breed;
fig. breeding; **racé, e** [raˈse]
thoroughbred (*a. fig.*); pure(bred).

racer [reˈsœːr] *m* racing-horse; *mot.*
racing-car.

rachat [raˈʃa] *m* repurchase; *goods:*
buying in; *annuity, covenant, loan,*
option, a. eccl.: redemption; *policy,*
value: surrender; **rachetable** [raʃ-
ˈtabl] † redeemable; *eccl.* atonable
(*sin*); **racheter** [ʌˈte] (1d) *v/t.* buy
back; † buy (*s.th.*) in; redeem (†
annuity, debt, loan, a. fig.); ransom
(*a prisoner*); atone for (*one's sins, a.*
fig.); † surrender (*a policy*); buy
more of (*s.th.*).

rachitique ✝ [raʃiˈtik] rachitic,
rickety; **rachitisme** ✝ [ʌˈtism] *m*
rachitis, rickets.

racinage [rasiˈnaːʒ] *m coll.* (edible)
roots *pl.*; *tex.* walnut dye; *book-*
binding: tree-marbling; **racine**
[ʌˈsin] *f* ♪, ♀, ⅄, *ling., a. fig.* root;
mountain: foot; **raciner** [ʌsiˈne]
(1a) *v/i.* ♀ (take) root; *v/t. tex.* dye
with walnut; *bookbinding:* marble.

racisme [raˈsism] *m* racialism,
racism; **raciste** [ʌˈsist] *adj., a. su.*
racialist, racist.

racle ⊕ [rɑːkl] *f* scraper.

raclée F [rɑˈkle] *f* hiding, thrashing,
dressing-down; **racler** [ʌˈkle] (1a)
v/t. scrape; make a clean sweep of; ✔
thin out; se ~ *la gorge* clear one's
throat; *v/i.:* ♪ ~ *du violon* scrape on
the fiddle; **raclette** [ʌˈklɛt] *f* ⊕
scraper; ✔ hoe; *phot.* squeegee; **ra-**
cloir ⊕ [ʌˈklwaːr] *m* scraper; **ra-**
cloire [ʌˈklwaːr] *f* ⊕ spokeshave;
tongue scraper; **raclure** [ʌˈklyːr] *f*
scrapings *pl.*

racolage [rakɔˈlaːʒ] *m* ✕, ⚓ recruiting; *fig.* enlisting; *prostitute:* solicit-
ing; **racoler** [ʌˈle] (1a) *v/t.* ✕, ⚓
recruit; *fig.* enlist; *fig.* tout for; *pros-*
titute: solicit; **racoleur** [ʌˈlœːr] *m*
tout; **racoleuse** [ʌˈløːz] *f* prostitute,
streetwalker.

raconter [rakɔˈte] (1a) *v/t.* tell,
relate; **raconteur** *m*, **-euse** *f*
[ʌˈtœːr, ʌˈtøːz] (story-)teller.

racornir [rakɔrˈniːr] (2a) *v/t.* hard-

en, toughen; se ~ harden; grow hard
or horny; *fig.* grow callous; *fig.*
shrivel up.

radar [raˈdaːr] *m* radar (set); **rada-**
riste [ʌdaˈrist] *m* radar operator.

rade ⚓ [rad] *f* roads *pl.*, roadstead;
fig. laisser en ~ abandon.

radeau [raˈdo] *m* raft; ~ *de sauvetage*
life raft.

radiaire [raˈdjɛːr] radiate(d);
radial, e, *m/pl.* **-aux** ⅄, *anat.*
[ʌˈdjal, ʌˈdjo] radial; **radiance**
[ʌˈdjãːs] *f* radiance; radiant heat;
radiant, e [ʌˈdjã, ʌˈdjãːt] *adj., a.*
su./m radiant; **radiateur** [ʌdja-
ˈtœːr] *m* radiator.

radiation[1] *phys.* [radjaˈsjɔ̃] *f* radiation.

radiation[2] [ʌ] *f* striking out; *debt*
etc.: cancellation; ♃ *solicitor:* striking off; *barrister:* disbarment.

radical, e, *m/pl.* **-aux** [radiˈkal,
ʌˈko] **1.** *adj.* radical (*a.* ⅄, ♀,
♏, *pol., gramm.*); **2.** *su./m* radical;
⅄ root(-sign); *gramm.* root; **radica-**
liser [ʌkaliˈze] (1a) *v/t.* radicalize;
intensify; **radicelle** ♀ [ʌˈsɛl] *f*
radicle.

radié, e [raˈdje] radiate(d), rayed.

radier[1] △ *etc.* [raˈdje] *m* floor, base,
bed; level; *basin, dock:* apron;
(*foundation-*)raft; *tunnel:* invert.

radier[2] [ʌ] (1o) *v/t.* strike out, erase;
delete; cancel.

radieusement [radjøzˈmã] radi-
antly; brilliantly; gloriously; **ra-**
dieux, -euse [ʌˈdjø, ʌˈdjøːz] radiant
(*a. fig.*).

radin *sl.* [raˈdɛ̃] stingy.

radio [raˈdjo] *su./f* radio; radio set; ✝
X-ray photograph; *à la* ~ on the
radio; *su./m* radio(tele)gram; radio
operator.

radio... [radjo] radio...; **~actif, -ve**
phys. [ʌakˈtif, ʌˈtiːv] radioactive;
~conducteur ⚡ [ʌkɔ̃dykˈtœːr] *m*
radio conductor; **~détection** [ʌde-
tɛkˈsjɔ̃] *f* radiodetection; **~diffuser**
[ʌdifyˈze] (1a) *v/t.* broadcast; **~dif-**
fusion [ʌdifyˈzjɔ̃] *f* broadcasting;
~électricité *radio, a. phys.* [ʌelɛk-
trisiˈte] *f* radioelectricity; **~élément**
phys. [ʌeleˈmã] *m* radioactive element; radio-element; **~goniomé-**
trie [ʌgɔnjɔmeˈtri] *f* direction-find-
ing; **~gramme** [ʌˈgram] *m* ♠ radiogram; ✝ X-ray photograph; skia-
graph; **~graphe** [ʌˈgraf] *su.* radiog-

rapher; **~graphie** ✵ [~gra'fi] *f* radiography; X-ray photograph(y); **~graphier** [~gra'fje] (1o) *v/t.* X-ray; **~guidage** [~gi'da:ʒ] *m* ⚓ radio control; *mot.* traffic news *pl.*; **~guidé, e** [~gi'de] radiocontrolled; **~journal** [~ʒur'nal] *m* radio: news bulletin; **~logie** ✵, *a. phys.* [~lɔ'ʒi] *f* radiology; **~logue** ✵ [~'lɔg] *m*, **~logiste** ✵ [~lɔ'ʒist] *m* radiologist; **~mètre** *phys.* [~'mɛtr] *m* radiometer; **~phare** ⚓ [~'fa:r] *m* radio beacon; **~phonie** [~fɔ'ni] *f* radiotelephony; **~phonique** [~fɔ'nik] wireless ...; radio...; **~phono** [~fɔ'no] *m instrument, furniture:* radiogram; **~repérage** [~rəpe'ra:ʒ] *m* radiolocation; **~reporter** [~rəpɔr'tɛ:r] *m* (radio) commentator; **~-réveil,** *pl.* **~s-réveils** [~re'vɛj] *m* clock radio; **~scopie** ✵ [~skɔ'pi] *f* radioscopy; **~télégramme** [~tele'gram] *m* radiotelegram; **~télégraphie** ✵ [~telegra'fi] *f* radiotelegraphy; **~téléphonie** [~telefɔ'ni] *f* radiotelephony; **~(-)télévisé, e** [~televi'ze] broadcast on both radio and television; **~thérapie** ✵ [~tera'pi] *f* radiotherapy.

radis ♀ [ra'di] *m* radish; F *ne pas avoir un ~* be penniless, F be broke.

radium ☢ [ra'djɔm] *m* radium; **~térapie** ✵ [~djɔmtera'pi] *f* radium treatment, radium-therapy.

radius *anat., a. zo.* [ra'djys] *m* radius.

radotage [radɔ'ta:ʒ] *m* drivel, twaddle; dotage; **radoter** [~'te] (1a) *v/i.* talk nonsense; drivel; be in one's dotage; **radoteur** *m*, **-euse** *f* [~'tœ:r, ~'tø:z] dotard; driveller.

radoub ⚓ [ra'du] *m* repair; *bassin m de ~* graving-dock, dry dock; **radouber** ⚓ [~du'be] (1a) *v/t.* repair the hull of; dock.

radoucir [radu'si:r] (2a) *v/t.* calm (*a. fig.*); make (*s.th.*) milder *or* softer; *se ~* become milder *or* softer.

rafale [ra'fal] *f* squall; *wind:* (strong) gust; ⚔ *gun-fire:* burst; **~ de pluie** cloud-burst.

raffermir [rafɛr'mi:r] (2a) *v/t.* harden, make firm(er); *fig.* strengthen; *fig.* fortify; *se ~* harden (*a.* ↑ *prices*); ↑ level off (*prices*); ✵ improve; **raffermissement** [~mis'mã] *m* hardening (*a.* ↑ *of prices*); *fig.* strengthening; *fig.* improvement.

raffinage ⊕ [rafi'na:ʒ] *m* sugar, petrol, etc.: refining; oil: distilling; **raffiné, e** [~fi'ne] refined (*sugar, petrol, a. fig.*); *fig.* subtle; **raffinement** [~fin'mã] *m* fig. refinement; *fig.* subtlety; ⊕ *sugar, petrol, etc.:* refining; oil: distilling; **raffiner** [~fi'ne] (1a) *v/t.* refine (*a.* ⊕, *a. fig.*); *v/i.* be punctilious *or* over-nice (on, upon *sur*); **raffinerie** [~fin'ri] *f* refinery; (sugar-)refining; oil distillery; **raffineur** *m*, **-euse** *f* ⊕ [~fi'nœ:r, ~'nø:z] refiner.

raffoler F [rafɔ'le] (1a) *v/i.*: **~ de** be passionately fond of, F be mad about; dote on.

raffut F [ra'fy] *m* row, din.

raffûter ⊕ [rafy'te] (1a) *v/t.* reset, sharpen (*a tool*).

rafiot ⚓ [ra'fjo] *m* skiff.

rafistoler F [rafistɔ'le] (1a) *v/t.* patch (*s.th.*) up.

rafle[1] ♀ [rɑ:fl] *f grapes etc.:* stalk; *maize:* cob.

rafle[2] [rɑ:fl] *f police etc.:* raid, round-up; swipe.

rafraîchir [rafrɛ'ʃi:r] (2a) *v/t.* cool; renovate; freshen up; refresh (*a. one's memory*); revive; brush up (*a subject*); restore (*a painting*); *v/i.* cool; grow cooler (*weather*); **rafraîchissement** [~ʃis'mã] *m* ⊕ *etc.* cooling; *memory:* refreshing; *subject:* brushing up; *painting etc.:* restoring; **~s** *pl.* refreshments; **rafraîchisseur** [~ʃi'sœ:r] *m*, **rafraîchissoir** [~ʃi'swa:r] *m* cooler.

ragaillardir F [ragajar'di:r] (2a) *v/t.* cheer (*s.o.*) up.

rage [ra:ʒ] *f* rage, fury; *fig.* mania; violent pain; ✵ rabies; *faire ~* rage, be raging; **rager** [ra'ʒe] (1l) *v/i.* rage; be infuriated; **rageur, -euse** [~'ʒœ:r, ~'ʒø:z] violent-tempered, choleric; angry.

raglan *cost.* [ra'glã] *m* raglan.

ragot[1], **e** [ra'go, ~'gɔt] **1.** *adj.* squat; stocky (*person, a. horse*); **2.** *su./m hunt.* boar in its third year.

ragot[2] F [ra'go] *m* tittle-tattle, gossip.

ragoût [ra'gu] *m cuis.* stew; † *fig.* relish, spice; **ragoûtant, e** [ragu'tã, ~'tã:t]: *peu ~* unsavo(u)ry; unpleasant; unpalatable.

ragréer [ragre'e] (1a) *v/t.* finish, polish; △ clean down (*brickwork*); ⚓ re-rig; *fig.* restore.

rai [rɛ] *m light:* ray; *wheel:* spoke.

raid [rɛd] *m* mot. long-distance run *or* ✈ flight; *mot.* (long-distance) endurance test; ✕, ✈ raid.

raide [rɛd] **1.** *adj.* stiff (*a. manner*); rigid; tight (*rope*); straight (*flight, hair*); steep (*path, slope, stair, a. fig. remark*); F *fig.* unyielding (*character*); **2.** *adv.* steep(ly); hard; *tomber* ~ *mort* drop stone dead; **raideur** [rɛ'dœːr] *f* stiffness (*a. of manner*); rigidity; *rope*: tautness; *path, slope, stair*: steepness; *character, temperament*: inflexibility; *avec* ~ violently; stubbornly; **raidir** [~'diːr] (2a) *v/t.* stiffen (*a. fig.*); tighten (*a rope*); se ~ brace o.s.; *v/i. a.* se ~ grow stiff; harden; **raidissement** [~dis'mã] *m* stiffening; tautening.

raie¹ [rɛ] *f* line; streak; stripe; scratch; *hair*: parting; ✎ furrow; *anat., a.* ✎ ridge.

raie² *icht.* [~] *f* skate, ray.

raifort ♣ [rɛ'fɔːr] *m* horse-radish.

rail [rɑːj] *m* rail; railway, *Am.* railroad; ~ *conducteur* live rail.

railler [rɑ'je] (1a) *v/t.* laugh at (*s.o.*); make fun of (*s.o.*); twit (*s.o.*); se ~ *de* make fun of; *v/i.* joke; **raillerie** [rɑj'ri] *f* banter; jest; scoffing; ~ *à part* joking aside; *entendre la* ~ be able to take a joke; *ne pas entendre* ~ be very touchy, be unable to take a joke; **railleur, -euse** [rɑ'jœːr, ~'jøːz] **1.** *adj.* bantering, mocking; **2.** *su.* scoffer; banterer.

rainette [rɛ'nɛt] *f zo.* tree-frog; ♣ *apple*: pippin.

rainure ⊕ [rɛ'nyːr] *f* groove; slot.

raire [rɛːr] (4ff) *v/i.* bell (*stag*).

rais [rɛ] *m see* rai.

raisin [rɛ'zɛ̃] *m* grape(s *pl.*); ~s *pl.* de *Corinthe* currants; ~s *pl.* de *Smyrne* sultanas; ~s *pl. secs* raisins; **raisiné** [~zi'ne] *m* grape jam.

raison [rɛ'zõ] *f* reason; sense; satisfaction; justice, right; proof, ground; justification; motive; ⚖ claim; ♣ ratio; ~ *sociale* name, style (*of a firm*); *à* ~ *de* at the rate of; *à plus forte* ~ so much *or* all the more; *avec* (*juste*) ~ rightly, with good reason; *avoir* ~ be right; *avoir* ~ *de* get the better of; get the upper hand of; *comme de* ~ as one might expect; of course; *en* ~ *de* in proportion to; because of; *parler* ~ talk sense; **raisonnable** [~zɔ'nabl] sensible, reasonable (*a.* ✝); rational; adequate; fair; **raisonné, e** [~zɔ'ne]

reasoned; descriptive (*catalogue*); **raisonnement** [~zɔn'mã] *m* reasoning; argument; *pas de* ~s! don't argue!; **raisonner** [rɛzɔ'ne] (1a) *v/i.* reason, argue (about, *sur*); *v/t.* reason with (*s.o.*); weigh (*actions*); **raisonneur, -euse** [~'nœːr, ~'nøːz] **1.** *adj.* reasoning; *fig.* argumentative; **2.** *su.* reasoner; *fig.* argumentative person; *su./m: faire le* ~ argue.

rait [rɛ] *p.p./inv. of* raire.

rajeunir [raʒœ'niːr] (2a) *v/t.* make younger, rejuvenate; renovate; se ~ make o.s. look younger; *v/i.* get *or* look younger; **rajeunissement** [~nis'mã] *m person:* rejuvenation; renovation.

rajouter [raʒu'te] (1a) *v/t.* add.

rajustement [raʒystə'mã] *m* readjustment, setting right; ✝ ~ *des salaires* wage adjustment; **rajuster** [~'te] (1a) *v/t.* readjust, set to rights; *fig.* settle (*a quarrel*).

râle [rɑːl] *m orn.* rail; (*a.* **râlement** [rɑl'mã] *m*) ✽ râle; *throat:* rattle; death-rattle.

ralenti [ralɑ̃'ti] *m* slow motion *or* speed; *au* ~ slow(ly *adv.*); *marcher au* ~ idle, tick over; **ralentir** [~'tiːr] (2a) *vt/i. a.* se ~ slow down; relax; **ralentissement** [~tis'mã] *m* slowing down, slackening; decrease.

râler [rɑ'le] (1a) *v/i.* groan; be in one's death agony; F grouse, fume (with anger, *de colère*); **râleur** *m*, **-euse** *f* F [~'lœːr, ~'løːz] grouser.

ralliement [rali'mã] *m* ✕ rally(ing); ✕, ⚓ assembly; *mot* ~ *de* ~ password; *point* *m* *de* ~ rallying-point; **rallier** [~'lje] (1o) *v/t.* ✕, ⚓ assemble (*troops, ships*); ✕, ⚓ rejoin (*a unit, a ship*); *fig.* win, attract (*support, votes, etc.*); se ~ *à* rally to; ⚓ hug (*the shore*).

rallonge [ra'lõːʒ] *f* ⊕ extension-piece; *table:* extension-leaf; ✝ additional sum *or* payment; *une* ~ *de* ... an additional ...; *table f à* ~s extension table; **rallongement** [~lõʒ'mã] *m* extension; **rallonger** [~lõ'ʒe] (1l) *v/t.* lengthen; eke out; *cuis.* thin (*a sauce*).

rallumer [raly'me] (1a) *v/t.* relight; *fig.* revive (*an emotion*); se ~ rekindle; break out again (*war*); *fig.* revive (*emotion*).

rallye *mot. etc.* [ra'li] *m* race-meeting, rally.

ramage [ra'ma:ʒ] *m tex.* floral design; *orn.* song, warbling; **ramager** *orn.* [~ma'ʒe] (11) *v/t.* sing, warble.

ramassage [rama'sa:ʒ] *m* gathering; collection; picking up; ~ *scolaire* school bus service; *point de* ~ pick-up point; **ramassé, e** [~'se] stocky (*person, horse*); ⊕, *a. fig.* compact; **ramasse-miettes** [~mas'mjɛt] *m/inv.* crumb-tray, crumb-scoop; **ramasser** [rama'se] (1a) *v/t.* gather (together); collect; pick up (*an object*); *fig.* ~ *une bûche* come a cropper; *se* ~ collect; pick o.s. up; *fig.* crouch (*animal*); *fig.* gather o.s. (*for an effort*); **ramassis** [~'si] *m* pile; F *people*: pack.

rame[1] ⚓ [ram] *f* oar.

rame[2] [~] *f* † *paper*: ream; 🚃 *coaches,* ⚓ *barges etc.*: string; 🚃 train.

rame[3] 🌱 [~] *f* stick, prop.

rameau [ra'mo] *m* 🌿 bough; 🌿 twig; *geog., a. family, science, etc.*: branch; 🍖 vein; *zo.* ~*x pl.* antlers; ~ *d'olivier* olive-branch (*a. fig.*); *eccl.* (*dimanche m des*) ♀*x* Palm Sunday; **ramée** [~'me] *f* leafy branches *pl.*, arbo(u)r; small wood (*for burning etc.*).

ramender [ramã'de] (1a) *v/t.* mend (*nets*); 🌱 manure again; renew the gilt of (*a picture-frame*).

ramener [ram'ne] (1d) *v/t.* bring back; 🍖, *a. fig.* reduce (to, *à*); draw (down, back, *etc.*); *fig.* restore (*peace*); *fig.* win (*s.o.*) over; *sl.* ~ *sa fraise* (*or gueule*), *la* ~ protest; talk big; *se* ~ amount, come down (to, *à*); F turn up, come (back).

ramequin *cuis.* [ram'kɛ̃] *m* ramekin, ramequin (= *mixture of cheese, eggs, etc.*).

ramer[1] 🌱 [ra'me] (1a) *v/t.* stick; prop (up).

ramer[2] [ra'me] (1a) *v/i.* row; **rameur, -euse** [~'mœ:r, ~'mø:z] *su.* rower; *su./m* oarsman; *su./f* oarswoman.

rameux, -euse 🌿 [ra'mø, ~'mø:z] ramose; branching; **ramier** *orn.* [~'mje] *m* ring-dove, wood-pigeon. **ramification** [~mifika'sjɔ̃] *f* ramification (*a. fig.*); branch(ing); **ramifier** [~mi'fje] (1o) *v/t.*: *se* ~ ramify; branch out; **ramille** [~'mi:j] *f* twig; ~*s pl.* fire-lighting; small wood *sg.*

ramolli, e [ramɔ'li] softened; F *fig.* soft-headed; **ramollir** [~'li:r] (2a) *v/t.* soften; *se* ~ soften, grow soft;

ramollissement [~lis'mã] *m* softening; 🍖 ~ *cérébral* softening of the brain.

ramoner [ramɔ'ne] (1a) *v/t.* sweep (*the chimney*); ⊕ scour, clear; *mount.* climb (*a chimney*); **ramoneur** [~'nœ:r] *m* (chimney-)sweep.

rampant, e [rã'pã, ~'pã:t] **1.** *adj.* ⚠ sloping; 🌿, *zo.* creeping; *zo.* crawling; *fig.* cringing; *fig.* pedestrian (*style*); **2.** *su./m* ⚠ sloping part; **rampe** [rã:p] *f* slope, incline; inclined plane; gradient, *Am. road*: grade; ⚠, 🚂, 🚋 ramp; *stairs*: handrail; *thea.* limelight (*a. fig.*); footlights *pl.*; 🚋 runway lights *pl.*; ~ *de lancement* launching ramp; **ramper** [rã'pe] (1a) *v/i.* creep (*a.* 🌿, *zo., a. person*); crawl (*zo., person, a.* F *fig.*); *fig.* fawn (*person*); 🌿 trail; *fig.* lurk.

ramponneau F [rãpɔ'no] *m* blow.

ramure [ra'my:r] *f* branches *pl.*; *stag*: antlers *pl.*

rancard *sl.* [rã'ka:r] *m* info, tip-off; meeting, date; **rancarder** *sl.* [~kar-'de] (1a) *v/t.* inform, tip (*s.o.*) off; make a date with, date (*s.o.*); *se* ~ get the info (about, *sur*).

rancart F [rã'ka:r] *m*: *mettre au* ~ discard; throw on the scrap-heap; F chuck out; shelve (*a project*); *admin.* retire (*s.o.*).

rance [rã:s] **1.** *adj.* rancid; **2.** *su./m*: *sentir le* ~ smell rancid.

ranch, *pl.* **ranches** [rã:ʃ] *m* ranch.

ranche [rã:ʃ] *f ladder*: peg; **rancher** [rã'ʃe] *m* peg-ladder, pole-ladder.

rancir [rã'si:r] (2a) *v/i.* become rancid; **rancissure** [~si'sy:r] *f* rancidness.

rancœur [rã'kœ:r] *f* ranco(u)r; resentment.

rançon [rã'sɔ̃] *f* ransom; *fig.* price; **rançonner** [rãsɔ'ne] (1a) *v/t.* hold to ransom; ransom (*s.o.*); † F fleece; **rançonneur, -euse** F [~-'nœ:r, ~'nø:z] extortionate.

rancune [rã'kyn] *f* grudge; *garder* (*de la*) ~ *à q.* bear s.o. a grudge (for, *de*); *sans* ~! no offence!; no hard feelings!; **rancunier, -ère** [~ky'nje, ~'njɛ:r] **1.** *adj.* spiteful; **2.** *su.* spiteful person; person bearing a grudge.

randonnée [rãdɔ'ne] *f* tour, excursion, (*long*) trip; outing; hike; **randonneur** *m*, **-euse** *f* [~'nœ:r, ~'nø:z] hiker; excursionist.

rang [rɑ̃] *m* row, line; order; class; tier; ✕, *a. fig.* rank; F *fig. de premier* ~ first-rate, first-class; **rangé, e** [rɑ̃'ʒe] **1.** *adj.* tidy; steady (*person*); orderly; (*a. bien* ~) well-ordered; ✕ pitched (*battle*); **2.** *su./f* row, line; *thea.* tier; *figures*: set; **ranger** [~] (11) *v/t.* (ar)range; ✕ draw up, marshal; put (*s.th.*) away; tidy (*objects, a room*); *fig.* rank (among, *parmi*); ⚓ hug (*the coast*); *fig.* steady (*s.o.*); restrain; keep back (*a crowd*); *mot.* park (*one's car*); se ~ line up, get into rows *or* line; *fig.* settle down (*in life, behaviour, etc.*); *mot.* pull over; *fig.* make way (*person*); *fig.* se ~ *à* fall in with, come round to.

ranimer [rani'me] (1a) *v/t. a.* se ~ revive; *fig.* cheer up.

rapace [ra'pas] rapacious (*a. fig.*); predatory; **rapacité** [~pasi'te] *f* rapacity; *avec* ~ rapaciously.

rapatriement [rapatri'mɑ̃] *m* repatriation; **rapatrier** [~'e] (1a) *v/t.* repatriate.

râpe [rɑ:p] *f* ⊕ rasp, rough file; *cuis.* grater; 🍇 *grapes etc.*: stalk; **râper** [rɑ'pe] (1a) *v/t.* ⊕ rasp; grind (*snuff*); *cuis.* grate; wear threadbare (*clothes*); *râpé* threadbare (*clothes*).

rapetasser F [rapta'se] (1a) *v/t.* patch up; cobble (*shoes*); *fig.* botch up.

rapetisser [rapti'se] (1a) *v/t.* make (*s.th.*) smaller; shorten (*clothes*); *v/i. a.* se ~ become smaller; shorten; *tex.* shrink.

râpeux, -euse [ra'pø, ~'pø:z] rough; raspy (*tongue*); harsh (*voice, wine*).

rapiat, e F [ra'pja, ~'pjat] **1.** *adj.* stingy; **2.** *su.* skinflint.

rapide [ra'pid] **1.** *adj.* rapid, fast, swift; steep (*slope*); **2.** *su./m geog.* rapid; 🚂 express (train); **rapidité** [~pidi'te] *f* swiftness, speed; *slope*: steepness.

rapiéçage [rapje'sa:ʒ] *m* patching (-up); patchwork; **rapiécer** [~'se] (1f *a.* 1k) *v/t.* patch.

rapière † [ra'pjɛːr] *f* rapier.

rapin † F [ra'pɛ̃] *m* art student; *pej.* dauber (= *painter*).

rapine [ra'pin] *f* rapine; *pej.* graft; **rapiner** [~pi'ne] (1a) *vt/i.* pillage.

rappareiller [raparɛ'je] (1a) *v/t.* match, complete (*a set*).

rapparier [rapa'rje] (1o) *v/t.* match, complete (*a pair*).

rappel [ra'pɛl] *m pol. etc.* recall; reminder; ✝ *money*: calling in; ✝ back pay; 💉 (*injection de* ~) booster (shot); *thea.* curtain call; call (*to order*); ⊕ backmotion; *fig.* touch, suspicion; *mount.* faire une descente en ~ rope down; *touche f de* ~ *typewriter*: backspacer; **rappeler** [~'ple] (1c) *pol., a. fig.* recall; *thea.* call for (*an actor*); remind (*s.o.* of s.th., *qch. à q.*); ⊕ draw back; *teleph.* ring back; *fig.* restore (*s.o. to health*); *parl.* ~ *à l'ordre* call to order; se ~ recall, remember (*s.th.*).

rappliquer [rapli'ke] (1m) *v/t.* reapply; *v/i.* F come *or* go back.

rapport [ra'pɔːr] *m* ✝, ⊕ return, yield; ✝ *etc.* report; statement, account; ⚕, *a. mot.* ratio; connection (with, *avec*); relation; *fig.* resemblance; ~s *pl.* intercourse *sg.*; *fig.* en ~ *avec* in keeping *or* touch with; F *faire des* ~s tell tales; *maison f de* ~ apartment house; *mettre q. en* ~ *avec* put s.o. in touch with; *par* ~ *à* in relation to; compared with; *sous tous les* ~s in every respect *or* way; **rapporter** [rapɔr'te] (1a) *v/t.* bring back; *hunt.* retrieve; ⚕ restore; ⚕ *admin.* revoke; ⊕ join, add; ✝ yield, produce; *fig.* get; report (*a fact, an observation, etc.*); *fig.* ~ *à* relate to; ascribe to; se ~ *à* relate to; *s'en* ~ *à* rely on; *v/i.* pay, be profitable; F tell tales; present a report (on, about *sur*); **rapporteur, -euse** [~'tœːr, ~'tøːz] **1.** *adj.* sneaking; **2.** *su.* sneak, telltale; *su./m committee, conference*: rapporteur; ✕, ⚕ judge advocate; ⚕ protractor.

rapprendre [ra'prɑ̃ːdr] (4aa) *v/t.* learn *or* teach (*s.th.*) again.

rapprochement [raprɔʃ'mɑ̃] *m* bringing together; comparison; connection; closeness; *fig.* reconciliation; *pol.* rapprochement, re-establishment of harmonious relations; **rapprocher** [~prɔ'ʃe] (1a) *v/t.* bring together; bring (*s.th.*) near again; bring (*things*) closer together; put (*s.th.*) nearer (to, *de*); compare, put together; *fig.* reconcile; se ~ get closer *or* draw near(er) (to, *de*); *fig.* become reconciled (with, *de*); *fig.* se ~ *de* be close to.

rapt F⁀ [rapt] *m* abduction of a minor; kidnapping.

râpure [rɑ'py:r] *f* filings *pl.*; raspings *pl.*

raquette [ra'kɛt] *f sp.* racket, ping-pong: snowshoe; ♣ prickly pear.

rare [ra:r] rare (*a.* ⁀, *phys.*, *fig.*); *fig.* singular, uncommon; ✿ slow (*pulse*); thin, scanty (*hair etc.*); **raréfaction** [rarefak'sjɔ̃] *f phys.* rarefaction; ✝ growing scarcity; **raréfier** [~'fje] (1o) *v/t. phys.* rarefy; ✝ *etc.* make scarce; se ~ rarefy; grow scarce(r); **rareté** [rar'te] *f phys.*, *a. fig.* rarity ✝, *a. fig.* scarcity; singularity; rare occurrence.

ras[1], **rase** [rɑ, rɑ:z] **1.** *adj.* close-cropped (*hair, head*); close-shaven (*cheek, chin, beard*); *fig.* blank, bare; open (*country*); full (*measure*); à ~ bord to the brim, brim-full; *faire table rase* make a clean sweep; *cuis. une cuillerée* ~e a level spoonful; **2.** *adv.:* coupé (*or* taillé) ~ cut short; **3.** *prp.:* à (*or* au)~ de level *or* flush with.

ras[2] [rɑ] *m see raz.*

rasade [rɑ'zad] *f* brim-full glass; *verser une* ~ à fill (*s.o.'s*) glass to the brim; **rasage** [~'za:ʒ] *m beard:* shaving; *tex. cloth:* shearing; **rasemottes** [~ ʒ 'mɔt] *m/inv.:* voler en ~ hedge-hop; **raser** [rɑ'ze] (1a) *v/t.* shave; *tex.* shear (*cloth*); F *fig.* bore (*s.o.*); ✗ raze (*to the ground*); *fig.* graze, skim; *crème f à* ~ shaving cream; se ~ shave; F *fig.* be bored; *rasé de près* clean-shaven, close-shaven; **raseur** *m*, **-euse** *f* [~'zœ:r, ~'zø:z] shaver; *tex.* shearer; F *fig.* bore; **rasibus** F [~zi'bys] *adv.* very close (to, de); **rasoir** [~'zwa:r] **1.** *su./m* razor; *tex.* knife; ~ *de sûreté* safety razor; *fig. au* ~ perfectly; **2.** *adj.* F boring.

rassasier [rasa'zje] (1o) *v/t.* satisfy; satiate (with, *de*); cloy (with, *de*); se ~ take one's fill.

rassemblement [rasɑ̃blə'mɑ̃] *m* collecting; gathering; crowd; ✗ parade; **rassembler** [~'ble] (1a) *v/t.* (re)assemble; gather together (again); *fig.* muster (*strength*); ✗ parade.   [down again.]

rasseoir [ra'swa:r] (3c) *v/t.:* se ~ sit)

rasséréner [rasere'ne] (1f) *v/t.:* se ~ become serene again.

rassis, e [ra'si, ~'si:z] settled, calm; sedate; stale (*bread*).

rassurer [rasy're] (1a) *v/t.* reassure; △ strengthen.

rastaquouère F [rasta'kwɛ:r] *m* flashy adventurer.

rat [ra] *m zo.* rat; F *fig.* miser; F *fig.* ~ *de bibliothèque* book-worm; ~ *de cave* exciseman; ~ *d'eglise* frequent church-goer; ~ *d'hôtel* hotel thief.

rata *sl.* [ra'ta] *m* stew.

ratage [ra'ta:ʒ] *m* failure, F washout, flop; messing-up.

ratatiner [ratati'ne] (1a) *v/t. a.* se ~ shrivel, shrink; crinkle up (*parchment*).

ratatouille *sl.* [rata'tu:j] *f* stew, skilly.

rate[1] [rat] *f anat.* spleen; *zo., anat.* milt; F *dilater la* ~ *de q.* make s.o. shake with laughter; F *ne pas se fouler la* ~ take things easy.

rate[2] *zo.* [~] *f (female)* rat.

raté, e [ra'te] **1.** *adj.* botched (*work*); miscarried; *coup m* ~ failure; **2.** *su. person:* failure; F washout; *su./m* ⊕, *mot.* misfire.

râteau [rɑ'to] *m* ✔ *etc.* rake; F large comb; ⊕ *lock:* wards *pl.*; **râteler** [rɑt'le] (1c) *v/t.* ✔ rake (up); **râtelier** [rɑtə'lje] *m* rack; F (set of) false teeth *pl.*, denture.

rater [ra'te] (1a) *v/i. mot.* misfire (*a. fig.*); fail to go off (*gun*); *fig.* fail; *v/t.* miss; mess up, spoil; fail in (*an examination, attempt, etc.*).

ratiboiser *sl.* [ratibwa'ze] (1a) *v/t.* pinch (= *steal*) (from s.o., *à q.*); clean (*s.o.*) out; ruin, wreck (*s.o.*).

ratière [ra'tjɛ:r] *f* rat-trap.

ratification [ratifika'sjɔ̃] *f* ratification; **ratifier** [~'fje] (1o) *v/t.* ratify; approve.

ratiner *tex.* [rati'ne] (1a) *v/t.* freeze (*cloth*).

ratiociner *pej.* [rasjɔsi'ne] (1a) *v/i.* reason, quibble.

ration [ra'sjɔ̃] *f* ration(s *pl.*), allowance; *physiol.* intake.

rationaliser [rasjɔnali'ze] (1a) *v/t.* rationalize; **rationalisme** *phls.* [~'lism] *m* rationalism; **rationaliste** *phls.* [~'list] *adj., a. su.* rationalist; **rationalité** [~li'te] *f* rationality.

rationnel, -elle [rasjɔ'nɛl] rational (*a.* Ⓐ); F *fig.* sensible.

rationnement [rasjɔn'mɑ̃] *m* rationing; **rationner** [~sjɔ'ne] (1a) *v/t.* ration (*a. fig.*).

ratisser [rati'se] (1a) *v/t.* ✔ rake; ✔

hoe; scrape (*skins, potatoes*); *fig.* comb (*police etc.*); F rake in, grab; F clean (*s.o.*) out; **ratissoire** [~'swa:r] *f* ✔ hoe; ✔ rake; scraper.

raton [ra'tɔ̃] *m zo.* little rat; F darling; *zo.* ~ *laveur* rac(c)oon.

rattachement [rataʃ'mɑ̃] *m* linking up; *pol.* union; **rattacher** [~ta'ʃe] (1a) *v/t.* (re)fasten; tie up (again); *fig.* connect; *fig.* bind; se ~ be fastened; *fig.* be connected (with, *à*).

rattraper [ratra'pe] (1a) *v/t.* catch again; recover (*one's health, one's money*); catch up on (*time*); overtake; *fig.* make good, make up for (*an error etc.*), compensate; ⊕ take up (*play*); se ~ *à* catch hold of (*a branch etc.*); *fig.* se ~ make up for it; catch up.

raturage [raty'ra:ʒ] *m* erasing; crossing out; **rature** [~'ty:r] *f* erasure; crossing out; **raturer** [~ty're] (1a) *v/t.* erase; cross out; scrape (*parchment*).

rauque [ro:k] hoarse; harsh.

ravage [ra'va:ʒ] *m* ravages *pl.*, havoc; **ravager** [~va'ʒe] (1l) *v/t.* ravage, lay waste; devastate; play havoc with.

ravalement [raval'mɑ̃] *m building:* re-surfacing, refurbishing; **ravaler** [~va'le] (1a) *v/t.* swallow (again *or* down); F *fig.* take back (*a statement*); ⊕, *fig.* reduce (to, *à*); *fig.* lower, disparage; ⚠ re-surface, refurbish (*a wall, a building*); ✔ cut back, trim; *fig.* se ~ lower o.s.

ravauder [ravo'de] (1a) *v/t.* mend, patch; darn (*socks etc.*); botch; **ravaudeur** *m*, **-euse** *f* [~'dœːr, ~'dø:z] mender; darner; botcher.

rave ⚘ [ra:v] *f* rape.

ravi, e [ra'vi] enraptured; F delighted (with s.th., *de qch.*; to *inf.*, *de inf.*).

ravier [ra'vje] *m* radish-dish, hors-d'œuvres dish; **ravière** ✔ [~'vjɛːr] *f* radish-bed; turnip-field.

ravigote *cuis.* [ravi'gɔt] *f* ravigote sauce; **ravigoter** F [~gɔ'te] (1a) *v/t.* revive, refresh, F buck (*s.o.*) up.

ravilir [ravi'liːr] (2a) *v/t.* degrade, debase.

ravin [ra'vɛ̃] *m*, **ravine** [~'vin] *f*, **ravinée** [ravi'ne] *f* ravine, gully; **raviner** [~] (1a) *v/t.* cut channels in (*the ground*).

ravir [ra'viːr] (2a) *v/t.* carry off, abduct; steal; *fig.* charm, delight; *à* ~ delightfully.

raviser [ravi'ze] (1a) *v/t.:* se ~ change one's mind; think again.

ravissant, e [ravi'sɑ̃, ~'sɑ̃:t] ravishing; enchanting; delightful, lovely; **ravissement** [~vis'mɑ̃] *m* carrying off; *fig.* rapture; **ravisseur** [~vi-'sœːr] *m* plunderer; abductor (*of a woman*); kidnapper (*of a child*).

ravitaillement [ravitaj'mɑ̃] *m* supplying (with, en); ⊕ refuel(l)ing; **ravitailler** [~ta'je] (1a) *v/t.* supply (with, en); *mot. etc.* refuel; se ~ get fresh supplies; ⊕ refuel; **ravitailleur** [~ta'jœːr] *m* ⚓ supply ship; ⚓ parent ship; ✈ refuelling aircraft.

raviver [ravi've] (1a) *v/t.* revive; brighten up; se ~ revive; break out again (*struggle*).

ravoir [ra'vwaːr] *v/t. occurs only in inf.* get (*s.th.*) back again; have (*s.th.*) again.

rayer [rɛ'je] (1i) *v/t.* scratch (*a surface*); stripe (*cloth etc.*); ⊕ groove (*a cylinder*); rifle (*a gun*); rule (*paper*); strike out, cross out.

rayon[1] [rɛ'jɔ̃] *m* book-case: shelf; store: department; *fig.* speciality, F line, field; ~ *de miel* honeycomb.

rayon[2] [rɛ'jɔ̃] *m phys.*, *a. fig.* ray; sun, light: beam; ⚡ radius (*a. fig.*); wheel: spoke; ✔ drill; ✔ lettuce etc.: row; ⚛ ~s *pl.* X X-rays; (*grand*) ~ *d'action* (long) range; **rayonnage** [rɛjɔ'na:ʒ] *m* set of shelves; **rayonnant, e** [~jɔ'nɑ̃, ~'nɑ̃:t] radiant (*heat, a. fig.*); *fig.* beaming (*face*); *phys.* radio-active (*matter*).

rayonne *tex.* [rɛ'jɔn] *f* rayon.

rayonnement [rɛjɔn'mɑ̃] *m phys.* radiation; *astr.*, *fig.* radiance; **rayonner** [~jɔ'ne] (1a) *v/i. phys. u. fig.* radiate; *fig.* shine (forth); *fig.* beam (with, de); tour, go touring.

rayure [rɛ'jyːr] *f tex.* stripe; streak; glass etc.: scratch; ⊕ groove; gun: rifling; erasure, striking out.

raz [rɑ] *m* strong current, race; ~ *de marée* tidal wave (*a. fig.*); *fig.* landslide; *fig.* flood.

razzia [ra(d)'zja] *f* raid, razzia.

re... [~rə], **ré...** [re] re-...; ... again; ... back.

ré ♪ [re] *m/inv.* re, note: D.

réacteur [reak'tœːr] *m* ⚛, *phys.* reactor; *mot.* choke; ✈ jet engine; F jet; **réactif, -ve** [~'tif, ~'ti:v] **1.** *adj.* reactive; test-(*paper*); **2.** *su./m* re-

agent; **réaction** [~'sjɔ̃] f *pol.*, ⊕
reaction; *rifle:* kick; ✗ jet; ⚙
physiol., etc. test; *phys.* ~ *en chaîne*
chain reaction; *avion* m à ~ jet
(plane); **réactionnaire** *pol.* [~sjɔ-
'nɛːr] *adj., a. su.* reactionary.

réadmettre [read'mɛtr] (4p) *v/t.* re-
admit; **réadmission** [~mi'sjɔ̃] f
readmittance.

réagir [rea'ʒiːr] (2a) *v/i.* react (to, à;
on, *sur*).

réalisable [reali'zabl] realizable;
available (*assets*); feasible (*plan*);
réalisateur, -trice[~za'tœːr,~'tris]
su. realizer; *shares:* seller; *plan:*
worker out; *su./m. cin.* director;
réalisation [~za'sjɔ̃] f realization;
shares: selling out; carrying out,
performing; production; **réaliser**
[~'ze] (1a) *v/t.* realize; achieve;
produce; sell out (*shares*); carry out
(*a plan*); *se* ~ be realized; come true;
réalisme [~'lism] m realism;
réaliste [~'list] **1.** *adj.* realist(ic);
2. *su.* realist; **réalité** [~li'te] f
reality; ~s *pl.* facts; *en* ~ really,
actually.

réanimation [reanima'sjɔ̃] f resus-
citation; **réanimer** [~'me] (1a) *v/t.*
resuscitate, revive.

réapparaître [reapa'rɛːtr] (4k) *v/i.*
reappear; **réapparition** [~ri'sjɔ̃] f
reappearance.

réapprovisionner [reaprɔvizjɔ'ne]
(1a) *v/t.* restock (with, *en*).

réarmement [rearmə'mã] m ✗
rearming; rearmement; ⚓ refitting;
réarmer [~'me] (1a) *v/t.* ✗ rearm;
reload (*a gun*); ⚓ refit.

réassigner ⚖ [reasi'ɲe] (1a) *v/t.* re-
summon.

réassortir ✝ [reasɔr'tiːr] (2a) *v/t.*
restock; match up.

réassurer ✝ [reasy're] (1a) *v/t.* re-
insure, reassure.

rebaptiser [rəbati'ze] (1a) *v/t.* re-
baptize (*child*); rename (*s.th.*).

rébarbatif, -ve [rebarba'tif, ~'tiːv]
forbidding, grim; *fig.* crabbed
(*style*); surly (*disposition*).

rebâtir [rəba'tiːr] (2a) *v/t.* △ rebuild; *fig.* reconstruct.

rebattre [rə'batr] (4a) *v/t.* beat
again; reshuffle (*cards*); F *fig.* repeat
over and over again; *avoir les oreilles rebattues de* be sick of hearing
(*s.th.*); *sentier* m *rebattu* beaten
track.

rebelle [rə'bɛl] **1.** *adj.* rebellious; ✗
obstinate; ⊕ refractory (*ore*); un-
ruly (*spirit*); **2.** *su.* rebel; **rebeller**
[~bɛ'le] (1a) *v/t.: se* ~ rebel, rise
(against, *contre*); **rébellion** [rebɛ-
'ljɔ̃] f rebellion, revolt, rising.

rebiffer F [rəbi'fe] (1a) *v/t.: se* ~
bristle (up); get one's back up.

reboisement [rəbwaz'mã] m reaf-
forestation; **reboiser** [~bwa'ze]
(1a) *v/t.* reafforest (*land*).

rebond [rə'bɔ̃] m bounce; rebound;
rebondi, e [rəbɔ̃'di] chubby;
plump; **rebondir** [~'diːr] (2a) *v/i.*
rebound; bounce; *fig.* get going
again.

rebord [rə'bɔːr] m edge, rim, border;
(*window-*)sill; ⊕ flange; *cost.* hem.

reboucher [rəbu'ʃe] (1a) *v/t.* stop
(*s.th.*) up again; recork (*a bottle*);
fill up.

rebours [rə'buːr] m: à (or au) ~
against the grain; *fig.* the wrong
way; backwards; contrary (to, de).

rebouter ✗ [rəbu'te] (1a) *v/t.* set
(*a broken leg*); **rebouteur** ✗ [~'tœːr]
m, **rebouteux** ✗ [~'tø] m bone-
setter.

rebras [rə'bra] m *glove:* gauntlet;
book jacket: flap.

rebrousse-poil [rəbrus'pwal] *adv.:*
à ~ against the nap; the wrong way
(*a.* F *fig.*); **rebrousser** [~bru'se]
(1a) *v/t.* brush up (*one's hair, tex.*);
ruffle up; F *fig.* rub (*s.o.*) the wrong
way; ~ *chemin* retrace one's steps;
turn back.

rebuffade [rəby'fad] f rebuff, snub.

rébus [re'bys] m picture-puzzle.

rebut [rə'by] m rejection; ✝ *etc.*
reject; ⊕ waste, rubbish; *fig.* scum;
post: dead letter; ✝ *marchandises*
f/pl. de ~ trash *sg.*; *mettre au* ~ discard; put on the scrap-heap; throw
out; ⊕ scrap; **rebutant, e** [rəby'tã,
~'tãːt] tiresome; forbidding; **rebuter** [~'te] (1a) *v/t.* repel; discourage,
take the heart out of; *se* ~ be(come)
discouraged.

récalcitrant, e [rekalsi'trã, ~'trãːt]
adj., a. su. recalcitrant.

recaler [rəka'le] (1a) *v/t.* wedge
again (*furniture*); ⊕ reset; F fail,
F plough (*a candidate*).

récapituler [rekapity'le] (1a) *v/t.*
recapitulate, sum up, summarize.

recel ⚖ [rə'sɛl] m, **recèlement** ⚖
[~sɛl'mã] m *stolen goods:* receiving;

criminal: harbo(u)ring; concealment; **receler** [rəs'le] (1d) *v/t.* ⚱ receive; harbo(u)r; conceal (*a. fig.*); **receleur** *m*, **-euse** *f* ⚱ [~'lœːr, ~'løːz] receiver (of stolen goods), F fence. [lately, of late.]

récemment [resa'mã] *adv.* recently,∫

recensement [rəsãːs'mã] *m admin.* census; *admin.* record; *admin. votes*: count(ing); ✝ (new) inventory; *fig.* review; ⚔ registration; **recenser** [rəsã'se] (1a) *v/t. admin.* take a census; count (*votes*); record; ⚔ register; ✝ inventory; **recension** [~'sjõ] *f text*: recension.

récent, e [re'sã, ~'sãːt] recent, fresh, new.

recéper [rəse'pe] (1f) *v/t.* ✂ cut down *or* back; ⊕ cut down to level.

récépissé ✝ [resepi'se] *m* receipt; acknowledgment.

réceptacle [resep'takl] *m* receptacle (*a.* ⚘); ⊕ steam, waters: collector; **récepteur, -trice** [~'tœːr, ~'tris] **1.** *adj.* receiving; *appareil m* ~ *tel., teleph.* receiver; *radio*: set; **2.** *su./m* ⊕, *tel., teleph.* receiver; *radio*: set; ⊕ *machine*: driven part; *teleph.* décrocher (raccrocher) le ~ lift (hang up) the receiver; **réceptif, -ve** [~'tif, ~'tiːv] receptive; **réception** [~'sjõ] *f* receipt; *tel., teleph., telev., a. hotel, a. at court*: reception; welcome; *thea.* acceptance (*of a new play*); **réceptionner** ✝ [~sjo'ne] (1a) *v/t.* check and sign for; **réceptionniste** [~sjo'nist] *su.* receptionist; **réceptivité** [~tivi'te] *f* receptivity; 💊 *en état de* ~ liable to infection.

récession [rese'sjõ] *f* recession (*a.* ✝).

recette [rə'sɛt] *f* ✝ receipts *pl.*, returns *pl.*; *thea. etc.* takings *pl.*; ✝ acceptance; receipt; *admin.* collectorship; *cuis.* recipe; ✝ bills, *debts*: collection; ⚔ landing; garçon *m* de ~ bank-messenger; *thea. etc.* faire ~ be a (box-office) hit; be a success.

recevable [rəsə'vabl] admissible (*a.* ⚱); ✝ fit for acceptance; **receveur, -euse** [~'vœːr, ~'vøːz] *su.* receiver; *admin.* collector; *tel.* addressee; *su./m bus, tram*: conductor; (post)master; *su./f* (post)mistress; *thea.* usherette; *bus, tram*: conductress; **recevoir** [~'vwaːr] (3a) *v/t.* receive; *fig.* welcome; admit (*pu-*

pils, a. fig. customs), promote (*to a higher class*); accept (*an excuse*); être reçu à (*inf.*) be permitted *or* authorized to (*inf.*); être reçu à un examen pass an examination; être reçu avocat (*médecin*) qualify as a barrister (doctor); *v/i.* hold a reception, be at home; **recevrai** [~'vre] *1st p. sg. fut. of* recevoir.

rechange [rə'ʃãːʒ] *m*: de ~ spare (*part etc.*); alternative (*plan etc.*); *des vêtements* de ~ a change of clothes; **rechanger** [~ʃã'ʒe] (11) *v/t.* (ex)change (*s.th.*) again.

rechaper *mot.* [rəʃa'pe] (1a) *v/t.* retread (*a tyre*).

réchapper [reʃa'pe] (1a) *v/i.*: ~ de escape from; get over (*s.th.*); 💊 recover from (*an illness*).

recharger [rəʃar'ʒe] (11) *v/t.* reload; ⚡ recharge; refill (*a pen, a lighter, etc.*).

réchaud [re'ʃo] *m* hot-plate; chafing-dish; ~ à alcool spirit-stove; ~ à gaz gas-oven, gas-cooker; ~ à pétrole oil-stove.

réchauffé [reʃo'fe] *m cuis.* warmed-up dish; *fig.* rehash; *fig.* old *or* stale news; **réchauffer** [~'fe] (1a) *v/t.* (re)heat; warm up *or Am.* over (*food*); *fig.* warm (*s.o.'s heart*); *fig.* reawaken (*s.o.'s enthusiasm etc.*); se ~ warm o.s. up; **réchauffeur** ⊕ [~'fœːr] *m* (pre-)heater; **réchauffoir** [~'fwaːr] *m* hot-plate.

rechausser [rəʃo'se] (1a) *v/t.* fit (*s.o.*) with new shoes; *mot.* fit (*a car*) with new tyres; ✂ bank up the foot of (*a tree etc.*); △ line the foot of (*a wall*).

rêche [rɛʃ] rough; difficult (*person*).

recherche [rə'ʃɛrʃ] *f* search; research, investigation; ⚱ enquiry; *fig.* style: studied elegance; ⚱ ~ de (la) paternité affiliation; à la ~ de in search of; *fig. sans* ~ unaffected, easy; **recherché, e** [rəʃɛr'ʃe] sought after; ✝ in demand; studied (*elegance, style*); *fig.* choice, exquisite (*dress etc.*); *fig.* strained (*interpretation, style*); **rechercher** [~] (1a) *v/t.* search for, seek; look for; *fig.* court (*praise, a woman*); try to obtain; ✝ find (*the value of s.th.*).

rechigné, e [rəʃi'ne] look sour (*look etc.*); sour-tempered, surly (*person*); **rechigner** [~] (1a) *v/i.* jib, balk (at, *devant*; at *ger.*, à *inf.*); look sour; *sans* ~ with a good grace.

rechute ♫, *eccl.* [rə'ʃyt] *f* relapse.

récidive [resi'diːv] *f* ♫ recurrence; ⚖ repetition of an offence; **récidiver** [~di've] (1a) *v/i.* ♫ recur; ⚖ commit an offence for the second time, relapse into crime; **récidiviste** ⚖ [~di'vist] *su.* second *or* habitual offender, recidivist.

récif ⚓, *geog.* [re'sif] *m* reef.

récipiendaire [resipjã'dɛːr] *su.* newly elected member; **récipient** [~'pjã] *m* container, receptable; ⊕ *air-pump etc.*: receiver; ⊕ cistern.

réciprocité [resiprɔsi'te] *f* reciprocity; interchange; **réciproque** [~-'prɔk] 1. *adj.* reciprocal (*a.* Å, *phls.*, *gramm.*), mutual; Å inverse (*ratio*), converse (*proposition*); *et* ~ment *and vice versa*.|*f* Å, *phls.* converse; *fig. la* ~ the same; the opposite, the reverse.

récit [re'si] *m* account; narrative; ♪ recitative; ♪ *organ:* swell-box; **récital**, *pl.* -als ♪ [~'tal] *m* recital; **récitant** *m*, e *f* [~'tã, ~'tãt] *radio*, *telev.*, *etc.*: narrator; **récitateur** *m*, -**trice** *f* [~ta'tœːr, ~'tris] reciter; **récitatif** ♪ [~ta'tif] *m* recitative; **récitation** [~ta'sjɔ̃] *f* recitation; **réciter** [~'te] (1a) *vt/i.* recite.

réclamant *m*, e *f* [rekla'mã, ~'mãːt] complainer; ⚖ claimant; **réclamation** [~ma'sjɔ̃] *f* complaint (*a. admin.*); objection; ⚖ claim; *bureau m des* ~s claims department; **réclame** [re'klaːm] *f* advertising; advertisement; *pej.* blurb; *typ.* catchword; ~ *lumineuse* illuminated sign; *faire de la* ~ advertise, boost one's goods; **réclamer** [~kla'me] (1a) *v/t.* claim (from, *à*); demand (*s.th.*) back; call for; require; *se* ~ *de* appeal to; *fig.* use (*s.o.*) as one's authority; *v/i.*: ~ *contre* complain of; protest against; ⚖ appeal against.

reclassement [rəklas'mã] *m* reclassifying, re-classification; regrouping; *admin.* regrading; **reclasser** [~kla'se] (1a) *v/t.* re-classify; regroup; regrade.

reclus, e [rə'kly, ~'klyːz] 1. *adj.* cloistered; 2. *su.* recluse; **réclusion** [rekly'sjɔ̃] *f* seclusion, retirement; ⚖ solitary confinement with hard labo(u)r.

récognition *phls.* [rekɔgni'sjɔ̃] *f* recognition.

recoiffer [rəkwa'fe] (1a) *v/t.* do (*s.o.'s*) hair (again); *se* ~ do one's hair (again); put one's hat on again.

recoin [rə'kwɛ̃] *m* nook, cranny.

reçois [rə'swa] *1st p. sg. pres. of recevoir*; **reçoivent** [~'swaːv] *3rd p. pl. pres. of recevoir*.

récolement ⚖ [rekɔl'mã] *m* verification; *depositions:* reading; **récoler** ⚖ [~kɔ'le] (1a) *v/t.* check; read over a deposition to (*a witness*).

récollection *eccl.* [rekɔlek'sjɔ̃] *f* recollection.

recoller [rəkɔ'le] (1a) *v/t.* re-glue; re-paste; F plough (again) (*in an examination*).

récolte [re'kɔlt] *f* harvest, crop; harvesting; F *fig.* collection; *fig.* profits *pl.*; **récolter** [~kɔl'te] (1a) *v/t.* harvest; gather in; *fig.* collect.

recommandable [rəkɔmã'dabl] to be recommended; estimable (*person*); *fig.* advisable; **recommandation** [~da'sjɔ̃] *f* recommendation; *fig.* instruction, advice; *post:* registration; **recommander** [~'de] (1a) *v/t.* recommend; *fig.* advise; *fig.* bring (*to s.o.'s attention*); *post:* register; *se* ~ *à* commend o.s. to; *se* ~ *de* give (*s.o.*) as a reference; *post:* *en recommandé* by registered post (*Am.* mail).

recommencer [rəkɔmã'se] (1k) *vt/i.* begin again, start afresh.

récompense [rekɔ̃'pãːs] *f* reward (for, *de*); *iro.* punishment; *show etc.:* prize, award; *en* ~ in return (for, *de*); **récompenser** [~pã'se] (1a) *v/t.* reward, recompense (for, *de*).

recomposer [rəkɔ̃po'ze] (1a) *v/t.* ♫ recompose; *typ.* reset.

recompter [rəkɔ̃'te] (1a) *v/t.* re-count, count again.

réconciliable [rekɔ̃si'ljabl] reconcilable; **réconciliateur** *m*, -**trice** *f* [~lja'tœːr, ~'tris] reconciler; **réconciliation** [~lja'sjɔ̃] *f* reconciliation; **réconcilier** [~'lje] (1o) *v/t.* reconcile; *se* ~ *à* make one's peace with (*a. eccl.*); make it up with (*s.o.*).

reconduction ⚖ [rəkɔ̃dyk'sjɔ̃] *f lease:* renewal; *tacite* ~ renewal of lease by tacit agreement; **reconduire** [~'dɥiːr] (4h) *v/t.* escort (*s.o.*) (back); lead back; show (*s.o.*) to the door; ⚖ renew (*a lease*); **reconduite** [~'dɥit] *f* escorting (s.o.) (back); showing (s.o.) to the door.

réconfort [rekɔ̃'fɔːr] m comfort, consolation; **réconfortant** ⚕ [~fɔr-'tɑ̃] m tonic, stimulant; **réconforter** [~fɔr'te] (1a) v/t. cheer (s.o.) up, comfort; strengthen.

reconnaissable [rəkɔnɛ'sabl] recognizable (by, from à); **reconnaissance** [~'sãːs] f recognition; ✕ etc. reconnaissance, reconnoitring; ✝ note of hand, F I.O.U.; ⚖ fig. acknowledgment; fig. gratitude; ⚖ bastard: affiliation; **reconnaissant, e** [~'sã, ~'sãːt] grateful (for, de; to, envers); **reconnaître** [rəkɔ-'nɛːtr] (4k) v/t. recognize (a. ⚖, a. pol. a government); know again; ✝ credit; fig. acknowledge; ✕, ✗, etc. reconnoitre; ⚓ identify (a ship); fig. be grateful for; fig. se ~ collect one's thoughts; get one's bearings.

reconquérir [rəkɔ̃ke'riːr] (2l) v/t. reconquer; win back (a. fig.); **reconquête** [~'kɛːt] f reconquest.

reconstituant, e ⚕ [rəkɔ̃sti'tɥɑ̃, ~'tɥãːt] adj., a. su./m tonic, restorative; **reconstituer** [~'tɥe] (1n) v/t. reconstitute or reconstruct (a crime); restore (⚕ an edifice, fig. s.o.'s health).

reconstruction [rəkɔ̃stryk'sjɔ̃] f reconstruction, rebuilding; **reconstruire** [~'trɥiːr] (4h) v/t. reconstruct, rebuild.

recoquiller [rəkɔki'je] (1a) v/t. a. se ~ curl up; shrivel; page f recoquillée dog-eared page.

record [rə'kɔːr] 1. su./m sp. etc. record; ⊕ maximum output; sp. détenir le ~ hold the record; 2. adj./inv. record...; bumper (crop).

recordman, pl. **-men** [~kɔrd-'man, ~'mɛn] m record-holder.

recoucher [rəku'ʃe] (1a) v/t. put (s.o.) to bed again; lay down again; se ~ go back to bed.

recoudre [rə'kudr] (4l) v/t. sew up or on again; fig. link up.

recoupe [rə'kup] f stone, metal, etc.: chips pl., chippings pl.; food: scraps pl.; ✿ second crop; ✝ flour: sharps pl.; **recouper** [~ku'pe] (1a) v/t. cut (again); intersect; ⚕ step; blend (wines); cross-check; confirm, support (a declaration etc.); se ~ intersect, overlap; match up, tally

(declarations etc); v/i. cards: cut again.

recourbement [rəkurbə'mã] m bending; **recourber** [~'be] (1a) v/t. bend (again or down).

recourir [rəku'riːr] (2i) v/i. run back; ~ à turn to (s.o.); resort to, have recourse to; **recours** [~'kuːr] m recourse; resort; ⚖ appeal (for mercy, en grâce).

recouvrement[1] [rəkuvrə'mã] m covering, coating.

recouvrement[2] [rəkuvrə'mã] m debt, health, strength, etc.: recovery; ~s pl. outstanding debts; **recouvrer** [~'vre] (1a) v/t. recover, regain; collect (a tax, a debt, etc.).

recouvrir [rəku'vriːr] (2f) v/t. recover, cover (s.th.) again (with, de); cover (a. fig.); coat; ⊕ overlap.

récréatif, -ve [rekrea'tif, ~'tiːv] recreational; entertaining; light (reading); **récréation** [~'sjɔ̃] f recreation; school: play.

recréer [rəkre'e] (1a) v/t. recreate; re-establish.

récréer [rekre'e] (1a) v/t. entertain, amuse; refresh; se ~ take some recreation.

recrépir [rəkre'piːr] (2a) v/t. ⚕ replaster; rough-cast again; F fig. patch up, touch up.

récrier [rekri'e] (1a) v/t.: se ~ (sur) cry out, exclaim (against); object (to).

récrimination [rekrimina'sjɔ̃] f remonstration; **récriminer** [~'ne] (1a) v/i. remonstrate (against, contre).

récrire [re'kriːr] (4q) v/t. rewrite; v/i. reply by letter.

recroître ✿ [rə'krwaːtr] (4o) v/i. grow again.

recroqueviller [rəkrɔkvi'je] (1a) v/t.: se ~ curl up, shrivel up (leaf etc.) curl or huddle o.s. up (person).

recrû, -crue [rə'kry] 1. su./m copsewood: new growth; 2. p.p. of recroître.

recrudescence [rəkrydɛ'sãːs] f recrudescence; fresh outbreak; **recrudescent, e** [~'sã, ~'sãːt] recrudescent.

recrue ✕, pol., fig. [rə'kry] f recruit; **recruter** [rəkry'te] (1a) v/t. recruit; se ~ be recruited; **recruteur** [~'tœːr] m recruiter; recruiting officer.

rectangle ⚖ [rɛk'tɑ̃:gl] 1. *adj.* right-angled; 2. *su./m* rectangle; **rectangulaire** ⚖ [~tɑ̃gy'lɛ:r] rectangular, right-angled.

recteur, -trice [rɛk'tœ:r, ~'tris] 1. *adj.* guiding; *orn.* tail(-*feather*); 2. *su./m univ.* rector, vice-chancellor.

rectificateur ⚙, ⚡ [rɛktifika'tœ:r] *m* rectifier; **rectificatif, -ve** [~'tif, ~'ti:v] 1. *adj.* rectifying; 2. *su./m* corrigendum (*to a circular*); **rectification** [~'sjɔ̃] *f* rectification; *alcohol:* rectifying; *fig.* correction; **rectifier** [rɛkti'fje] (1o) *v/t.* straighten; correct (*an error, a price,* ✗ *the range*); ⚙, ⚖, *a. fig.* rectify; *fig.* put (*s.th.*) right; ⊕ adjust (*a machine etc.*); ⊕ true up (*on the lathe*).

rectiligne [rɛkti'liɲ] rectilinear; linear (*movement*); *fig.* unswerving.

rectitude [rɛkti'tyd] *f* straightness; *fig.* rectitude; *fig.* correctness.

recto [rɛk'to] *m page:* recto; *book:* right-hand page.

reçu, e [rə'sy] 1. *su./m* receipt; *au ~ de* (up)on receipt of; 2. *adj.* received, accepted, recognized; 3. *p.p. of recevoir.*

recueil [rə'kœ:j] *m* collection; anthology; ⚖ compendium, digest; **recueillement** [~kœj'mɑ̃] *m* collectedness; meditation; **recueillir** [~kœ'ji:r] (2c) *v/t.* collect, gather; ✓, *a. fig.* reap; *fig.* give shelter to (*s.o.*), take (*s.o.*) in; obtain (*information*); *se ~* collect one's thoughts; meditate.

recuire [rə'kɥi:r] (4h) *v/t.* recook, cook (*s.th.*) again; ⊕ reheat; ⊕ anneal (*glass*), temper (*steel*).

recul [rə'kyl] *m* retirement; backward movement; *rifle:* kick; *cannon:* recoil; **reculade** [rəky'lad] *f* retreat (*a.* ✗, *fig.*), falling back; **reculé, e** [~'le] remote, distant; **reculer** [~'le] (1a) *v/i.* move or draw back; back (*car, horse*); *fig.* shrink (from, *devant*); *v/t.* move back; set back; *fig.* postpone; **reculons** [~'lɔ̃] *adv.:* à ~ backwards.

récupérateur ⊕ [rekypera'tœ:r] *m* regenerator; *oil:* extractor; **récupération** [~ra'sjɔ̃] *f loss:* recoupment; ⊕, *a.* ⚔ recovery; ⊕ retrieval, salvage, reprocessing; rehabilitation; **récupérer** [~'re] (1f) *v/t.*

recover; recoup (*a loss*); ⊕ retrieve, salvage, reprocess (*materials*); rehabilitate (*persons*); bring (*a satellite*) back to earth; *v/i. a. se ~* recuperate, recover.

récurer [reky're] (1a) *v/t.* scour; clean; **récureur** [~'rœ:r] *m* scourer.

reçus [rə'sy] *1st p. sg. p.s. of recevoir.*

récusable [reky'zabl] challengeable; impeachable (*evidence, witness*); **récuser** ⚖ [~'ze] (1a) *v/t.* challenge, object to (*a witness*); impeach (*s.o.'s evidence*); *se ~* declare o.s. incompetent, decline to give an opinion.

recyclage [rəsi'kla:ʒ] *m* reorientation; retraining; ⊕ recycling, reprocessing; **recycler** [~'kle] (1a) *v/t.* reorient; retrain; ⊕ recycle, reprocess.

rédacteur, -trice [redak'tœ:r, ~'tris] *su.* writer; author; drafter; *journ.* sub-editor; *su./m:* ~ *en chef* editor; **rédaction** [~'sjɔ̃] *f* drafting; *journ.* editorial staff; *journ.* editing; *journ.* (newspaper) office; *school:* composition, essay.

reddition [redi'sjɔ̃] *f* surrender; ✝ rendering (*of an account*).

redécouvrir [rədeku'vri:r] (2f) *v/t.* rediscover.

redemander [rədmɑ̃'de] (1a) *v/t.* ask for (*s.th.*) again or back; ask for more of (*s.th.*).

rédempteur, -trice [redɑ̃p'tœ:r, ~'tris] 1. *adj.* redeeming; 2. *su.* redeemer; **rédemption** [~'sjɔ̃] *f* redemption (*a. eccl.*).

redescendre [rədɛ'sɑ̃:dr] (4a) *v/i.* go or come down again; ⚓ back (*wind*); fall (*barometer*); *v/t.* bring down again; take (*s.th.*) down again; ~ *l'escalier* go downstairs again.

redevable [rəd'vabl] 1. *adj.* indebted (for, de); *être ~ de qch. à q.* owe s.o. s.th.; 2. *su.* debtor; **redevance** [~'vɑ̃:s] *f* charge, fee; (*author's*) royalty; *admin.* tax, dues *pl.*; **redevoir** [~'vwa:r] (3a) *v/t.* owe a balance of.

rédhibition ⚖ [redibi'sjɔ̃] *f* annulment of sale (*owing to latent defect*); **rédhibitoire** [~'twa:r] *adj.* ⚖ redhibitory (*defect*); *fig.* crippling, dooming (*defect etc.*); *vice m ~ a.* latent defect that makes a sale void.

rédiger [redi'ʒe] (1l) *v/t.* draw up, draft, write; *journ.* edit.

rédimer [redi'me] (1a) *v/t.* redeem; se ~ de redeem o.s. from; compound for (*a tax*).

redingote *cost.* [rədɛ̃'gɔt] *f* frock-coat.

redire [rə'diːr] (4p) *v/t.* repeat; say *or* tell again; *v/i.*: avoir (*or* trouver *or* voir) à ~ à find fault with; take exception to, criticize; **rediseur** *m*, **-euse** *f* [~di'zœːr, ~'zøːz] repeater; **redite** [~'dit] *f* repetition, tautology; **redites** [~'dit] 2nd *p. pl. pres.* of redire.

redondance [rədɔ̃'dɑ̃ːs] *f* redundancy; **redondant, e** [~'dɑ̃, ~'dɑ̃ːt] redundant.

redonner [rədɔ'ne] (1a) *v/t.* give (*s.th.*) again; restore (*s.th.*, *a. strength*); *v/i.* return, come on again; ~ dans fall back into; la pluie redonne de plus belle the rain is coming on again worse than ever.

redoubler [rədu'ble] (1a) *v/t.* redouble; *cost.* reline; ~ une classe school: stay down again; *v/i.* increase (*fever*); ~ d'efforts strive harder than ever.

redoutable [rədu'tabl] formidable; to be feared (by, à).

redoute [rə'dut] *f* ✕ redoubt; *dancing-hall*: gala evening.   [dread.]

redouter [rədu'te] (1a) *v/t.* fear,)

redressement [rədrɛs'mɑ̃] *m* *fig.* rectification; ⊕, *fig.* straightening; ⚡ rectifying; ✝, *opt.*, *phot.* correction; **redresser** [rədrɛ'se] (1a) *v/t.* re-erect (*a statue*); raise (*a pole*); ⚓ right (*a boat*); set right (*a wrong etc.*); ✕ lift the nose of; ⚡, *a. fig.* rectify; ⊕ straigthen out, true; se ~ stand up again; draw o.s. up; right itself (*boat*); ✕ flatten out; *fig.* mend one's ways; **redresseur** [~'sœːr] *m* ⚡ rectifier; ⚡ commutator; ⊕ straightener; *fig.* righter (*of wrongs*).

redû, -due [rə'dy] 1. *p.p.* of redevoir; 2. *su./m* ✝ balance due.

réducteur, -trice [redyk'tœːr, ~'tris] 1. *adj.* reducing; 2. *su./m* 🜍, *phot.* reducer; reducing camera *or* apparatus; ⊕, *mot.* reducing gear; **réductibilité** [~tibili'te] *f* reducibility; **réductible** [🜍, 🜍, ✝ [~'tibl] reducible; **réductif, -ve** [~ 🜍, ~'tiːv] reducing; **réduction** [~'sjɔ̃] *f* decrease; ✝, 🜍, 🜍, 🜍, metall., admin., phot., paint., a. fig. reduc-

tion, *taxes, wages, production, etc.*: a. cut; ⚡ voltage: stepping down; ⊕ gearing down; 🜍 sentence: mitigation; **réduire** [re'dɥiːr] (4h) *v/t.* reduce; lessen; cut down (*expenses*); subjugate; ⚡ step down; ⊕ gear down; se ~ à keep (o.s.) to; *fig.* come *or* F boil down to; **réduit** [~'dɥi] 1. *su./m* retreat, nook; *pej.* hovel; ✕ keep; 2. *adj./m*: à prix ~ at a reduced price.

réédifier [reedi'fje] (1o) *v/t.* rebuild; re-erect.

rééditer [reedi'te] (1a) *v/t.* republish; *cin.* remake (*a film*); **réédition** [~'sjɔ̃] *f* re-issue; *cin. a.* re-make.

rééducatif, -ve 🜍 [reedyka'tif, ~ 'tiːv] occupational (*therapy*); **rééducation** 🜍 [~ka'sjɔ̃] *f* re-education; rehabilitation; **rééduquer** 🜍 [~'ke] (1m) *v/t.* re-educate; rehabilitate.

réel, -elle [re'ɛl] 1. *adj.* real (*a.* 🜍 action, estate); actual; ✝ (in) cash; 2. *su./m* reality, the real.

réélection [reelɛk'sjɔ̃] *f* re-election; **rééligible** [~li'ʒibl] re-eligible; **réélire** [~'liːr] (4t) *v/t.* re-elect.

réescompte [rees'kɔ̃ːt] *m* rediscount; **réescompter** [~kɔ̃'te] (1a) *v/t.* rediscount.

réévaluation [reevalɥa'sjɔ̃] *f* revaluation; **réévaluer** [~'lɥe] (1n) *v/t.* revalue.

réexpédier [reɛkspe'dje] (1o) *v/t.* send back; forward, send on.

refaire [rə'fɛːr] (4r) *v/t.* remake; do *or* make (*s.th.*) again; mend, repair; 🜍 restore to health; F swindle, do (*s.o.*), dupe; F steal (from, à); se ~ 🜍 recuperate; ✝ retrieve one's losses; **refait, e** F [~'fɛ, ~'fɛt] duped.

réfection [refɛk'sjɔ̃] *f* remaking; ⚠ rebuilding; repair(ing); 🜍 recuperation; **réfectoire** [~'twaːr] *m* refectory, dining-hall.

refend [rə'fɑ̃] *m* splitting; ⊕ bois *m* de ~ wood in planks; ⚠ mur *m* de ~ partition-wall; **refendre** [~'fɑ̃ːdr] (4a) *v/t.* split; rip (*timber*); slit (*leather*).

référé 🜍 [refe're] *m* summary procedure; provisional order; **référence** [~'rɑ̃ːs] *f* reference (*a. of a servant*); ✝ pattern-book; ✝ sample-book; *fig.* allusion; ouvrage *m* de ~ reference book; **référendaire** [~-

rā'dɛ:r] *m* 🏛 *commercial court*: chief clerk; *hist. grand* ~ Great Referendary; **référendum** [ˌʀɛ̃-'dɔm] *m* referendum; strike ballot; **référer** [ˌ'ʀe] (1f) *v/t.* se ~ *à* refer to (*s.th.*); ask (*s.o.'s*) opinion; consult; *en* ~ *à q.* submit the matter to s.o.

refermer [ʀəfɛr'me] (1a) *v/t.* shut (again), close (again); se ~ close up (*wound*); shut (again).

réfléchi, e [refle'ʃi] thoughtful (*person*); considered (*action, opinion*); 🏛 premeditated (*crime*); *gramm.* reflexive; *tout* ~ everything considered; **réfléchir** [ˌ'ʃi:r] (2a) *v/t.* reflect; se ~ curl back; *phys.* be reflected; reverberate (*sound*); *v/i.* consider; reflect (on *à, sur*); **réfléchissement** *phys.* [ˌʃis'mã] *m* reflection; *sound:* reverberation; **réflecteur** [reflɛk'tœ:r] *m* ✝, *mot., phys.* reflector; *fig.* searchlight; **reflet** [ʀə'flɛ] *m* reflection; glint, gleam, glimmer; *picture, etc.*: highlight; **refléter** [ˌfle'te] (1f) *v/t.* reflect, throw back (*colour, light*); *fig.* se ~ *sur* be reflected on (*s.o.*).

réflexe *phys., physiol.* [re'flɛks] *adj., a. su./m* reflex; **réflexion** [ˌflɛk'sjɔ̃] *f phys., a. fig.* reflection; *fig.* thought; *toute* ~ *faite* everything considered.

refluer [ʀəfly'e] (1a) *v/i.* flow back; ebb (*tide*); *fig.* fall back; *fig.* pour (into, *dans*); **reflux** [ˌ'fly] *m tide:* ebb; ebbtide; flowing back; *fig. crowd etc.*: falling back.

refondre [ʀə'fɔ̃:dr] (4a) *v/t.* ⊕ remelt; *metall., a. fig.* recast; *fig.* remodel; ✝ refit (*a ship*); **refonte** [ˌ'fɔ̃:t] *f* remelting; recasting (*a. fig.*); reorganization; ✝ refit(ting).

réformable [refɔr'mabl] reformable; ✂ liable to discharge; 🏛 reversible; **réformateur, -trice** [ˌma'tœ:r, ˌ'tris] **1.** *adj.* reforming; **2.** *su.* reformer; **réformation** [ˌma'sjɔ̃] *f* reformation (*a. eccl.*); **réforme** [re'fɔrm] *f* reform(ation); ✂, ✝ discharge; *horse:* casting; *eccl. la* ♀ the Reformation; ✂ *mettre à la* ~ discharge (*s.o.*); cast (*a horse*); dismiss, cashier (*an officer*); **réformé, e** [refɔr'me] **1.** *su. eccl.* protestant; ✂ person invalided out of the service; **2.** *adj. eccl.* reformed; ✂ discharged (*soldier*).

reformer [ʀəfɔr'me] (1a) *v/t.* reform, form anew.

réformer [refɔr'me] (1a) *v/t.* reform, amend; ✂, ✝ invalid (*s.o.*) out of the service; dismiss; cashier (*an officer*); retire (*an officer*); cast (*a horse*); 🏛 reverse (*a judgment*).

refoulement [reful'mã] *m* driving back; *fig.* repression (*a. psych.*); **refouler** [rafu'le] (1a) *v/t.* drive back, repel; *fig.* repress (*a. psych.*), hold back, force back.

réfractaire [refrak'tɛ:r] **1.** *adj.* refractory (*a.* ⊕ *ore*), rebellious, recalcitrant; ⊕ fire-proof; proof (against, *à*); **2.** *su.* refractory person; ✂ defaulter, *Am.* draft-dodger.

réfraction *phys., opt.* [ˌ'sjɔ̃] *f* refraction; *indice m de* ~ refractive index.

refrain [ʀə'frɛ̃] *m* refrain (*a. fig.*); F *fig. le même* ~ the same old story.

refrènement [rəfrɛn'mã] *m instincts:* curbing; **refréner** [ˌfre'ne] (1f) *v/t.* curb, restrain.

réfrigérant, e [refriʒe'rã, ˌ'rã:t] **1.** *adj.* refrigerating, cooling; freezing; ⊕ refrigerant; ⊕ cooler-…; **2.** *su./m* ⚗ condenser; refrigerator; ✝ refrigerant; **réfrigérateur** [ˌra'tœ:r] *m* refrigerator; *fig. mettre qch. au* ~ put s.th. on ice *or* in cold storage; **réfrigératif, -ve** ✝ [ˌra'tif, ˌ'ti:v] *adj., a. su./m* refrigerant; **réfrigération** [ˌra'sjɔ̃] *f* refrigeration; *meat.:* chilling; **réfrigérer** [ˌ're] (1f) *v/t.* refrigerate; cool; chill (*meat*).

refroidir [rəfrwa'di:r] (2a) *v/t.* cool, chill; ⊕, *a. fig.* quench (*metal, a.* one's *enthusiasm,* one's *sympathy*); *sl.* kill; ⊕ *refroidi par l'air* air-cooled (*engine*); ✝ se ~ catch a chill; *v/i. a.* se ~ grow cold; cool off (*a. fig.*); **refroidissement** [ˌdis'mã] *m* cooling (down); ✝ chill; *temperature:* drop.

refuge [ʀə'fy:ʒ] *m* refuge; shelter (*a. admin.*); *birds:* sanctuary; *traffic* island; *mot.* lay-by; *fig.* pretext, F way out; **réfugié m, e** *f* [refy'ʒje] refugee; **réfugier** [ˌ] (1o) *v/t.:* se ~ take refuge; seek shelter; *fig.* have recourse (to, *dans*).

refus [ʀə'fy] *m* refusal; denial; rejection; ✝ ~ *m d'acceptation* non-acceptance; *essuyer un* ~ meet with a refusal; **refuser** [ˌfy'ze] (1a) *vt/i.* refuse, decline; *v/t.* ✂ reject (*a* *man*); fail (*a candidate*); ~ *de* (*inf.*), *se* ~ *à* (*inf.*) refuse to (*inf.*); *se* ~ *à qch.* resist s.th., object to s.th.

réfutation [refyta'sjɔ̃] *f* refutation; proof to the contrary; **réfuter** [~'te] (1a) *v/t.* refute; disprove.

regagner [rəga'ɲe] (1a) *v/t.* regain; win back; recover; return to (*a place*).

regain [rə'gɛ̃] *m* ✍ aftergrowth, second growth; *fig.* renewal, revival; ~ *de vie* new lease of (*Am.* on) life.

régal, *pl.* **-als** [re'gal] *m* treat; delight; **régalade** [~ga'lad] *f*: *boire à la* ~ drink without the lips coming into contact with the glass *or* bottle.

régalage ⊕ [rega'la:ʒ] *m* levelling.

régale [re'gal] **1.** *adj./f*: 🜍 *eau f* ~ aqua regia; **2.** *su./f hist.* royal prerogative. [ground).\

régaler¹ [rega'le] (1a) *v/t.* level (*the*)

régaler² [~] (1a) *v/t.* treat (*s.o.*) to a (fine) meal; ~ *q. de qch.* treat s.o. to s.th.; *se* ~ have a fine meal *etc.*; *fig.* enjoy o.s.; *se* ~ *de* feast on; treat o.s. to.

regard [rə'ga:r] *m* look, glance; sewer *etc.*: man-hole; inspection hole; peep-hole; *geol.* inlier; *fig.* attention, eyes *pl.*; *au* ~ *de* compared to; *en* ~ *de* opposite, facing; **regardant, e** F [rəgar'dã, ~'dã:t] stingy, niggardly; **regarder** [~'de] (1a) *v/t.* look at, watch; glance at; face, look on to; *telev.* look in; *fig.* consider (as, *comme*); *fig.* concern; ~ *fixement* stare at; *cela me regarde* that is my business; *v/i.* (have a) look; ~ *à* pay attention to (*s.th.*); look through (*s.th.*); ~ *par* (*à*) *la fenêtre* look through (in at) the window; ~ *fixement* stare.

régate [re'gat] *f* regatta; *cost.* sailor-knot tie.

regel [rə'ʒɛl] *m* renewed frost.

régence [re'ʒã:s] *f* regency; fob-chain.

régénération [reʒenera'sjɔ̃] *f* regeneration; ⊕ reclamation; ... *à* ~ regenerative ...; **régénérer** [~'re] (1f) *v/t.* regenerate; ⊕ reclaim.

régent, e [re'ʒã, ~'ʒã:t] *su.* regent; *su./m* † *collège*: form-master; **régenter** [~ʒã'te] (1a) *v/t.* † teach; F *fig.* lord it over.

régicide [reʒi'sid] **1.** *adj.* regicidal; **2.** *su. person*: regicide; *su./m crime*: regicide.

régie [re'ʒi] *f* administration; management; state control; excise-office.

regimber [rəʒɛ̃'be] (1a) *v/i.* balk (at, *contre*); kick (against, at *contre*).

régime [re'ʒim] *m* organization; regulations *pl.*; system; ⊕ *engine*: normal running; *mot.* speed; ✍ diet; *gramm.* object; ✤ *bananas etc.*: bunch; *hist.* Ancien ♀ Ancien Regime (*before 1789*); *gramm. cas m* ~ objective case; ✍ *mettre au* ~ put (*s.o.*) on a diet; *suivre un* ~ (follow a special) diet.

régiment [reʒi'mã] *m* ✕ regiment; F *fig.* host; **régimentaire** ✕ [~mã-'tɛ:r] regimental; army-...; troop (*train*).

région [re'ʒjɔ̃] *f* region (*a. anat.*); area; *phys.* field; ~ *désertique* desert region; ~ *vinicole* wine-producing district; **régional, e**, *m/pl.* **-aux** [~ʒjɔ'nal, ~'no] regional, local.

régir [re'ʒi:r] (2a) *v/t. pol.*, *gramm.*, *fig.* govern; ✝ direct, manage; **régisseur** [~ʒi'sœ:r] *m* manager; *thea.* stage-manager; *cin.* assistant director; ✍ *farm*: bailiff; *estate*: agent.

registre [rə'ʒistr] *m* register (*a.* ♪), record; ✝ account-book; ⊕ log-book; ⊕ *chimney etc.*: damper; ⊕ *steam engine*: throttle; ~ *de l'état civil* register of births, deaths and marriages; *tenir* ~ *de* keep a record of, note (down).

réglable [re'glabl] adjustable; **réglage** [~'gla:ʒ] *m* ⊕ regulating, adjustment; *speed*: control; *paper*: ruling; *radio*: tuning; **règle** [regl] *f* rule; ⊕ ruler, rule; *surv.* measuring rod; ✍ ~*s pl.* menses; ⩓ ~ *à calcul* slide rule; ⩓ ~ *de trois* rule of three; *de* ~ usual, customary; *en* ~ in order, straight; **réglé, e** [re'gle] regular; steady (*pace, person*); ⩓ uniform (*courses*); ruled (*paper*); fixed (*hour etc.*); **règlement** [reglə'mã] *m admin.*, ✕ *etc.* regulation(s *pl.*); rule; ✝ settlement; **réglementaire** [reglɔmã'tɛ:r] regular, prescribed; regulation-...; *pas* ~ against the rules; **réglementation** [~ta'sjɔ̃] *f* regulation; regulating, control; ~ *de la circulation* traffic regulations *pl.*; **réglementer** [~'te] (1a) *v/t.* regulate, control; make rules for; **régler** [re'gle] (1f) *v/t.* ⊕, *a. fig.* regulate; ⊕, ✝ adjust; *fig.* settle (*a quarrel, a question,* ✝ *an account*); ✝ settle (up), pay (up); rule (*paper*); *mot.* tune (*an engine*); ~ *sur* model on; adjust to.

réglet [re'glɛ] *m* carpenter's rule; ◬ reglet; **réglette** [~'glɛt] *f typ.* reglet; small rule; (*metal*) strip; *slide-rule:* slide; *mot.* ~*jauge* dipstick.

réglisse ♧, ⚘ [re'glis] *f* liquorice.

réglure [re'gly:r] *f paper:* ruling.

règne [rɛɲ] *m* ♧, zo. kingdom; *pol., a. fig.* reign; **régner** [re'ne] (1f) *v/i.* reign (*a. fig.*), rule; *fig.* prevail.

regorger [rəgɔr'ʒe] (1l) *v/i.* overflow; abound (in, *de*); be crowded (with, *de*); *v/t.* bring up (*food*); *fig.* disgorge.

regratter [rəgra'te] (1a) *v/t.* ◬ scrape, rub down (*a wall*); *v/i.* ✝ F huckster.

régresser [regre'se] (1a) *v/i.* decrease, decline, fall off; **régressif, -ve** [~'sif, ~'si:v] regressive; **régression** [~'sjɔ̃] *f* regression; *biol.* retrogression; *biol.* throw-back; *sales etc.:* drop.

regret [rə'grɛ] *m* regret (for, of *de*); *à* ~ regretfully, with regret; *avoir* ~ *de* (*inf.*) regret to (*inf.*); **regrettable** [rəgre'tabl] regrettable; unfortunate; **regretter** [~'te] (1a) *v/t.* regret; be sorry (that *ind.,* *que sbj.*; for *ger., de inf.*); miss, mourn (for).

regroupement [rəgrup'mɑ̃] *m* regrouping; **regrouper** [~gru'pe] (1a) *v/t.* regroup.

régulariser [regylari'ze] (1a) *v/t.* regularize; put (*s.th.*) in order; ⚖ put into legal form; **régularité** [~'te] *f* regularity; *temper:* evenness; punctuality; **régulateur, -trice** [regyla'tœ:r, ~'tris] **1.** *adj.* regulating; ✝ buffer-(*stocks*); **2.** *su./m* regulator; *watch:* balance-wheel; **régulier, -ère** [~'lje, ~'ljɛ:r] **1.** *adj.* regular (*a. gramm.*); steady; even, equable (*temper*); **2.** *su./m* ✕, *eccl.* regular.

régurgiter [regyrʒi'te] (1a) *v/t.* regurgitate.

réhabilitation [reabilita'sjɔ̃] *f* rehabilitation (*a. fig.*); *bankrupt:* discharge; ◬ modernization (*of buildings etc.*); **réhabiliter** [~'te] (1a) *v/t.* reinstate; discharge (*a bankrupt*); *fig.* rehabilitate; *fig.* bring back into

favo(u)r; ◬ modernize (*buildings etc.*); *se* ~ clear one's name.

réhabituer [reabi'tɥe] (1n) *v/t.* reaccustom (to, *à*).

rehaussement [rəos'mɑ̃] *m* raising (*a. prices*); *fig.* enhancing; **rehausser** [~o'se] (1a) *v/t.* raise; increase (*one's courage*); *fig.* enhance, set off (*one's beauty, a colour, one's merit*).

réimporter [reɛ̃pɔr'te] (1a) *v/t.* reimport.

réimposer [reɛ̃po'ze] (1a) *v/t.* reimpose (*a tax*); tax (*s.o.*) again.

réimpression [reɛ̃prɛ'sjɔ̃] *f* reprint (-ing); **réimprimer** [~pri'me] (1a) *v/t.* reprint.

rein [rɛ̃] *m anat.* kidney; ~*s pl.* back *sg.,* loins; ◬ *arch:* sides; ⚘ ~ *artificiel* kidney machine; ⚘ ~ *flottant* floating kidney; *avoir les* ~*s solides* be sturdy; F *fig.* be wealthy; *avoir mal aux* ~*s* have backache; *casser les* ~*s à q.* ruin s.o.

réincorporer [reɛ̃kɔrpɔ're] (1a) *v/t.* reincorporate.

reine [rɛn] *f* queen; ~**-claude,** *pl.* ~**s-claudes** ♧ [~'klo:d] *f* greengage; ~**-des-prés,** *pl.* ~**s-des-prés** ♧ [~de-'pre] *f* meadow-sweet; ~**-marguerite,** *pl.* ~**s-marguerites** ♧ [~mar-gə'rit] *f* china aster; **reinette** ♧ [rɛ'nɛt] *f apple:* pippin; ~ *grise* russet.

réinsérer [reɛ̃se're] (1f) *v/t.* reinsert; *fig.* reintegrate (*persons*); **réinsertion** [~sɛr'sjɔ̃] *f* reinsertion; *fig.* reintegration.

réintégration [reɛ̃tegra'sjɔ̃] *f* admin. person: reinstatement; ⚖ reintegration; ⚖ *conjugal rights:* restitution; *residence:* resumption; **réintégrer** [~'gre] (1f) *v/t.* admin. reinstate (*a person*); ⚖ reintegrate; return to, resume (*one's domicile*).

réitératif, -ve [reitera'tif, ~'ti:v] reiterative; second (*summons*); **réitérer** [~'re] (1f) *v/t.* repeat, reiterate.

reître [rɛtr] *m* ruffianly soldier.

rejaillir [rəʒa'ji:r] (2a) *v/i.* gush out; spurt; be reflected (*light*); spring; *fig.* fall (upon, *sur*), reflect (on, *sur*).

rejet [rə'ʒɛ] *m* throwing out; *food:* throwing up; ⚖ dismissal; *fig., parl.,* ⚘ *etc.* rejection; ✝ transfer; ⚘ shoot; **rejetable** [rəʒ'tabl] rejectable; **rejeter** [~'te] (1c) *v/t.* throw back *or* again; fling back (*a.* ✕ *the enemy*);

throw up (*a. food*); reject (*s.o.'s advice, parl. a. bill, an offer, a. ⚓ etc.*); ⚖ dismiss; ✝ transfer; cast off (*stitches*); shift (*a. fig. the blame etc.*); ⚓ throw out (*shoots*); ~ *la responsabilité sur* throw *or* cast the responsibility on; **rejeton** [~'tɔ̃] *m* ⚓ (off)shoot; *fig.* offspring, scion.

rejoindre [rə'ʒwɛ̃:dr] (4m) *v/t.* rejoin (*a.* ⚔); catch (*s.o.*) up; se ~ meet (again).

réjoui, e [re'ʒwi] **1.** *adj.* jolly, jovial, merry; **2.** *su./m:* gros ~ merry *or* jovial fellow; **réjouir** [~'ʒwi:r] (2a) *v/t.* cheer, delight; entertain, amuse (*the company*); se ~ rejoice (at, in *de*), be delighted (at, *de*); enjoy o.s., make merry; **réjouissance** [~ʒwi'sɑ̃:s] *f* rejoicing; ✝ makeweight.

relâche¹ [rə'lɑ:ʃ] *m* rest, respite; *thea.* ~! closed!; *thea.* faire ~ be closed; *sans* ~ without respite.

relâche² ⚓ [~] *f* (port of) call; *faire* ~ put into port.

relâché, e [rəlɑ'ʃe] relaxed; slack (*rope*); *fig.* loose; **relâchement** [~lɑʃ'mɑ̃] *m* relaxing, slackening; *fig.* relaxation (*a.* ⚓, *a. from work*); *bowels, conduct:* looseness; **relâcher** [~lɑ'ʃe] (1a) *v/t.* loosen (*a.* ⚓ *the bowels*), slacken; *fig.* release (*a prisoner*); ~ *le temps* make the weather milder; se ~ grow milder; *v/i.* ⚓ put into port.

relais [rə'lɛ] *m* ⚡ *radio:* relay; ⊕ shift; *mot.* ~ *des routiers* truck stop; *sp.* course *f* de (*or par*) ~ relay race; *prendre le* ~ (*de*) take over (from); *sans* ~ without rest.

relance [rə'lɑ̃s] *f* boost(ing), stimulation; revival, relaunching; **relancer** [rəlɑ̃'se] (1k) *v/t.* throw back *or* again; return (*a ball*); *hunt.* start (*the quarry*) again; *fig.* pester (*s.o.*); *mot.* restart (*the engine*); *fig.* boost, stimulate; *fig.* revive, relaunch.

relaps, e *eccl.* [rə'laps] **1.** *adj.* relapsed; **2.** *su.* apostate, relapsed heretic.

relater [rəla'te] (1a) *v/t.* relate, recount; report.

relatif, -ve [rəla'tif, ~'ti:v] relative (*a. gramm.*); ~ *à* referring to, connected with, related to; **relation** [~'sjɔ̃] *f* relation; connection; account, report; ~s *pl.* acquaintances; ✝ ~s *pl. publiques* public relations; **relativiser** [~tivi'ze] (1a) *v/t.* relativize; see

(*s.th.*) in (its true) perspective; **relativité** [~tivi'te] *f* relativity; *phys.* théorie *f* de la ~ relativity theory.

relaxer [rəlak'se] (1a) *v/t.* relax; ⚖ release; se ~ relax.

relayer [rəlɛ'je] (1i) *v/t.* relieve, take over from; take turns with; ⚡, *tel., radio:* relay; se ~ take turns; work in shifts; *v/i.* change horses.

relégation ⚖ [rəlega'sjɔ̃] *f* relegation; **reléguer** [~'ge] (1s) *v/t.* relegate; *fig.* banish; *fig.* remove.

relent [rə'lɑ̃] *m* musty smell *or* taste; unpleasant smell.

relevant, e [rəl'vɑ̃, ~'vɑ̃:t] *adj.:* ~ *de* dependent on; within the jurisdiction of.

relève [rə'lɛ:v] *f* ⚔, ⚓ relief; F relieving troops *pl.*; ⚔ guard: changing; **relevé, e** [rəl've] **1.** *adj.* raised (*head etc.*); turned up (*sleeve, trousers, etc.*); *fig.* high; lofty; noble (*sentiment*); *cuis.* highly seasoned; *fig.* spicy (*story*); **2.** *su./m* abstract, summary; ✝ statement; *admin.* return; survey; *cost.* tuck; *cuis.* remove (= *course after soup*); ~ *du gaz* gas-meter reading; *su./f* ✝ afternoon; **relèvement** [rəlɛv'mɑ̃] *m* raising again; picking up; *bankrate, temperature, wages:* rise; raising (*a.* ✝ *bank-rate etc.*), ⚓, *surv.* bearing, ✝, *fig.* recovery, improvement; ✝ *account:* making out; ⚔ *sentry:* relieving; *wounded:* collecting; **relever** [rəl've] (1d) *v/t.* raise (*a.* ✝ *prices, wages, etc.*); lift; pick up (*from the ground*); ⚓ rebuild; ⚓ take the bearings of; *surv.* survey; *fig.* bring into relief, set off, enhance; ✝ make out (*an account*), put up (*a price*); read (*the meter*); *fig.* call attention to, notice; *fig.* accept (*a challenge*); relieve, take over from (*s.o.*); *fig.* release (from, *de*); *cuis.* season; se ~ get up; rise (*a. fig.*); ✝, *a. fig.* revive, recover; take turns; *v/i.:* ~ *de* be dependent on; *admin.* be a matter for; pertain to; arise from; ⚓ have just recovered from.

reliage [rə'lja:ʒ] *m* binding; joining; *casks:* hooping.

relief [rə'ljɛf] *m* relief (*a. fig.*); *fig.* prominence; *en* ~ relief (*map*); *fig. mettre en* ~ set off, throw into relief.

relier [rə'lje] (1o) *v/t.* bind (*a. books*); join; connect (*a.* ⚡, *teleph.*, ⚓); tie *(s.th.)* up again; hoop *(a cask)*; **re-lieur, -euse** [rə'ljœːr, ~'ljøːz] *su.* (book)binder; *su./f* bookbinding machine.

religieux, -euse [rəli'ʒjø, ~'ʒjøːz] **1.** *adj.* religious; sacred *(music)*, church ...; **2.** *su./m* monk; *su./f* nun; **religion** [~'ʒjɔ̃] *f* religion; *fig.* sacred duty; *entrer en* ~ enter into religion, take the vows; **religiosité** [~ʒjozi-'te] *f* religiosity; *fig.* scrupulousness (in *ger.*, *à inf.*).

reliquaire [rəli'kɛːr] *m* reliquary, shrine.

reliquat [rəli'ka] *m* ⚕ residue; ✝ *account*: balance; ⚞ after-effects *pl.*

relique [rə'lik] *f* relic; F *fig. garder comme une* ~ *treasure.*

relire [rə'liːr] (4t) *v/t.* re-read.

reliure [rə'ljyːr] *f* (book)binding; ~ *en toile* cloth binding.

relouer [rəlu'e] (1a) *v/t.* re-let; renew the lease of.

reluire [rə'lɥiːr] (4u) *v/i.* gleam; glisten, glitter; *faire* ~ polish *(s.th.)*; **reluisant, e** [~lɥi'zɑ̃, ~'zɑ̃ːt] gleaming, shining; glittering; well-groomed *(horse)*.

reluquer [rəly'ke] (1m) *v/t.* eye, ogle; have one's eye on; covet.

remâcher [rəmɑ'ʃe] (1a) *v/t.* chew again; *fig.* turn *(s.th.)* over in one's mind; brood over.

remailler [rəmɑ'je] (1a) *v/t.* mend a ladder in *(a stocking)*.

remanent, e ⚡, *phys.* [rəmɑ'nɑ̃, ~'nɑ̃ːt] remanent, residual.

remaniement *pol.* [rəmani'mɑ̃] *m* reshuffle; **remanier** [~'nje] (1o) *v/t.* rehandle; ⌂ retile *(a roof)*, re-lay *(a pavement, pipes, etc.)*; *fig.* recast; *fig.* adapt *(a play etc.)*.

remarier [rəmɑ'rje] (1o) *v/t. a. se* ~ remarry, marry again.

remarquable [rəmar'kabl] remarkable (for, *par*); distinguished (by, *par*); outstanding (for, *par*); astonishing; **remarque** [~'mark] *f* re-mark; note; ⚓ landmark; **remarquer** [~mar'ke] (1m) *v/t.* notice, note; re-mark; remark, observe; *faire* ~ *qch. à q.* point s.th. out to s.o.; *se faire* ~ attract attention; make o.s. conspicuous.

remballer [rɑ̃bɑ'le] (1a) *v/t.* re-pack; pack up again.

rembarquer [rɑ̃bar'ke] (1m) *vt/i.* ⚓ re-embark; *v/i. a. se* ~ go to sea

again; *v/t.:* F *fig. se* ~ *dans* embark again upon *(s.th.)*.

remblai [rɑ̃'blɛ] *m* embankment; filling up *or* in; banking (up); *ma-terial*: filling; ⊕ slag dump; **rem-blayer** [~blɛ'je] (1i) *v/t.* fill (up); bank (up).

remboîter ⚕ [rɑ̃bwa'te] (1a) *v/t.* set *(a bone)*.

rembourrage [rɑ̃bu'raːʒ] *m* stuff-ing, padding; upholstering; **rem-bourrer** [~'re] (1a) *v/t.* stuff, pad, upholster.

remboursable ✝ [rɑ̃bur'sabl] re-payable; redeemable *(annuity, stock, etc.)*; **remboursement** ✝ [~sə'mɑ̃] *m* reimbursement, repayment; *an-nuity, stock*: redemption; *livraison f contre* ~ *post*: cash on delivery; **rembourser** [~'se] (1a) *v/t.* reim-burse, repay; redeem *(stocks etc.)*.

rembrunir [rɑ̃bry'niːr] (2a) *v/t.*: *se* ~ darken; cloud over; become gloomy.

remède [rə'mɛd] *m* remedy, cure (for, *à*) *(a. fig.)*; *porter* ~ *à* remedy; *sans* ~ beyond remedy; **remédiable** [rəme'djabl] remediable; **remédier** [~'dje] (1o) *v/i.*: ~ *à* remedy, cure; ⚕ stop *(a leak)*.

remembrement *admin.* [rəmɑ̃brə-'mɑ̃] *m* regrouping of lands.

remémorer [rəmemɔ're] (1a) *v/t.* remind (s.o. of s.th., *qch. à q.*); *se* ~ call *(s.th.)* to mind.

remerciements [rəmɛrsi'mɑ̃] *m/pl.* thanks; **remercier** [~'sje] (1o) *v/t.* thank (for, *de*); dismiss *(an em-ployee)*; *je vous remercie* thank you.

remettre [rə'mɛtr] (4v) *v/t.* put *(s.th.)* back again, replace; *cost.* put *(s.th.)* on again; return; restore; *fig.* calm *(s.o.'s mind)*, reassure *(s.o.)*; ⚕ set *(a bone)*; deliver; hand over *(a. a command, an office)*; tender *(one's resignation)*; pardon *(an of-fence)*; remit *(a penalty, a. sins)*; ✝ give a discount of, allow; *fig.* post-pone; ~ *au hasard* leave to chance; F ~ *ça* begin again; ~ *en état* over-haul; *se* ~ return; *fig.* recover (from, *de*); *s'en* ~ *à q.* rely on s.o. (for, *de*); leave it to s.o.

réminiscence [remini'sɑ̃ːs] *f* remi-niscence.

remise [rə'miːz] *su./f* putting back; postponement; *thea.* revival; *point-er*, ⚞ *bone*: setting; ✝ remittance; ✝ discount (of, *de*; on, *sur*); restoration; *post*: delivery; *debt, penalty*: remission; *duties, office, ticket*: handing over; *coach-house*: 🚋 (*engine-*)shed; ~ *à neuf* renovation; ~ *de bagages* luggage (*Am.* baggage) reclaim; F *sous la* ~ on the shelf; *su./m* livery carriage; **remiser** [~mi'ze] (1a) *v/t.* put (*a vehicle*) away; lay (*s.th.*) aside; F *fig.* superannuate (*s.o.*); F snub (*s.o.*); *hunt.* se ~ take cover.

rémissible [remi'sibl] remissible; **rémission** [~'sjɔ̃] *f debt, sin*: remission; ⚕ abatement, remission; *sans* ~ unremitting(ly *adv.*).

rémittence ⚕ [remi'tãːs] *f* abatement, remission; **rémittent, e** [~'tã, ~'tãːt] remittent.

remmailler [rãma'je] (1a) *v/t. see* **remailler.**

remodelage [rəmɔd'laːʒ] *m* remodelling; reorganization; **remodeler** [~'le] (1d) remodel, reshape; reorganize.

remontage [rəmɔ̃'taːʒ] *m* going up; *furniture*: assembling; ⚓ ascending; ⊕ *machine etc.*: (re)assembling, refitting; ↑ *shop*: restocking; *wine*: fortifying; *clock*: winding up; *shoes*: vamping; *à* ~ *automatique* self-winding (*watch*); **remontant, e** [~'tã, ~'tãːt] **1.** *adj.* ascending; ↑ *etc.* stimulating, tonic; **2.** *su./m* ⚕ stimulant, tonic, F pick-me-up; **remonte** [rə'mɔ̃ːt] *f salmon*: ascent, running; *coll. fish*: run; ✕ *cavalry*: remount(ing); **remontée** [~mɔ̃'te] *f road*: climb; ✕ climbing; **remonte-pente** *mount.* [~mɔ̃t'pãːt] *m see* monte-pente; **remonter** [rə-mɔ̃'te] (1a) *v/i.* go up (again) (*a.* ↑); get (*into a car, on a horse, etc.*) again; rise (*barometer*); re-ascend (the throne, *sur le trône*); get higher (*sun*); *fig.* date *or* go back (to, *à*); ⚓ flow (*tide*), come round (*wind*); *v/t.* go up (again), climb up (again); raise (up); take (*s.th.*) up; pull up (*socks, trousers*); ✕ remount (*s.o.*); wind up (*a watch*); ⊕ reassemble; refit, reset; ↑ restock; *thea.* put (*a play*) on again; refurnish (*a house*); F *fig.* cheer (*s.o.*) up; se ~ recover one's strength *or* spirits; get in a new supply (of, *de*); **remontoir** ⊕ [~'twaːr] *m watch*: winder; *clock, watch*: key.

remontrance [rəmɔ̃'trãːs] *f* reprimand, reproof.

remontrer [rəmɔ̃'tre] (1a) *v/t.* show (again); point out; *v/i.: en* ~ *à q.* show *or* prove one knows better than s.o., prove one's superiority to s.o.

remordre [rə'mɔrdr] (4a) *v/t.* bite again; *v/i.:* ~ *à* take up *or* tackle again; **remords** [~'mɔːr] *m* remorse; twinge of conscience.

remorque [rə'mɔrk] *f* ⚓, *mot.* tow(ing); tow-rope; ⚓ vessel in tow; *mot.* trailer; *prendre en* ~ tow; *être en* ~ be on tow; **remorquer** [rəmɔr'ke] (1m) *v/t.* ⚓, *mot.* tow; pull; **remorqueur, -euse** [~'kœːr, ~'køːz] **1.** *adj.* towing; 🚋 relief (*engine*); **2.** *su./m* tug(boat); towboat.

rémoulade *cuis.* [remu'lad] *f* remoulade-sauce.

rémouleur ⊕ [remu'lœːr] *m* (*scissors-, etc.*)grinder.

remous [rə'mu] *m water, wind*: eddy; *tide*: swirl; *crowd*: movement; ⚓ *ship*: wash; *river*: rise in level; ✈ slip-stream.

rempailler [rãpa'je] (1a) *v/t.* re-seat (*a rush-bottomed chair*); re-stuff (*with straw*).

rempart [rã'paːr] *m* △ rampart; *fig.* bulwark.

rempiler [rãpi'le] (1a) *v/t.* pile up again; *v/i.* ✕ *sl.* re-engage, re-enlist.

remplaçant, e [rãpla'sã, ~'sãːt] *person*: substitute, deputy; ✕, *eccl.* locum tenens, F locum; **remplacement** [~plas'mã] *m* replacement; substitution; ... *de* ~ refill ...; spare ...; *en* ~ *de* in place of; **remplacer** [~pla'se] (1k) *v/t.* replace (by, *par*); take the place of; supersede (*an official, a rule*); appoint a successor to (*an official, a diplomat*); deputize for.

rempli *cost.* [rã'pli] *m dress*: tuck; *hem or seam*: turning; **remplier** *cost.* [~pli'e] (1a) *v/t.* put a tuck in (*a dress etc.*); lay (*a hem, a seam*).

remplir [rã'pliːr] (2a) *v/t.* fill (up), refill (with, *de*); *admin.* complete, fill in *or* up (*a form*); *fig.* fulfil (*a hope, a promise*), perform (*a duty*), comply with (*formalities*); *thea.* play (*a part*); se ~ fill; **remplissage** [~pli'saːʒ] *m* filling (up); ✕ infilling; △ *etc.* filling (in); *fig.* padding, F radio: fill-up.

remploi [rã'plwa] *m* re-use, using again; re-employment; ⚖ reinvestment; **remployer** [~plwa'je] (1h) *v/t.* re-use; use again; employ (*s.o.*) again; reinvest (*money*).

remplumer [rɑ̃ply'me] (1a) *v/t.*: se ~ F put on flesh again, get better, recover; F get back on one's feet (*financially*); *orn.* grow new feathers.

rempocher [rɑ̃pɔ'ʃe] (1a) *v/t.* put (*s.th.*) back in one's pocket.

remporter [rɑ̃pɔr'te] (1a) *v/t.* take *or* carry back; carry off *or* away; *fig.* win, gain (*a prize, a victory*).

rempoter ✔ [rɑ̃pɔ'te] (1a) repot.

remuage [rə'mɥaːʒ] *m* moving, removal; shaking (up), stirring (up); *wine*: settling of the deposit; **remuant, e** [~'mɥɑ̃, ~'mɥɑ̃ːt] restless; bustling; **remue-ménage** [~myme-'naːʒ] *m/inv.* bustle, commotion, stir; **remue-méninges** [~myme-'nɛːʒ] *m/inv.* brainstorming; **remuement** [~my'mɑ̃] *m* moving; *furniture, earth*: removal; *fig.* stir, commotion; **remuer** [~'mɥe] (1n) *v/t.* move (*furniture, one's head, a. fig. s.o.'s heart, etc.*); stir (*coffee, tea*); *fig.* stir up (*a crowd*); *dog*: wag (*its tail*); se ~ move, stir; bestir o.s., F get a move on; *v/i.* move; budge; be loose (*tooth*).

remugle [rə'myːgl] *m* musty smell.

rémunérateur, -trice [remynera-'tœːr, ~'tris] **1.** *adj.* remunerative; profitable; **2.** *su.* rewarder; **rémunération** [~ra'sjɔ̃] *f* remuneration, payment (for, de); **rémunératoire** ✶✶ [~ra'twaːr] for services rendered; (*money*) by way of recompense; **rémunérer** [~re] (1f) *v/t.* remunerate, reward; pay for (*services*).

renâcler [rənɑ'kle] (1a) *v/i.* snort (*horse*); sniff (*person*); *fig.* turn up one's nose (at, à); F *fig.* be reluctant; jib (at, à).

renaissance [rənɛ'sɑ̃ːs] *f* rebirth; revival; *art etc.*: ♀ Renaissance, Renascence; **renaître** [~'nɛːtr] (4x) *v/i.* be born again; *fig.* reappear; *fig.* revive (*arts, hope, etc.*).

rénal, e, *m/pl.* **-aux** ✶, *anat.* [re'nal, ~'no] renal; *calcul m* ~ renal calculus.

renard [rə'naːr] *m zo.* fox; ⊕ *sl.* strike-breaker, F blackleg; ⊕, ⚓ dog(-hook); F *fig. fin* ~ sly dog; **renarde** *zo.* [~'nard] *f* vixen, she-fox; **renardeau** *zo.* [rənar'do] *m* fox-cub; **renardière** [~'djɛːr] *f* fox-hole, fox's earth, burrow.

renchéri, e [rɑ̃ʃe'ri] **1.** *adj.* dearer; F particular, fastidious; **2.** *su.* fastidious person; *su./m*: *faire le* ~ be squeamish; put on airs; **renchérir** [~'riːr] (2a) *v/t.* raise the price of; *v/i.* get dearer, go up in price; ~ *sur* go one better than (*s.o.*); improve upon (*s.th.*); **renchérissement** [~ris'mɑ̃] *m* increase *or* rise in price; **renchérisseur** [~ri'sœːr] *m* outdoer; outbidder; ✝ runner up of prices.

rencogner F [rɑ̃kɔ'ɲe] (1a) *v/t.* drive *or* push (*s.o.*) into a corner; se ~ huddle (o.s.) up.

rencontre [rɑ̃'kɔ̃ːtr] *f* ⚔, *person, streams*: meeting; ⚔, *persons*: encounter; 🚗, *mot.* collision; ⚔ skirmish; *fig.* occasion; *aller à la* ~ de go to meet; *de* ~ casual; chance ...; **rencontrer** [~kɔ̃'tre] (1a) *v/t.* meet; 🚗, *mot.* collide with; *fig.* come across; find; ⚔ encounter; *fig.* meet with, come up against; se ~ meet; 🚗, *mot.* collide; *fig.* happen; *fig.* appear (*person*); *fig.* agree (*persons, ideas*).

rendement [rɑ̃d'mɑ̃] *m* ✔, ✝, ⚔ yield; ⊕ *works, men*: output; ⊕ efficiency (*a. of machines*); ⊕, ⚓, *mot.* performance; *sp. time*: handicap; ~ *maximum* maximum output *or* speed.

rendez-vous [rɑ̃de'vu] *m* rendezvous (*a.* ⚔); appointment, F date; meeting-place; haunt; ~ *social* collective bargaining.

rendormir [rɑ̃dɔr'miːr] (2b) *v/t.* put to sleep again; se ~ fall asleep again.

rendre [rɑ̃ːdr] (4a) *v/t.* return, give back; restore (*s.o.'s liberty, s.o.'s health*); give (*an account, change,* ✶✶ *a verdict*); pay (*homage*); *fig.* convey (*the meaning*), translate; render (✝ *an account, services*); ✶✶ pronounce (*judgment*); ♩ perform, play; ✝ deliver; ✝, ✔, ⊕ yield, produce; ⚔ surrender (*a fortress*); ✶ throw up, vomit; ~ (*adj.*) make (*adj.*); ~ *compte de* account for; *fig.* ~ *justice* à do (*s.o.*) justice; ✶✶ ~ *la justice* dispense justice; ~ *les derniers devoirs* à pay (*s.o.*) the last hono(u)rs; ~ *nul* nullify; vitiate (*a contract*); se ~ go (to, à); *fig.* yield, give way; ⚔ surrender; *v/i.* be productive *or fig.* profitable; ✶ vomit; work, run (*engine*); ~ *à* lead to (*way*); **rendu, e** [rɑ̃'dy] **1.** *adj.* arrived;

rendurcir

exhausted; **2.** *su./m* paint. *etc.* rendering; ✝ returned article; F *un prêté pour un ~* tit for tat.

rendurcir [rãdyr'siːr] (2a) *v/t. a. se ~* harden.

rêne [rɛn] *f* rein (*a. fig.*); *lâcher* ~*s* slacken the reins; *give a horse its head.* [gade, turncoat.]

renégat *m*, e *f* [rəne'ga, ~'gat] rene-)

rénette ⊕ [re'nɛt] *f* tracing-iron; *leather*: race-knife; *horse's hoof*: paring-knife.

renfermé, e [rãfɛr'me] **1.** *adj. fig.* uncommunicative; **2.** *su./m* fustiness; *odeur f de ~* fusty *or* stale smell; *sentir le ~* smell fusty *or* stuffy; **renfermer** [~] (1a) *v/t.* shut *or* lock up (again); enclose; *fig.* contain, include; *fig.* confine (to *dans, en*); *fig.* hide; *se ~ (dans, en)* confine o.s. (to); withdraw (into *o.s., silence*).

renflé, e [rã'fle] bulging, swelling; **renflement** [rãflə'mã] *m* bulging, bulge, swelling; **renfler** [~'fle] (1a) *v/t.* swell (out); *se~* bulge (out), swell (out).

renflouer [rãflu'e] (1a) *v/t.* ⚓ refloat; *fig.* put in funds.

renfoncement [rãfõs'mã] *m* knocking in (*of s.th.*) again; ⚠ recess, hollow; denting; *paint.* effect of depth; **renfoncer** [~fõ'se] (1k) *v/t.* knock *or* push (further) in; ⚠ recess, set back; dent; pull down (*one's hat*).

renforçateur *phot.* [rãfɔrsa'tœːr] *m* intensifier; **renforcement** [~sə-'mã] *m* ⚠, ✕ strengthening (*a. fig. opinion*); reinforcing; *phys. sound*: magnification; *phot.* intensification; **renforcer** [~'se] (1k) *v/t.* reinforce; ⊕ *a.* strengthen; increase (*the sound, the expenditure*); *phot.* intensify; *phys.* magnify; **renfort** [rã'fɔːr] *m* ✕, ⊕, *etc.* reinforcement(s *pl.*); *de ~* stiffening ...; *à grand~ de* with a great deal of.

renfrogné, e [rãfrɔ'ɲe] sullen, sulky; **renfrogner** [~] (1a) *v/t.: se ~* scowl; frown.

rengager [rãga'ʒe] (1l) *v/t.* re-engage; *v/i., a. se ~* ✕ re-enlist.

rengaine F [rã'gɛːn] *f* old refrain, (*the same*) old story; **rengainer** [~gɛ'ne] (1a) *v/t.* ✝ put up (*the sword*); F withhold, hold back, save.

rengorger [rãgɔr'ʒe] (1l) *v/t.: se ~* puff o.s. up, give o.s. airs.

rengraisser [rãgrɛ'se] (1a) *v/t.* fatten up again; *v/i.* grow fat again.

renier [rə'nje] (1o) *v/t. eccl.* deny; abjure (*one's faith*); disown (*a friend, an opinion*); repudiate (*an action, an opinion*).

reniflement [rəniflə'mã] *m* sniff(ing); **renifler** [~'fle] (1a) *v/t.* sniff (*s.th.*) (up); *fig.* scent; *v/i.* sniff; snivel (*child*); **renifleur** *m*, **-euse** *f* [~'flœːr, ~'fløːz] sniffer.

rénitence ✱ [reni'tãːs] *f* resistance to pressure; **rénitent, e** [~'tã, ~'tãːt] renitent.

renne *zo.* [rɛn] *m* reindeer.

renom [rə'nõ] *m* fame, renown; **renommé, e** [rənɔ'me] **1.** *adj.* famed, renowned, famous (for, *pour*); **2.** *su./f* fame, renown; reputation; *esp.* ✱ report; rumo(u)r; **renommer** [~] (1a) *v/t.* re-elect, re-appoint; ✝ praise.

renoncement [rənõs'mã] *m* renouncing; renunciation (*a.* ✱); *~ à soi-même* self-denial; **renoncer** [rə-nõ'se] (1k) *v/i.:~ à* give up, renounce, abandon; waive (*a claim, a right*); **renonciation** [~sja'sjõ] *f* renunciation.

renoncule ♀ [rənõ'kyl] *f* ranunculus; *~ âcre* crowfoot; buttercup.

renouement [rənu'mã] *m* renewal; **renouer** [~'e] (1a) *v/t.* re-knot; tie up again; *fig.* renew; resume (*a conversation*).

renouveau [rənu'vo] *m* spring (-time); renewal; *~ catholique* Catholic (literary) revival; **renouveler** [~nuv'le] (1c) *v/t.* renew; revive (*a custom, a lawsuit, a quarrel*); *fig.* transform; ✝ repeat (*an order*); *mot.* fit a new set of (*tyres*); *se ~* be renewed; happen again; **renouvellement** [~nuvɛl'mã] *m* renovation; replacement; renewal; *fig.* increase.

rénovateur, -trice [renɔva'tœːr, ~'tris] **1.** *adj.* renovating; **2.** *su.* renovator, restorer; **rénovation** [~'sjõ] *f* renovation, restoration; renewal; reform; (*religious*) revival; **rénover** [~'ve] (1a) *v/t.* renovate, restore; renew; reform.

renseigné, e [rãsɛ'ɲe] (well-)informed (about, *sur*); **renseignement** [~sɛɲ'mã] *m* (piece of) information; *teleph. ~s pl.* inquiries; *bureau m de ~s* information bureau *or Am.* booth, inquiry office;

prendre des ⁓s *sur* make inquiries about; ✗ *service m de* ⁓s Intelligence Corps; **renseigner** [⁓sɛ'ɲe] (1a) *v/t.* inform (*s.o.*), give (*s.o.*) information (about, *sur*); give (*s.o.*) directions; se ⁓ inquire, find out (about, *sur*).

rentabiliser [rɑ̃tabili'ze] (1a) *v/t.* make profitable, make pay; **rentabilité** [rɑ̃tabili'te] *f* profitableness; **rentable** [rɑ̃'tabl] profitable.

rente [rɑ̃:t] *f* revenue; annuity, pension; stock(s *pl.*), bonds *pl.*; ⁓s *pl.* (private) income *sg.*; ⁓ *foncière* ground rent; ⁓ *perpétuelle* perpetuity; ⁓ *viagère* life annuity; **rentier** *m*, **-ère** *f* [⁓'tje, ⁓'tjɛ:r] stockholder; annuitant; person living on private means; *petit* ⁓ small investor.

rentrant, e [rɑ̃'trɑ̃, ⁓'trɑ̃:t] 1. *adj.* ↗ re-entrant; ✂ retractable; ⊕ inset; 2. *su. sp.* new player; **rentré, e** [rɑ̃'tre] suppressed (*anger*); sunken (*eyes, cheecks*); **rentrée** [⁓] *f* return, home-coming; re-entry (*a.* ♪); ✍ *crops*: gathering; *school etc.*: reopening; *parl.* re-assembly; ✚ *taxes etc.*: collection; ✚ *money*: receipt; *air etc.*: entry; *actor etc.*: comeback; **rentrer** [⁓] (1a) *v/i.* re-enter (*a. thea., a.* ♪); come *or* go in (again); return; come *or* go home; re-open (*school etc.*); *parl.* re-assemble; go back to school (*child*); ✚ come in (*money*); ⁓ *dans* be included in, be part of; get back, recover (*rights etc.*); crash into (*a wall, car, etc.*); ⁓ *en fonctions* resume one's duties; *v/t.* take *or* bring *or* get *or* pull in; put away; ✍ gather in (*crops*); ✚ re-enter (*in an account*); *fig.* suppress (*a desire, one's tears*); ✂ retract (*the undercarriage*).

renversable [rɑ̃vɛr'sabl] reversible; capsizable (*boat etc.*); **renversant, e** F [⁓'sɑ̃, ⁓'sɑ̃:t] staggering, stunning; **renverse** [rɑ̃'vɛrs] *f* ⚓ *tide*: turn; *à la* ⁓ backwards; **renversement** [rɑ̃vɛrsə'mɑ̃] *m* reversal (*a. phys.*); ♪, *opt., phls., geol.* inversion; ⊕ reversing; ⚓ *tide*: turn(ing); *wind*: shift(ing); overturning; *fig.* disorder; *fig., a. pol.* overthrow; **renverser** [⁓'se] (1a) *v/t.* reverse (*a.* ✗, ♪, ⊕ an engine, the steam, *mot.*); ♪, *opt., phls.* invert; turn upside down; knock down; knock over; overturn, upset; spill; *fig., a.*

pol. overthrow; F *fig.* amaze; F ⁓ *les rôles* turn the tables; se ⁓ fall over; overturn; lie back (*in a chair*); *v/i.* F spill over.

renvoi [rɑ̃'vwa] *m* return(ing), sending back, sending back; *tennis*: return; *heat, light*: reflecting; ✂ belch; ♪ repeat (sign); *servant*: dismissal; adjournment; ⚖, *pol., typ.* reference; ⚖ transfer; ⚖ remand; **renvoyer** [⁓vwa'je] (1r) *v/t.* return (*a. tennis*), send back; throw back (*a ball, a sound*); reflect (*heat, light*); dismiss (*s.o.*); postpone; adjourn; *pol.* refer; ⚖ defer; ⚖ remand.

réoccuper [reɔky'pe] (1a) *v/t.* reoccupy.

réorganiser [reɔrgani'ze] (1a) *v/t.* reorganize.

réouverture [reuver'ty:r] *f* reopening; resumption.

repaire [rə'pɛ:r] *m animals, a. fig.*: den; *fig. criminal*: haunt; hideout.

repaître [rə'pɛːtr] (4k) *v/t.* feed (*a. fig.*); se ⁓ eat one's fill; se ⁓ *de* feed on; *fig.* indulge in (*vain hopes*); wallow in (*blood*).

répandre [re'pɑ̃:dr] (4a) *v/t.* spill, shed; spread (*light, news*); scatter (*flowers, money, sand, etc.*); give off (*heat, a smell*); il s'est répandu que the rumo(u)r has spread that; *fig.* se ⁓ go out, be seen in society; **répandu, e** [⁓pɑ̃'dy] widespread, widely held (*opinion*); well known.

réparable [repa'rabl] reparable; *cost.* repairable; remediable.

reparaître [rəpa'rɛːtr] (4k) *v/i.* reappear; ✂ recur.

réparateur, -trice [repara'tœːr, ⁓'tris] 1. *adj.* repairing; restoring; 2. *su.* repairer; repairman; **réparation** [⁓ra'sjɔ̃] *f* repair(ing); *fig.* amends *pl.*; (*legal*) redress; ✗, ⁓s *pl.* reparations; ⚖ ⁓ *civile* compensation; *foot. coup m de pied de* ⁓ penalty kick; **réparer** [⁓'re] (1a) *v/t.* mend, repair, *Am.* fix; *fig.* make good (*losses, wear*); *fig.* make amends for, put (*s.th.*) right.

repartie [rəpar'ti] *f* repartee; retort; ⁓ *spirituelle* witty rejoinder; *avoir de la* ⁓, *avoir la* ⁓ *facile* be quick at repartee; **repartir** [⁓'tiːr] (2b) *v/i.* set out *or* leave again; retort, reply.

répartir [repar'tiːr] (2a) *v/t.* share out, distribute (amongst, *entre*);

admin. assess; ✝ allot (*shares*); **répartition** [ˌti'sjɔ̃] *f* distribution (*a.* ⚡); apportionment, division, sharing out; *errors*: frequency; *admin.* assessment; allocation; ✝ allotment.

repas [rə'pɑ] *m* meal; *petit* ∼ snack.

repassage [rəpɑ'saːʒ] *m* repassing; *water, mountains*: recrossing; *clothes*: ironing; *lessons*: revision; ⊕ sharpening; **repasser** [∼'se] (1a) *v/i.* pass again; call again (on s.o., *chez* q.); cross over again (to, en); *v/t.* repass; cross (*the sea etc.*) again; iron (*clothes*); go over (*in the mind, a lesson, an outline, accounts, etc.*); take (*s.o.*) back; ⊕ sharpen, whet; *fer m à* ∼ iron; **repasseur** [∼'sœ:r] *m* (*knife- etc.*)grinder; ⊕ examiner; **repasseuse** [∼'søːz] *f* woman, *a.* machine: ironer.

repayer [rəpɛ'je] (1i) *v/t.* repay; pay back.

repêchage [rəpe'ʃaːʒ] *m* fishing up *or* out; *fig.* giving a helping hand (to, de); *univ., school*: supplementary examination, ✝ resit; **repêcher** [∼'ʃe] (1a) *v/t.* fish up *or* out; *fig.* come to the rescue of, help (s.o.) out; give (s.o.) a second chance; *school*: let (s.o.) through, give (s.o.) a chance to scrape through.

repeindre [rə'pɛ̃:dr] (4m) *v/t.* repaint.

repenser [rəpɑ̃'se] (1a) *v/i.* think again (about, of à); *y* ∼ think it over.

repentant, e [rəpɑ̃'tɑ̃, ∼'tɑ̃:t] repentant; **repenti, e** [∼'ti] *adj., a. su.* repentant, penitent; **repentir** [∼'ti:r] **1.** (2b) *v/t.*: se ∼ (*de* qch.) repent ([of] s.th.), be sorry (for s.th.); **2.** *su./m* repentance.

repérage [rəpe'raːʒ] *m* marking with guide *or* reference marks; locating.

répercussion [repɛrky'sjɔ̃] *f* repercussion; consequences *pl.*; *phys. sound*: reverberation; **répercuter** [∼'te] (1a) *v/t.* reverberate; send *or* throw back, reflect (*heat, light, etc., a. fig.*); *fig.* pass on (*costs etc.*) (to, sur); se ∼ *phys.* reverberate; *fig.* have repercussions.

repère [rə'pɛ:r] *m* (reference *or* guide) mark; *surv.* benchmark; *cin.* synchronizing mark; *point m de* ∼ landmark (*a. fig.*); **repérer** [∼pe're] (1f) *v/t.* mark with guide *or* reference marks; fix *or* adjust by guide marks;

✖, ⚓ *etc.* locate; spot; se ∼ get *or* take one's bearings.

répertoire [repɛr'twa:r] *m* index, list; *thea., a. fig.* repertory; *thea.* repertoire; *fig.* ∼ *vivant* mine of information.

repeser [rəpə'ze] (1d) *v/t.* re-weigh.

répéter [repe'te] (1f) *v/t.* repeat; do *or* say again; con (*a lesson, thea. a part*); *thea.* rehearse (*a play*); *mirror*: reflect; **répéteur** [∼'tœ:r] *m teleph.* repeater; *phys.* reflector; reproducer; **répétiteur, -trice** [∼ti'tœ:r, ∼'tris] *su.* private tutor; *su./m school*: assistant-master; ⚓ repeating ship; *teleph.* repeater; *su./f school*: assistant-mistress; **répétition** [∼ti'sjɔ̃] *f* repetition; recurrence; private lesson; *thea.* rehearsal; *picture etc.*: reproduction, replica; *thea.* ∼ *générale* dress rehearsal; ✖ *fusil m à* ∼ repeating rifle; *montre f à* ∼ repeater (watch).

repeupler [rəpœ'ple] (1a) *v/t.* repeople; ⚘ replant; restock (*a pond, a river, etc.*).

repiquer [rəpi'ke] (1m) *v/t.* prick (s.th.) again; repair (*a road*); *cost.* restitch; ⚘ prick *or* plant out; *sl.* catch *or* F nab again; *v/i.*: F ∼ *au plat* have a second helping; F ∼ *au truc* begin again.

répit [re'pi] *m* respite; F *fig.* breather; *sans* ∼ incessant(ly *adv.*).

replacer [rəpla'se] (1k) *v/t.* replace; ✝ reinvest; find a new position for (*a servant*).

replanter [rəplɑ̃'te] (1a) *v/t.* replant.

replâtrer [rəplɑ'tre] (1a) *v/t.* ⚑ re-plaster; *fig.* patch up.

replet, -ète [rə'plɛ, ∼'plɛt] stoutish; **réplétion** [reple'sjɔ̃] *f* repletion.

repli [rə'pli] *m cost.* fold (*a. of ground*), crease; *rope, snake*: coil; *river*: bend, winding; ✖ falling back; **repliable** [rəpli'abl] folding; collapsible (*boat, chair*); **repliement** [∼'mɑ̃] *m* re-folding, turning up; bending back; ✖ falling back; *fig.* withdrawal (into o.s.); **replier** [∼'e] (1a) *v/t. a.* se ∼ fold up; coil up; bend back; ✖ withdraw (*outposts*); se ∼ ✖ fall back; *fig.* retire (within o.s., sur soi-même).

réplique [re'plik] *f* rejoinder, retort; *thea.* cue; *work of art etc.*: replica; *cin.* retake; ♪ *counterpoint*: answer; *fig. sans* ∼ unanswerable (*argument*);

répliquer [~pli'ke] (1m) *v/i.* retort; answer back.

reploiement [rəplwa'mã] *m see repliement.*

répondant [repɔ̃'dã] *m* ⚖ surety, guarantor; *eccl.* server; *servir de* ~ *à q.* stand surety for s.o.; F *avoir du* ~ have money behind one, *a. fig.* have something to fall back on; **répondeur** *teleph.* [~'dœːr] *m* (*a.* ~ *téléphonique*) answering machine; **répondre** [~'pɔ̃ːdr] (4a) *v/t.* answer, reply; *eccl.* make the responses at (*mass*); *v/i.* ⊕ etc., *a. fig.* respond; ~ *à* answer; comply with, satisfy; correspond to, match; ~ *de* answer for; be responsible for; guarantee; **réponse** [~'pɔ̃ːs] *f* answer, reply; *phys., physiol., a. fig.* response; *options:* declaration; ⚖~*s pl. de droit* judicial decisions; ~ *payée* reply paid.

report [rə'pɔːr] *m* ✝ carrying forward; ✝ amount carried forward; transfer; postponement; **reportage** *journ.* [rəpɔr'taːʒ] *m* report(ing); article, story; coverage; (live) commentary.

reporter[1] [rəpɔr'te] (1a) *v/t.* carry or take back; transfer (*a. phot.*), transmit; ✝ carry forward; ✝ *Stock Exchange:* continue; *fig.* postpone (to, until *à*).

reporter[2] *journ.* [rəpɔr'tɛːr] *m* reporter; ~ *sportif* sports reporter *or* commentator.

repos [rə'po] *m* rest, repose; peace (*of mind etc.*); ♪ pause; resting-place; *stair:* landing; ✕ ~! stand easy!; *au* ~ at rest (*a. machine*); still; **reposé, e** [~po'ze] **1.** *adj.* rested, refreshed; restful, quiet; fresh (*complexion*); *à tête* ~*e* at leisure; deliberately; **2.** *su./f animal:* lair; **repose-pied** [~poz'pje] *m/inv.* foot-rest; **reposer** [rəpo'ze] (1a) *v/t.* place, put, lay; 🚄 re-lay (*a track*); *fig.* rest; ✕ *reposez armes!* order arms!; *se* ~ (take a) rest; rely ([up]on, *sur*); settle (*bird, wine, etc.*); *fig. se* ~ *sur ses lauriers* rest on one's laurels; *v/i.* lie, rest; be at rest; *fig.* ~ *sur* rest on, be based on; *ici repose* here lies; **reposoir** *eccl.* [~'zwaːr] *m* temporary altar, station.

repoussant, e [rəpu'sã, ~'sãːt] repulsive; offensive, obnoxious (*odour*); **repousser** [~'se] (1a) *v/t.* push back *or* away, repel; ✕, *a. fig.*

repulse (*an attack, an offer*); *pol., a. fig.* reject (*a bill, overtures*); ⊕ chase (*metal*), emboss (*leather*); *v/i.* ⚘ shoot (up) again; grow again (*hair*); recoil (*gun*); resist (*spring*); **repoussoir** [~'swaːr] *m* cuticle remover; *paint.* strong piece of foreground; *fig.* foil.

répréhensible [repreã'sibl] reprehensible; **répréhension** [~'sjɔ̃] *f* reprehension.

reprendre [rə'prãːdr] (4aa) *v/t.* take again; recapture; get (*s.th.*) back; pick (*s.o.*) up (again); *fig.* recover (*senses, strength, taste, tongue*); take back (*an object, a gift, a promise, a servant, etc.*); resume (*a talk, one's work*); repeat (*an operation*); *thea.* revive (*a play*); *fig.* catch (*cold,* F *s.o.*) again; *fig.* reprove (*s.o.*); put on again (*one's summer clothes*); *v/i.* begin again; ⚘, ✝ improve; ⚕ heal again (*wound*); ⚘ take root (again); set again (*liquid*); reply; come in again (*fashion*).

représailles [rəpre'zaːj] *f/pl.* reprisal(s *pl.*) *sg.*; *user de* ~ make reprisals.

représentable [rəprezã'tabl] representable; *thea.* performable; **représentant, e** [~'tã, ~'tãːt] **1.** *adj.* representative; **2.** *su.* representative; *su./m* ✝ agent, traveller; ~ *exclusif de* sole agent for; **représentatif, -ve** [~ta'tif, ~'tiːv] representative (of, de); **représentation** [~ta'sjɔ̃] *f* ⚖, *paint., pol., fig.* representation; *thea.* performance, show; ✝ agency; *admin.* official entertainment; *fig.* protest; **représenter** [~'te] (1a) *v/t.* re-present; ⚖, ✝, *pol., fig.* represent; stand for; symbolize; *thea.* perform, give (*a play*), take the rôle of (*a character*); *paint.* depict, portray; *fig.* describe (as, *comme*); introduce (*s.o.*) again; recall (*s.o.*); point (*s.th.*) out (to, *à*); *fig. se* ~ *qch.* imagine *or* picture s.th.; *v/i.* have a good presence; keep up appearances.

répressif, -ve [repre'sif, ~'siːv] repressive; **répression** [~'sjɔ̃] *f* repression.

réprimable [repri'mabl] repressible.

réprimandable [reprimã'dabl] deserving (of) censure; **réprimande**

[~'mã:d] *f* reprimand, rebuke; **ré-primander** [~mã'de] (1a) *v/t.* reprimand, rebuke, reprove (for, de).

réprimer [repri'me] (1a) *v/t.* re-press.

repris, e [rə'pri, ~'pri:z] 1. *p.p. of re-prendre*; 2. *adj.* recaptured; 3. *su./m*: ~ *de justice* old offender; habitual criminal; F old lag, *Am.* repeater; *su./f* recapture, recovery; *talks, work*: resumption; *thea. play,* ✝ *business*: revival; *box.* round; *foot.* second half; ♪ repetition; *fig.* renewal; ⚡ fresh attack; *mot. engine*: pick-up; *cost.* darn(ing), mend(ing); repairing, mending; ~*e perdue* invisible mending; *à plusieurs* ~*es* again and again; on several occasions; ✝ *valeur f de* ~ trade-in value; ✝ *prendre qch. en* ~ take s.th. as a trade-in; **repriser** [~pri'ze] (1a) *v/t.* mend, darn; **repriseuse** [~'zø:z] *f* mender, darner.

réprobateur, -trice [reprɔba'tœ:r, ~'tris] reproachful; reproving; **ré-probation** [~'sjɔ̃] *f* reprobation, censure; *fig.* (howl of) protest.

reprochable [rəprɔ'ʃabl] reproach-able, blameworthy; **reproche** [~-'prɔʃ] *m* reproach; reproof; *sans* ~ blameless, unimpeachable; **repro-cher** [~prɔ'ʃe] (1a) *v/t.*: ~ *qch. à q.* reproach *or* blame s.o. for s.th.; grudge s.o. s.th.

reproducteur, -trice [rəprɔdyk-'tœ:r, ~'tris] 1. *adj.* reproductive; 2. *su./m* stud animal; **reproduc-tible** [~'tibl] reproducible; **repro-duction** [~'sjɔ̃] *f* ⚕, *zo., etc.* reproduction; ✝ reproducing; copy; replica; ⚖ *droits m/pl. de* ~ copyright *sg.*; **reproduire** [rəprɔ'dɥi:r] (4h) *v/t.* reproduce; produce (*s.th.*) again; copy; *se* ~ *fig.* recur; *zo. etc.* reproduce, breed.

reprographie [rəpɔgra'fi] *f* repro-graphy; **reprographier** [~'fje] (1o) *v/t.* reproduce, copy.

réprouvable [repru'vabl] blama-ble; blameworthy; **réprouvé, e** [~'ve] *su.* outcast; *su./m*: *eccl. les* ~*s pl.* the damned; **réprouver** [~'ve] (1a) *v/t.* reprobate (*a. eccl.*); *fig.* disapprove of; *eccl.* damn.

reps *tex.* [rɛps] *m* rep.

reptile *zo.* [rɛp'til] *adj., a. su./m* reptile.

repu, e [rə'py] 1. *p.p. of repaître*; 2. *adj.* satiated, full.

républicain, e [repybli'kɛ̃, ~'kɛn] *adj., a. su.* republican; **république** [~'blik] *f* republic (*a. fig.*).

répudier [repy'dje] (1o) *v/t.* repu-diate (*an opinion, one's wife*); ⚖ relinquish (*a succession*).

répugnance [repy'ɲɑ̃:s] *f* repug-nance; dislike (of, to *pour*); loath-ing (of, for *pour*); *fig.* reluctance (to *inf., à inf.*); *avec* ~ reluctantly; **répugnant, e** [~'ɲɑ̃, ~'ɲɑ̃:t] repug-nant, loathsome, disgusting; **répu-gner** [~'ɲe] (1a) *v/i.*: ~ *à q.* be re-pugnant to s.o., disgust s.o.; ~ *à faire qch.* be loath to do s.th.; *il me répugne de* (*inf.*) I am loath *or* reluctant to (*inf.*).

répulsif, -ve [repyl'sif, ~'si:v] re-pulsive; **répulsion** *phys., a. fig.* [~'sjɔ̃] *f* repulsion (for, *pour*).

réputation [repyta'sjɔ̃] *f* reputation, F character; (*good or bad*) name; *connaître q. de* ~ know s.o. by repu-tation; **réputer** [~'te] (1a) *v/t.* think, consider, hold.

requérant, e ⚖ [rəke'rɑ̃, ~'rɑ̃:t] 1. *su.* plaintiff; petitioner; appli-cant; 2. *adj.*: *partie f* ~*e* applicant; petitioner; claimant; **requérir** [~ke'ri:r] (2l) *v/t.* ask (for); claim, demand; *fig.* require; ⚔ requisi-tion; call upon (*s.o.*) for help; **re-quête** [~'kɛt] *f* request, petition; demand; ⚖ ~ *civile* appeal against a judgment.

requin *icht.* [rə'kɛ̃] *m* shark (*a.* F = *swindler*).

requis, e [rə'ki, ~'ki:z] 1. *adj.* re-quired, necessary, requisite; 2. *p.p. of requérir*; 3. *su./m* labo(u)r con-script.

réquisition [rekizi'sjɔ̃] *f* requisi-tion(ing) (*a.* ⚔); levy; demand; **réquisitionner** [~sjɔ'ne] (1a) *v/t.* requisition; seize, commandeer; **réquisitoire** ⚖ [~'twa:r] *m* charge, indictment.

rescapé, e [rɛska'pe] 1. *adj.* rescued; 2. *su.* survivor; rescued person.

rescinder ⚖ [rɛsɛ̃'de] (1a) *v/t.* re-scind, annul; avoid (*a contract*); **rescision** ⚖ [~si'sjɔ̃] *f* rescission, annulment; *contract*: avoiding.

rescousse [rɛs'kus] *f*: *aller* (*venir*) *à la* ~ *de* go (come) to the rescue of.

réseau [re'zo] *m* 🕸, *teleph., roads,*

lace, a. fig.: network; *teleph., fig.* area (served); ⚡ mains *pl.*; 🚗, *rivers, roads*: system; ✂ barbed wire *etc.*: entanglement; *opt.* diffraction grating; *anat. nerves*: plexus.

résection 🩺 [resek'sjɔ̃] *f* resection.

réséda ♀ [reze'da] *m* reseda.

réséquer 🩺 [rese'ke] (1s) *v/t.* resect.

réservation [rezerva'sjɔ̃] *f* reservation; 🚗 ~ *faite de* without prejudice to; **réserve** [~'zɛrv] *f* 🚗, 🚗, *eccl., a. fig.* reservation; ⚔, ⚓, ✝, 🚗, *pol.*, provisions, ⊕ *power*: reserve; *fig.* caution; 🚗 *(legal)* portion; ⚔ *officier m de* ~ reserve officer; *fig. sans* ~ unreserved(ly *adv.*), unstinted *(praise)*; 🚗 *sous* ~ without prejudice; *sous* ~ *de* subject to; **réservé, e** [rezɛr've] reserved; cautious; stand-offish; shy; 🚗 *tous droits* ~*s* all rights reserved; **réserver** [~'ve] (1a) *v/t.* reserve; set *(s.th.)* aside; save *(s.th.)* up; set apart *(money for a specific purpose)*; **réserviste** ⚔ [~'vist] *m* reservist; **réservoir** [~'vwa:r] *m* reservoir; container; *(fish-)*pond; ⊕, *mot.* tank; ⊕ *(grease-)*box, ✂, *mot.* ~ *de secours* reserve tank.

résidant, e [rezi'dɑ̃, ~'dɑ̃:t] resident; *eccl.* residentiary; **résidence** [~'dɑ̃:s] *f* residence; residential flats *pl.*; ~ *principale (secondaire)* main (second) home; **résident** *admin.* [~'dɑ̃] *m* resident; **résidentiel, -elle** [~dɑ̃'sjɛl] residential *(quarter)*; **résider** [~'de] (1a) *v/i.* live, dwell, reside (at, *à*; in, *dans*); *fig.* lie (in *dans, en*); **résidu** [~'dy] *m* 🔬, ⊕, 𝔸 residue; 𝔸 remainder.

résignation 🚗, *eccl. etc., a. fig.* [reziɲa'sjɔ̃] *f* resignation; **résigné, e** [~'ɲe] resigned (to, *à*); meek; **résigner** [~'ɲe] (1a) *v/t.* resign *(s.th.)*; give *(s.th.)* up; ~ *le pouvoir* abdicate *(king)*; lay down office; *se* ~ resign o.s. (to, *à*).

résilier 🚗 [rezi'lje] (1o) *v/t.* cancel, annul; terminate *(a contract)*.

résille [re'zi:j] *f* hair-net.

résine [re'zin] *f* resin; **résineux, -euse** [~zi'nø, ~'nø:z] resinous; coniferous *(forest)*.

résistance [rezis'tɑ̃:s] *f* ⚡, ⊕, ⚔, *pol., fig.* resistance; ⊕ *materials*: strength; *fig.* opposition; *fig.* stamina, endurance; *pol.* ♀ underground movement; ⚡ ~ *de fuite de grille*

radio: grid-leak; *faire* ~ offer *or* put up resistance; **résistant, e** [~'tɑ̃, ~'tɑ̃:t] **1.** *adj.* resistant; strong; tough; fast *(colour)*; hard-wearing; ⊕ *très* ~ *a.* heavy-duty ...; ~ *à la chaleur* heat-proof; **2.** *su. pol.* member of the *Résistance (1939—45 war)*; **résister** [~'te] (1a) *v/i.*: ~ *à* resist; ⚓ *weather (a storm)*; ⊕ *take (a stress)*; *fig.* bear; hold out against.

résolu, e [rezɔ'ly] **1.** *adj.* resolute; determined (to, *à*); **2.** *p.p. of* résoudre; **résolus** [~] *1st p. sg. p.s. of* résoudre; **résolutif, -ve** 🩺 [rezɔly'tif, ~'ti:v] *adj. a. su./m* resolvent; **résolution** [~'sjɔ̃] *f* 🔬, 𝔸, ♪, *admin., a. fig.* resolution; *fig.* resolve, determination; 🚗 *contract*: avoidance; termination; *prendre la* ~ *de* determine to; *admin. prendre une* ~ pass a resolution; **résolutoire** 🚗 [~'twa:r] *(condition)* of avoidance; **résolvons** [rezɔl'vɔ̃] *1st p. pl. pres. of* résoudre.

résonance [rezɔ'nɑ̃:s] *f* resonance; *radio a.* tuning; **résonnement** [~zɔn'mɑ̃] *m* resounding, reverberation, re-echoing; **résonner** [~zɔ'ne] (1a) *v/i.* resound, reverberate, ring; be resonant *(room)*; echo *(sound)*.

résorber 🩺 [rezɔr'be] (1a) *v/t.* re-(ab)sorb; **résorption** 🩺 [~zɔrp'sjɔ̃] *f* re(ab)sorption.

résoudre [re'zudr] (4bb) *v/t.* resolve *(a. ♪ a dissonance, a difficulty)*; 𝔸 solve *(a. fig. a problem)*; *fig.* decide on; settle *(a question)*; 🚗 rescind, avoid; *se* ~ *à (inf.)* decide to *(inf.)*, make up one's mind to *(inf.)*; **résous** 🔬 [~'zu] *p.p./m of* résoudre.

respect [rɛs'pɛ] *m* respect; ~ *de soi* self-respect; *sauf votre* ~ with all (due) respect; *saving your presence*; *tenir q. en* ~ keep s.o. at arm's length or in check; **respectable** [rɛspɛk-'tabl] respectable *(a. fig.)*; *fig. a.* fair-sized, sizeable; **respecter** [~'te] (1a) *v/t.* respect; *se* ~ have self-respect; **respectif, -ve** [~'tif, ~'ti:v] respective; **respectueux, -euse** [~'tɥø, ~'tɥø:z] respectful (towards, *envers*; of, *de*); dutiful *(child)*.

respirable [rɛspi'rabl] respirable; **respiration** [~ra'sjɔ̃] *f* respiration, breathing; **respiratoire** [~ra'twa:r] breathing; respiratory; *exercice m* ~ breathing exercise; **respirer** [~'re] (1a) *v/i.* breathe; *fig.* breathe again;

fig. take breath, get one's breath; *v/t.* breathe (in), inhale; *fig.* radiate, exude.

resplendir [rɛsplã'diːr] (2a) *v/i.* be resplendent, glitter (with, *de*); *fig.* glow (with, *de*); **resplendissant, e** [~di'sã, ~'sãːt] resplendent; **resplendissement** [~dis'mã] *m* splendo(u)r, resplendence, brightness.

responsabilité [rɛspõsabili'te] *f* responsibility, liability (*a.* ⚖️) (for, *de*); accountability; ⚖️ ~ *civile* civil liability; **responsable** [~'sabl] responsible, accountable (for s.th., *de qch.*; for s.o., *pour q.*; to *devant, envers*); *rendre q.* ~ *de* hold s.o. responsible for, blame s.o. for.

resquiller F [rɛski'je] (1a) *v/i.* get in on the sly; fiddle a free ride; *v/t.* avoid paying for.

ressac ⚓ [rə'sak] *m* backwash, undertow; surf.

ressaisir [rəsɛ'ziːr] (2a) *v/t.* recapture, seize again; recover possession of; *se* ~ recover o.s.; recover one's balance.

ressasser [rəsɑ'se] (1a) *v/t.* repeat (*a story etc.*) over and over; keep going back over (*a story etc.*); keep turning over (*memories etc.*).

ressaut [rə'so] *m* ⚙️ projection; shelf (*along a track*); *geol.* rockstep; *geog.* sharp rise.

ressemblance [rəsã'blãːs] *f* likeness; resemblance (to, *avec*); **ressemblant, e** [~'blã, ~'blãːt] lifelike, true to life; **ressembler** [~'ble] (1a) *v/i.:* ~ *à* resemble, look like; *ils se ressemblent* they are alike.

ressemeler [rəsəm'le] (1c) *v/t.* re-sole (*a shoe*).

ressentiment [rəsãti'mã] *m* resentment (against, *contre*; at, *de*); *avec* ~ resentfully; **ressentir** [~'tiːr] (2b) *v/t.* feel, experience (*an emotion, pain, etc.*); resent (*an insult etc.*); *fig. se* ~ *de* feel the (after)effects of.

resserre [rə'sɛr] *f* shed; **resserré, e** [rəsɛ're] narrow, confined; **resserrement** [~sɛr'mã] *m* contraction; tightening; closing up; narrowness; **resserrer** [~sɛ're] (1b) *v/t.* (*a. se* ~) tighten (up); contract; close (up); *se* ~ *a.* narrow, grow narrow(er); *se* ~ *autour de* close in on.

ressort¹ [rə'sɔːr] *m* elasticity; ⊕ spring; *fig.* incentive, motive; ~ *à boudin* (*à lames*) spiral (laminated)

spring; *faire* ~ act as a spring; be elastic; *fig. faire jouer tous les* ~s leave no stone unturned.

ressort² [~] *m* ⚖️ competence, jurisdiction; *fig.* scope; *en dernier* ~ ⚖️ without appeal; *fig.* in the last resort.

ressortir¹ [rəsɔr'tiːr] (2b) *v/i.* go *or* come out again; *fig.* stand out, be thrown into relief; *fig.* result, follow (from, *de*); *v/t.* bring *or* take out again.

ressortir² [rəsɔr'tiːr] (2a) *v/i.* ⚖️ be within the jurisdiction (of, *à*); *fig.* pertain (to, *à*); **ressortissant** *m*, -e *f* [~ti'sã, ~'sãːt] national (*of a country*), subject.

ressource [rə'surs] *f* resource(fulness); expedient; ⚔️ pull-out; ~s *pl.* resources, means; funds; *en dernière* ~ in the last resort.

ressouvenir [rəsuv'niːr] (2h) *v/t.:* *se* ~ *de* remember, recall.

ressuer [rə'sɥe] (1n) *v/i.* 🔺, *metall.* sweat; ⊕ *faire* ~ roast (*ore*).

ressusciter [resysi'te] (1a) *vt/i.* resuscitate, revive; *v/t.* raise from the dead; *v/i.* rise from the dead.

restant, e [rɛs'tã, ~'tãːt] 1. *adj.* remaining, left; ⚖️ surviving; 2. *su.* survivor; *su./m* remainder, rest; ♦ *account:* balance.

restaurant [rɛsto'rã] *m* restaurant; *manger au* ~ eat out; **restaurateur, -trice** [~ra'tœːr, ~'tris] *su.* restorer; *su./m* restaurateur, keeper of a restaurant; **restauration** [~ra'sjõ] *f* restoration; **restaurer** [~'re] (1a) *v/t.* restore; 🎨 *etc.* set (*s.o.*) up again; *se* ~ take refreshment; 🎨 feed up.

reste [rɛst] *m* rest, remainder, remnant(s *pl.*); ~s *pl.* ♦, *cuis.* remnants, leavings; left-overs; mortal remains; *au* ~, *du* ~ moreover; *de* ~ (*time, money, etc.*) to spare; *en* ~ ♦ in arrears; *fig.* indebted (to, *avec*); **rester** [rɛs'te] (1a) *v/i.* remain; be left (behind); stay; *en* ~ *là* leave it at that; (*il*) *reste à savoir si* it remains to be seen whether.

restituable [rɛsti'tɥabl] repayable; restorable; **restituer** [~'tɥe] (1n) *v/t.* restore (*a text, s.th. to s.o.*); return; restitute; ⚖️ reinstate (*s.o.*).

restitution [~ty'sjõ] *f* restoration (*of a text, a. of s.th. to s.o.*); ⚖️ restitution; return.   [side restaurant.)

restoroute (*TM*) [rɛsto'rut] *m* road-⌇

restreindre [rɛs'trɛ̃:dr] (4m) *v/t.* restrict, limit, cut down; *fig. se ~ à* limit o.s. to; **restrictif, -ve** [~trik-'tif, ~'ti:v] restrictive; **restriction** [~trik'sjɔ̃] *f* restriction (*a. fig.*); limitation; *fig. ~ mentale* mental reservation; **restringent, e** [~trɛ̃'ʒã, ~'ʒã:t] *adj., a. su./m* astringent.

restructurer [rəstrykty're] (1a) *v/t.* restructure.

résultante ⚡, *phys.* [rezyl'tã:t] *f* resultant; **résultat** [~'ta] *m* result (*a.* ⚡), issue; effect; *avoir pour ~* result in; **résulter** [~'te] (1a) *v/i.* (*3rd persons only*) result, follow (from, *de*); *il en résulte que* it follows that.

résumé [rezy'me] *m* summary, précis; *en ~* to sum up, in short; **résumer** [~] (1a) *v/t.* summarize; sum up (⚡, *arguments*, etc.); *se ~* sum up; *fig.* amount, F boil down (to, *à*).

résurrection [rezyrɛk'sjɔ̃] *f* resurrection; *fig.* revival.

retable ⚛, *eccl.* [rə'tabl] *m* reredos, altar-piece.

rétablir [reta'bli:r] (2a) *v/t.* re-establish, restore (*a.* ✕); reinstate (*an official*); ⚕ recover (*one's health*); *fig.* retrieve (*one's fortune, a position, one's reputation*); *se ~* recover (*a.* ⚕); ✝ revive; **rétablissement** [~blis'mã] *m* re-establishment; restoration; reinstatement; ⚕ recovery (*a. fig.*); ✝ revival.

retailler [rəta'je] (1a) *v/t.* recut (*a.* ⊕); resharpen (*a pencil*); prune (*a tree*) again.

rétamé, e F [reta'me] worn out; stoned (= *drunk*); broke; bust(ed); **rétamer** ⊕ [~'me] (1a) *v/t.* re-tin; re-coat; F *fig.* clean (*s.o.*) out; **rétameur** [~'mœ:r] *m* tinker.

retaper F [rəta'pe] *v/t.* touch up, recast; straighten (*a bed*); retrim (*a hat* etc.); *fig.* restore (*s.o.*); F buck (*s.o.*) up; plough (*a candidate*); *se ~* recover; F buck up.

retard [rə'ta:r] *m* delay; lateness; *child, harvest:* backwardness; ⚡, ⊕, ♣ lag; ♪ suspension; *être en ~* be late; be slow (*clock* etc.); be behind (with, *dans or pour*); be backward; *être en ~ sur* be behind (*the fashion, the times*); *ma montre est en ~ de cinq minutes* my watch is 5 minutes slow; **retardataire** [rətarda'tɛ:r] **1.** *adj.* late; ✝ backward in arrears; behindhand; backward

(*child, country,* etc.); **2.** *su.* latecomer; laggard; ✝ etc. person in arrears; ✕, ♣ defaulter; **retardadeur, -trice** [~'tœ:r, ~'tris] retarding; **retardation** *phys.* [~'sjɔ̃] *f* retardation, negative acceleration; **retardement** [rətardə'mã] *m* delay; retarding; F *à ~* after the event, afterwards; *bombe f à ~* delayed-action bomb; **retarder** [~'de] (1a) *v/t.* delay, retard; make late; defer (*an event, payment*); put back (*a clock*); *v/i.* be late; be slow, lose (*clock*); ⚡, ♣ lag; *~ sur son temps* be behind the times.

reteindre [rə'tɛ̃:dr] (4m) *v/t.* redye.

retéléphoner [rətelefɔ'ne] (1a) *v/i.: ~ (à q.)* phone (s.o.) again, call (s.o.) back.

retenir [rət'ni:r] (2h) *v/t.* hold back; detain (*s.o.*); keep; hold (*s.o., s.o.'s attention*); withhold (*wages*); *fig.* remember; book (*a seat, a room*); engage (*a servant* etc.); *fig.* repress, hold back (*a sob, tears, one's anger,* etc.); restrain (from *ger.*, *de inf.*); *se ~* control o.s.; refrain (from, *de*); *se ~ à* clutch at (*s.th.*); **rétention** [retã'sjɔ̃] *f* ✍, *a.* ⚖ *case:* retention; ⚖ *pledge:* retaining.

retentir [rətã'ti:r] (2a) *v/i.* (re-)sound, ring, echo; *fig. ~ sur* affect; **retentissement** [~tis'mã] *m* resounding, echoing; *fig.* repercussion (*of an event*); *fig.* stir.

retenu, e [rət'ny] restrained, reserved; discreet; low-key(ed); **retenue** [~] *f money:* deduction; stoppage; ✍ carry over; *school:* detention; holding back; reservoir; dam; ♣ guy(-rope); *fig.* discretion; modesty; *fig. actions, speech:* restraint.

réticence [reti'sã:s] *f* reticence; hesitation, reluctance.

réticule [reti'kyl] *m opt.* graticule; hand-bag, reticule; **réticulé, e** [~ky'le] reticulated.

rétif, -ve [re'tif, ~'ti:v] restive, stubborn (*a. fig.*).

rétine *anat.* [re'tin] *f eye:* retina; **rétinite** [~ti'nit] *f* ⚕ retinitis; *min.* pitchstone.

retiré, e [rəti're] retired, secluded, solitary; remote; in retirement; **retirer** [~] (1a) *v/t.* withdraw; take out; extract (*a bullet, a cork*); derive, get (*profit*); obtain; ✝ take up (*a bill*); *fig.* take back (*an insult, a* promise, *etc.*); *fig.* give shelter to (*s.o.*); *typ.* reprint (*a book*); fire (*a gun*) again; take out, *Am.* check out (*luggage*); ~ *de la circulation* call in (*currency*); se ~ retire, withdraw; ebb (*tide*), recede (*sea*), subside (*waters*).

retombée [rətɔ̃'be] *f* fallout; ⚛ *arch etc.*: springing; *fig.* ~s *pl.* repercussions, consequences, effect(s) (*sg.*); *fig.* spin-off (*sg.*); *phys.* ~s *pl.* radioactives fallout *sg.*; **retomber** [~] (1a) *v/i.* fall (down) again; fall (back); ~ *dans* lapse into; *fig.* ~ *sur* blame, *glory*: fall upon.

retoquer F [rətɔ'ke] (1m) *v/t.* fail, F plough (*a candidate*).

retordoir ⊕ [rətɔr'dwaːr] *m instrument*: twister; **retordre** [~'tɔrdr] (4a) *v/t.* wring out again; *tex.* twist; *fig. donner du fil à ~ à q.* give s.o. trouble.

retorquer [rətɔr'ke] (1m) retort; turn (*an argument*); cast back (*an accusation*).

retors, e [rə'tɔːr, ~'tɔrs] *tex.* twisted; curved (*beak*); *fig.* crafty; rascally.

retouche [rə'tuʃ] *f paint. etc.* retouch; *phot.* retouching; ⊕ finishing, dressing; **retoucher** [~tu'ʃe] (1a) *v/t. paint., phot., etc.* retouch; ⊕ finish, dress; *v/i.*: ~ *à* meddle with (*s.th.*) (again).

retour [rə'tuːr] *m* return (*a.* ⚛ *wall,* ✝, ✍, *sp., post, a. fig.*); going back; ✍, *life, feeling, fortune, opinion, rope*: turn; *fig. feeling, fortune, opinion, etc.*: change; ♪, ✍ recurrence; ✝ dishono(u)red bill; ⚖, *biol.* reversion; ✍ ~ *d'âge* critical age, change of life; *mot.* ~ *de flamme* back-fire; ✍ ~ *par la terre* earth return; *à son* ~ on his return; ✍ *billet m de* ~ return ticket; *en* ~ *de* in return *or* exchange for; *être de* ~ be back; *être sur le* ~ be past one's prime, F be getting on; *sp. match m* ~ return match; **retourne** [~'turn] *f cards*: turn-up; trumps *pl.*; **retourner** [~tur'ne] (1a) *v/i.* return; go back; *fig.* recoil (upon, *sur*); ⚖, *biol.* revert; *de quoi retourne-t-il?* what is it all about?; *il retourne cœur cards*: hearts are trumps; *v/t.* turn (*s.th.*) inside out; turn (*hay, one's head, omelette, ship, a. fig. argument, etc.*); turn over (*an*

idea, *the soil*); turn up (*a card*); twist (*s.o.'s arm*); *cuis.* mix (*salad*); *fig.* upset, disturb (*s.o.*); return (*s.th. to s.o., qch. à q.*); se ~ turn (round *or* over); round (on, *contre*); change (*opinion*); F *s'en* ~ go back.

retracer [rətra'se] (1k) *v/t.* retrace; mark (*s.th.*) out again; *fig.* bring to mind, recall; se ~ recur.

rétracter [retrak'te] (1a) *v/t.* retract; draw in; withdraw (*an opinion etc.*); ⚖ rescind (*a decree*); *tex.* shrink; ✍, *a. fig.* retract; **rétractile** [~'til] retractile; **rétraction** [~'sjɔ̃] *f* contraction; ✍ retraction.

retrait [rə'trɛ] *m* ⊕ *metal, wood, etc.*: shrinkage, contraction; withdrawal (*a.* ✝, *parl.*); licence, ticket, order, *etc.*: cancelling; ⚛ recess; ⚖ redemption; *en* ~ sunk (*panel*), recessed (*shelves*), set back (*house*); **retraite** [~'trɛt] *f* ✍, ⚓ retreat (*a. fig.*); withdrawal; ✍ tattoo; retirement, superannuation; pension, ✍, ⚓ retired pay; *animals*: lair; ✝ redraft; ⚛ offset; *caisse f de* ~ superannuation fund; *en* ~ retired; *mettre q. à la* ~ retire s.o., pension s.o. off; *prendre sa* ~ retire; **retraité, e** [rətrɛ'te] 1. *adj.* pensioned off, ✍, ⚓ on the retired list; 2. *su.* pensioner.

retraitement ⊕ [rətrɛt'mã] *m* reprocessing; **retraiter**[1] [rətrɛ'te] (1a) *v/t.* treat *or* handle again; ⊕ reprocess.

retraiter[2] [~] (1a) *v/t.* pension (*s.o.*) off, retire (*s.o.*), superannuate (*s.o.*); ✍, ⚓ place on the retired list.

retranchement [rətrãʃ'mã] *m* cutting off; *pension*: docking; suppression; ✍ entrenchment; **retrancher** [~trã'ʃe] (1a) *v/t.* cut off (from, *de*); remove (from, *de*); cut out (*a. fig.*); ✍ entrench; ⚖ deduct; se ~ retrench; ✍ entrench o.s.; dig o.s. in; *fig.* take refuge (behind, *derrière*).

retransmettre [rətrãs'mɛtrə] (4v) *v/t. radio*: broadcast; *telev.* show; **retransmission** [~mi'sjɔ̃] *f* broadcast; showing.

rétrécir [retre'siːr] (2a) *vt/i. a.* se ~ narrow; contract; *tex.* shrink; **rétrécissement** [~sis'mã] *m* narrowing; contraction (*a. opt.*); *tex.* shrinking; ✍ stricture.

retremper [rətrã'pe] (1a) *v/t.* soak

(*s.th.*) again; ⊕ retemper (*steel, a. fig. one's mind, etc.*); *fig.* strengthen (*s.o.*); **se ~** be toned up; get new strength.

rétribuer [retri'bɥe] (1n) *v/t.* pay, remunerate; **rétribution** [~by'sjɔ̃] *f* remuneration, payment; salary; *sans ~* honorary.

rétro [re'tro] 1. *adj.* reminiscent of times past; *la vogue ~* nostalgia; 2. *su./m* nostalgia; *mot.* (= *rétroviseur*) back-view mirror.

rétro... [retrɔ] retro...; **~actif, -ve** [~aktif, ~'ti:v] retroactive, retrospective; *avec effet ~* (ⓓ) backdated (to) (*measure etc.*); **~action** [~ak'sjɔ̃] *f* retroaction; ⚡, *radio*: feedback; **~céder** [~se'de] (1f) *v/t.* ⚖️ retrocede; redemise; ✝ return (*a commission*); **~fusée** ⚔️ [~fy'ze] *f* retrorocket; braking-rocket; **~grade** [~'grad] retrograde, backward; **~grader** [~gra'de] (1a) *v/i.* move backwards; regress; retrograde; fall back; *mot.* change (*Am.* shift) down (from ... to ..., de ... en ...); *v/t.* admin. ⚔️ etc. demote; **~pédalage** [~peda'la:ʒ] *m* bicycle: back-pedalling; **~spectif, -ve** [~spɛk'tif, ~'ti:v] retrospective.

retrousser [rətru'se] (1a) *v/t.* turn up (*a sleeve, one's trousers, one's moustache*); tuck up (*one's skirt*); curl up (*one's lips*); *nez m retroussé* turned-up or snub nose.

retrouvailles [rətru'vɑ:j] *f/pl.* reunion, reconciliation; **retrouver** [~'ve] (1a) *v/t.* find (again); rediscover (*s.th.*); meet (*s.o.*) again; return to (*a place*); recover (*one's health, one's strength*); *aller ~* go and see (*s.o.*) again; **se ~** find o.s. back; *a. s'y ~* find one's way.

rétro...: ~version ⚡ [retrɔvɛr'sjɔ̃] *f* retroversion; **~viseur** *mot.* [~vi-'zœ:r] *m* driving mirror, rear-view mirror.

rets *hunt.* [rɛ] *m* net.

réunifier [reyni'fje] (1o) *v/t.* reunify.

réunion [rey'njɔ̃] *f* reunion; meeting; ⚔️, *a. pol.* union; gathering; party, function; **réunir** [~'ni:r] (2a) *v/t.* (re)unite; join (to, with ⓓ); join together, link; collect (*money, water*); ⚔️ raise (*troops*).

réussir [rey'si:r] (2a) *v/i.* succeed (in *ger.*, ⓐ *inf.*; at or in s.th., *dans qch.*); be a success (*thea. etc.*); ♥ thrive; **~** ⓐ pass (*an examination*); *v/t.* be suc-

cessful in; carry (*s.th.*) out well; **réussite** [~'sit] *f* ✝ result, outcome; success; *cards*: patience.

revacciner ⚡ [rəvaksi'ne] (1a) *v/t.* revaccinate.

revaloir [rəva'lwa:r] (3l) *v/t.* pay back in kind; repay; **revalorisation** [rəvalɔriza'sjɔ̃] *f* ✝ revalorization, revaluation; *fig.* reassertion of the value of; **revaloriser** [~'ze] (1a) *v/t.* ✝ revalorize, revalue; *fig.* reassert the value of.

revanche [rə'vɑ̃:ʃ] *f* revenge; return; *en ~* in return; on the other hand; **revancher** [~vɑ̃'ʃe] (1a) *v/t.*: **se ~** have one's revenge; revenge o.s. (for, de).

rêvasser [rɛva'se] (1a) *v/i.* muse (on, ⓐ), day-dream (about, ⓐ); **rêvasserie** [~vas'ri] *f* musing, day-dream(ing); **rêvasseur *m*, -euse *f*** [~va'sœ:r, ~'sø:z] day-dreamer; **rêve** [rɛ:v] *m* dream (*a. fig.*); *faire un ~* have a dream.

revêche [rə'vɛʃ] harsh, rough; ⊕ difficult to work (*stone, wood*); brittle (*iron*); *fig.* cantankerous, crabby, sour (*face*).

réveil [re'vɛ:j] *m* waking, awakening; *religion*: revival; ⚔️ reveille; alarm(-clock); *fig. fâcheux ~* rude awakening; **réveille-matin** [~vɛjma'tɛ̃] *m/inv.* alarm(-clock); **réveiller** [revɛ'je] (1a) *v/t.* ⓐ(a)wake; waken (*a. fig.*); rouse (*a. fig.*); ⚔️ turn out; **se ~** wake up, awake (*person*); *fig.* be awakened or aroused; **réveillon** [~'jɔ̃] *m* midnight supper (*usu. on Christmas Eve and New Year's Eve*).

révélateur. -trice [revela'tœ:r, ~-'tris] 1. *adj.* revealing; tell-tale (*sign*); *phot.* developing (*bath*); 2. *su.* revealer; *su./m phot.* developer; ⊕ detector; **révélation** [~la-'sjɔ̃] *f* revelation; ✝ eye-opener; ⚖️ information; *bibl.* ♀ *pl. the* Revelation *sg.*; **révéler** [~'le] (1f) *v/t.* reveal (*a. eccl.*), disclose, F let out (*a secret*); *fig.* show; *phot.* develop.

revenant [rəv'nɑ̃] *m* ghost; F *fig.* stranger; *il y a des ~s ici* this place is haunted.

revendeur *m*, -euse *f* ✝ [rəvɑ̃'dœ:r, ~'dø:z] retailer; second-hand dealer.

revendication [rəvɑ̃dika'sjɔ̃] *f* claim, demand; **revendiquer** [~'ke] (1m) *v/t.* claim, demand; assume (*a* *responsibility*); claim (*an attempt, an attack, etc.*).

revendre [rə'vãːdr] (4a) *v/t.* resell; ✝ sell out; F *fig.* spare; *en ~ à* outwit (*s.o.*), be too much for (*s.o.*).

revenez-y [rəvne'zi] *m/inv.* renewal, revival, return; F *avoir un goût de ~* be very more-ish.

revenir [rəv'niːr] (2h) *v/i.* return, come back *or* again (*a. fig.*); recover (from, *de*); cost (*s.o., à q. à qch.*); *fig.* amount (to, *à*); *fig.* fall by right (to, *à*); *🐎 ~ à soi* come round; ~ *à qch.* amount *or* come down to s.th.; *cela revient au même* it amounts *or* comes to the same thing; ~ *de* get over (*s.th.*); ~ *sur* retrace (*one's steps*); go back on (*a decision, a promise*); go back over (*the past, an affair, etc.*); *cuis. faire ~* brown (*meat*); *... ne me revient pas* I don't like the look of ...; *I cannot recall ...; ne pas en ~* be unable to get over it.

revente [rə'vãːt] *f* re-sale; ✝ *stock:* selling-out.

revenu [rəv'ny] *m person:* income; *State:* revenue; ✝ yield; *metall.* tempering; *admin. impôt m sur le ~* income tax; **revenue** ✍ [~] *f* new growth; young wood.

rêver [rɛ've] (1a) *v/i.* dream (about, of *de*); ~ *à* think about, ponder over; ~ *de* long for; *v/t.* dream of; *fig.* imagine; *fig.* desire ardently.

réverbère [rever'bɛːr] *m heat, lamp, etc.:* reflector; street-lamp; **réverbérer** [~be're] (1f) *v/t.* reflect (*light*); re-echo (*a sound*).

reverdir [rəver'diːr] (2a) *v/t.* make *or* paint green again; *v/i.* turn green again; F *fig.* grow young again (*person*).

révérence [reve'rãːs] *f* reverence (*a. ♀ title*); bow; curtsey; F ~ *parler* with all due respect; *tirer sa ~* take one's leave; **révérenciel, -elle** [~rã'sjɛl] reverential; **révérencieux, -euse** [~rã'sjø, ~'sjøːz] ceremonious; over-polite (*person*); **révérend, e** *eccl.* [~'rã, ~'rãːd] Reverend; **révérendissime** *eccl.* [~rãdi-'sim] Most *or* Right Reverend; **révérer** [~'re] (1f) *v/t.* revere, (hold in) reverence.

rêverie [rev'ri] *f* reverie; dreaming.

revers [rə'vɛːr] *m coin, fencing, a. fig. fortune:* reverse; *hand, page:* back; *tex.* wrong side; *cost. coat:*

lapel; *trousers:* turn-up, *Am.* cuff; *stocking:* turn-down, top; ✂ *uniform:* facing; *fig.* set-back; back-handed blow; *sp.* back-hand stroke; **reverser** [rəvɛr'se] (1a) *v/t.* pour (*s.th.*) out again; pour (*s.th.*) back; *fig.* shift (on, to *sur*); ✝ transfer; **réversible** [rever'sibl] reversible; ⚖ revertible; **réversion** ⚖, *biol.* [~'sjõ] *f* reversion (to, *à*).

revêtement [rəvɛt'mã] *m* ⚙ facing, coating, sheathing; *road:* surface; ⚙, *a.* ✂ revetment; *🔩 flex:* cover; ⊕ *wood:* veneer(ing); ⚙ *mur m de* ~ retaining wall, revetment wall; **revêtir** [~ve'tiːr] (2g) *v/t.* (re-) clothe; dress (in, *de*); *fig.* invest (with, *de*); *cost.* put on; *fig.* assume (*a form, a shape, etc.*); ⚙ face, coat, cover; ⊕ lag (*a boiler*); ✂ revet; ✝ ~ *qch. de sa signature* sign s.th.; affix one's signature to s.th.

rêveur, -euse [rɛ'vœːr, ~'vøːz] **1.** *adj.* dreamy; dreaming; **2.** *su.* (day-)dreamer.

revient ✝ [rə'vjɛ̃] *m: prix m de ~* cost (price).

revirement [rəvir'mã] *m* ✝, *a. fig.* sudden change *or* turn; ✝ *debt etc.:* transfer; ⚓ going about; **revirer** [~vi're] (1a) *v/i.* ⚓ go about; *fig.* change sides.

réviser [revi'ze] (1a) *v/t.* revise; ✝ audit (*accounts*); ⚖ review; ⊕, *mot.* recondition, overhaul; inspect; **réviseur** [~'zœːr] *m* reviser; examiner; *typ.* proof-reader; ✝ auditor; **révision** [~'zjõ] *f* revision; audit(ing); ⚖ review; ⊕, *mot.* overhaul(ing); ⊕ inspection; *typ.* proof-reading; ✂ *conseil m de* ~ recruiting board, *Am.* draft board; military appeal court; **révisionnisme** *pol.* [~zjo-'nism] *m* revisionism.

revitaliser [rəvitali'ze] (1a) *v/t.* re-vitalize; *crème f revitalisante* nourishing cream.

revivifier [rəvivi'fje] (1o) *v/t.* revitalize, revive.

revivre [rə'viːvr] (4hh) *v/i.* live again, come alive again; *fig.* revive; *v/t.* live (*s.th.*) over again.

révocable [revo'kabl] revocable; removable (*official*); **révocation** [~ka'sjõ] *f* ⚖ *will:* revocation, *law:* repeal; *admin. order:* cancellation, *official:* removal, dismissal; **révocatoire** [~ka'twaːr] revocatory.

revoici F [rəvwa'si] *prp.*: *me* ~! here I am again!; **revoilà** F [~'la] *prp.*: *le* ~ *malade!* there he is, ill again!

revoir [rə'vwa:r] **1.** (3m) *v/t.* see again; meet (*s.o.*) again; revise; inspect; ⚔ review; *typ.* read (*proofs*); go over (*accounts etc.*) again; **2.** *su./m*: *au* ~ good-bye.

révoltant, e [revɔl'tã, ~'tã:t] shocking, revolting; **révolte** [~'vɔlt] *f* revolt, rebellion; ✕, ⚓ mutiny; **révolté, e** [revɔl'te] **1.** *adj.* in revolt; **2.** *su.* rebel, insurgent; ✕, ⚓ mutineer; **révolter** [~] (1a) *v/t.* rouse to rebellion, cause to revolt; F *fig.* revolt, shock, disgust; *se* ~ revolt, rebel (*a. fig.*); ✕, ⚓ mutiny.

révolu, e [revɔ'ly] past, bygone (*time*); full (*year*), completed (*period of time*); **révolution** [revɔly'sjɔ̃] *f* ⚕, *pol.*, *fig.* revolution; *astr.* rotation; **révolutionnaire** [~sjɔ'nɛ:r] *adj.*, *a. su.* revolutionary; **révolutionner** [~sjɔ'ne] (1a) *v/t.* revolutionize (*a. fig.*); F *fig.* stir up.

revolver [revɔl'vɛ:r] *m* revolver, gun; ⊕ *lathe*: turret.

révoquer [revɔ'ke] (1m) *v/t.* revoke, cancel (*an order*); dismiss, remove (*an official*); recall (*an ambassador*); ~ *en doute* question (*s.th.*), call (*s.th.*) in question.

revue [rə'vy] *f* review (= *survey*, *a.* ✕, *journ.*); inspection (*a.* ✕); *journ.* magazine, periodical; *thea.* revue; *nous sommes de* ~ we'll meet again; we often meet; *passer en* ~ review, run over (*s.th.*); ✕ be reviewed *or* inspected; **revuiste** *thea.* [~'vɥist] *su.* composer of revues.

révulsé, e [revyl'se] *adj.*: *l'œil* ~ with turned-up eyes; **révulsif, -ve** ⚕ [~'sif, ~'si:v] *adj.*, *a. su./m* revulsive; counter-irritant; **révulsion** ⚕ [~'sjɔ̃] *f* revulsion; counter-irritation.

rez-de-chaussée [retʃo'se] *m/inv.* street level; ground floor, *Am.* first floor; *au* ~ on the ground *or Am.* first floor.

rhabiller [rabi'je] (1a) *v/t.* dress (*s.o.*) again; provide (*s.o.*) with new clothing; *fig.* refurbish; ⊕ repair; △ renovate; *se* ~ get dressed again; F *il peut aller se* ~ he'd better give up; **rhabilleur** [~'jœ:r] *m* repairer; watch repairer.

rhénan, e [re'nã, ~'nan] Rhine ..., Rhenish.

rhéostat ⚡ [reɔs'ta] *m* rheostat.

rhétoricien † [retɔri'sjɛ̃] *m* rhetorician; **rhétorique** [~'rik] *f* rhetoric; † (*a. classe f de* ~) *school*: top classical form (*preparing for first part of the baccalauréat*).

Rhin *geog.* [rɛ̃] *m*: *vin m du* ~ hock.

rhino... [rinɔ] rhino...; **~céros** *zo.* [~se'rɔs] *m* rhinoceros; **~logie** ⚕ [~lɔ'ʒi] *f* rhinology; **~plastie** ⚕ [~plas'tie] *f* rhinoplasty; **~scopie** ⚕ [~skɔ'pi] *f* rhinoscopy.

rhodanien, -enne *geog.* [rɔda'njɛ̃, ~'njɛn] of the Rhone.

rhombe ⚕ [rɔ̃:b] *m* rhomb(us); **rhombique** [rɔ̃'bik] rhombic; **rhomboïdal, e**, *m/pl.* -aux [~bɔi'dal, ~'do] rhomboidal.

rhubarbe ♀ [ry'barb] *f* rhubarb.

rhum [rɔm] *m* rum.

rhumatisant, e ⚕ [rymati'zã, ~'zã:t] *adj.*, *a. su.* rheumatic; **rhumatismal, e**, *m/pl.* -aux ⚕ [~tis'mal, ~'mo] rheumatic; **rhumatisme** ⚕ [~'tism] *m* rheumatism, F rheumatics *pl.*; ~ *articulaire* rheumatoid arthritis.

rhume ⚕ [rym] *m* cold; ~ *de cerveau* (*poitrine*) cold in the head (on the chest); ~ *des foins* hayfever; *prendre un* ~ catch (a) cold.

ri [ri] *p.p. of rire* 1; **riant, e** [rjã, rjã:t] smiling (*person, face, a. countryside*); pleasant (*thought*).   [*su.* ribald.\
ribaud, e † [ri'bo, ~'bo:d] *adj.*, *a.*⟩

riblons ⊕ [ri'blɔ̃] *m/pl.* swarf *sg.*

ribote F [ri'bɔt] *f* drunken bout; *sl.* binge; *être en* ~ be tipsy; be on the spree.

ribouldingue F [ribul'dɛ̃:g] *f* spree.

ricaner [rika'ne] (1a) *v/i.* snigger; sneer; laugh derisively; **ricaneur, -euse** [~ka'nœ:r, ~'nø:z] **1.** *su.* sneerer; **2.** *adj.* derisive, sneering.

ric-(à-)rac F [rik(a)'rak] *adv.* strictly, exactly; punctually.

richard *m*, **e** *f* F [ri'ʃa:r, ~'ʃard] wealthy person; **riche** [riʃ] **1.** *adj.* rich (*in* en, de) (*a. fig.*); wealthy; *fig.* valuable, handsome (*present*); F *fig.* fine, first-class; **2.** *su.* rich person; *su./m*: *bibl.* le mauvais ~ Dives; *les* ~s *pl.* the rich; **richesse** [ri'ʃɛs] *f* wealth; riches *pl.*; *fig.* opulence; ✿ *soil*: richness; *vegetation*: exuberance; **richissime** F

[~ʃi'sɛ̃] extremely rich, F rolling in money.

ricin ♀ [ri'sɛ̃] *m* castor-oil plant; *huile f de* ~ castor oil.

ricocher [riko'ʃe] (1a) *v/i.* glance off; ricochet (*bullet etc.*); **ricochet** [~'ʃɛ] *m* rebound; ✕ ricochet; *fig. par* ~ indirectly; *faire* ~ rebound (*a. fig.*); *faire des* ~s play drakes and ducks.

rictus [rik'tys] *m* ▪ rictus; F grin.

ride [rid] *f face, forehead:* wrinkle; *geol. ground:* fold; *sand, water:* ripple; *sand:* ridge; ⚓ (shroud) lanyard; **rideau** [ri'do] *m* curtain, *Am. a.* drape; ✕, ⚓, △, *a. fig.* screen; *thea.* (drop-)curtain; ⊕ roll-top, roll-shutter; ~! that's enough!; ~ *de fer thea.* safety curtain; *pol.* Iron Curtain; *fig. tirer le* ~ *sur* draw a veil over.

ridelle [ri'dɛl] *f cart, truck:* rail.

rider [ri'de] (1a) *v/t.* wrinkle; ripple (*water, sand*); ⊕ corrugate (*metal*); ⚓ tighten (*the shrouds*).

ridicule [ridi'kyl] **1.** *adj.* ridiculous; **2.** *su./m* absurdity; ridiculous aspect; ridicule; *tourner en* ~ (hold up to) ridicule; **ridiculiser** [~kyli'ze] (1a) *v/t.* ridicule, deride.

rien [rjɛ̃] **1.** *su./m* mere nothing, trifle; F tiny bit; **2.** *pron./indef.* anything; nothing; not ... anything; ~ *de nouveau* nothing new; ~ *du tout* nothing at all; ~ *moins que* nothing less than; *cela ne fait* ~ that does not matter; *de* ~! don't mention it!; *en moins de* ~ in less than no time; *il ne dit jamais* ~ he never says a thing; *il n'y a* ~ *à faire* it can't be helped; *obtenir pour* ~ get for a song; *plus* ~ nothing more; *sans* ~ *dire* without (saying) a word.

rieur, -euse [rjœːr, ~'jøːz] **1.** *adj.* laughing; merry; mocking; **2.** *su.* laugher.

rififi *sl.* [rifi'fi] *m* fight, brawl; trouble.

riflard¹ F [ri'flaːr] *m* umbrella, F brolly.

riflard² [~] *m* ⊕ *metal:* coarse file; *wood:* jack-plane; paring chisel; plastering trowel.

rigide [ri'ʒid] rigid, stiff (*a. fig.*); fixed (*axle*); tense (*muscle, cord*); **ri-gidifier** [~ʒidi'fje] (1o) *v/t.* make rigid; harden; **rigidité** [~ʒidi'te] *f* rigidity, stiffness (*a. fig.*); tenseness.

rigolade F [rigɔ'lad] *f* fun, lark.

rigolage ✒ [rigɔ'la:ʒ] *m field:* trenching.

rigolard, e *sl.* [rigɔ'la:r, ~'lard] fond of a lark; full of fun, jolly.

rigole [ri'gɔl] *f* ✒ trench, ditch; ✒, ⊕ channel; ✕ trough.

rigoler F [rigɔ'le] (1a) *v/i.* laugh; enjoy o.s.; **rigoleur, -euse** [~'lœːr, ~'løːz] **1.** *adj.* jolly; fond of fun; **2.** *su.* jolly person; person fond of fun; laugher; **rigolo, -ote** F [~'lo, ~'lɔt] **1.** *adj.* funny, comical; queer, odd; **2.** *su./m* funny fellow; F card; F revolver, *Am.* gun.

rigorisme [rigɔ'rism] *m* rigorism, strictness; **rigoriste** [~'rist] **1.** *adj.* rigorous; strict; **2.** *su.* rigorist; rigid moralist; **rigoureux, -euse** [rigu'rø, ~'røːz] rigorous; strict; severe (*climate, punishment*); close (*reasoning*); **rigueur** [~'gœːr] *f* rigo(u)r, severity; *fig.* strictness; *fig. reasoning:* closeness, accuracy; *à la* ~ strictly; if really necessary, *sl.* at a push; *de* ~ obligatory, compulsory.

rillettes *cuis.* [ri'jɛt] *f/pl.* potted pork mince *sg.*

rimailler † [rima'je] (1a) *v/i.* write doggerel, dabble in poetry; **rimailleur** † [~'jœːr] *m* poetaster, rhymester; **rime** [rim] *f* rhyme; *fig. sans* ~ *ni raison* without rhyme or reason; **rimer** [ri'me] (1a) *v/t.* put into rhyme; *v/i.* rhyme (with, *avec*); **rimeur** [~'mœːr] *m* rhymer, versifier.

rinçage [rɛ̃'sa:ʒ] *m* rinsing.

rinceau [rɛ̃'so] *m* △ foliage; ☒ branch.

rince-bouteilles [rɛ̃sbu'tɛːj] *m/inv.* bottle washer; **rince-doigts** [~'dwa] *m/inv.* finger bowl; **rincée** [rɛ̃'se] *f sl.* thrashing; F downpour; **rincer** [~'se] (1k) *v/t.* rinse; *sl.* clean (*s.o.*) out; *rain:* soak (*s.o.*); *sl. se* ~ *la dalle* wet one's whistle; *sl. se* ~ *l'œil* get an eyeful; **rinceur** *m*, **-euse** *f* [~'sœːr, ~'søːz] washer, rinser; **rin-çure** [~'sy:r] *f* slops *pl.* (*a.* F = *very thin wine*).

ring *box.* [riŋ] *m* ring.

ringard ⊕ [rɛ̃'ga:r] *m* poker.

ripaille F † [ri'pɑ:j] *f* revelry; *faire* ~ carouse; **ripailleur** *m*, **-euse** *f* F † [~pɑ'jœːr, ~'jøːz] reveller, carouser.

ripoliner [ripɔli'ne] (1a) *v/t.* (paint with) enamel.

riposte [ri'pɔst] *f* retort, smart reply; *sp.* counter; **riposter** [ˌ.pɔs-'te] (1a) *v/i.* retort; *sp.* counter, riposte; *fig.* ~ *à* counteract.

riquiqui F [riki'ki] *m* shrimp (= *undersized man*).

rire [riːr] **1.** (4cc) *v/i.* laugh (at, de); jest, joke; smile (on, at *à*); make light (of, de); ~ *au nez de q.* laugh in s.o.'s face; ~ *dans sa barbe* chuckle to o.s.; ~ *jaune* give a sickly smile; *à crever de* ~ killingly funny; *éclater de* ~ burst out laughing; *je ne ris pas* I am in earnest; *pour* ~ for fun, as a joke; comic (*paper*); mock (*action, king*); *se* ~ *de* take (*s.th.*) in one's stride; † make fun of, laugh at; **2.** *su./m* laugh(ter); *fou* ~ uncontrollable laughter.

ris[1] ⚓ [ri] *m* reef (*in a sail*).

ris[2] *cuis.* [~] *m*: ~ *de veau* sweetbread.

ris[3] [ri] *1st p. sg. p.s. of rire 1*; **risée** [ri'ze] *f* derision; *person:* laughing stock; ⚓ light sqall; **risette** [~'zɛt] *f* (*child's*) smile; *faire* (*la*) ~ smile (at, *à*), give a smile; **risible** [~'zibl] ludicrous; ridiculous (*a. person*).

risotto *cuis.* [rizɔ'to] *m* risotto (*Italian rice dish*).

risque [risk] *m* risk; ~ *du métier* occupational hazard; ~ *pour la santé* health hazard; **risqué, e** [ris'ke] risky; daring, risqué (*joke, etc.*); † *à ses* ~*s et périls* at one's own risk; *à tout* ~ at all hazards; *au* ~ *de* (*inf.*) at the risk of (*ger.*); **risquer** [ris'ke] (1m) *v/t.* risk; venture (*a question etc.*); ~ *le coup* take a chance, chance it; *v/i.*: ~ *de* (*inf.*) run the risk of (*ger.*); be likely to (*inf.*); **risque-tout** [~kə'tu] *m/inv.* daredevil.

rissole *cuis.* [ri'sɔl] *f* rissole; (*fish-*)ball; **rissoler** *cuis.* [~sɔ'le] *vt/i.* brown (*meat*).

ristourne † [ris'turn] *f* repayment; refund; rebate; **ristourner** † [~tur'ne] (1a) *v/t.* repay; refund.

rite *eccl. etc.* [rit] *m* rite.

ritournelle [ritur'nɛl] *f* ♪ ritornello; F *fig. la même* ~ the same old story.

ritualiser [rityali'ze] (1a) *v/t.* ritualize; **rituel, -elle** [ri'tɥɛl] *adj., a. su./m* ritual, ceremonial.

rivage [ri'vaːʒ] *m river:* bank; *lake, sea:* shore, beach.

rival, e *m/pl.* **-aux** [ri'val, ~'vo] *adj., a. su.* rival; **rivaliser** [rivali'ze] (1a) *v/i.*: ~ *avec* rival; compete with,

vie with; **rivalité** [~'te] *f* rivalry, competition.

rive [riːv] *f river:* bank; *lake, river:* side; *lake,* † *sea:* shore; *forest:* edge.

river ⊕ [ri've] (1a) *v/t.* rivet; clinch (*a nail*); F ~ *son clou à q.* settle s.o.'s hash.

riverain, e [ri'vrɛ̃, ~'vrɛn] **1.** *adj.* riverside...; riparian; bordering on a road *etc.*; **2.** *su.* riverside resident; riparian owner; dweller along a road *etc.*

rivet ⊕ [ri've] *m* rivet; *nail:* clinch; **rivetage** ⊕ [riv'taːʒ] *m* riveting; clinching.

rivière [ri'vjɛːr] *f* river; stream (*a. fig.*); *sp.* water-jump; rivière (*of diamonds*).

rixe [riks] *f* brawl, fight; affray.

riz [ri] *m* rice; *cuis.* ~ *au lait* rice pudding; ~ *glacé* polished rice; **rizerie** [riz'ri] *f* rice-mill; **rizière** [ri'zjɛːr] *f* rice-field, rice-swamp.

roadster *mot.* [rɔds'tœːr] *m* two-seater, Am. roadster.

rob [rɔb] *m cards:* rubber; *faire un* ~ play a rubber.

robe [rɔb] *f* dress, frock; gown (*a.* ⚖, *a. univ.*); *animal:* coat; *bird:* plumage; *onion, potato, sausage:* skin; *cigar:* outer leaf; ⚖ legal profession; ~ *de chambre* dressing-gown; **robin** F *pej.* [rɔ'bɛ̃] *m* lawyer.

robinet [rɔbi'nɛ] *m* tap, Am. faucet; ~ *d'arrêt* stop cock; ~ *mélangueur* mixer tap; **robinetterie** [~nɛ'tri] *f* plumbing.

robot [rɔ'bo] *m* robot; ✈ pilotless plane; **robotiser** [rɔbɔti'ze] (1a) *v/t.* robotize; ⊕ *a.* automate; *fig. a.* turn (*s.o.*) into a robot.

robre [rɔbr] *m see* **rob**.

robuste [rɔ'byst] robust, sturdy; ⚘ hardy; *fig.* firm (*faith etc.*); **robustesse** [~bys'tɛs] *f* sturdiness; strength; hardiness.

roc [rɔk] *m* rock (*a. fig.*).

rocade [rɔ'kad] *f road:* bypass.

rocaille [rɔ'kaːj] *f* rock-work; rubble; † rococo; *jardin m de* ~ rock-garden; **rocailleux, -euse** [~ka'jø, ~'jøːz] rocky, stony, pebbly; *fig.* rugged, rough.

rocambolesque [rɔkɑ̃bɔ'lɛsk] fantastic.

roche [rɔʃ] *f* rock; boulder; ⚒ ~ *mère*

matrix, parent-rock; *fig.* cœur *m* de ~ heart of stone; **rocher** [rɔ'ʃe] *m* (mass of) rock; *anat.* otic bone.

rochet¹ *eccl.* [rɔ'ʃɛ] *m* rochet.

rochet² [~] *m* ⊕ ratchet; *tex.* bobbin; ⊕ *roue f à* ~ ratchet-wheel.

rocheux, -euse [rɔ'ʃø, ~'ʃøːz] rocky; stony.

rococo [rɔkɔ'ko] **1.** *su./m* rococo; **2.** *adj./inv.* rococo; *fig.* antiquated.

rodage [rɔ'daːʒ] *m* ⊕ grinding; *mot.*, *a. fig.* running in; **rodé, e** [~'de] ⊕ run in; *fig.* broken in; *fig.* running well *or* smoothly; **roder** [~'de] (1a) *v/t. mot.* run in (*an engine, a. fig.*); grind in (*valves*).

rôder [ro'de] (1a) *v/i.* loiter; prowl (about); ⚓ veer (at anchor, *sur son ancre*); **rôdeur** *m.* **-euse** *f* [~'dœːr, ~'døːz] prowler. [ging; bluster.〉

rodomontade [rɔdɔmɔ̃'tad] *f* brag-〉

rogations *eccl.* [rɔga'sjɔ̃] *f/pl.* Rogation days; **rogatoire** ⚖ [~'twaːr] rogatory; *commission f* ~ commission (*issued by foreign court*) to take evidence for that court, Commission Rogatoire.

rogatons [rɔga'tɔ̃] *m/pl. food:* scraps, left-overs.

rogne F [rɔɲ] *f* (bad) temper; *se mettre en* ~ blow one's top (*Am. a.* one's stack).

rogner [rɔ'ɲe] (1a) *v/t.* trim, pare; clip (*claws, a. fig. the wings*); cut down (*s.o.'s salary*); *v/i. sl.* be in a temper, be cross; grumble; **ro-gneuse** ⊕ [~'ɲøːz] *f* trimming-machine.

rognon *usu. cuis.* [rɔ'ɲɔ̃] *m* kidney.

rognures [rɔ'ɲyːr] *f/pl.* clippings, cuttings; trimmings; scraps.

rogomme F [rɔ'gɔm] *m* spirits *pl.*; *voix f de* ~ *drunkard:* husky voice.

rogue [rɔg] haughty, arrogant.

roi [rwa] *m* king (*a. cards, chess*); *jour m des* ♀s Twelfth-night.

roide [rwad] *see* raide. [wren.〉

roitelet [rwat'lɛ] *m* petty king; *orn.*〉

rôle [roːl] *m thea., a. fig.* part, rôle; *thea.* ~ *principal* title rôle; *thea.* ~ *secondaire* supporting part; *à tour de* ~ in turn.

romain, e [rɔ'mɛ̃, ~'mɛn] **1.** *adj.* Roman; **2.** *su./m ling.* Roman; *typ.* roman, primer; *su.* ♀ Roman.

romaine¹ [rɔ'mɛn] *f balance:* steel-yard.

romaine² ♀ [~] *f* Cos lettuce.

romaïque [rɔma'ik] *adj., a. su./m ling.* Romaic; modern Greek.

roman, e [rɔ'mɑ̃, ~'mɑ̃ːd] **1.** *adj.* Romance; ⚠ Norman (*in England*), Romanesque; **2.** *su./m ling.* Romance; novel; (*medieval*) romance; *usu.* ~s *pl.* fiction *sg.*; ~ *à thèse* tendenz novel.

romance ♪ [rɔ'mɑ̃ːs] *f* song, ballad; ~ *sans paroles* song without words.

romanche *ling.* [rɔ'mɑ̃ːʃ] *m* Ro(u)-mansh.

romancier *m,* **-ère** *f* [rɔmɑ̃'sje, ~'sjɛːr] novelist; fiction-writer; **roman-cycle,** *pl.* **romans-cycles** [~'sikl] *m* saga (novel).

romand, e *geog.* [rɔ'mɑ̃, ~'mɑ̃ːd] *adj.: la Suisse* ~e French(-speaking) Switzerland.

romanesque [rɔma'nɛsk] **1.** *adj.* romantic; **2.** *su./m fig.* romance; **roman-feuilleton,** *pl.* **romans-feuilletons** *journ.* [rɔmɑ̃fœj'tɔ̃] *m* serial (story); **roman-fleuve,** *pl.* **romans-fleuves** [~'flœːv] *m* saga (novel), river novel.

romanichel *m,* **-elle** *f* [rɔmani'ʃɛl] gipsy; Romany.

romaniser [rɔmani'ze] (1a) *vt/i.* Romanize (*a. eccl.*); **romaniste** [~'nist] *su. eccl., a. ling.* Romanist; *ling.* student of the Romance languages; **romantique** [rɔmɑ̃-'tik] **1.** *adj.* Romantic; *fig.* imaginative; **2.** *su.* Romantic; **roman-tisme** [~'tism] *m* Romanticism.

romarin ♀ [rɔma'rɛ̃] *m* rosemary.

rompre [rɔ̃ːpr] (4a) *v/t.* break (*s.th.*) in two; break (⚡ *circuit, one's neck, object, peace, promise, silence,* ✕ *step*); ⚖ *hist.* break on the wheel; break up (*an alliance,* ✕ *an attack, the road, etc.*); ✕ scatter (*a regiment*); break off (*a conversation, an engagement*); disrupt (✕ *an army, fig. unity*); burst (*an artery, the river banks*); break in (*an animal*); ✝ cancel; *fig.* disturb, upset; *fig.* interrupt; *fig.* deaden (*a shock*); *fig.* accustom (*s.o.*) (to, *à*); *se* ~ break; snap; accustom *or* harden o.s. (to, *à*); *v/i.* break; ✕, *a. sp.* give ground; ✕ *rompez!* dismiss!; **rompu, e** [rɔ̃'py] **1.** *p.p. of* rompre; **2.** *adj.* broken; broken in; ~ *à* used to, hardened to; experienced in (*business*); ~ *de fatigue* worn out; *à bâtons* ~s by fits and starts.

romsteck *cuis.* [rɔms'tɛk] *m* rump-steak.

ronce [rɔ̃:s] *f* ⚲ bramble branch; ⊕ *wood grain:* curl; F ~s *pl.* thorns; *fig.* difficulties; ~ *artificielle* barbed wire; **ronceraie** [~'rɛ] *f* ground covered with brambles.

ronchonner F [rɔ̃ʃɔ'ne] (1a) *v/i.* grumble, grouse; hum (*radio-set*); **ronchonneur** *m*, **-euse** *f* F [~'nœ:r, ~'nø:z] grumbler.

rond, ronde [rɔ̃, rɔ̃:d] **1.** *adj.* round; plump (*face, person*); *fig.* brisk (*wind*); *fig.* straight, honest (*person*); F tipsy, tight, *Am.* high; **2.** *rond adv.:* ⊕ *etc.*, *a. fig.* tourner ~ run smoothly; *fig.* qu'est-ce qui ne tourne pas ~ what's wrong?; **3.** *su./m* circle, round, ring; *bread etc.:* slice; *butter:* pat; ⊕ washer; F des ~s *pl.*, le ~ money, F cash; en ~ in a circle; *su./f* ⚔ *etc.*, *dance*, *a. song:* round; ♪ semibreve; *script:* round hand; à la ~e around; (*do s.th.*) in turn; **rond-de-cuir**, *pl.* **ronds-de-cuir** [~d-'kɥi:r] *m* round leather cushion; penpusher, clerk; bureaucrat; **rondeau** [rɔ̃'do] *m* poem: rondeau; ♪ rondo; ⊕ roller; **rondelet, -ette** [rɔ̃d'lɛ, ~'lɛt] plumpish; nice round (*sum*); **rondelle** [rɔ̃'dɛl] *f* disc; slice; ⊕ washer; ⊕ (*ball-*)race; **rondeur** [~'dœ:r] *f* roundness (*a. fig. style*); fullness; *figure:* curve; *fig.* straightforwardness, frankness; **rondin** [~'dɛ̃] *m* log; billet; *iron:* round bar; **rondpoint**, *pl.* **ronds-points** [rɔ̃'pwɛ̃] *m* road: mot. roundabout, *Am.* traffic circus.

ronflant, e [rɔ̃'flɑ̃, ~'flɑ̃:t] snoring (*person*); throbbing, roaring, rumbling (*noise*); resounding (*titles, voice*); *fig.* pretentious, bombastic; **ronflement** [~flə'mɑ̃] *m* snore; snoring; *noise:* roar(ing); boom (-ing); *machine, top, a. radio:* hum; **ronfler** [~'fle] (1a) *v/i.* snore (*sleeper*); roar, boom; hum; *sl.* prosper; **ronfleur, -euse** [~'flœ:r, ~'flø:z] *su.* snorer; *su./m* ⚡ buzzer.

rongeant, e [rɔ̃'ʒɑ̃, ~'ʒɑ̃:t] 🜍 corroding; ✎ rodent; *fig.* gnawing (*worries*); **ronger** [~'ʒe] (1l) *v/t.* gnaw; *worms etc.:* eat into; 🜍 corrode; pit (*metal*); *fig.* erode; *fig.* fret (*s.o.'s heart*); se ~ les ongles bite one's nails; *fig.* rongé de tormented by (*grief*); worn by (*care*); **rongeur,**

-euse [~'ʒœ:r, ~'ʒø:z] **1.** *adj.* zo., *a.* ✎ rodent; gnawing (*care, worry*); **2.** *su./m* zo. rodent.

ronron [rɔ̃'rɔ̃] *m* cat: purr(ing); F *machine:* hum; **ronronner** [~rɔ'ne] (1a) *v/i.* purr (*cat, engine*); ⊕, *radio, etc.:* hum.

roquer [rɔ'ke] (1m) *v/i.* chess: castle.

roquet [rɔ'kɛ] *m* pug(-dog); mongrel, *Am.* yellow dog.

roquette¹ ⚔ [rɔ'kɛt] *f* rocket.

roquette² ⚲ [~] *f* rocket.

rosace △ [ro'zas] *f* rose-window; (*ceiling-*)rose; **rosacé, e** [~za'se] **1.** *adj.* rosaceous; **2.** *su./f:* ~s *pl.* rosaceae; **rosage** ⚲ [~'za:ʒ] *m* rhododendron; **rosaire** *eccl.* [~'zɛ:r] *m* rosary; **rosâtre** [~'zɑ:tr] pinkish.

rosbif *cuis.* [rɔs'bif] *m* roast beef.

rose [ro:z] **1.** *su./f* ⚲ rose; △ rose-window; ~ *des vents* compass-card; ⚲ ~ *sauvage* dog-rose; *su./m* rose (*colo[u]r*), pink; *voir tout* (*or la vie*) *en* ~ see things (*or the world*) through rose-colo(u)red glasses; **2.** *adj.* pink; rosy; **rosé, e** [ro'ze] **1.** *adj.* rose-pink, rosy; rose, rosé (*wine*); **2.** *su./m wine:* rosé.

roseau [ro'zo] *m* ⚲ reed; *fig.* (broken) reed.

rose-croix [roz'krwa] *m/inv.* Rosicrucian.

rosée [ro'ze] *f* dew.

roseraie [roz'rɛ] *f* rose garden; **rosette** [ro'zɛt] *f ribbion:* bow; rosette (*a. = decoration*); red ink *or* chalk; ⊕ burr; **rosier** ⚲ [~'zje] *m* rose tree, rose bush.

rossard *sl.* [rɔ'sa:r] *m* skunk, beast (= *objectionable individual*).

rosse [rɔs] **1.** *su./f* † F *horse:* nag; *see* rossard; **2.** *adj.* nasty; beastly; cynical (*comedy*).

rossée F [rɔ'se] *f* thrashing; **rosser** F [~] (1a) *v/t.* give (*s.o.*) a thrashing.

rossignol [rɔsi'ɲɔl] *m orn.* nightingale; † F piece of junk, old stock; F white elephant; ⊕ skeleton-key; ♫ whistle.

rossinante F [rɔsi'nɑ:t] *f* worn-out old hack, Rosinante.

rossolis [rɔsɔ'li] *m* ⚲ sundew; *cordial:* rosolio.

rot *sl.* [ro] *m* belch.

rôt [~] *m* roast (meat).

rotateur, -trice [rɔta'tœ:r, ~'tris] **1.** *adj.* rotatory; **2.** *su./m anat.* rotator; *biol.* rotifer; **rotatif, -ve**

[ʌˈtif, ʌˈtiːv] **1.** *adj.* rotary; **2.** *su./f typ.* rotary (printing-)press; **rotation** [ʌˈsjɔ̃] *f* rotation (*a.* Å, ✎); ✝ ~ *du stock* merchandise turnover; **rotativiste** *typ.* [ʌtiˈvist] *m* rotary printer; **rotatoire** [ʌˈtwaːr] ⊕ rotatory (*a. phys. power*); rotational (*force*); *phys.* rotary (*polarization*).

roter *sl.* [rɔˈte] (1a) *v/i.* belch, bring up wind; *j'en rotais* it took my breath away.

rôti *cuis.* [roˈti] *m* roast (meat); ~ *de bœuf* (*porc*) roast beef (pork); **rôtie** [ʌ] *f* (round of) toast; ~ *à l'anglaise* Welch rarebit.

rotin [rɔˈtɛ̃] *m* ♀ rattan; rattan cane.

rôtir [roˈtiːr] (2a) *vt/i.* roast (*a. fig.*); *fig.* scorch; *cuis.* prêt(e) *à* ~ ovenready; *v/t.* toast (*bread*); **rôtissage** [ʌtiˈsaːʒ] *m* roasting; **rôtisserie** [ʌtisˈri] *f* cook-shop; **rôtisseur** *m*, -**euse** *f* [rotiˈsœːr, ʌˈsøːz] seller of roast meats; cook-shop keeper; **rôtissoire** *cuis.* [ʌˈswaːr] *f* Dutch oven; roaster.

rotonde [rɔˈtɔ̃d] *f* 🔺 rotunda; 🚂 engine shed; *en* ~ circular; **rotondité** [ʌtɔ̃diˈte] *f* rotundity; F stoutness.

rotor ✈, ⚙ [rɔˈtɔːr] *m* rotor.

rotule [rɔˈtyl] *f* anat. knee-cap; ⊕ ball-and-socket joint; *mot.* (*steering-*)knuckle.

roture [rɔˈtyːr] *f* commoner's condition; *coll.* commons *pl.*; **roturier**, -**ère** [ʌtyˈrje, ʌˈrjeːr] **1.** *adj.* common, plebeian; **2.** *su.* commoner; self-made man.

rouage ⊕ [rwaˈʒ] *m* wheels *pl.* (*a. fig.*); work(s *pl.*); cog-wheel, gearwheel; *fig.* cog.

rouan, -anne *zo.* [rwɑ̃, rwan] roan.

rouanne ⊕ [rwan] *f* rasing-knife; scribing-compass; carpenter's auger.

roublard, e F [ruˈblaːr, ʌˈblard] **1.** *adj.* wily, crafty; **2.** *su.* wily or crafty person; **roublardise** F [ʌblarˈdiːz] *f* cunning; piece of trickery.

rouble [rubl] *m Russian coinage:* r(o)uble.

roucouler [rukuˈle] (1a) *vt/i.* coo; *v/t. fig.* warble (*a song*).

roue [ru] *f* wheel; ~ *arrière* (*avant*) back (front) wheel; *mot.* ~ *de secours* spare wheel; ~ *directrice mot.* steering-wheel; *cycl.* front wheel;

~ *motrice* driving wheel; *faire la* ~ *orn.* spread its tail (*peacock etc.*); *sp.* turn cart-wheels; ✗ wheel about; *fig.* swagger; *mot. freins m/pl. sur quatre* ~*s* four-wheel brakes; **rouer** (*or jeter*) *des bâtons dans les* ~*s de q.* put a spoke in s.o.'s wheel; *sur* ~*s* wheeled, on wheels; **roué, e** [rwe] **1.** *su.* cunning *or* artful person; *su./m* rake, roué; **2.** *adj.* cunning, artful; exhausted; **rouelle** [rwɛl] *f* round slice; *veal:* fillet, *beef:* round.

rouennerie *tex.* [rwanˈri] *f* printed cotton goods *pl.*

rouer [rwe] (1p) *v/t.* coil (*a rope*); ⚖ *hist.* break (*s.o.*) on the wheel; *fig.* ~ *de coups* thrash (*s.o.*) soundly, beat (*s.o.*) black and blue; **rouerie** [ruˈri] *f* trick; piece of trickery; **rouet** [rwɛ] *m* small wheel; spinning-wheel; ⊕ pulley-wheel; ⊕ *pully:* sheave; *lock:* scutcheon; ⚓ gin.

rouge [ruːʒ] **1.** *adj.* red (with, de); ruddy (*cheek*); red-hot (*metal etc.*); ~ *brique* brick-red; ~ *sang* blood-red; **2.** *adv.:* *fig. voir* ~ see red; **3.** *su./m colour:* red; F red wine; ~ *à lèvres, bâton m de* ~ lipstick; ⊕ *au* ~ at red heat, red-hot; *porter au* ~ make (*s.th.*) red-hot; *se mettre du* ~ put on rouge; *traffic: passer au* ~ jump the lights; *su. pol. person:* red; **rougeâtre** [ruˈʒɑːtr] reddish; **rougeaud, e** [ʌˈʒo, ʌˈʒoːd] **1.** *adj.* red-faced; **2.** *su.* red-faced person; **rouge-gorge**, *pl.* **rouges-gorges** *orn.* [ruʒˈgɔrʒ] *m* robin (redbreast).

rougeole [ruˈʒɔl] *f* ♣ measles *sg.*; ♀ filed-cowwheat.

rouge-queue, *pl.* **rouges-queues** *orn.* [ruʒˈkø] *m* redstart; **rouget** [ruˈʒɛ] *m icht.* red mullet; gurnard; *vet.* swine-fever; *zo.* harvest-bug; **rougeur** [ʌˈʒœːr] *f* redness; *face:* blush, flush; blotch, red spot (*on the skin*); **rougir** [ʌˈʒiːr] (2a) *vt/i.* redden; turn red; *fig.* flush; *v/t.* make (*s.th.*) red-hot, bring (*s.th.*) to a red heat; *v/i.* blush.

rouille [ruːj] *f* rust (*a.* ✎); ♀ mildew; **rouillé, e** [ruˈje] rusty (*a. fig.*), rusted; ♀ mildewed; **rouiller** [ʌˈje] (1a) *v/t.* rust (*a.* ✎); ♀ mildew, blight; *se* ~ rust; ♀ go mildewed; *fig.* get out of practice; **rouillure** [ʌˈjyːr] *f* rustiness; ♀ rust, blight.

rouir [rwi:r] (2a) *v/t.* ret, steep (*flax etc.*); **rouissage** [rwi'sa:ʒ] *m* retting, steeping.

roulade [ru'lad] *f* roll; ♪ (vocal) flourish, roulade; **roulage** [ʌ'la:ʒ] *m* ♪⊃, *a. mot.* rolling; *goods*: carriage; haulage; cartage; (road) traffic; ♱ haulage firm; **roulant, e** [ʌ'lɑ̃, ʌ'lɑ̃:t] **1.** *adj.* rolling; sliding (*door*); good, smooth (*road*); smooth-running (*car*); ♱ floating, working (*capital*), going (*concern*); F screamingly funny; ✕, *fig.* feu *m* ʌ running fire; **2.** *su./m les ʌs* train *or* truck crews; **3.** *su./f* (*a. cuisine f ʌe*) field kitchen; **rouleau** [ʌ'lo] *m* roll; ⊕ *etc.* roller; *rope etc.*: coil; *phot.* spool; *tobacco*: twist; *hair*: curler, roller; (ʌ à pâtisserie) rolling pin; ʌ hygiénique toilet roll; *fig. être au bout de son ʌ* be at one's wit's end; **roulement** [rul'mɑ̃] *m* rolling; ⊕ *machine*: running; rumble, rattle; ⊕ (ʌ à billes) ball bearings *pl.*; ⊕ rolling (mechanism); race; ♪ *drum*: roll; ♱ *capital*: circulation; *fig.* alternation; ✍ run, taxying; *mot. bande f de ʌ* tread; ✍ *chemin m de ʌ* runway; *par ʌ* in rotation; **rouler** [ru'le] (1a) *v/t.* roll (along *or* about *or* up); *ling.* roll (one's *r's*), trill; *fig.* turn over (*in one's mind*); F cheat, fleece (*s.o.*); F ʌ *sa bosse* knock about the world; se ʌ roll; F se ʌ *par terre (de rire)* fall about laughing; *v/i.* roll (*a.* ♺); roll about *or* along *or* over; travel; wander; *mot.* ride, drive (along); ✍ taxi; ♱ run; ♱ circulate (*money*); take turns, rotate; vary (between, *entre*); ʌ *sur* turn upon, depend on; be rolling in (*money*).

roulette [ru'lɛt] *f* small wheel; *chair etc.*: caster, truckle; *tram*: trolley-wheel; ♱ *dentist's* drill; ♱ cycloid; *game*: roulette; bathchair; F *aller comme sur des ʌs* go like clockwork; *sp. patin m à ʌs* roller-skate.

rouleur, -euse [ru'lœ:r, ʌ'lø:z] *su.* travelling journeyman; worker who keeps changing jobs; *barrow*: wheeler; *su./m* ✕ trammer, haulier; *zo.* vine-weevil; *su./f zo.* leaf-roller; F low prostitute; **roulier, -ère** [ʌ'lje, ʌ'lje:r] **1.** *adj.* carrying; **2.** *su./m* carrier, carter; **roulis** ♺ [ʌ'li] *m* roll(ing); **roulotte** [ʌ'lɔt] *f* (gipsy-)van; *mot.* caravan, trailer;

roulure [ʌ'ly:r] *f* ⊕ *metal*: rolled edge; *timber*: cup-shake; *sl.* low prostitute.

roumain, e [ru'mɛ̃, ʌ'mɛn] **1.** *adj.* Rumanian; **2.** *su./m ling.* Rumanian; *su.* ♀ Rumanian.

roupie[1] [ru'pi] *f Indian coinage*: rupee.

roupie[2] [ʌ] *f* † drop of mucus; *fig.* bit of trash; F *ce n'est pas de la ʌ de sansonnet* that's not half bad.

roupiller F [rupi'je] (1a) *v/i.* snooze, doze; *sl.* sleep; **roupilleur** F [ʌ'jœ:r] *m* snoozer; **roupillon** F [ʌ'jɔ̃] *m* snooze; nap; *piquer un ʌ* have a snooze.

rouquin, e F [ru'kɛ̃, ʌ'kin] **1.** *adj.* red-haired, sandy-haired; **2.** *su.* red-haired *or* sandy-haired person, redhead.

rouspéter F [ruspe'te] (1f) *v/i.* resist, show fight; protest; complain; **rouspéteur** F [ʌ'tœ:r] *m* complainer; quarrelsome fellow; *Am. sl.* griper, sorehead.

roussâtre [ru'sa:tr] reddish; **rousseur** [ʌ'sœ:r] *f hair etc.*: redness; *tache f de ʌ* freckle.

roussi [ru'si] *m*: *sentir le ʌ* smell of burning; *fig.* smack of heresy (*opinion, statement*); be something of a heretic (*person*).

roussin † [ru'sɛ̃] *m* cart-horse; cob; *sl.* cop(per) (= *policeman*); *sl.* police-spy, *Am. sl.* stool pigeon.

roussir [ru'si:r] (2a) *vt/i.* turn brown; scorch, singe (*linen*); *cuis.* brown.

routage [ru'ta:ʒ] *m post*: sorting; routing.

route [rut] *f* road(way); path; route (*a.* ✕, ♺, ✍); course (*a.* ♺); ✕ *chanson f de ʌ* marching song; *en ʌ* on the way; ♱ on her course; ♱ on the road; *en ʌ!* off you go!; let's go!; ♺ right away!; ♱ full speed ahead!; *faire ʌ sur* make for; *faire fausse ʌ* go astray, take the wrong road; *fig.* be on the wrong track; *mettre en ʌ* start (up); *se mettre en ʌ* set out; ♺ get under way.

router [ru'te] (1a) *v/t. post*: sort; route.

routier, -ère [ru'tje, ʌ'tjɛr] **1.** *adj.* road-...; *carte f ʌère* road-map; réseau *m ʌ* highway network; *voie f ʌère* traffic lane; carriage-way; **2.** *su./m* track-chart; *mot.* long-distance driver; *cyclist*: (road) racer; *boy scout*: rover; F *vieux* ~ old stager; *su./f* roadster; road-map; traction-engine; **routine** [~'tin] *f* routine; red tape; *par* ~ as a matter of routine; *de* ~ routine ...; **routinier, -ère** [~ti'nje, ~'njɛːr] **1.** *adj.* routine (*activities*); who works to a routine (*person*); F in a rut; **2.** *su.* routinist; lover of routine; F *fig.* stick-in-the-mud.

rouvre ♦ [ruːvr] **1.** *adj.*: *chêne m* ~ = **2.** *su./m* Austrian *or* Russian oak, robur.

rouvrir [ruˈvriːr] (2f) *vt/i.* reopen.

roux, rousse [ru, rus] **1.** *adj.* russet; reddish(-brown); red (*hair*); *cuis.* brown(ed) (*butter, sauce*); *lune f rousse* April moon; *vents m/pl.* ~ cold winds of April; **2.** *su.* red-haired *or* sandy person; *su./m colour*: russet; reddish-brown; *cuis.* brown sauce; browning; brown(ed) butter.

royal, e, *m/pl.* **-aux** [rwaˈjal, ~'jo] royal, regal; kingly; crown (*prince*); *fig.* (*suivre*) *la voie* ~ (take) the royal road; **royaliste** [~jaˈlist] *adj., a. su.* royalist; **royaume** [~'joːm] *m* kingdom; realm (*a. fig.*); **royauté** [~jo'te] *f* royalty; kingship.

ru [ry] *m* water-course; gully; brook.

ruade [rɥad] *f horse*: kick, lashing out.

ruban [ryˈbɑ̃] *m* ribbon (*a.* ✂, *a. typewriter, decorations*), band; tape; measuring-tape; ~ *adhésif* adhesive tape; ~ *bleu* ♣ Blue Ribbon; *fig.* first place *or* prize; *fig.* (sign of) superiority; ~ *d'acier* steel band; *mot.* ~ *de frein* brake band; ⚡ ~ *isolant* insulating (*Am. a.* friction) tape; ~ *magnétique* (*or de magnétophone*) recording tape; ⊕ ~ *roulant* conveyor belt; ⊕ *scie f à* ~ band saw; **rubaner** [rybaˈne] (1a) *v/t.* trim (*s.th.*) with ribbons; cut (*s.th.*) (in)to ribbons; ⚡ tape (*a wire*); **rubanier, -ère** [~'nje, ~'njɛːr] ribbon-...

rubéfier ⚕ [rybeˈfje] (1o) *v/t.* rubefy; **rubicond, e** [~biˈkɔ̃, ~'kɔ̃ːd] florid, rubicund, redfaced.

rubigineux, -euse [rybiʒiˈnø, ~'nøːz] rusty, rust-colo(u)red.

rubis [ryˈbi] *m min.* ruby; *watch*: jewel; *faire* ~ *sur l'ongle* drain to the dregs; *montre f montée sur* ~ jewelled watch; *payer* ~ *sur l'ongle* pay to the last farthing *or Am.* last cent.

rubrique [ryˈbrik] *f journ.* column; heading, rubric.

ruche [ryʃ] *f* (bee-)hive; *cost.* ruching, ruche, frill; **rucher** [ryˈʃe] **1.** (1a) *v/t. cost.* ruche, frill; **2.** *su./m* apiary.

rude [ryd] rough (*cloth, path, sea, skin, wine*); hard (*blow, brush, climb, task, times, weather*); severe (*blow, cold, shock, trial, weather, a. fig.*); harsh (*voice, a. fig.*); primitive (*people etc.*); *fig.* brusque; F enormous; **rudement** [~'mɑ̃] *adv.* roughly *etc. see rude*; F extremely, awfully, real (= *very*).

rudesse [ryˈdɛs] *f* roughness; hardness; severity; harshness; primitiveness; brusqueness, abruptness.

rudiment [rydiˈmɑ̃] *m anat., biol., zo., etc.* rudiment; *fig.* ~s *pl. a.* grounding *sg.*; **rudimentaire** [~mɑ̃'tɛːr] rudimentary.

rudoyer [rydwaˈje] (1h) *v/t.* treat roughly; bully.

rue¹ [ry] *f* street, thoroughfare; ~ *à sens unique* one-way street; ~ *barrée!* no thoroughfare; ~ *commerçante* shopping street.

rue² ♦ [~] *f* rue.

ruée [rɥe] *f* rush, stampede.

ruelle [rɥɛl] *f* lane, alley; space between bed and wall.

ruer [rɥe] (1n) *v/i.* lash out, kick; *se* ~ (*sur*) fling o.s. (at); rush (at, to); **rueur, -euse** [rɥœːr, rɥøːz] **1.** *adj.* kicking (*horse*); **2.** *su. horse*: kicker.

rugby *sp.* [rygˈbi] *m* rugby (football).

rugir [ryˈʒiːr] (2a) *v/i.* roar (*a. fig.*); howl (*storm, wind*); **rugissement** [~ʒisˈmɑ̃] *m* roar(ing); *storm, wind*: howl(ing).

rugosité [rygoziˈte] *f* roughness, ruggedness; corrugation; *ground*: unevenness; **rugueux, -euse** [~'gø, ~'gøːz] rough, rugged; corrugated; gnarled (*tree, trunk*).

ruine [rɥin] *f* ruin (*a. fig.*); downfall (*a. fig.*); *fig.* fall; *tomber en* ~s fall in ruins; **ruiner** [rɥi'ne] (1a) *v/t.* ruin (*a. fig.*), destroy; ✝ bankrupt (*s.o.*); disprove (*a theory*); *se* ~ ruin o.s. (*person*); *fig.* go to ruin (*thing*); **ruineux, -euse** [~'nø, ~'nøːz] ruinous; *fig.* disastrous.

ruisseau [rɥi'so] *m* brook; stream (*a. fig. of blood*); *street, a. fig. pej.*: gutter; **ruisseler** [rɥis'le] (1c) *v/i.* stream (with, de), run (down);

trickle; drip; **ruisselet** [ˌ'lɛ] *m* rivulet, brooklet; **ruissellement** [rɥisɛl'mã] *m* streaming, running; trickling; dripping; *fig. jewels:* glitter, shimmer.

rumeur [ry'mœːr] *f* distant sound; confused noise; *traffic:* hum; uproar; *fig.* rumo(u)r, report.

ruminant, e *zo.* [rymi'nã, ˌ'nãːt] *adj., a. su./m* ruminant; **ruminer** [ˌ'ne] (1a) *v/t.* ruminate (*fig.* on an idea, *une idée*); *fig.* ponder; *v/i. zo., fig.* chew the cud, ruminate.

rune [ryn] *f* rune; **runique** [ry'nik] runic.

ruolz [ry'bls] *m* electroplate(d ware).

rupestre [ry'pɛstr] ♀ rupestral, rock-dwelling, rock-(*drawings*).

rupin, e F [ry'pɛ̃, ˌ'pin] **1.** *adj.* first-rate, *Am.* swell; wealthy (*person*); **2.** *su./m* swell, toff, nob.

rupteur ⚡ [ryp'tœːr] *m* circuit-breaker; **rupture** [ˌ'tyːr] *f dam:* breaking (*a.* ⚡ *circuit*), bursting; ⚡ *blood-vessel:* rupture; *bone:* fracture; *battle, engagement, negotiations:* breaking off; ⚖ *contract, promise:* breach; *road surface:* breaking up; *fig.* falling out, quarrel (*between persons*); 📷 ~ *de charge* dividing of load; ⚖ ~ *de promesse de mariage* breach of promise; *charge f de* ~ breaking load.

rural, e, *m/pl.* **-aux** [ry'ral, ˌ'ro] **1.** *adj.* rural, country...; **2.** *su.* peasant.

ruse [ryːz] *f* ruse, trick, wile; ✂ ~ *de guerre* stratagem; *en amour la* ~ *est de bonne guerre* all's fair in love and war; *user de* ~ practise deceit; **rusé, e** [ry'ze] artful, wily, crafty, cunning; **ruser** [ˌ] (1a) *v/i.* use guile; resort to trickery.

rush [rœʃ] *m sp.* (final) spurt, sprint; *fig.* rush.

russe [rys] **1.** *adj.* Russian; **2.** *su./m ling.* Russian; *su.* ♀ Russian; **russifier** [rysi'fje] (1o) *v/t.* Russianize.

russo... [rysɔ] Russo...; **~phile** [ˌ'fil] *adj., a. su.* Russophile.

rustaud, e [rys'to, ˌ'toːd] **1.** *adj.* boorish, loutish, uncouth; **2.** *su.* boor, lout; F bumpkin; **rusticité** [ˌtisi'te] *f* rusticity; boorishness; primitiveness; ♀ hardiness; **rustique** [ˌ'tik] **1.** *adj.* rustic (*a. fig.*); country...; *fig.* countrified, unrefined; ♀ hardy; **2.** *su./m* ⚒ bushhammer; **rustiquer** ⚒ [ˌti'ke] (1m) *v/t.* give a rustic appearance to; **rustre** [rystr] **1.** *adj.* boorish, loutish, churlish; **2.** *su./m* boor, lout, churl; F bumpkin.

rut [ryt] *m animals:* rut(ting), heat; *être en* ~ be in *or* on heat (*female*); rut (*male*).

rutilant, e [ryti'lã, ˌ'lãːt] glowing red; gleaming (*a. fig.*); ⚡ rutilant; *fig.* glittering; **rutiler** [ˌ'le] (1a) *v/i.* glow, gleam (red).

rythme [ritm] *m* rhythm; **rythmique** [rit'mik] rhythmic.

S

S, s [ɛs] *m* S, s; *s... sl.* = *sacré.*
sa [sa] *see* son¹.
sabbat [sa'ba] *m eccl.* Sabbath; *fig.*
witches' sabbath; F *fig.* din, racket;
sabbatique [ˌba'tik] sabbatical.
sabine ♀ [sa'bin] *f* savin(e).
sabir *ling.* [sa'biːr] *m Levant:* lingua
franca. [ing.)
sablage ⊕ [sɑ'blaːʒ] *m* sand-blast-)
sable¹ [sɑ:bl] *m* sand; ✻ gravel;
sand-glass; ~ *mouvant* quicksand; *bâ-*
tir sur le ~ build on sand; F *être sur le* ~
be broke; be down and out.
sable² *zo.* [~] *m* sable.
sablé *cuis.* [sɑ'ble] *m* shortbread;
sabler [~'ble] (1a) *v/t.* sand, gravel
(*a path*); ⊕ cast (*s.th.*) in a
sandmo(u)ld; ⊕ sand-blast; F *fig.*
swig (*a drink*); **sableur** [~'blœːr] *m*
⊕ sand-mo(u)lder; F *fig.* hard drinker; **sableux, -euse** [~'blø, ~'bløːz]
1. *adj.* sandy; 2. *su./f* ⊕ sand-jet;
sablier [~bli'e] *m* sand-man; sand-
box, sand-sifter; sand-glass; *cuis.*
egg-timer.
sablière¹ ⌂ [sɑbli'ɛːr] *f* plate;
stringer.
sablière² [sɑbli'ɛːr] *f* sand-pit;
gravel-pit; ⊕ sand-box; **sablon**
[~'blõ] *m* fine sand; **sablonner** [sɑ-
blɔ'ne] (1a) *v/t.* sand; *metall.* sprinkle with welding sand; **sablon-**
neux, -euse [~'nø, ~'nøːz] sandy;
gritty (*fruit*); **sablonnière** [~'njeːr]
f sand-pit, gravel-pit; *metall.* sand-
box.
sabord ⚓ [sa'bɔːr] *m* port(hole);
scuttle; **saborder** [~bɔr'de] (1a) *v/t.*
⚓ scuttle; *fig.* shut down, wind up (*a*
company etc.); *se* ~ ⚓ scuttle one's
ship; *fig.* shut down.
sabot [sa'bo] *m* sabot (*a.* ✻, ⊕);
wooden shoe *or* clog; *zo.* hoof; ⊕, ⚡,
mot. (brake-, contact-, *etc.*)shoe; F
dud; *toy:* top; *mot.* ~ (de Denver)
(TM) Denver shoe; *mot.* ~ de pare-
choc overrider; F *fig. dormir comme*
un ~ sleep like a log; **sabotage**
[sabɔ'taːʒ] *m work:* scamping, bun-
gling; scamped *or* bungled work;

(act of) sabotage (*during strikes etc.*);
saboter [~'te] (1a) *v/i.* bungle one's
work; commit acts of sabotage; *v/t.*
⊕ shoe (*a pile*); 🚂 chair (*a sleeper*);
fig. bungle (*one's work etc.*); ⊕ sabotage (*a job, machinery*); **saboteur**
m, **-euse** *f* [~'tœːr, ~'tøːz] ⊕ saboteur; *work:* bungler, botcher; **sa-**
botier [~'tje] *m* sabot-maker.
sabre [sɑːbr] *m* sabre, broadsword;
icht. sword-fish; ~ *au clair* (with)
drawn sword; *coup m de* ~ sabre cut;
slash; F *fig. traîneur m de* ~ sabre-
rattler; **sabrer** [~'bre] (1a) *v/t.*
sabre; slash; F botch, scamp (*one's*
work); F *fig.* make drastic cuts in (*a*
play etc.); **sabretache** ⚔ [~brə'taʃ] *f*
sabretache; **sabreur** [~'brœːr] *m* †
dashing cavalry officer; F *work:*
scamper.
sac¹ [sak] *m coal, flour, etc.:* sack; bag;
⚔ kit-bag, knapsack; rucksack; *zo.*
pouch; *anat.* sac; *geol.* pocket;
(wind-)cone; sackcloth; ~ *à main*
handbag, *Am. a.* purse; ~ *de couchage*
sleeping-bag; ~ *de voyage* travelling-
case; ~ *en bandoulière* shoulder-bag;
~ *en papier* paper-bag; F *homme m de*
~ *et de corde* thorough scoundrel; F
c'est dans le ~ it's in the bag; F *vider*
son ~ get it off one's chest.
sac² [~] *m* pillage, sacking.
saccade [sa'kad] *f* jerk; *par* ~*s* in
jerks; *fig.* by fits and starts; **sacca-**
dé, e [saka'de] jerky; irregular.
saccage [sa'kaːʒ] *m* sacking; havoc;
saccager [saka'ʒe] (1l) *v/t.* sack;
create havock in; upset; **saccageur**
m, **-euse** *f* [~'ʒœːr, ~'ʒøːz] plunderer.
saccharate 🜞 [sakka'rat] *m* saccharate; **saccharide** 🜞 [~'rid] *m*
saccharide; **saccharifier** 🜞 [~ri-
'fje] (1o) *v/t.* saccharify; **saccha-**
rin, e [~'rɛ̃, ~'rin] *adj., a. su./f* saccharine; **saccharose** 🜞 [~'roːz] *m*
saccharose.
sacerdoce [saser'dɔs] *m* priesthood
(*a. coll.*); **sacerdotal, e**, *m/pl.* **-aux**
[~dɔ'tal, ~'to] priestly; sacerdotal;
fig. priestlike.

sachant [sa'ʃɑ̃] *p.pr.* of *savoir* 1; **sache** [saʃ] *1st p. sg. pres. sbj.* of *savoir* 1.

sachée [sa'ʃe] *f* sackful, bagful; **sachet** [~'ʃɛ] *m* small bag; *scent*: sachet; ~ *de thé* teabag.

sacoche [sa'kɔʃ] *f* satchel, wallet; *mot., bicycle, etc.*: tool-bag; ✗ saddle-bag.

sacramental *eccl.* [sakramɑ̃'tal] *m* sacramental; **sacramentel, -elle** [~'tɛl] *eccl.* sacramental; *fig.* ritual.

sacre [sakr] *m king*: anointing, coronation; *bishop*: consecration.

sacraliser [sakrali'ze] (1a) *v/t.* make or consider (*s.th., s.o.*) sacred; **sacralité** [~'te] *f* sacredness; **sacré, e** [sa'kre] holy (*orders, scripture*); sacred (*spot, vessel, a. fig.*); *anat.* sacral; *sl.* (*before su.*) confounded, damned; **sacre-bleu!** [~krə'blø] *int.* damn (it)!; **sacrement** *eccl.* [~krə'mɑ̃] *m* sacrament; *derniers* ~s *pl.* last rites; *fréquenter les* ~s be a regular communicant; **sacrer** [~'kre] (1a) *v/t.* anoint, crown (*a king*); consecrate (*a bishop*); *v/i.* F curse.

sacrificateur *m*, **-trice** *f* † [sakrifika'tœːr, ~'tris] sacrificer; **sacrifice** [~'fis] *m* sacrifice (*a. fig.*); *eccl. saint* ~ Blessed Sacrament; **sacrifier** [~'fje] (1o) *v/t.* sacrifice (*a. ✝, a. fig.*); *fig.* give (*s.th.*) up to (for *à*); *se* ~ devote o.s. (to, *à*); *v/i.* sacrifice; conform (to, *à*); **sacrilège** [~'lɛːʒ] **1.** *adj.* sacrilegious, impious; **2.** *su.* sacrilegious person; *su./m* sacrilege.

sacripant [sakri'pɑ̃] *m* F scoundrel, knave; † braggart.

sacristain [sakris'tɛ̃] *m* sacristan; sexton; **sacristi!** [~'ti] *int.* Good Lord!; hang it!; **sacristie** *eccl.* [~'ti] *f* sacristy, vestry.

sacro... [sakrɔ] sacro-... (*a. anat.*); ~-**saint, e** [~'sɛ̃, ~'sɛ̃t] sacrosanct.

sacrum *anat.* [sa'krɔm] *m* sacrum.

sadique [sa'dik] **1.** *adj.* sadistic; **2.** *su.* sadist; **sadisme** [~'dism] *m* sadism.

safari [safa'ri] *m* safari; ~-**photo** photographic safari.

safran [sa'frɑ̃] **1.** *su./m* ♀, *cuis.* saffron; ♀ crocus; **2.** *adj./inv.* saffron (-colo[u]red); **safraner** *cuis.* [~fra-'ne] (1a) *v/t.* (colo[u]r *or* flavo[u]r with) saffron.

sagace [sa'gas] sagacious; shrewd; **sagacité** [~gasi'te] *f* sagacity; shrewdness; *avec* ~ sagaciously.

sage [sa:ʒ] **1.** *adj.* wise; prudent; discreet (*person, conduct*); well-behaved; good (*child*); modest (*woman*); **2.** *su./m* wise man, sage; ~-**femme**, *pl.* ~s-**femmes** [saʒ-'fam] *f* midwife; **sagesse** [sa'ʒɛs] *f* wisdom; discretion; good behavio(u)r; *woman*: modesty; *la* ~ (*d'*)*après coup* hindsight.

sagittaire [saʒi'tɛːr] *su./m hist.* archer; *astr. le* ♎ Sagittarius, the Archer; *su./f* ♀ sagittaria, arrowhead.

sagou *cuis.* [sa'gu] *m* sago.

sagouin, e [sa'gwɛ̃, ~'gwin] *su. zo.* squirrel-monkey; *su./m* F slovenly fellow; *su./f* F slattern, slut.

sagoutier ♀ [sagu'tje] *m* sago-palm.

saignant, e [sɛ'ɲɑ̃, ~'ɲɑ̃:t] bleeding; *cuis.* underdone, rare (*meat*); F *fig.* sensational, F hot; **saignée** [~'ɲe] *f* ✝ bleeding; *anat.* (~ *du bras*) bend of the arm; *drainage*: ditch; *fig. resources*: drain, loss(es *pl.*); ⊕ (*oil-*)groove; **saigner** [~'ɲe] (1b) *vt/i.* bleed (*a. fig.*); ⊕, *fig.* drain; tap.

saillant, e [sa'jɑ̃, ~'jɑ̃:t] **1.** *adj.* △ projecting; prominent; *fig.* outstanding, striking; **2.** *su./m* ✗ salient; **saillie** [~'ji] *f* spurt, bound; ✗ sally (*a. fig. wit*); *zo.* covering; *fig.* outburst; *paint.* prominence; △ projection; ⊕ lug; *en* ~ projecting; bay(-*window*); *faire* ~ project; protrude; *par* ~s by leaps and bounds.

saillir¹ [sa'jiːr] (2a) *v/i.* spurt out, gush out; ✗ (make a) sally; *v/t. zo.* cover (*a mare*).

saillir² [~] (2p) *v/i.* project; *paint. etc.* stand out.

sain, saine [sɛ̃, sɛn] healthy (*person, climate, a. sp.*); sound (*doctrine, horse, fruit, timber, views, ✝, ♂, etc.*); wholesome (*food*); ⚓ clear; ~ *et sauf* safe and sound; **sain(-)bois** ♀ [sɛ̃'bwa] *m* spurge-flax.

saindoux *cuis.* [sɛ̃'du] *m* lard.

sainfoin ♀, ✎ [sɛ̃'fwɛ̃] *m* sainfoin.

saint, sainte [sɛ̃, sɛ̃:t] **1.** *adj.* holy; *eccl.* saintly; consecrated (*building, ground, etc.*); ♀ *Jean* St. John; F *toute la sainte semaine* all the blessed week; **2.** *su.* saint; *su./m*: *les* ~s *pl. de glace* the Ice *or* Frost Saints; *le* ~ *des* ~s the Holy of

Holies; ~-bernard *zo.* [sɛbɛr-
ˈnaːr] *m/inv.* St. Bernard; ~-crépin
[⌣krɛˈpɛ̃] *m* shoemaker's tools *pl.*;
fig. possessions *pl.*; ♀-Esprit [⌣tɛs-
ˈpri] *m* Holy Ghost; sainteté [sɛ̃-
təˈte] *f* holiness, saintliness; *pej.*
sanctity.

saint...: ~-frusquin F [sɛ̃frysˈkɛ̃]
m/inv. possessions *pl.*; *tout le* ~ the
whole caboodle; ~-glinglin F
[⌣glɛ̃ˈglɛ̃]: *à la* ~ never; ~-office *eccl.*
[⌣tɔˈfis] *m* Holy Office; ♀-Père *eccl.*
[⌣ˈpɛːr] *m the* Holy Father, *the* Pope;
♀-Siège *eccl.* [⌣ˈsjɛːʒ] *m the* Holy
See; ♀-Sylvestre [⌣silˈvɛstrə]: *la* ~
New Year's Eve.

sais [sɛ] *1st p. sg. pres. of savoir* 1.

saisi ⚖ [sɛˈzi] *m* distrainee; saisie
[⌣] *f* seizure (*a.* ⚖); ⚖ distraint;
saisine [⌣ˈzin] *f* ⚖ livery of seisin;
♣ *etc.* lashing; *boat:* sling; saisir
[⌣ˈziːr] (2a) *v/t.* seize; catch hold
of; ⚖ attach; distrain upon (*goods*);
foreclose (*a mortgage*); ♣ stow
(*anchors, boats*); *cuis.* cook (*meat*)
at high temperature; *fig.* catch,
grasp; understand; ~ *q. de refer*
(*s.th.*) to s.o.; vest s.o. with; *se*
~ *de* seize upon (*a. fig.*); saisissable [⌣ziˈsabl] seizable; attachable; *fig.* distinguishable; saisissant, e [⌣ziˈsã, ⌣ˈsãːt] striking; gripping (*scene, spectacle, speech*); piercing (*cold*); saisissement [⌣zisˈmã]
m † seizure; sudden chill; shock,
emotion.

saison [sɛˈzɔ̃] *f* season; tourist
season; *time:* period; ~ *hivernale*
winter season; (*hors*) *de* ~ (un)sea-
sonable, (in)opportune; *la* ~ *bat son
plein* it is the height of the season;
saisonnier, -ère [⌣zɔˈnje, ⌣ˈnjɛːr]
1. *adj.* seasonal; 2. *su.* seasonal
worker.

salade [saˈlad] *f* salad; lettuce; *fig.*
confusion, jumble; *sl. panier m à* ~
Black Maria (= *prison van*); sala-
dier [⌣laˈdje] *m* salad-bowl.

salage [saˈlaːʒ] *m* salting; † salt-tax.
salaire [saˈlɛːr] *m* wage(s *pl.*) (*a. fig.*);
pay; *fig.* reward; ~ *de base* basic
wage; *les gros* ~s *pl.* the top earners.

salaison [salɛˈzɔ̃] *f* salting; *bacon:*
curing; salt provisions *pl.*; *marchand
m de* ~s dry-salter.

salamandre [salaˈmãːdr] *f zo.* sal-
amander; ⊕ slow-combustion stove.

salami [salaˈmi] *m* salami; *fig. métho-*

de f (ou tactique f) du ~ salami tactics
sg.

salangane *orn.* [salãˈgan] *f* salangane; *cuis.* nid *m de* ~ bird's nest.

salant [saˈlã] *adj./m* salt-...

salariat [salaˈrja] *m* salaried *or* wage-
earning classes *pl.*; salarié, e [⌣ˈrje]
1. *adj.* wage-earning (*person*); paid
(*work*); 2. *su.* wage-earner; *pej.* hireling; salarier [⌣ˈrje] (1o) *v/t.* pay
wages to (*s.o.*).

salaud *sl.* [saˈlo] *m* dirty person; *fig.*
bastard, *Br. a.* bugger; sale [sal]
dirty (*a. fig.*); *fig.* foul.

salé, e [saˈle] 1. *adj.* salt(ed); *fig.*
spicy, coarse (*story*); biting (*comment etc.*); F stiff (*price*, ⚖ *sentence*);
2. *su./m* salt pork; *petit* ~ pickled
pork.

salement [salˈmã] *adv.* dirtily;
meanly, nastily; *sl.* very, extremely.

saler [saˈle] (1a) *v/t.* salt (*a. fig.*);
cure (*bacon*); *fig.* fleece, overcharge
(*s.o.*).

saleté [salˈte] *f* dirt(iness), filth(iness);
fig. indecency; dirty story; *fig.* dirty
trick; *fig. dire des* ~s talk smut.

salicylate ⚗ [salisiˈlat] *m* salicylate;
salicylique ⚗ [⌣ˈlik] salicylic.

salière [saˈljɛːr] *f table:* salt-cellar,
Am. saltshaker; *kitchen:* salt-box.

saligaud *m, e f sl.* [saliˈgo, ⌣ˈgoːd]
dirty dog, skunk, rotter; sloven.

salin, e [saˈlɛ̃, ⌣ˈlin] 1. *adj.* saline,
salty; salt (*air*); 2. *su./m* salt-marsh;
⊕, ⚗ (crude) potash; 2. *su./f* salt-
pan, salt works *usu. sg*; rock-salt
mine; salinier [⌣liˈnje] *m* salter;
✝ salt merchant.

salir [saˈliːr] (2a) *v/t.* dirty, soil; *fig.*
sully; *se* ~ get dirty *or* soiled; *fig.*
tarnish one's reputation; salissant,
e [⌣liˈsã, ⌣ˈsãːt] dirty(ing); *tex. etc.*
easily soiled.

salivaire *anat.* [saliˈvɛːr] salivary;
salivation ⚕ [⌣vaˈsjɔ̃] *f* salivation;
salive [saˈliːv] *f* saliva; F *perdre sa*
~ waste one's breath; saliver [⌣li-
ˈve] (1a) *v/i.* salivate.

salle [sal] *f* hall; (*large*) room; *hospital:* ward; thea. (*a.* ~ *de spectacle*)
auditorium, F house; ~ *à manger*
dining-room; ~ *d'attente* waiting-
room; ~ *de bain(s)* bathroom; ~ *de
classe* class-room, schoolroom; ✗
~ *de police* guard-room; ~ *des pas
perdus* lobby, waiting-hall.

salmigondis [salmigɔ̃ˈdi] *m cuis.*

salmagundi, ragout; *fig.* hotch-potch.

salmis *cuis.* [sal'mi] *m* salmi; ragout (*of roasted game*).

saloir [sa'lwaːr] *m* salting-tub.

salon [sa'lɔ̃] *m* drawing-room; ⚓ *etc.* saloon, cabin; (*tea-*)room; ⚥ exhibition; *fig.* ⚓ *pl.* society *sg.*, fashionable circles; ⚥ *de l'automobile* motor-show; *fréquenter les* ⚓s move in high society; **salonnier** [⚓lɔ'nje] *m* art critic; critic of the *Salon* (*the annual art exhibition in Paris*).

salopard *sl.* [salɔ'paːr] *m* unprepossessing person; **salope** *sl.* [⚓'lɔp] *f* tart; bitch; **saloper** F [salɔ'pe] (1a) *v/t.* mess up, *sl.* goof up; **saloperie** F [salɔ'pri] *f* filth; rubbish, trash; mess; bungled piece of work; ⚓s *pl.* smut *sg.*, dirt *sg.*; *faire une* ⚓ *à* play a dirty trick on; **salopette** [⚓'pɛt] *f* overall(s *pl.*); dungarees *pl.*

salpêtre [sal'pɛːtr] *m* saltpetre, potassium nitrate, nitre.

salsifis ♀, *cuis.* [salsi'fi] *m* salsify.

saltimbanque [saltɛ̃'bɑ̃ːk] *m* (travelling) showman; *pol., fig.* charlatan, mountebank; † tumbler.

salubre [sa'lyːbr] salubrious, healthy; wholesome (*food etc.*); **salubrité** [⚓lybri'te] *f* salubrity, healthiness; *food etc.*: wholesomeness; ⚓ *publique* public health.

saluer [sa'lɥe] (1n) *v/t.* bow to; salute (*a.* ⚔, ⚓), greet (*s.o.*); *fig.* welcome; ⚓ ⚓ *du pavillon* dip the flag to. [(*of the sea air*).⟩

salure [sa'lyːr] *f* saltness; salt tang⟩

salut [sa'ly] *m* safety; *eccl., a. fig.* salvation; greeting; bow; ⚔ salute; ⚔ *flag*: dipping; ⚔ *colour*: lowering; *eccl.* Benediction (of the Blessed Sacrament); ⚓! hullo!; how do you do?; *Armée f du* ⚓ Salvation Army; **salutaire** [saly'tɛːr] salutary, wholesome, beneficent; **salutation** [⚓ta'sjɔ̃] *f* greeting; bow; *agréez mes meilleures* ⚓s *end of letter*: yours faithfully; **salutiste** [⚓'tist] *su.* Salvationist, member of the Salvation Army.

salve [salv] *f* ⚔ salvo; *guns*: salute; *fig.* round (*of applause*).

samedi [sam'di] *m* Saturday; ⚓ *saint* Holy Saturday, Saturday before Easter.

sanctificateur, -trice [sɑ̃ktifika-'tœːr, ⚓'tris] **1.** *adj.* sanctifying;

2. *su.* sanctifier; *su./m*: *le* ⚥ the Holy Ghost; **sanctification** [⚓fika'sjɔ̃] *f* sanctification; *Sabbath*: observance; **sanctifier** [⚓'fje] (1o) *v/t.* sanctify, make holy; observe (*the Sabbath*); *que votre nom soit sanctifié* hallowed be Thy name.

sanction [sɑ̃k'sjɔ̃] *f* sanction (*a. pol.*); approval; penalty, punishment; **sanctionner** [⚓sjɔ'ne] (1a) *v/t.* sanction; approve; punish.

sanctuaire [sɑ̃k'tɥɛːr] *m* sanctuary (*a. fig.*); **sanctus** *eccl.,* ♪ [⚓'tys] *m Mass*: sanctus.

sandal, *pl.* -**als** [sɑ̃'dal] *m see* santal.

sandale [sɑ̃'dal] *f* sandal; gym-shoe.

sandow (*TM*) [sɑ̃'dɔf] *m* elastic; *sp.* chest-expander.

sandre *icht.* [sɑ̃ːdr] *f* pike-perch.

sandwich, *pl. a.* -**es** [sɑ̃'dwitʃ] *m* sandwich; *fig.* ⚓ *play* gooseberry.

sang [sɑ̃] *m* blood; race, lineage; kinship, relationship; *biol. à* ⚓ *chaud* (*froid*) warm-blooded (cold-blooded) (*animal*); F *avoir le* ⚓ *chaud* be quick-tempered; ⚕ *coup m de* ⚓ (apoplectic) fit; *droit m du* ⚓ birthright; ⚕ *écoulement m de* ⚓ h(a)emorrhage; *être tout en* ⚓ be covered with blood; *se faire du mauvais* ⚓ worry; ⚓-*froid* [⚓'frwa] *m* composure, self-control; *de* ⚓ in cold blood, cold-bloodedly; *accompli de* ⚓ cold-blooded (*murder etc.*).

sanglant, e [sɑ̃'glɑ̃, ⚓'glɑ̃ːt] bloody; blood-covered; blood-red; *fig.* bitter (*attack, criticism, tears, etc.*); deadly (*insult*).

sangle [sɑ̃ːgl] *f* strap; (*saddle-*)girth; *fit m de* ⚓ camp-bed; **sangler** [sɑ̃'gle] (1a) *v/t.* strap; girth (*a horse*); strike (*s.o.*); fasten the webbing on (*a bed, a chair*).

sanglier *zo.* [sɑ̃gli'e] *m* wild boar.

sanglot [sɑ̃'glo] *m* sob; **sangloter** [⚓glɔ'te] (1a) *v/i.* sob.

sangsue *zo., fig.* [sɑ̃'sy] *f* leech.

sanguin, e [sɑ̃'gɛ̃, ⚓'gin] blood...; of blood; full-blooded (*person*); red-faced (*person*); **sanguinaire** [⚓gi'nɛːr] **1.** *adj.* bloodthirsty (*person*); bloody (*fight*); **2.** *su./f* ♀ blood-root; **sanguine** [⚓'gin] *f* blood-orange; red h(a)ematite, red chalk; *min.* bloodstone; *paint.* red chalk (*drawing*); **sanguinolent, e** [⚓ginɔ'lɑ̃, ⚓'lɑ̃ːt] blood-red; ⚕ sanguinolent.

sanie ⚓ [sa'ni] *f* pus, F matter;
sanieux, -euse ⚓ [~'njø, ~'njø:z]
sanious.

sanitaire [sani'tɛːr] **1.** *adj.* sanitary;
✗ hospital (*train*), ambulance (*aero-plane*); **2.** *su./m* (*a.* ~s *pl.*) sanitation;
(bathroom) plumbing; bathroom.

sans [sɑ̃] *prp.* without; free from
or of; ...less; un...; ~ *hésiter* without hesitating *or* hesitation; *non* ~
peine not without difficulty; ~ *plus
tarder* without further delay; ~
bretelles strapless; ~ *cesse* ceaseless; ~ *doute* doubtless, no doubt;
~ *exemple* unparalleled; ~ *faute*
without fail; faultless; ~ *le sou*
penniless; ~ *que* (*sbj.*) without (*ger.*);
~ *cela,* ~ *quoi* but for that; *see (ger.)*;
~**abri** [~za'bri] *m/inv.* homeless
person; ~**atout** [~za'tu] *m* cards:
no trumps; ~**cœur** F [~'kœːr] *su./
inv.* heartless person; ~**culotte**
hist. [~ky'lɔt] *m* sansculotte (= *extreme republican*); ~**façon** [~fa'sɔ̃]
m/inv. straightforwardness, blunt-
ness; ~**fil** [~'fil] *f/inv.* wireless
message; ~**filiste** [~fi'list] *su.* wireless enthusiast; wireless operator;
~**gêne** [~'ʒɛn] *su./inv.* off-handed
or unceremonious person; *su./m/
inv. pej.* off-handedness; F cheek;
~**le-sou** F [~lɔ'su] *su./inv.* penniless
person.

sansonnet *orn.* [sɑ̃sɔ'ne] *m* starling.
sans...: ~**parti** *pol.* [~par'ti] *su./inv.*
independent; ~**souci** [~sɑ̃su'si]
adj./inv. carefree; unconcerned; ~
travail [~tra'vaj] *su./inv.* jobless
person.

santal, *pl.* -**als** ⚕ [sɑ̃'tal] *m* sandal-
wood.

santé [sɑ̃'te] *f* health; *à votre* ~!
cheers!; your health!; *être en bonne* ~
be well; *maison f de* ~ private hospital, nursing home; mental hospital; *médecin m de (la)* ~ medical
officer of health, F M.O.H.; *service m
de (la)* ~ Health Service, ✗ medical
service, ⚓ quarantine service.

saoul [su] *see* soûl.

sape [sap] *f* ✗ *etc.* sap(ping); under-
mining (*a. fig.*); **saper** [sa'pe] (1a)
v/t. sap, undermine (*a. fig.*).

sapeur ✗ [sa'pœːr] *m* sapper;
pioneer; ~**pompier,** *pl.* ~**s-pom-
piers** [~pœrpɔ'pje] *m* fireman;
sapeurs-pompiers pl. fire-brigade.

saphir *min.,* *a. orn.* [sa'fiːr] *m* sap-

phire; **saphirine** *min.* [~fi'rin] *f*
sapphirine.

sapientiaux *bibl.* [sapjɑ̃'sjo] *adj./m/
pl.*: *Livres m/pl.* ~ wisdom-literature
sg.

sapin [sa'pɛ̃] *m* ⚕ fir(-tree), spruce;
✝ deal; F coffin; *faux* ~ pitch-pine;
F *toux f qui sent le* ~ churchyard
cough; **sapinière** ⚕ [~pi'njɛːr] *f*
fir-plantation.

saponacé, e [sapɔna'se] sapona-
ceous, soapy; **saponaire** ⚕ [~'nɛːr] *f*
saponaria, *usu.* soapwort; **saponi-
fier** [~ni'fje] (1o) *v/t. a. se* ~ saponify.

sapristi! ✝ [sapris'ti] *int.* Good
Lord!; hang it!

sarbacane [sarba'kan] *f* blow-pipe.
sarcasme [sar'kasm] *m* sarcasm;
sarcastic remark; **sarcastique** [~
kas'tik] sarcastic.

sarcelle *orn.* [sar'sel] *f* teal.
sarclage ✗ [sar'klaːʒ] *m* weeding;
sarcler [~'kle] *v/t.* ✗ weed; hoe
(up); *fig.* weed out; **sarcloir** ✗
[~'klwaːr] *m* hoe; **sarclure** ✗ [~
'klyːr] *f* (uprooted) weeds *pl.*

sarcome ⚓ [sar'koːm] *m* sarcoma;
sarcophage [sarkɔ'faːʒ] *m* sarcoph-
agus.

sarde [sard] **1.** *adj.* Sardinian; **2.**
su./m ling. Sardinian; *su.* ♀ Sardinian; **sardine** [sar'din] *f icht.* pil-
chard; ✝ sardine; ✗ F N.C.O.'s
stripe; **sardinerie** [~din'ri] *f* sar-
dine-packing factory *etc.*; **sar-
dinier, -ère** [~di'nje, ~'njɛːr] *su.*
sardine fisher; sardine packer *or*
curer; *su./m* sardine-net; sardine-
boat. [*bibl.* sardine stone.]
sardoine *min.* [sar'dwan] *f* sard;
sardonique [sardɔ'nik] sardonic.
sargasse ⚕ [sar'gas] *f* sargasso.
sarigue *zo.* [sa'rig] *m* sarigue;
South America: opossum.

sarment ⚕ [sar'mɑ̃] *m* vine-shoot;
bine; **sarmenteux, -euse** ⚕ [~mɑ̃-
'tø, ~'tøːz] sarmentous; *vine*: climbing.

sarrasin, e [sara'zɛ̃, ~'zin] **1.** *adj. hist.*
Saracen; **2.** *su. hist.* ♀ Saracen; *su./m*
✗ buckwheat; *su./f* ✗, ⚔ portcullis.

sarrau, *pl.* *a.* -**s** *cost.* [sa'ro] *m*
overall, smock.

sarriette ⚕ [sa'rjet] *f* savory.

sas ⊕ [sɑ] *m* sieve, riddle, screen;
(*air-*)lock; lock-chamber; ⚓ submarine: flooding-chamber; *passer
au* ~ sift, bolt (*s.th.*).

sasse [sɑːs] *f* ⚓ bailing-scoop, bailer; ⊕ *flour*: bolter.

sassement [sɑsˈmɑ̃] *m* ⚓ passing through a lock; ⊕ sifting, screening, *flour etc.*: bolting; **sasser** [sɑˈse] (1a) *v/t.* ⚓ pass (*a boat*) through a lock; ⊕ sift (*a. fig.*), screen, bolt (*flour etc.*); jig (*ore*); *fig.* examine in detail.

satané, e F [sataˈne] confounded; **satanique** [∼ˈnik] satanic; *fig.* diabolical.

satellisation [satɛllizaˈsjɔ̃] *f satellite*: putting into orbit; *fig.* making into or becoming a satellite; **satelliser** [∼liˈze] (1a) *v/t.* put (*a satellite*) into orbit; *fig.* make a satellite of (*a country etc.*); **satellite** [∼ˈlit] *m astr., phys., a. fig.* satellite.

satiété [sasjeˈte] *f* satiety; *à* ∼ to repletion, to satiety.

satin ⚘, *tex.* [saˈtɛ̃] *m* satin; *bois m de* ∼ satinwood; **satinade** ⚘, *tex.* [satiˈnad] *f silk*: satinette; **satinage** [∼ˈnaːʒ] *m* ⊕ glazing; *tex.* satining; *paper*: surfacing; *phot. print*: burnishing; **satiné, e** [∼ˈne] **1.** *adj.* satiny, glazed (*leather, paper*); *geol.* satin-(*spar, stone*); **2.** *su./m* gloss; **satiner** [∼ˈne] (1a) *v/t.* satin, glaze; *surface* (*paper*); press (*linen, paper*); *phot.* burnish; **satinette** ⚘, *tex.* [∼ˈnɛt] *f* (*cotton*) satinette, sateen; **satineur, -euse** *tex.* [∼ˈnœːr, ∼ˈnøːz] *su.* satiner, glazer; *su./f* satining-machine, glazing-machine.

satire [saˈtiːr] *f* satire (on, *contre*); lampoon; satirizing; **satirique** [satiˈrik] **1.** *adj.* satiric(al); **2.** *su./m* satirist; **satiriser** [∼riˈze] (1a) *v/t.* satirize.

satisfaction [satisfakˈsjɔ̃] *f* satisfaction (*a. fig.*); *fig.* amends *pl.* (for *pour, de*); *eccl.* atonement (for, de); **satisfaire** [∼ˈfɛːr] (4r) *v/t.* satisfy (*a. fig.*); make amends to (*s.o.*); *v/i. eccl.* make atonement; ∼ *à* satisfy; *fig.* meet (*an objection etc.*); *fig.* fulfil (*a duty*); **satisfaisant, e** [∼fəˈzɑ̃, ∼ˈzɑ̃ːt] satisfactory, satisfying; **satisfait, e** [∼ˈfɛ, ∼ˈfɛt] satisfied, pleased (with, de).

saturable ⚗, *phys.* [satyˈrabl] saturable; **saturer** [∼ˈre] (1a) *v/t.* ⚗, *phys.* saturate (with, de); *fig.* satiate.

saturnin, e ⚕ [satyrˈnɛ̃, ∼ˈnin]

lead-...; **saturnisme** ⚕ [∼ˈnism] *m* lead-poisoning.

satyre [saˈtiːr] *m myth.* satyr; *zo.* satyr butterfly.

sauce [soːs] *f cuis., a. tobacco*: sauce; *cuis.* gravy; *drawing*: lamp-black; ∼ *tomate* tomato sauce; F *dans la* ∼ in the soup; **saucée** F [soˈse] *f rain*: downpour; *fig.* dressing-down, F telling-off; **saucer** [∼ˈse] (1k) *v/t.* dip (*s.th.*) in the sauce; soak (*a.* F *fig.*); F scold, tell (*s.o.*) off; **saucière** [∼ˈsjɛːr] *f* sauce-boat; gravy-boat.

saucisse [soˈsis] *f* (*fresh*) sausage; *sl.* fat-head; idiot; F *ne pas attacher son chien avec des* ∼*s* be careful with one's money.

saucisson [sosiˈsɔ̃] *m* (*dry, smoked, etc.*) sausage; **saucissonnage** F *fig.* [∼sɔˈnaːʒ] *m* splitting (up); **saucissonner** [∼sɔˈne] (1a) *v/i.* have a snack; picknick.

sauf, sauve [sof, soːv] **1.** *adj.* safe, unhurt; unscathed; **2.** *sauf prp.* except, but; save; in the absence of; ∼ *à* (*inf.*) subject to (*ger.*); ∼ *erreur ou omission* errors and omissions excepted; ∼ *imprévu* except for unforeseen circumstances; ∼ *que* (*sbj.*) except that (*ind.*); ∼-**conduit** [sofkɔ̃ˈdɥi] *m* safe-conduct, pass.

sauge ⚘, *cuis.* [soːʒ] *f* sage.

saugrenu, e [sogrəˈny] preposterous, ridiculous.

saulaie ⚘ [soˈle] *f* willow-plantation; **saule** ⚘ [soːl] *m* willow; ∼ *pleureur* weeping willow; **saulée** [soˈle] *f* row of willows.

saumâtre [soˈmɑːtr] brackish; F nasty; sour (*person*).

saumon [soˈmɔ̃] **1.** *su./m icht.* salmon; ⊕ *lead*: pig; ⊕ *metal*: ingot, block; **2.** *adj./inv.* salmon-pink; **saumoné, e** [somɔˈne] salmon; *icht. truite f* ∼*e* salmon-trout; **saumoneau** *icht.* [∼ˈno] *m* young salmon; parr.

saumure [soˈmyːr] *f* pickling brine; pickle; **saumurer** [∼myˈre] (1a) *v/t.* pickle in brine; brine (*anchovies, meat*).

sauna [soˈna] *m* sauna.

saupoudrage [sopuˈdraːʒ] *m* sprinkling; *fig.* scattering; **saupoudrer** [∼ˈdre] (1a) *v/t.* sprinkle, powder (with, de); dust (with, de); *fig.* scatter; *fig.* stud (*the sky, a speech*) (with, de); **saupoudreuse** [∼ˈdrøːz] *f*,

saupoudroir [~'drwaːr] *m* sprinkler. [herring.\]

saur [sɔːr] *adj./m:* hareng *m* ~ red\}

saurai [sɔ're] *1st p. sg. fut. of savoir 1.*

saurer [so're] (1a) *v/t.* kipper, cure (*herrings*); **sauret** [~'rɛ] *adj./m* lightly cured (*herring*); **saurin** [~'rɛ̃] *m* bloater.

saut [so] *m* leap, jump; (*water*)fall; *sp.* ~ *à la perche* pole-jump; *sp.* ~ *d'ange* swallow-dive; *sp.* ~ *de haie* hurdling; *sp.* ~ *en hauteur* (*longueur*) high (long) jump; ~ *en parachute* parachute jump; *sp.* ~ *périlleux* somersault; F *au* ~ *du lit* on getting out of bed; *faire le* ~ give way; take the plunge; F *faire un* ~ *chez* pop round to (*a shop etc.*); *par* ~s *et par bonds* by leaps and bounds; *fig.* jerkily; ~**-de-lit**, *pl.* ~**s-de-lit** *cost.* [~d'li] *m* dressing-gown; **saute** [soːt] *f price, temperature:* jump; sudden change; *wind, a. fig.:* shift; **saute-mouton** *sp. etc.* [sotmu'tɔ̃] *m* leap-frog; *jouer à* ~ play leapfrog; **sauter** [so'te] (1a) **1.** *v/i.* jump, leap (*a. fig.* for joy, de joie); ⚓ shift, veer (*wind*); blow up (*explosive, mine, etc.*); ⚡ blow (*fuse*); ✝ go bankrupt, fail; ~ *aux yeux* be obvious; *faire* ~ blow (*s.th.*) up; ⚡ blow (*a fuse*); burst (*a boiler*); blast (*a rock*); spring (*a trap*); burst (*a button, a lock*); *fig.* dismiss, F fire (*an official*); *fig. pol.* bring down (*the government*); *v/t.* jump (over), leap (over); *fig.* skip, omit; ⚡ blow (*a fuse*); toss (*a child, a. cuis. a pancake*); *cuis.* fry quickly; **sauterelle** [~'trɛl] *f zo.* grasshopper; F *fig.* (*a. grande* ~) beanpole; **sauterie** [~'tri] *f* jumping, hopping, F (informal) dance, F hop; **sauteur, -euse** [~'tœːr, ~'tøːz] **1.** *adj.* jumping, leaping; *fig.* unreliable (*person*); **2.** *su.* jumper (*a. sp.*), leaper; *circus:* tumbler; *fig.* unreliable individual; *su./f cuis.* shallow pan; **sautiller** [~ti'je] (1a) *v/i.* hop, jump (about); throb (*heart*); *fig.* be jerky (*style*).

sautoir [so'twaːr] *m sp.* hurdle; St. Andrew's cross, ▨ saltire; *cost.* neckerchief (*worn crossed in front*); long chain worn round the neck; *en* ~ diagonal; *porter en* ~ wear (*s.th.*) crosswise; carry (*a haversack etc.*) with the straps crossed over the chest; *porter un ordre en* ~ wear an order round one's neck.

sauvage [so'vaːʒ] **1.** *adj.* wild (*a. zo., a.* ♟, *a. fig.*); savage; *fig.* shy; *fig.* unsociable; *fig.* unauthorized, illegal; wildcat (*strike*); **2.** *su.* (*f a.* **sauvagesse** [~va'ʒɛs]) savage; unsociable person; **sauvageon** ✒ [~va'ʒɔ̃] *m* wilding; *grafting:* wild stock; **sauvagerie** [~vaʒ'ri] *f* savagery; *fig.* unsociability; shyness; **sauvagine** [~va'ʒin] *su./f coll. orn.* waterfowl *pl.*; ✝ common pelts *pl.*

sauvegarde [sov'gard] *f* safeguard (*a. fig.*), protection; safety; safeconduct; ⚓ life-line; **sauvegarder** [~gar'de] (1a) *v/t.* safeguard, protect; keep up (*appearances*).

sauve-qui-peut [sovki'pø] *m* stampede; headlong flight; **sauver** [so've] (1a) *v/t.* save, rescue (from, de); keep up (*appearances*); ⚓ salvage, salve; *sauve qui peut!* every man for himself!; *se* ~ escape (from, de); ✝ recoup o.s.; *fig.* run away, F clear out, Am. F beat it; **sauvetage** [sov'taːʒ] *m* life-saving; rescue; ⚓ salvage; *bateau m* (*or canot m*) *de* ~ lifeboat; *ceinture f de* ~ lifebelt; **sauveteur** [~'tœːr] **1.** *su./m* rescuer; lifeboatman; ⚓ salvager; **2.** *adj./m: bateau m* ~ lifeboat; ⚓ salvage vessel; **sauvette** [so'vɛt]: *à la* ~ hurriedly, hastily, with undue haste; unauthorized, illicit (*hawking etc.*); *hawk etc.* illicitly, without authorization; **sauveur** [so'vœːr] *m* saver, preserver; *eccl.* ♀ Savio(u)r, Redeemer.

savamment [sava'mɑ̃] *adv.* learnedly; knowingly, wittingly; with full knowledge.

savane ✒ [sa'van] *f* savanna(h).

savant, e [sa'vɑ̃, ~'vɑ̃ːt] **1.** *adj.* learned (in, en); scholarly, erudite; performing (*dog*); *fig.* clever, skilful; **2.** *su.* scholar; scientist.

savate [sa'vat] *f* old shoe; *sp.* French *or* foot boxing; F bungler, clumsy workman; F *traîner la* ~ be down at heel; **savetier** ✝ [sav'tje] *m* cobbler.

saveur [sa'vœːr] *f* flavo(u)r, taste; *fig.* zest, pungency; *sans* ~ insipid, tasteless.

savoir [sa'vwaːr] **1.** (3i) *v/t.* know (of), be aware of, know how; be able to; learn, get to know; ~ *l'anglais* know English; ~ *vivre* know how to behave; *autant* (*pas*) *que je sache* as far as I know (not that I know of); *faire* ~ *qch. à q.* inform s.o. of s.th.; *je ne saurais* (*inf.*) I cannot (*inf.*), I could not (*inf.*); *ne ~ que* (*inf.*) not to know what to (*inf.*); *sans le ~* unintentionally; *v/i.* know; know how; (*à*) *~* to wit, namely; *c'est à ~ que* that remains to be seen; **2.** *su./m* knowledge, learning, erudition, scholarship; **~-faire** [savwar'fɛːr] *m/inv.* ability; knowhow; skill(s *pl.*); **~-vivre** [~'viːvr] *m/inv.* good manners *pl.*; (good) breeding.

savon [sa'vɔ̃] *m* soap; F *fig.* rebuke, F telling-off; *~ à barbe* shaving-soap; *~ de Marseille* yellow soap, scrubbingsoap; *bulle f de ~* soap bubble; *donner un coup de ~ à* give (*s.th.*) a wash; F *passer un ~ à q.* dress s.o. down, F tell s.o. off; *pain m de ~* cake of soap; **savonnage** [savɔ'naːʒ] *m* washing, soaping; **savonner** [~'ne] (1a) *v/t.* soap; wash (*clothes*); lather (*one's face before shaving*); F dress (*s.o.*) down; *tex. se ~* wash; **savonnette** [savɔ'nɛt] *f* cake of soap; **savonneux, -euse** [~'nø, ~'nøːz] soapy; **savonnier, -ère** [~'nje, ~'njɛːr] **1.** *adj.* soap...; **2.** *su./m* soap-maker; soap-berry(-tree).

savourer [savu're] (1a) *v/t.* enjoy; *fig.* savo(u)r; **savoureux, -euse** [~'rø, ~'røːz] tasty, savo(u)ry; *fig.* enjoyable; *fig.* racy (*story*).

savoyard, e [savwa'jaːr, ~'jard] *adj., a. su.* ♀ Savoyard.

saxe [saks] *m* Dresden china.

saxifrage ♀ [saksi'fraːʒ] *f* saxifrage.

saxon, -onne [sak'sɔ̃, ~'sɔn] *adj., a. su.* ♀ Saxon.

saynète *thea.* [sɛ'nɛt] *f* sketch; short comedy.

sbire [sbiːr] *m* henchman; F cop (= *policeman*).

scabieux, -euse ♀ [ska'bjø, ~'bjøːz] *adj., a. su./f* scabious.

scabreux, -euse ♀ [ska'brø, ~'brøːz] *fig.* scabrous (*behaviour, tale*); risky; difficult, F ticklish (*work*); delicate (*question*); indelicate (*allusion*); rough (*path*).

scaferlati [skafɛrla'ti] *m* ordinary cut tobacco.

scalène ⚕, *anat.* [ska'lɛn] *adj., a. su./m* scalene.

scalpe [skalp] *m trophy:* scalp.

scalpel ⚕ [skal'pɛl] *m* scalpel.

scandale [skã'dal] *m* scandal; *fig.* disgrace, shame; *faire ~* create a

scandal; **scandaleux, -euse** [skãda'lø, ~'løːz] scandalous, disgraceful; notorious; **scandaliser** [~ʌi'ze] (1a) *v/t.* shock, scandalize; *se ~ de* be shocked at.

scander [skã'de] (1a) *v/t.* scan (*a verse*); ♪ stress; *fig.* punctuate (with, *de*).

scandinave [skãdi'naːv] *adj., a. su.* ♀ Scandinavian.

scaphandre [ska'fãːdr] *m* diving suit; space suit; *~ autonome* aqualung; *casque m de ~* diver's helmet; **scaphandrier** [~fãdri'e] *m* deepsea diver.

scapulaire [skapy'lɛːr] *adj. anat., a. su./m eccl.* scapular.

scarabée *zo.* [skara'be] *m* beetle; *hist. Egypt.:* scarab.

scarificateur [skarifika'tœːr] *m* ✔ scarifier; ⚕ scarificator; **scarifier** [~'fje] (1o) *v/t.* scarify.

scarlatine ⚕ [skarla'tin] *f* (*a. fièvre f ~*) scarlet fever.

sceau [so] *m* seal (*a. fig.*); *fig.* mark; *admin. le ~ de l'État* the Great Seal.

scélérat, e [sele'ra, ~'rat] **1.** *adj.* villainous (*person*); outrageous (*act*); **2.** *su.* villain, scoundrel; **scélératesse** [~ra'tɛs] *f* villainy.

scellé ⚕? [se'le] *m* seal; **sceller** [~] (1a) *v/t.* seal; F ratify; ⚠ bed (*a post etc., in concrete etc.*); plug (*a nail in the wall etc.*).

scénario [sena'rjo] *m thea., cin.* scenario; *cin.* script; *cin.* screenplay; *fig. le ~ habituel* the usual pattern; **scénariste** [~'rist] *su.* scenario writer; *cin.* script-writer; **scène** [sɛn] *f thea.* stage; *fig.* drama; *play, a.* F *fig.:* scene; *fig. faire une ~* create a scene; *mettre en ~* stage (*a play*); *mise f en ~* production; (stage) setting; **scénique** [se'nik] scenic; stage...; *indications f/pl. ~s* stage directions.

sceptique [sɛp'tik] **1.** *adj.* sceptical, *Am.* skeptical; **2.** *su.* sceptic, *Am.* skeptic.

sceptre [sɛptr] *m* sceptre; *fig.* power.

schéma [ʃe'ma] *m* diagram; (sketch-) plan; design; **schématique** [~ma'tik] schematic.

schisme [ʃism] *m* schism.

schiste *geol.* [ʃist] *m* shale, schist; **schisteux, -euse** *geol.* [ʃis'tø, ~'tøːz] schistose; *coal:* slaty.

schlague [ʃlag] *f* ✗ † flogging; beating.

schlitte [ʃlit] *f* wood-sledge (*for transport of lumber down mountain*); *Am.* dray; **schlitteur** [ʃliˈtœːr] *m* lumberman (*in charge of a schlitte*).

schnaps F [ʃnaps] *m* brandy.

schnock *sl.* [ʃnɔk] *m* (old) fathead.

schooner ⚓ [skuˈnœːr] *m* schooner.

sciable ⊕ [sjabl] fit for sawing; **sciage** ⊕ [sjaːʒ] *m* sawing; (*a. bois m de* ~) sawn timber; **sciant, e** F [sjã, sjãːt] boring; *fig.* irritating.

sciatique ✦ [sjaˈtik] **1.** *adj.* sciatic; **2.** *su./m* sciatic nerve; *su./f* sciatica.

scie ⊕ [si] *f* saw; *sl.* bore, nuisance; *fig.* catchword, cliché; *fig.* catch tune, hit tune; ~ *à chantourner* compass-saw; ~ *à main* hand-saw; ~ *à manche* pad-saw; ~ *à ruban* band-saw; ~ *circulaire* circular saw, *Am.* buzz-saw; *trait m de* ~ sawcut.

sciemment [sjaˈmã] *adv.* knowingly, intentionally; **science** [sjãːs] *f* knowledge, learning; science; ~*s pl. naturelles* natural science *sg.*; *homme m de* ~ scientist, man of science; **science-fiction** [sjãsfik-ˈsjõ] *f* science fiction; **scientifique** [sjãtiˈfik] **1.** *adj.* scientific; **2.** *su.* scientist.

scier [sje] (1o) *v/t.* ⊕ saw; ✧ saw off (*a branch*); ✧ *le dos à qn* bore (*s.o.*) stiff; **scierie** ⊕ [siˈri] *f* saw-mill; **scieur** [sjœːr] *m* ⊕ sawyer; ~ *de long* pit sawyer.

scille [sil] *f* ♀ scilla; ✦ squills *pl.*

scindement [sɛ̃dˈmã] *m* splitting up; **scinder** [sɛ̃ˈde] (1a) *v/t.* split up, divide; *se* ~ split (*pol. party*).

scintillation [sɛ̃tillaˈsjõ] *f*, **scintillement** [~tijˈmã] *m* sparkling, scintillation (*a. fig.*); *star:* twinkling; *cin.* flicker(ing); **scintiller** [~tiˈje] (1a) *v/i.* sparkle, scintillate (*a. fig.*); twinkle (*star*); *cin.* flicker.

scion [sjõ] *m* ✧ shoot, scion; *fishing-rod:* tip.

scirpe ♀ [sirp] *m* bulrush, club-rush.

scissile *min.* [siˈsil] scissile; **scission** [~ˈsjõ] *f* scission, split, division; *faire* ~ secede; **scissipare** *biol.* [sisiˈpaːr] fissiparous, scissiparous; **scissiparité** *biol.* [~pariˈte] *f* fissiparity, scissiparity; **scissure** *anat. etc.* [siˈsyːr] *f* fissure, cleft.

sciure ⊕ [sjyːr] *f* (*saw*)dust.

scléreux, -euse ✦ [skleˈrø, ~ˈrøːz] sclerous; **sclérose** [~ˈroːz] *f* ✦

sclerosis; *fig.* ossification; **sclérosé, e** [~rɔˈze] ✦ sclerotic; *fig.* ossified; **sclérotique** *anat.* [rɔˈtik] *adj., a. su./f* sclerotic.

scolaire [skɔˈlɛːr] school...; **scolariser** [~lariˈze] (1a) *v/t.* provide with schools *or* schooling; **scolarité** [~lariˈte] *f* schooling; *années f/pl. de* ~ school years; **scolastique** *phls.* [~lasˈtik] **1.** *adj.* scholastic; **2.** *su./m* scholastic, schoolman; *su./f* scholasticism.

scolopendre [skɔlɔˈpãːdr] *f* *zo.* centipede; ♀ hart's-tongue.

sconse ✝ [skõːs] *m* skunk (fur).

scooter [skuˈtœːr] *m* scooter.

scorbut ✦ [skɔrˈby] *m* scurvy; **scorbutique** ✦ [~byˈtik] *adj., a. su.* scorbutic.

score *sp.* [skɔr] *m* score.

scorie [skɔˈri] *f* slag, scoria; *iron:* dross.

scorpion [skɔrˈpjõ] *m* *zo.* scorpion; *astr. le* ♏ Scorpio, the Scorpion.

scorsonère ♀ [skɔrsɔˈnɛːr] *f* scorzonera, black salsify.

scout, e [skut] **1.** *su./m* boy-scout; **2.** *adj.* scout...; **scoutisme** [skuˈtism] *m* boy-scout movement, scouting.

scribe [skrib] *m* *hist.* (*Jewish*) scribe; copyist; F pen-pusher.

script *cin.* [skript] *m* film-script; ~-**girl** *cin.* [~ˈgœːrl] *f* continuity-girl.

scriptural, e, *m/pl.* **-aux** [skriptyˈral, ~ˈro] scriptural; ✝ *monnaie f* ~e deposit currency.

scrofulaire ♀ [skrɔfyˈlɛːr] *f* fig-wort; **scrofule** ✦ [~ˈfyl] *f* scrofula; **scrofuleux, -euse** ✦ [~fyˈlø, ~ˈløːz] scrofulous (*person*); strumous (*tumour*).

scrupule [skryˈpyl] *m* weight, *a. fig.*: scruple; *avoir des* ~*s à* (*inf.*) have scruples about (*ger.*); *sans* ~ unscrupulous(ly *adv.*); **scrupuleux, -euse** [~pyˈlø, ~ˈløːz] scrupulous (about, over *sur*); punctilious; *peu* ~ unscrupulous.

scrutateur, -trice [skrytaˈtœːr, ~ˈtris] **1.** *adj.* searching; **2.** *su./m* scrutinizer, investigator; *pol. etc., ballot etc.:* teller; **scruter** [~ˈte] (1a) *v/t.* scrutinize; investigate; search (*one's memory*); **scrutin** [~ˈtɛ̃] *m* poll; *admin.* vote; voting; ~ *public* (*secret*) open (secret) vote;

dépouiller le ~ count the votes; *tour m de* ~ ballot.

sculpter [skyl'te] (1a) *v/t.* sculpture, carve (out of, *dans*); **sculpteur** [~'tœːr] *m* sculptor; ~ *sur bois* wood-carver; **sculpture** [~'tyːr] *f* sculpture; ~ *sur bois* wood-carving.

se [sə] **1.** *pron./rfl.* oneself; himself, herself, itself; themselves; *to express passive:* ~ *vendre* be sold; ~ *roser* be(come) pink; **2.** *pron./recip.* each other, one another.

séance [se'ãːs] *f* seat; sitting (*a. paint.*), session, meeting; *cin.* performance; ~ *plénière (de clôture)* plenary (closing) session; *fig.* ~ *tenante* immediately; **séant, e** [~'ã, ~'ãːt] **1.** *adj.* in session, sitting; *fig.* seemly, fitting; becoming (to, *à*); **2.** *su./m* F posterior; *se mettre sur son* ~ sit up (*in bed*).

seau [so] *m* pail, bucket; *biscuit:* barrel; ~ *à charbon* coal-scuttle; F *il pleut à* ~*x* it is raining in bucketfuls.

sébacé, e [seba'se] sebaceous.
sébile [se'bil] *f* wooden bowl.

sec, sèche [sɛk, sɛʃ] **1.** *adj.* dry (*a. wine, fig. remark*); dried (*cod, raisins*); lean (*person, horse*); sharp (*blow, answer, remark, tone*); *fig.* harsh, unsympathetic; barren; dead (*loss*); split (*peas*); hard (*cash*); *cards:* bare (*ace, king, etc.*); **2.** *sec adv.:* *boire* ~ drink neat; drink hard; *brûler* ~ burn like tinder; *parler* ~ not to mince one's words; *rire* ~ laugh harshly; *à* ~ dry; dried up; F hard-up, broke; **3.** *su./m être à* ~ be dried (up), be dry; F be broke; *mettre à* ~ dry (up *or* out); drain; F clean (*s.o.*) out; **4.** *su./f* ♪ flat; *sl.* fag (= *cigarette*); *sl. piquer une sèche* stumped (*in oral examination*), get no marks (*in examination*).

sécante ♫ [se'kãːt] *f* secant; **sécateur** ✂ [~ka'tœːr] *m* pruning shears *pl.*, secateurs *pl.*

sécession [sese'sjɔ̃] *f* secession; *faire* ~ secede (from, *de*); **sécessionniste** [~sjɔ'nist] *adj., a. su.* secessionist.

séchage [se'ʃaːʒ] *m* drying; ⊕ *wood:* seasoning; F *univ. lecture:* cutting; **sèche-cheveux** [sɛʃə'ʃvø] *m/inv.* hair-drier; **sécher** [se'ʃe] (1f) *v/i.* (become) dry; F waste away (with, *de*); F be stumped (*in an ex-*

amination); *sl.* smoke; *faire* ~ dry; ⊕ *season* (*wood*); *v/t.* dry; ⊕ *season* (*wood*); F *univ.* cut (*a lecture*); F fail (*a candidate*); **sécheresse** [seʃ'rɛs] *f* dryness; drought; *person, horse:* leanness; *answer, remark, tone:* curtness; *fig. heart:* coldness; *fig. style etc.:* bareness; **sécherie** [~'ri] *f* drying-floor; *machine:* drier; ✤ seed-kiln; **sécheur** ⊕ [se'ʃœːr] *m* drier; **sécheuse** [~'ʃøːz] *f* steam-drier; **séchoir** [~'ʃwaːr] *m* ⊕ drying-room; drying-ground; ⊕ drier; clothes-horse, airer.

second, e [sə'gɔ̃, ~'gɔ̃ːd] **1.** *adj.* second (*a. fig.*); **2.** *su.* (the) second; *su./m* second in command, principal assistant; ⚓ first mate, first officer, *sl.* number one; *box., a. duel:* second; ⚓ second floor, *Am.* third floor; ⚓ ~ *maître* petty officer; *su./f* ♪, ♪, time: second; ⬛ second (*class*); *secondary school:* (*approx.*) fifth form; *typ.* revise; **secondaire** [səgɔ̃'dɛːr] **1.** *adj.* secondary; *fig. a.* subordinate, minor; **2.** *su./m* ⚡ secondary winding; **seconder** [~'de] (1a) *v/t.* second, support; further (*s.o.'s interests*).

secouer [sə'kwe] (1p) *v/t.* shake (*a. fig.*); shake down *or* off; knock out (*a pipe*); F *fig.* rouse (*s.o.*); F *se* ~ get a move on; rouse o.s.

secourable [səku'rabl] helpful; ready to help; **secourir** [~'riːr] (2i) *v/t.* aid, succo(u)r, help; **secouriste** [~'rist] *su.* first-aid worker; voluntary ambulance worker; **secours** [sə'kuːr] *m* help, assistance; aid; ⚒ ~*pl.* relieving force *sg.*, relief troops; *au* ~! help!; *de* ~ relief-...; spare (*wheel*); emergency (*exit, landing-ground*); ⚒, ✂ *premier* ~ first aid.

secousse [sə'kus] *f* bump, jolt, jerk; ⚡, *a. fig.* shock.

secret, -ète [sə'krɛ, ~'krɛt] **1.** *adj.* secret, concealed; *fig.* reticent; **2.** *su./m* secret; secrecy; ⚖ solitary confinement; ⊕ *desk etc.:* secret spring; ~ *postal* secrecy of correspondence; *en* ~ in secret, in secrecy; privately; *su./f prayer:* secret; **secrétaire** [səkre'tɛːr] *su. person:* secretary; *su./m furniture:* secretaire, writing-desk; *orn.* secretary-bird; ~ *d'État* Secretary of State; ~ *particulier* private secretary;

secrétairerie [ˌtɛrəˈri] *f* secretary's staff; secretariat; *pol.* chancery, registry; **secrétariat** [ˌtaˈrja] *m* secretariat, secretary's office; secretaryship.

sécréter *physiol.* [sekreˈte] (1f) *v/t.* secrete; **sécréteur, -trice** *or* **-euse** *physiol.* [ˌˈtœːr, ˌˈtøːz] secretory; **sécrétion** *physiol.* [ˌˈsjɔ̃] *f* secretion; **sécrétoire** *physiol.* [ˌˈtwaːr] secretory.

sectaire [sɛkˈtɛːr] *adj., a. su.* sectarian; **secte** [sɛkt] *f* sect.

secteur [sɛkˈtœːr] *m* ᛒ, ⊕, ✕, *astr.* sector; *admin.* district, area; ⚡ mains *pl.*; ⚓ (*steering-*)quadrant.

section [sɛkˈsjɔ̃] *f* section (*a.* ᛒ, △); cutting, docking; ✕ *infantry:* platoon, *artillery:* section; ✕ *ammunition:* column; ⚓ subdivision; *admin.* branch; *bus, tram:* stage; *admin.* ~ de vote polling-district; **sectionnel, -elle** [sɛksjɔˈnɛl] sectional; **sectionner** [ˌˈne] (1a) *v/t.* divide into sections; cut, sever.

séculaire [sekyˈlɛːr] secular (= *once in 100 years*); century-old; *fig.* time-hono(u)red, ancient; **séculariser** [ˌlariˈze] (1a) *v/t.* secularize; convert (*a church etc.*) to secular use; **sécularité** [ˌlariˈte] *f* secularity; *eccl.* secular jurisdiction; **séculier, -ère** [ˌˈlje, ˌˈljɛːr] *adj., su./m* secular.

sécuriser [sekyriˈze] (1a) *v/t.* give (*s.o.*) a feeling of security, make (*s.o.*) feel (more) secure; **sécurité** [ˌˈte] *f* security; *admin., mot., a.* ⊕ safety; *pol.* ~ *collective* collective security; ~ *routière* road safety; ⊕ *etc.* de ~ safety ... [*a. su./m* sedative.] **sédatif, -ve** ✱ [sedaˈtif, ˌˈtiːv] *adj.,* **sédentaire** [sedɑ̃ˈtɛːr] sedentary (*life, profession*); settled, sedentary (*people etc.*); settled, fixed; *orn.* nonmigrant; **sédentariser** [ˌtariˈze] (1a) *v/t.* make sedentary, settle (*a tribe etc.*).

sédiment [sediˈmɑ̃] *m* sediment, deposit; **sédimentaire** *geol. etc.* [ˌmɑ̃ˈtɛːr] sedimentary; aqueous (*rock*); **sédimentation** [ˌmɑ̃taˈsjɔ̃] *f* sedimentation.

séditieux, -euse [sediˈsjø, ˌˈsjøːz] **1.** *adj.* seditious; mutinous; **2.** *su.* seditionist, fomenter of sedition; **sédition** [ˌˈsjɔ̃] *f* sedition; *en ~* in revolt.

séducteur, -trice [sedykˈtœːr, ˌˈtris] **1.** *adj.* seductive, alluring; tempting (*look, word*); **2.** *su.* seducer; **séductible** [ˌˈtibl] seducible; **séduction** [ˌˈsjɔ̃] *f* seduction (*a.* ᛒ); *fig.* attraction; **séduire** [seˈdɥiːr] (4h) *v/t.* seduce (*a.* ᛒ); suborn, bribe (*a witness*); *fig.* attract (*s.o.*), fascinate (*s.o.*); **séduisant, e** [ˌdɥiˈzɑ̃, ˌˈzɑ̃ːt] seductive, tempting; *fig.* attractive, fascinating.

segment [sɛgˈmɑ̃] *m* ᛒ, *zo.* segment; ⊕ (*piston-*)ring; *caterpillar tyre:* joint; **segmentaire** [ˌmɑ̃ˈtɛːr] ᛒ segmentary; △, *anat.* segmental; **segmenter** [ˌmɑ̃ˈte] (1a) *v/t. a.* se ~ segment, divide into segments.

ségrégation [segregaˈsjɔ̃] *f* segregation (*a. pol.*); isolation; **ségrég(u)é, e** [ˌˈge] segregated.

seiche *zo.* [sɛʃ] *f* cuttle-fish; *os m de* ~ cuttle-bone.

séide [seˈid] *m* henchman; blind supporter.

seigle 🌾 [sɛgl] *m* rye; ~ *ergoté* spurred rye.

seigneur [sɛˈɲœːr] *m* lord; noble; lord of the manor; *faire le* (*or vivre en*) *grand* ~ live like a lord; *eccl. le* ⵛ the Lord; **seigneurial, e,** *m/pl.* **-aux** † [sɛɲœˈrjal, ˌˈrjo] seigniorial, manorial; *maison f* ~*e* manor-house; **seigneurie** [ˌˈri] *f* lordship; manor.

seille [sɛːj] *f* pail, bucket.

sein [sɛ̃] *m* breast; bosom; *au* ~ *de* within; in the midst of.

seine [sɛn] *f fishing:* seine, dragnet.

seing ᛒ [sɛ̃] *m* signature, † sign manual; *acte m sous* ~ *privé* simple contract; private agreement.

séisme [seˈism] *m* earthquake, seism.

seize [sɛːz] *adj./num., a. su./m/inv.* sixteen; *date, title:* sixteenth; **seizième** [sɛˈzjɛm] **1.** *adj./num., a. su.* sixteenth.

séjour [seˈʒuːr] *m* stay; *place:* abode, residence, dwelling; ᛒ *interdiction f de* ~ prohibition from entering certain localities; *permis m de* ~ residence permit; **séjournant, e** [ˌʒurˈnɑ̃, ˌˈnɑ̃ːt] *su.* visitor, guest; **séjourner** [ˌʒurˈne] (1a) *v/i.* stay, reside; stop; remain.

sel [sɛl] *m* salt (*a.* 🜍); *fig.* wit; ~*s pl.* smelling-salts; *prendre qch. avec un* *grain de* ~ take s.th. with a grain of salt.

select F [se'lɛkt] select; *réunions f/pl. selects* exclusive parties.

sélecter F ✝ [selɛk'te] (1a) *v/t.* choose; **sélecteur** [~'tœːr] *m ⚡, a. radio:* selector; **sélectif, -ve** [~'tif, ~'tiːv] selective; **sélection** [~'sjɔ̃] *f* selection (*a. ♪, ⚡, radio, biol., a. sp.*); choice; **sélectionner** [~sjɔ'ne] (1a) *v/t.* select, choose; **sélectivité** [~tivi'te] *f radio:* selectivity.

sélénique ⚗, *astr.* [sele'nik] selenic; **sélénium** ⚗ [~'njɔm] *m* selenium; **sélénographie** [~nɔgra'fi] *f* selenography.

self [sɛlf] *f* F self-service restaurant; ⚡ (*a. bobine f de* ~) inductance-coil; **~-induction** ⚡ [~ɛ̃dyk'sjɔ̃] *f* self-induction; inductance.

selle [sɛl] *f* ⊕, *mot., cuis., horse, bicycle:* saddle; ⬛ plate; *physiol.* motion, stool; ~ *anglaise* hunting saddle; *physiol. aller à la* ~ go to stool; F *mettre q. en* ~ give s.o. a helping hand; **seller** [se'le] (1a) *v/t.* saddle (*a horse*); **sellette** [se'lɛt] *f* stool, seat; ⊕ slung cradle; *fig. mettre (or tenir) q. sur la* ~ cross-examine s.o., F carpet s.o.; **sellier** [se'lje] *m* saddler.

selon [sɔ'lɔ̃] **1.** *prp.* according to; ~ *moi* in my opinion; *c'est* ~ *!* it all *or* that depends!; **2.** *cj.:* ~ *que* according as, depending upon whether.

Seltz [sɛlts] *m: eau f de* ~ soda-water.

semailles [sə'mɑːj] *f/pl.* sowing *sg.*; seeds.

semaine [sə'mɛn] *f* week; ⊕, ✝ working week; ✗ *etc.* duty for the week; *week's pay;* ~ *anglaise* five and a half day (working) week; ~ *sainte* Holy Week; *à la* ~ by the week; *en* ~ during the week; *être de* ~ be on duty for the week.

sémantique [semɑ̃'tik] **1.** *adj.* semantic; **2.** *su./f* semantics *pl.*

sémaphore [sema'fɔːr] *m* semaphore; ⚓ signal-station (*on land*).

semblable [sɑ̃'blabl] **1.** *adj.* similar (to, à) (*a. ⯑ triangles*); alike; like (*a. ⯑ terms*); such; **2.** *su.* like, equal; fellow; *su./m: nos* ~*s pl.* our fellowmen; **semblablement** [~blablə'mɑ̃] *adv.* in like manner; **semblant** [~'blɑ̃] *m* appearance, look; *fig.* show (of, de); *faire* ~ pretend (to *inf.*, de *inf.*); make a show (of

s.th., de qch.); *faux* ~ pretence; *sans faire* ~ *de rien* as if nothing had happened; surreptitiously; **sembler** [~'ble] (1a) *v/i.* seem, appear; *il me semble* I think; *que vous en semble?* what do you think (about it)?

semelle [sə'mɛl] *f shoe:* sole; *stocking:* foot; *mot. tyre:* tread; ⊕ bed; ⚠ foundation; ~ *de liège* cork insole; *battre la* ~ stamp one's feet (to warm them); kick one's heels; *remettre des* ~*s à* re-sole.

semence [sə'mɑ̃ːs] *f* seed (*a. fig.*); *physiol.* semen; ⊕ (tin)tack; ~ *de perles* seed-pearls *pl.*; **semer** [~'me] (1d) *v/t.* ✔ sow (*a. fig. discord etc.*); scatter; *fig.* disseminate, spread (*a rumour*); squander (*one's money*); F lose; F shake off, drop (*s.o.*).

semestre [sə'mɛstr] *m* half-year; six months' duty *or* pay *or* ✗ leave of absence; *univ. etc.* semester; **semestriel, -elle** [~mɛstri'el] half-yearly, lasting six months.

semeur, -euse [sə'mœːr, ~'møːz] *su.* sower (*a. fig. of discord*); *fig.* spreader (*of rumours*).

semi... [səmi] semi...; **~-brève** ♪ [~'brɛːv] *f* semibreve, *Am.* whole note; **~-conducteur** ⚡ [~kɔ̃dyk-'tœːr] *m* semi-conductor; **~-coke** [~'kɔk] *m* coalite.

sémillant, e [semi'jɑ̃, ~'jɑ̃ːt] vivacious.

séminaire [semi'nɛːr] *m* seminary; *fig.* training centre; *fig.* colloque, symposium; *univ.* seminar; *petit* ~ secondary school run by priests.

séminal, e *m/pl.* **-aux** [semi'nal, ~'no] seminal.

semi-remorque [səmirə'mɔrk] *f* articulated truck, *Am.* trailer truck.

semis ✔ [sə'mi] *m* sowing; seedling; seed-bed.

semi-ton ♪ [səmi'tɔ̃] *m* semitone; **semi-voyelle** *gramm.* [~vwa'jɛl] *f* semivowel.

semoir ✔ [sə'mwaːr] *m* sowing-machine; seed-drill; seeder.

semonce [sə'mɔ̃ːs] *f fig.* reprimand; ⚓ *coup m de* ~ warning shot; **semoncer** (1k) *v/t.* ✝ reprimand, F read (*s.o.*) a lecture; ⚓ call upon (*a ship*) to heave to *or* to show her flag.

semoule *cuis.* [sə'mul] *f* semolina.

sempiternel, -elle [sɑ̃piter'nɛl] sempiternal, everlasting.

sénat [se'na] *m* senate(-house); **sé-nateur** [sena'tœ:r] *m* senator.

séneçon ♀ [sen'sɔ̃] *m* groundsel.

sénevé ♀ [sen've] *m* black mustard.

sénile ♂ [se'nil] senile; **sénilité** ♂ [₋nili'te] *f* senility, senile decay.

sens [sã:s] *m fig. smell etc.*: sense; *fig.* opinion; understanding; judg(e)-ment; meaning; direction (*a.* ⚡); way; ~ *de la musique* musicianship; ~ *de l'orientation* sense of direction; ~ *dessus dessous* upside down; ~ *devant derrière* back to front; ~ *interdit* no entry; ~ *moral* moral sense; ~ *unique* one-way street; *à mon* ~ in my view *or* opinion; *le bon* ~, *le* ~ *commun* common sense; *plaisirs m/pl. des* ~ sensual pleasures; **sensation** [sãsa-'sjɔ̃] *f* sensation; (*physical*) feeling; *à* ~ sensational (*news*); **sensationnel, -elle** [₋sjɔ'nɛl] sensational; *fig.* thrilling; *roman m* ~ thriller; **sensé, e** [sã'se] sensible, intelligent; practical.

sensibiliser [sãsibili'ze] (1a) *v/t.* sensitize; *fig.* make sensitive (to, *à*); *sensibilisé à* alive to; *...-minded*; **sensibilité** [₋'te] *f* sensitiveness (*a. phot.*); *fig.* feeling, compassion; **sensible** [sã'sibl] sensitive (*ear, instrument, phot. paper, skin, spot, a. fig. to pain etc.*); tender (*flesh, spot*); responsive; susceptible; *fig.* appreciative (of, *à*); *fig.* sympathetic; perceptible, real (*difference, progress*); *phot.* sensitized (*paper*); ♩ *note f* ~ leading note *or Am.* tone; **sensible-rie** [₋siblǝ'ri] *f* sentiment(ality); F sob-stuff.

sensitif, -ve [sãsi'tif, ₋'ti:v] 1. *adj.* sensitive; *anat.* sensory; 2. *su./f* ♀ sensitive plant; F very sensitive woman *or* girl; **sensitivité** [₋tivi'te] *f* sensitivity.

sensoriel, -elle [sãsɔ'rjɛl] sensorial, sensory.

sensualisme *phls.* [sãsɥa'lism] *m* sensualism; **sensualiste** *phls.* [₋'list] 1. *adj.* sensual; 2. *su.* sensualist; **sensualité** [₋li'te] *f* sensuality; sensuousness; **sensuel, -elle** [sã'sɥɛl] sensual; sensuous.

sentence [sã'tã:s] *f* maxim; ⚖ sentence; (*a.* ~ *arbitrale*) award; **sentencieux, -euse** [₋tã'sjø, ₋'sjø:z] sententious.

senteur *hunt.* [sã'tœ:r] *f* scent (*a. poet. = perfume*).

sentier [sã'tje] *m* footpath; path (*a. fig.*); ~ *battu* beaten track.

sentiment [sãti'mã] *m* feeling (*a. fig.*); emotion; consciousness, sense; *fig.* opinion, sentiment; ~ *d'infériori-té* sense of inferiority; *avoir le* ~ *de a.* be aware of; *voilà mon* ~ that is my opinion; **sentimental, e,** *m/pl.* **-aux** [₋mã'tal, ₋'to] sentimental; **sentimentalité** [₋mãtali'te] *f* sentimentality.

sentine ⚓ [sã'tin] *f ship*: well; cesspit (*a. fig.*); *fig.* sink of iniquity.

sentinelle ✕ [sãti'nɛl] *f* sentry; guard, watch; *faire* ~ mount guard; F *fig. faire la* ~ be on the watch.

sentir [sã'ti:r] (2b) *v/t.* feel; be conscious of, be alive to; smell (*a. fig.*); taste of, smack of (*s.th.*); F *je ne peux pas le* ~ I can't stand him; *vin m qui sent le bouchon* corked wine; *se* ~ feel; *ne pas se* ~ *de joie* be beside oneself with joy; *v/i.* smell (bad, *mauvais*; bon, good).

seoir [swa:r] (3k) *v/i.*: ~ *à q.* become s.o.

sépale ♀ [se'pal] *m* sepal.

séparable [sepa'rabl] separable (from, *de*); **séparateur, -trice** [separa'tœ:r, ₋'tris] 1. *adj.* separating, separative; 2. *su./m* ⊕ separator; **séparation** [₋'sjɔ̃] *f* ⊕, ⚙ ⚖, *a. fig.* separation (from, *d'avec*); parting; *fig. family, meeting*: breaking up; division; ⚖ *de biens* separate maintenance; ⚖ *de corps* judicial separation; *pol.* ~ *des pouvoirs* separation of powers; ⚠ *mur m de* ~ partition wall; **séparatiste** [₋'tist] 1. *adj.* separatist; 2. *su.* separatist, separationist; secessionist; **séparément** [separe'mã] *adv.* separately; **séparer** [₋'re] (1a) *v/t.* separate (from, *de*); part; drive apart; divide; *fig.* distinguish (from, *de*); *se* ~ part (company); break up (*assembly*); divide; *se* ~ *de* part with.

sépia [se'pja] *f zo., colour*: sepia; *zo.* cuttle-fish; *paint.* sepia drawing.

sept [sɛt] *adj./num., a. su./m/inv.* seven; *date, title*: seventh; **septain** [se'tɛ̃] *m* seven-line stanza; ⊕ seven-strand rope (*holding clock weights*); **septante** † [sep'tã:t] *adj./ num., a. su./m/inv.* seventy; *bibl. version des* ♀ Septuagint; **septem-bre** [₋'tã:br] *m* September; **sep-tembrisades** *hist.* [₋tãbri'zad] *f/pl.* September massacres (*1792 in Paris*); **septénaire** [ˌteˈnɛːr] *adj.*, *a. su./m* septenary; **septennal, e,** *m/pl.* **-aux** [ˌtɛnˈnal, ˌˈno] septennial; **septennat** [ˌtɛnˈna] *m* septennate.

septentrion *poet.* [sɛptɑ̃triˈɔ̃] *m* north; **septentrional, e,** *m/pl.* **-aux** [ˌˈnal, ˌˈno] 1. *adj.* north(ern); 2. *su.* northerner.

septicémie [septiseˈmi] *f* septic(a)emia; blood-poisoning; **septicémique** [ˌseˈmik] septic(a)emic; **septicité** [ˌsiˈte] *f* septicity.

septième [sɛˈtjɛm] 1. *adj./num.* seventh; 2. *su.* seventh; *su./m fraction:* seventh; *su./f* ♪ seventh; *school:* top form of lower school.

septique [sɛpˈtik] septic; *fosse f* ~ septic tank.

septuagénaire [sɛptɥaʒeˈnɛːr] *adj.*, *a. su.* septuagenarian.

septuple [sepˈtypl] *adj.*, *a. su./m* sevenfold; septuple; **septupler** [ˌtyˈple] (1a) *vt/i.* increase sevenfold, septuple.

sépulcral, e, *m/pl.* **-aux** [sepylˈkral, ˌˈkro] sepulchral; **sépulcre** [ˌˈpylkr] *m* sepulchre; *le saint* ~ the Holy Sepulchre.

sépulture [sepylˈtyːr] *f* burial; tomb; burial-place.

séquelles [seˈkɛl] *f/pl.* after-effects; aftermath *sg.*

séquence [seˈkɑ̃ːs] *f* sequence.

séquestration [sekɛstraˈsjɔ̃] illegal confinement; **séquestre** ⚖ [seˈkɛstr] *m* impoundment; *mettre sous* ~ impound; **séquestrer** [ˌkɛsˈtre] (1a) *v/t.* confine (*s.o.*) illegally; hold (*s.o.*) captive; ⚖ impound (*property*); *fig. se* ~ sequester o.s.

serai [səˈre] *1st p. sg. fut. of* être 1.

sérail [seˈraːj] *m* seraglio.

sérancer *tex.* [serɑ̃ˈse] (1k) *v/t.* heckle, comb (*flax*).

séraphin [seraˈfɛ̃] *m* seraph; ~s *pl.* seraphim; **séraphique** [ˌˈfik] seraphic.

serbe [sɛrb] 1. *adj.* Serb(ian); 2. *su./m ling.* Serb(ian); *su.* ♀ Serb(ian).

serein, e [səˈrɛ̃, ˌˈrɛn] 1. *adj.* serene, calm (*a. fig.*); *fig.* tranquil; ♨ *goutte f* ~e amaurosis; 2. *su./m* evening dew.

sérénade ♪ [sereˈnad] *f* serenade.

sérénissime [sereniˈsim] *title:* (Most) Serene; **sérénité** [ˌˈte] *f*

serenity (*a. title*); calmness; tranquillity.

séreux, -euse [seˈrø, ˌˈrøːz] serous.

serf, serve [sɛrf, sɛrv] 1. *adj.* in bondage; *condition f serve* serfdom; 2. *su.* serf; *su./m* bond(s)man; *su./f* bond(s)woman.

serfouette ✔ [sɛrˈfwɛt] *f* combined hoe and fork; **serfouir** ✔ [ˌˈfwiːr] (2a) *v/t.* hoe; loosen (*the soil*).

serge *tex.* [sɛrʒ] *f* serge.

sergent [sɛrˈʒɑ̃] *m* ✕ *etc.* sergeant; ⊕ cramp, clamp; ⚓ ~ *d'armes* (*approx.*) ship's corporal; † ~ *de ville* policeman; ✕ ~-*major*, ~-*chef infantry:* quartermaster-sergeant.

sériciculteur [serisikylˈtœːr] *m* silkworm breeder; **sériciculture** [ˌˈtyːr] *f* silkworm breeding.

série [seˈri] *f* series; sequence; *tools etc.:* set; *sp. race:* heat; *billiards:* break; *en* ~, *par* ~ in series; ✝ *fait en* ~ mass-produced; ✝ *fin f de* ~ remnants *pl.*; *fig. hors* ~ extraordinary; *fig. la* ~ *noire* one disaster after another, a run of hard luck; *fig.* ~ *noire* crime-thriller (*atmosphere, style, etc.*); eerie, sinister; **sérier** [ˌˈrje] (1o) *v/t.* arrange, classify.

sérieux, -euse [seˈrjø, ˌˈrjøːz] 1. *adj.* serious; grave; earnest; genuine (*offer, purchaser*); *fig. peu* ~ irresponsible (*person*); 2. *su./m* gravity, seriousness; *thea.* serious rôle; *garder son* ~ preserve one's gravity; *prendre au* ~ take (*s.th.*) seriously.

serin [səˈrɛ̃] *m orn.* serin; canary; F fool, *Am.* sap; greenhorn; **seriner** [səriˈne] (1a) *v/t.* teach (*a canary*) to sing; F *fig.* drum (*a rule etc.*) (into s.o., *à* q.); F ♪ thump out, grind out (*a tune*).

seringue [səˈrɛ̃ːg] *f* ✔, ♨ syringe; *mot.* ~ *à graisse* grease-gun; **seringuer** [ˌrɛ̃ˈge] (1m) *v/t.* syringe (*the ear etc.*), inject (*a drug*); squirt (*a liquid*).

serment [sɛrˈmɑ̃] *m* oath; *faux* ~ perjury; *prêter* ~ take an oath; *sous* ~ sworn (*evidence*).

sermon [sɛrˈmɔ̃] *m* sermon; *fig.* lecture; **sermonner** F [ˌmɔˈne] (1a) *vt/i.* sermonize; *v/t.* reprimand; **sermonneur, -euse** F [ˌmɔˈnœːr, ˌˈnøːz] 1. *adj.* fault-finding; 2. *su.* fault-finder.

sérosité *physiol.* [seroziˈte] *f* serosity; **sérothérapie** ⚕ [ˌrɔteraˈpi] f serotherapy.

serpe ✒ [sɛrp] f bill-hook.

serpent [sɛrˈpã] m ♪, zo., astr., fig. serpent; zo., fig. snake; ~ à lunettes cobra; ~ à sonnettes rattlesnake; **serpentaire** [sɛrpãˈtɛːr] su./m orn. secretary-bird; su./f ♀, ⚕ serpentaria, snake-root; **serpenteau** [ˌˈto] m zo. young snake; firework: serpent, squib; **serpenter** [ˌˈte] (1a) v/i. (a. aller en serpentant) wind, meander; **serpentin, e** [ˌˈtɛ̃, ˈtin] 1. adj. serpentine; 2. su./m ⊕ coil; ticker tape, paper streamer; su./f ♀ snake-wood; min. serpentine.

serpette ✒ [sɛrˈpɛt] f bill-hook; pruning-knife.

serpillière [sɛrpiˈjɛːr] f tex. packing-cloth; tex. dish-cloth; F apron made from sacking.

serpolet ♀ [sɛrpoˈlɛ] m wild thyme.

serrage ⊕ [sɛˈraːʒ] m tightening; gripping; mot. ~ des freins braking.

serre [sɛːr] f ✒ greenhouse, glasshouse, conservatory; ✒ (a. ~ chaude) hot-house; grip; orn. claw, talon; ⊕, ✒ clip; ⊕ mo(u)ld press.

serré, e [sɛˈre] 1. adj. tight; closegrained (wood); compact; narrow (defile etc.); close (buildings, ✗ order, reasoning, texture, translation, sp. finish); tightly packed (people etc.); 2. serré adv.: jouer ~ play cautiously; vivre ~ live on a tight budget.

serre...: ~**file** [sɛrˈfil] m/inv. ✗ file closer; ⚓ rear ship; marcher en ~ bring up the rear; ~**fils** [ˌˈfil] m/inv. ⚡ binding-srew; ⚡ clamp; ~**freins** [ˌˈfrɛ̃] m/inv. ⚡ brakesman; ⚡ brake-adjuster; ~**joint** ⊕ [ˌˈʒwɛ̃] m cramp; screw-clamp.

serrement [sɛrˈmã] m squeezing; ✗ dam; ~ de main handshake; hand pressure; fig. ~ de cœur pang; **serre-papiers** [sɛrpaˈpje] m/inv. file (for papers); **serrer** [sɛˈre] (1b) v/t. press, squeeze; grasp (s.o.'s hand), grip; put (away); tighten (a knot, ⊕ a screw); fig. compress, condense; ✗ close (the ranks); skirt (the coast, a wall); sp. jostle (other runners etc.); crowd (s.o.'s car); mot. ~ à droite keep (to the) right; ~ q. de près follow close behind s.o.; ~ la main à shake hands with; ~ les dents clench one's teeth; serrez-vous! sit closer!; F move up!; se ~ crowd, stand (sit etc.) close

together; tighten (lips); fig. feel a pang, contract (heart); **serre-tête** [sɛrˈtɛːt] m/inv. headband; skullcap.

serrure [sɛˈryːr] f lock; **serrurerie** [sɛryrəˈri] f locksmith's trade; locksmith's (shop); lock-mechanism; metal-work; **serrurier** [ˌˈrje] m locksmith; metal-worker.

serte [sɛrt] f gem: mounting or setting (in a bezel); **sertir** [sɛrˈtiːr] (2a) v/t. set (a gem) (in a bezel); set (window-panes) (in, de); **sertissage** [sɛrtiˈsaːʒ] m gem: setting; panes: setting in lead; **sertisseur** [ˌˈsœːr] m setter; **sertissure** [ˌˈsyːr] f bezel; setting.

sérum ⚕ [seˈrɔm] m serum.

servage [sɛrˈvaːʒ] m serfdom; bondage.

serval, pl. -als zo. [sɛrˈval] m serval, tiger-cat.

servant, e [sɛrˈvã, ˌˈvãːt] 1. adj. serving; eccl. lay (brother); 2. su./m ✗ gunner; tennis: server; su./f servant; dumb waiter, dinner-waggon; ⊕ prop; ⊕ (bench-)vice.

serveur [sɛrˈvœːr] m waiter; **serveuse** [ˌˈvøːz] f waitress.

serviabilité [sɛrvjabiliˈte] f obligingness; **serviable** [ˌˈvjabl] obliging, helpful (person); **service** [ˌˈvis] m service (a. ✗, ✝, eccl., tennis); ✗, ⚓ guard etc.: duty; hotel: service charge; ✝, admin. department; cuis. meal: course; tools: set; ~ compris service included; ~ de table dinner-service; ~ diplomatique diplomatic service, Am. corps; ~ divin divine service; ✗ ~ obligatoire compulsory (military) service; ~s pl. publics public services; ✗ être de ~ be on duty; ✝ libre ~ self-service; rendre (un) ~ à q. do s.o. a good turn.

serviette [sɛrˈvjɛt] f (table) napkin, serviette; towel; briefcase, portfolio; ~-éponge Turkish towel; ✒ hygiénique sanitary towel or Am. napkin.

servile [sɛrˈvil] servile; abject (to, envers); menial (duties); slavish (imitation); **servilité** [ˌviliˈte] f servility.

servir [sɛrˈviːr] (2b) v/t. serve (a dish, s.o. at table, ✝ a customer, one's country, a. tennis a ball); help, assist; be in the service of; wait on; cards: deal; ✝ supply; pay (a rent); eccl. ~ la messe serve at mass; hunt.

~ un sanglier au couteau dispatch a boar with a knife; se ~ help o.s. to food; se ~ de use; v/i. serve (a. ✕); be used (as, de); be in service; be useful; à quoi cela sert-il? what's the good of that?; à quoi cela sert-il de (inf.)?, à quoi sert de (inf.)? what is the good of (ger.)?; **serviteur** [~vi'tœːr] m servant; ~! no thank you; **servitude** [~vi'tyd] f servitude; slavery; fig. tyranny; 🏛 easement; fig. obligation.

servo... ⊕ [sɛrvo] servo(-assisted) ..., power(-assisted) ...; ~**commande** [~kɔ'mãd] f servo-control; ~**direction** [~dirɛk'sjɔ̃] f servo- or power steering; ~**moteur** [~mɔ'tœːr] m servo-motor.

ses [se] see son¹.

sessile ♀ etc. [sɛ'sil] sessile.

session 🏛, parl. [sɛ'sjɔ̃] f session.

set [sɛt] m tennis: set; table: place mat.

sétacé, e [seta'se] bristly, setaceous.

séton ✚, zo. [se'tɔ̃] m seton; plaie f en ~ flesh wound.

seuil [sœːj] m phys., psych., fig. fame, door: threshold; doorstep.

seul, seule [sœl] adj. before su. one, only, single; very, mere; after su. or verb alone, lonely; before art. only; ... alone; comme un ~ homme like one man; un homme ~ a single or lonely man; **seulement** [~'mã] adv. only; solely; but; ne ... pas ~ not even; si ... if only ...; **seulet, -ette** F [sœ'lɛ, ~'lɛt] alone; lonely.

sève [sɛːv] f ♀ sap; fig. vigo(u)r, pith.

sévère [se'vɛːr] severe (a. fig.); stern; strict (discipline, morals); hard (person, climate); **sévérité** [~veri'te] f severity (a. fig.); person, look: sternness; fig. taste: austerity; discipline, morals: strictness; 🏛 ~s pl. harsh sentences.

sévices [se'vis] m/pl. cruelty sg., ill treatment; **sévir** [~'viːr] (2a) v/i. rage (plague, war); ~ contre deal severely with.

sevrage [sə'vraːʒ] m child, lamb: weaning; **sevrer** [~'vre] (1d) v/t. wean (a child, a lamb); ✍ separate; fig. deprive (of, de).

sexagénaire [sɛksaʒe'nɛːr] adj., a. su. sexagenarian.

sex-appeal [sɛksa'piːl] m sex-appeal.

sexe [sɛks] m sex; F le beau ~, le ~ faible the fair or weaker sex, women

pl.; le ~ fort the strong sex, men pl.; des deux ~s of both sexes.

sextuor ♪ [sɛks'tɥɔːr] m sextet.

sextuple [sɛks'typl] adj., a. su./m sixfold, sextuple; **sextupler** [~ty-'ple] (1a) vt/i. increase sixfold, sextuple.

sexuel, -elle [sɛk'sɥɛl] sexual.

seyant, e [sɛ'jɑ̃, ~'jɑ̃ːt] becoming.

shake-hand [ʃɛk'hand] m/inv. handshake.

shaker [ʃɛ'kœːr] m cocktail-shaker.

shampooing [ʃɑ̃'pwɛ̃] m shampoo; faire un ~ à shampoo.

shooter [ʃu'te] (1a) v/i. foot. shoot; sl. se ~ shoot (up), fix (drug addict).

short cost. [ʃɔrt] m shorts pl.

shot foot. [ʃɔt] m shot.

shunt ⚡ [ʃœ̃ːt] m shunt; ~ de grille grid leak; **shunter** ⚡ [ʃœ̃'te] (1a) v/t. shunt.

si¹ [si] cj. if; whether; suppose; ~ ce n'est que were it not that; if it were not that; ~ je ne me trompe if I am not mistaken; ~ tant est que (sbj.) if it happens that (ind.).

si² [~] adv. so, so much; answer to negative question: yes; ~ bien que so that; with the result that; ~ fait! yes indeed!; ~ riche qu'il soit however rich he may be.

si³ ♪ [~] m/inv. si; note: B; ~ bémol B flat.

siamois, e [sja'mwa, ~'mwaːz] Siamese; ✳ frères m/pl. ~, sœurs f/pl. ~es Siamese twins.

sibérien, -enne [sibe'rjɛ̃, ~'rjɛn] Siberian.

sibilant, e ✚ [sibi'lɑ̃, ~'lɑ̃ːt] sibilant.

siccatif, -ve [sika'tif, ~'tiːv] **1.** adj. (quick-)drying, siccative; **2.** su./m siccative; quick-drying substance.

side-car [sajd'kaːr] m motor-cycle combination; side-car.

sidéral, e, m/pl. -aux [side'ral, ~'ro] astr. sidereal; **sidérer** F [~'re] (1a) v/t. stagger, shatter.

sidérose [side'roːz] f min. siderite; ✚ siderosis; **sidérostat** astr. [~ros'ta] m siderostat; **sidérotechnie** [~rɔtɛk'ni] f metallurgy of iron; **sidérurgie** [~ryr'ʒi] f metallurgy of iron; **sidérurgique** [~ryr'ʒik] ironworking; usine f ~ ironworks usu. sg.

siècle [sjɛkl] m century; eccl. world(ly life); fig. period, time, age;

F *il y a un* ⁓ *que it's ages since;* ♀ *des lumières* age of enlightenment; *Grand* ♀ *the* age of Louis XIV.

sied [sje] *3rd p. sg. pres. of* seoir.

siège [sjɛːʒ] *m* chair *etc.*, ⊕, *disease, government, parl.*: seat; centre (*of activity, learning, etc.*); ✝ office; ⚔ siege; ⚖ *judge*: bench; *eccl.* (*episcopal*) see; *chair*: bottom; *mot. etc.* ⁓ *arrière* back-seat; ⁓ *du cocher* coachman's box; ✝ ⁓ *social* head office, registered office; **siéger** [sje'ʒe] (1g) *v/i.* sit (⚖, *a.* in Parliament, *au parlement*); ✝ have its head office; ⚔ be seated; *eccl.* hold one's see (*bishop*).

sien, sienne [sjɛ̃, sjɛn] **1.** *pron./poss.*: *le* ⁓, *la* ⁓ne, *les* ⁓s *pl.*, *les* ⁓nes *pl.* his, hers, its, one's; **2.** *su./m* his *or* her *or* its *or* one's own; *les* ⁓s *pl.* his *or* her *or* one's (own) people; *su./f*: *faire des* ⁓nes lark (about).

sieste [sjɛst] *f* siesta; F nap; *faire la* ⁓ take a nap.

sieur ⚖ [sjœːr] *m*: *le* ⁓ ... Mr. ...

sifflant, e [si'flɑ̃, ⁓'flɑ̃ːt] **1.** *adj.* hissing; wheezing (*breath*); whistling (*note*); *gramm.* sibilant; **2.** *su./f gramm.* sibilant; **sifflement** [⁓flə'mɑ̃] *m person, a.* arrow, *bullet, wind*: whistle, whistling; *gas, goose, steam*: hiss(ing); *cuis., a.* ⚡ sizzling; *breathing*: wheezing; **siffler** [⁓'fle] (1a) *v/i.* whistle; hiss; *cuis., a.* ⚡ sizzle; ⚡ wheeze; blow a whistle; ⚓ pipe; *v/t.* whistle (*a tune*); whistle to (*a dog*); whistle for (*a taxi*); ⚓ pipe; *thea.* hiss, boo; F swig (*a drink*); **sifflet** [⁓'flɛ] *m* whistle, ⚓ pipe; *thea.* hiss, catcall; ⁓ *d'alarme* alarm-whistle; *coup m de* ⁓ (blast of the) whistle; *sl. couper le* ⁓ *à q.* cut s.o.'s throat; *fig.* nonplus s.o.; *donner un coup de* ⁓ blow a whistle; ⊕ *en* ⁓ slantwise; bevelled; **siffleur, -euse** [⁓'flœːr, ⁓'fløːz] **1.** *adj.* whistling; wheezy (*horse*); hissing (*serpent*); **2.** *su.* whistler; *thea.* hisser, booer; *su./m orn.* widgeon; **sifflotement** [⁓flɔt'mɑ̃] *m* soft whistling; **siffloter** [⁓flɔ'te] (1a) *vt/i.* whistle softly *or* under one's breath.

sigillaire [siʒil'lɛːr] sigillary; signet (-*ring*); **sigillé, e** [⁓'le] sigillate(d).

sigisbée ✝, *co.* [siʒis'be] *m* gallant.

sigle [sigl] *m shorthand*: outline; abbreviation; ⁓s *pl.* sigla (*in old manuscripts*).

signal [si'ɲal] *m* signal; *teleph.* (*dialling*) tone; ⁓ *à bras* hand signal, ⚔ *etc.* semaphore signal; 🚂 ⁓ *avancé* distant signal; ⁓ *d'alarme* alarm-signal, 🚂 communication cord; *teleph.* ⁓ *d'appel* calling signal; ⁓ *de danger* (*détresse*) danger (distress) signal; ⁓ *horaire radio*: time signal, F pips *pl.*; ⁓ *lumineux* traffic-light; **signalé, e** [siɲa'le] outstanding; *pej.* notorious; **signalement** [⁓ɲal'mɑ̃] *m* description; particulars *pl.*; **signaler** [siɲa'le] (1a) *v/t.* signal (*a train etc.*); *fig.* indicate; point out (*s.th.* to s.o., *qch. à q.*), draw attention to; describe, give a description of (*s.o.*); report (to, *à*); **signalétique** *admin.* [⁓le'tik] descriptive; **signalisation** [⁓liza'sjɔ̃] *f* signalling; signals *pl.*, signal system; *mot.* ⁓ *routière* road signs *pl.*; *panneau m de* ⁓ road sign.

signataire [siɲa'tɛːr] *su.* signatory; **signature** [siɲa'tyːr] *f* signature; *apposer sa* ⁓ *à* set one's hand to; **signe** [siɲ] *m* sign; (*bodily, punctuation*) mark; ⚔ insignia (*of rank*); ⁓ *de tête* (*des yeux*) nod (wink); *faire* ⁓ *à* beckon to; **signer** [si'ɲe] (1a) *v/t.* sign; *se* ⁓ cross o.s.; **signet** [⁓'ɲɛ] *m* bookmark.

significatif, -ve [siɲifika'tif, ⁓'tiːv] significant (*a.* ⚡ *figure*); **signification** [⁓'sjɔ̃] *f* meaning; sense; ⚖ notice, petition, writ, *etc.*: service; **signifier** [siɲi'fje] (1o) *v/t.* mean, signify (*a.* ⚖ serve (*a writ etc.*); ⁓ *qch. à q.* make s.th. known to s.o., inform s.o. of s.th.; *qu'est-ce que cela signifie?* what is the meaning of this? (*indicating disapproval*).

silence [si'lɑ̃ːs] *m* silence; stillness; *fig.* secrecy; ♪ rest; *garder le* ⁓ keep silent (about, *sur*); *passer qch. sous* ⁓ pass s.th. over in silence; say nothing about s.th.; **silencieux, -euse** [⁓lɑ̃'sjø, ⁓'sjøːz] **1.** *adj.* silent; still (*evening etc.*); **2.** *su./m mot.* silencer.

silex *min.* [si'lɛks] *m* flint, silex.

silhouette [si'lwɛt] *f* silhouette; outline; profile; **silhouetter** [⁓lwɛ'te] (1a) *v/t.* silhouette, outline; *phot.* block out; *se* ⁓ stand out (against, *contre*).

silicate ⚗ [sili'kat] *m* silicate; ⁓ *de potasse* water-glass; **silice** ⚗ [⁓'lis] *f* silica; **siliceux, -euse** [sili'sø,

~'sø:z] siliceous; **silicium** ⚛ [~-'sjɔm] *m* silicon; **siliciure** ⚛ [~-'sjy:r] *m* silicide.

sillage [si'ja:ʒ] *m* ⚓ wake; ✈, *fig.* trail; *fig. marcher dans le* ~ *de* follow in (*s.o.'s*) footsteps.

sillet ♩ [si'jɛ] *m violin etc.*: nut.

sillon [si'jɔ̃] *m* furrow; *anat.*, *a.* gram-ophone: groove; *poet.* ~s *pl.* fields; **sillonner** [~jɔ'ne] (1a) *v/t.* furrow (*a. one's forehead*); *fig.* criss-cross.

silo [si'lo] *m* silo; *potatoes:* clamp; **silotage** ✔ [~lɔ'ta:ʒ] *m* ensilage.

silphe *zo.* [silf] *m* carrion-beetle.

silure *icht.* [si'ly:r] *m* silurus, catfish.

simagrée F [sima'gre] *f* pretence; ~s *pl.* affectation *sg.*; affected airs; *faire des* ~s put on airs.

simien, -enne *zo.* [si'mjɛ̃, ~'mjɛn] *adj.*, *a. su./m* simian; **simiesque** [~'mjɛsk] simian; ape-like.

similaire [simi'lɛ:r] similar (*a.* ⚗); like; **similairement** [~lɛr'mɑ̃] *adv.* in like manner; **similarité** [~lari-'te] *f* similarity, likeness; **simili** [~'li] *m* imitation; **similitude** [~li-'tyd] *f* similitude; similarity (*a.* ⚗); *gramm.* simile.

simonie *eccl.* [simɔ'ni] *f* simony.

simoun [si'mun] *m wind:* simoom.

simple [sɛ̃:pl] **1.** *adj.* simple; single (*a.* ⛴ *ticket*); ⚔, ⚓ ordinary; *fig.* elementary; plain (*food, dress*); *fig.* simple(-minded); half-witted; **2.** *su./m the* simple; simple-minded person, simpleton; *tennis:* single; ⚕ ~s *pl.* medicinal herbs, simples; ~ *messieurs tennis:* men's single(s *pl.*); **simplicité** [sɛ̃plisi'te] *f* simplicity; *fig.* simple-mindedness; ~s *pl.* naïve remarks; **simplification** [~fika'sjɔ̃] *f* simplification; **simplifier** [~'fje] (1o) *v/t.* simplify; ⚗ reduce to its lowest terms; *se* ~ become simple(r); **simpliste** [sɛ̃'plist] **1.** *adj.* simplistic; over-simple; **2.** *su.* person who over-simplifies.

simulacre [simy'lakr] *m* image; *fig.* pretence, semblance; ✈ flight simulator; ~ *de combat* sham fight.

simulateur *m*, **-trice** *f* [simyla'tœ:r, ~'tris] shammer; ⚔ malingerer; ⊕ simulator; **simulation** [~'sjɔ̃] *f* sim-ulation; ⚔ malingering; **simulé, e** [simy'le] feigned (*illness*); fictitious; sham (*fight*); **simuler** [~] (1a) *v/t.* simulate; feign (*illness*).

simultané, e [simulta'ne] simul-taneous; **simultanéité** [~nei'te] *f* simultaneity; **simultanément** [~ne'mɑ̃] *adv. of* simultané.

sinapisme ⚕ [sina'pism] *m* mus-tard-plaster, sinapism.

sincère [sɛ̃'sɛ:r] sincere; **sincérité** [~seri'te] *f* sincerity, frankness; genuineness.

singe [sɛ̃:ʒ] *m zo.* monkey; *zo.* ape (*a.* F *fig.* = *imitator*); ⊕ hoist; F bully (*beef*); *sl.* boss; F *faire le* ~ monkey about; *laid comme un* ~ as ugly as sin; **singer** [sɛ̃'ʒe] (1l) *v/t.* mimic, ape; **singerie** [sɛ̃ʒ'ri] *f* monkey trick; grimace; ~s *pl. a.* airs and graces.

singulariser [sɛ̃gylari'ze] (1a) *v/t.* make (*s.o.*) conspicuous; render (*s.o.*) singular; *se* ~ make o.s. con-spicuous; **singularité** [~'te] *f* sin-gularity; peculiarity; eccentricity, oddness; **singulier, -ère** [sɛ̃gy'lje, ~'ljɛ:r] **1.** *adj.* singular (*a.* ⚗); pe-culiar; unusual; strange; conspic-uous; single (*combat*); **2.** *su./m gramm.* singular; *au* ~ in the sin-gular.

sinistre [si'nistr] **1.** *adj.* sinister; ominous, threatening; **2.** *su./m* dis-aster, catastrophe; fire; loss (*from fire etc.*); **sinistré, e** [~nis'tre] **1.** *adj.* (disaster-)stricken; shipwrecked; homeless (*through fire, bombs, etc.*); bomb-damaged (*house etc.*); **2.** *su.* victim (*of a disaster*).

sinon [si'nɔ̃] *cj.* otherwise, if not; except (that, *que*).

sinueux, -euse [si'nɥø, ~'nɥø:z] sinuous; winding (*path, river*); **sinuosité** [~nɥozi'te] *f* winding; meandering; bend (*in river*); **sinus** [~'nys] *m anat.* sinus; ⚗ sine; **sinu-site** ⚕ [~ny'zit] *f* sinusitis.

sionisme [sjɔ'nism] *m* Zionism.

siphon [si'fɔ̃] *m phys. etc.* siphon; ⚠ drain etc.: trap.

sire [si:r] *m king:* Sire, Sir; † lord; † *pauvre* ~ *person:* sorry specimen.

sirène [si'rɛn] *f* ⚓, ⊕, *myth.*, *zo.*, *fig.* siren; ⚓, ⊕ hooter; ⚓ foghorn.

sirocco [sirɔ'ko] *m wind:* sirocco.

sirop [si'ro] *m* syrup; (*fruit*) cordial; ⚕ *a.* mixture.

siroter [sirɔ'te] (1a) *v/t.* F sip; *v/i. sl.* tipple.

sirupeux, -euse [siry'pø, ~'pø:z] syrupy; F *fig.* sloppy, sentimental.

sis, e [si, si:z] *p.p. of* seoir.

sismique [sis'mik] seismic.

sismo...

sismo... [sismɔ] seismo...; **~graphe** [~'graf] *m* seismograph.

site [sit] *m* setting; site, spot; ⚠, ✗ lie of the ground; ~ *propre* bus lane; ✗ *angle m de* ~ angle of sight.

sitôt [si'to] *adv.* as *or* so soon; ~ *après* immediately after; ~ *dit,* ~ *fait* no sooner said than done; ~ *que* as soon as; *ne ... pas de* ~ not ... for a long time.

situation [sitɥa'sjɔ̃] *f* situation; position; *fig.* job, post; location; bearing; ✝, ✗, *admin.* return, report; ~ *économique* economic position; ~ *sociale* station in life; **situé, e** [si'tɥe] situated (at, *à*); **situer** [~] (1n) *v/t.* situate, place; locate (*a. fig.*).

six [sis; *before consonant* si; *before vowel and h mute* siz] *adj./num., a. su./m/inv.* six; *date, title:* sixth; *à la* ~*-quatre-deux* in a slapdash way; **sixain** [si'zɛ̃] *m prosody:* six-line stanza; *cards:* packet of six packs; **sixième** [~'zjɛm] **1.** *adj./num.* sixth; **2.** *su.* sixth; *su./m fraction:* sixth; *sixth floor,* *Am.* seventh floor; *su./f secondary school:* (*approx.*) first form; **sixte** ♩ [sikst] *f* sixth.

sizain [si'zɛ̃] *m see* **sixain**.

skating [ske'tiŋ] *m* roller-skating; skating-rink.

ski [ski] *m* ski; skiing; ~ *nautique* water skiing; *faire du* ~ = **skier** [~'e] (1a) *v/i.* ski; **skieur** *m*, **-euse** *f* [~'œːr, ~'øːz] skier.

slalom [sla'lɔm] *m sp.* slalom; *fig.* zigzag (movement); *sp.* descente en ~ slalom descent; *faire du* ~ = **slalomer** [~lɔ'me] (1a) *v/i. sp.* slalom; *fig.* zigzag (one's) way, dodge in and out.

slave [slaːv] **1.** *adj.* Slavonic; **2.** *su./m ling.* Slavonic; *su.* ♀ Slav; **slavisme** [sla'vism] *m* Slavism.

slip [slip] *m women:* panties *pl.*; *men:* (short) pants *pl.*

sloop ⚓ [slup] *m* sloop.

slovaque [slɔ'vak] *adj., a. su.* ♀ Slovak; **slovène** [~'vɛn] *adj., a. su.* ♀ Slovene.

smash [smaʃ] *m tennis:* smash.

smoking [smɔ'kiŋ] *m* dinner-jacket, *Am.* tuxedo.

snob [snɔb] **1.** *adj.* snobbish, swanky, swell; **2.** *su./m* snob; vulgar follower of fashion; **snober** [snɔ'be] (1a) *v/t.* look down on (*s.o.*); cold-shoulder, cut (*s.o.*); **snobisme**

[~'bism] *m* vulgar following of fashion; snobbery.

sobre [sɔbr] abstemious (*person*); sober; frugal (*eater, meal*); *fig.* ~ *de* sparing of; **sobriété** [sɔbrie'te] *f* abstemiousness; moderation (*in drinking, eating, speech*).

sobriquet [sɔbri'kɛ] *m* nickname.

soc ✔ [sɔk] *m* ploughshare.

sociabilité [sɔsjabili'te] *f* sociability; **sociable** [~'sjabl] sociable, companionable; *il est* ~ he is a good mixer.

social, e, *m/pl.* **-aux** [sɔ'sjal, ~'sjo] social; ✝ registered (*capital, name of company*); ✝ trading, financial (*year*); *assistante f* ~*e* social worker; ✝ *raison f* ~*e* (registered) name of company *or* firm; **socialisation** *pol.* [sɔsjaliza'sjɔ̃] *f* socialization; **socialiser** *pol.* [~li'ze] (1a) *v/t.* socialize; **socialisme** *pol.* [~'lism] *m* socialism; **socialiste** [~'list] **1.** *adj.* socialist; socialistic (*doctrine*); **2.** *su.* socialist.

sociétaire [sɔsje'tɛːr] *su.* (full) member; ✝ shareholder; **société** [~'te] *f* society; company (*a.* ✝); association, club; ~ *anonyme* company limited by shares; ~ *à responsabilité limitée* (*sort of*) limited company; ~ *d'abondance* affluent society; ~ *de consommation* consumer society; ~ *de masse* mass society; ♀ *des Nations* League of Nations; ~ *en commandite* (*par actions*) limited partnership; ~ *en nom collectif* firm; private company; ~ *filiale* daughter (company); ~ *par actions* company limited by shares; *acte m de* ~ deed of partnership.

sociologie [sɔsjɔlɔ'ʒi] *f* sociology; **sociologique** [~'ʒik] sociological; **sociologue** [~'lɔg] *su.* sociologist.

socle [sɔkl] *m* ⚠ base (*a. fig.*); *column:* plinth; *wall:* footing; ⊕ bed-plate (*of engine etc.*); bracket; stand.

socque [sɔk] *m* clog.

socquettes [sɔ'kɛt] *f/pl.* (*ladies'*) ankle socks.

soda [sɔ'da] *m* fizzy drink.

sodium ⚗ [sɔ'djɔm] *m* sodium.

sœur [sœːr] *f* sister (*a. eccl.*); *eccl.* nun; ~ *de lait* foster-sister.

sofa [sɔ'fa] *m* sofa, settee.

soi [swa] *pron.* oneself; himself; herself, itself; *amour m de* ~ self-love; *cela va de* ~ that goes without saying;

être chez ~ be at home; en (or de) ~ in itself; ~-**disant** [~di'zã] **1.** adj./inv. so-called; **2.** adv. supposedly, apparently; ostensibly.

soie [swa] f silk; (hog-)bristle; ⊕ crank: pin; ⊕ tool etc.: tongue; ✝ ~ artificielle artificial silk; ~ rayon; ~ grège raw silk; **soierie** ✝ [~'ri] f silk (fabric); silk trade; silk factory.

soif [swaf] f thirst (a. fig. for, de); avoir ~ be thirsty.

soigné, e [swa'ɲe] neat, trim; well-groomed (appearance); cuis. first-rate (meal); **soigner** [~'ɲe] (1a) v/t. look after; ✞ nurse (a sick person); ✞ doctor: attend (a patient); fig. elle soigne sa mise she dresses with care; ✞ se faire ~ have treatment; **soigneux, -euse** [~'ɲø, ~'ɲøːz] careful (of, de; to inf., de inf.); neat; painstaking.

soi-même [swa'mɛːm] oneself.

soin [swɛ̃] m care, pains pl.; neatness, tidiness; ~s pl. ✞ etc. attention pl.; aux bons ~s de post: care of, c/o.; par les ~s de thanks to; by courtesy of; premiers ~s pl. first aid sg.; avoir (or prendre) ~ de take care of (s.th.); take care to (do s.th.), be or make sure to (do s.th.).

soir [swaːr] m evening; afternoon; du matin au ~ from morning to night; le ~ in the evening; sur le ~ towards evening; tous les ~s every evening; **soirée** [swa're] f duration, period: evening; (evening) party; thea. evening performance; ~ d'adieu farewell party; ~ dansante dance; thea. ~ unique one-night stand.

sois [swa] 1st p. sg. pres. sbj. of être 1; soit **1.** adv. [swat] (let us) suppose...; say...; ~! all right!, agreed!; ainsi ~-il so be it!, amen!; tant ~ peu ever so little; **2.** cj. [swa]: ~ ... ~ ..., ~ ... ou ... either ... or ...; whether ... or ...; ~ que (sbj.) whether (ind.).

soixantaine [swasã'tɛn] f (about) sixty; la ~ the age of sixty, the sixties pl.; **soixante** [~'sãːt] adj./num., a. su./m/inv. sixty; **soixante-dix** [~sãt'dis; before consonant ~'di; before vowel and h mute ~'diz] adj./num., a. su./m/inv. seventy; **soixante-dixième** [~sãtdi'zjɛm] adj./num., a. su. seventieth; **soixantième** [~sã'tjɛm] adj./num., a. su. sixtieth.

soja ⚘ [sɔ'ʒa] m soya-bean, Am. soybean.   [f de ~ G-clef.\
sol[1] ♩ [sɔl] m/inv. sol; note: G; clef∫
sol[2] [sɔl] m earth, ground; ✔ soil; field; ~-**air** ⚔ [~'ɛːr] adj./inv. ground-to-air (missile).

solaire [sɔ'lɛːr] solar; sun(-dial, glasses); ✞ sun-ray (treatment).

soldat usu. ⚔ [sɔl'da] m soldier; ~ de plomb toy or tin soldier; ♀ inconnu the Unknown Warrior; les simples ~s pl. the rank sg. and file sg.; se faire ~ join the army; simple ~ private; **soldatesque** pej. [~da'tɛsk] **1.** adj. barrack-room ...; **2.** su./f soldiery.

solde[1] ⚔, ⚓ [sɔld] f pay.
solde[2] ✝ [~] m account: balance; job lot, remnant; ~s pl. (clearance) sale sg.; ~ créditeur (débiteur) credit (debit) balance.

solder[1] ⚔, ⚓ [sɔl'de] (1a) v/t. pay.
solder[2] [~] (1a) v/t. balance (accounts); settle (a bill, an account); sell off, clear (goods); remainder (a book); se ~ par (or en) show (a profit, deficit, etc.); end (up) in (failure etc.).

sole[1] ✒ [sɔl] f break.
sole[2] [~] f vet. sole; ⊕ bed-plate; ⊕ furnace: hearth; ⚠ sleeper; ⚓ boat: flat bottom.

sole[3] icht. [~] f sole.

solécisme gramm., a. fig. [sɔle'sism] m solecism.

soleil [sɔ'lɛːj] m sun; sunshine; eccl. monstrance; ⚘ sunflower; firework: Catherine-wheel; ✞ coup m de ~ sunstroke; sunburn; il fait (du) ~ the sun is shining; **soleilleux, -euse** [~lɛ'jø, ~'jøːz] sunny.

solennel, -elle [sɔla'nɛl] solemn; fig. grave (tone); **solenniser** [~ni'ze] (1a) v/t. solemnize; **solennité** [~ni'te] f solemnity; eccl. ceremony; ~s pl. celebrations.

solfège ♩ [sɔl'fɛːʒ] m sol-fa; **solfier** ♩ [~'fje] (1o) v/t. sol-fa.

solidage ⚘ [sɔli'daːʒ] m golden-rod.
solidaire [sɔli'dɛːr] ⊕ etc. interdependent; ⚖ joint and several; être ~ (de) show solidarity (with); ⊕ etc. be bound up (with); **solidariser** [sɔlidari'ze] (1a) v/t.: se ~ show solidarity (with, avec); make common cause; **solidarité** [~'te] f solidarity; ⚖ joint responsibility; grève f de ~ sympathetic strike.

solide [sɔ'lid] **1.** *adj.* solid (*body, earth, food, foundation, wall,* a. ⚹ *angle*); fast (*colour*); strong (*flow, cloth, building, person*); ✝ sound (*a. reason*); *fig.* reliable; **2.** *su./m* solid (*a.* ⚹); ⚹ solid ground *or* foundations *pl.*; **solidification** [sɔlidifika'sjɔ̃] *f* solidifying; **solidifier** [~'fje] (1o) *v/t. a.* se ~ solidify; **solidité** [~'te] *f* solidity; *building, friendship,* a. *tex.*: strength; *fig.* soundness (*of judgment,* a. ✝).

soliloque [sɔli'lɔk] *m* soliloquy.

solipède *zo.* [sɔli'pɛd] solid-ungulate; whole-hoofed.

soliste ♪ [sɔ'list] **1.** *su.* soloist; **2.** *adj.* solo (*violin etc.*).

solitaire [sɔli'tɛːr] **1.** *adj.* solitary, lonely; lonesome; ⚹ ver *m* ~ tapeworm; **2.** *su.* solitary, recluse; loner, lone wolf; *su./m diamond,* a. *game:* solitaire; *zo.* old boar.

solitude [sɔli'tyd] *f* solitude, loneliness; lonely spot.

solive ⚹ [sɔ'liːv] *f* beam, joist; **soliveau** ⚹ [~li'vo] *m* small joist.

sollicitation [sɔllisita'sjɔ̃] *f* entreaty, earnest request; ⚡ attraction, *magnet:* pull; ⚹⚹ application (*to the judge*); **solliciter** [~'te] (1a) *v/t.* seek, request, ask *or* beg for; appeal to; solicit; urge; attract; **solliciteur** *m,* -**euse** *f* [~'tœːr, ~'tøːz] applicant (for, de); petitioner; **sollicitude** [~'tyd] *f* concern, solicitude; anxiety (for, *pour*).

solo [sɔ'lo] **1.** *su./m* ♪ (*pl. a.* -**li** [~'li]) solo; **2.** *adj./inv.* solo (*cycle, violin, etc.*).

solstice [sɔls'tis] *m* solstice; **solsticial, e,** *m/pl.* -**aux** [~ti'sjal, ~'sjo] solstitial.

solubilité [sɔlybili'te] *f* solubility; *fig.* solvability; **soluble** [~'lybl] soluble (*a. fig.*); **solution** [~ly'sjɔ̃] *f* ⚛, ⚹, ⚹, a. *fig.* solution; resolution; ⚹⚹ discharge (*of obligation*); ~ **de continuité** gap; break; ⚡ fault.

solvabilité ✝ [sɔlvabili'te] *f* solvency; **solvable** ✝ [~'vabl] solvent; **solvant** ⚗ [~'vɑ̃] *m* solvent.

sombre [sɔ̃ːbr] dark, gloomy; dull, murky (*sky, weather*); dim (*light*); melancholy (*face, temperament, thoughts*).

sombrer [sɔ̃'bre] (1a) *v/i.* ⚓, a. *fig.* founder; sink; *fig.* fail.

sommaire [sɔ'mɛːr] **1.** *adj.* sum-

mary (*a.* ⚹⚹), brief, concise; *fig.* improvised; **2.** *su./m* summary, synopsis; **sommation** [~ma'sjɔ̃] *f* ⚹⚹ demand; notice; summons *sg.*; warning; ⚹ summation.

somme¹ [sɔm] *f* sum, amount; ~ **globale** lump *or* global sum; ~ **toute** ... on the whole ...; **en** ~ in short.

somme² [~] *f* burden; **bête** *f* **de** ~ beast of burden; *mulet m* **de** ~ pack-mule.

somme³ [sɔm] *m* nap; **faire un** ~ take a nap, F have a snooze; **sommeil** [sɔ'mɛːj] *m* sleep, slumber; sleepiness; *avoir* ~ feel *or* be sleepy; **sommeiller** [~mɛ'je] (1a) *v/i.* be asleep; doze; *fig.* lie dormant.

sommelier [sɔmə'lje] *m* butler; cellarman; *restaurant:* wine-waiter.

sommer¹ [sɔ'me] (1a) *v/t.* summon; call on (*s.o.*) (to *inf.,* de *inf.*); ⚔ call upon (*a place*) to surrender.

sommer² ⚹ [~] (1a) *v/t.* find the sum of.

sommes [sɔm] *1st p. pl. pres. of* être *1.*

sommet [sɔ'mɛ] *m* summit (*a. pol.*), top (*a. fig.*); ⚹, ⚹ apex; ⚹, ⚔ vertex; *head, arch:* crown; *wave:* crest; *fig.* zenith; height; ⚹ ~ **du poumon** apex of the lung; *pol.* **conférence** *f* **au** ~ summit conference.

sommier¹ [sɔ'mje] *m* ✝ cash-book; *admin.* register; *les* ~**s criminal records office.

sommier² [~] *m* pack-horse; ⚹ *arch:* springer; *floor:* cross-beam; *door:* lintel; ⊕ *machine:* bed; ⚹ bolster; ♪ *organ:* wind-chest; *piano:* stringplate; (*a.* ~ **élastique** *or* **à ressorts**) spring-mattress, box-mattress.

sommité [sɔmi'te] *f* ⚹ summit; tip; ⚘ top; *fig. person:* leading figure.

somnambule [sɔmnɑ̃'byl] **1.** *adj.* somnambulant; **2.** *su.* somnambulist, sleep-walker; **somnambulisme** [~nɑ̃by'lism] *m* somnambulism, sleep-walking; **somnifère** [~ni'fɛːr] **1.** *adj.* sleep-inducing; ⚹ soporific; F boring; **2.** *su./m* ⚹ sleeping drug; sleeping pill.

somnolence [sɔmnɔ'lɑ̃ːs] *f* sleepiness, somnolence; **somnolent, e** [~nɔ'lɑ̃, ~'lɑ̃ːt] sleepy, drowsy.

somptuaire [sɔ̃p'tɥɛːr] sumptuary; **somptueux, -euse** [~'tɥø, ~'tɥøːz] sumptuous; *fig.* magnificent; **somptuosité** [~tɥozi'te] *f* sumptuousness, magnificence.

467

sortie

son¹ *m*, sa *f*, *pl.* ses [sɔ̃, sa, se] *adj./poss.* his, her, its, one's.

son² [sɔ̃] *m* sound, noise; *phys.* mur *m* de ~ sound-barrier.

son³ ✒ [~] *m* bran; F *tache f* de ~ freckle.

sonate ♩ [sɔ'nat] *f* sonata; **sonatine** ♩ [~na'tin] *f* sonatina.

sondage [sɔ̃'da:ʒ] *m* ⚒ boring; ⚓ sounding; ⚙ probing; ⊕ drill-hole; *fig.* survey; (*a.* ~ d'opinion) poll; *enquête f par* ~ sampling survey; *fig.* faire des ~s make a spot check; **sonde** [sɔ̃:d] *f* sounding-rod; ⚙ lead; ⚓ sounding(s *pl.*); ⚙ probe; ⚒ drill(er), borer; **sonder** [sɔ̃'de] (1a) *v/t.* sound (⚓, ⚙ *a patient, a. fig.*); ⚙ probe (*a wound, a. fig.*); *fig.* investigate; *fig.* explore.

songe [sɔ̃:ʒ] *m* dream (*a. fig.*); ~-creux [sɔ̃ʒ'krø] *m/inv.* dreamer; **songer** [sɔ̃'ʒe] (1l) *v/i.* dream (of, de); think (of, à); *songez donc!* just fancy!; **songerie** [sɔ̃ʒ'ri] *f* reverie; (day)dream(ing); **songeur, -euse** [sɔ̃'ʒœ:r, ~'ʒø:z] 1. *adj.* pensive; dreamy; thoughtful; 2. *su.* dreamer.

sonique [sɔ'nik] sonic; sound ...; *barrière f* ~ sound barrier.

sonnaille [sɔ'na:j] *f* cattle-bell; **sonnailler** [~na'je] 1. *su./m* bell-wether; 2. (1a) *v/i.* ring the bell all the time; **sonnant, e** [~'nã, ~'nã:t] striking; *fig.* resounding; hard (*cash*); *à trois heures* ~es on the stroke of three; **sonner** [~'ne] (1a) *v/t.* sound (⚓, ⚒); ring (*a bell*); strike (*the hour*); ring for (*s.o., a. church service*); *fig.* ne pas ~ mot not to utter a word; *v/i.* sound; ring (*bell, coin*); strike (*clock*); *gramm.* be sounded *or* pronounced; *fig.* ~ bien (*creux*) sound well (hollow); *dix heures sonnent* it is striking 10; *dix heures sont sonnées* it has struck 10; *les vêpres sonnent* the bell is ringing for vespers; **sonnerie** [sɔn'ri] *f* bells: ringing; *church etc.:* bells *pl.*; alarm (mechanism); ⊕ striking mechanism; ⚡, *teleph.,* etc. bell; ✗ (bugle-)call.

sonnet [sɔ'nɛ] *m* sonnet.

sonnette [sɔ'nɛt] *f* (house-)bell; hand-bell; ⊕ pile-driver; *cordon m* de ~ bell-pull; *coup m* de ~ ring; **sonneur** [sɔ'nœ:r] *m* bell-ringer; *tel.* sounder; ✗ bugler.

sono F [sɔ'no] *f* P.A. (system); **sono-**

re [~'nɔ:r] resonant; *phys.* acoustic; resounding, loud; ringing (*voice*); *gramm.* voiced (*consonant*); *bande f* ~ sound track; *phys.* onde *f* ~ sound-wave; **sonorisation** [~nɔriza'sjɔ̃] *f* (fitting with a) P.A. (system); **sonorité** [~nɔri'te] *f* sonority; *instrument etc.:* tone, sound; *room:* acoustics *pl.*

sont [sɔ̃] 3rd *p. pl. pres.* of être 1.

sophisme [sɔ'fism] *m* sophism; *logic:* fallacy.

sophistication [sɔfistika'sjɔ̃] *f* use of sophistry; sophistication; † *wine etc.:* adulteration; **sophistique** [sɔfis'tik] 1. *adj.* sophistic(al); 2. *su./f* sophistry; **sophistiqué, e** [~ti'ke] sophisticated; highly developed; **sophistiquer** [~ti'ke] (1m) *v/t.* sophisticate; se ~ become (more) sophisticated; **sophistiqueur** [~ti'kœ:r] *m* quibbler. *[su./m soporific.]*

soporifique [sɔpɔri'fik] *adj., a.*

soprano, *pl. a.* -ni ♩ [sɔpra'no, ~'ni] *m* soprano (*voice, a. singer*).

sorbe ✿ [sɔrb] *f* rowanberry.

sorbet *cuis.* [sɔr'bɛ] *m* sorbet, water-ice; † sherbet.

sorbier ✿ [sɔr'bje] *m* sorb; ~ *sauvage* rowan(-tree), mountain-ash.

sorcellerie [sɔrsɛl'ri] *f* witchcraft, sorcery; **sorcier** [~'sje] *m* sorcerer; wizard; *fig.* brilliant mind; **sorcière** [~'sjɛ:r] *f* sorceress; witch; *fig.* vieille ~ old hag.

sordide [sɔr'did] sordid, squalid; filthy; *fig.* base; **sordidité** [~didi'te] *f* sordidness.

sornettes [sɔr'nɛt] *f/pl.* nonsense *sg.*; idle talk *sg.*; *conter des* ~ talk nonsense.

sort [sɔ:r] *m* fate, destiny; lot; chance, fortune; spell; *fig.* jeter un ~ sur cast a spell on *or* over; *tirer au* ~ draw lots; **sortable** [sɔr'tabl] presentable; **sorte** [sɔrt] *f* sort (*a. typ.*), kind; way, manner; *de la* ~ of that sort; in that way; *de* ~ que so that; *en quelque* ~ in a way, to some extent; *en* ~ que so that; *toutes* ~s de all sorts of.

sortie [sɔr'ti] *f* going out; exit; outlet (*a.* ⊕); ⊕ *a.* outflow; leaving; *admin. goods:* issue; ✝ export(ation); ✗ sortie, sally; outing, trip, excursion; *fig.* outburst; ~ *de secours* emergency exit; ✝ ~s *pl. de fonds* outgoings; *à la* ~ *de* on leaving; *cost.* ~ *de bain* bathrobe.

*30**

sortilège [sɔrti'lɛːʒ] *m* witchcraft; spell.

sortir[1] [sɔr'tiːr] **1.** (2b) *v/i.* go or come out, leave; ♀, ✎, *etc.* come up; come through (*tooth*); stand out, protrude (from, de); ~ de come from; come of (*a good family*); have been at (*a school*); get out of (*one's bed, a difficulty*); *fig.* deviate from (*a subject*); F ~ de (*inf.*) have just done or finished (*ger.*); ✍ ~ de l'hôpital be discharged from *or Am.* the hospital; 🚋 ~ des rails jump the metals; *être* sorti be out; *thea.* sort exit; *v/t.* bring *or* take *or* put *or* send out; ✝ bring out (*a product*), release (*a film etc.*), publish (*a book*); F throw (*s.o.*) out; F come out with (*a remark, joke, etc.*); **2.** *su./m*: au ~ de on leaving; *fig.* at the end of.

sortir[2] 🚋 [~] (2a, *3rd pers. only*) *v/t.* take, have (*effect*).

sosie F [sɔ'zi] *m* (*person's*) double.

sot, sotte [so, sɔt] **1.** *adj.* stupid, foolish; disconcerted; **2.** *su.* fool; **sottise** [sɔ'tiːz] *f* folly, stupidity; stupid act *or* saying; insult.

sou [su] *m* sou (= 5 *centimes*); *sans* le ~ penniless.

soubassement [subas'mɑ̃] *m* △ sub-foundation; base (*a.* △); ⊕ base-plate; *geol.* bed-rock; *bed:* valance; *fig.* substructure.

soubresaut [subrə'so] *m* jerk; sudden start; *vehicle:* jolt; ✍ ~s *pl.* trembling *sg.*

soubrette [su'brɛt] *f thea.* soubrette, maid-servant; F † maid.

souche [suʃ] *f* ✿ *tree etc.*: stump; ✿, *a. fig.* stock; ✚ *virus:* strain; △ (*chimney-*)stack; *eccl.* candle-stock; *fig.* blockhead; *fig.* head (*of a family*); ✝ *cheque, ticket:* counterfoil, stub; *carnet m à* ~s counterfoil book, *Am.* stub-book; *fig.* faire ~ found a family *or* a line.

souci[1] ♀ [su'si] *m* marigold.

souci[2] [su'si] *m* care; worry; concern; **soucier** [~'sje] (1o) *v/t.* trouble (*s.o.*); se ~ be anxious; ne se ~ de rien care for nothing; se ~ de trouble o.s. about; care for *or* about; mind about; **soucieux, -euse** [~'sjø, ~'sjøːz] anxious, concerned (about, de; to *inf.*, de *inf.*); *fig.* worried.

soucoupe [su'kup] *f* saucer; F ~ *volante* flying saucer.

soudable ⊕ [su'dabl] that can be soldered *or* welded; **soudage** ⊕ [~'daːʒ] *m* soldering; welding.

soudain, e [su'dɛ̃, ~'dɛn] **1.** *adj.* sudden; **2.** *soudain adv.* suddenly, all of a sudden; **soudaineté** [~dɛn-'te] *f* suddenness.

soudard *usu. pej.* [su'daːr] *m* † old soldier, F old sweat; *fig.* ruffian.

soude [sud] *f* ♠, ✝, ♀ soda; ♀ saltwort; ♠ ~ *caustique* caustic soda.

souder [su'de] (1a) *v/t.* ⊕ solder, weld; *fig.* join; *lampe f à* ~ blowlamp.

soudoyer [sudwa'je] (1h) *v/t.* hire (the services of); *fig.* bribe, buy (*s.o.*) (over).

soudure ⊕ [su'dyːr] *f* solder; soldering; welding; soldered joint; weld, (*welded*) seam; ✍, ⊕, *inner tube, etc.*: F join; *fig.* faire la ~ bridge the gap.

soue [su] *f* pigsty.

souffert, e [su'fɛːr, ~'fɛrt] *p.p.* of **souffrir**.

soufflage [su'flaːʒ] *m* ⊕ glass-blowing; ⊕ *furnace:* blast; **soufflante** ⊕ [~'flɑ̃ːt] *f* blower; **souffle** [sufl] *m* breath (*a.* ✍); breathing; blast; *fig.* inspiration; ✍ murmur; *sp., fig.* wind; à bout de ~ out of breath; trouver son second (*ou deuxième*) ~ *sp., a. fig.* get one's second wind; **soufflé** *cuis.* [su'fle] *m* soufflé; **soufflement** [~flə'mɑ̃] *m* blowing; **souffler** [~'fle] (1a) *v/i.* blow (*person, a. wind*); pant; get one's breath; *v/t.* blow (♪ *the organ,* ⊕ *glass*); inflate; blow up (*a balloon, a. the fire*); *thea.* prompt; *fig.* whisper; *fig.* breathe (*a word, a sound*); blow out (*a candle*); F trick (*s.o.* out of s.th., *qch. à q.*); F foment (*a strife*); *fig.* ~ le chaud et le froid blow hot and cold; **soufflerie** [~flə'ri] *f* forge, *a.* ♪ *organ:* bellows *pl.*; ⊕ *blower*; ⊕ *wind-tunnel;* **soufflet** [~'flɛ] *m* bellows *pl.* (*a. phot.*); ⊕ fan; 🚋 concertina vestibule; *carriage:* (*folding*) hood; ♪ *swell; cost.* gusset, gore; *fig.* slap, box on the ear; *fig.* affront; **souffleter** [~flə'te] (1c) *v/t.* slap (*s.o.*) in the face; *fig.* insult; **souffleur, -euse** [~'flœːr, ~'fløːz] *su.* blower; *thea. etc.* prompter; *vet. horse:* roarer; *su./m* ⊕ blower; ✍ blow-out; **soufflure** [~'flyːr] *f glass:* bubble; *metall.* flaw, blowhole; *paint:* blister.

souffrance [su'frɑ̃ːs] *f* suffering; ✝ sufferance; ✝ en ~ suspended (*busi-*

ness); held up (post etc.); outstanding (bill etc.); **souffrant, e** [ˌ'frã, ˌ'frãːt] suffering, in pain; ♣ unwell, ill; **souffre** [sufr] 1st p. sg. pres. of souffrir; **souffre-douleur** [ˌfrɔ-du'lœːr] su./inv. drudge; scapegoat; laughing-stock.

souffreteux, -euse [sufrɔ'tø, ˌ'tøːz] destitute; sickly (child etc.).

souffrir [su'friːr] (2f) vt/i. suffer; v/t. bear (a. fig.); permit, allow; v/i. fig. be grieved (to inf., de inf.); be injured.

soufre [sufr] m ♓ etc. sulphur; ~ en poudre, fleur f de ~ flowers pl. of sulphur; fig. sentir le ~ smack of heresy; **soufrer** [su'fre] (1a) v/t. treat with sulphur; ⊕, tex. sulphur (a. matches).

souhait [swɛ] m wish; à ~ to one's liking; **souhaitable** [swɛ'tabl] desirable; **souhaiter** [ˌ'te] (1a) v/t. wish.

souillard [su'jaːr] m ⊕ sink-hole; ⊕ sink-stone; ⚠ strut; **souillarde** [ˌ'jard] f scullery; **souille** [suːj] f (wild boar's) wallow; ⚓ bed; **souiller** [su'je] (1a) v/t. soil (with, de); pollute; stain (a. fig.); fig. tarnish (one's reputation etc.); **souillon** [ˌ'jɔ̃] su. sloven; woman: slut; **souillure** [ˌ'jyːr] f stain (a. fig.); spot; fig. blemish; ♓ impurity.

soûl, soûle F [su, sul] **1.** adj. drunk; surfeited (with, de); satiated; **2.** su./m fill (a. fig.); dormir tout son ~ have one's sleep out.

soulagement [sulaʒ'mã] m relief (a. ⊕); **soulager** [ˌla'ʒe] (1l) v/t. relieve; se ~ relieve o.s. (of a burden, a. F fig.); relieve one's mind.

soûlard m, e f [su'laːr, ˌ'lard], **soûlaud** m, e f [ˌ'lo, ˌ'loːd] drunkard, soaker; **soûler** [ˌ'le] (1a) v/t. satiate, glut (s.o.) (with, de); F make (s.o.) drunk; F get on (s.o.'s) nerves, bore (s.o.); F se ~ get drunk.

soulèvement [sulɛv'mã] m ground, stomach, a. fig. people: rising; ⚓ sea: swell(ing); fig. general protest; geol. upheaval; ♂ ~ de cœur nausea; **soulever** [sul've] (1d) v/t. raise (a. fig. an objection, a question, etc.); lift (up); fig. provoke (an emotion); fig. rouse (peole) to revolt; F steal, sl. lift; fig. ~ le cœur à q. make s.o. sick; se ~ rise (a. in revolt); raise o.s.; turn (stomach).

soulier [su'lje] m shoe; ~s pl. de ski ski-boots; ~ ferré (plat) spiked (low-heeled) shoe; ~ Richelieu lace-up shoe; être dans ses petits ~s be on pins and needles; be ill at ease.

soulignement [suliɲ'mã] m underlining; fig. stressing; **souligner** [ˌli'ɲe] (1a) v/t. underline; fig. stress, emphasize.

soumettre [su'mɛtr] (4v) v/t. subdue (s.o., one's feelings, a country); fig. subject (s.o. to s.th., q. à qch.); fig. submit (an idea, a plan, a request) (to s.o., à q.); se ~ à submit to, comply with; **soumis, e** [ˌ'mi, ˌ'miːz] submissive, obedient; dutiful; **soumission** [ˌmi'sjɔ̃] f ✕, pol. submission, surrender; obedience (to, à); ♦ tender (for, pour); **soumissionnaire** ♦ [sumisjɔ'nɛːr] m tenderer; finance: underwriter; **soumissionner** ♦ [ˌ'ne] (1a) v/t. tender for; finance: underwrite.

soupape ⊕ [su'pap] f valve; bath etc.: plug; fig. safety-valve; ~ à papillon throttle-valve; ~ d'admission intake valve; ~ d'échappement outlet valve; mot. exhaust-valve; ⚡ ~ électrique rectifier.

soupçon [sup'sɔ̃] m suspicion; fig. inkling, idea, hint; fig., a. cuis. touch, dash; liquid: drop; fig. pas un ~ de not a shadow of, not the ghost of; **soupçonner** [ˌsɔ'ne] (1a) v/t. suspect; surmise; **soupçonneux, -euse** [ˌsɔ'nø, ˌ'nøːz] suspicious.

soupe [sup] f soup; F, a. ✕ meal; F food, sl. grub; sop (for soaking in soup, wine, etc.); ~ à l'oignon onion-soup; F ~ populaire soup kitchen; F monter (or s'emporter) comme une ~ au lait flare up; F être ~ au lait be irritable; F être trempé comme une ~ be wet through.

soupente [su'pãːt] f ⊕ support; ⚠ loft, garret; closet.

souper [su'pe] **1.** v/i. (1a) have supper; sl. fig. j'en ai soupé I'm fed up with it; **2.** su./m supper.

soupeser [supɔ'ze] (1d) v/t. feel the weight of; weigh (s.th.) in the hand.

soupière [su'pjɛːr] f soup-tureen.

soupir [su'piːr] m sigh; ♪ crotchet rest; ♪ (demi-)quart m de ~ (demi-) semiquaver rest; ♪ quaver rest; **soupirail**, pl. -**aux** [supi'raːj, ˌ'ro] m air-hole; vent (in air-

shaft etc.); ventilator; **soupirant** F [ˌˈrɑ̃] suitor, admirer; **soupirer** [ˌˈre] (1a) *v/i.* sigh; ~ *après* (*or pour*) long *or* sigh for.

souple [supl] supple; flexible; *fig.* compliant, docile; **souplesse** [suˈplɛs] *f* suppleness; flexibility; *fig.* adaptability; *fig. character:* pliability.

souquenille † [sukˈniːj] *f* smock.

source [surs] *f* source (*a. fig.*); spring; *fig.* origin; ~ *jaillissante* gusher; *de bonne* ~ on good authority; *prendre sa* ~ *dans river:* rise in; **sourcier** [surˈsje] *m* water-diviner; **sourcil** [surˈsi] *m* eyebrow; *froncer les* ~*s* frown; **sourciller** [ˌsiˈje] (1a) *v/i.* knit one's brows, frown; *fig.* flinch; *ne pas* ~ F not to turn a hair, *Am.* never to bat an eyelid; **sourcilleux, -euse** [ˌsiˈjø, ˌˈjøːz] finicky, pernickety; supercilious.

sourd, sourde [suːr, surd] **1.** *adj.* deaf; dull (*blow, colour, noise, pain, thud*); low (*cry*); hollow (*voice*); *fig.* hidden, veiled (*hostility*); *fig.* underhand; *gramm.* voiceless; F ~ *comme un pot* deaf as a (door-)post; *faire la sourde oreille* turn a deaf ear; *lanterne f sourde* dark-lantern; **2.** *su.* deaf person.

sourdine [surˈdin] *f* ♪ mute; ♪ damper; *en* ~ ♪ muted; *fig.* softly; *fig.* on the quiet; *fig. mettre une* ~ *à qch.* tone s.th. down.

sourd-muet, sourde-muette [surˈmɥɛ, surdˈmɥɛt] **1.** *adj.* deaf-and-dumb; **2.** *su.* deaf-mute.

sourdre [surdr] (4dd) *v/i.* spring; *a. fig.* arise.

souriant, e [suˈrjɑ̃, ˌˈrjɑ̃ːt] smiling.

souriceau [suriˈso] *m* young mouse; **souricière** [ˌsjɛːr] *f* mouse-trap; *fig.* (police-)trap.

sourire [suˈriːr] **1.** (4cc) *v/i.* smile; *pej.* smirk; ~ *à q.* smile at s.o.; *fig.* appeal *or* be attractive to s.o.; **2.** *su./m* smile.

souris [suˈri] *f* mouse.

sournois, e [surˈnwa, ˌˈnwaːz] underhand; deceitful; **sournoiserie** [ˌnwazˈri] *f* underhand manner *or* trick; deceitfulness.

sous [su] *prp. usu.* under (*the table, s.o.'s command, etc.*); underneath; below; at (*the equator*); in (*the tropics, the rain, a favourable light*); within (*three months*); ~ *clé* under

lock and key; ~ *les drapeaux* with the colo(u)rs; ~ *enveloppe* under cover, in an envelope; ~ *le nom de* by the name of; ~ *peine de* on pain of; ~ *peu* before long, shortly; ~ *ce pli* enclosed; ~ *prétexte de* on the pretext of; ~ *le rapport de* in respect of; ~ (*le règne de*) *Louis XIV* under *or* in the reign of Louis XIV; *passer* ~ *silence* pass (*s.th.*) over in silence; ~ *mes yeux* before my eyes; *see cape; main.*

sous... [su; suz] sub..., under...; ~**-aide** [suˈzɛd] *su.* sub-assistant; ~**-alimenté, e** [ˌzalimɑ̃ˈte] undernourished, underfed; ~**-arrondissement** [ˌzarɔ̃disˈmɑ̃] *m* sub-district; ~**-bail** [suˈbaːj] *m* sub-lease; ~**-bois** [ˌˈbwɑ] *m* undergrowth.

souscripteur ♥ [suskripˈtœːr] *m* shares, *periodical, etc.:* subscriber; *cheque:* drawer; **souscription** [ˌˈsjɔ̃] *f* subscription (for shares, *à des actions*); signature; (*public*) fund; **souscrire** [susˈkriːr] (4q) *v/i.* ♥, *a. fig.* ~ *à* subscribe to; ~ *pour* subscribe (*a sum of money*); **souscrit, e** ♥ [ˌˈkri, ˌˈkrit] subscribed (*capital*).

sous...: ~**-cutané, e** ⚕ [sukytaˈne] subcutaneous; ~**-développé, e** [ˌdevlɔˈpe] underdeveloped; ~**-emploi** [suzɑ̃ˈplwa] *m* underemployment; ~**-entendre** [ˌzɑ̃ˈtɑ̃ːdr] (4a) *v/t.* understand (*a. gramm.*); imply; ~**-entendu** [ˌzɑ̃tɑ̃ˈdy] *m* implication; innuendo; allusion; overtone; ~**-entente** [ˌzɑ̃ˈtɑ̃ːt] *f* mental reservation; ~**-equipé, e** [ˌzekiˈpe] underequipped; ~**-estimer** [ˌzɛstiˈme] (1a) *v/t.* underestimate; ~**-exposer** *phot.* [ˌzɛkspoˈze] (1a) *v/t.* under-expose; ~**-fifre** F [suˈfifr] *m* underling; sidekick; ~**-locataire** [ˌlɔkaˈtɛːr] *su.* subtenant, sublessee; ~**-location** [ˌlɔkaˈsjɔ̃] *f* sub-letting; sub-lease; ~**-louer** [ˌˈlwe] (1p) *v/t.* sub-let; sub-lease; rent (*a house*) from a tenant; ~**-main** [ˌˈmɛ̃] *m/inv.* blotting-pad, writing-pad; *en* ~ secretly, behind the scenes; ~**-maître** [ˌˈmɛːtr] *m* assistant master; ~**-maîtresse** [ˌˈmɛtrɛs] *f* assistant mistress; ~**-marin, e** ⚓ [ˌmaˈrɛ̃, ˌˈrin] *adj., a. su./m* submarine; ~**-officier** [suzɔfiˈsje] *m*, F ~**-off** [ˌˈzɔf] *m* ✕ non-commissioned officer, N.C.O.; ⚓ petty officer; ~**-ordre**

[ʌˈzɔrdr] *m* ♀ sub-order; *admin.* subordinate; en ~ subordinate(ly *adv.*); ~-**payer** [ʌpɛˈje] (1i) *v/t.* underpay; ~-**pied** [suˈpje] *m* trouser-strap; *gaiters*: under-strap; ~-**préfet** [ʌpreˈfɛ] *m* sub-prefect; ~-**produit** ⊕ [ʌprɔˈdɥi] *m* by-product; spin-off; ~-**prolétariat** [ʌprɔletarˈja] *m* underprivileged class; ~-**secrétaire** [ʌsəkreˈtɛːr] *m* under-secretary of State, *d'État*; ~-**signé, e** [ʌsiˈɲe] **1.** *adj.* undersigned; **2.** *su.* undersigned; je ~ ... I the undersigned ...; ~-**sol** [ʌˈsɔl] *m* ✓ subsoil; △ basement; basement-flat; ⚒ underground; *richesses f/pl.* de ~ mineral resources; ~-**tendre** [ʌˈtɑ̃dr] (4a) *v/t.* ᴬ̶ subtend; *fig.* underlie.

soustraction [sustrakˈsjɔ̃] *f* removal, abstraction (*a.* 🕮); ᴬ̶ subtraction; **soustraire** [ʌˈtrɛːr] (4ff) *v/t.* remove; withdraw; ᴬ̶ subtract (from, *de*); *fig.* shield (s.o. from s.th., *q. à qch.*); se ~ *à* escape from; avoid (*a duty*).

sous...: ~-**traitance** [sutrɛˈtɑ̃ːs] *f* subcontracting; ~-**traitant** [ʌtrɛˈtɑ̃] *m* subcontractor; ~-**traiter** [ʌtrɛˈte] (1a) *v/t.* subcontract; ~-**ventrière** [ʌvɑ̃triˈɛːr] *f* saddle-girth; belly-band; ~-**verge** [ʌˈvɛrʒ] *m/inv.* offhorse; ✝ *fig.* underling; ~-**vêtement** [ʌvɛtmɑ̃] *m* undergarment.

soutache ✂, *a. cost.* [suˈtaʃ] *f* braid.

soutane *eccl.* [suˈtan] *f* cassock, soutane; *fig.* la ~ holy orders *pl.*, F the cloth.

soute [sut] *f* ⚓ store-room; ✕ ~ à *bombes* bomb-bay; ~ à *charbon* coal-bunker; ~ *aux poudres* (powder-)magazine.

soutenable [sutˈnabl] bearable; tenable (*opinion, theory, a.* ✕ ✝); **soutenance** [ʌˈnɑ̃ːs] *f thesis*: maintaining; **soutènement** [sutɛnˈmɑ̃] *m* support(ing); △ de ~ retaining (*wall*), relieving (*arch*); **souteneur** [sutˈnœːr] *m* procurer; **soutenir** [sutˈniːr] (2h) *v/t.* support; hold (*s.th.*) up; back (*s.o.*) (*financially*); keep up (*a conversation, a credit, a part*); maintain, assert (*a fact*); uphold (*an opinion, a theory, a thesis*); *fig.* endure, bear (*a. comparison*), stand; **soutenu, e** [ʌˈny] sustained; unflagging (*attention,*

effort, interest); ✝ steady (*market*); *fig.* lofty (*style*).

souterrain, e [sutɛˈrɛ̃, ʌˈrɛn] **1.** *adj.* underground; *a. fig.* subterranian; **2.** *su./m* underground passage.

soutien [suˈtjɛ̃] *m* support(ing); *person*: supporter; *fig.* mainstay; ~-**gorge**, *pl.* ~**s-gorge** *cost.* [ʌtjɛ̃ˈgɔrʒ] *m* brassière, F bra.

soutirer [sutiˈre] (1a) *v/t.* draw off (*wine etc.*); *fig.* get (s.th. out of s.o., *qch. à q.*).

souvenir [suvˈniːr] **1.** (2h) *v/t.*: se ~ *de* remember, recall; *v/impers.*: il me *souvient de* (*inf.*) I remember (*ger.*); **2.** *su./m* memory, remembrance; souvenir, keepsake.

souvent [suˈvɑ̃] *adv.* often; *assez* ~ fairly often; *peu* ~ seldom, not often.

souverain, e [suˈvrɛ̃, ʌˈvrɛn] **1.** *adj.* sovereign; supreme; **2.** *su.* sovereign; **souveraineté** [ʌvrɛnˈte] *f* sovereignty; territory (*of a sovereign*).

soviet *pol.* [sɔˈvjɛt] *m* Soviet; **soviétique** [ʌvjeˈtik] **1.** *adj.* Soviet; **2.** *su.* ⚥ Soviet citizen.

soya ♀ [sɔˈja] *m see soja*.

soyeux, -euse [swaˈjø, ʌˈjøːz] **1.** *adj.* silky, silken; **2.** *su./m* silk manufacturer.

soyons [swaˈjɔ̃] *1st p. pl. pres. sbj. of* être *1*.

spacieux, -euse [spaˈsjø, ʌˈsjøːz] spacious, roomy.

spadassin [spadaˈsɛ̃] *m* hired killer; ✝ swordsman.

spalter [spalˈtɛːr] *m painting*: graining-brush.

sparadrap ⚕ [sparaˈdra] *m* sticking *or* adhesive plaster, *Am. a.* Band-Aid (*TM*).

spasme ⚕ [spasm] *m* spasm; **spasmodique** ⚕ [spasmɔˈdik] spasmodic, spastic.

spath *min.* [spat] *m* spar; ~ *fluor* fluorite.

spatial, e, *m/pl.* -**aux** [spaˈsjal, ʌˈsjo] spatial; space ...; *navire m* ~ space craft.

spatule [spaˈtyl] *f* ⚕ spatula; ⊕ spoon tool; *sp.* ski-tip; *orn.* spoon-bill; **spatulé, e** [ʌtyˈle] spatulate.

speaker, speakerine [spiˈkœːr, ʌkəˈrin] *su. radio*: announcer; newscaster, newsreader; *su./m parl.* speaker.

spécial, e, *m*/*pl.* **-aux** [spe'sjal, ~-
'sjo] **1.** *adj.* special, particular; ⚔
armes *f*/*pl.* ~es technical arms;
2. *su.*/*f school:* higher mathematics
class; **spécialiser** [spesjali'ze] (1a)
v/*t.* particularize; ear-mark (*funds*);
se ~ *dans* specialize in, make a special study of, *Am.* major in; **spécialiste** [~'list] *su.* specialist (*a.* ⚙);
expert; ⚔ tradesman; **spécialité**
[~li'te] *f* speciality; special study;
⚓ special duty; ⚓ specialized
branch; ~ *pharmaceutique* patent
medicine.

spécieux, -euse [spe'sjø, ~'sjø:z]
specious; plausible.

spécification [spesifika'sjɔ̃] *f* speci-
fication; *raw material:* working up;
spécificité [~fisi'te] *f* specificity (*a.*
⚙); **spécifier** [~'fje] (1o) *v*/*t.* specify; lay down; stipulate; determine
(*s.th.*) specifically; **spécifique** [~-
'fik] **1.** *su.*/*m* specific (for, *de*); **2.** *adj.*
specific; *phys. poids m* ~ specific
gravity.

spécimen [spesi'mɛn] **1.** *su.*/*m*
specimen, sample; **2.** *adj.* specimen (*copy*).

spéciosité [spesjozi'te] *f* speciousness.

spectacle [spɛk'takl] *m* spectacle,
sight; *pej.* exhibition; *thea.* play,
show; «~s» *pl.* «entertainment»; *le
(monde du)* ~ show business; *fig. se
donner en* ~ make an ass of o.s.; *taxe f
sur les* ~s entertainment tax.

spectateur, -trice [spɛkta'tœ:r,
~'tris] *su.* spectator; witness (*of an
accident, an event, etc.*); *su.*/*m*: *thea.*
~s *pl.* audience *sg.*

spectral, e, *m*/*pl.* **-aux** [spɛk'tral,
~'tro] spectral (*a.* ⚛); spectrum
(*analysis*); *opt.* of the spectrum;
fig. ghostly; **spectre** [spɛktr] *m*
spectre; ghost (*a. fig.*); *opt.*, *a. phys.*
spectrum; **spectroscopie** *phys.*
[spɛktrɔskɔ'pi] *f* spectroscopy.

spéculaire [speky'lɛ:r] **1.** *adj.* spec-
ular; *psych.* mirror (*writing*); *pierre
f* ~ mica; **2.** *su.*/*f* ⚘ specularia.

spéculateur *m,* **-trice** *f* [spekyla-
'tœ:r, ~'tris] ✝, *a. fig.* speculator;
fig. theorizer; **spéculatif, -ve** [~'tif,
~'ti:v] ✝, *a. fig.* speculative; *fig.*
contemplative; **spéculation** [~'sjɔ̃]
f ✝, *a. fig.* speculation; *fig.* theory,
conjecture; *fig.* cogitation; **spéculer** [speky'le] (1a) *v*/*i.* ✝, *a. fig.*

speculate (*fig.* on, ✝ in *sur*; ✝
for, *à*).

spéléologie [speleɔlɔ'ʒi] *f* spel(a)e-
ology; cave hunting; F pot-holing;
spéléologue [~'lɔg] *m* spel(a)eolo-
gist; cave hunter; F pot-holer.

spencer *cost.* [spɛ̃'sɛ:r] *m* spencer.

sperme *physiol.* [spɛrm] *m* sperm,
semen.

sphère [sfɛ:r] *f* sphere (*a.* ⚗, *fig.*);
geog. globe; **sphéricité** [sferisi'te] *f*
sphericity, curvature; **sphérique**
[~'rik] **1.** *adj.* spherical (*a.* ⚗);
2. *su.*/*m* ⚛ spherical balloon.

sphinx [sfɛ̃:ks] *m* sphynx (*a. fig.*);
zo. hawk-moth.

spic ⚘ [spik] *m* spike-lavender.

spider *mot.* [spi'dɛ:r] *m* dick(e)y
(seat).

spinal, e, *m*/*pl.* **-aux** *anat.* [spi'nal,
~'no] spinal.

spinelle *min.* [spi'nɛl] *m* spinel.

spiral, e, *m*/*pl.* **-aux** [spi'ral, ~'ro]
1. *adj.* spiral; **2.** *su.*/*f* spiral; *en* ~
spiral(ly *adv.*), winding; *su.*/*m* ⊕
watch: hairspring; **spire** [spi:r] *f*
single turn, whorl (*a.* ⚡); ⚡ *bobbin:*
one winding.

spirée ⚘ [spi're] *f* spiraea.

spirite [spi'rit] **1.** *adj.* spiritualistic;
2. *su.* spiritualist; **spiritisme** [spi-
ri'tism] *m* spirit(ual)ism; **spiritualiser** [~tɥali'ze] (1a) *v*/*t.* spiritual-
ize; ⚗ ✝ distil; **spiritualité** [~tɥa-
li'te] *f* spirituality; **spirituel, -elle**
[~'tɥɛl] spiritual (*a. eccl., phls., etc.*);
fig. witty, humorous; **spiritueux,
-euse** ✝ [~'tɥø, ~'tɥø:z] **1.** *adj.*
spirituous; **2.** *su.*/*m* spirit(uous liquor); *les* ~ *pl.* spirits.

spleen ✝ [splin] *m* spleen, melancholy.

splendeur [splã'dœ:r] *f* splendo(u)r;
brilliance, brightness; *fig.* grandeur,
glory; **splendide** [~'did] splendid;
brilliant; *fig.* magnificent.

spoliateur, -trice [spɔlja'tœ:r, ~-
'tris] **1.** *adj.* spoliatory (*law,
measure*); **2.** *su.* despoiler; **spoliation** [~lja'sjɔ̃] *f* despoilment; **spo-
lier** [~'lje] (1o) *v*/*t.* despoil, rob (of,
de). [dee.\

spondée [spɔ̃'de] *m* *prosody:* spon-\

spongiaires [spɔ̃'ʒɛ:r] *m*/*pl.* spon-
giae; **spongieux, -euse** [~'ʒjø, ~-
'ʒjø:z] spongy; *anat.* ethmoid (*bone*);
spongiosité [~ʒjozi'te] *f* spongi-
ness.

spontané, e [spɔ̃ta'ne] spontaneous; ᵷᵗᵼ voluntary (*confession*); ⚓ self-sown; **spontanéite** [∿nei'te] *f* spontaneity; **spontanément** [∿ne-'mɑ̃] *adv. of* spontané.

sporadique ⚕, ⚓ [spɔra'dik] sporadic; **spore** ⚓, *biol.* [spɔːr] *f* spore.

sport [spɔːr] *m* sport; ∿s *pl. nautiques* aquatic sports; *le* ∿ *sports pl.*; **sportif, -ve** [spɔr'tif, ∿'tiːv] 1. *adj.* sporting; *sports...*; 2. *su.* follower of sports, F sports fan; *su./m* sportsman; *su./f* sportswoman; **sportsman, *pl.* sportsmen** [spɔrts'man, ∿'men] *m* sportsman; **sportswoman, *pl.* sportswomen** [∿wu'man, ∿'men] *f* sportswoman.

spot [spɔt] *m radio, TV, etc.*: spot; spot(light).

spoutnik [sput'nik] *m* sputnik.

sprat *icht.* [sprat] *m* sprat.

sprint *sp.* [sprint] *m* sprint; **sprinter** *sp.* 1. [sprin'tœːr] *su./m* sprinter; 2. [∿'te] (1a) *v/i.* sprint.

spumeux, -euse [spy'mø, ∿'møːz] frothy, foamy.

squale *icht.* [skwal] *m* dog-fish.

squame [skwam] *f skin*: scale; *bone*: exfoliation; squama; **squameux, -euse** [skwa'mø, ∿'møːz] ⚕, *anat.*, *etc.* scaly; squamous (*a.* ⚓).

square [skwaːr] *m* (public) square (with garden).

squelette [skə'lɛt] *m* skeleton (*a. fig.*); ⚓ carcass; *fig.* skeleton; *plot*: outline; **squelettique** [∿le'tik] skeletal; *fig.* skeleton-like.

stabilisateur, -trice [stabiliza'tœːr, ∿'tris] 1. *adj.* stabilizing; 2. *su./m* ✻ *etc.* stabilizer; **stabilisation** [∿za'sjɔ̃] *f* stabilization; ✻ standstill; ⊕ annealing; **stabiliser** [∿'ze] (1a) *v/t.* stabilize (*a.* ✝ *the currency*); ⊕ anneal; se ∿ become steady; **stabilité** [∿'te] *f* stability; **stable** [stabl] stable; steady; *fig.* lasting.

stade [stad] *m sp.* stadium; *sp.* athletic club; ✻, *a. fig.* stage, period.

stage [staːʒ] *m* (period of) probation; training period *or* course; ᵷᵗᵼ articles *pl.*; **stagiaire** [sta'ʒɛːr] *adj., su.* trainee.

stagnant, e [stag'nɑ̃, ∿'nɑ̃ːt] stagnant (*a.* ✝); **stagnation** [∿na'sjɔ̃] *f* stagnation (*a.* ✝); ⚓ *compass*: slowness; ✝ dullness.

stalle [stal] *f eccl., thea., stable, etc.*: stall; *stable*: box.

staminé, e ⚘ [stami'ne] stamened, staminate.

stance [stɑ̃ːs] *f* stanza.

stand [stɑ̃ːd] *m races, show, exhibition*: stand; ∿ *de tir* shooting-gallery, rifle range.

standard [stɑ̃'daːr] 1. *su./m teleph.* switchboard; *fig.* standard (of living, *de vie*); 2. *adj.* standard; **standardisation** ⊕ [stɑ̃dardiza'sjɔ̃] *f* standardization; **standardiser** ⊕ [∿di'ze] (1a) *v/t.* standardize; **standardiste** *teleph.* [∿'dist] *su.* switchboard operator.

standing [stɑ̃'diŋ] *m* (social) status, standing, reputation; (*de*) *grand* ∿ luxury (*flat, apartment, etc.*).

starter [star'tɛːr] *m sp.* starter; *mot.* choke.

station [sta'sjɔ̃] *f* ✕, ⚓, ⚡, radio, ⛴ underground: station; stop, halt; (*taxi-*)rank; *bus, tram*: (*fare*) stage; (*holiday*) resort; ⚡ ∿ *centrale* power station; ∿ *climatique* health resort; ∿ *de correspondance underground railway*: interchange station; *en* ∿ standing; *faire une* ∿ break one's journey; **stationnaire** [∿sjɔ'nɛːr] 1. *adj.* stationary; 2. *su./m* ⚓ guard ship; **stationnement** *mot.* [∿sjɔn'mɑ̃] *m* parking; ∿ *bilatéral* parking on both sides; ∿ *interdit road sign*: no parking; no waiting; ∿ *unilatéral* parking on one side only; **stationner** [∿sjɔ'ne] (1a) *v/i.* stop; halt; stand; park (*car*); ✕ be stationed; *défense f de* ∿ no parking; **station-service, *pl.* stations-service** *mot.* [∿sjɔ̃sɛr'vis] *f* service station; repair station.

statique [sta'tik] 1. *adj.* static; 2. *su./f* ⊕ statics *sg.*

statisticien [statisti'sjɛ̃] *m* statistician; **statistique** [∿'tik] 1. *adj.* statistical; 2. *su./f* statistics *sg.*

statuaire [sta'tɥɛːr] 1. *adj.* statuary; 2. *su./m person*: sculptor; *su./f art*: statuary; sculptress; **statue** [∿'ty] *f* statue; image.

statuer [sta'tɥe] (1n) *v/t.* decree, enact; rule; *v/i.*: ∿ *sur* q**ch.** decide s.th., give judgment on s.th.

stature [sta'tyːr] *f* stature; height.

statut [sta'ty] *m* ᵷᵗᵼ statute; regulation; charter; *pol.* status; constitution; **statutaire** [∿ty'tɛːr] statutory; ✝ qualifying (*share*).

stéarine ⚗ [stea'rin] *f* stearin(e); **stéarique** ⚗ [∿'rik] stearic.

steeple-chase sp. [stiplə'tʃez] m track: hurdle-race.

stellaire [stɛl'lɛːr] **1.** adj. astr. stellar; **2.** su./f ♀ starwort.

sténo... [stenɔ] steno...; **~dactylographe** [~daktilɔ'graf], F **~dactylo** [~dakti'lo] su. shorthand-typist; **~gramme** [~'gram] m shorthand report; **~graphe** [~'graf] su. shorthand writer; stenographer; **~graphie** [~gra'fi] f shorthand; **~type** [~'tip] su./m stenotype; su./f shorthand typewriter; **~typiste** [~ti-'pist] su. stenotypist.

stentor [stā'tɔːr] npr./m: fig. voix f de ~ stentorian voice.

steppe geog. [stɛp] f steppe.

stercoraire [stɛrkɔ'rɛːr] m zo. dung-beetle; orn. skua.

stère [stɛːr] m measure of wood: stere, cubic metre; bois m de ~ cordwood.

stéréo [stere'o] f, a. adj. short for stéréophonie, stéréophonique: stereo; en ~ (in) stereo.

stéréo... [stereɔ] stereo...; **~métrie** ⚕ [~me'tri] f stereometry; **~métrique** ⚕ [~me'trik] stereometric; **~phonie** [~fɔ'ni] f stereophony, stereo (sound); **~phonique** [~fɔ'nik] stereophonic; **~scope** opt. [stereɔ-s'kɔp] m stereoscope; **~scopique** [~skɔ'pik] stereoscopic; **~type** typ. [stereɔ'tip] **1.** adj. stereotype; stereotyped (book); **2.** su./m stereotype (plate); **~typer** [~ti'pe] (1a) v/t. stereotype; expression f stéréotypée hackneyed phrase; sourire m stéréotype fixed smile; **~typie** [~ti'pi] f stereotypy; stereotype foundry.

stérile [ste'ril] ✓, ♀, zo., a. fig. sterile, barren (a. woman); childless (marriage); fig. fruitless, vain (effort); **stériliser** [sterili'ze] (1a) v/t. sterilize (a. ⚗); **stérilité** [~'te] f sterility; barrenness (a. fig.).

sternum anat. [stɛr'nɔm] m sternum, breast-bone.

sternutation ⚗ [stɛrnyta'sjɔ̃] f sternutation, sneezing; **sternutatoire** ⚗ [~'twaːr] adj. sternutatory; sneezing(-powder).

stéthoscope ⚗ [stetɔs'kɔp] m stethoscope.

stick [stik] m ✕ swagger-stick; (riding-)switch.

stigmate [stig'mat] m ⚗, ♀, a. fig. stigma; ⚗ wound: scar, mark; small-pox: pock-mark; fig. stain (on

character); eccl. ~s pl. stigmata; **stigmatique** [~ma'tik] stigmatic; opt. anastigmatic; **stigmatiser** [~mati'ze] (1a) v/t. eccl., a. fig. stigmatize (with, de); ⚗ pock-mark (s.o.); fig. brand (s.o.).

stimulant, e [stimy'lɑ̃, ~'lɑ̃ːt] **1.** adj. stimulating; **2.** su./m ⚗ stimulant; fig. stimulus, incentive; **stimulateur, -trice** [~la'tœːr, ~'tris] **1.** adj. stimulative; **2.** su./m: ⚗ ~ cardiaque pacemaker; **stimuler** [~'le] (1a) v/t. stimulate; fig. incite, give a stimulus to; **stimulus** ⚗, biol. [~'lys] m stimulus.

stipendier pej. [stipɑ̃'dje] (1o) v/t. hire, buy (s.o.).

stipulation ⚖ [stipyla'sjɔ̃] f condition; stipulation; **stipuler** [~'le] (1a) v/t. stipulate.

stock ✝ [stɔk] m stock; **stockage** [stɔ'kaːʒ] m ✝ stocking; storing; **stocker** [~'ke] (1a) v/t. ✝ stock, store; ✕ stockpile (bombs).

stoïcien, -enne phls. [stɔi'sjɛ̃, ~'sjɛn] **1.** adj. stoic(al); **2.** su. stoic; **stoïcisme** phls., a. fig. [~i'sism] m stoicism; **stoïque** [~'ik] **1.** adj. fig. stoic(al); **2.** su. stoic.

stolon ♀ [stɔ'lɔ̃] f stolon, runner, sucker.

stomacal, e m/pl. -aux [stɔma'kal, ~'ko] gastric; stomach-(pump, tube); **stomachique** ⚗, anat. [~'ʃik] adj., a. su./m stomachic.

stop [stɔp] **1.** int. stop!; **2.** su./m mot. stop sign; brake light, Am. stoplight; F hitchhiking, hitching.

stoppage [stɔ'paːʒ] m cost. invisible mending; stockings: invisible darning; **stopper** [~'pe] (1a) v/t. stop; check; cost. repair by invisible mending; v/i. (come to a) stop; **stoppeur, -euse** [~'pœːr, ~'pøːz] su. cost. fine-darner, invisible mender; F hitchhiker.

store [stɔːr] m blind; awning.

strabique ⚗ [stra'bik] **1.** adj. squint-eyed, F cross-eyed; **2.** su. squinter; **strabisme** ⚗ [~'bism] m squinting, strabism(us).

strangulation [strɑ̃gyla'sjɔ̃] f strangulation.

strapontin [strapɔ̃'tɛ̃] m bus, taxi, thea.: folding seat, jump seat; fig. back seat, minor role.

strass [stras] m paste jewellery, strass.

stratagème ⚔, *a. fig.* [strataˈʒɛm] *m* stratagem.

stratégie ⚔, *a. fig.* [strateˈʒi] *f* strategy; **stratégiste** [ᴧˈʒist] *m* strategist.

stratifié, e [stratiˈfje] (1o) stratified; ⊕ laminated; **stratigraphie** *geol.* [ᴧtigraˈfi] *f* stratigraphy; **stratosphère** *meteor.* [ᴧtɔsˈfɛːr] *f* stratosphere.

stress *psych.* [strɛs] *m* stress; **stressant, e** [strɛˈsɑ̃, ᴧˈsɑ̃ːt] stress (*situation, etc.*), full of stress.

strict, stricte [strikt] strict (*a. fig.*); *fig.* severe; exact; **striction** [strikˈsjɔ̃] *f* 🖉 constriction; ⚕ striction.

strident, e [striˈdɑ̃, ᴧˈdɑ̃ːt] strident, harsh, shrill.

stridulant, e [stridyˈlɑ̃, ᴧˈlɑ̃ːt] stridulant, chirring; **stridulation** [ᴧlaˈsjɔ̃] *f* stridulation, chirring; **striduleux, -euse** 🖉 [ᴧˈlø, ᴧˈløːz] stridulous.

strie [stri] *f* groove; ⚕, ⚚, *anat., geol.* stria; *colour:* streak; **strier** [striˈe] (1a) *v/t.* score, scratch; ⚚, *geol.* striate; ⚕ flute, groove; ⊕ corrugate (*iron*); streak; **striure** [ᴧˈyːr] *f see* strie.   [strophe.⟩

strophe [strɔf] *f* stanza, verse;⟩

structure [strykˈtyːr] *f* structure; ᴧ(s) *d'accueil* reception facilities *pl.*; *psych.* ᴧ *de comportement* behavio(u)r pattern; ᴧ *gonflable* air hall; **structurel, -elle** [ᴧtyˈrɛl] structural.

strychnine 🜋 [strikˈnin] *f* strychnine.

stuc ⚕ [styk] *m* stucco; **stucateur** [stykaˈtœːr] *m* stucco-worker.

studieux, -euse [styˈdjø, ᴧˈdjøːz] studious; devoted to study.

studio [styˈdjo] *m radio, a. cin.:* studio; one-roomed flat, flatlet, *Am.* studio apartment.

stupéfaction [stypefakˈsjɔ̃] *f* stupefaction; amazement; **stupéfait, e** [ᴧˈfɛ, ᴧˈfɛt] stupefied; amazed (at, de); **stupéfiant, e** [ᴧˈfjɑ̃, ᴧˈfjɑ̃ːt] **1.** *adj.* stupefying (🖉, *a. fig.*); *fig.* astounding; **2.** *su./m* 🖉 drug, narcotic; **stupéfier** [ᴧˈfje] (1o) *v/t.* 🖉, *a. fig.* stupefy; *fig.* astound; **stupeur** [styˈpœːr] *f* stupor; *fig.* amazement.

stupide [styˈpid] **1.** *adj.* stupid, *Am.* dumb; dumbfounded; silly, foolish; **2.** *su.* stupid person; dolt; **stupidité** [ᴧpidiˈte] *f* stupidity; folly.

stuquer ⚕ [styˈke] (1m) *v/t.* stucco.

style [stil] *m* ⚚, ⚕, *fig., a. sun-dial:* style; etching-needle; *sun-dial:* gnomon; **styler** [stiˈle] (1a) *v/t.* train, form; ⨍ school (*s.o.*) (in, à).

stylet [stiˈlɛ] *m* stiletto; 🖉 stylet, probe.

styliser [stiliˈze] (1a) *v/t.* stylize; **styliste** [stiˈlist] *su.* stylist; **stylistique** [ᴧlisˈtik] *f* stylistics *sg.*

stylo [stiˈlo] *m* pen; ⨍ fountain pen; ᴧ (à) *bille*, ᴧ*-bille* ball-point pen; ᴧ(-)*feutre* felt-tip pen; **stylographe** [ᴧlɔˈgraf] *m* fountain pen.

styptique 🖉 [stipˈtik] *adj., a. su./m* styptic, astringent.

su, e [sy] **1.** *p.p. of savoir*; **2.** *su./m*: *au vu et au* ᴧ *de* to the knowledge of.

suaire [sɥɛːr] *m* shroud; *eccl. saint* ᴧ vernicle, veronica.

suant, e [sɥɑ̃, sɥɑ̃ːt] sweaty; *sl.* boring, deadly dull.

suave [sɥaːv] sweet; bland (*manner, tone*); soft (*shade*); mild (*cigar*); **suavité** [sɥaviˈte] *f* sweetness, softness; *manner, tone:* blandness, suavity.

sub... [syb] sub...

subalterne [sybalˈtɛrn] **1.** *adj.* subordinate; inferior; **2.** *su./m* underling; ⚔ subaltern.

subconscience [sybkɔ̃ˈsjaːs] *f* subconsciousness; **subconscient, e** [ᴧˈsjɑ̃, ᴧˈsjɑ̃ːt] **1.** *adj.* subconscious; **2.** *su./m*: *le* ᴧ the subconscious.

subdiviser [sybdiviˈze] (1a) *v/t.* subdivide; **subdivision** [ᴧˈzjɔ̃] *f* subdivision.

subéreux, -euse ⚚ [sybeˈrø, ᴧˈrøːz] suberose; corky; *enveloppe f* ᴧ*euse* cortex.

subir [syˈbiːr] (2a) *v/t.* undergo; suffer (*death, defeat, a penalty*); submit to (*a law, a rule*); come under (*an influence*); put up with, endure.

subit, e [syˈbi, ᴧˈbit] sudden, unexpected.

subjectif, -ve [sybʒɛkˈtif, ᴧˈtiːv] subjective.

subjonctif, -ve *gramm.* [sybʒɔ̃kˈtif, ᴧˈtiːv] **1.** *adj.* subjunctive; **2.** *su./m* subjunctive; *au* ᴧ in the subjunctive.

subjuguer [sybʒyˈge] (1m) *v/t.* captivate, thrill; † subdue (*a. fig.*); *fig.* master (*one's feelings*).

sublimation 🜋 *psych.* [syblimaˈsjɔ̃] *f* sublimation; **sublime** [ᴧˈblim] **1.** *adj.* sublime (*a. anat., fig.*); lofty; **2.** *su./m the* sublime; **sublimé** 🜋

sublimer

[sybli'me] *m* sublimate; **sublimer** [~] (1a) *v/t.* ⚗ sublimate (*a. psych.*), sublime; **sublimité** [syblimi'te] *f* sublimity.

submerger [sybmɛr'ʒe] (1l) *v/t.* submerge; flood (*a field, a village, a valley*); immerse (*an object in water*); swamp (*a boat, a field*); *fig.* inundate, overwhelm (with, *de*); *submergé de besogne* snowed under *or* inundated with work; **submersible** [~'sibl] *adj., su./m* ⚓ † submarine; **submersion** [~'sjɔ̃] *f* submersion, submergence; ⚓ sinking; ✦ flooding; *mort f par* ~ death by drowning.

subordination [sybɔrdina'sjɔ̃] *f* subordination; **subordonné, e** [~dɔ'ne] 1. *adj.* subordinate, dependent (*a. gramm.*); 2. *su.* subordinate, underling; **subordonner** [~dɔ'ne] (1a) *v/t.* subordinate; *fig.* regulate (according to, in the light of *à*).

suborner [sybɔr'ne] (1a) *v/t.* suborn (*a. ⚖ a witness etc.*); bribe; **suborneur, -euse** [~'nœːr, ~'nøːz] 1. *adj.* persuasive; 2. *su.* ⚖ suborner.

subreptice [sybrɛp'tis] surreptitious; clandestine; **subreption** ⚖ [~'sjɔ̃] *f* subreption.

subroger [sybrɔ'ʒe] (1l) *v/t.* subrogate; appoint (*s.o.*) as deputy; *subrogé tuteur m* surrogate guardian.

subséquemment [sypseka'mã] *adv.* subsequently; in due course; **subséquent, e** [~'kã, ~'kãːt] subsequent.

subside [syp'sid] *m* grant, allowance; **subsidiaire** [si'djɛːr] subsidiary, accessory, additional (to, *à*).

subsistance [sybzis'tãːs] *f* subsistence; keep; ~*s pl.* provisions, supplies; *mis en* ~ attached to another unit for rations; **subsistant, e** [~'tã, ~'tãːt] 1. *adj.* subsisting, extant; 2. *su./m* soldier attached (*to a unit*) for rations; **subsister** [~'te] (1a) *v/i.* subsist; exist, continue, be extant; live (on, *de*); *moyens m/pl. de* ~ means of subsistence.

substance [syps'tãːs] *f* substance (*a. fig.*); ⊕ *etc.* material; *fig.* gist; *anat.* ~ *grise* grey matter; *en* ~ substantially; **substantiel, -elle** [~tã'sjɛl] substantial; nourishing (*food*).

substantif, -ve [sypstã'tif, ~'tiːv] 1. *adj.* substantive (*a. gramm.*); 2. *su./m gramm.* substantive, noun.

substitué, e [sypsti'tɥe] supposititious (*child*); **substituer** [~'tɥe] (1n) *v/t.* substitute (for, *à*); *se* ~ *à* substitute for, act as substitute for (*s.o.*); take the place of; **substitut** [~'ty] *m* deputy; ⚖ locum tenens, F locum; ⚖ deputy public prosecutor; **substitution** [~ty'sjɔ̃] *f* substitution (for, *à*); mix-up.

substrat [syps'tra] *m* substratum.

substruction △ [sypstryk'sjɔ̃] *f* foundation, substructure; underpinning; **substructure** △ [~'tyːr] *f* substructure.

subterfuge [syptɛr'fyːʒ] *m* subterfuge; evasion, shift.

subtil, e [syp'til] subtle; fine, nice (*distinction, point*); **subtiliser** [syptili'ze] (1a) *v/t.* subtilize; F steal, filch, pinch; *v/i.:* ~ *sur* subtilize on (*a question*); **subtilité** [~'te] *f* subtlety; *distinction:* fineness; ~*s pl. a.* niceties.

suburbain, e [sybyr'bɛ̃, ~'bɛn] suburban.

subvenir [sybvə'niːr] (2h) *v/i.:* ~ *à* provide for; **subvention** [sybvã'sjɔ̃] *f* subsidy, subvention; **subventionnel, -elle** [~sjɔ̃'nɛl] subventionary; **subventionner** [~sjɔ̃'ne] (1a) *v/t.* subsidize.

subversif, -ve [sybvɛr'sif, ~'siːv] subversive, destructive (of, *de*); **subversion** [~'sjɔ̃] *f* subversion; overthrow.

suc [syk] *m* juice; ⚘ sap; *fig.* essence, pith.

succédané, e [sykseda'ne] *adj., a. su./m* substitute (for, *de*); **succéder** [~'de] (1f) *v/i.:* ~ *à* succeed, follow; replace; ⚖ come into (*a fortune*); ~ *au trône* succeed to the throne.

succès [syk'sɛ] *m* success; hit; *à* ~ successful; *avec* (*sans*) ~ *a.* (un)successfully.

successeur [sykse'sœːr] *m* successor (to, *of de*); **successible** ⚖ [~'sibl] entitled to inherit *or* succeed; **successif, -ve** [~'sif, ~'siːv] successive; in succession; ⚖ ... of succession; **succession** [~'sjɔ̃] *f* succession; series; ⚖ inheritance; **successivement** [~siv'mã] *adv.* in succession; one after another, consecutively; **successoral, e,** *m/pl.* -aux [~sɔ'ral, ~'ro] relating to a succession; death (*duties*).

succin [syk'sɛ̃] *m* yellow amber.

succinct, e [syk'sɛ̃, ‿'sɛ̃:(k)t] succinct, concise, brief.

succion [syk'sjɔ̃] f suction; sucking
(of a wound).

succomber [sykɔ̃'be] (1a) v/i. suc-
cumb (fig. to, à); fig. yield (to, à)
(grief, temptation, etc.); be overcome; die.

succube [sy'kyb] m succubus.

succulence [syky'lɑ̃:s] f succulence;
tasty morsel; **succulent, e** [‿'lɑ̃,
‿'lɑ̃:t] succulent (food, morsel, a. ♀,
a. fig. style); tasty (morsel).

succursale [sykyr'sal] f ✝ branch;
sub-office; magasin m à ‿s multiples multiple store, chain store.

sucer [sy'se] (1k) v/t. suck; fig.
avec le lait imbibe (s.th.) from infancy; **sucette** [‿'set] f ⊕ sucker;
✝ lollipop, F lolly; **suceur, -euse**
[‿'sœ:r, ‿'sø:z] 1. adj. sucking; zo.
suctorial; 2. su. sucker; su./m ⊕
vacuum cleaner: nozzle, sucker; zo.
‿s pl. suctoria; **suçoir** zo. [‿'swa:r]
m organ: sucker; **suçon** F [‿'sɔ̃] m
barley-sugar stick; kiss-mark, mark
left by sucking (on the skin); **suço-
ter** F [‿sɔ'te] (1a) v/t. suck (at).

sucrage ⊕ [sy'kra:ʒ] m sugaring,
sweetening; **sucrase** ⚗, ♀ [‿'krɑ:z]
f invert sugar; **sucrate** ✝ [‿'krat]
m sucrate; **sucre** [sykr] m sugar;
‿ de betterave beet sugar; ‿ de lait
lactose; ‿ de raisin grape sugar; ‿
en morceaux (poudre) lump (castor)
sugar; **sucré, e** [sy'kre] 1. adj. sweet;
2. su./f: faire la ‿e be all honey or
sweetness; **sucrer** [‿'kre] (1a) v/t.
sugar, sweeten; fig. a. sugar-coat;
sl. stop, cut; se ‿ help o.s. to sugar;
sl. line one's pockets; **sucrerie**
[‿krə'ri] f sugar-refinery; ‿s pl. confectionery sg., sweets, Am. candies;
sucrier, -ère [‿kri'e, ‿'ɛ:r] 1. adj.
sugar-...; 2. su. sugar-refiner, sugar-
boiler; su./m sugar-bowl, sugar-
basin; **sucrin** [‿'krɛ̃] m sugary
melon.

sud [syd] 1. su./m south; ⚓ south
wind; du ‿ south(ern); le ♀ the
south (of a country); vers le ‿ south-
ward(s), to the south; 2. adj./inv.
southern (latitudes); southerly
(wind).

sudation ⚕ [syda'sjɔ̃] f sudation,
sweating; **sudatoire** [‿'twa:r]
1. adj. sudatory; 2. su./m hot-air
bath; sweating-room.

sud-est [sy'dɛst] 1. su./m south-
east; 2. adj./inv. south-east; southeastern (region); south-easterly
(wind).

sudiste Am. hist. [sy'dist] 1. su./m
southerner (in Civil War); 2. adj.
southern.   [su./m sudorific.\
sudorifique ⚕ [sydɔri'fik] adj., a.\

sud-ouest [sy'dwɛst] 1. su./m south-
west; 2. adj./inv. south-west; southwestern (region); south-westerly
(wind).

suède ✝ [sɥɛd] m: de (or en) ‿ suède
(gloves); **suédois, e** [sɥe'dwa,
‿'dwa:z] 1. adj. Swedish; 2. su./m
ling. Swedish; su. ♀ Swede.

suée [sɥe] f F sweat(ing); sl. drag,
pain; **suer** [‿] (1n) v/i. sweat (a. wall,
a. fig. = toil); perspire; F faire ‿ q.
get on s.o.'s nerves; bore s.o.; make
s.o. sick; F se faire ‿ be bored, get
cheesed off; v/t. sweat (iron, a horse,
etc.); fig. reek of; fig. ‿ sang et eau toil
hard, F sweat blood; **suette** ⚕ [sɥet]
f fever; **sueur** [sɥœ:r] f sweat,
perspiration.

suffi [sy'fi] p.p. of suffire; **suffire**
[‿'fi:r] (4i) v/i. suffice, be sufficient;
fig. ‿ à meet (expenses); v/impers.: il
suffit que it is enough that; **suffi-
samment** [syfiza'mɑ̃] adv. sufficiently, enough; **suffisance** [‿'zɑ̃:s]
f sufficiency; pej. (self-)conceit, self-
importance; à (or en) ‿ in plenty;
suffisant, e [‿'zɑ̃, ‿'zɑ̃:t] 1. adj.
sufficient, adequate; pej. conceited,
self-important; 2. su. conceited
person; **suffisons** [‿'zɔ̃] 1st p. pl.
pres. of suffire.

suffixe gramm. [sy'fiks] 1. su./m
suffix; 2. adj. suffixed.

suffocant, e [syfɔ'kɑ̃, ‿'kɑ̃:t] suffo-
cating, stifling; **suffocation** [‿ka-
'sjɔ̃] f suffocation, choking; **suffoquer** [‿'ke] (1m) v/t. suffocate;
choke; v/i. choke (with, de).

suffragant, e [syfra'gɑ̃, ‿'gɑ̃:t] adj.,
a. su./m suffragan; **suffrage** [‿'fra:ʒ]
m pol., a. eccl. suffrage; pol. vote;
franchise; fig. approbation, approval.

suffusion ⚕ [syffy'zjɔ̃] f suffusion
(usu. of blood); flush.

suggérer [sygʒe're] (1f) v/t. suggest; inspire; **suggestif, -ve** [‿ʒes-
'tif, ‿'ti:v] suggestive; **suggestion**
[‿ʒes'tjɔ̃] f suggestion.

suicidaire [sɥisi'dɛ:r] 1. adj. suicidal; suicide-prone, with suicidal tendencies (*person*); 2. *su.* person with suicidal tendencies; **suicide** [sɥi'sid] suicide; **suicidé** *m*, e *f* [sɥisi'de] *person*: suicide; **suicider** [~] (1a) *v/t.*: se ~ commit suicide.

suie [sɥi] *f* soot.

suif [sɥif] *m* tallow; *cuis.* (*mutton*) fat; *sl.* **suiffer** [sɥi'fe] (1a) *v/t.* tallow; grease; **suiffeux, -euse** [~'fø,~'fø:z] tallowy; greasy.

suint [sɥɛ̃] *m* ⊕ yolk, wool grease; glass gall; *laines f/pl.* en ~ greasy wool *sg.*; **suintant, e** [sɥɛ̃'tɑ̃, ~'tɑ̃:t] oozing; sweating; **suinter** [~'te] (1a) *v/i.* ooze, sweat; ⚓ leak; exude; *v/t. fig.* ooze (*hatred*).

suis¹ [sɥi] *1st p. sg. pres.* of être 1.

suis² [~] *1st p. sg. pres.* of suivre.

suisse [sɥis] 1. *adj.* Swiss; 2. *su./m eccl.* beadle, (*approx.*) verger; *hotel*: porter; ♀ Swiss; les ♀s *pl.* the Swiss; *petit* ~ small cream cheese; **Suissesse** [sɥi'ses] *f* Swiss (woman).

suite [sɥit] *f* continuation; retinue, train, followers *pl.*; sequence, series; *fig.* result, consequence; sequel; *fig.* coherence; ✝ ~ à with reference to; ✗ à la ~ on pension; à la ~ de following (*s.th.*); in (*s.o.'s*) train; de ~ in succession, on end; F at once; *donner* ~ à give effect to, carry out (*a decision*); ✝ carry out (*an order*); *et ainsi de* ~ and so on; *manquer (d'esprit) de* ~ lack method or coherence; *par la* ~ later on, eventually; *par* ~ therefore, consequently; *par* ~ de as a result of, because of; *tout de* ~ at once, immediately.

suitée [sɥi'te] *adj./f: jument f* ~ mare and foal; wild sow with her young.

suivant, e [sɥi'vɑ̃, ~'vɑ̃:t] 1. *adj.* following, next; 2. *su.* follower; *su./m* attendant, follower; *su./f* lady's-maid; *thea.* soubrette; 3. *suivant prp.* following, along; *fig.* according to; ~ *que* according as; **suivi, e** [~'vi] *p.p.* of suivre; consistent; steady, regular; coherent (*speech, reasoning, story, etc.*); *très (peu)* ~ very popular (unpopular); (not) widely followed; well- (poorly) attended; **suivre** [sɥi:vr] (4ee) *v/t.* follow; take (*a course*); practise (*a profession*); succeed, come after; attend (*lectures etc.*); ~ *des yeux* look after (*s.o.*); ~ *la*

mode keep up with fashion; *v/i.* follow, come after; à ~ to be continued; *faire* ~ *post*: forward (*a letter*); (*prière de*) *faire* ~ please forward.

sujet, -ette [sy'ʒe, ~'ʒet] 1. *adj.* subject (to, à); 2. *su. pol.* subject; *su./m* subject (*a. gramm., ♪, a. fig.*); theme; (subject-)matter; reason (for, de); *fig.* individual, person; à ce ~ on this matter, about this; *au* ~ *de* about, concerning, with reference to (*a.* ✝); *mauvais* ~ *person*: bad lot; *school*: bad boy; **sujétion** [syʒe'sjɔ̃] *f* subjection; constraint.

sulfamide ✻ [sylfa'mid] *f* sulpha drug, sulphonamide; **sulfate** ⌂ₘ [~'fat] *m* sulphate; **sulfure** ⌂ₘ [~'fy:r] *m* sulphide; **sulfurer** [sylfy're] (1a) *v/t.* sulphurate; treat (*vines*) with sulphide; **sulfureux, -euse** [~'rø,~'rø:z] sulphureous; sulphurous; sulphur...; **sulfurique** ⌂ₘ [~'rik] sulphuric (*acid*).

sultan [syl'tɑ̃] *m* sultan; scent sachet; **sultanat** [~ta'na] *m* sultanate; **sultane** [~'tan] *f* sultana.

super [sy'pɛ:r] 1. *su./m* high-octane petrol or *Am.* gasoline, F super; 2. *adj./inv.* F super, fantastic, great.

super... [sypɛr] super-...

superbe [sy'pɛrb] 1. *adj.* superb; fine, magnificent; 2. † *su./f* pride, vainglory.

super...: ~**carburant** *mot.* [sypɛrkarby'rɑ̃] *m* high-octane petrol or *Am.* gasoline; ~**cherie** [~ʃə'ri] *f* swindle, fraud, deceit; ~**fétation** [~feta'sjɔ̃] *f physiol.* superfetation; *words etc.*: superfluity; ~**ficie** [~fi'si] *f* area; surface (*a. fig.*); ~**ficiel, -elle** [~fi'sjɛl] superficial (*a. fig.*); ~**fin, e** [~'fɛ̃, ~'fin] superfine; ~**flu, e** [~'fly] 1. *adj.* superfluous; useless; 2. *su./m* superfluity; ~**fluité** [~flɥi'te] *f* superfluity; *fig.* ~s *pl.* extras, F luxuries; ~**forteresse** ✈ [~fɔrtə'rɛs] *f* superfortress.

supérieur, e [sype'rjœ:r] 1. *adj.* superior (*a. fig.*); upper, higher (*a.* ✍, *zo.*); ✝ of superior quality; ~ à superior to; above; 2. *su.* superior; **supériorité** [~rjɔri'te] *f* superiority (*a. fig.*); *eccl.* superiorship; seniority (in age, d'âge).

super...: ~**latif, -ve** [sypɛrla'tif, ~'ti:v] 1. *adj.* superlative; 2. *su./m gramm.* superlative; *au* ~ *gramm.* in the superlative; *fig.* superlatively; **~marché** ✝ [~mar'ʃe] *m* supermarket; **~posable** [~po'zabl] super(im)posable; **~poser** [~po'ze] (1a) *v/t.* super(im)pose (on, *à*); **~position** [~pozi'sjɔ̃] *f* superimposition; ᴀ̸ superposition; *cin.* double exposure; **~(-)puissance** *pol.* [~pɥi'sɑ̃:s] *f* superpower; **~sonique** ✕̸ [~sɔ'nik] supersonic; *bang m* ~ sonic boom *or* bang; **~stitieux, -euse** [~sti'sjø, ~'sjø:z] superstitious; **~stition** [~sti'sjɔ̃] *f* superstition; *fig.* mania, obsession; **~structure** [~stryk'ty:r] *f* ⚙, ♣ superstructure; ⚙ permanent way; **~viser** [~vi'ze] (1a) *v/t.* supervise, control; **~vision** [~vi'zjɔ̃] *f* control, supervision.

supplanter [syplɑ̃'te] (1a) *v/t.* supplant, supersede.

suppléant, e [syple'ɑ̃, ~'ɑ̃:t] **1.** *adj.* deputy ...; acting ...; **2.** *su.* deputy; supply teacher; ⚖ locum; **~s** *pl. a.* temporary staff *sg.*; **suppléer** [~'e] (1a) *v/t.* supply; make up; complete; deputize for; replace, take the place of; *v/i.*: ~ *à* make up for; remedy; **supplément** [~'mɑ̃] *m* supplement (*a.* ᴀ̸, *a. book*); addition; extra charge, ⚙ excess (fare); *restaurant:* extra course; **supplémentaire** [~mɑ̃'tɛ:r] extra, additional; supplementary; ᴀ̸ supplemental; ♪ leger (*line*); ⊕ *heures f/pl.* **~s** overtime *sg.*; ⚙ *train m* ~ relief train; **supplétif, -ve** [~'tif, ~'ti:v] suppletive, suppletory; ✕ auxiliary.

suppliant, e [sypli'ɑ̃, ~'ɑ̃:t] **1.** *adj.* suppliant, pleading, imploring; **2.** *su.* suppli(c)ant; **supplication** [~ka'sjɔ̃] *f* supplication, entreaty.

supplice [sy'plis] *m* torture; *fig. a.* agony, torment; ⚖ *dernier* ~ capital punishment; *fig. être au* ~ be on tenterhooks; be agonized; **supplicier** [~pli'sje] (1o) *v/t. a. fig.* torture; torment.

supplier [sypli'e] (1a) *v/t.* beseech, implore, beg; **supplique** [sy'plik] *f* petition.

support [sy'pɔ:r] *m* support (*a. fig.*); stand, pedestal; **supportable** [sypɔr'tabl] tolerable, bearable; *fig.* fairly good, moderate; **supporter** [~'te] (1a) *v/t.* support; tolerate; withstand; bear, endure; put up with.

supposé, e [sypo'ze] supposed; es-

timated (*number etc.*); **supposer** [~'ze] (1a) *v/t.* suppose; imply, presuppose; *à* ~ *que, en supposant que* supposing (that); **supposition** [~zi'sjɔ̃] *f* supposition, surmise; ⚖ *will:* forging, setting up (*of a supposititious child*); production of forged document(s), assumption (*of a false name*).

suppositoire ⚕ [sypozi'twa:r] *m* suppository.

suppôt *fig.* [sy'po] *m* tool, instrument; henchman; ~ *du Satan* (*or du diable*) hellhound.

suppression [syprɛ'sjɔ̃] *f* suppression; ⚕ stoppage; *difficulty:* removal; ⚖ ~ *d'enfant* concealment of birth; **supprimer** [sypri'me] (1a) *v/t.* suppress; end; abolish; stop; cut out; do away with; *fig.* omit; *typ.* delete; ⚖ conceal; F kill (*s.o.*); cancel (*a train etc.*).

suppurant, e ⚕ [sypy'rɑ̃, ~'rɑ̃:t] suppurating; **suppuratif, -ve** [~ra'tif, ~'ti:v] *adj., a. su./m* suppurative; **suppuration** ⚕ [~ra'sjɔ̃] *f* suppuration, running; **suppurer** ⚕ [~'re] (1a) *v/i.* suppurate, run.

supputer [sypy'te] (1a) *v/t.* calculate, reckon; work out (*expenses, interest*).

supra... [sypra] supra..., super...

suprématie [syprema'si] *f* supremacy; **suprême** [~'prɛm] **1.** *adj.* supreme; highest; *fig.* last (*honours, hour, request*); **2.** *su./m cuis.* supreme.

sur¹ [syr] *prp. usu.* on (*a chair, the Thames, my word, my honour*), upon; *destination:* towards (*evening, old age*); *measurement:* by; *number:* out of; *succession:* after; *tomber* ~ *hit* upon; *donner* ~ *la rue* look on to the street; ~ *la droite* on *or* to the right; ~ *place* on the spot; *avoir de l'argent* ~ *soi* have money on *or* about one; ~ *ce* thereupon, and then; ~ *quoi* whereupon, and then; *un impôt* ~ a tax on; *travailler* ~ work on (*wood etc.*); *être* ~ *un travail* be at a task; *8* ~ *10* 8 out of 10; *measurement:* 8 by 10; *une fois* ~ *deux* every other time; *juger* ~ *les apparences* judge by appearances; *coup* ~ *coup* blow after blow; *revenir* ~ *ses pas* turn back; *fermer la porte* ~ *soi* close the door behind one; ~ *toute(s) chose(s)* above all; *lire qch.* ~ *le journal* read s.th. in the paper; ~ *un ton sévère* in a grave voice; *retenir* ~ keep (*s.th.*)

back out of; stop (*s.th.*) out of (*s.o.'s wages*); *autorité f* ~ authority over.

sur², **sure** [syːr] sour; tart.

sur... [syr] over-...; super...; supra...; sur...

sûr, sûre [syːr] sure (of, *de*); safe; reliable (*person*, ⊕, *information*, *a. weather*); *fig.* unerring; *fig.* certain, unfailing; ~ *de soi* self-confident; *à coup* ~ for certain, definitely; *bien* ~! certainly!; surely!, *Am.* sure!; *F pour* ~ of course.

surabondance [syrabɔ̃'dɑ̃ːs] *f* super-abundance; ✝ glut; **surabondant, e** [~'dɑ̃, ~'dɑ̃ːt] superabundant; superfluous; **surabonder** [~'de] (1a) *v/i.* overflow (with *de, en*); ✝ be glutted (with *de, en*).

suraigu, -guë [syre'gy] high-pitched, (very) shrill.

suranné, e [syra'ne] old-fashioned; superannuated; out of date.

surbaisser [syrbɛ'se] (1b) *v/t.* △ depress; *mot.* undersling.

surcharge [syr'ʃarʒ] *f* overload; extra *or* excess load; *fig.* extra work; ~ *de bagages* excess luggage (*Am.* baggage); *manuscript etc.*: alteration, correction; **surcharger** [~ʃar'ʒe] (1l) *v/t.* overload (*a. ⚡*), overburden; ⚡ overcharge (*an accumulator*); *post*: overprint (*a stamp*); *typ.* interline; write over (*other words in a line*); *fig.* overtax (*s.o.*).

surchauffe [syr'ʃof] *f* overheating; ⊕ superheat(ing); **surchauffer** [syrʃo'fe] (1a) *v/t.* overheat; super-heat (*steam*); burn (*iron*).

surchoix [syr'ʃwa] *m* finest quality.

surclasser *sp.* [syrkla'se] (1a) *v/t.* outclass.

surcontrer [syrkɔ̃'tre] (1a) *v/t. cards*: redouble.

surcoupe [syr'kup] *f cards*: over-trumping; **surcouper** [~ku'pe] (1a) *v/t. cards*: overtrump.

surcroît [syr'krwa] *m* increase; *un* ~ *de qch.* an added s.th.; *par* ~ in addition.

surdi-mutité ✱ [syrdimyti'te] *f* deaf-and-dumbness; **surdité** ✱ [~'te] *f* deafness.

surdos [syr'do] *m horse*: back-band; *porter*: carrying-pad.

surdoué, e [syr'dwe] exceptionally gifted.

sureau ♀ [sy'ro] *m* elder.

surélever [syrel've] (1d) *v/t.* △, ✝

heighten, raise; ✝ put up, boost (*prices*); *road-building*: bank (*a road bend*).

surenchère [syrɑ̃'ʃɛːr] *f auction*: higher bid, outbidding; overbid; *fig.* exaggerated promises *pl.*; *fig.* une ~ *de violences* ever-increasing violence; **surenchérir** [~ʃe'riːr] (2a) *v/i.* rise higher in price; *auction*: bid higher; ~ *sur q.* outbid s.o.; *fig. a.* go one better than s.o.; **surenchérisseur** *m*, **-euse** *f* [~ʃeri'sœːr, ~'søːz] out-bidder.

surentraînement *sp.* [syrɑ̃trɛn'mɑ̃] *m* over-training.

surestimer [syrɛsti'me] (1a) *v/t.* over-estimate; overrate (*s.o.*).

suret, -ette [sy'rɛ, ~'rɛt] sourish.

sûreté [syr'te] *f* safety; security (*a.* ✝); *fig.* blow, foot, hand, stroke: sureness; *judgment etc.*: soundness; *memory*: reliability; ~ *de soi* self-assurance; *de* ~ safety-...; *la* ♀ the Criminal Investigation Department, the C.I.D., *Am.* the Federal Bureau of Investigation, the F.B.I.

surexcitation [syrɛksita'sjɔ̃] *f* over-excitement; ✝ over-stimulation; **surexciter** [~'te] (1a) *v/t.* over-excite (*s.o.*); over-stimulate (*a. ✝*).

surexposer *phot.* [syrɛkspo'ze] (1a) *v/t.* over-expose.

surface [syr'fas] *f* surface; ⚓ surface area; area; ⚓ *faire* ~ surface (*sub-marine*).

surfaire [syr'fɛːr] (4r) *v/t.* overrate (*a book, a writer*); ✝ charge too much for.

surfer [sœr'fe] (1a) *v/i.* surf(ride); go surfing; **surfeur** *m*, **-euse** *f* [~'fœːr, ~'føːz] surfer, surfrider.

surgelé, e [syrʒə'le] deep-frozen; quick-frozen.

surgeon ♀ [syr'ʒɔ̃] *m* sucker; *pousser des* ~*s* sucker; **surgir** [~'ʒiːr] (2a) *v/i.* appear (suddenly); loom up; spring up; *fig.* arise.

surhausser [syro'se] (1a) *v/t.* △ raise; 🎯 cant; ✝ force up the price of.

surhomme [sy'rɔm] *m* superman; **surhumain, e** [~ry'mɛ̃, ~'mɛn] superhuman.

surimposer [syrɛ̃po'ze] (1a) *v/t.* superimpose; ✝ overtax, increase the tax on.

surimpression *phot.* [syrɛ̃prɛ'sjɔ̃] *f* double exposure.

surin *sl.* [sy'rɛ̃] *m* dagger, knife; **suriner** † *sl.* [ˌri'ne] (1a) *v/t.* knife (*s.o.*), murder (*s.o.*).

surintendant, e [syrɛ̃tɑ̃'dɑ̃, ˌdɑ̃:t] *su.* superintendent, overseer; *su./f* superintendent's wife; lady-in-waiting in chief.

surir [sy'ri:r] (2a) *v/i.* turn sour.

surjet [syr'ʒɛ] *m* seam: whipping; **surjeter** [ˌʒə'te] (1c) *v/t.* whip (a seam).   [once, on the spot.\

sur-le-champ [syrlə'ʃɑ̃] *adv.* at\

surlendemain [syrlɑ̃d'mɛ̃] *m* day after the morrow, second day (after s.th., de qch.).

surmenage [syrmə'na:ʒ] *m* over-work(ing); **surmener** [ˌ'ne] (1d) *v/t.* overwork; work (*s.o.*) too hard; override (a horse); ⊕, ⚡ overrun.

surmontable [syrmɔ̃'tabl] surmountable; **surmonter** [ˌ'te] (1a) *v/t.* rise above (a. fig.); surmount (a building, a. fig. feelings, an obstacle); fig. overcome (an enemy, feelings); se ˌ control o.s.; surmonté de crowned by, surmounted by.

surnager [syrna'ʒe] (1l) *v/i.* float on the surface; fig. linger (on).

surnaturel, -elle [syrnaty'rɛl] **1.** adj. supernatural; fig. uncanny, extraordinary; **2.** su./m: le ˌ the supernatural.

surnom [syr'nɔ̃] *m* nickname; appellation, name; hist. agnomen.

surnombre [syr'nɔ̃:br] *m* excess number; ˌ des habitants overpopulation; en ˌ extra; supernumerary.

surnommer [syrnɔ'me] (1a) *v/t.* call (*s.o. s.th., q. qch.*); nickname.

surnuméraire [syrnyme'rɛ:r] adj., a. su./m supernumerary.

suroffre † [sy'rɔfr] *f* better offer.

suroît ⚓ [sy'rwa] *m* south-west; hat, a. wind: sou'wester.

surpasser [syrpa'se] (1a) *v/t.* surpass (a. fig.); be higher than; be taller than (a person); fig. exceed, outdo.

surpaye [syr'pɛ:j] *f* overpayment; bonus, extra pay; **surpayer** [ˌpɛ-'je] (1i) *v/t.* overpay (*s.o.*); pay too much for (s.th.).

surpeuplé, e [syrpœ'ple] overpopulated (area); **surpeuplement** [ˌplə'mɑ̃] *m* overpopulation.

sur(-)place [syr'plas] *m*: faire du ˌ mark time.

surplis *eccl.* [syr'pli] *m* surplice.

surplomb [syr'plɔ̃] *m* overhang; en ˌ overhanging; **surplombement** [ˌplɔ̃b'mɑ̃] *m* overhang(ing); **surplomber** [ˌplɔ̃'be] (1a) *vt/i.* overhang; *v/t.* jut out over (s.th.).

surplus [syr'ply] *m* surplus, excess; remainder; au ˌ besides; moreover; en ˌ excess ..., surplus ...

surprenant, e [syrprə'nɑ̃, ˌ'nɑ̃:t] surprising, astonishing, amazing; **surprendre** [ˌ'prɑ̃:dr] (4aa) *v/t.* surprise; astonish, amaze; come upon (*s.o.*); catch (*s.o.*) (unawares); pay (*s.o.*) a surprise visit; overhear (a conversation, a remark); intercept (a glance, a letter); ˌ la bonne foi de q. abuse s.o.'s good faith.

surprime † [syr'prim] *f* insurance: extra premium.

surprise [syr'pri:z] *f* surprise; ⚔ surprise attack; fig. surprise-packet, lucky dip; par ˌ by surprise.

sur(-)prix [syr'pri] *m* excessive price; overcharge.

surproduction [syrprɔdyk'sjɔ̃] *f* overproduction.

surrégénérateur phys. [syreʒenera'tœ:r] *m*: (a. ˌ rapide) fast breeder.

sursalaire [syrsa'lɛ:r] *m* bonus; extra pay.

sursaturer ⚗ [syrsaty're] (1a) *v/t.* supersaturate.

sursaut [syr'so] *m* start, jump; s'éveiller en ˌ wake with a start.

surseoir [syr'swa:r] (3c) *v/i.*: ⚖ ˌ à stay (a judgment, proceedings), suspend (a judgment); defer, postpone; il a été sursis à qch. s.th. has been postponed; **sursis, e** [ˌ'si, ˌ'si:z] **1.** p.p. of surseoir; **2.** su./m ⚖ delay; suspension of sentence; ⚔ call-up: deferment; **sursitaire** ⚔ [ˌsi'tɛ:r] *m* deferred conscript.

surtaux [syr'to] *m* over-assessment.

surtaxe [syr'taks] *f* surtax; post: postage due, surcharge; admin. over-assessment; **surtaxer** [ˌtak-'se] (1a) *v/t.* surtax; post: surcharge (a letter); admin. over-assess, overtax.

surtout¹ [syr'tu] adv. above all; particularly, especially.

surtout² [ˌ] *m* dinner table: centrepiece; metall. mantle; light handcart; † overcoat.

surveillance [syrvɛ'jɑ̃:s] *f* supervision; ⊕ inspection; ⚖ surveillance; *sous la ~ de la police* under police supervision; **surveillant, e** [~'jã, ~'jãːt] *su.* supervisor, overseer; 🚇 inspector; ⛴ shop-walker, *Am.* floorwalker; *examination:* invigilator; *su./f* ⚖ *(ward-)*sister; **surveille** [syr've:j] *f: la ~ de* two days before ...; **surveiller** [~vɛ'je] (1a) *v/t.* supervise; superintend; tend *(a machine):* ⊕ inspect, test; *examination:* invigilate; *fig.* keep an eye on, watch; ⚖ *liberté f surveillée* probation.

survenir [syrvə'niːr] (2h) *v/i.* occur, happen; take place; set in *(complications etc.);* arrive unexpectedly *(person).*

survente ⛴ [syr'vãːt] *f* overcharge.

survie [syr'vi] *f* survival; ⚖ (presumption of) survivorship; ⛴ expectation of life; **survivance** [~vi'vãːs] *f* survival *(a. biol., a. fig.);* estate: reversion; **survivant, e** [~vi'vã, ~'vãːt] **1.** *adj.* surviving; **2.** *su.* survivor; **survivre** [~'viːvr] (4hh) *v/i.*: *~ à* outlive, survive.

survol [syr'vɔl] *m* ✈ flight over; *cin.* panning; **survoler** ✈ [~vɔ'le] (1a) *v/t.* fly over.

survolté, e [syrvɔl'te] ⚡ boosted; *fig.* (over)excited, worked up.

sus¹ [sy] *1st p. sg. p.s. of savoir 1.*

sus² [sy(s)] **1.** *adv.: courir ~ à* rush at *(s.o.);* *en ~ (de)* in addition (to); **2.** *int.* come on!; *~ à ...! at (s.o.)!,* away with *(s.th.)!*

susceptibilité [sysɛptibili'te] *f* susceptibility, sensitiveness, touchiness; **susceptible** [~'tibl] susceptible; sensitive, touchy; *~ de* capable of; liable to.

susciter [sysi'te] (1a) *v/t.* cause, give rise to; provoke, stir up *(a rebellion);* (a)rouse *(envy);* raise up.

suscription [syskrip'sjɔ̃] *f letter:* address.

susdit, e ⚖ [sys'di, ~'dit] *adj., a. su.* aforesaid, above-mentioned; **susmentionné, e** ⚖ [~mãsjɔ'ne] *see susdit.*

susnommé, e ⚖ [sysnɔ'me] *adj., a. su.* above-named, afore-named.

suspect, e [sys'pɛ, ~'pɛkt] **1.** *adj.* suspicious; suspect *(person);* *~ de* suspected of; **2.** *su.* suspect; **suspecter** [~pɛk'te] (1a) *v/t.* suspect *(s.o.);* doubt *(s.th.).*

suspendre [sys'pãːdr] (4a) *v/t.* suspend *(a. a judgment, payment);* hang up; *fig.* defer; *fig.* interrupt; **suspendu, e** [~pã'dy] hanging (on, from *à); mot. bien (mal) ~* with a good (poor) suspension *(car);* **suspens** [~'pã] *m: en ~* in suspense *(a. ⛴);* outstanding *(question, a. ⛴ bills);* **suspense** [sys'pɛns] *m* suspense; **suspensif, -ve** [syspã'sif, ~'siːv] suspensive; *gramm. points m/pl. ~s* points of suspension; **suspension** [~'sjɔ̃] *f* suspension; hanging *(a. ⚖);* (hanging) lamp; *mot.* springs *pl.;* *~ d'armes* truce; armistice; suspension of hostilities; ⚔ *en ~* in suspension; *gramm. points m/pl. de ~* points of suspension; **suspensoir** [~'swaːr] *m* suspensory bandage; jockstrap.

suspicion ⚖ *etc.* [syspi'sjɔ̃] *f* suspicion; *en ~* suspected.

sustentateur, -trice ✈ [systãta-'tœːr, ~'tris] lifting; main *(wing);* **sustentation** [~ta'sjɔ̃] *f* ✝ sustenance; ✈ lift(ing force); **sustenter** [~'te] (1a) *v/t.*: *F se ~* take sustenance.

susurrer [sysy're] (1a) *vt/i.* whisper, murmur.

suture [sy'tyːr] *f* ⚕, *anat.* suture; ⚕ *wound:* stitching; *fig. etc.* join.

suzerain, e [syz'rɛ̃, ~'rɛn] **1.** *adj.* paramount; **2.** *su.* suzerain; **suzeraineté** [~rɛn'te] *f* lordship; suzerainty; ⚖ suzerain (state).

svelte [svɛlt] slender, slim; **sveltesse** [svɛl'tɛs] *f* slenderness, slimness.

sweater *cost.* [swi'tœːr] *m* sweater.

swing ♪, *a. box.* [swiŋ] *m* swing; **swinguer** ♪ [swiŋ'ge] (1a) swing *(a. fig.).*

sybaritique [sibari'tik] sybaritic; voluptuary; **sybaritisme** [~'tism] *m* sybaritism.

sycomore ♣ [sikɔ'mɔːr] *m* sycamore.

sycophante [sikɔ'fãːt] *m* sycophant, F toady.

syllabaire [silla'bɛːr] *m* spelling book; **syllabe** [~'lab] *f* syllable; **syllabique** [~la'bik] syllabic.

sylphe [silf] *m,* **sylphide** [sil'fid] *f* sylph; *taille f de sylphide* sylph-like waist.

sylvain [sil'vɛ̃] *m* sylvan, silvan; *~s pl.* genii of the woods; **sylvestre** ♣ [~'vɛstr] woodland *(tree);* wood *(plant),* growing in the woods; **sylviculteur** [silvikyl'tœːr] *m* syl-

viculturist; **sylviculture** [ˌ~'tyːr] f
forestry, sylviculture.

symbiose [sɛ̃'bjoːz] f symbiosis.

symbole [sɛ̃'bɔl] m symbol; emblem;
eccl. ♀ creed; **symbolique** [sɛ̃bɔ'lik]
symbolic(al); **symboliser** [ˌ~li'ze]
(1a) *v/t.* symbolize; **symbolisme**
[ˌ~'lism] m symbolism; **symboliste**
[ˌ~'list] **1.** *adj.* symbolistic; **2.** *su.* sym-
bolist.

symétrie [sime'tri] f symmetry; *sans*
~ unsymmetrical; **symétrique**
[ˌ~'trik] symmetrical.

sympa F [sɛ̃'pa] *adj./inv.* nice, likable; **sympathie** [sɛ̃pa'ti] f sympathy (*a.* ✻, *physiol.*); *fig.* liking,
congeniality; **sympathique** [ˌ~'tik]
sympathetic (*a.* ✻, *physiol.*); nice,
likable (*person*); attractive; *fig.*
congenial (*task*, *work*); invisible
(*ink*); *il m'est* ~ I like him, I take to
him; **sympathisant, e** [ˌ~ti'zɑ̃,
ˌ~'zɑ̃ːt] **1.** *adj.* sympathizing; **2.** *su./m*
pol. fellow-traveller; sympathizer;
sympathiser [ˌ~ti'ze] (1a) *v/i. fig.*
blend, harmonize, go together; sympathize (with, *avec*).

symphonie ♪ [sɛ̃fo'ni] f symphony;
symphoniste ♪ [ˌ~'nist] m composer
of symphonies; orchestral player.

symposium [sɛ̃pɔ'zjɔm] m symposium.

symptôme [sɛ̃p'toːm] m ✻, *a. fig.*
symptom; *fig.* sign.

syn... [*before vowel* sin...; *before consonant* sɛ̃...] syn...; **~chronique**
[sɛ̃krɔ'nik] synchronological; syn-
chronistic; **~chronisateur** *mot.*
[ˌ~niza'tœːr] m synchromesh (device); **~chronisation** [ˌ~niza'sjɔ̃] f
synchronization; **~chroniser** [ˌ~-
ni'ze] (1a) *v/t.* synchronize (*a. cin.*);
∮ parallel; **~chronisme** [ˌ~'nism] m
synchronism; ∮, *phys.* step; syn-
chrony (*a. cin.*); **~cope** [sɛ̃'kɔp] f ✻,
gramm. syncope; ✻ fainting fit,
blackout; ♪ syncopation; ♪ syn-
copated note; **~coper** [ˌ~kɔ'pe] (1a)
v/t. ♪, *gramm.* syncopate.

syndic [sɛ̃'dik] m managing agent; ⚖
receiver; **syndical, e** m/pl. **-aux**
[sɛ̃di'kal, ˌ~'ko] trade-union (*movement*); ✝ *chambre f ~e* (*approx.*) Stock
Exchange Committee; **syndicali-**

sation [ˌ~kaliza'sjɔ̃] f unionization;
syndicaliser [ˌ~kali'ze] (1a) *v/t.* un-
ionize; **syndicalisme** [ˌ~ka'lism] m
trade unionism; **syndicaliste**
[ˌ~ka'list] *su.* trade unionist; **syndicat** [ˌ~'ka] m trade union; syndicate,
association; receivership, trusteeship (*in bankruptcy*); ~ *d'initiative*
tourist information bureau; **syndiqué, e** [ˌ~'ke] **1.** *adj.* associated; belonging to a (trade) union; union-...;
2. *su.* trade unionist; union member;
syndiquer [ˌ~'ke] (1m) *v/t.* un-
ionize; form (*men*) into a trade
union; *se* ~ combine; form a syndicate *or* trade-union.

syndrome [sɛ̃'drɔm] m syndrome.

synodal, e, m/pl. **-aux** [sinɔ'dal,
ˌ~'do] synodical; synodal (*examiner*);
synode *eccl.* [ˌ~'nɔd] m synod; **syno-
dique** [ˌ~nɔ'dik] synodic(al).

synonyme [sinɔ'nim] **1.** *adj.* syn-
onymous (with, *de*); **2.** *su./m* syn-
onym; **synonymie** [ˌ~ni'mi] f syno-
nymity; **synonymique** [ˌ~ni'mik] **1.**
adj. synonymic; **2.** *su./f* synonymy,
synonymics *sg.*

synoptique [sinɔp'tik] synoptic.

syntaxe *gramm.* [sɛ̃'taks] f syntax;
syntaxique *gramm.* [ˌ~tak'sik] syn-
tactic(al).

synthèse [sɛ̃'tɛːz] f synthesis; **synthétique** [sɛ̃te'tik] synthetic; **synthétiser** [ˌ~ti'ze] (1a) *v/t.* synthesize.

syntonisation [sɛ̃tɔniza'sjɔ̃] f *radio:*
tuning; *bobine f de* ~ tuning-coil;
syntoniser [ˌ~'ze] (1a) *v/t. radio:*
tune in.

syphilis ✻ [sifi'lis] f syphilis.

syrien, -enne [si'rjɛ̃, ˌ~'rjɛn] *adj., a.
su.* ♀ Syrian.

systématique [sistema'tik] systematic; methodical; *fig.* hide-bound;
systématiser [ˌ~ti'ze] (1a) *v/t.*
systematize; **système** [sis'tɛm] m
system; *phot.* (*back*, *front*) lens;
fig. device; ⊕ *etc.* set; F ~ D re-
sourcefulness; wangling; A ~ *décimal* (*métrique*) decimal (metric)
system; *anat.* ~ *nerveux* nervous
system; *fig. esprit m de* ~ pigheaded-
ness; **systémique** [ˌ~te'mik] sys-
temic.

systole ✻ [sis'tɔl] f systole.

T

T, t [te] *m* T, t; ⊕ *fer m en T* T-iron; tee; ⊕ *poutre f en double T* I-section, H-beam.

ta [ta] *see* ton¹.

tabac [ta'ba] **1.** *su./m* ♀, *a.* ✝ tobacco; ~ *à chiquer* chewing tobacco; ~ *à fumer* (smoking) tobacco; ~ *à priser* snuff; ⚭ *pl.* (State) Tobacco Department *sg.*; *bureau m* (or *débit m*) *de* ~ tobacconist's (shop); *sl. faire un* ~ be a hit; F *passer* (*q.*) *à* ~ *see tabasser; prendre du* ~ take snuff; **2.** *adj./inv.* snuff-colo(u)red; **tabagie** [taba'ʒi] *f* ✝ smoking-room; place smelling of stale tobacco-smoke; **tabagisme** [~'ʒism] *m* nicotine-poisoning; **tabasser** F [~'se] (1a) *v/t.* handle (*s.o.*) roughly, beat (*s.o.*) up.; **tabatière** [~'tjɛːr] *f* snuff-box.

tabernacle [tabɛr'nakl] *m* tabernacle.

table [tabl] *f* table; *stone*: slab, tablet; *teleph.* switchboard; index; ~ *à rallonges* extending table; ⚭ ~ *de multiplication* multiplication table; ~ *des matières* table of contents; ♪ ~ *d'harmonie violin*: belly; ~ *d'hôte* set dinner, table d'hôte; *pol. etc.* ~ *ronde* round table conference; *à* ~! dinner is served!; *mettre la* ~ lay the table; *sainte* ~ Lord's table, altar; *se mettre à* ~ sit down at table; *sl.* talk, come clean; **tableau** [ta'blo] *m paint. etc.* picture, painting; *thea.* tableau; *thea. a. fig.* scene; view; *notices, a.* ♀, *sp.*: board; *hotel*: key-board; (~ *noir*) blackboard; list, table; ♂, *a.* ⚖ *jurors*: panel; ⚖ *solicitors*: roll, *barristers*: list; *typ.* table; 🚂 train indicator; *fig.* description; ~ *d'annonces* notice-board; *Am.* bulletin-board; ~ *de bord mot.* dashboard; ⚡ instrument panel; ⚡ ~ *de distribution* switchboard; *mot.* ~ *de graissage* lubrication chart; F *au* ~ in the bag; **tableautin** [~blo'tɛ̃] *m* small picture; **tablée** [~'ble] *f* (tableful of) guests *pl.*; **tabler** [~'ble] (1a) *v/i.*: ~ *sur* count on.

tabletier ✝ [tablə'tje] *m* dealer in *or* maker of fancy articles and inlaid work; **tablette** [~'blɛt] *f* shelf; *stone*: slab; (window-)sill; *sideboard etc.*: (flat) top; *joist*: bearing surface; ⚡ plate; ♂ lozenge; *chocolate*: bar; ~ *de cheminée* mantelpiece; *rayez ça de vos* ~*s!* you can forget that!; don't count on that!; **tabletterie** [~blɛ'tri] *f* fancy-goods *pl.* (industry); inlaid work.

tablier [tabli'e] *m* apron, *child*: pinafore; *bridge*: road(way); ⊕ *etc.* shutter; *fig. rendre son* ~ resign; give notice.

tabou, e [ta'bu] **1.** *adj.* taboo; forbidden; **2.** *su./m* taboo.

tabouret [tabu'rɛ] *m* (foot)stool.

tabulaire [taby'lɛːr] *adj.* tabular; **tabulateur** [~la'tœːr] *m* tabulator; **tabulatrice** [~la'tris] *f machine*: tabulator.

tac [tak] *m mill*: clack; *sword-blades*: click; *riposter du* ~ *au* ~ *fencing*: parry with the riposte; *fig.* give tit for tat.

tache [taʃ] *f* stain (*a. fig.*), spot; mark; *ink, a. fig.*: blot; *colour*: blob, patch; *fig.* blemish; *fruit*: bruise; ~ *de naissance* birthmark; ~ *de rousseur face etc.*: freckle; ~ *de suie* smut; *fig. faire* ~ jar, be out of place.

tâche [tɑːʃ] *f* task, job; *ouvrier m à la* ~ jobbing workman; piece-worker; *prendre à* ~ *de* (*inf.*) undertake to (*inf.*), make a point of (*ger.*); *travailler à la* ~ do piece-work.

tacher [ta'ʃe] (1a) *v/t.* stain (*a. fig.*), spot; *fig.* tarnish (*s.o.'s reputation*); *se* ~ get one's clothes stained; stain, spot (*cloth*).

tâcher [tɑ'ʃe] (1a) *v/i.* try (to *inf.*, *de inf.*); labo(u)r, toil (at, *à*); ~ (*à ce*) *que* (*sbj.*) try to (*inf.*); **tâcheron** [tɑʃ'rɔ̃] *m* jobbing workman; ⚠ sub-contractor, jobber.

tacheter [taʃ'te] (1c) *v/t.* fleck, mottle speckle.

tachy... [taki] tachy...; tacho...; ~**mètre** ⊕ [~'mɛtr] *m* speedometer, tachometer.

tamis

tacite [ta'sit] tacit; implied; **taci-**
turne [~si'tyrn] taciturn; reserved;
close-mouthed.

tacot F [ta'ko] *m mot.* old rattletrap,
banger, crate.

tact [takt] *m* (sense of) touch; *fig.*
tact; *manque m de* ~ tactlessness.

tacticien ✕ *etc.* [takti'sjɛ̃] *m* tacti-
cian.

tactile [tak'til] tactile.

tactique [tak'tik] **1.** *adj.* tactical;
2. *su./f* ✕, *a. fig.* tactics *pl.*

taffetas *tex.* [taf'ta] *m* taffeta.

taie [tɛ] *f* (pillow-)case, slip; ✳
albugo, white speck (*on the eye*).

taillade [ta'jad] *f* slash, gash, cut;
taillader [~ja'de] (1a) *v/t.* slash (*a.
cost., a. fig.*); gash; **taillage** [~'ja:ʒ]
m file, gear: cutting; **taillant** [~'jɑ̃]
m blade, tool: (cutting) edge; **taille**
[tɑ:j] *f* cutting; ✔ *plant:* pruning;
hedge: clipping; *stone:* hewing; *hair,
tool, clothes:* cut; *blade:* edge; *fig.*
size, dimensions *pl.*; *person:* height,
stature; waist, figure; waist(line);
cost. à ~ *haute* (*basse*) high-waisted
(low-waisted); F *de* ~ big; *grandes* ~s
pl. outsizes; *par rang de* ~ in order of
size *or* height; *être de* ~ *à* (*inf.*) be
capable of (*ger.*); **taille-crayon**
[tajkrɛ'jɔ̃] *m/inv.* pencil sharpener;
taille-douce, *pl.* **tailles-douces**
[~'dus] *f* copperplate (engraving);
tailler [ta'je] (1a) *v/t.* cut (*gem, hair,
lawn, stone*); hew (*a stone*); trim
(*one's beard*); ✔ prune (*a plant*), clip
(*a hedge*); ⊕ mill (*gears*); sharpen (*a
pencil*); carve (*in a rock etc., a. fig. a
way*); hew (*the enemy to pieces*); *bien
taillé* well set-up (*person*); *cost.* well-
cut; *v/i. cards:* deal; **taillerie** [taj'ri]
f gem-cutting; gem-cutter's workshop; **tailleur** [ta'jœ:r] *m* ⊕ cutter;
cost. gaming: banker; *cost.* (*a.
costume m* ~) tailor-made costume; ~
pantalon m trouser suit, pant(s) suit;
taillis [~'ji] *m* copse; brushwood;
tailloir [taj'wa:r] *m* trencher; △
abacus.

tain ⊕ [tɛ̃] *m mirrors:* silvering; *iron:*
tin-bath; foil.

taire [tɛ:r] (4z) *v/t.* suppress, hush
(*s.th.*) up, say nothing about, not to
mention (*s.th.*); *faire* ~ silence, hush;
se ~ be silent, say nothing; stop
talking; *taisez-vous!* be quiet!; **tai-**
sons [tɛ'zɔ̃] *1st p. pl. pres. of taire*;
tait [tɛ] *3rd p. sg. pres. of taire*.

talc *min.* [talk] *m* talc; French chalk;
talcum powder; **talcique** [tal'sik]
talcose.

talent [ta'lɑ̃] *m* talent (*fig., a. ancient
weight*); aptitude; *de* ~ talented,
gifted; **talentueux, -euse** F [~lɑ̃-
'tɥø, ~'tɥø:z] talented.

talion [ta'ljɔ̃] *m* retaliation.

talisman [talis'mɑ̃] *m* talisman.

talle ✔ [tal] *f* sucker; *wheat etc.:*
tiller; **taller** ✔ [ta'le] (1a) *v/i.*
throw out suckers; tiller (*wheat*).

taloche [ta'lɔʃ] *f* ⊕ (*plasterer's*) hawk;
F cuff, clout; **talocher** F [~lɔ'ʃe] (1a)
v/t. cuff, clout.

talon [ta'lɔ̃] *m foot, shoe,* ⚓ *rudder,* ⊕
tool, rifle, mast, a. ♪ *violin bow:* heel;
spur; ⊕ catch; clip; *mot. tyre:*
bead(ing); ⊕ *axle, bayonet:* shoulder; *axle:* flange; *loaf:* end; *bread,
cheese:* remnant; *cards etc.:* stock,
pile; ✝ counterfoil, stub; ✝ ~s *pl.*
aiguille stiletto heels; *tourner les* ~s
take to one's heels; **talonner**
[talɔ'ne] (1a) *v/t.* follow (on the heels
of); dog (*s.o.*); spur on, urge on (*a
horse, a. fig. a person*); dun (*s.o.*); *v/i.*
⚓ touch; strike; **talonnette** [~'nɛt] *f*
heel.

talqueux, -euse *min.* [tal'kø, ~'kø:z]
talcose.

talus [ta'ly] *m* slope; bank, embankment; *en* ~ sloping.

talweg *geol.* [tal'veg] *m* thalweg.

tamanoir *zo.* [tama'nwa:r] *m* great
ant-eater.

tamarin ♀ [tama'rɛ̃] *m* tamarind;
tamarind-tree; **tamarinier** ♀ [~ri-
'nje] *m* tamarind-tree.

tambouille *sl.* [tɑ̃'bu:j] *f* kitchen
(staff); cooking.

tambour [tɑ̃'bu:r] *m* ♪, ✕, 🪚, ⊕
oil, ⚡ *cable, mot. brake,* △ *column:*
drum; *person:* drummer; ⚡ *coil:*
cylinder; △ *hotel etc.:* revolving
door; *embroidery:* frame; ♪ ~ *de
basque* tambourine (*with jingles*); ~
de ville town-crier; *fig. mener q.* ~
battant treat s.o. with a high hand;
sans ~ *ni trompette* quietly, on the
quiet; **tambourin** [tɑ̃bu'rɛ̃] *m* ♪
tambourine (*without jingles*); (*Provençal*) long, narrow drum; *ball-
games:* tambourine-like racquet;
tambouriner [~ri'ne] (1a) *vt/i.*
drum (*a. fig.*).

tamis [ta'mi] *m* sieve; *liquids:*
strainer; ⊕ screen; *cinders etc.:*

riddle; *flour*: bolter; *passer au* ~ sift (*a. fig.*); **tamiser** [tami'ze] (1a) *v/t.* sift, sieve; strain; filter (*air, light, a. liquid*); bolt (*flour*); *fig.* soften (*the light*); **lumière tamisée** subdued *or* soft(ened) light; **tamiseur** *m*, **-euse** *f* [~'zœːr, ~'zøːz] *person*: sifter, screener; strainer.

tampon [tɑ̃'pɔ̃] *m* ⚔ *wall*, ✷, *bath, wash-basin, cask, metall*: plug; *inking, polishing, a.* ✷ *cotton-wool*: pad; *paper, cotton-wool, etc.*: wad; rubber stamp; ⛨ (*a.* ~ *de choc*) buffer; ~ *buvard* hand-blotter; ~ *encreur* inking pad, stamp pad; *coup m de* ~ collision; F *fig.* thump; *pol.* État *m* ~ buffer State; **tamponnement** [~pɔn'mɑ̃] *m* ⛨, *mot.* collision; dabbing (*with pad*); F thumping; **tamponner** [~pɔ'ne] (1a) *v/t.* mop, dab (*with a handkerchief, a pad, etc.*); ✷ *etc.* collide with; *mot.* bump into; stamp (*a letter etc.*); ⊕ plug.

tam-tam [tam'tam] *m* ♪ tom-tom; ♪ (*Chinese*) gong; *fig.* fuss, to-do.

tan [tɑ̃] *m* tan, tanner's bark.

tancer [tɑ̃'se] (1k) *v/t.* scold, F tell (*s.o.*) off.

tanche *icht.* [tɑ̃ːʃ] *f* tench.

tandem [tɑ̃'dɛm] *m* tandem (*bicycle*); *fig.* twosome, pair, couple; *fig.* partnership; *fig.* combination; *en* ~ tandem; *fig.* together.

tandis [tɑ̃'di] *cj.*: ~ *que* whereas (*emphasizing difference*); while.

tangage ⚓, ✈ [tɑ̃'gaːʒ] *m* pitch (-ing).

tangent, e [tɑ̃'ʒɑ̃, ~'ʒɑ̃ːt] **1.** *adj.* ✕ tangent(ial) (*to, à*); **2.** *su./f* ✕ tangent; F *prendre la* ~*e, s'échapper par la* ~*e* make off; dodge the issue; wriggle out; **tangenter** [~ʒɑ̃'te] (1a) *v/t.* run along(side), border, skirt; **tangible** [~'ʒibl] tangible.

tanguer ⚓, ✈ [tɑ̃'ge] (1m) *v/i.* pitch, rock; be down by the head.

tanière [ta'njɛːr] *f* den, lair (*a. fig.*); (*fox-*)hole, earth.

tank ✕ [tɑ̃ːk] *m* tank; **tankiste** ✕ [tɑ̃'kist] *m* member of a tank crew.

tannant, e [ta'nɑ̃, ~'nɑ̃ːt] tanning; F tiresome; boring.

tanne [tan] *f* ✷ *face*: blackhead; ⊕ *leather*: spot.

tanné, e [ta'ne] **1.** *adj.* tan(ned); **2.** *su./m colour*: tan; **tanner** [~] (1a) *v/t.* ⊕ tan; F irritate; pester; F thrash (*s.o.*); F ~ *le cuir à q.* tan s.o.'s hide;

tannerie ⊕ [tan'ri] *f* tannery; *trade*: tanning; **tanneur** ⊕ [ta'nœːr] *m* tanner; **tan(n)in** [~'nɛ̃] *m* tannin; **tan(n)iser** ⊕ [~ni'ze] (1a) *v/t.* treat (*s.th.*) with tannin.

tan-sad [tɑ̃'sad] *m* pillion.

tant [tɑ̃] *adv.* so much; so *or* as many; so; as much, as hard (as, que); so *or* as long (as, que); ~ *bien que mal* somehow (or other); ~ *de fois* so often; ~ *heureuse qu'elle paraisse* however happy she may seem; ~ *il y a que* the fact remains, however, that; ~ *mieux!* so much the better!; F *good!*; ~ *pis!* so much the worse!; what a pity!; F *too bad!*; ~ *s'en faut* far from it; ~ *s'en faut que* (*sbj.*) far from (*ger.*); ~ *soit peu* ever so little; even a little; somewhat; *en* ~ *que* in so far as (+ *verb*); considered as (+ *su.*); *si* ~ *est que* if indeed.

tante [tɑ̃ːt] *f* aunt; *sl.* queer, nancyboy; F *chez ma* ~ pawned, in pawn.

tantième ✝ [tɑ̃'tjɛm] *m* percentage, share.

tantinet F [tɑ̃ti'ne] *m*: *un* ~ a little, a bit.

tantôt [tɑ̃'to] **1.** *adv.* presently, soon, by and by; a little while ago; just now; ~ ... ~ ... now ... now ...; sometimes ... sometimes ...; *à* ~! good-bye for the present!; F so long!; **2.** *su./m* F afternoon.

taon *zo.* [tɑ̃] *m* gad-fly, horse-fly.

tapage [ta'paːʒ] *m* noise; din; *fig.* row; fuss; F touching (*s.o. for money*); *faire du* ~ make a stir (*news*); **tapageur, -euse** [~pa'ʒœːr, ~'ʒøːz] **1.** *adj.* noisy, rowdy; *cost.* flashy; *fig.* blustering (*manner, speech*); **2.** *su.* rowdy, roisterer; brawler; noisy person; ⚖ disturber of the peace; **tape** [tap] *f* slap; F ✝ *ramasser une* ~ fail, F flop; **tapé, e** [ta'pe] **1.** *adj.* dried (*fruit*); *fig.* first-class; *sl.* crazy, nutty; *réponse f* ~*e* smart answer; **2.** *su./f* F lots *pl.*, heaps *pl.*; tons *pl.*; *children*: horde; **tape-à-l'œil** F [tapa'lœj] **1.** *adj.* showy, flashy; **2.** *su./m* show, window-dressing; **tapecul** [tap'ky] *m* see-saw, *Am.* teeter-totter; gig; *pej. carriage*: rattletrap; **taper** [ta'pe] (1a) *v/t.* plug, stop (up); F smack, slap; slam (*the door*); ♪ thump out (*a tune*), beat (*a drum*); type (*a letter etc.*); dab on (*paint*); F touch (*s.o.*) (*for, de*); *sl.*

se ~ qch. put s.th. away (= *eat, drink*); do s.th.; saddle o.s. with s.th.; *sl.* tu peux te ~! nothing doing!; *sl.* you've had it!; *v/i.* knock; hit; bang; ~ dans l'œil à take (*s.o. 's*) fancy; ~ du pied stamp (one's foot); ~ sur q. slate s.o., pitch into s.o.; F ~ sur le ventre à q. give s.o. a dig in the waistcoat; **tapette** [~'pɛt] *f* gentle tap; ⊕ bat (*for corking bottles*); fly-swatter; carpet-beater; F chatter-box; *sl.* queer, fairy, nancy-boy; F avoir une de ces ~s (or une fière ~) be a real chatterbox; **tapeur** F [~'pœːr] *m* cadger; piano strummer.

tapinois [tapi'nwa] *adv.*: en ~ quietly, on the sly.

tapioca [tapjɔ'ka] *m* tapioca; *cuis.* tapioca soup.

tapir[1] [ta'piːr] (2a) *v/t.*: se ~ crouch; hide (o.s. away); être tapi crouch; hide, be hidden; *fig.* lurk.

tapir[2] *zo.* [~] *m* tapir.

tapis [ta'pi] *m* carpet; cloth; ⚡ ~ chauffant electrically heated mat; ⊕ ~ roulant endless belt, assembly line; ~ vert (gaming) table; *fig.* mettre sur le ~ bring (*s.th.*) up (for discussion); **tapisser** [~pi'se] (1a) *v/t.* paper (*a room*); hang (*a wall*) with tapestry; *fig.* cover, line; **tapisserie** [~pis'ri] *f* tapestry, hangings *pl.*; tapestry-weaving; tapestry-work; wall-paper; *fig.* faire ~ be a wall-flower (*at a dance*); pantoufles *f/pl.* en ~ carpet-slippers; **tapissier, -ère** [~pi'sje, ~'sjeːr] *su.* tapestry-maker; *furniture:* uphol-sterer; crewel-worker; *su./f* deliv-ery-van; covered waggon.

tapon † [ta'pɔ̃] *m* plug, stopper; en ~ screwed up.

tapoter F [tapɔ'te] (1a) *v/t.* tap; pat; strum (*a tune*); drum (*on the table*).

taquer *typ.* [ta'ke] (1m) *v/t.* plane (down); **taquet** [~'ke] *m* ⊕ wedge, angle-block; *metall.* lug; ⚓ cleat.

taquin, e [ta'kɛ̃, ~'kin] 1. *adj.* (fond of) teasing; 2. *su.* tease; **taquiner** [~ki'ne] (1a) *v/t.* tease; *fig.* worry; **taquinerie** [~kin'ri] *f* teasing (disposition).

tarabiscoté, e [tarabiskɔ'te] ⊕ grooved; *fig.* over-elaborate (*style*).

tarabuster F [tarabys'te] (1a) *v/t.* pester (*person*); worry, bother (*thing, idea, etc.*).   [tare.

tarage † [ta'raːʒ] *m* allowance for

tarare ⚡ [ta'raːr] *m* winnower.

taratata! F [tarata'ta] *int.* fiddle-sticks!

taraud ⊕ [ta'ro] *m* (screw-)tap; **taraudage** ⊕ [taro'daːʒ] *m* nut etc.: tapping; screw-cutting; screw-pitch; **tarauder** [~'de] (1a) *v/t.* ⊕ tap, cut; *a. fig.* pierce; **taraudeuse** ⊕ [~'døːz] *f machine:* screw-cutter, thread-cutter.

tard [taːr] 1. *adv.* late; au plus ~ at the latest; il se fait ~ it is getting late; pas plus ~ que ... only ..., not later than ...; tôt ou ~ sooner or later; 2. *su./m:* sur le ~ late in the day; *fig.* late in life; **tarder** [tar'de] (1a) *v/i.* delay; il me tarde de (*inf.*) I am anxious to (*inf.*); ne pas ~ à (*inf.*) not to have to wait long be-fore (*ger.*); sans (plus) ~ without (further) delay; **tardif, -ve** [~'dif, ~'diːv] late; belated (*apology, re-gret*); *fig.* slow (to, à); backward (*fruit, a. fig. intelligence*); **tardi-grade** *zo.* [~di'grad] *adj., a. su./m* tardigrade; **tardillon** [~di'jɔ̃] *m animal:* latest born; *fig.* Benjamin (*of a family*); **tardiveté** [~div'te] *f* lateness; slowness; backwardness.

tare [taːr] *f* ✝ tare; *fig.* defect, flaw, taint; ✝ faire la ~ allow for the tare; **taré, e** [ta're] spoiled, damaged, with a defect; *a. fig.* tainted; *fig.* corrupt.

tarantelle ♪ *etc.* [tarɑ̃'tɛl] *f* taran-tella.

tarentule *zo.* [tarɑ̃'tyl] *f* tarantula; *fig.* être piqué (or mordu) de la ~ be very excited.

tarer ✝ [ta're] (1a) *v/t.* tare.

targette ⊕ [tar'ʒɛt] *f* sash-bolt; flat door-bolt.

targuer [tar'ge] (1m) *v/t.*: se ~ de pride o.s. on (s.th., qch.; doing, faire); claim (*a privilege*).

tarière ⊕ [ta'rjeːr] *f* auger; drill; ⚒ borer.

tarif [ta'rif] *m* price-list, tariff; rate(s *pl.*); schedule of charges; ~ différentiel (préférentiel) differential (preferential) tariff; ~ postal post-age (rates *pl.*); ~ réduit reduced tariff; plein ~ *goods:* full tariff; *per-son:* full fare; **tarifaire** [tari'feːr] tariff-...; **tarifer** [~'fe] (1a) *v/t.* fix the rate of (*a duty, a tariff*); fix the price of (*goods*); **tarification** [~fi-ka'sjɔ̃] *f* tariffing.

tarin *sl.* [taˈrɛ̃] *m* conk (= *nose*).

tarir [taˈriːr] (2a) *v/t.* dry up; *fig.* exhaust; *v/i. a. se* ~ dry up, run dry; *fig.* cease; **tarissement** [ˌrisˈmɑ̃] *m* drying up; *fig.* exhausting.

tarot [taˈro] *m cards*: tarot pack; ~s *pl. cards, game*: tarots.

tarse *anat.* [tars] *m* tarsus; F *human foot*: instep; **tarsien, -enne** *anat.* [tarˈsjɛ̃, ~ˈsjɛn] tarsal.

tartan *tex.* [tarˈtɑ̃] *m* tartan.

tartarinade F [tartariˈnad] *f* boast.

tarte *cuis.* [tart] *f* (open) tart; flan; **tartelette** *cuis.* [ˌˈlɛt] *f* tartlet; **tartine** [tarˈtin] *f* slice of bread and butter *or* jam *etc.*; F *fig.* rigmarole; long-winded speech *or* article *or* sermon; **tartiner** [ˌtiˈne] (1a) *v/t.* spread (*bread*) (with, de); butter (*bread*); spread (*butter etc.*) (on, sur); *fromage m à* ~ cheese spread.

tartrate ⚗ [tarˈtrat] *m* tartrate; **tartre** [tartr] *m* tartar (*a.* ⚗, *a. dental*); ⊕ *boiler*: scale, fur; **tartreux, -euse** [tarˈtrø, ~ˈtrøːz] tartarous; ⊕ furry, scaly; **tartrique** ⚗ [ˌˈtrik] tartaric (*acid*).

tartufe [tarˈtyf] *m* hypocrite; **tartuferie** [ˌtyˈfri] *f* (piece of) hypocrisy, cant.

tas [tɑ] *m* heap, pile (*a. fig. of things*); *fig.* crowd, lot; *lies, a. people*: pack; ⊕ hand *or* small anvil; *mettre en* ~ pile up; *sur le* ~ on the job, at work.

tasse [tɑːs] *f* cup; ~ *à café* coffee-cup; ~ *de café* cup of coffee.

tasseau [tɑˈso] *m* ⚠ bracket; (supporting) batten; brick foundation.

tassée [tɑˈse] *f* cupful.

tassement [tɑsˈmɑ̃] *m* sinking; settling; subsidence; ✝, *fig.* fall(-off), drop; **tasser** [tɑˈse] (1a) *v/t.* cram together; pack (tightly); shake down; *se* ~ crowd together; squeeze up; ⚠ settle; ⚠ sink, subside; ✝ weaken; shrink, grow smaller (*with age*) (*person*); F *fig.* settle down, come out in the wash.

tâter [tɑˈte] (1a) *v/t.* touch, feel; grope for (*s.th.*); *fig.* feel out, explore, try; ☞ feel (*the pulse*); *v/i.*: ~ *à* (*or* de) taste, try; *fig.* ~ *du* try (one's hand at) (*work*); **tâte-vin** [tɑtˈvɛ̃] *m/inv. instrument*: winetaster; sampling-tube.

tatillon, -onne F [tatiˈjɔ̃, ~ˈjɔn] **1.** *adj.* niggling, finicky; over-particular; **2.** *su.* fusspot; busybody; **tatillonner** F [ˌjɔˈne] (1a) *v/i.* niggle, fuss over details; be meddlesome.

tâtonner [tɑtɔˈne] (1a) *v/i.* feel one's way (*a. fig.*); grope; fumble; **tâtonneur** *m*, **-euse** *f* [ˌtɔˈnœːr, ~ˈnøːz] groper, fumbler; **tâtons** [ˌˈtɔ̃] *adv.*: *à* ~ gropingly; *marcher etc. à* ~ grope one's way.

tatou *zo.* [taˈtu] *m* armadillo.

tatouage [taˈtwaːʒ] *m* tattooing; *design*: tattoo; **tatouer** [ˌˈtwe] (1p) *v/t.* tattoo; **tatoueur** [ˌˈtwœːr] *m* tattooist.

taudis [toˈdi] *m* hovel; wretched room; squalid hole; ~ *pl.* slums.

taule [toːl] *f see* **tôle**.

taupe [toːp] *f zo.* mole; ✝ moleskin; F *myope comme une* ~ (as) blind as a bat; *sl. pej. vieille* ~ old hag; **taupinière** [ˌpiˈnjɛːr] *f* molehill.

taureau [tɔˈro] *m* bull; *astr. le* ♉ Taurus, the Bull; *avoir un cou de* ~ be bull-necked; *course f de* ~x bull-fight; **taurillon** [ˌriˈjɔ̃] *m* bull-calf; **tauromachie** [ˌrɔmaˈʃi] *f* bull-fighting. [redundancy.)

tautologie [totɔlɔˈʒi] *f* tautology,)

taux [to] *m* rate (*a.* ✝); ✝ fixed price; ⊕ ratio; ⚗ proportion, amount; ✝ ~ *de change* (rate of) exchange; ~ *de charge* load per unit area; ~ *de la mortalité* death-rate; ✝ ~ *d'escompte* bank rate; ✝ ~ *d'intérêt* rate of interest; *au* ~ at the rate of.

tavelé, e [tavˈle] marked; spotted, speckled; **tavelure** [ˌˈlyːr] *f* mark; spot, speckle.

taverne [taˈvɛrn] *f* tavern; public house, F pub; café-restaurant.

taxateur [taksaˈtœːr] *m* assessor; ⚖ taxing master; **taxation** [ˌˈsjɔ̃] *f* fixing of prices *etc.*; *admin., a.* ⚖ taxation; *admin.* assessment; **taxe** [taks] *f admin.* tax, duty; rate; fixed price; ✝ controlled price; **taxer** [takˈse] (1a) *v/t.* tax; put a tax on (*goods*); fix (*the price*); fix the price *or* rate of; *fig.* accuse (of, de).

taxi [takˈsi] *m* taxi(-cab), cab; ~mètre [ˌsiˈmɛtr] *m* taximeter; ~phone *teleph.* [ˌsiˈfɔn] *m* (public) call-box.

tayloriser ⊕ [tɛlɔriˈze] (1a) *v/t.* Taylorize; **taylorisme** ⊕ [ˌˈrism] *m* Taylorism.

tchécoslovaque [tʃekɔslɔ'vak] *adj.*, *a. su.* ♀ Czechoslovak; **tchèque** [tʃɛk] **1.** *adj.* Czech; **2.** *su./m ling.* Czech; *su.* ♀ Czech.

te [tə] **1.** *pron./pers.* you; to you; **2.** *pron./rfl.* yourself, to yourself.

té [te] *m letter*: T; T-square; △ tee-iron.

technicien *m*, **-enne** *f* [tɛkni'sjɛ̃, ~'sjɛn] technician; **techni(ci)ser** [~(si)'ze] (1a) *v/t.* ⊕ mechanize; *fig.* technicalize; **technicité** [~si'te] *f* technicality; **technique** [tɛk'nik] **1.** *adj.* technical; **2.** *su./f* technique; ~ électrique electrical engineering; **technocrate** [~'krat] *m* technocrat; **technocratie** [~nɔkra'si] *f* technocracy; **technocratique** [~nɔkra'tik] technocratic; **technologie** [~nɔb'ʒi] *f* technology; **technologique** [~nɔb'ʒik] technological.

te(c)k ♀, ♣ [tɛk] *m* teak.

tectrice *orn.* [tɛk'tris] *adj./f: plumes f/pl.* ~s tectrices.

tégument ♀, *anat.*, *zo.* [tegy'mɑ̃] *m* tegument.

teigne [tɛɲ] *f zo.* moth; ♣ tinea, scalp-disease; ♣ scurf; *vet.* thrush; F *fig.* pest; **teigneux, -euse** [tɛ'ɲø, ~'ɲøːz] **1.** *adj.* suffering from scalp-disease; **2.** *su.* person suffering from scalp-disease.

teignis [tɛ'ɲi] *1st p. sg. p.s. of teindre;* **teignons** [~'ɲɔ̃] *1st p. pl. pres. of teindre;* **teindre** [tɛ̃ːdr] (4m) *v/t.* dye (blue *etc.*, en bleu *etc.*); stain (*a. fig.*); se ~ dye one's hair; **teins** [tɛ̃] *1st p. sg. pres. of teindre;* **teint, teinte** [tɛ̃, tɛ̃ːt] **1.** *p.p. of teindre;* **2.** *su./m* dye, colo(u)r; complexion; *tex.* bon (*or* grand) ~ fast colo(u)r; *fig.* partisan m bon ~ staunch supporter; petit ~ fading dye; *su./f* tint, hue, shade; *fig.* touch, tinge; **teinter** [tɛ̃'te] (1a) *v/t.* tint; *fig.* tinge (with, de); **teinture** [~'tyːr] *f tex.*, *a. hair*: dye(ing); *phot. etc.* tinting; colo(u)r, hue; *fig.* touch; ♣ₘₛ ♣ tincture; **teinturerie** ⊕ [~tyr'ri] *f* (dry) cleaner's, cleaners *pl.*; dye-works *usu. sg.*; dyeing; **teinturier** [~ty'rje] *m* (dry) cleaner, dyer.

tel *m*, **telle** *f*, **tels** *m/pl.*, **telles** *f/pl.* [tɛl] **1.** *adj./indef.* such; so great; like; as; ~ maître, ~ valet like master, like man; ~ que (such) as; like; such that; ~ quel ordinary; just as he *or* it is *or* was; ♣ with all faults;

à telle ville in such and such a town; de telle sorte que in such a way that; il n'y a rien de ~ que there's nothing like; un ~ repas such a meal; **2.** *pron./indef.* (such a) one; some; Monsieur un ~ (*or* Un ♀) Mr. So-and-so; Madame une telle (*or* Une Telle) Mrs. So-and-so; ~ qui he who.

télautographe [telotɔ'graf] *m* telewriter.

télé F [te'le] television, *Br.* F telly. **télé...** [tele] tele...; **~commande** [~kɔ'mɑ̃ːd] *f* remote control; **~commander** [~kɔmɑ̃'de] (1a) *v/t.* operate by remote control; **~communication** [~kɔmynika'sjɔ̃] *f* telecommunication; **~distribution** [~distriby'sjɔ̃] *f* cable television; **~enseignement** [~ɑ̃sɛɲ'mɑ̃] *m* educational broadcast *or* television program(me)s *pl.*; **~férique** [~fe'rik] *m see* téléphérique; **~génique** *telev.* [~ʒe'nik] telegenous; **~gramme** [~'gram] *m* telegram, F wire; **~graphe** [~'graf] *m* telegraph; **~graphie** [~gra'fi] *f* telegraphy; ~ sans fil, *abbr.* T.S.F. wireless, radio; **~graphier** [~gra'fje] (1o) *vt/i.* telegraph, wire; **~graphique** [~gra'fik] telegraphic; mandat *m* ~ telegraph(ic) money order; poteau *m* ~ telegraph-pole; réponse *f* ~ reply by wire *or* cable; **~graphiste** [~gra'fist] *su.* telegraph operator; telegraph boy *or* messenger; **~guidé, e** [~gi'de] radio-controlled; guided (*missile*); **~imprimeur** [~ɛ̃pri'mœːr] *m* teleprinter; **~mètre** *phot.* [~'mɛtr] *m* rangefinder; **~objectif** *phot.* [~ɔbʒɛk'tif] *m* telephoto lens; **~phérique** [~fe'rik] *m* telpher railway; cableway; cable car; **~phone** [~'fɔn] *m* telephone, F phone; ~ intérieur house telephone; internal telephone, F intercom; annuaire *m* du ~ telephone directory *or* F book; appeler q. au ~ ring s.o. up; avez-vous le ~? are you on the phone?; **~phoner** [~fɔ'ne] (1a) *vt/i.* (tele)phone (s.o., à q.); **~phonie** [~fɔ'ni] *f* telephony; ~ sans fil radiotelephony; **~phonique** [~fɔ'nik] telephone...; telephonic; cabine *f* (*or* cabinet *m*) ~ telephone booth, call-box; **~phoniste** [~fɔ'nist] *su.* telephone operator.

télescopage [telɛskɔ'paːʒ] *m* smashing up; concertinaing; telescoping;

télescope

traffic: ~ *en serie* pile-up; **télescope**
[~'kɔp] *m* telescope; **télescoper** ⚙
etc. [~kɔ'pe] (1a) *v/t.* smash up, crash
into; *se* ~ concertina, telescope.

télé...: ~**scripteur** ✎ [teleskrip'tœːr]
m teleprinter; ~**spectateur** *m*, **-tri-**
ce *f* telev. [~spɛkta'tœːr, ~'tris]
(tele-)viewer; ~**viser** [~vi'ze] (1a)
v/t. televise; ~**viseur** [~vi'zœːr] *m*
television set; televisor; ~**vision**
[~vi'zjɔ̃] *f* television; ~ *en couleurs*
colo(u)r television; ~ *par câble* cable
television.

télex [te'lɛks] *m* telex; **télexer**
[~lɛk'se] (1a) *v/t.* telex.

tellement [tel'mɑ̃] *adv.* so, in such
a way; to such an extent.

tellure 🜍 [tel'lyːr] *m* tellurium;
tellureux, -euse 🜍 [telly'rø, ~-
'røːz] tellurous; **tellurien, -enne**
[~'rjɛ̃, ~'rjɛn] tellurian; earth...

téméraire [teme'rɛːr] **1.** *adj.* rash
(*a. fig. judgment etc.*), reckless; daring; **2.** *su.* rash person; dare-devil;
témérité [~ri'te] *f* temerity, rashness, recklessness; piece of daring;
bold speech.

témoignage [temwa'ɲaːʒ] *m* 🕮 *etc.*
evidence (*a. fig.*); 🕮 hearing (of
witness); *eccl.* witness; *fig.* proof;
fig. en ~ *de* as a token of; *porter* ~
certify; *rendre* ~ bear witness (to,
à); **témoigner** [~'ɲe] (1a) *vt/i.*
testify; *v/i.* bear witness; *v/t.* show;
bear witness to; **témoin** [tem'wɛ̃]
1. *su./m* witness; *duel:* second;
boundary mark; 🕮 reference solution; sample; *sp.* stick (*etc. in relay
race*); 🕮 *à charge (décharge)*
prosecution (defence) witness; ~
oculaire eye witness; **2.** *adj./inv.*
pilot..., test...; control...; *apparte-*
ment m ~ show flat; *lampe f* ~ warning
light.

tempe *anat.* [tɑ̃ːp] *f* temple.

tempérament [tɑ̃pera'mɑ̃] *m* temperament; constitution; disposition;
✝ *à* ~ by instal(l)ments, on the
instal(l)ment plan; *vente f à* ~ hire-
purchase; sale on the instalment
plan.

tempérance [tɑ̃pe'rɑ̃ːs] *f* temper-
ance, moderation; **tempérant, e**
[~'rɑ̃, ~'rɑ̃ːt] temperate, moderate;
🜍 sedative; **température** [~ra'tyːr]
f temperature; 🜍 (*boiling-, freez-*
ing-)point; *fig.* feeling; 🜍 *avoir de*
la ~ have a temperature; **tempéré, e**

[~'re] temperate, moderate (*climate,
a. fig. speech*); *fig.* sober, restrained;
♪ equally tempered; *geog.* zone *f* ~e
temperate zone; **tempérer** [~'re]
(1f) *v/t.* moderate, temper (*a. fig.*); *se*
~ moderate.

tempête [tɑ̃'pɛːt] *f* wind, *a. fig.*:
storm; ⚓ hurricane; **tempêter** F
[~pɛ'te] (1a) *v/i.* rant and rave, storm,
rage; **tempétueux, -euse** [~pe'tɥø,
~'tɥøːz] stormy, tempestuous (*a.
fig.*).

temple [tɑ̃ːpl] *m* temple (*a. hist.* ⚜);
protestantism: church, chapel; *free-*
masonry: lodge; **templier** [tɑ̃pli'e]
m Knight Templar; F *jurer comme*
un ~ swear like a trooper.

temporaire [tɑ̃pɔ'rɛːr] temporary;
provisional; ♪ *time(-value)*.

temporal, e, *m/pl.* **-aux** *anat.* [tɑ̃pɔ-
'ral, ~'ro] **1.** *adj.* temporal; **2.** *su./m*
temporal (bone).

temporalité *eccl.* ✝ [tɑ̃pɔrali'te] *f*
temporality; **temporel, -elle** [~-
'rɛl] **1.** *adj.* secular; temporal (=
not eternal, not spiritual); **2.** *su./m*
temporal power; revenue, tempo-
ralities *pl.* (*of a benefice*).

temporisateur, -trice [tɑ̃pɔriza-
'tœːr, ~'tris] **1.** *adj.* temporizing;
2. *su.* temporizer; ⊕ *welding:* timer;
temporisation [~za'sjɔ̃] *f* tempo-
rization, temporizing; **temporiser**
[~'ze] (1a) *v/i.* temporize, delay
action deliberately, play for time,
stall.

temps[1] [tɑ̃] *m* time (*a.* ♪); while;
times *pl.*; 🜍, ⊕ phase; *mot. etc.*
stroke; ♪ *a.* beat; *gramm.* tense; *à*
deux ~ two-stroke (*engine*); *à* ~ in (the
nick of) time; *avec le* ~ in (the course
of) time; *de mon* ~ in my time; *de* ~ *à*
autre (or en ~) now and then, from
time to time; *en même* ~ at the same
time; *en* ~ *de guerre* in wartime;
entre ~ meanwhile; *être de son* ~ keep
up with the times; *gagner du* ~ play
for time; *il est grand* ~ it is high time
(*to inf., de inf.; that ind., que sbj.*); *le*
bon vieux ~ the good old days *pl.*; *les* ~
pl. sont durs times are hard; *le* ~, *c'est*
de l'argent time is money; ♪ *mesure f*
à deux ~ duple time; (*ne pas*) *avoir le* ~
de (*inf.*) have (no) time to (*inf.*).

temps[2] [tɑ̃] *m* weather; *quel* ~ *fait-il?*
what is the weather like?; *il fait beau*
(*mauvais*) ~ the weather is fine (bad).

tenable [tə'nabl] ✖, *a. fig.* tenable;

habitable (*house*); *fig. pas* ~ unbearable.

tenace [tə'nas] tenacious; clinging
(*perfume, a.* 🐝); adhesive; stiff
(*soil*); tough (*metal*); *fig.* stubborn,
persistent; retentive (*memory*); **ténacité** [tenasi'te] *f* tenacity (*a.fig.*);
stickiness; *soil*: stiffness; *metal*:
toughness; *fig.* stubbornness; dog-
gedness; *memory*: retentiveness;
avec ~ tenaciously; stubbornly.

tenaille ⊕ [tə'nɑːj] *f* tongs *pl.*;
clamp; pliers *pl.*; pincers *pl.* (*a.* ✂️);
tenailler *fig.* [~nɑ'je] (1a) *v/t.*
torture.

tenancier [tənɑ'sje] *m* manager;
tenant-farmer; keeper; † freeholder;
tenant, e [~'nɑ̃, ~'nɑ̃ːt] 1. *adj.*: *séance f* ~*e* during the sitting; *fig.* then
and there; 2. *su./m* supporter; *sp. title
etc.*: holder; *bet*: taker; ⚖️ *d'un seul* ~
all in one block; continuous; ~*s pl.*
lands bordering on an estate; ~*s pl. et
aboutissants m/pl.* estate; adjacent
parts; *fig.* the full details, *the* ins and
outs.

tendance [tɑ̃'dɑ̃ːs] *f* tendency; lean-
ings *pl.*; drift, trend; *à* ~ tendentious
(*book*); *avoir* ~ *à* tend to, be inclined
to; **tendancieux, -euse** [~dɑ̃'sjø,
~'sjøːz] tendentious; ⚖️ leading
(*question*).

tender 🚂 [tɑ̃'dɛːr] *m* tender.

tenderie *hunt.* [tɑ̃'dri] *f* (*bird-*)
snare; setting of snares (*for birds*).

tendeur, -euse [tɑ̃'dœːr, ~'døːz] *su.*
carpet: layer; *wallpaper*: hanger;
hunt. snares: setter; *su./m* ⊕ tight-
ener; (*trouser- etc.*)stretcher; (*shoe-*)
tree; *mot.* tension-rod; ~ *de chaine*
chain-adjuster.

tendineux, -euse [tɑ̃di'nø, ~'nøːz]
anat. tendinous; *cuis.* stringy (*meat*).

tendoir [tɑ̃'dwaːr] *m* clothes-line;
tex. tenter.

tendon *anat.* [tɑ̃'dɔ̃] *m* tendon,
sinew.

tendre[1] [tɑ̃'dr] (4a) *v/t.* stretch;
hang (*wallpaper*), paper (*a room*);
lay (*a carpet, a snare*); pitch (*a
tent*); spread (*a net, a sail*); hold
out (*one's hand*); offer (*one's hand
etc.*); *fig.* strain; ~ *l'oreille* prick up
one's ears; *v/i.*: ~ *à* tend towards *s.th.*
or to *do s.th.*; aim at *s.th.* or to *do s.th.*

tendre[2] [tɑ̃'dr] tender (*heart, meat,
skin, years, youth*); soft (*colour,
grass, metal, pencil, stone, wood,*

etc.); early (*childhood, years*); *fig.*
affectionate, fond; **tendresse** [tɑ̃-
'drɛs] *f* tenderness; love; ~*s pl.*
caresses, endearments; **tendron**
[~'drɔ̃] *m* 🐝 tender shoot; *cuis.*
gristle; F *fig.* little *or* young girl.

tendu, e [tɑ̃'dy] 1. *p.p. of tendre*[1];
2. *adj.* stretched; tight; taut; tense,
strained (*a. fig.*).

ténèbres [te'nɛːbr] *f/pl.* darkness
sg. (*a. fig.*), gloom *sg.*; *eccl.* tenebrae;
ténébreux, -euse [~ne'brø, ~'brøːz]
dark, gloomy; lowering (*sky*); *fig.*
deep, sinister; obscure (*style*).

teneur[1], **-euse** [tə'nœːr, ~'nøːz] *su.*
holder; *su./m*: 🕊️ ~ *de livres* book-
keeper.

teneur[2] [tə'nœːr] *f* tenor (*of book,
conduct, etc.*); ⊕, 🔬 percentage,
amount; *solution*: strength; *min.*
grade; (*gold- etc.*)content; 🔬 ~ *en
alcool* alcoholic content.

ténia 🔬, *zo.* [te'nja] *m* taenia, tapeworm; **ténifuge** 🔬 [~ni'fyːʒ] *adj.,
a. su./m* t(a)enifuge.

tenir [tə'niːr] (2h) 1. *v/t.* hold (*a. a
meeting*); have, possess; grasp (*a. =
understand*); retain; *fig.* have in
hand, control; manage, run (*a
firm*); keep; contain (*a pint*); *fig.*
accommodate, seat (*200 persons*);
⚠️ support; occupy, take up; consider, think; regard (*as, pour*); ⚓
hug (*the coast*); *thea.* take, play
(*a rôle*); 🕊️ stock (*goods*); take (on)
(*a bet*); ~ *compte de* take (*s.th.*) into
account; ~ *en respect* hold in awe;
~ *l'eau* be watertight; ~ *le lit* stay
in bed; 🕊️ ~ *les livres* do the book-
keeping; ~ *sa langue* hold one's
tongue; ~ *sa promesse* keep one's
word; *mot.* ~ (*bien*) *la route* hold the
road well; ~ *son tempérament de son
père* have got one's temper from
one's father; ~ *tête à* resist; *tenez
votre droite* keep to the right; *se* ~
keep (*quiet*); remain (*standing*); be;
s'en ~ *à* keep to; be satisfied with; 2.
v/i. hold; hold firm; ⚔️ hold out;
remain; *fig.* last; 🕊️ be held (*market*);
⚖️ sit; border (on, *à*) (*land*); *fig.* be
joined (to, *à*); be keen (on *ger.*, *à
inf.*); ~ *à* value (*s.th.*); be due to,
depend on; ~ *à ce que* (*sbj.*) be
anxious that (*ind.*); ~ *bon* (*or ferme*)
stand firm; hold out; ⚓ hold tight; ~
de take after (*s.o.*), be akin to (*s.th.*); ~
pour be in favo(u)r of; *en* ~ *pour* be

fond of (s.o.), stick to (s.th.); je n'y tiens pas I don't care for it, F I am not keen (on it); ne pouvoir plus y ~ be unable to stand it; tiens!, tenez! look (here)!; here!; tiens! well!; really?

tennis [tɛ'nis] m (lawn) tennis; tennis court; pl. (a. chaussures f de ~) plimsolls, Am. sneakers; ~ de table table tennis.

tenon [tə'nɔ̃] m ⊕ tenon; ⊕ lug; ⚓ nut.

ténor ♩ [te'nɔ:r] m tenor; fort ~ heroic tenor.

tenseur [tɑ̃'sœːr] adj., a. su./m ♭, anat. tensor; **tension** [~'sjɔ̃] f phys., ⚡, etc., a. fig. tension; ⊕, ♒ blood, steam: pressure; ⚡ voltage; ✝ prices: hardness, firmness; ♒ (a. ~ artérielle) blood-pressure; ⚡ ~ de service operating potential; ♒ avoir de la ~ have high blood pressure; ⚡ sous ~ live (wire); **tensiomètre** [~sjɔ'mɛːtr] m blood pressure meter.

tentacule zo. [tɑ̃ta'kyl] m tentacle.

tentant, e [tɑ̃'tɑ̃, ~'tɑ̃:t] tempting, alluring; **tentateur, -trice** [tɑ̃ta-'tœːr, ~'tris] 1. adj. tempting; 2. su./m tempter; su./f temptress; **tentation** [~'sjɔ̃] f temptation (to inf., de inf.); **tentative** [~'tiːv] f attempt (at, de); ⚖ ~ d'assassinat attempted murder.

tente [tɑ̃:t] f tent; fair etc.: booth; ⚓ awning; dresser une ~ pitch a tent.

tenter [tɑ̃'te] (1a) v/t. tempt (s.o.); put to the test; ✗ ~ l'assaut de attempt (a place); être tenté de (inf.) be tempted to (inf.); v/i.: ~ de (inf.) try to (inf.), attempt to (inf.).

tenture [tɑ̃'tyːr] f (paper-)hanging; tapestry; hangings pl.; wallpaper.

tenu, e [tə'ny] 1. p.p. of tenir; 2. su./f holding (a. ⚖); ✝ books, shop, etc.: keeping; fig. shape; person: bearing; behavio(u)r; ⊕ maintenance; ⚖ etc. sitting; cost., a. ✗ dress; ✝ market, prices: firmness; ♩ sustained note; ✗ ~e de campagne battle-dress; ~ de détente leisure wear; mot. ~e de route road-holding qualities pl.; ~e de soirée evening dress; ~e de ville morning or street dress; ✗ walking-out dress; de la ~e! school etc.: behave yourself!; ✗ en grande (petite) ~e in full dress (undress); en petite ~, en ~ légère in light clothing; F scantily dressed.

ténu, e [te'ny] thin, slender; fig. fine; **ténuité** [~nɥi'te] f tenuousness; slenderness; thinness (a. of a liquid); sand, a. fig.: fineness.

ter [tɛːr] adv. three times, ♩ ter; for the third time; in house numbers: 3ter 3b.

tercet ♩ [tɛr'sɛ] m triplet (a. prosody).

térébenthène ♣ [terebɑ̃'tɛn] m terebenthene; **térébenthine** ♣ [~'tin] f turpentine.

térébrant, e [tere'brɑ̃, ~'brɑ̃:t] zo. boring; ♒ terebrating (pain).

tergiversation [tɛrʒivɛrsa'sjɔ̃] f equivocation; beating about the bush; **tergiverser** [~'se] (1a) v/i. shilly-shally; beat about the bush.

terme [tɛrm] m end, conclusion; statue: terminus; ⚖ quarter; quarter's rent; quarter day; ✗, ✝, ⚖ time; ✝ stocks etc.: settlement; delay (for payment); ✝ price: instalment; expression, ♭, phls., ⚖ contract: term; ⚖ ~ pl. wording sg.; conditions; ~ de métier technical term; à ~ in due time; à court (long) ~ ✝ short- (long-)dated; fig. short- (long-)term (policy etc.); ✝ demander un ~ de grâce ask for time to pay; en ~s de commerce in commercial language; en propres ~s in so many words; fig. être en bons ~s avec be on good terms with; ✝ opérations f/pl. à ~ forward deals; vente f (achat m) à ~ credit sale (purchase).

terminaison [tɛrminɛ'zɔ̃] f ending, termination (a. gramm.); **terminal, e**, m/pl. -aux adj., a. su./m [~'nal, ~'no] terminal; **terminer** [~'ne] (1a) v/t. terminate; end, finish, complete; se ~ come to an end; gramm. se ~ en end in.

terminologie [tɛrminɔlɔ'ʒi] f terminology; **terminologique** [~'ʒik] terminological.

terminus 🚂 etc. [tɛrmi'nys] 1. su./m terminus; 2. adj.: gare f ~ (railway) terminus.

termite zo. [tɛr'mit] m termite, white ant; **termitière** [~mi'tjɛːr] f termitary.

ternaire [tɛr'nɛːr] ♣, ♭ ternary; ♩ triple (measure). [two treys pl.\]

terne[1] [tɛrn] m lottery: tern; dice:\]

terne[2] [tɛrn] dull; colo(u)rless; tarnished (metal etc.); **ternir** [tɛr'niːr] (2a) v/t. tarnish (metal etc., a. fig. s.o.'s honour, s.o.'s reputation); fig. dull; se ~ become tarnished or dull;

ternissure [ˌnisyːr] *f* tarnish; dullness; *metal:* dull spot.
terrain [tɛˈrɛ̃] *m* ground; soil, land; terrain; ✕ (*parade-* etc.)ground; *foot.* field; *cricket:* ground; *golf:* course; ⚠ site; *geol.* rock formation; (*ne plus*) être sur son ~ be in one's element (out of one's depth).
terrasse [tɛˈras] *f* terrace; bank; ⚠ flat roof; *café:* pavement (area); *assis à la* ~ sitting outside the café; *en* ~ terraced; **terrassement** [ˌrasˈmɑ̃] *m* banking; earthwork; **terrasser** [ˌraˈse] (1a) *v/t.* embank, bank up; throw (*s.o.*) down, floor, down (*s.o.*); lay (*s.o.*) low; *fig.* overwhelm; **terrassier** [ˌraˈsje] *m* excavation *or* road worker.
terre [tɛːr] *f* earth (*a.* ⚡), ground; ✔ soil; ⊕ loam; clay; ⚓ land, shore; property, estate; *fig.* world; ~ à ~ prosaic; down-to-earth; ~ *cuite* terracotta; ~ *ferme* mainland; firm land, terra firma; ✕ armées *f/pl.* de ~ land forces; F *avoir les pieds sur* ~ have both feet firmly on the ground; *de* ~ earth(en)...; ⚡ *mettre à la* ~ earth; *mettre pied à* ~ alight; *toucher* ~ land; *se coucher par* ~ lie on the ground; *tomber par* ~ fall (flat).
terreau ✔ [tɛˈro] *m* vegetable-mo(u)ld; compost; leaf-mo(u)ld.
terre-neuvas [tɛrnœˈva] *m* Newfoundland fishing-boat *or* fisherman; **terre-neuve** *zo.* [ˌˈnœːv] *m/inv.* Newfoundland dog; **terreneuvien** [ˌnœˈvjɛ̃] *m see terre-neuvas.*
terre-plein [tɛrˈplɛ̃] *m* earth platform, terrace; 🚂 road-bed; ✕ terreplein.
terrer [tɛˈre] (1a) *v/t.* ✔ earth up; warp (*a field*); spread mo(u)ld over; ⊕ clay (*sugar*); *tex.* full; *se* ~ ✕ entrench o.s., ✕ lie flat on the ground; go to earth (*fox*); burrow (*rabbit*); **terrestre** [ˌˈrɛstr] ⚡, *zo.* terrestrial; ⚡ ground-...; ✕ land-... (*a. insurance*); *fig.* earthly, wordlly.
terreur [tɛˈrœːr] *f* terror (*a. fig.*), dread; *hist. la* ♀ the (Reign of) Terror.
terreux, -euse [tɛˈrø, ˌˈrøːz] earthy; *fig.* grubby, dirty; *fig.* muddy (*colour, complexion*).
terrible [tɛˈribl] terrible (*a. fig.*), dreadful, frightful.
terrien, -enne [tɛˈrjɛ̃, ˌˈrjɛn] **1.** *adj.*

landed (*proprietor*); country..., of the soil; **2.** *su.* earthling; ⚓ landsman, *pej.* land-lubber.
terrier [tɛˈrje] *m* (*rabbit-*)hole, (*fox-*) earth; *zo.* terrier.
terrifier [tɛriˈfje] (1o) *v/t.* terrify.
terri(l) ✕ [tɛˈri] *m* heap, tip.
terrine *cuis.* [tɛˈrin] *f* earthenware vessel *or* pot; potted meat; **terrinée** [ˌriˈne] *f* potful; panful.
territoire [tɛriˈtwaːr] *m* territory; area of jurisdiction; *anat.* area; **territorial, e,** *m/pl.* -aux [ˌtɔˈrjal, ˌˈrjo] **1.** *adj.* territorial; **2.** *su./m* ✕ territorial (soldier); *su./f* ✕ territorial army; **territorialité** [ˌtɔrjaliˈte] *f* territoriality.
terroir ✔ [tɛˈrwaːr] *m* soil; *sentir le* ~ smack of the soil.
terroriser [tɛrɔriˈze] (1a) *v/t.* terrorize; **terrorisme** [ˌˈrism] *m* terrorism; **terroriste** *pol.* [ˌˈrist] *adj., a. su.* terrorist.
tertiaire *geol. etc.* [tɛrˈsjɛːr] tertiary.
tertre [tɛrtr] *m* mound, hillock.
tes [te] *see* ton[1].
tessiture ♪ [tɛsiˈtyːr] *f* tessitura.
tesson [tɛˈsɔ̃] *m* potsherd; *glass etc.:* fragment.
test[1] 🐚 *etc.* [tɛst] *m* test; ~ *mental* intelligence test.
test[2] [tɛst] *m zo.* shell, test; ⚘ *seed:* testa, skin; **testacé, e** *zo.* [tɛstaˈse] testaceous.
testament [tɛstaˈmɑ̃] *m* ⚖ will, testament; *bibl.* Ancien (*Nouveau*) ♀ Old (New) Testament; **testamentaire** ⚖ [ˌmɑ̃ˈtɛːr] testamentary; **testateur** ⚖ [ˌˈtœːr] *m* testator *m*; **testatrice** ⚖ [ˌˈtris] *f* testatrix.
tester[1] ⚖ [tɛsˈte] (1a) *v/i.* make a will.
tester[2] 🐚 *etc.* [ˌ] (1a) *v/t.* test.
testicule *anat.* [tɛstiˈkyl] *m* testicle.
testimonial, e, *m/pl.* -aux [tɛstimɔˈnjal, ˌˈnjo] oral (*evidence*); deponed to by a witness; *lettre f* ~e testimonial.
têt 🍶 [tɛ] *m* small fire-clay cup, crucible.
tétanos [tetaˈnɔs] *m* 🐚 tetanus, lockjaw; *vet.* stag-evil.
têtard [tɛˈtaːr] *m zo.* tadpole; *sl.* child, kid; **tête** [tɛːt] *f* head (*a. = leader; a. = person*); *fig.* face; *fig.* intelligence; *fig.* memory; *fig.* selfpossession; *fig.* mind, reason; *page, class, tree, etc.:* top; *column, vehicle:*

tête-à-tête

front; *chapter*: heading; *foot.*
header; ~ *carrée* stubborn person, *sl.*
squarehead; ~ *chercheuse rocket etc.*:
homing device; *fig.* trail blazer; ~ *de
bielle* ⊕ crank-head; *mot.* big end; 💀
~ *de ligne* rail-head; ✗ ~ *de pont*
bridge-head; *iro.* ~ *d'œuf* egghead; ~
nue bareheaded; *agir* ~ *baissée* act
blindly; *avoir la* ~ *chaude (froide)* be
hot- (cool-)headed; *calculer de* ~
work (*s.th.*) out in one's head; *coup m
de* ~ rash action; *de* ~ from memory;
faire à sa ~ go one's own way; *en* ~ *à* ~
privately; *faire la* ~ *à* frown at; be
sulky with; *faire une* ~ look glum;
forte ~ strong-minded *or* unmanageable person; *sp. gagner d'une* ~
win by a head; *la* ~ *la première* head
first, headlong; *piquer une* ~ dive; *se
mettre en* ~ *de (inf.)* take it into one's
head to (*inf.*); *se monter la* ~ get
worked up; F *se payer la* ~ *de q.* make
fun of s.o.; take s.o. for a ride; *tenir* ~
à stand up to, hold one's own
against; *un homme m de* ~ a capable
man; ~-**à-tête** [tɛta'tɛːt] *m/inv.* tête-
à-tête; private interview; sofa; ~-
bêche [tɛt'bɛʃ] *adv.* head to tail; ~-
de-loup, *pl.* ~**s-de-loup** [~d'lu] *f*
wall-broom; longhandled brush.
tétée [te'te] *f (baby's)* feed; suck;
téter [~] (1f) *v/t.* baby: suck; *v/i.*
suck (*baby*).
têtière [tɛ'tjɛːr] *f* infant's cap; anti-
macasser; ⚓ *sail*: head; *horse*: head-
stall.
tétin [te'tɛ̃] *m* nipple; **tétine** [~'tin] *f
animal*: teat, dug; **téton** F [~'tɔ̃] *m
(woman's)* breast.
tétra... [tetra] tetra...; four-...; ~**èdre**
Ⓐ [~'ɛdr] 1. *adj.* tetrahedral; 2. *su./m*
tetrahedron; ~**phonie** [~fɔ'ni] *f*
quadrophony.
tétras *orn.* [te'trɑ] *m* grouse.
tette [tɛt] *f animal*: teat, dug.
têtu, e [te'ty] 1. *adj.* stubborn,
obstinate; 2. *su.* stubborn *or* obstinate person; *su./m* ⊕ granite-
hammer.
teuf-teuf [tœf'tœf] *m/inv.* puff-
puff (= *train*); motor-car, *Am.*
automobile.
teuton, -onne [tø'tɔ̃, ~'tɔn] 1. *adj.*
Teutonic; 2. ♀ Teuton; **teutonique** [~tɔ'nik] Teutonic (*a.* Order).
texte [tɛkst] *m* text.
textile [tɛks'til] 1. *adj.* textile;
2. *su./m* textile (industries *pl.*).

textuaire [tɛks'tɥɛːr] textual; **tex-
tuel, -elle** [~'tɥɛl] textual; word-
for-word (*quotation*); **texture** [~-
'tyːr] *f* texture; *fig.* construction,
make-up.
thalweg *geol.* [tal'vɛg] *m* thalweg.
thaumaturge [toma'tyrʒ] *m* mira-
cle-worker; thaumaturge; **thau-
maturgie** [~tyr'ʒi] *f* thaumaturgy.
thé [te] *m* tea; tea-party; *boîte f à* ~
tea-caddy, tea-canister; *heure f du* ~
tea-time.
théâtral, e, *m/pl.* -**aux** [tea'tral,
~'tro] theatrical; *fig.* spectacular; *pej.*
stagy; **théâtraliser** [~trali'ze] (1a)
v/t. put on the stage, dramatize;
théâtralisme [~tra'lism] *m* theatri-
calism, theatricalness; **théâtre**
[~'ɑːtr] *m* theatre, *Am.* theater (*a.* ✗
of war); stage, F boards *pl.*; scene (*a.
fig.*); *fig.* setting; dramatic art; plays
pl. (of s.o.); ~ *en plein air*, ~ *de verdure*
open-air theatre; *coup m de* ~ sensational development; *faire du* ~ go *or*
be on the stage; *fig.* playact.
thébaïde [teba'id] *f* solitary retreat;
wilderness; **thébaïque** ♎ [~'ik]
thebaic; opium...; **thébaïsme** ♒
[~'ism] *m* opium poisoning,
thebaism.
théière [te'jɛːr] *f* teapot.
théine ♎ [te'in] *f* theine.
théisme *phls.* [te'ism] *m* theism.
thématique [tema'tik] 1. *adj.* the-
matic; 2. *su./f* subject; **thème** [tɛm]
m theme (*a.* ♪); topic; ♪ subject;
gramm. stem; ✗, ⚓ scheme; *school*:
prose (composition).
théo... [teɔ] theo...; ~**cratie** [~kra'si]
f theocracy; ~**dolite** *surv.* [~dɔ'lit]
m theodolite; ~**logie** [~lɔ'ʒi] *f*
theology; *univ. a.* divinity; *docteur
m en* ~ doctor of divinity, D.D.;
~**logien** *m*, -**enne** *f* [~lɔ'ʒjɛ̃, ~'ʒjɛn]
theologian; ~**logique** [~lɔ'ʒik] the-
ological.
théorème Ⓐ [teɔ'rɛm] *m* theorem.
théoricien *m*, -**enne** *f* [teɔri'sjɛ̃,
~'sjɛn] theoretician, theorist; **théorie** [~'ri] *f* theory; **théorique** [~-
'rik] theoretical; **théoriser** [~ri'ze]
(1a) *vt/i.* theorize.
théosophe [teɔ'zɔf] *su.* theosophist.
thérapeute ♒ [tera'pøːt] *m* thera-
peutist; **thérapeutique** ♒ [~pø-
'tik] 1. *adj.* therapeutic; 2. *su./f*
therapy; therapeutics *pl.*; ~ *de choc*
shock-treatment; **thérapie** ♒ [~'pi]

f therapy; ~ *occupationnelle* occupational therapy; ~ *de groupe* group therapy.

thermal, e, *m/pl.* -aux [tɛr'mal, ~'mo] thermal; *eaux f/pl.* ~es hot springs; *station f* ~e spa; **thermalisme** [~ma'lism] *m* balneology; hydrotherapeutics *sg.*; running and organization of spas; **thermes** [tɛrm] *m/pl.* thermal baths; *hist.* *Greece and Rome:* thermae, public baths; **thermique** *phys.* [tɛr'mik] thermal, thermic; heat (*engine*).

thermo... [tɛrmɔ] thermo-...; ~**électrique** *phys.* [~elɛk'trik] thermo-electric(al); ~**gène** *physiol.* [~'ʒen] thermogenic; heat-producing; ✻ *ouate f* ♀ thermogene (wool); ~**mètre** [~'metr] *m* thermometer; ~**nucléaire** *phys.* [~nykle'ɛːr] thermonuclear; ~**siphon** *phys.* [~si'fɔ̃] *m* thermo-siphon; ~**stat** [~s'ta] *m* thermostat; ~**thérapie** ✻ [~tera'pi] *f* heat treatment.

thésauriser [tezɔri'ze] (1a) *v/i.* hoard; amass money; *v/t.* hoard, pile up, amass.

thèse [tɛːz] *f* thesis (*a. univ.*); argument.

thon *icht.* [tɔ̃] *m* tunny(-fish), tuna.

thoracique *anat.* [tɔra'sik] thoracic; **thorax** [~'raks] *m anat.* chest; thorax (*a. of insect*).

thrombose ✻ [trɔ̃'boːz] *f* thrombosis.

thuriféraire [tyrife'rɛːr] *m eccl.* thurifer, censer-bearer; *fig.* fawner; sycophant.

thym ♀ [tɛ̃] *m* thyme.

tiare [tjaːr] *f* (papal) tiara; papacy.

tibia *anat.* [ti'bja] *m* shin(-bone), tibia.

tic [tik] *m* ✻ tic, twitch; *fig.* mannerism.

ticket [ti'kɛ] *m* ticket; *cloak-room etc.:* check; (*ration-*)coupon; ⚓ ~ *de quai* platform ticket; ✻ ~ *modérateur* patient's contribution, portion paid by the insured.

tic-tac [tik'tak] *m/inv.* tick-tack; click-clack; *clock:* tick(-tock); *heart:* pit-a-pat; **tictaquer** [~ta'ke] (1m) *v/i.* tick (away) (*clock*); go pit-a-pat (*heart*).

tiède [tjed] tepid; lukewarm (*a. fig.*); warm (*wind*); **tiédeur** [tje'dœːr] *f* tepidity; lukewarmness (*a. fig.*); *fig.* indifference; **tiédir** [~'diːr] (2a) *v/i.*

become tepid *or* lukewarm; *v/t.* take the chill off; make tepid *or* lukewarm.

tien *m*, **tienne** *f* [tjɛ̃, tjɛn] **1.** *pron./ poss.:* le ~, la ~ne, les ~s *pl.*, les ~nes *pl.* yours; † thine; **2.** *su./m* your own; *les* ~s *pl.* your (own) people.

tiendrai [tjɛ̃'dre] *1st p. sg. fut. of tenir;* **tiennent** [tjɛn] *3rd p. pl. pres. of tenir;* **tiens** [tjɛ̃] *1st p. sg. pres. of tenir.*

tierce [tjɛrs] *f* ♪, ♀, *astr.* third; *eccl.* terce; *cards, fencing:* tierce; *typ.* final revise; **tiercé** [tjɛr'se] *m* bet to forecast the first three horses in a race; **tiers, tierce** [tjeːr, tjɛrs] **1.** *adj.* third; *hist.* ~ *état m* third estate, commonalty; ✻ *fièvre f tierce* tertian (ague); **2.** *su./m* third (part); third person; ⚖ third party; **Tiers-Monde** [tjeːr'mɔ̃d] *m: le* ~ the Third World; **tiers-point** [tjɛr'pwɛ̃] *m* ⊕ triangular file; △ *vaulting:* intersection of two ribs.

tige [tiːʒ] *f* ♀ stem, stalk; *tree:* trunk; *column:* shaft; ⊕ rod; *boot:* upper; ⚓ anchor, *a. key:* shank; *fig. family:* stock; ⊕ ~ *du piston* piston-rod.

tignasse F [ti'nas] *f hair:* mop.

tigre *zo.* [tigr] *m* tiger; **tigré, e** [ti'gre] striped (*fur*); spotted (*skin*); tabby (*cat*); **tigresse** *zo.* [~'grɛs] *f* tigress.

tilde *typ.* [tild] *m* tilde (~).

tillac ⚓ [ti'jak] *m* deck.

tilleul [ti'jœl] *m* ♀ linden, lime (-tree); *infusion:* lime-blossom tea.

timbale [tɛ̃'bal] *f* ♪ kettledrum; *cuis.* pie-dish; metal drinking-cup; F *décrocher la* ~ carry off the prize; ♪ *les* ~s *pl. orchestra:* the timpani; **timbalier** ♪ [~ba'lje] *m* kettledrummer; *orchestra:* timpanist.

timbre [tɛ̃:br] *m* date, postage, *etc.:* stamp; *bicycle, clock, etc.:* bell; *fig. voice etc.:* timbre; ~ *fiscal* revenue stamp; ~ *humide* rubber stamp; F *avoir le* ~ *fêlé* be cracked *or* crazy; **timbré, e** [tɛ̃'bre] sonorous (*voice*); *admin.* stamped (*paper*); ⊕ tested (*boiler*); F *fig.* cracked, crazy, daft; **timbre-poste,** *pl.* **timbres-poste** [~brə'pɔst] *m* postage stamp; **timbre-quittance,** *pl.* **timbres-quittance** [~brəki'tãːs] *m* receipt stamp; **timbrer** [~'bre] (1a) *v/t.* stamp (a *passport, paper*); post-mark (*a let-*

ter); ⊕ test (*a boiler*); **timbreur** [~'brœ:r] *m* stamper.

timide [ti'mid] timid; shy; apprehensive; **timidité** [~midi'te] *f* timidity; shyness; diffidence (in *ger.*, *à inf.*).

timon [ti'mɔ̃] *m* plough: beam; *vehicle*: pole; *fig.* helm; ⚓ † tiller; **timonerie** [~mɔn'ri] *f* ⚓ steering; ⚓ wheel-house; ⛴, *mot.* steering-gear, brake-gear; ⚓ *maître m de ~* quartermaster; *Royal Navy*: yeoman of signals; **timonier** [~mɔ'nje] *m vehicle*: wheel-horse; ⚓ helmsman; ⚓ quartermaster; ⚓ signalman.

timoré, e [timɔ're] timorous.

tinctorial, e, *m*/*pl.* **-aux** [tɛ̃ktɔ'rjal, ~'rjo] ⊕ tinctorial; dye(-stuffs, -woods).

tins [tɛ̃] *1st p. sg. p.s. of tenir*.

tintamarre F [tɛ̃ta'ma:r] *m* din, noise; *fig.* publicity, fuss; **tintement** [tɛ̃t'mã] *m bell*: ringing; *glasses, small bells*: tinkle; *coins*: jingle; ⚡ tinnitus, buzzing (*in the ears*); **tinter** [tɛ̃'te] (1a) *v/t.* ring, toll (*the bell*); ring the bell for (*mass etc.*); *v/i.* ring, toll (*bell*); tinkle (*glasses, small bells, etc.*); jingle (*coins*); ⚡ buzz (*ears*); *fig.* tingle, burn (*ears*); **tintouin** F [~'twɛ̃] *m* trouble, worry.

tique *zo.* [tik] *f* tick.

tiquer [ti'ke] (1m) *v/i.* vet. be a crib-biter, crib; F twitch (*face etc.*); wince; F *sans ~* without turning a hair.

tiqueté, e ♀, *orn., etc.* [tik'te] variegated, speckled.

tiqueur *m*, **-euse** *f* psych. [ti'kœ:r, ~'kø:z] person with a tic.

tir [ti:r] *m* shooting; musketry; *artillery*: gunnery; fire, firing; shooting-match; rifle-range; (*a. jeu m de ~*) shooting gallery; *~ à la cible* target-practice; *~ à volonté* individual fire; *~ sur zone* barrage; *à ~ rapide* quick-firing (*gun*); *ligne f de ~* line of fire.

tirade [ti'rad] *f* tirade; *thea.* long declamatory speech; ♪ run.

tirage [ti'ra:ʒ] *m* drawing, pulling, hauling; *chimney etc.*: draught, *Am.* draft; wire-drawing; *stone*: quarrying; *lottery*: draw; *typ., phot.* action, *a. number printed*: printing; *journ.* circulation; *book*: (print) run; *fig.* disagreement, friction; *~ à part* off-

print; *~ au sort* drawing lots; *cheval m de ~* draught horse; **tiraillement** [~raj'mã] *m* tugging, pulling; *fig.* disagreement, friction; ✽ *~s pl. d'estomac* pangs of hunger, F aching void *sg.*; **tirailler** [~ra'je] (1a) *v/t.* pull about; tug at; *fig.* pester (*s.o.*); *v/i.* blaze away, shoot at random; ⚔ *~ contre* snipe at; **tirailleur** [~ra'jœ:r] *m*⚔, *a. fig.* skirmisher; **tirant** [~'rã] *m* drawstring; bootstrap; *strap etc.*: pull; ⊕ rod; ⚓ tie-beam; tie-rod; ⚓ *~ d'eau* draught.

tire [ti:r] *f: voleur m à la ~* pickpocket.

tiré, e [ti're] **1.** *adj.* haggard, drawn; *fig. ~ par les cheveux* far-fetched; **2.** *su.*/*m* ✝ drawee; *su.*/*f:* F *une ~ a* long haul, quite a distance; quite a lot.

tire...: *~-au-flanc* sl. [tirɔ'flã] *m*/*inv.* skirker; *~-balle* ✽ [~'bal] *m* bullet-forceps; *~-botte* [~'bɔt] *m* bootjack; boot-hook; *~-bouchon* [~bu'ʃɔ̃] *m* corkscrew; *hair*: ringlet; *en ~* corkscrew (*curls*); *~-bouton* [~bu'tɔ̃] *m* button-hook; *~-clou* ⊕ [~'klu] *m* nail-puller; *~-d'aile* [~'dɛl] *adv.: à ~ at* full speed, swiftly; *~-fesses* F [~'fɛs] *m*/*inv.* ski tow; *~-larigot* F [~lari'go] *adv.: à ~ to* one's heart's content; *boire à ~ drink* heavily *or* like a fish; *~-ligne* [~'liɲ] *m* drawing pen; ⊕ scriber.

tirelire [tir'li:r] *f* moneybox; piggy bank; *sl.* tummy (= *stomach*); *sl.* nut (= *head*); *sl.* mug (= *face*).

tire-pied [tir'pje] *m* shoe-horn, shoe-lift; (*shoemaker's*) stirrup; **tirer** [ti're] (1a) **1.** *v/t.* pull, drag; draw (*a. a wire, a line, wine*); *a.* ✝ *a cheque, money*; *a.* ⚓ *10 feet*; *fig. lots*); tug; stretch; pull off (*boots*); raise (*one's hat*) (to, *devant*); ✽ pull out (*a tooth*); take out (*s.th. from somewhere*); *fig.* derive, get; fire (*a gun etc.*), let off (*a firearm*); *hunt.* shoot at (*an animal*); *typ.* pull (*a proof*), run off (*copies*); *gramm.* borrow (*a word*) (from Greek, *du grec*); *~ du sang à* take a blood specimen from (*s.o.*); *~ en longueur* stretch (*s.th.*) out; *~ la langue* put one's tongue out; *phot.* F *~ le portrait de* snap (*s.o.*); *~ les cartes* tell fortunes (by the cards); *~ les conséquences* draw the consequences; *~ plaisir* (*vanité*) *de* derive pleasure from (take pride in); *~ son origine* de spring from; ✝ ~ *une lettre de change sur* draw a bill on (*s.o.*); *film m tiré d'un roman* film adapted from a novel; *se* ~ extricate o.s. (from, *de*); F beat it; F *l'année se tire* the year is drawing to its close; *s'en* ~ get off; pull through; make ends meet; scrape through; *se* ~ *d'affaire* pull through, get out of trouble; **2.** *v/i.* pull (at, on *sur*); draw (*chimney, oven, etc.*); tend (to *à, sur*), verge (on *à, sur*); go, make (for, *vers*); shoot, fire (at, *sur*); ✝ ~ *à découvert* overdraw one's account; ~ *à sa fin* draw to a close; run low (*stock*); ✕ F ~ *au flanc* swing the lead, malinger; ~ *au large* ⚓ stand out to sea; F *fig.* beat it, clear off; ~ *au sort* draw lots; ~ *en longueur* drag on; ~ *sur le rouge* shade into *or* border on red; ~ *sur une cigarette* (*sa pipe*) draw on a cigarette (suck one's pipe); **tiret** *typ.* [~'rɛ] *m* hyphen; dash; **tirette** [~'rɛt] *f* draw-cords *pl.*, curtain cords *pl.*; *mot.* (bonnet) fastener; *desk*: writing-slide; **tireur, -euse** [~'rœ:r, ~'rø:z] *su.* ⊕, ✝, *a. beer, etc.*: drawer; *typ.* (*proof-*) puller; *gun*: firer; *shooter*; marksman, shot; *phot.* printer; pickpocket; *su./f phot.* printing-box; ~euse *de cartes* fortune-teller.

tiroir [ti'rwa:r] *m* desk, table, *etc.*: drawer; ⊕, *a.* slide-rule: slide; slide-valve; *à* ~s episodic (*play, novel*); F *nom m à* ~s double-barrel(l)ed name; **~-caisse**, *pl.* **~s-caisses** [~rwar'kɛs] *m* till.

tisane [ti'zan] *f* infusion; (*herb-*)tea; **tisanerie** [~zan'ri] *f hospital*: patients' kitchen.

tison [ti'zɔ̃] *m* fire-brand; half-burned log; fusee; **tisonné, e** [ti-zɔ'ne] with black spots (*horse's coat*); **tisonner** [~'ne] (1a) *vt/i.* poke, stir; *v/t. fig.* fan (a quarrel); **tisonnier** [~'nje] *m* poker; ⊕ ~s *pl.* firing tools.

tissage *tex.* [ti'sa:ʒ] *m* weaving, weave, mesh; cloth-mill; **tisser** *tex., a. fig.* [~'se] (1a) *v/t.* weave; **tisserand** *tex.* [tis'rɑ̃] *m* weaver; **tisserin** *orn.* [~'rɛ̃] *m* weaver-bird; **tisseur** *m*, **-euse** *f* [ti'sœ:r, ~'sø:z] weaver; **tissu, e** [~'sy] **1.** *adj. fig.* woven, made up; **2.** *su./m tex.* fabric, textile, cloth; *fig.* texture; *biol., a. fig.* lies *etc.*: tissue; **tissu-éponge**, *pl.* **tissus-éponges** [~sye-

'pɔ̃:ʒ] *m* terry (cloth), towelling; **tissure** *tex., a. fig.* [~'sy:r] *f* texture.

titane ♁ [ti'tan] *m* titanium; **titanesque** [~ta'nɛsk], **titanique** [~ta-'nik] titanic.

titiller [titil'le] (1a) *v/t.* tickle, titillate.

titrage [ti'tra:ʒ] *m* ♁, ⊕ titration; *métall.* assaying; ⊕ *thread, wire*: sizing; *cin.* insertion of the titles; **titre** [ti:tr] *m book, claim, eccl., gold, honour, nobility, office, song*: title; *book*: title-page; *chapter, page*: heading; *journ.* headline; *school*: certificate (*a.* ✝); *univ.* diploma; ✝ bond; *admin.* pass (*a.* ✕), voucher; ♁ deed; *fig.* claim; ♁ strength, *alcohol*: degree; *métall. ore*: content; *coinage*: standard; ⊕ *thread, wire*: size; ~s *pl.* qualifications (for, *à*); ✝ stocks and shares, securities; *typ.* ~ *courant* running headline; ~ *de créance* proof of debt; *à* ~ *de* by right *or* virtue of; as a (*friend*); *à* ~ *d'office* ex officio; *à* ~ *gratuit* free; as a favo(u)r; *à juste* ~ rightly, deservedly; *en* ~ titular; on the permanent staff; *fig.* acknowledged; *typ.* faux ~ half-title; *or m au* ~ standard gold; **titrer** [ti'tre] (1a) *v/t.* confer a title on (*s.o.*); give a title to; *cin.* title (*a film*); ♁ ⊕ titrate; *métall.* assay; *journ.* run as a headline; *wine etc.*: ~ 10° be 10° proof.

tituber [tity'be] (1a) *v/i.* stagger, lurch, reel.

titulaire [tity'lɛ:r] **1.** *adj.* titular (*a. eccl.*); full, regular (*member*); **2.** *su.* holder; *passport*: bearer; *su./m eccl.* incumbent; *univ.* regular professor.

toast [tɔst] *m* toast; *porter un* ~ propose a toast ((to, *à*); **toaster** [tɔs'te] (1a) *v/t.* toast (*s.o.*), drink to (*s.o.'s*) health.

toboggan [tɔbɔ'gɑ̃] *m* toboggan; *mot.* overpass; *piste f de* ~ toboggan-run.

toc [tɔk] **1.** *int.* tap, tap!; rat-rat! (*at door*); **2.** *su./m sound*: tap, rap; ⊕ (*lathe-*)carrier; ⊕ catch; F sham jewellery; ✝ *en* ~ pinchbeck; **3.** *adj./inv. sl.* touched, crazy.

tocante F [tɔ'kɑ̃:t] *f* watch, F ticker.

tocsin [tɔk'sɛ̃] *m* alarm(-bell, -signal).

toge [tɔ:ʒ] *f hist. Rome*: toga; ♁, *univ.* gown; ♁ robe.   [hubbub.)

tohu-bohu [tɔybɔ'y] *m* confusion;)

toi [twa] *pron./pers. subject*: you; *object*: you; (to) you; *à* ~ to you; yours.

toile [twal] *f* linen; cloth; *paint.* canvas; (oil) painting; (*spider's*) web; *thea.* curtain; ⚓ sail; ✗ tent; ~s *pl. hunt.* toils; ✝ ~ *à matelas* tick(ing); ~ *à sac* sackcloth; ~ *à voiles* sail-cloth; ~ *cirée* ✝ oilcloth, American cloth; ⚓ oilskin; ✝ ~ *de coton* cotton(-cloth); *thea., a. fig.* ~ *de fond* backdrop; ~ *métallique* wire gauze; *reliure f en* ~ cloth binding; **toilerie** ✝ [~'ri] *f* linen *or* textile trade; linen goods *pl.*;

toilettage [twale'ta:ʒ] *m* grooming (*of pets*); *fig.* touch-up; **toilette** [~'lɛt] *f* toilet, washing; dressing; dressing table; (*woman's*) dress, costume; wash-stand; ~s *pl.* toilet, lavatory; *faire sa* ~ have a wash, get washed; *objets pl. de* ~ toilet accessories; **toilier, -ère** [~'lje, ~'ljɛ:r] 1. *adj.* linen...; 2. *su./m* ✝ linen dealer *or* manufacturer. [yourself.⟩

toi-même [twa'mɛːm] *pron./rfl.*⟨

toise [twa:z] *f* measuring apparatus; *fig.* standard (of comparison); ✝ *measure*: fathom; **toiser** [twa'ze] (1a) *v/t.* measure; ⚠, *surv.* survey for quantities; *fig.* eye (*s.o.*) from head to foot, weigh (*s.o.*) up.

toison [twa'zɔ̃] *f* fleece; F *fig.* shock of hair.

toit [twa] *m* roof (*a.* ✗); house-top; *mot.* ~ *ouvrant* sunshine roof; *fig. crier sur les* ~s shout (*s.th.*) from the housetops; **toiture** [twa'ty:r] *f* roof (-ing).

tokai, tokay [tɔ'ke] *m wine*: Tokay.

tôle [to:l] *f* ⊕ sheet-metal, sheet-iron; (*galvanized, enamelled, etc.*) iron; plate; boiler-plate; *sl.* clink (= *prison*); ~ *ondulée* corrugated iron.

tolérable [tɔle'rabl] tolerable, bearable; **tolérance** [~'rɑ̃:s] *f* ⊕, ✗, *coinage, a. fig.*: tolerance; ⊕ limits *pl.*, margin; *admin.* allowance; (*religious*) toleration; **tolérant, e** [~'rɑ̃, ~'rɑ̃:t] tolerant; **tolérer** [~'re] (1f) *v/t.* tolerate (*a.* ✗ *a drug*); *fig.* overlook; F bear, endure.

tôlerie [tol'ri] *f* sheet-iron and steel-plate goods *pl. or* trade *or* works *usu. sg.*

tolet ⚓ [tɔ'lɛ] *m* thole-pin.

tôlier [to'lje] *m* ✝ sheet-iron merchant; sheet-iron worker; *sl.* innkeeper; *sl. hotel*: boss.

tomate ✿ [tɔ'mat] *f* tomato.

tombale [tɔ̃'bal] *adj./f*: *pierre f* ~ tombstone.

tombant, e [tɔ̃'bɑ̃, ~'bɑ̃:t] falling; drooping (*moustache, shoulders*); sagging (*branch*); flowing (*hair*); *à la nuit* ~*e* at nightfall.

tombe [tɔ̃:b] *f* tomb, grave; tombstone; **tombeau** [tɔ̃'bo] *m* tomb; *fig.* death.

tombée [tɔ̃'be] *f rain*: fall; *à la* ~ *de la nuit* (*or du jour*) at nightfall; **tomber** [~'be] (1a) 1. *v/i.* fall (*a.* ✗, *a. fig.* hair, night, government, *etc.*); tumble (down), fall (down); decline; drop (*a.* ✗ *fever*); decrease; subside (*rage, wind, a. fever*); die down (*feelings, fire, storm*); flag (*conversation*); *fig.* fail; *thea.* fall flat (*play*); ✗ crash; *fig.* become; *fig.* go out of fashion; *fig.* drop in (on, *chez*); ~ *à rien* come to nothing; ~ *bien* (*or juste*) happen *or* come at the right moment; ~ *d'accord* reach agreement, agree; ~ *dans le ridicule* make a fool of o.s.; ~ *de fatigue* be ready to drop; ~ *en disgrâce* fall into disgrace; ~ *le mardi* fall on a Tuesday (*festival*); ~ *mal* be inopportune; ~ *malade* (*mort, amoureux*) fall ill (dead, in love); ~ *sur* meet (with), run *or* come across; ✗ fall on (*the enemy*); *faire* ~ bring down; *cards*: drop; *il tombe de la neige* it is snowing; *laisser* ~ drop (*s.th., one's voice*, F *s.o.*); give up, discard; F *les bras m'en tombent* I am flabbergasted; 2. *v/t. wrestling*: throw (*s.o.*); ⊕ turn up *or* down (*the edge of a plate etc.*); *thea.* bring about the failure of, F kill; F ~ *la veste* slip off one's jacket; *sl.* ~ *une femme* lay a woman; **tombereau** [tɔ̃'bro] *m* (tip-)cart; ⚒ open truck; truckload; *hist.* tumbrel; ~ *à ordures* dust-cart; **tombeur** [~'bœ:r] *m sp.* wrestler; F ~ *de femmes* lady-killer.

tombola [tɔ̃bɔ'la] *f* lottery, raffle.

tome [tɔ:m] *m* tome, (large) volume.

ton[1] *m*, **ta** *f*, *pl.* **tes** [tɔ̃, ta, te] *adj./poss.* your.

ton[2] [tɔ̃] *m voice, paint., phot.*, ✗, *a.* ♩ *instrument, a. fig.* tone; *paint., phot.* tint; ✝ shade, colo(u)r; *fig.* (*good etc.*) form; ♩ pitch; ♩ key; ♩ mode; *fig. le bon* ~ good form; *être de bon* ~ be good form, be in good taste;

donner le ~ ♪ give the pitch; *fig.* set the tone *or* the fashion; *être dans le ton*, *avoir le* ~ ♪ be in tune; *fig.* tone in, match; *fig.* fit in; *ne pas être dans le* ~ ♪ be out of tune; *fig.* clash; *fig.* be out of place; ♂ *donner du* ~ (*à q.*) brace (s.o.) up, act as a tonic (on s.o.); **tonal, e** *m/pl.* **-als** ♪ [tɔ'nal] tonal; **tonalité** [~nali'te] *f* ♪, *paint.*, *phot.* tonality; *radio:* tone.

tondage [tɔ̃'daːʒ] *m vet.* dipping; shearing (*a. tex.*); **tondaille** [~'daːj] *f* (sheep-)shearing; **tondaison** [~dɛ'zɔ̃] *f see* tonte; **tondeur, -euse** [~'dœːr, ~'døːz] *su.* shearer; *vet.*, *a.* ♂ clipper; *su./f* shears *pl.*; ♂ lawn-mower; *hair, dog's coat:* clippers *pl.*; **tondre** [tɔ̃:dr] (4a) *v/t. vet.*, *a.* ⊕ shear; *sheep:* crop (*the grass*); clip (*dog, hair, hedge, horse*); *fig.* fleece (*s.o.*).

tonicité ♂ [tɔnisi'te] *f* tonicity; **tonifier** ♂ [~ni'fje] (1o) *v/t.* tone up, brace; **tonique** [~'nik] **1.** *adj.* tonic (♂, *a. gramm.*); *accent m* ~ stress, tonic; **2.** *su./m* ♂ tonic; *su./f* ♪ tonic, key-note.

tonitruant, e *fig.* [tɔnitry'ɑ̃, ~'ɑ̃:t] thundering; violent (*wind*); **tonitruer** *fig.* [~'e] (1a) *v/i.* thunder.

tonnage ⚓ [tɔ'naːʒ] *m* tonnage; displacement.

tonnant, e [tɔ'nɑ̃, ~'nɑ̃:t] thundering (*a. fig. voice*).

tonne [tɔn] *f measure:* metric ton; tun, cask; **tonneau** [tɔ'no] *m* cask, barrel; governess-cart; *mot.* tonneau; ✂ toll, horizontal spin; *au* ~ draught (*beer*); **tonnelage** [tɔn'laːʒ] *m* cooperage; ✝ marchandises *f/pl.* de ~ goods in barrels; **tonnelet** [~'le] *m* keg (*a.* ⚓); small cask; *oil:* drum; **tonnelier** ⊕ [tɔnə'lje] *m* cooper; **tonnelle** [~'nel] *f* △ barrel-vault, semicircular arch; *fig.* bower; *hunt.* tunnel-net; **tonnellerie** ⊕ [~nɛl'ri] *f* cooperage; cooper's shop.

tonner [tɔ'ne] (1a) *v/i.* thunder (*a. fig.*); *fig.* boom (out); **tonnerre** [~'nɛːr] *m* thunder (*a. fig.*); † thunderbolt, lightning; *coup m de* ~ thunderclap, peal of thunder; *fig.* thunderbolt; F *du* ~ (*de Dieu*) terrific, a hell of a ...

tonsure [tɔ̃'syːr] *f* tonsure; *fig.* priesthood; **tonsurer** [~sy're] (1a) *v/t.* tonsure.

tonte [tɔ̃:t] *f* (sheep-)shearing; shearing-time; *tex.* shearing; ♂ clipping; *lawn:* mowing.

tonton F [tɔ̃'tɔ̃] *m* uncle.

tonus [tɔ'nys] *m* ♂ tonus, tone; *fig.* energy.

topaze *min.* [tɔ'paːz] *f* topaz; ~ *brûlée* (*occidentale*) pink (false) topaz.

tope! [tɔp] *int.* agreed!; done!; **toper** *fig.* [tɔ'pe] (1a) *v/i.* agree; shake hands on it.

topinambour ♀, *cuis.* [tɔpinɑ̃'buːr] *m* Jerusalem artichoke.

topique [tɔ'pik] **1.** *adj.* local (*a.* ♂); *fig.* to the point, relevant; **2.** *su./m* ♂ local *or* topical remedy; *phls.* commonplace.

topographe [tɔpɔ'graf] *m* topographer; **topographie** [~gra'fi] *f* topography; surveying; topographical map *or* plan; **topographique** [~gra'fik] topographic(al); ordnance (*map, survey*).

toquade F [tɔ'kad] *f* passing craze, infatuation.

toquante F [tɔ'kɑ̃:t] *f* watch, F ticker.

toque *cost.* [tɔk] *f chef, jockey, univ.,* ⚖: cap; (*woman's*) toque.

toqué, e F [tɔ'ke] crazy, cracked, nuts; ~ *de* infatuated with, *sl.* mad about (*a hobby, a woman, etc.*); **toquer** [~] (1m) *v/t.* drive (*s.o.*) crazy; *fig.* infatuate; *se* ~ lose one's head (*over, de*).

torche [tɔrʃ] *f* torch; straw pad; **torcher** [tɔr'ʃe] (1a) *v/t.* wipe (*s.th.*) (clean); daub (*the wall*), cover (*the floor, the wall*) with cobmortar; F *fig.* polish off, do (*s.th.*) quickly; *pej.* botch, scamp (*one's work*); **torchère** [~'ʃɛːr] *f* candelabra; **torchette** [~'ʃet] *f* wisp of straw (*for cleaning*); house flannel; *tex.* hank; **torchis** △ [~'ʃi] *m* cob; **torchon** [~'ʃɔ̃] *m* (kitchen) cloth; (~ *à vaisselle*) dish towel; duster; floor cloth; F *fig.* rag (= *bad newspaper*); *coup de* ~ wipe; *a. fig.* clean-up; F *fig.* fight, quarrel; **torchonner** F [~ʃɔ'ne] (1a) *v/t.* wipe; *sl.* botch, scamp (*one's work*).

tordage [tɔr'daːʒ] *m* twisting; *tex. etc.* twist; **tordant, e** F [~'dɑ̃, ~'dɑ̃:t] screamingly funny; **tord-boyaux** F [tɔrbwa'jo] *m/inv.* strong (but poor) brandy, *sl.* rot-gut; rat poison; **tordeur, -euse** [tɔr'dœːr, ~'døːz] *su. tex. person:* twister; *su./f* ⊕ cable-twisting machine; *zo.* leafroller moth; **tordoir** ⊕ [ᴧˈdwaːr] *m* rope-twister, rack-stick; cable-twisting machine; *laundry*: wringer; oil-mill; **tordre** [tɔrdr] (4a) *v/t.* ⊕ twist; wring (*hands, s.o.'s neck, clothes, a. fig. s.o.'s heart*); distort, twist (*one's features, the mouth, the meaning*); ⊕ buckle (*metal*); se ~ twist, writhe; (*a. se ~ de rire*) roar with laughter; **tordu, e** [tɔrˈdy] twisted; bent; crooked; warped (*a. fig. mind*); F nuts, crazy, loony.

toréador [tɔreaˈdɔːr] *m* bull-fighter.

torgn(i)ole F [tɔrˈɲɔl] *f* slap, blow.

tornade [tɔrˈnad] *f* tornado; *fig.* torrent of abuse.

toron [tɔˈrɔ̃] *m rope*: strand; *straw*: wisp.

torpeur [tɔrˈpœːr] *f* torpor; **torpide** [ᴧˈpid] torpid.

torpille ⚓, ✂, *a. icht.* [tɔrˈpiːj] *f* torpedo; **torpiller** ⚓ [ᴧpiˈje] (1a) *v/t.* torpedo (*a ship, a. fig. a scheme*); **torpilleur** ⚓ [ᴧpiˈjœːr] *m* destroyer; *person*: torpedo man.

torréfacteur [tɔrrefakˈtœːr] *m* (coffee-)roaster; **torréfaction** [ᴧfakˈsjɔ̃] *f* (coffee-)roasting; torrefaction; **torréfier** [ᴧˈfje] (1o) *v/t.* roast (*coffee etc.*); torrefy; *sun*: scorch (*s.o.*).

torrent [tɔˈrɑ̃] *m* torrent (*a. fig.*); *fig. abuse, light, tears*: flood; **torrentiel, -elle** [tɔrɑ̃ˈsjɛl] torrential; **torrentueux, -euse** [ᴧˈtɥø, ᴧˈtɥøːz] torrent-like, torrential.

torride [tɔrˈrid] *geog.* torrid; *fig.* scorching (*heat*).

tors, torse [tɔːr, tɔrs] 1. *adj.* twisted, ▲ wreathed (*column*); crooked, bandy; *cou m* ~ wry neck; 2. *su./m rope etc.*: twist; (twisted) cord; **torsade** [tɔrˈsad] *f hair*: twist, coil; twisted cord; *en* ~ coiled (*hair*); **torsader** [ᴧsaˈde] (1a) *v/t.* twist (together); coil (*hair*).

torse [tɔrs] *m* trunk, torso; chest.

torsion [tɔrˈsjɔ̃] *f rope, wire, etc.*: twisting; *phys., ⚡, mot.* torsion; *moment m de* ~ torque.

tort [tɔːr] *m* wrong; mistake, error, fault; damage, harm; *à* ~ wrongly; *à* ~ *ou à raison* rightly or wrongly; *avoir* ~ be wrong; *dans* (*or en*) *son* ~ in the wrong, at fault; *donner* ~ *à* blame, lay the blame on; prove (to be) wrong; *faire* (*du*) ~ *à q.* harm s.o., do s.o. harm; be detrimental to s.o.

torticolis ⚕ [tɔrtikɔˈli] *m* crick (in the neck); stiff neck.

tortillard, e [tɔrtiˈjaːr, ᴧjard] *m* small local railway; **tortille** [ᴧˈtiːj] † *f* winding path (*in a wood etc.*); **tortillement** [ᴧtijˈmɑ̃] *m* twist(ing); *worm, a. fig.*: wriggling; *fig.* quibbling, subterfuge; **tortiller** [ᴧtiˈje] (1a) *v/t.* twist (up); twiddle; twirl (*one's moustache*); se ~ wriggle; writhe, squirm; *v/i.* F *fig.* wriggle (a)round; ~ *des hanches* swing *or* F wiggle one's hips; **tortillon** [ᴧtiˈjɔ̃] *m hair, paper*: twist; *market porter*: headpad.

tortionnaire [tɔrsjɔˈnɛːr] 1. *adj.* torture-..., of torture; *fig.* wicked; 2. *su./m* torturer.

tortis [tɔrˈti] *m* twisted threads *pl.*; torsel.

tortu, e † [tɔrˈty] crooked.

tortue [tɔrˈty] *f zo.* tortoise; F *à pas de* ~ at a snail's pace; *cuis. soupe f à la* ~ turtle-soup.

tortueux, -euse [tɔrˈtɥø, ᴧˈtɥøːz] tortuous (*a. fig. conduct*), winding; twisted (*tree*); *fig.* crooked (*conduct, person*); *fig.* wily (*person*).

torture [tɔrˈtyːr] *f* torture; **torturer** [ᴧtyˈre] (1a) *v/t.* torture; *fig.* twist, strain (*the sense, a text*); se ~ *l'esprit* rack one's brains.

torve [tɔrv] menacing; forbidding; *regard m* ~ grim look; scowl.

tôt [to] *adv.* soon; early; ~ *ou tard* sooner or later; *au plus* ~ at the earliest; *le plus* ~ *possible* as soon as possible; *pas de si* ~ not so soon.

total, e, *m/pl.* -aux [tɔˈtal, ᴧˈto] 1. *adj.* total, complete; 2. *su./m* (sum) total; *au* ~ on the whole; **totalisateur** [tɔtalizaˈtœːr] *m* adding-machine; *turf*: totalizator; **totalisation** [ᴧzaˈsjɔ̃] *f* totalization; totting up, adding up; **totalisatrice** [ᴧzaˈtris] *f* cash register; **totaliser** [ᴧˈze] (1a) *v/t.* totalize, tot up, add up; **totalitaire** [ᴧtɛːr] totalitarian; **totalitarisme** [ᴧtaˈrism] *m* totalitarianism; **totalité** [ᴧˈte] *f* whole, total; *en* ~ wholly.

toton [tɔˈtɔ̃] *m* teetotum; F *faire tourner q. comme un* ~ twist s.o. round one's little finger.

touage ⚓ [twaˈʒ] *m* chain-towage (dues *pl.*); kedging.

touaille [twaːj] *f* roller-towel.

toubib F [tuˈbib] *m* doctor, F doc.

touchant, e [tuˈʃɑ̃, ~ˈʃɑ̃:t] **1.** *adj.* touching, moving; **2.** *su./m* touching thing (about s.th., *de qch.*); **3.** † *touchant prp.* concerning, about, with regard to; **touchau** [tuˈʃo] *m* (*goldsmith's*) touch-needle, test-needle; **touche** [tuʃ] *f* touch (*a. paint., sp.*); *typewriter,* ♪ *piano*: key; ♪ *violin etc.*: fingerboard; *paint. etc., a. fig.* style, manner; *foot.* throw-in; *foot.* (*a. ligne f de ~*) touch-line; *fencing, billiards*: hit; ♪ *~s pl. guitar*: frets; *tel. ~ d'interruption* break-key; *arbitre m de ~ foot.* linesman; *rugby*: touch-judge; *pierre f de ~* touchstone (*a. fig.*); *sl. avoir une drôle de ~* look funny; *sur la ~ sp.* on the sidelines; *fig.* out in the cold; *fig.* aloof; **touche-à-tout** [tuʃaˈtu] *su./inv.* dabbler; meddler; Jack of all trades; **toucheau** [~ˈʃo] *m see touchau;* **toucher** [~ˈʃe] **1.** (1a) *v/t.* touch, hit (*a ball,* ✕ *the mark, an opponent*); feel; contact, reach (*s.o.*); receive, draw (*money*); ♰ collect (*a bill*); *fig.* move (*s.o.*) (*to tears etc.*); deal with, touch on, allude to (*a matter, a question*); strike (*a.* ⚓ *rock*); *v/i.: ~* ⚓ border on (*a place, a. fig.*); be in contact with (*s.th.*); be near to (*an age, a place, a. fig.*); reach to; *fig.* affect (*interests, question, welfare*); ⚓ call at; *~ à sa fin* be drawing to a close; *défense f de ~!* hands off!; F *touchez là!* shake hands on it!; F put it there!; shake!; **2.** *su./m* touch (*a.* ♪ *of a pianist*); feel; **touchette** ♪ [~ˈʃɛt] *f guitar etc.*: fret, stop; **toucheur** [~ˈʃœ:r] *m* (cattle-) drover.

toue ⚓ [tu] *f* river barge; **touée** [twe] *f* warping-cable; *cable, rope, ship at anchor*: scope; *fig.* stretch, length; **touer** ⚓ [~] (1p) *v/t.* chain-tow; take in tow.

touffe [tuf] *f grass, hair*: tuft; *hay, straw*: wisp; *flowers*: bunch; *trees*: clump; **touffeur** [tuˈfœ:r] *f room*: stifling heat; F fug; **touffu, e** [~ˈfy] bushy (*beard etc.*); thickly wooded (*scenery*); close, tangled (*thicket*); *fig.* abstruse; that is heavy reading (*book*).

toujours [tuˈʒu:r] *adv.* always, ever; still; nevertheless, anyhow; *~ est-il que* the fact remains that; *pour* (*or à*) *~* for ever.

toundra *geog.* [tunˈdra] *f* tundra.

toupet [tuˈpɛ] *m* tuft of hair; *person,* *a. horse*: forelock; F *fig.* impudence, cheek; *faux ~* toupet.

toupie [tuˈpi] *f* (spinning-)top; peg-top; ⊕ mo(u)lding lathe; *~ d'Allemagne* humming-top; F *vieille ~* old frump; **toupiller** [tupiˈje] (1a) *v/t.* ⊕ shape (*wood*); *v/i.* spin round; bustle about.

toupillon [tupiˈjɔ̃] *m* (*small*) bunch.

tour[1] [tu:r] *f* tower; *chess*: castle, rook; high-rise *or* tower block; *fig. ~ d'ivoire* ivory tower.

tour[2] [~] *m* ⊕ machine, key, phrase, order, *fig.*: turn; ⊕ revolution; (*potter's*) wheel; ⊕ lathe; circuit, circumference; *cost.* size, measurement; turning, winding; *face*: outline; *affairs*: course; trip, walk, stroll; ✂, *a. road*: twist; ✂ sprain; *sp. tennis*: round; *fig.* feat; trick; *fig.* manner, style; *~ à ~* by turns; *sp. ~ cycliste* cycle race; *~ de force* feat (*of strength or skill*); *~ de main* knack, skill; *fig.* tricks *pl.* of the trade; *sp. ~ de piste* lap; *cost. ~ de poitrine man*: chest measurement, *woman*: bust measurement; ✂ *~ de reins* crick in the back; *cost. ~ de taille* waist measurement; *à mon ~* in my turn; *à ~ de bras* with all one's might; *à ~ de rôle* in rotation; *c'est* (*à*) *son ~* it is his turn; *en un ~ de main* in a twinkling, straight away; ⚓ *faire le ~* swing the ship; capsize; *faire le ~ de* go round (*the world etc.*); *faire un mauvais ~ à q.* play a dirty trick on s.o.; *faire un ~* take a stroll; *fermer à double ~* double-lock (*a door*); *par ~ de faveur* out of (one's proper) turn.

touraille ⊕ [tuˈra:j] *f* malt-kiln.

tourbe[1] † *pej.* [turb] *f* mob, rabble.

tourbe[2] [turb] *f* peat, turf; **tour-beux, -euse** [turˈbø, ~ˈbø:z] ✿ peaty, boggy; *marais m ~* peat-bog; **tourbier** [~ˈbje] *m* peat-worker; **tourbière** [~ˈbjɛ:r] *f* peat-bog.

tourbillon [turbiˈjɔ̃] *m* whirlwind; *dust*: swirl; whirlpool; eddy; *astr., fig.* vortex; *fig.* whirl; *fig.* round; *~ de neige* snowstorm; **tourbillonner** [~jɔˈne] (1a) *v/i.* swirl; whirl round.

tourelle [tuˈrɛl] *f* ⌂, ✕, ⚓, ⊕, ✕ turret; ⊕ *lathe*: capstan.

tourie [tuˈri] *f* carboy.

tourisme [tuˈrism] *m* tourism; touring; holiday travel; tourist industry; *bureau m de ~* travel agency; *voiture f*

de ~ touring car; **touriste** [~'rist] *su.*
tourist; **touristique** [~ris'tik] travel
...; touristic, tourist ...
tourment [tur'mᾶ] *m* torment, torture (*a. fig.*); *fig.* agony, anguish; ~s
pl. hunger: pangs; **tourmente**
[~'mᾶːt] *f* storm (*a. fig.*); *fig.* turmoil;
~ de neige blizzard; **tourmenter**
[turmᾶ'te] (1a) *v/t.* torture, torment;
fig. worry, trouble; *fig.* pester, harry;
♫ wind: toss (*a ship*) about; *fig.* over-
elaborate (*a picture, a theme, etc.*); se
~ worry, fret; **tourmenteur, -euse**
[~'tœːr, ~'tøːz] tormenting; **tour-
mentin** ♫ [~'tɛ̃] *m* storm-jib.
tournage [tur'naːʒ] *m* ⊕ turning (*on
a lathe*); ♫ belaying; *cin.* shooting;
tournailler F [~na'je] (1a) *v/i.*
wander up and down *or* about;
tournant, e [~'nᾶ, ~'nᾶːt] 1. *adj.*
turning; revolving; winding (*path,
road*); spiral (*staircase*); 2. *su./m* road,
river: turning, bend; (*street*) corner;
winding; *mill:* water-wheel; *fig.*
turning point; F *fig.* avoir (*or* rattraper) q. au ~ pay s.o. back; **tournebroche** [turnə'brɔʃ] *m* roasting jack;
† turnspit; **tourne-disque** [~'disk]
m grammophone: turntable; **tournedos** *cuis.* [~'do] *m* tournedos; fillet
steak; **tournée** [tur'ne] *f admin.*, *a.*
♫ round; ⚡ circuit; *thea.* tour; *fig.*
round (of drinks); F *fig.* thrashing;
faire la ~ de visit, do the round of, F
do; **tournemain** † [~nə'mɛ̃] *m:* en
un ~ in a twinkling, straight away;
tourner [~'ne] (1a) 1. *v/t.* turn;
rotate (*a wheel*); turn round (*a
corner*); wind (*s.th. round s.th.*); ⊕
shape, fashion; *cuis.* stir (*a liquid*); ♫
make fast (*a hawser*); *cin.* shoot,
make (*a film*), actor: star in (*a film*);
⚡ outflank; *fig.* evade (*a difficulty, a
law*), get round (*a.* ⚡); *fig.* turn over
(*a. a page*), revolve (*a problem*);
convert (into, en); ~ la tête (*l'estomac*)
à q. turn s.o.'s head (stomach); se ~
turn (round); change (into, en); 2.
v/i. turn; go round, revolve; ⊕ run,
go; spin (*top*); wind (*path, road*); *fig.*
whirl (*head*); change (*weather, wind*);
shift (*wind*); *cin.* film; turn (sour)
(*milk etc.*); *fig.* turn out (*badly, well*);
fig. ~ à become, tend to(wards); ~ à
droite turn to the right; ~ au beau turn
fine; *mot.* ~ au ralenti idle, tick over;
bien tourné handsome, well set-up; il
tourne cœur cards: the turn-up is

hearts; la tête me tourne I feel giddy,
my head is spinning; mal ~ go to the
bad; **tournerie** ⊕ [~nə'ri] *f* turner's
shop.
tournesol [turnə'sɔl] *m* ♀ sunflower;
♣ litmus.
tournette [tur'nɛt] *f tex.* reel;
squirrel's cage; turn-table; ⊕ circular glass-cutter; **tourneur, -euse**
[~'nœːr, ~'nøːz] 1. *adj.* dancing (*dervish*); 2. *su./m* ⊕ turner; ⊕ lathe
operator; **tournevent** [~nə'vᾶ] *m*
chimney-jack; chimney-cowl; **tournevis** ⊕ [~nə'vis] *m* screwdriver.
tourniole ✦ F [tur'njɔl] *f* whitlow
(*round a nail*).
tourniquet [turni'kɛ] *m* turnstile; ✦
revolving stand; ✦ sprinkler; ⊕
catch; *shutter:* button; ⚡ vane;
tourniquet; ⚡ F passer au ~ be court-
martialled.
tournis *vet.* [tur'ni] *m sheep:* staggers
pl.
tournoi [tur'nwa] *m sp. etc.* tourna-
ment; *whist:* drive; **tournoiement**
[turnwa'mᾶ] *m* spinning, whirling;
water: swirling; *bird:* wheeling; ✦
dizziness; **tournoyer** [~'je] (1h) *v/i.*
spin; turn round and round, whirl;
swirl (*water*); wheel (*bird*); *fig.*
quibble.
tournure [tur'nyːr] *f fig.* turn (*of
events etc.*); shape; cast; *phrase:* turn;
⊕ lathe: turning(s *pl.*); ~ d'esprit cast
of mind; way of thinking; prendre
une meilleure ~ take a turn for the
better.
tourte [turt] *f cuis.* (covered) pie
or tart; F dolt, duffer; **tourteau**
[tur'to] *m* round loaf; cattle-cake,
oil-cake; edible crab; ⊕ centre-
boss.
tourtereau *orn.* [turtə'ro] *m* young
turtle-dove (*a. fig.*); **tourterelle**
orn. [~'rɛl] *f* turtle-dove.
tourtière *cuis.* [tur'tjɛːr] *f* pie-dish;
baking-tin.
tous [tu; tus] *see* tout.
Toussaint *eccl.* [tu'sɛ̃] *f:* la ~ All
Saints' Day; la veille de la ~ Hal-
lowe'en.
tousser [tu'se] (1a) *v/i.* cough;
tousseur *m*, -euse *f* [~'sœːr, ~'søːz]
cougher; **toussoter** [~sɔ'te] (1a)
v/i. give little coughs; have a slight
cough.
tous-temps [tu'tᾶ] *adj./inv.* all-
weather.

tout *m*, **toute** *f*, **tous** *m/pl.*, **toutes** *f/pl.* [tu, tut, tu, tut] **1.** *adj. before unparticularized noun*: all, any, every; sole, only; *intensive*: very, most, utmost, extreme; *before particularized su./sg.*: all, the whole (of); *before particularized su./pl.*: all, every, every one of; *with numerals*: all; *with numeral + su./pl.* every + *su./sg.*; ~ *homme* every or any man; *pour toute nourriture* as sole food; *de toute fausseté* completely false; *toute la (une) ville* the (a) whole town; ~ *le monde* everyone; ~ *Paris* all *or* the whole of Paris; *toutes les semaines* every week; *tous les cinq* all five; *tous les deux* both; *toutes les cinq (deux) semaines* every fifth (other) week; **2.** *pron./indef.* [*m/pl.* tus] all; everything; ~ *est là* everything is there; *après* ~ after all; *bonne f à* ~ *faire* maid of all work; *c'est (or voilà)* ~ that is all; *c'est* ~ *dire* that's the long and the short of it; *et* ~ *et* ~ and all the rest of it; *nous tous* all of us; *six fois en* ~ six times in all; **3.** *su./m the* whole, all; the main thing; ⚓ (*pl.* **touts** [tu]) total; *du* ~ *au* ~ completely, entirely; *pas du* ~ not at all; **4.** *adv.* (*before adj./f beginning with consonant or aspirate h, agrees as if adj.*) quite, completely; all; very; ready(*-cooked, -made, etc.*); right; stark (*naked, mad*); straight (*ahead, forward*); ~ *à coup* suddenly; ~ *à fait* completely; ~ *à l'heure* a few minutes ago; in a few minutes; ~ *au plus* at the very most; ~ *autant* quite as much *or* many; ~ *d'abord* at first; ~ *de même* all *or* just the same; ~ *de suite* at once, immediately; *restaurant*: in a moment; ~ *d'un coup* at one fell swoop; ~ *en* (*ger.*) while (*ger.*); ~ *petits enfants* very young children; ~ *sobre qu'il paraît* however sober he seems *or* may seem, sober though he seems *or* may seem; *à* ~ *à l'heure!* see you later!; *c'est* ~ *un* it's all the same; *elle est toute contente* (*honteuse*) she is quite content (a-shamed); *elle est tout étonnée* she is quite astonished.

tout-à-l'égout [tutale'gu] *m/inv.* main-drainage, direct-to-sewer drainage.

toute [tut] *see* **tout**; **~fois** [~'fwa]

cj. however, still, nevertheless; **~-puissance** *eccl.* [~pui̯'sã:s] *f* omnipotence.   [wow.\
toutou *ch.sp.* [tu'tu] *m* doggie, bow-⟨
tout(-)va F [tu'va]: *à* ~ enormous, unbounded, super; (*adv.*) enormously, F like crazy.

tout-venant [tuvə'nã] *m* ⁰ un-screened coal; ✝ ungraded products; *fig.* hoi polloi.

toux [tu] *f* cough; *accès m (or quinte f) de* ~ fit of coughing.

toxicité [tɔksisi'te] *f* toxicity; **toxicologie** 🐟 [~kɔlɔ'ʒi] *f* toxicology; **toxicomane** 🐟 [~kɔ'man] **1.** *su.* dope fiend; drug-addict; **2.** *adj.* drug-addicted; **toxicomanie** 🐟 [~kɔma'ni] *f* dope-habit; drug-habit; **toxine** 🐟 [tɔk'sin] *f* toxin; **toxique** [~'sik] **1.** *adj.* toxic; poisonous; **2.** *su./m* poison.

trac F [trak] *m* fright; *thea.* stage-fright; *avoir le* ~ get the wind up; *tout à* ~ without reflection.

tracas [tra'kɑ] *m* bother, worry, trouble; **tracasser** [~ka'se] (1a) *v/t.* bother, worry; *se* ~ worry, fret (about, *pour*); **tracasserie** [~kas'ri] *f* worry; harassment; **tracassier, -ère** [~ka'sje, ~'sjɛ:r] **1.** *adj.* vexatious; irksome; **2.** *su.* fussy person; troublesome person.

trace [tras] *f* trace; *vehicle*: track; *animal, person*: trail; footprints *pl.*; *fig.* footsteps *pl.*; *burn, suffering*: mark; *fig.* sign; **tracé** [tra'se] *m* tracing, sketching; *town etc.*: layout; *road*: lie; ⚓ graph; △ *etc.* outline, drawing, plan; **tracer** [~] (1k) *v/t.* trace; mark out; ⚓ plot (*a curve, a graph*); draw (*a line, a plan*); sketch (*an outline, a plan*); *fig.* open up (*a route etc.*); *fig.* show (*the way*); *v/i. sl.* get a move on; **traceret** ⊕ [tras'rɛ] *m* scriber, tracing-awl; **traceur, -euse** [tra'sœ:r, ~'sø:z] *su., a. adj.* ⊕, ✕, *etc.* tracer.

trachée [tra'ʃe] *f* 🐟, *zo.* trachea; ✿ duct; F *anat.* = **~-artère**, *pl.* **~s-artères** *anat.* [~ʃear'tɛ:r] *f* trachea, windpipe; **trachéite** [~ke'it] *f* tracheitis; **trachéotomie** [~keɔtɔ'mi] *f* tracheotomy; **trachome** 🐟 [~'kɔ:m] *m* trachoma.

traçoir ⊕ [tra'swa:r] *m see* **traceret**.
tract [trakt] *m* tract; leaflet.
tractations *pej.* [trakta'sjɔ̃] *m f/pl.* dealings.

tracté, e [trak'te] tractor-drawn; **tracteur** [~'tœːr] *m* tractor; **traction** [~'sjɔ̃] *f* traction; pulling; draught, *Am.* draft; *sp.* pull-up; *sp.* press-up, push-up; ⚙ rolling-stock department; *mot.* (*a.* ~ *avant*) car with front-wheel drive; ⊕ *etc. essai m de* ~ tension test; **tractoriste** [~tɔ-'rist] *su.* tractor driver.

tradition [tradi'sjɔ̃] *f* tradition; ⚖ delivery; folklore; *de* ~ traditional; **traditionaliste** [~sjɔna'list] *su.* traditionalist; **traditionnel, -elle** [~sjɔ'nɛl] traditional; standing (*joke etc.*); habitual.

traducteur *m*, **-trice** *f* [tradyk'tœːr, ~'tris] translator; **traduction** [~'sjɔ̃] *f* translation; interpretation; **traduire** [tra'dɥiːr] (4h) *v/t.* translate (into, en); *fig.* render, convey, express; ⚖ ~ *en justice* summon, sue, prosecute; *se* ~ *par* be translated by; *fig.* find it's expression in, be expressed by; **traduisible** [~dɥi'zibl] translatable; ⚖ ~ *en justice* liable to prosecution *or* to be sued.

trafic [tra'fik] *m* traffic (*a. fig. pej.*); trading; *teleph.* ~ *interurbain* trunk traffic; *faire le* ~ *de* traffic in; **traficotage** [~fikɔ'taːʒ] *m* trafficking, underhand(ed) dealings *pl.*; **trafiquant** [trafi'kɑ̃] *m* trader; trafficker (in de, en) (*a. pej.*); **trafiquer** [~'ke] (1m) *v/i.* trade, deal (in, en); *usu. pej.* traffic; *pej. fig.* ~ *de* make profit out of, sell; *v/t.* F doctor (*s.th.*) (up); **trafiqueur** *pej.* [~'kœːr] *m* trafficker (in de, en).

tragédie [traʒe'di] *f* tragedy (*a. fig.*); **tragédien** [~'djɛ̃] *m* tragedian, tragic actor; **tragédienne** [~'djɛn] *f* tragic actress, tragedienne; **tragicomique** [traʒikɔ'mik] tragi-comic; **tragique** [tra'ʒik] **1.** *adj.* tragic; F *ce n'est pas (si)* ~ *(que ça)* that's not so bad; **2.** *su./m* tragic aspect (*of an event*); tragedy (*a.* = *tragic art*); tragic poet; *prendre au* ~ make a tragedy of (*s.th.*).

trahir [tra'iːr] (2a) *v/t.* betray; disclose; deceive (*s.o.*); *fig. strength:* fail (*s.o.*); be false to (*one's oath*); not to come up to (*expectations, hopes*); **trahison** [~i'zɔ̃] *f* treachery, perfidy; betrayal (of, de); ⚖ treason; *haute* ~ high treason.

traille [traːj] *f* trail-ferry; ferry-cable.

train [trɛ̃] *m* ⚙ train; *vehicles etc.:* string; *tyres, wheels:* set; *admin. laws, decrees etc.:* set, batch, series; *metall.* rolls *pl.*; ⊕ gear; (*timber-, Am. lumber-*)raft, float; *zo. horse:* quarters *pl.*; pace (*a. sp.*), speed; *fig.* mood; ⚙~-*auto* car sleeper train; ⚙ ~ *correspondant* connection; ⚙ ~ *de banlieue* (*ceinture*) suburban (circle) train; ~ *de derrière* (*devant*) *horse:* hind- (fore-) quarters *pl.*; ⊕ ~ *de laminoir* rolling-mill; ⚙ ~ *de marchandises* (*plaisir, voyageurs*) goods, *Am.* freight (excursion, passenger) train; ⊕~ *d'engrenages* gear train; ⊕ ~ *de roues* wheel train; ⚙~ *direct* (*or express*) through *or* express train; ⚙ ~ *omnibus* slow *or Am.* accommodation train; ⚙ ~ *rapide* fast express (train); *fig. à fond de* ~ at top speed; *aller son petit* ~ jog along; *fig. dans le* ~ up to date, F in the swim; *en bon* ~ in a good state, doing *or* going well; *être en* ~ *de* (*inf.*) be (engaged in) (*ger.*); be in a mood for (*ger. or su.*); ✗ F *le* ♀ (*approx.*) (Royal) Army Service Corps; *mal en* ~ out of sorts; *fig. manquer le* ~ miss the bus; *mener grand* ~ live in great style; *sp. mener le* ~ set the pace; *mettre en* ~ set (*s.th.*) going; *typ.* make ready; *fig. monter dans* (*or prendre*) *le* ~ (*en marche*) jump on the bandwagon.

traînage [trɛ'naːʒ] *m* hauling; sleighing; sleigh transport; ⁰ haulage; *telev.* streaking; **traînant, e** [~'nɑ̃, ~'nɑ̃ːt] dragging; trailing (*robe*); *fig.* sluggish; **traînard, e** [~'naːr, ~'nard] *su.* dawdler, *Am.* F slowpoke; *su./m* ✗ straggler; ⊕ *lathe:* carriage; **traînasser** [~na'se] (1a) *v/t.* † drag out; spin out; *v/i.* hang about; dawdle; **traîne** [trɛːn] *f dress:* train; *fishing:* dragnet; *à la* ~ in tow (*a. fig.*); lagging behind; **traîneau** [trɛ'no] *m* sleigh, sledge; **traînée** [~'ne] *f blood, light, smoke, snail:* trail; *gunpowder:* train; *fishing:* ground-line; *sl.* prostitute; **traîner** [~'ne] (1b) *v/t.* draw, drag, pull; tow (*a barge*); drawl out (*words*); drag out (*an affair, an existence, a speech*); ~ *la jambe* limp; *se* ~ crawl; drag o.s. along; *fig.* linger; drag (*time*); *v/i.* trail; *fig.* linger on (*a. ✗ illness*); hang about; dawdle; lag behind; languish; flag; remain unpaid (*account*); lie around, lie about (*things*); ~ *en longueur* drag on;

traîneur, -euse [~'nœːr, ~'nøːz] *su.* dawdler; ~ *de cafés* person who is hanging about the cafés; *su./m* hauler, dragger; ~ *de sabre* swashbuckler; sabre-rattler.

train-poste, *pl.* **trains-poste(s)** [trɛ'post] *m* mail-train.

train-train F [trɛ̃'trɛ̃] *m* (daily) round; (humdrum) routine.

traire [trɛːr] (4ff) *v/t.* milk (*a cow*); draw (*milk*); **trait, traite** [trɛ, trɛt] 1. *p.p.* of traire; 2. *su./m* pull(ing); *arrow:* shooting; *dart:* throwing; arrow, dart; *pen:* stroke; mark, line; *liquid:* draught, *Am.* gulp; *light:* shaft, beam; *fig.* act; stroke (*of genius*); characteristic touch; trait (*of character*); *appearance:* feature; *fig.* reference, relation; *paint.* outline, contour; ~ *d'esprit* witticism; ~ *d'union* hyphen; *avoir* ~ *à* have reference to, refer to; *boire d'un seul* ~ drink (*s.th.*) at one gulp *or* F go; *cheval m de* ~ draught-horse, *Am.* draft-horse, cart-horse; *su./f road:* stretch; *journey:* stage; ✝ *bank:* bill, draft; *bill:* drawing; trade; milking; ~*e des blanches* white-slave traffic; ~*e des Noirs* slave-trade; *d'une (seule)* ~ at a stretch; in one go.

traitable [trɛ'tabl] treatable; manageable; *fig.* tractable.

traité [trɛ'te] *m* treatise (on *de, sur*); *pol. etc.* treaty, agreement.

traitement [trɛt'mɑ̃] *m* treatment (*a.* ⚙); salary; ✕ *etc.* pay; ⊕ *material:* processing; ~ *initial* starting *or* initial salary; *mauvais* ~ *pl.* illtreatment *sg.*; maltreatment *sg.*; ~ *des données* data processing; **traiter** [trɛ'te] (1a) *v/t.* treat (⚙, ⊕, *a. fig.*); call (*s.o. s.th., q. de qch.*); entertain (*s.o.*); deal with; discuss (*a subject*); negotiate (*business, a deal, a marriage, etc.*); ~ *q. de prince* address s.o. as prince; *v/i.* negotiate, treat (for *de, pour*; with, *avec*); ~ *de* deal with (*a subject*); **traiteur** [~'tœːr] *m banquet:* caterer; restaurant keeper.

traître, -esse [trɛːr, trɛ'trɛs] 1. *adj.* treacherous (*a. fig.*); *fig.* dangerous; vicious (*animal*); *ne pas dire un* ~ *mot* not to say a (single) word; 2. *su./m* traitor; *thea.* villain; *prendre q. en* ~ attack s.o. when he is off his guard; *su./f* traitress; **traîtreusement** [trɛtrøz'mɑ̃] *adv.* of traître 1; **traîtrise** [~'triːz] *f* treachery.

trajectoire *phys.,* ✈, *etc.* [traʒɛk-'twaːr] *su./f, a. adj.* trajectory.

trajet [tra'ʒɛ] *m* 🚢, *mot. etc.* journey; ⚓, *anat., tex.* passage; *channel etc.:* crossing; *mot. etc.* ride; ✈ flight; ✗, *a. phys.* artery, nerve, *projectile, etc.:* course.

tralala [trala'la] *m* ♪ tra la la; F *fig.* fuss, ceremony; *en grand* ~ all dressed up, F dressed up to the nines.

tram F [tram] *m* tram(car), *Am.* streetcar, trolley(-car).

trame [tram] *f tex.* woof, weft; *fig.* frame(work); *fig.* texture; *phot.* ruled screen; *telev.* frame; *fig.* plot; **tramer** [tra'me] (1a) *v/t. tex.* weave (*a. fig. a plot*); *fig.* plot; *fig.* hatch (*a plot*); *fig. il se trame qch.* s.th. is brewing.

traminot [trami'no] *m* tramway employee, *Am.* streetcar employee.

tramontane [tramɔ̃'tan] *f* ⚓ north wind; north; *astr.* North Star; *fig. perdre la* ~ lose one's bearings.

tramway [tram'wɛ] *m* tramway; tram(car), *Am.* streetcar, trolley (-car); *remorque f de* ~ trailer (of a tramcar).

tranchant, e [trɑ̃'ʃɑ̃, ~'ʃɑ̃ːt] 1. *adj.* cutting; sharp (*tool, edge, a. fig. tone, voice*); *fig.* trenchant (*argument etc*); glaring (*colour, a. fig. contradiction*); ⊕ *outil m* ~ edgetool; 2. *su./m* edge; *knife:* cutting edge; *fig.* argument *m à deux* ~*s* argument that cuts both ways; **tranche** [trɑ̃ːʃ] *f* bread, meat, *etc., a. fig.:* slice; *book, coin, plank:* edge; *wheel:* face; ⊕ *tools:* set; ✍ ridge; ✝ *shares:* block; *fig.* portion; ✗ *section; bacon:* rasher; *couper en* ~*s* slice; *en* ~*s* sliced, in slices; ⊕ *par la* ~ edgeways; *sl. s'en payer une* ~ have a lot of fun; **tranché, e** [trɑ̃'ʃe] 1. *adj.* distinct, sharp; ▨ tranché; 2. *su./f* trench (*a.* ✗); ✗, *forest etc.:* cutting; ✗ ~*es pl.* gripes; colic *sg.*; **tranchefil** [trɑ̃ʃ'fil] *m horse:* curbchain; **tranchefile** [~'fil] *f book:* headband; **tranchelard** *cuis.* [~'laːr] *m* cook's knife; **tranchemontagne** [~mɔ̃'taɲ] *m* blusterer, fire-eater; **tranche-pain** [~'pɛ̃] *m/inv.* breadcutter; **trancher** [trɑ̃'ʃe] (1a) *v/t.* slice, cut; cut off; *fig.* cut short; settle (*a question*) once and for all; settle (*a difficulty, a problem, a quarrel*); ~ *le mot* speak out, speak plainly; *v/i.* cut; contrast sharply (with, *sur*);

fig. take drastic action; † *fig.* ~ de set up for *or* as; **tranchoir** [~'ʃwaːr] *m* cutting board.

tranquille [trɑ̃'kil] tranquil; calm, still, quiet; *fig.* easy (*a.* ✝ *market*), untroubled (*mind*); *laissez-moi* ~ leave me alone; **tranquillisant** ✍ [trɑ̃kili'zɑ̃] *m* tranquil(l)izer; **tranquilliser** [~'ze] (1a) *v/t.* calm (*s.o., one's mind, etc.*); reassure (*s.o.*) (about, *sur*); se ~ calm down; *fig.* set one's mind at rest; **tranquillité** [~'te] *f* tranquil(l)ity, calm, stillness, quiet; peace (*of mind*).

trans... [trɑ̃s, trɑ̃z] trans...; **~action** [trɑ̃zak'sjɔ̃] *f* ✝ transaction; ✝ deal; ⚖ settlement, arrangement; ✝, ⚖ composition; compromise (*a. pej.*); **~s** *pl.* dealings; transactions (*of a learned society*); **~atlantique** [~zatlɑ̃'tik] **1.** *adj.* transatlantic; **2.** *su./m* Atlantic liner; deck-chair; **~bahuter** F [~bay'te] (1a) *v/t.* lug (along); shift (around); **~bordement** [trɑ̃sbɔrdə'mɑ̃] *m* ⚓ transshipment; *river:* ferrying across; ⛴ *goods, passengers:* transfer; *trucks etc.:* traversing; **~border** [~'de] (1a) *v/t.* ⚓ tranship; ferry across (*a river*); ⛴ transfer (*goods, passengers*); traverse; **~bordeur** [~'dœːr] *m* travelling platform; (*a. pont m* ~) transporter-bridge; ⛴ train-ferry; **~cendance** *phls.* [trɑ̃ssɑ̃'dɑ̃ːs] *f* transcendency, transcendence; **~cendant, e** [~'dɑ̃, ~'dɑ̃ːt] *phls., a. fig.* transcendent; 𝔄 transcendental.

transcription [trɑ̃skrip'sjɔ̃] *f* transcription (*a.* ♪); copy, transcript; **transcrire** [~'kriːr] (4q) *v/t.* transcribe (*notes, a. a text, a.* ♪); copy (out).

transe [trɑ̃ːs] *f* (hypnotic) trance; **~s** *pl.* fear *sg.*, fright *sg.*

transept 𝔄 *eccl.* [trɑ̃'sɛpt] *m* transept.

trans...: **~férer** [trɑ̃sfe're] (1f) *v/t.* transfer; (re)move from one place to another; relocate; move (*an appointment, a date*); *eccl.* translate (*a bishop*); ⚖ convey (*an estate*); **~fert** [~'fɛːr] *m* transference; transfer (*a. phot.,* ✝); relocation; ⚖ *estate:* conveyance; **~figuration** [~figyra-'sjɔ̃] *f* transfiguration; **~figurer** [~figy're] (1a) *v/t.* transfigure; se ~ be(come) transfigured; **~formable** [trɑ̃sfɔr'mabl] transformable; *mot.*

convertible; **~formateur, -trice** [~ma'tœːr, ~'tris] **1.** *adj.* transforming; **2.** *su./m* ⚡ transformer; **~formation** [~ma'sjɔ̃] *f* transformation (into, en); *phls.* conversion; de ~ ⚡ transformer ...; ⊕ processing ...; **~former** [~'me] (1a) *v/t.* transform, convert (*a. foot., a. phls.*), change (into, en); se ~ change, turn (into, en); **~formisme** *biol. etc.* [~'mism] *m* transformism; **~formiste** [~'mist] *su. phls. etc.* transformist; *thea.* quick-change artist; **~fuge** [trɑ̃s-'fyʒ] *m* renegade; defector; **~fuser** *usu.* ✍ [~fy'ze] (1a) *v/t.* transfuse; **~fusion** [~fy'zjɔ̃] *f:* (~ sanguine *or* de sang blood-)transfusion; **~gresser** [~grɛ'se] (1a) *v/t.* transgress, infringe, break (*a law etc.*); **~humer** [trɑ̃zy'me] (1a) *v/t.* move (*flocks*) to *or* from the Alpine pastures; *v/i.* move to *or* from the hills.

transi, e [trɑ̃'zi]: (~ de froid) chilled to the bone; ~ de peur paralyzed with fear.

transiger [trɑ̃zi'ʒe] (1l) *v/i.* compromise (*a. fig.*); come to terms (with, avec).

transir [trɑ̃'siːr] (2a) *v/t.* chill; benumb; *fig.* paralyse (with, de); *v/i.* be chilled to the bone; be paralysed with fear.

transistor [trɑ̃zis'tɔr] *m radio:* transistor; **transistoriser** [~tɔri'ze] (1a) *v/t.* transistorize.

transit [trɑ̃'zit] *m* ✝ transit; ⛴ through traffic; **transitaire** ✝ [trɑ̃zi'tɛːr] **1.** *adj.* relating to transit of goods; (*country*) across which goods are conveyed in transit; **2.** *su./m* forwarding *or* transport agent; **transiter** ✝ [~'te] (1a) *v/t.* convey (*goods*) in transit; *v/i.* be in transit; **transitif, -ve** [~'tif, ~'tiːv] *gramm.* transitive; positional; **transition** [~'sjɔ̃] *f* transition; ♪ modulation; *geol.* de ~ transitional; *geol.* transition; transitory; transient; temporary; *gramm.* glide (*consonant, vowel*).

trans...: **~lation** [trɑ̃sla'sjɔ̃] *f* transfer; ⊕, *eccl.* translation; ⊕ shifting; *tel.* retransmission; ⚖ conveyance; **~lucide** [~ly'sid] semi-transparent, translucent; **~lucidité** [~lysidi'te] *f* semi-transparency, translucence; **~metteur** [~mɛ'tœːr] *m* transmitter; ⚓ signals (officer) sg.; ⚓ ship's telegraph; **~mettre** [~'mɛtr] (4v) v/t. transmit (*tel., radio, a. heat, light, a message*); pass on (*a disease, a message*); hand down (*to other generations*); ~ convey, transfer; 🚊 assign (*a patent, shares*); **~migration** [~migra'sjɔ̃] f *people, soul:* transmigration; **~migrer** [~mi'gre] (1a) v/i. transmigrate; **~missibilité** [~misibili'te] f transmissibility; 🚊 transferability; **~missible** [~mi'sibl] transmissible; 🚊 *etc.* transferable; **~mission** [~mi'sjɔ̃] f *message, order, a.* ⊕, 🖉, *phys., radio, tel.:* transmission; *disease, message, order:* passing on; ⊕ drive, (transmission) gear, shafting; 🚊 transfer, conveyance; 🚊 *patent, shares:* assignment; *foot.* passing; ✕, ⚓ ~s *pl.* signals; *mot.* ~ *par chaîne* chain-drive; **~muable** [~'mɥabl] transmutable (into, en); **~muer** [~'mɥe] (1n) v/t. transmute (into, en); **~mutabilité** [~mytabili'te] f transmutability (into, en); **~mutable** [~my'tabl] transmutable (into, en); **~mutation** [~myta'sjɔ̃] f transmutation (into, en); **~océanique** [trãzɔsea'nik] transoceanic; **~paraître** [trãspa'rɛːtr] (4k) v/i. show through; **~parence** [~pa'rãːs] f transparency; **~parent, e** [~pa'rã, ~'rãːt] 1. adj. transparent (a. fig.); 2. su./m transparent screen; writing-pad: guide-lines pl.; **~percer** [~pɛr'se] (1k) v/t. pierce (through); run (s.o.) through; transfix; fig. pierce (s.o. to the heart, le cœur à q.); fig. rain: soak.

transpiration [trãspira'sjɔ̃] f 🖉 perspiring; perspiration, sweat; 🕭, phys., physiol., a. fig. transpiration; en ~ in a sweat; **transpirer** [~'re] (1a) v/i. ~ perspire, sweat; 🕭, physiol., a. fig. transpire; fig. leak (out) (news, secret).

trans...: **~plantable** 🕭, 🖉 [trãsplã-'tabl] transplantable; **~plantation** [~plãta'sjɔ̃] f transplanting, transplantation; **~planter** [~plã'te] (1a) v/t. transplant; **~port** [~'pɔːr] m 🕂 transport, carriage; 🖉, 🚊 conveyance; 🚊 assignment; 🕂 account: transfer, balance brought forward; ⚓ troop-ship, transport; fig. anger: (out)burst; delight, joy: transport, ecstasy; 🖉 ~ au cerveau brain-storm; light-headedness;

stroke; ~ d'aviation aircraft transport; 🚊 ~ sur les lieux visit to the scene (of the occurrence); 🕂 compagnie f de ~ forwarding company; ⊕ courroie f de ~ conveyor-belt; de ~ ⊕ conveyor-...; geol. alluvial (deposit); **~portable** [~pɔr'tabl] transportable; 🕭 fit to be moved (patient); **~portation** [~pɔrta'sjɔ̃] f 🕂 goods: conveyance; 🕂, 🚊 transportation; **~porter** [~pɔr'te] (1a) v/t. transport; carry, convey; bring; fig. carry (s.o.) away; transporté de joie beside o.s. with joy, enraptured; se ~ betake o.s.; 🚊 se ~ sur les lieux visit the scene (of the occurrence); **~porteur** [~pɔr'tœːr] m 🕂 carrier; ⊕ conveyor; ~ aérien overhead runway, cableway; **~posable** [~po'zabl] transposable; **~poser** [~po'ze] (1a) v/t. typ., ♪, 🅰, etc. transpose; **~positeur** ♪ [~pozi'tœːr] m (a. instrument m ~) transposing instrument; **~position** [~pozi'sjɔ̃] f transposition; cin. dubbing; **~sibérien, -enne** geog. [~sibe'rjɛ̃, ~'rjɛn] trans-Siberian; **~substantiation** eccl. [~sypstãsja-'sjɔ̃] f transubstantiation; **~suder** [~sy'de] (1a) v/t./i. transude; v/i. ooze through; fig. emanate (from, de); **~vasement** [~vaz'mã] m liquid: decanting; **~vaser** [~vɑ'ze] (1a) v/t. decant; se ~ siphon; **~versal, e**, m/pl. **-aux** [~vɛr'sal, ~'so] 1. adj. cross (-section), transverse (a. anat. muscle), transversal; ⚓ athwartship; 🅰 coupe f ~e cross-section; 2. su./f 🅰 transversal; **~versalement** [~vɛr-sal'mã] adv. transversely, crosswise; ⚓ athwartship.

trapèze [tra'pɛːz] m 🅰 trapezium; sp. trapeze; anat. (a. muscle m ~) trapezius; **trapéziste** sp. [~pe'zist] su. trapeze-artist; trapezist; **trapézoïde** 🅰 [~pezɔ'id] m trapezoid.

trappe [trap] f trap-door; thea., a. hunt. trap; ⊕ etc. hatch; **trappeur** [tra'pœːr] m trapper.

trapu, e [tra'py] thick-set, stocky, squat.

traque hunt. [trak] f game: beating; **traquenard** [~'naːr] m trap (a. fig.); pitfall; fig. être pris dans son propre ~ fall into one's own trap; **traquer** [tra'ke] (1m) v/t. beat (the wood) for game; beat up (game); track down (a criminal); surround, hem (s.o.) in; **traqueur** hunt. [~'kœːr] m beater.

trauma *psych.*, ✚ [tro'ma] *m* trauma;
traumatique [troma'tik] traumatic; **traumatiser** [~ti'ze] (1a) *v/t.*
traumatize; **traumatisme** [~'tism]
m traumatism; *psych.* traumatic experience.

travail[1] *vet.* [tra'va:j] *m* frame, sling.
travail[2], *pl.* -**aux** [tra'va:j, ~'vo] *m*
work; ✚, ⚙, *pol.* labo(u)r; ⊕,
physiol., *a. wine*: working; ✚ childbirth; employment; piece of work, F
job; workmanship; business; ⊕
power; ~ *à la tâche* piece-work; ~ *en
série* mass production; ~ *intellectuel
(manuel)* brain-work (manual work);
accident m du ~ accident at work; *être
sans* ~ be out of work; ⚙ *~aux pl.*
forcés hard labo(u)r *sg.*; **travailler**
[trava'je] (1a) *v/i.* work (on, *sur*); be
at work; strive, endeavo(u)r; practise (*musician etc.*); train; work, ferment (*wine*); warp, shrink (*wood*);
fade (*colour*); be active (*mind, volcano*); ⊕ be stressed (*beam*); strain
(*cable, ship, etc.*); ✝ produce interest
(*capital*); *v/t.* work (*a.* ✎, ⊕); torment (*s.o., s.o.'s mind*); ⊕ shape,
fashion; knead (*dough*); overwork (*a
horse*); work (hard) at, study (*a subject*); *phot.* work up; *fig.* tamper
with; **travailleur, -euse** [~'jœ:r,
~'jø:z] 1. *adj.* hard-working, industrious; 2. *su.* worker; *su./m* workman,
labo(u)rer; ~ *de force* heavy worker; ~
intellectuel (manuel) brain-worker
(manual worker); *su./f (lady's)* worktable; *zo.* worker (bee); **travaillisme** *pol.* [~'jism] *m* Labour; **travailliste** *pol.* [~'jist] 1. *adj.* Labour ...; 2.
su./m member of the Labour party;
parl. Labour member.

travée ⚙ [tra've] *f* bay (*a. of a bridge*);
span; row (of seats).

travers [tra'vɛːr] 1. *su./m* ✝ breadth;
fig. fault, failing; ✝ ~ *de doigt* finger's
breadth; 2. *adv.*: de ~ askew, awry;
(*look*) askance; *fig.* wrong; en ~ (de)
across (*s.th.*); 3. *prp.*: à ~, au ~ de
through (*s.th.*); à ~ *champs* across
country; **traversable** [~vɛr'sabl]
traversable; fordable (*river*); **traverse** [~'vɛrs] *f* ⚙ traverse beam *or*
girder; *ladder*: rung; transom; ⚙
sleeper, *Am.* tie; *mot. etc.* crossmember; ⊕ crosshead; ✖ groundsill; ⚓ *harbour*: bar; *fig.* set-back; (*a.
chemin m de* ~) crossroad, short cut;
cross-street; **traversée** [travɛr'se] *f*

⚓, ⚙ crossing; ⚓ voyage, passage;
mount. traverse; *fig.* ~ *du désert* time
in the wilderness; bad patch; low
ebb; **traverser** [~'se] (1a) *v/t.* cross
(*a. fig.*); pass *or* go through; △
bridge: span (*a river*); **traversier,
-ère** [~'sje, ~'sjɛ:r] cross-..., crossing; ferry(-*boat*); ⚓ leading (*wind*); ♪
transverse (*flute*); **traversin** [~'sɛ̃]
m carpentry: cross-bar, cross-piece;
balance: beam; *bed*: bolster; **traversine** [~'sin] *f* cross-bar, cross-beam;
⚓ gangplank.

travesti, e [travɛs'ti] 1. *adj.* disguised; fancy-dress (*ball*); burlesqued; 2. *su./m* fancy dress; *thea.*
man's part (played by a woman) (*or
vice versa*); transvestite; **travestir**
[~'ti:r] (2a) *v/t.* misrepresent, distort; se ~ put on fancy dress; dress up
(as, en); **travestisme** [~'tism] *m*
transvestism; **travestissement**
[~tis'mɑ̃] *m* disguise; disguising; *fig.*
travesty, misrepresentation (*of a
fact*).

trayeur [trɛ'jœ:r] *m* milker; **trayeuse** [~'jø:z] *f* milkmaid; milkingmachine; **trayon** [~'jɔ̃] *m cow*:
teat, dug.

trébuchant, e [treby'ʃɑ̃, ~'ʃɑ̃:t]
stumbling; staggering; of full
weight (*coin*); **trébucher** [~'ʃe] (1a)
v/i. stumble (*a. fig.*), stagger; turn
the scale (*coin*); *fig.* trip; *v/t.* test
(*a coin*) for weight; **trébuchet**
[~'ʃe] *m* assay *or* precision balance;
trap (*for small birds*).

tréfiler ⊕ [trefi'le] (1a) *v/t.* wiredraw; **tréfilerie** ⊕ [~fil'ri] *f* wiredrawing (mill); **tréfileur** ⊕ [~fi-
'lœːr] *m* wire-drawer.

trèfle [trɛfl] *m* ⚘ clover; △, ⚘ trefoil; *cards*: club(s *pl.*); ⚘ ~ *blanc*
shamrock; *mot.* croisement en ~
cloverleaf (crossing); *jouer* ~ play
a club, play clubs; **tréflière** ✎
[trefli'ɛ:r] *f* clover-field.

tréfonds [tre'fɔ̃] *m fig.* (inmost)
depths *pl.*

treillage [trɛ'ja:ʒ] *m* trellis; latticework; wire netting; wire fencing;
treillager [~ja'ʒe] (1l) *v/t.* trellis;
lattice (*a wall, a window*); enclose
with wire netting.

treille [trɛːj] *f* vine-arbo(u)r; ⚘
climbing vine, grape-vine; F *jus m de
la* ~ juice of the grape, wine.

treillis [trɛ'ji] *m* trellis(-work), lat-

tice; grid (*for maps etc.*); *tex.*
glazed calico; *tex.* coarse canvas,
sackcloth; ✕ fatigue-dress, fatigues
pl.; **treillisser** [~ji'se] (1a) *v/t. see*
treillager.

treize [trɛːz] **1.** *adj./num.* thirteen;
date, title: thirteenth; ~ *à la douzaine* baker's dozen; **2.** *su./m/inv.*
thirteen; **treizième** [trɛ'zjɛm] *adj./
num., a. su.* thirteenth.

tremblaie ♀ [trɑ̃'blɛ] *f* aspen grove;
tremblant, e [trɑ̃'blɑ̃, ~'blɑ̃ːt]
1. *adj.* trembling (with, de); quak-
ing, shaking (*ground, voice*); quavering (*voice*); flickering (*light*);
shaky (*bridge, a. fig. person*); quiv-
ering (*face*); **2.** *su./m* ♩ organ:
tremolo (stop); **tremble** ♀ [trɑ̃:bl]
m aspen; **tremblement** [trɑ̃blə-
'mɑ̃] *m* trembling, shaking, quiver-
ing; *voice:* quaver(ing); *fig. horror:*
shudder(ing); ♩ tremolo; *♬, a. fig.
emotion:* tremor; ~ *de terre* earthquake, earth tremor; F *tout le* ~
the whole shoot *or* caboodle; **trembler** [~'ble] (1a) *v/i.* tremble, shake,
quiver (with, de); quaver (♩, *a.
voice*); flicker (*light*); flutter (*bird's
wings*); *fig.* tremble, be afraid; ~
que (*sbj.*) be terrified lest (*cond.*);
trembleur, -euse [~'blœːr, ~'bløːz]
su. trembler; *fig.* timid *or* anxious
person; *su./m* ⚡ make-and-break;
tel., teleph. buzzer; **trembloter** F
[~blɔ'te] (1a) *v/i.* quiver; quaver
(*voice*); flicker (*light*); flutter
(*wings*); shiver (with, de).

trémière ♀ [tre'mjɛːr] *adj./f:* rose
f ~ hollyhock.

tremolo [tremɔ'lo] *m* ♩ tremolo; *fig.*
quaver.

trémousser [tremu'se] (1a) *v/t.:* se ~
wiggle; fidget (*child etc.*); jig about.

trempage [trɑ̃'paːʒ] *m* ⊕ soaking,
steeping; *typ. paper:* damping;
trempe [trɑ̃ːp] *f* ⊕ soaking, steeping; quenching; *metall.* tempering,
hardening; *steel:* temper; *fig.* calibre, stamp; F thrashing, hiding; ~ *de
surface* casehardening; **trempée**
[trɑ̃'pe] soaked, drenched, wet
(through); *metall.* tempered; *fig.*
sturdy, energetic; **tremper** [trɑ̃'pe]
(1a) *v/t.* soak; drench; dip (*the pen in
ink*); dip, *Am.* dunk (*bread, biscuit in
a liquid*); ⊕ *etc.* quench; *typ.* damp
(*paper*); dilute (*wine*) with water; *v/i.*
soak; *fig.* be a party (to, *dans*); **trem-**

pette [~'pɛt] *f: faire* ~ dunk a biscuit
etc. in one's wine *or* coffee *etc.*; F
have a dip.

tremplin [trɑ̃'plɛ̃] *m sp. etc.* spring-
board; diving-board; *ski:* platform;
fig. stepping-stone (to, *pour*).

trémulation [tremyla'sjɔ̃] *f* vibration, trepidation; ✽ tremor.

trentaine [trɑ̃'tɛn] *f* (about) thirty;
la ~ the age of thirty, the thirties *pl.*;
trente [trɑ̃ːt] *adj./num., a. su./m/inv.*
thirty; *date, title:* thirtieth; ~-*trois
tours m* long-playing record, album;
trentième [trɑ̃'tjɛm] *adj./num., a.
su.* thirtieth.

trépan [tre'pɑ̃] *m* ✽, ⊕ trepan; ⊕
rock-drill; *a.* = **trépanation** ✽
[~pana'sjɔ̃] *f* trepanning; **trépaner**
[~pa'ne] (1a) *v/t.* ✽ trepan; ⊕ drill *or*
bore into (*rock*).

trépas *poet.* [tre'pɑ] *m* death, decease; **trépassé, e** [trepa'se] *adj.,
a. su.* dead, departed, deceased; **trépasser** [~] (1a) *v/i.* die, pass away.

trépidation [trepida'sjɔ̃] *f* ✽, *a.
fig.* trembling; *fig.* flurry, agitation;
trepidation, vibration.

trépied [tre'pje] *m* tripod; *cuis.*
trivet.

trépigner [trepi'ɲe] (1a) stamp one's
feet; jump (for joy, de joie); dance
(with, de); *v/t.* trample (*the earth*).

trépointe [tre'pwɛ̃t] *f shoe:* welt.

très [trɛ] *adv.* very, most; very much.

trésaille [tre'zaːj] *f* ⊕ crosspiece.

Très-Haut [trɛ'o] *m/inv.: le* ~ the
Almighty, God.

trésor [tre'zɔːr] *m* treasure (*a. fig.*);
treasure-house; *eccl.* relics *pl.* and
ornaments *pl.*; ⚖ treasure-trove;
pol. ♀ Treasury; ~*s pl.* wealth *sg.*;
F *dépenser des* ~*s pour* spend a fortune on; **trésorerie** [~zɔr'ri] *f*
treasury; treasurer's office; treasurership; *pol.* ♀ Treasury; *Britain:*
Exchequer; **trésorier, -ère** [~zɔ-
'rje, ~'rjɛːr] *su.* treasurer; *su./m admin., a.* ✕ paymaster; *su./f admin.*
paymistress.

tressage [trɛ'saːʒ] *m* plaiting, braid-
ing.

tressaillement [trɛsaj'mɑ̃] *m* surprise: start; *fear:* shudder; *pleasure,
joy:* thrill; *pain:* wince; **tressaillir**
[~sa'jiːr] (2s) *v/i.* quiver, flutter
(*heart*); ~ *de* start (*etc.*) with; shudder with (*fear*); thrill with (*joy*);
wince with (*pain*).

tressauter [treso'te] (1a) *v/i.* jump (with fear, surprise, *etc.*); jolt, jump about (*things*).

tresse [trɛs] *f* hair, straw: tress, plait; yarn, *a.* ⚓: braid; **tresser** [trɛ'se] (1a) *v/t.* plait (*hair, straw*); braid (*yarn, a.* ⚓); weave (*a basket, flowers, a garland*); **tresseur** *m*, **-euse** *f* [∽'sœːr, ∽'søːz] braider, plaiter.

tréteau [tre'to] *m* trestle, support; *thea.* ∼x *pl.* stage *sg.*

treuil ⊕ [trœːj] *m* winch, windlass.

trêve [trɛːv] *f* truce; *fig.* respite; *sans* ∼ unremittingly, relentlessly; ∼ *de* ... enough of ..., no more ...; ∼ *de plaisanteries!* no more joking!

tri [tri] *m* sorting.

triade [tri'ad] *f* triad.

triage [tri'aːʒ] *m* sorting; selecting; ⚒ grading; 🚂 *gare f de* ∼ marshalling yard.

triangle [tri'ãːgl] *m* ♪, ♫, *astr.* triangle; ⚓ triangular flag; ♫ three-phase mesh; set square, *Am.* triangle; **triangulaire** [triãgy'lɛːr] triangular; *pol.* three-cornered (*contest*); **triangulation** *surv.* [∽la'sjõ] *f* triangulation.

trias *geol.* [tri'ɑːs] *m* trias; **triasique** *geol.* [∽a'zik] triassic.

tribal, e [tri'bal] tribal.

tribord ⚓ [tri'bɔːr] *m* starboard; *à (or par)* ∼ *to* starboard. [ily.)

tribu [tri'by] *f* tribe; *zo.* sub-fam-⟩

tribulation [tribyla'sjõ] *f* tribulation; *fig.* trial; F worry, trouble.

tribun [tri'bœ̃] *m hist.* tribune; *fig.* popular orator; demagogue.

tribunal [triby'nal] *m* ⚖, ⚔, *a. admin.* tribunal; *fig.* (law-)court; *judges:* bench; ∼ *arbitral (de commerce)* arbitration (commercial) court; ∼ *de première instance* court of first instance; (*approx.*) County Court; ∼ *de simple police* magistrate's court, F police-court; ∼ *pour enfants* juvenile court; **tribune** [∽'byn] *f* rostrum, (*speaker's*) platform; ⚙ (*organ*) loft; ⚖, *eccl., etc.* gallery; *turf:* grand stand; *fig.* forum; ∼ *de la presse* press galery; *parl. monter à la* ∼ address the House.

tribut [tri'by] *m* tribute (*a. fig.*); *fig.* reward; **tributaire** [∽by'tɛːr] tributary (*a. geog.*).

tricar *mot.* [tri'kaːr] *m* motor-tricycle; three-wheeler.

tricher [tri'ʃe] (1a) *vt/i.* cheat; **tricherie** [triʃ'ri] *f* cards *etc.*: cheating; trickery; **tricheur** *m*, **-euse** *f* [tri'ʃœːr, ∽'ʃøːz] cheat, trickster; *cards:* sharper.

trichine ⚕ [tri'ʃin, ∽'kin] *f* trichina; thread-worm; **trichinose** ⚕ [∽ki'noːz] *f* trichinosis.

trichromie *phot., typ.* [trikrɔ'mi] *f* three-colo(u)r process.

tricolore [trikɔ'lɔːr] tricolo(u)r(ed); *drapeau m* ∼ tricolo(u)r, French (national) flag.

tricorne [tri'kɔrn] **1.** *adj. zo.* three-horned; *cost.* tricorn (*hat*); **2.** *su./m* tricorn, three-cornered hat.

tricot [tri'ko] *m* knitting; *tex.* stockinet; ⚓ knitwear; jersey, sweater, pullover; (*a.* ∼ *de corps*) vest, *Am.* undershirt; **tricotage** [trikɔ'taːʒ] *m* knitting; **tricoter** [∽'te] (1a) *v/t.* knit; F *se* ∼ make off; *v/i.* F *fig.* move or walk fast; F dance; **tricoteur, -euse** [∽'tœːr, ∽'tøːz] *su.* knitter; *su./f* knitting-machine; ⊕ knitting-loom.

trictrac [trik'trak] *m* backgammon (-board); *dice:* rattle.

tricycle [tri'sikl] *m* tricycle; three-wheeled vehicle.

trident [tri'dã] *m myth. etc.* trident; ⚓ three-pronged pitch-fork; ♫ trident curve; fish-spear.

tridimensionnel, -elle [tridimãsjɔ-'nɛl] threedimensional.

trièdre ♫ [tri'edr] **1.** *adj.* trihedral; **2.** *su./m* trihedral, trihedron.

triennal, e, *m/pl.* **-aux** [trien'nal, ∽'no] triennial; **triennat** [∽'na] *m* triennium; three-year term of office.

trier [tri'e] (1a) *v/t.* sort (out); *tex.* pick; 🚂 marshal (*trucks*); *fig.* choose, select; **trieur, -euse** [∽-'œːr, ∽'øːz] *su. person:* sorter; *tex.* (*wool-*)picker; *su./m* ⊕ screening-machine; separator, sorter; *su./f* wool-picking machine; *computer:* sorter.

trifolié, e ♣ [trifɔ'lje] three-leaved, trifoliate.

trigone ♫ [tri'gɔn] trigonal, three-cornered; **trigonométrie** ♫ [∽gɔ-nɔme'tri] *f* trigonometry.

trilatéral, e, *m/pl.* **-aux** [trilate'ral, ∽'ro] trilateral, three-sided.

trilingue [tri'lɛ̃ːg] trilingual.

trille ♪ [tri'j] *m* trill; **triller** ♪ [tri'je] (1a) *vt/i.* trill.

trillion [tri'ljõ] *m* a million of billions, trillion, *Am.* a billion of billions, quintillion.

trilogie [trilɔ'ʒi] *f* trilogy.

trimard † *sl.* [tri'maːr] *m* high road; **trimarder** *sl.* [trimar'de] (1a) *v/i.* be on the tramp; *v/t.* carry, F lug; **trimardeur** *sl.* [ˌ'dœːr] *m* tramp, *Am.* hobo.

trimbaler F [trɛ̃ba'le] (1a) *v/t.* carry about, F tote about; trail (*s.o.*) along; have (*s.o.*) in tow; F lug (*s.th.*) about.

trimer F [tri'me] (1a) *v/i.* drudge, toil.

trimestre [tri'mɛstr] *m* quarter, three month; quarter's rent *or* salary; *univ., school:* term, *Am.* session; term's fees *pl., Am.* sessional fees *pl.*; **trimestriel, -elle** [ˌmɛstri'ɛl] quarterly; trimestrial.

trimoteur ✈ [trimɔ'tœːr] **1.** *adj./m* three-engined; **2.** *su./m* three-engined aeroplane.

tringle [trɛ̃ːgl] *f* rod; ⛴ bar; ⚓ *etc.* (*wooden*) batten; ⚠ square mo(u)lding, tringle.

trinité [trini'te] *f* trinity (*a.* ♀ *eccl.*).

trinôme ♀ [tri'noːm] *adj., a. su./m* trinomial.

trinquart ⚓ [trɛ̃'kaːr] *m* herring-boat.

trinquer [trɛ̃'ke] (1m) *v/i.* clink *or* touch glasses (with, *avec*); (have a) drink (with, *avec*); F *fig.* hobnob (with, *avec*); *sl.* get the worst of it, suffer.

trio [tri'o] *m* ♪ *etc.* trio.

triode [tri'ɔd] *f* (*a.* lampe *f* ~) radio: three-electrode lamp, triode.

triolet [triɔ'lɛ] *m* ♪ triplet; *prosody:* triolet.

triomphal, e, *m/pl.* **-aux** [triɔ̃'fal, ˌ'fo] triumphal; **triomphalement** [ˌfal'mã] *adv.* triumphantly; **triomphant, e** [ˌ'fã, ˌ'fãːt] triumphant; **triomphateur, -trice** [ˌfa-'tœːr, ˌ'tris] **1.** *adj.* triumphing; **2.** *su./m* (triumphant) victor; winner; **triomphe** [tri'ɔ̃ːf] *m* triumph; *arc m* de ~ triumphal arch; **triompher** [ˌɔ̃'fe] (1a) *v/i.* triumph (over, de); *fig.* rejoice, exult (over, de); ~ *dans* excel in *or* at; ~ *de a.* overcome, get over (*s.o.*).

tripaille F [tri'paːj] *f* garbage; (*butcher's*) offal.

triparti, e [tripar'ti], **tripartite** [ˌ'tit] tripartite; *pol.* three-party

(*government*), three-power; **tripartition** [ˌti'sjõ] *f* tripartition.

tripe [trip] *f cuis.* (*usu.* ~*s pl.*) tripe; *cigar:* core; F ~*s pl.* guts; *tex.* ~ de *velours* velveteen; **triperie** [tri'pri] *f* tripe-shop, tripe trade; **tripette** F [ˌ'pɛt] *f: ça ne vaut pas* ~ it's not worth a cent.

triphasé, e ⚡ [trifa'ze] three-phase, triphase.

tripier [tri'pje] *m* tripe-dealer, tripe-seller.

triple [tripl] **1.** *adj.* threefold, treble; triple (*a.* ♀, ⚗, *astr.*); F *fig.* out-and-out (*fool*); **2.** *su./m* treble; **triplé m, e** *f* [tri'ple] *children:* triplet; **tripler** [ˌ] (1a) *vt/i.* treble; increase threefold.

triporteur [tripɔr'tœːr] *m* carrier-tricycle; (*commercial*) tri-car.

tripot [tri'po] *m* gambling house, dive; **tripotage** [tripɔ'taːʒ] *m* messing about *or* round; *fig.* intrigue; tampering (*with accounts, the cash, etc.*); **tripotée** *sl.* [ˌ'te] *f* hiding, beating; lots *pl.* (*of people, things*); **tripoter** [ˌ'te] (1a) *v/i.* mess about *or* around; rummage about; *v/t.* finger, fiddle with, play with; meddle with (*s.th.*); paw (*s.o.*); *fig.* be up to; **tripoteur** [ˌ'tœːr] *m* intriguer; mischief-maker; shady speculator.

triptyque [trip'tik] *m art:* triptych; *admin.* triptyque; *fig.* three-part plan *etc.*

trique F [trik] *f* cudgel, big stick; *maigre* (*or sec*) *comme un coup de* ~ as thin as a rake.

triqueballe † [trik'bal] *m* timber-cart; logging-wheels *pl.*

triquer [tri'ke] (1m) *v/t.* sort (*timber*); beat, thrash (*s.o.*).

trisaïeul [triza'jœl] *m* great-great grandfather; **trisaïeule** [ˌ] *f* great-great grandmother.

trisannuel, -elle [triza'nɥɛl] triennial.

trisection [trisɛk'sjõ] *f* trisection.

trisser[1] *sl.* [tri'se] (1a) *v/t.: se* ~ clear off.

trisser[2] [ˌ] (1a) *v/i.* call for a second encore; *v/t.* encore twice.

triste [trist] sad; sorrowful, melancholy (*face, news, person*); downcast (*expression, face, person*); dull (*life, weather*); gloomy, dreary (*life, room, scene, weather*); painful (*duty,* *news*); *fig.* sorry, poor; **tristesse** [tris'tɛs] *f* sadness; gloom; *life, room, scene, weather*: gloominess, dreariness; *scenery*: bleakness.

triton[1] *zo.* [tri'tɔ̃] *m* water-salamander, newt; *mollusc*: trumpetshell.

triton[2] ♪ [~] *m* tritone.

trituration ⊕ [trityra'sjɔ̃] *f* trituration, grinding; **triturer** ⊕ [~'re] (1a) *v/t.* grind (up); knead, pommel; manipulate; F **se ~ la cervelle** rack one's brains.

trivalence 🜛 [triva'lɑ̃:s] *f* trivalence; **trivalent, e** 🜛 [~'lɑ̃, ~'lɑ̃:t] trivalent.

trivial, e, *m/pl.* **-aux** [tri'vjal, ~'vjo] trite, hackneyed; vulgar, coarse; **trivialité** [~vjali'te] *f* triteness; vulgarity, coarseness, vulgarism.

troc [trɔk] *m* barter, exchange; F swop(ping), *Am.* swap(ping).

trochée [trɔ'ʃe] *m prosody*: trochee.

troène ♀ [trɔ'ɛn] *m* privet.

troglodyte [trɔglɔ'dit] *m zo., orn.* troglodyte; *person*: caveman, cavedweller.

trogne [trɔɲ] *f* bloated face.

trognon [trɔ'ɲɔ̃] *m fruit*: core; *cabbage*: stump, stalk; *sl.* darling; F *fig.* **jusqu'au ~** completely, utterly.

trois [trwa] **1.** *adj./num.* three; *date, title*: third; **2.** *su./m/inv.* three; ♣ **règle f de ~** rule of three; **~-étoiles** [trwaze'twal] *adj.* (*a. su./inv.*) three-star (*restaurant or hotel, etc.*); **troisième** [~'zjɛm] **1.** *adj./num., a. su.* third; **2.** *su./m fraction*: third; third (*Am.* fourth) *floor*; *su./f secondary school*: (*approx.*) fourth form; **trois-mâts** ⚓ [trwɑ'mɑ] *m/inv.* three-master; **trois-pièces** *cost.* [~'pjɛs] *m/inv.* three-piece suit; **trois-quarts** ♣ [~'ka:r] *m/inv.* ♪ three-quarter violin; three-quarter length coat; *rugby*: three-quarter; **trois-six** ♣ [~'sis] *m* proof spirit.

trolley [trɔ'lɛ] *m* ⊕ trolley, runner; ⚡ trolley(-pole and wheel); **~bus** [~lɛ-'bys] *m* trolley-bus.

trombe [trɔ̃:b] *f meteor.* waterspout; *fig.* stream, torrent; **~ d'eau** cloudburst; *fig.* **en ~** like a whirlwind; *entrer* (*passer*) **en ~** burst in (dash by).

trombine *sl.* [trɔ̃'bin] *f* face; head.

trombone [trɔ̃'bɔn] *m* ♪ trombone; (wire) paper-clip; **tromboniste** ♪ [~bɔ'nist] *m* trombonist.

trommel ⊕, ⚒ [trɔ'mɛl] *m* revolving screen; drum.

trompe [trɔ̃:p] *f* ♪ horn (*a. mot.*); *zo.* proboscis, *elephant*: trunk; *anat.* tube; **~s** *pl. utérines* Fallopian tubes.

trompe-la-mort F [trɔ̃pla'mɔ:r] *su./inv.* death-dodger; **trompe-l'œil** [~'plœ:j] *m/inv. art*: trompe-l'œil; *fig.* eyewash, window dressing; **tromper** [~'pe] (1a) *v/t.* deceive; cheat; mislead; delude (about, *sur*); be unfaithful to (*one's husband or wife*); outwit, elude (*the law, a watch*); *fig.* beguile (*one's grief, one's hunger, the time*); *fig.* run counter to (*hopes, intentions*); **se ~** be wrong; make a mistake; **se ~ de chemin** take the wrong road; **tromperie** [~'pri] *f* deceit, deception; illusion; piece of deceit.

trompeter [trɔ̃p'te] (1c) *v/t.* trumpet abroad (*a. fig.*); *fig.* divulge; *v/i.* sound the trumpet; scream (*eagle*).

trompette [trɔ̃'pɛt] *su./f* trumpet; **en ~ turned-up** (*nose*); *su./m* = **trompettiste** [~pɛ'tist] *m* trumpeter.

trompeur, -euse [trɔ̃'pœ:r, ~'pø:z] **1.** *adj.* deceitful (*person*); lying (*tongue, words*); *fig.* deceptive (*appearance etc.*); **2.** *su.* deceiver; cheat; betrayer.

tronc [trɔ̃] *m* ⚘, △, *anat.* trunk; ♣ *tree*: bole; △ *column*: drum; *eccl.* collection-box; alms-box; ♣ frustum; ♣ **~ de cône** truncated cone; **tronche** *sl.* [trɔ̃ʃ] *f* head; **tronçon** [~'sɔ̃] *m* stump; piece; length; offcut; ⛭, *tel., etc.* section; **tronconique** ♣ [~kɔ'nik] in the shape of a truncated cone; **tronçonner** [~sɔ'ne] (1a) *v/t.* cut up; cut into lengths *or* sections.

trône [tro:n] *m* throne; **monter sur le ~** ascend the throne; **trôner** [tro'ne] (1a) *v/i.* sit enthroned; F *fig.* sit in state, lord it.

tronquer [trɔ̃'ke] (1m) *v/t.* △, ♣ truncate; *fig.* shorten; *fig.* cut down.

trop [tro] *adv.* too much *or* many; too, over-...; unduly; too long *or* far; too often; too well; **de ~** too many; **être de ~** be unwelcome, be in the way; **ne ... que ~** far too ..., only too ...; **par ~** altogether *or* really too ...

trophée [trɔ'fe] *m* trophy.

trophique *physiol.* [trɔ'fik] trophic; digestive (*trouble*).

tropical, e, *m/pl.* **-aux** [trɔpi'kal,

~'ko] tropical (*climate, heat, plant*);
tropique *astr.*, *geog.* [~'pik] *m*
tropic.

trop-plein [trɔ'plɛ̃] *m* overflow;
waste-pipe; overflow-pipe; *fig.* superabundance.

troquer [trɔ'ke] (1m) *v/t.* exchange,
barter, F swop, *Am.* swap (for,
contre).

troquet F [trɔ'kɛ] *m* (*small*) café.

trot [tro] *m* trot; *aller au* ~ trot; F
au ~ quickly; *prendre le* ~ break
into a trot; **trotte** F [trɔt] *f* (*a good*)
distance; **trotte-menu** † [~mə'ny]
adj./inv. scampering; *poet.* la *gent* ~
mice *pl.*; **trotter** [trɔ'te] (1a) *v/i.*
trot; scamper (about); F *fig.* be on the
move or go; ~ *par* (*or dans*) la tête de q.
haunt s.o. (*tune*); *v/t.*: F *se* ~ be off;
trotteur, -euse [~'tœːr, ~'tøːz] 1.
adj. walking(-*costume etc.*); 2. *su.*
horse: trotter; *fig.* quick walker; *su./f*
clock, watch: second hand; **trottiner** [~ti'ne] (1a) *v/i.* trot short
(*horse*); jog along (*on a horse*); *fig.*
toddle (*child*); *fig.* trot about; **trottinette** [~ti'nɛt] *f* scooter; **trottoir**
[~'twaːr] *m* pavement, footpath, *Am.*
sidewalk; ~ *cyclable* cycle path; F *pej.*
faire le ~ walk the streets.

trou [tru] *m* hole; *needle:* eye; gap (*a.
fig.*); *anat.* foramen; *thea.* (*prompter's*) box; ✈ ~ *d'air* air pocket; ⊕ ~ *de*
graissage oil-hole; *fig.* boucher un ~
pay off a debt; *faire* (*or créer*) le ~ *sp.*
break clear; *fig.* outdistance one's
rivals; F *faire un* ~ *à la lune* do a
moonlight flit; abscond.

troublant, e [tru'blɑ̃, ~'blɑ̃ːt] disturbing; disquieting; unsettling;
trouble [trubl] 1. *adj.* blurred,
hazy; cloudy (*liquid etc.*); confused;
murky (*light, sky, etc.*); dim (*eyes,
light*); 2. *su./m* confusion, disorder;
agitation, distress; discord, dissension; *fig.* uneasiness, turmoil; ~s *pl.*
pol. unrest *sg.*, disturbances; ✍
trouble *sg.*, disorders; **trouble-fête**
[trublə'fɛːt] *su./inv.* spoilsport; wet
blanket; **troubler** [~'ble] (1a) *v/t.*
disturb; cloud (*a liquid*); *fig.* interrupt; *fig.* perplex, disconcert; make
(*s.o.*) uneasy; ruffle (*s.o.*); *se* ~
become cloudy or overcast (*sky*);
falter (*voice*); become flustered
(*person*); show concern.

trouée [tru'e] *f* gap, break; ✍ breach,
break-through; **trouer** [~] (1a) *v/t.*

make a hole or holes in; *fig.* pit (with,
de); *fig.* make gaps in; *se* ~ wear into
holes, develop holes; *être troué* have a
hole or holes (in it).

trouille *sl.* [truːj] *f* fear, jitters *pl.*;
avoir la ~ have the wind up, be in a
blue funk.

troupe [trup] *f people:* troop (*a.* ✍),
band; *pej.* gang; *thea.* company,
troupe; ✍ regiment; ✍ men *pl.*;
cattle, deer, etc.: herd; *geese, sheep:*
flock; *flies:* swarm; *birds:* flight; ✍ ~s
pl. forces, troops; **troupeau** [tru-
'po] *m cattle etc.:* herd; *geese, sheep, a.
fig., eccl.:* flock; *fig.* set, pack; **troupier** † F [~'pje] *m* soldier; *jurer*
comme un ~ swear like a trooper.

trousse [trus] *f* † bundle; *hay:* truss;
⊕, ⚕ *instruments, tools:* case, kit; ~ *à*
pharmacie first-aid box or kit; ~ *de*
maquillage vanity case or bag; ~ *à*
outils toolkit; ~ *de réparation* repair
kit; ~ *de toilette* toilet bag, sponge
bag; ~ *de voyage* travelling case; *aux*
~s *de on* (*s.o.'s*) heels, after (*s.o.*);
trousseau [tru'so] *m keys etc.:*
bunch; outfit; *bride:* trousseau;
metall. sweep; **trousse-queue**
[trus'kø] *m/inv. horse:* tail-case;
trousser [tru'se] (1a) *v/t.* tuck up;
turn up (*one's trousers*); *cuis.* truss
(*fowl*); *metall.* sweep (*a mould*); F *fig.*
dash (*s.th.*) off.

trouvable [tru'vabl] that can be
found, findable; **trouvaille** [~'vɑːj]
f (lucky) find, godsend; **trouver**
[~'ve] (1a) *v/t.* find; discover; hit
or come upon; meet (with); *fig.*
consider, think; ~ *bon* (*mauvais*)
(dis)approve; ~ *bon de* (*inf.*) think
fit to (*inf.*); ~ *la mort* meet one's
death; *aller* (*venir*) ~ *q.* go (come)
and see s.o.; *comment trouvez-vous*
...? what do you think of ...?;
enfant m trouvé foundling; *objets*
m/pl. trouvés lost property *sg.*;
vous trouvez? do you think so ?; *se* ~
be (present, situated); feel (*better*
etc.); happen; *il se trouve que ...*
it happens that; **trouvère** [~'vɛːr]
m minstrel; **trouveur, -euse** *f*
[~'vœːr, ~'vøːz] discoverer; finder.

truand [try'ɑ̃] *m* crook, villain; †
begger; **truander** F [~ɑ̃'de] *v/t.* (1a)
swindle, do.   [shove-net.)

truble [trybl] *f fishing:* hoop-net.)

truc F [tryk] *m* knack, hang; dodge,
trick; thingummy, thing, gadget.

trucage [try'ka:ʒ] *m* faking; cheating; fake; F *accounts:* cooking; *cin.* trick picture; ✕ dummy work; *pol. elections:* gerrymandering.

truchement [tryʃ'mɑ̃] *m* † interpreter; *fig.* go-between; *fig.* means of expression; *par le ~ de* through.

trucider F [trysi'de] (1a) *v/t.* massacre, kill.

truc(k) 🚋 [tryk] *m* truck.

truculent, e [tryky'lɑ̃, ~'lɑ̃:t] colo(u)rful.

truelle [try'ɛl] *f* △, ⊕, *etc.* trowel; *cuis.* (fish-)slice; **truellée** [~ɛ'le] *f* trowelful.

truffe [tryf] *f* ♀, *cuis.* truffle; *dog:* nose; F idiot; **truffer** [try'fe] (1a) *v/t. cuis.* stuff with truffles; *fig. truffé de* full of, bristling with; **trufficulteur** [~fikyl'tœ:r] *m* truffle-grower; **truffier, -ère** [~'fje, ~'fjɛ:r] **1.** *adj.* truffle-...; **2.** *su./m* truffle-grower; *su./f* truffle-bed.

truie [trɥi] *f* sow.

truisme [try'ism] *m* truism.

truite *icht.* [trɥit] *f* trout; *~ saumonée* salmon trout; **truité, e** [trɥi'te] spotted; speckled; crackled (*china*).

trumeau [try'mo] *m* △ pier; pierglass; *cuis.* leg of beef.

truquage [try'ka:ʒ] *m see trucage*; **truquer** [~'ke] (1m) *v/t.* fake; F fiddle with, fix; cook (*accounts*); *pol.* gerrymander (*elections*); *v/i.* cheat; sham; **truqueur** *m*, **-euse** *f* [~'kœ:r, ~'kø:z] *person:* fraud, humbug; faker (*of antiques etc.*).

trust † [trœst] *m* trust; **truster** † [trœs'te] (1a) *v/i.* trust; *v/t.* monopolize (*a. fig.*).

tsar [tsa:r] *m* tsar, czar; **tsarine** [tsa'rin] *f* tsarina, czarina; **tsariste** [~'rist] *adj., a. su.* tsarist, czarist.

tsé-tsé *zo.* [tse'tse] *f* tsetse-fly.

tu¹ [ty] *pron./pers.* you.

tu², e [~] *p.p. of* taire.

tuable [tɥabl] fit for slaughter (*animal*); **tuant, tuante** F [tɥɑ̃, tɥɑ̃:t] killing (*work*); splitting (*headache*); *fig.* exasperating; boring (*person*).

tub [tœb] *m* tub, bath.

tuba [ty'ba] *m* ♪ tuba; *sp.* snorkel.

tubage [ty'ba:ʒ] *m* ⚙, ♣, *vet.* tubing; *shaft, well:* casing; **tube** [tyb] *m* ⚙, 🐾, ♣, ⊕ boiler, ⚓ torpedo, *anat., paint., phys., telev.,* † toothpaste, *etc.:* tube; ⊕, △ pipe; *radio:*

valve; *anat.* duct; *sl.* hit (song); *sl.* (tele)phone; 🐾 *~ à essai* test-tube; *telev. ~ de prise de vue* camera tube; *sl. coup de ~* phone call; F buzz.

tuber [ty'be] (1a) *v/t.* ⚙, ♣, *vet.* tube (*boiler, bore-hole, larynx, well*); ⊕ case (*a shaft*).

tubercule [tybɛr'kyl] *m* ♀ tuber; ♣ tubercle; **tuberculé, e** *biol.* [~ky'le] tubercled, tuberculate(d); **tuberculeux, -euse** [~ky'lø, ~'lø:z] **1.** *adj.* ♀ tubercular; ♣ tuberculous; **2.** *su.* ♣ tubercular patient; consumptive; **tuberculose** ♣ [~ky'lo:z] *f* tuberculosis.

tubéreux, -euse ♀ [tybe'rø, ~'rø:z] tuberose; **tubérosité** [~rozi'te] *f* tuberosity. [tubular.]

tubulaire ♀, △, ⊕, 🚋 [tyby'lɛ:r]

tubulure [tyby'ly:r] *f* pump *etc.:* pipe; nozzle; *bottle:* neck; *mot.* manifold.

tue-chien ♀ [ty'ʃjɛ̃] *m/inv.* meadow-saffron; **tue-mouches** [~'muʃ] *m/inv.* ♀ fly agaric; fly-swatter; (*a. papier m ~*) fly-paper; **tuer** [tɥe] (1n) *v/t.* kill (*a. fig. time*); *butcher:* slaughter; *fig.* bore (*s.o.*) to death; *fig.* while away (*one's time*); ✕ *tué à l'ennemi* killed in action; *se ~* kill o.s.; commit suicide; be killed; *fig.* wear o.s. out (in, with *à*); **tuerie** [ty'ri] *f fig.* slaughter, massacre; slaughter-house; **tue-tête** [~'tɛt] *adv.: à ~* at the top of one's voice; **tueur** *m*, **tueuse** *f* [tɥœ:r, tɥø:z] killer, slayer, slaughterer (*a. fig.*).

tuf [tyf] *m geol.* tufa; *fig.* foundation, bed-rock; *geol. ~ volcanique* tuff.

tuile [tɥil] *f* tile; F *fig.* (piece of) bad luck, blow; **tuileau** [tɥi'lo] *m* broken tile; piece of tile; **tuilerie** ⊕ [tɥil'ri] *f* tileworks *usu. sg.*, tilery; **tuilier** ⊕ [tɥi'lje] *m* tiler, tile maker.

tulipe [ty'lip] *f* ♀ tulip; ⚡ (tulip-shaped) lamp-shade; **tuilipier** ♀ [~li'pje] *m* tulip-tree.

tulle *tex.* [tyl] *m* tulle; net.

tuméfaction ♣ [tymefak'sjɔ̃] *f* swelling, tumefaction; **tuméfié, e** ♣ [~'fje] (1o) swollen.

tumeur ♣ [ty'mœ:r] *f* tumo(u)r, F growth; swelling.

tumulaire [tymy'lɛ:r] tomb-..., grave-...; tumular(y).

tumulte [ty'mylt] *m* tumult, uproar; *passions, politics:* turmoil; *business:* rush, bustle; riot; **tumultueux,**

-euse [~myl'tɥø, ~'tɥøːz] tumultuous, riotous; *fig.* noisy, rowdy.

tumulus [tymy'lys] *m* tumulus, barrow.

tungstène ⚛ *metall.* [tœ̃ks'tɛn] *m* tungsten, wolfram; *acier m au* ~ tungsten steel.

tunique [ty'nik] *f* ♀, ✂, *cost.* tunic; *eccl.* tunicle.

tunnel [ty'nɛl] *m* tunnel (*a. fig.*); ~ *aérodynamique* wind tunnel.

turban *cost.* [tyr'bɑ̃] *m* turban.

turbin F [tyr'bɛ̃] *m* work, job, F grind.

turbine ⊕ [tyr'bin] *f* turbine; *vacuum cleaner:* rotary fan.

turbiner F [tyrbi'ne] (1a) *v/i.* work, toil; *school:* swot, grind; **turbineur** F [~'nœːr] *m* hard worker.

turbocompresseur ⊕, ✈ [tyrbɔ-kɔ̃prɛ'sœːr] *m* turbo-compressor, turbo-supercharger; **turbopropulseur** ✈ [~prɔpyl'sœːr] *m* propeller turbine; *avion m à* ~ turboprop aircraft; **turboréacteur** ✈ [~reak-'tœːr] *m* turbo-jet engine.

turbot *icht.* [tyr'bo] *m* turbot.

turbulence [tyrby'lɑ̃ːs] *f* turbulence (*a. phys.*); *child:* boisterousness; *fig.* unruliness; **turbulent, e** [~lɑ̃, ~'lɑ̃ːt] turbulent; boisterous (*child, wind*); wild (*sea*); stormy (*life*); *fig.* unruly (*people*).

turc, turque [tyrk] **1.** *adj.* Turkish;† *fig.* hard-hearted, harsh; **2.** *su. ling.* Turkish; *su.* ♀ Turk; *tête f de 2* scapegoat; try-your-strength machine (*at a fair*).

turf [tyrf] *m* racecourse; turf, racing; **turfiste** [tyr'fist] *su.* racegoer.

turgide [tyr'ʒid] turgid, swollen.

turion ♀ [ty'rjɔ̃] *m* turion.

turlupin † [tyrly'pɛ̃] *m* buffoon, clown; **turlupinade** † [~pi'nad] *f* piece of low buffoonery; low pun; **turlupiner** [~pi'ne] (1a) *v/t.* F worry; bother; *v/i.* † play the clown, act the buffoon.

turlututu F [tyrlyty'ty] **1.** *su./m* (*sort of*) toy flute; **2.** *int.* fiddlesticks!; hoity-toity!

turne F [tyrn] *f* digs *pl.*; den, room; dilapidated house; *quelle* ~! what a hole!; what a dump!

turnep(s) ♀ [tyr'nɛp(s)] *m* kohlrabi.

turpitude [tyrpi'tyd] *f* turpitude; depravity; smut(ty talk *or* story); foul deed.

turquin [tyr'kɛ̃] *adj./m:* bleu ~ bluish-grey, slate-blue.

turquoise [tyr'kwaːz] **1.** *su./f stone:* turquoise; **2.** *adj./inv.* turquoise (*colour*).

tus [ty] *1st p. sg. p.s. of taire.*

tussilage ♀ [tysi'laːʒ] *m* coltsfoot.

tutélaire [tyte'lɛːr] tutelary; guardian ...; **tutelle** [~'tɛl] *f* ⚖ guardianship, tutelage; *pol.* trusteeship; *fig.* protection.

tuteur, -trice [ty'tœːr, ~'tris] *su.* ⚖ guradian; *fig.* protector; *su./m* ⚹ prop, stake; **tuteurage** ⚹ [~tœ'raːʒ] *m* staking.

tutoiement [tytwa'mɑ̃] *m* use of *tu* and *toi* (*as a sign of familiarity*); **tutoyer** [~'je] (1h) *v/t.* address (*s.o.*) as *tu;* be on familiar terms with (*s.o.*).

tutu [ty'ty] *m* ballet-skirt.

tuyau [tɥi'jo] *m* pipe, tube; *cost.* fluting, goffer; ♀ stalk; *pipe:* stem; *chimney:* flue; F *fig.* tip, wrinkle, hint; ~ *d'arrosage* garden-hose; *mot.* ~ *d'échappement* exhaust (pipe); tailpipe; ~ *d'écoulement* drain pipe; ~ *de jonction* (*or communication*) connecting pipe; ~ *de poêle* stovepipe; *sl.* top-hat; ~ *d'incendie* firehose; *fig. dire qch. à q. dans le* ~ *de l'oreille* whisper s.th. in s.o.'s ear; **tuyautage** [tɥijo'taːʒ] *m* ⊕ piping, tubing; pipes *pl.*; pipe-line; *cost.* fluting, goffering; F *fig.* tipping (off); **tuyauter** [~'te] (1a) *v/t.* flute (*linen*); F give (*s.o.*) a tip; *fer m à* ~ goffering iron *or* tongs *pl.*; **tuyauterie** [~'tri] *f* pipe and tube works *usu. sg. or* factory *or* trade; *cost.* fluting, goffering.

tuyère [tɥi'jɛːr] *f* ⊕ nozzle; ✈ ~ *d'éjection* outlet jet, *Am.* jet outlet.

tympan [tɛ̃'pɑ̃] *m* ⚿, *anat.* tympanum; *anat.* (ear-)drum; ⊕ pinion; *hydraulics:* scoop-wheel; treadmill; *typ.* tympan; *fig. crever le* ~ à q. split s.o.'s ears; **tympanisme** ⚕ [tɛ̃pa-'nism] *m* tympanites; **tympanon** ♪ [~'nɔ̃] *m* dulcimer.

type [tip] **1.** *su./m* type (*a. typ., fig.*); standard model *or* pattern; † sample; F fellow, chap, guy; **2.** *adj.* typical; standard ...; **typesse** *sl.* [ti-'pɛs] *f* female.

typhique ⚕ [ti'fik] typhous; **typhoïde** ⚕ [~fɔ'id] **1.** *adj.* typhoid; **2.** *su./f* typhoid (fever).

typhon *meteor.* [ti'fɔ̃] *m* typhoon.
typhus ⚕ [ti'fys] *m* typhus.
typique [ti'pik] typical (of, *de*); symbolical.
typographe [tipɔ'graf] *m* typographer, printer; **typographie** [ˌ⌣gra'fi] *f* typography; letterpress printing; printing-works *usu. sg.*; **typographique** [ˌ⌣gra'fik] typographical; *erreur f* ⌣ misprint.
tyran [ti'rɑ̃] *m* tyrant (*a. fig.*); *orn.* king-bird; **tyrannicide** [tirani'sid] *su. person*: tyrannicide; *su./m act*: tyrannicide; **tyrannie** [⌣'ni] *f* tyranny (*a. fig.*); **tyrannique** [⌣'nik] tyrannical (*a. fig.*); **tyranniser** [ˌ⌣ni'ze] (1a) *v/t.* tyrannize (*s.o.*); oppress (*s.o.*); rule (*s.o.*) with a rod of iron; *fig.* bully (*s.o.*).
tyrolien, -enne [tirɔ'ljɛ̃, ⌣'ljɛn] **1.** *adj.* Tyrolese; **2.** *su.* ♀ Tyrolese; *les* ♀*s m/pl.* the Tyrolese; *su./f* ♪ yodelled melody; ♪ Tyrolienne.
tzar [tsaːr] *etc. see tsar etc.*
tzigane [tsi'gan] *su.* Hungarian gipsy, Tzigane.

U

U, u [y] *m* U, u; ⊕ *fer m en U* U-girder.

ubiquité [ybikɥiˈte] *f* ubiquity; *avoir le don d'~* be everywhere at the same time.

ubuesque [ybyˈɛsk] grotesque.

ukase *pol.*, *a. fig.* [yˈkɑːz] *m* ukase, edict.

ulcération ✿ [ylseraˈsjɔ̃] *f* ulceration; **ulcère** ✿ [~ˈsɛːr] *m* ulcer; sore; *~ à l'estomac* stomach ulcer; **ulcérer** [ylseˈre] (1f) *v/t.* ✿ ulcerate; *fig.* embitter; **ulcéreux, -euse** [~ˈrø, ~ˈrøːz] ulcerated; ulcerous.

ultérieur, e [ylteˈrjœːr] ulterior; further; subsequent (to, *à*), later (*time*).

ultimatum [yltimaˈtɔm] *m* ultimatum; **ultime** [~ˈtim] ultimate, final; **ultimo** [~tiˈmo] *adv.* lastly, finally.

ultra *pol.* [ylˈtra] *m* extremist, ultra. **ultra...** [yltra] ultra...; **~court, e** *phys.* [~ˈkuːr, ~ˈkurt] ultra-short (*wave*); **~montain, e** [~mɔ̃ˈtɛ̃, ~ˈtɛn] 1. *adj. geog.*, *pol.*, *eccl.* ultramontane; 2. *su. eccl.*, *pol.* ultramontanist, Vaticanist; **~sensible** [~sɑ̃ˈsibl] high-speed (*film*); **~(-)son** *phys.* [~ˈsɔ̃] *m* ultra-sound; **~sonore** *phys.* [~sɔˈnɔːr] ultrasonic; supersonic; **~violet, -ette** *opt.* [~vjɔˈlɛ, ~ˈlɛt] ultraviolet.

ululer [ylyˈle] (1a) *v/i.* hoot (*owl*).

un, une [œ̃, yn] 1. *art./indef.* a, *before vowel*: an; *fig.* someone like; such a (*in int. as intensive*); *not translated before abstract nouns qualified by an adj.*: *avec une grande joie* with great joy; *~ de ces jours* one of these days; *~ jour ou l'autre* some day or other; 2. *adj./num./inv.* one; *une fois* once; *une heure* one o'clock; *~ jour sur deux* every other day; *c'est tout ~* it makes no difference; *de deux choses l'une* (it's) one thing or the other; 3. *su.* one; *~ à ~* one by one; *ne faire qu'~* be as one; be hand in glove; *su./f: journ. la une* page one; *su./m: le un* (number) one; *thea.* first act; 4. *pron./indef.* one; *les ~s les autres* one

another, each other; *les ~s ..., les autres ...* some ..., others ...; *l'~ l'autre* one another, each other.

unanime [ynaˈnim] unanimous (in s.th., *dans qch.*; in ger. *à*, *pour inf.*); **unanimité** [~nimiˈte] *f* unanimity; *à l'~* unanimously, with one voice.

uni, e [yˈni] 1. *p.p.* of *unir*; 2. *adj.* smooth; level, even (*ground*); regular; plain (*colour, a. tex.*); *fig.*, *a. pol.* united; close(-knit) (*family etc.*); 3. *su./m* plain *or* simple material.

unicellulaire ♥, *a. zo.* [yniselyˈlɛːr] unicellular.

unicité [ynisiˈte] *f* uniqueness; *phls.* oneness.

unicolore [ynikɔˈlɔːr] unicolo(u)red; one-colo(u)red.

unicorne [yniˈkɔrn] 1. *adj.* single-horned; 2. *su./m* 🐠, *zo.*, *myth.* unicorn.

unidirectionnel, -elle [ynidirɛksjɔˈnɛl] unidirectional.

unième [yˈnjɛm] *adj./num.*, *a. su. in compounds*: first; *vingt et ~* twenty-first.

unification [ynifikaˈsjɔ̃] *f* unification; ⊕, ✝ *companies*: amalgamation, merger; ✝ standardization; **unifier** [~ˈfje] (1o) *v/t.* unify; ⊕, ✝ amalgamate, merge (*companies*); ✝ standardize.

uniforme [yniˈfɔrm] 1. *adj.* uniform, unvarying; flat (*rate*); *fig.* monotonous; 2. *su./m* ✕, ⚓, *school, etc.*: uniform; **uniformément** [yniformeˈmɑ̃] *adv.* of *uniforme* 1; **uniformiser** [~miˈze] (1a) *v/t.* standardize; make (s.th.) uniform; **uniformité** [~miˈte] *f* uniformity; *fig.* consistency; evenness.

unijambiste [yniʒɑ̃ˈbist] *su.* one-legged person.

unilatéral, e, *m/pl.* -aux ♥, ⚖, *pol., etc.* [ynilateˈral, ~ˈro] unilateral.

union [yˈnjɔ̃] *f* union; combination; *admin.* association; marriage; ⊕ coupling, union-joint; *fig.* agreement.

unipare *biol.* [yni'paːr] uniparous.

uniphasé, e ⚡ [ynifɑ'ze] monophase; single-phase.

unipolaire ⚡ [ynipɔ'lɛːr] unipolar, single-pole ...

unique [y'nik] unique; single, alone; only; ✂, *pol.* united; *fig.* unrivalled; *fig. pej.* impossible; *seul et* ~ one and only; **uniquement** [ynik'mɑ̃] *adv.* solely; simply, merely.

unir [y'niːr] (2a) *v/t.* unite (with, à); combine (with, à); join in marriage; s'~ (à, *avec*) unite (with); combine (with); be joined in marriage.

unisson [yni'sɔ̃] *m* ♪ unison; *à l'*~ in unison (with, *de*); *fig.* in harmony *or* keeping (with, *de*).

unitaire [yni'tɛːr] unitary; unitarian (*a. eccl.*); ⚕, ✝ unit-...; **unitarisme** *eccl.* [~ta'rism] *m* Unitarianism; **unité** [~'te] *f* ✂, ⚕ unit; ⚕ one; ⚕, *phls., fig., thea.* unity; *fig.* consistency, uniformity; ✝ *prix m de l'*~ price of one.

univalent, e ⚗ [yniva'lɑ̃, ~'lɑ̃ːt] univalent, monovalent.

univers [yni'vɛːr] *m* universe; **universaliser** [ynivɛrsali'ze] (1a) *v/t.* universalize; **universalité** [~sali'te] *f* universality; whole (*a.* ⚕), entirety; **universel, -elle** [~'sɛl] universal (*a. phls.,* ⊕); ⊕ *etc. a.* all-purpose, general-purpose; world (-wide); ⚖ residuary (*legatee*); *fig. homme m*~ all-rounder; ⚕ *remède m*~ panacea.

universitaire [ynivɛrsi'tɛːr] **1.** *adj.* university ...; academic; **2.** *su.* academic; **université** [~'te] *f* university.

univoque [yni'vɔk] univocal; *fig.* unequivocal (*language, proof, words*); *fig.* uniform.

Untel [ɛ̃'tɛl] *m*: *Monsieur (Madame)* ~ Mr (Mrs) so-and-so.

uppercut *box.* [ypɛr'kyt] *m* uppercut.

uranate ⚗ [yra'nat] *m* uranate; **urane** ⚗ [y'ran] *m* uranium oxide; **uranite** *min.* [yra'nit] *f* uranite; **uranium** ⚗ [~'njɔm] *m* uranium.

urbain, e [yr'bɛ̃, ~'bɛn] urban; town ...; city ...; urbane; **urbaniser** [~ni'ze] (1a) *v/t.* urbanize; **urbanisme** [~'nism] *m* urbanism; town planning, *Am.* city planning; **urbaniste** [~'nist] *m* urbanist; town planner, *Am.* city planner; **urbanistique** [~ni'stik] urbanistic, town-planning ...; **urbanité** [~ni'te] *f* urbanity.

urée ⚗ [y're] *f* urea; **urémie** ⚗ [yre'mi] *f* ur(a)emia; **urétérite** ⚗ [~te'rit] *f* ureteritis; **urètre** *anat.* [y'rɛːtr] *m* urethra.

urgence [yr'ʒɑ̃ːs] *f* urgency; ⚕ *etc.* emergency; *affairs*: pressure; *d'*~ immediately; emergency...; *en cas d'*~ in case of *or* in an emergency; *il y a (grande)* ~ it is (very) urgent; **urgent, e** [~'ʒɑ̃, ~'ʒɑ̃ːt] urgent, pressing; ⚕ *cas m* ~ emergency; **urger** F [~'ʒe] (11) *v/i.* be urgent; *rien n'urge* there's no hurry.

urinaire *anat.* [yri'nɛːr] urinary; **urinal** ⚕ [~'nal] *m (day-, bed-)* urinal; **urine** *physiol.* [y'rin] *f* urine; **uriner** [yri'ne] (1a) *v/i.* urinate, make water; **urinoir** [~'nwaːr] *m* (public) urinal.

urique ⚗ [y'rik] uric.

urne [yrn] *f* urn; *(~ électorale)* ballot box; ~ *funéraire* cinerary urn; *aller (or se rendre) aux* ~s go to the polls.

urologie ⚗ [yrɔlɔ'ʒi] *f* urology; **urologiste** ⚗ [~'ʒist] *m* urologist.

urticacées ♣ [yrtika'se] *f/pl.* urticaceae; **urticaire** ⚕ [~'kɛːr] *f* urticaria, nettle-rash.

us [ys] *m/pl.*: ~ *et coutumes f/pl.* ways and customs.

usage [y'zaːʒ] *m* use (*a.* ⚖), employment; *cost., carpet, etc.*: service, wear; *fig.* custom; usage; *fig.* practice; ~ *du monde* good breeding; ⚕ ~ *externe* for external use; *à* ~s *multiples* multi-purpose; *à l'*~ *de* intended for; *faire* ~ *de* use; *faire bon* ~ *de* put to good use; *hors d'*~ disused; *il est d'*~ *de (inf.)* it is usual to *(inf.)*; **usagé, e** [yza'ʒe] second-hand; worn (*clothes*); used; **usager, -ère** [~'ʒe, ~'ʒɛːr] **1.** *su.* user; ⚖ *pasturage*: commoner; **2.** *adj.* in everyday use; ⚖ *customs*: for personal use; **usant, e** [y'zɑ̃, y'zɑ̃ːt] wearing; exhausting; tiresome (*person*); **usé, e** [y'ze] worn (out); *cost.* threadbare, shabby; frayed (*rope*); *fig.* hackneyed, commonplace; worn-out (*horse*); exhausted (*soil*); **user** [~] **1.** (1a) *v/t.* use up; consume (*fuel*); wear out; spoil (*one's eyes etc.*); waste (*one's youth*); s'~ wear away *or* out; *fig.* be spent; *v/i.*: ~ *de* use; make use of; resort to (*tricks, violence*).

usinage ⊕ [yzi'na:ʒ] *m* machining, tooling; **usine** [y'zin] *f* works *usu. sg.*, factory, plant; *tex., metall., paper*: mill; ~ *atomique* atomic plant; ~ *électrique* power station, powerhouse; ~ *hydraulique* waterworks *usu. sg.*; **usiner** [yzi'ne] (1a) *v/t.* ⊕ machine, tool; process.

usité, e [yzi'te] in use, current.

ustensile [ystɑ̃'sil] *m* utensil, implement; tool.

usuel, -elle [y'zɥɛl] usual, customary; common; *langue f* ~*elle* everyday language.

usufruit ⚖ [yzy'frɥi] *m* usufruct; life interest; **usufruitier, -ère** ⚖ [~frɥi'tje, ~'tjɛ:r] 1. *adj.* usufructuary; 2. *su.* tenant for life; usufructuary. [orbitant.)

usuraire [yzy'rɛ:r] usurious; ex-)

usure[1] [y'zy:r] *f* ⊕, *cost., furnishings, etc.*: wear (and tear); *geol., gramm.* erosion; ✗ *guerre f d'*~ war of attrition; F *avoir q. à l'*~ wear s.o. down (in the end).

usure[2] [y'zy:r] *f* usury; *fig. rendre avec* ~ repay (*s.th.*) with interest; **usurier** *m*, **-ère** *f* [yzy'rje, ~'rjɛ:r] usurer.

usurpateur, -trice [yzyrpa'tœ:r, ~'tris] 1. *adj.* usurping; *fig.* encroaching; 2. *su.* usurper; **usurpation** [~'sjɔ̃] *f* usurpation (of, *de*); *fig.* encroachment (upon, *de*); **usurpatoire** [~'twa:r] usurpatory; **usurper** [yzyr'pe] (1a) *v/t.* usurp (*the throne, a title*) (from, *sur*); *v/i. fig.* encroach (upon, *sur*).

ut ♩ [yt] *m/inv.* ut; *note*: C; *clef f d'*~ C-clef.

utérin, e [yte'rɛ̃, ~'rin] ⚕, ♀ uterine; ⚕ half(-*brother*, -*sister*) on the mother's side.

utile [y'til] 1. *adj.* useful; of service; *fig.* convenient; *en temps* ~ in (good) time; in due course; 2. *su./m the* useful; *joindre l'*~ *à l'agréable* combine business with pleasure; **utilisable** [ytili'zabl] usable; utilizable; available (*ticket*); **utilisateur** [~za-'tœ:r] *m* user; **utilisation** [~za'sjɔ̃] *f* utilization; turning (*of s.th.*) to account; use; **utiliser** [~'ze] (1a) *v/t.* make use of; use; utilize; **utilitaire** [~'tɛ:r] *adj., a. su.* utilitarian; **utilitarisme** [~ta'rism] *m* utilitarianism; **utilité** [~'te] *f* utility, usefulness; use; service, useful purpose; *thea.* small *or* minor part; *actor*: utility man.

utopie [ytɔ'pi] *f* utopia; *d'*~ utopian; **utopique** [~'pik] *adj., a. su.* utopian; **utopiste** [~'pist] *su.* utopian, utopist.

utricule *anat.* [ytri'kyl] *m* utricle.

uval, e, *m/pl.* **-aux** [y'val, ~'vo] grape-...

uvulaire *anat.* [yvy'lɛ:r] uvular.

V

V, v [ve] *m* V, v; *double v* W, w.
va! [va] *int.* to be sure!; believe me!;
well!; good!; ~ *pour cette somme!*
done (at that price)!; agreed (at that
figure)!
vacance [va'kã:s] *f* vacancy; vacant
post; ~s *pl.* holidays; vacation *sg.*
(*Am. a. univ.*), *parl.* recess *sg.*; *grandes* ~s long holidays *etc.*; **vacancier**
m, **-ière** *f* [~kã'sje, ~'sjɛːr] holiday-
maker, *Am.* vacationist; **vacant, e**
[~'kã, ~'kã:t] vacant, unoccupied
(*house, post, seat, etc.*); ½½ in abeyance
(*estate*).
vacarme [va'karm] *m* uproar, din,
racket, row.
vacation ½½ [vaka'sjɔ̃] *f* attendance,
sitting; *rights etc.*: abeyance; ~s *pl.*
fees; *law-courts*: vacation *sg.*
vaccin ✻ [vak'sɛ̃] *m* vaccine; **vaccinal, e**, *m/pl.* **-aux** ✻ [vaksi'nal, ~'no]
vaccinal; **vaccination** ✻ [~na'sjɔ̃] *f*
vaccination; inoculation; **vaccine**
✻ [vak'sin] *f* cowpox; **vacciner** ✻
[~si'ne] (1a) *v/t.* vaccinate; inoculate.
vache [vaʃ] **1.** *su./f* cow; ✝ cowhide;
sl. fat woman, V cow; *woman*: bitch;
sl. man etc.: swine; F *le plancher m des*
~s terra firma, dry land; F *fig. manger
de la ~ enragée* have a hard time of it;
F *parler français comme une ~ espagno-
le* murder the French language; **2.**
adj. sl. harsh; bad; mean, foul; **vachement** *sl.* [vaʃ'mã] terribly, real,
damned; (*rain etc.*) damned hard;
vacher *m*, **-ère** *f* [va'ʃe, ~'ʃɛːr] cowherd; **vacherie** [vaʃ'ri] *f* cowshed,
cowhouse; *sl.* dirty trick; nasty
remark; **vachette** ✝ [va'ʃɛt] *f* leather: calfskin.
vacillant, e [vasi'jã, ~'jã:t] unsteady;
swaying; staggering; flickering
(*flame*); shaky (*hand, ladder*); *fig.*
undecided; uncertain (*health*); **vacillation** [~ja'sjɔ̃] *f* unsteadiness;
flame: flickering; shakiness; *fig.*
wavering, vacillation; **vacillatoire**
[~ja'twaːr] vacillatory; **vaciller**
[~'je] (1a) *v/i.* be unsteady; sway (to
and fro); stagger; be shaky; flicker

(*light*); twinkle (*star*); *fig.* vacillate,
waver.
vacuité [vakɥi'te] *f* emptiness, vacu-
ity; **vacuum** [~'kɥɔm] *m* vacuum.
vade-mecum [vademe'kɔm] *m/inv.*
vade-mecum; companion (= *book*).
vadrouille [va'druːj] *f* ⚓ swab; F
stroll; **vadrouiller** F [vadru'je] (1a)
v/i. stroll *or* roam (about *or* around);
vadrouilleur, -euse [~'jœːr, ~'jøːz]
1. *adj.* strolling; roaming (the
streets); **2.** *su.* stroller; roamer.
va-et-vient [vae'vjɛ̃] *m/inv.* comings
and goings *pl.*; movement to and fro;
backward and forward motion, *Am.*
back and forth motion; ⚓ shuttle-
service; ⊕ reciprocating gear; ⚡
two-way switch; *faire le ~ entre* 🚌,
bus, etc.: ply between.
vagabond, e [vaga'bɔ̃, ~'bɔ̃:d] **1.** *adj.*
vagabond; wandering; roving (*a.
fig.*); **2.** *su.* vagabond; vagrant,
tramp; **vagabondage** [~bɔ̃'da:ʒ] *m*
wandering; vagrancy; **vagabonder**
[~bɔ̃'de] (1a) *v/i.* be a vagabond;
wander, roam (*a. fig.*).
vagin *anat.* [va'ʒɛ̃] *m* vagina.
vagir [va'ʒiːr] (2a) *v/i.* wail (*newborn
infant*); squeak (*hare*); **vagisse-
ment** [~ʒis'mã] *m* new-born infant:
vagitus, wail; *hare*: squeak(ing).
vague¹ [vag] *f* ⚓ wave (*a. fig., a.* ⚔);
billow; ⚡ current, *fig.* anger: surge;
fig. la nouvelle ~ the new wave; F *fig.
faire des ~s* cause a stir; F *fig. pas de
~s!* no fuss!
vague² [~] **1.** *adj.* vague; hazy; indeterminate; dim (*memory*); loose
(-fitting) (*garment*); **2.** *su./m* vagueness.
vague³ [~] **1.** *adj.* vacant, empty (*look,
stare*); **2.** *su./m* empty space; *fig.*
vacancy.
vaguemestre [vag'mɛstr] *m* ⚔ post-
orderly; ⚓ postman.
vaguer [va'ge] (1m) *v/i.* roam,
wander.
vaillamment [vaja'mã] *adv. of
vaillant;* **vaillance** [~'jã:s] *f* val-
o(u)r, courage, gallantry; **vaillant,**

e [~'jã, ~'jã:t] valiant, brave, courageous; ✕ gallant; stout (*heart*); F *fig.* in good health.

vaille [vaj] *1st p. sg. pres. sbj. of* valoir.

vain, vaine [vɛ̃, vɛn] **1.** *adj.* vain; empty (*promise, title, words, etc.*); useless (*effort*); conceited (*person*); **2.** *vain adv.*: en ~ vainly, in vain.

vainc [vɛ̃] *3rd p. sg. pres. of* vaincre.
vaincre [vɛ̃:kr] (4gg) *v/t.* conquer (*a. fig.* an emotion, hardship, *etc.*); defeat, beat (*s.o.*) (*a. sp.*); *fig.* outdo;
vaincu, e [vɛ̃'ky] **1.** *p.p. of* vaincre; **2.** *su.* defeated person *or* party; *etc.* loser; **vainqueur** [~'kœ:r] **1.** *su./m* victor, conqueror; *sp. etc.* winner; **2.** *adj.* victorious; **vainquis** [~'ki] *1st p. sg. p.s. of* vaincre; **vainquons** [~'kɔ̃] *1st p. pl. pres. of* vaincre.

vairon [vɛ'rɔ̃] **1.** *adj./m:* ♞, *vet.* walleyed; *yeux m/pl.* ~s eyes of different colo(u)rs; **2.** *su./m icht.* minnow.

vais [vɛ] *1st p. sg. pres. of* aller *1.*

vaisseau [vɛ'so] *m* ⚕, ♣, ♀, *anat., cuis.* vessel; ♣ ship; ♀, *anat.* duct, canal; ⚕ *building:* body; *church:* nave; *anat.* ~ sanguin blood-vessel; ~ spatial spacecraft; *fig.* brûler ses ~x burn one's boats; ~-école, *pl.* ~x-écoles [~soe'kɔl] *m* training ship.

vaisselier [vɛsə'lje] *m furniture:* dresser; **vaisselle** [~'sɛl] *f* dishes *pl.*; tableware; crockery, china; *eau f de* ~ dishwater; *faire la* ~ do the washingup, wash up, *Am.* wash the dishes.

val, *pl.* **vals,** *a.* **vaux** [val, vo] *m* vale, dale; *par monts et par vaux* up hill and down dale.

valable [va'labl] valid (*a. fig.*).

valdinguer *sl.* [valdɛ̃'ge] *v/i.* see dinguer.

valence ⚗ [va'lɑ̃:s] *f* valency.

valenciennes [valã'sjɛn] *f* Valenciennes (lace).

valériane ♣, ♀ [vale'rjan] *f* valerian; **valérianelle** ♀ [~rja'nɛl] *f* lamb's-lettuce.

valet [va'lɛ] *m* (man-)servant; *cards:* knave, jack; ⊕ door-counterweight; ⊕ clamp, dog; *mirror, etc., a.* ⚒: stand; *fig.* toady; ~ de chambre valet, man-servant; ♂ ~ de ferme farm-hand.

valétudinaire [valetydi'nɛ:r] *adj., a. su.* valetudinarian.

valeur [va'lœ:r] *f* value (*a.* ♬, ♠, ⚕, *phls., fig.*), worth; asset (*a. fig.*); ♪ *note:* length; ✕ valo(u)r, gallantry; ♠ ~s *pl.* shares, securities; ♠ ~s *pl.* actives assets; ✕ ~ militaire fighting qualities *pl.*; ⚓ ~ nautique seaworthiness; ♠ ~ nominale face value; de ~ valuable; *fig.* of value; able (*person*); mettre en ~ enhance the value of; develop (*the soil*); reclaim (*a marsh*); *fig.* emphasize, bring out; objets *m/pl.* de ~ valuables; **valeureux, -euse** ✕ [~lœ'rø, ~'rø:z] brave, gallant, valiant.

validation [valida'sjɔ̃] *f* validation; *law:* ratifying; **valide** [~'lid] valid; healthy; *fig.* sound; ✕ fit (*for service*); F *fig.* peu ~ off colo(u)r; **valider** [vali'de] (1a) *v/t.* validate; authenticate (*a document*); ratify (*a contract*); **validité** [~di'te] *f* validity.

valise [va'li:z] *f* suitcase; (*diplomatic*) bag; *faire sa* ~ (*or ses* ~s) pack one's suitcase(s) *or* one's bags (*a. fig.*).

vallée [va'le] *f* valley; **valleuse** [~'lø:z] *f* small dry valley; **vallon** [~'lɔ̃] *m* small valley; dale, vale; **vallonné, e** [~b'ne] undulating; **vallonnement** [~lɔn'mã] *m* undulation.

valoir [va'lwa:r] (3l) *v/i.* be worth; be profitable; be as good as; be equal to; apply, hold, be valid; ♠ à ~ on account (of, *sur*); *ça vaut la peine* (*de inf.*) it's worth while (*ger.*); *ça vaut le coup* it's worth trying; *faire* ~ make the most of (*s.th.*); ♠ invest profitably; ♠ exploit, make productive; *fig.* emphasize, bring out; *v/t.:* ~ qch. à q. earn *or* win s.o. s.th.; *se faire* ~ make the most of o.s.; *v/impers.:* il vaut mieux (*inf.*) it's better to (*inf.*); mieux vaut tard que jamais better late than never.

valorisation [valɔriza'sjɔ̃] *f* ♠, *fig.* increase in value *or* importance; **valoriser** [~'ze] (1a) *v/t.* increase the value *or* importance of; upgrade.

valse ♪ [vals] *f* waltz; F *aller* ~ go flying *or* crash (against, *contre*); F *envoyer* ~ send (*s.th.*) flying; send (*s.o.*) packing; F *faire* ~ juggle around; *faire* ~ *l'argent* spend money like water; **valseur, -euse** [~'sœ:r, ~'sø:z] **1.** *adj.* waltzing; **2.** *su.* dancer.

valu, e [va'ly] **1.** *p.p. of* valoir; **2.** *su./f see* moins-value; *plus*-value; **valus** [~] *1st p. sg. p.s. of* valoir.

valvaire ♀ *etc.* [val'vɛ:r] valvar, val-

vate; **valve** [valv] *f anat., mot.,
metall., radio,* ⚓, ✈: valve; **valvé, e** ⚓
[val've] valvate; **valvule** [~'vyl] *f*
valvule; *anat.* valve.

vamp [vã:mp] *f* vamp; **vamper**
[~'pe] (1a) *v/t.* vamp, seduce (by
coquetry).

vampire [vã'pi:r] *m zo., a. fig.* vampire; *fig.* blood-sucker; **vampiri-
que** [~pi'rik] vampiric; blood-
sucking.

van [vã] *m* ✔ winnowing-basket;
fan; winnowing-machine; ✕ van
(-ning-shovel); ✔ *passer au* ~ winnow.   [ism.]

vandalisme [vãda'lism] *m* vandal-⌋

vanesse *zo.* [va'nɛs] *f* vanessa.

vanille ♀, *cuis.* [va'ni:j] *f* vanilla;
à la ~ vanilla ...; **vanillé, e** *cuis.*
[~ni'je] vanilla(-flavo[u]red); **vanil-
lerie** ✔ [~nij'ri] *f* vanilla-planta-
tion; **vanillier** [vani'je] *m* vanilla
plant; **vanilline** ♠, ⊕ [~'jin] *f*
vanillin.

vanité [vani'te] *f* vanity; *fig.* futility;
pej. tirer ~ *de* pride o.s. on; **vaniteux, -euse** [~'tø, ~'tø:z] **1.** *adj.*
vain, conceited; **2.** *su.* conceited
person.

vannage¹ [va'na:ʒ] *m* ✔ winnowing,
sifting; ✕ *ore:* vanning; F *fig.* exhaustion.

vannage² ⊕ [~] *m water-gate:*
sluice-gates *pl.*; *turbine:* gating;
vanne [van] *f* sluice(-gate), water-
gate; *turbine:* gate; (overflow)
weir; *mot. etc.* valve; *fan, ventilator:*
shutter.

vanneau *orn.* [va'no] *m* lapwing,
(green) plover.

vanner¹ [va'ne] (1a) *v/t.* ✔ winnow,
sift; ✕ van; *fig.* exhaust, wear out,
tire out.

vanner² ⊕ [~] (1a) *v/t.* fit sluices
in; gate (*a turbine*).

vannerie [van'ri] *f* basket-making;
♦ wicker-work, basket-work.

vanneur [va'nœ:r] *m* ✔ winnower;
✕ vanner (*a. machine*); **vanneuse**
✔ [~'nø:z] *f* winnowing-machine.

vannier [va nje] *m* basket-maker.

vannure ✔ [va'ny:r] *f* chaff, husks
pl.

vantail, *pl.* **-aux** [vã'ta:j, ~'to] *m*
door, shutter, etc.: leaf.

vantard, e [vã'ta:r, ~'tard] **1.** *adj.*
boastful, bragging; **2.** *su.* bragger,
braggart; *Am. sl.* blow-hard, *Am.*

sl. wind-jammer; **vantardise** [~-
tar'di:z] *f* bragging; boasting; piece
of bluff; **vanter** [~'te] (1a) *v/t.*
vaunt, extol; F boost, crack up; *se*
~ (*de*) boast (of); **vanterie** [vã'tri] *f*
bragging; boast(ing).

va-nu-pieds [vany'pje] *m/inv.* tramp,
hobo; beggar.

vap(e)(s) *sl.* [vap] *f/(pl.):* etre dans la
vap(e) (*or les vap[e]s*) be in a daze.

vapeur [va'pœ:r] *su./f* steam;
vapo(u)r; fumes *pl.*; ⊕ *machine f à* ~
steam engine; *su./m* ⚓ steamer,
steamship; **vaporeux, -euse** [vapo-
'rø, ~'rø:z] vaporous, misty; steamy;
fig. hazy; *fig.* nebulous; **vaporisateur** [~riza'tœ:r] *m* vaporizer; atomizer; scent-spray; ⊕ evaporator; **vaporiser** [~ri'ze] (1a) *v/t.* vaporize;
atomize, spray (*a liquid*); F spray
(*s.th.*) with scent; *tex.* steam (*cloth*); se
~ vaporize; spray o.s.

vaquer [va'ke] (1m) *v/i.* † be vacant;
⚖ *parl.* not to be sitting; ~ *à* attend
to; be occupied with; see to; ~ *à ses
affaires a.* go about one's business.

varan *zo.* [va'rã] *m* varan, monitor.

varappe *mount.* [va'rap] *f* rock climbing; rock climb.

varech ♀ [va'rɛk] *m* seaweed, wrack.

vareuse [va'rø:z] *f* (pea *or* sports)
jacket; ✕ tunic.

variabilité [varjabili'te] *f* variability; *weather, a. fig.* mood: change-
ableness; **variable** [~'rjabl] **1.** *adj.*
♌, *astr., gramm., biol.* variable;
changeable (*weather, a. mood*); *fig.*
fickle; ♪ unequal (*pulse*); **2.** *su./f*
♌ variable; **variant, e** [~'rjã, ~-
'rjã:t] **1.** *adj.* variable, inconstant;
2. *su./f text:* variant, different reading; **variation** [~rja'sjõ] *f* variation
(*a.* ♪).

varice ♭ [va'ris] *f* varix; varicose
vein.   [varicella.]

varicelle ♭ [vari'sɛl] *f* chicken-pox,⌋

varié, e [va'rje] varied; various;
variegated (*colours etc.*); miscellaneous (*news, items, objects*); ⊕
variable (*motion*); **varier** [~'rje]
(1o) *v/t.* vary; variegate (*colours*);
♪ make variations on (*an air*); *v/i.*
vary; ♦ fluctuate (*market*); *fig.* ~
sur be at variance on, disagree over;
variété [~rje'te] *f* variety; *scenery:*
varied nature; *opinions:* diversity;
♦ range; *thea.* ~*s pl.* variety theatre
sg.

veille

variole [va'rjɔl] f 🩺 smallpox, variola; vet. (cow-, sheep-)pox; **variolé, e** [varjɔ'le] pock-marked; **varioleux, -euse** 🩺 [~'lø, ~'lø:z] 1. adj. variolous; 2. su. smallpox patient; sufferer from smallpox; **variolique** 🩺 [~'lik] variolous.

variomètre ⚡ [varjɔ'mɛtr] m variometer.

variqueux, -euse 🩺 [vari'kø, ~'kø:z] varicose.

varlope ⊕ [var'lɔp] f trying-plane; **varloper** ⊕ [~lɔ'pe] (1a) v/t. try up (a plank).

vasculaire 🩸, anat. [vasky'lɛːr], **vasculeux, -euse** 🩸, anat. [~'lø, ~'lø:z] vascular; 🩺 **pression** f vasculaire blood-pressure.

vase[1] [vɑːz] m vase; vessel, receptacle; ~ **de nuit** chamber; fig. **en ~ clos** in seclusion.

vase[2] [~] f mud, silt.

vaseline 🩺 [vaz'lin] f vaseline, petroleum jelly; Am. petrolatum; **enduire de ~** vaseline.

vaseux, -euse [va'zø, ~'zø:z] muddy, silty; F fig. woolly (ideas); sl. fig. seedy, ill.

vasistas [vazis'tas] m fanlight (over door), Am. transom.

vaso-moteur, -trice anat. [vazomɔ'tœːr, ~'tris] vaso-motor.

vasque [vask] f fountain: basin.

vassal, e, m/pl. **-aux** [va'sal, ~'so] 1. adj. vassal; ~ **de** (region) under the suzerainty of; 2. su. vassal; **vassalité** [~sali'te] f, **vasselage** [vas'la:ʒ] m vassalage; fig. bondage.

vaste [vast] 1. adj. vast, immense; comprehensive; anat. vastus; 2. su./m anat. vastus; **vastitude** [~i'tyd] f vastness; vastity.

va-t-en-guerre [vatɑ̃'gɛr] 1. su./inv. sabre-rattler; 2. adj. sabre-rattling.

vaticinateur, -trice [vatisina'tœːr, ~'tris] 1. adj. prophetic; 2. su./m prophet; su./f prophetess; **vaticination** [~na'sjɔ̃] f prophecy; pompous predictions pl.; **vaticiner** [~'ne] (1a) v/i. prophesy; make pompous predictions.

va-tout [va'tu] m/inv. the whole of one's stakes; **jouer son ~** stake one's all.

vaudeville [vod'vil] m light comedy.

vaudois, e [vo'dwa, ~'dwa:z] adj., a. su. ♀ Vaudois; eccl. hist. Waldensian.

vaudrai [vo'dre] 1st p. sg. fut. of valoir.

vau-l'eau [vo'lo] adv.: † **à ~** down-

stream; fig. **aller à ~** go to rack and ruin.

vaurien, -enne [vo'rjɛ̃, ~'rjɛn] su. bad lot; F child: rascal; su./m waster, ne'er-do-well; su./f worthless woman.

vautour orn. [vo'tuːr] m vulture (a. fig.).

vautrer [vo'tre] (1a) v/t.: **se ~** wallow (in, dans) (pig, a. fig. person); F fig. sprawl (on a sofa, etc.); revel (in, dans).

vau-vent hunt. [vo'vɑ̃] adv.: **à ~** down (the) wind; (fly) before the wind.

vaux [vo] 1st p. sg. pres. of valoir.

va-vite [va'vit]: **à la ~** in a hurry, hurriedly; carelessly.

veau [vo] m calf; meat: veal; ✝ calf(-leather); F person: clod, lout; F fig. gutless person or car; ~ **marin** seacalf, seal; fig. **adorer le ~ d'or** worship the golden calf; F **pleurer comme un ~** blubber; cuis. **tête f de ~** calf's-head.

vecteur Ⓐ [vɛk'tœːr] adj., a. su./m vector.

vécu, e [ve'ky] p.p. of vivre 1.

vécus [~] 1st p. sg. p. s. of vivre 1.

vedettariat thea. etc. [vɔdɛta'rja] m stardom; the stars (pl.); **vedette** [vɔ'dɛt] f thea., cin. etc. star; ⚓ patrol boat, scout; motor boat; **en ~** F fig. in the forefront; in the limelight; typ., journ. in bold type; **attraction** f ~ highlight.

végétal, e, m/pl. **-aux** [veʒe'tal, ~'to] 1. adj. plant(-life); vegetable (butter, kingdom); 2. su./m plant; **végétarien, -enne** [~ta'rjɛ̃, ~'rjɛn] adj., a. su. vegetarian; **végétarisme** [~ta'rism] m vegetarianism.

végétatif, -ve [veʒeta'tif, ~'tiːv] vegetative; **végétation** [~ta'sjɔ̃] f vegetation; growth; 🩺 **~s** pl. adénoïdes adenoids; **végéter** [~'te] (1d) v/i. † 🩸 grow; 🩸, a. fig. vegetate.

véhémence [vee'mɑ̃ːs] f vehemence; **avec ~** vehemently; **véhément, e** [~'mɑ̃, ~'mɑ̃:t] vehement; fig. violent.

véhiculaire [veiky'lɛːr] vehicular (language); **véhicule** [~'kyl] m vehicle (a. fig.); fig. a. medium; **véhiculer** [~ky'le] (1a) v/t. convey, carry; cart.

veille [vɛːj] f staying up (at night); wakefulness, waking; eccl. vigil; eve (of, de), day before; fig. verge, brink; (night) watch; fig. **à la ~ de** on the brink *or* eve *or* point of; *la* ∼ *de Noël* Christmas Eve; **veillée** [vɛˈje] *f* evening (spent in company); watch; *fig.* ∼ *d'armes* night before combat; **veiller** [∼ˈje] (1a) *v/i.* stay *or* sit up (late); remain *or* lie awake; *eccl.* keep vigil; ✕ watch, be on the lookout; stand by; ∼ *à* see to; attend to; ∼ *à ce que* (*sbj.*) see to it *or* make sure that (*ind.*); ∼ *sur* look after, watch over; *v/t.* watch over, attend to (*a patient etc.*); sit up with (*a patient, a corpse*); *Am.* wake (*a corpse*); **veilleur** [∼ˈjœːr] *m*: (∼ *de nuit* night) watchman; **veilleuse** [∼ˈjøːz] *f* watcher; night light; *mot.* sidelight; *gas:* pilot light; *mettre en* ∼ turn down (*the gas etc.*); dim (*a light*); *fig.* put (*a project etc.*) on ice.

veinard, e [vɛˈnaːr, ∼ˈnard] **1.** *adj.* lucky; **2.** *su.* lucky person; **veine** [vɛn] *f* ♀, *anat., geol., a. fig.* vein (*a.* = *marking in marble, wood, etc.*); ✕ *ore:* lode; *coal:* seam; *fig.* inspiration; *fig.* mood; F (good) luck; *avoir de la* ∼ be lucky; *être en* ∼ *de* ... be in a ... mood, be in the mood for ...; **veiné, e** [vɛˈne] veined; grained (*door*); **veiner** ⊕ [∼ˈne] (1a) *v/t.* grain, vein (*paintwork*); **veineux, -euse** [∼ˈnø, ∼ˈnøːz] ⊕ veiny (*wood etc.*); *anat., physiol.* venous; ♀ venose, veiny; **veinule** [∼ˈnyl] *f* *anat. etc.* veinlet; venule; ✕ thread (*of ore*).

vélaire *gramm.* [veˈlɛːr] **1.** *adj.* velar; uvular (*R*); **2.** *su./f* velar (consonant). **vêler** [vɛˈle] (1b) *v/i.* calve (*cow*). **vélin** [veˈlɛ̃] *m* vellum (paper). **velléité** [veleiˈte] *f* stray impulse; slight inclination; vague desire; *fig.* hint (*of a smile etc.*).

vélo F [veˈlo] *m* (push-)bike, wheel; *aller à* ∼ cycle, F bike, wheel. **vélocité** [velɔsiˈte] *f* speed, velocity; **vélodrome** [∼ˈdroːm] *m* cycle-racing track, velodrome; **vélomoteur** [∼mɔˈtœːr] *m* light motor-cycle; motor-assisted bicycle.

velours [vəˈluːr] *m* velvet; *gramm.* faulty liaison; *tex.* ∼ *à côtes* corduroy; ∼ *de coton* velveteen; ∼ *de soie* silk velvet; **velouté, e** [vəluˈte] **1.** *adj.* velvety; mellow (*wine*); downy (*cheek, peach*); *phot.* velvet-surface (*paper*); **2.** *su./m* softness, velvetiness; *fruit:* bloom; *tex.* velvet braid; *cuis.* rich thick gravy soup; *tex.* (*a.* ∼

de laine) velours; **velouter** [∼ˈte] (1a) *v/t.* give a soft *or* velvety appearance to (*s.th.*); *fig.* soften (*an outline*); *se* ∼ soften, mellow; **velouteux, -euse** [∼ˈtø, ∼ˈtøːz] soft, velvety; **veloutier** [∼ˈtje] *m* velvet-maker.

velu, e [vəˈly] hairy; ⚠ uncut, rough; ♀ pubescent, villous. **vélum** [veˈlɔm] *m* awning. **venaison** *cuis.* [vənɛˈzɔ̃] *f* venison. **vénal, e** *m/pl.* -aux [veˈnal, ∼ˈno] venal (*a. pej.*); *pej.* mercenary, corrupt(ible); † *valeur f* ∼*e* market value; **vénalité** [∼naliˈte] *f* venality; *pej.* corruptibility.

venant, e [vəˈnɑ̃, ∼ˈnɑ̃ːt] **1.** *adj.* thriving; **2.** *su./m*: *à tout* ∼ to all and sundry, to anyone. **vendable** [vɑ̃ˈdabl] saleable, marketable.

vendange [vɑ̃ˈdɑ̃ːʒ] *f* grape-gathering; wine-harvest; (*a.* ∼*s pl.*) *season:* vintage; **vendangeoir** [vɑ̃dɑ̃ˈʒwaːr] *m* grape-basket; **vendanger** [∼ˈʒe] (11) *vt/i.* vintage; *v/t.* gather the grapes of; *v/i.* harvest grapes; gather the grapes; **vendangeur** *m,* -euse *f* [∼ˈʒœːr, ∼ˈʒøːz] vintager; wine-harvester.

venderesse [vɑ̃ˈdrɛs] *f* vendor. **vendetta** [vɛ̃dɛtˈta] *f* vendetta. **vendeur** [vɑ̃ˈdœːr] *m* † vendor (*a.*), seller; shop assistant, *Am.* sales clerk; salesman; **vendeuse** † [∼ˈdøːz] *f* seller, shop assistant, *Am.* sales clerk; saleswoman; **vendre** [vɑ̃ːdr] (4a) *v/t.* sell (for, *à*); ∼ *à* for sale; *se* ∼ sell, be sold (at, for *à*). **vendredi** [vɑ̃drəˈdi] *m* Friday; *le* ∼ *saint* Good Friday. **vendu, e** [vɑ̃ˈdy] **1.** *su./m* traitor; **2.** *p.p. of* vendre.

venelle [vəˈnɛl] *f* alley. **vénéneux, -euse** [veneˈnø, ∼ˈnøːz] poisonous (*a.* ♀). **vénérable** [veneˈrabl] **1.** *adj.* venerable; **2.** *su./m* *freemasonry:* Worshipful Master; **vénération** [∼raˈsjɔ̃] *f* veneration; **vénérer** [∼ˈre] (1f) *v/t.* venerate; revere. **vénerie** [venˈri] *f* hunting; venery. **vénérien, -enne** ✚ [veneˈrjɛ̃, ∼ˈrjɛn] venereal. **venette** † *sl.* [vəˈnɛt] *f* funk. **veneur** [vəˈnœːr] *m* huntsman. **vengeance** [vɑ̃ˈʒɑ̃ːs] *f* revenge; vengeance; *tirer* ∼ *de* be revenged for (*s.th.*); take vengeance on (*s.o.*);

venu

venger [∼'ʒe] (11) v/t. avenge
(for, de); se ∼ take (one's) revenge
(for, de); be revenged (on s.o., de
q.); **vengeur, -eresse** [vã'ʒœ:r,
vãʒ'rɛs] **1.** su. avenger; **2.** adj.
avenging.

véniel, -elle eccl. [ve'njɛl] venial
(sin).

venimeux, -euse [vəni'mø, ∼'mø:z]
zo., a. fig. venomous; zo. poisonous
(serpent, bite); fig. malicious; **veni-
mosité** [∼mozi'te] f sting, a. fig.:
venomousness; **venin** zo., fig. [və-
'nɛ̃] m venom.

venir [və'ni:r] (2h) v/i. come, be
coming; arrive; grow (a. ♀, child,
tooth); fig. issue, be descended
(from, de); occur, happen (to inf.,
à inf.); ∼ à reach (maturity); ∼ à
bien be successful; ∼ au monde be
born; ∼ de ce que (ind.) result from
(ger.); ∼ de dire have just said; ∼
prendre come and fetch (s.o.); à ∼
future (event, state), (years) to
come; bien ∼ thrive; d'où cela
vient-il? what's the reason for
that?; en ∼ aux coups come to
blows; en ∼ aux faits get down to
business; être bien (mal) venu be
(un)welcome; typ. be well (badly)
produced (book); be (un)success-
ful; être mal venu à (inf.) be inap-
propriate or unseemly to (inf.);
faire ∼ send for; grow (wheat); où
voulez-vous en ∼? what are you
getting or driving at?; se faire bien
∼ de q. ingratiate o.s. with s.o.;
s'en ∼ come or go along; v/impers.
come; happen; occur; d'où vient-il
que (ind.)? how is it that (ind.)?; est-il
venu q.? has anyone called?; il est
venu quatre hommes four men have
come.

vénitien, -enne [veni'sjɛ̃, ∼'sjɛn] **1.**
adj. Venetian; blond m ∼ Titian red;
2. su. ♀ Venetian.

vent [vã] m wind; ∼ arrière tailwind; ∼
debout headwind; ∼ de travers cross-
wind; aller comme le ∼ go like the
wind; ⚓ au ∼ de to windward of; fig.
avoir ∼ de get wind of; coup m de ∼
gust of wind, squall; fig. en coup de ∼
very fast; F fig. dans le ∼ trendy, hip,
hep, with(-)it; ♪ instrument m à ∼
wind instrument; prendre le ∼ see
how the land lies.

vente [vã:t] f ♱ sale; ♱ fig. business;
timber; timber: felling; ∼ forcée com-

pulsory sale; ∼ publique public sale;
auction; de ∼ difficile hard to sell; en ∼
on sale; typ. out (book); en ∼ chez sold
by; en ∼ libre off the ration; un-
rationed; être de bonne ∼ sell well;
mettre en ∼ offer (s.th.) for sale;
publish, issue (a book).

venter [vã'te] (1a) v/impers.: il vente
it is windy, it is blowing; qu'il pleuve
ou qu'il vente (come) rain or shine, in
all weathers; **venteux, -euse** [∼'tø,
∼'tø:z] windy; windswept (region).

ventilateur [vãtila'tœ:r] m ventilator; ⚡ etc. fan; ∼ soufflant blower;
ventilation [∼la'sjɔ̃] f ventilation; ♱
apportionment; ♻ separate valuation; **ventiler** [∼'le] (1a) v/t. ventilate, air (a. fig.); ♱ apportion; ♻
value separately; mal ventilé stuffy
(room).

ventis [vã'ti] m/pl. wind-fallen trees.
ventosité ♻, vet. [vãtozi'te] f flatulence.

ventouse [vã'tu:z] f ♻ cupping glass;
⊕ etc. suction pad; zo. leech, octopus:
sucker; **ventouser** ♻ [∼tu'ze] (1a)
v/t. cup (a patient).

ventral, e, m/pl. **-aux** [vã'tral, ∼'tro]
ventral; **ventre** [vã:tr] m abdomen,
belly; stomach, paunch; pregnant
woman: womb; ⊕, furnace, ⚓ sail,
ship: belly; △, fig. bulge; ⚡, phys.
antinode; ∼ à terre at full speed;
à plat ∼ flat on one's face or one's
stomach; avoir (prendre) du ∼ be
(grow) stout; faire ∼ bulge (out) (⊕
vessel, △ wall); F fig. taper sur le ∼ à q.
be overfamiliar or chummy with
s.o.; **ventrebleu!** [vãtrə'blø] int.
zounds!; **ventrée** [vã'tre] f lambs:
fall; animals: litter; F bellyful.

ventricule anat. [vãtri'kyl] m ven-
tricle.

ventrière [vãtri'ɛ:r] f ♻ binder, abdominal belt; △ cross-tie, purlin;
⚓ bilge-block.

ventriloque [vãtri'lɔk] **1.** adj. ven-
triloquial, ventriloquous; **2.** su.
ventriloquist; **ventriloquie** [∼lɔ'ki]
f ventriloquism, ventriloquy.

ventripotent, e F [vãtripɔ'tã, ∼'tã:t]
big-bellied; corpulent.

ventru, e [vã'try] corpulent; big-
bellied (a. bottle); ⊕ dished (out-
wards).

venu, e [və'ny] **1.** p.p. of venir; **2.** adj.:
bien (mal) ∼ well- (poorly) devel-
oped; (un)timely (remark etc.); être

mal ~ *de* (*or à*) (*inf.*) be in no position to (*inf.*); *su.* (*first, last, new-*)comer; *le premier* ~ *a.* anybody; *su.*/*f* arrival; coming; *water:* inflow; *tree etc.:* growth; ~ *au monde* birth; *✔ d'une belle* ~ well-grown; *fig. tout d'une* ~ straight.

vêpres *eccl.* [vɛːpr] *f*/*pl.* vespers; evensong *sg.*

ver [vɛːr] *m* worm (*a. fig. person*); maggot, grub; ~ *à soie* silk-worm; ~ *blanc* grub; ~ *de terre* earthworm; ~ *luisant* glow-worm; *🐛* ~ *solitaire* tapeworm; *tirer les* ~*s du nez à q.* worm secrets out of s.o.

vérace [ve'ras] veracious; **véracité** [~rasi'te] *f* veracity, truth(fulness).

véranda ⚠ [verɑ̃'da] *f* veranda(h), *Am.* porch.

verbal, e, *m*/*pl.* **-aux** [vɛr'bal, ~'bo] verbal; *🕮* oral (*contract*); *see* procès-verbal; **verbalisation** *🕮* [vɛrbaliza-'sjɔ̃] *f* official entry of an offence; F taking of (*s.o.'s*) name and address (*by police*); **verbaliser** [~'ze] (1a) *v/i. admin.* draw up an official report (*of an offence etc.*); ~ *contre police:* take (*s.o.'s*) name and address; *vt/i.* verbalize; **verbe** [vɛrb] *m gramm.* verb; *eccl.* ♀ *the* Word; F *avoir le* ~ *haut* be loud of speech; *fig.* be over-bearing; **verbeux, -euse** [vɛr'bø, ~'bøːz] verbose, long-winded; **verbiage** [~'bja:ʒ] *m* verbosity; verbiage, wordiness, **verbosité** [~bozi-'te] *f* verbosity, wordiness.

verdâtre [vɛr'dɑːtr] greenish; **verdelet, -ette** [~də'lɛ, ~'lɛt] greenish; slightly acid (*wine*); **verdet** *🕮* [~'de] *m* verdigris; **verdeur** [~'dœːr] *f* greenness (*a. of wood*); *wine etc., a. fig. remarks:* acidity; *old person:* vigo(u)r.

verdict *🕮* [vɛr'dikt] *m* verdict (*against, contre*; for, *en faveur de*).

verdier *orn.* [vɛr'dje] *m* greenfinch; **verdir** [~'diːr] (2a) *v/t.* make *or* paint (*s.th.*) green; *v/i.* ♀ become green; *🕮* become covered with verdigris; **verdoyant, e** [vɛrdwa'jɑ̃, ~'jɑ̃:t] verdant, green; greenish (*colour*); **verdoyer** [~'je] (1h) *v/i.* become green; take on a green colo(u)r.

verdunisation [vɛrdyniza'sjɔ̃] *f water:* chlorination; **verduniser** [~'ze] (1a) *v/t.* chlorinate (*water*).

verdure [vɛr'dyːr] *f* greenness; ♀

greenery, verdure; *cuis.* greenstuff, pot-herbs *pl.*; **verdurier** [~dy'rje] *m* greengrocer.

véreux, -euse [ve'rø, ~'røːz] wormy (*fruit*); *fig.* bad (*debts*), shady (*company, firm, person*); shaky (*case*).

verge [vɛrʒ] *f* † rod; *anat.* penis.

vergé, e [vɛr'ʒe] **1.** *adj. tex.* streaky, unevenly dyed; *tex.* corded; laid (*paper*); **2.** *su.*/*m* ~ *blanc* cream-laid paper.

verger [vɛr'ʒe] *m* orchard.

vergeté, e [vɛrʒə'te] streaky; ⊘ paly; **vergette** [~'ʒɛt] *f* switch, cane; *drum:* hoop; *feathers, twigs:* whisk; ⊘ pallet.

verglacé, e [vɛrgla'se] iced-over, icy (*road*); **verglas** [~'gla] *m* black ice; thin coating of ice.

vergogne [vɛr'gɔɲ] *f* shame; *sans* ~ shameless(ly *adv.*).

vergue ⚓ [vɛrg] *f* yard; ~ *de misaine* foreyard; *bout m de* ~ yard-arm; *grande* ~ main yard.

véridique [veri'dik] veracious, truth-ful (*account, person*); **vérifiable** [~'fjabl] verifiable; **vérificateur, -trice** [verifika'tœːr, ~'tris] **1.** *su.*/*m weights etc.:* inspector, examiner; ⊕ ga(u)ge, calipers *pl.*; *mot.* ~ *de pression tyres:* pressure-ga(u)ge; ✝ ~ *comptable* auditor; **2.** *adj.* ⊕ testing; veri-fying; **vérificatif, -ve** [~'tif, ~'tiːv] verificatory; verifying-...; **vérifi-cation** [~'sjɔ̃] *f* checking, verifi-cation; check; confirming; confir-mation; **vérifier** [veri'fje] (1o) *v/t.* check, verify; confirm, bear out; ✝ audit (*accounts*).

vérin ⊕, *mot.* [ve'rɛ̃] *m* jack.

véritable [veri'tabl] true; real, genuine (*a. fig.*); *fig. usu. pej.* down-right.

vérité [veri'te] *f* truth; fact; *fig.* truthfulness, sincerity; *à la* ~ as a matter of fact; F *c'est la* ~ *vraie* it's the honest truth; *dire la* ~ tell the truth; *en* ~ really, truly.

verjus [vɛr'ʒy] *m* verjuice (*grape*); **verjuté, e** [~ʒy'te] acid, sour (*a. fig.*).

vermeil, -eille [vɛr'mɛːj] **1.** *adj.* ruby (*lips*), bright red; rosy (*cheek*); **2.** *su.*/*m* silver-gilt, vermeil; vermeil varnish.

vermicelle *cuis.* [vɛrmi'sɛl] *m* ver-micelli *pl.*

vermiculaire [vɛrmiky'lɛːr] ver-

micular (*a. physiol.*); *anat.* vermi-form (*appendix*); **vermiculé, e** [~ky'le] ⚕ vermiculate(d); *zo. etc.* vermiculate; **vermiculure** ⚕ *etc.* [~ky'ly:r] *f* vermiculation; **vermi-fuge** ⚕ [~'fy:ʒ] *adj., a. su./m* ver-mifuge.

vermillon [vɛrmi'jɔ̃] **1.** *su./m* ver-milion (*a. colour*); bright red; **2.** *adj./inv.* bright red; **ver-millonner** [~jɔ'ne] (1a) *v/t.* paint (*s.th.*) bright red; **rouge** (*one's cheeks*).

vermine [vɛr'min] *f* vermin (*usu.* = *lice, fleas*); *F fig.* rabble; **vermi-neux, -euse** ⚕ [vɛrmi'nø, ~'nø:z] caused by worms, verminous (*dis-ease*); **vermisseau** *zo.* [~'so] *m* small earthworm; **vermivore** *zo.* [~'vɔ:r] vermivorous; **vermouler** [vɛrmu'le] (1a) *v/t.: se ~* become worm-eaten (*wood*); **vermoulu, e** [~'ly] worm-eaten (*wood*); *fig.* de-crepit; out-of-date; **vermoulure** [~'ly:r] *f* worm-holes *pl.*; *wood*: worm-eaten state; wood dust (*from wormhole*); *fig.* decrepitude.

vermouth [vɛr'mut] *m* vermouth.

vernaculaire [vɛrnaky'lɛ:r] *adj., a. su./m* vernacular.

vernal, e, *m/pl.* **-aux** ♀, *astr., etc.* [vɛr'nal, ~'no] vernal.

verni, e [vɛr'ni] varnished; patent (*leather*); F lucky.

vernier ♀, *astr., surv.* [vɛr'nje] *m* vernier; sliding-ga(u)ge.

vernir [vɛr'ni:r] (2a) *v/t.* varnish; japan (*iron, leather*); polish (*furni-ture*); glaze (*pottery*); *fig.* gloss over; **vernis** [~'ni] *m* varnish; polish; gloss (*a. fig.*); glaze; ~ *à ongles* nail varnish; ~ *au tampon* French polish; **vernis-émail,** *pl.* **vernis-émaux** [vɛrnie'ma:j, ~'mo] *m* Japan enamel; **vernissage** [~'sa:ʒ] *m* ⊕ varnish (-ing) glaze; glazing; *exhibition*: varnishing-day; ~ *au tampon* French-polishing; **vernisser** ⊕ [~-'se] (1a) *v/t.* glaze (*pottery*).

vérole ⚕ [ve'rɔl] *f* ∨ pox (= *syphi-lis*); *petite ~ see variole*; **vérolé, e** ⚕ ∨ [~rɔ'le] poxed (= *syphilitic*).

véronal ⚕ᵐ [verɔ'nal] *m* veronal; bar-bitone.

véronique [verɔ'nik] *f* ♀ speedwell; *eccl.* veronica, vernicle.

verrai [vɛ're] *1st p. sg. fut. of voir.*

verrat *zo.* [vɛ'ra] *m* boar.

verre [vɛ:r] *m* glass; glassful; *opt.* lens; ~ *armé* wired *or* reinforced glass; ~ *à vin* wine glass; ⚗ ~ *de contact* contact lens; *mot.* ~ *de sûreté* safety glass; ~ *de vin* glass of wine; ~ *soluble* water-glass; *boire* (*or prendre*) *un* ~ have a drink; *se noyer dans un* ~ *d'eau* make a mountain out of a molehill; **verré, e** [vɛ're] *adj.: papier* *m* ~ glass-paper, sand-paper; **verre-rie** [vɛr'ri] *f* ⊕ glass-works *usu. sg.*; ⊕ glass-making; ⊕ glassware; *allant au four* flame-proof glassware; **verrier** [vɛ'rje] **1.** *su./m* glassmaker; glass-blower; glass-rack; **2.** *adj./m*: *peintre m* ~ artist in stained glass; **verrière** [~'rjɛ:r] *f* glass (casing); *eccl. etc.* stained glass window; ⊕ *station*: glass-roof; **verrine** [~'rin] *f* glass (casing); *barometer*: glass; ⚓ lantern; **verroterie** [~rɔ'tri] *f* glass trinkets *pl.*; small glassware; glass beads *pl.*

verrou [vɛ'ru] *m* bolt; *shot-gun*: breech-bolt; ⛓ ~ *de blocage* switch-lock; ⛓ *sous les* ~*s* under lock and key; **verrouiller** [~ru'je] (1a) *v/t.* bolt (*a door etc.*); ⊕ lock; lock (*s.o.*) in *or* up; *se* ~ bolt o.s. in.

verrue ⚕ [vɛ'ry] *f* wart; **ver-ruqueuse, -euse** [~ry'kø, ~'kø:z] ⚕ warty; ♀ warted; ⚕ verru-cose.

vers¹ [vɛ:r] *m poetry*: line, verse; ~ *pl. blancs* blank verse *sg.*

vers² [~] *prp. direction*: to, towards (*a place*); *time*: towards; about (*3 o'clock*), around (*noon, Easter*); ~ *l'époque* about the time; ~ *l'est* eastwards, towards the east.

versant [vɛr'sɑ̃] *m* slope; *hill etc.*: side; *canal etc.*: sloping bank.

versatile *fig.* [vɛrsa'til] changeable, fickle; **versatilité** [~tili'te] *f* change-ableness, fickleness, inconstancy.

verse [vɛrs] *adv.*: *à* ~ in torrents; *il pleut à* ~ it is pouring; **versé, e** [vɛr'se] versed, practised (in, *dans*); **Verseau** *astr.* [vɛr'so] *m*: *le* ~ Aquarius, the Water-bearer.

versement [vɛrsə'mɑ̃] *m liquid*: pouring (out); ✝ paying in, deposit, payment; instalment; *carnet m de* ~*s* paying-in book; *en* (*or par*) ~*s* (*éche-lonnés*) in *or* by instalments; **verser** [~'se] (1a) *v/t.* pour (out); overturn (*a vehicle etc.*); tip (*a truck*); shed (*blood, light, tears*); ✝ pay (in), de-

verset   528

posit (money); ✂ assign (men); v/i.
turn over; upset; fig. ~ dans lapse
into.

verset [vɛr'sɛ] m bibl. etc. verse; typ.
versicle.

verseur, -euse [vɛr'sœːr, ~'søːz] 1.
adj. ⊕ etc. pouring, pour-through; 2.
su. pourer; su./f coffee-pot.

versicolore [vɛrsikɔ'lɔːr] variegated,
versicolo(u)r(ed); chameleon-like.

versificateur m, **-trice** f [vɛrsifika-
'tœːr, ~'tris] versifier; **versification**
[~fika'sjɔ̃] f versification; **versifier**
[~'fje] (1o) v/t. write in verse; put
(prose) into verse; v/i. versify; write
poetry.

version [vɛr'sjɔ̃] f version; school:
translation into one's own language.

verso [vɛr'so] m verso, back (of a sheet
of paper); au ~ overleaf, on the back.

vert, verte [vɛːr, vɛrt] 1. adj. green;
unripe (fruit); sharp, young (wine);
raw (hide); callow (youth); hale and
hearty (old man); fig. severe (reprimand, punishment); sharp (reply);
smutty, spicy (story); haricots m/pl.
~s French beans; langue f ~e slang; en
dire (or raconter) des ~es (et de pas
mûres) tell some spicy things; 2.
su./m colour, ⚘ a. min.: green;
(green) grass; golf: putting-green;
wine: sharpness; inv. when used
adjectivally in compounds: une robe ~
foncé a dark green dress; des rideaux ~
olive olive-green curtains; ~-de-gris
[vɛrdə'gri] m verdigris; ~-de-grisé,
e [~gri'ze] coated or covered with
verdigris.

vertébral, e, m/pl. **-aux** anat. [vɛr-
te'bral, ~'bro] vertebral; colonne f
~e spine, backbone, spinal column;
vertèbre anat. [~'tɛːbr] f vertebra;
vertébré, e zo. [~te'bre] adj., a.
su./m vertebrate.

vertement [vɛrtə'mɑ̃] adv. sharply;
sternly.

vertical, e, m/pl. **-aux** [vɛrti'kal,
~'ko] 1. adj. vertical; perpendicular;
upright; 2. su./f ⋔ vertical; **verti-
calité** [~kali'te] f perpendicularity,
uprightness.

verticille ⚘ [vɛrti'sil] m verticil,
whorl; **verticillé, e** ⚘ [~si'le] ver-
ticillate, whorled.

vertige [vɛr'tiːʒ] m giddiness, dizziness, vertigo; fear of heights; avoir
le ~ feel dizzy; cela me donne le ~
it makes me (feel) dizzy; **vertigi-**

neux, -euse [~tiʒi'nø, ~'nøːz] dizzy,
giddy (hight, speed); breathtaking;
vertigo vet. [~ti'go] m (blind) staggers pl.

vertu [vɛr'ty] f virtue; chastity;
virtuous woman; substance: property; en ~ de by virtue of; because
of; in accordance with; thanks to;
faire de nécessité ~ make a virtue of
necessity; **vertueux, -euse** [~'tɥø,
~'tɥøːz] virtuous; chaste (woman).

verve [vɛrv] f (witty) eloquence; †
zest, verve, spirits pl., F go; être en ~
have got going, be in brilliant form.

verveine ⚘ [vɛr'vɛn] f verbena,
vervain.

vésanie † [veza'ni] f insanity; madness.

vesce ⚘ [vɛs] f vetch, tare.

vésicant, e ⚕ [vezi'kɑ̃, ~'kɑ̃ːt] see
vésicatoire 1; **vésicatoire** ⚕ [~ka-
'twaːr] 1. adj. vesicatory, blistering;
2. su./m blister, vesicatory; **vésicu-
laire** ⚘, zo. [~ky'lɛːr] vesicular (a.
⚕); bladder-like; **vésicule** [~'kyl] f
anat. etc. vesicle, bladder (a. icht.);
metall. blister; anat. ~ biliaire gall
bladder.

vespasienne [vɛspa'zjɛn] f street
urinal.

vespéral, e, m/pl. **-aux** [vɛspe'ral,
~'ro] 1. adj. evening-...; 2. su./m eccl.
vesperal.

vesse sl. [vɛs] f silent fart; ~-de-loup,
pl. ~s-de-loup ⚘ [~də'lu] f puffball.

vessie [ve'si] f anat., a. foot. bladder;
F blister (filled with serum); ⚕ ~ à
glace ice-bag; icht. ~ natatoire air-
bladder, swim(ming)-bladder; fig.
prendre des ~s pour des lanternes
believe that the moon is made of
green cheese, not to know chalk
from cheese.

vestale [vɛs'tal] f vestal (virgin).

veste cost. [vɛst] f short jacket; fig.
remporter une ~ fail; fig., pol. etc.
retourner sa ~ turn one's coat,
change sides or one's party; **vestiaire** [vɛs'tjɛːr] m thea. etc. cloak-
room, Am. check-room; hat-and-
coat rack; 🚂 robing-room; ✂, sp.
etc. changing-room.

vestibule [vɛsti'byl] m (entrance-)
hall; vestibule (a. anat.).

vestige [vɛs'tiːʒ] m relic, remnant,
vestige.

veston [vɛs'tɔ̃] m cost. (man's) jacket;
⚓ monkey-jacket; complet m ~

lounge suit; être en ~ wear a lounge suit.

vêtement [vɛt'mɑ̃] *m* garment; ~s *pl.* clothes; dress *sg.*; *eccl.* vestments; ~s *pl.* de dehors outdoor things; ~s *pl.* de dessous underwear; ~s *pl.* de deuil mourning *sg.*; window's weeds.

vétéran [vete'rɑ̃] *m* ✕ *etc.* veteran; *school etc.*: pupil repeating a course.

vétérinaire [veteri'nɛːr] **1.** *adj.* veterinary; **2.** *su./m* veterinary surgeon, F vet, *Am.* veterinarian.

vétillard *m*, **e** *f* † [veti'jaːr, ~'jard] *see* **vétilleur, -euse**; **vétille** [~'tiːj] *f* trifle; **vétiller** [~'je] *v/i.* † (1a) *v/i.* quibbler; niggler; **vétilleux, -euse** [~'jø, ~'jøːz] punctilious, particular (*person*).

vêtir [vɛ'tiːr] (2g) *v/t.* clothe, dress (in, de); se ~ dress o.s. (in, de); put on one's clothes.

veto [ve'to] *m/inv.* veto; *droit m de* ~ power of veto; *mettre son* ~ *à* veto (*s.th.*).

vêts [vɛ] *1st p. sg. pres. of* **vêtir**; **vêtu, e** [vɛ'ty] *p.p. of* **vêtir**; **vêture** [~'tyːr] *f* † clothing; † clothes *pl.*; *eccl.* taking of the habit (*monk*) *or* of the veil (*nun*).

vétuste [ve'tyst] timeworn; decrepit; **vétusté** [~tys'te] *f* decrepitude.

veuf, veuve [vœf, vœːv] **1.** *adj.* widowed; être (*or* rester) ~ *de* q. be left s.o.'s widow(er); bereft of; **2.** *su./m* widower; *su./f* widow; *orn.* widow-bird, whidah-bird.

veuille [vœj] *1st p. sg. pres. sbj. of* **vouloir 1.**

veule [vøːl] feeble, flabby (*person etc.*); drab (*life*); toneless, flat (*voice*); ♀ sickly (*plant*).

veulent [vœl] *3rd p. pl. pres. of* **vouloir 1.**

veulerie [vøl'ri] *f person etc.*: list-lessness, flabbiness; *life*: drabness; dullness; *voice*: flatness.

veuvage [vœ'vaːʒ] *m woman*: wid-owhood; *man*: widowerhood.

veux [vø] *1st p. sg. pres. of* **vouloir 1.**

vexant, e [vɛk'sɑ̃, ~'sɑ̃ːt] annoying, upsetting; **vexateur, -trice** [vɛksa-'tœːr, ~'tris] **1.** *adj.* vexatious; **2.** *su.* vexer; **vexation** [~'sjɔ̃] *f* humil-iation; harassing, harassment; **vexatoire** [~'twaːr] humiliating; harassing; **vexer** [vɛk'se] (1a) *v/t.* upset, annoy; se ~ get upset *or* an-noyed; se ~ become vexed *or* an-noyed *or* chagrined (at, de).

via [vi'a] *prp. before place-name*: via, by way of.

viabilité [vjabili'te] *f* viability; *road*: practicability; **viable** [vjabl] viable.

viaduc [vja'dyk] *m* viaduct.

viager, -ère [vja'ʒe, ~'ʒɛːr] **1.** *adj.* for life; life ...; *rente f* ~ère life annuity; *rentier m* ~ annuitant; **2.** *su./m* life income; en ~ at life income.

viande [vjɑ̃ːd] *f* meat; F substance; ~ fraîche (frigorifiée) fresh (frozen *or* chilled) meat; ~s *pl.* froides *restau-rant*: cold buffet; *conserve f de* ~ preserved meat. [(deer).\
viander *hunt.* [vjɑ̃'de] (1a) *v/i.* graze\

viatique [vja'tik] *m eccl.* viaticum, last sacrament; *fig.* money *or* provi-sions *pl.* for a journey; *fig.* resource.

vibrant, e [vi'brɑ̃, ~'brɑ̃ːt] vibrat-ing; *fig.* ringing, resonant (*voice*, *tone*); *fig.* rousing (*speech*); **vibra-teur** ⚡ [vibra'tœːr] *m* buzzer, vibra-tor; **vibration** [~'sjɔ̃] *f* vibration; ✈ flutter(ing); *voice*: resonance; **vi-brer** [vi'bre] (1a) *v/i.* vibrate; ⚡ *appel m vibré* buzzer call; *faire* ~ make (*s.th.*) vibrate; *fig.* thrill; **vibreur** ⚡ [~'brœːr] *m* vibrator, make-and-break; buzzer.

vibromasseur ⚡ [vibrɔma'sœːr] *m massage*: vibrator.

vicaire [vi'kɛːr] *m parish*: curate, assistant priest; † deputy; ~ *de Jésus-Christ the* Vicar of Christ, *the* Pope; ~ *général*, *grand* ~ vicar-general; **vi-cariat** *eccl.* [~ka'rja] *m* curacy; vicariate.

vice [vis] *m* vice; defect, fault; ~ *de conformation* defect in build; malfor-mation; ⚖ ~ *de forme* legal flaw; ~ *propre* inherent defect.

vice-... [vis] vice-...; ~**consul** [~kɔ̃-'syl] *m* vice-consul; ~**président** [~prezi'dɑ̃] *m* vice-president; ~**roi** [~'rwa] *m* viceroy.

vichy [vi'ʃi] *m* vichy water.

viciateur, -trice [visja'tœːr, ~'tris] vitiating; *fig.* contaminating; **vicia-tion** [~'sjɔ̃] *f* vitiation (*a.* ⚖); *air*: contamination; *fig. morals etc.*: corruption; **vicier** [vi'sje] (1o) *v/t.* vitiate (*a.* ⚖); corrupt, taint, spoil; *air m vicié* stale *or* foul air; se ~ become tainted; **vicieux, -euse** [~'sjø, ~'sjøːz] vicious (*a. fig. circle*); depraved (*person*); defective; faulty (*expression*, *reasoning*); restive, bad-tempered (*horse*).

vicinal, e, *m/pl.* **-aux** [visi'nal, ~'no] local, by(-road).

vicissitude [visisi'tyd] *f* vicissitude; ~s *pl.* ups and downs.

vicomte [vi'kɔ̃:t] *m* viscount; **vi-comté** [vikɔ̃'te] *m* viscountcy; vis-county; **vicomtesse** [~'tes] *f* vis-countess.

victime [vik'tim] *f* victim (*a. fig.*); *disaster*: casualty; être ~ de be a *or* the victim of; be down with (*bronchitis*); *fig.* labo(u)r under (*a delusion etc.*).

victoire [vik'twa:r] *f* victory; rem-porter la ~ gain a *or* the victory (over, *sur*); win the day; **victoria** [~tɔ'rja] *su./f carriage:* Victoria; *su./m:* ♀ ~ *regia* victoria regia, watermaize; **vic-torieux, -euse** [~tɔ'rjø, ~'rjø:z] victorious (over, *de*); triumphant (over, *de*); *fig.* decisive (*proof*).

victuailles F [vik'tɥɑ:j] *f/pl.* eat-ables, victuals.

vidage [vi'da:ʒ] *m* emptying; F *fig.* dismissal; **vidange** [~'dɑ̃:ʒ] *f* emp-tying; draining; *mot.* oil change; ~s *pl.* sewage *sg.*; en ~ broached (*cask*), opened (*bottle*); *mot. faire la* ~ change the oil; **vidanger** [vidɑ̃'ʒe] (11) *v/t.* empty; drain; clean out; **vidangeur** [~'ʒœ:r] *m* nightman; **vide** [vid] 1. *adj.* empty; blank (*space*); *fig.* vain; ~ de sens (de)void of meaning; *avoir le cerveau* ~ feel light-headed (*from lack of food*); 2. *su./m* (empty) space; blank (*in document*); gap (*between objects, a. fig.*); *phys.* vacuum, space; *fig.* vacancy, emptiness; *fig.* nothing-ness; à ~ empty; ⚡ no-load; ♦ em-ballé sous ~ vacuum-packed; frap-per à ~ miss (the mark, the nail, *etc.*); ⊕ *marcher* à ~ run light; *mot. tourner* à ~ tick over, idle; **vide-bouteille** [~bu'tɛ:j] *m* siphon; † country-lodge; **vide-citron** [~si'trɔ̃] *m* lemon-squeezer.

vidéo [vide'o] 1. *adj.* video(-)...; 2. *su./f* video; videofrequency; **vidéo-phone** [~ɔ'fɔn] *m* videophone.

vide-ordures [vidɔr'dy:r] *m/inv.* rubbish shoot; **vide-poches** [~'pɔʃ] *m/inv.* tidy; *mot.* glove compart-ment; **vide-pomme** [~'pɔm] *m/inv.* apple corer; **vider** [vi'de] (1a) *v/t.* empty; drain; clear out; clear (*a forest*); *fig.* exhaust; F *fig.* dismiss, sack (*s.o.*); F chuck (*s.o.*) out; gut, clean (*fish*); draw (*poultry*); stone (*fruit*), core (*an apple*); bail out (*a*

boat); *fig.* settle (*an argument, a ques-tion*); ♣ make up (*accounts*); ~ les arçons be thrown (*from a horse*); **videur** [~'dœ:r] *m* F bouncer.

vidimer [vidi'me] (1a) *v/t.* attest (*a copy*); **vidimus** [~'mys] *m* vidimus, attested copy.

viduité [vidɥi'te] *f* widowhood.

vidure [vi'dy:r] *f poultry:* entrails *pl.*, *fish:* guts *pl.*; ~s *pl.* rubbish *sg.*

vie [vi] *f* life; lifetime; way of life; livelihood, living; biography; *fig.* animation, spirit; ~ *moyenne* ex-pectation of life; ⊕ ~ *utile machine:* life; à ~ for life; de ma ~ in all my life; *donner la* ~ à give birth to (*a child, fig. a project*); être en ~ be alive; F *jamais de la* ~! never!; F not on your life!; sans ~ lifeless.

vieil [vjɛ:j] *see* vieux 1; **vieillard** [vjɛ'ja:r] *m* old man; ~s *pl.* old people; **vieille** [vjɛ:j] *see* vieux; ~ *fille f* old maid, spinster; **vieillerie** [vjɛj'ri] *f* old clothes *pl.*; old stuff (= *furniture etc.; a. fig.*); *fig.* out-dated ideas; **vieillesse** [vjɛ'jes] *f* old age; *coll.* old people *pl.*; *fig.* custom, manner, *etc.*: age; **vieillir** [~'ji:r] (2a) *v/t.* age; *v/i.* grow old; age; *fig.* go out of fashion; **vieil-lissement** [~jis'mɑ̃] *m* ageing; *fig.* obsolescence; **vieillot, -otte** F [~'jo, ~'jɔt] oldish; wizened (*face*); *fig.* old-fashioned.

vielle ♪ † [vjɛl] *f* hurdy-gurdy.

viendrai [vjɛ̃'dre] *1st p. sg. fut.* of venir; **viennent** [vjɛn] *3rd p. pl. pres.* of venir; **viens** [vjɛ̃] *1st p. sg. pres.* of venir.

vierge [vjɛrʒ] 1. *su./f* virgin, maiden; *astr.* la ♀ Virgo, the Virgin; 2. *adj.* virgin (*forest, gold, soil*); *fig.* clean, spotless, pure; blank (*page*); *phot.* unexposed (*film*); ~ de clear of.

vieux (*adj. before vowel or h mute* **vieil**) *m*, **vieille** *f*, *m/pl.* **vieux** [vjø, vjɛ:j, vjø] 1. *adj.* old; aged; ~ *jeu* old-fashioned; 2. *su./m* old man; old things *pl.*; mon ~! old boy!; *prendre un coup de* ~ grow old overnight; *su./f* old woman.

vif, vive [vif, vi:v] 1. *adj.* alive, living; *fig.* lively (*imagination*); brisk (*action, discussion, fire, game, pace*); sharp (*wind*); bright (*colour*); quick (*temper, wit*); de vive force by main force; eau *f* vive running water; vive arête sharp edge; vives

531

vins

eaux pl. spring tide *sg.*; **2.** *su./m* ⚡ living person; living flesh; *paint.* life; *fig. fight:* thick, heart; *blesser au ~* wound to the quick; *entrer dans le ~ du sujet* get to the heart of the matter; *pris sur le ~* taken from (real) life; lifelike; **vifargent** [vifar'ʒɑ̃] *m* quicksilver, mercury.

vigie [vi'ʒi] *f* look-out (post).

vigilamment [viʒila'mɑ̃] *adv. of vigilant;* **vigilance** [~'lɑ̃:s] *f* vigilance; caution; **vigilant, e** [~'lɑ̃, ~'lɑ̃:t] vigilant, watchful, alert; **vigile** [vi-'ʒil] *su./f eccl.* vigil; *su./m* watchman.

vigne [viɲ] *f* ⚘ vine; ✿ vineyard; ✿ ~ *blanche* clematis; ✿ ~ *de Judée* woody nightshade; ✿ ~ *vierge* Virginia creeper; ✿ ~ *vinestock;* *fig. dans les* ~*s du Seigneur* in one's cups (= *drunk*); **vigneron** [viɲə'rɔ̃] *m* wine-grower; vine-dresser; **vignette** [~'nɛt] *f* vignette; ✝ manufacturer's label; *typ.* engraving; *admin. packet of cigarettes etc.:* revenue band or seal; *mot.* (a. ~ *de l'impôt*) approx. road tax disc; **vignettiste** [viɲɛ'tist] *m* vignettist; **vigneture** [viɲə'ty:r] *f* ornamental border of vine-leaves (*round miniatures*); **vignoble** [vi-'ɲɔbl] **1.** *su./m* ✿ vineyard; vineyards *pl. (of a region);* **2.** *adj.* wine ...

vigogne *zo., a. tex.* [vi'gɔɲ] *f* vicuña.

vigoureux, -euse [vigu'rø, ~'rø:z] vigorous, strong; powerful (*blow*); *fig.* energetic; **vigueur** [~'gœ:r] *f* vigo(u)r, strength; *fig.* force; *en ~* in force; *entrer (mettre) en ~* come (put) into force.

vil, vile [vil] base (*a. metal*), vile; *à ~ prix* at a low price, F dirt cheap.

vilain, e [vi'lɛ̃, ~'lɛn] **1.** *adj.* ugly; nasty, unpleasant; dirty (*trick*); *fig.* mean (*person, deed*); **2.** *su.* blackguard, villain; ✝ villein; F naughty child; *su./m* F *fig.* trouble.

vilebrequin [vilbrə'kɛ̃] *m* ⊕ brace (and bit); wimble; ⊕, *mot.* crankshaft.

vilenie [vil'ni] *f* meanness; *fig.* abuse; vile story; dirty trick, mean action. [ify: run (*s.o.*) down.\
vilipender [vilipɑ̃'de] (1a) *v/t.* vil-\
villa [vi'la] *f* villa; country-house; cottage; **village** [~'la:ʒ] *m* village; **villageois, e** [~la'ʒwa, ~'ʒwa:z] **1.** *adj.* rustic, country-...; **2.** *su.* villager; *su./m* countryman; *su./f* countrywoman.

34*

ville [vil] *f* town, city; ~ *maritime* town on the sea, seaside town; ~ *natale* hometown; *à la ~* in town (= *not in the country*); *aller en ~* go (in)to town; *dîner en ~* dine out; *en ~ post:* Local.

villégiature [vileʒia'ty:r] *f* stay in the country; holiday (*away from town*); *en ~* on holiday.

vin [vɛ̃] *m* wine; ~ *chaud* mulled wine; ~ *de marque* vintage wine; ~ *de pays* local wine; ~ *ordinaire* table or dinner wine; *grand ~* wine from a famous vineyard; vintage wine; *gros (petit)* ~ full-bodied or heavy (light) wine; *offrir un ~ d'honneur à* give an official reception in hono(u)r of; *entre deux* ~*s* slightly tipsy; **vinage** [vi'na:ʒ] *m wine etc.:* fortifying; **vinaigre** [~'nɛ:gr] *m* vinegar; *tourner au ~* turn sour (*a. fig.*); **vinaigrer** [vinɛ'gre] (1a) *v/t.* season with vinegar; *fig.* give an acid edge to; **vinaigrerie** [~grə-'ri] *f* vinegar factory or trade; vinegar-making; **vinaigrette** *cuis.* [~'grɛt] *f* vinegar sauce; French dressing, oil and vinegar dressing; **vinaigrier** [~gri'e] *m* vinegar-maker; vinegar-merchant; vinegar-cruet; **vinasse** [~'nas] *f* poor, thin wine, F plonk; 🜍 residuary liquor.

vindicatif, -ve [vɛ̃dika'tif, ~'ti:v] vindictive; spiteful; ⚡ punitive; **vindicte** [~'dikt] *f* ⚡ prosecution; F *fig.* obloquy.

vinée [vi'ne] *f* wine-crop, vintage; ✿ fruit-branch of a vine; **viner** ⊕ [~'ne] (1a) *v/t.* fortify (*wine etc.*); **vineux, -euse** [~'nø, ~'nø:z] vinous; wine-flavo(u)red; wine-colo(u)red; full-bodied (*wine*); vintage (*year*).

vingt [vɛ̃; *before vowel and h mute, and when followed by another numeral* vɛ̃:t] *adj./num., a. su./m/inv.* twenty; *date, title:* twentieth; ~ *et un* twenty-one; ~*-deux* twenty-two; **vingtaine** [vɛ̃'tɛn] *f* (about) twenty; score; **vingtième** [~'tjɛm] *adj./num., a. su./m fraction:* twentieth.

vinicole [vini'kɔl] wine-growing; **viniculture** [~kyl'ty:r] *f* viniculture, wine-growing; **vinification** ⊕ [~fika'sjɔ̃] *f* vinification; **vinique** [vi'nik] vinic (*alcohol etc.*); **vinosité** [~nozi'te] *f wine:* flavo(u)r and strength, vinosity.

vins [vɛ̃] *1st p. sg. p.s. of venir.*

viol 🕮 [vjɔl] *m* rape; violation.
violacé, e [vjɔla'se] **1.** *adj.* purplish-blue; blue (*person*); **2.** *su./f:* ♀ ~s *pl.* violaceae; **violacer** [~] (1k) *v/i.* become covered with purplish spots; become purplish.
violateur, -trice [vjɔla'tœ:r, ~'tris] *su.* violator (*a. fig.*); *fig.* breaker (*of law, Sabbath, etc.*); *su./m* † 🕮 ravisher; **violation** [~'sjɔ̃] *f* violation (*a. fig.*); *fig.* breach; *Sabbath:* breaking; ~ **de domicile** violation of privacy (*of one's home*).
violâtre [vjɔ'lɑ:tr] purplish.
viole ♪ [vjɔl] *f* † viol; ~ **d'amour** viola d'amore.
violemment [vjɔla'mɑ̃] *adv.* of violent; **violence** [~'lɑ̃:s] *f* violence, force; 🕮 duress; *faire* ~ *à* do violence to (*a. fig.*); violate (*a woman*); **violent, e** [~'lɑ̃, ~'lɑ̃:t] violent (*a. death*); fierce; *fig.* intense; F *fig. c'est un peu* ~*!* that's a bit thick!; **violenter** [~lɑ̃'te] (1a) *v/t.* do violence to; 🕮 rape, ravish (*a woman*); **violer** [~'le] (1a) *v/t.* violate; *fig.* break; 🕮 rape, ravish (*a woman*).
violet, -ette [vjɔ'lɛ, ~'lɛt] **1.** *adj.* violet, purple; *inv. in compounds:* ~ **évêque** bishop's-purple; **2.** *su./m colour:* violet; *su./f* ♀ violet; *sl. faire sa* ~ play the shrinking violet.
violon [vjɔ'lɔ̃] *m* ♪ *instrument, a. player:* violin; F fiddle; ⊕ fiddle-block; F jail, *sl.* quod, clink; *fig.* ~ **d'Ingres** (*artistic*) hobby; *fig. aller plus vite que les* ~*s* jump the gun; **violoncelle** ♪ [~lɔ̃'sɛl] *m* (violon-)cello; cellist; **violoncelliste** ♪ [~lɔ̃-sɛ'list] *su.* (violon)cellist; **violoniste** ♪ [~lɔ'nist] *su.* violinist.
viorne ♀ [vjɔrn] *f* viburnum.
vipère [vi'pɛ:r] *f zo.* viper, adder; *fig. langue f de* ~ venomous tongue; **vipéridés** *zo.* [viperi'de] *m/pl.* viperidae, viper family *sg.*; **vipérin, e** [~'rɛ̃, ~'rin] **1.** *adj.* viperine; *fig.* venomous (*tongue*); **2.** *su./f zo.* viperine snake; ♀ viper's bugloss.
virage [vi'ra:ʒ] *m* turning; *road etc.:* turn, bend, corner; ✍, *mot., etc.* sweeping round; ✍ bank(ing); *sp. racing-track:* bank(ed corner); *mot.* turning space; ✈ going about; *phot.* toning; *tex.* changing of colo(u)r; ⚙ ♂ reversal; *fig.* change (of direction *or* policy); ~ *à droite* right turn; right-hand bend; ~ *à*

visibilité réduite blind corner; *prendre un* ~ take a corner; ~*-***fixage,** *pl.* ~*s-***fixages** *phot.* [~raʒfik'sa:ʒ] *m* combined toning and fixing.
viral, e *m/pl.* -**aux** [vi'ral, ~'ro] viral; virus (*disease*); infectious.
vire [vi:r] *f* winding mountain track.
virée [vi're] *f* trip, tour; joyride; **virement** [vir'mɑ̃] *m* ♣ tide, *a. fig.:* turn; ✝ transfer; *banque f de* ~ clearing bank; **virer** [vi're] (1a) *v/i.* turn; *mot.* (take a) corner; ✍ bank; ♣ heave; *phot.* tone; change colo(u)r; ~ *au bleu* turn blue; *v/t.* ✝ transfer (*money*); *phot.* tone; F chuck (*s.o.*) (out).
vireux, -euse [vi'rø, ~'rø:z] noxious, poisonous; malodorous; F stinking.
virevolte [vir'vɔlt] *f* half turn; spinning round; *fig.* sudden change, about-turn; **virevolter** [~vɔl'te] (1a) *v/i.* spin round.
virginal, e, *m/p.* -**aux** [virʒi'nal, ~'no] **1.** *adj.* virginal, maidenly; **2.** *su./m* ♪ virginal; **virginité** [~ni'te] *f* virginity; maidenhood.
virgule [vir'gyl] *f gramm.* comma; ✍ (decimal) point.
viril, e [vi'ril] *m* male (*clothing, sex*); *fig.* manly; virile; *âge m* ~ manhood; *anat. membre m* ~ penis; **viriliser** [virili'ze] (1a) *v/t.* make (*s.o.*) look like a man; make a man of (*s.o.*); **virilité** [~'te] *f* virility; manliness, manhood.
viro-fixateur *phot.* [virɔfiksa'tœ:r] **1.** *adj./m* toning and fixing; **2.** *su./m* toning and fixing bath.
virole [vi'rɔl] *f* ⊕ handle, stick, tube: ferrule; ⊕ *machine:* collar; *pipes:* thimble-joint; **viroler** [~rɔ'le] (1a) *v/t.* ferrule.
virtualité [virtɥali'te] *f* potentiality; virtuality; **virtuel, -elle** [~tɥ'ɛl] potential; virtual; **virtuellement** [~tɥɛl'mɑ̃] *adv.* potentially; virtually, practically.
virtuose [vir'tɥo:z] *su.* virtuoso; **virtuosité** [~tɥozi'te] *f* virtuosity.
virulence ⚕, *a. fig.* [viry'lɑ̃:s] *f* virulence; **virulent, e** ⚕, *a. fig.* [~'lɑ̃, ~'lɑ̃:t] virulent; **virus** ⚕ [vi'rys] *m* virus (*a. fig.*); *fig.* plague; *fig.* mania; ~ *filtrant* filterable virus; *maladie f à* ~ virus disease.
vis¹ [vis] *f* screw; ~ *de rappel* adjusting screw; ~ *sans fin* endless screw; *pas m*

de~ thread of screw; F *fig. serrer la* ~ *à q.* put the screw on s.o.

vis² [vi] *1st p. sg. pres. of* vivre 1.

vis³ [~] *1st p. sg. p.s. of* voir.

visa [vi'za] *m passport:* visa; *document:* signature; *supervisor etc.:* initials *pl.; cheque:* certification; *bill:* sighting; ~ *d'entrée* entry visa; ~ *de sortie* exit visa; ~ *de transit* transit visa.

visage [vi'za:ʒ] *m* face; countenance; *à* ~ *découvert* openly; *fig. à* ~ *humain* humane, fit for human beings; *faire bon (mauvais)* ~ *à* be friendly (unfriendly) towards, smile (frown) on (s.o.); F *trouver* ~ *de bois* find nobody at home; meet with a closed door; **visagiste** [viza'ʒist] *su.* beautician.

vis-à-vis [viza'vi] **1.** *adv.* opposite; **2.** *prp.:* ~ *de* opposite, facing; *fig.* in relation to, with respect to; **3.** *su./m* person opposite; partner *(at cards etc.);* S-shaped couch.

viscéral, e, *m/pl.* **-aux** *anat.* [vise'ral, ~'ro] visceral; **viscère** *anat.* [~'sɛːr] *m* internal organ; ~*s pl.* viscera.

viscose ⌒, ⊕, ⚕ [vis'ko:z] *f* viscose; **viscosité** [~kozi'te] *f* viscosity; stickiness.

visée [vi'ze] *f* aim *(a. fig.);* ✕, *surv.* aim(ing); sight(ing); ~*s pl.* aims, designs.

viser¹ [vi'ze] (1a) *v/i.* aim (at, *à*) *(a. fig.); v/t.* aim at *(a. fig.); surv.* sight; *fig.* relate to, have *(s.th.)* in view; *fig.* refer to *(s.o.),* allude to *(s.o.); sl.* (take a) look at; ~ *q. à la tête* aim at s.o.'s head.

viser² [~] (1a) *v/t.* visa *(a passport);* initial, sign *(a document);* certify *(a cheque);* 🎫 stamp *(the ticket when a journey is broken).*

viseur [vi'zœːr] *m gun:* sights *pl.; phot.* view-finder.

visibilité [vizibili'te] *f* visibility; conspicuousness *(of s.th.);* **visible** [~'zibl] visible; *fig.* evident, obvious; *fig.* able to receive (company), at home (to visitors) *(person).*

visière [vi'zjɛːr] *f helmet:* visor; *cap:* peak; eyeshade; ⊕ inspection-hole; *fig. rompre en* ~ *avec q.* contradict s.o. flatly; quarrel openly with s.o.

vision [vi'zjɔ̃] *f* vision *(a. eccl.);* sight; *fig.* fantasy; phantom; imagination; *trouble m de la* ~ eyesight

trouble; **visionnaire** [~zjɔ'nɛːr] *adj., a. su.* visionary.

visitation *eccl.* [vizita'sjɔ̃] *f:* la ♌ (the Feast of) the Visitation; **visite** [~'zit] *f* visit *(a. ✂);* (social or ceremonial) call; *admin.* inspection; *customs:* examination; ⚕ medical examination; 🕵 search; 🕵 ~ *domiciliaire* domiciliary visit; *heures f/pl. de* ~ calling hours; *hospital:* visiting hours; *rendre* ~ *à* pay (s.o.) a visit; **visiter** [vizi'te] (1a) *v/t.* visit; *admin.* inspect, examine; 🕵 search; **visiteur, -euse** [~'tœːr, ~'tøːz] **1.** *adj.* visiting; *infirmière f* ~*euse* visiting nurse; **2.** *su.* visitor, caller; ⊕, *admin., etc.* inspector; *customs:* searcher; ✝ representative; *su./f:* ~*euse de santé* health visitor.

vison [vi'zɔ̃] *m zo.* (American) mink; ✝ mink.

visqueux, -euse [vis'kø, ~'kø:z] viscous; sticky; gooey, slimy *(a. fig.).*

vissage ⊕ [vi'sa:ʒ] *m* screwing (on or down); **visser** [~'se] (1a) *v/t.* ⊕ screw (on, down, in, *etc.);* F clamp down on.

visualiser [vizɥali'ze] (1a) *v/t.* visualize; make visible; **visuel, -elle** [vi'zɥɛl] visual; *champ m* ~ field of vision.

vital, e, *m/pl.* **-aux** [vi'tal, ~'to] vital *(a. fig. question);* **vitaliser** [vitali'ze] (1a) *v/t.* vitalize; **vitalité** [~'te] *f* vitality.

vitamine [vita'min] *f* vitamin.

vite [vit] **1.** *adv.* quickly, rapidly, fast; soon; **2.** *adj.* fast, swift.

vitellus [vitɛl'lys] *m* ♀, *biol.* vitellus; *biol.* yolk.

vitesse [vi'tɛs] *f* speed; quickness; rapidity, swiftness; *phys. bullet, light, sound:* velocity, speed; *mot.* gear; ~ *imposée* prescribed speed; *mot.* ~ *limitée traffic sign:* speed limit, no speeding; *mot. boîte f de* ~*s* gear-box, *Am.* transmission; *grande (petite)* ~ high (low) speed; *mot. indicateur m de* ~ speedometer; *mot. première (quatrième)* ~ first (fourth) gear; bottom (top) gear; *à toute* ~ at top speed; *en* ~ quickly; in a hurry; *prendre q. de* ~ outrun s.o.

viticole [viti'kɔl] vine-...; viticultural; **viticulteur** [~kyl'tœːr] *m* vine-grower, viticulturist; **viticulture** [~kyl'ty:r] *f* vine-growing, viticulture.

vitrage [vi'tra:ʒ] *m* windows *pl.*; glass work; glass door; glass partition; glass roof; ⊕ glazing; net curtain; **vitrail**, *pl.* **-aux** [ʌ'tra:j, ʌ'tro] *m* leaded glass window; *eccl.* stained glass window; **vitre** [vitr] *f* pane (of glass); window-pane; F *fig.* *casser les* ʌs kick up a fuss; **vitré, e** [vi'tre] ⊕ glazed; ⚡, *anat.*, *etc.* vitreous; **vitrer** [ʌ'tre] (1a) *v/t.* ⊕ glaze (*a door, a window, etc.*); **vitrerie** [ʌtrə'ri] *f* glazing, glaziery; **vitreux, -euse** [ʌ'trø, ʌ'trø:z] vitreous (*a.* ⚡); glassy; **vitrier** [vitri'e] *m* glass maker; ⊕ glazier; **vitrière** [ʌ'ɛːr] *f* metal window framing; **vitrifiable** [ʌ'fjabl] vitrifiable; **vitrification** [ʌfika'sjɔ̃] *f* vitrification; **vitrifier** [ʌ'fje] (1o) *v/t.* vitrify; ʌ *par fusion* fuse; *se* ʌ vitrify; **vitrine** [vi'trin] *f* shop-window; glass case, showcase, display case.

vitriol ⚗ [vitri'ɔl] *m* vitriol (*a. fig.*); *fig. au* ʌ biting, caustic (*remark*); **vitriolé, e** ⚗ [ʌ'le] vitriolized; **vitrioler** [ʌ'le] (1a) *v/t.* vitriolize; throw vitriol at (*s.o.*); *tex.* sour (*fabric*); **vitrioleur** *m*, **-euse** *f* [ʌ'lœːr, ʌ'lø:z] vitriol-thrower.

vitupération [vitypera'sjɔ̃] *f* vituperation, abuse; **vitupérer** [ʌ're] (1f) *v/t.* abuse; ʌ *contre* rail against.

vivace [vi'vas] long-lived; ⚘ perennial; ⚘ hardy; *fig.* enduring; *fig.* inveterate; **vivacité** [ʌvasi'te] *f* promptness; alertness; *fig. combat, discussion:* heat; *fig.* hastiness; *colour, feelings, etc.:* vividness; *fig.* liveliness; *horse:* mettle; *avec* ʌ vivaciously.

vivandier, -ère † [vivɑ̃'dje, ʌ'djɛːr] *su.* canteen-keeper; *su./f* vivandière.

vivant, e [vi'vɑ̃, ʌ'vɑ̃:t] **1.** *adj.* living (*a. fig.*), alive; modern (*language*); *fig.* lively (*scene etc.*); vivid (*account, picture, etc.*); **2.** *su./m:* *les* ʌs the living; *bon* ʌ man who enjoys life; easy-going fellow; *de son* ʌ in his lifetime.

vivat [va'vat] **1.** *int.* hurrah!; **2.** *su./m* hurrah; ʌs *pl.* cheers.

vive *icht.* [viːv] *f* weever, sting-fish.

viveur [vi'vœːr] *m* pleasure-seeker; fast liver.

vivier [vi'vje] *m* fishpond, fish tank.

vivificateur, -trice [vivifika'tœːr, ʌ'tris] vivifying; invigorating; **vivi-**

fication [ʌ'sjɔ̃] *f* reviving; **vivifier** [vivi'fje] (1o) *v/t.* vitalize; enliven; give life to; invigorate; **vivipare** [ʌ'pa:r] **1.** *adj.* ⚘, *zo.* viviparous; **2.** *su. zo.* viviparous animal; **vivisection** [ʌsɛk'sjɔ̃] *f* vivisection.

vivoter [vivɔ'te] (1a) *v/i.* live from hand to mouth; rub *or* struggle along; **vivre** [viːvr] **1.** (4hh) *v/i.* live (on, *de*; at, in *à*); be alive; subsist, exist; *fig.* survive, last (*memory etc.*); F *apprendre à* ʌ *à* teach (*s.o.*) manners; *avoir beaucoup vécu* have seen life; *difficile à* ʌ difficult to get along with; ⚔ *qui vive?* who goes there?; *qui vivra verra* time will show; *se laisser* ʌ take life as it comes, take life *or* things easy; *vive ...!* long live ...!; hurrah for (*s.th.*)!; *v/t.* live (*one's life*); live through (*experiences*); **2.** *su./m* † living; food; ʌs *pl.* provisions; ⚔ rations; *le* ʌ *et le couvert* board and bed; *le* ʌ *et le logement* board and lodging.

vizir [vi'ziːr] *m* vizi(e)r.

vlan!, v'lan! [vlɑ̃] *int.* slap-bang!

vocable [vɔ'kabl] *m* word, term; *eccl. sous le* ʌ *de* dedicated to; **vocabulaire** [ʌkaby'lɛːr] *m* vocabulary; word-list.

vocal, e, *m/pl.* **-aux** [vɔ'kal, ʌ'ko] vocal (*a. anat.*, *a.* ♪); **vocalique** *gramm.* [vɔka'lik] vocalic, vowel-...; **vocalisation** *gramm.*, *a.* ♪ [ʌliza'sjɔ̃] *f* vocalization; **vocalise** ♪ [ʌ'liːz] *f* exercise in vocalization; *faire des* ʌs vocalize; **vocaliser** *gramm.*, *a.* ♪ [ʌli'ze] (1a) *vt/i.* vocalize; **vocalisme** *gramm.*, *a.* ♪ [ʌ'lism] *m* vocalism; **vocation** [ʌ'sjɔ̃] *f* vocation.

vociférations [vɔsifera'sjɔ̃] *f/pl.* shouts, yells; outcries; **vociférer** [ʌ're] (1f) *v/i.* shout, yell, scream (at, *contre*); vociferate (against, *contre*).

vodka [vɔd'ka] *f* vodka.

vœu [vø] *m* vow; *fig.* wish, desire.

vogue [vɔg] *f* fashion, F rage, craze; *dial. eccl.* patronal festival; *être en* ʌ be popular, be in fashion, F be in; *entrer (mettre) en* ʌ come (bring) into fashion.

voguer [vɔ'ge] (1m) *v/i.* sail (*boat, cloud*); float, drift; *fig. vogue la galère!* let's risk *or* chance it!

voici [vwa'si] *prp.* here is, here are; F ʌ! look!; ʌ *un an que je suis ici* I

have been here for a year; me ⁓!
here I am!

voie [vwa] *f* way (*a. fig.*), road;
path; *anat.* duct, tract; *fig.* means
pl., course; 🚂 railway, *Am.* railroad;
⚡ circuit; 🚗 (*dry, wet, etc.*) process; ⁓ *aérienne* air-route, airway;
⁓ *de communication* road, thoroughfare; line of communication;
✈ ⁓ *de départ* runway; ⁓*s pl. de
droit* legal channels; ⚖ ⁓*s pl. de
fait* assault *sg.* and battery *sg.*; *fig.*
⁓*s et moyens* ways and means;
🚿 ⁓*s pl.* respiratoires respiratory
tract *sg.*; ⚓ ⁓ *d'eau* leak; 🚂 *à deux
⁓s* double-track (*line*); 🚂 *à ⁓ normale* (*étroite*) standard-ga(u)ge
(narrow-ga[u]ge) (*line*); 🚂 *à ⁓
unique* single-track (*line*); *en ⁓ de*
in process of; under (*repair*); *par
⁓ de fig.* by (means of); 🚂 via;
par ⁓ ferrée by rail(way).

voilà [vwa'la] *prp.* there is, there are;
that is, those are; ⁓! here you are!; ⁓
ce que je dis that's what I say; ⁓ *qui est
drôle* that's funny; ⁓ *tout* that's all; ⁓
un an que je suis ici I have been here
for a year; *en ⁓ assez!* that's enough!;
me ⁓! here I am!

voilage [vwa'la:ʒ] *m* net curtain(s
pl.); *tex.* veiling, net; **voile** [vwal]
su./m veil (*a. fig., a. eccl.*); *fig.* cloak;
fig. blur; *tex.* voile; *phot.* fog; ⊕
buckle, warping; *anat.* ⁓ *du palais*
soft palate; *sous le ⁓ de* under the
cloak of; *su./f* ⚓ sail; *fig.* ship; *bateau
m à ⁓s* sailing boat; *faire ⁓* set sail (for,
pour); *grand-⁓* mainsail; ⚓ *mettre les
⁓s* clear out; **voiler** [vwa'le] (1a) *v/t.*
veil (*a.* ♪ *one's voice*); shade, dim (*the
light*); *fig.* cloak, hide; *phot.* fog; ⊕
buckle, warp; ⚓ rig (*a ship*) with
sails; *fig. voix f voilée* husky voice; *fig.
se ⁓* become overcast (*sky*); *v/i. a. se ⁓*
⊕ go out of true; warp (*wood*); **voi-
lerie** ⚓ [vwal'ri] *f* sail-making; sail-
loft; **voilette** *cost.* [vwa'let] *f* (hat-)
veil; **voilier** [⁓'lje] *m* ⚓ sailing ship,
sailing boat; sail-maker; *bâtiment m
bon ⁓* good sailer; **voilure** [⁓'ly:r] *f* ⚓
sails *pl.*; ✈ wings *pl.*, wing surface;
⊕ rod, wheel: buckling; *wood*:
warping.

voir [vwa:r] (3m) *v/t.* see; perceive;
watch; observe; remark; witness (*an
incident*); visit; inspect; examine; ⚕
attend (*a patient*); ⚕ consult (*a physician*); *fig.* consider, take a view of

(*s.th.*); *fig.* understand; *fig.* experience, go through (*misfortunes*); F
tolerate, stand; ⁓ *à* (*inf.*) see to it that
(*ind.*); ⁓ *le jour* be born; ⁓ *venir q.* see
s.o. coming; *fig.* see what s.o. is up
to; *à ce que je vois* from what I see;
aller ⁓ (go and) see (*s.o.*), look (*s.o.*)
up; visit; *cela se voit* that's obvious;
c'est à ⁓ that remains to be seen; F
écoutez ⁓ just listen; *être bien* (*mal*) *vu
de* be in s.o.'s good (bad) books; *faire
⁓* show; *laisser ⁓* betray, reveal;
n'avoir rien à ⁓ avec (*or à*) have
nothing to do with; ⚕ *se faire ⁓ par le
médecin* get examined; *venir ⁓* call on
(*s.o.*).

voire [vwa:r] *adv.* † truly; (*a. ⁓
même*) (and) even, indeed.

voirie [vwa'ri] *f* highway system;
system of roads; *admin.* Roads
Department, *Am.* Highway Divi-
sion; highway maintenance; refuse
(*Am.* garbage) collection; refuse
(*Am.* garbage) dump.

voisin, e [vwa'zɛ̃, ⁓'zin] **1.** *adj.* neigh-
bo(u)ring; adjacent; next (*building,
house, room, etc.*); ⁓ *de* in the vicinity
of; *fig.* similar to, akin to, approximating to; **2.** *su.* neighbo(u)r; **voisinage** [⁓zi'na:ʒ] *m* neighbo(u)rhood;
vicinity; surroundings *pl.*; *bon ⁓*
neighbo(u)rliness; **voisiner** [⁓zi'ne]
(1a) *v/i.* be adjacent, be side by side;
be neighbo(u)rly, be on friendly
terms (with, *avec*).

voiturage † [vwaty'ra:ʒ] *m* carriage,
conveyance; cost of conveyance;
voiture [⁓'ty:r] *f* carriage, conveyance, vehicle; *mot.* car, *Am. a.* automobile; ♦ van; ♦ cart; 🚌 coach,
Am. car; ♦ goods *pl.*, *Am.* freight; 🚂
⁓ *à marchandises* goods truck, *Am.*
freight car; ⁓ *carénée* streamlined car
or *Am.* automobile; ⁓ *de livraison*
delivery van; ⁓ *d'enfant* perambulator, F pram, *Am.* baby carriage; ⁓ *de
place* taxi; ⁓ *de remise* hired carriage;
⁓ *des quatre saisons* costermonger's
barrow; 🚌 ⁓ *directe* through carriage; F ⁓-*pie* radio patrol car; ⁓
publique public conveyance; 🚂
⁓-*restaurant* dining car, diner; *en ⁓!*
all aboard!; take your seats!; **voitu-
rée** [⁓ty're] *f people:* carriageful;
goods: cart-load, van-load; **voiturer**
[⁓ty're] (1a) *v/t.* convey, carry
(*goods*); *fig.* drive; **voiturette** [⁓ty-
'ret] *f mot.* baby car; light car; trap;

voiturier, -ère [ˌty'rje, ˌ'rjɛːr] **1.** *adj.* carriageable; carrying; carriage (*-drive*); **2.** *su./m* ✝ carrier.

voix [vwa] *f* voice (*a. gramm., a. ♪*); *♪* part; speech; tone; *fig.* opinion; *parl., pol.* vote; *à haute* ~ aloud; *à* ~ *basse* softly, in a low voice; *pol.* *aller aux* ~ vote; *de vive* ~ by word of mouth; *fig. demeurer sans* ~ remain speechless; *donner de la* ~ give tongue, bark (*hounds*); *mettre qch. aux* ~ put s.th. to the vote.

vol¹ ₰₰ [vɔl] *m* theft, larceny, robbery; ~ *à l'américaine* confidence trick; ~ *à l'étalage* shop-lifting; ~ *avec effraction* housebreaking and larceny.

vol² [vɔl] *m orn.*, ✈ flying; flight (*a. distance, a. fig., a. birds*); *locusts:* swarm; ~ *à voile* gliding; ~ *d'acrobatie* stunt flying; ~ *de nuit* night-flight; ~ *habité* manned spaceflight; ~ *plané* ✈ glide; *orn.* soaring flight; *à* ~ *d'oiseau* as the crow flies; bird's-eye (*view*); *au* ~ on the wing; *prendre son* ~ ✈ take off; *orn.* take wing, fly off; **volage** [vɔ'laːʒ] fickle, inconstant.

volaille [vɔ'laːj] *f* poultry; *cuis.* fowl; **volailler** [ˌla'je] *m* poulterer; poultry-yard.

volant, e [vɔ'lɑ̃, ˌ'lɑ̃ːt] **1.** *adj.* flying; *fig.* loose, floating (*dress*); portable; *ᵮ* wander(*-plug*); **2.** *su./m* game: shuttlecock; ⊕ fly-wheel; ⊕ *lathe etc.:* hand-wheel; *mot.* steering-wheel, F wheel; *cost.* flounce; ✝ ~ *de sécurité* reserve fund; *mot. prendre le* ~ drive, take the wheel.

volatil, e [vɔla'til] volatile.

volatile [ˌ] *m, a. f* fowl; ✝, *co.* bird, winged creature.

volatiliser [vɔlatili'ze] (1a) *v/t. a. se* ~ volatilize.

vol-au-vent *cuis.* [vɔlo'vɑ̃] *m/inv.* vol-au-vent (*small filled puff-pie*).

volcan [vɔl'kɑ̃] *m* volcano; **volcanique** [ˌka'nik] volcanic; *fig.* fiery; **volcanisme** *geol.* [ˌka'nism] *m* volcanism. [a slam *or* vole.)

vole [vɔl] *f:* faire la ~ *cards:* make)

volée [vɔ'le] *f* bird, bullet, stairs: flight; *birds:* flight, flock; ✕ volley, ⚓ broadside; *bells:* peal; *blows etc.:* shower; thrashing, hiding; ~ *basse tennis:* low volley; ~ *haute tennis:* smash; *à la* ~ in the air; *catch etc.* in mid air; *fig.* at random; *a. à toute* ~ with full force; *entre bond et* ~ *tennis:*

on the half-volley; *fig.* at a lucky moment; ✝ *fig. la haute* ~ the upper ten *pl.*; *fig. de haute* ~ top-flight, top-notch (*people*).

voler¹ ₰₰ [vɔ'le] (1a) *vt/i.* steal; *v/t.* rob (*s.o.*); swindle, cheat (*s.o.*).

voler² [ˌ] (1a) *v/i.* ✈, *orn.* fly (*a. fig.*); *fig.* rush; ~ *à voile* glide; *v/t. hunt.* fly (*a hawk*); fly at (*the quarry*).

volerie¹ ✝ [vɔl'ri] *f* robbery; larceny.

volerie² *hunt.* [ˌ] *f* hawking.

volet [vɔ'le] *m window, a. phot., mot., etc.:* shutter; *mot.* flap; *mot.* butterfly-valve; *ᵮ etc. indicator:* disk; sorting-board; *fig. trier sur le* ~ select (*persons*) carefully; screen (*candidates*).

voleter [vɔl'te] (1c) *v/i. orn.* flit (*a. fig. person*); flutter.

voleur, -euse [vɔ'lœːr, ˌ'løːz] **1.** *adj.* thieving; pilfering; *fig.* rapacious; **2.** *su.* thief; (*sheep- etc.*)stealer; *fig.* robber; *su./m: au* ~! stop thief!

volière [vɔ'ljɛːr] *f* aviary; large bird-cage; pigeon-run.

volige ⚠ [vɔ'liːʒ] *f* batten; lath; roofing-strip; **voliger** ⚠ [ˌli'ʒe] (11) *v/t.* batten; lath.

volitif, -ve [vɔli'tif, ˌ'tiːv] volitional; **volition** [ˌ'sjɔ̃] *f* volition.

volontaire [vɔlɔ̃'tɛːr] **1.** *adj.* voluntary; spontaneous; *fig.* self-willed, obstinate; **2.** *su./m* ✕ volunteer; **volonté** [ˌ'te] *f* will; will-power; *fig.* pleasure, desire; ~*s pl.* ₰₰ (*last*) will *sg.* and testament *sg.*; *fig.* whims; *à* ~ at pleasure, at will; *en faire à sa* ~ have one's own way; *montrer de la bonne* (*mauvaise*) ~ show (un)willingness; **volontiers** [ˌ'tje] *adv.* willingly, with pleasure; *fig.* readily, easily.

volt *ᵮ* [vɔlt] *m* volt; **voltage** *ᵮ* [vɔl'taːʒ] *m* voltage; **voltaïque** *ᵮ* [ˌ-ta'ik] voltaic.

voltaire [vɔl'tɛːr] *m* Voltaire chair (= *high-backed armchair*).

volte [vɔlt] *f* horsemanship, a. fencing: volt; *sp.* vaulting; ~**face** [ˌɔ-'fas] *f/inv.* volte-face; about-face; right-about turn.

voltige [vɔl'tiːʒ] *f* horsemanship: trick-riding; *sp.* exercises *pl.* on the flying trapeze; leaping-rope; **voltiger** [ˌti'ʒe] (11) *v/i. orn.* flit (*a. fig.*); fly about; flutter; *sp.* perform on the flying trapeze; *horsemanship:* do trick-riding; **voltigeur** [ˌti-

'ʒœːr] *m sp.* performer on the flying trapeze *(etc.)*; ✕ light infantryman.

volubile [vɔly'bil] ♥ voluble *(a. person)*, turning; *fig.* glib; fluent; **volubilis** ♥ [~bi'lis] *m* morning glory; **volubilité** [~bili'te] *f* volubility; *fig.* glibness.

volume [vɔ'lym] *m* volume; tome; ⚡, *phys., etc.* volume, mass; ✝, ♃ bulk; **volumineux, -euse** [~lymi-'nø, ~'nøːz] voluminous *(a. fig.)*; bulky, large.

volupté [vɔlyp'te] *f* (sensual) pleasure; **voluptueux, -euse** [~'tɥø, ~'tɥøːz] **1.** *adj.* voluptuous; **2.** *su.* sensualist.

volute [vɔ'lyt] *f shell, a.* △: volute; △, *a.* ♪ *violin:* scroll; *fig. smoke etc.:* curl.

vomique ♥, ✿ [vɔ'mik] *adj.:* noix *f* ~ nux vomica; **vomir** [~'miːr] (2a) *v/t.* ✿ vomit; *fig.* belch forth; *v/i.* be sick, ✿ vomit; **vomissement** ✿ [~mis'mã] *m action:* vomiting; vomit; **vomitif, -ve** ✿ [~mi'tif, ~'tiːv] *adj., a. su./m* emetic.

vont [vɔ̃] *3rd. p. pl. pres.* of aller 1.

vorace [vɔ'ras] voracious; **voracité** [~rasi'te] *f* voracity; *avec* ~ voraciously.   [(-ring).\

vortex [vɔr'tɛks] *m* whorl; vortex⌏

vos [vo] *pl.* of votre.

vosgien, -enne [vo'ʒjɛ̃, ~'ʒjɛn] of the Vosges.

votant, e [vɔ'tã, ~'tãːt] **1.** *adj.* voting; **2.** *su.* voter; *su./m:* liste *f* des ~s electoral roll; **votation** [~ta'sjɔ̃] *f* voting; **vote** [vɔt] *m* vote; voting; poll, ballot; *parl. bill:* division; passing (of a bill, *d'une loi)*; result (of the voting *or* ballot); **voter** [vɔ-'te] (1a) *v/i.* vote; *v/t.* vote *(money)*; pass *(a bill)*; ~ des remerciements *à* pass a vote of thanks to.

votif, -ve *eccl. etc.* [vɔ'tif, ~'tiːv] votive.

votre, *pl.* **vos** [vɔtr, vo] *adj./poss.* your.

vôtre [voːtr] **1.** *pron./poss.:* le *(la)* ~, les ~s *pl.* yours; F *à la* ~ cheerio!; your health!; je suis des ~s I am on your side; **2.** *su./m* yours, your own; les ~s *pl.* your (own) people.

voudrai [vu'dre] *1st p. sg. fut.* of vouloir 1.

vouer [vwe] (1p) *v/t.* dedicate; vow, pledge; *fig.* devote *(one's life, one's time)*.

vouloir [vu'lwaːr] **1.** (3n) *v/t.* want; need; require; claim; ~ *bien* be willing; ~ *dire* mean (to say); se ~ ... want *or* claim to be ...; be meant to be ...; je voudrais ... I would like ...; *Dieu veuille que* God grant that; je le veux bien I am quite willing; je veux que cela soit I insist that it shall be so; je veux que ce soit fait I want this to be done; le moteur ne voulut pas marcher the engine refused to work; sans le ~ unintentionally; veuillez me dire please tell me; *v/i.:* en ~ *à* bear *(s.o.)* a grudge; have designs on *(s.th.)*. **2.** *su./m* will; bon *(mauvais)* ~ good (ill) will; de son bon ~ of one's own accord; **voulu, e** [~'ly] *p.p.* of vouloir 1; **voulus** [~'ly] *1st p. sg. p.s.* of vouloir 1.

vous [vu] **1.** *pron./pers. subject:* you; *object:* you; (to) you; *à* ~ to you; yours; **2.** *pron./rfl.* yourself, yourselves; **3.** *pron./recip.* each other, one another; ~-même [~'mɛːm] *pron./rfl.* yourself; ~s *pl.* yourselves.

vousseau △ [vu'so] *m*, **voussoir** △ [~'swaːr] *m* arch-stone, voussoir; **voussure** △ [~'syːr] *f arch:* curve; *ceiling etc.:* arching; **voûte** [vut] *f* △ arch, vault *(a. fig.)*; archway; *anat. mouth:* roof, *skull:* dome; *fig.* ~ céleste canopy of heaven; ~ en berceau barrel vault(ing); ~ en ogive ogive vault; **voûté, e** [vu'te] △ vaulted, arched; *anat.* round *(shoulders)*; round-shouldered, bent *(person)*; **voûter** [~] (1a) *v/t. fig.* bend; *v/t. a.* se ~ vault; arch.

vouvoyer [vuvwa'je] (1h) *v/t.* address *(s.o.)* as vous.

voyage [vwa'jaːʒ] *m* journey; tour, trip; run *(in a car)*; ♃ voyage; ✈ flight; ~ *à pied* walk; ~ circulaire circular trip; ~ d'affaires business trip; ~ d'agrément pleasure trip; ~ de retour return journey; ~ surprise mystery tour; ~ touristique conducted tour; ... de ~ travelling-...; il est en ~ he is travelling; partir en ~ go on a journey, F go away; **voyager** [~ja'ʒe] (1l) *v/i.* travel *(a. ✝)*; (make a) journey; *fig.* get about; *orn.* migrate; il a beaucoup voyagé he has travelled widely; **voyageur, -euse** [~ja'ʒœːr, ~'ʒøːz] **1.** *su.* traveller; ♃, ✿, *etc.* passenger; fare *(in a taxi)*; ✝ *(a. commis* *m* ~) commercial traveller; **2.** *adj.* travelling; migratory (*bird*); *pigeon m* ~ homing pigeon, carrier-pigeon.

voyant, e [vwa'jɑ̃, ~'jɑ̃:t] **1.** *adj.* who can see (*person*); *fig.* loud, gaudy (*colour etc.*); conspicuous (*building, landmark, etc.*); **2.** *su.* sighted person, person who can see; clairvoyant; † seer; *su./m* mark; ⊕ sighting-slit; *surv.* sighting-board.

voyelle *gramm.* [vwa'jɛl] *f* vowel.

voyons [vwa'jɔ̃] *1st p. pl. pres. of* voir.

voyou [vwa'ju] *m* street-arab; hooligan, loafer, *Am.* hoodlum.

vrac [vrak] *m*: ✝ en ~ in bulk; loose; *fig.* higgledy-piggledy, in a jumble.

vrai, vraie [vrɛ] **1.** *adj.* true; truthful; sta(u)nch, loyal (*friend*); *fig.* real, genuine; *fig. usu. pej.* downright, regular; F (*pour*) de ~ really; in earnest; **2.** *vrai adv.* truly; really; *à* ~ dire as a matter of fact; strictly speaking; dire ~ tell the truth; ~ de ~! F honestly!; *sl.* cross my heart!; **3.** *su./m* truth; *au* ~ really; être dans le ~ be right; **vraiment** [~'mɑ̃] *adv.* really, truly; indeed; **vraisemblable** [~sɑ̃'blabl] **1.** *adj.* likely, probable; **2.** *su./m* probability; what is probable; **vraisemblance** [~sɑ̃'blɑ̃:s] *f* probability, likelihood; *story etc.:* verisimilitude; *selon toute* ~ in all probability.

vrille [vri:j] *f* ⊕ gimlet, borer; ♀ tendril; ✈ spin; ✈ tomber en ~ go into a spin; **vrillé, e** [vri'je] **1.** *adj.* ⊕ bored; ♀ tendrilled, with tendrils; *tex.* twisted, kinked; curled; **2.** *su./f* ♀ bindweed; **vriller** [~'je] (1a) *v/t.* ⊕ bore; *v/i. tex.* twist, kink; snarl; ascend in a spiral (*rocket etc.*); **vrillette** *zo.* [~'jɛt] *f* death-watch beetle.

vrombir [vrɔ̃'bi:r] (2a) *v/i.* buzz (*insect, engine*); ⊕, ✈ hum (*a. top*); throb; **vrombissement** [~bis'mɑ̃] *m insect, engine:* buzz(ing); ⊕, ✈, *top:* hum(ming); ⊕ throb(bing); *mot.* purr(ing).

vu, vue [vy] **1.** *p.p. of* voir; **2.** *vu prp.* considering, seeing (that, *que*); ~ *que a.* since; ⁂ whereas; **3.** *su./m* sight; *au* ~ *de tous* openly; *au* ~ *et au su de tous* to everybody's knowledge.

vue [~] *f* sight; eyesight; appearance, look; view; purpose, intention; idea, notion; *cin.* (lantern)slide; *à* ~ ♪, ✝ at sight; free-hand (*drawing*); *à* ~ *de* within sight of; *à* ~ *d'œil* visibly; *fig.* roughly, at a rough estimate; *à la* ~ *de* in the *or* at the sight of; *à première* ~ at first sight; ✝ *à trois jours de* ~ three days after sight; *fig. avoir des* ~*s sur* have one's eye(s) on; *avoir en* ~ have in mind; have it in mind (*to do*); *avoir la* ~ *courte* be shortsighted; *avoir* ~ *sur* look out on; face; *connaître q. de* ~ know s.o. by sight; *en* ~ in sight; *fig.* conspicuous; *fig.* prominent (*person*); *en* ~ *de* with a view to; for the purpose of; in order to; *garder q. à* ~ keep a close watch on s.o.; *perdre de* ~ lose sight of; *point m de* ~ point of view; *prise f de* ~*s* photography; *cin.* film-shooting.

Vulcain [vyl'kɛ̃] *m astr., myth.* Vulcan; *zo.* ♀ red admiral; **vulcaniser** ⊕ [~kani'ze] (1a) *v/t.* vulcanize, cure.

vulgaire [vyl'gɛ:r] **1.** *adj.* vulgar (*a. pej.*); common; general; *pej.* low, coarse; *langue f* ~ vernacular; **2.** *su./m* common people *pl.*; *fig. pej.* vulgarity; **vulgariser** [vylgari'ze] (1a) *v/t.* popularize; *pej.* coarsen; *se* ~ become common; grow vulgar; **vulgarité** [~'te] *f* vulgarity.

vulnérabilité [vylnerabili'te] *f* vulnerability; **vulnérable** [~'rabl] vulnerable; **vulnéraire** [~'rɛ:r] **1.** *adj.* ☞ vulnerary, healing; **2.** *su./f* ♀ kidney-vetch; **vulnérant, e** [~'rɑ̃, ~'rɑ̃:t] wounding.

vultueux, -euse ☞ [vyl'tɥø, ~'tɥø:z] bloated, red and puffy (*face*); **vultuosité** ☞ [~tɥozi'te] *f face:* puffiness.

vulve *anat.* [vylv] *f* vulva.

W

W, w [dublə've] *m* W, w.

wagon 🚃 [va'gɔ̃] *m* carriage, coach, *surt. Am.* car; *goods:* waggon, truck; ~ **de** *marchandises* goods-van, *Am.* freight-car; ~ *frigorifique* refrigerator van *or* car; *monter en* ~ get into *or* board the train; **~-bar,** *pl.* **~s-bars** [vagɔ̃'baːr] *m* refreshment-car; **~-citerne,** *pl.* **~s-citernes** [~si'tɛrn] *m* tank-car, tank-waggon; **~-lit,** *pl.* **~s-lits** [~'li] *m* sleeping-car, F sleeper, *Am.* pullman.

wagonnet [vagɔ'ne] *m* tip-truck, tip-waggon, *Am.* dump-truck.

wagon...: **~-poste,** *pl.* **~s-poste** [vagɔ̃'pɔst] *m* mail-van, *Am.* mail-car; **~-restaurant,** *pl.* **~s-restaurants** [~rɛstɔ'rɑ̃] *m* dining-car; restaurant-car; **~-salon,** *pl.* **~s-salons** [~sa'lɔ̃] *m* saloon(-car), *Am.* observation-car, parlor-car; **~-tombereau,** *pl.* **~s-tombereaux** [~tɔ̃'bro] *m* tipping-car.

wallon, -onne [va'lɔ̃, ~'lɔn] **1.** *adj.* Walloon; **2.** *su./m ling.* Walloon; *su.* ♀ Walloon.

waters F [wa'tɛːr] *m/pl.* water-closet *sg.*, W.C. *sg.*, toilet *sg.*

watt ⚡ [wat] *m* watt; **~-heure,** *pl.* **~s-heures** ⚡ [wa'tœːr] *m* watt-hour; **~man,** *pl.* **~men** [wat'man, ~'mɛn] *m electric tram or train:* driver, *Am.* motorman.

week-end [wi'kɛnd] *m* week-end; **weekendard** *m,* **e** *f* F [~kɛn'daːr, ~'dard] week-ender.

western *cin.* [wɛs'tœrn] *m* western (film).

wigwam [wig'wam] *m* wigwam.

wisigoth, e [vizi'go, ~'gɔt] **1.** *adj.* Visigothic; **2.** *su.* ♀ Visigoth.

X

X, x [iks] *m* X, x; *l'X sl.* the *École polytechnique; phys. rayons m/pl. X* X-rays; ✱ *passer aux rayons X* X-ray.

xénophobe [ksenɔ'fɔb] *adj., a. su.* xenophobe; **xénophobie** [~fɔ'bi] *f* xenophobia.

xérès [ke'rɛs] *m* sherry.

xylo... [ksilɔ] xylo...; **~graphe** [~'graf] *m* xylographer, wood-engraver; **~graphie** [~gra'fi] *f* wood-engraving; wood-cut; **~phage** *zo.* [~'fa:ʒ] **1.** *su./m* xylophagan, xylophage; **2.** *adj.* xylophagous; **~phone** ♪ [~'fɔn] *m* xylophone.

Y

Y, y [i'grɛk] *m* Y, y.

y [i] **1.** *adv.* there, here; *fig.* in, at home; *il y a* there is, there are; *il y a deux ans* two years ago; *je l'y ai rencontré* I met him there; *on y va!* come on!; **2.** *pron.* to *or* by *or* at *or* in it (him, her, them); *ça y est* that's it; *il n'y gagna rien* he gained nothing by it; *il n'y peut rien* there's nothing he can do about it; *il y va de* it is a matter of; *je n'y suis pour rien* I had nothing to do with it; *pendant que j'y pense* by the way; *vous y êtes?* do you follow?; F do you get it?

yacht ⚓ [jak] *m* yacht.

ya(c)k *zo.* [jak] *m* yak.

yaourt *cuis.* [ja'ur(t)] *m* yog(h)urt, yaourt.   [ilex.⟩

yeuse ♣ [jø:z] *f* holm-oak, holly-oak,⟩

yeux [jø] *pl. of œil.*   [Yiddish.⟩

yiddish [(j)i'diʃ] *adj., a. su./m*⟩

yodler ♪ [jɔd'le] (1a) *v/i.* yodel.

yoga [jɔ'ga] *m* yoga.

yogourt *cuis.* [jɔ'gurt] *m see yaourt.*

yole ⚓ [jɔl] *f* yawl, gig.

yougoslave [jugɔ'slaːv] *adj., a. su.* ♀ Jugoslav, Yugoslav.

youpin, e F *pej.* [ju'pɛ̃, ~'pin] **1.** *su.* Yid (= *Jew*); **2.** *adj.* Jewish.

youyou ⚓ [ju'ju] *m* dinghy.

ypérite ♠ [ipe'rit] *f* yperite, mustard-gas; **ypréau** ♣ [ipre'o] *m* wych-elm; white poplar.

Z

Z, z [zɛd] *m* Z, z.

zanzibar [zɑ̃zi'baːr] *m* dice-throwing (*for drinks*).

zazou F [za'zu] *m* hepcat.

zèbre [zɛbr] *m* zo. zebra; F chap, *Am.* guy; **zébrer** [ze'bre] (1f) *v/t.* streak; mark (*s.th.*) with stripes; **zébrure** [∿'bryːr] *f* stripe; zebra markings *pl.*, stripes *pl.*

zébu zo. [ze'by] *m* zebu.

zélateur, -trice [zela'tœːr, ∿'tris] **1.** *su.* zealot, zealous worker (for, de); **2.** *adj.* zealous; **zèle** [zɛːl] *m* zeal, enthusiasm (for, *pour*); F *faire du* ∿ make a show of zeal; go beyond one's orders; **zélé, e** [ze'le] **1.** *adj.* zealous; **2.** *su.* zealot; **zélote** *bibl.* [∿'lɔt] *m* zealot; **zélotisme** [∿lɔ-'tism] *m* zealotry.

zénith [ze'nit] *m* zenith (*a. fig.*).

zéphire *tex.* [ze'fiːr] *adj.*: *laine f* ∿ zephyr; **zéphyr** [∿'fiːr] *m* zephyr; soft breeze; **zéphyrien, -enne** [∿-fi'rjɛ̃, ∿'rjɛn] zephyr-like.

zéro [ze'ro] **1.** *su./m* nought, cipher; *scale*: zero; *sp. tennis*: love, *cricket*: duck; F nobody, nonentity; ∮ off (*on cooker etc.*); *fig. partir de* ∿ start from scratch; **2.** *adj./inv.*: *à* ∿ *heure* at midnight; **zérotage** *phys.* [∿rɔ-'taːʒ] *m* determination of the zero point; *thermometer etc.*: calibration.

zeste [zɛst] *m* lemon etc.: peel, twist; F *fig. cela ne vaut pas un* ∿ it's not worth a straw; **zester** [zɛs-'te] (1a) *v/t.* peel (*a lemon etc.*).

zézaiement [zeze'mɑ̃] *m* lisp(ing); **zézayer** [∿ze'je] (1i) *vt/i.* lisp.

zibeline zo., ⚕ [zi'blin] *f* sable.

zigouiller *sl.* [zigu'je] (1a) *v/t.* knife, kill; ✂ bayonet; cut to pieces.

zig(ue) *sl.* [zig] *m* chap, *Am.* guy.

zigzag [zig'zag] *m* zigzag (*a.* ✖, ⚓); ⊕ lazy-tongs *pl.*; ⊕ *disposé en* ∿ staggered; *en* ∿ zigzag...; forked (*lightning*); **zigzaguer** [∿za'ge] (1m) *v/i.* zigzag; flit about (*bat*); *mot.* drive erratically.

zinc [zɛ̃ːg] *m* zinc; ⚕ spelter; F counter, bar; ✈ *sl.* (heavy) aeroplane.

zinguer [zɛ̃'ge] (1m) *v/t.* metall. coat with zinc; galvanize (*iron*); △ etc. cover (*s.th.*) with zinc; **zingueur** [∿'gœːr] *m* ⊕ zinc-worker; △ zinc-roofer.

zinzin *sl.* [zɛ̃'zɛ̃] **1.** *su./m* thingummy, thingamajig, contraption; dance hall; **2.** *adj.* cracked, nuts.

zippé, e [zi'pe] with a zip(per).

zizanie [ziza'ni] *f* ⚘ zizania, Indian rice; *fig.* discord; *fig. semer* (*or mettre*) *la* ∿ stir up ill-feeling.

zodiacal, e, *m/pl.* **∿aux** *astr.* [zɔdja-'kal, ∿'ko] zodiacal; **zodiaque** *astr.* [∿'djak] *m* zodiac.

zona ⚕ [zɔ'na] *m* shingles *pl.*; **zone** [zoːn] *f* ⚕, ✖, *geog.* zone; ✖, *geog.* belt; *admin.* area; F outskirts *pl.* of Paris; *fig.* ∿ *sombre* grey zone; ∿ *de silence radio*: skip zone, silent zone.

zoo F [zɔ'ɔ] *m* zoo.

zoo... [zɔɔ] zoo...; **∿logie** [∿lɔ'ʒi] *f* zoology; **∿logique** [∿lɔ'ʒik] zoological; **∿phytes** *biol.* [∿'fit] *m/pl.* zoophytes; phytozoa; **∿tomie** [∿tɔ'mi] *f* zootomy, comparative anatomy.

zostère ⚘ [zɔs'tɛːr] *f* sea-wrack, grass-wrack, *Am.* eel-grass.

zouave ✖ *hist.* [zwa:v] *m* zouave (= *French colonial infantryman*).

zozoter F [zɔzɔ'te] (1a) *v/i.* lisp.

zut! *sl.* [zyt] *int.* anger, disappointment: hang it!; dash it!; darn it!

Proper names with pronunciation and explanation

Noms propres avec leur prononciation et notes explicatives

A

Abyssinie [abisi'ni] *f*: *l'~* Abyssinia (*former name of Ethiopia*).

Académie [akade'mi] *f*: *~ française* the French Academy.

Achille [a'ʃil] *m* Achilles.

Adam [a'dɑ̃] *m* Adam.

Adélaïde [adela'id] *f* Adelaide.

Adolphe [a'dɔlf] *m* Adolf, Adolphus.

Adour [a'du:r] *French river*.

Adriatique [adria'tik] *f*: *l'~* (*or la mer ~*) the Adriatic (*Sea*).

Afghanistan [afganis'tɑ̃] *m*: *l'~* Afghanistan.

Afrique [a'frik] *f*: *l'~* Africa; *l'~ du Sud* South Africa.

Agathe [a'gat] *f* Agatha.

Agen [a'ʒɛ̃] *capital of the department of Lot-et-Garonne.*

Agnès [a'nɛs] *f* Agnes.

Aimée [ɛ'me] *f* Amy.

Ain [ɛ̃] *French river; department of eastern France.*

Aisne [ɛn] *French river; department of northern France.*

Aix-en-Provence [ɛksɑ̃prɔ'vɑ̃:s] *former capital of the province of Provence.*

Ajaccio [aʒak'sjo] *capital of the department of Corse.*

Alain [a'lɛ̃] *m* Allen.

Alain-Fournier [alɛ̃fur'nje] *French writer.*

Albanie [alba'ni] *f*: *l'~* Albania.

Albert [al'bɛ:r] *m* Albert.

Albi [al'bi] *capital of the department of Tarn.*

Albion *poet.* [al'bjɔ̃] *f* Albion, Britain.

Alembert, d' [dalɑ̃'bɛ:r] *French philosopher and mathematician.*

Alençon [alɑ̃'sɔ̃] *capital of the department of Orne.*

Alexandre [alɛk'sɑ̃:dr] *m* Alexander.

Alger [al'ʒe] Algiers (*capital and port of Algeria*); Algier (*department of Algeria*).

Algérie [alʒe'ri] *f*: *l'~* Algeria.

Allemagne [al'maɲ] *f*: *l'~* Germany; *l'~ de l'Est* East Germany; *l'~ de l'Ouest* West Germany; *l'~ fédérale* the Federal Republic of Germany.

Allier [a'lje] *French river; department of central France.*

Alpes [alp] *f/pl.* Alps; *~-de-Haute-Provence* [alpdəotprɔ'vɑ̃:s] *f/pl. department of southeastern France;* **Hautes-~** [ot'salp] *f/pl. department of southeastern France;* **~-Maritimes** [~mari'tim] *f/pl. department of southeastern France.*

Alphonse [al'fɔ:s] *m* Alphonso; Alfonso.

Alsace [al'zas] *f*: *l'~* Alsace, Alsatia (*old province of France*).

Amboise [ɑ̃'bwa:z] *French town in the Loire valley with a famous castle.*

Amélie [ame'li] *f* Amelia.

Amérique [ame'rik] *f*: *l'~* America; *l'~ centrale* Central America; *l'~ du Nord* North America; *l'~ du Sud* South America.

Amiens [a'mjɛ̃] *capital of the department of Somme; former capital of the province of Picardie.*

Ampère [ɑ̃'pɛ:r] *French physicist.*

Anatole [ana'tɔl] *m Christian name.*

Andorre [ã'dɔ:r] f Andorra.

André [ã'dre] m Andrew.

Andrée [ã'dre] f Christian name.

Aneto [ane'to]: pic m d'~ highest peak of the Pyrénées.

Angers [ã'ʒe] capital of the department of Maine-et-Loire; former capital of the province of Anjou.

Angleterre [ãglə'tɛ:r] f: l'~ England.

Anglo-Normandes [ãglonɔr'mã:d]: les îles f/pl. ~ the Channel Islands.

Angoulême [ãgu'lɛm] capital of the department of Charente; former capital of the province of Angoumois.

Anjou [ã'ʒu] m old province of France.

Anne [ɑ:n] f Ann(e).

Annecy [an'si] capital of the department of Haute-Savoie; lac m d'~ French lake.

Annette [a'nɛt] f Annie, Nancy, Nanny, Nan.

Anouilh [a'nu:j] French writer.

Antarctique [ãtar(k)'tik] m: l'~ the Antarctic.

Antibes [ã'tib] French health resort on the Mediterranean.

Antoine [ã'twan] m Ant(h)ony.

Anvers [ã'vɛ:r; Belgian: ~'vɛrs] Antwerp.

Apennins [apɛn'nɛ̃] m/pl. Apennines.

Aquitaine [aki'tɛn] f old province of France.

Arabe [a'rab]: République f ♀ unie United Arab Republic.

Arabie [ara'bi] f: l'~ Arabia; l'~ Saoudite Saudi Arabia.

Aragon [ara'gɔ̃] French poet.

Archimède [arʃi'mɛd] m Archimedes (Greek scientist).

Arctique [ark'tik] m: l'~ the Arctic.

Ardèche [ar'dɛʃ] French river; department of southern France.

Ardennes [ar'dɛn] f/pl. department of northeastern France.

Argentine [arʒã'tin] f: l'~ Argentina, the Argentine.

Ariège [a'rjɛ:ʒ] French river; department of southern France.

Aristide [aris'tid] m Aristides.

Aristote [aris'tɔt] m Aristotle (Greek philosopher).

Arnaud [ar'no] m Christian name.

Arras [a'rɑ:s] capital of the department of Pas-de-Calais; former capital of the county of Artois.

Artus [ar'tys] m: le roi ~ King Arthur.

Artois [ar'twa] m former French county.

Asie [a'zi] f: l'~ Asia; l'~ Mineure Asia Minor.

Athènes [a'tɛn] f Athens.

Atlantique [atlã'tik] m: l'~ (or l'océan m ~) the Atlantic (Ocean).

Aube [o:b] French river; department of east-central France.

Auch [o:ʃ] capital of the department of Gers; former capital of the duchy of Gascogne.

Aude [o:d] French river; department of southern France.

Auguste [ɔ'gyst] m Augustus.

Aurigny [ɔri'ɲi] Alderney (one of the Channel Islands).

Aurillac [ɔri'jak] capital of the department of Cantal.

Australie [ɔstra'li] f: l'~ Australia.

Autriche [o'triʃ] f: l'~ Austria.

Auvergne [ɔ'vɛrɲ] f old province of France.

Auxerre [ɔ'sɛ:r] capital of the department of Yonne.

Aveyron [avɛ'rɔ̃] French river; department of southern France.

Avignon [avi'ɲɔ̃] capital of the department of Vaucluse.

Azay-le-Rideau [azɛlri'do] famous French castle.

B

Bahamas [baa'mas] f/pl.: les (îles f/pl.) ~ the Bahamas, the Bahama Islands.

Bâle [bal] Basle, Basel.

Balkans [bal'kã] m/pl.: les ~ the Balkan Peninsula sg.

Baltique [bal'tik]: la mer ~ the Baltic Sea.

Balzac [bal'zak] French writer.

Barbe [barb] f Barbara.

Bar-le-Duc [barlə'dyk] capital of the department of Meuse.

Barrès [ba'rɛs] French writer.

Barthélemy [bartelə'mi] m Bartholomew.

Basque [bask]: le pays ~ the Basque Provinces pl. (in Spain); the Basque Region (in France).

Basse-Terre [bɑs'tɛ:r] capital of the overseas department of Guadeloupe.

Bastille [bas'ti:j] f state prison destroyed in 1789.

Baudelaire [bod'lɛ:r] French poet.

Baudouin [bo'dwɛ̃] m Baldwin.

Bavière [ba'vjɛ:r] f: la ~ Bavaria.

Bayeux [ba'jø] *French town.*

Béarn [be'arn] *m old province of France.*

Beaumarchais [bomar'ʃɛ] *French writer.*

Beauvais [bo'vɛ] *capital of the department of Oise.*

Belfort [bɛl'fɔ:r] *capital of the Territoire de* ~; **Territoire** *m* **de** ~ [tɛritwardəbɛl'fɔ:r] *department of eastern France.*

Belgique [bɛl'ʒik] *f: la* ~ *Belgium.*

Belgrade [bɛl'grad] *capital of Yugoslavia.*

Benjamin [bɛ̃ʒa'mɛ̃] *m Benjamin.*

Benoît [bə'nwa] *m Benedict.*

Bergson [bɛrk'sɔn] *French philosopher.*

Berlin [bɛr'lɛ̃] *Berlin.*

Berlioz [bɛr'ljo:z] *French composer.*

Bernadotte [bɛrna'dɔt] *French Marshal.*

Bernanos [bɛrna'no:s] *French Catholic writer.*

Bernard [bɛr'na:r] *m Bernard.*

Berne [bɛrn] *Bern(e).*

Berry [bɛ'ri] *m old province of France.*

Berthe [bɛrt] *f Bertha.*

Bertrand [bɛr'trã] *m Bertram, Bertrand.*

Besançon [bəzãsɔ̃] *capital of the department of Doubs; former capital of the province of Franche-Comté.*

Beyrouth [be'rut] *Beirut.*

Birmanie [birma'ni] *f: la* ~ *Burma.*

Bizet [bi'zɛ] *French composer.*

Blanc [blã]: *mont m* ~ *highest peak of the Alpes.*

Blanche [blã:ʃ] *f Blanche.*

Blois [blwa] *capital of the department of Loir-et-Cher with a famous castle.*

Blum [blum] *French socialist.*

Bohême [bɔ'ɛm] *f: la* ~ *Bohemia.*

Bolivie [bɔli'vi] *f: la* ~ *Bolivia.*

Bonaparte [bɔna'part] *French (Corsican) family; see Napoléon.*

Bonn [bɔn] *capital of the Federal Republic of Germany.*

Bordeaux [bɔr'do] *capital of the department of Gironde.*

Bossuet [bɔ'sɥɛ] *French prelate, orator and writer.*

Bouches-du-Rhône [buʃdy'ro:n] *f|pl. department of southeastern France.*

Bouddha [bu'da] *m Buddha.*

Boulogne-sur-Mer [bulɔ̃syr'mɛ:r] *French port and town.*

Bourbons *hist.* [bur'bɔ̃] *m|pl.* Bourbons *(French royal house).*

Bourbonnais [burbɔ'nɛ] *m old province of France.*

Bourg [burk] *capital of the department of Ain.*

Bourges [burʒ] *capital of the department of Cher; former capital of the province of Berry.*

Bourget [bur'ʒɛ]: *lac m du* ~ *French lake;* **Le** ~ [ləbur'ʒɛ] *airport of Paris.*

Bourgogne [bur'gɔn] *f: la* ~ *Burgundy (old province of France).*

Braille [bra:j] *Frenchman who invented the alphabet named after him.*

Braque [brak] *French painter.*

Brésil [bre'zil] *m: le* ~ *Brazil.*

Brest [brɛst] *French port and town.*

Bretagne [brə'taɲ] *f: la* ~ *Brittany (old province of France).*

Briand [bri'ã] *French state man.*

Brigitte [bri'ʒit] *f Bridget.*

Broglie, de [də'brɔ:i] *name of two French physicists.*

Bruges [bry:ʒ] *Belgian port and town.*

Bruxelles [bry'sɛl] *Brussels.*

Bucarest [byka'rɛst] *Bucharest.*

Budapest [byda'pɛst] *capital of Hungary.*

Bulgarie [bylga'ri] *f: la* ~ *Bulgaria.*

C

Caen [kã] *capital of the department of Calvados.*

Cahors [ka'ɔ:r] *capital of the department of Lot.*

Caire, Le [lə'kɛ:r] *Cairo.*

Calais [ka'lɛ] *French port and town; le Pas de* ~ *the Straits pl. of Dover.*

Californie [kalifɔr'ni] *f: la* ~ *California.*

Calvados [kalva'do:s] *m department of northern France.*

Calvin [kal'vɛ̃] *famous French Protestant reformer.*

Camargue [ka'marg] *f region in the delta of the Rhône.*

Cambodge [kã'bɔdʒ] *m: le* ~ *Cambodia.*

Cambrai [kã'brɛ] *French town.*

Cameroun [kam'run] *m: le* ~ *Cameroon.*

Camus [ka'my] *French writer.*

Canada [kana'da] *m: le* ~ *Canada.*

Canaries [kana'ri] *f|pl.: les (îles f|pl.)* ~ *the Canary Islands.*

Cannes [kan] *French health resort on the Mediterranean.*

Cantal [kã'tal] *m department of central France.*

Cap [kap] *m: le* ~ *Cape Town.*

Capétiens *hist.* [kape'sjẽ] *m/pl.* Capetians (*French royal house*).

Caroline [karɔ'lin] *f* Caroline.

Carolingiens *hist.* [karɔlɛ̃'ʒjẽ] *m/pl.* Carolingians (*French royal house*).

Carpates [kar'pat] *f/pl.* Carpathians.

Catherine [ka'trin] *f* Catherine, Katharine, Katherine, Kathleen.

Caucase [kɔ'kaːz] *m* Caucasus.

Cayenne [ka'jɛn] *capital of the overseas department of Guyane française.*

Cécile [se'sil] *f* Cecilia, Cecily.

Centre ['sɑtr(ə)] *m: le* ~ *Central France.*

Cervin [sɛr'vẽ]: *le mont m* ~ *the Matterhorn.*

César [se'zaːr] *m: (Jules)* ~ *Julius Caesar.*

Cévennes [se'vɛn] *f/pl. mountain range of France.*

Cézanne [se'zan] *French painter.*

Chagall [ʃa'gal] *French painter.*

Châlons-sur-Marne [ʃalɔ̃syr'marn] *capital of the department of Marne.*

Chambéry [ʃãbe'ri] *capital of the department of Savoie; former capital of the province of Savoie.*

Chambord [ʃã'bɔːr] *famous French castle.*

Champagne [ʃã'paɲ] *f old province of France.*

Champ-de-Mars [ʃãd'mars] *m area of Paris between the École militaire and the Seine.*

Champs-Elysées [ʃãzeli'ze] *m/pl. famous Paris avenue.*

Chantilly [ʃãti'ji] *French town with famous castle; a. famous race course.*

Charente [ʃa'rãːt] *f French river; department of western France;* ~-**Maritime** [ʃarãtmari'tim] *f department of western France.*

Charles [ʃarl] *m* Charles.

Charlot [ʃar'lo] *m* Charlie, Charley; F *cin.* Charlie Chaplin.

Charlotte [ʃar'lɔt] *f* Charlotte.

Chartres [ʃartr] *capital of the department of Eure-et-Loir.*

Chartreuse [ʃar'trøːz] *f: la Grande-*~ *famous monastery near Grenoble.*

Chateaubriand [ʃatobri'ã] *French writer.*

Châteauroux [ʃato'ru] *capital of the department of Indre.*

Chaumont [ʃo'mɔ̃] *capital of the department of Haute-Marne.*

Chenonceaux [ʃənɔ̃'so] *famous French castle.*

Cher [ʃɛːr] *m French river; department of central France.*

Cherbourg [ʃɛr'buːr] *French port and town.*

Chili [ʃi'li] *m: le* ~ Chile, Chili.

Chine [ʃin] *f: la* ~ China.

Chirac [ʃi'rak] *French politician.*

Christine [kris'tin] *f* Christina, Christine.

Christophe [kris'tɔf] *m* Christopher.

Citroën [sitrɔ'ɛn] *French industrialist.*

Claire [klɛːr] *f* Clara, Clare.

Claudel [klo'dɛl] *French Catholic writer.*

Clemenceau [klemã'so] *French statesman.*

Clermont-Ferrand [klɛrmɔ̃fɛ'rã] *capital of the department of Puy-de-Dôme; former capital of the province of Auvergne.*

Cocteau [kɔk'to] *French writer.*

Cognac [kɔ'ɲak] *French town.*

Colbert [kɔl'bɛːr] *French statesman.*

Colette [kɔ'lɛt] *French authoress.*

Collège de France [kɔlɛʒdə'frãːs] *famous institution of higher education in Paris.*

Colmar [kɔl'maːr] *capital of the department of Haut-Rhin.*

Colombie [kɔlɔ̃'bi] *f: la* ~ Colombia.

Comédie-Française [kɔmedifrã-'sɛːz] *f National Theatre of France.*

Concorde [kɔ̃'kɔrd]: *place f de la* ~ *one of the most famous squares in Paris.*

Congo [kɔ̃'go] *m African river.*

Constance [kɔ̃s'tãːs] *m/f* Constance; *le lac m de* ~ *the lake of Constance.*

Copenhague [kɔpɛ'nag] Copenhagen.

Corée [kɔ're] *f: la* ~ Korea.

Corneille [kɔr'nɛːj] *French classical dramatist.*

Cornouailles [kɔr'nwaːj] *f/pl.: les* ~ Cornwall *sg.*

Corot [kɔ'ro] *French painter.*

Corrèze [kɔ'rɛːz] *f French river; department of central France.*

Corse [kɔrs] *f: la* ~ Corsica (*French island; department of France*).

Costa Rica [kɔstari'ka] *m* Costa Rica.

Côte d'Argent [kotdar'ʒã] *f part of French Atlantic coast.*

Côte d'Azur [kotda'zy:r] *f part of French Mediterranean coast.*

Côte d'Émeraude [kotdem'ro:d] *f part of French Channel coast.*

Côte-d'Ivoire [kotdi'vwa:r] *f: la ~ the Ivory Coast.*

Côte-d'Or [kot'dɔ:r] *f department of east-central France.*

Côtes-du-Nord [kotdy'nɔ:r] *f/pl. department of northwestern France.*

Coulomb, de [dəku'lɔ̃] *French physicist.*

Couperin [ku'prɛ̃] *family of French musicians.*

Courbet [kur'bɛ] *French painter.*

Couve de Murville [kuvdəmyr'vil] *French politician.*

Crète [krɛt] *f: la ~ Crete.*

Creuse [krø:z] *f French river; department of central France.*

Crimée [kri'me] *f: la ~ the Crimea.*

Cuba [ky'ba] *f: Cuba.*

Cupidon [kypi'dɔ̃] *m Cupid (Roman god of Love).*

Curie [ky'ri] *name of two eminent French physicists, discoverers of radium.*

D

Daguerre [da'gɛ:r] *French inventor of the earliest photographic process.*

Dalmatie [dalma'si] *f Dalmatia.*

Danemark [dan'mark] *m: le ~ Denmark.*

Daniel [da'njɛl] *m Daniel.*

Danton [dɑ̃'tɔ̃] *m French revolutionary.*

Danube [da'nyb] *m Danube.*

Dardanelles [darda'nɛl] *f/pl.: les ~ the Dardanelles.*

Daudet [do'dɛ] *French writer.*

Daumier [do'mje] *French lithographer.*

Dauphiné [dofi'ne] *m old province of France.*

David [da'vid] *m David (a. French painter).*

Deauville [do'vil] *French health resort on the Channel.*

Debré [də'bre] *French politician.*

Debussy [dəby'si] *French composer.*

Degas [də'ga] *French painter.*

Delacroix [dəla'krwa] *French painter.*

Denis [də'ni] *m Den(n)is.*

Descartes [de'kart] *French philosopher.*

Deux-Sèvres [dø'sɛ:vr] *department of western France.*

Diane [djan] *f Diana.*

Diderot [didə'ro] *French philosopher.*

Dieppe [djɛp] *French port and town.*

Digne [diɲ] *capital of the department of Alpes-de-Haute-Provence.*

Dijon [di'ʒɔ̃] *capital of the department of the Côte-d'Or; former capital of the province of Bourgogne.*

Dinard [di'na:r] *French health resort on the Channel.*

Dominicaine [dɔmini'kɛn]: *la République f ~ the Dominican Republic.*

Dominique [dɔmi'nik] *m Dominic.*

Don Quichotte [dɔ̃ki'ʃɔt] *m Don Quixote.*

Dordogne [dɔr'dɔɲ] *f French river; department of southwestern France.*

Dorothée [dɔrɔ'te] *f Dorothea, Dorothy.*

Doubs [du] *m French river; department of eastern France.*

Douvres [du:vr] *Dover.*

Draguignan [dragi'ɲɑ̃] *capital of the department of Var.*

Dresde [drɛsd] *Dresden.*

Dreyfus [drɛ'fys] *French army officer convicted of treason and imprisoned, but cleared in 1906.*

Drôme [dro:m] *f French river; department of southeastern France.*

Dublin [du'blɛ̃] *capital of the Republic of Ireland.*

Duhamel [dya'mɛl] *French writer.*

Dumas [dy'ma] *name of two French writers.*

Dunant [dy'nɑ̃] *Swiss merchant, founder of the Red Cross.*

Dunkerque [dœ̃'kɛrk] *Dunkirk (French port and town).*

Durance [dy'rɑ̃:s] *f French river.*

E

Écosse [e'kɔs] *f Scotland.*

Édimbourg [edɛ̃'bu:r] *Edinburgh.*

Edmond [ɛd'mɔ̃] *m Edmund.*

Édouard [e'dwa:r] *m Edward.*

Égée [e'ʒe] *f: la mer ~ the Aegaean Sea.*

Égypte [e'ʒipt] *f: l'~ Egypt.*

Eiffel [ɛ'fɛl] *French engineer.*

Elbe [ɛlb] *f: l'île d'~ Elba (scene of Napoleon's exile).*

Éléonore [eleɔ'nɔ:r] *f Eleanor, Elinor.*

Élisabeth [eliza'bɛt] *f* Elizabeth.

Elysée [eli'ze] *m* *palace in Paris, official residence of the President of the Republic.*

Émile [e'mil] *m Christian name.*

Émilie [emi'li] *f* Emily.

Épinal [epi'nal] *capital of the department of Vosges.*

Équateur [ekwa'tœːr] *m: l'~* Ecuador.

Escaut [ɛs'ko] *m the Scheldt.*

Ésope [e'zɔp] *m* Aesop *(Greek fabulist).*

Espagne [ɛs'paɲ] *f* Spain.

État français [etafrã'sɛ] *m name of the Pétain regime.*

États-Unis d'Amérique [etazynidame'rik] *m/pl. the* United States (of America), *the* U.S.A.

Éthiopie [etjɔ'pi] *f: l'~* Ethiopia.

Étienne [e'tjɛn] *m* Stephen.

Euclide [ø'klid] Euclid *(Greek mathematician).*

Eugène [ø'ʒɛn] *m* Eugene.

Eugénie [øʒe'ni] *f* Eugenia.

Euphrate [ø'frat] *m the* Euphrates.

Eure [œːr] *French river; department of northern France;* **~-et-Loir** [œre-'lwaːr] *department of northern France.*

Europe [ø'rɔp] *f: l'~* Europe.

Eustache [øs'taʃ] *m* Eustace.

Ève [ɛːv] *f* Eve, Eva.

Évreux [e'vrø] *capital of the department of* Eure.

Extrême-Orient [ɛkstrɛmɔr'jã] *m: l'~* the Far East.

F

Fauré [fɔ're] *French composer.*

Félix [fe'liks] *m* Felix.

Fénelon [fenə'lɔ̃] *French prelate and writer.*

Ferdinand [fɛrdi'nã] *m* Ferdinand.

Finistère [finis'tɛːr] *m department of northwestern France.*

Finlande [fɛ̃'lãːd] *f: la ~* Finland.

Flandre [flã:'dr] *f: la ~ (or les ~s)* Flanders *sg. (old province of France).*

Flaubert [flo'bɛːr] *French writer.*

Flessingue [fle'sɛ̃:g] Flushing.

Florence [flɔ'rãs] *f* Florence.

Foch [fɔʃ] *French Marshal.*

Foix [fwa] *capital of the department of* Ariège; *former county and its capital; old province of France.*

Fontainebleau [fɔ̃tɛn'blo] *famous French castle.*

Fort-de-France [fɔrdə'frãːs] *capital of the overseas department of Martinique.*

Fragonard [fragɔ'naːr] *French painter.*

France[1] [frãːs] *f: la ~* France.

France[2] [frãːs] *French writer.*

Franche-Comté [frãʃkɔ̃'te] *f old province of France.*

Franck [frãːk] *French composer.*

François [frã'swa] *m* Francis.

Françoise [frã'swaːz] *f* Frances.

Frédéric [frede'rik] *m* Frederick.

G

Gabon [gabɔ̃] *m: le ~* Gabon.

Gabriel [gabri'ɛl] *m* Gabriel.

Galles [gal] *f: le pays m de ~* Wales.

Gambetta [gãbe'ta] *French politician.*

Gand [gã] Ghent.

Gange [gãːʒ] *m the* Ganges.

Gap [gap] *capital of the department of* Hautes-Alpes.

Gard [gaːr] *m French river; department of southern France.*

Garonne [ga'rɔn] *f French river;* **Haute-~** [otga'rɔn] *f department of southwestern France.*

Gascogne [gas'kɔɲ] *f: la ~* Gascony; *le golfe de ~* the Bay of Biscay.

Gauguin [go'gɛ̃] *French painter.*

Gaule [goːl] *f: la ~* Gaul.

Gaulle, de [də'goːl] *French general and president.*

Gautier [go'tje] *French poet.*

Gay-Lussac [gɛly'sak] *French scientist.*

Gênes [ʒɛn] *f* Genoa.

Genève [ʒə'nɛːv] *f* Geneva.

Geneviève [ʒən'vjɛːv] *f* Genevieve, Winifred.

Geoffroi [ʒɔ'frwa] *m* Geoffrey, Jeffery, Godfrey.

Georges [ʒɔrʒ] *m* George.

Gérard [ʒe'raːr] *m* Gerald.

Germaine [ʒɛr'mɛn] *f Christian name.*

Gers [ʒɛːr] *m French river; department of southwestern France.*

Gertrude [ʒɛr'tryd] *f* Gertrude.

Gévaudan [ʒevo'dã] *m former French county.*

Ghana [ga'na] *m: le ~* Ghana.

Gide [ʒid] *French writer.*

Gilbert [ʒil'bɛːr] *m* Gilbert.

Gilles [ʒil] *m* Giles.

Giraudoux [ʒiro'du] *French writer.*

Gironde [ʒi'rɔ̃:d] *f French river; department of southwestern France.*

Giscard d'Estaing [ʒiskardɛs'tɛ̃] *French president.*

Gobelins, les [lego'blɛ̃] *m/pl. famous tapestry factory in Paris.*

Goncourt [gɔ̃'ku:r] *name of two French writers.*

Gounod [gu'no] *French composer.*

Grande-Bretagne [grɑ̃dbrə'taɲ] *f: la ~ Great Britain.*

Grandlieu [grɑ̃'ljø]: *lac m de ~ French lake.*

Grèce [grɛs] *f: la ~ Greece.*

Grégoire [gre'gwa:r] *m Gregory.*

Grenoble [grə'nɔbl] *capital of the department of Isère; former capital of the province of Dauphiné.*

Greuze [grø:z] *French painter.*

Grisons [gri'zɔ̃] *m/pl.: les ~ (the Canton of) Grisons.*

Groenland [grɔɛn'lɑ̃:d] *m: le ~ Greenland.*

Groningue [grɔ'nɛ̃:g] *Groningen.*

Guadeloupe [gwad'lup] *f French overseas department.*

Guatemala [gwatema'la] *m: le ~ Guatemala.*

Guebwiller [gɛbvi'lɛ:r]: *ballon m de ~ highest peak of the Vosges.*

Guéret [ge'rɛ] *capital of the department of Creuse; former capital of the province of Marche.*

Guernesey [gɛrnə'zɛ] *Guernsey (one of the Channel Islands).*

Gui [gi] *m Guy.*

Guillaume [gi'jo:m] *m William, Will.*

Guillotin [gijo'tɛ̃] *French physician who first proposed the use of the guillotine.*

Guinée [gi'ne] *f: la ~ Guinea.*

Guise, de [də'gi:z] *French noble family.*

Guitry [gi'tri] *French actor and playwright.*

Guizot [gi'zo] *French statesman and historian.*

Guy [gi] *m Guy.*

Guyane [gɥi'jan] *f: la ~ Guiana; ~ française [gɥijanfrɑ̃'sɛ:z] f French overseas department.*

Guyenne [gɥi'jɛn] *f: la ~ Guienne; ~ et Gascogne [gɥijɛnegas'kɔɲ] old province of France.*

H

Hainaut [*ɛ'no] *m province of southern Belgium.*

Haïti [ai'ti] *f Haiti.*

Halles [*al] *f/pl: les ~ quarter of Paris, formerly with the principal market.*

Hambourg [ɑ̃'bu:r] *f Hamburg.*

Haussmann [os'man] *French administrator.*

Havane [*a'van] *f: la ~ Havana.*

Havre, Le [lə'*ɑ:vr] *m French port and town.*

Haye, La [la'*ɛ] *the Hague.*

Hélène [e'lɛn] *f Helen.*

Helsinki [ɛlsin'ki] *capital of Finland.*

Henri [ɑ̃'ri] *m Henry.*

Henriette [ɑ̃'rjɛt] *f Harriet.*

Hérault [e'ro] *m French river; department of southern France.*

Hercule [ɛr'kyl] *m Hercules.*

Hilaire [i'lɛ:r] *m Hilary.*

Hildegarde [ildə'gard] *f Hildegard.*

Hippolyte [ipɔ'lit] *m Christian name.*

Hoche [*ɔʃ] *French revolutionary general.*

Hollande [*ɔ'lɑ̃:d] *f: la ~ Holland.*

Homère [ɔ'mɛ:r] *m Homer (Greek poet).*

Honduras [*ɔ̃dy'ra:s] *m: le ~ Honduras.*

Hongrie [*ɔ̃'gri] *f: la ~ Hungary.*

Hortense [ɔr'tɑ̃:s] *f Hortense.*

Hôtel-Dieu [otɛl'djø] *m name of the oldest hospital in Paris.*

Hugo [*y'go] *French writer.*

Hugues [yg] *m Hugh.*

I

Ibert [i'bɛ:r] *French composer.*

If [if] *m small island near Marseilles, former state prison.*

Île-de-France [ildə'frɑ̃:s] *f old province of France.*

Ille-et-Vilaine [ilevi'lɛn] *department of northwestern France.*

Inde [ɛ̃:d] *f: l'~ India.*

Indien [ɛ̃'djɛ̃]: *océan m ~ Indian Ocean.*

Indochine [ɛ̃dɔ'ʃin] *f: l'~ Indo-China.*

Indonésie [ɛ̃dɔne'zi] *f: l'~ Indonesia.*

Indre [ɛ̃:dr] *French river; department*

* Before the so-called aspirate h, marked *, there is neither elision nor liaison.

550

of central France; ~-et-Loire [ɛ̃dre-'lwa:r] department of central France.
Indus [ɛ̃'dys] m the Indus.
Ingres [ɛ̃:gr] French painter.
Invalides, Les [lezɛ̃va'lid] m/pl. army pensioners' hospital in Paris; its church contains the tomb of Napoleon.
Iphigénie [ifiʒe'ni] f Iphigenia.
Irak, Iraq [i'rak] m: l'~ Irak, Iraq.
Iran [i'rɑ̃] m: l'~ Iran.
Irène [i'rɛn] f Irene.
Irlande [ir'lɑ̃:d] f: l'~ Ireland; l'~ du Nord Northern Ireland.
Isabelle [iza'bɛl] f Isabel.
Isère [i'zɛ:r] French river; department of southeastern France.
Islande [is'lɑ̃:d] f: l'~ Iceland.
Israël [isra'ɛl] m Israel.
Italie [ita'li] f: l'~ Italy.

J

Jacquard [ʒa'ka:r] inventor of the loom named after him.
Jacqueline [ʒa'klin] f Jacqueline.
Jacques [ʒa:k] m James.
Jamaïque [ʒama'ik] f: la ~ Jamaica.
Japon [ʒa'pɔ̃] m: le ~ Japan.
Jaurès [ʒɔ'rɛs] French politician and orator.
Jean [ʒɑ̃] m John; ~-**Jacques** [~'ʒa:k] m Christian name; ~-**Paul** [~'pɔl] m Christian name; ~ **sans Terre** [~sɑ̃-'tɛ:r] m John Lackland (English king).
Jeanne [ʒa:n] f Jean, Joan; ~ **d'Arc** [ʒan'dark] f Joan of Arc.
Jeanneton [ʒan'tɔ̃] f Jenny.
Jeannette [ʒa'nɛt] f Jenny, Janet.
Jeannot [ʒa'no] m Jack, Johnny.
Jérôme [ʒe'ro:m] m Jerome.
Jersey [ʒɛr'zɛ] one of the Channel Islands.
Jérusalem [ʒeryza'lɛm] Jerusalem.
Jésus [ʒe'zy], **Jésus-Christ** [ʒezy-'kri] m Jesus (Christ).
Joliot-Curie [ʒɔljoky'ri] name of two French physicists.
Jordanie [ʒɔrda'ni] f: la ~ Jordan.
Joseph [ʒɔ'zɛf] m Joseph.
Joséphine [ʒɔze'fin] f Josephine (first wife of Napoleon I).
Jourdain [ʒur'dɛ̃] m: le ~ the Jordan.
Juin [ʒɥɛ̃] French Marshal.
Jules [ʒyl] m Julius.
Julie [ʒy'li] f Julia, Juliet, Gill, Jill.
Julien [ʒy'ljɛ̃] m Julian.
Julienne [ʒy'ljɛn] f Juliana; Gillian.

Juliette [ʒy'ljɛt] f Juliet.
Jura [ʒy'ra] m mountain department of eastern France.

K

Karpates [kar'pat] f/pl. Carpathians.
Kenya [ke'nja] m: le ~ Kenya.
Kléber [kle'bɛ:r] French general.
Koweït [kɔ'wɛjt] Kuweit.
Kremlin [krɛm'lɛ̃] m the Kremlin.

L

La Boétie [labɔe'si] French writer.
La Bruyère [labry'jɛ:r] French moralist.
La Chaise [la'ʃɛ:z] French Jesuit.
Laclos [la'klo] French writer.
La Fayette, de [dəlafa'jɛt] French general and statesman; French woman writer.
Laffitte [la'fit] French financier.
La Fontaine [lafɔ̃'tɛn] French fabulist.
Lamarck [la'mark] French naturalist.
Lamartine [lamar'tin] French poet.
Lamennais [lam'nɛ] French philosopher.
La Motte-Picquet [lamɔtpi'kɛ] French naval commander.
Landes [lɑ̃:d] f/pl. department of southwestern France.
Languedoc [lɑ̃g'dɔk] m old province of France.
Laon [lɑ̃] capital of the department of Aisne.
Laos [la'o:s] m: le ~ Laos.
Laplace [la'plas] French physicist.
Laponie [lapɔ'ni] f: la ~ Lapland.
La Rochefoucauld [larɔʃfu'ko] French moralist.
Larousse [la'rus] French lexicographer.
Laure [lɔ:r] f Laura.
Laurent [b'rɑ̃] m Laurence.
Lausanne [lo'zan] Swiss town.
Laval [la'val] capital of the department of Mayenne; French politician.
Lavoisier [lavwa'zje] French chemist.
Law [lo; Fr. la:s] Scottish financier, controller-general of the French finances.
Lazare [la'za:r] m Lazarus.
Leconte de Lisle [ləkɔ̃tdə'lil] French poet.
Le Corbusier [ləkɔrby'zje] French architect.

Léman [le'mɑ̃] *m*: *le lac m~* the lake of Geneva, Lake Leman.
Leningrad [lenin'grad] *town of the U.S.S.R.*
Léon [le'ɔ̃] *m* Leo.
Léonard [leɔ'na:r] *m* Leonard.
Léopold [leɔ'pɔl] *m* Leopold.
Lesage [lə'sa:ʒ] *French writer.*
Lesseps [le'sɛps] *French diplomat who conceived the idea of the Suez Canal.*
Leyde [lɛd] Leyden.
Liban [li'bɑ̃] *m*: *le ~* Lebanon.
Libéria [liber'ja] *m*: *le ~* Liberia.
Libye [li'bi] *f*: *la ~* Libya.
Liège [ljɛ:ʒ] *Belgian town.*
Lille [lil] *capital of the department of Nord.*
Limoges [li'mɔ:ʒ] *capital of the department of Haute-Vienne; former capital of the province of Limousin; renowned for its porcelain.*
Limousin [limu'zɛ̃] *m old province of France.*
Lisbonne [liz'bɔn] *f* Lisbon.
Lise [li:z], **Lisette** [li'zɛt] *f* Betty; Lizzie.
Lisieux [li'zjø] *French town, place of pilgrimage.*
Littré [li'tre] *French lexicographer.*
Livourne [li'vurn] Leghorn.
Loire [lwa:r] *f French river; department of central France;* **Haute-~** [ot'lwa:r] *f department of central France;* **~-Atlantique** [lwaratlɑ̃'tik] *f department of northwestern France.*
Loiret [lwa'rɛ] *m French river; department of central France.*
Loir-et-Cher [lware'ʃɛ:r] *department of central France.*
Londres [lɔ̃:dr] London.
Lons-le-Saunier [lɔ̃ləso'nje] *capital of the department of Jura.*
Lorrain [lɔ'rɛ̃] *French painter.*
Lorraine [lɔ'rɛn] *f old province of France.*
Lot [lɔt] *m French river; department of southern France;* **~-et-Garonne** [~ega-'rɔn] *department of southwestern France.*
Loti [lɔ'ti] *French writer.*
Louis [lwi] *m* Lewis.
Louise [lwi:z] *f* Louisa, Louise.
Lourdes [lurd] *French town, place of pilgrimage.*
Louvre [lu:vr] *m former royal palace in Paris, now famous museum.*
Lozère [lo'zɛ:r] *f department of southeastern France.*

Luc [lyk] *m* Luke.
Lucette [ly'sɛt] *f diminutive of Lucie.*
Lucie [ly'si] *f* Lucy; Lucia.
Lucien [ly'sjɛ̃] *m* Lucian.
Lucienne [ly'sjɛn] *f Christian name.*
Lully [lyl'li] *French composer.*
Lumière [ly'mjɛ:r] *name of two French chemists, inventors of the cinematograph.*
Luxembourg [lyksɑ̃'bu:r] *m* Luxemb(o)urg; *palace and gardens in Paris.*
Lydie [li'di] *f* Lydia.
Lyon [ljɔ̃] Lyons (*capital of the department of Rhône; former capital of the province of Lyonnais*).
Lyonnais [ljɔ'nɛ] *m old province of France.*

M

Mac-Mahon [makma'ɔ̃] *French Marshal.*
Mâcon [mɑ'kɔ̃] *capital of the department of Saône-et-Loire.*
Madagascar [madagas'ka:r] *f* Madagascar.
Madeleine [mad'lɛn] *f* Madeleine; *bibl.* Magdalen.
Madelon [mad'lɔ̃] *f diminutive of Madeleine.*
Madère [ma'dɛ:r] *f* Madeira.
Madrid [ma'drid] *capital of Spain.*
Maeterlinck [meter'lɛ̃:k] *Belgian writer.*
Maginot [maʒi'no] *French politician.*
Mahomet [maɔ'mɛ] *m* Mahomet.
Maillol [ma'jɔl] *French sculptor.*
Maine [mɛn] *f French river; m old province of France;* **~-et-Loire** [~e-'lwa:r] *department of western France.*
Mainfroi [mɛ̃'frwa] *m* Manfred.
Maintenon, de [dəmɛ̃t'nɔ̃] *French marquise, secret wife of Louis XIV.*
Majorque [ma'ʒɔrk] *f* Majorca.
Malaisie [male'zi] *f*: *la ~* Malaysia.
Malaysia [male'zja] *f*: *la ~* Malaysia.
Malebranche [mal'brɑ̃:ʃ] *French metaphysician.*
Malherbe [ma'lɛrb] *French poet.*
Mallarmé [malar'me] *French poet.*
Malmaison [malmɛ'zɔ̃] *residence of Joséphine after her divorce from Napoleon I.*
Malraux [mal'ro] *French writer.*
Malte [malt] *f* Malta.
Manche [mɑ̃:ʃ] *f*: *la ~* the English

Channel; *department of northwestern France.*

Manet [ma'nɛ] *French painter.*

Manon [ma'nɔ̃] *f Moll.*

Mans, Le [lɔ'mɑ̃] *capital of the department of Sarthe; former capital of the province of Maine.*

Marat [ma'ra] *French revolutionary.*

Marc [mark] *m Mark.*

Marcel [mar'sɛl] *m Christian name.*

Marche [marʃ] *f old province of France.*

Margot [mar'go] *f Maggie, Margot, Peg(gy).*

Marguerite [margə'rit] *f Margaret.*

Marie [ma'ri] *f Mary.*

Maritain [mari'tɛ̃] *French philosopher.*

Marivaux [mari'vo] *French playwright.*

Marne [marn] *f French river; department of northeastern France;* **Haute-~** [ot'marn] *f department of northeastern France.*

Maroc [ma'rɔk] *m: le ~ Morocco.*

Marseille [mar'sɛ:j] *Marseilles (capital of the department of Bouches-du-Rhône).*

Marthe [mart] *f Martha.*

Martin du Gard [martɛ̃dy'ga:r] *French writer.*

Martinique [marti'nik] *f French overseas department.*

Massif central [masifsɑ̃'tral] *m upland area of France.*

Mathilde [ma'tild] *f Mathilda, Maud.*

Matignon [mati'ɲɔ̃]: *l'hôtel m ~ residence of the French Prime Minister.*

Matisse [ma'tis] *French painter.*

Mat(t)hieu [ma'tjø] *m Mat(t)hew.*

Maupassant [mopa'sɑ̃] *French writer.*

Mauriac [mɔ'rjak] *French writer.*

Maurice [mɔ'ris]: *l'île f ~ Mauritius.*

Mauritanie [mɔrita'ni] *f: la ~ Mauritania.*

Maurois [mɔ'rwa] *French writer.*

Maurras [mɔ'ras] *French writer.*

Maxime [mak'sim] *m Christian name.*

Maximilien [maksimi'ljɛ̃] *m Maximilian.*

Mayenne [ma'jɛn] *f French river; department of northwestern France.*

Mecque [mɛk] *f: la ~ Mecca.*

Médicis [medi'sis] *Medici (Florentine noble family).*

Méditerranée [meditɛra'ne] *f: la ~ the Mediterranean.*

Melun [mə'lœ̃] *capital of the department of Seine-et-Marne.*

Mende [mɑ̃:d] *capital of the department of Lozère.*

Menton [mɑ̃'tɔ̃] *French tourist centre on the Mediterranean.*

Mérimée [meri'me] *French writer.*

Mérovingiens *hist.* [merovɛ̃'ʒjɛ̃] *m/pl. Merovingians (French royal family).*

Metz [mɛs] *capital of the department of Moselle.*

Meurthe [mœrt] *f French river; former department of northeastern France;* **~-et-Moselle** [~emo'zɛl] *department of northeastern France.*

Meuse [mø:z] *f French river; department of northeastern France.*

Mexico [mɛksi'ko] *Mexico City.*

Mexique [mɛk'sik] *m: le ~ Mexico.*

Mézières [me'zjɛ:r] *capital of the department of Ardennes.*

Michel [mi'ʃɛl] *m Michael.*

Michelet [miʃ'lɛ] *French historian.*

Milan [mi'lɑ̃] *m Milan.*

Millet [mi'lɛ; mi'jɛ] *French painter.*

Minorque [mi'nɔrk] *f Minorca.*

Mirabeau [mira'bo] *revolutionary orator.*

Mistral [mis'tral] *Provençal poet.*

Mitterand [mitɛ'rɑ̃] *French president.*

Mohammed [mɔa'mɛd] *see Mahomet.*

Molière [mɔ'ljɛ:r] *French writer of comedies.*

Mollet [mo'lɛ] *French politician.*

Monaco [mɔna'ko] *m Monaco.*

Monet [mɔ'nɛ] *French painter.*

Mongolie [mɔ̃gɔ'li] *f: la ~ Mongolia.*

Monique [mɔ'nik] *f Monica.*

Montaigne [mɔ̃'tɛɲ] *French moralist.*

Montalembert [mɔ̃talɑ̃'bɛ:r] *French politician and writer.*

Montauban [mɔ̃to'bɑ̃] *capital of the department of Tarn-et-Garonne.*

Montcalm, de [dəmɔ̃'kalm] *French general in Canada.*

Mont-de-Marsan [mɔ̃dmar'sɑ̃] *capital of the department of Landes.*

Montespan [mɔ̃tɛs'pɑ̃] *mistress of Louis XIV.*

Montesquieu [mɔ̃tɛs'kjø] *French writer and constitutionalist.*

Montherlant [mɔ̃tɛr'lɑ̃] *French writer.*

Montmartre [mɔ̃'martr] *part of Paris famous for its night life.*

Montparnasse [mɔ̃par'nɑːs] *famous artistic quarter of Paris.*

Montpellier [mɔ̃pə'lje] *capital of the department of Hérault.*

Montréal [mɔ̃re'al] Montreal.

Moravie [mɔra'vi] *f: la ~* Moravia.

Morbihan [mɔrbi'ɑ̃] *m department of western France.*

Morvan [mɔr'vɑ̃] *m mountain range of France.*

Moscou [mɔs'ku] Moscow.

Moselle [mɔ'zɛl] *f French river; department of northeastern France.*

Moulins [mu'lɛ̃] *capital of the department of Allier; former capital of the province of Bourbonnais.*

Moyen-Orient [mwaɛnɔr'jɑ̃] *m: le ~* the Middle East.

Mozambique [mozɑ̃'bik] *m: le ~* Mozambique.

Munich [my'nik] *m* Munich.

Musset [my'sɛ] *French writer.*

N

Nancy [nɑ̃'si] *capital of the department of Meurthe-et-Moselle.*

Nanette [na'nɛt] *f* Nancy.

Nantes [nɑ̃ːt] *French port; capital of the department of Loire-Atlantique.*

Naples ['naplə] *m, f* Naples.

Napoléon [napɔle'ɔ̃]: *~ Iᵉʳ* Napoleon I *(emperor of the French).*

Navarre [na'vaːr] *f former kingdom.*

Necker [ne'kɛːr] *French financier.*

Neige [nɛːʒ]: *crêt m de la ~ highest peak of the Jura.*

Népal [ne'pal] *m: le ~* Nepal.

Nerval [nɛr'val] *French writer.*

Nevers [nə'vɛːr] *capital of the department of Nièvre; former capital of the province of Nivernais.*

Nicaragua [nikara'gwa] *m: le ~* Nicaragua.

Nice [nis] *capital of the department of Alpes-Maritimes.*

Nicolas [nikɔ'lɑ] *m* Nicholas.

Nicolette [nikɔ'lɛt] *f Christian name.*

Nièvre [njɛːvr] *f French river; department of central France.*

Niger [ni'ʒɛːr] *m* Niger.

Nigeria [niʒɛr'ja] *m, f: le (or la) ~* Nigeria.

Nil [nil] *m* Nile.

Nîmes [nim] *capital of the department of Gard.*

Ninon [ni'nɔ̃] *f* Nina.

Niort [njɔːr] *capital of the department of Deux-Sèvres.*

Nivernais [nivɛr'nɛ] *m old province of France.*

Nord [nɔːr] *m department of northern France; la mer du ~* the North Sea.

Normandie [nɔrmɑ̃'di] *f: la ~* Normandy *(old province of France).*

Norvège [nɔr'vɛːʒ] *f: la ~* Norway.

Notre-Dame [nɔtrə'dam] *metropolitan church of Paris.*

Nouvelle-Calédonie [nuvɛlkaledɔ'ni] *f: la ~* New Caledonia.

Nouvelle-Zélande [nuvɛlze'lɑ̃d] *f: la ~* New Zealand.

O

Océanie [ɔsea'ni] *f: l'~* Oceania.

Oise [waːz] *French river; department of northern France.*

Olivier [ɔli'vje] *m* Oliver.

Oran [ɔ'rɑ̃] *town and department of Algeria.*

Orléanais [ɔrlea'nɛ] *m old province of France.*

Orléans [ɔrle'ɑ̃] *capital of the department of Loiret; former capital of the province of Orléanais; hist. branch of the French royal house of Bourbon.*

Orly [ɔr'li] *airport of Paris.*

Orne [ɔrn] *French river; department of northern France.*

Orphée [ɔr'fe] *m* Orpheus.

Oslo [ɔs'lo] *capital of Norway.*

Ottawa [ɔta'wa] *capital of Canada.*

Ouganda [ugɑ̃'da] *m: l'~* Uganda.

Oural [u'ral] Ural.

P

Pacifique [pasi'fik] *m: le (or l'océan) ~* the Pacific (Ocean).

Pagnol [pa'nɔl] *French writer.*

Pakistan [pakis'tɑ̃] *m: le ~* Pakistan.

Palestine [palɛs'tin] *f: la ~* Palestine.

Panamá [pana'ma] *m: le ~* Panama.

Panthéon [pɑ̃te'ɔ̃] *m Pantheon (building in Paris in the crypt of which are buried some of France's greatest men).*

Paraguay [para'gɛ] *m: le ~* Paraguay.

Paris [pa'ri] *m capital of France; capital of the department of Seine; former capital of the province of Ile-de-France.*

554

Parmentier [parmɑ̃'tje] *French economist and agronomist.*
Pascal [pas'kal] *French mathematician, physicist, and philosopher.*
Pas-de-Calais [pɑdka'lɛ] *m department of northern France.*
Pasteur [pas'tœːr] *French chemist and biologist.*
Patrice [pa'tris], **Patrick** [pa'trik] *m* Patrick.
Pau [po] *capital of the department of Basses-Pyrénées; former capital of the province of Béarn.*
Paul [pɔl] *m* Paul.
Pays-Bays [pei'bɑ] *m/pl.:* les ~ the Netherlands.
Pékin [pe'kɛ̃] Pekin(g).
Père-Lachaise [pɛrla'ʃɛːz] *m main cemetery of Paris, named after La Chaise.*
Périgord [peri'gɔr] *m former county of France.*
Périgueux [peri'gø] *capital of the department of Dordogne; former capital of the county of Périgord.*
Pérou [pe'ru] *m:* le ~ Peru.
Perpignan [pɛrpi'ɲɑ̃] *capital of the department of Pyrénées-Orientales; former capital of the province of Roussillon.*
Perrault [pɛ'ro] *French writer of fairy tales.*
Perrier [pɛ'rje] *French naturalist.*
Perse hist. [pɛrs] *f:* la ~ Persia.
Persique [pɛr'sik]: le golfe ~ Persian Gulf.
Pétain [pe'tɛ̃] *French Marshal and politician.*
Peugeot [pø'ʒo] *French industrialist.*
Phèdre [fɛdr] *f* Phaedra.
Philippe [fi'lip] *m* Philip.
Philippines [fili'pin] *f/pl.:* les ~ the Philippines.
Picardie [pikar'di] *f old province of France.*
Picasso [pika'so] *Spanish painter.*
Piccard [pi'kaːr] *Swiss physicist.*
Pierre [pjɛːr] *m* Peter.
Pissarro [pisa'ro] *French painter.*
Platon [pla'tɔ̃] *m* Plato (*Greek philosopher*).
Pleyel [plɛ'jɛl] *family of musicians.*
Poincaré [pwɛ̃kɑ're] *French statesman.*
Poitiers [pwa'tje] *capital of the department of Vienne; former capital of the province of Poitou.*

Poitou [pwa'tu] *m old province of France.*
Pologne [pɔ'lɔɲ] *f:* la ~ Poland.
Polynésie [pɔline'zi] *f:* la ~ Polynesia.
Pompadour [pɔ̃pa'duːr] *mistress of Louis XV.*
Pompidou [pɔ̃pi'du] *French president.*
Port-Royal [pɔrrwa'jal] *French abbey, centre of jansenism.*
Portugal [pɔrty'gal] *m:* le ~ Portugal.
Poussin [pu'sɛ̃] *French painter.*
Prague [prag] *capital of Czechoslovakia.*
Prévost [pre'vo] *French writer.*
Privas [pri'va] *capital of the department of Ardèche.*
Proche-Orient [prɔʃɔr'jɑ̃] *m:* le ~ the Near East.
Proudhon [pru'dɔ̃] *French philosopher.*
Proust [prust] *French writer.*
Provence [prɔ'vɑ̃ːs] *f old province of France.*
Prud'hon [pry'dɔ̃] *French painter.*
Prusse [prys] *f:* la ~ Prussia.
Puy [pui]: Le ~ *capital of the department of Haute-Loire;* ~**-de-Dôme** [~d'doːm] *m department of central France.*
Pyrénées [pire'ne] *f/pl.* Pyrenees; **Basses-**~ [bɑspire'ne] *f/pl. department of southwestern France;* **Hautes-**~ [otpire'ne] *f/pl. department of southwestern France;* ~**Orientales** [pirenezɔrjɑ̃'tal] *f/pl. department of southwestern France.*

Q

Quai d'Orsay [kedɔr'sɛ] *m French Ministry of Defence.*
Quartier latin [kartjela'tɛ̃] *m the student quarter of Paris.*
Quatre-Cantons [katrəkɑ̃'tɔ̃]: le lac *m* des ~ the Lake of Lucerne.
Québec [ke'bɛk] Quebec.
Queneau [kə'no] *French writer.*
Quesnay [ke'nɛ] *French physiocrat.*
Quimper [kɛ̃'pɛːr] *capital of the department of Finistère; former capital of the county of Cornouaille.*

R

Rabelais [ra'blɛ] *French writer.*
Rachel [ra'ʃɛl] *f* Rachel.

Racine [ra'sin] *French classical dramatist.*

Rambouillet [rãbu'jɛ] *French town with a famous castle.*

Rameau [ra'mo] *French composer.*

Raoul [ra'ul] *m Ralph; Rudolph.*

Ravel [ra'vɛl] *French composer.*

Raymond [rɛ'mɔ̃] *m Raymond.*

Réaumur [reo'my:r] *French naturalist and physicist.*

Récamier [reka'mje] *French woman whose salon under the Restoration was famous.*

Reims [rɛ̃:s] Rheims (*French town*).

Renan [rə'nã] *French writer.*

Renaud [rə'no] *m Reginald.*

Renault [rə'no] *French industrialist.*

René [rə'ne] *m Christian name.*

Renée [rə'ne] *f Christian name.*

Rennes [rɛn] *capital of the department of Ille-et-Vilaine; former capital of the province of Bretagne.*

Renoir [rə'nwa:r] *French painter.*

Réunion [rey'njɔ̃] *f French overseas department.*

Reykjavik [rɛkja'vik] *capital of Iceland.*

Rhénanie [rena'ni] *f: la ~ the Rhineland.*

Rhin [rɛ̃] *m Rhine;* **Bas-~** [bɑ'rɛ̃] *m department of eastern France;* **Haut-~** [o'rɛ̃] *m department of eastern France.*

Rhodésie [rɔde'zi] *f: la ~ Rhodesia.*

Rhône [ro:n] *m French river; department of southeastern France.*

Richard [ri'ʃa:r] *m Richard;* **~ Cœur de Lion** [riʃarkœrdə'ljɔ̃] *m Richard the Lionhearted.*

Richelieu [riʃə'ljø] *French cardinal and statesman.*

Rimbaud [rɛ̃'bo] *French poet.*

Rivarol [riva'rɔl] *French writer.*

Robert [rɔ'bɛ:r] *m Robert.*

Robespierre [rɔbɛs'pjɛ:r] *French revolutionary.*

Rochelle, La [larɔ'ʃɛl] *capital of the department of Charente-Maritime; former capital of the province of Aunis.*

Roche-sur-Yon, La [larɔʃsy'rjɔ̃] *capital of the department of Vendée.*

Rodez [rɔ'dɛ:z] *capital of the department of Aveyron; former capital of the province of Rouergue.*

Rodin [rɔ'dɛ̃] *French sculptor.*

Rodolphe [rɔ'dɔlf] *m Ralph, Rudolph.*

Roger [rɔ'ʒe] *m Roger.*

Rohan [rɔ'ã] *French general and Calvinist leader; French cardinal.*

Roland [rɔ'lã] *French woman and republican whose salon had considerable influence in the 18th century.*

Rolland [rɔ'lã] *French writer.*

Romains [rɔ'mɛ̃] *French writer.*

Rome [rɔm] *f Rome.*

Ronsard [rɔ̃'sa:r] *French poet.*

Rostand [rɔs'tã] *French dramatist.*

Rouault [rwo] *French painter.*

Roubaix [ru'bɛ] *French town.*

Rouen [rwã] *French port; capital of the department of Seine-Maritime; former capital of the province of Normandie.*

Rouergue [rwɛrg] *m old province of France.*

Rouget de Lisle [ruʒɛd'lil] *author of the Marseillaise.*

Roumanie [ruma'ni] *f: la ~ Rumania.*

Rousseau [ru'so] *Swiss-born French philosopher.*

Roussillon [rusi'jɔ̃] *old province of France.*

Ruanda [rwã'da, rwan'da] *m: le ~ Rwanda.*

Rude [ryd] *French sculptor.*

Russie [ry'si] *f: la ~ Russia.*

S

Sade [sad] *French writer.*

Sahara [saa'ra] *m: le ~ the Sahara.*

Saint-Barthélemy, la [lasɛ̃bartelə-mi] *f Massacre of St. Bartholomew.*

Saint-Brieuc [sɛ̃bri'ø] *capital of the department of Côtes-du-Nord.*

Saint-Cloud [sɛ̃'klu] *French town with famous race-course.*

Saint-Denis-de-la-Réunion [sɛ̃-dnidəlarey'njɔ̃] *capital of the overseas department of Réunion.*

Sainte-Beuve [sɛ̃t'bœ:v] *French writer.*

Sainte-Hélène [sɛ̃te'lɛn] *f Saint Helena.*

Saintes [sɛ̃:t] *former capital of the province of Saintonge.*

Saint-Etienne [sɛ̃te'tjɛn] *capital of the department of Loire.*

Saint-Exupéry [sɛ̃tɛksype'ri] *French writer.*

Saint-Germain-des-Prés [sɛ̃-ʒɛrmɛde'pre] *very old church and* *popular quarter of Paris*; **Saint-Germain-en-Laye** [ѵɑ̃'lɛ] *French town with a famous castle.*

Saint-Just [sɛ̃'ʒyst] *French revolutionary.*

Saint-Laurent [sɛlɔ'rɑ̃] *m the St. Lawrence.*

Saint-Lô [sɛ̃'lo] *capital of the department of Manche.*

Saint-Malo [sɛma'lo] *French port and town.*

Saint-Marin [sɛma'rɛ̃] *m San Marino.*

Saintonge [sɛ̃'tɔ̃:ʒ] *old province of France.*

Saint-Pétersbourg [sɛpetɛr'sbu:r] St. Petersburg (*former name of Leningrad*).

Saint-Saëns [sɛ̃'sɑ̃:s] *French composer.*

Saint-Simon [sɛ̃si'mɔ̃] *French economist and philosopher.*

Salvador, El [ɛlsalva'dɔ:r] *m* El Salvador.

Salzbourg [salz'bu:r] *f* Salzburg.

Sancy [sɑ̃'si]: *puy m de ѵ highest peak of the Massif central.*

Sand [sɑ̃, sɑ̃:d] *French woman writer.*

Saône [so:n] *f French river*; **Haute-ѵ** [ot'so:n] *f department of eastern France*; **ѵ-et-Loire** [sone'lwa:r] *department of east-central France.*

Sardaigne [sar'dɛɲ] *f: la ѵ Sardinia.*

Sarre [sar] *f: la ѵ the Saar.*

Sarthe [sart] *f French river; department of northwestern France.*

Sartre [sartr] *French philosopher.*

Savoie [sa'vwa] *f: la ѵ Savoy (department of southeastern France; old province of France)*; **Haute-ѵ** [otsa'vwa] *f department of eastern France.*

Saxe [saks] *f: la ѵ Saxony.*

Scandinavie [skɑ̃dina'vi] *f: la ѵ Scandinavia.*

Scudéry [skyde'ri] *French woman writer.*

Ségur [se'gy:r] *French woman writer.*

Seine [sɛn] *f French river; department of northern France*; **ѵ-et-Marne** [ѵe'marn] *department of northern France*; **ѵ-et-Oise** [ѵe'wa:z] *department of northern France*; **ѵ-Maritime** [ѵmari'tim] *department of northern France.*

Serbie [sɛr'bi] *f: la ѵ Serbia.*

Seurat [sø'ra] *French painter.*

Sévigné [sevi'ɲe] *French woman writer.*

Sévres [sɛ:vr] *French town renowned for its porcelain.*

Sibérie [sibe'ri] *f: la ѵ Siberia.*

Sicile [si'sil] *f: la ѵ Sicily.*

Sieyès [sje'jɛs] *French politician.*

Silésie [sile'zi] *f: la ѵ Silesia.*

Sisley [sis'lɛ] *French painter.*

Slovaquie [slɔva'ki] *f: la ѵ Slovakia.*

Sluter [sly'tɛ:r] *Burgundian sculptor.*

Sofia [sɔ'fja] *capital of Bulgaria.*

Somme [sɔm] *f French river; department of northern France.*

Sophie [sɔ'fi] *f Sophia, Sophy.*

Sorbonne [sɔr'bɔn] *f seat of the faculties of letters and science of the University of Paris.*

Soubise [su'bi:z]: *hôtel m de ѵ the National Archives in Paris.*

Soudan [su'dɑ̃] *m: le ѵ the Sudan.*

Staël [stɑl] *French woman writer.*

Stendhal [stɛ̃'dal] *French writer.*

Stockholm [stɔ'kɔlm] *capital of Sweden.*

Strasbourg [straz'bu:r] Strasb(o)urg (*capital of the department of Bas-Rhin; former capital of the province of Alsace*).

Suède [sɥɛd] *f: la ѵ Sweden.*

Suez [sɥe:z] *m Suez.*

Suisse [sɥis] *f: la ѵ Switzerland.*

Sully [syl'li] *French politician.*

Sully Prudhomme [syllipry'dɔm] *French poet.*

Suzanne [sy'zan] *f Susan, F Sue.*

Sylvestre [sil'vɛstr] *m Sylvester.*

Syrie [si'ri] *f: la ѵ Syria.*

T

Taine [tɛn] *French philosopher and historian.*

Talleyrand-Périgord [talɛrɑ̃peri'gɔ:r] *French statesman.*

Tamise [ta'mi:z] *f: la ѵ the Thames.*

Tanger [tɑ̃'ʒe] Tangier.

Tarbes [tarb] *capital of the department of Hautes-Pyrénées.*

Tarn [tarn] *m French river; department of southern France*; **ѵ-et-Garonne** [ѵega'rɔn] *department of southwestern France.*

Tchad [tʃad] *m: le ѵ the Republic of Chad.*

Tchécoslovaquie [tʃekɔslɔva'ki] *f: la ѵ Czechoslovakia.*

Téhéran [tee'rã] *m* Teheran.
Teilhard de Chardin [tɛjardǝʃar-'dɛ̃] *French Jesuit and philosopher.*
Tel-Aviv [tɛla'vif] *city in West Israel.*
Terre de Feu [tɛrdeˈfø] *f: la ~* Tierra del Fuego.
Terre-Neuve [tɛrˈnœːv] Newfoundland.
Texas [tɛkˈsas] *m: le ~* Texas.
Thaïlande [tajˈlãːd] *f: la ~* Thailand.
Théophile [teɔˈfil] *m* Theophilus.
Thérèse [teˈrɛːz] *f* Theresa.
Thibau(l)t [tiˈbo] *m* Theobald.
Thierry [tjɛˈri] *m* Theodoric (*Christian name*); *French historian.*
Thomas [tɔˈma] *m* Thomas.
Tibet [tiˈbɛ] *m: le ~* Tibet.
Tigre [tigr] *m the* Tigris.
Tirana [tiraˈna] *capital of Albania.*
Tocqueville [tɔkˈvil] *French politician and writer.*
Tokyo [tɔˈkjo] *m* Tokyo.
Toulon [tuˈlɔ̃] *French port and town.*
Toulouse [tuˈluːz] *capital of the department of Haute-Garonne; former capital of the province of Languedoc;*
~-Lautrec [tuluzloˈtrɛk] *French painter.*
Touraine [tuˈrɛn] *f old province of France.*
Tours [tuːr] *capital of the department of Indre-et-Loire; former capital of the province of Touraine.*
Trocadéro [trɔkadeˈro] *m formerly building on the heights of Passy, Paris, replaced by the Palais de Chaillot.*
Trouville [truˈvil] *French health resort on the Channel.*
Troyes [trwa] *capital of the department of Aube; former capital of the province of Champagne.*
Tuileries [tɥilˈri] *f/pl.: les ~ gardens and former royal palace in Paris.*
Tulle [tyl] *capital of the department of Corrèze.*
Tunisie [tyniˈzi] *f: la ~* Tunisia.
Turquie [tyrˈki] *f: la ~* Turkey.

U

Union soviétique [ynjɔ̃sɔvjeˈtik] *f: l'~* the Soviet Union.
Uruguay [yryˈgɛ] *m: l'~* Uruguay.
Utrillo [ytriˈjo] *French painter.*

V

Valadon [valaˈdɔ̃] *French woman painter.*

Valence [vaˈlãːs] *m capital of the department of Drôme; f* Valencia (*Spain*).
Valéry [valeˈri] *French writer.*
Valois *hist.* [vaˈlwa] *m/pl. French royal house.*
Van Gogh [vanˈgɔg] *Dutch painter.*
Vanne [van] *f French river.*
Vannes [van] *f capital of the department of Morbihan.*
Var [vaːr] *m French river; department of southeastern France.*
Varsovie [varsɔˈvi] Warsaw.
Vatican [vatiˈkã] *m: le ~* the Vatican.
Vaucluse [voˈklyːz] *department of southeastern France.*
Vaud [vo] *m: le canton de ~* Vaud.
Vaugelas [voʒˈla] *French grammarian.*
Vauvenargues [vovˈnarg] *French moralist.*
Vendée [vãˈde] *f French river; department of western France.*
Venezuela [venezɥeˈla] *m: le ~* Venezuela.
Venise [vǝˈniz] *f* Venice.
Verdun [vɛrˈdɛ̃] *French town.*
Verhaeren [vɛˈrarǝn] *Belgian poet.*
Verlaine [vɛrˈlɛn] *French poet.*
Véronique [verɔˈnik] *f* Veronica.
Versailles [vɛrˈsaːj] *capital of the department of Seine-et-Oise with famous royal palace.*
Vesoul [vǝˈzul] *capital of the department of Haute-Saône.*
Vichy [viˈʃi] *French health resort; seat of Pétain government.*
Victor [vikˈtɔːr] *m* Victor.
Vienne [vjɛn] *f* Vienna (*capital of Austria*); *French river; department of west-central France; m town of Isère, near Grenoble;* **Haute-~** [otˈvjɛn] *f department of central France.*
Viêt-nam [vjɛtˈnam] *m: le ~* Vietnam.
Vigny [viˈɲi] *French writer.*
Vilaine [viˈlɛn] *f French river.*
Villon [viˈlɔ̃, viˈjɔ̃] *French poet.*
Vincennes [vɛ̃ˈsɛn] *suburb of Paris; famous castle and wood.*
Vlaminck [vlaˈmɛ̃ːk] *French painter.*
Voltaire [vɔlˈtɛːr] *French philosopher.*
Vosges [voːʒ] *f/pl. mountain range; department of eastern France.*

W

Wallonie [walɔˈni] *f French speaking part of Belgium.*

Waterloo [vatɛr'lo] *Belgian village, scene of famous defeat of Napoleon.*
Watteau [va'to] *French painter.*
Weygand [ve'gɑ̃] *Belgian-born French general.*

Y

Yémen [je'mɛn] *m*: le ~ Yemen.
Yonne [jɔn] *f French river; department of central France.*
Yougoslavie [jugɔsla'vi] *f*: la ~ Yugoslavia, Jugoslavia.
Ypres [ipr] *Belgian town.*
Yves [i:v] *m Christian name.*

Z

Zaïre [za'i:r] *m*: le ~ Zaïre.
Zambèze [zɑ̃'bɛ:z] *m the* Zambezi.
Zambie [zɑ̃'bi] *f*: la ~ Zambia.
Zola [zɔ'la] *French writer.*
Zurich [zy'rik] *m* Zurich.

Common French Abbreviations
Abréviations françaises usuelles

A

A *ampère* ampere.

A 2 *Antenne deux* channel two (*on French television*).

A.A. *antiaérien* A.A., anti-aircraft.

ac., à cte. *acompte* payment on account.

a.c. *argent comptant* ready money.

A.C.F. *Automobile Club de France* Automobile Association of France.

act. *action* share.

A.D.A.V. *avion à décollage et atterrissage vertical* V.T.O.(L.), vertical take-off (and landing) (aircraft).

à dr. *à droite* on *or* to the right.

A.d.S. *Académie des Sciences* Academy of Science.

AELE *Association européenne de libre échange* EFTA, European Free Trade Association.

AF *Air France* (*French airline*); *anciens francs* old francs.

A.F. *Allocations familiales* family allowance.

A.F.P. *Agence France-Presse* French press agency.

A.G. *Assemblée générale* general meeting; G.A., General Assembly.

à g. *à gauche* on *or* to the left.

AIH *Association internationale de l'hôtellerie* IHA, International Hotel Association.

A.J. *auberge de la jeunesse* youth hostel.

AME *Accord monétaire européen* EMA, European Monetary Agreement.

A.N.P.E. *Agence nationale pour l'emploi* national employment bureau.

A.O.C. *appellation d'origine controlée* guaranteed vintage.

A.P. *à protester* to be protested; *Assistance publique* Public Assistance.

ap. J.-C. *après Jesus-Christ* A.D., anno Domini.

arr. *arrondissement* district.

A.S. *Assurances sociales* social insurance; *association sportive* sports club.

a/s. *aux soins de* c/o., care of.

av. *avenue* avenue; *avoir* credit.

av. J.-C. *avant Jésus-Christ* B.C., before Jesus Christ.

B

B *bougie* candle-power.

B. *balle* bale; *billet* bill.

B.C.G. *vaccin bilié Calmette-Guérin* (*antitubercular vaccine*).

B.D. *bande dessinée* cartoon; comic.

Bd. *boulevard* boulevard.

BENELUX *Belgique-Nederland-Luxembourg* BENELUX, Belgium, Netherlands, Luxemb(o)urg.

B. ès L. (*or* **Sc.**) *Bachelier ès Lettres* (*or Sciences*) (*approx.*) Advanced Level of the General Certificate of Education in Arts (*or* Science).

B.F. *Banque de France* Bank of France.

B.O. *Bulletin officiel* Official Bulletin.

B.P. *boîte postale* POB, Post Office Box.

B.P.F. *bon pour francs* value in francs.

B.R.I. *Banque de règlements internationaux* B.I.S., Bank for International Settlements.

B.S.G.D.G. *breveté sans garantie du gouvernement* patent.

C

C *cent* hundred; **°C** *degré Celsius* degree centigrade.

c. *centime* (*hundredth part of a franc*).

C.A. *courant alternatif* A.C., alternating current; *chiffre d'affaires* turnover.

560

c.-à-d. *c'est-à-dire* i.e., that is to say.

C.A.F. *coût, assurance, fret* c.i.f., cost, insurance, freight.

cal *calorie* calory.

C.A.P. *Certificat d'aptitude profession-nelle* (*certificate granted to a qualified apprentice*).

C.C. *corps consulaire* consular corps; *compte courant* a/c, current account.

CCI *Chambre de Commerce Internatio-nale* ICC, International Chamber of Commerce.

C.C.P. *compte chèques postaux* postal cheque account.

C.D. *corps diplomatique* diplomatic corps.

CE *Conseil de l'Europe* Council of Europe.

CECA *Communauté européenne du charbon et de l'acier* E.C.S.C., European Coal and Steel Community.

CED *Communauté européenne de dé-fense* E.D.C., European Defence Community.

CEE *Communauté économique euro-péenne* E.E.C., European Economic Community.

CEEA *Commission européenne de l'énergie atomique* EURATOM, European Atomic Energy Commis-sion.

C.E.G. *collège d'enseignement général* (*Secondary Modern School*).

CERN *Organisation européenne pour la recherche nucléaire* European Organ-isation for Nuclear Research.

C.E.S. *collège d'enseignement secon-daire* (*Secondary School*).

C.E.T. *collège d'enseignement tech-nique* (*a technical college*).

Cf. *conférez* cf., compare.

C.F.D.T. *Confédération française* (et) *démocratique du travail* (*a major asso-ciation of French trade unions*).

C.F.T.C. *Confédération française des travailleurs chrétiens* French Confed-eration of Christian Workers.

C.G.A. *Confédération générale de l'agriculture* General Confederation of Agriculture.

C.G.C. *Confédération générale des cadres* General confederation of higher administrative staffs.

C.G.T. *Confédération générale du travail* General confederation of Labour, (*approx.*) T.U.C., Trade Union(s) Congress.

ch *cheval(-vapeur)* H.P., h.p., horse-power.

ch.d.f. *chemin de fer* Ry., railway.

ch.-l. *chef-lieu* capital.

CICR *Comité international de la Croix-Rouge* ICRC., International Com-mittee of the Red Cross.

Cie., Cie. *Compagnie* Co., Company.

CIO *Comité international olympique* IOC., International Olympic Com-mittee.

CISL *Confédération internationale des syndicats libres* ICFTU, Internation-al Confederation of Free Trade Unions.

cl *centilitre* centilitre, *Am.* centiliter.

cm *centimètre* centimetre, *Am.* centi-meter.

C.N.P.F. *Conseil national du patronat français* (*employers' association*).

C.N.R. *Conseil national de la Resistance* National Resistance Council.

C.N.R.S. *Centre national de la recher-che scientifique* (*approx.*) S.R.C., Scientific Research Centre.

COE *Conseil œcuménique des églises* WCC, World Council of Churches.

cour. *courant* inst., instant.

C.Q.F.D. *ce qu'il fallait démontrer* Q.E.D., quod erat demonstrandum which was to be proved.

C.-R.F. *Croix-Rouge française* French Red Cross.

CRI *Croix-Rouge internationale* IRC, International Red Cross.

C.R.S. *Compagnies républicaines de sécurité* (*state security police; member of the C.R.S.*).

cᵗ. *courant* inst., instant.

C.V. *cheval-vapeur* H.P., h.p., horse-power; *cette ville* this town.

D

D.A.T. *Défense aérienne du territoire* Air Space Defence.

D.C.A. *défense contre avions* A.A., anti-aircraft (defence).

D.D.T. *Dichlorodiphényltrichloroéthane* DDT, dichlorodiphenyltrichloro-ethane.

dép. *départ* departure; *député(e)* member of Parliament, *Am.* repre-sentative.

dépt. *département* administrative department.

der. *dernier* ult., ultimo.

dest. *destinataire* addressee, consignee.

D.E.U.G. [døg] *diplôme d'études universitaires générales* certificate of general studies at university level.

D.G.S.E. *Direction générale de la sécurité extérieure* (*counterintelligence agency*).

D.I.T. *défense intérieure du territoire* (*internal defence*).

div. *dividende* dividend.

D.M. *Docteur Médecin* Doctor of Medicine.

dº *dito* ditto.

D.O.M. *départements d'outre-mer* overseas administrative departments.

D.O.M.-T.O.M., Dom–Tom [dɔm-ˈtɔm] *départements, territoires d'outre-mer* overseas administrative departments and territories.

D.P.L.G. *Diplômé par le gouvernement* state certificated.

Dr *Docteur* Dr., Doctor (*university degree*).

dr. *droit* right.

D.S.T. *Direction de la surveillance du territoire* (*counterintelligence service*).

dt *doit* debit.

dz *douzaine* doz., dozen.

E

E. *est* E., east.

E.-M. *État-major* H.Q., Headquarters.

E.N.A. *École nationale d'administration* national administrative school.

E.N.S. *École normale supérieure* Training College for secondary school teachers.

E.N.S.I. *Écoles nationales supérieures d'ingénieurs* state colleges of advanced engineering.

env. *environ* about.

e.o.o.e. *erreur ou omission exceptée* E. & O.E., errors and omissions excepted.

etc. *et cætera* etc., etcetera.

Éts *établissements* establishments.

É.-U. *États-Unis* U.S.A., United States.

E.V. *en ville* Local (*on envelopes*).

ex. *exemple* example; *exercice* year's trading.

ex. att. *exercice attaché* cum dividend.

Exc. *Excellence* Excellency (*title*).

exD. *ex-dividende* ex div., ex dividend.

exp. *expéditeur* consigner.

ext. *externe* external; *extérieur* exterior.

F

F *franc* franc; **°F** *degré Fahrenheit* degree Fahrenheit.

F.A.B. *franco à bord* f.o.b., free on board.

FB *franc(s) belge(s)* Belgian franc(s).

f.c(t). *fin courant* at the end of this month.

Fco *franco* free, carriage paid.

F.E.N. *Fédération de l'éducation nationale* National Education Federation (*autonomous professional union*).

FF *franc(s) français* French franc(s).

F.F.I. *Forces françaises de l'intérieur* French Forces of the Interior.

F.F.L. *Forces françaises libres* Free French Forces.

F.I.A.A. *Fédération internationale d'athlétisme amateur* I.A.A.F., International Amateur Athletic Federation.

FIFA *Fédération internationale de football association* (*federation controlling international football competitions*).

fig. *figure* figure.

FISE *Fonds des Nations Unies pour l'enfance* UNICEF, United Nations Children's Fund.

FIT *Fédération internationale des traducteurs* IFT, International Federation of Translators.

F.M. *fréquence modulée, modulation de fréquence* F.M., frequency modulation.

FMI *Fond monétaire international* IMF, International Monetary Fund.

FMPA *Fédération mondiale pour la protection des animaux* WFPA, World Federation for the Protection of Animals.

F.N.A.C. *Fédération nationale d'achats des cadres* (*department store* [*chain*] *for high-quality goods*).

F.O. *Force Ouvrière* (*a Socialist trade union*).

fº *franco* free, carriage paid.

F.O.Q. *franco à quai* f.a.s., free alongside ship.

F.O.R. *franco sur rail* f.o.r., free on rail.

F.O.T. *franco en wagon* f.o.t., free on truck.

562

f.p. *fin prochain* at the end of next month.
fque *fabrique* make.
FR 3 *France trois* channel three (*on French television*).
fro *franco* free, carriage paid.
Frs *Frères* Bros., Brothers.
FS *franc(s) swisse(s)* Swiss franc(s).
F.S. *faire suivre* please forward (*on letters*).
F.S.M. *Fédération syndicale mondiale* WFTU, World Federation of Trade Unions.

G

g *gramme* gramme, *Am.* gram; *gravité* gravity.
g. *gauche* left.
G.C. (*route de*) *grande communication* (*approx.*) B-road.
G(r.)C. *Grand'Croix* Grand Cross (*of the Legion of Honour*).
G.D.F. *Gaz de France* (*French Gas Board*).
G.O. *grandes ondes* L.W., long wave(s).
G.V. *grande vitesse* per passenger train.

H

h *heure* hour, o'clock.
ha *hectare* hectare.
H.B.M. *habitations à bon marché* property to let at low rents.
H.C. *hors concours* not competing.
H.E.C. (*École des*) *Hautes Études commerciales* School of Advanced Commercial and Management Studies, Paris; *heure de l'Europe Centrale* CET, Central European Time.
H.F. *haute fréquence* high frequency.
H.L.M. *habitations à loyer modéré* property to let at moderate rents.
H.T. *haute tension* high tension.

I

Ibid. *ibidem* ibid., in the same place, ibidem.
Id. *idem* id., same, idem.
I.D.S. *Initiative de défense stratégique* S.D.I., Strategic Defense Initiative.
I.F.O.P. [i'fɔp] *Institut français d'opinion publique* (*state institute monitoring public opinion*).
ing(én.). *ingénieur* engineer.

I.N.P.I. [in'pi] *Institut national de la propriété industrielle* French Patent office.
I.N.S.E. [in'se] *Institut national des statistiques et des études économiques* national institute for statistics and economic research.
int. *interne* internal; *intérieur* interior.
I.U.T. *Institut universitaire de technologie* (*a technical college*).
I.V.G. *interruption volontaire de grossesse* voluntary termination of pregnancy.

J

j *jour* day.
J.A.C. *Jeunesse agricole chrétienne* Christian Agricultural Youth.
J.-B. *Jean-Baptiste* John the Baptist.
J.-C. *Jésus-Christ* J.C., Jesus (Christ).
Je *Jeune* Jun., Junior.
J.E.C. *Jeunesse étudiante chrétienne* Y.C.S., Young Christian Students.
J.-J. *Jean-Jacques* John James.
J.O. *Journal officiel* Official Gazette.
J.O.C. *Jeunesse ouvrière chrétienne* YCW, Young Christian Workers.

K

kg *kilogramme* kilogramme, *Am.* kilogram.
km *kilomètre* kilometre, *Am.* kilometer.
km:h *kilomètres par heure* kilometres (*Am.* -meters) per hour.
kV *kilovolt* k.v., kilovolt.
kW *kilowatt* k.w., kilowatt.
kWh *kilowatt-heure* kilowatt-hour.

L

l *litre* litre, *Am.* liter.
lat. *latitude* latitude.
L. ès L. *licencié ès lettres* (*approx.*) B.A., Bachelor of Arts.
L. ès Sc. *licencié ès sciences* (*approx.*) B.Sc., Bachelor of Science.
Lieut. *lieutenant* Lieut., Lieutenant.
ll. *lignes* ll., lines.
loc. cit. *loco citato* at the place cited.
long. *longitude* longitude.
Lt *lieutenant* Lt., Lieutenant.
Lt-Col. *lieutenant-colonel* Lt.-Col., Lieutenant-Colonel.

M

M. *Monsieur* Mr., Mister.
m *mètre* metre, *Am.* meter.
m. *mort* died.
mb *millibar* millibar.
md(e) *marchand(e)* merchant.
Me *Maître* (*barrister's title of address*).
mg *milligramme* milligramme, *Am.* milligram.
Mgr *Monseigneur* Monsignor.
M.L.F. *Mouvement de libération des femmes* Women's Liberation Movement.
Mlle *Mademoiselle* Miss.
Mlles *Mesdemoiselles* the Misses.
MM. *Messieurs* Messrs.
mm *millimètre* millimetre, *Am.* millimeter.
Mme *Madame* Mrs., Mistress.
Mmes *Mesdames* Mesdames.
mn *minute* minute.
Mon *maison* firm.
M.R.P. *Mouvement Républicain Populaire* Popular Republican Movement.
M/S *navire à moteur Diesel* M.S., motorship.
ms *manuscrit* MS., manuscript.
mss *manuscrits* MSS, manuscripts.
M.T.S. *mètre-tonne-seconde* metre (*Am.* meter)-ton-second.
MV *maladie vénérienne* V.D., venereal disease.
mV *millivolt* millivolt.

N

N. *nord* N., North; *nom* name.
n/... *notre, nos* our.
n. *notre* our.
N.B. *notez bien* N.B., note well.
N.-D. *Notre-Dame* Our Lady.
N.D.L.R. *note de la rédaction* editor's note.
N.E. *nord-est* N.E., north-east.
NF *nouveaux francs* new francs.
N.F. *norme française* French Standard.
No., no *numéro* number.
N.O., N.W. *nord-ouest* N.W., North-west.
n/sr. *notre sieur* ... our Mr. ...
N.U. *Nations Unies* U.N., United Nations.
n/v. *notre ville* our town.

O

O. *ouest* W., west; *officier* Officer (*of an Order*).

OAA *Organisation pour l'alimentation et l'agriculture* F.A.O., Food and Agriculture Organization.
OACI *Organisation de l'aviation civile internationale* ICAO, International Civil Aviation Organization.
OAS *Organisation de l'Armée Secrète* Secret Army Organization.
O.C. *ondes courtes* s.w., short wave(s).
OCDE *Organisation de coopération et de développement économiques* O.E.C.D., Organization for Economic Co-operation and Development.
OECE *Organisation européenne de coopération économique* O.E.E.C., Organization for European Economic Co-operation.
OIC *Organisation internationale du commerce* ITO, International Trade Organization.
OIN *Organisation internationale de normalisation* ISO, International Organization for Standardization.
OIPC *Organisation internationale de police criminelle* ICPO, INTERPOL, International Criminal Police Organization.
OIR *Organisation internationale pour les réfugiés* IRO, International Refugee Organization.
OIT *Organisation internationale du travail* ILO, International Labour Organization.
O.L.P. *Organisation de libération de la Palestine* PLO, Palestine Liberation Organization.
OMS *Organisation mondiale de la santé* WHO, World Health Organization.
O.N.M. *Office national météorologique* Meteorological Office.
ONU *Organisation des Nations Unies* UNO, United Nations Organization.
op. cit. *opere citato* in the work quoted.
O.P.E.P. [ɔ'pep] *Organisation des pays exportateurs de pétrole* OPEC, Organization of Petroleum Exporting Countries.
O.S *ouvrier spécialisé* semi-skilled worker.
OTAN *Organisation du Traité de l'Atlantique Nord* NATO, North Atlantic Treaty Organization.
OTASE *Organisation du Traité de défense collective pour l'Asie du Sud-Est*

SEATO, Southeast Asia Treaty Organization.

OTC *onde très courte* VHF, very high frequency.

P

P. *Père* Fr., Father.

p. *pour* per; *par* per; *page* page.

P.C. *Parti Communiste* Communist Party; *poste de commandement* Headquarters.

p.c. *pour cent* $^0/_0$, per cent.

p/c. *pour compte* on account.

P.C.B. *physique, chimie, biologie* physics, chemistry, biology.

P.C.C., p.c.c. *pour copie conforme* true copy.

P.C.V. [pese've] *paiement contre vérification* (*a. communication f en* ∿) reverse charge call.

p.d. *port dû* carriage forward.

P.(-)D.G. *président-directeur général* chairman (of the board).

P. et T. *postes et télécommunications* (*approx.*) The Post Office.

p.ex. *par exemple* e.g., for example.

P.G. *Prisonnier de guerre* P.O.W., Prisoner of War.

P.J. *Police judiciaire* (*approx.*) C.I.D., Criminal Investigation Department.

pl. *planche* plate, full-page illustration.

P.M. *police militaire* MP, M.P., Military Police.

p.m. *poids mort* dead weight.

P.M.E. *petites et moyennes entreprises* small businesses.

PMI *Protection maternelle et infantile* MCH, Maternal and Child Health; *petites et moyennes industries* small industries.

P.M.U. *Pari mutuel urbain* local tote.

P.N.B. *produit national brut* gross national product.

P.O. *par ordre* by order.

pp. *pages* pages.

p.p. *port payé* carriage paid.

P.p.c. *pour prendre congé* to take leave.

prov. *province* province.

P.-S. *post-scriptum* P.S., postscript.

P.S.V. *pilotage sans visibilité* instrument flying, blind flying.

P.T.T. *Postes, Télégraphes, Téléphones* (*French*) G.P.O., General Post Office.

P.V. *petite vitesse* per goods train.

P.-V. *procès-verbal* (*see main dictionary*).

Q

q. *carré* square; *quintal* quintal.

Q.G. *Quartier général* H.Q., Headquarters.

Q.I. *quotient intellectuel* I.Q., intelligence quotient.

qq. *quelque* some; *quelqu'un* someone.

qqf. *quelquefois* sometimes.

Q.S. *quantité suffisante* sufficient quantity.

R

R, r. *rue* Rd., road, street.

R.A.T.P. *régie autonome des transports parisiens* (*Paris Public Transport Board*).

R.A.U. *République arabe unie* United Arab Republic.

RB (*envoi*) *contre remboursement* C.O.D., cash on delivery.

R.C. *registre du commerce* register of trade.

r.d. *rive droite* right bank.

R.D.A. *République démocratique allemande* G.D.R., German Democratic Republic.

Rem. *remarque* annotation.

R.E.R. *Réseau express régional* (*commuter-train network*).

R.F. *République française* French Republic.

R.F.A. *République fédérale d'Allemagne* G.F.R., German Federal Republic.

r.g. *rive gauche* left bank.

R.N. *route nationale* (*approx.*) National Highway.

R.P. *réponse payée* R.P., reply paid; *Révérend Père* Rev. Fr., Reverend Father; *Représentation proportionnelle* P.R., proportional representation.

R.P.F. *Rassemblement du Peuple Français* Rally of the French People (*de Gaull's party*).

R.P.R. *Rassemblement pour la Republique* Rally for the Republic (*Gaullist party*).

R.S.V.P. *répondez, s'il vous plaît* the favour of an answer is requested.

Rte *route* road.

R.T.F. *Radiodiffusion-télévision française* French Radio and Television.

S

S. *sud* S., south; *Saint* St., Saint.

s. *seconde* s., second.

S.A. *Société anonyme* Co Ltd., limited company; *Am.* Inc., Incorporated.
S.A.R.L. *société à responsabilité limitée* limited liability company.
s.b.f. *sauf bonne fin* under usual reserve.
S.C.E. *service contre-espionnage* C.I.C., Counter Intelligence Corps.
s.d. *sans date* n.d., no date.
SDN *Société des Nations* L of N, League of Nations.
S.-E. *sud-est* S.E., southeast.
s.e. ou o. *sauf erreur ou omission* E. & O.E., errors and omissions excepted.
S.E. *Son Excellence* His Excellency *(Minister's title of address).*
S.F. *sans frais* no expenses; *sience-fiction* science fiction.
S.F.I.O. *Section française de l'internationale ouvrière* French section of the Workers' International *(unified Socialist Party).*
SG *Secrétaire général* SG, Secretary General.
S.G.D.G. *sans garantie du gouvernement (patent)* without government guarantee.
S.I. *Syndicat d'initiative* Travel and Tourist Bureau *or* Association.
S.I.D.A. [si'da] *syndrome immuno-déficitaire acquis* AIDS, Acquired Immunity Deficiency Syndrome.
S.J. *Société de Jésus* SJ, Society of Jesus.
s.l.n.d. *sans lieu ni date* n. p. or d., no place or date.
S.M. *Sa Majesté* H.M., His (Her) Majesty.
S.M.E. *Système monétaire européen* European Monetary System.
S.M.I.G. *salaire minimum interprofessionnel garanti* guaranteed minimum wage.
S.N.C.F. *Société nationale des chemins de fer français* French National Railways.
S.-O. *sud-ouest* S.W., southwest.
S.O.F.R.S. [sɔ'frɛs] *Société française d'enquêtes par sondage (a French institute for opinion-polling and market research).*
S.P.A. *Société protectrice des animaux (French)* Society for the Prevention of Cruelty to Animals.
S.R. *service de renseignement* Intelligence (Service *or* Department).
SS. *Saints* Saints.
S.S. *Sa Sainteté* His Holiness; *sécurité sociale* Social Security.

S/S *navire à vapeur* S.S., steamship.
st *stère* cubic metre, *Am.* meter.
St(e) *Saint(e)* St., Saint.
Sté *société* company.
S.V.P., s.v.p. *s'il vous plaît* please.

T

t *tonne* ton.
t. *tour* revolution; *tome* volume.
TB *tuberculose* TB, tuberculosis.
T.C.F. *Touring Club de France* Touring Club of France.
tél. *téléphone* telephone.
TF 1 *Télévision française un* channel one *(on French television).*
T.G.V. *train à grande vitesse* high-speed train.
T.N.P. *Théâtre National Populaire (one of the Paris theatres subsidized by the State).*
T.N.T. *trinitrotoluène* TNT, trinitro-toluene.
t.p.m. *tours par minute* r.p.m., revolutions per minute.
tr/s *tours par seconde* revolutions per second.
T.S.F. *Télégraphie sans fil* wireless telegraphy; wireless (set).
T.S.V.P. *tournez, s'il vous plaît* P.T.O., please turn over.
T.T.C. *toutes taxes comprises* all taxes included.
T.U. *temps universel* G.M.T., Greenwich mean time.
T.V. *télévision* TV, television.
T.V.A. *taxe à la valeur ajoutée* V.A.T., value-added tax.

U

UEO *Union européenne occidentale* WEU, Western European Union.
UEP *Union européenne de paiements* EPU, European Payments Union.
U.E.R. *unité d'enseignement et de recherche* area of study.
U.H.T. *ultra-haute température* ultra-high temperature.
UIE *Union internationale des étudiants* IUS, International Union of Students.
UIJS *Union internationale de la jeunesse socialiste* IUSY, International Union of Socialist Youth.
UIP *Union interparlementaire* IPU, Inter-parliamentary Union.

UIT *Union internationale des télécom-munications* ITU, International Tele-communication Union.

U.N.E.D.I.C. *Union nationale pour l'emploi dans l'industrie et le commerce (unemployment insurance scheme).*

U.N.E.F. *Union nationale des étudiants de France* French National Union of Students.

UNESCO *Organisation des Nations Unies pour l'éducation, la science et la culture* UNESCO, United Nations Educational, Scientific, and Cultural Organization.

U.R.S.S. [yrs] *Union des républiques socialistes soviétiques* U.S.S.R., Union of Soviet Socialist Republics.

V

V *volt* V, volt.

v. *votre, vos* your; *voir, voyez* see; *vers* verse; *verset* versicle.

v/ *votre, vos* your.

Var. *variante* variant.

V.D.Q.S. *vin délimité de qualité supérieure (medium-quality wine).*

Ve *veuve* widow.

vo *verso* verso, back of the page.

vol. *volume* volume.

V/Réf. *votre référence* your reference.

vv. *vers* ll., lines.

Vve *veuve* widow.

W

W *watt* watt.

W. *ouest* W., west.

Wh *watt-heure* watt-hour.

W.L. *Wagons-lits* sleeping cars.

W.R. *Wagons-restaurants* dining cars.

X

X. *anonym* anonymous.

X.P. *exprès payé* express paid.

Z

Z.I. *zone industrielle* industrial area.

Z.U.P. *zone à urbaniser en priorité* priority development area *or* zone.

Numerals
Nombres

Cardinal Numbers — Nombres cardinaux

0 zéro *nought, zero, cipher*
1 un, une *one*
2 deux *two*
3 trois *three*
4 quatre *four*
5 cinq *five*
6 six *six*
7 sept *seven*
8 huit *eight*
9 neuf *nine*
10 dix *ten*
11 onze *eleven*
12 douze *twelve*
13 treize *thirteen*
14 quatorze *fourteen*
15 quinze *fifteen*
16 seize *sixteen*
17 dix-sept *seventeen*
18 dix-huit *eighteen*
19 dix-neuf *nineteen*
20 vingt *twenty*
21 vingt et un *twenty-one*
22 vingt-deux *twenty-two*
30 trente *thirty*
40 quarante *forty*
50 cinquante *fifty*
60 soixante *sixty*
70 soixante-dix *seventy*
71 soixante et onze *seventy-one*
72 soixante-douze *seventy-two*
80 quatre-vingts *eighty*
81 quatre-vingt-un *eighty-one*
90 quatre-vingt-dix *ninety*
91 quatre-vingt-onze *ninety-one*
100 cent *a or one hundred*
101 cent un *one hundred and one*
200 deux cents *two hundred*
211 deux cent onze *two hundred and eleven*
1000 mille *a or one thousand*
1001 mille un *one thousand and one*
1100 onze cents *eleven hundred*
1967 dix-neuf cent soixante-sept *nineteen hundred and sixty-seven*
2000 deux mille *two thousand*
1 000 000 un million *a or one million* [*million*}
2 000 000 deux millions *two*}
1 000 000 000 un milliard *one thousand millions,* Am. *one billion*

Ordinal Numbers — Nombres ordinaux

1ᵉʳ le premier, 1ʳᵉ la première *the first*
2ᵉ le deuxième, la deuxième *the second*
3ᵉ le *or* la troisième *the third*
4ᵉ quatrième *fourth*
5ᵉ cinquième *fifth*
6ᵉ sixième *sixth*
7ᵉ septième *seventh*
8ᵉ huitième *eighth*
9ᵉ neuvième *ninth*
10ᵉ dixième *tenth*
11ᵉ onzième *eleventh*
12ᵉ douzième *twelfth*
13ᵉ treizième *thirteenth*
14ᵉ quatorzième *fourteenth*
15ᵉ quinzième *fifteenth*
16ᵉ seizième *sixteenth*
17ᵉ dix-septième *seventeenth*
18ᵉ dix-huitième *eighteenth*
19ᵉ dix-neuvième *ninteenth*
20ᵉ vingtième *twentieth*
21ᵉ vingt et unième *twenty-first*
22ᵉ vingt-deuxième *twenty-second*
30ᵉ trentième *thirtieth*
31ᵉ trente et unième *thirty-first*
40ᵉ quarantième *fortieth*
41ᵉ quarante et unième *forty-first*
50ᵉ cinquantième *fiftieth*
51ᵉ cinquante et untième *fifty-first*
60e soixantième *sixtieth*

61ᵉ	soixante et unième *sixty-first*
70ᵉ	soixante-dixième *seventieth*
71ᵉ	soixante et onzième *seventy-first*
72ᵉ	soixante-douzième *seventy-second*
80ᵉ	quatre-vingtième *eightieth*
81ᵉ	quatre-vingt-unième *eighty-first*

90ᵉ	quatre-vingt-dixième *nine-tieth*
91ᵉ	quatre-vingt-onzième *ninety-first*
100ᵉ	centième *hundredth*
101ᵉ	cent unième *hundred and first*
200ᵉ	deux centième *two hundredth*
1000ᵉ	millième *thousandth*

Fractions — Fractions

½ (un) demi *one half;* la moitié (*the*) half
1½ un et demi *one and a half*
⅓ un tiers *one third*
⅔ (les) deux tiers *two thirds*
¼ un quart *one quarter*
¾ (les) trois quarts *three quarters*

⅕ un cinquième *one fifth*
⅝ (les) cinq huitièmes *five eighths*
⁹⁄₁₀ (les) neuf dixièmes *nine tenths*
0,45 zéro, virgule, quarante-cinq *point four five*
17,38 dix-sept, virgule, trente-huit *seventeen point three eight*

French weights and measures
Mesures françaises

Linear Measures — Mesures de longueur

km	*kilomètre*	=	1000 m	0.6214 mi.
hm	*hectomètre*	=	100 m	109 yd. 1 ft. 1 in.
dam	*décamètre*	=	10 m	32.808 ft.
m	*mètre*	=	1 m	3.281 ft.
dm	*décimètre*	=	¹⁄₁₀ m	3.937 in.
cm	*centimètre*	=	¹⁄₁₀₀ m	0.394 in.
mm	*millimètre*	=	¹⁄₁₀₀₀ m	0.039 in.
μm or **μ**	*micron*	=	¹⁄₁ ₀₀₀ ₀₀₀ m =	0.000039 in.
	mille marin	=	1852 m	6080 ft.

Square Measures — Mesures de surface

km²	*kilomètre carré*	=	1 000 000 m²	0.3861 sq. mi.
hm²	*hectomètre carré*	=	10 000 m²	2.471 acres
dam²	*décamètre carré*	=	100 m²	119.599 sq. yd.
m²	*mètre carré*	=	1 m²	1.196 sq. yd.
dm²	*décimètre carré*	=	¹⁄₁₀₀ m²	15.5 sq. in.
cm²	*centimètre carré*	=	¹⁄₁₀ ₀₀₀ m²	0.155 sq. in.
mm²	*millimètre carré*	=	¹⁄₁ ₀₀₀ ₀₀₀ m²	0.002 sq. in.

Land Measures — Mesures de surfaces agraires

ha	*hectare*	=	100 a *or*	10 000 m² =	2.471 acres
a	*are*	=	dam² *or*	100 m² =	119.599 sq. yd.
ca	*centiare*	=	¹⁄₁₀₀ a *or*	1 m² =	1.196 sq. yd.

Cubic Measures — Mesures de volume

m³	*mètre cube*	=	1 m³	35.32 cu. ft.
dm³	*décimètre cube*	=	¹⁄₁₀₀₀ m³	61.023 cu. in.
cm³	*centimètre cube*	=	¹⁄₁ ₀₀₀ ₀₀₀ m²	0.061 cu. in.
mm³	*millimètre cube*	=	¹⁄₁ ₀₀₀ ₀₀₀ ₀₀₀ m³	0.00006 cu. in.

Measures of Capacity — Mesures de capacité

hl	*hectolitre*	=	100 l	22.01 gals.
dal	*décalitre*	=	10 l	2.2 gals.
l	*litre*	=	1 l	1.76 pt.
dl	*décilitre*	=	¹⁄₁₀ l	0.176 pt.
cl	*centilitre*	=	¹⁄₁₀₀ l	0.018 pt.
ml	*millilitre*	=	¹⁄₁₀₀₀ l	0.002 pt.
st	*stère*	=	1 m³	35.32 cu. ft. (*of wood*)

Weights — Poids

t	tonne	=	1 t or 1000 kg =	19.68	cwt.
q	quintal	=	¹⁄₁₀ t or 100 kg =	1.968	cwt.
kg	kilogramme	=	1000 g =	2.205	lb.
hg	hectogramme	=	100 g =	3.527	oz.
dag	décagramme	=	10 g =	5.644	dr.
g	gramme	=	1 g =	15.432	gr.
dg	décigramme	=	¹⁄₁₀ g =	1.543	gr.
cg	centigramme	=	¹⁄₁₀₀ g =	0.154	gr.
mg	milligramme	=	¹⁄₁₀₀₀ g =	0.015	gr.

Former Measures — Anciennes mesures

aune f	=	1,188 m	ell*
pied m	=	0,3248 m	foot
pouce m	=	¹⁄₁₂ pied or 27,07 mm	inch
ligne f	=	¹⁄₁₂ pouce or 2,258 mm	line
livre f	=	489,50 g; F 500 g	pound
lieue f	=	4 km	league
arpent m	=	42,21 a	acre

Conjugation of French verbs
Conjugaison des verbes français

In this section specimen verb-tables are set out. Within the body of the Dictionary every infinitive is followed by a number in brackets, *e.g.* (1a), (2b), (3c), *etc.* This number refers to the appropriate model or type in the following pages. (1a), (2a), (3a), (4a) are the **regular** verbs of their conjugation. Others have some irregularity or other special feature.

How to Form the Tenses

Impératif. Take the 2nd person singular and the 1st and 2nd persons plural of the *Indicatif présent*. In verbs of the 1st Conjugation the singular imperative has no final **s** unless followed by *en* or *y*.

Imparfait. From the 1st person plural of the *Indicatif présent:* replace **-ons** by **-ais** etc.

Participe présent. From the 1st person plural of the *Indicatif présent:* replace **-ons** by **-ant.**

Subjonctif présent. From the 3rd person plural of the *Indicatif présent:* replace **-ent** by **-e** etc.

Subjonctif imparfait. To the 2nd person singular of the *Passé simple* add **-se** etc.

Future simple. To the *Infinitif présent* add **-ai** etc.

Conditionnel présent. To the *Infinitif présent* add **-ais** etc.

---

*The English 'translation' given does not mean that the English measure of that name is exactly the same length, etc., as the French, e.g. the French *pouce* is 27,07 mm and the English *inch* is 25,4 mm.

Auxiliary Verbs

(1) être

A. Indicatif

I. Simple Tenses

Présent

- sg. je suis / tu es / il est
- pl. nous sommes / vous êtes / ils sont

Imparfait

- sg. j'étais / tu étais / il était
- pl. nous étions / vous étiez / ils étaient

Passé simple

- sg. je fus / tu fus / il fut
- pl. nous fûmes / vous fûtes / ils furent

Futur simple

- sg. je serai / tu seras / il sera
- pl. nous serons / vous serez / ils seront

Conditionnel présent

- sg. je serais / tu serais / il serait
- pl. nous serions / vous seriez / ils seraient

Participe présent

etant

Participe passé

été

II. Compound Tenses

Passé composé

j'ai été

Plus-que-parfait

j'avais été

Passé antérieur

j'eus été

Futur antérieur

j'aurai été

Conditionnel passé

j'aurais été

Participe composé

ayant été

Infinitif passé

avoir été

B. Subjonctif

I. Simple Tenses

Présent

- sg. que je sois / que tu sois / qu'il soit
- pl. que nous soyons / que vous soyez / qu'ils soient

Imparfait

- sg. que je fusse / que tu fusses / qu'il fût
- pl. que nous fussions / que vous fussiez / qu'ils fussent

Impératif

sois — soyons — soyez

II. Compound Tenses

Passé

que j'aie été

Plus-que-parfait

que j'eusse été

Auxiliary Verbs

(1) avoir

A. Indicatif

I. Simple Tenses

Présent

sg. j'ai
tu as
il a[1]

pl. nous avons
vous avez
ils ont

Imparfait

sg. j'avais
tu avais
il avait

pl. nous avions
vous aviez
ils avaient

Passé simple

sg. j'eus
tu eus
il eut

pl. nous eûmes
vous eûtes
ils eurent

[1] a-t-il?

Futur simple

sg. j'aurai
tu auras
il aura

pl. nous aurons
vous aurez
ils auront

Conditionnel présent

sg. j'aurais
tu aurais
il aurait

pl. nous aurions
vous auriez
ils auraient

Participe présent

ayant

Participe passé

eu (f eue)

II. Compound Tenses

Passé composé

j'ai eu

Plus-que-parfait

j'avais eu

Passé antérieur

j'eus eu

Futur antérieur

j'aurai eu

Conditionnel passé

j'aurais eu

Participe composé

ayant eu

Infinitif passé

avoir eu

B. Subjonctif

I. Simple Tenses

Présent

sg. que j'aie
que tu aies
qu'il ait

pl. que nous ayons
que vous ayez
qu'ils aient

Imparfait

sg. que j'eusse
que tu eusses
qu'il eût

pl. que nous eussions
que vous eussiez
qu'ils eussent

Impératif

aie — ayons — ayez

II. Compound Tenses

Passé

que j'aie eu

Plus-que-parfait

que j'eusse eu,

(1 a) blâmer

First Conjugation

I. Simple Tenses

Présent

sg. je blâme
tu blâmes
il blâme[1]

pl. nous blâmons
vous blâmez
ils blâment

Passé simple

sg. je blâmai
tu blâmas
il blâma

pl. nous blâmâmes
vous blâmâtes
ils blâmèrent

Participe passé

blâmé, e

Infinitif présent

blâmer

[1] blâme-t-il?

Impératif

blâme[2]
blâmons
blâmez

Imparfait

sg. je blâmais
tu blâmais
il blâmait

pl. nous blâmions
vous blâmiez
ils blâmaient

Participe présent

blâmant

Futur simple

sg. je blâmerai
tu blâmeras
il blâmera

pl. nous blâmerons
vous blâmerez
ils blâmeront

[2] blâmes-en
blâmes-y

Conditionnel présent

sg. je blâmerais
tu blâmerais
il blâmerait

pl. nous blâmerions
vous blâmeriez
ils blâmeraient

Subjonctif présent

sg. que je blâme
que tu blâmes
qu'il blâme

pl. que nous blâmions
que vous blâmiez
qu'ils blâment

Subjonctif imparfait

sg. que je blâmasse
que tu blâmasses
qu'il blâmât

pl. que nous blâmassions
que vous blâmassiez
qu'ils blâmassent

II. Compound Tenses

(*Participe passé* with the help of **avoir** and **être**)

1. Actif

Passé composé: j'ai blâmé
Plus-que-parfait: j'avais blâmé
Passé antérieur: j'eus blâmé
Futur antérieur: j'aurai blâmé
Conditionnel passé: j'aurais blâmé

2. Passif

Présent: je suis blâmé
Imparfait: j'étais blâmé
Passé simple: je fus blâmé
Passé composé: j'ai été blâmé
Plus-que-parf.: j'avais été blâmé
Passé antérieur: j'eus été blâmé
Futur simple: je serai blâmé
Futur antérieur: j'aurai été blâmé
Conditionnel présent: je serais blâmé
Conditionnel passé: j'aurais été blâmé
Impératif: sois blâmé
Participe présent: étant blâmé
Participe composé: ayant été blâmé
Infinitif présent: être blâmé
Infinitif passé: avoir été blâmé

Infinitif	Remarks	Présent — de l'indicatif	Présent — du subjonctif	Passé simple	Futur simple	Impératif	Participe passé
(1 b) aimer	Unstressed ai- may be pronounced [ɛ] or [e]	aime aimes aime aimons aimez aiment	aime aimes aime aimions aimiez aiment	aimai aimas aima aimâmes aimâtes aimèrent	aimerai aimeras aimera aimerons aimerez aimeront	aime aimons aimez	aimé, e
(1 c) appeler	The final consonant of the stem is doubled and [ə] becomes [ɛ] before a mute syllable (including the fut. and cond.)	apelle appelles appelle appelons appelez appellent	appelle appelles appelle appelions appeliez appellent	appelai appelas appela appelâmes appelâtes appelèrent	appellerai appelleras appellera appellerons appellerez appelleront	appelle appelons appelez	appelé, e
(1 d) amener	The e [ə] of the stem becomes è when stressed and also in the fut. and cond.	amène amènes amène amenons amenez amènent	amène amènes amène amenions ameniez amènent	amenai amenas amena amenâmes amenâtes amenèrent	amènerai amèneras amènera amènerons amènerez amèneront	amène amenons amenez	amené, e
(1 e) arguer	In this particular verb a mute e after the u is written ë and an ï after the u is written ï	arguë arguës arguë arguons arguez arguënt	arguë arguës arguë arguïons arguïez arguënt	arguai arguas argua arguâmes arguâtes arguèrent	arguërai arguëras arguëra arguërons arguërez arguëront	arguë arguons arguez	argué, e

	Infinitif	Remarks	Présent de l'indicatif	Présent du subjonctif	Passé simple	Futur simple	Impératif	Participe passé
(1f)	céder	The **é** of the stem becomes **è** when stressed, i.e. **not** in the *fut.* or *cond.*	cède cèdes cède cédons cédez cèdent	cède cèdes cède cédions cédiez cèdent	cédas cédas céda cédâmes cédâtes cédèrent	céderai céderas cédera céderez céderons céderont	cède cédons cédez	cédé, e
(1g)	abréger	The **é** of the stem becomes **è** when stressed, i.e. **not** in the *fut.* or *cond.* In addition, between the g and a or o, an e is inserted in the spelling but is not pronounced	abrège abrèges abrège abrégeons abrégez abrègent	abrège abrèges abrège abrégions abrégiez abrègent	abrégeas abrégeas abrégea abrégeâmes abrégeâtes abrégèrent	abrégerai abrégeras abrégera abrégerons abrégerez abrégeront	abrège abrégeons abrégez	abrégé, e
(1h)	employer	The **y** of the stem becomes **i** when followed by a mute **e** (including the *fut.* and *cond.*)	emploie emploies emploie employons employez emploient	emploie emploies emploie employions employiez emploient	employai employas employa employâmes employâtes employèrent	emploierai emploieras emploiera emploierons emploierez emploieront	emploie employons employez	employé, e

Infinitif	Remarks	Présent de l'indicatif	Présent du subjonctif	Passé simple	Futur simple	Impératif	Participe passé
(1i) payer	The **y** of the stem may be written **y** or **i** when followed by a mute **e** (including the *fut.* and *cond.*)	paie, paye paies, payes paie, paye payons payez paient, -yent	paie, paye paies, payes paie, paye payions payiez paient, -yent	payai payas paya payâmes payâtes payèrent	paierai, paye.. paieras paiera paierons paierez paieront	paie, paye payons payez	payé, e
(1k) menacer	**c** takes a cedilla (ç) before **a** and **o** to preserve the [s] sound	menace menaces menace menaçons menacez menacent	menace menaces menace menacions menaciez menacent	menaçai menaças menaça menaçâmes menaçâtes menacèrent	menacerai menaceras menacera menacerons menacerez menaceront	menace menaçons menacez	menacé, e
(1l) manger	Between the **g** of the stem and an ending beginning **a** or **o**, a mute **e** is inserted to preserve the [ʒ] sound	mange manges mange mangeons mangez mangent	mange manges mange mangions mangiez mangent	mangeai mangeas mangea mangeâmes mangeâtes mangèrent	mangerai mangeras mangera mangerons mangerez mangeront	mange mangeons mangez	mangé, e
(1m) conjuguer	The mute **u** at the end of the stem remains throughout, even before **a** and **o**.	conjugue conjugues conjugue conjuguons conjuguez conjuguent	conjugue conjugues conjugue conjuguions conjuguiez conjuguent	conjuguai conjuguas conjugua conjuguâmes conjuguâtes conjuguèrent	conjuguerai conjugueras conjuguera conjuguerons conjuguerez conjugueront	conjugue conjuguons conjuguez	conjugué, e

	Infinitif	Remarks	Présent de l'indicatif	Présent du subjonctif	Passé simple	Futur simple	Impératif	Participe passé
(1 n)	saluer	The **u** of the stem, pronounced [ɥ], becomes [y] when stressed and in the *fut.* and *cond.*	salue salues salue saluons saluez saluent	salue salues salue saluions saluiez saluent	saluai saluas salua saluâmes saluâtes saluèrent	saluerai salueras saluera saluerons saluerez salueront	salue saluons saluez	salué, e
(1 o)	châtier	The **i** of the stem, pronounced [j], becomes [i] when stressed and in the *fut.* and *cond.* The 1st and 2nd persons pl. of the *pres. sbj.* and of the *impf. ind.* are **-tions, -tiez.**	châtie châties châtie châtions châtiez châtient	châtie châties châtie châtiions châtiiez châtient	châtiai châtias châtia châtiâmes châtiâtes châtièrent	châtierai châtieras châtiera châtierons châtierez châtieront	châtie châtions châtiez	châtié, e
(1 p)	allouer	The **ou** of the stem, pronounced [w], becomes [u] when stressed and in the *fut.* and *cond.*	alloue alloues alloue allouons allouez allouent	alloue alloues alloue allouions allouiez allouent	allouai allouas alloua allouâmes allouâtes allouèrent	allouerai alloueras allouera allouerons allouerez alloueront	alloue allouons allouez	alloué, e
(1 q)	aller		vais vas va allons allez vont	aille ailles aille allions alliez aillent	allai allas alla allâmes allâtes allèrent	irai iras ira irons irez iront	va (vas-y) allons allez	allé, e

	Infinitif	Remarks	Présent de l'indicatif	Présent du subjonctif	Passé simple	Futur simple	Impératif	Participe passé
(1r)	envoyer	Like (1h) but with an irregular *fut.* and *cond.*	envoie envoies envoie envoyons envoyez envoient	envoie envoies envoie envoyions envoyiez envoient	envoyai envoyas envoya envoyâmes envoyâtes envoyèrent	enverrai enverras enverra enverrons enverrez enverront	envoie envoyons envoyez	envoyé, *e*
(1s)	léguer	The **é** of the stem becomes **è** when stressed, i.e. **not** in the *fut.* or *cond.* In addition, the mute **u** at the end of the stem remains throughout, even before **a** and **o.**	lègue lègues lègue léguons léguez lèguent	lègue lègues lègue léguions léguiez lèguent	léguai léguas légua léguâmes léguâtes léguèrent	léguerai légueras léguera léguerons léguerez légueront	lègue léguons léguez	légué, *e*

Second Conjugation

(2a) punir[2],

Note the cases in which the verb stem is lengthened by ...**iss**...

I. Simple Tenses

Présent

sg. je punis
tu punis
il punit

pl. nous punissons
vous punissez
ils punissent

Passé simple

sg. je punis
tu punis
il punit

pl. nous punîmes
vous punîtes
ils punirent

Participe passé

puni, e

Infinitif présent

punir

Impératif

punis
punissons
punissez

Imparfait

sg. je punissais
tu punissais
il punissait

pl. nous punissions
vous punissiez
ils punissaient

Participe présent

punissant

Futur simple

sg. je punirai
tu puniras
il punira

pl. nous punirons
vous punirez
ils puniront

Conditionnel présent

sg. je punirais
tu punirais
il punirait

pl. nous punirions
vous puniriez
ils puniraient

Subjonctif présent

sg. que je punisse
que tu punisses
qu'il punisse

pl. que nous punissions
que vous punissiez
qu'ils punissent

Subjonctif imparfait

sg. que je punisse
que tu punisses
qu'il punît

pl. que nous punissions
que vous punissiez
qu'ils punissent

II. Compound Tenses

Participe passé with the help of **avoir** and **être**; see (1 a)

Participe passé with the help of **avoir** and **être**; see (1 a). P.pr. **saillant**

---

[1] **saillir** is used only in the 3rd persons of the simple tenses. P.pr. **saillant**

Infinitif	Remarks	Présent		Passé simple	Futur simple	Impératif	Participe passé
		de l'indicatif	du subjonctif				
(2b) sentir	No stem lengthening by ...**iss**... The last consonant of the stem is lost in the 1st and 2nd persons sg. of the *pres. ind.* and the sg. *imper.*	sens sens sent sentons sentez sentent	sente sentes sente sentions sentiez sentent	sentis sentis sentit sentîmes sentîtes sentirent	sentirai sentiras sentira sentirons sentirez sentiront	sens sentons sentez	senti, *e*
(2c) cueillir	*Pres., fut.* and derivatives like (1 a)	cueille cueilles cueille cueillons cueillez cueillent	cueille cueilles cueille cueillions cueilliez cueillent	cueillis cueillis cueillit cueillîmes cueillîtes cueillirent	cueillerai cueilleras cueillera cueillerons cueillerez cueilleront	cueille cueillons cueillez	cueilli, *e*
(2d) fuir	No stem lengthening by ...**iss**... Note the alternation between the **y** and **i**: **y** appears in 1st and 2nd persons pl. of *pres. ind.*, *pres. sbj.*, and *imper.*, in the *p.-pr.* and throughout the *impf. ind.*	fuis fuis fuit fuyons fuyez fuient	fuie fuies fuie fuyions fuyiez fuient	fuis fuis fuit fuîmes fuîtes fuirent	fuirai fuiras fuira fuirons fuirez fuiront	fuis fuyons fuyez	fui, *e*

	Infinitif	Remarks	Présent de l'indicatif	Présent du subjonctif	Passé simple	Futur simple	Impératif	Participe passé
(2e)	bouillir	Pres. *ind.* and derivatives like (4a)	bous bous bout bouillons bouillez bouillent	bouille bouilles bouille bouillions bouilliez bouillent	bouillis bouillis bouillit bouillîmes bouillîtes bouillirent	bouillirai bouilliras bouillira bouillirons bouillirez bouilliront	bous bouillons bouillez	bouilli, *e*
(2f)	couvrir	Pres. and derivatives like (1a); *p.p.* in **-ert**	couvre couvres couvre couvrons couvrez couvrent	couvre couvres couvre couvrions couvriez couvrent	couvris couvris couvrit couvrîmes couvrîtes couvrirent	couvrirai couvriras couvrira couvrirons couvrirez couvriront	couvre couvrons couvrez	couvert, *e*
(2g)	vêtir	As (2b) but keeps the final consonant of the stem throughout the pres. *ind.* and the *im-per.* and has *p.p.* in **-u**	vêts vêts vêt vêtons vêtez vêtent	vête vêtes vête vêtions vêtiez vêtent	vêtis vêtis vêtit vêtîmes vêtîtes vêtirent	vêtirai vêtiras vêtira vêtirons vêtirez vêtiront	vêts vêtons vêtez	vêtu, *e*
(2h)	venir	Note that the ...**en**... of the *inf*... becomes ...**ien**... in the *fut.* and *cond.*, and when stressed except in the *p.s.* where it becomes ...**in**... [ɛ̃]. Note too the ...**d**... inserted in the *fut.* and *cond.*	viens viens vient venons venez viennent	vienne viennes vienne venions veniez viennent	vins vins vint vînmes vîntes vinrent	viendrai viendras viendra viendrons viendrez viendront	viens venons venez	venu, *e*

Infinitif	Remarks	Présent de l'indicatif	Présent du subjonctif	Passé simple	Futur simple	Impératif	Participe passé
(2i) courir	Pres., p.p., fut. and derivatives as in (4a); p.s. like (3a); ...rr... in fut. and cond.	cours cours court courons courez courent	coure coures coure courions couriez courent	courus courus courut courûmes courûtes coururent	courrai courras courra courrons courrez courront	cours courons courez	couru, e
(2k) mourir	Pres., fut. and derivatives as in (4a) with change of ...ou... to ...eu... in the sg. and the 3rd person pl. of the pres.; p.s. like (3a); ...rr... in fut. and cond.	meurs meurs meurt mourons mourez meurent	meure meures meure mourions mouriez meurent	mourus mourus mourut mourûmes mourûtes moururent	mourrai mourras mourra mourrons mourrez mourront	meurs mourons mourez	mort, e
(2l) acquérir	Pres. and derivatives as in (4a) with change of ...ér... to ...ièr... (ind.) and ..ièr... (sbj.) [jɛːr] when stressed; p.p in ..is; fut. and cond. in ..err..., not ..érir...	acquiers acquiers acquiert acquérons acquérez acquièrent	acquière acquières acquière acquérions acquériez acquièrent	acquis acquis acquit acquîmes acquîtes acquirent	acquerrai acquerras acquerra acquerrons acquerrez acquerront	acquiers acquérons acquérez	acquis, e

	Infinitif	Remarks	Présent de l'indicatif	Présent du subjonctif	Passé simple	Futur simple	Impératif	Participe passé
(2m)	haïr	Regular except that it loses trema from the **i** in the sg. of the *pres. ind.* and of the *imper.* with a corresponding change of pronunciation	hais [ɛ] hais hait haïssons haïssez haïssent	haïsse haïsses haïsse haïssiez haïssent	hais [aˈ] hais haït haïmes haïtes haïrent	haïrai haïras haïra haïrons haïrez haïront	hais [ɛ] haïssons haïssez	haï, *e*
(2n)	faillir	Defective verb			faillis faillis faillit faillîmes faillîtes faillirent	faillirai failliras faillira faillirons faillirez failliront		failli, *e*
(2o)	fleurir	Regular (like 2a) but in the sense of *prosper* has *p.pr.* **florissant** and *impf. ind.* **florissais**, etc.	fleuris fleuris fleurit fleurissons fleurissez fleurissent	fleurisse fleurisses fleurisse fleurissiez fleurissent	fleuris fleuris fleurit fleurîmes fleurîtes fleurirent	fleurirai fleuriras fleurira fleurirons fleurirez fleuriront	fleuris fleurissons fleurissez	fleuri, *e*
(2p)	saillir	Defective verb. *P.pr.* **saillant**	saille saillent	saille saillent		saillera sailleront		sailli, *e*

	Infinitif	Remarks	Présent de l'indicatif	Présent du subjonctif	Passé simple	Futur simple	Impératif	Participe passé
(2q)	gésir	Defective verb. Used only in *pres.* and *impf.* *ind.* *P.pr.* gisant	— — gît gisons gisez gisent					
(2r)	ouïr	Defective verb						ouï, e
(2s)	assaillir	*Pres.* and occasionally *fut.* and their derivatives like (1a)	assaille assailles assaille assaillons assaillez assaillent	assaille assailles assaille assaillions assailliez assaillent	assaillis assaillis assaillit assaillîmes assaillîtes assaillirent	assaillirai assailliras assaillira assaillirons assaillirez assailliront	assaille assaillons assaillez	assailli, e
(2t)	défaillir	Like (2s). But there is an old 3rd person sg. *pres. ind.* défaut in addition	défaille défailles défaille défaillons défaillez défaillent	défaille défailles défaille défaillions défailliez défaillent	défaillis défaillis défaillit défaillîmes défaillîtes défaillirent	défaillirai défailliras défaillira défaillirons défaillirez défailliront	défaille défaillons défaillez	défailli, e
(2u)	férir	Defective verb						féru, e
(2v)	querir	Defective verb						

Third Conjugation

(3a) **recevoir**

I. Simple Tenses

Présent

sg.
- je reçois
- tu reçois
- il reçoit

pl.
- nous recevons
- vous recevez
- ils reçoivent

Passé simple

sg.
- je reçus
- tu reçus
- il reçut

pl.
- nous reçûmes
- vous reçûtes
- ils reçurent

Participe passé[1]

reçu, e

Infinitif présent

recevoir

Impératif

- reçois
- recevons
- recevez

Imparfait

sg.
- je recevais
- tu recevais
- il recevait

pl.
- nous recevions
- vous receviez
- ils recevaient

Participe présent

recevant

Futur simple

sg.
- je recevrai
- tu recevras
- il recevra

pl.
- nous recevrons
- vous recevrez
- ils recevront

Conditionnel présent

sg.
- je recevrais
- tu recevrais
- il recevrait

pl.
- nous recevrions
- vous recevriez
- ils recebraient

Subjonctif présent

sg.
- que je reçoive
- que tu reçoives
- qu'il reçoive

pl.
- que nous recevions
- que vous receviez
- qu'ils reçoivent

Subjonctif imparfait

sg.
- que je reçusse
- que tu reçusses
- qu'il reçût

pl.
- que nous reçussions
- que vous reçussiez
- qu'ils reçussent

II. Compound Tenses

Participe passé with the help of **avoir** and **être;** *see* (1a)

---

[1] **devoir** and its derivative **redevoir** have **dû, due,** *m/pl.* **dus** and **redû, redue,** *m/pl.* **redus**

Infinitif	Remarks	Présent de l'indicatif	Présent du subjonctif	Passé simple	Futur simple	Impératif	Participe passé
(3b) apparoir	Defective verb	il appert					
(3c) asseoir	There are alternative forms; *pres. ind.* **assois, assoie** etc.; *pres. sbj.* **assoie** etc.; *fut.* **assoirai** etc.; *imper.* **assois, assoyons, assoyez;** *p.pr.* **assoyant;** *impf. ind.* **assoyais**	assieds assieds assied asseyons asseyez asseyent	asseye asseyes asseye asseyions asseyiez asseyent	assis assis assit assîmes assîtes assirent	assiérai assiéras assiéra assiérons assiérez assiéront	assieds asseyons asseyez	assis, e
surseoir		sursois sursois sursoit sursoyons sursoyez sursoient	sursoie sursoies sursoie sursoyions sursoyiez sursoient	sursis sursis sursit sursîmes sursîtes sursirent	surseoirai surseoiras surseoira surseoirons surseoirez surseoiront	sursois sursoyons sursoyez	sursis, e
(3d) choir	Defective verb. No p.pr. There are alternative forms: *fut.* **cherrai** etc.	chois chois choit		chus chus chut chûmes châtes churent	choirai choiras choira choirons choirez choiront		chu, e

Infinitif	Remarks	Présent de l'indicatif	Présent du subjonctif	Passé simple	Futur simple	Impératif	Participe passé
déchoir	Defective verb. No impf. ind. and no p.pr.	déchois déchois déchoit déchoyons déchoyez déchoient	déchoie déchoies déchoie déchoyions déchoyiez déchoient	déchus déchus déchut déchûmes déchûtes déchurent	déchoirai déchoiras déchoira déchoirons déchoirez déchoiront		déchu, e
échoir	Defective verb. *P.pr.* **il échéant.** *Impf. ind.* **il échoyait** or **échéait.** There are alternative forms: *fut.* **il écherra, ils écherront**	il échoit ils échoient	qu'il échoie	il échut ils échurent	il échoira ils échoiront		échu, e
(3 e) falloir	Impersonal verb	il faut	qu'il faille	il fallut	il faudra		fallu *inv.*
(3 f) mouvoir	The **...ou...** of the stem becomes **...eu...** when stressed. **Promouvoir** is used chiefly in the *inf.,* *p.p.* (**promu,** *p.p.* **e**) and compound tenses; **émouvoir** has *p.p.* **ému, e**	meus meus meut mouvons mouvez meuvent	meuve meuves meuve mouvions mouviez meuvent	mus mus mut mûmes mûtes murent	mouvrai mouvras mouvra mouvrons mouvrez mouvront	meus mouvons mouvez	mû, mue

	Infinitif	Remarks	Présent de l'indicatif	Présent du subjonctif	Passé simple	Futur simple	Impératif	Participe passé
(3g)	pleuvoir	Impersonal verb	il pleut	qu'il pleuve	il plut	il pleuvra		plu *inv.*
(3h)	pouvoir	In the *pres. ind.* the 1st person can also be **je puis** and the interrogative is **puis-je** not **peux-je**. No *imper.* In the sg. and 3rd person pl. the **...ou...** of the stem becomes **...eu...** when stressed	peux peux peut pouvons pouvez peuvent	puisse puisses puisse puissions puissiez puissent	pus pus put pûmes pûtes purent	pourrai pourras pourra pourrons pourrez pourront		pu *inv.*
(3i)	savoir	*P.pr.* **sachant**	sais sais sait savons savez savent	sache saches sache sachions sachiez sachent	sus sus sut sûmes sûtes surent	saurai sauras saura saurons saurez sauront	sache sachons sachez	su, e
(3k)	seoir	Defective verb. *P.pr.* **seyant** or **séant.** *Impf. ind.* is **il seyait, ils seyaient**	il sied ils siéent	il siée ils siéent		il siéra ils siéront		sis, e

589

Infinitif	Remarks	Présent de l'indicatif	Présent du subjonctif	Passé simple	Futur simple	Impératif	Participe passé
(31) valoir	**Prévaloir** forms its pres. sbj. regularly: **que je prévale**, etc. Note the fut. and cond. with **...d...**	vaux vaux vaut valons valez valent	vaille vailles vaille valions valiez vaillent	valus valus valut valûmes valûtes valurent	vaudrai vaudras vaudra vaudrons vaudrez vaudront		valu, e
(3m) voir	Alternation between **i** and **y** as in (2d). **Pourvoir** and **prévoir** have fut. and cond. in **...oir...**; **pourvoir** has p.s. **pourvus**	vois vois voit voyons voyez voient	voie voies voie voyions voyiez voient	vis vis vit vîmes vîtes virent	verrai verras verra verrons verrez verront	vois voyons voyez	vu, e
(3n) vouloir	The **...ou...** of the stem becomes **...eu...** when stressed. Note the fut. and cond. with **...d...**	veux veux veut voulons voulez veulent	veuille veuilles veuille voulions vouliez veuillent	voulus voulus voulut voulûmes voulûtes voulurent	voudrai voudras voudra voudrons voudrez voudront	veuille veuillons veuillez	voulu, e

Fourth Conjugation

In the regular 4th Conjugation verbs, the stem does not change

(4a) vendre

I. Simple Tenses

Présent[1]

sg. je vends
tu vends
il vend[2]

pl. nous vendons
vous vendez
ils vendent

Passé simple

sg. je vendis
tu vendis
il vendit

pl. nous vendîmes
vous vendîtes
ils vendirent

Participe passé

vendu, e

Infinitif présent

vendre

Impératif

vends
vendons
vendez

Imparfait

sg. je vendais
tu vendais
il vendait

pl. nous vendions
vous vendiez
ils vendaient

Participe présent

vendent

Futur simple

sg. je vendrai
tu vendras
il vendra

pl. nous vendrons
vous vendrez
ils vendront

Conditionnel présent

sg. je vendrais
tu vendrais
il vendrait

pl. nous vendrions
vous vendriez
ils vendraient

Subjonctif présent

sg. que je vende
que tu vendes
qu'il vende

pl. que nous vendions
que vous vendiez
qu'ils vendent

Subjonctif imparfait

sg. que je vendisse
que tu vendisses
qu'il vendît

pl. que nous vendissions
que vous vendissiez
qu'ils vendissent

II. Compound Tenses

Participe passé with the help of **avoir** and **être;** *see* (1 a)

---

[1] **battre** and its derivatives have **bats, bats, bat** in the sg.; the pl. is regular: **battons,** etc.
[2] **rompre** and its derivatives have **il rompt.**

	Infinitif	Remarks	Présent de l'indicatif	Présent du subjonctif	Passé simple	Futur simple	Impératif	Participe passé
(4b)	boire	Note the ...v... in some forms and the ...u...u... [y] which appears instead of ...oi... The *p.s.* endings are as in (3a). *P.pr.* **buvant**	bois bois boit buvons buvez boivent	boive boives boive buvions buviez boivent	bus bus but bûmes bûtes burent	boirai boiras boira boirons boirez boiront	bois buvons buvez	bu, *e*
(4c)	braire	Defective verb. *Impf. ind.* is **il brayait**	il brait ils braient			il braira ils brairont		brait
(4d)	bruire	Defective verb. *Impf. ind.* is **bruissait** or **bruyait**	il bruit ils bruissent			il bruira		
(4e)	circoncire	Goes like (4i) except for *p.p.* **circoncis, e**	circoncis circoncis circoncit circoncisons circoncisez circoncisent	circoncise circoncises circoncise circoncisions circoncisiez circoncisent	circoncis circoncis circoncit circoncîmes circoncîtes circoncirent	circoncirai circonciras circoncira circoncirons circoncirez circonciront	circoncis circoncisons circoncisez	circoncis, *e*
(4f)	clore	Defective verb. Note the circumflex in the 3rd person sg. *pres. ind.* **clôt. Enclore** is conjugated like **clore,** but has all forms of the *pres. ind.*	je clos tu clos il clôt	close closes close closions closiez closent		clorai cloras clora clorons clorez cloront	clos	clos, *e*

Infinitif	Remarks	Présent de l'indicatif	Présent du subjonctif	Passé simple	Futur simple	Impératif	Participe passé
(4 g) éclore	Defective verb	il éclôt ils éclosent	qu'il éclose qu'ils éclosent		il éclora ils écloront		éclos, e
conclure	P.s. as in (3a). **Reclure** is used only in the *inf.*; the p.p. (**reclus, e**) and the *compound tenses*	conclus conclus conclut concluons concluez concluent	conclue conclues conclue concluions concluiez concluent	conclus conclus conclut conclûmes conclûtes conclurent	conclurai concluras conclura conclurons conclurez concluront	conclus concluons concluez	conclu, e
(4h) conduire	**Luire, reluire, nuire** have not **t** in the *p.p.*	conduis conduis conduit conduisons conduisez conduisent	conduise conduises conduise conduisions conduisiez conduisent	conduisis conduisis conduisit conduisîmes conduisîtes conduisirent	conduirai conduiras conduira conduirons conduirez conduiront	conduis conduisons conduisez	conduit, e
(4i) suffire	**Confire** has p.p. **confit, e**	suffis suffis suffit suffisons suffisez suffisent	suffise suffises suffise suffisions suffisiez suffisent	suffis suffis suffit suffîmes suffîtes suffirent	suffirai suffiras suffira suffirons suffirez suffiront	suffis suffisons suffisez	suffi *inv.*

Infinitif	Remarks	Présent de l'indicatif	Présent du subjonctif	Passé simple	Futur simple	Impératif	Participe passé
(4k) connaître	The î keeps its circumflex only in the 3rd person sg. pres. ind. and in the fut. and cond.; p.s. ends as in (3a). **Repaître** goes like **connaître, paître** has no p.s. and no p.p.	connais connais connaît connaissons connaissez connaissent	connaisse connaisses connaisse connaissions connaissiez connaissent	connus connus connut connûmes connûtes connurent	connaîtrai connaîtras connaîtra connaîtrons connaîtrez connaîtront	connais connaissons connaissez	connu, e
(4l) coudre	Note that ...s... replaces ...d... before a vowel	couds couds coud cousons cousez cousent	couse couses couse cousions cousiez cousent	cousis cousis cousit cousîmes cousîtes cousirent	coudrai coudras coudra coudrons coudrez coudront	couds cousons cousez	cousu, e
(4m) craindre	Note alternation of nasal **n** and **n mouillé** (gn); also ...d... before the ...r... only in the inf., fut. and cond. **Oindre** has only inf. fut. and cond.; **poindre** has 3rd person sg. pres. ind., fut. and cond., and the compound tenses	crains crains craint craignons craignez craignent	craigne craignes craigne craignions craigniez craignent	craignis craignis craignit craignîmes craignîtes craignirent	craindrai craindras craindra craindrons craindrez craindront	crains craignons craignez	craint, e

	Infinitif	Remarks	Présent de l'indicatif	Présent du subjonctif	Passé simple	Futur simple	Impératif	Participe passé
(4n)	croire	P.s. ends as in (3a). Accroire occurs only in the inf.	crois crois croit croyons croyez croient	croie croies croie croyions croyiez croient	crus crus crut crûmes crûtes crurent	croirai croiras croira croirons croirez croiront	crois croyons croyez	cru, e
(4o)	croître	The î keeps its circumflex only in the pres. ind. sg., imper. sg., and the fut. and cond. Décroître and accroître have no circumflex in p.s. or p.p.	croîs croîs croît croissons croissez croissent	croisse croisses croisse croissions croissiez croissent	crûs crûs crût crûmes crûtes crûrent	croîtrai croîtras croîtra croîtrons croîtrez croîtront	croîs croissons croissez	crû, crue m/pl. crus
(4p)	dire	Redire is conjugated like dire. The other derivatives of dire have ...disez in the 2nd person pl. pres. ind. and imper., except maudire which is conjugated like (2a) but has p.p. maudit, e	dis dis dit disons dites disent	dise dises dise disions disiez disent	dis dis dit dîmes dîtes dirent	dirai diras dire dirons direz diront	dis disons dites	dit, e

	Infinitif	Remarks	Présent de l'indicatif	Présent du subjonctif	Passé simple	Futur simple	Impératif	Participe passé
(4q)	écrire	Note the ...v... which appears when the verb-ending begins with a vowel	écris écris écrit écrivons écrivez écrivent	écrive écrives écrive écrivions écriviez écrivent	écrivis écrivis écrivit écrivîmes écrivîtes écrivirent	écrirai écriras écrira écrirons écrirez écriront	écris écrivons écrivez	écrit, e
(4r)	faire	Malfaire is used only in the inf. and forfaire and parfaire only in the inf., p.p. and compound tenses	fais fais fait faisons faites font	fasse fasses fasse fassions fassiez fassent	fis fis fit fîmes fîtes firent	ferai feras fera ferons ferez feront	fais faisons faites	fait, e
(4s)	frire	Defective verb	fris fris frit			frirai friras frira frirons frirez friront	fris	frit, e
(4t)	lire	P.s. ends as in (3a)	lis lis lit lisons lisez lisent	lise lises lise lisions lisiez lisent	lus lus lut lûmes lûtes lurent	lirai liras lira lirons lirez liront	lis lisons lisez	lu, e

	Infinitif	Remarks	Présent de l'indicatif	Présent du subjonctif	Passé simple	Futur simple	Impératif	Participe passé
(4u)	luire	See (4h). *P.s.* and *impf. sbj.* are rarely used						*mis, e*
(4v)	mettre	Note that one **t** drops in the *pres. ind.* sg. and *imper.* sg.	mets mets met mettons mettez mettent	mette mettes mette mettions mettiez mettent	mis mis mit mîmes mîtes mirent	mettrai mettras mettra mettrons mettrez mettront	mets mettons mettez	
(4w)	moudre	Note that ...**l**... replaces ...**d**... before a vowel	mouds mouds moud moulons moulez moulent	moule moules moule moulions mouliez moulent	moulus moulus moulut moulûmes moulûtes moulurent	moudrai moudras moudra moudrons moudrez moudront	mouds moulons moulez	*moulu, e*
(4x)	naître	Note that ...**ss**... replaces ...**t**... in the *pres. ind.* pl. and its derivatives; note the circumflex in **il naît** and in the *fut.* and *cond.*, and the *p.p.* **né.** In **renaître** the *p.p.* and the compound tenses are not used	nais nais naît naissons naissez naissent	naisse naisses naisse naissions naissiez naissent	naquis naquis naquit naquîmes naquîtes naquirent	naîtrai naîtras naîtra naîtrons naîtrez naîtront	nais naissons naissez	*né, e*

Infinitif	Remarks	Présent de l'indicatif	Présent du subjonctif	Passé simple	Futur simple	Impératif	Participe passé
(4y) occire	Defective verb						occis, e
(4z) plaire	P.s. ends as in (3a). **Taire** has no circumflex **il tait**; *p.p.* **tu, e**	plais plais plait plaisons plaisez plaisent	plaise plaises plaise plaisions plaisiez plaisent	plus plus plut plûmes plûtes plurent	plairai plairas plaira plairons plairez plairont	plais plaisons plaisez	plu *inv.*
(4aa) prendre		prends prends prend prenons prenez prennent	prenne prennes prenne prenions preniez prennent	pris pris prit prîmes prîtes prirent	prendrai prendras prendra prendrons prendrez prendront	prends prenons prenez	pris, e
(4bb) résoudre	**Absoudre** has *p.p.* **absous, absoute,** but no *p.s.* or *impf. sbj.* **Dissoudre** goes like **absoudre**	résous résous résout résolvons résolvez résolvent	résolve résolves résolve résolvions résolviez résolvent	résolus résolus résolut résolûmes résolûtes résolurent	résoudrai résoudras résoudra résoudrons résoudrez résoudront	résous résolvons résolvez	résolu, *e* In ⚡ résous
(4cc) rire	*P.p.* as in (2a)	ris ris rit rions riez rient	rie ries rie riions riiez rient	ris ris rit rîmes rîtes rirent	rirai riras rira rirons rirez riront	ris rions riez	ri *inv.*

	Infinitif	Remarks	Présent de l'indicatif	Présent du subjonctif	Passé simple	Futur simple	Impératif	Participe passé
(4dd)	sourdre	Defective verb. The past tenses are rare.	il sourd ils sourdent	qu'il sourde qu'ils sourdent	il sourdit ils sourdirent	il sourdra ils sourdront		
(4ee)	suivre	Note the p.p. **suivi, e.** *S'ensuivre* occurs only in the 3rd person of each tense.	suis suis suit suivons suivez suivent	suive suives suive suivions suiviez suivent	suivis suivis suivit suivîmes suivîtes suivirent	suivrai suivras suivra suivrons suivrez suivront	suis suivons suivez	suivi, *e*
(4ff)	traire	Defective verb. No *impf. sbj.*; **raire** goes like **traire**; *p.p.* **rait** is *inv.*	trais trais trait trayons trayez traient	traie traies traie trayions trayiez traient		trairai trairas traira trairons trairez trairont	trais trayons trayez	trait, *e*
(4gg)	vaincre	No **t** in the 3rd person sg. *pres. ind.* Note **c** is replaced by **qu** before a vowel except in the *p.p.* **vaincu, e**	vaincs vaincs vainc vainquons vainquez vainquent	vainque vainques vainque vainquions vainquiez vainquent	vainquis vainquis vainquit vainquîmes vainquîtes vainquirent	vaincrai vaincras vaincra vaincrons vaincrez vaincront	vaincs vainquons vainquez	vaincu, *e*
(4hh)	vivre	Note omission of the final **v** of the stem in the *pres. ind. sg,* the *p.s.* and the *p.p.*	vis vis vit vivons vivez vivent	vive vives vive vivions viviez vivent	vécus vécus vécut vécûmes vécûtes vécurent	vivrai vivras vivra vivrons vivrez vivront	vis vivons vivez	vécu, *e*

Second Part

English-French

Contents

Table des matières

Preface

Language has two faces: one looking back, one looking forward. This revised edition of the "Standard French Dictionary" has tried to take both of these aspects into account: In retaining some of yesterday's speech, it will help the user to grapple with the great 19th century authors, whether for school or for pleasure. At the same time, he will find language's path into the future staked out by such words as: *acceleration lane, acid rain, antipollution device, cassette recorder, chat show, deejay, ecocide, typing pool, etc., etc.*

Needless to say, a great deal of the material old and new is made up of phrases and phraselike expressions covering all registers of speech from everyday language down to slang. Irregular forms of verbs and nouns have been put in their proper alphabetic position to help the beginner.

After each entry word the phonetic transcription has been given, using the system of the International Phonetic Association. For English entry words syllabification has been indicated by centred dots. American English, both spelling and usage, has been the object of particular attention.

We recommend the user to read carefully pages 603–604 – instructions on how to use the dictionary, which should increase its practical value. On page 605 ff. there is the explanation of the devices used to save space without sacrificing clarity.

A series of appendices to the dictionary proper gives lists – of proper names, of common abbreviations, of numerals, weights and measures – as well as a list of irregular verbs and an introduction to the conjugations of English verbs.

LANGENSCHEIDT

Préface

La langue a deux visages: l'un est tourné vers le passé, l'autre vers le futur. Cette nouvelle édition du «Standard French Dictionary» s'efforce de tenir compte de ces deux aspects: En gardant une certaine partie du vocabulaire d'hier, il aidera l'utilisateur dans la lecture des auteurs classiques, que ce soit à l'école ou pour son plaisir personnel; mais d'autre part, pour rendre son dû à l'aspect «futuriste» de la langue, de nombreux «mots nouveaux» ont été introduits, comme par ex.: *acceleration lane, acid rain, antipollution device, cassette recorder, chat show, deejay, ecocide, typing pool*, etc., etc.

Il va sans dire qu'une bonne partie de ce dictionnaire consiste en phrases et expressions idiomatiques appartenant à tous les niveaux de langue. Les formes irrégulières des verbes et des substantifs sont mises à leur place alphabétique pour aider les débutants.

À la suite de chaque mot-souche la prononciation est indiquée entre crochets selon le système de l'Association Phonétique Internationale. En outre, pour les mots-souches anglais la division en syllabes est marquée par des points à l'intérieur des mots. L'américain, tant dans son orthographe que dans ses idiotismes, a été l'objet d'une attention spéciale et détaillée.

Nous recommandons la lecture attentive des pages 603/604 – indications pour l'emploi du dictionnaire qui en releveront la valeur pratique. A la page 605 ss. on trouvera l'explication des expédients auxquels on a eu recours pour gagner de la place sans nuire à la clarté.

En complément du dictionnaire proprement dit on trouvera des listes – de noms propres, d'abréviations usuelles, de nombres, de poids, de mesures, – ainsi qu'une liste des verbes irréguliers et une introduction aux conjugaisons des verbes anglais.

LANGENSCHEIDT

Directions for the use of this dictionary
Indications pour l'emploi de ce dictionnaire

1. **Arrangement.** The alphabetic order of the entry words has been observed throughout. Hence you will find, in their proper alphabetic order:

a) the irregular forms of verbs, nouns, comparatives and superlatives;

b) the various forms of the pronouns;

c) compounds.

2. **Homonyms** of different etymologies have been subdivided by exponents;

e.g. *March*[1] mars ...
march[2] marche ...
march[3] marche ...

3. **Vocabulary.** Some of the numerous nouns ending in *...er*, *...ing*, *...ism*, *...ist* or *...ness* and adjectives formed with *in...* or *un...* have not been listed in this dictionary. In order to find out their meanings, look up the radical.

4. **Differences in meaning.** The different senses of English words have been distinguished by:

a) explanatory additions given in italics after a translation;

e.g. **a·bate** ...(ra)baisser (*le prix*); ... tomber (*vent*); ...
an·cient 2. the ~s *pl.* les anciens *m/pl.* (*grecs et romains*);

b) symbols and abbreviations before the particular meaning (see list on pages 605–607). If, however, the symbol or abbreviation applies to all translations alike, it is placed

---

1. **Classement.** L'ordre alphabétique des mots-souches a été rigoureusement observé. Ainsi on trouvera dans leur ordre alphabétique:

a) les formes irrégulières des verbes, des noms, des comparatifs et des superlatifs;

b) les formes diverses des pronoms;

c) les mots composés.

2. Les **homonymes** d'étymologie différente font l'objet d'articles différents distingués par un chiffre placé en haut derrière le mot en question;

p.ex. *March*[1] mars ...
march[2] marche ...
march[3] marche ...

3. **Vocabulaire.** De nombreux noms à terminaison en *...er*, *...ing*, *...ism*, *...ist* ou *...ness*, ainsi que beaucoup d'adjectifs formés à l'aide des préfixes *in...* ou *un...* n'ont pas été inclus dans ce dictionnaire. Pour trouver leurs sens il faut chercher les radicaux appropriés.

4. **Distinction de sens.** Les différents sens des mots anglais se reconnaissent grâce à:

a) des additions explicatives, en italique, placées à la suite des versions proposées;

p.ex. **a·bate** ...(ra)baisser (*le prix*); ... tomber (*vent*); ...
an·cient 2. the ~s *pl.* les anciens *m/pl.* (*grecs et romains*);

b) des symboles ou des définitions en abrégé qui les précèdent (voir liste pages 605–607). Si, cependant, les symboles ou abréviations se rapportent à l'ensemble des tra-

between the entry word and its phonetic transcription.

A semicolon separates a given meaning from another one which is essentially different.

5. **Letters in brackets** within an entry word indicate that in most cases in British English the word is spelt with the letter bracketed, in American English without.

6. The **indication of the parts of speech** has been omitted when it is obvious.

7. **Syllabification** has been indicated by centred dots in all entry words of more than one syllable. If, however, a syllabification dot coincides with a stress mark the former is left out.

8. In order to save space we have omitted:

a) *to* before English infinitives;

b) the phonetic transcriptions of compounds whose component parts are separate entry words with transcriptions;

c) the phonetic transcriptions of entry words having one of the endings listed on page 611. In this case the entry word itself takes the stress mark.

9. **Preterite and past participle** of irregular verbs have been given as separate entries. [*irr.*] given after the infinitive of each irregular verb refers to the list of the strong and irregular weak verbs at the end of this volume (pages 1257–1260). Irregular forms of compound verbs, however, have not been listed; instead, their infinitive has been supplemented by [*irr.*] and the respective radical in round brackets;

e.g. **un·der·stand** [*irr.* (*stand*)].

ductions, ils sont intercalés entre le mot-souche et la transcription phonétique.

Le point-virgule sépare une acception d'une autre essentiellement différente.

5. Les **lettres entre parenthèses** dans les mots-souches indiquent que dans la plupart des cas en anglais britannique le mot s'écrit avec cette lettre, pendant qu'en anglais américain sans cette lettre.

6. L'**indication des différentes fonctions des mots** est omise lorsqu'elle est évidente.

7. Les **points de séparation de syllabes** à l'intérieur des mots-souches de plus d'une syllabe indiquent après quelles syllabes le mot peut se diviser. Si, cependant, le point de séparation coïncide avec l'apostrophe d'accentuation, on laisse de côté le point.

8. Afin de gagner de la place, nous avons omis:

a) *to* devant les infinitifs anglais;

b) la transcription phonétique de mots composés dont les parties composantes sont données en tant que mots-souches individuels avec leurs transcriptions;

c) les transcriptions phonétiques de mots-souches possédant l'une des terminaisons mentionnées page 611. L'apostrophe d'accentuation de ces mots se trouve à l'intérieur même du mot-souche.

9. Le **prétérite et le participe passé** des verbes irréguliers se trouvent dans le vocabulaire sous forme de mots-souches individuels. [*irr.*] après l'infinitif de chaque verbe irrégulier renvoie à la liste des verbes forts et des verbes faibles irréguliers à la fin de ce dictionnaire (pages 1257–1260). Les formes irrégulières des verbes composés sont supprimées; au lieu de quoi leurs infinitifs sont supplementés par [*irr.*] et leurs radicaux;

p.ex. **un·der·stand** [*irr.* (*stand*)].

Key to the symbols and abbreviations
Explication des symboles et des abréviations

1. Symbols

The tilde (~, ~) serves as a mark of repetition. To save space, compound entry words are often given with a tilde replacing one part.

The tilde in bold type (~) replaces the entry word at the beginning of the entry;

e.g. **day** ...; '**~·book** = daybook.

The simple tilde (~) replaces:

a) the entry word immediately preceding (which itself may contain a tilde in bold type);

    e.g. **half** ...; ~ *a crown* = half a crown;
    day ...; '**~·light** ...; *~-saving time* = daylight-saving time;

b) within the phonetic transcription, the whole of the pronunciation of the preceding entry word, or of some part of it which remains unchanged;

    e.g. **bill**¹ [bil] ...; **bill**² [~] ...; **pil·lar** ['pilə] ...; **pil·lared** ['~ləd] = ['piləd].

The tilde with a circle (2, 2).

When the first letter changes from small to capital or vice-versa, the usual tilde is replaced by a tilde with circle (2, 2);

e.g. **grand** ...; 2 *Duchess* = Grand Duchess; **can·dle** ...; '2·**mas** = Candlemas.

□ after an adjective indicates that the adjective takes the regular adverbial form;

e.g. **bit·ter** □ = bitterly;
    a·ble □ = ably;
    hap·py □ = happily.

1. Symboles

Le tilde (~, ~) est le signe de la répétition. Afin de gagner de la place, souvent le mot-souche ou un de ses éléments a été remplacé par le tilde.

Le tilde en caractère gras (~) remplace le mot-souche qui se trouve au début de l'article;

p.ex. **day** ...; '**~·book** = daybook.

Le tilde simple (~) remplace:

a) le mot-souche qui précède (qui d'ailleurs peut également être formé à l'aide du tilde en caractère gras);

    p.ex. **half** ...; ~ *a crown* = half a crown;
    day ...; '**~·light** ...; *~-saving time* = daylight-saving time;

b) dans la transcription phonétique, la prononciation entière ou la partie qui demeure inchangée;

    p.ex. **bill**¹ [bil] ...; **bill**² [~] ...; **pil·lar** ['pilə] ...; **pil·lared** ['~ləd] = ['piləd].

Le tilde avec cercle (2, 2).

Quand la première lettre se transforme de minuscule en majuscule ou vice versa, le tilde normal est remplacé par le tilde avec cercle (2, 2);

p.ex. **grand** ...; 2 *Duchess* = Grand Duchess; **can·dle** ...; '2·**mas** = Candlemas.

□ placé après un adjectif signifie qu'à partir de lui un adverbe régulier peut se former;

p.ex. **bit·ter** □ = bitterly;
    a·ble □ = ably;
    hap·py □ = happily.

(∿*ally*) after an adjective indicates that an adverb is formed by affixing -ally to the entry word;

e.g. **ar·o·mat·ic** (∿*ally*) = aromatically.

When there is but one adverbial form for adjectives ending in both -*ic* and -*ical*, this is indicated in the following way:

his·tor·ic, his·tor·i·cal □,

i.e. historically is the adverb of both adjectives.

The other symbols used in this dictionary are:

F	*familier*, colloquial.	
V	*vulgaire*, vulgar.	
†	*vieilli*, obsolete.	
⚘	*botanique*, botany.	
⊕	*technologie*, technology; *mécanique*, mechanics.	
⚒	*mines*, mining.	
✕	*militaire*, military.	
⚓	*nautique*, nautical; *marine*, navy.	
✝	*commerce*, commercial; *finances*, finance.	

(∿*ally*) placé après un adjectif signifie qu'à partir de lui un adverbe peut se former en ajoutant -ally au mot-souche;

p.ex. **ar·o·mat·ic** (∿*ally*) = aromatically.

Quand il n'y a qu'un seul adverbe pour des adjectifs à terminaison en -*ic* et -*ical*, c'est indiqué de manière suivante:

his·tor·ic, his·tor·i·cal □,

c.-à-d. historically est l'adverbe des deux adjectifs.

Les autres symboles employés dans ce dictionnaire sont:

⚞	*chemin de fer*, railway, *Am.* railroad.	
✈	*aviation*, aviation.	
♪	*musique*, music.	
△	*architecture*, architecture.	
⚡	*électricité*, electricity.	
⚖	*droit*, law.	
A	*mathématique*, mathematics.	
✔	*agriculture*, agriculture.	
⚗	*chimie*, chemistry.	
✚	*médecine*, medicine.	
▨	*blason*, heraldry.	

2. Abbreviations – Abréviations

a.	*aussi*, also.	*co.*	*comique*, comical.
abr.,	*abréviation*, abbreviation.	*coll.*	*collectif*, collective.
abbr.		*comp.*	*comparatif*, comparative.
adj.	*adjectif*, adjective.	*cond.*	*conditionnel*, conditional.
admin.	*administration*, administration.	*cons.*	*consonne*, consonant.
		cost.	*costume*, costume.
adv.	*adverbe*, adverb.	*cuis.*	*cuisine*, culinary art.
alp.	*alpinisme*, mountaineering.	*cycl.*	*cyclisme*, cycling.
Am.	Americanism, *américanisme*.	*dém.*	*démonstratif*, demonstrative.
anat.	*anatomie*, anatomy.		
Angl.	*Angleterre*, England.	*dial.*	*dialectal*, dialectal.
approx.	*approximativement*, approximately.	*eccl.*	*ecclésiastique*, ecclesiastical.
		écoss.	*écossais*, Scottish.
art.	*article*, article.	*enf.*	*enfantin*, childish speech.
astr.	*astronomie*, astronomy.	*èquit.*	*èquitation*, horsemanship.
attr.	*attribut*, attributively.	*etc.*	*et cætera*, and so on.
bibl.	*biblique*, biblical.	*É.-U.*	*États-Unis*, U.S.A.
biol.	*biologie*, biology.	*f*	*féminin*, feminine.
box.	*boxe*, boxing.	*fig.*	figuratively, *sens figuré*.
Brit.	British, *britannique*.	*foot.*	*football*, football.
cin.	*cinéma*, cinema.	*Fr.*	French, *français*.
cj.	*conjonction*, conjunction.	*fut.*	*futur*, future.

géog.	*géographie,* geography.	*p.pr.*	*participe présent,* present participle.
géol.	*géologie,* geology.		
gér.	*gérondif,* gerund.	*préf.*	*préfixe,* prefix.
gramm.	*grammaire,* grammar.	*prét.*	*prétérit,* preterite.
gymn.	*gymnastique,* gymnastics.	*pron.*	*pronom,* pronoun.
hist.	*histoire,* history.	*prov.*	*provincialisme,* provincialism.
icht.	*ichtyologie,* ichthyology.		
impér.	*impératif,* imperative.	*prp.*	*préposition,* preposition.
impf.	*imparfait,* imperfect.	*p.s.*	*passé simple,* past tense.
ind.	*indicatif,* indicative.	*psych.*	*psychologie,* psychology.
indéf.	*indéfini,* indefinite.	*q., q.*	*quelqu'un,* someone.
inf.	*infinitif,* infinitive.	*qch.,*	*quelque chose,* something.
int.	*interjection,* interjection.	*qch.*	
interr.	*interrogatif,* interrogative.	*qqfois*	*quelquefois,* sometimes.
inv.	*invariable,* invariable.	*rel.*	*relatif,* relative.
Ir.	Irish, *irlandais.*	*sbj.*	*subjonctif,* subjunctive.
iro.	*ironiquement,* ironically.	*sc.*	scilicet, namely, *c'est-à-dire.*
irr.	*irrégulier,* irregular; *see page 604.*	*sg.*	*singulier,* singular.
		sl.	slang, *argot.*
journ.	*journalisme,* journalism.	*s.o.*	someone, *quelqu'un.*
ling.	*linguistique,* linguistics.	*souv.*	*souvent,* often.
m	*masculin,* masculine.	*sp.*	*sport,* sports.
mes.	*mesure,* measure.	*s.th.*	something, *quelque chose.*
métall.	*métallurgie,* metallurgy.	*str.*	strictly taken, *au sens étroit.*
météor.	*météorologie,* meteorology.		
min.	*minéralogie,* mineralogy.	*su.*	*substantif,* substantive; *nom,* noun.
mot.	motoring, *automobilisme.*		
myth.	*mythologie,* mythology.	*sup.*	*superlatif,* superlative.
n	*neutre,* neuter.	*surt.*	*surtout,* especially.
nég.	*négatif,* negative.	*surv.*	surveying, *arpentage.*
npr.	nom propre, proper name.	*tél.*	*télégraphie,* telegraphy.
opt.	*optique,* optics.	*téléph.*	*téléphonie,* telephony.
orn.	*ornithologie,* ornithology.	*télév.*	*télévision,* television.
o.s.	oneself, *soi-même.*	*tex.*	*industries textiles,* textiles.
parl.	*parlement,* parliament.	*théâ.*	*théâtre,* theatre.
peint.	*peinture,* painting.	*(TM)*	trademark, *marque déposée.*
péj.	*sens péjoratif,* pejoratively.	*typ.*	*typographie,* typography.
pers.	*personnel,* personal.	*univ.*	*université,* university.
p.ex.	*par exemple,* for example.	*usu.*	usually, *d'ordinaire.*
p.ext.	*par extension,* more widely taken.	*v/aux.*	*verbe auxiliaire,* auxiliary verb.
pharm.	*pharmacie,* pharmacy.	*vét.*	*vétérinaire,* veterinary.
phls.	*philosophie,* philosophy.	*v/i.*	*verbe intransitif,* intransitive verb.
phot.	*photographie,* photography.		
phys.	*physique,* physics.	*v/impers.*	*verbe impersonnel,* impersonal verb.
physiol.	*physiologie,* physiology.		
pl.	*pluriel,* plural.	*v/rfl.*	*verbe réfléchi,* reflexive verb.
poét.	*poétique,* poetic.	*v/t.*	*verbe transitif,* transitive verb.
pol.	*politique,* politics.		
poss.	*possessif,* possessive.	*vt/i.*	*verbe transitif et intransitif,* transitive and intransitive verb.
p.p.	*participe passé,* past participle.		
		zo.	*zoologie,* zoology.

The phonetic symbols
of the International Phonetic Association

Signes phonétiques
de l'Association Phonétique Internationale

A. Voyelles et Diphtongues

[ɑ:] a long, clair, postérieur, comme dans pâte, âme, pâle: *far* [fɑ:], *father* ['fɑ:ðə].

[ʌ] n'existe pas en français. A bref, obscur, sans que les lèvres ne s'arrondissent. Se forme à l'avant de la bouche, ouvertement: *butter* ['bʌtə], *come* [kʌm], *colour* ['kʌlə], *blood* [blʌd], *flourish* ['flʌriʃ], *twopence* ['tʌpəns].

[æ] clair, plutôt ouvert, pas trop bref. On relève la langue vers la partie antérieure du palais dur, en appliquant les lèvres contre les dents: *fat* [fæt], *man* [mæn].

[ɛə] e ouvert, semi-long, pas trop ouvert; ne se trouve en anglais que devant le r qui apparaît en tant que [ə] après l'e ouvert: *bare* [bɛə], *pair* [pɛə], *there* [ðɛə].

[ai] a clair entre le [ɑ:] et le [æ], et un i plus faible. La langue s'élève à demi comme pour prononcer l'i: *I* [ai], *lie* [lai], *dry* [drai].

[au] a clair entre le [ɑ:] et le [æ], et un [u] plus faible, ouvert: *house* [haus], *now* [nau].

[e] e court à demi ouvert, un peu moins pur que l'e dans paix: *bed* [bed], *less* [les].

[ei] e à demi ouvert, tendant à finir en i; la langue se soulève à demi comme pour prononcer l'i: *date* [deit], *play* [plei], *obey* [o'bei].

[ə] son glissant, semblable à l'e muet du français debout, mais plus rapide: *about* [ə'baut], *butter* ['bʌtə], *connect* [kə'nekt].

[i:] i long, comme dans vie, bible, mais un peu plus ouvert qu'en français; se prononce avec redoublement dans le sud de l'Angleterre, la langue se soulevant lentement pour prononcer l'i: *scene* [si:n], *sea* [si:], *feet* [fi:t], *ceiling* ['si:liŋ].

[i] i court, ouvert, qui n'existe pas en français; s'articule avec les lèvres lâches: *big* [big], *city* ['si-ti].

[iə] i à demi ouvert, semi-long, finissant en [ə]: *here* [hiə], *hear* [hiə], *inferior* [in'fiəriə].

[ɔ:] son ouvert, long, entre l'a et l'o: *fall* [fɔ:l], *nought* [nɔ:t], *or* [ɔ:], *before* [bi'fɔ:].

[ɔ] son ouvert, court, entre l'a et l'o, un peu comme [ɑ:] très bref, les muscles peu tendus: *god* [gɔd], *not* [nɔt], *wash* [wɔʃ], *hobby* ['hɔ-bi].

[ɔi] o ouvert et i ouvert plus faible. La langue se soulève à demi comme pour prononcer l'i: *voice* [vɔis], *boy* [bɔi], *annoy* [ə'nɔi].

[o] o fermé rapide: *obey* [o'bei], *molest* [mo'lest].

[ou] o long, à demi ouvert, finissant en [u] faible; lèvres non arrondies, langue non soulevée: *note*

[nout], *boat* [bout], *below* [bi'lou].

[ə:] n'existe pas en français; un peu comme l'[œ:] dans peur, mais les lèvres ne s'avancent ni s'arrondissent: *word* [wə:d], *girl* [gə:l], *learn* [lə:n], *murmur* ['mə:mə].

[u:] [u] long comme dans poule, mais sans que les lèvres s'arrondissent; se prononce souvent comme [u] long, à demi ouvert, se terminant en [u] fermé: *fool* [fu:l], *shoe* [ʃu:], *you*

[ju:], *rule* [ru:l], *canoe* [kə'nu:].

[u] [u] rapide: *put* [put], *look* [luk], *careful* ['kɛəful].

[uə] [u] à demi ouvert et à demi long, se terminant en [ə]: *poor* [puə], *sure* [ʃuə], *allure* [ə'ljuə].

Parfois on emploie les nasales françaises suivantes: [ã] comme dans *détente*, [ɔ̃] comme dans *bonbon*, et [ɛ̃] comme dans *vin*.

La longueur d'une voyelle se traduit par [:], p.ex. *ask* [ɑ:sk], *astir* [əs'tə:].

B. Consonnes

[r] ne se prononce que devant les voyelles. Tout à fait différent du r vélaire français. Le bout de la langue forme avec la partie antérieure du palais un passage étroit, par lequel le souffle, voisé, passe, sans pourtant que le son soit roulé. A la fin d'un mot, r ne se prononce qu'en liaison avec la voyelle initiale du mot suivant: *rose* [rouz], *pride* [praid], *there is* [ðɛər'iz].

[ʒ] ch sonore, comme g dans génie, j dans journal: *gentle* ['dʒentl], *jazz* [dʒæz], *large* [lɑ:dʒ], *azure* ['æʒə].

[ʃ] ch sourd, comme dans champ, cher: *shake* [ʃeik], *fetch* [fetʃ], *chivalrous* ['ʃivlrəs].

[θ] n'existe pas en français; résulte de l'application de la langue contre les incisives supérieures: *thin* [θin], *path* [pɑ:θ], *method* ['meθəd].

[ð] le même son sonorisé: *there* [ðɛə], *breathe* [bri:ð], *father* ['fɑ:ðə].

[s] sifflante sourde, comme dans sourd, sot: *see* [si:], *hats* [hæts], *decide* [di'said].

[z] sifflante sonore, comme dans chose, zèle: *zeal* [zi:l], *rise* [raiz], *horizon* [hə'raizn].

[ŋ] n'existe pas en français (sauf dans quelques mots empruntes à l'anglais comme *meeting*); se prononce comme pour une voyelle nasale mais en abaissant le voile du palais vers la fin, de sorte à produire une espèce de n guttural: *ring* [riŋ], *singer* ['siŋə], *finger* ['fiŋgə], *ink* [iŋk].

[w] [u] rapide, prononcé lèvre contre lèvre; se forme avec la bouche dans la même position que u elle allait prononcer [u:]: *will* [wil], *swear* [swɛə], *queen* [kwi:n].

[f] labiale sourde: *fat* [fæt], *tough* [tʌf], *effort* ['efət].

[v] labiale sonore: *vein* [vein], *velvet* ['velvit].

[j] son rapide comme l'i dans diable ou l'y dans yeux: *onion* ['ʌnjən], *yes* [jes], *filial* ['filjəl].

La prononciation des autres consonnes correspond à peu près à celle du français, mais en anglais les occlusives sont plus plosives.

C. Apostrophes d'accentuation

L'accentuation des mots anglais est indiquée par le signe ['] devant la syllabe à accentuer; p.ex. **on·ion** ['ʌnjən]. Si deux des syllabes d'un mot donné se trouvent pourvues d'une apostrophe d'accentuation, à faut les accentuer également tous les deux; p.ex. **up·stairs** ['ʌp'stɛəz], cependant, souvent on n'accentue que l'une des deux syllabes, selon la position du mot dans l'ensemble de la phrase, ou en langue emphatique; p.ex. *upstairs* dans *"the upstairs rooms"* [ði ˈʌpstɛəz ˈrumz] et *"on going upstairs"* [ɔn ˈgouiŋ ʌpˈstɛəz].

Dans les mots-souches composés, dont les éléments sont donnés dans le dictionnaire en tant que mots-souches indépendants avec leurs transcriptions phonétiques, et dans les mots-souches qui possèdent l'une des terminaisons mentionnées sous D, l'apostrophe d'accentuation est donnée dans le mot-souche lui-même. L'accentuation est indiquée également dans le mot-souche, si on ne donne qu'une partie de la transcription phonétique et que l'accent ne porte pas sur la première syllabe de la partie phonétique remplacée par un tilde; p.ex. ad′min·is·tra·tor [~tə]. Si, cependant, l'accent porte sur la première syllabe ou sur une partie phonétique transcrite, l'apostrophe d'accentuation n'est pas donnée dans le mot-souche, mais se trouve dans la partie entre crochets; p.ex. ac·cu·rate [ˈ~rit], ad·a·man·tine [~ˈmæntain].

D. Syllabes finales sans symboles phonétiques

Afin de gagner de la place, nous donnerons ici les terminaisons les plus fréquentes des mots-souches avec leur transcription phonétique; par conséquent, ils figurent, sauf exception, dans le dictionnaire sans transcription phonétique. Ces terminaisons ne se trouvent pas transcrites non plus, quand elles sont précédées d'une consonne qui n'a pas été donnée dans les symboles phonétiques du mot précédent, mais qui en français, comme en anglais, demande le même signe phonétique; p.ex. -tation, -ring.

-ability [-əbiliti]	-ent [-e(ə)nt]	-ize [-aiz]
-able [-əbl]	-er [-ə]	-izing [-aiziŋ]
-age [-idʒ]	-ery [-əri]	-less [-lis]
-al [-(ə)l]	-ess [-is]	-ly [-li]
-ally [-(ə)li]	-fication [-fikeiʃ(ə)n]	-ment(s) [-mənt(s)]
-an [-(ə)n]	-ial [-(ə)l]	-ness [-nis]
-ance [-(ə)ns]	-ible [-əbl]	-oid [-ɔid]
-ancy [-ənsi]	-ian [-(jə)n]	-oidic [-ɔidik]
-ant [-ənt]	-ic(s) [-ik(s)]	-or [-ə]
-ar [-ə]	-ical [-ik(ə)l]	-ous [-əs]
-ary [-(ə)ri]	-ily [-ili]	-ry [-ri]
-ation [-eiʃ(ə)n]	-iness [-inis]	-ship [-ʃip]
-cious [-ʃəs]	-ing [-iŋ]	-(s)sion [-ʃ(ə)n]
-cy [-si]	-ish [-iʃ]	-sive [-siv]
-dom [-dəm]	-ism [-iz(ə)m]	-ties [-tiz]
-ed [-d; -t; -id]★	-ist [-ist]	-tion [-ʃ(ə)n]
-edness [-dnis;	-istic [-istik]	-tious [-ʃəs]
-tnis; -idnis]	-ite [-ait]	-trous [-trəs]
-ee [-i:]	-ity [-iti]	-try [-tri]
-en [-n]	-ive [-iv]	-y [-i]
-ence [-(ə)ns]	-ization [-aizeiʃ(ə)n]	

Pour la prononciation de l'américain, voir à la page 613.

★ [-d] après voyelles et consonnes sonores; [-t] après consonnes sourdes; [-id] après d et t finals.

The spelling of American English

L'orthographe de l'américain

L'orthographe de l'anglais de l'Amérique (AA) se distingue de l'anglais britannique (AB) par les particularités suivantes:

1. L'**u** tombe dans la terminaison **-our**; p.ex. col*o*r, hum*o*r, hon*o*rable, fav*o*r.

2. **-er** au lieu de l'AB **-re** dans les syllabes finales; p.ex. cent*er*, fib*er*, theat*er*, mais pas dans massacre.

3. Le redoublement de la consonne finale **l** ne se produit que quand l'accent principal porte sur la syllabe finale; d'où p.ex. AA counci*l*or, jewe*l*ry, quarre*l*ed, trave*l*ed, woo*l*en au lieu de l'AB councillor, jewellery, quarrelled, travelled, woollen; d'autre part on trouve en AA enroll(s), fulfill(s), skillful, installment au lieu de l'AB enrol(s), fulfil(s), skilful, instalment.

4. En AA **s** au lieu du **c** en AB, surtout dans la syllabe finale **-ence**; p.ex. def*e*nse, off*e*nse, lic*e*nse, mais aussi en AA practice et practise en tant que verbe.

5. On simplifie et on abandonne couramment les terminaisons d'origine étrangère; p.ex. dialog(*ue*), prolog(*ue*), catalog(*ue*), program(*me*), envelop(*e*).

6. La simplification d'**ae** et d'**œ** ou **oe** en **e** est également courante; p.ex. an(*a*)emia, an(*a*)esthesia, man*e*uvers = AB manœuvers, subp(*o*)ena.

7. On préfère la terminaison **-ction** à **-xion**; p.ex. conne*ction*, infle*ction*.

8. On trouve fréquemment une simplification des consonnes; p.ex. wag*o*n, kidna*p*er, worshi*p*er, benefi*t*ed pour l'AB waggon, kidnapper, worshipper, benefitted.

9. L'AA préfère **o** à **ou**; p.ex. mo(*u*)ld, smo(*u*)lder, pl*o*w au lieu de l'AB plough.

10. L'**e** muet disparaît dans des mots comme abridg(*e*)ment, judg(*e*)ment, acknowledg(*e*)ment.

11. L'AA utilise le préfixe **in-** au lieu de **en-** plus souvent que l'AB; p.ex. *in*close, *in*case.

12. L'AA préfère l'orthographe suivante dans des cas particuliers: *check* = AB cheque, *hello* = AB hallo, *cozy* = AB cosy, *mustache* = AB moustache, *skeptic* = AB sceptic, *peddler* = AB pedlar, *gray* = AB grey, *tire* = AB tyre.

13. A côté de although, through, on trouve les formules familières *altho*, *thru*.

The pronunciation of American English
La prononciation de l'américain

L'anglais de l'Amérique (AA), en ce qui concerne l'intonation, le rythme et le son, se distingue de l'anglais britannique (AB) par les particularités suivantes:

1. **Intonation:** L'AA est plus monotone que l'AB.

2. **Rythme:** Des mots à une ou plusieurs syllabes après la syllabe principale accentuée [ˈ] ont en AA un accent secondaire très marqué [ˌ], que les mots en AB n'ont pas ou n'ont que dans une faible mesure; p.ex. dictionary [AA ˈdikʃəˌnɛri = AB ˈdikʃənri], secretary [AA ˈsekrəˌtɛri = AB ˈsekrətri]; en AA, les voyelles courtes accentuées s'allongent (*American drawl*); p.ex. food [AA fuːd = AB fud], capital [AA ˈkæːpətəl = AB ˈkæpitl]; en AA, la syllabe inaccentuée (après une syllabe accentuée) subit un affaiblissement qui adoucit p, t, k en b, d, g; p.ex. property [AA ˈprabərti = AB ˈprɔpəti], united [AA juˈnaidid = AB juːˈnaitid].

3. Une autre particularité courante dans la façon de parler américaine, par opposition à l'AB, c'est la **nasalisation** avant et après une consonne nasale [m, n, ŋ] (*nasal twang*), ainsi que la prononciation plus fermée de [e] et de [o] en tant que premier élément d'une diphtongue; p.ex. home [AA hoːm], take [AA teːk].

4. Le **r** écrit à la finale après une voyelle, ou entre une voyelle et une consonne, se prononce clairement (r rétrofléchi); p.ex. car [AA kɑːr = AB kɑː], care [AA kɛr = AB kɛə], border [AA ˈbɔːrdər = AB ˈbɔːdə].

5. L'**o** [AB ɔ] se prononce en AA un peu comme l'**a** voilé [AA ɑ]; p.ex. dollar [AA ˈdɑlər = AB ˈdɔlə], college [AA ˈkɑlidʒ = AB ˈkɔlidʒ], lot [AA lɑt = AB lɔt], problem [AA ˈprɑbləm = AB ˈprɔbləm]; dans de nombreux cas [ɑ] et [ɔ] peuvent exister simultanément.

6. L'**a** [AB ɑː] donne [æ] ou [æː] en AA dans des mots du genre pass [AA pæ(ː)s = AB pɑːs], answer [AA ˈæ(ː)nsər = AB ˈɑːnsə], dance [AA dæ(ː)ns = AB dɑːns], half [AA hæ(ː)f = AB hɑːf], laugh [AA læ(ː)f = AB lɑːf].

7. L'**u** [AB juː] après consonne dans les syllabes qui portent l'accent principal donne en AA [uː]; p.ex. Tuesday [AA ˈtuːzdi = AB ˈtjuːzdi], student [AA ˈstuːdənt = AB ˈstjuːdənt], mais pas dans music [AA, AB = ˈmjuːzik], fuel [AA, AB = ˈfjuːəl].

8. Le suffixe **-ile** (en AB de préférence [-ail]) s'abrège en AA très souvent en [-əl] ou [-il]; p.ex. futile [AA ˈfjuːtəl = AB ˈfjuːtail], textile [AA ˈtekstil = AB ˈtekstail]; quant à [-əl] ou [-il] il n'y a pas de prononciation obligatoire.

9. La terminaison **-ization** (AB le plus souvent [-aiˈzeiʃən]) se prononce en AA de préférence [-əˈzeiʃən]. Cette différence de sons correspond au rapport des prononciations AA (préférée) [ə] et AB (standard) [i]; p.ex. editor [AA ˈedətər = AB ˈeditə], basket [AA ˈbæ(ː)skət = AB ˈbɑːskit].

A

A, a [ei] A *m*, a *m*.

a *gramm.* [ei; ə] *article*: un(e *f*); *20 miles a day* 20 milles par jour; *2 shillings a pound* 2 shillings la livre.

A 1 ['ei'wʌn] F de première qualité.

a·back [ə'bæk] masqué (*voile*); F *taken ~* déconcerté, interdit, étonné.

ab·a·cus ['æbəkəs], *pl.* -ci ['~sai] boulier *m* compteur; △ abaque *m*.

a·baft ⚓ [ə'bɑːft] **1.** *adv.* sur l'arrière; **2.** *prp.* en arrière de.

a·ban·don [ə'bændən] abandonner (*a. sp.*), délaisser (*q.*), renoncer à (*un projet*); *~ o.s. to* se livrer à; **a'ban·doned** *adj.* dévergondé; abandonné; **a'ban·don·ment** abandon (-nement) *m*.

a·base [ə'beis] abaisser; F ravaler (*q.*); **a'base·ment** abaissement *m*; humilité *f*.

a·bash [ə'bæʃ] confondre, déconcerter, interdire; *~ed at* confus de; **a'bash·ment** confusion *f*, embarras *m*.

a·bate [ə'beit] *v/t.* diminuer; faire cesser (*la douleur*); (r)abattre (*l'orgueil*); (ra)baisser (*le prix*); ⚖ annuler; mettre fin à (*un abus*); *v/i.* diminuer, s'affaiblir, s'apaiser, se modérer; tomber (*vent*); baisser (*prix*); **a'bate·ment** diminution *f*, affaiblissement *m*; *prix, eaux*: baisse *f*; *tempête*: apaisement *m*.

ab·a(t)·tis ⚔ [ə'bætis] abattis *m*.

ab·at·toir ['æbətwɑː] abattoir *m*.

ab·ba·cy ['æbəsi] dignité *f* d'abbé; **'ab·bess** abbesse *f*; **ab·bey** ['æbi] abbaye *f*; **ab·bot** ['æbət] abbé *m*, supérieur *m*.

ab·bre·vi·ate [ə'briːvieit] abréger (*a.* Ⓐ); **ab·bre·vi'a·tion** abréviation *f*.

ABC ['ei'biː'siː] ABC *m*; ⛟ indicateur *m* alphabétique; abécédaire *m*; *~ warfare* guerre *f* atomique, bactériologique (*ou* microbienne) et chimique.

ab·di·cate ['æbdikeit] *v/t.* abdiquer (*le trône*); renoncer à (*un droit*); ré-

signer (*une fonction*); *v/i.* abdiquer; **ab·di'ca·tion** abdication *f*, démission *f*.

ab·do·men *anat.* ['æbdəmen; ⚕ æb'doumen] abdomen *m*; ventre *m*; **ab·dom·i·nal** [æb'dɔminl] abdominal (-aux *m/pl.*).

ab·duct [æb'dʌkt] enlever; **ab'duc·tion** enlèvement *m*; **ab'duc·tor** ravisseur *m*.

a·be·ce·dar·i·an [eibiːsiː'dɛəriən] **1.** abécédaire; ignorant; **2.** élève *mf* d'une classe élémentaire.

a·bed [ə'bed] au lit, couché.

ab·er·ra·tion [æbə'reiʃn] aberration *f*.

a·bet [ə'bet] encourager; prêter assistance à; (*usu. aid and ~*) être le complice de; **a'bet·ment** encouragement *m*; complicité *f* (dans, *in*); **a'bet·tor** complice *mf*; fauteur (-trice *f*) *m* (de, *in*).

a·bey·ance [ə'beiəns] suspension *f*; ⚖ *in ~* en suspens, pendant; vacant (*estate*).

ab·hor [əb'hɔː] abhorrer; **ab·hor·rence** [əb'hɔrns] horreur *f*, aversion *f* (pour, *of*); *hold in ~* avoir en horreur; **ab'hor·rent** □ répugnant (à, *to*); incompatible (avec, *to*); contraire (à, *to*).

a·bide [ə'baid] [*irr.*] *v/i.* demeurer; *~ by* rester fidèle à (*une promesse*), maintenir; *v/t.* attendre; *I cannot ~ him* je ne peux pas le sentir *ou* supporter; **a'bid·ing** □ permanent.

a·bil·i·ty [ə'biliti] capacité *f*; *to the best of one's ~* de son mieux; **a'bil·i·ties** *pl.* intelligence *f*; aptitude *f*.

ab·ject □ ['æbdʒekt] misérable; servile; **ab'jec·tion**, **ab'ject·ness** abjection *f*, misère *f*.

ab·jure [əb'dʒuə] abjurer; renoncer à.

a·blaze [ə'bleiz] en flammes; *a. fig.* enflammé (de, *with*).

a·ble □ ['eibl] capable; habile; compétent; ⚖ apte; *be ~ to* (*inf.*) être à même de (*inf.*); pouvoir (*inf.*); *~ to* *pay* en mesure de payer; **~-bod·ied** ['~'bɔdid] robuste; ✕ bon pour le service; ⚓ ~ *seaman* matelot *m* de deuxième classe.

ab·lu·tion [ə'blu:ʃn] ablution *f*.

ab·ne·gate ['æbnigeit] renoncer à; faire abnégation de (*droits etc.*); **ab·ne'ga·tion** renoncement *m*; désaveu *m*; (*a. self-~*) abnégation *f* de soi.

ab·nor·mal □ [æb'nɔːml] anormal (-aux *m/pl.*); **ab·nor'ma·li·ty** caractère *m* anormal; difformité *f*.

a·board ⚓ [ə'bɔːd] à bord (de); *Am.* 🚋, ✕, *bus, tram: all~!* en voiture!; ⚓ embarquez!

a·bode [ə'boud] **1.** *prét. et p.p. de abide;* **2.** demeure *f*; résidence *f*; séjour *m*.

a·bol·ish [ə'bɔliʃ] abolir, supprimer; **a'bol·ish·ment**, **ab·o·li·tion** [æbə'liʃn] abolissement *m*, suppression *f*; **ab·o'li·tion·ist** abolitionniste *mf*.

A-bomb ['eibɔm] *see atomic bomb.*

a·bom·i·na·ble □ [ə'bɔminəbl] abominable; **a·bom·i'na·tion** abomination *f*, horreur *f*.

ab·o·rig·i·nal [æbə'ridʒənl] □ aborigène, indigène, primitif (-ive *f*); **ab·o'rig·i·nes** [~ni:z] *pl.* aborigènes *m/pl.*

a·bort *biol.* [ə'bɔːt] avorter; ✕, *espace: ~ a mission* interrompre *ou* abandonner une mission; **a'bor·tion** avortement *m*; *fig.* œuvre *f* manquée; monstre *m*; *procure ~* faire avorter; **a'bor·tive** □ abortif (-ive *f*); avorté (*projet*); mort-né (*projet*).

a·bound [ə'baund] abonder (en *with, in*); foisonner (de *with, in*).

a·bout [ə'baut] **1.** *prp.* autour de; environ, presque; au sujet de; *~ the house* quelque part dans la maison; *~ the streets* dans les rues; *I had no money ~ me* je n'avais pas d'argent sur moi; *~ ten o'clock* vers 10 heures; *he is ~ my height* il a à peu près la même taille que moi; *talk ~ business* parler affaires; *what are you ~?* qu'est-ce que vous faites là?; *send s.o. ~ his business* envoyer promener q.; **2.** *adv.* tout autour; en tour; çà et là; de ci, de là; *be ~ to do* être sur le point de faire; *a long way ~* un long détour; *bring ~* accomplir; faire naître; *come ~* arriver; *right ~!* demi-tour!; *~ turn!* demitour à droite!

a·bove [ə'bʌv] **1.** *prp.* au-dessus de, par-dessus; au delà de; *fig.* supérieur à; *~ 300* plus de 300; *~ all (things)* surtout; *be ~ s.o.* le surpasser q. par (*l'intelligence etc.*); *fig. it is ~ me* cela me dépasse; **2.** *adv.* en haut; là-haut; au-dessus; *over and ~* en outre; **3.** *adj.* précédent; *the ~ points* ce qui a été mentionné plus haut, les remarques précédentes; **4.** *su.: the ~* le susdit; **a'bove-'board** loyal (-aux *m/pl.*), franc(he *f*); **a'bove-'ground** au-dessus de terre; vivant; **a'bove-'men·tioned** susmentionné, (cité) ci-dessus.

ab·ra·ca·dab·ra [æbrəkə'dæbrə] baragouin *m*.

ab·rade [ə'breid] user par le frottement; écorcher (*la peau*).

ab·ra·sion [ə'breiʒn] frottement *m*; attrition *f*; 🩹 écorchure *f*, excoriation *f*; *monnaies:* frai *m*; **ab'ra·sive** ⊕ abrasif *m*.

a·breast [ə'brest] de front; côte à côte; *~ of (ou with)* à la hauteur de; *keep ~ of* marcher de pair avec.

a·bridge [ə'bridʒ] abréger; *fig.* restreindre; **a'bridg(e)·ment** raccourcissement *m*; abrégé *m*, résumé *m*; restriction *f*.

a·broad [ə'brɔːd] à l'étranger, en voyage; sorti (*de la maison*); *there is a report ~* le bruit court que; *the thing has got ~* la nouvelle s'est répandue; *F he is all ~* il est tout désorienté.

ab·ro·gate ['æbrogeit] abroger; **ab·ro'ga·tion** abrogation *f*.

ab·rupt □ [ə'brʌpt] brusque, précipité; saccadé, abrupt (*style*); à pic (*montagne*); **ab'rupt·ness** brusquerie *f*; *chemin:* raideur *f*.

ab·scess ['æbsis] abcès *m*.

ab·scond [əb'skɔnd] s'évader (de, *from*), s'enfuir; se soustraire à la justice; *F* décamper, filer.

ab·sence ['æbsns] absence *f*, éloignement *m* (de, *from*); *~ of mind* distraction *f*; *leave of ~* permission *f*, congé *m*.

ab·sent 1. □ ['æbsnt] absent, manquant; *fig. = '~-'mind·ed* □ distrait; **2.** [æb'sent]: *~ o.s.* s'absenter (de, *from*); **ab·sen·tee** [æbsn'ti:] absent(e *f*) *m*; *~ ballot* vote *m* par correspondance; *~ voter* électeur (-trice *f*) *m* par correspondance; **ab'sen·tee·ism** absence *f* de l'ate-

lier; absentéisme *m*; F carottage *m*.
ab·sinth ['æbsinθ] absinthe *f*.
ab·so·lute □ ['æbsəluːt] absolu; autoritaire; ⚖ irrévocable; F achevé (*coquin etc.*); **'ab·so·lute·ness** caractère *m* absolu; **ab·so'lu·tion** absolution *f*; **'ab·so·lut·ism** *hist.* absolutisme *m*.
ab·solve [əb'zɔlv] absoudre (de, *from*), remettre (*un péché*); dispenser, affranchir (de, *from*).
ab·sorb [əb'sɔːb] absorber; amortir (*un choc*); résorber (*un excédent*); *fig.* engloutir; ~ed in absorbé dans; tout entier à; **ab'sorb·ent** absorbant (*a. su./m*).
ab·sorp·tion [əb'sɔːpʃn] absorption *f*; *choc*: amortissement *m*; *fig.* engloutissement *m*; *esprit*: absorbement *m*.
ab·stain [əb'stein] s'abstenir (de, *from*); ~ *from meat* faire maigre; *parl.* ~ (*from voting*) s'abstenir (de voter); **ab'stain·er** (*souv. total* ~) abstème *mf*.
ab·ste·mi·ous □ [əb'stiːmiəs] sobre, tempérant.
ab·sten·tion [æb'stenʃn] abstinence *f* (de, *from*); *parl.* abstention *f*.
ab·ster·gent [əb'stəːdʒnt] **1.** abstergent (*a. su./m*); **2.** ✚ détersif *m*.
ab·sti·nence ['æbstinəns] abstinence *f* (de, *from*); *total* ~ abstinence *f* complète; **'ab·sti·nent** □ abstinent, sobre.
ab·stract 1. ['æbstrækt] □ abstrait; F abstrus; **2.** [~] abstrait *m*; résumé *m*, abrégé *m*; *gramm.* ~ (*noun*) nom *m* abstrait; *in the* ~ du point de vue abstrait, en théorie; **3.** [æb'strækt] *v/t.* soustraire (à, *from*); détourner (*l'attention*); dérober (à, *from*); résumer (*un livre*); ⚗ extraire; **ab'stract·ed** □ *fig.* distrait, rêveur (-euse *f*); **ab'strac·tion** *papiers etc.*: soustraction *f*; vol *m*; *phls.* abstraction *f*; distraction *f* (*d'esprit*); ⚗ extraction *f*.
ab·struse □ [əb'struːs] *fig.* abstrus, obscur; caché; **ab'struse·ness** obscurité *f*, caractère *m* abstrus *etc.*
ab·surd □ [əb'səːd] absurde, déraisonnable; F idiot; **ab'surd·i·ty** absurdité *f*; absurde *m*.
a·bun·dance [ə'bʌndəns] abondance *f*, affluence *f*; épanchement *m* (*du cœur*); **a'bun·dant** □ abondant, copieux (-euse *f*); ~ *in* abondant

en; **a'bun·dant·ly** abondamment.
a·buse 1. [ə'bjuːs] abus *m*; insultes *f/pl.*; **2.** [~z] abuser de, mésuser de, faire abus de; maltraiter (*q.*); dénigrer (*q.*); injurier; **a'bu·sive** □ abusif (-ive *f*); injurieux (-euse *f*) (*propos*); *be* ~ dire des injures (à, *to*).
a·but [ə'bʌt] aboutir (à, *upon*), confiner (à, *upon*); △ s'appuyer (contre *on*, *against*); **a'but·ment** △ arc-boutant (*pl.* arcs-boutants) *m*; *pont*: butée *f*; *voûte*: pied-droit (*pl.* pieds-droits) *m*; **a'but·ter** propriétaire *m* limitrophe.
a·bysm [ə'bizm] *see abyss*; **a'bys·mal** □ insondable; **a·byss** [ə'bis] abîme *m*, gouffre *m*.
a·ca·cia ♀ [ə'keiʃə] acacia *m*.
ac·a·dem·ic, ac·a·dem·i·cal □ [ækə'demik(l)] académique; *academic freedom* liberté *f* de l'enseignement; *academic year* année *f* universitaire; **a·cad·e'mi·cian** [əkædə-'miʃn] académicien *m*; **ac·a'dem·ics** *pl.* discussion *f* abstraite.
a·cad·e·my [ə'kædəmi] académie *f*.
a·can·thus [ə'kænθəs] ♀ acanthe *f*; △ (feuille *f* d')acanthe *f*.
ac·cede [æk'siːd]: ~ *to* accueillir (*une demande*); entrer en possession de (*une charge*); monter sur (*le trône*).
ac·cel·er·ate [æk'seləreit] (s')accélérer; *v/t. fig.* activer; **ac·cel·er'a·tion** accélération *f*; *mot.* ~ *lane* rampe *f* d'accès; **ac'cel·er·a·tor** *mot.* accélérateur *m*.
ac·cent 1. ['æksnt] accent *m*; ♪ temps *m* fort; temps *m* marqué; ton *m*; voix *f*; **2.** [æk'sent] accentuer (*a. fig.*) appuyer sur, souligner.
ac·cen·tu·ate [æk'sentjueit] accentuer; faire ressortir; **ac·cen·tu'a·tion** accentuation *f*.
ac·cept [ək'sept] accepter; agréer (*des vœux*); (*ou* ~ *of*) ✝ accepter, prendre en recette; admettre; **ac·cept·a·ble** □ [ək'septəbl] acceptable, agréable (à, *to*); **ac'cept·a·ble·ness** acceptabilité *f*; **ac'cept·ance** acceptation *f*; accueil *m* favorable; réception *f*; ✝ *article*: réception *f*; *traite*: acceptation *f*; **ac·cep·ta·tion** [ækəsep'teiʃn] acception *f*, signification *f* (*d'un mot*); **ac'cept·ed** □ reconnu, admis; **ac'cept·er, ac'cept·or** acceptant(e *f*) *m*; ✝ tiré *m*; accepteur *m*.

access   618

ac·cess ['ækses] 1. accès *m* (*a.* 🖥, *a. ordinateur*), abord *m* (à, *to*); entrée *f*; *easy of* ~ abordable; ~ *to power* accession *f* au pouvoir; 2. *ordinateur*: accéder à; **ac'ces·sa·ry** complice *m*, fauteur *m* (de, *to*); *see accessory* 2; **ac·ces·si·bil·i·ty** [~i'biliti] accessibilité *f*; **ac'ces·si·ble** □ [~əbl] accessible (à, *to*); **ac'ces·sion** admission *f* (*d'air*); entrée *f* en fonctions; arrivée *f* (*à un âge*); accroissement *m*; ~ *to the throne* avènement *m* au trône. **ac·ces·so·ry** [æk'sesəri] 1. □ ~ accessoire, subsidiaire (à, *to*); 2. accessoire *m*; *accesories pl.* objets *m/pl.* de toilette; accessoires *m/pl.* (*a. théâ.*); *see accessary.*

ac·ci·dence *gramm.* ['æksidəns] morphologie *f*.

ac·ci·dent ['æksidənt] accident *m*; *terrain*: inégalité *f*; *machine*: avarie *f*; ~ *insurance* assurance *f* contre les accidents; *by* ~ accidentellement; par hasard; *be killed in an* ~ perdre la vie dans un accident; **ac·ci·den·tal** [æksi'dentl] 1. □ accidentel(le *f*), fortuit; accessoire; ♪ *death mort f* accidentelle; 2. accessoire *m*; ♪ signe *m* accidentel, accident *m*.

ac·claim [ə'kleim] acclamer.

ac·cla·ma·tion [æklə'meiʃn] acclamation *f*; *by* ~ par acclamation.

ac·cli·mate *surt. Am.* [ə'klaimit] *see acclimatize.*

ac·cli·ma·ti·za·tion [əklaimətai-'zeiʃn] acclimatation *f*; **ac'cli·ma·tize** acclimater; habituer.

ac·cliv·i·ty [ə'kliviti] montée *f*; côte *f*; rampe *f*; pente *f*.

ac·com·mo·date [ə'kɔmədeit] accommoder, conformer; adapter; arranger (*une querelle*); prêter (qch. à q., *s.o. with s.th.*); recevoir, loger; ~ *o.s. to* s'accommoder à; **ac'com·mo·dat·ing** □ complaisant; peu difficile (sur, *about*); **ac·com·mo·da·tion** adaptation *f*; arrangement *m*; *dispute*: ajustement *m*; compromis *m*; logement *m*; prêt *m* (*d'argent*); *Am.* ~*s pl.* hébergement *m*, hôtels *m/pl.*; ✝ ~ *bill* billet *m* de complaisance; *seating* ~ nombre *m* de places assises; *Am.* ~ *train* train *m* omnibus.

ac·com·pa·ni·ment [ə'kʌmpəni-mənt] accompagnement *m*; accessoires *m/pl.*; **ac'com·pa·nist** ♪ accompagnateur (-trice *f*) *m*; **ac'com·pa·ny** accompagner; accompanied with accompagné de, par.

ac·com·plice [ə'kɔmplis] complice *mf* (de, *in*), fauteur (-trice *f*) *m* (de, *in*).

ac·com·plish [ə'kɔmpliʃ] accomplir; venir à bout de; mener à bonne fin (*une tâche etc.*); réaliser (*un projet*); **ac'com·plished** achevé; doué; **ac'com·plish·ment** accomplissement *m*; réalisation *f*; *usu.* ~*s pl.* talents *m/pl.*, arts *m/pl.* d'agrément.

ac·cord [ə'kɔːd] 1. accord *m*, consentement *m*; ⚖ consentement *m* mutuel; *with one* ~ d'un commun accord; *of one's own* ~ de sa propre volonté; 2. *v/i.* concorder (avec, *with*); *v/t.* concéder; **ac'cord·ance** conformité *f*, accord *m*; *in* ~ *with* conformément à, suivant; **ac'cord·ant** □ (*with, to*) conforme (à), d'accord (avec); **ac'cord·ing**: ~ *to* selon, suivant, d'après; ~ *as* selon que; **ac'cord·ing·ly** en conséquence; donc.

ac·cor·di·on ♪ [ə'kɔːdjən] accordéon *m*.

ac·cost [ə'kɔst] aborder, accoster.

ac·cou·cheur [æku:'ʃɔː], **ac·cou·'cheuse** [~z] accoucheur (-euse *f*) *m*.

ac·count [ə'kaunt] 1. calcul *m*, compte *m*, note *f*; récit *m*, relation *f*; valeur *f*; *blocked* ~ compte *m* bloqué; *current* ~ compte *m* courant; ~ *agreed upon* compte *m* arrêté; *payment on* ~ acompte *m*, versement *m* à compte; *sale for the* ~ vente *f* à terme; *statement of* ~ relevé *m* de compte; *of no* ~ de peu d'importance; *on no* ~ dans aucun cas; *on his* ~ à cause de lui, pour lui; *on* ~ *of* à cause de; *sl. be no* ~ ne pas compter; *find one's* ~ *in* trouver son compte à; *have (ou hold) an* ~ *with* avoir un compte chez; *have a bank* ~ avoir un compte en banque; *lay one's* ~ *with* compter sur; *place to s.o.'s* ~ verser au compte de q.; *take into* ~, *take* ~ *of* tenir compte de; *leave out of* ~ négliger; *turn to* ~ tirer parti de; *keep* ~*s* tenir les livres; *call to* ~ demander compte (*à q. de qch.*); *give (ou render) an* ~ *of* rendre raison de; faire un rapport sur; expliquer (*qch.*); *F give a good* ~ *of o.s.* s'acquitter bien; *make (little)* ~ *of* faire (peu de) cas de; 2. *v/i.*

~ *for* expliquer (*qch.*); rendre raison de; justifier (de); *sp.* avoir à son actif; *v/t.* estimer, tenir pour; *be much* (*little*) ~ *ed of* être beaucoup (peu) estimé; **ac·count·a'bil·i·ty** responsabilité *f*; **ac'count·a·ble** □ responsable; redevable (de, *for*); **ac'count·ant** comptable *m*; *chartered* ~, *Am.* certified *public* ~ expert *m* comptable diplômé; **ac'count-book** livre *m* de comptes.

ac·cou·tred [ə'ku:təd] accoutré; équipé; **ac·cou·tre·ments** [ə'ku:təmənts] *pl.* équipement *m*.

ac·cred·it [ə'kredit] accréditer (*q.*, *qch.*), *a. un ambassadeur auprès d'un gouvernement*); ~ *s.th. to s.o.*, ~ *s.o. with s.th.* mettre qch. sur le compte de q.   [ment *m.*}

ac·cre·tion [æ'kri:ʃn] accroisse-}

ac·crue [ə'kru:] provenir, dériver (de, *from*); ✝ s'accumuler (*intérêts*).

ac·cu·mu·late [ə'kju:mjuleit] (s')accumuler; (s')amonceler; *v/t.* amasser (*de l'argent*); **ac·cu·mu·la·tion** accumulation *f*, amoncellement *m*; amas *m*; **ac·cu·mu·la·tive** □ [ə'kju:mjulətiv] qui s'accumule; **ac'cu·mu·la·tor** accumulateur (-trice *f*) *m*; *phys.* accumulateur *m*.

ac·cu·ra·cy ['ækjurəsi] exactitude *f*; fidélité *f*; **ac·cu·rate** □ ['~rit] exact, juste; fidèle.

ac·curs·ed [ə'kə:sid], **ac·curst** [ə'kə:st] *usu.* F *fig.* maudit; exécrable.

ac·cu·sa·tion [ækju:'zeiʃn] accusation *f*; ⚖ incrimination *f*; **ac·cu·sa·tive** *gramm.* [ə'kju:zətiv] (*a.* ~ *case*) accusatif *m*; **ac·cu·sa·to·ry** [ə'kju:zətəri] accusateur (-trice *f*); **ac·cuse** [ə'kju:z] accuser (q. de qch., *s.o. of s.th.*), ⚖ incriminer (*q.*) (auprès de *before, to*); *the* ~*d* le (la) prévenu(e *f*) *m*; **ac'cus·er** accusateur (-trice *f*) *m*.

ac·cus·tom [ə'kʌstəm] accoutumer (à, *to*); **ac'cus·tomed** habitué, accoutumé (à, *to*); *be* ~ *to do*(*ing*) *a.* avoir coutume *ou* avoir l'habitude de faire; *get ou become* ~ *to* (*doing*) *s.th.* s'habituer *ou* s'accoutumer à (faire) qch.

ace [eis] as *m* (*a. sl. fig.*, *usu. un aviateur*); *Am.* F ~ *in the hole fig.* encore une ressource; *within an* ~ *of* à deux doigts de.

a·cer·bi·ty [ə'sə:biti] aigreur *f*; *ton:* âpreté *f*.

ac·e·tate 🜍 ['æsiteit] acétate *m*; **a·cetic** [ə'si:tik] acétique; ~ *acid* acide *m* acétique; **a·cet·i·fy** [ə'setifai] (s')acétifier; **ac·e·tone** ['æsitoun] acétone *f*; **ac·e·tous** ['~təs] acéteux (-euse *f*); *fig.* aigre; **a·cet·y·lene** [ə'setili:n] acétylène *m*.

ache [eik] **1.** faire mal à; **2.** douleur *f*.

a·chieve [ə'tʃi:v] atteindre à, parvenir à; réaliser (*un but*); accomplir (*un exploit*); acquérir (*de l'estime*); **a'chieve·ment** accomplissement *m*; *projet:* exécution *f*; exploit *m*.

ach·ing ['eikiŋ] **1.** □ douloureux (-euse *f*); **2.** douleur *f*, mal *m*.

ach·ro·mat·ic [ækro'mætik] (~*ally*) achromatique.

ac·id ['æsid] **1.** aigre; ~ *rain* pluies *f/pl.* acides; **2.** acide *m* (*a.* = LSD); **'ac·id·head** *sl.* acidomane *mf*; **a·cid·i·fy** [ə'sidifai] (s')acidifier; **a'cid·i·ty** acidité *f*; *fig.* aigreur *f*; **ac·i·do·sis** [æsi'dousis] acidose *f*; **a·cid·u·late** [ə'sidjuleit] aciduler; ~*d drops* bonbons *m/pl.* acidulés *ou* anglais; **a·cid·u·lous** [ə'sidjuləs] acidulé.

ac·knowl·edge [ək'nɔlidʒ] reconnaître (pour, *as*); répondre à (*un salut*); accuser réception de (*une lettre*); s'avouer; **ac'knowl·edg(e)·ment** reconnaissance *f*; aveu *m*; ~*s pl.* remerciements *m/pl.*; *usu.* ✝ accusé *m* de réception; reçu *m*, quittance *f*.

ac·me ['ækmi] comble *m*; apogée *m*.

ac·ne ⚕ ['ækni] acné *f*.

a·cock [ə'kɔk] d'un air de défi.

ac·o·nite ⚘ [ə'kɔnait] aconit *m*.

a·corn ⚘ ['eikɔ:n] gland *m*.

a·cous·tic, **a·cous·ti·cal** [ə'ku:stik(l)] acoustique; sonore; **a'cous·tics** *usu. sg.* acoustique *f*.

ac·quaint [ə'kweint] informer; ~ *s.o. with s.th.* apprendre qch. à q.; *be* ~*ed with* connaître; *become* ~*ed with* faire *ou* lier connaissance avec; **ac'quaint·ance** connaissance *f*; ~ *with* connaissance de.

ac·qui·esce [ækwi'es] (*in*) acquiescer (à); accepter (*qch.*); **ac·qui·es·cence** (*in*) acquiescement *m* (à); assentiment *m* (à); soumission *f* (à); **ac·qui·es·cent** □ consentant; résigné.

ac·quire [ə'kwaiə] acquérir (*a. fig.*), ~*d taste* goût *m* acquis; **ac'quire·ment** acquisition *f* (de, *of*); talent *m*; *usu.* ~*s pl.* connaissances *f/pl.*

ac·qui·si·tion [ækwi'ziʃn] acquisition *f*; **ac·quis·i·tive** □ [æ'kwizitiv] apte *ou* âpre au gain.

ac·quit [ə'kwit] acquitter, absoudre (de, *of*); ~ *o.s. of* s'acquitter de; ~ *o.s. well* (*ill*) se bien (mal) acquitter; **ac'quit·tal** ⚖ décharge *f*; *devoir*: exécution *f*; **ac'quit·tance** †, ⚖ acquit *m*, acquittement *m*.

a·cre ['eikə] acre *f*; (*approx.*) arpent *m*; † champ *m*.

ac·rid □ ['ækrid] âcre; mordant (*style*).

ac·ri·mo·ni·ous □ [ækri'mounjəs] acrimonieux (-euse *f*), atrabilaire; **ac·ri·mo·ny** ['ækriməni] acrimonie *f*, aigreur *f*.

ac·ro·bat ['ækrobæt] acrobate *mf*; **ac·ro'bat·ic** (~*ally*) acrobatique; **ac·ro'bat·ics** *pl.* acrobatie *f*; ✈ acrobaties *f/pl.* aériennes.

a·cross [ə'krɔs] **1.** *adv.* à travers, en travers; de l'autre côté; en croix; **2.** *prp.* à travers, sur; en travers de; *come* ~, *run* ~ rencontrer; tomber sur.

act [ækt] **1.** *v/i.* agir (en, *as*; sur, on); prendre des mesures; se comporter; fonctionner; opérer; *théâ.* jouer; ~ (*up*)*on* exercer une action sur, agir sur; *Am.* F ~ *up* devenir insoumis; *v/t.* représenter, jouer (*un rôle, une pièce*); **2.** acte *m*; action *f*; *théâ.* acte *m*; loi *f*, décret *m*; ~*s pl.* actes *m/pl.*; ♀ *of God* force *f* majeure; ♀*s pl. of the Apostles les* Actes *m/pl.* des Apôtres; **'act·a·ble** jouable; **'act·ing 1.** action *f*; *théâ.* acteur: jeu *m*; *pièce*: exécution *f*; **2.** suppléant; intérimaire; provisoire; gérant.

ac·tion ['ækʃn] action *f* (*a. théâ.*); acte *m*; *cheval*: allure *f*; *procès m*; combat *m*, bataille *f*; mécanisme *m*; *couleurs*: jeu *m*; gestes *m/pl.*; ~ *radius* rayon *m* d'action; *bring an* ~ *against* intenter une action *ou* un procès à *ou* contre; *take* ~ prendre des mesures; **'ac·tion·a·ble** actionnable, sujet(te *f*) à procès.

ac·tiv·ate ['æktiveit] activer; *phys.* rendre radioactif (-ive *f*).

ac·tive □ ['æktiv] actif (-ive *f*); alerte; agile; vif (vive *f*); ✝ ~ *partner* commandité *m*; **ac'tiv·i·ty** (*souv. pl.*) activité *f*; occupation *f*; *surt.* ✝ mouvement *m*; *in full* ~ en pleine activité; *intense* ~ activité *f* intense.

ac·tor ['æktə] acteur *m*; **ac·tress** ['æktris] actrice *f*.

ac·tu·al □ ['æktjuəl] réel(le *f*), véritable; actuel(le *f*), présent; **ac·tu·al·i·ty** [æktju'æliti] réalité *f*; actualité *f*; **ac·tu·al·ize** ['æktjuəlaiz] réaliser; **ac·tu·al·ly** ['ækʃuəli] en fait; réellement; en réalité; à vrai dire.

ac·tu·ar·y ['æktjuəri] actuaire *m*.

ac·tu·ate ['æktjueit] mettre en action; animer (q. à, s.o. *to*).

a·cu·men [ə'kju:men] finesse *f* (d'esprit). [puncture *f*.]

ac·u·punc·ture ['ækjupʌŋtʃə] acu-

a·cute □ [ə'kju:t] aigu (-uë *f*) (*a.* ♪, *a. angle, pointe, accent, son*); vif (vive *f*) (*douleur*); fin (*ouïe, esprit*); qui sévit (*crise*); **a'cute·ness** angle: aiguïté *f*; son: acuité *f*; *douleur etc.*: intensité *f*; *ouïe*: finesse *f*; *esprit*: pénétration *f*.

ad F [æd] *see advertisement.*

ad·age ['ædidʒ] maxime *f*.

ad·a·mant ['ædəmənt] *fig.* inflexible; insensible (à, *to*); **ad·a·man·tine** [~'mæntain] adamantin; *fig. see adamant.*

a·dapt [ə'dæpt] adapter (à *to*, *for*); accommoder; adapter (*un texte*) (de, *from*); **a·dapt·a'bil·i·ty** souplesse *f*; **a'dapt·a·ble** adaptable; commode; **ad·ap'ta·tion** adaptation *f* (à, *to*); appropriation *f*; **a'dap·ter** *radio*: (bouchon *m* de) raccord *m*; *télév.* adaptateur *m*.

add [æd] *v/t.* ajouter; joindre; ~ *in* inclure; ~ *up* additionner; *v/i.* ~ *to* augmenter; accentuer; ~ *up to* se totaliser.

ad·den·dum [ə'dendəm], *pl.* **-da** [~də] addenda *m*; supplément *m*.

ad·der ['ædə] vipère *f*.

ad·dict 1. [ə'dikt]: ~ *o.s.* s'adonner (à, *to*), se livrer (à, *to*); **2.** ['ædikt] (*opium etc.* ~) -mane *mf*; **ad'dict·ed** adonné (à, *to*); *become* ~ *to* s'adonner à (*la boisson etc.*), s'abandonner à (*un vice*).

add·ing ['ædin] (d')arithmétique.

ad·di·tion [ə'diʃn] addition *f*; adjonction *f*; *bâtiment*: rajout *m*; *ville*: extension *f*; *Am. terrain*: agrandissement *m*; ~ *to* addition à; *he had an* ~ *to his family* sa famille vient d'augmenter; *in* ~ en outre; *in* ~ *to* en plus de; **ad'di·tion·al** additionnel(le *f*), supplémentaire; nouveau

(-el *devant une voyelle ou un h muet*; -elle *f*; -aux *m/pl.*); de plus.

ad·di·tive ['æditiv] additif *m*.

ad·dle ['ædl] 1. (se) pourrir (*œufs*); *v/t. fig.* troubler (*le cerveau, la tête etc.*); 2. pourri (*œuf*); trouble, brouillé (*cerveau*).

ad·dress [ə'dres] 1. adresser; haranguer (*une foule*); (*a. ~ o.s. to*) adresser la parole à (*q.*); ~ *o.s. to s.th.* entreprendre qch.; se mettre à qch.; 2. adresse *f*; habileté *f*; *parl.* profession *f* de foi; supplique *f*; abord *m*; discours *m*; *give an ~* faire une allocution; *pay one's ~es to* faire la cour à (*une femme*); **ad·dress·ee** [ædre'si:] destinataire *mf*; **ad·dress tag** étiquette *f* d'adresse.

ad·e·noids ['ædinɔidz] *pl.* végétations *f/pl.* adénoïdes.

ad·ept ['ædept] 1. expert (à *at, in*); versé (dans *at, in*); 2. adepte *mf*; initié(e *f*) *m*; expert *m* (en, *in*); F *be an ~ at* être expert à.

ad·e·qua·cy ['ædikwəsi] suffisance *f*; **ad·e·quate** □ ['~kwit] suffisant; juste; raisonnable.

ad·here [əd'hiə] (*to*) adhérer (à), se coller (à); *fig.* persister (dans), s'en tenir (à); observer (*une règle etc.*); donner son adhésion (à) (*un parti etc.*); **ad'her·ence** (*to*) adhérence *f*, adhésion *f* (à); fidélité *f* (à) (*un parti*); observance *f* (de) (*une règle*); **ad'her·ent** 1. adhérent; 2. adhérent(e *f*) *m*; partisan *m*.

ad·he·sion [əd'hi:ʒn] *see* adherence; *fig.* adhésion *f*; *phys.* adhérence *f*; *give one's ~* donner son adhésion (à, *to*).

ad·he·sive [əd'hi:siv] adhésif (-ive *f*) collant; tenace; ~ *plaster*, ~ *tape* sparadrap *m*, emplâtre *m* adhésif.

a·dieu [ə'dju:] 1. adieu!; 2. adieu *m*.

ad·i·pose ['ædipous] adipeux (-euse *f*); gras(se *f*).

ad·it ['ædit] accès *m*; ⚒ galerie *f*.

ad·ja·cen·cy [ə'dʒeisənsi] contiguïté *f*; adjacencies *pl.* voisinage *m* immédiat; **ad'ja·cent** □ (*to*) contigu (-uë *f*) (à), attenant (à); limitrophe (de).

ad·jec·ti·val □ [ædʒek'taivl] adjectif (-ive *f*); **ad·jec·tive** ['ædʒiktiv] adjectif *m*.

ad·join [ə'dʒɔin] avoisiner (*qch.*), toucher (à); **ad'join·ing** contigu (-uë *f*); avoisinant.

ad·journ [ə'dʒə:n] (s') ajourner; *v/t.* remettre, différer; lever (*une séance*) (jusque, *to*); **ad'journ·ment** ajournement *m*; remise *f*.

ad·judge [ə'dʒʌdʒ] juger; ⚖ décider, déclarer (*coupable etc.*); condamner (à, *to*); **ad'judge·ment** décision *f*.

ad·ju·di·cate [ə'dʒu:dikeit] *see* adjudge; **ad·ju·di·ca·tion** jugement *m*; décision *f*; arrêt *m*.

ad·junct ['ædʒʌŋkt] accessoire *m*; adjoint(e *f*) *m*; *gramm.* complément *m*.

ad·ju·ra·tion [ædʒuə'reiʃn] adjuration *f*; **ad·jure** [ə'dʒuə] conjurer (de, *to*).

ad·just [ə'dʒʌst] ajuster; arranger; arrêter (*un compte*); régler (*un différend*); agencer (*une machine*); ajuster (*une balance*); *fig.* ~ *to* adapter à; ~*ing screw* vis *f* de serrage; **ad'just·a·ble** □ réglable, ajustable; **ad'just·ment** ajustement *m*; arrangement *m*; règlement *m*; réglage *m*; correction *f*; accommodement *m*.

ad·ju·tan·cy ⚔ ['ædʒutənsi] fonctions *f/pl.* de capitaine adjudant major; **ad·ju·tant** capitaine *m* adjudant major.

ad-lib *Am.* F [æd'lib] improviser.

ad·meas·ure·ment [æd'meʒəmənt] mensuration *f*; mesurage *m*.

ad·min·is·ter [əd'ministə] *v/t.* administrer (*pays, affaires, sacrement, médicament*); assermenter; appliquer (*la loi*); ~ *justice*, ~ *the law* dispenser *ou* rendre la justice; *v/i.* pourvoir aux besoins (de *q.*, *to s.o.*); **ad·min·is'tra·tion** administration *f*; gestion *f*; prestation *f* (*d'un serment*); *surt. Am.* administration *f*, Gouvernement *m*; ~ *of justice* administration *f* de la justice; **ad'min·is·tra·tive** [~trətiv] administratif (-ive *f*); d'administration; **ad'min·is·tra·tor** [~treitə] administrateur *m*; gérant *m*; ⚖ curateur *m*.

ad·mi·ra·ble □ ['ædmərəbl] admirable, excellent.

ad·mi·ral ['ædmərəl] amiral *m*; ♀ *of the Fleet* amiral *m* commandant en chef; **'ad·mi·ral·ty** amirauté *f*; *First Lord of the* ♀ ministre *m* britannique de la marine.

ad·mi·ra·tion [ædmi'reiʃn] admiration *f*.

ad·mire [əd'maiə] admirer; s'extasier devant; **ad'mir·er** admirateur (-trice *f*) *m*; adorateur (-trice *f*) *m*.

ad·mis·si·bil·i·ty [ədmisə'biliti] admissibilité *f*; **ad'mis·si·ble** □ admissible; recevable; **ad'mis·sion** admission *f*, accès *m* (à, to); entrée *f*; confession *f*, aveu *m*; F prix *m* d'entrée.

ad·mit [əd'mit] *v/t.* admettre (à, dans to, into); laisser entrer; avoir de la place pour; reconnaître (*une faute etc.*); 🏛 surt. Am. ~ to the bar inscrire au tableau des avocats; *v/i.*: ~ of permettre, comporter; it ~s of no excuse il est sans excuse; **ad'mit·tance** entrée *f*; accès *m*; no ~! entrée interdite!; **ad'mit·ted·ly** de l'aveu de tous; de son propre aveu.

ad·mix·ture [əd'mikstʃə] mélange *m*, dosage *m*; *pharm.* mixtion *f*.

ad·mon·ish [əd'mɔniʃ] admonester; exhorter (à, to); prévenir (de, of); **ad·mo·ni·tion** [ædmə'niʃn] remontrance *f*; avertissement *m*; **ad·mon·i·to·ry** □ [əd'mɔnitəri] de remontrances; d'avertissement.

a·do [ə'du:] agitation *f*, activité *f*, embarras *m*, bruit *m*; difficulté *f*; *without much* ~ sans difficulté; sans embarras.

a·do·be [ə'doubi] adobe *m*.

ad·o·les·cence [ædo'lesns] adolescence *f*; **ad·o'les·cent** *adj., a. su./mf* adolescent(e *f*) *m*.

a·dopt [ə'dɔpt] adopter; *fig.* choisir, adopter, embrasser; *fig.* F chiper; ~ed country pays *m* ou patrie *f* d'adoption; **a'dop·tion** adoption *f*; choix *m*; **a'dop·tive** adoptif (-ive *f*); ~ country pays *m* ou patrie *f* d'adoption.

a·dor·a·ble [ə'dɔ:rəbl] adorable; **ad·o·ra·tion** [ædɔ:'reiʃn] adoration *f*; F amour *m*; **a·dore** [ə'dɔ:] adorer; **a'dor·er** adorateur (-trice *f*) *m*.

a·dorn [ə'dɔ:n] orner, parer; **a'dorn·ment** ornement *m*, parure *f*; ornementation *f*.

a·drift [ə'drift] ⚓ à la dérive; *fig.* loin du compte; *turn s.o.* ~ abandonner q., mettre q. sur le pavé.

a·droit [ə'drɔit] adroit; **a'droit·ness** adresse *f*.

ad·u·late ['ædjuleit] aduler, flatter (*q.*); **ad·u'la·tion** adulation *f*; **'ad·u·la·tor** adulateur (-trice *f*) *m*;

'ad·u·la·to·ry adulateur (-trice *f*).

a·dult ['ædʌlt] *adj., a. su./mf* adulte *mf*.

a·dul·ter·ant [ə'dʌltərənt] adultérant *m*; **a'dul·ter·ate 1.** [~reit] adultérer; *fig.* altérer; **2.** [~it] adultéré; falsifié; altéré; **a·dul·ter·a·tion** [ədʌltə'reiʃn] adultération *f*; altération *f*; **a'dul·ter·a·tor** falsificateur (-trice *f*) *m*; **a'dul·ter·er** adultère *m*; **a'dul·ter·ess** adultère *f*; **a'dul·ter·ous** □ adultère; **a'dul·ter·y** adultère *m*.

ad·um·brate ['ædʌmbreit] ébaucher, esquisser; laisser entrevoir; † voiler; **ad·um'bra·tion** ébauche *f*, esquisse *f*; pressentiment *m*.

ad·vance [əd'va:ns] **1.** *v/i.* s'avancer; avancer (*en âge*); monter (*en grade*); hausser (*prix*); *biol.* évoluer; *v/t.* avancer; mettre en avant (*des opinions*); augmenter, hausser (*le prix*); élever (*en grade*); faire avancer; **2.** marche *f* en avant; ✕ avance *f*; progrès *m*; avancement *m* (*en grade*); *prix:* hausse *f*; *in* ~ d'avance, en avance; en avant; *be in* ~ *of s.o.* devancer q.; **3.** avant-; **ad'vanced** *adj.* avancé; supérieur (*cours, école, etc.*); ~ *English* anglais *m* supérieur; **ad'vance·ment** avancement *m*; progrès *m*.

ad·van·tage [əd'va:ntidʒ] avantage *m* (*a. au tennis*); dessus *m*; profit *m*; *gain an* ~ *over* se procurer un avantage sur; *gain the* ~ *over* l'emporter sur; *take* ~ *of* profiter de (*qch.*); abuser de (la crédulité de) (*q.*); *to* ~ avantageusement; **ad·van·ta·geous** □ [ædvən'teidʒəs] avantageux (-euse *f*) (pour, to) (*qch.*); utile.

ad·vent ['ædvənt] arrivée *f*; ♀ *eccl.* Avent *m*; **ad·ven·ti·tious** □ [ædven'tiʃəs] adventice; accidentel(le *f*); accessoire.

ad·ven·ture [əd'ventʃə] **1.** aventure *f*, entreprise *f*; ✝ spéculation *f* hasardée; **2.** (se) hasarder; **ad'ven·tur·er** aventurier *m*; spéculateur *m*; **ad'ven·tur·ess** [~əris] intrigante *f*; **ad'ven·tur·ous** □ aventureux (-euse *f*); audacieux (-euse *f*); entreprenant (*personne*).

ad·verb ['ædvə:b] adverbe *m*; **ad·ver·bi·al** □ [əd'və:bjəl] adverbial (-aux *m/pl.*).

ad·ver·sar·y ['ædvəsəri] adversaire *m*; ennemi(e *f*) *m*; **ad·verse** □

['ˌ‿vəːs] adverse; contraire; ennemi (de, *to*), hostile (à, *to*); opposé; défavorable; ~ *balance* déficit *m*; **ad·ver·si·ty** [əd'vəːsiti] adversité *f*, infortune *f*.

ad·vert [əd'vəːt]: ~ *to* faire allusion à; parler de.

ad·ver·tise ['ædvətaiz] faire de la réclame (pour); *v/t.* annoncer, faire savoir, faire connaître; *v/i.* insérer une annonce; ~ *for* chercher par voie d'annonce; **ad·ver·tise·ment** [əd-'vəːtismənt] publicité *f*; *journal:* annonce *f*; affiche *f* (*sur un mur*); réclame *f*; **ad·ver·tis·er** ['ædvətaizə] auteur *m* d'une annonce; faiseur *m* de réclame; **'ad·ver·tis·ing:** ~ *agency* agence *f* de publicité; ~ *campaign* campagne *f* publicitaire; ~ *designer* dessinateur *m* publicitaire; ~ *film* film *m* publicitaire; ~ *manager* chef *m* de la publicité; ~ *media* supports *m/pl.* publicitaires; ~ *medium* organe *m* de publicité.

ad·vice [əd'vais] conseil *m*, -s *m/pl.*; avis *m*; ✝ lettre *f ou* note *f* d'avis; *usu.* ~s *pl.* nouvelles *f/pl.*; *on the* ~ *of* sur le conseil de, suivant les conseils de; *take medical* ~ consulter un médecin; **ad'vice-boat** ⚓ aviso *m*.

ad·vis·a·ble □ [əd'vaizəbl] recommandable; **ad'vise** *v/t.* recommander (*qch.*); conseiller (*q.*); conseiller (à q. de *inf.*, *s.o. to inf.*); prévenir (de, *of*; que, *that*); ✝ aviser de; *v/i.* se consulter; ~ *with* consulter (*q.*), se consulter avec (*q.*); ~ *on* renseigner (*q.*) sur; **ad'vised** □ réfléchi (*acte*); **ad'vis·ed·ly** [ˌidli] à dessein; **ad'vis·er** conseiller (-ère *f*) *m*; **ad'vi·so·ry** [ˌəri] consultatif (-ive *f*); ♀ *Board* conseil *m* consultatif.

ad·vo·ca·cy ['ædvəkəsi] fonction *f* d'avocat; appui *m* (donné à une cause); **ad·vo·cate 1.** ['ˌkit] avocat *m*; *fig.* défenseur *m*, partisan *m*; **2.** ['ˌkeit] plaider en faveur de (*qch.*); appuyer (*une cause*); préconiser.

adze ⊕ [ædz] (h)erminette *f*.

ae·gis ['iːdʒis] *fig.* égide *f*.

ae·on ['iːɔn] éon *m*; *fig.* éternité *f*.

a·er·at·ed ['eiəreitid] aéré (*pain*); gazeux (*-euse f*) (*eau*).

a·e·ri·al ['eəriəl] **1.** □ aérien(ne *f*); ~ *camera* aérophoto *m*; ~ *survey* prise *f*

de vue aérienne; ~ *view* vue *f* aérienne; **2.** *radio, télév.:* antenne *f*; *high* ~ antenne *f* haute; *mains* ~ antenne *f* secteur; *outdoor* ~ antenne *f* d'extérieur; ~ *mast* mât *m* d'antenne.

a·e·rie ['eəri] aire *f*.

aero... [eərə] aéro-; **a·er·o·bat·ics** [ˌ'bætiks] *pl.* acrobaties *f/pl.* (aériennes); **a·er·o·drome** ['eərədroum] aérodrome *m*; **a·er·o·gram** ['ˌgræm] radiogramme *m*; **a·er·o·lite** ['ˌlait] aérolithe *m*; **a·er·o·naut** ['ˌnɔːt] aéronaute *m*; **a·er·o'nau·tic, a·er·o'nau·ti·cal** □ aéronautique; **a·er·o'nau·tics** *sg.* aéronautique *f*; **a·er·o·plane** ['ˌplein] aéroplane *m*, avion *m*; **a·er·o·sol (can)** ['ˌsɔl] aérosol *m*, atomiseur *m*; **a·er·o·space in·du·stry** industrie *f* aérospatiale; **a·er·o·stat** ['ˌoustæt] aérostat *m*; **a·er·o'sta·tic** aérostatique.

aes·thete ['iːsθiːt] esthète *mf*; **aes·thet·ic, aes·thet·i·cal** □ [iːs-'θetik(l)] esthétique; **aes'thet·ics** *sg.* esthétique *f*.

a·far [ə'fɑː] (*surt.* ~ *off*) au loin, éloigné; *from* ~ de loin.

af·fa·bil·i·ty [æfə'biliti] affabilité *f*; **af·fa·ble** □ ['æfəbl] affable, courtois.

af·fair [ə'fɛə] affaire *f*; *love* ~ affaire *f* de cœur; F affaire *f*, chose *f*; ~ *of honour* affaire *f* d'honneur; duel *m*.

af·fect [ə'fekt] atteindre, attaquer, toucher; influer sur (*qch.*); affliger; concerner; altérer (*la santé*); ✱ intéresser (*un organe*); affecter (*une manière*); *he* ~s *the freethinker* il pose au libre penseur; *he* ~s *to sleep* il affecte de dormir; **af·fec·ta·tion** [æfek'teiʃn] affectation *f*, simulation *f* (de, *of*); *langage:* afféterie *f*; *style:* mièvrerie *f*; **af·fect·ed** □ [ə'fektid] atteint (*santé*); disposé (pour q., *towards s.o.*); ému; touché; affecté, maniéré (*style, maintien, etc.*); simulé (*-ère f*) (*personne*); simulé; **af'fec·tion** affection *f* (a. ✱⁸) (pour *for*, *towards*); tendresse *f* (pour, *for*); impression *f*; **af'fec·tion·ate** □ [ˌkʃənit] affectueux (-euse *f*), aimant; **af'fec·tive** affectif (-ive *f*).

af·fi·ance [ə'faiəns] **1.** confiance *f* (en, *in*); **2.** fiancer (avec, *to*).

af·fi·da·vit [æfi'deivit] attestation *f*

par écrit; *make an* ~ faire une déclaration sous serment.

af·fil·i·ate [ə'filieit] affilier (*un membre*) (*à une société* to, with a so*ciety*); ⚖, *a. fig.* attribuer la paternité de (*q., a. qch.*) (à, on); ~ *o.s.* with s'affilier à; *Am.* fraterniser avec; ~d company filiale *f*; **af·fil·i·a·tion** affiliation *f* (*à une société etc.*); ⚖ légitimation *f*; *Am. usu.* ~s *pl.* attaches *f*/*pl.* (*politiques*).

af·fin·i·ty [ə'finiti] parenté *f*; affinité *f* (*a.* ⚖, *a. fig.*).

af·firm [ə'fə:m] affirmer, soutenir; ⚖ confirmer; **af·fir·ma·tion** [æfə:-'meiʃn] affirmation *f*; assertion *f*; ⚖ confirmation *f*; **af·firm·a·tive** □ [ə'fə:mətiv] **1.** affirmatif (-ive *f*); **2.** affirmative *f*; *answer in the* ~ répondre affirmativement *ou* que oui.

af·fix 1. ['æfiks] addition *f*; **2.** [ə'fiks] attacher (à, to); apposer (*un sceau, un timbre*) (sur, à).

af·flict [ə'flikt] affliger, tourmenter; ~ed with affligé de; **af·flic·tion** affliction *f*; calamité *f*; infirmité *f*.

af·flu·ence ['æfluəns] affluence *f*; abondance *f*; **'af·flu·ent** □ **1.** abondant, riche (en, *in*); opulent, riche; **2.** affluent *m*.

af·flux ['æflʌks] afflux *m*; concours *m* (*de gens*).

af·ford [ə'fɔ:d] avoir les moyens de; être en mesure de; disposer de (*le temps*); offrir; *I can* ~ *it* mes moyens me le permettent.

af·for·est [æ'fɔrist] (re)boiser; **af·for·est·a·tion** (re)boisement *m*.

af·fran·chise [ə'fræntʃaiz] affranchir.

af·fray [ə'frei] bagarre *f*; rixe *f*.

af·front [ə'frʌnt] **1.** offenser; faire rougir (*q.*); **2.** affront *m*, offense *f*; *put an* ~ *upon, offer an* ~ *to* faire (un) affront *ou* une avanie à (*q.*).

a·fi·cio·na·do [əfisjə'nɑ:dou] aficionado *m*, amateur *m*, fana *m*.

a·field [ə'fi:ld] aux champs; à la campagne; *far* ~ très loin.

a·fire [ə'faiə] en feu, embrasé; *set* ~ mettre le feu à.

a·flame [ə'fleim] en flammes, embrasé; *set* ~ mettre en flammes, faire brûler.

a·float ⚓ *a. fig.* [ə'flout] à flot (*a. fig.* = *quitte de dettes*); sur l'eau, à la mer; à bord; en circulation (*idée, bruit*); ⚓ en cours; *keep* ~ se maintenir à flot; *set* ~ lancer (*un navire, un journal, etc.*).

a·foot [ə'fut] à pied; en mouvement, sur pied; *be* ~ être en route *ou* marche *ou* train.

a·fore ⚓ [ə'fɔ:] *see before*; **a·fore·men·tioned** [~menʃnd], **a·fore·named** [~neimd], **a·fore·said** susdit, précité; **a·fore·thought** prémédité; *with malice* ~ avec préméditation.

a·fraid [ə'freid] pris de peur, effrayé; *be* ~ *of* avoir peur de, craindre (*q., qch.*); F *I am* ~ *I have to go* je crains bien que je doive partir.

a·fresh [ə'freʃ] de *ou* à nouveau.

Af·ri·caans [æfri'kɑ:ns] africaans *m* (= *patois hollandais parlé au Cap*); **Af·ri·can** ['~kən] **1.** africain; **2.** African(e *f*) *m*; *surt. Am.* nègre; **Af·ri·can·der** [~'kændə] Afrikander *m*.

Af·ro ['æfrou] **1.** afro; **2.** coiffure *f* afro.

aft ⚓ [ɑ:ft] à *ou* sur l'arrière.

aft·er ['ɑ:ftə] **1.** *adv.* après; plus tard; ensuite; **2.** *prp. temps:* après; *lieu:* après; à la suite de; *manière:* suivant, selon, d'après; ~ *all* après tout, enfin; *I'll go* ~ *him* j'irai le chercher; *time* ~ *time* à maintes reprises; ~ *having seen him* après l'avoir vu; **3.** *cj.* après que; **4.** *adj.* subséquent; futur; ⚓ arrière; '~·**birth** arrière-faix *m*/*inv.*; '~·**crop** regain *m*; seconde récolte *f*; '~·**din·ner** d'après dîner; '~·**ef·fect** répercussion *f*; '~·**glow** dernières lueurs *f*/*pl.* du couchant; '~·**grass**, '~·**math** ✍ regain *m*; *fig.* suites *f*/*pl.*; '~·**hours** le temps *m* après la fermeture (des magasins, cafés, *etc.*); '~·**noon** après-midi *m*/*inv.*; *fig.* ~ (*of life*) déclin *m* de la vie; *this* ~ cet après-midi.

aft·ers F ['ɑ:ftəz] *pl.* dessert *m*.

after...: '~·**sales serv·ice** service *m* après-vente; '~·**sea·son** arrière-saison *f*; '~·**shave (lo·tion)** lotion *f* après-rasage, after-shave *m*; '~·**taste** arrière-goût *m*; '~·**thought** réflexion *f* après coup; '~·**wards** ['~wədz] après, plus tard, ensuite; par la suite.

a·gain [ə'gen] encore; encore une fois, de nouveau; en outre, d'autre part; ~ *and* ~, *time and* ~ maintes et maintes fois; *as much* (*ou many*) ~ deux fois autant; *twice as much* ~

trois fois autant; *now and* ~ de temps en temps; de temps à autre.

a·gainst [ə'genst] *prp.* contre; à l'encontre de; *fig.* en prévision de; *as* ~ comparé à; ~ *the wall* contre le mur; ~ *a background* sur un fond; *over* ~ vis-à-vis de; F *run* ~ rencontrer (*q.*) par hasard.

a·gape [ə'geip] bouche *f* bée.

ag·ate *min.* ['ægət] agate *f*; *Am.* marbre *m*; *Am. typ. see* ruby.

a·ga·ve ♀ [ə'geivi] agave *m*.

age [eidʒ] **1.** âge *m*; époque *f*, siècle *m*; génération *f*; F éternité *f*; (*old*) ~ vieillesse *f*; *at the* ~ *of* à l'âge de; *in the* ~ *of Queen Anne* à l'époque de *ou* du temps de la reine Anne; *of* ~ majeur; *over* ~ trop âgé; *under* ~ mineur; *what is your* ~? quel âge avez-vous?; *when I was your* ~ quand j'avais ton âge, à ton âge; *act ou be your* ~! tu n'es plus un(e) enfant!; F *wait for* ~s attendre des éternités; *come of* ~ atteindre sa majorité; **2.** vieillir; **age brack·et** groupe *m ou* catégorie *f ou* tranche *f* d'âge; **a·ged** ['~id] âgé, vieux (vieil *devant une voyelle ou un h muet*); vieille *f*; vieux *m/pl.*); [eidʒd]: ~ *twenty* âgé de vingt ans; **age group** → **age bracket**; **'age·less** toujours jeune; **'age·old** séculaire.

a·gen·cy ['eidʒənsi] action *f*, opération *f*; entremise *f*, intermédiaire *m*; agent *m* (*naturel*); agence *f*, bureau *m*.   [du jour.]

a·gen·da [ə'dʒendə] *sg.* ordre *m*)

a·gent ['eidʒənt] agent *m*, représentant(e *f*) *m*; régisseur *m* (*d'une propriété*); mandataire *mf*; commis *m* voyageur; 🚂 *Am.* chef *m* de gare; ⚗ agent *m*.

ag·glom·er·ate [ə'gləmə reit] (s')agglomérer; **ag·glom·er'a·tion** agglomération *f*.

ag·glu·ti·nate 1. [ə'glu:tineit] (s'ag-) glutiner (*a. ⚗, gramm.*); **2.** [~nit] agglutiné; **ag·glu·ti·na·tion** [~ 'neiʃn] agglutination *f* (*a. ⚗, gramm.*).

ag·gran·dize [ə'grændaiz] agrandir; exagérer; **ag'gran·dize·ment** [~ dizmənt] agrandissement *m*.

ag·gra·vate ['ægrəveit] aggraver; empirer; envenimer (*une querelle*); F agacer (*q.*); **ag·gra'va·tion** aggravation *f*; envenimement *m*; F agacement *m*.

ag·gre·gate 1. ['ægrigeit] (s')agréger (à, to); *v/i.* F s'élever à *ou* au total de; **2.** □ ['~git] collectif (-ive *f*); global (-aux *m/pl.*), total (-aux *m/pl.*); ⚙, *géol., etc.* agrégé; **3.** [~] ensemble *m*, total *m*; masse *f*; *in the* ~ dans l'ensemble; **ag·gre·ga·tion** [~'geiʃn] agrégation *f*; assemblage *m*.

ag·gres·sion [ə'greʃn] agression *f*; **ag'gres·sive** □ [ə'gresiv] agressif (-ive *f*); militant; casseur (*air*); ~ *war* guerre *f* offensive; *take* (*ou assume*) *the* ~ prendre l'offensive; **ag'gres·sive·ness** agressivité *f*; **ag'gres·sor** agresseur *m*.

ag·grieve [ə'gri:v] chagriner, blesser.

ag·gro *Brit. sl.* ['ægrou] agressivité *f*; violences *f/pl.*

a·ghast [ə'gɑ:st] consterné; stupéfait (de, *at*).

ag·ile □ ['ædʒail] agile, leste.

a·gil·i·ty [ə'dʒiliti] agilité *f*

ag·i·o ♱ ['ædʒiou] agio *m*; **ag·i·o·tage** ♱ ['ædʒiotidʒ] agiotage *m*.

ag·i·tate ['ædʒiteit] *v/t.* agiter, remuer; agiter (*une question*); *fig.* émouvoir, troubler; *v/i.* faire de l'agitation (*en faveur de, for*); **ag·i'ta·tion** agitation *f*; mouvement *m*; émotion *f*, trouble *m*; discussion *f*; *insidious* ~ menées *f/pl.* insidieuses; **'ag·i·ta·tor** agitateur *m*; meneur *m*; fauteur *m* de troubles.

ag·let ['æglit] ferret *m*.

a·glow [ə'glou] enflammé; *fig.* resplendissant.

ag·nail ⚕ ['ægneil] envie *f*.

ag·nate ['ægneit] **1.** agnat(e *f*) *m*; **2.** agnat.

a·go [ə'gou]: *a year* ~ il y a un an; *it is a year* ~ il y a un an (que, *since*); *long* ~ il y a longtemps.

a·gog [ə'gɔg] en émoi; dans l'expectative (de, *for*).

ag·o·nize ['ægənaiz] *v/t.* torturer, mettre au supplice; *v/i.* être au supplice *ou* au martyre; **'ag·o·niz·ing** □ atroce; navrant.

ag·o·ny ['ægəni] angoisse *f*; paroxysme *m* (*de joie*); (~ *of death, mortal* ~) agonie *f*; *journ.* F ~ *column* annonces *f/pl.* personnelles.

a·grar·i·an [ə'grɛəriən] **1.** agrarien(ne *f*) *m*; **2.** agraire.

a·gree [ə'gri:] *v/i.* consentir; tomber d'accord; s'accorder; (*upon, on*) convenir (de), accepter (*qch.*);

tomber d'accord (sur); admettre (que, *that*); être du même avis (que q., *with s.o.*); ~ to consentir à, accepter (*qch.*); ~ to *differ* différer à l'amiable; *v/t.* ✝ faire accorder (*les livres*), faire cadrer (*un compte*); *be* ~d être d'accord (sur, on; que, *that*), ~d! d'accord!, soit!; a'**gree-a-ble** □ agréable (à, *to*); aimable (envers, *to*); F consentant (à, *to*); a'**gree-a-ble-ness** amabilité *f*; endroit: agrément *m*; a'**gree-ment** accord *m*; conformité *f*, concordance *f*; convention *f*, contrat *m*; traité *m*; *come to an* ~ arriver à une entente; *make an* ~ passer un contrat (avec *q.*, *with s.o.*).

ag·ri·cul·tur·al [ægri'kʌltʃərəl] agricole (*produit, nation*); agriculteur (*peuple*); **ag·ri·cul·ture** ['ǁtʃə] agriculture *f*; **ag·ri·cul·tur·ist** [ǁtʃərist] agriculteur *m*, agronome *m*.

a·ground ⚓ [ə'graund] échoué; *run* ~ échouer; mettre (*un navire*) à la côte.

a·gue ['eigjuː] fièvre *f* (intermittente); '**a·gu·ish** fiévreux (-euse *f*); impaludé (*personne*); *fig.* frissonnant.

ah [ɑː] ah!, ha!, heu!

a·head [ə'hed] en avant, sur l'avant; *straight* ~ droit devant; ~ *of s.o.* en avant de q.; *go* ~ aller de l'avant, avancer; *go* ~! marchez!; allez-y!; continuez!

a·hoy ⚓ [ə'hɔi] ho *ou* ohé, du canot!

aid [eid] 1. aider, secourir; venir en aide à; 2. aide *f*, secours *m*; *by* (*ou with*) *the* ~ *of* avec l'aide de (*q.*); à l'aide de (*qch.*); ~*s and appliances* moyens *m/pl.*

aide-de-camp ⚔ ['eiddə'kɑ̃:ŋ], *pl.* **aides-de-camp** ['eidzdə'kɑ̃:ŋ] officier *m* d'ordonnance.

ai·grette ['eigret] aigrette *f*.

ai·guil·lette ⚔ [eigwi'let] aiguillette *f*.

ail [eil] *v/i.* être souffrant; *v/t.* faire souffrir (*q.*); *what* ~*s him?* qu'est-ce qu'il a?; '**ail·ing** souffrant, indisposé; '**ail·ment** mal *m*, maladie *f*.

aim [eim] 1. *v/i.* viser (*qch.*); *fig.* ~ *at* viser (à *inf.*; *qch.*, *s.th.*); *surt. Am.* ~ *to* (*inf.*) aspirer à (*inf.*); *v/t.*: ~ *a gun* (*ou blow*) *at* viser (*q.*); ~ *remarks at* parler à l'adresse de; 2. action *f* de viser; but *m*; *fig.*

dessein *m*, visées *f/pl.*, but *m*; *take* ~ viser; '**aim·less** □ sans but.

ain't F [eint] = *are not, am not, is not, have not, has not.*

air[1] [ɛə] 1. air *m*; souffle *m*; brise *f*; *by* ~ en avion, par la voie des airs; *in the open* ~ au grand air; *castles in the* ~ châteaux *m/pl.* en Espagne; *be in the* ~ être en l'air; *fig.* se préparer; *war in the* ~ guerre *f* aérienne; *on the* ~ radiodiffusé; à la radio; *be on* (*off*) *the* ~ (ne pas) radiodiffuser; *go on* (*off*) *the* ~ commencer (terminer) une émission; *put on the* ~ mettre en ondes, émettre; ~ *supply* entrée *f* d'air; *take the* ~ prendre l'air; 🛬 décoller; 2. aérer (*une chambre, le linge*); mettre à l'air; bassiner (*un lit*); ventiler (*une question*); faire parade de (*son savoir, ses opinions*); ~ *o.s.* prendre l'air.

air[2] [~] air *m*, mine *f*, apparence *f*; *give o.s.* ~*s* se donner des airs; *with an* ~ d'un grand geste; ~*s and graces* minauderies *f/pl.*

air[3] ♪ [~] air *m*, mélodie *f*.

air...: '~-**base** base *f* d'aviation; '~-**bath** bain *m* d'air; '~-**bed** matelas *m* pneumatique; '~-**blad·der** vésicule *f* (aérienne); vessie *f* natatoire; '~-**borne** 🛬 en vol; ⚔ aéroporté; '~-**brake** frein *m* à air comprimé; ~-**bus** aérobus *m*, airbus *m*; ~-**car·go** fret *m* aérien; '~-**cham·ber** *biol.* chambre *f* à air; ⊕ cloche *f* d'air; '~-**con·di-tioned** climatisé; '~-**con·di·tion·er** climatiseur *m*; '~-**cooled** (*moteur*) à refroidissement par l'air; '~-**craft** avion *m*, -s *m/pl.*; ~ *carrier* porteavions *m/inv.*; '~-**cush·ion** coussin *m* à air; '~-**drop** 1. parachuter; 2. parachutage *m*; '~-**field** champ *m* d'aviation; '~-**force** aviation *f*; ♀ **Force** armée *f* de l'air; ~ **freight** fret *m* aérien; transport *m* par air; *by* ~ par voie aérienne, par avion; '~-**gun** fusil *m* à vent; ~ *host·ess see* stewardess.

air·i·ness ['ɛərinis] situation *f* aérée; bonne ventilation *f*; *fig.* légèreté *f* d'esprit, gaieté *f*.

air·ing ['ɛəriŋ] ventilation *f*; aérage *m*; *vêtements*: éventage *m*; *give s.th. an* ~ aérer qch.; *that room needs an* ~ il faut aérer cette pièce; *take an* ~ faire un (petit) tour, prendre l'air.

air...: '~-**jack·et** gilet *m* de sauve-

align

tage; ⊕ chemise *f* d'air; ~ **let·ter**
lettre *f* par avion, aérogramme *m*; '~-
lift pont *m* aérien; '~-**line** ligne *f*
aérienne; service *m* de transports
aériens; trajet *m* à vol d'oiseau; ~
lin·er avion *m* de ligne; ~ **mail** poste
f aérienne; '~-**man** aviateur *m*; '~-
me'chan·ic mécanicien *m* d'avion;
'~-**mind·ed** ayant le sens de l'air; '~-
pas·sen·ger passager (-ère *f*) *m*; '~-
pipe ⊕ tuyau *m* d'air; '~-**plane** *surt.*
Am. avion *m*; ~ *pilot* pilote *m*
(d'avion); '~-**pock·et** ✖ trou *m*
d'air; '~-**port** aéroport *m*; '~-**pump**
pompe *f* à air; '~-**raid** ✖ raid *m*
aérien; ~ *precautions* défense *f* antiaérienne; ~ *shelter* abri *m*; '~-**ship**
dirigeable *m*; '~-**sick**: be ~ avoir la
nausée; *fig.* mal de *f* d'atterrissage;
~ **ter·mi·nal** ✖ aérogare *f*; '~-**tight**
(à clôture) hermétique; *sl.* ~ *case*
thèse *f* inébranlable; '~-**traf·fic**
con'trol·ler contrôleur *m* de la
navigation aérienne, aiguilleur *m* du
ciel; '~-**tube** tuyau *m* à air; '~-**way**
voie *f* aérienne; '~-**wom·an** aviatrice
f; '~-**wor·thy** navigable.

air·y ☐ ['ɛəri] bien aéré; léger
(-ère *f*); désinvolte; *fig.* en l'air.

aisle △ [ail] nef *f* latérale; bas-côté
m; passage *m* (*entre bancs*).

aitch [eitʃ] h *m*.

aitch·bone ['eitʃboun] culotte *f* (de
bœuf).

a·jar [ə'dʒɑ:] entrouvert, entre-
bâillé; *fig.* en désaccord (avec, *with*).

a·kim·bo [ə'kimbou] (les poings)
sur les hanches.

a·kin [ə'kin] apparenté (à, avec *to*).

al·a·bas·ter ['æləbɑ:stə] **1.** albâtre
m; **2.** d'albâtre.

a·lack † [ə'læk] hélas!; ~-*a-day!* ô
jour malheureux!

a·lac·ri·ty [ə'lækriti] empressement
m, alacrité *f*; promptitude *f*.

a·larm [ə'lɑ:m] **1.** alarme *f*, alerte *f*;
avertisseur *m*, signal *m*; *fig.* agitation *f*; réveille-matin *m/inv.*; ~-*gun*
canon *m* d'alarme; *give the* ~, *raise*
an ~ donner l'alarme, alerter;
2. alarmer (*a. fig.*); alerter; **a'larm-**
bell tocsin *m*; timbre *m* avertisseur; **a'larm-clock** réveille-
matin *m/inv.*, réveil *m*; **a'larm-cord**
cordon *m* de la sonnette d'alarme;
a'larm·ist alarmiste *mf* (*a. adj.*).

a·lar·um [ə'lɛərəm] alerte *f*; réveille-matin *m/inv.*; timbre *m*.

a·las [ə'lɑ:s] hélas!, las!

alb *eccl.* [ælb] aube *f*.

Al·ba·ni·an [æl'beinjən] **1.** albanais;
2. Albanais(e *f*) *m*.

al·be·it [ɔ:l'bi:it] quoique, bien que.

al·bi·no *biol.* [æl'bi:nou] **1.** albinos
mf; **2.** blanc(he *f*) (*animal*).

al·bum ['ælbəm] album *m* (*a.* =
disque).

al·bu·men, al·bu·min ⚗ ['ælbju-
min] albumen *m*; blanc *m* d'œuf;
al'bu·mi·nous albumineux (-eu-
se *f*).

al·chem·ic, al·chem·i·cal ☐ [æl-
'kemik(l)] alchimique; **al·che·mist**
['ælkimist] alchimiste *m*; **'al·che-**
my alchimie *f*.

al·co·hol ['ælkəhɔl] alcool *m*; **al·co-**
'hol·ic alcoolique (*adj., mf*); **'al·co-**
hol·ism alcoolisme *m*; **al·co·hol-**
ize ['~laiz] alcooliser.

al·cove ['ælkouv] alcôve *f*; niche *f*;
tonnelle *f* (de jardin).

al·der ♀ ['ɔ:ldə] aune *m*.

al·der·man ['ɔ:ldəmən] alderman
m, magistrat *m* municipal; **al·der-**
man·ship ['~mənʃip] fonctions *f/pl.*
d'alderman; magistrature *f*.

ale [eil] ale *f*; bière *f* anglaise.

a·lee ⚓ [ə'li:] sous le vent.

a·lem·bic ⚗ [ə'lembik] alambic *m*.

a·lert [ə'lɔ:t] **1.** ☐ alerte, éveillé;
actif (-ive *f*); **2.** alerte *f*; *on the* ~
sur le qui-vive; éveillé; **a'lert-**
ness vigilance *f*; promptitude *f*.

al·fal·fa ✖ [æl'fælfə] luzerne *f*.

al·ga ♀ ['ælgə], *pl.* -**gae** [~dʒi:]
algue *f*.

al·ge·bra ⚕ ['ældʒibrə] algèbre *f*;
al·ge·bra·ic [~'breiik] algébrique.

a·li·as ['eiliæs] **1.** autrement nommé;
2. nom *m* d'emprunt.   [excuse *f*.]

al·i·bi ['ælibai] alibi *m*; *Am.* F]

al·ien ['eiljən] **1.** étranger (-ère *f*);
fig. ~ *to* contraire à; qui répugne à;
2. étranger (-ère *f*) *m*; **'al·ien·a·ble**
aliénable, mutable; **al·ien·ate** ['~-
eit] aliéner (*des biens*); *fig.* détacher,
éloigner (de, *from*), (s')aliéner (*q.*);
al·ien·a·tion *biens, cœur*: aliénation *f*; désaffection *f*; ~ *of mind*
égarement *m* d'esprit; **'al·ien·ist** ⚕
aliéniste *m*.

a·light¹ [ə'lait] allumé; en feu.

a·light² [~] descendre; mettre pied
à terre; se poser (*oiseau*); ✖ atterrir; amerrir.

a·lign [ə'lain] *v/t.* aligner (*a. surv.*);

mettre en ligne; ~ o.s. with se ranger du côté de; v/i. s'aligner; a'lign·ment alignement m (a. surv.).

a·like [ə'laik] 1. adj. semblable, pareil(le f); 2. adv. semblablement; de la même manière; de même.

al·i·ment ['ælimənt] aliment m; al·i·men·ta·ry [~'mentəri] alimentaire; ~ canal tube m ou canal m alimentaire; al·i·men'ta·tion alimentation f.

al·i·mo·ny ['æliməni] pension f alimentaire; aliments m/pl.

a·line(·ment) [ə'lain(mənt)] see align(ment).

al·i·quot ⚹ ['ælikwɔt] (partie f) aliquote f.

a·live [ə'laiv] vivant, en vie; sensible (à, to), conscient (de, to); fig. éveillé; ⚡ sous tension; no man ~ personne au monde; F look ~! dépêchez-vous!; F man ~! par exemple!; grand Dieu!; be ~ to avoir conscience de; be ~ with grouiller de.

al·ka·li ⚹ ['ælkəlai] alcali m; al·ka·line ['~lain] alcalin; make ~ alcaliser.

all [ɔːl] 1. adj. tout; sans exception; entier (-ère f); ~ day (long) (pendant) toute la journée; ~ kind(s) of books toutes sortes de livres; for ~ that toutefois, cependant; see above; after; 2. su. tout m; totalité f; my ~ mon tout; ~ of them eux tous; at ~ quoi que ce soit; aucunement; not at ~ (pas) du tout; for ~ (that) I care pour ce que cela me fait; for ~ I know autant que je sache; 3. adv. tout; entièrement; ~ at once tout à coup; tout d'un coup; ~ the better tant mieux; ~ but à peu près, presque; ~ right en règle; en bon état; entendu!; bon!; c'est ça!

all-A·mer·i·can [ɔːlə'merikən] 1. relevant entièrement des É.-U., de; 2. sp. champion m américain.

al·lay [ə'lei] apaiser, calmer; modérer; dissiper (des soupçons); apaiser (la faim, la soif).

al·le·ga·tion [æle'geiʃn] allégation f; al·lege [ə'ledʒ] alléguer; prétendre; al'leged prétendu; présumé.

al·le·giance [ə'liːdʒns] fidélité f (à, to), obéissance f (à, to); oath of ~ serment m d'allégeance.

al·le·gor·ic, al·le·gor·i·cal □ [æle-

'gɔrik(l)] allégorique; al·le·go·rize ['æligəraiz] allégoriser; 'al·le·go·ry allégorie f.

al·le·lu·ia [æli'luːjə] alléluia m.

al·ler·gic [ə'ləːdʒik] a. fig. allergique (à to); al'ler·gy ['ælədʒi] allergie f.

al·le·vi·ate [ə'liːvieit] alléger, soulager; apaiser (la soif); al·le·vi'a·tion allègement m, soulagement m; adoucissement m.

al·ley ['æli] jardin: allée f; ruelle f, ville: passage m; Am. ruelle f latérale; see back ~; see blind; a. skittle-~; F that is right down his ~ c'est son rayon; F '~·way Am. ruelle f.

All Fools' Day [ɔːl'fuːlzdei] le premier avril.

al·li·ance [ə'laiəns] alliance f; apparentage m; form an ~ s'allier (avec, with).

al·li·ga·tor zo. ['æligeitə] alligator m.

all-in ['ɔːl'in] mixte; ... tous risques; tout compris; Am. F fini, sl. fichu.

al·lit·er·ate [ə'litəreit] allitérer; al·lit·er'a·tion allitération f.

all-met·al ⊕ ['ɔːl'metl] tout métal.

al·lo·cate ['æləkeit] allouer, assigner; distribuer; al·lo'ca·tion allocation f; répartition f (des dépenses); part f assignée. [tion f.]

al·lo·cu·tion [ælo'kjuːʃn] allocu-]

al·lo·di·al □ [ə'loudjəl] allodial (-aux m/pl.).

al·lop·a·thist ⚹ [ə'lɔpəθist] allopathe mf; al'lop·a·thy allopathie f.

al·lot [ə'lɔt] assigner, attribuer; affecter (qch.) (à, for); répartir; al'lot·ment attribution f; somme: affectation f; ⚔ délégation f de solde; partage m; distribution f; portion f; terre: lopin m.

all-out ['ɔːl'aut] avec toute son énergie, de toutes ses forces.

al·low [ə'lau] permettre; admettre; tolérer; laisser; Am. F opiner; he is ~ed to be on lui reconnaît (su.); ~ for tenir compte de; avoir égard à; F it ~s of no excuse c'est impardonnable; al'low·a·ble □ admissible, admis, légitime; al'low·ance 1. tolérance f; pension f alimentaire; rente f; argent m de poche; ⚔ nourriture: indemnité f; frais m/pl.; rabais m, remise f; marge f; ⊕ tolérance f; make ~ for s.o. se montrer indulgent envers q.; make ~ for s.th. faire la part de qch.; 2. faire une rente à; rationner (le pain etc.).

al·loy [ə'lɔi] **1.** alliage *m*; *fig.* mélange *m*; **2.** (s')allier; *v/t. fig.* altérer, diminuer, porter atteinte à.

all...: '**~-'pur·pose** universel(le *f*), à tout faire; '**~-'red** entièrement britannique; '**~-'round** universel(le *f*); complet (-ète *f*); à tout usage; ✝ global (-aux *m/pl.*).

All Saints' Day ['ɔ:l'seintsdei] la Toussaint *f*.

All Souls' Day ['ɔ:l'soulzdei] la fête *f* des morts.

all-star *sp. Am.* ['ɔ:l'sta:] composé de joueurs de premier ordre.

al·lude [ə'lu:d] faire allusion (à, *to*).

al·lure [ə'ljuə] attirer; séduire; **al-'lure·ment** attrait *m*; appât *m*; séduction *f*; **al'lur·ing** □ attrayant, séduisant.

al·lu·sion [ə'lu:ʒn] allusion *f* (à, *to*); **al'lu·sive** □ allusif (-ive *f*); faisant allusion (à, *to*).

al·lu·vi·al [ə'lu:vjəl] alluvial (-aux *m/pl.*) (*terrain*); alluvien(ne *f*) (*gîte*); **al'lu·vi·on** [~ən] alluvion *f*; **al'lu·vi·um** [~əm], *pl.* **-ums, -vi·a** [~vjə] alluvion *f*; lais *m*.

all-weath·er ['ɔ:l'weðə] tous-temps; *sp.* ~ *court* (terrain *m* en) quick *m* (*TM*).

al·ly¹ 1. [ə'lai] (s')allier (à, avec *to, with*); *v/t.* apparenter (*des familles*); *allied to fig.* allié à *ou* avec; de la même nature que; **2.** ['ælai] allié *m*, coallié *m*.

al·ly² ['æli] grosse bille *f*; calot *m*.

al·ma·nac ['ɔ:lmənæk] almanach *m*.

al·might·i·ness [ɔ:l'maitinis] toute-puissance *f*; **al'might·y 1.** □ tout-puissant (toute-puissante *f*); **2.** F rudement; **3.** ♀ *le* Tout-Puissant.

al·mond ['ɑ:mənd] amande *f*.

al·mon·er ['ɑ:mənə] aumônier (-ère *f*) *m*.

al·most ['ɔ:lmoust] presque, à peu près.

alms [ɑ:mz] *usu. sg.* aumône *f*; '**~-bag** aumônière *f*; '**~-house** asile *m* de vieillards *ou* d'indigents.

al·oe ♀, *a. pharm.* ['ælou] aloès *m*.

a·loft [ə'lɔft] ♨ en haut (*dans la mâture*); *fig.* en l'air; ✈ en vol.

a·lone [ə'loun] seul; *let (ou leave)* ~ laisser (*q.*) tranquille; *let it* ~! n'y touchez pas!; *let* ~ sans compter; sans parler de.

a·long [ə'lɔŋ] **1.** *adv.*: *move* ~ avancer; *come* ~! venez donc; *stride* ~ avancer à grandes enjambées; *all* ~ depuis longtemps; tout le temps; ~ *with* avec; F *get* ~ *with you!* filez!; allons donc!; **2.** *prp.* le long de; **a'long·shore** le long de la côte; **a'long·side 1.** ♨ *adv.* bord à bord, contre à contre; **2.** *prp.* ♨ accosté le long de; *fig.* tout près de.

a·loof [ə'lu:f] à l'écart; distant; ♨ au large; *keep* ~ se tenir éloigné (de, *from*); *stand* ~ s'abstenir; **a'loof·ness** réserve *f* (à l'égard de, *from*).

a·loud [ə'laud] à haute voix; tout haut.

alp [ælp] **1.** alpe *f*; **2.** *the* ~s *pl.* les Alpes *f/pl.*; **al·pen·stock** ['ælpinstɔk] alpenstock *m*; bâton *m* ferré.

al·pha·bet ['ælfəbit] alphabet *m*; **al-pha·bet·ic, al·pha·bet·i·cal** □ [~-'betik(l)] alphabétique.

Al·pine ['ælpain] alpin; alpestre (*climat etc.*); ☀ ~ *sun* rayons *m/pl.* ultraviolets; **al·pin·ist** ['~pinist] alpiniste *mf*.

al·read·y [ɔ:l'redi] déjà; dès à présent.

Al·sa·tian [æl'seiʃjən] **1.** alsacien (-ne *f*); **2.** Alsacien(ne *f*) *m*; (a. ~ *wolf-hound*) chien-loup (*pl.* chiens-loups) *m*.

al·so ['ɔ:lsou] aussi; encore; également; *équit.* ~ *ran* non classé.

al·tar ['ɔ:ltə] autel *m*; '**~-piece** retable *m*; tableau *m* d'autel.

al·ter ['ɔ:ltə] changer; *v/t.* modifier; remanier (*un texte*); *Am.* F châtrer (*un animal*); '**al·ter·a·ble** variable; modifiable; **al·ter·a·tion** [~'reiʃn] changement *m*, modification *f* (à, *to*); remaniement *m*.

al·ter·cate ['ɔ:ltə:keit] se quereller; **al·ter·ca·tion** dispute *f*, querelle *f*.

al·ter·nate 1. ['ɔ:ltə:neit] (faire) alterner; ⚡ *alternating current* courant *m* alternatif; **2.** □ [ɔ:l'tə:nit] alternatif (-ive *f*), alterné; *on* ~ *days* tous les deux jours; **3.** [~] *Am.* suppléant(e *f*) *m*; remplaçant(e *f*) *m*; **al·ter·na·tion** [~'neiʃn] alternation *f*; alternance *f*; **al'ter·na·tive** [~nətiv] **1.** □ alternatif (-ive *f*); second, autre; ⊕ *d'emprunt* (*route*); **2.** alternative *f*; autre parti *m* (*entre deux*); *I have no* ~ je n'ai pas le choix; **al·ter·na·tor** ⚡ ['~neitə] alternateur *m*.

al·though [ɔ:l'ðou] quoique, bien que.

al·tim·e·ter [æl'timitə] altimètre m.

al·ti·tude ['æltitjuːd] altitude f; élévation f; hauteur f; ~ recorder altitraceur m.   [contralto m.]

al·to ♪ ['æltou] alto m; femme:∫

al·to·geth·er [ɔːltə'geðə] 1. tout à fait, entièrement; en tout; somme toute, F tous ensemble; 2. F in the ~ tout nu, F à poil.

al·tru·ism ['æltruizm] altruisme m; 'al·tru·ist altruiste mf; al·tru'is·tic (~ally) altruiste.

al·um ⚗ ['æləm] alun m; a·lu·mi·na [ə'ljuːminə] alumine f; al·u·min·i·um [ælju'minjəm], Am. al·u·mi·num [ə'luːminəm] aluminium m; ~ acetate acétate m d'aluminium; a'lu·mi·nous [ə'ljuːminəs] alumineux (-euse f).

a·lum·nus [ə'lʌmnəs], pl. -ni [~nai] m; a'lum·na [~nə], pl. -nae [~niː] f élève mf (d'un collège); étudiant(e f) m (à une université); gradué(e f) m; Am. sp. ancien équipier m.

al·ve·o·lar [æl'viələ] alvéolaire.

al·ways ['ɔːlwəz] toujours; tout le temps; as ~ comme toujours, F comme d'habitude.

a·mal·gam [ə'mælgəm] amalgame m; a'mal·gam·ate [~meit] (s')amalgamer; fusionner; a·mal·gam·'a·tion amalgamation f; mélange m; ✝ fusion f.

a·man·u·en·sis [əmænju'ensis], pl. -ses [~siːz] secrétaire mf.

am·a·ranth ⚘ ['æmərænθ] amarante f.

a·mass [ə'mæs] amasser, accumuler.

am·a·teur ['æmətə:] amateur m; dilettante m; am·a'teur·ish d'amateur.

am·a·tive ['æmətiv], am·a·to·ry ['~təri] amoureux (-euse f); érotique; d'amour.

a·maze [ə'meiz] stupéfier, confondre; a'maze·ment stupéfaction f, stupeur f; a'maz·ing □ stupéfiant, étonnant.

Am·a·zon ['æməzn] Amazone f; fig. ♀ femme f hommasse; Am·a·zo·ni·an [~'zounjən] d'Amazone; géog. de l'Amazone.

am·bas·sa·dor [æm'bæsədə] ambassadeur m; am·bas·sa·do·ri·al [~'dɔːriəl] ambassadorial (-aux m/pl.), d'ambassadeur; am'bas·sa·dress [~dris] ambassadrice f.

am·ber ['æmbə] 1. ambre m; 2. ambré; jaune; d'ambre; am·ber·gris ['~griːs] ambre m gris.

am·bi·dex·trous □ ['æmbi'dekstrəs] ambidextre; fig. fourbe.

am·bi·ent ['æmbiənt] ambiant.

am·bi·gu·i·ty [æmbi'gjuiti] ambiguïté f; équivoque f; am'big·u·ous □ ambigu(ë f), équivoque; incertain; obscur.

am·bi·tion [æm'biʃn] ambition f (de, to); ~s pl. ambitions f/pl.; visées f/pl.; am'bi·tious □ ambitieux (-euse f) (de of, to); prétentieux (-euse f) (style).

am·ble ['æmbl] 1. amble m, entrepas m; 2. aller (à) l'amble; traquenarder; fig. marcher d'un pas tranquille; ~ up s'approcher d'un pas tranquille; 'am·bler flâneur (-euse f) m; cheval m ambleur.

am·bro·si·a [æm'brouziə] ambroisie f; am'bro·si·al □ ambrosiaque; fig. délicieux (-euse f).

am·bu·lance ['æmbjuləns] ambulance f; hôpital m ambulant; attr. sanitaire; ~ box infirmerie f portative; Am. F ~ chaser avoué qui guette les accidents pour faire poursuivre le responsable en dommages-intérêts; ~ man ambulancier m; ~ station poste m d'ambulance; poste m de secours; 'am·bu·lant ambulant.

am·bu·la·to·ry ['æmbjulətəri] 1. ambulant, mobile; ✚ ambulatoire; 2. promenoir m, préau m; eccl. déambulatoire m.

am·bus·cade [æmbəs'keid], am·bush ['æmbuʃ] 1. guet-apens (pl. guets-apens) m; embuscade f; lay (ou make) an ~ dresser une embuscade (à q., for s.o.); 2. v/t. attirer (q.) dans un piège; v/i. s'embusquer.

a·mel·io·rate [ə'miːliəreit] (s')améliorer; a·mel·io·ra·tion amélioration f.

a·men ['ɑː'men] amen; ainsi soit-il.

a·me·na·ble □ [ə'miːnəbl] soumis, docile (à, to); ⚖ justiciable.

a·mend [ə'mend] v/t. amender; réformer; ⚖ corriger; parl. modifier, amender; v/i. s'amender; a'mend·ment modification f; ⚖ rectification f; parl. amendement m (Am. a. article ajouté à la Constitution des É.-U.); a'mends [~dz] sg. réparation *f*; make ~ for réparer (*un tort*); compenser (*un défaut*).

a·men·i·ty [ə'mi:niti] *lieu*: aménité *f*; charme *m*; amabilité *f*; amenities *pl.* commodités *f/pl.* (*de l'existence*); civilités *f/pl.*

a·merce † [ə'mə:s] confisquer (*des terres*); mettre à l'amende.

A·mer·i·can [ə'merikən] **1.** américain; ~ cloth toile *f* cirée; ~ leather molesquine *f*; *Am.* ~ Legion association *f* des anciens combattants des deux guerres mondiales; *tourisme*: ~ plan pension *f* complète; **2.** Américain(e *f*) *m*; **a'mer·i·can·ism** américanisme *m*; **a'mer·i·can·ize** (s')américaniser.

Am·er·in·di·an [æmər'indjən], **Am·er·ind** ['æmərind] Indien *m* indigène de l'Amérique.

am·e·thyst *min.* ['æmiθist] améthyste *f*.

a·mi·a·bil·i·ty [eimjə'biliti] amabilité *f* (envers, to); **'a·mi·a·ble** □ aimable (envers, to).

am·i·ca·ble □ ['æmikəbl] amical (-aux *m/pl.*); bien disposé; **am·i·ca·ble·ness** disposition *f* amicale.

a·mid(st) [ə'mid(st)] *prp.* au milieu de; parmi; entre.

a·mid·ships ⚓ [ə'midʃips] par le travers, au milieu du navire.

a·miss [ə'mis] mal; de travers; mal à propos; take ~ prendre (*qch.*) en mauvaise part; it would not be ~ (*for him*) to il ne (lui) ferait pas mal de; what is ~ with him? qu'est-ce qu'il a?

am·i·ty ['æmiti] amitié *f*; concorde *f*.

am·me·ter ⚡ ['æmitə] ampèremètre *m*.

am·mo·ni·a [ə'mounjə] ammoniaque *f*; liquid ~ (solution *f* aqueuse d'ammoniaque *f*; F alcali *m* volatil); **am'mo·ni·ac** [~æk], **am·mo·ni·a·cal** [æmo'naiəkl] ammoniac (-aque *f*); see sal.

am·mu·ni·tion ⚔ [æmju'niʃn] **1.** munitions *f/pl.* de guerre; **2.** d'ordonnance; ~ boots chaussures *f/pl.* de munition; ~ bread pain *m* de guerre.

am·nes·ty ['æmnesti] **1.** amnistie *f*; **2.** amnistier.

a·moe·ba *zo.* [ə'mi:bə] amibe *f*.

a·mong(st) [ə'mʌŋ(st)] *prp.* parmi, entre; from ~ d'entre; be ~ être du nombre de; they have it ~ them ils l'ont en commun.

a·mor·al [æ'mɔrəl] amoral (-aux *m/pl.*).

am·o·rous □ ['æmərəs] amoureux (-euse *f*) (de, of); érotique (*poésie*).

a·mor·phous [ə'mɔ:fəs] *min.* amorphe; *fig.* sans forme; vague.

am·or·ti·za·tion [əmɔ:ti'zeiʃn] amortissement *m*; **am'or·tize** [~-taiz] amortir.

a·mount [ə'maunt] **1.** ~ to s'élever à, monter à; revenir à; se réduire à; **2.** somme *f*, montant *m*, total *m*; quantité *f*; valeur *f*; to the ~ of à la valeur de; jusqu'à concurrence de.

a·mour [ə'muə] intrigue *f* galante.

am·pere ⚡ ['æmpɛə] ampère *m*.

am·phet·a·mine [æm'fetəmi:n] amphétamine *f*.

am·phib·i·an ✈, *zo.* [æm'fibiən] **1.** amphibie *m*; **2.** = **am'phib·i·ous** □ amphibie.

am·phi·the·a·tre ['æmfiθiətə] amphithéâtre *m*.

am·ple □ ['æmpl] ample, large; vaste; gros(se *f*); grand; abondant; **'am·ple·ness** ampleur *f*; abondance *f*.

am·pli·fi·ca·tion [æmplifi'keiʃn] amplification *f* (*a. poét., a. phys.*); *gramm.* attribut: extension *f*; **am·pli·fi·er** ['~faiə] *radio*: amplificateur *m*; haut-parleur *m*; **am·pli·fy** ['~fai] *v/t.* amplifier (*a. radio*); développer; exagérer; *v/i.* discourir; *radio*: ~ing valve lampe *f* amplificatrice; **am·pli·tude** ['~tju:d] amplitude *f* (*a. phys.*); ampleur *f*.

am·poule ['æmpu:l] ampoule *f*.

am·pu·tate ✚ ['æmpjuteit] amputer, faire l'amputation de; **am·pu·ta·tion** amputation *f*.

a·muck [ə'mʌk]: run ~ tomber dans la folie meurtrière de l'amok; *fig.* faire les cent coups; run ~ at (*ou on ou against*) *fig.* s'emballer contre.

am·u·let ['æmjulit] amulette *f*.

a·muse [ə'mju:z] amuser, divertir, faire rire, égayer; distraire; **a'muse·ment** amusement *m*; divertissement *m*; distraction *f*; ~ arcade luna-park *m*; ~ park parc *m* d'attraction; fête *f* foraine; for ~ pour se distraire; pour (faire) rire; **a'mus·ing** □ amusant, divertissant (pour, to).

am·y·la·ceous [æmi'leiʃəs] amylacé.

an *gramm.* [æn; ən] *article*: un(e *f*).

an·a·bap·tist [ænə'bæptist] anabaptiste *mf*.

a·nach·ro·nism [ə'nækrənizm] anachronisme *m*.

a·n(a)e·mi·a [ə'niːmjə] anémie *f*; **a'n(a)e·mic** anémique.

an·(a)es·the·si·a [ænis'θiːzjə] anesthésie *f*; **an·(a)es·thet·ic** [ᴧ'θetik] (ᴧally) anesthésique (*a. su./m*); **a·n(a)es·the·tist** [æ'niːsθitist] anesthésiste *mf*; **a·n(a)es·the·tize** [æ'niːsθitaiz] anesthésier, insensibiliser.

an·a·log·ic, an·a·log·i·cal □ [ænə'lɔdʒik(l)] analogique; **a·nal·o·gous** [ə'næləgəs] analogue (à *with, to*); **a'nal·o·gy** analogie *f* (avec *with, to*; entre *between*).

an·a·lyse [ænəlaiz] analyser; faire l'analyse de (*a. gramm.*); **a·nal·y·sis** [ə'næləsis], *pl.* -ses [ᴧsiːz] analyse *f*; *compte*: dépouillement *m*; *gramm.* analyse *f* logique; **an·a·lyst** [ænəlist] analyste *mf*; *public* ᴧ analyste *m* officiel.

an·a·lyt·ic, an·a·lyt·i·cal □ [ænə'litik(l)] analytique.

an·ar·chic, an·ar·chi·cal □ [æ'nɑːkik(l)] anarchique; **an·ar·chism** [ænəkizm] anarchisme *m*; **an·arch·ist** [ænəkist] anarchiste *mf*; **'an·arch·y** anarchie *f*; désordre *m*.

a·nath·e·ma [ə'næθimə] anathème *m*; malédiction *f*; **a'nath·e·ma·tize** anathématiser, frapper d'anathème; F maudire.

an·a·tom·i·cal □ [ænə'tɔmikl] anatomique; **a·nat·o·mist** [ə'nætəmist] anatomiste *mf*; **a'nat·o·mize** anatomiser; disséquer; **a'nat·o·my** anatomie *f*; dissection *f*; F *fig.* squelette *m*.

an·ces·tor [ænsistə] ancêtre *m*; aïeul (*pl.* -eux) *m*; **an·ces·tral** [ᴧ'sestrəl] *biol.* ancestral (-aux *m/pl.*); héréditaire, de famille; **an·ces·tress** [ænsistris] ancêtre *f*; aïeule *f*; **'an·ces·try** race *f*; lignage *m*; aïeux *m/pl.*

an·chor [æŋkə] ⚓, *a. fig.* **1.** ancre *f*; *at* ᴧ à l'ancre; mouillé; **2.** *v/t.* ancrer, mettre à l'ancre; *v/i.* jeter l'ancre, mouiller; **'an·chor·age** ancrage *m*, mouillage *m*.

an·cho·ret [æŋkəret], **an·cho·rite** ['ᴧrait] anachorète *m*.

an·chor·man [æŋkə'mæn] *radio*, *télév.*: présentateur-réalisateur *m* (*pl.* présentateurs-réalisateurs).

an·cho·vy [æn'tʃouvi] anchois *m*.

an·cient ['einʃənt] **1.** ancien(ne *f*); antique; **2.** *the* ᴧs *pl.* les anciens *m/pl.* (*grecs et romains*); **'an·cient·ly** anciennement; jadis.

an·cil·lar·y [æn'siləri] *fig.* subordonné, ancillaire (à, *to*); accessoire (à, *to*).

and [ænd; ənd] et; *thousands* ᴧ *thousands* des milliers et des milliers; *there are flowers* ᴧ *flowers* il y a des fleurs et encore des fleurs; *try* ᴧ *take it* tâchez de le prendre.

and·i·ron [ændaiən] landier *m*; chenet *m*.

an·ec·do·tal [ænek'doutl], **an·ec·dot·i·cal** [ᴧ'dɔtikl] □ anecdotique; **an·ec·dote** [ænikdout] anecdote *f*.

an·e·lec·tric *phys.* [æni'lektrik] anélectrique.

an·e·mom·e·ter [æni'mɔmitə] anémomètre *m*.

a·nem·o·ne [ə'neməni] anémone *f*.

an·er·oid [ænərɔid] (baromètre *m*) anéroïde *m*.

a·new [ə'njuː] de nouveau; à nouveau.

an·gel ['eindʒl] ange *m*; **an·gel·ic, an·gel·i·cal** □ [æn'dʒelik(l)] angélique.

an·ger [æŋgə] **1.** colère *f*; emportement *m* (contre, *at*); **2.** irriter, mettre (*q.*) en colère.

an·gi·na ⚕ [æn'dʒainə] angine *f*; ᴧ *pectoris* angine *f* de poitrine.

an·gle [æŋgl] **1.** angle *m*; *fig.* point *m* de vue; **2.** pêcher à la ligne; ᴧ *for* F quêter; **'an·gler** pêcheur (-euse *f*) *m* à la ligne.

An·gles [æŋglz] *pl.* Angles *m/pl.*

An·gli·can [æŋglikən] **1.** anglican; *Am. a.* anglais; **2.** anglican(e *f*) *m*.

An·gli·cism [æŋglisizm] anglicisme *m*; idiotisme *m* anglais.

an·gling [æŋgliŋ] pêche *f* à la ligne.

An·glo-Sax·on [æŋglou'sæksn] **1.** Anglo-Saxon(ne *f*) *m*; **2.** anglo-saxon(ne *f*).

an·go·ra [æŋ'gɔːrə] (laine *f*) angora *m*; (*a.* ᴧ *cat*) (chat *m*) angora *m*.

an·gry [æŋgri] fâché, irrité, courroucé (contre *q.*, *with s.o.*; de qch. *about s.th.*); ⚕ irrité, enflammé.

an·guish [æŋgwiʃ] angoisse *f*; douleur *f*; *fig.* supplice *m*.

an·gu·lar [æŋgjulə] angulaire; anguleux (-euse *f*) (*visage*); *fig.* maigre, décharné; ᴧ *point* ⚭ sommet *m*; **an·gu·lar·i·ty** [ᴧ'læriti] angu-

larité *f*; *fig.* caractère *m* anguleux.
an·hy·drous ⚗ [æn'haidrəs] anhydre; sec (sèche *f*), tapé (*fruits*).
an·ile ['einail] de vieille femme.
an·i·line ⚗ ['ænili:n] aniline *f*; ∼
dyes pl. colorants *m/pl.* d'aniline.
an·i·mad·ver·sion [ænimæd'və:ʃn]
censure *f*, blâme *m*; **an·i·mad·vert**
[∼'və:t] critiquer, censurer, blâmer
(qch., *on s.th.*).
an·i·mal ['æniməl] **1.** animal *m*;
bête *f*; **2.** animal (-aux *m/pl.*); *Brit.* ∼
home asyle *m* pour animaux; *zo.* ∼
kingdom règne *m* animal; ∼ *lover*
ami(e *f*) *m* des animaux; *Am.* ∼ *shelter*
asyle *m* pour animaux; ∼ *spirits pl.*
verve *f*, entrain *m*; **an·i·mal·cule**
[∼'mælkju:l] animalcule *m*; **an·i·**
mal·ism [∼'məlizm] animalité *f*;
biol. animalisme *m*; **an·i·mal·i·ty**
animalité *f*.
an·i·mate 1. ['ænimeit] animer;
stimuler; mouvementer; **2.** [∼'mit],
usu. **an·i·mat·ed** [∼'meitid] animé
(*a. fig.*); doué de vie; ∼ *cartoon*
dessins *m/pl.* animés.
an·i·ma·tion [æni'meiʃn] animation
f; vivacité *f*; chaleur *f*; entrain *m*;
stimulation *f*.
an·i·mos·i·ty [æni'mɔsiti], *a.* **an·i·**
mus ['æniməs] animosité *f*.
an·ise ⚘ ['ænis] anis *m*; **an·i·seed**
['∼si:d] (graine *f* d')anis *m*; *attr.* à
l'anis.   [astragale *m.*⟩
an·kle ['æŋkl] cheville *f*; ∼ *bone*⟩
an·klet ['æŋklit] bracelet *m* de
jambe; manille *f* (de forçat); F
socquette *f*.
an·nals ['ænlz] *pl.* annales *f/pl.*; *fig.*
archives *f/pl.*
an·neal ⊕ [ə'ni:l] recuire, adoucir
(*un métal etc.*); *fig.* tremper.
an·nex 1. [ə'neks] annexer (à, *to*);
ajouter; joindre; ∼ *to* poser (*des
conditions*) à; **2.** ['æneks] annexe *f*;
dépendance *f*; adjonction *f*; **an·**
nex'a·tion annexion *f* (de, *of*);
mainmise *f* (sur, *of*).
an·ni·hi·late [ə'naiəleit] anéantir;
annihiler; *see annul*; **an·ni·hi·la·**
tion anéantissement *m*; annihilation *f*; *see annulment.*
an·ni·ver·sa·ry [æni'və:səri] anniversaire *m*.
an·no·tate ['ænouteit] annoter; commenter; accompagner de remarques; **an·no'ta·tion** annotation *f*;
commentaire *m*; note *f*.

an·nounce [ə'nauns] annoncer;
faire connaître; **an'nounce·ment**
annonce *f*; avis *m*; faire-part *m/inv.*;
an'nounc·er *radio*: speaker *m*.
an·noy [ə'nɔi] contrarier; gêner;
molester; vexer; **an'noy·ance** contrariété *f*; chagrin *m*; ennui *m*; **an-**
'noyed contrarié, ennuyé, vexé;
an'noy·ing □ contrariant, ennuyeux (-euse *f*), ennuyant.
an·nu·al ['ænjuəl] **1.** □ annuel(le *f*)
(*a.* ⚘); ∼ *ring* ⚘ couche *f* annuelle;
2. ⚘ plante *f* annuelle; *livre*: annuaire *m*.
an·nu·i·tant [ə'njuitənt] rentier
(-ère *f*) *m*; **an'nu·i·ty** rente *f* (annuelle); ✝ (*a.* ∼ *bond*) obligation *f*;
see life.
an·nul [ə'nʌl] annuler, résilier; dissoudre (*un mariage*); abroger (*une
loi*).
an·nu·lar □ ['ænjulə] annulaire.
an·nul·ment [ə'nʌlmənt] annulation *f*, résiliation *f*; dissolution *f*;
abrogation *f*.
an·nun·ci·a·tion [ənʌnsi'eiʃn] proclamation *f*, annonce *f*; *eccl.* Annonciation *f*; **an'nun·ci·a·tor**
[∼ʃieitə] annonciateur *m*; *Am.* bouton *m* (*de sonnerie*).
an·ode ⚡ ['ænoud] **1.** anode *f*;
2. de plaque; ∼ *potential* tension *f*
de plaque.
an·o·dyne ⚕ ['ænodain] anodin (*a.
su./m*); calmant (*a. su./m*).
a·noint [ə'nɔint] *surt. eccl.* oindre;
sacrer; *fig.* graisser.
a·nom·a·lous □ [ə'nɔmələs] ano-
mal (-aux *m/pl.*); F exception-
nel(le *f*), anormal (-aux *m/pl.*),
irrégulier (-ère *f*); **a'nom·a·ly**
anomalie *f*.
a·non [ə'nɔn] bientôt, tout à l'heure;
ever and ∼ de temps en temps.
an·o·nym·i·ty [ænə'nimiti] anonymat *m*, anonyme *m*; **a·non·y·mous**
□ [ə'nɔniməs] anonyme; inconnu.
an·oth·er [ə'nʌðə] encore un(e);
un(e) autre; un(e) second(e); *just
such* ∼ un autre du même genre; F *tell
me ou us* ∼! à d'autres!, tu ne le crois
pas toi-même!
an·swer ['ɑ:nsə] **1.** *v/t.* répondre
(qch.) (à q., *s.o.*); faire réponse à;
remplir (*un but*); obéir (*à la barre*);
répondre à (*une accusation*); ∼ *the bell*
(*ou door*) aller *ou* venir ouvrir; *v/i.*
répondre (à q., *to s.o.*; à qch., *to s.th.*;

à une question, *to a question*); ne pas réussir; F ~ *back* répliquer, répondre avec impertinence; *don't* ~ *back!* ne réponds pas!; ~ *for* être responsable de; répondre de (*q.*), se porter garant de (*q., qch.*); ~ *to the name of* s'appeler; **2.** réponse *f* (à, *to*); ⚡ solution *f*; ⚡ réplique *f*, réfutation *f*; **'an·swer·a·ble** □ responsable; comptable.

ant [ænt] fourmi *f*.

an't [ɑ:nt] F = *are not, am not*; *sl. ou prov.* = *is not.*

an·tag·o·nism [æn'tægənizm] antagonisme *m* (entre, de *between*); opposition *f* (à, *to*; avec, *with*); **an'tag·o·nist** adversaire *m*; antagoniste *m*; **an·tag·o'nis·tic** (~*ally*) opposé, contraire (à, *to*); adverse; **an'tag·o·nize** éveiller l'hostilité de (*q.*); s'opposer à; contrarier (*une force*).

ant·arc·tic [ænt'ɑ:ktik] antarctique; ♀ *Circle* cercle *m* polaire antarctique.

an·te *Am.* ['ænti] *poker:* **1.** première mise *f*; **2.** F (*usu.* ~ *up*) *v/t., a. v/i.* ouvrir (le jeu); *v/i. fig.* donner son obole.

an·te·ced·ence [ænti'si:dəns] priorité *f*; antériorité *f*; *astr.* antécédence *f*; **an·te'ced·ent 1.** □ antécédent; antérieur (à, *to*); **2.** antécédent *m* (*a. gramm.*); thème *m*; *his* ~*s pl.* les ancêtres *m/pl.*; son passé *m*.

an·te·cham·ber ['æntitʃeimbə] antichambre *f*.

an·te·date ['ænti'deit] antidater (*un document*); précéder, venir avant.

an·te·di·lu·vi·an ['æntidi'lu:vjən] antédiluvien(ne *f*) (*a. su./mf*).

an·te·lope *zo.* ['æntiloup] antilope *f*.

an·te·na·tal [ænti'neitl] prénatal.

an·ten·na [æn'tenə], *pl.* **-nae** [~ni:] *zo., radio, télév.:* antenne *f*; limaçon: corne *f*.

an·te·ri·or [æn'tiəriə] antérieur (à, *to*).

an·te·room ['æntirum] antichambre *f*, vestibule *m*.

an·them ['ænθəm] *eccl.* antienne *f*, motet *m*; hymne *m*.

ant-hill ['ænthil] fourmilière *f*.

an·thol·o·gy [æn'θɔlədʒi] *fig.* anthologie *f*, florilège *m*.

an·thra·cite *min.* ['ænθrəsait] anthracite *m*; F houille *f* sèche; **an·thrax** ['ænθræks] *vét.* charbon *m*.

an·thro·poid ['ænθrəpoid] anthropoïde (*a. su./m*); **an·thro·po·log·i-**cal □ [ænθrəpə'lɔdʒikəl] anthropologique; **an·thro·pol·o·gist** [~'pɔlədʒist] anthropologiste *mf*, -logue *mf*; **an·thro'pol·o·gy** [~dʒi] anthropologie *f*; **an·thro·poph·a·gy** [ænθrə'pɔfədʒi] anthropophagie *f*.

anti... [ænti] *préf.* anti-; anté-; contre-.

an·ti-air·craft ['ænti'ɛəkrɑ:ft]: ~ *alarm* alerte *f* (aux avions); ~ *defence* défense *f* contre avions; D.C.A.; ~ *gun* canon *m* antiaérien.

an·ti·bi·ot·ic ⚕ ['æntibai'ɔtik] antibiotique (*a. su./m*).

an·tic ['æntik] **1.** □ † grotesque; **2.** bouffonnerie *f*, singerie *f*; ~*s pl.* gambades *f/pl.*

An·ti·christ ['æntikraist] Antéchrist *m*.

an·tic·i·pate [æn'tisipeit] anticiper (*un paiement; sur les événements*); devancer; prévoir; s'attendre à; se promettre; escompter (*un résultat*); **an·tic·i·pa·tion** anticipation *f*; prévision *f*; attente *f*; expectative *f*; *payment by* ~ paiement *m* par anticipation; *in* ~ d'avance; *Thanking you in* ~ Avec mes *ou* nos remerciements anticipés; **an'tic·i·pa·to·ry** [~peitəri] anticipé, anticipatif (-ive *f*); par anticipation.

an·ti·cler·i·cal ['ænti'klerikəl] anticlérical.

an·ti·cli·max ['ænti'klaimæks] anticlimax *m*.

an·ti·cor·ro·sive a·gent ['æntikə-'rousiv'eidʒənt] antirouille *m*.

an·ti·cy·clone *météor.* ['ænti'saikloun] anticyclone *m*.

an·ti·daz·zle *mot.* ['ænti'dæzl] antiaveuglant; ~ *headlights pl.* phares-code *m/pl.*

an·ti·dote ['æntidout] antidote *m*, contrepoison *m* (de, contre *against*, *for, to*).

an·ti·freeze *mot.* ['ænti'fri:z] antigel *m*.

an·ti·fric·tion ['ænti'frikʃn] antifriction *f*; *attr.* ⊕ antifriction.

an·ti·ha·lo *phot.* ['ænti'heilou] antihalo *m* (*a. su./m*).

an·ti·ic·er ⊕, ✈ ['ænti'aisə] antigivreur *m*.

an·ti·knock *mot.* ['ænti'nɔk] (produit *m*) antidétonant.

an·ti·mo·ny *min.* ['æntiməni] antimoine *m*.

an·tip·a·thy [æn'tipəθi] antipathie *f*

apology

(pour, contre *against*, *to*); aversion *f* (pour q., *against* s.th.).

an·tip·o·dal [æn'tipədl] situé aux antipodes; **an·ti·pode** ['~poud], *pl.* **an·tip·o·des** [~'tipədi:z] chose *f* diamétralement opposée; rebours *m*; ~s *pl.* *géog.* antipodes *m*/*pl.*

an·ti·pol·lu·tion de·vice ['æntipə-'luʃəndi'vais] équipement *m* anti-pollution.

An·ti·py·rin [ænti'paiərin] antipyrine *f*, analgésine *f*.

an·ti·quar·i·an □ [ænti'kwɛəriən] archéologique, de l'antique; **an·ti·quar·y** ['~kwəri] archéologue *m*; amateur *m* d'antiquités; antiquaire *m*; **an·ti·quat·ed** ['~kweitid] vieilli; désuet (-ète *f*); suranné, démodé. **an·tique** [æn'ti:k] **1.** □ antique; ancien(ne *f*); suranné; **2.** antiquité *f*; objet *m* antique; **an·tiq·ui·ty** [~'tikwiti] antiquité *f* (*romaine etc.*); ancienneté *f*; *antiquities pl.* antiquités *f*/*pl.*

an·ti·rust ['ænti'rʌst] antirouille *m*.

an·ti·sem·ite [ænti'si:mait] antisémite (*a. su.*/*mf*); **an·ti-Se·mit·ic** ['~si'mitik] antisémite; **an·ti-sem·i·tism** [~'semitizm] antisémitisme *m*.

an·ti·sep·tic [ænti'septik] antiseptique (*a. su.*/*m*).

an·ti·skid *mot.* ['ænti'skid] anti-dérapant.

an·tith·e·sis [æn'tiθisis], *pl.* -ses [~si:z] antithèse *f*; contraire *m*; **an·ti·thet·ic**, **an·ti·thet·i·cal** □ [~'θetik/əl] antithétique.

ant·ler ['æntlə] *cerf etc.*: andouiller *m*; ~s *pl.* bois *m* (*pl.*).

an·to·nym *gramm.* ['æntənim] antonyme *m*.

A num·ber 1 *Am.* F *see* A 1.

a·nus *anat.* ['einəs] anus *m*.

an·vil ['ænvil] enclume *f*; *fig.* chantier *m*, métier *m*.

anx·i·e·ty [æŋ'zaiəti] inquiétude *f*; soucis *m*/*pl.*; *fig.* désir *m* (de *inf.*; *to inf.*); *fig.* sollicitude *f* (pour, for); ✤ anxiété *f*; ~ *dream* rêve *m* anxieux.

anx·ious □ ['æŋkʃəs] inquiet (-ète *f*), soucieux (-euse *f*) (sur, de, au sujet de *about*); désireux (-euse *f*) (de *inf.*, to *inf.*); impatient (de *inf.*, to *inf.*).

an·y ['eni] **1.** *adj.*, *a.* *pron.* un(e *f*); tout(e *f*); n'importe quel(le *f*);

n'importe lequel (laquelle *f*); *are there* ~ *nails?* y a-t-il des clous?; *not* ~ aucun, nul; **2.** *adv.* *ne se traduit pas d'ordinaire*; '~·**bod·y**, '~·**one** quelqu'un(e *f*); n'importe qui; tout le monde; quiconque; (*avec négation*) personne; *not* ~ personne; '~·**how** **1.** *cj.* en tout cas; **2.** *adv.* n'importe comment; '~·**thing** quelque chose; (*avec négation*) rien; ~ *but* rien moins que; '~·**way** *see* anyhow; '~·**where** n'importe où.

a·pace [ə'peis] vite; à grands pas.

a·part [ə'pɑ:t] à part; de côté; écarté; ~ *from* en dehors de; hormis que; *joking* ~ plaisanterie à part; *set* ~ *for* mettre de côté pour; réserver à; **a'part·ment** salle *f*, chambre *f*; pièce *f*; *Am.* appartement *m*; ~s *pl.* logement *m*; *Am.* ~ *hotel* hôtel *m* meublé avec *ou* sans service; *Am.* ~ *house* maison *f* de rapport.

ap·a·thet·ic [æpə'θetik] (~ally) indifférent; '**ap·a·thy** apathie *f*, indifférence *f*; nonchalance *f*.

ape [eip] **1.** (grand) singe *m*; *Am.* F *go* ~ devenir fou (folle *f*); **2.** imiter, singer.

a·peak ⚓ [ə'pi:k] à pic, dérapé (*ancre*).

a·pe·ri·ent [ə'piəriənt] **1.** laxatif (-ive *f*); relâchant; **2.** laxatif *m*; relâchant *m*.

ap·er·ture ['æpətjuə] ouverture *f*.

a·pex ['eipeks], *pl.* '**a·pex·es**, **a·pi·ces** ['eipisi:z] sommet *m*; *fig.* apogée *m*.

aph·o·rism ['æfərizm] aphorisme *m*; **aph·o'ris·tic** (~ally) aphoristique.

a·pi·ar·y ['eipiəri] rucher *m*; **a·pi·cul·ture** ['~kʌltʃə] apiculture *f*.

a·piece [ə'pi:s] chacun(e *f*); la pièce.

ap·ish □ ['eipiʃ] simiesque; imitateur (-trice *f*).

A·poc·ry·pha *bibl.* [ə'pɔkrifə] *pl.* *les Apocryphes m*/*pl.*; **a'poc·ry·phal** apocryphe.

ap·o·gee *astr.* ['æpodʒi:] apogée *m*.

a·pol·o·get·ic [əpɔlə'dʒetik] **1.** (~ally) d'excuse; *eccl.* apologétique (*livre*); **2.** *eccl.* *usu.* ~s *pl.* apologétique *f*; **a'pol·o·gist** apologiste *m*, défenseur *m*; **a'pol·o·gize** s'excuser (de, for; auprès de, to); **a'pol·o·gy** excuses *f*/*pl.*; apologie *f*, justification *f* (de, *for*); *fig.* semblant *m* (de, *for*); F (mauvais) substitut *m* (de, *for*); **make an ~** présenter des excuses.

ap·o·plec·tic, ap·o·plec·ti·cal □ [æpə'plektik(l)] apoplectique (*personne*); d'apoplexie; **'ap·o·plex·y** apoplexie *f*; congestion *f* cérébrale.

a·pos·ta·sy [ə'pɔstəsi] apostasie *f*; **a'pos·tate** [~stit] apostat (*a. su./m*); relaps(e *f*) *m*; **a'pos·ta·tize** [~stətaiz] apostasier (qch., *from s.th.*).

a·pos·tle [ə'pɔsl] apôtre *m*; **ap·os·tol·ic, ap·os·tol·i·cal** □ [æpə-'stɔlik(l)] apostolique.

a·pos·tro·phe *gramm., a. rhétorique*: [ə'pɔstrəfi] apostrophe *f*; **a'pos·tro·phize** apostropher; *gramm.* mettre une apostrophe à.

a·poth·e·car·y † [ə'pɔθikəri] apothicaire *m*, pharmacien *m*.

a·poth·e·o·sis [əpɔθi'ousis] apothéose *f*.

ap·pal [ə'pɔːl] épouvanter; consterner; **ap'pall·ing** épouvantable, effroyable.

ap·pa·ra·tus [æpə'reitəs], *pl.* -tus·es [~təsiz] appareil *m*, dispositif *m*; attirail *m*; **~ exercises** *pl.* gymnastique *f* aux agrès.

ap·par·el [ə'pærəl]: **wearing ~** vêtements *m/pl.*, habits *m/pl.*

ap·par·ent □ [ə'pærənt] apparent, évident, manifeste; *see* **heir**; **ap·pa·ri·tion** [æpə'riʃn] apparition *f*; fantôme *m*, revenant *m*.

ap·peal [ə'piːl] **1.** faire appel (à, *to*); demander (qch., *for s.th.*; à, *to*); interjeter appel; se pourvoir en cassation; **~ to** attirer, séduire; ⚖ invoquer l'aide de (*la loi*); appeler de (*un jugement*); *see* **country**; **2.** appel *m*; recours *m*; *fig.* prière *f*, supplication *f*; attrait *m*; ⚖ **court of ~** cour *f* d'appel; **lodge** *ou* **file an ~** interjeter appel, se pourvoir en appel; **notice of ~** intimation *f*; **right of ~** droit *m* d'appel; **~ for mercy** demande *f* de grâce; **ap'peal·ing** □ suppliant; émouvant; sympathique.

ap·pear [ə'piə] paraître (*a. livres*); se montrer; se présenter; apparaître; sembler; ⚖ comparaître; **~ for** plaider pour (*q.*); **ap'pear·ance** apparition *f*; entrée *f*; livre: parution *f*; apparence *f*; ⚖ comparution *f*; **~s** *pl.* dehors *m/pl.*; **keep up** (*ou* **save**) **~s** sauver *ou* garder les apparences; **make one's ~** débuter;

paraître; **put in an ~** faire acte de présence; **to all ~s** selon toute apparence.

ap·pease [ə'piːz] apaiser, calmer (*l'agitation, une douleur*); assouvir (*la faim*); **ap'pease·ment** apaisement *m*; assouvissement *m*; **~ policy** politique *f* d'apaisement.

ap·pel·lant [ə'pelənt] appelant(e *f*) (*a. su./mf*); **ap'pel·late** [~lit] d'appel; **ap·pel·la·tion** [æpe'leiʃn] appellation *f*, nom *m*, désignation *f*, titre *m*; **ap'pel·la·tive** *gramm.* [ə'pelətiv] (*a.* **~ name**) nom *m* commun *ou* générique.

ap·pend [ə'pend] attacher, joindre; apposer (*une signature, un sceau*); annexer (*un document*); **ap'pend·age** accessoire *m*, apanage *m* (de, *to*); annexe *f*; *anat.* appendice *m*; **ap·pen·dec·to·my** *Am.* [~-'dektəmi] appendicectomie *f*; **ap·pen·di·ci·tis** [~di'saitis] appendicite *f*; **ap'pen·dix** [~diks], *pl.* -dix·es, -di·ces [~disiːz] appendice *m*; ⚕ appendice *m* (vermiculaire).

ap·per·tain [æpə'tein]: **~ to** appartenir à; incomber à; convenir à.

ap·pe·tence, ap·pe·ten·cy ['æpitəns(i)] (*for, after, of*) appétence *f*; désir *m* (de); convoitise *f* (pour).

ap·pe·tite ['æpitait] (*for*) appétit *m* (de); *fig.* désir *m* (de), soif *f* (de); **~ suppressant** coupe-faim *m/inv.*, anorexigène *m*.

ap·pe·tiz·er ['æpitaizə] apéritif *m*; **'ap·pe·tiz·ing** alléchant, appétissant.

ap·plaud [ə'plɔːd] *v/i.* applaudir, battre des mains; *v/t.* applaudir (*q.; aux efforts de q.*).

ap·plause [ə'plɔːz] applaudissements *m/pl.*; approbation *f*.

ap·ple ['æpl] pomme *f*; **'~-cart** voiture *f* à bras; F **upset s.o.'s ~** bouleverser les plans de q.; **~ pie** tourte *f* aux pommes; **'~-pie**: F **in ~ order** rangé en ordre parfait; **'~-pol·ish** *sl.* flatter, flagorner (*q.*); **'~-sauce** compote *f* de pommes; *Am. sl.* flagornerie *f*; *int.* chansons!; **'~-tree** pommier *m*.

ap·pli·ance [ə'plaiəns] appareil *m*; instrument *m*; dispositif *m*; **~s** *pl.* attirail *m*.

ap·pli·ca·bil·i·ty [æplikə'biliti] applicabilité *f*; **'ap·pli·ca·ble** (à, *to*) applicable; approprié; **'ap·pli·cant**

candidat(e f) m (à, for); postulant(e f) m (de, for); **ap·pli'ca·tion** (to) application f (à, sur); apposition f (à); frein: serrage m; assiduité f; demande f (de, for); sollicitation f (de, for); ~ form bulletin m de demande; ~ for external ~ pour l'usage externe; (letter of) ~ (lettre f de) demande f d'emploi; make an ~ formuler ou faire une demande.

ap·ply [ə'plai] v/t. (to) appliquer (qch. sur qch.); faire l'application de (qch. à qch.); coller (sur); serrer (le frein); mettre en pratique; affecter (un paiement) (à); ~ o.s. to s'attacher à; v/i. (to) s'appliquer (à); s'adresser (à); avoir recours (à); ~ for poser sa candidature à, solliciter (qch.); applied science science f appliquée ou expérimentale.

ap·point [ə'point] nommer (q. gouverneur, s.o. governor); désigner(pour inf., to inf.); fixer, assigner (l'heure, un endroit); arrêter (un jour); prescrire (que, that); well ~ed bien installé, bien équipé; **ap'point·ment** rendez-vous m; entrevue f; nomination f; désignation f; charge f, emploi m; ~s pl. aménagement m, installation f; équipement m; † émoluments m/pl.; ~ book agenda m, calepin m; by special ~ to (fournisseur) breveté ou attitré de.

ap·por·tion [ə'po:ʃn] répartir; assigner (à, to); **ap'por·tion·ment** partage m, répartition f; allocation f.

ap·po·site □ ['æpəzit] approprié (à, to); juste; be ~ to convenir à; **'ap·po·site·ness** justesse f, à-propos m.   [tion f.]

ap·po·si·tion [æpə'ziʃn] apposi-

ap·prais·al [ə'preizl] évaluation f; **ap·praise** [~'preiz] priser, estimer; **ap'praise·ment** évaluation f, estimation f; **ap'prais·er** estimateur m, priseur m.

ap·pre·ci·a·ble □ [ə'pri:ʃəbl] appréciable; sensible; **ap'pre·ci·ate** [~ʃieit] v/t. apprécier, faire cas de; estimer; évaluer; hausser la valeur de; v/i. augmenter de valeur; **ap·pre·ci·a'tion** appréciation f (de, of); estimation f (de, of); évaluation f; amélioration f; hausse f; plus-value f; **ap'pre·ci·a·tive** □ [~ətiv], **ap'pre·ci·a·to·ry** [~ətəri] appréciateur (-trice f); sensible (à, of); be ~ of apprécier; être sensible à.

ap·pre·hend [æpri'hend] arrêter; saisir; poét. comprendre; poét. redouter; **ap·pre·hen·si·ble** □ [~'hensəbl] appréhensible; perceptible; **ap·pre'hen·sion** arrestation f; prise f de corps; perception f; compréhension f; appréhension f, crainte f; **ap·pre'hen·sive** □ perceptif (-ive f); timide, craintif (-ive f); be ~ redouter (qch., of s.th.); craindre (qch., of s.th.; pour q., for s.o.; que, that).

ap·pren·tice [ə'prentis] 1. apprenti(e f) m; 2. placer en apprentissage (chez, to); ~d to en apprentissage chez; **ap'pren·tice·ship** [~tiʃip] apprentissage m.

ap·prise [ə'praiz]: ~ s.o. of s.th. apprendre qch. à q.; prévenir q. de qch.   [condition.]

ap·pro † ['æprou]: on ~ à l'essai, à

ap·proach [ə'proutʃ] 1. v/i. (s')approcher; fig. approcher (de, to); ⚓ atterrir; v/t. (s')approcher de; aborder (q.); entrer en communication avec (q.); fig. faire une démarche auprès de (q.) (au sujet de, about); fig. s'attaquer à, aborder (un problème); 2. approche f; approches f/pl.; venue f; voie f d'accès; accès m; abord m; fig. rapprochement m; **ap'proach·a·ble** accessible; abordable.

ap·pro·ba·tion [æpro'beiʃn] approbation f; consentement m.

ap·pro·pri·ate 1. [ə'prouprieit] (s')approprier; s'emparer de; parl. affecter, consacrer (à to, for); 2. □ [~iit] (to) approprié (à); convenable, propre (à); à propos; **ap·pro·pri·a·tion** appropriation f; crédit m, budget m; affectation f de fonds; parl. ♀ Committee commission f du budget.

ap·prov·a·ble [ə'pru:vəbl] louable; **ap'prov·al** approbation f; ratification f; on ~ à l'essai, à l'examen; **ap'prove** approuver; ratifier; (a. ~ of) agréer; ~ o.s. faire ses preuves; **ap'proved** □ autorisé; approuvé; **ap'prov·er** ⚖ complice m qui dénonce ses camarades.

ap·prox·i·mate 1. [ə'prɔksimeit] (se) rapprocher (de, to); 2. □ [~mit] rapproché, proche, voisin (de, to); approximatif (-ive f); **ap'prox·i·mate·ly** [~mitli] environ, à peu près; **ap·prox·i·ma·tion** [~'meiʃn] rapprochement m; approximation f; **ap·prox·i·ma·tive** □ [~mətiv] approximatif (-ive f).

ap·pur·te·nance [ə'pə:tinəns] usu. ~s pl. accessoires m/pl., attirail m.

a·pri·cot ♀ ['eiprikɔt] abricot m; arbre: abricotier m.

A·pril ['eiprəl] avril m; make an ~-fool of s.o. faire un poisson d'avril à q.

a·pron ['eiprən] tablier m (a. mot.); théâ. avant-scène f; '~-string cordon m de tablier; fig. be tied to her ~s être pendu à ses jupes; être tenu en laisse.

ap·ro·pos ['æprəpou] 1. à propos (de, of), opportun; 2. à-propos m.

apt □ [æpt] juste, fin; heureux (-euse f) (expression etc.); enclin (à, to); susceptible (de, to); habile (à, at); intelligent; apte, propre (à, to); ~ to take fire sujet à prendre feu; qui prend feu facilement; **ap·ti·tude** ['~titju:d], **'apt·ness** justesse f, à-propos m; penchant m, tendance f (à, to); talent m (pour, for); aptitude test test m d'aptitude.

aq·ua for·tis ⚗ ['ækwɔ'fɔ:tis] eau-forte (pl. eaux-fortes) f.

aq·ua·lung ['ækwəlʌŋ] scaphandre m autonome.

aq·ua·ma·rine min. [ækwəmə'ri:n] aigue-marine (pl. aigues-marines) f.

aq·ua·plane ['ækwəplein] 1. aquaplane m; 2. faire de l'aquaplane; mot. faire de l'aquaplaning; **aq·ua·plan·ing** mot. [~'pleiniŋ] aquaplaning m.

aq·ua·relle [ækwə'rel] aquarelle f.

a·quar·i·um [ə'kwɛəriəm], pl. **-ums, -i·a** [~iə] aquarium m.

A·quar·i·us astr. [ə'kwɛəriəs] le Verseau.

a·quat·ic [ə'kwætik] 1. aquatique; ~ sports see aquatics; 2. plante f ou animal m aquatique; **a'quat·ics** pl. sports m/pl. nautiques.

aq·ua·tint ['ækwətint] aquatinte f.

aq·ue·duct ['ækwidʌkt] aqueduc m.

a·que·ous ['eikwiəs] □ aqueux (-euse f); géol. sédimentaire.

aq·ui·line nose ['ækwilain'nouz] nez m aquilin ou busqué.

Ar·ab ['ærəb] Arabe mf; (cheval m) arabe m; sl. street ⚥ gamin m des rues; gavroche m; **ar·a·besque** [~'besk] 1. usu. pl. arabesque f, -s f/pl.; 2. arabesque, dans le style ara-

be; **A·ra·bi·an** [ə'reibjən] 1. arabe; The ~ Nights les Mille et Une Nuits; 2. Arabe mf; **Ar·a·bic** ['ærəbik] 1. arabe; gum ⚥ gomme f arabique; 2. ling. arabe m.

ar·a·ble ['ærəbl] 1. labourable; 2. (ou ~ land) terre f arable ou labourable.

a·rach·nid [ə'ræknid] arachnide m.

ar·bi·ter ['ɑ:bitə] arbitre m (a. fig.); **ar·bi·trage** ✝ [ɑ:bi'trɑ:ʒ] arbitrage m; **'ar·bi·tral tri'bu·nal** tribunal m arbitral; **ar'bit·ra·ment** [~trəmənt] arbitrage m; **'ar·bi·trar·i·ness** arbitraire m; **'ar·bi·trar·y** □ arbitraire; **ar·bi·trate** ['~treit] arbitrer (a. v/i.); juger; trancher (un différend); **ar·bi'tra·tion** arbitrage m; procédure f arbitrale; ~ court tribunal m arbitral; ✝ ~ of exchange arbitrage m du change; **'ar·bi·tra·tor** ['~ treitə] ⚖ arbitre m; arbitre-juge m; **ar·bi·tress** ['~tris] femme: arbitre m.

ar·bor ['ɑ:bə] ⊕, roue, meule: arbre m; tour: mandrin m; ⚥ Day Am. jour m où on est tenu de planter un arbre; **ar·bo·re·al** [ɑ:'bɔ:riəl], **ar·'bo·re·ous** [~riəs] d'arbre(s); arboricole (animal); **ar·bo·res·cent** □ [ɑ:bo·'resnt] arborescent; **ar·bo·ri·cul·ture** ['ɑ:borikʌltʃə] arboriculture f.

ar·bour ['ɑ:bə] tonnelle f, charmille f; vine ~ treille f.

arc ⚡, astr., etc. [ɑ:k] arc m (⚡ électrique); **ar·cade** [ɑ:'keid] arcade f, -s f/pl.; galerie f, -s f/pl.; passage m.

ar·ca·num [ɑ:'keinəm], pl. **-na** [~nə] arcane m, secret m.

arch¹ [ɑ:tʃ] 1. surt. ⚓ voûte f, arc m; cintre m; pont: arche f; ~-support cambrure f; 2. (se) voûter; v/t. bomber (a. v/i.); arquer, cintrer; cambrer.

arch² [~] □ espiègle; malin (-igne f); malicieux (-euse f).

arch³ [~] insigne, grand; archi-.

ar·ch(a)e·o·log·i·cal □ [ɑ:kiə'lɔdʒikəl] archéologique; **ar·ch(a)e·ol·o·gist** [ɑ:ki'ɔlədʒist] archéologue su./mf; **ar·ch(a)e·ol·o·gy** archéologie f.

ar·cha·ic [ɑ:'keiik] (~ally) archaïque; **'ar·cha·ism** archaïsme m.

arch·an·gel ['ɑ:keindʒl] archange m. **arch·bish·op** ['ɑ:tʃ'biʃəp] archevêque m; **arch'bish·op·ric** [~rik] archevêché m; archiépiscopat m.

arch·dea·con [ˈɑːtʃˈdiːkən] archidiacre *m.*

arch·duch·ess [ˈɑːtʃˈdʌtʃis] archiduchesse *f.*; **'arch'duch·y** archiduché *m.*

arch·duke [ˈɑːtʃˈdjuːk] archiduc *m.*

arch·er [ˈɑːtʃə] archer *m.*; **'arch·er·y** tir *m* à l'arc.

ar·chi·di·ac·o·nal [ɑːkidaiˈækənl] d'archidiacre.

ar·chi·e·pis·co·pal [ɑːkiiˈpiskəpl] archiépiscopal (-aux *m/pl.*); métropolitain.

ar·chi·pel·a·go [ɑːkiˈpeligou] *géog.* archipel *m.*

ar·chi·tect [ˈɑːkitekt] architecte *m*; *fig.* auteur *m*, artisan *m*; **ar·chi·tec·ton·ic** [⁓ˈtɔnik] (⁓*ally*) architectonique; architectural (-aux *m/pl.*); *fig.* directeur (-trice *f*); **ar·chi·tec·ture** [ˈ⁓tʃə] architecture *f.*

ar·chives [ˈɑːkaivz] *pl.* archives *f/pl.*

arch·ness [ˈɑːtʃnis] espièglerie *f*; malice *f.*

arch·way [ˈɑːtʃwei] passage *m* voûté; porte *f* cintrée; portail *m.*

arc·lamp ⚡ [ˈɑːklæmp] lampe *f* à arc.

arc·tic [ˈɑːktik] **1.** arctique; *fig.* glacial (-als *m/pl.*); ♀ *Circle* cercle *m* polaire; ♀ *Ocean* (océan *m*) Arctique *m*; **2.** ⁓s *pl.* snowboots *m/pl.*

ar·den·cy [ˈɑːdənsi] ardeur *f*; **'ar·dent** □ *usu. fig.* ardent; *fig.* fort; ⁓ *spirits pl.* alcool *m*, spiritueux *m/pl.*

ar·do(u)r [ˈɑːdə] *fig.* ardeur *f*; chaleur *f.*

ar·du·ous [ˈɑːdjuəs] ardu (*sentier*, *travail*); rude (*travail*); escarpé (*chemin*); pénible; laborieux (-euse *f*).

a·re·a [ˈɛəriə] aire *f*, superficie *f*; surface *f*; région *f*, territoire *m*; terrain *m* vide; *cinéma etc.*: parterre *m*; cour *f* d'entrée en sous-sol; zone *f*; *Am. téléph.* ⁓ code numéro *m* de présélection; *danger* ⁓ zone *f* dangereuse; *foot. goal* ⁓ surface *f* de but; 🏒 *judicial* ⁓ ressort *m* judiciaire; *foot. penalty* ⁓ surface *f* de réparation; *prohibited* ⁓ zone *f* interdite; ⁓ *bell* sonnette *f* de la porte de service.

a·re·na [əˈriːnə] arène *f*; champ *m* (*a. fig.*); *fig.* théâtre *m.*

aren't F [ɑːnt] = *are not.*

a·rête *alp.* [æˈreit] arête *f.*

ar·gent [ˈɑːdʒənt] argenté; ⧅ (d')argent.

Ar·gen·tine [ˈɑːdʒəntain] argentin; Argentin(e *f*) *m.*

ar·gil [ˈɑːdʒil] argile *f*; **ar·gil·la·ceous** [⁓ˈleiʃəs] argileux (-euse *f*), argillacé.

Ar·go·naut [ˈɑːgənɔːt] argonaute *m*; *Am.* chercheur *m* d'or en Californie.

ar·gu·a·ble [ˈɑːgjuəbl] discutable; soutenable; **ar·gue** [ˈ⁓gjuː] *v/t.* discuter, débattre; raisonner sur; prouver, démontrer; ⁓ *s.o. into doing s.th.* persuader à q. de faire qch.; ⁓ *s.o. out of doing s.th.* dissuader q. de faire qch.; *v/i.* argumenter (sur, *about*); discuter; raisonner; (se) disputer; plaider; ⁓ *from* tirer argument de.

ar·gu·ment [ˈɑːgjumənt] argument *m*; raisonnement *m*; débat *m*, discussion *f*, dispute *f*; **ar·gu·men·ta·tion** [⁓menˈteiʃn] argumentation *f*; **ar·gu'men·ta·tive** □ [⁓tətiv] disposé à argumenter; critique.

a·ri·a ♪ [ˈɑːriə] aria *f.*

ar·id [ˈærid] aride (*a. fig.*); **a'rid·i·ty** aridité *f.*

Ar·ies *astr.* [ˈɛəriəs] le Bélier.

a·right [əˈrait] bien, correctement.

a·rise [əˈraiz] [*irr.*] *fig.* s'élever, surgir (de, *from*); se produire; *bibl.* ressusciter; **a'ris·en** *p.p. de arise.*

ar·is·toc·ra·cy [ærisˈtɔkrəsi] aristocratie *f*; *fig.* élite *f*; **a·ris·to·crat** [ˈ⁓təkræt] aristocrate *mf*; **a·ris·to'crat·ic**, **a·ris·to'crat·i·cal** □ aristocratique.

a·rith·me·tic [əˈriθmətik] arithmétique *f*, calcul *m*; **ar·ith·met·i·cal** □ [⁓ˈmetikl] arithmétique; **a·rith·me·ti·cian** [⁓məˈtiʃən] arithméticien(ne *f*) *m.*

ark [ɑːk] arche *f*; *bibl.* ♀ *of the Covenant* Arche *f* d'alliance.

arm[1] [ɑːm] bras *m*; *fauteuil:* accoudoir *m*; *within* ⁓*'s reach* à portée de la main; *keep s.o. at* ⁓*'s length* tenir q. à distance; *infant in* ⁓*s* bébé *m*; F poupon *m*; *take s.o. to* (*ou in*) *one's* ⁓*s* prendre q. dans ses bras.

arm[2] [⁓] **1.** arme *f*; ⁓*s pl.* armes *f/pl.*; ⧅ armes *f/pl.*, armoiries *f/pl.*; *see coat 1;* ⁓*s race* course *f* aux armements; ⁓*s reduction* désarmement *m*; ⁓*s* (*reduction*) *talks* pourparlers *m/pl. ou* négociations *f/pl.* sur le désarmement; *be* (*all*) *up in* ⁓*s* être en révolte; se gendarmer *ou* s'élever (contre, *against*); *take up* ⁓*s* prendre les armes; 2. (s')armer; *fig.* (se) nantir de; *v/t.* ⊕ armer; renforcer; ⚓ ~ed spinifère.

ar·ma·da [ɑːˈmɑːdə] flotte *f* de guerre; *hist.* the (*Invincible*) ♀ l'(Invincible) Armada *f*.

ar·ma·ment [ˈɑːməmənt] armement *m*; munitions *f/pl.* de guerre; ⚓ artillerie *f*; (*a. naval* ~) armements *m/pl.* navals; flotte *f* navale; ~s *industry* industrie *f* d'armements; **ar·ma·ture** [ˈ~tjuə] armure *f* (*a.* ⚓, *zo.*); △, *phys.* armature *f*; *phys.* induit *m*.

arm·chair [ˈɑːmˈtʃɛə] fauteuil *m*; ~ *strategist*, ~ *politician* stratège *m* du café du commerce.

armed [ɑːmd] à *ou* aux bras ...

Ar·me·ni·an [ɑːˈmiːnjən] 1. arménien(ne *f*); 2. Arménien(ne *f*) *m*.

arm·ful [ˈɑːmful] brassée *f*.

ar·mi·stice [ˈɑːmistis] armistice *m* (*a. fig.*).

arm·let [ˈɑːmlit] bracelet *m*; brassard *m* (*de parti politique etc.*).

ar·mo·ri·al [ɑːˈmɔːriəl] armorial (-aux *m/pl.*), héraldique.

ar·mo(u)r [ˈɑːmə] 1. ✕ armure *f*, blindés *m/pl.*; cuirasse *f* (*a. fig.*, *zo.*); scaphandre *m*; 2. cuirasser; blinder; ~ed *car* automitrailleuse *f*, char *m* blindé; ~ed *train* train *m* blindé; ~ed *turret* tourelle *f* blindée; '~-**clad**, '~-**plat·ed** blindé, cuirassé; ˈar·mo(u)r·er armurier *m* (*a.* ✕, ⚓); ˈar·mo(u)r·y magasin *m* d'armes; *caserne*: armurerie *f*; *fig.* arsenal *m*; *Am.* fabrique *f* d'armes; *Am.* salle *f* d'exercice.

arm·pit [ˈɑːmpit] aisselle *f*; ˈ**arm·rest** accoudoir *m*, accotoir *m*.

ar·my [ˈɑːmi] armée *f*; *fig.* foule *f*; ~ *chaplain* aumônier *m* militaire; ~ *command staff* état-major (*pl.* étatsmajors) *m*; *Salvation* ♀ Armée *f* du Salut; *see service*, '~-**a·gent**, '~-**bro·ker**, '~-**con·trac·tor** fournisseur *m* de l'armée; '~-**corps** corps *m* d'armée; '~-ˈ**list** ✕ Annuaire *m* militaire.

a·ro·ma [əˈroumə] arôme *m*; bouquet *m*; **ar·o·mat·ic** [ærouˈmætik] (~*ally*) aromatique; balsamique.

a·rose [əˈrouz] *prét.* de arise.

a·round [əˈraund] 1. *adv.* autour, à l'entour; d'alentour; *Am.* F par ici, dans ces parages; *Am.* sur pied;

2. *prp.* autour de; *surt. Am.* F environ, presque.

a·rouse [əˈrauz] *usu. fig.* éveiller; stimuler (*q.*); soulever (*une passion*).

ar·rack [ˈærək] arac(k) *m*.

ar·raign [əˈrein] accuser, inculper; traduire en justice; *fig.* s'en prendre à; **ar·raign·ment** mise *f* en accusation; interpellation *f* de l'accusé.

ar·range [əˈreindʒ] *v/t.* arranger; ranger; régler (*des affaires*); ♪ adapter, arranger; fixer (*un jour*); ménager (*des effets*); ♗ ordonner; *v/i.* prendre ses dispositions (pour *for*, *to*); convenir (de, *to*); s'arranger (pour *for*, *to*); ~ *for s.th. to be there* prendre les mesures pour que qch. soit là; **ar·range·ment** arrangement *m*, disposition *f*, aménagement *m*; ♪ arrangement *m*, adaptation *f*; accord *m*; ♱ compromis *m*; *make one's* ~*s* prendre ses dispositions.

ar·rant □ [ˈærənt] insigne, achevé; ~ *knave* franc coquin *m*.

ar·ray [əˈrei] 1. rangs *m/pl.*; *fig.* étalage *m*, rangée *f*; *poét.* atours *m/pl.*, parure *f*; 2. ranger, mettre en ordre; déployer (*des troupes etc.*); *poét.* revêtir, parer (de, *in*).

ar·rear [əˈriə] arrérages *m/pl.*; arriéré *m*; ~*s of rent* arriéré *m* de loyer; *be in* ~*s* s'arriérer; **ar·rear·age** retard *m*; *Am.* ~*s pl.* arrérages *m/pl.*, dettes *f/pl.*

ar·rest [əˈrest] 1. arrestation *f*; prise *f* de corps; ✕, ⚓ arrêts *m/pl.*; suspension *f*, *mouvement*: arrêt *m*; *under* ~ aux arrêts; 2. arrêter (*criminel*, *mouvement*, *regard*, *attention*, *etc.*); appréhender (*q.*) au corps; fixer (*l'attention*, *le regard*); surseoir (*un jugement*).

ar·riv·al [əˈraivl] arrivée *f*; ♱ arrivage *m*; ⚓ entrée *f* (*du vaisseau*); ~*s pl.* nouveaux venus *m/pl.* *ou* arrivés *m/pl.*; ~ *platform* quai *m* de débarquement; *on* ~ à l'arrivée; *To await* ~ ne pas faire suivre; **ar·rive** arriver; *parvenir*; ~ *at* arriver à; atteindre (*a. un âge*); parvenir à.

ar·ro·gance [ˈærəgəns] arrogance *f*; morgue *f*; ˈ**ar·ro·gant** □ arrogant; **ar·ro·gate** [ˈærogeit] (s')attribuer (*qch.*) (à tort) (*usu.* ~ *to o.s.*) s'arroger, usurper (*qch.*).

ar·row [ˈærou] flèche *f*; *surv.* flèche *f* d'arpenteur; '~-**head** pointe *f* de flèche; *broad ~* marque *f* de l'État (*britannique*); **~·root** ['ærəru:t] ⚓ marante *f*; *cuis.* arrow-root *m*; **ar·row·y** ['æroui] en forme de flèche.

arse *sl.* [ɑ:s] derrière *m*; *sl.* cul *m*.

ar·se·nal ['ɑ:sinl] arsenal *m*.

ar·se·nic ['ɑ:snik] arsenic *m*; **ar·sen·ic** ⚗ [ɑ:'senik] arsénique; **ar'sen·i·cal** arsenical (-aux *m/pl.*).

ar·son ['ɑ:sn] crime *m* d'incendie.

art¹ [ɑ:t] art *m*; adresse *f*, habileté *f*; *fig.* artifice *m*; finesse *f*; *péj.* astuce *f*; ~ *critic* critique *mf* d'art; ~ *dealer* marchand *m* d'objets d'art; *Master of ~s* (*abbr.* M.A.) maître *m* ès arts, agrégé *m* de lettres; *applied ~s* arts *m/pl.* industriels; *fine ~s* les beaux-arts *m/pl.*; *liberal ~s* arts *m/pl.* libéraux; *~s and crafts* arts *m/pl.* et métiers *m/pl.*; *Faculty of ~s* Faculté *f* des Lettres; *journal: ~s page* page *f* littéraire.

art² † [~] *tu* es.

ar·te·ri·al [ɑ:'tiəriəl] artériel(le *f*); ~ *road* artère *f*, grande voie *f* de communication; **ar·te·ri·o·scle·ro·sis** [ɑ:'tiəriouskliə'rousis] artériosclérose *f*; **ar·ter·y** ['ɑ:təri] artère *f* (*a. fig.*); *traffic ~* artère *f* de circulation.

ar·te·sian well [ɑ:'ti:zjən'wel] puits *m* artésien.

art·ful ['ɑ:tful] adroit, habile, ingénieux (-euse *f*); rusé.

ar·thrit·ic 🐟 [ɑ:'θritik] arthritique; **ar·thri·tis** [ɑ:'θraitis] arthrite *f*.

ar·ti·choke ['ɑ:titʃouk] artichaut *m*; *Jerusalem ~* topinambour *m*.

ar·ti·cle ['ɑ:tikl] 1. 🐟, 🕮, ✝, *eccl.*, *gramm.*, *etc.* article *m*; ⚔, ⚓ code *m*; objet *m*; ~ *of clothing* vêtement *m*, article *m* ou pièce *f* d'habillement; *~s pl. of apprenticeship* contrat *m* d'apprentissage; *~s pl. of association* acte *m* de société; contrat *m* de société; 2. placer comme apprenti (chez, *to*); accuser (de, *for*); *be ~ed* faire son apprentissage (chez *to*, *with*).

ar·tic·u·late 1. [ɑ:'tikjuleit] *v/t.* articuler (*anat.*, *a. mots*); énoncer (*des mots*); *v/i.* s'articuler (*os*); 2. □ [~lit], *a.* **ar'tic·u·lat·ed** [~leitid] net(te *f*), distinct; *surt. zo.* articulé (*a. langage*); *Brit. mot.* ~ *lorry* semi-remorque *m*; **ar·tic·u·la·tion** articulation *f*; netteté *f* d'énonciation.

ar·ti·fice ['ɑ:tifis] artifice *m*, ruse *f*;

adresse *f*, habileté *f*; **ar'tif·i·cer** artisan *m*, ouvrier *m*; ✕ artificier *m*; ⚓ mécanicien *m*; **ar·ti·fi·cial** □ [~'fiʃəl] artificiel(le *f*); simili-; factice (*larmes*); ~ *manure* engrais *m/pl.* chimiques; 🕮 ~ *person* personne *f* juridique *ou* morale; ~ *respiration* respiration *f* artificielle; ~ *silk* soie *f* artificielle; ~ *stone* simili *m*.

ar·til·ler·y [ɑ:'tiləri] artillerie *f*; **ar'til·ler·y·man** artilleur *m*.

ar·ti·san [ɑ:ti'zæn] artisan *m*, ouvrier *m*.

art·ist ['ɑ:tist] artiste *mf*, *surt.* (artiste-)peintre [*pl.* (artistes-)peintres] *m*; **ar·tiste** [ɑ:'ti:st]artiste *mf*; **ar·tis·tic**, **ar·tis·ti·cal** □ [~'tistik(l)] artistique; artiste (*tempérament*).

art·less □ ['ɑ:tlis] sans art; naturel (-le *f*), sans artifice; naïf (-ïve *f*), candide; **'art·less·ness** naturel *m*, simplicité *f*; naïveté *f*, candeur *f*.

art·y ['ɑ:ti] prétentieux (-euse *f*); *péj.* pseudo-artistique.

Ar·y·an ['ɛəriən] 1. aryen(ne *f*), japhétique; 2. Aryen(ne *f*) *m*.

as [æz, əz] 1. *adv.*, *a. cj.* aussi, si; comme; puisque, étant donné que; tout ... que; au moment où; (au-) tant que; ~ *good* ~ aussi bon que; ~ *far* ~ aussi loin que; autant que; ~ *if*, ~ *though* comme si; *as if* (*gér.*) comme pour (*inf.*); ~ *it were* pour ainsi dire; ~ *well* aussi, également; opportun; ~ *well* ~ de même que; comme; ~ *yet* jusqu'ici, jusqu'à présent; (~) *cold* ~ *ice* glacé, glacial (-als *m/pl.*); *fair* ~ *she is* si belle qu'elle soit; *so kind* ~ *to do* assez aimable pour faire; *such* ~ *to* (*inf.*) de sorte à (*inf.*), de façon que; *such* ~ *tel* que, tel; par exemple; 2. *prp.* ~ *for*, ~ *to* quant à; ~ *from* à partir de (*telle date*), depuis; ✝ ~ *per* conformément à, suivant. [amiante *m.*)

as·bes·tos [æz'bestɔs] asbeste *m*,∫

as·cend [ə'send] *v/i.* monter, s'élever (à, jusqu'à *to*); remonter (*généalogie*); *v/t.* monter (*un escalier*); gravir (*une colline etc.*); monter sur (*le trône*); remonter (*un fleuve*); **as'cend·an·cy**, **as'cend·en·cy** ascendant *m*, pouvoir *m*, influence *f* (sur, *over*); suprématie *f*; **as'cend·ant**, **as'cend·ent** 1. ascendant; 2. *see* ascendancy; *astr.* ascendant *m*; F position *f* prééminente; *be in the ~* être à l'ascendant; prédominer.

as·cen·sion [ə'senʃn] *surt. astr., Am. a. montagne, ballon, etc.*: ascension *f*; ♀ (*Day*) jour *m* de l'Ascension.

as·cent [ə'sent] *montagne, ballon*: ascension *f*; montée *f*; pente *f*, rampe *f*.

as·cer·tain [æsə'tein] constater; s'informer de; **as·cer'tain·a·ble** □ vérifiable; dont on peut s'assurer; **as·cer'tain·ment** constatation *f*; vérification *f*.

as·cet·ic [ə'setik] **1.** (*∼ally*) ascétique; **2.** ascète *mf*; **as'cet·i·cism** [∼tisizəm] ascétisme *m*.

as·crib·a·ble [əs'kraibəbl] imputable, attribuable; **as'cribe** imputer, attribuer.

a·sep·tic ⚕ [æ'septik] aseptique (*a. su./m*).

ash¹ [æʃ] ♀ frêne *m*; *mountain* ∼ sorbier *m* sauvage.

ash² [∼] *usu. ∼es pl.* cendre *f*, -s *f/pl.*; *Ash Wednesday* mercredi *m* des Cendres.

a·shamed [ə'ʃeimd] honteux (-euse *f*), confus; *be* (*ou feel*) ∼ *of* avoir honte de; *être honteux (-euse f) de*; *be* ∼ *of o.s.* avoir honte.

ash-can *Am.* ['æʃkæn] boîte *f* à ordures, poubelle *f*.

ash·en¹ ['æʃn] de frêne, en frêne.

ash·en² [∼] de cendres; cendré; gris; terreux (-euse *f*) (*visage*); blême.

ash·lar ['æʃlə] pierre *f* de taille; moellon *m* d'appareil.

a·shore [ə'ʃɔ:] à terre; échoué; *run* ∼, *be driven* ∼ s'échouer; faire côte.

ash-tray ['æʃtrei] cendrier *m*.

ash·y ['æʃi] cendreux (-euse *f*); couvert de cendres; gris; blême.

A·si·at·ic [eiʃi'ætik] **1.** asiatique, d'Asie; **2.** Asiatique *mf*.

a·side [ə'said] **1.** de côté; à part; à l'écart; *théâ.* en aparté; ∼ *from Am.* à part, en plus de; **2.** à-côté *m*; *théâ.* aparté *m*.

as·i·nine ['æsinain] asine; F stupide.

ask [ɑ:sk] *v/t.* demander (qch., *s.th.*; qch. à q., *s.o. s.th.*; que *that*); *a.* inviter (à, *to*); solliciter (qch. de q., *s.o.* for *s.th.*); prier (q. de *inf., s.o. to inf.*); ∼ (*s.o.*) *a question* poser une question (à q.); *v/i.*: ∼ *about* se renseigner sur; ∼ *after* s'informer de, demander des nouvelles de; ∼ *for* demander (*qch.*); demander à voir (*q.*); *sl.* he ∼s for it il ne l'a pas volé;

it is to be had for the ∼*ing* il n'y a qu'à le demander.

a·skance [əs'kæns], **a'skant**, **askew** [əs'kju:] de côté, de travers, obliquement; *fig.* de guingois.

a·slant [ə'slɑ:nt] de biais, de travers.

a·sleep [ə'sli:p] endormi, plongé dans le sommeil; engourdi (*pied etc.*); *be* ∼ être endormi, dormir; *see fall*.

a·slope [ə'sloup] en pente, en talus.

asp¹ *zo.* [æsp] aspic *m*.

asp² [∼] *see aspen*.

as·par·a·gus ♀ [əs'pærəgəs] asperge *f*, *cuis.* -s *f/pl.*

as·pect ['æspekt] exposition *f*, vue *f*; aspect *m*, air *m*; point *m* de vue; *the house has a southern* ∼ la maison est exposée au sud *ou* a une exposition sud.

as·pen ['æspən] tremble *m*; *attr.* de tremble.

as·per·gill ['æspədʒil], **as·per·gil·lum** *eccl.* [∼'dʒiləm] goupillon *m*.

as·per·i·ty [æs'periti] âpreté *f*; sévérité *f*; rudesse *f*; aspérité *f* (*du style, a. fig.*).

as·perse [əs'pə:s] asperger; *fig.* calomnier, dénigrer; salir (*la réputation*); **as·per·sion** [əs'pə:ʃn] aspersion *f*; *fig.* calomnie *f*.

as·phalt ['æsfælt] **1.** asphalte *m*; F bitume *m*; **2.** d'asphalte; bitumé.

as·phyx·i·a ⚕ [æs'fiksiə] asphyxie *f*; **as'phyx·i·ate** [∼ieit] asphyxier; **as·phyx·i·a·tion** asphyxie *f*.

as·pic ['æspik] aspic *m*; ♀ grande lavande *f*.

as·pir·ant [əs'paiərənt] aspirant(e *f*) *m* (à *to, after, for*); candidat(e *f*) *m*; ∼ *officer* candidat *m* au rang d'officier; **as·pi·rate** ['æspərit] **1.** *gramm.* aspiré; **2.** *gramm.* aspirée *f*; **3.** ['∼reit] aspirer (*a.* ⊕, ⚕); **as·pi'ra·tion** aspiration *f* (*a.* ⊕, ⚕); ambition *f*; visée *f*; **as'pire** [əs'paiə] aspirer, viser (à *to, after, at*); ambitionner (*qch.*).

as·pi·rin *pharm.* ['æspərin] aspirine *f*; F comprimé *m* d'aspirine.

as'pir·ing □ [əs'paiəriŋ] ambitieux (-euse *f*).

ass¹ [æs] âne(sse *f*) *m*; *make an* ∼ *of o.s.* faire des âneries; se donner en spectacle.

ass² *Am. sl.* [æs] derrière *m*, *sl.* cul *m*.

as·sail [ə'seil] assaillir, attaquer; *fig.* s'attaquer à; accabler de; *crainte*, *doute, etc.*: saisir, envahir (*q.*); frapper (*l'œil etc.*); ~ *s.o. with questions* assaillir *ou* harceler *ou* bombarder q. de questions; **as'sail·a·ble** attaquable; mal défendable; **as'sail·ant, as'sail·er** assaillant(e *f*) *m*; agresseur *m*.

as·sas·sin [ə'sæsin] assassin *m*; **as·'sas·si·nate** [~neit] assassiner; **as·sas·si'na·tion** assassinat *m*.

as·sault [ə'sɔ:lt] **1.** assaut *m* (*a.* ✕); ✕ attaque *f*; ⚖ tentative *f* de voie de fait; agression *f*; *see* battery; *indecent*; **2.** attaquer, assaillir; ⚖ se livrer à des voies de fait sur (*q.*); ✕ livrer l'assaut à.

as·say [ə'sei] **1.** *métal etc.*: essai *m*; **2.** *v/t.* essayer, titrer; *v/i. Am.* titrer; **as'say·er** essayeur *m*.

as·sem·blage [ə'semblidʒ] réunion *f*; rassemblement *m*; ⊕ montage *m*, assemblage *m*; **as'sem·ble** (s')assembler; (se) rassembler (*troupes*); (se) réunir; *v/t.* ⊕ assembler, monter; **as'sem·bler** ⊕ monteur (-euse *f*) *m*; ajusteur (-euse *f*) *m*; **as'sem·bly** assemblée *f*; assemblement *m*, réunion *f*; ✕ (sonnerie *f* du) rassemblement *m*; ⊕ montage *m*, assemblage *m*; (*a.* ~ *shop*) salle *f ou* atelier *m* de montage; *moving* ~ *belt* chaîne *f* de montage; *Am.* ~ *line* banc *m* de montage; *Am. pol.* ~ *man* député *m*.

as·sent [ə'sent] **1.** assentiment *m*, consentement *m*; **2.**: ~ *to* acquiescer, accéder à; admettre (*qch.*).

as·sert [ə'sɔ:t] affirmer (que, *that*); (*surt.* ~ *o.s.*) soutenir ses droits; (~ *o.s. s'*) imposer; **as·ser'tion** assertion *f*, affirmation *f*; revendication *f* (*de droits*); **as'ser·tive** □ péremptoire; *gramm.* assertif (-ive *f*); impérieux (-euse *f*); **as'ser·tor** celui (celle *f*) qui affirme; défenseur *m*.

as·sess [ə'ses] estimer, évaluer; répartir (*un impôt*); fixer (*une somme*); coter, taxer (à *in, at*); **as'sess·a·ble** □ évaluable (*dommage*); imposable (*propriété*); **as'sess·ment** répartition *f*; évaluation *f*; cotisation *f*; côte *f*; **as'ses·sor** assesseur *m*; contrôleur *m* (*des contributions*).

as·set ['æset] ✝ avoir *m*, actif *m*; *fig.* atout *m*, avantage *m*, valeur *f*; ~*s pl.* biens *m/pl.*; ✝ actifs *m/pl.*; ~*s pl. and liabilities pl.* actif et passif *m*.

as·sev·er·ate [ə'sevəreit] affirmer; **as·sev·er'a·tion** affirmation *f*.

as·si·du·i·ty [æsi'djuiti] assiduité *f*, diligence *f* (à, *in*); *assiduities pl.* petits soins *m/pl.*; **as·sid·u·ous** □ assidu; diligent.

as·sign [ə'sain] **1.** assigner; consacrer; attribuer; donner (*la raison de qch.*); ⚖ transférer, céder; **2.** ⚖ ayant droit (*pl.* ayants droit) *m*; **as·'sign·a·ble** □ assignable, attribuable; cessible; **as·sig·na·tion** [æsig'neiʃn] attribution *f*; rendez-vous *m*; *see* assignment; **as·sign·ee** [æsi'ni:] *see* assign 2; délégué(e *f*) *m*; ⚖ syndic *m*; ⚖ séquestre *m*; **as·sign·ment** [ə'sainmənt] allocation *f*; citation *f*; *surt. Am.* désignation *f*, nomination *f*; *univ.* tâche *f* assignée, devoir *m*; ⚖ transfert *m*, cession *f*; **as·sign·or** [æsi'nɔ:] ⚖ cédant(e *f*) *m*.

as·sim·i·late [ə'simileit] (*to, with*) (s')assimiler (à) (*a. physiol.*); *v/t.* comparer (à); **as·sim·i·la·tion** assimilation *f* (*a. physiol.*); comparaison *f*.

as·sist [ə'sist] *v/t.* aider; prêter assistance à; secourir; *v/i.* ~ *at* prendre part à; assister à; **as'sist·ance** aide *f*, secours *m*, assistance *f*; **as'sist·ant 1.** qui aide; adjoint (à, *to*); sous-; **2.** adjoint(e *f*) *m*, auxiliaire *m/f*; ✝ commis *m*, employé(e *f*) *m*.

as·size ⚖ [ə'saiz] assises *f/pl.*; ~*s pl.* (cour *f* d')assises *f/pl*.

as·so·ci·a·ble [ə'souʃjəbl] associable (à, *with*); **as'so·ci·ate 1.** [~ʃieit] (s')associer (avec, *with*); *v/i.* s'affilier (à, *with*); ~ *in* s'associer pour (*qch.*); fréquenter (*q.*); **2.** [~ʃiit] associé; adjoint; **3.** [~] associé *m* (*a.* ✝); adjoint *m*; compagnon *m*, camarade *m/f*; membre *m* correspondant (*d'une académie*); professeur *m* adjoint; **as·so·ci·a·tion** [~si'eiʃən] association *f* (*a. d'idées*); fréquentation *f*; société *f*, amicale *f* (*d'étudiants etc.*); ~ *football* football *m* association.

as·so·nance ['æsənəns] assonance *f*.

as·sort [ə'sɔ:t] *v/t.* assortir; classer, ranger; ✝ assortir; *v/i.* (*with*) (s')assortir (avec); aller ensemble; **as'sort·ment** assortiment *m*; classement *m*; ✝ assortiment *m*, choix *m*.

as·suage [ə'sweidʒ] apaiser (*la faim, un désir, etc.*); calmer; sou-

lager; assouper (*la souffrance*); **as-**
'suage·ment apaisement *m*, soulagement *m*, adoucissement *m*.

as·sume [ə'sju:m] prendre; affecter; revêtir; assumer (*une charge
etc.*); simuler; présumer, supposer;
as'sum·ing □ présomptueux
(-euse *f*); **as·sump·tion** [ə'sʌmpʃn]
action *f* de prendre; entrée *f* en
fonctions; affectation *f*; arrogance
f; hypothèse *f*; *eccl.* ♀ Assomption
f; **on the ~ that** en supposant que;
as'sump·tive □ hypothétique;
admis; arrogant.

as·sur·ance [ə'ʃuərəns] affirmation
f; promesse *f*; assurance *f* (*a.* =
sûreté; *aplomb*); *péj.* hardiesse *f*;
Brit. **life ~** assurance-vie *f* (*pl.* assurances-vie); **as'sure** assurer; assurer la vie de; s'assurer sur la vie; **~ s.o.
of s.th.** assurer q. de qch., assurer
qch. à q.; **as'sured 1.** assuré (*a.* =
certain; *a.* = *sûr de soi*); *péj.* affronté;
2. assuré(e *f*) *m*; **as'sur·ed·ly** [~ridli]
assurément, sans aucun doute; avec
assurance, d'un ton assuré; **as'sur·**
er [~rə] assuré(e *f*) *m*.

As·syr·i·an [ə'siriən] **1.** assyrien(ne
f); **2.** Assyrien(ne *f*) *m*.

as·ter ♀ ['æstə] aster *m*; **as·ter·isk**
['~ərisk] *typ.* astérisque *m*.

a·stern ⚓ [ə'stə:n] à *ou* sur
l'arrière.

asth·ma ['æsmə] asthme *m*; **asth-**
mat·ic [~'mætik] **1.** *a.* **asth'mat·i-**
cal □ asthmatique; **2.** asthmatique *mf*.

as·tig·mat·ic [æstig'mætik] (~*ally*)
opt. astigmate; **a'stig·ma·tism**
[~mətizm] astigmatisme *m*.

a·stir [ə'stə:] animé; debout; agité.

as·ton·ish [ə'stɔniʃ] étonner, surprendre; **be ~ed** être étonné,
s'étonner (de *at*, *to*); **as'ton·ish-**
ing □ étonnant, surprenant; **as-**
'ton·ish·ment étonnement *m*, surprise *f*. [stupéfier.\
as·tound [ə'staund] confondre;∫
as·tra·gal △ ['æstrəgəl] astragale *m*,
chapelet *m*.

as·tra·khan [æstrə'kæn] *fourrure:*
astrakan *m*.

as·tral ['æstrəl] astral (-aux *m/pl.*).

a·stray [ə'strei] égaré; *péj.* dévoyé;
go ~ s'égarer; *péj.* se dévoyer.

a·stride [ə'straid] à califourchon
(sur, *of*); **ride ~** aller jambe deçà,
jambe delà (*sur un cheval etc.*).

as·trin·gent □, ⚕ [əs'trindʒənt] astringent (*a. su./m*); styptique (*a.
su./m*).

as·trol·o·ger [əs'trɔlədʒə] astro-
logue *m*; **as·trol·o·gy** [əs'trɔlədʒi]
astrologie *f*; **as·tro·naut** ['æstro-
nɔ:t] astronaute *mf*; **as·tro·nau·tics**
[æstrə'nɔ:tiks] *sg.* astronautique *f*;
as·tron·o·mer [əs'trɔnəmə] astro-
nome *m*; **as·tro·nom·i·cal** □
[æstrə'nɔmikl] astronomique; **as-**
tron·o·my [əs'trɔnəmi] astronomie
f.

as·tute □ [əs'tju:t] avisé, fin; *péj.*
rusé, astucieux (-euse *f*); **as'tute-**
ness finesse *f*, pénétration *f*; *péj.*
astuce *f*.

a·sun·der [ə'sʌndə] éloignés l'un de
l'autre; en deux.

a·sy·lum [ə'sailəm] asile *m*, refuge
m; hospice *m*; F maison *f* d'aliénés.

a·sym·me·try [æ'simitri] asymétrie
f, dissymétrie *f*.

at [æt; ət] *prp.* à; en (*guerre*, *mer*);
(au)près de; sur (*demande*); *après
certains verbes comme rire, se réjouir,
s'étonner de:* de; **~ the door** à la porte;
~ the seuil; **~ my expense** à mes frais;
~ my aunt's chez ma tante; **run ~ s.o.**
se jeter sur q.; **~ day-break** au jour
levant; **~ night** la nuit; **~ table** à
table; **~ a low price** à un bas prix;
~ all events en tout cas; **~ school** à
l'école; **2 ~ a time** 2 par 2; **~ peace**
en paix; **~ the age of** à l'âge de; **~
one blow** d'un seul coup; **~ five
o'clock** à cinq heures; **~ Christmas**
à Noël. [visme *m.*\
at·a·vism *biol.* ['ætəvizm] ata-∫
a·tax·y ⚕ [ə'tæksi] ataxie *f*, incoordi-
nation *f*.

ate [et] *prét. de* eat 1.

a·the·ism ['eiθiizm] athéisme *m*;
'a·the·ist athée *mf*; **a·the·is·tic,**
a·the'is·ti·cal □ athéistique; athée.

ath·lete ['æθli:t] athlète *m*; ⚕ **~'s
foot** pied *m* de l'athlète; **~'s heart**
cardiectasie *f*; **ath·let·ic** [~'letik]
athlétique; F sportif (-ive *f*); **~ heave**
effort *m* vigoureux; **~ sports** *pl.*
sports *m/pl.* athlétiques; **ath'let·ics**
pl., **ath'let·i·cism** [~tisizm] athlétisme *m*.

at-home [ət'houm] réception *f*;
soirée *f*.

a·thwart [ə'θwɔ:t] **1.** *prp.* en travers
de; **2.** *adv.* en travers (*a.* ⚓); ⚓ par
le travers.

a-tilt [ə'tilt] incliné, penché; sur l'oreille (*chapeau*).

At·lan·tic [ət'læntik] **1.** atlantique; **2.** (*a.* ~ Ocean) (océan *m*) Atlantique *m*.

at·las ['ætləs] atlas *m*; ⚠ atlante *m*.

at·mos·phere ['ætməsfiə] atmosphère *f* (*a. fig.*); **at·mos·pher·ic,** **at·mos·pher·i·cal** □ [~'ferik(l)] atmosphérique; **at·mos'pher·ics** *pl.* radio: parasites *m/pl.*, perturbations *f/pl.* atmosphériques.

at·oll *géog.* [ə'təl] atoll *m*; île *f* de corail.

at·om ⚛, *phys.* ['ætəm] atome *m* (*a. fig.*); **a·tom·ic** [ə'təmik] atomique; ~ *age* (*bomb, energy, number, warfare, weight*) âge *m* (bombe *f*, énergie *f*, nombre *m*, guerre *f*, poids *m*) atomique; ~ *fission* fission *f* de l'atome; ~-*powered* actionné par l'énergie atomique; ~ *pile* (*ou reactor*) pile *f* atomique, réacteur *m* nucléaire; ~ *research* recherche *f* atomique, recherches *f/pl.* nucléaires; ~ *waste* déchets *m/pl.* nucléaires; **at·om·ism** ['ætəmizm] atomisme *m*; **at·om'is·tic** (~*ally*) atomistique; **'at·om·ize** pulvériser (*un liquide*); vaporiser; **'at·om·iz·er** pulvérisateur *m*, atomiseur *m*; **'at·o·my** *surt. fig.* squelette *m*.

a·tone [ə'toun]: ~ *for* expier (*qch.*), racheter (*qch.*); **a'tone·ment** expiation *f*, réparation *f*.

a·ton·ic [æ'tənik] ⚕ atonique; *gramm.* atone; **at·o·ny** ['ætəni] atonie *f*; F aveulissement *m*.

a·top F [ə'təp] en haut, au sommet; ~ *of* en haut de.

a·tro·cious □ [ə'trouʃəs] atroce; F affreux (-euse *f*); **a·troc·i·ty** [ə'trəsiti] atrocité *f* (*a. fig.*).

at·ro·phy ['ætrəfi] **1.** atrophie *f*; contabescence *f*; **2.** (s')atrophier.

at·tach [ə'tætʃ] *v/t.* (*to*) attacher (*chose, valeur, sens, etc.*) (à); lier, fixer (à); annexer (*un document*) (à); imputer (*une responsabilité*) (à); ajouter (*de la foi*) (à); prêter (*de l'importance*) (à); ⚖ arrêter (*q.*); saisir (*qch.*); ~ *o.s.* to s'attacher à; ~ *value to* attacher du prix à; ~ *o.s.* s'attacher (à, *to*); **at'tach·a·ble** qui peut être attaché (à, *to*); ⚖ saisissable; **at·ta·ché** [ə'tæʃei] attaché *m*; ~ *case* mallette *f* (*pour documents*); **at·tached** [ə'tætʃt]: *be* ~ *to* être atta-

ché à, tenir à; faire parti de, être adjoint à; ~ *house* maison *f* individuelle standard; **at'tach·ment** action *f* d'attacher; attachement *m* (pour, *for*); attache *f*, lien *m*; affection *f* (pour, *for*); ⊕, *machine*: accessoire *m*; attelage *m*; ⚖ saisie-arrêt (*pl.* saisies-arrêts) *f*; contrainte *f* par corps.

at·tack [ə'tæk] **1.** attaquer (*a. fig.*); s'attaquer à (*un travail, un repas, etc.*); *maladie*: s'attaquer à (*q.*); **2.** assaut *m*; attaque *f* (*a.* ⚔); attentat *m* (*à la vie*); ⚕ crise *f*; accès *m*; *heart* ~ crise *f* cardiaque; **at'tack·er** agresseur *m*; attaquant(e *f*) *m*.

at·tain [ə'tein] *v/t.* atteindre, arriver à (*a. fig.*); acquérir (*des connaissances*); *v/i.:* ~ *to* atteindre à; atteindre (*un âge*); **at'tain·a·ble** accessible; **at'tain·der** ⚖ confiscation *f* de biens et mort *f* civile; **at'tain·ment** arrivée *f*; *fig.* réalisation *f*; ~*s pl.* connaissance *f*, -s *f/pl.*, savoir *m*.

at·taint [ə'teint] frapper (*q.*) de mort civile; *fig.* attaquer; souiller.

at·tar ['ætə] essence *f* de roses.

at·tem·per [ə'tempə] tremper; adoucir; modérer; accorder (avec, *to*).

at·tempt [ə'tempt] **1.** essayer (de, *to*), tâcher (de, *to*); ~ *the life of* attenter à la vie de; **2.** tentative *f*, essai *m*, effort *m* (de, *to*); attentat *m* (contre la vie de *q.*, [*up*]*on s.o.'s life*).

at·tend [ə'tend] *v/t.* assister à; aller à; servir; visiter; soigner (*un malade*); accompagner; suivre (*un cours*); *v/i.* faire attention; assister; se charger (de, *to*); s'appliquer (à, *to*); ~ *on* visiter, soigner (*un malade*); ~ *to* s'occuper de (*affaires etc.*); **at'tend·ance** *hôtel, magasin, etc.*: service *m*; présence *f*; assistance *f* (à, *at*); ⚔ soins *m/pl.* (pour, *on*), visites *f/pl.* (à, *on*); assiduité *f* (*aux cours, à l'école*); *hours pl. of* ~ heures *f/pl.* de présence; *be in* ~ être de service (auprès de, *on*); F *dance* ~ faire les trente-six volontés (de, *on*); **at'tend·ant 1.** qui accompagne, qui sert, qui suit (*q.*, [*up*]*on s.o.*); qui assiste; concomitant; **2.** serviteur *m*, domestique *mf*; surveillant(e *f*) *m*; *théâ.* ouvreuse *f*; gardien(ne *f*) *m*; appariteur *m*; ⊕ surveillant *m*, soigneur *m*; ~s *pl.* personnel *m*.

at·ten·tion [ə'tenʃn] attention *f* (*a. fig.* = *civilité*); ✕ ~! garde à vous!; *see* call; give; pay; **at'ten·tive** □ attentif (-ive *f*) (à, to); soucieux (-euse *f*) (de, to); *fig.* empressé (auprès de, to).

at·ten·u·ate [ə'tenjueit] atténuer (*a. fig.*); amincir; raréfier (*un gaz etc.*); **at'ten·u·at·ed** atténué; amaigri; ténu; **at·ten·u'a·tion** atténuation *f*; amaigrissement *m*.

at·test [ə'test] attester, certifier (*a. fig.*); (*a. v/i.* ~ to) témoigner de; affirmer sous serment; ⚖ assermenter (*q.*); *surt.* ✕ faire prêter serment à (*q.*); **at·tes·ta·tion** [ætes-'teiʃn] attestation *f*; témoignage *m*; prestation *f* de serment; *surt.* ✕ assermentation *f*; **at'test·er, at'test·or** [ə'testə] témoin *m* (⚖ instrumentaire); ⚖ certificateur *m*.

At·tic ['ætik] **1.** attique; **2.** ♀ mansarde *f*, F grenier *m*; ♀s *pl.* combles *m/pl.*; étage *m* mansardé.

at·tire *poét.* [ə'taiə] **1.** vêtir; parer; **2.** costume *m*, vêtements *m/pl.*

at·ti·tude ['ætitju:d] attitude *f* (envers, to[wards]); pose *f*; position *f* (*d'un avion en vol*); *strike an ~* poser, prendre une attitude dramatique; ~ *of mind* disposition *f* d'esprit; manière *f* de penser; **at·ti'tu·di·nize** poser; faire des grâces.

at·tor·ney [ə'tɔ:ni] mandataire *mf*; *Am.* avoué *m*; ⚖ *Am.* circuit ~, *district* ~ procureur *m* de la République; *letter* (*ou warrant*) *of* ~ procuration *f*; *power of* ~ pouvoirs *m/pl.*; ♀ *General* avocat *m* du Gouvernement; procureur *m* général; *Am.* chef *m* du Ministère de Justice.

at·tract [ə'trækt] attirer (*a. l'attention*); *fig.* séduire; avoir de l'attrait pour; **at'trac·tion** [~kʃn] attraction *f*; *fig.* attrait *m*; *théâ.* attraction *f*; clou *m* (*du spectacle*); **at'trac·tive** [~tiv] □ *usu. fig.* attrayant, attirant; *théâ.* alléchant; **at'trac·tive·ness** attrait *m*, charme *m*.

at·trib·ut·a·ble [ə'tribjutəbl] imputable; **at·tri·bute 1.** [ə'tribju:t] imputer, attribuer; prêter (*une qualité, des vertus*); **2.** ['ætribju:t] attribut *m*, qualité *f*; apanage *m*; symbole *m*; *gramm.* épithète *f*; **at·tri·bu·tion** [ætri'bju:ʃn] attribution

f, imputation *f* (à, to); affectation *f* (à *un but*); compétence *f*; **at'trib·u·tive** *gramm.* [ə'tribjutiv] **1.** □ qualificatif (-ive *f*); **2.** épithète *f*.

at·tri·tion [ə'triʃn] attrition *f*; usure *f* par le frottement; ⊕ usure *f*, *machine*: fatigue *f*; *war of* ~ guerre *f* d'usure.

at·tune [ə'tju:n] ♪ accorder, *fig.* harmoniser (avec, to).

au·burn ['ɔ:bən] châtain roux, blond ardent; acajou.

auc·tion ['ɔ:kʃn] **1.** (*a. sale by* ~) vente *f* aux enchères; vente *f* à l'encan; *sell by* (*Am. at*) ~, *put up for* ~ vendre aux enchères; vente à la criée (*du poisson etc.*); **2.** (*usu.* ~ *off*) vendre aux enchères; **auc·tion·eer** [~ʃə'niə] commissaire-priseur *m* (*pl.* commissaires-priseurs) *m*.

au·da·cious □ [ɔ:'deiʃəs] audacieux (-euse *f*), hardi; *péj.* effronté, cynique; **au·dac·i·ty** [ɔ:'dæsiti] audace *f*; hardiesse *f* (*a. péj.*); *péj.* effronterie *f*, cynisme *m*.

au·di·bil·i·ty [ɔ:di'biliti] perceptibilité *f*; **au·di·ble** ['ɔ:dəbl] perceptible; intelligible (*voix etc.*).

au·di·ence ['ɔ:djəns] audience *f* (avec of, with); assistance *f*, assistants *m/pl.* (à *une réunion*); public *m*, spectateurs *m/pl.* (*au théâtre*); auditeurs *m/pl.* (*au concert*).

audio... ['ɔ:diou] audio-; **au·di·o·fre·quen·cy** [~'fri:kwənsi] *radio:* audiofréquence *f*; **au·di·o·phile** ['~fail] amateur *m* de hi-fi; **au·di·o·vis·u·al aids** [~'vizjuəl eidz] support *m* audio-visual.

au·dit ['ɔ:dit] **1.** *comptes:* vérification *f*; **2.** vérifier, apurer (*des comptes*); *univ.* † assister à (*un cours*); **au·di·tion** audition *f*; **'au·di·tor** commissaire *m* aux comptes; expert *m* comptable; auditeur *m* (*surt. univ.*); **au·di·to·ri·um** [~'tɔ:riəm] salle *f*; *eccl.* parloir *m*; *Am.* salle *f* (*de concert, de conférence, etc.*); **au·di·to·ry** ['~təri] **1.** auditif (-ive *f*); de l'ouïe; **2.** auditoire *m*; auditeurs *m/pl.*; *see* auditorium.

au·ger ⊕ ['ɔ:gə] perçoir *m*; tarière *f*.

aught [ɔ:t] quelque chose *m*; *for* ~ *I care* pour ce qui m'importe; *for* ~ *I know* autant que je sache.

aug·ment [ɔ:g'ment] *v/t.* augmenter, accroître; *v/i.* augmenter, s'accroître; **aug·men'ta·tion** augmen tation *f*, accroissement *m*; **aug·'ment·a·tive** □ [ˌtətiv] augmentatif (-ive *f*).

au·gur ['ɔ:gə] **1.** augure *m*; **2.** augurer; prédire; *v/i.* être de bon *ou* de mauvais augure; **au·gu·ry** ['ɔ:gjuri] augure *m*; F présage *m*; science *f* des augures.

Au·gust 1. ['ɔ:gəst] août *m*; **2.** ♀ □ [ɔ:'gʌst] auguste, imposant; **Au·gus·tan** [ɔ:'gʌstən] d'Auguste; *littérature anglaise:* de la reine Anne.

auk *orn.* [ɔ:k] pingouin *m*.

aunt [ɑ:nt] tante *f*; ♀ *Sally* jeu *m* de massacre; **aunt·ie, aunt·y** F ['ˌti] tata *f*; ma tante.

au pair [əu'pɛə] (*a. ~ girl*) jeune fille *f* au pair.

au·ral ['ɔ:rəl] de l'oreille.

au·re·ole ['ɔ:rioul] *eccl., astr.* auréole *f*; *saint:* gloire *f*.

au·ri·cle *anat.* ['ɔ:rikl] auricule *f*; **au·ric·u·la** ♀ [ə'rikjulə] auricule *f*; **au·ric·u·lar** □ [ɔ:'rikjulə] auriculaire; de l'oreille, des oreillettes du cœur; *~witness* témoin *m* auriculaire.

au·rif·er·ous [ɔ:'rifərəs] aurifère.

au·rist ⚕ ['ɔ:rist] auriste *m*.

au·rochs *zo.* ['ɔ:rɔks] bœuf *m* urus.

au·ro·ra [ɔ:'rɔ:rə] Aurore *f* (*fig.* ♀); *~ borealis* aurore *f* boréale; **au'ro·ral** auroral (-aux *m/pl.*); de l'aurore.

aus·cul·ta·tion ⚕ [ɔ:skəl'teiʃn] auscultation *f*.

aus·pice ['ɔ:spis] augure *m*; *~s pl.* auspices *m/pl.*; **aus·pi·cious** □ [ˌ'piʃəs] propice; prospère, heureux (-euse *f*).

Aus·sie F ['ɔsi] **1.** Australien(ne *f*) *m*; **2.** australien(ne *f*).

aus·tere □ [ɔs'tiə] austère; frugal (-aux *m/pl.*) (*repas*); sans luxe (*chambre etc.*); cénobitique (*vie*); **aus·ter·i·ty** [ˌ'teriti] austérité *f*; sévérité *f* de goût; absence *f* de luxe; *~ budget* budget *m* d'austérité.

aus·tral ['ɔ:strəl] austral (-als *ou* -aux *m/pl.*).

Aus·tra·lian [ɔs'treiljən] **1.** australien(ne *f*); **2.** Australien(ne *f*) *m*.

Aus·tri·an ['ɔstriən] **1.** autrichien (-ne *f*); **2.** Autrichien(ne *f*) *m*.

au·tar·chy [ɔ:'tɑ:ki] autarchie *f* (= *souveraineté*); *Am. see* autarky.

au·tark·y ['ɔ:tɑ:ki] autarcie *f*.

au·then·tic [ɔ:'θentik] (*~ally*) authentique; digne de foi; **au'then·ti·cate** [ˌkeit] certifier, légaliser,

valider, viser (*un acte etc.*); établir l'authenticité de; **au·then·ti·ca·tion** certification *f*; validation *f*; **au·then·tic·i·ty** [ˌ'tisiti] authenticité *f*; crédibilité *f*.

au·thor ['ɔ:θə] auteur *m* (*a. fig.*); écrivain *m*; **au·thor·ess** ['ɔ:θəris] femme *f* auteur; femme *f* écrivain; **au·thor·i·tar·i·an** [ɔ:θɔri'tɛəriən] autoritaire (*a. su./m*); **au'thor·i·ta·tive** □ [ˌtətiv] autoritaire; péremptoire; qui fait autorité (*document*); de bonne source; **au'thor·i·ta·tive·ness** autorité *f*; ton *m* autoritaire; **au'thor·i·ty** autorité *f* (sur, over); ascendant *m* (sur, over); domination *f*; autorisation *f*, mandat *m* (de *inf.*, to *inf.*); qualité *f* (pour *inf.*, to *inf.*); expert *m* (dans qch., on *s.th.*); source *f* (de renseignements); *surt. ~s pl.* l'administration *f*; *on good ~* de bonne source; *on the ~ of* sur la foi de (*q.*); *I have it on the ~ of* Mr. X je le tiens de Monsieur X; **au·thor·i·za·tion** [ɔ:θərai'zeiʃn] autorisation *f*; pouvoir *m*; mandat *m*; **'au·thor·ize** autoriser, sanctionner; donner mandat à; **'au·thor·ship** profession *f ou* qualité *f* d'auteur; *livre:* paternité *f*.

au·tism ['ɔ:tizm] autisme *m*; **au·tis·tic** [ɔ:'tistik] autistique.

au·to ['ɔ:tou] auto(mobile) *f*.

auto... [ɔ:to] auto-.

au·to·bi·og·ra·pher [ɔ:tobai'ɔgrəfə] autobiographe *m*; **'au·to·bi·o·'graph·ic, 'au·to·bi·o·'graph·i·cal** □ [ˌo'græfik(l)] autobiographique; **au·to·bi·og·ra·phy** [ˌ'ɔgrəfi] autobiographie *f*.

au·to·cade *Am.* [ɔ:'toukeid] *see* mo-|
[torcade.

au·to·car ['ɔ:toukɑ:] autocar *m*.

au·toch·thon [ɔ:'tɔkθən] autochthone *m* (= *aborigène*); **au'toch·tho·nous** autochthone.

au·toc·ra·cy [ɔ:'tɔkrəsi] autocratie *f*; **au·to·crat** ['ɔ:təkræt] autocrate *m*; **au·to'crat·ic, au·to'crat·i·cal** □ autocratique; autocrate (*personne*); absolu (*caractère*).

au·tog·e·nous weld·ing ⊕ [ɔ:'tɔdʒənəs'weldiŋ] soudure *f* (à l')autogène.

au·to·gi·ro ✈ ['ɔ:tou'dʒaiərou] autogyre *m*.

au·to·graph ['ɔ:təgrɑ:f] **1.** autographe *m*; *~ album* keepsake *m*; **2.** signer; dédicacer; ⊕ autographier; **au·to·graph·ic** [~'græfik] (*ally*) autographe; ⊕ autographique; **au·tog·ra·phy** [ɔ:'tɔgrəfi] autographe *m*; ⊕ autographie *f*.

au·to·mat *Am.* ['ɔtəmæt] restaurant *m* à distributeurs automatiques; **aut·o·mate** ['~meit] automatiser; **au·to·mat·ic** [~'mætik] (~*ally*) **1.** automatique; inconscient; ~ *machine* distributeur *m*; ~ *telephone* (téléphone *m*) automatique *m*; *mot.* ~ *transmission* transmission *f* automatique; **2.** *Am.* automatique *m*; **au·tom'a·tion** ⊕ automatisation *f*; **au·tom·a·ton** [ɔ:'tɔmətən], *pl.* -tons, -ta [~tə] automate *m* (*a. fig.*).

au·to·mo·bile *surt. Am.* ['ɔ:təmə-bi:l] automobile *f*; F voiture *f*.

au·ton·o·mous [ɔ:'tɔnəməs] autonome; **au'ton·o·my** autonomie *f*.

au·top·sy ['ɔ:təpsi] autopsie *f*.

au·to·type ⊕ ['ɔ:tətaip] fac-similé *m*.

au·tumn ['ɔ:təm] automne *m*; **au·tum·nal** [ɔ:'tʌmnəl] automnal (-aux *m/pl.*); d'automne.

aux·il·i·a·ry [ɔ:g'ziljəri] **1.** auxiliaire, subsidiaire (à, to); **2.** (*a.* ~ *verb*) *gramm.* verbe *m* auxiliaire; *auxiliaries pl.* (troupes *f/pl.*) auxiliaires *m/pl.*

a·vail [ə'veil] **1.** servir (à), être utile (à) (*q.*); ~ *o.s. of* profiter de (*qch.*); user de (*qch.*); saisir (*une opportunité*); **2.** avantage *m*, utilité *f*; *of no* ~ inutile; *of what* ~ *is it?* à quoi bon?; à quoi sert (de *inf.*, *to inf.*)?; **a·vail-a'bil·i·ty** disponibilité *f*; billet: durée *f*, validité *f*; **a'vail·a·ble** □ disponible; libre; accessible; valable, bon(ne *f*), valide; **a'vail-ments** *pl.* disponibilités *f/pl.*

av·a·lanche ['ævəlɑ:nʃ] avalanche *f*.

av·a·rice ['ævəris] avarice *f*; mesquinerie *f*; **av·a'ri·cious** □ avare, avaricieux (-euse *f*).

a·venge [ə'vendʒ] venger; prendre la vengeance de (*q.*); ~ *o.s.* (*ou be* ~*d*) (*up*)*on* se venger de *ou* sur; *avenging angel* divinité *f* vengeresse; **a'veng·er** vengeur (-eresse *f*) *m*.

av·e·nue ['ævinju:] avenue *f*; chemin *m* d'accès; promenade *f* plantée d'arbres; *Am.* boulevard *m*.

a·ver [ə'və:] avérer, affirmer, déclarer; ⚖ prouver; alléguer.

av·er·age ['ævəridʒ] **1.** moyenne *f*; ⚓ avarie *f*; ⚓ *general* ~ avaries *f/pl.* communes; ⚓ *particular* ~ avarie *f*

particulière; *on an* ~ en moyenne; **2.** □ moyen(ne *f*); *fig.* ordinaire, normal (-aux *m/pl.*); **3.** prendre *ou* faire *ou* établir la moyenne (de, of); donner une moyenne (de, at).

a·ver·ment [ə'və:mənt] affirmation *f*; ⚖ allégation *f*; preuve *f*.

a·verse □ [ə'və:s] opposé (à *to*, *from*); ennemi (de); **a'verse·ness**, **a'ver·sion** aversion *f* (pour *to*, *from*); répugnance *f* (à); *he is my aversion* il est mon cauchemar.

a·vert [ə'və:t] détourner (*a. fig.*); écarter.

a·vi·ar·y ['eivjəri] volière *f*.

a·vi·ate ⚡ ['eivieit] voler; **a·vi'a-tion** aviation *f*; vol *m*; ~ *ground* aérodrome *m*; **'a·vi·a·tor** aviateur (-trice *f*) *m*.

av·id □ ['ævid] avide (de *of*, *for*); **a·vid·i·ty** [ə'viditi] avidité *f* (de, pour *for*).

av·o·ca·do ⚘ [ævou'ka:dou] (*a.* ~ *pear*) avocat *m*.

av·o·ca·tion [ævo'keiʃn] occupation *f*; vocation *f*; profession *f*; métier *m*.

a·void [ə'vɔid] éviter; se soustraire à; se dérober à; ⚖ résoudre, annuler, résilier (*un contrat etc.*); **a'void-a·ble** évitable; **a'void·ance** action *f* d'éviter; *usu. eccl.* vacance *f*; ⚖ *contrat etc.*: résolution *f*, annulation *f*, résiliation *f*.

av·oir·du·pois ✝ [ævədə'pɔiz] poids *m* du commerce; *Am. sl.* poids *m*, pesanteur *f*.

a·vouch [ə'vautʃ] garantir; reconnaître; *see avow*.

a·vow [ə'vau] reconnaître; s'avérer; déclarer; **a'vow·al** aveu *m*; **a'vow-ed·ly** [~idli] franchement, ouvertement.

a·wait [ə'weit] attendre (*a. fig.*).

a·wake [ə'weik] **1.** éveillé; attentif (-ive *f*); *be* ~ *to* avoir conscience de; *wide* ~ bien *ou* tout éveillé; *fig.* averti, avisé; **2.** [*irr.*] *v/t.* (*usu.* **a'wak·en**) éveiller; réveiller; ~ *s.o. to* ouvrir les yeux à q. sur; *v/i.* se réveiller, s'éveiller; prendre conscience (de qch., *to s.th.*).

a·ward [ə'wɔ:d] **1.** adjudication *f*, sentence *f* arbitrale; récompense *f*; *Am.* bourse *f*; ⚖ dommages-intérêts *m/pl.*; **2.** adjuger, décerner; accorder; conférer (*un titre etc.*).

a·ware [ə'wɛə]: *be* ~ avoir connaissance (de, *of*); avoir conscience (de, *of*); ne pas ignorer (qch., *of s.th.*; que, *that*); become ~ *of* prendre connaissance *ou* conscience de; se rendre compte de; **a'ware·ness** conscience *f.*

a·wash ⚓ [ə'wɔʃ] à fleur d'eau; ras (*écueil*); *fig.* inondé.

a·way [ə'wei] (au) loin; dans le lointain; absent; à une distance de; *do ~ with* supprimer; ~ *with it!* emportez-le!;~ *with you!* allez-vouz-en!; *Am.* F ~ *back* il y a (déjà) longtemps; dès (*une date*); *I cannot~ with it* je ne peux pas sentir cela.

awe [ɔː] crainte *f*, terreur *f* (de, *of*); *qqfois* respect *m* (pour, *of*); terreur *f* religieuse; effroi *m* religieux; **awe·some** ['~səm] *see awful*; **'awe-struck** frappé d'une terreur profonde religieuse *ou* mystérieuse; intimidé.

aw·ful ☐ ['ɔːful] redoutable, effroyable; F fameux (-euse *f*); fier (-ère *f*), affreux (-euse *f*); **'aw·ful·ness** caractère *m* terrible; solennité *f.*

a·while [ə'wail] un moment; pendant quelque temps.

awk·ward ☐ ['ɔːkwəd] gauche, maladroit; gêné; fâcheux (-euse *f*), gênant; incommode, peu commode; **'awk·ward·ness** gaucherie *f*; maladresse *f*; manque *m* de grâce; embarras *m*; inconvénient *m.*

awl [ɔːl] alêne *f*, poinçon *m.*

awn ♀ [ɔːn] barbe *f*, barbelure *f.*

awn·ing ['ɔːniŋ] ⚓, *a. voiture:* tente *f*; *boutique:* banne *f*; *théâtre, hôtel:* marquise *f*; ⚓ tendelet *m.*

a·woke [ə'wouk] *prét. et p.p. de awake* 2.

a·wry [ə'rai] de travers; de guingois; *go* ~, *turn* ~ aller de travers.

axe [æks] **1.** hache *f*; F *the* ~ coupe *f*; *traitement, personnel, etc.*: réductions *f/pl.*; *have an* ~ *to grind* avoir un intérêt personnel à servir; **2.** *v/t.* F faire des coupes dans; mettre à pied (*des fonctionnaires*).

ax·i·om ['æksiəm] *principe:* axiome *m*; **ax·i·o'mat·ic** (~ally) axiomatique; F évident.

ax·is ['æksis], *pl.* **ax·es** ['~siːz] axe *m.*

ax·le ⊕ ['æksl] tourillon *m*; arbre *m*; (*a.* ~*-tree*) essieu *m.*

ay(e) [ai] **1.** *parl.* oui; ⚓ ~, ~! bien (monsieur)!; **2.** oui *m*; *parl.* voix *f* pour; *the* ~*s have it* le vote est pour.

a·za·lea ♀ [ə'zeiljə] azalée *f.*

az·i·muth *astr.* ['æziməθ] azimut *m*; ~ *instrument* compas *m* de relèvement; **az·i·muth·al** [~'mjuːθl] azimutal (-aux *m/pl.*).

a·zo·ic *géol.* [ə'zouik] azoïque.

az·ure ['æʒə] **1.** d'azur, azuré; **2.** azur *m.*

B

B, b [biː] B *m*, b *m*.

baa [bɑː] **1.** bêler; **2.** bêlement *m*.

Bab·bitt *Am.* [ˈbæbit] philistin *m*; affreux bourgeois *m*; ⊕ ♀ *metal* métal *m* blanc antifriction.

bab·ble [ˈbæbl] **1.** babiller; jaser; murmurer; gazouiller; raconter (*qch.*) en babillant; **2.** babil(lage) *m*, babillement *m*; bavardage *m*, jaserie *f*; murmure *m*; **'bab·bler** bavard(e *f*) *m*; jaseur (-euse *f*) *m*.

babe [beib] *poét.* petit(e) enfant *m*(*f*).

Ba·bel [ˈbeibl] *bibl.* Tour *f* de Babel; *fig.* brouhaha *m*, vacarme *m*.

ba·boon *zo.* [bəˈbuːn] babouin *m*.

ba·by [ˈbeibi] **1.** bébé *m*; poupon(ne *f*) *m*; poupard *m*; F *it's your ~* c'est votre affaire; F *be left holding the ~* rester avec l'affaire sur les bras; **2.** d'enfant, de bébé, petit; *~ act usu.* plead (*ou* play) the *~ Am.* plaider son inexpérience; appuyer sa défense sur sa minorité; *~ boom* montée *f* en flèche des naissances; **'~-car·riage** *Am.* voiture *f* d'enfant; **'~-farm·er** personne *f* qui prend des enfants en nourrice; *péj.* faiseuse *f* d'anges; *~ grand* ♩ piano *m* (à) demi-queue; **'ba·by·hood** [ˈ~hud] première enfance *f*; bas âge *m*; **'ba·by·ish** □ puéril; de bébé.

Bab·y·lo·ni·an [bæbiˈlounjən] **1.** babylonien(ne *f*); **2.** Babylonien(ne *f*) *m*.

ba·by...: **'~-mind·er** nourrice *f*; **'~-sit** [*irr.* (sit)] veiller sur un enfant; faire du baby-sitting; **'ba·by'sit·ter** baby-sitter *m*, garde-bébé *mf* (*pl.* gardes-bébés).

bac·ca·lau·re·ate [bækəˈlɔːriit] baccalauréat *m*; *univ. usu.* licence *f* (*ès lettres, ès sciences, etc.*).

Bac·cha·nal [ˈbækənl] *see* Bacchant; **'Bac·cha·nals** *pl.*, **Bac·cha·na·li·a** [ˌ~ˈneiljə] *pl.* bacchanales *f*/*pl.*; **Bac·cha·na·li·an** **1.** bachique; **2.** *fig.* noceur *m*.

Bac·chant [ˈbækənt] adorateur *m* de Bacchus; (*a.* **Bac·chante** [bəˈkænti]) bacchante *f*.

bach·e·lor [ˈbætʃələ] célibataire *m*, garçon *m*; *hist.* bachelier *m*; *univ.* licencié(e *f*) *m*; *~ girl* garçonne *f*; **bach·e·lor·hood** [ˈ~hud] célibat *m*; vie *f* de garçon.

bac·il·la·ry [bəˈsiləri] bacillaire; **ba·'cil·lus** [ˌ~əs], *pl.* **-li** [ˌ~lai] bacille *m*.

back [bæk] **1.** *su. personne, animal:* dos *m*; reins *m*/*pl.*; revers *m*; *chaise:* dossier *m*; *salle, armoire, scène:* fond *m*; *tête, maison:* derrière *m*; *foot., maison:* arrière *m*; (*at the*) *~ of* au fond de; *put one's ~ into it* y aller de tout son cœur; F *put s.o.'s ~ up* mettre q. en colère; faire rebiffer q.; **2.** *adj.* arrière, de derrière; sur le derrière (*pièce*); sur la cour (*chambre d'hôtel*); *gramm.* vélaire; *~ formation* dérivation *f* régressive; *~ issue* ancien numéro *m*, ancien volume *m*; *~ pay* (*ou* salary) rappel *m* de traitement; **3.** *adv.* en arrière; de retour; **4.** *v*/*t.* renforcer (*un mur, une carte*); endosser (*un livre*); parier sur, miser sur (*un cheval*); appuyer, (*a. ~ up*) soutenir; servir de fond à; reculer (*une charrette*); faire (re)culer (*un cheval*); refouler (*un train*); mettre en arrière (*une machine*); ✝ endosser (*un effet*); financer (*q.*); ⚓ *~ the sails* masquer les voiles; *~ water, ~ the oars* ramer à rebours; scier; *~ up* prêter son appui à (*qch., q.*); *v*/*i.* aller en arrière; marcher à reculons; reculer (*cheval*); faire marche arrière (*voiture*); ravaler (*vent*); F se dégager (de, *out of*); F *~ down* en rabattre; rabattre (de, *from*); *~ al·ley Am.* rue *f* misérable (*dans le bas quartier*); **'~-bas·ket** hotte *f*; **'~-bench·er** membre *m* du Parlement sans portefeuille; **'~-bend** *sp.* pont *m*; **'~-bite** [*irr.* (bite)] médire de (*q.*); **'~-board** dossier *m*; ✠ planche *f* à dos; **'~-bone** échine *f*; colonne *f* vertébrale; *fig.* caractère *m*, fermeté *f*; *to the ~ fig.* à la moelle des os; **'~-chat** impertinence *f*, répliques *f*/*pl.* impertinentes; **'~-cloth** *théâ.*

toile *f* de fond; '~·**date** antidater; ~*d to* avec effet rétroactif à, avec rappel à compter de; '~-'**door** porte *f* de derrière; *fig.* petite porte *f*; '~·**drop** *théâ.* toile *f* de fond; **backed** à dos, à dossier; *phot.* ocré (*plaque*); ~ **entrance** entrée *f* de derrière; '**back·er** parieur (-euse *f*) *m*; partisan *m*; ✝ donneur *m* d'aval; commanditaire *m*. **back**...: '~-'**fire** *mot.* 1. pétarde *f*; 2. pétarder; ~'**gam·mon** trictrac *m*; jacquet *m*; '~·**ground** fond *m*, arrière-plan *m*; '~-'**hand** 1. coup *m* fourré; *tennis:* revers *m*; 2. déloyal (-aux *m/pl.*); de revers; '~-'**hand·ed** renversé; *fig.* équivoque; '~-'**hand·er** *see* back-hand 1; riposte *f* inattendue; '~·**lash** contre-coup *m*, répercussion(s *pl.*) *f*, *fig. a.* réaction *f* brutale; '~·**log** réserve *f*; arriéré *m*; '~·**pack** sac *m* à dos; '~·**pay** rappel *m* de salaire; '~-'**ped·al** contre-pédaler; ~ling brake frein *m* par contrepédalage; '~'**side** derrière *m*; '~·**sight** hausse *f*; *surv.* coup *m* arrière; '~-**slap·per** *Am.* luron *m*; '~·**slide** [*irr.* (*slide*)] retomber dans l'erreur *m*; rechuter; '~·**slid·er** relaps(e *f*) *m*; '~·**slid·ing** récidive *f*; '~·**stage** derrière la scène, dans les coulisses; '~·**stairs** escalier *m* de service; '~·**stitch** 1. point *m* arrière; 2. coudre à points de piqûre; ~ **street** rue *f* latérale, petite rue *f*; ~ **abortionist** faiseuse *f* d'anges; '~·**stroke** (*ou* ~ *swimming*) nage *f* sur le dos; ~ **talk** *Am.* impertinence *f*; ~ **to back** *sp. Am.* F l'un après l'autre; ~ **to front** sens devant derrière; '~·**track** *Am.* F *fig.* s'en retourner (*chez soi etc.*).
back·ward ['bækwəd] 1. *adj.* attardé, arrière (*personne*); en arrière, rétrograde; en retard; peu empressé (à *inf.*, *in gér.*); 2. *adv.* (*a.* '**back·wards**) en arrière; *walk backwards and forwards* aller et venir; **back·ward'a·tion** ✝ *Br.* déport *m*; '**back·ward·ness** retard *m*; hésitation *f*, lenteur *f* (*a. d'intelligence*); tardiveté *f*.
back...: '~·**wa·ter** eau *f* arrêtée; bras *m* de décharge; remous *m*; '~·**wheel** roue *f* arrière; roue *f* motrice; ~ **drive** pont *m* arrière; '~·**woods** *pl.* forêts *f/pl.* de l'intérieur (de l'Amérique du Nord); '~·**woodsman** colon *m* des forêts (de l'Amérique du Nord).

ba·con ['beikən] lard *m*; F *save one's* ~ sauver sa peau; se tirer d'affaire; *sl. bring home the* ~ revenir triomphant; décrocher la timbale.
bac·te·ri·al □ [bæk'tiəriəl] bactérien(ne *f*); **bac·te·ri·o·log·i·cal** □ [bæktiəriə'lɔdʒikl] bactériologiqῠe; **bac·te·ri·ol·o·gist** [~'ɔlədʒist] bactériologiste *mf*; **bac'te·ri·um** [~iəm], *pl.* -**ri·a** [~riə] bactérie *f*.
bad □ [bæd] mauvais; triste (*affaire*); avarié (*viande*); piteux (-euse *f*) (*état*); méchant (*enfant*); grave (*accident*); malade; faux (fausse *f*) (*monnaie*); vilain (*mot. a. Am.*); F *not* ~ pas mal du tout; *not too* ~ comme ci comme ça; *things are not so* ~ ça ne marche pas si mal; *he is* ~*ly off* il est mal loti; ~*ly wounded* gravement blessé; F *want* ~*ly* avoir grand besoin de.
bade [beid] *prét. de* bid 1.
badge [bædʒ] insigne *m*; *fig.* symbole *m*.
badg·er ['bædʒə] 1. *zo.* blaireau *m*; 2. tracasser, harceler, importuner.
bad·lands *Am.* ['bæd'lændz] *pl.* terres *f/pl.* incultivables.
bad·min·ton *sp.* ['bædmintən] badminton *m*.
bad·ness ['bædnis] mauvaise qualité *f*; mauvais état *m*; méchanceté *f* (*d'une personne*).
bad-tem·pered ['bæd'tempəd] grincheux (-euse *f*); acariâtre.
baf·fle ['bæfl] dérouter (*q., des soupçons*); faire échouer (*un projet etc.*); confondre; dépister; *it* ~*s description* il défie toute description; **baf·fling** déconcertant.
bag [bæg] 1. sac *m*; sacoche *f*; bourse *f*; F poche *f* (*sous l'œil*); *chasse:* tableau *m*; *sl.* ~*s pl.* pantalon *m*; *Am.* F *it's in the* ~ c'est dans le sac; *depart* ~ *and baggage* emporter ses cliques et ses claques; 2. (se) gonfler, bouffer; *v/t.* mettre en sac; F chiper, voler; *chasse:* abattre, tuer.
bag·a·telle [bægə'tel] bagatelle *f*; billard *m* anglais.
bag·gage ['bægidʒ] *Am.* bagages *m/pl.*; ~ **al·low·ance** franchise *f* de bagages; ~ **car** 🚉 fourgon *m* aux bagages; '~-**check** bulletin *m* de bagages; ~ **rack** *auto:* galerie *f*, 🚉 porte-bagages *m/inv.*; ~ **re·claim** (guichet *m* de) remise *f* des bagages; ~ **room** consigne *f*.

bag·ging ['bægiŋ] mise *f* en sac; toile *f* à sac.

bag·gy ['bægi] bouffant; pendant (*joues*); formant poches (*pantalon*).

bag...: '**~·man** F commis *m* voyageur; '**~·pipe** cornemuse *f*; '**~·snatch·er** voleur *m* à la tire.

bail¹ [beil] **1.** garant *m*; caution *f*; ⚖ *admit to ~* accorder la liberté provisoire sous caution à (*q.*); *be* (*ou go ou stand*) *~ for* fournir caution pour; **2.** cautionner; *~ out* se porter caution pour (*q.*).

bail² ⚓ [~] écoper.

bail³ [~] *cricket:* *~s pl.* bâtonnets *m/pl.*, barrettes *f/pl.*

bail⁴ [~] *baquet etc.:* poignée *f*.

bail·a·ble ⚖ ['beiləbl] admettant l'élargissement *m* sous caution.

bail·ee ⚖ [bei'li:] dépositaire *m*; emprunteur (-euse *f*) *m*.

bail·er ⚓ ['beilə] **1.** écope *f*; **2.** écoper.

bail·iff ['beilif] 🖊 régisseur *m*, intendant *m*; ⚖ agent *m* de poursuites, huissier *m*.

bail·ment ⚖ ['beilmənt] dépôt *m* (*de biens*); mise *f* en liberté sous caution.

bail·or ⚖ ['beilə] déposant *m*; prêteur (-euse *f*) *m*; ⚖ caution *f*.

bairn *écoss.* [beən] enfant *mf*.

bait [beit] **1.** amorce *f*; appât *m* (*a. fig.*); *a. fig. take the ~* mordre à l'hameçon; **2.** *v/t.* amorcer (*un piège, une ligne, etc.*); faire manger (*un cheval pendant une halte*); *fig.* harceler; importuner; *v/i.* se restaurer; s'arrêter pour se rafraîchir.

bait·ing ['beitiŋ] harcèlement *m*; amorcement *m*.

baize 🖊 [beiz] serge *f*; tapis *m* vert.

bake [beik] **1.** (faire) cuire; *v/i.* boulanger; F brûler; *~d potatoes pl.* pommes *f/pl.* (de terre) au four; **2.** soirée *f*; '**~·house** fournil *m*, boulangerie *f*.

ba·ke·lite ⊕ ['beikəlait] bakélite *f*.

bak·er ['beikə] boulanger *m*; '**bak·er·y** boulangerie *f*; '**bak·ing** rôtissant, desséchant (*soleil*); F brûlant; *~ hot* torride; '**bak·ing-pow·der** poudre *f* à lever; '**bak·ing-soda** bicarbonate *m* de soude.

bak·sheesh ['bækʃi:ʃ] bakchich *m*.

bal·a·lai·ka ♩ [bælə'laikə] balalaïka *f*.

bal·ance ['bæləns] **1.** balance *f*; *fig.* équilibre *m*, aplomb *m*; *montre:* balancier *m*, *a. horloge:* régulateur *m*;

🕈 solde *m*; bilan *m*; *surt. Am.* F reste *m*; *~ in hand* solde *m* créditeur; *~ of payments* balance *f* des paiements; *~ of power* balance *f* politique; *~ of trade* balance *f* commerciale; *see strike* 2; **2.** *v/t.* balancer; équilibrer, stabiliser; compenser; faire contrepoids à; 🕈 balancer, solder; dresser le bilan de; *v/i.* se faire équilibre; se balancer; '**~-sheet** 🕈 bilan *m*.

bal·co·ny ['bælkəni] balcon *m*; *théâ.* deuxième balcon *m*.

bald [bɔ:ld] chauve; *fig.* nu; dénudé.

bal·da·chin ['bɔ:ldəkin] baldaquin *m*.

bal·der·dash ['bɔ:ldədæʃ] bêtises *f/pl.*, balivernes *f/pl.*

bald...: '**~-head**, '**~-pate** tête *f* chauve; '**~-'head·ed** à la tête chauve; *go ~ into* faire (*qch.*) tête baissée; '**bald·ness** calvitie *f*; *fig.* nudité *f*; *surt. style:* sécheresse *f*.

bale¹ 🕈 [beil] balle *f*, ballot *m*.

bale² ⚓ [~] *v/t.* écoper; *v/i.* ✈ *~ out* sauter en parachute.

bale·fire ['beilfaiə] † feu *m* d'alarme; *see bonfire*; bûcher *m* funéraire.

bale·ful □ ['beilful] sinistre; funeste.

balk [bɔ:k] **1.** bande *f* de délimitation; billon *m*; *fig.* obstacle *m*; **2.** *v/t.* contrarier; entraver; éviter (*un sujet*); se soustraire à; frustrer; *v/i.* refuser; reculer (devant, *at*); regimber (contre, *at*).

Bal·kan ['bɔ:lkən] balkanique, des Balkans.

ball¹ [bɔ:l] **1.** *cricket, tennis, hockey, fusil, etc.:* balle *f*; *croquet, neige:* boule *f*; *foot., enfant:* ballon *m*; *billard:* bille *f*; *laine, ficelle:* pelote *f*, peloton *m*; *canon:* boulet *m*; *Am. baseball:* coup *m* manqué; F *be on the ~* être à la hauteur (de la situation); connaître son affaire; *keep the ~ rolling* soutenir la conversation; *Am.* F *play ~* coopérer (avec, *with*); **2.** (s')agglomérer.

ball² [~] (*pl.* -s) *m*; F *fig. have a ~* s'amuser bien; *open the ~* ouvrir le bal (*a. fig.*).

bal·lad ['bæləd] ballade *f*; ♩ romance *f*; '**~-mon·ger** chansonnier *m*.

ball-and-sock·et ⊕ ['bɔ:lən'sɔkit]: *~ joint* joint *m* à rotule.

bal·last ['bæləst] **1.** ⚓ lest *m*; *fig.* esprit *m* rassis; 🚂 ballast *m*, empierrement *m*; *mental* ~ sens *m* rassis; 2. lester; 🚢 ballaster.

ball...: '~-'**bear·ing**(*s pl.*) ⊕ roulement *m* à billes; '~-**boy** *tennis*: ramasseur *m* de balles.

bal·let ['bælei] ballet *m*.

bal·lis·tics [bə'listiks] *usu. sg.* balistique *f*.

bal·loon [bə'luːn] 1. 🎈, *a.* ⚗ ballon *m*; ⚠ pomme *f*; *mot.* ~ tyre pneu *m* ballon *ou* confort; 2. monter en ballon; bouffer, se ballonner; **bal'loon fab·ric** entoilage *m*; **bal·'loon·ist** aéronaute *m*, aérostier *m*.

bal·lot ['bælət] 1. (tour *m* de) scrutin *m*; vote *m*; *parl.* tirage *m* au sort; 2. voter au scrutin; tirer au sort; ~ *for* tirer (*qch.*) au sort; tirer au sort pour; '~-**box** urne *f*.

ball-point-pen ['bɔːlpɔint'pen] stylo *m* à bille.

ball-room ['bɔːlrum] salle *f* de bal; *hôtel*: salle *f* de danse.

bal·ly·hoo *Am.* ['bæli'huː] grosse réclame *f*; battage *m*.   [dêver (*q.*).]

bal·ly·rag F ['bæliræg] faire enrager.

balm [baːm] baume *m* (*a. fig.*).

bal·mor·al [bæl'mɔrl] (béret *m*) balmoral *m*; (brodequin *m*) balmoral *m*.

balm·y □ ['baːmi] balsamique; *fig.* embaumé, doux (douce *f*); F toqué.

ba·lo·ney *Am. sl.* [bə'louni] sottises *f/pl.*; foutaise *f*.

bal·sam ['bɔːlsəm] baume *m*; **bal·sam·ic** [~'sæmik] (~*ally*) balsamique.

bal·us·ter ['bæləstə] balustre *m*.

bal·us·trade [bæləs'treid] balustrade *f*; *fenêtre etc.*: accoudoir *m*; garde-corps *m/inv.*

bam·boo [bæm'buː] bambou *m*.

bam·boo·zle F [bæm'buːzl] frauder (de, *out of*); amener par ruse (à, *into*).

ban [bæn] 1. ban *m*, proscription *f*; *eccl.* interdit *m*; 2. interdire (qch. à q., *s.o. from s.th.*); mettre (*un livre*) à l'index.

ba·nan·a 🍌 [bə'naːnə] banane *f*; *Am.* ~ split banane *f* à la glace.

band [bænd] 1. bande *f*; lien *m*; *chapeau etc., frein*: ruban *m*; raie *f*; *deuil*: brassard *m*; ⊕ *roue*: bandage *m*; *reliure*: nerf *m*, nervure *f*; *radio*: bande *f*; ♪ orchestre *m*, musique *f* (*militaire*); 2. bander; fretter (*un four etc.*); ~ *o.s.*, *be* ~*ed* se bander; *péj.* s'ameuter.

band·age ['bændidʒ] 1. bandage *m*; bande *f*; bandeau *m*; pansement *m*; *first aid* ~ bandage *m*; pansement *m*; 2. bander; mettre un pansement à (*une plaie*).   [sparadrap *m*.]

Band-Aid (*TM*) *Am.* ['bændeid]

ban·dan·(n)a [bæn'dænə] foulard *m*; F mouchoir *m*.

band·box ['bændbɔks] carton *m* à chapeaux; carton *m* de modiste; *look as if one came out of a* ~ être tiré à quatre épingles.

ban·dit ['bændit] bandit *m*, brigand *m*; '**ban·dit·ry** brigandage *m*.

band·mas·ter ['bændmaːstə] chef *m* d'orchestre *ou* de musique *etc.*

ban·dog † ['bændɔg] mâtin *m*.

ban·do·leer [bændə'liə] bandoulière *f*; cartouchière *f*.

bands·man ['bændzmən] musicien *m*; fanfariste *m*; '**band·stand** kiosque *m* à musique; '**band·wag·on** *Am.* F *pol.* char *m* des musiciens; *fig.* cause *f* victorieuse; *get into* (*ou on*) *the* ~ se ranger du bon côté.

ban·dy ['bændi] 1. *sp.* jeu *m* de crosse; ~-*ball* hockey *m*; 2. (se) renvoyer (*balle, paroles, reproches, etc.*); échanger (*des coups, des plaisanteries*); (*a.* ~ *about*) faire courir (*des bruits*); '~-**leg·ged** bancal (~als *m/pl.*).

bane [bein] *fig.* tourment *m*, malheur *m*; † poison *m*; **bane·ful** □ ['beinful] *fig.* funeste; pernicieux (-euse *f*).

bang [bæŋ] 1. boum! pan!; *go* ~ éclater; 2. exactement, pile; directement, en plein; 3. coup *m*; détonation *f*; *porte*: claquement *m*; 4. frapper; (faire) claquer *ou* heurter à (*la porte*); F faire baisser (*le prix*); *sl.* baiser; '**bang·er** pétard *m*; F vieux tacot *m*; F saucisse; ~*s and mash* saucisses *f/pl.* à la purée.

ban·gle ['bæŋgl] bracelet *m* de poignet *ou* de cheville.

bang-on F ['bæŋ'ɔn] exactement, tout juste; *it's* ~ *a.* c'est au poil; *il tombe pile;* ~ *time* à l'heure pile.

bangs *Am.* [bæŋz] *pl. coiffure:* franges *f/pl.*

bang-up F ['bæŋ'ʌp] première classe; chic *adj./inv. en genre.*

ban·ish ['bæniʃ] bannir; proscrire; '**ban·ish·ment** exil *m*, proscription *f*.

ban·is·ters ['bænistəz] *pl.* balustres *m/pl.*; rampe *f*.

ban·jo ♩ ['bændʒou] banjo *m*.

bank [bæŋk] **1.** talus *m*; terrasse *f*; *sable, brouillard, huîtres*: banc *m*; *rivière*: berge *f*; *nuages*: couche *f*; ✝, *a. jeu*: banque *f*; ~ *of deposit* banque *f* de dépôt; ~ *of issue* banque *f* d'émission; *joint-stock* ~ banque *f* sous forme de société par actions; **2.** *v/t.* endiguer; terrasser; ⊕ surhausser (*un virage*); ✝ déposer en banque; ✍ pencher; incliner sur l'aile; *v/i.* s'entasser, s'amonceler; avoir un compte de banque (*chez, with*); ✍ virer, pencher l'avion; ~ *on* compter sur, miser sur; ~ *up* (s')amonceler; **'bank·a·ble** bancable, négociable en banque; **'bank-ac·count** compte *m* en banque; **'bank-bill** effet *m*; *Am. see* banknote; **'bank·er** banquier *m* (*a. jeu*); *jeu*: tailleur *m*; **bank hol·i·day** jour *m* férié; **'bank·ing 1.** (affaires *f/pl.* de) banque *f*; ✍ virage *m* incliné; **2.** de banque, en banque; ~ *charges pl.* frais *m/pl.* de banque; ~ *hours pl.* heures *f/pl.* d'ouverture des banques; ~ *house* maison *f* de banque; **'bank·note** billet *m* de banque; **'bank·rate** taux *m* officiel *ou* de la Banque *ou* de l'escompte; **bankrupt** ['~rəpt] **1.** (commerçant *m*) failli *m*; *fraudulent* ~ banqueroutier (-ère *f*) *m*; ~*'s estate* masse *f* des biens (de la faillite); *go* ~ faire faillite; **2.** failli; banqueroutier (-ère *f*); *fig.* ~ *in* (*ou of*) dépourvu de (*une qualité*); **3.** mettre (*q.*) en faillite; **bank·rupt·cy** ['~rəptsi] faillite *f*; *fraudulent* ~ banqueroute *f*; *declaration of* ~ déclaration *f* de faillite.

ban·ner ['bænə] **1.** bannière *f* (*a. eccl.*); étendard *m*; **2.** *Am.* excellent, de première classe; principal (-aux *m/pl.*).

banns [bænz] *pl.* bans *m/pl.* (*de mariage*); *put up the* ~ (faire) publier les bans; *call the* ~ *of* annoncer le mariage de (*q.*).

ban·quet ['bæŋkwit] **1.** banquet *m*; dîner *m* de gala; **2.** *v/t.* offrir un banquet *etc.* à (*q.*); *v/i.* F faire festin; ~*ing hall* salle *f* de banquet; **'ban·quet·er** banqueteur (-euse *f*) *m*.

ban·shee *écoss., Ir.* [bæn'ʃiː] fée *f* de mauvais augure.

ban·tam ['bæntəm] coq *m* (poule *f*)

Bantam; *fig.* nain *m*; *sp.* ~ *weight* poids *m* coq.

ban·ter ['bæntə] **1.** badinage *m*; raillerie *f*; **2.** badiner; railler; **'ban·ter·er** railleur (-euse *f*) *m*.

bap·tism ['bæptizm] baptême *m*; ~ *of fire* baptême *f* du feu; **bap·tismal** [bæp'tizməl] de baptême; baptistaire (*registre*).

bap·tist ['bæptist] (*ana*)baptiste *mf*; **bap·tis·ter·y** ['~tistri] baptistère *m*; **bap·tize** [~'taiz] baptiser (*a. fig.*).

bar [bɑː] **1.** barre *f* (*a. métal, a. sable, port*); traverse *f*; bar *m*, estaminet *m*; *savon*: brique *f*; *or*: lingot *m*; ♪ barre *f*; mesure *f*; ♪ lame *f*; ⚖ barre *f* (*des accusés*), barreau *m* (*des avocats*); *théâ. etc.*: buvette *f*; *fig.* empêchement *m*; *sp. horizontal* ~ barre *f* fixe; ⚖ *be called to the* ~ être reçu avocat; *prisoner at the* ~ accusé(e *f*) *m*; *stand at the* ~ paraître à la barre; **2.** barrer; griller (*une fenêtre*); bâcler (*une porte*); interdire, exclure (de, *from*); rayer (*de lignes*); empêcher (q. de *inf.*, *s.o. from gér.*); ~ *out* barrer la porte à; **3.** excepté, sauf, à l'exception de; ~ *none* sans exception; ~ *one* sauf un(e).

barb [bɑːb] *hameçon*: barbillon *m*; *flèche*: barbelure *f*; *plume*: barbe *f*; *fig.* trait *m* acéré; ⚕ ~*s pl.* arêtes *f/pl.*

bar·bar·i·an [bɑː'bɛəriən] barbare (*a. su./mf*); **bar·bar·ic** [~'bærik] (~*ally*) barbare, rude; **bar·ba·rism** ['~bərizm] barbarie *f*, rudesse *f*, grossièreté *f*; *ling.* barbarisme *m*; **bar·bar·i·ty** [~'bæriti] barbarie *f*, cruauté *f*; **bar·ba·rize** ['~bəraiz] barbariser; **'bar·ba·rous** ▢ barbare; cruel(le *f*), inhumain.

bar·be·cue ['bɑːbikjuː] **1.** grand châssis *m* pour le rôtissage; animal *m* rôti tout entier; *Am.* grande fête *f* (*en plein air*) où on rôtit des animaux tout entiers; **2.** griller au charbon de bois (*de la viande*); rôtir tout entier (*un animal*).

barbed barbelé; ⚕ aristé, hameçonné; ~ *wire* fil *m* de fer barbelé; ~*-wire fence* haie *f* barbelée, haie *f* de barbelés.

bar·bel *icht.* ['bɑːbl] barbeau *m*.

bar·bell *sp.* ['bɑːbel] barre *f* à sphères *ou* à boules.

bar·ber ['bɑːbə] coiffeur *m*; barbier

m; *surt. Am.* ~ **shop** salon *m* de coiffure.

bar·bi·tu·rate [baː'bitjuərət] barbiturique *m*.

bard [baːd] barde *m*; F poète *m*.

bare [bɛə] **1.** nu; dénudé; vide; dégarni; sec (sèche *f*) (*as, valet, etc.*); *the* ~ *idea* la seule pensée; **2.** mettre à nu, découvrir; '~**·back(ed)** à nu, à poil; '~**·faced** □ F éhonté, cynique; '~**·fac·ed·ness** effronterie *f*, cynisme *m*; '~**·foot·ed** aux pieds nus; nu-pieds; '~**·'head·ed** nutête, (la) tête nue; '**bare·ly** à peine, tout juste; '**bare·ness** nudité *f*, dénuement *m*; *style:* pauvreté *f*.

bar·gain ['baːgin] **1.** marché *m*, affaire *f*; emplette *f*; occasion *f*; *une* véritable occasion; *a good* (*bad*) ~ une bonne (mauvaise) affaire; *a* ~ *is a* ~ marché conclu reste conclu; F *it's a* ~! entendu!, convenu!; *into the* ~ en plus, pardessus le marché; *make* (*ou strike*) *a* ~ conclure un marché (*avec, with*); ~ *basement* coin *m ou* sous-sol *m* des bonnes affaires; ~ *price* prix *m* de solde; ~ *sale* soldes *m/pl.*; **2.** négocier; traiter (de, *for*); marchander (qch., *about s.th.*); ~ *for* F s'attendre à.

barge [baːdʒ] **1.** chaland *m*, péniche *f*; gabarre *f* (*à voiles*); barge *f* de parade; ♱ deuxième canot *m*; **2.** F se heurter (contre, *into*); bousculer (*q.*); ~ *in* faire irruption; ~ *into the conversation* se mêler à la conversation; **barg'gee**, '**barge·man** chalandier *m*; gabarier *m*; F batelier *m*.

bar·i·ron ['baːaiən] fer *m* en barres.

bar·i·tone ♪ ['bæritoun] baryton *m*.

bar·i·um ♱ ['bɛəriəm] baryum *m*.

bark¹ [baːk] **1.** écorce *f*; *inner* ~ liber *m*; ⊕ tan *m*; **2.** écorcer, décortiquer; F écorcher (*la peau*).

bark² [~] **1.** aboyer (après, contre *at*); glapir (*renard*); F tousser; F *be* ~*ing up the wrong tree* faire fausse route; **2.** aboiement *m*, aboi *m*; glapissement *m*; F toux *f*.

bark³ [~] ♱ *see barque; poét.* barque *f*.

bar-keep(·er) ['baːkiːp(ə)] cabaretier *m*; tenancier *m* d'un bar.

bark·er ['baːkə] aboyeur (-euse *f*) *m* (*a. fig.*); F revolver *m*.

bar·ley ['baːli] orge *f*.

barm [baːm] levure *f*, levain *m* de bière.

bar·maid ['baːmeid] barmaid *f*.

bar·man ['baːmən] *see bartender.*

barm·y ['baːmi] en fermentation; *sl.* toqué.

barn [baːn] grange *f*; *Am.* étable *f*, écurie *f*.

bar·na·cle¹ ['baːnəkl] *orn.* bernacle *f*; oie *f* marine; *zo.* bernache *f*; *ana*tife *m*; *fig.* individu *m* cramponnant.

bar·na·cle² [~] *vét. usu.* ~*s pl.* morailles *f/pl.*; *iro.* ~*s pl.* besicles *f/pl.*

barn·storm *Am. pol.* ['baːnstɔːm] faire une tournée de discours électoraux.

ba·rom·e·ter [bə'rɔmitə] baromètre *m*; **bar·o·met·ric, bar·o·met·ri·cal** □ [bærə'metrik(l)] barométrique.

bar·on ['bærən] baron *m*; ~ *of beef* selle *f* de bœuf; *coal etc.* ~ (haut) baron *m* du charbon *etc.*; '**bar·on·age** baronnage *m*; barons *m/pl.*; annuaire *m* de la noblesse; '**bar·on·ess** baronne *f*; **bar·on·et** ['~it] baronnet; **bar·on·et·cy** ['~si] dignité *f* de baronnet; **ba·ro·ni·al** [bə'rouniəl] de baron; F seigneurial (-aux *m/pl.*); **bar·o·ny** ['bærəni] baronnie *f*.

ba·roque [bə'rouk] baroque (*a. su./ m*), rococo (*a. su./m*).

barque ♱ [baːk] trois-mâts barque *m*.

bar·rack ['bærək] **1.** *usu.* ~*s pl.* caserne *f*; ~ *room* chambrée *f*; **2.** *v/t. sl.* conspuer (*q.*); *v/i.* chahuter; '~**·square**, '~**·yard** cour *f* du quartier.

bar·rage ['bæraːʒ] barrage *m*; ✕ tir *m* de barrage *ou* sur zone; *creeping* ~ barrage *m* rampant.

bar·rel ['bærl] **1.** tonneau *m*, futaille *f*, *vin etc.*: fût *m*; *fusil etc.*: canon *m*; *serrure:* cylindre *m*; *montre:* barillet *m*; ♪ cylindre *m* noté; *anat.* caisse *f* (du tympan); *harengs:* caque *f*; **2.** mettre (*qch.*) en fût; enfûtailler; (*souv.* ~ *off*, ~*up*) encaquer; '**bar·relled** en tonneau(x); en caque (*harengs*); bombé; '**bar·rel·or·gan** ♪ orgue *m* mécanique *ou* de Barbarie; piano *m* mécanique.

bar·ren □ ['bærən] stérile; aride (*a. fig.*); peu fertile (*a. fig.*); ✝ improductif (-ive *f*) (*argent*); '**bar·ren·ness** stérilité *f*; *fig.* aridité *f*.

bar·ri·cade [bæri'keid] **1.** barricade *f*; **2.** barricader.

bar·ri·er ['bæriə] barrière f; obstacle m (a. fig.); muraille f (de glace); 🚂 portillon m d'accès.

bar·ring ['bɑːriŋ] prp. excepté, sauf; à part.

bar·ris·ter ['bæristə] (a. ~-at-law) avocat m.

bar·row¹ ['bærou] tumulus m; tertre m funéraire.

bar·row² [~] see hand-~, wheel-~; ~·man marchand m des quatre saisons.

bar·tend·er ['bɑːtendə] buvetier m; garçon m de comptoir, barman m.

bar·ter ['bɑːtə] 1. échange m; troc m; ~ shop boutique f pour l'échange de marchandises; 2. échanger, troquer (contre, for); péj. faire trafic de; a. fig. ~ away vendre.

bar·y·tone ♪ ['bæritoun] baryton m.

ba·salt ['bæsɔːlt] basalte m.

base¹ □ [beis] bas(se f), vil; indigne, ignoble; faux (fausse f) (monnaie).

base² [~] 1. base f (a. 🔬, ⚗); fondement m; △ soubassement m; ⊕ socle m; phot. support m; lampe, cartouche: culot m; 2. fig. baser, fonder (sur, [up]on); ⚓ baser; ~ o.s. on se baser ou fonder sur; be ~d (up)on dépendre de; être fondé sur.

base...: '~-ball Am. base-ball m; '~-less sans base ou fondement; '~-line ⚓ base f d'approvisionnement; sp. ligne f de fond; surv. base f; 'base·ment soubassement m; sous-sol m. [(fig.).\
base·ness ['beisnis] bassesse f (a.).⌐
bash·ful □ ['bæʃful] timide; modeste.

bash F [bæʃ] 1. frapper ou cogner dur ou fort; 2. coup m violent; have a ~ at s.th. essayer qch., s'essayer à qch.; have a ~ at it essayer le coup.

ba·sic ['beisik] (~ally) fondamental (-aux m/pl.); de base; 🔬 basique; ♀ English (= British, American, Scientific, International, Commercial English) l'anglais m basique, le basic m; ~ iron fer m basique; **bas·ics** pl.: the ~ l'essentiel m, les éléments m/pl.
ba·sil·i·ca △ [bə'zilikə] basilique f.
bas·i·lisk ['bæzilisk] 1. basilic m; 2. de basilic.

ba·sin ['beisn] bassin m; soupe: écuelle f, bol m; lait: jatte f; cuvette f; lavabo m; ⚓, géog. bassin m.

ba·sis ['beisis], pl. -ses ['~siːz] base f; fondement m; impôt: assiette f; ⚔ base f; ⚓ station f; take as ~ se baser sur.

bask [bɑːsk] se chauffer au soleil, prendre un bain de soleil; F jouir (de, in).

bas·ket ['bɑːskit] corbeille f; panier m; '~-ball basket-ball m; ~·din·ner, ~ sup·per Am. souper m en piquenique; 'bas·ket·ful plein panier m; 'bas·ket-work vannerie f.

bass¹ ♪ [beis] basse f.
bass² [bæs] liber m; tille f, filasse f; '~-broom balai m.
bas·si·net [bæsi'net] berceau m; voiture f d'enfant.
bas·so ♪ ['bæsou] basse f.
bas·soon ♪ [bə'suːn] basson m.
bast [bæst] liber m; tille f.
bas·tard ['bæstəd] 1. □ bâtard; faux (fausse f), corrompu; 2. bâtard(e f) m; enfant mf naturel(le f); 'bas·tar·dy bâtardise f.
baste¹ [beist] arroser (de graisse) (un rôti); F bâtonner (q.).
baste² [~] bâtir, baguer.
bas·ti·na·do [bæsti'neidou] 1. bastonnade f; 2. donner la bastonnade à (q.).
bas·tion ⚔ ['bæstiən] bastion m.

bat¹ [bæt] chauve-souris (pl. chauves-souris) f; be blind as a ~ ne pas y voir plus clair qu'une taupe.
bat² [~] 1. cricket: batte f; pingpong: raquette f; baseball: at ~ (être) à la batte; Am. F come (go) to ~ for porter secours à; off one's own ~ fig. de sa propre initiative; 2. manier la batte; être au guichet.
batch [bætʃ] pain, a. fig.: fournée f; papiers: paquet m; lot m.
bate [beit] diminuer; rabattre (le prix); baisser (la voix); with ~d breath en retenant son souffle.
Bath¹ [bɑːθ]: ~ brick brique f anglaise; ~ chair fauteuil m roulant.
bath² [~] 1. (pl. baths [bɑːðz] bain m (de boue, de pieds, de soleil, de trempe, de vapeur, ~ douche); ~ foam mousse f de bain; ~ house cabines f/pl. de bains; 2. (se) baigner.
bathe [beið] 1. (se) baigner; 2. bain m (de mer etc.); baignade f.
bath·ing ['beiðiŋ] bains m/pl. (de mer etc.); baignades f/pl.; attr. de bain(s); ~ beau·ty belle baigneuse f; '~-cap bonnet m de bain; '~-cos-

'**tume** maillot *m* de bain; '**~-hut** cabine *f* de bains (de plage); **~ re'sort** station *f* balnéaire, plage *f*; '**~-suit** maillot *m* de bain; '**~-trunks** *pl.* caleçon *m* de bain.

ba·thos ['beiθɔs] ampoulé *m*; enflure *f*; anticlimax *m*.

bath...: '**~-robe** *Am.* peignoir *m* de bain; '**~-tow·el** serviette *f* de bain; '**~-tub** baignoire *f*; '**~-wa·ter** eau *f* de bain.

ba·tiste † [bæ'ti:st] batiste *f*.

bat·man ['bætmən] brosseur *m*; ordonnance *mf*.

ba·ton ['bætɔn] *maréchal, chef d'orchestre, police:* bâton *m*; *police:* matraque *f*.

ba·tra·chi·an [bə'treikjən] batracien *m*.

bats·man ['bætsmən] *cricket etc.:* batteur *m*.

bat·tal·ion [bə'tæljən] bataillon *m*.

bat·ten ['bætn] **1.** couvre-joint *m*; latte *f* (*a.* ⚓); **2.** *v/t.* latter; (⚓ ~*down*) assujettir; *v/i.* repaître (de, [up]on).

bat·ter ['bætə] **1.** *cricket:* batteur *m*; *cuis.* pâte *f* lisse; **2.** battre; (*a.* ~ *at*) frapper avec violence; bossuer (*un chapeau etc.*); rouer (*q.*) de coups; ⊕ battre en brèche; *fig. critique:* démolir (*q.*); '**bat·ter·ed** délabré, bossué; maltraité; ~ *babies* enfants *m/pl.* martyrs; '**bat·ter·ing-ram** bélier *m*; '**bat·ter·y** batterie *f*; *Am. baseball: the* ~ le lanceur et le batteur; ✗ *a.* ⊕ batterie *f*; ⚡ pile *f*; accumulateur *m*; ⚖ voie *f* de fait; rixe *f*; *assault and* ~ (menaces *f/pl.* et) voies *f/pl.* de fait; '**bat·ter·y-charg·ing 'sta·tion** ⚡ station *f* de charge; '**bat·ter·y-'op·er·at·ed** ⚡ à piles.

bat·tle ['bætl] **1.** bataille *f*, combat *m*; ~ *royal* bataille *f* en règle; mêlée *f* générale; **2.** se battre, lutter (pour, *for*; avec, *with*; contre, *against*); '**~-axe** hache *f* d'armes; *Am. fig.* mégère *f*.

bat·tle·dore ['bætldɔ:] *lessive:* battoir *m*; raquette *f*.

bat·tle·field ['bætlfi:ld], **bat·tle-ground** ['~graund] champ *m* de bataille.

bat·tle·ments ['bætlmənts] *pl.* créneaux *m/pl.*; parapet *m*.

bat·tle...: '**~-plane** ✗ avion *m* de combat; '**~-ship** ✗ cuirasse *m* (de ligne).

bat·tue [bæ'tu:] battue *f*; F carnage *m*.

bau·ble ['bɔ:bl] babiole *f*; fanfreluche *f*.

baulk [bɔ:k] *see* balk.

baux·ite *min.* ['bɔ:ksait] bauxite *f*.

baw·bee *écoss.* [bɔ:'bi:] *see* halfpenny.

bawd [bɔ:d] procureuse *f*; '**bawd·y** obscène; ordurier (-ère *f*) (*propos*).

bawl [bɔ:l] brailler; hurler; crier à tue-tête; F beugler; ~*out* brailler *etc.*; gueuler; *Am. sl.* injurier; F engueuler (*q.*).

bay¹ [bei] bai (*cheval*); isabelle; **2.** cheval *m* bai; isabelle *m*.

bay² [~] baie *f*; golfe *m*; anse *f*; échancrure *f*; ~ *salt* sel *m* de mer; *cuis.* gros sel *m*.

bay³ △ [~] travée *f*; claire-voie (*pl.* claires-voies) *f*; enfoncement *m*; ⛴ quai *m* subsidiaire.

bay⁴ [~] laurier *m*.

bay⁵ [~] **1.** aboyer; hurler (*chien*); ~ *at* hurler *etc.* à; **2.** *stand at* ~ s'acculer à *ou* contre (*qch.*); être aux abois; *bring to* ~, *keep* (*ou hold*) *at* ~ acculer (*un cerf*).

bay·o·net ✗ ['beiənit] **1.** baïonnette *f*; **2.** percer d'un coup de baïonnette; passer (*des gens*) à la baïonnette; '**~-catch** ⊕ encliquetage *m*.

bay·ou *géog. Am.* ['baiu:] bras *m* marécageux (*de rivière*).

bay win·dow ['bei'windou] fenêtre *f* en saillie; *Am. sl.* bedaine *f*.

ba·zaar [bə'zɑ:] bazar *m*; vente *f* de charité.

be [bi:; bi] (*irr.*) **1.** être; se trouver; *there is, there are* il y a; *here's to you(r health)!* à votre santé!; *here you are again!* vous revoilà!; ~ *about* (*gér.*) être occupé à (*inf.*), de (*qch.*); ~ *after* venir après (*q.*); F être en quête de (*q.*); ~ *at* s'occuper de (*qch.*); ~ *off* s'en aller; partir; finir; couper (*courant*); ~ *off with you!* allez-vous-en!; filez!; ~ *on* at *s.o.* harceler *q.*; ~ *on to* être en contact avec; être sur la piste de; être aux trousses de (*q.*); **2.** *v/aux. et p.pr. pour exprimer la durée ou une action incomplète:* ~ *reading* (être en train de) lire; **3.** *v/aux. et inf. pour exprimer le devoir, l'intention ou la possibilité:* I *am to inform you* je suis chargé de vous faire savoir; *it is (not) to* ~ *seen* on (ne) peut (pas) le voir *ou* visiter; *if* *he were to die's'il mourait; 4. v/aux. et p.p. à la voix passive: se rend ordinairement par on et la voix active, ou par la voix passive, ou par un verbe réfléchi; I am asked on me demande.*

beach [biːtʃ] **1.** plage *f*, grève *f*; **2.** ⚓ échouer; tirer à sec; '~-**ball** ballon *m* de plage; '~-**comb·er** F rôdeur *m* de grève; *sl.* propre *m* à rien; '~-**head** ⚔ tête *f* de pont.

bea·con ['biːkn] **1.** † feu *m* d'alarme; feu *m* de joie; ⚓ phare *m*, fanal *m*; balise *f*; **2.** baliser; éclairer.

bead [biːd] **1.** perle *f* (*d'émail etc.*); goutte *f* (*de sueur etc.*); *pneu:* talon *m*; *chapelet:* grain *m*; *fusil:* guidon *m*; ~**s** *pl. a.* chapelet *m*; **2.** *v/t.* couvrir *ou* orner de perles; ⊕ appliquer une baguette sur; *v/i.* perler; '**bead·ing** ⊕, △ baguette *f*.

bea·dle ['biːdl] bedeau *m*; *univ.* appariteur *m*.

bead·y ['biːdi] qui perle; percé en vrille (*yeux*).

beak [biːk] bec *m*; F nez *m* crochu; '**beaked** à bec; crochu (*nez*).

beak·er ['biːkə] gobelet *m*; coupe *f*.

beam [biːm] **1.** *bois:* poutre *f*, solive *f*; *charrue:* flèche *f*, *fig.* rayon *m*; éclat *m*; ⊕ balancier *m*; ⚓ bau *m*, barrot *m* de pont; *chasse:* merrain *m* (*bois de cerf*); *radio:* (*wireless* ~) faisceau *m* hertzien; *phare:* faisceau *m*; F *fig.* be off (*the*) ~ faire fausse route, faire erreur; F *fig.* be on (*the*) ~ être sur la bonne voie; **2.** *v/i. a. fig.* rayonner (*fig.* de with); *v/t.* émettre (*des ondes etc.*); transmettre (par ondes dirigées); '~-**ends** *pl.*: *the ship is on her* ~ le navire est engagé; F *fig.* be on one's ~ F être à la côte.

bean [biːn] fève *f*; grain *m* (*de café*); *Am. sl.* tête *f*, caboche *f*; F *full of* ~*s* plein d'entrain; *sl. give s.o.* ~*s* laver la tête à q.; '~-**feast**, **bean·o** *sl.* ['biːnou] régal *m*; *sl.* bombe *f*.

bear¹ [bɛə] **1.** ours(e *f*) *m*; *fig.* homme *m* maussade; † *sl.* baissier *m*; **2.** † spéculer à la baisse; prendre position à la baisse.

bear² [~] (*irr.*) **1.** *v/t.* porter (*qch., épée, nom, date, amour etc.*); jouir de (*une réputation*); supporter (*poids, frais, conséquences*); soutenir (*un poids*); souffrir (*une douleur etc.*); tolérer, supporter, souffrir; ~ *away* (r)emporter, enlever; ~ *down* vaincre; accabler; ~ *out* emporter;

confirmer (*une assertion*); ~ *up* soutenir; résister à; **2.** *v/i.* endurer; avoir rapport (à, *upon*); porter; ⚓ (*avec adv.*) faire route; ⚓ ~ *to the right* courir sur (*qch.*); ~ *up* tenir bon; ~ *up! courage!;* ~ (*up*)on porter sur; peser sur; ~ *with* se montrer indulgent pour; supporter; *bring to* ~ mettre (*qch.*) en action; braquer (*une lunette*) (sur, [*up*]on); **bear·a·ble** ['bɛərəbl] supportable.

beard [biəd] **1.** barbe *f*; ⚘ arête *f*; **2.** *v/t.* braver, défier, narguer (*q.*); '**beard·ed** barbu; '**beard·less** imberbe; sans barbe.

bear·er ['bɛərə] porteur (-euse *f*) *m*; *passeport:* titulaire *mf*; † *chèque:* porteur *m*; ⊕ support *m*.

bear·ing ['bɛəriŋ] port *m* (d'armes, de nouvelles; *a.* = *maintien*); allure *f*, maintien *m*; capacité *f* de supporter; appui *m*; ⚓ relèvement; ⊕ *souv.* ~*s pl.* palier *m*; coussinet *m*, -s *m/pl.*; ~*s pl.* ⃠ armoiries *f/pl.*, blason *m*; *lose one's* ~*s* perdre le nord, être désorienté; *take one's* ~*s* s'orienter, se repérer.

bear·ish ['bɛəriʃ] d'ours; bourru (*personne*); à la baisse (*tendance*).

beast [biːst] bête *f*; *fig. a.* animal *m*, brute *f*; ~*s pl.* bétail *m*; '**beast·li·ness** bestialité *f*, brutalité *f*; F saleté *f*; '**beast·ly** bestial (-aux *m/pl.*), brutal (-aux *m/pl.*); F sale, dégoûtant; *fig. adv.* terriblement.

beat [biːt] **1.** [*irr.*] *v/t.* battre (*a. chasse: un bois; a.* ♪ *la mesure*); donner des coups de bâton à; cogner à (*une porte*); *oiseau:* battre de (*l'aile*); dépasser (*q.*); (*a.* ~ *out*) aplatir; marteler (*un métal*); frayer, battre (*un chemin*); F assommer; F devancer (*q.*); *Am.* F rouler, refaire (*q.*); *Am. sl.* ~ *it!* filez!; ~ *the air* F taper dans le vide; *Am.* F *it* ~*s the band* ça c'est le comble; ~ *one's brains* se creuser la cervelle; ⚔ ~ *a retreat* battre en retraite; *Am.* F ~ *one's way* to gagner (*un endroit, souv. sans payer*); ~ *down* (r)abattre; donner à plomb (sur, [*up*]on); † faire baisser le prix à (*q.*); marchander (avec) ~ *up* fouetter (*œufs, crème etc.*); recruter (*des partisans*); *Am.* F rosser (*q.*); *v/i.* battre; ~ *about the bush* tourner autour du pot; **2.** battement *m* (*a. phys.*); pulsation *f*; *tambour:* batterie *f*; ♩ mesure *f*, temps *m*; *police*: ronde *f*; *chasse*: battue *f*; *radio*: battement *m*; *Am.* reportage *m* sensationnel que l'on est le premier à publier; *fig.* domaine *m*; **3.** F battu, confondu; F ~ *out* épuisé; **'beat·en** *p.p.* de beat 1; *adj.* battu (*chemin, métal*); **'beat·er** batteur (-euse *f*) *m*; battoir *m* (de laveuse); *chasse*: rabatteur *m*, traqueur *m*.

be·a·tif·ic [biə'tifik] béatifique; *wear a ~ smile* rire aux anges; **be·at·i·fi·ca·tion** *eccl.* [bi:ætifi'keiʃn] béatification *f*; **be'at·i·fy** *eccl.* béatifier; **be'at·i·tude** [~tju:d] béatitude *f*.

beau [bou], *pl.* **beaux** [bouz] galant *m*, prétendant *m*; dandy *m*, élégant *m*; ~ *ideal* idéal *m*.

beau·ti·cian [bju:'tiʃən] esthéticien(ne *f*)*m*, visagiste *mf*.

beau·ti·ful □ ['bju:təful] beau (bel *devant une voyelle ou un h muet*; belle *f*; beaux *m/pl.*); *the ~ people* les gens chic; *the ~ people of Paris a.* le Tout-Paris.

beau·ti·fy ['bju:tifai] embellir.

beau·ty ['bju:ti] beauté *f* (*a. = belle femme*); F drôle *m* de type; *Sleeping* ♀ *Belle f* au bois dormant; ~ *par-lo(u)r,* ~ *shop* institut *m* de beauté; ~ *spot* mouche *f* (*collée sur le visage*); *lieu*: coin *m* pittoresque.

bea·ver ['bi:və] *zo.* castor *m*; † chapeau *m* de castor; F barbu *m*; *casque*: visière *f*.

be·calm [bi'ka:m] abriter, déventer (*un navire*); *poét.* calmer; ⚓ ~*ed* accalminé.

be·came [bi'keim] *prét.* de become.

be·cause [bi'kɔz] parce que; ~ *of* à cause de.

beck [bek] signe *m* (*de tête etc.*).

beck·on ['bekn] faire signe (à *q.*).

be·cloud [bi'klaud] ennuager, voiler.

be·come [bi'kʌm] [*irr.* (come)] *v/i.* devenir; se faire; advenir (de *q., of s.o.*); *v/t.* convenir à, aller (bien) à; **be'com·ing** □ convenable, bienséant; seyant (*costume etc.*).

bed [bed] **1.** lit *m* (*a. d'un fleuve etc.*); banc *m* (*d'huîtres*); tanière *f* (*d'un animal*); ✿ *fleurs*: parterre *m*; *légumes*: planche *f*; ⊕ sommier *m*; assise *f*; *chaussée etc.*: assiette *f*; ~ *and breakfast* chambre(s *pl.*)*f* (*avec petit déjeuner*); **2.** mettre au lit; faire la litière à (*un cheval etc.*); ✿ ~ (*out*) dépoter.

be·daub [bi'dɔ:b] barbouiller (de peinture).

be·daz·zle [bi'dæzl] aveugler, éblouir.

bed-clothes ['bedklouðz] *pl.* draps *m/pl.* de lit.

bed·ding ['bediŋ] literie *f*; litière *f*; ~(*-out*) *plantes*: dépotage *m*.

be·deck [bi'dek] parer, orner.

be·dev·il [bi'devl] ensorceler; *fig.* tourmenter, lutiner; **be·dev·il·ment** ensorcellement *m*; vexation *f*.

be·dew [bi'dju:] humecter de rosée; *poét.* baigner.

be·dim [bi'dim] obscurcir.

be·diz·en [bi'daizn] attifer; chamarrer (*a. fig.*).

bed·lam ['bedləm] F maison *f* de fous; **bed·lam·ite** ['~mait] F fou *m*, folle *f*.

bed·lin·en ['bedlinin] draps *m/pl.* de lit et taies *f/pl.*

bed·ou·in ['beduin] **1.** bédouin(e *f*); **2.** Bédouin(e *f*) *m*.

bed-pan ['bedpæn] bassin *m* de lit.

be·drag·gle [bi'drægl] tacher de boue; crotter.

bed...: '~**·rid**(·**den**) cloué au lit; '~-'rock *géol.* roche *f* de fond; tuf *m*; *fig.* fondement *m*, fond *m*; '~**room** chambre *f* (à coucher); '~**·side:** *at the ~* au chevet (*de q.*); ⚕ *good ~ manner* bonne manière *f* professionnelle; ~ *lamp* lampe *f* de chevet; ~ *rug* descente *f* de lit; '~-'sit·ting-room pièce *f* unique avec lit *ou* divan; '~**sore** ⚕ escarre *f*; '~**·space** *hôtel etc.*: lits *m/pl.*; '~**spread** dessus *m* de lit; '~**stead** châlit *m*; '~**straw** ♀ gaillet *m*; '~**tick** toile *f* à matelas; '~**time** heure *f* du coucher.

bee [bi:] abeille *f*; *Am.* réunion *f* pour travaux en commun; F *have a ~ in one's bonnet* avoir une araignée au plafond.

beech ♀ [bi:tʃ] hêtre *m*; '~**·nut** faine *f*.

beef [bi:f] **1.** bœuf *m*; F muscle *m*; **2.** *Am.* F grommeler, se plaindre; '~**eat·er** hallebardier *m* (*à la Tour de Londres*); ~**steak** ['bi:f'steik] bifteck *m*; ~ **tea** *cuis.* jus *m* de viande de bœuf; consommé *m*; '**beef·y** F musculeux (-euse *f*).

bee...: '~·**hive** ruche *f*; '~·**keep·er**
apiculteur *m*; '~·**keep·ing** apiculture *f*; '~·**line** ligne *f* à vol d'oiseau;
Am. *make a* ~ *for* aller droit vers
(*qch.*); '~·**mas·ter** apiculteur *m*.

been [bi:n, bin] *p.p. de* be.

beer [biə] bière *f*; ~ *on tap* bière *f* à la
pression; *small* ~ petite bière *f*; F
détail *m*, petite affaire *f*; ~ **can** boîte *f*
de bière; ~ **en·gine** pompe *f* à bière;
'**beer·y** F un peu gris.

bees·wax ['bi:zwæks] cire *f* d'abeilles.

beet ♀ [bi:t] betterave *f*; *white* ~
bette *f*, poirée *f*; betterave *f* à sucre;
red ~ betterave *f* rouge.

bee·tle¹ ['bi:tl] **1.** mailloche *f*; maillet *m*; **2.** damer.

bee·tle² [~] coléoptère *m*.

bee·tle³ [~] **1.** bombé (*front*);
touffu (*sourcils*); **2.** *v/i.* surplomber.

beet·root ['bi:tru:t] *Brit.* betterave *f*.

beet-sug·ar ['bi:t∫ugə] sucre *m* de
betterave.

be·fall [bi'fɔ:l] [*irr.* (*fall*)] arriver *ou*
survenir à (*q.*).

be·fit [bi'fit] convenir *ou* seoir à (*q.*,
qch.).

be·fog [bi'fɔg] envelopper de brouillard; *fig.* obscurcir.

be·fool [bi'fu:l] duper, mystifier.

be·fore [bi'fɔ:] **1.** *adv.* *lieu:* en
avant; devant; *temps:* auparavant;
avant; **2.** *cj.* avant que; **3.** *prp.*
lieu: devant; *temps:* avant; *be* ~ *one's
time* être en avance; *be* ~ *s.o.* être en
présence de q.; *fig.* attendre q.; devancer q.; ~ *long* avant longtemps;
~ *now* déjà; **be'fore·hand** préalablement; d'avance.

be·foul [bi'faul] souiller, salir.

be·friend [bi'frend] venir en aide à
(*q.*); secourir (*q.*).

beg [beg] *v/t.* mendier; solliciter;
prier; supplier (*q. de faire qch.*); *I* ~
your pardon je vous demande pardon; plaît-il?; ~ *the question* supposer vrai ce qui est en question; *v/i.*
mendier (*qch. à q.*, *for s.th. of s.o.*);
demander, prier; faire le beau
(*chien*); ✝ *I* ~ *to inform you* j'ai
l'honneur de vous faire savoir.

be·gan [bi'gæn] *prét. de* begin.

be·get [bi'get] [*irr.* (*get*)] engendrer;
be'get·ter père *m*; F auteur *m* (de,
of).

beg·gar ['begə] **1.** mendiant(e *f*) *m*;
F individu *m*; diable *m*; **2.** *de* men-

diant; **3.** réduire (*q.*) à la mendicité;
it ~*s all description* cela ne peut pas
se décrire, cela défie toute description; '**beg·gar·ly** chétif (-ive *f*);
mesquin; '**beg·gar·y** mendicité *f*,
misère *f*; *reduce to* ~ réduire à la
mendicité.

be·gin [bi'gin] [*irr.*] *v/i.* commencer
(à, *de to*; par, à *at*); se mettre (à *inf.*,
to inf.); ~ (*up*)*on s.th.* entamer qch.;
to ~ *with* pour commencer; (tout)
d'abord; *to* ~ *by* (*gér.*) commencer
par (*inf.*); *v/t.* commencer; **be'gin·
ner** commençant(e *f*) *m*; **be'gin·
ning** commencement *m*; début *m*;
from the ~ dès le commencement.

be·gird [bi'gə:d] [*irr.* (*gird*)] ceindre, entourer (de, *with*).

be·gone [bi'gɔn] partez!, hors d'ici!

be·go·ni·a ♀ [bi'gounjə] bégonia *m*.

be·got, be·got·ten [bi'gɔt(n)] *prét.
et p.p. de* beget.

be·grime [bi'graim] noircir, salir.

be·grudge [bi'grʌdʒ] envier, mesurer (*qch. à q.*, *s.o. s.th.*).

be·guile [bi'gail] enjôler, tromper;
distraire; soutirer (*qch. à q.*, *s.o.
out of s.th.*); faire passer (*le temps*);
~ *s.o. into* (*gér.*) induire q. à (*inf.*).

be·gun [bi'gʌn] *p.p. de* begin.

be·half [bi'hɑ:f]: *on* (*ou in*) ~ *of* au
nom de; de la part de; en faveur de;
✝ au compte de.

be·have [bi'heiv] se conduire, se
comporter (*bien, mal, etc.*); ~ *yourself* (*yourselves*)! sois (soyez) sa-
ge(s)!; **be'hav·io(u)r** [~jə] conduite
f (avec, envers *to*[*wards*]); tenue *f*
(*a. d'une voiture*); *machine:* allure *f*,
fonctionnement *m*; *be on one's best*
~ se surveiller; **be'hav·io(u)r·al**
[~jərəl] de comportement; behavio-
riste; ~ *pattern* type *m* de comportement; ~ *psychology* psychologie *f* du
comportement.

be·head [bi'hed] décapiter; **be-
'head·ing** décapitation *f*.

be·hest *poét.* [bi'hest] ordre *m*.

be·hind [bi'haind] **1.** *adv.* (par) derrière; en arrière; en retard; *be* ~ *with
s.th.* être en retard dans qch.; **2.** *prp.*
derrière; en arrière de; en retard sur;
see time; **3.** F derrière *m*, postérieur
m.

be·hold [bi'hould] [*irr.* (*hold*)]
voir, apercevoir; ~! voyez!; **be-
'hold·en** redevable (à, *to*); **be'hold·
er** témoin *m*; spectateur (-trice *f*) *m*.

be·hoof [bi'hu:f]: *to (for, on) (the)* ~ *of* au profit de, à l'avantage de.

be·hove [bi'houv]: *it* ~*s s.o. to (inf.)* il appartient à q. de (*inf.*).

beige [bei3] **1.** *tex.* beige *f*; **2.** beige; blond.

be·ing ['bi:iŋ] être *m*; existence *f*; *in* ~ vivant; existant; *come into* ~ prendre naissance; se produire.

be·la·bo(u)r F [bi'leibə] rouer (*q.*) de coups.

be·laid [bi'leid] *prét. et p.p. de* belay.

be·lat·ed [bi'leitid] attardé (*personne*); tardif (-ive *f*) (*regret, heure, etc.*).

be·laud [bi'lɔ:d] combler (*q.*) de louanges.

be·lay [bi'lei] [*irr.*] ⚓ tourner, amarrer; *alp.* assurer; **be'lay·ing** tournage *m*.

belch [beltʃ] éructer; *sl.* roter; ~ *forth (ou out)* vomir(*des flammes etc.*).

bel·dam ['beldəm] mégère *f*; vieille sorcière *f*.

be·lea·guer [bi'li:gə] assiéger.

bel·fry ['belfri] beffroi *m*, clocher *m*.

Bel·gian ['beld3ən] **1.** belge, de Belgique; **2.** Belge *mf*.

be·lie [bi'lai] démentir; donner un démenti à; faire mentir.

be·lief [bi'li:f] croyance *f* (à, *in*; en Dieu, *in God*); *fig.* confiance *f*; *past all* ~ incroyable; *to the best of my* ~ autant que je sache.

be·liev·a·ble [bi'li:vəbl] croyable.

be·lieve [bi'li:v] *v/i.* croire (à, en *in*); F (*not*) ~ *in* (ne pas) être partisan de (*qch.*); (ne pas) avoir confiance dans (*qch.*); *v/t.* croire; **be'liev·er** croyant(e *f*) *m*.

Be·li·sha bea·con [bə'li:ʃə'bi:kən] globe *m* orange (*indiquant un passage clouté*).

be·lit·tle [bi'litl] *fig.* décrier, amoindrir.

bell[1] [bel] **1.** cloche *f*; sonnette *f*; timbre *m*; sonnerie *f* (*électrique*); ♀ clochette *f*; ⚠ campane *f*; vase *m*; ⚓ coup *m*; ♪ *trompette*: pavillon *m*; **2.** *v/t.* ~ *the cat* attacher le grelot.

bell[2] *chasse*: [~] **1.** bramer; **2.** bramement *m*.

bell·boy *Am.* ['belbɔi] *see* bellhop.

belle [bel] beauté *f*.

bell...: '~-**flow·er** campanule *f*; '~-**found·er** fondeur *m* de cloches; '~-**hop** *Am. sl.* chasseur *m*.

bel·li·cose ['belikous] belliqueux

(-euse *f*); **bel·li·cos·i·ty** [~'kɔsiti] bellicosité *f*; humeur *f* belliqueuse.

bel·lied ['belid] ventru.

bel·lig·er·ent [bi'lid3ərənt] belligérant(e *f*) (*a. su./mf*).

bel·low ['belou] **1.** beugler; mugir (*a.* F); **2.** beuglement *m*; F hurlement *m*.

bel·lows ['belouz] *pl.*: (*a pair of*) ~ (un) soufflet *m*; *sg. phot.* soufflet *m*.

bell...: '~-**pull** cordon *m* de sonnette; '~-**push** *poussoir*: bouton *m*; '~-**weth·er** sonnailler *m*; '~-**wire** fil *m* à sonnerie.

bel·ly ['beli] **1.** ventre *m*; ~ *button* F nombril *m*; ~ *flop* plat-ventre *m*/*inv.*; ✈ ~ *landing* atterrissage *m* sur le ventre; ~ *laugh* gros rire *m*; **2.** (s')enfler, (se) gonfler.

be·long [bi'lɔŋ] appartenir (à, *to*); faire partie (de, *to*); être (à, de *to a place*); *Am.* ~ *with* aller avec; **be'long·ings** [~iŋz] *pl.* affaires *f*/*pl.*; effets *m*/*pl.*

be·lov·ed [bi'lʌvd] **1.** aimé; **2.** chéri (-e *f*) *m*; bien-aimé(e *f*) *m*.

be·low [bi'lou] **1.** *adv.* en bas, (au-) dessous; *poét.* ici-bas; **2.** *prp.* au-dessous de; *fig.* ~ *me* indigne de moi (*de inf., to inf.*).

belt [belt] **1.** ceinture *f*; porte-jarretelles *m*; *fig.* zone *f*, bande *f*; ✕ ceinturon *m*; ⊕ courroie *f*; ⚓ ceinture *f* cuirassée; *box. below the* ~ déloyal (-aux *m*/*pl.*) (*coup*); *green* ~ ceinture *f* verte; *mot. seat* ~ ceinture *f* de sécurité; **2.** ceindre; entourer (*qch.*) d'une ceinture; *Am.* F ~ *out* faire retentir *ou* éclater.

bel·ve·dere ['belvidiə] ⚠ belvédère *m*; mirador *m*; pavillon *m*.

be·moan [bi'moun] pleurer, déplorer (*qch.*).

be·mused □ [bi'mju:zd] confus, embrouillé; rêveur(-euse *f*).

bench [bentʃ] banc *m*; banquette *f*; siège *m* (*du juge*); magistrature *f*; menuiserie: établi *m*; *see* treasury; '**bench·er** membre *m* du conseil d'une École de droit.

bend [bend] **1.** tournant *m*; *chemin*: coude *m*; courbure *f*; courbe *f*; *fleuve*: sinuosité *f*; ⛊ bande *f*; ⚓ nœud *m*; **2.** [*irr.*] (se) courber; *v/i.* tourner (*route*); *v/t.* plier; fléchir; baisser (*la tête*); tendre (*un arc*); fixer (*les regards*); porter (*les pas* *vers qch.*); appliquer (*l'esprit*); ⚓ enverguer.

be·neath [bi'ni:θ] *see below.*

ben·e·dick ['benidik] nouveau marié *m* (*surt. vieux garçon*).

Ben·e·dic·tine [beni'diktin] *eccl.* Bénédictin(e *f*) *m*; [ˌtiːn] *liqueur:* Bénédictine *f*.

ben·e·dic·tion *eccl.* [beni'dikʃn] bénédiction *f*; bénédicité *m* (*avant les repas*).

ben·e·fac·tion [beni'fækʃn] bienfait *m*; donation *f*; œuvre *f* de charité; **'ben·e·fac·tor** bienfaiteur *m*; **ben·e·fac·tress** ['ˌtris] bienfaitrice *f*.

ben·e·fice ['benifis] bénéfice *m*; **be·nef·i·cence** [bi'nefisns] bienfaisance *f*; **be'nef·i·cent** □ bienfaisant; salutaire.

ben·e·fi·cial □ [beni'fiʃl] avantageux (-euse *f*), salutaire, utile; ~ *interest* usufruit *m*; ⚖ ~ *owner* usufruitier (-ère *f*) *m*; **ben·e'fi·ci·ar·y** ⚖, *eccl.* bénéficier (-ère *f*) *m*; bénéficiaire *mf*; ayant droit (*pl.* ayants droit) *m*.

ben·e·fit ['benifit] **1.** avantage *m*, profit *m*; *théâ.* représentation *f* au bénéfice (*de q.*); indemnité *f* (*de chômage*); ~ *of the doubt* bénéfice *m* du doute; *for the* ~ *of* à l'intention de; *au bénéfice de;* **2.** *v/t.* profiter à; être avantageux (-euse *f*) à; faire du bien à; *v/i.* profiter (de *by, from*).

be·nev·o·lence [bi'nevələns] bienveillance *f*, bonté *f*; **be'nev·o·lent** □ (*envers, to*) bienveillant; charitable; ~ *society* association *f* de bienfaisance.

Ben·gal [beŋ'gɔːl] du Bengale; **Ben'gal·i** [ˌli] **1.** bengali; **2.** *ling.* bengali *m*; Bengali *mf*.

be·night·ed [bi'naitid] anuité; surpris par la nuit; *fig.* aveugle; plongé dans l'ignorance.

be·nign □ [bi'nain] bénin (-igne *f*) (*a.* ✞); doux (douce *f*); favorable; **be·nig·nant** □ [bi'nignənt] bénin (-igne *f*); bienveillant; **be'nig·ni·ty** bienveillance *f*, bonté *f*; ✞, *a. climat:* bénignité *f*.

bent¹ [bent] **1.** *prét. et p.p. de* bend 2; ~ *on* acharné à; **2.** penchant *m*, disposition *f* (pour, *for*); *to the top of one's* ~ tant qu'on peut.

bent² ✿ [ˌ] jonc *m*; agrostide *f*; prairie *f*.

be·numb [bi'nʌm] engourdir (*a.* F); transir.

ben·zine ⚗ ['benziːn] benzine *f*.

ben·zol(e) ⚗ ['benzɔl] benzol *m*.

be·queath [bi'kwiːð] léguer.

be·quest [bi'kwest] legs *m*.

be·rate [bi'reit] réprimander.

be·reave [bi'riːv] [*irr.*] priver; *be* ~*d of* perdre (*q. par la mort*); ~*d* affligé; **be'reave·ment** perte *f* (*d'un père etc.*); deuil *m*.

be·reft [bi'reft] *prét. et p.p. de* bereave.

be·ret ['berei] béret *m*.

Ber·lin [bəː'lin] **1.** de Berlin; ~ *black* vernis *m*; **2.** *voiture:* berline *f*; (*usu.* ~ *glove*) gant *m* de laine de Berlin; (*usu.* ~ *wool*) laine *f* de Berlin.

ber·ry ['beri] ✿ baie *f*.

berth [bəːθ] **1.** ⚓ évitée *f*; couchette *f*; *fig.* place *f*; emploi *m*; *give s.o. a wide* ~ éviter q.; **2.** *v/t.* accoster (*un navire*) le long du quai; *v/i.* mouiller; aborder à quai.

ber·yl *min.* ['beril] béryl *m*.

be·seech [bi'siːtʃ] [*irr.*] supplier (*q. de inf., s.o. to inf.*); implorer; **be'seech·ing** □ suppliant.

be·seem [bi'siːm]: *it* ~*s* il sied (à *q. de inf., s.o. to inf.*).

be·set [bi'set] [*irr.* (set)] assaillir; serrer de près; assiéger; ~*ting sin* péché *m* d'habitude.

be·side [bi'said] **1.** *adv. see* besides; **2.** *prp.* à côté de (*a. fig.*); auprès de; ~ *o.s.* transporté (de *joie etc., with*); *be* ~ *the purpose* ne pas entrer dans les intentions (*de q.*); ~ *the question* en dehors du sujet; **be'sides** [ˌdz] **1.** *adv.* en plus, en outre; d'ailleurs; **2.** *prp. fig.* sans compter; en plus de; excepté.

be·siege [bi'siːdʒ] assiéger (*a. fig.*); faire le siège de; *fig.* entourer; **be'sieg·er** assiégeant *m*.

be·slav·er [bi'slævə] baver sur; *fig.* flagorner.

be·slob·ber [bi'slɔbə] prodiguer des baisers à (*q.*).

be·smear [bi'smiə] barbouiller.

be·smirch [bi'sməːtʃ] salir.

be·som ['biːzm] balai *m*.

be·sot·ted [bi'sɔtid] assoté; abruti (par, *with*) (*a. fig.*).

be·sought [bi'sɔːt] *prét. et p.p. de* } [beseech.} beseech.

be·spat·ter [bi'spætə] éclabousser; *fig.* salir le nom de; accabler (de, *with*).

be·speak [bi'spi:k] [*irr.* (*speak*)] commander; retenir; *fig.* annoncer; *usu. poét.* s'adresser à, parler à.

be·spoke [bi'spouk] **1.** *prét. de bespeak;* **2.** *adj.:* ~ *tailor* tailleur *m* à façon; ~ *work* travail *m* sur commande; **be'spoken** *p.p. de* bespeak.

be·sprin·kle [bi'spriŋkl] arroser.

best [best] **1.** *adj.* meilleur; F *la crème de;* ~ *man* garçon *m* d'honneur; *at* ~ au mieux; *see seller;* **2.** *adv.* le mieux; **3.** *su.* meilleur *m;* mieux *m; all the* ~! bonne chance!; *Sunday* ~ habits *m/pl.* du dimanche; *for the* ~ pour le mieux; *to the* ~ *of my knowledge* autant que je sache; *make the* ~ *of* s'accommoder de; *make the* ~ *of a bad job* faire bonne mine à mauvais jeu; *the* ~ *of the way* la plus grande partie du chemin; *at* ~ pour dire le mieux; **4.** *v/t.* F l'emporter sur (*q.*).

be·stead [bi'sted] [*irr.*] aider.

be·ste(a)d [~] : *hard* ~ serré de près; *ill* ~ F en mauvaise passe.

bes·tial □ ['bestjəl] bestial (-aux *m/pl.*); **bes·ti·al·i·ty** [besti'æliti] bestialité *f.*

be·stir [bi'stə:] : ~ *o.s.* se remuer.

be·stow [bi'stou] accorder, octroyer (à, [*up*]*on*); † déposer; **be'stow·al,** **be'stow·ment** don *m,* octroi *m.*

be·strew [bi'stru:] [*irr.*] joncher, parsemer (de, *with*).

be·strid·den [bi'stridn] *p.p. de* bestride.

be·stride [bi'straid] [*irr.*] être à cheval sur; enjamber (*un endroit*); enfourcher (*un cheval*).

be·strode [bi'stroud] *prét. de* bestride.

bet [bet] **1.** pari *m;* **2.** [*irr.*] parier; F *you* ~ pour sûr; F *I* ~ *you a shilling* F je vous parie 50 francs.

be·take [bi'teik] [*irr.* (*take*)]: ~ *o.s. to* se rendre à; *fig.* se livrer à.

be·think [bi'θiŋk] [*irr.* (*think*)]: ~ *o.s.* se rappeler (qch. *of s.th.*); ~ *o.s. to* (*inf.*) s'aviser de (*inf.*).

be·tide [bi'taid]: *whate'er* ~ advienne que pourra; *woe* ~ *him!* gare à lui!

be·times [bi'taimz] de bonne heure.

be·to·ken [bi'toukn] être signe de, révéler; présager.

be·tray [bi'trei] trahir (*a. fig.* = *laisser voir*); séduire (*une femme*); **be'tray·al** trahison *f;* ~ *of trust* abus

m de confiance; **be'tray·er** traître(sse *f*) *m;* trompeur (-euse *f*) *m.*

be·troth [bi'trouð] fiancer (à, avec *to*); *the* ~*ed* le fiancé *m;* la fiancée *f; pl.* les fiancés *m/pl.;* **be'troth·al** fiançailles *f/pl.*

bet·ter[1] ['betə] **1.** *adj.* meilleur; mieux; *he is* ~ il va mieux; *get* ~ s'améliorer; se remettre; *for* ~ *or* (*for*) *worse* pour le meilleur ou pour le pire; **2.** *su.* meilleur *m;* mieux *m;* ~*s pl.* supérieurs *m/pl.; get the* ~ *of* l'emporter sur (*q.*); rouler (*q.*) (= *duper*); surmonter (*un obstacle*); maîtriser (*une émotion*); *he is my* ~ il est plus fort que moi; **3.** *adv.* mieux; *be* ~ *off* être plus à son aise (*matériellement*); *so much the* ~ tant mieux; *you had* ~ *go* vous feriez mieux de vous en aller *ou* de partir; *I know* ~ j'en sais plus long; *think* ~ *of it* se raviser; revenir de; **4.** *v/t.* améliorer; surpasser; ~ *o.s.* améliorer sa position (*etc.*); *v/i.* s'améliorer.

bet·ter[2] [~] parieur (-euse *f*) *m.*

bet·ter·ment ['betəmənt] amélioration *f.*

bet·ting ['betiŋ] paris *m/pl.;* cote *f;* mise *f;* ~*-debt* dette *f* d'honneur.

be·tween [bi'twi:n] (*poét. et prov. a.* **be·twixt** [bi'twikst]) **1.** *adv.* entre les deux; betwixt and between entre les deux; **2.** *prp.* entre; ~ *ourselves* entre nous, de vous à moi; *they bought it* ~ *them* ils l'ont acheté à eux deux (trois *etc.*); **be'tween-decks** ⚓ entrepont *m; adv.* sous barrots; **be'tween-maid** aide *f* de maison.

bev·el ['bevl] **1.** oblique; **2.** ⊕ biseau *m,* biais *m;* conicité *f;* **3.** *v/t.* biseauter; *v/i.* biaiser; aller de biais; aller en biseau; '~-**wheel** ⊕ roue *f* dentée conique; pignon *m* conique.

bev·er·age ['bevəridʒ] boisson *f.*

bev·y ['bevi] bande *f,* troupe *f.*

be·wail [bi'weil] *v/t.* pleurer (qch.); *v/i.* se lamenter.

be·ware [bi'wɛə] se méfier (de q., *of s.o.*); se garder (de qch., *of s.th.*); ~ *of the dog!* chien méchant!

be·wil·der [bi'wildə] égarer, désorienter; F ahurir; abasourdir; **be'wil·der·ment** trouble *m,* confusion *f;* ahurissement *m;* abasourdissement *m.*

be·witch F [bi'witʃ] ensorceler; F

enchanter; **be'witch·ment** ensor-cellement *m*; charme *m*.

be·yond [bi'jɔnd] **1.** *adv.* au-delà, par-delà, plus loin; **2.** *prp.* au-delà de; par-delà; au-dessus de; excepté; en dehors de; autre ... que; ~ *endurance* intolérable; ~ *measure* outre mesure; ~ *dispute* incontestable; ~ *words* au-delà de toute expression; *get* ~ *s.o.* dépasser q.; *go* ~ *one's depth* ne pas avoir pied; *it is* ~ *me* cela me dépasse; je n'y comprends rien.

bi... [bai] bi(s)-; di(s)-; semi-.

bi·an·nu·al □ [bai'ænjuəl] semes-triel; biennal (-aux *m/pl.*).

bi·as ['baiəs] **1.** *adj. et adv.* oblique (-ment); en biais, de biais; *couture*: coupé de biais, en biais; **2.** *couture*: biais *m*; *boules*: décentrement *m*; déviation *f*; *radio*: polarisation *f*; *fig.* parti *m* pris; penchant *m*; **3.** dé-centrer (*une boule*); *fig.* rendre par-tial; prévenir (contre, *against*; en faveur de, *towards*); ~sed partial (-aux *m/pl.*).

bib [bib] bavette *f* (*d'enfant*); *ta-blier*: baverette *f*.

bib·cock ['bibkɔk] robinet *m* coudé.

Bi·ble ['baibl] Bible *f*.

bib·li·cal □ ['biblikl] biblique.

bib·li·og·ra·pher [bibli'ɔgrəfə] bi-bliographe *m*; **bib·li·o·graph·ic**, **bib·li·o·graph·i·cal** [‿o'græfik(l)] bibliographique; **bib·li·og·ra·phy** [‿'ɔgrəfi] bibliographie *f*; **bib·li·o·ma·ni·a** [‿o'meinjə] bibliomanie *f*; **bib·li·o·ma·ni·ac** [‿niæk] biblio-mane *m*; **bib·li·o·phile** ['‿ofail] bibliophile *m*.

bib·u·lous □ ['bibjuləs] adonné à la boisson; absorbant (*chose*).

bi·car·bon·ate [bai'kɑːbənit] bi-carbonate *m*.

bi·ceps *anat.* ['baiseps] biceps *m*.

bick·er ['bikə] se quereller; être toujours en zizanie; trembloter (*lumière*); murmurer (*ruisseau etc.*); **'bick·er·ing(s** *pl.*) querelles *f/pl.*; bisbille *f*.

bi·cy·cle ['baisikl] **1.** bicyclette *f*, F vélo *m*; *folding* ~ bicyclette *f* pliante; ~ *bell* timbre *m* ou sonnette *f* de bicyclette; ~ *rack* porte-vélos *m/inv.*; râtelier *m* à bicyclettes; ~ *track* piste *f* cyclable; **2.** faire de la bicyclette *ou* du vélo; aller à bicyclette; **'bi·cy·clist** (bi)cycliste *mf*.

bid [bid] **1.** [*irr.*] *v/t.* commander, ordonner; inviter (*à dîner*); *cartes*: appeler; *fig.* ~ *fair* promettre de; s'annoncer; ~ *farewell* faire ses adieux; ~ *up* surenchérir; ~ *welcome* souhaiter la bienvenue; *v/i.* (*prét. et p.p.* bid) faire une offre (pour, *for*); **2.** offre *f*, mise *f*, enchère *f*; *cartes*: appel *m*; *a* ~ *to* (*inf.*) un effort pour (*inf.*); *cartes*: *no* ~ Parole!; **'bid·den** *p.p. de* bid **1**; **'bid·der** enchérisseur *m*; *cartes*: demandeur (-euse *f*) *m*; *see high* **1**, *low*¹ **1**; **'bid·ding** ordre *m*; invitation *f*; enchères *f/pl.*; *cartes*: enchère *f*.

bide [baid] attendre (*le moment*).

bi·en·ni·al [bai'enjəl] **1.** biennal (-aux *m/pl.*); **2.** ♀ plante *f* bisan-nuelle.

bier [biə] civière *f* (*pour un cercueil*).

bi·fo·cals [bai'foukəlz] *pl.* lunettes *f/pl.* bifocales.

bi·fur·cate ['baifəːkeit] (se) bifur-quer; **bi·fur'ca·tion** bifurcation *f*.

big [big] grand; gros(se *f*); *fig.* lourd, gros(se *f*) (de, *with*); enceinte *f* (*grosse d'enfant*); *fig.* hautain, fanfaron (-ne *f*); ♀ *Apple* surnom de *New York City*; F ♀ *Ben* grosse cloche du *Palais du Parlement à Londres*; ~ *business* grosses affaires *f/pl.*; F *fig.* ~ *shot* chef *m* de file; personnage *m* important, *sl.* grosse légume *f*; *Am.* ~ *stick fig.* F trique *f*; *hit ou make the* ~ *time* réussir, arriver; *Am.* ~ *top cirque*: chapiteau *m*, *a. fig.* cirque *m*; *talk* ~ faire l'important; fanfaronner.

big·a·mous ['bigəməs] bigame; **'big·a·my** bigamie *f*.

bight ♣ [bait] crique *f*; golfe *m*.

big·mouth F ['bigmauθ] gueulard(e *f*) *m*.

big·ness ['bignis] grandeur *f*; gros-seur *f*.

big·ot ['bigət] bigot(e *f*) *m*; *fig.* fana-tique *mf*; sectaire *mf*; **'big·ot·ed** fanatique; *fig.* à l'esprit sectaire; **'big·ot·ry** fanatisme *m*; zèle *m* outré.

'big-time ['bigtaim] de première catégorie, important; de grande envergure; extraordinaire; magnifi-que.

big·wig F ['bigwig] gros bonnet *m*; *sl.* grosse légume *f*.

bike F [baik] vélo *m*.

bi·lat·er·al □ [bai'lætərl] bilatéral (-aux *m/pl.*).

bil·ber·ry ♀ ['bɪlbəri] airelle *f*, myrtille *f*.

bile [baɪl] bile *f* (*fig.* = *colère*).

bilge [bɪldʒ] bouge *m* (*de barrique*); ⚓ fond *m* de cale; bouchain *m*; *sl.* bêtises *f/pl.*

bi·lin·gual [baɪ'lɪŋgwəl] bilingue.

bil·ious □ ['bɪljəs] bilieux (-euse *f*); *fig.* colérique.

bilk [bɪlk] F tromper, escroquer.

bill¹ [bɪl] 1. *oiseau, ancre, géog.*: bec *m*; serpette *f* (*pour tailler*); 2. (*a. fig.* ~ *and coo*) se becqueter.

bill² [~] 1. note *f*, facture *f*; *restaurant*: addition *f*; ✝ effet *m*; ✝ (*a.* ~ *of exchange*) traite *f*; *Am.* billet *m* (*de banque*); *théâ. etc.* affiche *f*; *parl.* projet *m* de loi; ~ *of costs* compte *m* de frais; ~ *of expenses* note *f* de(s) frais; ~ *of fare* carte *f* du jour; ⚓ ~ *of health* patente *f* de santé; ~ *of lading* connaissement *m*, police *f* de chargement; ⚖ ~ *of sale* acte *m* de vente; ✝ ~ *of sight* déclaration *f* d'entrée; ♀ *of Rights Brit.* Déclaration *f* des Droits du citoyen (1689); *Am. les* amendements *m/pl.* (1791) à la constitution des É.-U.; 2. facturer (*des marchandises*); afficher.

bill·board *Am.* ['bɪl'bɔːd] panneau *m* d'affichage.

bil·let ['bɪlɪt] 1. ✕ (billet *m* de) logement *m*; bûche *f*; billette *f* (*a. métall.*); 2. ✕ loger (*des troupes*) (*chez on, with*).

bill·fold ['bɪlfould] porte-billets *m/inv.*

bil·liard ['bɪljəd] *attr.* de billard; '~-**cue** queue *f* de billard; '**bil·liards** *sg. ou pl.* (jeu *m* de) billard *m*.

bil·lion ['bɪljən] billion *m*; *Am.* milliard *m*.

bil·low ['bɪlou] 1. lame *f* (de mer), grande vague *f*; 2. se soulever en vagues; ondoyer (*foule etc.*); '**bil·low·y** houleux (-euse *f*).

bill-stick·er ['bɪlstɪkə] afficheur *m*; placardeur *m*.

bil·ly *Am.* ['bɪli] bâton *m* (*de police*); '~-**cock** chapeau *m* melon; '~-**goat** F bouc *m*.

bi-mo·tored ✈ ['baɪmoutəd] bimoteur.

bin [bɪn] coffre *m*; casier *m*; F poubelle *f*.

bi·na·ry ['baɪnəri] binaire; *biol.* ~ *fission* division *f* binaire *ou* cellulaire.

bin·au·ral [baɪn'ɔːrəl] binauriculaire; stéréophonique.

bind [baɪnd] [*irr.*] *v/t.* lier, attacher; (res)serrer; garrotter; rendre constipé; ratifier, confirmer (*un marché*); border (*une étoffe*); relier (*des livres*); fixer (*un ski*); bander (*une blessure*); lier, agglutiner (*le sable*); ~ *over* sommer (*q.*) d'observer une bonne conduite; *fig.* be bound with être engagé (à to, with); ~ *s.o.* apprentice to mettre q. en apprentissage chez; *I'll* be bound je m'engagerai (à, to); F j'en suis sûr!; *v/i.* se lier; durcir; '**bind·er** lieur (-euse *f*) *m*; lien *m*; ceinture *f*; ⊕ liant *m*; relieur *m* (*de livres*); '**bind·ing** 1. obligatoire (pour, on); agglomératif (-ive *f*); 2. agglutination *f*; serrage *m*; lien *m*; *étoffe*: bordure *f*; *livres*: reliure *f*; '**bind·weed** ♀ liseron *m*.

binge *sl.* [bɪndʒ] bombe *f*, ribote *f*.

bin·na·cle ⚓ ['bɪnəkl] habitacle *m*.

bin·o·cle ['bɪnɔkl] binoculaire *m*; **bin·oc·u·lar** 1. [baɪ'nɔkjulə] binoculaire; 2. [bɪ'nɔkjulə] jumelle *f*, -s *f/pl.*

bi·o·chem·i·cal ['baɪo'kemɪkl] biochimique; '**bi·o'chem·is·try** biochimie *f*.

bi·og·ra·pher [baɪ'ɔgrəfə] biographe *m*; **bi·o·graph·ic, bi·o·graph·i·cal** □ [~o'græfik(l)] biographique; **bi·og·ra·phy** [~'ɔgrəfi] biographie *f*.

bi·o·log·ic, bi·o·log·i·cal □ [baɪə-'lɔdʒik(l)] biologique; **bi·ol·o·gist** [~'ɔlədʒist] biologiste *mf*; **bi·ol·o·gy** biologie *f*.

bi·par·tite [baɪ'pɑːtaɪt] biparti(te *f*); ⚖ rédigé en double. [*su./m*).\
bi·ped *zo.* ['baɪped] bipède (*a.*)\
bi·plane ✈ ['baɪpleɪn] biplan *m*.

birch [bəːtʃ] 1. ♀ (*ou* ~-tree) bouleau *m*; (*a.* ~-rod) verge *f*; 2. de bouleau; '**birch·en** de bouleau.

bird [bəːd] oiseau *m*; ~ *of passage* oiseau *m* de passage; ~ *of prey* oiseau *m* de proie; F *that's for the* ~s ça ne vaut rien; *tell a child about the* ~s and the bees expliquer à un enfant comment font les petits oiseaux; *kill two* ~s with one stone faire d'une pierre deux coups; '~-**cage** cage *f* à oiseaux; '~-**fan·ci·er** oiselier *m*; marchand(e *f*) *m* d'oiseaux; connaisseur (-euse *f*) *m* en oiseaux; '~-**lime** glu *f*; '~-**nest** 1. see bird's nest; 2.

dénicher des oiseaux; **'bird's-eye view** perspective *f* à vol d'oiseau; **'bird's nest** nid *m* d'oiseaux; ~ *soup* soupe *f* aux nids d'hirondelles; ~ **sanc·tu·ar·y** refuge *m* d'oiseaux.

bi·ro (*TM*) ['baiərou] stylo *m* (à bille).

birth [bə:θ] naissance *f*; accouchement; *animaux*: mise *f* bas; *bring to* ~ faire naître, engendrer; *come to* ~ naître, prendre naissance; '~-**control** limitation *f* des naissances; '~-**day** anniversaire *m*; jour *m* natal; ~ *cake* gâteau *m* d'anniversaire; *Brit.* ~ *honours pl.* distinctions *f/pl.* honorifiques accordées à l'occasion de l'anniversaire du monarque; ~ *present* cadeau *m* d'anniversaire; '~-**place** lieu *m* de naissance; '~-**rate** natalité *f*; '~-**right** droit *m* de naissance; droit *m* d'aînesse.

bis·cuit ['biskit] biscuit *m* (*a. poterie*).

bi·sect ᚛ [bai'sekt] bissecter (*un angle*); couper en deux parties égales (*une ligne, un angle*); **bi'sec·tion** bissection *f*.

bish·op ['biʃəp] évêque *m*; *échecs*: fou *m*; **'bish·op·ric** évêché *m*.

bis·muth ⚗ ['bizməθ] bismuth *m*.

bi·son *zo.* ['baisn] bison *m*.

bis·sex·tile [bi'sekstail] **1.** bissextil; ~ *year* = **2.** année *f* bissextile.

bit [bit] **1.** morceau *m*; bout *m* (*de papier etc.*); *monnaie:* pièce *f*; *cheval, tenaille:* mors *m*; ⊕ mèche *f*; percevoir: bit *m*; ~ *by* ~ peu à peu; F *be a* ~ *of a coward* être plutôt lâche; **2.** mettre le mors à, brider; **3.** *prét. de bite* 2.

bitch [bitʃ] **1.** chienne *f*; *sl.* garce *f*; renarde *f*; louve *f*; **2.** F gâcher.

bite [bait] **1.** coup *m* de dent; morsure *f*; *sauce:* piquant *m*; *poisson:* touche *f*; ⊕ mordant *m*; **2.** [*irr.*] mordre (*a. poisson, ancre, outil, acide, etc.*); piquer (*insecte, poivre*); ronger (*rouille*); F *fig.* ~ *the dust* mordre la poussière (= *mourir*); ~ *one's nails* se ronger les ongles; *v/i.* adhérer (*roues*); ⚓ crocher (*ancre*); ~ *at* rembarrer (*q.*); **'bit·er** *animal etc.* qui mord; *the* ~ *bit* le trompeur trompé.

bit·ing □ ['baitiŋ] mordant; perçant (*froid*); cinglant (*vent*).

bit·ten ['bitn] *p.p. de bite* 2; *be* ~ *fig.* se faire attraper; F *be* ~ *with s'en-*

ticher de; *once* ~ *twice shy* chat échaudé craint l'eau froide.

bit·ter ['bitə] **1.** □ amer (-ère *f*); aigre; glacial (-als *m/pl.*) (*vent*); ~ *sweet* aigre-doux (-douce *f*); **2.** bière *f* amère.

bit·tern *orn.* ['bitə:n] butor *m*.

bit·ter·ness ['bitənis] amertume *f*; âpreté *f*; rancune *f*.

bit·ters ['bitəz] *pl.* bitter *m*, -s *m/pl.*, amer *m*, -s *m/pl.*

bitts ⚓ [bits] *pl.* bittes *f/pl.*

bi·tu·men ['bitjumin] bitume *m*; **bi·tu·mi·nous** [ˌ'tjuːminəs] bitumineux (-euse *f*); gras(se *f*) (*houille*).

biv·ouac ['bivuæk] **1.** bivouac *m*; **2.** bivouaquer.

biz F [biz] affaire *f*, -s *f/pl.*

bi·zarre [bi'zaː] bizarre.

blab F [blæb] **1.** (*a.* **'blab·ber**) jaseur (-euse *f*) *m*; indiscret (-ète *f*) *m*; **2.** *v/i.* jaser, bavarder; *v/t.* divulguer (*un secret*).

black [blæk] **1.** □ noir; *fig.* sombre, triste; ~ *cattle* bœufs *m/pl.* de race écossaise ou galloise; ~ *eye* œil *m* poché; *see frost*; ~ *ice* verglas *m*; ~ *market* marché *m* noir; ~ *marketeer* profiteur (-euse *f*) *m*; ~ *marketing* vente *f* ou achats *m/pl.* au marché noir; ~ *sheep fig.* brebis *f* galeuse; **2.** noircir; *v/t.* cirer (*des bottes*); F *poche* (*l'œil*); ~ *out v/t.* obscurcir; *v/i.* couper la lumière; **3.** noir *m* (*a. vêtements*); noir(e *f*) *m* (= *nègre*); flocon *m* de suie.

black...: ~**a·moor** † [ˌ'~əmuə] nègre *m*, négresse *f*; '~-**ball** blackbouler; '~-**ber·ry** ♀ mûre *f* (sauvage); '~-**bird** merle *m*; '~-**board** tableau *m* noir; '~-**coat·ed** vêtu de noir; '~-**cock** *orn.* tétras *m*; **'black·en** *v/t.* noircir (*a. fig.*); *fig.* calomnier; *v/i.* (se) noircir; s'assombrir.

black...: ~**guard** ['blægaːd] **1.** vaurien *m*; ignoble personnage *m*; **2.** (*a.* '~**guard·ly**) □ ignoble, canaille; **3.** adjectiver (*q.*); ~**head** ᚛ ['blækhed] comédon *m*; **'black·ing** cirage *m*; **'black·ish** □ noirâtre, tirant sur le noir.

black...: '~**jack 1.** *surt. Am.* assommoir *m*; **2.** assener un coup d'assommoir (*q.*); '~**lead 1.** plombagine *f*; crayon *m* (de mine de plomb); **2.** passer à la mine de plomb; '~**leg** renard *m*; jaune *m*; '~**let·ter** *typ.* caractères *m/pl.* gothiques; '~·**list** 1. liste *f* noire; 2. mettre sur la liste noire; '~·**mail** 1. extorsion *f* sous menace; chantage *m*; 2. faire chanter (*q*.); '~·**mail·er** maître *m* chanteur; '**black·ness** noirceur *f*; obscurité *f*.

black...: '~-**out** black-out *m*; *fig.* syncope *f*, amnésie *f* passagère; '~·**smith** forgeron *m*; '~·**thorn** ♀ épine *f* noire; '**black·y** F nègre *m*; moricaud *m*.

blad·der ['blædə] *anat.*, *a. foot.* vessie *f*; *anat.*, ♀ vésicule *f*.

blade [bleid] *herbe*: brin *m*; *couteau, rasoir, scie, épée*: lame *f*; *langue*: plat *m*; *aviron*: pale *f*; *hélice*: aile *f*; *ventilateur*: vanne *f*; F gaillard *m*; (*a.* ~-**bone**) *anat.* omoplate *f*.

blain [blein] pustule *f*.

blam·a·ble □ ['bleiməbl] blâmable; répréhensible; '**blam·a·ble·ness** caractère *m* répréhensible.

blame [bleim] 1. reproches *m/pl.*; blâme *m*; faute *f*; 2. blâmer; *he is not to* ~ *for* il n'y a pas de faute de sa part; *he is to* ~ *for* il y a de sa faute; il est responsable de; ~ *s.th. on s.o.* imputer (la faute de) qch. à q.

blame·ful ['bleimful] blâmable; répréhensible; '**blame·less** □ innocent; irréprochable; '**blame·less·ness** innocence *f*; irréprochabilité *f*; '**blame·wor·thi·ness** caractère *m* blâmable *ou* répréhensible; '**blame·wor·thy** blâmable; répréhensible.

blanch [blɑːntʃ] blanchir; pâlir; ~ *over* pallier; F blanchir.

blanc-mange *cuis.* [blə'mɔnʒ] blancmanger (*pl.* blancs-mangers) *m*.

bland □ [blænd] doux (douce *f*); débonnaire; narquois (*sourire*); '**blan·dish** cajoler, flatter; '**blandish·ment** flatterie *f*.

blank [blæŋk] 1. □ blanc(he *f*); vierge (*page*); sans expression, étonné (*regard*); ✗ ~ *cartridge* cartouche *f* à blanc; ✝ ~ *cheque* (*Am.* check) cheque *m* en blanc; *fig.* give *s.o. a* ~ *cheque* donner carte blanche à q. (pour faire, *to do*); ✗ *fire* ~ tirer à blanc; 2. blanc *m*; vide *m*; lacune *f*; *mémoire*: trou *m*; *loterie*: billet *m* blanc; ⊕ flan *m*; F *fig.* draw a ~ échouer.

blan·ket ['blæŋkit] 1. *lit.*, *cheval*: couverture *f*; F *neige, fumée*: nappe *f*; *typ.* blanchet *m*; *fig.* wet ~ trouble-fête *m/inv.*; rabat-joie

m/inv.; 2. mettre une couverture à; ⚓ déventer; F étouffer, supprimer; *Am.* éclipser; 3. *Am.* général (-aux *m/pl.*), d'une portée générale.

blank·ness ['blæŋknis] vide *m*; air *m* confus.

blare [blɛə] *v/i.* sonner, cuivrer (*trompette*); *v/t.* faire retentir.

blar·ney ['blɑːni] 1. patelinage *n*; 2. cajoler, enjôler.

blas·pheme [blæs'fiːm] blasphémer; ~ *against* outrager; **blas-'phem·er** blasphémateur (-trice *f*) *m*; **blas·phe·mous** □ ['blæsfiməs] blasphémateur (-trice *f*) (*personne*); blasphématoire (*propos*); '**blas·phe·my** blasphème *m*.

blast [blɑːst] 1. *vent*: rafale *f*; *vent, explosion*: souffle *m*; *trompette*: sonnerie *f*; sifflet, sirène, *mot.* coup *m*; explosion *f*; ⊕ soufflerie *f*; ♀ cloque *f*; *at full* ~ en pleine activité; 2. *v/t.* faire sauter, pétarder; flétrir; *fig.* ruiner, briser; *v/i.* cuivrer; ~ (*it*)! sacrebleu!; '~-**fur·nace** ⊕ haut fourneau *m*; '**blast·ing** abattage *m* à la poudre; travail *m* aux explosifs; '**blast-off** *espace*: lancement *m*, mise *f* à feu (*d'une fusée*).

bla·tan·cy ['bleitənsi] vulgarité *f* criarde; '**bla·tant** □ d'une vulgarité criarde; criant (*tort etc.*).

blath·er *Am.* ['blæðə] 1. bêtises *f/pl.*; 2. débiter des inepties.

blaze [bleiz] 1. flamme *f*; feu *m*; conflagration *f*; éclat *m*; étoile *f* (*au front d'un cheval*); *arbre*: griffe *f*; *pl.* F enfer *m*; 2. *v/i.* flamber; flamboyer (*soleil, couleurs*); étinceler; ~ *away* tirer sans désemparer (sur, at); *chasse*: *blazing scent* piste *f* toute fraîche; *v/t.* (*usu.* ~ *abroad*) répandre, publier; griffer (*un arbre*); '**blaz·er** blazer *m*.

bla·zon ['bleizn] 1. blason *m*; armoiries *f/pl.*; 2. ⃠ blasonner; marquer (*qch.*) aux armoiries (*de q.*); *fig.* célébrer, exalter; F publier; '**bla·zon·ry** blasonnement *m*; science *f* héraldique; *fig.* ornementation *f*.

bleach [bliːtʃ] 1. blanchir; *v/i.* blondir (*cheveux*); 2. décolorant *m*; '**bleach·er** blanchisseur (-euse *f*) *m*; *Am.* ~*s pl.* places *f/pl.* découvertes d'un terrain de baseball; '**bleaching** blanchiment *m*; '**bleach·ingpow·der** poudre *f* à blanchir.

bleak □ [bliːk] sans abri, exposé au

vent; *fig.* froid; triste, morne; **'bleak·ness** froidure *f*; aspect *m* morne.

blear [bliə] **1.** chassieux (-euse *f*) (*surt. des yeux*); **2.** rendre trouble; estomper (*des couleurs*); **~-eyed** ['bliəraid], **'blear·y** aux yeux chassieux.

bleat [bli:t] **1.** bêlement *m*; **2.** bêler.

bleb [bleb] bouton *m*, (petite) ampoule *f*.

bled [bled] *prét. et p.p. de* bleed.

bleed [bli:d] [*irr.*] *v/i.* saigner, perdre du sang; *v/t.* saigner; ~ white saigner (*q.*) à blanc; **'bleed·ing** écoulement *m* de sang; *&* saignée *f*.

blem·ish ['blemiʃ] **1.** défaut *m*, imperfection *f*; tache *f*; **2.** tacher, souiller; abîmer.

blench [blentʃ] blêmir, pâlir.

blend [blend] **1.** (se) mêler (à, avec with); (se) mélanger (*thé, café*); *v/t.* couper (*le vin*); *fig. v/i.* s'allier; se marier (*voix, couleurs*); **2.** mélange *m*.

blende *min.* [blend] blende *f*.

bless [bles] bénir; consacrer; ~ s.o. with accorder à q. le bonheur de; F ~ me!, ~ my soul! tiens, tiens!; ~ you! à vos souhaits!; **bless·ed** □ [*p.p.* blest; *adj.* 'blesid] bienheureux (-euse *f*); saint; *sl.* fichu; be ~ with jouir de; ~ event heureux événement *m* (= naissance); **bless·ed·ness** ['~sidnis] félicité *f*, béatitude *f*; live in single ~ vivre dans le bonheur du célibat; **'bless·ing** bénédiction *f*; bienfait *m*; aux repas: bénédicité *m*.

blest *poét.* [blest] *see* blessed.

bleth·er ['bleðə] *see* blather.

blew [blu:] *prét. de* blow² *et* blow³ 1.

blight [blait] **1.** *&* nielle *f* (*des céréales*); cloque *f* (*du fruit*); *fig.* influence *f* néfaste; **2.** nieller; brouir; *fig.* flétrir; **'blight·er** *sl.* bon *m* à rien; individu *m*; poor ~ pauvre hère *m*; lucky ~ veinard *m*.

Blight·y *≥ sl.* ['blaiti] la patrie (*usu.* l'Angleterre); a ~ (one) la bonne blessure.

blind □ [blaind] **1.** aveugle; sans issue (*chemin*); faux (fausse *f*) (*porte*); be ~ to ne pas voir (*qch.*); the ~ *pl.* les aveugles *m/pl.*; ~ alley impasse *f* (*a. fig.*); ~ corner tournant *m* encaissé; virage *m* masqué; ~ flying vol *m* sans visibilité, vol *m* en P.S.V.; *anat.* ~ gut cæcum *m*; *&*,

≥ ~ shell obus *m* qui a raté; ~ spot *anat.* point *m* aveugle, papille *f* optique; *radar etc.*: angle *m* mort; *fig.* côté *m* faible (*d'une personne*); that's your ~ spot c'est là où vous n'y voyez pas clair; c'est là où vous refusez de voir clair; ~ story conte *m* en l'air; ~ly *fig.* aveuglément; à l'aveuglette; **2.** store *m*; jalousie *f*; abat-jour *m/inv.*; banne *f*; *≥* blinde *f*; *Am. cheval*: œillère *f*; masque *m*, prétexte *m*; **3.** aveugler (sur, to); *fig.* éblouir; *min.* blinder.

blind...: '**~-fold 1.** aveuglément; **2.** bander les yeux (à *ou* de q., s.o.); '**~-man's-'buff** colin-maillard *m*; '**blind·ness** cécité *f*.

blink [bliŋk] **1.** clignotement *m* des paupières; lueur *f* momentanée; signal *m* optique; F *fig.* on the ~ abîmé, détraqué; **2.** *v/i.* *&* battre *ou* cligner des paupières; papilloter (*lumière*); *v/t. fig.* fermer les yeux sur; dissimuler; **'blink·er** clignotant *m*; *cheval*: œillère *f*; **'blink·ing** F sacré.

bliss [blis] félicité *f*, béatitude *f*; **bliss·ful** □ ['blisful] bienheureux (-euse *f*); serein; **'bliss·ful·ness** félicité *f*, béatitude *f*; bonheur *m*.

blis·ter ['blistə] **1.** ampoule *f*; *peint.*, *peau*: cloque *f*; *&* vésicatoire *m*; **2.** (se) couvrir d'ampoules; (se) cloquer (*peinture*).

blithe □ ['blaið], **~some** ['blaiðsəm] *surt. poét.* joyeux (-euse *f*), gai.

blith·er *sl.* ['bliðə] dire des bêtises; **~ing** F sacré.

blitz [blits] **1.** F bombardement *m* aérien; **2.** détruire par un bombardement.

bliz·zard ['blizəd] tempête *f* de neige.

bloat [blout] gonfler; boursoufler; bouffir (*a. fig.*), saurer (*des harengs*); ~ed boursouflé, gonflé; bouffi (*a. fig.*); **'bloat·er** hareng *m* saur.

blob [blɔb] tache *f*; pâté *m*; goutte *f* d'eau.

block [blɔk] **1.** *marbre, fer, papier, etc.*: bloc *m*; *bois*: tronçon *m*; *roche*: quartier *m*; *mot.*: tin *m*; sabot *m* (*de frein*); (a. ~ of flats) pâté *m* (*de maisons*); (a. dead ~) embouteillage *m*; blocus *m*; ~ letter *typ.* caractère *m* gras; majuscule *f*; **2.** bloquer; entraver; fermer (*une voie, un jeu*); ~ in esquisser à grands traits; (*usu.* ~ up) bloquer, obstruer; murer (*une porte*); ♱ bâcler (*un port*); ~ **out** caviarder (*une censure*).

block·ade [blɔ'keid] **1.** blocus *m*; **2.** bloquer; faire le blocus de; **block'ade-run·ner** forceur *m* de blocus.

block…: '~·**bust·er** F ⚔ bombe *f* de très gros calibre; *fig.* succès *m* fou; *fig.* personne *f* ou chose *f* d'une efficacité à tout casser; '~·**head** sot *m*; tête *f* de bois; '~·**house** blockhaus *m*.

bloke F [blouk] type *m*, individu *m*.

blond(e *f*) [blɔnd] **1.** blond; **2.** blondin(e *f*) *m*; ✝ (*a.* blonde *lace*) blonde *f*.

blood [blʌd] sang *m* (*a.* = *descendance*); race *f*; ✝ dandy *m*; *in cold* ~ de sang-froid; *see* run.

blood…: ~ **bank** banque *f* du sang; ~ **bath** *fig.* bain *f* de sang; ~ **clot** caillot *m* de sang; '~·**cur·dling** à (vous) figer le sang (*histoire etc.*); '~'**do·nor** donneur (-euse *f*) *m* sang; ~ **group** groupe *m* sanguin; '~·**guilt·i·ness** culpabilité *f* d'avoir versé du sang; '~·**heat** température *f* du sang; '~·**horse** cheval *m* de race, pur-sang *m*/*inv.*; '~·**hound** limier *m*; '**blood·i·ness** état *m* sanglant; disposition *f* sanguinaire; '**blood·less** ☐ exsangue, anémié; sans effusion de sang; *fig.* pâle; sans énergie; sans courage.

blood…: '~·**let·ting** saignée *f*; '~·**poi·son·ing** ⚕ empoisonnement *m* du sang; '~·**pres·sure** pression *f* vasculaire; ~ **sam·ple** prélèvement *m* de sang; '~·**shed** carnage *m*; '~·**shot** éraillé (*œil*); ~ **sports** *pl.* sports *m*/*pl.* sanguinaires; '~·**stanch·ing** styptique; ~ **test** analyse *f* de sang; '~·**thirst·y** avide de sang; ~ **trans·fu·sion** transfusion *f* de sang; '~·**ves·sel** vaisseau *m* sanguin; '**blood·y** l. ☐ ensanglanté; sanguinaire; *sl.* sacré; **2.** *sl.* vachement; '**blood·y'mind·ed** *sl.* mauvais coucher (-euse *f*); *she's just being* ~ elle le fait rien que pour nous emmerder.

bloom¹ [blu:m] **1.** fleur *f* (*a. fig.*); épanouissement *m*; duvet *m* (*d'un fruit*); *fig.* incarnat *m*; **2.** fleurir.

bloom² *métall.* [~] loupe *f*.

bloom·er *sl.* ['blu:mə] gaffe *f*, bévue *f*; *usu.* ~s *pl.* culotte *f* bouffante.

bloom·ing ☐ ['blu:miŋ] fleurissant,

en fleur; florissant, prospère; *sl.* sacré; *souv. ne se traduit pas.*

blos·som ['blɔsəm] **1.** fleur *f* (*surt. des arbres*); **2.** fleurir; ~ **into** devenir.

blot [blɔt] **1.** tache *f* (*a. fig.*); pâté *m* (*d'encre*); **2.** *v/t.* tacher; ternir (*a. fig.*); sécher, passer le buvard sur (*l'encre*); (*usu.* ~ out) effacer, *fig.* masquer; *v/i.* faire des pâtés (*plume*); boire l'encre (*buvard*).

blotch [blɔtʃ] tache *f*; pustule *f*; *peau*: tache *f* rouge.

blot·ter ['blɔtə] buvard *m*; *Am.* registre *m* d'arrestations *etc.*

blot·ting…: '~·**book** bloc *m* buvard; '~·**pad** bloc *m* buvard, sous-main *m*/*inv.*; '~·**pa·per** papier *m* buvard.

blot·to *sl.* ['blɔtou] soûl perdu.

blouse [blauz] blouse *f*; ⚔, *a. Am.* vareuse *f*.

blow¹ [blou] coup *m* (de poing, de bâton, *etc.*); *at one* ~ d'un (seul) coup; *come to* ~s en venir aux coups.

blow² [~] [*irr.*] s'épanouir.

blow³ [~] **1.** [*irr.*] *v/i.* souffler; faire du vent; claquer (*ampoule*); sauter (*plomb*); ~ **in** entrer; ~ **over** se calmer; ~ **up** éclater, sauter; *Am.* F entrer en colère; *v/t.* souffler (*a. une verre*); *vent:* pousser; vider (*un œuf*); sonner (*un instrument*); *mouches:* gâter (*la viande*); évacuer (*une chaudière*); ⚡ faire sauter (*les plombs*); *sl.* manger (*son argent*); F louper (*une chance*); *sl.* ~ me!, l'm ~ed! zut alors!; F ~ *s.o. a kiss* envoyer un baiser à q.; ~ *one's nose* se moucher; F ~ *one's top* sortir de ses gonds; ~ **up** faire sauter; gonfler (*un pneu*); *sl.* semoncer, tancer; *phot.* agrandir; **2.** coup *m* de vent, souffle *m*; '~·**dry** sécher (au sèche-cheveux); '**blow·er** souffleur (-euse *f*) *m*; rideau *m* (*de cheminée*); ⊕ machine *f* à vent; *sl.* téléphone *m*.

blow…: '~·**fly** mouche *f* à viande; '~·**hole** évent *m* (*de baleine*; *a.* ⊕); ventilateur *m*.

blown [bloun] *p.p. de* blow³ 1.

'**blow·lamp** lampe *f* à souder, chalumeau *m*; **blow·out** *mot.* éclatement *m* (*de pneu*); *sl.* gueuleton *m*; '**blow·pipe** sarbacane *f*; *métall.* chalumeau *m*; '**blow·torch** *see* blowlamp; '**blow·up** explosion *f*; *phot.* agrandissement *m*; F accès *m* de colère; *sl.* engueulade *m*; '**blow·y** venteux (-euse *f*); tempétueux (-euse *f*).

blowz·y ['blauzi] rougeaud; ébouriffé.

blub·ber ['blʌbə] 1. graisse *f* de baleine; 2. *v/i.* pleurnicher; *v/t.* dire en pleurant; barbouiller de larmes.

bludg·eon ['blʌdʒn] 1. matraque *f*; 2. assener un coup de matraque à.

blue [blu:] 1. □ bleu; F triste, sombre; 2. bleu (*pl.* -s) *m*; azur *m*; *pol.* conservateur (-trice *f*) *m*; *out of the* ~ à l'improviste, sans crier gare; 3. bleuir; azurer (*le linge*); ~ **ba·by** 🖈 enfant *mf* bleu(e); '~**ber·ry** myrtille *f*, airelle *f*; '~**book** *Am.* registre *m* des employés de l'État; '~**bot·tle** ⚕ bl(e)uet *m*; *zo.* mouche *f* à viande; ~ **dev·ils** F *pl.* cafard *m*; '~**jack·et** col-bleu (*pl.* cols-bleus) *m* (= *matelot*); ~ **jeans** *sg. ou pl.* blue-jean(s) *m(pl.)*; ~ **laws** *Am.* lois *f/pl.* inspirées par le puritanisme; '**blue·ness** couleur *f* bleue; '**blue·print** dessin *m* négatif; *fig.* projet *m*; **blues** *pl.*, *a. sg.* humeur *f* noire, cafard *m*; ♪ *Am.* blues *m*; '**blue·stock·ing** *fig.* bas-bleu *m*.

bluff [blʌf] 1. □ escarpé (*falaise etc.*); brusque (*personne*); 2. bluff *m*; menaces *f/pl.* exagérées; *géog.* cap *m* à pic; 3. bluffer; *v/i.* faire du bluff.

blu·ish ['blu:iʃ] bleuâtre; bleuté.

blun·der ['blʌndə] 1. bévue *f*; erreur *f*; faux pas *m*; 2. faire une bévue *ou* une gaffe; ~ *into* heurter (*q.*), se heurter contre (*q.*); F ~ *out* laisser échapper (*un secret*) par maladresse; '**blun·der·er**, '**blun·der·head** maladroit(e *f*) *m*; lourdaud (-e *f*) *m*.

blunt [blʌnt] 1. □ émoussé; épointé; obtus (*angle*); *fig.* brusque, carré; 2. émousser (*un couteau*); épointer (*un crayon*); '**blunt·ness** état *m* épointé; manque *m* de tranchant; *fig.* franchise *f*.

blur [blə:] 1. tache *f*; *fig.* brouillard *m*; apparence *f* confuse; 2. *v/t.* barbouiller; brouiller, troubler; estomper (*les lignes*); ~*red surt. phot.* mal réussi, flou.

blurb [blə:b] *livre*: bande *f* de publicité.

blurt [blə:t]: ~ *out* trahir (*qch.*) par maladresse.

blush [blʌʃ] 1. rougeur *f*; incarnat *m* (*d'une rose*); prémices *f/pl.* (*de la jeunesse*); *at the first* ~ à l'abord; 2. rougir (*de for, with, at*); ~ *to*

(*inf.*) avoir honte de (*inf.*); '**blush·ing** □ rougissant.

blus·ter ['blʌstə] 1. fureur *f*, fracas *m*; rodomontades *f/pl.*; 2. souffler en rafales (*vent*); faire du fracas; faire le rodomont; '**blus·ter·er** rodomont *m*, bravache *m*.

bo·a *zo.*, 🖈 ['bouə] boa *m*.

boar [bɔ:] verrat *m*; sanglier *m*.

board [bɔ:d] 1. planche *f*; madrier *m*; tableau *m* (*d'annonces etc.*); carton *m*; *reliure*: emboîtage *m*; table *f*; pension *f*; *admin.* commission *f*; 🖈 conseil *m*; *pol.* ministère *m*; ⚓ bord *m*; ~*s pl. box.* canevas *m*; *théâ.* scène *f*, tréteaux *m/pl.*; *see director*; ♀ *of Trade* Ministère *m* du Commerce; *on* ~ *a ship* (*a train etc.*) à bord d'un navire (dans un train, en wagon, *etc.*); *above* ~ dans les règles; *across the* ~ général; 2. *v/t.* planchéier; cartonner (*un livre*); nourrir (*des élèves*); (*a.* ~ *out*) mettre en pension; ⚓ aller à bord de (*un navire*); ⚓ accoster; *surt. Am.* monter (en, dans); ~ *up* boucher (*une fenêtre*); couvrir *ou* entourer de planches; *v/i.* être en pension (chez, *with*); '**board·er** pensionnaire *mf*.

board·ing ['bɔ:diŋ] planchéiage *m*; cartonnage *m*; planches *f/pl.*; pension *f*; ⚓ accostage *m*; '~**house** pension *f* de famille; '~**school** pensionnat *m*, internat *m*.

board...: '~**wag·es** *pl.* indemnité *f* de logement *ou* de nourriture; '~**walk** *surt. Am.* trottoir *m* (en planches), caillebotis *m*.

boast [boust] 1. vanterie *f*; *fig.* orgueil *m*; 2. *v/i.* (*of, about* de) se vanter, se faire gloire; *v/t. fig.* (se glorifier de) posséder (*qch.*); '**boast·er** vantard(e *f*) *m*, fanfaron(ne *f*) *m*; **boast·ful** □ ['~ful] vantard.

boat [bout] 1. bateau *m*; embarcation *f*; navire *m* (*marchand*); *be in the same* ~ être logé(s) à la même enseigne; 2. aller en bateau; faire du canotage; '**boat·hook** gaffe *f*; '**boat·house** hangar *m* à bateaux; '**boat·ing** canotage *m*; '**boat·race** régate *f*, -s *f/pl.*; **boat·swain** ['bousn] maître *m* d'équipage.

bob [bɔb] 1. *pendule*: lentille *f*; plomb *m*; *pêche*: bouchon *m*; *cheval*: queue *f* écourtée; *sl.* shilling *m*; *Am. traîneau*: patin *m*; chignon *m*; petite révérence *f*; *see* ~*bed hair*; 2.

v/t. écourter; couper (*les cheveux*); ~**bed hair** cheveux *m/pl.* à la Jeanne d'Arc; *v/i.* s'agiter, danser; faire une petite révérence; *fig.* ~ **for** chercher à saisir avec les dents.

bob·bin ['bɔbin] bobine *f*; ⚡ corps *m* de bobine; fuseau *m* pour dentelles; '~**·lace** dentelle *f* aux fuseaux.

bob·ble *Am.* ['bɔbl] gaffe *f*.

bob·by *Brit. sl.* ['bɔbi] agent *m* de police; '~**·pin** pince *f* à cheveux; '~**·socks** *pl.* socquettes *f/pl.*; '~**·sox·er** *Am. sl.* adolescente *f*.

bob·sled ['bɔbsled], **bob·sleigh** ['bɔbslei] bobsleigh *m*.

bob·tail ['bɔbteil] queue *f* écourtée; cheval *m ou* chien *m* à queue écourtée; F canaille *f*.

bode [boud] présager; ~ **well** (*ill*) être de bon (mauvais) augure.

bod·ice ['bɔdis] corsage *m*; brassière *f* (*d'enfant*).

bod·i·less ['bɔdilis] sans corps.

bod·i·ly ['bɔdili] corporel(le *f*), physique; ⚖ ~ *harm* lésion *f* corporelle.

bod·kin ['bɔdkin] passe-lacet *m*; poinçon *m*; grande épingle *f*; F *sit* ~ être en lapin.

bod·y ['bɔdi] **1.** corps *m*; consistance *f*; *vin*: sève *f*; foule *f*; *église*: vaisseau *m*; fond *m* (*de chapeau*); (*a. dead* ~) cadavre *m*; ✈ fuselage *m*; ⊕ bâti *m*, corps *m*; *mot.* (*a.* ~**-work**) carrosserie *f*; ✕ troupe *f*, bande *f*; *astr.* astre *m*; F personne *f*, type *m*; ~ *odo(u)r* odeur *f* corporelle; *in a* ~ en masse, en corps; **2.** ~ *forth* donner une forme à; '~**-guard** garde *f* du corps.

Boer [buə] **1.** Boer *mf*; **2.** boer.

bog [bɔg] **1.** marécage *m*; **2.** embourber; *be* ~*ged* s'embourber.

bog·gle ['bɔgl] rechigner (devant *at*, *over*; à *inf. at*, *about* gér.).

bog·gy ['bɔgi] marécageux (-euse *f*).

bo·gie ['bougi] 🚂 bog(g)ie *m*; *a. see* bogy.

bo·gus ['bougəs] faux (fausse *f*); feint.

bo·gy ['bougi] épouvantail *m*; croque-mitaine *m*.

bo(h) [bou] bou.

Bo·he·mi·an [bou'hi:mjən] **1.** bohémien(ne *f*); **2.** Bohémien(ne *f*) *m*; *fig.* bohème *m*.

boil [bɔil] **1.** *v/i.* bouillir (*a. fig.*); *v/t.* faire bouillir; cuire à l'eau; ~*ed egg* œuf *m* à la coque; **2.** ébullition *f*;

furoncle *m*, F clou *m*; '**boil·er** chaudière *f*; bain-marie (*pl.* bains-marie) *m*; ~ *suit* bleu(s) *m(pl.)* (de travail); '**boil·ing** ébullition *f*; *sl. the whole* ~ tout le bazar.

bois·ter·ous □ ['bɔistərəs] bruyant; violent; tumultueux (-euse *f*); tempétueux (-euse *f*); '**bois·ter·ous·ness** violence *f*; turbulence *f*.

bold □ [bould] hardi, courageux (-euse *f*); assuré; à pic, escarpé (*côte etc.*); *péj.* effronté; *typ.* en vedette; *make* (*so*) ~ (*as*) *to* (*inf.*) s'enhardir jusqu'à (*inf.*); '**bold·face** *typ.* charactères *m/pl.* gras; '**bold·ness** hardiesse *f etc.*; *péj.* effronterie *f*.

bole [boul] fût *m*, tronc *m* (*d'arbre*).

boll 🌿 [boul] capsule *f*.

bol·lard ⚓ ['bɔləd] pieu *m* d'amarrage; *à bord:* bitte *f*.

bo·lo·ney [bə'louni] *see* baloney.

Bol·she·vism ['bɔlʃivizm] bolchevisme; '**Bol·she·vist** bolchevik (*a. su./mf*), bolcheviste (*a. su./mf*).

bol·ster ['boulstə] **1.** traversin *m*; ⊕ matrice *f*; coussinet *m*; **2.** (*usu.* ~ *up*) soutenir; F appuyer.

bolt¹ [boult] **1.** *arbalète:* carreau *m*; *porte:* verrou *m*; *serrure:* pêne *m*; *fig., a. poét.* coup *m* de foudre; *fig.* élan *m* soudain, fuite *f*; ~ *upright* tout droit; **2.** *v/t.* verrouiller; bâcler; F gober; *Am. pol.* abandonner (*son parti, q.*); *v/i.* partir au plus vite; F s'emballer (*cheval*); filer, décamper (*personne*).

bolt² [~] tamiser.

bolt·er¹ ['boultə] cheval *m* porté à s'emballer; déserteur *m*.

bolt·er² [~] blutoir *m*.

bolt-hole ['boulthoul] *animal:* trou *m* de refuge; *fig.* échappée *f*.

bomb [bɔm] **1.** *surt.* ✕ bombe *f*; F grenade *f* à main; *hydrogen* ~ bombe *f* H; *incendiary* ~ bombe *f* incendiaire; **2.** lancer des bombes sur; ~*ed out* sinistré par suite des bombardements.

bom·bard [bɔm'ba:d] bombarder (*a. fig.*); **bom'bard·ment** bombardement *m*.

bom·bast ['bɔmbæst] emphase *f*, enflure *f*; **bom'bas·tic**, **bom'bas·ti·cal** □ enflé, ampoulé (*style*).

bomb·er ✕ ['bɔmə] bombardier *m* (*a. personne*).

bomb-proof ['bɔmpru:f] à l'épreuve des bombes; blindé (*abri*).

bo·na fi·de ['bəunə'faidi] **1.** de bonne foi; sérieux (-euse *f*) (*offre etc.*); **2.** de bonne foi.

bo·nan·za F [bo'nænzə] **1.** *fig.* vraie mine *f* d'or; **2.** prospère, favorable.

bon-bon ['bɔnbɔn] bonbon *m*.

bond [bɔnd] **1.** lien *m* (*a. fig.*); attache *f* (*a. fig.*); contrat *m*; ⊕ joint *m*; ✝ bon *m*; ✝ in ~ entreposé; **2.** liaisonner; appareiller (*un mur*); ✝ entreposer, mettre en dépôt; ~ed *warehouse* entrepôt *m* de la douane; '**bond·age** esclavage *m*, servitude *f*, asservissement *m*; ✝ servage *m*; *fig.* in ~ to s.o. sous la férule de q.; '**bond(s)·man** *hist.* serf *m*; F esclave *m*; '**bond(s)·wom·an** *hist.* serve *f*; F esclave *f*.

bone [bəun] **1.** os *m*; arête *f* (*de poisson*); ~s *pl. a.* ossements *m/pl.* (*des morts*); ~ *of contention* pomme *f* de discorde; *feel in one's* ~s en avoir le pressentiment; *frozen to the* ~ glacé jusqu'à la moelle, transi de froid; F *have a* ~ *to pick with* avoir maille à partir avec (*q.*); F *make no* ~s *about* (*gér.*) ne pas se gêner pour (*inf.*); **2.** désosser; ôter les arêtes de; garnir de baleines (*un corset*); *Am.* F (*a.* ~ *up*) potasser; **3.** d'os; **boned** à (aux) os ...; *désossé etc.*; '~·**i·dle**, '~·**la·zy** paresseux (-euse *f*) comme une couleuvre; '**bone-meal** engrais *m* d'os; '**bon·er** *Am. sl.* bourde *f*; '**bone·set·ter** rebouteur *m*; F renoueur *m*.

bon·fire ['bɔnfaiə] feu *m* de joie; feu *m* (de jardin); F conflagration *f*.

bon·kers *Brit. sl.* ['bɔŋkəz] cinglé, dingue.

bon·net ['bɔnit] **1.** bonnet *m*; béret *m*; chapeau *m* à brides (*de femme*); béguin *m* (*d'enfant*); capote *f* de cheminée; ⊕ capot *m*; *fig.* compère *m*, complice *mf*; ⚓ bonnette *f* maillée; **2.** mettre un béret *ou* chapeau à; F enfoncer le chapeau sur la tête à (*q.*).

bon·ny *surt. écoss.* ['bɔni] joli, gentil(le *f*).

bo·nus ✝ ['bəunəs] prime *f*; boni *m*; *actions:* bonus *m*.

bon·y ['bəuni] osseux (-euse *f*); anguleux (-euse *f*), décharné (*personne*); plein d'os *ou* d'arêtes.

boo [bu:] huer, conspuer (*q.*).

boob *Am.* [bu:b] rigaud(e *f*) *m*, benêt *m*.

boo·by ['bu:bi] *orn.* fou *m*; *a. see boob*; ~ *prize* prix *m* décerné à celui qui vient en dernier; ~ **trap** attrape-niais *m/inv.*; ✕ mine-piège *f*.

boo-hoo F [bu'hu:] pleurnicher.

book [buk] **1.** livre *m*; volume *m*; tome *m*; registre *m*; carnet *m* (*de billets etc.*); cahier *m* (*d'écolier*); ✝ *stand in the* ~s at ... être porté pour ... dans les livres; *fig. be in s.o.'s good* (*bad*) ~s être bien (mal) dans les papiers de q.; **2.** *v/t.* inscrire (*une commande, un voyageur à l'hôtel*); délivrer un billet à (*q.*); prendre (*un billet*); retenir (*une chambre, une place*); louer (*une place*); enregistrer; *v/i.* s'inscrire; prendre un billet; ~ *through* prendre un billet direct (pour, to); '~·**bind·er** relieur (-euse *f*) *m*; '~·**burn·er** *Am.* F fanatique *mf*; zélateur (-trice *f*) *m*; '~·**case** bibliothèque *f*; ~ **end** serre-livres *m/inv.*; **book·ie** F *sp.* ['buki] bookmaker *m*; '**book·ing-clerk** employé(e *f*) *m* du guichet; '**book·ing-of·fice** ☎, *théâ.* guichet *m*; guichets *m/pl.*; '**book·ish** ☐ studieux (-euse *f*); livresque (*style*); '**book-keep·er** comptable *m*, teneur *m* de livres; '**book-keep·ing** tenue *f* des livres; comptabilité *f*; **book·let** ['~lit] livret *m*; opuscule *m*.

book...: '~·**mak·er** faiseur *m* de livres; *sp.* bookmaker *m*; '~·**mark** signet *m*; '~·**plate** ex-libris *m*; '~·**sell·er** libraire *m*; *wholesale* ~ libraire-éditeur (*pl.* libraires-éditeurs*) *m*; '~·**worm** *zo.* gerce *f*, teigne *f*; *fig.* rat *m* de bibliothèque.

boom¹ ⚓ [bu:m] bout-dehors (*pl.* bouts-dehors) *m*; gui *m*; *port:* barrage *m*.

boom² [~] **1.** ✝ hausse *f* rapide; boom *m*; vogue *f*; ~ *and bust* prospérité *f* économique suivie d'une crise sévère; **2.** *v/i.* être en hausse; *fig.* aller très fort; *v/t.* faire du battage autour de (*q., qch.*).

boom³ [~] gronder, mugir; bourdonner (*insectes*).

boon¹ [bu:n] faveur *f*; bienfait *m*.

boon² [~] gai, joyeux (-euse *f*); ~ *companion* bon vivant *m*.

boor *fig.* [buə] rustre *m*, rustaud *m*; butor *m*.

boor·ish ☐ ['buəriʃ] rustre, rustaud, grossier (-ère *f*); malappris; '**boor-**

ish·ness grossièreté *f*; manque *m* de savoir-vivre.

boost [buːst] faire de la réclame pour; F chauffer; ⚡ survolter; ~ *business* augmenter les affaires; **'boost·er** ⚡ survolteur *m*; *radio*: amplificateur *m*; ⊕ (*a.* ~ *rocket*) fusée *f* de lancement; ✚ ~ *shot* injection *f ou* piqûre *f* de rappel, rappel *m* (de vaccination).

boot[1] [buːt]: *to* ~ en sus, de plus.

boot[2] [~] chaussure *f*; *mot.* caisson *m*; F *get the* ~ se faire flanquer à la porte; *give s.o. the* ~ flanquer q. à la porte; **'~·black** *Am. see* shoeblack; **'boot·ed** chaussé; **boot·ee** ['buːtiː] bottine *f* (d'intérieur) (*de dame*); bottine *f* d'enfant.

booth [buːð] baraque *f*, tente *f* (*de marché etc.*).

boot···: **'~·jack** tire-botte *m*; **'~·lace** lacet *m*; **'~·leg** *surt. Am.* 1. de contrebande (*alcool*); 2. faire la contrebande de l'alcool; **'~·leg·ger** contrebandier *m* de boissons alcooliques; *p.ext.* profiteur *m*.

boots [buːts] *sg. hôtel*: garçon *m* d'étage.

boot-tree ['buːttriː] tendeur *m*.

boo·ty ['buːti] butin *m*.

booze *sl.* [buːz] 1. faire ribote; 2. boisson *f* alcoolique; **'booz·y** *sl.* soûlard; pompette.

bo·rax ⚗ ['bɔːræks] borax *m*.

bor·der ['bɔːdə] 1. bord *m*; *bois*: lisière *f*; *chemin*: marge *f*; *région*: frontière *f*, confins *m/pl.*; *tableau*: bordure *f*; platebande *f* (*de gazon*); ~ *state* état *m* limitrophe; 2. *v/t.* border; encadrer; *v/i.* confiner (à, [up] on); **'bor·der·er** frontalier (-ère *f*) *m*; **'bor·der·land** *usu. fig.* pays *m* limitrophe *ou* frontière.

bore[1] [bɔː] 1. *tuyau, arme à feu*: calibre *m*; *min.* trou *m* de sonde *ou* de mine; 2. creuser.

bore[2] [~] 1. importun(e *f*) *m*; ennui *m*; 2. ennuyer, F raser, assommer.

bore[3] [~] mascaret *m*; raz *m* de marée.

bore[4] [~] *prét. de* bear[2].   [*m/pl.*).\

bo·re·al ['bɔːriəl] boréal (-aux/

bore·dom ['bɔːdəm] ennui *m*.

bor·er ['bɔːrə] perceur *m*; outil *m* de perforation.

bo·ric ⚗ ['bɔːrik] borique.

bor·ing ['bɔːriŋ] d'alésage; de perçage; à aléser.

born [bɔːn] *p.p. de* bear[2] naître.

borne [bɔːn] *p.p. de* bear[2] porter.

bo·ron ⚗ ['bɔːrɔn] bore *m*.

bor·ough ['bʌrə] bourg *m*; commune *f*; *Am. a.* quartier *m de New York City*; *municipal* ~ ville *f* (avec municipalité).

bor·row ['bɔrou] emprunter (à, *from*); **'bor·row·er** emprunteur (-euse *f*) *m*; **'bor·row·ing** emprunts *m/pl.*; *ling.*: emprunt *m*.

Bor·stal in·sti·tu·tion ['bɔːstl in·sti'tjuːʃn] maison *f* de redressement, école *f* de réforme.

bos·cage ['bɔskidʒ] *poét.* bocage *m*.

bosh F [bɔʃ] bêtises *f/pl.*; blague *f*.

bos·om ['buzəm] sein *m*, giron *m*; poitrine *f*; *fig.* cœur *m*; ~*friend* ami(e *f*) *m* de cœur; intime *mf*.

boss[1] [bɔs] 1. protubérance *f*, △ bosse *f*; ⊕ mamelon *m*; moyeu *m* de l'hélice; 2. relever en bosse.

boss[2] [~] 1. F patron *m*, chef *m*; *pol. Am.* grand manitou *m* (*d'un parti*); 2. mener; *sl.* commander, régenter.

boss·y ['bɔsi] F autoritaire, tyrannique.

Bos·ton ['bɔstən] *cartes, danse*: boston *m*.

bo·tan·ic, bo·tan·i·cal □ [bo'tænik(l)] botanique; **bot·a·nist** ['bɔtənist] botaniste *mf*; **bot·a·nize** ['~naiz] botaniser, herboriser; **'bot·a·ny** botanique *f*.

botch [bɔtʃ] 1. F travail *m* mal fait; travail *m* bousillé; 2. bousiller, saboter; rafistoler (*des souliers*); **'botch·er** bousilleur (-euse *f*) *m*; *fig.* savetier *m*.

both [bouθ] tous (toutes *f*) (les) deux; l'un(e) et l'autre; ~ ... *and* ... et ... et ...; ~ *of them* tous (toutes) (les) deux.

both·er F ['bɔðə] 1. ennui *m*; tracas *m*; 2. *v/t.* gêner, tracasser; *v/i.* s'inquiéter (de, *about*); ~ *it!* zut!; quelle scie!; **both·er'a·tion** F ennui *m*, vexation *f*; **'~!** zut!

bot·tle ['bɔtl] 1. bouteille *f*; flacon *m*; botte *f* (*de foin*); 2. mettre en bouteille(s); *fig.* ~ *up* embouteiller (*une flotte etc.*); F étouffer (*des sentiments*); ~*d beer* bière *f* en canette; **'~·neck** *fig. circulation*: embouteillage *m*; ⚙ col *m* de bouteille; **'~·o·pen·er** ouvre-bouteilles *m/inv.*

bot·tom ['bɔtəm] 1. *colline, escalier,*

page: bas *m*; *boîte, mer, cœur, na-vire, jardin*: fond *m*; *chaussée*: assiette *f*; *verre, assiette*: dessous *m*; *classe*: queue *f*; *chaise*: siège *m*; *terrain*: creux *m*; F derrière *m*, postérieur *m*; *at the ⁓ (of)* au fond (de); *au bas bout* (de); *fig. (a. su.⁓)* au fond; *get to the ⁓ of a matter* aller au fond d'une chose; examiner une chose à fond; *jealousy is at the ⁓ of it* c'est la jalousie qui en est la cause; **2.** inférieur; en bas; du bas; dernier (-ère *f*); ⁓ *drawer* trousseau *m* (de mariage), F trésor *m*, cache *f*; **3.** (re)mettre un fond à; fonder (sur, *upon*); ⚓ toucher le fond; **'bot-tomed** à fond ...; à siège (de)...; **'bot·tom·less** sans fond; *fig.* insondable; **'bot·tom·ry** ⚓ (emprunt *m* à la) grosse aventure *f*.

bough [bau] branche *f*, rameau *m*.

bought [bɔːt] *prét. et p.p. de* buy.

bou·gie [ˈbuːʒiː] bougie *f* (*a. ⚕*).

boul·der [ˈbouldə] bloc *m* de pierre roulé; *géol.* bloc *m* erratique.

bounce [bauns] **1.** rebond *m*; bond *m*; rebondissement *m*; F jactance *f*, vantardise *f*; bluff *m*; **2.** *v/i.* rebondir; F faire de l'épate; *v/t.* faire rebondir; ⁓ *in (out)* entrer (sortir) en coup de vent; ⁓ *s.o. out of s.th.* obtenir qch. de q. à force de bluff *ou* d'intimidation; **3.** boum!, v(')lan!; **'bounc·er** F vantard *m*, épateur *m*; mensonge *m* effronté; *sl.* chèque *m* sans provision; *Am. sl.* agent *m* du service d'ordre; *Am. sl.* videur *m*; **'bounc·ing** F plein de vie, plein de santé.

bound¹ [baund] **1.** *prét. et p.p. de* bind; **2.** *adj.* obligé; *be ⁓ to do* être obligé de faire, devoir faire; *I will be ⁓* je vous le promets.

bound² [⁓] en partance, en route (pour, *for*).

bound³ [⁓] **1.** limite *f*, borne *f*; *in ⁓s* accès permis (à, *to*); *out of ⁓s* accès interdit (à, *to*), *sp.* hors du jeu; **2.** borner, limiter.

bound⁴ [⁓] **1.** bond *m*, saut *m*; **2.** bondir, sauter; *fig.* sursauter.

bound·a·ry [ˈbaundəri] limite *f*; frontière *f*; ⁓ *line* ligne *f* frontière.

bound·less □ [ˈbaundlis] sans bornes; illimité.

boun·te·ous □ [ˈbauntiəs], **boun·ti·ful** □ [ˈ⁓tiful] généreux (-euse *f*); libéral (-aux *m/pl.*).

boun·ty [ˈbaunti] générosité *f*; libéralité *f*; don *m*; ✝ indemnité *f*; prime *f* (*a. ✕, ⚓*).

bou·quet [ˈbukei] *fleurs etc., vin*: bouquet *m*.

bour·geois¹ *péj.* [ˈbuəʒwɑː] bourgeois(e *f*) (*a. su./mf*).

bour·geois² *typ.* [bəːˈdʒɔis] petit romain *m*. [geoisie *f*.\
bour·geoi·sie [buəʒwɑːˈziː] bour-]

bout [baut] tour *m*, *jeux*: reprise *f*; *lutte*: assaut *m*; *maladie*: accès *m*, attaque *f*, crise *f*.

bo·vine [ˈbouvain] **1.** bovin; F lourd; **2.** ⁓*s pl.* bovidés *m/pl.*

bov·ver *sl.* [ˈbɔvə] bagarre *f*, *sl.* rififi *m*.

bow¹ [bau] **1.** révérence *f*; salut *m*; inclination *f* de tête; **2.** *v/i.* s'incliner (devant, *to*); saluer (q., *to s.o.*); *fig.* se plier (à, *to*); *have a ⁓ing acquaintance* connaître (q.) pour lui dire bonjour; *v/t.* incliner, baisser (*la tête*); fléchir (*le genou*); voûter (*le dos*).

bow² [⁓] ⚓ avant *m*; *poét.* proue *f*; *dirigeable*: nez *m*.

bow³ [bou] arc *m*; *ruban*: nœud *m*; ♪ archet *m*; **2.** ♪ gouverner l'archet; faire des coups d'archet.

bowd·ler·ize [ˈbaudləraiz] expurger (*un texte*).

bow·els [ˈbauəlz] *pl.* intestins *m/pl.*; entrailles *f/pl.* (*a. fig.*); *fig.* sein *m*.

bow·er [ˈbauə] tonnelle *f*; *poét.* boudoir *m*; ⚓ ancre *f* de bossoir.

bow·ie·knife [ˈbouinaif] couteau *m* de chasse.

bow·ing ♪ [ˈbouiŋ] manière *f* de gouverner l'archet *m*.

bowl¹ [boul] bol *m*, jatte *f*; sébile *f* (*de mendiant*); coupe *f*; *pipe*: fourneau *m*; *lampe*: culot *m*.

bowl² [⁓] **1.** boule *f*; ⁓*s pl.* (jeu *m* de) boules *f/pl.*; *Am.* (jeu *m* de) quilles *f/pl.*; **2.** *v/t.* rouler; *cricket*: bôler; ⁓ *out* renverser (q., *le guichet de q.*); *v/i.* rouler rapidement; servir la balle; rouler la boule.

bow-legged [ˈboulegd] bancal (-als *m/pl.*), aux jambes arquées.

'bowl·er *cricket*: bôleur *m*; joueur *m* de boules; (*chapeau m*) melon *m*.

bowl·ing [ˈbouliŋ] bowling *m*; jeu *m* de boules; ⁓ **al·ley** bowling *m*.

bow-wow [ˈbauˈwau] ouâ-ouâ!

box¹ [bɔks] **1.** boîte *f* (*a. d'essieu*); coffret *m*; caisse *f*; *voyage*: malle *f*;

chapeaux: carton *m*; siège *m* (*de cocher*); 🚂 cabine *f* (*de signaleur*), wagon *m* à chevaux; ⊕ moyeu *m* de roue; *mot.* carter *m*; *théâ.* loge *f*; ⚖ banc *m* (*du jury*), barre *f* (*des témoins*); *écurie*: stalle *f*; 2. emboîter, encaisser; mettre en boîte; *fig.* (*a. ~up*) serrer, renfermer.

box² [~] 1. *sp.* boxer; ~ *on the ear* gifler q.; 2. ~ *on the ear* gifle *f*, claque *f*; '~**calf** ⊕, 🐂 veau *m* chromé; '**box·er** boxeur *m*, pugiliste *m*.

box·ing ['bɔksiŋ] boxe *f*; ~ *gloves* gants *m/pl.* de boxe; ~ *match* match *m* de boxe; ~ *ring* ring *m*.

Box·ing-day ['bɔksiŋdei] lendemain *m* de Noël.

box...: '~**keep·er** ouvreuse *f* de loges; '~**of·fice** bureau *m* de location; caisse *f*; ~ *hit* (spectacle *m etc.* à) succès *m*; *be a ~ hit a.* faire recette; ~ *room Brit.* (cabinet (*m* de) débarras *m*.

box(·wood) ['bɔkswud] (bois *m*) buis *m*.

boy [bɔi] 1. garçon *m*; *école:* élève *m*; domestique *m*; 2. garçon ...; jeune; ~ *scout* boy-scout *m*.

boy·cott ['bɔikɔt] 1. boycotter; 2. mise *f* en interdit; boycottage *m*.

boy·hood ['bɔihud] enfance *f*, (première) jeunesse *f*.

boy·ish □ ['bɔiiʃ] puéril, enfantin, d'enfant, de garçon.

bra F [brɑ:] *see* brassière.

brace [breis] 1. ⊕ vilebrequin *m*; armature *f*; *mur:* bracon *m*; ancre *f*; ♪, *typ.* accolade *f*; *chasse:* couple *f* (*de perdrix etc.*); laisse *f* (*de lévriers*); paire *f* (*de pistolets*); ⚓ bras *m* (*de vergue*); ~*s pl.* pantalon: bretelles *f/pl.*; *tambour:* corde *f*; 2. ancrer; accolader; tendre (*les jarrets*); ⚓ brasser; *fig.* fortifier.

brace·let ['breislit] bracelet *m*.

brack·en ♣ ['brækn] fougère *f* arborescente.

brack·et ['brækit] 1. △ corbeau *m*; console *f*; support *m*; *typ.* [ ] crochet *m*; ( ) parenthèse *f*; applique *f* (*électrique, à gaz, etc.*); ⚓ courbaton *m*; support *m*; 2. mettre entre crochets *etc.*; *fig.* placer ex aequo.

brack·ish ['brækiʃ] saumâtre.

bract ♣ [brækt] bractée *f*.

brad [bræd] pointe *f*, clou *m* étêté.

brag [bræg] 1. vanterie *f*; 2. se vanter (*de of, about*).

brag·gart ['brægət] fanfaron (*a. su./m*); vantard (*a. su./m*).

Brah·man ['brɑ:mən], *usu.* **Brahmin** ['~min] brahmane *m*, brame *m*.

braid [breid] 1. *cheveux:* tresse *f*; galon *m* (*a.* ✂), ganse *f*; 2. tresser; galonner; passementer.

brail ⚓ [breil] cargue *f*.

braille [breil] alphabet *m* des aveugles; système *m* Braille.

brain [brein] 1. *anat.* cerveau *m*; F cervelle *f* (*a. cuis.*); *p.ext. usu.* ~*s pl.* tête *f*, intelligence *f*, esprit *m*; *have s.th. on the* ~ être hanté par qch.; avoir l'obsession de qch.; F *pick* (*ou suck*) *s.o.'s* ~ exploiter les connaissances de q.; 2. défoncer le crâne à (*q.*); '~**child** F idée *f*; invention *f*; ~ **drain** exode *m* des cerveaux; **~ed:** *dull-*~ à l'esprit lourd.

brain...: '~**fag** épuisement *m* cérébral; ~ **fe·ver** fièvre *f* cérébrale; '~**less** sans cervelle, stupide; *fig.* irréfléchi; '~**pan** (boîte *f* du) crâne *m*; '~**storm** transport *m* au cerveau; **brain(s) trust** brain-trust *m*.

brain...: '~**twist·er** problème *m* à faire casser la tête à q.; '~**wash** (subir) un lavage de cerveau à (*q.*); '~**wash·ing** lavage *m* de cerveau; *media etc.:* bourrage *m* de crâne; '~**wave** F idée *f* lumineuse; '~**work** travail *m* cérébral; '**brain·y** intelligent.

braise [breiz] *cuis.* braiser; **braised** *cuis.* en daube, en casserole.

brake¹ [breik] fougère *f* arborescente *ou* impériale; fourré *m*.

brake² [~] 1. *lin. etc.:* brisoir *m*; ⊕ frein *m* (*a. fig.*); ~ *fluid* liquide *m* pour freins; ~ *lining* garniture *f* de frein; ~ *pedal* pédale *f* de frein; 2. briser, broyer (*le lin etc.*); *mot.* serrer le frein; '**brake(s)·man** 🚂 serrefreins *m/inv.*; *Am.* chef *m* de train; '**brak·ing** ~ *distance* distance *f* de freinage; ~ *power* puissance *f* de freinage.

bram·ble ♣ ['bræmbl] ronce *f* sauvage; mûrier *m* sauvage.

bran [bræn] son *m*.

branch [brɑ:ntʃ] 1. *arbre, famille, fleuve:* branche *f*; *arbre, montagnes:* rameau *m*; *fleuve:* bras *m*; 🚂, *route:* embranchement *m*; (*ou local* ~) succursale *f*, filiale *f*; *chief of* ~ chef *m* de service; 2. (*a.* ~ *out*) se ramifier; (*a. ~ off*) (se) bifurquer (sur, *from*), se partager (à, *at*); '**branch-line** embranchement *m*; **branch of·fice** agence *f*; bureau *m* de quartier; '**branch·y** branchu; rameux (-euse *f*).

brand [brænd] **1.** brandon *m*, tison *m*; fer *m* chaud; marque *f*; stigmate *m*; ♀ rouille *f*; *poét.* flambeau *m*; *poét.* glaive *m*; ~ *name* marque *f* (de fabrique); **2.** marquer au fer chaud; *fig.* flétrir, stigmatiser (*q.*).

bran·dish ['brændiʃ] brandir.

bran(d)-new ['bræn(d)'nju:] tout (battant) neuf (neuve *f*).

bran·dy ['brændi] cognac *m*, eau-de-vie (*pl.* eaux-de-vie) *f*.

brash □ ['bræʃ] impertinent, éffronté; présomptueux (-euse *f*); impétueux (-euse *f*); indiscret (-ète *f*).

brass [brɑːs] cuivre *m* jaune; laiton *m*; *fig.* impertinence *f*, *sl.* toupet *m*; F argent *m*, galette *f*; ♪ *les* cuivres *m/pl.*; ~ *band* fanfare *f*; ~ *hat* ✕ *sl.* officier *m* d'état-major; *Am.* ~ *knuckles pl.* coup-de-poing (*pl.* coups-de-poing) *m* américain; *sl.* ~ *tacks pl.* les faits *m/pl.*; *get down to* ~ *tacks* en venir au fait.

bras·sière ['bræsiɛə] soutien-gorge (*pl.* soutiens-gorge) *m*.

bras·sy ['brɑːsi] qui ressemble au cuivre; *usu. fig.* cuivré; *sl.* effronté.

brat F [bræt] marmot *m*, mioche *mf*.

bra·va·do [brə'vɑːdou], *pl.* -dos, does [~douz] bravade *f*.

brave [breiv] **1.** courageux (-euse *f*), brave; **2.** braver; défier (*q.*); '**brav·er·y** courage *m*, bravoure *f*; vaillance *f*.

bra·vo ['brɑː'vou] **1.** (*pl.* -vos, -voes ['~vouz]) bravo *m*; spadassin *m*; **2.** bravo!

brawl [brɔːl] **1.** rixe *f*, bagarre *f*, querelle *f*; **2.** brailler; se chamailler; '**brawl·er** braillard(e *f*) *m*; tapageur (-euse *f*) *m*.

brawn [brɔːn] *cuis.* fromage *m* de cochon; muscles *m/pl.*; *fig.* force *f* corporelle; '**brawn·i·ness** carrure *f* musclée; force *f*; '**brawn·y** musculeux (-euse *f*); musclé (*personne*).

bray[1] [brei] **1.** âne *m*; braiment *m*; fanfare *f*; *trompette:* son *m* strident; **2.** braire (*âne*); émettre un son strident.

bray[2] [~] broyer, piler.

braze ⊕ [breiz] souder au laiton.

bra·zen □ ['breizn] d'airain; *fig.* (*a.* ~-*faced*) effronté.

bra·zier ['breizjə] *personne:* chaudronnier *m*; brasero *m* (*à charbon de bois*).

Bra·zil·ian [brə'ziljən] **1.** brésilien (-ne *f*); **2.** Brésilien(ne *f*) *m*.

Bra·zil-nut [brə'zil'nʌt] noix *f* du Brésil.

breach [briːtʃ] **1.** rupture *f*; *fig.* infraction *f* (à, *of*); ✕ brèche *f*; ~ *of contract* rupture *f* de contrat; ~ *of duty* violation *f* des devoirs; ~ *of peace* attentat *m* contre l'ordre public; **2.** *v/t.* ouvrir une brèche dans; *v/i.* se rompre.

bread [bred] pain *m* (*a.* = *subsistance*); *sl.* fric *m*; ~ *and butter* pain *m* beurré; *take the* ~ *out of s.o.'s mouth* ôter le pain à q.; *know which side one's* ~ *is buttered* savoir d'où vient le vent; '~-**bas·ket** corbeille *f* à pain; *sl.* estomac *m*; '~-**bin**, '~-**box** boîte *f* à pain; '~-**crumb** *cuis.* **1.** paner (*une escalope etc.*), gratiner (*une sole etc.*); **2.** miette *f*; '~-**knife** couteau *m* à pain.

breadth [bredθ] largeur *f* (*a. de pensées, d'esprit*); *style:* ampleur *f*; *étoffe:* lé *m*.

bread-win·ner ['bredwinə] gagne-pain *m/inv.*; chef *m* de famille.

break [breik] **1.** rupture *f*; fracture *f*; percée *f*, brèche *f*; éclaircie *f* (*à travers les nuages*); lacune *f*; ♀ *Am.* baisse *f* (*de prix*); *voitures:* break *m*; voiture *f* de dressage (*des chevaux*); *billard:* série *f* de carambolages; ⚡ rupture *f* (*du circuit*); *école:* récréation *f*; *voix:* mue *f* (*dans la puberté*), *émotion:* altération *f*; *temps:* changement *m*; répit *m*; ~ *of day* point *m* du jour; *see brake*[2] *1*; F *a bad* ~ une sottise *f*; F *give s.o. a* ~ agir loyalement avec q.; mettre q. à l'essai; **2.** [*irr.*] *v/t.* briser, casser; enfoncer (*une porte*); rompre (*chose, pain, rangs, cheval*); entamer (*la peau*); résilier (*un contrat*); faire sauter (*la banque*); s'évader de (*la prison*); ⚡ interrompre (*le courant*), rompre (*un circuit*); ⚡ défricher; ✕ casser (*un officier*); violer (*une loi, une trêve*); ~ *down* abattre, démolir; ⚗ décomposer; ~ *in* enfoncer; défoncer (*un tonneau*); dresser (*un cheval*); rompre (à, *to*); ~ *up* mettre (qch.) en morceaux; disperser (une foule); rompre; démolir; **3.** [irr.] v/i. (se) casser, se briser, se rompre; déferler (vagues); crever (abcès); se dissiper (nuages); se briser, se fendre (cœur); changer (temps); s'altérer (voix); ~ away se détacher (de, from); s'évader (de prison); ~ down échouer (projet); fondre en larmes; mot. avoir une panne; ~ up entrer en vacances; see a. broken; **'break·a·ble** fragile; **'break·age** rupture f; verre: fracture f; ✝ a. ~s pl. casse f; **'break-down** rupture f; service: arrêt m complet; insuccès m; débâcle f de la santé; mot. panne f; ~ lorry dépanneuse f; ~ service service m de dépannage; ~ truck dépanneuse f; **'break·er** casseur (-euse f) m; ⚓ brisant m.

break...: ~**fast** ['brekfəst] **1.** petit déjeuner m; **2.** déjeuner m; ~**neck** ['breiknek] à se casser le cou; **'~-out** évasion f; **'~-through** ⚔, a. fig. percée f; fig. a. bond m en avant; découverte f; solution f; réussite f; **'~-'up** dissolution f, fin f; affaisement m; école: entrée f en vacances; temps: changement m; **'~-wa·ter** brise-lames m/inv.; môle m.

bream icht. [bri:m] brème f.

breast [brest] **1.** sein m; mamelle f; poitrine f; make a clean ~ of it dire ce qu'on a sur la conscience; **2.** affronter; lutter contre, faire front à; **'breast·ed** à poitrine ...

breast...: **'~-feed** donner le sein à (un bébé); élever au sein; **'~-pin** épingle f de cravate; **'~-stroke** brasse f sur le ventre; **'~-work** ⚔ parapet m.

breath [breθ] haleine f, souffle m, respiration f; bad ~ mauvaise haleine f; under (ou below) one's ~ à voix basse, à mi-voix; **'breath·a·lyse** mot. [~əlaiz] faire subir l'alcootest à (q.); **breath·a·lys·er** ['~əlaizə] alcootest m; **breathe** [bri:ð] v/i. respirer, souffler; fig. vivre; v/t. respirer, exhaler (un soupir); murmurer (une prière); aspirer (l'air, un son); **'breath·er** F moment m de repos; brin m d'air; répit m.

breath·ing ['bri:ðiŋ] **1.** vivant (portrait); **2.** respiration f; souffle m; **'~-space**, **'~-time** répit m; intervalle m de repos.

breath·less □ ['breθlis] essoufflé;

fig. fiévreux (-euse f); **'breath·less-ness** essoufflement m.

breath-tak·ing ['breθteikiŋ] F ahurissant.

bred [bred] prét. et p.p. de breed 2.

breech ⊕ [bri:tʃ] fusil, canon: culasse f, tonnerre m; **breech·es** ['~iz] pl.: (a pair of)~ (une) culotte f; F (un) pantalon m; **'breech-load·er** ⊕ fusil m se chargeant par la culasse.

breed [bri:d] **1.** race f; péj. espèce f; Am. métis(se f) m; **2.** [irr.] v/t. produire, engendrer; élever (du bétail); v/i. se reproduire; multiplier; **'breed·er** reproducteur (-trice f) m; éleveur m (d'animaux); **'breed-ing** reproduction f; élevage m (d'animaux); bonnes manières f/pl.

breeze¹ [bri:z] **1.** brise f; F querelle f; altercation f; **2.** Am. F s'en aller (à la hâte).

breeze² zo. [~] œstre m.

breeze³ ⊕ [~] braise f de houille; fraisil m.

breez·y ['bri:zi] venteux (-euse f); jovial (-als, -aux m/pl.) (personne).

breth·ren eccl. ['breðrin] pl. frères m/pl.; my ~ mes très chers frères.

breve [bri:v] syllabe: brève f.

bre·vet ⚔ ['brevit] brevet m (avancement d'un officier sans augmentation de solde); ~ rank grade m honoraire; ~ colonel lieutenant-colonel m faisant fonction de colonel.

bre·vi·ar·y eccl. ['bri:vjəri] bréviaire m.

brev·i·ty ['breviti] brièveté f.

brew [bru:] **1.** vt/i. brasser; fig. (se) tramer; v/i. s'infuser; couver (orage, tempête); **2.** brassage m; brassin m; infusion f; **'brew·age** poét. see brew 2; **'brew·er** brasseur m; **'brew·er·y** brasserie f.

bri·ar ['braiə] see brier¹ et brier².

bribe [braib] **1.** paiement m illicite; **2.** corrompre, acheter (pour que, to); **'brib·er** corrupteur (-trice f) m; **'brib·er·y** corruption f; ⚖ subornation f (d'un témoin); ⚖ ~ and corruption corruption f; be open to ~ être corruptible.

bric-a-brac ['brikəbræk] bric-à-brac m.

brick [brik] **1.** brique f; F a regular ~ un chic type; sl. drop a ~ faire une gaffe; **2.** briqueter; ~ up murer (une fenêtre etc.); **'~-bat** briqueton m; **'~-kiln** four m à briques; **'~-lay·er**

maçon *m*; '**~-works** *usu. sg.* briqueterie *f*; '**brick·y** de *ou* en brique; comme une brique.

brid·al ['braidl] **1.** □ nuptial (-aux *m*/*pl.*), de noce(s); **2.** *usu. poét.* noce *f*, -s *f*/*pl.*

bride [braid] future *f* (*sur le point de se marier*); (nouvelle) mariée *f*; '**~·groom** futur *m* (*sur le point de se marier*); (nouveau) marié *m*; '**brides·maid** demoiselle *f* d'honneur; '**brides·man** garçon *m* d'honneur; **bride-to-'be** future fiancée *f ou* épouse *f*.

bride·well *Brit.* ['braidwəl] maison *f* de correction.

bridge[1] [bridʒ] **1.** pont *m*; ⚓ passerelle *f*; **2.** jeter un pont sur; *fig.* relier, combler.

bridge[2] [~] *cartes*: bridge *m*.

bridge...: '**~-head** tête *f* de pont; '**~-work** bridge-work *m* (*dentaire*).

bri·dle ['braidl] **1.** bride *f*; *fig.* frein *m*; **2.** *v/t.* brider (*a. fig.*); *v/i.* (*a. ~ up*) redresser la tête; se rebiffer; '**~-path** piste *f* cavalière.

bri·doon [bri'du:n] bridon *m*.

brief [bri:f] **1.** □ bref (brève *f*); court; passager (-ère *f*); **2.** dossier *m* (*d'avocat*); abrégé *m*; *p.ext.* ordres *m*/*pl.*; *eccl.* bref *m*; hold a ~ for défendre; prendre le parti de; ⚖ take a ~ for accepter de représenter (*q.*) en justice; **3.** ⚖ confier une cause à (*un avocat*); ✗ munir d'instructions; fournir des directives à; '**~-bag**, '**~-case** serviette *f*; '**brief·ing** instructions *f*/*pl.*; séance *f* d'information; '**brief·ness** brièveté *f*.

bri·er[1] ⚘ ['braiə] bruyère *f* arborescente; églantier *m*.

bri·er[2] [~] (*a. ~ pipe*) pipe *f* en bruyère.

brig ⚓ [brig] brick *m*.

bri·gade ✗ [bri'geid] **1.** brigade *f*; **2.** embrigader; **brig·a·dier** [brigə'diə] général *m* de brigade.

brig·and ['brigənd] brigand *m*, bandit *m*; '**brig·and·age** brigandage *m*; briganderie *f*.

bright □ [brait] brillant; éclatant; vif (vive *f*); clair; animé; F intelligent; '**bright·en** *v/t.* faire briller; fourbir (*un métal*); *fig.* égayer; *v/i.* s'éclaircir; *yeux:* s'allumer; '**bright·ness** éclat *m*; clarté *f*; vivacité *f*; intensité *f*; intelligence *f*; *télév.* ~

control (dispositif *m* de) réglage *m* de la luminosité.

brill *icht.* [bril] barbue *f*.

bril·lian·cy ['briljənsi] brillant *m*; éclat *m*; '**bril·liant 1.** □ brillant, éclatant; lumineux (-euse *f*) (*idée*); **2.** brillant *m*.

brim [brim] **1.** bord *m*; **2.** *v/t.* remplir jusqu'au bord; *v/i.* déborder (de, *with*); '**~·ful**, '**~-full** plein jusqu'aux bords; débordant (de, *of*).

brim·stone ['brimstən] ⚗ soufre *m* (brut); *zo.* (*ou ~ butterfly*) papillon *m* citrin.

brin·dle(d) ['brindl(d)] tacheté, tavelé.

brine [brain] **1.** saumure *f*; eau *f* salée; *poét.* mer *f*, océan *m*; **2.** saumurer.

bring [briŋ] [*irr.*] amener; apporter; intenter (*un procès*); avancer (*des arguments*); ~ about amener, occasionner; (*a. ~ to pass*) entraîner; ~ along amener (*qch.*); ~ down faire baisser (*le prix*); avilir (*les prix*); *théâ.* ~ down the house faire crouler la salle; ~ forth produire; mettre au monde; mettre bas (*des petits*); ~ forward (faire) avancer; produire; † reporter; ~ s.th. home to s.o. faire sentir qch. à q.; prouver qch. contre q.; ~ in introduire; rapporter (*une somme*); ~ in guilty déclarer coupable; ~ off ramener à terre *ou* à bord; réussir; ~ on occasionner; faire pousser (*une plante*); ~ out apporter dehors; publier; mettre en relief; faire valoir; lancer (*une actrice etc.*); ~ round ramener à la vie; convertir (*q.*); ~ s.o. to (*inf.*) amener q. à (*inf.*); ⚓ ~ to mettre en panne; ~ s.o. to himself faire reprendre connaissance à q.; ranimer q.; ~ under assujettir; ~ up approcher; élever (*un enfant*); citer en justice; vomir; (faire) monter; ⚓ mouiller.

bring·er ['briŋə] porteur (-euse *f*) *m*.

brink [briŋk] bord *m* '**~·man·ship** politique *f* du bord du gouffre.

brin·y ['braini] **1.** saumâtre, salé; **2.** F mer *f*.

bri·quette [bri'ket], **bri·quet** ['brikit] briquette *f*; aggloméré *m*.

brisk [brisk] **1.** □ vif (vive *f*), alerte, plein d'entrain, animé; *feu:* vif (vive *f*); ✗ nourri; *air:* vivifiant; **2.** (*usu. ~ up*) (s')animer.

bris·ket ['briskit] poitrine *f* (*de bœuf*).

brisk·ness ['brisknis] vivacité *f*, entrain *m*; *air*: fraîcheur *f*.

bris·tle ['brisl] 1. soie *f*; *barbe*: poil *m* raide; 2. (*souv.* ~ up) se hérisser; F se rebiffer (*personne*); *fig.* ~ with être hérissé de; '**bris·tled,** '**bris·tly** hérissé; poilu; garni de soies.

Bri·tan·nic [bri'tænik] britannique.

Brit·ish ['britiʃ] 1. anglais; britannique; 2. the ~ *pl.* les Britanniques *m/pl.*; '**Brit·ish·er** *surt.* Am. natif (-ive *f*) *m* de la Grande-Bretagne.

Brit·on *hist., poét.* ['britən] Anglais(e *f*) *m*.

brit·tle ['britl] fragile, cassant; cendreux (-euse *f*) (*acier*); '**brittle·ness** fragilité *f* etc.

broach [broutʃ] 1. broche *f*; ⚕ flèche *f*, aiguille *f*; 2. percer, entamer (*un fût*); aborder (*un sujet*); entrer en (*matière*).

broad □ [brɔːd] large; plein, grand (*jour*); peu voilé (*avis, allusion*); hardi, risqué (*histoire*); épanoui (*sourire*); prononcé (*accent*); ~ly speaking généralement parlant; '~·axe ⊕ doloire *f*; '~·cast 1. ⚡ semé à la volée; *fig.* (radio)diffusé; répandu; 2. (*irr.* [cast]) *v/t.* ⚡ semer à la volée; *fig.* répandre; radiodiffuser; transmettre; *v/i.* parler etc. à la radio; ~(ing) station poste *m* émetteur; station *f* de radiodiffusion; 3. émission *f*; '~·cloth drap *m* noir fin; Am. popeline *f*; '**broad·en** (s')élargir; '**broad·'mind·ed** tolérant; à l'esprit large; '**broad·ness** largeur *f*; grossièreté *f*; ~ of speech accent *m* prononcé.

broad...: '~·sheet placard *m*; *hist.* canard *m*; '~·side ⚓ flanc *m*, travers *m*; bordée *f*, feu *m* de travers; *a. see* broadsheet; '~·sword latte *f*; sabre *m*.

bro·cade † [bro'keid] brocart *m*; **bro'cad·ed** broché; de brocart.

broc·co·li ♀ ['brɔkəli] brocoli *m*.

bro·chure [brou'ʃjuə] brochure *f*.

brock *zo.* [brɔk] blaireau *m*.

brogue [broug] soulier *m* de golf; accent *m* (*surt.* irlandais).

broil [brɔil] 1. querelle *f*, bagarre *f*; 2. griller (*a. fig.*); (faire) cuire sur le gril; ~ing brûlant; torride; '**broil·er** gril *m*; poulet *m* à rôtir.

broke [brouk] *prét. de* break 2.

bro·ken ['broukn] *p.p. de* break 2; ~ health santé *f* délabrée *ou* ruinée; ~ stones *pl.* pierraille *f*, cailloutis *m*; ~ weather temps *m* variable; speak ~ English écorcher l'anglais; '~·'heart·ed navré de douleur; au cœur brisé; '**bro·ken·ly** par saccades; sans suite; à mots entrecoupés; '**bro·ken-'wind·ed** *vét.* poussif (-ive *f*).

bro·ker ['broukə] † courtier *m*; agent *m* de change; '**bro·ker·age** † courtage *m*; frais *m/pl.* de courtage.

bro·mide ⚗ ['broumaid] bromure *m*; *sl.* banalité *f*; **bro·mine** ⚗ ['~miːn] brome *m*.

bron·chi·al *anat.* ['brɔŋkjəl] bronchial (-aux *m/pl.*); des bronches; **bron·chi·tis** ⚕ [brɔŋ'kaitis] bronchite *f*.

Bronx cheer *Am. sl.* ['brɔŋks'tʃiə] sifflement *m* (*de mépris*).

bronze [brɔnz] 1. bronze *m*; 2. de *ou* en bronze; 3. (se) bronzer; (se) brunir.

brooch [broutʃ] broche *f*, épingle *f*.

brood [bruːd] 1. couvée *f*; volée *f*; F enfants *m/pl.*; ~·hen couveuse *f*; ~·mare poulinière *f*; 2. couver; *v/i.* F broyer du noir; *v/t.* F ruminer (*une idée*); *fig.* planer sur; '**brood·er** couveuse *f* (Am. artificielle).

brook¹ [bruk] ruisseau *m*.

brook² [~] *usu. au nég.* souffrir.

brook·let ['bruklit] ruisselet *m*.

broom ♀ [bruːm] genêt *m*; [brum] balai *m*; ~·stick ['brumstik] manche *m* à balai.

broth [brɔθ] bouillon *m*.

broth·el ['brɔθl] bordel *m*, maison *f* de tolérance.

broth·er ['brʌðə] frère *m*; younger ~ cadet *m*; ~·hood ['~hud] fraternité *f*; confraternité *f*; *eccl.* confrérie *f*; '~-in-law beau-frère (*pl.* beaux-frères) *m*; '**broth·er·ly** fraternel(le *f*).

brougham ['bruːəm] coupé *m*; *mot.* coupé *m* (de ville).

brought [brɔːt] *prét. et p.p. de* bring; ~-in capital capital *m* d'apport.

brow [brau] sourcil *m*; arcade *f* sourcilière; front *m*; *précipice*: bord *m*; *colline*: croupe *f*; '~·beat [*irr* (beat)] rabrouer; rudoyer.

brown [braun] 1. brun, marron(ne

f)); châtain (*cheveux*); jaune (*chaussures*); ~ *bread* pain *m* bis; ~ *paper* papier *m* gris; *be in a ~ study* être plongé dans ses réflexions; 2. brun *m*, marron *m*; 3. (se) brunir; **brown·ie** ['~i] farfadet *m*; **'brown·ish** brunâtre; **'brown·ness** couleur *f* brune; **'brown·stone** *Am.* 1. grès *m* de construction; 2. ... des gens prospères.

browse [brauz] 1. jeunes pousses *f/pl.*; 2. (*a.* ~ *on*) brouter, paître, *fig.* feuilleter (des livres).

bruise [bru:z] 1. bleu *m*, meurtrissure *f*; *fruit*: talure *f*; 2. (se) meurtrir; *v/t.* broyer (*une substance*); **'bruis·er** *sl.* boxeur *m* (brutal).

Brum·ma·gem ['brʌmədʒəm] de camelote, en toc.

bru·nette [bru:'net] brunette *f*.

brunt [brʌnt] choc *m*; attaque *f*; violence *f*; *the ~ of* le plus fort de.

brush [brʌʃ] 1. brosse *f*; pinceau *m*; *renard*: queue *f*; coup *m* de brosse (*aux vêtements*); échauffourée *f* (*avec un ennemi*); ⚡ faisceau *m* de rayons; *commutateur*: balai *m*; *Am. see ~wood*; *see backwoods*; *give s.o. a ~* brosser q.; *have a ~ with s.o.* froisser les opinions de q.; 2. *v/t.* brosser; balayer (*un tapis etc.*); frôler, toucher légèrement; ~ *away* (*ou off*) enlever (*qch.*) d'un coup de brosse *ou* de balai; essuyer (*des larmes*); écarter (*un avis, une pensée*); ~ *down* donner un coup de brosse à (*q.*); ~ *up* donner un coup de brosse à (*qch.*); *fig.* se remettre à, dérouiller; *v/i.* ~ *against* frôler *ou* froisser (*q.*) en passant; ~ *by* (*ou past*) passer rapidement auprès de (*q.*); frôler (*q.*) en passant; **'~-off** *sl.*: *give s.o. the ~* envoyer promener q.; **'~·wood** broussailles *f/pl.*; bois *m* taillis; menu bois *m*.

brusque □ [brusk] brusque; *ton*: bourru.

Brus·sels ['brʌslz]: ⚘ ~ *sprouts pl.* choux *m/pl.* de Bruxelles.

bru·tal □ ['bru:tl] brutal (-aux *m/pl.*); de brute; animal (-aux *m/pl.*); **bru·tal·i·ty** [bru:'tæliti] brutalité *f*; **bru·tal·ize** ['bru:təlaiz] abrutir; animaliser; **brute** [bru:t] 1. brut; vif (vive *f*), brutal (-aux *m/pl.*) (*force*); 2. bête *f* brute; brute *f* (*a. fig.* = *homme brutal*); F animal *m*; *a ~ of a ...* un(e) ... de chien; **'brut-**

ish □ *see brute 1*; **'brut·ish·ness** bestialité *f*; abrutissement *m*.

bub·ble ['bʌbl] 1. bulle *f*; *fig.* projet *m* chimérique; tromperie *f*; 2. bouillonner; glouglouter (*en versant*).

buc·ca·neer [bʌkə'niə] 1. F pirate *m*; flibustier *m* (*a. hist*); 2. faire le boucanier; flibuster.

buck [bʌk] 1. *zo.* daim *m*; chevreuil *m*; mâle (*du lapin etc.*); *Am. sl.* dollar *m*; *Am.* F *pass the ~* passer la décision (à, *to*); se débrouiller sur le voisin; 2. *Am.* F résister, opposer; *Am.* F chercher à prendre le dessus de; *Am.* ~ *for* viser; essayer d'obtenir (*qch.*); F ~ *up* (se) ragaillardir.

buck·et ['bʌkit] seau *m*; *a mere drop in the ~* une goutte d'eau dans la mer; *sl. kick the ~* casser sa pipe (= *mourir*); 2. surmener (*un cheval*); **'~·ful** plein seau *m*; **'~-shop** bureau *m* d'un courtier marron.

buck·le ['bʌkl] 1. boucle *f*, agrafe *f*; 2. *v/t.* boucler; attacher; ceindre (*l'épée*); *v/i.* ⊕ (se) gondoler, arquer; se voiler (*tôle*); ~ *to v/t.* s'appliquer à (*un travail*); *v/i.* s'y atteler; **'buck·ler** bouclier *m*.

buck·ram ['bʌkrəm] bougran *m*; *fig.* raideur *f*.

buck...: **'~·skin** (peau *f* de) daim *m*; **'~·wheat** ⚘ blé *m* noir.

bud [bʌd] 1. ⚘ bourgeon *m*; œil (*pl.* yeux) *m*; bouton *m*; *fig.* germe *m*; *Am.* débutante *f*; *sl.* jeune fille *f*; *in ~* qui bourgeonne; *fig. in the ~* en germe, en herbe; 2. *v/t.* écussonner; *v/i.* bourgeonner; boutonner (*fleur*); *~ding lawyer* juriste *m* en herbe.

bud·dy *Am.* F ['bʌdi] ami *m*; copain *m*.

budge [bʌdʒ] *v/i.* bouger, céder; reculer; *v/t.* bouger. [che *f*.]

budg·er·i·gar ['bʌdʒəriga:] perru-⟩

budg·et ['bʌdʒit] collection *f*; recueil *m*; budget *m*; *usu. fig.* plein sac *m*; *draft ~* budget *m* du ménage; *open the ~* présenter le budget; **'budg·et·ar·y** budgétaire.

buff¹ [bʌf] 1. (peau *f* de) buffle *m*; cuir *m* épais; couleur *f* chamois; *in (one's) ~* tout nu; 2. jaune clair; 3. polir (*au buffle*).

buff² [bʌf] (~) enthousiaste *m/f*, mordu(e *f*) *m*.

buf·fa·lo *zo.* ['bʌfəlou], *pl.* **-loes** ['~louz] buffle *m*; *Am.* F bison *m*.

buff·er ['bʌfə] 🚂 tampon *m*; (*a. ~ stop*) butoir *m*; tampon *m* d'arrêt; *sl.* vieux bonze *m*; ~ *state* état *m* tampon.

buf·fet¹ ['bʌfit] 1. coup *m* (de poing); *poét.* soufflet *m*; 2. flanquer une torgn(i)ole à (*q.*); bourrer (*q.*) de coups.

buf·fet² [*meuble*: 'bʌfit; *autres sens*: 'bufei] buffet *m*.

buf·foon [bʌ'fu:n] bouffon *m*, paillasse *m*; **buf'foon·er·y** bouffonneries *f/pl.*

bug [bʌg] punaise *f*; *Am.* insecte *m*; bacille *m*; loup *m* (de fabrication); *Am. sl.* fou *m*, folle *f*; maboul(e *f*) *m*; F appareil *m* d'écoute; microphone *m* clandestin; **bug·a·boo** ['~əbu:], **'bug·bear** objet *m* d'épouvante; F cauchemar *m*; F bête *f* noire; **'bug·ger** *sl.* pédéraste *m*; con *m*, salaud *m*; bougre *m*; *poor* ~! pauvre bougre!; *a* ~ *of a job* un boulot infernal; *little* ~ petit bonhomme; **'bug·ging de·vice** appareil *m* d'écoute (clandestine); **bug·gy** ['bʌgi] boghei *m*.   [*m*.]

bu·gle¹ ['bju:gl] (*a. ~horn*) clairon]

bu·gle² [~] verroterie *f* noire.

bu·gler ✗ ['bju:glə] (sonneur *m* de) clairon *m*.

buhl [bu:l] *meubles*: boul(l)e *m*.

build [bild] 1. [*irr.*] bâtir; édifier; construire; *fig.* fonder (sur, [up]on); faire construire; ~ *in* murer, boucher; ~ *up* affermir (*la santé*); bâtir; *be ~ing* être en construction; 2. construction *f*; taille *f*; **'build·er** entrepreneur *m* en bâtiments; constructeur *m*; **'build·ing** construction *f*; bâtiment *m*; maison *f*; édifice *m*; *attr.* de construction; ~ *contractor* entrepreneur *m* en *ou* de bâtiment(s); ~*site* chantier *m*; ~*(p)lot* terrain *m* à bâtir; ~*society Brit.* coopérative *f* de construction; ~ *trade* industrie *f* du bâtiment; **'build-up** construction *f*; échafaudage *m*.

built [bilt] 1. *prét. et p.p. de build* 1; 2. *adj.* ... bâti; de construction ...; **'built-'up 'a·re·a** agglomération *f* urbaine.

bulb [bʌlb] ♀ bulbe *m*, oignon *m*; *thermomètre, a. ⚡* ampoule *f*; **'bulb·ous** ♀ bulbeux (-euse *f*).

Bul·gar ['bʌlgɑ:] Bulgare *mf*; **Bul·gar·i·an** [bʌl'gɛəriən] 1. bulgare; 2. *ling.* bulgare *m*; Bulgare *mf*.

bulge [bʌldʒ] 1. bombement *m*; saillie *f*; ⚓, *a. fig.* hausse *f*; 2. bomber; faire saillie; se déjeter (*mur etc.*).

bulk [bʌlk] masse *f*, grosseur *f*, volume *m*; *fig.* gros *m* (*a.* ⚓); ⚓ charge *f*; chargement *m* arrimé; *in* ~ en bloc, en vrac; *in the* ~ en bloc, en gros; ~ *goods* marchandise *f ou* marchandises *f/pl.* en masse; **'~·head** ⚓ cloison *f*; **'bulk·i·ness** grosseur *f*; volume *m* (excessif); **'bulk·y** gros(se *f*); volumineux (-euse *f*), encombrant.

bull¹ [bul] 1. taureau *m*; ✝ *sl.* haussier *m*; F ~ *session* réunion *f* d'hommes; 2. ✝ *sl.* spéculer à la hausse; chercher à faire hausser (*les cours*).

bull² *eccl.* [~] bulle *f*.

bull³ [~] bévue *f*; F, *a. Am.* bêtises *f/pl.*; *Irish* ~ inconséquence *f*.

bull·dog ['buldɔg] bouledogue *m*; chienne *f* de bouledogue; F *univ.* appariteur *m*.

bull·doze *Am.* F ['buldouz] intimider; **'bull·doz·er** ⊕ machine *f* à cintrer; bulldozer *m*.

bul·let ['bulit] *fusil, revolver*: balle *f*.

bul·le·tin ['bulitin] bulletin *m*, communiqué *m*; *radio*: informations *f/pl.*; *Am.* ~ *board* tableau *m* d'affichage (*des nouvelles du jour*).

bul·let-proof ['bulitpru:f] blindé, pare-balles *inv.*

bull...: **'~·fight** course *f* de taureaux; **'~·finch** *orn.* bouvreuil *m*; haie *f* (*avec fossé*); **'~·frog** *zo.* grenouille *f* mugissante; **'~·head·ed** F entêté.

bul·lion ['buljən] or *m* en barres; or *m ou* argent *m* en lingot; ✗ franges *f/pl.*

bull·ock ['bulək] bœuf *m*.

bull-pen *Am.* ['bul'pen] F salle *f* de détention.

bull's-eye ['bulzai] ⚓ (verre *m* de) hublot *m*; *cible*: noir *m*, centre *m*, blanc *m*; ~ *pane* carreau *m* à boudine.

bull·shit V ['bulʃit] merde *f*.

bul·ly¹ ['buli] 1. brute *f*, brutal *m*, tyran *m*; *école*: brimeur *m*; bravache *m*; 2. bravache; *surt. Am.* F fameux (-euse *f*); *a. int.* bravo; 3. brutaliser, rudoyer, intimider.

bul·ly² [~] (*a.* ~ *beef*) bœuf *m* en conserve; F singe *m*.

bul·rush ♀ ['bulrʌʃ] jonc *m*.

bulwark   682

bul·wark ['bulwək] *usu. fig.* rempart *m*; ~s *pl.* ⚓ pavois *m*.

bum¹ *sl.* [bʌm] derrière *m*, cul *m*.

bum² *Am.* F [~] 1. fainéant *m*; chemineau *m*; (be) go on the ~ fainéanter; vagabonder; 2. *v/t.* mendier; resquiller (*le trajet*); 3. misérable.

bum·ble-bee ['bʌmblbi:] bourdon *m*.

bum·boat ['bʌmbout] bateau *m* à provisions.

bump [bʌmp] 1. choc *m*; coup *m*, heurt *m*; *fig.* bosse *f* (de, of); 2. (se) cogner; (se) heurter; *v/t.* entrer en collision avec (*qch.*); *Am. sl.* ~ off assassiner, supprimer (*q.*); *v/i.* ~ against buter contre; F ~ into s.o. rencontrer q. par hasard.

bump·er ['bʌmpə] 1. verre *m* plein; rasade *f*, *mot.* pare-chocs *m/inv.*; *théâ.* (a. ~ house) salle *f* comble *ou* bondée; ~ sticker autocollant *m*; 2. plein ...; magnifique; F exceptionnel(le *f*) (*récolte*).

bump·kin ['bʌmpkin] rustre *m*.

bump·tious □ F ['bʌmpʃəs] arrogant, présomptueux (-euse *f*), suffisant.

bump·y ['bʌmpi] cahoteux (-euse *f*); couvert de bosses; ⚡ chahuté.

bun [bʌn] petit pain *m* au lait; *cheveux:* chignon *m*.

bunch [bʌntʃ] 1. botte *f*; *fleurs:* bouquet *m*; *personnes:* groupe *m*; ~ of grapes grappe *f* de raisin; 2. (se) grouper; *v/t.* lier.

bun·combe *Am.* ['bʌnkəm] blague *f*; paroles *f/pl.* vides.

bun·dle ['bʌndl] 1. paquet *m*; ballot *m*; *bois:* fagot *m*; 2. *v/t.* (a. ~ up) empaqueter; F ~ away *ou* off se débarrasser de (*q.*); *v/i.* ~ off s'en aller sans cérémonie.

bung [bʌŋ] 1. *fût:* bondon *m*; 2. bondonner (*un fût*); boucher (*un trou*); F ~ed up poché (*œil*).

bun·ga·low ['bʌŋgəlou] bungalow *m*.

bung-hole ['bʌŋhoul] bonde *f*.

bun·gle ['bʌŋgl] 1. gâchis *m*; maladresse *f*; 2. bousiller; *sl.* rater; **'bun·gler** bousilleur (-euse *f*) *m*; maladroit(e *f*) *m*; **'bun·gling** 1. □ maladroit; 2. *see* bungle 1.

bun·ion ⚕ ['bʌnjən] oignon *m* (*callosité au gros orteil*).

bunk¹ *surt. Am. sl.* [bʌŋk] blague *f*; balivernes *f/pl.*

bunk² [~] ⚓, ⚙ couchette *f*.

bunk·er ⚓ ['bʌŋkə] 1. soute *f* (à charbon); 2. mettre en soute; F *fig.* be ~ed se trouver dans une impasse.

bun·kum ['bʌŋkəm] *see* buncombe.

bun·ny ['bʌni] F Jeannot lapin *m*.

bunt *Am.* [bʌnt] *baseball:* coup *m* qui arrête la balle.

bunt·ing¹ *orn.* ['bʌntiŋ] bruant *m*.

bunt·ing² [~] *tex.* étamine *f*; *p.ext.* pavillons *m/pl.*

buoy ⚓ [bɔi] 1. bouée *f*; 2. baliser (*le chenal*); (*usu.* ~ up) faire flotter; *fig.* soutenir, appuyer.

buoy·an·cy ['bɔiənsi] flottabilité *f*; *fig.* élasticité *f* de caractère; *fig.* entrain *m*; **'buoy·ant** □ flottable; léger (-ère *f*); *fig.* allègre, optimiste; *fig.* élastique (*pas*); ✝ soutenu.

bur ⚕ [bə:] capsule *f* épineuse; teigne *f* (*de bardane*); *personne:* crampon *m*.

Bur·ber·ry ['bə:bəri] imperméable *m* (*marque Burberry*).

bur·bot *icht.* ['bə:bət] lotte *f*, barbot *m*.

bur·den¹ ['bə:dn] refrain *m*.

bur·den² ['bə:dn] 1. fardeau *m*, charge *f* (a. ⚖); ⚓ charge *f*, contenance *f*; *discours:* substance *f*; 2. charger; *fig.* accabler; **'bur·densome** onéreux (-euse *f*); fâcheux (-euse *f*).

bur·dock ⚕ ['bə:dɔk] bardane *f*.

bu·reau [bjuə'rou], *pl.* -reaux [~'rouz] *surt. Am.* bureau *m*; service *m* (*du gouvernement*); *meuble:* secrétaire *m*, bureau *m*; *Am.* commode *f*; **bu·reauc·ra·cy** [~'rɔkrəsi] bureaucratie *f*; **bu·reau·crat** ['bjuəərokræt] bureaucrate *mf*; **bu·reau·'crat·ic** (~ally) bureaucratique; **bu·reauc·ra·tize** [bjuə'rɔkrətaiz] bureaucratiser.

bur·gee ⚓ ['bə:dʒi:] guidon *m*.

bur·geon *poét.* ['bə:dʒən] 1. bourgeon *m*; bouton *m*; 2. bourgeonner; commencer à éclore.

bur·gess ['bə:dʒis] bourgeois *m*, citoyen *m*; *hist.* représentant *m* d'un bourg (*au Parlement*).

burgh *écoss.* ['bʌrə] bourg *m*.

bur·glar ['bə:glə] cambrioleur *m* (*nocturne*); ~ alarm sonnerie *f* d'alarme *ou* antivol; **bur·glar·i·ous** □ [bə:'glɛəriəs] de cambriolage; **'bur·glar-proof** à l'épreuve de l'infraction; incrochetable (*serrure*); **bur-**

gla·ry [ˈ‿əri] vol *m* nocturne avec effraction; **bur·gle** [ˈbəːgl] cambrioler.

bur·gun·dy [ˈbəːgəndi] (vin *m* de) bourgogne *m*.

bur·i·al [ˈberiəl] enterrement *m*; ˈ‿ **ground** cimetière *m*.

bu·rin ⊕ [ˈbjuərin] burin *m*.

burke [bəːk] étouffer (*un scandale*); escamoter (*une question*).

burl *tex.* [bəːl] nope *f*.

bur·lap [ˈbəːləp] toile *f* d'emballage.

bur·lesque [bəːˈlesk] **1.** burlesque; **2.** burlesque *m*; parodie *f*; **3.** travestir, parodier; tourner (*qch.*) en ridicule.   [dement bâti.\

bur·ly [ˈbəːli] de forte carrure; soli-\

Bur·mese [bəːˈmiːz] **1.** birman; **2.** Birman(e *f*) *m*.

burn [bəːn] **1.** brûlure *f*; **2.** [*irr.*] brûler; cuire; ˈ**burn·er** brûleur (-euse *f*) *m*; bec *m* de gaz; ˈ**burn·ing** □ brûlant, ardent.

bur·nish [ˈbəːniʃ] brunir, (se) polir; ˈ**bur·nish·er** *personne*: brunisseur (-euse *f*) *m*; ⊕ brunissoir *m*.

burnt [bəːnt] *prét. et p.p. de* burn 2; ~ almond amande *f* grillée; praline *f*; mot. ~ gas gaz *m* d'échappement; ~ offering holocauste *m*.

burr [bəː] **1.** r *m* de la gorge; **2.** prononcer l'r de la gorge.

bur·row [ˈbʌrou] **1.** terrier *m* (*de lapin, de renard*); **2.** *v/t.* creuser; *v/i.* se terrer; *fig.* fouiller.

bur·sa·ry [ˈbəːsəri] bourse *f* (*d'études*).

burst [bəːst] **1.** éclat(ement) *m*; jaillissement *m*; coup *m*; *fig.* poussée *f*; rafale *f*; emballage *m* (*de vitesse*); **2.** [*irr.*] *v/i.* éclater, exploser; crever (*abcès, pneu, rire, boîte, etc.*); *fig.* déborder (de, with); ⚙ éclore (*bouton*); s'épanouir (*fleur*); ~ from s'affranchir de; ~ forth (*ou* out) jaillir; s'exclamer; apparaître (*soleil*); ~ into a gallop prendre le galop; ~ into flame s'enflammer brusquement; ~ into leaf (se) feuiller; ~ into tears fondre en larmes; ~ out laughing éclater de rire; *v/t.* faire éclater; enfoncer (*une porte*).   [tenance *f*.\

bur·then ⚓ [ˈbəːðn] charge *f*, con-\

bur·y [ˈberi] enterrer, ensevelir; inhumer; ⚓ immerger; *fig.* plonger.

bus F [bʌs] **1.** autobus *m*; sl. bagnole *f*; sl. fig. miss the ~ laisser échapper l'occasion; *Am.* ~ boy garçon *m* de restaurant qui débarrasse la table après le repas; ~ driver conducteur *m* d'autobus; **2.** ~ it aller *ou* venir *ou* voyager en autobus.

bus·by ✕ [ˈbʌzbi] colback *m*.

bush [buʃ] buisson *m*; fourré *m*; ⊕ fourrure *f* métallique; **bush·el** [ˈbuʃl] boisseau *m* (*a. mesure*); F (grande) quantité *f*; **bush league** *Am. baseball*: ligue *f* de second ordre; ˈ**bush-rang·er** broussard *m*.

bush·y [ˈbuʃi] touffu; broussailleux (-euse *f*); buissonnant (*arbrisseau*).

busi·ness [ˈbiznis] affaire *f*, besogne *f*; occupation *f*; devoir *m*; affaires *f/pl.* (*a.* ✝); ✝ entreprise *f*; maison *f* (de commerce); fonds *m* de commerce; ~ address adresse *f* du bureau (*de q.*); ~ of the day ordre *m* du jour; agenda *m*; ~ end côté *m* opérant (*d'un outil etc.*), tranchant *m* (*d'un couteau etc.*); ~ hours *pl.* heures *f/pl.* d'ouverture; ~man homme *m* d'affaires; ~ quarter quartier *m* commerçant; ~ research étude *f* du mouvement des prix *ou* des cycles économiques; *surt. Am.* ~ suit *see* lounge suit; ~ tour, ~ trip voyage *m* d'affaires; on ~ pour affaires; have no ~ to (*inf.*) ne pas avoir le droit de (*inf.*); get down to ~ en venir au fait; mind one's own ~ s'occuper de ses affaires; send s.o. about his ~ F envoyer promener q.; that's none of your ~ cela ne vous regarde pas; ˈ~-like pratique; sérieux (-euse *f*) (*manière*); capable.

bus·kin [ˈbʌskin] antiquité, théâ.: cothurne *m*; *fig.* tragédie *f*.

bus·man [ˈbʌsmən] conducteur *m* *ou* receveur d'autobus; ~'s holiday congé *m* passé à exercer son métier.   [trine *f*.\

bust[1] [bʌst] buste *m*, gorge *f*, poi-\

bust[2] sl. [bʌst] **1.** fiasco *m*, four *m* (noir); faillite *f*; coup *m* (violent); bringue *f*, bombe *f*; go on the ~, have a ~ faire la bombe; **2.** casser; (faire) crever; abîmer; arrêter, choper (*un criminel etc.*); **3.** foutu; fauché; abîmé; go ~ faire faillite; s'abîmer.

bus·tard *orn.* [ˈbʌstəd] outarde *f*.

bus·tle [ˈbʌsl] **1.** mouvement *m*, confusion *f*; remue-ménage *m/inv.*; va-et-vient *m/inv.*; *cost.* tournure *f*; **2.** *v/i.* s'affairer; s'activer; faire l'empressé; se dépêcher; *v/t.* faire dépêcher (*q.*); bousculer; ˈ**bus·tler** personne *f* très active; homme *m* expéditif; **'bus·tling** □ affairé; empressé.

bust-up *sl.* [ˈbʌstˈʌp] grabuge *f*; engueulade *f*; débâcle *f*; faillite *f*; *surt. Am.* rupture *f* (*d'un mariage etc.*).

bus·y □ [ˈbizi] **1.** occupé (à, de *at*, *with*); affairé; actif (-ive *f*); mouvementé (*rue*); diligent; ~ *packing* occupé à faire ses malles; ~*body* officieux (-euse *f*) *m*; **2.** (*usu.* ~ *o.s.*) s'occuper (à *with*, *in*, *about*; à, de *inf.* *with gér.*); **'bus·y·ness** affairement *m*; activité *f*.

but [bʌt] **1.** *cj.* mais; or; sauf que; (*a.* ~ *that*) sans que; et cependant; toutefois; **2.** *prp.* sans; *the last* ~ *one* l'avant-dernier (-ère *f*); *the next* ~ *one* le (la) deuxième; ~ *for* sans; ne fût-ce pour; **3.** *après négation:* que (*sbj.*); qui (*sbj.*); *there is no one* ~ *knows* il n'y a personne qui ne sache (*qch.*); **4.** *adv.* ne ... que; seulement; ~ *just* tout à l'heure; tout récemment; ~ *now* à l'instant; il n'y a qu'un instant que; *all* ~ presque; *nothing* ~ rien que; *I cannot* ~ (*inf.*) il m'est impossible de ne pas (*inf.*); je ne peux m'empêcher de (*inf.*).

bu·tane [ˈbjuːtein] butane *m*.

butch·er [ˈbutʃə] **1.** boucher *m* (*a. fig.*); *fig.* massacreur *m*; 🐂 *Am.* F vendeur *m* de fruits *etc.*; **2.** égorger; massacrer (*a. fig.*); ~('s) *shop* boucherie *f*; **'butch·er·y** (*a.* ~ *business*) boucherie *f* (*a. fig.*); F massacre *m*; abattoir *m*.

but·ler [ˈbʌtlə] maître *m* d'hôtel; † sommelier *m*.

butt¹ [bʌt] **1.** coup *m* de corne (*d'un bélier*); (*a.* ~*-end*) gros bout *m*; *arbre, chèque:* souche *f*; *fusil:* couche *f*, crosse *f*; ✗ butte *f*; *fig.* souffre-douleur *m*/*inv.*; F mégot *m*; ⊕ bout *m*; *about* ~; ~*s pl.* butte *f*; *fig.* but *m*; *fig.* objectif *m*; **2.** *v/t.* donner un coup de corne *ou* de tête à; *v/i.* F ~ *in* intervenir sans façon.

butt² [~] futaille *f*; (*gros*) tonneau *m*.

but·ter [ˈbʌtə] **1.** beurre *m*; *fig.* flatterie *f*, F pommade *f*; F *he looks as if* ~ *would not melt in his mouth* il fait la sainte nitouche; **2.** beurrer; (*a.* ~ *up*) F flatter; **'~·cup** bouton-d'or (*pl.* boutons-d'or) *m*; **'~·dish** beurrier *m*; **'~·fin·gered** maladroit, empoté; **'~·fly** papillon *m* (*a. fig.*); F *have butterflies in one's stomach* avoir

le trac; *avoir l'estomac serré;* **'but·ter·y 1.** de beurre; butyreux (-euse *f*); graisseux (-euse *f*); **2.** *univ.* dépense *f*.

but·tock [ˈbʌtək] fesse *f*; *usu.* ~*s pl.* fesses *f/pl.*, derrière *m*.

but·ton [ˈbʌtn] **1.** bouton *m* (*a.* ♀); **2.** (se) boutonner; (*usu.* ~ *up*) *fig.* renfermer; mettre les boutons à; **'~·hole 1.** boutonnière *f*; (*fleur f* portée à la) boutonnière *f*; **2.** festonner; F accrocher (*q.*) au passage; **'~·hook** tire-bouton *m*.

but·tress [ˈbʌtris] contrefort *m*; butoir *m* (*d'une chaîne de montagnes*); *fig.* pilier *m*.

bux·om [ˈbʌksəm] dodu; rondelet(te *f*) (*femme*); grassouillet(te *f*).

buy [bai] [*irr.*] *v/t.* acheter (à, *from*); prendre (*un billet*); *fig.* payer, F suborner; ~ *back* racheter; *v/i.* (*a.* ~ *and sell*) brocanter; *order to* ~ ordre *m* d'achat; **'buy·er** acheteur (-euse *f*) *m*; acquéreur *m*; ✝ acquisiteur *m*, acheteur *m*, chef *m* de rayon.

buzz [bʌz] **1.** bourdonnement *m*; *conversation:* brouhaha *m*; ✈ ronflement *m*; *Am.* ~ *saw* scie *f* circulaire; F *give s.o. a* ~ donner un coup de fil à q. (*téléphoner*); **2.** *v/i.* bourdonner, vrombir; *v/t.* lancer, jeter.

buz·zard *orn.* [ˈbʌzəd] buse *f*, busard *m*.

buzz·er ✧ [ˈbʌzə] appel *m*; sonnerie *f*.

by [bai] **1.** *prp.* *lieu:* (au)près de, à côté de; au bord de (*la mer*); *direction:* par; *temps:* avant, pour; *moyen:* par, de; à (*la main, la machine, bicyclette, cheval, etc.*); en (*auto, tramway*); *auteur:* de; *serment:* au nom de (*qch.*); *mesures:* sur; selon; *North* ~ *East* nord quart nord-est; *side* ~ *side* côte à côte; ~ *day* de jour, le jour; ~ *name* de nom; (*connu*) sous le nom de; ~ *now* déjà, à l'heure qu'il est; ~ *the time* (*that*) quand; avant que (*sbj.*); *a play* ~ *Shaw* une pièce de Shaw; ~ *lamplight* à (la lumière de) la lampe; ~ *the dozen* à la douzaine; ~ *far* de beaucoup; *50 feet* ~ *20* cinquante pieds sur vingt; ~ *half* de moitié; F beaucoup; ~ *o.s.* seul; à l'écart; ~ *land* par terre; ~ *rail* par le chemin de fer; *day* ~ *day* de jour en jour; ~ *twos* deux par deux; **2.** *adv.* près;

de côté; ~ and ~ tout à l'heure, tantôt, bientôt, par la suite; ~ the ~ à
propos ...; *close* ~ tout près; *go* ~
passer; ~ *and large* à tout prendre;
3. *adj.* latéral (-aux *m*/*pl.*); écarté;
supplémentaire.

bye [bai] *cricket*: balle *f* passée;
tennis: exemption *f* (*d'un match
dans un tournoi, accordée à un joueur
qui ne tire pas d'adversaire*); *be
a* ~ se trouver exempt d'un match.

bye-bye F ['bai'bai] au revoir!;
adieu!; *go to* ~ F aller faire dodo.

by...: '~•e·lec·tion élection *f* par-
tielle; '~•gone **1.** écoulé, d'autrefois; **2.** ~s *pl.* passé *m*; *let* ~s *be* ~s
oublions le passé!; sans rancune!;
'~•law arrêté *m* municipal; '~•line
Am. rubrique *f* d'un article qui en

nomme l'auteur; '~•name sobri-
quet *m*; '~•pass **1.** *gaz*: veilleuse *f*;
route *f* de contournement; **2.** F éviter; dévier (*la circulation*); '~•path
sentier *m* écarté; '~•play *théâ.* jeu *m*
accessoire; aparté *m* mimé; '~•
prod·uct dérivé *m*; '~•road chemin
m détourné; chemin *m* vicinal.

By·ron·ic [bai'rɔnik] (~ally) byro-
nien.

by...: '~•stand·er assistant *m*; spec-
tateur(-trice *f*) *m*; '~•street ruelle *f*;
rue *f* écartée; '~•way chemin *m* détourné; détour *m* (*a. péj.*); *fig.* à-côté
m; '~•word proverbe *m*; *be a* ~ *for*
être passé en proverbe pour; *be the*
~ *of* être la fable de.

By·zan·tine [bi'zæntain] **1.** byzantin; **2.** Byzantin(e *f*) *m*.

C

C, c [siː] C *m*, c *m*.

cab [kæb] 1. taxi *m*; fiacre *m*; *camion, grue, etc.*: guérite *f*; ⚙ poste *m* de conduite; 2. de fiacres, de taxis; 3. F ~ *it* aller *ou* venir en taxi.

ca·bal [kə'bæl] 1. cabale *f*, brigue *f*; 2. cabaler; comploter.

cab·a·ret ['kæbərei] cabaret *m*; concert *m* genre music-hall.

cab·bage ['kæbidʒ] chou *m*; ~ *butterfly* piéride *f* du chou; ~ *lettuce* laitue *f* pommée.

cab·by F ['kæbi] cocher *m*.

cab·in ['kæbin] 1. cabane *f*; ⚓ cabine *f*; ⚙ guérite *f*; 2. enfermer; '~-boy** mousse *m*.

cab·i·net ['kæbinit] meuble *m* à tiroirs; *étalage etc.*: vitrine *f*; *radio*: coffret *m*; *phot.* format *m* album; *pol.* cabinet *m*, ministère *m*; ♀ *Council* conseil *m* des ministres; '~-mak·er** ébéniste *m*.

ca·ble ['keibl] 1. ⚓, *a. tél.* câble *m*; ⚓ chaîne *f*; câble-chaîne (*pl.* câbles-chaînes) *m*; *buried* ~ câble *m* souterrain; 2. *tél.* câbler; '~-car** téléphérique *m*; *sur rail*: funiculaire *m*; '~-gram** câblogramme *m*; ~ **rail·way** funiculaire *m*; ~ **tel·e·vi·sion** télédistribution *f*, télévision *f* par câble(s).

cab·man ['kæbmən] cocher *m* de fiacre.

ca·boo·dle *sl.* [kə'buːdl]: *the whole* ~ tout le bazar.

ca·boose [kə'buːs] ⚓ cuisine *f*; ⚙ *Am.* fourgon *m*.

cab·ri·o·let *surt. mot.* [kæbrio'lei] cabriolet *m*.

cab·stand ['kæbstænd] station *f* de voitures.   [perlée.\

ca'can·ny [kɔːˈkæni] faire la grève\

ca·ca·o [kə'kɑːou] cacao *m*; *arbre*: cacaotier *m*.

cache [kæʃ] cache *f*, cachette *f*.

cack·le ['kækl] 1. caquet *m* (*a. fig.*); ricanement *m*; 2. caqueter (*a. fig.*); ricaner; carder (*oie*); '**cack·ler** poule *f* qui caquette; *fig.* caqueteur (-euse *f*) *m*; ricaneur (-euse *f*) *m*.

cac·tus ♣ ['kæktəs] cactus *m*.

cad F [kæd] goujat *m*; canaille *f*.

ca·das·tre [kə'dæstə] cadastre *m*.

ca·dav·er·ous [kə'dævərəs] cadavéreux (-euse *f*); *fig.* exsangue.

cad·die ['kædi] *golf*: cadet *m*.

cad·dish F □ ['kædiʃ] voyou; digne d'un goujat.

cad·dy ['kædi] boîte *f* à thé.

ca·dence ['keidəns] ♪ cadence *f*; intonation *f*; rythme *m*.

ca·det [kə'det] cadet *m*; ~ *corps* bataillon *m* scolaire.

cadge [kædʒ] colporter; mendier; chiner (*qch.*); '**cadg·er** colporteur *m*; mendiant(e *f*) *m*; chineur (-euse *f*) *m*.

ca·du·cous ♣, *a. zo.* [kə'djuːkəs] caduc (-uque *f*).

cae·cum *anat.* ['siːkəm] cæcum *m*.

Cae·sar ['siːzə] César *m*; **C(a)e·sar·i·an** (*sec·tion*) ⚕ [siːˈzɛəriən ('sekʃən)] césarienne *f*.

cae·su·ra [siˈzjuərə] césure *f*.

ca·fé ['kæfei] café(-restaurant) *m*.

caf·e·te·ri·a *Am.* [kæfi'tiəriə] cafeteria *f*, restaurant *m* de libre service *m*.

caf·e·to·ri·um *Am.* [kæfi'tɔːriəm] salle *f* des festins, restaurant *m*.

caf·fe·ine ♣ ['kæfiːn] caféine *f*.

cage [keidʒ] 1. cage *f*; *oiseau*: cage *f*, volière *f*; ⚒ cage *f* (de puits); 2. encager (*a. fig.*); mettre en cage.

cag·ey □ F ['keidʒi] peu communicatif (-ive *f*); prudent; *be* ~ *about a.* ne pas vouloir parler de, cacher.

cairn [kɛən] cairn *m*.

cais·son [kə'suːn] ⚔ caisson *m* (à munitions); *hydraulique*: caisson *m*, batardeau *m*.

ca·jole [kə'dʒoul] enjôler; cajoler; persuader (à q. de *inf.*, *s.o. into gér.*); **ca'jol·er** cajoleur (-euse *f*) *m*; **ca'jol·er·y** cajolerie *f*, -s *f/pl.*; enjôlement *m*.

cake [keik] 1. gâteau *m*; pâtisserie *f*; *chocolat*: tablette *f*; *savon*: pain *m*; 2. faire croûte; se coller; se cailler (*sang*).

cal·a·bash ['kæləbæʃ] calebasse *f.*

cal·a·mine *min.* ['kæləmain] calamine *f.*

ca·lam·i·tous □ [kə'læmitəs] calamiteux (-euse *f*), désastreux (-euse *f*); **ca'lam·i·ty** calamité *f*, infortune *f*; désastre *m*; catastrophe *f*; **ca'lam·i·ty-howl·er** *surt. Am.* pessimiste *mf*; prophète *m* de malheur; **ca'lam·i·ty-howl·ing** *surt. Am.* défaitisme *m*; prophéties *f/pl.* de malheur.

ca·lash [kə'læʃ] calèche *f.*

cal·care·ous *min.* [kæl'kɛəriəs] calcaire.

cal·ci·fi·ca·tion [kælsifi'keiʃn] calcification *f*; **cal·ci·fy** ['⁓fai] (se) calcifier; **cal·ci·na·tion** ⚗ [kælsi'neiʃn] calcination *f*; cuisson *f*; **cal·cine** ['kælsain] *v/t.* ⚗ calciner; cuire; *v/i.* se calciner; **'cal·cite** *min.* calcite *f*; **cal·ci·um** ⚗ ['⁓siəm] calcium *m.*

cal·cu·la·ble ['kælkjuləbl] calculable; **cal·cu·late** ['⁓leit] *v/t.* calculer; estimer; faire le compte de; ⁓d propre (à, to), fait (pour, to); *v/i.* compter (sur, on); *Am.* F supposer; *calculating-machine* machine *f* à calculer; **cal'cu·la·tion** calcul *m*; **cal·cu·la·tor** calculateur (-trice *f*) *m*; machine *f* à calculer, calculatrice *f*; **'cal·cu·lus** ✿, ⚕ ['⁓ləs] calcul *m.*

cal·dron ['kɔːldrən] *see* cauldron.

cal·en·dar ['kælində] **1.** calendrier *m*; ⚖ rôle *m* des assises; *univ.* annuaire *m*; **2.** inscrire sur un calendrier *ou* sur une liste.

cal·en·der ⊕ ['⁓] **1.** calandre *f*; laminoir *m*; **2.** calandrer; laminer.

calf [kɑːf], *pl.* **calves** [kɑːvz] veau *m*; *fig.* petit(e *f*) *m*; (*a.* ⁓-leather) veau *m*, vachette *f*; ⚙ reliure *f* en veau; *anat.* mollet *m*; *in* ⁓, *with* ⁓ pleine (*vache*); F ⁓-love amours *f/pl.* enfantines; '⁓skin (cuir *m* de) veau *m.*

cal·i·brate ⊕ ['kælibreit] étalonner; calibrer (*un tube*); **cal·i·bre** ['⁓bə] calibre *m* (*a. fig.*); alésage *m.*

cal·i·co ✝ ['kælikou] calicot *m*; *surt. Am.* indienne *f.*

Cal·i·for·nian [kæli'fɔːnjən] **1.** californien(ne *f*); de Californie; **2.** Californien(ne *f*) *m.*

ca·liph ['kælif] calife *m*; **cal·iph·ate** ['⁓eit] califat *m.*

calk¹ [kɔːk] *peint.* décalquer.

calk² [⁓] *see* caulk.

calk³ [⁓] **1.** *a.* **calk·in** ['kælkin] crampon *m*, clou *m* à glace; **2.** ferrer (*un cheval*) à glace.

call [kɔːl] **1.** appel *m* (*a. téléph., bridge, etc.*); cri *m* (*a. oiseau*); *téléph., clairon, etc.*: coup *m*; *théâ.* rappel *m*; *bridge*: annonce *f*; visite *f*; demande *f* (de, for); vocation *f*; invitation *f*, nomination *f* (à un poste, à une chaire, etc.); *Bourse*: appel *m* de fonds; option *f*; ✝ ⁓-money prêts *m/pl.* au jour le jour; *port of* ⁓ port *m* d'escale; ✝ *on* ⁓ sur demande; au jour le jour; *give s.o. a* ⁓ donner un coup de fil à q.; **2.** *v/t.* appeler (*a.* ⚖), crier; convoquer (*une réunion*); héler (*un taxi*); faire venir (*un médecin*); appeler, attirer (*l'attention*) (sur, to); *théâ.* rappeler; réveiller; *cartes:* déclarer; décréter (*une grève*); qualifier de (*un titre*); injurier; *fig.* nommer (à, to); *be* ⁓ed s'appeler; ⁓ *s.o. names* injurier q.; ⁓ *down* injurier; reprendre (*q.*); ⁓ *forth* produire, évoquer; faire appel à (*le courage*); ⁓ *in* retirer (*une monnaie*) de la circulation; faire (r)entrer (*q.*); ⁓ *over* faire l'appel de (*les noms*); ⁓ *up* évoquer; ✕ mobiliser, appeler sous les drapeaux; appeler au téléphone; **3.** *v/i.* téléphoner; faire une visite, passer (chez *at, on*); ⁓ *at a port* faire escale; ⁓ *for* faire venir (*q.*) *ou* apporter (*qch.*); commander; *théâ.* rappeler, réclamer; venir chercher (*q., qch.*); *to be* (*left till*) ⁓ed poste restante; à remettre au messager; poste restante; ⁓ *on* invoquer; réclamer (qch. à q., *s.o. for s.th.*) requérir (*q.*) (de, *to inf.*) ⁓ *to* crier à (*q.*); ⁓ *upon see* ⁓ *on*; **'call·a·ble** ✝ au jour le jour (*prêt*); **'call·box** cabine *f* téléphonique; **'call·er** personne *f* qui appelle; visiteur (-euse *f*) *m*; *téléph.* demandeur (-euse *f*) *m.*

cal·li·graph·ic [kæli'græfik] (⁓ally) calligraphique; **cal·lig·ra·phy** [kə'ligrəfi] calligraphie *f*, belle écriture *f.*

call-in ['kɔːlin] *radio, télév.* programme *m ou* émission *f* avec participation des assistants, programme *m* à ligne ouverte.

call·ing ['kɔːliŋ] appel *m*; convocation *f*; métier *m*; visite *f* (à, on); *Am.* ⁓ *card* carte *f* de visite.

cal·(l)i·pers *pl.* ['kælipəz] compas *m* d'épaisseur.

cal·lis·then·ics [kælis'θeniks] *usu. sg.* callisthénie *f.*

call-of·fice ['kɔːlɔfis] bureau *m* téléphonique.

cal·los·i·ty [kæ'lɔsiti] callosité *f;* cal *(pl.* -s) *m; fig.* dureté *f;* '**cal·lous** ☐ calleux (-euse *f); fig.* insensible, dur.

cal·low ['kælou] sans plumes; *fig.* imberbe, sans expérience.

call-up [kɔl'ʌp] appel *m* (⚔ sous les drapeaux).

cal·lus ['kaləs] callosité *f.*

calm [kɑːm] **1.** ☐ calme, tranquille *(a. fig.);* **2.** tranquillité *f;* calme *m (a. fig., a.* ⚓); sérénité *f;* **3.** (~ *down* se) calmer; apaiser; adoucir; '**calm·ness** tranquillité *f;* calme *m;* sérénité *f.*

ca·lor·ic *phys.* [kə'lɔrik] calorique *m;* **cal·o·rie** *phys.* ['kæləri] calorie *f;* **cal·o·rif·ic** [kælə'rifik] calorifique, calorifiant.

cal·trop ['kæltrəp] ⚘ chardon *m* étoilé; ⚔ *hist.* chausse-trape *f.*

ca·lum·ni·ate [kə'lʌmnieit] calomnier; **ca·lum·ni·a·tion** calomnie *f;* **ca·lum·ni·a·tor** calomniateur (-trice *f) m;* **ca·lum·ni·ous** ☐ calomnieux (-euse *f);* **cal·um·ny** ['kæləmni] calomnie *f.*

Cal·va·ry ['kælvəri] *le* Calvaire *m.*

calve [kɑːv] vêler *(a. géol.);* **calves** [kɑːvz] *see* **calf.** [nisme *m.*)

Cal·vin·ism ['kælvinizm] calvi-∫

ca·lyx ['keiliks], *pl. a.* **ca·ly·ces** ['~lisiːz] ⚘, *a. zo.* calice *m.*

cam ⊕ [kæm] came *f;* excentrique *m;* ~ *gear* distribution *f* à came(s).

cam·ber ⊕ ['kæmbə] **1.** *poutre:* cambrure *f; chaussée:* bombement *m;* **2.** (se) cambrer; bomber.

cam·bric ✝ ['keimbrik] batiste *f.*

came [keim] *prét. de* come.

cam·el *zo., a.* ⚓ ['kæml] chameau *m;* **ca·mel·li·a** ⚘ [kə'miːljə] camélia *m.*

cam·e·o ['kæmiou] camée *m.*

cam·er·a ['kæmərə] *phot.* appareil *m;* ♊ *in* ~ à huis clos; '**~-man** caméraman *m;* preneur *m* de vues.

cam·i·knick·ers [kæmi'nikəz] *pl.* chemise-culotte *(pl.* chemises-culottes) *f.*

cam·o·mile ⚘ ['kæməmail] camomille *f;* ~ *tea* (tisane *f* de) camomille *f.*

cam·ou·flage ⚔ ['kæmuflɑːʒ] **1.** camouflage *m;* **2.** camoufler.

camp [kæmp] **1.** camp *m;* campement *m;* ~*-bed* lit *m* de camp; ~*-chair,* ~*-stool* chaise *f* pliante; pliant *m;* **2.** camper; ~ *out* camper; faire du camping.

cam·paign [kæm'pein] **1.** campagne *f (a. pol., a. fig.); election* ~ campagne *f* électorale; **2.** faire une (des) campagne(s); **cam'paign·er:** F *old* ~ vieux routier *m;* vétéran *m.*

camp·er ['kæmpə] campeur (-euse *f) m; Am. a.* caravane *f.*

cam·phor ['kæmfə] camphre *m;* **cam·phor·at·ed** ['~reitid] camphré.

camp·ing ['kæmpiŋ] camping *m;* ⚔ campement *m.*

camp·site ['kæmpsait] (terrain *m* de) camping *m.*

cam·pus *Am.* ['kæmpəs] terrains *m/pl. (d'une université).*

cam·shaft ⊕ ['kæmʃɑːft] arbre *m* à cames.

can¹ [kæn] [*irr.*] *v/aux. (défectif)* je peux *etc., je* suis *etc.* capable de *(inf.).*

can² [~] **1.** bidon *m,* broc *m,* pot *m; Am. conserves:* boîte *f;* canette *f* en métal; ~ *opener* ouvre-boîtes *m/inv.;* F *carry the* ~ rester avec l'affaire sur les bras; **2.** *Am.* conserver *(qch.)* en boîte; *Am. sl.* ~ *it!* la ferme!

Ca·na·di·an [kə'neidjən] **1.** canadien(ne *f);* **2.** Canadien(ne *f) m.*

ca·nal [kə'næl] canal *m (a.* ♊); **ca·nal·i·za·tion** [kænəlai'zeiʃn] canalisation *f;* '**ca·nal·ize** (se) canaliser.

ca·nard [kæ'nɑːd] canard *m,* fausse nouvelle *f.*

ca·nar·y [kə'nɛəri] *(a.~bird)* serin *m.*

can·cel ['kænsl] biffer; annuler; *fig. (a.* ~ *out)* éliminer; **can·cel·la·tion** [kænse'leiʃn] annulation *f;* résiliation *f;* révocation *f.*

can·cer ['kænsə] *astr. le* Cancer *m;* ♋ cancer *m; attr.* cancéreux (-euse *f);* '**can·cer·ous** cancéreux (-euse *f).*

can·did ☐ ['kændid] franc(he *f);* sincère; impartial (-aux *m/pl.).*

can·di·date ['kændidit] candidat *m,* aspirant *m* (à, *for);* **can·di·da·ture** ['~ʃə] candidature *f.*

can·died ['kændid] candi; confit.

can·dle ['kændl] bougie *f;* chandelle *f;* cierge *m;* ~*-power* bougie *f,* -s *f/pl.;* **2·mas** *eccl.* [~'məs] la Chandeleur *f;* '~*-stick* chandelier *m;* bougeoir *m.*

cap

can·do(u)r ['kændə] franchise *f*, sincérité *f*; impartialité *f*.

can·dy ['kændi] 1. sucre *m* candi; *Am.* bonbons *m/pl.*; confiseries *f/pl.*; ~ floss barbe *f* à papa; 2. *v/t.* faire candir *(du sucre)*; glacer *(des fruits)*; *v/i.* se cristalliser.

cane [kein] 1. ♀ jonc *m*; canne *f*; *pour sièges*: rotin *m*; 2. battre à coups de canne; canner *(une chaise)*.

ca·nine ['keinain] 1. de chien, canin; 2. ['kænain] *a.* ~ tooth canine *f*.

can·is·ter ['kænistə] boîte *f* (*en fer blanc*).

can·ker ['kæŋkə] 1. ✻, *a.* ♀ chancre *m* (*a. fig. = influence corruptrice*); 2. ronger; *fig.* corrompre; **'can·kered** *fig.* plein d'amertume; **'can·ker·ous** chancreux (-euse *f*).

can·na·bis ['kænəbis] chanvre *m*; cannabis *m*.

canned *Am.* [kænd] (conservé) en boîte; ~ music musique enregistrée *ou* en conserve.

can·ner·y *Am.* ['kænəri] conserverie *f*.

can·ni·bal ['kænibl] cannibale (*a. su./mf*).

can·non ['kænən] 1. ✕ canon *m*; pièce *f* d'artillerie; *billard*: carambolage *m*; 2. caramboler; *fig.* ~ against (*ou* with) se heurter contre; **cannon·ade** [~'neid] canonnade *f*; **'can·non·ball** boulet *m* de canon.

can·not ['kænɔt] *je ne peux pas etc.*

can·ny □ *écoss.* ['kæni] prudent, finaud.

ca·noe [kə'nu:] 1. canoë *m*; pirogue *f*; périssoire *f*; *paddle one's own* ~ se débrouiller tout seul, diriger seul sa barque; 2. faire du canoë *ou* de la périssoire; aller en canoë.

can·on ['kænən] *eccl., a.* ♪ canon *m*; F règle *f*, critère *m*; canon *m*; *eccl. personne*: chanoine *m*; *typ.* gros canon *m*; ⚖ ~ *law* droit *m* canon; **can·on·i·za·tion** [~nai'zeiʃn] canonisation *f*; **'can·on·ize** canoniser (*q.*); sanctionner (*un usage*); **'can·on·ry** canonicat *m*.

can·o·py ['kænəpi] 1. dais *m*; baldaquin *m*; marquise *f*; *fig.* voûte *f*; ⚙ gable *m*; 2. couvrir d'un dais *etc.*

cant¹ [kænt] 1. inclinaison *f*, dévers *m*; ⚙ pan *m* coupé; 2. (s')incliner; pencher; *v/i.* ⚓ éviter; ~ over se renverser.

cant² [~] 1. jargon *m*, argot *m* (*des mendiants, criminels, etc.*); langage *m* hypocrite; boniments *m/pl.*; 2. faire le cafard; parler avec hypocrisie (*de, about*).

can't F [kɑ:nt] *see cannot.*

can·ta·loup ♀ ['kæntəlu:p] cantaloup *m*.

can·tan·ker·ous F □ [kən'tæŋkərəs] revêche, acariâtre.

can·teen [kæn'ti:n] cantine *f*; *coutellerie*: service *m* de table en coffre; ✕ bidon *m*; ✕ gamelle *f*.

can·ter ['kæntə] 1. petit galop *m*; 2. aller au petit galop.

can·ter·bur·y ['kæntəbəri] casier *m* à musique; ♀ *bell* ♀ campanule *f*.

can·tha·ris *zo.* ['kænθəris], *pl.* **-thar·i·des** [~'θæridi:z] cantharide *f*.

can·ti·cle ['kæntikl] cantique *m*; *bibl.* ♀*s pl.* le Cantique des Cantiques.

can·ti·le·ver ⚙ ['kæntili:və] encorbellement *m*; cantilever *m*.

can·to ['kæntou] chant *m* (*d'un poème*).

can·ton 1. ['kæntɔn] canton *m*; 2. ✕ [kən'tu:n] cantonner; **'can·ton·ment** ✕ cantonnement *m*.

can·vas ['kænvəs] (grosse) toile *f*; toile *f* de tente; *navire*: voiles *f/pl.*; *peint.* toile *f*; *p.ext.* tableau *m*.

can·vass [~] 1. sollicitation *f* de suffrages; tournée *f* électorale; *Am. a.* dépouillement *m* (*des voix*); 2. *v/t.* discuter; solliciter (*des suffrages,* ✝ *des commandes*); *v/i. pol.* faire une tournée électorale; ✝ faire la place; **'can·vass·er** solliciteur (-euse *f*) *m*; ✝ placier *m*; *pol.* courtier *m* électoral; *Am. a.* scrutateur *m* (*du scrutin*).

caou·tchouc ['kautʃuk] caoutchouc *m*.

cap [kæp] 1. casquette *f*; béret *m*; *univ.* toque *f*, mortier *m*; ⊕ *etc.* chapeau *m*, capuchon *m*; ⊕ *pompe*: calotte *f*; ~ *and gown* toque *f* et toge *f*, costume *m* académique; ~ *in hand* le bonnet à la main; *set one's* ~ *at s.o.* entreprendre la conquête de q.; 2. *v/t.* coiffer; choisir comme membre de la première équipe; capsuler (*une bouteille etc.*); *fig.* couronner; F surpasser; *sp. be* ~ped être admis *ou* jouer dans l'équipe nationale; *v/i.* F se découvrir (devant q., [to] *s.o.*).

ca·pa·bil·i·ty [keipə'biliti] capacité *f* (pour *inf.*, *of gér.*); faculté *f* (de *inf.*, *of gér.*); **'ca·pa·ble** capable, susceptible (de, *of*).

ca·pa·cious □ [kə'peiʃəs] vaste; ample; **ca·pac·i·tate** [ˌ~'pæsiteit] rendre capable (de, *for*); **ca'pac·i·ty** capacité *f* (pour *inf.*, *for gér.*); volume *m*, contenance *f*; *locomotive*: rendement *m*; *rivière*: débit *m*; qualité *f* (*professionnelle*); *disposing* (*ou legal*) ~ capacité *f* juridique; *in my* ~ *as* en ma qualité de.

cap-à-pie [kæpə'pi:] de pied en cap.

ca·par·i·son [kə'pærisn] caparaçon *m*; *fig.* parure *f* somptueuse.

cape¹ [keip] cap *m*, promontoire *m*.

cape² [ˌ~] pèlerine *f*, cape *f*.

ca·per¹ ⚕ ['keipə] câpre *f*; *plante*: câprier *m*.

ca·per² [ˌ~] **1.** cabriole *f*, entrechat *m* (*a. fig.*); *cut* ~*s* = **2.** faire des entrechats *ou* des cabrioles; gambader.

ca·pi·as ⚖ ['keipiæs]: *writ of* ~ mandat *m* d'arrêt.

cap·il·lar·i·ty [kæpi'læriti] capillarité *f*; **cap·il·lar·y** [kə'piləri] **1.** capillaire; **2.** *anat.* (vaisseau *m*) capillaire *m*.

cap·i·tal ['kæpitl] **1.** □ capital (-aux *m/pl.*) (*lettre, peine, crime, ville*); *le plus haut*; F excellent, fameux (-euse *f*); **2.** capitale *f*; ✝ capital *m*, fonds *m/pl.*; *typ.* (*ou* ~ *letter*) majuscule *f*, capitale *f*; ✝ ~ *assets pl.* actif *m* immobilisé; ✝ ~ *gains* (*tax*) (impôt *m* sur les) plus-values *f/pl.* (en capital); **3.** △ chapiteau *m*; **'cap·i·tal·ism** capitalisme *m*; **'cap·i·tal·ist** capitaliste *mf*; **cap·i·tal'is·tic** capitaliste; **cap·i·tal·i·za·tion** [kəpitəlai'zeiʃn] capitalisation *f*; **'cap·i·tal·ize** capitaliser; écrire avec une majuscule.

cap·i·ta·tion [kæpi'teiʃn] capitation *f* (*a.* ⚕); *attr.* par tête.

Cap·i·tol ['kæpitl] Capitole *m*.

ca·pit·u·late [kə'pitjuleit] capituler; **ca·pit·u·la·tion** capitulation *f*, reddition *f*.

ca·pon ['keipən] chapon *m*, poulet *m*.

ca·price [kə'pri:s] caprice *m* (*a.* ♪), lubie *f*; **ca·pri·cious** capricieux (-euse *f*); **ca'pri·cious·ness** humeur *f* capricieuse.

Cap·ri·corn *astr.* ['kæprikɔ:n] *le* Capricorne *m*.

cap·ri·ole ['kæprioul] cabriole *f*.

cap·size ⚓ [kæp'saiz] *v/i.* chavirer; *fig.* se renverser; *v/t.* faire chavirer.

cap·stan ⚓ ['kæpstən] cabestan *m*.

cap·su·lar ['kæpsjulə] capsulaire; **cap·sule** ⚕, ⚘ ['ˌ~sju:l] capsule *f*.

cap·tain ['kæptin] capitaine *m*, chef *m*; *sp.* chef *m* d'équipe; ✕, ⚓ capitaine *m*; ✖ *group* ~ colonel *m*; ~ *of horse* capitaine *m* de cavalerie; ~ *of industry* chef *m* de l'industrie; **'cap·tain·cy**, **'cap·tain·ship** grade *m* de capitaine; *sp.* commandement *m* de l'équipe; *entreprise*: conduite *f*.

cap·tion ['kæpʃn] **1.** en-tête *m*; légende *f*; *journal*: rubrique *f*; *cin.* sous-titre *m*; **2.** *v/t. Am.* fournir d'en-têtes *etc.*

cap·tious □ ['kæpʃəs] captieux (-euse *f*); pointilleux (-euse *f*) (*personne*).

cap·ti·vate ['kæptiveit] *fig.* captiver, charmer; **cap·ti·va·tion** séduction *f*; **'cap·tive 1.** captif (-ive *f*); ~ *balloon* ballon *m* captif; **2.** captif (-ive *f*) *m*; prisonnier (-ère *f*) *m*; **cap·tiv·i·ty** [ˌ~'tiviti] captivité *f*.

cap·tor ['kæptə] preneur *m*; ⚓ capteur *m*; **cap·ture** ['ˌ~tʃə] **1.** capture *f*; prise *f* (*a.* ⚓); **2.** capturer, s'emparer de (*un malfaiteur*); prendre (*une ville*); ⚓ capturer.

Cap·u·chin *eccl.* ['kæpjuʃin] capucin *m*.

car [kɑ:] *mot.* automobile *f*, voiture *f*; 🚋 *Am.* voiture *f*, wagon *m*; *Am.* ascenseur: cabine *f*; *poét.* char *m*; *ballon*: nacelle *f*; ~ *park* parking *m*, parc *m* de stationnement; ~ *port* auvent *m* *ou* abri *m* pour voitures; ~ *wash* lave-auto *m*, tunnel *m* de lavage.

car·a·cole ['kærəkoul] *équit.* **1.** caracole *f*; **2.** caracoler.

ca·rafe [kə'rɑ:f] carafe *f*.

car·a·mel ['kærəmel] caramel *m*; bonbon *m* au caramel.

car·at ['kærət] *mesure*: carat *m*.

car·a·van [kærə'væn] caravane *f* (*a. mot.*); roulotte *f*; ~ *site* camping *m* pour caravanes; **car·a·van·se·rai** [ˌ~serai] caravansérail *m*.

car·a·way ⚕ ['kærəwei] carvi *m*.

car·bide 🜍 ['kɑ:baid] carbure *m*.

car·bine ['kɑ:bain] carabine *f*.

car·bo·hy·drate 🜍 ['kɑ:bou'haidreit] hydrate *m* de carbone.

car·bol·ic ac·id [kɑ:'bɔlik'æsid] phénol *m*.

691   **carnivore**

car·bon ['kɑ:bən] 🜍 carbone m; ⚡ charbon m; ~ *copy* copie f *ou* double m au carbone; (*ou* ~ *paper*) papier m carbone; **car·bo·na·ceous** [~-'neiʃəs] *géol.* charbonneux (-euse f); **car·bon·ate** ['~bənit] carbonate m; **car·bon·ic** [~'bɔnik] carbonique; ~ *acid* anhydride m carbonique; **car·bon·i·zation** [~bənai'zeiʃn] carbonisation f; **'car·bon·ize** carboniser.

car·boy ['kɑ:bɔi] bonbonne f.

car·bun·cle ['kɑ:bʌŋkl] min. escarboucle f; ⚕ anthrax m.

car·bu·ret 🜍 ['kɑ:bjuret] carburer; **'car·bu·ret·ter**, usu. **'car·bu·ret·tor** mot. carburateur m.

car·case, car·cass ['kɑ:kəs] *homme, animal:* cadavre m; *animal, maison:* carcasse f; *fig.* squelette m, carcasse f.

car·ci·no·ma ⚕ [kɑ:sinoumə] carcinome m; **car·cin·o·gen·ic** [~nə-'dʒenik] cancérigène.

card¹ ⊕ [kɑ:d] 1. carde f, peigne m; 2. carder, peigner (*la laine*).

card² [~] carte f; ~ *catalogue* fichier m; F *house of* ~*s* château m de cartes; *sl. queer* ~ drôle m de type *ou* de numéro.

car·dan ⊕ ['kɑ:dən]: ~ *joint* joint m de cardan, joint m universel; ~ *shaft* arbre m à cardan.

card...: **'~·board** carton m; cartonnage m; ~ *box* carton m; **'~·case** porte-cartes m/inv.

car·di·ac ⚕ ['kɑ:diæk] 1. cardiaque, cardiaire; ~ *arrest* arrêt m du coeur; ~ *stimulant* stimulant m cardiaque; 2. cordial m.

car·di·gan ['kɑ:digən] cardigan m.

car·di·nal □ ['kɑ:dinl] 1. cardinal (-aux m/pl.); principal (-aux m/pl.); ~ *number* nombre m cardinal; 2. *eccl.* cardinal m (a. *orn.*); **car·di·nal·ate** ['~eit] cardinalat m.

card...: **'~·in·dex** fichier m, classeur m; **'~·sharp·er** tricheur m, escroc m.

care [kɛə] 1. souci m; soin m, attention f; charge f; tenue f; *medical* ~ soins m/pl. médicaux; ~ *of the mouth* hygiène f orale; ~ *of the nails* soin m des ongles; ~ *of* (abbr. c/o) aux bons soins de; chez; *take* ~ faire attention; *take* ~ (*of yourself*)! fais bien attention (à toi); *take* ~ *to do* faire attention *ou* prendre soin de faire; *take* ~ *of* s'occuper de;

garder; *with* ~! fragile!; 2. se soucier; s'inquiéter; ~ *for* soigner; aimer; se soucier de; *usu. au nég.:* tenir à; être important à (*q.*); F *I don't* ~ (*if I do*)! ça m'est égal; *I don't* ~ *what he said* peu m'importe ce qu'il a dit.

ca·reen ⚓ [kə'ri:n] v/t. caréner; v/i. donner de la bande.

ca·reer [kə'riə] 1. carrière f; *fig.* course f précipitée; ~ *diplomat* diplomate m de carrière; 2. *fig.* courir rapidement; **ca·reer·ist** [kə'riərist] arriviste mf.

care·free ['kɛəfri:] insouciant; exempt de soucis.

care·ful □ ['kɛəful] soigneux (-euse f) (de of, for); attentif (-ive f) (à, of); prudent; soigné; *be* ~ *to* (inf.) avoir soin de (inf.); *be* ~ *not to fall!* prenez garde de tomber; **'care·ful·ness** soin m, attention f; prudence f.

care·less □ ['kɛəlis] sans soin; négligent; inconsidéré; nonchalant; insouciant (de of, about); **'care·less·ness** inattention f; insouciance f; manque m de soin.

ca·ress [kə'res] 1. caresse f; 2. caresser; *fig.* mignoter.

care·tak·er ['kɛəteikə] concierge mf; gardien(ne f) m; *école:* dépensier (-ère f) m.

care·worn ['kɛəwɔ:n] usé par le chagrin.

car·fare Am. ['kɑ:fɛə] prix m du voyage.

car·go ⚓ ['kɑ:gou] cargaison f; *mixed* (*ou general*) ~ cargaison f mixte; *shifting* ~ cargaison f volante.

car·i·ca·ture [kærikə'tjuə] 1. caricature f; 2. caricaturer; **car·i·ca·tur·ist** [kærikə'tjuərist] caricaturiste m.

car·i·es ⚕ ['kɛərii:z] carie f; **'car·i·ous** carié; gâté (*dent etc.*).

car·man ['kɑ:mən] charretier m.

car·mine ['kɑ:main] 1. carmin m; 2. carmin adj./inv., carminé.

car·nage ['kɑ:nidʒ] carnage m; **'carnal** □ charnel(le f); de la chair; sensuel(le f); sexuel(le f); mondain; **car·nal·i·ty** [~'næliti] sensualité f; **car·na·tion** [~'neiʃn] 1. incarnat m; ✿ œillet m; 2. incarnat.

car·ni·val ['kɑ:nivl] carnaval (pl. -s) m; *fig.* réjouissances f/pl.

car·ni·vore ['kɑ:nivɔ:] carnassier m;

44*

car·niv·o·rous [~'nivərəs] carnassier (-ère f) (animal); carnivore (plante, personne).

car·ol ['kærl] **1.** chant m, chanson f; noël m; **2.** chanter joyeusement.

ca·rot·id anat. [kə'rɔtid] (a. ~ artery) carotide f.

ca·rouse [kə'rauz] **1.** a. **ca'rous·al** buverie f; F bombe f; **2.** faire la fête.

carp¹ [ka:p] carpe f.

carp² [~] gloser, épiloguer; ~ at trouver à redire à.

car·pen·ter ['ka:pintə] **1.** charpentier m; menuisier m; **2.** v/i. faire de la charpenterie; v/t. charpenter; **'car·pen·try** charpente(rie) f.

car·pet ['ka:pit] **1.** tapis m (a. fig.); bring on the ~ soulever (une question); F ~-dance sauterie f; **2.** recouvrir d'un tapis; F mettre (q.) sur la sellette; **'~-bag·ger** parl. candidat m étranger à la circonscription; **'~-beat·er** tapette f.

car·pet·ing ['ka:pitiŋ] tapis m/pl. en pièce; pose f de tapis.

car·pet-sweep·er ['ka:pitswi:pə] balai m mécanique.

car·riage ['kærid3] port m; transport m; (a. ⊕) voiture f, wagon m; ⚔ affût m; personne: allure f; machine à écrire: chariot m; voiture: train m; **'car·riage·a·ble** charriable (objet); praticable (chemin).

car·riage...: '~-**and**-'**pair** voiture f à deux chevaux; '~-**door** porte f cochère; '~-**drive** allée f; avenue f pour voitures; '~-**free**, ~'**paid** franc(he f) ou franco de port, envoi franco; '~-**road**, '~-**way** chaussée f; route f carrossable.

car·ri·er ['kæriə] porteur (-euse f) m (a. ⚕); ⚔ ravitailleur m; ✝ camionneur m, voiturier m; bicyclette: porte-bagages m/inv.; '~-**bag** sac m (en plastique); '~-**pi·geon** pigeon m voyageur.

car·ri·on ['kæriən] **1.** charogne f; **2.** pourri.

car·rot ['kærət] carotte f; **'car·rot·y** F roux (rousse f).

car·ry ['kæri] **1.** v/t. porter; transporter; conduire (q.); mener (q.); mener à bonne fin (une entreprise); (rap)porter (intérêt); remporter (un prix); élever (un mur); (sup)porter (une poutre); faire adopter (une proposition); ⚖ retenir (un chiffre); bien supporter (du vin); avoir en magasin (des marchandises); ⚔ enlever (une forteresse); be carried être voté; être adopté; univ. ~ a course suivre un cours; ~ away emmener (q.); emporter (a. fig.); ~ everything before one triompher sur toute la ligne; ✝ ~ forward (ou over) reporter (une somme); transporter (un solde); ~ on continuer; entretenir; exercer (un métier); poursuivre (un procès); ~ out porter dehors; exécuter; mener à bonne fin; ~ through exécuter, réaliser; **2.** v/i. porter (son, fusil); faire une trajectoire (balle); ~ on persister; F faire des scènes; F se comporter; F ~ on with flirter avec (q.); ~ing capacity charge f utile; **3.** fusil: portée f; trajet m.

cart [ka:t] **1.** charrette f; ⚔ fourgon m; ~ grease cambouis m; fig. put the ~ before the horse mettre la charrue devant les bœufs; sl. in the ~ dans le pétrin; **2.** charrier, charroyer; **'cart·age** charroi m; (prix m du) charriage m.

car·tel [ka:'tel] cartel m; ✝ syndicat m de producteurs; ⚔ convention f pour l'échange de prisonniers.

car·ter ['ka:tə] charretier m, camionneur m.

car·ti·lage ['ka:tilid3] cartilage m; **car·ti·lag·i·nous** [~'læd3inəs] cartilagineux (-euse f).

cart-load ['ka:tloud] charretée f; charbon: tombereau m.

car·tog·ra·pher [ka:'tɔgrəfə] cartographe m; **car'tog·ra·phy** cartographie f.

car·ton ['ka:tən] carton m; a ~ of cigarettes une cartouche de cigarettes.

car·toon [ka:'tu:n] **1.** peint. carton m; ⊕ dessin m (sur page entière), surt. portrait m caricaturé; cin. dessin m animé; **2.** faire la caricature de.

car·touche [ka:'tuʃ] cartouche m.

car·tridge ['ka:trid3] cartouche f; '~-**belt** ceinture: cartouchière f.

cart-wheel ['ka:twi:l] roue f de charrette; gymn. roue f; co. Am. dollar m d'argent.

cart·wright ['ka:trait] charron m.

carve [ka:v] v/t. découper (de la viande), tailler; se frayer (un chemin); vt./i. sculpter (dans, in); graver (sur, in); **'carv·er** couteau m à découper; personne: découpeur m;

serveur *m*; ciseleur *m*; ⁓*s pl.* service *m* à découper.

carv·ing ['kɑːviŋ] 1. sculpture *f*, gravure *f*; découpage *m* de la viande; 2. à découper; à sculpter.

cas·cade [kæs'keid] chute *f* d'eau; cascade *f*.

case¹ [keis] 1. caisse *f*; colis *m*; (*a. cartridge-*⁓) étui *m*; *instruments*: trousse *f*; *violon*: boîte *f*; *montre*: boîtier *m*; *magasin*: vitrine *f*; *livre*: couverture *f*; *typ.* casse *f*; 2. encaisser; cartonner (*un livre*); ⊕ chemiser (*une chaudière*); envelopper (de, with).

case² [⁓] cas *m* (*a.* ✵, ⚖, *gramm.*); ✵ *a.* malade *mf*; *Am.* F original *m*; ⚖ *a.* cause *f*, affaire *f*; exposé *m* des faits; réclamation *f*; *a* ⁓ *for* (*gér.*) des raisons de (*inf.*); *have a strong* ⁓ être dans son droit; avoir des raisons sérieuses (pour, for); *as the* ⁓ *may* be selon le cas; *in* ⁓ au cas où; *à* tout hasard; *in any* ⁓ en tout cas; '⁓**-book** dossier *m* médical; rapports *m/pl.* de cas sociaux.

case·hard·en ⊕ ['keishɑːdn] aciérer; *fig.* ⁓*ed* endurci.

ca·se·in ⚗ ['keisiiːn] caséine *f*.

case-knife ['keisnaif] couteau *m* à gaine.

case·mate ✕ ['keismeit] casemate *f*.

case·ment ['keismənt] fenêtre *f* à deux battants; croisée *f*; ⁓ *cloth* tissu *m* de rideaux.

case-shot ['keisʃɔt] mitraille *f*.

cash [kæʃ] 1. espèces *f/pl.*; argent *m* comptant; ⁓ *down, for* ⁓ argent comptant; *in* ⁓ en espèces; *be in* (*out of*) ⁓ (ne pas) être en fonds; ⁓ *payment* paiement *m* (au) comptant; ⁓ *on delivery* livraison *f* contre remboursement; ⁓ *dispenser* changeur *m* de monnaie; ⁓ *price* prix *m* au comptant; ⁓ *register* caisse *f* enregistreuse; 2. encaisser (*un coupon*); toucher (*un chèque*); '⁓**-book** livre *m* de caisse; sommier *m*; '⁓**-cheque** chèque *m* ouvert; '⁓**-desk** caisse *f*; *théâ. etc.* guichet *m*; **cash·ier** [kæ'ʃiə] 1. caissier (-ère *f*) *m*; 2. ✕ casser (*un officier*); '**cash·less** sans argent; F à sec.   [*m*.]

cash·mere [kæʃ'miə] *tex.* cachemire

cas·ing ['keisiŋ] encaissement *m*; enveloppe *f*; *livre*: cartonnage *m*; *cylindre*: chemise *f*; *turbine*: bâche *f*; ▲ revêtement *m*.

ca·si·no [kə'siːnou] casino *m*.

cask [kɑːsk] fût *m*, tonneau *m*.

cas·ket ['kɑːskit] cassette *f*, coffret *m*; *Am.* cercueil *m* (de luxe).

cas·sa·tion ⚖ [kæ'seiʃn] cassation *f*.

cas·se·role ['kæsəroul] *cuis.* daubière *f*; ⌂ casserole *f*; ⁓ *of chicken* poulet *m* en cocotte.

cas·sette [kə'set] cassette *f*; ⁓ **deck** platine *f* à cassettes; ⁓ **play·er** lecteur *m* de cassettes; ⁓ **re·cord·er** magnétophone *m* à cassettes.

cas·si·a ⚕ ['kæsiə] casse *f* (*a. pharm.*); *arbre*: casier *m*.

cas·sock ['kæsək] soutane *f*.

cas·so·war·y *orn.* ['kæsəwɛəri] casoar *m*; *New Holland* ⁓ émeu *m*.

cast [kɑːst] 1. jet *m*; coup *m*; ⊕ *metall.* coulée *f*; moulage *m*; ⚓ coup *m* (*de sonde*); bas *m* de ligne; *théâ.* troupe *f*; distribution *f* des rôles; ✝ additon *f*; *fig.* trempe *f*, tournure *f* (*d'esprit*); 2. [*irr.*] *v/t.* jeter (*a.* ⚓ *l'ancre*), lancer; donner (*son suffrage*); *zo.* jeter (*sa dépouille*); *orn.* (*usu.* ⁓ *its feathers*) muer; perdre (*les dents*); jeter (*un regard*); projeter (*une lumière, une ombre, etc.*); *métall.* couler; *typ.* clicher (*une page*); *théâ.* distribuer les rôles de (*une pièce*), assigner (un rôle à q., s.o. *for a part*); ✝, ▲ (*a.* ⁓ *up*) additionner, faire le total; ⁓ *iron* fonte *f* (de fer); ⁓ *steel* fonte *f* d'acier; ⚖ *be* ⁓ *in costs* être condamné aux frais; ⚖ *be* ⁓ *in a lawsuit* perdre un procès, être débouté; ⁓ *lots* tirer au sort (pour, for); ⁓ *one's skin* se dépouiller; ⁓ *s.th. in s.o.'s teeth* reprocher qch. à q.; ⁓ *away* rejeter; ⚓ *be* ⁓ *away* faire naufrage; ⁓ *down* jeter bas; baisser (*les yeux*); *be* ⁓ *down* être découragé; ⁓ *up* lever au ciel; ✵ rejeter; ✝ ⁓ *up* (*accounts*) additionner, faire le total; 3. *v/i.* se voiler; ⊕ se couler; ⁓ *about for* chercher; briguer; ⚓ ⁓ *off* abattre sous le vent; démarrer.

cas·ta·net [kæstə'net] castagnette *f*.

cast·a·way ['kɑːstəwei] 1. rejeté; ⚓ naufragé; 2. naufragé(e *f*) *m*; *fig.* proscrit(e *f*) *m*; exilé(e *f*) *m*.

caste [kɑːst] caste *f*; *fig.* rang *m*, classe *f*; ⁓ *feeling* esprit *m* de caste.

cas·tel·lan ['kæstələn] châtelain *m*; **cas·tel·lat·ed** ['kæsteleitid] crénelé; bâti dans le style féodal.

cas·ter ['kɑːstə] *see castor²*.

castigate

694

cas·ti·gate ['kæstigeit] châtier; *fig.* critiquer sévèrement; **cas·ti'ga·tion** châtiment *m*, correction *f*; *fig.* critique *f* sévère.

cast·ing ['kɑːstiŋ] **1.** ~ vote voix *f* prépondérante; **2.** jet *m*; moulage *m*, fonte *f*; *théâ.* distribution *f* des rôles; ✝ addition *f*; ~s *pl.* pièces *f/pl.*

cast-i·ron ['kɑːst'aiən] en fonte; *fig.* de fer, rigide; ~ *alibi* alibi *m* de fer.

cas·tle ['kɑːsl] **1.** château *m* (fort); *échecs:* tour *f*; **2.** *échecs:* roquer.

cas·tor[1] ['kɑːstə] *pharm.* castoréum *m*; ✝ chapeau *m* castor; ~ *oil* huile *f* de ricin.

cas·tor[2] [~] roulette *f* (*de meuble*); *sucre etc.:* saupoudroir *m*; ~s *pl.* huilier *m*; ✝ ~ *sugar* sucre *m* en poudre.

cas·trate [kæs'treit] châtrer; **cas'tra·tion** castration *f*; éviration *f*; *fig.* émasculation *f*.

cas·u·al ['kæʒjuəl] **1.** □ fortuit, accidentel (le *f*); F insouciant; ~ *labo(u)rer* homme *m* à l'heure, manœuvre *m* d'emploi intermittent; ~ *pauper* = **2.** indigent (e *f*) *m* de passage; **'cas·u·al·ty** accident *m*; ✕ *casualties pl.* pertes *f/pl.*

cas·u·ist ['kæzjuist] casuiste *m* (*a. péj.*); **'cas·u·ist·ry** casuistique *f* (*a. péj.*).

cat [kæt] **1.** chat(te *f*) *m*; *Am. sl.* fanatique *mf* du jazz; **2.** *sl.* renarder.

cat·a·clysm ['kætəklizm] cataclysme *m*.

cat·a·comb ['kætəkoum] catacombe *f*.

cat·a·logue, *Am. a.* **cat·a·log** ['kætələg] **1.** catalogue *m*, répertoire *m*; *univ. Am.* annuaire *m*; prospectus *m*; **2.** cataloguer.

cat·a·lʏ·sis [kə'tælisis], *pl.* **ca'tal·y·ses** [~siːz] catalyse *f*; **cat·a·lyst** ['kætəlist] catalyseur *m*.

cat·a·pult ['kætəpʌlt] catapulte *f* (*a.* ✈); ~ *launching* catapultage *m*.

cat·a·ract ['kætərækt] cataracte *f* (*a. fig., a.* ✚).

ca·tarrh [kə'tɑː] catarrhe *m*; F *surt.* rhume *m* de cerveau; **ca·tarrh·al** [kə'tɑːrəl] catarrhal (-aux *m/pl.*).

cat·as·tro·phe [kə'tæstrəfi] catastrophe *f*, désastre *m*; **cat·a·stroph·ic** [kætə'strɔfik] (~ally) désastreux (-euse *f*).

cat...: '~·bur·glar cambrioleur *m*

par escalade; '~·call **1.** *théâ. etc.* sifflet *m*; **2.** siffler; chahuter.

catch [kætʃ] **1.** prise *f*; *porte, fenêtre:* loqueteau *m*; attrape *f*, tromperie *f*; *fig.* aubaine *f*; F bon parti *m* (*à épouser*); ♪ chant *m* à reprises, canon *m*; ⊕ crochet *m* d'arrêt; cliquet *m*; *cricket:* prise *f* au vol; *see* ~ *word*; **2.** [*irr.*] *v/t.* attraper, prendre; saisir; F obtenir, gagner; rencontrer (*un regard*); *son:* frapper (*l'oreille*); recueillir (*de l'eau*); prendre; ne pas manquer (*le train etc.*); attraper, être atteint de (*une maladie*); flanquer (*un coup*) à (*q.*); prendre (*un poisson*); accrocher (*sa robe*); attirer (*l'attention*); contracter (*une habitude*); *orage etc.:* surprendre (*q.*); *fig.* entendre, comprendre; F ~ *it* se faire attraper (par, *from*); ~ *in the act* prendre (*q.*) en flagrant délit; prendre (*q.*) sur le fait; ~ *me!* F pas si bête!; ~ *cold* prendre froid; s'enrhumer; ~ *one's breath* avoir un sursaut; ~ *s.o.'s eye* attirer l'attention de q.; *parl.* ~ *the Speaker's eye* obtenir la parole; ~ *up* ramasser vivement; F couper la parole à (*q.*), interrompre; rattraper (*q.*); **3.** [*irr.*] *v/i.* prendre; ⊕ mordre; s'engager (*verrou etc.*); *cuis.* attacher; ~ *at* s'accrocher à; saisir; F ~ *on* avoir du succès, prendre; *Am.* F comprendre; ~ *up with* rattraper (*q.*) '~·all *Am.* fourre-tout *m/inv.*; '~·as-catch-can *sp.* catch *m*; '**catch·er** *baseball:* rattrapeur *m*; '**catch·ing** ♪ entraînant; ✚ contagieux (-euse *f*); infectieux (-euse *f*); '**catch·ment ba·sin** bassin *m* de réception.

catch...: '~·pen·ny ✝ **1.** d'attrape; **2.** camelote *f* de réclame; attrapenigaud *m*; '~·phrase F scie *f*, rengaine *f*; devise *f*; '~·pole huissier *m*; '~·word *pol.* mot *m* de ralliement; F scie *f*; *théâ.* réplique *f*; *typ.* mot-souche (*pl.* mots-souches) *m*; '**catch·y** *fig.* F entraînant; insidieux (-euse *f*) (*question etc.*).

cat·e·chism ['kætikizm] catéchisme *m*; **cat·e·chize** ['~kaiz] catéchiser; **cat·e·chu·men** [~'kjuːmən] catéchumène *mf*.

cat·e·gor·i·cal □ [kæti'gɔrikl] catégorique; **cat·e·go·ry** ['~gəri] catégorie *f*.

cat·e·nar·y [kə'tiːnəri] **1.** caténaire;

⅄ ~ *curve* funiculaire *f*; **2.** caténaire *f*; chaînette *f*.

ca·ter ['keitə]: ~ *for* approvisionner; *fig.* pourvoir à; **'ca·ter·er** approvisionneur (-euse *f*) *m*; fournisseur *m*; *banquet*: traiteur *m*; **'ca·ter·ing** approvisionnement *m*.

cat·er·pil·lar ['kætəpilə] chenille *f*; ~ *wheel* roue *f* à chenille.

cat·er·waul ['kætəwɔːl] miauler.

cat·gut ['kætɡʌt] corde *f* à boyau.

ca·the·dral [kə'θiːdrl] **1.** *su.* cathédrale *f*; **2.** *adj.* cathédral (-aux *m/pl.*).

Cath·er·ine-wheel ⚙ ['kæθərin-wiːl] rosace *f* rayonnante; *pièce d'artifice*: soleil *m*; roue *f* à feu.

cath·e·ter ['kæθitə] sonde *f* creuse, cathéter *m*.

cath·ode ⚡ ['kæθoud] **1.** cathode *f*; **2.** cathodique.

cath·o·lic ['kæθəlik] **1.** (~[*al*]*ly*) universel(le *f*); catholique; **2.** catholique *mf*; **ca·thol·i·cism** [kə'θɔlisizm] catholicisme *m*.

cat·kin ⚘ ['kætkin] chaton *m*.

cat·nap ['kætnæp] **1.** petit somme *m*; **2.** faire un petit somme.

cat's...: ~ *eye* cataphote *m*; **'~-paw** ['kætspɔː] *fig.* dupe *f*; *be s.o.'s* ~ tirer les marrons du feu pour q.

cat·sup ['kætsəp] *Am. see* ketchup.

cat·tle ['kætl] bétail *m*; bestiaux *m/pl.*; **'~-plague** peste *f* bovine; **'~-rus·tler** *Am.* voleur *m* de bétail; **'~-show** comice *m* agricole; concours *m* d'élevage.

cat·walk ['kætwɔːk] passerelle *f*.

Cau·ca·sian [kɔː'keiziən] **1.** caucasien(ne *f*); du Caucase; **2.** Caucasien(ne *f*) *m*.

cau·cus ['kɔːkəs] comité *m* électoral; *usu. péj.* clique *f* politique; *pol. Am.* réunion *f* préliminaire (*d'un comité électoral*).

cau·dal *zo.* ['kɔːdl] caudal (-aux *m/pl.*); **cau·date** ['~deit] caudifère.

cau·dle ['kɔːdl] chaudeau *m*.

caught [kɔːt] *prét. et p.p. de* catch 2, 3.

ca(u)l·dron ['kɔːldrən] chaudron *m*; ⊕ chaudière *f*.

cau·li·flow·er ⚘ ['kɔliflauə] chou-fleur (*pl.* choux-fleurs) *m*.

caulk ⚓ [kɔːk] calfater; **'caulk·er** calfat *m*.

caus·al □ ['kɔːzl] causal (*sg. seulement*); causatif (-ive *f*); **caus·al·i·ty** [~'zæliti] causalité *f*; **'caus·a·tive**

causatif (-ive *f*); **cause** [kɔːz] **1.** cause *f*; raison *f*, motif *m*; ⚖ cause *f*; procès *m*; *fig.* querelle *f*; *with good* ~ pour cause; **2.** occasionner, causer; faire (faire qch. à q., *s.o. to do s.th.*); **'cause·less** □ sans cause, sans motif.

cause·way ['kɔːzwei], *a.* **cau·sey** ['~zei] chaussée *f*, digue *f* (*à travers des marécages*).

caus·tic ['kɔːstik] **1.** caustique *m*; *phys.* caustique *f*; **2.** (~[*al*]*ly*) caustique; *fig. a.* mordant.

cau·ter·i·za·tion ⚕ [kɔːtərai'zeiʃn] cautérisation *f*; **'cau·ter·ize** cautériser; **'cau·ter·y** cautère *m*.

cau·tion ['kɔːʃn] **1.** précaution *f*; prudence *f*; avertissement *m*; réprimande *f*; F drôle *m* de pistolet; ⚖ caution *f*, garant *m*; ~ *money* cautionnement *m*; **2.** avertir (contre, *against*); **'cau·tion·ar·y** d'avertissement, avertisseur (-euse *f*).

cau·tious □ ['kɔːʃəs] prudent, circonspect; **'cau·tious·ness** prudence *f*, circonspection *f*.

cav·al·cade [kævl'keid] cavalcade *f*.

cav·a·lier [kævə'liə] **1.** cavalier *m*; F galant *m*; **2.** □ désinvolte, cavalier (-ère *f*).

cav·al·ry ⚔ ['kævlri] cavalerie *f*.

cave [keiv] **1.** caverne *f*, antre *m*; grotte *f*; des cavernes; **3.**: ~ *in v/i.* s'effondrer; F céder (*personne*); *v/t.* F aplatir.

ca·ve·at ⚖ ['keiviæt] opposition *f*.

cave-man ['keivmən] troglodyte *m*; F homme *m* à la manière forte.

cav·en·dish ['kævəndiʃ] tabac *m* foncé édulcoré.

cav·ern ['kævən] caverne *f* (*a.* ⚕); souterrain *m*; **'cav·ern·ous** caverneux (-euse *f*) (*a. fig.*).

cav·i·ar(e) ['kæviɑː] caviar *m*.

cav·il ['kævil] **1.** argutie *f*; **2.** pointiller (sur *at, about*); **'cav·il·ler** chicaneur (-euse *f*) *m*.

cav·i·ty ['kæviti] cavité *f*; creux *m*; trou *m*.

ca·vort *Am.* F [kə'vɔːt] cabrioler; faire des galopades.

ca·vy *zo.* ['keivi] cobaye *m*, cochon *m* d'Inde.   [ment *m*.]

caw [kɔː] **1.** croasser; **2.** croasse-]

cay·enne [kei'en], **cay·enne pep·per** ['keien] poivre *m* de Cayenne.

cay·man *zo.* ['keimən], *pl.* **-mans** caïman *m*.

cay·use *Am.* ['kaiju:s] petit cheval *m* (indien).

cease [si:s] *v/i.* cesser (de, *from*); *v/t.* cesser (*a.* ✕ *le feu*); '~-'**fire** ✕ cessez-le-feu *m/inv.*; '**cease·less** □ incessant; sans arrêt.

ce·dar ⚘ ['si:də] cèdre *m*.

cede [si:d] céder.

ceil [si:l] plafonner (*une pièce*); † lambrisser; '**ceil·ing** plafond *m* (*a. fig.*); ⚓ vairage *m*; ~ *lighting* illumination *f* de plafond; ~ *price* prix *m* maximum.

cel·an·dine ⚘ ['seləndain] éclaire *f*.

cel·e·brate ['selibreit] célébrer (*a. eccl., a. fig. = glorifier*); '**cel·e·brat·ed** célèbre (par, *for*); renommé (pour, *for*); **cel·e'bra·tion** célébration *f* (*a. eccl.*); *in* ~ *of* pour commémorer *ou* fêter (*qch.*); ~ *of May-day* fête *f* du premier mai; '**cel·e·bra·tor** célébrateur *m*.

ce·leb·ri·ty [si'lebriti] célébrité *f* (*a. personne*).

ce·ler·i·ty [si'leriti] célérité *f*.

cel·er·y ⚘ ['seləri] céleri *m*.

ce·les·tial □ [si'lestjəl] céleste.

cel·i·ba·cy ['selibəsi] célibat *m*; **cel·i·bate** ['~bit] **1.** célibataire, de célibataire; **2.** célibataire *mf*.

cell [sel] cellule *f*; ⚡ élément *m* de pile.

cel·lar ['selə] **1.** cave *f*; **2.** mettre en cave *ou* en chai; '**cel·lar·age** emmagasinage *m*; caves *f/pl.*; '**cel·lar·et** cave *f* à liqueurs.

celled [seld] à cellule(s); ⚡ à pile(s).

cel·list ♪ ['tʃelist] violoncelliste *mf*; **cel·lo** ['tʃelou] violoncelle *m*.

cel·lo·phane ['selofein] cellophane *f*.

cel·lu·lar ['seljulə] cellulaire; **cel·lule** ['~ju:l] cellule *f*; **cel·lu·loid** ['~juloid] celluloïd *m*; **cel·lu·lose** ['~lous] cellulose *f*.

Celt [kelt] Celte *mf*; '**Celt·ic** celte; celtique.

ce·ment [si'ment] **1.** ciment *m*; *anat., a. métall.* cément *m*; **2.** cimenter (*a. fig.*); coller; *métall.* cémenter; ~ *mixer* bétonnière *f*; **ce·men·ta·tion** [si:men'teiʃn] cimentage *m*; collage *m*; *métall.* cémentation *f*.

cem·e·ter·y ['semitri] cimetière *m*.

cen·o·taph ['senətɑ:f] cénotaphe *m*.

cense [sens] encenser; '**cen·ser** encensoir *m*.

cen·sor ['sensə] **1.** censeur *m*; **2.** interdire; expurger; **cen·so·ri·ous** □ [sen'sɔ:riəs] porté à censurer; sévère; **cen·sor·ship** ['~səʃip] censure *f*; contrôle *m*.

cen·sur·a·ble □ ['senʃərəbl] censurable, blâmable; **cen·sure** ['senʃə] **1.** censure *f*, blâme *m*; réprimande *f*; **2.** censurer; blâmer publiquement.

cen·sus ['sensəs] recensement *m*.

cent [sent] *Am.* cent *m* (= $^1/_{100}$ *dollar*); F sou *m*; *per* ~ pour cent.

cen·taur *myth.* ['sentɔ:] centaure *m*.

cen·tau·ry ⚘ ['sentɔ:ri] centaurée *f*.

cen·te·nar·i·an [senti'nɛəriən] centenaire (*a. su./m*); **cen·te·nar·y** [sen'ti:nəri] centenaire *m*.

cen·ten·ni·al [sen'tenjəl] centennal (-aux *m/pl.*); *Am. see centenary*.

cen·tes·i·mal □ [sen'tesiml] centésimal (-aux *m/pl.*).

centi... [senti]: '~**grade** centigrade; '~**gramme** centigramme *m*; '~**me·tre** centimètre *m*; ~**pede** *zo.* ['~pi:d] centipède *m*; F mille-pattes *m/inv.*

cen·tral ['sentrəl] □ central (-aux *m/pl.*); ~ *heating* chauffage *m* central; ~ *office*, ⚡ *station* centrale *f*; *téléph. Am.* central *m*; **cen·tral·i·za·tion** [~lai'zeiʃn] centralisation *f*; '**cen·tral·ize** (se) centraliser.

cen·tre, *Am.* **cen·ter** ['sentə] **1.** centre *m* (*a.* ✕, *pol.*), milieu *m*; *foot.* ~ *forward* avant-centre *m*; *foot.* ~ *half* demi-centre *m*; **2.** central (-aux *m/pl.*), du centre; **3.** *v/t.* placer au centre; centrer (*a. foot.*); concentrer; *v/i.* se concentrer (dans, *in*; sur, *on*; autour de, *round*); '~-**bit** ⊕ mèche *f* anglaise.

cen·tric, cen·tri·cal □ ['sentrik(l)] central (-aux *m/pl.*), du centre; **cen·trif·u·gal** □ [sen'trifjugl] centrifuge; **cen'trip·e·tal** □ [~pitl] centripète.

cen·tu·ple ['sentjupl] **1.** □ centuple (*a. su./m*); **2.** centupler.

cen·tu·ry ['sentʃuri] siècle *m*; *cricket:* centaine *f*.

ce·ram·ic [si'ræmik] céramique; **ce'ram·ics** *v/i.* céramique *f*.

ce·re·al ['siəriəl] **1.** céréale; **2.** céréale *f*; *usu.* ~s *pl.* céréales *f/pl.* en flocons.

cer·e·bel·lum *anat.* [seri'beləm] cervelet *m*; **cer·e·bral** ['seribrəl] cérébral (-aux *m/pl.*); **ce·re·brum** ['seribrəm] cerveau *m*.

cere·cloth ['siəklɔθ] toile *f* d'embaumement.

cer·e·mo·ni·al [seri'mounjəl] **1.** □ (*a.* **cer·e'mo·ni·ous** □) cérémonieux (-euse *f*), de cérémonie; **2.** cérémonial (*pl.* -s) *m*; **cer·e·mo·ny** ['serimⱥni] cérémonie *f*; formalité *f*; *Master of Ceremonies* maître *m* des cérémonies; *without* ~ sans cérémonie, sans façon; *stand on* ~ faire des façons.

cer·tain □ ['sⱥ:tn] certain, sûr; infaillible; *see some* 2; **'cer·tain·ty** certitude *f*; chose *f* certaine; conviction *f*.

cer·tif·i·cate 1. [sⱥ'tifikit] certificat *m*, attestation *f*; diplôme *m*; brevet *m*; ~ *of birth* (*death, marriage*) acte *m* de naissance (de décès, de mariage); ~ *of employment* certificat *m* de travail; *medical* ~ certificat *m* médical; **2.** [~keit] diplômer, breveter; délivrer un certificat *etc.* à (*q.*); ~ed diplômé; **cer·ti·fi·a·ble** ['sⱥ:tifaiⱥbl] qu'on peut certifier; bon(ne *f*) à enfermer, fou (folle *f*); **cer·ti·fi'ca·tion** certification *f*; **cer·ti·fy** ['~fai] certifier, attester; diplômer; authentiquer; *this is to* ~ je soussigné certifie; **cer·ti·tude** ['~tju:d] certitude *f*.　　　[*m/pl.*)]

cer·vi·cal ['sⱥ:vikl] cervical (-aux)

ces·sa·tion [se'seiʃn] cessation *f*, arrêt *m*.

ces·sion ['seʃn] cession *f*; abandon *m*.

cess·pool ['sespu:l] fosse *f* d'aisance.

ce·ta·cean *zo.* [si'teiʃiən] **1.** cétacé *m*; **2.** (*a.* **ce'ta·ceous**) cétacé.

chafe [tʃeif] *v/t.* frictionner; user par le frottement; écorcher (*la peau*); irriter; *v/i.* s'user par le frottement; s'écorcher; s'irriter (*contre, against*); s'érailler (*corde*); *chafing dish* réchaud *m* (*de table*).

chaff [tʃɑ:f] **1.** balle *f* (*de grain*); menue paille *f*; paille *f* hachée; *fig.* vétilles *f/pl.*; F raillerie *f*; **2.** hacher (*de la paille*); F railler, plaisanter (*q.*); **'~-cut·ter** hache-paille *m/inv.*

chaf·fer ['tʃæfⱥ] marchander (*q., with s.o.*).

chaf·finch *zo.* ['tʃæfintʃ] pinson *m*.

cha·grin ['ʃægrin] **1.** chagrin *m*; **2.** chagriner.

chain [tʃein] **1.** chaîne *f* (*a. fig.*);

suite *f* (*des événements*); chaînette *f*; *surt. Am.* ~-*store* succursale *f* de grand magasin; *mot.* ~ *drive* transmission *f* par chaînes; **2.** attacher par des chaînes; enchaîner; ~ **re·ac·tion** *phys.* réaction *f* en chaîne; **'~-smoke** fumer une cigarette après l'autre; **'~-smok·er** fumeur (-euse *f*) *m* invétéré(e) (qui fume sans arrêt).

chair [tʃɛə] **1.** chaise *f*, siège *m*; fauteuil *m*; (*a. professorial* ~) chaire *f*; 🚊 coussinet *m*; ⚖ *Am.* fauteuil *m* électrique; *see chair(wo)man*; ~! ~! à l'ordre! à l'ordre!; *be in the* ~ présider; **2.** *v/i.* prendre la présidence; *v/t.* porter (*q.*) en triomphe; **'~-man** président *m*; **'~-wom·an** présidente *f*.

chaise [ʃeiz] cabriolet *m*, chaise *f*.

chal·dron ['tʃɔ:ldrən] *mesure à charbon de 36 boisseaux (72 à Newcastle) anglais.*

chal·ice ['tʃælis] calice *m*.

chalk [tʃɔ:k] **1.** craie *f*; *billard*: blanc *m*; *red* ~ sanguine *f*; F *by a long* ~ de beaucoup; *see chair(wo)man*; ~! ~! talquer; (*usu.* ~ *up*) écrire à la craie; ~ *out* tracer (*un plan*); **'chalk·y** crayeux (-euse *f*), crétacé; terreux (-euse *f*) (*teint*).

chal·lenge ['tʃælindʒ] **1.** défi *m*; provocation *f* (*en duel, to a duel*); ⚖ interpellation *f*; récusation *f*; **2.** défier, provoquer (*q.*); *sp.* porter un défi à; ⚖ interpeller; récuser; disputer; mettre en doute; **'chal·leng·er** provocateur (-trice *f*) *m*; *sp.* lanceur *m* d'un challenge.

cha·lyb·e·ate 🜨 [kə'libiit] ferrugineux (-euse *f*).

cham·ber ['tʃeimbⱥ] ⚕, ⊕, *poét., parl., zo., Am.* chambre *f*; ~s *pl.* appartement *m* de garçon; cabinet *m*, étude *f*; *see* ~*-pot*; **cham·ber·lain** ['~lin] chambellan *m*; **'cham·ber·maid** *hôtel.:* femme *f* de chambre; **'cham·ber·pot** vase *m* de nuit.

cha·me·le·on *zo.* [kə'mi:ljən] caméléon *m*.

cham·fer △ ['tʃæmfⱥ] **1.** biseau *m*; **2.** biseauter; canneler (*une colonne*).

cham·ois ['ʃæmwɑ:; *pl.* -wɑ:z] *zo.* chamois *m*; ⊕ (*ou* ~ *leather*) [*souv.* 'ʃæmi] (peau *f* de) chamois *m*.

champ[1] [tʃæmp] (*at*) mâcher bruyamment; ronger (*le mors*).

champ[2] *Am. sl.* [~] *see champion* 1.

cham·pagne [ʃæm'pein] champagne *m.*

cham·paign ['tʃæmpein] campagne *f* ouverte.

cham·pi·on ['tʃæmpjən] **1.** champion *m (a. sp.); sp.* recordman *(pl.* recordmen) *m;* **2.** soutenir, défendre; **'cham·pi·on·ship** défense *f; sp.* championnat *m.*

chance [tʃɑːns] **1.** chance *f,* hasard *m;* occasion *f* (de, *of*); *surt. Am.* risque *m; by ~* par hasard; *take a* (*ou* one's) *~* encourir un risque; **2.** fortuit, accidentel(le *f);* de rencontre; **3.** *v/i.: ~ to see* voir par hasard; avoir l'occasion de voir; *~ upon* rencontrer par hasard; *v/t.* F risquer.

chan·cel ['tʃɑːnsəl] chœur *m;* sanctuaire *m;* **'chan·cel·ler·y** chancellerie *f;* **'chan·cel·lor** chancelier *m; see exchequer;* **'chan·cel·lor·ship** dignité *f* de chancelier.

chan·cer·y ⚖ ['tʃɑːnsəri] cour *f* de la chancellerie; *fig. in ~* en danger; dans une situation difficile.

chanc·y F ['tʃɑːnsi] risqué.

chan·de·lier [ʃændi'liə] lustre *m.*

chan·dler ['tʃɑːndlə] marchand *m* (de couleurs), droguiste *m;* **'chan·dler·y** épicerie-droguerie *f.*

change [tʃeindʒ] **1.** changement *m;* revirement *m (d'opinion etc.);* monnaie *f; Bourse:* change *m;* **2.** *v/t.* changer (de) *(qch.);* échanger; modifier; relever *(la garde);* échanger (contre, *for); ~one's mind* changer d'avis; *v/i.* (se) changer (en, *into*); varier; changer de vêtements; 🚂 (*ou ~ trains*) changer de) **'Change** [~] Bourse *f.* [train.]

change·a·bil·i·ty [tʃeindʒə'biliti] *temps:* variabilité *f;* versatilité *f; caractère:* mobilité *f;* **'change·a·ble** □ changeant; variable; mobile; **'change·less** □ immuable; fixe; **'change·ling** enfant *m* changé en nourrice; **'change·o·ver** changement *m; pol.* renversement *m.*

chan·nel ['tʃænl] **1.** *géog.* canal *m;* conduit *m; rivière:* lit *m; port:* passe *f; irrigation:* rigole *f; télév.* chaîne *f; fig.* voie *f (diplomatique);* artère *f; by the official ~s* par (la) voie hiérarchique; **2.** creuser des rigoles dans; canneler.

chant *eccl.* [tʃɑːnt] **1.** plain-chant *(pl.* plains-chants) *m;* psalmodie *f;* chant *m* monotone; **2.** psalmodier; *fig.* chanter *(des louanges);* **'chan·try** *eccl.* chapelle *f,* chantrerie *f.*

cha·os ['keiɔs] chaos *m;* **cha'ot·ic** (~*ally*) chaotique, sans ordre.

chap[1] [tʃæp] **1.** gerçure *f,* crevasse *f;* **2.** gercer, crevasser.

chap[2] [~] bajoue *f (d'un animal,* F *d'une personne).*

chap[3] F [~] garçon *m,* type *m,* individu *m.*

chap-book ['tʃæpbuk] livre *m* de colportage.

chap·el ['tʃæpl] chapelle *f;* oratoire *m; typ.* atelier *m* (syndiqué).

chap·er·on ['ʃæpəroun] **1.** chaperon *m;* **2.** chaperonner.

chap-fall·en ['tʃæpfɔːlən] abattu.

chap·lain ['tʃæplin] aumônier *m;* **'chap·lain·cy** aumônerie *f.*

chap·let ['tʃæplit] guirlande *f; eccl.* chapelet *m.*

chap·ter ['tʃæptə] chapitre *m (a. eccl.); Am.* filiale *f (d'une société);* régionale *f; Brit. ~ of accidents* suite *f* de malheurs, serie *f* noire; *give (ou quote) ~ and verse* citer ses autorités; fournir des preuves.

char[1] *icht.* [tʃɑː] ombre *m.*

char[2] [~] (se) carboniser.

char-à-banc ['ʃærəbæŋ] autocar *m;* F car *m.*

char·ac·ter ['kæriktə] caractère *m (a. typ.);* marque *f* distinctive; réputation *f;* genre *m; domestique:* certificat *m* de moralité; *métier:* qualité *f; typ. a.* lettre *f; théâ.,* *roman:* personnage *m; théâ. a.* rôle *m;* F personnalité *f;* F type *m,* original *m;* F mauvais sujet *m;* ~ *assassination* assassinat *m* moral; *that's in (out of) ~ for him* cela (ne) lui ressemble (pas); **char·ac·ter'is·tic** **1.** (~*ally*) caractéristique (de, *of*); particulier(-ère *f) (signe);* ✽ diacritique; ♪ de genre; **2.** trait *m* caractéristique *ou* de caractère; propre *m;* **char·ac·ter·i·za·tion** [~rai'zeiʃn] caractérisation *f;* **'char·ac·ter·ize** caractériser; être caractéristique de.

cha·rade [ʃə'rɑːd] charade *f.*

char·coal ['tʃɑːkoul] charbon *m* (de bois); *peint.* fusain *m;* **'~-burn·er** charbonnier *m.*

chare [tʃɛə] **1.** faire des ménages en ville; travailler à la journée; **2.** *usu.* ~*s pl.* travaux *m/pl.* domestiques.

charge [tʃɑːdʒ] **1.** ✕, ⚖, ⚒, ♪, *foot.,*

wagon, cartouche: charge *f* (*a. fig.*) (de, *of*); emploi *m*, fonction *f*; *eccl.* cure *f*; devoir *m*; soin *m*, garde *f*; recommandation *f*; *arme à feu*: décharge *f*; ✕ *a.* attaque *f*; *foot. a.* choc *m*; ⚖ plainte *f*, chef *m* d'accusation, réquisitoire *m*; *fig.* privilège *m* (sur, *on*); prix *m*; *admin.* droits *m/pl.*; ✝ ~s *pl.* frais *m/pl.*; tarif *m*; ✝ ~ *account* compte *m* crédit d'achats; *be in* ~ *of* être préposé à la garde de (*qch.*); *take* ~ *of* se charger de; *free of* ~ exempt de frais; franco; à titre gratuit; **2.** *v/t.* charger (*a.* ✕); passer (à, *to*) (*dépense*); débiter (des marchandises à un client, *goods to a customer*); accuser, inculper (q. de qch., *s.o. with s.th.*); ⚖ *the jury* faire le résumé des débats; ~ *on, upon* foncer sur (*q.*); porter sur (*la note*); ~ *s.o. a price* demander un prix à q. (pour qch., *for s.th.*); **'charge·a·ble** □ inculpable (de, *with*); imputable (à, *to*); à la charge (de, *to, on*).

char·gé d'af·faires *pol.* ['ʃɑːʒei dæˈfɛə] chargé *m* d'affaires.

charg·er ✕, *poét.* ['tʃɑːdʒə] cheval *m* de bataille, cheval *m* d'armes.

char·i·ot *poét., hist.* ['tʃæriət] char *m*; **char·i·ot·eer** [~'tiə] conducteur *m* de char.

char·i·ta·ble □ ['tʃæritəbl] charitable; indulgent (*personne*); de charité (*œuvre*); ~ *society* société *f* de bienfaisance.

char·i·ty ['tʃæriti] charité *f*; bienfaisance *f*, aumônes *f/pl.*; œuvre *f* de bienfaisance; fondation *f* pieuse; *sister of* ~ fille *f* de la Charité, sœur *f* de charité; ~ *begins at home* charité bien ordonnée commence par soi-même; **'~·child** enfant *mf* élevé(e) dans un orphelinat; **'~·school** orphelinat *m*.

char·la·tan ['ʃɑːlətən] charlatan *m*; **'char·la·tan·ry** charlatanerie *f*.

char·lotte *cuis.* ['ʃɑːlət] charlotte *f*.

charm [tʃɑːm] **1.** charme *m* (*a. fig.*); porte-bonheur *m/inv.*; sortilège *m*; **2.** jeter un sort sur; *fig.* charmer; ~ *away etc.* charmer (*les ennuis etc.*); *bear a* ~*ed life* F être verni; **'charm·er** *fig.* charmeur (-euse *f*) *m*; F jolie femme *f*; **'charm·ing** □ charmant, ravissant.

char·nel-house ['tʃɑːnlhaus] charnier *m*, ossuaire *m*.

chart [tʃɑːt] **1.** ⚓ carte *f* marine; ⊕ graphique *m*; tableau *m*; **2.** dresser la carte de; porter sur une carte.

char·ter ['tʃɑːtə] **1.** charte *f*; privilège *m* (*a. fig.*); ⚓ affrètement *m*; (*usu.* ~*·party*) charte-partie (*pl.* chartes-parties) *f*; *Am.* ~ *member* membre *m* fondateur; **2.** instituer (*une compagnie*) par charte; ~*ed accountant* expert *m* comptable.

char·wom·an ['tʃɑːwumən] femme *f* de journée *ou* de ménage.

char·y □ ['tʃɛəri] (*of*) circonspect; chiche (de).

chase[1] [tʃeis] **1.** chasse *f* (*a.* = *proie*), poursuite *f* (*a. fig.*); *beasts of* ~ bêtes *f/pl.* fauves; **2.** chasser; poursuivre (*a. fig.*); *fig.* donner la chasse à (*q.*); *v/i.* (*usu.* ~ *off*) partir à la hâte.

chase[2] [~] ciseler; sertir (*un bijou*).

chase[3] *typ.* [~] châssis *m*.

chas·er[1] ['tʃeisə] chasseur (-euse *f*) *m* (*a.* ✈); ⚓ (*navire m*) chasseur *m*.

chas·er[2] [~] ciseleur *m*.

chasm ['kæzm] gouffre *m* béant; gorge *f*; fissure *f*; abîme *m* (*a. fig.*); *fig.* immense lacune *f*.

chas·sis ['ʃæsi], *pl.* -sis [-siz] châssis *m*.

chaste □ [tʃeist] chaste, pudique; pur (*a. style*).

chas·ten ['tʃeisn] châtier (*q., son style, ses passions*); assagir (*q.*).

chas·tise [tʃæs'taiz] corriger; **chas·tise·ment** ['~tizmənt] châtiment *m*.

chas·ti·ty ['tʃæstiti] chasteté *f*; *fig.* pureté *f*.

chas·u·ble *eccl.* ['tʃæzjubl] chasuble *f*.

chat [tʃæt] **1.** causerie *f*; *télév.* ~ *show* causerie *f* télévisée; **2.** causer, bavarder.

chat·tels ['tʃætlz] *pl.* (*usu. goods and* ~) biens *m/pl.* et effets *m/pl.*; meubles *m/pl.*

chat·ter ['tʃætə] **1.** bavarder; caqueter (*personne, a. oiseau*); jaser (*oiseau, a. personne*); claquer (*dents*); **2.** caquet(age) *m*; bavardage *m*; **'~·box** F babillard(e *f*) *m*; **'chat·ter·er** bavard(e *f*) *m*.

chat·ty ['tʃæti] causeur (-euse *f*) (*personne*); sur le ton de la conversation (*article*).

chauf·feur ['ʃoufə] chauffeur *m*; **chauf·feuse** [~'fɔːz] chauffeuse *f*.

chau·vin·ism ['ʃouvinizm] chauvinisme *m*; **'chau·vin·ist** chauvin(e f) m; **'chau·vin·is·tic** (~ally) chauvin, chauviniste.

chaw sl. [tʃɔ:] mâcher; Am. sl. ~ up usu. fig. démolir; massacrer.

cheap □ [tʃi:p] bon marché, pas cher (chère f); à prix réduits; fig. trivial (-aux m/pl.), vulgaire; F feel ~ ne pas être dans son assiette; hold ~ faire peu de cas de; F on the ~ à peu de frais; ⨂ jack camelot m; ⨁~ money policy politique f de facilités d'escompte; **'cheap·en** v/t. baisser le prix de; v/i. diminuer de prix; **'cheap·skate** Am. sl. radin m.

cheat [tʃi:t] 1. trompeur (-euse f) m; escroc m; jeux: tricheur (-euse f) m; 2. tromper; frauder; frustrer (q. de qch., s.o. [out] of s.th.); fig. échapper à; **'cheat·ing** tromperie f; jeux: tricherie f.

check [tʃek] 1. échec m (a. jeu, a. ⨂); revers m (a. ⨂); arrêt m; frein m; contrôle m; billet m, ticket m; Am. bulletin m (de bagages); ✝ Am. see cheque; Am. restaurant: addition f; tex. étoffe m en damier; carreau m; ~ pattern damier m; Am. F pass (ou hand) in one's ~s mourir, avaler sa chique; keep s.o. in ~ tenir q. en échec; 2. faire échec à (a. jeu): contenir; arrêter; retenir; refréner; vérifier (un compte); pointer (des noms); (souv. ~ up on) contrôler, vérifier; (faire) enregistrer (ses bagages); Am. déposer (son chapeau au vestiaire); v/i. s'arrêter (devant, at); refuser (cheval); ~ in arriver; descendre à un hôtel; s'inscrire sur le registre d'un hôtel; aéroport: se présenter à l'enregistrement; ~ off cocher, pointer; ~ out v/i. partir; régler son compte ou la note en quittant un hôtel; v/t. retirer (ses bagages etc.); surt. Am. vérifier, contrôler; ~ up v/t. contrôler (des renseignements); v/i. faire la vérification; **~ ac·count** Am. compte m courant; **'~·book** Am. carnet m de chèques, chéquier m; **'check·er** contrôleur m; ~s pl. Am. jeu m de dames; see chequer; **'check·er·board** Am. damier m; équiquier m; **'check·ered** Am. see chequered; **check·'in** aéroport: enregistrement m; ~ counter (guichet m d')enregistrement m; ~ desk hôtel: réception f; your ~ time is at ... présentez-vous à l'enregistrement à ...; **'check·ing** répression f;

contrôle m; enregistrement m; **'check(·ing)·room** vestiaire m; ⨂ Am. consigne f; **'check·list** liste f de contrôle, checklist f; **'check'mate** 1. échec et mat m; 2. mater; faire échec et mat à (a. fig.); **check·'out** (a. ~ counter) caisse f (à la sortie d'un self-service etc.); **'check·up** vérification f; F visite f médicale.

cheek [tʃi:k] 1. joue f; F toupet m; ⨁ poulie: joue f; manivelle: bras m; étau: mâchoire f; see jowl; 2. F faire l'insolent avec; **'cheek·y** F insolent, effronté.

cheep [tʃi:p] piauler.

cheer [tʃiə] 1. (bonne) disposition f; encouragement m; bonne chère f; hourra m; bravos m/pl.; applaudissements m/pl.; be of good ~ prendre courage; three ~s! un ban (pour, for)!; vive (q.)!; 2. v/t. applaudir (q.); (a. ~ up) égayer, relever le moral de; (a. ~ on) encourager; v/i. applaudir; pousser des vivats; (a. ~ up) reprendre sa gaieté; **cheer·ful** □ ['~ful] gai; allègre; riant; **'cheer·ful·ness**, **'cheer·i·ness** gaieté f; **cheer·i·o** ['~ri'ou] F à bientôt!; à la vôtre!; □ **'cheer·less** triste, sombre; **'cheer·y** □ gai, joyeux (-euse f).

cheese [tʃi:z] fromage m; hard ~ sl. ça, c'est de la déveine; **'~·cake** talmouse f; **'~·mon·ger** marchand(e f) m de fromage; **'~·par·ing** pelure f de fromage; fig. lésine f. **chees·y** ['tʃi:zi] caséeux (-euse f); de fromage.

chef [ʃef] chef m de cuisine.

chem·i·cal ['kemikl] 1. □ chimique; 2. ~s pl. produits m/pl. chimiques.

che·mise [ʃi'mi:z] chemise f (de femme).

chem·ist ['kemist] chimiste mf; (ou pharmaceutical ~) pharmacien (-ne f) m; **'chem·is·try** chimie f.

chem·o·ther·a·py ⚕ [kemo'θerəpi] chimiothérapie f.

cheque ✝ [tʃek] chèque m; not negotiable (ou crossed) ~ chèque m barré; ~ ac·count compte m courant; **'~·book** carnet m de chèques, chéquier m.

cheq·uer ['tʃekə] 1. usu. ~s pl. quadrillage m; 2. quadriller; **'chequered** à carreaux, en échiquier; diapré; fig. accidenté (vie).

cher·ish ['tʃeriʃ] chérir; fig. caresser.

che·root [ʃə'ru:t] manille *m*.

cher·ry ['tʃeri] **1.** cerise *f*; *arbre*: cerisier *m*; **2.** cerise *adj./inv.*; vermeil(le *f*) (*lèvres*).

cher·ub ['tʃerəb], *pl.* -ubs, -u·bim ['⁓əbim] chérubin *m*; **che·ru·bic** [tʃə'ru:bik] chérubique; de chérubin.

cher·vil ♧ ['tʃə:vil] cerfeuil *m*.

chess [tʃes] (jeu *m* d')échecs *m/pl.*; '⁓·board échiquier *m*; '⁓·man *jeu d'échecs*: pièce *f*.

chest [tʃest] caisse *f*, coffre *m*; *anat.* poitrine *f*; ⁓ *of drawers* commode *f*; ♪ ⁓ *note* note *f* de poitrine; *get it off one's* ⁓ dire ce qu'on a sur le cœur.

chest·nut ['tʃesnʌt] **1.** châtaigne *f*, marron *m*; *arbre*: châtaignier *m* (commun); marronnier *m*; *fig.* vieille histoire *f*; **2.** châtain (-aine *f*).

chest·y F ['tʃesti] de poitrine (*toux etc.*); qui a la poitrine bien développée.

che·val-glass [ʃə'vælglɑ:s] psyché *f*.

chev·a·lier [ʃevə'liə] chevalier *m*.

chev·i·ot *tex.* ['tʃeviət] cheviotte *f*.

chev·ron ✕ ['ʃevrən] chevron *m* (*d'ancienneté de service*); galon *m* (*de grade*).

chev·y F ['tʃevi] **1.** poursuite *f*; *sp.* (jeu *m* de) barres *f/pl.*; **2.** poursuivre; relancer (*q.*).

chew [tʃu:] *v/t.* mâcher; F ⁓ *the fat* bavarder; F ⁓ *the rag Brit.* ronchonner, *Am.* bavarder; *v/i. fig.* méditer (*sur* [up]*on, over*); '**chew·ing·gum** chewing-gum *m*.

chi·cane [ʃi'kein] **1.** chicane *f*; **2.** chicaner; **chi'can·er·y** chicanerie *f*; *fig.* arguties *f/pl.*

chick, chick·en ['tʃik(in)] **1.** poussin *m*, poulet *m*; **2.** *sl. chicken out* se dégonfler, flancher, caner.

chicken...: '⁓-feed *Am.* mangeaille *f*; *sl.* petite monnaie *f*; '⁓-heart·ed, '⁓-liv·ered froussard; '⁓-pox ✿ varicelle *f*; ⁓ **run**, *Am.* ⁓ **yard** poulailler *m*.

chick...: '⁓-pea ♧ pois *m* chiche; '⁓-weed ♧ mouron *m* des oiseaux.

chic·o·ry ['tʃikəri] chicorée *f*.

chid [tʃid] *prét. et p.p.*, '**chid·den** *p.p.* de chide.

chide *poét.* [tʃaid] [*irr.*] gronder.

chief [tʃi:f] **1.** □ principal (-aux *m/pl.*); premier (-ère *f*); en chef; ⁓ *clerk* chef *m* de bureau; premier

clerc *m*; **2.** chef *m*; F patron *m*; ...-in-⁓ ... en chef; **chief·tain** ['⁓tən] chef *m* de clan.

chil·blain ['tʃilblein] engelure *f*.

child [tʃaild] enfant *mf*; *be a good* ⁓ être sage; *from a* ⁓ dès mon *etc.* enfance; *with* ⁓ enceinte; '⁓·bed couches *f/pl.*; '⁓·birth accouchement *m*; '**child·hood** enfance *f*; '**child·ish** □ enfantin; *péj.* puéril; '**child·ish·ness** *péj.* enfantillage *m*; puérilité *f*; '**child·less** sans enfant(s); '**child·like** enfantin; *fig.* naïf (-ïve *f*); **chil·dren** ['tʃildrən] *pl.* de child; **child's play** *fig.* jeu *m* d'enfant.

chill [tʃil] **1.** froid, glacé; **2.** froideur *f*; froid *m* (*a. fig.*); ✿ coup *m* de froid; *take the* ⁓ *off* dégourdir (*un liquide*), chambrer (*le vin*); **3.** *v/t.* refroidir, glacer; *fig.* donner le frisson à (*q.*); *métall.* tremper en coquille; ⁓*ed meat* viande *f* frigorifiée; *v/i.* se refroidir, se glacer; '**chill·ness**, '**chill·i·ness** froid *m*, fraîcheur *f*; (*a. fig.*) froideur *f*; '**chill·y** froid; frais (fraîche *f*).

chime [tʃaim] **1.** carillon *m*; *fig.* harmonie *f*; **2.** carillonner; *v/i. fig.* s'accorder, s'harmoniser (avec, *with*); ⁓ *in* intervenir.

chi·me·ra [kai'miərə] chimère *f*; **chi·mer·i·cal** □ [⁓'merikl] chimérique, imaginaire.

chim·ney ['tʃimni] cheminée *f* (*a. alp.*); *lampe*: verre *m*; '⁓-piece (chambranle *m* de) cheminée *f*; '⁓-pot mitre *f* ou pot *m* de cheminée; F *fig. chapeau*: tuyau *m* de poêle; '⁓-stack, '⁓-stalk souche *f*; (corps *m* de) cheminée *f*; cheminée *f* d'usine; '⁓-sweep(·er) ramoneur *m*.

chim·pan·zee *zo.* [tʃimpən'zi:] chimpanzé *m*.

chin[1] [tʃin] **1.** menton *m*; **2.** *gymn. Am.* (*usu.* ⁓ *o.s.*) faire une traction à la barre fixe.

chin[2] *sl.* [⁓] discourir, jaboter.

chi·na ['tʃainə] porcelaine *f*; ♀·**man** Chinois *m*.

chine [tʃain] *anat.* échine *f*; *cuis.* échinée *f*; *géog.* arête *f*.

Chi·nese ['tʃai'ni:z] **1.** chinois; **2.** *ling.* chinois *m*; Chinois(e *f*) *m*.

chink[1] [tʃiŋk] fente *f*; *mur*: lézarde *f*; *porte*: entrebâillement *m*.

chink[2] [⁓] **1.** *métal, verre*: tintement *m*; **2.** (faire) sonner (*son argent*); (faire) tinter.

chink³ *sl.* [~] Chinois *m*.

chintz *tex.* [tʃints] perse *f*, indienne *f*.

chin·wag *sl.* ['tʃinwæg] causerie *f*.

chip [tʃip] **1.** éclat *m*; *bois*: copeau *m*; *jeu*: jeton *m*; *ordinateur*: chip *m*; *cuis.* (potato) ~s *pl.* Brit. (pommes *f/pl.* de terre) frites *f/pl.*, Am. chips *m/pl.*; F have a ~ on one's shoulder chercher noise à tout le monde; **2.** *v/t.* tailler par éclats; doler (*du bois*); ébrécher (*un couteau*); enlever un morceau à (*qch.*); *v/i.* s'écailler, s'ébrécher; F ~ in(to) intervenir dans; se mêler à; **chip·muck** ['tʃipmʌk], **chip·munk** ['tʃipmʌŋk] tamias *m*; '**chip·pan** friteuse *f*; '**chip·py** sec (sèche *f*); sans saveur.

chi·rop·o·dist [ki'rɔpədist] pédicure *mf*; **chi'rop·o·dy** chirurgie *f* pédicure.

chirp [tʃə:p] **1.** gazouiller, pépier, ramager; grésiller (*grillon*); **2.** gazouillement *m*; *grillon*: grésillement *m*; '**chirp·y** F d'humeur gaie.

chirr [tʃə:] grésiller.

chir·rup ['tʃirəp] **1.** gazouillement *m etc.*; **2.** gazouiller *etc.*

chis·el ['tʃizl] **1.** ciseau *m*; burin *m*; **2.** ciseler; buriner (*du métal*); *sl.* filouter; '**chis·el·er** ciseleur *m*; *sl.* escroc *m*.

chit [tʃit] mioche *mf*; a ~ of a girl une simple gosse *f*.

chit-chat ['tʃittʃæt] bavardages *m/pl.*

chiv·al·rous □ ['ʃivlrəs] chevaleresque; courtois; '**chiv·al·ry** chevalerie *f*; courtoisie *f*.

chive ♀ [tʃaiv] ciboulette *f*.

chiv·y F ['tʃivi] *see* chevy.

chlo·ral ⚗ ['klɔ:rl] chloral *m*; **chlo·ride** ['~aid] chlorure *m*; **chlo·rine** ['~i:n] chlore *m*; **chlo·ro·form** ['~əfɔ:m] **1.** chloroforme *m*; **2.** chloroformer.

chock ⊕ [tʃɔk] **1.** cale *f*; **2.** caler; '~-a-'block F bondé (de, with); '~-'full comble.

choc·o·late ['tʃɔkəlit] chocolat *m*; ~ cream chocolat *m* fourré à la crème.

choice [tʃɔis] **1.** choix *m*; for ~ de préférence; leave s.o. no ~ ôter à q. toute alternative; make (ou take) one's ~ faire son choix; **2.** □ (bien) choisi; d'élite; de choix; surfin; † surchoix; † ~ quality première qualité *f*.

choir △, ♪ ['kwaiə] chœur *m*; '~-

mas·ter chef *m* de chœur; ~ **stalls** *pl.* stalles *f/pl.* (de chœur).

choke [tʃouk] **1.** *v/t.* étouffer; suffoquer (*a. fig.*); étrangler; ⊕ engorger; (*usu.* ~ up) obstruer, boucher; (*usu.* ~ down) étouffer, ravaler; fermer (*le gaz*); ~ off se débarrasser de; décourager; *v/i.* étouffer, se boucher; **2.** étranglement *m*; ⊕ étrangleur *m*; starter *m*; ⚡ ~ coil bobine *f* de réactance; self *f*; '~-**bore** ⊕ (fusil *m* de chasse à) choke-bore *m*; '~-**damp** ⚒ mofette *f*; '**chok·er** F *co.* foulard *m* (d'ouvrier); cravate *f* de fourrure; col *m* montant; *perles*: collier *m* court.

chol·er·a ♨ ['kɔlərə] choléra *m*; '**chol·er·ic** colérique; irascible.

cho·les·te·rol [kə'lestərəl] cholestérol *m*.

choose [tʃu:z] [*irr.*] choisir; *v/t.* opter pour; *v/i.* ~ to (*inf.*) vouloir que (*sbj.*), aimer mieux (*inf.*); '**choos·y** F difficile.

chop¹ [tʃɔp] **1.** coup *m* de hache; *cuis.* côtelette *f*; ~s *pl.* bajoues *f/pl.*; babines *f/pl.*; ⊕ mâchoires *f/pl.*; ~s and changes vicissitudes *f/pl.*; girouetteries *f/pl.*; **2.** *v/t.* couper, fendre, hacher; (*souv.* ~ up) couper en morceaux; ~ down abattre; *v/i.* clapoter (*mer*); ~ about changer; ~ and change girouetter; tergiverser; ~ping sea mer *f* clapoteuse.

chop² † [~] marque *f*; first ~ (de) première qualité *f*.

chop-house ['tʃɔphaus] restaurant *m* populaire; '**chop·per** couperet *m*; *sl.* moulin *m*, banane *f* (*hélicoptère*); '**chop·ping-block** hachoir *m*; '**chop·py** variable; clapoteux (-euse *f*) (*mer*); '**chop·stick** baguette *f*, bâtonnet *m* (*des Chinois*).

cho·ral □ ['kɔ:rl] choral (-als *ou* -aux *m/pl.*); chanté en chœur; **cho·ral(e)** ♪ [kɔ'rɑ:l] choral (*pl.* -als) *m*.

chord [kɔ:d] ♪, ♪, poét., fig. corde *f*; ♪ accord *m*; anat. corde *f* (vocale), cordon *m*.

chore *surt.* Am. [tʃɔ:] *see* chare.

chor·e·og·ra·phy [kɔri'ɔgrəfi] choréographie *f*.

chor·is·ter ['kɔristə] choriste *mf*; *eccl.* enfant *m* de chœur; *Am. a.* chef *m* de chœur.

cho·rus ['kɔ:rəs] **1.** chœur *m*; refrain *m*; **2.** répéter en chœur; ~ **girl** girl *f*.

chose [tʃouz] *prét.*, **'cho·sen** *p.p. de*
choose.

chough *orn.* [tʃʌf] crave *m.*

chouse F [tʃaus] **1.** filouterie *f*;
2. filouter.

chow *Am. sl.* [tʃau] mangeaille *f.*

chrism ['krizm] chrême *m.*

Christ [kraist] le Christ *m*, Jésus-
Christ *m*; *for* ~'s sake pour l'amour de
Dieu; F *for* ~'s sake!, ~! Bon Dieu de
Bon Dieu!

chris·ten ['krisn] baptiser; **Chris-
ten·dom** ['~dəm] chrétienté *f*;
'chris·ten·ing 1. de baptême;
2. baptême *m.*

Chris·tian ['kristjən] **1.** □ chré-
tien(ne *f*); ~ *name* prénom *m*, nom
m de baptême; **2.** chrétien (ne *f*) *m*;
Chris·ti·an·i·ty [.tiˈæniti] christianisme *m*; **Chris·tian·ize** ['~-
tjənaiz] convertir au christianisme;
christianiser.

Christ·mas ['krisməs] **1.** Noël *m*,
(fête *f* de) Noël *f*; **2.** de Noël; ~ **box**
étrennes *f/pl.*; gratification *f*; ~ **Day**
le jour de Noël; ~ **Eve** la veille de
Noël; ~ **pres·ent** cadeau *m* de Noël;
~ **tide**, ~ **time** (saison *f* de) Noël; ~
tree arbre *m* de Noël.

chro·mat·ic ♪, *phys.* [krəˈmætik]
1. (~ally) chromatique; **2.** ~s *sg.*
chromatique *f.*

chrome 🜍 [kroum] *teinture:* bi-
chromate *m* de potasse; **chro·mi-
um** ['~jəm] chrome *m*; **'chro·mi-
um-plat·ed** chromé; **chro·mo-
lith·o·graph** ['kroumouˈliθəgrɑːf]
chromolithographie *f.*

chron·ic ['krɔnik] (~ally) (*usu.* ✚)
chronique, constant; *sl.* insupportable; **chron·i·cle** ['~kl] **1.** chronique
f; **2.** enregistrer, faire la chronique
de; **'chron·i·cler** chroniqueur *m.*

chron·o·log·i·cal □ [krɔnəˈlɔdʒikl]
chronologique; ~*ly* par ordre de
dates; **chro·nol·o·gy** [krəˈnɔlədʒi]
chronologie *f.*   [nomètre *m.*]

chro·nom·e·ter [krəˈnɔmitə] chro-⌋

chrys·a·lis *zo.* ['krisəlis], *pl. a.* **chrys-
al·i·des** [~ˈsælidiːz] chrysalide *f.*

chrys·an·the·mum ♀ [kriˈsænθə-
məm] chrysanthème *m.*

chub *icht.* [tʃʌb] chabot *m* de
rivière; **'chub·by** F potelé; jouflu
(*visage*); rebondi (*joues*).

chuck¹ [tʃʌk] **1.** gloussement *m*;
my ~! mon petit chou!; **2.** glousser;
3. petit!, petit! (*appel aux poules*).

chuck² F [~] **1.** lancer; ~ *out* flanquer
(*q.*) à la porte; ~ *under the chin* donner une tape sous le menton; **2.** congé *m*; lancement *m.*

chuck³ ⊕ [~] mandrin *m.*

chuck·le ['tʃʌkl] rire tout bas.

chum F [tʃʌm] **1.** camarade *mf*;
copain *m*, copine *f*; *be great* ~*s* être
(amis) intimes; **2.** se lier d'amitié
(avec, *with*).

chump F [tʃʌmp] tronçon *m* de
bois; tête *f*; nigaud(e *f*) *m*; *Brit. sl.*
off one's ~ timbré; fou (fol *devant
une voyelle ou un h muet*; folle *f*);
déboussolé.

chunk F [tʃʌŋk] gros morceau *m*;
pain *a.* quignon *m.*

church [tʃəːtʃ] **1.** église *f*; *protestantisme:* temple *m*; *attr.* d'église; *be
of* l'Église; ♀ *of England* Église *f* anglicane; ~ *rate* dîme *f*; ~ *service* office *m*; **2.** *be* ~*ed* faire ses relevailles (*femme après ses couches*); '~-
go·er pratiquant(e *f*) *m*; **'church-
ing** relevailles *f/pl.* (*d'une femme
après ses couches*); **'church'ward-
en** marguillier *m*; pipe *f* hollandaise; **'church·y** F bigot; **'church-
'yard** cimetière *m.*

churl [tʃəːl] manant *m*; *fig.* rustre *m*;
F grincheux (-euse *f*) *m*; **'churl·ish**
□ mal élevé; grincheux (-euse *f*),
hargneux (-euse *f*).

churn [tʃəːn] **1.** baratte *f*; **2.** *v/t.* baratter; *fig.* agiter (*qch.*); *v/i.* faire du
beurre.

chute [ʃuːt] chute *f* d'eau; *sp.* glissière *f*; ✈ couloir *m.*

chut·ney ['tʃʌtni] chutney *m.*

chyle *physiol.* [kail] chyle *m.*

chyme ✚ [kaim] chyme *m.*

ci·ca·da *zo.* [siˈkɑːdə] cigale *f.*

cic·a·trice ['sikətris] cicatrice *f*;
'cic·a·trize (se) cicatriser.

cic·e·ro·ne [tʃitʃəˈrouni], *pl.* **-ni**
[~ni:] cicérone *m.*

ci·der ['saidə] cidre *m.*

ci·gar [siˈgɑː] cigare *m*; **ci'gar-case**
étui *m* à cigares; **ci'gar-cut·ter**
coupe-cigares *m/inv.*

cig·a·rette [sigəˈret] cigarette *f*;
cig·a·rette-case étui *m* à cigarettes; **cig·a·rette-end** mégot *m*; **cig-
a·rette-hold·er** fume-cigarette
m/inv.; **cig·a·rette-pa·per** papier
m à cigarettes.

ci·gar-hold·er [siˈgɑːhouldə] fume-
cigare *m/inv.*

cil·i·ar·y ['siliəri] ciliaire.

cinch *Am. sl.* [sintʃ] certitude *f*; chose *f* certaine.

cinc·ture ['siŋktʃə] ceinture *f*.

cin·der ['sində] cendre *f*; ~s *pl. a.* escarbilles *f/pl.*; **Cin·der·el·la** [ə'relə] Cendrillon *f* (*a. fig.*); '**cin·der-track** *sp.* piste *f* cendrée.

cin·e·cam·er·a ['sini'kæmərə] caméra *f*; **cin·e·film** ['sinifilm] film *m* de format réduit.

cin·e·ma ['sinimə] cinéma *m*; F ciné *m*; '~-**go·er** amateur *m* de cinéma, cinéphile *mf*; **cin·e·mat·o·graph** [~'mætəgra:f] 1. cinématographe *m*, F cinéma *m*; 2. filmer; **cin·e·mat·o·graph·ic** [~mætə'græfik] (~ally) cinématographique.

cin·er·ar·y ['sinərəri] cinéraire.

cin·na·bar ['sinəba:] cinabre *m*; vermillon *m*.

cin·na·mon ['sinəmən] 1. cannelle *f*; *arbre*: cannelier *m*; 2. cannelle *adj./inv.* (*couleur*).

cinque [siŋk] *dés*: cinq *m*.

ci·pher ['saifə] 1. zéro *m* (*a. fig.*); *fig.* nullité *f*; *code secret*: chiffre *m*; message *m* chiffré; 2. chiffrer.

cir·cle ['sə:kl] 1. cercle *m* (*a. fig.*); *fig.* milieu *m*, monde *m*, coterie *f*; *théât.* galerie *f*; 🎭 ceinture *f*; 2. *v/t.* ceindre; *v/i.* tournoyer, circuler; **cir·clet** ['~klit] petit cercle *m*; anneau *m*.

circs F [sə:ks] *see* circumstances.

cir·cuit ['sə:kit] ⚡, *sp.* circuit *m*; 🚗 tournée *f*, circonscription *f*; *soleil*: révolution *f*; *ville*: pourtour *m*; 🚗 parcours *m*; ⚡ integrated ~ circuit *m* intégré; *radio*: ⚡ short ~ courtcircuit (*pl.* courts-circuits) *m*; ⚡ ~ breaker coupe-circuit *m/inv.*; **cir·cu·i·tous** □ [sə'kju:itəs] détourné, sinueux (-euse *f*).

cir·cu·lar ['sə:kjulə] 1. □ circulaire; de cercle; ~ letter (lettre *f*) circulaire *f*; ✝ ~ note lettre *f* de crédit circulaire; ~ railway chemin *m* de fer de ceinture; ~ saw scie *f* circulaire; 2. (lettre *f*) circulaire *f*.

cir·cu·late ['sə:kjuleit] *v/i.* circuler; *v/t.* faire circuler (*un bruit, l'air, le vin*); mettre en circulation; ✝ transmettre par voie d'endossement; '**cir·cu·lat·ing**: ~ decimal fraction *f* périodique; ~ library bibliothèque *f* circulante; **cir·cu·la·tion** circulation *f*; *fonds*: roulement *m*; *journal*: tirage *m*; '**cir·cu·la·to·ry** circulatoire; ✻ ~ system appareil *m* circulatoire; ~ troubles *pl.* troubles *m/pl.* de la circulation.

circum... [sə:kəm] circon..., circum...; **cir·cum·cise** ['~saiz] circoncire (*le prépuce*); **cir·cum·ci·sion** [~'siʒn] circoncision *f*; **cir·cum·fer·ence** [sə'kʌmfərəns] circonférence *f*; périphérie *f*; **cir·cum·flex** ['sə:kəmfleks] accent *m* circonflexe; **cir·cum·ja·cent** [~'dʒeisnt] circonjacent; **cir·cum·lo·cu·tion** [~lə'kju:ʃn] circonlocution *f*; ambages *f/pl.*; **cir·cum·nav·i·gate** [~'nævigeit] faire le tour de; **cir·cum·nav·i·ga·tor** circumnavigateur *m*; **cir·cum·scribe** ⚡ [~'skraib] circonscrire; *fig.* limiter; **cir·cum·scrip·tion** [~'skripʃn] ⚡ circonscription *f*; *fig.* restriction *f*; **circum·spect** □ ['~spekt] circonspect; prudent; **cir·cum·spec·tion** [~'spekʃn] circonspection *f*; prudence *f*; **cir·cum·stance** ['~stəns] circonstance *f*; détail *m*; *in* (*ou under*) *the* ~s puisqu'il en est ainsi; ~ *dans une ... situation*; **cir·cum·stan·tial** [~'stænʃl] circonstanciel(le *f*); détaillé; ⚖ ~ evidence preuves *f/pl.* indirectes; **cir·cum·stan·ti·al·i·ty** ['~stænʃi'æliti] abondance *f* de détails; détail *m*; **cir·cum·val·la·tion** [~və'leiʃn] retranchements *m/pl.*; **cir·cum·vent** [~'vent] circonvenir.

cir·cus ['sə:kəs] cirque *m*; *place*: rond-point (*pl.* ronds-points) *m*.

cir·rho·sis ✻ [si'rousis] cirrhose *f*.

cir·rous ['sirəs] cirreux (-euse *f*); **cir·rus** ['~rəs], *pl.* -ri ['~rai] *nuages*: cirrus *m*; ⚘ vrille *f*.

cis·tern ['sistən] réservoir *m* à eau; citerne *f* (*souterraine*).

cit·a·del ['sitədl] citadelle *f*.

ci·ta·tion [sai'teiʃn] citation *f* (*a.* ⚖); *Am. souv.* citation *f* à l'ordre du jour; **cite** [sait] citer; assigner (*un témoin*).

cit·i·zen ['sitizn] citoyen(ne *f*) *m*; bourgeois(e *f*) *m*; *a. Am.* civil *m*; *attr.* civique; '**cit·i·zen·ship** droit *m* de cité; nationalité *f*.

cit·ric ac·id ['sitrik'æsid] acide *m* citrique; **cit·ron** ['~rən] cédrat *m*; *arbre*: cédratier *m*; **cit·rus** ['~rəs] agrumes *m/pl.*

cit·y ['siti] 1. ville *f*; *Londres*: the ♀

la Cité; *fig.* les affaires *f/pl.*; 2. urbain, municipal (-aux *m/pl.*); *Am.* ~ *editor* rédacteur *m* chargé des nouvelles locales; *Am.* ~ *father* conseiller *m* municipal; ~ *hall* hôtel *m* de ville; *Am.* ~ *manager* chef *m* des services municipaux.

civ·ic ['sivik] 1. civique; municipal (-aux *m/pl.*); ~ *rights pl.* droits *m/pl.* de citoyen, droits *m/pl.* civiques; 2. ~*s pl.* instruction *f* civique.

civ·il □ ['sivl] civil (*a.* 🏛️); poli, courtois; civique (*droits*); ~ *engineering* travaux *m/pl.* publics; ~ *rights movement* mouvement *m* de défense des droits du citoyen; ♀ *Servant* fonctionnaire *m/f*; ♀ *Service Administration f*; **ci·vil·ian** ⚔️ [si'viljən] civil *m*; ~ *population* civils *m/pl.*; **ci·vil·i·ty** civilité *f*; politesse *f*; **civ·i·li·za·tion** [~lai'zeiʃn] civilisation *f*; *fig.* culture *f*; **'civ·i·lize** civiliser.

clack [klæk] 1. claquement *m*; *fig.* caquet *m*; ⊕ (soupape *f* à) clapet *m*; 2. claquer; *fig.* caqueter.

clad [klæd] *prét. et p.p. de clothe.*

claim [kleim] 1. demande *f*; revendication *f*; droit *m*, titre *m* (à, to); 🏛️ réclamation *f*; *dette*: créance *f*; ⚒️ concession *f*; *surt. Am.* terrain *m* revendiqué par un chercheur d'or *etc.*; *lay* ~ *to* prétendre à; 2. réclamer; revendiquer; prétendre à; ~ *to be* se prétendre (*qch.*); **'claim·a·ble** revendicable, exigible; **'claim·ant** prétendant(e *f*) *m*; réclamant(e *f*) *m*.

clair·voy·ance [klɛə'vɔiəns] voyance *f*; *fig.* clairvoyance *f*; **clair'voy·ant** voyant(e *f*) *m*.

clam *zo.* [klæm] peigne *m*.

cla·mant *poét.* ['kleimənt] criant; urgent.

clam·ber ['klæmbə] grimper.

clam·mi·ness ['klæminis] moiteur *f* froide; **'clam·my** □ moite; froid et humide; collant.

clam·or·ous □ ['klæmərəs] bruyant; vociférant (*foule etc.*); **'clam·o(u)r** 1. clameur *f*; cris *m/pl.*; 2. vociférer; réclamer à grands cris (qch., for s.th.).

clamp ⊕ [klæmp] 1. crampon *m*; *étau*: mordache *f*; 2. agrafer; cramponner; *fig.* fixer.

clan [klæn] clan *m*; *p.ext.* tribu *f*; *fig.* coterie *f*.

clan·des·tine □ [klæn'destin] clandestin.

clang [klæŋ] 1. bruit *m* métallique *ou* retentissant; 2. (faire) retentir; (faire) résonner; **clang·or·ous** ['klæŋgərəs] retentissant, strident; **'clang·o(u)r** *see clang 1.*

clank [klæŋk] 1. bruit *m* sec; cliquetis *m*; 2. *v/i.* rendre un bruit métallique; *v/t.* faire sonner.

clan·nish *péj.* ['klæniʃ] imbu de l'esprit de coterie; exclusif (-ive *f*).

clap [klæp] 1. battement *m* de mains; applaudissements *m/pl.*; 💊 *sl.* chaude-pisse *f*; 2. *vt/i.* applaudir; *v/t.* donner à (*q.*) une tape (dans le dos, *on the back*); ~ *one's hands* battre des mains; **'~·board** *Am.* bardeau *m*; **'~·net** *chasse*: tirasse *f*; **'clap·per** claquet *m*; *cloche*: battant *m*; **'clap·trap** 1. boniment *m*; phrases *f/pl.* à effet; 2. sans sincérité; creux (creuse *f*).

clar·et ['klærət] bordeaux *m* (rouge); *sl.* sang *m* (*usu. du nez*).

clar·i·fi·ca·tion [klærifi'keiʃn] clarification *f*; *fig.* mise *f* au point; **clar·i·fy** ['~fai] *v/t.* clarifier; *fig.* éclaircir; *v/i.* s'éclaircir.

clar·i·(o·)net [klæri(o)'net] clarinette *f*.

clar·i·ty ['klæriti] clarté *f*.

clash [klæʃ] 1. choc *m*; fracas *m*; *couleurs*: disparate *f*; 2. (faire) résonner; (se) heurter; (s')entrechoquer; *v/i.* faire disparate (*couleurs*).

clasp [klɑːsp] 1. *médaille, broche*: agrafe *f*; *livre, bourse*: fermoir *m*; *collier*: fermeture *f*; *fig.* étreinte *f*; serrement *m* de mains; 2. *v/t.* agrafer; *fig.* étreindre; serrer (*les mains*); ~ *s.o.'s hand* serrer la main à q.; *v/i.* s'agrafer; **'~·knife** couteau *m* pliant; F eustache *m*.

class [klɑːs] 1. classe *f*; cours *m*; genre *m*, sorte *f*, catégorie *f*; *univ. Am.* année *f*; 2. classer; ranger par classes; ~ *with* assimiler à; **'~·'con·scious** conscient de sa classe; imbu de l'esprit de caste.

clas·sic ['klæsik] 1. classique *m*; humaniste *m/f*; ~ *pl.* études *f/pl.* classiques, humanités *f/pl.*; 2. = **'clas·si·cal** □ classique.

clas·si·fi·ca·tion [klæsifi'keiʃn] *plantes etc.*: classification *f*; codification *f*; *navire*: cote *f*; *papiers*:

classement *m*; **clas·si·fied** [ˈ~faid] classifié; secret (-ète *f*); ~ *ads pl.* petites annonces *f/pl.*; **clas·si·fy** [ˈ~fai] classifier; classer; ranger par classes.

class...: '~**mate** camarade *mf* de classe; '~**room** salle *f* de classe; ~ **strug·gle**, ~ **war(fare)** lutte *f* des classes.

clas·sy F [ˈklæsi] chic *inv.*

clat·ter [ˈklætə] **1.** vacarme *m*; bruit *m* (*de tasses etc.*); *fig.* brouhaha *m*; **2.** *v/i.* faire du bruit; retentir; *fig.* bavarder; *v/t.* faire retentir.

clause [klɔːz] clause *f*, article *m*; *gramm.* membre *m* de phrase; proposition *f*.

claus·tral [ˈklɔːstrəl] claustral (-aux *m/pl.*).

claus·tro·pho·bi·a *psych.* [klɔːstrəˈfoubiə] claustrophobie *f*.

clav·i·cle *anat.* [ˈklævikl] clavicule *f*.

claw [klɔː] **1.** griffe *f*; *aigle etc.:* serre *f*; *écrevisse:* pince *f*; ⊕ *étau:* mordache *f*; coup *m* de griffe *etc.*; **2.** griffer; s'accrocher à (*qch.*); **clawed** [~d] armé de griffes *etc.*

clay [klei] argile *f*, glaise *f*; *sp.* ~ *pigeon* pigeon *m* artificiel; **clay·ey** [ˈkleii] argileux (-euse *f*), glaiseux (-euse *f*).

clean [kliːn] **1.** *adj.* □ propre; net (-te *f*) (*assiette, cassure, a. fig.*); **2.** *adv.* tout à fait, absolument; **3.** *v/t.* nettoyer; balayer; faire (*une chambre*); cirer (*les souliers*); ~ *up* nettoyer; *v/i.* faire le nettoyage; F se débarbouiller; '~-'**cut** net(te *f*), bien défini; '**clean·er** nettoyeur *m* (-euse *f*); femme *f* de ménage; ~'s (*shop*) ~s *pl.* teinturerie *f*; *take to the* ~s donner (*qch.*) à la teinturerie; F nettoyer (*q.*), mettre (*q.*) à sec; '**clean·ing** nettoyage *m*; dégraissage *m*; ~ *woman* femme *f* de ménage; **clean·li·ness** [ˈklenlinis] propreté *f*; netteté *f*; **clean·ly 1.** *adv.* [ˈklenli] proprement, nettement; **2.** *adj.* [ˈklenli] propre; **clean·ness** [ˈkliːnnis] propreté *f*; netteté *f*; **cleanse** [klenz] nettoyer (*a.* ⚕); assainir; purifier; '**cleans·er** [ˈklenzə] détergent *m*; démaquillant *f*; **clean·shav·en** [ˈkliːnˈʃeivən] rasé de près; **clean-up** [ˈkliːnˈʌp] nettoyage *m*; *pol.* épuration *f* (*de personnel etc.*).

clear [kliə] **1.** □ *usu.* clair; net(te *f*) (*idée, vision, conscience*); évident;

dégagé; lucide; certain (*de, about*); *fig.* libre (*de, of*); débarrassé (*de, of*); disculpé (*de, of*) (*un soupçon*); ✝ net(te *f*); ~ *of* libre de; exempt de; *as* ~ *as day* clair comme le jour; *get* ~ *of* quitter, sortir de; se dégager de; *steer* ~ *of* éviter, s'écarter de; **2.** ⚓ *in the* ~ en terrain découvert; **3.** *v/t.* éclaircir (*a. fig.*); nettoyer; *fig.* dépeupler; déblayer (*le terrain*) (*a. fig.*); rafraîchir (*l'air*); écarter (*un obstacle*); désencombrer (*une salle*); défricher (*un terrain*); dégager (*une route, une voie*); acquitter (*une dette*); clarifier (*un liquide*); (*a.* ~ *away*) enlever, ôter; disculper (*de of, from*); ✝ *see* ~ *off*; ✝ faire (*un bénéfice net*); arrêter (*un compte*); ⚖ innocenter (*de of, from*); ✝ ~ *off* solder (*des marchandises*); ~ *a port* sortir d'un port; ~ *a ship for action* faire le branle-bas de combat; ~ *one's throat* s'éclaircir la voix; ~ *one's throat* se racler la gorge; *v/i.* (*a.* ~ *up*) s'éclaircir; (*a.* ~ *off*) se dissiper (*nuages, brouillard*); '**clear·ance** dégagement *m*; déblaiement *m*; *boîte à lettres:* levée *f*; ✝ compensation *f* (*d'un chèque*); ⚓, ✝ dédouanement *m*; ⚓ départ *m*; ✝ solde *m*; ⊕ jeu *m*, espace *m* libre; ~ *sale* vente *f* de soldes; '**clear·'cut** net(te *f*); '**clear·ing** éclaircissement *m etc.* (*see clear 3*); *forêt:* clairière *f*; ✝ *see clearance*; ~ *procedure* voie *f* de compensation; ~ *bank* banque *f* de virement; ⚖ *House* chambre *f* de compensation.

cleat ⚓ [kliːt] agrafe *f*; taquet *m*.

cleav·age [ˈkliːvidʒ] fendage *m*; *fig.* scission *f*; *min.* clivage *m*.

cleave[1] [kliːv] [*irr.*] (se) fendre (*a. eau, air*).

cleave[2] [kliːv] *fig.* [~] adhérer, être fidèle (*à, to*); ~ *together* rester fidèles l'un à l'autre. [*ret m* (*de viande*).]

cleav·er [ˈkliːvə] fendoir *m*; coupe-⌡

cleek *sp.* [kliːk] cleek *m*.

clef ♪ [klef] clef *f*, clé *f*.

cleft [kleft] **1.** fente *f*, fissure *f*, crevasse *f*; **2.** *prét. et p.p. de cleave*[1].

clem·en·cy [ˈklemənsi] clémence *f*; '**clem·ent** □ clément.

clench [klentʃ] (se) serrer (*lèvres, dents, poings*); (se) crisper (*mains*).

cler·gy [ˈklɜːdʒi] (membres *m/pl.* du) clergé *m*; '~**man** ecclésiastique *m*; *protestantisme:* pasteur *m*.

close

cler·i·cal ['klerikl] **1.** □ *eccl.* clérical
(-aux *m/pl.*); de bureau; ~ *error*
faute *f* de copiste; **2.** *pol.* clérical *m.*
clerk [klɑːk] employé(e *f*) *m* de bureau; ✝ commis *m*, employé(e *f*) *m*
de magasin; *surt. Am.* vendeur
(-euse *f*) *m* (*de magasin*); *eccl.* clerc
m.
clev·er □ ['klevə] habile, adroit; intelligent; ~ **dick** *Brit. sl.* gros malin
m, je-sais-tout *m*; **'clev·er·ness**
habileté *f*, adresse *f*; intelligence.
clew [kluː] *see* clue.
cli·ché ['kliːʃei] cliché *m.*
click [klik] **1.** cliquetis *m*, bruit *m*
sec; ⊕ cliquet *m*; déclic *m*; **2.** *v/i.*
cliqueter; faire tic tac; se plaire du
premier coup; *v/t.* (faire) claquer
(*les talons*).
cli·ent ['klaiənt] client(e *f*) *m*; **cli-
en·tele** [kliːɑːnˈteil] clientèle *f.*
cliff [klif] falaise *f*; escarpement *m.*
cli·mac·ter·ic [klaiˈmæktərik] **1.**
climatérique; **2.** ménopause *f*, retour
d'âge *m*; *fig.* tournant *m.*
cli·mate ['klaimit] climat *m*; **cli-
mat·ic** [klaiˈmætik] (*~ally*) cli-
mat(ér)ique.
cli·max ['klaimæks] gradation *f*; *fig.*
apogée *m*, plus haut point *m.*
climb [klaim] monter; gravir, grimper à; escalader; **'climb·er** ascensionniste *mf*; *fig.* arriviste *mf*; ♣
plante *f* grimpante; **'climb·ing**
montée *f*, escalade *f*; **'climb·ing-
i·ron** crampon *m.*
clinch [klintʃ] **1.** ⊕ rivet *m*, accrochage *m*; *fig.* étreinte *f*; *box.* corps-
à-corps *m*; **2.** *v/t.* river; confirmer
(*un argument etc.*); conclure (*un
marché*); *see* clench; *v/i.* s'accrocher;
'clinch·er ⊕ crampon *m*; *fig.* argument *m* sans réplique.
cling [kliŋ] [*irr.*] (à, to) s'accrocher,
se cramponner, s'attacher; adhérer;
coller (*robe*); **'cling·ing** qui s'accro-
che *etc.*; collant (*robe*).
clin·ic ['klinik] **1.** clinique *f*; **2.** =
'clin·i·cal □ clinique; ~ *thermometer* thermomètre *m* médical.
clink [kliŋk] **1.** tintement *m*, choc *m*;
épées: cliquetis *m*; **2.** *v/i.* tinter
(*verres*); *v/t.* faire tinter, faire résonner; ~ *glasses with* trinquer
avec; **'clink·er** escarbilles *f/pl.*;
sl. chose *f* ou chose *f* épatante;
'clink·ing *Brit. sl.* **1.** *adj.* épatant;
2. *adv. sl.* très.

45*

clip¹ [klip] **1.** tonte; *Am.* F *at one ~*
d'un seul coup; **2.** tondre; rogner;
tailler; écourter (*un mot*).
clip² [~] attache *f*, pince *f*; *paper-~*
agrafe *f* de bureau; trombone *m.*
clip·per ['klipə] tondeur (-euse *f*) *m*;
(*a pair of*) *~s pl.* (une) tondeuse *f*;
F *cheval m* qui va comme le vent;
⚓ fin voilier *m*; ✈ (*flying ~*) clipper
m; *sl.* type *m* épatant; **'clip·pings**
pl. tonte *f*; *ongles etc.:* rognures
f/pl.; *Am. presse:* coupures *f/pl.*
clique [kliːk] coterie *f*; F clan *m.*
cloak [klouk] **1.** manteau *m* (*a. fig.*);
fig. voile *m*; **2.** revêtir d'un manteau; *fig.* masquer, voiler; **'~room**
vestiaire *m*; ⚑ consigne *f.*
clob·ber *sl.* ['klɔbə] **1.** battre; rosser;
2. *Brit.* frusques *f/pl.*, barda *m.*
clock [klɔk] **1.** horloge *f*; *moins
grand:* pendule *f*; *bas:* coin *m*; *sp. sl.*
chronomètre *m* à déclic; **2.** *v/t. sp.
sl.* chronométrer; *v/i.:* ~ *in* (*out*)
pointer à l'arrivée (au départ) (*ouvrier etc.*); **'~face** cadran *m*; ~
ra·di·o radio-réveil *m* (*pl.* radios-
réveils); **'~wise** à droite; dans le
sens des aiguilles d'une montre.
clod [klɔd] motte *f* (de terre); *fig.*
terre *f*; (*a. ~-hopper*) lourdaud *m.*
clog [klɔg] **1.** entrave *f*; *fig.* empêchement *m*; galoche *f*; sabot *m*;
2. entraver; *fig.* (se) boucher, (s')obs-
truer; **'clog·gy** collant.
clois·ter ['klɔistə] **1.** cloître *m*;
2. cloîtrer.
close 1. [klouz] fin *f*, conclusion *f*;
clôture *f*; [klous] clos *m*, enclos
m; *cathédrale:* enceinte *f*; **2.** [klouz]
v/t. fermer; barrer; terminer; arrêter (*un compte*); *~d shop* atelier
etc. qui n'admet pas de travailleurs
non syndiqués; ~ *down* fermer (*une
usine etc.*); ~ *one's eyes to* fermer les
yeux sur; *v/i.* (se) fermer; se terminer, finir; se prendre corps à
corps (avec, *with*); ✝ ~ *with* conclure le marché avec; ~ *in* cerner de près; tomber (*nuit*); ~ *on*
(*prp.*) se (re)fermer sur; **3.** □ [klous]
bien fermé; clos; avare; peu communicatif (-ive *f*); étroit (*vêtement etc.*);
exclusif (-ive *f*) (*société*); serré (*style,
rangs, lutte*); *typ.* compact; soutenu
(*attention*); minutieux (-euse *f*)
(*étude*); vivement contesté (*lutte*);
lourd (*temps*); impénétrable (*secret*);
intime (*ami*); fidèle (*traduction*); ~ *by*

(*ou* to) tout près (de); ~ *fight* (*ou combat ou quarters*) combat *m* corps à corps; *have a* ~ *call* (*ou shave*) l'échapper belle, y échapper de justesse; *that was a* ~ *call* (*ou shave ou thing*) il était moins une; *at* ~ *quarters* de près; ~(*d*) *season* (*ou time*) *chasse*: chasse *f* fermée; *shave* ~*ly* (se) raser de près; '~**knit** étroitement lié, très uni; '~**meshed** à petites mailles; '**close·ness** proximité *f*; exactitude *f*; *temps*: lourdeur *f*; manque *m* d'air; réserve *f*.

clos·et ['klɔzit] **1.** cabinet *m*; armoire *f*, placard *m*; *see water-*~; **2.** *be* ~*ed with* être enfermé avec (*q.*), être en tête avec (*q.*).

close-up *cin.* ['klousʌp] premier plan *m*; gros plan *m*.

clos·ing ['klouziŋ] **1.** fermeture *f*; clôture *f*; **2.** dernier (-ère *f*), final; *de fermeture*; *the* ~ *days* les derniers jours *m/pl.*; ~ *time* heure *f* de fermeture; ~ *time!* on ferme!

clo·sure ['klouʒə] **1.** fermeture *f*; clôture *f*; *parl. move the* ~ voter la clôture; *apply the* ~ clôturer le débat; **2.** clôturer (*un débat etc.*).

clot [klɔt] **1.** *sang*: caillot *m*; *encre*: bourbillon *m*; **2.** figer (*le sang*); cailler (*le lait*).

cloth [klɔθ], *pl.* **cloths** [klɔθs] étoffe *f* de laine; drap *m*; toile *f*; linge *m*; tapis *m*; (*a. table-*~) nappe *f*; habit *m* (*surt.* ecclésiastique); F *the* ~ le clergé; *lay the* ~ mettre la nappe *ou* le couvert; *bound in* ~ relié toile; ~*-binding* reliure *f* en toile.

clothe [klouð] [*irr.*] vêtir, habiller (*de in*, *with*); revêtir (*de*, *with*) (*a. fig.*).

clothes [klouðz] *pl.* vêtements *m/pl.*, habits *m/pl.*; (*a. suit of* ~) complet *m*; linge *m* (*propre*, *sale*, *etc.*); '~**bas·ket** panier *m* à linge; '~**brush** brosse *f* à habits; ~ **hang·er** cintre *m*; ~ **horse** séchoir *m* (à linge); '~**line** corde *f* à linge; '~**peg** pince *f*; fichoir *m*; '~**pin** *surt. Am.* pince *f*; '~**press** armoire *f* à linge.

cloth·ier ['klouðiə] drapier *m*; marchand *m* de confections.

cloth·ing ['klouðiŋ] vêtements *m/pl.*

cloud [klaud] **1.** nuage *m* (*a. fig.*); *fig.* voile *m*; *liquide*: turbidité *f*; *poét.*, *a. sauterelle*: nuée *f*; *be under a* ~ être l'objet de soupçons; **2.** (se)

couvrir, (se) voiler; *fig.* s'assombrir; ⊕ ~*ed* nuageux (-euse *f*) (*joyau*); nuagé (*poil*); tacheté (*marbre*); '~**burst** rafale *f* de pluie; trombe *f*; ~**'cuck·oo-land** pays *m* utopique *ou* imaginaire; *live in* ~ être *ou* planer dans les nuages; '**cloud·less** ☐ sans nuages; **cloud·let** ['~lit] petit nuage *m*; '**cloud·y** ☐ nuageux (-euse *f*), assombri; couvert (*temps*); trouble (*liquide*); *fig.* fumeur (-euse *f*).

clout [klaut] **1.** rapiécer; F flanquer une taloche à (*q.*); **2.** chiffon *m*, torchon *m*; F taloche *f*, claque *f*.

clove[1] [klouv] clou *m* de girofle; gousse *f* (*d'ail*).

clove[2] [~] *prét. de* cleave[1]; **clo·ven** **1.** *p.p. de* cleave[1]; **2.** *adj.* fendu, fourchu.

clo·ver ♣ ['klouvə] trèfle *m*; '~**leaf** ♣ feuille *f* de trèfle; *mot.* (*a.* ~ *crossing*) croisement *m* en trèfle.

clown [klaun] *théâ.* bouffon *m*; *cirque*: clown *m*; rustre *m*; *poét.* paysan *m*; '**clown·ish** ☐ de bouffon; de clown; gauche; grossier (-ère *f*).

cloy [klɔi] rassasier (de, *with*) (*a. fig.*); affadir.

club [klʌb] **1.** massue *f*, assommoir *m*; *sp.* crosse *f*; cercle *m*, club *m*; ~*s pl. cartes*: trèfle *m*; **2.** *v/t.* frapper avec une massue; ~ *together* mettre en commun; *v/i.* (*usu.* ~ *together*) s'associer (*pour faire qch.*); '**club·ba·ble** sociable; '**club·'foot** ☞ pied-bot (*pl.* pieds-bots) *m*; '**club·law** la loi du plus fort.

cluck [klʌk] glousser (*poule*).

clue [klu:] *fig.* indication *f*, indice *m*; *mots croisés*: définition *f*.

clump [klʌmp] **1.** bloc *m*; *arbres*: groupe *m*; *fleurs*: massif *m*; F taloche *f*; (*a.* ~*sole*) semelle *f* supplémentaire; **2.** marcher lourdement; ajouter des patins à (*des chaussures*).

clum·si·ness ['klʌmzinis] gaucherie *f*, maladresse *f*; '**clum·sy** ☐ gauche, maladroit; informe.

clung [klʌŋ] *prét. et p.p. de* cling.

clus·ter ['klʌstə] **1.** ♣ *fleurs*: massif *m*, bouquet *m*; *arbres*: groupe *m*; *raisins*: grappe *f*; **2.** (se) grouper; (se) rassembler.

clutch [klʌtʃ] **1.** griffe *f*; *aigle etc.*: serre *f*; ⊕ embrayage *m*; *in his* ~*es* dans ses griffes, sous sa patte; *mot.* ~ *pedal* pédale *f* d'embrayage; **2.** *v/t.*

saisir, empoigner; *v/i.* se raccrocher (à, *at*).

clut·ter ['klʌtə] **1.** méli-mélo (*pl.* mélis-mélos) *m*, encombrement *m*; désordre *m*; **2.** (*a.* ~ *up*) encombrer (de, *with*); mettre le désordre dans.

clys·ter ['klistə] clystère *m*.

coach [koutʃ] **1.** carrosse *m*; ☞ voiture *f*, wagon *m*; *Am.* autocar *m*; *univ.* répétiteur *m*; *sp.* entraîneur *m*; **2.** *v/i.* aller en carrosse; *v/t. univ.* donner des leçons particulières à; *sp.* entraîner; '~-**box** siège *m* (du cocher); '~-**build·er** carrossier *m*; '~-**house** remise *f*; '~-**man** cocher *m*; '~-**work** carrosserie *f*.

co·ad·ju·tor *surt. eccl.* [kou'ædʒutə] coadjuteur *m*.

co·ag·u·late [kou'ægjuleit] (se) figer; (se) cailler (*lait*); **co·ag·u·la·tion** coagulation *f*, figement *m*.

coal [koul] **1.** charbon *m*; houille *f*; morceau *m* de charbon; *carry* ~*s to Newcastle* porter de l'eau à la mer; *haul* (*ou call*) *s.o. over the* ~*s fig.* semoncer q.; **2.** (s')approvisionner de charbon; ~*ing station* port *m* à charbon; '~-**bed** couche *f* de houille, couche *f* carbonifère; '~-**dust** charbon *m* en poussière.

co·a·lesce [kouə'les] se fondre; se combiner; fusionner; **co·a·les·cence** coalescence *f*; fusion *f*; combinaison *f*.

co·a·li·tion [kouə'liʃn] coalition *f*; *pol.* cartel *m*.

coal-field ['koulfi:ld] bassin *m* houiller.

coal…: '~-**pit** houillère *f*; '~-**scut·tle** seau *m* à charbon.

coarse ☐ [kɔːs] grossier (-ère *f*) (*a. fig.*); gros(se *f*); rude; '**coarse·ness** grossièreté *f*; rudesse *f*.

coast [koust] **1.** côte *f*, rivage *m*; plage *f*; littoral *m*; *cycl.* descente *f* en roue libre; *surt. Am.* piste *f* (*de toboggan*); **2.** suivre la côte; descendre (en toboggan, en roue libre, *mot.* le moteur débrayé); '**coast·er** *Am.* bobsleigh *m*; ⚓ caboteur *m*; **coast·er brake** *Am.* frein *m* à contre-pédalage; '**coast-guard** garde-côte (*pl.* gardes-côtes) *m*; '**coast·ing** navigation *f* côtière; cabotage *m*; ~ *trade* commerce *m* caboteur; cabotage *m*.

coat [kout] **1.** *hommes:* habit *m*; *femmes:* manteau *m*, jaquette *f*

(*courte*); robe *f*, poil *m*; *animaux:* peau *f*, fourrure *f*; *peinture:* couche *f*; ~ *of arms* armoiries *f/pl.*; écusson *m*; ~ *of mail* cotte *f* de mailles; *cut the* ~ *according to the cloth* subordonner ses dépenses à son revenu; **2.** enduire (de, *with*); revêtir, couvrir (de, *with*); '~-**hang·er** cintre *m*; '**coat·ing** enduit *m*, revêtement *m*; enveloppe *f*; couche *f*; *tex.* étoffe *f* pour habits; '**coat-rack** portemanteau *m*.

coax [kouks] cajoler, enjôler; encourager (*q.*) à force de cajoleries (à *inf., into gér.*); ~ *s.th. out of s.o.* soutirer qch. à q. en le cajolant.

cob [kɔb] cob *m*, bidet *m*; cygne *m* mâle; △ pisé *m*; *Am.* épi *m* de maïs; *see* ~*nut*; ~*s pl.* charbon: gaillette *f*; ~*loaf* miche *f*.

co·balt *min.* [kə'bɔːlt] cobalt *m*.

cob·ble ['kɔbl] **1.** galet *m*; ~*s pl.* gaillette *f*, -s *f/pl.*; **2.** paver en cailloutis; carreler (*des chaussures*); '**cob·bler** cordonnier *m*; *fig.* rapetasseur *m*; *Am.* boisson *f* rafraîchissante.

cob·nut ⚘ ['kɔbnʌt] grosse noisette *f*.

cob·web ['kɔbweb] toile *f* d'araignée.

co·caine ⚕ [kə'kein] cocaïne *f*.

coch·i·neal ['kɔtʃiniːl] cochenille *f*.

cock [kɔk] **1.** coq *m* (*a. fig.*); oiseau *m* mâle; chien *m* (*de fusil*); meulon *m* (*de foin*); robinet *m*; **2.** (*souv.* ~ *up*) (re)lever; dresser (*les oreilles*); armer le chien de (*un fusil*); retrousser (*le chapeau*); mettre (*le chapeau*) de travers; ~ *one's eye at s.o.* lancer une œillade à q.; ~ *one's nose at s.o.* toiser q.; ~*ed hat* tricorne *m*.

cock·ade [kɔ'keid] cocarde *f*.

Cock·aigne [kɔ'kein] pays *m* de cocagne.

cock-and-bull sto·ry ['kɔkənd'bulstɔːri] histoire *f* de pure invention.

cock·a·too [kɔkə'tuː] cacatoès *m*.

cock·a·trice ['kɔkətrais] basilic *m*.

cock·boat ⚓ ['kɔkbout] petit canot *m*.

cock·chaf·er ['kɔktʃeifə] hanneton *m*.

cock-crow(·ing) ['kɔkkrou(iŋ)] (premier) chant *m* du coq; aube *f*.

cock·er¹ ['kɔkə]: ~ *up* câliner.

cock·er² [~] (épagneul *m*) cocker *m*.

cock·er·el ['kɔkərəl] jeune coq *m*.

cock...: '**~-eyed** [ˈkɔkaid] *sl.* qui louche; de biais; *Am.* gris (*ivre*); '**~-fight(·ing)** combat, -s *m/pl.* de coqs; '**~-'horse** cheval *m* de bois.

cock·le¹ ⚘ [ˈkɔkl] nielle *f* des blés.

cock·le² [~] **1.** *zo.* bucarde *f*; pli *m*; **2.** *v/t.* recoquiller (*les pages d'un livre*); faire goder (*une étoffe*); *v/i.* se recroqueviller; goder.

cock·ney [ˈkɔkni] londonien(ne *f*) (*a. su./mf*); '**cock·ney·ism** locution *f ou* prononciation *f* londonienne.

cock·pit [ˈkɔkpit] arène *f* de combats de coqs; ⚓ poste *m* des blessés; ✈ baquet *m*, carlingue *f*; poste *m* du pilote. [*f*; F cafard *m*.]

cock·roach *zo.* [ˈkɔkroutʃ] blatte)

cocks·comb [ˈkɔkskoum] crête *f* de coq; ⚘ crête-de-coq (*pl.* crêtes-de-coq) *f*; '**cock-'sure** F outrecuidant; '**cock·tail** demi-sang *m/inv.* † parvenu *m*; cocktail *m*; '**cock-up** *sl.* pagaille *f*; *make a* ~ *of* saloper, gâcher; '**cock·y** □ F outrecuidant, suffisant, effronté.

co·co [ˈkoukou] cocotier *m*.

co·coa [ˈkoukou] cacao *m*.

co·co·nut [ˈkoukənʌt] noix *f* de coco.

co·coon *zo.* [kəˈkuːn] cocon *m*.

cod *icht.* [kɔd] morue *f*; dried ~ merluche *f*; cured ~ morue *f* salée.

cod·dle [ˈkɔdl] gâter, câliner; douilletter; ~ *up* élever dans la ouate.

code [koud] **1.** code *m*; *secret:* chiffre *m*; **2.** *tél.* codifier; chiffrer.

co·de·ine ⚕ [ˈkoudiːn] codéine *f*.

cod·fish [ˈkɔdfiʃ] *see* cod.

codg·er F [ˈkɔdʒə] vieux bonhomme *m*.

cod·i·cil [ˈkɔdisil] codicille *m*; **cod·i·fi·ca·tion** [~fiˈkeiʃn] codification *f*; **cod·i·fy** [~fai] codifier (*des lois*).

cod·ling [ˈkɔdliŋ] ⚘ pomme *f* à cuire; *icht.* petite morue *f*.

cod-liv·er oil [ˈkɔdlivərˈɔil] huile *f* de foie de morue.

co-ed *Am.* [ˈkouˈed] élève *f* d'une école coéducationelle.

co·ed·u·ca·tion [kouedjuˈkeiʃn] *école mixte:* coéducation *f*.

co·ef·fi·cient [kouiˈfiʃnt] coefficient *m*; facteur *m* (*de sûreté*).

co·erce [kouˈəːs] contraindre; forcer; **co·er·ci·ble** contraignable; coercible (*gaz*); **co·er·cion** [~ʃn] contrainte *f*; *under* ~ par contrainte; à son corps défendant; **co·er·cive** □ [~siv] coercitif (-ive *f*).

co·e·val □ [kouˈiːvəl] (*with*) de l'âge (de); contemporain (de).

co·ex·ist [ˈkouigˈzist] coexister (avec, with); '**co·ex·ist·ence** coexistence *f*; '**co·ex·ist·ent** coexistant.

cof·fee [ˈkɔfi] café *m*; ~ **bar** café *m*, cafétéria *f*; '**~-'bean** grain *m* de café; '**~-grounds** *pl.* marc *m* de café; '**~-pot** cafetière *f*; '**~-room** *hôtel:* salle *f* à manger; ~ **shop** *Am.* café *m*, cafétéria *f*; ~ **ta·ble** table *f* basse.

cof·fer [ˈkɔfə] coffre *m*; △ caisson *m*; ~*s pl.* coffres *m/pl.*; fonds *m/pl.*

cof·fin [ˈkɔfin] **1.** cercueil *m*; **2.** mettre en bière.

cog ⊕ [kɔg] dent *f* (*d'une roue*).

co·gen·cy [ˈkoudʒənsi] force *f*; '**co·gent** □ valable, incontestable.

cogged ⊕ [kɔgd] à dents, denté.

cog·i·tate [ˈkɔdʒiteit] *v/i.* réfléchir, méditer (sur, [*up*]on); *v/t.* méditer (*qch.*); **cog·i·ta·tion** réflexion *f*.

co·gnac [ˈkounjæk] cognac *m*.

cog·nate [ˈkɔgneit] **1.** (*with*) parent (de), analogue (à); **2.** cognat *m*.

cog·ni·tion [kɔgˈniʃn] connaissance *f*.

cog·ni·za·ble [ˈkɔgnizəbl] (re)connaissable; ⚖ du ressort du tribunal; '**cog·ni·zance** connaissance *f* (*a.* ⚖); ⚖ compétence *f*, ressort *m* (*de la cour*); '**cog·ni·zant** (*of*) ayant connaissance (de); instruit (de).

cog·no·men [kɔgˈnoumen] nom *m* de famille; sobriquet *m*, surnom *m*.

cog-wheel ⊕ [ˈkɔgwiːl] roue *f* dentée.

co·hab·it [kouˈhæbit] cohabiter; **co·hab·i·ta·tion** cohabitation *f*.

co-heir [ˈkouˈɛə] cohéritier *m*; **co-heir·ess** [ˈkouˈɛəris] cohéritière *f*.

co·here [kouˈhiə] se tenir (ensemble); **co·her·en·cy** cohérence *f*; **co·her·ent** □ cohérent; conséquent; **co·her·er** cohéreur *m*.

co·he·sion [kouˈhiːʒn] cohésion *f*; **co·he·sive** cohésif (-ive *f*).

coif·feur [kwɑːˈfəː] coiffeur *m*; **coif·fure** [~ˈfjuə] **1.** coiffure *f*; **2.** coiffer.

coign of van·tage [kɔinəvˈvɑːntidʒ] position *f* avantageuse.

coil [kɔil] **1.** *corde*, *fil métallique*, *cheveux:* rouleau *m*; *câble:* roue *f*; ⚡ bobine *f*; *serpent:* repli *m*; ⊕ *tube:* serpentin *m*; ~ *spring* ressort *m* en spirale; **2.** (*souv.* ~ *up*) *v/t.*

(en)rouler; *v/i.* serpenter; s'enrouler.

coin [kɔin] **1.** (pièce *f* de) monnaie *f*; *false* ~ fausse monnaie *f*; *small* ~ monnaie *f* divisionnaire; **2.** frapper (*de la monnaie*); *fig.* inventer; *fig.* ~ *money* faire des affaires d'or; ~*ed money* argent *m* monnayé; '**coin·age** monnayage *m*; monnaie *f*, -s *f/pl.*; *fig.* invention *f*.

co·in·cide [kouin'said] (*with*) coïncider (avec); *fig.* s'accorder (avec); **co·in·ci·dence** [kou'insidəns] coïncidence *f*; *fig.* rencontre *f*, concours *m*; **co'in·ci·dent** □ coïncident; *fig.* d'accord.

coin·er [kɔinə] monnayeur *m*; *souv.* faux-monnayeur *m*; *fig.* inventeur (-trice *f*) *m*.

coir ['kɔiə] fibre *f* de coco; coir *m*.

coke [kouk] **1.** coke *m* (*a. sl.* = *cocaine*); *Am.* F Coca-Cola *f*; **2.** (se) cokéfier.

col·an·der ['kʌləndə] *cuis.* passoire *f*.

cold [kould] **1.** □ froid (*a. fig.*); ~ *meat* viande *f* froide; *give s.o. the* ~ *shoulder see* ~*-shoulder*; F *have* ~ *feet* avoir le trac (= *avoir peur*); **2.** froid *m*; froideur *f*; (*souv.* ~ *in the head*) rhume *m*; '~-'**blood·ed** *zo.* à sang froid; *fig.* insensible, sans pitié (*personne*); accompli de sang-froid (*action*); ~ **cream** crème *f* de beauté, cold-cream *m*; '~-'**heart·ed** au cœur froid, sans pitié; '**cold·ness** froideur *f*; *climat:* froidure *f*.

cold...: '~-**shoul·der** battre froid à (*q.*); tourner le dos à (*q.*); ~ **stor·age** conservation *f* par le froid; glacière *f*; '~-'**stor·age** frigorifique; ~ **store** entrepôt *m* frigorifique.

cole ♀ [koul] chou-marin (*pl.* choux-marins) *m*.

cole·seed ♀ ['koulsi:d] (graine *f* de) colza *m*.

cole·slaw ['koulslɔ:] *Am.* salade *f* de choux.

col·ic ⚕ ['kɔlik] colique *f*.

col·lab·o·rate [kə'læbəreit] collaborer; **col·lab·o'ra·tion** collaboration *f*; **col'lab·o·ra·tor** collaborateur (-trice *f*) *m*.

col·lapse [kə'læps] **1.** s'affaisser; s'écrouler; s'effondrer (*prix, a. personne*); **2.** affaissement *m* etc.; **col'laps·i·ble** pliant, démontable; ~ *boat* canot *m* pliant, berthon *m*.

col·lar ['kɔlə] **1.** *robe:* col *m*; *manteau:* collet *m*; *chemise:* (faux) col *m*; *ordre:* collier *m*; ⊕ anneau *m*, collet *m*; **2.** saisir au collet; ⊕ baguer; *cuis.* rouler (*de la viande*) pour la ficeler; '~-**bone** *anat.* clavicule *f*.

col·late [kɔ'leit] collationner (*des textes*).

col·lat·er·al [kɔ'lætərəl] **1.** □ collatéral (-aux *m/pl.*); accessoire; additionnel(le *f*); concomitant; **2.** garantie *f* accessoire.

col·la·tion [kɔ'leiʃn] *textes, cuis., a. eccl.* collation *f*.

col·league ['kɔli:g] collègue *mf*.

col·lect 1. ['kɔlekt] *prière:* collecte *f*; **2.** [kə'lekt] *v/t.* (r)assembler; amasser; collectionner (*des timbres*); percevoir (*des impôts*); faire rentrer (*une créance*); quêter (*pour les pauvres*); ~ *one's thoughts* se reprendre; se recueillir; ~*ing business* service *m* d'encaissement; *v/i.* s'assembler; ~ *call Am. téléph.* PCV (= Per-Ce-Voir), communication *f* téléphonique payable par le destinateur; **col'lect·ed** □ *fig.* plein de sang-froid; **col'lect·ed·ness** *fig.* sang-froid *m*; **col'lec·tion** rassemblement *m*; recouvrement *m*; perception *f*; *billet:* encaissement *m*; *eccl.* quête *f*; *forcible* ~ réquisition *f*; **col'lec·tive** collectif (-ive *f*); multiple (*fruit*); ⚖ ~ *ownership* possession *f* en commun; ~ *bargaining* convention *f* collective; **col'lec·tive·ly** collectivement; en commun; **col'lec·tiv·ism** collectivisme *m*; **col'lec·tor** quêteur (-euse *f*) *m*; encaisseur *m*; collectionneur (-euse *f*) *m*; *contributions indirectes:* receveur *m*, *directes:* percepteur *m*; ⊕ contrôleur *m* de billets; ⚡ prise *f* de courant; ~*'s item* pièce *f* de collection.

col·leen *Ir.* ['kɔli:n; *Ir.* kɔ'li:n] jeune fille *f*.

col·lege ['kɔlidʒ] collège *m*; *souv.* université *f*; école *f* secondaire, lycée *m*; école *f* (*militaire ou navale*); **col·le·gi·an** [kə'li:dʒiən] étudiant(e *f*) *m*; lycéen(ne *f*) *m*; élève *mf*; **col·le·gi·ate** [~dʒiit] collégial (-aux *m/pl.*); de collège.

col·lide [kə'laid] se heurter; entrer en collision (avec, *with*); ~ *with* heurter (*qch.*) (*a. fig.*).

col·lie ['kɔli] colley *m*.

col·lier [ˈkɔliə] houilleur *m*, mineur *m*; ⚓ charbonnier *m*; **col·lier·y** [ˈkɔljəri] houillère *f*; mine *f* de charbon.

col·li·sion [kəˈliʒn] collision *f* (*a. fig.*); rencontre *f*; *fig.* conflit *m*.

col·lo·ca·tion [kɔloˈkeiʃn] collocation *f*, arrangement *m*.

col·lo·di·on [kəˈloudiən] collodion *m*.

col·lo·qui·al □ [kəˈloukwiəl] familier (-ère *f*); de (la) conversation; **col·lo·qui·al·ism** expression *f* familière.

col·lo·quy [ˈkɔləkwi] colloque *m*.

col·lude [kəˈljuːd] s'entendre (avec, *with*); **col·lu·sion** [kəˈluːʒn] collusion *f*; ⚖ complicité *f*, connivence *f*.

col·ly·wob·bles F [ˈkɔliwɔblz]: *have the* ~ se sentir mal; avoir le trac.

col·o·cynth ⚘ [ˈkɔlɔsinθ] coloquinte *f*.

co·lon [ˈkoulən] *typ.* deux-points *m/inv.*; *anat.* côlon *m*.

colo·nel ⚔ [ˈkəːnl] colonel *m*; **colo·nel·cy** grade *m* de colonel.

co·lo·ni·al [kəˈlounjəl] colonial (-aux *m/pl.*) (*a. su./m*); **col·o·nist** [ˈkɔlənist] colon *m*; **col·o·ni·za·tion** colonisation *f*; **col·o·nize** *v/t.* coloniser; *v/i.* former une colonie.

col·on·nade [kɔləˈneid] colonnade *f*.

col·o·ny [ˈkɔləni] colonie *f* (*a. fig.*).

col·o·pho·ny [kɔˈlɔfəni] colophane *f*.

col·or *see* colo(u)r.

Col·o·ra·do bee·tle [kɔləˈraːdouˈbiːtl] doryphore *m*.

co·los·sal □ [kəˈlɔsl] colossal (-aux *m/pl.*).

col·o(u)r [ˈkʌlə] **1.** couleur *f*; pigment *m*; *visage:* teint *m*; *nuance:* teinte *f*; *fig.* couleur *f*, prétexte *m*; ⚔ ~s *pl.* drapeau *m*; ~ *bar*, ~ *line* discrimination *f* raciale; ~ *problem* problème *m* racial; ~ *supplement* supplément illustré (*d'un journal*); ~ *television* télévision *f* (en) couleur; ~ *television set* téléviseur *m* couleur; *local* ~ couleur *f* locale; **2.** *v/t.* colorer; colorier; teindre; *fig.* imager (*son style*); présenter sous un faux jour; *v/i.* se colorer; rougir (*personne*); **col·o(u)r·a·ble** □ plausible; trompeur; **col·o(u)r-blind** daltonien(ne *f*); **col·o(u)r blind·ness** daltonisme *m*; **col·o(u)red** coloré; de couleur; en couleurs; ~ *film* film *m* en couleurs; ~ *pencil* crayon *m* de cou-

leur; ~ (*wo*)*man* homme *m* (femme *f*) de couleur; **col·o(u)r·fast** bon teint; **col·o(u)r·ful** [ˈ~ful] coloré; **col·o(u)r·ing 1.** colorant; ~ *matter* colorant *m*; **2.** coloration *f*; *peint.* coloris *m*; *visage:* teint *m*; *nuance:* teinte *f*; *fig.* apparence *f*; **col·o(u)r·ist** coloriste *m*; **col·o(u)r·less** □ sans couleur; terne; pâle.

colt [koult] poulain *m*, pouliche *f*; *fig.* débutant(e *f*) *m*; **colts·foot** ⚘ tussilage *m*.

col·um·bine ⚘ [ˈkɔləmbain] ancolie *f*.

col·umn [ˈkɔləm] colonne *f* (*a. typ., a.* ⚔); *journ. a.* rubrique *f*; **co·lum·nar** [kɔˈlʌmnə] en forme de colonne; en colonnes; **col·um·nist** [ˈkɔləmnist] *Am. journ.* collaborateur *m* régulier d'un journal.

col·za ⚘ [ˈkɔlzə] colza *m*.

co·ma¹ ⚕ [ˈkoumə] coma *m*.

co·ma² [~], *pl.* **-mae** [ˈ~miː] ⚘ barbe *f*, *astr.* chevelure *f*.

comb [koum] **1.** peigne *m*; *coq, vague, colline:* crête *f*; ⊕ peigne *m*, carde *f*; *curry*-~ *see honey*, ~ **2.** *v/t.* peigner; *a.* carder (*la laine*); ~ *out fig.* F éplucher; *v/i.* déferler (*vague*).

com·bat [ˈkɔmbæt] **1.** combat *m*; **2.** combattre (contre, *with*; pour, *for*); **com·bat·ant** combattant *m*; **com·bat·ive** □ combattif (-ive *f*); agressif (-ive *f*).

comb·er [ˈkoumə] ⊕ peigneuse *f*; ⚓ vague *f* déferlante.

com·bi·na·tion [kɔmbiˈneiʃn] combinaison *f*; association *f*; ⚙ combiné *m*; *fig.* mélange *m*; *usu.* ~s *pl. cost.* combinaison *f*; ~ *lock* serrure *f* à combinaison; **com·bine 1.** [ˈ~bain] (se) réunir; (s')allier; **2.** [ˈ~bain] ⚙ entente *f* industrielle; cartel *m*; *surt. Am.* moissonneuse-batteuse (*pl.* moissonneuses-batteuses) *f*.

comb·ings [ˈkoumiŋz] *pl.* peignures *f/pl.*

com·bus·ti·ble [kəmˈbʌstəbl] **1.** combustible, comburable; inflammable (*foule etc.*); **2.** ~s *pl.* matière *f* inflammable; *mot.* combustibles *m/pl.*; **com·bus·tion** [kəmˈbʌstʃn] combustion *f*.

come [kʌm] [*irr.*] venir, arriver; ~! allons!; voyons!; ~ *to* ~ futur, à venir, qui vient; F *how* ~? comment ça?; ~ *about* arriver, se passer; ~ *across*

s.o. tomber sur q.; ~ *along* se dépêcher; arriver; ~ *at* se jeter sur;
parvenir à (*la vérité*); ~ *by* passer
par; obtenir; ~ *down* descendre;
fig. s'abaisser; déchoir; ~ *down
upon s.o.* blâmer q. sévèrement; ~
down with F se fendre de (*une somme*);
Am. F être frappé par (*une maladie*);
~ *for* venir chercher; ~ *in* entrer; ⚓
arriver; être de saison; devenir la
mode; ~ *in!* entrez!; ~ *off* tomber
(de); se détacher (*bouton*); s'enlever
(*tache*); avoir lieu; réussir; tomber
(*cheveux*); ~ *on* s'avancer; survenir;
~ *on!* allons-y!; ~ *out* sortir (de, *of*);
se développer; débuter; ~ *out right*
donner la solution juste; ~ *round
fig.* reprendre connaissance; ~ *to
adv. see* ~ *to o.s.*; ⚓ venir sur
bâbord *ou* tribord; *prp.* arriver à;
~ *to o.s.* (*ou to one's senses*) revenir à
soi; reprendre ses sens; ~ *to anchor*
s'ancrer, mouiller; ~ *to know* en
venir à connaître *ou* savoir; ~ *up*
monter; surgir; pousser (*plante*);
paraître; ~ *up to* répondre à (*une
attente*); s'élever jusqu'à; s'approcher de (*q.*); égaler; ~ *up with*
rattraper, rejoindre (*q.*); ~ *upon*
tomber sur (*q.*); rencontrer par
hasard; venir à l'esprit de (*q.*);
~-'at·a·ble F accessible; '~-back
rentrée *f*; retour *m* en vogue *ou* au
pouvoir; *Am.* revanche *f*; *Am. sl.*
réplique *f*.

co·me·di·an [kə'miːdjən] comé-
dien(ne *f*) *m*; *music-hall*: comique *m*.

com·e·dy ['kɔmidi] comédie *f*.

come·li·ness ['kʌmlinis] mine *f*
avenante; **'come·ly** avenant.

come-off F ['kʌmɔːf] résultat *m*;
issue *f*.

com·er ['kʌmə] arrivant(e *f*) *m*;
venant(e *f*) *m*.

co·mes·ti·ble [kə'mestibl] *usu.* ~s
pl. comestible *m*, -s *m/pl.*

com·et ['kɔmit] comète *f*.

com·fort ['kʌmfət] **1.** soulagement
m; consolation *f*; bien-être *m*; confort *m*; aisance *f*; agrément *m*; *fig.*
réconfort *m*; **2.** soulager; consoler;
réconforter; **'com·fort·a·ble** □
confortable; à son aise (*personne*);
tranquille; *I am* ~ je suis à mon
aise; je suis bien; **'com·fort·er**
consolateur (-trice *f*) *m*; *fig.* cache-
nez *m/inv.*; *Am.* couvre-pied *m*

piqué; *Brit.* sucette *f*; **'com·fort-
less** □ incommode; dépourvu de
confort.

com·frey ⚘ ['kʌmfri] consoude *f*.

com·fy □ F ['kʌmfi] *see comfortable.*

com·ic ['kɔmik] (~*ally*) comique;
fig. (*usu.* '**com·i·cal** □) ~ *journal*
(*ou paper*) journal *m* pour rire;
journ. Am. comic strip bande *f*
dessinée; **'com·ics** *pl. journ. Am.*
bandes *f/pl.* dessinées (*souvent humo-
ristiques*).

com·ing ['kʌmiŋ] **1.** futur, qui
vient; ~, *Sir!* tout de suite, monsieur!; **2.** venue *f*; approche *f*.

com·i·ty ['kɔmiti]: ~ *of nations* bon
accord *m* entre les nations; courtoisie *f* internationale.

com·ma ['kɔmə] virgule *f*; *inverted* ~s *pl.* guillemets *m/pl.*

com·mand [kə'maːnd] **1.** ordre *m*;
maîtrise *f* (*d'une langue*); ✕ commandement *m* (*souv.* ♀, *p.ex.* Sou-
thern ♀); *at* (*ou by*) ~ *of* d'après les
ordres de, suivant l'ordre de; *have*
~ *of* commander; dominer; *be
(have) at* ~ être à la (avoir à sa)
disposition; ✕ *be in* ~ *of* commander; **2.** ordonner; commander,
inspirer (*un sentiment*); forcer
(*l'attention*); dominer (*une vallée*);
fig. être maître de, maîtriser; disposer de; **com·man·dant** ✕ [kɔmən'dænt] commandant *m*; **com·man·deer** [~'diə] ✕
réquisitionner; **com·mand·er** ✕
[kə'maːndə] commandant *m*; chef
m de corps; ⚓ capitaine *m* de frégate; *ordres:* commandeur *m*;
com'mand·er-in-'chief commandant *m* en chef; **com'mand·ing**
commandant; en chef; *fig.* d'autorité; imposant; éminent (*lieu*);
~ *point* point *m* stratégique; **com-
'mand·ment** commandement *m*.

com·mem·o·rate [kə'meməreit]
commémorer; célébrer le souvenir
de; **com·mem·o'ra·tion** commémoration *f*; **com'mem·o·ra·tive**
[~rətiv] □ commémoratif (-ive *f*)
(de, *of*).

com·mence [kə'mens] commencer;
initier; entamer; ⚖ intenter (*un
procès*); **com'mence·ment** commencement *m*, début *m*.

com·mend [kə'mend] recommander; confier; louer; F ~ *me to* ...

saluez ... de ma part; **com·mend·a·ble** □ louable; digne d'éloges; **com·men·da·tion** [kɔmen'deiʃn] éloge *m*, louange *f*; **com·mend·a·to·ry** [~ətəri] élogieux (-euse *f*).

com·men·su·ra·ble □ [kə'menʃə-rəbl] commensurable (avec *with, to*); *see* commensurate; **com·men·su·rate** □ [~rit] proportionné (à *with, to*); coétendu (à, *with*).

com·ment ['kɔmənt] **1.** commentaire *m*; critique *f*, glose *f*, observation *f* (sur, *on*); **2.** (*upon*) commenter, critiquer (*qch.*); faire le commentaire (de); **com·men·tar·y** ['~təri] commentaire *m*, glose *f*; radioreportage *m*; **'com·men·ta·tor** ['~teitə] commentateur (-trice *f*) *m*; radioreporter *m*.

com·merce ['kɔmə:s] commerce *m*; affaires *f/pl.*; *Chamber of* ♀ Chambre *f* de Commerce; **com·mer·cial** □ [kə'mə:ʃəl] **1.** commercial (-aux *m/pl.*); mercantile; marchand; de (du) commerce; ~ *traveller* commis *m* voyageur; représentant(e *f*) *m*; **2.** *Brit. F see* ~ *traveller*; *surt. Am. radio*: réclame *f*; **com·'mer·cial·ism** esprit *m* commercial; **com'mer·cial·ize** commercialiser.

com·mis·er·ate [kə'mizəreit] s'apitoyer sur le sort de (*q.*); **com·mis·er'a·tion** compassion *f* (pour, *with*).

com·mis·sar·i·at ✕ [kɔmi'seəriət] intendance *f*; **com·mis·sar·y** ['~səri] commissaire *m*; ✕ intendant *m* général d'armée.

com·mis·sion [kə'miʃn] **1.** commission *f*; ordre *m*, mandat *m*; délégation *f* (*d'autorité, de devoirs*); *crime*: perpétration *f*; ✕ brevet *m* (*d'officier*), grade *m* d'officier; ♣ *navire*: armement *m*; commission *f*, pourcentage *m*; on ~ à la commission; **2.** commissionner; déléguer; charger; ✕ nommer (*un officier*); ♣ armer; **com·mis·sion·aire** [~ʃə-'neə] commissionnaire *m*; *hôtel*: chasseur *m*; **com'mis·sion·er** [~ʃnə] commissaire *m*; délégué *m* d'une commission.

com·mit [kə'mit] commettre (*a. un crime, une erreur*); confier; engager (*sa parole*); coucher (*par écrit*); *pol.* renvoyer à une commission; ~ (*o.s. s'*)engager (à, *to*); se compromettre; ~ (*to prison*) envoyer en prison,

écrouer (*q.*); ~ *for trial* renvoyer aux assises; **com'mit·ment** délégation *f*; *pol.* renvoi *m* à une commission; mise *f* en prison; renvoi *m* aux assises; engagement *m* financier; **com'mit·tal** *see* commitment; mise *f* en terre (*d'un cadavre*); *crime*: perpétration *f*; ~ *order* mandat *m* de dépôt; **com'mit·tee** comité *m*, commission *f*.

com·mode [kə'moud] commode *f*; chaise *f* percée; **com'mo·di·ous** □ [~djəs] spacieux (-euse *f*); **com·mod·i·ty** [kə'mɔditi] (*usu.* ~*s pl.*) marchandise *f*, -s *f/pl.*; denrée *f*, -s *f/pl.*; ~ *value* valeur *f* vénale.

com·mo·dore ♣ ['kɔmədɔ:] chef *m* de division; commodore *m*.

com·mon ['kɔmən] **1.** □ commun; public (-ique *f*); courant; ordinaire; vulgaire; trivial (-aux *m/pl.*); *gramm.* ~ *noun* nom *m* commun; ♀ *Council* conseil *m* municipal; *Book of* ♀ *Prayer* rituel *m* de l'Église anglicane; ~ *law* droit *m* commun *ou* coutumier; ~ *room* salle *f* commune; salle *f* des professeurs; ~ *sense* sens *m* commun, bon sens *m*; ✝ ~ *stock* actions *f/pl.* ordinaires; ~ *weal* bien *m* public; *in* ~ en commun (avec, *with*); **2.** pâtis *m*; terrain *m* communal; **com·mon·al·ty** ['~nlti] le commun des hommes; **'com·mon·er** bourgeois *m*; homme *m* du peuple; *qqfois* membre *m* de la Chambre des Communes; *univ.* étudiant *m* ordinaire; **'com·mon·place 1.** lieu *m* commun; **2.** banal (-aux *m/pl.*); terre à terre; médiocre; **com·mons** ['~z] *pl.* le peuple *m*; le tiers état *m*; ordinaire *m* (*de la table*); *short* ~ maigre chère *f*; (*usu. House of*) ♀ Chambre *f* des Communes; **'com·mon·sense** sensé, raisonnable; **'com·mon·wealth** État *m*; *souv.* republique *f*; chose *f* publique; the *British* ♀? l'Empire *m* Britannique; the ♀ *of Australia* le Commonwealth *m* d'Australie.

com·mo·tion [kə'mouʃn] agitation *f*; troubles *m/pl.*; brouhaha *m*.

com·mu·nal □ ['kɔmjunl] communal (-aux *m/pl.*); ~ *estate* 🏛 communauté *f* de biens; **com·mu·nal·ize** ['~nəlaiz] mettre en commun.

com·mu·ni·ca·bil·i·ty [kəmju:nikə-'biliti] communicabilité *f*; **com-**

'mu·ni·ca·ble □ communicable; ⚕ contagieux (-euse *f*); **com'mu-ni·cant** *eccl.* communiant(e *f*) *m*; **com'mu·ni·cate** [‿keit] *v/t.* communiquer (à, to); *v/i.* communiquer (avec, with; par, by); *eccl.* recevoir la communion; **com·mu·ni'ca-tion** communication *f* (*a.* ✕, *téléph.*, *voie*); voie *f* d'accès; 🚂 ‿ cord signal *m* d'alarme; *be in* ‿ *with* être en relation avec; **com'mu·ni-ca·tive** □ communicatif (-ive *f*); expansif (-ive *f*); **com'mu·ni·ca-tor** débiteur (-euse *f*) *m* (*de nou-velles*); ⊕ communicateur *m*.

com·mun·ion [kəm'ju:njən] rap-port *m*; relations *f/pl.*; *eccl.* communion *f*.

com·mu·ni·qué [kəm'ju:nikei] com-muniqué *m*.

com·mu·nism ['kɔmjunizm] com-munisme *m*; **'com·mu·nist 1.** com-muniste *mf*; **2.** = **com·mu'nis·tic** (‿ally) communiste.

com·mu·ni·ty [kəm'ju:niti] com-munauté *f* (*a. eccl.*); solidarité *f*; *the* ‿ l'État *m*; *he public m*; ‿ *ownership* collectivité *f*; ‿ *service* service *m* public; ‿ *spirit* sens *m* du groupe; ‿ *work* travail *m* en com-mun.

com·mu·nize ['kɔmjunaiz] collec-tiviser; rendre communiste.

com·mut·a·ble [kəm'ju:təbl] per-mutable; commuable (*peine*); **com-mu·ta·tion** [kɔmju:'teiʃn] commu-tation *f* (en *into*, for); *Am.* ‿ *ticket* carte *f* d'abonnement; **com·mu·ta·tive** [kə'mju:tətiv] commutatif (-ive *f*); **com·mu·ta·tor** ⚡ ['kɔm-ju:teitə] commutateur *m*; **com-mute** [kə'mju:t] *v/t.* échanger (pour, contre for, into); commuer (*une peine*) (en, into); racheter (*qch.*) (par, into) (*une rente, une servitude*); *v/i. Am.* prendre un abonnement; **com'mut·er** *Am.* abonné(e *f*) *m*.

com·pact 1. ['kɔmpækt] convention *f*; poudrier *m*; **2.** [kəm'pækt] com-pact; serré; formé (de, of); **3.** [‿] *v/t.* rendre compact; **com'pact-ness** compacité *f*; *style*: concision *f*.

com·pan·ion [kəm'pænjən] com-pagnon *m*, compagne *f*; manuel *m*; pendant *m*; *ordre*: compagnon *m*; ⚓ capot *m* (d'échelle); ‿ *in arms* compagnon *m* d'armes; **com'pan-ion·a·ble** □ sociable; **com'pan-**

ion·ship camaraderie *f*; compag-nie *f*.

com·pa·ny ['kʌmpəni] compagnie *f* (*a.* ✝, *a.* ✕); assemblée *f*; bande *f*; *invités*: monde *m*; ✝ *a.* société *f*; ⚓ équipage *m*; *théâ.* troupe *f*; *good* (*bad*)‿ bonne (mauvaise) compagnie *f*; *bear s.o.* ‿ tenir compagnie à q.; *have* ‿ avoir du monde; *keep* ‿ *with* sortir avec.

com·pa·ra·ble □ ['kɔmpərəbl] com-parable (avec, à with, to); **com'par-a·tive** [kəm'pærətiv]. □ compa-ratif (-ive *f*); comparé; relatif (-ive *f*); ‿ *degree* = **2.** *gramm.* com-paratif *m*; **com·pare** [‿'pɛə] **1.**: *beyond* (*ou without ou past*) ‿ sans pareil(le *f*) *m*; **2.** *v/t.* comparer (avec, à with, to); confronter (avec, with); *gramm.* former les degrés de com-paraison de; (*as*) ‿*d with* en com-paraison de; *v/i.* être comparable (à, with); **com·par·i·son** [‿'pærisn] comparaison *f* (*a. gramm.*); con-frontation *f*; *in* ‿ *with* en com-paraison de; auprès de.

com·part·ment [kəm'pɑ:tmənt] compartiment *m* (*a.* ♠, *a.* 🚂); *tiroir*: case *f*; *bagages*: soute *f*.

com·pass ['kʌmpəs] **1.** boussole *f*; limite *f*, -s *f/pl.*; ♪ registre *m*; (*a pair of*) ‿*es pl.* (un) compas *m*; **2.** faire le tour de; entourer; comploter (*la mort, la ruine*); atteindre (*un but*).

com·pas·sion [kəm'pæʃn] compas-sion *f*; *have* ‿ *on* avoir compassion de; **com'pas·sion·ate** □ [‿ʃənit] compatissant (à, pour to[wards]).

com·pat·i·bil·i·ty [kəmpætə'biliti] compatibilité *f*; **com'pat·i·ble** □ compatible (avec, with).

com·pa·tri·ot [kəm'pætriət] com-patriote *mf*.

com·peer [kɔm'piə] égal *m*, pair *m*; compagnon *m*.

com·pel [kəm'pel] contraindre, for-cer, obliger (q. à *inf.*, *s.o. to inf.*).

com·pen·di·ous □ [kəm'pendiəs] abrégé, concis; **com'pen·di·ous-ness** concision *f*; forme *f* succincte.

com·pen·di·um [kəm'pendiəm] ab-régé *m*; recueil *m*.

com·pen·sate ['kɔmpenseit] *v/t.* dé-dommager (de, for); compenser (*a.* ⊕) (avec with, by); *v/i.* ‿ *for* racheter (*qch.*); compenser (*qch.*); **com·pen'sa·tion** compensation *f*; dédommagement *m*; indemnité *f*;

réparation *f*; *Am.* appointements *m/pl.*; ⊕ compensation *f*, rattrapage *m*; **'com·pen·sa·tive**, **'com·pen·sa·to·ry** compensatoire, -teur (-trice *f*).

com·pete [kəm'piːt] concourir (pour qch., *for s.th.*); disputer (qch. à q., *with s.o. for s.th.*); rivaliser (avec q. de qch., *with s.o. in s.th.*); faire concurrence (à q., *with s.o.*).

com·pe·tence, **com·pe·ten·cy** ['kɔmpitəns(i)] compétence *f* (en in, at) (*a.* ⚖); moyens *m/pl.* (*d'existence*); attributions *f/pl.*; **'com·pe·tent** □ capable; compétent (*a.* ⚖); suffisant (*connaissances*).

com·pe·ti·tion [kɔmpi'tiʃn] rivalité *f*; concurrence *f* (*a.* ✝); concours *m*; *échecs*: tournoi *m*; *sp.* meeting *m*; rifle ~ concours *m* de tir; **com·pet·i·tive** □ [kəm'petitiv] de concurrence; de concours; **com·pet·i·tor** concurrent(e *f*) *m*; rival(e *f*) *m*; compétiteur (-trice *f*) *m*.

com·pi·la·tion [kɔmpi'leiʃn] compilation *f*; recueil *m*; **com·pile** [kəm-'pail] compiler; composer, établir (de, *from*); recueillir.

com·pla·cence, **com·pla·cen·cy** [kəm'pleisns(i)] satisfaction *f*; contentement *m* de soi-même; **com·pla·cent** □ content de soi-même; suffisant.

com·plain [kəm'plein] se plaindre (de of, *about*; à, *to*; que, *that*); porter plainte (contre *against*, *about*); *poét.* se lamenter; **com·plain·ant** plaignant(e *f*) *m*; **com·plain·er** réclamant(e *f*) *m*; mécontent(e *f*) *m*; **com·plaint** grief *m*; plainte *f*; doléances *f/pl.*; maladie *f*, mal *m*.

com·plai·sance [kəm'pleizns] complaisance *f*, obligeance *f*; **com·plai·sant** □ complaisant, obligeant.

com·ple·ment 1. ['kɔmplimənt] effectif *m* (complet); plein *m*; *gramm.* attribut *m*; *livre*, *a.* ⚓ complément *m*; 2. ['~ment] compléter; **com·ple·men·tal**, **com·ple·men·ta·ry** complémentaire; *be* ~ (*to*) compléter.

com·plete [kəm'pliːt] 1. □ complet (-ète *f*); entier (-ère *f*); total (-aux *m/pl.*); achevé, parfait; 2. compléter; achever; remplir (*un bulletin*); **com·ple·tion** achèvement *m*; *contrat*: signature *f*; réalisation *f*; accomplissement *m*.

com·plex ['kɔmpleks] 1. □ complexe; *fig.* compliqué; 2. tout *m*, ensemble *m*; *psych.* complexe *m*; **com·plex·ion** [kəm'plekʃn] teint *m*; aspect *m*, caractère *m*, jour *m*; **com'plex·i·ty** complexité *f*.

com·pli·ance [kəm'plaiəns] acquiescement *m* (à, *with*); obéissance *f*; *péj.* basse complaisance *f*; in ~ with en conformité de; suivant; **com'pli·ant** □ accommodant, obligeant.

com·pli·cate ['kɔmplikeit] compliquer; **com·pli·ca·tion** complication *f* (*a.* ⚕).

com·plic·i·ty [kəm'plisiti] complicité *f* (à, in).

com·pli·ment 1. ['kɔmplimənt] compliment *m*; honneur *m*; ~s *pl. a.* hommages *m/pl.*, amitiés *f/pl.*; galanteries *f/pl.*; 2. ['~ment] *v/t.* féliciter, complimenter (de, on); **com·pli·men·ta·ry** flatteur (-euse *f*); ✝ à titre gracieux, en hommage; ~ copy livre *m* offert en hommage; give s.o. a ~ dinner donner un dîner *m* en l'honneur de q.; ~ ticket billet *m* de faveur.

com·ply [kəm'plai] *v/i.* ~ with se conformer à; se soumettre à; accéder à; accomplir (*une condition*); observer (*une règle*).

com·po·nent [kəm'pounənt] 1. partie *f* constituante; composant *m*; 2. constituant; composant; ~ part see ~ 1.

com·port [kəm'pɔːt] *v/i.* convenir (à, with); *v/t.*: ~ o.s. se comporter.

com·pose [kəm'pouz] composer (*a. typ.*); arranger; disposer; régler (*un différend*); calmer (*l'esprit*); rasseoir; **com'posed**, *adv.* **com'pos·ed·ly** [~zidli] calme, tranquille; composé (*visage*); **com'pos·er** auteur *m*; ♪ compositeur (-trice *f*) *m*; **com'pos·ing** 1. calmant; 2. composition *f*; ~-machine composeuse *f*; ~-room atelier *m* de composition; **com·pos·ite** ['kɔmpəzit] 1. composé; mixte; ⌂ composite; 2. (corps *m*) composé; ♀ composée *f*; **com·po·si·tion** composition *f* (*a.* ♪, *peint.*, ⌂); mélange *m*; *exercice*: dissertation *f*, rédaction *f*; thème *m*; *fig.* caractère *m*; ✝ arrangement *m*; **com·pos·i·tor** [kəm-'pɔzitə] compositeur *m*, typographe *m*; **com·post** ['kɔmpɔst] compost *m*; **com·po·sure** [kəm'pouʒə] sang-froid *m*, calme *m*.

com·pote ['kɔmpout] compote *f*.

com·pound[1] **1.** ['kɔmpaund] composé; ⚕ ~ *fracture* fracture *f* compliquée; ~ *interest* intérêts *m/pl.* composés; **2.** composé *m* (*a.* ⚗); ⊕ mastic *m*; *gramm.* (*a.* ~ *word*) mot *m* composé; **3.** [kəm'paund] *v/t.* mélanger; arranger (*un différend*); *v/i.* s'arranger; transiger (*avec q., avec sa conscience*); ✝ se rédimer (de, *for*); s'accommoder.

com·pound[2] ['kɔmpaund] enceinte *f*; ⚔ camp *m* de concentration.

com·pre·hend [kɔmpri'hend] comprendre; se rendre compte de.

com·pre·hen·si·ble □ [kɔmpri-'hensəbl] compréhensible; **com·pre'hen·sion** compréhension *f*; entendement *m*; **com·pre'hen·sive** □ compréhensif (-ive *f*); ~ *insurance* assurance *f* tous risques; **com·pre'hen·sive·ness** étendue *f*.

com·press 1. [kəm'pres] comprimer; condenser (*un discours*); **2.** ['kɔmpres] ⚕ compresse *f*; **com·press·i·bil·i·ty** [kɔmpresi'biliti] compressibilité *f*; **com'press·i·ble** [~presəbl] compressible; **com·pres·sion** [~'preʃn] compression *f* (*a. phys.*); **com·pres·sor** [~'presə] ⊕ compresseur *m*.   [dre, contenir.\

com·prise [kəm'praiz] compren-\

com·pro·mise ['kɔmprəmaiz] **1.** compromis *m*; *fig.* accommodement *m*; **2.** *v/t.* compromettre; arranger (*un différend*); *v/i.* aboutir à un compromis; transiger (sur, *on*); s'accommoder.

com·pul·sion [kəm'pʌlʃn] contrainte *f*; **com'pul·sive** [~siv] compulsif (-ive *f*); **com'pul·so·ry** [~səri] obligatoire; forcé; par contrainte.

com·punc·tion [kəm'pʌŋkʃn] remords *m*; componction *f*.

com·put·a·ble [kəm'pjuːtəbl] calculable; **com·pu·ta·tion** [kɔmpjuː-'teiʃn] calcul *m*, estimation *f*; **com·pute** [kəm'pjuːt] calculer, computer, estimer (à, *at*); **com·put·er** ⊕ [kəm'pjuːtə] ordinateur *m*; ~ *age* ère *f* de l'ordinateur *ou* de l'informatique; ~-*controlled* commandé par ordinateur; ~ *language* langage *m* machine; ~ *science* informatique *f*; ~ *scientist* informaticien(ne *f*) *m*.

com·rade ['kɔmrid] camarade *m*, compagnon *m*.   [leçon).\

con[1] [kɔn] étudier; répéter (*une*\

con[2] ⚓ [~] gouverner (*un navire*); diriger la manœuvre.

con[3] [~] *abr. de contra*; *pro and* ~ pour et contre; *the pros and* ~*s* le pour et le contre.

con[4] *Am. sl.* [~] **1.** *mots composés:* *abr. de confidence*; **2.** duper, tromper.

con·cat·e·nate [kɔn'kætineit] *usu. fig.* enchaîner; **con·cat·e'na·tion** enchaînement *m*; *circonstances:* concours *m*.

con·cave □ ['kɔn'keiv] concave, incurvé; **con·cav·i·ty** [~'kæviti] concavité *f*; *qqfois* creux *m*.

con·ceal [kən'siːl] cacher (*a. fig.*); celer; taire (à, *from*); masquer; voiler; **con'ceal·ment** dissimulation *f*; action *f* de (se) cacher; (*a. place of* ~) cachette *f*, retraite *f*.

con·cede [kən'siːd] concéder; admettre; **con'ced·ed·ly** [~idli] *Am.* reconnu (pour, comme).

con·ceit [kən'siːt] vanité *f*, suffisance *f*; (*ou self-*~) amour-propre (*pl.* amours-propres) *m*, infatuation *f*; *out of* ~ *with* dégoûté de; **con'ceit·ed** □ vaniteux (-euse *f*), prétentieux (-euse *f*); **con'ceit·ed·ness** vanité *f*, suffisance *f*.

con·ceiv·a·ble □ [kən'siːvəbl] imaginable, concevable; **con'ceive** *v/i.* devenir enceinte; ~ *of s.th.* (s')imaginer qch.; *v/t.* concevoir (*un enfant, un projet, de l'amour*); rédiger.

con·cen·trate 1. ['kɔnsentreit] *v/t.* concentrer (*a. fig.*); ⚔ faire converger (*les feux*); *v/i.* se concentrer; **2.** ['~trit] concentré *m*; **con·cen·'tra·tion** concentration *f* (*a.* ⚗); ⚔ convergence *f*; **con'cen·tre**, **con'cen·ter** [~tə] (se) réunir; (se) concentrer; **con'cen·tric** (~*ally*) concentrique.

con·cep·tion [kən'sepʃn] *biol.* enfant, idée: conception *f*; idée *f*, imagination *f*; **con·cep·tu·al** □ [kən'septjuəl] conceptuel(le *f*).

con·cern [kən'sɔːn] **1.** rapport *m*; affaire *f*; intérêt *m* (dans, *in*); souci *m*, inquiétude *f* (à l'égard de, *about*); ✝ entreprise *f*; maison *f* de commerce; F appareil *m*; **2.** concerner, regarder, intéresser (*q.*, *qch.*); ~ *o.s. with* s'occuper de; ~

o.s. about (ou for) s'intéresser à, s'inquiéter de; **con'cerned** □ inquiet (-ète *f*) (de *at, about*; au sujet de *about, for*); soucieux (-euse *f*); impliqué (dans, *in*); those ~ les intéressés; be ~ être en cause; be ~ that s'inquiéter que (*sbj.*); be ~ to (*inf.*) tâcher de (*inf.*), chercher à (*inf.*); be ~ with s'occuper de; s'intéresser à; **con'cern·ing** *prp.* au sujet de, concernant, touchant, en ce qui concerne.

con·cert 1. ['kɔnsət] concert *m* (*a. ♪*); accord *m*; **2.** [kən'sɔːt] *v/t.* concerter; *fig.* arranger; *v/i.* se concerter (avec, *with*); ♪ ~ed concertant, d'ensemble; **con·cer·ti·na** ♪ [kɔnsə'tiːnə] accordéon *m* hexagonal, concertina *f*; '**con·cert-pitch** ♪ diapason *m* de concert.

con·ces·sion [kən'seʃn] opinion, *terrain:* concession *f*; make ~s to sacrifier à; **con·ces·sion·aire** [kənseʃə'nɛə] concessionnaire *m*.

con·ces·sive □ [kən'sesiv] concessif } **conch** [kɔŋk] conque *f*. [(-ive *f*).}

con·cil·i·ate [kən'silieit] (ré)concilier; gagner (*q.*) à son parti; se concilier (*la faveur de q.*); **con·cil·i·'a·tion** conciliation *f*; arbitrage *m*; **con'cil·i·a·tor** conciliateur (-trice *f*) *m*; **con'cil·i·a·to·ry** [~ətəri] conciliant, conciliatoire; ~ *proposal* offre *f* de conciliation.

con·cin·ni·ty [kən'siniti] élégance *f* (*de style*).

con·cise □ [kən'sais] concis; bref (brève *f*); serré (*style*); **con'cise·ness** concision *f*.

con·clave ['kɔŋkleiv] *eccl.* conclave *m*; *fig.* conseil *m*; assemblée *f*.

con·clude [kən'kluːd] *v/t.* conclure; terminer, achever; arranger, régler (*une affaire*); to be ~d in our next la fin au prochain numéro; *v/i.* conclure, estimer; *Am.* ~ to (*inf.*) décider de (*inf.*); **con'clud·ing** final (-als *m/pl.*).

con·clu·sion [kən'kluːʒn] conclusion *f*, fin *f*; *séance:* clôture *f*; conclusion *f*, décision *f*; try ~s with se mesurer contre *ou* avec; **con·clu·sive** □ [kən'kluːsiv] concluant, décisif (-ive *f*).

con·coct [kən'kɔkt] confectionner; *fig.* imaginer; tramer; **con'coc·tion** confection *f*; mixtion *f*; *fig. plan etc.:* élaboration *f*.

con·com·i·tance, con·com·i·tan·cy [kən'kɔmitəns(i)] concomitance *f* (*a. eccl.*); **con'com·i·tant 1.** □ concomitant (de, *with*); **2.** accessoire *m*, accompagnement *m*.

con·cord 1. ['kɔŋkɔːd] concorde *f*; harmonie *f* (*a. ♪*); *gramm.* concordance *f*; *fig.* accord *m*; **2.** [kən'kɔːd] concorder, s'accorder; être d'accord; **con'cord·ance** accord *m* (avec, *with*); concordance *f* (*a. eccl.*); **con'cord·ant** □ concordant (avec, *with*); qui s'accorde (avec, *with*); ♪ consonant; **con'cor·dat** *eccl.* [~dæt] concordat *m*.

con·course ['kɔŋkɔːs] foule *f*; rassemblement *m*; carrefour *m*; concours *m*; *Am.* hall *m* (*de gare*).

con·crete [kɔnkriːt] **1.** □ concret (-ète *f*); de *ou* en béton; **2.** △ béton *m*, ciment *m*; *phls., gramm.* concret *m*; in the ~ sous forme concrète; **3.** [kən'kriːt] (se) concréter; (se) solidifier; ['kɔn-kriːt] *v/t.* bétonner; **con·cre·tion** [kən'kriːʃn] concrétion *f*.

con·cu·bi·nage [kɔn'kjuːbinidʒ] concubinage *m*; **con'cu·bine** ['kɔŋkjubain] concubine *f*.

con·cu·pis·cence [kən'kjuːpisns] concupiscence *f*; **con'cu·pis·cent** libidineux (-euse *f*), lascif (-ive *f*).

con·cur [kən'kəː] coïncider; être d'accord (avec, *with*); concourir (à, *in*); contribuer (à, *to*); **con·cur·rence** [~'kʌrəns] concours *m*; coopération *f*; simultanéité *f*; accord *m*; approbation *f*; in ~ with en commun avec; d'accord avec; **con'cur·rent** □ concourant; simultané; unanime.

con·cus·sion [kən'kʌʃn] secousse *f*; commotion *f* (*cérébrale*).

con·demn [kən'dem] condamner (*a. fig.*); condamner à mort; déclarer coupable; *fig.* blâmer; ~ed cell cellule *f* des condamnés; **con'dem·na·ble** condamnable, blâmable; **con·dem·na·tion** [kɔndem'neiʃn] condamnation *f*; censure *f*; blâme *m*; **con·dem·na·to·ry** □ [kən'demnətəri] condamnatoire.

con·den·sa·ble [kən'densəbl] condensable; **con·den·sa·tion** [kɔnden'seiʃn] condensation *f*; liquide *m* condensé; **con·dense** [kən'dens] (se) condenser; *v/t.* concentrer; **con-**

'dens·er condenseur *m* (*a.* ⊕); ⊕, *a.* ⚡ condensateur *m*.

con·de·scend [kɔndi'send] s'abaisser; condescendre; con·de'scend·ing □ condescendant (envers, *to*); con·de'scen·sion condescendance *f*; complaisance *f*.

con·dign □ [kən'dain] mérité; exemplaire.

con·di·ment ['kɔndimənt] condiment *m*.

con·di·tion [kən'diʃn] 1. condition *f*; stipulation *f*; état *m*, situation *f*; on ~ *that* à condition que; 2. soumettre à une condition; stipuler; conditionner (*l'air, la laine*; *a. psych.*); con'di·tion·al [~ʃənl] 1. □ conditionnel(le *f*); dépendant (de, [up]on); ~ *mood* = 2. *gramm.* conditionnel *m*; *in the* ~ au conditionnel; con·di·tion·al·i·ty [~'æliti] état *m* conditionnel; con'di·tion·al·ly [~ʃnəli] sous certaines conditions; con'di·tioned conditionné; en ... état.

con·dole [kən'doul] (*with s.o.*) partager la douleur (de q.); exprimer ses condoléances (à q.); con'do·lence condoléance *f*.

con·do·min·i·um [kɔndə'miniəm] condominium *m*; *Am.* immeuble *m* en copropriété.

con·do·na·tion [kɔndou'neiʃn] pardon *m*; indulgence *f* (pour, of); con·done [kən'doun] pardonner; *action*: racheter (*une offense*).

con·duce [kən'dju:s] contribuer (à, *to*); favoriser (qch., *to s.th.*); con'du·cive (*to*) favorable (à); qui contribue (à).

con·duct 1. ['kɔndʌkt] conduite *f*; *affaire*: gestion *f*; manière *f* de se conduire; 2. [kən'dʌkt] conduire; (a)mener (*q.*); accompagner (*une excursion*); diriger (♪, *une opération*); mener, gérer (*une affaire*); *phys.* être conducteur (-trice *f*) de; ~ *o.s.* se comporter (*bien, mal, etc.*); con·duct·i·bil·i·ty [kəndʌkti'biliti] *phys.* conductibilité *f*; con'duct·i·ble [~təbl] *phys.* conductible; con'duct·ing conducteur (-trice *f*); con'duc·tion conduction *f*; con'duc·tive □ *phys.* conducteur (-trice *f*); con·duc·tiv·i·ty [kɔndʌk'tiviti] *phys.* conductivité *f*; conductibilité *f*; con·duc·tor [kən'dʌktə] conducteur *m* (*a. phys.*);

accompagnateur *m*; *tramway etc.*: receveur; *Am.* 🚂 chef *m* de train; ♪ chef *m* d'orchestre; ⚡ (conducteur *m* de) paratonnerre *m*; con'duc·tress conductrice *f*; *tramway etc.*: receveuse *f*.

con·duit ['kɔndit] conduit *m*; tuyau *m* conducteur.

cone [koun] cône *m*; ⊕ cloche *f*; ♀ pomme *f*, cône *m*; *glace*: cornet *m*.

co·ney ['kouni] (peau *f* de) lapin *m*.

con·fab F ['kɔnfæb] 1. (= con·fab·u·late [kən'fæbjuleit]) causer (*entre intimes*); 2. (= con·fab·u'la·tion) causerie *f* intime.

con·fec·tion [kən'fekʃn] confection *f* (*de qch.*, *a. pharm.*); *cost.* (vêtement *m* de) confection *f*; friandise *f*; con'fec·tion·er confiseur (-euse *f*) *m*; con'fec·tion·er·y confiserie *f*; bonbons *m/pl.*

con·fed·er·a·cy [kən'fedərəsi] confédération *f*; *fig.* entente *f*; *surt. Am.* the ♀ les Confédérés *m/pl.* (= *les sudistes pendant la guerre de Sécession 1860—65*); ⚖ conspiration *f*; con'fed·er·ate [~rit] 1. confédéré; 2. confédéré *m*; complice *m*; 3. [~reit] (se) confédérer; con·fed·er'a·tion confédération *f*; *surt. Am.* the ♀ la Confédération *f* des 11 États sécessionnistes.

con·fer [kən'fəː] *v/t.* (à, on) conférer; accorder (*une faveur*); décerner (*un honneur*); *v/i.* conférer; entrer en consultation (avec, *with*; sur *about*, on); con·fer·ence ['kɔnfərəns] conférence *f*; consultation *f*; entretien *m*; congrès *m*.

con·fess [kən'fes] *v/t.* confesser; avouer (*qch.*; que, *that*; *inf.*, *to* gér.); *v/i. eccl.* se confesser; con'fess·ed·ly [~idli] de l'aveu général; franchement; con·fes·sion [~'feʃn] confession *f* (*a. eccl.*); aveu *m*; *go to* ~ aller à confesse; con'fes·sion·al 1. confessionnel(le *f*); 2. confessionnal *m*; con'fes·sor [~sə] celui (celle) qui avoue; confesseur *m*.

con·fi·dant [kɔnfi'dænt] confident *m*; con·fi'dante [~] confidente *f*.

con·fide [kən'faid] confier; se (con)fier (à q., *in s.o.*); avouer (*qch.*) en confidence (à q., *to s.o.*); con·fi·dence ['kɔnfidəns] confiance *f* (en, *in*); assurance *f*, hardiesse *f*; confidence *f*; ~ *man* escroc *m*; ~ *trick* vol *m* à l'américaine; *man of* ~

homme *m* de confiance; **'con·fi·dent** □ assuré, sûr (de, of); *péj.* effronté; **con·fi·den·tial** [ˌ‿'denʃl] □ confidentiel(le *f*); ~ clerk clerc *m* de confiance; ~ agent homme *m* de confiance.

con·fig·u·ra·tion [kənfigjuˈreiʃn] configuration *f*.

con·fine 1. [ˈkɔnfain] *usu.* ~s *pl.* confins *m/pl.*; **2.** [kənˈfain] (r)enfermer (dans, to); borner, limiter (à, to); *be* ~d *to bed* être alité, garder le lit; *be* ~d faire ses couches; accoucher (*d'un fils etc.*); **con'fine·ment** emprisonnement *m*, réclusion *f*; alitement *m*; restriction *f*; *femme:* couches *f/pl.*, accouchement *m*.

con·firm [kənˈfəːm] confirmer (*a. eccl.*); affermir (*un pouvoir*); ✝ entériner; **con·fir·ma·tion** [kənfəˈmeiʃn] confirmation *f*; affermissement *m*; **con·firm·a·tive** □ [kənˈfəːmətiv], **con'firm·a·to·ry** [ˌ‿təri] confirmatif (-ive *f*); confirmatoire; **con'firmed** invétéré; endurci; incorrigible (*surt.* ✝) chronique.

con·fis·cate [ˈkɔnfiskeit] confisquer; F voler; **con·fis'ca·tion** confiscation *f*; F *fig.* vol *m*; **con'fis·ca·to·ry** [ˌ‿kətəri] de confiscation.

con·fla·gra·tion [kɔnfləˈgreiʃn] conflagration *f*; incendie *m*.

con·flict 1. [ˈkɔnflikt] conflit *m*, lutte *f*; *intérêts:* antagonisme *m*; **2.** [kənˈflikt] (*with*) être en conflit *ou* désaccord *ou* contradiction (avec); se heurter (à).

con·flu·ence [ˈkɔnfluəns], **con·flux** [ˈ‿flʌks] *voies, rivières, etc.:* confluent *m*; concours *m* (*d'hommes etc.*); **con·flu·ent** [ˈ‿fluənt] **1.** qui confluent; qui se confondent; **2.** *fleuve:* affluent *m*.

con·form [kənˈfɔːm] *v/t.* conformer; *v/i.:* ~ *to* se conformer à; obéir à; s'adapter à; ~ *with* se soumettre à; **con'form·a·ble** □ (*to*) conforme (à); docile, soumis (à); **con·for·ma·tion** [kɔnfɔːˈmeiʃn] conformation *f*, structure *f*; **con·form·ist** [kənˈfɔːmist] conformiste *m*; adhérent *m* de l'Église anglicane; **con'form·i·ty** conformité *f* (à *with*, to); *in* ~ *with* conformément à.

con·found [kənˈfaund] confondre (*q., un plan*); déconcerter; bouleverser; F ~ *it!* zut!; **con'found·ed** □ F maudit, sacré.

con·fra·ter·ni·ty [kɔnfrəˈtəːniti] confrérie *f*; confraternité *f*.

con·front [kənˈfrʌnt] être en face de; faire face à; confronter (avec, with); *find o.s.* ~ed *with* se trouver en présence de; **con·fron·ta·tion** [kɔnfrʌnˈteiʃn] confrontation *f*.

con·fuse [kənˈfjuːz] confondre (*a. fig.*); mêler, brouiller; embrouiller; troubler; **con'fus·ed** □ embrouillé; bouleversé; confus; interdit; **con'fu·sion** confusion *f*; désordre *m*; *poét.* déconfiture *f*.

con·fut·a·ble [kənˈfjuːtəbl] réfutable; **con·fu·ta·tion** [kɔnfjuːˈteiʃn] réfutation *f*; **con·fute** [kənˈfjuːt] réfuter; convaincre (*q.*) d'erreur.

con·gé [ˈkɔːnʒei] congé *m*.

con·geal [kənˈdʒiːl] (se) congeler; (se) cailler; (se) figer; geler; **con'geal·a·ble** congelable.

con·ge·la·tion [kɔndʒiˈleiʃn] congélation *f*.

con·ge·ner [ˈkɔndʒinə] congénère (*a. su./mf*) (de, to).

con·gen·ial □ [kənˈdʒiːnjəl] sympathique (*esprit*); agréable; convenable (à, to); ~ *with* du même caractère que; **con·ge·ni·al·i·ty** [ˌ‿niˈæliti] communauté *f* de goûts; accord *m* d'humeur *etc.*

con·gen·i·tal [kənˈdʒenitl] congénital (-aux *m/pl.*), de naissance; **con'gen·i·tal·ly** de naissance.

con·ge·ri·es [kɔnˈdʒiəriːz] *sg. et pl.* amas *m*, accumulation *f*.

con·gest [kənˈdʒest] ✽ (se) congestionner; *v/t.* encombrer; **con'ges·tion** encombrement *m*; ✽ congestion *f*; ~ *of population* surpeuplement *m*; ~ *of traffic* encombrement *m* de circulation.

con·glo·bate [ˈkɔŋɡlobeit] **1.** (se) conglober; **2.** conglobé.

con·glom·er·ate [kənˈɡlɔmərit] **1.** congloméré; **2.** conglomérat *m*; aggloméré *m*; **3.** [ˌ‿reit] (se) conglomérer; **con·glom·er·a·tion** conglomération *f*; *roches:* agrégation *f*.

con·grat·u·late [kənˈɡrætjuleit] féliciter (*q. de qch., s.o.* [*up*]*on s.th.*); **con·grat·u·la·tion** félicitation *f*; **con·grat·u·la·tor** congratulateur (-trice *f*) *m*; **con'grat·u·la·to·ry** [ˌ‿lətəri] de félicitation(s).

con·gre·gate [ˈkɔŋɡrigeit] (se) rassembler; **con·gre'ga·tion** *eccl.* assistance *f*, paroissiens *m/pl.*; **con-**

gre·ga·tion·al en assemblée; *eccl.* congrégationaliste.

con·gress ['kɔŋgres] réunion *f*; congrès *m*; ♀ Congrès *m* (*assemblée des représentants aux É.-U.*); **con·gres·sion·al** [ˌ'greʃənl] du congrès; **congressionnel(le** *f*); **'Con·gress·man**, **'Con·gress·wo·man** *Am.* membre *m* du Congrès.

con·gru·ence, con·gru·en·cy ['kɔŋ-gruəns(i)] *see* **congruity**; ♭ congruence *f*; **'con·gru·ent** *see* **congruous**; ♭ congruent; **con'gru·i·ty** conformité *f*, convenance *f*; **'con·gru·ous** □ conforme (à *to, usu.* with).

con·ic ['kɔnik] conique; ♭ ∼ section section *f* conique; **'con·i·cal** □ *see* **conic**.

co·ni·fer ['kounifə] conifère *m*; **co'nif·er·ous** conifère.

con·jec·tur·al □ [kən'dʒektʃərəl] conjectural (-aux *m/pl.*); **con'jec·ture 1.** hypothèse *f*, supposition *f*; conjecture *f*; **2.** conjecturer; supposer.

con·join [kən'dʒɔin] *v/t.* conjoindre; *v/i.* s'unir; **con'joint** conjoint, associé; **con'joint·ly** conjointement, ensemble.

con·ju·gal □ ['kɔndʒugl] conjugal (-aux *m/pl.*); **con·ju·gate 1.** ['ˌgeit] *v/t.* conjuguer; *v/i. biol.* se conjuguer; **2.** [ˌgit] ⚕ conjugué; **con·ju·ga·tion** [ˌ'geiʃn] conjugaison *f*.

con·junct □ [kən'dʒʌŋkt] conjoint, associé; **con'junc·tion** conjonction *f* (*a. astr., a. gramm.*); **con·junc·ti·va** *anat.* [kɔndʒʌŋk'taivə] conjonctive *f*; **con·junc·tive** [kən'dʒʌŋk-tiv] conjonctif (-ive *f*); ∼ *mood gramm.* (mode *m*) conjonctif *m*; **con·'junc·tive·ly** conjointement, ensemble; **con·junc·ti·vi·tis** [ˌˈvai-tis] conjonctivite *f*; **con'junc·ture** [ˌtʃə] conjoncture *f*, circonstance *f*, occasion *f*, rencontre *f*.

con·ju·ra·tion [kɔndʒuə'reiʃn] conjuration *f*; **con·jure** [kən'dʒuə] *v/t.* conjurer (*q. de inf., s.o. to inf.*); ['kʌndʒə] *v/t.* conjurer (*un démon*); ∼ *up* évoquer (*a. fig.*); *v/i.* faire des tours de passe-passe; **'con·jur·er**, **'con·jur·or** † conjurateur *m*; prestidigitateur *m*, illusionniste *mf*; **con·jur·ing trick** tour *m* de passe-passe.

conk F [kɔŋk] avoir des ratés; flancher (*moteur*); ∼ *out* (se) caler.

con·ker F *Brit.* ['kɔŋkə] marron *m*.

con man F ['kɔnmæn] escroc *m*.

con·nate ['kɔneit] ⚘ inné; ⚘, *a. anat.* conné, coadné; **con·nat·u·ral** [kə'nætʃrl] de la même nature (que, to).

con·nect [kə'nekt] (se) (re)lier, (se) joindre; *v/t.* ⚡ (inter)connecter; brancher (*une lampe*); **con'nect·ed** □ connexe; apparenté (*personne*); suivi (*discours*); *be* ∼ *with* être allié à *ou* avec; se rattacher à; avoir des rapports avec; *be well* ∼ être de bonne famille; **con'nect·ing** de connexion (*fil*); de communication; qui relie; ∼ *rod* bielle *f* (motrice); **con'nec·tion** *see* **connexion**; **con'nec·tive** □ connectif (-ive *f*); *anat.* ∼ *tissue* tissu *m* cellulaire connectif.

con·nex·ion [kə'nekʃn] rapport *m*, liaison *f*; *idées:* suite *f*; ⚡ connexion *f*; ⚡ contact *m*; prise *f* de courant; ⊕ raccord *m*; ⚡ correspondance *f*; *eccl.* secte *f*; *famille:* parenté *f*, parent(e *f*) *m*; allié(e *f*) *m*; *personne:* relations *f/pl.*; ♱ clientèle *f*; relation *f* (entre, between); ∼*s pl.* belles relations *f/pl.*; amis *m/pl.* influents.

conn·ing-tow·er ⚓ ['kɔniŋtauə] *sous-marin:* capot *m*; *cuirassé:* tourelle *f* de commandement.

con·niv·ance [kə'naivəns] complicité *f* (dans *at, in*); connivence *f* (avec, with); **con'nive:** ∼ *at* fermer les yeux sur; être fauteur de (*un crime*).

con·nois·seur [kɔni'səː] connaisseur (-euse *f*) *m* (en *of, in*).

con·no·ta·tion [kɔnou'teiʃn] signification *f*; *phls.* compréhension *f*; **'con·not·a·tive** □ compréhensif (-ive *f*); **con'note** *phls.* comporter; F signifier.

con·nu·bi·al □ [kə'njuːbjəl] conjugal (-aux *m/pl.*).

con·quer ['kɔŋkə] vaincre; *v/t.* conquérir; *fig.* subjuguer; **con'quer·a·ble** qui peut être vaincu *ou* conquis; **'con·quer·or** conquérant(e *f*) *m*; vainqueur *m*; *cartes:* la belle *f*.

con·quest ['kɔŋkwest] conquête *f*.

con·san·guin·e·ous [kɔnsæŋ'gwini-əs] consanguin; F parent; **con·san·'guin·i·ty** consanguinité *f*; parenté *f* (du côté du père).

con·science ['kɔnʃns] conscience *f*;

F *in all* ~ certes, en vérité; *have the* ~ *to* (*inf.*) avoir l'audace de (*inf.*); ~ *money* restitution *f* anonyme au fisc; **'con·science·less** sans conscience.

con·sci·en·tious □ [kɔnʃi'enʃəs] consciencieux (-euse *f*); de conscience; ~ *objector* objecteur *m* de conscience; **con·sci'en·tious·ness** conscience *f*; droiture *f*.

con·scious □ ['kɔnʃəs] conscient; *be* ~ *of* avoir conscience de; *be* ~ *that* sentir que; **'con·scious·ness** conscience *f*; ✻ connaissance *f*.

con·script 1. ✗ [kən'skript] (*ou* **con·scribe** [~'skraib]) enrôler par la conscription; **2.** ['kɔnskript] conscrit (*a.* ✗ *su./m*); **con·scrip·tion** ✗ [kən'skripʃn] conscription *f*; *industrial* ~ conscription *f* industrielle.

con·se·crate ['kɔnsikreit] consacrer (*a. fig.*); bénir; sacrer (*un évêque, un roi*); **con·se'cra·tion** consécration *f*; *fig.* dévouement *m*; *roi:* sacre *m*; **'con·se·cra·tor** consacrant *m*.

con·sec·u·tive [kən'sekjutiv] consécutif (-ive *f*) (*a.* ♪, *a.* gramm.); de suite; qui se suivent; **con'sec·u·tive·ly** de suite; consécutivement.

con·sen·sus [kən'sensəs] consensus *m*; unanimité *f*.

con·sent [kən'sent] **1.** consentement *m*, assentiment *m* (à, to); accord *m*; *with one* ~ d'un commun accord; **2.** consentir (à, to); accepter (qch. to, in s.th.); **con·sen·ta·ne·ous** □ [kɔnsen'teiniəs] (to) d'accord (avec); en harmonie (avec); **con·sen·tient** [kən'senʃnt] unanime (sur, in); consentant (à, to).

con·se·quence ['kɔnsikwəns] (to) conséquence *f*; suites *f/pl.*; importance *f* (pour *q.*, à qch.); *in* ~ *of* par suite de; en conséquence de; **'con·se·quent 1.** résultant; logique; *be* ~ *on* résulter de; **2.** ⅋ conséquent *m*; *phls.* conclusion *f*; **con·se·quen·tial** □ [~'kwenʃl] conséquent (à to, [up]on); consécutif (-ive *f*) (à, to); *personne:* suffisant; **con·se·quent·ly** ['~kwəntli] par conséquent; donc.

con·ser·va·tion [kɔnsə'veiʃn] conservation *f*; **con'ser·va·tion·ist** partisan(e *f*) *m* de la défense de l'environnement; **con·serv·a·tism** [kən'sə:vətizm] conservatisme *m*;

con·serv·a·tive □ **1.** conservateur (-trice *f*) (*a.* pol.) (de, of); préservateur (-trice *f*) (de, from); prudent (*évaluation*); **2.** conservateur (-trice *f*) *m*; **con'ser·va·toire** [~twa:] ♪ conservatoire *m*; **con'ser·va·tor** conservateur (-trice *f*) *m*; **con·serv·a·to·ry** [~tri] serre *f*; conservatoire *m*; **con'serve** conserver; préserver.

con·sid·er [kən'sidə] *v/t.* considérer (*une question*); envisager (*une possibilité*); étudier, examiner (*une proposition*); estimer, regarder (= penser); prendre en considération; avoir égard à; *v/i.* réfléchir; **con'sid·er·a·ble** □ considérable, important; **con'sid·er·ate** [~rit] □ plein d'égards (pour, envers to[wards]); **con·sid·er·a·tion** [~'reiʃn] considération *f*; égard *m*, -s *m/pl.*; compensation *f*, rémunération *f*; pourboire *m*; *fig.* importance *f*; ✝ prix *m*; cause *f* (*d'un billet*); *be under* ~ être en délibération *ou* à l'examen; *take into* ~ prendre en considération; tenir compte de; *money is no* ~ l'argent n'est rien; l'argent n'entre pas en ligne de compte; *on no* ~ sous aucun prétexte; **con'sid·er·ing** □ **1.** *prp.* en égard à, étant donné ...; **2.** *F adv.* somme toute, malgré tout.

con·sign [kən'sain] remettre, livrer; reléguer; déposer (*de l'argent*); **con·sig·na·tion** [kɔnsai'neiʃn], **con·sign·ment** [kən'sainmənt] ✝ expédition *f*; envoi *m*; consignation *f*; **con·sign·ee** [kɔnsai'ni:] destinataire *m*; **con'sign·er, con·sign·or** [kən'sainə] consignateur *m*, expéditeur *m*.

con·sist [kən'sist] consister (en, dans of; à *inf.*, in *gér.*); se composer (de, of); **con'sist·ence, con'sist·en·cy** *sirop, esprit:* consistance *f*; *sol:* compacité *f*; *conduite:* uniformité *f*; logique *f*; **con'sist·ent** □ conséquent; logique; compatible (avec, with); ~*ly a.* uniformément; **con'sis·to·ry** [~təri] *eccl.* consistoire *m*.

con·sol·a·ble [kən'souləbl] consolable; **con·so·la·tion** [kɔnsə'leiʃn] consolation *f*; *sp.* ~ *goal* but *m* qui sauve l'honneur; **con·sol·a·to·ry** [kən'sɔlətəri] consolateur (-trice *f*); consolant; de consolation; **con·sole 1.** ['kɔnsoul] console *f* (*a.*

consult

$\triangle$); ~-table (table *f*) console *f*; **2.** [kən'soul] consoler; **con'sol·er** consolateur (-trice *f*) *m*.

con·sol·i·date [kən'sɔlideit] (se) consolider (*a. fig.*); (se) tasser (*chaussée*); *v/t.* affermir; solidifier; unir (*des entreprises, des propriétés, etc.*); **con·sol·i·da·tion** consolidation *f*; affermissement *m*; tassement *m*; unification *f*.

con·sols [kən'sɔlz] *pl.* fonds *m/pl.* consolidés; *3 per cent* ~ consolidés *m/pl.* trois pour cent.

con·so·nance ['kɔnsənəns] consonance *f*; accord *m* (*a. ♪*); **'con·so·nant 1.** □ *♪* harmonieux (-euse *f*); consonant; conforme (à *with, to*); **2.** consonne *f*; ~ *shift* mutation *f* consonantique.

con·sort 1. ['kɔnsɔːt] époux *m*, épouse *f*; *reine:* consort *m*; ⚓ conserve *f*; **2.** [kən'sɔːt] (*with*) fréquenter (*q.*); frayer (avec).

con·spic·u·ous □ [kən'spikjuəs] apparent, bien visible, manifeste; *fig.* frappant; insigne; *be* ~ *by one's absence* briller par son absence.

con·spir·a·cy [kən'spirəsi] conspiration *f*; **con'spir·a·tor** [~tə] conspirateur (-trice *f*) *m*; **con'spir·a·tress** [~tris] conspiratrice *f*; **con·spire** [~'spaiə] conspirer (contre, *against*); comploter (de, *to*); *fig.* concourir (à, *to*).

con·sta·ble ['kʌnstəbl] gardien *m* de la paix; *château:* gouverneur *m*; *hist.* connétable *m*; *chief* ~ commissaire *m* de police; **con·stab·u·lar·y** [kən'stæbjuləri] police *f*; *county* ~ gendarmerie *f*.

con·stan·cy ['kɔnstənsi] constance *f*, fermeté *f*; fidélité *f*; régularité *f*; **'con·stant 1.** □ constant; ferme; fidèle; invariable; continuel(le *f*); assidu; **2.** ⚕ constante *f*.

con·stel·la·tion *astr.* [kɔnstə'leiʃn] constellation *f* (*a. fig.*).

con·ster·na·tion [kɔnstə'neiʃn] consternation *f*; atterrement *m*.

con·sti·pate ⚕ ['kɔnstipeit] constiper; **con·sti'pa·tion** ⚕ constipation *f*.

con·stit·u·en·cy [kən'stitjuənsi] circonscription *f* électorale; électeurs *m/pl.*; **con'stit·u·ent 1.** constituant, constitutif (-ive *f*); composant; ~ *body see constituency*); **2.** élément *m* (constitutif); ⚕ constituant *m*; *pol.*

électeur (-trice *f*) *m*; ~s *pl.* commettants *m/pl.*, électeurs *m/pl.*

con·sti·tute ['kɔnstitjuːt] constituer; faire (*le bonheur de q.*); constituer, nommer (*q. arbitre, s.o. judge*); **con·sti·tu·tion** constitution *f* (*de qch., a.* = *santé, a. pol.*); *chose:* composition *f*; ⚕s *pl. hist.* arrêts *m/pl.*; **con·sti·tu·tion·al 1.** □ constitutionnel(le *f*) (*a. ⚕*); *fig.* hygiénique; naturel(le *f*); ~ *law* droit *m* constitutionnel; **2.** F promenade *f* hygiénique *ou* quotidienne; **con·sti·tu·tion·al·ist** historien *m* des constitutions politiques; *pol.* constitutionnel *m*; **con·sti·tu·tive** □ [kən'stitjutiv] constitutif (-ive *f*).

con·strain [kən'strein] contraindre (à, de *inf. to inf.*); retenir de force; **con'straint** contrainte *f* (*a. ⚕*); retenue *f*.

con·strict [kən'strikt] (res)serrer; rétrécir; gêner; **con'stric·tion** resserrement *m*; ⚕ *artères:* strangulation *f*; **con'stric·tor** *anat.* constricteur *m*; *zo.* (*a. boa* ~) boa *m* constricteur.

con·strin·gent [kən'strindʒnt] constringent; ⚕ astringent.

con·struct [kən'strʌkt] construire; bâtir; établir (*un chemin de fer*); *fig.* confectionner; **con'struc·tion** construction *f*; *machine:* établissement *m*; édifice *m*, bâtiment *m*; *fig.* interprétation *f*; ~ *site* chantier *m*; *under* ~ en construction; **con'struc·tive** □ constructif (-ive *f*); *esprit:* créateur; de construction; ⚕ implicite; par interprétation; **con'struc·tor** constructeur *m*; *constructions navales:* ingénieur *m*.

con·strue [kən'struː] *gramm.* analyser; décomposer (*une phrase*); faire le mot à mot de (*un texte*); interpréter (*une conduite, des paroles, etc.*).

con·sue·tu·di·nar·y [kɔnswi'tjuːdinəri] coutumier (-ère *f*).

con·sul ['kɔnsl] consul *m*; ~ *general* consul *m* général; **con·su·lar** ['kɔnsjulə] consulaire; *de ou* du consul; **con·su·late** ['~lit] consulat *m* (*a. bâtiment*); ~ *general* consulat *m* général; **con·sul·ship** ['kɔnslʃip] consulat *m*.

con·sult [kən'sʌlt] *v/t.* consulter (*a. fig.*); avoir égard à (*la sensibilité*); ~*ing engineer* ingénieur-conseil (*pl.* ingénieurs-conseils) *m*; *v/i.* consulter (avec q., *s.o.*); (*a.* ~ *together*) délibérer; **con'sult·ant** médecin *m* etc. consultant; ⊕ expert-conseil (*pl.* experts-conseils) *m*; **con·sul·ta·tion** [kɔnsəl'teiʃn] ⚕, ⚖, *livre:* consultation *f*; délibération *f*; **con·sult·a·tive** [kən'sʌltətiv] consultatif (-ive *f*); **con'sult·ing** consultant; ~-*hours* heures *f/pl.* de consultation; ~ *physician* médecin *m* consultant; ~ *room* cabinet *m* de consultation.

con·sum·a·ble [kən'sjuːməbl] consumable (*feu*); consommable; **con'sume** *v/t.* consumer (*a. feu*), dévorer; consommer (*des vivres*); *fig.* absorber, brûler; dévorer; *v/i.* se consumer; **con'sum·er** consommateur (-trice *f*) *m*; abonné(e *f*) *m* (*au gaz etc.*); ~ *association* association *f* des consommateurs; ~ *demand* demande *f*; ~ *durables pl.* biens *m/pl.* de consommation durables; ~(*s'*) *goods pl.* biens *m/pl.* de consommation; ~ *resistance* résistance *f* du consommateur; ~ *society* société *f* de consommation.

con·sum·mate 1. □ [kən'sʌmit] achevé; **2.** ['kɔnsʌmeit] consommer (*un sacrifice, le mariage*); **con·sum·ma·tion** [~'meiʃn] *mariage, crime:* consommation *f*; achèvement *m*; fin *f*; *fig.* but *m*, comble *m*.

con·sump·tion [kən'sʌmpʃn] *vivres, charbon:* consommation *f*; *charbon, chaleur:* dépense *f*; ⚕ phtisie *f*; tuberculose *f*; **con'sump·tive** □ poitrinaire (*a. su./mf*); tuberculeux (-euse *f*); phtisique (*a. su./mf*).

con·tact 1. ['kɔntækt] contact *m* (*a. ⚡*); ⚡ ~ *breaker* interrupteur *m*; *opt.* ~ *lenses pl.* lentilles *f/pl.* cornéennes, verres *m/pl.* de contact; *phot.* ~ *print* négatif *m* contact; ⚡ *make* (*break*) ~ établir (rompre) le contact; **2.** [kən'tækt] contacter (*q.*).

con·ta·gion ⚕ [kən'teidʒn] contagion *f*; maladie *f* contagieuse; **con'ta·gious** □ contagieux (-euse *f*).

con·tain [kən'tein] contenir; renfermer; ⚔ maintenir, contenir (*l'ennemi*); *fig.* retenir, maîtriser; ~ *o.s.* se contenir; **con'tain·er** récipient *m*, boîte *f*; ✝ conteneur *m*; **con'tain·er·ize** conteneuriser; **con'tain·ment** *conduite:* retenue *f*; ⚔ échec *m*.

con·tam·i·nate [kən'tæmineit] contaminer; *fig.* corrompre; vicier;

con·tam·i'na·tion *textes, a. ling.:* contamination *f*; souillure *f*.

con·tan·go ✝ [kən'tæŋgou] intérêt *m* de report.

con·tem·plate ['kɔntempleit] *v/t.* contempler, considérer; *v/i.* méditer; **con'tem'pla·tion** contemplation *f*; méditation *f*; *have in* ~ projeter; **con'tem·pla·tive** □ [kən'templətiv] contemplatif (-ive *f*); recueilli; songeur (-euse *f*).

con·tem·po·ra·ne·ous □ [kɔntempə'reinjəs] contemporain; ⚖ ~ *performance* exécution *f* simultanée; **con'tem·po·rar·y 1.** contemporain (de, *with*); **2.** contemporain(e *f*) *m*; confrère *m*.

con·tempt [kən'tempt] mépris *m*, dédain *m*; ~ *of court* contumace *f*, outrage *m* à la Cour; *hold in* ~ mépriser; *in* ~ *of* au *ou* en mépris de; **con'tempt·i·ble** □ méprisable; bas(se *f*); **con'temp·tu·ous** □ [~juəs] dédaigneux (-euse *f*) (de, *of*); méprisant, de mépris.

con·tend [kən'tend] *v/i.* lutter; contester (qch., *for s.th.*; à q., *with s.o.*); *v/t.* soutenir (que, *that*).

con·tent¹ ['kɔntent] *vase etc:* contenance *f*; *min.* teneur *f*; ~*s pl.* contenu *m*.

con·tent² [kən'tent] **1.** satisfait (de, *with*); *parl.* pour; oui; non ~ contre; **2.** contenter, satisfaire; ~ *o.s.* se contenter (de, *with*); se borner à; **3.** contentement *m*; *to one's heart's* ~ à souhait; **con'tent·ed** □ content, satisfait (de, *with*); *be* ~ *to* (*inf.*) se contenter de (*inf.*).

con·ten·tion [kən'tenʃn] dispute *f*, débat *m*; affirmation *f*, prétention *f*; **con'ten·tious** □ contentieux (-euse *f*); disputeur (-euse *f*) (*personne*).

con·tent·ment [kən'tentmənt] contentement *m* (de son sort).

con·ter·mi·nous [kɔn'təːminəs] limitrophe (de *to*, *with*); de même étendue *ou* durée (que, *with*).

con·test 1. ['kɔntest] lutte *f*; concours *m*; *sp.* match (*pl.* matchs, matches) *m*; **2.** [kən'test] (se) disputer; contester, débattre; *pol.* ~ *a seat* se poser candidat pour un siège; **con'test·a·ble** contestable; débattable; **con'test·ant** contestant(e *f*) *m*; concurrent(e *f*) *m*; **con'test·ed** disputé.

con·text ['kɔntekst] *texte:* contexte

m; **con·tex·tu·al** □ [kən'tekstjuəl]
d'après le contexte; **con'tex·ture**
[‿tʃə] *os, tissu:* texture *f; poème,
discours:* facture *f.*

con·ti·gu·i·ty [kɔnti'gjuiti] contiguïté *f;* **con·tig·u·ous** □ [kən-
'tigjuəs] contigu(ë *f*), attenant (à,
to).

con·ti·nence ['kɔntinəns] continence *f,* chasteté *f;* **'con·ti·nent**
1. □ continent, chaste; **2.** continent
m; the ♀ l'Europe *f* (continentale);
con·ti·nen·tal □ [‿'nentl] continental (-aux *m/pl.*); F de l'Europe;
∼ quilt duvet *m;* **con·ti'nen·tal·ize**
continentaliser.

con·tin·gen·cy [kən'tindʒənsi] éventualité *f;* cas *m* imprévu; **con'tin·**
gen·cies *pl.* imprévu *m;* ✝ faux
frais *m/pl.;* **con'tin·gent 1.** □ éven-
tuel(le *f*); accidentel(le *f*); aléatoire; conditionnel(le *f); be ∼ on* dépendre de; **2.** ✕ contingent *m.*

con·tin·u·al □ [kən'tinjuəl] conti-
nuel(le *f*), incessant; **con'tin·u·**
ance continuation *f;* durée *f;* **con·**
tin·u'a·tion continuation *f;* suite *f;*
prolongement *m;* ✝ report *m; sl. ∼s*
pl. pantalon *m;* guêtres *f/pl.; ∼*
school école *f* du soir, cours *m* complémentaire; **con'tin·ue** *v/t.* continuer; prolonger; reprendre;
maintenir; *∼ reading* continuer à *ou*
de lire; *to be ∼d* à suivre; *v/i.* (se)
continuer; se prolonger; persévérer;
se poursuivre; *∼ (in) a business* continuer dans une affaire; **con·ti·nu·**
i·ty [kɔnti'njuiti] continuité *f; ∼-*
girl script-girl *f;* **con·tin·u·ous** □
[kən'tinjuəs] continu; suivi; ⚡ *∼*
current courant *m* continu.

con·tort [kən'tɔːt] tordre; contourner; **con'tor·tion** contorsion *f;*
con'tor·tion·ist contorsionniste *m.*

con·tour ['kɔntuə] contour *m,* profil *m; plan:* tracé *m; ∼ line* courbe *f*
de niveau.

con·tra ['kɔntrə] contre; ✝ *per ∼*
par contre.

con·tra·band ['kɔntrəbænd] **1.** de
contrebande; **2.** contrebande *f.*

con·tract 1. [kən'trækt] *v/t.* contracter (*habitudes, maladie, dettes,
mariage, muscles*); prendre (*des
habitudes, un goût*); *v/i.* se resserrer,
se contracter (*a. ling.*); traiter (pour,
for); entreprendre (de, *to*); *∼ for*
entreprendre (*qch.*); *∼ing party* con-

tractant(e *f*) *m;* **2.** ['kɔntrækt]
pacte *m,* contrat *m;* entreprise *f;*
by ∼ par contrat; *under ∼* engagé
par contrat; *∼ work* travail *m* à forfait; **con·tract·ed** □ [kən'træktid]
contracté; *fig.* rétréci; **con·tract·i·**
'bil·i·ty contractilité *f;* **con'tract·**
i·ble contractile; **con'trac·tile** ⚕
[‿tail] contractile; de contraction;
con'trac·tion contraction *f (a.
gramm.*), rétrécissement *m; crédit:*
amoindrissement *m; habitudes:*
prise *f;* **con'trac·tor** *bâtiments:*
entrepreneur *m; armée, gouvernement:* fournisseur *m; anat.* (muscle
m) fléchisseur *m;* **con'trac·tu·al** [‿-
tjuəl] contractuel(le *f*).

con·tra·dict [kɔntrə'dikt] contredire (*q., qch.*); **con·tra'dic·tion**
contradiction *f;* **con·tra·dic·tious**
contredisant; ergoteur (-euse *f*);
con·tra'dic·to·ri·ness [‿tərinis]
nature *f* contradictoire; esprit *m* de
contradiction; **con·tra'dic·to·ry** □
contradictoire; opposé (à, to).

con·tral·to ♪ [kən'træltəu] **1.** contralto *m;* **2.** (de) contralto.

con·tra·dis·tinc·tion [kɔntrədis-
'tiŋkʃn] opposition *f,* contraste *m.*

con·trap·tion *sl.* [kən'træpʃn] dispositif *m,* machin *m;* invention *f*
baroque.

con·tra·ri·e·ty [kɔntrə'raiəti] contrariété *f;* **con·tra·ri·ly** ['‿rili]
contrairement; **'con·tra·ri·ness** esprit *m* contrariant *ou* de contradiction; contrariété *f;* **con·tra·ri·**
wise ['‿waiz] au contraire; d'autre
part; en sens opposé; **'con·tra·ry**
1. contraire, opposé; F [*a.* kən-
'treəri] indocile, revêche; *∼ to* contraire à, contre, à l'encontre de;
2. contraire *m; on (ou to) the ∼* au
contraire; *to the ∼ a.* à l'encontre.

con·trast 1. ['kɔntræst] contraste *m*
(avec *to,* with); *in ∼ to* par contraste avec; *by ∼* en opposition;
comme contraste; **2.** [kən'træst]
v/t. faire contraster (avec, *with*);
opposer; mettre en contraste (avec,
with); *v/i.* contraster, faire contraste (avec, with).

con·tra·vene [kɔntrə'viːn] enfreindre, transgresser; contrevenir à;
aller à l'encontre de; **con·tra·ven·**
tion [‿'venʃn] contravention *f,* infraction *f* (à, of); violation *f* (de, of).

con·trib·ute [kən'tribjuːt] *v/t.* con-

contribution

tribuer pour (une somme); payer; écrire (des articles); v/i. contribuer, aider (à, to); collaborer (à un journal); **con·tri'bu·tion** [kɔntri'bjuːʃn] contribution f; cotisation f; ✝ apport m (de capitaux), versement m; journal: article m; ✕ contribution f, réquisition f; **con'trib·u·tor** [kən-'tribjutə] contribuant(e f) m; collaborateur (-trice f) m (d'un journal, to a newspaper); **con'trib·u·to·ry** contribuant.

con·trite □ ['kɔntrait] contrit, pénitent; **con·tri·tion** [kən'triʃn] contrition f, pénitence f.

con·triv·ance [kən'traivəns] invention f; combinaison f; artifice m; appareil m, dispositif m; F truc m; **con'trive** v/t. inventer, imaginer, combiner; pratiquer; v/i. se débrouiller; se tirer d'affaire; s'arranger; trouver moyen (de inf., to inf.); **con'triv·er** inventeur (-trice f) m; péj. machinateur (-trice f) m.

con·trol [kən'troul] **1.** autorité f; maîtrise f, contrainte f; empire m; contrôle m; train, navire: manœuvre f; mot. (a. ~ lever) manette f de commande; surveillance f; ⊕ commande f; contrôleur (-euse f) m (d'un médium); exchange ~ contrôle m des changes; attr. de commande, de contrôle; ✈ ~ surfaces pl. empennage m; remote (ou distant) ~ commande f à distance; ✈ ~ board commutateur m; ✈ ~ column levier m de commande; ⊕ ~ desk pupitre m de commande; ~ knob bouton m de réglage; ✈ ~ panel tableau m de bord; ✈ ~ tower tour f de contrôle; be in ~ commander (qch., of s.th.); avoir de l'autorité (sur, of); put s.o. in ~ charger q. du contrôle ou de la direction (de, of); **2.** diriger; régler; tenir (ses élèves); maîtriser; gouverner (a. fig.); dompter (ses passions); réglementer (la circulation); retenir (ses larmes); ⊕ commander (a. ✈); ✝ ~ling interest participation majoritaire; **con'trol·la·ble** contrôlable; maniable, manœuvrable; maîtrisable; **con'trol·ler** contrôleur (-euse f) m; appareil, a. ✈ contrôleur m; affaire: gérant m.

con·tro·ver·sial □ [kɔntrə'vəːʃl] controversable; polémique; personne: disputailleur (-euse f) m; **con·tro·ver·sy** ['~si] controverse f;

polémique f; **con·tro·vert** ['~vəːt] controverser (une question); disputer (qch.); **con·tro'vert·i·ble** □ controversable.

con·tu·ma·cious □ [kɔntju:'meiʃəs] rebelle, récalcitrant; ✝✝ contumace; **con·tu·ma·cy** ['kɔntjuməsi] obstination f, entêtement m; ✝✝ contumace f.

con·tu·me·li·ous [kɔntju:'miːliəs] insolent, dédaigneux (-euse f); **con·tu·me·ly** ['kɔntjumli] insolence f; mépris m; honte f.

con·tuse ✕ [kən'tjuːz] contusionner; **con'tu·sion** contusion f.

co·nun·drum [kə'nʌndrəm] devinette f; fig. énigme f.

con·va·lesce [kɔnvə'les] être en convalescence; **con·va·les·cence** convalescence f; **con·va·les·cent** □ convalescent(e f) (a. su./mf).

con·vec·tion [kən'vekʃn] phys. convection f.

con·vene [kən'viːn] (s')assembler, (se) réunir; v/t. convoquer (une assemblée); ✝✝ citer (devant, before).

con·ven·ience [kən'viːnjəns] commodité f, convenance f; plaisir m; (a. public ~) cabinets m/pl. d'aisance, commodités f/pl.; at your earliest ~ au premier moment favorable; make a ~ of s.o. abuser de la bonté de q.; marriage of ~ mariage m de convenance; **con'ven·ient** □ commode; à proximité (de to, for).

con·vent ['kɔnvənt] couvent m (surt. de femmes); **con·ven·ti·cle** [kən'ventikl] conciliabule m; conventicule m (surt. de dissidents); **con·ven·tion** convention f; accord m; usu. ~s pl. bienséances f/pl.; **con'ven·tion·al** conventionnel(le f); de convention; courant (a. ✕ armes); **con'ven·tion·al·ism** respect m des convenances; art: formalisme m; **con·ven·tion·al·i·ty** [~'næliti] convention f; conventions f/pl. sociales; **con'ven·tu·al** [~tjuəl] □ conventuel(le f) (a. su./mf).

con·verge [kən'vəːdʒ] v/i. converger (sur, on); v/t. faire converger; **con'ver·gence**, **con'ver·gen·cy** convergence f; **con'ver·gent**, **con'verg·ing** convergent.

con·vers·a·ble [kən'vəːsəbl] sociable; de commerce agréable; **con'ver·sant** familier (-ère f) (avec q., with s.o.); versé (dans with, in); compétent (en with, in); **con·ver·sa·tion** [ˌvəˈseiʃn] conversation f, entretien m; **con·verˈsa·tion·al** de (la) conversation; **con·verse** [ˈkɔnvəːs] 1. contraire; 2. conversation f; relations f/pl., commerce m; ⚖ proposition f réciproque; phls. proposition f converse; 3. [kənˈvəːs] causer; s'entretenir (avec, with); **con·verˈsion** ⊕, phls., eccl., pol., † rentes: conversion f (à, to; en into); transformation f (a. ⚡); ⚖ détournement m (de fonds); accommodation f (d'une usine aux usages de qch.).

con·vert 1. [ˈkɔnvəːt] converti(e f) m; 2. [kənˈvəːt] transformer (a. ⚡); changer; convertir (a. ⊕, eccl., pol., phls.); sp. transformer (un essai); † détourner (des fonds); ⚖ détourner (des fonds); † accommoder (une usine etc.); **con·vertˈer** convertisseur (-euse f) m; ⊕, a. ⚡ convertisseur m; radio: adapteur m; **con·vertˈi·bilˈi·ty** [ˌvəˈbiliti] convertibilité f; **con·vertˈi·ble** □ convertissable (personne); convertible (en, into) (chose); interchangeable (termes), réciproque; mot. décapotable, transformable.

con·vex □ [ˈkɔnˈveks] convexe; **con·vexˈi·ty** convexité f.

con·vey [kənˈvei] (trans)porter; conduire; (a)mener (q.); communiquer (une pensée, une nouvelle, etc.); transmettre (phys., a. odeur, son, ordre, remerciements, etc.); ⚖ faire cession de; dresser l'acte translatif de propriété de; **con·veyˈance** transport m; moyen(s) m(pl.) de transport; transmission f (a. ⚖, a. phys.); communication f; voiture f; véhicule m; ⚖ transfert m, cession f; ⚖ acte m translatif de propriété; ⚡ transmission f; transport m (d'énergie); public ~ voiture f publique; **con·veyˈanc·er** notaire m (qui dresse des actes translatifs de propriété); **con·veyˈor** ⊕ (a. ~ belt) bande f transporteuse.

con·vict 1. [ˈkɔnvikt] forçat m; 2. [kənˈvikt] convaincre (de, of); **con·vicˈtion** conviction f; ⚖ condamnation f; previous ~s dossier m du prévenu.

con·vince [kənˈvins] persuader,

convaincre (q. de qch., s.o. of s.th.).

con·viv·i·al [kənˈviviəl] joyeux(-euse f), jovial (-als ou -aux m/pl.), bon vivant; **con·viv·i·alˈi·ty** [ˌviˈæliti] franche gaieté f; sociabilité f.

con·vo·caˈtion [kɔnvəˈkeiʃn] convocation f; eccl. assemblée f.

con·voke [kənˈvouk] convoquer.

con·vo·luˈtion [kɔnvəˈluːʃn] ⚔ circonvolution f; fig. repli m, sinuosité f.   [volubilis m.\ **con·volˈvu·lus** ♣ [kənˈvɔlvjuləs]∫

con·voy 1. [ˈkɔnvɔi] convoi m; escorte f; 2. [kənˈvɔi] convoyer, escorter.

con·vulse [kənˈvʌls] fig. bouleverser; be ~d with laughter se tordre de rire; **con·vulˈsion** usu. ~s pl. convulsion f, -s f/pl.; fig. bouleversement m; go off in ~s of laughter se tordre de rire; **con·vulˈsive** □ convulsif (-ive f).

coo [kuː] 1. roucouler; 2. roucoulement m.

cook [kuk] 1. cuisinier (-ère f) m; (a. head ~) chef m; 2. v/t. (faire) cuire; F cuisiner (les comptes etc.); v/i. faire la cuisine; **'~·book** Am. livre m de cuisine; **'cookˈer** cuisinière f; pomme f ou fruit m à cuire; F falsificateur (-trice f) m des comptes; pressure~ marmite f express; **'cookˈer·y** cuisine f; **cookˈie** [ˈ~i] Am. galette f; **'cookˈing** cuisson f; cuisine f; attr. de cuisine.

cool [kuːl] 1. □ frais (fraîche f); froid, tiède (sentiments); fig. calme, de sang-froid; péj. sans gêne, peu gêné; F a ~ thousand pounds mille livres bien comptées; 2. frais m; 3. (se) rafraîchir; **'coolˈer** rafraîchisseur m; vin: glacière f; sl. prison f; **'coolˈ'head·ed** à l'esprit calme; de sang-froid; imperturbable.

coo·lie [ˈkuːli] coolie m.

cool·ing ⊕ [ˈkuːliŋ] refroidissement m; attr. de réfrigération; **'coolˈness** fraîcheur f; fig. personne: froideur f; sang-froid m; flegme m; **coolth** F ou co. Brit. [kuːlθ] frais m.

coomb(e) géog. [kuːm] combe f.

coon Am. F [kuːn] zo. abr. de rac(c)oon; nègre m; type m; he is a gone ~ c'en est fait de lui; ~ song chanson f nègre.

coop [kuːp] 1. cage f à poules;

poussinière *f*; **2.** ~ *up* (*ou in*) enfermer; tenir enfermé.

co-op F [kou'ɔp] *see* co(-)operative store; co(-)operative society.

coop·er ['ku:pə] tonnelier *m*; *dry* ~ boisselier *m*; *vins:* embouteilleur *m*; **'coop·er·age** tonnellerie *f*.

co(-)op·er·ate [kou'ɔpəreit] coopérer (avec, *with*); concourir (à, *in*); *ready to* ~ prêt à aider; **co(-)op·er·a·tion** coopération *f*, concours *m* (à, *in*); **co(-)'op·er·a·tive** [~pərətiv] **1.** coopératif (-ive *f*); ~ *society* société *f* coopérative; ~ *store* société *f* coopérative de consommation; F coopérative *f*; **2.** *see* ~ *store*; **co·'op·er·a·tor** [~reitə] coopérateur (-trice *f*) *m*.

co-opt [kou'ɔpt] coopter; **co-op'ta·tion** cooptation *f*.

co-or·di·nate [kou'ɔ:dinit] **1.** □ coordonné; **2.** A coordonnée *f*; **3.** [~neit] coordonner (à, *with*); **co-or·di'na·tion** coordination *f*.

coot [ku:t] *orn.* foulque *f* noire; F niais(e *f*) *m*; **cooties** ['~i] *sl.* pou (*pl.* poux) *m*.

cop *sl.* [kɔp] **1.** pincer (=*attraper*); ~ *it* (se faire) attiger; recevoir un savon; **2.** sergot *m*, flic *m*.

co·par·ce·nar·y ['kou'pa:sinəri] copartage *m*; copropriété *f*; **'co'par·ce·ner** indivisaire *m/f*.

co·part·ner ['kou'pa:tnə] coassocié(e *f*) *m*; **'co'part·ner·ship** coassociation *f*; coparticipation *f*; actionnariat *m* ouvrier.

cope¹ [koup] **1.** *eccl.* chape *f*; *fig.* voile *m*, manteau *m*; voûte *f* (*céleste*); **2.** recouvrir d'une voûte; chaperonner (*un mur*).

cope² [~] se débrouiller, s'en tirer; ~ *with* tenir tête à, faire face à; s'occuper de; venir à bout de.

cop·i·er ['kɔpiə] machine *f* à photocopier.

cope·stone ['koupstoun] *usu. fig.* couronnement *m*.

cop·ing A ['koupiŋ] chaperon *m* (*d'un mur*).

co·pi·ous □ ['koupjəs] copieux (-euse *f*), abondant; **'co·pi·ous·ness** profusion *f*, abondance *f*.

cop·per¹ ['kɔpə] **1.** cuivre *m* (rouge); pièce *f* de deux sous; lessiveuse *f*; ~*s pl.* petite monnaie *f*; **2.** de *ou* en cuivre; **3.** cuivrer; doubler (*un navire*).

cop·per² [~] *Brit. sl. see* cop 2.

cop·per·as 🜍 ['kɔpərəs] couperose *f* verte.

cop·per...: '**~plate** plaque *f* de cuivre; ~ *writing* écriture *f* moulée; '**~works** *usu. sg.* fonderie *f* de cuivre; **'cop·per·y** cuivreux (-euse *f*).

cop·pice ['kɔpis], **copse** [kɔps] taillis *m*, hallier *m*.

cop·u·late *zo.* ['kɔpjuleit] s'accoupler; **cop·u'la·tion** coït *m*; *zo.* accouplement *m*; **cop·u·la·tive** ['~lətiv] **1.** *anat.*, *physiol.* copulateur (-trice *f*); *gramm.* copulatif (-ive *f*); **2.** copulative *f*.

cop·y ['kɔpi] **1.** copie *f*; reproduction *f*; transcription *f*; *livre:* exemplaire *m*; *journal:* numéro *m*; *écriture:* modèle *m*; *imprimerie:* manuscrit *m*; *journ.* matière *f* à reportage; (*a. carbon* ~) double *m*; *fair* (*ou clean*) ~ copie *f* au net; *fig.* corrigé *m*; *rough* (*ou foul*) ~ brouillon *m*; **2.** copier; reproduire; transcrire; ~ *fair* mettre au net; *phot.* ~*ing stand* porte-copie *m/inv.*; '**~book** cahier *m* d'écriture; '**~cat** F imitateur *m* (-trice *f*); ~ **ed·i·tor** secrétaire *mf* de rédaction; '**~hold** 🏛 tenure *f* censitaire; '**cop·y·ing·ink** encre *f* à copier; '**cop·y·ing·press** presse *f* à copier; '**cop·y·ist** copiste *mf*; scribe *m*; '**cop·y·right** propriété *f* littéraire; droit *m* d'auteur; *attr.* protégé par des droits d'auteur; qui n'est pas dans le domaine public (*livre*); **cop·y writ·er** rédacteur (-trice *f*) *m* publicitaire.

co·quet [kou'ket] faire la coquette; **co·quet·ry** ['~kitri] coquetterie *f*; **co·quette** [~'ket] coquette *f*; **co·quet·tish** □ provocant; coquet(te *f*) (*chapeau etc.*); flirteur (-euse *f*) (*femme*).

cor·al ['kɔrəl] **1.** corail (*pl.* -aux) *m*; anneau *m* de corail (*pour bébé*); **2.** (*a.* **cor·al·line** ['~lain]) corallien (-ne *f*); corallin (*couleur*).

cor·bel A ['kɔ:bl] corbeau *m*, console *f*.

cord [kɔ:d] **1.** corde *f*; cordon *m* (*a.* ♪); ficelle *f*; *bois de chauffage:* corde *f*; *fig.* lien *m*; *anat.* corde *f* (*vocale*); cordon *m* (*médullaire, ombilical*); *see* corduroy; **2.** corder; attacher *ou* lier avec une corde; '**cord·ed** *tex.* côtelé; '**cord·age** cordages *m/pl.*

cor·dial ['kɔ:djəl] **1.** □ cordial (-aux *m/pl.*); chaleureux (-euse *f*); **2.** cordial *m*; **cor·dial·i·ty** [ˌ~diˈæliti] cordialité *f*.

cord-mak·er ['kɔ:dmeikə] cordier *m*.

cor·don ['kɔ:dən] **1.** △, ✕, etc. cordon *m*; **2.** ~ *off* isoler par un cordon (*de police etc.*).

cor·do·van ['kɔ:dəvən] (cuir *m*) de Cordoue.

cor·du·roy ['kɔ:dərɔi] *tex.* velours *m* côtelé; ~s *pl.* pantalon *m ou* culotte *f* de velours à côtes; ~ *road Am.* chemin *m* de rondins.

core [kɔ:] **1.** ♀ *pomme:* trognon *m*; *bois:* cœur *m*; *fig.* cœur *m*; intérieur *m*; *abcès:* bourbillon *m*; ✕ carotte *f*; ⊕ noyau *m*; ~ *time* temps *m* de présence obligatoire; **2.** enlever le cœur de (*une pomme*); '**cor·er** (*a. apple-~*) vide-pomme *m/inv.*

co·re·li·gion·ist ['kouriˈlidʒənist] coreligionnaire *mf*.

Co·rin·thi·an [kəˈrinθiən] **1.** corinthien(ne *f*); **2.** Corinthien(ne *f*) *m*.

cork [kɔ:k] **1.** liège *m*; *bouteille:* bouchon *m*; **2.** boucher; *fig.* (*a.* ~ *up*) étouffer; '**cork·age** bouchage *m*; débouchage *m*; *restaurant:* droit *m* de débouchage; '**corked** qui sent le bouchon (*vin*); '**cork·er** *sl.* dernier cri *m*; type *m etc.* épatant; mensonge *m* un peu fort; '**cork·ing** *Am.* F fameux (-euse *f*); bath.

cork...: '~-**jack·et** gilet *m* de sauvetage; '~-**screw** **1.** tire-bouchon *m*; ~ *curl cheveux:* tire-bouchon *m*; **2.** *v/i.* vriller (*fil*); tourner en vrille (*escalier*); '~-**tree** ♀ chêne-liège (*pl.* chênes-lièges) *m*; '**cork·y** semblable au liège; *fig.* enjoué.

cor·mo·rant *orn.* ['kɔ:mərənt] cormoran *m*, F corbeau *m* de mer.

corn[1] [kɔ:n] **1.** grain *m*; blé *m*; *Am.* (*a. Indian* ~) maïs *m*; *Am.* ~ *bread* pain *m* de maïs; *Am.* ~*-flakes* paillettes *f/pl.* de maïs; **2.** saler; ~*ed beef* bœuf *m* de conserve.

corn[2] ✿ [~] *orteil:* cor *m*; *pied:* oignon *m*.

corn...: '~-**chan·dler** *Brit.* marchand *m* de grains; '~-**cob** *Am.* épi *m* de maïs.

cor·ne·a *anat.* ['kɔ:niə] *œil:* cornée *f*.

cor·nel ♀ ['kɔ:nl] cornouille *f*; *arbre:* cornouiller *m*.

cor·nel·ian *min.* [kɔ:ˈni:ljən] cornaline *f*.

cor·ne·ous ['kɔ:niəs] corné.

cor·ner ['kɔ:nə] **1.** coin *m*, angle *m*; tournant *m*; *mot.* virage *m*; *fig.* dilemme *m*, impasse *f*; ♰ monopole *m*; ♰ trust *m* d'accapareurs; *foot.* (*a.*~ *kick*) corner *m*; **2.** mettre dans un coin (*fig.* une impasse); acculer (*q.*); mettre (*un animal*) à l'accul; ♰ accaparer; '**cor·nered** à angles, à coins.

corner...: '~-**house** maison *f* du coin; '~-**stone** pierre *f* angulaire (*a. fig.*).

cor·net ['kɔ:nit] ♪ cornet *m* à pistons; *papier:* cornet *m*; *glaces:* plaisir *m*.

corn...: '~-**ex·change** bourse *f* des céréales; halle *f* aux blés; '~-**flow·er** bl(e)uet *m*; ~ *blue* bleu barbeau.

cor·nice ['kɔ:nis] △, *alp.* corniche *f*; chapiteau *m* d'armoire.

Cor·nish ['kɔ:niʃ] cornouaillais, de Cornouailles.

corn...: ~ *meal Am.* farine *f* de maïs; '~-**pop·py** ✿ coquelicot *m*; pavot *m* rouge.

cor·nu·co·pi·a [kɔ:njuˈkoupjə] corne *f* d'abondance.

corn·y ['kɔ:ni] abondant en blé; *sl.* suranné, rebattu; *sent. Am.* ♪ sentimental (-aux *m/pl.*); gnangnan *inv.*

co·rol·la ♀ [kəˈrɔlə] corolle *f*; **cor·ol·la·ry** corollaire *m*; *fig.* conséquence *f*.

co·ro·na [kəˈrounə], *pl.* -nae [ˌ~ni:] *astr.* couronne *f*; △ larmier *m*; **co·ro·nal** ['kɔrənl] *anat.* coronal (-aux *m/pl.*); **cor·o·nar·y** ⚕ ['kɔrənəri] **1.** coronaire; ~ *thrombosis* infarctus *m* du myocarde; **2.** infarctus *m*; **cor·o·na·tion** couronnement *m*, sacre *m*; '**cor·o·ner** ⚖ coroner *m*; **cor·o·net** ['~nit] cercle *m*, couronne *f*; *dame:* diadème *m*.

cor·po·ral ['kɔ:pərəl] **1.** □ corporel (-le *f*); **2.** ✕ *infanterie:* caporal *m*; *artillerie, cavalerie:* brigadier *m*; **cor·po·rate** ['~rit] □ constitué; ~ *body* corps *m* constitué; personne *f* civile; **cor·pó·ra·tion** corporation *f*, corps *m* constitué; personne *f* civile; municipalité *f*; *Am.* société *f* par actions; F gros ventre *m*; **cor·po·ra·tive** ['~rətiv] corporatif (-ive *f*); **cor·po·re·al** □ [~-

'pɔːriəl] corporel(le f); matériel(le f) (a. ⚖️); **cor·po·re·i·ty** [ˌpɔːˈriːiti] corporéité f.

corps [kɔː], pl. **corps** [kɔːz] corps m.

corpse [kɔːps] cadavre m; corps m.

cor·pu·lence, cor·pu·len·cy ['kɔːpjuləns(i)] corpulence f; **'cor·pu·lent** corpulent.

cor·pus ['kɔːpəs], pl. **-po·ra** [ˌpərə] corpus m, recueil m; ♀ **Chris·ti** ['kɔːpəsˈkristi] la Fête-Dieu f; **corpus·cle** ['kɔːpʌsl] corpuscule m; sanguin: globule m; fig. atome m.

cor·ral surt. Am. [kɔːˈraːl] 1. corral (pl. -als) m; 2. renfermer dans un corral; fig. s'emparer de; parquer (des chariots) en rond.

cor·rect [kəˈrekt] 1. adj. □ correct; juste; bienséant; be ~ avoir raison; fig. être en règle; 2. v/t. corriger; rectifier (une erreur); neutraliser (une influence); reprendre (un enfant); **cor'rec·tion** correction f; rectification f; châtiment m, punition f; house of ~ maison f de correction; I speak under ~ je le dis sous toutes réserves, sauf correction; **cor'rect·i·tude** [ˌitjuːd] correction f; **cor'rec·tive** 1. correctif (-ive f), rectificatif (-ive f); punitif (-ive f); 2. correctif m; **cor'rec·tor** correcteur (-trice f) m; typ. corrigeur (-euse f) m; ⊕ appareil m etc. correcteur.

cor·re·late ['kɔrileit] 1. v/t. mettre en corrélation (avec, with); v/i. correspondre (à with, to); 2. corrélatif m; **cor·re'la·tion** corrélation f; **cor·rel·a·tive** □ ['ˌrelətiv] corrélatif (-ive f); en corrélation (avec, with).

cor·re·spond [kɔrisˈpɔnd] (with, to) correspondre (avec, à); être conforme (à); (s')écrire (à); **cor·re·'spond·ence** correspondance f; courrier m; **cor·re'spond·ent** 1. □ conforme; 2. correspondant(e f) m (a. ✝); journ. envoyé(e f) m.

cor·ri·dor ['kɔridɔː] couloir m, corridor m; 🚂 ~ train train m à inter-circulation.

cor·ri·gi·ble □ ['kɔridʒəbl] corrigible.

cor·rob·o·rant [kəˈrɔbərənt] 1. corroborant; corroboratif (-ive f); 2. corroborant m; fortifiant m; **cor·'rob·o·rate** [ˌreit] corroborer, confirmer; **cor·rob·o'ra·tion** corrobo-

ration f, confirmation f; **cor'rob·o·ra·tive** [ˌrətiv] corroboratif (-ive f); corroborant.

cor·rode [kəˈroud] corroder, ronger (un métal, a. fig.); **cor'ro·dent** corrodant (a. su./m); **cor'ro·sion** corrosion f; qqfois rouille f; ⚡ sulfatage m (des bornes); **cor'ro·sive** [ˌsiv] 1. □ corrosif (-ive f) (a. fig.); corrodant; 2. corrosif m, corrodant m; **cor'ro·sive·ness** corrosivité f; mordant m.

cor·ru·gate ['kɔrugeit] ⊕ strier de nervures; ~d cardboard carton m ondulé; ~d iron tôle f ondulée.

cor·rupt [kəˈrʌpt] 1. □ corrompu, altéré (a. texte); fig. dépravé; vénal (-aux m/pl.) (presse); pol. ~ practices brigues f/pl.; abus m; trafic m d'influence; 2. v/t. corrompre, altérer (a. texte); fig. dépraver, dévoyer; v/i. se corrompre; s'altérer; **cor'rupt·er** corrupteur (-trice f) m; démoralisateur (-trice f) m; **cor·rupt·i·bil·i·ty** [ˌəˈbiliti] corruptibilité f; vénalité f; **cor'rupt·i·ble** □ corruptible; vénal (-aux m/pl.); **cor'rup·tion** corruption f (a. fig.); dépravation f; subornation f (d'un témoin); **cor'rup·tive** □ corruptif (-ive f).

cor·sage [kɔːˈsaːʒ] corsage m; Am. bouquet m.

cor·sair ['kɔːsɛə] homme, vaisseau: corsaire m; pirate m.

cors(e)·let ['kɔːslit] corselet m.

cor·set ['kɔːsit] corset m; **'cor·set·ed** corseté.

cor·ti·cal ['kɔːtikl] cortical (-aux m/pl.); fig. extérieur.

cor·ti·sone ['kɔːtizoun] cortisone f.

co·run·dum min. [kəˈrʌndəm] corindon m.

cor·us·cate ['kɔrəskeit] scintiller; briller; **cor·us'ca·tion** vif éclat m; fig. ~s of wit paillettes f/pl. d'esprit.

cor·vette ⚓ [kɔːˈvet] corvette f.

cor·vine ['kɔːvain] orn. corvin.

cor·y·phae·us [kɔriˈfiːəs], pl. **-phae·i** [ˌfiːai] coryphée m (a. fig.); fig. chef m de secte etc.; **co·ry·phée** [ˌfei] ballet: première danseuse f.

cosh·er ['kɔʃə] dorloter, gâter.

co·sig·na·to·ry ['kouˈsignətəri] cosignataire (a. su.).

co·sine ⅄ ['kousain] cosinus m.

co·si·ness ['kouzinis] confortable m; chaleur f agréable.

cos·met·ic [kɔz'metik] (~ally) cosmétique (a. su./m).

cos·mic, cos·mi·cal □ ['kɔzmik(l)] cosmique.

cos·mo·naut ['kɔzmənɔːt] cosmonaute m.

cos·mo·pol·i·tan [kɔzmə'pɔlitən], **cos·mop·o·lite** [~'mɔpəlait] cosmopolite (a. su./mf).

Cos·sack ['kɔsæk] cosaque (a. su.).

cos·set ['kɔsit] **1.** (agneau m) favori m; **2.** dorloter, gâter.

cost [kɔst] **1.** coût m; frais m/pl.; dépens m/pl.; prix m; ⚖ ~s pl. frais m/pl. d'instance; les frais m/pl. et dépens m/pl.; first (ou prime) ~ prix m coûtant; prix m de revient; ~ of living coût m de la vie; to my ~ à mes dépens; as I know to my ~ (comme) je l'ai appris pour mon malheur; **2.** [irr.] coûter; ✝ établir le prix de revient de (un article); ~ dear coûter cher (à q., s.o.).

co-star cin. ['kou'staː] **1.** partenaire mf, acteur m (actrice f) qui partage la vedette; **2.** partager la vedette.

cos·ter F ['kɔstə], **'~·mon·ger** marchand m des quatre-saisons.

cost·ing ['kɔstiŋ] établissement m du prix de revient.

cos·tive □ ['kɔstiv] constipé.

cost·li·ness ['kɔstlinis] prix m élevé; meubles: somptuosité f; **'cost·ly** de grand prix; riche (meubles); coûteux (-euse f).

cost-price ✝ ['kɔstprais] prix m coûtant, prix m de revient, prix m de fabrique.

cos·tume ['kɔstjuːm] **1.** costume m (pour dames: tailleur); ~ play pièce f historique; **2.** costumer; **cos'tum·i·er** [~miə] costumier m.

co·sy ['kouzi] **1.** □ chaud, commode, confortable; **2.** cosy m (pour œufs à la coque); couvre-théière m; molleton m.

cot [kɔt] lit m d'enfants; lit m de camp; ⚓ hamac m à cadre.

co·te·rie ['koutəri] coterie f; cénacle m (littéraire etc.).

cot·tage ['kɔtidʒ] chaumière f; petite maison f de campagne; Am. résidence f d'été; Am. ~ cheese fromage m blanc; ~ industry industrie f à domicile; ~ piano petit piano m droit; **'cot·tag·er** paysan(ne f) m; habitant(e f) m d'une chaumière; Am. estivant(e f) m.

cot·ter ⊕ ['kɔtə] clavette f, goupille f.

cot·ton ['kɔtn] **1.** coton m; arbre: cotonnier m; toile f ou fil m de coton; fil m à coudre; **2.** de coton; Am. ~ candy barbe f à papa; ~ wool ouate f; **3.** F s'accorder, faire bon ménage (avec, with); se sentir attiré (par, to); F ~ on (to s.th.) piger (qch.); ~ to s.th. s'accommoder à qch.; ~ up faire des avances (à to, with); **'~-grass** linaigrette f; **'cot·ton·y** cotonneux (-euse f).

couch [kautʃ] **1.** canapé m, divan m; chaise f longue; poét. lit m; **2.** v/t. coucher; mettre (sa lance) en arrêt; envelopper (sa pensée); rédiger (une lettre, une réclamation); abaisser (une cataracte); v/i. se coucher; se tapir; **'~-grass** ♀ chiendent m.

cou·gar zo. ['kuːgaː] couguar m, puma m.

cough [kɔf] **1.** toux f; ~ drop pastille f pour la toux; ~ mixture sirop m pour la toux; **2.** v/i. tousser; v/t. ~ down réduire (q.) au silence à force de tousser; ~ up cracher (a. sl. = payer).

could [kud] prét. de can[1].

couldn't ['kudnt] = could not.

coul·ter ['koultə] coutre m (de charrue).

coun·cil ['kaunsl] conseil m; eccl. concile m; **coun·ci(l)·lor** ['~ilə] conseiller m; membre m du conseil.

coun·sel ['kaunsəl] **1.** consultation f; conseil m; dessein m; ⚖ avocat m; conseil m; ~ for the defence défenseur m; avocat m du défendeur; ~ for the prosecution avocat m de la partie publique; keep o.'s (own) ~ observer le silence; take ~ with consulter avec; **2.** conseiller, recommander (à q. de inf., s.o. to inf.); **coun·se(l)·lor** ['~lə] conseiller m.

count[1] [kaunt] **1.** compte m, calcul m; votes: dépouillement m; dénombrement m; ⚖ chef m (d'accusation); box. compte m; parl. (a. ~out) ajournement m; lose ~ perdre le compte (de, of); **2.** v/t. compter; dénombrer; fig. tenir (q.) pour; box. be ~ed out rester sur le plancher pour le compte; F être compté dehors; v/i. compter (sur, on; pour as, for; au nombre de, among); avoir de l'importance; ~ for little compter pour peu, ne compter guère.

count² [ˏ] *titre étranger*: comte *m*.

count·down [ˈkauntdaun] *fusée*: compte *m* à rebours.

coun·te·nance [ˈkauntinəns] **1.** visage *m*, figure *f*, mine *f*; expression *f* (du visage); faveur *f*; **2.** approuver; encourager, appuyer.

count·er¹ [ˈkauntə] compteur (-euse *f*) *m*; ⊕ compteur *m*; *jeux*: fiche *f* (*carrée*), jeton *m* (*rond*); *boutique*: comptoir *m*; *banque etc.*: guichets *m*/*pl.*; caisse *f*; *phys.* compteur *m* Geiger. Geiger ~ compteur *m* Geiger.

count·er² [ˏ] **1.** *adj.* contraire, opposé (à, *to*); **2.** *adv.* à contresens; contrairement; **3.** *su.* contre *m*; *box.* coup *m* d'arrêt; **4.** *v/t.* aller à l'encontre de; contrecarrer (*des desseins*); *box.* parer.

coun·ter·act [kauntəˈrækt] neutraliser; parer à; **coun·ter'ac·tion** action *f* contraire; neutralisation *f*; contre-mesure *f*.

coun·ter·at·tack [ˈkauntərətæk] contre-attaque *f*.

coun·ter·bal·ance 1. [ˈkauntəbæ-ləns] contrepoids *m*; **2.** [ˌˏˈbæləns] contrebalancer; compenser; ✝ équilibrer.

coun·ter·blast [ˈkauntəblɑːst] riposte *f*.

coun·ter·change [kauntəˈtʃeindʒ] échanger (pour, contre *for*).

coun·ter·charge [ˈkauntətʃɑːdʒ] contre-accusation *f*.

coun·ter·check [ˈkauntətʃek] force *f* opposée *ou* antagoniste; riposte *f*.

coun·ter·clock·wise [ˈkauntəˈklɔk-waiz] en sens inverse des aiguilles d'une montre.

coun·ter·cur·rent [ˈkauntəˈkʌrənt] contre-courant *m*.

coun·ter·es·pi·onage [ˈkauntərespi-əˈnɑːʒ] contre-espionnage *m*.

coun·ter·feit [ˈkauntəfit] **1.** ☐ contrefait; faux (fausse *f*); simulé; ~ money fausse monnaie *f*; **2.** contrefaçon *f*; *document*: faux *m*; F fausse monnaie *f*; **3.** contrefaire; simuler; feindre (*une émotion*); **'coun·ter·feit·er** contrefacteur *m*; faux-monnayeur *m*; simulateur (-trice *f*) *m*.

coun·ter·foil [ˈkauntəfɔil] souche *f*, *chèque*: talon *m*.

coun·ter·fort ⚠ [ˈkauntəfɔːt] contrefort *m*.

coun·ter·in·tel·li·gence [ˈkauntərintelidʒəns] *see* counter-espionage.

coun·ter·jump·er F [ˈkauntə-dʒʌmpə] commis *m*; calicot *m*.

coun·ter·mand [kauntəˈmɑːnd] **1.** contrordre *m*, contremandement *m*; **2.** contremander; révoquer; ✝ décommander.

coun·ter·march [ˈkauntəmɑːtʃ] **1.** contremarche *f*; **2.** (faire) contremarcher.

coun·ter·mark [ˈkauntəmɑːk] contremarque *f*.

coun·ter·meas·ure [ˈkauntəmeʒə] contre-mesure *f*.

coun·ter·mine [ˈkauntəmain] **1.** contre-mine *f*; **2.** contre-miner (*a. fig.*).

coun·ter·or·der [ˈkauntərɔːdə] contrordre *m*.

coun·ter·pane [ˈkauntəpein] couvre-lit *m*; courtepointe *f*.

coun·ter·part [ˈkauntəpɑːt] contrepartie *f*; double *m*.

coun·ter·point ♪ [ˈkauntəpɔint] contrepoint *m*.

coun·ter·poise [ˈkauntəpɔiz] **1.** contrepoids *m*; équilibre *m*; **2.** contrebalancer; faire contrepoids à (*a. fig.*).

coun·ter·pro·duc·tive [ˈkauntə-prəˈdʌktiv] improductif (-ive *f*); inutile; absurde; be ~ *a*. n'aboutir à rien.

coun·ter·scarp ✕ [ˈkauntəskɑːp] contrescarpe *f*.

coun·ter·sign [ˈkauntəsain] **1.** contreseing *m*; mot *m* d'ordre; **2.** contresigner.

coun·ter·sink ⊕ [kauntəˈsiŋk] [*irr.*] fraiser; noyer (*la tête d'une vis*); encastrer (*la tête d'un rivet*).

coun·ter·stroke [ˈkauntəstrouk] retour *m* offensif.

coun·ter·ten·or ♪ [ˈkauntəˈtenə] haute-contre (*pl.* hautes-contre) *f*; alto *m*.

coun·ter·vail [ˈkauntəveil] *v/t.* compenser; *v/i.* prévaloir (contre, *against*).

coun·ter·weight [ˈkauntəweit] contrepoids *m* (à, *to*).

coun·ter·work [ˈkauntəwɔːk] contrarier; contrecarrer.

count·ess [ˈkauntis] comtesse *f*.

count·ing-house [ˈkauntiŋhaus] (bureau *m* de la) comptabilité *f*.

count·less [ˈkauntlis] innombrable.

coun·tri·fied ['kʌntrifaid] aux allures agrestes; province *inv.* (*personne*).

coun·try ['kʌntri] 1. pays *m*; région *f*; patrie *f*; campagne *f*; province *f*; *appeal* (*ou go*) *to the* ~ en appeler au pays; 2. campagnard; *de ou* à la campagne; ~ *policeman* garde *m* champêtre; ~ **dance** dance *f* rustique; '~**man** campagnard *m*, paysan *m*; compatriote *m*; '~**side** campagnes *f/pl.*; (population *f* de la) région *f*; '~**wom·an** campagnarde *f*, paysanne *f*; compatriote *f*.

coun·ty ['kaunti] comté *m*; ~ **town**, *Am.* ~ **seat** chef-lieu (*pl.* chefslieux) *m* de comté.

coup [kuː] coup *m* (audacieux).

cou·ple ['kʌpl] 1. couple *m*, deux ...; couple *f* (*a. d'œufs, de pigeons*); 2. *v/t.* coupler; associer; ⊕ engrener; 🚗 atteler, accrocher; ⚡ brancher (sur, *to*), interconnecter; *v/i.* s'accoupler (*personne*); ~ *back* coupler à réaction; '**cou·pler** *radio*: accouplement *m*; **cou·plet** ['~lit] distique *m*.

cou·pling ⊕ ['kʌpliŋ] accouplement *m*; 🚗 accrochage *m*; ⚡ couplage *m*; *radio*: accouplement *m*; *attr.* d'accouplement.

cou·pon ['kuːpɔn] coupon *m* (*a.* ⚕); ticket *m* (*de carte alimentaire*).

cour·age ['kʌridʒ] courage *m*; **cou·ra·geous** □ [kə'reidʒəs] courageux (-euse *f*).

cour·gette [kuə'ʒet] courgette *f*.

cour·i·er ['kuriə] courrier *m*, messager *m*.

course [kɔːs] 1. *événements, fleuve, temps, univ.*: cours *m*; *événements*: marche *f*; direction *f*, route *f* (*a.* ⚓); *affaires*: courant *m*; *balle*: trajet *m*; *repas*: plat *m*, service *m*; *fig.* chemin *m*; *fig.* parti *m*; *sp.* piste *f*; *sp.* champ *m* de course(s); *golf*: parcours *m*; ⚓ cap *m*; ⚓ basse voile *f*; ⚓ cote *f* (*des changes*); ⚙ traitement *m*; ⊕ *piston*: course *f*; △ assise *f*; *cours d'eau*: lit *m*; ~ *of action* ligne *f* de conduite; *in due* ~ en temps utile; *of* ~ (bien) entendu, naturellement; *be a matter of* ~ aller de soi; ~ *of exchange* cote *f* des changes; 2. *v/t. chasse*: (faire) courir; *v/i.* courir, couler (*liquide, surt. sang*).

cours·ing ['kɔːsiŋ] chasse *f* (à courre) au lièvre.

court [kɔːt] 1. cour *f* (*royale, a.* ⚖); ⚖ tribunal *m*; ruelle *f*; ⚔, ⚓ commission *f* (d'enquête); *sp.* court *m* (*de tennis*); terrain *m*; *Am.* General ⚹ Parlement *m* (*des États de Vermont et New Hampshire*); *at* ~ à la cour; *pay* (*one's*) ~ faire la cour (à, *to*); 2. courtiser; faire la cour à (*une femme*); solliciter (*qch.*); rechercher (*qch.*); aller au-devant de (*un échec, un danger*); '~**card** *cartes*: figure *f*, carte *f* peinte; '~**day** jour *m* d'audience; **cour·te·ous** □ ['kɔːtiəs] courtois, poli (envers, *to*); **cour·te·san**, *a.* **cour·te·zan** [kɔːti'zæn] courtisane *f*; **cour·te·sy** ['kɔːtisi] courtoisie *f*, politesse *f*; ~ *call* visite *f* de politesse; *mot.* ~ *light* plafonnier *m*; **court-house** ['kɔːthaus] palais *m* de justice; *Am. a.* administration *f* (d'un département); **cour·ti·er** ['~jə] courtisan *m*; '**court·li·ness** courtoisie *f*; élégance *f*; '**court·ly** courtois; élégant.

court...: ~ *mar·tial*, *pl.* ~*s mar·tial* ⚔ conseil *m* de guerre; '~-'*mar·tial* faire passer en conseil de guerre; '~-'**plas·ter** taffetas *m* gommé; '~-**ship** cour *f* (*faite à une femme*); '~'**yard** cour *f* (*d'une maison*).

cous·in ['kʌzn] cousin(e *f*) *m*; *first* ~, ~ *german* cousin(e *f*) *m* germain(e *f*); '**cous·in·ly** de bon cousinage; **cous·in·hood** ['~hud], '**cous·in·ship** cousinage *m*; parenté *f*.

cove[1] [kouv] 1. anse *f*; petite baie *f*; △ grande gorge *f*; voûte *f* (*de plafond*); 2. voûter.

cove[2] *sl.* ['~] type *m*, individu *m*.

cov·e·nant ['kʌvinənt] 1. ⚖ convention *f*, contrat *m*; *bibl.* alliance *f*; *pol.* pacte *m*; 2. *v/t.* accorder par contrat; stipuler (*de l'argent*); *v/i.* convenir (de qch. avec q., *with s.o. for s.th.*).

Cov·en·try ['kɔvəntri]: *send s.o. to* ~ mettre q. en quarantaine.

cov·er ['kʌvə] 1. couverture *f*; *table*: tapis *m*; *buffet*: dessus *m*; couvercle *m*; abri *m*; *poste*: enveloppe *f*; *fig.* masque *m*, voile *m*; *mot., bicyclette, etc.*: bâche *f*; ⚕ provision *f*, marge *f*; *repas*: couvert *m*; (*ou* ~ *address*) adresse *f* de convenance; *Am.* ~ *charge* couvert *m*; *journ.* ~ *story* article *m* principal; 2. recouvrir; couvrir (de, *with*) (q., qch., ⚕ *risque*,

⚓ *retraite, dépenses*); envelopper; revêtir; dominer (*une vue, un terrain*); parcourir (*une distance*); tapisser (*un mur*); combler (*un déficit*); ⚡ guiper (*un fil*); assurer le compte-rendu de (*un journal*); F couvrir, dissimuler; *fig.* tenir compte de, comprendre; ~ed button bouton *m* d'étoffe; ~ed court *tennis*: court *m* couvert; ~ed wire fil *m* guipé; '**cov·er·ing** recouvrement *m*; couverture *f* (*a. de lit*); enveloppe *f*; ⚡ fil *etc.*: guipage *m*; *meubles*: housse *f*; ⚓ bâche *f*; *floor* ~ linoléum *m*; **cov·er·let** ['~lit] couvre-lit *m*; dessus *m* de lit.

cov·ert ['kʌvət] **1.** □ voilé, caché, secret (-ète *f*); ♁ en puissance de mari; **2.** *chasse*: abri *m*, couvert *m*, fourré *m*; retraite *f*; **cov·er·ture** ['~tjuə] abri *m*; ♁ condition *f* de la femme mariée.

cov·er-up ['kʌvərʌp] dissimulation *f*; tentatives *f/pl.* pour étouffer *ou* dissimuler un scandale.

cov·et ['kʌvit] convoiter; aspirer à; '**cov·et·ous** □ avide (de, *of*); avare; cupide; '**cov·et·ous·ness** convoitise *f*; cupidité *f*.

cov·ey ['kʌvi] vol *m ou* couvée *f* (*de perdrix etc.*).

cov·ing △ ['kouviŋ] plafond *etc.*: voussure *f*; saillie *f*.

cow[1] [kau] vache *f*.

cow[2] [~] intimider, dompter.

cow·ard ['kauəd] **1.** □ lâche; **2.** lâche *m/f*; '**cow·ard·ice**, '**cow·ard·li·ness** lâcheté *f*; '**cow·ard·ly 1.** lâche; **2.** lâchement.

cow·boy ['kaubɔi] jeune vacher *m*; *Am.* cow-boy *m*; '**cow-catch·er** 🚂 *Am.* chasse-pierres *m/inv.*

cow·er ['kauə] se blottir, se tapir; *fig.* trembler (devant, *before*).

cow·herd ['kauhə:d] vacher *m*; bouvier *m*; '**cow·hide 1.** (peau *f* de) vache *f*; **2.** *Am.* donner le fouet à (*q.*).

cowl [kaul] *moine, cheminée*: capuchon *m*; *cheminée*: mitre *f*; ✈, ⚓ capot *m*.

cow...: '**~·man** *Am.* éleveur *m* de bétail; '**~·pars·ley** ♣ cerfeuil *m* sauvage; '**~·pars·nip** ♀ berce *f*; '**~·pox** variole *f* des vaches; '**~·punch·er** *Am.* F cow-boy *m*.

cow·rie ['kauri] porcelaine *f*; *argent*: cauris *m*.

cow...: '**~-shed** étable *f*; '**~-slip** ♀ (*fleur f* de) coucou *m*.

cox F [kɔks] **1.** *see* coxswain; **2.** diriger, gouverner.

cox·comb ['kɔkskoum] petit-maître (*pl.* petits-maîtres) *m*; fat *m*; **cox·'comb·i·cal** □ fat.

cox·swain ['kɔkswein; 'kɔksn] barreur *m*; ⚓ patron *m* (*d'une chaloupe*).

coy [kɔi] □ modeste, farouche, réservé; '**coy·ness** modestie *f*, réserve *f*.

coz·en ['kʌzn] tromper; '**coz·en·age** tromperie *f*.

co·zy ['kouzi] *see* cosy.

crab[1] [kræb] crabe *m*, cancre *m*; *astr. le* Cancer *m*; ⊕ treuil *m*; chèvre *f*; *sl. see* crab-louse; *catch a* ~ faire fausse rame; F *turn out* ~*s* échouer.

crab[2] [~] **1.** pomme *f* sauvage; F personne *f* revêche; critique *f*; grognon(ne *f*) *m*; **2.** *v/t.* dénigrer; *v/i.* trouver à redire (à, *about*); **crab·bed** ['kræbid] □ maussade, grognon(ne *f*); pénible (*style*); illisible (*écriture*); **crab-louse** ['kræblaus] pou *m* du pubis.

crack [kræk] **1.** craquement *m*; fente *f*; fissure *f*; lézarde *f*; *cloche, verre, porcelaine, etc.*: fêlure *f*; F coup *m* sec; *écoss.* F cousette *f*; *sp. sl.* crack *m*, as *m*; *sl.* cambriolage *m*; *sl.* toqué(e *f*) *m*; *surt. Am. sl.* remarque *f* mordante, observation *f* satirique; plaisanterie *f*; *in a* ~ en un clin d'œil; **2.** F fameux (-euse *f*), de premier ordre; **3.** clac!; pan!; **4.** *v/t.* faire claquer (*un fouet*); fêler; crevasser; fendre; casser (*une noisette*); ⚗ fractionner (*une huile lourde*); ~ *a bottle* déboucher *ou* entamer *ou* boire une bouteille; ~ *a joke* faire une plaisanterie; F ~ *up* vanter (*q., qch.*); *v/i.* craquer; claquer; se fêler; se crevasser; se lézarder; se gercer (*peau*); se casser (*voix etc.*); *Am. sl.* ~ *down on s.o.* F laver la tête à q.; prendre des mesures sévères contre q.; '**~-brained** (au cerveau) timbré; '**~-down** *Am. sl.* razzia *f*; '**cracked** fêlé, fendu *etc.*; F timbré, toqué; '**crack·er** papillote *f* à pétard; pétard *m*; F mensonge *m*; *Am.* craquelin *m*, croquet *m*; biscuit *m* dur; '**crack·er·jack** *Am.*

F as *m*, expert *m*; '**crack·jaw** F (mot *m*) à vous décrocher la mâchoire; '**crack·le** craqueter; crépiter; pétiller (*feu*); (se) fendiller; '**crack·ling** *porc rôti*: peau *f* croquante; couenne *f*; **crack·nel** ['⁓nl] craquelin *m*; '**crack·pot** 1. type *m* cinglé; 2. cinglé; '**crack-up** collision *f*; ✗ crash *m*; '**crack·y** *see* cracked.

cra·dle ['kreidl] 1. berceau *m* (*a. fig.*); *fig.* première enfance *f*; ⚓ ber *m* (de lancement); chantier *m*; *téléph.* étrier *m* du récepteur; 2. mettre dans un berceau *etc.*

craft [krɑːft] habileté *f*; ruse *f*, artifice *m*; métier *m* manuel; profession *f*; corps *m* de métier; *coll. pl.* embarcations *f/pl.*, petits navires *m/pl.*; the gentle ⁓ la pêche à la ligne, *fig. co.* le noble art; '**craft·i·ness** ruse *f*, astuce *f*; '**crafts·man** artisan *m*, ouvrier *m*; artiste *m* dans son métier; '**crafts·man·ship** exécution *f* merveilleuse; dextérité *f* manuelle; '**craft·y** □ astucieux (-euse *f*), rusé.

crag [kræg] rocher *m* à pic; *alp.* varappe *f*; '**crag·gy** rocailleux (-euse *f*); escarpé; '**crags·man** varappeur *m*.

crake *orn.* [kreik] (cri *m* du) râle *m*.

cram [kræm] 1. fourrer, bourrer; empâter (*de la volaille*); *fig.* empiffrer; F bûcher (*un sujet*), bourrer; *v/i.* s'entasser; se gorger de nourriture; préparer un examen; 2. F chauffage *m* (*pour un examen*); F mensonge *m*; '⁓-'**full** regorgeant (de, of), bondé; '**cram·mer** chauffeur *m*; F mensonge *m*.

cramp [kræmp] 1. ✂ crampe *f*; ⊕ crampon *m*; presse *f* à vis; *fig.* contrainte *f*; 2. ⊕ cramponner, agrafer; serrer à (*l'étau*); *fig.* gêner; '**cramped** gêné; à l'étroit; '**cramp-frame** ⊕ serre-joint *m*; presse *f* à main; '**cramp-i·ron** crampon *m*, agrafe *f*.

cram·pon ['kræmpən] crampon *m* à glace.

cran·ber·ry ⚘ ['krænbəri] airelle *f*; canneberge *f*.

crane [krein] 1. grue *f* (*a.* ⊕); 2. tendre *ou* allonger (*le cou*); ⊕ hisser *ou* descendre au moyen d'une grue; ⁓ *at* refuser *ou* reculer devant; **crane·fly** *zo.* ['⁓flai] tipule *f*;

crane's-bill ⚘ bec-de-grue (*pl.* becs-de-grue) *m*.

cra·ni·um *anat.* ['kreiniəm] crâne *m*.

crank [kræŋk] 1. ⊕ détraqué, délabré; ⚓ instable, mal équilibré; 2. manivelle *f*; *meule à aiguiser*: cigogne *f*; coude *m*; *cloche*: bascule *f*; starting ⁓ mot. (manivelle *f* de) mise *f* en marche; 3. *v/t.* ⁓ off bobiner (*un film*); *mot.* ⁓ up lancer (*une auto, un moteur*); '⁓-**case** carter *m* (du moteur); '**crank·i·ness** humeur *f* difficile; excentricité *f*; '**crank-shaft** ⊕ vilebrequin *m*; '**crank·y** d'humeur difficile; excentrique; capricieux (-euse *f*).

cran·nied ['krænid] lézardé, crevassé; '**cran·ny** fente *f*, crevasse *f*, niche *f*.

crape [kreip] 1. crêpe *m* noir; 2. draper de crêpe.

craps *Am.* [kræps] *pl.* dés *m/pl.*

crap·u·lence ['kræpjuləns] crapule *f*; F débauche *f*.

crash[1] [kræʃ] 1. fracas *m*; catastrophe *f*; ✝ krach *m*; ✗ crash *m*; ⁓-helmet casque *m* protecteur; ⁓-landing atterrissage *m* brutal, crash *m*; 2. *v/i.* retentir; éclater avec fracas; ✗ s'écraser; atterrir brutalement; *v/t.* jeter avec fracas; 3. F à exécuter rapidement; ⁓ *course* cours *m* intensif; ⁓ *diet* régime *m* radical (*pour maigrir*).

crash[2] [⁓] toile *f* à serviettes.

crass [kræs] grossier (-ère *f*); stupide.

crate [kreit] caisse *f* à claire-voie.

cra·ter ['kreitə] *volcan, a.* ⚡ cratère *m*; ✗ entonnoir *m*.

cra·vat [krə'væt] foulard *m*; † cravate *f*.

crave [kreiv] *v/t.* implorer avec instance (de, from), solliciter; *v/i.* (for) désirer avidement (*qch.*).

cra·ven ['kreivn] 1. poltron(ne *f*), lâche; 2. poltron(ne *f*) *m*, lâche *mf*.

crav·ing ['kreiviŋ] désir *m* ardent, besoin *m*, passion *f*, appétit *m* insatiable (de, for).

craw [krɔː] jabot *m* (*d'oiseau*).

craw·fish ['krɔːfiʃ] 1. eau *douce*: écrevisse *f*; *mer*: langouste *f*; 2. *Am.* F se dérober; *sl.* caner.

crawl [krɔːl] 1. rampement *m*; *personne*: mouvement *m* traînant; *nage*: crawl *m*; 2. ramper; se traîner; grouiller (de, with); marauder; '**crawl·er** reptile *m*; *personne*:

traînard(e f) m; fig. plat valet m; taxi m en maraude; nage: crawleur m; vêtement pour enfants: barboteuse f.

cray·fish ['kreifiʃ] eau douce: écrevisse f; mer: langouste f.

cray·on ['kreiən] **1.** craie f à dessiner; surt. (crayon m de) pastel m; fusain m; blue (red) ~ crayon m bleu (rouge); **2.** dessiner au pastel; crayonner.

craze [kreiz] manie f (de, for); fig. fureur f (de); be the ~ faire fureur; **'crazed** affolé (de, with); **'cra·zi·ness** folie f, démence f; maison: délabrement m; **'cra·zy** □ fou (fol devant une voyelle ou un h muet; folle f) (de with, about, for); affolé (de, with); branlant; délabré (maison); irrégulier (-ère f); en pièces rapportées.

creak [kri:k] **1.** grincement m; **2.** grincer, crier; **'creak·y** □ qui crie, qui grince.

cream [kri:m] **1.** crème f (a. fig.); fig. le plus beau (de l'histoire); cold ~ crème f, cold-cream m; ~ of tartar crème f de tartre; **2.** (souv. ~-colo(u)red) crème inv.; **3.** v/t. écrémer; ajouter de la crème à; battre (du beurre) en crème; v/i. se couvrir de crème; mousser; **'cream·er·y** crémerie f; **'cream·y** □ crémeux (-euse f); fig. velouté.

crease [kri:s] **1.** (faux) pli m; tex. ancrure f; papier: fronce f; cricket: ligne f de limite; **2.** (se) plisser; (se) froisser.

cre·ate [kri'eit] v/t. créer (qch., q. chevalier, théâ. rôle, difficulté, mode); faire; produire; faire naître; v/i. sl. faire une scène (à propos de, about); **cre·a·tion** création f (a. mode); **cre·a·tive** créateur (-trice f); **cre·a·tor** créateur (-trice f) m; **cre·a·tress** créatrice f; **crea·ture** ['kri:tʃə] créature f (a. péj.); être m (vivant); animal m, bête f; ~ comforts pl. l'aisance f matérielle.

cre·dence ['kri:dəns] foi f, croyance f; give ~ to ajouter foi à; letter of ~ lettre f de créance; **cre·den·tials** [kri'denʃlz] pl. lettres f/pl. de créance; domestique: certificat m; papiers m/pl. d'identité.

cred·i·bil·i·ty [kredi'biliti] crédibilité f; **cred·i·ble** □ ['kredəbl] croyable; digne de foi.

cred·it ['kredit] **1.** foi f, croyance f, créance f; réputation f, crédit m (a. ✝); mérite m; honneur m; banque: crédit m, actif m; Am. école: unité f de valeur, U.V. f; ✝ on ~ à crédit, à terme; ✝ ~ balance solde m créditeur; ✝ ~ card carte f de crédit; ✝ ~ note f ou facture f d'avoir; ✝ ~ rate degré m de solvabilité; ✝ ~ rating limite f de crédit; do s.o. ~ honorer q., faire honneur à q.; get ~ for s.th. se voir attribuer le mérite de qch.; give s.o. ~ for s.th. attribuer (le mérite de) qch. à q.; put (ou place ou pass) to s.o.'s ~ porter (qch.) au crédit de s.o.; **2.** ajouter foi à; attribuer, prêter (une qualité à q., s.o. with a quality); ✝ créditer (q. d'une somme s.o. with a sum, a sum to s.o.); porter (une somme) au crédit; ~ s.o. with s.th. prêter qch. à q.; **'cred·it·a·ble** □ honorable, estimable; be ~ to faire honneur à; **'cred·i·tor 1.** créancier (-ère f) m; **2.** créditeur (-trice f).

cre·du·li·ty [kri'dju:liti] crédulité f; **cred·u·lous** □ ['kredjuləs] crédule.

creed [kri:d] crédo m (a. pol.); croyance f. [m; petite vallée f.]

creek [kri:k] crique f; Am. ruisseau

creel [kri:l] panier m de pêche; casier m à homards; ⊕ râtelier m (à bobines).

creep [kri:p] **1.** [irr.] ramper; se traîner; se glisser (a. fig.); fig. entrer doucement; ⊕ glisser; **2.** glissement m; ~s pl. chair f de poule; **'creep·er** F homme m rampant; femme f rampante; ♀ plante f rampante ou grimpante; **'creep·y** rampant; qui donne la chair de poule.

creese [kri:s] criss m (= poignard malais).

cre·mate [kri'meit] incinérer (un mort); **cre·ma·tion** incinération f; crémation f; **crem·a·to·ri·um** [kremə'tɔ:riəm], pl. -ums, -ri·a [~riə], **cre·ma·to·ry** ['~təri] crématorium m; four m crématoire.

cren·el·(l)at·ed ['krenileitid] crénelé.

cre·ole ['kri:oul] créole (a. su.).

cre·o·sote ↗ ['kriəsout] créosote f.

crep·i·tate ['krepiteit] crépiter; **crep·i·ta·tion** crépitation f.

crept [krept] prét. et p.p. de creep 1.

cre·pus·cu·lar [kri'pʌskjulə] crépusculaire, du crépuscule.

crock

cres·cent ['kresnt] **1.** (en forme de) croissant; **2.** croissant m (a. *pâtisserie*); rue f en arc de cercle; ⚥ *City* la Nouvelle-Orléans f.

cress ⚥ [kres] cresson m.

cres·set ['kresit] *tour*, *phare*: fanal m.

crest [krest] △, *casque*, *coq*, *montagne*, *vague*: crête f; *arête* f, *colline*: sommet m; *alouette*: huppe f; *paon*: aigrette f; *blason*: timbre m; *sceau*: armoiries f/pl.; *casque*: cimier m; **'crest·ed** à crête etc.; *casque*: orné d'un cimier; ~ *lark* cochevis m; **'crest·fall·en** abattu, découragé; penaud (*air*).

cre·ta·ceous [kri'teiʃəs] crétacé, crayeux (-euse f).

cre·tin ['kretin] crétin(e f) m.

cre·vasse [kri'væs] crevasse f (*glaciaire*); *Am.* fissure f.

crev·ice ['krevis] fente f; lézarde f; fissure f.

crew¹ [kru:] ⚓ équipage m; *ouvriers*: équipe f; *péj.* bande f; ~ *cut* cheveux m/pl. en brosse.

crew² [~] *prét. de* crow 2.

crew·el ⴕ ['kru:il] laine f à broder *ou* à tapisserie.

crib [krib] **1.** mangeoire f; lit m d'enfant; *eccl.* crèche f; F *école*: clef f; F plagiat m; *sl.* emploi m; *surt.* *Am.* huche f (*pour le maïs etc.*); *sl.* *crack a* ~ cambrioler une maison); **2.** † enfermer; F plagier (*qch.*); F copier; F tuyauter; **'crib·bage** cribbage m; **'crib·ble** crible m; **crib-bit·er** ['~baitə] tiqueur (-euse f) m.

crick [krik] **1.** crampe f; ~ *in the neck* torticolis m; **2.** se donner un torticolis *ou* un tour de reins.

crick·et¹ *zo.* ['krikit] grillon m.

crick·et² [~] **1.** *sp.* cricket m; F *not* ~ déloyal (-aux m/pl.); ne pas (*être*) de jeu; **2.** jouer au cricket; **'crick·et·er** joueur m de cricket, cricketeur m.

cri·er ['kraiə] crieur m (public).

crime [kraim] crime m, délit m.

Cri·me·an War [krai'miən wɔ:] guerre f de Crimée.

crim·i·nal ['kriminl] criminel(le f) (a. *su./mf*); **crim·i·nal·i·ty** [~'næliti] criminalité f; **crim·i·nate** ['~neit] incriminer, accuser; convaincre d'un crime; **crim·i·na·tion** incrimination f.

crimp¹ ⚓, ✂ [krimp] **1.** racoleur m,

embaucheur m; **2.** racoler, embaucher.

crimp² [~] gaufrer, friser.

crim·son ['krimzn] **1.** cramoisi (a. *su./m*); **2.** *v/t.* teindre en cramoisi; *v/i.* s'empourprer.

cringe [krindʒ] **1.** se faire tout petit, se blottir; *fig.* s'humilier, ramper (*devant to*, *before*); **2.** *fig.* courbette f servile.

crin·kle ['kriŋkl] **1.** pli m, ride f; **2.** (se) froisser; onduler (a. *cheveux*).

crin·o·line ['krinəli:n] crinoline f.

crip·ple ['kripl] **1.** boiteux (-euse f) m, estropié(e f) m; **2.** estropier; *fig.* disloquer.

cri·sis ['kraisis], *pl.* -ses ['~si:z] crise f.

crisp [krisp] **1.** crêpé, frisé (*cheveux etc.*); croquant (*biscuit*); vif (vive f), froid (*air*, *vent*); net(te f) (*profil*); tranchant (*ton*); nerveux (-euse f) (*style*); **2.** (se) crêper (*cheveux*); (se) froncer; *v/t.* donner du croustillant à.

criss-cross ['kriskrɔs] **1.** entrecroisement m; enchevêtrement m; **2.** entrecroisé; **3.** (s')entrecroiser.

cri·te·ri·on [krai'tiəriən], *pl.* -ri·a [~riə] critérium m, critère m.

crit·ic ['kritik] critique (*littéraire etc.*) m; censeur m (*de conduite*); critiqueur m; **'crit·i·cal** □ critique; ⚕ dangereux (-euse f); *be* ~ *of* critiquer; regarder d'un œil sévère; ⚕ *in* ~ *condition* dans un état critique; **crit·i·cism** ['~sizm], **cri·tique** [kri'ti:k] critique f (de, sur *of*); **crit·i·cize** ['~saiz] critiquer, faire la critique de; censurer.

croak [krouk] **1.** *v/i.* coasser (*grenouille*); croasser (*corbeau*); *fig.* grogner; *sl.* casser sa pipe (= *mourir*); *v/t.* *sl.* descendre (= *tuer*); **2.** c(r)oassement m; **'croak·er** *fig.* prophète m de malheur; **'croak·y** □ rauque, enroué (*voix*).

Cro·at ['krouət] **1.** croate; **2.** Croate mf.

cro·chet ['krouʃei] **1.** crochet m; **2.** *v/t.* faire (*qch.*) au crochet; *v/i.* faire du crochet.

crock [krɔk] **1.** pot m de terre; cruche f; F cheval m claqué; F *auto*: tacot m; F bonhomme m fini; F patraque f (= *personne maladive*); **2.** *sl.* (*usu.* ~ *up*) tomber malade, se faire abîmer; **'crock·er·y** faïence f, poterie f.

croc·o·dile zo. ['krɔkədail] crocodile m; fig. ~ tears pl larmes f/pl. de crocodile.

cro·cus ♀ ['kroukəs] crocus m.

croft·er Brit. ['krɔftə] petit fermier m.

crom·lech ['krɔmlek] dolmen m.

crone F [kroun] commère f, vieille f.

cro·ny F ['krouni] copain m; ami(e f) m intime.

crook [kruk] **1.** croc m, crochet m; berger: houlette f; eccl. crosse f; fig. angle m; chemin etc.: détour m, coude m; sl. escroc m; sl. fraude f; on the ~ malhonnête(ment); **2.** (se) recourber; **crooked** ['ⁿkt] (re-) courbé; à béquille (canne); ['ⁿkid] □ fig. tordu; tortueux (-euse f) (chemin); contourné (jambe, arbre); F déshonnête; oblique (moyen).

croon [kru:n] fredonner, chanter à demi-voix; **'croon·er** chanteur (-euse f) m de charme.

crop [krɔp] **1.** oiseau: jabot m; fouet: manche m; stick m (de chasse); récolte f, moisson f; fruits: cueillette f; fig. tas m; cheveux: coupe f; ~ failure mauvaise récolte f; F ~ of hair chevelure f; **2.** v/t. tondre, tailler, couper; brouter, paître (l'herbe); v/i. donner une récolte; ~ up géol. affleurer; F surgir; **'~-eared** essorillé (chien); hist. aux cheveux coupés ras; **'crop·per** tondeur m etc. (see crop 2); (pigeon m) boulant m; F planté f qui donne bien ou mal; F culbute f; Am. sl. métayer m.

cro·quet ['kroukei] **1.** (jeu m de) croquet m; **2.** (a. tight-) croquer; (a. loose-~) roquer.

cro·sier eccl. ['krouʒə] crosse f.

cross [krɔs] **1.** croix f (a. médaille, a. fig.); croisement m (de races); métis(se f) m; sl. escroquerie f; **2.** □ (entre)croisé; mis en travers; oblique; contraire; maussade (personne); fâché (de qch., at s.th.); contre q., with s.o.); de mauvaise humeur; sl. illicite, déshonnête; be at ~ purposes y avoir malentendu; **3.** v/t. croiser (deux choses, ~aces, q. dans la rue); traverser; passer (la mer); franchir (le seuil); barrer (un chèque); mettre les barres à (ses t); fig. contrarier, contrebarrer (q., un projet); ~ o.s. se signer, faire le signe de la croix; ~ out biffer, rayer (un mot etc.); v/i. se croiser; passer; faire la traversée; **'~-bar** foot. barre f; **'~-beam** △ sommier m; **'~'bench** parl. Centre m; **'~-bow** arbalète f; **'~-breed** race f croisée; F métis(se f) m; **'~-check 1.** contre-épreuve f; **2.** vérifier par contre-épreuve; **'~'coun-try** à travers champs; ~ running le cross-country m; ~ runner crossman (pl. -men) m; ~ skiing ski m de randonnée; **'~-cut saw** scie f de travers; **'~-ex·am·i'na·tion** interrogatoire m contradictoire; **~-ex·am·ine** ['krɔsig'zæmin] contre-interroger; **'~-fer·ti·li'za·tion** ♀ fécondation f croisée; fig. fécondation f mutuelle; **'~-grained** tortillard (bois); fig. revêche; bourru; **'cross·ing** passage m (pour piétons); intersection f (de voies); 🚉 passage m à niveau; croisement m (de lignes); traversée f; **'cross·legged** les jambes croisées; **'cross·ness** mauvaise humeur f.

cross...: **'~-patch** F grincheux (-euse f) m; grognon mf; ~ **ref·er·ence** renvoi m, référence f; **'~-'road** chemin m de traverse; ~s pl. ou sg. carrefour m (a. fig.); croisement m de routes; **'~-sec·tion** coupe f en travers; ~ **talk** répliques f/pl., échange m de propos; radio etc.: interférence f; **'~-walk** Am. passage m clouté; **'~-wind** vent m de travers; **'~-wise** en croix, en travers; **'~-word puz·zle** mots m/pl. croisés.

crotch [krɔtʃ] fourche f; **crotch·et** ['ⁿit] crochet m; ♪ noire f; F lubie f; **'crotch·et·y** F capricieux (-euse f); (à l'humeur) difficile.

crouch [krautʃ] se blottir, s'accroupir (devant, to).

croup[1] [kru:p] croupe f (de cheval).

croup[2] ⚕ [~] croup m.

crou·pi·er ['kru:piə] croupier m.

crow [krou] **1.** corneille f; chant m du coq; Am. F eat ~ avaler des couleuvres; have a ~ to pick with avoir maille à partir avec; as the ~ flies à vol d'oiseau; **2.** [irr.] chanter; fig. chanter victoire (sur, over); gazouiller (enfant); **'~-bar** levier m, pied-de-biche (pl. pieds-de-biche) m.

crowd [kraud] 1. foule *f*, rassemblement *m*, affluence *f*; F tas *m*; F bande *f*; *péj.* monde *m*; 2. *v/t.* serrer; remplir (de, with); *v/i.* se presser (en foule); s'attrouper; ~ **out** *v/t.* ne pas laisser de place à; *v/i.* sortir en foule; ⊕ ~ **sail** (on) faire force de voiles; ~ed hours *pl.* heures *f/pl.* de pointe.

crow·foot ♀ ['kroufut] renoncule *f*.

crown [kraun] 1. *roi, dent, fleurs, monnaie, etc.*: couronne *f*; *bonheur etc.*: comble *m*; *carrière*: couronnement *m*; *chapeau*: forme *f*; *tête*: sommet *m*; *arbre*: cime *f*; *mot.* axe *m* (de la chaussée); 2. couronner; sacrer (*roi*); F mettre le comble à; '**crown·ing** *fig.* suprême; final (-als *m/pl.*).

crow's... [krouz]: '~-**foot** patte *f* d'oie (*au coin de l'œil*); '~-**nest** ⊕ nid *m* de pie.

cru·cial □ ['kru:ʃjəl] décisif (-ive *f*); critique; **cru·ci·ble** ['kru:sibl] creuset *m* (*a. fig.*); **cru·ci·fix** ['~fiks] crucifix *m*; **cru·ci·fix·ion** [~'fikʃn] crucifixion *f*; mise *f* en croix; '**cru·ci·form** cruciforme; **cru·ci·fy** ['~fai] crucifier (*a. fig.*).

crude □ [kru:d] (à l'état) brut (*métal, matériel, huile, etc.*); cru (*a. lumière, couleur*); vert, aigre (*fruit*); brutal (-aux *m/pl.*); grossier (-ère *f*) (*style*); fruste (*manières*); ⚕ non encore développé (*maladie*), non assimilé (*aliment*); '**crude·ness**, **cru·di·ty** ['~iti] crudité *f* (*a. fig.*).

cru·el □ ['kruəl] cruel(le *f*) (*a. fig.*); '**cru·el·ty** cruauté *f*.

cru·et ['kru:it] burette *f*; '~-**stand** ménagère *f*.

cruise ⊕ [kru:z] 1. croisière *f*; voyage *m* d'agrément; ✕ ~ **missile** engin *m* atmosphérique; 2. ⊕ croiser; *cruising speed* vitesse *f* économique; '**cruis·er** ⊕ croiseur *m*; *light* ~ contre-torpilleur *m*; *Am.* voiture *f* cellulaire; *box.* ~ **weight** poids *m* mi-lourd.

crul·ler *Am.* ['krʌlə] *cuis.* roussette *f*.

crumb [krʌm] 1. *pain*: miette *f*; *fig.* brin *m*; 2. *cuis.* paner (*la viande etc.*); *a.* = **crum·ble** ['~bl] (s')émietter (*pain*); *v/t. fig.* réduire en miettes (*aliment*); s'écrouler (*maison etc.*); s'ébouler (*sol*); '**crum·bling**, '**crum·bly** friable, ébouleux (-euse

f); **crumb·y** ['krʌmi] qui s'émiette; couvert de miettes.

crum·my *sl.* ['krʌmi] minable, moche.

crump *sl.* [krʌmp] chute *f*; coup *m* violent; ✕ obus *m* qui éclate.

crum·pet ['krʌmpit] *sorte de brioche grillée* (*plate et poreuse*); *sl.* caboche *f* (= *tête*); *be off one's* ~ être maboul (= *fou*).

crum·ple ['krʌmpl] *v/t.* froisser, friper; *v/i.* se froisser; se recroqueviller (*parchemin, feuilles*); *fig.* s'effondrer.

crunch [krʌntʃ] *v/t.* croquer, broyer (*avec les dents*); écraser; *v/i.* craquer; s'écraser.

cru·ral ['kruərəl] *anat.* crural (-aux *m/pl.*).

cru·sade [kru:'seid] 1. croisade *f*; (*a. fig.*); 2. aller *ou* être en croisade; *fig.* mener une campagne (*contre* qch.); **cru·sad·er** croisé *m*.

crush [krʌʃ] 1. écrasement *m*; F presse *f*, foule *f*; *sl. have a* ~ avoir un béguin (pour, on); ~ *hat* claque *m*; *Am.* chapeau *m* mou; 2. *v/t.* écraser, aplatir; froisser (*une robe*); *fig.* anéantir; accabler (*de douleur etc.*); † vider (*une bouteille*); ~ **out** *fig.* étouffer; *v/i.* se presser en foule; *Am. sl.* flirter; '**crush·er** broyeur *m*; F malheur *m etc.* accablant; coup *m* d'assommoir; '**crush-room** *théâ.* foyer *m*.

crust [krʌst] 1. croûte *f*; *Am. sl.* toupet *m*; 2. (se) couvrir d'une croûte; '**crust·ed** qui a du dépôt (*vin*); *fig.* invétéré; '**crust·y** □ qui a une forte croûte; *fig.* bourru.

crutch [krʌtʃ] béquille *f*; '**crutched** à béquille; à poignée à croisillon.

crux [krʌks] *fig.* nœud *m*; point *m* capital.

cry [krai] 1. cri *m*; plainte *f*; pleurs *m/pl.*; *it is a far* ~ *from ... to* il y a loin de ... à (*a. fig.*); *within* ~ à portée de voix; 2. crier; *v/i.* s'écrier, pousser un cri *ou* des cris; pleurer; ~ *for* demander en pleurant; crier à (*le secours*); réclamer; ~ *off* se dédire; s'excuser; annuler (*une affaire*); ~ **out** *v/t.* crier; *v/i.* s'écrier, pousser des cris; se récrier (contre, *against*); ~ *up* prôner, vanter; '~-**ba·by** pleurard(e *f*) *m*; '**cry·ing** *fig.* criant, urgent; scandaleux (-euse *f*).

crypt [kript] crypte *f*; **'cryp·tic** occulte, secret (-ète *f*); énigmatique.

crys·tal ['kristl] **1.** cristal *m*; *surt. Am.* verre *m* de montre; **2.** cristallin, limpide; **'~-clear** clair comme le jour *ou* comme de l'eau de roche; **crys·tal·line** ['~təlain] cristallin, de cristal; **crys·tal·i·za·tion** cristallisation *f*; **'crys·tal·lize** cristalliser; **~d** candi (*fruits*).

cub [kʌb] **1.** petit *m* (*d'un animal*); *ours:* ourson *m*; lionceau *m*, louveteau *m*, renardeau *m*, *etc.*; **2.** *v/t.* mettre bas (*des petits*); *v/i.* faire des petits.

cu·bage ['kju:bidʒ] cubage *m*.

cub·by·hole ['kʌbihoul] retraite *f*; placard *m*.

cube ♣ ['kju:b] **1.** cube *m*; **~ root** racine *f* cubique; **2.** cuber.

cub·hood ['kʌbhud] adolescence *f*.

cu·bic, cu·bi·cal □ ['kju:bik(l)] cubique.

cu·bi·cle ['kju:bikl] *dortoir:* alcôve *f*; *piscine etc.:* cabine *f*.

cuck·old ['kʌkəld] **1.** cocu *m*; **2.** cocufier (*son mari*).

cuck·oo ['kuku:] **1.** coucou *m*; **2.** *sl.* maboul, loufoque (= *fou*).

cu·cum·ber ['kju:kəmbə] concombre *m*.

cu·cur·bit [kju:'kɔ:bit] ♣ courge *f*; *alambic:* cucurbite *f*.

cud [kʌd] bol *m* alimentaire; **chew the ~** ruminer (*a. fig.*).

cud·dle ['kʌdl] **1.** F embrassade *f*; **2.** *v/t.* serrer doucement dans ses bras; *v/i.* se peloter.

cudg·el ['kʌdʒl] **1.** gourdin *m*; **take up the ~s for** prendre fait et cause pour; **2.** bâtonner; **~ one's brains** se creuser la cervelle (pour *inf.*, **for** *gér.*; pour, **about**).

cue [kju:] *billard:* queue *f*; *surt. théâ.* réplique *f*; avis *m*, mot *m*; **take the ~ from** *s.o.* prendre exemple sur q.

cuff[1] [kʌf] **1.** calotte *f*, taloche *f*; **2.** calotter, flanquer une taloche à (*q.*).

cuff[2] [~] *chemise:* poignet *m*; manchette *f* (*empesée*); *jaquette etc.:* parement *m*; *Am. pantalon:* bord *m* relevé.

cui·rass [kwi'ræs] cuirasse *f*.

cui·sine [kwi'zi:n] cuisine *f*.

cu·li·nar·y ['kʌlinəri] culinaire.

cull [kʌl] (re)cueillir; choisir (dans, **from**).

cul·ly *sl.* ['kʌli] copain *m*, camaro *m*.

culm [kʌlm] ♣ chaume *m*, tige *f*.

cul·mi·nate ['kʌlmineit] *astr.* culminer; *fig.* atteindre son apogée; *fig.* terminer (par, **in**); **cul·mi·na·tion** *astr.* culmination *f*; *fig.* point *m* culminant.

cu·lottes [kju:'lɔts] *pl.* (**a pair of ~** une) jupe-culotte *f* (*pl.* jupes-culottes).

cul·pa·bil·i·ty [kʌlpə'biliti] culpabilité *f*; **'cul·pa·ble** □ coupable; digne de blâme.

cul·prit ['kʌlprit] coupable *mf*; prévenu(e *f*) *m*.

cult [kʌlt] culte *m*.

cul·ti·va·ble ['kʌltivəbl] cultivable.

cul·ti·vate ['kʌltiveit] *usu.* cultiver; *biol.* faire une culture de (*un bacille*); **cul·ti·va·tion** culture *f*; **'cul·ti·va·tor** *personne:* cultivateur (-trice *f*) *m*; *machine:* cultivateur *m*, extirpateur *m*; *fig.* ami *m*.

cul·tur·al □ ['kʌltʃərəl] culturel (-le *f*); ✍ cultural (-aux *m/pl.*).

cul·ture ['kʌltʃə] culture *f*; **'cul·tured** cultivé, lettré; **cul·ture me·di·um**, *pl.* **-di·a** *biol.* bouillon *m* de culture; **'cul·ture-pearl** perle *f* japonaise.

cul·vert ['kʌlvət] ponceau *m*, canal *m*; ✍ conduit *m* souterrain.

cum·ber ['kʌmbə] encombrer, gêner (de, **with**); **~some** ['~səm], **cum·brous** □ ['~brəs] encombrant, gênant; difficile à remuer; lourd; entravant.

cum·in ♣ ['kʌmin] cumin *m*.

cu·mu·la·tive □ ['kju:mjulətiv] cumulatif (-ive *f*); **cu·mu·lus** ['~ləs], *pl.* **-li** ['~lai] cumulus *m*.

cu·ne·i·form ['kju:niifɔ:m] cunéiforme.

cun·ning ['kʌniŋ] **1.** □ rusé; astucieux (-euse *f*); malin (-igne *f*); *Am.* mignon(ne *f*); **2.** ruse *f*; *péj.* astuce *f*.

cup [kʌp] **1.** tasse *f*; *métal:* gobelet *m*; *soutien-gorge:* bonnet *m*; *Am. cuis.* demi-pinte *f*; calice *m* (*a.* ♣, *a. fig.*); *sp.* coupe *f*; *sp.* **~ final** finale *f* de la coupe; *sp.* **~ tie** match *m* de coupe; **2.** ✍ ventouser; mettre (*la main*) en cornet *ou* en porte-voix; **~board** ['kʌbəd] armoire *f*; *mur:* placard *m*; F **~ love** amour *m* intéressé.

Cu·pid ['kju:pid] Cupidon *m*, Amour *m*.

cu·pid·i·ty [kju'piditi] cupidité *f*.

cu·po·la ['kju:pələ] coupole *f* (*a*. ⨯, ⚓); dôme *m*.

cup·ping-glass ⚕ ['kʌpiŋglɑ:s] ventouse *f*.

cu·pre·ous ['kju:priəs] cuivreux (-euse *f*).

cur [kə:] roquet *m*; chien *m* sans race; F cuistre *m*.

cur·a·bil·i·ty [kjuərə'biliti] curabilité *f*; **'cur·a·ble** guérissable.

cu·ra·cy ['kjuərəsi] vicariat *m*; **cu·rate** ['⁓rit] vicaire *m*; **cu·ra·tor** [⁓'reitə] *musée*: conservateur *m*.

curb [kə:b] **1.** gourmette *f*; *fig.* frein *m*; (*a.* ⁓stone) bordure *f* (*de trottoir*); margelle *f* (*de puits*); **2.** gourmer (*un cheval*); *fig.* contenir, refréner; ⁓ **mar·ket** *Am. Bourse*: coulisse *f*; ⁓ **roof** toit *m* en mansarde.

curd [kə:d] **1.** (lait *m*) caillé *m*; **2.** (*usu.* **cur·dle** ['⁓dl]) se cailler (*lait*); F se figer (*sang*).

cure [kjuə] **1.** guérison *f*; cure *f* (*de raisins, de lait, etc.*); remède *m*; ⁓ of souls cure *f* d'âmes; **2.** guérir; saurer (*des harengs*); saler (*les peaux, la viande*); fumer (*la viande*); '⁓**all** panacée *f*.

cur·few ['kə:fju:] couvre-feu *m* (*a. pol.*); ring the ⁓(*-bell*) sonner le couvre-feu.

cu·ri·o ['kjuəriou] curiosité *f*; bibelot *m*; **cu·ri·os·i·ty** [⁓'ɔsiti] curiosité *f*; F excentrique *m*; **'cu·ri·ous** ☐ curieux (-euse *f*); singulier (-ère *f*); *péj.* indiscret (-ète *f*).

curl [kə:l] **1.** *cheveux*: boucle *f*; *fumée, vague*: spirale *f*; **2.** boucler; *v/t.* friser; ⁓ one's *lip* faire la moue; *v/i.* s'élever en spirales (*fumée*); ⁓ up (*ou* ⁓ o.s. up) se mettre en boule (*chat etc.*); **'curl·er** bigoudi *m*, rouleau *m*.

curl·ing ['kə:liŋ] *sp.* curling *m*; '⁓-**i·ron**, '⁓-**tongs** *pl.* fer *m* à friser, frisoir *m*; **'curl·y** bouclé, frisé; en spirale.

cur·mudg·eon [kə:'mʌdʒn] bourru *m*; grippe-sou (*pl.* grippe-sou[s]) *m*.

cur·rant ['kʌrənt] groseille *f* (*a.* dried ⁓) raisin *m* de Corinthe.

cur·ren·cy ['kʌrənsi] circulation *f*, cours *m*; † (terme *m* d')échéance *f*; † espèces *f*/*pl.* de cours; monnaie *f*; *fig.* vogue *f*, *idées*: crédit *m*; **'cur-**

rent 1. ☐ en cours, courant (*argent, compte, mois, prix, opinion, etc.*); reçu (*opinion*); qui court (*bruit*); ⁓ events *pl.* actualités *f*/*pl.*; ⁓ hand (-*writing*) (écriture *f*) courante *f*; pass ⁓ avoir cours, être accepté *ou* en vogue; ⁓ issue dernier numéro *m* (*d'une publication*); ⁓ problem question *f* d'actualité; **2.** courant *m* (*a.* ⚡, *a.* d'air); fil *m* de l'eau; *fig.* cours *m*, marche *f*; ⊕ jet *m* (*d'air*); ⚡ ⁓ impulse impulsion *f* de courant; ⁓ junction prise *f* de courant.

cur·ric·u·lum [kə'rikjuləm], *pl.* -la [⁓lə] programme *m* ou plan *m* d'études.

cur·ri·er ['kʌriə] corroyeur *m*.

cur·rish ☐ ['kə:riʃ] *fig.* chien *m* de; qui ne vaut pas mieux qu'un roquet.

cur·ry¹ ['kʌri] **1.** *poudre, plat*: cari *m*, curry *m*; **2.** apprêter au cari; curried eggs *pl.* œufs *m*/*pl.* à l'indienne.

cur·ry² [⁓] corroyer (*le cuir*); étriller (*un cheval*); ⁓ favo(u)r with s'insinuer dans les bonnes grâces de (*q.*); '⁓-**comb** étrille *f*.

curse [kə:s] **1.** malédiction *f*, anathème *m*; juron *m*; *fig.* fléau *m*; **2.** *v/i.* blasphémer, jurer; *v/t.* maudire; **curs·ed** ☐ ['kə:sid] maudit; F sacré.

cur·sive ['kə:siv] cursif (-ive *f*); ⁓ handwriting cursive *f*.

cur·so·ry ☐ ['kə:səri] rapide; superficiel(le *f*).

curt ☐ [kə:t] brusque; sec (sèche *f*); cassant.

cur·tail [kə:'teil] raccourcir; tronquer; *fig.* restreindre; *fig.* enlever (de, of); **cur'tail·ment** raccourcissement *m*; restriction *f*.

cur·tain ['kə:tn] **1.** rideau *m* (*a. fig.*); *fig.* voile *m*; ⨯ courtine *f*; rideau *m* (*de feu*); **2.** garnir de rideaux; ⁓ off séparer *ou* dissimuler par des rideaux; '⁓-**fire** ⨯ (tir *m* de) barrage *m*; ⁓ lec·ture F semonce *f* conjugale; '⁓-**rais·er** *théâ.*, *a. fig.* lever *m* de rideau.

curt·s(e)y ['kə:tsi] **1.** révérence *f*; drop a ⁓ = **2.** faire une révérence (à, to).

cur·va·ture ['kə:vətʃə] courbure *f*; ⁓ of the spine déviation *f* de la colonne vertébrale.

curve [kə:v] **1.** courbe *f*; *rue*: tournant *m*; *mot.* virage *m*; *Am. base-*

ball: balle *f* qui a de l'effet; **2.** (se) courber; *v/i.* décrire une courbe.

cush·ion ['kuʃn] **1.** coussin *m*; bourrelet *m*; *billard*: bande *f*; *mot.* ~ *tyre* bandage *m* plein avec canal à air; **2.** garnir de coussins; rembourrer; *fig.* amortir (*des coups*); ⊕ matelasser.

cush·y *sl.* ['kuʃi] facile; F pépère.

cusp [kʌsp] pointe *f*; *lune*: corne *f*; ⚕ cuspide *f*; A̶ point *m* de rebroussement, sommet *m*.

cuss *Am.* F [kʌs] **1.** juron *m*; *co.* type *m*; *it's not worth a* ~ ça ne vaut pas chipette; **2.** jurer; **'cuss·ed** ['kʌsid] sacré; têtu.

cus·tard ['kʌstəd] crème *f*; œufs *m/pl.* au lait.

cus·to·di·an [kʌs'toudjən] gardien (-ne *f*) *m*; *musée*: conservateur *m*; **cus·to·dy** ['kʌstədi] garde *f*; emprisonnement *m*, détention *f*.

cus·tom ['kʌstəm] coutume *f*, usage *m*, habitude *f*; ⚖ droit *m* coutumier; ✝ clientèle *f*; patronage *m* (*du client*); **cus·tom·ar·y** ['~əri] □ habituel(le *f*); d'usage; coutumier (-ère *f*) (*droit*); **'cus·tom·er** client(e *f*) *m*; *boutique*: chaland(e *f*) *m*; F type *m*; **'cus·tom-house** (bureau *m* de la) douane *f*; ~ *officer* douanier *m*; **'cus·tom-made** *Am.* fait sur commande; **'cus·toms** *pl.* douane *f*; ~ *clearance* dédouanement *m*, expédition *f* douanière; ~ *duty* droits *m/pl.* de douane; ~ *inspection* visite *f* douanière; ~ *officer* douanier *m*.

cut [kʌt] **1.** coupe *f* (*a. vêtements*); coupure *f* (*théâ., a. blessure*); *sp.*, *épée, fouet*: coup *m*; *pierre*, ⊕ *lime*: taille *f*; réduction *f* (*de salaire*); gravure *f* (sur bois); *cuis.* morceau *m*; *unkindest* ~ *of all* coup *m* de pied de l'âne; (*a. short-*~) raccourci *m*; *cheveux*: taille *f*, coupe *f*; ⚡ coupure *f* (*de courant*); ~ *havage m*; ⚕ incision *f*; ⚔ enture *f*; *cartes*: tirage *m* (*pour les places*); F revers *m*; F absence *f* sans permission; *iro.* sarcasme *m* blessant; *fig.* refus *m* de saluer; *cuis.* cold ~*s pl.* tranches *f/pl.* de viande froide; F *give s.o. the* ~ (*direct*) passer près de q.; tourner le dos à q.; **2.** [*irr.*] *v/t.* couper (*a. cartes*), tailler; (*a.* ~ *in slices*) trancher; hacher (*le tabac*); ⚓ filer (*le câble*); réduire (*le prix*); *mot.* prendre (*un virage*); F

manquer exprès à; F sécher (*une classe*); F abandonner; ~ *s.o. dead* passer q. sans le saluer, tourner le dos à q.; ~ *one's finger* se couper le *ou* au doigt; *he is* ~*ting his teeth* ses dents percent; F ~ *a figure* faire figure; ~ *short* couper la parole à (*q.*); *to* ~ *a long story short* pour abréger, en fin de compte; *v/i.* (se) couper; percer (*dent*); ~ *and come again* revenir au plat; F ~ *and run* déguerpir, filer; ~ *back* rabattre (*un arbre*); F rebrousser chemin; ~ *down* abattre; couper (*un arbre, le blé*); réduire (*une distance, le prix*); (ra)baisser (*le prix*); restreindre (*la production*); raccourcir (*une jupe*); abréger (*un livre etc.*); ~ *in v/i.* intervenir; *mot.* couper; ~ *off* couper (*a. fig., a. téléph.*) (de, *from*); trancher; *fig.* priver; *fig.* déshériter; ~ *out* couper, découper (*des images*); tailler (*une robe, une statue*); *Am.* détacher (*des bêtes*) d'un troupeau; *fig.* supplanter (*q.*); évincer (*auprès de, with*); *fig.* cesser; supprimer; abandonner; ⚡ mettre hors circuit; faire taire (*la radio*), supprimer; ⚕ exciser; *be* ~ *out for* être taillé pour (*qch.*); *have one's work* ~ *out* avoir de quoi faire; *he had his work* ~ *out for him* on lui avait taillé de la besogne; *sl.* ~ *it out!* pas de ça!; ça suffit!; ~ *up* (dé)couper; tailler (*par morceaux, en pièces*); *fig.* affliger; critiquer sévèrement; ~ *up rough* se fâcher; **3.** coupé *etc.*; *sl.* ivre; *flowers pl.* fleurs *f/pl.* coupées; ~ *glass* cristal *m* taillé; ~ *and dry* (*ou* dried) tout fait; tout taillé (*travail*).

cu·ta·ne·ous [kju'teinjəs] cutané.

cut·a·way ['kʌtəwei] (*a.* ~ *coat*) jaquette *f*.

cut·back ['kʌtbæk] *cin.* retour *m* en arrière.

cute □ F [kju:t] malin (-igne *f*); *Am.* F gentil(le *f*), coquet(te *f*).

cu·ti·cle ['kju:tikl] *anat.* épiderme *m*; ⚕ cuticule *f*; ~ *scissors pl.* ciseaux *m/pl.* de manucure.

cut-in ['kʌt'in] *cin.* scène *f* raccord; ⚡ conjoncteur *m*.

cut·lass ['kʌtləs] ⚓ sabre *m* d'abordage; *Am.* couteau *m* de chasse.

cut·ler ['kʌtlə] coutelier *m*; **'cut·ler·y** coutellerie *f* (✝ et argenterie *f* de table); *canteen of* ~ ménagère *f*.

cut·let ['kʌtlit] *mouton, agneau*: côtelette *f*; *veau*: escalope *f*.

cut...: '**~-off** *Am.* raccourci *m*; *attr.* ⊕ de détente; *cin.* de sûreté; d'obscuration; '**~-out** *mot.* clapet *m* d'échappement libre; ⚡ coupe-circuit *m/inv.*; *cin.* déchet *m* de film; *Am.* décor *m etc.* découpé; '**~-price**, '**~-rate** ✝ à prix réduit; '**cut·ter** coupeur *m* (*a. de vêtements*); *pierre etc.*: tailleur *m*; *cin.* monteur (-euse *f*) *m*; ⚒ *personne*: abatteur *m* (*de charbon*); haveur *m*; *machine*: haveuse *f*; ⊕ coupoir *m*, couteau *m*; ⚓ canot *m*; patache *f* (*de la douane*); *Am.* traîneau *m*; '**cut-throat** coupe-jarret *m*; F rasoir *m* à manche; **2.** de coupe-jarret; *fig.* acharné; ~ *bridge* bridge *m* à trois; '**cut·ting 1.** □ tranchant; cinglant (*vent*); ⊕ a. de coupe, à couper; ~ *edge* coupant *m*; *outil*: fil *m*; ~ *nippers pl.* pinces *f/pl.* coupantes; **2.** coupe *f*; ⊕ cisaillage *m*; *bijou, vêtement*: taille *f*; ⚒ déblai *m*; tranchée *f*; ⚘ bouture *f*; *journal*: coupure *f*; ~s *pl.* bouts *m/pl.*; ⊕ copeaux *m/pl.*; rognures *f/pl.*

cut·tle *zo.* ['kʌtl] (*usu.* ~-*fish*) seiche *f*, sépia *f*; '**~-bone** os *m* de seiche; biscuit *m* de mer.

cy·a·nide ⚗ ['saiənaid] cyanure *m*; ~ *of potassium* prussiate *m* de potasse.

cyc·la·men ['sikləmən] cyclamen *m*.

cy·cle ['saikl] **1.** cycle *m*; période *f*; ⊕ cycle *m* (d'opérations); ✝ *a.* ~s *pl.* (*periode f* de) vogue *f*; bicyclette *f*; *mot.* four-~ *engine* moteur *m* à quatre temps; **2.** faire de la *ou* aller à bicyclette; **cy·clic, cy·cli·cal** □ ['siklik(l)] cyclique; **cy·cling** ['saikliŋ] **1.** cycliste; de cyclisme; **2.** cyclisme *m*; '**cy·clist** cycliste *mf*.

cy·clone ['saikloun] cyclone *m*.

cy·clo·p(a)e·di·a [saiklə'pi:djə] encyclopédie *f*.

cyg·net ['signit] jeune cygne *m*.

cyl·in·der ['silində] cylindre *m*; *revolver*: barillet *m*; *machine à écrire*: rouleau *m* porte-papier; **cy'lin·dric, cy'lin·dri·cal** □ cylindrique.

cym·bal ♪ ['simbl] cymbale *f*.

cyn·ic ['sinik] **1.** (*a.* '**cyn·i·cal** □) cynique; sceptique; **2.** *phls.* cynique *m*; sceptique *m*; **cyn·i·cism** ['~sizm] *phls.* cynisme *m*; scepticisme *m* railleur.

cy·no·sure *fig.* ['sinəsjuə] point *m* de mire.

cy·press ⚘ ['saipris] cyprès *m*.

cyst [sist] sac *m*; ⚕, *a.* ⚘ kyste *m*; '**cyst·ic** kystique, cystique; **cys·ti·tis** [sis'taitis] cystite *f*.

Czar [za:] tsar *m*.

Czech [tʃek] **1.** tchèque; **2.** *ling.* tchèque *m*; Tchèque *mf*.

Czech·o·Slo·vak ['tʃekou'slouvæk] **1.** tchécoslovaque; **2.** Tchécoslovaque *mf*.

D

D, d [di:] D *m*, d *m*.

'd F *see had; would.*

dab [dæb] **1.** coup *m* léger; tape *f*;
tache *f*; petit morceau *m* (*de beurre*);
icht. limande *f*; F expert *m*; *sl.* ⁓s *pl.*
empreintes *f/pl.* digitales; *be a* ⁓
(*hand*) *at* être passé maître en (*qch.*);
2. lancer une tape à; tapoter; appliquer légèrement (*des couleurs*); *typ.*
clicher.

dab·ble ['dæbl] *v/t.* humecter,
mouiller; *v/i.* ⁓ *in* barboter dans;
fig. s'occuper un peu de; **'dab·bler**
dilettante *mf.*

dac·ty·lo·gram [dæk'tilogræm]
dactylogramme *m.*

dad(·dy) F ['dæd(i)] papa *m.*

dad·dy-long·legs *zo.* F ['dædi'lɔŋ-
legz] tipule *f.*

daf·fo·dil ♀ ['dæfədil] narcisse *m*
sauvage *ou* des bois.

dag·ger ['dægə] poignard *m*; *be at*
⁓s *drawn* être à couteaux tirés; *look* ⁓s
at s.o. foudroyer q. du regard.

dag·gle ['dægl] (*se*) mouiller.

da·go *Am. sl. péj.* ['deigou] Espagnol
m, Portugais *m*, *surt.* Italien *m.*

dahl·ia ♀ ['deiljə] dahlia *m.*

Dail Eir·eann ['dail'ɛərən] *Chambre
des députés de l'État libre d'Irlande.*

dai·ly ['deili] **1.** quotidien (*ne f*);
F ⁓ *dozen* gymnastique *f* quotidienne; **2.** quotidien *m*, journal *m*;
domestique *f* à la journée.

dain·ti·ness ['deintinis] délicatesse
f, raffinement *m*; *taille*: mignon-
nesse *f*; **'dain·ty** □ **1.** délicat (*personne, a. chose*); friand (*mets*); exquis (*personne*); F mignon(ne *f*);
2. friandise *f*; morceau *m* de choix.

dair·y ['dɛəri] laiterie *f* (*a. boutique*);
crémerie *f*; **'⁓-farm** vacherie *f*; **'⁓-
maid** fille *f* de laiterie; **'⁓-man**
nourrisseur *m*; ✝ laitier *m*, crémier
m.

da·is ['deiis] estrade *f*; dais *m.*

dai·sy ['deizi] ♀ marguerite *f*; F
pâquerette *f*; F personne *f ou*
chose *f* épatante; (*as*) *fresh as a* ⁓ frais
(fraîche *f*) comme une rose; F *push up*

the daisies manger les pissenlits par la
racine (= *être mort*).

dale [deil] vallée *f*, vallon *m.*

dal·li·ance ['dæliəns] échange *m* de
tendresses; flirtage *m*; badinage *m*;
dal·ly ['⁓li] flirter (avec, *with*); caresser (qch., *with s.th.*); badiner; *fig.*
tarder.

dam¹ [dæm] mère *f* (*d'animaux*).

dam² [⁓] **1.** barrage *m* de retenue;
digue *f*; ✗ serrement *m*; *rivière*:
décharge *f*; **2.** (*a.* ⁓ *up*) contenir,
endiguer; obstruer.

dam·age ['dæmidʒ] **1.** dégâts *m/pl.*;
⚖ ⁓s *pl.* dommages-intérêts *m/pl.*;
2. endommager; abîmer; *fig.* nuire à
(*q.*); **'dam·age·a·ble** avariable.

dam·a·scene ['dæməsi:n] damasquiner; **dam·ask** ['dæməsk] **1.** damas *m*; *couleur*: incarnat *m*; **2.** rose
foncé *adj./inv.*; vermeil(le *f*); **3.** damasquiner (*l'acier*); damasser (*une
étoffe*).

dame [deim] dame *f* (*a. titre*); *sl.*
femme *f*; madame *f.*

damn [dæm] **1.** condamner; ruiner;
eccl. damner; *théâ.* éreinter (*une
pièce*); ⁓ *it!* zut!, sapristi!; **2.** juron
m, gros mot *m*; *I don't care a* ⁓! je
m'en moque pas mal!, je m'en
fiche!; **dam·na·ble** □ ['⁓nəbl]
damnable; F maudit; **dam·na·tion**
[⁓'neiʃn] damnation *f*; *théâ.* éreintement *m*; ⁓! sacrebleu!; **dam·na·to-
ry** ['⁓nətəri] □ qui condamne;
damned ['dæmd] *adj. et adv.*
damné, F sacré (*a.* = *très, bigrement*); **damn·ing** ['dæmiŋ] accablant (*fait*).

damp [dæmp] **1.** humide; moite;
2. humidité *f*; *peau*: moiteur *f*;
fig. froid *m*; nuage *m* de tristesse;
✗ (*a.* choke-⁓) mofette *f*; ⌂, ⊕ ⁓
course couche *f* isolante; **3.** (*a.*
'damp·en) mouiller; étouffer;
assourdir (*un son*); étouffer (*le feu*);
refroidir (*le courage etc.*); décourager; **'damp·er** rabat-joie *m/inv.*; *fig.*
froid *m*; *mot.* amortisseur *m*; ♪ étouffoir *m*; *foyer*: registre *m*; **'damp·ish**

un peu humide *ou* moite; **'damp-proof** imperméable.

dam·son ♀ ['dæmzn] prune *f* de Damas.

dance [dɑːns] **1.** danse *f*; bal (*pl.* -s) *m*; F sauterie *f*; *lead s.o. a* ~ donner du fil à retordre à q.; faire danser q.; **2.** danser; **'danc·er** danseur (-euse *f*) *m*.

danc·ing ['dɑːnsiŋ] danse *f*; *attr.* de danse; **'~-girl** bayadère *f*; **'~-les-son** leçon *f* de danse; **'~-room** dancing *m*.

dan·de·li·on ♀ [dændi'laiən] pissenlit *m*.

dan·der *sl.* ['dændə]: *get s.o.'s* ~ *up* mettre q. en colère; *get one's* ~ *up* prendre la mouche.

dan·dle ['dændl] dodeliner (*un enfant*); faire sauter (*un enfant sur ses genoux*).

dan·driff ['dændrif], **dan·druff** ['dændrəf] pellicules *f/pl.*

dan·dy ['dændi] **1.** dandy *m*, gommeux *m*; **2.** *int. surt. Am.* F chic *inv.* en genre, chouette, *sl.* bath; **dan·dy·ish** ['~diiʃ] élégant, gommeux (-euse *f*); **'dan·dy·ism** dandysme *m*.   [danois *m*.]

Dane [dein] Danois(e *f*) *m*; *chien:*]

dan·ger ['deindʒə] danger *m*, péril *m*; ~ *list*: F *be on the* ~ être dans un état grave; **'dan·ger·ous** □ dangereux (-euse *f*); **dan·ger sig·nal** 🚂 (signal *m* à l')arrêt *m*.

dan·gle ['dæŋgl] (faire) pendiller, pendre; balancer; ~ *about* (*ou after ou round*) tourner autour de (*q.*); **'dan·gler** (*ou* ~ *after women*) soupirant *m*.

Dan·ish ['deiniʃ] **1.** danois; **2.** *ling.* danois *m*; *the* ~ *pl.* les Danois *m/pl.*

dank [dæŋk] humide.

dap·per □ F ['dæpə] pimpant, coquet(te *f*), correct; sémillant.

dap·ple ['dæpl] **1.** (se) tacheter; *v/i.* se pommeler (*ciel*); **2.** tache(ture) *f*; **'dap·pled** tacheté, pommelé; **'dap·ple-'grey** (cheval *m*) gris pommelé.

dare [dɛə] *v/i.* oser; *I* ~ *say* je (le) crois bien; sans doute; peut-être bien; *v/t.* oser faire; braver, risquer (*la mort*); défier (*q.*); **'~-dev·il** casse-cou *m/inv.*; **'dar·ing** □ **1.** audacieux (-euse *f*); **2.** audace *f*, hardiesse *f*.

dark [dɑːk] **1.** □ *usu.* sombre; obscur; triste; foncé (*couleur*); basané

(*teint*); ténébreux (-euse *f*); *the* ~ *ages* l'âge *m* des ténèbres; ~ *horse* cheval *m* dont on ne sait rien; *fig.* concurrent *m* que l'on ne croyait pas dangereux; ~ *lantern* lanterne *f* sourde; ~ *room* chambre *f* noire; **2.** obscurité *f*, ténèbres *f/pl.*; *fig.* ignorance *f*; *leap in the* ~ saut *m* dans l'inconnu; **'dark·en** (s')obscurcir; (s')assombrir; *v/t.* attrister; embrumer; *never* ~ *s.o.'s door* ne plus remettre les pieds chez q.; **'dark·ish** un peu sombre; **'dark·ness** obscurité *f*, ténèbres *f/pl.*; **dark·some** *poét.* ['~səm] *see* dark 1; **'dark·y** F moricaud(e *f*) *m*.

dar·ling ['dɑːliŋ] **1.** bien-aimé *m*; chéri(e *f*) *m*; **2.** bien-aimé, chéri(te *f*).

darn[1] *sl.* [dɑːn] *see* damn *etc.*, *int.* sacré.

darn[2] [~] **1.** reprise *f*; **2.** repriser, raccommoder; (*a. fine-*~) stopper; **'darn·er** repriseur (-euse *f*) *m etc.*

darn·ing ['dɑːniŋ] reprise *f*; **'~-nee·dle** aiguille *f* à repriser; **'~-wool** laine *f* à repriser.

dart [dɑːt] **1.** dard *m*, trait *m* (*a. fig.*); *couture:* pince *f*, ponce *m*; élan *m*, mouvement *m* soudain en avant; **2.** *v/t.* darder; lancer; *v/i. fig.* se précipiter, foncer (*sur at*, [*up*]*on*).

Dar·win·ism ['dɑːwinizm] darwinisme *m*.

dash [dæʃ] **1.** coup *m*, heurt *m*; attaque *f* soudaine; trait *m* (*de plume*, *a. tél.*); ♪ brio *m*; *typ.* tiret *m*; ♯ prime; *couleur:* touche *f*, tache *f*; *fig.* brillante figure *f*; élan *m*, entrain *m*, fougue *f*; élan *m* (vers *for*, to); *fig. sel etc.:* soupçon *m*, *liquide:* goutte *f*; *cut a* ~ faire de l'effet; *at first* ~ du premier coup; **2.** *v/t.* lancer violemment; éclabousser (de boue, *with mud*); (*usu.* ~ *to pieces*) fracasser; anéantir (*une espérance*); jeter, flaquer; déconcerter, confondre; abattre (*le courage*, *l'entrain*); ~ *down* (*ou off*) enlever, exécuter à la vavite (*une lettre etc.*); *sl.* ~ *it!* zut!; *v/i.* se précipiter, s'élancer (sur, *at*); courir; se jeter (contre, *against*); ~ *off* partir en vitesse; ~ *through* traverser (*une pièce etc.*) en toute hâte; ~ *up* monter à toute vitesse; **'~-board** garde-boue *m/inv.*, 🚂, *mot.* tableau *m* de bord; **'dash·er** F élégant *m*, *péj.* épateur *m*; **'dash·ing** □ plein d'élan; fougueux (-euse *f*) (*cheval*); *fig.* brillant, beau (bel *devant une voyelle ou un h muet*); belle *f*; beaux *m/pl.*).

das·tard ['dæstəd] **1.** □ (*a.* **'das·tard·ly**) lâche, ignoble; **2.** lâche *m*; personnage *m* ignoble.

da·ta ['deitə] *pl.*, *Am. a. sg.* donnée *f*, -s *f/pl.*; éléments *m/pl.* d'information; ~ *bank* banque *f* de données; ~ *file* fichier *m* de données; *personal* ~ détails *m/pl.* personnels.

date¹ [deit] ♀ datte *f*; *arbre*: dattier *m*.

date² [~] **1.** date *f*; jour *m*, temps *m*; ♀ terme *m*, échéance *f*; *surt. Am.* F rendez-vous *m*; celui *m* ou celle *f* avec qui on a rendez-vous; *make a* ~ fixer un rendez-vous; *out of* ~ démodé; *to* ~ à ce jour; *up to* ~ au courant, à jour; F à la page; **2.** dater; assigner une date à; *surt. Am.* F fixer un rendez-vous avec; ~ *back* antidater; *v/i.* dater, être démodé; ~*d* démodé; ~ *from*, ~ *back to* remonter à; **'~-block** calendrier *m* à effeuiller; **'~-less** sans date; **'~-line** ligne *f* de changement de date; **'~-stamp** (timbre *m*) dateur *m*.

da·tive *gramm.* ['deitiv] (*ou* ~ *case*) datif *m*.

da·tum ['deitəm], *pl.* -ta ['~tə] donnée *f*; ~-*point* point *m* de repère.

daub [dɔ:b] **1.** enduit *m*; *peint.* croûte *f*; **2.** barbouiller (de, *with*) (*a. peint.*); **'daub·(st)er** barbouilleur (-euse *f*) *m*.

daugh·ter ['dɔ:tə] fille *f*; ♀ ~ *company* société *f* filiale; **~-in-law** ['dɔ:tərinlɔ:] belle-fille (*pl.* belles-filles) *f*; **'daugh·ter·ly** filial (-aux *m/pl.*).

daunt [dɔ:nt] intimider, décourager; **'~-less** intrépide.

dav·it ♣ ['dævit] bossoir *m*, davier *m*.

da·vy¹ ⚒ ['deivi] (*a.* ~-*lamp*) lampe *f* Davy (= *lampe de sûreté*).

da·vy² *sl.* [~] *see* affidavit; *take one's* ~ donner sa parole *ou* son billet.

daw *orn.* [dɔ:] choucas *m*.

daw·dle F ['dɔ:dl] *v/i.* flâner; *v/t.* gaspiller (*son temps*); **'daw·dler** F flâneur (-euse *f*) *m*; *fig.* lambin(e *f*) *m*.

dawn [dɔ:n] **1.** aube *f* (*a. fig.*), aurore *f*; point *m* du jour; **2.** poindre; se lever (*jour*); *fig.* venir à l'esprit (de, *upon*).

day [dei] jour *m* (*a.* = *aube*); journée *f*; *souv.* ~*s pl.* temps *m*; vivant *m*; âge *m*; ~ *off* jour *m* de congé; *carry* (*ou win*) *the* ~ remporter la victoire; *this* ~ aujourd'hui; *the other* ~ l'autre jour; *this* ~ *week* (d')aujourd'hui en huit; *the next* ~ le lendemain; *the* ~ *before* la veille (de qch., *s.th.*); **'~-book** ♀ journal *m*; **'~-break** point *m* du jour; aube *f*; **'~-care cen·ter** *Am.* crèche *f*; **'~-dream** rêverie *f*; **'~-fly** éphémère *m*; **'~-la·bo(u)r·er** journalier *m*; **'~-light** (lumière *f* du) jour *m*; ~-*saving time* heure *f* d'été; *sl. beat the living* ~*s out of* tabasser, rosser; **'~-nur·se·ry** garderie *f*, crèche *f*; **'~-star** étoile *f* du matin; soleil *m*; **'~-time** jour *m*, journée *f*; **'~-times** de jour.

daze [deiz] **1.** étourdir (*coup*); stupéfier (*narcotique*); **2.** étourdissement *m*, stupéfaction *f*.

daz·zle ['dæzl] éblouir, aveugler.

dea·con ['di:kn] diacre *m*; **dea·con·ess** ['di:kənis] diaconesse *f*; **'dea·con·ry** diaconat *m*.

dead [ded] **1.** *adj. usu.* mort; de mort (*silence, sommeil*); sourd (*douleur, son*); engourdi (*par le froid*); subit (*halte*); profond (*secret*); perdu (*puits*); terne (*couleur*); mat (*or*); aveugle (*fenêtre*); sans éclat (*yeux*); éventé (*boissons*); éteint (*charbon*); *sl.* vide (*bouteille*); ⊕ fixe (*essieu*); sourd (à, *to*), mort (à, *to*); ⚡ hors courant; sans courant; épuisé (*pile etc.*); ~ *bargain* véritable occasion *f*; *at a* ~ *bargain* à un prix risible; ~ *calm* calme *m* plat; *fig.* silence *m* de mort; ⊕ ~ *centre* (*ou point*) point *m* mort; centre *m* fixe; ~ *heat* manche *f* nulle; course *f* à égalité; ~ *letter* lettre *f* de rebut; *fig.* lettre morte (*loi etc.*); ~-*letter office* bureau *m* des rebuts; ~ *level* niveau *m* parfait; ~ *lift* effort *m* extrême; ~ *load* poids *m* mort; charge *f* constante; ~ *loss* perte *f* sèche; *sl. un* bon à rien *m*; ~ *man* mort *m*; *sl.* bouteille *f* vide; ~ *march* marche *f* funèbre; *play* ~ faire le mort; ~ *set fig.* attaque *f* furieuse; F *make a* ~ *set at* se jeter à la tête de (*q.*); *a* ~ *shot* tireur *m* sûr de son coup, tireur *m* qui ne rate jamais son coup; ~ *stock* fonds *m/pl.* de boutique; ~ *wall* mur *m* orbe; ~ *water* remous *m* de sillage; ~ *weight* poids *m* mort; *fig.* poids *m* inutile; *cut out the ~ wood* élaguer le personnel; **2.** *adv.* absolument; complètement; ~ *against* absolument opposé à; ~ *asleep* profondément endormi; ~ *broke* fauché; ~ *drunk* ivre mort; ~ *sure* absolument certain; ~ *tired* mort de fatigue; **3.** *su.* the ~ *pl.* les morts *m/pl.*; les trépassés *m/pl.*; *in the ~ of winter* au cœur de l'hiver; *in the ~ of night* au plus profond de la nuit; **'~-a'live** (à moitié) mort; sans animation; **'~-'beat 1.** épuisé; *≠* apériodique (*instrument*); **2.** *Am. sl.* chemineau *m*; quémandeur *m*; filou *m*; chevalier *m* d'industrie; **'dead·en** amortir (*un coup*); assourdir (*un son*); *fig.* feutrer (*le pas*); émousser (*les sens*); ⊕ hourder (*le plancher etc.*); **'dead-'end:** ~ (*street*) cul-de-sac (*pl.* culs-de-sac) *m*; *Am.* ~ *kids pl.* gavroches *m/pl.*; **'dead-'end·ed sid·ing** voie *f* (de garage) à bout fermé.

dead...: **'~-head** personne *f* munie d'un billet de faveur; *métall.* masselotte *f*; ⊕ contre-pointe *f*; **'~-line** *Am.* limites *f/pl.* (*d'une prison pour forçats etc.*); date *f* limite; délai *m* de rigueur; **'~-lock** impasse *f* (*a. fig.*); situation *f* insoluble; **'dead·ly** mortel(le *f*); ~ *pale* d'une pâleur mortelle; **'dead·ness** torpeur *f*; *membres:* engourdissement *m*; indifférence *f* (envers, *to*); † stagnation *f*.

dead...: **'~-net·tle** ortie *f* blanche; **~ pan** *Am. sl.* acteur *m etc.* sans expression.

deaf □ [def] sourd (à, *to*); *turn a ~ ear* faire la sourde oreille (à, *to*); **~ aid** appareil *m* acoustique, audiophone *m*; **'deaf·en** rendre sourd; assourdir; **'deaf-'mute** sourd(e *f*)-muet(te *f*) *m*.

deal¹ [di:l] madrier *m*; planche *f*; (bois *m* de) sapin *m*.

deal² [~] **1.** *cartes:* donne *f*, main *f*; *fig.* marché *m*, affaire *f*, † coup *m* (*de Bourse*); *Am. usu. péj.* tractation *f*; *a good* ~ quantité *f*, beaucoup; *a great* ~ (grande) quantité *f*, beaucoup; *give a square* ~ *to* agir loyalement envers; **2.** [*irr.*] *v/t.* distribuer, répartir, partager (entre *to*, *among*); *cartes:* donner, faire; distribuer; porter, donner (*un coup*) (à, *to*); *v/i.* faire le commerce (de,

in); *cartes:* donner; en user (*bien ou mal*) (avec q., *by s.o.*); ~ *with* avoir affaire à *ou* avec (q.); s'occuper de; conclure (*une affaire*); faire justice à, négocier avec; *have ~t with* avoir pris des mesures à l'égard de (q.); **'deal·er** *cartes:* donneur *m*; † négociant(e *f*) *m* (en, *in*); marchand *f*) *m* (de, *in*); *plain* ~ homme *m* franc et loyal; *sharp* ~ *un* fin matois; **'deal·ing** *usu.* ~s *pl.* distribution *f*; commerce *m*; conduite *f*; relations *f/pl.*; *péj.* tractations *f/pl.*

dealt [delt] *prét. et p.p. de* deal² 2.

dean [di:n] doyen *m*; **'dean·er·y** doyenné *m*; résidence *f* du doyen.

dear [diə] **1.** □ cher (chère *f*); coûteux (-euse *f*); **2.** F *o(h)* ~! oh là là!; hélas; ~ *me!* mon Dieu!; vraiment?; **'dear·ness** cherté *f*; tendresse *f*; **dearth** [də:θ] disette *f*; *fig.* dénuement *m*; **dear·y** ['diəri] F mon chéri *m*, ma chérie *f*.

death [deθ] mort *f*; décès *m*; *journ.* ~s *pl.* nécrologie *f*; ~ *penalty* peine *f* capitale; *tired to* ~ mort de fatigue; épuisé; **'~-bed** lit *m* de mort; **'~-blow** coup *m* fatal *ou* mortel; **'~-du·ty** droit *m* de succession; **'~-less** □ immortel(le *f*); **'~-like** de mort; semblable à la mort; **'death·ly 1.** *adj. see* deathlike; **2.** *adv.* comme la mort; **'death-rate** (taux *m* de la) mortalité *f*; **'death-roll** liste *f* des morts; **'death's-head** tête *f* de mort; **'death-war·rant** ⚖ ordre *m* d'exécution.

dé·bâ·cle [dei'ba:kl] débâcle *f*.

de·bar [di'ba:] exclure, priver (q. de qch., *s.o. from s.th.*); défendre (à q. de *inf.*, *s.o. from gér.*).

de·bar·ka·tion [di:ba:'keiʃn] débarquement *m*.

de·base [di'beis] avilir; rabaisser (*son style*); altérer (*la monnaie*); **de-'base·ment** avilissement *m*, dégradation *f*; *monnaie:* altération *f*.

de·bat·a·ble □ [di'beitəbl] discutable; contestable; **de'bate 1.** débat *m*, discussion *f*; **2.** discuter, disputer (sur qch., [*on*] *s.th.*; avec q., *with s.o.*); **de'bat·er** orateur *m*.

de·bauch [di'bɔ:tʃ] **1.** débauche *f*; **2.** débaucher; *fig.* corrompre; **deb·au'chee** débauché(e *f*) *m*; **de-'bauch·er·y** débauche *f*.

de·ben·ture [di'bentʃə] obligation *f*; certificat *m* de drawback.

de·bil·i·tate [di'biliteit] débiliter; **de·bil·i·ta·tion** débilitation *f*; **de·'bil·i·ty** débilité *f*.

deb·it ✝ ['debit] **1.** débit *m*, doit *m*; ~ *balance* solde *m* débiteur; **2.** débiter; porter (*une somme*) au débit (de q. *to*, *against* s.o.).

de·bouch [di'bautʃ] déboucher (*dans*, *into*).

de·bris ['debri:] débris *m/pl.*; *géol.* détritus *m/pl.*

debt [det] dette *f*; créance *f*; ~ *collector* agent *m* de recouvrement; *active* ~ dette *f* active; *pay the* ~ *of nature* payer le tribut à l'humanité (= *mourir*); **'debt·or** débiteur (-trice *f*) *m*.

de·bug F [di:'bʌg] remettre en ordre, réparer.

de·bunk F *surt. Am.* [di:'bʌŋk] débronzer; déboulonner.

de·bus [di:'bʌs] (faire) débarquer d'un autobus; (faire) descendre.

dé·but ['deibu:] début *m*; entrée *f* dans le monde.

dec·ade ['dekəd] décade *f*; (période *f* de) dix ans *m/pl. ou* jours *m/pl.*

de·ca·dence ['dekədəns] décadence *f*; **'de·ca·dent** décadent; en décadence.

de·caf·fei·nat·ed [di:'kæfineitid] décaféiné.

dec·a·log(ue) ['dekələg] décalogue *m*; *les* dix commandements *m/pl.*

de·camp [di'kæmp] ✗ lever le camp; F décamper, filer.

de·cant [di'kænt] décanter, transvaser; tirer au clair; **de'cant·er** carafe *f*; carafon *m*. [*obus*).]

de·cap [di:'kæp] désamorcer (*un*/ **de·cap·i·tate** [di'kæpiteit] décapiter; *Am.* congédier, F liquider; **de·cap·i'ta·tion** décapitation *f*.

de·cath·lon *sp.* [di'kæθlɔn] décathlon *m*.

de·cay [di'kei] **1.** décadence *f*; délabrement *m*; déclin *m*; pourriture *f*; *dents*: carie *f*; **2.** tomber en décadence; pourrir; se carier (*dents*); *fig.* décliner, se perdre; ~*ed with age* rongé par le temps.

de·cease *surt.* ⚖ [di'si:s] **1.** décès *m*; **2.** décéder; *the* ~*d* le défunt *m*, la défunte *f*; *pl.* les défunts *m/pl.*

de·ceit [di'si:t] tromperie *f*; fourberie *f*; **de'ceit·ful** □ trompeur (-euse *f*); faux (fausse *f*); mensonger (-ère *f*) (*regard etc.*); **de'ceit·ful·ness** fausseté *f*; nature *f* trompeuse.

de·ceiv·a·ble [di'si:vəbl] facile à tromper; **de·ceive** [di'si:v] tromper; en imposer à (*q.*); amener (*q.*) par supercherie (à *inf.*, *into gér.*); *be* ~*d* se tromper; **de'ceiv·er** trompeur (-euse *f*) *m*; fourbe *m*.

de·cel·er·ate [di:'seləreit] ralentir; **de·cel·er·a·tion** ralentissement *m*; *mot. a.* décélération *f*.

De·cem·ber [di'sembə] décembre *m*.

de·cen·cy ['di:snsi] bienséance *f*; pudeur *f*; decencies *pl.* les convenances *f/pl.*

de·cen·ni·al [di'senjəl] décennal (-aux *m/pl.*); **de'cen·ni·um** [~jəm] décennie *f*, période *f* de dix ans.

de·cent □ ['di:snt] convenable; honnête; assez bon(ne *f*); *sl.* très bon(ne *f*), brave.

de·cen·tral·i·za·tion [di:sentrəlai'zeiʃn] décentralisation *f*; **de'cen·tral·ize** décentraliser.

de·cep·tion [di'sepʃn] tromperie *f*; fraude *f*; supercherie *f*; **de'cep·tive** □ trompeur (-euse *f*); mensonger (-ère *f*).

de·cide [di'said] *v/i.* décider (*de*, *to*); se décider (pour in *favour of*, *for*; à *inf.*, on *gér.*); prendre son parti; *v/t.* trancher (*une question*); (*a.* ~ on) déterminer (qch.); **de'cid·ed** □ décidé; arrêté (*opinion*); résolu; **de'cid·er** *sp.* course *f ou* match *m* de décision; *la* belle *f*.

de·cid·u·ous ♀, *zo.* □ [di'sidjuəs] caduc (-uque *f*); ~ *tree* arbre *m* à feuilles caduques.

dec·i·mal ['desiml] **1.** décimal (-aux *m/pl.*); ⚞ ~ *point* virgule *f*; **2.** décimale *f*; **dec·i·mate** ['~meit] décimer; **dec·i'ma·tion** décimation *f*.

de·ci·pher [di'saifə] déchiffrer; transcrire en clair; **de'ci·pher·a·ble** [~rəbl] déchiffrable; **de'ci·pher·ment** déchiffrement *m*.

de·ci·sion [di'siʒn] décision *f* (*a.* ⚖); ⚖ jugement *m*, arrêt *m*; *fig. caractère*: fermeté *f*, résolution *f*; *take a* ~ prendre une décision *ou* un parti; **de·ci·sive** [di'saisiv] □ décisif (-ive *f*); tranchant (*ton*).

deck [dek] **1.** ⚓ pont *m*; tillac *m*; *top* ~ impériale *f*; *surt. Am.* paquet *m* de cartes; *Am.* F on ~ prêt; **2.** parer, orner; ⚓ ponter; **'~·'chair**

chaise *f* longue; F transat(lantique) *m*; **'deck·er:** *double-* (*single-*)~ autobus *m etc.* à (sans) impériale.

de·claim [di'kleim] déclamer (contre, *against*).

dec·la·ma·tion [deklə'meiʃn] déclamation *f*; **de·clam·a·to·ry** [di-'klæmətəri] déclamatoire.

de·clar·a·ble [di'klɛərəbl] déclarable; à déclarer; **dec·la·ra·tion** [deklə'reiʃn] déclaration *f* (en douane); **make a** ~ déclarer, proclamer; émettre une déclaration; **de·clar·a·tive** [di'klærətiv] qui déclare, qui annonce (*qch.*); **de-'clar·a·to·ry** [~təri] déclaratoire; **de·clare** [di'klɛə] *v/t.* déclarer (*qch. à q., la guerre, qch. en douane, q. coupable, etc.*); annoncer; ~ **o.s.** prendre parti; faire sa déclaration (*amant*); ~ **off** rompre (*un marché*); *v/i.* se déclarer, se prononcer (pour, *for*; contre, *against*); F **well, I** ~! par exemple!; eh bien, alors!; **de-'clared** □ ouvert, avoué, déclaré.

de·clen·sion [di'klenʃn] déclin *m*, décadence *f*; *caractère etc.*: altération *f*; *gramm.* déclinaison *f*.

de·clin·a·ble [di'klainəbl] déclinable; **dec·li·na·tion** [dekli'neiʃn] † pente *f*, déclin *m*; *Am.* refus *m*; *astr., phys.* déclinaison *f*; **de·cline** [di'klain] **1.** déclin *m* (*a. fig.*); prix: baisse *f*; ~ consommation *f*; **2.** *v/t.* refuser (courtoisement); *gramm.* décliner; *v/i.* décliner (*santé, soleil*); baisser; s'incliner (*terrain*); tomber en décadence; s'excuser.

de·cliv·i·ty [di'kliviti] pente *f*, déclivité *f*; **de'cliv·i·tous** [~təs] escarpé.

de·clutch ['di:'klʌtʃ] *mot.* débrayer.

de·coct [di'kɔkt] faire bouillir; **de-'coc·tion** décoction *f*; *pharm.* décocté *m*.

de·code ['di:'koud] déchiffrer.

dé·col·le·té [dei'kɔltei] **1.** décolletage *m*; **2.** décolleté.

de·col·o(u)r·ize [di:'kʌləraiz] décolorer.

de·com·pose [di:kəm'pouz] (se) décomposer; *v/t.* analyser; *v/i.* pourrir; **de·com·po·si·tion** [di:kɔmpə-'ziʃn] décomposition *f*; désintégration *f*; putréfaction *f*.

de·com·pres·sor [di:kəm'pre-sə] décompresseur *m*.

de·con·tam·i·nate [di:kən'tæmi-neit] désinfecter; **de·con·tam·i-'na·tion** désinfection *f*.

de·con·trol ['di:kən'troul] libérer (*qch.*) des contraintes du gouvernement; ~ **the price of** détaxer (*qch.*).

dec·o·rate ['dekəreit] décorer (*a. d'une médaille*); orner; pavoiser (*une rue*); remettre une décoration à (*q.*); **dec·o·ra·tion** décoration *f*; remise *f* d'une décoration (*à q.*); *appartement etc.*: décor *m*; *Am.* ♀ **Day** le 30 mai; **dec·o·ra·tive** ['dekərətiv] décoratif (-ive *f*); **dec·o-ra·tor** ['~reitə] décorateur (-trice *f*) *m*; (*a. house* ~) peintre *m* décorateur.

dec·o·rous □ ['dekərəs] bienséant; **de·co·rum** [di'kɔ:rəm] bienséance *f*.

de·cor·ti·cate [di'kɔ:tikeit] décortiquer.

de·coy [di'kɔi] **1.** leurre *m*, appât *m*; (*a.* ~-*duck*) oiseau *m* de leurre; moquette *f*; canard *m* privé; *fig.* compère *m* (*d'un escroc*); **2.** piper; leurrer (*a. fig.*).

de·crease 1. ['di:kri:s] diminution *f*; **2.** [di:'kri:s] diminuer; (s')amoindrir.

de·cree [di'kri:] **1.** *admin., a. eccl.:* décret *m*; arrêté *m*; ordonnance *f* (*royale*); ⚖ jugement *m*; **2.** décréter, ordonner.

dec·re·ment ['dekrimənt] décroissement *m*; perte *f*.

de·crep·it [di'krepit] décrépit (*personne*); qui tombe en ruine (*chose*); **de'crep·i·tude** [~tju:d] décrépitude *f*; vermoulure *f*.

de·cres·cent [di'kresnt] en décroissance.

de·cry [di'krai] dénigrer, décrier.

dec·u·ple ['dekjupl] **1.** décuple (*a. su./m*); **2.** (se) décupler.

ded·i·cate ['dedikeit] dédier (*a. fig.*); **ded·i·ca·tion** dédicace *f*; **'ded·i-ca·tor** dédicateur (-trice *f*) *m*; **'ded·i·ca·to·ry** dédicatoire.

de·duce [di'dju:s] déduire, conclure (de, *from*); **de'duc·i·ble** que l'on peut déduire.

de·duct [di'dʌkt] retrancher (de, *from*); **de'duc·tion** déduction *f*; *salaire:* retenue *f*, imputation *f* (sur, *from*); **de'duc·tive** déductif (-ive *f*).

deed [di:d] **1.** action *f*, acte *m*; fait *m*; ⚖ acte *m* (notarié); **2.** *Am.* transférer par un acte.

dee-jay F ['di:'dʒei] disc-jockey *m*; animateur *m*.

deem [di:m] *v/t.* juger, considérer, estimer.

deep [di:p] **1.** □ profond (*a. fig.*); foncé, sombre (*couleur*); *fig.* vif (vive *f*); difficile à pénétrer; malin (-igne *f*) (*personne*); plongé (dans, in); *box.* ~ hit coup *m* bas; **2.** abîme *m*; *poét.* océan *m*; '~-'**breath·ing** respiration *f* à pleins poumons; '**deep·en** (s')approfondir; rendre *ou* devenir plus profond; rendre *ou* devenir plus intense (*sentiment*); *v/t.* foncer; *v/i.* devenir plus foncé (*couleur*); '~-'**freeze 1.** surgeler; **2.** *a.* '~-'**freez·er** congélateur *m*; '~-'**fro·zen** surgelé; '~-'**fry** faire frire *ou* cuire dans la friture; ~*ing pan* friteuse *f*; '**deep·ness** profondeur *f*; '**deep·-'root·ed** profondément enraciné; '**deep·-'seat·ed** enraciné.

deer [diə] cerf *m*; *coll.* cervidés *m/pl.*; '~-'**lick** *Am.* roches *f/pl.* couvertes de sel; '~-**skin** *cuir*: daim *m*; '~-**stalk·er** chasseur *m* à l'affût.

de-es·ca·late [di:'eskəleit] réduire; limiter; **de-es·ca'la·tion** reduction *f*; limitation *f*; désescalade *f*.

de·face [di'feis] défigurer; mutiler; oblitérer (*un timbre*); **de'face·ment** défiguration *f etc.*

de·fal·cate [di:'fælkeit] détourner des fonds; **de·fal'ca·tion** détournement *m* de fonds; fonds *m/pl.* manquants; '**de·fal·ca·tor** détourneur *m* de fonds.

def·a·ma·tion [defə'meiʃn] diffamation *f*; **de·fam·a·to·ry** [di-'fæmətəri] diffamatoire; diffamant; **de·fame** [di'feim] diffamer; **de·'fam·er** diffamateur (-trice *f*) *m*.

de·fault [di'fɔ:lt] **1.** manquement *m*; ✝, ⚖ défaut *m*; *droit criminel*: contumace *f*; *sp.* forfait *m*; ⚖ *judgement by* ~ jugement *m* par défaut; *in* ~ *of which* faute de quoi; au défaut duquel *etc.*; *make* ~ faire défaut; être en état de contumace; **2.** *v/i.* manquer à ses engagements; ⚖ faire défaut; être en état de contumace; *v/t.* condamner (*q.*) par défaut; **de'fault·er** délinquant(e *f*) *m*; ✝ défaillant(e *f*) *m*; auteur *m* de détournements de fonds; ⚖ contumace *mf*; ✕ retardataire *m*; consigné *m*.

de·fea·sance [di'fi:zns] annulation *f*.

de·feat [di'fi:t] **1.** défaite *f*; insuccès *m*; *suffer a* ~ essuyer une défaite; **2.** ✕ battre, vaincre; faire échouer; *parl.* qqfois renverser; mettre en minorité; **de'feat·ist** défaitiste *mf*.

def·e·cate ['defikeit] déféquer, aller à la selle; **de·fe·ca·tion** défécation *f*.

de·fect [di'fekt] défaut *m*; manque *m*; imperfection *f*; **de'fec·tion** défection *f*; *eccl.* apostasie *f*; **de'fec·tive** □ défectueux (-euse *f*); imparfait; anormal (-aux *m/pl.*); en mauvais état; *gramm.* défectif (-ive *f*); *be* ~ *in* manquer de; **de'fec·tor** transfuge *m*.

de·fence [di'fens] défense *f*; protection *f*; ~ *mechanism physiol.* mécanisme *m* de défense; *psych.* défenses *f/pl.*; ✕ ~ *spending* dépenses *f/pl.* pour la défense; *witness for the* ~ témoin *m* à décharge; **de'fence·less** sans défense; désarmé.

de·fend [di'fend] défendre, protéger (contre *against, from*); justifier (*une opinion*); **de'fen·dant** défenseur (-eresse *f*) *m*; accusé(e *f*) *m*; **de'fend·er** défenseur *m*.

de·fense·(·less) [di'fens(lis)] *Am.* see *defence(·less)*.

de·fen·si·ble [di'fensəbl] défendable; soutenable (*opinion*); **de·'fen·sive 1.** □ défensif (-ive *f*); de défense; **2.** défensive *f*; *be (ou stand) on the* ~ se tenir sur la défensive.

de·fer¹ [di'fə:] différer; *v/t. a.* remettre; ajourner; ✕ mettre en sursis; ~*red annuity* rente *f* à paiement différé; ~*red payment* paiement *m* par versements échelonnés.

de·fer² [~] (*to*) déférer (à); se soumettre (à); s'incliner (devant); **de'fer·ence** ['defərəns] déférence *f*; respect *m*; *in* ~ *to, out of* ~ *to* par déférence pour; **def·er·en·tial** □ [~'renʃl] de déférence.

de·fer·ment [di'fə:mənt] ajournement *m* (*a.* ✕); remise *f*; ✕ *be on* ~ être en sursis.

de·fi·ance [di'faiəns] défi *m*; *bid* ~ *to* porter un défi à; *in* ~ *of* en dépit de (*q.*); **de'fi·ant** □ provocant; intraitable; *be* ~ *of* braver (*qch.*).

de·fi·cien·cy [di'fiʃənsi] manque *m*, défaut *m*; insuffisance *f*; *a.* see *deficit*; **de'fi·cient** défectueux

deliberate

(-euse *f*); insuffisant; à petite mentalité (*personne*); be ~ in manquer de; être au-dessous de.

def·i·cit ['defisit] déficit *m*.

de·fi·er [di'faiə] provocateur (-trice *f*) *m*.

de·file¹ 1. ['difail] défilé *m*; gorge *f*; **2.** [di'fail] défiler (*troupes etc.*).

de·file² [di'fail] souiller, salir; polluer (*une église, les mœurs*); **de'file·ment** souillure *f*; pollution *f*.

de·fin·a·ble [di'fainəbl] définissable; **de'fine** définir; délimiter (*un territoire*); **def·i·nite** ['definit] □ défini; bien déterminé; **def·i'ni·tion** définition *f*; † délimitation *f*; *opt.* netteté *f*; by ~ par définition; **de·fin·i·tive** □ [di'finitiv] définitif (-ive *f*).

de·flate [di:'fleit] dégonfler (*un ballon, fig. une personne*); ✝ amener la déflation de (*la monnaie*); **de'fla·tion** dégonflement *m*; ✝ déflation *f*; **de'fla·tion·a·ry** de déflation.

de·flect [di'flekt] dévier, défléchir; **de'flec·tion**, *souv.* **de·flexion** [di-'flekʃn] *lumière:* déflexion *f*; *compas:* déviation *f*; déformation *f*; ⊕ flèche *f*.

de·flow·er [di:'flauə] défleurir (*une plante*); *fig.* déflorer (*un paysage, un sujet, une jeune fille*).

de·fo·li·ate [di:'foulieit] (se) défeuiller.

de·form [di'fɔ:m] déformer; ~ed contrefait, difforme; **de·for·ma·tion** [di:fɔ:'meiʃn] déformation *f*; **de·form·i·ty** [di'fɔ:miti] difformité *f*; † *caractère etc.:* laideur *f*.

de·fraud [di'frɔ:d] frustrer (q. de qch., *s.o. of s.th.*); ✝, ✝ frauder.

de·fray [di'frei] couvrir (*les frais de q.*); défrayer (*q.*); [givreur *m.*]

de·freez·er *mot.* [di:'fri:zə] dé-]

de·frost ['di:'frost] dégivrer; décongeler; **de'frost·er** dégivreur *m*.

deft □ [deft] adroit, habile.

de·funct [di'fʌŋkt] **1.** défunt; décédé; *fig.* désuet (-ète *f*); **2.** défunt(e *f*) *m*.

de·fy [di'fai] défier; mettre (*q.*) au défi.

de·gen·er·a·cy [di'dʒenərəsi] dégénération *f*; **de'gen·er·ate 1.** [~reit] dégénérer (en, *into*); **2.** □ [~rit] dégénéré; **de·gen·er·a·tion** [~'reiʃn] dégénération *f*; dégénérescence *f*.

deg·ra·da·tion [degrə'deiʃn] dégradation *f*; avilissement *m*; ✂ cassation *f*; **de·grade** [di'greid] *v/t.* dégrader (*a. fig.*, ✂, *géol.*); ✂ casser (*un officier*); *géol.* effriter; *fig.* avilir; *v/i.* dégénérer; *géol.* se dégrader.

de·gree [di'gri:] degré *m* (*a.* ♈, *géog., gramm., phys.*); ♪ *gamme:* échelon *m*; *autel:* marche *f*; *univ.* grade *m*; *fig.* rang *m*, condition *f*; by ~s petit à petit; par degrés; in no ~ pas le moins du monde; in some ~ dans une certaine mesure; F to a ~ éminemment; take one's ~ prendre ses grades.

de·hy·drat·ed [di:'haidreitid] déshydraté (*pommes de terre, légumes, etc.*); en poudre (*œufs*).

de·ice ✈ ['di:'ais] dégivrer; **de-'ic·er** dégivreur *m*.

de·i·fi·ca·tion [di:ifi'keiʃn] déification *f*; **de·i·fy** ['di:ifai] déifier.

deign [dein] daigner (à, *to*).

de·ism ['di:izm] déisme *m*; **'de·ist** déiste *mf*; **de'is·tic**, **de'is·ti·cal** □ déiste.

de·i·ty ['di:iti] divinité *f*; dieu *m*, déesse *f*.

de·ject [di'dʒekt] décourager; **de-'ject·ed** □ abattu, déprimé; **de-'ject·ed·ness**, **de'jec·tion** découragement *m*, tristesse *f*.

dek·ko *Brit. sl.* ['dekou] (petit) coup d'œil; have a ~ jeter un (coup d')œil.

de·la·tion [di'leiʃn] dénonciation *f*.

de·lay [di'lei] **1.** délai *m*, retard *m*; arrêt *m*; sursis *m*; **2.** *v/t.* retarder, différer; retenir; arrêter; ~ing tactics *pl.* moyens *m/pl.* dilatoires; ~ed-action... ... à retardement; *v/i.* tarder (à *inf., in gér.*); s'attarder.

de·lec·ta·ble □ [di'lektəbl] délicieux (-euse *f*); **de·lec·ta·tion** [di:lek'teiʃn] délectation *f*.

del·e·ga·cy ['deligəsi] délégation *f*; **del·e·gate 1.** ['~geit] déléguer; **2.** ['~git] délégué(e *f*) *m*; **del·e·ga·tion** [~'geiʃn] délégation *f* (*a. parl. Am.*); députation *f*.

de·lete [di'li:t] rayer, supprimer; **del·e·te·ri·ous** □ [deli'tiəriəs] nuisible (à la santé); **de·le·tion** [di-'li:ʃn] suppression *f*; passage *m* supprimé.

delf(t) ✝ [delf(t)] faïence *f* de Delft.

de·lib·er·ate 1. [di'libəreit] *v/i.* délibérer (de, sur *on*); *v/t.* délibérer

deliberateness   752

au sujet de; **2.** □ [⌐rit] prémédité, voulu; réfléchi, avisé (*personne*); lent, mesuré (*pas etc.*);
de'lib·er·ate·ness intention *f* marquée; mesure *f*; **de·lib·er·a·tion**
[⌐'reiʃn] délibération *f*; circonspection *f*; lenteur *f* réfléchie; **de-
'lib·er·a·tive** □ [⌐rətiv] de réflexion; délibératif (-ive *f*); délibé-
rant.
del·i·ca·cy ['delikəsi] délicatesse *f*
(*a. fig.*); sensibilité *f*; *santé*:
faiblesse *f*; friandise *f*; *fig.* scrupule
m; *touche*: légèreté *f*; **del·i·cate**
['⌐kit] □ délicat (*a. fig.*); fin (*esprit*);
raffiné (*sentiment*); léger (-ère *f*)
(*touche*); épineux (-euse *f*) (*question*); faible (*santé*); **del·i·ca·tes-
sen** *Am.* [delikə'tesn] *pl.* charcuterie
f.   [(-euse *f*).\
de·li·cious [di'liʃəs] délicieux\
de·light [di'lait] **1.** délices *f/pl.*,
délice *m*; joie *f*; **2.** *v/t.* enchanter,
ravir; *v/i.* se délecter (à, *in*); se
complaire (à *inf.*, *in gér.*); ~ *to*
(*inf.*) mettre son bonheur à (*inf.*);
de'light·ful □ [⌐ful] ravissant;
charmant; délicieux (-euse *f*); **de-
'light·ful·ness** délices *f/pl.*; charme
m.
de·lim·it [di:'limit], **de'lim·i·tate**
[⌐teit] délimiter; **de·lim·i'ta·tion**
délimitation *f*.
de·lin·e·ate [di'linieit] tracer; dessiner; délinéer; **de·lin·e'a·tion**
tracé *m*; délinéation *f*; **de'lin·e·a·
tor** dessinateur *m*; instrument *m*
traceur.
de·lin·quen·cy [di'liŋkwənsi] culpabilité *f*; délit *m*; délinquance *f*; **de-
'lin·quent 1.** délinquant; coupable; **2.** délinquant(e *f*) *m*.
del·i·quesce [deli'kwes] fondre; ⌐
se liquéfier; *fig.* tomber en dé-
liquescence.
de·lir·i·ous □ [di'liriəs] en délire;
délirant; F fou (fol *devant une
voyelle ou un h muet*; folle *f*) (de,
with); **de'lir·i·ous·ness** délire *m*;
de'lir·i·um [⌐əm] délire *m*; fièvre *f*
délirante; ~ *tremens* [⌐'tri:menz]
delirium *m* tremens.
de·liv·er [di'livə] délivrer (de,
from); (*a.* ~ *up*) restituer, rendre,
livrer; faire (*une commission, une
conférence*); exprimer (*une opinion*);
prononcer (*un discours*); livrer (*un
assaut, des marchandises*); ⚕ (faire)

accoucher (de, *of*); distribuer (*des
lettres*), remettre (*un paquet*); porter, donner (*un coup*); lancer (*une
attaque, une balle*); ⚕ be ⌐ed of accoucher de; **de'liv·er·a·ble** [⌐rəbl]
livrable; **de'liv·er·ance** délivrance
f; libération *f*; expression *f*; **de-
'liv·er·er** libérateur (-trice *f*) *m*;
✝ livreur (-euse *f*) *m*; **de'liv·er·y**
remise *f*; *discours*: prononciation *f*;
orateur: diction *f*; ⚕ accouchement
m; *lettres*: distribution *f*; *colis, a.* ✝
livraison *f*; ⚖ signification *f* (*d'un
acte*); *cricket*: envoi *m* (*de la balle*);
⚔ *ville, prisonnier*: reddition *f*; ✝ ~
charge frais *m/pl.* de livraison; ~ *man*
livreur *m*; ⚕ ~ *room* salle *f* d'accouchement; ~ *truck*, ~ *van* voiture *f*
de livraison; *special* ~ envoi *m* par
exprès; *on* ~ *of* au reçu de; **de'liv-
er·y-note** bulletin *m* de livraison;
de'liv·er·y-truck, **de'liv·er·y-
van** voiture *f* de livraison.
dell [del] vallon *m*, combe *f*.
de·louse [di:'laus] épouiller.
del·ta ['deltə] delta *m*.
de·lude [di'lu:d] abuser (au point
de *inf.*, *into gér.*); tromper; duper.
de·luge ['delju:dʒ] **1.** déluge *m* (*a.
fig.*); ⌐ *le Déluge m*; **2.** inonder (de,
with) (*a. fig.*).
de·lu·sion [di'lu:ʒn] illusion *f*, erreur *f*; action *f* de duper; **de'lu-
sive** [⌐siv] □, **de'lu·so·ry** [⌐səri]
illusoire; trompeur.
dem·a·gog·ic, **dem·a·gog·i·cal**
[demə'gɔgik(l)] démagogique;
dem·a·gogue ['⌐gɔg] démagogue
m; **'dem·a·gog·y** démagogie *f*.
de·mand [di'ma:nd] **1.** demande *f*,
réclamation *f*; ⚖ requête *f* (*a on, to*);
✝ *in* ~ très demandé; *on* ~ à vue,
sur demande; *make* ~*s* faire des
demandes (à q., *on s.o.*); ~ *note*
avertissement *m*; **2.** demander
(formellement); exiger (de, *from*);
insister (pour *inf.*, *to inf.*); ⚖ réclamer (à, *from*).
de·mar·cate ['di:ma:keit] délimiter; **de·mar'ca·tion** démarcation *f*;
(*usu. line of* ~) ligne *f* de démarcation;
délimitation *f*.   [baisser.\
de·mean¹ [di'mi:n] (*usu.* ~ *o.s.*) s')a-\
de·mean² [~]: ~ *o.s.* se comporter;
de'mean·o(u)r [⌐ə] air *m*, tenue *f*.
de·ment·ed [di'mentid] fou (fol
devant une voyelle ou un h muet;
folle *f*).

de·mer·it [di:'merit] démérite *m.*
de·mesne [di'mein] possession *f*;
domaine *m* (*a. fig.*).
demi... [demi] demi-.
dem·i·john ['demidʒɔn] dame-
jeanne (*pl.* dames-jeannes) *f*; bouteille *f* clissée; bac *m* à acide.
de·mil·i·ta·ri·za·tion ['di:militərai-
'zeiʃn] démilitarisation *f*; **de'mil·i-
ta·rize** démilitariser.
de·mise [di'maiz] **1.** F décès *m*; ⚏
cession *f*; transfert *m*; *terrain*:
affermage *m*; **2.** céder, transmettre.
de·mob *sl.* [di:'mɔb] *see demobilize*;
de·mo·bi·li·za·tion ['di:moubilai-
'zeiʃn] démobilisation *f*; **de'mo·bi-
lize** démobiliser.
de·moc·ra·cy [di'mɔkrəsi] démocratie *f*; **dem·o·crat** ['deməkræt]
démocrate *mf*; **dem·o'crat·ic,**
dem·o'crat·i·cal □ démocratique;
de·moc·ra·tize [di'mɔkrətaiz] (se)
démocratiser.
de·mol·ish [di'mɔliʃ] démolir (*a.
fig.*); F dévorer, avaler; **dem·o·li-
tion** [demo'liʃn] démolition *f*.
de·mon ['di:mən] démon *m*; diable
m; **de·mo·ni·ac** [di'mouniæk] **1.** (*a.*
de·mo·ni·a·cal □ [di:mə'naiəkl])
démoniaque; diabolique; **2.** démoniaque *mf*; **de·mon·ic** [di:-
'mɔnik] diabolique; du Démon.
de·mon·stra·ble □ ['demənstrəbl]
démontrable; **dem·on·strate** ['⁓-
streit] *v/t.* démontrer; expliquer,
décrire (*un système*); *v/i.* manifester;
✕ faire une démonstration; **demon'stra·tion** démonstration *f* (*a.*
✕); *sentiments*: témoignage *m*, démonstration *f*, effusion *f*; *pol.*
manifestation *f*; ✝ *mot.* ⁓ *car* voiture
f de démonstration; **de·mon·stra-
tive** [di'mɔnstrətiv] **1.** □ démonstratif (-ive *f*) (*a. gramm.*); *a.* expansif (-ive *f*) (*personne*); démontrable
(*vérité etc.*); **2.** *gramm.* pronom *m*
etc. démonstratif; **dem·on·stra·tor**
['demənstreitə] démonstrateur *m* (*a.
anat.*); *univ.* préparateur *m*; *pol.*
manifestant *m.*
de·mor·al·i·za·tion [dimɔrəlai-
'zeiʃn] démoralisation *f*; **de'mor·
al·ize** corrompre; démoraliser.
de·mote *Am.* [di:'mout] réduire à
un grade inférieur *ou* à une classe
inférieure; *école*: faire descendre
d'une classe; **de'mo·tion** réduction *f* à un grade inférieur *etc.*

de·mur [di'mə:] **1.** hésitation *f*; objection *f*; **2.** hésiter; soulever des
objections (contre *to*, *at*).
de·mure [di'mjuə] grave; réservé;
d'une modestie affectée; F (*air*) de
sainte nitouche; **de'mure·ness**
gravité *f*; modestie *f* (affectée); air
m de sainte nitouche.
de·mur·rage [di'mʌridʒ] ⚓ sures-
tarie *f*, -s *f/pl.*; 🏬 magasinage *m*;
de'mur·rer ⚏ fin *f* de non-
recevoir.
de·my ✝ [di'mai] *papier*: coquille *f*.
den [den] tanière *f*, antre *m*; *fig.*
retraite *f*; F cabinet *m* de travail; F
bouge *m.*   [dénationaliser.)
de·na·tion·al·ize [di:'næʃnəlaiz]/
de·na·ture ⚗ [di'neitʃə] dénaturer.
de·ni·a·ble [di'naiəbl] niable; **de-
'ni·al** déni *m*, refus *m*; dénégation *f*,
démenti *m*; **de'ni·er** dénégateur
(-trice *f*) *m.*
den·i·grate ['denigreit] diffamer
(*q.*); noircir (*la réputation*); dénigrer (*q.*, *un projet*).
den·im ['denim] *tex.* étoffe *f* croisée
de coton (*pour salopette*); F ⁓s *pl.*
bleus *m/pl.*
den·i·zen ['denizn] habitant(e *f*) *m.*
de·nom·i·nate [di'nɔmineit] dénommer; **de·nom·i'na·tion** dénomination *f*; catégorie *f*; *eccl.*
secte *f*, culte *m*; **de·nom·i'na-
tion·al** confessionnel(le *f*), sectaire; **de'nom·i·na·tive** [⁓nətiv]
dénominatif (-ive *f*); **de'nom·i·na-
tor** ⅍ [⁓neitə] dénominateur *m*;
common ⁓ dénominateur *m* commun.
de·no·ta·tion [di:nou'teiʃn] désignation *f*; signification *f*; *fig.* indication *f*; **de·no·ta·tive** [di'noutətiv]
indicatif (-ive *f*) (de, of); **de'note**
dénoter; signifier; indiquer.
de·nounce [di'nauns] dénoncer (*q.*,
un traité, etc.); démasquer (*un imposteur*); s'élever contre (*un abus*);
✝ prononcer (*un jugement*); **de-
'nounce·ment** dénonciation *f*.
dense □ [dens] épais(se *f*); profond
(*obscurité etc.*); lourd (*esprit*); *fig.*
stupide; *phot.* opaque; **'dense·ness**
épaisseur *f*; *population*: densité *f*;
fig. stupidité *f*; **'den·si·ty** *phys.*
densité *f*; *a. see* denseness.
dent [dent] **1.** bosselure *f*; *lame*:
brèche *f*; **2.** bosseler, bossuer;
ébrécher (*une lame*).

den·tal ['dentl] **1.** dentaire; *gramm.*
dental (-aux *m/pl.*); ~ *science* chirurgie *f* dentaire; **2.** *gramm.* den-
tale *f*; **den·tate** ['~teit] ⚕ denté;
dentelé; **den·ti·frice** ['~tifris] dentifrice *m*; **'den·tist** dentiste *mf*;
'den·tist·ry art *m* dentaire; **den-
'ti·tion** dentition *f*; **den·ture**
['~tʃə] dentier *m*; *zo.* denture *f*.

den·u·da·tion [di:nju:'deiʃn] dénu-
dation *f*; *géol.* érosion *f*; **de'nude**
(*of*) dénuder; dépouiller (de); *fig.*
dégarnir (de).

de·nun·ci·a·tion [dinʌnsi'eiʃn] dénonciation *f*; condamnation *f*; accusation *f* publique; **de'nun·ci·a-
tor** dénonciateur (-trice *f*) *m*.

de·ny [di'nai] nier; dénier (*un crime*);
repousser (*une accusation*); démentir
(*une nouvelle*); renier (*sa foi*); refuser (qch. à q. *s.o.* s.th., *s.*th. *to s.o.*);
~ *o.s.* s.th. se refuser qch.; ~ *o.s.*
fermer sa porte (à q., *to s.o.*).

de·o·dor·ant [di:'oudərənt] désodorisant *m*; **de·o·dor·ize** [di:'oudə-
raiz] désodoriser; **de'o·dor·iz·er**
désodorisateur *m*.

de·part [di'pɑ:t] *v/i.* partir (pour,
for), s'en aller (à, *for*); quitter (un
lieu, *from a place*); F sortir (de,
from); s'écarter (de, *from*); démordre (de, *from*); mourir; *the ~ed* le
défunt *m*, la défunte *f*; *pl.* les morts
m/pl.; *v/t.* ~ *this life* quitter ce monde; **de'part·ment** département *m*
(*a. géog.*); service *m*; ✝ rayon *m*,
comptoir *m*; *Am.* ministère *m*;
♀ *of Education* (*and Science*) Ministère
m de l'Éducation nationale *ou de*
l'Instruction publique; ♀ *of the*
Environment Ministère *m* de l'Environnement; *State* ♀ Ministère *m* des
Affaires étrangères; ~ *store* grand
magasin *m*; **de·part·men·tal** [~-
'mentl] départemental (-aux *m/pl.*);
de'par·ture [~tʃə] départ *m* (*a.* 🚢,
✈); déviation (de, *from*); *a new* ~ une
nouvelle tendance *f*; une nouveauté
f; une nouvelle orientation *f*; *aéroport:* ~ *lounge* salle *f* de départ; ~
platform (quai *m* de) départ *m*;
embarcadère *m*.

de·pend [di'pend] † pendre (à,
from); ⚖ être pendant; ~ (*up*)*on*
dépendre de; se trouver à la charge
de; compter sur; se fier à (*qch.*);
F *it* ~*s* cela dépend, F c'est selon;
de'pend·a·ble bien fondé; digne

de confiance (*personne*); **de'pendant** protégé(e *f*) *m*; pensionnaire
mf; ~*s pl.* charges *f/pl.* de famille;
de'pend·ence dépendance *f* (de,
[*up*]*on*); confiance *f* (en, on); **de-
'pend·en·cy**, *souv.* dependencies *pl.*
dépendance *f*; **de'pend·ent 1.** □
(*on*) dépendant (de); à la charge (de);
be ~ *on charity* subsister d'aumônes;
2. *see* dependant; **de'pend·ing** ⚖
be ~ être pendant.

de·pict [di'pikt] (dé)peindre.

de·pil·a·to·ry [de'pilətəri] **1.** (d)épi-
latoire; **2.** dépilatoire *m*.

de·plane [di:'plein] descendre d'a-
vion.

de·plete [di'pli:t] épuiser (*a. fig.*); ✕
dégarnir (*une garnison*); **de'ple·tion**
épuisement *m*; ✕ dégarnissement
m; **de'ple·tive** épuisant, qui
épuise.

de·plor·a·ble □ [di'plɔ:rəbl] déplorable; lamentable; **de·plore** [di-
'plɔ:] déplorer; regretter vivement.

de·ploy ✕ [di'plɔi] (se) déployer;
de'ploy·ment ✕ déploiement *m*.

de·plume [di'plu:m] déplumer.

de·po·nent [di'pounənt] ⚖ déposant *m*; *gramm.* (verbe *m*) déponent
m.

de·pop·u·late [di:'pɔpjuleit] (se) dépeupler; **'de·pop·u'la·tion** *pays:*
dépopulation *f*; *forêt:* dépeuplement *m*.

de·port [di'pɔ:t] expulser (*un étranger*); ~ *o.s.* se conduire; **de·por'tation** expulsion *f*; **de·port·ee** [di:-
pɔ:'ti:] détenu(e *f*) *m*; **de'port-
ment** tenue *f*; conduite *f*.

de·pos·a·ble [di'pouzəbl] capable
d'être déposé; **de'pose** déposer; ⚖
témoigner (que, *that*; de qch., *to*
s.th.).

de·pos·it [di'pozit] **1.** *géol.* gisement
m, couche *f*; ⚕ encroûtement *m*;
🜍 précipité *m*, sédiment *m*; ✝
acompte *m*, somme *f* en gage,
arrhes *f/pl.*; dépôt *m* (*en banque*);
✝ ~ *account* compte *m* d'épargne (à
terme); **2.** de dépôts; **3.** déposer (*qch.*
sur qch., des œufs, de l'argent, *a.* 🜍);
consigner (*de l'argent*); cautionner
(*des droits de douane*); **de'pos·i·ta·ry**
dépositaire *m*; **dep·o·si·tion** [depə-
'ziʃn] déposition *f*; témoignage *m*; 🜍
dépôt *m*; *eccl.* Descente *f* de Croix;
de·pos·i·tor [di'pozitə] déposant *m*;
de'pos·i·to·ry dépôt *m*, entrepôt *m*;

garde-meuble (*pl.* garde-meuble[s]) *m*; *fig.* mine *f*, trésor *m*.

de·pot ['depou] ✕, ⚓, ⚓ dépôt *m*; ⚓ entrepôt *m*; *Am.* gare *f*.

dep·ra·va·tion [deprə'veiʃn] dépravation *f*; see *depravity*; **de·prave** [di'preiv] dépraver; **de'praved** dépravé (*a. goût*); **de·prav·i·ty** [di'præviti] perversité *f*; dépravation *f*.

dep·re·cate ['deprikeit] désapprouver, désavouer, déconseiller (*une action*); **dep·re'ca·tion** désapprobation *f*; désaveu *m*; *eccl.* † déprécation *f*; **dep·re·ca·to·ry** ['⌣kətəri] déprécatif (-ive *f*).

de·pre·ci·ate [di'priːʃieit] *v/t.* déprécier (*a. fig.*); avilir; *fig.* dénigrer; *v/i.* se déprécier; diminuer de valeur; **de·pre·ci·a·tion** dépréciation *f* (*a.* ⚓); dénigrement *m*; ⚓ amortissement *m*; **de'pre·ci·a·to·ry** [⌣ətəri] dépréciateur (-trice *f*).

dep·re·da·tion [depri'deiʃn] déprédation *f*; pillage *m*; **'dep·re·da·tor** déprédateur (-trice *f*) *m*; **dep·re·da·to·ry** [di'predətəri] de déprédation.

de·press [di'pres] abaisser (*a.* ✕); baisser; abattre (*les forces*); faire languir (*le commerce*); faire baisser (*le prix*); baisser le ton de (*la voix*); appuyer sur (*la pédale*); *fig.* attrister, décourager; **de'press·ing** *fig.* déprimant; **de'pressed** *fig.* triste; abattu; **de·pres·sion** [di'preʃn] abaissement *m* (*a. phys.*); ⚓, *astr.*, *géog.*, *météor.* dépression *f*; ⚓ abattement *m*; ⚓ affaissement *m* (*a.* ⚓); ⊕ trou *m*, godet *m*; *géog.* creux *m*; *météor.* baisse *f*; *tir.* pointage *m* négatif; *fig.* découragement *m*.

dep·ri·va·tion [depri'veiʃn] privation *f*; ✕, *admin.* retrait *m* (*d'emploi*); *eccl.* révocation *f*, destitution *f*; **de·prive** [di'praiv] priver (q. de qch., *s.o.* of *s.th.*); déposséder (*q.*) d'une charge; *eccl.* destituer; **de'prived** déshérité.

depth [depθ] profondeur *f*; *forêt*, *eau*: fond *m*; *couche*: épaisseur *f*; *couleur*: intensité *f*; *son*: gravité *f*; *intelligence*: portée *f*; ~ **bomb** (*ou* charge) grenade *f* sous-marine; *phot.* ~ **of field**, ~ **of focus** profondeur *f* de foyer; **go beyond one's** ~ perdre fond; *a.* **be out of one's** ~ avoir perdu pied; *fig.* sortir de sa compétence; *fig.* **in** ~ profond, en profondeur.

dep·u·ta·tion [depju'teiʃn] délégation *f*, députation *f*; **de·pute** [di'pjuːt] déléguer, députer; **dep·u·tize** ['depjutaiz] remplacer (*q.*); ~ **for** faire l'intérim de; **'dep·u·ty 1.** remplaçant(e *f*) *m*; ⚖ fondé *m* de pouvoir; substitut *m* (*d'un juge*); suppléant(e *f*) *m*; délégué(e *f*) *m*; **2.** sous-; suppléant.

de·rac·i·nate [di'ræsineit] déraciner.

de·rail 🚂 [di'reil] (faire) dérailler; **de'rail·ment** déraillement *m*.

de·range [di'reindʒ] déranger; désorganiser; ⊕ fausser (*une machine*); aliéner (*l'esprit*); **de'ranged** détraqué (*cerveau*); dérangé (*estomac*); **de'range·ment** dérèglement *m* (de *l'esprit*); dérangement *m*; troubles *m/pl.* (*de digestion*).

de·rate [diː'reit] dégrever.

Der·by *sp.* ['daːbi] le Derby *m*; **'der·by** *Am.* chapeau *m* melon.

der·e·lict ['derilikt] **1.** abandonné, délaissé; *surt. Am.* négligent; **2.** objet *m* abandonné; épave *f*; **der·e'lic·tion** [deri'likʃn] abandon *m*, délaissement *m*; ~ **of duty** manquement *m* au devoir.

de·ride [di'raid] tourner en dérision; se moquer de; railler.

de·ri·sion [di'riʒn] dérision *f*; ridicule *m*; **de·ri·sive** [di'raisiv] ☐, **de'ri·so·ry** [⌣səri] moqueur (-euse *f*); *fig.* dérisoire (*offre*).

de·riv·a·ble ☐ [di'raivəbl] dérivable; que l'on peut tirer (de, from); **der·i·va·tion** [deri'veiʃn] dérivation *f* (*a.* ✕, ⚓); **de·riv·a·tive** [di'rivətiv] **1.** ☐ dérivé; **2.** dérivé *m*; ✕ dérivée *f*; **de·rive** [di'raiv] (from) tirer (de); prendre (*du plaisir etc.*) (à); devoir (*qch.*) (à); **be** ~**ed from** dériver de.   [matite *f*.]

der·ma·ti·tis [dəːmə'taitis] der-∫
der·ma·tol·o·gy [dəːmə'tɔlədʒi] dermatologie *f*.

der·o·gate ['derəgeit] déroger (à sa dignité, from one's *dignity*); diminuer (qch., from *s.th.*); **der·o'ga·tion** dérogation *f* (à une loi, of *a law*); atteinte *f* (portée à qch., from *s.th.*); **de·rog·a·to·ry** ☐ [di'rɔgətəri] (**to**) dérogatoire (à); attentatoire (à); qui déroge (à).

der·rick ['derik] ⊕ chevalement *m*; ⚓ mât *m* de charge; ✕ chevalement *m* de sondage.

de·sal·i·nate ['di:'sælineit] dessaler; **de·sal·i'na·tion** dessalage *m*.

des·cant [dis'kænt] discourir, s'étendre (sur, [up]on).

de·scend [di'send] descendre; *v/i.* tomber (*pluie*); s'abaisser; tirer son origine (de, *from*); ~ (up)on s'abattre sur, tomber sur, descendre sur; ~ to passer à (*q. par héritage*); descendre jusqu'à (*bassesse etc.*); ~ (*a. be ~ed*) *from* descendre de; **de·'scend·ant** descendant(e *f*) *m*.

de·scent [di'sent] *usu.* descente *f*; pente *f*; chute *f*; abaissement *m*; déchéance *f*; descendance *f*; ⚕ transmission *f* par héritage; atterrissage *m* (*p.ex. forcé, d'un avion*).

de·scrib·a·ble [dis'kraibəbl] descriptible; **de'scribe** décrire, dépeindre.

de·scrip·tion [dis'kripʃn] description *f*; *police etc.:* signalement *m*; ⚕ désignation *f*; espèce *f*, sorte *f*; **de'scrip·tive** □ descriptif (-ive *f*); raisonné (*catalogue*).

de·scry [dis'krai] apercevoir, aviser.

des·e·crate ['desikreit] profaner; **des·e'cra·tion** profanation *f*.

de·seg·re·gate *Am.* [di'segrigeit] abolir les distinctions légales *ou* sociales entre les blancs et les races de couleur dans (*une école etc.*); **'de·seg·re'ga·tion** déségrégation *f*.

de·sen·si·tize ['di:'sensitaiz] désensibiliser.

des·ert¹ ['dezət] **1.** désert; désertique (*flore*); aride (*sujet*); **2.** désert *m*; **3.** [di'zə:t] *v/t.* déserter; *fig.* abandonner, délaisser (*q.*); *v/i.* faire défection; ✗ déserter.

de·sert² [di'zə:t], *a.* ~s *pl.* mérite *m*, -s *m/pl.*; dû *m*; ce qu'on mérite.

de·sert·er [di'zə:tə] déserteur *m*; *pol.* F saxon *m*; **de'ser·tion** abandon *m*; ⚕ abandon *m* criminel; ✗ désertion *f*; *pol.* défection *f*.

de·serve [di'zə:v] mériter (de, *of*); être digne de; **de'serv·ed·ly** [~vidli] à juste titre; **de'serv·ing** méritant (qch., *of s.th.*); méritoire (*action*).

des·ic·cate ['desikeit] dessécher; **des·ic'ca·tion** dessèchement *m*; **'des·ic·ca·tor** dessiccateur *m*.

de·sid·er·ate [di'zidəreit] soupirer après; sentir le besoin de; **de·sid·er·a·tum** [~'reitəm], *pl.* -ta [~tə] desiderata *m/pl.*

de·sign [di'zain] **1.** dessein *m* (*péj. a.* ~s *pl.*); projet *m*; intention *f*; dessin *m* d'ornement; plan *m*; modèle *m* (*a. mot.*, ⊕); ⊕ dessin *m*, étude *f*; by ~ à dessein; with the ~ dans le dessein (de *inf.*, of *gér.*); **2.** préparer; construire; étudier (*une machine*); destiner (à, *for*); projeter (de *inf.*, to *inf.*); créer (*des modes*); ~ed to (*inf.*) conçu pour, fait pour (*inf.*).

des·ig·nate 1. ['dezigneit] nommer; désigner (pour, comme *as*, for); qualifier (de, *as*); indiquer (*qch.*); **2.** ['~nit] *après le su.* (*p.ex. bishop* ~): désigné; **des·ig'na·tion** désignation *f*; nomination *f*; nom *m*.

de·sign·ed·ly [di'zainidli] à dessein; **de'sign·er** dessinateur (-trice *f*) *m*; inventeur (-trice *f*) *m*; concepteur-projeteur *m* (*pl.* concepteurs-projeteurs); *théa.* décorateur *m*; *fig.* intrigant(e *f*) *m*; **de'sign·ing** □ artificieux (-euse *f*).

de·sir·a·ble □ [di'zaiərəbl] désirable; avantageux (-euse *f*); attrayant; **de·sire** [di'zaiə] **1.** désir *m* (de, *for*; de *inf.*, to *inf.*); souhait *m*; envie *f* (de *inf.*, to *inf.*); at s.o.'s ~ selon le désir de q.; **2.** désirer; avoir envie de; vouloir (que q. *sbj.*, s.o. *to inf.*); ~ to (*inf.*) désirer (*inf.*); **de·sir·ous** □ [di'zaiərəs] désireux (-euse *f*) (de *inf.* of *gér.*, to *inf.*).

de·sist [di'zist] cesser (de *inf.*, from *gér.*); renoncer (à qch., *from s.th.*).

desk [desk] pupitre *m*; bureau *m*; ⚕ caisse *f*; ~ pad sous-main *m* (*pl.* sous-mains); bloc-notes *m* (*pl.* blocs-notes).

des·o·late 1. ['desəleit] ravager; affliger (*q.*); **2.** □ ['~lit] désert, morne; affligé (*personne*); **des·o·la·tor** ['~leitə] dévastateur (-trice *f*) *m*; **des·o'la·tion** désolation *f* (*a. fig.*).

de·spair [dis'pɛə] **1.** désespoir *m*; **2.** désespérer (de, *of*); **de'spair·ing** □ [dis'pɛəriŋ] désespéré.

des·patch *see* dispatch.

des·per·a·do [despə'rɑ:dou] risque-tout *m/inv.*; tête *f* brûlée; bandit *m*.

des·per·ate □ ['despərit] *adj.* désespéré; *fig.* acharné; *fig.* épouvantable; **des·per·a·tion** [despə'reiʃn] désespoir *m*.

des·pi·ca·ble □ ['despikəbl] méprisable.

de·spise [dis'paiz] mépriser; dédaigner.

de·spite [dis'pait] **1.** *poét.* dépit *m*; in ~ of en dépit de; **2.** *prp.* (*a.* ~ *of*) en dépit de; **de'spite·ful** □ [~ful] *poét.* dédaigneux (-euse *f*).

de·spoil [dis'pɔil] dépouiller (de, of); **de'spoil·ment** spoliation *f*.

de·spond [dis'pɔnd] perdre courage; ~ of envisager (*qch.*) sans espoir; **de'spond·en·cy** [~dənsi] découragement *m*, abattement *m*; **de'spond·ent** □, **de'spond·ing** □ découragé, abattu.

des·pot ['despɔt] despote *m*; tyran *m*; **des'pot·ic** (~*ally*) despotique; **des·pot·ism** ['~pətizm] despotisme *m*.

des·qua·ma·tion [deskwə'meiʃn] exfoliation *f*.   [entremets *m*.]

des·sert [di'zɔːt] dessert *m*; *Am.*

des·ti·na·tion [desti'neiʃn] destination *f*; **des·tine** ['~tin] destiner (a for, to); be ~d to (*inf.*) être destiné à (*inf.*); **'des·ti·ny** destin *m*, destinée *f*; sort *m*.

des·ti·tute □ ['destitjuːt] dépourvu, dénué (de, of); sans ressources; **des·ti'tu·tion** dénuement *m*; misère *f*.

de·stroy [dis'trɔi] détruire; anéantir; tuer; **de'stroy·er** destructeur (-trice *f*) *m*; ⚓ torpilleur *m*.

de·struc·ti·bil·i·ty [distrʌkti'biliti] destructibilité *f*; **de'struct·i·ble** [~əbl] destructible; **de'struc·tion** destruction *f*; anéantissement *m*; *feu, tempête*: ravages *m/pl.*; *fig.* perte *f*; **de'struc·tive** □ destructeur (-trice *f*); destructif (-ive *f*); fatal (à, of); **de'struc·tive·ness** effet *m* destructeur; penchant *m* à tout briser; **de'struc·tor** incinérateur *m* (*d'ordures*).

des·ue·tude [di'sjuːitjuːd] désuétude *f*.

des·ul·to·ri·ness ['desəltərinis] manque *m* de méthode *ou* de suite; décousu *m*; **'des·ul·to·ry** □ décousu, sans suite.

de·tach [di'tætʃ] détacher (*a.* ✂); séparer; dételer (*des wagons*); **de'tach·a·ble** détachable; amovible; mobile; **de'tached** détaché (*a. maison*); à part; séparé; désintéressé (*personne*); désinvolte (*manière*); ✂ isolé (*poste*); **de'tach·ment** séparation *f* (de, from); indifférence *f* (envers, from); détachement *m* (*d'esprit*; *a.* ✂).

de·tail ['diːteil] **1.** détail *m*; particularité *f*; ⊕ organe *m*; ✂ détachement *m* (*de corvée*); ~s *pl.* détails *m/pl.*; accessoires *m/pl.*; in ~ de point en point, en détail; go into ~ entrer dans tous les détails; **2.** détailler; raconter en détail; ✂ affecter (à un service, *for a duty*); **'de·tailed** détaillé.

de·tain [di'tein] retenir; arrêter; empêcher de partir; consigner (*un élève*); ⚖ détenir; **de·tain·ee** [~'niː] détenu(e *f*) *m*; **de'tain·er** détention *f*; ⚖ ordre *m* d'incarcération.

de·tect [di'tekt] découvrir; apercevoir; détecter (*radio*); **de'tect·a·ble** discernable; **de'tec·tion** découverte *f*; *radio:* détection *f*; **de'tec·tive 1.** révélateur (-trice *f*); de détective; policier (-ère *f*) (*roman etc.*); **2.** agent *m* de la sûreté; policier *m*; **de'tec·tor** découvreur (-euse *f*) *m*; signal *m* d'alarme; ⊕, *a. radio:* détecteur *m*.

de·tent ⊕ [di'tent] détente *f*, arrêt *m*.

dé·tente [dei'tãːnt] *pol.* détente *f*.

de·ten·tion [di'tenʃn] détention *f*; arrêt *m*; retenue *f* (*d'un élève*); retard *m*; ~ camp camp *m* d'internement; house of ~ maison *f* d'arrêt.

de·ter [di'tɔː] détourner (de, from).

de·ter·gent [di'tɔːdʒənt] **1.** détersif (-ive *f*), détergent; **2.** détersif *m*, détergent *m*.

de·te·ri·o·rate [di'tiəriəreit] (se) détériorer; *v/i.* diminuer de valeur; dégénérer (*race*); **de·te·ri·o'ra·tion** détérioration *f*; diminution *f* de valeur; *race:* dégénération *f*.

de·ter·ment [di'tɔːmənt] action *f* de détourner.

de·ter·mi·na·ble □ [di'tɔːminəbl] déterminable; ⚖ résoluble; **de'ter·mi·nant** déterminant (*a. su./m*); **de'ter·mi·nate** □ [~nit] déterminé; défini; définitif (-ive *f*); **de·ter·mi'na·tion** détermination *f*, résolution *f* (*a. d'un contrat etc.*); décision *f*; délimitation *f*; **de'ter·mi·na·tive** [~nətiv] **1.** déterminant; *gramm.* déterminatif (-ive *f*); **2.** *gramm.* déterminatif *m*; **de'ter·mine** [~min] *v/t.* déterminer, fixer; décider (de, to); *surt.* ⚖ décider (*une question*), résoudre (*un contrat*); *v/i.* décider (de *inf.*, to *inf.*); se décider (à *inf.* on *gér.*, to *inf.*);

determined   758

de'ter·mined déterminé; résolu
(*personne*); **de'ter·min·er** *gramm.*
déterminant *m.*
de·ter·rent [di'terənt] **1.** préventif
(-ive *f*); ✕ ~*weapon* arme *f* de dissuasion; **2.** préventif *m.*
de·test [di'test] détester; **de'test·a-
ble** □ détestable; **de·tes'ta·tion**
détestation *f* (de, *of*); horreur *f*;
he is my ~ c'est ma bête noire.
de·throne [di'θroun] détrôner; **de-
'throne·ment** détrônement *m.*
det·o·nate ['detouneit] (faire) détoner; **'det·o·nat·ing** détonant, explosif (-ive *f*); **det·o·na·tion** détonation *f*; explosion *f*; **det·o·na-
tor** ['~tə] 🚂 pétard *m*; ✕ détonateur *m*; amorce *f.*
de·tour [di'tuə], **dé·tour** ['deituə]
détour *m*; *Am.* déviation *f* (*d'itinéraire*).
de·tract [di'trækt] diminuer, amoindrir (qch., *from s.th.*); **de'trac·tion**
détraction *f*, dénigrement *m*; **de-
'trac·tive** détracteur (-trice *f*); **de-
'trac·tor** détracteur (-trice *f*) *m.*
de·train [di:'trein] débarquer.
det·ri·ment ['detrimənt] détriment
m, dommage *m*; préjudice *m* (de,
to); **det·ri·men·tal** □ [detri'mentl]
nuisible (à, *to*).   [*m.*⟩
de·tri·tus *géol.* [di'traitəs] détritus⟩
deuce [dju:s] *jeu:* deux *m*; *tennis:*
égalité *f*; F diable *m*; *the ~!* diable!;
(*the*) *~ a one* personne, pas un;
'deu·ced F satané, fichu.
de·val·u·ate ['di:'vӕljueit] dévaluer;
de·val·u·a·tion [di:vӕlju'eiʃn] dévaluation *f*; **de'val·ue** [~ju:] dévaluer.
dev·as·tate ['devəsteit] dévaster, ravager; **'dev·as·tat·ing** dévastateur
(-trice *f*), écrasant (*critique etc.*);
irrésistible (*charme etc.*); **dev·as'tation** dévastation *f.*
de·vel·op [di'veləp] (se) développer;
v/t. manifester; exploiter (*une région*); contracter (*une habitude, une
maladie*); *Am.* mettre à jour; *v/i.*
prendre une nouvelle tournure; apprendre (que, *that*); **de'vel·op·er**
phot. révélateur *m*; **de'vel·op·ing**
phot. développement *m*; *attr.* de
ou à développement; **de'vel·op-
ment** développement *m*; exploitation *f*; événement *m*, fait *m* nouveau; déroulement *m* (*des événements*).

de·vi·ate ['di:vieit] (*from*) s'écarter
(de); dévier (de); **de·vi'a·tion** déviation *f* (*a. boussole*); écart *m.*
de·vice [di'vais] expédient *m*, moyen
m; ruse *f*, stratagème *m*; plan *m*; appareil *m*; emblème *m*, devise *f*;
leave s.o. to his own ~s livrer q. à lui-
même.
dev·il ['devl] **1.** diable *m* (*a. fig.*);
démon *m*; F mauvaise passion *f*,
élan *m*; bruit *m* infernal; *fig.* nègre
m; ⊕ dispositif *m* à dents *ou* à pointes; *cuis.* plat *m* grillé et poivré; *the
~!* diable!; *play the ~ with* ruiner;
2. *v/t.* faire griller et poivrer fortement; ⊕ effilocher; *Am.* harceler
(de, *with*); *v/i.* F servir de nègre (à,
for); **'dev·il·ish** □ diabolique; F
maudit; **'dev·il-may-'care 1.** F
insouciant; téméraire (*a. su./m*); **2.**
tête *f* brûlée; **'dev·il·(t)ry** diablerie *f*; magie *f* (noire); *fig.* mauvais
coup *m.*
de·vi·ous □ ['di:viəs] tortueux
(-euse *f*); détourné (*a. fig.*); *~ path*
détour *m*; chemin *m* tortueux.
de·vis·a·ble [di'vaizəbl] imaginable;
de'vise 1. ⚖ legs *m* (immobilier);
dispositions *f/pl.* testamentaires de
biens immobiliers; **2.** imaginer;
combiner; ⚖ disposer par testament
de (*biens immobiliers*); **dev·i·see** ⚖
[devi'zi:] légataire *mf*; **de·vis·er**
[di'vaizə] inventeur (-trice *f*) *m*;
de·vi·sor ⚖ [devi'zɔ:] testateur
(-trice *f*) *m.*   [ser.⟩
de·vi·tal·ize [di:'vaitəlaiz] dévitali-⟩
de·void [di'vɔid] dénué, dépourvu,
exempt (de, *of*).
dev·o·lu·tion [di:və'lu:ʃn] ⚖ dévolution *f*; transmission *f*; *parl.* délégation *f*; décentralisation *f* administrative; *biol.* dégénération *f*; **devolve** [di'vɔlv] (*upon, to*) *v/t.* déléguer, transmettre (*qch. à q.*); *v/i.*
incomber (à); ⚖ être dévolu (à).
de·vote [di'vout] consacrer, vouer;
de'vot·ed □ dévoué, attaché; **dev-
o·tee** [devou'ti:] fervent(e *f*) *m*;
fanatique *m* (de, *of*); **de·vo·tion**
[di'vouʃn] dévouement *m* (à, pour
q., *to s.o.*); dévotion *f* (*à Dieu*); assiduité *f* (*au travail*); *~s pl.* dévotions
f/pl., prières *f/pl.*; **de'vo·tion·al** □
de dévotion, de prière.
de·vour [di'vauə] dévorer (*a. fig.*);
~ed with dévoré de, rongé de; **de-
'vour·ing** □ dévorateur (-trice *f*).

de·vout □ [di'vaut] dévot, pieux (-euse *f*); fervent; **de'vout·ness** dévotion *f*, piété *f*.

dew [dju:] 1. rosée *f*; 2. humecter de rosée; *fig.* mouiller (de, *with*); '~-**drop** goutte *f* de rosée; '~**lap** fanon *m* (*de la vache*); '**dew·y** humecté *ou* couvert de rosée.

dex·ter·i·ty [deks'teriti] dextérité *f*; **dex·ter·ous** □ ['~tərəs] adroit, habile (à *inf.*, *in gér.*).

di·a·be·tes ✆ [daiə'bi:ti:z] diabète *m*; glycosurie *f*; **di·a·bet·ic** [~'betik] diabétique (*adj.*, *mf*).

di·a·bol·ic, **di·a·bol·i·cal** □ [daiə-'bɔlik(l)] diabolique; infernal (-aux *m*/*pl.*).

di·a·dem ['daiədem] diadème *m*.

di·ag·nose ✆ ['daiəgnouz] diagnostiquer; **di·ag'no·sis** [~sis], *pl.* -ses [~si:z] diagnostic *m*.

di·ag·o·nal [dai'ægənl] 1. □ diagonal (-aux *m*/*pl.*); 2. diagonale *f* (*a. tex.*).

di·a·gram ['daiəgræm] diagramme *m*, tracé *m*, schéma *m*; graphique *m*; **di·a·gram·mat·ic** [daiəgrə'mætik] (~ally) schématique.

di·al ['daiəl] 1. *usu.* cadran *m*; *téléph.* tabulateur *m*; *sl.* visage *m*; ⚓ rose *f* (*des vents*); ~ *light* lampe *f* de cadran; 2. *téléph.* *v*/*i.* composer un numéro; *v*/*t.* appeler.

di·a·lect ['daiəlekt] dialecte *m*, parler *m*, idiome *m*; **di·a'lec·tic**, **di·a-'lec·ti·cal** □ de dialecte, dialectal (-aux *m*/*pl.*); **di·a'lec·tics** *usu. sg.* dialectique *f*.

di·a·logue, *Am. a.* **di·a·log** ['daiə-lɔg] dialogue *m*.

di·al...: '~-**plate** *téléph.* tabulateur *m*; *montre*: cadran *m*; '~-**sys·tem** téléphone *m* automatique; '~-**tone** *téléph.* signal *m* de numérotage.

di·am·e·ter [dai'æmitə] diamètre *m*; **di·a·met·ri·cal** □ [daiə'metrikl] diamétral (-aux *m*/*pl.*).

di·a·mond ['daiəmənd] 1. diamant *m*; losange *m*; *Am. baseball*: terrain *m* (*de baseball*); *cartes*: carreau *m*; ~ *cut* ~ à malin malin et demi; 2. de diamant; à diamants; en losange; '~-'**cut·ter** tailleur *m* de diamants.

di·a·pa·son ♩ [daiə'peisn] *voix, ton*: diapason *m*; *orgue*: principaux jeux *m*/*pl.* de fond; *poét.* harmonie *f*.

di·a·per ['daiəpə] 1. toile *f* gaufrée; serviette *f* ouvrée; couche *f*, maillot

m (*des bébés*); 2. ouvrer (*le linge*); gaufrer (*la toile*); emmailloter (*un bébé*).

di·aph·a·nous [dai'æfənəs] diaphane.

di·a·phragm ['daiəfræm] diaphragme *m* (*a.* ⊕, *a. opt.*); *téléph.* membrane *f*.

di·a·rist ['daiərist] personne *f* qui tient un journal; **'di·a·rize** *v*/*i.* tenir son journal; *v*/*t.* noter (*qch.*) dans son journal.

di·ar·rhoe·a ✆ [daiə'riə] diarrhée *f*.

di·a·ry ['daiəri] journal *m* intime; agenda *m*.

di·a·ther·my ✆ ['daiəθə:mi] diathermie *f*.

di·a·tribe ['daiətraib] diatribe *f*.

dib·ble ['dibl] 1. plantoir *m*; 2. repiquer au plantoir.

dibs *sl.* [dibz] *pl.* argent *m*; *sl.* pépette *f*.

dice [dais] 1. *pl. de* die²; F no ~ rien à faire; 2. *v*/*i.* jouer aux dés; *v*/*t.* *cuis.* couper en cubes; **dic·ey** F ['daisi] risqué.

dick *Am. sl.* [dik] agent *m* de la sûreté; policier *m*; *take one's* ~ jurer.

dick·ens F ['dikinz] diable *m*.

dick·er *Am.* ['dikə] marchander.

dick·(e)y ['diki] âne *m*; (*a.* ~-*bird*) F petit oiseau *m*; siège *m* de derrière; *mot.* spider *m*; *chemise*: faux plastron *m*.

dic·ta·phone ['diktəfoun] dictaphone *m* (*marque*); machine *f* à dicter.

dic·tate 1. ['dikteit] commandement *m*, ordre *m*; dictamen *m*; 2. [dik-'teit] dicter; *fig.* prescrire; **dic'ta·tion** dictée *f*; ordres *m*/*pl.*; **dic'ta·tor** celui *m* ou celle *f* qui dicte; *pol.* dictateur *m*; **dic·ta·to·ri·al** □ [diktə'tɔ:riəl] dictatorial(-aux*m*/*pl.*); impérieux (-euse *f*) (*ton etc.*); **dic·ta·tor·ship** [dik'teitəʃip] dictature *f*.

dic·tion ['dikʃn] style *m*; diction *f*; **dic·tion·ar·y** ['dikʃənri] dictionnaire *m*; glossaire *m*.

dict·um ['diktəm], *pl.* -**ta** ['~tə] affirmation *f*; maxime *f*, dicton *m*.

did [did] *prét. de* do 1, 2, 3.

di·dac·tic [di'dæktik] (~ally) didactique.

did·dle ['didl] duper; rouler (q. de qch., *s.o. out of s.th.*).

didn't ['didnt] = did not.

die[1] [dai] (*p.pr. dying*) mourir (de *of*, *from*); périr; crever (*animal*); brûler (de *inf.*, *to inf.*); tomber, languir (de, *of*); ~ *away* s'éteindre (*voix*); s'affaiblir (*son*); s'effacer (*couleur*); disparaître (*lumières*); ~ *down* s'éteindre; se calmer; baisser; ~ *out* s'éteindre; disparaître; F ~ *hard* vendre chèrement sa vie; être dur à tuer (*abus*); F *never say* ~! il ne faut pas jeter le manche après la cognée.

die[2] [~] (*pl. dice*) dé m.

die[3] [~], *pl.* **dies** [daiz] matrice f; étampe f; monnaie: coin m; lower ~ matrice f; *as straight as a* ~ d'une droiture absolue.

die...: '~-a'way langoureux (-euse f); '~-cast·ing ⊕ moulage m sous pression; '~-hard conservateur m à outrance; jusqu'au-boutiste m.

di·e·lec·tric [daii'lektrik] diélectrique (*a. su./m*).

Die·sel en·gine ['di:zl'endʒin] moteur m Diesel.   [d'étampes.\
die-sink·er ['daisiŋkə] graveur m∫

di·et[1] ['daiət] 1. nourriture f; régime m; be on a ~ être au régime; put on a ~ mettre (*q.*) au régime; 2. v/t. mettre (*q.*) au régime; v/i. être au régime.

diet[2] [~] diète f.

di·e·tar·y ['daiətəri] 1. régime m; 2. diététique; alimentaire.

dif·fer ['difə] différer (de *in, from*); être différent (de); ne pas s'accorder (sur, *about*); **dif·fer·ence** ['difrəns] différence f (*a. Ȧ*), écart m (*entre, between*); dispute f; différend m (*a. ✝*); ⚕, *théâ., etc.* supplément m; *split the* ~ partager le différend; '**dif·fer·ent** □ différent (de *from, to*); divers; autre (que, *from*); **dif·fer·en·ti·a** [~fə'renʃiə], *pl.* -ti·ae [~ʃii:] attribut m distinctif; **dif·fer·en·tial** [~ʃl] 1. différentiel(le f); distinctif (-ive f); ~ *calculus* calcul m différentiel; 2. *mot.* différentiel m; Ȧ différentielle f; **dif·fer·en·ti·ate** [~ʃieit] (se) différencier; Ȧ différentier.

dif·fi·cult □ ['difikəlt] difficile (*a. caractère etc.*); malaisé; **dif·fi·cul·ty** difficulté f; obstacle m; ennui m; embarras m.

dif·fi·dence ['difidəns] manque m d'assurance; '**dif·fi·dent** □ qui manque d'assurance.

dif·fract *phys.* [di'frækt] diffracter; **dif·frac·tion** diffraction f.

dif·fuse 1. [di'fju:z] (se) répandre; (se) diffuser; 2. □ [~s] diffus (*lumière, style, etc.*); prolixe (*style*); **dif·fu·sion** [~ʒn] diffusion f (*a. ⚛*); *phys.* dispersion f; **dif·fu·sive** □ [~siv] diffusif (-ive f); diffus (*style*).

dig [dig] 1. [*irr.*] vt/i. creuser; v/t. bêcher, retourner (*la terre*); enfoncer; F cogner; F loger en garni; ~ *in* enterrer; ~ *into* creuser (*qch.*); mordre dans; ~ *up* déraciner, arracher; (*fig. a.* ~ *out*) mettre à jour; v/i. travailler la terre; ~ *for* fouiller pour trouver (*qch.*); ~ *in* ⚔ se terrer; *fig.* s'assurer; 2. F coup m (*de coude etc.*); sarcasme m.

di·gest 1. [di'dʒest] v/t. mettre en ordre; faire un résumé de; digérer, élaborer (*un projet*); ⚕ digérer (*a. une insulte*); v/i. se digérer; 2. ['daidʒest] abrégé m, résumé m, sommaire m; ⚖ recueil m de lois, digeste m; **di·gest·er** [di'dʒestə] rédacteur m d'un résumé *etc.*; marmite f (*de Papin*); **di·gest·i·bil·i·ty** [~ə'biliti] digestibilité f; **di'gest·i·ble** digestible; **di'ges·tion** digestion f; **di'ges·tive** digestif m.

dig·ger ['digə] bêcheur m; *Am. sl.* exploiteuse f d'hommes riches; **dig·gings** F ['~iŋz] *pl.* logement m, garni m; *Am.* placer m.

dig·it ['didʒit] doigt m (*a. de pied*); Ȧ chiffre m; '**dig·it·al** digital (-aux m/pl.); numérique (*ordinateur, montre etc.*).

dig·ni·fied ['dignifaid] digne; plein de dignité; **dig·ni·fy** ['~fai] revêtir d'un air de majesté; donner de la dignité à; *fig.* décorer (d'un titre).

dig·ni·tar·y *usu. eccl.* ['dignitəri] dignitaire m; '**dig·ni·ty** dignité f.

di·gress [dai'gres] faire une digression (de, *from*); **di'gres·sion** [~ʃn] digression f, écart m; **di'gres·sive** □ digressif (-ive f).

dike[1] [daik] 1. digue f, levée f; chaussée f surélevée; 2. protéger par des digues.

dike[2] *sl.* [~] gouine f.

di·lap·i·date [di'læpideit] (se) délabrer; **di·lap·i·dat·ed** délabré, décrépit; **di·lap·i·da·tion** délabrement m; ~s *pl.* ⚖ détériorations f/pl.

di·lat·a·bil·i·ty *phys.* [daileitəˈbiliti] dilatabilité *f*; **diˈlat·a·ble** dilatable; **dil·aˈta·tion** dilatation *f*; **diˈlate** (se) dilater; ~ *upon* s'étendre sur (*qch.*); **diˈla·tion** *see dilatation*; **dil·a·to·ri·ness** [ˈdilətərinis] lenteur *f* (à agir); **ˈdil·a·to·ry** □ lent (à agir); tardif (-ive *f*) (*action*).

di·lem·ma *phls.* [diˈlemə] dilemme *m*; *fig.* embarras *m*.

dil·et·tan·te [diliˈtænti], *pl.* **-ti** [~ti:] dilettante *mf*.

dil·i·gence [ˈdilidʒəns] assiduité *f*; **ˈdil·i·gent** □ assidu, diligent, appliqué.

dill ⚘ [dil] aneth *m*.

dil·ly-dal·ly F [ˈdilidæli] traînasser.

dil·u·ent [ˈdiljuənt] délayant (*a. su./m*); **di·lute** [daiˈlju:t] **1.** diluer; arroser; délayer; *fig.* atténuer; couper avec de l'eau; **2.** dilué; délayé; *fig.* atténué; **diˈlu·tion** dilution *f*; délayage *m*; *fig.* atténuation *f*; mouillage *m*.

di·lu·vi·al [daiˈlu:vjəl], **diˈlu·vi·an** *géol.* diluvien(ne *f*); diluvial (-aux *m/pl.*).

dim [dim] **1.** □ faible; effacé (*couleur*); vague (*mémoire*); **2.** *v/t.* obscurcir; réduire (*la lumière*); ternir (*un miroir, a. fig.*); *mot.* baisser (*les phares*); *Am. mot.* ~ *the headlights a.* se mettre en code; *v/i.* s'obscurcir; baisser.

dime *Am.* [daim] dime *f*; ~ *novel* roman *m* à quatre sous; ~ *store* magasin *m* uniprix.

di·men·sion [diˈmenʃn] dimension *f*; ⊕ cote *f*; ~*s pl. a.* encombrement *m* hors tout.

di·min·ish [diˈminiʃ] (se) réduire; *vt/i.* diminuer; **dim·i·nu·tion** [dimiˈnju:ʃn] diminution *f*; amoindrissement *m* (de, *in*); **diˈmin·u·tive** [~jutiv] **1.** □ *gramm.* diminutif (-ive *f*); *fig.* minuscule; **2.** *gramm.* diminutif *m*.

dim·mer [ˈdimə] ⚡ rhéostat *m*, interrupteur *m* à gradation de lumière; *Am. mot.* ~*s pl.* phares *m/pl.* code; feux *m/pl.* de position.

dim·ple [ˈdimpl] **1.** fossette *f*; ride *f* (*dans l'eau*); **2.** *v/t.* former des fossettes dans; *v/i.* se former en fossettes; onduler (*eau*); **ˈdim·pled** à fossette(s).

din [din] **1.** fracas *m*, vacarme *m*; **2.** *v/i.* retentir; *v/t.* ~ *s.th. into s.o.* (*'s ears*) corner qch. aux oreilles à q.

dine [dain] dîner; ~ *out* dîner en ville; **ˈdin·er** dîneur (-euse *f*) *m*; 🚃 *surt. Am.* wagon-restaurant (*pl.* wagons-restaurants) *m*; **di·nette** [daiˈnet] aire *f* de repas.

ding [diŋ] retentir, résonner; **~-dong** [ˈ~ˈdɔŋ] **1.** digue-don; **2.** digue-don *m/inv.*; **3.** *sp.* durement disputé.

din·gey, din·ghy [ˈdiŋgi] canot *m*, youyou *m*; *rubber* ~ berthon *m*.

din·gle [ˈdiŋgl] vallon *m* (boisé).

din·gus *Am. sl.* [ˈdiŋgəs] machin *m*, truc *m*.

din·gy □ [ˈdindʒi] qui manque d'éclat; terne; sale; défraîchi (*meubles*).

din·ing... [ˈdainiŋ]: **ˈ~-car** 🚃 wagon-restaurant (*pl.* wagons-restaurants) *m*; **ˈ~-room** salle *f* à manger.

dink·ey *Am.* [ˈdiŋki] locomotive *f* de manœuvres.

dink·y [ˈdiŋki] F coquet(te *f*), mignon(ne *f*).

din·ner [ˈdinə] dîner *m*; banquet *m*; F déjeuner *m*; **ˈ~-jack·et** smoking *m*; **ˈ~-pail** *Am.* potager *m* (*d'ouvrier*); **ˈ~-par·ty** dîner *m* (par invitations); **ˈ~-set** service *m* de table; **ˈ~-suit** smoking *m*; **~ ta·ble** table *f* de salle à manger; **ˈ~-wag·(g)on** *fourniture*: servante *f*.

dint [dint] **1.** marque *f* de coup; creux *m*; *by* ~ *of* à force de; **2.** bosseler; ébrécher (*une lame*).

di·o·ce·san *eccl.* [daiˈɔsisn] diocésain (*a. su./m*); **di·o·cese** [ˈdaiəsis] diocèse *m*.

di·ode ⚡ [ˈdaioud] diode *f*; *light-emitting* ~ diode *f* lumineuse.

di·op·tric *opt.* [daiˈɔptrik] **1.** dioptrique; **2.** dioptrie *f*; ~*s pl.* dioptrique *f*.

di·o·ra·ma [daiəˈrɑ:mə] diorama *m*.

dip [dip] **1.** *v/t.* plonger; tremper; immerger; baisser subitement; écoper (dans *from, out of*); teindre (*une étoffe*); baigner (*les moutons*); ⚓ saluer avec (*son pavillon*); *mot.* baisser (*les phares*); *mot.* ~ *the headlights a.* se mettre en code; *v/i.* plonger; baisser (*soleil*); incliner; s'abaisser (*terrain*); *géol.* s'incliner; ~ *into* puiser dans (*une bourse*); effleurer (*un sujet*); feuilleter (*un livre*); **2.** plongement *m*, immersion *f*; pente *f*, déclivité *f*; chandelle *f* plongée; ⚓ salut *m*; *géol.* pendage *m*; dépression *f (de l'horizon)*; bain *m* parasiticide *(pour moutons)*; *aiguille aimantée:* inclinaison *f*; F coup *m* d'œil; F baignade *f*; F *have ou take a* ~ prendre un bain rapide, faire trempette; ⚓ *at the* ~ à mi-drisse.

diph·the·ri·a [dif'θiəriə] diphtérie *f*.

diph·thong ['difθɔŋ] diphtongue *f*.

di·plo·ma [di'ploumə] diplôme *m*; **di'plo·ma·cy** diplomatie *f*; **di'plo·maed** [~məd] diplômé; **dip·lo·mat** ['dipləmæt] diplomate *m*; **dip·lo'mat·ic**, **dip·lo'mat·i·cal** □ diplomatique; **dip·lo'mat·ics** *pl.* diplomatique *f*; **di·plo·ma·tist** [di'ploumətist] diplomate *m*.

dip·per ['dipə] plongeur (-euse *f*) *m*; *orn.* merle *m* d'eau; *mot.* basculeur *m*; *Am.* cuiller *f* à pot; *Am.* Great (*ou* Big) ♀ *astr. la* Grande Ourse; **'dip·py** *sl.* maboul.

dip·so·ma·ni·a ⚕ [dipsou'meinjə] dipsomanie *f*; **dip·so'ma·ni·ac** [~niæk] dipsomane *mf*.

dip...: '~**rod** *Am.*, '~**stick** *mot.* jauge *f* (de niveau d'huile); '~**switch** *mot.* alternateur *m* phares-code.

dire ['daiə] néfaste; affreux (-euse *f*).

di·rect [di'rekt] **1.** □ direct; absolu; franc(he *f*) *(personne)*; catégorique *(réponse)*; ✗ de plein fouet *(tir)*; ⚡ ~ **current** courant *m* continu; *téléph.* ~ *dial(l)ing* (numéro *m* interurbain) automatique *m*; *gramm.* ~ *speech* discours *m ou* style *m* direct; ~ *train* train *m* direct; **2.** tout droit; *see* ~*ly* 1; **3.** diriger (vers *at*, to[*wards*]); conduire *(les affaires, un orchestre)*; gérer, régir, administrer; adresser *(une lettre* à q., *to s.o.);* ordonner (à q. de *inf.*, *s.o. to inf.);* indiquer (qch. à q., *s.th. to s.o.);* **di'rec·tion** direction *f*; administration *f*; sens *m*; adresse *f*; instruction *f*; **di'rec·tion·al** dirigeable *(radio)*; radiogoniométrique; **di'rec·tion-find·er** *radio:* radiogoniomètre *m*; **di'rec·tion-find·ing** *radio:* radiogoniométrie *f*; *attr.* radiogoniométrique; ~ *set* radiogoniomètre *m*; **di·rec·tion-in·di·ca·tor** *mot.* clignotant *m*; flèche *f* lumineuse; signalisateur *m* de direction; ⚞ indicateur *m* de direction; **di'rec·tive** [~tiv] directif (-ive *f*); **di'rect·ly 1.** *adv.* directement, tout droit; tout de suite; tout à fait; **2.** *cj.* aussitôt que;

di'rect·ness direction *f ou* mouvement *m* en droite ligne; *fig.* franchise *f*.

di·rec·tor [di'rektə] directeur *m*, administrateur *m*; membre *m* d'un conseil d'administration; *théâ.*, *cin.* metteur *m* en scène; *cin.* réalisateur *m*; **di'rec·to·rate** [~rit] (conseil *m* d')administration *f*; *(a.* **di'rec·tor·ship**) directorat *m*; **di'rec·to·ry** répertoire *m* d'adresses; *téléph.* annuaire *m* (des téléphones); *en France:* le Bottin *m*; *téléph. Am.* ~ *assistance, Brit.* ~ *enquiries* (service *m* des) renseignements *m/pl.*

di·rec·tress [di'rektris] directrice *f*.

dire·ful □ ['daiəful] néfaste.

dirge [də:dʒ] hymne *m* funèbre.

dir·i·gi·ble ['diridʒəbl] dirigeable *m (a. adj.)*.

dirk [də:k] **1.** poignard *m*; **2.** poignarder.

dirt [də:t] saleté *f*; boue *f (surt. fig. péj.)*; langage *m* ordurier; terre *f*, sol *m*; *Am. sl.* do (one) ~ jouer un vilain tour (à q.); '~*cheap* F à vil prix; donné; ~ *road Am.* chemin *m ou* route *f* non macadamisé(e); '~*track sp.* (piste *f* en)cendrée *f*; **'dirt·y 1.** □ sale *(a. fig.);* **2.** (se) salir.

dis·a·bil·i·ty [disə'biliti] incapacité *f*; infirmité *f*; ⚖ inhabilité *f*; *admin.* invalidité *f*.

dis·a·ble [dis'eibl] mettre hors de service *ou* de combat; mettre (*q.*) hors d'état (de *inf. from*, for *gér.*); **dis'a·bled** estropié, mutilé; hors de service *ou* de combat *ou* d'état; **dis'a·ble·ment** mise *f* hors de combat; incapacité *f*; invalidité *f*.

dis·a·buse [disə'bju:z] désabuser (de, *of*).

dis·ac·cord [disə'kɔ:d] être en désaccord (avec, *with*).

dis·ac·cus·tom ['disə'kʌstəm] déshabituer (q. de qch., *s.o. to s.th.*).

dis·ad·van·tage [disəd'vɑ:ntidʒ] désavantage *m*, inconvénient *m*; *sell to* ~ vendre à perte; **dis·ad·van·ta·geous** □ [disædvɑ:n'teidʒəs] défavorable.

dis·af·fect·ed □ [disə'fektid] désaffectionné, mal disposé (à l'égard de, envers *to*, *towards*); **dis·af'fec·tion** désaffection *f*.

dis·af·firm ⚖ [disə'fə:m] annuler.

dis·a·gree [disə'gri:] *(with)* ne pas être d'accord, être en désaccord (avec); donner tort (à); ne pas convenir (à *q.*); se brouiller (avec); **dis·a'gree·a·ble** □ désagréable (*a. fig.*); **dis·a'gree·ment** différence *f*; désaccord *m* (avec q. sur qch., with s.o. in s.th.); querelle *f*, différend *m*; mésentente *f*.

dis·al·low ['disə'lau] ne pas admettre; ne pas permettre; interdire.

dis·ap·pear [disə'piə] disparaître; **dis·ap·pear·ance** [~'piərəns] disparition *f*.

dis·ap·point [disə'pɔint] décevoir; désappointer; manquer de parole à; **dis·ap'point·ment** déception *f*; mécompte *m*.

dis·ap·pro·ba·tion [disæpro'beiʃn], **dis·ap·prov·al** [disə'pruːvl] désapprobation *f*; **dis·ap'prove** désapprouver (qch., *of* s.th.).

dis·arm [dis'ɑːm] *vt/i.* désarmer (*a. fig.*); **dis'ar·ma·ment** [~məmənt] désarmement *m*.

dis·ar·range ['disə'reindʒ] mettre en désordre, déranger; **dis·ar-'range·ment** désordre *m*; dérangement *m*.

dis·as·sem·bly ⊕ [disə'sembli] démontage *m*.

dis·as·ter [di'zɑːstə] désastre *m*; sinistre *m*; catastrophe *f*; **dis'as·trous** □ désastreux (-euse *f*).

dis·a·vow ['disə'vau] désavouer; renier; **dis·a'vow·al** désaveu *m*; reniement *m*.

dis·band [dis'bænd] ✕ *v/t.* licencier; *v/i.* se débander; être licencié; **dis'band·ment** licenciement *m*.

dis·bar [dis'bɑː] rayer (*un avocat*) du tableau de l'ordre.

dis·be·lief ['disbi'liːf] incrédulité *f* (à l'égard de, *in*); refus *m* de croire (à, *in*); **dis·be·lieve** ['disbi'liːv] *v/i.* ne pas croire (à, *in*); *v/t.* refuser créance à (*q.*); **'dis·be'liev·er** incrédule *mf*.

dis·bur·den [dis'bəːdn] décharger (d'un fardeau, *of a burden*); déposer (*un fardeau*); ouvrir (*son cœur*); *fig.* décharger.

dis·burse [dis'bəːs] débourser; **dis-'burse·ment** déboursement *m*; ~s *pl.* débours *m/pl.*

disc [disk] *see* disk.

dis·card [dis'kɑːd] 1. se défaire de; abandonner (*une théorie etc.*); laisser de côté, mettre au rebut (*des vêtements*); *bridge:* se défausser (de qch., *s.th.*); 2. *bridge:* défausse *f*; *surt. Am.* (pièce *f* de) rebut *m*.

dis·cern [di'səːn] discerner; distinguer; apercevoir; **dis'cern·i·ble** perceptible; **dis'cern·ing** 1. □ pénétrant; judicieux (-euse *f*) (*personne*); 2. discernement *m*; pénétration *f*; **dis'cern·ment** discernement *m*; jugement *m*.

dis·charge [dis'tʃɑːdʒ] 1. *v/t.* décharger (a. ⚓ *un navire*, ⚡, ⚡ *un fusil*); ⚓ débarquer (*un équipage*); lancer (*un projectile*); jeter (*du pus*); renvoyer (*un malade*); congédier (*un employé*), débaucher (*un ouvrier*); s'acquitter de (*un devoir*); verser (*du chagrin*); déverser (*du mépris*); acquitter (*un accusé, une dette, etc.*); libérer (*q. d'une obligation*); payer, apurer (*un compte*); *v/i.* se dégorger; suppurer; se déverser; partir (*fusil*); 2. décharge *f* (a. ⚡); ⚓ déchargement *m*; *cargaison:* débardage *m*; *employé:* renvoi *m*; ✕ libération *f*; *prisonnier:* élargissement *m*; *accusé:* acquittement *m*; *dette:* paiement *m*; *devoir:* accomplissement *m*; *fonctions:* exercice *m*; ⚡ écoulement *m*; **dis'charg·er** ⚡ excitateur *m*.

dis·ci·ple [di'saipl] disciple *mf*; élève *mf*; **dis'ci·ple·ship** qualité *f* de disciple.

dis·ci·plin·a·ble ['disiplinəbl] disciplinable; docile; **'dis·ci·pli·nal** disciplinaire; **dis·ci·pli·nar·i·an** [~-'neəriən] 1. (*a.* **dis·ci·pli·nar·y** ['~əri]) disciplinaire; de discipline; 2. disciplinaire *mf*; **dis·ci·pline** ['~plin] 1. discipline *f* (a. = *sujet d'étude*); 2. discipliner; former, élever; dresser (*un animal*).

dis·claim [dis'kleim] renoncer à; renier; désavouer; **dis'claim·er** renonciation *f*; déni *m*; désaveu *m*.

dis·close [dis'klouz] révéler, découvrir; divulguer; **dis'clo·sure** [~ʒə] révélation *f*; divulgation *f*.

dis·col·o(u)r·a·tion [diskʌlə'reiʃn] décoloration *f*; **dis'col·o(u)r** (se) décolorer; (se) ternir.

dis·com·fit [dis'kʌmfit] déconfire; F déconcerter; **dis'com·fi·ture** [~tʃə] déconfiture *f* (*d'une armée*); *personne:* déconvenue *f*.

dis·com·fort [dis'kʌmfət] 1. inconfort *m*; malaise *m*, gêne *f*; 2. incommoder.

dis·com·pose [diskəm'pouz] troubler; **dis·com'po·sure** [~ʒə] trouble *m*; perturbation *f*.

dis·con·cert [diskən'sə:t] déconcerter; troubler.

dis·con·nect ['diskə'nekt] disjoindre (de *from*, *with*); ⊕ débrayer; ⚡ déconnecter; couper; **'dis·con'nect·ed** □ détaché; décousu (*style etc.*); **'dis·con'nec·tion** séparation *f*; ⊕ débrayage *m*.

dis·con·so·late □ [dis'kɔnsəlit] désolé; triste.

dis·con·tent ['diskən'tent] **1.** † *see* ~ed; **2.** mécontentement *m*; **'dis·con'tent·ed** □ mécontent (de, *with*); peu satisfait.

dis·con·tin·u·ance ['diskən'tinju-əns] discontinuation *f*; abandon *m*; **'dis·con'tin·ue** [~nju:] discontinuer; cesser (*a. v/i.*); se désabonner à (*un journal*); **'dis·con'tin·u·ous** □ discontinu; ⚕ discret (-ète *f*).

dis·cord ['diskɔ:d], **dis'cord·ance** discorde *f*; ♪ dissonance *f*, accord *m* dissonant; **dis'cord·ant** □ discordant; en désaccord (avec *to*, *from*, *with*); ♪ dissonant.

dis·co·theque ['diskoutek] discothèque *f*.

dis·count ['diskaunt] **1.** ✝ remise *f*, rabais *m*; *banque etc.*: escompte *m*; ~ **rate** taux *m* de l'escompte; ~ **store** magasin *m* à demi-gros; *at a* ~ en perte; *fig.* en défaveur, peu estimé; **2.** ✝ escompter; faire l'escompte de; *fig.* ne pas tenir compte de; faire peu de cas de; envisager (*un événement*); **dis'count·a·ble** escomptable; à négliger.

dis·coun·te·nance [dis'kauntinəns] déconcerter; désapprouver; **dis-'coun·te·nanced** décontenancé.

dis·cour·age [dis'kʌridʒ] décourager (de, *from*); abattre; détourner (de, *from*); **dis'cour·age·ment** découragement *m*; désapprobation *f*.

dis·course [dis'kɔ:s] **1.** allocution *f*; discours *m*; dissertation *f*; **2.** (*on*, *upon*, *about*) discourir (sur); s'entretenir (de).

dis·cour·te·ous □ [dis'kə:tiəs] impoli; **dis'cour·te·sy** [~tisi] impolitesse *f*.

dis·cov·er [dis'kʌvə] trouver, découvrir; *poét.* révéler; **dis'cov·er·a·ble** □ que l'on peut découvrir; **dis'cov·er·er** découvreur (-euse *f*)

m; **dis'cov·er·y** découverte *f*; *poét.* révélation *f*.

dis·cred·it [dis'kredit] **1.** discrédit *m*; doute *m*; **2.** mettre en doute; ne pas croire; discréditer; **dis'cred·it·a·ble** □ (*to*) indigne, peu digne (de); qui ne fait pas honneur (à).

dis·creet □ [dis'kri:t] discret (~ète *f*); avisé.

dis·crep·an·cy [dis'krepənsi] divergence *f*; désaccord *m*; écart *m*.

dis·crete □ † [dis'kri:t] discret (-ète *f*); distinct; *phls.* abstrait.

dis·cre·tion [dis'kreʃn] discrétion *f*; sagesse *f*, jugement *m*, prudence *f*; silence *m* judicieux; *at s.o.'s* ~ à la discrétion de q.; *age* (*ou years*) *of* ~ âge *m* de raison; *surrender at* ~ se rendre à discrétion; **dis'cre·tion·al** □, **dis'cre·tion·ar·y** discrétionnaire.

dis·crim·i·nate [dis'krimineit] distinguer; ~ *against* faire des distinctions contre (*q.*); **dis'crim·i·nat·ing** □ avisé; plein de discernement; différentiel(le *f*) (*tarif*); **dis·crim·i'na·tion** discernement *m*; jugement *m*; distinction *f*; **dis'crim·i·na·tive** [~nətiv] □ avisé; plein de discernement; différentiel(le *f*); **dis'crim·i·na·to·ry** ⚖, ✝ [dis'kriminətəri] qui fait la distinction des personnes.

dis·cur·sive □ [dis'kə:siv] décousu, sans suite; *phls.* discursif (-ive *f*).

dis·cus ['diskəs] *sp.* disque *m*.

dis·cuss [dis'kʌs] discuter; *co.* expédier (*un plat*), vider (*une bouteille*); **dis'cuss·i·ble** [~əbl] discutable; **dis'cus·sion** discussion *f*; débat *m*.

dis·dain [dis'dein] **1.** dédain *m* (de, *of*); mépris *m*; **2.** dédaigner; **dis'dain·ful** □ [~ful] dédaigneux (-euse *f*) (de, *of*).

dis·ease [di'zi:z] maladie *f*; mal *m*; **dis'eased** malade; morbide.

dis·em·bark ['disim'bɑ:k] débarquer; **dis·em·bar·ka·tion** [disembɑ:'keiʃn] débarquement *m*.

dis·em·bar·rass ['disim'bærəs] débarrasser (de, *of*); dégager (de, *from*).

dis·em·bod·y ['disim'bɔdi] désincorporer; ⚔ licencier (*des troupes*).

dis·em·bogue [disim'boug] *v/t.* verser; *v/i.* déboucher (*rivière*); déboucher (*navire*). [cérer.]

dis·em·bow·el [disim'bauəl] évis-⌡

dis·en·chant [ˈdisinˈtʃɑːnt] désenchanter; désabuser.

dis·en·cum·ber [ˈdisinˈkʌmbə] débarrasser (de *of, from*); désencombrer (*q.*).

dis·en·gage [ˈdisinˈgeidʒ] (se) dégager; ⊕ (se) déclencher; *v/t.* débrayer; **'dis·en'gaged** libre; **dis·en'gage·ment** dégagement *m*; rupture *f* de fiançailles.

dis·en·tan·gle [ˈdisinˈtæŋgl] (se) démêler; *fig.* dépêtrer (de, *from*); **dis·en'tan·gle·ment** débrouillement *m*.

dis·en·tomb [disinˈtuːm] exhumer.

dis·es·tab·lish [ˈdisisˈtæbliʃ] séparer (*l'Église*) de l'État; **dis·es'tab·lish·ment** séparation *f* de l'Église et de l'État.

dis·fa·vo(u)r [ˈdisˈfeivə] 1. défaveur *f*; disgrâce *f*; désapprobation *f*; 2. voir avec défaveur; désapprouver.

dis·fig·ure [disˈfigə] défigurer; gâter; **dis'fig·ure·ment** défiguration *f*.

dis·fran·chise [ˈdisˈfræntʃaiz] priver (*q.*) du droit électoral; priver (*un bourg*) de ses droits de représentation; **dis'fran·chise·ment** [disˈfræntʃizmənt] privation *f* du droit de vote *ou* des droits civiques.

dis·gorge [disˈgɔːdʒ] rendre (= *vomir*); (*a.* ~ *o.s.*) dégorger; décharger (*rivière*).

dis·grace [disˈgreis] 1. disgrâce *f*; honte *f*; déshonneur *m*; 2. déshonorer; disgracier (*q.*); *be* ~*ed* être disgracié; **dis'grace·ful** □ [~ful] honteux (-euse *f*); scandaleux (-euse *f*).

dis·grun·tled [disˈgrʌntld] maussade; mécontent (de, *at*).

dis·guise [disˈgaiz] 1. déguiser; masquer (*une odeur*); dissimuler (*une émotion*); 2. déguisement *m*; fausse apparence *f*; feinte *f*; *blessing in* ~ bienfait *m* insoupçonné.

dis·gust [disˈgʌst] 1. (*at, for*) dégoût *m* (pour); répugnance *f* (pour); *fig. in* ~ dégoûté; 2. dégoûter, écœurer; ~*ed with* profondément mécontent de; **dis'gust·ing** □ dégoûtant.

dish [diʃ] 1. plat *m*; récipient *m*; *cuis.* plat *m* (*de viande etc.*), mets *m*; *fig. standing* ~ plat *m* de tous les jours; 2. (*usu.* ~ *up*) servir (*a. fig.*), dresser; *sl.* enfoncer, rouler (*q.*).

dis·ha·bille [disæˈbiːl] négligé *m*, déshabillé *m*; *in* ~ en déshabillé.

dis·har·mo·ny [disˈhɑːməni] dissonance *f*; désaccord *m*.

dish-cloth [ˈdiʃklθ] torchon *m*; lavette *f*.

dis·heart·en [disˈhɑːtn] décourager.

di·shev·el(l)ed [diˈʃevld] échevelé; ébouriffé; en désordre.

dis·hon·est □ [disˈɔnist] malhonnête; déloyal (-aux *m/pl.*); **dis'hon·es·ty** malhonnêteté *f*.

dis·hon·o(u)r [disˈɔnə] 1. déshonneur *m*; honte *f*; 2. déshonorer; manquer à (*sa parole*); † ne pas honorer; **dis'hon·o(u)r·a·ble** □ déshonorant, honteux (-euse *f*); sans honneur (*personne*).

dish...: '~-**pan** *Am.* cuvette *f*; '~-**rag** *Am.* see dish-cloth; '~-**wa·ter** eau *f* de vaisselle; *sl.* lavasse *f*.

dish·y F [ˈdiʃi] appétisant.

dis·il·lu·sion [disiˈluːʒn] 1. désillusion *f*, désabusement *m*; 2. *a.* **dis·il'lu·sion·ize** désillusionner, désabuser; **dis·il'lu·sion·ment** *see* disillusion 1.

dis·in·cli·na·tion [disinkliˈneiʃn] répugnance *f* (pour *for, to*); manque *m* d'empressement (à, *to*); **dis·in·cline** [ˈ~ˈklain] détourner (de *for, to*); **'dis·in'clined** peu disposé (à *for, to*).

dis·in·fect [ˈdisinˈfekt] désinfecter; **dis·in'fect·ant** désinfectant (*a. su./m*); **dis·in'fec·tion** désinfection *f*.

dis·in·gen·u·ous □ [disinˈdʒenjuəs] sans franchise; faux (fausse *f*).

dis·in·her·it [ˈdisinˈherit] déshériter; **dis·in'her·it·ance** déshéritement *m*; ⚖ exhérédation *f*.

dis·in·te·grate [disˈintigreit] (se) désagréger; (se) désintégrer (*minerai*); **dis·in·te'gra·tion** désagrégation *f*; effritement *m*.

dis·in·ter [ˈdisinˈtəː] déterrer, exhumer.

dis·in·ter·est·ed □ [disˈintristid] désintéressé.

dis·join [disˈdʒɔin] disjoindre; **dis·joint** [~t] démembrer, disjoindre; désassembler; ⚕ désarticuler; **dis'joint·ed** disjoint, disloqué; *fig.* décousu.

dis·junc·tion [disˈdʒʌŋkʃn] disjonction *f*; **dis'junc·tive** □ 1. disjonctif (-ive *f*) (*a. gramm.*); 2. *gramm.* disjonctive *f*.

disk [disk] disque *m*; plaque *f* (*d'identité*); *mot*. ~ *brakes* freins *m/pl.* à disque; *mot*. ~ *clutch* embrayage *m* par disque unique; ⚙ *slipped* ~ hernie *f* discale; *Am. sl.* ~ *jockey* radio: présenteur *m ou* présentatrice *f* du disque des auditeurs.

dis·like [dis'laik] **1.** aversion *f*, répugnance *f* (pour *for*, *of*, *to*); **2.** ne pas aimer; détester; trouver mauvais; ~*d* mal vu.

dis·lo·cate ['dislokeit] disloquer; déboîter (*un membre*); *fig.* désorganiser; **dis·lo·ca·tion** dislocation *f* (*a. géol., a. anat.*); *fig.* désorganisation *f*. [tacher.\

dis·lodge [dis'lɔdʒ] déloger; dé-\
dis·loy·al ['] ['dis'lɔiəl] infidèle; déloyal (-aux *m/pl.*); **'dis·loy·al·ty** infidélité *f*; déloyauté *f*.

dis·mal [ ] ['dizməl] **1.** *fig.* sombre, triste; morne; lugubre; **2.**: *the* ~*s pl.* le cafard *m*.

dis·man·tle [dis'mæntl] dégarnir, dépouiller (de, *of*); démanteler (*une forteresse*, ⚓ *un vaisseau de guerre*); ⚓ dégréer (*un navire*); ⊕ démonter (*une machine*), déséquiper (*une grue etc.*); **dis'man·tling** dégarnissement *m etc.*; ⊕ démontage *m*.

dis·mast ⚓ [dis'mɑːst] démâter.

dis·may [dis'mei] **1.** consternation *f*; épouvante *f*; **2.** consterner; épouvanter.

dis·mem·ber [dis'membə] démembrer; écarteler (*un corps*); **dis'member·ment** démembrement *m*.

dis·miss [dis'mis] *v/t.* congédier; renvoyer; éconduire (*un importun etc.*); relever (*q.*) de ses fonctions; quitter (*un sujet*); *cricket*: mettre hors jeu; ⚖ acquitter (*un accusé*), rejeter (*une demande*); *be* ~*ed* the *service* être renvoyé du service; *v/i.* ✗ ~! rompez (les rangs)!; **dis-'miss·al** congédiement *m*; renvoi *m*; ⚖ acquittement *m* (*d'un accusé*); fin *f* de non-recevoir.

dis·mount ['dis'maunt] *v/t.* faire descendre (*q.*) de cheval; ⊕ démonter (*a. un canon*); *v/i.* descendre (de cheval, de voiture).

dis·o·be·di·ence [disə'biːdjəns] désobéissance *f* (à *to*, *of*); **dis·o'be·di·ent** [ ] désobéissant; **'dis·o'bey** désobéir à; enfreindre; *I will not be* ~*ed* je ne veux pas qu'on me désobéisse.

dis·o·blige ['disə'blaidʒ] désobliger (*q.*); **'dis·o'blig·ing** [ ] désobligeant, peu complaisant (envers, *to*); **'dis·o'blig·ing·ness** désobligeance *f*.

dis·or·der [dis'ɔːdə] **1.** désordre *m* (*a.* ⚕); confusion *f*; tumulte *m*; ⚕ affection *f*; *mental* ~ dérangement *m* d'esprit; **2.** déranger (*a.* ⚕); mettre le désordre dans; **dis'or·dered** [ ] en désordre; désordonné; ⚕ dérangé (*estomac etc.*); **dis'or·der·ly** en désordre; désordonné (*a. personne*); qui manque d'ordre; turbulent (*foule etc.*).

dis·or·gan·i·za·tion [disɔːgənai'zeiʃn] désorganisation *f*; **dis'or·gan·ize** désorganiser.

dis·own [dis'oun] désavouer; renier.

dis·par·age [dis'pæridʒ] déprécier, dénigrer; discréditer; **dis'par·age·ment** dénigrement *m*, dépréciation *f*; déshonneur *m*; **dis'par·ag·ing** [ ] dépréciateur (-trice *f*); peu flatteur (-euse *f*).

dis·pa·rate [ ] ['dispərit] **1.** disparate; **2.** ~*s pl.* disparates *f/pl.*; **dis·par·i·ty** [dis'pæriti] inégalité *f*; différence *f*.

dis·part [dis'pɑːt] *poét. ou* † (se) fendre; (se) séparer; *v/t.* ⊕ distribuer.

dis·pas·sion·ate [ ] [dis'pæʃnit] impartial (-aux *m/pl.*); calme; sans passion.

dis·patch [dis'pætʃ] **1.** expédition *f*; envoi *m*; promptitude *f*, diligence *f*; dépêche *f*; mise *f* à mort; *bearer of* ~*es* messager *m*; *mentioned in* ~*es* cité à l'ordre du jour; *by* ~ par exprès; **2.** expédier (*a.* = *mettre à mort*); envoyer; dépêcher (*un courrier*); ~**·box** valise *f* diplomatique; ~ **note** bulletin *m ou* bordereau *m* d'expédition; ~**·rid·er** ✗ estafette *f*.

dis·pel [dis'pel] dissiper, chasser (*a. fig.*).

dis·pen·sa·ble [dis'pensəbl] dont on peut se passer; *eccl.* dispensable; **dis'pen·sa·ry** pharmacie *f*; policlinique *f*; *hôpital*: dépense *f*; **dis·pen·sa·tion** [dispen'seiʃn] distribution *f*; décret *m*; *eccl.* dispense *f*; fait *m* d'être dispensé (de, *from*).

dis·pense [dis'pens] *v/t.* dispenser, distribuer; administrer (*la loi*); préparer (*un médicament*); exécuter (*une ordonnance*); ~ *from* dispenser

de; *v/i.* ~ **with** se passer de; supprimer (*une main-d'œuvre*); ne pas exiger; **dis'pens·er** dispensateur (-trice *f*) *m*; pharmacien(ne *f*) *m*.
dis·perse [dis'pəːs] (se) disperser; *v/t.* dissiper; répandre; ⚡ résoudre; **dis'per·sion, dis'per·sal** dispersion *f* (*a. opt.*); **dis'per·sive** □ dispersif (-ive *f*) (*a. opt.*).
dis·pir·it [dis'pirit] décourager; **dis'pir·it·ed** □ découragé, abattu.
dis·place [dis'pleis] déplacer; évincer (*q.*); supplanter, remplacer; ~**d person** (*abr. D.P.*) personne *f* déplacée; **dis'place·ment** déplacement *m* (*a.* ⚓); changement *m* de place; remplacement *m*; *géol.* dislocation *f*.
dis·play [dis'plei] **1.** étalage *m* (*a.* ✝); manifestation *f*; exposition *f*; parade *f*, apparat *m*; **2.** étaler, exposer; afficher; montrer; faire preuve de; révéler; ~ **case** vitrine *f* (d'exposition); ~ **stand** présentoir *m*.
dis·please [dis'pliːz] déplaire (à q., *s.o.*); *fig.* contrarier; **dis'pleased** □ mécontent (de *at, with*); **dis'pleas·ing** □ désagréable, déplaisant (à, *to*); **dis'pleas·ure** [~'pleʒə] mécontentement *m* (de *at, over*); déplaisir *m*. [tir; s'ébattre.]
dis·port [dis'pɔːt]: ~ *o.s.* se diver-∫
dis·pos·a·ble [dis'pouzəbl] disponible; **dis'pos·al** disposition *f*; action *f* de disposer (de, *of*); expédition *f* (*d'une affaire*); résolution *f* (*d'une question*); ✝ délivrance *f*; *at s.o.'s* ~ à la disposition de q.; **dis'pose** *v/t.* disposer (*a.* q. à, *s.o. to*); arranger; incliner (q. à, *s.o. to*; q. à qch., *s.o.for s.th.*); *v/i.* ~ *of* disposer de; se défaire de; vaincre; expédier; ✝ vendre, écouler; trancher (*une question*); résoudre (*un problème*); **dis'posed** □ porté, enclin (à *to, for*); disposé (à, *to*) (*bien, mal*) intentionné (envers, pour, à l'égard de *towards*); **dis'pos·er** dispensateur (-trice *f*) *m*; ordonnateur (-trice *f*) *m*; vendeur (-euse *f*) *m*; **dis·po·si·tion** [~pə'ziʃn] disposition *f* (*a. testamentaire*); arrangement *m*; humeur *f*, naturel *m*, caractère *m*; tendance *f* (à, *to*); *at my* ~ à ma disposition, à mon service; *make* ~*s* prendre des dispositions (pour, *to*).

dis·pos·sess [dispə'zes] (*of*) déposséder (de); expropier; ✝ délivrer (de); ⚖ dessaisir (de); **dis·pos·ses·sion** [~'zeʃn] dépossession *f*; expropriation *f*; ⚖ dessaisissement *m*.
dis·praise [dis'preiz] **1.** blâme *m*; dépréciation *f*; **2.** blâmer; dénigrer.
dis·proof ['dis'pruːf] réfutation *f*.
dis·pro·por·tion ['dispro'pɔːʃn] disproportion *f*; **dis·pro'por·tion·ate** □ [~it] disproportionné (à, *to*); hors de proportion (avec, *to*); **dis·pro'por·tion·ate·ness** disproportion *f*.
dis·prove ['dis'pruːv] réfuter.
dis·pu·ta·ble [dis'pjuːtəbl] contestable; **dis'pu·tant** discuteur (-euse *f*) *m*; *écoles:* disputant *m*; **dis·pu·ta·tion** [~'teiʃn] débat *m*; discussion *f*; **dis·pu'ta·tious** □ chicanier (-ère *f*); **dis'pute 1.** contestation *f*, controverse *f*; querelle *f*; *beyond* ~ incontestable; *in* ~ contesté; **2.** *v/t.* contester; débattre; disputer (qch. à q., *s.th. with s.o.*); *v/i.* se disputer (sur, au sujet de *about*).
dis·qual·i·fi·ca·tion [diskwɔlifi'keiʃn] incapacité *f*; mise *f* en état *ou* cause *f* d'incapacité; *sp.* disqualification *f*; ⚖ inhabilité *f*; **dis'qual·i·fy** [~fai] rendre incapable (de *inf., for gér.*); *sp.* disqualifier.
dis·qui·et [dis'kwaiət] **1.** inquiétude *f*; agitation *f*; **2.** inquiéter; troubler; ~*ing* alarmant; **dis'qui·e·tude** [~'kwaiitjuːd] inquétude *f*; agitation *f*. [tation *f* (sur, *on*).]
dis·qui·si·tion [diskwi'ziʃn] disser-∫
dis·re·gard ['disri'gɑːd] **1.** indifférence *f* (à l'égard de *of, for*); inobservation *f* (*de la loi*); **2.** ne tenir aucun compte de; négliger.
dis·rel·ish [dis'reliʃ] **1.** dégoût *m*, aversion *f* (pour, *for*); **2.** éprouver du dégoût pour; trouver mauvais.
dis·re·pair ['disri'pɛə] délabrement *m*; *fall into* ~ tomber en ruines; *in* ~ en mauvais état.
dis·rep·u·ta·ble □ [dis'repjutəbl] honteux (-euse *f*); minable; de mauvaise réputation (*personne*); **dis·re·pute** ['~ri'pjuːt] discrédit *m*, mépris *m*.
dis·re·spect ['disris'pekt] manque *m* de respect *ou* d'égards (envers, *for*); **dis·re·spect·ful** [~'pektful] □ irrespectueux (-euse *f*), irrévérencieux (-euse *f*).

dis·robe ['dis'roub] (aider à) se dévêtir de sa robe; (se) déshabiller.
dis·root [dis'ru:t] déraciner.
dis·rupt [dis'rʌpt] rompre, disloquer; démembrer; **dis'rup·tion**
rupture *f*; dislocation *f*; démembrement *m*; **dis'rup·tive** perturbateur
(-trice *f*).
dis·sat·is·fac·tion ['dissætis'fækʃn]
mécontentement *m* (de *with*, *at*);
dissatisfaction *f*; **'dis·sat·is'fac-
to·ry** [ˌ.təri] peu satisfaisant; **dis-
'sat·is·fy** [ˌ.fai] mécontenter; ne
pas satisfaire (*q.*).
dis·sect [di'sekt] disséquer (*a. anat.*);
découper; ⚕ exciser (*une tumeur
etc.*); **dis·sec·tion** [di'sekʃn] dissection *f*; découpage *m*.
dis·semble [di'sembl] *v/t.* dissimuler; passer sous silence; feindre;
v/i. déguiser sa pensée; user de
dissimulation.
dis·sem·i·nate [di'semineit] disséminer; **dis·sem·i·na·tion** dissémination *f*. [désaccord *m*.]
dis·sen·sion [di'senʃn] dissension *f*,
dis·sent [di'sent] 1. dissentiment *m*;
avis *m* contraire; *eccl.* dissidence *f*;
2. différer (de, *from*); *eccl.* être
dissident; **dis'sent·er** dissident(e *f*)
m; **dis·sen·tient** [di'senʃiənt] dissi-
dent(e *f*) *m* (*a. adj.*).
dis·ser·ta·tion [disə'teiʃn] dissertation *f* (sur, *on*).
dis·serv·ice ['dis'sə:vis] mauvais
service *m* (rendu à, *to*).
dis·sev·er [di'sevə] (se) séparer,
(se) désunir; **dis'sev·er·ance** [ˌ.
ərəns] séparation *f*.
dis·si·dence ['disidəns] dissidence *f*;
'dis·si·dent 1. dissident; 2. membre *m* dissident; dissident(e *f*) *m*.
dis·sim·i·lar □ [di'similə] (to)
différent (de); dissemblable (à);
dis·sim·i·lar·i·ty [ˌ.'læriti] dissemblance *f*, dissimilitude *f* (de, *to*).
dis·sim·u·late [di'simjuleit] *see* **dissemble**; **dis·sim·u'la·tion** dissimulation *f*.
dis·si·pate ['disipeit] (se) dissiper;
v/i. F mener une vie dissipée; **'dis·si-
pat·ed** dissipé; **dis·si'pa·tion** dissipation *f*; gaspillage *m*; divertissement *m*; F vie *f* désordonnée.
dis·so·ci·ate [di'souʃieit] désasso-
cier; ⚕ dissocier; ˷ *o.s.* se désintéresser (de, *from*); **dis·so·ci'a·tion**
désassociation *f*; ⚕ dissociation *f*;

psych. dédoublement *m* de la
personnalité.
dis·sol·u·bil·i·ty [disɔlju'biliti] dis-
solubilité *f*; **dis·sol·u·ble** [di-
'sɔljubl] dissoluble (dans, *in*).
dis·so·lute □ ['disəlu:t] dissolu, débauché; **dis·so'lu·tion** dissolution
f; fonte *f*; mort *f*.
dis·solv·a·ble [di'zɔlvəbl] dissoluble; **dis'solve** 1. *v/t.* (faire) dissoudre (*a. fig.*); *v/i.* se dissoudre;
fondre (*a. fig.*); se dissiper; 2. *Am.
cin.* fondu *m*; **dis'solv·ent** 1. † dissolvant; 2. dissolvant *m*.
dis·so·nance ['disənəns] ♩ dissonance *f*; désaccord *m*; **'dis·so·nant**
♩ dissonant; en désaccord (avec,
from, *to*).
dis·suade [di'sweid] dissuader, détourner (de, *from*); **dis·sua·sion**
[di'sweiʒn] dissuasion *f*; **dis·sua-
sive** [di'sweisiv] □ dissuasif (-ive *f*).
dis·taff ['dista:f] quenouille *f*; *attr.*
fig. du côté féminin.
dis·tance ['distəns] 1. *lieu, temps:*
distance *f*; éloignement *m*; lointain
m; intervalle *m*; *fig.* réserve *f*; *at a* ˷
de loin; à une distance (de, *of*);
dans le lointain; *in the* ˷ au loin,
dans le lointain; de loin; *a great* ˷
away très loin, à une grande distance; *striking* ˷ portée *f* (de la
main); 2. éloigner; *fig.* reculer;
'˷-con·trolled commandé à distance; **'dis·tant** □ éloigné; lointain; à distance; réservé, distant
(*personne*); *two miles* ˷ à deux
milles de distance; ˷ *control* commande *f* à distance; ˷ *relative* cousin
m (cousine *f*) éloigné(e).
dis·taste ['dis'teist] dégoût *m* (de,
for); aversion *f* (pour, *for*); **dis-
'taste·ful** □ [ˌ.ful] désagréable,
antipathique (à, *to*).
dis·tem·per¹ [dis'tempə] 1. détrempe *f*; badigeon *m*; 2. peindre
(*un tableau*, *un mur*) en détrempe;
badigeonner (*un mur*) en couleur.
dis·tem·per² [ˌ.] † maladie *f*; *vét.*
maladie *f* des chiens; *pol.* † désordre *m*; **dis'tem·pered** troublé,
dérangé (*esprit*).
dis·tend [dis'tend] (se) dilater; (se)
distendre; *v/t.* gonfler; *v/i.* enfler;
dis'ten·sion dilatation *f*.
dis·tich ['distik] distique *m*.
dis·til(l) [dis'til] *usu.* (se) distiller;
(laisser) tomber goutte à goutte;

v/t. raffiner (*le pétrole*); *fig.* faire couler; **dis·til·late** ['~it] distillat *m*; **dis·til·la·tion** [~'leiʃn] distillation *f*; **dis'till·er** distillateur *m*; **dis'till·er·y** distillerie *f*.

dis·tinct □ [dis'tiŋkt] distinct (de, *from*); net(te *f*); clair; marqué; **dis'tinc·tion** distinction *f*; *draw a ~ between* faire une distinction entre; *have the ~ of* (*gér.*) avoir l'honneur de (*inf.*); **dis'tinc·tive** □ distinctif (-ive *f*); d'identification; **dis'tinct·ness** clarté *f*, netteté *f*; différence *f* totale.

dis·tin·guish [dis'tiŋgwiʃ] *v/t.* distinguer; différencier (de, *from*); *v/i.* faire une *ou* la distinction (entre, *between*); **dis'tin·guish·a·ble** que l'on peut distinguer; perceptible; **dis'tin·guished** distingué; de distinction *ou* marque; remarquable (par, *for*); *~ by* connu pour; reconnu à (*sa marche etc.*).

dis·tort [dis'tɔːt] tordre; déformer; *fig.* fausser, défigurer; *~ing mirror* miroir *m* déformant; **dis'tor·tion** distorsion *f*; déformation *f* (*a. opt., a. tél.*).

dis·tract [dis'trækt] distraire, détourner; affoler (*q.*); brouiller (*l'esprit*); **dis'tract·ed** □ affolé, éperdu (de, *with*); **dis'tract·ing** □ affolant; tourmentant; **dis'trac·tion** distraction *f*; confusion *f*; affolement *m*, folie *f*.

dis·train [dis'trein]: *~ upon* saisir; exécuter (*q.*); **dis'train·a·ble** saisissable; **dis'traint** saisie *f*.

dis·tress [dis'tres] 1. détresse *f*, angoisse *f*; embarras *m*; gêne *f*; *see distraint*; ⚓ *~ rocket* signal *m* de détresse; 2. affliger, chagriner; épuiser; **dis'tressed** affligé, désolé; épuisé; *fig.* ruiné, réduit à la misère; **dis'tress·ing** □, *poét.* **dis'tress·ful** □ [~ful] angoissant, affligeant.

dis·trib·ut·a·ble [dis'tribjutəbl] répartissable, partageable; **dis'trib·ute** [~juːt] distribuer (*a. typ.*); répartir; **dis·tri'bu·tion** (mise *f* en) distribution *f*; répartition *f* (*a. des dettes*); *typ.* mise *f* en casse; **dis'trib·u·tive** 1. □ distributif (-ive *f*) (*a. gramm.*); 2. *gramm.* distributif *m*; **dis'trib·u·tor** distributeur *m* (*a.* ⊕); ✝ concessionnaire *m*.

dis·trict ['distrikt] région *f*, contrée *f*; district *m* (*a. admin.*); quartier *m*

(*de ville*); circonscription *f* (*électorale*); *~ council* conseil *m* départemental; *Am.* ⚖ *~ court* cour *f* fédérale; ✝ *~ manager* directeur (-trice *f*) *m* régional(e).

dis·trust [dis'trʌst] 1. méfiance *f*, défiance *f* (de, *of*); 2. se méfier *ou* défier de; **dis'trust·ful** □ [~ful] méfiant, défiant; soupçonneux (-euse *f*); *~ of o.s.* timide.

dis·turb [dis'təːb] déranger; troubler; agiter; inquiéter; **dis'turb·ance** trouble *m*; agitation *f*; tapage *m*; émeute *f*; ⚖ trouble *m* de jouissance; **dis'turbed** *psych.* inadapté.

dis·un·ion ['dis'juːnjən] désunion *f*; séparation *f*; **dis·u·nite** ['disjuː'nait] (se) désunir; (se) séparer; **dis·u·ni·ty** [dis'juːniti] désunion *f*.

dis·use 1. ['dis'juːs] désuétude *f*; *fall into ~* tomber en désuétude; *F être mis au rancart*; 2. ['dis'juːz] cesser d'employer; abandonner.

di·syl·lab·ic ['disi'læbik] (*~ally*) dissyllabe (*mot*); dissyllabique (*vers*); **di·syl·la·ble** [di'siləbl] dissyllabe *m*.

ditch [ditʃ] 1. fossé *m*; *Am.* Canal *m* de Panama; *die in the last ~* résister jusqu'à la dernière extrémité; 2. *v/t.* entourer de fossés; *sl.* se débarrasser de, plaquer; *mot.* verser dans le fossé; *v/i.* curer les fossés; *sl.* faire un amerrissage forcé; **'ditch·er** cureur *m* de fossés.

dith·er F ['diðə] trembloter; s'agiter sans but.

dith·y·ramb ['diθiræmb] dithyrambe *m*.

dit·to ['ditou] 1. idem; de même; 2. ✝ dito *m/inv.*; (*suit of*) *~s pl.* complet *m*.

dit·ty ['diti] chanson(nette *f*) *f*.

di·ur·nal □ [dai'əːnl] diurne.

di·va·gate ['daivəgeit] diverger, divaguer, s'éloigner du sujet; **di·va·ga·tion** [daivə'geiʃn] divagation *f*.

di·van [di'væn] divan *m*.

di·var·i·cate [dai'værikeit] diverger; bifurquer.

dive [daiv] 1. plonger (dans, *into*); ⚸, *a. fig.* piquer (du nez); F *~ into* s'enfoncer dans, entrer précipitamment dans; plonger (la main) dans (*la poche*); 2. plongeon *m*; sous-marin: plongée *f*; ⚸ (vol *m*) piqué *m*; *Am.* F cabaret *m* borgne;

gargote *f*; boîte *f*; **'div·er** plongeur *m*; scaphandrier *m*; orn. plongeon *m*.

di·verge [dai'və:dʒ] diverger, s'écarter; **di'ver·gence, di'ver·gen·cy** divergence *f*; écart *m*; biol. variation *f*; **di'ver·gent** □ divergent.

di·verse □ [dai'və:s] divers, différent; varié; **di·ver·si·fi·ca·tion** [⁓sifi'keiʃn] variation *f*; **di'ver·si·fy** [⁓fai] diversifier, varier; **di'ver·sion** [⁓ʃn] détournement *m*; ✕ diversion *f* (*a. de l'esprit*); *fig.* divertissement *m*, distraction *f*; **di'ver·si·ty** [⁓siti] diversité *f*.

di·vert [dai'və:t] détourner; écarter; divertir; distraire.

di·vest [dai'vest] dévêtir; *fig.* dépouiller, priver; ⁓ *o.s. of* renoncer à; **di'vest·ment** dévêtement *m*; *fig.* privation *f*.

di·vide [di'vaid] **1.** *v/t.* diviser (*a.* ✕); (*souv.* ⁓ *up*) démembrer; partager, répartir (entre, *among*); séparer (de, *from*); *parl.* ⁓ *the house* aller aux voix; *v/i.* se diviser, se partager (en, *into*); se séparer; ✕ être divisible (par, *by*); fourcher (*chemin*); *parl.* aller aux voix; **2.** *Am.* ligne *f* de partage des eaux; **div·i·dend** ['dividend] ✝, *a.* ✕ dividende *m*; **di·vi·der** [di'vaidə] *Am.* mot. bande *f* médiane; ✕ ⁓*s pl.* compas *m* à pointes sèches; **di·vid·ing** [di'vaidiŋ] de démarcation; mitoyen(ne *f*) (*mur*).

div·i·na·tion [divi'neiʃn] divination *f*; **di·vine** [di'vain] **1.** □ divin (*a. fig.*); ⁓ *service* office *m* divin; **2.** théologien *m*; **3.** deviner, prédire (l'avenir); **di'vin·er** devin(eresse *f*) *m*; divinateur (-trice *f*) *f*.

div·ing ['daiviŋ] action *f* de plonger; *attr.* de plongeurs; à plonger; **'⁓-bell** cloche *f* à ou de plongeur.

di·vin·ing-rod [di'vainiŋrɔd] baguette *f* divinatoire.

di·vin·i·ty [di'viniti] divinité *f* (*a. = dieu*); théologie *f*.

di·vis·i·bil·i·ty [divizi'biliti] divisibilité *f*; **di'vis·i·ble** □ [⁓zəbl] divisible; **di'vi·sion** [⁓ʒn] division *f* (*a. = désunion, a.* ✕, ✝); partage *m* (en, *into*); biol. classe *f*; *parl.* vote *m*; *parl.* circonscription *f* (*électorale*); **di'vi·sion·al** ✕ *etc.* divisionnaire; **di'vi·sive** [di'vaisiv] qui désunit; qui sème la discorde; **di'vi·sor** ✝ [⁓zə] diviseur *m*.

di·vorce [di'vɔ:s] **1.** divorce *m* (*a. fig.*); **2.** divorcer d'avec (*sa femme, son mari*); F *a. fig.* séparer (de, *from*), détacher (de, *from*); **di'vor·cee** divorcé(e *f*) *m*.

di·vulge [dai'vʌldʒ] divulguer; révéler.

dix·ie ✕ *sl.* ['diksi] gamelle *f*; *Am.* ♀ États *m/pl.* du Sud; ♀crat *Am. pol.* démocrate *m* dissident des États du Sud.

diz·zi·ness ['dizinis] vertige *m*; **'diz·zy 1.** □ pris de vertige (*personne*); *sl.* étourdi, écervelé; vertigineux (-euse *f*) (*chose*); ⁓ *spell* étourdissement *m*; **2.** étourdir.

do [du:] (*see a. done*) **1.** *v/t.* [*irr.*] *usu.* faire; (faire) cuire; s'acquitter de; finir; jouer (*une pièce*); F duper, refaire (*q.*); *sl.* ⁓ *London* visiter Londres; *sl.* ⁓ *s.o.* traiter, soigner *q.*; fêter *q.*; *what is to be done?* que faire?; ⁓ *the polite etc.* faire l'aimable *etc.*; *have done reading* avoir fini de lire; ⁓ (*over*) *again* refaire; F ⁓ *down* rouler, enfoncer (*q.*); F ⁓ *in* tuer; ⁓ *into* traduire en (*une langue*); ⁓ *out* nettoyer; ⁓ *over* couvrir (*de peinture etc.*); ⁓ *up* envelopper, ficeler; emballer; boutonner; décorer, réparer; F éreinter (*q.*); F ⁓ *o.s. up* faire toilette; **2.** *v/i.* [*irr.*] faire l'affaire; aller; suffire; convenir; *that will* ⁓ c'est bien; cela va; cela suffira; *that won't* ⁓ cela ne va *ou* n'ira pas; *how* ⁓ *you* ⁓? comment allez-vous?; comment vous portez-vous?; F ça va?; ⁓ *well* aller bien; réussir; ⁓ *badly* aller mal; ne pas réussir; *have done!* finissez donc!; *cela suffit!*; ⁓ *away with* abolir; détruire; F tuer; ⁓ *for* faire le ménage de (*q.*); tuer (*q.*); ⁓ *with* s'accommoder de; *I could* ⁓ *with some coffee* je prendrais volontiers du café; *I have done with him* j'ai rompu avec lui; ⁓ *without* se passer de; **3.** *v/aux.* [*irr.*] *interr.:* ⁓ *you know him?* le connaissez-vous?; *avec not: I* ⁓ *not know him* je ne le connais pas; *accentué: I* ⁓ *feel better* je me sens vraiment mieux; ⁓ *come and see me* venez me voir, je vous en prie; ⁓ *be quick* dépêchez-vous donc; *remplaçant un verbe déjà exprimé: do you like London?* — *I* ⁓ aimez-vous Londres?

— **Oui;** *you write better than I* ~ vous écrivez mieux que moi; *I take a bath every day.* — *So* ~ *I* je prends un bain tous les jours. — Moi aussi; **4.** F *su.* attrape *f*; réception *f*, dîner *m*; *make* ~ *with* s'accommoder de.

doc F [dɔk] *abr. de* doctor *1.*

doc·ile ['dousail] docile; **do·cil·i·ty** [dou'siliti] docilité *f*.

dock¹ [dɔk] écourter; *fig.* diminuer; retrancher (qch. à q., *s.o. of s.th.*).

dock² [~] **1.** ⚓ bassin *m*; *surt. Am.* quai *m*; ⚖ banc *m* des prévenus; ⚓ ~*s pl.* docks *m/pl.*; *dry* ~ cale *f* sèche; *floating* ~ dock *m* flottant; *wet* ~ bassin *m* à flot; **2.** ⚓ (faire) entrer au bassin; *espace:* (s')amarrer; ~ *hand,* 'dock·er travailleur *m* aux docks.

dock·et ['dɔkit] **1.** fiche *f*; étiquette *f*; ⚖ registre *m* des jugements rendus, *Am.* rôle *m* des causes; ⊕ bordereau *m*; **2.** étiqueter; classer.

dock·yard ['dɔkja:d] chantier *m* de construction de navires; arsenal *m* maritime.

doc·tor ['dɔktə] **1.** docteur *m*; médecin *m*; ~*'s certificate* certificat *m* médical; **2.** F soigner; F droguer; (*a.* ~ *up*) réparer; fausser; frelater (*du vin*); **doc·tor·ate** ['~rit] doctorat *m*.

doc·tri·naire [dɔktri'nɛə] **1.** idéologue *m*; **2.** pédant; de théoriciens; **doc·tri·nal** □ ['~trainl] doctrinal (-aux *m/pl.*); **doc·trine** ['~trin] doctrine *f*; dogme *m*.

doc·u·ment 1. ['dɔkjumənt] document *m*; pièce *f*; **2.** ['~ment] documenter; **doc·u·men·tal** *see* documentary *1*; **doc·u·men·ta·ry 1.** □ documentaire; **2.** (*a.* ~ *film*) documentaire *m*; **doc·u·men·ta·tion** documentation *f*.

dod·der ['dɔdə] **1.** ♀ cuscute *f*; **2.** trembloter; branler.

dodge [dɔdʒ] **1.** mouvement *m* de côté; *sp.* esquive *f*; ruse *f*, F truc *m*; **2.** *v/t.* esquiver; éviter; éluder (*une question*); *v/i.* se jeter de côté; *sp.* éviter; *fig.* user d'artifices; 'dodg·er malin *m*; *Am.* prospectus *m*; *Am.* (*sorte de*) biscuit *m* dur; **dodg·y** ['dɔdʒi] épineux (-euse *f*); délicat; difficile; risqué; louche.

doe [dou] daine *f*; lapine *f*; hase *f*.

do·er ['du:ə] faiseur (-euse *f*) *m*; auteur *m*.

does [dʌz] (*il, elle*) fait.

doe·skin ['douskin] (peau *f* de) daim *m*.

dog [dɔg] **1.** chien *m* (*qqfois a.* chienne *f*); renard *m etc.* mâle; ⊕ cliquet *m*; agrafe *f*, serre *f*; (*a.* fire-~) chenet *m*; ✂ (*landing-~*) taquets *m/pl.*; (*safety* ~) chambrière *f*; F type *m*; *Am.* F épate *f*; *Am.* F ✝ billet *m* à ordre; ~ *show* exposition *f* canine; *go to the* ~*s* marcher à la ruine; se débaucher; ✝ aller à vau-l'eau; *lead a* ~*'s life* mener une vie de chien; *lead s.o. a* ~*'s life* faire une vie de chien à q.; **2.** filer (*q.*); suivre (*q.*) à la piste; '~**cart** charrette *f* anglaise; '~**cheap** à vil prix; '~**col·lar** collier *m* de chien; ✝ F col *m* de pasteur; '~**days** *pl.* canicule *f*.

doge [doudʒ] doge *m*.

dog·ged □ ['dɔgid] tenace.

dog·ger·el ['dɔgərəl] **1.** (*a.* ~ *rhymes pl.*) vers *m/pl.* de mirliton; **2.** de mirliton.

dog·gie ['dɔgi] *see* doggy.

dog·gish ['dɔgiʃ] qui ressemble à un chien; qui a un air de chien; **dog·go** *sl.* ['dɔgou]: *lie* ~ se tenir coi; '**dog·gy 1.** toutou *m*; **2.** de chien; canin; *Am.* F affichant; à effet; **dog lat·in** latin *m* de cuisine.

dog·ma ['dɔgmə] dogme *m*; **dog·mat·ic, dog·mat·i·cal** □ [dɔg·'mætik(l)] dogmatique; *fig.* autoritaire, tranchant; **dog'mat·ics** *sg.* dogmatique *f*; **dog·ma·tism** ['~mə·tizm] dogmatisme *m*; *fig.* ton *m ou* esprit *m* autoritaire; '**dog·ma·tist** dogmatiste *m*; *fig.* individu *m* positif; **dog·ma·tize** ['~taiz] dogmatiser.

dog('s)-ear F ['dɔg(z)iə] corne *f* (*dans un livre*).

dog-tired ['dɔg'taiəd] éreinté.

doi·ly ['dɔili] dessus *m* d'assiette; petit napperon *m*.

do·ing ['du:iŋ] **1.** *p.pr. de* do *1, 2*; *nothing* ~ rien à faire; ✝ le marché est mort; **2.** action *f* de faire; fait *m*; ~*s pl.* faits *m/pl.*; événements *m/pl.*; conduite *f*; *péj.* agissements *m/pl.*; *sl.* machin *m*, truc *m*.

doit [dɔit] F sou *m*, liard *m*; bagatelle *f*.

dol·drums ['dɔldrəmz] *pl.* cafard *m*; ✝ marasme *m*; ⚓ zone *f* des calmes.

dole [doul] **1.** aumône *f*; ✝ portion *f*; F allocation *f* de chômage; *be (ou* *go) on the* ~ ne vivre que des allocations de chômage; **2.** (*usu.* ~ *out*) distribuer avec parcimonie.

dole·ful □ ['doulful] lugubre; douloureux (-euse *f*); triste; '**dole·ful·ness** tristesse *f*, chagrin *m*; caractère *m* contristant.

doll [dɔl] **1.** poupée *f*; *Am.* jeune fille *f*; **2.** F ~*ed up* en grand tralala.

dol·lar ['dɔlə] dollar *m*; *Am.* F ~*s to doughnuts* très probable.

dol·lop F ['dɔləp] morceau *m* informe.

doll·y ['dɔli] poupée *f*.

dol·o·mite *min.* ['dɔləmait] dolomi(t)e *f*.

dol·o·rous □ ['dɔlərəs] *usu. poét.*, *co.* douloureux (-euse *f*); plaintif (-ive *f*); triste.

dol·phin *icht.* ['dɔlfin] dauphin *m*.

dolt [doult] benêt *m*; *sl.* cruche *f*; '**dolt·ish** □ lourdaud, sot(te *f*).

do·main [də'mein] domaine *m* (*a. fig.*); propriété *f*; terres *f/pl.*

dome [doum] dôme *m* (*a. fig.*); ⊕ couronne *f*, dôme *m*.

do·mes·tic [də'mestik] **1.** (~*ally*) domestique; de ménage; de famille; intérieur (*commerce etc.*); casanier (-ère *f*); ~ *appliance* appareil *m* ménager; ~ *bliss* bonheur *m* familial *ou* de ménage; ~ *coal* houille *f* de ménage; ✈ ~ *flight* vol *m* intérieur; ~ *science* enseignement *m* ménager; **2.** domestique *mf*; **do'mes·ti·cate** [~keit] apprivoiser, domestiquer (*un animal*); ⚕ *zo.* acclimater; rendre (*q.*) casanier (-ère *f*); **do·mes·ti·ca·tion** domestication *f*; acclimatation *f*; **do·mes·tic·i·ty** [doumes'tisiti] vie *f* de famille; goûts *m/pl.* domestiques.

dom·i·cile ['dɔmisail] **1.** *surt.* ⚖ domicile *m*; **2.** ✝ domicilier (*un effet*); F résider, s'établir (dans); '**dom·i·ciled** domicilié, demeurant (à, *at*); **dom·i·cil·i·ar·y** [dɔmi'siljəri] domiciliaire (*visite etc.*).

dom·i·nance ['dɔminəns] (pré-) dominance *f*; '**dom·i·nant 1.** dominant; **2.** ♪ dominante *f*.

dom·i·nate ['dɔmineit] dominer; **dom·i'na·tion** domination *f*; '**dom·i·na·tor** dominateur (-trice *f*) *m*; **dom·i·neer** [dɔmi'niə] se montrer autoritaire; ~ *over* tyranniser; **dom·i'neer·ing** □ autoritaire; tyrannique.

do·min·i·cal [də'minikl] dominical (-aux *m/pl.*) (*oraison*).

Do·min·i·can [də'minikən] dominicain(e *f*) *m* (*a. adj.*).

do·min·ion [də'minjən] domination *f*, maîtrise *f*; *souv.* ~*s pl.* dominion *m*, -s *m/pl.*; possessions *f/pl.*; colonie *f*, -s *f/pl.*; ♀ Dominion *m*.

dom·i·no ['dɔminou], *pl.* -**noes** ['~nouz] domino *m*; ~*s sg.* jeu: dominos *m/pl.*

don [dɔn] professeur *m* d'université.

do·nate *Am.* [dou'neit] donner; faire un don à; **do'na·tion, don·a·tive** ['dounətiv] don *m*, donation *f*.

done [dʌn] **1.** *p.p. de do 1, 2; be* ~ *souv.* se faire; **2.** *adj.* fait; cuit; (*ou* ~ *up*) éreinté, fourbu; *well* ~ bien cuit; *he is* ~ *for* c'est un homme coulé; **3.** *int.* d'accord!

do·nee ⚖ [dou'ni:] donataire *mf*.

don·jon ['dɔndʒən] cachot *m*.

don·key ['dɔŋki] âne(sse *f*) *m*; *attr.* qqfois auxiliaire; '~**work** F le gros (du) travail.

do·nor ['dounə] donateur (-trice *f*) *m*; ⚕ donneur (-euse *f*) *m* de sang.

do-noth·ing F ['du:nʌθiŋ] fainéant(e *f*) (*a. su./mf*).

don't [dount] **1.** = do not; *impér.* ne fai(te)s pas ça!; **2.** défense *f*.

doo·dle ['du:dl] **1.** griffonnage *m*; griffonner.

doom [du:m] **1.** *surt. péj.* sort *m*, destin *m*; mort *f*; ruine *f*; **2.** condamner; **dooms·day** ['du:mzdei] (jour *m* du) jugement *m* dernier.

door [dɔ:] porte *f*; *auto, wagon, etc.*: portière *f*; *next* ~ (*to*) à côté (de); *fig.* approchant (de); *two* ~*s off* deux portes plus loin; (*with*)*in* ~*s* chez soi; *out of* ~*s* dehors; en plein air; *turn s.o. out of* ~*s* mettre q. à la porte; *lay s.th. to* (*ou at*) *s.o.'s* ~ imputer qch. à q.; '~**bell** sonnette *f*; '~**han·dle** poignée *f* de port(ièr)e); '~**keep·er** concierge *mf*; portier *m*; ~ **knob** poignée *f* *ou* bouton *m* de porte; '~**man** concierge *m*; portier *m*; '~**way** porte *f*; portail *m*.

dope [doup] **1.** liquide *m* visqueux; ✈ enduit *m*; *mot.* laque *f*; F stupéfiant *m*; narcotique *m*; *Am. sl.* tuyau *m*; renseignement *m*; imbécile *mf*; idiot(e *f*) *m*; type *m*; ~ *fiend* toxicomane *mf*, drogué(e *f*) *m*; ~ *peddler*, ~ *pusher* revendeur (-euse *f*) *m* de stupéfiants; **2.** *v/t.*

enduire; administrer un narcotique à; *sp.* doper (*a. un combustible*); narcotiser (*une cigarette*); *v/i.* F prendre des stupéfiants; **'dope·y** *Am. sl.* stupide; hébété.

dor·mant ['dɔːmənt] *usu. fig.* endormi, assoupi; en repos; tombé en désuétude; ♀, ▨ dormant; ✝ ∼ *partner* commanditaire *m.*

dor·mer ['dɔːmə] (*a.* ∼*-window*) lucarne *f*; (fenêtre *f* en) mansarde *f.*

dor·mi·to·ry ['dɔːmitri] dortoir *m*; *surt. Am.* maison *f* d'étudiants.

dor·mouse ['dɔːmaus], *pl.* -**mice** [∼mais] loir *m*; lérot *m.*

dor·sal ☐ ['dɔːsl] dorsal (-aux *m/pl.*); **'dor·ser** hotte *f.*

dose [dous] **1.** dose *f*; **2.** médicamenter (q. avec qch., *s.o. with s.th.*); doser (*le vin etc.*).

doss *Brit. sl.* [dɔs] **1.** pieu *m* (*lit*); roupillon *m* (*sommeil*); somme *m*; **2.** ∼ *down* se pieuter (*se coucher*); crécher (*coucher, loger*); **'∼·house** asile *m* de nuit.

dos·si·er ['dɔsiei] dossier *m*, documents *m/pl.*

dot [dɔt] **1.** point *m*; mioche *mf*; on the ∼ F à l'heure tapante; argent comptant; **2.** mettre un point sur; pointiller (*a.* ∼ *about*) *fig.* (par-)semer (de, *with*); ♩ pointer; marquer (*une surface*) avec des points.

dot·age ['doutidʒ] seconde enfance *f*; radotage *m*; **do·tard** ['∼təd] radoteur (-euse *f*) *m*; gâteux (-euse *f*) *m*; **dote** [dout] radoter; tomber dans la sénilité; ∼ ([up]on) aimer (q.) à la folie; **'dot·ing** sénile; qui aime follement (q., on *s.o.*).

dot·ty *sl.* ['dɔti] toqué, maboul.

dou·ble ☐ ['dʌbl] **1.** double; à deux personnes *ou* choses (*chambre*); deux (*lettres*); ∼ *tooth* grosse dent *f*; **2.** double *m* (*a. tennis*); deux fois autant; *fleuve, lièvre:* détour *m*; ✕ pas *m* de course; **3.** *v/t.* doubler (*a.* ♴); serrer (*le poing*); *bridge:* contrer; plier en deux (*un papier*); *théâ.* jouer deux (*rôles*); ∼ *up* replier; faire plier (*q.*) en deux; ∼*d up* ployé; *v/i.* (se) doubler; ✕ prendre le pas de course; (*a.* ∼ *back*) faire un brusque crochet (*animal*); *cartes:* contrer; **'∼-bar·relled** à deux coups (*fusil*); *fig.* (*nom*) à charnière; ∼ **bass** ♩ contrebasse *f*; ∼ **bend** virage *m* en S;

'∼-'breast·ed croisé (*gilet etc.*); **'∼-check** revérifier; **'∼-'cross** *Am. sl.* tromper, duper; **'∼-'deal·er** homme *m* à deux visages; fourbe *m*; **'∼-'deal·ing** duplicité *f*, fourberie *f*; **'∼-'deck·er** autobus *m* à impériale; *cuis.* sandwich *m* double; **'∼-'edged** à deux tranchants; ∼ **en·try** ✝ comptabilité *f* en partie double; ∼ **fea·ture** *cin. Am.* programme *m* double; **'∼-'glaz·ing** doubles fenêtres *f/pl.*; double vitrage *m*; **'∼-'head·er** *Am. baseball:* deux parties *f/pl.* de suite; **'∼-'joint·ed** désarticulé; ∼ **line** ⚏ ligne *f* à voie double; **'dou·ble·ness** état *m* double; duplicité *f* (*a. fig.*); *fig.* mauvaise foi *f*, fausseté *f*; **'dou·ble·park** *Am.* stationner contrairement à la loi; **'dou·ble-'quick** ✕ (au) pas *m* gymnastique.

dou·blet ['dʌblit] pourpoint *m*; doublet *m* (*a. gramm.*); ∼*s pl.* doublet *m* (*aux dés*).

dou·ble...: **'∼-'talk** paroles *f/pl.* trompeuses *ou* ambiguës; ∼ **take** F do a ∼ y regarder à deux fois; ∼ **time** ✕ pas *m* gymnastique; **'∼-'track** à voie double.

doub·ling ['dʌbliŋ] doublement *m*; doublage *m*; détour *m*, crochet *m.*

doubt [daut] **1.** *v/i.* hésiter; douter; *v/t.* douter de (*q., qch.*); révoquer (*qch.*) en doute; **2.** doute *m*; incertitude *f*; no ∼ sans (aucun) doute; **'doubt·er** sceptique *mf*, douteur (-euse *f*) *m*; **doubt·ful** ☐ ['∼ful] douteux (-euse *f*); incertain; équivoque; suspect; **'doubt·fulness** incertitude *f*; ambiguïté *f*; irrésolution *f*; **'doubt·less** sans doute.

douche [duːʃ] **1.** douche *f* (*a.* 🎯); **2.** (se) doucher.

dough [dou] pâte *f* (*à pain*); *Am. sl.* argent *m*; **'∼·boy** *Am.* F simple soldat *m*; **'∼-·nut** pet *m* de nonne; **'dough·y** pâteux (-euse *f*); *fig.* terreux (-euse *f*).

dour *écoss.* ['duə] austère; obstiné.

douse [daus] tremper; arroser; doucher.

dove [dʌv] colombe *f* (*a. fig.*); **'∼·cot** colombier *m*; **'∼·tail** ⊕ **1.** queue-d'aronde (*pl.* queues-d'aronde) *f*; **2.** *v/t.* adenter; *fig.* opérer le raccord entre; *v/i.* se raccorder.

dow·a·ger ['dauədʒə] douairière *f.*

dow·dy F ['daudi] **1.** sans élégance; **2.** femme *f* mal habillée.

dow·el ⊕ ['dauəl] goujon *m*; cheville *f* (en bois).

dow·er ['dauə] **1.** douaire *m*; *fig.* don *m*, apanage *m*; **2.** assigner un douaire à (*une veuve*); doter (*une jeune fille*).

dow·las ['dauləs] toile *f* commune.

down¹ [daun] duvet *m*; *oreiller*: plume *f*.

down² [~] *see* dune; ~s *pl.* hautes plaines *f/pl.* du Sussex etc.

down³ [~] **1.** *adv.* vers le bas; en bas; (*vu*) d'en haut; par terre; ~ *and out fig.* ruiné, à bout de ressources; be ~ être en baisse (*prix*); être de chute (*cartes*); F be ~ *upon* en vouloir à (*q.*); être toujours sur le dos de (*q.*); ~ *in the country* à la campagne; **2.** *prp.* vers le bas de; en bas de; au fond de; en descendant; le long de; ~ *the river* en aval; ~ *the wind* à vau-vent; **3.** *int.* à bas!; **4.** *adj.* ✝ ~ *payment* acompte *m*, arrhes *f/pl.*; ~ *platform* quai *m* montant; ~ *train* train *m* montant; **5.** F *v/t.* abattre; terrasser; ~ *tools* se mettre en grève; **6.** *su. see* up **5**; '~-and-'out clochard *m*; sans-le-sou *m/inv.*; '~·cast abattu; baissé (*regard*); ⌐-'East·er *Am.* habitant(e *f*) *m* de la Nouvelle-Angleterre, *surt.* du Maine; '~·fall chute *f* (*a. fig.*); *fig.* ruine *f*; écroulement *m*; '~·grade *Am.* déprécier; dégrader; '~-'heart·ed déprimé, découragé; '~·hill **1.** en descendant; **2.** incliné; en pente; '~·pour grosse averse *f*; déluge *m*; '~·right □ **1.** *adv.* tout à fait; carrément; nettement; **2.** *adj.* franc(he *f*); direct; carré; éclatant (*mensonge*); pur (*bêtises*); véritable; '~·right·ness franchise *f*; droiture *f*; '~·stairs **1.** d'en bas, du rez-de-chaussée (*pièce*); **2.** en bas (de l'escalier); '~·stream en aval, à l'aval; '~·stroke *écriture*: jambage *m*; ⊕ mouvement *m* de descente; '~-to-'earth terre-à-terre; '~·town *surt. Am.* centre *m* des affaires municipales; '~·ward **1.** de haut en bas; descendant; *fig.* fatal, vers la ruine; dirigé en bas (*regard*); **2.** (*a.* '~·wards) de haut en bas; '~·wash ⚔ *etc.* remous *m* d'air descendant.

down·y ['dauni] duveteux (-euse *f*); velouté (*fruit*); *sl.* rusé.

dow·ry ['dauəri] dot *f* (*a. fig.*).

dowse ['daus] **1.** *see* douse; **2.** faire de l'hydroscopie; '**dows·er** hydroscope *m*; homme *m* à baguette; radiesthésiste *mf*; '**dows·ing-rod** baguette *f* divinatoire.

doze [douz] **1.** sommeiller; ~ *away* passer (*le temps*) à sommeiller; **2.** petit somme *m*.

doz·en ['dʌzn] douzaine *f*.

doz·y ['douzi] somnolent; F gourde.

drab [dræb] **1.** gris brunâtre; beige; *fig.* terne; **2.** drap *m* beige; toile *f* bise; *couleur*: gris *m* brunâtre; *fig.* monotonie *f*.

drachm [dræm] (*poids*), **drach·ma** ['drækmə] (*monnaie*) drachme *f*.

draff [dræf] ✝ lie *f* de vin; ✝ lavure *f*; drêche *f*.

draft [drɑːft] **1.** *see* draught; ✝ traite *f*; lettre *f* de change; ⚔ détachement *m*; *Am.* conscription *f*; ~ *agreement* projet *m* de contract; *Am.* ⚔ ~ *dodger* insoumis *m*; **2.** rédiger; faire le brouillon de; désigner (à, pour to); ⚔ détacher; envoyer (*des troupes*) en détachement; *Am.* appeler sous les armes; **draft·ee** ⚔ [drɑːf'tiː] *Am.* conscrit *m*; '**drafts·man** dessinateur *m*, traceur *m*.

drag [dræg] **1.** filet *m* à la trôle, drague *f*; traîneau *m*; herse *f*; sabot *m*; drag *m*; résistance *f*; *fig.* obstacle *m*, entrave *f*; *fig.* corvée *f*; F casse-pieds *m*; *sl.* travesti *m* (*vêtements de femme*); **2.** *v/t.* (en)traîner, tirer; ⚓ chasser sur (*ses ancres*); draguer; ⚘ herser; enrayer (*une roue*); *see* dredge¹ **2**; ~ *along* (en)traîner; ~ *out one's life* traîner sa vie (jusqu'à sa fin); *v/i.* traîner; draguer (à la recherche de, *for*); pêcher à la drague; ✝ languir.

drag·gle ['drægl] traîner dans la boue; '~·tail F souillon *f*.

drag·on ['drægən] dragon *m*; '~-fly libellule *f*.

dra·goon [drə'guːn] **1.** dragon *m*; **2.** dragonner; *fig.* tyranniser.

drain [drein] **1.** tranchée *f*; caniveau *m*; égout *m*; F saignée *f*, fuite *f*; **2.** *v/t.* assécher, dessécher; vider (*un étang*, *un verre*, *etc.*); égoutter (*des légumes*); *fig.* épuiser; (*a.* ~ *off*) faire écouler; évacuer (de, *of*); *v/i.* s'écouler; '**drain·age** écoulement *m*; ⚘ drainage *m*; '**drain·ing**

1. d'écoulement; **2.** *see* drainage; ~s *pl.* égoutture *f*; '**drain·pipe** tuyau *m* d'écoulement; gouttière *f*; ~ trousers pantalon-cigarette *m* (*pl.* pantalons-cigarette).

drake [dreik] canard *m*, malard *m*.

dram [dræm] *poids*: drachme *f*; goutte *f*; petit verre *m*.

dra·ma ['drɑːmə] drame *m*; **dra-mat·ic** [drə'mætik] (~ally) dramatique; **dram·a·tist** ['dræmətist] auteur *m* dramatique; '**dram·a·tize** dramatiser; adapter (*qch.*) à la scène; **dram·a·tur·gy** ['~təːdʒi] dramaturgie *f*.

drank [dræŋk] *prét. de* drink 2.

drape [dreip] *v/t.* draper, tendre (de *with, in*); *v/i.* se draper; '**drap·er** marchand *m* d'étoffes; '**dra·per·y** draperie *f*; nouveautés *f/pl.*

dras·tic ['dræstik] (~ally) énergique.

draught [drɑːft] tirage *m*; pêche *f*; courant *m* d'air; plan *m*, tracé *m*, ébauche *f*; *boisson*: coup *m*, trait *m*; ✚ potion *f*; ⚓ tirant *m* d'eau; ~s *pl.* dames *f/pl.*; *see* draft; ~ beer bière *f* au tonneau; *at a* ~ d'un seul trait; '~-**board** damier *m*; '~-**horse** cheval *m* de trait; '**draughts·man** dessinateur *m*, traceur *m*; '**draught·y** exposé; plein de courants d'air.

draw [drɔː] **1.** [*irr.*] *v/t.* souv. tirer; attirer (*une foule*); tracer; dessiner; établir (*une distinction*); faire infuser (*le thé*); *chasse*: battre (*le couvert*); vider (*un poulet*); toucher (*de l'argent*); dresser, rédiger (*un contrat, un acte*); aspirer (*l'air*); arracher (*des larmes*) (à, *from*); *sp.* faire partie nulle; *v/i.* s'approcher de; ⚓ tirer; *the battle was* ~n la bataille resta indécise; ~ *away* entraîner; détourner; ~ *down* baisser; faire descendre; ~ *forth* faire paraître; susciter; ~ *near* s'approcher (de); ~ *on* mettre; *fig.* attirer; ~ *out* tirer; allonger; prolonger; ~ *up* tirer en haut; faire monter; ✗ ranger; ⚕ dresser, rédiger; ~ (*up*)*on* fournir (*une traite*) sur (*q.*); tirer (*un chèque*); *fig.* faire appel à; **2.** tirage *m*; loterie *f*, tombola *f*; *sp.* partie *f* nulle; F attraction *f*; '~-**back** dés-avantage *m*, inconvénient *m*; ✚ drawback *m*; *Am.* remboursement *m*; '~-**bridge** pont-levis *m* (*pl.* pont-levis) *m*; **draw'ee** ✚ tiré *m*; payeur *m*; '**draw·er** dessinateur *m*; tireur

m (*a.* ✚); tiroir *m*; (*a pair of*) ~s *pl.* (un) pantalon *m* (*de femme*); (un) caleçon *m* (*d'homme*); (*usu. chest of* ~s) commode *f*.

draw·ing ['drɔːiŋ] tirage *m*; puise-ment *m*; attraction *f*; tirage *m* au sort, loterie *f*; dessin *m*; ébauche *f*; ✚ *effets*: traite *f*; *chèque*: tirage *m*; *out of* ~ mal dessiné; ~ *instruments pl.* instruments *m/pl.* de dessin; '~-**ac·count** compte *m* en banque; '~-**board** planche *f* à dessin; '~-**pen** tire-ligne *m*; '~-**pin** punaise *f*; '~-**room** salon *m*; réception *f*.

drawl [drɔːl] **1.** *v/t.* (*souv.* ~ *out*) dire (*qch.*) avec une nonchalance affec-tée; *v/i.* parler d'une voix traînante; **2.** voix *f* traînante; débit *m* traîn-ant.

drawn [drɔːn] **1.** *p.p. de* draw 1; **2.** *adj.* tiré; ⊕ étiré; *sp.* égal; *cuis. Am.* ~ *butter* beurre *m* fondu (aux fines herbes).

draw-well ['drɔːwel] puits *m* à pou-lie.

dray [drei] (*a.* ~-*cart*) camion *m* (*surt.* de brasseur); '~·**man** livreur *m* de brasserie.

dread [dred] **1.** terreur *f*, épouvante *f*; **2.** redouter; **dread·ful** □ ['~ful] **1.** redoutable; terrible; atroce; **2.** *penny* ~ roman *m* à sensation; '**dread·nought** ['~nɔːt] *tex.* frise *f*; ⚓ dreadnought *m*.

dream [driːm] **1.** rêve *m*; songe *m*; **2.** [*irr.*] rêver (de, *of*); ~ *away* pas-ser à rêver; '**dream·er** rêveur (-euse *f*) *m*; '**dream-read·er** inter-prète *m* des rêves; **dreamt** [dremt] *prét. et p.p. de* dream 2; **dream·y** ['driːmi] □ rêveur (-euse *f*); lan-goureux (-euse *f*).

drear·i·ness ['driərinis] tristesse *f*; aspect *m* morne; '**drear·y** □ triste; morne.

dredge[1] [dredʒ] **1.** (filet *m* de) dra-gue *f*; **2.** draguer (*fig.* à la recherche de); (*a.* ~ *up*, ~ *out*) dévaser.

dredge[2] [~] *cuis.* saupoudrer.

dredg·er[1] ['dredʒə] drague *f*; *per-sonne*: dragueur *m*.

dredg·er[2] [~] saupoudroir *m*.

dregs [dregz] *pl.* lie *f*.

drench [drentʃ] **1.** *vét.* breuvage *m*, purge *f*; F *see* drencher; **2.** tremper, mouiller (*de, with*); *vét.* donner un breuvage à; '**drench·er** F pluie *f* battante.

dress

dress [dres] **1.** robe *f*, toilette *f*, costume *m*; *fig.* habillement *m*, habits *m/pl.*; *théâ.* ~ *rehearsal* répétition *f* générale; *full* ~ grande tenue *f*; **2.** (s')habiller, (se) vêtir; ✕ (s')aligner; *v/t.* orner; panser (*une blessure*); tailler (*une vigne*); ⊕ dresser, parer (*des pierres*); *cuis.* apprêter; ✔ donner une façon à (*un champ*); *théâ.* costumer; *v/i.* faire sa toilette; ~ **circle** *théâ.* (premier) balcon *m*; '~-'**coat** frac *m*; '**dress·er** ⊕, *cuis.* apprêteur (-euse *f*) *m*; buffet *m* de cuisine; panseur (-euse *f*) *m*; *théâ.* habilleur (-euse *f*) *m*; *Am.* dressoir *m*.

dress·ing ['dresiŋ] habillement *m*, toilette *f*; pansement *m* (*d'une blessure*); ✕ alignement *m*; *cuis.* sauce *f* mayonnaise; ⊕ apprêt *m*; dressage *m* (*de pierres*); ✔ façon *f*; fumages *m/pl.*; ~*s pl.* ⚙ moulures *f/pl.*; ⚕ pansements *m/pl.*; ~ *down* F semonce *f*; '~-**case** mallette *f* garnie; sac *m* de toilette; ⚙ trousse *f* de pansement; '~-'**down** F réprimande *f*; F engueulade *f*; *get a* ~ se faire passer un savon; *give s.o. a (good)* ~ passer un savon à q.; '~-**glass** miroir *m* de toilette; psyché *f*; '~-**gown** robe *f* de chambre; '~-**jack·et** camisole *f*; '~-**ta·ble** (table *f* de) toilette *f*.

dress...: '~-**mak·er** couturier (-ère *f*) *m*; '~-**mak·ing** couture *f*; '~-**shield** dessous-de-bras *m/inv.*; '~-'**suit** habit *m* (de soirée); '**dress·y** F élégant; chic *inv. en genre*; coquet(te *f*) (*femme*).

drew [dru:] *prét. de* draw 1.

drib·ble ['dribl] dégoutter; baver (*enfant etc.*); *foot.* dribbler.

drib·(b)let ['driblit] chiquet *m*; *in* ~*s* petit à petit.

dribs and drabs F ['dribzən'dræbz] *pl.*: *in* ~ petit à petit, peu à peu.

dried [draid] (des)séché; ~ *fruit* fruits *m/pl.* secs; ~ *vegetables pl.* légumes *m/pl.* déshydratés.

drift [drift] **1.** mouvement *m*; direction *f*, sens *m*; ⚓ dérive *f*; *fig.* cours *m*; *fig.* portée *f*, tendance *f*; *neige:* amoncellement *m*; *pluie:* rafale *f*; ⊕ poinçon *m*; *géol.* apport *m*, ~*s m/pl.*; ✕ galerie *f* (*chassante*); ~ *from the land* dépeuplement *m* des campagnes; **2.** *v/t.* flotter; entasser;

v/i. flotter; être entraîné; ⚓ dériver; se laisser aller (*a. fig.*); '**drift·er** ⚓ chalutier *m*; *fig.* vagabond(e *f*) *m*; '**drift-ice** glaces *f/pl.* flottantes.

drill¹ [dril] **1.** foret *m*; perçoir *m*; vilebrequin *m*; ✔ rayon *m*; semeuse *f*; ✕ manœuvre *f*, -s *f/pl.*; exercice *m*, -s *m/pl.* (*a. fig.*); ~ *ground* terrain *m* d'exercice; **2.** ✕ (faire) faire l'exercice (*a. fig.*); *v/t.* forer; percer; buriner (*une dent*); ✔ semer en rayons.

drill² [~], **drill·ing** ['~iŋ] *tex.* coutil *m*, treillis *m*.

drink [driŋk] **1.** boire *m*; boisson *f*; consommation *f*; *in* ~ ivre; **2.** [*irr.*] *vt/i.* boire; *v/i.* être adonné à la boisson; ~*s.o.'s health* boire à la santé de q.; ~ *away* boire; ~ *in* absorber; ~ *to* boire à; ~ *off*, ~ *out*, ~ *up* vider; achever de boire; avaler; '**drink·a·ble** buvable; potable (*eau*).

drink·ing ['driŋkiŋ] boire *m*; *fig.* boisson *f*; ivrognerie *f*; '~-**bout** ribote *f*; '~-**foun·tain** borne-fontaine (*pl.* bornes-fontaines) *f*; poste *m* d'eau potable; '~-**song** chanson *f* à boire; '~-**wa·ter** eau *f* potable.

drip [drip] **1.** (d)égouttement *m*; goutte *f*; F nouille *f* (*personne*); ⚙ (*be on the* ~ avoir le) goutte-à-goutte *m/inv.*; **2.** (laisser) tomber goutte à goutte; *v/i.* dégoutter; ~*ping wet* trempé; '**drip·ping** (d)égouttement *m*; *cuis.* ~*s pl.* graisse *f* (de rôti).

drive [draiv] **1.** promenade *f* en voiture; course *f*; avenue *f*; *tennis:* drive *m*; *cartes:* tournoi *m*; *sp.* coup *m* droit; *mot.* prise *f*; traction *f*; ⊕ attaque *f*; commande *f*; propulsion *f*; *chasse:* battue *f*; *fig.* énergie *f*; urgence *f*; *Am.* campagne *f* de propagande; **2.** [*irr.*] *v/t.* chasser, passer; conduire; faire marcher; surmener; exercer (*un métier*); contraindre (à, [*in*]to); (*a.* ~ *away*) éloigner; *v/i.* chasser; ⚓ dériver; *chasse:* battre un bois; *mot.* rouler; ~ *at* viser (*qch.*); travailler à (*qch.*) sans relâche; ~ *on v/t.* pousser; *v/i.* continuer sa route; ~ *up to* s'approcher de (*qch.*).

drive-in *Am.* ['draiv'in] *usu. attr.* (restaurant *m ou* cinéma *m*) où l'on accède en voiture.

driv·el ['drivl] **1.** baver; **2.** bave *f*; F balivernes *f/pl.*

driv·en ['drivn] *p.p. de* drive 2.

driv·er ['draivə] conducteur (-trice f) m (a. mot.); 🚋 mécanicien m; tramway: wattman (pl. -men) m; ⊕ poinçon m; heurtoir m (d'une soupape); Am. ~'s license permis m de conduire.

drive·way ['draivwei] allée f; entrée f (pour voitures).

driv·ing ['draiviŋ] conduite f etc.; attr. de transmission; conducteur (-trice f); a. fig. ~ force force f motrice ou agissante; fig. a. moteur m; ~ instructor moniteur m de conduite; ~ licence permis m de conduire; ~ mirror rétroviseur m; ~ school auto-école f; '~·belt courroie f de commande; '~·gear transmission f; '~·wheel roue f motrice.

driz·zle ['drizl] 1. bruine f; 2. bruiner.

droll [droul] (adv. drolly) drôle; 'droll·er·y drôlerie f.

drom·e·dar·y zo. ['drʌmədəri] dromadaire m.

drone¹ [droun] 1. zo. faux bourdon m; fig. fainéant m; 2. fainéanter.

drone² [~] 1. bourdonnement m; ♪ bourdon m; 2. bourdonner; parler d'un ton monotone.

drool [dru:l] 1. baver; F radoter; 2. Am. F radotage m.

droop [dru:p] v/t. baisser; laisser pendre; v/i. pendre; languir; s'affaisser; (se) pencher; 'droop·ing □ (re)tombant; (a)baissé; languissant.

drop [drɔp] 1. goutte f; bonbon: pastille f; chute f; pendant m; échafaud: trappe f; théâ. rideau m d'entracte; ✝ baisse f; Am. F get (ou have) the ~ on prendre (q.) au dépourvu; ~ light lampe f suspendue; 2. v/t. lâcher; laisser tomber (qch., une question, la voix); mouiller (l'ancre); lancer (une bombe); jeter à la poste (une lettre); verser (des larmes); laisser (un sujet); glisser (un mot à q.); laisser échapper (une remarque); déposer (un passager); baisser (la voix, les yeux, le rideau); supprimer (une lettre, une syllabe); abattre (le gibier); tirer (une révérence); perdre (de l'argent); ~ s.o. a line écrire un mot à q.; F ~ it! assez!; v/i. tomber; dégoutter; s'égoutter; s'abaisser (terrain); se laisser tomber (dans un fauteuil); baisser (prix, température); se calmer; ~ in entrer

en passant (à, chez at, [up]on); attraper (q., [up]on s.o.); ~ off tomber, se détacher; F s'endormir; ~ out v/t. omettre; v/i. tomber dehors; renoncer; rester en arrière; **drop·let** ['drɔplit] gouttelette f; 'drop·ping dégouttement m; abandon m; ~s pl. fiente f (d'animaux); 'drop-scene théâ. toile f de fond; rideau m d'entracte; fig. dernier acte m.

drop·si·cal □ ['drɔpsikl] hydropique; 'drop·sy hydropisie f.

dross [drɔs] scories f/pl.; déchet m; fig. rebut m.

drought [draut] sécheresse f; 'drought·y aride, sec (sèche f).

drove [drouv] 1. troupeau m (de bœufs) (en marche); fig. bande f, foule f; 2. prét. de drive 2; 'dro·ver conducteur m ou marchand m de bestiaux.

drown [draun] v/t. noyer (a. fig.); submerger; étouffer, couvrir (un son); v/i. (ou be ~ed) se noyer; être noyé.

drowse [drauz] v/i. somnoler, s'assoupir; v/t. assoupir; 'drow·si·ness somnolence f; 'drow·sy somnolent, assoupi; soporifique.

drub [drʌb] battre, rosser; 'drub·bing volée f de coups; F tripotée f.

drudge [drʌdʒ] 1. fig. cheval m de bât; esclave mf; 2. peiner; mener une vie d'esclave; 'drudg·er·y travail m ingrat; fig. esclavage m.

drug [drʌg] 1. drogue f; stupéfiant m; be a ~ in the market être invendable; ~ abuse abus m des drogues; ~ pusher (ou peddler) revendeur (-euse f) m de stupéfiants; ~ traffic(king) trafic m des stupéfiants; 2. v/t. donner ou administrer des stupéfiants à (q.); v/i. s'adonner aux stupéfiants; **drug·gist** ['drʌgist] Am., a. écoss. pharmacien m; **drug·gist's shop**, Am. 'drug·store pharmacie f; Am. p.ext. débit m de boissons non alcoolisés et de casse-croûte.

drum [drʌm] 1. tambour m (a. ⊕); tonneau m; anat. tympan m; 2. battre du tambour; tambouriner (a. fig.); '~·fire ⚔ tir m de barrage; '~·head peau f de tambour; 'drum·mer tambour m; Am. F commis m voyageur; 'drum·stick baguette f de tambour; cuis. pilon m.

drunk [drʌŋk] 1. p.p. de drink 2;

2. ivre, soûl (de, with); get ~ s'enivrer, se soûler; **drunk·ard** ['ʌəd] ivrogne(sse f) m; **'drunk·en** ivre; ~ driving conduite f en état d'ivresse; **'drunk·en·ness** ivresse f; ivrognerie f.

drupe ♣ [dru:p] drupe m.

dry [drai] 1. □ usu. sec (sèche f) (F a. = prohibitionniste); aride (sujet, terrain); tari; à sec (maçonnerie, puits, etc.); mordant, caustique (esprit); be ~ F avoir le gosier sec; ⚡ ~ cell pile f sèche; ~ goods pl. F Am. tissus m/pl.; articles m/pl. de nouveauté; 2. Am. F prohibitionniste m; 3. vt/i. sécher; v/t. faire sécher; essuyer (les yeux); v/i. (a. ~ up) tarir, se dessécher; F ~ up! taisez-vous!

dry·ad ['draiəd] dryade f.

dry-clean ['drai'kli:n] nettoyer à sec; **'dry-'clean·ing** nettoyage m à sec.

dry...: '**~-nurse** 1. nourrice f sèche; 2. élever au biberon; '**~-rot** carie f sèche; fig. désintégration f; '**~-shod** à pied sec.

du·al □ ['dju:əl] 1. double; jumelé (pneus); 2. gramm. duel m; **'du·al·ism** dualité f; phls. dualisme m.

dub [dʌb] adouber (q.) chevalier; donner l'accolade à; F qualifier (q.) de (qch.); préparer (le cuir) avec le dégras; cin. doubler; **dub·bing** ['~iŋ] hist. adoubement m; (a. **dub·bin** ['~in]) dégras m.

du·bi·ous □ ['dju:bjəs] douteux (-euse f); incertain (de of, about, over); **'du·bi·ous·ness** incertitude f.

du·cal ['dju:kl] de duc; ducal (-aux m/pl.).

du·cat ['dʌkət] ducat m.

duch·ess ['dʌtʃis] duchesse f.

duch·y ['dʌtʃi] duché m.

duck¹ [dʌk] canard m; cane f; Am. sl. type m, individu m; cricket: zéro m; ⚔ camion m amphibie.

duck² [~] 1. plongeon m; courbette f; box. esquive f; 2. plonger dans l'eau; faire (faire) une courbette; v/t. Am. éviter; v/i. F partir, quitter.

duck³ F [~] (mon) petit chou m; poulet(te f) m; chat(te f) m.

duck⁴ [~] toile f fine (pour voiles).

duck·ling ['dʌkliŋ] caneton m.

duck·y F ['dʌki] 1. see duck³; 2. mignon(ne f); chic inv. en genre.

duct [dʌkt] conduit m; ♣, anat. canal m.

duc·tile □ ['dʌktail] malléable; fig. a. docile; **duc·til·i·ty** [~'tiliti] malléabilité f; fig. souplesse f.

dud sl. [dʌd] 1. ⚔ obus m non éclaté; type m nul; raté m; chèque m sans provision; fausse monnaie f; crétin m; ~s pl. frusques f/pl.; 2. faux (fausse f); sl. moche.

dude Am. [dju:d] gommeux m; Am. ~ ranch ranch m d'opérette.

dudg·eon ['dʌdʒn] colère f.

due [dju:] 1. échu; exigible; mérité; in ~ time en temps utile; the train is ~ at le train arrive ou doit arriver à; in ~ course en temps et lieu; be ~ to être dû (due f) à, être causé par; be ~ to (inf.) devoir (inf.); Am. être sur le point de (inf.); ✝ fall ~ échoir, venir à échéance; ~ date échéance f; 2. adv. ⚓ droit; ~ east est franc, droit vers l'est; 3. dû m; droit m; usu. ~s pl. droits m/pl.; frais m/pl.; cotisation f.

du·el ['dju:əl] 1. duel m; 2. se battre en duel; **'du·el·list** duelliste m.

du·et(t) [dju:'et] duo m.

duf·fel ['dʌfəl]: ~ bag sac m marin; ~ coat duffel-coat m.

duff·er F ['dʌfə] cancre m; sp. maladroit(e f) m.

dug [dʌg] 1. prét. et p.p. de dig 1; 2. mamelle f; '**~-out** ⚔ abri m (blindé); canot: pirogue f; Am. baseball: (sorte de) fosse f où se tiennent les joueurs en attendant leur tour. [duché m; titre m de duc.]

duke [dju:k] duc m; **'duke·dom**\

dull [dʌl] 1. □ terne (a. style), mat (couleur); sans éclat (œil); atone (regard); dur (oreille); peu sensible (ouïe); sourd (bruit, douleur); lourd (esprit, temps); sombre (temps); émoussé (ciseau); ✝ inactif (-ive f) (marché); triste, ennuyeux (-euse f); ⚓ calme; 2. v/t. émousser; assourdir; ternir; amortir (une douleur); engourdir (l'esprit); hébéter (q.); v/i. se ternir; s'engourdir; **dull·ard** ['~əd] lourdaud(e f) m; **'dull·ness** manque m d'éclat ou de tranchant; lenteur f de l'esprit; dureté f (d'oreille); tristesse f, ennui m; bruit m sourd; ✝ marasme m, inactivité f.

du·ly ['dju:li] see due 1; dûment; convenablement; en temps voulu.

dumb □ [dʌm] muet(te f); interdit; Am. F sot(te f); bête; deaf and ~ sourd(e f)-muet(te f); see show 2;

strike ~ rendre muet; ~-*waiter* meu-*ble*: servante *f*; *Am.* monte-plats *m/inv.*; '~-**bell** haltère *m*; *Am. sl.* imbécile *mf*; ~'**found** F interdire; abasourdir; '**dumb·ness** mutisme *m*; silence *m*.

dum·my ['dʌmi] chose *f* factice; mannequin *m*; *fig.* muet(te *f*) *m*; *fig.* homme *m* de paille; *fig.* sot(te *f*) *m*; *cartes*: mort *m*; sucette *f* (*de bébé*); *attr.* faux (fausse *f*); factice; ~ *whist* whist *m* avec un mort.

dump [dʌmp] **1.** déposer (*a. fig.*); jeter (*des ordures*); décharger, vider; ✝ écouler à perte, faire du dumping; *fig.* laisser lourdement; **2.** coup *m* sourd; tas *m*; ✗ *etc.*: halde *f*; chantier *m*; décharge *f*; dépôt *m* (*de vivres, a.* ✗ *de munitions*); (*a. refuse* ~) voirie *f*; *see* ~*ing*; *fig.* ~*s pl.* cafard *m*; '**dump·ing** basculage *m*; dépôt *m*; ✝ dumping *m*; '**dump·ing-ground** (lieu *m* de) décharge *f*; dépotoir *m* (*a. fig.*); '**dump·ling** boulette *f*; '**dump·y** trapu, replet (-ète *f*).

dun¹ [dʌn] **1.** brun foncé; **2.** (*cheval m*) gris louvet *m*.

dun² [~] **1.** demande *f* pressante; créancier *m* importun; **2.** importuner, harceler (*un débiteur*); ~*ning letter* demande *f* pressante.

dunce [dʌns], **dun·der·head** ['dʌndəhed] F crétin(e *f*) *m*; lourdaud(e *f*) *m*.

dune [dju:n] dune *f*; ~ *buggy* buggy *m*.

dung [dʌŋ] **1.** fiente *f*; ✍ engrais *m*; **2.** fumer (*un champ*).

dun·geon ['dʌndʒn] cachot *m*.

dung·hill ['dʌŋhil] fumier *m*.

dunk *Am.* F [dʌŋk] *v/t.* tremper (dans son café *etc.*); *v/i.* faire la trempette.

du·o ['dju:ou] duo *m*.

du·o·dec·i·mal [dju:ou'desiml] duodécimal *f*; **du·o'dec·i·mo** [~mou] *typ.* in-douze *m/inv.*

dupe [dju:p] **1.** dupe *f*; **2.** duper, tromper; '**dup·er·y** duperie *f*.

du·plex ⊕ ['dju:pleks] double; *tél.* duplex; *Am.* maison *f* comprenant deux appartements indépendants.

du·pli·cate ['dju:plikit] **1.** double; en double; **2.** double *m*; *cin.*, *phot.* contretype *m*; **3.** ['~keit] reproduire; copier; **du·pli·ca·tion** [~'keiʃn] reproduction *f*; dédoublement *m*; '**du·pli·ca·tor** duplicateur

m; **du·plic·i·ty** [dju:'plisiti] duplicité *f*; mauvaise foi *f*.

du·ra·bil·i·ty [djuərə'biliti] durabilité *f*; stabilité *f*; ⊕ résistance *f*; '**du·ra·ble** □ durable; résistant; '**dur·ance** *poét.* captivité *f*; **du·ra·tion** [~'reiʃn] durée *f*.

du·ress(e) ⚖ [dju'res] contrainte *f*, violence *f*; captivité *f*.

dur·ing ['djuəriŋ] *prp.* pendant.

durst [də:st] *prét. de* dare.

dusk [dʌsk] demi-jour *m/inv.*; crépuscule *m*; (*a.* '**dusk·i·ness**) obscurité *f*; '**dusk·y** □ obscur, sombre; noirâtre; brun foncé (*teint*); moricaud.

dust [dʌst] **1.** poussière *f*; **2.** épousseter (*la table, une pièce*); saupoudrer (de, *with*); '~**·bin** boîte *f* à ordures; poubelle *f*; ~ *liner* sac *m* à poussière; '~**·bowl** *Am.* étendue *f* désertique et inculte (*États de la Prairie*); '~**·cart** tombereau *m* aux ordures; '~**·cloak**, '~**·coat** cache-poussière *m/inv.*; '**dust·er** torchon *m*; chiffon *m*; ⚓ F pavillon *m*; *Am.* cache-poussière *m/inv.*; '**dust·i·ness** état *m* poudreux *ou* poussiéreux; '**dust·ing** *sl.* raclée *f*, frottée *f*; '**dust·jack·et** *Am. livre*: jaquette *f*; '**dust·man** boueur *m*; F marchand *m* de sable; '**dust·pan** pelle *f* à ordures *ou* à poussière; '**dust·up** F querelle *f*; scène *f*; '**dust·y** □ poussiéreux (-euse *f*), poudreux (-euse *f*).

Dutch [dʌtʃ] **1.** hollandais, de Hollande ~ *courage* courage *m* puisé dans la bouteille; *Am.* F ~ *treat* repas *m* où chacun paie sa part; *go* ~ (*with s.o.*) partager les frais (avec q.); *Am.* F *in* ~ (*with s.o.*) en défaveur (auprès de q.); **2.** *ling.* hollandais *m*; *the* ~ *pl.* les Hollandais *m/pl.*; *double* ~ baragouin *m*; F hébreu *m*; '**Dutch·man** Hollandais *m*; '**Dutch·wom·an** Hollandaise *f*.

du·ti·a·ble ['dju:tjəbl] taxable; F déclarable; **du·ti·ful** □ ['~tiful] respectueux (-euse *f*); soumis; obéissant; '**du·ti·ful·ness** soumission *f*, obéissance *f*.

du·ty ['dju:ti] devoir *m* (envers, *to*); respect *m*; obéissance *f*; fonction *f*, -s *f/pl.*; douane *etc.*: droit *m*, -s *m/pl.*; service *m*; *on* ~ de service; *off* ~ libre; ~ *call* visite *f* obligée *ou* de politesse; *in* ~ *bound de* (*mon*) devoir; *do* ~ *for* remplacer; *fig.* servir de; '~-'**free** exempt de droits.

du·vet ['dju:vei] édredon *m*.

dwarf [dwɔ:f] **1.** nain(e *f*) *m*; **2.** rabougrir; *fig.* rapetisser; **'dwarf·ish** □ (de) nain; chétif (-ive *f*); **'dwarf·ish·ness** nanisme *m*; petite taille *f*.

dwell [dwel] [*irr.*] habiter; demeurer (dans, à); se fixer; ～ (*up*)*on* s'étendre sur, insister sur; **'dwell·ing** demeure *f*; **'dwell·ing-house** maison *f* d'habitation.

dwelt [dwelt] *prét. et p.p de* dwell.

dwin·dle ['dwindl] diminuer; dépérir; se réduire (à, [*in*]*to*); **'dwin·dling** diminution *f*.

dye [dai] **1.** teint(ure *f*) *m*; *fig.* of deepest ～ fieffé; endurci; **2.** teindre; **'dy·er** teinturier *m*; **'dye-stuff** matière *f* colorante; **'dye-works** *usu. sg.* teinturerie *f*.

dy·ing ['daiiŋ] (*see die*[1]) **1.** mourant, moribond; **2.** mort *f*.

dy·nam·ic [dai'næmik] **1.** (*a.* **dy·'nam·i·cal** □) dynamique; **2.** force *f* dynamique; **dy'nam·ics** *usu. sg.* dynamique *f*; **dy·na·mite** ['dainəmait] **1.** dynamite *f*; **2.** faire sauter à la dynamite; **'dy·na·mit·er** dynamiteur *m*; **dy·na·mo** ['dainəmou] dynamo *f*.

dy·nas·tic [di'næstik] (～*ally*) dynastique; **dy·nas·ty** ['dinəsti] dynastie *f*.

dyne *phys.* [dain] dyne *f*.

dys·en·ter·y ✻ ['disntri] dysenterie *f*.

dys·lex·i·a [dis'leksiə] dyslexie *f*.

dys·pep·sia ✻ [dis'pepsiə] dyspepsie *f*; **dys'pep·tic** (～*ally*) dyspepsique, dyspeptique (*a. su.*/*mf*).

E

E, e [iː] E m, e m.

each [iːtʃ] adj. chaque; pron. chacun (-e f); ~ other l'un(e) l'autre, les un(e)s les autres; devant verbe: se; they cost a shilling ~ ils coûtent un shilling chacun.

ea·ger □ ['iːgə] passionné; avide (de after, for); fig. vif (vive f); acharné; **'ea·ger·ness** ardeur f; vif désir m; empressement m.

ea·gle ['iːgl] aigle mf; pièce f de 10 dollars; **ea·glet** ['iːglit] aiglon m.

ea·gre ['eigə] mascaret m.

ear¹ [iə] blé: épi m.

ear² [~] oreille f; sens: ouïe f; ⊕ anse f; be all ~s être tout oreilles; surt. Am. keep an ~ to the ground se tenir aux écoutes; play by ~ ♪ jouer à l'oreille; fig. décider quoi faire le moment venu; turn a deaf ~ to faire la sourde oreille à; **~ache** ['iəreik] mal m ou maux m/pl. d'oreille; **~deaf·en·ing** ['~defniŋ] assourdissant; **'~drum** anat. tympan m.

earl [əːl] comte m (d'Angleterre); ⧉ Marshal grand maréchal m; **earl·dom** ['~dəm] comté m.

ear·li·ness ['əːlinis] heure f peu avancée; précocité f.

ear·lobe ['iəloub] lobe m.

ear·ly ['əːli] 1. adj. matinal (-aux m/pl.); premier (-ère f); précoce; be an ~ bird être matinal, se lever de bonne heure; Brit. it's ~ closing (day) today aujourd'hui les magasins sont fermés l'après-midi; ~ life jeunesse f; ✕ ~ warning system système m de pré-alerte; 2. adv. de bonne heure; tôt; as ~ as dès; not plus tard que.

ear...: '~mark 1. bétail: marque f à l'oreille; fig. marque f distinctive; 2. marquer (les bestiaux) à l'oreille; fig. faire une marque distinctive à; affecter (qch. à une entreprise); réserver (une somme); '~muffs pl. protège-oreilles m/inv., cache-oreilles m/inv.

earn [əːn] gagner; acquérir (de, for); **~ed income** revenu m du travail.

ear·nest¹ ['əːnist] (a. ~-money) arrhes f/pl.; garantie f, gage m.

ear·nest² [~] 1. sérieux (-euse f); sincère; délibéré; 2. sérieux m; be in ~ être sérieux; **'ear·nest·ness** (caractère m) sérieux m; ardeur f.

earn·ings ['əːniŋz] pl. gages m/pl., salaire m; gain m; profits m/pl.

ear...: '~phones pl. radio: casques m/pl. (d'écoute); '~pick cure-oreille m; '~piece téléph. écouteur m; '~pierc·ing qui vous perce les oreilles; '~plugs pl. boules f/pl. Quiès (TM); '~ring boucle f d'oreille; '~shot portée f de la voix; within ~ à portée de voix; '~split·ting assourdissant, à vous fendre les oreilles.

earth [əːθ] 1. terre f (a. ⚡); sol m; monde m; renard etc.: terrier m; radio: (a. earth-connection) contact m à la terre; 2. v/t. ⚡ relier à la terre ou mot. à la masse; ⚡ ~ up butter, terrer; v/i. se terrer; **'earth·en** de ou en terre; **'earth·en·ware** poterie f; **'earth·i·ness** nature f terreuse; **'earth·ing** ⚡ mise f à la terre (mot. à la masse); **'earth·li·ness** nature f terrestre; mondanité f; **'earth·ly** terrestre; F imaginable; no ~ pas le ou la moindre; **'earth·quake** tremblement m de terre; **'earth·worm** lombric m; fig. piètre personnage m; **'earth·y** terreux (-euse f); de terre; fig. grossier (-ère f); terre à terre inv.

ear...: '~trum·pet cornet m acoustique; '~wax cérumen m.

ease [iːz] 1. repos m, bien-être m, aise f; tranquillité f (d'esprit); soulagement m; loisir m; oisiveté f; manières: aisance f; facilité f; simplicité f; at ~ tranquille; à son etc. aise; ill at ~ mal à l'aise; ✕ stand at ~! repos!; take one's ~ prendre ses aises; with ~ facilement; live at ~ vivre à l'aise; 2. adoucir, soulager (la douleur); calmer; ⚓ larguer (une amarre), mollir (une barre); débarrasser (de, of); it ~d the situation la situation se détendit; ~ *nature* faire ses besoins; **ease·ful** □ ['~ful] tranquille; calmant; doux (douce *f*).

ea·sel ['iːzl] chevalet *m*.

ease·ment ⚖ ['iːzmənt] *charges*: servitude *f*.

eas·i·ness ['iːzinis] commodité *f*, bien-être *m*; aisance *f*; facilité *f*; douceur *f*; complaisance *f*; ~ *of belief* facilité *f* à croire.

east [iːst] **1.** *su.* est *m*, orient *m*; *the* ⚹ *Am.* les États *m/pl.* de l'Est (*des É.-U.*); **2.** *adj.* d'est, de l'est; oriental (-aux *m/pl.*); **3.** *adv.* à ou vers l'est; '~·bound (allant) en direction de l'est.

East·er ['iːstə] Pâques *m/pl.*; *attr.* de Pâques; ~ *egg* œuf *m* de Pâques.

east·er·ly ['iːstəli] de *ou* à l'est; **east·ern** ['~tən] de l'est; oriental (-aux *m/pl.*); '**east·ern·er** oriental(e *f*) *m*; habitant(e *f*) *m* de l'est; **east·ern·most** ['iːstənmoust] *le* plus à l'est.

east·ing ⚓ ['iːstiŋ] chemin *m* est; route *f* vers l'est.

east·ward ['iːstwəd] **1.** *adj.* à ou de l'est; **2.** *adv. a.* **east·wards** ['~dz] vers l'est.

eas·y □ ['iːzi] **1.** à l'aise; tranquille; aisé (*air, style, tâche*); libre; facile (*personne, style, tâche*); doux (douce *f*); ample (*vêtement*); ✝ calme; *in* ~ *circumstances* dans l'aisance; *Am.* *on* ~ *street* très à l'aise, F bien renté; ✝ *on* ~ *terms* avec facilités de paiement; *make o.s.* ~ se rassurer (sur, *about*); *take it* ~ F se la couler douce; *take it* ~! doucement!; ⚔ *Brit.* stand ~ repos!; **2.** halte *f*; ~ **chair** fauteuil *m*; bergère *f*; '~·**go·ing** *fig.* accommodant; insouciant; d'humeur facile.

eat [iːt] **1.** [*irr.*] *v/t.* manger; déjeuner, dîner, souper; prendre (*un plat*); ~ *up* manger jusqu'à la dernière miette; consumer; dévorer (*a. fig.*); *v/i.* manger; déjeuner *etc.*; ~ *out* manger au restaurant; **2.** *Am. sl.* ~*s pl.* manger *m*; mangeaille *f*; **eat·a·ble 1.** mangeable; **2.** ~*s pl.* comestibles *m/pl.*; '**eat·en** *p.p. de* eat 1; '**eat·er** mangeur (-euse *f*) *m*; *be a great* (*poor*) ~ être gros (petit) mangeur; '**eat·ing** manger *m*; '**eat·ing·house** restaurant *m*.

eaves [iːvz] *pl.* avance *f*; gouttières *f/pl.*; '~·**drop** écouter à la porte;

être aux écoutes; '~·**drop·per** écouteur (-euse *f*) *m* aux portes.

ebb [eb] **1.** (*a.* ~-*tide*) reflux *m*; *fig.* déclin *m*; *at a low* ~ très bas; **2.** baisser (*a. fig.*); refluer; *fig.* décroître; être sur le déclin.

eb·on·ite ['ebənait] ébonite *f*; '**eb·on·y** (bois *m* d')ébène *f*.

e·bri·e·ty [iːˈbraiəti] ivresse *f*.

e·bul·li·ent [iˈbʌljənt] bouillonnant; *fig.* débordant (de, *with*); **eb·ul·li·tion** [ebəˈliʃn] ébullition *f*; *surt. fig.* débordement *m*; insurrection *f*.

ec·cen·tric [ikˈsentrik] **1.** (*a.* **ec·cen·tri·cal** □) excentrique (*a. fig.*); *fig.* original (-aux *m/pl.*); **2.** ⊕ excentrique *m*; original(e *f*) *m*; **ec·cen·tric·i·ty** [eksenˈtrisiti] excentricité *f*.

ec·cle·si·as·tic [ikliːziˈæstik] **1.** ✝, *usu.* **ec·cle·si·as·ti·cal** □ ecclésiastique; **2.** ecclésiastique *m*.

ech·e·lon ⚔ ['eʃəlɔn] **1.** échelon *m*; **2.** échelonner.

e·chi·nus *zo.* [eˈkainəs] oursin *m*.

ech·o ['ekou] **1.** écho *m*; **2.** *v/t.* répéter; *fig.* se faire l'écho de; *v/i.* faire écho; retentir; '~·**sound·er** ['~saundə] sondeur *m* acoustique.

é·clat ['eiklɑː] éclat *m*, gloire *f*.

ec·lec·tic [ekˈlektik] éclectique (*a. su./mf*); **ec·lec·ti·cism** [~tisizm] éclectisme *m*.

e·clipse [iˈklips] **1.** éclipse *f* (*a. fig.*); *fig.* ombre *f*; *in* ~ éclipsé; *orn.* dans son plumage d'hiver; **2.** *v/t.* éclipser; *v/i.* être éclipsé; **e·clip·tic** *astr.* écliptique (*a. su./f*).

ec·logue ['eklɔg] églogue *f*.

e·co·cid·al ['iːkouˈsaidl] nuisible à l'environnement; **e·co·cide** ['~said] destruction de l'environnement.

e·co·log·i·cal [iːkəˈlɔdʒikl] écologique; **e·col·o·gist** [iːˈkɔlədʒist] écologiste *mf*; **e·col·o·gy** écologie *f*; ~ *movement* mouvement *m* écologique, écologisme *m*.

e·co·nom·ic, e·co·nom·i·cal □ [iːkəˈnɔmik(l)] économique; économe (*personne*); *economic aid* aide *f* économique; ~ *growth* croissance *f* économique; ~ *summit* sommet *m* économique; **e·co·nom·ics** *sg.* économie *f* politique; **e·con·o·mist** [iˈkɔnəmist] économiste *m*; personne *f* économe (de, *of*); **e·con·o·mize** économiser (qch. *in, on, with s.th.*); **e·con·o·my** économie *f*; economies *pl.* économies *f/pl.*; épargnes *f/pl.*; *political* ~ économie *f* politique; ~ *class* classe *f* touriste; ~ *drive* (mesures *f/pl.*) restrictions *f/pl.*; ~ *pack* paquet *m* économique.

e·co·sys·tem ['i:kousistəm] écosystème *m*.

ec·sta·size ['ekstəsaiz] *v/t.* ravir; *v/i.* s'extasier (devant, *over*); '**ec·sta·sy** transport *m*; extase *f* (*religieuse etc.*); *go into ecstasies* s'extasier (devant, *over*); **ec·stat·ic** [eks'tætik] (~*ally*) extatique.

e·cu·men·i·cal [i:kju:'menikl] œcuménique.

ec·ze·ma ✽ ['eksimə] eczéma *m*.

e·da·cious [i'deiʃəs] vorace.

ed·dy ['edi] **1.** remous *m*; tourbillon *m*; **2.** faire des remous; tourbillonner.

e·den·tate *zo.* [i'denteit] édenté (*a. su./m*).

edge [edʒ] **1.** tranchant *m*; angle *m*; crête *f*; *livre, shilling*: tranche *f*; *forêt*: lisière *f*, orée *f*; *étoffe, table, lac, etc.*: bord *m*; *be on* ~ être nerveux (-euse *f*); *surt. Am.* F *have the* ~ *on* être avantagé par rapport à; *put an* ~ *on* aiguiser; *lay on* ~ mettre de champ; *set s.o.'s teeth on* ~ faire grincer les dents à q.; énerver q.; *stand on* ~ mettre de champ; **2.** *v/t.* aiguiser; border; *v/i.* (se) faufiler; ~ *in* (se) glisser dans; ~ *forward* avancer tout doucement; ~ *off v/t.* amincir; *v/i. fig.* s'écarter tout doucement; **edged** [edʒd] tranchant, acéré; à ... tranchant(s).

edge ...: '~·**less** dépourvu de bords; émoussé; '~·**tool** outil *m* tranchant; '~·**ways**, '~·**wise** de côté; de *ou* sur champ.

edg·ing ['edʒiŋ] bordure *f*; *robe*: liséré *m*, ganse *f*.

edg·y ['edʒi] anguleux (-euse *f*); F énervé, agacé.

ed·i·ble ['edibl] **1.** bon(ne *f*) à manger; **2.** ~*s pl.* comestibles *m/pl.*

e·dict ['i:dikt] édit *m*.

ed·i·fi·ca·tion [edifi'keiʃn] édification *f*; **ed·i·fice** ['~fis] édifice *m*; **ed·i·fy** ['~fai] édifier; '**ed·i·fy·ing** ☐ édifiant.

ed·it ['edit] éditer (*un livre*); diriger (*un journal, une série*); **e·di·tion** [i'diʃn] édition *f*; *fig.* double *m*; **ed·i·tor** ['editə] éditeur *m*; direc-

teur *m*; rédacteur *m* en chef; *letters pl. to the* ~ courrier *m* des lecteurs; **ed·i·to·ri·al** [~'tɔ:riəl] **1.** éditorial (-aux *m/pl.*) (*a. su./m*); ~ *office* (bureau *m* de) rédaction *f*; ~ *staff* la rédaction; **2.** article *m* de fond; **ed·i·tor·ship** ['~təʃip] direction *f*; travail *m* d'éditeur.

ed·u·cate ['edjukeit] instruire; pourvoir à l'instruction de; former; éduquer (*un animal*); **ed·u·ca·tion** éducation *f*; enseignement *m*; instruction *f*; *elementary* ~ enseignement *m* primaire; *secondary* ~ enseignement *m* secondaire; *Ministry of* ~ Ministère *m* de l'Éducation nationale; **ed·u·ca·tion·al** ☐ d'enseignement; pédagogique; ~ *film* film *m* éducatif; ~ *policy* politique *f* d'enseignement; **ed·u·ca·tion(·al)·ist** [~'keiʃn(ə)list] pédagogue *mf*; spécialiste *mf* de pédagogie; **ed·u·ca·tive** ['~kətiv] *see educational*; **ed·u·ca·tor** ['~keitə] éducateur (-trice *f*) *m*.

e·duce [i'dju:s] dégager (*a.* 🜍); déduire; évoquer.

e·duc·tion [i'dʌkʃn] extraction *f*; déduction *f*; ⊕ échappement *m*.

eel [i:l] anguille *f*.

e'en [i:n] *see even*[1] 2.

e'er [ɛə] *see ever*.

ee·rie, **ee·ry** ['iəri] mystérieux (-euse *f*); étrange; qui donne le frisson.

ef·face [i'feis] effacer (*a. fig.*); *fig.* éclipser; **ef·face·a·ble** effaçable; **ef·face·ment** effacement *m*.

ef·fect [i'fekt] **1.** effet *m*; action *f* (*a.* ⊕); conséquence *f*; vigueur *f* (𝔵𝔷 *d'une loi*); réalisation *f*; sens *m*, teneur *f*; ~*s pl.* effets *m/pl.* (*théâ., a. d'un mort*); ✝ provision *f*; *bring to* ~ exécuter; *take* ~, *be of* ~ produire un effet; entrer en vigueur; *deprive of* ~ rendre ineffectif (-ive *f*); *of no* ~ sans effet, inefficace; *in* ~ en effet; en réalité; *to the* ~ portant (que, *that*); *to this* ~ dans ce sens; **2.** réaliser, effectuer; *be* ~*ed* s'opérer, intervenir; **ef·fec·tive 1.** ☐ efficace; utile; effectif (-ive *f*) (*a.* ⊕); 𝔵𝔷 en vigueur; *fig.* frappant; ✖, ⚓ valide; ⊕ ~ *capacity* rendement *m*; ~ *date* date *f* d'entrée en vigueur; ~ *range* portée *f* utile; **2.** ✖ *usu.* ~*s pl.* effectifs *m/pl.*; **ef·fec·tu·al** [~juəl] efficace; valide;

en vigueur; ef'fec·tu·ate [~jueit] effectuer; réaliser.

ef·fem·i·na·cy [i'feminəsi] caractère m efféminé; ef'fem·i·nate [~nit] □ efféminé.

ef·fer·vesce [efə'ves] entrer en effervescence, mousser; ef·fer-'ves·cence effervescence f; ef·fer-'ves·cent effervescent; ~ drink boisson f gazeuse.

ef·fete [e'fi:t] caduc (-uque f); épuisé.

ef·fi·ca·cious □ [efi'keiʃəs] efficace; ef·fi·ca·cy ['~kəsi] efficacité f.

ef·fi·cien·cy [e'fiʃnsi] efficacité f; capacité f; valeur f; ⊕ rendement m; bon fonctionnement m; Am. ~ expert expert m de l'organisation rationnelle (de l'industrie); ef'fi·cient [~ʃnt] □ efficace; effectif (-ive f); à bon rendement.

ef·fi·gy ['efidʒi] effigie f.

ef·flo·resce [eflɔː'res] ♀ fleurir (a. fig.); ⤳ (s')effleurir; ef·flo'res·cence efflorescence f (a. ⤳); fleuraison f; ef·flo'res·cent efflorescent; ♀ en fleur.

ef·flu·ence ['efluəns] émanation f, effluence f; 'ef·flu·ent 1. effluent (a. su./m.); 2. cours m d'eau dérivé; ef·flu·vi·um [e'flu:vjəm], pl. -vi·a [~vjə] effluve m; exhalaison f; ef·flux ['eflʌks] flux m, écoulement m.

ef·fort ['efət] effort m (pour inf., at gér.); fig. œuvre f; 'ef·fort·less □ sans effort; facile.

ef·fron·ter·y [e'frʌntəri] effronterie f; fig. toupet m.

ef·ful·gence [e'fʌldʒns] splendeur f; éclat m; ef'ful·gent □ resplendissant.

ef·fuse [e'fju:z] (se) répandre; ef·fu·sion [i'fju:ʒn] effusion f, épanchement m (a. fig.); ef'fu·sive □ [~siv] expansif (-ive f); ef'fu·sive·ness effusion f; volubilité f.

eft [eft] see newt.

egg[1] [eg] (usu. ~ on) pousser, inciter.

egg[2] [~] œuf m; buttered (ou scrambled) ~s pl. œufs m/pl. brouillés; boiled ~s pl. œufs m/pl. à la coque; fried ~s pl. œufs m/pl. sur le plat; sl. bad ~ vaurien m, bon m à rien; as sure as ~s aussi sûr que deux et deux font quatre; '~-beat·er batteur m à œufs; '~-cup coquetier m; '~-flip, '~-nog flip m; '~-head Am. sl. intellectuel m; '~-plant

aubergine f; '~-shell coquille f; '~-whisk fouet m (à œufs).

eg·lan·tine ♀ ['eglantain] églantine f; buisson: églantier m.

e·go ['egou] le moi; e·go·cen·tric [~'sentrik] égocentrique; 'e·go·ism égotisme m; culte m du moi; phls. égoïsme m; 'e·go·ist égotiste mf; égoïste mf; e·go·is·tic, e·go·is·ti·cal □ égotiste; fig. vaniteux (-euse f); e·go·tism ['egoutizm] égotisme m; 'e·go·tist égotiste mf; e·go·tis·tic, e·go·tis·ti·cal □ égotiste.

e·gre·gious iro. □ [i'gri:dʒəs] insigne; fameux (-euse f).

e·gress ['i:gres] sortie f, issue f; ⊕ échappement m.

e·gret ['i:gret] orn. aigrette f (a. ♀); héron m argenté.

E·gyp·tian [i'dʒipʃn] 1. égyptien(ne f); 2. Égyptien(ne f) m.

eh [ei] eh!; hé!; hein?

ei·der ['aidə] (a. ~-duck) eider m; '~-down duvet m d'eider; (a. ~ quilt) édredon m piqué.

eight [eit] 1. huit; 2. huit m; ⚓ équipe f de huit rameurs; huit m de pointe; Am. fig. behind the ~ ball dans une position précaire; eight·een ['ei'ti:n] dix-huit; 'eight-'eenth [~θ] dix-huitième; 'eight·fold octuple; adv. huit fois autant; eighth [eitθ] huitième (a. su./m.); 'eighth·ly en huitième lieu; eight-hour day ['~'auədei] journée f de huit heures; eight·i·eth ['~iiθ] quatre-vingtième; 'eight·y quatre-vingt(s); ~-two quatre-vingt-deux; ~-first quatre-vingt-unième.

ei·ther ['aiðə, 'i:ðə] 1. adj. chaque; l'un(e f) et l'autre de; l'un(e f) ou l'autre de; 2. pron. chacun(e f); l'un(e) et ou ou l'autre; 3. cj. ~ ... or ... ou ... ou ...; soit ... soit ...; not (...) ~ ne ... non plus.

e·jac·u·late [i'dʒækjuleit] éjaculer; lancer; proférer; e·jac·u·la·tion ⚕, eccl. éjaculation f; exclamation f.

e·ject [i'dʒekt] émettre; expulser (un agitateur, un locataire); e'jec·tion flammes: jet m; expulsion f; éviction f; e'ject·ment ⚖ réintégrande f; expulsion f; e'jec·tor ⊕ éjecteur m.

eke [i:k]: ~ out suppléer à l'insuffisance de (en y ajoutant, with); allonger (un liquide); faire du remplissage (avec, with); ~ out a

elementary

miserable existence gagner une maigre pitance.

el *Am.* F [el] *abr. de* elevated 2.

e·lab·o·rate 1. [i'læbərit] □ compliqué; travaillé (*style*); recherché; soigné; **2.** [ˌ~reit] élaborer (*a. physiol.*) (en, *into*); travailler (*son style*); **e'lab·o·rate·ness** [ˌ~ritnis] soin *m*, minutie *f*; **e·lab·o·ra·tion** [ˌ~'reiʃn] élaboration *f*.

e·lapse [i'læps] (se) passer; s'écouler.

e·las·tic [i'læstik] **1.** (ˌ~ally) élastique (*a. fig.*); flexible; *he is* ~ il a du ressort; **2.** élastique *m*; **e·las·tic·i·ty** [ˌ~'tisiti] élasticité *f*; souplesse *f*; *fig.* ressort *m*.

e·late [i'leit] **1.** □ élevé; (*usu.* ˌ~ed) transporté (de, *with*); **2.** exalter, transporter; **e'la·tion** exaltation *f*; gaieté *f*.

el·bow ['elbou] **1.** coude *m* (*a.* ⊕); *route:* tournant *m*; ⊕ genou *m*, jarret *m*; *at one's* ~ tout à côté; tout près; *out at* ~s troué aux coudes; *fig.* déguenillé; **2.** coudoyer; pousser du coude; ~ *one's way through* se frayer un passage à travers; ~ *out* évincer (de, *of*); '~-'**chair** fauteuil *m*; '~-**grease** F huile *f* de bras (= *travail, énergie*); '~-**room:** *have* ~ avoir du champ.

eld·er¹ ['eldə] **1.** plus âgé, aîné; *cartes:* ~ *hand* premier *m* en main; ~ *statesman* vétéran *m* de la politique, homme *m* d'État chevronné; **2.** plus âgé(e*f*) *m*; aîné(e*f*) *m*; *eccl.* ancien *m*; *my* ~s *pl.* mes aînés *m/pl.*

el·der² ♀ [ˌ~] sureau *m*; '~-**ber·ry** baie *f* de sureau.

eld·er·ly ['eldəli] assez âgé.

eld·est ['eldist] aîné.

e·lect [i'lekt] **1.** élu (*a. eccl.*); futur; *bride* ~ la future *f*; **2.** élire; *eccl.* mettre parmi les élus; choisir (de *inf.*, *to inf.*); **e'lec·tion** élection *f*; ~ *address ou speech* discours *m* électoral; **e·lec·tion·eer** [ˌ~ʃə'niə] solliciter des voix; **e·lec·tion'eer·ing** propagande *f* électorale; **e'lec·tive 1.** □ électif (-ive*f*); électoral (-aux *m/pl.*); *Am. univ. etc.* facultatif (-ive *f*); **2.** *Am.* cours *m ou* sujet *m* facultatif; **e'lec·tive·ly** par choix; **e'lec·tor** électeur *m*; *Am.* membre *m* du Collège électoral; **e'lec·tor·al** électoral (-aux *m/pl.*); ~ *address ou speech* discours *m* électoral; ~ *campaign*

campagne *f* électorale; ~ *district ou division* circonscription *f* électorale;~ *roll* liste *f* électorale; **e'lec·tor·ate** [ˌ~rit] corps *m* électoral; votants *m/pl.*; **e'lec·tress** électrice *f*.

e·lec·tric [i'lektrik] électrique; *fig.* électrisant; ⚡ ~ *arc* arc *m* voltaïque; ~ *blue* bleu électrique; ~ *circuit* circuit *m*; *zo.* ~ *eel* anguille *f* électrique; ~ *eye* cellule *f* photoélectrique; **e'lec·tri·cal** □ électrique; ~ *engineer* ingénieur *m* électricien; ~ *engineering* technique *f* électrique; **e·lec·tri·cian** [ˌ~'triʃn] (monteur-) électricien *m*; **e·lec'tric·i·ty** [ˌ~siti] électricité *f*; ~ *works* centrale *f* électrique; **e·lec·tri·fi·ca·tion** [ˌ~fi-'keiʃn] électrisation *f*; ⚙ électrification *f*; **e'lec·tri·fy** [ˌ~fai], **e'lec·trize** électriser (*a. fig.*); ⚙ électrifier.

electro... [ilektrou] électro-; **e'lec·tro·cute** [ˌ~trəkjuːt] électrocuter; **e·lec·tro'cu·tion** électrocution *f*; **e'lec·trode** [ˌ~troud] électrode *f*; **e·lec·tro·dy'nam·ics** [ˌ~troud] électrodynamique *f*; **e·lec·tro·lier** [ˌ~'liə] lustre *m* électrique; **e'lec·tro·lyse** [ˌ~trolaiz] électrolyser; **e·lec'trol·y·sis** [ˌ~'trolisis] électrolyse *f*; **e'lec·tro'mag·net** électro-aimant *m*; **e·lec·tro'met·al·lur·gy** électrométallurgie *f*; **e'lec·tro'mo·tor** électromoteur *m*.

e·lec·tron [i'lektrən] électron *m*; *attr.* à électrons, électronique; ~-*ray tube* oscillographe *m* cathodique; **e·lec'tron·ic 1.** électronique; ~ *data processing* traitement électronique de(s) données *f*; **2.** ~s *sg.* électronique *f*.

e·lec·tro·plate [i'lektroupleit] **1.** plaquer; argenter; **2.** articles *m/pl.* argentés *ou* plaqués; **e·lec·tro·type** [i'lektrotaip] électrotype *m*; (cliché *m*) galvano *m*.

e·lec·tu·ar·y ✚ [i'lektjuəri] électuaire *m*.

el·e·gance ['eligəns] élégance *f*; '**el·e·gant** □ élégant; *Am.* excellent.

e·le·gi·ac [eli'dʒaiæk] élégiaque.

el·e·gy ['elidʒi] élégie *f*.

el·e·ment ['elimənt] élément *m* (*a.* ⚡, *eccl.*, *temps*, *fig.*); partie *f*; 🜍 corps *m* simple; ~s *pl.* rudiments *m/pl.*, éléments *m/pl.*; **el·e·men·tal** [ˌ~'mentl] □ élémentaire; des éléments; *fig.* premier (-ère *f*); **el·e-**

'men·ta·ry [~təri] □ élémentaire; simple; ~ *school* école *f* primaire.

el·e·phant ['elifənt] éléphant *m* (*mâle, femelle*); white ~ objet *m* inutile qui occupe trop de place; el·e·phan·tine [~'fæntain] éléphantin; éléphantesque; *fig.* lourd.

el·e·vate ['eliveit] élever; lever; relever; 'el·e·vat·ed 1. élevé, haut; F un peu ivre; 2. (*a. ~ railroad ou train*) *Am.* F chemin *m* de fer aérien; el·e·'va·tion élévation *f* (*a.* ⊕, △, *astr., eccl., colline*); altitude *f*, hauteur *f*; *fig.* noblesse *f*; 'el·e·va·tor ⊕ élévateur *m*; *Am.* ascenseur *m*; ✞ gouvernail *m* d'altitude; *Am.* (*grain*) ~ silo *m* à élévateur pneumatique; *Am.* ~ *shaft* cage *f* d'ascenseur.

el·ev·en [i'levn] onze (*a. su./m*); e'lev·en·ses *Brit.* F [~ziz] pause-café *f*, (*pl.* pauses-café) casse-croûte *m*/*inv.* dans la matinée; e'lev·enth [~θ] onzième.

elf [elf], *pl.* elves [elvz] elfe *m*; lutin(e *f*) *m*; elf·in ['~in] d'elfe, de lutin; 'elf·ish des elfes, de lutin; espiègle (*enfant*).   [tir; obtenir.)

e·lic·it [i'lisit] faire jaillir, faire sor-∫ e·lide *gramm.* [i'laid] élider.

el·i·gi·bil·i·ty [elidʒə'biliti] acceptabilité *f*; éligibilité *f*; 'el·i·gi·ble □ admissible; éligible; F bon(ne *f*) (*parti*), acceptable; be ~ for a. avoir droit à (*qch.*).

e·lim·i·nate [i'limineit] éliminer (*surt.* ⚕, ⚗, ⚙); supprimer; e·lim·i'na·tion élimination *f*.

e·li·sion [i'liʒn] *gramm.* élision *f*.

é·lite [ei'li:t] élite *f*, (fine) fleur *f*, choix *m*; é'lit·ist [~ist] élitiste, élitaire.

e·lix·ir [i'liksə] élixir *m*.

E·liz·a·be·than [ilizə'bi:θn] élisabéthain.

elk *zo.* [elk] élan *m*.

ell *hist.* [el] aune *f*; aunée *f* (*de drap*).

el·lipse ⅄ [i'lips] ellipse *f*; *gramm.* el'lip·sis [~sis], *pl.* -ses [~si:z] ellipse *f*; el'lip·tic, el'lip·ti·cal □ elliptique.

elm ⚘ [elm] orme *m*.

el·o·cu·tion [elə'kju:ʃn] élocution *f*, diction *f*; el·o'cu·tion·ar·y de diction; oratoire; el·o'cu·tion·ist déclamateur *m*; professeur *m* d'élocution.

e·lon·gate ['i:lɔŋgeit] (s')allonger; e·lon'ga·tion allongement *m*; prolongement *m*; *astr.* élongation *f*.

e·lope [i'loup] s'enfuir (avec un amant); ~ *with* se faire enlever par; e'lope·ment fuite *f* amoureuse; enlèvement *m* (consenti).

el·o·quence ['eləkwəns] éloquence *f*; 'el·o·quent □ éloquent.

else [els] 1. *adv.* autrement; ou bien; 2. *adj.* autre; encore; *all* ~ tout le reste; *anyone* ~ quelqu'un d'autre; *what* ~? quoi encore?; *or* ~ ou bien; 'else·where ailleurs.

e·lu·ci·date [i'lu:sideit] éclaircir, élucider; e·lu·ci'da·tion éclaircissement *m*, élucidation *f*; e'lu·ci·da·to·ry [~təri] éclaircissant.

e·lude [i'lu:d] éviter; échapper à; éluder (*une question*).

e·lu·sion [i'lu:ʒn] esquive *f*; évasion *f*; e'lu·sive [~siv] insaisissable; évasif (-ive *f*) (*réponse*); e'lu·sive·ness nature *f* insaisissable; caractère *m* évasif; e'lu·so·ry [~səri] évasif (-ive *f*).

elves [elvz] *pl. de* elf.

E·ly·si·um [i'liziəm] l'Élysée *m*.

em *typ.* [em] cadratin *m*.

e·ma·ci·ate [i'meiʃieit] amaigrir; émacier; e·ma·ci'a·tion [imeisi'eiʃn] amaigrissement *m*, émaciation *f*.

em·a·nate ['eməneit] émaner (de, from); em·a'na·tion émanation *f* (*a. phys., a. fig.*); effluve *m*.

e·man·ci·pate [i'mænsipeit] émanciper; affranchir; e·man·ci'pa·tion émancipation *f*; affranchissement *m*; e'man·ci·pa·tor émancipateur (-trice *f*) *m*; affranchisseur *m*.

e·mas·cu·late 1. [i'mæskjuleit] émasculer, châtrer (*un texte*); efféminer (*le style*); 2. [~lit] émasculé, châtré; énervé; e·mas·cu·la·tion [~'leiʃn] émasculation *f*.

em·balm [im'ba:m] embaumer (*a. fig.*); *fig.* parfumer; be ~ed in *fig.* être perpétué par *ou* dans.

em·bank [im'bæŋk] endiguer; remblayer (*une route*); em'bank·ment endiguement *m*; remblayage *m*; digue *f*; talus *m*; remblai *m*; quai *m*.

em·bar·go [em'ba:gou] 1. *pl.* -goes [~gouz] embargo *m*, séquestre *m*, arrêt *m*; *put an* ~ *on fig.* interdire; 2. mettre l'embargo sur, séquestrer (*un navire etc.*); réquisitionner.

eminent

em·bark [im'baːk] (s')embarquer (*a. fig.* dans, [up]on); *v/t.* prendre (*qch.*) à bord; *v/i.*: ~ (up)on *s.th.* entreprendre qch.; **em·bar·ka·tion** [embaː'keiʃn] embarquement *m*.

em·bar·rass [im'bærəs] embarrasser, gêner; déconcerter; ~ed embarrassé, gêné; dans l'embarras; **em'bar·rass·ing** □ embarrassant; gênant; **em'bar·rass·ment** embarras *m*, gêne *f*.

em·bas·sy ['embəsi] ambassade *f*.

em·bat·tle ✕ [im'bætl] ranger en bataille; ~d crénelé. [châsser.)

em·bed [im'bed] enfoncer; en-)

em·bel·lish [im'beliʃ] embellir, orner; enjoliver (*un conte*); **em'bel·lish·ment** embellissement *m*, ornement *m*; enjolivure *f*.

em·ber-days ['embədeiz] *pl.* les Quatre-Temps *m/pl.*

em·bers ['embəz] *pl.* cendres *f/pl.* ardentes; *fig.* cendres *f/pl.*

em·bez·zle [im'bezl] détourner, s'approprier; **em'bez·zle·ment** détournement *m* de fonds; **em'bez·zler** détourneur *m* de fonds.

em·bit·ter [im'bitə] remplir d'amertume; envenimer (*une querelle etc.*).

em·bla·zon(·ry) [im'bleizn(ri)] *see* blazon(ry).

em·blem ['embləm] emblème *m*; *sp.* insigne *m*; ⌀ devise *f*; **em·blem·at·ic**, **em·blem·at·i·cal** □ [embli'mætik(l)] emblématique.

em·bod·i·ment [im'bɔdimənt] incorporation *f*; personnification *f*; incarnation *f*; **em'bod·y** incarner; personnifier; incorporer (dans, *in*); réaliser; ✕ rassembler. [in).)

em·bog [im'bɔg] embourber (dans,)

em·bold·en [im'bouldn] enhardir.

em·bo·lism ⚕ ['embəlizm] embolie *f*.

em·bos·om [im'buzəm] cacher dans son sein; serrer contre son sein.

em·boss [im'bɔs] graver en relief; repousser (*du métal, du cuir*); **em'bossed** gravé en relief; repoussé, estampé.

em·bow·el [im'bauəl] éventrer.

em·brace [im'breis] **1.** *v/t.* embrasser (*a. une carrière*); saisir, profiter de (*une occasion*); adopter (*une cause, une philosophie*); contenir (dans, *in*); comprendre; envisager tous les aspects de; *v/i.* s'embrasser; **2.** étreinte *f*.

em·bra·sure [im'breiʒə] embrasure *f*.

em·bro·cate ['embrokeit] frictionner (à, *with*); **em·bro'ca·tion** embrocation *f*.

em·broi·der [im'brɔidə] broder (*a. fig.*); **em'broi·der·y** broderie *f* (*a. fig.*).

em·broil [im'brɔil] brouiller; embrouiller; **em'broil·ment** brouillement *m*; embrouillement *m*; brouille *f* (*entre personnes*).

em·bry·o ['embriou] **1.** embryon *m*; in ~ embryonnaire; F en herbe; **2.** (*ou* **em·bry·on·ic** [~'ɔnik]) *fig.* F en germe.

em·bus [im'bʌs] *v/t.* embarquer en autobus; *v/i.* s'embarquer dans un autobus.

em·cee F [em'siː] animateur (-trice *f*) *m*, présentateur (-trice *f*) *m*.

e·men·da·tion [iːmen'deiʃn] émendation *f*; correction *f*; **e·men·da·tor** correcteur *m*; **e'mend·a·to·ry** [~dətəri] rectificatif (-ive *f*).

em·er·ald ['emərəld] **1.** émeraude *f*; **2.** vert d'émeraude.

e·merge [i'məːdʒ] émerger, surgir, déboucher (de, *from*); *fig.* apparaître, surgir; **e'mer·gence** émergence *f*; **e'mer·gen·cy** urgence *f*; cas *m* imprévu; circonstance *f* critique; ~ *brake* frein *m* de secours; *téléph.* ~ *call* appel *m* urgent; ~ *exit* sortie *f* de secours; ~ *fund* masse *f* de secours; ~ *house* habitation *f* provisoire; ✈ ~ *landing* atterrissage *m* forcé; ~ *man* ouvrier *m* supplémentaire; remplaçant *m*; ~ *measure* mesure *f* extraordinaire; ~ *number* police-secours *f*; ~ *service* service *m* des urgences; **e'mer·gent 1.** émergent; surgissant; **2.** résultat *m*.

e·mer·sion [i'məːʃn] émersion *f*.

em·er·y ['eməri] émeri *m*; ~ *board* lime *f* émeri; **'~-pa·per** papier *m* d'émeri.

e·met·ic [i'metik] émétique (*a su./m*).

em·i·grant ['emigrənt] émigrant(e *f*) (*a. su./mf*); **em·i·grate** ['~greit] (faire) émigrer; **em·i·gra·tion** émigration *f*; **em·i·gra·to·ry** ['~grətəri] émigrant.

em·i·nence ['eminəns] éminence *f* (*titre*: ⌀); grandeur *f*; élévation *f*; monticule *m*; saillie *f*; **'em·i·nent**

□ *fig.* éminent, célèbre (pour *in*, *for*); '**em·i·nent·ly** par excellence.
em·is·sar·y ['emisəri] émissaire *m*; **e·mis·sion** [i'miʃn] émission *f* (*a. phys.,* ✝); lancement *m*.
e·mit [i'mit] dégager; lancer; laisser échapper; émettre (*une opinion, a.* ✝).   [(*a. su./m*).]
e·mol·li·ent [i'mɔliənt] émollient]
e·mol·u·ment [i'mɔljumənt] émolument *m*; ~s *pl.* appointements *m/pl.*
e·mo·tion [i'mouʃn] émotion *f*; émoi *m*; **e'mo·tion·al** □ émotionnable; facile à émouvoir; ✝ émotif (-ive *f*); **e·mo·tion·al·i·ty** [~'næliti] émotivité *f*; **e'mo·tive** émotif (-ive *f*); émouvant.
em·pan·el [im'pænl] inscrire (*q.*) sur la liste du jury.
em·per·or ['empərə] empereur *m*.
em·pha·sis ['emfəsis], *pl.* -ses [~si:z] force *f*; accentuation *f*; insistance *f*; accent *m* (*a. gramm.*); **em·pha·size** ['~saiz] accentuer; appuyer sur; souligner; faire ressortir; **em·phat·ic** [im'fætik] (~ally) énergique; positif (-ive *f*); autoritaire; *be* ~ *that* faire valoir que.
em·pire ['empaiə] empire *m*.
em·pir·ic [em'pirik] **1.** empirique *m*, empiriste *m*; *péj.* charlatan *m*; **2.** (*usu.* **em'pir·i·cal** □) empirique.
em·place·ment ⚔ [im'pleismənt] emplacement *m*.   [en avion.]
em·plane [im'plein] (faire) monter]
em·ploy [im'plɔi] **1.** employer; faire usage de; ~ *oneself* s'occuper (à *in, on, for*); **2.** emploi *m*; *in the* ~ *of* au service de; **em·ploy·é** [ɔm'plɔiei] employé *m*; **em·ploy·ée** [~] employée *f*; **em·ploy·ee** [em·plɔi'i:] employé(e *f*) *m*; ~s' *spokesman* porte-parole *m* des employés; **em·ploy·er** [im'plɔiə] patron(ne *f*) *m*; maître(sse *f*) *m*; employeur *m*; **em'ploy·ment** emploi *m*; occupation *f*; situation *f*, place *f*; travail *m*; ~ *agency* bureau *m* de placement; *full* ~ plein(-)emploi *m*; *place of* ~ emploi *m*; bureau *m*, atelier *m etc.*; ♀ *Exchange* Bourse *f* du Travail.
em·po·ri·um [em'pɔ:riəm] entrepôt *m*; marché *m*; F grand magasin *m*.
em·pow·er [im'pauə] autoriser; donner (plein) pouvoir à (*q.*) (pour *inf., to inf.*); rendre capable (de *inf., to inf.*).

em·press ['empris] impératrice *f*.
emp·ti·er ['emptiə] videur *m*; '**emp·ti·ness** vide *m*; *fig.* néant *m*, vanité *f*; **emp·ty** □ **1.** vide; *fig.* vain; F creux (creuse *f*), affamé; **2.** (se) vider; (se) décharger; **3.** bouteille *f* ou caisse *f ou* ✝ emballage *m* vide; '**emp·ty-hand·ed** les mains vides; *return* ~ *a.* revenir bredouille.
em·pur·ple [im'pə:pl] empourprer.
e·mu *orn.* ['i:mju:] émeu *m*.
em·u·late ['emjuleit] imiter; rivaliser avec; **em·u·la·tion** émulation *f*; '**em·u·la·tive** ['~lətiv] qui tente de rivaliser (avec, *of*); **em·u·la·tor** ['~leitə] émule *mf*; '**em·u·lous** □ émulateur (-trice *f*) (de, *of*).
e·mul·sion ⚗ [i'mʌlʃn] émulsion *f*.
en·a·ble [i'neibl] rendre capable, mettre à même (de, *to*); donner pouvoir à (*q.*) (de *inf., to inf.*).
en·act [i'nækt] décréter (*une loi, une mesure*); *théâ.* jouer, représenter; *be* ~*ed* se dérouler; **en'ac·tive** décrétant; représentant; **en'act·ment** promulgation *f*; loi *f*; décret *m*.
en·am·el [i'næml] **1.** émail (*pl.* -aux) *m*; (peinture *f* au) vernis *m*; F ripolin *m*; **2.** émailler; peindre au ripolin; *poét.* embellir, orner.
en·am·o(u)r [i'næmə] rendre amoureux (-euse *f*); ~*d* épris, amoureux (-euse *f*) (de, *of*).
en·cage [in'keidʒ] mettre en cage.
en·camp ⚔ [in'kæmp] camper; **en'camp·ment** camp(ement) *m*.
en·case [in'keis] enfermer (dans, *in*); F revêtir (de, *with*); **en'case·ment** revêtement *m*; enveloppe *f*.
en·cash·ment ✝ [in'kæʃmənt] recette *f*; encaissement *m*.
en·caus·tic [en'kɔ:stik] encaustique (*a. su./f*).
en·chain [in'tʃein] enchaîner.
en·chant [in'tʃɑ:nt] ensorceler; *fig.* enchanter, ravir; **en'chant·er** enchanteur *m*; **en'chant·ing** ravissant; **en'chant·ment** enchantement *m*; **en'chant·ress** enchanteresse *f*.
en·chase [in'tʃeis] enchâsser (*a. fig.*); sertir (*une pierre précieuse*); graver; incruster.
en·ci·pher [in'saifə] chiffrer.
en·cir·cle [in'sə:kl] ceindre; entourer; *surt.* ⚔ envelopper; **en'cir·cle·ment** *pol.* encerclement *m*.
en·close [in'klouz] enclore; en-

tourer; renfermer; joindre (à une lettre, *in a letter*); *eccl.* cloîtrer; ~**d** herewith sous ce pli, ci-joint; **en'clo·sure** [~ʒə] clôture *f* (*a. eccl.*); (en)clos *m*; ✝ pièce *f* annexée *ou* jointe.

en·code [in'koud] chiffrer.

en·co·mi·ast [en'koumiæst] panégyriste *m*; **en'co·mi·um** [~mjən] panégyrique *m*, éloge *m*.

en·com·pass [in'kʌmpəs] entourer; renfermer.

en·core [ɔŋ'kɔ:] 1. bis!; 2. bisser; crier bis; 3. bis *m*.

en·coun·ter [in'kauntə] 1. rencontre *f*; duel *m*; combat *m*; *fig.* assaut *m* (*d'esprit*); 2. rencontrer; éprouver (*des difficultés*); affronter.

en·cour·age [in'kʌridʒ] encourager; inciter; aider, soutenir; favoriser; **en'cour·age·ment** encouragement *m*; **en'cour·ag·er** celui (celle *f*) qui encourage.

en·croach [in'krəutʃ] empiéter (sur, [up]on), léser (les droits de *q.*); ~ *upon s.o.'s kindness* abuser de la bonté de *q.*; **en'croach·ment** ([up]on) empiétement *m* (sur); anticipation *f* (sur), usurpation *f* (de).

en·crust [in'krʌst] (s')incruster.

en·cum·ber [in'kʌmbə] encombrer (de, *with*); gêner; grever (*une propriété*); **en'cum·brance** embarras *m*; charge *f* (*a. fig.*); servitude *f*; *without* ~ sans charges de famille.

en·cy·clo·p(a)e·di·a [ensaiklo'pi:djə] encyclopédie *f*; **en·cy·clo·'p(a)e·dic** encyclopédique.

end [end] 1. bout *m*, extrémité *f*; fin *f*; limite *f*; but *m*, dessein *m*; *be at an* ~ être au bout (de qch., *of s.th.*); être fini; *no* ~ *of* une infinité de, infiniment de, ... sans nombre; *have s.th. at one's fingers'* ~*s* savoir qch. sur le bout du doigt; *in the* ~ à la fin, enfin; à la longue; *on* ~ de suite; debout; *stand on* ~ se dresser (sur la tête); *to the* ~ *that* afin que (*sbj.*), afin de (*inf.*); *to no* ~ en vain; *to this* ~ dans ce but; *make an* ~ *of*, *put an* ~ *to* mettre fin à, achever; *make both* ~*s meet* joindre les deux bouts; s'en tirer; 2. finir, (se) terminer, (s')achever.

en·dan·ger [in'deindʒə] mettre en danger.

en·dear [in'diə] rendre cher; **en-**

'**dear·ing** qui rend sympathique; attirant; **en'dear·ment** (*ou term of* ~) mot *m* tendre; attrait *m*.

en·deav·o(u)r [in'devə] 1. effort *m*, tentative *f*; 2. (*to inf.*) essayer (de *inf.*); chercher (à *inf.*); s'efforcer (de *inf.*).

en·dem·ic ✻ [en'demik] 1. (*a.* en-'dem·i·cal □) endémique; 2. maladie *f* endémique.

end·ing ['endiŋ] fin *f*; achèvement *m*; *gramm.* terminaison *f*.

en·dive ✿ ['endiv] chicorée *f*; *a.* endive *f*.

end·less □ ['endlis] sans fin (*a.* ⊕); infini; continuel(le *f*).

end-of-term [endəv'tə:m] *école*: de fin de semestre.

en·dorse ✝ [in'dɔ:s] endosser (*un document*); mentionner (*qch.*) au verso de; avaliser (*un effet*); viser (*un passeport*); *fig.* appuyer; *endorsing ink* encre *f* à tampon; **en·dor·see** ✝ [endɔ:'si:] endossataire *mf*; **en·dorse·ment** [in'dɔ:smənt] ✝ endos(sement) *m*; *fig.* approbation *f*; adhésion *f*; **en'dors·er** ✝ endosseur *m*.

en·dow [in'dau] doter (*une église etc.*); fonder; *fig.* douer; **en'dow·ment** dotation *f*; fondation *f*; *fig.* don *m* (= qualité); ~ *assurance* assurance *f* à terme fixe.

en·due [in'dju:] revêtir (*un vêtement*; *q.* de, *with*); *usu. fig.* investir; douer.

en·dur·a·ble [in'djuərəbl] supportable; **en'dur·ance** endurance *f*, résistance *f*; patience *f*; *past* ~ insupportable; ~ *flight* vol *m* d'endurance; ~ *run* course *f* d'endurance; **en·dure** [in'djuə] *v/t.* supporter, souffrir (*qch.*); *v/i.* durer, rester, persister.

end·way(s) ['endwei(z)], **end·wise** ['~waiz] debout; bout à bout.

en·e·ma ✻ ['enimə] lavement *m*; irrigateur *m*.

en·e·my ['enimi] 1. ennemi(e *f*) *m*; *the* ♀ le diable *m*; *sl. how goes the* ~? quelle heure est-il?; 2. ennemi(e *f*).

en·er·get·ic [enə'dʒetik] (~*ally*) énergique; **'en·er·gize** stimuler; ⚡ aimanter; amorcer (*un dynamo*); **'en·er·gy** énergie *f* (*a. phys.*); force *f*; vigueur *f*; ~ *crisis* crise *f* de l'énergie; **'en·er·gy-sav·ing** qui économise de l'énergie, à faible consommation d'énergie.

en·er·vate ['enɔ:veit] énerver, affaiblir; **en·er'va·tion** affaiblissement m; mollesse f.

en·fee·ble [in'fi:bl] affaiblir; **en·'fee·ble·ment** affaiblissement m.

en·feoff [in'fef] investir d'un fief; inféoder (*une terre*); **en'feoff·ment** inféodation f.

en·fi·lade ✕ [enfi'leid] **1.** enfilade f; **2.** battre d'enfilade.

en·fold [in'fould] envelopper.

en·force [in'fɔ:s] faire valoir (*un argument*); exécuter (*une loi*); rendre effectif (-ive f); faire observer; imposer (à q., *upon s.o.*); **en'force·ment** application f; exécution f; contrainte f; mise f en force.

en·fran·chise [in'fræntʃaiz] donner le droit de vote à (q.) *ou* de cité à (*une ville*); affranchir (*un esclave*); **en'fran·chise·ment** [~tʃizmɔnt] admission f au suffrage; affranchissement m.

en·gage [in'geidʒ] *v/t.* engager (*l'honneur, la parole, un domestique*); embaucher (*un ouvrier*); retenir, réserver, louer (*une place*); mettre en prise (*un engrenage*); fixer (*l'attention*); attaquer (*l'ennemi*); attirer (*l'affection*); be ~d être fiancé; être pris; être occupé (*a. téléph.*); be ~d in être occupé à; prendre part à; lier (*une conversation*); *v/i.* s'engager; s'obliger (à, to); s'embarquer (dans, in); ✕ livrer combat, en venir aux mains; **en'gaged sig·nal** *ou* **tone** téléph. signal m d'occupé *ou* pas libre; **en·gage·ment** engagement m; promesse f; poste m, situation f; rendez-vous m; invitation f; fiançailles f/pl.; ⊕ mise f en prise; ✕ action f, combat m.

en·gag·ing □ [in'geidʒiŋ] *fig.* attrayant, séduisant.

en·gen·der [in'dʒendɔ] *fig.* faire naître; engendrer; produire.

en·gine ['endʒin] machine f, appareil m; 🚂 locomotive f; ⊕ moteur m; *fig.* engin m, instrument m; **'en·gined** ✕ à ... moteurs.

en·gine...: '~-**driv·er** 🚂 mécanicien m; '~-**fit·ter** ajusteur m mécanicien.

en·gi·neer [endʒi'niɔ] **1.** ingénieur m; *fig.* agenceur (-euse f) m, *péj.* machinateur (-trice f) m; ✕ soldat m du génie, ~s pl. le génie m; ⚓ ingénieur m maritime; 🚂 *Am.* mécanicien m; **2.** construire; F machiner, manigancer; **en·gi'neer·ing** art m de l'ingénieur; génie m; technique f; construction f mécanique; F manœuvres f/pl.; *attr.* du génie; ~ college école f des arts et métiers.

en·gine·man ['endʒinmɔn] machiniste m; 🚂 mécanicien m; **en·gine·ry** ['~nɔri] machines f/pl.; *fig.* machinations f/pl.

en·gird [in'gɔ:d] [*irr.* (gird)] ceindre (de, with).

Eng·lish ['iŋgliʃ] **1.** anglais; the ~ Channel la Manche; **2.** *ling.* anglais m; the ~ pl. les Anglais m/pl.; ~-speaking anglophone (*pays etc.*), qui parle anglais (*personne*); **'Eng·lish·man** Anglais m; **'Eng·lish·wom·an** Anglaise f. [tir.]

en·gorge [in'gɔ:dʒ] dévorer, englou-

en·graft ✗ [in'grɑ:ft] greffer (sur in[to], [up]on); *fig.* inculquer (à, in).

en·grain [in'grein] teindre grand teint; *fig.* enraciner; **en'grained** encrassé; enraciné.

en·grave [in'greiv] graver (*a. fig.*); **en'grav·er** *personne:* graveur m; *outil:* burin m; ~ on *copper* chalcographe m; **en'grav·ing** gravure f (*sur bois, acier*); estampe f.

en·gross [in'grous] écrire en grosse; rédiger; absorber (*l'attention, q.*); s'emparer de; ~ing hand écriture f en grosse; **en'gross·ment** 🏛 (rédaction f de la) grosse f; absorption f (dans, in).

en·gulf [in'gʌlf] *fig.* engloutir, engouffrer; be ~ed *a.* être sombré.

en·hance [in'hɑ:ns] rehausser; augmenter; relever; **en'hance·ment** rehaussement m; augmentation f; ✝ *prix:* hausse f.

e·nig·ma [i'nigmɔ] énigme f; **e·nig·mat·ic, e·nig·mat·i·cal** □ [enig'mætik(l)] énigmatique.

en·join [in'dʒɔin] enjoindre, imposer; recommander (à q., [up]on s.o.); ~ s.o. from (*gér.*) interdire à q. de (*inf.*).

en·joy [in'dʒɔi] prendre plaisir à; goûter; jouir de; ~ o.s. s'amuser; se divertir; I ~ my dinner je trouve le dîner bon; **en'joy·a·ble** agréable; excellent; **en'joy·ment** plaisir m; 🏛 jouissance f.

en·kin·dle [in'kindl] allumer; *fig.* enflammer.

en·lace [in'leis] enlacer.

en·large [in'lɑːdʒ] *v/t.* agrandir (*a. phot.*); élargir; augmenter; *v/i.* s'agrandir, s'élargir, s'étendre (sur, [up]on); **en'large·ment** agrandissement *m* (*a. phot.*); élargissement *m*; accroissement *m*; **en'larg·er** *phot.* agrandisseur *m*.

en·light·en [in'laitn] *fig.* éclairer (q. sur qch., s.o. on s.th.); **en'light·en·ment** éclaircissements *m/pl.*

en·list [in'list] *v/t.* enrôler (*un soldat*); engager, rattacher (à, in); ✕ ﹏ed man (simple) soldat *m*; *v/i.* s'enrôler; s'engager (dans in).

en·liv·en [in'laivn] animer; *fig.* égayer, stimuler (*surt.* ♱).

en·mesh [in'meʃ] prendre dans un piège; empêtrer.

en·mi·ty ['enmiti] inimitié *f.*

en·no·ble [i'noubl] anoblir; *fig.* ennoblir.

e·nor·mi·ty [i'nɔːmiti] énormité *f*; **e'nor·mous** □ énorme.

e·nough [i'nʌf] assez; *sure* ﹏! assurément!; c'est bien vrai!; *well* ﹏ passablement; très bien; *be kind* ﹏ *to* (*inf.*) avoir la bonté de (*inf.*).

e·nounce [i'nauns] *see* enunciate.

en·quire [in'kwaiə] *see* inquire.

en·rage [in'reidʒ] enrager, rendre furieux (-euse *f*); **en'raged** furieux (-euse *f*) (contre, at).

en·rap·ture [in'ræptʃə] ravir.

en·rich [in'ritʃ] enrichir; ✔ fertiliser (*le sol*); **en'rich·ment** enrichissement *m*.

en·rol(l) [in'roul] *v/t.* immatriculer (*un étudiant*); inscrire (*dans une liste*); engager (*des ouvriers*); ✕ enrôler, encadrer; *v/i.* (*ou* ﹏ *o.s.*) s'engager; s'inscrire (à une société, in a society); se faire inscrire; **en'rol(l)·ment** enrôlement *m*; engagement *m*.

en route [ɑ̃ːnˈruːt] en route.

en·sconce [in'skɔns] cacher; ﹏ *o.s.* se camper, se blottir (dans, in).

en·shrine [in'ʃrain] enchâsser (*a. fig.*) (dans, in). [ensevelir.]

en·shroud [in'ʃraud] envelopper,]

en·sign ['ensain] étendard *m*, drapeau *m*; ♣ ['ensn] pavillon *m*; *Am.* enseigne *m*.

en·si·lage ['ensilidʒ] 1. ensil(ot)age *m*; 2. (*a.* **en·sile** [in'sail]) ensil(ot)er.

en·slave [in'sleiv] réduire à l'esclavage; asservir; **en'slave·ment** asservissement *m*; **en'slav·er** *surt. fig.* ensorceleuse *f.*

en·snare [in'snɛə] prendre au piège (*a. fig.*); *fig.* séduire (*une femme*).

en·sue [in'sjuː] s'ensuivre (de from, on).

en·sure [in'ʃuə] (*against, from*) garantir (de), assurer (contre).

en·tab·la·ture △ [en'tæblətʃə] entablement *m.*

en·tail [in'teil] 1. substitution *f*; bien *m* substitué; 2. (*on*) substituer (*un bien*) (au profit de); entraîner (*des conséquences*) (pour); comporter (*des difficultés*) (pour).

en·tan·gle [in'tæŋgl] emmêler; enchevêtrer (*a. fig.*); *fig.* empêtrer; **en'tan·gle·ment** embrouillement *m*, enchevêtrement *m*; embarras *m*; ✕ barbelé *m*, -s *m/pl.*

en·ter ['entə] *v/t.* entrer dans, pénétrer dans; monter dans (*un taxi etc.*); inscrire, porter (*un nom*) dans une liste; entrer à (*l'armée, une école*); s'inscrire à (*une université etc.*); prendre part à (*une discussion, une querelle*); ♱ déclarer en douane, ♱ inscrire (*au grand livre*); faire (*des protestations*); dresser (*un animal*); ♱ ﹏ *up v/t.* inscrire (à un compte); *v/i.* entrer, s'inscrire, *sp.* s'engager (pour, for); entrer (à, at school etc.); ﹏ *into* entrer dans (*les affaires, les détails*); entrer en (*conversation*); prendre part à; partager (*des idées, des sentiments*); *fig.* contracter (*un mariage*), conclure (*un marché*), fournir (*des explications*); ﹏ (*up*)*on* entrer en (*fonctions*); entreprendre; embrasser (*une carrière*); entrer dans (*une année*); entamer (*un sujet*); s'engager dans (*qch.*); ♱♱ entrer en possession de (*qch.*); *théâ.* ﹏ *Macbeth* entre Macbeth; **en'ter·a·ble** ♱ importable; **en'ter·ing** entrée *f*; inscription *f*; *attr.* d'entrée, d'attaque, de pénétration.

en·ter·ic 🕮 [en'terik] entérique; **en·ter·i·tis** [⸝⸜tə'raitis] entérite *f.*

en·ter·prise ['entəpraiz] entreprise *f*; *fig.* initiative *f*; ♱ *private* ﹏ entreprise *f* privée; le secteur privé; **'en·ter·pris·ing** □ entreprenant.

en·ter·tain [entə'tein] *v/t.* amuser; divertir; recevoir (*des invités*); fêter; accepter, accueillir (*une proposition*

etc.); entretenir (*la correspondance*);
avoir (*des doutes, une opinion*); être
animé de (*un sentiment*); v/i.
recevoir, donner une réception;
en·ter'tain·er hôte(sse *f*) *m*; comique *m*; diseur (-euse *f*) *m*; **en·ter-
'tain·ing** □ amusant, divertissant;
en·ter'tain·ment hospitalité *f*;
soirée *f*; spectacle *m*; divertissement *m*, *a.* accueil *m*; ~ tax taxe *f*
sur les spectacles.
en·thral(l) [in'θrɔ:l] asservir; *fig.*
captiver, charmer.
en·throne [in'θroun] mettre sur le
trône; introniser (*un roi, un évêque*);
en'throne·ment, **en·thron·i·za-
tion** [enθronai'zeiʃn] intronisa-
tion *f*.
en·thuse F [in'θju:z] s'enthousiasmer (de, pour *about*, over).
en·thu·si·asm [in'θju:ziæzm] enthousiasme *m*; **en'thu·si·ast** [~æst]
enthousiaste *mf* (de, for); **en·thu·
si'as·tic** (~ally) enthousiaste (de *at*,
about); passionné.
en·tice [in'tais] séduire, attirer; **en-
'tice·ment** séduction *f*; attrait *m*;
en'tic·er séducteur (-trice *f*) *m*;
en'tic·ing □ séduisant; attrayant.
en·tire [in'taiə] **1.** □ entier (-ère *f*)
(*a. cheval*), complet (-ète *f*), tout;
intact; **2.** entier *m*; totalité *f*; **en-
'tire·ly** entièrement, tout entier;
du tout au tout; **en'tire·ness** inté-
gralité *f*; **en'tire·ty** intégr(al)ité *f*.
en·ti·tle [in'taitl] intituler; donner à
(*q.*) le droit (à, to).
en·ti·ty *phls.* ['entiti] entité *f*; *legal* ~
personne *f* juridique.
en·tomb [in'tu:m] ensevelir; **en-
'tomb·ment** ensevelissement *m*.
en·to·mol·o·gy *zo.* [entə'mɔlədʒi]
entomologie *f*.
en·trails ['entreilz] *pl.* entrailles
f/pl.
en·train ✕ [in'trein] (s')embarquer
en chemin de fer.
en·trance[1] ['entrəns] entrée *f* (dans,
into); *a.* en fonctions, into [ou upon]
office); accès *m*; pénétration *f*; (*a.* ~
fee) prix *m* d'entrée; *théâ.* entrée *f*
en scène; ~ examination examen *m*
d'entrée.
en·trance[2] [in'trɑ:ns] ravir, extasier.
en·trant ['entrənt] débutant(e *f*) *m*;
sp. inscrit(e *f*) *m*.
en·trap [in'træp] prendre au piège;

amener (*q.*) par ruse (à *inf.*, into
gér.).
en·treat [in'tri:t] supplier, prier;
demander instamment (à, of); **en-
'treat·y** prière *f*, supplication *f*.
en·trench ✕ [in'trentʃ] retrancher;
~ upon empiéter sur; **en'trench-
ment** retranchement *m*.
en·tre·pre·neur [ɔntrəprə'nə:]
entrepreneur *m* (de); **en·tre-
pre·neur·i·al** [~'nə:riəl] des entre-
preneurs.
en·trust [in'trʌst] confier (qch. à *q.*,
s.th. to s.o.); charger (*q.* de qch.,
s.o. with s.th.).
en·try ['entri] entrée *f*; inscription *f*;
✝ prise *f* de possession, entrée *f*
en jouissance (de, [up]on); ✝ comptabilité: partie *f*, compte: article *m*;
sp. liste *f* des inscrits; *sp.* inscription
f; ⚓ élément *m* (*du journal*); *Am.*
commencement *m*; no ~ entrée
interdite; *rue*: sens interdit; ~ permit permis *m* d'entrée; ~ visa visa *m*
d'entrée; make an ~ of s.th. passer
qch. en écriture; bookkeeping by
double (single) ~ tenue *f* des livres *ou*
comptabilité *f* en partie double
(simple).
en·twine [in'twain], **en·twist** [in-
'twist] (s')entrelacer.
e·nu·mer·ate [i'nju:məreit] énumérer; **e·nu·mer'a·tion** énumération *f*.
e·nun·ci·ate [i'nʌnsieit] prononcer,
articuler; énoncer, exprimer (*une
opinion*); **e·nun·ci·a·tion** prononciation *f*, articulation *f*; *opinion*:
énonciation *f*; *problème*: énoncé *m*.
en·vel·op [in'veləp] envelopper (*a.*
✕); *fig.* voiler; **en·ve·lope** ['envi-
loup], *Am. a.* **en·vel·op** [in'veləp]
enveloppe *f*; ⚕, *biol.* tunique *f*; in
an ~ sous enveloppe; **en·vel·op-
ment** [in'veləpmənt] enveloppement *m*; *biol.* enveloppe *f*.
en·ven·om [in'venəm] empoisonner; *fig.* envenimer.
en·vi·a·ble □ ['enviəbl] enviable,
digne d'envie; **'en·vi·er** envieux
(-euse *f*) *m*; **'en·vi·ous** envieux
(-euse *f*) (de, of).
en·vi·ron [in'vaiərən] entourer, environner (de with); **en'vi·ron·ment**
environnement *m*; milieu *m*; ambiance *f*; **en·vi·ron·men·tal**
[~'mentl] du milieu; de l'environnement; écologiste; **en·vi·ron'men-**

tal·ist environnementaliste *mf*; **en·vi·rons** [ˈenvirənz] *pl.* environs *m/pl.*, alentours *m/pl.*; voisinage *m*.

en·vis·age [inˈvizidʒ] envisager (*un danger*); faire face à; se proposer (*un but*).

en·vi·sion [inˈviʒən] prévoir.

en·voy [ˈenvɔi] envoyé *m*.

en·vy [ˈenvi] **1.** envie *f* (au sujet de qch. *of*, *at s.th.*; de q., *of s.o.*); **2.** envier (qch. à q., *s.o. s.th.*); porter envie à (*q.*).

en·wrap [inˈræp] envelopper, enrouler.

en·zyme *biol.* [ˈenzaim] enzyme *m*.

e·pergne [iˈpəːn] surtout *m* (*de table*).

e·phem·er·a *zo.* [iˈfemərə], **eˈphem·er·on** [ˌ.rɔn], *pl. a.* **-er·a** [ˌ.ərə] éphémère *m*; *fig.* chose *f* éphémère; **eˈphem·er·al** éphémère; passager (-ère *f*).

ep·ic [ˈepik] **1.** (*a.* **ˈep·i·cal** □) épique; **2.** épopée *f*.

ep·i·cure [ˈepikjuə] gourmet *m*, gastronome *m*; **ep·i·cu·re·an** [ˌ.ˈriən] épicurien(ne *f*) (*a. su./mf*).

ep·i·dem·ic ⚕ [epiˈdemik] **1.** (ˌ.ally) épidémique; ~ *disease* = **2.** épidémie *f*.   [derme *m.*]

ep·i·der·mis *anat.* [epiˈdəːmis] épi-⌡

ep·i·gram [ˈepigræm] épigramme *f*; **ep·i·gram·mat·ic**, **ep·i·gram·mat·i·cal** □ [ˌ.grəˈmætik(l)] épigrammatique.

ep·i·lep·sy [ˈepilepsi] épilepsie *f*; **ep·i·lep·tic** □ épileptique (*a. su./mf*).

ep·i·logue [ˈepilɔg] épilogue *m*.

E·piph·a·ny [iˈpifəni] Épiphanie *f*; F jour *m* des Rois.

e·pis·co·pa·cy [iˈpiskəpəsi] épiscopat *m*; gouvernement *m* par les évêques; **eˈpis·co·pal** épiscopal (-aux *m/pl.*); **e·pis·co·pa·li·an** [ˌ.ˈpeiljən] membre *m* de l'Église épiscopale; **eˈpis·co·pate** [ˌ.pit] épiscopat *m*; évêques *m/pl.*; évêché *m*.

ep·i·sode [ˈepisoud] épisode *m*; **ep·i·sod·ic**, **ep·i·sod·i·cal** □ [ˌ.ˈsodik(l)] épisodique.

e·pis·tle [iˈpisl] épître *f*; *fig.* lettre *f*; **eˈpis·to·lar·y** [ˌ.tələri] épistolaire.

ep·i·taph [ˈepitaːf] épitaphe *f*.

ep·i·thet [ˈepiθet] épithète *f*.

e·pit·o·me [iˈpitəmi] abrégé *m*, résumé *m*; **eˈpit·o·mize** abréger, résumer.

ep·och [ˈiːpɔk] époque *f*.

Ep·som salts [ˈepsəmˈsɔːlts] *pl.* sulfate *m* de magnésie; sels *m/pl.* anglais.

eq·ua·bil·i·ty [ekwəˈbiliti] uniformité *f*, égalité *f*; **ˈeq·ua·ble** □ uniforme; égal (-aux *m/pl.*) (*a. fig.*).

e·qual [ˈiːkwl] **1.** □ égal (-aux *m/pl.*); ~ *to* à la hauteur de; égal à; ~ *opportunities pl.* égalité *f* des chances, chances *f/pl.* égales; ~ *rights pl.* égalité *f* des droits; **2.** égal (-e *f*) *m*; *my* ~*s pl.* mes pareil(le)s; **3.** égaler; *not to be* ~*led* sans égal; **eˈqual·i·ty** [iˈkwɔliti] égalité *f*; **eˈqual·i·za·tion** [iːkwəlaiˈzeiʃn] égalisation *f*; compensation *f*; **ˈe·qual·ize** *v/t.* égaliser (avec *to*, *with*); *v/i. sp.* marquer égalité de points; **ˈe·qual·iz·er** *sp.* but *m* égalisateur.

e·qua·nim·i·ty [iːkwəˈnimiti] sérénité *f*; tranquillité *f* d'esprit.

e·quate [iˈkweit] égaler (à *to*, *with*); Å mettre en équation; **eˈqua·tion** égalisation *f*; Å, *astr.* équation *f*; **eˈqua·tor** équateur *m*; *at the* ~ sous l'équateur; **e·qua·to·ri·al** □ [ekwəˈtɔːriəl] équatorial (-aux *m/pl.*).

e·quer·ry [iˈkweri] écuyer *m*.

e·ques·tri·an [iˈkwestriən] **1.** équestre; d'équitation; **2.** cavalier (-ère *f*) *m*.   [équilatéral (-aux *m/pl.*).]

e·qui·lat·er·al □ [ˈiːkwiˈlætərəl]⌡

e·qui·li·brate [iːkwiˈlaibreit] *v/t.* mettre en équilibre; contrebalancer; *v/i.* être en équilibre; **eˈquil·i·brist** [iːˈkwilibrist] équilibriste *mf*; danseur (-euse *f*) *m* de corde; **eˈquil·ib·ri·um** [ˌ.əm] équilibre *m*.

e·quine [ˈiːkwain] équin; du cheval; chevalin (*race*).

e·qui·noc·tial [iːkwiˈnɔkʃl] équinoxial (-aux *m/pl.*); **e·qui·nox** [ˈ.nɔks] équinoxe *m*.

e·quip [iˈkwip] équiper; monter (*une maison, une usine*); **eq·ui·page** [ˈekwipidʒ] équipement *m*; *véhicule:* équipage *m*; † suite *f*; **eˈquip·ment** [iˈkwipmənt] équipement *m*; *maison:* aménagement *m*; ⊕ outillage *m*.

e·qui·poise [ˈekwipɔiz] **1.** équilibre *m*; poids *m* égal; **2.** équilibrer.

eq·ui·ta·ble □ [ˈekwitəbl] équitable; **ˈeq·ui·ty** justice *f*; ⚖ équité *f*, droit *m* équitable.

e·quiv·a·lence [iˈkwivələns] équivalence *f*; **eˈquiv·a·lent** équivalent (à, *to*) (*a. su./m*).

e·quiv·o·cal □ [i'kwivəkl] équivoque; ambigu(ë *f*); **e·quiv·o·cal·i·ty** [‿'kæliti] caractère *m ou* expression *f* équivoque; **e'quiv·o·cate** [‿keit] ˙équivoquer; tergiverser; **e·quiv·o'ca·tion** équivocation *f*, tergiversation *f*.

eq·ui·voque, eq·ui·voke ['ekwivouk] équivoque *f*; jeu *m* de mots.

e·ra ['iərə] ère *f*; époque *f*; âge *m*.

e·rad·i·cate [i'rædikeit] déraciner; **e·rad·i'ca·tion** déracinement *m*; *fig.* extirpation *f*.

e·rase [i'reiz] effacer (*a. fig.*), gratter, raturer; *fig.* oblitérer; **e'ras·er** grattoir *m*; gomme *f*; **e'ra·sure** [‿ʒə] rature *f*; suppression *f*.

ere † [ɛə] **1.** *cj.* avant que (*sbj.*); **2.** *prp.* avant; ~ *this* déjà; ~ *long* sous peu; ~ *now* déjà, auparavant.

e·rect [i'rekt] **1.** □ droit; debout; **2.** dresser; ériger; élever (*une statue*); édifier (*une théorie etc.*); **e'rec·tion** dressage *m*; construction *f*; érection *f*; édifice *m*; **e'rect·ness** attitude *f* droite; position *f* perpendiculaire; **e'rec·tor** constructeur *m*; ⊕ monteur *m*; *anat.* érecteur *m*.

er·e·mite ['erimait] ermite *m*; **er·e·mit·ic** [‿'mitik] érémitique.

erg *phys.* [ə:g] mesure: erg *m*.

er·go·nom·ics [ə:gou'nɔmiks] *sg.* ergonomie *f*.

er·got ⚕ ['ə:gət] ergot *m*.

er·mine *zo.* ['ə:min] hermine *f* (*a. fourrure*); *fig.* (dignité *f* de) juge *m*.

e·rode [i'roud] éroder; ronger.

e·rog·e·nous [i'rɔdʒinəs] érogène.

e·ro·sion [i'rouʒn] érosion *f*; *mer etc.*: affouillement *m*; *chaudière*: usure *f*; **e'ro·sive** [‿siv] érosif (-ive *f*).

e·rot·ic [i'rɔtik] (poème *m*) érotique; **e'rot·i·cism** [‿sizm] érotisme *m*.

err [ə:] errer, se tromper; s'égarer (de, from).

er·rand ['erənd] commission *f*, course *f*; message *m*; *go* (*on*) ~s faire des commissions; '~-boy garçon *m* de courses; *hôtel*: chasseur *m*.

er·rant □ ['erənt] errant; *see knight-*~; **'er·rant·ry** vie *f* errante (*des chevaliers*).

er·rat·ic [i'rætik] (‿ally) capricieux (-euse *f*); irrégulier (-ère *f*); *géol.*, ⚕ erratique; ~ *fever* fièvre *f* inter-

mittente; **er·ra·tum** [i'reitəm], *pl.* -**ta** [‿tə] erratum *m* (*pl.* -ta).

er·ro·ne·ous □ [i'rounjəs] erroné.

er·ror ['erə] erreur *f*, faute *f*; ~ *of judgement* erreur *f* de jugement; ~ *rate* pourcentage *m* de fautes; ~*s and omissions excepted* sauf erreur ou omission.

e·ruc·ta·tion [i:rʌk'teiʃn] éructation *f*, renvoi *m*.

er·u·dite ['erudait] érudit, savant; **er·u·di·tion** [‿'diʃn] érudition *f*.

e·rupt [i'rʌpt] entrer en éruption (*volcan etc.*); percer (*dent*); **e'rup·tion** *volcan, a. fig., a.* ⚕ éruption *f*; *fig.* éclat *m*, accès *m*; **e'rup·tive** éruptif (-ive *f*).

er·y·sip·e·las ⚕ [eri'sipiləs] érysipèle *m*, érésipèle *m*.

es·ca·lade ⚔ [eskə'leid] escalade *f*.

es·ca·late ['eskəleit] (s')intensifier; monter (en flèche); **es·ca'la·tion** intensification *f*; montée *f* (en flèche).

es·ca·la·tor ['eskəleitə] escalier *m* roulant, escalator *m*.

es·ca·pade [eskə'peid] escapade *f*; **es·cape** [is'keip] **1.** *v/t.* échapper à, éviter; faillir (*inf., gér.*); *v/i.* s'échapper, s'évader (de, from); se dégager (*gaz etc.*); **2.** évasion *f*, fuite *f*; *vapeur*: échappement *m*; *attr.* d'échappement; ~ *hatch* trappe *f* de secours; *have a narrow* ~ l'échapper belle; **es'cape·ment** ⊕ *pendule etc.*: échappement *m*.

es·carp [is'ka:p] **1.** (*a.* **es'carp·ment**) talus *m*; escarpement *m*; **2.** escarper; taluter.

es·cheat ⚖ [is'tʃi:t] **1.** déshérence *f*; dévolution *f* d'héritage à l'État; **2.** *v/i.* tomber en déshérence; *v/t.* confisquer.

es·chew [is'tʃu:] éviter, renoncer à.

es·cort 1. ['eskɔ:t] escorte *f*; *bal:* cavalier *m*; **2.** [is'kɔ:t] escorter; accompagner.

es·cri·toire [eskri'twa:] secrétaire *m*.

es·cu·lent ['eskjulənt] comestible (*a. su./m*). [(*a.* ⊕, ♣).)

es·cutch·eon [is'kʌtʃn] écusson *m*)

Es·ki·mo ['eskimou] Esquimau (*pl.* -aux) *m*, Esquimaude *f*.

es·pal·ier ✔ [is'pæljə] espalier *m*.

es·pe·cial [is'peʃl] spécial (-aux *m/pl.*); particulier (-ère *f*); **es·pe·cial·ly** particulièrement, surtout; spécialement.

es·pi·al [is'paiəl] espionnage *m*; vue *f*. [nage *m*.]

es·pi·o·nage [espiə'na:3] espion-

es·pous·al [is'pauzl] *fig.* adoption *f* (de, of); **es'pouse** [~z] † donner en mariage; épouser (*a. fig.*); *fig.* embrasser.

es·py [is'pai] apercevoir, entrevoir.

es·quire [is'kwaiə] † écuyer *m*; *adresse:* Monsieur.

es·say 1. [e'sei] essayer; mettre à l'épreuve; **2.** ['esei] essai *m*; tentative *f* (de, at); *école:* composition *f*, dissertation *f*; **'es·say·ist** essayiste *mf*.

es·sence ['esns] essence *f*; extrait *m*; *fig.* fond *m*; **es·sen·tial** [i'senʃl] **1.** □ essentiel(le *f*), indispensable; ~ *likeness* ressemblance *f* fondamentale; ~ *oil* huile *f* essentielle; **2.** essentiel *m*; qualité *f* indispensable.

es·tab·lish [is'tæbliʃ] établir; fonder; créer; confirmer (*dans un emploi*); ratifier; démontrer; ~ *o.s.* s'établir; *2ed Church* Église *f* Établie; ~*ed merchant* marchand *m* patenté; **es'tab·lish·ment** établissement *m* (*a.* ⚓); création *f*; fondation *f*; ⚓ maison *f*; confirmation *f*; ménage *m*; ⚔, ⚓ effectif *m*.

es·tate [is'teit] état *m* (*a. pol.*), condition *f*; terre *f*, propriété *f*; ⚖ immeuble *m*, bien *m*, domaine *m*; ⚖ succession *f*; rang *m*; *personal* ~ biens *m/pl.* mobiliers; *real* ~ biens-fonds *m/pl.*, propriété *f* immobilière; ~ *agent* agent *m* de location; administrateur *m* foncier; ~ *duty* droits *m/pl.* de succession.

es·teem [is'ti:m] **1.** estime *f*, considération *f*; **2.** estimer; priser; considérer (comme, as).

Es·tho·ni·an [es'tounjən] **1.** Estonien(ne *f*) *m*; **2.** estonien(ne *f*).

es·ti·ma·ble ['estiməbl] estimable, digne d'estime.

es·ti·mate 1. ['estimeit] estimer; évaluer (à, at); **2.** ['~mit] calcul *m*, estimation *f*; évaluation *f*; appréciation *f*; † devis *m*; *parl.* ~*s pl.* prévisions *f/pl.* budgétaires; **es·ti·ma·tion** [~'meiʃn] jugement *m*; opinion *f*; considération *f*; **'es·ti·ma·tor** appréciateur *m*; estimateur *m*.

es·trange [is'treindʒ] aliéner l'estime (de q., *from s.o.*); ~*d couple* époux *m/pl.* séparés; **es'trange·ment** aliénation *f*; brouille *f*.

es·tro·gen *biol.* ['estrədʒen] œstrogène *m*.

es·tu·ar·y ['estjuəri] estuaire *m*.

et·cet·er·as [it'setrəz] *pl.* extra *m/inv.*

etch [etʃ] *v/t.* graver à l'eau-forte; *v/i.* faire de la gravure à l'eau-forte; **'etch·ing** (gravure *f* à l')eau-forte (*pl.* eaux-fortes) *f*; art *m* de graver à l'eau-forte.

e·ter·nal □ [i'tə:nl] éternel(le *f*); *fig.* sans fin; **e'ter·nal·ize** [~nəlaiz] éterniser; **e'ter·ni·ty** éternité *f*; **e·ter·nize** [i:'tə:naiz] éterniser.

e·ther ['i:θə] éther *m* (*a.* ⚗); **e·the·re·al** □ [i:'θiəriəl] éthéré; *fig.* impalpable; **'e·ther·ize** éthériser; endormir.

eth·i·cal □ ['eθikl] éthique; moral (-aux *m/pl.*); **'eth·ics** *usu. sg.* morale *f*, éthique *f*.

E·thi·o·pi·an [i:θi'oupjən] **1.** éthiopien(ne *f*); **2.** Éthiopien(ne *f*) *m*.

eth·nog·ra·phy [eθ'nɔgrəfi] ethnographie *f*; **eth·nol·o·gy** [~lədʒi] ethnologie *f*.

e·ti·o·late ['i:tioleit] (s')étioler.

et·i·quette [eti'ket] étiquette *f*; protocole *m*; cérémonial *m* (*souv.* de cour).

E·ton crop ['i:tn'krɔp] cheveux *m/pl.* à la garçonne; cheveux *m/pl.* garçon.

et·y·mo·log·i·cal □ [etimə'lɔdʒikl] étymologique; **et·y·mol·o·gy** [~'mɔlədʒi] étymologie *f*.

eu·cha·rist ['ju:kərist] eucharistie *f*.

Eu·clid [⚗ 'ju:klid] géométrie *f*.

eu·gen·ic *biol.* ['ju:'dʒenik] **1.** (~*ally*) eugénésique; **2.** ~*s sg.* eugénique *f*; eugénisme *m*.

eu·lo·gist ['ju:lədʒist] panégyriste *m*; **eu·lo·gize** ['~dʒaiz] faire l'éloge de, louer; **eu·lo·gy** ['~dʒi] éloge *m*.

eu·nuch ['ju:nək] eunuque *m*, castrat *m*.

eu·phe·mism ['ju:fimizm] euphémisme *m*; **eu·phe'mis·tic**, **eu·phe'mis·ti·cal** □ euphémique.

eu·phon·ic, **eu·phon·i·cal** □ [ju:'fɔnik(l)] euphonique; **eu·pho·ny** ['ju:fəni] euphonie *f*.

eu·phu·ism ['ju:fjuizm] euphuisme *m*; *fig.* préciosité *f*.

Eu·ro·cheque ['juərətʃek] eurochèque *m*; **Eu·ro·crat** [~'kræt] eurocrate *mf*.

Eu·ro·pe·an [juərə'pi:ən] **1.** européen(ne f); ~ *Community* Communauté f Économique Européenne; ~ *Parliament* Assemblée f européenne; **2.** Européen(ne f) m.

Eu·ro·pol·i·tics [ˈjuərəpɔlitiks] *sg.* politique f européenne.

eu·tha·na·si·a [juːθəˈneizjə] euthanasie f.

e·vac·u·ate [iˈvækjueit] évacuer (*région, ville, blessés, ventre*); *mot.* expulser (*des gaz brûlés*); **e·vac·u·a·tion** évacuation f; **e·vac·u·ee** évacué(e f) m.

e·vade [iˈveid] éviter, échapper à; éluder (*question, justice, obstacle*).

e·val·u·ate *surt.* Ⱥ [iˈvæljueit] évaluer; **e·val·u·a·tion** évaluation f.

ev·a·nesce [iːvəˈnes] s'effacer; **ev·a·nes·cence** évanouissement m; nature f éphémère; **ev·a·nes·cent** évanescent.

e·van·gel·ic, **e·van·gel·i·cal** □ [iːvænˈdʒelik(l)] évangélique; **e·van·ge·list** [iˈvændʒilist] évangéliste m; **e·van·ge·lize** prêcher l'évangile (à q.).

e·vap·o·rate [iˈvæpəreit] *v/t.* (faire) évaporer; *v/i.* s'évaporer (*a. fig.*); **~d** *fruit* fruits m/pl. secs; **~d** *milk* lait m concentré; **e·vap·o·ra·tion** évaporation f, vaporisation f.

e·va·sion [iˈveiʒn] évasion f, évitement m; subterfuge m; **e·va·sive** □ [~siv] évasif (-ive f); *fig.* be ~ faire une réponse évasive.

eve [iːv] veille f; *poét.* soir m; on the ~ of sur le point de; à la veille de.

e·ven¹ [ˈiːvn] **1.** *adj.* □ égal (-aux m/pl.); uni; plat, uniforme; régulier (-ère f); calme; pair (*nombre*); ~ *with the ground* au ras du sol, à fleur de terre; be ~ *with* être quitte avec (q.); *odd or* ~ pair ou impair; ✝ *of* ~ *date* de même date; **2.** *adv.* même; *devant comp.:* encore; *avec négation:* seulement, même; *not* ~ pas même; ~ *though*, ~ *if* quand même; **3.** *v/t.* égaliser, rendre égal.

e·ven² *poét.* [~] soir m.

e·ven...: '**~·hand·ed** impartial (-aux m/pl.); '**~·tem·pered** d'humeur égale.

eve·ning [ˈiːvniŋ] soir m; soirée f; ~ *class* cours m du soir; ~ *dress* tenue f *ou* toilette f de soirée; habit m (à queue); ~ *star* étoile f du berger.

e·ven·ness [ˈiːvənnis] égalité f; ré-

gularité f; sérénité f; impartialité f.

e·ven·song [ˈiːvənsɔŋ] office m du soir; vêpres f/pl.

e·vent [iˈvent] événement m; cas m; *fig.* résultat m, issue f; *sp.* réunion f sportive; *sp.* épreuve f; *box.* rencontre f; *athletic* ~s *pl.* concours m athlétique; *table of* ~s programme m; *at all* ~s en tout cas; quoi qu'il arrive; *in any* ~ en tout cas; *in the* ~ *of* dans le cas où (*cond.*); **e·vent·ful** [~ful] mémorable.

e·ven·tu·al □ [iˈventjuəl] éventuel (-le f); définitif (-ive f); **~·ly** à la fin, en fin de compte; par la suite; **e·ven·tu·al·i·ty** [~ˈæliti] éventualité f; **e·ven·tu·ate** [~eit] se terminer (par, *in*); aboutir (à, *in*).

ev·er [ˈevə] jamais; toujours; ~ *so* très, infiniment; ... au possible; *as soon as* ~ *I can* aussitôt que je pourrai; le plus vite possible; ~ *after*, ~ *since* depuis lors; depuis le jour où ...; ~ *and anon* de temps en temps; *for* ~, *a. for* ~ *and* ~, *for* ~ *and a day* à tout jamais; *liberty for* ~! vive la liberté!; F ~ *so much* infiniment; *for* ~ *so much* pour rien au monde; *I wonder who* ~ je me demande qui donc *ou* diable; F *the best* ~ le meilleur *etc.* du monde; *formule finale d'une lettre:* ~ *yours* bien cordialement; '**~·glade** *Am.* région f marécageuse; '**~·green** (arbre m) toujours vert; **~·last·ing 1.** □ éternel(le f); inusable; **2.** éternité f; ♀ immortelle f; '**~·more** toujours; éternellement.

ev·er·y [ˈevri] chaque; tous (toutes f/pl.) m/pl. les; ~ *bit as much* tout autant que; ~ *now and then* de temps à autre; par moments; **~·one** chacun(e f); ~ *other day* tous les deux jours; un jour sur deux; ~ *twenty years* tous les vingt ans; *her* ~ *movement* son moindre mouvement; '**~·bod·y**, '**~·one** chacun; tout le monde; '**~·day** de tous les jours; '**~·thing** tout; '**~·way** sous tous les rapports; de toutes les manières; '**~·where** partout.

e·vict [iˈvikt] évincer, expulser; **e·vic·tion** éviction f, expulsion f.

ev·i·dence [ˈevidəns] **1.** évidence f; preuve f; témoignage m; *fig.* signe m; *in* ~ présent, en évidence; *furnish* ~ *of* fournir des preuves de;

give ~ témoigner (de, *of*; en faveur de, *for*; contre, *against*); **2.** *v/t.* manifester, prouver (*qch.*); *v/i.* porter témoignage; **'ev·i·dent** □ évident, clair; patent; **ev·i·den·tial** □ [~-'denʃl] indicateur (-trice *f*) (de, *of*).

e·vil ['i:vl] **1.** □ mauvais; méchant; sinistre; malfaisant; *the* ~ *eye* le mauvais œil *m*; *the* ♀ *One* le Malin *m*, le Mauvais *m*, le diable *m*; **2.** mal *m*; malheur *m*; **'~-'do·er** malfaiteur (-trice *f*) *m*.   [moigner.\

e·vince [i'vins] manifester, té-⌐

e·vis·cer·ate [i'visəreit] éviscérer.

ev·o·ca·tion [evo'keiʃn] évocation *f*; **e·voc·a·tive** [i'vɔkətiv] évocateur (-trice *f*).

e·voke [i'vouk] évoquer.

ev·o·lu·tion [i:və'lu:ʃn] développement *m*; évolution *f* (a. ✕); ♣ extraction *f* (*d'une racine*).

e·volve [i'vɔlv] (se) développer; (se) dérouler; (se) dégager (*gaz*).

ewe [ju:] brebis *f*.

ew·er ['ju:ə] pot *m* à eau; broc *m*.

ex [eks] **1.** ♣ dégagé de, hors de; ~ *store* en magasin; *bourse*: ex-; ~ *officio* de droit, (à titre) d'office; **2.** *devant su.*: ancien(ne *f*); *ex-minister* ex-ministre *m*.

ex·ac·er·bate [eks'æsəbeit] exaspérer, irriter; aggraver.

ex·act [ig'zækt] **1.** □ exact; précis; juste; **2.** exiger (*un impôt*); extorquer; réclamer; **ex'act·ing** exigeant; astreignant (*travail*); **ex'ac·tion** exaction *f*; **ex'act·i·tude** [~ti-tju:d] exactitude *f*; **ex'act·ly** exactement; à vrai dire; ~! précisément! *not* ~ *ne* ... *pas* à proprement parler; **ex'act·ness** *see* exactitude.

ex·ag·ger·ate [ig'zædʒəreit] exagérer; **ex·ag·ger·a·tion** exagération *f*; **ex'ag·ger·a·tive** □ [~ətiv] exagératif (-ive *f*); exagéré (*personne*).

ex·alt [ig'zɔ:lt] élever; louer; **ex·al·ta·tion** [egzɔ:l'teiʃn] élévation *f*; exaltation *f*; émotion *f* passionnée; **ex·alt·ed** [ig'zɔ:ltid] élevé; haut; exalté.

ex·am F [ig'zæm] *école*: examen *m*.

ex·am·i·na·tion [igzæmi'neiʃn] examen *m*; *douane*: visite *f*; interrogatoire *m*; inspection *f*; épreuve *f* (*écrite*, *orale*); *competitive* ~ *examen*: concours *m*; **ex'am·ine** [~min] examiner (*q.*, *qch.*); faire une enquête sur (*qch.*); visiter; contrôler; interroger; **ex·am·i'nee** candidat(e *f*) *m*; **ex'am·in·er** examinateur (-trice *f*) *m*; **ex'am·in·ing 'bod·y** jury *m* d'examen.

ex·am·ple [ig'zɑ:mpl] exemple *m*; précédent *m*; *beyond* ~ sans précédent; *for* ~ par exemple; *make an* ~ *of* faire un exemple de (*q.*).

ex·as·per·ate [ig'zɑ:spəreit] exaspérer; irriter; aggraver (*la douleur etc.*); **ex·as·per'a·tion** exaspération *f*; aggravation *f* (de, *of*).

ex·ca·vate ['ekskəveit] *v/t.* creuser; approfondir; *v/i.* faire des fouilles; **ex·ca'va·tion** excavation *f*; fouille *f*; **'ex·ca·va·tor** excavateur *m*; fouilleuse *f*.

ex·ceed [ik'si:d] *v/t.* excéder, dépasser, outrepasser; surpasser (en, *in*), *v/i.* prédominer; **ex'ceed·ing** excessif (-ive *f*); **ex'ceed·ing·ly** extrêmement, excessivement.

ex·cel [ik'sel] *v/t.* surpasser; *v/i.* exceller (à *in*, *at*); **ex·cel·lence** ['eksələns] excellence *f*; perfection *f*; mérite *m*; **'Ex·cel·len·cy** Excellence *f*; **'ex·cel·lent** □ excellent, parfait.

ex·cept [ik'sept] **1.** *v/t.* excepter, exclure; *v/i.* faire des objections; **2.** *cj.* à moins que; excepté que; **3.** *prp.* excepté, à l'exception de, sauf; ~ *for* à part; **ex'cept·ing** *prp.* à l'exception de; **ex'cep·tion** exception *f*; objection *f* (à, *to*); *take* ~ *to* s'offenser de; objecter (*qch.*) (à *q.*, *in s.o.*); **ex'cep·tion·a·ble** récusable; blâmable; **ex'cep·tion·al** □ exceptionnel(le *f*); ~*ly* par exception.

ex·cerpt 1. [ek'sə:pt] extraire (*un passage*) (de, *from*); **2.** ['eksə:pt] extrait *m* (de, *from*); emprunt *m* (à).

ex·cess [ik'ses] excès *m*; excédent *m*; surpoids *m*; *attr.* en surpoids; en excédent; *in* ~ *of* au-dessus de; *carry to* ~ pousser (*qch.*) trop loin; ~ *charge* supplément *m*; ~ *fare* supplément *m*; ~ *luggage* excédent *m* de bagages; ~ *money* argent *m* en surplus; ~ *postage* surtaxe *f* postale; ~ *profit* surplus *m* des bénéfices; **ex'ces·sive** □ excessif (-ive *f*); immodéré; ~*ly* à l'excès.

ex·change [iks'tʃeindʒ] **1.** échanger (contre, *for*); faire un échange de; **2.** échange *m*; ♣ change *m*; (*bill of* ~) traite *f*; (a. ♀) Bourse *f*; *téléph.*

central *m*; *foreign* ∼(*s pl.*) devises *f/pl.* étrangères *ou* sur l'étranger; *in* ∼ *for* en échange de; ∼ *control* contrôle *m* des changes; ∼ *list* bulletin *m* des changes; ∼ *market* marché *m* des changes; ∼ *office* bureau *m* de change; *free* ∼ libre-échange *m*; *par of* ∼ pair *m* du change; (*rate of*) ∼ cours *m ou* taux *m* du change; **ex-ʼchange-a-ble** échangeable (contre, *pour for*); ∼ *value* valeur *f* d'échange; ✝ contre-valeur *f*.

ex-cheq-uer [iks'tʃekə] Trésor *m* public; F budget *m*; Ministère *m* des Finances; *Chancellor of the* ♀ Ministre *m* des Finances (*britannique*); ∼ *bill* bon *m* du Trésor.

ex-cise¹ [ek'saiz] **1.** régie *f*; contributions *f/pl.* indirectes; **2.** imposer; frapper d'une imposition.

ex-cise² [∼] retrancher; **ex-ci-sion** [ek'siʒn] excision *f*; incision *f*.

ex-cit-a-bil-i-ty [iksaitə'biliti] émotivité *f*; **ex-ʼcit-a-ble** émotionnable; mobile (*foule*); **ex-cit-ant** ['eksitənt] stimulant *m*; **ex-ci-ta-tion** [eksi'teiʃn] excitation *f*; **ex-cite** [ik'sait] provoquer, soulever, exciter; animer; **ex-ʼcite-ment** agitation *f*; émotion *f*; excitation *f*; **ex-ʼcit-er** instigateur (-trice *f*) *m*; ⚕ excitant *m*; ⚡ excitateur *m*.

ex-claim [iks'kleim] *v/i.* s'exclamer; s'écrier; ∼ *against* se récrier contre; *v/t.* crier.

ex-cla-ma-tion [ekskləʼmeiʃn] exclamation *f*; *note* (*ou* mark *ou* point) *of* ∼, ∼ *mark* point *m* d'exclamation; **ex-clam-a-to-ry** □ [∼-ʼklæmətəri] exclamatif (-ive *f*).

ex-clude [iks'klu:d] exclure; *fig.* écarter.

ex-clu-sion [iks'klu:ʒn] exclusion *f*; refus *m* d'admission (à, *from*); **ex-ʼclu-sive** □ [∼siv] exclusif (-ive *f*); en exclusivité (*film*); seul, unique; très fermé (*cercle*); ∼ *of* non compris; *be mutually* ∼ s'exclure mutuellement.

ex-cog-i-tate [eks'kɔdʒiteit] combiner; *péj.* machiner; **ex-cog-i-ʼta-tion** excogitation *f*; méditation *f*.

ex-com-mu-ni-cate [ekskəʼmju:nikeit] excommunier; **ex-com-mu-ni-ca-tion** excommunication *f*.

ex-co-ri-ate [eks'kɔ:rieit] excorier, écorcher (*la peau*).

ex-cre-ment ['ekskrimənt] excrément *m*; **ex-cre-men-tal** [∼ʼmentl], **ex-cre-men-ti-tious** [∼ʼtiʃəs] excrémen(ti)tiel(le *f*).

ex-cres-cence [iks'kresns] excroissance *f*; excrescence *f*; **ex-ʼcres-cent** qui forme une excroissance; superflu.

ex-crete [eks'kri:t] excréter; sécréter; **ex-ʼcre-tion** excrétion *f*; sécrétion *f*; **ex-ʼcre-tive**, **ex-ʼcre-to-ry** [∼təri] excréteur (-trice *f*); excrétoire.

ex-cru-ci-ate [iks'kru:ʃieit] torturer; **ex-ʼcru-ci-at-ing** □ atroce; **ex-cru-ci-ʼa-tion** torture *f*, supplice *m*.

ex-cul-pate ['ekskʌlpeit] disculper, exonérer; justifier (*q.*); **ex-cul-ʼpa-tion** exonération *f*; justification *f*; **ex-ʼcul-pa-to-ry** [∼pətəri] justificatif (-ive *f*).

ex-cur-sion [iks'kə:ʃn] excursion *f*; partie *f* de plaisir; *mot.* randonnée *f*; ∼ *train* train *m* de plaisir; **ex-ʼcur-sion-ist** excursionniste *mf*.

ex-cur-sive □ [eks'kə:siv] digressif (-ive *f*); vagabond.

ex-cus-a-ble □ [iks'kju:zəbl] excusable; **ex-cuse** [∼ʼkju:z] **1.** excuser; pardonner (qch. à q., *s.o. s.th.*); **2.** [∼ʼkju:s] excuse *f*, prétexte *m*.

ex-di-rec-to-ry [eksdi'rektəri] qui n'est pas dans l'annuaire téléphonique.

ex-e-cra-ble □ ['eksikrəbl] exécrable; **ex-e-crate** ['∼kreit] exécrer, détester; **ex-e-ʼcra-tion** exécration *f*; malédiction *f*.

ex-e-cu-tant ♩ [ig'zekjutənt] exécutant(e *f*) *m*; **ex-e-cute** ['eksikju:t] exécuter (*projet, ordre, testament*, ♩, ⚖); ✝ effectuer (*un transfert*); ⚖ souscrire (*un acte*); **ex-e-ʼcu-tion** exécution *f* (*see* execute); ⚖ souscription *f* (*d'un acte*), saisie-exécution (*pl.* saisies-exécutions) *f*; jeu *m* (*d'un musicien*); *fig.* carnage *m*; *a man of* ∼ un homme *m* énergique; *take out an* ∼ *against* faire une exécution sur; ⚔, *a. fig. do* ∼ causer des ravages; **ex-e-ʼcu-tion-er** bourreau *m*; **ex-ec-u-tive** [ig'zekjutiv] **1.** □ exécutif (-ive *f*); ∼ *committee* bureau *m* (*d'une société*), commission *f* exécutive (*d'un parti*); ∼ *editor* rédacteur *m* en chef; ∼ *suite* bureaux *m/pl.* de la direction;

2. (pouvoir *m*) exécutif *m*; bureau *m*; *Am.* président *m*; *pol.* gouverneur *m*; ✝ directeur *m* (*commercial*); **ex'ec·u·tor** [∼tə] exécuteur *m* testamentaire; **ex'ec·u·to·ry** exécutif (-ive *f*); ⚖ exécutoire, en vigueur; non encore exécuté.

ex·em·plar [ig'zemplə] exemplaire *m*; **ex'em·pla·ri·ness** exemplarité *f*; **ex'em·pla·ry** exemplaire; typique.

ex·em·pli·fi·ca·tion [igzemplifi-'keiʃn] démonstration *f*; exemple *m*; ⚖ copie *f* authentique; **ex'em·pli·fy** [∼fai] démontrer, expliquer; servir d'exemple; donner un exemple de; ⚖ faire une ampliation de.

ex·empt [ig'zempt] **1.** exempt, franc(he *f*), dispensé (de, *from*); **2.** exempter, dispenser (de, *from*); **ex'emp·tion** exemption *f*, dispense *f* (de, *from*).

ex·e·quies ['eksikwiz] *pl.* convoi *m* funèbre; obsèques *f/pl.*

ex·er·cise ['eksəsaiz] **1.** exercice *m* (*d'une faculté, a. école, ♪, etc.*); ✂, ⚓ évolution *f*; *école:* devoir *m*, thème *m*; ∼ *book école:* cahier *m*; take ∼ prendre de l'exercice; *Am.* ∼s *pl.* cérémonies *f/pl.*; **2.** *v/t.* exercer (*corps, esprit, influence, métier, faculté*); pratiquer; user de; promener (*un cheval*); tracasser; *v/i.* s'entraîner; ✂ faire l'exercice; **'ex·er·cis·er** exerciseur *m*.

ex·ert [ig'zə:t] exercer (*de l'influence etc.*); employer (*de la force*); ∼ *o.s.* s'employer; s'efforcer (de, *to*); **ex'er·tion** effort *m*; emploi *m*.

ex·e·unt *théâ.* ['eksiʌnt] ... sortent.

ex·fo·li·ate [eks'foulieit] (s')exfolier; (se) déliter (*pierre*).

ex·ha·la·tion [ekshə'leiʃn] exhalaison *f*; *souffle:* expiration *f*; **ex·hale** [∼'heil] *v/t.* exhaler (*odeur, souffle, prière, rage*); *fig.* respirer; *v/i.* s'exhaler.

ex·haust [ig'zɔ:st] **1.** épuiser (*a. fig.*); vider (de, *of*); aspirer (*l'air, du gaz, etc.*); ∼ *the air* faire le vide (dans, *in*); **2.** ⊕ échappement *m*; ∼ *box* pot *m* d'échappement; silencieux *m*; ∼ *cut-out* (*ou muffler*) soupape *f* d'échappement libre; silencieux *m*; ∼ *fumes pl.*, ∼ *gas* gaz *m* d'échappement; ∼ *pipe* tuyau *m* d'échappement; ∼ *steam* vapeur *f*

d'échappement; ∼ *valve* soupape *f* d'échappement; **ex'haust·ed** *usu.* épuisé (*a. fig.*), usé; vide d'air; **ex'haust·i·ble** épuisable; **ex-'haust·ing** □ épuisant; ⊕ d'épuisement; **ex'haus·tion** épuisement *m*; **ex'haus·tive** □ *see* exhausting; approfondi.

ex·hib·it [ig'zibit] **1.** exhiber (*a. ⚖*); montrer; offrir; exposer; **2.** objet *m* exposé; exposition *f*; ⚖ pièce *f* à l'appui; on ∼ exposé; **ex·hi·bi·tion** [eksi'biʃn] exposition *f*; étalage *m*; démonstration *f*; *cin.* présentation *f*; ⚖ exhibition *f*; *make an* ∼ *of o.s.* faire spectacle; on ∼ exposé; **ex·hi·'bi·tion·er** boursier (-ère *f*) *m*; **ex·hib·i·tor** [ig'zibitə] exposant(e *f*) *m*; *cin.* exploitant *m* d'un cinéma.

ex·hil·a·rate [ig'ziləreit] égayer; ranimer; **ex·hil·a·ra·tion** gaieté *f*, joie *f* de vivre.

ex·hort [ig'zɔ:t] exhorter; **ex·hor·ta·tion** [egzɔ:'teiʃn] exhortation *f*; **ex·hor·ta·tive** [ig'zɔ:tətiv], **ex-'hor·ta·to·ry** [∼təri] exhortatif (-ive *f*), exhortatoire.

ex·hu·ma·tion [ekshju:'meiʃn] exhumation *f*; **ex'hume** déterrer.

ex·i·gence, ex·i·gen·cy ['eksidʒəns(i)] exigence *f*; nécessité *f*; situation *f* critique; **'ex·i·gent** urgent, pressant; exigeant; *be* ∼ *of* exiger.

ex·ig·u·ous [eg'zigjuəs] exigu (-üe *f*); modique (*revenu etc.*).

ex·ile ['eksail] **1.** exil *m*; *personne:* exilé(e *f*) *m*; **2.** exiler, bannir.

ex·ist [ig'zist] exister; être; se trouver; vivre; **ex'ist·ence** existence *f*; vie *f*; *phls.* être *m*; *in* ∼ = **ex'ist·ent** existant; actuel(le *f*).

ex·it ['eksit] **1.** sortie *f*; *fig.* fin *f*, mort *f*; ∼ *permit* permis *m* de sortie; ∼ *visa* visa *m* de sortie; **2.** *théâ.* ... sort.   [*fig.* sortie *f.*]

ex·o·dus ['eksədəs] *bibl.* exode *m*;

ex·on·er·ate [ig'zɔnəreit] exonérer, disculper, dispenser (de, *from*); **ex·on·er·a·tion** exonération *f*, décharge *f*.

ex·or·bi·tance, ex·or·bi·tan·cy [ig-'zɔ:bitəns(i)] énormité *f*; **ex'or·bi·tant** □ exorbitant, excessif (-ive *f*).

ex·or·cism ['eksɔ:sizm] exorcisme *m*; **'ex·or·cist** exorciste *m*; **ex·or·cize** ['∼saiz] exorciser (*un démon, un possédé*); chasser (de, *from*).   [que.⟩

ex·ot·ic [eg'zɔtik] (plante *f*) exoti-⟨

ex·pand [iks'pænd] (s')étendre; (se) déployer (ailes); (se) dilater (yeux, gaz, solide); (se) développer (abrégé, poitrine, formule); amplifier; (s')élargir; **ex'pand·er** extenseur m; ⊕ mécanisme m d'expansion; **ex·panse** [~'pæns] étendue f; **ex·pan·si·bil·i·ty** [~sə'biliti] expansibilité f; phys. dilatabilité f; **ex'pan·si·ble** expansible; phys. dilatable; **ex'pan·sion** expansion f (a. pol.); dilatation f; ⊕ détente f; **ex'pan·sive** □ expansif (-ive f) (a. fig.); dilatable; étendu; **ex'pan·sive·ness** expansibilité f (a. d'une personne); dilatabilité f.

ex·pa·ti·ate [eks'peiʃieit] s'étendre (sur, on); **ex·pa·ti·a·tion** long discours m; prolixité f.

ex·pa·tri·ate [eks'pætrieit] expatrier, bannir; **ex·pa·tri·a·tion** expatriation f.

ex·pect [iks'pekt] attendre (de of, from); compter sur; s'attendre à; F penser, croire; **ex'pect·an·cy** attente f, espoir m; **ex'pect·ant 1.** qui attend; be ~ of attendre (qch.); be ~ attendre un bébé; ~ mother future maman f; **2.** aspirant (-e f) m; **ex·pec·ta·tion** attente f; espérance f; probabilité f; ⚖ expectative f d'héritage; beyond ~ au-delà de mes etc. espérances; on (ou in) ~ of dans l'attente de; **ex'pect·ing** see expectant 1.

ex·pec·to·rate [eks'pektəreit] v/t. expectorer; v/i. cracher; **ex·pec·to·ra·tion** expectoration f; crachat m.

ex·pe·di·ence, ex·pe·di·en·cy [iks'pi:djəns(i)] convenance f, à-propos m; péj. opportunisme m; **ex'pe·di·ent 1.** □ expédient, avantageux (-euse f); pratique; **2.** expédient m, moyen m, ressource f; **ex·pe·dite** ['ekspidait] expédier; accélérer, hâter; **ex·pe·di·tion** [~'diʃn] promptitude f; diligence f; ✕ etc.: expédition f; **ex·pe'di·tion·ar·y** expéditionnaire; **ex·pe'di·tious** □ prompt; rapide; expéditif (-ive f).

ex·pel [iks'pel] expulser, chasser; renvoyer (q. de l'école, s.o. [from] the school).

ex·pend [iks'pend] dépenser (de l'argent); consacrer (le temps) (à on s.th., in inf.); épuiser (les forces, les ressources); **ex'pend·a·ble** dépensable; **ex'pend·i·ture** [~itʃə] dé-

pense f (d'argent etc.); consommation f; dépense f, -s f/pl.; **ex·pense** [~'pens] dépense f; frais m/pl.; prix m; dépens m/pl.; ~s pl. dépenses f/pl., frais m/pl.; indemnité f; at my ~ à mes frais; à mes dépens; at the ~ of aux dépens de; at great ~ à grands frais; **ex'pen·sive** □ coûteux (-euse f), cher (chère f).

ex·pe·ri·ence [iks'piəriəns] **1.** expérience f; aventure f; **2.** éprouver; essuyer (des insultes); **ex'pe·ri·enced** éprouvé; averti; expérimenté; exercé (à, in); consommé.

ex·per·i·ment 1. [iks'perimənt] expérience f; épreuve f; **2.** [~ment] expérimenter (sur, avec on, with); faire des expériences; **ex·per·i·men·tal** □ [eksperi'mentl] expérimental (-aux m/pl.); d'expérience; d'essai; d'épreuve; **ex·per·i'men·tal·ist** [~təlist], **ex·per·i·men·ter** [iks'perimentə] expérimentaliste m; expérimentateur (-trice f) m.

ex·pert ['ekspə:t] **1.** □ préd. eks-'pə:t] expert (en at, in), adroit, habile; ~ opinion avis m d'expert; expertise f; ~ worker ouvrier m spécialisé; homme m du métier; **2.** expert m; spécialiste m; **'ex·pert·ness** adresse f (à, in); expertise f.

ex·pi·a·ble ['ekspiəbl] expiable; **ex·pi·ate** ['~pieit] expier; **ex·pi·a·tion** expiation f; **ex·pi·a·to·ry** ['~piətəri] expiatoire.

ex·pi·ra·tion [ekspaiə'reiʃn] expiration f; cessation f; fin f; ✝ échéance f; **ex·pir·a·to·ry** [iks'paiərətəri] expirateur; **ex'pire** v/t. expirer; v/i. expirer (a. temps, contrat, etc.); mourir; s'éteindre (feu); fig. s'évanouir.

ex·plain [iks'plein] expliquer; éclaircir; élucider; justifier (une conduite); **ex'plain·a·ble** explicable; justifiable (conduite).

ex·pla·na·tion [eksplə'neiʃn] explication f, éclaircissement m; **ex·plan·a·to·ry** □ [iks'plænətəri] explicatif (-ive f).

ex·ple·tive [eks'pli:tiv] **1.** □ explétif (-ive f); **2.** gramm. explétif m; fig. juron m.

ex·pli·ca·ble ['eksplikəbl] explicable; justifiable (conduite); **ex·pli·cate** ['~keit] développer; **ex·pli·ca-**

tive ['ˌkətiv], **ex·pli·ca·to·ry** ['ˌ~təri] explicatif (-ive f).
ex·plic·it □ [iks'plisit] explicite; formel(le f), clair; fig. franc(he f).
ex·plode [iks'ploud] (faire) sauter; (faire) éclater (de, with); v/t. discréditer; **ex'plod·ed** éclaté; discrédité (théorie).
ex·ploit 1. [iks'plɔit] exploiter (a. fig.); **2.** ['eksplɔit] exploit m; **ex·ploi'ta·tion** exploitation f.
ex·plo·ra·tion [eksplɔː'reiʃn] exploration f (a. ⚙); reconnaissance f (du terrain); **ex'plor·a·to·ry** [ˌ~rətəri] d'exploration; de découverte; **ex·plore** [iks'plɔː] explorer; aller à la découverte dans (un pays); reconnaître (un terrain); **ex'plor·er** explorateur (-trice f) m.
ex·plo·sion [iks'plouʒn] explosion f (a. fig.); détonation f; **ex'plo·sive** [ˌ~siv] **1.** □ explosif (-ive f); explosible (arme etc.); **2.** explosif m.
ex·po·nent [eks'pounənt] interprète mf; explicateur (-trice f) m; ⅍ exposant m.
ex·port 1. [eks'pɔːt] exporter; **2.** ['ekspɔːt] marchandise f exportée; exportation f; ~s pl. articles m/pl. d'exportation; exportation f; **ex'port·a·ble** exportable; **ex·por·ta·tion** [ˌ~'teiʃn] exportation f; **ex'port·er** exportateur (-trice f) m.
ex·pose [iks'pouz] exposer (a. phot.); étaler; démasquer; mettre à découvert; dévoiler; **ex·po·si·tion** [ekspə'ziʃn] exposition f; exposé m; **ex·pos·i·tive** [ˌ~'pɔzitiv] expositoire; **ex'pos·i·tor** interprète mf; commentateur (-trice f) m.
ex·pos·tu·late [iks'pɔstjuleit] reprocher (amicalement) (qch. à q., with s.o. for s.th); sermonner (sur, [up]on); **ex·pos·tu·la·tion** remontrance f, -s f/pl.
ex·po·sure [iks'pouʒə] exposition f (au danger, au froid, d'un bébé); étalage m (d'articles); fig. dévoilement m, mise f à nu; phot. pose f; ~ meter photomètre m; ~ time temps m de pose; ~ table tableau m de temps de pose; death from ~ mort f de froid.
ex·pound [iks'paund] expliquer; exposer (une doctrine).
ex·press [iks'pres] **1.** □ exprès (-esse f); formel(le f); 🚄 rapide; ~ company Am. compagnie f de

messageries; Am. ~way autostrade f; **2.** exprès m; (a ~ train) rapide m, express m; by ~ = **3.** adv. en toute hâte; sans arrêt; send s.th. ~ poste: envoyer qch. exprès; **4.** exprimer (un sentiment, du jus, etc.); énoncer (un principe); émettre (une opinion); not ~ed sous-entendu; **ex'press·i·ble** exprimable; **ex'pres·sion** [ˌ~preʃn] ♪, ⅍, gramm., peint., visage: expression f; **ex'pres·sive** [ˌ~siv] expressif (-ive f); be ~ of exprimer (qch.); **ex'press·ly** expressément; exprès.
ex·pro·pri·ate [eks'prouprieit] exproprier (q. de qch., s.o. from s.th.); **ex·pro·pri'a·tion** expropriation f.
ex·pul·sion [iks'pʌlʃn] expulsion f; **ex'pul·sive** expulsif (-ive f).
ex·punge [eks'pʌndʒ] effacer, biffer.
ex·pur·gate ['ekspəːgeit] expurger (un livre); épurer (un texte); supprimer (un passage); **ex·pur'ga·tion** expurgation f; épuration f.
ex·qui·site ['ekskwizit] **1.** □ exquis; ravissant; délicieux (-euse f); délicat; vif (vive f), atroce (douleur etc.); **2.** dandy m; **'ex·qui·site·ness** perfection f; exquisité f; finesse f; douleur etc.: acuité f.
ex-serv·ice·man ⚔ ['eks'sɔːvismən] ancien combattant m.
ex·tant [eks'tænt] existant, qui existe.
ex·tem·po·ra·ne·ous □ [ekstempə'reinjəs], **ex·tem·po·rar·y** [iks'tempərəri], **ex·tem·po·re** [eks'tempəri] impromptu, improvisé; **ex·tem·po·rize** [iks'tempəraiz] improviser; **ex'tem·po·riz·er** improvisateur (-trice f) m.
ex·tend [iks'tend] v/t. étendre (a. fig., la bonté, etc.); tendre (la main); agrandir (un territoire); reculer (des frontières); prolonger (une ligne, un billet, une période); transcrire (de la sténographie); ✝ proroger; ⚔ déployer; in ~ed order en fourrageurs; v/i. s'étendre, se prolonger; continuer.
ex·ten·si·bil·i·ty [ikstensə'biliti] extensibilité f; **ex'ten·si·ble** extensible; **ex'ten·sion** extension f; prolongation f; table: (r)allonge f; gramm. complément m; annexe f; téléph. poste m; ⚡ ~ cord allonge f de câble; ~ ladder échelle f coulissante; University ♀ cours m populaire

organisé par une université; **ex·ten·sive** □ [~siv] étendu, vaste; **ex·'ten·sive·ness** étendue f.

ex·tent [iks'tent] étendue f; importance f; to the ~ of au point de; prêt d'argent etc.: jusqu'à concurrence de; to a certain ~ jusqu'à un certain point; to some ~ dans une certaine mesure; to that ~ à ce point-là; grant ~ for atermoyer.

ex·ten·u·ate [eks'tenjueit] atténuer; † amaigrir; **ex·ten·u·a·tion** atténuation f; affaiblissement m extrême.

ex·te·ri·or [eks'tiəriə] **1.** □ extérieur (à, to); en dehors (de, to); ⯑ externe; **2.** extérieur m (a. cin.).

ex·ter·mi·nate [eks'tə:mineit] exterminer; **ex·ter·mi·na·tion** extermination f; **ex·'ter·mi·na·tor** exterminateur (-trice f) m.

ex·ter·nal [eks'tə:nl] **1.** □ extérieur (à, to); du dehors; ⯑, ⯑ externe; ~ to en dehors de; **2.** ~s pl. dehors m (a. pl.); fig. apparence f; **ex·'ter·nal·ize** extérioriser.

ex·tinct [iks'tiŋkt] éteint (a. fig.); **ex·'tinc·tion** extinction f (a. fig.).

ex·tin·guish [iks'tiŋgwiʃ] éteindre (a. fig.); abolir (un office, une loi, etc.); exterminer; réduire (q.) au silence; **ex·'tin·guish·er** lampe etc.: éteignoir m; personne: éteigneur (-euse f) m; see fire-~; **ex·'tin·guish·ment** extinction f.

ex·tir·pate ['ekstə:peit] extirper, déraciner (a. ⯑); **ex·tir·pa·tion** extirpation f, éradication f; **'ex·tir·pa·tor** extirpateur (-trice f) m.

ex·tol [iks'tɔl] louer, vanter.

ex·tort [iks'tɔ:t] extorquer, arracher (à, from); **ex·'tor·tion** extorsion f; **ex·'tor·tion·ate** [~ʃnit] exorbitant; **ex·'tor·tion·er** extorqueur (-euse f) m; exacteur m.

ex·tra ['ekstrə] **1.** adj. en plus, à part; supplémentaire; ~ pay salaire m etc. supplémentaire; sp. ~ time prolongation f; **2.** adv. extra-; plus que d'ordinaire; **3.** su. supplément m; numéro m etc. supplémentaire; cin. figurant(e f) m; journ. édition f spéciale; ~s pl. frais m/pl. ou dépenses f/pl. supplémentaires; ~ special deuxième édition f spéciale (d'un journal du soir); ~-special F d'extra; supérieur.

ex·tract 1. ['ekstrækt] extrait m;

concentré m (a. ⯑); **2.** [iks'trækt] extraire (a. ⯑, ⯑, une dent, un passage); tirer (argent, aveu, doctrine, plaisir, sons) (de, from); arracher (argent, aveu, dent) (à, from); **ex·'trac·tion** extraction f; origine f; **ex·'trac·tive 1.** extractif (-ive f); **2.** extractif m; **ex·'trac·tor** arracheur (-euse f) m; ⊕ pince f; extracteur m.

ex·tra·cur·ric·u·lar ['ekstrəkə'rikjulə] hors programme.

ex·tra·dit·a·ble ['ekstrədaitəbl] qui justifie l'extradition; passible d'extradition (personne); **ex·tra·dite** ['~dait] extrader; obtenir l'extradition de; **ex·tra·di·tion** [~'diʃn] extradition f.

extra...: '~·**ju·di·cial** officieux (-euse f); extra-légal (-aux m/pl.); '~**mar·i·tal** extra-conjugal (-aux m/pl.); '~**mu·ral** en dehors de la ville; univ. hors faculté (professeur, cours, etc.).

ex·tra·ne·ous [eks'treinjəs] étranger (-ère f) (à, to).

ex·tra·or·di·nar·y [iks'trɔ:dnri] extraordinaire; remarquable; F prodigieux (-euse f). [trapoler.]

ex·trap·o·late [ek'stræpouleit] ex-)

ex·tra·ter·res·tri·al ['ekstrəti'restriəl] extraterrestre.

ex·trav·a·gance [iks'trævigəns] extravagance f, exagération f; prodigalité f, gaspillage m (d'argent); **ex·'trav·a·gant** □ extravagant, exagéré; prodigue (personne); exorbitant (prix); **ex·trav·a·gan·za** [ekstrævə'gænzə] théâ. œuvre f (musicale) fantaisiste.

ex·treme [iks'tri:m] **1.** □ extrême; très grand ou haut; dernier (-ère f) (point, supplice); eccl. ~ unction extrême onction f; **2.** extrême m; in the ~ au dernier degré; **ex·'trem·ist** extrémiste mf, ultra m; **ex·trem·i·ty** [~'tremiti] extrémité f, bout m, point m extrême; gêne f; extremities pl. extrémités f/pl. (du corps); be reduced to extremities être dans la plus grande gêne.

ex·tri·cate ['ekstrikeit] dégager, tirer; ⯑ libérer; **ex·tri·ca·tion** dégagement m, délivrance f; ⯑ libération f.

ex·trin·sic [eks'trinsik] (~ally) extrinsèque; ~ to en dehors de.

ex·tro·vert ['ekstrouvə:t] extroverti(e f) m.

ex·trude [eks'tru:d] *v/t.* expulser; ⊕ refouler; *v/i.* géol. s'épancher.

ex·u·ber·ance [ig'zju:bərəns] exubérance *f*; richesse *f*; surabondance *f* (*en idées*); **ex'u·ber·ant** exubérant; débordant, surabondant; riche.

ex·u·da·tion [eksju:'deiʃn] exsudation *f*; écoulement *m*; **ex·ude** [ig'zju:d] exsuder; s'écouler (*sève*).

ex·ult [ig'zʌlt] exulter, se réjouir (de qch. *at, in s.th.*); triompher (de qch., *at s.th.*; sur q., *over s.o.*); **ex-'ult·ant** exultant; triomphant; **ex·ul·ta·tion** [egzʌl'teiʃn] exultation *f*; triomphe *m*.

ex·u·vi·ate [ig'zju:vieit] (se) dépouiller (*peau etc.*).

eye [ai] **1.** œil (*pl.* yeux) *m* (*a.* ⚿, *outil*); regard *m*; aiguille: trou *m*; *have an ~ for* s'y connaître en; *sl. my ~(s)!* mince alors!; *sl. it's all my ~!* c'est de la blague!; *mind your ~!* gare à vous!; *with an ~ to* en vue de; **2.** observer, regarder; suivre des yeux; mesurer (*q.*) des yeux; '**~·ball** prunelle *f*; globe *m* de l'œil; '**~·brow** sourcil *m*; '**~·catch·er** F attraction *f*; **eyed** [aid] aux yeux ...; ocellé (*plume, aile*).

eye ...: '**~·drops** *pl.* gouttes *f/pl.* pour les yeux; '**~·ful** F coup *m* d'œil; *be (quite) an ~ a.* valoir le coup d'œil; *get an ~* se rincer l'œil; *get an ~ of* viser (= *regarder*); '**~·glass** monocle *m*; (*a pair of*) *~es pl.* (un) pince-nez *m/inv.*, (un) binocle *m*, (un) lorgnon *m*; '**~·hole** œillet *m*; △ judas *m*; ⚛ cavité *f* de l'œil; '**~·lash** cil *m*; **eye·let** ['ailit] œillet *m*; petit trou *m*; aile: ocelle *m*.

eye ...: '**~·lid** paupière *f*; '**~·o·pen·er** révélation *f*; surprise *f*; '**~·piece** *opt.* oculaire *m*; **~ shad·ow** fard *m* à paupières; '**~·shot** portée *f* de (la) vue; '**~·sight** vue *f*; portée *f* de la vue; '**~·sore** *fig.* chose *f* qui offense le regard; horreur *f*; '**~·tooth** dent *f* œillère; '**~·wash 1.** collyre *m*; *sl.* boniment *m*, bourrage *m* de crâne; **2.** *sl.* jeter de la poudre aux yeux de (*q.*); '**~·'wit·ness** témoin *m* oculaire.

ey·ot [eit] îlot *m*.

eyre *hist.* [ɛə]: *justices in ~* juges *m/pl.* en tournée.

ey·rie, ey·ry ['aiəri] *see* aerie.

F

F, f [ef] F *m*, f *m*.

fa·ble ['feibl] **1.** fable *m*, conte *m*; *fig.* mythe *m*, invention *f*.

fab·ric ['fæbrik] édifice *m*, bâtiment *m*; *eccl.* fabrique *f*; étoffe *f*, tissu *m*; **fab·ri·cate** ['ˌkeit] fabriquer (*usu. fig.*); inventer; **fab·ri·ca·tion** fabrication *f*; *fig.* invention *f*; contrefaçon *f*; **'fab·ri·ca·tor** inventeur *m*; *mensonge:* forgeur *m*; *document:* contrefacteur *m*.

fab·u·list ['fæbjulist] fabuliste *m*; *fig.* menteur (-euse *f*) *m*; **'fab·u·lous** □ légendaire.

fa·çade △ [fa'sɑːd] façade *f*.

face [feis] **1.** face *f*; visage *m*, figure *f*; air *m*, mine *f*; *horloge:* cadran *m*; *étoffe:* endroit *m*; aspect *m*; *fig.* impudence *f*, front *m*; *in (the)* ~ *of* devant; en présence de; ~ *to* ~ *with* vis-à-vis de; *save one's* ~ sauver la face; *on the* ~ *of it* à première vue; *set one's* ~ *against* s'opposer à, s'élever contre; ✝ ~ *value* valeur *f* nominale; **2.** *v/t.* affronter, braver; donner sur (*la cour etc.*); parer (*un habit*); envisager (*les faits*); revêtir (*un mur*); faire face à (*q.*); *be* ~*d with* être menacé de, se heurter à; *v/i.* être exposé *ou* tourné *ou* orienté; ~ *about* faire demi-tour; ✕ *left* ~! à gauche, gauche!; *about* ~! volteface!; ~ *up to* affronter (*un danger etc.*); **face card** *cartes:* figure *f*; **faced** (*with*) à revers (de *qch.*); contre-plaqué (de *bois*); **'face·down** épreuve *f* de force; **'face·less** *fig.* anonyme; **'face-lift·ing** remontée *f* du visage; lifting *m*; **'fac·er** gifle *f*, F tuile *f*.

fac·et ⊕ ['fæsit] facette *f*; **'fac·et·ed** à facettes.

fa·ce·tious □ [fə'siːʃəs] facétieux (-euse *f*), plaisant.

fa·cial ['feiʃl] facial (-aux *m/pl.*); du [visage.]

fac·ile ['fæsail] facile; complaisant (*personne*); **fa·cil·i·tate** [fə'siliteit] faciliter; **fa·cil·i·ta·tion** action *f* de faciliter; **fa'cil·i·ty** facilité *f*; souplesse *f* de caractère.

fac·ing ['feisiŋ] ⊕ revêtement *m*; *moule:* poncif *m*; ✕ conversion *f* (à droite *etc.*); ~*s pl.* ✕ parement *m*.

fac·sim·i·le [fæk'simili] fac-similé *m*; ✍ copie *f* figurée; ~ *broadcast* (-*ing*) téléphotographie *f*.

fact [fækt] fait *m*, action *f*; réalité *f*; ~*s pl.* (*of the case*) faits *m/pl.* (de la cause), vérité *f*; *after the* ~ par assistance; *before the* ~ par instigation; *in (point of)* ~ au fait, en vérité; *tell s.o. about the* ~*s of life* apprendre à q. les choses de la vie; **'~-find·ing** pour établir les faits.

fac·tion ['fækʃn] *péj.* cabale *f*, faction *f*; dissension *f*; **'fac·tion·ist** factieux (-euse *f*) *m*, partisan *m*.

fac·tious □ ['fækʃəs] factieux (-euse *f*); **'fac·tious·ness** esprit *m* factieux.

fac·ti·tious □ [fæk'tiʃəs] factice, contrefait; faux (fausse *f*).

fac·tor ['fæktə] Å, *fig.* facteur *m*; ✝ agent *m*, commissionnaire *m* en gros; **'fac·to·ry** fabrique *f*, usine *f*.

fac·to·tum [fæk'toutəm] factotum *m*, homme *m* à tout faire.

fac·tu·al ['fæktjuəl] effectif (-ive *f*), positif (-ive *f*), réel(le *f*); ~ *knowledge* connaissance *f* des faits.

fac·ul·ty ['fækəlti] pouvoir *m*; faculté *f* (*a. univ.*); *fig.* talent *m*; *eccl.* autorisation *f*; ⚖ droit *m*; *Am.* corps *m* enseignant.

fad F [fæd] lubie *f*, marotte *f*, dada *m*; **'fad·dish**, **'fad·dy** maniaque; capricieux (-euse *f*); **'fad·dist** maniaque *mf*.

fade [feid] (se) faner, flétrir; (se) décolorer (*tissu*); s'affaiblir; (*a.* ~ *out*) s'évanouir, s'éteindre; ~ *down* (*ou out*) *cin.* (faire) partir dans un fondu; *radio:* faire fondre dans le lointain; ~ *in* (faire) arriver dans un fondu; **'fade·less** ineffaçable; *tex.* bon teint; **'fad·ing 1.** □ qui se fane *etc.*; **2.** *radio:* fading *m*, évanouissement *m*; *cin.* fondu *m*.

fae·ces *pl.* ['fiːsiːz] fèces *f/pl.*; matières *f/pl.* fécales.

fag F [fæg] **1.** corvée f, travail m pénible; école: petit m (élève) qui fait les corvées d'un grand; sl. sèche f, cigarette f; **2.** v/i. travailler dur; faire les corvées d'un grand élève; v/t. éreinter, fatiguer; '~-'end F bout m; queue f; sl. mégot m.

fag·ot, fag·got ['fægət] fagot m; ⊕ faisceau m, paquet m; Am. F pédé m.

Fahr·en·heit ['færənhait]: ~ thermometer thermomètre m Fahrenheit.

fail [feil] **1.** v/i. faire défaut, faillir; manquer (cœur, force, pluie, voix, etc.); diminuer; être refusé, échouer (à un examen); faire faillite; mot. rester en panne; baisser (jour, lumière, santé); he ~ed to do (a. in doing) manquer de faire; omettre de faire; he cannot ~ to il ne peut manquer de; v/t. manquer (à); abandonner; manquer à ses engagements envers (q.); refuser (un candidat); his heart ~ed him le cœur lui manqua; **2.** without ~ sans faute; à coup sûr; '**fail·ing 1.** su. défaut m; faiblesse f; **2.** prp. faute de, à défaut de; ~ which faute de quoi; '**fail·ure** ['feiljə] manque m; défaut m; insuccès m; mot. panne f; affaiblissement m; fiasco m; faillite f; personne: raté(e f) m.

fain [fein] **1.** adj. bien disposé; trop heureux (-euse f) (de, to); **2.** adv. avec plaisir.

faint [feint] **1.** □ faible; léger (-ère f); feel ~ se sentir mal; **2.** s'évanouir; fig. mourir (de, with); **3.** évanouissement m; ~-**heart·ed** □ ['~'hɑːtid] timide; lâche; '~-'heart·ed·ness pusillanimité f; '**faint·ness** faiblesse f.

fair¹ [fɛə] **1.** adj. beau (bel devant une voyelle ou un h muet); belle f; beaux m/pl.); juste; blond; ~ loyal; assez bon(ne f); **2.** adj., a. adv. poli(ment); doux (douce f), adv. doucement; favorable(ment); loyal(ement); école: passable, assez bien (mention); passablement; ~ copy copie f au net; corrigé m; ~ dealing probité f, loyauté f; ~ play jeu m loyal, franc jeu m; traitement m juste; our ~ readers nos aimables lectrices f/pl.; the ~ pl. (a. the ~ sex) le beau sexe; ~ and softly tout doucement; ✝ ~ trade système m réciproque de libre échange; bid ~ to promettre de; speak s.o. ~ parler poliment à q.; strike ~ frapper carrément.

fair² [~] foire f; grand marché m; '~-**ground** champ m de foire; '**fair·ing** † cadeau m acheté à la foire; ✄ entoilage m; profilage m.

fair·ly ['fɛəli] adv. de fair³; honnêtement, loyalement; avec impartialité; passablement, assez; '**fair·ness** beauté f; cheveux: couleur f blonde; teint m blond; blancheur f; loyauté f; probité f; sp. franc jeu m; '**fair·spo·ken** à la parole courtoise; '**fair·way** ✄ passage m, chenal m; '**fair-weath·er friend** ami m jusqu'à la bourse.

fair·y ['fɛəri] **1.** féerique; des fées; ~ lamp, ~ light lampion m; **2.** fée f; '**fair·y·land** pays m ou royaume m des fées; fig. pays m enchanté; '**fair·y·like** féerique; de fée; '**fair·y-tale** conte m de fées; fig. conte m bleu.

faith [feiθ] foi f (à qch., en Dieu); confiance f (en, in); croyance f; religion f; parole f; in good ~ de bonne foi; '~-**cure** guérison f par (auto)suggestion; '**faith·ful** □ ['~-ful] fidèle; loyal (-aux m/pl.); exact; the ~ pl. les fidèles m/pl.; yours ~ly Agréez l'expression de mes sentiments distingués; '**faith·ful·ness** loyauté f (envers, to), fidélité f; exactitude f; '**faith·less** □ infidèle; perfide; incrédule; '**faith·less·ness** infidélité f; déloyauté f; perfidie f.

fake sl. [feik] **1.** chose f truquée; article m faux; (Am. a. '**fak·er**) personne: simulateur (-trice f) m; **2.** (a. ~ up) truquer.

fal·con ['fɔːlkən] faucon m; '**fal·con·er** fauconnier m; '**fal·con·ry** fauconnerie f.

fald·stool ['fɔːldstuːl] prie-dieu m/inv.; siège m d'évêque; pliant m.

fall [fɔːl] **1.** chute f (a. d'eau, du jour, d'une ville); baromètre, eaux, théâ., rideau, température: baisse f; nuit: tombée f; pente f; descente f; arbres: abattis m; surt. Am. automne m; pluie, neige, etc.: quantité f; usu. ~s pl. chute f d'eau, cascade f; voix: cadence f; perte f, ruine f; ✄ usu. ~s pl. garants m/pl.; the ♀ (of Man) la chute de l'homme; have a ~ tomber; **2.** [irr.] tomber (a. gouvernement, nuit, vent); baisser (jour, prix, etc.); arriver; capituler (ville);

(*avec adj.*) devenir, tomber; naître (*animal*); (se) calmer (*mer*); retomber (*blâme, responsabilité, etc.*); s'effondrer (*bâtiment*); aller en pente, descendre; se projeter (*ombre*); *his countenance fell* sa figure s'allongea; *his spirits fell* il perdit courage; ~ *asleep* s'endormir; ~ *away* s'abaisser; déserter; ~ *back* tomber en arrière; reculer; se rabattre (sur, *upon*); ~ *behind* rester en arrière; se laisser devancer; ~ *between two stools* demeurer entre deux selles; ~ *down* tomber (par terre); s'écrouler; F échouer; ~ *due* venir à échéance; *surt. Am.* F ~ *for* tomber amoureux de; adopter (*qch.*) avec enthousiasme; ~ *from* (re)tomber de; ~ *ill* (*ou* ~ *sick*) tomber malade; ~ *in* s'effondrer; ✕ former les rangs; ⚖ expirer (*bail*); arriver à échéance (*dette*); ~ *in with* se prêter à (*un projet*); rencontrer (*q.*); s'accorder avec; ~ *in love with* tomber amoureux de; ~ *into* tomber dans (*l'eau*); contracter (*une habitude*); être induit en (*erreur*); dégénérer en; ~ *into line* se mettre en rangs; rentrer dans les rangs; ~ *off* tomber; faire défection; *fig.* décliner, diminuer; ~ *on* ✕ attaquer; fondre sur; se jeter sur; tomber sur (*q.*); ~ *out* se brouiller (avec, *with*); se passer, arriver; ✕ quitter les rangs; ~ *short* tomber en deçà (de, *of*); ~ *short of* ne pas atteindre, être audessous de; ~ *to see* ~ *on*; *a.* se mettre au travail; commencer; ~ *under* entrer dans (*une catégorie*).

fal·la·cious ☐ [fəˈleiʃəs] illusoire; trompeur (-euse *f*); **falˈla·ciousness** fausseté *f*.

fal·la·cy [ˈfæləsi] sophisme *m*; erreur *f*; faux raisonnement *m*.

fall·en [ˈfɔːlən] *p.p. de fall 2.*

fall guy *Am. sl.* [ˈfɔːlˈgai] bouc *m* émissaire.

fal·li·bil·i·ty [fæliˈbiliti] faillibilité *f*; **fal·li·ble** ☐ [ˈfæləbl] faillible.

fall·ing [ˈfɔːliŋ] baisse *f*; chute *f* etc.; ˈ~ˈoff chute *f*; défection *f*; décroissement *m*; déclin *m*; ~ **star** étoile *f* filante. [radioactives.]

fall·out [ˈfɔːlaut] retombées *f/pl.*

fal·low [ˈfælou] 1. *zo.* fauve; en friche; 2. ✔ jachère *f*, friche *f*; 3. ✔ jachérer, défricher; ˈ~-**deer** *zo.* daim *m*.

false ☐ [fɔːls] 1. *adj.* faux (fausse *f*); artificiel(le *f*); erroné; infidèle (à, to); *be* ~ *to* trahir; tromper; ~ *imprisonment* détention *f* illégale; ~ *key* crochet *m*, rossignol *m*; ~ *teeth pl.* dentier *m*; 2. *adv. play s.o.* ~ trahir q.; **false·hood** [ˈ~hud] mensonge *m*; fausseté *f*; faux *m*; **ˈfalse·ness** fausseté *f*; *femme etc.*: infidélité *f*.

fal·set·to ♩ [fɔːlˈsetou] fausset *m*.

fal·si·fi·ca·tion [ˈfɔːlsifiˈkeiʃn] falsification *f*; altération *f*; **fal·si·fi·er** [ˈ~faiə] falsificateur (-trice *f*) *m*; **fal·si·fy** [ˈ~fai] falsifier; altérer; rendre vain; tromper; **fal·si·ty** [ˈ~ti] fausseté *f*.

fal·ter [ˈfɔːltə] *v/i.* chanceler; *fig.* hésiter, trembler (*voix*); défaillir (*courage, personne*); *v/t.* balbutier.

fame [feim] renom(mée *f*) *m*; **famed** célèbre, renommé (pour, for).

fa·mil·iar [fəˈmiljə] 1. ☐ familier (-ère *f*) (à, to); intime; bien connu (de, to); au courant (de, with); 2. ami(e *f*) *m* intime; (*a.* ~ *spirit*) démon *m* familier; **fa·mil·i·ar·i·ty** [~liˈæriti] familiarité *f*; connaissance *f* (de, with); **fa·mil·iar·i·za·tion** [~ljəraiˈzeiʃn] accoutumance *f* (à, with), habitude *f* (de, with); **fa·mil·iar·ize** rendre familier.

fam·i·ly [ˈfæmili] 1. famille *f*; 2. de famille, familial (-aux *m/pl.*); *in the* ~ *way* enceinte (*f*); ~ *allowance* allocation *f* familiale; ~ *doctor* médecin *m* de famille; ~ *man* père *m* de famille; ~ *tree* arbre *m* généalogique.

fam·ine [ˈfæmin] famine *f*; disette *f*.

fam·ish [ˈfæmiʃ] *v/t.* affamer; réduire à la famine; *v/i.* être affamé.

fa·mous ☐ [ˈfeiməs] célèbre (pour, for); F fameux (-euse *f*), parfait.

fan¹ [fæn] 1. éventail *m* (*a.* ♣); ventilateur *m*; ✔ *van m*; *mot.* ~ *belt* courroie *f* de ventilateur; 2. éventer; ✔ vanner; souffler (*le feu*); *fig.* exciter.

fan² F [~] *sp. etc.* fervent(e *f*) *m*; *cin.* fanatique *mf*; *radio:* sans-filiste *mf*; *mots composés:* -ophile *mf*.

fa·nat·ic [fəˈnætik] 1. (*a.* faˈnat·i·cal ☐ [~kl]) fanatique; 2. fanatique *mf*; **faˈnat·i·cism** [~isizm] fanatisme *m*.

fan·ci·er [ˈfænsiə] amateur (-trice *f*) *m* (d'oiseaux *etc.*).

fan·ci·ful □ [ˈfænsiful] fantastique; fantasque, imaginaire (*personne*).

fan·cy [ˈfænsi] **1.** fantaisie *f*, imagination *f*; idée *f*; caprice *m*, goût *m*; lubie *f*; the ~ les amateurs *m/pl.* de boxe; *take a* ~ *to* prendre goût à (*qch.*); s'éprendre de (*q.*); **2.** de fantaisie; de luxe; de pure imagination; ~ *apron* tablier *m* de fantaisie; ~ *ball* bal *m* travesti; ~ *dress* travesti *m*, costume *m*; ~ *fair* vente *f* de charité; ~ *goods pl.* nouveautés *f/pl.*, articles *m/pl.* de fantaisie; *sl.* ~ *man* souteneur *m*; ~ *price* prix *m* exagéré *ou* de fantaisie; **3.** s'imaginer, se figurer; croire, penser; avoir envie de (*qch.*); se sentir attiré vers (*q.*); *just* ~! figurez-vous (ça)!; '~-**free** libre comme l'air; '~-**work** broderie *f*; ouvrages *m/pl.* de dames.

fan·fare [ˈfænfeə] fanfare *f*; sonnerie *f*; **fan·fa·ron·ade** [ˌfærə-ˈnɑːd] fanfaronnade *f*, vanterie *f*.

fang [fæŋ] *chien*: croc *m*; *vipère*: crochet *m*; ⊕ soie *f*.

fan·ner [ˈfænə] ✒ van *m* mécanique; ⊕ ventilateur *m*.

fan·ta·sia ♩ [fænˈteizjə] fantaisie *f*; **fan·tas·tic** [ˌˈtæstik] (ˌally) fantastique, bizarre; **fan'tas·ti·cal·ness** [ˌklnis] bizarrerie *f*; **fan·ta·sy** [ˈˌtəsi] fantaisie *f*, caprice *m*.

far [fɑː] *adj.* lointain, éloigné; *adv.* loin, au loin; beaucoup, fort, bien; ~ *better* beaucoup mieux; ~ *the best* de beaucoup le meilleur; *as* ~ *as* jusqu'à; *by* ~ de beaucoup; ~ *from* (*gér.*) loin de (*inf.*); *in so* ~ *as* dans la mesure où; ~-**a·way** [ˈfɑːrəwei] lointain; *fig.* vague.

farce *théâ.* [fɑːs] farce *f* (*a. cuis.*); **far·ci·cal** □ [ˈˌikl] burlesque; *fig.* grotesque.

fare [feə] **1.** prix *m* (du voyage, de la place, *etc.*); chère *f*, manger *m*; *personne*: client(e *f*) *m*; **2.** voyager; aller (*bien ou mal*); ~ *well!* adieu!; '~-**in·di·ca·tor** tarif *m*; '~-**well 1.** adieu!; **2.** adieu *m*, -x *m/pl.*; **3.** d'adieu; ~ *party* soirée *f* d'adieu.

far... [fɑː]: '~-**fetched** *fig.* tiré par les cheveux, recherché, forcé; '~-**flung** *fig.* vaste, très étendu; ~ *gone* F (dans un état) avancé.

far·i·na·ceous [færiˈneiʃəs] farinacé; ~ *food* (aliment *m*) farineux *m*.

farm [fɑːm] **1.** ferme *f*; *see* ~ *house*; élevage *m* de volaille en grand; **2.**

v/t. cultiver; (*a.* ~ *out*) donner à ferme, affermer; exploiter (*un terrain*); mettre en nourrice (*des enfants*); *v/i.* être fermier, cultiver la terre; '**farm·er** fermier *m*; '**farm·hand** ouvrier (-ère *f*) *m* agricole; '**farm'house** (maison *f* de) ferme *f*; '**farm·ing 1.** cultivateur (-trice *f*); à ferme; aratoire *f*; **2.** agriculture *f*; exploitation *f*; culture *f*; '**farm·stead** [ˈˌsted] ferme *f*; '**farm'yard** basse-cour (*pl.* basses-cours) *f*; cour *f* de ferme.

far·o [ˈfeərou] *cartes*: pharaon *m*.

far...: ~-**off** [ˈfɑːˈɔːf] lointain, éloigné; penser; extravagant; super. ~-**out** [ˈfɑːˈraut] insolite; extravagant; super.

far·ra·go [fəˈreigou] méli-mélo (*pl.* mélis-mélos) *m*; fatras *m*.

far·ri·er [ˈfæriə] vétérinaire *m*; ✗ maréchal-ferrant (*pl.* maréchaux-ferrants) *m*; '**far·ri·er·y** art *m* vétérinaire; ✗ maréchalerie *f*.

far·row [ˈfærou] **1.** cochonnée *f*; **2.** *vt/i.* mettre bas; *v/i.* cochonner.

far·sight·ed [ˈfɑːˈsaitid] ✗ presbyte; *fig.* prévoyant.

fart V [fɑːt] **1.** pet *m*; **2.** péter.

far·ther [ˈfɑːðə], **far·thest** [ˈˌðist] *comp.*, *a. sup.* de far.

far·thing [ˈfɑːðiŋ] F sou *m* (¹/₄ penny).

fas·ci·a [ˈfæʃiə], *pl.* **fas·ci·ae** [ˈˌii] *anat.* fascia *m*; △ fasce *f*, bande (-lette) *f*.

fas·ci·nate [ˈfæsineit] fasciner, charmer; **fas·ci·na·tion** fascination *f*; charme *m*, attrait *m*.

fas·cine [fæˈsiːn] fascine *f*.

Fas·cism *pol.* [ˈfæʃizm] fascisme *m*; '**Fas·cist** fasciste (*a. su./mf*).

fash·ion [ˈfæʃn] **1.** mode *f*; vogue *f*; façon *f*, manière *f*; forme *f*; habitude *f*; *sl. rank and* ~ le gratin *m*; *in* ~ à la mode; *out of* ~ démodé; *set the* ~ mener la mode; donner le ton; **2.** façonner, former; confectionner (*une robe*); '**fash·ion·a·ble** □ à la mode, de bon ton; élégant; '**fash·ion·a·ble·ness** vogue *f*; élégance *f*; '**fash·ion·pa·rade** présentation *f* de collections; '**fash·ion-plate** gravure *f* de modes.

fast[1] [fɑːst] **1.** *adj.* rapide; résistant, bon teint (*drap etc.*); en avance (*montre etc.*); fidèle, constant (*ami*); dissolu (*vie*); ~ *to light* résistant; *phys.* ~ *breeder* surrégénérateur *m* rapide; 🚂 ~ *train* rapide *m*, train *m* express; 2. *adv.* ferme; vite.

fast² [␣] **1.** jeûne *m*; **2.** jeûner; '**~-day** jour *m* maigre.

fas·ten ['fɑːsn] *v/t.* attacher (à, to); amarrer (*un bateau*); fermer (*la porte*); assurer; fixer (*a.* les yeux sur, *one's eyes* [up]on); *v/i.* s'attacher; se fixer; se fermer; ~ *upon fig.* saisir (*qch.*); s'arrêter sur; '**fas·ten·er** (*a.* '**fas·ten·ing**) attache *f*; *robe:* agrafe *f; bourse, livre:* fermoir *m; fenêtre etc.:* fermeture *f; patent* ~ bouton-pression (*pl.* boutons-pression) *m*.

fas·tid·i·ous □ [fæs'tidiəs] difficile; délicat; exigeant; blasé; **fas'tid·i·ous·ness** délicatesse *f;* goût *m* difficile.

fast·ness ['fɑːstnis] fermeté *f; couleurs:* solidité *f;* vitesse *f;* légèreté *f* de conduite; ⚔ forteresse *f*.

fat [fæt] **1.** □ gras(se *f*); gros(se *f*); **2.** graisse *f; viande:* gras *m;* **3.** (s')engraisser.

fa·tal □ ['feitl] fatal (-als *m/pl.*); mortel(le *f*); funeste (à, to); **fa·tal·ism** ['~əlizm] fatalisme *m;* '**fa·tal·ist** fataliste *m; **fa·tal·i·ty** [fə'tæliti] fatalité *f;* mort *f;* destin *m;* accident *m* mortel, sinistre *m*.

fate [feit] destin *m;* sort *m;* fatalité *f; the* ♀s les Parques *f/pl.;* **fat·ed** ['~id] destiné; fatal (-als *m/pl.*); infortuné; '**fate·ful** □ ['~ful] décisif (-ive *f*).

fat·head *sl.* ['fæthed] idiot(e *f*) *m*.

fa·ther ['fɑːðə] **1.** père *m;* **2.** engendrer; adopter; avouer la paternité de; servir de père à; ~ *s.th. upon s.o.* imputer qch. à q.; '**fa·ther·hood** ['~hud] paternité *f;* '**fa·ther-in-law** beau-père (*pl.* beaux-pères) *m;* '**fa·ther·land** patrie *f;* '**fa·ther·less** sans père; '**fa·ther·ly** paternel(le *f*).

fath·om ['fæðəm] **1.** *mes.* toise *f;* ⚓ brasse *f;* ⚓ 216 pieds *m/pl.* cubes; **2.** ⚓ (*a. fig.*) sonder; *fig.* approfondir; '**fath·om·less** sans fond.

fa·tigue [fə'tiːg] **1.** fatigue *f;* ⚔ corvée *f;* ~*s pl.* ⚔ tenue *f* de corvée; **2.** fatiguer, lasser; **fa'tigue-par·ty** ⚔ (détachement *m* de) corvée *f*.

fat·ling ['fætliŋ] jeune bête *f* engraissée; '**fat·ness** graisse *f; personne:* embonpoint *m; sol:* fertilité *f;*

'**fat·ten** (s')engraisser; devenir *ou* rendre gras; *v/t.* fertiliser (*le sol*); '**fat·ty** **1.** graisseux (-euse *f*); gras(se *f*) (*sol*); ~ *degeneration* stéatose *f;* **2.** F gros (bonhomme) *m*.

fa·tu·i·ty [fə'tjuiti] sottise *f;* imbécillité *f;* **fat·u·ous** □ ['fætjuəs] sot(te *f*), imbécile.

fau·cet ⊕ *surt. Am.* ['fɔːsit] robinet *m*.

faugh [fɔː] pouah!

fault [fɔːlt] faute *f* (*a. tennis*); imperfection *f;* défaut *m* (*a.* ⚡, ⊕); ⊕ *métal:* paille *f;* *géol.* faille *f; to a* ~ à l'excès; *find* ~ *with* trouver à redire à; *be at* ~ être en défaut; *be his* ~ être (de) sa faute; '**~-find·er** épilogueur (-euse *f*); censeur (-euse *f*); '**~-find·ing 1.** sermonneur (-euse *f*); grondeur (-euse *f*); **2.** censure *f*, critique *f;* disposition *f* à critiquer; '**fault·i·ness** imperfection *f;* '**fault·less** □ sans défaut; sans faute; parfait; '**faults·man** *tel., téléph.* surveillant *m* de ligne (*qui recherche les dérangements*); '**fault·y** □ défectueux (-euse *f*) imparfait.

fa·vo(u)r ['feivə] **1.** faveur *f;* permission *f;* bonté *f;* nœud *m* de rubans, couleurs *f/pl.;* † *your* ~ † votre honorée *f ou* estimée *f;* † *in great* ~ très recherché; *in* ~ *of* en faveur de; *I am (not) in* ~ *of it* moi je suis pour (contre); *under* ~ *of night* à la faveur de la nuit; **2.** être en faveur de; approuver; honorer (de, *with*); **fa·vo(u)r·a·ble** □ ['~vərəbl] (to) favorable (à); bon(ne *f*); '**fa·vo(u)r·a·ble·ness** caractère *m* favorable; **fa·vo(u)red** ['~vəd] favorisé; *well-*~ beau (bel *devant une voyelle ou un h muet*); belle *f;* beaux *m/pl.*); **fa·vo(u)r·ite** ['~vərit] **1.** favori(te *f*), préféré; **2.** favori(te *f*) *m; sp.* favori *m;* '**fa·vo(u)r·it·ism** favoritisme *m; sl.* piston *m*.

fawn¹ [fɔːn] **1.** *zo.* faon *m;* (couleur *f*) fauve *m;* **2.** mettre bas (un faon).

fawn² [␣] *chien:* caresser (q., [up]on *s.o.*); *personne:* aduler (q.); '**fawn·er** adulateur (-trice *f*) *m;* '**fawn·ing** caressant; servile.

faze *surt. Am.* F [feiz] bouleverser.

fe·al·ty ['fiːəlti] féauté *f;* fidélité *f*.

fear [fiə] **1.** peur *f*, crainte *f; through (ou from)* ~ *of* de peur de; *for* ~ *of* (*gér.*) de crainte de (*inf.*); go in ~ of one's life craindre pour sa vie; **2.** craindre; *v/t.* redouter, avoir peur de; *v/i.* avoir peur; **fear·ful** □ ['ˏful] craintif (-ive *f*); timide; affreux (-euse *f*); **'fear·ful·ness** caractère *m* épouvantable; timidité *f*; **'fear·less** □ intrépide; sans peur (de, *of*); **'fear·less·ness** intrépidité *f*, courage *m*.

fea·si·bil·i·ty [fiːzəˈbiliti] possibilité *f*; **'fea·si·ble** possible, faisable.

feast [fiːst] **1.** fête *f* (*a. eccl.*); festin *m*; *fig.* régal *m*; **2.** *v/t.* fêter; ~ one's eyes on assouvir ses yeux de; *v/i.* faire bonne chère; se régaler (de, [*up*]on).

feat [fiːt] exploit *m*, haut fait *m*.

feath·er ['feðə] **1.** plume *f*; *aile, queue*: penne *f*; *chasse*: gibier *m* à plumes; ✕ plumet *m*; F show the white ~ caner, manquer de courage; that is a ~ in his cap c'est une perle à sa couronne; in high ~ d'exellente humeur; **2.** *v/t.* emplumer; empenner (*une flèche*); ⚓ ramener à plat (*l'aviron*); *v/i.* nager plat; ~ one's nest faire sa pelote; '~-brained,'~-head·ed étourdi, écervelé; **'feath·ered** emplumé, empenné (*flèche*); **'feath·er-edge** ⊕ biseau *m*; morfil *m* (*d'un outil*); **'feath·er·ing** plumage *m*; empennage *m*; biseautage *m*; nage *f* plate; **'feath·er-stitch** point *m* d'arêtes; **'feath·er-weight** *box.* poids *m* plume; **'feath·er·y** plumeux (-euse *f*); léger (-ère *f*.)

fea·ture ['fiːtʃə] **1.** trait *m* (*a. du visage*); caractéristique *f*; spécialité *f*; *cin.* film *m*; *journ. Am.* article *m*; ~s *pl.* physionomie *f*; *pays.*: topographie *f*; *œuvre*: caractère *m*; **2.** marquer, caractériser; dépeindre; *journ.* mettre en manchette; *cin.* tourner (*un rôle*), représenter (*q.*); mettre en vedette; a film featuring N.N. un film avec N.N. en vedette; ~ film grand film *m* du programme; **'fea·ture·less** sans traits bien marqués; peu intéressant.

feb·ri·fuge ['febrifjuːdʒ] fébrifuge *m*.

fe·brile ['fiːbrail] fiévreux (-euse *f*).

Feb·ru·ar·y ['februəri] février *m*.

feck·less ['feklis] propre à rien, incapable.

fec·u·lence ['fekjuləns] féculence

f; saleté *f*; **'fec·u·lent** féculent; sale.

fe·cun·date ['fiːkʌndeit] féconder; **fe·cun·da·tion** fécondation *f*; **fe·cun·di·ty** [fiˈkʌnditi] fécondité *f*.

fed [fed] *prét. et p.p. de* feed **2**; be ~ up with en avoir assez de; well ~ bien nourri.

fed·er·al ['fedərəl] fédéral (-aux *m/pl.*); **'fed·er·al·ism** fédéralisme *m*; **'fed·er·al·ist** fédéraliste *mf*; **'fed·er·al·ize** (se) fédérer; **fed·er·ate 1.** ['ˏreit] (se) fédérer; **2.** ['ˏrit] fédéré; allié; **fed·er·a·tion** fédération *f*; *ouvriers etc.*: syndicat *m*; **fed·er·a·tive** ['ˏrətiv] fédératif (-ive *f*).

fee [fiː] **1.** honoraires *m/pl.*; *école*: frais *m/pl.*; droit *m*; taxe *f*; *hist.* fief *m*; pourboire *m*; ~ simple propriété *f* libre; **2.** payer des honoraires (à q., *s.o.*); donner un pourboire à (*q.*).

fee·ble □ ['fiːbl] faible; '~-'mind·ed à l'esprit faible; **'fee·ble·ness** faiblesse *f*.

feed [fiːd] **1.** alimentation *f* (*a.* ⊕); pâturage *m*; *cheval*: fourrage *m*; *avoine etc.*: picotin *m*; nourriture *f*; F repas *m*; ⊕ entraînement *m*; *attr.* d'alimentation *etc.*; auxiliaire; **2.** [*irr.*] *v/t.* nourrir (*q., l'esprit*); alimenter (⊕, *sp.*, *machine, chaudière, feu, famille*); faire paître (*les vaches etc.*); manger (*a. q. des yeux, one's eyes on s.o.*); introduire (*des matières premières dans une machine*); *théâ.* donner la réplique à; ~ off (*ou* down) pâturer (*un pré*); ~ up engraisser; see fed; *v/i.* manger, paître, se nourrir (de, [*up*]on); '~-back **1.** ⚡ réaction *f*; **2.** ⊕ alimenter en retour; **'feed·er** mangeur (-euse *f*) *m*; *surt. Am.* nourrisseur *m* de bestiaux; *enfant*: bavette *f*; *bébé*: biberon *m*; canal *m* d'alimentation; ⊕ alimentateur *m*; ⚡ artère *f* ou conducteur *m* alimentaire; **feed·er line** 🚂 embranchement *m*; **'feed·ing** alimentation *f*; pâture *f*; ⊕, ⚡ avance *f*; *attr.* du repas; alimentateur (-trice *f*); high ~ vie *f* de luxe; **'feed·ing-bottle** biberon *m*; **'feed·ing-stuff** fourrage *m*.

fee-faw-fum ['fiːˈfɔːˈfʌm] pouah!

feel [fiːl] **1.** [*irr.*] *v/t.* sentir; tâter (*a.* ✕); ressentir (*une douleur, une émotion*); éprouver; penser; être sensible à; avoir conscience de; *v/i.* être ... au toucher (*chose*); sembler, paraître; se sentir (*personne*); se trouver; ~ *cold* avoir froid (*personne*), être froid (au toucher) (*chose*); *I* ~ *like* (*gér.*) j'ai envie de (*inf.*); je me sens d'humeur à (*inf.*); ~ *for* avoir de la sympathie pour; **2.** toucher *m*; sensation *f*; **'feel·er** *fig.* ballon *m* d'essai; *zo.* antenne *f*; *escargot:* corne *f*; *mollusque etc.:* tentacule *m*; *chat:* moustache *f*; ⚔ éclaireur *m*; **'feel·ing 1.** □ sensible; ému; **2.** toucher *m*; émotion *f*; sentiment *m*; sensibilité *f*; *good* ~ bonne entente *f*; sympathie *f*.

feet [fi:t] *pl. de* **foot 1.**

feign [fein] feindre, faire semblant (de *inf.*, *to inf.*); ~ *mad* faire semblant d'être fou; **'feigned** feint, simulé; contrefait; déguisé; **feign·ed·ly** ['~idli] avec feinte.

feint [feint] **1.** feinte *f*; ⚔ fausse attaque *f*; **2.** feinter; ⚔ faire une fausse attaque.

fe·lic·i·tate [fi'lisiteit] féliciter (de, sur *on*); **fe·lic·i'ta·tion** félicitation *f*; **fe'lic·i·tous** □ heureux (-euse *f*); à propos; **fe'lic·i·ty** félicité *f*, bonheur *m*; à-propos *m*.

fe·line ['fi:lain] félin, de chat.

fell¹ [fel] **1.** *prét. de* **fall 2**; **2.** abattre; assommer.

fell² *poét.* [~] cruel(le *f*); funeste.

fell³ [~] peau *f*; toison *f*.

fell⁴ [~] colline *f* rocheuse.

fel·loe ['felou] jante *f*.

fel·low ['felou] personne *f*; camarade *m*; compagnon *m*, compagne *f*; collègue *m*; semblable *m*, pareil *m*; *univ.* agrégé(e *f*) *m*; *société:* membre *m*; *F* homme *m*, type *m*; *péj.* individu *m*; *attr.* compagnon de; co(n)-; *F a* ~ on; *F old* ~ mon vieux *m*; *the* ~ *of a glove* l'autre gant *m*; *he has not his* ~ il n'a pas son pareil *ou* de rival; **'~-'be·ings** *pl.* semblables *m/pl.*; **'~-'cit·i·zen** concitoyen(ne *f*) *m*; **'~-'coun·try·man** compatriote *mf*; **'~-'crea·ture** semblable *m*; prochain *m*; **'~-'feel·ing** sympathie *f*; **~ship** ['~ʃip] communauté *f*; association *f*; (*a. good* ~) camaraderie *f*, solidarité *f*; association *f*, société *f*; fraternité *f*; *univ.* dignité *f* d'agrégé (*d'un collège universitaire*); titre *m* de membre (*d'une société savante*); ~ **sol·dier**

compagnon *m* d'armes; **'~-'stu·dent** camarade *mf* d'études; **'~-'trav·el·ler** compagnon *m* (compagne *f*) de voyage; *pol.* communisant(e *f*) *m*.

fel·ly ['feli] jante *f*.

fel·on ['felən] ⚕ criminel(le *f*) *m*; ⚕ panaris *m*; **fe·lo·ni·ous** □ ⚕ [fi'lounjəs] criminel(le *f*); délictueux (-euse *f*); **fel·o·ny** ⚕ ['feləni] crime *m*.

felt¹ [felt] *prét. et p.p. de* **feel 1.**

felt² [~] **1.** feutre *m*; **2.** (se) feutrer; **~-tip(ped) pen** ['~tip(t) pen] crayon *m* feutre.

fe·male ['fi:meil] **1.** féminin (*personne*); femelle (*animal*); ~ *child* enfant *m* du sexe féminin; ~ *screw* vis *f* femelle; **2.** femme *f*; *animal:* femelle *f*.

fem·i·nine □ ['feminin] féminin; *gramm.* du féminin; *souv. péj.* de femme; **fem·i'nin·i·ty** féminité *f*; *péj.* caractère *m* féminin; **'fem·i·nism** féminisme *m*; **'fem·i·nist** féministe (*a. su. mf*); **fem·i·nize** ['~naiz] (se) féminiser.

fen [fen] marais *m*, marécage *m*.

fence [fens] **1.** clôture *f*; palissade *f*; ⊕ guide *m*; garde *f*; *sp.* haie *f*; *Am.* mur *m* de clôture; *sl.* receleur (-euse *f*) *m*; *sit on the* ~ attendre d'où vient le vent; **2.** *v/t.* (*a.* ~ *in*) enclore, entourer; protéger (contre, *from*); *sl.* receler; *v/i.* faire de l'escrime; *fig.* parer (qch., *with s.th.*); *sp.* sauter les haies; *sl.* faire le recel; **'fence·less** ouvert, sans clôture.

fenc·ing ['fensiŋ] clôture *f*, palissade *f*; escrime *f*; ⊕ garde *f*; *attr.* d'armes; **'~-foil** fleuret *m*; **'~-mas·ter** maître *m* d'armes.

fend [fend]: ~ *off* détourner; *F* ~ *for* pourvoir à; ~ *for o.s.* se débrouiller; **'fend·er** △ bouteroue *f*; garde-feu *m/inv.*; *mot. Am.* aile *f*; *mot.* pare-chocs *m/inv.*; ⚓ défense *f*.

Fe·ni·an ['fi:niən] **1.** fénian; **2.** fénian *m* (*membre d'une association d'Irlandais aux É.-U. partisans de l'Indépendance de l'Irlande*).

fen·nel ♀ ['fenl] fenouil *m*.

fen·ny ['feni] marécageux (-euse *f*).

feoff [fef] fief *m*; **feoff·ee** [fe'fi:] fieffataire *mf*; **'feoff·ment** inféodation *f*; don *m* en fief; **feof·for** [fe'fɔ:] fieffant(e *f*) *m*.

fer·ment 1. ['fə:ment] ferment *m*; *fig.* agitation *f*; **2.** [fə'ment] (faire) fermenter; *fig.* (s')échauffer; **fer·**'**ment·a·ble** fermentable; **fer·men·ta·tion** [fə:men'teiʃn] fermentation *f*; *fig.* effervescence *f*; **fer·**'**ment·a·tive** [‿tətiv] fermentatif (-ive *f*).

fern ♀ [fə:n] fougère *f*.

fe·ro·cious □ [fə'rouʃəs] féroce; **fe·roc·i·ty** [fə'rɔsiti] férocité *f*.

fer·ret ['ferit] **1.** *zo.* furet *m* (*a. fig.*); **2.** *v/t.* fureter (*un terrier*); ~ **out** découvrir, dénicher; *fig.* déterrer; *v/i.* chasser au furet.

fer·ric ⚗ ['ferik] ferrique; **fer·rif·er·ous** [fe'rifərəs] ferrifère.

Fer·ris wheel ['feriswi:l] *foire*: grande roue *f*.

fer·ru·gi·nous [fe'ru:dʒinəs] ferrifère; **fer·ro·con·crete** ⊕ ['ferou-'kɔŋkri:t] béton *m* armé; **fer·rous** ⚗ ['ferəs] ferreux (-euse *f*).

fer·rule ['feru:l] bout *m* ferré; virole *f*.

fer·ry ['feri] **1.** passage *m*; bac *m*; **2.** passer la rivière en bac; '~-**boat** bac *m*; '**fer·ry·man** passeur *m*.

fer·tile □ ['fə:tail] (*a. fig.*) fertile, fécond (en *of*, *in*); **fer·til·i·ty** [fə'tiliti] fertilité *f* (*a. fig.*); **fer·ti·li·za·tion** [‿tilai'zeiʃn] fertilisation *f*; ♀ pollinisation *f*; '**fer·ti·lize** (*a.* ♀) fertiliser, féconder; amender (*la terre*); '**fer·ti·liz·er** engrais *m*.

fer·ule † ['feru:l] férule *f* (*a.* ♀).

fer·ven·cy ['fə:vənsi] (*usu. fig.*) ferveur *f*; ardeur *f*; '**fer·vent** □ ardent (*a. fig.*); *fig.* fervent, vif (vive *f*).

fer·vid □ ['fə:vid] *see* fervent.

fer·vo(u)r ['fə:və] *see* fervency.

fes·tal □ ['festl] de fête; joyeux (-euse *f*).

fes·ter ['festə] **1.** (faire) suppurer; (s')ulcérer; *fig.* couver; **2.** inflammation *f* avec suppuration.

fes·ti·val ['festəvl] fête *f*; ♪, *théâ.* festival *m*; **fes·tive** □ ['‿iv] de fête, joyeux (-euse *f*); **fes'tiv·i·ty** fête *f*, réjouissance *f*, festivité *f*.

fes·toon [fes'tu:n] **1.** feston *m*; **2.** festonner.

fetch [fetʃ] *v/t.* apporter (*qch.*); amener (*q.*); aller chercher; rapporter (*un prix*); F captiver; F flanquer (*un coup*); pousser (*un soupir*); tirer (*des larmes*); ~ **up** faire monter; vomir; *v/i.*: ~ **and carry** être aux ordres (de *q.*, for *s.o.*); ~ **up** s'arrêter; *usu. Am.* aboutir (à, *at*); '**fetch·ing** F □ ravissant, séduisant.

fête [feit] **1.** fête *f* (*a. eccl.*); **2.** fêter.

fet·id □ ['fetid] fétide, puant.

fe·tish ['fi:tiʃ] fétiche *m*.

fet·ter ['fetə] **1.** chaîne *f*; **2.** enchaîner.   [dition *f*.]

fet·tle ['fetl] forme *f*; bonne con-]

fe·tus ['fi:təs] *see* foetus.

feud [fju:d] inimitié *f*; fief *m*; **feu·dal** □ ['‿dl] féodal (-aux *m/pl.*); **feu·dal·ism** ['‿dəlizm] féodalité *f*; **feu·dal·i·ty** [‿'dæliti] féodalité *f*; fief *m*; **feu·da·to·ry** ['‿dətəri] feudataire (*a. su./m*), vassal (-aux *m/pl.*) (*a. su./m*).

fe·ver ['fi:və] fièvre *f*; **fe·vered** ['fi:vəd] *surt. fig.* fiévreux (-euse *f*); '**fe·ver·ish** □ fiévreux (-euse *f*) (*a. fig.*).

few [fju:] **1.** *adj.* peu de; quelques; **2.** *pron.*: *a* ~ quelques-uns (-unes *f*); *a good* ~ pas mal (de); **3.** *su.* petit nombre *m*; **the** ~ la minorité.

fi·at ['faiæt] décret *m*; consentement *m*; *Am.* ~ **money** monnaie *f* fiduciaire (*billets de banque*).

fib [fib] **1.** petit mensonge *m*; blague *f*; **2.** mentir; blaguer; '**fib·ber** menteur (-euse *f*) *m*; blagueur (-euse *f*) *m*.

fi·bre, *Am.* **fi·ber** ['faibə] fibre *f* (*a.* ⊕); ♀ radicelle *f*; *fig.* nature *f*, trempe *f*; **fi·brin** ['‿brin] ⚗, *physiol.* fibrine *f*; **fi·bro·si·tis** ['‿brou'saitis] cellulite *f*; '**fi·brous** □ fibreux (-euse *f*).

fib·u·la *anat.* ['fibjulə], *pl.* -**lae** [‿li:], -**las** péroné *m*.

fick·le ['fikl] inconstant, volage; changeant; '**fick·le·ness** inconstance *f*; humeur *f* volage.

fic·tile ['fiktail] plastique, céramique (*argile*).

fic·tion ['fikʃn] fiction *f* (*a.* ⚖); (*a.* works of ~) romans *m/pl.*, littérature *f* d'imagination; '**fic·tion·al** □ de romans; d'imagination.

fic·ti·tious □ [fik'tiʃəs] fictif (-ive *f*); imaginaire; inventé; feint; '**fic·tive** fictif (-ive *f*), imaginaire.

fid·dle ['fidl] **1.** violon *m*; **2.** *v/i.* jouer du violon; tripoter; *v/t.* jouer (*un air*) sur le violon; *souv. Am.* truquer; ~ **away** perdre (*son temps*);

fid·dle·de·dee ['ˌdi'di:] quelle blague!; **fid·dle·fad·dle** F ['ˌfædl] **1.** fadaises f/pl.; ~! quelle blague!; **2.** musard; **3.** baguenauder; '**fid·dler** joueur m du violon; '**fid·dle·stick** archet m; ~s! quelle bêtise!

fi·del·i·ty [fi'deliti] fidélité f, loyauté f (à, envers to, towards).

fidg·et F ['fidʒit] **1.** usu. ~s pl. agitation f, énervement m; personne: énervé(e f) m; have the ~s ne pas tenir en place; **2.** (s')énerver; (se) tourmenter; v/i. s'agiter; '**fidg·et·y** agité, nerveux (-euse f), impatient.

fi·du·ci·ar·y [fi'dju:ʃiəri] **1.** fiduciaire; **2.** héritier (-ère f) m fiduciaire; dépositaire mf.

fie [fai] fi (donc)!

fief [fi:f] fief m.

field [fi:ld] **1.** champ m; pré m; sp. terrain m; course: champ m; fig. domaine m; † marché m; ✕ champ m de bataille; glace: banc m; hold the ~ ✕ se maintenir sur ses positions; fig. être toujours en faveur; **2.** cricket: v/i. tenir le champ; v/t. arrêter et relancer (la balle); '~-**day** ✕ jour m de grandes manœuvres ou de revue; fig. grande occasion f, grand jour m; Am. réunion f athlétique; Am. journée f d'expédition en pleine campagne; '**field·er** cricket: chasseur m.

field ...: '~-**fare** litorne f; '~-**glass** jumelle f, -s f/pl.; '~-**jack·et** anorak m; '2-**Mar·shal** feld-maréchal m; '~-**sports** pl. chasse f et pêche f; '~-**work** travaux m/pl. ou recherches f/pl. sur le terrain ou sur les lieux; † démarchage m auprès de la clientèle; sociologie: travail m avec des cas sociaux.

fiend [fi:nd] démon m, esprit m malin; diable m; fig. monstre m; fig. fanatique mf (de); '**fiend·ish** □ diabolique; infernal (-aux m/pl.).

fierce □ [fiəs] féroce; violent; furieux (-euse f); '**fierce·ness** férocité f; violence f; fureur f.

fi·er·i·ness ['faiərinis] ardeur f (a. fig.); '**fi·er·y** □ de feu; enflammé; ardent; emporté (personne).

fife [faif] **1.** fifre m; **2.** v/t. fifrer; v/i. jouer du fifre; '**fif·er** (joueur m de) fifre m.

fif·teen ['fif'ti:n] quinze; '**fif'teenth** [~θ] quinzième (a. su./m); **fifth** [fifθ] cinquième (a. su./m); '**fifth·ly** en cinquième lieu; **fif·ti·eth** ['~tiiθ] cinquantième (a. su./m); '**fif·ty** cinquante; '**fif·ty-'fif·ty** chacun(e f) la moitié; go ~ être de moitié.

fig[1] [fig] figue f; arbre: figuier m; a ~ for ...! zut pour ...!; I don't care a ~ for him je m'en fiche (de lui).

fig[2] F [~] **1.** forme f; gala f; in full ~ en grande toilette ou tenue; in good ~ en bonne forme; **2.** ~ out attifer.

fight [fait] **1.** combat m, bataille f; box. assaut m; (a. free ~) bagarre f; fig. lutte f; make a ~ for lutter pour; put up a good ~ se bien acquitter; show ~ offrir de la résistance; **2.** [irr.] v/t. se battre avec ou contre; combattre; lutter contre; ~ off repousser, résister à; v/i. se battre; combattre; lutter; ~ against combattre (q., qch.); ~ back résister à, repousser; ~ for se battre pour; ~ shy of éviter; ~ing fit frais et dispos; en parfaite santé; '**fight·er** combattant m, guerroyeur m; ~ plane avion m de chasse, chasseur m; '**fight·ing** combat m; attr. de combat.   [vention f.]

fig·ment ['figmənt] fiction f, in-]

fig-tree ['figtri:] figuier m.

fig·u·rant ['figjurənt] figurant m.

fig·u·ra·tion [figju'reiʃn] (con-) figuration f; ♪ embellissement m; **fig·u·ra·tive** □ ['~rətiv] figuratif (-ive f); figuré; en images.

fig·ure ['figə] **1.** figure f (a. ♪, danse, géométrie, livre); taille f, forme f; ♣ chiffre m; image f; tissu: dessin m; F what's the ~? ça coûte combien?; at a high ~ à un prix élevé; **2.** v/t. écrire en chiffres; ♪ chiffrer; brocher (un tissu); (a. ~ to o.s., se) figurer, représenter; Am. estimer; ~ up (ou out) calculer; ~ out résoudre (un problème); v/i. chiffrer, calculer; ~ as représenter; ~ on se trouver sur; Am. compter sur; ~ out at (se) monter à; '~-**head** ⚓ figure f de proue; fig. personnage m purement décoratif; prête-nom m; '~-**skat·ing** tracé m des figures sur la glace.

fig·u·rine ['figjuri:n] figurine f.

fil·a·ment ['filəmənt] filament m (a. ⚡); ⚡, zo., phys. filet m; attr. ⚡, radio: de chauffage.

fil·bert ♀ ['filbə:t] aveline *f*; *arbre*: avelinier *m*.

filch [filtʃ] chiper (à, *from*).

file¹ [fail] **1.** dossier *m* (*a.* 🕮), *lettres*: classeur *m*; *papiers*: liasse *f*; crochet *m* à papiers; fichier *m*; ✂ file *f*; *in single* ~ en file indienne; *Am.* ~ *case* classeur *m*; fichier *m*; *Am.* ~ *clerk* documentaliste *mf*; ~*-leader* chef *m* de file; **2.** ✕ (faire) marcher en ligne de file; ✕ ~ *off* (faire) défiler; *v/t.* enfiler; classer; ranger; joindre au dossier; enregistrer (*une enquête*); *Am.* déposer (*une plainte*); *filing cabinet* fichier *m*; classeur *m*; *filing clerk* documentaliste *mf*.

file² [~] **1.** lime *f*; *sl. deep* ~ fin matois *m*; **2.** limer; **'**~*-cut·ter** tailleur *m* de limes.

fil·i·al □ ['filjəl] filial (-aux *m/pl.*);

fil·i·a·tion [fili'eiʃn] filiation *f*.

fil·i·bus·ter ['filibʌstə] **1.** (*ou* **fil·i-'bus·ter·er**) flibustier *m*; *Am.* obstructionniste *m*; **2.** flibuster; *Am.* faire de l'obstruction.

fil·i·gree ['filigri:] filigrane *m*.

fil·ings *pl.* ['failiŋz] limaille *f*.

fill [fil] **1.** (se) remplir (de, *with*); (se) combler; *v/t.* plomber (*une dent*); occuper (*un poste*); charger, satisfaire (*un besoin, un désir*); *Am.* ♀, *pharm.* exécuter; *Am.* répondre à; ~ *s.o.'s glass* verser à boire à q.; ~ *in* combler (*un trou etc.*); remplir (*un bulletin, une formule*); libeller (*un chèque*); ~ *out* (s')enfler; grossir; ~ *up* (se) remplir, (se) combler; libeller (*un chèque*); **2.** suffisance *f*; soûl *m*; plein *m* de pipe; plumée *f*; *eat* (*drink*) *one's* ~ manger à sa faim (boire à sa soif).

fill·er ['filə] remplisseur (-euse *f*) *m*; remplissage *m*.

fil·let ['filit] **1.** △, *cheveux*: filet *m*; *cuis.* filet *m* (*de bœuf etc.*); ⚕ bandelette *f*; ruban *m*; *veau*: rouelle *f*; △ fasce *f*; **2.** orner d'un filet; *cuis.* détacher les filets de.

fill·ing ['filiŋ] remplissage *m*; charge *f*; *dent*: plombage *m*; *mot.* ~ *station* poste *m* d'essence.

fil·lip ['filip] **1.** *doigt*: chiquenaude *f*; encouragement *m*, stimulant *m*; **2.** donner une chiquenaude à; stimuler.

fil·ly ['fili] pouliche *f*; F jeune fille *f*.

film [film] **1.** pellicule *f* (*a. phot.*); voile *m*; peau *f* (*du lait chaud*); *cin.* film *m*, bande *f*; *œil*: taie *f*; ~ *cartoon* dessin *m* animé; ~ *cartridge phot.* (pellicule *f* en) bobine *f*; *take a* ~ tourner un film; **2.** (se) couvrir d'une pellicule *ou* d'un voile; *v/t. phot., cin.* filmer; *v/i. fig.* se voiler; **'film·y** □ *fig.* voilé; transparent.

fil·ter ['filtə] **1.** filtre *m*; ~ *tip* bout *m* filtre; cigarette *f* à bout filtre; **2.** *v/t.* filtrer; *v/i. fig.* s'infiltrer; ~ *in* changer de file; **'fil·ter·ing** filtrage *m*; **fil·ter-tipped** ['filtətipt] à bout filtre.

filth [filθ] saleté *f*; **'filth·y** □ sale, dégoûtant; crapuleux (-euse *f*).

fil·trate ['filtreit] **1.** (s'in)filtrer; **2.** ⚗ filtrat *m*; **fil'tra·tion** filtration *f*; *pharm.* colature *f*.

fin [fin] nageoire *f*; *sl.* main *f*; ✈ plan *m* fixe; *mot.* ailette *f*.

fi·nal ['fainl] **1.** □ final (-als *m/pl.*) (*a. gramm.*); dernier (-ère *f*); définitif (-ive *f*); sans appel; *sp.* ~ *whistle* coup *m* de sifflet final; **2.** *a.* ~*s pl.* examen *m* final; *sp.* finale *f*; **fi·nal·ist** ['~nəlist] *sp.* finaliste *mf*; **fi·nal·i·ty** [~'næliti] caractère *m* définitif; décision *f*; **fi·nal·ize** ['~nəlaiz] terminer, mener (*qch.*) à bonne fin; mettre la dernière main à; rendre (*qch.*) définitif (-ive *f*).

fi·nance [fai'næns] **1.** finance *f*; **2.** *v/t.* financer; *v/i.* être dans la finance; **fi'nan·cial** □ [~ʃl] financier (-ère *f*); ~ *year* année *f* budgétaire; **fin'an·cier** [~siə] financier *m*; *fig.* bailleur *m* de fonds.

finch *orn.* [fintʃ] pinson *m*.

find [faind] **1.** [*irr.*] trouver; découvrir; constater; retrouver; croire; fournir, procurer; 🕮 déclarer, prononcer (*coupable etc.*); ~ *o.s.* se trouver; se pourvoir soi-même; *all found* tout fourni; ~ *out* découvrir; se renseigner (sur, *about*); inventer; *I cannot* ~ *it in my heart* je n'ai pas le cœur (de *inf.*, *to inf.*); **2.** trouvaille *f*, découverte *f*; **'find·er** trouveur (-euse *f*) *m*; *phot.* viseur *m*; *opt.* chercheur *m*; **'find·ing** découverte *f*; *a.* ~*s pl.* trouvaille *f*; 🕮 conclusion *f*; verdict *m*.

fine¹ □ [fain] **1.** fin, pur; raffiné, subtil; bon(ne *f*); excellent; petit; beau (bel *devant une voyelle ou un h muet*); belle *f*; beaux *m/pl.*) (*a. temps*); joli; élégant; *you are a* ~ *fellow! iro.* vous êtes joli, vous!; ~

arts pl. beaux arts *m/pl.*; **2.** *adv.* finement; admirablement; *cut ~* tout juste (*temps*); au plus bas (*prix*); **3.** *météor.* beau temps *m*; **4.** (se) clarifier (*bière*); *~ away* (*ou down ou off*) (s')amincir; rendre *ou* devenir effilé.

fine² [~] **1.** amende *f*; *in ~* bref; enfin; **2.** mettre (*q.*) à l'amende; frapper (*q.*) d'une amende (d'une livre, *a pound*).

fine-draw ['fain'drɔ:] rentraire; *~n fig.* amaigri; subtil.

fine·ness ['fainnis] finesse *f*; pureté *f*; subtilité *f*; beauté *f*; élégance *f*.

fin·er·y ['fainəri] parure *f*; atours *m/pl.*; ⊕ (af)finerie *f*.

fi·nesse [fi'nes] finesse *f*; ruse *f*; *cartes:* impasse *f*.

fine-tooth(ed) comb ['fain'tu:θ(t) koum] peigne *m* fin; *go through ou over s.th. with a ~* passer qch. au peigne fin.

fin·ger ['fiŋgə] **1.** doigt *m*; *have a ~ in the pie* être mêlé à *ou* se mêler de l'affaire; *see end 1*; **2.** manier, toucher; tâter; ♪ doigter; tapoter sur (*un piano*); '~-**board** ♪ *piano etc.:* clavier *m*; *violon etc.:* touche *f*; '~-**bowl** rince-doigts *m*; '**fin·gered** aux doigts ...; '**fin·ger·ing** maniement *m*; ♪ doigté *m*; grosse laine *f* à tricoter.

fin·ger...: '~-**lan·guage** langage *m* mimique; '~-**nail** ongle *m*; ~ **pol·ish** vernis *m* à ongles; '~-**post** poteau *m* indicateur; '~-**print 1.** empreinte *f* digitale; **2.** prendre les empreintes digitales de (*q.*); '~-**stall** doigtier *m*.

fin·i·cal □ ['finikl], **fin·ick·ing** ['~kiŋ], **fin·ick·y** ['~ki], **fin·i·kin** ['~kin] difficile; méticuleux (-euse *f*) (*personne*).

fin·ish ['finiʃ] **1.** *v/t.* finir; terminer; casser; (*a. ~ off, up*) achever, mener à terme; ⊕ usiner; *tex.* apprêter; *~ed goods pl.* articles *m/pl.* apprêtés; *sp. ~ing line* ligne *f* d'arrivée; *~ing touch* dernière main *f*; *v/i.* finir; se terminer; prendre fin; **2.** achèvement *m*; ⊕ apprêtage *m*; ⊕ finissage *m*; ✝ fini *m*, apprêt *m*; '**fin·ish·er** ⊕ finisseur (-euse *f*) *m*, apprêteur (-euse *f*) *m*; F coup *m* de grâce.

fi·nite □ ['fainait] borné, limité; fini (*a.* ✿); *gramm. ~ verb* verbe *m* à un mode fini; '**fi·nite·ness** nature *f* limitée.

fink *Am. sl.* [fiŋk] jaune *m*.

Fin·land·er ['finləndə], **Finn** [fin] Finlandais(e *f*) *m*; Finnois(e *f*) *m*.

Finn·ish ['finiʃ] finlandais; *ling.* finnois *m*.

fin·ny ['fini] à nageoires.

fir [fə:] sapin *m*; *Scotch ~* pin *m* rouge; '~-**cone** pomme *f* de sapin.

fire ['faiə] **1.** feu *m*; incendie *m*; ✕ tir *m*; *fig.* ardeur *f*; radiateur *m* (à gaz, électrique); *~!* au feu!; *come under ~* (*from*) ✕ essuyer le feu (de *l'ennemi etc.*); *fig.* être vivement attaqué (*par q.*); *on ~* en flammes, en feu; **2.** *v/t.* mettre le feu à; (*a. ~ off*) ✕ tirer; cuire (*des briques etc.*); *fig.* enflammer; F congédier, renvoyer; ⊕ chauffer (*le four etc.*); *~ up* allumer; chauffer; *v/i.* prendre feu; s'enflammer (*a. fig.*); partir; tirer (sur *at*, [*up*]on); F *~ away!* allez-y!; *~ up* s'emporter (contre, *at*); '~-**a·larm** signal *m* d'incendie; '~-**arms** *pl.* armes *f/pl.* à feu; '~-**ball** *météor.* aérolithe *m*; éclair *m* en boule; ✕ balle *f* à feu; '~-**box** ⊕ boîte *f* à feu; '~-**brand** F brandon *m* (de discorde); '~-**bri·gade** sapeurs-pompiers *m/pl.*; '~-**bug** *Am.* F incendiaire *m*; '~-**crack·er** pétard *m*; '~-**cur·tain** *théâ.* rideau *m* métallique; '~-**damp** ✕ grisou *m*; '~-**de·part·ment** *Am.* sapeurs-pompiers *m/pl.*; '~-**dog** chenet *m*; landier *m*; '~-**door** porte *f* anti-incendie *ou* coupe-feu; ~ **drill** exercice *f* anti-incendie; '~-**en·gine** ⊕ pompe *f* à incendie; '~-**es·cape** échelle *f* *ou* escalier *m* de sauvetage; '~-**ex·tin·guish·er** extincteur *m* (d'incendie); '~-**fight·er** pompier *m* (volontaire); lutteur (-euse *f*) *m* contre l'incendie; '~-**fly** luciole *f*; F mouche *f* à feu; '~-**gre·nade** grenade *f* extinctrice; '~-**in·sur·ance** assurance *f* contre l'incendie; '~-**i·rons** *pl.* garniture *f* de foyer; '~-**light·er** allume-feu *m/inv.*; '~-**man** (sapeur-)pompier *m*; ⊕ chauffeur *m*; '~-**of·fice** bureau *m* d'assurance contre l'incendie; '~-**place** cheminée *f*; foyer *m*; '~-**plug** bouche *f* d'incendie; '~-**proof** ignifuge; '~-**rais·ing** incendie *f* volontaire; pyromanie *f*; '~-**screen** devant *m* de cheminée; '~-**side 1.** cheminée *f*, foyer *m*; coin *m* du feu; **2.** de *ou* au coin du feu; '~-**sta·tion** poste *m* de pompiers; '~-**wall**

cloison *m* pare-feu; '~-**war·den** responsable *mf* de la lutte anti-incendie; guetteur *m* d'incendies; '~-**wood** bois *m* à brûler; '~-**work(s** *pl. fig.*) feu *m* d'artifice; '~-**work** pièce *f* d'artifice.

fir·ing ['faiəriŋ] chauffage *m*; ⊕ chauffe *f*; brisques etc.: cuite *f*; ✗ tir *m*; ~ *squad* peleton *m* d'exécution.

fir·kin ['fə:kin] *mesure*: quartaut *m* (45,5 litres); tonnelet *m*.

firm [fə:m] **1.** □ ferme; solide; inébranlable; **2.** maison *f* (de commerce); raison *f* sociale.

fir·ma·ment ['fə:məmənt] firmament *m*.   [solidité *f*.)

firm·ness ['fə:mnis] fermeté *f*;)

first [fə:st] **1.** *adj.* premier (-ère *f*); ~ *aid* premiers secours *m/pl. ou* soins *m/pl.*, soins *m/pl.* d'urgence; ✝ ~ *cost* prix *m* coûtant *ou* initial *ou* de revient; *Am.* ~ *floor see* ground floor; ~ *name* prénom *m*; ~ *night théâ.* première *f*; *Am.* ~ *papers pl.* déclaration *f* de naturalisation; **2.** *adv.* premièrement, d'abord; pour la première fois; plutôt; *at* ~, ~ *of all* pour commencer; tout d'abord; ~ *and last* en tout et pour tout; **3.** *su.* premier (-ère *f*) *m*; ✝ ~ *of exchange* première *f* de change; *from the* ~ dès le premier jour; *go* ~ passer devant; prendre le devant; 🚋 voyager en première; '~-'**aid box** *ou* **kit** trousse *f* de premiers secours *ou* à pharmacie; '~-'**aid post** poste *m* de secours; '~-**born** premier-né (premier-née *ou* première-née *f*); '~-**class** de première classe; de première qualité; '~-**fruits** *pl.*, **first·lings** *pl.* ['~liŋz] prémices *f/pl.*; '**first·ly** premièrement; d'abord; '**first-rate** de premier ordre; *see* first-class.

firth [fə:θ] estuaire *m*, golfe *m*.

fis·cal ['fiskl] fiscal (-aux *m/pl.*); financier (-ère *f*).

fish [fiʃ] **1.** poisson *m*; *coll.* poissons *m/pl.*; 🚋 éclisse *f*; F type *m*; *odd* ~ drôle *m* de type; *have other* ~ *to fry* avoir d'autres chats à fouetter; **2.** *v/i.* pêcher (qch., *for s.th.*); aller à la pêche (de, *for*); *v/t.* pêcher; 🚋 éclisser; ~ *out* tirer; sortir; '~-**bone** arête *f*; '~-**cake** *cuis.* croquette *f* de poisson.

fish·er·man ['fiʃəmən] pêcheur *m*; '**fish·er·y** pêche *f*; *lieu:* pêcherie *f*.

fish...: ~ **fin·gers** *pl. cuis.* bâtonnets *m/pl.* de poisson; ~ **hook** hameçon *m*.

fish·ing ['fiʃiŋ] pêche *f*; '~-**line** ligne *f* de pêche; '~-**rod** canne *f* à pêche; '~-**tack·le** attirail *m* de pêche.

fish...: ~ **line** *Am.* ligne *f* de pêche; '~-**mon·ger** marchand(e *f*) *m* de poisson; ~ **pole** *Am.* canne *f* à pêche; ~ **pond** étang *m* à poissons; ~ **sticks** *pl. Am. see* fish fingers; ~ **sto·ry** *Am.* F histoire *f* incroyable; '~-**wife** marchande *f* de poisson; '**fish·y** de poisson; vitreux (-euse *f*) (œil); F louche; véreux (-euse *f*).

fis·sion ['fiʃn] fission *f*; *see* atomic; **fis·sion·a·ble** *phys.* ['~əbl] fissile; **fis·sure** ['fiʃə] **1.** fissure *f*, fente *f*; **2.** fendre.

fist [fist] poing *m*; F main *f*; F écriture *f*; **fist·i·cuffs** ['~ikʌfs] *pl.* coups *m/pl.* de poing.

fis·tu·la 🩺 ['fistjulə] fistule *f*.

fit[1] [fit] **1.** □ bon, propre, convenable (à, *for*); digne (de); en bonne santé; capable; F prêt (à, *for*); *sp.* en forme, en bonne santé; *it is not* ~ il ne convient pas; F ~ *as a fiddle* en parfaite santé; **2.** *v/t.* adapter, ajuster, accommoder (à *to, for*); préparer; s'accorder avec; aller à (*q.*), (*a.* ~ *together*) assembler (*des pièces*); ⊕ (*a.* ~ *in*) emboîter; pourvoir (de, *with*); ~ *out* équiper (de, *with*); ~ *up* monter; établir; appareiller; *v/i.* s'ajuster; aller (*robe etc*) convenir; **3.** coupe *f*, costume *etc.*: ajustement *m*; *it is a bad* ~ il est mal ajusté.

fit[2] [~] 🩺 attaque *f*, crise *f*, colère: accès *m*; *by* ~*s and starts* par boutades, à bâtons rompus; *give s.o. a* ~ F donner un coup de sang à q.

fitch·ew *zo.* ['fitʃu:] putois *m*.

fit·ful □ ['fitful] irrégulier (-ère *f*); capricieux (-euse *f*); d'humeur changeante; '**fit·ment** meuble *m*; ⊕ montage *m*; '**fit·ness** convenance *f*; aptitude *f*; justesse *f*; santé *f*; '**fit-out** équipement *m*; '**fit·ted:** ~ *carpet* tapis *m* ajusté, moquette *f*; ~ *sheet* drap-housse *m*; '**fit·ter** monteur *m*; appareilleur *m*; *cost. etc.* essayeur (-euse *f*) *m*; '**fit·ting 1.** □ convenable, propre; *cost. etc.* essayage *m*; ~ *pl. chambre:* garniture *f*; installations *f/pl.*; *gaz, électri-*

cité: appareillage *m*; **'fit-up** F scène *f* démontable; accessoires *m/pl.*

five [faiv] **1.** cinq (*a. su./m*); **2.** ~s *sg.* (jeu *m* de) balle *f* au mur; **'fivefold** quintuple.

fix [fiks] **1.** *v/t.* fixer (*a. phot., a. les yeux sur q.*); attacher (*a. un regard sur q.*); nommer (*un jour*); régler; déterminer; *surt. Am.* F arranger, faire (*le lit etc.*); réduire à quia; graisser la patte à; ~ *o.s.* s'établir; ~ *up* arranger; installer; *Am.* réparer; *v/i.* s'installer; se fixer; se décider (pour, *on*); **2.** F embarras *m*, difficulté *f*; **fix'a·tion** fixation *f*; *phot.* fixage *m*; **fix·a·tive** ['~ətiv], **fix·ature** ['~ətfə] fixatif *m*; **fixed** ['~t] (*adv.* **fix·ed·ly** ['~idli]) fixe; arrêté; permanent; invariable; figé (*sourire*); ~ *quota* contingent *m* (déterminé); ~ *star* étoile *f* fixe; **fixedin·ter·est** ✝ à intérêt fixe; **fix·edness** ['~idnis] fixité *f*; constance *f*; **'fix·er** *phot.* fixateur *m*; bain *m* de fixage; **'fix·ing** fixage *m*; *tex.* bousage *m*; *Am.* ~s *pl.* équipement *m*; garniture *f*; **'fix·i·ty** fixité *f*; fermeté *f*; **fix·ture** ['~tfə] meuble *m* fixe; appareil *m* fixe; *sp.* engagement *m*; ~s *pl.* meubles *m/pl.* fixes; appareil *m* (*à gaz etc.*).

fizz [fiz] **1.** pétiller; cracher (*vapeur*); **2.** pétillement *m*; F champagne *m*; mousseux *m*; **'fiz·zle 1.** pétiller; siffler; (*usu.* ~ *out*) faire fiasco, avorter; **2.** pétillement *m*; fiasco *m*; **'fiz·zy** ☐ pétillant; gazeux (-euse *f*).

flab·ber·gast F ['flæbəgɑːst] abasourdir; *be* ~*ed* (*en*) rester interdit.

flab·by ☐ ['flæbi] flasque, mou (mol *devant une voyelle ou un h muet*; molle *f*).

flac·cid ☐ ['flæksid] flasque, mou (mol *devant une voyelle ou un h muet*; molle *f*).

flag¹ [flæg] **1.** drapeau *m*; ⚓ pavillon *m*; ~ *of truce* drapeau *m* parlementaire; *black* ~ pavillon *m* noir; **2.** pavoiser; transmettre par signaux; *sp.* ~ *out* jalonner.

flag² [~] carreau *m*; dalle *f*.

flag³ ♀ [~] iris *m*.

flag⁴ [~] languir; traîner.

flag-day ['flægdei] jour *m* de quête; *Am. Flag Day* le quatorze juin (*anniversaire de l'adoption du drapeau national*).

flag·el·late ['flædʒeleit] flageller; **flag·el·la·tion** flagellation *f*.

fla·gi·tious ☐ [flə'dʒiʃəs] infâme, abominable.

flag·on ['flægən] flacon *m*; ✝ *vin*: pot *m* à anse; *bière*: grosse bouteille *f*.

flag·pole ['flægpoul] *see* flagstaff.

fla·grant ☐ ['fleigrənt] infâme; flagrant, énorme.

flag...: '~**ship** vaisseau *m* amiral; '~**staff** mât *m* ou hampe *f* de drapeau; ⚓ mât *m* de pavillon; '~**stone** pierre *f* à paver; dalle *f*; '~**wag·ging** ✕, ⚓ signalisation *f*; *sl.* chauvinisme *m*.

flail 🗡 [fleil] fléau *m*. [*for*).\
flair [flɛə] flair *m*; F aptitude *f* (à,\
flake [fleik] **1.** flocon *m*; *savon*: paillette *f*; *métal*: écaille *f*; **2.** (s')écailler; (s')épaufrer (*pierre*); **'flak·y** floconneux (-euse *f*); écailleux (-euse *f*); feuilleté (*pâte*).

flam F [flæm] blague *f*; charlatanerie *f*.

flam·boy·ant [flæm'bɔiənt] flamboyant; éclatant; voyant.

flame [fleim] **1.** flamme *f*; feu *m*; *fig.* passion *f*; F béguin *m*; **2.** flamber (*a. fig.*); s'enflammer; ~ *out (ou up*) jeter des flammes; s'enflammer.

flam·ma·ble *surt. Am.* ['flæməbl] inflammable.

flan *Brit.* [flæn] tarte *f*.

flange ⊕ [flændʒ] *roue*: boudin *m*; *pneu*: talon *m*; *poutre*: semelle *f*.

flank [flæŋk] **1.** flanc *m* (*a.* ✕, *a. fig.*); **2.** flanquer (de *by*, *with*); ✕ prendre de flanc.

flan·nel ['flænl] *tex.* flanelle *f*; *attr.* de flanelle; ~s *pl.* flanelles *f/pl.*; pantalon *m* de flanelle; *face-*~ gant *m* de toilette.

flap [flæp] **1.** patte *f*; pan *m*; *table*: battant *m*; *chaussure*: oreille *f*; léger coup *m*; clapotement *m*; F affolement *m*, panique *f*; F *be ou get in a* ~ s'affoler, paniquer; **2.** *v/t.* frapper légèrement; battre de (*les ailes, les bras, etc.*); *v/i.* battre; claquer; ballotter; **'flap·per** battoir *m*; claquette *f*; *sl.* jeune fille *f*; *see* flap 1.

flare [flɛə] **1.** flamboyer; brûler avec une lumière inégale; s'évaser (*jupe, tube, etc.*); ~ *up* s'enflammer; s'emporter (*personne*); **2.** flamme *f* vacillante; ✕ fusée *f* éclairante; ✕ feu *m*; *jupe*: godet *m*.

flash [flæʃ] **1.** voyant; contrefait, faux (fausse f); **2.** éclair m; éclat m; fig. saillie f; rayon m; surt. Am. dernière nouvelle f; nouvelle f brève; in a ~ en un clin d'œil; ~ of wit boutade f; ~ in the pan feu m de paille; **3.** v/i. lancer des étincelles; briller; étinceler; v/t. faire étinceler; faire parade de; diriger, projeter (un rayon de lumière); darder (un regard); télégraphier; riposter; it ~ed on me l'idée me vint tout d'un coup; '**~back** cin. scène f de rappel; '**~bulb** phot. ampoule f (de) flash; '**~cube** phot. cube-flash m (pl. cubes-flash); '**~gun** phot. flash m; '**~light** phot. lumière-éclair f; Am. lampe f de poche; **~point** point m d'inflammabilité; '**flash·y** □ voyant; superficiel(le f); tapageur (-euse f).

flask [flɑːsk] flacon m; poire f à poudre; vacuum ~ thermos m.

flat [flæt] **1.** □ plat, uni; étendu; insipide; catégorique; ✝ net(te f); languissant; mat (peinture); ♩ faux (fausse f); ♩ bémol inv.; calme (bourse); ~ price prix m unique; fall ~ rater, manquer; sing ~ chanter faux; **2.** pays m plat; plaine f; théâ. ferme f; paroi f; appartement m; ♩ bas-fond m; ♩ bémol m; F benêt m, niais(e f) m; mot. sl. pneu m à plat; '**~foot** pied m plat; souv. Am. agent m, flic m; '**~'foot·ed** à pieds plats; Am. F formel(le f); franc(he f); '**~·i·ron** fer m à repasser; **flat·let** ['~lit] studio m; '**flat·ness** nature f plate; égalité f; fig. monotonie f; franchise f; ✝ langueur f, marasme m; **flat out** F **1.** à toute allure; work ~ travailler d'arrache-pied; **2.** épuisé, à plat, vidé; '**flat·ten** (s')aplatir; ✗ ~ out se redresser; allonger le vol.

flat·ter ['flætə] flatter; '**flat·ter·er** flatteur (-euse f) m; '**flat·ter·y** flatterie f.

flat·u·lence, flat·u·len·cy ['flætjuləns(i)] flatuosité f, flatulence f; '**flat·u·lent** □ flatulent.

flaunt [flɔːnt] faire étalage (de).

flau·tist ['flɔːtist] flûtiste mf.

fla·vo(u)r ['fleivə] **1.** saveur f; goût m; arome m; vin: bouquet m; fig. atmosphère f; **2.** assaisonner (de, with); parfumer; '**fla·vo(u)red** vanilla-~ (parfumé) à la vanille; '**fla·vo(u)r·less** insipide, fade.

flaw [flɔː] **1.** défaut m, défectuosité f; imperfection f; ⊕ paille f; ♩♩ vice m de forme; fig. tache f; ♩ grain m; **2.** (se) fêler; fig. (s')endommager; '**flaw·less** □ sans défaut; parfait.

flax ♀ [flæks] lin m (a. tex.); '**flax·en**, '**flax·y** de lin; F blond.

flay [flei] écorcher; fig. rosser; '**flay·er** écorcheur m.

flea [fliː] puce f; '**~bane** ♀ érigéron m; '**~bite** morsure f de puce; '**~pit** F ciné(ma) de quartier.

fleck [flek] **1.** petite tache f; **2.** tacheter (de, with).

flec·tion ['flekʃn] see flexion.

fled [fled] prét. et p. de flee.

fledge [fledʒ] v/i. s'emplumer; v/t. pourvoir de plumes; **fledg(e)·ling** ['~liŋ] oisillon m; fig. novice mf.

flee [fliː] [irr.] v/i. s'enfuir (de, from); v/t. (a. ~ from) fuir.

fleece [fliːs] **1.** toison f; tex. nappe f; ♀ molleton m; **2.** tondre; écorcher; '**fleec·y** floconneux (-euse f); moutonné (nuage, vagues).

fleer [fliə] **1.** ✝ ricanement m; **2.** se moquer (de, at), railler (q., at s.o.).

fleet [fliːt] **1.** □ poét. rapide; léger (-ère f); **2.** flotte f; fig. série f; ♀ Street la presse f (à Londres); **3.** passer rapidement; '**fleet·ing** □ fugitif (-ive f); passager (-ère f).

Flem·ing ['flemiŋ] Flamand(e f) m; '**Flem·ish 1.** flamand; **2.** ling. flamand m; Flamand(e f) m.

flesh [fleʃ] chair f (a. eccl., a. des fruits); viande f; make s.o.'s ~ creep donner la chair de poule à q.; **2.** donner le goût (fig. le baptême) du sang à; '**~brush** brosse f à friction; **flesh·ings** ['~iŋz] pl. théâ. maillot chair m/inv.; '**flesh·ly** charnel(le f); sensuel(le f); '**flesh·y** charnu; gras(se f).

flew [fluː] prét. de fly 2.

flex ⚡ [fleks] flexible m, cordon m souple; **flex·i·bil·i·ty** [~ə'biliti] souplesse f (a. fig.); '**flex·i·ble** □ flexible; souple; pliant; ~ working hours pl. horaire m souple; **flex·ion** ['flekʃn] flexion f; courb(ur)e f; gramm. (in)flexion f; **flex·or** ['~ksə] anat. (muscle m) fléchisseur m; **flex·u·ous** ['fleksjuəs] flexueux (-euse f); **flex·ure** ['flek'ʃə] flexion f; géol. pli m.

flick [flik] **1.** effleurer (un cheval etc.); (a. ~ at) donner une chiquenaude à; **2.** petit coup *m*; chique-naude *f*; ~s *pl. sl.* ciné *m.*

flick·er ['flikə] **1.** trembler, vaciller; clignoter; **2.** tremblement *m*; battement *m*; *Am.* évanouissement *m.*

fli·er ['flaiə] *see* flyer.

flight [flait] vol *m* (*a.* ✍); essor *m* (*a. fig.*); *abeilles:* essaim *m*; *oiseaux:* volée *f*; fuite *f* (*a.* ✍); ✍ ligne *f*; (~ *of stairs*) escalier *m*, perron *m*; *put to* ~ mettre (*q.*) en déroute; *take* (*to*) ~ prendre la fuite; '~-**com-'mand·er** commandant *m* de groupe; '~-**lieu'ten·ant** capitaine *m* aviateur; '~-**re'cord·er** enregistreur *m* de vol; '**flight·y** □ frivole, étourdi; volage; inconstant.

flim·flam *Am.* F ['flimflæm] **1.** boniments *m/pl.*, baratin *m*; **2.** tromper, duper, F rouler.

flim·sy ['flimzi] **1.** tenu; fragile; léger (-ère *f*); frivole; **2.** papier *m* pelure; F fafiot *m* (=*billet de banque*); télégramme *m*; *journ.* copie *f.*

flinch [flintʃ] broncher; reculer (devant, from); tressaillir.

fling [fliŋ] **1.** coup *m*, jet *m*; *cheval:* ruade *f*; *fig.* essai *m*; *have one's* ~ jeter sa gourme (*q.*); **2.** [*irr.*] *v/i.* s'élancer, se précipiter; (*a.* ~ *out*) ruer (*cheval*); étendre; *v/t.* jeter, lancer; ~ *o.s.* se précipiter; ~ *away* jeter de côté; gaspiller (*l'argent*); ~ *out* jeter dehors; F flanquer à la porte; ~ *open* ouvrir tout grand; ~ *out* étendre (*les bras*).

flint [flint] caillou (*pl.* -x) *m*; *géol.* silex *m*; pierre *f* à briquet; '**flint·y** cailouteux (-euse *f*); *fig.* insensible.

flip [flip] **1.** chiquenaude *f*; petite secousse *f* vive; ✍ *sl.* petit tour *m* de vol; *boisson:* flip *m*; *the* ~ *side* (*of a record*) l'autre face *ou* le revers (*d'un disque*); **2.** donner une chiquenaude à; donner une petite secousse à; claquer (*le fouet*).

flip-flap ['flipflæp] **1.** *su.* saut *m* périlleux; **2.** *adv.* flic flac.

flip-flops ['flipflɔps] *pl.* tongs *f/pl.* (*TM*).

flip·pan·cy ['flipənsi] légèreté *f*; '**flip·pant** □ léger (-ère *f*); irrévérencieux (-euse *f*). [main *f.*]

flip·per ['flipə] *zo.* nageoire *f*; *sl.*⏋

flirt [flə:t] **1.** coquette *f*; flirteur *m*; **2.** *v/i.* flirter; faire la coquette; *v/t. see* flip 2; **flir'ta·tion** flirt *m*; coquetterie *f.*

flit [flit] voltiger; s'en aller; passer rapidement; déménager.

flitch [flitʃ] flèche *f* de lard.

flit·ter ['flitə] voltiger.

fliv·ver *Am.* F ['flivə] **1.** voiture *f* bon marché, F tacot *m*; **2.** subir un échec.

float [flout] **1.** ⊕, *pêche:* flotteur *m*; *filet:* galet *m*; masse *f* flottante; *théâ.* paroi *f* mobile; *théâ.* rampe *f*; radeau *m*; wagon *m* en plate-forme; char *m* de cortège; **2.** *v/t.* flotter; transporter dans les airs; inonder (*un terrain*); *fig.* émettre, faire circuler; ✝ lancer, fonder, monter; *v/i.* flotter, nager; ⚓ être à flot; *nage:* faire la planche; '**float-a·ble** flottable; '**float·age** flottement *m*; **float'a·tion** *see* flotation; '**float·ing** flottant; à flot; sur mer; ✝ courant (*dette*); ~ *bridge* pont flottant; ✝ ~ *capital* capital disponible; ~ *ice* glace *f* flottante; ~ *kidney* rein *m* mobile; ~ *light* bateau-feu (*pl.* bateaux-feux) *m*; ✝ ~ *rate* taux *m* de change flottant; *pol.* ~ *voter* électeur *m* (*-trice f*) non engagé(e).

flock[1] [flɔk] **1.** bande *f* (*a. fig.*); troupeau *m*; *oiseaux:* volée *f*; *eccl.* ouailles *f/pl.*; *fig.* foule *f*; **2.** s'attrouper; aller (entrer *etc.*) en foule.

flock[2] [~] flocon *m*; *coussin etc.:* bourre *f* de laine.

floe [flou] glaçon *m* (flottant).

flog [flɔg] fouetter; battre à coups de verge; '**flog·ging** (coups *m/pl.* de) fouet *m*; F bastonnade *f.*

flood [flʌd] **1.** (*a.* ~-*tide*) marée *f* montante; flux *m*; déluge *m*; inondation *f*; *rivière:* débordement *m*; *the* ♀ le Déluge; **2.** *v/t.* inonder (de, with); noyer (*a. mot.*); *v/i.* déborder; '~-**dis·as·ter** inondation *f*; '~-**gate** écluse *f*; vanne *f*; '~-**light 1.** lumière *f* à grands flots; illumination *f* par projecteurs; **2.** [*irr.* (*light*)] illuminer par projecteurs.

floor [flɔ:] **1.** plancher *m*; parquet *m* (*a. parl., a. sl. Bourse*); ✍ *blé:* airée *f*; *maison:* étage *m*; ~ *lamp* lampadaire *m*; *Am.* ~ *leader* chef *m* de parti (*qui dirige les votes dans l'hémicycle*); ~ *manager* ✝ chef *m* de rayon; *télév.* régisseur *m*; ~ *price* prix *m* minimum; *restaurant etc.:* ~ *show* attractions *f/pl.*; *hold the* ~ *parl.* avoir la parole; F accaparer la conversation; *take the* ~ prendre la parole; *se* joindre aux danseurs; 2. planchéier; terrasser; F réduire à quia; '~-**cloth** linoléum *m*; torchon *m* à laver; '**floor·er** F coup *m* qui (*vous etc.*) terrasse; '**floor·ing** planchéiage *m*; plancher *m*; dallage *m*; renversement *m*; '**floor-walk·er** *Am.* see shopwalker; '**floor-wax** cire *f* (à parquet), encaustique *f*.

floo·zy *sl.* ['fluːzi] poule *f*, pouffiasse *f*.

flop F [flɔp] 1. faire floc; se laisser tomber; pendre (*bords d'un chapeau*); *sl.* échouer; *Am. pol.* tourner casaque; 2. bruit *m* sourd; coup *m* mat; fiasco *m*; *Am. sl.* lit *m*; *Am. sl.* ~ *house* see doss-house; hôtel *m* borgne; 3. patapouf!; '**flop·py** pendant, flasque; lâche; F veule.

flo·ral ['flɔːrəl] floral (-aux *m/pl.*).

flo·res·cence [flɔːˈresns] floraison *f*.

flor·id □ ['flɔrid] fleuri; flamboyant; rubicond (*visage*); '**flor·id·ness** style *m* fleuri; flamboyant *m*; teint: rougeur *f*. [deux shillings.]

flor·in ['flɔrin] florin *m*; pièce *f* de|

flo·rist ['flɔrist] fleuriste *mf*.

floss [flɔs] (*a.* ~ *silk*) bourre *f* de soie; soie *f* floche; '**floss·y** soyeux (-euse *f*).

flo·ta·tion [flouˈteiʃn] ⚓ flottaison *f*; flottage *m*; ✝ lancement *m*.

flot·sam ⚓ ['flɔtsəm] épave(s) *f(pl.)* flottante(s).

flounce¹ [flauns] 1. *cost. etc.* volant *m*; 2. garnir de volants.

flounce² [~] s'élancer; se débattre; ~ *in* (*out*) entrer (sortir) brusquement.

floun·der¹ *icht.* ['flaundə] flet *m*.

floun·der² [~] patauger (*a. fig.*).

flour ['flauə] 1. farine *f*; 2. saupoudrer de farine.

flour·ish ['flʌriʃ] 1. geste *m*; *discours*: fleurs *f/pl.*; brandissement *m*; trait *m* de plume; ♪ fanfare *f*; ornement *m*; 2. *v/i.* fleurir; prospérer; *v/t.* brandir; agiter; *fig.* faire parade de.

flout [flaut] *v/t.* narguer; se moquer de; *v/i.* se railler (de, *at*).

flow [flou] 1. (é)coulement *m*; courant *m*, cours *m*; passage *m*; flux *m*; ~ *chart* organigramme *m*; ~ *of spirits* fonds *m* de gaieté; 2. couler; s'écouler; monter (*marée*); circuler; flotter (*cheveux*); découler (de, *with*); ~ *from* dériver de.

flow·er ['flauə] 1. fleur *f*; élite *f*; *plantes*: fleuraison *f*; ~ *girl* marchande *f* de fleurs, bouquetière *f*; ~ *shop* (boutique *f* de) fleuriste *m*; *say it with* ~*s* exprimez vos sentiments avec des fleurs; 2. fleurir; '**flow·er·i·ness** style *m* fleuri; fleurs *f/pl.* de rhétorique; '**flow·er·pot** pot *m* à fleurs; '**flow·er·y** fleuri, de fleurs.

flown [floun] *p.p. de fly* 2.

flu F [fluː] *see* influenza.

flub·dub *Am.* ['flʌbdʌb] 1. radotage *m*; 2. ridicule.

fluc·tu·ate ['flʌktjueit] varier; **fluc·tu'a·tion** fluctuation *f*.

flue¹ [fluː] conduite *f*; tuyau *m*; cheminée *f*; ♪ *tuyau d'orgue*: bouche *f*.

flue² [~] duvet *m*, peluches *f/pl.*

flu·en·cy ['fluːənsi] *parole etc.*: facilité *f*; '**flu·ent** □ courant, facile.

fluff [flʌf] peluche *f*; duvet *m*; '**fluff·y** pelucheux (-euse *f*); duveteux (-euse *f*); *sl.* pompette (= *ivre*); ~ *hair* cheveux *m/pl.* flous.

flu·id ['fluːid] 1. fluide; liquide; 2. liquide *m*, fluide *m*; **flu'id·i·ty** fluidité *f*.

fluke¹ [fluːk] ancre: patte *f*.

fluke² F [~] coup *m* de veine.

flum·mer·y ['flʌməri] *cuis.* crème *f* aux œufs; F flagornerie *f*.

flung [flʌŋ] *prét. et p.p. de fling* 2.

flunk *Am.* F [flʌŋk] *v/i.* échouer (à *un examen*); *v/t.* recaler (*q.*).

flunk·(e)y ['flʌŋki] laquais *m*; '**flunk·ey·ism** servilité *f*; flagornerie *f*.

flu·o·res·cence *phys.* [fluəˈresns] fluorescence *f*.

flur·ry ['flʌri] 1. agitation *f*; ⚓ brise *f* folle; *Am.* rafale *f* (de neige); averse *f*; 2. agiter; bouleverser.

flush [flʌʃ] 1. ⊕ de niveau, affleuré; très plein; abondant; F en fonds; 2. rougeur *f*; abondance *f*; *W.-C.*: chasse *f* d'eau; *fig.* fraîcheur *f*; transport *m*; *cartes*: flush *m*; 3. *v/t.* inonder; laver à grande eau; lever (*le gibier*); donner une chasse à; rincer; *v/i.* rougir; jaillir.

flus·ter ['flʌstə] 1. confusion *f*; 2. *v/t.* agiter, ahurir; ✝ griser; *v/i.* s'agiter; s'énerver.

flute [fluːt] 1. ♪ flûte *f*; △ cannelure *f*; *linge*: tuyau *m*; 2. jouer de la flûte; flûter; jouer (*qch.*) sur la flûte; parler d'une voix flûtée; '**flut·ist** flûtiste *mf*.

flut·ter ['flʌtə] 1. *ailes*: battement *m*; palpitation *f*; agitation *f*; F petit pari *m*; spéculation *f*; 2. *v/t.* agiter; *v/i.* battre des ailes; s'agiter; palpiter.

flux [flʌks] *fig.* flux *m* (*a.* ⚕); *fig.* changement *m* continuel; ~ *and reflux* flux *m* et reflux *m*.

fly [flai] 1. mouche *f*; voiture *f* de place; *pantalon*: braguette *f*; *Am. mot.* volant *m*; *Am. baseball*: balle *f* lancée en chandelle; *théâ.* flies *pl.* cintres *m/pl.*; 2. [irr.] *v/i.* voler; voyager en avion; flotter (*pavillon*); passer rapidement (*temps*); courir; ~ *at* s'élancer sur; ~ *in s.o.'s face* défier q.; ~ *into a passion* se mettre en colère; ~ *off* s'envoler; ~ *on instruments* piloter sans visibilité; ~ *out* s'emporter contre; ~ *open* s'ouvrir subitement; *v/t.* battre (*un pavillon*); *see* flee; ~ *the Atlantic* survoler l'Atlantique.

fly-blow ['flaiblou] 1. *fig.* souillures *f/pl.*; œufs *m/pl.* de mouche; 2. couvrir d'œufs de mouche; *fig.* souiller.

fly·er ['flaiə] *surt.* ⚔ aviateur (-trice *f*) *m*; bon coureur *m*; oiseau *m* qui vole; *Am.* express *m*; *take a* ~ être projeté; *Am. sl.* s'engager dans une opération risquée à la Bourse.

fly-flap ['flaiflæp] tue-mouches *m/inv.*

fly·ing ['flaiiŋ] volant; d'aviation; rapide; ~ *boat* hydravion *m* (à coque); ⚓ ~ *buttress* arc-boutant (*pl.* arcs-boutants) *m*; ~ *deck* pont *m* d'atterrissage; ~ *field* champ *m* d'aviation; ~ *jump* saut *m* avec élan; ~ *machine* avion *m*; ~ *school* école *f* de pilotage; *police*: ~ *squad* brigade *f* mobile; ~ *start* départ *m* lancé; ~ *visit* courte visite *f*; *come off with* ~ *colo(u)rs* s'en tirer brillamment; remporter une victoire magnifique; ⚲ **Of·fi·cer** lieutenant *m* aviateur.

fly...: '~-**leaf** *typ.* feuille *f* de garde; '~-**sheet** feuille *f* volante; *camping*: double toit *m*; '~-**weight** *box.* poids *m* mouche; '~-**wheel** volant *m* (de commande).

foal [foul] 1. poulain *m*, pouliche *f*; 2. *v/t.* mettre bas (*un poulain*); *v/i.* pouliner.

foam [foum] 1. écume *f*; mousse *f*; 2. écumer; mousser; ~ **bath** bain *m* moussant; ~ **rub·ber** caoutchouc *m*

mousse; '**foam·y** écumeux (-euse *f*); mousseux (-euse *f*).

fob¹ [fɔb] *pantalon*: gousset *m*; (*ou* ~-*seal*) breloque *f*; (*ou* ~-*chain*) régence *f*. [*s.th. on s.o.*)]

fob² [~]: ~ *off fig.* refiler (qch. à q.).)

fo·cal ['foukl] focal (-aux *m/pl.*); *phot.* ~ *distance* distance *f* focale; *phot.* ~ *plane shutter* obturateur *m* à rideau.

fo·cus ['foukəs] 1. foyer *m*; *fig. a.* siège *m*; 2. (faire) converger; *v/t.* concentrer (*des rayons, a. l'attention*); *opt.* mettre au point.

fod·der ['fɔdə] 1. fourrage *m*; 2. donner le fourrage à.

foe *poét.* [fou] ennemi(e *f*) *m*, adversaire *m*.

foe·tus *biol.* ['fi:təs] fœtus *m*.

fog [fɔg] 1. brouillard *m* (*a. fig.*); ⚓ brume *f*; *phot.* voile *m*; 2. *v/t.* embrumer; *fig.* embrouiller; *phot.* voiler; *v/i.* se voiler.

fo·g(e)y F ['fougi]: *old* ~ ganache *f*; vieille baderne *f*.

fog·gy □ ['fɔgi] brumeux (-euse *f*); *phot.* voilé; *fig.* confus; '**fog-horn** corne *f* de brume. [marotte *f*.)]

foi·ble ['fɔibl] *fig.* faible *m*; F)

foil¹ [fɔil] feuille *f*; lame *f*; *glace*: tain *m*; *escrime*: fleuret *m*; *fig.* repoussoir *m*.

foil² [~] faire échouer; déjouer.

foist [fɔist] imposer (à, on); refiler (qch. à q., *s.th. on s.o.*).

fold¹ [fould] 1. enclos *m*; *fig.* sein *m*; (*a. sheep-*~) parc *m* à moutons; 2. (em)parquer.

fold² [~] 1. pli *m*, repli *m*; *porte*: battant *m*; 2. -uple; 3. *v/t.* plier; plisser; croiser (*les bras*); serrer (dans, in); ~ *in three* plier en trois doubles; ~ *down* retourner; plier; ~ *up* plier; fermer; *v/i.* se (re)plier; *Am.* F fermer boutique; '**fold·er** plieur (-euse *f*) *m*; plioir *m*; dépliant *m*; chemise *f*; (*a pair of*) ~*s pl.* (un) pince-nez *m/inv.* pliant.

fold·ing ['fouldiŋ] pliant; repliable; '~-**bed** lit *m* pliant; '~-**boat** canot *m* pliable; '~-**cam·er·a** *phot.* appareil *m* pliant; '~-**chair** pliant *m*; '~-**cot** lit *m* pliant; '~-**door(s** *pl.*) porte *f* à deux battants; '~-**hat** (chapeau *m*) claque *m*; '~-**screen** paravent *m*; '~-**seat** pliant *m*; *théâ. etc.* strapontin *m*; '~-**ta·ble** table *f* pliante.

fo·li·age ['fouliidʒ] feuillage *m*; **fo·li·at·ed** ['ˏeitid] feuilleté, folié; lamellaire, lamelleux (-euse *f*); **fo·li·a·tion** *plante:* frondaison *f*; *miroir:* étamage *m*; *métal:* laminage *m*.

fo·li·o ['fouliou] folio *m*; feuille *f*; *volume:* in-folio *m*/*inv.*

folk [fouk] peuple *m*; gens *mf*/*pl.*; F ˜*s pl.* famille *f*.

folk·lore ['fouklɔ:] folklore *m*; légendes *f*/*pl.* populaires; **'folk-song** chanson *f* populaire.

fol·low ['folou] *v*/*t.* suivre; poursuivre (*a. les plaisirs*); succéder à; exercer (*un métier*); être partisan de; comprendre; *it* ˜*s that* il s'ensuit que; ˜ *out* poursuivre (*qch.*) jusqu'à sa conclusion; *cartes:* ˜ *suit* jouer dans la couleur; *fig.* en faire autant; ˜ *up* (pour)suivre; *v*/*i.* (s'en)suivre; *to* ˜ à suivre; **'fol·low·er** serviteur *m*; disciple *m*; sectateur (-trice *f*) *m*; ⊕ plateau *m*; F amoureux (-euse *f*) *m*; **'fol·low·ing** suite *f*; partisans *m*/*pl.*; *the* ˜ *pl.* les suivant(e)s *mf*/*pl.*; ˜ *wind* vent *m* arrière; **'fol·low-up** poursuite *f*; rappel *m*, contrôle *m*; ☞ soins *m*/*pl.* post-hospitaliers.

fol·ly ['fɔli] folie *f*, sottise *f*.

fo·ment [fou'ment] ☞ fomenter (*a. une discorde*); *fig.* exciter; **fo·men·ta·tion** fomentation *f*; stimulation *f*; **fo'ment·er** *fig.* fauteur (-trice *f*) *m*.

fond □ [fɔnd] affectueux (-euse *f*); amateur (de, of); *be* ˜ *of* aimer; *be* ˜ *of dancing* aimer danser.

fon·dle ['fɔndl] caresser, câliner.

fond·ness ['fɔndnis] (pour, for) tendresse *f*; penchant *m*; goût *m*.

font *eccl.* [fɔnt] fonts *m*/*pl.* baptismaux.

food [fu:d] nourriture *f* (*a. fig.*); vivres *m*/*pl.*; aliment(s) *m*(*pl.*); manger *m*; *fig.* matière *f*; ˜ *hall* *magasin:* rayon *m* d'alimentation; '˜-**stuffs** *pl.* produits *m*/*pl.* alimentaires; '˜-**val·ue** valeur *f* nutritive.

fool¹ [fu:l] **1.** fou (folle *f*) *m*; sot(te *f*) *m*; imbécile *mf*; idiot(e *f*) *m*; *make a* ˜ *of s.o.* se moquer de q.; duper q.; *make a* ˜ *of o.s.* se rendre ridicule; *live in a* ˜*'s paradise* se bercer d'un bonheur illusoire; **2.** *Am.* F stupide; imbécile de; **3.** *v*/*t.* duper, berner; escamoter (*qch.* à

q., *s.o.* out of s.th.); F ˜ *away* gaspiller; *v*/*i.* faire la bête; ˜ *about, surt. Am.* ˜ *(a)round* baguenauder; gâcher son temps.

fool² [ˏ] marmelade *f* à la crème.

fool·er·y ['fu:ləri] bêtise *f*; **'fool-hard·y** □ téméraire; **'fool·ish** □ insensé, étourdi; **'fool·ish·ness** folie *f*, sottise *f*; **'fool-proof** ⊕ indétraquable; à toute épreuve; **fool's-cap** ['ˏzkæp] bonnet *m* de fou; **fools·cap** ['ˏskæp] papier *m* ministre.

foot [fut] **1.** (*pl.* feet) *homme, bas, échelle, lit, arbre:* pied *m* (*a. mesure 30,48 cm*); *chat, chien, insecte, oiseau:* patte *f*; *marche f*; ✕ infanterie *f*; *page:* bas *m*; *on* ˜ à pied; *sur pied,* en train (*affaire*); *put one's* ˜ *down* faire acte d'autorité; opposer son veto (à, *upon*); F *I have put my* ˜ *into it* j'ai mis le pied dans le plat; j'ai dit *ou* fait une sottise; *set on* ˜ mettre en train; *set* ˜ *on* mettre pied sur; **2.** *v*/*t.* mettre un pied à; (*usu.* ˜ *up*) additionner (*le compte*); F ˜ *the bill* payer la note; *v*/*i.* ˜ *it* danser; marcher; **'foot·age** longueur *f* en pieds; métrage *m*; **'foot-and-'mouth dis·ease** fièvre *f* aphteuse; **'foot·ball** ballon *m*; football *m*; *Am.* rugby *m*; **'foot-board** *mot.* marchepied *m*; **'foot-boy** *hôtel:* chasseur *m*; **'foot-brake** frein *m* à pied; **'foot-bridge** passerelle *f*; **'foot·ed** swift-˜ aux pieds légers; **'foot·fall** (bruit *m* de) pas *m*; **'foot-gear** chaussures *f*/*pl.*; **'foot-guards** ✕ *pl.* gardes *m*/*pl.* à pied; **'foot-hills** *pl.* collines *f*/*pl.* avancées; **'foot-hold** prise *f* pour le pied; *fig.* pied *m*.

foot·ing ['futiŋ] place *f* pour le pied; point *m* d'appui; situation *f* sûre; condition *f*; △ base *f*; *fig.* entrée *f*; ✝ addition *f*; *upon the same* ˜*as* sur un pied d'égalité avec; *get a* ˜ prendre pied; *lose one's* ˜ perdre pied; *pay (for) one's* ˜ payer sa bienvenue.

foo·tle F ['fu:tl] **1.** *v*/*t.* gâcher (*le temps*); *v*/*i.* s'occuper de choses futilités; **2.** bêtise *f*, niaiserie *f*.

foot ˜: '˜-**lights** *pl. théâ.* rampe *f*; '˜-**loose** (*and fancy-free*) libre comme l'air; '˜-**man** laquais *m*; '˜-**note** note *f* au bas d'une page; '˜-**pace** pas *m*; '˜-**pas·sen·ger** piéton *m*; '˜-

path sentier *m*; *ville*: trottoir *m*; '~-
print empreinte *f* de pas; pas *m*; '~-
-**race** course *f* à pied; '~-**rule** règle *f*.
foot·sie F ['futsi]: *play* ~ (*with*) faire
du pied (à, avec); *fig.* s'entendre.
foot...: '~-**slog** *sl.* marcher; '~-**sore**
aux pieds endoloris; '~-**stalk** ⚲
pétiole *m*; pédoncule *m*; '~-**step** pas
m; trace *f*; ⊕ butée *f*; '~-**stool**
tabouret *m*; '~-**wear** *see* foot-gear; '~-
work *sp.* jeu *m* de pieds *ou* de
jambes.
fop [fɔp] fat *m*, dandy *m*; '**fop·per·y**
dandysme *m*; '**fop·pish** □ fat;
affecté.
for [fɔː; fə] **1.** *prp. usu.* pour (*a. destination*); comme; à cause de; de
(*peur, joie, etc.*); par (*exemple, charité, etc.*); avant (*3 jours*), d'ici (à)
(*2 mois*); pendant (*une semaine*);
depuis, il y a (*un an*); *distance*: jusqu'(à), pendant (*10 km*); contre, en
échange de; en, dans; malgré, en
dépit de; *destination*: à (*Londres*);
vers, envers, ⚓ allant à; *he is* ~ *London* il va à Londres; ~ *example* (*ou
instance*) par exemple; *were it not* ~
that sans cela; *he is a fool* ~ *doing
that* il est sot de faire cela; *I walked*
~ *a mile* j'ai fait un mille; ~ *3 days*
pour *ou* pendant 3 jours; ~ *all that*
en dépit de *ou* malgré tout; *come* ~
dinner venir dîner; *I* ~ *one* moi entre
autres; *go* ~ aller chercher (*q.*); *it is
good* ~ *us to* (*inf.*) il est bon que nous
(*sbj.*); *the snow was too deep* ~ *them
to come* la neige était trop profonde
pour qu'ils viennent; *it is* ~ *you to
decide* c'est à vous à décider; ~ *sure!*
bien sûr! *pour* for *après verbe voir le
verbe simple*; **2.** *cj.* car.
for·age ['fɔridʒ] **1.** fourrage *m*;
2. fourrager (pour, for).
for·as·much [fɔrəz'mʌtʃ]: ~ *as* puisque, vu que, d'autant que.
for·ay ['fɔrei] incursion *f*, raid *m*.
for·bade [fə'beid] *prét. de* forbid.
for·bear[1] ['fɔːbɛə] ancêtre *m*.
for·bear[2] [fɔː'bɛə] [*irr.*] *v/t.* s'abstenir de; *v/i.* s'abstenir (de, from);
montrer de la patience; **for'bear-
ance** patience *f*, indulgence *f*;
abstention *f*.
for·bid [fə'bid] [*irr.*] défendre (qch.
à q., *s.o. s.th.*); interdire (qch. à q.,
s.o.s.th.); *God*~! à Dieu ne plaise!;
for'bid·den *p.p. de* forbid; **for'bidding** □ sinistre; menaçant.

for·bore, for·borne [fɔː'bɔː(n)]
prét. et p.p. de forbear[2].
force [fɔːs] **1.** force *f*, violence *f*;
puissance *f*, autorité *f*; intensité *f*;
effort *m*; énergie *f*; *the* ~ la police;
armed ~*s pl.* forces *f/pl.* armées; *by* ~
de vive force; *come* (*put*) *in* ~ entrer
(mettre) en vigueur; **2.** *usu.* forcer;
contraindre, obliger; prendre par
force; violer (*une femme*); faire
avancer; pousser (*a.* F *un élève*);
imposer (qch. à q., *s.th.* [*up*]*on s.o.*);
~ *one's way* se frayer un chemin; ~
back repousser; ✈ ~ *down* forcer à
atterrir; ~ *on* forcer à avancer; ~
open enfoncer; ouvrir de force;
'**forced** (*adv.* **forc·ed·ly** ['~idli])
forcé; obligatoire; contraint; ~ *loan*
emprunt *m* forcé; ~ *landing* atterrissage *m* forcé; ~ *march* marche *f*
forcée; ~ *sale* vente *f* forcée; '**force-
feed** alimenter (*q.*) de force; **force-
ful** □ ['~ful] énergique; plein de
force; vigoureux (-euse *f*); violent.
'**force·meat** ['fɔːsmiːt] *cuis.* farce *f*.
for·ceps ⚕, *zo.* ['fɔːseps] *sg. ou pl.*
pince *f*; *dentiste*: davier *m*.
force-pump ['fɔːspʌmp] pompe *f*
foulante.
forc·er ⊕ ['fɔːsə] plongeur *m*.
for·ci·ble □ ['fɔːsəbl] de force, forcé; vigoureux (-euse *f*); énergique.
forc·ing-house ['fɔːsiŋhaus] forcerie *f*.
ford [fɔːd] **1.** gué *m*; **2.** passer à gué;
'**ford·a·ble** guéable.
fore [fɔː] **1.** *adv.* ⚓ ~ *and aft* de
l'avant à l'arrière; *to the* ~ en évidence; présent; *bring* (*come*) *to the*~
(se) mettre en évidence; **2.** *adj.* de
devant; antérieur; pré-; '~**arm**
avant-bras *m*; ~'**bode** présager;
pressentir (*personne*); ~'**bod·ing**
présage *m*; pressentiment *m*; '~**cast**
1. prévision *f*; *weather* ~ prévisions
f/pl. météorologiques; **2.** [*irr.*
(*cast*)] prédire; prévoir; '~**cas·tle**
⚓ ['fouksl] gaillard *m* d'avant;
poste *m* de l'équipage; ~'**close**
exclure (de, from), empêcher (de
from, to); saisir (*un immeuble
hypothéqué*); '~**date** antidater; ~-
'**doom** condamner d'avance; présager; '~**fa·ther** aïeul (*pl.* -eux) *m*;
'~**fin·ger** index *m*; '~**foot** pied *m*
antérieur; '~**front** F premier rang
m; ~'**go** [*irr.* (*go*)] aller devant;
~*ing* précédent; ~'**gone** passé; ~

conclusion chose *f* prévue; '**~-ground** premier plan *m*; '**~·hand** avant-main *f*; **~·head** ['fɔrid] front *m*.

for·eign ['fɔrin] étranger (-ère *f*) (*a. fig.*); **~** *affairs pl.* Affaires *f/pl.* étrangères; **~** *exchange* devises *f/pl.* étrangères; *the* ⚥ *Office* le Ministère des Affaires étrangères; **~** *policy* politique *f* extérieure; ⚥ *Secretary* Ministre *m* des Affaires étrangères; **~** *trade* commerce *m* extérieur; '**for·eign·er** étranger (-ère *f*) *m*; '**for·eign·ness** caractère *m* ou air *m* étranger.

fore...: **~'judge** préjuger; **~'know** [*irr.* (*know*)] prévoir; savoir d'avance; '**~·land** promontoire *m*; '**~·leg** patte *f* ou jambe *f* de devant; '**~·lock** mèche *f* sur le front; *take time by the* **~** saisir l'occasion aux cheveux; '**~·man** *ⁿ* chef *m* du jury; ⊕ chef *m* d'équipe; contremaître *m*; '**~·mast** ⚓ mât *m* de misaine; '**~·most 1.** *adj.* premier (-ère *f*), le plus avancé; **2.** *adv.* tout d'abord; '**~·noon** matinée *f*.

fo·ren·sic [fə'rensik] judiciaire; légal (-aux *m/pl.*); **~** *medicine* médecine *f* légale.

fore...: '**~·run·ner** avant-courrier (-ère *f*) *m*, -coureur *m*, précurseur *m*; **~·sail** ['~seil, ⚓ '~sl] (voile *f* de) misaine *f*; **~'see** [*irr.* (*see*)] prévoir; **~'see·a·ble** qu'on peut prévoir; prévisible; **~'shad·ow** présager, laisser prévoir; '**~·shore** plage *f*; **~'short·en** dessiner en raccourci; **~'show** [*irr.* (*show*)] préfigurer; '**~·sight** prévoyance *f*; prévision *f*; *arme* à *feu*: guidon *m*; '**~·skin** prépuce *m*.

for·est ['fɔrist] **1.** forêt *f*; **2.** boiser. **fore·stall** [fɔː'stɔːl] anticiper, prévenir.

for·est·er ['fɔristə] (garde-)forestier *m*; habitant(e *f*) *m* d'une forêt; '**for·est·ry** sylviculture *f*.

fore...: '**~·taste** avant-goût *m*; **~'tell** [*irr.* (*tell*)] prédire, présager; '**~·thought** prévoyance *f*; préméditation *f*; '**~·top** ⚓ hune *f* de misaine; **~'warn** avertir, prévenir; '**~·wom·an** première ouvrière *f*; contremaîtresse *f*; '**~·word** avant-propos *m/inv.*; préface *f*.

for·feit ['fɔːfit] **1.** confisqué; **2.** confiscation *f*; amende *f*; gage *m*;

punition *f*; ✝ dédit *m*; *sp.* forfait *m*; *jeu:* **~s** *pl.* gages *m/pl.*; **3.** confisquer, perdre; forfaire à (*l'honneur*); '**for·feit·a·ble** confiscable; '**for·fei·ture** ['~tʃə] confiscation *f*, perte *f*.

for·gath·er [fɔː'gæðə] s'assembler.

for·gave [fə'geiv] *prét. de forgive.*

forge¹ [fɔːdʒ] (*usu.* **~** *ahead*) avancer à toute vitesse *ou* à travers les obstacles.

forge² [fɔːdʒ] **1.** forge *f*; **2.** forger (*a. fig. une excuse etc.*); contrefaire (*une signature etc.*); inventer; '**forg·er** forgeron *m*; faussaire *mf*; fauxmonnayeur *m*; '**forg·er·y** falsification *f*; contrefaçon *f*; faux *m*.

for·get [fə'get] [*irr.*] oublier; F *I* **~** j'ai oublié, ça m'échappe; **for'get·ful** □ [~ful] oublieux (-euse *f*); **for'get·ful·ness** oubli *m*; négligence *f*; **for'get-me-not** ⚘ myosotis *m*, F ne-m'oubliez-pas *m*.

for·give [fə'giv] [*irr.*] pardonner (à *q.*, *s.o.*); faire remise de (*une dette*); **for'giv·en** *p.p. de forgive*; **for'give·ness** pardon *m*; clémence *f*; **for'giv·ing** □ clément; peu rancunier (-ère *f*).

for·go [fɔː'gou] [*irr.* (*go*)] renoncer à; s'abstenir de.

for·got [fə'gɔt], **for'got·ten** [~n] *prét. et p.p. de forget.*

fork [fɔːk] **1.** *table:* fourchette *f*; ✔, *routes:* fourche *f*; *tuning* **~** diapason *m*; **2.** fourcher; F **~** *out* *v/t.* allonger (*de l'argent*); *v/i.* casquer, cracher; '**forked** fourchu; en fourche.

for·lorn [fə'lɔːn] abandonné, perdu; désespéré; **~** *hope* ⚔ enfants *m/pl.* perdus; troupe *f* sacrifiée; *fig.* tentative *f* désespérée.

form [fɔːm] **1.** forme *f*; taille *f*; formule *f*, bulletin *m*, feuille *f* (*d'impôts*); *école:* classe *f*; banc *m*; *lièvre:* gîte *m*; *sp. in* **~** en forme; *in good* **~** en haleine; *that is bad* **~** c'est de mauvais ton; *cela ne se fait pas*; **2.** *v/t.* former, faire; organiser; établir; contracter (*une alliance, une habitude*); arrêter (*un plan*); ⚔ se mettre en; *v/i.* se former; prendre forme; ⚔ se ranger; **~** *up* se former en rangs.

for·mal [fɔː'mel] □ ['fɔːml] cérémonieux (-euse *f*); formel(le *f*); en règle; régulier (-ère *f*) (*jardin*); '**for·mal·ist** formaliste *mf*; **for·mal·i·ty**

[fɔ:'mæliti] formalité *f*; *maintien*: raideur *f*; cérémonie *f*; **for·mal·ize** ['fɔ:məlaiz] donner une forme (conventionnelle) à.

for·ma·tion [fɔ:'meiʃn] formation *f* (*a.* ✕, *a. géol.*); disposition *f*, ordre *m*; ✕ vol *m* de groupe; **form·a·tive** ['fɔ:mətiv] formateur (-trice *f*).

form·er[1] ['fɔ:mə] façonneur (-euse *f*) *m*; ⊕ gabarit *m*.

for·mer[2] [◡] précédent; ancien(ne *f*); antérieur; premier (-ère *f*); **'for·mer·ly** autrefois, jadis.

for·mic ['fɔ:mik]: ◡ *acid* acide *m* formique.

for·mi·da·ble ◻ ['fɔ:midəbl] formidable (*a. fig.*), redoutable.

form·less ◻ ['fɔ:mlis] informe.

for·mu·la ['fɔ:mjulə], *pl.* **-lae** ['◡li:], **-las** formule *f*; **for·mu·lar·y** ['◡ləri] **1.** rituel(le *f*); prescrit; **2.** formulaire *m*; **for·mu·late** ['◡leit] formuler; **for·mu·la·tion** formulation *f*.

for·ni·cate ['fɔ:nikeit] forniquer; **for·ni·ca·tion** fornication *f*.

for·sake [fə'seik] [*irr.*] abandonner, délaisser; renoncer à; **for·sak·en** *p.p. de* forsake.

for·sook [fə'suk] *prét. de* forsake.

for·sooth *iro.* [fə'su:θ] ma foi!

for·swear [fɔ:'swɛə] [*irr. (swear)*] renier, répudier; ◡ *o.s.* se parjurer; **for'sworn** parjure.

fort [fɔ:t] ✕ fort *m*; forteresse *f*.

forte [◡] *fig.* fort *m*.

forth [fɔ:θ] *lieu*: en avant; *temps*: désormais; *and so* ◡ et ainsi de suite; *from this day* ◡ à partir de ce jour; dès maintenant; **'◡·com·ing** qui arrive; futur; prochain; prêt à paraître; *be* ◡ paraître; ne pas se faire attendre; **'◡·right 1.** *adj.* franc(he *f*); **2.** *adv.* carrément; **'◡·with** tout de suite.

for·ti·eth ['fɔ:tiiθ] quarantième (*a. su./m*).

for·ti·fi·ca·tion [fɔ:tifi'keiʃn] fortification *f* (*a.* ✕); **for·ti·fi·er** ['◡faiə] fortificateur *m*; *boisson etc.*: fortifiant *m*; **for·ti·fy** ['◡fai] ✕ fortifier (*a. fig.*); **for·ti·tude** ['◡tju:d] courage *m*, fortitude *f*.

fort·night ['fɔ:tnait] quinze jours *m/pl.*; quinzaine *f*; *this day* ◡ d'aujourd'hui en quinze; **'fort·night·ly 1.** *adj.* bimensuel(le *f*); **2.** *adv.* tous les quinze jours.

for·tress ['fɔ:tris] forteresse *f*.

for·tu·i·tous ◻ [fɔ:'tjuitəs] fortuit; **for'tu·i·tous·ness, for'tu·i·ty** fortuité *f*; casualité *f*.

for·tu·nate ['fɔ:tʃnit] heureux (-euse *f*); ◡*ly usu.* par bonheur, heureusement.

for·tune ['fɔ:tʃn] fortune *f*; sort *m*, destinée *f*; chance *f*; richesses *f/pl.*; ♀ ['fɔ:tju:n] Fortune *f*, Destin *m*; *good* ◡ bonheur *m*; *bad* ◡, *ill* ◡ malheur *m*, mauvaise chance *f*; *marry a* ◡ faire un riche mariage; **'◡-hunt·er** coureur *m* de dots; **'◡-tel·ler** diseur (-euse *f*) *m* de bonne aventure.

for·ty ['fɔ:ti] quarante (*a. su./m*); *Am.* ◡*-niner* chercheur *m* d'or de 1849; F ◡ *winks pl.* petit somme *m*.

fo·rum ['fɔ:rəm] forum *m*; F tribunal *m*.

for·ward ['fɔ:wəd] **1.** *adj.* de devant, d'avant; avancé; précoce; effronté; impatient; ✝ à terme; **2.** *adv.* en avant; sur l'avant; ✝ *carried* ◡ à reporter; *from this time* ◡ désormais, à l'avenir; **3.** *su. foot.* avant *m*; **4.** *v/t.* avancer, favoriser; expédier; faire suivre; *poste*: *please* ◡ prière de faire suivre; **'for·ward·er** expéditeur (-trice *f*) *m*.

for·ward·ing ['fɔ:wədiŋ] expédition *f*, avancement *m*; ◡ *address* adresse *f* (pour faire suivre le courrier); ◡ *agent* expéditeur *m*; entrepreneur *m* de transports.

for·ward·ness ['fɔ:wədnis] empressement *m*; précocité *f*; hardiesse *f*; présomption *f*; **for·wards** ['fɔ:wədz] en avant.

fosse [fɔs] ✕ fossé *m*; *anat.* fosse *f*.

fos·sil ['fɔsl] fossile (*a. su./m.*).

fos·ter ['fɔstə] **1.** *fig.* nourrir, encourager; ◡ *up* élever; **2.** adoptif (-ive *f*) (*p.ex.* ◡*-brother*); ◡ *home* famille *f* adoptive *ou* nourricière; **'fos·ter·age** mise *f* en nourrice; fonctions *f/pl.* de nourrice; **'fos·ter·er** parent *m* adoptif; *fig.* promoteur (-trice *f*) *m*; **'fos·ter·ling** nourrison(ne *f*) *m*.

fought [fɔ:t] *prét. et p.p. de* fight.

foul [faul] **1.** ◻ infect (*a. haleine*); sale (*a. temps*, *a.* ⚓ carène); *fig.* dégoûtant; ⚓ engagé (*ancre etc.*); ⚓ gros(se *f*) (*temps*); ⚓ contraire (*vent*); *box.* bas(se *f*) (*coup*); encrassé (*fusil*); déloyal (-aux *m/pl.*)

franchise

(jeu); bourbeux (-euse *f*) *(eau)*; atroce, infâme *(action)*; impur *(pensée)*; grossier (-ère *f*) *(mot. etc.)*; ~ tongue langage *m* ordurier; *fall (ou run)* ~ of ⚓ entrer en collision avec; *fig.* se brouiller avec; **2.** ⚓ collision *f*; *sp.* faute *f*; *box.* coup *m* bas; *foot.* poussée *f* irrégulière; **3.** (s')engager; (s')encrasser; *v/t.* salir; souiller; *sp.* commettre une faute contre; ⚓ entrer en collision avec; **~-mouthed** ['~'mauðd] mal embouché; au langage ordurier.

found[1] [faund] *prét. et p.p. de* find 1.

found[2] [~] fonder *(a. fig.)*; établir.

found[3] ⊕ [~] fondre; mouler *(la fonte)*.

foun·da·tion [faun'deiʃn] fondation *f*; △, *a. fig.* fondement *m*; base *f*; établissement *m*; **foun'da·tion-school** école *f* dotée; **foun'da·tion-stone** première pierre *f*.

found·er[1] ['faundə] fondateur *m*; auteur *m*; fondeur *m*; ~ member membre *m* fondateur.

found·er[2] [~] *v/i.* ⚓ sombrer, couler à fond; *fig.* échouer; s'effondrer *(cheval, maison, etc.)*; s'enfoncer; *v/t.* ⚓ couler; outrer *(un cheval)*.

found·ling ['faundliŋ] enfant *mf* trouvé(e).

found·ress ['faundris] fondatrice *f*.

found·ry ⊕ ['faundri] fonderie *f*.

fount [faunt] *poét.* source *f*; *typ.* [*usu.* fɔnt] fonte *f*.

foun·tain ['fauntin] fontaine *f*; jet *m* d'eau; *fig.* source *f*; ⊕ distributeur *m*; **'~'head** source *f* *(a. fig.)*; **'~-'pen** stylographe *m*, F stylo *m*.

four [fɔː] quatre *(a. su./m)*; **'four-eyes** *sg.* F binoclard(e *f*) *m*; **'four-'flush·er** *Am. sl.* bluffeur *m*, vantard *m*; **'four-fold** quadruple; **'four-in-hand** voiture *f* à quatre chevaux; **'four-'let·ter word** mot *m* obscène, obscénité *f*; **'four-'square** carré (-ment *adv.*); *fig.* inébranlable (devant, to); **'four-'stroke** *mot.* à quatre temps; **four·teen** ['~'tiːn] quatorze *(a. su./m)*; **four'teenth** ['~'tiːnθ] quatorzième *(a. su./m)*; **fourth** [fɔːθ] quatrième *(a. su./m)*; ♩ quart *m*; **'fourth·ly** en quatrième lieu; **'four'wheel·er** fiacre *m*.

fowl [faul] **1.** poule *f*; volaille *f* *(a. cuis.)*; **2.** faire la chasse au gibier; oiseler *(au filet)*; **'fowl·er** oiseleur *m*.

fowl·ing ['fauliŋ] chasse *f* aux oiseaux; **'~-piece** fusil *m* de chasse.

fox [fɔks] **1.** renard *m*; **2.** *sl.* tromper; **'~-brush** queue *f* de renard; **'~-earth** terrier *m*; **foxed** ['~t] piqué *(papier, bière, etc.)*.

fox...: **'~-glove** ♀ digitale *f*; F gantelée *f*; **'~-hole** ✕ nid *m* d'embusqués; **'~-hound** chien *m* courant; fox-hound *m*; **'~-hunt** chasse *f* au renard; **'~-trot** fox-trot *m/inv.*; **'fox·y** rusé; astucieux (-euse *f*); roux (rousse *f*); piqué.

fra·cas ['fræka:] fracas *m*; *sl.* bagarre *f*.

frac·tion ♠ ['frækʃn] fraction *f*; *fig.* fragment *m*; **'frac·tion·al** □ fractionnaire; ⚗ fractionné.

frac·tious □ ['frækʃəs] revêche; difficile; maussade.

frac·ture ['fræktʃə] **1.** fracture *f* *(souv.* 🩹*)*; **2.** briser; 🩹 fracturer.

frag·ile □ ['frædʒail] fragile; *fig.* faible; **fra·gil·i·ty** [frə'dʒiliti] fragilité *f*; faiblesse *f*.

frag·ment ['frægmənt] fragment *m*; morceau *m*; **'frag·men·tar·y** □ fragmentaire; *géol.* clastique.

fra·grance ['freigrəns] parfum *m*; bonne odeur *f*; **'fra·grant** □ parfumé, odoriférant.

frail[1] □ [freil] peu solide; fragile; frêle *(personne)*; délicat; **'frail·ty** *fig.* faiblesse *f* morale; défaut *m*.

frail[2] [~] cabas *m*.

frame [freim] **1.** construction *f*, forme *f*; cadre *m* *(a. ⚓ de l'hélice)*; ⊕ charpente *f*; métier *m*; ✈ fuselage *m*; ⚓ carcasse *f* *(d'un navire)*; ⚓ couple *m*; fenêtre: chambranle *m*; ⚞ châssis *m*; *télév.* trame *f*; ~ *aerial* antenne *f* en cadre; ~ *house* maison *f* à charpente de bois; ~ *of mind* état *m* d'esprit; **2.** former; construire; encadrer *(a. fig.)*; ⊕ faire la charpente de *(un toit)*; *fig.* imaginer; fabriquer; *surt.* *Am.* ~ *up* monter une accusation contre *(q.)*; truquer *(qch.)*; **'fram·er** auteur *m*; encadreur *m*; **'frame-up** *surt.* *Am.* F coup *m* monté; **'frame·work** ⊕ squelette *m*; △ bâti *m*; charpente *f*; *fig.* cadre *m*.

fran·chise ⚖ ['fræntʃaiz] franchise *f*, privilège *m*; *pol.* droit *m* de vote; *admin.* droit *m* de cité.

Fran·cis·can *eccl.* [fræn'siskən] franciscain(e *f*) *m* (*a. adj.*).

fran·gi·ble ['frændʒibl] frangible, fragile.

Frank¹ [fræŋk] Franc (Franque *f*) *m*; *npr.* François *m*.

frank² □ [∼] franc(he *f*); sincère; ouvert.

frank·furt·er *Am.* ['fræŋkfətə] saucisse *f* de Francfort.

frank·in·cense ['fræŋkinsens] encens *m*. [sincérité *f*.\]

frank·ness ['fræŋknis] franchise *f*.\

fran·tic ['fræntik] (∼ally) frénétique; fou (fol *devant une voyelle ou un h muet*); folle *f*) (de, with).

fra·ter·nal □ [frə'tə:nl] fraternel(le *f*); **fra'ter·ni·ty** fraternité *f*; confrérie *f*; *Am. univ.* association *f* estudiantine; **frat·er·ni·za·tion** [frætənai'zeiʃn] fraternisation *f*; **'frat·er·nize** fraterniser (avec, with).

frat·ri·cide ['freitrisaid] fratricide *m*; *personne*: fratricide *mf*.

fraud [frɔːd] fraude *f*; F déception *f*, duperie *f*; imposteur *m*; **fraud·u·lence** ['∼juləns] caractère *m* frauduleux; **'fraud·u·lent** □ frauduleux (-euse *f*).

fraught *poét.* [frɔːt]: ∼ with plein de; gros(se *f*) de; fertile en.

fray¹ [frei] (s')érailler; (s')effiler; s'effranger (*faux col*).

fray² [∼] bagarre *f*.

fraz·zle *surt. Am.* F ['fræzl] 1. état *m* usé; *beat to a* ∼ battre (*q.*) à plates coutures; 2. (s')érailler.

freak [friːk] caprice *m*; tour *m*; F excentrique *mf*, un drôle de type; F mordu *m*, fana *mf*; *a film* ∼ un mordu du film; ∼ *of nature* monstre *m*; phénomène *m*; **'freak·ish** □ capricieux (-euse *f*); fantasque; **freak out** *sl.* se défoncer.

freck·le ['frekl] 1. tache *f* de rousseur; *fig.* point *m*; 2. marquer *ou* se couvrir de taches de rousseur.

free [friː] 1. □ libre; en liberté; franc(he *f*); gratuit; exempt, débarrassé, affranchi (de *from*, of); prodigue (de, with); † franco; ∼ *of debt* etc. exempt ou quitte de dettes etc.; *he is* ∼ *to* (*inf.*) il lui est permis de (*inf.*); ∼ *and easy* sans gêne; † ∼ *enterprise* libre entreprise *f*; ∼ *fight* mêlée *f* générale; bagarre *f*; ∼ *port* port *m* franc; ∼ *trade* libre échange *m*; ∼ *wheel* roue *f* libre; *make* ∼ prendre

des libertés (avec q., with s.o.); *make* ∼ *to* (*inf.*) se permettre de (*inf.*); *make* ∼ *with s.th.* se servir de qch. sans se gêner; *make s.o.* ∼ *of a city* créer q. citoyen d'honneur; ⊕ *run* ∼ marcher à vide; *set* ∼ libérer; 2. (*from*, of) libérer (de); dégager (de); débarrasser (de); exempter (de), affranchir (*un esclave*); **'∼boot·er** flibustier; F maraudeur *m*; **'free·dom** liberté *f*; indépendance *f*; franchise *f*; facilité *f*; familiarité *f*; ∼ *of a city* citoyenneté *f* d'honneur d'une ville; ∼ *of a company* maîtrise *f* d'une corporation; ∼ *of the press* liberté *f* de la presse; ∼ *of speech* franc-parler *m*; ∼ *of worship* liberté *f* religieuse.

free...: **'∼hold** ⅃⅃ propriété *f* foncière (perpétuelle et libre); **'∼hold·er** propriétaire *m* foncier; **'∼kick** *foot.* coup *m* franc; **'∼man** homme *m* libre; citoyen *m* (d'honneur); **'∼ma·son** franc-maçon (*pl.* francs-maçons) *m*; **'∼ma·son·ry** franc-maçonnerie *f*; **'∼stone** grès *m*; **'∼style** nage *f* libre; **'∼'think·er** libre penseur (-euse *f*) *m*; **'∼'think·ing**, **'∼thought** libre pensée *f*; **'∼way** *Am. mot.* autoroute *f*.

freeze [friːz] [*irr.*] 1. *v/i.* (se) geler; se figer; ∼ *to death* mourir de froid; *v/t.* (con)geler; glacer; bloquer (*les prix*, *les fonds*); geler (*des capitaux*); *sl.* ∼ *out* évincer; 2. gel *m* (*a. fig.*, *a.* † *des crédits*); gelée *f*; † *etc. a.* blocage *m*; *price (wage)* ∼ blocage *m* des prix (des salaires); **'∼dry** lyophiliser; **'freez·er** congélateur *m*; sorbetière *f*; **'freez·ing** □ réfrigérant; glacial (-als *m/pl.*); ∼ *of prices* blocage *m* des prix; ∼ *compartment* congélateur *m*, compartiment *m* de congélation; **∼mixture** *phys.* mélange *m* réfrigérant; **∼point** point *m* de congélation.

freight [freit] 1. fret *m* (*a. prix*); cargaison *f*; *attr. Am.* de marchandises; ∼ *out* (*home*) fret *m* de sortie (de retour); ∼ *plane* avion-cargo *m* (*pl.* avions-cargo); *Am.* ∼ *train* train *m* de marchandises; ∼ *yard* dépôt *m* des marchandises; 2. (af)fréter; **'freight·age** *see* freight 1; **'freight·car** *Am.* ⅅ wagon *m* de marchandises; **'freight·er** affréteur *m*; navire *m* de charge; *Am.* consignateur (-trice *f*) *m*; *Am.* convoi *m*; *Am. see* freight-car.

French [frentʃ] 1. français; ∼ *beans*

haricots *m/pl.* verts; *cuis.* ~ *dressing* vinaigrette *f*; *cuis.* ~ *fried potatoes*, *Am. a.* ~ fries (pommes *f/pl.* [de terre]) frites *f/pl.*; *take* ~ *leave* filer à l'anglaise; ~ *window* portefenêtre (*pl.* portes-fenêtres) *f*; **2.** *ling.* français *m*, langue *f* française; *the* ~ *pl.* les Français *m/pl.*; '~-**man** Français *m*; '~-**wom·an** Française *f*.

fren·zied ['frenzid] forcené; fou (fol *devant une voyelle ou un h muet*; folle *f*); '**fren·zy** frénésie *f*; *fig.* transport *m*; ✽ délire *m*.

fre·quen·cy ['fri:kwənsi] fréquence *f* (*a.* ✍); **fre·quent 1.** □ ['~kwənt] fréquent; très répandu; **2.** [~'kwent] fréquenter; hanter; **fre·quen·ta·tion** fréquentation *f* (de, of); **fre·quent·er** habitué(e *f*) *m*; familier (-ère *f*) *m*.

fres·co ['freskou], *pl.* -**co(e)s** ['~kouz] (peinture *f* à) fresque *f*.

fresh [freʃ] **1.** □ frais (fraîche *f*); récent; nouveau (-el *devant une voyelle ou un h muet*; -elle *f*; -eaux *m/pl.*); éveillé; *Am. sl.* effronté; ~ *water* eau *f* fraîche; eau *f* douce (= *non salée*); **2.** fraîcheur *f* (*du matin etc.*); crue *f*; '**fresh·en** *vt/i.* rafraîchir; '**fresh·er** *Brit. sl. pour* freshman; **fresh·et** ['~it] courant *m* d'eau douce; inondation *f*; '**fresh-fro·zen** frais (fraîche *f*) frigorifié; '**fresh·man** *univ.* étudiant(e *f*) *m* de première année; '**fresh·ness** fraîcheur *f*; nouveauté *f*; '**fresh-wa·ter** d'eau douce; *Am.* ~ *college* petit collège *m* de province.

fret[1] [fret] **1.** agitation *f*; irritation *f*; **2.** (se) ronger; (se) frotter; (s')irriter, (s')inquiéter; *v/i.* s'agiter (*eau*); *v/t.* érailler (*un cordage*); ~ *away*, ~ *out* éroder.

fret[2] [~] **1.** ⚓ frette *f*; **2.** sculpter; *fig.* bigarrer.

fret[3] [~] ♪ touche(tte) *f*; ~ted *instrument* instrument *m* à touchettes.

fret·ful □ ['fretful] chagrin.

fret-saw ['fretsɔ:] scie *f* à découper.

fret·work ['fretwɔːk] ouvrage *m* à claire-voie; découpage *m*.

Freud·i·an ['frɔidjən] freudien(ne *f*); ~ *slip* lapsus *m*.

fri·a·bil·i·ty [fraiə'biliti] friabilité *f*; '**fri·a·ble** friable.

fri·ar ['fraiə] moine *m*, frère *m*; '**fri·ar·y** monastère *m*; couvent *m*.

frib·ble ['fribl] **1.** baguenauder; gaspiller (*de l'argent*); **2.** frivolité *f*; *personne*: baguenaudier *m*.

fric·as·see [frikə'si:] **1.** fricassée *f*; **2.** fricasser.

fric·tion ['frikʃn] friction *f* (✽, *a. fig.*); frottement *m*; *Am.* ~ *tape* chatterton *m*, ruban *m* isolant; '**fric·tion·al** à *ou* de frottement *ou* friction; '**fric·tion·less** □ sans frottement.

Fri·day ['fraidi] vendredi *m*.

fridge *Brit.* F [fridʒ] frigo *m*.

friend [frend] ami(e *f*) *m*; connaissance *f*; ♀ Quaker(esse *f*) *m*; *his* ~*s pl. souv.* ses connaissances *f/pl.*; *make* ~*s with* se lier d'amitié avec; '**friend·less** sans ami(s); abandonné; '**friend·ly** amical (-aux *m/pl.*); ami; bienveillant; *fig.* intime; ♀ *Society Brit.* société *f* de secours mutuel; '**friend·ship** amitié *f*.

frieze [fri:z] frise *f* (*tex., a.* △).

frig·ate ⚓ ['frigit] frégate *f*.

fright [frait] peur *f*, effroi *m*, épouvante *f*; F épouvantail *m*; '**fright·en** effrayer, faire peur à; *be* ~ed *at* (*ou of*) avoir peur de; **fright·ful** □ ['~ful] affreux (-euse *f*); '**fright·ful·ness** horreur *f*.

frig·id □ ['fridʒid] glacial (-als *m/pl.*); froid (*a. fig.*); **fri·gid·i·ty** frigidité *f*; (grande) froideur *f*.

frill [fril] **1.** ruche *f*; jabot *m*; F *fig. put on* ~*s* faire des façons; **2.** plisser, rucher.

fringe [frindʒ] **1.** frange *f*; bord (-ure *f*) *m*; *forêt:* lisière *f*; *a.* ~*s pl.* cheveux *m/pl.* à la chien; ~ *benefits pl.* avantages *m/pl.* supplémentaires; ~ *group* groupe *m* marginal; **2.** franger; border.

frip·per·y ['fripəri] **1.** camelote *f*; faste *m*; **2.** sans valeur; de camelote.

frisk [frisk] **1.** gambade *f*, cabriole *f*; **2.** gambader; '**frisk·i·ness** vivacité *f*; '**frisk·y** □ vif (vive *f*); fringant (*cheval*); animé.

frith [friθ] *see* firth.

frit·ter ['fritə] **1.** beignet *m*; **2.** ~ *away* gaspiller.

fri·vol·i·ty [fri'vɔliti] frivolité *f*; légèreté *f* d'esprit; **friv·o·lous** □ ['frivələs] frivole; léger (-ère *f*); futile, vain; évaporé (*personne*).

frizz [friz] frisotter; *cuis.* faire frire; *a. see* frizzle 2; **friz·zle** ['~l] **1.** cheveux *m/pl.* crêpelés; **2.** (*a.* ~ *up*) frisotter; *v/t.* cuis. griller (*qch.*); *v/i.* grésiller; **'friz·z(1)y** crêpelé, frisotté.

fro [frou]: *to and* ~ çà et là, de long en large.

frock [frɔk] *moine:* froc *m*; (*usu.* ~*-coat*) *femme, enfant:* robe *f*; redingote *f*; ✕ tunique *f* de petite tenue.

frog [frɔg] grenouille *f*; *cost.* soutache *f*; 🏥 (cœur *m* de) croisement *m*; ✕ porte-épée *m/inv.*; **'~·man** homme-grenouille (*pl.* hommes-grenouilles) *m*.

frol·ic ['frɔlik] **1.** gambades *f/pl.*; ébats *m/pl.*, jeu *m*; escapade *f*; divertissement *m*; **2.** folâtrer, gambader; **frol·ic·some** □ ['~səm] folâtre, gai, joyeux (-euse *f*).

from [frɔm; frəm] *prp.* de; depuis; à partir de; par suite de; de la part de; par; *defend* ~ protéger contre; *draw* ~ *nature* dessiner d'après nature; *drink* ~ boire dans; *hide* ~ cacher à; *remove* ~ enlever à; ~ *above* d'en haut; ~ *amidst* d'entre; ~ *before* dès avant.

front [frʌnt] **1.** devant *m*; premier rang *m*; façade *f*; *boutique:* devanture *f*; promenade *f* (*au bord de la mer*); ✕ front *m*; *chemise:* plastron *m*; F prête-nom *m* (*pl.* prête-noms), façade *f*; *in* ~ *of* devant, en face de; *two-pair* ~ chambre *f* sur le devant au deuxième; *fig.* come *to the* ~ se faire connaître; arriver au premier rang; **2.** antérieur, de devant; ✕ *u. fig.* ~ *line* line front *m*, première ligne *f*, ligne *f* de contact; *mot.* ~ *wheel drive* traction *f* avant; ~ *yard* Am. jardin *m* de devant; **3.** *v/t.* (*a.* ~ *on, towards*) faire face à; donner sur; braver; *Am.* F prêter son nom à, agir en homme de paille pour; *v/i.* faire front; **'front·age** △ façade *f*; **'fron·tal 1.** frontal (-aux *m/pl.*); de face; de front; **2.** △ façade *f*; *eccl.* devant *m* d'autel; **fron·tier** ['~jə] frontière *f*; *surt. Am. hist.* frontière *f* des États occidentaux; **'fron·tier·run·ner** passeur *m* de frontière; **fron·tiers·man** ['~jezmən] frontalier *m*; *hist. Am.* broussard *m*; **fron·tis·piece** ['~ispi:s] △, *a. typ.* frontispice *m*; **front·let** ['~lit] *cost.* bandeau *m*; **front page** *journ.* première page *f*; **'front-page** en première page.

frost [frɔst] **1.** (*a.* hoar ~, white ~)

gelée *f* blanche, givre *m*; F fiasco *m*, déception *f*; *black* ~ froid *m* noir; **2.** geler; saupoudrer; givrer; dépolir (*un verre*); ⊕ glacer (*le métal*); ~*ed glass* verre *m* dépoli; **'~-bite** gelure *f*; **'frost-bit·ten** gelé; 🌿 brûlé par le froid; **'frost·i·ness** froid *m* glacial; *fig.* froideur *f*; **'frost·y** □ gelé; glacial (-als *m/pl.*) (*a. fig.*); couvert de givre.

froth [frɔθ] **1.** écume *f*; mousse *f*; *fig.* paroles *f/pl.* creuses; **2.** écumer, mousser; moutonner (*mer*); **'froth·i·ness** état *m* écumeux *etc.*; *fig.* manque *m* de substance; **'froth·y** □ écumeux (-euse *f*); moutonneux (-euse *f*) (*mer*); vide, creux (creuse *f*).

frown [fraun] **1.** froncement *m* de sourcils; air *m* désapprobateur; **2.** *v/t.* ~ *down* imposer le silence à (*q.*) d'un regard sévère; *v/i.* froncer les sourcils; se renfrogner; avoir l'air menaçant (*montagne etc.*); ~ *at,* ~ (*up*)*on* regarder en fronçant les sourcils; *fig.* désapprouver.

frowst F [fraust] odeur *f* de renfermé; atmosphère *f* qui sent le renfermé; **'frowst·y** □, **frowz·y** ['frauzi] qui sent le renfermé; mal tenu, sale.

froze [frouz] *prét. de* freeze; **'frozen 1.** *p.p. de* freeze; **2.** *a. adj.* gelé; frigorifié; bloqué (*capital*); ~ *locker Am.* chambre *f* frigorifique; ~ *meat* viande *f* frigorifiée.

fruc·ti·fi·ca·tion [frʌktifi'keiʃn] fructification *f*; **fruc·ti·fy** ['~fai] *v/t.* féconder; *v/i.* fructifier (*a. fig.*).

fru·gal □ ['fru:gəl] frugal (-aux *m/pl.*); économe; simple; **fru·gal·i·ty** [fru'gæliti] frugalité *f*; sobriété *f*.

fruit [fru:t] **1.** fruit *m* (*a. fig.* = résultat); *coll.* fruits *m/pl.*; ~ *cocktail* macedoine *f* de fruits; ~ *cup* coupe *f* de fruits rafraîchis; ~ *knife* couteau *m* à fruits; **2.** porter des fruits; **'fruit·age** fructification *f*; *coll.* fruits *m/pl.*; **frui·ta·ri·an** [fru:'tɛərjən] fruitarien(ne *f*) *m*; **'fruit-cake** cake *m*, gâteau *m* de fruits confits; **'fruit·er** arbre *m* fruitier; **'fruit·er·er** fruitier (-ère *f*) *m*; **fruit·ful** □ ['~ful] fructueux (-euse *f*); (*a. fig.* = *profitable*); fécond, fertile (en *of, in*); **fru·i·tion** [fru'iʃn] *projet etc.*: réalisation *f*;

come to ~ porter fruit; **'fruit·less** ☐ stérile; *fig.* vain; **'fruit·y** de fruit; fruité; *fig.* corsé.

frump [frʌmp] *fig.* femme *f* fagotée; **'frump·ish**, **'frump·y** mal attifée (*femme*).

frus·trate [frʌs'treit] frustrer; déjouer; **frus'tra·tion** frustration *f*; anéantissement *m*.

fry [frai] **1.** *cuis.* friture *f*; **2.** frai *m*, fretin *m*; F *small* ~ petites gens *f/pl.*; gosses *m/pl.*; **3.** (faire) frire; *see egg*; *fried potatoes* (pommes *f/pl.* de terre) frites *f/pl.*; **'fry·ing-pan** poêle *f*; *get out of the* ~ *into the fire* sauter de la poêle sur la braise.

fuch·sia ♀ ['fju:ʃə] fuchsia *m*.

fuck V [fʌk] **1.** baiser; **2.** merde (de la merde)!, putain!

fud·dle ['fʌdl] **1.** *v/t.* griser; hébéter; *v/i.* riboter; F se pocharder; **2.** ribote *f*.

fudge F [fʌdʒ] **1.** bousiller; cuisiner (*les comptes*); **2.** bousillage *m*; *bonbon*: fondant *m*; ~*!* quelle blague!

fu·el ['fjuəl] **1.** combustible *m*; carburant *m*; *mot.* essence *f*; *mot.* ~ *ga(u)ge* jauge *f* d'essence; ~ *oil* fueloil *m*; mazout *m*; ~ *tank* réservoir *m* d'essence; **2.** *v/t.* pourvoir de combustibles; *v/i.* obtenir du combustible; *mot.* s'approvisionner en essence.

fug [fʌg] **1.** touffeur *f*; forte odeur *f* de renfermé; **2.** rester enfermé.

fu·ga·cious [fju:'geiʃəs] fugace; éphémère.

fu·gi·tive ['fju:dʒitiv] **1.** fugitif (-ive *f*) (*a. fig.*); **2.** fugitif (-ive *f*) *m*; exilé(e *f*) *m*.

fu·gle·man ✕ ['fju:glmæn] chef *m* de file; *fig.* chef *m*; porte-parole *m/inv.*

fugue ♪ [fju:g] fugue *f*.

ful·crum ['fʌlkrəm], *pl.* -**cra** ['ʌkrə] ⊕ pivot *m*; *fig.* point *m* d'appui.

ful·fil [ful'fil] remplir; accomplir; s'acquitter de; réaliser; **ful'fil·er** celui (celle *f*) *m* qui remplit *etc.*; **ful'fil·ment** accomplissement *m*.

ful·gent *poét.* ['fʌldʒənt] resplendissant.

full¹ [ful] **1.** *adj.* ☐ plein; rempli; entier(-ère *f*); complet(-ète *f*); comble; *cost.* large, ample; *at* ~ *length* tout au long; ~ *employment* plein-emploi *m*; *of* ~*age* majeur; ~ *stop*

gramm. point *m*; **2.** *adv.* tout à fait; en plein; précisément; parfaitement; bien; ~ *nigh* tout près; F ~ *up* au complet, comble; **3.** *su.* plein *m*; cœur *m*, fort *m*; apogée *f*; *in* ~ intégralement; *in extenso*; en toutes lettres; *pay in* ~ payer intégralement; *to the* ~ complètement, tout à fait.

full² ⊕ [~] (re)fouler.

full...: **'~-'blown** épanoui; **'~-'bod·ied** corsé (*vin*); ~ *dress* grande tenue *f*; **'~-'dress** de cérémonie; solennel(le *f*); ~ *rehearsal* répétition *f* générale *ou* des couturières.

full·er ⊕ ['fulə] fouleur (-euse *f*) *m*.

full-fledged ['ful'fledʒd] qui a toutes ses plumes (*oiseau*); *fig.* qualifié, achevé.

full·ing-mill ['fuliŋmil] foulon *m*.

full-length ['ful'leŋθ] (portrait *m*) en pied; ~ *film* film *m* principal.

ful(l)·ness ['fulnis] plénitude *f*.

full...: **'~-'orbed** dans son plein (*lune*); **'~-'time** de toute la journée; à pleines journées; à temps plein.

ful·mi·nate ['fʌlmineit] fulminer (*a. fig.* contre, *against*); faire explosion; **ful·mi'na·tion** fulmination *f* (*a. fig.*); **ful·mi·na·to·ry** ['~ətəri] fulminatoire.

ful·some ☐ ['fulsəm] excessif (-ive *f*); répugnant (*flatterie*).

fum·ble ['fʌmbl] fouiller, tâtonner; **'fum·bler** maladroit(e *f*) *m*.

fume [fju:m] **1.** fumée *f*, vapeur *f*; *in a* ~ en rage, furieux (-euse *f*); **2.** *v/i.* fumer (*a. fig.*); s'exhaler; *v/t.* exposer à la fumée.

fu·mi·gate ['fju:migeit] fumiger; désinfecter; **fu·mi'ga·tion** fumigation *f*.

fum·ing ☐ ['fju:miŋ] *fig.* enragé, bouillonnant de colère.

fun [fʌn] amusement *m*, gaieté *f*; *have* ~ s'amuser; *make* ~ *of* se moquer de; *for* ~, *in* ~ pour rire, par plaisanterie, pour s'amuser.

func·tion ['fʌŋkʃn] **1.** fonction *f* (*a. physiol., a.* ᴀ); réception *f*, soirée *f*; cérémonie *f*; **2.** fonctionner; **'func·tion·al** ☐ fonctionnel(le *f*); **'func·tion·ar·y** fonctionnaire *m*.

fund [fʌnd] **1.** fonds *m*; *fig.* trésors *m/pl.*; ~*s pl.* fonds *m(pl.)*; capital *m*; ressources *f/pl.* pécuniaires; *banque*: provision *f*; **2.** consolider (*une dette*);

placer (*de l'argent*) dans les fonds publics.

fun·da·ment ['fʌndəmənt] fondement *m*; **fun·da·men·tal 1.** □ [ˌ~ˈmentl] fondamental (-aux *m/pl.*); essentiel(le *f*); **2.** ~s *pl.* principe *m*; premiers principes *m/pl.*

fu·ner·al ['fjuːnərəl] **1.** funérailles *f/pl.*, obsèques *f/pl.*; **2.** funèbre; des morts; ~ *pile* bûcher *m* funéraire; **fu·ne·re·al** □ [ˌ~ˈnɪərɪəl] funéraire; *fig.* lugubre, funèbre.

fun-fair foire *f* aux plaisirs; parc *m* d'attractions.

fun·gous ['fʌŋɡəs] fongueux (-euse *f*); **fun·gus** [~], *pl.* -gi ['~ɡaɪ] ♣ champignon *m* mycète; ⚕ fongus *m*.

fu·nic·u·lar [fjuːˈnɪkjulə] **1.** funiculaire; ~ *railway* = **2.** funiculaire *m*.

funk *sl.* [fʌŋk] **1.** frousse *f*, trac *m*; *personne*: caneur (-euse *f*) *m*; *blue* ~ peur *f* bleue; **2.** caner; avoir peur de (*qch.*); **'funk·y** *sl.* froussard.

fun·nel ['fʌnl] entonnoir *m*; ⊕ trémie *f*; ⚓, 🚂 cheminée *f*.

fun·ny □ ['fʌnɪ] **1.** drôle, comique; curieux (-euse *f*); **2.** *funnies* pl. see comics; '~-bone ⚚ F petit juif *m*.

fur [fəː] **1.** fourrure *f*; *lapin*: pelage *m*; *bouilloire*: dépôt *m*; *langue*: enduit *m*; ~s *pl.* peaux *f/pl.*; ~ *coat* manteau *m* de fourrure; **2.** à *ou* en *ou* de fourrure; **3.** ⊕ (s')incruster; *v/t.* fourrer, garnir de fourrure; ~*red tongue* langue *f* chargée.

fur·be·low ['fəːbɪlou] falbala *m*; *usu.* ~s *pl. iro.* fanfreluches *f/pl.*

fur·bish ['fəːbɪʃ] polir, nettoyer; mettre à neuf.

fur·ca·tion [fəːˈkeɪʃn] bifurcation *f*.

fu·ri·ous □ ['fjuərɪəs] furieux (-euse *f*).

furl [fəːl] *v/t.* ferler (*une voile*); rouler (*un parapluie*); replier (*les ailes*); *v/i.* se rouler.

fur·long ['fəːlɔŋ] *mesure*: furlong *m* (201 mètres).

fur·lough ['fəːlou] **1.** permission *f*, congé *m*; **2.** ✕ envoyer (*q.*) en permission; *Am.* accorder un congé à.

fur·nace ['fəːnɪs] four(neau) *m*; *chaudière*: foyer *m*; *fig.* brasier *m*.

fur·nish ['fəːnɪʃ] fournir, munir, pourvoir (de, *with*); meubler, garnir (*une maison*); ~*ed rooms* meublé *m*; **'fur·nish·er** fournisseur *m*; marchand *m* d'ameublement; '**fur-**

nish·ing fourniture *f*; provision *f*; ~s *pl.* ameublement *m*.

fur·ni·ture ['fəːnɪtʃə] meubles *m/pl.*; ameublement *m*; mobilier *m*; *typ.* garniture *f*; ⚓ matériel *m*.

fur·ri·er ['fʌrɪə] pelletier *m*; '**fur·ri·er·y** pelleterie *f*.

fur·row ['fʌrou] **1.** sillon *m* (*a. fig.*); ⊕ cannelure *f*; **2.** labourer; sillonner; ⊕ canneler; rider profondément.

fur·ry ['fəːrɪ] qui ressemble à (de) la fourrure.

fur·ther ['fəːðə] **1.** *adj. et adv.* plus éloigné; see *furthermore*; **2.** avancer; servir; '**fur·ther·ance** avancement *m*; appui *m*; '**fur·ther·er** celui (celle *f*) *m* qui aide à l'avancement (*de qch.*); '**fur·ther·more** en outre, de plus, d'autre part; '**fur·ther·most** le plus lointain, le plus éloigné.

fur·thest ['fəːðɪst] see *furthermost*; *at* (*the*) ~ au plus tard.

fur·tive □ ['fəːtɪv] furtif (-ive *f*).

fu·ry ['fjuərɪ] furie *f*, fureur *f*; acharnement *m*.

furze ♣ [fəːz] ajonc *m*, genêt *m* épineux.

fuse [fjuːz] **1.** (se) fondre; (se) réunir par fusion; *v/t.* pourvoir d'une fusée; *v/i.* ⚡ sauter (*plombs*); **2.** ⚡ plomb *m*; fusible *m*; ✕ fusée *f*.

fu·see [fjuːˈziː] *montre etc.*: fusée *f*; tison *m*.

fu·se·lage ['fjuːzɪlɑːʒ] 🛩 fuselage *m*.

fu·si·bil·i·ty [fjuːzəˈbɪlɪtɪ] fusibilité *f*; **fu·si·ble** ['fjuːzəbl] fusible.

fu·sil·ier ✕ [fjuːzɪˈlɪə] fusilier *m*.

fu·sil·lade [fjuːzɪˈleɪd] fusillade *f*.

fu·sion ['fjuːʒn] fusion *f*; fonte *f*.

fuss F [fʌs] **1.** agitation *f*, F potin *m*; façons *f/pl.*; *kick up a* ~ faire un tas d'histoires; **2.** *v/t.* tracasser, agiter; *v/i.* se tracasser (de, *over*); faire des histoires; faire l'empressé; '~-pot F enquiquineur (-euse *f*) *m*; coupeur (-euse *f*) *m* de cheveux en quatre; '**fuss·y** □ F tracassier (-ère *f*) tatillon(ne *f*).

fus·tian ['fʌstɪən] ✝ futaine *f*; *fig.* emphase *f*.

fust·i·ness ['fʌstɪnɪs] odeur *f* de renfermé; *fig.* caractère *m* démodé; '**fust·y** □ qui sent le renfermé *ou* moisi; *fig.* démodé.

fu·tile □ ['fjuːtaɪl] futile; vain; puéril; **fu·til·i·ty** [fjuˈtiliti] futilité *f*; vanité *f*; puérilité *f*.

fu·ture [ˈfjuːtʃə] **1.** futur; à venir; **2.** avenir *m*; *in the ~* à l'avenir; **✝** *~s pl.* livraisons *f/pl.* à terme; **ˈfu·tur·ism** *peint.* futurisme *m*;

fu·tu·ri·ty [fjuˈtjuəriti] avenir *m*.
fuzz [fʌz] **1.** duvet *m*; *a ~ of hair* des cheveux bouffants; *sl. the ~* les flics *m/pl.*, la flicaille; **2.** (faire) bouffer; (faire) frisotter; **ˈfuzz·y** □ bouffant; frisotté; flou (*a. phot.*).

G

G, g [dʒiː] G *m*, g *m*.

gab F [gæb] faconde *f*; *the gift of the* ~ la langue bien pendue.

gab·ble ['gæbl] **1.** bredouillement *m*; caquet *m*; **2.** bredouiller; caqueter; **'gab·bler** bredouilleur (-euse *f*) *m*; caquetage *m*.

gab·by ['gæbi] bavard.

gab·er·dine ['gæbədiːn] *tex.* gabardine *f*.

ga·ble ['geibl] (*a.* ~-end) pignon *m*.

ga·by ['geibi] nigaud *m*, benêt *m*.

gad [gæd]: ~ *about* courir (le monde *etc.*); ⚓ *poét.* errer; **'gad·a·bout** F coureur (-euse *f*) *m*.

gad·fly *zo.* ['gædflai] taon *m*; œstre *m*.

gadg·et F ['gædʒit] dispositif *m*; machin *m*, truc *m*.

Gael·ic ['geilik] gaélique (*a. ling. su./m*).

gaff [gæf] gaffe *f*; ⚓ corne *f*; *sl.* théâtre *m* de bas étage; *blow the* ~ *sl.* vendre la mèche.

gaffe F [gæf] bêtise *f*; faux pas *m*.

gaf·fer F ['gæfə] † ancien *m*; contremaître *m*; patron *m*.

gag [gæg] **1.** bâillon *m* (*a. fig.*); *parl.* clôture *f*; *théâ.* improvisation *f*; plaisanterie *f*; F blague *f*; *sl. what's the* ~? à quoi vise tout cela?; **2.** *v/t.* bâillonner (*a. fig. la presse*); *pol.* clôturer (*un débat*); *v/i. théâ.* improviser; plaisanter.

gage [geidʒ] gage *m*, garantie *f*; F défi *m*.

gai·e·ty ['geiəti] gaieté *f*; réjouissances *f/pl.*

gai·ly ['geili] *adv. de gay.*

gain [gein] **1.** gain *m*; *surt.* ⚓ ~s *pl.* profit *m*; **2.** gagner, profiter; ~ *on* gagner sur; ~ *s.o. over* gagner q. à sa cause; **'gain·er** gagnant(e *f*) *m*; gagneur (-euse *f*) *m* (*d'argent*); **gain·ful** □ ['~ful] profitable; ~ *employment* travail *m* rémunéré; *be* ~*ly occupied* avoir un travail rémunéré; **gain·ings** ['~iŋz] *pl.* gain *m*, -s *m/pl.*; profit *m*. [nier (qch.).\
gain·say † [gein'sei] contredire;⟩

---

gait [geit] allure *f*; *cheval:* train *m*.

gai·ter ['geitə] guêtre *f*.

gal *Am. sl.* [gæl] jeune fille *f*.

ga·la ['gɑːlə] fête *f*, gala *m*.

gal·ax·y ['gæləksi] *astr.* voie *f* lactée; *fig.* essaim *m*; constellation *f*.

gale [geil] grand vent *m*; tempête *f*.

gall¹ [gɔːl] fiel *m* (*a. fig.*); *surt. Am. sl.* audace *f*; toupet *m*; ~ *bladder* vésicule *f* biliaire; ~ *stone* calcul *m* biliaire.

gall² ♀ [~] galle *f*.

gall³ [~] **1.** écorchure *f*; *fig.* blessure *f*; **2.** écorcher; *fig.* froisser, blesser; irriter.

gal·lant ['gælənt] **1.** □ vaillant; superbe; galant; **2.** galant *m*; *péj.* coureur *m* de femmes; **3.** faire le galant; **'gal·lant·ry** vaillance *f*; galanterie *f* (auprès des femmes).

gal·ler·y ['gæləri] galerie *f* (*a.* ✂).

gal·ley ['gæli] ⚓ † galère *f*; ⚓ cuisine *f*; *typ.* galée *f*; **'~-proof** *typ.* placard *m*.

Gal·lic ['gælik] gaulois; **Gal·li·can** ['~kən] *eccl.* gallican.

gal·li·vant [gæli'vænt] courailler.

gall-nut ♀ ['gɔːlnʌt] noix *f* de galle.

gal·lon ['gælən] gallon *m* (*4,54 litres, Am. 3,78 litres*).

gal·loon [gə'luːn] galon *m*.

gal·lop ['gæləp] **1.** galop *m*; **2.** (faire) aller au galop.

gal·lows ['gælouz] *usu. sg.* potence *f*.

ga·lore [gə'lɔː] à foison.

ga·losh [gə'lɔʃ] galoche *f*; ~s *pl.* caoutchoucs *m/pl.*

gal·van·ic [gæl'vænik] (~*ally*) galvanique; **gal·va·nism** ['gælvənizm] galvanisme *m*; **'gal·va·nize** galvaniser (*a. fig.*); **gal·va·no·plas·tic** [gælvəno'plæstik] galvanoplastique.

gam·ble ['gæmbl] **1.** *v/i.* jouer de l'argent; *v/t.* ~ *away* perdre (qch.) au jeu; **2.** F jeu *m* de hasard; *fig.* affaire *f* de chance; **'gam·bler** joueur (-euse *f*) *m*; † spéculateur (-trice *f*) *m*; **'gam·bling-house** maison *f* de jeu. [gutte (*pl.* gommes-guttes) *f*.\
gam·boge ♀ [gæm'buːʒ] gomme-⟩

gam·bol ['gæmbl] 1. cabriole *f*; 2. cabrioler; s'ébattre.

game [geim] 1. jeu *m*; amusement *m*; *cartes*: partie *f*; *péj.* manège *m*; *cuis. etc.* gibier *m*; *play the* ~ jouer franc jeu; *fig.* agir loyalement; 2. F courageux (-euse *f*); *die* ~ mourir crânement; 3. jouer; '~-**cock** coq *m* de combat; '~-**keep·er** garde-chasse (*pl.* gardes-chasse[s]) *m*; '~-**li·cence** permis *m* de chasse; **game·ster** ['~stə] joueur (-euse *f*) *m*.

gam·mer ['gæmə] vieille *f*.

gam·mon[1] ['gæmən] 1. quartier *m* de lard fumé; jambon *m* fumé; 2. saler et fumer.

gam·mon[2] [~] 1. bredouille *f* (*au jeu*); blague *f*; *sl.* ~! quelle bêtise!; 2. blaguer.

gam·my F ['gæmi] estropié; boiteux (-euse *f*).

gam·ut ♪ ['gæmət] gamme *f* (*a. fig.*).

gam·y ['geimi] giboyeux (-euse *f*); *cuis.* faisandé.

gan·der ['gændə] jars *m*; *Am. sl.* coup *m* d'œil.

gang [gæŋ] 1. groupe *m*; troupe *f*; bande *f*; équipe *f*; *péj.* clique *f*; 2. ~ *up* se liguer (contre *against*, on); '~-**board** ♣ planche *f* à débarquer; **gang·er** ['gæŋə] chef *m* d'équipe.

gan·grene ⚕ ['gæŋgri:n] gangrène *f*, mortification *f*.

gang·ster *Am.* ['gæŋstə] bandit *m*, gangster *m*.

gang·way ['gæŋwei] passage *m*, couloir *m*; ♣ passerelle *f* de service; ♣ coupée *f*.

gaol [dʒeil] *see* jail.

gap [gæp] trou *m* (*a. fig.*); ouverture *f*; brèche *f*; interstice *m*.

gape [geip] rester bouche bée (devant, at); s'ouvrir tout grand (*abîme*); [rage *m*; 2. *mot.* garer.\

ga·rage ['gæra:ʒ; 'gærid ʒ] 1. ga-

garb [gɑ:b] costume *m*, vêtement *m*.

gar·bage *surt. Am.* ['gɑ:bidʒ] ordures *f*/*pl.*; immondices *f*/*pl.*; ~ *can* boîte *f* aux ordures; ~ *collector* (é)boueur *m*, boueux *m*; ~ *pail* poubelle *f*.

gar·ble ['gɑ:bl] fausser; tronquer.

gar·den ['gɑ:dn] 1. jardin *m*; 2. *v/i.* jardiner, faire du jardinage; *v/t.* entretenir; '**gar·den·er** jardinier *m*; '**gar·den·ing** jardinage *m*; horticulture *f*.

gar·gan·tu·an [gɑ:'gæntjuən] gargantuesque.

gar·gle ['gɑ:gl] 1. se gargariser; 2. gargarisme *m*.

gar·goyle △ ['gɑ:gɔil] gargouille *f*.

gar·ish □ ['gɛəriʃ] voyant; cru (*lumière*).

gar·land ['gɑ:lənd] 1. guirlande *f*, couronne *f*; 2. (en)guirlander.

gar·lic ♀ ['gɑ:lik] ail (*pl.* aulx, ails) *m*.

gar·ment ['gɑ:mənt] vêtement *m*.

gar·ner ['gɑ:nə] 1. grenier *m*; *fig.* recueil *m*; 2. mettre en grenier.

gar·net *min.* ['gɑ:nit] grenat *m*.

gar·nish ['gɑ:niʃ] garnir, orner, embellir (de, with); '**gar·nish·ing** garnissage *m*; *cuis.* garniture *f*.

gar·ni·ture ['gɑ:nitʃə] garniture *f*.

gar·ret ['gærit] mansarde *f*.

gar·ri·son ✕ ['gærisn] 1. garnison *f*; 2. mettre une garnison dans; mettre (*des troupes*) en garnison; garnir; *be* ~*ed* être en garnison.

gar·ru·li·ty [gæ'ru:liti] loquacité *f*; *style*: verbosité *f*; **gar·ru·lous** □ ['gæruləs] loquace; verbeux (-euse *f*).

gar·ter ['gɑ:tə] jarretière *f*; *Am.* jarretelles *f*/*pl.*; *Order of the* ♀ Ordre *m* de la jarretière.

gas [gæs] 1. gaz *m*; F bavardage *m*; *Am. see* gasoline; *mot.* step on the ~ appuyer sur le champignon; *fig.* se dépêcher; 2. asphyxier; ✕ gazer; F jaser; '~-**bag** 🎈 enveloppe *f* à gaz; F grand parleur *m*; phraseur *m*; ~ **brack·et** applique *f* à gaz; '~-**burn·er** bec *m* de gaz; '~-**cook·er** cuisinière *f* à gaz; **gas·e·lier** [~ə'liə] lustre *m* à gaz; '**gas-en·gine** moteur *m* à gaz; **gas·e·ous** ['geiziəs] gazeux (-euse *f*); '**gas-fit·ter** gazier *m*; poseur *m* d'appareils à gaz; '**gas-fit·tings** *pl.* appareillage *m* pour le gaz.

gash [gæʃ] 1. entaille *f* (*dans la chair*); taillade *f*; balafre *f* (*dans la figure*); coup *m* de couteau *etc.*; 2. entailler.

gas·ket ['gæskit] ♣ garcette *f*; ⊕ joint *m* en étoupe *etc.*

gas...: '~-**light** lumière *f* du gaz; '~-**light·er** allume-gaz *m*/*inv.*; '~-**man·tle** manchon *m*; '~-**mask** masque *m* à gaz; '~-**me·ter** compteur *m* (à gaz); **gas·o·line** *Am. mot.* ['gæsəli:n] essence *f*; **gas·om·e·ter** [gæ'sɔmitə] gazomètre *m*, réservoir *m* à gaz; **'gas·ov·en** four *m* à gaz.

gasp [gɑ:sp] **1.** sursaut *m*; *fig.* souffle *m*; **2.** sursauter; (*ou* ~ *for breath*) suffoquer.

gas-proof ['gæs'pru:f] à l'épreuve du *ou* des gaz; **'gas-range** cuisinière *f* à gaz; **gassed** [gæst] asphyxié; ✕ gazé; **'gas-sta·tion** *Am.* poste *m* d'essence, station *f* service; **'gas-stove** four *m* ou réchaud *m* à gaz; ⚡ radiateur *m* à gaz; **'gas·sy** gazeux (-euse *f*); mousseux (-euse *f*) (*vin*); *fig.* bavard.

gas·tric ⚕ ['gæstrik] gastrique; **gas·tri·tis** [gæs'traitis] gastrite *f*.

gas·tron·o·mist [gæs'trɔnəmist] gastronome *m*; **gas'tron·o·my** gastronomie *f*.

gas-works ['gæswə:ks] *usu. sg.* usine *f* à gaz.

gate [geit] porte *f* (*a. fig.*); barrière *f*; grille *f*; *sp.* public *m*; *see* ~-money; **'~-crash·er** *sl.* intrus(e *f*) *m*; **'~-keep·er** portier *m* (-ière *f*); **'~-leg(ged) ta·ble** table *f* à abattants; **'~-man** 🚂 garde-barrière (*pl.* gardes-barrière[s]) *m*; **'~-mon·ey** *sp.* recette *f*; **'~-way** entrée *f*, porte *f*.

gath·er ['gæðə] **1.** *v/t.* (r)assembler; ramasser; (re)cueillir; retrousser (*ses jupes*); percevoir (*des impôts*); conclure; *cost.* froncer; *see* information; ~ speed prendre de la vitesse; *v/i.* se rassembler; se réunir; s'accumuler; se préparer (*orage*); ⚕ abcéder; (⚕ *a.* ~ *to a head*) mûrir (*a. fig.*); **2.** ~s *pl.* fronces *f/pl.*; **'gath·er·ing** rassemblement *m*; cueillette *f*; accumulation *f*; froncement *m*; assemblée *f*.

gaud·y ['gɔ:di] **1.** □ voyant, criard; fastueux (-euse *f*); **2.** *univ.* banquet *m* anniversaire.

gauge [geidʒ] **1.** calibre *m*; jauge *f*; vérificateur *m*; indicateur *m*; 🚂 largeur *f* de la voie; ⚓ tirant *m* d'eau; **2.** calibrer; mesurer; *fig.* estimer; **'gaug·er** jaugeur *m*, mesureur *m*.

Gaul [gɔ:l] Gaulois(e *f*) *m*; *pays:* la Gaule *f*.

gaunt □ [gɔ:nt] décharné; désolé.

gaunt·let ['gɔ:ntlit] gant *m* à crispins; *fig.* gant *m*; *run the* ~ ✕ passer par les bretelles; *fig.* soutenir un feu roulant (de, *of*).

gauze [gɔ:z] gaze *f*; *wire* ~ tissu *m* métallique; **'gauz·y** diaphane.

gave [geiv] *prét. de* give 1, 2.

gav·el *Am.* ['gævl] marteau *m* (*du commissaire-priseur*).

gawk F [gɔ:k] godiche *mf*; personne *f* gauche; **'gawk·y** gauche; godiche.

gay □ [gei] gai, allègre; brillant; F homo; *Am. sl.* effronté.

gaze [geiz] **1.** regard *m* (fixe); **2.** regarder fixement; ~ *at* (*ou* on) contempler, considérer.

ga·zelle *zo.* [gə'zel] gazelle *f*.

gaz·er ['geizə] contemplateur (-trice *f*) *m*; curieux (-euse *f*) *m*.

ga·zette [gə'zet] **1.** journal *m* officiel; **2.** publier dans un journal officiel; *be* ~*d* être publié à l'Officiel;

gaz·et·teer [gæzi'tiə] répertoire *m* géographique.

gear [giə] **1.** accoutrement *m*; effets *m/pl.* personnels; ustensiles *m/pl.*; attirail *m*, appareil *m*; harnais *m*; ⊕ transmission *f*, commande *f*; *mot.* (low première, high grande) vitesse *f*; *top* ~ prise *f* directe; *in* ~ en jeu; *mot.* engrené; *out of* ~ hors d'action; *mot.* débrayé, désengrené; **2.** *v/t.* gréer; engrener; ⊕ ~ *up* (down) multiplier (démultiplier); ~ *into* engrener (*qch.*) dans; *v/i.* s'engrener; ~ *with* (s')engrener dans; **'~-box, '~-case** ⊕ carter *m*; *mot.* boîte *f* de vitesses; **'gear·ing** ⊕ engrenage *m*; transmission *f*; *cycl.* développement *m*; **'gear-le·ver, surt.** *Am.* **'gear-shift** levier *m* de(s) vitesse(s).

gee [dʒi:] hue!, huhau!; *Am.* sapristi!; sans blague!

geese [gi:s] *pl. de* goose.

gee·zer *sl.* ['gi:zə] bonhomme *m*; vieille taupe *f*.

gei·sha ['geiʃə] geisha *f*.

gel·a·tin(e) ['dʒeləti:n] gélatine *f*; **ge·lat·i·nize** [dʒi'lætinaiz] (se) gélatiniser; **ge'lat·i·nous** gélatineux (-euse *f*).

geld [geld] [*irr.*] hongrer (*un cheval*); châtrer; **'geld·ing** (cheval *m*) hongre *m*.

gel·id ['dʒelid] glacial (-als *m/pl.*).

gelt [gelt] *prét. et p.p. de* geld.

gem [dʒem] **1.** pierre *f* précieuse; gemme *f*; joyau *m* (*a. fig.*); **2.** orner de pierres précieuses.

Gem·i·ni *astr.* ['dʒeminai] *pl.* les Gémaux *m/pl.*

gen *Brit. sl.* [dʒen] **1.** informations *f/pl.*, renseignements *m/pl.*; **2.** ~ *up* renseigner, F rancarder.

gen·der *gramm.* ['dʒendə] genre *m*; F sexe *m*.

gen·e·a·log·i·cal □ [dʒi:niə'lɔdʒikl] généalogique; **gen·e·al·o·gy** [dʒi:-ni'ælədʒi] généalogie *f*.

gen·er·a ['dʒenərə] *pl. de* genus.

gen·er·al ['dʒenərəl] **1.** □ général (-aux *m/pl.*); commun; grand (*public etc.*); en chef; ⚕ ~ an(a)esthetic anesthésie *f* générale; ~ election élections *f/pl.* générales; ~ practitioner médecin *m* de médecine générale, (médecin *m*) généraliste; médecin *m* de famille; ✕ ~ staff état-major *m* (*pl.* états-majors); *Am.* ~ store magasin *m* qui vend de tout; **2.** ✕ général *m*; ~ général en chef; **gen·er·al·i·ty** [~'ræliti] généralité *f*; *la* plupart; **gen·er·al·i·za·tion** [~rəlai'zeiʃn] généralisation *f*; **'gen·er·al·i·ze** généraliser; populariser; **'gen·er·al·ly** généralement; universellement; F pour la plupart; **'gen·er·al·'pur·pose** universel(le *f*); **'gen·er·al·ship** ✕ généralat *m*; stratégie *f*.

gen·er·ate ['dʒenəreit] engendrer; produire; *generating station* station *f* génératrice; **gen·er·a·tion** génération *f*; ⚕ engendrement *m*; **gen·er·a·tive** [~ətiv] générateur (-trice *f*); producteur (-trice *f*); **'gen·er·a·tor** ['~eitə] générateur (-trice *f*) *m*; ⊕ générateur *m*; *surt. mot. Am.* dynamo *f* d'éclairage.

ge·ner·ic [dʒi'nerik] générique.

gen·er·os·i·ty [dʒenə'rɔsiti] générosité *f*; libéralité *f*; **'gen·er·ous** □ généreux (-euse *f*) (*a. vin*); libéral (-aux *m/pl.*); magnanime; riche.

gen·e·sis ['dʒenisis] genèse *f*; origine *f*; *bibl.* ♀ (la) Genèse; **ge·net·ic** [dʒi'netik] **1.** (~ally) génétique; génésique (*instinct*); F *see* generative; **2.** ~s *sg.* génétique *f*.

gen·ial □ ['dʒi:njəl] doux (douce *f*) (*climat*); propice; génial (-aux *m/pl.*) (*talent*); jovial (-als *ou* -aux *m/pl.*) (*personne*); **ge·ni·al·i·ty** [~ni-'æliti] douceur *f*; bienveillance *f*.

gen·i·tals *anat.* ['dʒenitlz] *pl.* organes *m/pl.* génitaux. [*case*] génitif *m*.]

gen·i·tive *gramm.* ['dʒenitiv] (*ou* ~)

gen·ius ['dʒi:njəs] génie *m*; *pl.* **gen·i·i** ['~niai] démon *m*, esprit *m*; *pl.* **~ius·es** ['~jəsiz] génie *m*; F don *m*, aptitudes *f/pl.* naturelles.

gen·o·cide ['dʒenousaid] extermination *f* d'une race.

gent F [dʒent] homme *m*, monsieur *m*.

gen·teel □ *sl. ou iro.* [dʒen'ti:l] comme il faut; maniéré.

gen·tian ♀ ['dʒenʃiən] gentiane *f*.

gen·tile ['dʒentail] **1.** gentil *m*; **2.** païen(ne *f*); *Am.* non mormon.

gen·til·i·ty *souv. iro.* [dʒen'tiliti] prétention *f* au bon ton; haute bourgeoisie *f*.

gen·tle □ ['dʒentl] *usu.* doux (douce *f*); modéré; léger (-ère *f*); cher (chère *f*) (*lecteur*); *co.* noble; † bien né; bon(ne *f*) (*naissance*); '**~·folk(s)** personnes *f/pl.* de bonne famille; '**~·man** monsieur *m* (*pl.* messieurs) *m*; homme *m* comme il faut; 🎩 rentier *m*; *sp.* amateur *m*; *bal:* cavalier *m*; † gentilhomme (*pl.* gentilshommes) *m*; *gentlemen!* messieurs!; ~'s agreement convention *f* verbale (*qui n'engage que la parole d'honneur des partis*); '**~·man·like,** '**~·man·ly** comme il faut; bien élevé; '**gen·tle·ness** douceur *f*; '**gen·tle·wom·an** dame *f ou* demoiselle *f* bien née.

gen·try ['dʒentri] petite noblesse *f*; *péj.* individus *m/pl.*

gen·u·flec·tion, gen·u·flex·ion [dʒenju'flekʃn] génuflexion *f*.

gen·u·ine □ ['dʒenjuin] authentique; véritable; franc(he *f*); sincère.

ge·nus ['dʒi:nəs] (*pl. genera*) genre *m* (*a. fig.*).

ge·od·e·sy [dʒi'ɔdisi] géodésie *f*.

ge·og·ra·pher [dʒi'ɔgrəfə] géographe *m*; **ge·o·graph·i·cal** □ [dʒiə-'græfikl] géographique; **ge·og·ra·phy** [~'ɔgrəfi] géographie *f*.

ge·o·log·ic, ge·o·log·i·cal □ [dʒiə-'lɔdʒik(l)] géologique; **ge·ol·o·gist** [dʒi'ɔlədʒist] géologue *mf*; **ge·ol·o·gy** géologie *f*.

ge·om·e·ter [dʒi'ɔmitə] géomètre *m*; **ge·o·met·ric, ge·o·met·ri·cal** □ [dʒiə'metrik(l)] géométrique; **ge·om·e·try** [~'ɔmitri] géométrie *f*.

ge·o·phys·ics [dʒiə'fiziks] *usu. sg.* géophysique *f*.

ge·ra·ni·um ♀ [dʒi'reinjəm] géranium *m*.

germ [dʒə:m] **1.** germe *m*; **2.** germer.

Ger·man¹ ['dʒə:mən] **1.** allemand; ⚕ ~ measles rubéole *f*; ~ Ocean mer *f* du Nord; ⊕ ~ silver argentan *m*, maillechort *m*; ~ steel acier *m* brut; ~ text caractères *m/pl.* gothiques; ~ *toys pl.* jouets *m/pl.* de Nuremberg; **2.** *ling.* allemand *m*; Allemand(e *f*) *m*.

ger·man² [~]: *brother etc.* ~ frère *m etc.* germain; **ger·mane** [dʒɔ:'mein] (*to*) approprié (à); se rapportant (à). **Ger·man·ic** [dʒɔ:'mænik] allemand; *hist.* germanique.

germ-car·ri·er ['dʒɔ:mkæriɔ] porteur *m* de bacilles.

ger·mi·nal ['dʒɔ:minl] germinal (-aux *m/pl.*); *fig.* en germe; **ger·mi·nate** ['~neit] (faire) germer; **ger·mi·na·tion** germination *f*.

germ-proof ['dʒɔ:mpru:f] aseptique.

ger·ry·man·der *pol.* ['dʒerimændə] truquage *m* électoral.

ger·und *gramm.* ['dʒerənd] gérondif *m*.

ges·ta·tion ✻, *vet.* [dʒes'teiʃn] gestation *f*.

ges·tic·u·late [dʒes'tikjuleit] *v/i.* gesticuler; *v/t.* exprimer par des gestes; **ges·tic·u·la·tion** gesticulation *f*.

ges·ture ['dʒestʃə] geste *m*; signe *m*.

get [get] [*irr.*] **1.** *v/t.* obtenir, procurer; gagner; prendre; se faire (*une réputation etc.*); recevoir; aller chercher; attraper (*un coup, une maladie*); faire parvenir; faire (*inf., p.p.*); *Am.* F saisir; ~ *a wife* prendre femme; *have got* avoir; F *you have got to obey* il faut que vous obéissiez; ~ *one's hair cut* se faire couper les cheveux; ~ *me the book!* allez me chercher le livre!; ~ *by heart* apprendre par cœur; ~ *with child* faire un enfant à; ~ *away* arracher; éloigner; ~ *down* descendre (*qch.*); avaler (*une pilule etc.*); mettre (*qch.*) par écrit; ~ *in* rentrer; placer (*un mot*); donner (*un coup*); ~ *off* ôter (*un vêtement*); expédier (*une lettre*); ~ *on* mettre (*qch.*); ~ *out* arracher, tirer; (faire) sortir; ~ *over* faire passer (*qch.*) par-dessus; en finir avec (*qch.*); ~ *through* terminer; assurer le succès de; *parl.* faire adopter; ~ *up* faire monter; organiser; préparer; F (*se*) faire beau (belle); ~ *up steam* faire monter la pression; chauffer; **2.** *v/i.* devenir, se faire; aller, se rendre (à, *to*); en arriver (à *inf.*, *to inf.*); se mettre; ~ *ready* se préparer; ~ *about* circuler; être sur pied; ~ *abroad* se

répandre; ~ *ahead* prendre de l'avance; ~ *along* s'avancer; faire du chemin; ~ *along with* s'accorder avec, s'entendre bien avec; ~ *around* to en venir à, trouver le temps de; ~ *at* atteindre; parvenir à; ~ *away* partir; s'échapper; ~ *away with it* réussir; faire accepter la chose; ~ *down to* descendre jusqu'à; *fig.* en venir à; F se mettre à; ~ *in* rentrer; placer (*un coup*); ~ *into* entrer ou monter dans; mettre (*une robe etc.*); ~ *off* descendre (*de qch.*); se tirer d'affaire; F attraper un mari; ✻ décoller; ~ *off with* faire la conquête de; ~ *on* monter sur; s'avancer (vers *qch.*); s'approcher (de, *to*); prendre de l'âge; s'entendre (bien), s'accommoder (avec, *with*); ~ *out* (of, *from*) sortir (de); s'échapper (de); se soustraire (à); ~ *over* franchir; passer par-dessus; *fig.* guérir de (*une maladie*); ~ *it over with* en finir avec; ~ *through* passer; *téléph.* obtenir la communication; ~ *to hear* (*ou know ou learn*) apprendre; ~ *up* se lever; grossir (*mer*); monter; s'élever (*prix etc.*); **get-at-a·ble** [get'ætəbl] accessible; d'accès facile; **get-a·way** ['getəwei] *sp.* départ *m*; démarrage *m*; *Am.* fuite *f*; *make one's* ~ s'échapper; **'get·ter** acquéreur *m*; *zo.* reproducteur *m*; **'get·ting** acquisition *f*; mise *f*; ✻ extraction *f*; **get-to·geth·er** F réunion *f*; **get-'up** tenue *f*; ✝ habillage *m*; *Am.* F entrain *m*; esprit *m* entreprenant.

gew·gaw ['gju:gɔ:] babiole *f*, bagatelle *f*; ~s *pl.* afféteries *m/pl.*

gey·ser ['gaizə] *géog.* geyser *m*; ['gi:zə] chauffe-bain *m*; chauffe-eau *m/inv.* à gaz.

ghast·li·ness ['gɑ:stlinis] horreur *f*; pâleur *f* mortelle; **'ghast·ly** horrible; affreux (-euse *f*); blême.

gher·kin ['gə:kin] cornichon *m*.

ghost [goust] fantôme *m*, spectre *m*, revenant *m*; F nègre *m* (*d'un auteur*); *Holy* ⚥ Saint-Esprit *m*; **'ghost·like**, **'ghost·ly** spectral (-aux *m/pl.*); **'ghost·write** *Am.* écrire un article *etc.* qui paraîtra sous la signature d'autrui.

gi·ant ['dʒaiənt] géant *m* (*a. su./m*).

gib·ber ['dʒibə] baragouiner; **'gib·ber·ish** baragouin *m*, charabia *m*.

gib·bet ['dʒibit] **1.** gibet *m*; ⊕

flèche *f* de grue; **2.** pendre; *fig.* clouer au pilori.

gib·bos·i·ty [gi'bɒsiti] gibbosité *f*, bosse *f*; **gib·bous** ['gibəs] gibbeux (-euse *f*); bossu (*personne*).

gibe [dʒaib] **1.** railler (q., *at s.o.*); se moquer (de q., *at s.o.*); **2.** raillerie *f*; moquerie *f*; brocard *m*.

gib·lets ['dʒiblits] *pl.* abatis *m*.

gid·di·ness ['gidinis] vertige *m*; *fig.* étourderie *f*; frivolité *f*; **'gid·dy** □ pris de vertige (*personne*); étourdi (*a. fig.*); *fig.* frivole; vertigineux (-euse *f*), qui donne le vertige.

gift [gift] **1.** don *m*; cadeau *m*, présent *m*; ✝ prime *f* (*à un acheteur*); *deed of ~* (*acte m de*) donation *f* entre vifs; *~ shop surt. Am.* magasin *m* de nouveautés; *never look a ~ horse in the mouth* à cheval donné on ne regarde pas la bride; **2.** douer (de, *with*); donner en présent; **'gift·ed** bien doué; de talent.

gig [gig] cabriolet *m*; ⚓ petit canot *m*.

gi·gan·tic [dʒai'gæntik] (*~ally*) géant, gigantesque.

gig·gle ['gigl] **1.** rire nerveusement; **2.** petit rire *m* nerveux.

gild [gild] [*irr.*] dorer; **'gild·er** doreur (-euse *f*) *m*; **'gild·ing** dorure *f*.

gill¹ [dʒil] (*approx.*) huitième *m* de litre.

gill² [gil] *icht.* ouie *f*; *fig. usu.* *~s* *pl.* bajoue *f*, *-s f/pl.*; *champignon*: lame *f*; *tex.* peigne *m*; ⊕ ailette *f*.

gill³ [dʒil] jeune fille *f*; bonne amie *f*.

gilt [gilt] **1.** *prét. et p.p. de gild*; **2.** dorure *f*; doré *m*; **'~-edged** doré sur tranche; ✝ de premier ordre; ✝ *~ securities* (*ou shares ou stock*) valeurs *f/pl.* de tout repos.

gim·crack ['dʒimkræk] **1.** article *m* de pacotille *ou* en toc; **2.** de pacotille (*meuble*); en toc (*bijou*); de carton (*maison*).

gim·let ⊕ ['gimlit] vrille *f*.

gim·mick *Am. sl.* ['gimik] truc *m*; tour *m*.

gin¹ [dʒin] genièvre *m*.

gin² [~] **1.** piège *m*, trébuchet *m*; ⊕ chèvre *f*; **2.** ⊕ égrener.

gin·ger ['dʒindʒə] **1.** gingembre *m*; F entrain *m*, énergie *f*; **2.** F (*souv. ~ up*) secouer; mettre du cœur au ventre de; **3.** roux (rousse *f*) (*cheveux*); **~ ale**, **~ beer** boisson *f*

gazeuse au gingembre; **'~·bread** pain *m* d'épice; **~ group** *pol.* groupe *m* de pression; **'gin·ger·ly 1.** *adj.* délicat; **2.** *adv.* délicatement; **'ginger-nut** biscuit *m* au gingembre.

gip·sy ['dʒipsi] bohémien(ne *f*) *m*.

gi·raffe *zo.* [dʒi'rɑːf] girafe *f*.

gir·an·dole ['dʒirəndoul] girandole *f*.

gird¹ [gəːd] **1.** raillerie *f*; brocard *m*; **2.** railler (q., *at s.o.*); se moquer (de, *at*).

gird² [~] [*irr.*] ceindre (de, *with*); encercler (de, *with*).

gird·er ⊕ ['gəːdə] poutre *f*.

gir·dle ['gəːdl] **1.** ceinture *f*; gaine *f*; **2.** entourer, ceindre.

girl [gəːl] jeune fille *f*; F employée *f*; domestique *f*; *~ Friday* aide *f* de bureau; *Brit. ~ guide*, *Am. ~ scout* éclaireuse *f*; **girl·hood** ['~hud] jeunesse *f*; adolescence *f*; **'girl·ish** □ de jeune *ou* petite fille; **'girl·ishness** air *m* de petite fille; **'girl·y** *Am.* F magazine *m* (*de beautés légèrement vêtues*).

girt [gəːt] **1.** *prét. et p.p. de gird²*; **2.** ⊕ circonférence *f*.

girth [gəːθ] **1.** sangle *f* (*de selle*); circonférence *f*; **2.** sangler (*un cheval*).

gist [dʒist] ⚖ principal motif *m*; F essence *f*; point *m* essentiel; fond *m*.

give [giv] **1.** [*irr.*] *v/t. usu.* donner; remettre; causer; faire (*attention, aumône, peine, plaisir, saut, etc.*); pousser (*un soupir etc.*); présenter (*des compliments*) porter (*un coup*); prononcer (*un arrêt*); céder (*une place*); *~ attention* to faire attention à; *~ battle* donner bataille; *~ birth to* donner le jour à; prononcer naissance à (*a. fig.*); *~ chase to* donner la chasse à; *~ credit to* ajouter foi à; *~ ear* to prêter l'oreille à; *~ one's mind to* s'appliquer à; *~ it to s.o.* rosser q.; semoncer vertement q.; *~ away* donner; F trahir; *~ away the bride* conduire la mariée à l'autel; *~ back* rendre; *~ forth* émettre; dégager; *~ in* donner; remettre; *~ out* distribuer; annoncer; exhaler (*une odeur etc.*); émettre; *~ over* abandonner; remettre; *~ up* rendre (*une proie*); abandonner (*affaire, malade, prétention*); *~ o.s. up* se livrer (à, *to*); se constituer prisonnier; **2.** [*irr.*] *v/i. ~ (in)* céder;

se rendre; ~ *into*, ~ (*up*)*on* donner sur (*la rue etc.*); ~ *out* manquer; faire défaut; être à bout; s'épuiser; ~ *over* finir; **3.** *su.* élasticité *f*; **give-and-take** ['givən'teik] concessions *f/pl.* mutuelles; **give-a·way** ['givə-'wei] F trahison *f*; *radio, télév., surt. Am.* ~ *show* (*ou program*) audition *f* où on décerne des prix à des concurrents; '**giv·en** *p.p. de* give; ~ *name Am.* nom *m* de baptême; ~ *to* adonné à; ~ (*that*) étant donné (que); '**giv·er** donneur (-euse *f*) *m*; † *lettre de change:* tireur *m*.

giz·zard ['gizəd] gésier *m*.

gla·cé ['glæsei] glacé.

gla·ci·al □ ['gleisiəl] glacial (-als *m/pl.*); *géol.* glaciaire; ⌒ cristallisé; **gla·cier** ['glæsjə] glacier *m*; **gla·cis** ⚔ ['glæsis] glacis *m*.

glad □ [glæd] heureux (-euse *f*), content, bien aise (de *of, at, to*); joyeux (-euse *f*); ~*ly* volontiers, avec plaisir; F give s.o. the ~ *eye* lancer des œillades à q.; **glad·den** ['~dn] réjouir.

glade [gleid] clairière *f*; *Am.* région *f* marécageuse.

glad·i·a·tor ['glædieitə] gladiateur *m*.

glad·ness ['glædnis] joie *f*; **glad·some** ['~səm] heureux (-euse *f*), joyeux (-euse *f*).

Glad·stone ['glædstən] (*a.* ~ *bag*) sac *m* américain.

glair [glɛə] **1.** glaire *f*; **2.** glairer.

glam·or·ize ['glæməraiz] faire apparaître sous de belles couleurs; glorifier, magnifier; embellir; **glam·or·ous** ['~əs] magnifique; brillant; enchanteur (-eresse *f*); *fig.* éblouissant; **glam·o(u)r** ['~mə] **1.** charme *m*, enchantement *m*; ~ *girl* jeune beauté *f* fascinante; **2.** fasciner.

glance [glɑːns] **1.** ricochet *m*; regard *m*; coup *m* d'œil; **2.** jeter un regard (*sur, at*); lancer un coup d'œil (à, *at*); refléter; ~ *aside* (*ou off*) ricocher, dévier; ~ *over* parcourir, examiner rapidement.

gland *anat.*, ♀ [glænd] glande *f*; **glan·dered** *vét.* ['~əd] morveux (-euse *f*); **glan·ders** *vét.* ['~əz] *pl.* morve *f*; **glan·du·lar** ['~julə] glandulaire.

glare [glɛə] **1.** éclat *m*, clarté *f*; éblouissement *m*; regard *m* fixe et furieux; **2.** briller d'un éclat

éblouissant; lancer un regard furieux (à, *at*); **glar·ing** □ ['~riŋ] éblouissant, aveuglant; *fig.* manifeste; flagrant.

glass [glɑːs] **1.** verre *m*; miroir *m*, glace *f*; (*a. reading-*~) loupe *f*; baromètre *m*; *coll.* verrerie *f*; (*a pair of*) ~*es pl.* (*des*) lunettes *f/pl.*; **2.** de *ou* en verre; **3.** vitrer; '~**-blow·er** souffleur *m* de verre; verrier *m*; **glass·ful** ['~ful] (plein) verre *m*; '**glass·i·ness** aspect *m* vitreux.

glass...: '~**-roofed court** cour *f* vitrée; '~**-shade** cloche *f*; '~**works** ⊕ *usu. sg.* verrerie *f*; '**glass·y** □ vitreux (-euse *f*).

glaze [gleiz] **1.** vernis *m*; *cuis.* glace *f*; *peint.* glacis *m*; **2.** (se) glacer; *v/t.* vitrer; vernir; lisser; *v/i.* devenir vitreux (*œil*); ~*d paper* papier *m* brillant; ~*d veranda* véranda *f* vitrée; **gla·zier** ['~iə] vitrier *m*; '**glaz·ing** pose *f* des vitres; vernissage *m*; vitrerie *f*; '**glaz·y** glacé.

gleam [gliːm] **1.** lueur *f* (*a. fig.*); reflet *m*; **2.** (re)luire; miroiter (*eau*).

glean [gliːn] *v/t.* glaner; *v/i.* faire la glane; '**glean·er** glaneur (-euse *f*) *m*; **glean·ings** ['~iŋz] *pl.* glanure *f*, -s *f/pl.*

glebe [gliːb] terre *f* assignée à un bénéfice; *poét.* terrain *m*, glèbe *f*.

glee [gliː] joie *f*, allégresse *f*; ♪ petit chant *m* (à 3 *ou* 4 parties) sans accompagnement; (*male*) ~ *club* chorale *f*; **glee·ful** □ ['~ful] allègre, joyeux (-euse *f*).

glen [glen] vallon *m*.

glib □ [glib] † glissant; *péj.* spécieux (-euse *f*); beau parleur (*personne*); '**glib·ness** spéciosité *f*; faconde *f*.

glide [glaid] **1.** glissement *m*; *danse:* glissade *f*; ✈ vol *m* plané; *gramm.* son *m* transitoire; **2.** (faire) glisser, couler; *v/i.* ✈ faire du vol plané; '**glid·er** planeur *m*, glisseur *m*; ~ *pilot* pilote *m* de planeur; '**glid·ing** glissement *m*; vol *m* plané.

glim·mer ['glimə] **1.** faible lueur *f*; miroitement *m*; *min.* mica *m*; **2.** entreluire, jeter une faible lueur; miroiter (*eau*).

glimpse [glimps] **1.** vision *f* momentanée; **2.** entrevoir; ~ *at* avoir la vision fugitive de; jeter un rapide coup d'œil sur.

glint [glint] **1.** étinceler, entreluire; **2.** éclair *m*, reflet *m*.

glis·sade *alp.* [gliˈsɑːd] **1.** faire une descente en glissade; **2.** glissade *f*.

glis·ten [ˈglisn], **glit·ter** [ˈglitə] étinceler, (re)luire; scintiller; *fig.* briller.

gloam·ing [ˈgloumiŋ] crépuscule *m*.

gloat [glout] ([*up*]*on, over*) savourer (*qch.*); se réjouir (de); triompher (de).

glob·al [ˈgloubl] global (-aux *m/pl.*); mondial (-aux *m/pl.*); universel(le *f*); **globe** [gloub] globe *m* (*a. anat.*); sphère *f*; terre *f*; ˈ**globe-trot·ter** globe-trotter *m*; **glo·bose** [ˈ‿ous] ♀ globeux (-euse *f*); **glo·bos·i·ty** [‿ˈbɔsiti] caractère *m* globuleux *etc.*; **glob·u·lar** □ [ˈglɔbjulə] globuleux (-euse *f*); globulaire; **glob·ule** [ˈ‿juːl] globule *m*.

gloom [gluːm] **1.** obscurité *f*, ténèbres *f/pl.*; mélancolie *f*; **2.** *v/i.* se renfrogner; s'assombrir; *v/t.* obscurcir; assombrir; ˈ**gloom·i·ness** obscurité *f*; mélancolie *f*, tristesse *f*; ˈ**gloom·y** □ sombre, obscur, ténébreux (-euse *f*); morne.

glo·ri·fi·ca·tion [glɔːrifiˈkeiʃn] glorification *f*; **glo·ri·fy** [ˈ‿fai] glorifier; ˈ**glo·ri·ous** □ glorieux (-euse *f*); resplendissant; *fig.* magnifique.

glo·ry [ˈglɔːri] **1.** gloire *f*; renommée *f*; splendeur *f*, éclat *m*; *Am.* F **Old ⚲** drapeau *m* des É.-U.; **2.** (*in*) se glorifier (de); être fier (-ère *f*) (de); F se réjouir (de).

gloss¹ [glɔs] **1.** glose *f*; commentaire *m*; **2.** gloser sur; F expliquer.

gloss² [‿] **1.** vernis *m*, lustre *m*; **high ~ painting** ripolin *m*; **2.** lustrer, glacer; **~ over** glisser sur, farder.

glos·sa·ry [ˈglɔsəri] glossaire *m*, lexique *m*.

gloss·i·ness [ˈglɔsinis] vernis *m*, lustre *m*; ˈ**gloss·y** □ lustré, brillant, glacé.

glot·tis *anat.* [ˈglɔtis] glotte *f*.

glove [glʌv] gant *m*; *see* hand 1; *mot.* ~ compartment boîte *f* à gants; ˈ**glov·er** gantier (-ère *f*) *m*.

glow [glou] **1.** lueur *f*; chaleur *f*; **2.** rayonner; rougir; ˈ**~-worm** ver *m* luisant; luciole *f*.

gloze [glouz] (*usu.* ~ *over*) glisser sur, pallier.

glu·cose ♑ [ˈgluːkous] glucose *m*.

glue [gluː] **1.** colle *f*; **2.** coller (*a. fig.*); ~ one's eyes on ne pas quitter (*qch.*) des yeux; ˈ**glue·y** gluant, poisseux (-euse *f*).

glum □ [glʌm] renfrogné, maussade, morne.

glut [glʌt] **1.** excès *m*; surabondance *f*; † encombrement *m* (du marché); **2.** inonder, encombrer; ~ o.s. se rassasier.

glu·ten ♀ [ˈgluːtən] gluten *m*; **glu·ti·nous** □ [ˈgluːtinəs] glutineux (-euse *f*).

glut·ton [ˈglʌtn] gourmand(e *f*) *m*; glouton(ne *f*) *m*, goulu(e *f*) *m*; *zo.* glouton *m*; ~ for work bourreau *m* de travail; ˈ**glut·ton·ous** □ glouton(ne *f*); ˈ**glut·ton·y** gourmandise *f*.

G-man *Am.* [ˈdʒiːmæn] agent *m* armé du F.B.I.

gnarl [nɑːl] nœud *m*, loupe *f*; **gnarled**, *a.* ˈ**gnarl·y** noueux (-euse *f*); tordu.

gnash [næʃ] grincer (*les dents*).

gnat [næt] moustique *m*, moucheron *m*. [(geur *m*).]

gnaw [nɔː] ronger; ˈ**gnaw·er** ron-⌐

gnome¹ [ˈnoumiː] maxime *f*, aphorisme *m*.

gnome² [noum] gnome *m*; gobelin *m*; ˈ**gnom·ish** de gnome.

go [gou] **1.** [*irr.*] aller; se rendre; faire une promenade *ou* un voyage; marcher (*machine, cœur, affaire*); visiter (qch., *to* s.th.); sonner (*cloche*); passer (*temps*); aboutir (*affaire, guerre*); partir (de, *from*); s'en aller; disparaître; se casser; s'épuiser; *avec adj.:* devenir; se rendre; s'étendre (jusqu'à, *to*); adjuger (à, *for*) (*lot*); ~ *bad* se gâter; *see* mad, sick; (*this dog etc.*) *must* ~ il faut absolument qu'on se débarrasse de (*ce chien etc.*); *the story* ~*es that* on dit que; *sl.* here~*es!* allons-y!; *sl.* ~ *it!* vas-y!; allez-y!; *as men etc.* ~ étant donné les hommes *etc.*; *let* ~ lâcher; laisser aller; ~ *shares* partager; ~ *to* (*ou and*) *see* aller voir; *just* ~ *and try!* essayez toujours!; ~ *about* circuler, aller çà et là; se mettre à (*une tâche*); ~ *abroad* voyager à l'étranger; émigrer; ~ *ahead* avancer; faire des progrès; persister; ~ *at* s'attaquer à; ~ *back* rentrer; retourner; ~ *back from* (*ou* F *on*) revenir sur (*une promesse*); ~ *before* *fig.* devancer; ~ *behind* revenir sur (*qch.*); ~ *between* servir de médiateur entre (... *et* ...); passer entre; ~ *by* (*adv.*) passer; (*prp.*) se régler sur; ~ *by the name of* être connu sous le nom de; ~ *down* descendre; F prendre (avec, *with*), être (*bien ou mal*) reçu (de, *with*); ~ *for* aller chercher; F tomber sur; F s'en prendre à (*q.*); ~ *for* (aller) faire (*une promenade, un voyage, etc.*); ~ *in* entrer, rentrer; se cacher (*soleil*); ~ *in for* se mêler de, s'adonner à; ~ *in for an examination* se présenter à *ou* passer un examen; ~ *into* entrer dans; examiner (*une question*); ✿ diviser; ~ *off* partir (*a. fusil etc.*), s'en aller; s'écarter; se passer; se détériorer; passer (*beauté*); tourner (*lait*); ~ *on* continuer sa route; continuer (de *inf., gér.*); marcher; passer (à, *to*); F se passer; F se conduire; ~ *on!* avancez!; *iro.* allons donc!; ~ *out* sortir; disparaître; baisser (*marée*); s'éteindre (*feu*); *pol.* quitter le pouvoir; ~ *over* passer (à, *to*) (*un parti etc.*); traverser; ~ *through* passer par; traverser; remplir; subir (*une épreuve*); examiner; ~ *through with* aller jusqu'au bout de; ~ *to* aller à; ~ *to expense* se mettre en dépense; ~ *up* monter; sauter; ✝ subir une hausse; ~ *up to town* aller à la ville; ~ *with* accompagner; s'accorder avec; ~ *without* se passer de; 2. F aller *m*; entrain *m*, coup *m*, essai *m*; F ✿ accès *m*; *sl.* dernier cri *m*; *sl.* affaire *f*; *univ. sl. little* ~ premier examen *m*; *great* ~ examen *m* final; *on the* ~ à courir, remuant; *it is no* ~ ça ne prend pas; *is it a* ~? entendu?; *in one* ~ d'un seul coup; *have a* ~ essayer (de *inf., at gér.*).

goad [goud] 1. aiguillon *m* (*a. fig.*); 2. aiguillonner, piquer (*a. fig.*).

go-a·head F ['gouəhed] 1. entreprenant; actif (-ive *f*); 2. *surt. Am.* F esprit *m* entreprenant; *Am. sl.* voie *f* libre.

goal [goul] but *m* (*a. sp., a. foot.*); '~-ar·e·a *foot.* surface *f* de but; **goal·ie** F ['gouəli] = '~-**keep·er** *foot.* gardien *m* de but; F **goal** *m*; ~ **kick** *foot.* coup *m* de pied de but.

goat [gout] *zo.* chèvre *f*; he-~ bouc *m*; *fig.* imbécile *m*; *sl.* get s.o.'s ~ irriter q.; **goat'ee** barbiche *f*; bouc *m*; '**goat·ish** de bouc; lascif.

gob [gɔb] *sl.* crachat *m*; ⚒ remblai *m*; *Am.* F marin *m*; **gob·bet** ['~it] grosse bouchée *f*.

gob·ble ['gɔbl] dévorer; glouglouter (*dindon*); **gob·ble·dy·gook** *Am. sl.* ['gɔbldiguk] style *m* ampoulé; jargon *m* (*des fonctionnaires*); '**gob·bler** avaleur (-euse *f*) *m*; dindon *m*.

go-be·tween ['goubitwi:n] intermédiaire *mf*.

gob·lin ['gɔblin] gobelin *m*, lutin *m*.

go-by ['goubai]: *give s.o. the* ~ éviter q.; se dérober à q.

go-cart ['goukɑ:t] poussette *f*, charrette *f* (*pour bébés*).

god [gɔd] *eccl.* ♀ dieu *m*; *fig.* idole *f*; '**god·child** filleul(e *f*) *m*; '**god·dess** déesse *f*; '**god·fa·ther** parrain *m*; '**god·for·sak·en** perdu (*endroit*); '**god·head** divinité *f*; '**god·less** impie; athée; '**god·like** de dieu; divin; '**god·li·ness** piété *f*; '**god·ly** saint; pieux (-euse *f*), dévot; '**god·moth·er** marraine *f*; '**god·send** aubaine *f*; bienfait *m* du ciel; '**god-'speed** bon voyage *m*, adieu *m*.

go·er ['gouə] passant *m*; *play*~ habitué(e *f*) *m* du cinéma *ou* théâtre; *cheval:* marcheur *m*; F homme *m* énergique.

gof·fer ['goufə] gaufrer; tuyauter.

go-get·ter *Am. sl.* ['gou'getə] arriviste *mf*; homme *m* d'affaires *etc.* énergique.

gog·gle ['gɔgl] 1. (*a.* ~ *one's eyes*) rouler de gros yeux; 2. (*a pair of*) ~*s* *pl.* lunettes *f/pl.*; '~-**box** *sl.* télé *f*.

go·ing ['gouiŋ] 1. qui marche; qui va (*sur*); qui soit; F actuel(le *f*); *be* ~ *to* (*inf.*) être sur le point de (*inf.*); aller (*inf.*); avoir l'intention de (*inf.*); *keep* ~ aller toujours; *set* (*a-*)~ mettre en train; *a* ~ *concern* une affaire *etc.* en pleine activité; ~, ~, *gone!* une fois, deux fois, adjugé!; 2. allée *f*; départ *m*; recours *m*; *sp.* état *m* du sol; *be heavy* ~ être difficile; '**go·ings-'on** *pl.* F conduite *f*.

goi·tre ✿ ['gɔitə] goitre *m*; **goi·trous** ['gɔitrəs] goitreux (-euse *f*).

gold [gould] 1. or *m*; 2. d'or; *sl.* ~ *brick* escroquerie *f*; attrape-nigaud *m*; *Am. sl.* ~*brick* se défiler, tirer au flanc; '**~-dig·ger** *Am.* chercheur *m* d'or; *sl.* maîtresse *f* coûteuse; '**gold·en** † d'or; *fig.* précieux (-euse *f*); '**gold·finch** *orn.* chardonneret *m*; '**gold-plat·ed** plaqué or; '**gold·smith** orfèvre *m*.

golf [gɔlf] *sp.* golf *m*; '**~·ball** balle *f* de golf; '**~·club** club *m* de golf; crosse *f* de golf; '**golf·er** golfeur (-euse *f*) *m*; joueur (-euse *f*) *m* de golf; '**golf·links** *pl.* terrain *m* de golf.

gol·li·wog(g) ['gɔliwɔg] poupée *f* grotesque; *fig.* objet *m* d'épouvante.

go·losh [gə'lɔʃ] caoutchouc *m*.

gon·do·la ⚓, ⚔ ['gɔndələ] gondole *f*.

gone [gɔn] **1.** *p.p. de go 1*; **2.** *adj.* absent; mort; F épris, amoureux (-euse *f*) (de, on); *sl.* filez-vous-en!; *sl.* filez!; *sl.* ~ **on** épris de (*q.*), emballé sur (*q.*); '**gon·er** *sl.* homme *m* fichu *ou* mort.

gong [gɔŋ] gong *m*.

good [gud] **1.** *usu.* bon(ne *f*); valable (*excuse*); excellent; avantageux (-euse *f*) (*mariage, prix, etc.*); ~ **and** *Am.* très, tout à fait; ⚹ *Friday* (le) Vendredi *m* saint; *the* ~ *Samaritan* le bon Samaritain; ~ *at* bon *ou* fort en; *in* ~ *earnest* pour (tout) de bon; ~ *afternoon* bonjour!; *plus tard*; ~ *evening* bonsoir!; ~ *morning* bonjour!; ~ *night* bonne nuit!; **2.** bien *m*; ~*s pl.* articles *m/pl.*; marchandises *f/pl.*; ⚏ biens *m/pl.*; *Am.* F avantage *m* (sur, on); *that's no* ~ cela ne vaut rien; *it is no* ~ *talking* inutile de parler; *for* ~ pour de bon; ~*s station* (*train*) gare *f* (train *m*) de marchandises; ~*s in process produits m/pl.* semi-fabriqués; ~*s in short supply* marchandises *f/pl.* qui manquent; ~*bye* **1.** [gud'bai] adieu *m*; **2.** [gud'bai] au revoir!, adieu!; '**~-for-noth·ing 1.** bon(ne *f*) à rien; sans valeur; **2.** bon(ne *f*) *m* à rien; vaurien(ne *f*) *m*; '**good-hu·mo(u)red** de bonne humeur; jovial, bonhomme; '**good·li·ness** beauté *f*; '**good-look·ing** joli; '**good·ly** beau (bel *devant une voyelle ou un h muet*; belle *f*; beaux *m/pl.*); ample; considérable; '**good-'na·tured** bon(ne *f*); au bon naturel; '**good·ness** bonté *f*; bonne qualité *f*; *int.* dieu *m*!; *see gracious*; '**good-sized** assez grand; '**good·wife** maîtresse *f* de la maison; '**good·will** bonne volonté *f*; bienveillance *f* (envers, pour towards); † clientèle *f*; † achalandage *m*.

good·y¹ ['gudi] bonbon *m*.

good·y² [~] **1.** *adj.* édifiant; d'une piété affectée; **2.** *int. Am.* F chouette!

goo·ey F ['gu:i] gluant; sentimental.

goof F [gu:f] **1.** idiot(e *f*) *m*; gaffe *f*; **2.** *a.* ~ **up** saloper, gâcher, bousiller; '**goof·y** F idiot, toqué.

goon *Am. sl.* [gu:n] voyou *m*.

goose [gu:s] (*pl.* geese) oie *f*; *fig.* sot(te *f*) *m*; (*pl.* gooses) carreau *m* (*à repasser*).

goose·ber·ry ['guzbəri] groseille *f* verte; *buisson:* groseillier *m*; F *play* ~ se trouver en tiers; *sl.* faire sandwich.

goose...: '**~-flesh**, *surt. Am.* '**~-pim·ples** *pl. fig.* chair *f* de poule; '**~-step** pas *m* de l'oie; '**goos·ey**, '**goos·ie** F oison *m*.

go·pher *surt. Am.* ['goufə] saccophore *m*; chien *m* de prairie.

Gor·di·an ['gɔ:diən] gordien; *fig.* difficile, compliqué.

gore¹ [gɔ:] sang *m* coagulé.

gore² [~] **1.** *cost.* godet *m*; soufflet *m*; ⚓ pointe *f*; **2.** blesser avec les cornes; découdre; *cost.* faire goder.

gorge [gɔ:dʒ] **1.** gorge *f* (*a. géog.*); gosier *m*; *my* ~ *rises at it* j'en ai des nausées; **2.** (se) rassasier; (se) gorger.

gor·geous □ ['gɔ:dʒəs] magnifique; superbe; '**gor·geous·ness** splendeur *f*.

gor·get ⚔ ['gɔ:dʒit] hausse-col *m*.

gor·man·dize ['gɔ:məndaiz] *vt/i.* bâfrer; *v/i.* goinfrer.

gorm·less *Brit.* F ['gɔ:mlis] bête; lourdaud; bouché.

gorse ⚘ [gɔ:s] genêt *m* épineux.

gor·y □ ['gɔ:ri] ensanglanté.

gosh F [gɔʃ] sapristi!

gos·hawk *orn.* ['gɔshɔ:k] autour *m*.

gos·ling ['gɔzliŋ] oison *m*.

gos·pel ['gɔspl] évangile *m*.

go-slow [gou'slou] grève *f* perlée; travail *m* au ralenti.

gos·sa·mer ['gɔsəmə] filandres *f/pl.*; † gaze *f* légère.

gos·sip ['gɔsip] **1.** causerie *f*; *péj.* cancans *m/pl.*; *personne:* bavard(e *f*) *m*; *journ.* ~ *column* échos *m/pl.*!; **2.**

bavarder; faire des cancans (sur, *about*).

got [gɔt] *prét. et p.p. de* get.

Goth [gɔθ] *hist.* Goth *m* (*a. fig.*); *fig.* vandale *m*; **'Goth·ic** gothique.

got·ten † *ou Am.* ['gɔtn] *p.p. de* get.

gouge [gaudʒ] **1.** ⊕ gouge *f*; **2.** (*usu.* ~ out) creuser à la gouge; *fig.* faire sauter (un œil à *q.*); *Am.* F duper, refaire.

gourd ♀ ['guəd] courge *f*; gourde *f* (*a. bouteille*).

gout ✞ [gaut] goutte *f*; podagre *f*; **'gout·y** □ goutteux (-euse *f*); podagre.

gov·ern ['gʌvən] *v/t.* gouverner, régir (*a. gramm.*); *fig.* maîtriser; *v/i.* gouverner; ~*ing body* conseil *m* d'administration; **'gov·ern·a·ble** □ gouvernable; **'gov·ern·ess** gouvernante *f*; institutrice *f*; **'gov·ern·ment** gouvernement *m*; régime *m*; ministère *m*; *Am.* conseil *m* municipal; *attr.* public, d'État, gouvernemental (-aux *m/pl.*); **gov·ern·men·tal** [~'mentl] gouvernemental(-aux *m/pl.*); **'gov·er·nor** gouverneur *m* (*Am. d'un État des É.-U.*); F patron *m*; F vieux *m*; ⊕ régulateur *m*.

gown [gaun] **1.** robe *f*; *univ.*, ⚖ toge *f*; **2.** *v/t.* revêtir d'une robe; *v/i.* revêtir sa robe; **gowns·man** ['~zmən] étudiant *m*; civil *m*.

grab F [græb] **1.** *v/t.* saisir, empoigner; *v/i.* ~ *at* s'agripper à; **2.** mouvement *m* vif de la main (*pour saisir q. etc.*); ⊕ benne *f* preneuse; *surt. Am.* ~-*bag* sac *m* à surprise; **'grab·ber** accapareur (-euse *f*) *m*.

grace [greis] **1.** grâce *f*; bénédicité *m*; † délai *m*; *style:* aménité *f*; ~*s pl.* agréments *m/pl.*; ♪ ~-*note* note *f* d'agrément; *myth.* the ♀s *pl.* les Grâces *f/pl.*; *act of* ~ faveur *f*; *with (a) good (bad)* ~ avec bonne (mauvaise) grâce; *Your* ♀ votre Grandeur *f*; *good* ~*s pl.* bonnes grâces *f/pl.*; **2.** embellir, orner; honorer (de, *with*); **grace·ful** □ ['~ful] gracieux (-euse *f*); **'grace·ful·ness** élégance *f*, grâce *f*; **'grace·less** □ impie; F effronté; inélégant.

gra·cious □ ['greiʃəs] gracieux (-euse *f*); bienveillant; miséricordieux (-euse *f*); *good(ness)* ~! bonté

divine!; mon Dieu!; **'gra·cious·ness** grâce *f*; bienveillance *f*.

gra·da·tion [grə'deiʃn] gradation *f*.

grade [greid] **1.** grade *m*, rang *m*, degré *m*; qualité *f*; *surt. Am. see* gradient; *Am.* classe *f*; *Am. make the* ~ arriver; surmonter les difficultés; *surt. Am.* ~ *crossing* passage *m* à niveau; *surt. Am.* ~(*d*) *school* école *f* primaire; **2.** classer; graduer; ⚞ ménager la pente de; améliorer (*le bétail*) par le métissage.

gra·di·ent ['greidiənt] ⚞ *etc.* rampe *f*, pente *f*.

grad·u·al □ ['grædjuəl] progressif (-ive *f*); graduel(le *f*); doux (douce *f*); **grad·u·ate 1.** ['~eit] *v/t.* graduer; *v/i. Am.* recevoir son diplôme; *univ.* passer sa licence; prendre ses grades; **2.** ['~it] *univ.* gradué(e *f*) *m*; **grad·u·a·tion** [~'eiʃn] gradation *f*; ⚕, ✞ graduation *f*; *Am.* remise *f* d'un diplôme; *univ.* réception *f* d'un grade.

graft[1] [grɑ:ft] **1.** ✿ greffe *f*; **2.** ✿ greffer (*a.* ✞), enter (*a. fig.*) (sur *in, upon*).

graft[2] *Am.* [~] **1.** corruption *f*, gratte *f*; rabiot *m*; **2.** F rabioter, gratter; **'graft·er** F *surt. pol.* rapineur *m*, F tripoteur *m*.

grail, *a.* ♀ [greil] (Saint-)Graal *m*.

grain [grein] grain *m* (*a. fig., a. mesure, a. bois*); *coll.* grains *m/pl.*, céréales *f/pl.*; *fig.* brin *m*; *in* ~ invétéré, fieffé; *dyed in the* ~ (teint) grand teint; *against the* ~ contre le fil; *fig.* à contrecœur.

gram·i·na·ceous ♀ [greimi'neiʃəs] graminé.

gram·ma·logue ['græməlɔg] sténogramme *m*.

gram·mar ['græmə] grammaire *f* (*a. livre*); ~-*school* école *f* secondaire, collège *m*, lycée *m*; *Am.* école *f* primaire; **gram·mar·i·an** [grə'mɛəriən] grammairien *m*; **gram·mat·i·cal** □ [grə'mætikl] grammatical (-aux *m/pl.*).

gram(me) [græm] gramme *m*.

gram·o·phone ['græməfoun] phonographe *m*; ~ *pick-up* pick-up *m/inv.*; ~ *record* disque *m*.

gran·a·ry ['grænəri] grenier *m*.

grand □ [grænd] **1.** *fig.* grand; grandiose, magnifique (-aux *m/pl.*); F excellent; ♀ *Duchess* grande-duchesse (*pl.* grandes-du-

843 gratify

chesses) *f*; ♀ Duke grand-duc (*pl.*
grands-ducs) *m*; *Am.* ♀ Old Party
parti *m* républicain; *sp.* ~ stand
grande *f* tribune; **2.** ♪ (*a.* ~ *piano*)
piano *m* à queue; *Am. sl.* mille dollars *m/pl.*; *miniature* ~ piano *m* demi-queue; **gran·dam(e)** ['~dæm]
† grand-mère (*pl.* grand[s]-mères)
f; **'grand·child** petit-fils (*pl.* petits-
fils) *m*; petite-fille (*pl.* petites-filles)
f; ~ren *pl.* petits-enfants *m/pl.*;
gran(d)·dad F ['grændæd] bon-
papa (*pl.* bons-papas) *m*, grand-
papa (*pl.* grands-papas) *m*; **'grand·
daugh·ter** petite-fille (*pl.* petites-
filles) *f*; **gran·dee** [græn'di:] grand
m (*d'Espagne*); *fig.* grand personnage *m*.
gran·deur ['grændʒə] grandeur *f*;
noblesse *f*; splendeur *f*; **'grand·
fa·ther** grand-père (*pl.* grands-
pères) *m*; ~'s clock horloge *f* de parquet.
gran·dil·o·quence [græn'diləkwəns]
emphase *f*; **gran'dil·o·quent** □
grandiloquent; emphatique.
gran·di·ose □ ['grændious] grandiose, magnifique; pompeux (-euse
f); **gran·di·os·i·ty** [~'ɔsiti] grandiose *m*; caractère *m* pompeux.
grand·moth·er ['grænmʌðə] grand-
mère (*pl.* grand[s]-mères) *f*; **'grand·
ness** *see* grandeur.
grand...: '~**par·ents** *pl.* grands-
parents *m/pl.*; ~**sire** ['~saiə] † *ou*
animal: grand-père (*pl.* grands-pè-
res) *m*; aïeul (*pl.* -eux) *m*; '~**son**
petit-fils (*pl.* petits-fils) *m*; '~**stand**
tribune *f*.
grange [greindʒ] manoir *m*, château
m; *Am.* fédération *f* agricole.
gran·ite ['grænit] granit *m*; **gra·nit·
ic** [græ'nitik] granitique, graniteux
(-euse *f*).
gran·ny F ['græni] bonne-maman *f*
(*pl.* bonnes-mamans).
grant [grɑ:nt] **1.** concession *f*; subvention *f* (*pécuniaire*); ⚖ don *m*,
cession *f*; **2.** accorder; céder; admettre; ⚖ faire cession de; *take for*
~ed prendre pour avéré, présupposer; ~*ing this* (*to*) *be so* admettant
qu'il en soit ainsi; ceci posé; *God*
~...! Dieu veuille ...!; **gran'tee** ⚖
cessionnaire *mf*; donataire *mf*;
grant-in-aid ['grɑ:ntin'eid] subvention *f* de l'État; **grant·or** ⚖
[~'tɔ:] donateur (-trice *f*) *m*.

gran·u·lar ['grænjulə] granuleux
(-euse *f*); **gran·u·late** ['leit] (se)
cristalliser; (se) grenailler; **gran·u·
'la·tion** granulation *f*; **gran·ule**
['~ju:l] granule *m*; **gran·u·lous**
['~juləs] granuleux (-euse *f*), granulaire.
grape [greip] (grain *m* de) raisin *m*;
unfermented ~ *juice* jus *m* de raisin
(*infermenté*); '~**fruit** ♀ pamplemousse *m* ou *f*; ⚕ grape-fruit *m*;
'~**sug·ar** sucre *m* de raisin; '~**vine**
vigne *f*; rumeur *f* publique; *hear s.th.*
through ou on the ~ apprendre qch.
par le téléphone arabe.
graph [græf] graphique *m*, courbe *f*;
'**graph·ic**, '**graph·i·cal** □ graphique; *fig.* pittoresque, vivant; ~ *arts*
pl. graphique *f*; **graph·ite** *min.*
['~fait] graphite *m*; **graph·ol·o·gy**
[~'fɔlədʒi] graphologie *f*.
grap·nel ['græpnəl] ⚓ grappin *m*;
⚔ ancre *f*.
grap·ple ['græpl] **1.** ⚓ grappin *m*;
⊕ araignée *f*; **2.** *v/t.* accrocher; *v/i.*
fig. en venir aux prises (avec, *with*),
s'attaquer (à, *with*).
grasp [grɑ:sp] **1.** poigne *f*; prise *f*;
étreinte *f*; *fig.* compréhension *f*;
2. *v/t.* saisir; empoigner; *fig.* comprendre; *v/i.:* ~ *at* chercher à saisir
(*qch.*); saisir avidement (*une offre*
etc.); '**grasp·ing** □ tenace; F avare.
grass [grɑ:s] herbe *f*; pâture *f*;
gazon *m*; *sl.* herbe *f* (*marijuana*); *at* ~
au vert (*a. fig.* = *en congé*); *send to* ~ F
étendre (*q.*) par terre; '~**hop·per**
sauterelle *f*; '~**plot** pelouse *f*; '~**
roots** **1.** émanant du peuple, populaire; **2.** *pol. etc.* base *f*; *fig. les faits*
m/pl. fondamentaux; '~**wid·ow** F
veuve *f* temporaire; femme *f* séparée
(de son mari); '~**wid·ow·er** F veuf
m temporaire; homme *m* séparé (de
sa femme); '**grass·y** herbeux (-euse
f), herbu.
grate¹ [greit] grille *f* (*du foyer, a.*⊕);
âtre *m*; *fig.* foyer *m*.
grate² [~] *v/t.* râper; grincer de (*ses*
dents); *v/i.* grincer, crier; ~ (*up*)*on*
fig. choquer (*les oreilles*), agacer (*les*
nerfs).
grate·ful □ ['greitful] reconnaissant; agréable (*chose*); bienfaisant.
grat·er ['greitə] râpe *f*.
grat·i·fi·ca·tion [grætifi'keiʃn] satisfaction *f*, plaisir *m*; **grat·i·fy**
['~fai] satisfaire; faire plaisir à;

'**grat·i·fy·ing** flatteur (-euse *f*), agréable.

grat·ing ['greitiŋ] **1.** □ grinçant, discordant; **2.** treillis *m*; grillage *m*; grincement *m*.

gra·tis ['greitis] gratuit, gratis.

grat·i·tude ['grætitju:d] reconnaissance *f*, gratitude *f* (envers, *to*).

gra·tu·i·tous □ [grə'tju:itəs] gratuit; sans motif; bénévole; injustifié; **gra'tu·i·ty** gratification *f*; F pourboire *m*.   [*m*, fondement *m*.]

gra·va·men ₤₤ [grə'veimen] fond)

grave[1] □ [greiv] grave; sérieux (-euse *f*); *gramm.* ~ accent accent *m* grave.

grave[2] [~] **1.** tombe(au *m*) *f*; **2.** [*irr.*] *usu. fig.* graver; '~-**dig·ger** fossoyeur *m*.

grav·el ['grævl] **1.** gravier *m*; ⚕ gravelle *f*; **2.** graveler; sabler; F réduire (*q.*) à quia; '**grav·el·ly** graveleux (-euse *f*).

grav·en ['greivən] *p.p. de* grave[2] **2.**

grav·er ⊕ ['greivə] échoppe *f*.

grave...: '~**side**: *at his* ~ au bord de son tombeau; '~**stone** pierre *f* tombale; '~**yard** cimetière *m*.

grav·ing dock ⚓ ['greiviŋ'dɔk] cale *f* sèche; bassin *m* de radoub.

grav·i·tate ['græviteit] graviter (vers, *to*[*wards*]); **grav·i'ta·tion** gravitation *f*; **grav·i'ta·tion·al** [~ʃənl] de gravitation (*force etc.*); *phys.* ~ **pull** gravitation *f*.

grav·i·ty ['græviti] gravité *f* (*phys., a. fig.*); *fig.* sérieux *m*; centre *of* ~ centre *m* de gravité; *phys. specific* ~ poids *m* spécifique.

gra·vy ['greivi] jus *m*; sauce *f* au jus; '~-**boat** saucière *f*.

gray [grei] gris; blême (*teint*); *Am.* F moyen(ne *f*); *see a.* grey.

graze[1] [greiz] **1.** *vt/i.* paître; *v/t.* vaches: pâturer (*un champ*).

graze[2] [~] **1.** écorcher; *fig.* raser; **2.** écorchure *f*.

gra·zier ['greiziə] éleveur *m*.

grease 1. [gri:z] graisser; **2.** [gri:s] graisse *f*; *wool* ~ suint *m*; '~-**cup** *mot.* graisseur *m*; '~-**gun** *mot.* pompe *f* à graisse; '~-**pa·per** papier *m* parcheminé; papier *m* jambon; '~-**proof** parcheminé; **greas·er** *Am. sl.* ['gri:zə] Mexicain *m*, Américain *m* du Sud; **greas·y** □ ['gri:zi] graisseux (-euse *f*); taché de graisse; gras(se *f*).

great □ [greit] **1.** *usu.* grand; *qqfois* magnifique; important; F fameux (-euse *f*); ~ **grandchild** arrière-petit-fils *m*, arrière-petite-fille *f* (*pl.* ~**grandchildren** arrière-petits-enfants *m/pl.*) ~ **grandfather** arrière-grand-père (*pl.* arrière-grands-pères) *m*; *see* deal, many; **2.** the ~ *pl.* les grands (hommes) *m/pl.*, les célébrités *f/pl.*; *Am.* no ~ nullement; '~-**coat** pardessus *m*; '**great·ly** beaucoup, fortement; '**great·ness** grandeur *f*; importance *f*.

greave [gri:v] jambière *f*.   [*m/pl.*]

greaves [gri:vz] *pl. cuis.* cretons)

Gre·cian ['gri:ʃn] grec(que *f*).

greed [gri:d], '**greed·i·ness** cupidité *f*; gourmandise *f*; '**greed·y** □ avide (de *of, for*); gourmand.

Greek [gri:k] **1.** grec(que *f*); **2.** *ling.* grec *m*; Grec(que *f*) *m*; *that is* ~ *to* me c'est de l'hébreu pour moi.

green [gri:n] **1.** □ vert (*a.* ⊕); inexpérimenté, jeune; naïf (-ïve *f*); frais (fraîche *f*); blême (*teint*); **2.** vert *m*; gazon *m*, pelouse *f*; *fig.* première jeunesse *f*; ~s *pl.* légumes *m/pl.* verts; '~-**back** *Am.* billet *m* d'un dollar *m*; '~-**baize ta·ble** tapis *m* vert, table *f* de jeu; '**green·er·y** verdure *f*, feuillage *m*.

green...: '~-**gage** ⚘ reine-claude (*pl.* reines-claudes) *f*; '~-**gro·cer** marchand(e *f*) *m* de légumes; fruitier (-ère *f*) *m*; '~-**gro·cer·y** commerce *m* de légumes; légumes *m/pl.* et fruits *m/pl.*; '~-**horn** F blanc-bec (*pl.* blancs-becs) *m*, bleu *m*; '~-**house** serre *f* (chaude); '**green·ish** verdâtre.

Green·land·er ['gri:nləndə] Groenlandais(e *f*) *m*; **Green·land·man** ⚓ ['~ləndmən] baleinière *f* (*des pêcheries du Groenland*).

green light F voie *f* libre; *fig.* permission *f*; '**green·ness** verdeur *f*; verdure *f*; immaturité *f*; naïveté *f*.

green...: '~-**room** *théâ.* foyer *m* des artistes; '~-**sick·ness** ⚕ chlorose *f*; '~-**sward** gazon *m*.

greet [gri:t] saluer; accueillir; '**greet·ing** salut(ation *f*) *m*; accueil *m*; ~s *card* carte *f* de vœux.

gre·gar·i·ous □ [gre'gɛəriəs] grégaire.

gre·nade ⚔ [gri'neid] grenade *f* (à main, extinctrice); **gren·a·dier** [grenə'diə] grenadier *m*.

grew [gru:] *prét. de* grow.

grey □ [grei] **1.** gris; *fig.* ~ *area* zone *f*
sombre; ♀ *Friar* frère *m* mineur;
Franciscain *m*; ~ *matter* anat. substance *f* grise (du cerveau); *fig.* intelligence *f*; **2.** gris *m*; cheval *m* gris; **3.**
grisailler; *v/i.* grisonner (*cheveux*);
'~-**haired** aux cheveux gris, grisonnant; '~-**hound** lévrier *m*, levrette
f; '**grey-ish** grisâtre; grisonnant
(*cheveux*).

grid [grid] grille *f*, grillage *m*; réseau *m*; treillis *m*; *national* ~ caisse *f*
nationale de l'énergie; *foot. Am.* (*a.*
~ *iron*) terrain *m* de rugby; *see a.*
gridiron; '**grid-i-ron** *cuis.* gril *m*;
cycl. F bicyclette *f*.

grief [gri:f] douleur *f*, chagrin *m*;
fig. accident *m*.

griev-ance ['gri:vəns] grief *m*; injustice *f*; **grieve** [gri:v] (s')affliger;
(se) chagriner; '**griev-ous** □ pénible; cruel(le *f*); grave; '**griev-ous-
ness** gravité *f*.

grif-fin ['grifin] *myth.* griffon *m* (*a.*
chien).

grig [grig] petite anguille *f*; grillon
m.

grill [gril] **1.** griller; *v/t. sl.* cuisiner
(*q.*); **2.** gril *m*; *cuis.* grillade *f*; '~-
room grill-room *m.*

grim □ [grim] sinistre; sévère; farouche; ~ *facts* faits *m/pl.* brutaux;
~ *humo(u)r* humour *m* macabre.

gri-mace [gri'meis] **1.** grimace *f*;
2. grimacer.

gri-mal-kin [gri'mælkin] mistigri
m; *femme:* mégère *f*.

grime [graim] **1.** saleté *f*; poussière *f*
de charbon *etc.*; **2.** noircir, salir;
'**grim-y** □ noirci, sale; barbouillé.

grin [grin] **1.** large sourire *m*; sourire d'une oreille à l'autre; ~ *at*
adresser un large sourire à (*q.*).

grind [graind] **1.** [*irr.*] *v/t.* moudre;
broyer; dépolir (*un verre*); ⊕ meu-
ler; aiguiser (*une lame*); *fig.* opprimer; *Am. sl.* faire enrager; *sl.* faire
travailler; ~ *one's teeth* grincer des
dents; ~ *out* tourner (*un air*); dire entre les dents; *v/i.* grincer, crisser; *sl.*
potasser; bûcher; **2.** grincement *m*;
sl. turbin *m*; '**grind-er** pileur (-euse
f) *m*; (*dent f*) molaire *f*; moulin *m* (à
café); ⊕ rectifieuse *f*; *sl.* joueur *m*
d'orgue de Barbarie; '**grind-ing**
fig. déchirant, rongeur (-euse *f*); ⊕
à roder; '**grind-stone** meule *f* à

aiguiser; *keep s.o.'s nose to the* ~
faire travailler q. sans relâche.

grip [grip] **1.** empoigner; saisir (*a.*
fig.); *fig.* ~*ping* passionnant; **2.** prise
f, serrement *m*; poignée *f* (*a. cycl.*);
Am. see gripsack; *get to* ~*s with* en
venir aux prises avec.

gripe [graip] **1.** saisissement *m*;
étreinte *f*; poignée *f*; ~*s pl.* colique
f; *surt. Am.* plaintes *f/pl.*; **2.** *v/t.*
saisir, empoigner; donner la coli-
que à; *v/i. surt. Am.* F rouspéter,
se plaindre.

grip-sack *Am.* ['gripsæk] petite valise *f* à main.   [frayant.\

gris-ly ['grizli] affreux (-euse *f*); ef-\

grist [grist] blé *m* moulu *ou* à moudre; *fig. bring* ~ *to the mill* faire
venir l'eau au moulin.

gris-tle ['grisl] cartilage *m*; '**gris-tly**
cartilagineux (-euse *f*).

grit [grit] **1.** grès *m*; sable *m*; *pierre*
grain *m*; ⊕ impuretés *f/pl.*; F cou-
rage *m*; **2.** ~ *one's teeth* grincer des
dents; '**grit-ty** sablonneux (-euse
f); graveleux (-euse *f*) (*a. poire*);
Am. sl. qui a du cran.

griz-zle F ['grizl] grognonner; pleurnicher; '**griz-zled** *see* grizzly *1*;
'**griz-zly 1.** grisonnant (*cheveux*
etc.); ~ *bear* = **2.** ours *m* grizzlé.

groan [groun] **1.** gémissement *m*,
plainte *f*; **2.** gémir; pousser des gé-
missements; † ~ *for* languir après.

groat [grout] *not worth a* ~ qui ne
vaut pas un liard.

groats [grouts] *pl.* gruau *m* d'a-
voine *ou* de froment.

gro-cer ['grousə] épicier (-ère *f*) *m*;
'**gro-cer-y** épicerie *f*; *Am.* boutique
f d'épicier; *Am.* débit *m* de boissons; *groceries pl.* (articles *m/pl.*
d'épicerie *f*.   [celant; soûl.\

grog [grɔg] grog *m*; '**grog-gy** chan-\

groin [grɔin] **1.** *anat.* aine *f*; △ arête
f; nervure *f*; **2.** △ fournir d'arêtes;
tailler les nervures sur.

groom [grum] **1.** valet *m* (*du roi etc*);
valet *m* d'écurie; laquais *m*; *see*
bridegroom; **2.** panser (*un cheval*);
Am. pol. dresser (*un candidat*); *well*
~*ed* bien entretenu; élégant, bien
soigné (*personne*); **grooms-man**
['~zmən] garçon *m* d'honneur.

groove [gru:v] **1.** rainure *f*; cannelure *f*; *vis:* creux *m*; *disque:*
sillon *m*; *fig.* routine *f*; ~*s pl. canon*
etc.: rayures *f/pl.*; *fig. in the* ~ rangé;

dans la bonne voie; **2.** rainer, canneler; rayer.

grope [group] tâtonner.

gross [grous] **1.** □ gros(se f); gras (-se f); grossier (-ère f); global (-aux m/pl.); ✝ brut; ✝ ~ *national product* revenu m national brut; **2.** grosse f (*12 douzaines*); *Am.* recette f brute; *in the* ~ à tout prendre; '**gross·ness** grossièreté f; énormité f.

gro·tesque □ [grou'tesk] grotesque.

grot·to ['grɔtou] grotte f.

grouch *Am.* F [grautʃ] **1.** rouspéter; ronchonner; **2.** maussaderie f; plainte f; *personne:* grogneur (-euse f) m; '**grouch·y** grognon(ne f).

ground¹ [graund] *prét. et p.p. de* grind¹; ~ *glass* verre m dépoli; *phot.* (châssis m à) glace f dépolie.

ground² [~] **1.** fond m; terre f; terrain m (*a. sp.*); raison f, cause f; base f; sol m; ⚡ terre f, masse f; ~s pl. parc m, terrains m/pl.; motifs m/pl.; raisons f/pl.; marc m de café; *on the* ~(*s*) *of* pour *ou* en raison de; *fall to the* ~ tomber par *ou* à terre; *fig.* ne pas aboutir; *give* ~ lâcher pied; *stand one's* ~ tenir bon; **2.** *v/t.* fonder, baser; enseigner à fond; ⊕ donner la première couche de peinture à, préparer; ⚡ mettre à la terre *ou* masse; ⚓ jeter à la côte; *v/i.* ⚓ (s')échouer; *well* ~ed bien fondé; '**ground·age** ⚓ droits m/pl. de mouillage *ou* d'ancrage.

ground...: '~-**con·nex·ion** ⚡ prise f de terre; *mot.* mise f à la masse; '~-'**floor** rez-de-chaussée m/inv.; '~-**hog** *surt. Am.* marmotte f d'Amérique; '~-**less** □ sans fondement; '~-**nut** arachide f; '~-'**plan** plan m de fondation.

ground·sel ['graunsl] séneçon m.

ground...: '~-**sheet** tapis m de sol; '~s·**man** gardien m de stade; ~ **staff** ✈ personnel m rampant *ou* nonnavigant; ~ **swell** houle f de fond; ~-**wire** ⚡ fil m de terre *ou* masse; '~-**work** fond(ement) m; *poét.* canevas m.

group [group] **1.** groupe m; peloton m; *psych.* ~ *therapy* thérapie f de groupe; **2.** (se) grouper.

grouse¹ *orn.* [graus] tétras m; lagopède m rouge.

grouse² F [~] ronchonner, grogner (contre *at*, *about*).

grout [graut] **1.** ⚗ coulis m; **2.** jointoyer (avec du mortier liquide).

grove [grouv] bosquet m, bocage m.

grov·el ['grɔvl] *usu. fig.* ramper; '**grov·el·(l)er** *usu. fig.* flagorneur (-euse f) m; '**grov·el·(l)ing 1.** rampant (*usu. fig.*); *fig.* abject; **2.** rampement m; *fig.* aplatissement m.

grow [grou] [*irr.*] *v/i.* croître, pousser; devenir; grandir (*personne*); ~ *in* s'incarner (*ongle*); ~ *into fashion* devenir de mode; ~ *out of use* se perdre; être abandonné; ~ (*up*)*on* s.o. plaire à q. de plus en plus; ~ *up* grandir; *fig.* naître, se répandre; *v/t.* cultiver; faire venir; laisser pousser; '**grow·er** cultivateur (-trice f) m; planteur m.

growl [graul] **1.** grondement m, grognement m; **2.** gronder, grogner.

growl·er ['graulə] *fig.* grognon(ne f) m; *Am. sl.* cruche f à bière.

grown [groun] **1.** *p.p. de* grow; **2.** *adj.* (*a.* ~-*up*) grand, fait; (*a.* ~-*over*) (re)couvert; **growth** [grouθ] croissance f; accroissement m; augmentation f; extension f; poussée f; ✚ tumeur f; *of one's own* ~ indigène; qu'on a cultivé soimême.

grub [grʌb] **1.** larve f; ver m; *péj.* gratte-papier m/inv.; *sl.* mangeaille f; **2.** *v/i.* (*a.* ~ *away*) fouiller (pour trouver qch., *for s.th.*); *sl.* bouffer (= *manger*); *v/t.* ~ *up* essarter; déraciner; (*usu.* ~ *out*) arracher; '**grub·by** malpropre; '**grub·stake** *Am.* avances f/pl.; équipement m (*que fournit un commanditaire à un prospecteur*); fonds m/pl. (*fournis à un entrepreneur*).

grudge [grʌdʒ] **1.** rancune f; *bear s.o. a* ~ garder rancune à q.; avoir une dent contre q.; **2.** accorder à contrecœur; voir d'un mauvais œil; ~ *no pains* ne pas marchander sa peine; '**grudg·er** envieux (-euse f) m; '**grudg·ing·ly** ['~iŋli] à contrecœur, en rechignant.

gru·el ['gruəl] gruau m (d'avoine); *sl. get* (*ou have*) *one's* ~ avaler sa médecine; '**gru·el·(l)ing** éreintant.

grue·some □ ['gru:səm] macabre.

gruff □ [grʌf] bourru, revêche, rude.

grum·ble ['grʌmbl] grommeler; grogner; gronder (*tonnerre*); '**grumbler** *fig.* mécontent(e f) m.

grump·y □ F ['grʌmpi] maussade; grincheux (-euse *f*).

grunt [grʌnt] **1.** grognement *m*; **2.** grogner; **'grunt·er** porc *m*.

guar·an·tee [gærən'tiː] **1.** garant(e *f*) *m*, caution *f*; garanti(e *f*) *m*; *see* **guaranty**; **2.** garantir; se porter caution pour; **guar·an·tor** [ˌ'tɔː] garant(e *f*) *m*; **'guar·an·ty** garantie *f*; caution *f*, gage *m*.

guard [gɑːd] **1.** garde *f* (*a.* ✕); protecteur *m* (*d'une machine*), carter *m* (*d'engrenages*); 🖷 chef *m* de train; ✕ ♀s *pl.* Garde *f*; *be off* ⁓ être pris au dépourvu; ⁓ *of honour* haie *f* d'honneur; ✕ *mount* ⁓ monter la garde; ✕ *relieve* ⁓ relever la garde; **2.** *v/t.* protéger (*a.* ⊕); garder (de *from*, *against*); *v/i.* se garder (de, *against*); **'guard·ed** □ prudent, réservé, mesuré; **'guard·i·an** gardien(ne *f*) *m*; 🕮 tuteur (-trice *f*) *m*; *attr.* tutélaire; ⁓ *of the poor* administrateur (-trice *f*) *m* de l'Assistance publique; **'guard·i·an·ship** garde *f*; tutelle *f*; **'guard·rail** barrière *f* de sécurité; **guards·man** ✕ ['gɑːdzmən] officier *m ou* soldat *m* de la Garde.

gudg·eon ['gʌdʒən] *icht.*, ⊕ goujon *m*; *fig.* benêt *m*.

guer·don *poét.* ['gəːdən] **1.** récompense *f*; **2.** récompenser.

gue(r)·ril·la [gə'rilə] (*souv.* ⁓ *war*) guerre *f* d'embuscades *ou* de partisans.

guess [ges] **1.** conjecture *f*; **2.** *v/t.* deviner; *surt. Am.* croire, supposer; *v/i.* deviner; estimer (qch., *at s.th.*); **'guess·work** conjecture *f*, estime *f*.

guest [gest] invité(e *f*) *m*; pensionnaire *mf*; **'⁓·house** pension *f* de famille; **'⁓·room** chambre *f* d'amis.

guf·faw [gʌ'fɔː] **1.** gros rire *m*; **2.** pouffer de rire.

guid·a·ble ['gaidəbl] dirigeable; **guid·ance** ['gaidəns] conduite *f*; gouverne *f*; direction *f*; orientation *f*.

guide [gaid] **1.** guide *m* (*a.* ⊕); *see* ⁓*book*; *attr.* directeur (-trice *f*); **2.** guider; conduire; diriger; *guiding principle* principe *m* directeur, gouverne *f*; **'⁓·book** guide *m*; ⁓ **dog** chien *m* d'aveugle; **'⁓·lines** *pl.* directives *f/pl.*; **'⁓·post** poteau *m* indicateur; **'⁓·rope** ⚓ guiderope *m*.

gui·don ✕ ['gaidən] guidon *m*.

guild [gild] association *f*; corps *m* (*de métier*); *hist.* corporation *f*; **'Guild'hall** hôtel *m* de ville.

guile [gail] ruse *f*, astuce *f*; **guile-ful** □ ['ˌful] rusé; **'guile·less** □ candide; franc(he *f*); **'guile·less-ness** candeur *f*; franchise *f*.

guil·lo·tine [gilə'tiːn] guillotine *f*; ⊕ presse *f* à rogner.

guilt [gilt], *a.* **'guilt·i·ness** culpabilité *f*; **'guilt·less** □ innocent (de, *of*); *fig.* vierge (de, *of*); **'guilt·y** □ coupable; *plead* ⁓ s'avouer coupable.

guin·ea ['gini] guinée *f* (*21 shillings*); **'⁓·fowl** pintade *f*; **'⁓·pig** cobaye *m*, cochon *m* d'Inde.

guise [gaiz] † costume *m*; forme *f*; apparence *f* (*a. fig.*).

gui·tar ♪ [gi'tɑː] guitare *f*.

gulch *Am.* [gʌltʃ] ravin *m* étroit.

gulf [gʌlf] *géog.* golfe *m*; abysse *m* (*de la mer*); abîme *m*, gouffre *m*.

gull¹ *orn.* [gʌl] mouette *f*, goéland *m*.

gull² [ˌ] **1.** jobard *m*, dupe *f*; **2.** jobarder, duper; amener (*q.*) par ruse (à *inf.*, *into gér.*).

gul·let ['gʌlit] œsophage *m*; F gosier *m*; † ravin *m*.

gul·li·bil·i·ty [gʌli'biliti] crédulité *f*; **gul·li·ble** □ [ˌ'ˌəbl] crédule; facile à duper.

gul·ly ['gʌli] ravine *f*; *ruisseau:* ru *m*; ⊕ caniveau *m*; (*a.* ⁓*hole*) bouche *f* d'égout.

gulp [gʌlp] **1.** coup *m* (de gosier); **2.** avaler (à pleine gorge).

gum¹ [gʌm] *usu.* ⁓s *pl.* gencive *f*.

gum² [ˌ] **1.** gomme *f*; colle *f*; *Am.* gomme *f* à mâcher; ⁓s *pl. Am.* caoutchouc *m/pl.*, bottes *f/pl.* de caoutchouc; **2.** gommer; coller.

gum·boil ['gʌmbɔil] abcès *m* à la gencive, ⊕ parulie *f*.

gum·my ['gʌmi] gommeux (-euse *f*) gluant; chassieux (-euse *f*) (*yeux*).

gump·tion ['gʌmpʃn] jugeotte *f*; sens *m* pratique.

gun [gʌn] **1.** canon *m*; fusil *m* (de chasse); ⊕ injecteur *m* (à graisse); *peint.* pistolet *m*; *surt. Am.* revolver *m*, pistolet *m*; *Am. mot. sl.* accélérateur *m*; F *big* (*ou great*) ⁓ grand personnage *m*; **2.** *Am.* chasser au tir; *fig.* pourchasser; **'⁓·boat** (chaloupe *f*) canonnière *f*; **'⁓·car·riage** ✕ affût *m*; **'⁓·cot·ton** coton *m* azotique; **'⁓·li·cence** *Am.* permis *m* de port d'armes; **'⁓·man** *surt. Am.*

bandit *m*, gangster *m*, terroriste *m*;
'gun·ner ✕, ⚓ canonnier *m*.

gun...: '~**·pow·der** poudre *f* (*à
canon*); '~**·run·ning** contrebande *f*
d'armes; '~**·shot** coup *m* de fusil *ou*
de feu; portée *f* de fusil; '~**·shy** qui
a peur du coup de fusil; '~**·smith**
armurier *m*; *Am. sl.* professeur *m* de
vol à la tire; '~**·stock** fût *m* (*de
fusil*); '~**·tur·ret** tourelle *f*.

gur·gle ['gə:gl] glouglouter.

gush [gʌʃ] **1.** jaillissement *m*; jet *m*;
débordement *m* (sentimental); **2.**
jaillir (de, *from*); bouillonner; *fig.*
sortir à flots; *fig.* faire de la sensiblerie; **'gush·er** *fig.* personne *f*
expansive; puits *m* jaillissant;
'gush·ing, gush·y □ exubérant,
expansif (-ive *f*).

gus·set ['gʌsit] *cost.* soufflet *m*;
gousset *m*.

gust [gʌst] rafale *f*, bourrasque *f*,
coup *m* de vent; bouffée *f* (*de colère*).

gus·ta·to·ry ['gʌstətəri] gustatif
(-ive *f*).

gus·to ['gʌstou] délectation *f*;
entrain *m*.

gus·ty ['gʌsti] à rafales; venteux
(-euse *f*).

gut [gʌt] **1.** boyau *m*, intestin *m*; ♩
corde *f* de boyau; *fig.* passage *m*
étroit; ~s *pl. sl.* cran *m* (= *courage*);
2. vider (*un poisson*); *fig.* résumer;
incendie: ne laisser que les murs de
(*une maison*); piller; **'gut·less** F mou
(molle *f*), lâche, qui manque de cran;
'guts·y F qui a du cran; qui a du
punch.

gut·ter ['gʌtə] **1.** gouttière *f* (*d'un
toit*); *rue*: ruisseau *m*; *chaussee*:
caniveau *m*; **2.** *v/t.* sillonner, raviner; rainer (*une tôle etc.*); *v/i.*
couler (*bougie*); ~ **press** bas-fonds

m/pl. du journalisme; '~**·snipe**
gavroche *m*; gamin(e *f*) *m* des rues.

gut·tur·al *anat., a. gramm.* ['gʌtərəl]
1. □ guttural (-aux *m/pl.*); **2.** gut-
turale *f*.

guy[1] [gai] **1.** F épouvantail *m*; *surt.
Am.* F type *m*, individu *m*; **2.** se
moquer de; travestir.

guy[2] [~] retenue *f*; ⚓ étai *m*,
hauban *m*.

guz·zle ['gʌzl] boire avidement;
v/t. bouffer; *v/i.* goinfrer.

gym *sl.* [dʒim] *abr. de gymnasium, gymnastics.*

gym·kha·na [dʒim'kɑːnə] gymkhana
m.

gym·na·si·um [dʒim'neizjəm] gymnase *m*; **gym·nast** ['dʒimnæst]
gymnaste *m*; **gym'nas·tic 1.** (~ally)
gymnastique; ~ *competition* concours *m* de gymnastique; **2.** ~s *pl.*
gymnastique *f*; éducation *f* physique; *heavy* ~s *pl.* gymnastique *f*
aux agrès; *light* ~s callisthénie *f*.

gyn·ae·col·o·gist ✿ [gaini'kɔlədʒist]
gynécologiste *m*; **gyn·ae'col·o·gy**
gynécologie *f*.

gyp *sl.* [dʒip] *Am.* voler; tromper.

gyp·se·ous ['dʒipsiəs] gypseux (-euse
f).

gyp·sum *min.* ['dʒipsəm] gypse *m*.

gy·rate [dʒaiə'reit] tourn(oy)er;
gy'ra·tion giration *f*, révolution *f*;
gy·ra·to·ry ['dʒaiərətəri] giratoire.

gy·ro·com·pass *phys.* ['gaiəro-
'kʌmpəs] gyrocompas *m*; **gy·ro·
scope** ['gaiərəskoup] gyroscope *m*;
gy·ro·scop·ic sta·bi·liz·er [gaiə-
rəs'kɔpik'steibilaizə] gyrostat *m* (*de
bateau*); toupie *f* gyroscopique.

gyve *poét.* [dʒaiv] **1.**: ~s *pl.* fers
m/pl., chaînes *f/pl.*; **2.** enchaîner,
mettre les fers à.

H

H, h [eitʃ] H *m*, h *m*; *drop one's hs* ne pas aspirer les h.

ha [hɑ:] ha!; ah!

ha·be·as cor·pus ⚖ ['heibjəs-'kɔːpəs] (*a. writ of* ~) habeas corpus *m*.

hab·er·dash·er ['hæbədæʃə] mercier (-ère *f*) *m*; *surt. Am.* chemisier *m*; **'hab·er·dash·er·y** mercerie *f*; *surt. Am.* chemiserie *f*.

ha·bil·i·ments [hə'bilimənts] *pl.* vêtements *m/pl.* de cérémonie.

hab·it ['hæbit] 1. habitude *f*; disposition *f* (*d'esprit*); habit *m* (*de moine*); *be in the* ~ *of* (*gér.*) avoir l'habitude de (*inf.*); *see riding-*~; 2. vêtir; **'hab·it·a·ble** habitable; **hab·i·tat** ♀, *zo.* ['~tæt] habitat *m*; aire *f* d'habitation; **hab·i'ta·tion** habitation *f*; demeure *f*.

ha·bit·u·al □ [hə'bitjuəl] habituel(le *f*); invétéré; **ha'bit·u·ate** [~eit] habituer (à, *to*); **hab·i·tude** ['hæbitjuːd] habitude *f*.

hack¹ [hæk] 1. ⊕ pic *m*, pioche *f*; taillade *f*; *foot.* coup *m* de pied; 2. hacher; couper; *foot.* (*ou v/i.* ~ *at*) donner à (*q.*) un coup de pied sur le tibia; ~*ing cough* toux *f* sèche.

hack² [~] 1. cheval *m* de louage *ou* de selle à toutes fins; *fig.* homme *m* de peine; (*souv.* ~ *writer*) nègre *m*; 2. à la tâche; *fig.* banal (-als *m/pl.*); 3. banaliser.

hack·le ['hækl] 1. ⊕ peigne *m*; *orn.* plume *f* de cou *ou* de dos; 2. (se) taillader; *v/t.* peigner.

hack·ney ['hækni] *see hack²*; ~ *coach* voiture *f* de louage; **'hack·neyed** banal (-als *m/pl.*).

hack·saw ['hæksɔː] scie *f* à métaux.

had [hæd, həd] *prét. et p.p. de have* 1, 2.

had·dock *icht.* ['hædək] aiglefin *m*; *finnan* ~ haddock *m*.

hae·mal ✷ ['hiːml] hémal (-aux *m/pl.*); **haemo...** [hiːmo] hém(o)-.

haem·or·rhage ['hemɔridʒ] hémorragie *f*; **haem·or·rhoids** ['~rɔidz] *pl.* hémorroïdes *f/pl.*

haft [hɑːft] manche *m*, poignée *f*.

hag [hæg] sorcière *f*; *fig. sl.* vieille taupe *f*.

hag·gard □ ['hægəd] hagard; hâve.

hag·gle ['hægl] marchander; chicaner (sur, *over*).

hag·rid·den ['hægridn] tourmenté par les cauchemars.

hail¹ [heil] 1. grêle *f*; 2. *v/impers.* grêler; *v/t. fig.* faire pleuvoir.

hail² [~] 1. *v/t.* saluer; héler; *v/i.:* ~ *from* venir de; être originaire de; 2. appel *m*; ~! salut!; *within* ~ à portée de (la) voix.

hail-fel·low ['heilfelou] très gentil pour *ou* avec tous.

hail·stone ['heilstoun] grêlon *m*; **'hail·storm** abat *m* de grêle.

hair [hɛə] cheveu *m*, -x *m/pl.* (*sur la tête*); poil *m*; *sl. keep your* ~ *on!* calmez-vous!; ~*'s breadth* = **'~-breadth** épaisseur *f* d'un cheveu; *by* (*ou within*) *a* ~ à un cheveu (de), à deux doigts (de); ~ *cream* crème *f* à coiffer; **'~-cut** taille *f* (de cheveux); *have a* ~ se faire couper les cheveux; **'~-do** F coiffure *f*; **'~-dress·er** coiffeur (-euse *f*) *m*; **'~-dry·er** sèche-cheveux *m/inv.*; séchoir *m*; **'~-dye** teinture *f* pour les cheveux; **'haired** aux cheveux ...; à pelage ...; **'hair·i·ness** aspect *m* hirsute.

hair...: **'~-less** sans cheveux, chauve; **'~-line** naissance *f* des cheveux; *écriture:* délié *m*; ~ *crack* fissure *f* fine; **'~-piece** postiche *m*; **'~-pin** épingle *f* à cheveux; ~ *bend* lacet *m*; **'~-rais·ing** horripilant, horrifique; **'~-re·mov·er** dépilatoire *m*; **'~-re·stor·er** régénérateur *m* des cheveux; **'~-split·ting** ergotage *m*; **'~-spray** laque *f* (en aérosol); **'~-style** coiffure *f*; ~ **'styl·ist** coiffeur *m* (-euse *f*); **'hair·y** chevelu, poilu, velu.   [colin *m*.]

hake [heik] *icht.* merluche *f*; F⌡

ha·la·tion *phot.* [hə'leiʃn] halo *m*.

hal·berd ✕ *hist.* ['hælbəd] hallebarde *f*.

hal·cy·on ['hælsiən] **1.** *orn.* alcyon *m*; martin-pêcheur (*pl.* martins-pêcheurs) *m*; **2.** *fig.* calme, serein.
hale [heil] vigoureux (-euse *f*); robuste; ~ *and hearty* frais et gaillard.
half [hɑːf] **1.** demi; *adv.* à moitié; ~ *a crown* une demi-couronne *f*; *a pound and a* ~ une livre et demie; *F not* ~ *and comment!*; *it isn't* ~ *bad* ce n'est pas mauvais du tout; **2.** moitié *f*; ⚔ demi *m*; *see* ~*year*; ⚔ parti *m*; *too clever by* ~ beaucoup trop malin; *by halves* à demi; *go halves* se mettre de moitié (avec q., *with s.o.*), partager; ~-**back** ['~bæk] *foot.* demi(-arrière) *m*; ~-**baked** ['~'beikt] *fig.* inexpérimenté; niais; incomplet (-ète *f*); '~-**bind·ing** demi-reliure *f* à petits coins; '~-**blood** parenté *f* d'un seul côté; '~-'**bound** en demi-reliure à petits coins; '~-'**bred** demi-sang *m*/*inv.*; '~-**breed** métis(se *f*) *m*; '~-**broth·er** demi-frère *m*; '~-**caste** métis(se *f*) *m*; '~-**court line** *tennis:* ligne *f* médiane; '~-'**crown** demi-couronne *f*; '~-'**fare 1.** demi-tarif *m*; **2.** à demi-tarif; '~-'**heart·ed** ☐ tiède; hésitant; '~-'**length** (*a.* ~ *portrait*) *fig.* portrait *m* en buste; '~-'**mast** *(at)* ~ à mimât; en berne *(pavillon)*; '~-'**moon** demi-lune *f*; '~-'**mourn·ing** demi-deuil *m*; ~ *note* ♩ blanche *f*; '~-'**pay** demi-solde *f*; ~**pen·ny** ['heipni] **1.** demi-penny *m*; **2.** à un sou; '~-'**price:** *at* ~ à moitié prix; ~**seas·o·ver** F ['hɑːfsiːz'ouvə] à moitié ivre; '~-'**time** *sp.* mi-temps *f*; '~-**tone proc·ess** ⊕ simili(gravure) *f* (tramée); '~-**truth** demi-vérité *f*; '~-'**way** à mi-chemin; ~ *house* maison *f* à demi-étape; *fig.* compromis *m*; '~-**wit** simple *mf*, faible *mf* d'esprit; '~-'**wit·ted** simple; niais; '~-'**year** semestre *m*.
hal·i·but *icht.* ['hælibət] flétan *m*.
hal·i·to·sis [hæli'təusis] mauvaise haleine *f*.
hall [hɔːl] grande salle *f*; vestibule *m*; hall *m* *(hôtel)*; château *m*; *univ.* maison *f* estudiantine, foyer *m*; réfectoire *m*; *see* guild-~, music-~.
hal·le·lu·jah [hæli'luːjə] alléluia *m*.
hall...: '~-'**mark 1.** contrôle *m*; *fig.* cachet *m*, empreinte *f*; **2.** contrôler; '~-'**stand** porte-parapluies *m*/*inv.*
hal·loo [hə'luː] **1.** holà!; **2.** ohé *m*;

chasse: huée *f*; **3.** *v*/*i.* crier (taïaut); *v*/*t.* encourager.
hal·low ['hælou] sanctifier, consacrer; **Hal·low·mas** ['~mæs] la Toussaint *f*.
hal·lu·ci·na·tion [həluːsi'neiʃn] hallucination *f*, illusion *f*.
halm [hɑːm] *see* haulm.
ha·lo ['heilou] *astr.*, *anat.* halo *m*; auréole *f* (*a. eccl.*, *a. fig.*).
halt [hɔːlt] **1.** halte *f* (*a.* 🚉), arrêt *m*; **2.** faire halte; s'arrêter; *fig.* hésiter, balancer; **3.** boiteux (-euse *f*).
hal·ter ['hɔːltə] *cheval:* licou *m*; corde *f* *(au cou)*.
halve [hɑːv] diviser en deux; **halves** [~z] *pl.* de half.
hal·yard ⚓ ['hæljəd] drisse *f*.
ham [hæm] jambon *m*; *Am. sl.* (*a.* ~ *actor ou fatter)* cabotin *m*; *(souv. radio)* amateur *m*.
ham·burg·er ['hæmbəːgə] hamburger *m*, bifteck *m* haché; viande *f* de bœuf hachée.
ham-fist·ed ['hæmfistid], **ham-hand·ed** ['~hændid] gauche, maladroit.
ham·let ['hæmlit] hameau *m*.
ham·mer ['hæmə] **1.** marteau *m*; *armes à feu:* chien *m*; F ~ *and tongs* tant qu'on peut; **2.** *v*/*t.* marteler, battre au marteau; *bourse:* exécuter *(un agent)*; F critiquer; ~ *out* gironner; F forger; *v*/*i.* ~ *at* heurter à; s'acharner à.
ham·mock ['hæmək] hamac *m*; ~ *chair* transatlantique *m*.
ham·per ['hæmpə] **1.** panier *m*, banne *f*; **2.** embarrasser, gêner; entraver.
ham·string ['hæmstrin] **1.** *anat.* tendon *m* du jarret; **2.** couper le jarret à; *fig.* couper les moyens à.
hand [hænd] **1.** main *f* (*a. zo.*, *a. fig.* = *aide*, *autorité*, *possession*, *protection)*; montre: aiguille *f*; ouvrier (-ère *f*) *m*; ⚓ matelot *m*; côté *m*; *cartes:* joueur (-euse *f*) *m*; *cartes:* jeu *m*; *mesure:* paume *f*; écriture *f*; signature *f*; *typ.* index *m*; *baromètre etc.:* indicateur *m*; ♀ régime *m* *(de fruits)*; *at* ~ sous la main; à portée de la main; tout près; *at first* ~ de première main; *a good (poor)* ~ *at* bon (piètre) joueur de; *fort à* (faible en); *be* ~ *and glove* être d'intelligence (avec, *with)*; être comme les deux doigts de la main;

by ~ à la main; *change* ~*s* changer de propriétaire *ou* de mains; *get out of* ~ s'indiscipliner, devenir impossible; *have a* ~ *in* prendre part à; *in* ~ en main; au poing; à la main; en question; en préparation; *sp.* de retard; ✝ en caisse; en magasin; *lay* ~*s on* faire violence à; s'emparer de; mettre les mains sur; *lend a* ~ aider; donner un coup de main (à); *off* ~ brusque; tout de suite; ~*s off!* n'y touchez pas!; *on* ~ en main; ✝ en magasin; *surt. Am.* tout près; prêt; *on one's* ~*s* à sa charge; *on all* ~*s* de tous les côtés; de toutes parts; *on the one* ~ d'une part; *on the other* ~ d'autre part; par contre; *have one's* ~ *out* avoir perdu l'habitude; *out of* ~ sur-le-champ; indiscipliné; ~ *over fist* main sur main; rapidement; *take a* ~ *at* faire une partie de (*bridge etc.*); *to (one's)* ~ sous la main; ~ *to* ~ corps à corps; *come to* ~ parvenir, arriver; *put one's* ~ *to* entreprendre; *he can turn his* ~ *to anything* c'est un homme à toute main; ~*s up!* haut les mains!; *see high 1;* **2.** passer; ~ *about* faire circuler; ~ *down* descendre (*qch.*); transmettre; ~ *in* remettre; présenter (*une demande*); ~ *out* distribuer; tendre; ~ *over* remettre; céder; '~-**bag** sac *m* à main; '~-**bar·row** brancard *m*, civière *f*; '~-**bell** sonnette *f*; '~-**bill** affiche *f* à la main; ✝ prospectus *m*; '~-**brake** ⊕ frein *m* à main; '~-**cuff** **1.**: ~*s pl.* menottes *f/pl.*; **2.** mettre les menottes à (*q.*); '**hand·ed** à ... mains; aux mains ...; **hand·ful** ['~ful] poignée*f*; F enfant *mf* terrible; '**hand-glass** loupe *f* à main; miroir *m* à main.

hand·i·cap ['hændikæp] **1.** *sp.* handicap *m*; *fig.* désavantage *m*; **2.** *sp.* handicaper; *fig.* gêner; *fig.* désavantager; '**hand·i·capped 1.** handicapé; **2.**: *the (mentally ou physically)* ~ les handicapés (mentaux *ou* physiques); '**hand·i·cap·per** *sp.* handicapeur *m*.

hand·i·craft ['hændikrɑːft] travail *m* manuel; métier *m* manuel; '**hand·i·crafts·man** artisan *m*, ouvrier *m*; '**hand·i·ness** commodité *f*; adresse *f*, dextérité *f*; '**hand·i·work** travail *m* manuel; ouvrage *m* (*a. fig.*).

hand·ker·chief ['hæŋkətʃif] mouchoir *m*; foulard *m* (*pour le cou*).

han·dle ['hændl] **1.** épée, *porte*: poignée *f*; *outil*: manche *m*; *seau, cruche*: anse *f*; *pompe*: balancier *m*; *Am.* F *fly off the* ~ s'emporter; *sl.* sortir de ses gonds; **2.** manier; manœuvrer (*un navire*); traiter; prendre en main; '~-**bar** *cycl.* guidon *m*; *dropped* ~ guidon *m* course.

hand...: '~-'**made pa·per** papier *m* à la cuve; '~-**maid** *fig.* servante *f*; '~-**me-downs** *Am.* F *pl.* costume *m* de confection; décrochez-moi-ça *m/inv.*; '~-**out** *Am.* F aumône *f*; '~-**rail** main *f* courante; garde-fou *m*; '~-**saw** scie *f* à main; égoïne *f*; **hand·sel** ['hænsl] **1.** étrenne *f*; ✝ première vente *f*; arrhes *f/pl.*; **2.** donner des étrennes à; ✝ donner des arrhes à; inaugurer; '**hand·shake** poignée *f* de main; **hand·some** □ ['hænsəm] beau (bel *devant une voyelle ou un h muet*); belle *f*; beaux *m/pl.*); élégant; noble; riche.

hand...: '~-**spike** ⊕ levier *m* de manœuvre; '~-**work** travail *m* à la main; '~-**writ·ing** écriture *f*; '**hand·y** □ adroit; habile; commode (*chose*); maniable; ~**man** homme *m* à tout faire; factotum *m*, bricoleur *m*; F débrouillard *m*.

hang [hæŋ] **1.** [*irr.*] *v/t.* (*sus*)pendre (à *from*, *on*); tapisser (de, *with*); accrocher (à *from*, *on*); coller (*un papier à tapisser*); (*usu. prét. et p.p.* ~*ed*) pendre; F *I'll be* ~*ed if* ... que le diable m'emporte si ...; F ~ *it!* zut alors!; F ~ *fire* traîner; ~ *out* *vt/i.* pendre au dehors; ~ *up* accrocher, pendre; *téléph.* raccrocher (*le récepteur*); *fig.* ajourner; *v/i.* pendre, être suspendu (à, *on*); *fig.* planer (sur, *over*); ~ *about* flâner; rôder; ~ *back* rester en arrière; *fig.* hésiter; ~ *on* s'accrocher, se cramponner (à, *to*); *fig.* tenir bon; *téléph.* ~ *up* raccrocher; **2.** pente *f*; *cost.* ajustement *m*; F façon *f*; F *get the* ~ *of* comprendre, saisir le truc de (*qch.*); *sl. I don't care a* ~ je m'en moque pas mal.

hang·ar ['hæŋə] hangar *m*.

hang-dog ['hæŋdɔg] **1.** F gibier *m* de potence; **2.** patibulaire (*mine*).

hang·er ['hæŋə] *personne*: tendeur *m*; crochet *m*; porte-vêtements *m/inv.*; ⊕ suspenseur *m*; *Am.*

pancarte *f*; **~-on** [ˈ~rˈɔn], *pl.* ˈ~s-ˈon *fig.* parasite *m*; dépendant *m*.

hang-glid·ing [ˈhæŋglaidiŋ] vol *m* libre.

hang·ing [ˈhæŋiŋ] **1.** suspendu; tombant; *peint.* **~** *committee* jury *m* d'admission (des tableaux); **2.**: **~s** *pl.* tenture *f*, tapisserie *f*; rideaux *m/pl.*

hang·man [ˈhæŋmən] bourreau *m*.

hang·nail ⚕ [ˈhæŋneil] envie *f*.

hang·out *Am. sl.* [ˈhæŋˈaut] repaire *m*, nid *m* (*de gangsters etc.*).

hang·over *sl.* [ˈhæŋouvə] gueule *f* de bois.

hang·up *sl.* [ˈhæŋʌp] problème *m*; complexe *m*.   [neau *m*.]

hank [hæŋk] écheveau *m*; ⚓ an-)

han·ker [ˈhæŋkə]: **~** *after* soupirer après, désirer vivement; être assoiffé de; **ˈhan·ker·ing** vif désir *m*, soif *f*.

Han·o·ve·ri·an [hæno'viəriən] **1.** hanovrien(ne *f*); **2.** Hanovrien(ne *f*) *m*.

Han·sard [ˈhænsəd] compte *m* rendu officiel des débats parlementaires.

han·som [ˈhænsəm], (*a.* **~-cab**) cab *m*; hansom *m*.

hap † [hæp] hasard *m* (malencontreux); destin *m*; **ˈhapˈhaz·ard 1.** hasard *m*; *at* **~** au petit bonheur; **2.** fortuit; **~** *chaos* tohu-bohu *m*; **ˈhap·less** □ infortuné, malheureux (-euse *f*).

ha'p'orth F [ˈheipəθ] (valeur *f* d')un sou *m*; *a* **~** *of* ... ... pour un sou.

hap·pen [ˈhæpən] arriver, se passer; *he* **~***ed to be at home* il se trouvait chez lui; **~** (*up*)*on* tomber sur; rencontrer par hasard; *Am.* F **~,** **~** *in*(*to*) entrer en passant; **ˈhap·pen·ing** événement *m*.

hap·pi·ness [ˈhæpinis] bonheur *m*; félicité *f* (*a. d'expression*).

hap·py □ [ˈhæpi] *usu.* heureux (-euse *f*); content; joyeux (-euse *f*); F un peu parti *ou* gris; **ˈ~-go-luck·y** F insouciant.

ha·rangue [həˈræŋ] **1.** harangue *f*; **2.** *v/t.* haranguer; *v/i.* prononcer une harangue.

har·ass [ˈhærəs] harceler; tourmenter (de, *with*); tracasser; accabler (de dettes, *with debt*); **ˈharass·ment** harcèlement *m*; tracassement *m*.

har·bin·ger [ˈhɑːbindʒə] **1.** *fig.* avant-coureur *m*; **2.** annoncer.

har·bo(u)r [ˈhɑːbə] **1.** port *m*; *fig.* asile *m*; **2.** *v/t.* héberger; receler (*un criminel*); entretenir (*un soupçon*); garder (*une rancune etc.*); *v/i.* se réfugier; **~** asile *m*; ⚓ mouillage *m*.

hard [hɑːd] **1.** *adj. usu.* dur; sévère; fort (*gelée*); rigoureux (-euse *f*) (*temps*); pénible; cruel(le *f*); rude; difficile; *surt. Am.* incorrigible; *surt. Am.* riche (en alcool); ferme (*rendez-vous*); **~** *cash* espèces *f/pl.* sonnantes; **~** *coal* anthracite *m*; **~** *core* noyau *m* dur; *tennis:* **~** *courts pl.* terrains *m/pl.* de tennis; **~** *currency* devises *f/pl.* fortes; **~** *drink* (*ou liquor*) alcool *m* fort; *the* **~** *facts* les faits brutaux; **~** *hat* casque *m*; *pol.* **~** the ligne *f* dure; F **~** *luck* déveine *f*, malchance *f*; **~** *sell* promotion *f* de vente agressive; *mot.* **~** *shoulder* accotement *m* stabilisé; **~** *of hearing* dur d'oreille; **~** *to deal with* peu commode; intraitable; *be* **~** (*up*)*on s.o.* être sévère envers q.; traiter q. sévèrement; *give s.o. a* **~** *time* donner du mal à q.; faire passer un mauvais quart d'heure à q.; faire la vie dure à q.; **2.** *adv.* fort; dur; durement; avec peine; **~** *by* tout près; **~** *up* sans moyens; dans la gêne; à court (de, *for*); *be* **~** *put to it* avoir beaucoup de mal (à to); *ride* **~** chevaucher à toute vitesse; **3.** F travaux *m/pl.* forcés; **~s** *pl.* gêne *f*; **ˈ~-ˈbit·ten** F tenace; dur à cuire; **ˈ~-ˈboiled** dur (*œuf*); tenace; *surt. Am.* expérimenté, dur à cuire; **ˈhard·en** (se) durcir; (s')endurcir; rendre *ou* devenir dur; *v/i.* ↑, *bourse:* se raffermir; *v/t.* ⊕ tremper (*l'acier*); **ˈhard·en·ing** durcissement *m*.

hard...: **ˈ~-ˈfea·tured** aux traits durs *ou* sévères; **ˈ~-ˈfist·ed** dur à la détente; **ˈ~-ˈhead·ed** pratique; positif (-ive *f*); **ˈ~-ˈheart·ed** □ au cœur dur; **har·di·hood** [ˈ~ihud] hardiesse *f*; **ˈhar·di·ness** vigueur *f*, robustesse *f*; **ˈhard·lin·er** partisan *m* d'une ligne dure; **ˈhard-ˈluck·stor·y** F récit *m* de misères; **ˈhard·ly** durement; avec difficulté; à peine; ne ... guère; **ˈhard·ˈmouthed** dur de bouche; **ˈhard·ness** dureté *f*, difficulté *f* (*a. fig.*); rudesse *f*; *temps:* rigueur *f*; *acier:* trempe *f*.

hard...: **ˈ~-ˈpan** *Am.* sol *m* résistant;

'~-'set fort gêné; affamé; durci; '~·shell à carapace dure; à coque dure; *fig.* dur à cuire; 'hard·ship privation *f*; gêne *f*; épreuve *f*, tribulation *f*; 'hard·ware quincaillerie *f*; *ordinateur*: hardware *m*, matériel *m*; 'har·dy □ robuste, endurci; hardi; ⚱ de pleine terre.

hare [heə] lièvre *m*; '~·bell jacinthe *f* des prés; clochette *f*; '~-brained étourdi, écervelé; '~·lip *anat.* bec-de-lièvre (*pl.* becs-de-lièvre) *m*.

ha·rem ['heərem] harem *m*.

har·i·cot ['hærikou] *cuis.* haricot *m* (*de mouton*); ⚱ (*a.* ~ bean) haricot *m*.

hark [ha:k] (to) écouter; prêter l'oreille (à); ~! écoutez!; ~ back *chasse*: prendre le contre-pied; *fig.* en revenir (à, sur to).

har·lot ['ha:lət] prostituée *f*; 'har·lot·ry prostitution *f*.

harm [ha:m] 1. mal *m*; tort *m*; danger *m*; 2. faire du mal *ou* tort à; nuire à; harm·ful □ ['~ful] nuisible; 'harm·less □ inoffensif (-ive *f*); innocent.

har·mon·ic [ha:'mɔnik] (~ally) harmonique; har'mon·i·ca [~ikə] harmonica *m*; har·mo·ni·ous □ [ha:'mounjəs] harmonieux (-euse *f*) (*a. fig.*); har·mo·nize ['ha:mənaiz] *v/t.* harmoniser (*a.* ♪); faire accorder; *v/i.* s'harmoniser; s'assortir; 'har·mo·ny harmonie *f*.

har·ness ['ha:nis] 1. harnais *m*; attelage *m*; die in ~ mourir à la besogne; 2. harnacher; atteler; *fig.* aménager; '~-mak·er sellier *m*, bourrelier *m*.

harp ♪ [ha:p] 1. harpe *f*; 2. jouer de la harpe; ~ (up)on rabâcher (*qch.*); be always ~ing on the same string réciter toujours la même litanie; 'harp·er, 'harp·ist harpiste *mf*.

har·poon [ha:'pu:n] 1. harpon *m*; 2. harponner.

har·py ['ha:pi] *myth.* harpie *f* (*a. fig.* = *vieille mégère*); *fig.* personne *f* rapace.

har·ri·dan ['hæridən] vieille mégère *f*.

har·ri·er ['hæriə] *chasse*: braque *m*; *sp.* coureur *m*.

har·row 🖊 ['hærou] 1. herse *f*; 2. herser; *fig.* ravager, piller.

har·ry ['hæri] ravager, piller, mettre à sac; *fig.* harceler, tourmenter.

harsh □ [ha:ʃ] rude; âpre (*goût*); rauque; discordant (*son*); rigoureux (-euse *f*); dur; 'harsh·ness rudesse *f*; âpreté *f*; rigueur *f*; sévérité *f*.

hart *zo.* [ha:t] cerf *m*.

har·um-scar·um F ['heərəm'skeərəm] 1. étourdi, écervelé (*a. su./mf*); 2. étourneau *m*; hurluberlu *m*.

har·vest ['ha:vist] 1. moisson *f* (*a. fig.*); récolte *f*; ~ festival actions *f/pl.* de grâces pour la récolte; 2. *v/t.* moissonner; récolter; *v/i.* rentrer la moisson; 'har·vest·er moissonneur (-euse *f*, *a. machine*) *m*; har·vest-home ['~'houm] fête *f* de la moisson.

has [hæz, həz] (*il, elle*) a; '~-been F vieux ramollot *m*; homme *m* etc. fini.

hash[1] [hæʃ] 1. hachis *m*; *Am.* F mangeaille *f*, boulot *m*; *fig.* gâchis *m*; *fig.* réchauffé *m*; F make a ~ of faire un joli gâchis de; 2. hacher (*de la viande*).

hash[2] *sl.* [~] hachich *m*, hash *m*.

hash·ish ['hæʃi:ʃ] hachich *m*.

hasp [ha:sp] 1. moraillon *m*; loquet *m*; fermoir *m*; 2. cadenasser.

has·sle F ['hæsl] chamaillerie *f*; affaire *f*, histoire *f*.   [*eccl.* coussin *m*.)

has·sock ['hæsək] touffe *f* d'herbe;)

hast † [hæst] (*tu*) as.

haste [heist] hâte *f*; diligence *f*; make ~ se dépêcher, se hâter; more ~ less speed, make ~ slowly hâtez-vous lentement; has·ten ['heisn] (se) hâter, (se) presser; *v/t.* avancer (*qch.*); 'hast·i·ness ['heistinis] précipitation *f*, hâte *f*; emportement *m* (*de colère* etc.); 'hast·y □ précipité; fait à la hâte; irré-fléchi; emporté; rapide.

hat [hæt] chapeau *m*; sl. my ~! pigez-moi ça!; F hang up one's ~ with s.o. s'introniser chez q.; talk through one's ~ extravaguer; exagérer.

hatch[1] [hætʃ] 1. *poussins*: couvée *f*; demi-porte *f*; ♻, ⚓ panneau *m*, écoutille *f*; ⚓ serving ~ passe-plats *m*; under ~es dans la cale; *fig.* mort et enterré; 2. (faire) éclore; *v/t. fig.* tramer, ourdir.

hatch[2] [~] hach(ur)er.

hatch·back *mot.* ['hætʃbæk] (voiture *f* à) hayon *m* arrière.

hat·check girl *Am.* ['hætʃek'gə:l] dame *f* du vestiaire.

hatch·et ['hætʃit] hachette *f; bury the ~* enterrer la hache de guerre; '**~-face** visage *m* en lame de couteau.

hatch·way ⚓ ['hætʃwei] écoutille *f.*

hate [heit] **1.** *poét.* haine *f* (de, contre *to[wards]*); **2.** détester, haïr; **hate·ful** □ ['~ful] odieux (-euse *f*), détestable; '**hat·er** haïsseur (-euse *f*); **ha·tred** ['heitrid] haine *f* (de, contre *of*).

hat·ter ['hætə] chapelier (-ère *f*) *m.*

haugh·ti·ness ['hɔːtinis] arrogance *f*, morgue *f*; '**haugh·ty** □ arrogant, hautain.

haul [hɔːl] **1.** amenée *f*; effort *m; pêche:* coup *m* de filet; prise *f; Am.* trajet *m; a. fig. long ~* long voyage *m*, longue route *f*; **2.** *v/t.* tirer (sur, *at*); traîner; ⚓ haler sur; transporter par camion(s); ✗ hercher; ⚓ repiquer dans (*le vent*); *v/i.* haler (*vent*); '**haul·age** traction *f*; (frais *m/pl.* de) roulage *m*, (frais *m/pl.* de) transport *m*; ✗ herchage *m; ~ contractor* entrepreneur *m* de transports.

haulm [hɔːm] fane *f* (*de légume*); *coll.* chaume *m.*

haunch [hɔːnʃ] hanche *f; cuis.* cuissot *m*, quartier *m*; ⌂ voûte: rein *m.*

haunt [hɔːnt] **1.** lieu *m* fréquenté; repaire *m*; **2.** fréquenter; hanter (*a. revenants*); *fig.* obséder, troubler; *the house is ~ed* il y a des revenants dans la maison; *~ed house* maison *f* hantée; '**haunt·er** *fig.* habitué(e *f*) *m.*

haut·boy ♪ ['ouboi] hautbois *m.*

Ha·van·a [hə'vænə] (*ou ~ cigar*) havane *m.*

have [hæv; həv] **1.** [*irr.*] *v/t.* avoir, posséder; tenir; prendre (*un bain, un repas*); faire (*une promenade etc.*); obtenir; affirmer; F rouler; *~ to* (*inf.*) être obligé de (*inf.*); *I ~ my hair cut* je me fais couper les cheveux; *he had his leg broken* il s'est cassé la jambe; *I would ~ you know that ... sachez que ...*; *he will ~ it that ...* il soutient que ...; *I had as well* (*inf.*) j'aurais pu aussi bien (*inf.*); *I had better* (*best*) (*inf.*) je ferai(s) mieux de (*inf.*); *I had rather* (*inf.*) j'aime(rais) mieux (*inf.*); *let s.o. ~ s.th.* céder qch. à q.; *~ about one* avoir sur soi; *~ on* porter; *~ it out with* s'expliquer avec; F

~ s.o. up citer q. en justice (pour, *for*); *v/i. ~ at him!* à l'attaque; **2.** [*irr.*] *v/aux.* avoir; *qqfois* être; *~ come* être venu; **3.** riche *m.*

ha·ven ['heivn] havre *m*, port *m; fig.* asile *m*, abri *m.*

have-not ['hævnɔt] pauvre *m.*

haven't ['hævnt] = *have not.*

hav·er·sack ['hævəsæk] ✗ musette *f; touriste etc.:* havresac *m.*

hav·ing ['hæviŋ] (*souv. ~s pl.*) possession *f; pl. a.* biens *m/pl.*

hav·oc ['hævək] dévastation *f*, dégâts *m/pl.*, ravage *m; make ~ of, play ~ with* (*ou among*) faire de grands dégâts dans; massacrer.

haw[1] ♀ [hɔː] cenelle *f.*

haw[2] [~] **1.** toussoter, bredouiller; **2.** hem *m* (*a. int.*).

haw-haw ['hɔː'hɔː] rire bruyamment.

hawk[1] [hɔːk] **1.** *orn.* faucon *m; fig.* vautour *m; attr. fig.* d'aigle (*yeux*); **2.** chasser au faucon; *~ at* fondre sur.

hawk[2] [~] graillonner.

hawk[3] [~] colporter, cameloter; **hawk·er** ['hɔːkə] colporteur *m*; marchand(e *f*) *m* ambulant(e *f*).

hawk·ing ['hɔːkiŋ] chasse *f* au faucon.

hawse ⚓ [hɔːz] (*a. ~-hole*) écubier *m.*

haw·ser ⚓ ['hɔːzə] (h)aussière *f*; amarre *f.*

haw·thorn ♀ ['hɔːθɔːn] aubépine *f.*

hay [hei] **1.** foin *m; ~ fever* rhume *m* des foins; *make ~ of* faire un gâchis de; démolir; **2.** faire les foins; '**~-box** (*ou ~ cooker*) marmite *f* norvégienne; '**~-cock** meulon *m ou* meule *f* de foin; '**~-fe·ver** rhume *m* des foins; '**~-loft** grenier *m* à foin; '**~-mak·er** *sl.* coup *m* de poing balancé; '**~-mak·ing** fenaison *f*; '**~-rick** *see ~cock*; '**~-seed** graine *f* de foin; *fig. Am.* paysan *m*; '**~-stack** *see ~cock*; '**~-wire** *Am. sl.:* *go ~* ne tourner plus rond; avorter (*projet*).

haz·ard ['hæzəd] **1.** hasard *m*; risque *m; golf:* accident *m* de terrain; *tennis:* trou *m* gagnant; jeu *m* de hasard; *run a ~* courir un risque; **2.** hasarder; risquer; '**haz·ard·ous** □ risqué; hasardeux (-euse *f*). [obscurité *f.*]

haze[1] [heiz] brume *f* légère; *fig.*/

haze[2] [~] ⚓ harasser (*q.*) de corvées; *Am.* brimer.

ha·zel ['heizl] **1.** ♀ noisetier *m*; **2.** couleur noisette; '**~-nut** noisette *f*.

ha·zy □ ['heizi] brumeux (-euse *f*), embrumé; estompé (*contour etc.*); *fig.* vague, nébuleux (-euse *f*).

H-bomb ['eitʃbɔm] bombe *f* H.

he [hi:] **1.** il, *accentué:* lui; ~ (who) celui qui; **2.** *attr.* mâle.

head [hed] **1.** *anat.*, *cuis.*, *sp.*, *arbre*, *chasse*, *cortège*, *fleur*, *furoncle*, *humérus*, *intelligence*, *légume*, *liste*, *sculpture*, *violon*, *volcan*, *etc.*: tête *f*; *chasse*: bois *m*; ⚓ *voile*: envergure *f*; *torpille*: cône *m*; nez *m*, avant *m*, *navire*: cap *m*; ⚔, *mine*: carreau *m*; *puits de mine*: gueule *f*; *mot.* capote *f*; ⊕ *eau*: charge *f*, *vapeur*: volant *m*; ⊕ culasse *f*; *asperge*: pointe *f*; *céleri*: pied *m*; *blé*: épi *m*; *chou*: pomme *f*; *escalier*, *page*: haut *m*; *lit*: chevet *m*; *table*: haut bout *m*; *bière*: mousse *f*; *rivière*: source *f*; *tambour*: peau *f*; *géog.* cap *m*; *personne*: chef *m*; ✝, *école*: directeur (-trice *f*) *m*; patron(ne *f*) *m*; *fig.* cervelle *f*, esprit *m*, entendement *m*, mémoire *f*; *fig.* crise *f*; *fig.* point *m*, rubrique *f*; ~ restraint mot. appui-tête *m* (*pl.* appuis-tête); ~ *and shoulders above the rest* dépassant les autres de la (*a. fig.*); *bring to a* ~ faire aboutir (*a. fig.*); *come to a* ~ aboutir (*abcès*); mûrir; *gather* ~ monter en pression; augmenter; prendre de l'importance; *get it into one's* ~ *that* se mettre dans la *ou* en tête que; ~(s) *or tail(s)?* pile ou face?; ~ *over heels* à la renverse; *over* ~ *and ears* surchargé, débordé; *make* ~ *against* faire tête à; *I can't make* ~ *or tail of it* je n'y comprends rien, je m'y perds; *take the* ~ prendre la tête; **2.** premier (-ère *f*); principal (-aux *m/pl.*); ... en chef; ~ *office* bureau *m ou* siège *m* central; ~ *start sp.* avance *f*; ~ *waiter* maître *m* d'hôtel; **3.** *v/t.* mener, être en tête de; être à la tête de; conduire; mettre une tête à; mettre *ou* porter en tête (de); *foot.* jouer de la tête; *be* ~*ed* se diriger (vers, for); ~ *off* intercepter; *v/i.* ⚓ avoir le cap (sur, for); *Am.* prendre sa source (à, at); *fig.* ~ *for* se diriger vers; '**head·ache** mal *m ou* maux *m/pl.* de tête; '**head·ach·y** sujet(te *f*) aux maux de tête, migraineux (-euse *f*); '**head-dress** coiffure *f*; garniture *f* de tête; '**head·ed** à

... tête(s); aux cheveux; '**head·er** ⚓ boutisse *f*; F plongeon *m*; *foot.* coup *m* de tête; '**head-gear** garniture *f* de tête; coiffure *f*; chapeau *m*; '**head-hunt·er** chasseur *m* de têtes; '**head-i·ness** emportement *m*, impétuosité *f*; *vin*: qualité *f* capiteuse; '**head·ing** entête *m*; rubrique *f*; manchette *f*; titre *m*; ⚔ (galerie *f* d')avancement *m*; *sp.* (jeu *m* de) tête *f*; '**head·land** cap *m*, promontoire *m*; '**head·less** sans tête; *fig.* sans chef.

head...: '**~light** 🔦 feu *m* d'avant; *mot.* phare *m*; '**~-line** titre *m*; manchette *f*; *typ.* titre *m* courant, entête *m*; F *he hits the* ~*s* il est en vedette; il défraye la chronique; '**~-long** *adj.* précipité; impétueux (-euse *f*); *adv.* la tête la première; '**~-man** chef *m*; '**~-mas·ter** directeur *m*; *lycée*: proviseur *m*; '**~-mis·tress** directrice *f*; '**~-most** au premier rang; '**~-on** de front; frontal (-aux *m/pl.*); '**~-phone** *radio*: écouteur *m*; casque *m*; '**~-piece** casque *m* (*a. radio*); F tête *f*; *typ.* fleuron *m* de tête; en-tête *m*; '**~-quar·ters** *pl.* ⚔ quartier *m* général; ✝ *etc.* siège *m* (social); '**~-rest** appui-tête *m* (*pl.* appuis-tête); '**~-set** *radio*: casque *m*; '**head·ship** première place *f*; direction *f*; '**head-shrink·er** F psy(chiatre) *m*; '**heads·man** bourreau *m*; ⚓ patron *m*.

head...: '**~-strong** entêté; obstiné; '**~-wa·ters** *pl.* cours *m* supérieur d'une rivière; '**~-way** progrès *m*; *make* ~ avancer, faire des progrès; '**~-wind** vent *m* contraire; '**~-work** travail *m* intellectuel; *foot.* jeu *m* de tête; '**head·y** □ capiteux (-euse *f*) (*vin etc.*); emporté (*personne*).

heal [hi:l] guérir (de, of); ~ *up* (se) guérir, se cicatriser; '**~-all** panacée *f*; '**heal·ing 1.** □ curatif (-ive *f*); cicatrisant; *fig.* calmant; **2.** guérison *f*; cicatrisation *f*.

health [helθ] santé *f* (*a. toast*); *Board of* ♀ Ministère *m* de la santé publique; ~ *certificate* certificat *m* médical; ~ *food(s pl.)* aliments *m/pl.* naturels; ~ *food shop ou store* magasin *m* diététique; ~ *hazard* risque *m* pour la santé; ~ *service* (Service *m* de Santé de la) Sécurité *f* Sociale; '**health·ful** □ ['~ful] salubre; salutaire; '**health-i·ness** salubrité *f*; '**health-re·sort** station *f* estivale *ou* thermale;

'**health·y** □ en bonne santé; *see* healthful.

heap [hi:p] **1.** tas *m* (*a. fig.*), monceau *m*; F ⁓s *pl.* beaucoup (de, of); *sl.* F *struck all of a* ⁓ stupéfait; **2.** (*a.* ⁓ *up*) entasser, mettre en tas; accabler (de, with); ⁓*ed spoon* cuiller *f* à dos d'âne.

hear [hiə] [*irr.*] entendre; écouter; recevoir des nouvelles (de, from); apprendre; faire répéter (*une leçon etc.*); ⁓ *of* entendre parler de; ⁓ *that* entendre dire que; **heard** [hə:d] *prét. et p.p. de hear*; **hear·er** ['hiərə] auditeur (-trice *f*) *m*; '**hear·ing** *sens*: ouïe *f*; audition *f* (*a.* ♫); ♪♪ audience *f*; ⁓ *aid* appareil *m* acoustique, audiophone *m*; **hearken** ['hɑ:kən] écouter (qch., *to s.th.*); **hear·say** ['hiəsei] ouï-dire *m/inv.*

hearse [hə:s] corbillard *m*.

heart [hɑ:t] cœur *m* (*fig. = courage,* *enthousiasme, etc.*); fond *f/pl.* cartes: ⁓s *pl.* cœur *m*; (*a. dear* ⁓) *see* sweetheart; ⁓ *and soul* corps et âme, de tout son cœur; *I have a matter at* ⁓ j'ai qch. à cœur; *by* ⁓ par cœur; *in good* ⁓ bien entretenu (*sol*); en train (*personne*); *in his* ⁓ (*of* ⁓s) au plus profond de son cœur; *out of* ⁓ effrité (*sol*); découragé (*personne*); *with all my* ⁓ de tout mon cœur; *lose* ⁓ perdre courage; *take* ⁓ prendre courage; *take* (*ou lay*) *to* ⁓ prendre (*qch.*) à cœur; '⁓**ache** chagrin *m*; '⁓**beat** battement *m* du cœur; '⁓**break** déchirement *m* de cœur; '⁓**break·ing** □ navrant; '⁓**broken** le cœur brisé, navré; '⁓**burn** ♫ aigreurs *f/pl.*; '⁓**burn·ing** rancune *f*; jalousie *f*; '⁓**com·plaint,** '⁓**dis·ease** maladie *f* de cœur; ...⁓ '**heart·ed** au cœur ...; '**heart·en** *v/t.* encourager; *v/i.* reprendre courage; '**heart-fail·ure** arrêt *m* du cœur; '**heart·felt** sincère; profond.

hearth [hɑ:θ] foyer *m*, âtre *m*; '⁓**rug** tapis *m* de foyer; '⁓**stone** foyer *m*; pierre *f* de la cheminée.

heart·i·ness ['hɑ:tinis] cordialité *f*; chaleur *f*; vigueur *f*; '**heart·less** □ insensible; cruel(le *f*); '**heartrend·ing** navrant.

heart...: '⁓**sick** *fig.* découragé; désolé; '⁓**strings** *pl. fig.* sensibilité *f*, cœur *m*; '⁓**throb** F idole *f*; ⁓**trans·plant** ♫ greffe *f* du cœur; ⁓**troub·le** troubles *m/pl.* cardiaques;

have ⁓ *a.* être cardiaque, souffrir du cœur; '⁓**whole** au cœur libre; *fig.* sincère; *fig.* aucunement ébranlé; '**heart·y 1.** □ cordial (-aux *m/pl.*); sincère; vigoureux (-euse *f*), robuste; gaillard; ⁓ *eater* gros mangeur *m*, belle fourchette *f*; **2.** ♫ brave *m*; *univ.* sportif *m*.

heat [hi:t] **1.** chaleur *f*; *phys. a.* calorique *m*; ardeur *f*; *fig.* colère *f*; *animal:* rut *m*; *sp.* épreuve *f*, manche *f*; *dead* ⁓ manche *f* nulle; course *f* à égalité; **2.** (s')échauffer (*a. fig.*); *v/t.* chauffer (*de l'eau etc.*); '**heat·ed** □ chauffé; chaud (*a. fig.*); '**heat·er** ⊕ bouilleur *m*; four *m*; radiateur *m*; *Am. sl.* revolver *m*.

heath [hi:θ] bruyère *f*, brande *f* (*a.* ♀); '⁓**cock** petit coq *m* de bruyère.

hea·then ['hi:ðən] païen(ne *f*) (*a.* *su./mf*); '**hea·then·dom** paganisme *m*; '**hea·then·ish** □ *usu. fig.* barbare, grossier (-ère *f*); '**hea·then·ism** paganisme *m*; barbarie *f*.

heath·er ['heðə] bruyère *f*, brande *f*; '⁓**bell** ♀ cloche *f* de bruyère.

heat·ing ['hi:tin] chauffage *m*; *attr.* de chaleur; ⁓ *battery* batterie *f* de four *etc.*; ⁓ *cushion*, ⁓ *pad* coussin *m* chauffant *ou* électrique.

heat...: ⁓ **light·ning** *Am.* éclairs *m/pl.* de chaleur; '⁓**re·sist·ant** résistant à la chaleur; '⁓**stroke** ♫ coup *m* de chaleur; ⁓ **treat·ment** ♫ thermothérapie *f*; '⁓**val·ue** pouvoir *m* calorifique; '⁓**wave** *phys.* onde *f* calorifique; *météor.* vague *f* de chaleur.

heave [hi:v] **1.** soulèvement *m*; effort *m*; palpitation *f* (*du sein*); ♫ houle *f*; **2.** [*irr.*] *v/t.* (sou)lever; lancer, jeter; pousser (*un soupir*); ⁓ *the anchor* déraper; ♫ ⁓ *down* caréner; ♫ ⁓ *out* déferler; *v/i.* se soulever (*a. vagues, poitrine*); haleter; s'agiter (*mer*); palpiter (*sein*); avoir des haut-le-cœur; ⁓ *for breath* panteler; ♫ ⁓ *at haler sur*; ♫ ⁓ *in sight* paraître; ♫ ⁓ *to* se mettre à la cape.

heav·en ['hevn] ciel *m*, cieux *m/pl.*; ⁓s *pl.* ciel *m*; ⁓! juste ciel!; '**heaven·ly** céleste; divin; **heav·enward(s)** ['⁓wəd(z)] vers le ciel.

heav·er ['hi:və] (dé)chargeur *m*; ⊕ levier *m* de manœuvre.

heav·i·ness ['hevinis] pesanteur *f*, lourdeur *f*; *fig.* tristesse *f*, abattement *m*; *mot.* mauvais état *m* (*des routes*).

heav·y □ ['hevi] *usu.* lourd; pesant; gros(se *f*) (*cœur*, *pluie*, *rhume*, *etc.*); triste; violent; pénible; profond; gras(se *f*) (*sol*); ✗ lourd, de gros calibre, gros(se *f*); ⚡ ~ current courant *m* fort; '~-**du·ty** ⊕ à grande puissance; très résistant; '~-**hand·ed** qui a la main lourde; gauche, maladroit; '~-**heart·ed** qui a le cœur gros, accablé; '~-**lad·en** lourdement chargé; *fig.* chargé de soucis; '~-**weight** *box.* poids *m* lourd.

heb·dom·a·dal □ [heb'dɔmədl], **heb·dom·a·da·ry** hebdomadaire.

He·bra·ic [hi'breiik] (~*ally*) hébraïque.

He·brew ['hi:bru:] 1. hébraïque, is-raélite; 2. *ling.* hébreu *m*; *bibl.* Hébreu(e *f*) *m*; Israélite *mf*.

hec·a·tomb ['hekətoum] hécatombe *f*.

heck·le ['hekl] *see* hackle; *pol.* inter-rompre par des questions embarras-santes.

hec·tic 🖉 ['hektik] 1. hectique; *fig.* fiévreux (-euse *f*); 2. rougeur *f* (*usu.* ~ *fever*) fièvre *f* hectique.

hec·tor ['hektə] *v/t.* rudoyer, dra-gonner; *v/i.* prendre un ton autori-taire; faire de l'esbroufe.

hedge [hedʒ] 1. haie *f*; *attr. souv.* ignorant, interlope (*p.ex.* ~-*priest*); 2. *v/t.* entourer d'une haie; enfer-mer; ~ *off* séparer par une haie; ~ *up* clore d'une haie; ~ *a bet* parier pour et contre; *v/i.* éviter de se compro-mettre; '~-**bill** serpe *f*; '~-**hog** *zo.* hérisson *m*; *Am.* porc-épic *m*; '~-**hop** *sl.* 🖅 voler en rase-mottes; '~-**row** bordure *f* de haies; haie *f*; '~-'**spar·row** *orn.* fauvette *f*.

heed [hi:d] 1. attention *f* (à, *to*), soin *m*; compte *m* (de, *to*); *take* ~ *of* tenir compte de, prendre garde à; *take no* ~ *of* ne tenir aucun compte de; 2. faire attention à, observer; tenir compte de; **heed·ful** □ ['~ful] at-tentif (-ive *f*) (à, *of*); '**heed·less** □ insouciant.

hee-haw ['hi:'hɔ:] 1. hi-han *m*; *fig.* ricanement *m*; 2. braire; *fig.* ri-caner.

heel[1] ⚓ [hi:l] *v/i.* se coucher sur le flanc; avoir de la bande.

heel[2] [~] 1. talon *m*; *surt. Am. sl.* gouape *f*; *be at* (*on*) *s.o.'s* ~*s* être

aux trousses de q.; marcher sur les talons de q.; *down at* ~ éculé; *fig.* minable, de pauvre apparence; *take to one's* ~*s* prendre ses jambes à son cou; s'enfuir; 2. mettre un talon à; *foot.* ~ *out* talonner le ballon (*pour le sortir de la mêlée*); '**heeled** *Am.* F pourvu d'argent; muni d'un revol-ver; '**heel·er** *pol. Am. sl.* partisan *m* servile.

heel-tap ['hi:ltæp] ⊕ rondelle *f* de hausse; ~*s pl.* fonds *m/pl.* de verre; *no* ~! vidons les verres.

heft [heft] 1. poids *m*; effort *m*; *Am.* F gros *m* (de la récolte); 2. *Am.* soupeser; '**heft·y** F solide; *Am.* lourd.

he·gem·o·ny [hi'geməni] hégémo-nie *f*.

he-goat ['hi:gout] bouc *m*.

heif·er ['hefə] génisse *f*.

heigh-ho [hei'hou] ah!

height [hait] hauteur *f*, élévation *f*; comble *m*, apogée *m*; *personne:* taille *f*; altitude *f*; cœur *m* (*d'été*); '**height·en** augmenter (*a. fig.*); re-hausser; *fig.* relever.

hei·nous □ ['heinəs] atroce; odieux (-euse *f*); '**hei·nous·ness** énor-mité *f*.

heir [ɛə] héritier (-ère *f*) *m* (de, *to*); ~ *apparent* héritier *m* présomptif; ~-*at-law* héritier *m* légitime; '**heir·dom** droit *m* de succession; † héri-tage *m*; '**heir·ess** héritière *f*; '**heir·less** sans héritier; **heir·loom** ['~lu:m] meuble *m* ou bijou *m* de famille; *fig.* apanage *m*; '**heir·ship** qualité *f* d'héritier.

held [held] *prét. et p.p. de* hold 2.

hel·i·bus *Am.* F ['helibʌs] hélicoptère *m qui fait le service de communication entre l'aéroport et la ville.*

hel·i·cal ⊕ ['helikl] en spirale.

hel·i·cop·ter ['helikɔptə] hélicop-tère *m*.

helio... [hi:liou] hélio-; **he·li·o·graph** ['~ougrɑ:f] héliographe *m* (*a. phot.*); héliogravure *f*; **he·li·o·graph·ic** [~'græfik] héliographi-que; ~ *calking* (reproduction *f* par) héliogravure *f*; **he·li·o·gra·vure** ['hi:liougrəvjuə] héliogravure *f*; **he·li·o·trope** ['heljətroup] ♀ hélio-trope *m* (*a. couleur*).

hel·i·port ['helipɔ:t] héliport *m*.

he·lix ['hi:liks], *pl. usu.* **hel·i·ces** ['helisi:z] ⚕, ⊕, *zo.* hélice *f*; △ spirale *f*, volute *f*; *anat.* hélix *m*, ourlet *m*.

hell [hel] enfer *m*; *attr.* de l'enfer; *like ~* infernal (-aux *m/pl.*); oh *~!* diable!; sapristi!; *go to ~* aller en enfer; F *what the ~ ...?* que diable...?; *a ~ of a noise* un bruit infernal; *raise ~* faire un bruit infernal; faire une scène; *ride ~ for leather* aller au triple galop; *'~·'bent Am. sl.* résolu; acharné; *'~·cat fig.* mégère *f*. [*m.*]

hel·le·bore ♀ ['helibɔ:] ellébore]
Hel·lene ['heli:n] Hellène *mf*.
hell·ish □ ['heliʃ] infernal (-aux *m/pl.*); diabolique.
hel·lo [he'lou] holà!; *téléph.* allô!
helm ⚓ [helm] (barre *f* du) gouvernail *m*; timon *m* (*a. fig.* de l'État); *fig.* direction *f*.
hel·met ['helmit] casque *m*; **'hel·met·ed** casqué.
helms·man ⚓ ['helmzmən] homme *m* de barre; timonier *m*.
hel·ot *hist.* ['helət] ilote *m*; *fig.* esclave *m*.
help [help] **1.** aide *f*; secours *m*; remède *m*; *surt. Am.* domestique *mf*; *lady ~* dame *f* (de bonne maison) qui aide aux soins du ménage; *mother's ~* jeune fille *f* qui aide dans le soin des enfants; *by the ~ of* à l'aide de; **2.** *v/t.* aider; secourir; prêter son concours à; faciliter; *à table*: servir (q., *s.o.*) qch., *s.th.*; qch. à q., *s.o.* to *s.th.*); *~ o.s.* se servir (de, *to*); s'aider; *I could not ~ laughing* je ne pouvais m'empêcher de rire; *v/i.* aider, servir, contribuer (à, *to*); **'help·er** aide *mf*; assistant(e *f*) *m*; ⚙ machine *f* de secours; **'help·ful** □ ['~ful] utile; salutaire; serviable (*personne*); **'help·ing** portion *f*; **'help·less** □ sans ressource; impuissant; **'help·less·ness** faiblesse *f*; **'help·mate**, **'help·meet** aide *mf*; compagnon *m*, compagne *f*.
hel·ter-skel·ter ['heltə'skeltə] *adv.* pêle-mêle; à la débandade.
helve [helv] manche *m*.
Hel·ve·tian [hel'vi:ʃiən] **1.** helvétien (-ne *f*), suisse; **2.** Helvétien(ne *f*) *m*, Suisse *mf*.
hem¹ [hem] **1.** *cost.* bord *m*; ourlet *m*; **2.** border; ourler; *~ in* entourer.
hem² [~] **1.** toussoter; **2.** hem!
he-man *Am. sl.* ['hi:mæn] homme *m* viril.

hem·i·sphere ['hemisfiə] hémisphère *m*.
hem·lock ♀ ['hemlɔk] ciguë *f*.
hemo... [hi:mo] *see haemo...*
hemp [hemp] chanvre *m*; **'hemp·en** de chanvre.
hem·stitch ['hemstitʃ] **1.** ourlet *m* à jour; **2.** ourler à jour.
hen [hen] poule *f*; femelle *f* (*d'oiseau*); *~'s egg* œuf *m* de poule.
hen·bane ['henbein] jusquiame *f*.
hence [hens] (*souv. from ~*) d'ici; à partir d'aujourd'hui, désormais; de là, ce qui explique...; *~!* hors d'ici!; va-t'en d'ici!; *a year ~* dans un an; **'~·'forth**, **'~·'for·ward** désormais, à l'avenir.
hench·man ['hentʃmən] F partisan *m*; homme *m* de confiance.
hen...: **'~·'par·ty** F assemblée *f* de jupes; **'~·pecked** dominé par sa femme; **'~·roost** juchoir *m*.
hep *Am. sl.* [hep]: *be ~* être dans le vent; **'~·cat** *Am. sl.* fanatique *mf* du jazz.
he·pat·ic *anat.* [hi'pætik] hépatique.
hepta... [heptə] hepta-; **hep·ta·gon** ['~gən] heptagone *m*.
her [hə:; hə] **1.** *accusatif:* la; *datif:* lui; à elle; se, soi; celle; **2.** son, sa, ses.
her·ald ['herəld] **1.** héraut *m*; *fig.* avant-coureur *m*; **2.** annoncer; *~ in* introduire; **he·ral·dic** [he-'rældik] (*~ally*) héraldique; **her·ald·ry** ['herəldri] blason *m*.
herb [hə:b] herbe *f*; **her·ba·ceous** ['~'beiʃəs] herbacé; **'herb·age** herbage *m*; herbes *f/pl.*; ⚖ droit *m* de pacage; **'herb·al 1.** d'herbes; **2.** herbier *m*; **'herb·al·ist** botaniste *m*; guérisseur *m*; ⚘ herboriste *mf*; **her·bar·i·um** ['~'beəriəm] herbier *m*; **her·biv·o·rous** ['~'bivərəs] herbivore; **her·bo·rize** ['~bəraiz] herboriser. [léen(ne *f*); d'Hercule.]
Her·cu·le·an [hə:kju'li:ən] hercu-]
herd [hə:d] **1.** troupeau *m* (*a. fig.*); **2.** *v/t.* assembler; *v/i.* (*a. ~ together*) s'assembler en troupeau; s'attrouper; **'herds·man** bouvier *m*.
here [hiə] ici; *~ is* voici; *~'s to ...!* à la santé de ...!
here-a·bout(s) ['hiərəbaut(s)] près d'ici; **here·aft·er** [hiər'ɑ:ftə] **1.** dorénavant; **2.** avenir *m*; *l'*au-delà *m*, la vie *f* à venir; **'here·by** par là; ⚖ par les présentes.

her·e·dit·a·ment ⚖️ [heri'ditəmənt] bien *m* transmissible par héritage; *fig.* patrimoine *m*; **he·red·i·tar·y** [hi'reditəri] héréditaire; **he'red·i·ty** hérédité *f*.

here·in ['hiər'in] ici; en ceci; **here·in·be'fore** ci-dessus; **here·of** [hiər-'ɔv] de ceci.

her·e·sy ['herəsi] hérésie *f*.

her·e·tic ['herətik] **1.** (*usu.* **he·ret·i·cal** □ [hi'retikl]) hérétique; **2.** hérétique *mf*.

here·to·fore ['hiətu'fɔː] jusqu'ici; **here·up·on** ['hiərə'pɔn] là-dessus; sur ce; **'here'with** avec ceci; ci-joint.

her·it·a·ble ['heritəbl] héréditaire; héritable (*propriété*); **'her·it·age** héritage *m*, patrimoine *m*.

her·maph·ro·dite ⚕️, *zo.* [hɔː'mæfrədait] hermaphrodite (*a. su./m*).

her·met·ic, her·met·i·cal □ [hɔː-'metik(l)] hermétique.

her·mit ['hɔːmit] ermite *m*; **'her·mit·age** ermitage *m*.

her·ni·a ⚕️ ['hɔːnjə] hernie *f*; **'her·ni·al** herniaire.

he·ro ['hiərou], *pl.* **-roes** ['⁓z] héros *m*; **he·ro·ic** [hi'rouik] (⁓ally) héroïque; épique; **her·o·ine** ['herouin] héroïne *f*; **'her·o·ism** héroïsme *m*.

her·on *orn.* ['herən] héron *m*.

her·ring *icht.* ['heriŋ] hareng *m*; **'her·ing-bone** arête *f* de hareng; point *m* de chausson.

hers [hɔːz] le sien, la sienne, les siens, les siennes; à elle.

her·self [hɔː'self] elle-même; réfléchi: se, *accentué*: soi.

hes·i·tance, hes·i·tan·cy ['hezitəns(i)] hésitation *f*, irrésolution *f*; **hes·i·tate** ['⁓teit] hésiter (à, to; sur *about, over*; entre, *between*); **hes·i·'ta·tion** hésitation *f*.

het·er·o·dox ['hetərədɔks] hétérodoxe; **'het·er·o·dox·y** hétérodoxie *f*; **het·er·o·dyne** ['⁓dain] *radio:* hétérodyne (*a. su./m*); **het·er·o·ge·ne·i·ty** [⁓rodʒi'niːiti] hétérogénéité *f*; **het·er·o·ge·ne·ous** □ ['⁓ro'dʒiːnjəs] hétérogène; F disparate.

het up F [het'ʌp] excité, agité, nerveux (-euse *f*).

hew [hjuː] [*irr.*] couper; tailler (*a.* ⊕); ⊕ abattre; ⊕ dresser; **'hew·er** tailleur *m*; abatteur *m* (*d'arbres*); ⚒️

piqueur *m*; **hewn** [hjuːn] *p.p. de* hew.

hexa... [heksə] hex(a)-; **hex·a·gon** ['⁓gən] hexagone *m*; **hex·ag·o·nal** □ [hek'sægənl] hexagonal (-aux *m/pl*.); **hex·am·e·ter** [hek'sæmitə] hexamètre *m*.

hey [hei] hé!; holà!; hein?

hey·day ['heidei] **1.** tiens!; **2.** *fig.* apogée *m*; fleur *f* de l'âge; beaux jours *m/pl*.

hi [hai] hé!; holà!; ohé!

hi·a·tus [hai'eitəs] ⚕️, *gramm.* hiatus *m*; lacune *f*.

hi·ber·nate ['haibəːneit] hiberner; hiverner (*a. personne*); **hi·ber'na·tion** hibernation *f*.

hic·cup, a. hic·cough ['hikʌp] **1.** hoquet *m*; **2.** avoir le hoquet; hoqueter.

hick F [hik] paysan *m*, rustaud *m*; *attr.* de province.

hick·o·ry ['hikəri] noyer *m* d'Amérique.

hid [hid] *prét. et p.p. de* hide²; **hid·den** ['hidn] *p.p. de* hide².

hide¹ [haid] **1.** peau *f*; ✝ cuir *m*; **2.** F tanner le cuir à (*q.*).

hide² [⁓] [*irr.*] (se) cacher (à, *from*); (se) dérober (à, *from*); **'hide-and-'seek** cache-cache *m*; *play* (at) ⁓ jouer au cache-cache; **'hide·a·way** F cachette *f*, F planque *f*.

hide·bound *fig.* ['haidbaund] aux vues étroites; rigide.

hid·e·ous □ ['hidiəs] affreux (-euse *f*); horrible; **'hid·e·ous·ness** laideur *f*, horreur *f*.

hide·out ['haidaut] cachette *f*.

hid·ing¹ F ['haidiŋ] rossée *f*; tripotée *f*.

hid·ing² [⁓]: *go into* ⁓ se cacher; *in* ⁓ caché; **'⁓-place** cachette *f*.

hie *poét.* [hai] (*p.pr.* hying) se rendre (à la hâte).

hi·er·arch·y ['haiərɑːki] *admin., eccl., etc.* hiérarchie *f*.

hi·er·o·glyph ['haiəroglif] hiéroglyphe *m*; **hi·er·o'glyph·ic** (*a.* **hi·er·o'glyph·i·cal** □) hiéroglyphique; **hi·er·o'glyph·ics** *pl.* hiéroglyphes *m/pl*.

hi-fi *Am.* ['hai'fai] (*abr. de high fidelity*) de haute fidélité (*reproduction*).

hig·gle ['higl] marchander.

hig·gle·dy-pig·gle·dy F ['higldi-'pigldi] en pagaïe, sans ordre.

high [hai] **1.** *adj.* □ *(see a.* ⁓*ly) usu.*
haut; élevé; fort, violent *(vent)*;
grand *(vitesse)*; faisandé *(gibier)*;
avancé *(viande)*; fort *(beurre)*; *attr.*
de fête; solennel(le *f*); F ivre: parti,
par la drogue: drogué, camé; F get ⁓
se défoncer; ⁓*est bidder le* plus
offrant *m*; *with a* ⁓ *hand* arbitraire-
ment; tyranniquement; de façon
cavalière; ⁓ *spirits pl.* gaieté *f*, entrain
m; ♀ *Church* haute Église *f* (anglicane); ⁓ *colo(u)r* vivacité *f* de teint
(d'une personne); couleur *f* vive; ⁓
dive plongeon *m* de haut vol; ⁓
frequency haute fréquence *f*; *surt.*
Am. sl. ⁓*hat* gommeux *m*; *v/t.* traiter
d'une manière hautaine; *v/i.* se
donner de grands airs; ⁓ *life* la vie *f*
mondaine; ⁓ *noon* plein midi; ⁓ *street*
grand-rue *f*, rue *f* principale; *see tea*;
⚡ *tension* haute tension *f*; *it is* ⁓ *time*
il est grand temps; ⁓ *treason* lèse-
majesté *f*; haute trahison *f*; ⁓ *water*
marée *f* haute; ⁓ *wind* gros vent *m*; ⁓
words paroles *f/pl.* dures; **2.** *su.*
météor. aire *f* anticyclonique; *surt.*
Am. ♀ *see High School;* ⁓ *and low* les
grands et les petits; *on* ⁓ en haut; **3.**
adv. haut; en haut; fort(ement); '⁓-
'**backed** à grand dossier; '⁓-**ball**
Am. whisky *m* et soda *m*; '⁓-**born** de
haute naissance; '⁓-**boy** *Am.* commode *f*; '⁓-**bred** de race; '⁓-**brow** F
1. intellectuel(le *f*) *m*; **2.** *iro.* prétendu intellectuel(le *f*); '⁓-**class** de première classe *ou* qualité; '⁓-**day** jour
m de fête; '⁓-ex'**plo·sive** brisant; à
haut explosif; '⁓-**fa·lu·tin(g)** ['⁓fə'lu:-
tiŋ, -iŋ] **1.** prétentieux (-euse *f*); **2.**
discours *m* pompeux; '⁓-**flown**
ampoulé; ambitieux (-euse *f*); '⁓-
grade de qualité supérieure; '⁓-
'**hand·ed** arbitraire; ⁓ **jump** saut *m*
en hauteur; '⁓-**land·er** montagnard
m écossais; soldat *m* d'un régiment
écossais; '⁓-**lands** hautes terres *f/pl.*;
'⁓-**lev·el** *adj.:* alp. ⁓ *climb* ascension *f*
à haute altitude; '⁓-**light 1.** *peinture:*
rehaut; reflet *m*; *fig.* point *m* marquant, F clou *m*; **2.** mettre en
lumière, mettre en vedette; souligner; '⁓-**liv·ing** bonne chère *f*;
'**high·ly** fort(ement); très; bien; extrêmement; *speak* ⁓ *of* parler en termes très flatteurs de; vanter; ⁓ *de-*
scended de haute naissance; '**high-**
'**mind·ed** magnanime; généreux
(-euse *f*); '**high·ness** élévation

f; *fig.* grandeur *f*; ♀ *titre:* Altesse *f*.
high...: '⁓ **oc·tane pet·rol** essence *f*
à haut indice d'octane; '⁓-'**pitched**
aigu(ë *f*) *(ton etc.)*; à forte inclinaison
(toit etc.); '⁓-**pow·er:** ⁓ *station* station *f* génératrice de haute puissance; ⁓ *radio station* poste *m* de
grande portée; '⁓-**priced** coûteux
(-euse *f*), cher; '⁓-**rank·ing** haut, de
haut rang; '⁓-'**rise** tour *f* d'habitation; '⁓-'**road** grand-route *f*; grand
chemin *m*; '⁓-**speed** à grande vitesse; ⊕ à marche rapide; '⁓-'**spir·it-**
ed plein d'ardeur; fougueux (-euse
f); '⁓-'**step·ping** qui trousse *(che-*
val); *Am. sl.* noceur (-euse *f*); '⁓-
'**strung** (au tempérament) nerveux;
'⁓-'**toned** *surt. Am.* F chic, élégant; '⁓-
wa·ter marée *f* haute; '⁓-**way**
grand-route *f*; grand chemin *m*; *fig.*
bonne voie *f*; chemin *m*; '⁓-**way-**
man voleur *m* de grand chemin.

hi·jack ['haidʒæk] **1.** détourner *(un*
avion); **2.** détournement *(d'un*
avion); '**hi·jack·er** pirate *m* (de
l'air).

hike F [haik] **1.** faire du footing;
2. excursion *f* à pied; *surt. Am.* F
hausse *f* *(des prix)*; '**hik·er** excursionniste *mf* à pied.

hi·lar·i·ous □ [hi'lɛəriəs] joyeux
(-euse *f*).

hi·lar·i·ty [hi'læriti] hilarité *f*.

Hil·a·ry ['hiləri]; ⚖️ᴬ *a. univ.* ⁓
Term session *f* de la Saint-Hilaire
(janvier à mars).

hill [hil] colline *f*, coteau *m*; côte *f*;
⁓-**bil·ly** *Am.* F ['⁓bili] montagnard
m; '⁓-**climb·ing** *mot.* montée *f* des
côtes; ⁓ *contest* course *f* de côte;
'**hill·i·ness** nature *f* accidentée
(d'une région); **hill·ock** ['⁓ɔk] petite
colline *f*; '**hill·y** montueux (-euse
f); accidenté *(terrain)*.

hilt [hilt] *épée:* poignée *f*; *up to the* ⁓
jusqu'à la garde; *fig.* complètement,
sans réserve.

him [him] *accusatif:* le; *datif:* lui;
se, soi; celui.

him·self [him'self] lui-même; *ré-*
fléchi: se, *accentué:* soi; *of* ⁓ de lui-
même; de son propre choix; *by* ⁓
tout seul.

hind[1] *zo.* [haind] biche *f*.

hind[2] [⁓] valet *m* de ferme; paysan *m*.

hind[3] [⁓]: ⁓ *leg* jambe *f ou* patte *f*
derrière; = '**hind·er** de derrière;
postérieur; arrière-...

hin·der ['hində] v/t. empêcher (q.) (de, from); gêner; retarder.

hind·most ['haindmoust] dernier (-ère f); **hind·quar·ters** ['haindkwɔːtəz] pl. arrière-train m (pl. arrière-trains).

hin·drance ['hindrəns] empêchement m; obstacle m.

hind·sight ['haindsait] sagesse f (d')après coup; with ~ (en réfléchissant) après coup.

Hin·du, a. **Hin·doo** ['hin'duː] 1. hindou; 2. Hindou(e f) m.

Hin·du·sta·ni ling. [hindu'stæni] hindoustani m.

hinge [hindʒ] 1. gond m; charnière f; fig. pivot m; off the ~s hors de ses gonds; 2. ~ upon fig. dépendre de; ~d lid couvercle m à charnière(s).

hin·ny zo. ['hini] bardot m.

hint [hint] 1. avis m; allusion f; signe m; 2. suggérer, insinuer; faire allusion (à, at).

hip¹ [hip] 1. hanche f; ~ bath bain m de siège; ~ flask flacon m plat; 2. coxal (-aux m/pl.); de la hanche; sur les hanches.

hip² ⚕ [~] cynorrhodon m; F gratte-cul m/inv.

hip³ [~] 1. mélancolie f; 2. attrister; F donner le cafard à.

hip⁴ [~]: int. ~, ~, hurra(h)! hip! hip! hourra!

hipped F [hipt] mélancolique; Am. sl. obsédé.

hip·po F ['hipou] = **hip·po·pot·a·mus** [hipə'pɔtəməs], pl. a. ~mi [~mai] hippopotame m.

hip-roof ⌂ ['hipruːf] toit m en croupe.

hip-shot ['hipʃɔt] (d)éhanché.

hire ['haiə] 1. louage m; maison: location f; gages m/pl.; ~ charge prix m de (la) location; on ~ en location; à louer; à louage; for ~ libre (taxi); 2. louer; arrêter; engager (un domestique); ~ out louer; Am. entrer en service; **hire·ling** péj. ['~liŋ] mercenaire (a. su./m); **hire·pur·chase** vente f à tempérament; on the ~ system à tempérament.

hir·sute ['həːsjuːt] hirsute, velu; fig. grossier (-ère f).

his [hiz] 1. son, sa, ses; 2. le sien, la sienne, les siens, les siennes; à lui.

hiss [his] 1. sifflement m; 2. v/i. siffler; chuinter (vapeur etc.); v/t. siffler; ~ off chasser à coups de sifflets.

hist [sːt] chut; pour attirer l'attention: pst!

his·to·ri·an [his'tɔːriən] historien m; **his·tor·ic, his·tor·i·cal** □ [~'tɔrik(l)] historique; de l'histoire; **his·to·ri·og·ra·pher** [~tɔːri'ɔgrəfə] historiographe m; **his·to·ry** ['~təri] histoire f; manuel m d'histoire; théâ. drame m historique.

his·tri·on·ic [histri'ɔnik] théâtral (-aux m/pl.); péj. histrionique.

hit [hit] 1. coup m; touche f; trait m satirique, coup m de patte; théâ. (pièce f à) succès m; ♪ succès m; 2. [irr.] v/t. frapper; heurter; atteindre (un but); porter (un coup); trouver (le mot juste); Am. F arriver à; ~ it off with s'accorder avec; ~ off imiter exactement; ~ one's head against se cogner la tête contre; ~ s.o. a blow porter un coup à q.; v/i. ~ at décocher un coup à; ~ or miss à tout hasard; ~ out détacher des coups (à, at); ~ (up)on découvrir; trouver; tomber sur; '~-and-'run driv·er mot. chauffard m.

hitch [hitʃ] 1. saccade f; ♣ nœud m, clef f; fig. empêchement m soudain; accroc m; radio etc.: technical ~ incident m technique; 2. remuer par saccades; accrocher; nouer; attacher (un cheval etc.); ♣ amarrer; ~ up remonter (le pantalon); Am. atteler (des chevaux); Am. sl. get ~ed se marier; '~-hike Am. F faire de l'auto-stop; '~-hik·ing Am. F auto-stop m.

hith·er poét. ['hiðə] ici; le plus rapproché; **hith·er·to** ['~'tuː] jusqu'ici.

hive [haiv] 1. ruche f (a. fig.); essaim m; fig. fourmilière f; ⚕ ~s pl. urticaire f; varicelle f pustuleuse; croup m; 2. v/t. mettre dans une ruche; ~ up accumuler; v/i. entrer dans la ruche; fig. vivre ensemble.

ho [hou] ho!; hé!; ♣ en vue!

hoar [hɔː] 1. see hoarfrost; 2. chenu (personne).

hoard [hɔːd] 1. amas m; accumulation f secrète; F argent: magot m; 2. (a. ~ up) amasser; accumuler; thésauriser (de l'argent).

hoard·ing¹ ['hɔːdiŋ] resserre f; accumulation f; thésaurisation f.

hoard·ing² [~] clôture f de bois; panneau m d'affichage.

hoar·frost [ˈhɔːˈfrɔst] gelée f blanche, givre m.

hoar·i·ness [ˈhɔːrinis] blancheur f; vieillesse f.

hoarse □ [hɔːs] rauque, enroué; **'hoarse·ness** enrouement m.

hoar·y [ˈhɔːri] blanchi (cheveux); chenu (personne); fig. séculaire.

hoax [houks] **1.** tour m, mystification f, farce f; supercherie f; journ. canard m; **2.** attraper, jouer un tour à, mystifier.

hob[1] [hɔb] cheminée: plaque f de côté; fiche f de but (au jeu de palets).

hob[2] [~] see hobgoblin; surt. Am. F raise ~ faire du raffut; rouspéter fort.

hob·ble [ˈhɔbl] **1.** clochement m, boitillement m; F embarras m; **2.** v/i. clocher, boitiller, clopiner; v/t. entraver; F embarrasser.

hob·ble·de·hoy F [ˈhɔbldiˈhɔi] jeune homme m gauche; F grand dadais m.

hob·by [ˈhɔbi] fig. marotte f, dada m; **'~-horse** † petit cheval m de selle; cheval m de bois; dada m.

hob·gob·lin [ˈhɔbgɔblin] lutin m.

hob·nail [ˈhɔbneil] clou m à ferrer; caboche f.

hob·nob [ˈhɔbnɔb] ~ with être à tu et à toi avec (q.); fréquenter (q.).

ho·bo Am. [ˈhoubou] ouvrier m ambulant; F chemineau m.

hock[1] [hɔk] **1.** zo. jarret m; **2.** couper le jarret à.

hock[2] [~] vin m du Rhin.

hock[3] sl. [~] **1.** gage m; prison f; **2.** engager.

hock·ey sp. [ˈhɔki] hockey m.

hock-shop [ˈhɔkʃɔp] mont m de piété; F ma tante f.

ho·cus [ˈhoukəs] duper; droguer (q., qch.); narcotiser (une boisson); **~-po·cus** [ˈ~ˈpoukəs] **1.** (tour m de) passe-passe m/inv.; tromperie f; **2.** v/i. faire des tours de passe-passe; v/t. mystifier; escamoter (qch.).

hod [hɔd] oiseau m (de maçon); seau m à charbon.

hodge-podge [ˈhɔdʒpɔdʒ] see hotchpotch.

hod·man [ˈhɔdmən] aide-maçon (pl. aides-maçons) m.

hoe ⚏ [hou] **1.** houe f; **2.** houer.

hog [hɔg] **1.** porc m (châtré); fig. goinfre m; sl. go the whole ~ aller jusqu'au bout; F accaparer, monopoliser; mot. ~ the road tenir toute la route; **hogged** [hɔgd] fortement bombé; en brosse; **hog·get** [ˈhɔgit] agneau m antenais; **hog·gish** □ [ˈ~iʃ] de cochon; grossier (-ère f); **'hog·gish·ness** grossièreté f; gloutonnerie f; **hogs·head** [ˈ~zhed] tonneau m; mesure: fût m (240 litres); Am. grosse balle f de tabac (de 750 à 1200 livres); **'hog·skin** peau f de porc; **'hog·wash** eaux f/pl. grasses; F lavasse f.

hoi(c)k [hɔik] ⚏ (faire) monter en chandelle; F lever d'un coup sec.

hoist [hɔist] **1.** (coup m de) treuil m; **2.** hisser; guinder.

hoi·ty-toi·ty [ˈhɔitiˈtɔiti] **1.** susceptible; qui fait l'important; **2.** taratata!

ho·kum Am. sl. [ˈhoukəm] balivernes f/pl.; absurdité f, fumisterie f.

hold [hould] **1.** su. prise f; appui m; empire m, pouvoir m; influence f; box. tenu m; tanière f (d'une bête fauve); ⚓ cale f; catch (ou get ou lay ou take) ~ of saisir, s'emparer de; have a ~ of (ou on) tenir; keep ~ of ne pas lâcher (qch.); **2.** [irr.] v/t. usu. tenir; retenir (l'attention, l'haleine, dans la mémoire); contenir; maintenir; détenir; tenir pour; professer (une opinion); avoir (une idée); arrêter; célébrer (une fête); tenir (une séance); faire (une enquête); ⚖ décider (que, that); surt. Am. ~ down a job occuper un emploi; se montrer à la hauteur d'un emploi; ~ one's own tenir bon; défendre sa position; téléph. ~ the line ne pas quitter; ~ water être étanche; fig. tenir debout; ~ off tenir à distance; ⚏ intercepter; ~ on maintenir; tenir (qch.) en place; ~ out tendre; offrir; ~ over remettre à plus tard; ~ up lever en l'air; soutenir; relever (la tête); offrir (comme modèle); arrêter; entraver; tourner (en ridicule); exposer; **3.** [irr.] v/i. tenir (bon); se maintenir; persister; être vrai; ~ forth pérorer, disserter (sur, on); ~ good (ou true) être valable; ne pas se démentir; ~ hard! arrêtez!; halte là!; ⚓ baste!; ~ in se maîtriser; ~ off se tenir à distance; ⚓ tenir le large; ~ on se cramponner (à, to); ne pas lâcher; F ~ on! tenez ferme!; attendez un instant!; *téléph.* ne quittez pas!; ~ to s'en tenir à; ~ *up* se maintenir; se soutenir; 'hold·all fourre-tout *m/inv.*; 'hold·er *maison*: possesseur *m*; locataire *mf*; *médaille, poste*: titulaire *mf*; *sp.*, ✝ détenteur (-trice *f*) *m*; ~ *of shares* actionnaire *mf*; 'hold·fast crampon *m* (*a.* ⚓); serre-joint *m*; 'hold·ing tenue *f*; possession *f*; ⊕ serrage *m*; ✝ portefeuille *m* effets, dossier *m*; *small* ~ petite propriété *f*; ~ *company* société *f* de portefeuille; 'hold·o·ver *Am.* survivance *f*, restant *m*; 'hold·up *Am.* F coup *m* à main armée; hold-up *m*; *mot.* emboutéillage *m*, bouchon *m*.

hole [houl] **1.** trou *m* (*a. fig.*); ouverture *f*; F *fig.* embarras *m*, difficulté *f*; F *fig.* embarras *m*, difficulté *f*; *find* ~*s in* critiquer); **2.** trouer, percer, faire un trou dans; *golf*: poter; *billard*: blouser; '~-and-'cor·ner clandestin, secret (-ète *f*); obscur.

hol·i·day ['hɔlədi] jour *m* de fête; congé *m*; ~*s pl.* vacances *f/pl.*; *on* ~ vacances; '~-mak·er vacancier (-ère *f*) *m*.

ho·li·ness ['houlinis] sainteté *f*.

hol·la ['hɔlə], **hol·lo(a)** ['hɔlou] **1.** holà!; tiens!; *souv.* bonjour!; **2.** crier holà.

hol·land ['hɔlənd] (*a. brown* ~) toile *f* de Hollande, toile *f* écrue.

hol·ler *Am.* F ['hɔlə] **1.** crier (à tue-tête); **2.** grand cri *m*.

hol·low ['hɔlou] **1.** *adj.* □ creux (creuse *f*); vide; faux (fausse *f*); sourd (*bruit*); **2.** F *adv.* (*a. all* ~) complètement; (*sonner*) creux; **3.** *su.* creux *m*, cavité *f*; *terrain*: dénivellation *f*, enfoncement *m*; ⊕ évidure *f*; **4.** *v/t.* creuser, évider; 'hol·low·ness creux *m*; *fig.* fausseté *f*.

hol·ly ⚘ ['hɔli] houx *m*.

hol·ly·hock ⚘ ['hɔlihɔk] rose *f* trémière.

holm [houm] îlot *m*; rive *f* plate; ⚘ yeuse *f*.

hol·o·caust ['hɔləkɔːst] holocauste *m*; *fig.* massacre *m*.   [volver.\]

hol·ster ['houlstə] étui *m* de re-\]

ho·ly ['houli] saint; pieux (-euse *f*); ♀ *of Holies* le saint *m* des saints; ♀ *Thursday le* jeudi *m* saint; ~ *water* eau *f* bénite; ♀ *Week la* semaine *f* sainte.

hom·age ['hɔmidʒ] hommage *m*; *do* (*ou pay ou render*) ~ rendre hommage (à, to).

home [houm] **1.** *su.* foyer *m*; maison *f*, demeure *f*; asile *m*; patrie *f*; *at* ~ chez moi (lui, elle, *etc.*); **2.** *adj.* domestique, de famille; qui porte (*coup*); bien senti (*vérité*); ~ *affairs pl.* affaires *f/pl.* intérieures; ~ *help* aide *f* ménagère; ♀ *Office* Ministère *m* de l'Intérieur; ~ *rule* autonomie *f*; ♀ *Secretary* Ministre *m* de l'Intérieur; ~ *straight*, ~ *stretch sp.* dernière ligne droite; F *fig.* phase *f* finale; ~ *trade* commerce *m* intérieur; F *tell s.o. a few* ~ *truths* dire ses quatre verités à q.; **3.** *adv.* à la maison, chez moi *etc.*; à son pays; à la patrie; à fond; ~ *delivery* livraison *f* à domicile; *be* ~ être chez soi; être de retour; *bring* (*ou press*) *s.th.* ~ *to s.o.* faire sentir qch. à q.; convaincre q. de qch.; *come* ~ retourner au pays; rentrer; *it came* ~ *to her fig.* elle s'en rendit compte; *hit* (*ou strike*) ~ frapper juste; **4.** *v/i.* revenir au foyer (*pigeon*: au colombier); '~-'baked de ménage; fait à la maison; '~'bred indigène; *fig.* naturel(le *f*); '~·com·ing retour *m* (au foyer ou au pays); rentrée *f*; '~·croft petite ferme *f*; ~ e·co'nom·ics *sg. Am.* économie *f* domestique; '~-felt dans son for intérieur; profond; '~-'grown indigène, du cru (*vin*); 'home·less sans foyer, sans asile; 'home·like qui rappelle le foyer; intime; 'home·li·ness simplicité *f*; *Am.* manque *m* de beauté; 'home·ly □ *fig.* simple, modeste, ordinaire; *Am.* sans beauté.

home...: '~-made fait à la maison; du pays; '~-mak·er mère *f* de famille, ménagère *f*; '~-sick nostalgique; '~-sick·ness nostalgie *f*; '~-spun **1.** filé à la maison; *fig.* simple, rude; **2.** gros drap *m*; '~-stead ferme *f* avec dépendances; *Am.* bien *m* de famille; '~-town ville *f* natale; '~-ward **1.** *adv.* (*ou* '~-wards) vers la maison; vers son pays; **2.** *adj.* de retour; '~-work travail *m* fait à la maison; *école*: devoirs *m/pl.*; *do one's* ~ faire ses devoirs; *fig.* se bien préparer.

hom·i·cide ['hɔmisaid] homicide *m*; meurtre *m*; *personne*: homicide *mf*.

hom·i·ly ['hɔmili] homélie *f*.

hom·ing [ˈhoumiŋ] retour *m* à la maison; ✈ retour *m* par radioguidage; ~ *instinct* instinct *m* qui ramène au foyer; ~ *pigeon* pigeon *m* voyageur. [maïs.)

hom·i·ny [ˈhɔmini] semoule *f* de)

ho·mo F [ˈhoumou] homo *m*, pédé *m*.

ho·moe·o·path [ˈhoumiopæθ] homéopathe *mf*; **ho·moe·o'path·ic** (~*ally*) homéopathique; homéopathe (*médecin*); **ho·moe·op·a·thist** [~ˈɔpəθist] homéopathe *mf*; **ho·moe'op·a·thy** homéopathie *f*.

ho·mo·ge·ne·i·ty [hɔmodʒeˈniːiti] homogénéité *f*; **ho·mo·ge·ne·ous** □ [~ˈdʒiːnjəs] homogène; **ho·mog·en·ized** [həˈmɔdʒənaizd] homogénéisé; **ho·mol·o·gous** [hɔˈmɔləgəs] homologue; **ho'mol·o·gy** [~dʒi] homologie *f*; **hom·o·nym** [ˈhɔmənim] homonyme *m*; **ho·mo·sex·u·al** [ˈhoumouˈseksjuəl] homosexuel(le *f*).

hom·y F [ˈhoumi] *see* homelike.

hone ⊕ [houn] **1.** pierre *f* à aiguiser; **2.** aiguiser; repasser (*un rasoir*).

hon·est □ [ˈɔnist] honnête, sincère, loyal (-aux *m/pl.*); intègre; ~ *truth* exacte vérité *f*; **'hon·es·ty** honnêteté *f*, probité *f*, loyauté *f*.

hon·ey [ˈhʌni] miel *m*; *my* ~! chéri(e *f*)!; **'~·comb** rayon *m* de miel; **'~·combed** alvéolé; criblé; **hon·eyed** [ˈhʌnid] emmiellé; *fig.* mielleux (-euse *f*); **'hon·ey·moon 1.** lune *f* de miel; **2.** passer la lune de miel; **hon·ey·suck·le** ♀ [ˈ~sʌkl] chèvrefeuille *m*.

honk *mot.* [hɔŋk] **1.** cornement *m*; **2.** corner, klaxonner.

honk·y-tonk *Am. sl.* [ˈhɔŋkitɔŋk] beuglant *m*.

hon·o·rar·i·um [ɔnəˈrɛəriəm] honoraires *m/pl.*; **hon·or·ar·y** [ˈɔnərəri] honoraire, d'honneur.

hon·o(u)r [ˈɔnə] **1.** honneur *m*; distinction *f* honorifique; *fig.* gloire *f*; ~*s pl.* honneurs *m/pl.*; distinctions *f/pl.*; *your* ♀ Monsieur le juge; *in* ~ *of s.o.* en honneur de q., à la gloire de q.; *do the* ~*s of the house* faire les honneurs de sa (*etc.*) maison; **2.** honorer; faire honneur à (*a.* ✝).

hon·o(u)r·a·ble □ [ˈɔnərəbl] honorable; *Right* ♀ (le) très honorable; **'hon·o(u)r·a·ble·ness** honorabilité *f*; caractère *m* honorable.

hooch *Am. sl.* [huːtʃ] gnôle *f*.

hood [hud] capuchon *m*; ⚡ cloche *f*; ⊕ *forge etc.*: hotte *f*; *univ.* chaperon *m*; *mot.* capote *f*; *Am. mot.* capot *m* (*du moteur*); **'hood·ed** encapuchonné (*personne*), ♀ capuchonné; *cost.* à capuchon; *fig.* couvert.

hood·lum *Am.* F [ˈhuːdləm] voyou *m*; gangster *m*; galapiat *m*.

hoo·doo *surt. Am.* [ˈhuːduː] **1.** déveine *f*, guigne *f*; porte-malheur *m/inv.*; **2.** porter la guigne à; jeter un sort sur.

hood·wink [ˈhudwiŋk] ✝ bander les yeux à; *fig.* tromper.

hoo·ey *Am. sl.* [ˈhuːi] bêtise *f*.

hoof [huːf] sabot *m*; F pied *m*; **hoofed** [huːft] à sabots.

hook [huk] **1.** croc(het) *m*; *robe:* agrafe *f*; *vestiaire:* patère *f*; *pêche:* hameçon *m*; ~*s and eyes* agrafes et œillets; *by* ~ *or by crook* coûte que coûte; *Am.* F ~, *line and sinker* sans exception, totalement; sans réserve; **2.** *v/t.* accrocher; agrafer (*une robe*); prendre (*un poisson*); courber (*le doigt*); *fig.* crocher (*le bras*); *sl.* voler à la tire; attraper; *sl.* ~ *it* attraper; ficher le camp; *sl.* ~ *up* agrafer (*une robe*); suspendre; *v/i.* (*a.* ~ *on*) s'accrocher; **hooked** [~t] crochu (*a. nez*); muni de crochets *etc.*; *sl.* toxicomane; **'hook·er** ♣ hourque *f*; *Am. sl.* pouffiasse *f* (= *prostituée*); **'hook-up** combinaison *f*, alliance *f*; *radio:* relais *m* radiophonique; postes *m/pl.* conjugués; **'hook·y:** *Am. play* ~ faire l'école buissonnière.

hoo·li·gan [ˈhuːligən] gouape *f*, voyou *m*.

hoop [huːp] **1.** *tonneau:* cercle *m*; ⊕ *roue:* jante *f*; *cost.* panier *m*; cerceau *m* (*d'enfant*); *Am. sl.* bague *f*; **2.** cercler; garnir de jantes; **'hoop·er** tonnelier *m*, cerclier *m*.

hoop·ing-cough [ˈhuːpiŋkɔf] coqueluche *f*.

hoo·poe *orn.* [ˈhuːpuː] huppe *f*.

hoose·gow *Am. sl.* [ˈhuːsgau] prison *f*; cabinets *m/pl.*

hoot [huːt] **1.** *su.* hibou: ululement *m*; *personne:* huée *f*; *mot.* cornement *m*; coup *m* de sifflet; **2.** *v/i.* ululer; huer; *mot.* klaxonner; *fig.* siffler; *v/t.* huer; (*a.* ~ *at*, ~ *out*, ~ *away*) chasser (*q.*) par des huées; **'hoot·er**

sirène *f*; avertisseur *m*; *mot.* klaxon *m*.

hop¹ [hɔp] **1.** *su.* ♀ houblon *m*; ~s *pl.* houblon *m*; **2.** *v/t.* houblonner (*la bière*); *v/i.* cueillir le houblon.

hop² [~] **1.** saut *m*; gambade *f*; 🏇 étape *f*; *sl.* sauterie *f* (= *bal*); **2.** sauter; *v/t. sl.* ~ it ficher le camp, filer; se débiner; *v/i.* sautiller; 🏇 ~ off décoller, partir.

hope [houp] **1.** espoir *m* (de, of); espérance *f*; of great ~s qui promet; **2.** espérer (qch., for s.th.); ~ in mettre son espoir en; **hope·ful** □ [ˈ~ful] plein d'espoir; qui promet; be ~ that avoir bon espoir que; **ˈhope·ful·ly** *surt. Am.* on espère (que); **ˈhope·less** □ désespéré; sans espoir; incorrigible; inutile.

hop-o'-my-thumb [ˈhɔpəmiˈθʌm] le Petit Poucet; *fig.* petit bout *m* d'homme.

hop·per [ˈhɔpə] ⊕ *moulin*: trémie *f*, huche *f*; ✍ semoir *m*; ⚓ marie-salope (*pl.* maries-salopes) *f*.

horde [hɔːd] horde *f*.

ho·ri·zon [həˈraizn] horizon *m*; on the ~ à l'horizon; **hor·i·zon·tal** □ [hɔriˈzɔntl] horizontal (-aux *m/pl.*).

hor·mone *biol.* [ˈhɔːmoun] hormone *f*.

horn [hɔːn] *usu.* corne *f*; *zo.* antenne *f*; *hibou*: aigrette *f*; ♪ cor *m*; ♪ ♩ instrument *m* à vent; *radio etc.*: pavillon *m*; † corne *f* à boire; *mot.* klaxon *m*; trompe *f*; (*stag's*) ~s *pl.* bois *m*; ~ of plenty corne *f* d'abondance; **horned** [ˈ~id; hɔːnd] à ... cornes, cornu.

hor·net *zo.* [ˈhɔːnit] frelon *m*.

horn·less [ˈhɔːnlis] sans cornes; **ˈhorn·pipe** (*a. sailor's* ~) *danse*: matelote *f*; **horn·swog·gle** *Am. sl.* [ˈ~swɔgl] escroquer, tromper (*q.*); **ˈhorn·y** □ corné; de *ou* en corne; calleux (-euse *f*) (*main*); ∨ excité, en chaleur.

hor·o·loge [ˈhɔrələdʒ] horloge *f*; **hor·o·scope** [ˈ~skoup] horoscope *m*; cast s.o's ~ dresser l'horoscope de q.

hor·ren·dous [həˈrendəs] terrible, horrible.

hor·ri·ble □ [ˈhɔrəbl] horrible, affreux (-euse *f*); **hor·rid** □ [ˈhɔrid] horrible, affreux (-euse *f*); **hor·rif·ic** [hɔˈrifik] horrifique; **hor·ri·fy** [ˈ~fai] horrifier; *fig.*

scandaliser; **hor·ror** [ˈhɔrə] horreur *f* (de, of); *chose f* horrible; F the ~s *pl.* delirium *m* tremens.

horse [hɔːs] **1.** *su.* cheval *m*; *coll.* cavalerie *f*; séchoir *m*; take ~ monter à cheval; ~ artillery artillerie *f* montée; **2.** *v/t.* fournir des chevaux à; mettre des chevaux à; *v/i.* chevaucher; **ˈ~·back**: on ~ à cheval; sur un cheval; be (*ou* go) on ~ aller à cheval; get on ~ monter à cheval; **ˈ~·bean** féverole *f*; **ˈ~·box** 🚋 wagon *m* à chevaux; fourgon *m* pour le transport des chevaux; **ˈ~·break·er** dresseur *m* de chevaux; **ˈ~·deal·er** marchand *m* de chevaux; ♀ **Guards** *pl.* la cavalerie de la Garde; **ˈ~·hair** crin *m* (de cheval); **ˈ~·laugh** F gros rire *m* bruyant; **ˈ~·man** cavalier *m*; **ˈ~·man·ship** manège *m*, équitation *f*; **ˈ~·op·er·a** *Am.* Western *m*; **ˈ~·play** jeu *m* de main(s), jeu *m* brutal; **ˈ~·pond** abreuvoir *m*; **ˈ~·pow·er** *mesure*: cheval-vapeur (*pl.* chevaux-vapeur) *m*; **ˈ~·race** course *f* de chevaux; **ˈ~·rad·ish** ♀ raifort *m*; **ˈ~·sense** gros bon sens *m*; **ˈ~·shoe** fer *m* à cheval; **ˈ~·whip** cravache *f*; **ˈ~·wom·an** amazone *f*, cavalière *f*.

hors·y [ˈhɔːsi] chevalin; hippomane (*personne*).

hor·ta·tive □ [ˈhɔːtətiv], **hor·ta·to·ry** [ˈ~təri] exhortatif (-ive *f*).

hor·ti·cul·tur·al [hɔːtiˈkʌltʃərəl] d'horticulture; **ˈhor·ti·cul·ture** horticulture *f*; **hor·ti·cul·tur·ist** horticulteur *m*.

hose [houz] **1.** † bas *m/pl.*; *jardin*: tuyau *m*; manche *f* à eau; **2.** *v/t.* arroser au tuyau.

ho·sier † [ˈhouʒə] bonnetier (-ère *f*) *m*; **ˈho·sier·y** † bonneterie *f*.

hos·pice [ˈhɔspis] hospice *m*.

hos·pi·ta·ble □ [ˈhɔspitəbl] hospitalier (-ère *f*).

hos·pi·tal [ˈhɔspitl] hôpital *m*; hospice *m*; ♀ Sunday dimanche *m* de quête pour les hôpitaux; **hos·pi·tal·i·ty** [~ˈtæliti] hospitalité *f*; **hos·pi·tal·ize** [ˈ~təlaiz] hospitaliser; envoyer à l'hôpital; **hos·pi·tal·(l)er** [ˈ~tlə] hospitalier *m*; *qqfois* aumônier *m*; **ˈhos·pi·tal·train** ✕ train *m* sanitaire.

host¹ [houst] hôte *m* (*a. zo.*, ♀); hôtelier *m*, aubergiste *m*; *radio, télév.* présentateur (-trice *f*) *m*.

host² [~] *fig.* foule *f*, multitude *f*; *bibl.* Lord of ~s le Dieu des armées.
host³ *eccl.* [~] hostie *f*.
hos·tage ['hɔstidʒ] otage *m*.
hos·tel ['hɔstəl] † hôtellerie *f*; *univ.* foyer *m*; **youth ~** auberge *f* de la jeunesse.
host·ess ['houstis] hôtesse *f*.
hos·tile ['hɔstail] hostile, ennemi; **hos·til·i·ty** [hɔs'tiliti] hostilité *f* (contre, *to*); animosité *f*.
hos·tler ['ɔslə] valet *m* d'écurie.
hot [hɔt] **1.** chaud; brûlant, cuisant; violent (*colère*); piquant (*sauce*); *sl.* volé; *Am.* remarquable; *Am. sl.* radio-actif (-ive *f*); F ~ **air** discours *m/pl.* vides; *Am.* F ~ **dog** petit pain *m* fourré d'une saucisse chaude; **go** (*ou* **sell**) **like ~ cakes** se vendre comme des petits pains; *pol.* ~ **line** téléphone *m* rouge; ~ **spot** point *m* névralgique; boîte *f* de nuit; *sl.* ~ **stuff** as *m*; viveur *m*; marchandise *f* récemment volée; **2.** F chauffer; **hot·bed** couche *f* à ou de fumier; *fig.* foyer *m*.
hotch·potch ['hɔtʃpɔtʃ] salmigondis *m*; hochepot *m*; *fig.* méli-mélo (*pl.* mélis-mélos) *m*.
ho·tel [hou'tel] hôtel *m*.
hot...: '~**foot 1.** à toute vitesse; **2.** F se dépêcher; '~**head** tête *f* chaude, impétueux (-euse *f*) *m*; '~**house** serre *f* chaude; '**hot·ness** chaleur *f*; violence *f*; *moutarde etc.:* force *f*.
hot...: '~**plate** chauffe-assiettes *m/inv.*, réchaud *m*; '~**pot** hochepot *m*, (*sorte de*) ragoût *m*; '~**press** satiner (*le papier*), *tex.* calandrer; ~ **rod** mot. *Am. sl.* bolide *m*; '~**spur** cerveau *m* brûlé; tête *f* chaude; '~-'**wa·ter:** ~ **bottle** bouillotte *f*.
hough [hɔk] *see* hock¹.
hound [haund] **1.** chien *m* (*usu.* de chasse); *fig.* (*sale*) type *m*; **2.** chasser; *fig.* s'acharner après; exciter (contre *at*, on *s.th.*).
hour ['auə] heure *f*; *fig. a.* moment *m*; ~s *pl.* heures *f/pl.* de bureau *etc.*; *eccl.* heures *f/pl.*; '~-**glass** sablier *m*; '~-**hand** petite aiguille *f*; '**hour·ly** (*adj.*) de) toutes les heures; d'heure en heure.
house 1. *su.* [haus], *pl.* **hous·es** ['hauziz] maison *f*, habitation *f*, demeure *f*; † maison *f* (de commerce); *parl.* Chambre *f*; *théâ.* salle *f*; *fig.* ~ **of cards** château *m* de cartes; *fig.* **put ones ~ in order** mettre de

l'ordre dans ses affaires; **2.** [hauz] *v/t.* loger; mettre à l'abri; *v/i.* habiter, loger; ~-**a·gent** ['haus~] agent *m* de location; ~ **ar·rest** assignation *f* à domicile; **put s.o. under ~** assigner q. à domicile; '~-**boat** barge *f* de parade; '~-**break·er** voleur *m* avec effraction, cambrioleur *m*; démolisseur *m*; '~-**bro·ken** *Am.* propre (*animal*), docile, obéissant (*personne*); '~-**check** perquisition *f* à domicile; '~-**fly** mouche *f* commune; '~-**hold** ménage *m*, famille *f*; domestiques *m/pl.*; *attr.* domestique, de *ou* du ménage; **King's ~** Maison *f* du roi; ~ **troops** *pl.* la Garde *f*; ~ **word** mot *m* d'usage courant; '~-**hold·er** propriétaire *m*, locataire *m*; chef *m* de famille; '~-**hunt·ing** F recherche *f* d'un appartement *ou* d'une maison; '~-**keep·er** ménagère *f*; gouvernante *f*; '~-**keep·ing 1.** ménage *m*; **2.** du ménage; '~-**less** sans domicile *ou* abri; '~-**maid** bonne *f*; fille *f* de service; '~-**mas·ter** *école:* professeur *m* directeur (*d'une pension officielle*); '~-**paint·er** peintre *m* décorateur; '~-**proud:** be ~ être (une) ménagère très méticuleuse; '~-**room** logement *m*, place *f*; **give s.o. ~** loger q.; '~-**to-house:** ~ **collection** *etc.* quête *f etc.* à domicile; '~-**trained** *Brit. see* housebroken; '~-**warm·ing** (*ou* ~-**party**) pendaison *f* de la crémaillère; ~ **wife** ['~waif] ménagère *f*, maîtresse *f* de maison; ['hazif] trousse *f* de couture; '~-**wife·ly** ['~waifli] ménager (-ère *f*); de *ou* du ménage; '~-**wif·er·y** ['~wifəri] économie *f* domestique; travaux *m/pl.* domestiques; '~-**wreck·er** démolisseur *m*.
hous·ing¹ ['hauziŋ] logement *m*; *récolte, moutons, etc.:* rentrée *f*; † emmagasinage *m*; ~ **conditions** *pl.* état *m* du logement; ~ **estate** (*ou* **project** *ou* **scheme**) cité *f*, grand ensemble *m*; ~ **shortage** crise *f* du logement.
hous·ing² [~] caparaçon *m*.
hove [houv] *prét. et p.p. de* heave 2.
hov·el ['hɔvl] taudis *m*, masure *f*.
hov·er ['hɔvə] planer, se balancer; *fig.* hésiter.
how [hau] comment; ~ **much** (*ou* **many**) combien (de); ~ **large a room!** que la pièce est grande!; ~ **about ...?** et ...?; si on ...?; ~-**d'ye-do** *sl.* ['~djə'du:] affaire *f*;

pétrin *m*; ~·**'ev·er 1.** *adv.* de quelque manière que (*sbj.*); *devant adj. ou adv.*: quelque ... que (*sbj.*), tout ... que (*ind.*); F comment diable?; **2.** *conj.* cependant, toutefois, pourtant.

how·itz·er ⚔ ['hauitsə] obusier *m*.

howl [haul] **1.** hurler; **2.** hurlement *m*; mugissement *m*; huée *f*; *radio*: réaction *f* dans l'antenne; **'howl·er** hurleur (-euse *f*) *m*; *sl.* gaffe *f*, perle *f*; **'howl·ing 1.** hurlant; F énorme; **2.** hurlement *m*.

hoy [hɔi] **1.** hé!; holà!; **2.** ⚓ bugalet *m* (= *petit vaisseau côtier*).

hoy·den ['hɔidn] jeune fille *f* garçonnière.

hub [hʌb] moyeu *m*; *fig.* centre *m*.

hub·ble-bub·ble ['hʌblbʌbl] glouglou *m*; bruit *m* confus de voix, brouhaha *m*.

hub·bub ['hʌbʌb] brouhaha *m*, vacarme *m*, tohu-bohu *m*.

hub(·by) F ['hʌb(i)] mari *m*.

huck·a·back ✝ ['hʌkəbæk] toile *f* grain d'orge; toile *f* ouvrée.

huck·le ['hʌkl] hanche *f*; **'~·ber·ry** ♀ airelle *f* myrtille; **'~·bone** os *m* de la hanche; jointure *f* du doigt.

huck·ster ['hʌkstə] **1.** *su.* regrattier (-ère *f*) *m*; **2.** *v/t.* colporter; *v/i.* marchander; trafiquer; regratter.

hud·dle ['hʌdl] **1.** *v/t.* entasser (pêle-mêle); *v/i.* (*a. ~ together, ~ up*) s'entasser, s'empiler; ~ *on* mettre à la hâte; **2.** *su.* tas *m* confus; mélimélo (*pl.* mélis-mélos) *m*; *Am.* conclave *m*, conférence *f* confidentielle.

hue[1] [hju:] teinte *f*, couleur *f*.

hue[2] [~]: ~ *and cry* clameur *f* de haro; clameur *f* publique.

huff [hʌf] **1.** *su.*: take (the) ~ se froisser; **2.** *v/t.* froisser; *dames*: souffler (*un pion*); *v/i.* ✝ haleter; se fâcher; *dames*: souffler; **'huff·ish** □ irascible; susceptible; **'huff·i·ness**, **'huff·ish·ness** mauvaise humeur *f*, susceptibilité *f*; **'huff·y** □ irascible; susceptible; fâché.

hug [hʌg] **1.** étreinte *f*; **2.** étreindre, embrasser; serrer dans ses bras; tenir à, ne pas démordre de; chérir; serrer (*le trottoir, un mur*); ~ *o.s.* se féliciter (de *inf.*, on *gér.*).

huge □ [hju:dʒ] immense, énorme, vaste; **'huge·ness** immensité *f*.

hug·ger-mug·ger F ['hʌgəmʌgə] **1.** *adj.* sans ordre; en désordre (*a.*

adv.); **2.** *v/t.* (*a. ~ up*) étouffer, supprimer; *v/i.* patauger; agir sans méthode; vivre sans ordre; **3.** *su.* confusion *f*, pagaïe *f*.

Hu·gue·not *hist.* ['hju:gənɔt] huguenot(e *f*) *m* (*a. adj.*).

hulk ⚓ [hʌlk] ponton *m* (*carcasse de navire*); *fig.* lourdaud *m*, gros pataud *m*; **'hulk·ing** lourd, gros(se *f*).

hull [hʌl] **1.** ♀ cosse *f*; *fig.* enveloppe *f*; ⚓, ✈ coque *f*; **2.** écosser (*des pois*), décortiquer (*de l'orge, du riz*), monder (*de l'orge*); ⚓ percer la coque de.

hul·la·ba·loo [hʌləbə'lu:] vacarme *m*, brouhaha *m*.

hul·lo ['hʌ'lou] ohé!; tiens!; *téléph.* allô!

hum [hʌm] **1.** bourdonnement *m* (*des abeilles ou fig.*); ronflement *m*; murmure *m*; F supercherie *f*; **2.** hmm!; **3.** *v/i.* bourdonner; ronfler; fredonner; ~ *and ha* bredouiller; tourner autour du pot; F *make things* ~ faire ronfler les choses; *v/t.* fredonner (*un air*).

hu·man ['hju:mən] **1.** □ humain; ~*ly* en être humain; ~*ly possible* possible à l'homme; ~*ly speaking* humainement parlant; ~ *rights pl.* droits *m/pl.* de l'homme; **2.** F être *m* humain; **hu·mane** □ [hju:'mein] humain, compatissant; humanitaire; ~ *learning* humanités *f/pl.*; **hu·man·ism** ['hju:mənizm] humanisme *m*; **'hu·man·ist** humaniste (*a. su./m*); **hu·man·i·tar·i·an** [hjumæni'tɛəriən] humanitaire (*a. su./mf*); **hu·man·i·ty** humanité *f*; nature *f* humaine; genre *m* humain, hommes *m/pl.*; *humanities pl.* humanités *f/pl.*, lettres *f/pl.*; **hu·man·i·za·tion** [hju:mənai'zei∫n] humanisation *f*; **'hu·man·ize** (s')humaniser; **hu·man·kind** ['hju:mən'kaind] le genre *m* humain, les hommes *m/pl.*

hum·ble ['hʌmbl] **1.** □ humble; modeste; *in my* ~ *opinion* à mon humble avis; *your* ~ *servant* votre humble serviteur *m*; *eat* ~ *pie* s'humilier, se rétracter; **2.** humilier; rabaisser.

hum·ble-bee ['hʌmblbi:] bourdon *m*.

hum·ble·ness ['hʌmblnis] humilité *f*.

hum·bug ['hʌmbʌg] **1.** charlatan

(-isme) *m*; blagues *f/pl.*; *personne*: blagueur (-euse *f*) *m*; bonbon *m* glacé à la menthe; 2. mystifier; conter des blagues à; enjôler (*q.*).

hum·drum ['hʌmdrʌm] 1. monotone; banal (-aux *m/pl.*); ennuyeux (-euse *f*); 2. monotonie *f*.

hu·mer·al *anat.* ['hju:mərəl] huméral (-aux *m/pl.*).

hu·mid ['hju:mid] humide; moite (*peau, chaleur*); **hu'mid·i·ty** humidité *f*.

hu·mil·i·ate [hju'milieit] humilier; mortifier; **hu·mil·i'a·tion** humiliation *f*; affront *m*.

hu·mil·i·ty [hju'militi] humilité *f*.

hum·mer ['hʌmə] *surt. téléph.* appel *m* vibré; sonnerie *f*; *sl.* brasseur *m* d'affaires; personne *f* très active.

hum·ming F ['hʌmiŋ] bourdonnant; vrombissant; '**~-bird** *orn.* colibri *m*, oiseau-mouche (*pl.* oiseaux-mouches) *m*; '**~-top** toupie *f* d'Allemagne.

hum·mock ['hʌmək] mamelon *m*, coteau *m*; *glace*: monticule *m*.

hu·mor·ist ['hju:mərist] humoriste *m*; comique *m*; farceur (-euse *f*) *m*.

hu·mor·ous □ ['hju:mərəs] comique, drôle; facétieux (-euse *f*); '**hu·mor·ous·ness** drôlerie *f*; humeur *f* facétieuse.

hu·mo(u)r ['hju:mə] 1. *usu.* humeur *f*; plaisanterie *f*; caractère *m*; *out of* ~ mécontent (de, *with*); 2. complaire à (*q.*); laisser faire (*q.*); flatter les caprices de; '**hu·mo(u)r·less** froid, austère; **hu·mo(u)r·some** □ ['~səm] capricieux (-euse *f*).

hump [hʌmp] 1. bosse *f*; *sl.* cafard *m*; *give s.o. the* ~ embêter *q.*; 2. courber, arquer; F embêter (*q.*); *Am. sl.* ~ *o.s.* se fouler; '**hump·back(ed)** *see* hunchback(ed).

humph [mm] hmm!

Hum·phrey ['hʌmfri]: *dine with Duke* ~ dîner par cœur.

hump·ty-dump·ty F ['hʌmpti-'dʌmpti] petite personne *f* boulotte.

hump·y ['hʌmpi] couvert de protubérances.

hunch [hʌntʃ] 1. *see* hump; gros morceau *m*; *pain*: quignon *m*; *Am.* F pressentiment *m*; 2. (*a.* ~ *out*, ~ *up*) voûter; '**hunch·back** bossu(e*f*) *m*; '**hunch·backed** bossu.

hun·dred ['hʌndrəd] 1. cent; 2. cent *m*; centaine *f* (de); *admin.* canton *m*; '**hun·dred·fold** centuple; **hun·dredth** ['~θ] centième (*a. su./m*); '**hun·dred·weight** quintal *m* (50,802 kg, *Am.* 45,359 kg).

hung [hʌŋ] 1. *prét. et p.p. de* hang 1; 2. *adj.* faisandé (*gibier, viande*).

Hun·gar·i·an [hʌŋ'gɛəriən] 1. hongrois; 2. Hongrois(e *f*) *m*; *ling.* hongrois *m*.

hun·ger ['hʌŋgə] 1. *su.* faim *f*; *fig.* ardent désir *m* (de, *for*); 2. *v/i.* avoir faim; *fig.* avoir soif (de *for, after*); *v/t.* affamer; contraindre par la faim (à *inf., into gér.*); ~ **strike** grève *f* de la faim; *go on* (*a*) ~ faire la grève de la faim.

hun·gry □ ['hʌŋgri] affamé (de *for, after*); avide (*œil*); maigre (*sol*).

hunk F [hʌŋk] gros morceau *m*; *pain*: quignon *m*; '**hun·kers** *pl.*: *on one's* ~ à croupetons.

hunks F [hʌŋks] grippe-sou *m*, avare *m*.

hunk·y(-do·ry) *Am. sl.* ['hʌŋki (-'dɔːri)] parfait; d'accord.

hunt [hʌnt] 1. *su.* chasse *f*; terrain *m* de chasse; recherche *f* (de, *for*); vénerie *f*; 2. *v/t.* chasser; poursuivre; ~ *out*, ~ *up* déterrer; découvrir; *v/i.* chasser (au chien courant *ou* à courre); aller à la recherche (de *for, after*); '**hunt·er** chasseur *m*; tueur *m* (*de lions etc.*); chien *m* de chasse; '**hunt·ing** 1. chasse *f*; poursuite *f*; vénerie *f*; 2. de chasse; '**hunt·ing-box** pavillon *m* de chasse; muette *f*; '**hunt·ing-ground** terrain *m* de chasse; '**hunt·ress** chasseuse *f*; '**hunts·man** chasseur *m* (à courre).

hur·dle ['hɜːdl] claie *f*, clôture *f*; *sp.* haie *f*; '**hur·dler** *sp.* sauteur *m* de haies; '**hur·dle-race** *sp.*, *turf*: course *f* de haies; steeple-chase *m*.

hur·dy-gur·dy ['hɜːdiɡɜːdi] † vielle *f*.

hurl [hɜːl] 1. lancement *m*; 2. lancer (*a. fig.*), jeter.

hurl·y-burl·y ['hɜːlibɜːli] brouhaha *m*, tintamarre *m*.

hur·ra(h) *int.* [hu'rɑː] hourra! (*a. su./m*). [♣ tempête *f*.]

hur·ri·cane ['hʌrikən] ouragan *m*;)

hur·ried □ ['hʌrid] pressé, précipité.

hur·ry ['hʌri] **1.** hâte *f*; précipitation *f*; empressement *m*; *in a* ~ à la hâte; *be in a* ~ être pressé; *is there any* ~? est-ce que cela presse?; F *not ... in a* ~ ne ... pas de sitôt; **2.** *v/t.* hâter, presser; ~ *on*, ~ *up* faire hâter le pas à; pousser; *v/i.* (*a.* ~ *up*) se hâter, se dépêcher; presser le pas; ~ *over s.th.* expédier qch.; faire qch. à la hâte; '~**scur·ry 1.** désordre *m*; débandade *f*; **2.** à la débandade; pêle-mêle.

hurt [hə:t] **1.** *su.* mal *m*; blessure *f*; tort *m*; **2.** [*irr.*] *v/t.* faire du mal à; *fig.* nuire à; blesser (*a. les sentiments*); faire de la peine à; gâter, abîmer; *v/i.* faire mal; offenser; F s'abîmer; **hurt·ful** □ ['~ful] (*to*) nuisible (à); préjudiciable (à).

hur·tle ['hə:tl] *v/t.* heurter; *v/i.* se précipiter.

hus·band ['hʌzbənd] **1.** mari *m*, époux *m*; **2.** ménager; ✔ cultiver; '**hus·band·man** cultivateur *m*; laboureur *m*; '**hus·band·ry** agronomie *f*; industrie *f* agricole; *good* ~ bonne gestion *f*; *bad* ~ gaspillage *m*.

hush [hʌʃ] **1.** *int.* silence!; chut!; **2.** *su.* silence *m*; **3.** *v/t.* calmer; faire taire; étouffer (*un bruit*); ~ *up* étouffer; *v/i.* se taire; '~**mon·ey** prix *m* du silence (*de q.*).

husk [hʌsk] **1.** ✔ cosse *f*, gousse *f*; brou *m*; *fig.* carcasse *f*; **2.** écosser (*des pois*); décortiquer; '**husk·i·ness** enrouement *m*, raucité *f*.

husk·y[1] □ ['hʌski] cossu (*pois*); enroué (*voix*); altéré par l'émotion (*voix*); F fort, costaud.

hus·ky[2] [~] Esquimau *mf*; chien *m* esquimau.

hus·sar ✕ [hu'za:] hussard *m*.

hus·sy ['hʌsi] coquine *f*; garce *f*.

hus·tings *hist.* ['hʌstiŋz] *pl.* estrade *f*, tribune *f*; élection *f*.

hus·tle ['hʌsl] **1.** *v/t.* bousculer; pousser; *v/i.* se dépêcher, se presser; **2.** *su.* bousculade *f*; hâte *f*; activité *f* énergique; ~ *and bustle* animation *f*; remue-ménage *m/inv.*; '**hus·tler** homme *m* d'expédition.

hut [hʌt] **1.** hutte *f*, cabane *f*; ✕ baraquement *m*; **2.** (se) baraquer; loger.

hutch [hʌtʃ] coffre *m*, huche *f*; cage *f* (*à lapins*); *fig.* logis *m* étroit; pétrin *m*.

hut·ment ✕ ['hʌtmənt] (camp *m* de)

baraques *f/pl.*; baraquements *m/pl.*

huz·za *int.* [hu'za:] hourra!; vivat! (*a. su./m*).

hy·a·cinth ⚘ ['haiəsinθ] jacinthe *f*.

hy·a(e)·na *zo.* [hai'i:nə] hyène *f*.

hy·brid ['haibrid] **1.** *biol.* hybride*m*; *personne*: métis(se *f*) *m*; **2.** hybride; hétérogène; '**hy·brid·ism** hybridité *f*; '**hy·brid·ize** (s')hybrider.

hy·drant ['haidrənt] prise *f* d'eau;

hy·drate 🜅 ['haidreit] hydrate *m*.

hy·drau·lic [hai'drɔ:lik] **1.** (~*ally*) hydraulique; **2.** ~*s pl.* hydraulique *f*, hydromécanique *f*.

hydro... [haidro] hydr(o)-; '~**·a·er·o·plane** hydravion *m*; '~**·car·bon** 🜅 hydrocarbure *m*; '~**·chlo·ric ac·id** acide *m* chlorhydrique; '~**·dy'nam·ics** *pl.* hydrodynamique*f*; '~**·e'lec·tric** hydroélectrique; ~ *generating station* centrale *f* hydroélectrique; '~**·foil** hydrofoil *m*; **hy·dro·gen** 🜅['haidridʒən] hydrogène *m*; **hy·dro·gen·at·ed** [hai'drɔdʒineitid] hydrogéné; **hy'drog·e·nous** hydrogénique; **hy'drog·ra·phy** [~grəfi] hydrographie *f*; **hy·dro·path·ic** ['haidro'pæθik] **1.** hydrothérapique; hydropathe (*personne*); **2.** (*a.* ~ *establishment*) établissement *m* hydrothérapique; **hy·drop·a·thy** [hai'drɔpəθi] hydropathie *f*.

hydro...: ~'**pho·bi·a** hydrophobie *f*; '~**plane** hydravion *m*; bateau *m* glisseur; ~'**stat·ic 1.** hydrostatique; ~ *press* presse *f* hydraulique; **2.** ~*s pl.* hydrostatique *f*.

hy·giene ['haidʒi:n] hygiène *f*; **hy'gien·ic 1.** (~*ally*) hygiénique; **2.** ~*s pl. see* hygiene.

hy·grom·e·ter *phys.* [hai'grɔmitə] hygromètre *m*.

Hy·men ['haimen] *myth.* Hymen *m*.

hymn [him] **1.** *eccl.* hymne *f*, cantique *m*; hymne *m* (*national, de guerre, etc.*); **2.** glorifier, louer; **hym·nal** ['~nəl] **1.** qui se rapporte à un cantique; **2.** (*ou* '**hymn·book**) recueil *m* d'hymnes.

hy·per·bo·la ⅄ [hai'pə:bələ] hyperbole *f*; **hy'per·bo·le** [~li] *rhétorique*: hyperbole *f*; **hy·per·bol·ic** ⅄ [~'bɔlik] hyperbolique; **hy·per·bol·i·cal** □ hyperbolique; **hy·per·crit·i·cal** □ ['~'kritikl] hypercritique; difficile; **hy'per·tro·phy** [~trəfi] hypertrophie *f*.

hy·phen ['haifən] **1.** trait *m* d'union;

typ. division *f*; **2.** écrire avec un trait d'union; **hy·phen·ate** ['ˌeit] mettre un trait d'union à; **~d** *Americans pl.* étrangers *m/pl.* naturalisés (*qui conservent leur sympathie pour leur pays d'origine*).

hyp·no·sis [hip'nousis], *pl.* **-ses** [ˌsiːz] hypnose *f*.

hyp·not·ic [hip'nɔtik] **1.** (*ˌally*) hypnotique; **2.** narcotique *m*; **hyp·no·tism** ['ˌnətizm] hypnotisme *m*; **'hyp·no·tist** hypnotiste *mf*; **hyp·no·tize** ['ˌtaiz] hypnotiser.

hy·po·chon·dri·a [haipo'kɔndriə] hypocondrie *f*; F spleen *m*; **hy·po·'chon·dri·ac** [ˌdriæk] **1.** hypocondriaque; **2.** hypocondre *mf*; **hy·poc·ri·sy** [hi'pɔkrəsi] hypocrisie *f*; **hyp·o·crite** ['hipokrit] hypocrite *mf*; F *homme:* tartufe *m*, *femme:* sainte nitouche *f*; **hyp·o·'crit·i·cal** □ hypocrite; **hy·po·der·mic** [haipo'dəːmik] **1.** sous-cutané (*injection*); **~** *needle* canule *f*; **2.** seringue *f* hypodermique; **hy·pot·e·nuse** ⩗ [hai'pɔtinjuːz] hypoténuse *f*; **hy'poth·e·car·y** [ˌθikəri] ⅔ hypothécaire; **hy'poth·e·cate** [ˌθikeit] hypothéquer; **hy·'poth·e·sis** [ˌθisis], *pl.* **-ses** [ˌsiːz] hypothèse *f*; **hy·po·thet·ic**, **hy·po·thet·i·cal** □ [ˌpo'θetik(l)] hypothétique, supposé.

hys·te·ri·a ⚕ [his'tiəriə] hystérie *f*; F crise *f* de nerfs; **hys·ter·ic**, *usu.* **hys·ter·i·cal** □ [his'terik(l)] hystérique; **hys'ter·ics** *pl.* crise *f ou* attaque *f* de nerfs; *go into* **~** avoir une crise de nerfs.

I

I, i [ai] I *m*, i *m*.

I [ai] *je; accentué:* moi.

i·am·bic [ai'æmbik] **1.** iambique;
2. *(ou* **'i·amb, i'am·bus** [ᴧbəs]*)*
iambe *m*.

i·bex *zo.* ['aibeks] bouquetin *m*.

ice [ais] **1.** glace *f (a. cuis.)*; F cut no ᴧ
ne faire aucune impression (sur,
with); F ne pas compter; *fig. skate on
thin* ᴧ être *ou* s'engager dans une
situation dangereuse; **2.** (con)geler;
v/i. être pris dans les glaces; *v/t.* ☒
(a. ᴧ *up)* givrer; *cuis.* glacer *(un
gâteau)*; frapper *(le vin)*; '**ᴧ-age**
période *f* glaciaire; '**ᴧ-axe** piolet *m*;
ice·berg ['ᴧbəːg] iceberg *m*.

ice...: '**ᴧ-bound** fermé *ou* retenu
par les glaces; '**ᴧ-box,** *surt. Am.* '**ᴧ-
chest** glacière *f*; sorbetière *f*; '**ᴧ-
'cream** (crème *f* à la) glace *f*; '**ᴧ-
cube** glaçon *m*, cube *:n* de glace; '**ᴧ-
'hock·ey** hockey *m* sur glace.

Ice·land·er ['aisləndə] Islandais(e
f) *m*.

ice...: '**ᴧ-pack** embâcle *m* (de glaç-
çons); '**ᴧ-rink** patinoire *f*; '**ᴧ-show**
spectacle *m* sur glace; '**ᴧ-skate 1.**
patinage *m* (sur glace); **2.** patiner,
faire du patinage (sur glace).

ich·thy·ol·o·gy [ikθi'ɔlədʒi] ichtyo-
logie *f*.

i·ci·cle ['aisikl] glaçon *m*.

i·ci·ness ['aisinis] froid *m* glacial;
fig. froideur *f* glaciale.

ic·ing ['aisiŋ] glaçage *m*; glacé *m*
(de sucre); ☒ givrage *m*; ᴧ *sugar* sucre
m glace.

i·con·o·clast [ai'kɔnəklæst] iconoclaste *mf*.

i·cy □ ['aisi] glacial (-als *m/pl.*).

i·de·a [ai'diə] idée *f*; notion *f*;
intention *f*; *form an* ᴧ *of* se faire une
idée de; **i'de·al 1.** □ idéal (-als, -aux
m/pl.); optimum; *le* meilleur; F
parfait; **2.** idéal *(pl.* -als, -aux) *m*);
i'de·al·ism idéalisme *m*; **i'de·al-
ist** idéaliste *mf*; **i·de·al'is·tic**
(ᴧally) idéaliste; **i'de·al·ize** [ᴧaiz]
idéaliser.

i·den·ti·cal □ [ai'dentikl] identique

(à, *with*), même; **i'den·ti·cal·ness**
see identity; **i·den·ti·fi·ca·tion** [ᴧfi-
'keiʃn] identification *f*; ᴧ *card* carte
f d'identité; ᴧ *mark* ⸸ estampille
f; **i'den·ti·fy** [ᴧfai] identifier;
établir *ou* constater l'identité de;
reconnaître (pour, *as*); F découvrir;
i'den·ti·kit [ᴧkit] portrait-robot *m*
(pl. portraits-robots); **i'den·ti·ty**
identité *f*; ᴧ *card* carte *f* d'identité; ⚔
ᴧ *disk* plaque *f* d'identité.

id·e·o·log·i·cal □ [aidiə'lɔdʒikl]
idéologique; **id·e·ol·o·gy** [ᴧ'ɔlədʒi]
idéologie *f*.

id·i·o·cy ['idiəsi] idiotie *f*; idiotisme
m; *fig.* bêtise *f*.

id·i·om ['idiəm] idiotisme *m*; *région:*
idiome *m*; locution *f*; style *m*;
♪, *peint.* manière *f* de s'exprimer;
id·i·o·mat·ic [idiə'mætik] (ᴧally)
idiomatique.

id·i·o·syn·cra·sy [idiə'siŋkrəsi] 🔬
idiosyncrasie *f*; *fig.* petite manie *f*.

id·i·ot ['idiət] idiot(e *f*) *m*, imbécile *mf* (a. F); **id·i·ot·ic** [idi'ɔtik]
(ᴧally) idiot; inepte; stupide, bête.

i·dle ['aidl] **1.** □ paresseux (-euse *f*);
inoccupé; en chômage; *fig.* inutile,
vain, sans fondement; dormant
(capital, fonds); ⊕ arrêté *(machine)*, parasite *(roue)*; ᴧ *hours pl.*
heures *f/pl.* perdues; ᴧ *motion* mot.
mouvement *m* perdu; ⊕ *run* ᴧ
marcher à vide; **2.** *v/t.* (*usu.* ᴧ *away*)
perdre; *v/i.* fainéanter; muser;
'i·dle·ness paresse *f*; oisiveté *f*;
chômage *m*; *fig.* inutilité *f*; **'i·dler**
fainéant(e *f*) *m*; flâneur (-euse *f*) *m*.

i·dol ['aidl] idole *f* (a. *fig.*); **i·dol·a-
ter** [ai'dɔlətə] idolâtre *m*; **i'dol·a-
tress** idolâtre *f*; **i'dol·a·trous** □
idolâtre; **i'dol·a·try** idolâtrie *f*;
i·dol·ize ['aidəlaiz] idolâtrer.

i·dyl(l) ['idil] idylle *f*; **i'dyl·lic**
(ᴧally) idyllique.

if [if] **1.** si; *even* ᴧ quand même;
ᴧ *not* sinon; ᴧ *so* s'il en est ainsi;
as ᴧ *to say* comme pour dire; **2.** si
m/inv.; **'if·fy** *Am.* F plein de si,
douteux (-euse *f*).

ig·ne·ous ['igniəs] igné.

ig·nis fat·u·us ['ignis'fætjuəs] feu *m* follet.

ig·nit·a·ble [ig'naitəbl] inflammable; **ig'nite** *v/t.* mettre le feu à, allumer; ⚗ enflammer; *v/i.* prendre feu; **ig·ni·tion** [⁓'niʃn] ignition *f*; ⚡, *mot.* allumage *m*; *attr.* d'allumage; *mot.* ⁓ **key** clef *f* de contact.

ig·no·ble □ [ig'noubl] ignoble; vil, infâme; de basse naissance.

ig·no·min·i·ous □ [ignə'miniəs] ignominieux (-euse *f*); méprisable; **'ig·no·min·y** ignominie *f*, honte *f*; infamie *f*.

ig·no·ra·mus F [ignə'reiməs] ignorant(e *f*) *m*; F bourrique *f*; **ig·no·rance** ['ignərəns] ignorance *f*; **'ig·no·rant** ignorant (de, of); étranger (à, of); **ig·nore** [ig'nɔː] ne tenir aucun compte de; feindre de ne pas voir; ⚖ rejeter (*une plainte*).

Il·i·ad ['iliəd] Iliade *f* (*a. fig.*).

ill [il] **1.** *adj.* mauvais; malade, souffrant; *see* ease; **2.** *adv.* mal; **3.** *su.* mal (*pl.* maux) *m*; malheur *m*; dommage *m*; tort *m*.

I'll [ail] = *I will*, shall.

ill…: '⁓-**ad'vised** impolitique; malavisé (*personne*); '⁓-'**bred** mal élevé; '⁓-**con'di·tioned** en mauvais état; de mauvaise mine (*personne*); méchant; '⁓-**dis'posed** malintentionné; mal disposé (envers, to).

il·le·gal □ [i'liːgəl] illégal (-aux *m/pl.*); **il·le·gal·i·ty** [ili'gæliti] illégalité *f*.

il·leg·i·ble □ [i'ledʒəbl] illisible.

il·le·git·i·ma·cy [ili'dʒitiməsi] illégitimité *f*; **il·le'git·i·mate** □ [⁓mit] illégitime (*a. enfant*); non autorisé; bâtard (*enfant*).

ill…: '⁓-**fat·ed** malheureux (-euse *f*); infortuné; '⁓-**'fa·vo(u)red** laid; '⁓-**'feel·ing** ressentiment *m*, rancune *f*; '⁓-'**got·ten** mal acquis; '⁓-**'hu·mo(u)red** de mauvaise humeur; maussade.

il·lib·er·al □ [i'libərəl] grossier (-ère *f*); illibéral (-aux *m/pl.*); borné (*esprit*); **il·lib·er·al·i·ty** [ilibə'ræliti] illibéralité *f*; petitesse *f*; manque *m* de générosité.

il·lic·it □ [i'lisit] illicite; clandestin.

il·lim·it·a·ble □ [i'limitəbl] illimité; illimitable.

il·lit·er·ate □ [i'litərit] **1.** illettré; ignorant; **2.** analphabète *mf*.

ill…: '⁓-'**judged** malavisé; peu sage; '⁓-'**man·nered** malappris, mal élevé; '⁓-'**na·tured** □ méchant; désagréable.

ill·ness ['ilnis] maladie *f*.

il·log·i·cal □ [i'lɔdʒikl] illogique.

ill…: ⁓-**o·mened** ['il'oumend] de mauvais augure; '⁓-'**starred** malheureuse (-euse *f*); '⁓-'**tem·pered** de mauvaise humeur; de méchant caractère (*a. animal*); '⁓-'**timed** mal à propos; '⁓-'**treat** maltraiter.

il·lu·mi·nant [i'ljuːminənt] illuminant, éclairant (*a. su./m*); **il'lu·mi·nate** [⁓neit] éclairer (*a. fig.*); illuminer (*de dehors*); enluminer (*un manuscrit etc.*); *fig.* embellir (*une action*); ⁓d advertising enseigne *f* lumineuse, enseignes *f/pl.* lumineuses; **il'lu·mi·nat·ing** lumineux (-euse *f*); qui éclaire (*a. fig.*); **il·lu·mi'na·tion** éclairage *m*; illumination *f* (*de dehors*); *manuscrit:* enluminure *f*; **il'lu·mi·na·tive** [⁓nətiv] éclairant; d'éclairage; **il'lu·mi·na·tor** [⁓neitə] illuminateur (-trice *f*) *m*; enlumineur (-euse *f*) *m*; dispositif *m* d'éclairage; **il'lu·mine** [⁓min] *see* illuminate.

ill-use [il'juːz] maltraiter.

il·lu·sion [i'luːʒn] illusion *f*, tromperie *f*; **il'lu·sive** □ [⁓siv], **il'lu·so·ry** □ [⁓səri] illusoire, trompeur (-euse *f*).

il·lus·trate ['iləstreit] expliquer; éclairer; illustrer; **il·lus'tra·tion** exemple *m*; explication *f*; **'il·lus·tra·tive** □ qui sert d'exemple; be ⁓ **of** expliquer; éclaircir; **'il·lus·tra·tor** illustrateur *m*.

il·lus·tri·ous □ [i'lʌstriəs] illustre; célèbre.

ill will ['il'wil] rancune *f*, malveillance *f*.

I'm [aim] = *I am*.

im·age ['imidʒ] **1.** *tous les sens:* image *f*; idole *f*; portrait *m*; idée *f*; **2.** représenter par une image; tracer le portrait de; be ⁓d se refléter; **'im·age·ry** idoles *f/pl.*; images *f/pl.*; langage *m* figuré.

im·ag·i·na·ble □ [i'mædʒinəbl] imaginable; **im'ag·i·nar·y** imaginaire, de pure fantaisie; **im·ag·i·na·tion** [⁓'neiʃn] imagination *f*; **im'ag·i·na·tive** □ [⁓nətiv] d'imagination; imaginatif (-ive *f*) (*personne*); **im'ag·ine** [~dʒin] imaginer; concevoir; se figurer.

im·be·cile □ ['imbisiːl] imbécile (*a. su./mf*); **im·be·cil·i·ty** [~'siliti] imbécillité *f*; faiblesse *f* (d'esprit).

im·bibe [im'baib] boire; absorber (*a. fig.*); *fig.* s'imprégner de.

im·bro·glio [im'brouliou] imbroglio *m*.

im·brue [im'bruː] tremper (dans)⌉
im·bue [im'bjuː] imbiber; imprégner; *fig.* pénétrer (de, with).

im·i·ta·ble ['imitəbl] imitable; **im·i·tate** ['~teit] imiter; copier (*a.* ⊕); singer (*q.*); **im·i'ta·tion** imitation *f*; copie *f*; ⊕ contrefaçon *f*; *attr.* simili-; factice; artificiel(le *f*); ~ *leather* similicuir *m*; **im·i·ta·tive** □ ['~tətiv] imitatif (-ive *f*); imitateur (-trice *f*) (*personne*); ~ *of* qui imite; **im·i·ta·tor** ['~teitə] imitateur (-trice *f*) *m*; † contrefacteur *m*.

im·mac·u·late □ [i'mækjulit] immaculé; impeccable.

im·ma·nent ['imənənt] immanent.

im·ma·te·ri·al □ [imə'tiəriəl] immatériel(le *f*); peu important; sans conséquence; indifférent (à, to).

im·ma·ture [imə'tjuə] pas mûr(i); **im·ma'tu·ri·ty** immaturité *f*.

im·meas·ur·a·ble □ [i'meʒərəbl] immesurable; infini.

im·me·di·ate □ [i'miːdjət] immédiat; sans intermédiaire; instantané; urgent; **im'me·di·ate·ly** **1.** *adv.* tout de suite, immédiatement; **2.** *cj.* dès que.

im·me·mo·ri·al □ [imi'mɔːriəl] immémorial (-aux *m/pl.*).

im·mense □ [i'mens] immense; vaste; *sl.* magnifique; **im'men·si·ty** immensité *f*.

im·merse [i'məːs] immerger, plonger; *fig.* ~ *o.s. in* se plonger dans; ~*d in* plongé dans (*un livre*); accablé de (*dettes*); **im'mer·sion** immersion *f*; submersion *f*; *fig.* absorption *f*; ~ *heater* thermo-plongeur *m*.

im·mi·grant ['imigrənt] immigrant(e *f*) *m*, -gré(e *f*) *m*; **im·mi·grate** ['~greit] *v/i.* immigrer; *v/t.* introduire des étrangers (dans, [in]to); **im·mi'gra·tion** immigration *f*.

im·mi·nence ['iminəns] imminence *f*, proximité *f*; **'im·mi·nent** □ imminent, proche.

im·mit·i·ga·ble □ [i'mitigəbl] que l'on ne saurait adoucir; implacable.

im·mo·bile [i'moubail] immobile; fixe; **im·mo·bil·i·ty** [imo'biliti] immobilité *f*; fixité *f*; **im·mo·bi·lize** [i'moubilaiz] immobiliser (*a. des espèces monnayées*); rendre indisponible (*un capital*).

im·mod·er·ate □ [i'mɔdərit] immodéré, excessif (-ive *f*).

im·mod·est □ [i'mɔdist] immodeste; † impudent; **im'mod·es·ty** immodestie *f*; † impudence *f*.

im·mo·late ['imoleit] immoler; **im·mo'la·tion** immolation *f*; **'im·mo·la·tor** immolateur *m*.

im·mor·al □ [i'mɔrəl] immoral (-aux *m/pl.*); **im·mo·ral·i·ty** [imo-'ræliti] immoralité *f*.

im·mor·tal □ [i'mɔːtl] immortel(le *f*); **im·mor·tal·i·ty** [~'tæliti] immortalité *f*; **im'mor·tal·ize** [~təlaiz] immortaliser; perpétuer.

im·mov·a·ble [i'muːvəbl] **1.** □ immobile; inébranlable; **2.** ~*s pl.* biens *m/pl.* immeubles.

im·mune [i'mjuːn] à l'abri (de) (*a.* 🐝); inaccessible (à, from); 🐝 immunisé (contre from, against); **im'mu·ni·ty** exemption *f* (de, from); 🐝 immunité *f* (contre); **im·mu·nize** ['~aiz] 🐝 immuniser.

im·mure [i'mjuə] enfermer.

im·mu·ta·bil·i·ty [imjuːtə'biliti] immu(t)abilité *f*; **im'mu·ta·ble** □ immuable; inaltérable.

imp [imp] diablotin *m*; petit démon *m*; lutin *m*; petit(e *f*) espiègle *m*(*f*).

im·pact ['impækt] choc *m*; impact *m*; collision *f*.

im·pair [im'pɛə] altérer; endommager; diminuer; affaiblir (*la santé*).

im·pale [im'peil] empaler (*un criminel*); enclore d'une palissade; *fig.* fixer.

im·pal·pa·ble □ [im'pælpəbl] impalpable; *fig.* insaisissable; subtil.

im·pan·(n)el [im'pænl] *see* empanel.

im·part [im'pɑːt] communiquer; annoncer; donner.

im·par·tial □ [im'pɑːʃl] impartial (-aux *m/pl.*); **im·par·ti·al·i·ty** ['~ʃi'æliti] impartialité *f* (envers, to).

im·pass·a·ble □ [im'pɑːsəbl] infranchissable (*rivière*); impraticable (*chemin*).

im·passe [æm'pɑːs] impasse *f*.

im·pas·si·ble □ [im'pæsibl] impassible; insensible (à, to).

im·pas·sion [im'pæʃn] passionner; exalter; enivrer (de passion).

im·pas·sive □ [im'pæsiv] impassible; insensible (aux émotions); **im'pas·sive·ness** impassibilité f; insensibilité f.

im·pa·tience [im'peiʃns] impatience f; intolérance f (de of, with); **im'pa·tient** □ impatient; intolérant (de at, of, with); avide (de, for); be ~ of (inf.) être impatient de(inf.); F brûler de (inf.).

im·peach [im'pi:tʃ] accuser (de of, with); attaquer; dénoncer; mettre (qch.) en doute; **im'peach·a·ble** accusable; blâmable; récusable (témoin); **im'peach·ment** accusation f; dénigrement m; ½ mise f en accusation.

im·pec·ca·bil·i·ty [impekə'biliti] impeccabilité f; **im'pec·ca·ble** □ impeccable, irréprochable.

im·pe·cu·ni·ous [impi'kju:njəs] impécunieux (-euse f), besogneux (-euse f).

im·pede [im'pi:d] empêcher, entraver.

im·ped·i·ment [im'pedimənt] empêchement m (à, to); ~ in one's speech empêchement m de la langue; **im·ped·i·men·ta** ⚔ [~-'mentə] pl. impedimenta m/pl.; attirail m; F bagages m/pl.

im·pel [im'pel] pousser (à, to); **im'pel·lent 1.** moteur (-trice f); impulsif (-ive f); **2.** moteur m; force f motrice.

im·pend [im'pend] être suspendu (sur, over); fig. menacer (q., over s.o.); être imminent; **im'pend·ence** imminence f; proximité f; **im'pend·ent** imminent; menaçant.

im·pen·e·tra·bil·i·ty [impenitrə-'biliti] impénétrabilité f (a. fig.); **im'pen·e·tra·ble** □ impénétrable (à to, by); fig. insondable.

im·pen·i·tence [im'penitəns] impénitence f; **im'pen·i·tent** □ impénitent.

im·per·a·tive [im'perətiv] **1.** □ péremptoire; impérieux (-euse f); urgent; impératif (-ive f); ~ mood = **2.** gramm. (mode m) impératif m.

im·per·cep·ti·ble □ [impə'septəbl] imperceptible; fig. insensible.

im·per·fect [im'pə:fikt] **1.** □ impar-

fait, défectueux (-euse f); △ surbaissé; ~ tense = **2.** gramm. (temps m) imparfait m; in the ~ à l'imparfait; **im·per·fec·tion** [~pə'fekʃn] imperfection f; fig. a. faiblesse f.

im·pe·ri·al [im'piəriəl] **1.** □ impérial (-aux m/pl.); fig. majestueux (-euse f); **2.** impériale f; papier: grand jésus m; **im'pe·ri·al·ism** impérialisme m; césarisme m; pol. colonialisme m; **im'pe·ri·al·ist** impérialiste m; césariste m; pol. colonialiste m; **im·pe·ri·al'is·tic** impérialiste.

im·per·il [im'peril] mettre en péril.

im·pe·ri·ous □ [im'piəriəs] impérieux (-euse f); arrogant; péremptoire.

im·per·ish·a·ble □ [im'periʃəbl] impérissable.

im·per·me·a·ble □ [im'pə:mjəbl] imperméable.

im·per·son·al □ [im'pə:snl] impersonnel(le f); **im·per·son·al·i·ty** [~sə'næliti] impersonnalité f.

im·per·son·ate [im'pə:səneit] personnifier; se faire passer pour; théâ. représenter; **im·per·son·'a·tion** personnification f; théâ. interprétation f; ½ supposition f de personne.

im·per·ti·nence [im'pə:tinəns] impertinence f; insolence f; **im'per·ti·nent** □ impertinent (a. ½); insolent.

im·per·turb·a·bil·i·ty ['impətə:bə-'biliti] imperturbabilité f; flegme m; **im·per'turb·a·ble** □ imperturbable, flegmatique.

im·per·vi·ous □ [im'pə:vjəs] inaccessible (à, to) (a. fig.); imperméable (à).

im·pet·u·os·i·ty [impetju'ɔsiti] impétuosité f; **im'pet·u·ous** □ impétueux (-euse f); emporté; **im·pe·tus** ['~pitəs] élan m, poussée f; fig. impulsion f.

im·pi·e·ty [im'paiəti] impiété f.

im·pinge [im'pindʒ] entrer en collision (avec [up]on, against); empiéter (sur, on) (a. ½); **im'pinge·ment** heurt m; collision f (avec [up]on, against); empiètement m (sur, on) (a. fig., a. ½).

im·pi·ous □ ['impiəs] impie.

imp·ish □ ['impiʃ] de démon; (d')espiègle.

im·pla·ca·bil·i·ty [implækə'biliti]

implacabilité *f*; **im·pla·ca·ble** □ [ˌˈplækəbl] implacable (à, pour *towards*).

im·plant [imˈplɑːnt] *usu. fig.* implanter (dans, *in*); inculquer (à, *in*).

im·plau·si·ble [imˈplɔːzəbl] peu plausible.

im·ple·ment 1. [ˈimplimənt] instrument *m*, outil *m*; **2.** [ˌˈment] exécuter (*un contrat, une promesse*); accomplir; suppléer à; **im·ple·men'ta·tion** [ˌˈteiʃn] exécution *f*; mise *f* en œuvre.

im·pli·cate [ˈimplikeit] impliquer, mêler (dans, *in*); compromettre; **im·pli'ca·tion** implication *f*; insinuation *f*; ~*s pl.* portée *f*.

im·plic·it □ [imˈplisit] implicite; tacite; *fig.* aveugle, parfait.

im·plied □ [imˈplaid] implicite; sous-entendu.

im·plore [imˈplɔː] implorer; supplier; **im'plor·ing** [ˌriŋ] suppliant.

im·ply [imˈplai] impliquer; emporter; signifier, vouloir dire.

im·pol·i·cy [imˈpɔlisi] mauvaise politique *f*; *fig.* maladresse *f*.

im·po·lite □ [impəˈlait] impoli.

im·pol·i·tic □ [imˈpɔlitik] impolitique.

im·pon·der·a·ble [imˈpɔndərəbl] **1.** impondérable; **2.** ~*s pl.* impondérables *m/pl.*

im·port 1. [ˈimpɔːt] ✝ importation *f*; signification *f*, sens *m*; portée *f*; importance *f*; ✝ ~*s pl.* marchandises *f/pl. ou* articles *m/pl.* d'importation, importations *f/pl.*; ~ duty droits *m/pl.* d'importation; **2.** [imˈpɔːt] importer (*des marchandises*); signifier, indiquer; déclarer; **im'por·tance** importance *f*; F conséquence; **im'por·tant** □ important; **im·por·ta·tion** [ˌˈteiʃn] importation *f*; **im'port·er** importateur (-trice *f*) *m*.

im·por·tu·nate □ [imˈpɔːtjunit] importun, ennuyeux (-euse *f*); **im·por·tune** [ˌˈpɔːtjuːn] importuner; presser; **im·por'tu·ni·ty** importunité *f*.

im·pose [imˈpouz] *v/t.* imposer (à, [up]on) ; *v/i.* ~ upon en imposer à; tromper; abuser de; **im'pos·ing** □ imposant; grandiose; **im·po·si·tion** [ˌpəˈziʃn] *eccl., typ.* imposition *f*; impôt *m*; tromperie *f*, imposture *f*; *école:* pensum *m*.

im·pos·si·bil·i·ty [impɔsəˈbiliti] im-

possibilité *f*; **im'pos·si·ble** □ impossible.

im·post [ˈimpoust] impôt *m*; taxe *f*; tribut *m*; **im·pos·tor** [imˈpɔstə] imposteur *m*; **im'pos·ture** [ˌtʃə] imposture *f*, supercherie *f*.

im·po·tence [ˈimpətəns] impuissance *f* (*a. physiol.*); faiblesse *f*; **'im·po·tent** impuissant; faible.

im·pound [imˈpaund] confisquer; enfermer; mettre en fourrière (*une auto, un animal*).

im·pov·er·ish [imˈpɔvəriʃ] appauvrir; dégraisser (*le sol*).

im·prac·ti·ca·bil·i·ty [impræktikəˈbiliti] impraticabilité *f*, impossibilité *f*; **im'prac·ti·ca·ble** □ impraticable; infaisable; intraitable (*personne*).

im·pre·cate [ˈimprikeit] lancer des imprécations (contre, *upon*); **im·pre'ca·tion** imprécation *f*, malédiction *f*; **im·pre·ca·to·ry** [ˌˈkeitəri] imprécatoire.

im·preg·na·bil·i·ty [impregnəˈbiliti] caractère *m* imprenable *ou* F invincible; **im'preg·na·ble** □ imprenable; F invincible; **im·preg·nate** [ˌˈneit] **1.** ♀, ♫, *biol.* imprégner; imbiber, saturer; pénétrer (*a. fig.*); **2.** [imˈpregnit] imprégné, fécondé; **im·preg'na·tion** fécondation *f*; imprégnation *f*; ⊕ injection *f*.

im·pre·sa·ri·o [impreˈsɑːriou] imprésario *m*.

im·pre·scrip·ti·ble [imprisˈkriptəbl] imprescriptible.

im·press 1. [ˈimpres] impression *f*; empreinte *f*; *fig.* marque *f*, cachet *m*; **2.** [imˈpres] imprimer (à, on); graver (dans la mémoire, on the memory); inculquer (*une idée*) (à, on); faire bien comprendre (qch. à q. *s.th. on s.o., s.o. with s.th.*); ⊕ empreindre (qch. sur qch. *s.th. on s.th., s.th. with s.th.*); *fig.* impressionner, en imposer à; ⚓ ✝ presser (*les marins*); *fig.* réquisitionner; **im'press·i·ble** susceptible de recevoir une empreinte; *a. see* impressionable; **im'pres·sion** [ˌʃn] impression *f* (*a. fig.*); ⊕, *a. typ.* caractères: empreinte *f*; *livre:* impression *f*; *be under the ~ that* avoir l'impression que; **im'pres·sion·a·ble** impressionnable, susceptible, sensible; **im'pres·sive** □

impressionnant; **im·press·ment** ⚓
† *marines*: presse *f*.

im·print 1. [im'print] imprimer (sur,
on); *fig.* graver (dans on, in);
2. ['imprint] empreinte *f* (*a. fig.*);
typ. nom *m* (*de l'imprimeur*); rubrique *f* (*de l'éditeur*).

im·pris·on [im'prizn] emprisonner;
mettre en prison; enfermer; **im-
'pris·on·ment** emprisonnement *m*.

im·prob·a·bil·i·ty [imprɔbə'biliti]
improbabilité *f*; invraisemblance *f*;
im'prob·a·ble □ improbable; invraisemblable.

im·pro·bi·ty [im'proubiti] improbité *f*; manque *m* d'honnêteté.

im·promp·tu [im'prɔmtju:] **1.** *adv.*
(à l')impromptu; **2.** *adj.* impromptu; **3.** *su.* (*discours m etc.*) impromptu *m*.

im·prop·er □ [im'prɔpə] incorrect;
malséant, malhonnête, indécent;
déplacé; ⅋ ~ *fraction* expression *f*
fractionnaire; **im·pro·pri·e·ty** [im-
prə'praiəti] impropriété *f*; inexactitude *f*; inconvenance *f*, indécence
f.

im·prov·a·ble □ [im'pru:vəbl]
améliorable; bonifiable (*sol*).

im·prove [im'pru:v] *v/t.* améliorer;
perfectionner; cultiver (*l'esprit*);
bonifier (*le sol*); *v/i.* s'améliorer;
faire des progrès; ~ *upon* surpasser;
enchérir sur; **im'prove·ment** amélioration *f*; perfectionnement *m*;
culture *f* (*de l'esprit*); progrès *m*
(*pl.*); supériorité *f* (à, [up]on); **im-
'prov·er** réformateur (-trice *f*) *m*;
⊕ apprenti(e *f*) *m*; *cost.* petite
main *f*.

im·prov·i·dence [im'prɔvidəns] imprévoyance *f*; **im'prov·i·dent** □
imprévoyant; prodigue.

im·pro·vi·sa·tion [imprəvai'zeiʃn]
improvisation *f*; **im·pro·vise** ['~-
vaiz] improviser; **'im·pro·vised**
improvisé; impromptu *inv.*

im·pru·dence [im'pru:dəns] imprudence *f*; **im'pru·dent** □ imprudent.

im·pu·dence ['impjudəns] impudence *f*, insolence *f*; **'im·pu·dent**
□ effronté, insolent.

im·pugn [im'pju:n] attaquer, contester; **im'pugn·a·ble** contestable.

im·pulse ['impʌls], **im·pul·sion**
impulsion *f*; choc *m* propulsif; *fig.*
mouvement *m* (spontané); **im-**

'pul·sive □ impulsif (-ive *f*); *fig.*
irréfléchi, spontané, involontaire.

im·pu·ni·ty [im'pju:niti] impunité *f*;
with ~ impunément.

im·pure □ [im'pjuə] impur (*a. fig.*);
im'pu·ri·ty [~riti] impureté *f*.

im·put·a·ble [im'pju:təbl] imputable, attribuable (à, to); **im·pu·ta-
tion** [~'teiʃn] imputation *f*; **impute** [~'pju:t] imputer, attribuer.

in [in] **1.** *prp.* dans (*les circonstances,
la foule, la maison, la rue, l'eau*); en
(*un mot, soie, anglais, Europe, juin,
été, réponse*); à (*l'église, la main de q.,
la campagne, le crayon*); au (*lit, Canada, désespoir, soleil, printemps*);
de (*cette manière*); par (*groupes,
soi-même, ce temps, écrit*); sur (*un
ton*); sous (*le règne de*); chez
(*les Anglais, Corneille*); pendant
(*l'hiver de 1812, la journée*); comme;
~ *a few words* en peu de mots;
~ *all probability* selon toutes pro-
babilités; ~ *crossing the road* en
traversant la rue; *the thing* ~ *itself*
la chose en elle-même *ou phls.* en
soi; *trust* ~ *s.o.* avoir confiance en
q., se fier à q.; *professor* ~ *the university* professeur à l'université;
wound ~ *the head* blessure à la tête;
engaged ~ (*gér.*) occupé à (*inf.*);
~ *a ... voice* d'une voix ...; *blind* ~
one eye borgne; ~ *length* de long;
~ *our time* de nos jours; *at two*
(o'clock) ~ *the morning* à deux heures du matin; ~ *the rain* à *ou* sous
la pluie; ~ *the paper* dans le journal;
one ~ *ten* un sur dix; ~ *the firm of*
sous firme de; ~ *the press* sous
presse; ~ *excuse of* comme excuse
de; ~ *1966* en 1966; *two days* ~ *three*
deux jours sur trois; *there is nothing*
~ *it* il est sans fondement; F cela n'a
pas d'importance; l'un vaut l'autre;
it is not ~ *her to* (*inf.*) il n'est pas de sa
nature de (*inf.*); *he hasn't it* ~ *him* il
n'en est pas capable; ~ *that* puisque,
vu que; **2.** *adv.* dedans; au dedans; rentré; au pouvoir; *be* ~ être
chez soi, être à la maison, y être;
être élu; être au pouvoir; *sport,
train*: être arrivé; brûler encore
(*feu*); *be* ~ *for* en avoir pour
(*qch.*); être inscrit pour (*un examen etc.*); F *be* ~ *with* avoir de belles
relations avec, être en bons termes
avec; **3.** *adj.* intérieur; F en vogue, à
la mode, dans le vent; **4.** *su. parl. the*

~s *pl.* le parti au pouvoir; ~s *and outs* méandres *m/pl.*, coins *m/pl.* et recoins *m/pl.*; tous les détails *m/pl.*

in·a·bil·i·ty [inə'biliti] impuissance *f* (à, *to*), incapacité *f* (de, *to*).

in·ac·ces·si·bil·i·ty ['inæksesə'biliti] inaccessibilité *f*; in·ac'ces·si·ble □ inaccessible.

in·ac·cu·ra·cy [in'ækjurəsi] inexactitude *f*; in·ac·cu·rate □ [~rit] inexact; incorrect.

in·ac·tion [in'ækʃn] inaction *f*.

in·ac·tive □ [in'æktiv] inactif (-ive *f*); ✝ en chômage; ♎ inerte; in·ac'tiv·i·ty inactivité *f*; inertie *f*.

in·ad·e·qua·cy [in'ædikwəsi] insuffisance *f*; imperfection *f*; in'ad·e·quate □ [~kwit] insuffisant; incomplet (-ète *f*).

in·ad·mis·si·bil·i·ty ['inədmisə'biliti] inadmissibilité *f*; in·ad'mis·si·ble □ inadmissible; ⚖ irrecevable.

in·ad·vert·ence, in·ad·vert·en·cy [inəd'vəːtəns(i)] inadvertance *f*; étourderie *f*; mégarde *f*; in·ad·'vert·ent inattentif (-ive *f*); négligent; involontaire; ~ly par inadvertance. [inaliénable; indisponible.\

in·al·ien·a·ble □ [in'eiljənəbl]∫

in·al·ter·a·ble □ [in'ɔːltərəbl] immuable; inaltérable (*couleur*).

in·am·o·ra·ta [inæmə'rɑːtə] amante *f*; amoureuse *f*; in·am·o'ra·to [~tou] amant *m*, amoureux *m*.

in·ane □ [i'nein] *usu. fig.* stupide, inepte, bête, niais.

in·an·i·mate □ [in'ænimit] inanimé, sans vie (*a. fig.*).

in·a·ni·tion [inə'niʃn] ✿ inanition *f*.

in·an·i·ty [i'næniti] inanité *f*, niaiserie *f*.

in·ap·pli·ca·bil·i·ty ['inæplikə'biliti] inapplicabilité *f*; in'ap·pli·ca·ble □ inapplicable (à, *to*); étranger (-ère *f*) (à).

in·ap·po·site □ [in'æpəsit] sans rapport (avec, *to*); hors de propos; inapplicable (à, *to*).

in·ap·pre·ci·a·ble □ [inə'priːʃəbl] inappréciable.

in·ap·pre·hen·si·ble □ [inæpri-'hensəbl] insaisissable, incompréhensible.

in·ap·proach·a·ble [inə'proutʃəbl] inabordable; incomparable.

in·ap·pro·pri·ate □ [inə'prouprijt] peu approprié; déplacé.

in·apt □ [in'æpt] inapte; incapable; inhabile; peu approprié; in'apt·i·tude [~itjuːd], in'apt·ness inaptitude *f* (à, *for*); incapacité *f*.

in·ar·tic·u·late □ [inɑː'tikjulit] muet(te *f*); bégayant (de, *with*); *zo.* inarticulé; in·ar'tic·u·late·ness mutisme *m*; défaut *m* d'articulation.

in·as·much [inəz'mʌtʃ] *adv.*: ~ *as* vu que, puisque; ✝ dans la mesure que.

in·at·ten·tion [inə'tenʃn] inattention *f*; in·at'ten·tive □ inattentif (-ive *f*) (à, *to*); négligent (de); peu attentionné (pour, *to[wards]*).

in·au·di·ble □ [in'ɔːdəbl] imperceptible; faible (*voix*).

in·au·gu·ral [i'nɔːgjurəl] inaugural (-aux *m/pl.*); in'au·gu·rate [~reit] inaugurer; commencer; mettre en vigueur; in·au·gu'ra·tion inauguration *f*; commencement *m*; ♀ *Day Am.* entrée *f* en fonction du nouveau président des É.-U.

in·aus·pi·cious □ [inɔːs'piʃəs] peu propice; fâcheux (-euse *f*).

in·board ⚓ ['inbɔːd] 1. *adj.* intérieur; 2. *adv.* en abord; 3. *prp.* en abord de.

in·born ['in'bɔːn] inné.

in·breathe ['in'briːð] inspirer (à, *into*).

in·bred ['in'bred] inné; consanguin (*chevaux etc.*).

in·breed·ing ['in'briːdiŋ] consanguinité *f*.

in·cal·cu·la·ble □ [in'kælkjuləbl] incalculable.

in·can·des·cence [inkæn'desns] incandescence *f*; *métall.* chaleur *f* blanche; in·can'des·cent incandescent; ~ *light* lumière *f* à incandescence).

in·can·ta·tion [inkæn'teiʃn] incantation *f*; charme *m*.

in·ca·pa·bil·i·ty [inkeipə'biliti] incapacité *f*; ⚖ inéligibilité *f*; in'ca·pa·ble □ incapable (de, *of*); non susceptible (de, *of*); ⚖ inéligible; en état d'ivresse manifeste; in·ca·pac·i·tate [inkə'pæsiteit] rendre incapable (de *for, from*); ⚖ frapper d'incapacité; in·ca'pac·i·ty incapacité *f* (de, *for, to*).

in·car·cer·ate [in'kɑːsəreit] incarcérer; in·car·cer'a·tion incarcération *f*.

in·car·nate 1. [in'kɑːnit] fait chair; incarné (a. fig.); **2.** ['inkɑːneit] incarner; **in·car'na·tion** incarnation f (a. fig.).

in·case [in'keis] see encase.

in·cau·tious □ [in'kɔːʃəs] imprudent; inconsidéré.

in·cen·di·ar·y [in'sendjəri] **1.** incendiaire (a. fig.); ~ bomb bombe f incendiaire; **2.** incendiaire m; auteur m d'un incendie; F see ~ bomb.

in·cense¹ ['insens] **1.** encens m; **2.** encenser; fig. embaumer.

in·cense² [in'sens] exaspérer, courroucer, irriter (contre, with).

in·cen·tive [in'sentiv] **1.** provocant; stimulant; **2.** stimulant m, encouragement m.

in·cep·tion [in'sepʃn] commencement m; **in'cep·tive** initial (-aux m/pl.); gramm. inchoatif (-ive f) (a. su./m). [titude f.\
in·cer·ti·tude [in'səːtitjuːd] incer-\
in·ces·sant □ [in'sesnt] incessant, continuel(le f).

in·cest ['insest] inceste m; **in·ces·tu·ous** □ [in'sestjuəs] incestueux (-euse f).

inch [intʃ] pouce m (2,54 cm); fig. pas m; ~es pl. a. taille f; by ~es peu à peu, petit à petit; **inched** [~t] de ... pouces.

in·cho·a·tive ['inkoueitiv] initial (-aux m/pl.); gramm. inchoatif (-ive f).

in·ci·dence ['insidəns] incidence f; angle of ~ angle m d'incidence; **'in·ci·dent 1.** (à, to) qui arrive; qui appartient; qui tient; **2.** incident m; événement m; pièce, roman: épisode m; ⚖ servitude f ou privilège m attachés à une tenure; **in·ci·den·tal** □ [~'dentl] accidentel(le f), fortuit; inséparable (de, to); be ~ to résulter de, appartenir à; ~ly incidemment.

in·cin·er·ate [in'sinəreit] incinérer (a. Am. un mort); réduire en cendres; **in·cin·er'a·tion** incinération f; **in'cin·er·a·tor** incinérateur m; Am. four m crématoire.

in·cip·i·ence [in'sipiəns] commencement m; **in'cip·i·ent** naissant, qui commence.

in·cise [in'saiz] inciser (a. ✚), faire une incision dans; **in·ci·sion** [~'siʒn] incision f (a. ✚); ✎ enture f; **in·ci·sive** □ [~'saisiv] incisif (-ive f); mordant; pénétrant; **in'ci·sor** [~zə] (dent f) incisive f.

in·ci·ta·tion [insai'teiʃn] see incitement; **in'cite** inciter; pousser; animer (à, to); **in'cite·ment** incitation f, encouragement m; stimulant m, aiguillon m; mobile m.

in·ci·vil·i·ty [insi'viliti] incivilité f.

in·clem·en·cy [in'klemənsi] inclémence f, rigueur f; temps: intempérie f; **in'clem·ent** inclément; rigoureux (-euse f).

in·cli·na·tion [inkli'neiʃn] tête, a. fig.: inclination f; inclinaison f, pente f; fig. penchant m; **in·cline** [~'klain] **1.** v/i. s'incliner, se pencher (personne); incliner, pencher (chose); fig. avoir un penchant (pour qch., to s.th.; à inf., to inf.); être disposé (à, to); incliner (à, to); v/t. (faire) pencher; fig. disposer; ~d plane plan m incliné; **2.** pente f, déclivité f; ⚒ oblique f.

in·close [in'klouz] see enclose.

in·clude [in'kluːd] renfermer; comprendre.

in·clu·sion [in'kluːʒn] inclusion f; **in'clu·sive** □ qui renferme; qui comprend; tout compris; be ~ of comprendre, renfermer (qch.); ~ terms prix tout compris.

in·cog F [in'kɔg], **in'cog·ni·to** [~ni·tou] **1.** incognito, sous un autre nom; **2.** incognito m.

in·co·her·ence,   in·co·her·en·cy [inkou'hiərəns(i)] incohérence f; manque m de suite; **in·co'her·ent** □ incohérent; sans suite; décousu.

in·com·bus·ti·ble □ [inkəm'bʌstəbl] incombustible.

in·come ['inkəm] revenu m; **in·com·er** ['inkʌmə] entrant m; immigrant(e f) m; ⚖ successeur m; **in·come-tax** ['inkəmtæks] impôt m sur le revenu; ~ form feuille f d'impôts.

in·com·ing ['inkʌmiŋ] **1.** entrée f; ~s pl. recettes f/pl., revenus m/pl.; ✝ rentrées f/pl.; **2.** qui entre, qui arrive.

in·com·men·su·ra·bil·i·ty ['inkəmenʃərə'biliti] incommensurabilité f; **in·com'men·su·ra·ble** □ incommensurable.

in·com·mode [inkə'moud] incommoder, gêner, déranger; **in·com'mo·di·ous** □ [~jəs] incommode; peu confortable.

in·com·mu·ni·ca·bil·i·ty ['inkə-mju:nikə'biliti] incommunicabilité *f*; **in·com'mu·ni·ca·ble** □ incommunicable; **in·com'mu·ni·ca·do** *surt. Am.* [inkəmjuni'kɑ:dou] sans contact avec l'extérieur; **in·com'mu·ni·ca·tive** □ [ˌ↳kətiv] taciturne; peu communicatif (-ive *f*).

in·com·mut·a·ble □ [inkə'mju:təbl] non-interchangeable; immuable.

in·com·pa·ra·ble □ [in'kɔmpərəbl] incomparable.

in·com·pat·i·bil·i·ty ['inkəmpætə-'biliti] incompatibilité *f*; inconciliabilité *f*; **in·com'pat·i·ble** □ incompatible, inconciliable.

in·com·pe·tence, in·com·pe·ten·cy [in'kɔmpitəns(i)] incompétence *f* (*a.* ⚖); insuffisance *f*; **in'com·pe·tent** □ incompétent (*a.* ⚖); incapable; ⚖ inhabile.

in·com·plete □ [inkəm'pli:t] incomplet (-ète *f*); inachevé; imparfait.

in·com·pre·hen·si·bil·i·ty [inkəm-prihensə'biliti] incompréhensibilité *f*; **in·com·pre'hen·si·ble** □ incompréhensible.

in·com·press·i·bil·i·ty ['inkəm-presə'biliti] incompressibilité *f*; **in·com'press·i·ble** incompressible.

in·con·ceiv·a·ble □ [inkən'si:vəbl] inconcevable.

in·con·clu·sive □ [inkən'klu:siv] peu *ou* non concluant.

in·con·gru·i·ty [inkɔŋ'gruiti] incongruité *f*, absurdité *f*; désaccord *m*; inconséquence *f*; inconvenance *f*; **in'con·gru·ous** □ incongru, absurde; qui ne s'accorde pas (avec, *with*); sans rapport (avec *to, with*).

in·con·se·quence [in'kɔnsikwəns] inconséquence *f*; manque *m* de logique; **in·con·se·quen·tial** [ˌ↳'kwenʃl] sans importance; illogique.

in·con·sid·er·a·ble □ [inkən'sidərəbl] insignifiant; **in·con'sid·er·ate** □ [ˌ↳rit] irréfléchi, inconsidéré; sans égards (pour, *towards*); **in·con'sid·er·ate·ness** irréflexion *f*, imprudence *f*; manque *m* d'égards.

in·con·sist·en·cy [inkən'sistənsi] inconséquence *f*; inconsistance *f*; incompatibilité *f*; **in·con'sist·ent** □ incompatible; contradictoire (à,

with); en désaccord (avec, *with*); illogique, inconséquent (*personne*).

in·con·sol·a·ble □ [inkən'souləbl] inconsolable (de, *for*).

in·con·so·nant [in'kɔnsənənt] en désaccord (avec, *with*).

in·con·spic·u·ous □ [inkən'spikjuəs] discret (-ète *f*); insignifiant; peu frappant.

in·con·stan·cy [in'kɔnstənsi] inconstance *f*; instabilité *f*; **in'con·stant** □ inconstant, variable.

in·con·test·a·ble □ [inkən'testəbl] incontestable; irrécusable.

in·con·ti·nence [in'kɔntinəns] incontinence *f*; ⚕ ~ *of urine* incontinence *f* d'urine; **in'con·ti·nent** □ incontinent; ⚕ qui ne peut retenir son urine; ~ *of speech* bavard; ~*ly* sur-le-champ, incontinent; incontinemment.

in·con·tro·vert·i·ble □ ['inkɔntrə-'və:təbl] indisputable.

in·con·ven·ience [inkən'vi:njəns] **1.** inconvénient *m*; embarras *m*; incommodité *f*; **2.** incommoder, gêner, déranger; **in·con'ven·ient** □ incommode; inopportun; gênant.

in·con·vert·i·bil·i·ty ['inkənvə:tə-'biliti] (*a.* ✝) non-convertibilité *f*; **in·con'vert·i·ble** □ inconvertible; ✝ *a.* non convertible.

in·con·vin·ci·ble □ [inkən'vinsəbl] impossible à convaincre.

in·cor·po·rate 1. [in'kɔ:pəreit] *v/t.* incorporer (à *in*[to], with; avec, *with*); mêler, unir (à, avec *with*); ériger (*une ville*) en municipalité; ⚖ constituer en société commerciale; *v/i.* s'incorporer (en, *in*; à, avec *with*); **2.** [ˌ↳rit] incorporé; faisant corps; **in'cor·po·rat·ed** [ˌ↳reitid] *see incorporate* 2; ~ *company* société *f* constituée, *Am.* société *f* anonyme (*abbr.* S.A.); **in·cor·po·'ra·tion** incorporation *f* (à, avec, dans *in*[to], with); incorporation *f* communale; constitution *f* en société commerciale.

in·cor·po·re·al □ [inkɔ:'pɔ:riəl] incorporel(le *f*).

in·cor·rect □ [inkə'rekt] incorrect; inexact; défectueux (-euse *f*); **in·cor'rect·ness** incorrection *f*; inexactitude *f*.

in·cor·ri·gi·bil·i·ty [inkɔridʒə'biliti] incorrigibilité *f*; **in'cor·ri·gi·ble** □ incorrigible.

in·cor·rupt·i·bil·i·ty ['inkərʌptə-'biliti] incorruptibilité *f*; **in·cor·'rupt·i·ble** □ incorruptible; **in·cor'rupt·ness** incorruption *f*.

in·crease 1. [in'kri:s] *v/i.* augmenter (de, *in*); s'augmenter; grandir; croître, s'accroître; grossir; se multiplier; *v/t.* augmenter; agrandir; accroître; grossir; **2.** ['inkri:s] augmentation *f*; accroissement *m*; *effort:* redoublement *m*; multiplication *f*.

in·cred·i·bil·i·ty [inkredi'biliti] incrédibilité *f*; **in'cred·i·ble** □ incroyable.

in·cre·du·li·ty [inkri'dju:liti] incrédulité *f*; **in'cred·u·lous** □ [in-'kredjuləs] incrédule.

in·cre·ment ['inkrimənt] *see increase* 2; profit *m*; ~ *value* plus-value *f*.

in·crim·i·nate [in'krimineit] incriminer; impliquer; **in'crim·i·na·to·ry** [~əri] tendant à incriminer.

in·crust [in'krʌst] *see encrust;* **in·crus'ta·tion** incrustation *f*; ⊕ *chaudière:* entartrage *m*, tartre *m*.

in·cu·bate ['inkjubeit] *v/t.* couver (*a. fig.*); *v/i.* être soumis à l'incubation; ♒ couver; **in·cu'ba·tion** incubation *f* (*a. biol., a.* ♒); ~ *period* période *f* d'incubation; **'in·cu·ba·tor** incubateur *m*, couveuse *f*; **in·cu·bus** ['~bəs] *myth.* incube *m*; F fardeau *m*; cauchemar *m*.

in·cul·cate ['inkʌlkeit] inculquer (à q., *upon s.o.;* dans l'esprit, *in the mind*); **in·cul'ca·tion** inculcation *f*.

in·cul·pate ['inkʌlpeit] inculper, incriminer; mêler à une affaire; **in·cul'pa·tion** inculpation *f*; **in'cul·pa·to·ry** [~pətəri] tendant à inculper; accusateur (-trice *f*).

in·cum·ben·cy [in'kʌmbənsi] *eccl.* charge *f*; période *f* d'exercice d'une charge; **in'cum·bent 1.** étendu, appuyé; *be* ~ *on s.o.* incomber à q.; **2.** *eccl.* titulaire *m* d'une charge.

in·cu·nab·u·la [inkju'næbjulə] *pl.* incunables *m/pl.*

in·cur [in'kə:] encourir, s'attirer; contracter (*une dette*); courir (*un risque*); faire (*des dépenses*).

in·cur·a·bil·i·ty [inkjuərə'biliti] incurabilité *f*; **in'cur·a·ble 1.** □ inguérissable; **2.** incurable *mf*.

in·cu·ri·ous □ [in'kjuəriəs] sans curiosité, indifférent.

in·cur·sion [in'kə:ʃn] incursion *f*; descente *f* (dans, *into*).

in·cur·va·tion [inkə:'veiʃn] incurvation *f*; courbure *f*; **'in'curve** s'incurver, se courber en dedans.

in·debt·ed [in'detid] endetté; *fig.* redevable (à q. de qch., *to s.o. for s.th.*); **in'debt·ed·ness** dette *f* (*a. fig.*), dettes *f/pl.*

in·de·cen·cy [in'di:snsi] indécence *f*; ⁂ attentat *m* aux mœurs; **in'de·cent** □ indécent, peu décent; ~ *assault* attentat *m* à la pudeur.

in·de·ci·pher·a·ble [indi'saifərəbl] indéchiffrable.

in·de·ci·sion [indi'siʒn] indécision *f*, irrésolution *f*; **in·de·ci·sive** □ [~-'saisiv] peu concluant; indécis (*personne, a. bataille*), irrésolu.

in·de·clin·a·ble *gramm.* [indi'klainəbl] indéclinable.

in·dec·o·rous □ [in'dekərəs] malséant; inconvenant; **in'dec·o·rous·ness,** *a.* **in·de·co·rum** [indi'kɔ:rəm] inconvenance *f*; manque *m* de maintien.

in·deed [in'di:d] **1.** *adv.* en effet; en vérité; même, à vrai dire; **2.** *int.* effectivement!; vraiment?

in·de·fat·i·ga·ble □ [indi'fætigəbl] infatigable, inlassable.

in·de·fea·si·ble □ [indi'fi:zəbl] irrévocable; ⁂ indestructible (*intérêt*).

in·de·fect·i·ble □ [indi'fektəbl] indéfectible; impeccable.

in·de·fen·si·ble □ [indi'fensəbl] ⚔ indéfendable; *fig.* insoutenable.

in·de·fin·a·ble □ [indi'fainəbl] indéfinissable; *fig.* vague.

in·def·i·nite □ [in'definit] indéfini (*a. gramm.*); imprécis.

in·del·i·ble □ [in'delibl] ineffaçable, indélébile; ~ *ink* encre *f* indélébile; ~ *pencil* crayon *m* à copier.

in·del·i·ca·cy [in'delikəsi] indélicatesse *f*; manque *m* de délicatesse; grossièreté *f*, inconvenance *f*; **in·'del·i·cate** □ [~kit] peu délicat; indélicat; inconvenant; risqué; qui manque de tact.

in·dem·ni·fi·ca·tion [indemnifi-'keiʃn] indemnisation *f*; **in'dem·ni·fy** [~fai] indemniser, dédommager (de, *for*); garantir (contre *against, from*); compenser; **in'dem·ni·ty** garantie *f*, assurance *f*; indemnité *f*, dédommage-

ment *m*; *act of* ~ bill *m* d'indemnité.
in·dent [in'dent] **1.** denteler; découper; ⊕ adenter; *typ.* faire un alinéa; ⚏ passer (*un contrat etc.*) en partie double; ♱ passer une commande pour; ~ *upon* s.o. *for* s.th. réquisitionner qch. de q.; **2.** denteler *f*; découpure *f*; *littoral*: échancrure *f*; ♱ ordre *m* d'achat; ⚒ ordre *m* de réquisition; *see* indenture; **in·den·'ta·tion** découpage *m*; impression *f*; dentelure *f*; découpure *f*; *littoral*: échancrure *f*; **in'den·tion** *typ.* renfoncement *m*; **in'den·ture** [~t∫ə] **1.** contrat *m* bilatéral; ~s *pl.* contrat *m* d'apprentissage; **2.** lier par contrat; engager par un contrat d'apprentissage.
in·de·pend·ence [indi'pendəns] indépendance *f* (à l'égard de, *of*); *État*: autonomie *f*; *Am.* ♀ Day le 4 juillet; **in·de·'pend·ent** □ **1.** indépendant; autonome (*État*); ~ *means* fortune *f* personnelle; rentes *f/pl*; **2.** indépendant *m*.
in·depth [in'depθ] en profondeur.
in·de·scrib·a·ble □ [indis'kraibəbl] indescriptible; indicible.
in·de·struct·i·ble □ [indis'trʌktəbl] indestructible.
in·de·ter·mi·na·ble □ [indi'tə:minəbl] indéterminable; interminable (*dispute*); **in·de'ter·mi·nate** □ [~nit] indéterminé; *fig.* imprécis; **in·de'ter·mi·nate·ness**, **in·de·ter·mi·na·tion** [~'nei∫n] indétermination *f*; *fig.* irrésolution *f*.
in·dex ['indeks] **1.** (*pl. a.* indices) *eccl., volume*: index *m*; *cadran etc.*: aiguille *f*; indice *m*, signe *m*; ⚡ exposant *m*; *opt.* indice *m*; (*ou* ~ *finger*) index *m*; (*ou* ~ *number*) coefficient *m*; ~ *card* fiche *f*; ~ *figure* indice *m*; **2.** dresser l'index de (*un volume*); classer; répertorier.
In·di·a ['indjə] Inde *f*; ~ *paper* papier *m* indien, papier *m* bible; ~ *rubber* gomme *f* (à effacer); caoutchouc *m*; **'In·di·a·man** ⚓ long-courrier *m* des Indes.
In·di·an ['indjən] **1.** indien(ne *f*); de l'Inde; des Indes; *gymn.* ~ *club* bouteille *f* en bois; ~ *corn* maïs *m*; *in* ~ *file* en file indienne; *Am.* F ~ *giver* personne *f* qui fait un cadeau dans l'intention d'en demander à son tour; ~ *ink* encre *f* de Chine; *surt. Am.* ~ *summer* été *m* de la Saint-

Martin; **2.** Indien(ne *f*) *m*; F Hindou(e *f*) *m*; (*usu.* Red ~) *a.* Peau-Rouge (*pl.* Peaux-Rouges) *m*.
in·di·cate ['indikeit] indiquer; signaler; montrer; témoigner; faire savoir; **in·di'ca·tion** indication *f*; indice *m*, signe *m*; **in·dic·a·tive** [in'dikətiv] **1.** □ indicatif (-ive *f*) (de, *of*); *be* ~ *of* dénoter; ~ *mood* = **2.** *gramm.* indicatif *m*; **in·di·ca·tor** ['~keitə] indicateur (-trice *f*) *m* (*a.* ⊕, *tél. su./m*); aiguille *f*; **in'di·ca·to·ry** [~kətəri] indicateur (-trice *f*) (de, *of*).
in·di·ces ['indisi:z] *pl. de* index 1.
in·dict [in'dait] inculper (de *for*, *on a charge of*); **in'dict·a·ble** inculpable; ~ *offence* délit *m*; **in'dict·ment** inculpation *f*; *document*: acte *m* d'accusation.
in·dif·fer·ence [in'difrəns] indifférence *f* (*pour*, à l'égard de *to*, *towards*); **in'dif·fer·ent** □ indifférent (à, *to*); médiocre, passable; ♱ impartial (-aux *m/pl*.); ⚡ neutre.
in·di·gence ['indidʒəns] indigence *f*; F misère *f*.
in·di·gene ['indidʒi:n] indigène *mf*; **in·dig·e·nous** [in'didʒinəs] indigène (à, *to*); du pays.
in·di·gent ['indidʒənt] indigent; nécessiteux (-euse *f*).
in·di·gest·ed [indi'dʒestid] mal digéré; **in·di'gest·i·ble** □ indigeste (*a. fig.*); **in·di'ges·tion** dyspepsie *f*; indigestion *f*.
in·dig·nant □ [in'dignənt] indigné (de, *at*); d'indignation; **in·dig·'na·tion** indignation *f* (contre *with*, *against*); ~ *meeting* meeting *m* de protestation; **in'dig·ni·ty** [~niti] indignité *f*; affront *m*; honte *f*.
in·di·rect □ [indi'rekt] indirect (*a. gramm.*); détourné (*moyen*).
in·dis·cern·i·ble [indi'sə:nəbl] indiscernable; imperceptible.
in·dis·creet □ [indis'kri:t] indiscret (-ète *f*); imprudent, peu judicieux (-euse *f*); inconsidéré; **in·dis·cre·tion** [~'kre∫n] indiscrétion *f*; manque *m* de discrétion; imprudence *f*; F faux pas *m*.
in·dis·crim·i·nate □ [indis'kriminit] au hasard, à tort et à travers; (*a.* **in·dis'crim·i·nat·ing** □ [~'neitiŋ], **in·dis'crim·i·na·tive** [~nətiv]) sans discernement; *fig.* aveugle;

'in·dis·crim·i·na·tion manque *m* de discernement.

in·dis·pen·sa·ble □ [indis'pensəbl] obligatoire; indispensable (à, to).

in·dis·pose [indis'pouz] indisposer, prévenir (contre, *towards*); détourner (de, *from*); rendre peu propre (à qch., *for s.th.*); rendre incapable (de *inf.*, *for gér.*); rendre peu disposé (à *inf.*, *to inf.*); in·dis·po·si·tion [indispə'ziʃn] indisposition *f* (à l'égard de, to[wards]); aversion *f* (pour); malaise *m*, indisposition *f*.

in·dis·pu·ta·ble □ ['indis'pju:təbl] incontestable; hors de controverse.

in·dis·so·lu·bil·i·ty ['indisɔlju'biliti] indissolubilité *f*; ⌐ insolubilité *f*; in·dis·so·lu·ble □ [ˌ'sɔljubl] indissoluble.

in·dis·tinct □ [indis'tiŋkt] indistinct, vague, confus; in·dis'tinct·ness indistinction *f*, vague *m*.

in·dis·tin·guish·a·ble □ [indis-'tiŋgwiʃəbl] indistinguible; imperceptible; insaisissable.

in·dite [in'dait] composer (*un poème*); rédiger (*une lettre*).

in·di·vid·u·al [indi'vidjuəl] **1.** □ individuel(le *f*); particulier (-ère *f*); ⌐ *drive* commande *f* séparée; **2.** individu *m*; in·di·vid·u·al·i·ty [ˌ‑'æliti] individualité *f*; personnalité *f*; in·di'vid·u·al·ize [ˌəlaiz] individualiser.

in·di·vis·i·bil·i·ty ['indivizi'biliti] indivisibilité *f*; in·di'vis·i·ble □ indivisible; ⋏ insécable.

Indo... [indou] indo-; Indo-.

in·doc·ile [in'dousail] indocile; in·do·cil·i·ty [ˌdo'siliti] indocilité *f*.

in·doc·tri·nate [in'dɔktrineit] instruire; endoctriner; ⌐ *s.o. with s.th.* inculquer qch. à q.

in·do·lence ['indələns] indolence *f* (*a.* 𝔰); paresse *f*; 'in·do·lent □ indolent (*a.* 𝔰); paresseux (-euse *f*).

in·dom·i·ta·ble □ [in'dɔmitəbl] indomptable.

in·door ['indɔ:] de maison; d'intérieur; intérieur; *sp.* de salle, de salon; ⌐ *aerial* antenne *f* d'appartement; ⌐ *game* jeu *m* de salle *ou* de salon *ou* de société; ⌐ *plant* plante *f* d'appartement; ⌐ *relief* assistance *f* des pauvres hospitalisés; ⌐ *swimming-bath* piscine *f*; in·doors

['in'dɔ:z] à la maison; à l'intérieur.

in·dorse *etc.* [in'dɔ:s] *see* endorse.

in·du·bi·ta·ble □ [in'dju:bitəbl] indubitable, incontestable.

in·duce [in'dju:s] persuader (à q., *s.o.*); amener; occasionner, produire; 𝔡 amorcer, induire; 𝔡 ⌐d *current* courant *m* induit *ou* d'induction; in'duce·ment motif *m*; attrait *m*; raison *f*.

in·duct *eccl.* [in'dʌkt] installer; in'duct·ance 𝔡 inductance *f*; ⌐-coil (bobine *f* de) self *f*; bobine *f* d'inductance; in'duc·tion *eccl.*, fonctionnaire: installation *f*; ⋏, phls., phys. induction *f*; 𝔡 production *f*; in'duc·tive □ qui induit (à, to); ⋏, phls. inductif (-ive *f*) (*a.* 𝔡 *charge*); 𝔡 inducteur (-trice *f*).

in·dulge [in'dʌldʒ] *v/t.* gâter (*q.*), avoir de l'indulgence pour (*q.*); se livrer à, s'adonner à; donner libre cours à (*ses passions, ses caprices*); F boire; ⌐ *s.o. with s.th.* accorder qch. à q.; ⌐ *o.s. in* se livrer à, s'adonner à (*qch.*); *v/i.* se permettre (à, *in*); se livrer, s'adonner (à, *in*); in'dul·gence indulgence *f* (*a. eccl.*); complaisance *f* (envers, to); assouvissement *m* (de of, *in*); abandon *m* (à, *in*); ✝ délai *m* de paiement; in'dul·gent □ indulgent (envers, à, pour to); faible.

in·du·rate ['indjuəreit] (s')endurcir; durcir; 𝔰 (s')indurer; in·du·ra·tion (*fig.* en)durcissement *m*; 𝔰 induration *f*.

in·dus·tri·al [in'dʌstriəl] **1.** □ industriel(le *f*); professionnel (*le f*); de l'industrie; ⌐ *art* art *m* mécanique; ⌐ *court* tribunal *m* industriel; ⌐ *disease* maladie *f* professionnelle; ⌐ *espionage* espionnage *m* industriel; ⌐ *school* école *f* des arts et métiers; école *f* professionnelle de rééducation; ⌐ *tribunal* conseil *m* de prud'hommes; **2.** *see* industrialist; ⌐s *pl.* ✝ valeurs *f/pl.* industrielles; in'dus·tri·al·ist industriel *m*, industrialiste *m*; in'dus·tri·al·ize [ˌaiz] industrialiser; *become* ⌐d s'industrialiser; in'dus·tri·ous □ travailleur (-euse *f*), laborieux (-euse *f*), assidu.

in·dus·try ['indəstri] assiduité *f* au travail, diligence *f*; travail *m*; ⊕ industrie *f*; *heavy industries pl.* industries *f/pl.* lourdes.

in·dwell ['in'dwel] [*irr.* (*dwell*)] demeurer dans; habiter (*un lieu*); *fig.* reposer dans.

in·e·bri·ate 1. [i'ni:brieit] enivrer; **2.** [i'ni:briit] ivre, enivré; **3.** ivrogne *mf*; **in·e·bri·a·tion**, **in·e·bri·e·ty** [ini:'braiəti] ivresse *f*; alcoolisme *m*; enivrement *m*.

in·ed·i·ble [in'edibl] immangeable.

in·ed·it·ed [in'editid] inédit; publié sans notes.

in·ef·fa·ble □ [in'efəbl] ineffable, indicible.

in·ef·face·a·ble □ [ini'feisəbl] ineffaçable.

in·ef·fec·tive [ini'fektiv], **in·ef·fec·tu·al** □ [‿tjuə!] inefficace, sans effet, sans résultat; ✕ inapte au service.

in·ef·fi·ca·cious □ [inefi'keiʃəs] inefficace; **in·ef·fi·ca·cy** [‿kəsi] inefficacité *f*.

in·ef·fi·cien·cy [ini'fiʃənsi] incapacité *f*; incompétence *f*; inefficacité *f*; **in·ef·fi·cient** □ [‿ʃiənt] incapable; incompétent; inefficace.

in·el·e·gance [in'eligəns] inélégance *f*; **in·el·e·gant** □ sans élégance (*personne*); inélégant (*style*).

in·el·i·gi·bil·i·ty [inelidʒə'biliti] inéligibilité *f*; caractère *m* peu acceptable; **in·el·i·gi·ble** □ inéligible; indigne d'être choisi; *fig.* peu acceptable; ✕ inapte.

in·ept □ [i'nept] inepte; déplacé; mal à propos; ⚖ de nul effet; **in'ept·i·tude** [‿itju:d], **in'ept·ness** manque *m* d'à-propos *ou* de justesse; inaptitude *f*; sottise *f*.

in·e·qual·i·ty [ini'kwɔliti] inégalité *f*; *sol, bois*: rugosité *f*; irrégularité *f*.

in·eq·ui·ta·ble □ [in'ekwitəbl] inéquitable, injuste; **in'eq·ui·ty** injustice *f*.

in·e·rad·i·ca·ble □ [ini'rædikəbl] indéracinable.

in·ert □ [i'nə:t] inerte; **in·er·tia** [i'nə:ʃjə], **in'ert·ness** inertie *f*.

in·es·cap·a·ble [inis'keipəbl] inévitable, inéluctable.

in·es·sen·tial ['ini'senʃl] négligeable; non essentiel(le *f*) (à, to).

in·es·ti·ma·ble □ [in'estiməbl] inestimable; incalculable.

in·ev·i·ta·ble □ [in'evitəbl] inévitable, inéluctable; immanquable; fatal (-als *m/pl.*); **in'ev·i·ta·ble·ness** inévitabilité *f*.

in·ex·act □ [inig'zækt] inexact; **in·ex'act·i·tude** [‿itju:d], **in·ex'act·ness** inexactitude *f*.

in·ex·cus·a·ble □ [iniks'kju:zəbl] inexcusable, sans excuse.

in·ex·haust·i·bil·i·ty [inigzɔ:stə'biliti] nature *f* inépuisable; **in·ex·'haust·i·ble** □ inépuisable; intarissable (*source*).

in·ex·o·ra·bil·i·ty [ineksərə'biliti] inexorabilité *f*; caractère *m* implacable; **in'ex·o·ra·ble** □ inexorable, implacable.

in·ex·pe·di·en·cy [iniks'pi:diənsi] inopportunité *f*; **in·ex'pe·di·ent** □ inopportun, malavisé.

in·ex·pen·sive □ [iniks'pensiv] bon marché; peu coûteux (-euse *f*); pas cher (chère *f*).

in·ex·pe·ri·ence [iniks'piəriəns] inexpérience *f*; **in·ex'pe·ri·enced** inexpérimenté, sans expérience.

in·ex·pert □ [ineks'pə:t] inexpert; peu habile (à, in).

in·ex·pi·a·ble □ [in'ekspiəbl] inexpiable; † impitoyable.

in·ex·pli·ca·ble □ [in'eksplikəbl] inexplicable; inconcevable.

in·ex·press·i·ble [iniks'presəbl] **1.** □ inexprimable; indicible; **2.** *co. ou* † ‿s *pl.* pantalon *m*, culotte *f*.

in·ex·pres·sive □ [iniks'presiv] inexpressif (-ive *f*); sans expression.

in·ex·pug·na·ble □ [iniks'pʌgnəbl] inexpugnable; *fig.* inattaquable.

in·ex·tin·guish·a·ble □ [iniks'tiŋgwiʃəbl] inextinguible.

in·ex·tri·ca·ble □ [in'ekstrikəbl] inextricable.

in·fal·li·bil·i·ty [infælə'biliti] infaillibilité *f*; **in'fal·li·ble** □ infaillible; sûr.

in·fa·mous □ ['infəməs] infâme; mal famé; abominable; **in·fa·my** ['‿mi] (note *f* d')infamie *f*.

in·fan·cy ['infənsi] première enfance *f*; ⚖ minorité *f*; **in·fant** ['‿fənt] **1.** enfant *mf*; ⚖ mineur(e*f*) *m*; ‿ *school* école *f* maternelle *ou* enfantine; ‿ *welfare* puériculture *f* sociale; **2.** d'enfance; enfantin.

in·fan·ta [in'fæntə] infante *f*; **in'fan·te** [‿ti] infant *m*.

in·fan·ti·cide [in'fæntisaid] infanticide *m*; *personne*: infanticide *mf*; **in·fan·tile** ['infəntail] d'enfant; ⚕ infantile; *péj.* enfantin; ‿ *paralysis*

poliomyélite *f*; **in·fan·tine** ['ᴗtain]
see infantile.

in·fan·try ✕ ['infəntri] infanterie *f*;
'**in·fan·try·man** soldat *m* d'infanterie; fantassin *m*.

in·fat·u·ate [in'fætjueit] infatuer,
affoler; enticher; **in·fat·u·a·tion**
infatuation *f*, engouement *m*; béguin *m* (pour, *for*).

in·fect [in'fekt] infecter; ⚕ contaminer; *fig.* inculquer (qch. à q.,
s.o. with s.th.); become ᴗed se con-
tagionner; **in'fec·tion** ⚕, *fig.* infection *f*, contagion *f*; contamination
f; **in'fec·tious** □, **in'fec·tive** ⚕ infectieux (-euse *f*); *fig.* contagieux
(-euse *f*).

in·fe·lic·i·tous [infi'lisitəs] malheureux (-euse *f*); mal trouvé; **in-
fe'lic·i·ty** infélicité *f*; manque *m*
de justesse; gaffe *f*.

in·fer [in'fə:] déduire, conclure (de,
from); impliquer; **in'fer·a·ble**
qu'on peut inférer; qu'on peut déduire; **in·fer·ence** ['infərəns] infé-
rence *f*, conclusion *f*; **in·fer·en·tial**
□ [ᴗ'renʃl] déductif (-ive *f*); ob-
tenu par déduction; ᴗly par déduction.

in·fe·ri·or [in'fiəriə] **1.** inférieur (à,
to); ♀ infère; **2.** inférieur *m*;
subordonné(e *f*) *m*; **in·fe·ri·or·i·ty**
[ᴗri'ɔriti] infériorité *f* (par rapport
à, *to*); ᴗ *complex* complexe *m*
d'infériorité.

in·fer·nal □ [in'fə:nl] infernal
(-aux *m/pl.*); des enfers; de l'enfer;
F diabolique, infernal (-aux *m/pl.*);
ᴗ *machine* machine *f* infernale.

in·fer·tile [in'fə:tail] stérile; **in·fer-
til·i·ty** [ᴗ'tiliti] stérilité *f*, infer-
tilité *f*.

in·fest [in'fest] infester (de, *with*)
(*fig.*); **in·fes'ta·tion** infestation *f*.

in·fi·del ['infidəl] infidèle (*a. su./mf*);
péj. incroyant(e *f*) (*a. su.*); **in·fi-
del·i·ty** [ᴗ'deliti] infidélité *f*.

in·fight(·ing) ['infait(iŋ)] *box.* corps
à corps *m*; *fig.* guerre *f* intestine.

in·fil·trate ['infiltreit] *v/t.* infiltrer;
imprégner; pénétrer dans; *v/i.*
s'infiltrer (dans, *into*; à travers,
through); **in·fil'tra·tion** infiltration *f*.

in·fi·nite □ ['infinit] infini; illimité;
astr. sans nombre; **in'fin·i·tive** (*a.
ᴗ mood*) *gramm.* infinitif *m*; **in-
'fin·i·tude** [ᴗtju:d], **in'fin·i·ty** in-

finité *f*, infinitude *f*; A infini *m*.

in·firm □ [in'fə:m] débile, infirme,
faible; (*a. ᴗ of purpose*) irrésolu,
flottant; **in'fir·ma·ry** infirmerie *f*;
hôpital *m*; **in'fir·mi·ty** [ᴗiti] infirmité *f*; faiblesse *f* (*a. fig.*).

in·fix [in'fiks] implanter; *gramm.*
infixer; *fig.* inculquer.

in·flame [in'fleim] (s')enflammer (*a.
fig.*, *a.* ⚕); (s')allumer (*a. fig.*); *v/t.*
mettre le feu à; *v/i.* prendre feu.

in·flam·ma·bil·i·ty [inflæmə'biliti]
inflammabilité *f*; **in'flam·ma·ble**
1. □ inflammable; **2.** ᴗ*s pl.* substan-
ces *f/pl.* inflammables; **in·flam-
ma·tion** [inflə'meiʃn] inflammation
f; **in·flam·ma·to·ry** [in'flæmətəri]
incendiaire; ⚕ inflammatoire.

in·flate [in'fleit] gonfler (*a. fig.*); ✝
grossir; ✝ hausser (*le prix*); **in-
'flat·ed** gonflé, enflé; ✝ exagéré;
ampoulé (*style*); **in'fla·tion** gonflement *m*; ⚕, ✝ inflation *f*; ✝ *prix:*
hausse *f*; *fig.* enflure *f*; **in'fla·tion-
ar·y** d'inflation, inflationniste.

in·flect [in'flekt] fléchir; moduler
(*la voix*); ♪ altérer; *gramm.* conjuguer (*un verbe*), décliner (*un substantif*); **in'flec·tion** *see* inflexion.

in·flex·i·bil·i·ty [infleksə'biliti] inflexibilité *f* (*a. fig.*); **in'flex·i·ble** □
inflexible (*a. fig.*); **in'flex·ion** [ᴗʃn]
inflexion *f*; *voix:* modulation *f*;
gramm. flexion *f*.

in·flict [in'flikt] donner (*un coup*)
(à, *on*); infliger (*une punition*) (à,
on); ᴗ *o.s.* (*ou one's company*) on
imposer sa compagnie à; **in'fliction** infliction *f*; châtiment *m*, peine
f; *fig.* vexation *f*.

in·flo·res·cence ♀ [inflo'resns] inflorescence *f*; floraison *f*.

in·flow ['infləu] *see* influx.

in·flu·ence ['influəns] **1.** influence *f*
(sur, [*up*]on; auprès de, *with*);
2. influencer; influer sur; **in·flu-
en·tial** □ [ᴗ'enʃl] influent.

in·flu·en·za ⚕ [influ'enzə] grippe *f*.

in·flux ['inflʌks] affluence *f*, entrée
f; *fig.* invasion *f*, inondation *f*.

in·form [in'fɔ:m] *v/t.* informer (de,
of); renseigner (sur, *about*); avertir; faire part à; mettre au courant;
well ᴗed bien renseigné; *keep s.o.*
ᴗed tenir q. au courant (de, *of*);
v/i. dénoncer (q., *against s.o.*).

in·for·mal □ [in'fɔ:ml] sans cérémonie; officieux (-euse *f*); irrégu-

lier (-ère f); **in·for·mal·i·ty** [~'mæ-liti] absence f de cérémonie; irrégularité f.

in·form·ant [in'fɔ:mənt] informateur (-trice f) m; ⚖ déclarant(e f) m; see informer; **in·for·ma·tion** [infə-'meiʃn] renseignements m/pl.; informations f/pl.; instruction f; ⚖ dénonciation f (contre, against); ~ film documentaire m; ~ science informatique f; gather ~ recueillir des renseignements (sur, about); **in·form·a·tive** [in'fɔ:mətiv] instructif (-ive f); **in·form·er** dénonciateur (-trice f), F mouchard m.

in·frac·tion [in'frækʃn] infraction f; contravention f.

in·fra…: ~ **dig** F au-dessous de la dignité (de q.), déshonorant; '~**red** phys. infrarouge; '~**struc·ture** infrastructure f.

in·fre·quen·cy [in'fri:kwənsi] rareté f; **in'fre·quent** □ rare, infréquent.

in·fringe [in'frindʒ] v/t. enfreindre, violer (la loi, un serment); v/i. empiéter (sur, upon) (un brevet etc.); **in'fringe·ment** infraction f; contrefaçon f.

in·fu·ri·ate [in'fjuərieit] rendre furieux (-euse f).

in·fuse [in'fju:z] infuser (du thé) (à, into); faire infuser (le thé); inspirer (qch. à q., s.o. with s.th.); pharm. macérer; **in'fu·sion** [~ʒn] infusion f (a. fig.); **in·fu·so·ri·a** zo. [infju-'sɔ:riə] pl. infusoires m/pl.

in·gath·er·ing ['ingæðəriŋ] rentrée f; récolte f.

in·gen·ious □ [in'dʒi:njəs] ingénieux (-euse f); **in·ge·nu·i·ty** [indʒi'nju:iti] ingéniosité f; **in·gen·u·ous** □ [in'dʒenjuəs] ingénu, naïf (-ïve f); franc(he f).

in·gle ['iŋgl] foyer m; feu m.

in·glo·ri·ous □ [in'glɔ:riəs] honteux (-euse f); ignominieux (-euse f); humble, obscur.

in·go·ing ['ingouiŋ] **1.** entrée f; **2.** qui entre, entrant; nouveau (nouvel devant une voyelle ou un h muet; -elle f; -eaux m/pl.) (locataire).

in·got ['iŋgət] lingot m; étain: saumon m; '~**steel** acier m en lingots.

in·grain ['in'grein] teindre grand teint; **'in'grained** fig. imprégné; invétéré (personne).

in·gra·ti·ate [in'greiʃieit]: ~ o.s.

s'insinuer (dans les bonnes grâces de, with); **in·grat·i·tude** [~'græ-titju:d] ingratitude f.

in·gre·di·ent [in'gri:diənt] ingrédient m; 🍴 principe m.

in·gress ['ingres] entrée f; droit m d'accès.

in·gui·nal anat. ['iŋgwinl] inguinal (-aux m/pl.).

in·gur·gi·tate [in'gə:dʒiteit] ingurgiter, avaler.

in·hab·it [in'hæbit] habiter; **in'hab·it·a·ble** habitable; **in'hab·it·an·cy** habitation f; résidence f; **in'hab·it·ant** habitant(e f) m.

in·ha·la·tion [inhə'leiʃn] aspiration f; ⚕ inhalation f; **in·hale** [~'heil] aspirer; respirer; ⚕ inhaler; **in-'hal·er** ⚕ inhalateur m.

in·har·mo·ni·ous □ [inha:'mou-njəs] inharmonieux (-euse f).

in·here [in'hiə] (in) être inhérent (à); appartenir (à); exister (dans); **in-'her·ence, in'her·en·cy** [~rəns(i)] inhérence f (à, in); **in'her·ent** □ inhérent, propre (à, in).

in·her·it [in'herit] hériter de (qch.); succéder à; tenir (de, from); **in-'her·it·a·ble** □ dont on peut hériter; transmissible (a. ⚕); **in'her·it·ance** succession f; héritage m; biol. hérédité f; **in'her·i·tor** héritier m; **in'her·i·tress** héritière f.

in·hib·it [in'hibit] empêcher (q. de, s.o. from); défendre (à q. de inf., s.o. from gér.); psych. inhiber; **in-hi·bi·tion** [~'biʃn] défense f expresse; eccl. interdit m; psych. inhibition f; **in'hib·i·to·ry** [~təri] prohibitif (-ive f); physiol., psych. inhibiteur (-trice f).

in·hos·pi·ta·ble □ [in'hɔspitəbl] inhospitalier (-ère f); **in·hos·pi·tal·i·ty** ['~'tæliti] inhospitalité f.

in·hu·man □ [in'hju:mən] inhumain; barbare; **in·hu·mane** □ [~'mein] inhumain, cruel(le f); **in·hu·man·i·ty** [~'mæniti] inhumanité f; cruauté f.

in·hu·ma·tion [inhju:'meiʃn] inhumation f; enterrement m; **in-hume** [in'hju:m] inhumer, enterrer.

in·im·i·cal □ [i'nimikl] ennemi, hostile; contraire (à, to).

in·im·i·ta·ble □ [i'nimitəbl] inimitable.

in·iq·ui·tous □ [i'nikwitəs] inique; **in'iq·ui·ty** iniquité f.

initial

886

in·i·tial [i'niʃl] 1. □ initial (-aux *m/pl.*); premier (-ère *f*); du début; ~ *payment* acompte *m*; ~ *salary* salaire *m* initial *ou* du début; 2. initiale *f*; paraphe *m*; 3. parafer; viser; **in·i·ti·ate** 1. [i'niʃiit] initié(e *f*) (*a. su.*); 2. [i'niʃieit] commencer (*une entreprise etc.*); inaugurer; initier (à, *into*); **in·i·ti·a·tion** début *m*; commencement *m*; inauguration *f*; initiation *f*; *surt. Am. société:* ~ *fee* droits *m/pl.* d'admission; **in·i·ti·a·tive** [~ətiv] 1. préliminaire, préparatoire; 2. initiative *f*; *on one's own* ~ de sa propre initiative; *take the* ~ prendre l'initiative (pour *inf.*, *in gér.*); **in·i·ti·a·tor** [~eitə] initiateur (-trice *f*) *m*; lanceur *m* (*d'une mode etc.*); **in·i·ti·a·to·ry** [~ətəri] préliminaire, préparatoire, premier (-ère *f*).

in·ject [in'dʒekt] injecter (dans, *into*; de, *with*); **in·jec·tion** injection *f*.

in·ju·di·cious □ [indʒu'diʃəs] malavisé, peu judicieux (-euse *f*).

in·junc·tion [in'dʒʌŋkʃn] injonction *f*, ordre *m*.

in·jure ['indʒə] nuire à, faire du mal à, faire du tort à; gâter; endommager; **in·ju·ri·ous** □ [in'dʒuəriəs] nuisible, préjudiciable (à, *to*); injurieux (-euse *f*) (*langage*); **in·ju·ry** ['indʒəri] tort *m*; mal *m*; dommage *m*; blessure *f*.

in·jus·tice [in'dʒʌstis] injustice *f*.

ink [iŋk] 1. encre *f*; (*usu. printer's* ~) noir *m* d'imprimerie; *attr.* à encre, d'encre; 2. noircir d'encre; *typ.* encrer.

ink·ling ['iŋkliŋ] soupçon *m* (*a. fig.*).

ink...: '~**pot** encrier *m*; '~**stand** grand encrier *m*; '**ink·y** taché *ou* barbouillé d'encre.

in·land ['inlənd] 1. du pays, intérieur (*commerce etc.*); ♀ *Revenue* fisc *m*; 2. intérieur *m*; 3. [in'lænd] dans les terres; vers l'intérieur; **in·land·er** ['inləndə] habitant(e *f*) *m* de l'intérieur.

in·laws ['inlɔːz] *pl.* parents *m/pl.* par alliance; beaux-parents *m/pl.*

in·lay ['in'lei] 1. [*irr.* (*lay*)] incruster (de, *with*); marqueter (*une table*); parqueter (*un plancher*) en mosaïque; 2. incrustation *f*; marqueterie *f*; *livre:* encartage *m*.

in·let ['inlet] entrée *f*; bras *m* de mer; crique *f*; ⊕ arrivée *f*, admission *f*.

in·mate ['inmeit] habitant(e *f*) *m*; *aliéné:* pensionnaire *mf*; *hospice etc.:* hôte *m*.

in·most ['inmoust] le plus profond.

inn [in] auberge *f*; *ville:* hôtellerie *f*; ♀s *pl.* of *Court* écoles *f/pl.* de droit (*Londres*).

in·nate □ ['i'neit] inné.

in·ner ['inə] intérieur; interne, de dedans; intime; *cycl., mot.* ~ *tube* chambre *f* à air, boudin *m* d'air; '**in·ner·most** le plus profond *ou* intime.

in·ner·vate ['inəːveit] *physiol.* innerver.

in·nings ['iniŋz] *pl. ou sg. sp.* tour *m* de batte; tournée *f*; *have one's* ~ être au guichet, *fig.* être au pouvoir, prendre son tour.

inn·keep·er ['inkiːpə] aubergiste *mf*; hôtelier (-ère *f*) *m*.

in·no·cence ['inəsns] innocence *f*; naïveté *f*, candeur *f*; '**in·no·cent** 1. □ innocent (de, *of*); dépourvu (de); pur, sans péché; F ~ *of* sans; 2. innocent(e *f*) *m*; naïf (-ïve *f*) *m*; idiot(e *f*) *m*.

in·noc·u·ous □ [i'nɔkjuəs] inoffensif (-ive *f*).

in·nom·i·nate [i'nɔminit] *anat.* innominé; ♫ innommé.

in·no·vate ['inoveit] innover; **in·no·va·tion** innovation *f*; nouveauté *f*; '**in·no·va·tor** (in)novateur (-trice *f*) *m*.

in·nox·ious □ [i'nɔkʃəs] inoffensif (-ive *f*).

in·nu·en·do [inju'endou] insinuation *f*; allusion *f*.

in·nu·mer·a·ble □ [i'njuːmərəbl] innombrable.

in·nu·tri·tious [inju'triʃəs] peu nourrissant; peu nutritif (-ive *f*).

in·ob·serv·ance [inəb'zəːvəns] (*of*) inobservance *f* (de); *promesse:* inobservation *f* (de); inattention *f* (à).

in·oc·u·late [i'nɔkjuleit] ↗ greffer; ✿ inoculer (qch. à q. *s.o. with s.th.*, *s.th. into s.o.*; contre, *against*); **in·oc·u·la·tion** ↗ greffe *f*; ✿ inoculation *f*; **in·oc·u·la·tor** inoculateur (-trice *f*) *m*.

in·o·dor·ous [in'oudərəs] sans [odeur, inodore.]

in·of·fen·sive □ [inə'fensiv] inoffensif (-ive *f*).

in·of·fi·cial [inə'fiʃl] inofficieux (-euse *f*).

in·op·er·a·tive [in'ɔpərətiv] inopérant.

in·op·por·tune □ [in'ɔpətjuːn] inopportun; hors de saison.

in·or·di·nate □ [i'nɔːdinit] démesuré, immodéré; effréné.

in·or·gan·ic [inɔː'gænik] inorganique.

in·pa·tient ['inpeiʃənt] hospitalisé(e f) m.

in·put ⊕, surt. ⚡ ['input] puissance f; entrée f de courant.

in·quest ⚕ ['inkwest] enquête f (sur, on); coroner's ~ enquête f judiciaire après mort d'homme.

in·qui·e·tude [in'kwaiitjuːd] agitation f, inquiétude f.

in·quire [in'kwaiə] demander (qch., for s.th.); se renseigner (sur about, after), s'informer (de qch.); ~ into faire des recherches ou une enquête sur; **in'quir·er** investigateur (-trice f) m; **in'quir·ing** □ curieux (-euse f); interrogateur (-trice f); **in'quir·y** enquête f, investigation f; demande f (a. ⚡); make inquiries prendre des renseignements (sur about, on); s'informer (auprès de, of); **in'quir·y-of·fice** bureau m de renseignements; Service m des renseignements.

in·qui·si·tion [inkwi'ziʃn] investigation f; ⚕ enquête f; hist. 2 Inquisition f; **in'quis·i·tive** □ questionneur (-euse f); curieux (-euse f); **in'quis·i·tive·ness** curiosité f (indiscrète); **in'quis·i·tor** enquêteur m; hist. Inquisiteur m; **in·quis·i·to·ri·al** □ [ˌ·'tɔːriəl] inquisitorial (-aux m/pl.).

in·road ['inroud] ✕ incursion f, irruption f; fig. empiétement m (sur, upon); make ~s upon (ou in) ébrécher, harceler.

in·sa·lu·bri·ous [insə'luːbriəs] malsain; insalubre.

in·sane [in'sein] fou (fol devant une voyelle ou un h muet; folle f); insensé; **in·san·i·tar·y** □ [ˌ·'sænitəri] insalubre; malsain; **in'san·i·ty** folie f, démence f.

in·sa·ti·a·bil·i·ty [inseiʃjə'biliti] insatiabilité f; **in'sa·ti·a·ble** □, **in'sa·ti·ate** [ˌ·ʃiit] inassouvissable; insatiable (de, of).

in·scribe [in'skraib] inscrire (a. Å, a. ✝ actions); graver (un nom sur qch., s.th. with a name); fig.

inscrire (sur, on; dans, in); dédier.

in·scrip·tion [in'skripʃn] inscription f (✝ au grand livre); fig. dédicace f.

in·scru·ta·bil·i·ty [inskruːtə'biliti] inscrutabilité f; **in'scru·ta·ble** □ inscrutable, impénétrable; fermé (visage).

in·sect ['insekt] insecte m; **in'sec·ti·cide** [ˌ·isaid] insecticide (a. su./m); **in·sec·tiv·o·rous** [ˌ·'tivərəs] insectivore.

in·se·cure □ [insi'kjuə] peu sûr; incertain; **in·se'cu·ri·ty** [ˌ·riti] insécurité f; danger m.

in·sen·sate [in'senseit] insensé; insensible (matière); **in·sen·si·bil·i·ty** [ˌ·sə'biliti] défaillance f; insensibilité f (à, to); indifférence f (pour, to); **in'sen·si·ble** □ insensible (à of, to); indifférent (à of, to); évanoui, sans connaissance; **in'sen·si·tive** insensible (à, to).

in·sen·ti·ent [in'senʃiənt] insensible.

in·sep·a·ra·bil·i·ty [insepərə'biliti] inséparabilité f; **in'sep·a·ra·ble** □ inséparable.

in·sert 1. [in'səːt] usu. insérer (dans, in[to]); introduire; intercaler (une ligne, un mot); 2. ['insəːt] insertion f; pièce f rapportée; **in'ser·tion** insertion f, introduction f; cost. incrustation f; dentelle: entre-deux m/inv.

in·set ['inset] typ. encart m; feuillet m; hors-texte m/inv.; médaillon m; attr. en médaillon.

in·shore ⚓ ['in'ʃɔː] 1. adj. côtier (-ère f); 2. adv. près de terre.

in·side [in'said] 1. su. dedans m, intérieur m; F entrailles f/pl.; 2. adj. (d')intérieur; interne; mot. ~ drive conduite f intérieure; sp. ~ lane piste f intérieure; foot. ~ left intérieur m gauche; 3. adv. en dedans; Am. a. ~ of en moins de (temps); 4. prp. à l'intérieur de; **'in'sid·er** initié(e f) m.   [(-euse f).\
in·sid·i·ous □ [in'sidiəs] insidieux⌡

in·sight ['insait] perspicacité f; fig. aperçu m (de, into).

in·sig·ni·a [in'signiə] pl. insignes m/pl.; signes m/pl. etc. distinctifs.

in·sig·nif·i·cance, a. **in·sig·nif·i·can·cy** [insig'nifikəns(i)] insignifiance f; **in·sig'nif·i·cant** insignifiant; sans importance.

insincere

888

in·sin·cere □ [insin'siə] peu sincère; faux (fausse *f*); **in·sin·cer·i·ty** [~'seriti] manque *m* de sincérité; fausseté *f*.

in·sin·u·ate [in'sinjueit] insinuer; laisser entendre; donner à entendre; glisser (dans, *into*); ~ *o.s. into* s'insinuer dans; **in'sin·u·at·ing** □ insinuant; suggestif (-ive *f*) (*propos etc.*); **in·sin·u·a·tion** insinuation *f* (*a. fig.*); introduction *f*.

in·sip·id □ [in'sipid] insipide, fade; **in·si'pid·i·ty** insipidité *f*; fadeur *f*.

in·sist [in'sist] insister; ~ (*up*)*on* insister sur, appuyer sur; revendiquer (*un droit*); insister pour (*inf.*); vouloir (*qch.*) absolument; ~ *that* insister pour que (*sbj.*), exiger que (*sbj.*); **in'sist·ence** insistance *f*; protestations *f/pl.* (de, on); *at his* ~ devant son insistance; puisqu'il insistait; **in'sist·ent** □ qui insiste (sur, [*up*]*on*); instant; importun.

in·so·bri·e·ty [inso'braiəti] intempérance *f*.

in(·)so(·)far as [insə'fɑ:rəz] tant que, dans la mesure où.

in·so·la·tion [inso'leiʃn] insolation *f* (⚕, *a. phot.*); ⚕ coup *m* de soleil.

in·so·lence ['insələns] insolence *f*, effronterie *f* (envers, *to*); **'in·so·lent** □ insolent (envers, *to*).

in·sol·u·bil·i·ty [insɔlju'biliti] insolubilité *f*; **in'sol·u·ble** □ [~jubl] insoluble (*a. fig.*).

in·sol·ven·cy [in'sɔlvənsi] insolvabilité *f*; faillite *f*; **in'sol·vent** **1.** insolvable; en faillite; **2.** débiteur *m* insolvable; failli *m*.

in·som·ni·a [in'sɔmniə] insomnie *f*.

in·so·much [insou'mʌtʃ]: ~ *that* au point que; tellement que.

in·spect [in'spekt] examiner; contrôler; **in'spec·tion** inspection *f*; examen *m*; contrôle *m*; visite *f*; ✝ *for* ~ à l'essai; **in'spec·tor** inspecteur *m*; surveillant *m*; **in'spec·tor·ate** [~tərit] *office*: inspectorat *m*; *corps m d'inspecteurs.

in·spi·ra·tion [inspə'reiʃn] inspiration *f*; **in·spire** [~'spaiə] aspirer, inspirer; *fig.* inspirer (qch. à q. *s.th. in[to] s.o., s.o. with s.th.*); aiguillonner (*q.*); **in·spir·it** [~'spirit] animer, encourager.

in·spis·sate [in'spiseit] (s')épaissir.

in·sta·bil·i·ty [instə'biliti] instabi-

lité *f*; manque *m* de solidité; *fig.* inconstance *f*.

in·stall [in'stɔ:l] installer (dans, *in*) (*a.* ⊕); ⊕ monter (*un atelier, une machine*); **in·stal·la·tion** [instə-'leiʃn] installation *f* (*a.* ⚡); ⊕, *radio:* montage *m*; poste *m* (*de T.S.F.*).

in·stal(l)·ment [in'stɔ:lmənt] ✝ fraction *f*; acompte *m*; versement *m*; *ouvrage:* fascicule *m*; *monthly* ~ mensualité *f*; *by* ~s par paiements à termes; *fig.* peu à peu; ~ **plan** ✝ système *m* de crédit; *buy s.th. on the* ~ acheter qch. à tempérament.

in·stance ['instəns] **1.** instance *f* (*a.* ⚖); exemple *m*, cas *m*; *for* ~ par exemple; *in the first* ~ en premier lieu; *at the* ~ *of* à la demande de; sur l'instance de; **2.** citer (*qch.*) en exemple.

in·stant □ ['instənt] **1.** instant, urgent; pressant; immédiat; *on the 10th* ~ le 10 courant; **2.** instant *m*, moment *m*; *in an* ~, *on the* ~ sur-le-champ, tout de suite; *the* ~ *you come* dès que vous viendrez; **in·stan·ta·ne·ous** □ [~'teinjəs] instantané; **in·stan·ter** [in'stæntə], **in·stant·ly** ['instəntli] immédiatement, sur-le-champ.

in·state [in'steit] établir (dans, *in*).

in·stead [in'sted] au lieu de cela; ~ *of* (*gér.*) au lieu de (*inf.*).

in·step ['instep] cou-de-pied (*pl.* cous-de-pied) *m*; *soulier:* cambrure *f*.

in·sti·gate ['instigeit] exciter, inciter, provoquer (à, *to*); **in·sti'ga·tion** instigation *f*; **'in·sti·ga·tor** instigateur (-trice *f*) *m*; auteur *m* (*d'une révolte*).

in·stil(l) [in'stil] instiller; *fig.* inculquer (à, *into*), inspirer (à, *into*); **in·stil·la·tion** [insti'leiʃn], **in·'stil(l)·ment** instillation *f*; inspiration *f*; inculcation *f*.

in·stinct 1. ['instiŋkt] instinct *m*; **2.** [in'stiŋkt] plein; ~ *with life* plein ou doué de vie; **in'stinc·tive** □ instinctif (-ive *f*).

in·sti·tute ['institju:t] **1.** institut *m*; cercle *m*; ✝ institution *f*; ⚥ *of Justinian Institutes f/pl.* de Justinien; **2.** instituer, établir (*q.*); fonder; intenter (*un procès*); investir (*q.*) (de, [*in*]*to*), ⚖ instituer (*q.*) (héritier, *as heir*); **in·sti'tu·tion** institution *f*, établissement *m* (*a. édifice*); commencement *m*; association *f* (*d'ingénieurs etc.*); hospice *m* (*de charité*); *eccl.* investiture *f*; ⚖ institution *f*; **in·sti'tu·tion·al·ize** [~əlaiz] faire une institution de (*qch.*); **'in·sti·tu·tor** fondateur (-trice *f*) *m*; auteur *m*.

in·struct [in'strʌkt] instruire; enseigner (*qch. à q., s.o. in s.th.*); charger (de, *to*); **in'struc·tion** instruction *f*, enseignement *m*; ordre *m*; **in'struc·tion·al** d'instruction; ✕ ~ **school** école *f* d'application; **in·'struc·tive** □ instructif (-ive *f*); **in'struc·tor** maître *m*; précepteur *m*; ♩ moniteur *m*; *Am. univ.* chargé *m* de cours; **in'struc·tress** maîtresse *f*, préceptrice *f*.

in·stru·ment ['instrumənt] (♪, ♩, ⚖, *a. fig.*) instrument *m*; appareil *m*; ⚖ *a.* acte *m* juridique; ✎, mot. ~ **board** *ou* **panel** tablier *m* des instruments; ✈ **fly on** ~**s** voler en P.S.V.; **in·stru·men·tal** □ [~'mentl] contributif (-ive *f*), qui contribue (à, *in*); *gramm., a.* ♩ instrumental (-aux *m/pl.*); **be** ~ **to** contribuer à (*qch. ou inf.*); **in·stru·men·tal·i·ty** [~'tæliti] moyen *m*, concours *m*, intermédiaire *m*.

in·sub·or·di·nate [insə'bɔːdnit] insubordonné; mutin; **'in·sub·or·di·'na·tion** insubordination *f*, insoumission *f*.

in·suf·fer·a·ble □ [in'sʌfərəbl] insupportable, intolérable.

in·suf·fi·cien·cy [insə'fiʃənsi] insuffisance *f*; **in·suf'fi·cient** □ insuffisant.

in·su·lar □ ['insjulə] insulaire; *fig.* borné, étroit; **in·su·lar·i·ty** [~'læriti] insularité *f*; *fig.* esprit *m* borné, étroitesse *f* de vues; **in·su·late** ['~leit] faire une île de; ⚡, *a. fig.* isoler; *phys.* calorifuger, protéger (contre, *against*); **'in·su·lat·ing** isolant; ~ **tape** chatterton *m*; **in·su'la·tion** isolement *m* (*a. phys.*); *a.* = **'in·su·la·tor** *phys.* isolant *m*.

in·sult 1. ['insʌlt] insulte *f*, affront *m*; **2.** [in'sʌlt] insulter, affronter.

in·su·per·a·bil·i·ty [insju:pərə'biliti] caractère *m* *ou* nature *f* insurmontable; **in'su·per·a·ble** □ insurmontable; infranchissable.

in·sup·port·a·ble □ [insə'pɔːtəbl] insupportable, intolérable.

in·sup·press·i·ble [insə'presəbl] irrépressible.

in·sur·ance [in'ʃuərəns] assurance *f*; *attr.* d'assurance; ~ **fraud** escroquerie *f* à l'assurance; **in'sur·ant** assuré(e *f*) *m*; **in·sure** [in'ʃuə] (faire) assurer; *fig. a.* garantir; **in'sured** assuré(e *f*) *m*; **in'sur·er** assureur *m*.

in·sur·gent [in'sɜːdʒənt] insurgé, révolté (*a. su./mf*).

in·sur·mount·a·ble □ [insə'mauntəbl] insurmontable (*a. fig.*).

in·sur·rec·tion [insə'rekʃn] insurrection *f*, soulèvement *m*; **in·sur·'rec·tion·al** insurrectionnel(le *f*); **in·sur'rec·tion·ist** [~ʃnist] insurgé(e *f*) *m*.

in·sus·cep·ti·ble [insə'septəbl] non susceptible (de, *of*), inaccessible (à, *of*); insensible (à, *to*).

in·tact [in'tækt] intact, indemne.

in·take ['inteik] prise *f* (*d'eau etc.*); ⊕ ~ **valve** soupape *f* d'admission.

in·tan·gi·bil·i·ty [intændʒə'biliti] intangibilité *f*; *traité:* inviolabilité *f*; **in'tan·gi·ble** □ [~dʒəbl] intangible; immatériel(le *f*); *fig.* impondérable.

in·te·ger ['intidʒə] totalité *f*; ♲ nombre *m* entier; **in·te·gral** ['~grəl] **1.** □ intégrant; total; entier (-ère *f*); ♲ intégral; **2.** ♲ intégrale *f*; **in·te·grant** ['~grənt] intégrant; **in·te·grate** ['~greit] rendre entier; ♲ intégrer; **be** ~**d into** s'intégrer dans; ⚡ ~**d circuit** circuit *m* intégré; **in·te'gra·tion** intégration *f*; **in·teg·ri·ty** [in'tegriti] intégrité *f*; probité *f*; totalité *f*.

in·teg·u·ment [in'tegjumənt] (in)tégument *m*, enveloppe *f* (*a.* ♧).

in·tel·lect ['intilekt] intelligence *f*, esprit *m*, intellect *m*; **in·tel'lec·tu·al** [~tjuəl] **1.** □ intellectuel(le *f*); **2.** intellectuel(le *f*) *m*; **in·tel·lec·tu·al·i·ty** ['~æliti] intellectualité *f*.

in·tel·li·gence [in'telidʒəns] intelligence *f*; esprit *m*; renseignements *m/pl.*, nouvelles *f/pl.*; informations *f/pl.*; ~ **department**, ✕, ⚓ *a.* ~ **service** service *m* des renseignements; **in'tel·li·genc·er** informateur (-trice *f*) *m*; espion *m*.

in·tel·li·gent □ [in'telidʒənt] intelligent; avisé; † ~ **of** au courant de; **in·tel·li·gent·si·a** [~'dʒentsiə] la classe *f* des intellectuels *m/pl.*; élite *f* intellectuelle; **in·tel·li·gi·bil·i·ty**

[~dʒə'biliti] intelligibilité f; **in'tel·li·gi·ble** □ intelligible.

in·tem·per·ance [in'tempərəns] intempérance f; alcoolisme m; **in-'tem·per·ate** □ [~rit] immodéré, intempérant; adonné à la boisson.

in·tend [in'tend] avoir l'intention de, se proposer de, compter; entendre (par, by); ~ for destiner à; **in-'tend·ant** intendant m; **in'tend·ed 1.** projeté; intentionnel(le f); ~ husband fiancé m, prétendu m; **2.** F fiancé(e f) m, prétendu(e f) m, futur(e f) m.

in·tense □ [in'tens] intense; vif (vive f) (a. couleur); fort; **in'tense·ness** intensité f; violence f; force f. **in·ten·si·fi·ca·tion** [intensifi'keiʃn] renforcement m (a. phot.); **in'ten·si·fy** [~fai] (s')augmenter; (s')intensifier; v/t. phot. renforcer.

in·ten·sion [in'tenʃn] tension f (d'esprit); phls. compréhension f; **in-'ten·si·ty** see intenseness; **in'tensive** □ see intense; intensif (-ive f); ⚕ ~ care unit service m de réanimation ou de soins intensifs.

in·tent [in'tent] **1.** □ tout entier (-ère f) (à, on); acharné (à, on); fixe (regard); **2.** intention f, but m, dessein m; to all ~s and purpose à toutes fins utiles; with ~ to kill dans l'intention de tuer; **in'ten·tion** intention f; dessein m; but m; **in'ten·tion·al** □ [~ʃnl] voulu, intentionnel (-le f); fait exprès; **in'ten·tioned** (bien ou mal) intentionné; **in'tent·ness** application f; tension f d'esprit; attention f soutenue (du regard).

in·ter [in'tə:] enterrer, ensevelir.

inter... [intə] entre-; inter-; réciproque.

in·ter·act 1. ['intərækt] théâ. entracte m; intermède m; **2.** [~'ækt] agir l'un sur l'autre; **in·ter'ac·tion** action f réciproque.

in·ter·breed ['intə'bri:d][irr.(breed)] (s')entrecroiser; v/t. accoupler (des animaux).

in·ter·ca·lar·y [in'tə:kələri] intercalaire; géol. intercalé (couche); **in-'ter·ca·late** [~leit] intercaler; **in-ter·ca'la·tion** intercalation f.

in·ter·cede [intə'si:d] intercéder, plaider (auprès de, with); **in·ter-'ced·er** intercesseur m; médiateur (-trice f) m.

in·ter·cept [intə'sept] intercepter (une lettre, un navire, un message); couper (la retraite); ⚔ comprendre (un espace); **in·ter'cep·tion** interception f; téléph. etc. captation f; **inter'cep·tor** celui (celle f) m qui intercepte; ✈ ~ fighter intercepteur m.

in·ter·ces·sion [intə'seʃn] intercession f; médiation f; **in·ter·ces·sor** [~'sesə] intercesseur m; médiateur (-trice f) m.

in·ter·change 1. [intə'tʃeindʒ] v/t. échanger; mettre (qch.) à la place de (qch. d'autre); v/i. s'interchanger; **2.** ['~'tʃeindʒ] échange m; alternance f; ⚡ interversion f; **in·ter-'change·a·ble** interchangeable, permutable.

in·ter·com·mu·ni·cate [intəkə-'mju:nikeit] communiquer (entre eux ou elles); **'in·ter·com·mu·ni-'ca·tion** communication f réciproque; rapports m/pl.; ⚙ intercirculation f; **in·ter·com'mun·ion** [~jən] rapports m/pl. intimes; eccl. intercommunion f.

in·ter·con·nect ['intəkə'nekt] communiquer (réciproquement).

in·ter·con·ti·nen·tal ['intəkənti-'nentl] intercontinental (-aux m/pl.).

in·ter·course ['intəkɔ:s] commerce m, relations f/pl.

in·ter·de·nom·i·na·tion·al [intədi-nɔmi'neiʃənl] interconfessionnel(le f).

in·ter·de·pend·ent [intədi'pendənt] solidaire (de, with).

in·ter·dict 1. [intə'dikt] interdire (qch. à q., s.th. to s.o.; à q. de inf., s.o. from gér.); prohiber; **2.** ['intədikt], **in·ter'dic·tion** interdiction f, défense f; eccl. interdit m.

in·ter·est ['intrist] **1.** usu. intérêt m; participation f (à, in); fig. groupe m, parti m, monde m; profit m, avantage m; † influence f, crédit m (auprès de, with); ⚕ intérêt m; revenu m; be of ~ to intéresser (q.); take an ~ in s'intéresser à; **2.** usu. intéresser (dans, in); éveiller l'intérêt de (q.); be ~ed in s'intéresser à; s'occuper de; ⚕ être intéressé dans; ~ o.s. s'intéresser (à, in); **'in·ter·est·ed** □ intéressé; intéressant (regard); **'in·ter-est-free** ⚕ sans intérêts; **'in·ter-est·ing** □ intéressant.

in·ter·fere [intə'fiə] se mêler (de,

with); toucher (à, *with*); intervenir (dans, *in*); gêner, déranger (qch., *with s.th.*); **in·ter'fer·ence** intervention *f*, ingérence *f* (dans, *in*); *phys.* interférence *f*; *radio*: interférences *f/pl.*; ~ *elimination radio*: filtrage *m* à interférences; ~ *suppressor* antiparasite *m*.

in·ter·flow [intə'flou] se mélanger.

in·ter·flu·ent [in'tə:fluənt] se mélangeant; mêlant leurs eaux.

in·ter·fuse [intə'fju:z] (se) mélanger, (se) confondre.

in·ter·im ['intərim] **1.** *su.* intérim *m*; *ad* ~ par intérim; *in the* ~ sur ces entrefaites; **2.** *adv.* en attendant, entretemps; **3.** *adj.* intérimaire.

in·te·ri·or [in'tiəriə] **1.** □ (de l')intérieur; *fig.* intime; ⚕ interne; **2.** intérieur *m* (*tous les sens*); ~ *decorator* ensemblier *m*, artiste *mf* décorateur (-trice *f*).

in·ter·ja·cent [intə'dʒeisənt] intermédiaire, interjacent.

in·ter·ject [intə'dʒekt] interrompre; faire (*une remarque*); **in·ter'jec·tion** interjection *f*; **in·ter'jec·tion·al** □ interjectionnel(le *f*).

in·ter·lace [intə'leis] (s')entrelacer, (s')entrecroiser, (s')entremêler.

in·ter·lard [intə'lɑːd] *fig.* piquer (de, *with*).

in·ter·leave [intə'liːv] interfolier (*un livre*).

in·ter·line [intə'lain] écrire (qch.) entre les lignes; *typ.* interligner; **in·ter·lin·e·ar** [intə'liniə] (à traduction) interlinéaire; **in·ter·lin·e·a·tion** ['..lini'eiʃn] interlinéation *f*, entre-ligne *m*; intercalation *f* de mots *etc.* dans un texte.

in·ter·lock [intə'lɔk] (s')emboîter; 🚂 (s')enclencher; (s')engrener.

in·ter·lo·cu·tion [intələ'kju:ʃn] interlocution *f*; **in·ter·loc·u·tor** [~'lɔkjutə] interlocuteur *m*; **in·ter'loc·u·to·ry** en forme de dialogue; ⚖ interlocutoire.

in·ter·lope [intə'loup] faire intrusion; † vendre sans autorisation; **'in·ter·lop·er** intrus(e *f*) *m*; † commerçant *m* interlope.

in·ter·lude ['intəluːd] intermède *m*.

in·ter·mar·riage [intə'mæridʒ] intermariage *m*; **in·ter'mar·ry** se marier entre parents *ou* entre membres de races *etc.* différentes.

in·ter·med·dle [intə'medl] s'ingérer

(dans *with*, *in*); **in·ter'med·dler** *fig.* officieux (-euse *f*) *m*.

in·ter·me·di·ar·y [intə'miːdiəri] intermédiaire (*a. su./m*); **in·ter·me·di·ate** □ [~'miːdiət] intermédiaire; intermédiat; moyen(ne *f*); 🎓 ~ *landing* escale *f*; *Am.* ~ *school* école *f* secondaire; ~ *trade* commerce *m* intermédiaire.   [ment *m*.]

in·ter·ment [in'tə:mənt] enterre-)

in·ter·mi·na·ble □ [in'tə:minəbl] sans fin, interminable.

in·ter·min·gle [intə'miŋgl] (s')entremêler.

in·ter·mis·sion [intə'miʃn] interruption *f*, intervalle *m*; pause *f*; *Am. théâ.* entracte *m*.

in·ter·mit [intə'mit] (s')interrompre; *v/t.* suspendre; **in·ter'mit·tent 1.** □ intermittent; ~ *fever* ⚕ **2.** ⚕ fièvre *f* intermittente; **in·ter'mit·ting·ly** par intervalles.

in·ter·mix [intə'miks] (s')entremêler, (se) mélanger; **in·ter'mix·ture** [~tʃə] mélange *m*; mixtion *f*.

in·tern [in'tə:n] interner.

in·tern(e) ['intə:n] interne *m* (*des hôpitaux*).

in·ter·nal □ [in'tə:nl] interne; intérieur; intime, secret (-ète *f*); *Am.* ✝ ~ *revenue* revenu *m* fiscal; *le* fisc *m*; ~-**com'bus·tion en·gine** moteur *m* à combustion interne.

in·ter·na·tion·al [intə'næʃnəl] **1.** □ international (-aux *m/pl.*); ~ *data line* ligne *f* de changement de date; 🎓 ~ *departures pl.* départ *m* vols internationaux; ~ *exhibition* exposition *f* internationale; 🎓 ~ *flight* vol *m* international; ~ *law* droit *m* international *ou* des gens; **2.** *pol.* F Internationale *f*; *sp.* international(e *f*) *m*; **in·ter·na·tion·al·i·ty** [~'næliti] internationalité *f*; **in·ter'na·tion·al·ize** [~əlaiz] internationaliser.

in·ter·ne·cine war [intə'ni:sain'wɔ:] guerre *f* d'extermination réciproque.

in·tern·ee [intə:'ni:] interné(e *f*) *m*; **in'tern·ment** internement *m*; ~ *camp* camp *m* d'internement.

in·ter·pel·late [in'tə:peleit] interpeller; **in·ter·pel·la·tion** interpellation *f*.

in·ter·phone ['intəfoun] téléphone *m* privé; 🎓 téléphonie *f* de bord.

in·ter·plan·e·tar·y [intə'plænitəri] interplanétaire.

in·ter·play ['intə'plei] effet *m* réciproque; jeu *m*.

in·ter·po·late [in'tə:poleit] interpoler; intercaler; **in·ter·po'la·tion** interpolation *f*.

in·ter·pose [intə'pouz] *v/t.* interposer; faire (*une observation*); *v/i.* s'interposer, intervenir; **in·ter·po·si·tion** [intə:pə'ziʃn] interposition *f*; intervention *f*.

in·ter·pret [in'tə:prit] interpréter; **in·ter·pre'ta·tion** interprétation *f*; **in'ter·pre·ta·tive** [ˌtətiv] interprétatif (-ive *f*); qui explique (qch., *of* s.th.); **in'ter·pret·er** interprète *mf*.

in·ter·ro·gate [in'terogeit] interroger, questionner; **in·ter·ro'ga·tion** interrogation *f*; *police:* interrogatoire *m*; question *f*; note (*ou* mark *ou* point) of ~ point *m* d'interrogation; **in·ter·rog·a·tive** [ˌtə'rɔgətiv] **1.** □ interrogateur (-trice *f*); *gramm.* interrogatif (-ive *f*); **2.** *gramm.* pronom *m* interrogatif; **in·ter'rog·a·to·ry** [ˌtəri] **1.** interrogateur (-trice *f*); **2.** *ɡ̃ʑ* question *f*; interrogatoire *m*.

in·ter·rupt [intə'rʌpt] interrompre; **in·ter'rupt·ed·ly** de façon interrompue; **in·ter'rupt·er** interrupteur (-trice *f*) *m*; *ⵁ* interrupteur *m*, *a.* coupe-circuit *m/inv.*; **in·ter'rup·tion** interruption *f*.

in·ter·sect [intə'sekt] (s')entrecouper, (s')entrecroiser; *ⵁ* (se) couper; **in·ter'sec·tion** intersection *f* (**⟦** *de voies*); *chemins:* carrefour *m*.

in·ter·space ['intə'speis] espacement *m*; *temps:* intervalle *m*.

in·ter·sperse [intə'spə:s] entremêler (de, *with*); parsemer (de, *with*).

in·ter·state *Am.* ['intə'steit] entre États.

in·ter·stel·lar [intə'stelə] interstellaire.

in·ter·stice [in'tə:stis] interstice *m*; **in·ter·sti·tial** □ [intə'stiʃl] interstitiel(le *f*).

in·ter·twine [intə'twain], **in·ter·twist** [intə'twist] (s')entrelacer.

in·ter·val ['intəvəl] intervalle *m* (*a.* de temps, *a.* ♪); distance *f*; *sp.* mitemps *f*; *théâ.* entracte *m*; *école:* récréation *f*.

in·ter·vene [intə'vi:n] intervenir, s'interposer; s'écouler (*années*); séparer; arriver, survenir; **in·ter·ven·tion** [ˌ'venʃn] intervention *f*; interposition *f*.

in·ter·view ['intəvju:] **1.** entrevue *f*; *journ.* interview *f*; **2.** avoir une entrevue avec; *journ.* interviewer; **in·ter·view·ee** [ˌi:] personne *f* interviewée, interviewé(e *f*) *m*; **'in·ter·view·er** interviewer *m*.

in·ter·weave [intə'wi:v] [*irr.* (weave)] (s')entrelacer; *fig.* (s')entremêler.

in·tes·ta·cy *ɡ̃ʑ* [in'testəsi] absence *f* de testament; **in'tes·tate** *ɡ̃ʑ* [ˌtit] intestat (*usu. su./m*); ~ succession succession *f* ab intestat.

in·tes·ti·nal *anat.* [in'testinl] intestinal (-aux *m/pl.*); **in'tes·tine** [ˌtin] intestin (*a. su./m*).

in·ti·ma·cy ['intiməsi] intimité *f*; *péj.* accointances *f/pl.*; *ɡ̃ʑ* relations *f/pl.* charnelles; **in·ti·mate 1.** ['ˌmeit] signifier; indiquer, suggérer; intimer (*un ordre*); **2.** ['ˌmit] □ intime; *fig.* approfondi; **3.** ['ˌmit] intime *mf*; **in·ti·ma·tion** [ˌ'meiʃn] avis *m*; indication *f*; suggestion *f*.

in·tim·i·date [in'timideit] intimider; **in·tim·i'da·tion** intimidation *f*; *ɡ̃ʑ* menaces *f/pl.*

in·tim·i·ty [in'timiti] intimité *f*.

in·to ['intu, 'intə] *prp.* dans, en; à; entre (*les mains*).

in·tol·er·a·ble □ [in'tɔlərəbl] intolérable, insupportable; **in'tol·er·ance** intolérance *f*; **in'tol·er·ant** □ intolérant.

in·to·na·tion [intou'neiʃn] ♪, *voix:* intonation *f*; *eccl.* psalmodie *f*; cadence *f*, *voix:* ton *m*; **in·to·nate** ['ˌneit], **in·tone** [in'toun] psalmodier; entonner.

in·tox·i·cant [in'tɔksikənt] **1.** enivrant; **2.** boisson *f* alcoolique; **in'tox·i·cate** [ˌkeit] enivrer; **in·tox·i'ca·tion** ivresse *f*; *fig.* enivrement *m*; *ⵁ* poison: intoxication *f*.

in·trac·ta·bil·i·ty [intræktə'biliti] indocilité *f*; *terrain:* nature *f* incultivable; **in'trac·ta·ble** □ intraitable, obstiné, difficile; incultivable; ingrat. [l'intérieur de la ville.⟩

in·tra·mu·ral ['intrə'mjuərəl] dans⟨

in·tran·si·gent *pol.* [in'trænsidʒənt] intransigeant(e *f*) (*a. su.*).

in·tran·si·tive □ [in'trænsitiv] intransitif (-ive *f*).

in·tra·state *Am.* [intrə'steit] intérieur de l'État; qui ne concerne que l'État.

in·tra·ve·nous *ⵁ* [intrə'vi:nəs] intraveineux (-euse *f*).

in·trep·id □ [in'trepid] intrépide, courageux (-euse *f*); **in·tre·pid·i·ty** [intri'piditi] intrépidité *f*, courage *m*.

in·tri·ca·cy ['intrikəsi] complication *f*; complexité *f*; **in·tri·cate** □ ['ˏkit] compliqué; confus; embrouillé.

in·trigue [in'triːg] **1.** intrigue *f* (*a. théâ.*); liaison *f* (*amoureuse*); cabale *f*; **2.** *v/i.* intriguer (*a. v/t.*); mener des intrigues; *v/t. fig.* piquer la curiosité de (*q.*); **in'tri·guer** intrigant(e *f*) *m*.

in·trin·sic, in·trin·si·cal □ [in'trinsik(l)] intrinsèque.

in·tro·duce [intrə'djuːs] introduire, faire entrer; présenter (q. à q., s.o. to s.o.; *a. parl. un projet de loi*); faire connaître (*un livre*); initier (q. à qch., s.o. to s.th.); établir; commencer (*une phrase*); **in·tro·duc·tion** [ˏ'dʌkʃn] introduction *f*; présentation *f*; avant-propos *m|inv.*; letter of ~ lettre *f* de recommandation; **in·tro'duc·to·ry** [ˏtəri] préliminaire; de recommandation (*lettre*); ✝ ~ price prix *m* de lancement.

in·tro·spec·tion [intro'spekʃn] introspection *f*; **in·tro'spec·tive** □ introspectif (-ive *f*).

in·tro·vert 1. [intro'vəːt] 🕮 retourner, introvertir (*a. psych.*); **2.** ['introvəːt] caractère *m* introverti.

in·trude [in'truːd] *v/t.* introduire de force (dans, *into*); imposer (à, [up]on); *v/i.* faire intrusion (auprès de, [up]on); empiéter (sur, *on*); être importun; **in'trud·er** intrus(e *f*) *m*; importun(e *f*) *m*; F resquilleur (-euse *f*) *m* (à une soirée).

in·tru·sion [in'truːʒn] intrusion *f*, empiétement *m*.

in·tru·sive □ [in'truːsiv] importun (*personne*); *géol.* d'intrusion; *gramm.* intrusif (-ive *f*).

in·trust [in'trʌst] see entrust.

in·tu·it [in'tjuːit] savoir intuitivement; **in·tu·i·tion** [intju'iʃn] intuition *f*; **in·tu·i·tive** □ [ˏ'tjuitiv] intuitif (-ive *f*).

in·un·date ['inʌndeit] inonder (de, with); **in·un'da·tion** inondation *f*.

in·ure [i'njuə] habituer (à, to); **in·'ure·ment** habitude *f* (de, to); endurcissement *m* (à, to).

in·u·til·i·ty [inju'tiliti] inutilité *f*.

in·vade [in'veid] envahir; faire une invasion dans (*un pays*); *fig.* violer; empiéter sur (*un droit*); **in'vad·er** envahisseur *m*; *fig.* intrus(e *f*) *m*; transgresseur *m* (*d'un droit*).

in·val·id¹ [in'vælid] invalide; nul (-le *f*).

in·val·id² ['invəliːd] **1.** malade (*a. su./mf*); infirme (*a. su./mf*); **2.** ⚔, ♟ invalide *m*; **3.** *v/t.* rendre malade ou infirme; ⚔, ♟ réformer; *v/i.* être réformé.

in·val·i·date [in'vælideit] rendre nul, invalider; ⚖ casser (*un jugement*); **in·val·i'da·tion** invalidation *f*; cassation *f*.

in·va·lid·i·ty [invə'liditi] invalidité *f*.

in·val·u·a·ble □ [in'væljuəbl] inestimable.

in·var·i·a·ble □ [in'vɛəriəbl] invariable.

in·va·sion [in'veiʒn] invasion *f* (*a. ⚔*), envahissement *m*; *fig.* violation *f* (*a. ⚖*) (de, *of*); ⚖ empiétement *m* (sur, *of*); **in'va·sive** [ˏsiv] envahissant; d'invasion.

in·vec·tive [in'vektiv] invective *f*, injures *f/pl.*

in·veigh [in'vei]: ~ against déclamer ou fulminer contre, maudire (*qch.*).

in·vei·gle [in'viːgl] séduire; attirer (dans, *into*); **in'vei·gle·ment** séduction *f*; leurre *m*.

in·vent [in'vent] inventer; **in'ven·tion** invention *f* (*a. fig.*); *fig.* mensonge *m*; **in'ven·tive** □ inventif (-ive *f*); **in'ven·tive·ness** fécondité *f* d'invention; imagination *f*; **in'ven·tor** inventeur (-trice *f*) *m*; **in·ven·to·ry** ['invəntri] **1.** inventaire *m*; **2.** inventorier; dresser l'inventaire de.

in·verse □ ['in'vəːs] inverse; **in·ver·sion** [in'vəːʃn] renversement *m*; *gramm.*, 🎵, 🔍, *etc.* inversion *f*.

in·vert 1. [in'vəːt] renverser; invertir; 🎵 intervertir; ~ed commas *pl.* guillemets *m/pl.*; 🐝 ~ed flight vol *m* renversé *ou* sur le dos; **2.** ['invəːt] inverti(e *f*) *m*.

in·ver·te·brate [in'vəːtibrit] **1.** invertébré; *fig.* flasque, faible; **2.** *zo.* invertébré *m*; *fig.* personne *f* qui manque de caractère.

in·vest [in'vest] *v/t.* revêtir (de with, in); *fig.* investir (q. de qch., s.o. with s.th.; *a. de l'argent*); prêter (qch. à q., s.o. with s.th.); ⚔ investir, cerner; ⚓ investir, placer (*des fonds*) (dans, *in*); *v/i.* ⚓ placer de l'argent (dans, *in*); F ~ *in s.th.* acheter qch., se payer qch.

in·ves·ti·gate [in'vestigeit] examiner, étudier, rechercher; *investigating committee* commission *f* d'enquête; **in·ves·ti·ga·tion** investigation *f*, recherches *f/pl.*; **in·ves·ti·ga·tor** [~tə] investigateur (-trice *f*) *m*.

in·ves·ti·ture [in'vestitʃə] remise *f* de décorations; *eccl.* investiture *f*; *poét.* (re)vêtement *m*; **in'vest·ment** placement *m* (*de fonds*); ⚔ investissement *m*; **in'vest·or** capitaliste *mf*; spéculateur *m*; *small* ~ petit rentier *m*.

in·vet·er·a·cy [in'vetərəsi] caractère *m* invétéré; **in'vet·er·ate** □ [~rit] invétéré, enraciné (*chose*); acharné (*personne*).

in·vid·i·ous □ [in'vidiəs] odieux (-euse *f*), haïssable; qui excite la haine *ou* l'envie *ou* la jalousie.

in·vig·or·ate [in'vigəreit] *v/t.* fortifier, donner de la vigueur à; **in·vig·or·a·tion** invigoration *f*.

in·vin·ci·bil·i·ty [invinsi'biliti] invincibilité *f*; **in'vin·ci·ble** □ invincible.

in·vi·o·la·bil·i·ty [invaiələ'biliti] inviolabilité *f*; **in'vi·o·la·ble** □ inviolable; **in'vi·o·late** [~lit] inviolé.

in·vis·i·bil·i·ty [invizə'biliti] invisibilité *f*; **in'vis·i·ble** □ invisible.

in·vi·ta·tion [invi'teiʃn] invitation *f*; **in·vite** [in'vait] 1. inviter (q. à *inf.*, *s.o. to inf.*); convier (*a. à dîner*); solliciter (*qch.*); provoquer (*une critique, un danger, etc.*); 2. F invitation *f*.

in·vo·ca·tion [invo'keiʃn] invocation *f*; **in·voc·a·to·ry** [in'vɔkətəri] invocatoire.

in·voice ⚓ ['invɔis] 1. facture *f*; 2. facturer.

in·voke [in'vouk] invoquer (*Dieu, la mémoire, un esprit*); appeler.

in·vol·un·tar·y □ [in'vɔləntəri] involontaire.

in·vo·lute ['invəlu:t] 1. ♀ involuté; ♉ de *ou* à développante; 2. ♉ développante *f*; **in·vo'lu·tion** complication *f*; enchevêtrement *m*; ♀, ♉, *biol.* involution *f*.

in·volve [in'vɔlv] envelopper (dans, *in*); embarrasser; impliquer (dans, *in*); engager (dans, *in*); entraîner; comprendre; **in'volve·ment** impli-

cation *f*; confusion *f*; embarras *m/pl.* pécuniaires.

in·vul·ner·a·bil·i·ty [invʌlnərə'biliti] invulnérabilité *f*; **in'vul·ner·a·ble** □ invulnérable.

in·ward ['inwəd] 1. *adj.* intérieur (*a. fig.*); interne; vers l'intérieur; 2. *adv.* (*usu.* **in·wards** ['~z]) vers l'intérieur; ⚓ pour l'importation; *fig.* dans l'âme; 3. *su. fig.* ~*s pl.* entrailles *f/pl.*, ventre *m*; **'in·ward·ly** intérieurement (*a. fig.*); dans *ou* vers l'intérieur; **'in·ward·ness** essence *f*, signification *f* intime; spiritualité *f*.

in·weave ['in'wi:v] [*irr.* (*weave*)] brocher (de, *with*); tisser (dans, *into*).

in·wrought ['in'rɔ:t] broché, ouvragé (de, *with*; dans, *into*).

i·od·ic ♁ [ai'ɔdik] iodique; **i·o·dide** ['aiədaid] iodure *m*; **i·o·dine** ['~di:n] iode *m*; **i·o·do·form** ♁ [ai'ɔdəfɔ:m] iodoforme *m*.

i·on *phys.* ['aiən] ion *m*.

I·o·ni·an [ai'ouniən] 1. ionien(ne *f*); 2. Ionien(ne *f*) *m*.

I·on·ic[1] [ai'ɔnik] △ ionique; ♪, *ling.* ionien(ne *f*).

i·on·ic[2] *phys.* [~] ionique; **i·on·ize** *phys.* ['aiənaiz] (s')ioniser.

i·o·ta [ai'outə] iota *m* (*a. fig.*).

I O U ['aiou'ju:] (*abr. de I owe you*) reconnaissance *f* de dette.

ip·e·cac·u·an·ha ♀ [ipikækju'ænə] ipécacuana *m*, *abr.* ipéca *m*.

I·ra·ni·an [ai'reinjən] 1. iranien(ne *f*); 2. Iranien(ne *f*) *m*.

i·ras·ci·bil·i·ty [iræsi'biliti] irascibilité *f*; tempérament *m* colérique; **i'ras·ci·ble** □ [~sibl] irascible; colérique (*tempérament*).

i·rate [ai'reit] en colère, furieux (-euse *f*).

ire *poét.* ['aiə] colère *f*; courroux *m*.

ire·ful □ ['aiəful] plein de colère.

ir·i·des·cence [iri'desns] irisation *f*; *plumage etc.*: chatoiement *m*; **ir·i·des·cent** irisé; chatoyant.

I·ris ['aiəris] *myth.* Iris *f*; ♀ ♀, *anat.*, *cin.*, *opt.* iris *m*; *phot.* ~ *diaphragm* diaphragme *m* iris.

I·rish ['aiəriʃ] 1. irlandais; d'Irlande; 2. *ling.* irlandais *m*; *the* ~ les Irlandais *m/pl.*; **'I·rish·ism** locution *f* irlandaise; **'I·rish·man** Irlandais *m*; **'I·rish·wom·an** Irlandaise *f*.

irk † [ə:k] ennuyer; en coûter à (*q.*).

irk·some □ ['ə:ksəm] ennuyeux (-euse f); ingrat; '**irk·some·ness** caractère m ingrat; ennui m.

i·ron ['aiən] **1.** fer m (a. fig.); fig. souv. airain m; cast ~ fonte f; (qqfois flat-~) fer m à repasser; ~s pl. fers m/pl.; **2.** de fer (a. fig.); en fer; ⊕ de fonte; **3.** repasser; donner un coup de fer à; garnir de fer; mettre (q.) aux fers; '~·**bound** cerclé de fer; fig. sévère, inflexible; à pic (côte); '~·**clad** cuirassé (a. su./m); '**i·ron·er** repasseur (-euse f) m; '**i·ron-found·ry** fonderie f de fonte; '**i·ron-heart·ed** fig. dur, sans pitié.

i·ron·ic, i·ron·i·cal □ [ai'rɔnik(l)] ironique.

i·ron·ing ['aiəniŋ] **1.** repassage m; **2.** à repasser.

i·ron...: ~ **lung** ⚕ poumon m d'acier; '~·**mas·ter** maître m de forges; '~·**mon·ger** quincaillier (-ère f) m; '~·**mon·ger·y** quincaillerie f; '~·**mould** tache f de rouille; '~·**willed** à la volonté de fer; '~·**work** construction f en fer; serrurerie f; ~s usu. sg. ⊕ fonderie f (de fonte).

i·ro·ny[1] ['aiəni] de ou en fer; qui ressemble au fer.

i·ro·ny[2] ['aiərəni] ironie f.

ir·ra·di·ance, ir·ra·di·an·cy [i'reidiəns(i)] rayonnement m; éclat m (a. fig.); **ir'ra·di·ant** rayonnant (de, with).

ir·ra·di·ate [i'reidieit] irradier; v/i. rayonner (de, with); v/t. rayonner sur; a. éclairer; illuminer; faire rayonner; **ir·ra·di'a·tion** rayonnement m, éclat m (a. fig.); phys. irradiation f; fig. illumination f.

ir·ra·tion·al □ [i'ræʃnəl] déraisonnable; dépourvu de raison; & irrationnel(le f); **ir·ra·tion·al·i·ty** [~ʃə'næliti] déraison f; absurdité f.

ir·re·claim·a·ble □ [iri'kleiməbl] incorrigible; ⁏ incultivable.

ir·rec·og·niz·a·ble □ [i'rekəgnaizəbl] méconnaissable.

ir·rec·on·cil·a·ble □ [i'rekənsailəbl] incompatible (avec, with); implacable (haine etc.).

ir·re·cov·er·a·ble □ [iri'kʌvərəbl] irrécouvrable; irréparable (perte).

ir·re·deem·a·ble □ [iri'di:məbl] irrachetable (faute, fonds); irrémédiable (désastre etc.); ✝ non amortissable; incorrigible (coquin).

ir·re·duc·i·ble □ [iri'dju:səbl] irréductible.

ir·ref·ra·ga·bil·i·ty [irefrəgə'biliti] caractère m irréfragable etc.; **ir'ref·ra·ga·ble** □ irréfragable; irréfutable.

ir·ref·u·ta·ble □ [i'refjutəbl] irréfutable; irrécusable.

ir·reg·u·lar [i'regjulə] **1.** □ irrégulier (-ère f); anormal (-aux m/pl.); inégal (-aux m/pl.); saccadé (mouvement etc.); **2.** ~s pl. troupes f/pl. irrégulières, irréguliers m/pl.; **ir·reg·u·lar·i·ty** [~'læriti] irrégularité f.

ir·rel·a·tive [i'relətiv] sans rapport (avec, to), étranger (-ère f) (à, to).

ir·rel·e·vance, ir·rel·e·van·cy [i'relivəns(i)] inconséquence f; inapplicabilité f; **ir'rel·e·vant** □ hors de propos; étranger (-ère f) (à, to).

ir·re·li·gion [iri'lidʒn] irréligion f, indévotion f; **ir·re'li·gious** □ [~dʒəs] irréligieux (-euse f).

ir·re·me·di·a·ble □ [iri'mi:djəbl] irrémédiable; sans remède.

ir·re·mis·si·ble □ [iri'misəbl] impardonnable; irrémissible.

ir·re·mov·a·ble □ [iri'mu:vəbl] inébranlable; bien ancré; inamovible (juge etc.).

ir·rep·a·ra·ble □ [i'repərəbl] irréparable; irrémédiable.

ir·re·press·i·ble □ [iri'presəbl] irrésistible; irrépressible.

ir·re·proach·a·ble □ [iri'proutʃəbl] irréprochable; **ir·re'proach·a·ble·ness** caractère m irréprochable.

ir·re·sist·i·bil·i·ty ['irizistə'biliti] irrésistibilité f; **ir·re'sist·i·ble** □ irrésistible.

ir·res·o·lute □ [i'rezəlu:t] irrésolu; indécis; hésitant; **ir'res·o·lute·ness, ir·res·o'lu·tion** irrésolution f; indécision f.

ir·re·solv·a·ble [iri'zɔlvəbl] insoluble; indécomposable.

ir·re·spec·tive □ [iris'pektiv] (of) indépendant (de); adv. sans tenir compte (de).

ir·re·spon·si·bil·i·ty ['irisponsə'biliti] étourderie f; ⚖ irresponsabilité f; **ir·re'spon·si·ble** □ étourdi, irréfléchi; ⚖ irresponsable.

ir·re·triev·a·ble □ [iri'tri:vəbl] irréparable, irrémédiable.

ir·rev·er·ence [i'revərəns] irrévérence f; manque m de respect (pour, envers *towards*); **ir'rev·er·ent** □ irrévérent; irrévérencieux (-euse *f*). **ir·re·vers·i·ble** [iri'və:səbl] irrévocable; *mot.* irréversible. **ir·rev·o·ca·bil·i·ty** [irevəkə'biliti]irrévocabilité *f*; **ir'rev·o·ca·ble** □ irrévocable. **ir·ri·gate** ['irigeit] arroser; ✍, ⚕ irriguer; **ir·ri'ga·tion** arrosage *m*; ✍, ⚕ irrigation *f*. **ir·ri·ta·bil·i·ty** [iritə'biliti] irritabilité *f*; **'ir·ri·ta·ble** □ irritable; **'ir·ri·tant** irritant (*a. su./m*); **ir·ri·tate** ['⁓teit] irriter; agacer; **'ir·ri·tat·ing** □ irritant; agaçant; **ir·ri'ta·tion** irritation *f*; *biol.* stimulation *f*. **ir·rup·tion** [i'rʌpʃn] irruption *f*. **is** [iz] *il, elle, etc.* est. **i·sin·glass** ['aiziŋglɑ:s] ichtyocolle *f*; gélatine *f*. **Is·lam** ['izlɑ:m] Islam *m*. **is·land** ['ailənd] île *f*; îlot *m* (*a. fig.*); (*a. traffic-⁓*) refuge *m*; **'is·land·er** insulaire *mf*. **isle** [ail] *poét. ou géogr. devant npr.* île *f*; **is·let** ['ailit] îlot *m*. **ism** *usu. péj.* [izm] théorie *f*, doctrine *f*. **isn't** ['iznt] = *is not.* **iso...** [aiso] *préf.* is(o)-. **i·so·late** ['aisəleit] isoler; ⚕, ⚙ dégager; **i·so'la·tion** isolement *m*; ⁓ *hospital* hôpital *m* de contagieux; **i·so'la·tion·ist** *Am. pol.* isolationniste (*a. su./mf*). **i·so·met·rics** [aisou'metriks] *pl.* exercices *f/pl.* isométriques. **i·so·tope** ⚙ ['aisotoup] isotope *m*. **Is·ra·el·ite** ['izriəlait] Israélite *mf*; **'Is·ra·el·it·ish** israélite. **is·sue** ['isju:; 'iʃu:] **1.** sortie *f*; *fleuve*: embouchure *f*; résultat *m*, dénouement *m*, fin *f*; perte *f*, *sang*: épanchement *m*; ⚖ progéniture *f*, postérité *f*; ⚖ cause *f*; question *f*; distribution *f* (*de vivres etc.*); ⚕ émission *f* (*des billets de banque etc.*); publication *f* (*d'un livre*; *a.* ⚔, ⚓ *d'ordres*); numéro *m*, *journal*: édition *f*; *prospectus*: lancement *m*; passeport *etc.*: délivrance *f*; ⁓ *of fact* question *f* de fait; ⁓ *of law* question *f* de droit; *force an* ⁓ forcer une décision; amener une crise; *join (the)* ⁓ différer d'opinion; F relever le gant; *join* ⁓ *with s.o.* contredire q., discuter l'opinion de q.; *be at* ⁓ être en débat (sur, *on*); être en question;

2. *v/i.* sortir, jaillir (de, *from*); provenir (de, *from*); se terminer (par, *in*); *v/t.* publier (*a. des livres*); distribuer (*qch.* à q., *s.o. with s.th.*); lancer (*un mandat d'arrêt*); donner (*un ordre*); ⚕ émettre (*des billets de banque*); **'⁓·de·part·ment** section *f* émettrice (*de la Banque d'Angleterre*); **'is·sue·less** sans enfants. **isth·mus** ['isməs] isthme *m*. **it** [it] **1.** *pron.* il, *accentué:* lui; elle (*a. accentué*); ce, *accentué:* cela; *accusatif:* le, la; *datif:* lui; *of (ou from)* ⁓ en; to (*ou at*) ⁓ y; *how is* ⁓ *with?* comment va *etc.?*; *see lord 2, foot 2*; F go ⁓ aller grand train; *sl.* *go* ⁓! vas-y!; allez-y!; *we had a very good time of* ⁓ nous nous sommes bien amusés; **2.** *adj. préd.* F épatant; **3.** *su.* F quelque chose; F *abr. de Italian* vermouth. **I·tal·ian** [i'tæljən] **1.** italien(ne *f*); ⁓ *warehouse* magasin *m* de comestibles, épicerie *f*; **2.** *ling.* italien *m*; Italien(ne *f*) *m*. **i·tal·ics** *typ.* [i'tæliks] italiques *m/pl.* **itch** [itʃ] **1.** ⚕ gale *f*; démangeaison *f* (*a. fig.*, *de inf. for, to inf.*); **2.** démanger; *personne:* éprouver des démangeaisons; *fig.* avoir une démangeaison (de *inf. for, to inf.*); *be* ⁓*ing to* (*inf.*) brûler de (*inf.*); **'itch·ing** ⚕ prurit *m*; démangeaison *f* (*a. fig.*); *fig.* grande envie *f*; **'itch·y** ⚕ galeux (-euse *f*). **i·tem** ['aitem] **1.** item; de plus; **2.** article *m*, détail *m*; question *f*; *journ.* fait *m* divers; ⚕ poste *m*; **3.** noter; **i·tem·ize** ['aitəmaiz] *surt. Am.* détailler, donner les détails de. **it·er·ate** ['itəreit] réitérer; **it·er'a·tion** réitération *f*, répétition *f*; **it·er·a·tive** □ ['itərətiv] itératif (-ive *f*). **i·tin·er·ant** □ [i'tinərənt] ambulant; **i·tin·er·ar·y** [ai'tinərəri] itinéraire (*a. su./m*); **i·tin·er·ate** [i'tinəreit] voyager (de lieu en lieu). **its** [its] son, sa; ses. **it's** F [its] = *it is; it has.* **it·self** [it'self] lui-même, elle-même; *réfléchi:* se, *accentué:* soi; *of* ⁓ tout seul; de lui-même, d'elle-même; *in* ⁓ en lui-même *etc.*; en soi, de soi; *by* ⁓ à part; tout seul. **I've** F [aiv] = *I have.*

i·vied ['aivid] couvert de lierre.
i·vo·ry ['aivəri] **1.** ivoire *m*; F *ivories*
pl. touches *f/pl.* de piano; ♪ *tickle the*
ivories jouer du piano; **2.** en ivoire;
d'ivoire; *fig.* ~ *tower* tour *f* d'ivoire.
i·vy ✤ ['aivi] lierre *m*.

J

J, j [dʒei] J *m,* j *m.*

jab F [dʒæb] **1.** piquer (*q., qch.*) du bout (de qch., *with s.th.*); *box.* lancer un coup sec à; **2.** coup *m* de pointe; *box.* coup *m* sec.

jab·ber ['dʒæbə] **1.** *vt/i.* baragouiner; *v/i.* jacasser; **2.** baragouinage *m;* jacasserie *f.*

Jack [dʒæk] Jean *m;* ~ *Frost* bonhomme *m* Hiver; ~ *and Jill* Jeannot et Colette; ~ *Ketch* le bourreau; ~ *Pudding* bouffon *m;* ~ *Rake* noceur *m,* roué *m;* ~ *Sprat* nabot *m;* ♣ *Tar* matelot *m;* F mathurin *m.*

jack [dʒæk] **1.** *cartes:* valet *m;* ♣ pavillon *m* de beaupré; *mot.* cric *m;* tournebroche *m; icht.* brocheton *m; boules:* cochonnet *m; horloge:* jaquemart *m;* tire-botte *m; Am. sl.* argent *m, sl.* fric *m; zo.* ~ *rabbit* gros lièvre *m;* **2.** soulever (avec un cric); *sl.* ~ *up* abandonner; *surt. Am.* F augmenter rapidement (*les prix*).

jack·al ['dʒækɔːl] *zo.* chacal (*pl.* -als) *m* (*a. fig.*).

jack·a·napes ['dʒækəneips] petit(*e f*) vaurien(-ne *f*) *m;* impertinent *m;* '**jack·ass** baudet *m; fig.* imbécile *m;* '**jack·boots** bottes *f/pl.* de cavalier; '**jack·daw** *orn.* choucas *m.*

jack·et ['dʒækit] veston *m* (*d'homme*); jaquette *f* (*de femme*); veste *f* (*d'un garçon de café*); ⊕ chemise *f* (*a. de documents*); *livre:* couverture *f;* *potatoes in their* ~*s* pommes *f/pl.* de terre en robe de chambre.

jack...: '~-**in-'of·fice** bureaucrate *m;* '~-**in-the-box** diable *m* à ressort; '~-**knife** couteau *m* pliant; '~-**of-'all-trades** maître Jacques *m;* '~-**of-'all-work** factotum *m;* '~-**o'-'lan·tern** feu *m* follet; '~-**pot** *poker:* pot *m; Am.* F *hit the* ~ décrocher la timbale; '~-'**tow·el** essuie-mains *m/inv.* à rouleau.

Jac·o·bin *hist.* ['dʒækobin] jacobin(e *f*) *m;* **Jac·o·bite** *hist.* ['~bait] jacobite *mf.*

jade¹ [dʒeid] **1.** rosse *f,* haridelle *f; péj.* drôlesse *f; fickle* ~ oiseau *m*

volage; **2.** *v/t.* éreinter; fatiguer; *v/i.* languir.

jade² *min.* [~] jade *m.*

jag [dʒæg] **1.** pointe *f,* saillie *f; sl.* bombe *f,* noce *f,* ivresse *f;* **2.** déchiqueter; **jag·ged** □ ['~id] *surt. Am. sl.* soûl, gris; '**jag·gy** déchiqueté, ébréché.

jail [dʒeil] **1.** prison *f;* **2.** mettre en prison; '~-**bird** F gibier *m* de potence; '~-**break** évasion *f* de prison; **jail·er** ['dʒeilə] gardien *m* de prison.

ja·lop·(p)y *mot. surt. Am.* F [dʒə'lɔpi] bagnole *f;* ✈ avion *m* de transport.

jam¹ [dʒæm] confiture *f.*

jam² [~] **1.** presse *f,* foule *f;* ⊕ arrêt *m* (de fonctionnement); *radio:* brouillage *m; traffic* ~ embouteillage *m; sl. be in a* ~ être en difficulté; ~ *session* séance *f* de jazz improvisé; **2.** *v/t.* serrer, presser; enfoncer de force; obstruer (*un passage*); *radio:* brouiller; ⊕ coincer; ~ *the brakes* freiner brusquement; *v/i.* s'enrayer (*fusil*); se caler (*roue*); ⊕ se coincer.

Ja·mai·ca [dʒə'meikə] (*a.* ~ *rum*) rhum *m* de la Jamaïque.

jamb [dʒæm] chambranle *m.*

jam·bo·ree [dʒæmbə'ri] *sl.* bombance *f;* congrès *m* bruyant; *boy-scouts:* jamboree *m.*

jam·my *Brt. sl.* ['dʒæmi] facile comme tout; veinard, verni; ~ *fellow* veinard *m.*

jam-packed F ['dʒæmpækt] plein à craquer, bondé.

jan·gle ['dʒæŋgl] **1.** (faire) rendre des sons discordants (à qch.); *v/i.* s'entrechoquer; *v/t.* (faire) entrechoquer; (*a.* ~ *upon*) agacer; **2.** sons *m/pl.* discordants; cliquetis *m;* '**jangling** cacophonique, discordant.

jan·i·tor ['dʒænitə] concierge *m.*

Jan·u·ar·y ['dʒænjuəri] janvier *m.*

Jap F *péj.* [dʒæp] Japonais(e *f*) *m.*

ja·pan [dʒə'pæn] **1.** laque *m;* vernis *m* japonais; **2.** du Japon; **3.** laquer; vernir (*du cuir*).

jet-black

Jap·a·nese [dʒæpə'niːz] **1.** japonais; **2.** *ling.* japonais *m*; Japonais(e *f*) *m*; the ~ *pl.* les Japonais *m/pl.*

ja·pan·ner [dʒə'pænə] vernisseur *m*.

jar¹ [dʒɑː] pot *m* (*pour la moutarde etc.*); bocal *m*; récipient *m*; ⚡ verre *m*; *phys.* Leyden ~ bouteille *f* de Leyde.

jar² [~] **1.** choc *m*; secousse *f*; discorde *f*; **2.** heurter, cogner; vibrer; être en désaccord; ♪ détonner (*note*); ~ upon choquer, agacer; taper sur (*les nerfs*); ~ with jurer avec.

jar³ F [~]: *on the* ~ *see ajar.*

jar·gon ['dʒɑːgən] jargon *m*; *péj.* charabia *m*.

jas·min(e) ♀ ['dʒæsmin] jasmin *m*.

jas·per. ['dʒæspə] jaspe *m*.

jaun·dice ['dʒɔːndis] jaunisse *f*; *fig.* prévention *f*; **'jaun·diced** ictérique; *fig.* prévenu; *fig.* ~ eye regard *m* envieux.

jaunt [dʒɔːnt] **1.** balade *f*, randonnée *f*, sortie *f*; **2.** faire une petite excursion; **'jaun·ti·ness** désinvolture *f*; air *m* effronté; **'jaun·ty** □ désinvolte, insouciant; vif (vive *f*); effronté.

jave·lin ['dʒævlin] javeline *f*; javelot *m* (*a. sp.*); *throwing the* ~ lancement *m* du javelot.

jaw [dʒɔː] **1.** mâchoire *f*; F caquet *m*; F sermon *m*; ~s *pl.* mâchoire *f*, -s *f/pl.*; *fig.* bras *m/pl.* (*de la mort*); ⊕ *étau:* mors *m*; *clef anglaise:* bec *m*; **2.** *v/i.* F caqueter; *v/t.* F chapitrer (*q.*); **'~-bone** os *m* maxillaire; mâchoire *f*; **'~-break·er** F mot *m* à vous décrocher la mâchoire.

jay [dʒei] *orn.* geai *m*; F jobard *m*; gogo *m* (de, *at*); **'~-walk** traverser (la rue) sans regarder; **'~-walk·er** badaud *m*; piéton *m* imprudent.

jazz [dʒæz] **1.** ♪ jazz *m*; **2.** F bariolé; discordant; tapageur (-euse *f*); **3.** jouer *ou* danser le jazz; F ~ up animer, égayer, mettre de l'animation dans (*qch.*); rajeunir (*une robe etc.*); **'~-band** jazz-band *m*.

jeal·ous □ ['dʒeləs] jaloux (-ouse *f*) (de, *of*); **'jeal·ous·y** jalousie *f*.

jeep ⚔, *mot. Am.* [dʒiːp] jeep *f*.

jeer [dʒiə] **1.** huée *f*; raillerie *f*; **2.** se moquer (de, *at*), se railler (de, *at s.th.*); railler (*q.*, *at s.o.*); huer; **'jeer·er** railleur (-euse *f*) *m*, mo-

queur (-euse *f*) *m*; **'jeer·ing** □ railleur (-euse *f*),moqueur (-euse *f*).

je·june □ [dʒi'dʒuːn] stérile, aride; *a.* maigre (*sol*).

jell [dʒel] *cuis.* épaissir, prendre; F *fig.* prendre forme, se réaliser, réussir.

jel·ly ['dʒeli] **1.** gelée *f*; **2.** *v/t.* faire prendre en gelée; *v/i.* se prendre en gelée; **'~-fish** *zo.* méduse *f*.

jem·my ['dʒemi] pince-monseigneur (*pl.* pinces-monseigneur) *f* (*du cambrioleur*), rossignol *m*.

jen·ny ⊕ ['dʒeni] machine *f* à filer; chariot *m* de roulement.

jeop·ard·ize ['dʒepədaiz] mettre en péril, exposer au danger; **'jeop·ard·y** danger *m*, péril *m*.

jer·e·mi·ad [dʒeri'maiəd] jérémiade *f*.

jerk [dʒəːk] **1.** *su.* saccade *f*, secousse *f*; ⚕ réflexe *m* tendineux; tic *m*; *Am. sl.* nigaud *m*; *by* ~s par à-coups; *sl. put a* ~ *in it!* mets-y-en!; dépêchez-vous!; **2.** *v/t.* donner une secousse *ou* une saccade à; tirer d'un coup sec; *v/i.* se mouvoir brusquement; *avec adv. ou prp.:* lever, arracher; **'~-wa·ter** *Am.* **1.** petit train *m*, tortillard *m*; **2.** F petit, de province, sans importance; **'jerk·y 1.** □ saccadé; **2.** *Am.* viande *f* conservée; charqui *f*; *sl.* singe *m*.

jer·ry-build·ing ['dʒeribildiŋ]construction *f* de maisons de pacotille; **'jer·ry-built** de pacotille, de boue et de crachat (*maison*).

jer·sey ['dʒəːzi] jersey *m*; chandail *m*; *foot.* maillot *m*.

jes·sa·mine ♀ ['dʒesəmin] jasmin *m*.

jest [dʒest] **1.** plaisanterie *f*, badinage *m*; **2.** plaisanter (sur, *about*); badiner; **'jest·er** railleur (-euse *f*) *m*; *hist.* bouffon *m*.

Jes·u·it ['dʒezjuit] jésuite *m*; **Jes·u·'it·ic, Jes·u'it·i·cal** □ *péj.* jésuitique.

jet¹ *min.* [dʒet] jais *m*.

jet² [~] **1.** jet *m* (*d'eau etc.*); bec *m* (*de gaz*); ⊕ gicleur *m*; ⊕ brûleur *m*; ~ age époque *f* des avions à réaction; ✈ ~ fighter chasseur *m* à réaction; ~ lag (troubles *m/pl.* dus au) décalage *m* horaire; ~ propulsion propulsion *f* par réaction; ~ set jet-set *m*; **2.** (faire) s'élancer en jet.

jet-black ['dʒet'blæk] noir comme du jais.

jet...: '~-**plane** avion *m* à réaction, jet *m*; '~-**pro·pelled** à réaction.

jet·sam ['dʒetsəm] épaves *f/pl.* jetées à la côte; marchandise *f* jetée à la mer.

jet·ti·son ['dʒetisn] **1.** jet *m* (de marchandises) à la mer; **2.** jeter à la mer; se délester de (*a. fig.*).

jet·ty ⚓ ['dʒeti] jetée *f*, digue *f*; estacade *f*.

Jew [dʒuː] juif *m*; *attr.* juif (-ive *f*), des juifs; ~'s *harp* guimbarde *f*.

jew·el ['dʒuːəl] **1.** bijou (*pl.* -x) *m*, joyau (*pl.* -x) *m*; *horloge:* rubis *m*; *fig. personne:* perle *f*; **2.** orner de bijoux; monter (*un horloge*) sur rubis; 'jew·el·(l)er bijoutier *m*; 'jew·el·ry, 'jew·el·ler·y bijouterie *f*.

Jew·ess ['dʒuːis] juive *f*; 'Jew·ish juif (-ive *f*); **Jew·ry** ['dʒuəri] Juiverie *f*.

jib [dʒib] **1.** ⚓ foc *m*; ⊕ volée *f* (de grue); ~ *door* porte *f* dérobée; **2.** *vt/i.* gambier, coiffer (*voile*); regimber (devant, *at*); 'jib·ber cheval *m* rétif; *fig.* récalcitrant(e *f*) *m*; 'jib-'boom ⚓ bout-dehors (*pl.* bouts-dehors) *m* de foc.

jibe *Am.* F [dʒaib] s'accorder, F coller.

jif·fy F ['dʒifi] instant *m*, clin *m* d'œil; *in a* ~ en un clin d'œil; F en cinq sec.

jig [dʒig] **1.** ♪ gigue *f*; **2.** danser la gigue; *fig.* se trémousser.

jig·ger *Am.* ['dʒigə] **1.** machin *m*, truc *m*; petite mesure *f* (*pour spiritueux*); **2.** *sl.* sautiller (= *danser*).

jig·gered ['dʒigəd]: *I'm* ~ *if* ... du diable si ...

jig·gle F ['dʒigl] *v/t.* secouer légèrement; *v/i.* sautiller.

jig-saw ['dʒigsɔː] scie *f* à chantourner; ~ *puzzle* puzzle *m*.

jilt [dʒilt] **1.** coquette *f*; **2.** laisser là (*un amoureux*).

Jim Crow [dʒim'krou] *Am. sl.* nègre *m* (*a. attr.*); discrimination *f* (entre races blanche et noire).

jim·my ['dʒimi] *see jemmy.*

jimp *sl.* [dʒimp] diable *m*.

jin·gle ['dʒiŋgl] **1.** cliquetis *m*; *grelot:* tintement *m*; **2.** (faire) tinter *ou* cliqueter.

jin·go ['dʒiŋgou], *pl.* -goes ['~z] chauvin(e *f*) *m*; patriotard *m*; F *by* ~*!* nom de nom!; 'jin·go·ism chauvinisme *m*.

jinks [dʒiŋks] *pl.*: F *high* ~ ébats *m/pl.* bruyants.

jinx *Am. sl.* [~] porte-malheur *m/inv.*

jit·ney *Am. sl.* ['dʒitni] pièce *f* de 5 cents; tacot *m*.

jit·ter F ['dʒitə] **1.** frétiller (de nervosité), être nerveux (-euse *f*); **2.** *sl.* ~s *pl.* nervosité *f*, crise *f* nerveuse; ~·**bug** ['~bʌg] **1.** fanatique *m* du swing; *danse:* swing *m*; paniquard *m*; **2.** faire du *jitterbug*; 'jit·ter·y *sl.* nerveux (-euse *f*) à l'excès.

jiu-jit·su [dʒuː'dʒitsuː] jiu-jitsu *m*.

jive *Am. sl.* [dʒaiv] hot jazz *m*; jargon *m* des musiciens swing.

Job[1] [dʒoub]: ~'s *comforter* consolateur *m* pessimiste, ami *m* de Job; ~'s *news* nouvelle *f* fatale.

job[2] [dʒɔb] **1.** tâche *f*, travail (*pl.* -aux) *m*, besogne *f*; F emploi *m*; *sl.* chose *f*, article *m*; ~ *soldes m/pl.*, marchandise *f* d'occasion; *péj.* intrigue *f*; *typ.* travail (*pl.* -aux) *m* de ville; ~ *analysis* analyse *f* des tâches *ou* des postes de travail; *by the* ~ à la pièce, à forfait; *make a* (*good*) ~ *of s.th.* bien faire qch., réussir à qch.; *a bad* ~ une mauvaise *ou* triste affaire, un malheur; *odd* ~s *pl.* petits travaux *m/pl.*; métiers *m/pl.* à part; ~ *horse* cheval *m* loué; ~ *lot soldes m/pl.*; *on the* ~ *training* apprentissage *m ou* formation *f* sur le tas; ~ *printer* imprimeur *m* à façon; imprimeur *m* de travaux de ville; ~ *work* travail (*pl.* -aux) *m* à la pièce *ou* tâche; **2.** *v/t.* louer (*un cheval etc.*); ✝ marchander; donner *ou* prendre à forfait (*un travail*); *v/i.* faire des petits travaux, bricoler; travailler à la tâche; ✝ agioter.

job·ber ['dʒɔbə] ouvrier (-ère *f*) *m* à la tâche; intermédiaire *m* revendeur; *péj.* tripoteur (-euse *f*) *m*; ✝ marchand *m* de titres; 'job·ber·y tripotages *m/pl.*; ✝ *a.* agiotage *m*; *a piece of* ~ une affaire maquignonnée; 'job·bing ouvrage *m* à la tâche; ✝ courtage *m*; ✝ vente *f* en demi-gros; *see jobbery;* 'job-'hunt·ing chasse *f* à l'emploi; 'job·less sans emploi, en chômage, chômeur (-euse *f*).

jock·ey ['dʒɔki] **1.** *su.* jockey *m*; **2.** *v/t.* tromper, duper; *v/i.* manœuvrer; intriguer.

jock·strap ['dʒɔkstræp] suspensoir *m.*

jo·cose □ [dʒə'kous] facétieux (-euse *f*); jovial (-aux *m/pl.*); **jo'cose·ness** jocosité *f*; humeur *f* joviale.

joc·u·lar ['dʒɔkjulə], **joc·u·lar·i·ty** [‿'læriti] *see* jocose(ness).

joc·und □ ['dʒɔkənd] gai; jovial (·als *ou* -aux *m/pl.*).

Joe [dʒou]: ~ *Miller* vieille plaisanterie *f*; plaisanterie *f* usée.

jog [dʒɔg] 1. *su.* secousse *f*, cahot *m*; coup *m* de coude; petit trot *m*; 2. *v/t.* pousser le coude à; donner un coup de coude à; *fig.* rafraîchir (*la mémoire à q.*); secouer; *v/i.* (*usu.* ~ *along*, ~ *on*) aller son petit train; aller au petit trot; *be* ~*ging* se (re)mettre en route.

jog·gle ['dʒɔgl] 1. secouer (*qch.*); branler; ⊕ goujonner; 2. petite secousse *f*; ⊕ (joint *m* à) goujon *m*.

jog-trot ['dʒɔg'trɔt] 1. petit trot *m*; *fig.* train-train *m*; 2. routinier (-ère *f*); monotone.

John [dʒɔːn]: ~ *Bull* l'Anglais; *Am.* ~ *Hancock* signature *f (de q.*); ♀ *Am.* F cabinets *m/pl.*, toilette *f*.

john·ny F ['dʒɔni] type *m*, individu *m*; *surt. Am.* ~ *cake* galette *f* de farine de maïs.

join [dʒɔin] 1. *v/t.* joindre (*a.* ⊕), (ré)unir; (re)nouer; se joindre à, rejoindre; ajouter; ⊕ raboutir; ✕, ♲ rallier; s'affilier à; s'enrôler dans; *v/i.* s'unir, se (re)joindre (à, *with*); (*a.* ~ *together*) se réunir; ~ *battle* livrer bataille (à, *with*); ~ *company* se joindre (à, *with*); ~ *hands* se donner la main; *fig.* se joindre (à, *with*); ~ *a ship* rallier le bord; ~ *in* prendre part à; se mettre de la partie; s'associer à; ~ *up* s'engager dans l'armée; *I* ~ *with you* je me joins avec *ou* à vous (pour *inf.*, *in gér.*); 2. *su.* joint *m*, jointure *f*; ligne *f* de jonction.

join·er ['dʒɔinə] menuisier *m*; **'join·er·y** menuiserie *f (travail, a. endroit).*

joint [dʒɔint] 1. joint *m* (*a. du genou*), jointure *f*; ⊕ assemblage *m*; *livre:* mors *m*; *anat.* articulation *f*; *doigt:* phalange *f*; *cuis.* quartier *m*, rôti *m*; ♀ nœud *m*; *Am. sl.* boîte *f*, bistrot *m*; *put out of* ~ disloquer; *fig. out of* ~ détraqué;

2. □ (*en*) commun; combiné; collectif (-ive *f*); co-; ~ *heir* cohéritier *m*; ~ *ownership* copropriété *f*; ~ *production* coproduction *f*; ~ *venture* entreprise *f* commune; 3. joindre, assembler (*a.* ⊕); *cuis.* découper; *anat.* (s')articuler; **'joint·ed** articulé (*a. zo.*, *a.* ♀); ~ *doll* poupée *f* articulée; **'joint-stock:** ~ *company* société *f* par actions; **join·ture** ♫ ['‿tʃe] douaire *m*.

joist [dʒɔist] 1. solive *f*, poutre *f*; 2. poser le solivage de; assujettir (*les ais*) sur le solivage.

joke [dʒouk] 1. *su.* plaisanterie *f*; farce *f*; 2. *v/i.* plaisanter, badiner; *v/t.* railler; **'jok·er** farceur (-euse *f*) *m*; *cartes:* joker *m*; F type *m*; *Am. sl.* clause *f* ambiguë; **'jok·y** □ facétieux (-euse *f*).

jol·li·fi·ca·tion F [dʒɔlifi'keiʃn] partie *f* de plaisir; **'jol·li·ness**, **'jol·li·ty** gaieté *f*.

jol·ly ['dʒɔli] 1. □ gai, joyeux (-euse *f*); F fameux (-euse *f*); 2. F *adv.* rudement; 3. F railler; flatter.

jol·ly-boat ♲ ['dʒɔlibout] canot *m*.

jolt [dʒoult] 1. cahoter; *v/t.* secouer. 2. cahot *m*, secousse *f*; **'jolt·y** cahotant; cahoteux (-euse *f*) (*chemin*).

Jon·a·than ['dʒɔnəθən]: *Brother* ~ l'Américain.

jon·quil ♀ ['dʒɔŋkwil] jonquille *f*.

jo·rum ['dʒɔːrəm] bol(ée *f*) *m*.

josh *Am. sl.* [dʒɔʃ] 1. blague *f*; 2. blaguer; taquiner.

joss [dʒɔs] idole *f* chinoise; ~ *stick* bâton *m* d'encens.

jos·tle ['dʒɔsl] 1. *v/t.* coudoyer; *v/i.* jouer des coudes; 2. *su.* bousculade *f*; coudoiement *m*.

jot [dʒɔt] 1. iota *m*; atome *m*; 2. ~ *down* prendre note de; **'jot·ting** note *f*.

jour·nal ['dʒəːnl] journal *m*; revue *f*; ♱ (*livre m*) journal *m*; ♲ journal *m* de bord; ⊕ tourillon *m*; ⊕ fusée *f*; **jour·nal·ese** F ['‿nə'liːz] style *m* de journaliste; **'jour·nal·ism** journalisme *m*; **'jour·nal·ist** journaliste *mf*; **jour·nal·is·tic** (‿ally) journalistique; **'jour·nal·ize** tenir un journal de; ♱ porter au journal.

jour·ney ['dʒəːni] 1. voyage *m*; trajet *m (d'autobus etc.*); parcours *m*; 2. voyager; **'‿man** compagnon *m*; ouvrier *m*; '**~-work** travail (*pl.* -aux) *m* à la journée; *fig.* dure besogne *f*.

joust [dʒaust] **1.** joute *f*; **2.** jouter.

Jove [dʒouv]: *by* ~*!* parbleu!

jo·vi·al □ ['dʒouviəl] jovial (-als *ou* -aux *m/pl.*); enjoué; **jo·vi·al·i·ty** [~'æliti] jovialité *f*; bonne humeur *f*.

jowl [dʒaul] mâchoire *f*; joue *f*; *cheek by* ~ côte à côte.

joy [dʒɔi] joie *f*, allégresse *f*; **joy·ful** □ ['~ful] joyeux (-euse *f*); heureux (-euse *f*); enjoué; **joy·ful·ness** joie *f*; **joy·less** □ triste, sans joie; **joy·ous** □ joyeux (-euse *f*), heureux (-euse *f*); **joy·ride** *mot.* F balade *f* en auto (*souv.* à l'insu du propriétaire); **joy·rid·er** baladeur (-euse *f*) *m*; **joy·stick** ✈ *sl.* manche *m* à balai.

ju·bi·lant ['dʒu:bilənt] joyeux (-euse *f*); réjoui, exultant (*personne*); **ju·bi·late** ['~leit] se réjouir, exulter; **ju·bi·la·tion** allégresse *f*; **ju·bi·lee** ['~li:] jubilé *m*; cinquantenaire *m*.

Ju·da·ism ['dʒu:deiizm] judaïsme *m*.

Ju·das ['dʒu:dəs] *fig.* Judas *m*; traître *m*; '**2**(-**hole**) judas *m*.

judge [dʒʌdʒ] **1.** *su.* juge *m* (*a. fig., a. sp.*); président *m* du tribunal; *fig.* connaisseur (-euse *f*) *m*; *Am.* magistrat *m*; *sp.* arbitre *m*; *commercial* ~ juge *m* préposé au tribunal commercial; **2.** *v/i.* juger (d'après, par *from*, *by*; de, of); estimer; *v/t.* juger (par, by); estimer; arbitrer (à qch., *s.th.*).

judg(e)·ment ['dʒʌdʒmənt] jugement *m*; arrêt *m*, décision *f* judiciaire; *fig.* avis *m*; *fig.* discernement *m*; *in my* ~ à mon avis; *pronounce* ~ rendre un arrêt; *sit in* ~ juger; *eccl.* ~-*day* jugement *m* dernier.

judge·ship ['dʒʌdʒʃip] fonctions *f/pl.* de juge.

ju·di·ca·ture ['dʒu:dikətʃə] judicature *f*; (cour *f* de) justice *f*; *coll.* magistrature *f*.

ju·di·cial □ [dʒu:'diʃl] judiciaire; de juge; de bonne justice; légal (-aux *m/pl.*); *fig.* impartial (-aux *m/pl.*); ~ *murder* assassinat *m* judiciaire; ~ *system* système *m* judiciaire.

ju·di·cious □ [dʒu:'diʃəs] judicieux (-euse *f*), sensé; **ju·di·cious·ness** discernement *m*.

jug [dʒʌg] **1.** cruche *f*; pot *m*; *sl.* prison *f*; **2.** étuver; ~*ged hare* civet *m* de lièvre.

Jug·ger·naut ['dʒʌgənɔ:t] *fig.* poids *m* écrasant; roues *f/pl.* meurtrières.

jug·gins F ['dʒʌginz] niais *m*.

jug·gle ['dʒʌgl] **1.** jonglerie *f*; tour *m* de passe-passe; *fig.* supercherie *f*; **2.** jongler; faire des tours de passe-passe; escamoter (à q., *out of s.o.*); **jug·gler** jongleur (-euse *f*) *m*; prestidigitateur *m*; escamoteur (-euse *f*) *m*; **jug·gler·y** jonglerie *f*; prestidigitation *f*; *fig.* supercherie *f*.

Ju·go·slav ['ju:gou'slɑ:v] **1.** Yougoslave *m/f*; **2.** yougoslave.

jug·u·lar *anat.* ['dʒʌgjulə] jugulaire; ~ *vein* (veine *f*) jugulaire *f*; **ju·gu·late** ['~leit] *fig.* étrangler; supprimer.

juice [dʒu:s] jus *m* (*a. mot. sl., a. ⚡ F*); *mot. sl.* essence *f*; ⚡ courant *m*; **juic·i·ness** ['~inis] succulence *f*; **juic·y** □ succulent; F savoureux (-euse *f*).

ju·jube ['dʒu:dʒu:b] ♀ jujube *f*; *pharm.* boule *f* de gomme.

juke-box *Am.* F ['dʒu:kbɔks] pick-up *m/inv.* à sous.

ju·lep ['dʒu:lep] ♀ julep *m*; *surt. Am.* boisson *f* alcoolique glacée.

Ju·ly [dʒu'lai] juillet *m*.

jum·ble ['dʒʌmbl] **1.** *su.* méli-mélo (*pl.* mélis-mélos) *m*; fatras *m*; **2.** *v/t.* (*a.* ~ *up*) brouiller, mêler; *v/i.* se brouiller; ~ *along* avancer en cahotant; '~-*sale* vente *f* d'objets usagés.

jum·bo ['dʒʌmbou] *fig.* éléphant *m*; *attr.* (*a.* ~-*sized*) géant.

jump [dʒʌmp] **1.** *su.* saut *m* (*a. sp.*); bond *m*; sursaut *m*; *sp.* obstacle *m*; *surt. Am.* F *get* (*ou have*) *the* ~ *on* devancer; *give a* ~ sursauter (*q.*); faire un saut; **2.** *v/i.* sauter, bondir; sursauter; *poét.* être d'accord; ~ *at fig.* saisir, sauter sur; ~ *to conclusions* conclure à la légère, juger trop vite; *v/t.* franchir, sauter; faire sauter (*un cheval etc.*); saisir à l'improviste; 🚂 quitter (*les rails*); *Am.* F usurper; voler; ~ *the gun sp.* partir avant le départ; F *fig.* (ré)agir prématurément; *mot.* ~ *the lights* brûler le feu (rouge), passer au rouge; ~ *the queue* (*Am. line*) passer avant son tour; ~ *a train* sauter dans un train en marche;

'**jump·er** sauteur (-euse f) m (a. = cheval, insecte); ⚓ chemise f; (a. knitted ~) casaque f, jumper m (de femme); barre f à mine; '**jump·ing-board** tremplin m; '**jump·ing-'off** fig. départ m; '**jump·seat** strapontin m; '**jump·y** nerveux (-euse f), agité.

junc·tion ['dʒʌŋkʃn] jonction f; bifurcation f; rivières: confluent m; 🚂 gare f d'embranchement; ⚡ ~ box boîte f de dérivation; **junc·ture** ['~tʃə] jointure f; jonction f (de rivières); conjoncture f (de circonstances); at this ~ of things à ce moment critique.

June [dʒuːn] juin m.

jun·gle ['dʒʌŋgl] jungle f; fig. confusion f.

jun·ior ['dʒuːnjə] 1. cadet(te f); plus jeune (que, to); second; univ. Am. de troisième année (étudiant); Am. ~ high school (sorte d')école f secondaire (moyennes classes); ~ partner second associé m, associé m en second; 2. cadet(te f) m; rang: subalterne m, second associé m; Am. élève mf de troisième année dans un collège; F le jeune m; he is my ~ by four years, he is four years my ~ il est plus jeune que moi de quatre ans; **jun·ior·i·ty** [dʒuːni-'ɔriti] infériorité f d'âge; position f moins élevée.

ju·ni·per ♀ ['dʒuːnipə] genièvre m; arbuste: genévrier m.

junk[1] ⚓ [dʒʌŋk] jonque f.

junk[2] [~] ⚓ vieux cordages m/pl.; ⚓ bœuf m salé; 🐟 rossignol m, camelote f; déchets m/pl.; fig. bêtises f/pl.; pej. pacotille f; sl. came f, drogue f; ~ heap dépotoir m.

jun·ket ['dʒʌŋkit] 1. lait m caillé; festin m, banquet m; Am. partie f de plaisir; voyage m d'agrément aux frais de l'État ou du gouvernement; 2. faire bombance; festoyer; F ~ing party pique-nique m.

junk·ie sl. ['dʒʌŋki] camé(e f) m, drogué(e f) m.

junk·yard ['dʒʌŋkjaːd] dépotoir m.

jun·ta ['dʒʌntə] junte f; (a. **jun·to** ['~tou]) cabale f.

ju·rid·i·cal □ [dʒuə'ridikl] juridique, judiciaire.

ju·ris·dic·tion [dʒuəris'dikʃn] juridiction f; compétence f, ressort m;

ju·ris·pru·dence ['~pruːdəns] jurisprudence f; '**ju·ris·pru·dent** légiste m.

ju·rist ['dʒuːrist] juriste m; Am. avocat m.

ju·ror 🏛 ['dʒuərə] membre m du jury.

ju·ry 🏛 ['dʒuəri] jury m; jurés m/pl.; '~**box** banc m du jury; '~**man** membre m du jury.

ju·ry-mast ⚓ ['dʒuərimaːst] mât m de fortune.

just □ [dʒʌst] 1. adj. juste, équitable; légitime; impartial (-aux m/pl.); exact; 2. adv. juste; précisément, justement; tout près (de, by); tout à fait; seulement; ~ as au moment où; ~ as ... so ... de même que ... de même ...; be ~ (p.pr.) être en train de (inf.); have ~ (p.p.) venir de (inf.); ~ now actuellement; tout à l'heure; ~ over (below) juste au-dessus (au-dessous) (de qch., s.th.); ~ let me see! faites(-moi) voir!; it's ~ splendid! c'est vraiment magnifique!

jus·tice ['dʒʌstis] justice f; personne: juge m; magistrat m; ⚖ of the Peace juge m de paix; court of ~ tribunal m, cour f de justice; do ~ to rendre justice à (q.); '**jus·tice·ship** fonctions f/pl. de juge; magistrature f.

jus·ti·fi·a·bil·i·ty [dʒʌstifaiə'biliti] caractère m justifiable; justice f; '**jus·ti·fi·a·ble** □ justifiable; légitime.

jus·ti·fi·ca·tion [dʒʌstifi'keiʃn] justification f; **jus·ti·fi·ca·to·ry** ['~təri] justificatif (-ive f); justificateur (-trice f).

jus·ti·fi·er typ. ['dʒʌstifaiə] justificateur m; **jus·ti·fy** ['~fai] justifier (a. typ. une ligne); typ. parangonner (les caractères).

just·ly ['dʒʌstli] avec justice ou justesse.

just·ness ['dʒʌstnis] justice f (d'une cause); justesse f (d'une observation).

jut [dʒʌt] 1. (a. ~out) être en ou faire saillie; 2. saillie f.

Jute[1] [dʒuːt] Jute mf.

jute[2] ♀, 🌿 [~] jute m.

ju·ve·nes·cence [dʒuːvi'nesns] adolescence f; jeunesse f; **ju·ve·nes·cent** adolescent; **ju·ve·nile** ['~nail] 1. juvénile; de (la) jeunesse; pour enfants; ♀ *Court* tribunal *m* pour enfants; ~ *delinquent* mineur(e *f*) *m* délinquant(e); *théâ.* ~ *lead* jeune premier *m*; 2. jeune *mf*; ~*s pl.* livres *m*/*pl.* pour enfants *ou* pour la jeu-nesse; **ju·ve·nil·i·ty** [~'niliti] jeu-nesse *f*, juvénilité *f*.

jux·ta·pose [dʒʌkstə'pouz] juxta-poser; **jux·ta·po·si·tion** [~pə'ziʃən] juxtaposition *f*.

K

K, k [kei] K *m*, k *m*.

Kaf·(f)ir [ˈkæfə] Cafre *mf*.

kale [keil] chou (*pl.* -x) *m* (frisé); *Am. sl.* argent *m*, pognon *m*; *Scotch* ∼ chou *m* rouge.

ka·lei·do·scope *opt.* [kəˈleidəskoup] kaléidoscope *m*.

kan·ga·roo *zo.* [kæŋgəˈruː] kangourou *m*.

ka·o·lin *min.* [ˈkeiəlin] kaolin *m*.

ka·put *sl.* [kəˈpuːt] fichu, foutu.

keck [kek] avoir des haut-le-cœur; ∼ at F rejeter avec dégoût.

kedge ⚓ [kedʒ] 1. ancre *f* de touée; ancre *f* à jet; 2. haler sur une ancre à jet.

keel ⚓ [kiːl] 1. quille *f*; on an even ∼ sans différence de calaison; *fig.* symétrique(ment); 2. ∼ over chavirer; F s'évanouir; **'keel·age** ⚓ droits *m/pl.* de mouillage; **'keeled** ⚓ caréné; **keel·haul** ⚓ [ˈ∼hɔːl] † donner la grande cale à; **keel·son** ⚓ [ˈkelsn] carlingue *f*.

keen □ [kiːn] aiguisé; perçant (*froid, œil, vent, etc.*); vif (vive *f*) (*froid, plaisir, vent, etc.*); mordant (*satire*); zélé, ardent; vorace (*appétit*); be ∼ on hunting être chasseur enthousiaste, avoir la passion de la chasse; ∼-edged [ˈ∼edʒd] tranchant, bien affilé; **'keen·ness** acuité *f*, finesse *f*; froid: âpreté *f*; *fig.* zèle *m*, ardeur *f*.

keep [kiːp] 1. *su.* frais *m/pl.* de subsistance; nourriture *f*; *hist.* donjon *m*, réduit *m*; F surt. *Am.* for ∼s pour de bon; 2. [*irr.*] *v/t. usu.* tenir (*p.ex. boutique, comptes, école, journal, promesse, scène, a. devant adj.*); garder (*sp. but, lit, provisions, qch. pour q.*); avoir (*une auto*); (*a.* ∼ up) maintenir (*la discipline, l'ordre*); contenir; conserver (*sa sveltesse etc.*); préserver (de, *from*); retenir (*q. à dîner, en prison; l'attention*); suivre (*une règle*); célébrer, observer (*une fête*); subvenir aux besoins de; cacher (*qch. à q., s.th. from s.o.*); ∼ *s.o. company* tenir compagnie à q.; ∼ *company with* sortir avec; ∼ *silence*

garder le silence; ∼ *one's temper* se contenir; ∼ *time* être exact (*montre*); ♪ suivre la mesure; ⚔ être au pas; ∼ *watch* monter la garde, veiller; ∼ *s.o. waiting* faire attendre q.; ∼ *away* tenir éloigné; ∼ *down* empêcher de monter; réprimer; maintenir (*les prix*) bas; ∼ *s.o. from* (*gér.*) empêcher q. de (*inf.*); préserver q. de; ∼ *in* retenir; contenir (*la colère*); consigner, mettre en retenue (*un élève*); entretenir (*un feu*); ∼ *s.o. in money* fournir de l'argent à q.; ∼ *in view* ne pas perdre de vue; ∼ *off* éloigner; ∼ *on* garder; ∼ *out* empêcher d'entrer; se garantir de (*le froid, la pluie*); ∼ *up* tenir haut; maintenir (*un prix etc.*); entretenir (*la correspondance*); sauver (*les apparences*); 3. [*irr.*] *v/i.* rester, se tenir; se conserver (*fruit etc.*); continuer; F ne rien perdre (pour attendre); ∼ *clear of* éviter, rester à distance de; ∼ *doing* ne pas cesser de faire, continuer de faire; ∼ *away* se tenir éloigné *ou* à l'écart; ∼ *from* s'abstenir de; ∼ *in with* rester bien avec, cultiver; ∼ *off* se tenir éloigné; ∼ *on* (*gér.*) continuer de (*inf.*), s'obstiner à (*inf.*); ∼ *to* s'en tenir à; observer; suivre; ∼ *up* se maintenir; ∼ *up with* aller de pair avec; *fig.* se maintenir au niveau de.

keep·er [ˈkiːpə] garde *m*, gardien (-ne *f*) *m*, surveillant(e *f*) *m*; *musée:* conservateur *m*; troupeaux: gardeur (-euse *f*) *m*; **'keep·ing** observation *f*; célébration *f*; garde *f*; be in (out of) ∼ with (ne pas) être en accord avec; **keep·sake** [ˈ∼seik] souvenir *m* (*cadeau etc.*).

keg [keg] harengs: caque *f*; alcool: barillet *m*.

kel·son ⚓ [ˈkelsn] see keelson.

ken [ken] connaissance *f*, -s *f/pl.*

ken·nel¹ [ˈkenl] ruisseau *m* (*de rue*).

ken·nel² [∼] 1. niche *f* (*de chien*); *chien de chasse:* chenil *m*; *chasse:* la meute *f*; 2. *fig.* enfermer.

kept

906

kept [kept] *prét. et p.p.* de *keep* 2.

kerb(·stone) ['kə:b(stoun)] *see* **curb (-stone)**.

ker·chief ['kə:tʃif] fanchon *f*, mouchoir *m* de tête; fichu *m*.

kerf [kə:f] trait *m* ou voie *f* de scie; bout *m* coupé (*d'un arbre abattu*).

ker·nel ['kə:nl] *noisette etc.*: amande *f*; *céréales*: grain *m*; *fig.* fond *m*, essentiel *m*.

ker·o·sene ['kerəsi:n] kérosène *m*, pétrole *m* lampant.

kes·trel *orn.* ['kestrəl] émouchet *m*.

ketch·up ['ketʃəp] sauce *f* tomate très relevée.

ket·tle ['ketl] bouilloire *f*; '**~-drum** ♪ timbale *f*; *Am.* F thé *m* ou réception *f* sans cérémonie.

key [ki:] 1. clé *f*, clef *f* (*a. fig.*); ⊕ clavette *f*, coin *m*, cale *f*; *machine à écrire, piano*: touche *f*; *flûte etc.*: clef *f*; ♩ fiche *f*; ♪ ton *m* (*a. fig.*); *école*: corrigé *m*; *pendule etc.*: remontoir *m*; ♪ ~s *pl.* instruments *m/pl.* à clavier *ou* à touches; ~ **industry** industrie *f* clef; ~ **money** pas *m* de porte; ~ **punch** poinçonneuse *f*; ♪ *signature* armature *f*; ⊕ ~ **saw** scie *f* à guichet; 2. claveter; coincer; adenter (*une planche*); ♪ accorder; ~ **up** hausser; *fig.* stimuler; *be* ~ed **up** être tendu; '**~-bit** panneton *m* de clef; '**~·board** clavier *m*; porte-clefs *m/inv.*, '**~-bu·gle** ♪ bugle *m*; '**~-hole** trou *m* de serrure; '**~·less** sans clef; ~ **watch** montre *f* à remontoir; '**~·man** pivot *m*; '**~-note** tonique *f*; *fig.* note *f* dominante; '**~·stone** clef *f* de voûte.

khak·i ['kɑ:ki] *tex.*, *a. couleur*: kaki *m* (*a. adj./inv.*).

kib·butz [ki'buts], *pl.* **-but·zim** [~'butsim] kibboutz (*pl.* kibboutzim) *m*.

kibe [kaib] gerçure *f*.

kib·itz·er *Am.* F ['kibitsə] je sais tout *m* (*qui donne des conseils à des joueurs aux cartes sans qu'on les lui demande*).

ki·bosh *sl.* ['kaibɔʃ] bêtises *f/pl.*; *put the* ~ *on* faire son affaire à (*q.*); bousiller (*qch.*).

kick [kik] 1. coup *m* de pied; *arme à feu*: recul *m*, réaction *f*; F vigueur *f*, énergie *f*; résistance *f*; *surt. Am.* F plaintes *f/pl.*, protestation *f*; *foot. see* ~er; F *do s.th. for* ~s faire qch. pour le plaisir *ou* pour s'amuser; F *get a* ~ *out of* éprouver du plaisir à; *sl. it's got a* ~ *to it* ça vous remonte; 2. *v/t.*

donner des coups *ou* un coup de pied à; F congédier (*q.*); *sl.* ~ *the bucket* casser sa pipe (= *mourir*); ~ *s.o. downstairs* faire dégringoler l'escalier à q.; F ~ *one's heels* faire le pied de grue (= *attendre*); F ~ *out ficher à la porte*; *sl.* ~ *up a row* faire du chahut; *fig.* faire un scandale; *v/i.* donner un coup de pied; reculer (*arme à feu*); ruer (*animal*); rechigner (à *against, at*); *sl.* rouspéter; F ~ *around ou about* traîner (*quelque part*); *Am. sl.* ~ *in with* contribuer (*de l'argent*); '**kick-back** *surt. Am.* F réaction *f* violente; *Am. sl.* ristourne *f*; '**kick·er** cheval *m* qui rue; *sp.* joueur *m*; *Am. sl.* rouspéteur (-euse *f*) *m*; '**kick-'off** *foot.* coup *m* d'envoi; commencement *m*; **kick-shaw** ['kikʃɔ:] bagatelle *f*; *cuis.* friandise *f*; '**kick-'up** *sl.* boucan *m*.

kid [kid] 1. chevreau (-ette *f*) *m*; (peau *f* de) chevreau *m*; *sl.* gosse *mf*; ~ *glove* gant *m* de chevreau; gant *m* glacé; 2. mettre bas (*v/t. un chevreau*) *v/i. sl.* plaisanter, taquiner; *v/t.* en conter à; tromper; '**kid·dy** F gosse *mf*, petit(e *f*) *m*.

kid·nap ['kidnæp] kidnapper, enlever (*surt. un enfant*); ✂, ⚓ prendre par la presse; enlever; '**kid·nap·(p)er** ravisseur (-euse *f*) *m* (*d'enfant*), kidnappeur *m*.

kid·ney ['kidni] *anat.* rein *m*; *cuis.* rognon *m*; F *bean m*; ~ *bean* ⚘ haricot *m* nain; ⚕ ~ *machine* rein *m* artificiel.

kike *Am. sl. péj.* [kaik] juif *m*.

kill [kil] tuer, faire mourir; abattre (*une bête*); amortir (*un son*); *fig.* supprimer; *parl.* couler (*un projet de loi*); ~ *off* exterminer; ~ *time* tuer le temps; '**kill·er** tueur (-euse *f*) *m*; meurtrier (-ère *f*) *m*; '**kill·ing** 1. meurtrier (-ère *f*); écrasant (*travail etc.*); F tordant; 2. *Am.* F opération *f* lucrative; succès *m* (*financier*); '**kill-joy** rabat-joie *m/inv.*

kiln [kiln] four *m*; séchoir *m*, étuve *f*; meule *f* (*de charbon de bois*); '**~-dry** sécher (*qch.*) au four *etc.*

kil·o·cy·cle *phys.* ['kilosaikl] kilocycle *m*; **kil·o·gram(me)** ['~ogræm] kilogramme *m*; F kilo *m*; **kil·o·me·ter, kil·o·me·tre** ['~mi:tə] kilomètre *m*.

kilt [kilt] 1. *écoss.* kilt *m* (*jupe courte*

et plissée); **2.** plisser; retrousser (*ses jupes*).

kin [kin] **1.** parents *m/pl.*; *the next of* ~ le parent le plus proche; F la famille; **2.** apparenté (avec, to).

kind [kaind] **1.** □ bon(ne *f*) (pour, to); aimable (à, of); **2.** espèce *f*; sorte *f*; genre *m*; nature *f*; *people of all* ~*s* monde *m* de tous les genres; des gens de toutes sortes; *different in* ~ qui diffère(nt) en nature; *pay in* ~ payer en nature; *fig.* payer de la même monnaie; F *I* ~ *of expected it* je m'en doutais presque.

kin·der·gar·ten [ˈkindəgɑːtn] jardin *m* d'enfants; école *f* maternelle; ~ *teacher* jardinière *f* d'enfants; institutrice *f* d'école maternelle.

kind-heart·ed [ˈkaindˈhɑːtid] bienveillant, bon(ne *f*).

kin·dle [ˈkindl] (s')allumer; (s')enflammer; *fig.* susciter.

kind·li·ness [ˈkaindlinis] bonté *f*, bienveillance *f*.

kin·dling [ˈkindliŋ], *a.* ~*s pl.* petit bois *m*; bois *m* d'allumage.

kind·ly [ˈkaindli] **1.** *adj.* bienveillant, bon(ne *f*); doux (douce *f*) (*climat*); **2.** *adv.* avec bonté; ~ *do s.th.* avoir la bonté de faire qch.

kind·ness [ˈkaindnis] bonté *f* (pour, to); bienveillance *f*; amabilité *f* (envers, to).

kin·dred [ˈkindrid] **1.** analogue; de la même nature; **2.** parenté *f*; *coll.* parents *m/pl.*; affinité *f* (avec, with).

ki·net·ic *phys.* [kaiˈnetik] **1.** cinétique; **2.** ~*s pl.* cinétique *f*.

king [kiŋ] roi *m*; *jeu de dames:* dame *f*; ♀'s *English* anglais *m* correct; ✠ ~'s *evil* scrofule *f*; écrouelles *f/pl.*; **ˈking·craft** art *m* de régner; **ˈking·cup** ♣ bouton *m* d'or; **ˈking·dom** royaume *m*; *surt.* ♣, *zo.* règne *m*; **ˈking·fish·er** martin-pêcheur (*pl.* martins-pêcheurs) *m*; **king·let** [ˈ~lit] roitelet *m*; **ˈking·like** royal (-aux *m/pl.*), de roi; **ˈking·li·ness** prestance *f* royale; noblesse *f*; **ˈking·ly** royal (-aux *m/pl.*), de roi; **ˈking·post** ⌂ poinçon *m*, aiguille *f*; **ˈking·ship** royauté *f*; **ˈking-size** F de taille *etc.* exceptionnelle.

kink [kiŋk] **1.** *corde etc.:* tortillement *m*, nœud *m*; *fil de fer:* faux pli *m*; *tex.* boucle *f*; *fig.* lubie *f*, point *m* faible; F *have a* ~ être un peu toqué;

2. (se) nouer, tortiller; **ˈkink·y** crépu (*cheveux*); F bizarre, excentrique.

kins·folk [ˈkinzfouk] *pl.* parenté *f*, famille *f*; **ˈkin·ship** parenté *f*; **ˈkins·man** [ˈ~zmən] parent *m*; allié *m*; **ˈkins·wom·an** parente *f*; alliée *f*.

ki·osk [kiˈɔsk] kiosque *m*.

kip *Brit. sl.* [kip] **1.** roupillon *m* (= *sommeil*); pieu *m* (= *lit*); *have a* ~ piquer un roupillon; **2.** coucher; roupiller (*dormir*); ~ *down* se pieuter (= *se coucher*).

kip·per [ˈkipə] **1.** hareng *m* fumé *ou* doux; *sl.* jeune personne *f*; **2.** saurer, saler et fumer (*des harengs*).

kirk [kɔːk] *écoss.* église *f*.

kiss [kis] **1.** baiser *m*; *fig.* frôlement *m*; **2.** (s')embrasser; **ˈ~-proof** indélébile.

kit [kit] seau *m*; ✗, ⚓ petit équipement *m*; ✗ bagage *m*; ⚓ sac *m*; ⊕ trousse(au *m*) *f*; F effets *m/pl.*; **ˈ~-bag** ✗ musette *f*; sac *m* (de voyage); ⊕ trousse *f* d'outils.

kitch·en [ˈkitʃin] cuisine *f*; **ˈkitch·en·er** cuisinière *f*; **kitch·en·ette** [ˌ~'net] cuisine *f* miniature.

kitch·en...: ~ *gar·den* (jardin *m*) potager *m*; **ˈ~-maid** fille *f* de cuisine; **ˈ~-range** cuisinière *f* anglaise; **ˈ~-sink** évier *m*.

kite [kait] *orn.* milan *m*; *fig.* vautour *m*; cerf-volant (*pl.* cerfs-volants) *m*; *fig.* ballon *m* d'essai; † *sl.* traite *f* de complaisance; ✗ ~ *balloon* ballon *m* captif.   [rents.]

kith [kiθ]: ~ *and kin* amis et pa-)

kit·ten [ˈkitn] **1.** chaton *m*, petit(e *f*) chat(te *f*) *m*; **2.** *chatte:* mettre bas (*v/t. des petits*); **ˈkit·ten·ish** coquet(te *f*); enjoué.

kit·tle [ˈkitl] *fig.* difficile (à manier); ~ *cattle* gens *m/pl.* difficiles à manier.

Klans·man *Am.* [ˈklænzmən] membre *m* du Ku-Klux-Klan.

klax·on *mot.* [ˈklæksn] klaxon *m*.

klep·to·ma·ni·a [kleptoˈmeinjə] kleptomanie *f*; **klep·to'ma·ni·ac** [ˌ~niæk] kleptomane (*a. su./mf*).

knack [næk] tour *m* de main; F truc *m*; *get the* ~ *of* (*gér.*) attraper le chic pour (*inf.*).

knack·er [ˈnækə] *Brit.* équarrisseur *m*; entrepreneur *m* de démolitions; **ˈknack·ered** *Brit. sl.* éreinté; **ˈknack·er·y** *Brit.* abattoir *m* de chevaux.

knack·y ['næki] adroit, habile.

knag [næg] nœud *m*; **'knag·gy** noueux (-euse *f*).

knap·sack ['næpsæk] (havre)sac *m*; ✕ sac *m* d'ordonnance.

knar [nɑ:] nœud *m* saillant.

knave [neiv] fripon *m*; *cartes*: valet *m*; **knav·er·y** ['⌐əri] friponnerie *f*, fourberie *f*; **'knav·ish** □ fourbe; **'knav·ish·ness** fourberie *f*.

knead [ni:d] pétrir (*a.* ✱); travailler (*la pâte etc.*).

knee [ni:] 1. genou (*pl.* -x) *m* (*a.* ⊕); 2. pousser du genou; F fatiguer (*un pantalon*) aux genoux; **'⌐-cap**, **'⌐-pan** rotule *f*; **'⌐-joint** articulation *f* du genou; ⊕ rotule *f*; **kneel** [ni:l] [*irr.*] s'agenouiller, se mettre à genoux (devant, *to*); **'kneel·er** personne *f* à genoux.

knell [nel] glas *m*.

knelt [nelt] *prét. et p.p. de* kneel.

knew [nju:] *prét. de* know 1.

knick·er·bock·ers ['nikəbɔkəz] *pl.* culotte *f* (bouffante); **'knick·ers** F *pl.* culotte *f*, pantalon *m* (*de femme*); *see* knickerbockers.

knick·knack ['niknæk] babiole *f*, bibelot *m*; **⌐s** *pl.* afféteries *f/pl.*

knife [naif] 1. (*pl.* knives) couteau *m*; 2. poignarder; **'⌐-bat·tle** rixe *f* entre gens armés de poignards; **'⌐-grind·er** repasseur *m* de couteaux.

knight [nait] 1. chevalier *m*; *échecs*: cavalier *m*; 2. créer chevalier; **'knight·age** corps *m* des chevaliers; **knight er·rant** ['nait'erənt], *pl.* **knights er·rant** chevalier *m* errant; **knight·hood** ['⌐hud] chevalerie *f*; titre *m* de chevalier; **'knight·li·ness** caractère *m* chevaleresque; air *m* de chevalier; **'knight·ly** chevaleresque, de chevalier.

knit [nit] [*irr.*] *v/t.* tricoter; joindre; *v/i.* se nouer; **⌐** *the brows* froncer les sourcils; **'knit·ter** tricoteur (-euse *f*) *m*; **'knit·ting** tricot *m*; *action*: tricotage *m*; soudure *f* (*d'os*); 2. à tricoter; **⌐-needle** aiguille *f* à tricoter; **'knit·wear** tricot *m*.

knives [naivz] *pl. de* knife 1.

knob [nɔb] bosse *f*; *tiroir, porte*: bouton *m*; *canne*: pomme *f*; *charbon, sucre, etc.*: morceau *m*; **'knob·by** plein de bosses; loupeux (-euse *f*) (*arbre*); **'knob·stick** canne *f* à

pommeau; gourdin *m*; ✝ F jaune *m*.

knock [nɔk] 1. coup *m*, heurt *m*, choc *m*; 2. *v/i.* frapper; taper (sur, *at*); *mot.* cogner, taper; F se heurter (à, *against*); F **⌐** *about* se balader, flâner; **⌐** *off sl.* cesser le travail; **⌐** *under* se rendre; *v/t.* frapper, cogner, heurter; *Am. sl.* critiquer; **⌐** *down* renverser, abattre; *vente aux enchères*: adjuger; ⊕ démonter; *be* **⌐ed** *down* être renversé par une auto; **⌐** *off* faire tomber de; rabattre (*qch. du prix*); F voler, chiper; *box.* **⌐** *out* knockouter, F endormir; **⌐** *up* faire sauter (en l'air); construire à la hâte; réveiller; *fig.* éreinter, épuiser; **'⌐-a·bout** 1. violent; vagabond; de tous les jours (*habits*); *théâ.* de bateleur, de clown; 2. *Am.* rixe *m*; **'⌐-'down** de réclame, minimum (*prix*); **'knock·er** frappeur (-euse *f*) *m*; marteau *m* (*de porte*); *Am. sl.* critique *m* impitoyable; *Brit. sl.* **⌐s** *pl.* nénés *f/pl.* (= *seins*); **'knock-kneed** cagneux (-euse *f*); panard (*cheval*); **'knock-'out** *box.* (*a.* **⌐** *blow*) knock-out *m*; *sl.* chose *f* ou personne *f* épatante.

knoll[1] [noul] tertre *m*, butte *f*.

knoll[2] [⌐] ✝ sonner; tinter.

knot [nɔt] 1. nœud *m* (*a. fig., a.* ⚓, ⛴); *gens*: groupe *m*; *cheveux*: chignon *m*; *sailor's* **⌐** nœud *m* régate; F *be tied up in* **⌐s** ne savoir plus que faire *ou* dire; 2. (se) nouer; *v/t.* froncer (*les sourcils*); **'⌐-hole** trou *m* (*provenant d'un nœud d'arbre*); **'knot·ti·ness** nodosité *f*; *bois*: caractère *m* noueux; *fig.* complexité *f*; **'knot·ty** plein de nœuds; noueux (-euse *f*) (*bois*); *fig.* épineux (-euse *f*); **'knot·work** *couture*: macramé *m*.

knout [naut] 1. knout *m*; 2. knouter.

know [nou] 1. [*irr.*] savoir (*un fait*); connaître (*q., un endroit*); reconnaître; distinguer (de, d'avec *from*); **⌐** *French* connaître *ou* parler le français; *come to* **⌐** apprendre; 2. F *be in the* **⌐** être au courant (de l'affaire); être dans le secret; **know·a·ble** ['nouəbl] (re)connaissable; **'know-all** 1. omniscient; 2. je sais tout *m*; **'know-how** savoir-faire *m/inv.*; connaissances *f/pl.* techniques; **'know·ing** 1. □ instruit; intelligent; habile; rusé, malin (-igne *f*); F chic *inv. en genre*; 2. connaissance *f*, compréhension *f*; **knowl·edge**

['nɔlidʒ] connaissance *f*; savoir *m*, connaissances *f/pl.*; *to my* ~ autant que je sache; à mon vu et su; **known** [noun] *p.p.* *de* know 1; *come to be* ~ se répandre (*bruit*); se faire connaître; se savoir; *make* ~ faire connaître; signaler.

knuck·le ['nʌkl] **1.** (*a.* ~-*bone*) articulation *f* du doigt; *veau:* jarret *m*; **2.** ~ *down* (*ou under*) se soumettre; céder; '~-**dust·er** coup-de-poing (*pl.* coups-de-poing) *m* américain.

knur [nə:] nœud *m*.

knut F [(k)nʌt] gommeux *m*.

ko·dak *phot.* ['koudæk] **1.** kodak *m*; **2.** photographier avec un kodak.

Ko·ran [kɔ'rɑːn] Koran *m*, Coran *m*.

ko·tow ['kou'tau] **1.** prosternation *f* (à la chinoise); **2.** saluer à la chinoise; *fig.* faire des courbettes (devant, *to*).

krem·lin ['kremlin] Kremlin *m*.

ku·dos *co.* ['kjuːdɔs] gloriole *f*.

Ku-Klux-Klan *Am.* ['kjuːˈklʌks-ˈklæn] *association secrète de l'Amérique du Nord, hostile aux Noirs.*

L

L, l [el] L *m*, l *m*.

lab F [læb] laboratoire *m*.

la·bel ['leibl] **1.** étiquette *f*; *fig.* désignation *f*, titre *m*; ⚖ queue *f*; △ larmier *m*; **2.** étiqueter; adresser; attacher une étiquette à; ✝ marquer le prix de; *fig.* qualifier (du nom de, *as*). [*m*/*pl.*); **2.** labiale *f*.\
la·bi·al ['leibjəl] **1.** labial (-aux)

lab·o·ra·to·ry [lə'bɔrətəri] laboratoire *m*; ~ *assistant* préparateur (-trice *f*) *m*.

la·bo·ri·ous □ [lə'bɔːriəs] laborieux (-euse *f*); pénible; travailleur (-euse *f*).

la·bo(u)r ['leibə] **1.** travail (*pl.* -aux) *m*, peine *f*, labeur *m*; main-d'œuvre (*pl.* mains-d'œuvre) *f*, travailleurs *m*/*pl.*; *pol.* les travaillistes *m*/*pl.*; ✚ couches *f*/*pl.*; *Ministry of* ♀ Ministère *m* du Travail; *hard* ~ travail *m* forcé; travaux *m*/*pl.* forcés; **2.** travailliste (*parti*); du travail; ♀ *Day* fête *f* du travail; ~ *dispute* conflit *m* social *ou* du travail; ~ *Exchange* Bourse *f* du Travail; ~ *force* les employés *m*/*pl.*, le personnel *m*; ♀ *Office* bureau *m* de placement; *surt. Am.* ~ *union* syndicat *m* ouvrier; **3.** *v/i.* travailler; peiner (*a. fig.*); ~ *under* être courbé sous; avoir à lutter contre; ~ *under a delusion* être victime d'une illusion; *v/t.* travailler; **'la·bo(u)r·age** paie *f*; **'la·bo(u)r-cre·a·tion** création *f* des emplois; **'la·bo(u)red** travaillé (*style*); pénible (*respiration*); **'la·bo(u)r·er** travailleur *m*; manœuvre *m*; *heavy manual* ~ travailleur *m* de force; **'la·bo(u)r·ing** ouvrier (-ère *f*); haletant (*poitrine*); palpitant (*cœur*); ~ *force* effectif *m* de la main-d'œuvre; **la·bo(u)r·ist** ['~rist], **la·bo(u)r·ite** ['~rait] membre *m* du parti travailliste.

la·bur·num ♣ [lə'bəːnəm] cytise *m*.

lab·y·rinth ['læbərinθ] labyrinthe *m*, dédale *m*; **lab·y·rin·thi·an** [~'rin-θiən], *usu.* **lab·y·rin·thine** [~'rin-θain] labyrinthique.

lac [læk] (gomme *f*) laque *f*; (*souv.* ~ *of rupees*) lack *m*; 100 000 de roupies.

lace [leis] **1.** lacet *m*; cordon *m*; *tex.* dentelle *f*; **2.** lacer (*un soulier*); entrelacer (de, *avec with*); arroser (*une boisson*) (à, *with*); garnir de dentelle(s); *fig.* (*a.* ~ *into s.o.*) rosser, battre; ~-**'pil·low** coussin(et) *m* à dentelle.

lac·er·ate 1. ['læsəreit] lacérer; *fig.* déchirer; **2.** ['~rit] lacéré; **lac·er·a·tion** lacération *f*; déchirement *m* (*a. fig.*); ✚ déchirure *f*.

lach·ry·mal *anat.* ['lækriml] lacrymal (-aux *m*/*pl.*); **lach·ry·ma·to·ry** ['~mətəri] lacrymatoire; lacrymogène (*gaz*); **lach·ry·mose** ['~mous] larmoyant.

lack [læk] **1.** *su.* manque *m*, défaut *m*, absence *f*; **2.** *v/t.* manquer de; ne pas avoir; *he* ~*s money* il n'a pas d'argent, l'argent lui fait défaut; *v/i.* be ~*ing* manquer, faire défaut; be ~*ing in* ... manquer de ...

lack·a·dai·si·cal □ [lækə'deizikl] apathique; affecté.

lack·ey ['læki] **1.** laquais *m*; **2.** *fig.* faire le plat valet auprès de (*q.*).

lack...: '~**land** sans terre (*a. su./m*/ *inv.*); '~**lus·ter**, '~**lus·tre** terne.

la·con·ic [lə'kɔnik] (~*ally*) laconique, bref (brève *f*).

lac·quer ['lækə] **1.** vernis *m* du Japon; laque *m*; **2.** laquer; F vernir.

lac·ta·tion [læk'teifn] lactation *f*.

lac·te·al ['læktiəl] lacté; laiteux (-euse *f*) (*suc*).

la·cu·na [lə'kjuːnə] lacune *f*, hiatus *m*.

lac·y ['leisi] de dentelle; fin comme de la dentelle.

lad [læd] garçon *m*; jeune homme *m*.

lad·der ['lædə] **1.** échelle *f* (*a. fig.*, *a.* ⚓); *bas:* maille *f* qui file, éraillure *f*; **2.** se démailler; '~-**proof** indémaillable (*bas etc.*).

lade [leid] [*irr.*] charger (de, *with*); puiser de l'eau (à, *from*); **'lad·en** chargé.

lad·ing ['leidiŋ] chargement m; embarquement m.

la·dle ['leidl] **1.** cuiller f à pot; poche f (a. métall.); ⊕ puisoir m; **2.** servir (avec une louche); métall. couler; ⊕ (a. ~ out) pucher.

la·dy ['leidi] dame f; titre: Lady, F milady, madame de ...; my ~ madame; ladies! mesdames!; young ~ demoiselle f; jeune dame f (mariée); ♀ Day (fête f de) l'Annonciation f (le 25 mars); ~ doctor femme f docteur, doctoresse f; ~'s maid femme f de chambre; ~'s (ou ladies') man galant m; '~-bird coccinelle f, F bête f à bon Dieu; '~-kill·er bourreau m des cœurs; don Juan m; '~-like distingué; péj. efféminé; '~-love bienaimée f; '~-ship: her ~, Your ♀ madame (la comtesse etc.).

lag¹ [læg] **1.** traîner; (a. ~ behind) rester en arrière; **2.** retard m.

lag² sl. [~] **1.** forçat m; **2.** condamner aux travaux forcés.

lag³ [~] garnir d'un calorifuge.

la·ger (beer) ['la:gə (biə)] bière f blonde.

lag·gard ['lægəd] **1.** lent, paresseux (-euse f); **2.** traînard m.

la·goon [lə'gu:n] atoll: lagon m; Adriatique: lagune f.

la·ic ['leiik] **1.** a. 'la·i·cal □ laïque; **2.** laïque mf; **la·i·cize** ['laiəsaiz] laïciser.

laid [leid] prét. et p.p. de lay⁴ **2.** ~ up alité, au lit; ~ paper papier m vergé.

lain [lein] p.p de lie² **2.**

lair [lɛə] tanière f, repaire m (d'une bête fauve).

laird écoss. [lɛəd] propriétaire m foncier; F châtelain m.

la·i·ty ['leiiti] laïques m/pl.

lake¹ [leik] lac m; ornamental ~ bassin m.

lake² [~] peint. laque f.

lake-dwel·lings ['leikdweliŋz] pl. habitations f lacustres.

lam sl. [læm] v/t. (a. ~ into) rosser, étriller; v/i. s'évader, s'enfuir.

lamb [læm] **1.** agneau m; ~ chop côtelette f d'agneau; **2.** agneler.

lam·baste sl. [læm'beist] donner une râclée à.

lam·bent ['læmbənt] blafard (yeux, étoile); chatoyant (style, esprit).

lamb·kin ['læmkin] agnelet m; 'lamb·like doux (douce f) comme un agneau; 'lamb·skin peau f d'a-

gneau; fourrure: agnelin m; 'lambs-wool laine f d'agneau.

lame [leim] **1.** □ boiteux (-euse f); estropié; fig. faible, piètre (excuse etc.); ~ duck fig. faible mf; ✝ failli m; Am. député m non réélu; **2.** rendre boiteux (-euse f); estropier; 'lame·ness boitement m; cheval: boiterie f; fig. faiblesse f.

la·ment [lə'mənt] **1.** lamentation f; **2.** se lamenter (sur, for), pleurer (q., for s.o.); **lam·en·ta·ble** □ ['læmən-təbl] lamentable, déplorable; **lam·en'ta·tion** lamentation f.

lam·i·na ['læminə], pl. **-nae** ['~ni:] lam(ell)e f; ♣ feuillet m; ♀ limbe m; 'lam·i·nar laminaire; **lam·i·nate** ['~nit], **lam·i·nat·ed** ['~neitid] à feuilles; contre-plaqué (bois).

lamp [læmp] lampe f; mot. lanterne f; head ~ phare m; '~-chim·ney verre m de lampe; '~-light lumière f de la (ou d'une) lampe; '~-light·er allumeur m de réverbères, lampiste m.

lam·poon [læm'pu:n] **1.** satire f, libelle m, brocard m; **2.** lancer des libelles etc. contre; chansonner (q.); **lam'poon·er, lam'poon·ist** libelliste m, satiriste m.

lamp-post ['læmppoust] (poteau m de) réverbère m.

lam·prey icht. ['læmpri] lamproie f.

lamp·shade ['læmpʃeid] abat-jour m/inv.

lance [la:ns] **1.** lance f; ✁ bistouri m; free ~ soldat m mercenaire; parl. politique m indépendant; journ. journaliste m indépendant; couch a ~ mettre une lance en arrêt; **2.** percer (a. ✁); '~-'cor·po·ral ✕ caporal m; **lan·ce·o·late** surt. ♀ ['læn-siəlit] lancéolé; **lanc·er** ['la:nsə] ✕ lancier m; ~s pl. danse anglaise: lanciers m/pl.

lan·cet ['la:nsit] bistouri m, lancette f; ~ arch △ arc m à lancette.

land [lænd] **1.** terre f; sol m; terrain m; pays m; propriété f foncière; ~s pl. terres f/pl., terrains m/pl.; ~ reclamation mise f en valeur (des marais); ~ défrichement m (d'un terrain); ~ reform réforme f agraire; ~ register cadastre m; fig. see how the ~ lies prendre le vent, tâter le terrain; **2.** v/t. mettre à terre; ⚓ débarquer (a. v/t.); ✈ atterrir (a. v/i.); F porter (un coup); F remporter (un *prix*); amener à terre (*un poisson*); '**~-a·gent** intendant *m* (*d'un domaine*); courtier *m* en immeubles; '**land·ed** foncier (-ère *f*) (*propriété*); terrien(ne *f*) (*personne*).

land...: '**~·fall** ⚓ atterrissage *m*; '**~-forc·es** *pl.* armée *f* de terre; '**~-grab·ber** accapareur *m* de terre; '**~·grave** landgrave *m*; '**~·hold·er** propriétaire *m* foncier.

land·ing ['lændiŋ] débarquement *m*; ✕, ⚓ descente *f*; ✈ atterrissage *m*; amerrissage *m*; ✈ ~ *gear* train *m* d'atterrissage; ~ *ground* terrain *m* d'atterrissage; ✈ ~ *run* distance *f* d'atterrissage; '**~-net** épuisette *f*; '**~-stage** débarcadère *m*, embarcadère *m*.

land...: '**~·la·dy** propriétaire *f*; *pension etc.*: logeuse *f*; aubergiste *f*, F patronne *f*; '**~-locked** entouré de terre; intérieur (*lac etc.*); '**~·lop·er** vagabond *m*; '**~·lord** propriétaire *m*; *pension etc.*: logeur *m*; aubergiste *m*, F patron *m*; '**~·lord·ism** landlordisme *m*; '**~·lub·ber** ⚓ *péj.* marin *m* d'eau douce; terrien *m*; '**~·mark** *surt.* ⚓ indice *m*; point *m* coté (*sur une carte*); borne *f* limite; *fig.* point *m* de repère; *fig.* événement *m* marquant; '**~·own·er** propriétaire *mf* foncier (-ère *f*); ~**scape** ['læn-skeip] paysage *m*; ~ *architecture ou design* architecture *f* de paysage; ~ *gardener* jardinier *m* paysagiste; ~ *gardening* jardinage *m* paysagiste; '**~-slide** éboulement *m* (de terrain); *fig.* catastrophe *f*; *pol.* débâcle *f*, *Am.* victoire *f* écrasante; '**~-slip** éboulement *m* (de terrain); ~**s·man** ⚓ ['~zmən] terrien *m*; '**~-sur·vey·or** arpenteur *m*; '**~-tax** impôt *m* foncier; ~**ward** ['~wəd] vers la terre; du côté de la terre.

lane [lein] chemin *m* (vicinal); *ville*: ruelle *f*, passage *m*; ⚓ route *f* de navigation; *mot.* voie *f*.

lang syne *écoss.* ['læŋ'sain] **1.** jadis; **2.** le temps *m* jadis; les jours *m/pl.* d'autrefois.

lan·guage ['læŋgwidʒ] langue *f*; langage *m*; ~ *laboratory* laboratoire *m* de langues; *bad* ~ langage *m* grossier; *strong* ~ langage *m* violent; injures *f/pl.*

lan·guid □ ['læŋgwid] languissant, langoureux (-euse *f*); mou (mol *devant une voyelle ou un h muet*; molle

f); faible; '**lan·guid·ness** langueur *f*, faiblesse *f*.

lan·guish ['læŋgwiʃ] languir (*après, pour for*); dépérir; ⚕ s'étioler; ✝ traîner (*affaires*); '**lan·guish·ing** □ languissant, langoureux (-euse *f*); ✝ faible.

lan·guor ['læŋgə] langueur *f*; '**lan·guor·ous** langoureux (-euse *f*).

lank □ [læŋk] maigre; sec (sèche *f*); efflanqué (*personne, a. bête*); plat (*cheveux*); '**lank·y** □ grand et maigre.

lans·que·net ✕ ['lænskinet] lansquenet *m* (*a. cartes*).

lan·tern ['læntən] lanterne *f*; ⚓ fanal *m*; ⚠ lanterne(au *m*) *f*; *dark* ~ lanterne *f* sourde; '**~-jawed** aux joues creuses; '**~-slide** (diapositive *f* de) projection *f*; ~ *lecture* conférence *f* avec projections.

lan·yard ⚓ ['lænjəd] aiguillette *f*.

lap[1] [læp] **1.** *su. cost.* pan *m*; genoux *m/pl.*; ⊕ recouvrement *m*; *corde etc.*: tour *m*; *sp.* tour *m*, circuit *m*; ⚡ guipage *m*; *sp.* ~ *of hono(u)r* tour *m* d'honneur; **2.** *v/t.* enrouler; entourer, envelopper (q. de qch. *s.o. about with s.th., s.th. round s.o.*); ⊕ enchevaucher (*des planches*); ⚡ guiper; *v/i.* (*usu.* ~ *over*) dépasser, chevaucher.

lap[2] [~] **1.** gorgée *f*; coup *m* de langue; *vagues*: clapotis *m*; **2.** laper; *fig.* avaler; clapoter (*vagues*).

lap-dog ['læpdɔg] chien *m* de manchon.

la·pel *cost.* [lə'pel] revers *m*.

lap·i·dar·y ['læpidəri] lapidaire (*a. su./m*).

lap·pet ['læpit] *cost.* pan *m*; revers *m*; *oreille*: lobe *m*.

lapse [læps] **1.** erreur *f*; faux pas *m*; laps *m* (de temps); délai *m* (de *temps*); défaillance *f* (*de la mémoire*); ⚖ déchéance *f*; *eccl.* apostasie *f*; chute *f*; **2.** déchoir; *au sens moral*: tomber (dans, *into*); manquer à ses devoirs; ✝ cesser d'être en vigueur; *fig.* rentrer (dans le silence, *into silence*); ⚖ tomber en désuétude; s'abroger (*loi*).

lap·wing *orn.* ['læpwiŋ] vanneau *m*.

lar·ce·ny ⚖ ['lɑːsni] larcin *m*, vol *m* insignifiant; *grand* ~ vol *m*; *petty* ~ vol *m* simple.

larch ♣ [lɑːtʃ] mélèze *m*.

lard [lɑːd] **1.** saindoux *m*, graisse *f* de porc; **2.** larder (de, *with*) (*a.*

fig.); '**lard·er** garde-manger *m*/*inv.*; '**lard·ing-nee·dle**, '**lard·ing-pin** lardoire *f*; '**lard·y** lardeux (-euse *f*).

large □ [lɑːdʒ] grand; gros(se *f*); fort; nombreux (-euse *f*); large; ~ *farmer* gros fermier *m*; *at* ~ en liberté, libre; en général; en détail; *talk at* ~ parler au hasard; parler longuement (sur qch.); *in* ~ en grand; '**large·ly** en grande partie; pour la plupart; pour une grande part; '**large·ness** grandeur *f*; grosseur *f*; *fig.* largeur *f*; '**large-'mind·ed** à l'esprit large; tolérant; '**large-'scale** de grande envergure; '**large-'sized** de grandes dimensions.

lar·gess(e) *poét.* ['lɑːdʒes] largesse *f*.

lark[1] *orn.* [lɑːk] alouette *f*.

lark[2] [~] **1.** farce *f*, blague *f*; **2.** rigoler, faire des farces; **lark·some** ['~səm] *see* larky.

lark·spur ♀ ['lɑːkspəː] pied *m* d'alouette.

lark·y F ['lɑːki] espiègle; folichon(ne *f*).

lar·va *zo.* ['lɑːvə], *pl.* -vae ['~viː] larve *f*; **lar·val** ['~vl] larvaire; ♂ latent.

lar·ynx ['læriŋks] larynx *m*.

las·civ·i·ous □ [lə'siviəs] lascif (-ive *f*).

la·ser ['leizə] laser *m*; ~ *beam* rayon *m* laser.

lash [læʃ] **1.** coup *m* de fouet; lanière *f*; *fig.* supplice *m* du fouet; œil: cil *m*; **2.** fouailler; cingler (*a. pluie*); fouetter; *fig.* flageller, cingler; attacher, lier (à, to); ⚓ amarrer; ~ *out* ruer (*cheval*); *fig.* se livrer (à, *into*); ~ *out at* lâcher un coup à.

lass [læs] jeune fille *f*; **las·sie** ['~i] fillette *f*.

las·si·tude ['læsitjuːd] lassitude *f*.

last[1] [lɑːst] **1.** *adj.* dernier (-ère *f*); ~ *but one* avant-dernier (-ère *f*); ~ *night* hier soir; la nuit dernière; *the* ~ *two* les deux derniers (-ères *f*); **2.** *su.* dernier (-ère *f*) *m*; bout *m*; fin *f* (= *mort*); *my* ~ ma dernière lettre; *mon dernier m*, ma dernière *f* (*enfant*); *at* ~ enfin; à la fin; *at long* ~ enfin; à la fin (des fins); *breathe one's* ~ rendre le dernier soupir; **3.** *adv.* la dernière fois; le (la) dernier (-ère *f*); ~, *but not least* et mieux encore ...; le dernier, mais non le moindre.

last[2] [~] durer, se maintenir; (*a.* ~ *out*) aller (*comestibles etc.*); faire (*robe etc.*); soutenir (*une allure*).

last[3] [~] forme *f* (*à chaussures*).

last[4] ⚓ [~] *mesure:* last(e) *m*.

last-ditch [lɑːst'ditʃ] ultime, désespéré (*efforts etc.*); **last-ditch·er** jusqu'auboutiste *mf*.

last·ing ['lɑːstiŋ] **1.** □ durable; résistant; **2.** *tex.* lasting *m*; '**last·ing·ness** durabilité *f*, permanence *f*.

last·ly ['lɑːstli] en dernier lieu; pour finir.

last-min·ute [lɑːst'minit] de dernière minute *ou* heure.

latch [lætʃ] **1.** loquet *m*; serrure *f* de sûreté; *on the* ~ au loquet; fermé à demi-tour; **2.** fermer au loquet *ou* à demi-tour; '**~-key** clef *f* de maison; passe-partout *m*/*inv.*

late [leit] en retard; retardé; tard; tardif (-ive *f*) (*fruit etc.*); ancien(ne *f*), ex-; feu (= *mort*); récent; *at (the)* ~*st* au plus tard; tout au plus; *as* ~ *as* pas plus tard que; *of* ~ récemment; *of* ~ *years* ces dernières années; depuis quelques années; ~*r on* plus tard; *be* ~ être en retard; ☂ avoir du retard *ou* un retard de ...; *keep* ~ *hours* se coucher tard; rentrer tard; '**~-com·er** retardataire *mf*; tard-venu(e *f*) *m*; '**late·ly** dernièrement, récemment; depuis peu.

la·ten·cy ['leitənsi] état *m* latent.

late·ness ['leitnis] arrivée *f* tardive; date *f* récente; heure *f* avancée; *fruit etc.:* tardiveté *f*.

la·tent □ ['leitənt] caché; latent.

lat·er·al □ ['lætərəl] latéral (-aux *m*/*pl.*).

lath [lɑːθ] **1.** latte *f*; *toit:* volige *f*; jalousie: lame *f*; **2.** latter; voliger (*un toit*).

lathe [leið] ⊕ tour *m*; *tex., métier:* battant *m*.

lath·er ['lɑːðə] **1.** *su.* mousse *f* de savon; écume *f*; **2.** *v/t.* savonner; F rosser (*q.*), fouailler (*un cheval*); *v/i.* mousser (*savon*); jeter de l'écume (*cheval*).

lath·y ['lɑːθi] latté; *fig.* long et mince.

Lat·in ['lætin] **1.** latin; **2.** Latin(e *f*) *m*; *ling.* latin *m*; ~ **A·mer·i·ca** Amérique *f* latine; '**Lat·in·ism** latinisme *m*, tournure *f* latine.

lat·i·tude ['lætitjuːd] latitude *f* (*a.*

latitudinal 914

fig., géog., astr.); *fig. a.* étendue *f;* liberté *f* d'action; *~s pl.* latitudes *f/pl.,* F parages *m;* **lat·i·tu·di·nal** [*~inl*] latitudinal (-aux *m/pl.);* **lat·i·tu·di·nar·i·an** [*'~'nεəriən*] **1.** latitudinaire (*a. su./mf*); **2.** partisan(e *f*) *m* du tolérantisme.

lat·ter ['lætə]: *the ~* le dernier *m,* la dernière *f;* celui-ci *m* (celle-ci *f,* ceux-ci *m/pl.,* celles-ci *f/pl.);~* end fin *f;* '*~-day* récent, moderne; '**lat·ter·ly** dans les derniers temps; dans la suite; récemment.

lat·tice ['lætis] **1.** (*a. ~-work*) treillage *m,* treillis *m;* **2.** treillager, treillisser.

Lat·vi·an ['lætviən] **1.** lettonien(ne *f*); **2.** Lettonien(ne *f*) *m.*

laud [lɔːd] louer, chanter les louanges de; **laud·a'bil·i·ty** caractère *m* louable; '**laud·a·ble** □ louable, digne d'éloges; **lau'da·tion** louange *f;* **laud·a·to·ry** □ ['~ətəri] élogieux (-euse *f*).

laugh [lɑːf] **1.** rire *m;* **2.** (*at*) rire (de); se moquer (de); *~ off* traiter (*qch.*) en plaisanterie; *~ out of* faire renoncer à force de plaisanteries; *see sleeve;* '**laugh·a·ble** □ risible, ridicule; '**laugh·er** rieur (-euse *f*) *m;* '**laugh·ing 1.** rires *m/pl.;* **2.** □ riant; rieur (-euse *f*); '**laugh·ing-stock** objet *m* de risée; '**laugh·ter** rire *m,* -s *m/pl.*

launch [lɔːntʃ] **1.** ⚓ lancement *m;* chaloupe *f;* motor *~* vedette *f;* **2.** *v/t.* lancer (*a. un navire, une fusée*); débarquer (*un canot*); ⚔ déclencher; *fig.* mettre en train; lancer; *v/i. ~ out* lancer un coup (à *at, against*); ⚓ mettre à la mer; *~ (out) into* se lancer dans; '**launch·ing 1.** lancement *m;* **2.** *~ pad* (site *etc.*) rampe *f* (aire *f etc.*) de lancement.

laun·dress ['lɔːndris] blanchisseuse *f;* '**laun·dry** blanchisserie *f;* lessive *f.*

lau·re·ate ['lɔːriit] **1.** lauréat; *poet ~* = **2.** poète *m* lauréat.

lau·rel ⚘ ['lɔrl] laurier *m; fig.* win *~s* cueillir des lauriers; '**lau·relled** couronné (de lauriers).

la·va ['lɑːvə] lave *f.*

lav·a·to·ry ['lævətəri] lavabo *m;* cabinet *m* de toilette; *public ~* cabinets *m/pl.*

lave [leiv] *usu. poét.* laver; ⚕ bassiner.

lav·en·der ⚘ ['lævində] lavande *f.*

lav·ish ['læviʃ] **1.** □ prodigue (de *in, of*); abondant; **2.** prodiguer; '**lav·ish·ness** prodigalité *f.*

law [lɔː] loi *f;* droit *m;* code *m;* législation *f;* justice *f;* règle *f; at ~* en justice, en procès; *go to ~* avoir recours à la justice; *have the ~ of s.o.* faire un procès à q., poursuivre q. en justice; *necessity knows no ~* nécessité n'a point de loi; *lay down the ~* expliquer la loi; F dogmatiser; *practise ~* exercer le droit; '**~-a·bid·ing** ⚖ ami de l'ordre; '**~-court** cour *f* de justice; tribunal *m;* '**law·ful** □ légal (-aux *m/pl.*); licite, permis; légitime; juste; valide (*contrat etc.*); '**law·giv·er** législateur *m;* '**law·less** □ sans loi; désordonné.

lawn[1] [lɔːn] *tex.* batiste *f;* linon *m.*

lawn[2] [~] pelouse *f;* gazon *m;* '**~-mow·er** tondeuse *f;* '**~-'sprin·kler** arrosoir *m* de pelouse; *~ ten·nis* (lawn-)tennis *m.*

law·suit ['lɔːsjuːt] procès *m;* **law·yer** ['~jə] homme *m* de loi; juriste *m;* jurisconsulte *m; see a. solicitor, barrister.*

lax [læks] mou (mol *devant une voyelle ou un h muet;* molle *f*); flasque; relâché; négligent; facile (*morale*); **lax·a·tive** ['~ətiv] **1.** laxatif (-ive *f*); **2.** laxatif *m;* '**lax·i·ty,** '**lax·ness** mollesse *f;* relâchement *m;* inexactitude *f.*

lay[1] [lei] *prét. de lie*[2] 2.

lay[2] [~] lai *m,* chanson *f; poét.* poème *m.*

lay[3] [~] laïque, lai.

lay[4] [lei] **1.** *su. cordage:* commettage *m; terrain:* configuration *f; sl.* spécialité *f;* **2.** [*irr.*] *v/t.* coucher; abattre (*q., la poussière*); exorciser (*un fantôme*); mettre (*couvert, qch. sur qch., enjeu, impôt, nappe*); parier (*une somme, fig. que, that*); faire (*un pari*); pondre (*un œuf*); porter (*une plainte*); poser (*des fondements, un tapis, qch. sur qch.*); *~ bare* mettre à nu; dévoiler; découvrir; *~ before* exposer, présenter à (*q.*); *~ by* mettre de côté; *~ down* déposer; rendre (*les armes*); résigner (*un office*); donner (*la vie*); étaler (*les cartes*); poser (*qch., voie, câble, principe*); imposer (*une condition*); formuler (*un principe*); *~ in* s'approvisionner de; ⚓ emmagasiner; *~*

in stock s'approvisionner; ~ *low* étendre, abattre; ~ *off* congédier; *peint.* lisser (avec la brisse; faire la contre-partie de (*un pari*); *Am. sl.* en finir avec (*q., qch.*), laisser (*tranquille*); ~ *on* imposer; étendre (*un enduit*); ne pas ménager (*des couleurs*); appliquer; porter (*des coups*); amener (*de l'eau*); installer (*le gaz etc.*); *fig.* ~ *it on* (*thick*) flatter (*grossièrement*); ~ *open* exposer; ~ (*o.s.*) *open to* (s')exposer à (*qch.*); ~ *out* arranger, étaler (*devant les yeux*); disposer (*le jardin*); dépenser (*l'argent*); F aplatir (*q.*); ~ *o.s. out* faire de son mieux (*pour fire, to*); ~ *up* accumuler, amasser (*de l'argent, des provisions*); amasser (*des connaissances*); mettre (*qch.*) en réserve; mettre (*la terre*) en jachère; ⚓ mettre en rade; ⚓ désarmer; ~ *with* coucher avec; **3.** [*irr.*] *v/i.* pondre (*des œufs*); ~ *a wager*) parier; ⚓ être (à l'ancre); mettre la table (*pour, for*); ~ *about one* frapper de tous côtés; *sl.* ~ *into* rosser (*q.*); F ~ (*it*) *on* porter des coups.

lay...: '~·**a·bout** *Brit.* F fainéant(e *f*) *m*, paresseux (-euse *f*) *m*; '~·**by** *Brit. mot.* petite aire *f* de stationnement.

lay·er 1. *su.* ['leiə] poseur *m*; parieur *m*; *poule:* pondeuse *f*; *peint.* etc. couche *f*; *géol.* assise *f*, strate *f*; **2.** *v/t.* ✍ ['lɛə] marcotter; *v/i.* se coucher (*blé*).

lay·ette [lei'et] layette *f*.

lay fig·ure mannequin *m*.

lay·ing ['leiiŋ] *câble, rail, tuyau, etc.*: pose *f*; *fondements:* assise *f*; *œufs:* ponte *f*.   [laïque *m*.]

lay·man ['leimən] profane *m*; *eccl.*]

lay...: '~·**off** *Am.* période *f* de chômage; vacances *f/pl.* (*d'un ouvrier*); '~·**out** disposition *f*; tracé *m*.

laz·a·ret, *usu.* **laz·a·ret·to** [læzə-'ret(ou)] léproserie *f*; ⚓ lazaret *m*.

laze F [leiz] fainéanter; baguenauder; '**la·zy 1.** paresseux (-euse *f*), fainéant; **2.** = '**la·zy-bones** fainéant(e *f*) *m*, F flémard(e *f*) *m*.

lea *poét.* [li:] prairie *f*.

leach [li:tʃ] *v/t/i.* filtrer.

lead[1] [led] **1.** plomb *m*; ⚓ (plomb *m* de) sonde *f*; *typ.* interligne *f*; *crayon:* mine *f*; ~*s pl.* plombs *m/pl.*; ~ *pencil* crayon *m* (à la mine de

plomb); **2.** plomber; garnir de plomb; *typ.* interligner.

lead[2] [li:d] **1.** *su.* conduite *f*, exemple *m*; tête *f*; *théâ.* premier rôle *m*, vedette *f*; *cartes:* main *f*, couleur *f*; ⚡ câble *m*, connexion *f*; *chien:* laisse *f*; *journ.* ~ *story* article *m* de tête; *cartes:* *it's my* ~ à moi de jouer; *take the* ~ prendre la tête; *fig.* gagner les devants (*sur of, over*); **2.** [*irr.*] *v/t.* mener, conduire (à, *to*); amener; induire (en, *into*); guider; entamer de (*cartes*); ~ *on* entraîner; *fig.* encourager (à parler); *v/i.* mener, conduire; ~ *to* produire; ~ *off* commencer (par, *with*); *sp.* jouer le premier; ~ *up to* donner accès à; *fig.* introduire, amener.

lead·en ['ledn] de plomb (*a. fig.*).

lead·er ['li:də] chef *m* (*a.* ✖); conducteur (-trice *f*) *m*; guide *m*; ♪ chef *m* d'attaque; *journ.* article *m* de fond; *cin.* bande *f* amorce; **lead·er·ette** [~'ret] article *m* de fond succinct; '**lead·er·ship** conduite *f*; ✖ commandement *m*; direction *f*.

lead·ing ['li:diŋ] **1.** premier (-ère *f*), principal (-aux *m/pl.*); de tête; ~ *article* article *f* de fond; ~ *spécialité *f* de réclame; ‡‡ ~ *case* cas *m* d'espèce qui fait autorité; *théâ.* ~ *man* (*lady*) vedette *f*, premier rôle *m*; ‡‡ ~ *question* question *f* tendancieuse; **2.** conduite *f*, direction *f*; ✖ commandement *m*; '~-**strings** *pl.* lisière *f*.

leaf [li:f] (*pl. leaves*) ♀ feuille *f* (*a. or etc., papier*); *fleur:* F pétale *m*; *livre:* feuillet *m*; *porte, table:* battant *m*; *table:* rallonge *f*; '**leaf·age** feuillage *m*; '**leaf·less** sans *ou* dépourvu de feuilles; **leaf·let** [~'lit] feuillet *m*; feuille *f* volante; papillon *m* (*de publicité*); ♀ foliole *f*; '**leaf·y** feuillu; couvert de feuilles; de feuillage.

league[1] [li:g] lieue *f* (marine) (= 4,8 km.).

league[2] [~] **1.** ligue *f*; *sp.* ♀ *match* match *m* de championnat; ♀ *of Nations* Société *f* des Nations; **2.** se liguer; '**lea·guer** ligueur (-euse *f*) *m*.

leak [li:k] **1.** écoulement *m*; ⚓ voie *f* d'eau; **2.** couler, fuir; se perdre; ⚓ faire eau; ~ *out* couler; *fig.* s'ébruiter; transpirer; '**leak·age** fuite *f*, perte *f*; ✝ coulage *m*; *fig.* secrets:

fuite *f*; 'leak·y qui coule; qui prend l'eau; *fig.* peu fidèle, peu discret (-ète *f*).

lean¹ [li:n] maigre (*a. su./m*).

lean² [~] 1. [*irr.*] *v/t.* appuyer (contre, *against*); *v/i.* s'appuyer (sur, *on*; contre, *against*); s'adosser (à, contre *against*); s'accouder (à, contre *against*); se pencher (sur, *over*; vers, *towards*); pencher (*mur etc.*), incliner (*a. fig.*); 2. inclinaison *f*; *fig.* (*a.* 'lean·ing) penchant *m* (pour, *to* [*wards*]); tendance *f* (à, *to*[*wards*]).

lean·ness ['li:nnis] maigreur *f*.

leant [lent] *prét. et p.p. de* lean² 1.

lean-to ['li:n'tu:] appentis *m*.

leap [li:p] 1. *su.* saut *m*, bond *m*; by ~s and bounds par bonds et par sauts; 2. [*irr.*] *v/i.* sauter (*a. fig.*); jaillir (*flamme etc.*); *v/t.* franchir d'un saut; sauter; '~-frog 1. saute-mouton *m*; 2. sauter comme à saute-mouton; leapt [lept] *prét. et p.p. de* leap 2; 'leap-year année *f* bissextile.

learn [lə:n] [*irr.*] apprendre; ~ from mettre (*qch.*) à profit; learn·ed □ ['~id] instruit, savant; 'learn·er-driv·er conducteur *m* novice; 'learn·ing étude *f*; action *f* d'apprendre; érudition *f*; learnt [lə:nt] *prét. et p.p. de* learn.

lease [li:s] 1. bail (*pl.* baux) *m*; terre: bail *m* à ferme; *fig.* concession *f*; let (out) on ~ louer à bail; a new ~ of life un renouveau *m* de vie; 2. donner *ou* prendre à bail; louer; affermer (*une terre*); '~hold tenure *f ou* propriété *f* à bail; *attr.* tenu à bail; '~hold·er bailleur *m*.

leash [li:ʃ] 1. laisse *f*, attache *f*; *chasse:* harde *f* (= 3 *chiens*); 2. mettre à l'attache.

least [li:st] 1. *adj.* le (*la*) moindre; le (*la*) plus petit(e); 2. *adv.* (le) moins; not ~ pas le moindre; 3. *su.:* at (the) ~ au moins; du moins; at the very ~ tout au moins; not in the ~ pas du tout; to say the ~ pour ne pas dire plus.

leath·er ['leðə] 1. cuir *m*; F foot. ballon *m*; ~s *pl.* culotte *f ou* guêtres *f/pl.* de cuir; 2. de *ou* en cuir; 3. garnir de cuir; F tanner le cuir à, rosser; leath·er·ette [~'ret] simili-cuir *m*; leath·ern ['leðən] de cuir, en cuir; 'leath·er·y qui ressemble au cuir; coriace (*viande*).

leave [li:v] 1. permission *f*, autorisation *f*; (*a.* ~ of absence) mois: congé *m*, jours: permission *f*; by your ~ si vous le voulez bien; 2. [*irr.*] *v/t.* laisser; abandonner; déposer (à la consigne); léguer (*une fortune etc.*); quitter (*un endroit*); sortir de; F ~ it at that en demeurer là; *see* call; ~ behind laisser (*a. des traces*), oublier; devancer, distancer; ~ off cesser; renoncer à (*une habitude*); cesser de porter (*un vêtement*); *v/i.* partir (pour, *for*).

leaved [li:vd] aux feuilles...; feuillu; à ... battants (*porte*); à ... rallonges (*table*).

leav·en ['levn] 1. levain *m*; 2. faire lever; *fig.* modifier (par, *with*); 'leav·en·ing ferment *m*; *fig.* addition *f*, nombre *m*.

leaves [li:vz] *pl. de* leaf.

leav·ings ['li:viŋz] *pl.* restes *m/pl.*

lec·tern *eccl.* [lektən] lutrin *m*.

lec·ture ['lektʃə] 1. conférence *f* (sur, *on*); leçon *f* (de, *on*); give a ~ faire une conférence; attend ~s suivre un cours; *see* curtain ~; read *s.o.* a ~ faire une semonce à q.; 2. *v/i.* faire une conférence (sur, *on*); faire un cours (de, *on*); *v/t.* F semoncer, sermonner; 'lec·tur·er conférencier (-ère *f*) *m*; *univ.* maître *m* de conférences; chargé *m* de cours; professeur *m*; 'lec·ture·ship poste *m* de conférencier (-ère *f*); *univ.* maîtrise *f* de conférences.

led [led] *prét. et p.p. de* lead² 2.

ledge [ledʒ] rebord *m*; saillie *f*; corniche *f*; banc *m* de récifs.

ledg·er ['ledʒə] ✝ grand livre *m*; *Am.* registre *m*; ⊕ échafaudage: filière *f*.

lee ⚓ [li:] côté *m* sous le vent.

leech [li:tʃ] *zo.* sangsue *f* (*a. fig.*); *fig.* crampon *m*.

leek ♣ [li:k] poireau *m*.

leer [liə] 1. œillade *f* en dessous; regard *m* paillard; 2. ~ at lorgner d'un air méchant; lancer des œillades à; 'leer·y □ *sl.* malin(-igne *f*), rusé; soupçonneux (-euse *f*).

lees [li:z] *pl.* lie *f* (*a. fig.*). [vent.\]

lee·ward ⚓ ['li:wəd] sous le

lee·way ⚓ ['li:wei] dérive *f*; make ~ dériver; *fig.* traîner; *fig.* make up ~ rattraper le temps perdu.

left¹ [left] *prét. et p.p. de* leave 2; be ~ rester.

lens

left² [~] adj. gauche; 2. adv. à gauche; 3. su. gauche f; '~-'**hand** de ou à gauche; mot. ~ drive conduite f à gauche; '~-'**hand·ed** □ gaucher (-ère f) (personne); fig. gauche; douteux (-euse f) (compliment); ⊕ à gauche. [mf].)
left·ist pol. ['leftist] gauchiste (adj.,)
left...: '~-'**lug·gage lock·er** casier m à consigne automatique; '~-'**luggage of·fice** consigne f; '~-o'**vers** pl. restes m/pl.
Left-Wing pol. ['left'wiŋ] de gauche.
leg [leg] jambe f; chien, oiseau, etc.: patte f; table: pied m; ⅄ branche f; course: étape f; ~ of mutton gigot m; give s.o. a ~ up faire la courte échelle à q.; F donner un coup d'épaule à q.; F be on one's last ~s être à bout de ses ressources; pull s.o.'s ~ se payer la tête de q., faire marcher q.
leg·a·cy ['legəsi] legs m; '~-'**hunt·er** coureur (-euse f) m d'héritages.
le·gal □ ['li:gəl] légal (-aux m/pl.); juridique; judiciaire; de droit; de loi;~ adviser conseiller m juridique;~ aid assistance f judiciaire; ~ capacity capacité f de contracter; ~ costs pl. dépens m/pl., frais m/pl. de justice; ✝ ~ department service m du contentieux; ~ dispute litige m, procès m; ~ entity personne f morale; ~ remedy voie f de recours; ~ status capacité f juridique; see tender² 1; **le·gal·i·ty** [li'gæliti] légalité f; **le·gal·i·za·tion** [li:gəlai'zeiʃn] légalisation f; '**le·gal·ize** rendre légal; autoriser; authentiquer (un document).
leg·ate ['legit] légat m (du pape).
leg·a·tee ⚏ [legə'ti:] légataire mf.
le·ga·tion [li'geiʃn] légation f.
leg-bail ['leg'beil]: give ~ F s'évader; filer à l'anglaise.
leg·end ['ledʒənd] légende f (a. = inscription); explication f; '**leg·end·ar·y** légendaire.
leg·er·de·main ['ledʒədə'mein] passe-passe m/inv.; prestidigitation f.
legged [legd] à ou aux jambes; short-~ aux jambes courtes; **leggings** ['~z] pl. guêtres f/pl.; '**leg·gy** aux longues jambes.
leg·horn [le'gɔ:n] chapeau m de paille d'Italie; poule: leghorn f.
leg·i·bil·i·ty [ledʒi'biliti] lisibilité f; **leg·i·ble** ['ledʒəbl] □ lisible.

le·gion ['li:dʒən] légion f (a. fig.); '**le·gion·ar·y** légionnaire (a. su./m).
leg·is·late ['ledʒisleit] faire des lois; **leg·is·la·tion** législation f; '**leg·is·la·tive** □ législatif (-ive f); '**leg·is·la·tor** législateur m; **leg·is·la·ture** ['~tʃə] législature f; corps m législatif.
le·git·i·ma·cy [li'dʒitiməsi] enfant, opinion, etc.: légitimité f; **le·git·i·mate 1.** [~mit] □ légitime; F vrai; **2.** [~meit] (a. **le·git·i·mize**) légitimer; **le·git·i·ma·tion** légitimation f; légalisation f.
leg·room ['legrum] place f pour les jambes.
leg·ume ['legju:m] fruit m d'une légumineuse; **le·gu·mi·nous** légumineux (-euse f).
lei·sure ['leʒə] loisir m, -s m/pl.; ~ activities pl. loisirs m/pl.; ~ time temps m libre, loisir m;~ wear tenue f de détente; be at ~ être de loisir; at your ~ à (votre) loisir; '**lei·sured** de loisir; désœuvré; '**lei·sure·ly 1.** adj. posé, tranquille; qui n'est pas pressé; **2.** adv. posément; à loisir.
lem·on ['lemən] **1.** citron m; sl. saloperie f; **2.** jaune citron adj./inv.; **lem·on·ade** [~'neid] limonade f; **lem·on squash** citron m pressé; citronnade f; '**lem·on-squeez·er** presse-citron m/inv.
lend [lend] [irr.] prêter (a. secours); ~ out louer; ~ o.s. to se prêter à; ~ing library bibliothèque f de prêt; '~-'Lease Act loi f prêt-bail (américaine); '**lend·er** prêteur (-euse f) m.
length [leŋθ] longueur f; morceau m; pièce f; temps: durée f; at ~ enfin, à la fin; at (great) ~ d'un bout à l'autre; go all ~s aller jusqu'au bout; go (to) great ~s se donner bien de la peine (pour, to); he goes the ~ of saying it va jusqu'à dire; '**length·en** (s')allonger; (se) prolonger; v/i. augmenter; '**length·ways**, '**length·wise** □ en longueur, en long; '**length·y** assez long; plein de longueurs (discours etc.).
le·ni·ence, le·ni·en·cy ['li:njəns(i)], **len·i·ty** ['leniti] clémence f; douceur f; **le·ni·ent** □ ['li:njənt] clément, indulgent (pour, envers to [-wards]); '**len·i·tive** ✚ **1.** lénitif (-ive f); **2.** lénitif m.
lens [lenz] loupe f; opt. lentille f,

verre *m*; *phot.* objectif *m*; *phot.* ~ *system* objectif *m*.

lent¹ [lent] *prét. et p.p. de* lend.

Lent² [~] carême *m*.

Lent·en ['lentən] de carême (*a. fig.*).

len·tic·u·lar □ [len'tikjulə] lentiforme, lenticulaire.

len·til ♀ ['lentil] lentille *f*.

Leo *astr.* ['li:ou] le Lion.

leop·ard ['lepəd] léopard *m*.

le·o·tard ['li:əta:d] collant *m*, maillot *m*.

lep·er ['lepə] lépreux (-euse *f*) *m*.

lep·ro·sy ✻ ['leprəsi] lèpre *f*; **'lep·rous** lépreux (-euse *f*).

les·bi·an ['lezbiən] 1. lesbien; 2. lesbienne *f*; **'les·bi·an·ism** lesbianisme *m*.

lese-maj·es·ty ⚖ ['li:z'mædʒisti] lèse-majesté *f*.

le·sion ⚖, ✻ ['li:ʒən] lésion *f*.

less [les] 1. *adj.* moindre; plus petit; moins de; inférieur; † moins important, mineur; *no* ~ *a person than* ne … rien moins que; 2. *adv.* moins; 3. *prp.* ⅍ moins; † sans; 4. *su.* moins *m*; *no* ~ *than* ne … rien moins que; autant que.

les·see [le'si:] locataire *mf*; concessionnaire *mf*.

less·en ['lesn] *v/t.* amoindrir, diminuer; ralentir; raccourcir; *fig.* atténuer; *v/i.* diminuer, s'amoindrir; *fig.* s'atténuer.

less·er ['lesə] petit; moindre.

les·son ['lesn] 1. leçon *f* (*a. eccl., a. fig.*); exemple *m*; ~*s pl.* leçons *f/pl.*; cours *m*; 2. faire la leçon à, enseigner.

les·sor ⚖ [le'sɔ:] bailleur (-eresse *f*) *m*.

lest [lest] de peur *ou* de crainte que … ne (*sbj.*) *ou* de (*inf.*).

let¹ [let] [*irr.*] *v/t.* permettre, laisser; faire (*inf.*); louer (*une maison etc.*); ~ *alone* laisser tranquille *ou* en paix; laisser (*q.*) faire; ne pas se mêler de (*qch.*); *adv.* sans parler de …; ~ *down* baisser; F laisser (*q.*) en panne; ~ *s.o. down gently* refuser qch. à q. *ou* corriger q. avec tact; ~ *fly* lancer; décocher; ~ *go* lâcher; ⚓ mouiller (*l'ancre*); ~ *into* laisser entrer; *cost.* incruster; mettre (dans un secret, *into a secret*); ~ *loose* lâcher; ~ *off* tirer; décocher (*a. fig. une épigramme*); *fig.* dispenser (de *inf., from gér.*); *see* steam; ~ *out*

laisser sortir; laisser échapper; *cost.* rélargir; (*a.* ~ *on hire*) louer; *v/i.* se louer (à *at, for*); ~ *on* rapporter, trahir; ~ *up* diminuer; cesser.

let² [~] *tennis:* (*a.* ~ *ball*) balle *f* de filet; *without* ~ *or hindrance* sans entrave, en toute liberté.

let·down F ['letdaun] déception *f*.

le·thal □ ['li:θl] mortel(le *f*).

le·thar·gic, le·thar·gi·cal □ [le-'θɑ:dʒik(l)] léthargique (*a. fig.*); **leth·ar·gy** ['leθədʒi] léthargie *f*; *fig.* inaction *f*, inertie *f*.

let·ter ['letə] 1. lettre *f*; caractère *m*; missive *f*; ~*s pl.* (belles-)lettres *f/pl.*; littérature *f*; *by* ~ par lettre, par correspondance; *man of* ~*s* homme *m* de lettres, littérateur *m*; *to the* ~ au pied de la lettre; 2. marquer avec des lettres; ⚖ coter; mettre le titre à (*un livre*); **'~-bal·ance** pèse-lettre *m*; **'~-box** boîte *f* aux lettres; **'~-car·ri·er** *Am.* facteur *m*; **'~-case** portefeuille *m*; **'~-cov·er** enveloppe *f*; **'let·tered** marqué avec des lettres; *fig.* lettré; **'let·ter-file** classeur *m* de lettres; relieur *m*; **'let·ter-found·er** fondeur *m* *typographie*; **let·ter-gram** *Am.* ['~græm] télégramme *m* à tarif réduit; **'let·ter-head** en-tête *m* (*pl.* en-têtes); **'let·ter-ing** lettrage *m*; inscription *f*.

let·ter…: '~-o·pen·er ouvre-lettres *m/inv.*; **'~-pa·per** papier *m* à lettres; **'~'per·fect** *théâ.:* *be* ~ savoir son rôle par cœur; **'~-press** *typ.* impression *f* typographique; texte *m*; ~ *printing* typographie *f*; **'~-press** presse *f* à copier; **'~-weight** presse-papiers *m/inv.*

let·tuce ♀ ['letis] laitue *f*.

let·up F ['letʌp] relâchement *m*, diminution *f*; arrêt *m*; *without* (*a*) ~ *a.* sans s'arrêter, d'affilé.

leuco… [lju:ko] leuco-; **leu·co·cyte** ['~sait] leucocyte *m*.

le·vant [li'vænt] F décamper sans payer.

lev·ee¹ ['levi] réception *f* royale; *hist.* lever *m*.

lev·ee² *Am.* [~] digue *f*, endiguement *m*, levée *f* (*d'une rivière*).

lev·el ['levl] 1. *adj.* égal (-aux *m/pl.*); à *ou* de niveau; *fig.* équilibré; ~ *with* à fleur de; *my* ~ *best* tout mon possible; 🚈 ~ *crossing* passage *m* à niveau; *cuis. a* ~ *spoonful* une cuille-

licence

rée rase; **2.** *su.* niveau *m* (*a.* ⊕, *a. fig.*); terrain *m ou* surface *f* de niveau; hauteur *f*; 🚂, *mot.* palier *m*; ⚔ galerie *f* (de niveau); ~ *of the sea* niveau *m* de la mer; *on a* ~ *with de* niveau avec, à la hauteur de; *fig.* au niveau de (*q.*); *dead* ~ franc niveau *m*, 🚂 palier *m* absolu; *fig.* uniformité *f*; *on the* ~ loyal (-aux *m/pl.*); tout à fait sincère; **3.** *v/t.* niveler, aplatir, égaliser; *surv.* déniveler; pointer (*un fusil*); braquer (*un canon*); *fig.* raser (*une ville*); *fig.* lancer (contre, *at*); ~ *with* (*ou to*) *the ground* raser (*qch.*); ~ *down* araser; *fig.* abaisser à son niveau; ~ *up* élever (*qch.*) au niveau (de *qch.*, *to s.th.*); *v/i.* ~ *at* (*ou against*) viser; ~ *off* cesser de monter, se raffermir (*prix*); '~-'**head·ed** à la tête bien équilibrée; (à l'esprit) rassis; '**lev·el·(l)er** *surv.* niveleuse *f* de route; *personne:* niveleur (-euse *f*) *m*; *pol.* égalitaire *mf*; '**lev·el·(l)ing** de nivellement.

le·ver ['liːvə] **1.** *su.* levier *m*; **2.** *v/t.* soulever au moyen d'un levier; *v/i.* manœuvrer un levier; '**le·ver·age** force *f* de levier; *fig.* prise *f*.

lev·er·et ['levərit] levraut *m*.

le·vi·a·than [li'vaiəθən] *bibl.* Léviathan *m*; *fig.* navire *m* monstre.

lev·i·gate *pharm.* ['levigeit] réduire en poudre; délayer (avec, *with*).

lev·i·tate ['leviteit] *spiritisme:* (se) soulever (par lévitation).

lev·i·ty ['leviti] légèreté *f*, manque *m* de sérieux.

lev·y ['levi] **1.** *impôt, a.* ⚔ *troupes:* levée *f*; ⚔ *chevaux:* réquisition *f*; impôt *m*, contribution *f*; *capital* ~ prélèvement *m* sur le capital; **2.** lever, percevoir (*un impôt*); imposer (*une amende*); ⚔ lever (*des troupes*); réquisitionner; faire (*la guerre, du chantage*).

lewd □ [luːd] lascif (-ive *f*); impudique; '**lewd·ness** impudicité *f*; débauche *f*.

lex·i·cal □ ['leksikl] lexicologique.

lex·i·cog·ra·pher [leksi'kɔgrəfə] lexicographe *mf*; **lex·i·co·graph·i·cal** □ [ˌleksikoˈgræfikl] lexicographique; **lex·i·cog·ra·phy** [ˌ~'kɔgrəfi] lexicographie *f*.

li·a·bil·i·ty [laiə'biliti] responsabilité *f* (*a.* ⚖); risque *m* (de, *to*); *fig.* disposition *f*, tendance *f* (à, *to*);

liabilities pl. engagements *m/pl.*; ✝ ensemble *m* des dettes; passif *m*.

li·a·ble □ ['laiəbl] ⚖ responsable (de, *for*); passible (de, *for*) (*une amende, un impôt*); sujet(te *f*), apte (à, *to*); susceptible (de *inf.*, *to inf.*); *Am.* probable; *be* ~ *to* avoir une disposition à; être sujet(te *f*) à; ~ *to duty* assujetti à un impôt; ~ *to punishment* punissable.

li·aise F [li'eiz] entrer *ou* rester en liaison; **li·ai·son** [li'eizɔ̃ːŋ] liaison *f* (*a.* ⚔); *attr.* de liaison.

li·ar ['laiə] menteur (-euse *f*) *m*.

li·bel ['laibl] **1.** diffamation *f*, calomnie *f* (contre, on); ⚖ écrit *m* diffamatoire; **2.** calomnier; ⚖ diffamer (par écrit); '**li·bel·(l)ous** □ diffamatoire; *fig.* peu flatteur (-euse *f*).

lib·er·al ['libərəl] **1.** □ libéral (-aux *m/pl.*) (*a. pol.*); généreux (-euse *f*); prodigue (de, *of*); abondant; **2.** *pol.* libéral (-aux *pl.*) *m*; '**lib·er·al·ism** libéralisme *m*; **lib·er·al·i·ty** [~ˈræliti] libéralité *f*; générosité *f*.

lib·er·ate ['libəreit] libérer (*a.* 🜛); mettre en liberté; délivrer (de, *from*); affranchir (*un esclave*); '**lib·er·a·tor** libérateur (-trice *f*) *m*; '**lib·er·a·to·ry** libératoire.

lib·er·tar·i·an [libə'tɛəriən] libertaire *mf*.

lib·er·tine ['libətain] **1.** libertin, débauché (*a. su./m*); **2.** libre penseur *m*; **lib·er·tin·ism** ['ˌtinizm] libertinage *m*, débauche *f*.

lib·er·ty ['libəti] liberté *f*; permission *f*; *take liberties* prendre des libertés (avec, *with*); *be at* ~ être libre (de, *to*).

li·bid·i·nous □ [li'bidinəs] libidineux (-euse *f*), lascif (-ive *f*); **li·bi·do** [li'biːdou] libido *f*.

li·brar·i·an [lai'brɛəriən] bibliothécaire *m*; **li·brar·y** ['laibrəri] bibliothèque *f*; ~ *science* bibliothéconomie *f*.

lice [lais] *pl. de louse* 1.

li·cence ['laisəns] *admin.* permis *m*, autorisation *f*, patente *f*; permission *f*; *fig.* licence *f* (*a. morale, a. univ.*); *driving* ~ permis *m* de conduire; *mot.* ~ *number* numéro *m* d'immatriculation; *mot.* ~ *plate* plaque *f* d'immatriculation *ou* minéralogique.

li·cense [~] 1. see licence; 2. accorder un permis à; † patenter (q.); autoriser la parution de (un livre, une pièce de théâtre, etc.); Brit. (fully) ~d autorisé à vendre des boissons alcooliques; **li·cen·see** [~'si:] patenté(e f) m; concessionnaire mf; **'li·cens·er** concesseur m; théâ. etc.: censeur m.

li·cen·ti·ate univ. [lai'senʃiit] licence f; personne: licencié(e f) m.

li·cen·tious □ [lai'senʃəs] licencieux (-euse f); dévergondé.

li·chen ♥, a. ✿ ['laikən] lichen m.

lich-gate ['litʃgeit] porche m (couvert) de cimetière.

lick [lik] 1. coup m de langue; Am. terrain m salifère; sl. † coup m; F vitesse f; 2. lécher; F battre, rosser; ~ the dust mordre la poussière; ~ into shape façonner; mettre au point; **'lick·er** celui m (celle f) qui lèche; ⊕ lécheur m; **'lick·er·ish** friand; gourmand, avide (de, after); **'lick·ing** lèchement m; F raclée f; F défaite f; **'lick·spit·tle** flagorneur m.

lic·o·rice ♥ Am. ['likəris] réglisse f.

lid [lid] couvercle m; sl. chapeau m; paupière f.

lie[1] [lai] 1. mensonge m; give s.o. the ~ donner un démenti à q.; tell a ~ mentir; white ~ mensonge m innocent; 2. mentir.

lie[2] [~] 1. (dis)position f; ⚓, géol. gisement m; 2. [irr.] être couché; se tenir, rester; se trouver; ⚓ être recevable; ~ by rester inactif (-ive f); être en réserve; se tenir à l'écart; ~ down se coucher; take it lying down se laisser faire, ne pas dire mot; ~ in (adv.) être en couches; (prp.) être situé dans; ~ in wait for se tenir à l'affût de (q.); † ~ over différer l'échéance de; ⚓ ~ to être à la cape; ~ under être dominé par; encourir (un déplaisir); être sous le coup de (une accusation); ~ up rentrer dans l'inactivité; garder le lit; it ~s with you il vous incombe (de inf., to inf.).

lie-a-bed ['laiəbed] grand(e f) dormeur (-euse f) m; paresseux (-euse f) m.

liege [li:dʒ] hist. 1. lige; 2. (a. ~lord) suzerain m; (a. ~man) vassal m.

li·en ⚖ ['li:ən] privilège m.

lieu [lju:]: in ~ of au lieu de.

lieu·ten·an·cy [lef'tenənsi; ⚓ le't-; Am. lu:'tenənsi] grade m de lieutenant (⚓ de vaisseau); hist. lieutenance f.

lieu·ten·ant [lef'tenənt; ⚓ le't-; Am. lu:'tenənt] lieutenant m (⚓ de vaisseau); fig. délégué m, premier adjoint m; **'~-'colo·nel** lieutenant-colonel (pl. lieutenants-colonels) m; **'~-com'mand·er** capitaine m de corvette; lieutenant m de vaisseau; **'~-'gen·er·al** général m de division; Am. † commandant m en chef; **'~-'gov·er·nor** sous-gouverneur m; vice-gouverneur m (d'un État des É.-U.).

life [laif] (pl. lives) vie f; vivant m; biographie f; ~ and limb corps et âme; for ~ à vie, à perpétuité; for one's (ou for dear) ~ de toutes ses (etc.) forces; to the ~ naturel(le f); **'~ an·nu·i·ty** rente f viagère; **'~-as·sur·ance** assurance f sur la vie, assurance-vie (pl. assurances-vie) f; **'~-belt** ceinture f de sauvetage; **'~-blood** sang m; fig. âme f; **'~-boat** canot m de sauvetage; **'~-buoy** bouée f de sauvetage; ~ ex·pect·an·cy espérance f de vie; **'~-guard** garde f du corps; **'~-guard** Am. sauveteur m (à la plage); ~ in·sur·ance see life assurance; ~ in·ter·est usufruit m (de, in); **'~-'jack·et** ⚓ brassière f de sauvetage; **'~·less** □ sans vie; mort; fig. sans vigueur, inanimé; **'~·less·ness** absence f de vie; manque m d'animation; **'~-like** vivant; **'~-line** ligne f de sauvetage; à bord: sauvegarde f; **'~-long** de toute la vie; **'~-pre·serv·er** ⚓ appareil m de sauvetage; canne f plombée; casse-tête m/inv.; **'~-raft** radeau m de sauvetage; ~ sen·tence † condamnation f à vie; **'~-'size** de grandeur naturelle; **'~-'span** (durée f de) vie f; **'~-strings** pl. ce qui est nécessaire à l'existence; **'~-time** vie f, vivant m.

lift [lift] 1. su. haussement m; levée f (a. ⊕); ⊕ hauteur f de levage; ✿ poussée f; fig. élévation f; ascenseur m; give s.o. a ~ donner un coup de main à q.; mot. conduire q. un bout; 2. v/t. (souv. ~ up) usu. lever; soulever; redresser; relever; élever (la voix); sl. plagier; sl. voler; v/i. s'élever; ✿ décoller; **'~-at·tend·ant** liftier (-ère f) m; **'lift·er**

921   lilt

souleveur *m*; ⊕ came *f*; **'lift·ing** ⊕ de levée; de levage; de suspension; **'lift-off** décollage *m*.

lig·a·ment *anat.* ['ligəmənt] ligament *m*.

lig·a·ture ['ligətʃuə] **1.** ✍, *typ.* ligature *f*; ♩ liaison *f*; **2.** ✍ ligaturer; lier.

light[1] [lait] **1.** *su.* lumière *f*; jour *m* (*a. fig.*); lampe *f*; feu *m*, phare *m*; fenêtre *f*; éclairage *m*; *fig.* ~s *pl.* lumières *f/pl.*; *phot.* ~ meter photomètre *m*; ~ wave onde *f* lumineuse; ~ year année-lumière *f* (*pl.* années-lumière); *in the* ~ *of* à la lumière de (*a. fig.*); *bring to* ~ mettre à jour; *come to* ~ se révéler; *will you give me a* ~ voudriez-vous bien me donner du feu?; *put a* ~ *to* allumer; *see the* ~ voir le jour (= *naître*); *fig.* comprendre, *Am.* être convaincu; **2.** *adj.* clair; éclairé; blond; ~ *blue* bleu clair *inv.*; **3.** [*irr.*] *v/t.* (*souv.* ~ *up*) allumer; éclairer; illuminer (*la rue, un visage, etc.*); ~ *up to* éclairer (*q.*) jusqu'à (*en*); *v/i.* (*usu.* ~ *up*) s'allumer; s'éclairer; *Am. sl.* ~ *out* détaler, ficher le camp.

light[2] [~] **1.** □ *usu.* léger (-ère *f*); frivole; amusant; facile; ~ *car* voiturette *f*; ~ *reading* lecture *f* distrayante; *make* ~ *of* faire peu de cas de; prendre à la légère; **2.** *see* lights; **3.** ~ *on* s'abattre sur (*a. oiseau*); tomber sur (*a. fig.*); rencontrer; trouver par hasard.   [faire des éclairs.]

light·en[1] ['laitn] (s')éclairer; *v/i.*⌐

light·en[2] [~] *v/t.* alléger (*a. fig.*); réduire le poids de; *v/i.* être soulagé.

light·er[1] ['laitə] *personne:* allumeur (-euse *f*) *m*; (*a. petrol-*~) briquet *m*.

light·er[2] ⚓ [~] péniche *f*, chaland *m*.

light...: '~-'fin·gered aux doigts agiles; '~-'fit·ting plafonnier *m*; *mur:* applique *f*; '~-'foot·ed au pied léger, leste; '~-'head·ed étourdi; *feel* ~ avoir le cerveau vide; '~-'heart·ed □ allègre; au cœur léger; ~-'heav·y·weight *sp.* (poids *m*) mi-lourd *m*; '~-'house phare *m*.

light·ing ['laitiŋ] *mot.* (*a.* ~-*up*), *a. bâtiment:* éclairage *m*; ⚡ ~ *point* prise *f* de courant (d'éclairage).

light·less ['laitlis] sans lumière.

light·ly ['laitli] *adv.* légèrement; à la légère; à bon marché; '**light-'mind·ed** frivole, étourdi; '**light-ness** légèreté *f*.

light·ning ['laitniŋ] **1.** éclairs *m/pl.*, foudre *f*; **2.** de paratonnerre; *fig.* foudroyant, rapide; '~-ar'rest·er parafoudre *m*; '~-con·duc·tor, '~-rod (tige *f* de) paratonnerre *m*; '~-strike grève *f* surprise.

lights [laits] *pl.* mou *m* (*de veau etc.*).

light·ship ['laitʃip] bateau-feu (*pl.* bateaux-feux) *m*; '**light-treat-ment** ✍ photothérapie *f*.

light weight *sp.* ['lait'weit] poids *m* léger; '**light-weight** *sp.* léger (-ère *f*).

lig·ne·ous ['ligniəs] ligneux (-euse *f*); **lig·nite** ['lignait] lignite *m*.

like [laik] **1.** *adj.*, *adv.* pareil(le *f*), semblable, tel(le *f*); ~ *a man* digne de l'homme; qui ressemble à un homme; F *he is* ~ *to die* il est en cas de mourir; *such* ~ similaire, de la sorte; F *feel* ~ (*gér.*) se sentir d'humeur à (*inf.*); avoir envie de (*inf.*); *s.th.* ~ qch. d'approchant à; environ (*2 mois, 100 francs*); ~ *that* de la sorte; *what is he* ~? comment est-il?; *that's more* ~ *it* à la bonne heure!; *cela en approche plus*; cela laisse moins à désirer; **2.** *su.* semblable *mf*, pareil(le *f*) *m*; ~*s pl.*; sympathies *f/pl.*; *his* ~ ses congénères; *the* ~ chose *f* pareille; F *the* ~(*s*) *of* des personnes *ou* choses comme; **3.** *v/t.* aimer; avoir de la sympathie pour; souhaiter, vouloir; *how do you* ~ *London?* comment trouvez-vous Londres?, vous vous plaisez à Londres?; *I should* ~ *time* il me faut du temps; *I should* ~ *to know* je voudrais bien savoir.

lik(e)·a·ble ['laikəbl] sympathique, agréable.

like·li·hood ['laiklihud] probabilité *f*; '**like·ly** probable; susceptible (de, to); *be* ~ *to* (*inf.*) être en cas de (*inf.*).

like...: '~-'mind·ed du même avis; '**lik·en** comparer (à, avec to); '**like-ness** ressemblance *f*; apparence *f*; image *f*, portrait *m*; *have one's* ~ *taken* se faire peindre *ou* photographier; '**like·wise** de plus, aussi.

lik·ing ['laikiŋ] (*for*) goût *m* (de), penchant *m* (pour); *to one's* ~ à souhait; à son gré.

li·lac ['lailək] **1.** lilas *adj./inv.*; **2.** ⚘ lilas *m*.

lilt [lilt] **1.** chanter gaiement; **2.** rythme *m*, cadence *f*; chant *m* gai.

lil·y ⚘ ['lili] lis *m*; ~ *of the valley* muguet *m*; *gild the* ~ orner la beauté même.

limb[1] [lim] membre *m* (*du corps*); ⚘ branche *f*; F suppôt *m*.

limb[2] *astr.*, ⚘ [~] limbe *m*, bord *m*; *fig.* go out on a ~ aller jusqu'au bout.

limbed [limd] aux membres ...

lim·ber[1] ['limbə] souple, agile.

lim·ber[2] ⚔ [~] **1.** avant-train *m*; **2.** atteler à l'avant-train; ~ *up* mettre l'avant-train.

lim·bo ['limbou] limbes *m/pl.*; *sl.* prison *f*; *fig.* oubli *m*.

lime[1] [laim] **1.** chaux *f*; (*a. bird~*) glu *f*; **2.** ✗ chauler; gluer (*des ramilles*).

lime[2] ⚘ [~] lime *f*; (*a. ~-tree*) tilleul *m*. [*m* de limon.)

lime[3] ⚘ [~] limon *m*; '~**-juice** jus)

lime...: '~**-kiln** four *m* à chaux; '~**-light** lumière *f* oxhydrique; *théâ.* rampe *f*; *fig. in the* ~ très en vue.

lim·er·ick ['limərik] (*sorte de*) petit poème *m* comique (*en 5 vers*).

lime·stone *géol.* ['laimstoun] calcaire *m*.

lim·it ['limit] **1.** limite *f*, borne *f*; *in (off)* ~*s* accès *m* permis (interdit); F *that is the* ~! ça, c'est le comble!; ça, c'est trop fort!; *Am.* F *go the* ~ aller jusqu'au bout; risquer le tout; **2.** limiter, borner (à); '**lim·i·tar·y** qui sert de limite (à, *of*); **lim·i·ta·tion** restriction *f*, limitation *f*; entrave *f*; ⚖ prescription *f*; '**lim·it·ed** limité, restreint (à, *to*); ~ (*liability*) *company* (*abbr.* Co.Ltd.) société *f* à responsabilité limitée; société *f* anonyme; ~ *in time* à terme; de durée restreinte; *surt. Am.* ~ (*express train*) rapide *m*; train *m* de luxe; '**lim·it·less** ☐ illimité, sans bornes.

limn [lim] dessiner, peindre.

lim·ou·sine ['limu(ː)ziːn] limousine *f*.

limp[1] [limp] **1.** boiter (*a. fig.*); **2.** boitement *m*, clochement *m*.

limp[2] [~] flasque; mou (mol *devant une voyelle ou un h muet*; molle *f*); *fig.* sans énergie.

lim·pet ['limpit] *zo.* patelle *f*; *fig.* crampon *m*; fonctionnaire *m* ancré dans son poste.

lim·pid ☐ ['limpid] limpide, clair; **lim'pid·i·ty**, '**lim·pid·ness** limpidité *f*, clarté *f*.

lim·y ['laimi] gluant; ✗ calcaire.

lin·age *journ.* ['lainidʒ] nombre *m* de lignes; paiement *m* à la ligne.

linch·pin ['lintʃpin] esse *f*; cheville *f* d'essieu.

lin·den ⚘ ['lindən] (*a. ~-tree*) tilleul *m*.

line[1] [lain] **1.** *su.* ⚓, ✗, 🚂, armes, démarcation, dessin, pêche, personne, téléph., télév., tennis, typ., phys. (*de force*): ligne *f*; △ alignement *m*; ✝ articles *m/pl.*; ✗, ⚓ ligne *f* de bataille; 🚂 voie *f*; téléph. fil *m*; peint. cimaise *f*; surv. cordeau *m*; dessin, phys. (*du spectre*): raie *f*; dessin, visage: trait *m*; front: ride *f*; véhicules: file *f*, colonne *f*; objets, personnes: rangée *f*; fig. emploi *m*; fig. mot *m*; *Am. fig.* tuyaux *m/pl.*; F mesure *f*; ~*s pl.* modèle *m*; (*bonne, mauvaise*) voie *f*; formes *f/pl.*; F acte *m* de mariage; ✗ rangs *m/pl.*; ~ *of battle* ligne *f* de bataille; ~ *of business* genre *m* d'affaires; ~ *of conduct* ligne *f* de conduite; ~ *of danger* zone *f* dangereuse; *ship of the* ~ vaisseau *m* de ligne; *hard* ~*s pl.* mauvaise chance *f*; *all down the* ~ sur toute la ligne; *in* ~ *with* d'accord avec; *position*: de pair avec; *that is not in my* ~ ce n'est pas mon métier; *stand in* ~ se tenir en ligne; *fall into* ~ s'aligner; *fig.* se conformer (à, *with*); **2.** *v/t.* ligner, régler; rayer; border (*allée, chemin, rive, etc.*); ~ *the streets* faire la haie; ~ *out* ✗ repiquer; tracer; ~ *through* biffer, rayer; *v/i. sp.* ~ *out* se mettre en lignes parallèles pour la touche; ~ *up* s'aligner; faire la queue.

line[2] [~] *cost. etc.* doubler; *fig.* ~ *one's pocket* faire sa pelote.

lin·e·age ['liniidʒ] lignée *f*; F famille *f*; **lin·e·al** ☐ ['liniəl] linéal (-aux *m/pl.*); direct; **lin·e·a·ment** ['~iəmənt] trait *m*, linéament *m*; **lin·e·ar** ['~iə] linéaire.

lin·en ['linin] **1.** toile *f* (*de lin*); linge *m*; **2.** *de ou* en toile; de lin (*fil*); '~**-bas·ket** panier *m* à linge; '~**-clos·et**, '~**-cup·board** lingerie *f*; armoire *f* à linge; '~**-drap·er** marchand(e *f*) *m* de toiles.

lin·er ['lainə] paquebot *m* (*de ligne*); grand avion *m* de transport; *personne*: traceur *m* de filets; *cost.* doubleur (-euse *f*) *m*; **lines·man** ['lainzmən] ✗ soldat *m* de la ligne; 🚂

garde-ligne *m*; *sp.* arbitre *m* de ligne; **'line-'up** mise *f* en rang; *sp.* rassemblement *m*; *sp. Am.* composition *f* d'une équipe.

ling[1] *icht.* [liŋ] morue *f* longue.

ling[2] ♀ [~] bruyère *f* commune.

lin·ger ['liŋgə] tarder; s'attarder (sur, over [up]on); traîner (*a. malade*); flâner (*dans la rue*); subsister (*doute*); ~ *at* (*ou about*) s'attarder sur *ou* à (*qch.*) *ou* dans (*un endroit*).

lin·ge·rie ✝ ['lɛ̃:nʒəri] lingerie *f* (de dame).

lin·ger·ing □ ['liŋgəriŋ] prolongé; persistent (*espoir*); qui traîne (*a. maladie*).

lin·go ['liŋgou] jargon *m*. [*m*/*pl.*].)

lin·gual ['liŋgwəl] lingual (-aux)

lin·guist ['liŋgwist] linguiste *mf*; **lin'guis·tic** (~ally) linguistique; **lin'guis·tics** *usu. sg.* linguistique *f*.

lin·i·ment ✱ ['linimənt] liniment *m*.

lin·ing ['lainiŋ] vêtement: doublage *m*; *robe*: doublure *f*; *mur*: incrustation *f*; ⊕ *fourneau, cylindre*: chemise *f*.

link [liŋk] **1.** *su* chaînon *m*; *chaîne*: anneau *m*; *fig.* lien *m*; *cuff-*~ bouton *m* de manchette; **2.** (se) joindre; *v/t. a.* relier, enchaîner.

links [liŋks] *pl.* dunes *f*/*pl.*; lande *f* sablonneuse; (*a. golf-*~) terrain *m* de golf.

link·up ['liŋkʌp] connexion *f*; lien *m*, rapport *m*; jonction *f*.

lin·net *orn.* ['linit] linot(te *f*) *m*.

lin·o·type *typ.* ['lainotaip] linotype *f*.

lin·seed ['linsi:d] graine *f* de lin; ~ oil huile *f* de lin.

lin·sey-wool·sey ✝ ['linzi'wulzi] tiretaine *f*.

lint ✱ [lint] charpie *f* anglaise; lint *m*.

lin·tel △ ['lintl] linteau *m*.

lin·y ['laini] strié de lignes; ridé.

li·on ['laiən] lion *m* (*zo., astr. a. fig.*); F ~*s pl. of a place* curiosités *f*/*pl.* d'un endroit; **'li·on·ess** lionne *f*; **'li·on·ize** visiter les curiosités de (*un endroit*); faire une célébrité de (*q.*).

lip [lip] lèvre *f* (*a.* ♀, *a. plaie*); *animal*: babine *f*; *tasse*: (re)bord *m*, saillie *f*; F insolence *f*; **'~-read** lire sur les lèvres; **'~-serv·ice** hommages *m*/*pl.* peu sincères; **'~-stick** rouge *m* à lèvres, bâton *m* de rouge.

liq·ue·fac·tion [likwi'fækʃn] liquéfaction *f*; **liq·ue·fi·a·ble** [~'faiəbl]

liquéfiable; **liq·ue·fy** ['~fai] (se) liquéfier.

li·queur [li'kjuə] liqueur *f*; **'~-choc·o·late** chocolat *m* aux liqueurs.

liq·uid ['likwid] **1.** □ liquide (*a. gramm.*); doux (douce *f*) (*son*); ♀ disponible; limpide (*œil etc.*); **2.** liquide *m*; *gramm.* liquide *f*.

liq·ui·date ['likwideit] ✝ liquider (*une dette*); mobiliser (*des capitaux*); **liq·ui·da·tion** liquidation *f*; **'liq·ui·da·tor** liquidateur *m*; **'liq·uid·iz·er** *cuis.* centrifugeuse *f*.

liq·uor ['likə] **1.** ⚗, *pharm.* solution *f*; boisson *f* alcoolique; *in* ~ ivre; **2.** *sl. v/i.* chopiner; *v/t.* (*a.* ~ *up*) enivrer.

liq·uo·rice ♀ ['likəris] réglisse *f*.

lisp [lisp] **1.** zézayement *m*; **2.** zézayer.

lis·som(e) ['lisəm] souple, agile.

list[1] [list] **1.** *su.* △ lisière *f* (*a. tex.*); liste *f*, répertoire *m*; carte *f* (*des vins*); **2.** enregistrer; inscrire (*des noms*); dresser la liste de; cataloguer; ~*ed a.* classé, historique (*édifice*).

list[2] ♣ [~] **1.** bande *f*, gîte *f*; **2.** donner de la bande; prendre de la gîte.

lis·ten ['lisn] (*to*) écouter; prêter l'oreille (à); faire attention (à); ~ *in radio*: se mettre à l'écoute; écouter (*qch., to s.th.*); **'lis·ten·er** auditeur (-trice *f*) *m*; ✂ *a. péj.* écouteur *m*; *radio*: ~*s' requests* disques *m*/*pl.* des auditeurs; **'lis·ten·er-'in** (*pl.* **'lis·ten·ers-'in**) *radio*: auditeur (-trice *f*) *m*.

lis·ten·ing ['lisniŋ] d'écoute; ~ *apparatus* appareil *m* d'écoute; **'~-in** *radio*: écoute *f*; **'~-post** poste *m* d'écoute.

list·less □ ['listlis] apathique, sans énergie; indifférent; **'list·less·ness** apathie *f*, manque *m* d'énergie; indifférence *f*.

lists [lists] *pl.* lice *f*.

lit [lit] *prét. et p.p. de* **light**[1] 3; ~ *up sl.* ivre, soûl.

lit·a·ny *eccl.* ['litəni] litanie *f*.

lit·er·al □ ['litərəl] littéral (-aux *m*/*pl.*) (*a.* ✗); propre (*sens*); sans imagination (*personne*); **'lit·er·al·ism**, **'lit·er·al·ness** littéralité *f*.

lit·er·ar·y □ ['litərəri] littéraire; de lettres; **'lit·er·ate** [~it] **1.** qui sait lire et écrire; lettré; **2.** lettré *m*; *eccl.* prêtre *m* sans grade universitaire; **lit·e·ra·ti** [litə'rɑ:ti:] *pl.* hommes *m/pl.* de lettres, littérateurs *m/pl.*; **lit·e·ra·tim** [~'rɑːtim] mot à mot; **lit·er·a·ture** ['litəritʃə]littérature *f*; écrits *m/pl.*; ✝ prospectus *m/pl.*

lithe(·some) ['laið(səm)] souple, agile, leste.

lith·o·graph ['liθəgrɑːf] 1. lithographie *f*; 2. lithographier; **li·thog·ra·pher** [li'θɒgrəfə] lithographe *m*; **lith·o·graph·ic** [liθə'græfik] (~ally) lithographique; **li·thog·ra·phy** [li-'θɒgrəfi] lithographie *f*, procédés *m/pl.* lithographiques.

Lith·u·a·ni·an [liθju'einjən] 1. lituanien(ne *f*); 2. Lituanien(ne *f*) *m*.

lit·i·gant 🖭 ['litigənt] 1. plaidant; 2. plaideur (-euse *f*) *m*; **lit·i·gate** ['~geit] *v/i.* plaider; être en procès; *v/t.* contester; **lit·i·ga·tion** litige *m*, procès *m*; **li·ti·gious** □ [li'tidʒəs] litigieux (-euse *f*) (*cas, a. personne*).

lit·mus 🖭 ['litməs] tournesol *m*.

lit·ter ['litə] 1. litière *f* (*véhicule, a. de paille*); civière *f*; désordre *m*; ordures *f/pl.*; *zo.* portée *f*; 2. mettre en désordre; joncher (de, *with*); *zo.* mettre bas; (*a. ~ down*) faire la litière à; joncher (*qch.*) de paille; **'~·bag** *Am.*, **'~·bas·ket**, **'~·bin** boîte *f* à ordures.

lit·tle ['litl] 1. *adj.* petit; peu de ...; mesquin (*esprit*); *a ~* one un(e *f*) petit(e *f*) (*enfant*); F *my ~ Mary* mon estomac *m*; *his ~ ways* ses petites manies *f/pl.*; *~ people* les fées *f/pl.*; 2. *adv.* peu; *a ~ red* un *ou* quelque peu rouge; 3. *su.* peu *m* (de chose); *~ by ~, by ~ and ~* peu à peu; petit à petit; *for a ~* pendant un certain temps; *not a ~* beaucoup; **'lit·tle·ness** petitesse *f*.

lit·to·ral ['litərəl] 1. du littoral; 2. littoral *m*.

lit·ur·gy *eccl.* ['litə(ː)dʒi] liturgie *f*.

liv·a·ble ['livəbl] F habitable (*maison etc.*); supportable (*vie*); F (*usu. ~ with*) accommodant, sociable (*personne*).

live 1. [liv] vivre (de, *on*); se nourrir (de, [*up*]*on*); demeurer, habiter; durer; *v/t.* mener (*une vie*); *~ to see* vivre assez longtemps pour voir (*qch.*); *~ down* faire oublier; surmonter; *~ off one's capital* manger son capital; *~ out* passer; durer (jusqu'à la fin de); *~ up to one's promise* remplir sa promesse; *~ up*

to a standard atteindre un niveau *etc.*; 2. [laiv] vivant, en vie; ardent (*charbon*); *fig.* actuel(le *f*); utile (*poids*); ⚡ chargé (*cartouche etc.*); ⚡ sous tension; *télév., radio:* en direct; *fig. ~ wire* homme *m etc.* très entreprenant; **'live·a·ble** *see livable*; **lived** [livd]: *short-~* éphémère; **live·li·hood** ['laivlihud] vie *f*; gagne-pain *m/inv.*; **live·li·ness** ['~linis] vivacité *f*, entrain *m*; **live·long** *poét.* ['livlɒŋ]: *~ day* toute la (sainte) journée; **live·ly** ['laivli] vif (vive *f*); animé; vivant.

liv·en ['laivn] *souv. ~ up v/t.* animer, égayer; *v/i.* s'aminer; s'activer.

liv·er¹ ['livə] vivant *m*; celui *m* (celle *f*) qui vit; *fast ~* viveur (-euse *f*) *m*; débauché(e *f*) *m*; *good ~* amateur *m* de bonne chère.

liv·er² [~] foie *m*.

liv·er·y ['livəri] 🖭 mise *f* en possession; (*a. ~ company*) corporation *f* d'un corps de métier; *cost.* livrée *f*; *at ~* en pension (*cheval*); **'~·man** membre *m* d'une corporation (*see livery company*); **~ sta·ble** écuries *f/pl.* de louage.

lives [laivz] *pl. de life*; **'live·stock** bétail *m*, bestiaux *m/pl.*; **'live·weight** poids *m* utile.

liv·id ['livid] blême, livide; plombé (*ciel*); **li·vid·i·ty** lividité *f*.

liv·ing ['liviŋ] 1. □ vivant; vif (vive *f*); ardent (*charbon*); *within ~ memory* de mémoire d'homme; 2. vie *f*; séjour *m*; *train m ou* niveau *m* de vie; *eccl.* bénéfice *m*, cure *f*; **'~·room** salle *f* de séjour; **~ space** espace *m* vital; **~ 'stan·dard** niveau *m* de vie.

Li·vo·ni·an [li'vounjən] 1. livonien (-ne *f*); 2. Livonien(ne *f*) *m*.

liz·ard ['lizəd] lézard *m*.

Liz·zie *Am. co.* ['lizi] (*a. tin ~*) vieille Ford *f*.

lla·ma *zo.* ['lɑːmə] lama *m*.

Lloyd's [lɔidz] la Société *f* Lloyd; *approx.* le Véritas *m*.

load [loud] 1. *su.* fardeau *m* (*a. fig.*); ⊕, *a. armes:* charge *f*; *test ~* charge *f* d'essai; 2. *v/t.* charger (de, *with*); *fig.* combler (de, *with*); *v/i.* (*a. ~ up*) prendre charge; **'load·ed** plombé (*canne etc.*); *~ dice pl.* dés *m/pl.* pipés; *fig. ~ question* question-piège *f* (*pl.* questions-piège); **'load·er** chargeuse *f*; *personne:* chargeur *m*; **'load·ing**

1. de chargement; **2.** chargement *m*; **'load-line** ⚓ ligne *f* de charge; **'load-star** étoile *f* polaire; *fig.* point *m* de mire; **'load-stone** pierre *f* d'aimant; aimant *m* naturel.

loaf¹ [louf] (*pl.* **loaves**) pain *m* (*a. de sucre*); miche *f* (*de pain*).

loaf² [~] fainéanter, flâner.

loaf-er ['loufə] flâneur *m*; voyou *m*.

loaf-sug-ar ['louf ʃugə] sucre *m* en pain.

loam [loum] ✒ terre *f* grasse; *métall.* glaise *f*; **'loam-y** ✒ gras(se *f*); *métall.* argileux (-euse *f*).

loan [loun] **1.** prêt *m*; avance *f*; emprunt *m*; on ~ à titre d'emprunt; détaché (auprès de, to) (*personne*); ask s.o. for the ~ of s.th. demander à emprunter qch. à q.; put out to ~ prêter; **2.** *surt. Am.* prêter; **'~word** mot *m* d'emprunt.

loath □ [louθ] peu disposé; be ~ for s.o. to do s.th. ne pas vouloir que q. fasse qch.; nothing ~ très volontiers; **loathe** [louð] détester; abhorrer; **loath-ing** ['~ðiŋ] aversion *f*, répugnance *f* (pour for, of); **loath-some** ['~səm] dégoûtant; **'loath-some-ness** caractère *m ou* nature *f* dégoûtant(e).

loaves [louvz] *pl.* de *loaf*¹.

lob [lɔb] *tennis:* **1.** lob *m*; **2.** lober (*la balle*).

lob-by ['lɔbi] **1.** vestibule *m* (*a. parl.*); *parl.* salle *f* des pas perdus; *théâ.* foyer *m*, entrée *f*; *parl. Am.* groupe *m* d'intrigants; **2.** *surt. Am. parl.* faire les couloirs; influencer certains députés *etc.*; **'lob-by-ist** *parl. surt. Am.* faiseur *m* des couloirs.

lobe *anat.*, ⚕ [loub] lobe *m*; ⊕ nez *m*; F oreille *f*.

lob-ster ['lɔbstə] homard *m*.

lo-cal □ ['loukəl] **1.** local (-aux *m/pl.*), régional (-aux *m/pl.*); de la localité, du pays; *see branch*; ✒ an(a)esthetic anesthésique *m* local; *téléph.* ~ call communication *f* interurbaine *ou* locale; ~ colour couleur *f* locale; ~ elections (élections *f/pl.*) municipales *f/pl.*; ~ government administration *f* décentralisée; **2.** *journ.* nouvelles *f/pl.* de la région; 🚂 (*a.* ~ train) train *m* d'intérêt local; F tortillard *m*; ~s *pl.* habitants *m/pl.* de l'endroit; **lo-cale** [lou'kɑ:l] scène *f* (*des événements*); **lo-cal-i-ty** [~'kæli-

ti] localité *f*; région *f*; **lo-cal-ize** ['~kəlaiz] localiser.

lo-cate [lou'keit] *v/t.* localiser; déterminer la situation de; établir; repérer (*une épave etc.*); *Am.* fixer l'emplacement de; be ~d être situé; it was ~d on le trouva; *v/i. Am.* s'établir; **lo'ca-tion** situation *f*, emplacement *m*; établissement *m*; 🚗 location *f*; *Am.* concession *f* minière; *cin.* extérieurs *m/pl.*

loch *écoss.* [lɔx] lac *m*; bras *m* de mer.

lock¹ [lɔk] **1.** *su.* porte *etc.:* serrure *f*, fermeture *f*; *fusil:* platine *f*; écluse *f*; ⊕ roue: enrayure *f*; verrou *m* (*a. fig.*); *sp. lutte:* clef *f*; *mot.* (*a. steering* ~) angle *m* de braquage; **2.** *v/t.* fermer à clef; (*a.* ~ up) enfermer; ⊕ enrayer (*une roue*); écluser (*un bateau*); verrouiller (*des armes*); *fig.* serrer; ~ the door against fermer sa porte à (*q.*); ~ in enfermer à clef; mettre sous clef; ~ out fermer la porte à *ou* sur; ⊕ lock-outer; ~ up bloquer, immobiliser (*des capitaux*); *v/i.* se fermer à clef; s'enrayer (*roues*); s'enclencher (*pièces d'un mécanisme*).

lock² [~] cheveux: boucle *f*; laine: flocon *m*.

lock-age ['lɔkidʒ] éclusage *m*; droit *m* d'écluse; **'lock-er** armoire *f*, coffre *m* (*fermant à clef*); ⚓ caisson *m*; ⚓ soute *f*; **lock-et** ['~it] médaillon *m*.

lock...: '~-**gate** porte *f* d'écluse; '~-**jaw** ✚ trisme *m*; F tétanos *m*; '~-**keep-er** gardien *m* d'écluse, éclusier *m*; '~-**nut** ⊕ contre-écrou *m*; '~-**out** lock-out *m/inv.*; '~-**smith** serrurier *m*; '~-**stitch** point *m* de navette; '~-**up** **1.** *su. surt. école:* fermeture *f* des portes; hangar *m ou* magasin *m etc.* fermant à clef; F poste *m* de police; ✝ immobilisation *f* (*de capital*); **2.** *adj.* fermant à clef.

lo-co *Am. sl.* ['loukou] toqué, fou (fol *devant une voyelle ou un h muet*; folle *f*).

lo-co-mo-tion [loukə'mouʃn] locomotion *f*; **lo-co-mo-tive** ['~tiv] **1.** locomotif (-ive *f*); *co.* voyageur (-euse *f*); **2.** 🚂 (*ou* ~ engine) locomotive *f*.

lo-cum-ten-ens ['loukəm'ti:nenz] remplaçant(e *f*) *m*; **lo-cus** ['loukəs], *pl.* -ci [~sai] Å lieu *m* géométrique.

lo·cust ['loukəst] *zo.* grande saute-relle *f*; ♀ caroube *f*; ~*-tree* carou-bier *m*; faux acacia *m*.

lo·cu·tion [lo'kju:ʃn] locution *f*.

lode ⚒ [loud] veine *f*.

lodge [lɔdʒ] **1.** *su.* pavillon (*de chasse, d'entrée*); concierge, francs-maçons: loge *f*; maison *f* (de garde-chasse); **2.** *v/t.* loger (*q., une balle*); avoir (*q.*) comme locataire; *v/i.* (*usu.* se) loger; demeurer (chez, *with*); être en pen-sion (chez, *with*); '**lodge·ment** *see* lodgment; '**lodg·er** locataire *mf*; pensionnaire *mf*; '**lodg·ing** héber-gement *m*; *argent etc.*: dépôt *m*; ~s *pl.* logement *m*, logis *m*, apparte-ment *m* meublé; *souv.* chambre *f*; '**lodg·ing-house** hôtel *m* garni; pension *f*; '**lodg·ment** prise *f*; ✕ logement *m*; ⚔ dépôt *m*, remise *f*.

loft [lɔft] grenier *m*; *église etc.*: gale-rie *f*; ⊕ atelier *m*; colombier *m*; **loft·i·ness** ['~inis] hauteur *f* (*a. fig.*); élévation *f* (*a. du style, des sen-timents, etc.*); '**loft·y** □ haut, élevé; hautain (*personne, a. air*).

log [lɔg] (grosse) bûche *f*; ⚓ loch *m*; *see a.* log-book. [rithme *m.*]
log·a·rithm ⚕ ['lɔgəriθm] loga-]
log...: '**~-book** ⚓ livre *m* de loch; journal *m* de bord; *mot.* carnet *m* de route; ✈ livre *m* de vol; ~ **cab·in** cabane *f* de bois; **logged** [lɔgd] im-bibé (d'eau); **log·ger** ['lɔgə] bûche-ron *m*; **log·ger·head** ['lɔgəhed]: *be at* ~*s* être en bisbille (avec, *with*); '**log-house**, '**log-hut** cabane *f* de bois.

log·ic ['lɔdʒik] logique *f*; '**log·i·cal** □ logique; **lo·gi·cian** [lo'dʒiʃən] logicien(ne *f*) *m*.

lo·gom·a·chy *poét.* [lɔ'gɔməki] logo-machie *f*, dispute *f* de mots.

log-roll *pol. surt. Am.* ['lɔgroul] échanger des faveurs, se prêter une entraide intéressée; **log·roll·ing** échange *m* de faveurs mutuelles.

log·wood ['lɔgwud] bois *m* de cam-pêche.

loin [lɔin] *cuis.* filet *m* (*de mouton ou de veau*), aloyau *m* (*de bœuf*), longe *f* (*de veau*); ~s *pl.* reins *m/pl.*; *anat.* lombes *m/pl.*

loi·ter ['lɔitə] traîner, flâner; ⚖ rôder; ~ *away one's time* perdre son temps à flâner; '**loi·ter·er** flâneur (-euse *f*) *m*; ⚖ rôdeur *m*.

loll [lɔl] *v/t.* pencher; laisser pendre;

v/i. pendre; être étendu (*personne*); se renverser nonchalamment; ~ *about* fainéanter, flâner; ~ *out* (*v/t.* laisser) pendre (*langue*).

lol·li·pop F ['lɔlipɔp] sucette *f*; *usu.* ~s *pl.* bonbons *m/pl.*; sucreries *f/pl.*

lol·lop F ['lɔləp] se traîner; marcher lourdement. [(= *argent*).]
lol·ly *Brit.* F *see* lollipop; *sl.* fric *m*)

Lom·bard ['lɔmbəd] Lombard(e *f*) *m*; ~ *Street* centre des opérations de banque à Londres.

Lon·don ['lʌndən] de Londres; '**Lon·don·er** Londonien(ne *f*) *m*, habitant(e *f*) *m* de Londres.

lone *poét.* [loun] solitaire, seul; ~ *wolf* solitaire *mf*; '**lone·li·ness** soli-tude *f*, isolement *m*; '**lone·ly** □ *see* lonesome; '**lon·er** solitaire *mf*; **lone-some** □ ['~səm] solitaire, isolé.

long¹ [lɔŋ] **1.** *su.* longueur *f*; F ~*s pl.* les grandes vacances *f/pl.*; *before* ~ sous peu; avant peu; *for* ~ pendant longtemps; *take* ~ = *be* ~ (*see* ~ 2); *the* ~ *and the short of it* le fort et le fin de l'affaire; en un mot comme en mille; **2.** *adj.* long(ue *f*); F *see tall*; ✝ ~ *figure* gros chiffre *m*; ~ *firm* bande *f* noire; F ~ *johns* caleçon *m* long; *sp.* ~ *jump* saut *m* en longueur; ✝ ~ *price* prix *m* élevé; *radio:* ~ *waves* grandes ondes *f/pl.*; ✝ *at* ~ *date* à longue échéance; *in the* ~ *run* à la longue; avec le temps; en fin de compte; *be* ~ prendre du temps (*chose*); tarder (à *inf., to inf.*; [*in*] *gér.*) (*personne*); **3.** *adv.* longtemps; depuis longtemps; *as* ~ *ago as* 1900 dès 1900; *I have* ~ *sought* je cherche depuis longtemps, voilà longtemps que je cherche; ~*er* plus longtemps; *no* ~*er* ne ... plus; *no* ~*er ago than* ... pas plus tard que ...

long² [~] désirer ardemment (*qch., for s.th.*); brûler (de, *to*).

long...: '~-**chair** chaise *f* longue; '~-'**dat·ed** à longue échéance; '~-'**dis·tance** à longue distance; *sp.* de fond (*coureur, course*); ~ *flight* raid *m*; *radio:* ~ *reception* réception *f* à longue distance; **lon·gev·i·ty** [lɔn'dʒeviti] longévité *f*; '**long-hair** *Am.* F amateur *m* de la musique classique; adversaire *mf* du jazz *etc.*; intellectuel(le *f*) *m*; '**long-hand** écriture *f* courante.

long·ing ['lɔŋiŋ] **1.** □ impatient, avide; **2.** désir *m* ardent, grande envie *f* (de, *for*).

long·ish ['lɔŋiʃ] assez *ou* plutôt long.
lon·gi·tude *géog.* ['lɔndʒitju:d] longitude *f*; **lon·gi'tu·di·nal** □ [ˌ.inl] en long; longitudinal (-aux *m/pl.*).
long...: '~-'**range** à longue *ou* grande portée (*a.* ✕); ✈ à grand rayon d'action; '~-**shore·man** débardeur *m*; docker *m*; ~ **shot** *cin.* plan *m* lointain; '~-'**sight·ed** presbyte; *fig.* prévoyant; '~-'**suf·fer·ing 1.** patient; longanime; **2.** patience *f*; longanimité *f*; '~-'**term** à long terme; ~ *memory* mémoire *f* à long terme; '~-'**ways** en long(ueur); '~-**wind·ed** □ interminable; diffus, intarissable (*personne*).
loo [lu:] *cartes:* mouche *f*.
loo·by ['lu:bi] nigaud *m*.
look [luk] **1.** *su.* regard *m*; air *m*, aspect *m*; (*usu.* ~s *pl.*) mine *f*; new ~ nouvelle mode *f*; *have a* ~ *at s.th.* jeter un coup d'œil sur qch., regarder qch.; *I like the* ~ *of him* sa figure me revient; **2.** *v/i.* regarder (qch., *at s.th.*); par, *out of*); avoir l'air (*malade etc.*); sembler (*que* ...); paraître; porter la mine (de qch., [*like*] *s.th.*); *it* ~*s like rain* on dirait qu'il va pleuvoir; *he* ~*s like winning* on dirait qu'il va gagner; ~ *about* chercher (q., *for s.o.*) des yeux; regarder autour de soi; ~ *after* soigner; s'occuper de; ~ *at* regarder; examiner; ~ *for* chercher; ~ *forward to* s'attendre à, attendre; ~ *in* faire une petite visite (à, *on*), entrer en passant (chez, *on*); *télév.* recevoir une émission, regarder; ~ *into* examiner, étudier; ~ *out!* attention!; ~ *out for* être à la recherche de; guetter; ~ *over* jeter un coup d'œil sur (*qch.*); ~ *to* voir à, s'occuper de; compter sur; ~ *to s.o. to* (*inf.*) compter sur q. pour (*inf.*); ~ *up* regarder en haut, lever les yeux, s'améliorer (*affaires, prix, etc.*); F ~ *up to* respecter; *fig.* ~ (*up*)*on* regarder, envisager (comme, *as*); **3.** *v/t.*: ~ *s.o. in the face* regarder q. en face; ~ *one's age* paraître *ou* accuser son âge; ~ *disdain* lancer un regard dédaigneux; ~ *over* revoir (*qch.*); jeter un coup d'œil sur; parcourir; ~ *up* (re)chercher; consulter; F aller voir (*q.*).
look-a·like ['lukəlaik] double *m*.
look·er-on ['lukər'ɔn] spectateur (-trice *f*) *m* (de, *at*); assistant *m* (à, *at*).

look·ing-glass ['lukiŋglɑ:s] miroir *m*, glace *f*.
look...: '~-'**out** guet *m*, surveillance *f*; ✕ guetteur *m*; ♣ vigie *f*; *fig.* qui-vive *m/inv.*; ♣ *keep a* ~ être en vigie; *be on the* ~ ♣ être de veille; *fig.* être sur ses gardes; *that is my* ~ ça c'est mon affaire; '~-o·ver F examen *m* superficiel; coup *m* d'œil; *give s.th. a* ~ examiner qch. rapidement; jeter un coup d'œil à qch.
loom¹ [lu:m] métier *m* (à tisser).
loom² [~] se dessiner, s'estomper; se dresser; surgir (*du brouillard*).
loon¹ *écoss.* [lu:n] garçon *m*; vaurien *m*; lourdaud *m*.
loon² *orn.* [~] grand plongeon *m*.
loon·y *sl.* ['lu:ni] dingue (= *fou*) (*adj., mf*); ~ *bin* maison *f* de fous.
loop [lu:p] **1.** *su.* boucle *f*; œil *m*, ganse *f*; *rideau:* embrasse *f*; sinuosité *f*; ⊕ boucle *f* d'évitement; *radio:* ~ *aerial* antenne *f* en cadre; **2.** *v/t.* boucler; enrouler; ~ *up* retrousser, relever (*les cheveux, la robe*); retenir (*un rideau*) avec une embrasse; ✈ ~ *the* ~ boucler la boucle; *v/i.* faire une boucle, boucler; '~-**hole** trou *m*, ouverture *f*; *fig.* échappatoire *f* (à, *for*); ✕ meurtrière *f*; '~-**line** ⊕ voie *f* de dérivation; *tél.* ligne *f* dérivée.
loose [lu:s] **1.** □ branlant; détaché; défait; échappé; libre; mobile; ✝ en vrac; mou (mol *devant une voyelle ou un h muet*; molle *f*); lâche; meuble (*terre*); vague (*terme etc.*); débauché; dissolu; ⚡ *connection* contact *m* intermittent; *at a* ~ *end* désœuvré; **2.** *v/t.* défaire (*un nœud etc.*); dénouer (*les cheveux, une ficelle, etc.*); détacher; ♣ larguer (*a.* ~ *off*) décocher, tirer; lâcher (*une prise*); ~ *one's hold on* lâcher (*qch.*); *v/i.* tirer (sur q., *at s.o.*); **3.** *su.:* *give* (*a*)~ *to* donner libre cours à; '~-**leaf**: ~ *book* album *m* à feuilles mobiles.
loos·en ['lu:sn] (se) défaire, délier; (se) relâcher; (se) desserrer; '**loose·ness** état *m* branlant; jeu *m*; *robe etc.:* ampleur *f*; relâchement *m* (*a.* ⚕); *sol:* inconsistance *f*; imprécision *f*; *morale:* licence *f*.
loot [lu:t] **1.** piller; voler; **2.** pillage *m*; butin *m*.
lop¹ [lɔp] tailler, émonder (*un arbre*); (*usu.* ~ *away ou off*) élaguer, couper.
lop² [~] pendre flasque; retomber.

lope [loup]: ～ along courir à petits bonds.

lop...: '～-**ears** pl. oreilles f/pl. pendantes; '～-'**sid·ed** de guingois; déjeté; qui manque de symétrie.

lo·qua·cious [loˈkweiʃəs] loquace; **lo·quac·i·ty** [loˈkwæsiti] loquacité f.

lord [lɔːd] **1.** seigneur m, maître m; titre: lord m; the ♀ le Seigneur (= Dieu); my ～ monsieur le baron etc.; parl. the (House of)♀s la Chambre des Lords; ♀ Mayor maire m; the ♀'s Prayer l'oraison f dominicale, le Pater m; the ♀'s Supper la Cène f; **2.** ～ it faire l'important; ～ it over en imposer à (q.); '**lord·li·ness** dignité f; péj. orgueil m; '**lord·ling** petit seigneur m; '**lord·ly** de grand seigneur; magnifique; majestueux (-euse f) péj. hautain; '**lord·ship** suzeraineté f (de, over); titre: seigneurie f.

lore [lɔː] science f, savoir m.

lor·ry [ˈlɔri] 🚚 lorry m; motor ～ camion m.

lose [luːz] [irr.] v/t. usu. perdre; égarer; gaspiller (le temps); montre: retarder de (cinq minutes); manquer (le train); coûter; ～ o.s. s'égarer, se perdre; fig. s'absorber; ～ sight of s.th. perdre qch. de vue; v/i. subir une perte, perdre; retarder (montre); Am. ～ out échouer; perdre; '**los·er** battu(e f) m, vaincu(e f) m; celui m (celle f) qui perd; sp. perdant(e f) m; come off a ～ échouer; '**los·ing** perdant; de vaincu.

loss [lɔs] perte f; † ～ leader article-réclame m (pl. articles-réclame); at a ～ désorienté; embarrassé (pour inf., to inf.); † à perte; be at a ～ for ne savoir trouver (qch.); be at a ～ what to say ne savoir que dire.

lost [lɔst] prét. et p.p. de lose; be ～ être perdu (a. fig.); être désorienté; sl. get ～! fiche le camp!; this won't be ～ on me j'en prendrai bonne note; je comprends; be ～ upon s.o. être en pure perte en ce qui concerne q.; '～-'**prop·er·ty of·fice** (service m des) objets m/pl. trouvés.

lot [lɔt] **1.** sort m (a. fig.); fig. destin m, destinée f, fortune f; † lot m; partie f; F quantité f; monde m; beaucoup; Am. terrain m; cin. Am. terrain m de studio; F a ～ (ou ～s pl.) of beaucoup; bien des; draw ～s for s.th. tirer qch. au sort; fall to s.o.'s ～ revenir à q. (de, to); tomber en partage à q.; throw in one's ～ with unir sa destinée à celle de; s'attacher à la fortune de; **2.** (usu. ～ out) lotir; Am. ～ upon compter sur.

lo·tion [ˈlouʃn] lotion f.

lot·ter·y [ˈlɔtəri] loterie f.

loud □ [laud] bruyant; retentissant; criard (couleur); haut (a. adv.); '～-**mouth** gueulard(e f) m, grande gueule f; '**loud·ness** caractère m bruyant; grand bruit m; force f; radio: volume m; '**loud·speak·er** radio: haut-parleur m (pl. haut-parleurs).

lounge [laundʒ] **1.** flâner; s'étendre à son aise; s'étaler; **2.** flânerie f; maison: salon m; hôtel: hall m; théâ. foyer m; promenoir m; (a. ～ chair) chaise f longue; sl. ～-lizard gigolo m, greluchon m; ～ suit complet m veston; ～ coat veston m; '**loung·er** flâneur (-euse f) m.

lour [ˈlauə] se renfrogner (personne); menacer (orage); s'assombrir (ciel); '**lour·ing** □ renfrogné; menaçant.

louse 1. [laus] (pl. lice) pou (pl. -x) m; **2.** [lauz] † épouiller; **lous·y** [ˈlauzi] pouilleux (-euse f); plein de poux; F sale.

lout [laut] rustre m, lourdaud m; '**lout·ish** rustre, lourdaud.

lou·vre, Am. **lou·ver** [ˈluːvə] persienne f.

lov·a·ble □ [ˈlʌvəbl] aimable; digne d'être aimé.

love [lʌv] **1.** amour m (de, pour, envers of, for, to[wards]); tendresse f; personne: ami(e f) m; Amour m, Cupidon m; sp. rien m, zéro m; attr. d'amour; F a ～ of a dress un amour de robe; for the ～ of God pour l'amour de Dieu; play for ～ jouer pour l'honneur; sp. four (to) ～ quatre à zéro; give (ou send) one's ～ to envoyer son affectueux souvenir ou ses meilleures amitiés à (q.); in ～ with amoureux (-euse f) de; make ～ to faire la cour à; neither for ～ nor money à aucun prix; **2.** aimer (d'amour), affectionner; ～ to do aimer à faire; '～-**af·fair** affaire f de cœur; intrigue f galante; '～-**bird** psittacule m, inséparable m; '～-**child** enfant m naturel; ～ **game** sp. jeu m blanc; '**love·less** sans amour; '**love·let·ter** billet m d'amour; '**love·li·ness** beauté f; '**love·lock** accroche-cœur m; '**love·ly** beau

ist loyaliste *mf*; '**loy·al·ty** fidélité *f*;
loyauté *f*.

loz·enge ['lɔzindʒ] losange *m*;
pharm. pastille *f*, tablette *f*.

lub·ber ['lʌbə] lourdaud *m*; ⚓ maladroit *m*; '**lub·ber·ly** lourdaud *m*;
gauche.

lu·bri·cant ['lu:brikənt] lubrifiant
(*a. su./m*); **lu·bri·cate** ['⁓keit]
graisser; **lu·bri·ca·tion** lubrification *f*, ⊕ graissage *m*; '**lu·bri·ca·-
tor** ⊕ graisseur *m*; **lu·bric·i·ty**
[lu:'brisiti] onctuosité *f*; *fig.* lubricité *f*.

lu·cid □ ['lu:sid] lucide, clair; ⚹ luisant; *poét.* brillant; *poét.* transparent; ⚕ ⁓ *interval* intervalle *m* de
lucidité; **lu'cid·i·ty**, '**lu·cid·ness**
lucidité *f*.

Lu·ci·fer ['lu:sifə] Lucifer *m* (*a.
bibl.*); *astr. a.* Vénus *f*; ⚸ allumette *f*.

luck [lʌk] hasard *m*, fortune *f*,
chance *f*; *good* ⁓ bonne chance *f*;
bad (*ou hard ou ill*) ⁓ mauvaise fortune *f*, malheur *m*; *be down on one's*
⁓ avoir de la déveine; '**luck·i·ly** par
bonheur; '**luck·i·ness** bonheur *m*;
chance *f*; '**luck·less** infortuné;
malencontreux (*-euse f*) (*jour etc.*);
'**luck·y** □ fortuné; heureux (*-euse
f*); ⁓ *hit* (*ou break*) coup *m* de bonheur; '**luck·y-bag**, '**luck·y-dip**
boîte *f* à surprises.

lu·cra·tive □ ['lu:krətiv] lucratif
(*-ive f*); **lu·cre** ['lu:kə] lucre *m*.

lu·cu·bra·tion [lu:kju'breiʃn] *usu.* ⁓s
pl. élucubration *f*, -s *f/pl.*

lu·di·crous □ ['lu:dikrəs] grotesque,
risible.

lu·do ['lu:dou] jeu *m* des petits chevaux.

luff ⚓ [lʌf] **1.** *su.* lof *m*; ralingue *f*
du vent; **2.** *v/i.* lofer; *v/t.* (*a.* ⁓ *up*)
faire lofer.

lug [lʌg] **1.** traîner, tirer; *fig.* ⁓ *in*
amener (*qch.*) à toute force; **2.** ⊕
a. F oreille *f*; *casquette:* oreillette *f*.

luge [lu:ʒ] **1.** luge *f*; **2.** luger; faire de
la luge.

lug·gage ['lʌgidʒ] bagage *m*, -s
m/pl.; '**⁓-car·ri·er** *cycl.*, *mot.* porte-
bagages *m/inv.*; '**⁓-grid** *mot.* porte-
bagages *m/inv.*; '**⁓-of·fice** 🚂 consigne *f*; '**⁓-rack** filet *m* (à bagages);
'**⁓-van** 🚂 fourgon *m* aux bagages.

lug·ger ⚓ ['lʌgə] lougre *m*.

lu·gu·bri·ous □ [lu:'gju:briəs] lugubre.

(bel *devant une voyelle ou un h muet*;
belle *f*; beaux *m/pl.*); ravissant; F
charmant; '**love-mak·ing** cour *f*
(amoureuse); '**love-match** mariage
m d'amour; '**love-po·tion** philtre *m*;
'**lov·er** amoureux *m*; fiancé *m*;
amant *m*; *fig.* ami(*e f*) *m*; *pair of*
⁓s deux amoureux *m/pl.*; '**love-set**
sp. six jeux *m/pl.* à zéro; '**love-sick**
féru d'amour; qui languit d'amour;
'**love-to·ken** gage *m* d'amour.

lov·ing □ ['lʌviŋ] affectueux (*-eu-
se f*).

low¹ (□ †) [lou] **1.** bas(se *f*), peu
élevé, petit (*classe, vitesse, etc.*);
lent (*fièvre*); grave (*son*); décolleté
(*robe*); (*a. in* ⁓ *spirits*) abattu; *fig.*
bas(se *f*), vil; *adv.* bas; ⁓*est bidder*
le moins disant m; *in a* ⁓ *voice* à voix
basse, doucement; *bring* ⁓ abattre;
humilier; *lie* ⁓ se tapir; se tenir coi; **2.**
météor. aire *f* de basses pressions;
surt. Am. niveau *m* le plus bas.

low² [⁓] **1.** meugler (*vache*); **2.** meuglement *m*.

low...: '**⁓-brow 1.** peu intellectuel
(-le *f*), terre à terre; **2.** homme
m etc. terre à terre; *péj.* philis-
tin(e *f*) *m*; '**⁓-cost** (à) bon marché;
'**⁓-'down** *sl.* **1.** bas(se *f*); ignoble; **2.**
['⁓] tuyau *m*, renseignement *m*; substance *f*, fond *m*.

low·er¹ ['louə] **1.** *adj.* plus bas(se *f*)
etc. (*see low¹* 1.); inférieur; d'en bas
inv.; **2.** *v/t.* baisser; abaisser (*chapeau, paupières, voile, etc.*); rabaisser
(*le prix, q.*); diminuer; (faire) descendre; *v/i.* descendre, s'abaisser;
baisser (*prix etc.*).

low·er² ['lauə] *see* **lour**.

low·er·most ['louəmoust] le (la) plus
bas(se *f*); '**low-in·come** à revenus
modérés; '**low-key(ed)** discret (-ète
f), retenu, modéré; '**low·land** plaine *f* basse; pays *m* plat; '**low·li·ness**
humilité *f*; '**low·ly** *adj.*, † *adv.*
humble, sans prétention, modeste;
'**low-'necked** décolleté (*robe*);
'**low·ness** manque *m* de hauteur;
petitesse *f*; *son:* gravité *f*; *conduite:*
bassesse *f*; ⁓ *of spirits* abattement *m*,
découragement *m*; '**low-'pres·sure**
basse pression *f*; '**low-shoe** soulier
m; '**low-'spir·it·ed** abattu, découragé; '**low-'wa·ter** basse mer *f ou*
marée *f*.

loy·al □ ['lɔiəl] (*to*) loyal (-aux
m/pl.) (envers); fidèle (à); '**loy·al·-**

luke·warm ['lu:kwɔ:m] tiède (a. fig.); **'luke·warm·ness** tiédeur f.
lull [lʌl] **1.** v/t. endormir (a. fig.); calmer; bercer; v/i. se calmer; s'apaiser; tomber (vent etc.); **2.** su. moment de calme; ⚓ accalmie f.
lull·a·by ['lʌləbai] berceuse f.
lum·ba·go ⚕ [lʌm'beigou] lumbago m.
lum·ber ['lʌmbə] **1.** su. fatras m; vieux meubles m/pl.; surt. Am. bois m de charpente; **2.** v/t. (usu. ~ up) encombrer; v/i. aller lourdement ou à pas pesants; Am. débiter (le bois); **'lum·ber·er, 'lum·ber·man** bûcheron m; **'lum·ber·ing** lourd; **'lum·ber·jack** bûcheron m; **'lum·ber-room** fourre-tout m/inv.
lu·mi·nar·y ['lu:minəri] corps m lumineux; astre m; fig. lumière f; **'lu·mi·nous** ☐ lumineux (-euse f) (a. fig.); fig. illuminant; ~ **clock** horloge f à cadran lumineux; ~ **dial** cadran m lumineux; ~ **paint** peinture f lumineuse.
lump [lʌmp] **1.** su. pierre, sucre, etc.: morceau m; bloc m; masse f; bosse f (au front etc.); fig. personne: lourdaud m, empoté m; in the ~ en bloc; en gros; ~ **sugar** sucre m en morceaux; ~ **sum** somme f globale; **2.** v/t. mettre en bloc ou en tas; fig. réunir; ~ **together** réunir en bloc; v/i. former des mottes; sl. ~ **it** s'arranger; **'lump·er** ⚓ déchargeur m, débardeur m; **'lump·ing** F énorme; gros(se f); **'lump·ish** (ba)lourd; à l'esprit lent; **'lump·y** ☐ rempli de mottes; couvert de bosses; grumeleux (-euse f) (sauce); houleux (-euse f) (mer).
lu·na·cy ['lu:nəsi] folie f; ⚖ démence f.
lu·nar ['lu:nə] de (la) lune; lunaire; ~ **caustic** caustique m lunaire; ~ **landing** alunissage m; ~ **module** module m lunaire.
lu·na·tic ['lu:nətik] **1.** de fou(s); fou (fol devant une voyelle ou un h muet; folle f); ~ **asylum** maison f d'aliénés; F pol. ~ **fringe** les outranciers m/pl.; les ultras m/pl.; **2.** fou (folle f) m; aliéné(e f) m.
lunch [lʌntʃ] **1.** (abr. de **lunch·eon** ['~ən]) su. déjeuner m; Am. a. cassecroûte m/inv.; ~ **basket, packed ~** panier-repas m (pl. paniers-repas); **2.** v/i. déjeuner; Am. prendre un

petit repas; v/t. offrir un déjeuner à (q.); ~ **hour, '~·time** heure f du déjeuner.
lung [lʌŋ] poumon m; animal tué: mou m; ⚕ **iron ~** poumon m d'acier.
lunge [lʌndʒ] **1.** su. escrime: botte f; fig. mouvement m en avant; **2.** v/i. lancer un coup (à, at); escrime: porter une botte (à, at), se fendre; fig. se précipiter; v/t. darder, lancer.
lung·er sl. ['lʌŋə] tuberculeux (-euse f) m.
lu·pin(e) ⚘ ['lu:pin] lupin m.
lurch[1] [lə:tʃ] **1.** ⚓ embardée f; fig. pas m titubant; **2.** ⚓ embarder (a. F); fig. marcher en titubant.
lurch[2] [~]: **leave in the ~** laisser (q.) dans l'embarras; planter là (q.).
lurch·er ['lə:tʃə] chien m croisé d'un lévrier avec un chien de berger.
lure [ljuə] **1.** leurre m; fig. piège m; fig. attrait m; **2.** leurrer; fig. séduire.
lu·rid ['ljuərid] blafard; fig. corsé; haut en couleur (langage).
lurk [lə:k] se cacher; rester tapi; **'lurk·ing-place** cachette f.
lus·cious ☐ ['lʌʃəs] succulent; péj. trop sucré ou fleuri; **'lus·cious-ness** succulence f; douceur f extrême.
lush [lʌʃ] plein de sève; luxuriant.
lust poét. [lʌst] **1.** appétit m; luxure f; fig. soif f; **2.** ~ **after** convoiter; avoir soif de; **'lust·ful** ☐ lubrique, lascif (-ive f); plein de convoitise.
lust·i·ness ['lʌstinis] vigueur f.
lus·tra·tion eccl. [lʌs'treiʃn] lustration f.
lus·tre, Am. lus·ter ['lʌstə] éclat m, brillant m; lustre m (a. fig.); **'lus·tre·less** terne (a. fig.); fig. sans éclat.
lus·trine ['lʌstrin] lustrine f.
lus·trous ☐ ['lʌstrəs] brillant; tex. lustré.
lust·y ☐ ['lʌsti] vigoureux (-euse f), robuste; fig. puissant.
lu·ta·nist, lut·ist ['lu:t(ən)ist] joueur (-euse f) m de luth, luthiste mf.
lute[1] ♪ [lu:t] luth m.
lute[2] [~] **1.** lut m, mastic m; **2.** luter, mastiquer; métall. brasquer.
lute·string ['lu:tstriŋ] see lustrine.
Lu·ther·an ['lu:θərən] luthérien(ne f) (a. su./mf); **'Lu·ther·an·ism** luthéranisme m.
lux·ate ⚕ ['lʌkseit] luxer; déboîter

lux·u·ri·ance [lʌgˈzjuəriəns] exubérance *f*; **lux'u·ri·ant** □ exubérant;
lux'u·ri·ate [‿rieit] croître avec
exubérance; *fig.* jouir avec délices
(de, *in*); vivre (dans, *in*); **lux'u·ri-
ous** □ [‿riəs] luxueux (-euse *f*); F
voluptueux (-euse *f*); **lux'u·ri·ous-
ness** somptuosité *f*; luxe *m*; **lux-
u·ry** [ˈlʌkʃəri] luxe *m*; objet *m* de
luxe.

ly·ce·um [laiˈsiəm] Lycée *m*.

lye ⚗ [lai] lessive *f*.

ly·ing [ˈlaiiŋ] **1.** *p.pr. de* lie[1]
et lie[2]; **2.** *adj.* menteur (-euse
f); '‿-'in couches *f/pl.*, accouche-

ment *m*; ‿ *hospital* maternité *f*.

lymph ⚕ [limf] vaccin *m*; lymphe *f*;
lym·phat·ic [‿ˈfætik] **1.** (‿*ally*)
lymphatique; **2.** ‿*s pl.* (vaisseaux
m/pl.) lymphatiques *m/pl.*

lynch [lintʃ] lyncher; ‿ **law** loi *f*
de Lynch; lynchage *m*.

lynx *zo.* [liŋks] lynx *m*; loup-
cervier (*pl.* loups-cerviers) *m*.

lyre [laiə] lyre *f*; *orn.* ‿-*bird* ménure
m.

lyr·ic [ˈlirik] **1.** lyrique; **2.** poème *m*
lyrique; chanson *f*; ‿*s pl.* lyrisme
m; **'lyr·i·cal** □ lyrique.

ly·sol *pharm.* [ˈlaisɔl] lysol *m*.

M

M, m [em] M *m*, m *m*.
ma F [mɑ:] maman *f*.
ma'am [mæm; *sl.* məm] *see* madam.
mac·ad·am [mə'kædəm] macadam
m; **mac'ad·am·ize** macadamiser.
mac·a·ro·ni [mækə'rouni] macaroni *m/inv.*
mac·a·roon [mækə'ru:n] macaron
m.
mace¹ [meis] *hist.* masse *f* d'armes;
masse *f* (portée devant un fonctionnaire).
mace² [~] ✝ fleur *f* de muscade.
mac·er·ate ['mæsəreit] (faire) macérer; **mac·er'a·tion** macération *f*.
mach·i·na·tion [mæki'neiʃn] complot *m*, intrigue *f*; ~s *pl.* agissements
m/pl., intrigues *f/pl.*; **mach·i·na-
tor** ['~tə] machinateur (-trice *f*) *m*;
intrigant(e *f*) *m*; **ma·chine** [mə-
'ʃi:n] **1.** machine *f*; appareil *m* (*a.*
= *avion*); bicyclette *f*; *fig.* automate
m; *pol.* organisation *f*; *attr.* des
machines, à la machine; ~ *fitter*
assembleur *m*, ajusteur *m*; ✖ ~-*gun*
mitrailleuse *f*; ~ *translation* traduction *f* automatique; **2.** façonner; usiner; coudre à la machine; **ma-
'chine·made** fait à la machine;
ma'chin·er·y mécanisme *m*; machines *f/pl.*; appareil *m*, -s *m/pl.*;
ma'chine-shop atelier *m* de construction mécanique; atelier *m* d'usinage; **ma'chine-tool** machine-outil (*pl.* machines-outils) *f*; **ma-
'chine-wash·a·ble** lavable en machine; **ma'chin·ist** machiniste *m*;
mécanicien(ne *f*) *m*.
mack·er·el *icht.* ['mækrəl] maquereau *m*; ~ *sky* ciel *m* pommelé.
mack·i·naw *Am.* ['mækinɔ:] couverture *f* épaisse.
mack·in·tosh ['mækintɔʃ] imperméable *m*; caoutchouc *m*.
macro... [mækro] macro-; ~·**bi·ot·ic**
[~bai'ɔtik] macrobiotique; ~·**bi·ot-
ics** *sg.* macrobiotisme *m*; ~·**cosm**
['~kɔzəm] macrocosme *m*.
mac·u·lat·ed ['mækjuleitid] maculé.
mad ☐ [mæd] fou (fol *devant une*

voyelle *ou un h muet*; folle *f*) (*a.*
fig.), aliéné; enragé (*a. chiens etc.*);
fig. éperdu, affolé, ivre (de *about*,
with, *on*); *Am.* fâché (contre, *with*);
F furieux (-euse *f*), furibond; *go* ~
devenir fou; *drive* ~ rendre fou;
affoler (*a. fig.*).
mad·am ['mædəm] madame *f*;
mademoiselle *f*.
mad·cap ['mædkæp] écervelé (*a.*
su./mf); **mad·den** ['mædn] rendre
fou, exaspérer; *it is* ~*ing* c'est exaspérant.
mad·der ♀, ⊕ ['mædə] garance *f*.
made [meid] *prét. et p.p. de* make
1, 2.
made-to-meas·ure ['meidtə'meʒə]
fait sur mesure; **made-to-ord·er**
['~'ɔ:də] fait sur commande.
made-up ['meid'ʌp] assemblé; arti-
ficiel(le *f*); tout fait (*vêtement*);
maquillé (*femme*); faux (fausse *f*),
inventé (*histoire etc.*).
mad·house ['mædhaus] maison *f*
de fous; asile *m* d'aliénés; **'madman** fou *m*, aliéné *m*, insensé *m*;
'mad·ness folie *f*; démence *f*; *vét.*
rage *f*; hydrophobie *f*; *Am.* colère *f*;
rage *f*; **'mad·wom·an** folle *f*,
aliénée *f*, insensée *f*.
mael·strom ['meilstroum] *géog.*
le Malstrom *m*; *fig.* tourbillon *m*.
mag·a·zine [mægə'zi:n] *fusil*: magasin *m*; ✖ magasin *m* d'armes, de
vivres, *etc.*; ✖ dépôt *m* de munitions; (revue *f*) périodique *m*;
magazine *m* (*illustré*).
mag·da·len ['mægdəlin] fille *f*
repentie.
mag·got ['mægɔt] asticot *m*; *fig.*
lubie *f*; F ver *m*; **'mag·got·y** plein
de vers; *fig.* capricieux (-euse *f*).
Ma·gi ['meidʒai] *pl.*: *the* ~ les Rois
m/pl. Mages.
mag·ic ['mædʒik] **1.** (*a.* **'mag·i·cal**
☐) magique, enchanté; **2.** magie *f*,
enchantement *m*; **ma·gi·cian** [mə-
'dʒiʃn] magicien(ne *f*) *m*.
mag·is·te·ri·al ☐ [mædʒis'tiəriəl]
magistral (-aux *m/pl.*); *a. péj.* de

maître; de magistrat; **mag·is·tra-cy** ['ˌtrəsi] magistrature *f*; les magistrats *m/pl.*; **mag·is·trate** ['ˌtrit] magistrat *m*, juge *m*; *usu.* juge *m* de paix.

mag·na·nim·i·ty [mægnə'nimiti] magnanimité *f*; **mag·nan·i·mous** □ [ˌ'nænɪməs] magnanime.

mag·nate ['mægneit] magnat *m*.

mag·ne·sia 🜎 [mæg'ni:ʃə] magnésie *f*.

mag·net ['mægnit] aimant *m*; **mag·net·ic** [ˌ'netik] (ˌally) magnétique; aimanté; ~ *field* (*pole*) champ *m* (pôle *m*) magnétique; **mag·net·ism** ['ˌnitizm] magnétisme *m*; **mag·net·i·za·tion** [ˌtai'zeiʃn] aimantation *f*; **'mag·net·ize** aimanter; F magnétiser; **'mag·net·iz·er** *phys.* dispositif *m* d'aimantation; *personne:* magnétiseur *m*; **mag·ne·to** [mæg'ni:tou] ⊕ *etc.* magnéto *m*.

mag·nif·i·cence [mæg'nifisns] magnificence *f*; **mag'nif·i·cent** magnifique; somptueux (-euse *f*); **mag·ni·fi·er** ['mægnifaiə] loupe *f*, verre *m* grossissant; **mag·ni·fy** ['ˌfai] *v/t.* grossir (*a. fig.*); *~ing glass* loupe *f*, verre *m* grossissant; **mag·nil·o·quence** [mæg'nilokwəns] emphase *f*, grandiloquence *f*; **mag'nil·o·quent** □ emphatique, grandiloquent; **mag·ni·tude** ['ˌtju:d] grandeur *f*; *star of the first ~* étoile *f* de première magnitude.

mag·pie *orn.* ['mægpai] pie *f*; *a. fig.* bavard(e *f*) *m*.

mahl·stick *peint.* ['mɔ:lstik] appui(e)-main (*pl.* appuis-main, appuie-main) *m*.

ma·hog·a·ny [mə'hɔgəni] acajou *m*; *attr.* en acajou.

maid [meid] †, *co.* pucelle *f*; † demoiselle *f*; † jeune fille *f*; (*ou* ~-*servant*) bonne *f*, domestique *f*, servante *f*; *old* ~ vieille fille *f*; ~ *of all work* bonne *f* à tout faire; ~ *of hono(u)r* fille *f* d'honneur; *Am.* première demoiselle *f* d'honneur.

maid·en ['meidn] **1.** *prov.*, *co. see* maid; **2.** de jeune fille; non mariée; *fig.* premier, de début; ~ *name* nom *m* de jeune fille; ~ *speech* discours *m* de début; ~ *voyage* ⚓ premier voyage *m*; ⚔ premier vol *m*; ⚕ capillaire *m*; '~·**head**, '~·**hood** virginité *f*; célibat *m* (*de fille*); '~·**like**,

'maid·en·ly virginal (-aux *m/pl.*); modeste.

mail¹ [meil] mailles *f/pl.*

mail² [ˌ] **1.** *poste:* courrier *m*; poste *f*; départ *m* du courrier; **2.** envoyer par la poste; expédier; ~*ing list* liste *f* d'adresses; '**mail·a·ble** *Am.* transmissible par la poste.

mail...: '~·**bag** sac *m* de dépêches *ou* de poste; '~·**boat** courrier *m* postal; paquebot *m*; '~·**box** *surt. Am.* boîte *f* aux lettres; '~·**car·ri·er** *Am.* facteur *m*; '~·**clad** revêtu de mailles; '~·**coach**, *Brit.* '~·**cart** wagon-poste (*pl.* wagons-poste) *m*; '~·**man** *Am.* facteur *m*; '~·**or·der firm**, surt. *Am.* '~·**or·der house** maison *f* qui vend par correspondance; '~·**train** train-poste (*pl.* trains-poste[s]) *m*.   [(*a. fig.*).

maim [meim] estropier, mutiler╎

main [mein] **1.** principal (-aux *m/pl.*); premier (-ère *f*), essentiel(le *f*); grand (*route*); ~ *chance* son propre intérêt; *téléph.* ~ *station* table *f* (principale); *by* ~ *force* de vive force; ⚔ ~ *plane* voilure *f*; **2.** vigueur *f*; ⊕ canalisation *f* maîtresse; ⚡ conducteur *m* principal; *poét.* océan *m*; ~*s pl.* ⚡ secteur *m*; ⚡ *rising* ~ conducteur *m* principal montant; ~*s aerial* antenne *f* secteur; ~*s receiving set* poste *m* secteur; *in the* ~ en général, à tout prendre; '~·**land** terre *f* ferme; continent *m*; '**main·ly** surtout.

main...: '~·**mast** ['ˌmɑ:st; ⚓ '~məst] grand mât *m*; '~·**sail** ['ˌseil; ⚓ '~sl] grand-voile *f*; '~·**spring** ressort *m* moteur; *fig.* mobile *m* essentiel; '~·**stay** ⚓ étai *m* de grand mât; *fig.* soutien *m* principal; '~·**stream** *fig.* tendance *f* principale; ⚻·**Street** *Am.* grand-rue *f*; habitants *m/pl.* d'une petite ville.

main·tain [men'tein] maintenir; soutenir (*opinion, famille, conversation, cause, guerre*); entretenir (*famille, correspondance, route, relations*); défendre (*ses droits, une cause*); conserver (*l'allure, la santé*); garder (*l'attitude, l'avantage*); ~ *that* affirmer *ou* maintenir que; **main'tain·a·ble** (sou)tenable.

main·te·nance ['meintinəns] maintien *m*; entretien *m*; défense *f*; appui *m*; subsistance *f*; ~ *costs pl.* frais *m/pl.* d'entretien.

main·top ⚓ ['meintɔp] grand-hune f.

maize ♀ [meiz] maïs m.

ma·jes·tic [mə'dʒestik] (⁓ally) majestueux (-euse f); **ma·jes·ty** ['mædʒisti] majesté f.

ma·jor ['meidʒə] **1.** majeur(e f); le plus grand; mot. de priorité (route); principal (-aux m/pl.) (a. couleurs aux cartes); ♪ A ⁓ la m majeur; ♪ ⁓ third tierce f majeure; ♪ ⁓ key ton m majeur; Am. baseball: ⁓ league ligue f majeure; **2.** ✕ commandant m; ✕ chef m de bataillon (infanterie ou d'escadron (cavalerie); personne: majeur(e f) m; phls. majeure f; Am. univ. sujet m principal; **3.** Am. (in) se spécialiser (en) (un sujet); être reçu à l'examen supérieur (de); '⁓-'gen·er·al général m de brigade; **ma·jor·i·ty** [mə'dʒɔriti] majorité f (a. âge); le plus grand nombre; la plus grande partie; ✕ (a. **ma·jor·ship** ['meidʒəʃip]) grade m de commandant; ⁓ decision décision f prise à la majorité; pol. ⁓ rule gouvernement m majoritaire ou de la majorité; join the ⁓ mourir, s'en aller ad patres.

make [meik] **1.** [irr.] v/t. faire (qch., distinction, amis, paix, guerre, discours, testament, thé, bruit, faute, fortune, etc.); fabriquer; confectionner (des vêtements); conclure (un marché); fixer (les conditions); établir (une règle); subir (une perte); conclure (la paix, un traité); battre (les cartes); ✝ fermer (le circuit); nommer (un juge, un professeur, etc.); ⁓ the best of it prendre son parti; ⁓ capital out of tirer parti de; ⁓ good réparer (un tort), tenir (sa parole), établir (son droit à qch.); Am. F ⁓ it réussir (à qch.); arriver à temps; ⚓ ⁓ the land atterrir; ⁓ or mar s.o. faire la fortune ou la ruine de q.; ⁓ one joindre, unir; do you ⁓ one of us? êtes-vous des nôtres?; ⚓ ⁓ a port arriver à un port; ⁓ shift s'accommoder (de qch.); ⁓ sure of s'assurer de (un fait); s'assurer (une place etc.); ⁓ sure that s'assurer que; F être persuadé que; ⁓ way faire du chemin; ⁓ way for faire place à (q.) (a. fig.); ⁓ into transformer en; ⁓ out dresser (une liste, un compte); faire (un chèque); prouver; discerner;

démêler (les raisons de q.); déchiffrer (une écriture); F feindre; ⁓ over céder; transférer; ⁓ up compléter; combler (un déficit); faire (un paquet); préparer; façonner (une robe etc.); dresser (une liste, un compte); établir (un compte); inventer (une excuse, une histoire); composer (un ensemble); accommoder (un différend); made up of composé de; see ⁓ up for (v/i.); ⁓ up one's mind se décider (à, to; pour for, in favo[u]r of); prendre son parti; **2.** [irr.] v/i. ⚡ se fermer (circuit); monter (marée); ⁓ as if faire mine de; faire semblant de; ⁓ after s'élancer sur ou après; ⁓ against s'opposer à; ⁓ at se ruer sur (q.); ⁓ away s'éloigner; ⁓ away with enlever; détruire; dérober (de l'argent); ⁓ for se diriger vers; s'élancer sur; ⚓, ✕ mettre le cap sur; favoriser; ⁓ off se sauver; décamper; ⁓ up compenser; se réconcilier; se maquiller; ⁓ up for réparer; se rattraper de (une perte); suppléer à (un manque); compenser; ⁓ up to s'approcher de; F faire la cour à; **3.** fabrication f; façon f; taille f (de q.); ✝ marque f; ⚡ circuit: fermeture f; our own ⁓ de notre marque; of poor ⁓ de qualité inférieure; '⁓-be·lieve **1.** semblant m; feinte f; trompe-l'œil m/inv.; **2.** fictif (-ive f), imaginaire, feint; **'mak·er** faiseur (-euse f) m; ✝ fabricant m; constructeur m; the ♀ le Créateur m (= Dieu).

make...: '⁓-shift **1.** pis-aller m/inv.; **2.** de fortune; '⁓-up see make 3; composition f; maquillage m; invention f; ⁓ charge façon f; '⁓-weight complément m de poids; fig. supplément m.

mak·ing ['meikiŋ] fabrication f; création f; F ⁓s pl. recettes f/pl.; petits profits m/pl.; in the ⁓ en train de se faire; have the ⁓s of avoir ce qu'il faut pour.

mal·a·chite min. ['mæləkait] malachite f; cendre f verte.

mal·ad·just·ment ['mælə'dʒʌstmənt] ajustement m défectueux; dérèglement m.

mal·ad·min·is·tra·tion ['mælədminis'treiʃn] mauvaise administration f ou gestion f.

mal·a·droit ['mælə'drɔit] maladroit.

mal·a·dy ['mælədi] maladie f.

mal·ap·ro·pos ['mæl'æprəpou] **1.**

adv. mal à propos; **2.** *adj.* inopportun.

ma·lar·i·a ✵ [məˈlɛərɪə] malaria *f*, paludisme *m*; **ma·lar·i·al** paludéen(ne *f*).

ma·lar·key *Am.* F [məˈlɑːki] baliverne(s) *f/(pl.)*, blague(s) *f/(pl.)*, baratin *m*.

mal·con·tent [ˈmælkəntent] mécontent (*a. su./mf*).

male [meil] **1.** mâle; ~ *child* enfant *m* mâle; ~ *screw* vis *f* mâle *ou* pleine; **2.** mâle *m*; homme *m*.

mal·e·dic·tion [mæliˈdikʃn] malédiction *f*; anathème *m*.

mal·e·fac·tor [ˈmælifæktə] malfaiteur (-trice *f*) *m*.

ma·lef·i·cence [məˈlefisns] malfaisance *f*; **ma·lef·i·cent** malfaisant (envers, *to*); criminel(le *f*).

ma·lev·o·lence [məˈlevələns] malveillance *f* (envers, *to[wards]*); **ma·lev·o·lent** □ malveillant (envers, *to[wards]*).

mal·for·ma·tion [ˈmælfɔːˈmeiʃn] malformation *f*; défaut *m* de conformation.

mal·func·tion [mælˈfʌŋkʃən] **1.** fonctionnement *m* défectueux, dérèglement *m*; **2.** fonctionner mal.

mal·ice [ˈmælis] malice *f*; malveillance *f*; méchanceté *f*; ⚖ intention *f* criminelle; *bear s.o.* ~ vouloir du mal à q., en vouloir à q.; ⚖ *with* ~ *aforethought* avec intention criminelle.

ma·li·cious □ [məˈliʃəs] méchant; malveillant; ⚖ avec intention criminelle; **ma·li·cious·ness** malice *f etc.*

ma·lign [məˈlain] **1.** □ pernicieux (-euse *f*), nuisible; ✻ malin (-igne *f*); **2.** calomnier, diffamer; **ma·lig·nan·cy** [məˈlignənsi] malignité *f* (*a.* ✻); virulence *f*; **ma·lig·nant** □ malin (-igne *f*) (*a.* ✻); méchant; **2.** *hist.* ~*s pl.* dissidents *m/pl.*; **ma·lig·ni·ty** malignité *f*; méchanceté *f*; *souv.* ✻ malignité *f*.

ma·lin·ger [məˈliŋgə] faire le malade; **ma·lin·ger·er** faux malade *m*, fausse malade *f*.

mall *Am.* [mɔːl] centre *m* commercial.

mal·lard *orn.* [ˈmæləd] malard *m*; canard *m* sauvage.

mal·le·a·bil·i·ty [mæliəˈbiliti] malléabilité *f*; *fig.* souplesse *f*; **mal·**

le·a·ble malléable; *fig.* complaisant.

mal·let [ˈmælit] maillet *m*.

mal·low ♀ [ˈmælou] mauve *f*.

malm·sey [ˈmɑːmzi] Malvoisie *f*.

mal·nu·tri·tion [ˈmælnjuːˈtriʃn] sous-alimentation *f*; alimentation *f* défectueuse.

mal·o·dor·ous □ [mæˈloudərəs] malodorant.

mal·prac·tice [ˈmælˈpræktis] méfait *m*; ✻ négligence *f*; ⚖ malversation *f*.

malt [mɔːlt] **1.** malt *m*; ~ *liquor* bière *f*; **2.** (se) convertir en malt; *v/t.* malter.

Mal·tese [ˈmɔːˈtiːz] **1.** maltais; **2.** Maltais(e *f*) *m*.

malt·ing [ˈmɔːltiŋ] maltage *m*.

mal·treat [mælˈtriːt] maltraiter, malmener; **mal·treat·ment** mauvais traitement *m*.

malt·ster [ˈmɔːltstə] malteur *m*.

mal·ver·sa·tion [mælvəˈseiʃn] malversation *f*; mauvaise administration *f*.

ma(m)·ma [məˈmɑː] maman *f*.

mam·mal [ˈmæməl] mammifère *m*; **mam·ma·li·an** [məˈmeiljən] mammifère (*a. su./m*).

mam·mon [ˈmæmən] Mammon *m*.

mam·moth [ˈmæməθ] **1.** *zo.* mammouth *m*; **2.** géant, monstre.

mam·my F [ˈmæmi] maman *f*; *Am.* nourrice *f* noire.

man [mæn; *mots composés:* -mən] **1.** (*pl.* men) homme *m* (*a.* ✖); domestique *m*, valet *m*; ouvrier *m*; F mari *m*; *échecs:* pièce *f*; *dames:* pion *m*; *attr.* d'homme(s); *to a* ~ jusqu'au dernier; ✖ ~ *on leave* permissionnaire *m*; **2.** ✖, ⚓ garnir d'hommes; armer, équiper; ~ *o.s.* faire appel à tout son courage.

man·a·cle [ˈmænəkl] **1.** menotte *f*; **2.** mettre les menottes à (*q.*).

man·age [ˈmænidʒ] *v/t.* manier (*un outil*); conduire (*une auto, une entreprise*); régir (*une propriété*); gérer (*une banque, une affaire*); manœuvrer (*un navire*); gouverner (*une banque*); maîtriser (*un animal*); venir à bout de (*qch.*); *v/i.* s'arranger; se débrouiller; ~ *to* (*inf.*) venir à bout de (*inf.*); réussir à (*inf.*); ~ *without s.th.* se passer de qch.; **'man·age·a·ble** □ maniable; traitable (*personne*); **'man·age·ment** maniement *m*; direction f; conduite f; gestion f; savoir-faire m/inv.; administrateurs m/pl.; **'man·ag·er** directeur m; régisseur m; gérant m; chef m (du service etc.); journal: administrateur m; théâ. imprésario m; departmental ~ chef m de rayon; chef m de service; sales ~ directeur m commercial; she is a good (bad) ~ elle est bonne (mauvaise) ménagère f; **'man·ag·er·ess** directrice f, gérante f; **man·a·ge·ri·al** □ [~ə'dʒiəriəl] directorial (-aux m/pl.).

man·ag·ing ['mænidʒiŋ] 1. directeur (-trice f); gérant; fig. entreprenant; F autoritaire; ~ clerk m clerk m de bureau; ⚖ premier clerc m; 2. direction f; conduite f; gestion f.

man·da·mus ⚖ [mæn'deiməs] commandement m (à une cour inférieure).

man·da·rin ['mændərin] mandarin m; ♀ (ou **'man·da·rine** [~]) mandarine f.

man·da·tar·y ⚖ ['mændətəri] mandataire mf; **man·date** ['~deit] 1. pol. mandat m; poét. commandement m, ordre m; 2. attribuer sous mandat; **man'da·tor** mandant m; **man·da·to·ry** ['~dətəri] 1. mandataire; 2. état m mandataire.

man·di·ble ['mændibl] mandibule f; anat. mâchoire f inférieure.

man·do·lin(e) ♪ ['mændəlin] mandoline f. [dragore f.\
man·drake ♀ ['mændreik] man-\
man·drel ⊕ ['mændril] mandrin m.\
man·drill zo. ['mændril] mandrill m.\
mane [mein] crinière f.

man·eat·er ['mæni:tə] mangeur m d'hommes; personne: cannibale m.

ma·nes ['meini:z] pl. antiquité romaine: mânes m/pl.

ma·neu·ver [mə'nu:və] Am. see manœuvre.

man·ful □ ['mænful] viril; hardi; **'man·ful·ness** virilité f; vaillance f.

man·ga·nese ⚗ ['mæŋgə'ni:z] manganèse m; **man·gan·ic** [~'gænik] manganique. [rogne f.\
mange vét. [meindʒ] gale f; F\
man·ger ['meindʒə] crèche f; F dog in the ~ chien m du jardinier.

man·gle¹ ['mæŋgl] 1. calandre f; 2. calandrer; cylindrer.

man·gle² [~] déchirer; mutiler (a. fig.); fig. massacrer.

man·gler ['mæŋglə] machine f à calandrer.

man·gy ['meindʒi] galeux (-euse f); fig. minable.

man...: '~**han·dle** manutentionner, transporter à force de bras; sl. malmener; bousculer; '~**hat·er** misanthrope m; '~**hole** ⊕ trou m de regard; bouche f d'accès; '~**hood** humanité f; âge m viril, âge m d'homme; '~-**hours** pl. heures f/pl. de travail (par homme).

ma·ni·a ['meinjə] manie f; folie f; F passion f; suffixe: -manie f; **ma·ni·ac** ['~iæk] 1. fou (folle f) m enragé(e f) m; 2. (a. **ma·ni·a·cal** □ [mə'naiəkl]) de fou (folle f); furieux (-euse f).

man·i·cure ['mænikjuə] 1. soin m des mains; toilette f des ongles; 2. soigner les mains; '~-**case** trousse f de manucure.

man·i·cur·ist ['mænikjuərist] personne: manucure mf.

man·i·fest ['mænifest] 1. □ manifeste, évident, clair; 2. ♣ manifeste m (de sortie); 3. v/t. manifester, témoigner; ♣ déclarer (qch.) en douane; v/i. manifester; **man·i·fes'ta·tion** manifestation f; **man·i·fes·to** [~'festou] pol. etc. manifeste m.

man·i·fold □ ['mænifould] 1. divers, varié; nombreux (-euse f); 2. mot. intake ou inlet (exhaust) ~ collecteur m d'admission (d'échappement); 3. polycopier; ~ **writ·er** appareil m à polycopier.

man·i·kin ['mænikin] petit homme m; homoncule m.

ma·nip·u·late [mə'nipjuleit] manipuler (qch.); ⊕ manœuvrer; agir sur (une pédale, ✝ le marché); **ma·nip·u·la·tion** manipulation f; ⊕ manœuvre f; tripotages m/pl. en Bourse; ✝ exploration f; **ma·'nip·u·la·tive** de manipulation; **ma·'nip·u·la·tor** manipulateur m; ✝ agioteur m.

man·kind [mæn'kaind] le genre m humain; ['mænkaind] les hommes m/pl.; **'man·like** see manly; mannish; **'man·li·ness** caractère m viril; virilité f; **'man·ly** viril, d'homme; **'man-made** artificiel(le f); ~ fibre fibre f synthétique.

man·ne·quin ['mænikin] mannequin m; ~ parade défilé m de mannequins.

man·ner ['mænə] manière f (a. art,

a. littérature); façon *f*; *peinture*: style *m*; ~s *pl.* mœurs *f/pl.*, usages *m/pl.*; manières *f/pl.*; tenue *f*; *no* ~ *of doubt* aucune espèce de doute; *in a* ~ d'une façon; *in such a* ~ *that* de manière que, de sorte que; **'mannered** aux manières ...; *littérature, art:* maniéré; recherché; **'man·ner·ism** maniérisme *m*; particularité *f*; **'man·ner·li·ness** courtoisie *f*, politesse *f*; **'man·ner·ly** courtois, poli.   [masse (*femme*).]

man·nish ['mænɪʃ] d'homme; hom-⌉ **ma·nœu·vra·ble,** *Am. a.* **ma·neu·ver·a·ble** [mə'nu:vrəbl] manœuvrable, maniable; **ma'nœu·vre,** *Am. a.* **ma'neu·ver** [~və] **1.** manœuvre *f* (*a. fig.*); *fig.* ~s *pl.* F intrigues *f/pl.*; **2.** (faire) manœuvrer.

man-of-war ['mænəv'wɔ:] vaisseau *m* de guerre *ou* de ligne.

ma·nom·e·ter ⊕, *phys.* [mə-'nɔmɪtə] manomètre *m*.

man·or ['mænə] seigneurie *f*; *see* ~-**house**; *lord of the* ~ seigneur *m*; châtelain *m*; **'~-house** château *m* seigneurial; manoir *m*; **ma·no·ri·al** [mə'nɔ:riəl] seigneurial (-aux *m/pl.*); de seigneur.

man-pow·er ['mænpauə] ⊕ force *f* des bras; main-d'œuvre (*pl.* mains-d'œuvre) *f*; ✕ effectifs *m/pl.*

manse *écoss.* [mæns] presbytère *m*.

man-serv·ant ['mænsə:vənt] domestique *m*, valet *m*.

man·sion ['mænʃn] château *m*; hôtel *m* particulier (*en ville*); ~s *pl.* maison *f* de rapport.

man·slaugh·ter ['mænslɔ:tə] homicide *m* par imprudence.

man·tel ['mæntl] manteau *m* de cheminée; ~**piece,** ~**shelf** dessus *m* de cheminée; F cheminée *f*.

man·tel·et ['mæntlit] mantelet *m*; ✕ pare-balles *m/inv.*

man·til·la [mæn'tilə] mantille *f*.

man·tle ['mæntl] **1.** manteau *m* (*a.* △, *anat.*, *zo.*); △ parement *m* (*d'un mur*); *fig.* voile *m*, manteau *m*; (*a. incandescent* ~) manchon *m*; **2.** *v/t.* vêtir d'un manteau; *fig.* couvrir; revêtir; ~ *on* recouvrir; *v/i.* rougir (*joues*); se couvrir (de, with).

mant·let ['mæntlit] *see* mantelet.

man·trap ['mæntræp] piège *m* à hommes *ou* à loups.

man·u·al ['mænjuəl] **1.** □ manuel

(-le *f*); fait à la main; ✕ ~ *exercise* maniement *m* des armes; *sign* ~ seing *m*; **2.** manuel *m*; aide-mémoire *m/inv.*; *orgue:* clavier *m*; *instruction* ~ manuel *m* d'entretion.

man·u·fac·to·ry [mænju'fæktəri] fabrique *f*, usine *f*.

man·u·fac·ture [mænju'fæktʃə] **1.** fabrication *f*; confection *f*; *p.ext.* industrie *f*; **2.** fabriquer; confectionner; ~d *article* produit *m* industriel; ~d *goods pl.* produits *m/pl.* fabriqués; **man·u'fac·tur·er** fabricant *m*; industriel *m*; **man·u'fac·tur·ing** manufacturier (-ère *f*); industriel(le *f*).

ma·nure [mə'njuə] **1.** engrais *m*; **2.** fumer, engraisser.

man·u·script ['mænjuskript] **1.** manuscrit *m*; **2.** manuscrit, écrit à la main.

Manx [mæŋks] **1.** manxois, mannois; **2.** *ling.* mannois *m*; Mannois(e *f*) *m*; *the Manx pl.* les Mannois *m/pl.*

man·y ['meni] **1.** beaucoup de; bien des; plusieurs; ~ *a* maint(e *f*); bien des; ~ *a one* bien des gens; *one too* ~ un(e) de trop; **2.** beaucoup (de gens); un grand nombre; *a good* ~ pas mal de; un assez grand nombre (de gens); *a great* ~ un grand nombre (*de personnes*); **'~-'sid·ed** *fig.* complexe, divers.

map [mæp] **1.** *géog.* carte *f*; *ville:* plan *m*; F *off the* ~ ne plus de saison; *on the* ~ d'actualité; **2.** dresser une carte *etc.* (de qch., s.th.); ~ *out* dresser.

ma·ple ♀ ['meipl] érable *m*.

map·per ['mæpə] cartographe *m*.

mar [mɑ:] gâter; déparer; troubler (*la joie*); ruiner.

mar·a·bou *orn.* ['mærəbu:] marabout *m*.

Mar·a·thon ['mærəθən] *sp.* (*a.* ~ *race*) marathon *m*.

ma·raud [mə'rɔ:d] marauder; **ma'raud·er** maraudeur *m*.

mar·ble ['mɑ:bl] **1.** marbre *m*; *jeu:* bille *f*; **2.** de marbre; *fig.* dur; **3.** marbrer.

March¹ [mɑ:tʃ] mars *m*.

march² [~] **1.** marche *f* (*a.* ♪, *événements*); *civilisation, événements:* progrès *m*; ✕ ~ *past* défilé *m*; **2.** *v/i.* marcher; *fig.* avancer; faire des progrès; *v/t.* faire marcher; ✕ ~ *off* *v/t.* emmener (*un prisonnier*); *v/i.* se mettre en marche; ~ *past* défiler.

march³ [~] **1.** *hist.* marche *f; usu.* ~es *pl.* pays *m* limitrophe; **2.** confiner (à, *with*).

march·ing ['mɑːtʃiŋ] **1.** marche *f;* ~ *order* tenue *f* de route; ~ *orders pl.* feuille *f* de route; *fig.* congé *m; in heavy* ~ *order* en tenue de campagne; **2.** ~ *past* défilé *m.*

mar·chion·ess ['mɑːʃənis] marquise *f.*

march·pane ['mɑːtʃpein] massepain *m.*

mare [mɛə] jument *f; fig.* ~'s *nest* canard *m,* découverte *f* illusoire.

mar·ga·rine [mɑːdʒə'riːn] margarine *f.*

mar·gin ['mɑːdʒin] marge *f; bois:* lisière *f; rivière:* rive *f;* écart *m;* ~ *of error* tolérance *f;* ~ *of profit* bénéfice *m,* marge *f; safety* ~, ~ *of safety* marge *f* de sécurité; **'mar·gin·al** □ marginal (-aux *m/pl.*); en marge.

mar·grave ['mɑːgreiv] margrave *m;* **mar·gra·vine** ['~grəviːn] margrave *f,* margravine *f.*

Ma·ri·a [mə'raiə]: F *Black* ~ panier *m* à salade (= *voiture cellulaire*).

mar·i·gold ♀ ['mærigould] souci *m.*

mar·i·jua·na [mɑːri'hwɑːnə] marihuana *f.*

ma·ri·nade [mæri'neid] **1.** marinade *f;* **2.** mariner.

ma·rine [mə'riːn] **1.** marin; de mer; de (la) marine; **2.** soldat *m* de l'infanterie de marine; marine *f* (*a. peint.*); *tell that to the* ~s! allez conter ça ailleurs!; **mar·i·ner** *usu.* ⚓ ['mærinə] marin *m.*

mar·i·o·nette [mæriə'net] marionnette *f.*

mar·i·tal □ [mə'raitl] marital (-aux *m/pl.*); matrimonial (-aux *m/pl.*); ~ *status* état *m* familial.

mar·i·time ['mæritaim] maritime; naval (-als *m/pl.*); ~ *affairs pl.* affaires *f/pl.* maritimes.

mar·jo·ram ♀ ['mɑːdʒərəm] origan *m,* marjolaine *f.*

mark¹ [mɑːk] *monnaie:* mark *m.*

mark² [~] **1.** marque *f;* but *m;* signe *m; école:* note *f; école:* point *m* (*a. ponctuation*); *sp.* ligne *f* de départ; croix *f* (*au lieu de signature*); ✝ cote *f* (*d'une valeur*); marque *f* (*d'un produit*); *vét.* marque *f; a man*

of ~ un homme *m* marquant; *fig. up to the* ~ à la hauteur; dans son assiette (*santé*); *hit the* ~ frapper juste; *make one's* ~ se faire une réputation; *miss the* ~ manquer le but; *we are not far from the* ~ *in saying that* nous ne sommes pas loin de compte en disant que; **2.** *v/t.* (*a.* ~ *out*) tracer; estampiller (*des marchandises*); marquer ([*les points de*] *un jeu*); ✝ marquer; chiffrer; mettre le prix à; piquer (*les cartes*); coter (*un devoir*); indiquer; témoigner (*son approbation etc.*); guetter; observer; ~ *down* baisser de prix; repérer (*le gibier, un point*); ~ *off* séparer; mesurer (*une distance*); ~ *out* délimiter, tracer; borner (*un champ*); jalonner; ✕ ~ *time* marquer le pas; **marked** [mɑːkt], **mark·ed·ly** *adv.* ['mɑːkidli] marqué; *fig.* sensible; accusé (*accent*); **'mark·er** *billard:* marqueur *m;* pointeur *m.*

mar·ket ['mɑːkit] **1.** marché *m;* place *f* du marché; halle *f,* -s *f/pl.;* débouché *m* (pour, *for*); *Bourse:* cours *m/pl.; be in the* ~ être au marché; être acheteur; *come into the* ~ être mis en vente; *condition of the* ~ le marché; ~ *gardener* maraîcher (-ère *f*) *m; Am. sl. play the* ~ spéculer (*à la Bourse*); **2.** *v/t.* lancer (*qch.*) sur le marché; trouver des débouchés pour (*qch.*); *v/i.* faire son marché *ou* ses emplettes; **'mar·ket·a·ble** □ vendable; marchand (*valeur etc.*); **mar·ket·eer** [~'tiə] *see black 1;* **'mar·ket·ing** achat *m ou* vente *f* au marché; **'mar·ket·val·ue** valeur *f* marchande; cours *m.*

mark·ing ['mɑːkiŋ] marquage *m; usu.* -s *pl.* marque *f,* tache *f;* rayure *f;* '~-**ink** encre *f* à marquer.

marks·man ['mɑːksmən] bon tireur *m;* **'marks·man·ship** adresse *f* au tir.

marl [mɑːl] **1.** *géol.* caillasse *f;* ✍ marne *f;* **2.** ✍ marner.

mar·ma·lade ['mɑːməleid] confiture *f* d'oranges.

mar·mo·re·al □ *poét.* [mɑː'mɔːriəl] marmoréen(ne *f*).

mar·mot *zo.* ['mɑːmət] marmotte *f.*

ma·roon¹ [mə'ruːn] marron pourpré *inv.;* châtain.

ma·roon² [~] **1.** nègre *m* marron, négresse *f* marronne; **2.** abandonner (*q.*) sur une île déserte.

mar·plot ['mɑ:plɔt] brouille-tout *m/inv.*   [quise *f.*]

mar·quee [mɑ:'ki:] (tente-)mar-

mar·quess ['mɑ:kwis], *usu.* **mar·quis** ['mɑ:kwis] marquis *m.*

mar·que·try ['mɑ:kitri] marqueterie *f.*

mar·riage ['mærɪdʒ] mariage *m*; *fig.* union *f*; *civil* ~ mariage *m* civil; *by* ~ par alliance; *related by* ~ allié de près; *take in* ~ épouser (*q.*); prendre (*q.*)en mariage; ~*-guidance* guidance *f* de mariage; ~ *counsellor* raccommodeur *m* de ménages; **'mar·riage·a·ble** nubile; à marier; d'âge à se marier; ~ *person* parti *m.*

mar·riage...: **'~-lines** *pl.* acte *m* de mariage; **'~-'mar·ket**: *in the* ~ mariable; **'~-'por·tion** dot *f* (*de la femme*).

mar·ried ['mærid] marié (*personne*); conjugal (-aux *m/pl.*) (*vie*); ~ *couple* ménage *m.*

mar·row ['mærou] moelle *f* (*a. fig.*); *fig.* essence *f*; ♀ *vegetable* ~ courge *f* à la moelle; **'~-bone** os *m* à moelle; ~*s pl. co.* genoux *m/pl.*; **'mar·row·y** plein de moelle (*a. fig.*).

mar·ry ['mæri] *v/t.* marier (*q.* à *q.*, *s.o. to s.o.*); se marier avec, épouser (*q.*); *v/i.* se marier (*à*, *to*).

marsh [mɑ:ʃ] **1.** marais *m*, marécage *m*; **2.** des marais, ~*-fever* paludisme *m*, fièvre *f* paludéenne; ~ *gas* gaz *m* des marais.

mar·shal ['mɑ:ʃəl] **1.** maréchal *m*; ✠ général *m*; maître *m* des cérémonies; *Am.* chef *m* de (la) police (*d'un comté*); **2.** placer en ordre; ranger (*les troupes*); 🚂 classer, trier (*des wagons*); **'mar·shal·ship** maréchalat *m.*

marsh·i·ness ['mɑ:ʃinis] état *m* marécageux (*du terrain*); **marsh mal·low** ♀ guimauve *f*, althée *f*; bonbon *m* à la guimauve; **marsh mar·i·gold** souci *m* d'eau; **'marsh·y** marécageux (-euse *f*).

mar·su·pi·al *zo.* [mɑ:'sju:piəl] marsupial (-aux *m/pl.*) (*a. su./m*).

mart [mɑ:t] marché *m*; salle *f* de vente; centre *m* de commerce.

mar·ten *zo.* ['mɑ:tin] mart(r)e *f.*

mar·tial □ ['mɑ:ʃəl] martial (-aux *m/pl.*); guerrier (-ère *f*); ~ *law* loi *f* martiale; *state of* ~ *law* état *m* de siège; ~ *music* musique *f* militaire.

mar·tin¹ *zo.* ['mɑ:tin] martinet *m.*

Mar·tin² [~]: *St.* ~*'s summer* été *m* de la Saint-Martin.

mar·ti·net [mɑ:ti'net] F exploiteur *m*; F gendarme *m*; garde-chiourme (*pl.* gardes-chiourme) *m.*

Mar·tin·mas ['mɑ:tinməs] la Saint-Martin *f* (*le 11 novembre*).

mar·tyr ['mɑ:tə] **1.** martyr(e *f*) *m*; **2.** martyriser; **'mar·tyr·dom** martyre *m*; **'mar·tyr·ize** martyriser.

mar·vel ['mɑ:vəl] **1.** merveille *f*; **2.** ~ *at* s'émerveiller de; s'étonner de. **mar·vel·(l)ous** □ ['mɑ:viləs] merveilleux (-euse *f*), étonnant; **'mar·vel·(l)ous·ness** merveilleux *m.*

Marx·ism ['mɑ:ksizm] marxisme *m*; **Marx·ist** marxiste (*adj., fm*).

mas·cot ['mæskət] mascotte *f*; porte-bonheur *m/inv.*

mas·cu·line ['mɑ:skjulin] **1.** □ masculin; mâle; **2.** *gramm.* masculin *m.*

mash [mæʃ] **1.** mélange *m*; pâte *f*; *brassage*: fardeau *m*; 🐎 *chevaux*: mâche *f*; *chiens, volaille*: pâtée *f*; **2.** écraser; brasser; démêler (*le moût*); F faire infuser (*le thé*); ~*ed potatoes pl.* purée *f* (de pommes de terre); *sl. be* ~*ed on* avoir un béguin pour (*q.*); **'mash·er** broyeur *m*; *pommes de terre*: presse-purée *m/inv.*; *sl.* dandy *m*; gommeux *m*; **'mash(·ing)-tub** cuve-matière (*pl.* cuves-matière) *f*; 🐎 barbotière *f.*

mask [mɑ:sk] **1.** masque *m*; *renard*: face *f*; *see* masque; **2.** masquer; *fig.* cacher, déguiser; **masked** masqué; caché; ~ *ball* bal *m* masqué; **'mask·er** *personne*: masque *m.*

ma·son ['meisn] maçon *m*; franc-maçon (*pl.* francs-maçons) *m*; **ma·son·ic** [mə'sɔnik] des francs-maçons; **'ma·son·ry** maçonnerie *f.*

masque [mɑ:sk] † masque *m*; **mas·quer·ade** [mæskə'reid] **1.** mascarade *f*; bal *m* masqué; F déguisement *m*; **2.** *fig.* se déguiser (en, *as*).

mass¹ *eccl.* [mæs] messe *f*; *High* ⚭ grand-messe *f*; *Low* ⚭ messe *f* basse.

mass² [~] **1.** masse *f*, amas *m*; ~ *meeting* réunion *f* en masse; ~ *production* fabrication *f* en série; **2.** (se) masser.   [*m*; **2.** massacrer.]

mas·sa·cre ['mæsəkə] **1.** massacre]

mas·sage ['mæsɑ:ʒ] **1.** massage *m*; **2.** masser (*le corps*); malaxer (*les muscles*).

mas·seur [mæ'sə:] masseur *m*; **masseuse** [~'sə:z] masseuse *f.*

mas·sive □ ['mæsiv] massif (-ive f); énorme; solide; 'mas·sive·ness massiveté f; aspect m massif.

mass...: ~ **me·di·a** pl. media m/pl.; ~ **psy·chol·o·gy** psychologie f des foules; ~ **so·ci·e·ty** société f de masse.

mas·sy ['mæsi] massif (-ive f); solide; lourd.

mast¹ ⚓ [mɑːst] **1.** mât m; radio: pylône m; **2.** mâter.

mast² [~] faines f/pl.; glands m/pl.

mas·ter¹ ['mɑːstə] **1.** maître m (a. art, propriété, navire de commerce, a. peint., a. fig.); patron m (d'employés, d'un navire de commerce); école: instituteur m; lycée: professeur m; univ. (di)recteur m; titre: monsieur m; ♀ of Arts maître m ès arts, agrégé m des lettres; ♀ of Ceremonies maître m des cérémonies; ~ copy original m; be one's own ~ ne dépendre que de soi; **2.** maître m; de maître; fig. magistral (-aux m/pl.), supérieur, dominant; **3.** dompter, maîtriser; régir (une maison etc.).

mas·ter² ⚓ [~] à mât(s); three-~ trois-mâts m/inv.

mas·ter-at-arms ⚓ ['mɑːstərət-'ɑːmz] capitaine m d'armes; 'mas·ter-'build·er entrepreneur m de bâtiments; **mas·ter·ful** □ ['~ful] impérieux (-euse f); autoritaire; 'mas·ter-key passe-partout m/inv.; 'mas·ter·less sans maître; indiscipliné; 'mas·ter·li·ness domination f, autorité f; caractère m magistral; 'mas·ter·ly magistral (-aux m/pl.), de maître; '~mind **1.** fig. cerveau m (d'une entreprise etc.); **2.** organiser, diriger.

mas·ter...: '~piece chef-d'œuvre (pl. chefs-d'œuvre) m; '~ship maîtrise f (de over, of); autorité f (sur, over); poste m de professeur ou de maître; '~stroke coup m de maître; 'mas·ter·y maîtrise f (de over, of); domination f (sur over, of); dessus m; connaissance f approfondie (d'une langue etc.).

mas·tic ['mæstik] mastic m; ♀ lentisque m.

mas·ti·cate ['mæstikeit] mastiquer; **mas·ti·ca·tion** mastication f; **mas·ti·ca·to·ry** ['~təri] masticateur (-trice f).

mas·tiff ['mæstif] mâtin m; dogue m anglais.

mat¹ [mæt] **1.** paille: natte f; laine etc.: tapis m; **2.** (s')emmêler (cheveux); v/t. natter.

mat² ⊕ [~] mat; mati.

mat³ ⊕ sl. [~] matrice f.

match¹ [mætʃ] allumette f; min. canette f; mèche f.

match² [~] **1.** égal(e f) m, pareil(le f) m; couleurs: assortiment m; mariage m, alliance f; sp. partie f, match (pl. matchs, matches) m; personne: parti m; be a ~ for pouvoir le disputer à (q.); meet one's ~ trouver à qui parler; trouver son homme; **2.** v/t. égaler (q.); rivaliser avec (q.); assortir (des couleurs); apparier (des gants); unir (q.) (à, with); sp. matcher (des adversaires); ⊕ bouveter (des planches); ~ s.o. against opposer q. à (q.); well ~ed bien assorti; v/i. s'assortir, s'harmoniser; ~ with aller avec; to ~ à l'avenant; assorti.

match-box ['mætʃbɔks] boîte f à ou d'allumettes.

match·less □ ['mætʃlis] incomparable; sans pareil; 'match-mak·er marieur (-euse f) m.

match·wood ['mætʃwud] bois m d'allumettes; fig. miettes f/pl.

mate¹ [meit] faire échec et mat (échecs); mater.

mate² [~] **1.** camarade mf; compagnon m, compagne f; oiseau: mâle m, femelle f; personne: époux m, épouse f; école: condisciple m, camarade mf; ⚓ second maître m; marine marchande: officier m; **2.** (s')accoupler; (s')unir (personne); 'mate·less seul, sans compagnon.

ma·te·ri·al □ [mə'tiəriəl] **1.** matériel(le f); grossier (-ère f); essentiel(le f) (pour, to); pertinent (fait); sensible (service); **2.** matière f; étoffe f, tissu m; matériaux m/pl. (a. fig.); ✗ matériel m; ~s pl. fournitures f/pl.; working ~ matière f première de base; writing ~s pl. de quoi écrire; **ma'te·ri·al·ism** matérialisme m; **ma'te·ri·al·ist** matérialiste mf; **ma·te·ri·al·is·tic** (~ally) matérialiste; matériel(le f) (plaisirs); **ma·te·ri·al·i·ty** [~ri'æliti] matérialité f; ⅍ pertinence f; **ma·te·ri·al·i·za·tion** [~riəlai'zeiʃn] matérialisation f; projet etc.: aboutissement m; **ma'te·ri·al·ize** (se) matérialiser; v/i. F se réaliser; aboutir (projet etc.).

ma·ter·nal □ [mə'təːnl] maternel

(-le *f*); de mère; d'une mère; **ma-'ter·ni·ty** [ˌ.niti] maternité *f*; (*a.* ~ *hospital*) maternité *f*; ~ *benefit* allocation *f* de maternité; ~ *dress* robe *f* pour futures mamans; ~ *ward* salle *f* des accouchées.

math·e·mat·i·cal □ [mæθi'mætikl] mathématique; **math·e·ma·ti·cian** [ˌmə'tiʃn] mathématicien(ne *f*) *m*; **math·e·mat·ics** [ˌ'mætiks] *usu. sg.* mathématiques *f/pl.*

mat·in ['mætin] **1.** *poét.* matinal (-aux *m/pl.*), de grand matin; **2.** *eccl.* ~s *pl.* matines *f/pl.*; *poét. a.* ~s *pl.* chant *m* des oiseaux au point du jour.

mat·i·née ['mætinei] matinée *f*.

mat·ing *biol.* ['meitiŋ] accouplement *m*; ~ *season* saison *f* des amours.

ma·tri·cide ['meitrisaid] matricide *m*; *personne*: matricide *mf*.

ma·tric·u·late [mə'trikjuleit] *v/t.* immatriculer; *v/i.* prendre ses inscriptions; **ma·tric·u·la·tion** inscription *f*.

mat·ri·mo·ni·al □ [mætri'mounjəl] matrimonial (-aux *m/pl.*); conjugal (-aux *m/pl.*); **mat·ri·mo·ny** ['mætriməni] mariage *m*; vie *f* conjugale.

ma·trix ['meitriks] *anat., géol.* matrice *f*; ⊕ (*a.* ['mætriks]) matrice *f*, moule *m*.

ma·tron ['meitrən] matrone *f*; mère *f* de famille; *institution*: intendante *f*; *hôpital*: infirmière *f* en chef; **'ma·tron·ly** matronal (-aux *m/pl.*); de matrone; domestique; *fig.* brave; **ma·tron-of-hon·o(u)r** dame *f* d'honneur.

mat·ter ['mætə] **1.** matière *f*; substance *f*; sujet *m*; chose *f*, affaire *f*; ⚕ matière *f* purulente; *typ.* copie *f*; *printed* ~ imprimés *m/pl.*; *in the* ~ *of* quant à; *what's the* ~? qu'est-ce qu'il y a?; *what's the* ~ *with you?* qu'est-ce que vous avez?; *no* ~ n'importe; cela ne fait rien; *no* ~ *who* qui que ce soit; *as a* ~ *of course* comme de raison; *for that* ~ quant à cela; *d'ailleurs;* ~ *of fact* question *f* de(s) fait(s); *as a* ~ *of fact* en effet; à vrai dire; ~ *in hand* chose *f* en question; **2.** avoir de l'importance; importer (à, *to*); *it does not* ~ n'importe; cela ne fait rien; **'~-of-'course** de raison, naturel(le *f*); **'~-of-'fact** pratique; prosaïque.

mat·ting ['mætiŋ] natte *f*, -s *f/pl.*; paillassons *m/pl.*

mat·tock ['mætək] hoyau *m*; pioche *f*.

mat·tress ['mætris] matelas *m*.

ma·ture [mə'tjuə] **1.** □ mûr; d'âge mûr; ✝ échu (*traite etc.*); **2.** mûrir; affiner (*vin, fromage*); ✝ échoir; **ma·tu·ri·ty** maturité *f*; ✝ échéance *f*.

ma·tu·ti·nal □ [mætju'tainl] matu-(tu)tinal (-aux *m/pl.*); du matin.

maud·lin □ ['mɔ:dlin] larmoyant, pleurard (*souv. état d'ivresse*).

maul [mɔ:l] meurtrir, malmener; *usu.* ~ *about* tirer de ci de là.

maul·stick ['mɔ:lstik] *see* mahlstick.

maun·der ['mɔ:ndə] radoter, divaguer; flâner; se trimbaler.

Maun·dy Thurs·day ['mɔ:ndi-'θə:zdi] jeudi *m* saint.

mau·so·le·um [mɔ:sə'li:əm] mausolée *m*.

mauve [mouv] **1.** mauve *m*; **2.** mauve.

mav·er·ick *Am.* ['mævərik] bouvillon *m* errant sans marque de propriétaire; *pol.* indépendant(e *f*) *m*.

maw [mɔ:] caillette *f* (*de ruminant*); jabot *m* (*d'oiseau*); gueule *f* (*de lion*); *co.* panse *f*.

mawk·ish □ ['mɔ:kiʃ] insipide; sentimental (-aux *m/pl.*); **'mawk·ish·ness** fadeur *f*; fausse sentimentalité *f*.

maw·worm ['mɔ:wə:m] ver *m* intestinal, ascaride *m*.

max·il·lar·y [mæk'siləri] maxillaire.

max·im ['mæksim] maxime *f*, dicton *m*; **'max·i·mal** □ ['ˌ.əl] maximal; **'max·i·mize** ['ˌ.aiz] maxim(al)iser, porter (*qch.*) ou maximum; **max·i·mum** ['ˌ.əm] **1.** *pl. usu.* -ma [ˌ.mə] maximum (*pl. a.* -ma) *m*; **2.** maximum; limite; ~ *wages* salaire *m* maximum.

May¹ [mei] **1.** mai *m*; ♀ ♣ aubépine *f*; **2.** *go* ♀*ing* fêter le premier mai.

may² [ˌ] [*irr.*] *v/aux.* (*défectif*) je peux *etc.*; il se peut que.

may·be ['meibi:] peut-être.

May·day ['meidei] le premier mai; ♀ mayday *m*, S.O.S. *m*.

may·hem ['meihem] *Am.* ⚖ mutilation *f*; F chaos *m*, tohu-bohu *m*, grabuge *m*.

may·or [mɛə] maire *m*; **'may·or·al** de maire, du maire; **'may·or·al·ty** mairie *f*; (temps *m* d')exercice *m* des fonctions de maire; **'may·or·ess** femme *f* du maire; mairesse *f*.

may·pole ['meipoul] mai *m*.

maze [meiz] **1.** labyrinthe *m*, dédale *m*; *fig.* enchevêtrement *m*; *be in a* ~ ne savoir où donner de la tête; **2.** embarasser, désorienter; *be* ~d être désorienté; **'ma·zy** labyrinthique; sinueux (-euse *f*); *fig.* compliqué.

Mc Coy *Am. sl.* [mə'kɔi]: *the real* ~ authentique. [moi.\
me [mi:; mi] *accusatif:* me; *datif:*∫

mead[1] [mi:d] hydromel *m*.

mead[2] [~] *poét. see* meadow.

mead·ow ['medou] pré *m*, prairie *f*; **'~-'saf·fron** ♀ safran *m* des prés; **'mead·ow·y** de prairie; herbu; herbeux (-euse *f*).

mea·ger, mea·gre □ ['mi:gə] maigre (*a. fig.*); peu copieux (-euse *f*); *fig.* pauvre; **'mea·ger·ness, 'mea·gre·ness** maigreur *f*; pauvreté *f*.

meal[1] [mi:l] repas *m*; ~s *pl.* on wheels repas *m/pl.* livrés à domicile.

meal[2] [~] farine *f* d'avoine, d'orge etc.; **meal·ies** ['~iz] *usu. pl.* maïs *m*.

meal-time ['mi:ltaim] heure *f* du repas.

meal·y ['mi:li] farineux (-euse *f*); **~-mouthed** doucereux (-euse *f*), patelin.

mean[1] □ [mi:n] misérable; mesquin, bas(se *f*), méprisable; méchant; avare; pauvre.

mean[2] [~] **1.** moyen(ne *f*); *in the* ~ *time see* ~time; **2.** milieu *m*; moyen terme *m*; ⅋ moyenne *f*; ~s *pl.* moyens *m/pl.*, ressources *f/pl.*; ~s *sg.* voie *f*, moyen *m*, -s *m/pl.* (*de faire qch.*); *a* ~s of (*gér.*) *ou* to (*inf.*) un moyen (*de inf.*); *by all* (*manner of*) ~s par tous les moyens; mais certainement!; *by no* (*manner of*) ~s en aucune façon; *by this* ~s *sg.* par ce moyen; ainsi; *by* ~s *of* au moyen de.

mean[3] [~] [*irr.*] avoir l'intention (de *inf.*, to *inf.*); se proposer (de *inf.*, to *inf.*); vouloir; vouloir dire; entendre (par, *by*); destiner (pour, *for*); ~ *well* (*ill*) vouloir du bien (mal) (à, *by*).

me·an·der [mi'ændə] **1.** méandre *m*, repli *m*; sinuosité *f*; **2.** serpenter.

mean·ing ['mi:niŋ] **1.** □ significatif (-ive *f*); d'intelligence (*sourire*); *well-*~ bien intentionné; **2.** sens *m*, acception *f*; *astr.* signification *f*; **'mean·ing·less** dénué de sens; qui ne signifie rien.

mean·ness ['mi:nnis] médiocrité *f*, pauvreté *f*; bassesse *f*; avarice *f*; *see* mean[1].

meant [ment] *prét. et p.p. de* mean[3].

mean·time ['mi:ntaim], **mean·while** ['min:wail] en attendant, dans l'intervalle.

mea·sle F ['mi:zl] être atteint de rougeole; **'mea·sled** *vét.* ladre; **'mea·sles** *pl.* ᵍ rougeole *f*; *vét.* ladrerie *f*; *German* ⚥ rubéole *f*; **'mea·sly** rougeoleux (-euse *f*); *vét.* ladre; *sl.* misérable.

meas·ur·a·ble □ ['meʒərəbl] me(n)-surable.

meas·ure ['meʒə] **1.** mesure *f* (*a.* ♪, *a. fig.*); *fig.* limite *f*; ~ *of capacity* mesure *f* de capacité; *beyond* ~ outre mesure; *in some* ~ jusqu'à un certain point; *in a great* ~ en grande partie; *made to* ~ fait sur mesure; *take s.o.'s* ~ prendre les mesures de q.; *fig.* prendre la mesure de q. **2.** mesurer (pour, *for*); métrer (*un mur*); faire l'arpentage de (*un terrain*); *Am.* ~ *up to s.th.* se montrer à la hauteur de qch.; **'measure·less** □ infini, illimité; **'measure·ment** mesurage *m*; mesure *f*; tour *m* (*de tête, de hanches*); ⚓ tonnage *m*.

meas·ur·ing ['meʒəriŋ] de mesure; d'arpentage.

meat [mi:t] viande *f*; †, *prov.* nourriture *f*; *fig.* moelle *f*; *butcher's* ~ grosse viande *f*; *cold* ~ rôti *m* froid; *fresh-killed* ~ viande *f* fraîche; *preserved* ~ viande *f* de conserve; *green* ~ fourrages *m/pl.* verts; *roast* ~ viande *f* rôtie; rôti *m*; ~ *tea* thé *m* de viande; bouillon *m*; **'~-ball** boulette *f* de viande; **'~-fly** mouche *f* à viande; **'~-head** *Am. sl.* idiot(e *f*) *m*; **'~-safe** garde-manger *m/inv.*; **'meat·y** charnu; *fig.* étoffé.

mec·ca·no [me'kɑ:nou] jeu *m* mécanique (*pour enfants*).

me·chan·ic [mi'kænik] artisan *m*, ouvrier *m*; ⊕ mécanicien *m*; **me-'chan·i·cal** □ mécanique; *fig.* machinal (-aux *m/pl.*), automatique; ~ *engineering* construction *f* mécanique; **me'chan·i·cal·ness** caractère *m* machinal; **mech·a·ni·cian** [mekə-'niʃn] mécanicien *m*; **me·chan·ics** [mi'kæniks] *usu. sg.* mécanique *f*.

mech·a·nism ['mekənizm] mécanisme *m*; *biol., pol.* machinisme *m*;

mech·a·nize [ˈ‿naiz] mécaniser (a. ✕); ✕ motoriser.

med·al [ˈmedl] médaille f; décoration f; ˈmed·al(l)ed medaillé; décoré; **me·dal·lion** [miˈdæljən] médaillon m; **med·al·(l)ist** [ˈmedlist] médailliste mf; graveur: médailleur m; médaillé(e f) m.

med·dle [ˈmedl] (with, in) se mêler (de); s'immiscer (dans); toucher (à); ˈmed·dler officieux (-euse f) m; intrigant(e f) m; touche-à-tout m/inv.; **med·dle·some** [ˈ‿səm] □ officieux (-euse f), intrigant; qui touche à tout; ˈmed·dle·some·ness tendance f à se mêler des affaires d'autrui.

me·di·a [ˈmiːdjə] pl. les media m/pl.

me·di·ae·val [mediˈiːvəl] see medieval.

me·di·al □ [ˈmiːdjəl], ˈme·di·an 1. médial (-als, -aux m/pl.); médian; 2. médiale f; médiane f.

me·di·an strip Am. mot. [ˈmiːdjən-ˈstrip] bande f médiane.

me·di·ate 1. □ [ˈmiːdiit] intermédiaire; 2. [ˈ‿eit] s'interposer; agir en médiateur; **me·di·a·tion** médiation f; **me·di·a·tor** [ˈ‿tə] médiateur (-trice f) m (a. école); **me·di·a·to·ri·al** □ [‿əˈtɔːriəl], **me·di·a·to·ry** [ˈ‿təri] médiateur (-trice f); **me·di·a·trix** [ˈ‿eitriks] médiatrice f.

med·ic F [ˈmedik] étudiant: carabin m; médecin: toubib m.

Med·ic·aid Am. [ˈmedikeid] assistance f médicale aux économiquement faibles.

med·i·cal □ [ˈmedikəl] médical (-aux m/pl.); de médecine; ~ board conseil m de santé; ~ certificate attestation f de médicin; ~ evidence témoignage m des médecins; ~ jurisprudence médecine f légale; ~ man médecin m; ~ officer médecin m militaire; ~ specialist spécialiste mf; ~ student étudiant m en médecine; ♀ Superintendent médecin m en chef; **me·dic·a·ment** médicament m.

Med·i·care Am. [ˈmedikɛə] assistance f médicale aux personnes agées.

med·i·cate [ˈmedikeit] médicamenter; traiter; rendre médicamenteux (du vin); **med·i·ca·tion** médication f; emploi m de medicaments; **med·i·ca·tive** [ˈmedikətiv] médicateur (-trice f).

me·dic·i·nal □ [meˈdisinl] médicinal (-aux m/pl.) (bains etc.); médicamenteux (-euse f) (vin etc.); **med·i·cine** [ˈmedsin] art, profession, médicament: médecine f; médicament m, remède m; F drogue f; ~-chest (coffret m de) pharmacie f.

me·di·e·val □ [mediˈiːvəl] médiéval (-aux m/pl.); du Moyen Âge; **me·di·ˈe·val·ism** médiévisme m; culture f médiévale; **me·di·ˈe·val·ist** médiéviste mf.

me·di·o·cre [ˈmiːdioukə] médiocre; **me·di·oc·ri·ty** [‿ˈɔkriti] médiocrité f.

med·i·tate [ˈmediteit] v/i. méditer (sur, [up]on); se recueillir; v/t. méditer (qch.; de faire qch., doing s.th.); projeter; avoir l'intention (de faire qch., doing s.th.); **med·i·ta·tion** méditation f; recueillement m; (profondes) pensées f/pl.; **med·i·ta·tive** □ [ˈ‿tətiv] méditatif (-ive f).

me·di·um [ˈmiːdiəm] 1. pl. -di·a [‿djə], -di·ums milieu m; ambiance f (sociale); intermédiaire m; moyen m; phys. milieu m, véhicule m; ♠ agent m; biol. bouillon m; spiritisme: médium m; élément: milieu m; 2. moyen(ne f); radio: ~ wave onde f moyenne; ˈ‿-ˈsized de grandeur ou de taille moyenne.

med·lar ♀ [ˈmedlə] nèfle f; arbre: néflier m.

med·ley [ˈmedli] mélange m; couleurs etc.: bigarrure f; péj. idées etc.: bariolage m; ♪ pot-pourri (pl. pots-pourris) m.

me·dul·la [meˈdʌlə] épinière: moelle f; **med·ul·lar·y** médullaire f.

meed poét. [miːd] récompense f.

meek □ [miːk] doux (douce f); humble; soumis; ˈmeek·ness humilité f; soumission f.

meer·schaum [ˈmiəʃəm] (pipe f en) écume f de mer.

meet[1] [miːt] † convenable; séant.

meet[2] [‿] 1. [irr.] v/t. rencontrer, aller à la rencontre de; faire la connaissance de; fréquenter; croiser (dans la rue); aller chercher (q. à la gare); se conformer à (des opinions); satisfaire à, répondre à (des désirs, des besoins); faire face à (des demandes, des besoins, la mort); trouver (la mort); faire honneur à (ses engagements); prévenir (une objection); subvenir à (des frais);

rivières: confluer avec; *fig.* ~ *s.o. half-way* faire la moitié des avances; *come* (*go, run*) *to* ~ *s.o.* venir (aller, courir) à la rencontre de q.; *they are well met* ils sont bien assortis; ils font la paire; *v/i.* se rencontrer; se voir; se réunir (*société, gens*); se joindre; confluer (*rivières*); ~ *with* rencontrer, éprouver (*des difficultés*); essuyer (*un refus*); faire (*des pertes*); trouver (*un accueil*); être victime de (*un accident*); *make both ends* ~ joindre les deux bouts, arriver à boucler son budget; **2.** *sp.* réunion *f*; assemblée *f* de chasseurs.

meet·ing ['miːtiŋ] rencontre *f*; réunion *f*; assemblée *f*; *rivières:* confluent *m*; *pol., sp.* meeting *m*; '~-**place** rendez-vous *m*; lieu *m* de réunion.

meg·a·fog ['megəfɔg] très fort signal *m* de brume; **meg·a·lo·ma·ni·a** ['~lou'meinjə] 🌢 mégalomanie *f*; **meg·a·lop·o·lis** [~'lɔpəlis] conurbation *f*; **meg·a·phone** [~'foun] portevoix *m/inv.*; *sp.* mégaphone *m*; **meg·a·ton** ['~tʌn] mégatonne *f*.

me·grim ['miːgrim] migraine *f*; ~*s pl.* vapeurs *f/pl.*; spleen *m*.

mel·an·chol·ic [melən'kɔlik] mélancolique; **mel·an·chol·y** ['~kəli] **1.** mélancolie *f*; tristesse *f*; **2.** mélancolique; triste.

mê·lée ['melei] mêlée *f*; bagarre *f*.

mel·io·rate ['miːljəreit] (s')améliorer.

mel·lif·lu·ent [me'lifluənt], *usu.* **mel·lif·lu·ous** mielleux (-euse *f*); melliflu (*éloquence*).

mel·low ['melou] **1.** ☐ mûr (*a. esprit, caractère*); moelleux (-euse *f*); doux (douce *f*) (*ton, lumière, vin*); velouté (*vin*); *fig.* doux (douce *f*), tendre (*couleur*); débonnaire (*personne*); *sl.* un peu gris *ou* ivre; **2.** (faire) mûrir; (s')adoucir (*personne*); *v/i.* prendre de la patine; '**mel·low·ness** *fruit, sol:* maturité *f*; *vin, voix:* moelleux *m*; *caractère:* douceur *f*.

me·lo·di·ous ☐ [mi'loudjəs] mélodieux (-euse *f*), harmonieux (-euse *f*); **me·lo·di·ous·ness** mélodie *f*; **mel·o·dist** ['melədist] mélodiste *mf*; '**mel·o·dize** rendre mélodieux (-euse *f*); mettre en musique; *v/i.* chanter; faire des mélo-

dies; **mel·o·dra·ma** ['~drɑːmə] mélodrame *m*; '**mel·o·dy** mélodie *f*, chant *m*, air *m*.

mel·on ♀ ['melən] melon *m*; *water-*~ melon *m* d'eau; pastèque *f*.

melt [melt] fondre; *fig.* (se) dissoudre; *v/t.* attendrir (*le cœur*); *v/i.:* ~ *away* fondre complètement; *fig.* se dissiper; ~ *down* fondre; ~ *into tears* fondre en larmes.

melt·ing ☐ ['meltiŋ] fondant; *fig.* attendri (*voix*); '~-**point** point *m* de fusion; '~-**pot** creuset *m*; *be in the* ~ tout remettre en question.

mem·ber ['membə] membre *m* (*a. gramm.*); organe *m*; ⊕ pièce *f*; député *m*; membre *m* de la Chambre des Communes; *make s.o. a* ~ élire q. membre (de, *of*); '**mem·ber·ship** qualité *f* de membre; nombre *m* des membres; ~ *card* carte *f* de membre; ~ *fee* cotisation *f*.

mem·brane ['membrein] membrane *f*; enveloppe *f* (*d'un organe*); **mem'bra·nous, mem'bra·ne·ous** [~jəs] membraneux (-euse *f*).

me·men·to [mi'mentou] souvenir *m*, mémento *m*.

mem·oir ['memwɑː] mémoire *m*; notice *f* biographique; ~*s pl.* mémoires *m/pl.*; mémorial *m*; autobiographie *f*.

mem·o·ra·ble ☐ ['memərəbl] mémorable.

mem·o·ran·dum [memə'rændəm] mémorandum *m* (*a. pol.*); acte *m* (*de société*); *pol.* note *f* (*diplomatique*).

me·mo·ri·al [mi'mɔːriəl] **1.** mémoratif (-ive *f*); commémoratif (-ive *f*) (*monument*); *Am.* ♀ *Day* jour *m* des morts au champ d'honneur; **2.** monument *m* (*commémoratif*); pétition *f*; **me'mo·ri·al·ist** pétitionnaire *mf*; auteur *m* de mémoires; **me'mo·ri·al·ize** commémorer; pétitionner.

mem·o·rize ['meməraiz] apprendre par cœur.

mem·o·ry ['meməri] mémoire *f* (*a. ordinateur*); souvenir *m*; *commit to* ~ apprendre par cœur; se mettre dans la mémoire; *beyond the* ~ *of man* de temps immémorial; *within the* ~ *of man* de mémoire d'homme; *in* ~ *of* à la mémoire de; en souvenir de.

men [men] (*pl. de man*) hommes *m/pl.*; l'homme *m*, le genre *m* humain, l'humanité *f*; *sp.* ~'s doubles *pl.* double *m* messieurs.

men·ace ['menəs] **1.** menacer; **2.** *poét.* menace *f*.

me·nag·er·ie [mi'nædʒəri] ménagerie *f*.

mend [mend] **1.** *v/t.* raccommoder (*un vêtement*); réparer (*un outil, une machine*); rectifier, corriger; hâter (*le pas*); ~ the fire arranger le feu; ~ one's ways changer de conduite, se corriger; *v/i.* se corriger; s'améliorer; **2.** raccommodage *m*; amélioration *f*; on the ~ en voie de guérison, en train de se remettre.

men·da·cious □ [men'deiʃəs] menteur (-euse *f*), mensonger (-ère *f*); **men·dac·i·ty** [~'dæsiti] penchant *m* au mensonge; fausseté *f*.

mend·er ['mendə] raccommodeur (-euse *f*) *m*; *invisible* ~ stoppeur (-euse *f*) *m*.

men·di·can·cy ['mendikənsi] mendicité *f*; **men·di·cant** mendiant (*a. su./m*); **men'dic·i·ty** [~siti] mendicité *f*.

men·folk F ['menfouk] hommes *m/pl.* (*de la famille*).

men·hir ['menhiə] menhir *m*.

me·ni·al *usu. péj.* ['mi:njəl] **1.** □ servile, bas(se *f*); **2.** domestique *mf*; laquais *m*.

men·in·gi·tis 𝔤 [menin'dʒaitis] méningite *f*.

men·o·pause ['menoupɔ:z] ménopause *f*.

men·ses ['mensi:z] *pl.* menstrues *f/pl.*, époques *f/pl.*; *see* menstruation; **men·stru·al** ['~struəl] menstruel(le *f*); **men·stru·ate** ['~strueit] avoir ses règles; **men·stru'a·tion** menstruation *f*; règles *f/pl.*, époques *f/pl.*

men·su·ra·tion [mensjuə'reiʃn] mesurage *m*; 𝔸 mensuration *f*.

men·tal □ ['mentl] mental (-aux *m/pl.*); de l'esprit; ~ *arithmetic* calcul *m* de tête; ~ *home* (*ou hospital ou institution*) hôpital *m ou* clinique *f* psychiatrique; maison *f* de santé; ~*ly ill* aliéné; **men·tal·i·ty** [~'tæliti] mentalité *f*; esprit *m*.

men·thol *pharm.* ['menθɔl] menthol *m*.

men·tion ['menʃn] **1.** mention *f*; allusion *f*; **2.** mentionner, faire allusion à, citer; *don't* ~ *it!* je vous en prie!; il n'y a pas de quoi!; *not to* ~ sans parler de; sans compter;

men·tion·a·ble ['menʃn·a·ble] digne de mention; dont on peut parler.

men·tor ['mentɔ:] mentor *m*, guide *m*.

men·u ['menju:] menu *m*; carte *f*.

me·phit·ic [me'fitik] méphitique; **me·phi·tis** [~'faitis] méphitisme *m*.

mer·can·tile ['mə:kəntail] mercantile, marchand; commercial (-aux *m/pl.*), de commerce; commerçant.

mer·ce·nar·y ['mə:sinəri] **1.** □ mercenaire, intéressé; **2.** ✕ mercenaire *m*.

mer·cer ['mə:sə] marchand(e *f*) *m* de soieries; † mercier (-ère *f*) *m*; **mer·cer·ize** mercerimer; **mer·cer·y** (commerce *m* des) soieries *f/pl.*; † mercerie *f*.

mer·chan·dise ['mə:tʃəndaiz] **1.** marchandise *f*, -s *f/pl.*; **2.** *Am.* commercer.

mer·chant ['mə:tʃənt] **1.** négociant *m*; commerçant *m*; *Am.* marchand(e *f*) *m*; boutiquier (-ère *f*) *m*; **2.** marchand; de *ou* du commerce; ~ *bank* banque *f* de commerce; *law* ~ droit *m* commercial; *Am.* ~ *marine, Brit.* ~ *navy* marine *f* marchande; **mer·chant·a·ble** vendable; négociable; **mer·chant·man** navire *m* marchand *ou* de commerce.

mer·ci·ful □ ['mə:siful] miséricordieux (-euse *f*) (pour, to); clément (envers, to); **mer·ci·ful·ness** miséricorde *f*; clémence *f*; pitié *f*.

mer·ci·less □ ['mə:silis] impitoyable, sans pitié; **mer·ci·less·ness** caractère *m* impitoyable; manque *m* de pitié.

mer·cu·ri·al [mə:'kjuəriəl] *astr.* de Mercure; 🜍 mercuriel(le *f*); *fig.* vif (vive *f*); inconstant, changeant.

Mer·cu·ry ['mə:kjuri] *astr.* Mercure; *fig.* messager *m*; 🜍 ♀ mercure *m*.

mer·cy ['mə:si] miséricorde *f*; clémence *f*; pitié *f*; be at s.o.'s ~ être à la merci de q.; *at the* ~ *of the waves* au gré des flots; *it is a* ~ *that* c'est un bonheur que; *for* ~'s *sake* par pitié; *poét., co.* have ~ (up)on avoir pitié de; ~ *killing* euthanasie *f*.

mere □ [miə] simple, seul, pur; ~(st) *nonsense* extravagance *f* pure et simple; ~ *words* vaines paroles *f/pl.*; rien que des mots; ~*ly* simplement; tout bonnement.

mer·e·tri·cious □ [meri'triʃəs] de courtisane; *fig.* factice; d'un éclat criard.

merge [mə:dʒ] (*in*) *v/t.* fondre (dans); amalgamer (avec); *v/i.* se fondre, se perdre (dans); s'amalgamer; *mot.* s'enfiler; **'merg·er** fusion *f*.

me·rid·i·an [mə'ridiən] **1.** méridien(ne *f*); *fig.* culminant, le plus haut; **2.** *géog.* méridien *m*; *fig.* point *m* culminant, apogée *m*; **me'rid·i·o·nal** □ [~iənl] méridional(-aux *m/pl.*); du midi.

me·ringue [mə'ræŋ] meringue *f*.

mer·it ['merit] **1.** mérite *m*; valeur *f*; *usu.* ⚖ ~s *pl.* bien-fondé *m*; le pour et le contre (*de qch.*); *on the* ~s *of the case* (*juger qch.*) au fond; *on its* (*own*) ~s selon ses mérites; *make a* ~ *of* se faire un mérite de; **2.** *fig.* mériter; **mer·i·to·ri·ous** □ [~'tɔːriəs] méritoire; méritant (*personne*).

mer·maid ['mə:meid] sirène *f*.

mer·ri·ment ['merimənt] gaieté *f*, réjouissance *f*.

mer·ry □ ['meri] joyeux (-euse *f*), gai; jovial (~als, -aux *m/pl.*); *make* ~ se réjouir; se divertir; ~ **an·drew** paillasse *m*, bouffon *m*; **'~-go-round** carrousel *m*; chevaux *m/pl.* de bois; **'~-mak·ing** réjouissances *f/pl.*, fête *f*; **'~-thought** lunette *f* (*d'une volaille*).

mes·en·ter·y *anat.* ['mesəntəri] mésentère *m*.

mesh [meʃ] **1.** maille *f*; *fig. usu.* ~es *pl.* réseau *m*; ⊕ *be in* ~ être en prise (avec, *with*); **2.** *fig.* (s')engrener; **meshed** [~t] à ... mailles; **'mesh-work** réseau *m*; treillis *m*.

mes·mer·ism ['mezmərizm] mesmérisme *m*, hypnotisme *m*; **'mesmer·ize** hypnotiser; magnétiser.

mess¹ [mes] **1.** désordre *m*; gâchis *m*, fouillis *m*; saleté *f*; F *a fine* ~ *of things* du joli, une belle équipée, un chef-d'œuvre; F *look a* ~ être dans un état épouvantable; *make a* ~ *of* gâcher, bousiller; **2.** *v/t. a.* ~ *up* gâcher, galvauder, abîmer; salir; *v/i.* F ~ *about* patauger (*dans la boue*); gaspiller son temps.

mess² [~] **1.** † plat *m*, mets *m*; ✕, ⚓ *officiers:* mess *m*, table *f*; ✕ *hommes:* ordinaire *m*, ⚓ plat *m*; **2.** manger à la même table.

mes·sage ['mesidʒ] message *m*;

commission *f*; F *get the* ~ comprendre, F piger; *give s.o. the* ~ faire la commission à q.; *take a* ~ faire la commission.

mes·sen·ger ['mesindʒə] messager (-ère *f*) *m*; ~ *boy hôtel:* chasseur *m*, *télégraphes:* facteur *m*.

Mes·si·ah [mi'saiə] Messie *m*.

Mes·sieurs, *usu.* **Messrs.** ['mesəz] ✝ Messieurs *m/pl.*; maison *f*.

mess-room ['mesrum] ✕ salle *f* de mess; ⚓ carré *m* (des officiers); **'mess-tin** ✕ gamelle *f*, ⚓ quart *m*.

mess-up F ['mesʌp] gâchis *m*; pagaille; embrouillement *m*, embrouillamini *m*; malentendu *m*; **mess·y** ['mesi] embrouillé, en désordre; sale, malpropre.

met [met] *prét. et p.p. de meet²* 1.

met·a·bol·ic [metə'bɔlik] métabolique; **me·tab·o·lism** *physiol.* [me-'tæbəlizm] métabolisme *m*.

met·age ['mi:tidʒ] mesurage *m*.

met·al ['metl] **1.** métal *m*; ⊕ empierrement *m*; *route:* cailloutis *m*, pierraille *f*; ⛁ F ~s *pl.* rails *m/pl.*; **2.** empierrer, caillouter; **me·tal·lic** [mi'tælik] (~ally) métallique; métallin; de métal; **met·al·lif·er·ous** [metə'lifərəs] métallifère; **met·al·line** ['metəlain] métallin; **'met·allize** métalliser; vulcaniser (*le caoutchouc*); **met·al·log·ra·phy** [~'lɔgrəfi] métallographie *f*; **met·al·lur·gic**, **met·al·lur·gi·cal** □ [~'lə:dʒik(l)] métallurgique; **'met·al·lur·gy** métallurgie *f*.

met·a·mor·phose [metə'mɔ:fouz] métamorphoser, transformer (en, [*in*]*to*); **met·a·mor·pho·sis** [~fə-sis], *pl.* -ses [~si:z] métamorphose *f*.

met·a·phor ['metəfə] métaphore *f*; image *f*; **met·a·phor·ic**, *usu.* **met·a·phor·i·cal** □ [~'fɔrik(l)] métaphorique.

met·a·phys·ic [metə'fizik] **1.** (*usu.* **met·a·phys·i·cal** □) métaphysique; **2.** ~s *souv. sg.* métaphysique *f*; ontologie *f*.

mete [mi:t] *litt.* mesurer; (*usu.* ~ *out*) assigner; décerner, distribuer.

me·te·or ['mi:tiə] météore *m* (*a. fig.*); **me·te·or·ic** [mi:ti'ɔrik] météorique; *fig.* rapide; **me·te·or·ite** ['mi:tjərait] météorite *mf*; aérolithe *m*; **me·te·or·o·log·i·cal** □ [mi:-tjərə'lɔdʒikl] météorologique, aérologique; **me·te·or·ol·o·gist** [~'rɔlədʒist] météorologiste *mf*, -logue *mf*; **me·te·or·ol·o·gy** météorologie *f*, aérologie *f*.

me·ter ['mi:tə] (*a. gas* ~) compteur *m*; jaugeur *m*; '~**maid** *Am*. F contractuelle *f*.

me·thinks [mi'θiŋks] (*prét. me·thought*) il me semble.

meth·od ['meθəd] méthode *f*; système *m*; manière *f*; procédé *m* (pour *for*, *of*); **me·thod·ic**, **me·thod·i·cal** □ [mi'θɔdik(l)] méthodique; **Meth·od·ism** *eccl*. ['meθədizm] méthodisme *m*; '**meth·od·ist** *péj*. qui a le souci exagéré de la méthode; *eccl*. ♀ méthodiste *mf*; '**meth·od·ize** ordonner, régler.

meth·yl ⚗ ['meθil] méthyle *m*; **meth·yl·at·ed spir·it** ['meθileitid 'spirit] alcool *m* à brûler.

me·tic·u·lous □ [mi'tikjuləs] méticuleux (-euse *f*).

me·tre ['mi:tə] mètre *m*, mesure *f*; mètre *m* (*39,37 inches*).

met·ric ['metrik] (~*ally*) métrique; '**met·ri·cal** □ métrique; en vers; '**met·rics** *sg*. métrique *f*.

me·trop·o·lis [mi'trɔpəlis] métropole *f*; **me·tro·pol·i·tan** [metrə'pɔlitən] 1. métropolitain; ♀ *Railway* chemin *m* de fer métropolitain; 2. métropolitain *m*, archevêque *m*.

met·tle ['metl] *personne*: ardeur *f*, courage *m*, feu *m*; tempérament *m*, caractère *m*; *cheval*: fougue *f*; *be on one's* ~ se piquer d'honneur; *faire de son mieux*; *put s.o. on his* ~ piquer q. d'honneur; stimuler le zèle de q.; *horse of* ~ cheval *m* fougueux; '**met·tled**, **met·tle·some** ['~səm] fougueux (-euse *f*) (*cheval*); ardent (*personne*).

mew[1] *poét*. [mju:] mouette *f*.

mew[2] [~] 1. miaulement *m*; 2. miauler.

mew[3] [~] 1. mue *f*, cage *f* (*pour les faucons*); 2. *v/i*. se cloîtrer; *v/t*. (*usu.* ~ *up*) renfermer.   [miauler.⟩

mewl [mju:l] vagir, piailler; F⟩

mews [mju:z] *sg*., † *pl*. écuries *f/pl*.; *Londres*: impasse *f*, ruelle *f*.

Mex·i·can ['meksikən] 1. mexicain; 2. Mexicain(e *f*) *m*.

mi·aow [mi'au] 1. miaulement *m*, miaou *m*; 2. miauler.

mi·as·ma [mi'æzmə], *pl*. -**ma·ta** [~mətə], -**mas** miasme *m*; **mi·as·mal** □ miasmatique.

mi·aul [mi'ɔ:l] miauler.

mi·ca *min*. ['maikə] mica *m*; **mi·ca·ce·ous** [~'keiʃəs] micacé.

mice [mais] *pl. de* mouse 1.

Mich·ael·mas ['miklməs] la Saint-Michel *f* (*le 29 septembre*).

mick·ey *sl*. ['miki] (*a.* ~ *finn*) boisson *f* droguée; *take the* ~ *out of s.o.* se payer la tête de q.

micro... [maikro] micro-.

mi·crobe ['maikroub] microbe *m*; **mi·cro·bi·al** [~iəl] microbien(ne *f*).

mi·cro·cosm ['maikrəkɔzəm] microcosme *m*; **mi·crom·e·ter** [mai'krɔmitə] micromètre *m*; **mi·cro·phone** ['maikrəfoun] microphone *m*; F micro *m*; **mi·cro·proc·es·sor** ['~prə'sesə] microprocesseur *m*, chip *m*; **mi·cro·scope** ['~skoup] microscope *m*; **mi·cro·scop·ic**, **mi·cro·scop·i·cal** □ [~s'kɔpik(l)] microscopique; *au microscope* (*examen*); F minuscule, très petit; **mi·cro·wave** ⚡ ['maikrəweiv] micro-onde *f*.

mid [mid] *see middle* 2; *mi-*; *poét. see amid*; ~'**air**: *in* ~ entre ciel et terre; '~**course**: *in* ~ en pleine carrière; '~**day**: 1. midi *m*; 2. de midi, méridien(ne *f*).

mid·den ['midn] (*tas m de*) fumier *m*.

mid·dle ['midl] 1. milieu *m*, centre *m*; *fig*. taille *f*, ceinture *f*; ✝ ~*s pl*. qualité *f* moyenne; 2. ordinaire; bon(ne *f*); du milieu, central (-aux *m/pl*.); moyen(ne *f*), intermédiaire; ♀ *Ages pl.* Moyen Âge *m*; ~ *class(es pl.)* classe *f* moyenne; bourgeoisie *f*; '~'**aged** F entre deux âges; '~'**class** bourgeois; '~**man** F entremetteur *m*; ✝ intermédiaire *m*; '~**most** central (-aux *m/pl*.); le plus au milieu; '~**sized** de grandeur *ou* taille moyenne; '~**weight** *box*. poids *m* moyen.

mid·dling ['midliŋ] 1. *adj*. médiocre; passable, assez bon(ne *f*); moyen(ne *f*); ✝ de qualité moyenne; 2. *adv*. (*a.* ~*ly*) passablement, assez bien; 3. *su*. ✝ ~*s pl*. marchandises *f/pl*. de qualité moyenne.

mid·dy F ['midi] *see midshipman*.

midge [midʒ] moucheron *m*; **midg·et** ['~it] nain(e *f*) *m*; nabot(e *f*) *m*.

mid·land ['midlənd] 1. entouré de terre; intérieur (*mer*); 2. *the* ♀*s pl*.

les Midlands *m/pl.*; '**mid·most** central (-aux *m/pl.*); le plus près du milieu; '**mid·night 1.** minuit *m*; **2.** de minuit; **mid·riff** ['ⁿrif] diaphragme *m*; '**mid·ship·man** ⚓ aspirant *m*; *Am.* enseigne *m*; '**mid·ships** ⚓ par le travers; **midst** [midst] **1.** *su.* milieu *m*; *in the ~ of* au milieu de; parmi; *in our ~* au milieu de nous, parmi nous; **2.** *prp. poét. see amidst;* '**mid·sum·mer** milieu *m* de l'été; solstice *m* d'été; ♀ *Day* la Saint-Jean *f*; ~ *holidays pl.* vacances *f/pl.* d'été; '**mid·way 1.** *su. Am.* allée *f* centrale (*d'une exposition*); **2.** *adj.* du milieu, central (-aux *m/pl.*), intermédiaire; **3.** *adv.* à mi-chemin; '**mid·wife** sage-femme (*pl.* sages-femmes) *f*; **mid·wife·ry** ['midwifri] obstétrique *f*; '**mid-win·ter** milieu *m* de l'hiver; solstice *m* d'hiver.

mien *poét.* [mi:n] mine *f*, air *m*.

miff F [mif] boutade *f*; accès *m* d'humeur.

might [mait] **1.** puissance *f*, force *f*, -s *f/pl.*; *with ~ and main* de toutes mes (*etc.*) forces; **2.** *prét. de* may²; **might·i·ness** ['ⁿinis] puissance *f*, force *f*, grandeur *f*; '**might·y** (☐ †) **1.** *adj.* puissant, fort; vaste; F considérable; **2.** F *adv.* très, extrêmement.

mi·grant ['maigrənt] **1.** *see migratory;* **2.** (*ou ~ bird*) migrateur (-trice *f*) *m*.

mi·grate [mai'greit] émigrer; passer; **mi'gra·tion** migration *f*, émigration *f*; **mi·gra·to·ry** ['ⁿgrətəri] migrateur (-trice *f*) (*personne, a. oiseau*); nomade (*personne*); de passage (*oiseau*).

mike *sl.* [maik] microphone *m*, F micro *m*.

Mil·an·ese [milə'ni:z] **1.** milanais; **2.** Milanais(e *f*) *m*.

milch [miltʃ] à lait, laitière (*vache*).

mild ☐ [maild] doux (douce *f*); tempéré (*climat*); peu sévère; peu rigoureux (-euse *f*); bénin (-igne *f*); *to put it ~ly* pour m'exprimer avec modération.

mil·dew ['mildju:] **1.** *pain etc.:* chancissure *f*; *froment etc.:* rouille *f*; *vignes etc.:* mildiou *m*; moisissure *f*; **2.** chancir (*le pain*); rouiller, moisir (*la plante etc.*); piquer (*le papier etc.*).

mild·ness ['maildnis] douceur *f*; *maladie:* bénignité *f*.

mile [mail] mille *m* (anglais) (*1609,33 m*).

mil(e)·age ['mailidʒ] distance *f ou* vitesse *f* en milles; *fig.* parcours *m*.

mile·stone ['mailstoun] borne *f* milliaire *ou* kilométrique.

mil·foil ⚹ ['milfɔil] mille-feuille *f*.

mil·i·tan·cy ['militənsi] esprit *m* militant; *pol.* activisme *m*; '**mil·i·tant** ☐ militant; activiste; **mil·i·tar·i·ness** ['militərinis] caractère *m* militaire; **mil·i·ta·rism** ['ⁿrizəm] militarisme *m*; '**mil·i·tar·y 1.** ☐ militaire; de guerre; de soldat; ~ *college* école *f* militaire; ♀ *Government* gouvernement *m* militaire; ~ *map* carte *f* d'état-major; ~ *service* service *m* militaire; *of ~ age* en âge de servir; **2.** *les militaires m/pl.*; l'armée *f*; **mil·i·tate** ['ⁿteit]: ~ *in favo(u)r of* (*against*) militer en faveur de (contre); **mi·li·tia** [mi'liʃə] milice *f*; garde *f* nationale.

milk [milk] **1.** lait *m*; *powdered* (*whole*) ~ lait *m* en poudre (non écrémé); *Brit.* ~ *float* voiture *f* de laitier; ~ *tooth* dent *f* de lait; **2.** traire; *fig.* dépouiller; *⚡, a. tél.* capter; '**milk-and-'wa·ter** F insipide, fade; '**milk·er** *personne:* trayeur (-euse *f*) *m*; *vache:* laitière *f*; *machine:* trayeuse *f*; **milk·i·ness** ['ⁿinis] lactescence *f*; couleur *f* laiteuse; *fig.* douceur *f*.

milk...: '~**maid** laitière *f*, crémière *f*; trayeuse *f*; '~**man** laitier *m*, crémier *m*; '~'**shake** shake *m* (*mélange de lait, crème glacée et sirop battus ensemble*); '~**sop** F poule *f* mouillée; peureux (-euse *f*) *m*; '**milk·y** laiteux (-euse *f*) *m*, lactescent; *fig.* blanchâtre; *astr.* ♀ *Way* Voie *f* lactée.

mill¹ [mil] **1.** moulin *m*; usine *f*; fabrique *f*; filature *f*; *sl.* combat *m* à coups de poings; **2.** *v/t.* moudre; ⊕ fraiser; créneler (*la monnaie*); fouler (*un drap*); mousser (*une crème*); broyer (*le minerai*); *sl.* rouer de coups; F *v/i.* fourmiller.

mill² *Am.* [ⁿ] millième *m* (*de dollar*).

mill·board ['milbɔ:d] carton-pâte (*pl.* cartons-pâtes) *m*; carton *m* épais; '**mill-dam** barrage *m* de moulin.

mil·le·nar·i·an [mili'nɛəriən], **mil-**

len·ni·al [mi'leniəl] millénaire; **mil·le·nar·y** ['⁓əri] millénaire (*a. su./m*); **mil'len·ni·um** [⁓iəm] *eccl.* millénium *m*; mille ans *m/pl.*

mil·le·pede *zo.* ['milipi:d] mille-pieds *m/inv.*; mille-pattes *m/inv.*

mill·er ['milə] meunier *m*; ⊕ fraiseur *m*; *machine:* fraiseuse *f.*

mil·les·i·mal [mi'lesiməl] millième (*a. su./mf*).

mil·let ♀ ['milit] millet *m.*

mill-hand ['milhænd] ouvrier (-ère *f*) *m* d'usine.

mil·li·ard ['miljɑ:d] milliard *m.*

mil·li·gram ['miligræm] milligramme *m.*

mil·li·me·tre ['milimi:tə] millimètre *m.*

mil·li·ner ['milinə] modiste *f*; **'mil·li·ner·y** (articles *m/pl.* de) modes *f/pl.*

mill·ing ['miliŋ] meunerie *f*; moulage *m*; broyage *m*; foulage *m*; ⊕ ⁓ *cutter* fraise *f*, fraiseuse *f*; ⁓ *plant* moulin *m*; laminerie *f*; ⁓ *machine* machine (*f* à fraiser; ⁓ *product* produit *m* de moulin.

mil·lion ['miljən] million *m*; **mil·lion·aire** [⁓'nɛə] millionnaire *mf*; **mil·lionth** ['miljənθ] millionième (*a. su./m*).

mill...: '⁓**·pond** réservoir *m* de moulin; '⁓**·race** bief *m* de moulin; '⁓**·stone** meule *f*; F *see through a* ⁓ voir à travers les murs; '⁓**·wright** constructeur *m* de moulins.

milt¹ [milt] laitance *f* (*des poissons*).

milt² [⁓] rate *f.*   [laité.\

milt·er *icht.* ['miltə] poisson *m*

mime [maim] 1. mime *m*; 2. mimer.

mim·e·o·graph ['mimiəgrɑ:f] 1. autocopiste *m*, machine *f* à polycopier; 2. polycopier.

mim·ic ['mimik] 1. mimique; imitateur (-trice *f*); 2. mime *m*; imitateur (-trice *f*) *m*; 3. imiter; contrefaire; F singer (*q.*); **'mim·ic·ry** mimique *f*, imitation *f*; *zo.* mimétisme *m.*

min·a·to·ry ['minətəri] menaçant.

mince [mins] 1. *v/t.* hacher; *he does not* ⁓ *matters* il ne mâche pas ses mots; ⁓ *one's words* minauder, parler du bout des lèvres; ⁓*d meat* hachis *m*; *v/i.* marcher *etc.* d'un air affecté; 2. hachis *m*; '⁓**·meat** compôte *f* de raisins secs, de pommes, d'amandes *etc.*; *make* ⁓ *of* F rédu-

ire (*q.*) en chair à pâté; ⁓ **pie** petite tarte *f* au *mincemeat*; **'minc·er** hachoir *m.*

minc·ing □ ['minsiŋ] affecté, minaudier (-ère *f*); '⁓**·ma·chine** hachoir *m.*

mind [maind] 1. esprit *m*, âme *f*; pensée *f*, idée *f*, avis *m*; mémoire *f*, souvenir *m*; raison *f*; *to my* ⁓ à mon avis, selon moi, à ce que je pense; ⁓*'s eye* idée *f*, imagination *f*; *out of one's* ⁓ hors de son bon sens; insensé; *time out of* ⁓ de temps immémorial; *change one's* ⁓ changer d'avis; se raviser; *bear s.th. in* ⁓ se rappeler qch.; tenir compte de qch.; F *blow s.o.'s* ⁓ bouleverser q., renverser q.; *have (half) a* ⁓ *to* avoir (bonne) envie de; *have s.th. on one's* ⁓ avoir qch. sur sa conscience; *have in* ⁓ avoir (*qch.*) en vue; (*not*) *know one's own* ⁓ (ne pas) savoir ce qu'on veut; *make up one's* ⁓ se décider, prendre son parti; *put s.o. in* ⁓ *of* rappeler (*qch. ou q.*) à q.; 2. faire attention à; s'occuper de; ne pas manquer de (*inf.*); prendre garde à (*qch.*); soigner (*un enfant*), garder (*un chien etc.*); ⁓! attention!; *never* ⁓! n'importe!; ne vous inquiétez pas!; ⁓ *the step!* attention à la marche!; *I don't* ⁓ (*it*) cela m'est égal; peu (m')importe; *do you* ⁓ *smoking?* la fumée ne vous gêne pas?; *would you* ⁓ *taking off your hat?* voudriez-vous bien ôter votre chapeau?; ⁓ *your own business!* mêlez-vous de ce qui vous regarde!; '⁓**·bend·ing** F halluzinant; '⁓**·blow·ing** F renversant, bouleversant; halluzinant; '⁓**·bog·gling** F inimaginable, inconcevable; **'mind·ed** disposé, enclin; à l'esprit...; sensibilisé à *ou* sur ...; **'mind·er** surveillant(e *f*) *m*; gardeur (-euse *f*) *m* (*d'animaux*); **'mind·ful** □ (*of*) attentif (-ive*f*) (à); soigneux (-euse *f*) (de); **'mind·ful·ness** attention *f* (à, *of*); soin *m* (de, *of*); **'mind·less** □ sans esprit; insouciant (de, *of*); indifférent (à, *of*); oublieux (-euse *f*) (de, *of*); **'mind-read·er** liseur (-euse *f*) *m* de pensées.

mine¹ [main] 1. le mien, la mienne, les miens, les miennes; à moi; 2. les miens *m/pl.*

mine² [⁓] ⚒, *a.* ⚔ mine *f*; *fig.* trésor *m*, bureau *m*; 2. *v/i.* fouiller (sous) la terre; *v/t.* miner, saper; ⚒ exploiter (le charbon); creuser; ⚒ miner, saper; ⚓ miner, semer des mines dans; '~·**lay·er** ⚓, ⚒ poseur m ou mouilleur m de mines; '**min·er** mineur m (a. ⚒).

min·er·al ['minərəl] **1.** minerai m; ~s pl. eaux f/pl. minérales; F boissons f/pl. gazeuses; **2.** minéral (-aux m/pl.); ~ **jelly** vaseline f; '**min·er·al·ize** minéraliser; **min·er·al·o·gist** [~'rælədʒist] minéralogiste m; **min·er·al·o·gy** minéralogie f.

mine·sweep·er ⚓ ['mainswi:pə] dragueur m de mines.

min·gle ['miŋgl] (se) mêler (avec, à with); ~ mélanger (avec, with).

min·i... [mini] mini-.

min·i·a·ture ['minjətʃə] **1.** miniature f; **2.** en miniature, en raccourci; petit modèle; minuscule; ~ **camera** appareil m de petit format; ~ **grand piano** m à queue écourtée; ~ **rifle shooting** tir m au fusil de petit calibre.

min·i·bus ['minibʌs] minibus m.

min·i·kin ['minikin] **1.** mignon(ne f); affecté; **2.** homuncule m.

min·im ['minim] ♪ blanche f; mesure: goutte f; F bout m d'homme; '**min·i·mize** réduire au minimum; fig. mettre au minimum l'importance de (qch.); **min·i·mum** ['~məm] **1.** pl. -**ma** [~mə] minimum (pl. -s, -ma) m; **2.** minimum (qqfois -ma f).

min·ing ['mainiŋ] **1.** minier (-ère f); de mine(s); ✝ de mine; ⚒, ⚓ de mouilleur de mines; **2.** exploitation f des mines, travaux m/pl. de mines; ⚒ sape f; ⚓ pose f de mines.

min·ion ['minjən] favori(te f) m; typ. mignonne f; F ~ **of the law** sbire m.

mini-skirt ['miniskə:t] mini-jupe f.

min·is·ter ['ministə] **1.** ministre m (a. pol., a. eccl.); eccl. pasteur m (protestant); **2.** v/t. ✝ fournir; v/i. ~ **to** soigner (q.); subvenir aux besoins de (q.); aider à (qch.); **min·is·te·ri·al** □ [~'tiəriəl] accessoire; pol. ministériel(le f); exécutif (-ive f); gouvernemental (-aux m/pl.); eccl. sacerdotal (-aux m/pl.); **min·is'te·ri·al·ist** ministériel m.

min·is·trant ['ministrənt] **1.** qui subvient à (q.); **2.** eccl. officiant m; **min·is'tra·tion** service m; ministère m; eccl. saint ministère m, sa-cerdoce m; '**min·is·try** ministère m; pol. a. gouvernement m.

min·i·ver ['minivə] petit-gris (pl. petits-gris) m (a. fourrure).

mink zo. [miŋk] vison m.

min·now icht. ['minou] vairon m.

mi·nor ['mainə] **1.** petit, mineur; peu important; d'importance secondaire; ♪ mineur; A ~ **la** m mineur; ~ **third** tierce f mineure; ~ **key** mineur m; **2.** mineur(e f) m; le plus jeune (de deux frères); phls. mineure f, petit terme m; Am. univ. sujet m (d'étude) secondaire; **mi·nor·i·ty** [mai'nɔriti] minorité f (a. ⚖); ~ **government** gouvernement m minoritaire.

min·ster ['minstə] cathédrale f; église f abbatiale.

min·strel ['minstrəl] ménestrel m; F musicien m; ~s pl. (troupe f de) chanteurs m/pl. déguisés en nègres; **min·strel·sy** ['~si] chants m/pl. ou art m des ménestrels.

mint[1] ♪ [mint] menthe f; ~ **sauce** vinaigrette f à la menthe.

mint[2] [~] **1.** Hôtel m de la Monnaie; source f; **a ~ of money** une somme f fabuleuse; **2.** (à l'état) neuf (neuve f) (volume etc.); fig. intrinsèque; **3.** monnayer; battre monnaie; '**mint·age** monnayage m; fabrication f; espèces f/pl. monnayées; empreinte f.

min·u·et ♪ [minju'et] menuet m.

mi·nus ['mainəs] **1.** prp. moins; F sans; **2.** adj. négatif (-ive f).

min·ute[1] ['minit] **1.** minute f; fig. moment m; instant m; projet m; note f; ~s pl. procès-verbal (pl. procès-verbaux) m; ~-**hand** grande aiguille f; **just a** ~! minute!; **2.** faire la minute de (un contrat); prendre note de; dresser le procès-verbal de.

mi·nute[2] □ [mai'nju:t] tout petit; minuscule; détaillé; ~**ly** dans ses moindres détails; **mi'nute·ness** petitesse f; exactitude f minutieuse.

mi·nu·ti·a [mai'nju:ʃiə], pl. -**ti·ae** [~ʃii:] petits détails m/pl.

minx [miŋks] friponne f, coquine f.

mir·a·cle ['mirəkl] miracle m; F prodige m; **to a** ~ à merveille; **mi·rac·u·lous** □ [mi'rækjuləs] miraculeux (-euse f); F merveilleux (-euse f); **mi'rac·u·lous·ness** miraculeux m.

mi·rage ['mira:ʒ] mirage m.

mire ['maiə] **1.** boue *f*, fange *f*; bourbier *m*; vase *f* (*de fleuve*); **2.** be ⌐d s'embourber; F s'avilir.

mir·ror ['mirə] **1.** miroir *m*, glace *f*; **2.** refléter (*a. fig.*).

mirth [mə:θ] gaieté *f*; hilarité *f*; **mirth·ful** □ ['⌐ful] gai, joyeux (-euse *f*); '**mirth·less** □ triste.

mir·y ['maiəri] bourbeux (-euse *f*), fangeux (-euse *f*); vaseux (-euse *f*).

mis... [mis] mé-, més-, mal-, mauvais ...; faux (fausse *f*).

mis·ad·ven·ture ['misəd'ventʃə] mésaventure *f*, contretemps *m*; ⚖ accident *m*.   [liance *f*.]

mis·al·li·ance [misə'laiəns] mésal-⌐

mis·an·thrope ['mizənθroup] misanthrope *m*; **mis·an·throp·ic**, **mis·an·throp·i·cal** □ [⌐'θrɔpik(l)] misanthrope (*personne*), misanthropique (*humeur*); **mis·an·thro·pist** [mi'zænθrəpist] misanthrope *m*; **mis'an·thro·py** misanthropie *f*.

mis·ap·pli·ca·tion ['misæpli'keiʃn] mauvaise application *f*; mauvais usage *m*; détournement *m* (*de fonds*); **mis·ap·ply** ['⌐ə'plai] mal appliquer; détourner (*des fonds*).

mis·ap·pre·hend ['misæpri'hend] mal comprendre; '**mis·ap·pre·'hen·sion** malentendu *m*, méprise *f*.

mis·ap·pro·pri·ate ['misə'prouprieit] détourner, distraire (*des fonds*); '**mis·ap·pro·pri·a·tion** détournement *m*, distraction *f* (*de fonds*).

mis·be·come ['misbi'kʌm] messeoir à (*q.*), mal convenir à (*q.*); '**mis·be'com·ing** malséant.

mis·be·got(·ten) ['misbi'gɔt(n)] illégitime, bâtard; F misérable.

mis·be·have ['misbi'heiv] se conduire mal; '**mis·be'hav·io(u)r** [⌐jə] mauvaise conduite *f*, inconduite *f*.

mis·be·lief ['misbi'li:f] fausse croyance *f*; opinion *f* erronée; **mis·be·lieve** ['⌐'li:v] être infidèle; '**mis·be'liev·er** infidèle *mf*.

mis·cal·cu·late ['mis'kælkjuleit] *v/t.* mal calculer; *v/i.* se tromper (sur, *about*); '**mis·cal·cu'la·tion** faux calcul *m*; mécompte *m*.

mis·car·riage [mis'kæridʒ] *lettre:* perte *f*; avortement *m*; ⚕ fausse couche *f*; ⌐ *of justice* erreur *f* judiciaire; **mis'car·ry** avorter; échouer; s'égarer (*lettre*); ⚕ faire une fausse couche.

mis·cel·la·ne·ous □ [misi'leinjəs] mélangé, varié, divers; **mis·cel·la·ne·ous·ness** variété *f*, diversité *f*.

mis·cel·la·ny [mi'seləni] mélange *m*; collection *f* d'objets variés; *miscellanies pl.* mélanges *m/pl.*

mis·chance [mis'tʃɑːns] malchance *f*; malheur *m*, accident *m*.

mis·chief ['mistʃif] mal *m*, dommage *m*, dégât *m*; F discorde *f*, trouble *m*; malice *f*; bêtises *f/pl.* (*d'un enfant*); *personne:* fripon(ne *f*) *m* what *etc.* the ⌐ ...? que *etc.* diantre ...?; '⌐**mak·er** brandon *m* de discorde.

mis·chie·vous □ ['mistʃivəs] méchant, espiègle, malin (-igne *f*) (*personne*); mauvais, nuisible; '**mis·chie·vous·ness** méchanceté *f*; espièglerie *f*, malice *f*; caractère *m* nuisible (*de qch.*).

mis·con·ceive ['miskən'siːv] mal concevoir; mal comprendre; **mis·con·cep·tion** ['⌐'sepʃn] idée *f* fausse; malentendu *m*.

mis·con·duct 1. ['mis'kɔndəkt] mauvaise conduite *f* (*d'une personne*); mauvaise gestion *f ou* administration *f* (*d'une affaire*); **2.** ['⌐kən'dʌkt] mal diriger *ou* gérer; ⌐ *o.s.* se conduire mal.

mis·con·struc·tion ['miskən'strʌkʃn] fausse interprétation *f*; **mis·con·strue** ['⌐'struː] mal interpréter.

mis·count ['mis'kaunt] **1.** mal compter; se tromper; **2.** faux calcul *m*; erreur *f* d'addition.

mis·cre·ant ['miskriənt] scélérat (*a. su./m*); misérable (*a. su./mf*).

mis·date ['mis'deit] **1.** erreur *f* de date; **2.** mal dater.

mis·deal ['mis'diːl] *cartes* **1.** [*irr.* (*deal*)] faire maldonne; **2.** maldonne *f*.

mis·deed ['mis'diːd] méfait *m*.

mis·de·mean·ant ⚖ ['misdi'miːnənt] délinquant(e *f*) *m*; **mis·de·mean·o(u)r** ⚖ [⌐nə] délit *m* correctionnel.

mis·di·rect ['misdi'rekt] mal diriger; mal adresser (*une lettre*); '**mis·di'rec·tion** renseignement *m* erronné; fausse adresse *f*.

mis·do·ing ['mis'duːiŋ] méfait *m*.

mis·doubt ['mis'daut] se douter de (*qch.*, *q.*); soupçonner.

mi·ser ['maizə] avare *mf*.

mis·er·a·ble □ ['mizərəbl] malheureux (-euse *f*); triste; misérable; déplorable; **'mis·er·a·ble·ness** état *m* malheureux *ou* misérable.

mi·ser·ly ['maizəli] avare; sordide.

mis·er·y ['mizəri] souffrance *f*; misère *f*, détresse *f*.

mis·fea·sance ⚖ ['mis'fi:zəns] infraction *f* à la loi; abus *m* d'autorité.

mis·fire ['mis'faiə] 1. *fusil*: raté *m*; *mot.* raté *m* d'allumage; 2. rater (*a. mot.*).

mis·fit ['mis'fit] vêtement *m ou* soulier *m* manqué; F inapte *mf*.

mis·for·tune [mis'fɔ:tʃn] malheur *m*, infortune *f*, calamité *f*.

mis·give [mis'giv] [*irr.* (*give*)] avoir des inquiétudes; *my heart misgave me* j'avais de mauvais pressentiments; **mis·giv·ing** pressentiment *m*, doute *m*, crainte *f*.

mis·gov·ern ['mis'gʌvən] mal gouverner; **'mis·gov·ern·ment** mauvais gouvernement *m*; mauvaise administration *f*.

mis·guide ['mis'gaid] mal guider *ou* conseiller.

mis·han·dle ['mis'hændl] malmener, maltraiter (*q.*); traiter mal (*un sujet*).

mis·hap ['mishæp] mésaventure *f*; *mot.* panne *f*.

mis·hear [mis'hiə] [*irr.* (*hear*)] mal entendre; mal comprendre.

mish·mash ['miʃmæʃ] fatras *m*.

mis·in·form ['misin'fɔ:m] mal renseigner; **'mis·in·for·ma·tion** faux renseignement *m*, -s *m/pl.*

mis·in·ter·pret ['misin'tə:prit] mal interpréter; mal comprendre; **'mis·in·ter·pre'ta·tion** fausse interprétation *f*.

mis·judge ['mis'dʒʌdʒ] mal juger; se tromper sur; **'mis'judg(e)·ment** jugement *m* erroné.

mis·lay [mis'lei] [*irr.* (*lay*)] égarer.

mis·lead [mis'li:d] [*irr.* (*lead*)] tromper, induire en erreur; fourvoyer.

mis·man·age ['mis'mænidʒ] mal administrer; mal conduire; **'mis·man·age·ment** mauvaise administration *f ou* gestion *f*.

mis·no·mer ['mis'noumə] faux nom *m*; erreur *f* de nom.

mi·sog·y·nist [mai'sɔdʒinist] misogyne *m*; **mi·sog·y·ny** misogynie *f*.

mis·place ['mis'pleis] déplacer (*qch.*); mal placer (*sa confiance*); **'mis'place·ment** déplacement *m*.

mis·print 1. [mis'print] imprimer incorrectement; 2. ['mis'print] faute *f* d'impression.

mis·pri·sion ⚖ [mis'priʒn] nonrévélation *f* (*d'un crime*); négligence *f* (coupable).

mis·pro·nounce ['mисprə'nauns] mal prononcer; **mis·pro·nun·ci·a·tion** ['ˌprənʌnsi'eiʃn] mauvaise prononciation *f*.

mis·quo·ta·tion ['miskwou'teiʃn] citation *f* inexacte; fausse citation *f*; **'mis'quote** citer inexactement.

mis·read ['mis'ri:d] [*irr.* (*read*)] mal lire *ou* interpréter.

mis·rep·re·sent ['misrepri'zent] mal représenter; dénaturer (*les faits*); **'mis·rep·re·sen'ta·tion** faux rapport *m*; ⚖ fausse déclaration *f*; ⚖ réticence *f*.

mis·rule ['mis'ru:l] 1. confusion *f*, désordre *m*; mauvaise administration *f*; 2. mal gouverner.

miss¹ [mis] mademoiselle (*pl.* mesdemoiselles) *f*; *co.* demoiselle *f*; adolescente *f*.

miss² [ˌ] 1. coup *m* manqué, perdu *ou* raté; 2. *v/t.* manquer; F rater (*le but, une occasion, le train*); ne pas trouver; ne pas saisir; se tromper de (*chemin*); ne pas avoir; sauter; remarquer *ou* regretter l'absence de; (*gér.*) faillir (*inf.*); ~ *one's footing* poser le pied à faux; ~ *one's hold* lâcher prise; ne pas saisir; *v/i.* manquer le coup; frapper à vide; ~ *out on s.th.* louper qch., rater qch.

mis·sal *eccl.* ['misəl] missel *m*.

mis·shap·en ['mis'ʃeipən] difforme, contrefait; déformé (*chapeau etc.*).

mis·sile ['misail] projectil *m*; ~ *site* base *f* de lancement; *ballistic* ~ engin *m* balistique.

miss·ing ['misiŋ] absent, perdu; *surt.* ✕ disparu; *be* ~ manquer; être égaré *ou* perdu.

mis·sion ['miʃn] mission *f* (*a. eccl., a. fig.*); **'mis·sion·ar·y** 1. missionnaire *m*; 2. missionnaire; de missionnaires; des missions.

mis·sis F ['misiz] femme *f*, dame *f*.

mis·sive ['misiv] lettre *f*, missive *f*.

mis·spell ['mis'spel] [*irr.* (*spell*)] mal épeler *ou* écrire (*un mot*).

mis·spend ['mis'spend] [*irr.* (*spend*)]

mal employer (*son temps, son argent*).

mis·state ['mis'steit] exposer incorrectement; altérer (*des faits*); '**mis·state·ment** exposé *m* inexact; erreur *f* de fait.

mis·sus F ['misəz] femme *f*, dame *f*.

miss·y F ['misi] mademoiselle (*pl. mesdemoiselles*) *f*.

mist [mist] **1.** brume *f*; buée *f* (*sur une glace*); *fig. in a* ~ désorienté, perdu; **2.** (se) couvrir de buée (*glace*); *v/i.* disparaître sous la brume.

mis·tak·a·ble [mis'teikəbl] sujet(te *f*) à méprise; facile à confondre; **mistake** [~'teik] **1.** [*irr.* (take)] *v/t.* se tromper; se méprendre sur; mal comprendre; confondre (avec, for); *be* ~*n* se tromper; *v/i.* se tromper; **2.** erreur *f*, méprise *f*, faute *f*; *by* ~ par méprise; *and no* ~ décidément; **mis'tak·en** □ erroné; mal compris; ~ *identity* erreur *f* sur la personne.

mis·ter ['mistə] (*abr.* **Mr.**) monsieur (*pl.* messieurs) *m*.

mis·time ['mis'taim] mal calculer; faire (*qch.*) mal à propos; '**mis·timed** inopportun.

mist·i·ness ['mistinis] état *m* brumeux; brouillard *m*; obscurité *f* (*a. fig.*).

mis·tle·toe ♀ ['misltou] gui *m*.

mis·trans·late ['mistræns'leit] mal traduire; '**mis·trans·la·tion** traduction *f* inexacte; contresens *m*.

mis·tress ['mistris] maîtresse *f*; patronne *f*; *lycée:* professeur *m*; *école primaire:* institutrice *f*; (*abr.* **Mrs.** ['misiz]) madame (*pl.* mesdames) *f*.

mis·trust ['mis'trʌst] **1.** se méfier de; **2.** méfiance *f*, défiance *f* (de *in*, of); '**mis'trust·ful** □ [~ful] méfiant, soupçonneux (-euse *f*) (à l'endroit de, of).

mist·y □ ['misti] brumeux (-euse *f*); *fig.* vague, confus.

mis·un·der·stand ['misʌndə'stænd] [*irr.* (stand)] mal comprendre *ou* interpréter; '**mis·un·der·stand·ing** malentendu *m*; mésentente *f*.

mis·use 1. ['mis'ju:z] faire mauvais emploi *ou* usage de; maltraiter; **2.** ['~'ju:s] abus *m*; mauvais emploi *m ou* usage *m*.

mite¹ *zo.* [mait] mite *f*; acarien *m*.

mite² [~] denier *m*, obole *f*; *personne:* mioche *mf*; petit(e *f*) *m*; *a* ~

of *a child* un(e *f*) enfant haut(e *f*) comme ma botte.

mit·i·gate ['mitigeit] adoucir, atténuer (*a. fig.*); **mit·i'ga·tion** adoucissement *m*, atténuation *f*.

mi·tre, mi·ter ['maitə] **1.** *eccl.* mitre *f*; ⊕ onglet *m*; **2.** *eccl.* mitrer; ⊕ tailler *ou* assembler à onglet; '~·wheel ⊕ roue *f* dentée conique.

mitt [mit] mitaine *f*; *baseball:* gant *m*; *sl.* patte *f* (= *main*).

mit·ten ['mitn] mitaine *f*; F *get the* ~ recevoir son congé.

mix [miks] (se) mêler (à, avec *with*); (se) mélanger; (s')allier (*couleurs*); *v/i.:* ~ *in society* fréquenter la société; ~*ed* mêlé, mélangé, mixte; confus (*a. fig.*); ~*ed bathing* bains *m/pl.* mixtes; ~*ed marriage* mariage *m* mixte; ~*ed mathematics* mathématiques *f/pl.* appliquées; ~*ed pickles pl.* variantes *f/pl.*; pickles *m/pl.* assortis; ~ *up* mêler; confondre; embrouiller; ~*ed up with* mêlé à, engagé dans (*une affaire*); ~*ed with* accointé avec; impliqué dans; '**mix·er** ⊕ brasseur *m*; garçon *m* de bar (*qui prépare des cocktails*), F barman *m*; *cuis.* mixe(u)r *m*; *radio:* opérateur *m* des sons, *machine:* mélangeur *m* des sons; *be a good* (*bad*) ~ (ne pas) savoir s'adapter à son entourage; **mix·ture** ['~tʃə] mélange *m* (*a. fig.*), *pharm.* mixtion *f*, mixture *f*; '**mix-'up** confusion *f*; embrouillement *m*.

miz·(z)en ⚓ ['mizn] artimon *m*; *attr.* d'artimon; de fougue (*perroquet*).

miz·zle ['mizl] bruiner, crachiner.

mne·mon·ic [ni'mɔnik] **1.** (~*ally*) mnémonique; **2.** ~*s pl.* mnémonique *f*, mnémotechnie *f*.

moan [moun] **1.** gémissement *m*; **2.** gémir; se lamenter.

moat [mout] fossé *m*; douve *f*; '**moat·ed** entouré d'un fossé.

mob [mɔb] **1.** foule *f*, ameutement *m*; populace *f*; **2.** *v/t.* assiéger; *v/i.* s'attrouper; '**mob·bish** de la populace; canaille; tumultueux (-euse *f*).

mob·cap ['mɔbkæp] petite coiffe *f*; cornette *f*; F charlotte *f*.

mo·bile ['moubail] mobile (*a.* ✕); changeant; ~ *police* (policiers *m/pl.* de la) brigade *f* mobile; *télév.* ~ *unit* motard *m*; **mo·bil·i·ty** [mo'biliti] mobilité *f*; **mo·bi·li·za·tion** [moubilai'zeiʃn] mobilisation *f*; **'mo·bi·lize** ✕ mobiliser.

mob-law ['mɔblɔ:] loi *f* de la populace; loi *f* de Lynch.

mob·oc·ra·cy [mɔ'bɔkrəsi] F voyoucratie *f*.

moc·ca·sin ['mɔkəsin] mocassin *m*.

mock [mɔk] **1.** dérision *f*; (sujet *m* de) moquerie *f*; **2.** faux (fausse *f*); contrefait; d'imitation; ~ *fight* simulacre *m* de combat; **3.** *v/t.* imiter, singer; tromper; *v/i.* se moquer (de, *at*); **'mock·er** moqueur (-euse *f*) *m*; **'mock·er·y** raillerie *f*; (sujet *m* de) moquerie *f*; objet *m* de risée; simulacre *m*; **'mock-he'ro·ic** héroï-comique; burlesque.

mock·ing ['mɔkiŋ] **1.** raillerie *f*, moquerie *f*; **2.** ▢ moqueur (-euse *f*); **'~-bird** *orn.* moqueur *m*.

mock...: **'~-king** roi *m* pour rire; **'~-'tur·tle soup** potage *m* (à la) fausse tortue; **'~-up** ⊕ maquette *f*.

mod·al ▢ ['moudl] modal (-aux *m/pl.*); ✝ conditionnel(le *f*); **mo·dal·i·ty** [mou'dæliti] modalité *f*.

mode [moud] méthode *f*, manière *f*, façon *f*, mode *m* (*a.* ♪, *gramm.*, *phls.*); mode *f* (= *coutume*).

mod·el ['mɔdl] **1.** modèle *m* (*a.fig.*); maquette *f*; figurine *f* (*de cire*); *personne:* mannequin *m*, modèle *mf*; *attr.* modèle; *act as a* ~ servir de modèle; **2.** modeler (sur *after*, [*up*]*on*) (*a. fig.*); **mod·el·(l)er** ['mɔdlə] modeleur (-euse *f*) *m*.

mod·er·ate 1. ▢ ['mɔdərit] modéré; raisonnable; moyen(ne *f*); médiocre; **2.** ['~reit] (se) modérer; *v/t.* tempérer; **mod·er·ate·ness** ['~ritnis] modération *f*; *prix:* modicité *f*; médiocrité *f*; **mod·er·a·tion** [~'reiʃn] modération *f*, mesure *f*; *langage:* sobriété *f*; *in* ~ modérément; frugalement; *univ.* ~*s pl.* premier examen *m* pour le B.A. (*Oxford*); **'mod·er·a·tor** *assemblée, jury, etc.:* président *m*; *univ.* examinateur *m* (*Oxford*); *phys.* modérateur *m*.

mod·ern ['mɔdən] **1.** moderne; **2.** *the* ~*s pl.* les modernes *m/pl.*; **'mod·ern·ism** modernité *f*; goût *m* du moderne; *eccl.* modernisme *m*; *gramm.* néologisme *m*; **mo·der·ni·ty** [mɔ'də:niti] modernité *f*; **'mod·ern·ize** moderniser.

mod·est ▢ ['mɔdist] modeste; sans prétentions; honnête, chaste;

'mod·es·ty modestie *f*; modération *f*; simplicité *f*; honnêteté *f*.

mod·i·cum ['mɔdikəm] faible quantité *f*.

mod·i·fi·a·ble ['mɔdifaiəbl] modifiable; **mod·i·fi·ca·tion** [~fi'keiʃn] modification *f*; atténuation *f*; **mod·i·fy** ['~fai] modifier (*a. gramm.*); apporter des modifications à; atténuer.

mod·u·late ['mɔdjuleit] moduler (*v/i. a.* ♪); ajuster; **mod·u·la·tion** modulation *f*; **'mod·u·la·tor** modulateur (-trice *f*) *m*; ~ *of tonality cin.* modulateur *m* de tonalité.

Mo·gul [mo'gʌl]: *the Great* (*ou Grand*) ~ le Grand Mogol *m*.

mo·hair ['mouhɛə] mohair *m*.

Mo·ham·med·an [mo'hæmidən] **1.** Mahométan(e *f*) *m*; **2.** mahométan.

moi·e·ty ['mɔiəti] moitié *f*; part *f*.

moil [mɔil] peiner.

moire [mwa:] moire *f*; ~ *crêpe* crêpe *m* ondé.

moi·ré ['mwɑ:rei] moiré (*a. su./m*).

moist [mɔist] humide; moite; **mois·ten** ['mɔisn] (se) mouiller, (s')humecter; **'moist·ness, mois·ture** ['~tʃə] humidité *f*; *peau:* moiteur *f*; **mois·tur·ize** ['~tʃəraiz] humidifier (*air*); hydrater (*peau*); **mois·tur·iz·ing cream** crème *f* hydratante.

moke *sl.* [mouk] âne *m*; bourrique *f*.

mo·lar ['moulə] (*ou* ~ *tooth*) molaire *f*.

mold [mould] *see* mould *etc.*

mo·las·ses [mə'læsiz] mélasse *f*.

mole[1] *zo.* [moul] taupe *f*.

mole[2] [~] grain *m* de beauté; nævus (*pl.* -vi) *m*.

mole[3] [~] mole *m*; brise-lames *m/inv.*

mo·lec·u·lar [mo'lekjulə] moléculaire; **mol·e·cule** *phys.* ['mɔlikju:l] molécule *f*.

mole·hill ['moulhil] taupinière *f*; **'mole·skin** (peau *f* de) taupe *f*; ✝ velours *m* de coton.

mo·lest [mo'lest] rudoyer; ✝ molester; **mo·les·ta·tion** [moules'teiʃn] molestation *f*; voies *f/pl.* de fait.

moll F [mɔl] catin *f*.

mol·li·fy ['mɔlifai] adoucir; apaiser.

mol·lusc *zo.* ['mɔləsk] mollusque *m*; **mol·lus·cous** [mɔ'lʌskəs] de(s) mollusque(s); *fig.* mollasse.

mol·ly·cod·dle ['mɔlikɔdl] **1.** douillet *m*; petit chéri *m* à sa maman; **2.** dorloter.

mol·ten ['moultən] en fusion; fondu.

mom *Am.* F [mɔm] maman *f*; **~-and-pop store** épicerie *f* du coin.

mo·ment ['moumənt] moment *m*; instant *m*; *see* momentum; *at (ou for) the* **~** pour le moment; en ce moment; *of* **~** important; **'mo·men·tar·y** □ momentané, passager (-ère *f*); **'mo·ment·ly** *adv.* d'un moment à l'autre; momentanément; **mo·men·tous** □ [~'mentəs] important; grave; **mo'men·tum** *phys.* [~təm] force *f* vive; vitesse *f* acquise.   [chisme *m.*]

mon·a·chism ['mɔnəkizm] mona-]

mon·arch ['mɔnək] monarque *m*; **mo·nar·chic, mo·nar·chi·cal** □ [mɔ'nɑːkik(l)] monarchique; **mon·arch·y** ['mɔnəki] monarchie *f*.

mon·as·ter·y ['mɔnəstri] monastère *m*; **mo·nas·tic, mo·nas·ti·cal** □ [mɔ'næstik(l)] monastique; monacal (-aux *m/pl.*).

Mon·day ['mʌndi] lundi *m*.

mon·e·tar·y ['mʌnitəri] monétaire.

mon·ey ['mʌni] argent *m*; monnaie *f*; **~ matters** pl. affaires *f/pl.* financières; *ready* **~** argent *m* comptant; F *out of* **~** à sec; *keep s.o. out of his* **~** frustrer q. de son argent; *make* **~** faire de l'argent; **'~-box** caisse *f*, cassette *f*; **'~-chang·er** changeur *m*, cambiste *m*; **mon·eyed** ['mʌnid] riche; qui a de l'argent.

mon·ey...: **'~-grub·ber** grippe-sou (*pl.* grippe-sou[s]) *m*; **'~-of·fice** caisse *f*; **'~-or·der** mandat-poste (*pl.* mandats-poste) *m*; **'~-'s-worth:** *get one's* **~** en avoir pour son argent.

mon·ger ['mʌŋgə] marchand(e *f*) *m* (de).

Mon·gol ['mɔŋgɔl], **Mon·go·lian** [~'gouljən] **1.** mongol; mongolique; *🎗* idiot; **2.** Mongol(e *f*) *m*.

mon·grel ['mʌŋgrəl] **1.** métis(se *f*) *m*; bâtard(e *f*) *m*; **2.** métis(se *f*).

mo·ni·tion [mo'niʃn] avertissement *m*; **mon·i·tor** ['mɔnitə] moniteur (-trice *f*) *m*; *⚓* monitor *m*; *radio:* contrôleur *m* d'enregistrement; *télév.* moniteur *m*, écran *m* de contrôle; **'mon·i·tor·ing** monitoring *m*; service *m* d'écoute; **'mon·i·to·ry** d'avertissement, d'admonition; monitoire.

monk [mʌŋk] moine *m*, religieux *m*; **'monk·er·y** *usu. péj.* moinerie *f*.

mon·key ['mʌŋki] **1.** singe *m*; *fig.* polisson *m*, espiègle *mf*; ⊕ mouton *m*; *sl.* monnaie: cinq cents livres *f/pl.* *ou Am.* dollars *m/pl.*; *sl.* **~'s allow-ance** plus de coups que de pain; F *put s.o.'s* **~** *up* mettre q. en colère; F **~ business, ~ tricks** *pl.* affaire *f* peu loyale; procédé *m* irrégulier; fumisterie *f*; **2.** F faire des tours de singe; **~ about with** tripoter (*qch.*); **'~-en·gine** ⊕ (*sorte de*) sonnette *f* (à mouton); **'~-puz·zle** araucaria *m*; **'~-wrench** ⊕ clé *f* anglaise; *Am. sl.* throw *a* **~** *in s.th.* saboter une affaire.

monk·hood ['mʌŋkhud] mona-chisme *m*; moinerie *f*; **'monk·ish** *usu. péj.* de moine, monacal (-aux *m/pl.*).

mon·o ┤ ['mɔnou] **1.** mono(phonique); **2.** (*in* **~** en) monophonie *f*; F disque *m* mono.

mono- [mɔno] mon(o)-; **mon·o·cle** ['mɔnɔkl] monocle *m*; **mo'noc·u·lar** [~kjulə] monoculaire; **mo'nog·a·my** [~gəmi] monogamie *f*; **mon·o·gram** ['mɔnəgræm] monogramme *m*; **mon·o·graph** ['~grɑːf] monographie *f*; **mon·o·lith** ['mɔnoliθ] monolithe *m*; **mon·o·lith·ic** monolithe; *a. fig.* monolithique; gigantesque; **mon·o·logue** ['mɔnəlɔg] monologue *m*; **mon·o·ma·ni·a** ['mɔno'meinjə] monomanie *f*; **mon·o'ma·ni·ac** [~niæk] monomane *mf*; **mon·o·plane** *🞲* ['mɔnəplein] monoplan *m*; **mo·nop·o·list** [mə'nɔpəlist] accapareur (-euse *f*) *m*; **mo'nop·o·lize** [~laiz] monopoliser; *fig.* s'emparer de; **mo'nop·o·ly** monopole *m* (de, *of*); **mon·o·syl·lab·ic** ['mɔnəsi'læbik] (~ally) monosyllabe, monosyllabique; **mon·o·syl·la·ble** ['~ləbl] monosyllabe *m*; **mon·o·the·ism** ['mɔnoθi:izm] monothéisme *m*; **mon·o·tone** ['mɔnətoun] **1.** débit *m* monotone; *in* **~** d'une voix uniforme *ou* monotone; **2.** chanter sur le même ton; **mo·not·o·nous** □ [mə'nɔtənəs] monotone; *fig.* fastidieux (-euse *f*); **mo'not·o·ny** [~təni] monotonie *f*; **mon·o·type** *typ.* ['mɔnətaip] monotype *f*.

mon·soon [mɔn'suːn] mousson *f*.

mon·ster ['mɔnstə] **1.** monstre *m* (*a. fig.*); monstruosité *f*; avorton *m*; F géant(e f) m; **2.** F monstre; colossal (-aux m/pl.).

mon·strance eccl. ['mɔnstrəns] ostensoir m.

mon·stros·i·ty [mɔns'trɔsiti] monstruosité f; **'mon·strous** □ monstrueux (-euse f); colossal (-aux m/pl.).

mon·tage cin., phot. [mɔn'tɑːʒ] montage m.

month [mʌnθ] mois m; **'month·ly 1.** mensuel(le f); ~ season ticket (carte f d')abonnement m (valable pour un mois); **2.** revue f mensuelle.

mon·u·ment ['mɔnjumənt] monument m; pierre f tombale; **mon·u·men·tal** □ [~'mentl] monumental (-aux m/pl.); F colossal (-aux m/pl.), prodigieux (-euse f).

moo [muː] **1.** meuglement m, beuglement m; **2.** meugler, beugler.

mooch F [muːtʃ]: v/i. ~ about flâner; ~ along traîner.

mood[1] gramm., a. ♪ [muːd] mode m.

mood[2] [~] humeur f, disposition f.

mood·i·ness ['muːdinis] morosité f; humeur f changeante; **'mood·y** □ maussade; mal luné.

moon [muːn] **1.** lune f; poét. mois m; F once in a blue ~ tous les trentesix du mois; F be over the ~ être aux anges; cry for the ~ demander la lune; promise s.o. the ~ promettre la lune ou monts et merveilles à q.; **2.** (usu. ~ about) F muser; **'moon·less** sans lune; **'moon·light** clair m de lune; clarté f de la lune; **'moon·light·ing** travail m noir; **'moon·lit** éclairé par la lune.

moon…: '~-shine clair m de lune; F balivernes f/pl.; alcool m de contrebande; '~-shin·er Am. F contrebandier m de boissons alcooliques; bouilleur m de contrebande; '~-struck halluciné; F hébété; **moon·y** □ de ou dans la lune; F rêveur (-euse f); vague.

Moor[1] [muə] Maure m, Mauresque f.

moor[2] [~] lande f, bruyère f; † ou prov. terrain m marécageux.

moor[3] ⚓ [~] (s')amarrer; **moor·age** ['muəridʒ] amarrage m, mouillage m.

moor-game ['muəgeim] lagopède m rouge d'Écosse.

moor-ing-mast ['muəriŋmɑːst] mât m d'amarrage.

moor-ings ⚓ ['muəriŋz] pl. amarres f/pl.; corps-morts m/pl.

Moor·ish ['muəriʃ] mauresque.

moose zo. [muːs] (a. ~-deer) élan m, orignal m.

moot [muːt] **1.** hist. assemblée f du peuple; **2.** ~ case (ou point) point m litigieux; **3.** soulever (une question).

mop [mɔp] **1.** balai m à franges; cheveux: tignasse f; **2.** essuyer, (a. ~up) éponger (de l'eau); engloutir (les bénéfices); ✗ F nettoyer; sl. aplatir (q.).

mope [moup] **1.** fig. cafardeux (-euse f) m; ~s pl. idées f/pl. noires; F cafard m; **2.** v/i. voir tout en noir, s'ennuyer; v/t. ~ o.s., be ~d languir.

mo·ped ['mouped] cyclomoteur m, mobylette f (TM).

mop·ing □ ['moupiŋ], **'mop·ish** □ morose, mélancolique, triste.

mo·raine géol. [mɔ'rein] moraine f.

mor·al ['mɔrəl] **1.** □ moral (-aux m/pl.); conforme aux bonnes mœurs; **2.** morale f; moralité f (d'un conte); ~s pl. mœurs f/pl.; conduite f; **mo·rale** [mɔ'rɑːl] usu. ✗ moral m; **mor·al·ist** ['mɔrəlist] moraliste mf; **mo·ral·i·ty** [mɔ-'ræliti] moralité f; sens m moral; probité f; bonnes mœurs f/pl.; péj. sermon m; théâ. hist. moralité f; **mor·al·ize** ['mɔrəlaiz] v/i. faire de la morale (sur, [up]on); v/t. moraliser (q.); indiquer la morale de.

mo·rass [mə'ræs] marais m, marécage m; fig. bourbier m.

mor·bid □ ['mɔːbid] morbide; malsain; **'mor·bid·i·ty**, **'mor·bid·ness** morbidité f; état m maladif.

mor·dant ['mɔːdənt] **1.** mordant; **2.** mordant m.

more [mɔː] **1.** adj. plus (de); **2.** adv. plus, davantage; once ~ encore une fois; de nouveau; two ~ deux de plus; so much (ou all) the ~ d'autant plus; à plus forte raison; no ~ ne … plus; ~ and ~ de plus en plus; **3.** su. plus m.

mo·rel ♧ [mɔ'rel] morelle f.

more·o·ver [mɔː'ouvə] d'ailleurs, du reste.

Mo·resque [mɔ'resk] **1.** mauresque; **2.** Mauresque f; arabesque f.

mor·ga·nat·ic [mɔːgə'nætik] (~ally) morganatique.

morgue [mɔːg] morgue f; dépôt m mortuaire.

mor·i·bund ['mɔribʌnd] moribond.
Mor·mon ['mɔːmən] mormon(e f)
m.
morn poét. [mɔːn] matin m.
morn·ing ['mɔːniŋ] **1.** matin m;
matinée f; in the ~ le matin; du
matin; tomorrow ~ demain matin;
2. du matin; matinal (-aux m/pl.);
~ coat jaquette f; ~ dress tenue f de
ville; femmes: négligé m; ~ performance matinée f.
Mo·roc·can [mə'rɔkən] marocain.
mo·roc·co [mə'rɔkou] (ou ~ leather)
maroquin m.
mo·ron ['mɔːrɔn] faible mf d'esprit;
F idiot(e f) m.
mo·rose □ [mə'rous] morose,
chagrin; **mo'rose·ness** morosité f.
mor·phi·a ['mɔːfjə], **mor·phine**
['mɔːfiːn] morphine f.
mor·pho·log·i·cal [mɔːfə'lɔdʒikl]
morphologique.
mor·row ['mɔrou] usu. poét. lendemain m; good ~! bonjour!
mor·sel ['mɔːsəl] (petit) morceau m;
terre: lopin m.
mor·tal ['mɔːtl] **1.** adj. □ mortel(le
f); fig. funeste, fatal (-s m/pl.); à outrance (combat); **2.** adv. F très; **3.** su.
mortel(le f) m, être m humain;
mor·tal·i·ty [mɔː'tæliti] mortalité
f; les mortels m/pl.
mor·tar ['mɔːtə] mortier m (a. ✕);
enduit m.
mort·gage ['mɔːgidʒ] **1.** hypothèque f; (a. ~-deed) contrat m hypothécaire; **2.** hypothéquer; **mort-
ga·gee** [ˌmɔːgə'dʒiː] créancier m hypothécaire; **mort·ga·gor** [ˌmɔː'dʒɔː]
débiteur m hypothécaire.
mor·tice ['mɔːtis] see mortise.
mor·ti·cian Am. [mɔː'tiʃn] entrepreneur m de pompes funèbres.
mor·ti·fi·ca·tion [mɔːtifi'keiʃn] ⚕
mortification f; gangrène f; déconvenue f, mortification f; humiliation f; **mor·ti·fy** ['ˌfai] v/t.
mortifier; humilier; ⚕ gangrener;
v/i. se gangrener.
mor·tise ⊕ ['mɔːtis] **1.** mortaise f;
serrure f encastrée; **2.** mortaiser.
mort·main ⚖ ['mɔːtmein] main-
morte f.
mor·tu·ar·y ['mɔːtjuəri] **1.** mortuaire; **2.** dépôt m mortuaire;
morgue f.
mo·sa·ic¹ [mə'zeiik] mosaïque f.
Mo·sa·ic² [~] mosaïque, de Moïse.

mo·selle [mə'zel] vin m de Moselle,
moselle m.
Mos·lem ['mɔzlem] musulman (a.
su.); mahométan (a. su.).
mosque [mɔsk] mosquée f.
mos·qui·to zo. [məs'kiːtou], pl.
-toes [ˌtouz] moustique m.
moss [mɔs] ⚘ mousse f; tourbière f;
'**moss·y** moussu.
most [moust] **1.** adj. □ le plus de;
la plupart de; for the ~ part pour la
plupart; **2.** adv. le plus; surtout;
très, fort, bien; **3.** su. le plus; la plupart d'entre eux (elles); at (the) ~
tout au plus; make the ~ of tirer le
meilleur parti possible de; faire
valoir.
most·ly ['moustli] pour la plupart;
le plus souvent.
mote [mout] atome m de poussière;
bibl. paille f.
mo·tel ['moutel] motel m.
mo·tet ♪ [mou'tet] motet m.
moth [mɔθ] mite f, teigne f des
draps; papillon m de nuit; '**~-eat·en**
rongé des mites.
moth·er ['mʌðə] **1.** mère f; ♀'s Day
la fête des Mères; **2.** servir de mère
à; fig. dorloter; **moth·er·hood**
['ˌhud] maternité f; '**moth·er-in-
law** belle-mère (pl. belles-mères) f;
'**moth·er·less** sans mère; '**moth-
er·li·ness** affection f maternelle;
'**moth·er·ly** maternel(le f).
moth·er...: ~ of pearl nacre f;
'~-of-pearl en ou de nacre; '~-ship
Brit. ravitailleur m; navire-atelier
(pl. navires-ateliers) m; '~-tongue
langue f maternelle.
moth·y ['mɔθi] mité.
mo·tif [mou'tiːf] motif m.
mo·tion ['mouʃn] **1.** mouvement m,
marche f (a. ⊕); signe m; parl. proposition f, motion f; ⚕ selle f;
parl. bring forward (agree upon) a ~
présenter (adopter) une motion;
set in ~ mettre en train; **2.** v/t.
faire signe à (q.) (de inf., to inf.);
v/i. faire un signe ou geste; '**mo-
tion·less** immobile; '**mo·tion-
pic·ture** Am. film m; ~s pl. films
m/pl.; projection f animée; attr.
ciné...
mo·ti·vate ['moutiveit] motiver;
mo·ti'va·tion motivation f.
mo·tive ['moutiv] **1.** moteur (-trice
f); **2.** motif m; mobile m; **3.** motiver; '**mo·tive·less** immotivé.

motivity 958

mo·tiv·i·ty [mo'tiviti] motilité *f*.
mot·ley ['mɔtli] bariolé; bigarré.
mo·tor ['moutə] **1.** moteur *m*; mécanisme *m*; *see* ~*-car*; **2.** moteur
(-trice *f*); à *ou* par moteur;
d'automobile; ~ *ambulance* auto-
ambulance *f*; *Am.* ~ *court see*
~ *park*; ~ *goggles pl.* lunettes *f/pl.*
d'automobiliste; ~ *mechanic* (*ou*
fitter) mécanicien *m* automobiliste;
~ *park Am. usu.* stationnement *m*;
garage *m* pour autos; ~ *school* auto-
école *f*; **3.** *v/i.* voyager *ou* aller en
auto; *v/t.* conduire (*q.*) en auto;
~ **bi·cy·cle** motocyclette *f*; '~**boat**
canot *m* automobile; vedette *f* à
moteur; '~-'**bus** autobus *m*; ~ **cab**
autotaxi *m*; '~**cade** *Am.* ['~keid]
défilé *m* d'automobiles; '~**car**
auto(mobile) *f*; voiture *f*; ~ **cy-**
cle motocyclette *f*; ~ **cy·clist**
motocycliste *mf*; **mo·to·ri·al** [mo-
'tɔːriəl] moteur (-trice *f*); **mo·tor-**
ing ['moutəriŋ] automobilisme *m*;
tourisme *m* en auto; '**mo·tor·ist**
automobiliste *mf*; **mo·tor·i·za-**
tion [~rai'zeiʃn] motorisation *f*;
'**mo·tor·ize** motoriser; '**mo·tor-**
launch vedette *f*; bateau *m* automobile; '**mo·tor·less** sans moteur.
mo·tor...: '~-'**lor·ry** (auto-)camion
m; '~-**man** *Am.* wattman (*pl.*
-men) *m*; '~-**plough** charrue *f* automobile; '~-**pool** autos *f/pl.* communes; '~-**road** autostrade *f*; ~
scoot·er scooter *m*; '~-**truck** *Am.*
(auto-)camion *m*; '~-**way** autoroute
f.
mot·tled ['mɔtld] marbré; pommelé; madré (*bois, savon*).
mot·to ['mɔtou], *pl.* -toes ['~touz]
devise *f*; ⊘ mot *m*.
mo(u)ld¹ [mould] terre *f* végétale;
terreau *m*.
mo(u)ld² [~] **1.** moule *m* (*a. fig.*);
typ. matrice *f*; *cuis.* crème *f* ren-
versée; △ moulure *f*; **2.** mouler,
façonner (sur, [up]on); pétrir (*le
pain*).
mo(u)ld·er¹ ['mouldə] mouleur *m*;
façonneur *m*.
mo(u)ld·er² [~] s'effriter; (*a.*~*away*)
tomber en poussière.
mo(u)ld·i·ness ['mouldinis] (état*m*)
moisi *m*.
mo(u)ld·ing ['mouldiŋ] moulage *m*;
moulure *f*; F formation *f*; △ *square*
~ baguette *f*; *plain* ~ bandeau *m*;

grooved ~ moulure *f* à gorge; *attr.*
de mouleur; à moulurer *etc.*
mo(u)ld·y ['mouldi] moisi; chanci
(*pain, confiture*).
moult [moult] **1.** mue*f*; **2.** *v/i.* muer;
vt/i. fig. perdre (ses cheveux).
mound [maund] tertre *m*; monceau
m, tas *m*.
mount [maunt] **1.** montagne *f*;
poét., a. géog. mont *m*; (carton *m* de)
montage *m*; monture *f* (= *cheval*);
⊕ *machine*: armement *m*; **2.** *v/i.*
monter; monter à cheval, se mettre
en selle; s'élever (à, to); (*usu.* ~ *up*)
augmenter; *v/t.* monter sur (*un
banc, un cheval*); monter, gravir
(*une colline etc.*); ✗ affûter (*une
pièce*); ⊕ installer; entoiler, coller
(*un tableau*); monter (*un bijou*);
théâ. mettre à la scène; *see guard 1.*
moun·tain ['mauntin] **1.** montagne
f; *make a* ~ *out of a molehill* (se) faire
d'une mouche un éléphant; **2.** des
montagnes; montagneux (-euse *f*);
moun·tain·eer [~'niə] monta-
gnard(e *f*) *m*; alpiniste *mf*; **moun-**
tain·eer·ing 1. alpinisme *m*; **2.**
alpin; '**moun·tain·ous** montagneux (-euse *f*); **moun·tain rail-**
way chemin *m* de fer de montagne;
moun·tain range chaîne *f* de montagnes; **moun·tain sick·ness** mal
m des montagnes.
moun·te·bank ['mauntibæŋk] saltimbanque *m*; *fig.* charlatan *m*.
mount·ing ⊕ ['mauntiŋ] montage
m; entoilage *m*.
mourn [mɔːn] (se) lamenter; *v/i.*
porter le deuil; *v/t.* (*ou* ~ *for, over*)
pleurer (*q.*), déplorer (*qch.*);
'**mourn·er** affligé(e *f*) *m*; **mourn-**
ful □ ['~ful] lugubre; mélancolique; '**mourn·ful·ness** aspect *m*
lugubre; air *m* désolé; tristesse *f*.
mourn·ing ['mɔːniŋ] **1.** □ de deuil;
en deuil; qui pleure; **2.** deuil *m*,
affliction *f*; '~-**bor·der**, '~-**edge**
bordure *f* noire; '~-**pa·per** papier
m deuil.
mouse 1. [maus] (*pl.* mice) souris
f; **2.** [mauz] chasser les souris.
mous·tache [məs'taːʃ] moustache *f*,
-s *f/pl.*
mous·y ['mausi] gris souris; de
souris; effacé, timide (*personne*); *péj.*
peu distingué.
mouth [mauθ] **1.** *pl.* **mouths**
[mauðz] bouche *f*; chien, four, sac:

gueule f; *fleuve, clarinette*: embouchure f; *bouteille*: goulot m; *port, tunnel, trou*: entrée f; *entonnoir*: pavillon m; *fig.* grimace f; *by word of ~* de vive voix; *down in the ~* déprimé; *keep one's ~ shut* ne pas souffler mot, rester bouche cousue; *shut your ~!, keep your ~ shut!* ferme ta bouche!, F la ferme!; *stop s.o.'s ~* faire taire q.; fermer la bouche à q.; 2. [mauð] *vt/i.* déclamer (des phrases); *v/i.* faire des grimaces; **mouthed** [mauðd] embouché (*cheval*); *clean-~* au langage honnête; **mouth·ful** ['~ful] bouchée f; F mot m long d'une aune.

mouth...: '~-**or·gan** harmonica m; '~-**piece** ♪ bec m, embouchure f; *porte-voix*: embout m; *fig.* porte-parole m/inv.; '~-**wash** (eau f) dentifrice m; '~-**wa·ter·ing** qui fait venir l'eau à la bouche, appétissant.

move [mu:v] 1. *vt/t.* déplacer (*qch.*); bouger (*qch.*); remuer (*la tête etc.*); émouvoir (*q.*); toucher (*q.*); exciter (*la pitié*); faire changer d'avis à (*q.*); proposer (*une motion*); mouvoir; *~ on* faire circuler; *v/i.* se déplacer, se mouvoir; circuler; faire un mouvement, bouger; s'avancer; déménager; marcher (*échecs*); *~ for s.th.* demander qch.; *~ in* entrer; emménager; *~ on* avancer, continuer son chemin; 2. mouvement m; déménagement m; échecs: coup m; *fig.* démarche f, pas m; *on the ~* en marche; F *get a ~ on* se dépêcher, se presser; *make a ~* faire un mouvement (*vers qch.*); F *partir*, prendre congé; **mov(e)·a·ble** ['mu:vəbl] 1. mobile; 2. *~s pl.* mobilier m; biens m/pl. mobiliers; **'mov(e)·a·ble·ness** mobilité f; **'move·ment** mouvement m (*a.* ♪); geste m; ⊕ mécanisme m; ⚙ selle f; **'mov·er** moteur m; mobile m; inspirateur (-trice f) m; auteur m.

mov·ie F ['mu:vi] 1. de ciné(ma); de vues; 2. *~s pl.* ciné(ma) m; films m/pl.; '~-**go·er** amateur m de cinéma, cinéphile mf.

mov·ing □ ['mu:viŋ] en mouvement; en marche; mobile; moteur (-trice f); *fig.* émouvant; *~-band production* travail m à la chaîne; *~ pictures pl. see motion-pictures*; *~ staircase* escalier m roulant.

mow¹ [mau] meule f (*de foin*); tas m (*de blé*) (*en grange*).

mow² [mou] [*irr.*] faucher; **'mow·er** faucheur (-euse f) m; tondeuse f (*de gazon*); **'mow·ing** fauchage m; *gazon*: tondaison f; fauchée f; **'mow·ing-ma·chine** faucheuse f; *gazon*: tondeuse f; **mown** *p.p. de* mow².

much [mʌtʃ] 1. *adj.* beaucoup de, bien du (*etc.*); 2. *adv.* beaucoup, bien, fort; *as ~ more* (*ou again*) encore autant; *as ~ as* autant que; *not so ~ as* ne ... pas (au)tant que; ne ... pas même; *nothing ~* peu de chose; F *pas fameux*; *~ less* moins encore; *bien moins*; *~ as I would like* pour autant que je désire *ou* veuille; *I thought as ~* je m'y attendais; *make ~ of* faire grand cas de; *I am not ~ of a dancer* F je ne suis pas fameux comme danseur; **'much·ness** F grandeur f; *much of a ~* c'est bonnet blanc et blanc bonnet.

mu·ci·lage ['mju:silidʒ] mucilage m; *surt. Am.* colle f, gomme f; **mu·ci·lag·i·nous** [~'lædʒinəs] mucilagineux (-euse f).

muck *sl.* [mʌk] 1. fange f; fumier m; saletés f/pl. (*a. fig.*); 2. souiller; (*usu. ~ up*) F gâcher; **'muck·er** *sl.* culbute f; *come* (*ou go*) *a ~* faire la culbute; **muck-rake** ['~reik] râteau m à fumier; racloir m à boue; **'muck·rake** *Am.* déterrer des scandales; **'muck·rak·er** *Am.* déterreur m de scandales; **'muck·y** sale, crotté.

mu·cous ⚕ ['mju:kəs] muqueux (-euse f); *~ membrane* ⚕ muqueuse f.

mu·cus [~] mucus m, glaire f.

mud [mʌd] boue f, bourbe f; *fleuve*: vase f; **'mud·di·ness** saleté f; *liquide*: turbidité f; **mud·dle** ['mʌdl] 1. *v/t.* brouiller; emmêler; (*a. ~ up, together*) embrouiller; *v/i.* s'embrouiller; F lambiner; 2. confusion f, embrouillement m; F pagaille f; *get into a ~* s'embrouiller; **'mud·dle-head·ed** à l'esprit confus; brouillon(ne f); **'mud·dy** 1. □ boueux (-euse f); fangeux (-euse f); vaseux (-euse f) (*fleuve*); trouble (*liquide*); brouillé (*teint*); 2. crotter; troubler; (em)brouiller (*l'esprit*).

mud...: '~-**guard** garde-boue *m/inv.*; pare-boue *m/inv.*; '~-**lark** F gamin *m* des rues; '~-**sling·er** F médisant(e *f*) *m*, calomniateur (-trice *f*) *m*; '~-**sling·ing** F médisance *f*; calomnies *f/pl.*

muff¹ [mʌf] **1.** F empoté *m*; *sl.* andouille *f*; *sp.* coup *m* raté; **2.** F rater, manquer.

muff² [~] manchon *m*; **muf·fe·tee** [mʌfi'ti:] miton *m*.

muf·fin ['mʌfin] *petit pain mollet qui se mange beurré à l'heure du thé*; **muf·fin·eer** [~'niə] saupoudroir *m*.

muf·fle ['mʌfl] **1.** ⊕ moufle *m*; **2.** (*souv.* ~ *up*) (s')emmitoufler; amortir (*un son*); assourdir (*les avirons, un tambour*); *tapis*: étouffer (*le bruit*); '**muf·fler** cache-nez *m/inv.*; F moufle *f*; ♪ étouffoir *m*; *mot.* pot *m* d'échappement, silencieux *m*.

muf·ti ['mʌfti] costume *m* de ville; *in* ~ en civil.

mug [mʌg] **1.** chope *f*, pot *m*; *sl.* binette *f* (= *visage*); *sl.* nigaud *m*, dupe *f*; **2.** agresser; '**mug·ger** agresseur *m*; '**mug·ging** (vol *m* avec) agression *f*.

mug·gy ['mʌgi] chaud et humide, lourd.

mug·wump *Am. iro.* ['mʌgwʌmp] personnage *m* important, gros bonnet *m*; *pol.* indépendant *m*; *sl.* rouspéteur *m*.

mu·lat·to [mju'lætou] mulâtre(sse *f*) *m*.

mul·ber·ry ['mʌlbəri] mûre *f*; *arbre*: mûrier *m*.

mulct [mʌlkt] **1.** amende *f*; **2.** frapper d'une amende; imposer une amende (de, *in*); priver (de, *of*).

mule [mju:l] mulet *m*, mule *f*; métis(se *f*) *m*; (*a.* ~-*jenny*) mule-jenny *f*; **mu·le·teer** [~li'tiə] muletier *m*; '**mule-track** piste *f* muletière. [têtu, entêté.)

mul·ish □ ['mju:liʃ] de mulet; *fig.*)

mull¹ ⊕ [mʌl] mousseline *f*.

mull² F [~] **1.** F bousiller; rater; *Am.* ~ *over* ruminer; **2.** gâchis *m*; *make a* ~ *of* gâcher, F bousiller.

mulled [mʌld] chaud (et) épicé (*bière, vin*).

mul·le(i)n ⊕ ['mʌlin] molène *f*.

mul·let *icht.* ['mʌlit] muge *m*; grey ~ mulet *m*; red ~ rouget *m*.

mul·li·gan *Am.* F ['mʌligən] rata-touille *f*; **mul·li·ga·taw·ny** [mʌligə'tɔ:ni] potage *m* au curry.

mul·li·grubs *sl.* ['mʌligrʌbz] *pl.* cafard *m*; colique *f*.

mul·lion ▲ ['mʌljən] meneau *m*; '**mul·lioned** à meneau(x).

mul·ti·far·i·ous □ [mʌlti'fɛəriəs] varié; multiple; **mul·ti·form** ['~fɔ:m] multiforme; **mul·ti·lat·er·al** □ [~'lætərəl] multilatéral (-aux *m/pl.*); complexe; **mul·ti·mil·lion·aire** ['~miljə'nɛə] milliardaire *mf*; **mul·ti·na·tion·al** ['~'næʃənl] multinationale *f*; **mul·ti·ple** ['mʌltipl] **1.** multiple; ~ *firm* maison *f* à succursales multiples; ~ *shop* succursale *f*; ⚡ ~ *switchboard* commutateur *m* (multiple); **2.** multiple *m*; **mul·ti·plex** ['~pleks] multiplex; **mul·ti·pli·cand** ⅍ [~'kænd] multiplicande *m*; **mul·ti·pli·ca·tion** multiplication *f*; *compound* (*simple*) ~ multiplication *f* de nombres complexes (de chiffres); ~ *table* table *f* de multiplication; **mul·ti·plic·i·ty** [~'plisiti] multiplicité *f*; **mul·ti·pli·er** ['~plaiə] multiplicateur *m*; **mul·ti·pur·pose** ['~'pə:pəs] universel(le *f*), à usages multiples, multi-usages *inv.*; **mul·ti·ply** ['~plai] (se) multiplier; **mul·ti·ra·cial** [~'reiʃəl] multiracial (-aux *m/pl.*); **mul·ti·tude** ['~tju:d] multitude *f*; foule *f*; multiplicité *f*; **mul·ti·tu·di·nous** [~dinəs] □ innombrable; de toutes sortes.

mum¹ [mʌm] **1.** silencieux (-euse *f*); **2.** chut!; **3.** mimer.

mum² F [~] maman *f*.

mum·ble ['mʌmbl] *v/t.* marmotter; *v/i.* manger ses mots.

mum·mer *péj.* ['mʌmə] cabotin(e *f*) *m*; '**mum·mer·y** *péj.* momerie *f*; † pantomime *f*.

mum·mied ['mʌmid] momifié.

mum·mi·fi·ca·tion [mʌmifi'keiʃn] momification *f*; **mum·mi·fy** ['~fai] momifier.

mum·my¹ ['mʌmi] momie *f*; F *beat to a* ~ battre (*q.*) comme plâtre.

mum·my² F [~] maman *f*.

mump [mʌmp] mendier; '**mump·ish** maussade; **mumps** [mʌmps] *sg.* ⚕ oreillons *m/pl.*; parotidite *f* épidémique.

munch [mʌntʃ] mâcher, mâchonner.

mun·dane □ ['mʌndein] mondain; terrestre.

mu·nic·i·pal □ [mju:'nisipl] municipal (-aux *m/pl.*); de (la) ville; interne (*droit*); **mu·nic·i·pal·i·ty** [~'pæliti] municipalité *f*; administration *f* municipale; **mu'nic·i·pal·ize** [~pəlaiz] municipaliser.

mu·nif·i·cence [mju:'nifisns] munificence *f*; **mu'nif·i·cent** □ munificent, généreux (-euse *f*).

mu·ni·ments ['mju:nimənts] *pl.* titres *m/pl.*; chartes *f/pl.*

mu·ni·tion [mju:'niʃn] 1. de munitions de guerre; 2. ~*s pl.* munitions *f/pl.*; armements *m/pl.*

mu·ral ['mjuərəl] 1. mural (-aux *m/pl.*); 2. peinture *f* murale.

mur·der ['mə:də] 1. assassinat *m*, meurtre *m*; F *fig.* get away with (blue) ~ pouvoir faire n'importe quoi impunément; 2. assassiner; *fig.* massacrer; écorcher; **'mur·der·er** assassin *m*, meurtrier *m*; **'mur·der·ess** assassine *f*, meurtrière *f*; **'mur·der·ous** meurtrier (-ère *f*); *fig.* sanguinaire.

mure [mjuə] (*usu.* ~ up) murer.

mu·ri·at·ic ac·id 🜍 [mjuəri'ætik-'æsid] acide *m* chlorhydrique.

murk·y □ ['mə:ki] ténébreux (-euse *f*); obscur.

mur·mur ['mə:mə] 1. murmure *m* (*a.* 🖤); bruissement *m*; 2. murmurer (contre *at*, *against*); bruire (*ruisseau*); **'mur·mur·ous** □ murmurant. [épizootie *f.*]

mur·rain ['mʌrin] † peste *f*; *vét.*]

mus·ca·dine ['mʌskədin], **mus·cat** ['~kət], **mus·ca·tel** [~'tel] muscat *m*.

mus·cle ['mʌsl] 1. muscle *m*; 2. Am. sl. ~ in s'immiscer dans (*usu. dans la spécialité d'un escroc*); **mus·cu·lar** ['mʌskjulə] musculaire; musculeux (-euse *f*), musclé (*personne*).

Muse¹ [mju:z] Muse *f.*

muse² [~] méditer (sur, [*up*]on); **'mus·er** rêveur (-euse *f*) *m*; rêvasseur (-euse *f*) *m.*

mu·se·um [mju:'ziəm] musée *m.*

mush *surt.* Am. [mʌʃ] bouillie *f* de farine de maïs; *fig.* sottises *f/pl.*

mush·room ['mʌʃrum] 1. champignon *m*; *fig.* parvenu(e *f*) *m*; 2. de champignons, à champignon, à tête de champignon; *fig.* parvenu; champignon *inv.* (*ville*); 3. F (s')aplatir (*balle de fusil, cigarette, etc.*); *v/i.* faire champignon; se répandre (*flammes etc.*).

mu·sic ['mju:zik] musique *f*, harmonie *f* (*a. fig.*); set to ~ mettre en musique; F face the ~ affronter la tempête; **'mu·si·cal** 1. □ musical (-aux *m/pl.*); musicien(ne *f*) (*personne*); *fig.* harmonieux (-euse *f*); ~ box boîte *f* à musique; ~ clock horloge *f etc.* à carillon; ~ instrument instrument *m* de musique; 2. (*ou* ~ comedy) comédie *f* musicale.

mu·sic...: **'~-book** cahier *m* de musique; **'~-box** boîte *f* à musique; **'~-hall** music-hall *m.*

mu·si·cian [mju:'ziʃn] musicien(ne *f*) *m*; **~-ship** sens *m* de la musique.

mu·si·col·o·gy [mju:zi'kɔlədʒi] musicologie *f.*

mu·sic...: **'~-pa·per** papier *m* à *ou* de musique; **'~-stand** pupitre *m* à musique; **'~-stool** tabouret *m* de piano.

musk [mʌsk] musc *m* (*a.* 🌸); (*a.* ~-deer) *zo.* porte-musc *m/inv.*

mus·ket ['mʌskit] mousquet *m*; **mus·ket·eer** *hist.* [~'tiə] mousquetaire *m*; **'mus·ket·ry** ✕ mousqueterie *f*; tir *m*; mousquets *m/pl.*

musk·y ['mʌski] musqué, de musc.

Mus·lim ['mʌzlim] *see* Moslem.

mus·lin 🐞 ['mʌzlin] mousseline *f.*

mus·quash ['mʌskwɔʃ] *zo.* rat *m* musqué; 🐞 castor *m* du Canada.

muss *surt.* Am. F [mʌs] 1. désordre *m*; 2. déranger; *fig.* confondre.

mus·sel ['mʌsl] moule *f.*

Mus·sul·man ['mʌslmən] musulman (*a. su.*).

must¹ [mʌst] 1. *v/aux.* (*défectif*): I ~ (*inf.*) je dois *etc.*, il faut que je (*sbj.*), il est nécessaire que je (*sbj.*); I ~ not (*inf.*) il ne faut pas que je (*sbj.*); 2. impératif *m*; nécessité *f* absolue.

must² [~] moût *m*, vin *m* doux.

must³ [~] moisi *m*; moisissure *f.*

mus·tache Am. [məs'tæʃ] *see* moustache.

mus·tard ['mʌstəd] moutarde *f.*

mus·ter ['mʌstə] 1. ✕ revue *f*; ⚓ appel *m*; rassemblement *m*; inspection *f*; ✕ (*usu.* ~-roll) contrôles *m/pl.*; *fig.* assemblée *f*, réunion *f*; pass ~ être passable, passer; 2. *v/t.* ✕ passer en revue; ⚓ faire l'appel de; (*fig. usu.* ~ up) rassembler; ~ in compter; *v/i.* se rassembler.

mus·ti·ness ['mʌstinis] goût *m ou* odeur *f* de moisi; moisi *m*; relent *m*;

'**mus·ty** de moisi; be ~ sentir le renfermé.

mu·ta·bil·i·ty [mju:tə'biliti] mutabilité f; inconstance f; '**mu·ta·ble** □ muable, variable; **mu'ta·tion** mutation f (a. gramm.).

mute [mju:t] 1. □ muet(te f); 2. muet(te f) m; théâ. personnage m muet; ♪ sourdine f; gramm. consonne f sourde; 3. surt. ♪ assourdir.

mu·ti·late ['mju:tileit] mutiler (a. fig.); **mu·ti'la·tion** mutilation f.

mu·ti·neer [mju:ti'niə] révolté; '**mu·ti·nous** □ rebelle, mutin; '**mu·ti·ny** 1. révolte f; 2. se révolter.

mutt sl. [mʌt] nigaud m.

mut·ter ['mʌtə] 1. murmure m; 2. marmotter; murmurer (contre, against).

mut·ton ['mʌtn] mouton m; leg of ~ gigot m; '~-'chop côtelette f de mouton; ~s pl., ~ whiskers pl. favoris m/pl. en côtelette.

mu·tu·al □ ['mju:tjuəl] mutuel(le f), réciproque; commun; ~ insurance company (compagnie f d'assurance) mutuelle f; Am. ~ fund société f d'investissement; by ~ consent par consentement mutuel; **mu·tu·al·i·ty** [~'æliti] mutualité f, réciprocité f.

muz·zle ['mʌzl] 1. animal: museau m; chien: muselière f; arme à feu: bouche f; 2. museler (a. fig.); '~-load·er ⚔ pièce f se chargeant par la bouche.

muz·zy □ ['mʌzi] estompé; confus

(idées); brumeux (-euse f) (temps).

my [mai; a. mi] mon, ma, mes.

my·ope 🖋 ['maioup] myope mf; **my·op·ic** [~'ɔpik] (~ally) (de) myope; **my·o·pi·a** [~'oupjə], **my·o·py** ['~əpi] myopie f.

myr·i·ad ['miriəd] 1. myriade f; 2. innombrable.

myr·mi·don ['mə:midən] myrmidon m; F assassin m à gages; ~s pl. of the law sbires m/pl.

myrrh ♀ [mə:] myrrhe f.

myr·tle ♀ ['mə:tl] myrte m.

my·self [mai'self] moi-même; réfléchi: me, accentué: moi.

mys·te·ri·ous □ [mis'tiəriəs] mystérieux (-euse f); fig. a. incompréhensible; **mys'te·ri·ous·ness** mystère m; caractère m mystérieux.

mys·ter·y ['mistəri] mystère m (a. eccl.); hist. (a. ~-play) mystère m; Am. (ou ~ story) roman m policier; mysteries pl. arcanes m/pl.; '~-ship piège m à sous-marin(s).

mys·tic ['mistik] 1. (a. 'mys·ti·cal □) mystique; ésotérique (rite); occulte; 2. eccl. mystique mf; initié(e f) m; **mys·ti·cism** ['~sizm] mysticisme m; **mys·ti·fi·ca·tion** [~fi'keiʃn] mystification f; embrouillement m; **mys·ti·fy** ['~fai] mystifier; désorienter; fig. intriguer.

myth [miθ] mythe m; **myth·ic**, **myth·i·cal** □ ['~ik(l)] mythique. **myth·o·log·ic**, **myth·o·log·i·cal** □ [miθə'lɔdʒik(l)] mythologique; **my·thol·o·gy** [~'θɔlədʒi] mythologie f.

N

N, n [en] N *m*, n *m*.

nab *sl.* [næb] saisir, arrêter.

na·bob ['neibɔb] nabab *m*; *fig.* richard *m*.

na·celle ✈ [nə'sel] nacelle *f*.

na·cre ['neikə] nacre *f*; **na·cre·ous** ['ᴧkriəs] nacré.

na·dir ['neidiə] *astr.* nadir *m*; *fig.* stade *m* le plus bas.

nag¹ F [næg] petit cheval *m*, bidet *m*.

nag² [ᴧ] *v/i.* chamailler; criailler (contre, *at*); *v/t.* harceler (*q.*); '**ᴧ-ging** criailleries *f/pl.*; harcèlement *m*.

nail [neil] **1.** *doigt, orteil:* ongle *m*; ⊕ clou *m*; ᴧ *clippers pl.* pince *f* à ongles; ᴧ *file* lime *f* à ongles; *Am.* ᴧ *polish* vernis *m* à ongles; ᴧ *scissors pl.* ciseaux *m/pl.* à ongles, ᴧ *varnish* vernis *m* à ongles/ *fig.* hit the ᴧ on the head frapper juste; **2.** clouer (*a.* les yeux sur *q.*); clouter (*la porte, les chaussures*); *fig.* attraper; ᴧ **down** clouer; *fig.* ᴧ **s.o. down** to ne pas laisser à *q.* le moyen d'échapper à (*qch.*); ᴧ **to** the counter démontrer la fausseté de; '**nail·er** cloutier *m*; *sl.* bon type *m*; passé maître *m* (en, *at*); '**nail·er·y** clouterie *f*; '**nail·ing 1.** clou(t)age *m*; **2.** *sl.* (*souv.* ᴧ *good*) épatant.

na·ïve □ [nɑːˈiːv], **na·ive** □ [neiv] naïf (-ïve *f*); ingénu; **na·ïve·té** [nɑːˈiːvtei], **na·ive·ty** ['neivti] naïveté *f*.

na·ked □ ['neikid] nu; sans vêtements; dénudé (*pays etc.*); dépouillé (*arbre*); *fig.* découvert; *poét.* sans protection; ᴧ *facts pl.* faits *m/pl.* bruts; with the ᴧ *eye* à l'œil nu; '**na·ked·ness** nudité *f*; F pauvreté *f*.

nam·by-pam·by ['næmbi'pæmbi] **1.** maniéré; fade; **2.** F pouille *f* mouillée.

name [neim] **1.** nom *m*; *navire:* devise *f*; *fig.* réputation *f*; *of* (*ou* F *by*) the ᴧ *of* du nom de, nommé; *Christian* ᴧ prénom *m*; *call s.o.* ᴧ*s* injurier *q.*; *know s.o. by* ᴧ connaître

q. de nom; **2.** nommer; désigner par son nom; dénommer; citer; fixer (*un jour*); '**name-day** fête *m*; '**name·less** □ sans nom; inconnu; anonyme; *fig.* indicible; '**name·ly** (*abr. viz.*) c'est-à-dire; '**name-plate** plaque *f*; écusson *m*; '**name-sake** homonyme *m*.

nan·keen [næŋ'kiːn] nankin *m*; ᴧ*s pl.* pantalon *m* de nankin.

nan·ny ['næni] nounou *f*; bonne *f* (d'enfant); '**ᴧ-goat** chèvre *f*, bique *f*.

nap¹ [næp] *velours etc.:* poil *m*.

nap² [ᴧ] **1.** petit somme *m*; **2.** sommeiller; *catch s.o.* ᴧ*ping* surprendre la vigilance de *q.*; surprendre *q.* en faute.

nap³ [ᴧ] *cartes:* go ᴧ jouer son va-tout.

nape [neip] (*usu.* ᴧ *of* the *neck*) nuque *f*.

naph·tha ⚗ ['næfθə] naphte *m*.

nap·kin ['næpkin] (*souv.* table-ᴧ) serviette *f*; (*a.* baby's ᴧ) couche *f*; '**ᴧ-ring** rond *m* de serviette.

na·poo(h) *sl.* [nɑːˈpuː] épuisé; inutile; mort; fini; *sl.* fichu.

nar·co·sis ⚕ [nɑːˈkousis] narcose *f*.

nar·cot·ic [nɑːˈkɔtik] **1.** (ᴧ*ally*) narcotique; **2.** stupéfiant *m*; narcotique *m*; **nar·co·tize** ['nɑːkətaiz] narcotiser.

nard [nɑːd] nard *m*.

nar·rate [næ'reit] raconter; **nar-ˈra·tion** narration *f*; récit *m*; **nar-ra·tive** ['ᴧrətiv] **1.** □ narratif (-ive *f*); **2.** récit *m*; **nar·ra·tor** [ᴧ'reitə] narrateur (-trice *f*) *m*.

nar·row ['nærou] **1.** □ étroit; encaissé (*vallon*); borné (*esprit*); faible (*majorité*); *see escape*; **2.** ᴧ*s pl.* passe *f* étroite; *port:* goulet *m*; **3.** *v/t.* resserrer; rétrécir; restreindre; limiter; *v/i.* devenir plus étroit; se resserrer; se rétrécir; '**ᴧ-'chest-ed** à poitrine étroite; '**ᴧ-gauge** 🚂 à voie étroite; '**ᴧ-'mind·ed** □ borné; '**nar·row·ness** étroitesse *f* (*a. fig.*); petitesse *f*; limitation *f*.

nar·whal *zo.* ['nɑːwəl] narwal(*pl.* -s) *m.*

na·sal ['neizl] **1.** □ nasal (-aux *m/pl.*); nasillard (*accent*); **2.** *gramm.* nasale *f*; **na·sal·i·ty** [~'zæliti] nasalité *f*; **na·sal·ize** ['~zəlaiz] nasaliser; *v/i.* parler du nez; nasiller.

nas·cent ['næsnt] naissant.

nas·ti·ness ['nɑːstinis] goût *m* ou odeur *f* désagréable; méchanceté *f* (*d'une personne*); *fig.* saleté *f*; **'nas·ty** □ désagréable; dégoûtant; sale; méchant, désagréable (*personne*); *fig.* malpropre.

na·tal ['neitl] natal (-als *m/pl.*); **na·tal·i·ty** [nə'tæliti] natalité *f*.

na·ta·tion [nei'teiʃn] natation *f*.

na·tion ['neiʃn] nation *f*, peuple *m*; member ~ État *m* membre.

na·tion·al ['næʃənl] **1.** □ national (-aux *m/pl.*); de l'État; ~ grid caisse *f* nationale de l'énergie; **2.** national (-e *f*) *m*); **'na·tion·al·ism** nationalisme *m*; **'na·tion·al·ist** nationaliste *mf*; **na·tion·al·i·ty** [næʃə'næliti] nationalité *f*; caractère *m* ou esprit *m* national; **na·tion·al·ize** ['næʃnəlaiz] nationaliser; naturaliser; ~d undertakings entreprises *f/pl.* nationalisées.

na·tion-wide ['neiʃnwaid] répandu par tout le pays; *souv.* général (-aux *m/pl.*).

na·tive ['neitiv] **1.** □ indigène, originaire (de, to) (*personne, plante*); naturel(le *f*), inné (*qualité*); de naissance, natal (-als *m/pl.*) (*lieu*); à l'état natif (*métaux*); ~ language langue *f* maternelle; **2.** natif (-ive *f*) *m*; indigène *mf*; a ~ of Ireland Irlandais *m* de naissance.

na·tiv·i·ty [nə'tiviti] nativité *f*; horoscope *m*.

na·tron ['neitrən] natron *m*.

nat·ty ['næti] coquet(te *f*); pimpant; bien ménagé.

na·tu·ral ['nætʃrəl] **1.** □ naturel(le *f*); de la nature; inné, natif (-ive *f*); illégitime, naturel(le *f*) (*enfant*); ~ disaster catastrophe *f* naturelle; ~ gas gaz *m* naturel; ~ history histoire *f* naturelle; ♩ ~ note note *f* naturelle; ~ philosopher physicien *m*; ~ philosophy physique *f*; ~ reserve réserve *f* naturelle; ~ science sciences *f/pl.* naturelles; **2.** idiot(e *f*) *m*; ♩ bécarre *m*; **'nat·u·ral·ism** naturalisme *m*; *arts:* naturisme *m*; **'nat·u·ral·ist** natura-

liste *mf*; naturiste *mf*; **nat·u·ral·i·za·tion** [~lai'zeiʃn] naturalisation *f*; **'nat·u·ral·ize** naturaliser; ♣, *zo.* acclimater; **'nat·u·ral·ness** naturel *m*.

na·ture ['neitʃə] nature *f*; caractère *m*, essence *f*; naturel *m*, tempérament *m*; espèce *f*, genre *m*; by ~ de ou par nature; **'na·tured** au cœur ...; de caractère ...

na·tur·ism ['neitʃərizəm] naturisme *m*; **'na·tur·ist** naturiste *mf*.

naught [nɔːt] rien *m*, néant *m*; bring to ~ faire échouer; come to ~ échouer, n'aboutir à rien; set at ~ ne tenir aucun compte de; **naugh·ti·ness** ['~tinis] mauvaise tenue *f*; désobéissance *f*; **'naugh·ty** □ méchant, vilain.

nau·se·a ['nɔːsiə] nausée *f*; mal *m* de mer; *fig.* dégoût *m*; **nau·se·ate** ['~sieit] *v/i.* avoir la nausée (de, at); *v/t.* dégoûter; donner des nausées à (*q.*); **nau·se·ous** □ ['~siəs] dégoûtant.

nau·ti·cal □ ['nɔːtikl] nautique, marin; de marine; ~ mile mille *m* marin.

na·val ['neivəl] naval (-als *m/pl.*); de marine; ~ architect ingénieur *m* des constructions navales; ~ base port *m* de guerre; base *f* navale; ~ staff officiers *m/pl.* de l'état-major; **'na·val·ly** au point de vue naval.

nave[1] △ [neiv] nef *f*, vaisseau *m*.

nave[2] [~] *roue:* moyeu *m*.

na·vel ['neivəl] nombril *m*; *fig.* centre *m*; ~ orange (orange *f*) navel *f*; *anat.* ~ string cordon *m* ombilical.

nav·i·ga·ble □ ['nævigəbl] navigable; ~ balloon ballon *m* dirigeable.

nav·i·gate ['~geit] *v/i.* naviguer; *v/t.* naviguer sur (*la mer*); gouverner (*un navire*); **nav·i'ga·tion** navigation *f*; *ballon, navire:* conduite *f*; **'nav·i·ga·tor** navigateur *m*.

nav·vy ['nævi] terrassier *m*; (*a. steam-*~) piocheuse *f*.

na·vy ['neivi] marine *f* de guerre; marine *f* de l'État; **'~-'blue** bleu *m* marine *inv.*

nay [nei] **1.** † ou *prov.* non; pour mieux dire; **2.** non *m*; refus *m*.

Naz·a·rene [næzə'riːn] Nazaréen (-ne *f*) *m*. [*m.*]

naze [neiz] cap *m*, promontoire

neap [niːp] (*a.* ~-*tide*) marée *f* de morte-eau; **'neaped** ♣: be ~ être amorti.

Ne·a·pol·i·tan [niə'pɔlitən] 1. napo-
litain; 2. Napolitain(e f) m.

near [niə] 1. adj. proche; voisin; à
peu près juste; intime (ami); (le
plus) court (chemin); chiche (personne); serré (traduction); mot.
gauche (côté); montoir (cheval);
have (ou be) a ~ escape l'échapper
belle; ~ at hand tout près; ~ beer
bière f faible; ~ horse cheval m de
gauche (Am. de droite); it was a ~
miss (ou thing) il s'en est fallu de peu,
le coup est passé très près; 2. adv.
près, proche; 3. prp. (a.: ~ to) (au)près
de; 4. v/t. (s')approcher de; **near·by**
['~bai] tout près (de); tout proche
(de); **'near·ly** (de) près; presque; à
peu près; près de; **'near·ness** proximité f; fidélité f; parcimonie f;
'near-'sight·ed myope.

neat[1] □ [ni:t] bien rangé ou tenu;
soigné; élégant; pur, sans eau, sec
(sèche f) (boisson); net(te f) (écriture).

neat[2] † [~] bête f bovine; **'~'s-foot**
de pied de bœuf; **'~'s-leath·er** cuir
m de vache; **'~'s-tongue** langue f
de bœuf.

neat·ness ['ni:tnis] bon ordre m;
simplicité f; bon goût m; adresse f.

neb·u·la astr. ['nebjulə], pl. -lae
['~li:] nébuleuse f; **'neb·u·lar** né-
bulaire; **neb·u·los·i·ty** [~'lɔsiti]
nébulosité f; **'neb·u·lous** nébuleux
(-euse f) (a. fig.).

nec·es·sar·y □ ['nesisəri] 1. nécessaire, indispensable (à, for); inévitable (résultat); 2. nécessaire m;
usu. necessaries pl. nécessités f/pl.;
ne·ces·si·tate [ni'sesiteit] nécessiter (qch.); rendre (qch.) nécessaire;
ne'ces·si·tous nécessiteux (-euse
f); **ne'ces·si·ty** nécessité f; obligation f; besoin m; usu. necessities pl.
nécessaire m; nécessités f/pl.; the
bare necessities pl. (of life) les choses
f/pl. essentielles à la vie; of ~ de toute
nécessité.

neck [nek] 1. cou m; cuis. collier m
(de bœuf), collet m (de mouton);
bouteille: goulot m; robe: encolure f;
~ of land langue f de terre); ~ and ~
à égalité; F ~ and crop tout entier;
à corps perdu; F ~ or nothing à corps
perdu; (jouer) le tout pour le tout;
F be up to one's ~ in s.th. être dans qch.
jusqu'au cou; be up to one's ~ in work
a. avoir du travail par-dessus la tête;

sl. get it in the ~ en prendre pour son
compte; F stick one's ~ out prendre
des risques, s'avancer; se compromettre; 2. Am. sl. (se) caresser; v/t.
peloter; **'~-band** col m; encolure f;
neck·er·chief ['nekətʃif] foulard m;
neck·lace ['~lis] collier m; **neck·let**
['~lit] see necklace; tour m de cou (en
fourrure); **'neck·line** encolure f;
'neck·tie cravate f.

ne·crol·o·gy [ne'krɔlədʒi] nécrologe
m (d'une église etc.); nécrologie f;
nec·ro·man·cy ['nekromænsi] né-
cromancie f.

nec·tar ['nektə] nectar m.

née [nei]: Mrs. X, ~ Y Mme X,
née Y.

need [ni:d] 1. besoin m, nécessité f
(de of, for); adversité f; indigence f;
one's own ~s pl. son (propre) compte
m; if ~ be au besoin; le cas échéant;
be (ou stand) in ~ of avoir besoin de;
2. avoir besoin de; réclamer, demander (qch.); être obligé de;
need·ful ['~ful] 1. □ nécessaire;
2. F nécessaire m, souv. argent m
nécessaire; **'need·i·ness** indigence
f, nécessité f.

nee·dle ['ni:dl] 1. aiguille f; 2. surt.
Am. irriter, agacer; F ajouter de
l'alcool à, renforcer (une consommation); **'~-case** étui m à aiguilles; **'~-**
craft couture f; **'~-gun** fusil m à
aiguille; **'~-mak·ing** aiguillerie f.

need·less □ ['ni:dlis] inutile; ~ly
inutilement, sans raison; **'need-**
less·ness inutilité f.

nee·dle...: **'~-tel·e·graph** télégraphe
m à cadran; **'~-wom·an** couturière
f; **'~-work** travail (pl. -aux) m à
l'aiguille.

needs [ni:dz] adv. de nécessité; I
must ~ (inf.) force m'est de (inf.);
'need·y □ nécessiteux (-euse f).

ne'er [nɛə] = never; **~-do-well**
['~du:wel] propre-à-rien mf (pro-
pres-à-rien), vaurien(ne f) m.

ne·far·i·ous □ [ni'fɛəriəs] infâme,
scélérat.

ne·gate [ni'geit] nier; **ne'ga·tion**
négation f; **neg·a·tive** ['negətiv]
1. □ négatif (-ive f); 2. négative f;
gramm. négation f; phot. négatif m,
cliché m; answer in the ~ répondre
par la négative; 3. rejeter, s'opposer
à; nier; annuler; neutraliser.

neg·lect [ni'glekt] 1. manque m de
soin; mauvais entretien m; négli-

gence *f*; **2.** négliger; manquer de soins pour; laisser échapper (*une occasion*); **neg'lect·ful** □ [`-ful`] négligent; insoucieux (-euse *f*) (de, of).

neg·li·gence ['neglidʒəns] incurie *f*; négligence *f*; **'neg·li·gent** □ négligent; ~ *of* insoucieux (-euse *f*) de; ~ *attire* tenue *f* négligée.

neg·li·gi·ble ['neglidʒəbl] négligeable.

ne·go·ti·a·bil·i·ty [nigouʃiə'biliti] négociabilité *f*, commercialité *f*; **ne'go·ti·a·ble** □ négociable, commerciable; franchissable (*montagne*); praticable (*chemin*); ~ *cheque* chèque *m* barré; **ne'go·ti·ate** [-ʃeit] *v/t.* négocier (*affaire, effet, traité*); prendre (*un virage*); franchir (*une montagne*);*fig.* surmonter; *v/i.* traiter (avec q. de *ou* pour, *with s.o. for*); **ne·go·ti·at·ing ta·ble** table *f* de conférence; *at the* ~ par des négotiations, par voie de négociations; **ne·go·ti·a·tion** *effets, traite:* négociation *f*; pourparlers *m/pl.*; *fig.* franchissement *m*; *under* ~ en négociation; **ne'go·ti·a·tor** négociateur (-trice *f*) *m*.

ne·gress ['ni:gris] négresse *f*; **ne·gro** ['ni:grou], *pl.* -groes [-z] nègre *m*; **ne·groid** ['ni:grɔid] négroïde.

ne·gus ['ni:gəs] vin *m* chaud et épicé.

neigh [nei] **1.** hennissement *m*; **2.** hennir.

neigh·bo(u)r ['neibə] **1.** voisin(e *f*) *m*; *bibl.* prochain *m*; **2.** être le voisin de (*personne*); avoisiner (*terrain*); **'neigh·bo(u)r·hood** voisinage *m*; **'neigh·bo(u)r·ing** avoisinant, voisin, proche; **'neigh·bo(u)r·ly** de bon voisinage; obligeant.

nei·ther ['naiðə] **1.** *adj. ou pron.* ni l'un(e) ni l'autre; aucun(e *f*); **2.** *adv.* ~ ... *nor* ... ni ... ni ...; *not* ... ~ (ne ... pas) ... ne ... pas non plus. [gisme *m*.]

ne·ol·o·gism [ni'ɔlədʒism] néolo-

ne·on [nɪ] ['ni:ən] néon *m*; ~ *lamp* lampe *f* au néon; ~ *light(ing)* éclairage *m* au néon; ~ *sign* enseigne *m* au néon.

ne·o·phyte ['ni(:)oufait] néophyte *mf*; *fig.* débutant(e *f*) *m*.

neph·ew ['nevju(:)] neveu *m*.

nep·o·tism ['nepətizm] népotisme *m*.

nerve [nə:v] **1.** nerf *m*; ⚕, ⚕ nervure *f*; *fig.* courage *m*, sang-froid *m*; *fig.* vigueur *f*; F audace *f*, aplomb *m*; F *be all* ~s être un paquet de nerfs; F *have the* ~ *do to s.th.* avoir le toupet de faire qch.; *lose one's* ~s perdre son sang-froid *ou* son calme; **2.** fortifier; donner du courage à (*q.*); ~ *o.s.* s'armer de courage (pour, *to*); **'nerved** ⚕ nervé; **'nerve·less** □ inerte, sans force; **'nerve·rack·ing** énervant.

nerv·ine [ni] ['nə:vain] nervin (*a. su./m.*).

nerv·ous □ ['nə:vəs] timide, peureux (-euse *f*); inquiet (-ète *f*); excitable; *anat.* nerveux (-euse *f*), des nerfs; ⚕ ~ *breakdown* dépression *f* nerveuse; ~ *system* système *m* nerveux; **'nerv·ous·ness** timidité *f*; état *m* nerveux.

nerv·y *sl.* ['nə:vi] irritable; énervé; nerveux (-euse *f*), saccadé (*mouvement*).

nes·ci·ence ['nesiəns] ignorance *f*; **'nes·ci·ent** ignorant.

ness [nes] promontoire *m*, cap *m*.

nest [nest] **1.** nid *m* (*a. fig.*); nichée *f* (*d'oiseaux*); *fig.* série *f*; **2.** (se) nicher; **'nest·ed** niché; emboîté (*caisses etc.*); **'nest-egg** nichet *m*; argent *m* mis de côté; gentille petite somme *f*; **nes·tle** ['nesl] *v/i.* se nicher; *fig.* se blottir; se serrer (contre, [*up*] to); *v/t.* serrer; **nest·ling** ['neslin] oisillon *m*.

net¹ [net] **1.** filet *m* (*a. fig.*); *tex.* tulle *m*; mousseline *f*; ~ *courtains pl.* voilage *m*; **2.** prendre (*qch.*) au filet. **net²** [-] **1.** net(te*f*); sans déduction; **2.** rapporter *ou* toucher net.

neth·er ['neðə] inférieur; **'-most** le plus profond, le plus bas.

net·ting ['netin] pêche *f* au filet; pose *f* de filets; *tex.* tulle *m*; *fig.* réseau *m*.

net·tle ['netl] **1.** ⚕ ortie *f*; **2.** † fustiger avec des orties; *fig.* piquer, irriter; **'-rash** ⚕ urticaire *f*.

net·work ['netwə:k] réseau *m* (*a. fig.*); ouvrage *m* en filet; *national* ~ réseau *m* national.

neu·ral·gia ⚕ [njuə'rældʒə] névralgie *f*; *facial* ~ tic *m* douloureux; **neu·ras·the·ni·a** [njuərəs'θi:njə] ⚕ neurasthénie *f*; **neu·ras·then·ic** [-'θenik] neurasthénique (*a. su/mf*); **neu·ri·tis** ⚕ [njuə'raitis] névrite *f*;

neu·rol·o·gy ✻ [ˌ~'rɔlədʒi] neurologie f, névrologie f; **neu·ron** ['njuə-rɔn] neurone m; **neu·ro·path·ic** [njuəro'pæθik] 1. névropathique; 2. névropathe mf; **neu·ro·sis** ✻ [ˌ~'rousis] névrose f; **neu·rot·ic** [ˌ~'rɔtik] névrosé (a. su./mf.).

neu·ter ['nju:tə] 1. neutre; 2. animal m châtré; abeille f etc. asexuée; gramm. neutre m.

neu·tral ['nju:trəl] 1. □ neutre (a. ⚛); indéterminé, moyen(ne f); 2. neutre m; **neu·tral·i·ty** [nju(:)-'træliti] neutralité f; **neu·tral·i·za·tion** [nju:trəlai'zeiʃn] neutralisation f (a. ⚛); **'neu·tral·ize** neutraliser (a. ⚛); rendre inutile ou inoffensif (-ive f).

neu·tron phys. ['nju:trɔn] neutron m; ⚔ ~ bomb bombe f à neutrons.

né·vé géol. ['neivei] névé m.

nev·er ['nevə] ne ... jamais; jamais (de la vie); ~ so quelque (adj.) que (sbj.); '~·more (ne ...) plus jamais; (ne ...) jamais plus; ~·the·less [ˌ~ðə'les] néanmoins, quand même, pourtant.

new [nju:] nouveau (-el devant une voyelle ou un h muet); -elle f; -eaux m/pl.); neuf (neuve f); frais (fraîche f); 'new'com·er nouveau venu m; nouvel arrivé m; **new·fan·gled** ['ˌ~fæŋgld] péj. d'une modernité outrée; **'new·ly** récemment, nouvellement; **'new·ness** nouveauté f; état m neuf; inexpérience f.

news pl. ou sg. [nju:z] nouvelle f, -s f/pl.; what's the ~? quelles nouvelles?; F quoi de neuf?; break the (bad) ~ to s.o. annoncer les nouvelles à q. (avec ménagement); F he is much in the ~ il défraye la chronique; '~·a·gen·cy agence f d'informations; '~·a·gent marchand m de journaux; '~·boy vendeur m de journaux; '~·butch·er ✻ Am. vendeur m ambulant de journaux; '~·cast (bulletin m d')informations f/pl.; '~·cast·er speaker(ine f) m; ~ flash radio: flash m; ~ let·ter bulletin m, circulaire f; ~ mag·a·zine revue f; '~·mon·ger débiteur (-euse f) m de nouvelles; '~·pa·per journal m; attr. de journaux; '~·print papier m de journal; Brit. ~ read·er speaker(ine f) m; '~·reel film m d'actualité; actualités f/pl.; '~·room salle f des journaux; journ.

Am. salle f de rédaction; '~·stall, Am. '~·stand étalage m de marchand de journaux; France: kiosque m (à journaux); '~·ven·dor vendeur m de journaux; **news·y** ['nju:zi] F plein de nouvelles.

newt zo. [nju:t] triton m, F lézard m d'eau.

new-year, usu. **New year** ['nju:'jə:] nouvel an m; nouvelle année f; ~'s day le jour de l'an; ~'s eve la Saint-Sylvestre f; ~'s gift étrennes f/pl.

next [nekst] 1. adj. prochain; voisin; le plus proche; suivant; ~ but one le deuxième; '~·door voisin; ~ door maison f d'à côté; fig. ~ door to approchant de; the ~ of kin la famille; ⚛ le(s) parent(s) le(s) plus proche(s); ~ to contigu(ë f) à ou avec; à côté de; ~ to nothing ne ... presque rien; what ~? et ensuite?; F par exemple!; 2. adv. ensuite, après.

nex·us ['neksəs] lien m, rapport m.

nib [nib] 1. bec m (de plume); 2. mettre une plume à (un porte-plume).

nib·ble ['nibl] v/t. grignoter (qch.); mordiller; mouton: brouter; v/i. ~ at grignoter (qch.); mordre à (a. fig.); fig. être attiré par.

nice □ [nais] aimable, gentil(le f), sympathique (naturel); délicat (question, oreille); juste, sensible (oreille, œil); fin, subtil (distinction); joli (repas, montre, etc.); difficile (pour, about); scrupuleux (-euse f) (quant à, about); ~ and warm bien (au) chaud; **'nice·ness** gentillesse f, amabilité f; délicatesse f; finesse f; justesse f; **nice·ty** ['ˌ~iti] exactitude f; subtilité f; délicatesse f exagérée; méticulosité f; to a ~ à merveille; exactement; stand upon niceties faire des façons.

niche [nitʃ] niche f.

Nick¹ [nik]: F Old ~ le diable m.

nick² [ˌ~] 1. entaille f; fente f; in the (very) ~ of time juste à temps; à pic; 2. entailler; sl. choper.

nick·el ['nikl] 1. min. nickel m (Am. a. pièce f de 5 cents); Am. ~-in-the-slot machine distributeur m automatique; 2. nickeler.

nick·el·o·de·on Am. [nikl'oudiən] pick-up m/inv. à sous.

nick-nack ['niknæk] see knicknack.

nick·name ['nikneim] 1. surnom m;

sobriquet *m*; 2. surnommer; donner un sobriquet à.

nic·o·tine ['nikəti:n] nicotine *f*.

nid-nod ['nidnɔd] dodeliner ⟨de⟩ la tête.

niece [ni:s] nièce *f*.

niffed F [nift] offensé.

nif·ty *Am.* ['nifti] 1. élégant; pimpant; 2. remarque *f* bien à propos.

nig·gard ['nigəd] 1. grippe-sou *m*; pingre *m*, avare *mf*; 2. avare, parcimonieux (-euse *f*); '**nig·gard·li·ness** pingrerie *f*; parcimonie *f*; '**nig·gard·ly** *adj.* (*a. adv.*) chiche (-ment); mesquin(ement).

nig·ger F *usu. péj.* ['nigə] nègre *m*, négresse *f*; *Am. sl. that's the ~ in the woodpile* il y a anguille sous roche!

nig·gle ['nigl] vétiller; '**nig·gling** insignifiant; fignolé (*travail*); tatillon(ne *f*) (*personne*).

nigh † *ou prov.* [nai] *see near* 1, 2, 3.

night [nait] nuit *f*, soir *m*; obscurité *f*; *by ~* de nuit; *in the ~* (pendant) la nuit; *at ~* la nuit; *~ out* soir *m* de sortie; *make a ~ of it* faire la noce toute la nuit; '**~·cap** bonnet *m* de nuit; *fig.* grog *m* (avant de se coucher); '**~·club** boîte *f* de nuit; '**~-dress** chemise *f* de nuit (*de femme*); '**~·fall** tombée *f* de la nuit; '**~-gown** *see night-dress*; **night·in·gale** *orn.* ['ˌnaiŋgeil] rossignol *m*; '**night·ly** de nuit, nocturne; (de) tous les soirs.

night·...: '**~·mare** cauchemar *m*; '**~·school** classe *f* du soir; '**~-shade** ♀ morelle *f* noire; *deadly ~* belladone *f*; '**~-shift** équipe *f* de nuit; poste *m* de nuit; *be on ~* être (au poste) de nuit; '**~-shirt** chemise *f* de nuit (*d'homme*); '**~-spot** *Am.* F boîte *f* de nuit; '**~·time** nuit *f*; *~ watch·man* gardien *m* de nuit.

ni·hil·ism ['naiilizm] nihilisme *m*; '**ni·hil·ist** nihiliste *mf*.

nil [nil] rien *m*; *sp.* zéro *m*; *~ return* état *m* néant.

nim·ble □ ['nimbl] agile, leste; délié (*esprit*); '**nim·ble·ness** agilité *f*; vivacité *f* (*d'esprit*); '**nim·ble-wit·ted** à l'esprit vif; qui a la répliique facile, qui a de la repartie.

nim·bus ['nimbəs], *pl.* -**bi** [~bai], -**bus·es** nimbe *m*, auréole *f*; *météor.* nimbus *m*.

nim·i·ny-pim·i·ny ['nimini'pimini] maniéré; mignard.

nin·com·poop F ['ninkəmpu:p] nigaud *m*, benêt *m*, niais *m*.

nine [nain] 1. neuf; *~ days' wonder* merveille *f* d'un jour; 2. neuf *m*; '**~-fold** nonuple, neuf fois; '**~-pins** *pl.* quilles *f/pl.*; **nine·teen** ['~'ti:n] dix-neuf (*a. su./m*); **'nine'teenth** [~θ] dix-neuvième; **nine·tieth** ['~tiiθ] quatre-vingt-dixième(*a.su./m*); '**nine·ty** quatre-vingt-dix.

nin·ny F ['nini] niais(e *f*) *m*.

ninth [nainθ] 1. neuvième; 2. neuvième *m*; ♪ neuvième *f*; '**ninth·ly** en neuvième lieu.

nip¹ [nip] 1. pincement *m*; morsure *f*; ♦ coup *m* de gelée; 2. pincer; piquer, mordre (*froid*); brûler (*gelée*); *~ in the bud* tuer dans l'œuf; faire avorter (*un complot*).

nip² [~] 1. goutte *f*, doigt *m* (*d'alcool*); 2. boire *ou* une goutte.

nip³ *sl.* [~] chiper, choper, refaire.

nip·per ['nipə] F gamin *m*, gosse *m*; homard *etc.*: pince *f*; (*a pair of*) *~s pl.* (une) pince *f*; (des) tenailles *f/pl.*

nip·ple ['nipl] mamelon *m*; bout *m* de sein; ⊕ raccord *m*.

nip·py F ['nipi] vif (vive *f*); âpre; piquant.

Ni·sei *Am.* ['ni'sei] (*a. pl.*) japonais *m* (*né aux É.-U.*).

nit [nit] œuf *m* de pou; '**~-pick·ing** F qui coupe les cheveux en quatre.

ni·tre, ni·ter 🜍 ['naitə] nitre *m*, salpêtre *m*.

ni·tric ac·id 🜍 ['naitrik'æsid] acide *m* nitrique *ou* azotique.

ni·tro·gen 🜍 ['naitrədʒən] azote *m*; **ni·trog·e·nous** [~'trɔdʒinəs] azoté.

ni·tro·glyc·er·in(e) ['naitrouglisə-'ri:n] nitroglycérine *f*.

ni·trous 🜍 ['naitrəs] azoteux (-euse *f*).

nit·ty-grit·ty *sl.* ['nitigriti]: *the ~* l'essentiel; *come* (*ou get down*) *to the ~* en venir au fait; en venir au fond.

nit·wit F [nitwit] imbécile *mf*.

nix *sl.* [niks] 1. rien *m* (du tout), F peau *f* de balle; 2. non!; rien à faire!; 3. dire non à (*qch.*).

no [nou] 1. *adj.* aucun, pas de; *in ~ time* en un clin d'œil; *~ man's land* zone *f* neutre; *~ one* personne (... ne); 2. *adv.* peu; non; *avec comp.*: pas (plus); 3. *su. m/inv.*: **noes** [nouz] *pl.* les non *m/pl.*; voix *f/pl.* contre.

nob[1] *sl.* [nɔb] caboche *f* (= *tête*); ⊕ bouton *m.*   [rupins *m/pl.*)
nob[2] *sl.* [ʌ] aristo *m*; the ~*s pl.* les)
nob·ble *sl.* ['nɔbl] écloper (*un cheval*); soudoyer (*q.*); pincer (*un criminel*); filouter (*de l'argent*).
nob·by *sl.* ['nɔbi] élégant, chic.
No·bel prize [nou'bel'praiz] Prix *m* Nobel; *Nobel peace prize* Prix *m* Nobel de la paix; ~ *winner* (lauréat *m* du) Prix Nobel *m.*
no·bil·i·ar·y [nou'biliəri] nobiliaire.
no·bil·i·ty [nou'biliti] noblesse *f* (*a. fig.*).
no·ble ['noubl] **1.** □ noble (*q. sentiment, métal, joyau*); sublime; grand (*vin, âme, etc.*); admirable; **2.** noble *mf*, aristocrate *mf*; '~·**man** noble *m*, gentilhomme (*pl.* gentilshommes) *m*; '~-'**mind·ed** à l'âme noble; généreux (-euse *f*); '**no·ble·ness** noblesse *f* (*a. fig.*); '**no·ble·wom·an** noble *f*, aristocrate *f.*
no·bod·y ['noubədi] **1.** personne, aucun (... ne); **2.** zéro *m*, nullité *f.*
nock [nɔk] (en)coche *f.*
no-claims bo·nus ['nou'kleimz bounəs] *assurance:* bonification *f* pour non-sinistre.
noc·tur·nal [nɔk'tə:nl] nocturne.
nod [nɔd] **1.** *v/i.* faire signe que oui; incliner la tête; dodeliner de la tête; somnoler; *fig.* danser; *have a ~ding acquaintance* se connaître vaguement; ~ *off* somnoler; *v/t.* incliner (*la tête*); ~ *s.o.* out fai re sortir q. d'un signe de la tête; **2.** signe *m* de (la) tête; penchement *m* de tête (*au sommeil*).
nod·dle F ['nɔdl] caboche *f* (= *tête*).
nod·dy F ['nɔdi] niais(e *f*) *m.*
node [noud] nœud *m* (*a. ♀, a. astr.*); ⊕ nodosité *f.*
nod·u·lar ['nɔdjulə] nodulaire.
nod·ule ['nɔdjuːl] nodule *m.*
nog [nɔg] cheville *f* de bois; **nog·gin** ['~in] (petit) pot *m* (*en étain etc.*); **nog·ging** △ ['~in] hourdage *m.*
no·how F ['nouhau] en aucune façon.
noil [nɔil] *tex.* blousse *f.*
noise [nɔiz] **1.** bruit *m*, tapage *m*, fracas *m*, vacarme *m*; son *m*; ~ *abatement* lutte *f* anti-bruit *ou* contre le bruit; ~ *level* niveau *m* des bruits; *surt. Am.* F big ~ gros bonnet *m*; **2.** ~ *about*, ~ *abroad* ébruiter; crier sur les toits.

noise·less □ ['~lis] sans bruit; silencieux (-euse *f*); '**noise·less·ness** silence *m*, absence *f* de bruit.
nois·i·ness ['nɔizinis] caractère *m* bruyant; tintamarre *m.*
noi·some ['nɔisəm] fétide, infect; *fig.* désagréable; '**noi·some·ness** fétidité *f*, puanteur *f.*
nois·y □ ['nɔizi] bruyant, tapageur (-euse *f*); turbulent (*enfant*).
no·mad ['nɔməd] nomade *mf*; **no·mad·ic** [no'mædik] (~*ally*) nomade; **no·mad·ize** ['nɔmədaiz] *v/t.* nomadiser; *v/i.* vivre en nomade(s).
no·men·cla·ture [nou'menklətʃə] nomenclature *f*; recueil *m* de noms propres.
nom·i·nal □ ['nɔminl] nominal (-aux *m/pl.*); fictif (-ive *f*) (*prix, valeur*); ✕ nominatif (-ive *f*); ~ *value* valeur *f* fictive *ou* nominale; **nom·i·nate** ['~neit] nommer, désigner; proposer; **nom·i·na·tion** nomination *f*; présentation *f* (*d'un candidat*); in ~ nommé; proposé; **nom·i·na·tive** *gramm.* ['~nətiv] (*a.* ~ *case*) nominatif *m*, cas *m* sujet; **nom·i·na·tor** ['~neitə] présentateur *m*; **nom·i·nee** [~'ni:] candidat *m* désigné *ou* choisi.
non ... [nɔn] non-; in-; sans ...
non-ac·cept·ance ['nɔnək'septəns] non-acceptation *f.*
non·age ['nounidʒ] minorité *f.*
non·a·ge·nar·i·an ['nɔnədʒi'neəriən] nonagénaire (*a. su./mf*).
non-ag·gres·sion ['nɔnə'greʃn] ~ *pact* pacte *m* de non-agression.
non-al·co·hol·ic ['nɔnælkə'hɔlik] sans alcool; non alcoolique.
non-a·ligned ['nɔnə'laind] neutraliste, non aligné; '**non-a·lign·ment** neutralisme *m*, non-alignement *m.*
non-ap·pear·ance ⚖ ['nɔnə'piərəns] non-comparution *f*; *souv.* défaut *m.*
non-at·tend·ance ⚖ ['nɔnə'tendəns] absence *f.*
nonce [nɔns] *for the* ~ pour l'occasion; ~ *word* mot *m* de circonstance.
non·cha·lance ['nɔnʃələns] nonchalance *f*, indifférence *f*; '**non·cha·lant** □ nonchalant, indifférent.
non-com·mis·sioned ['nɔnkə'miʃənd] sans brevet; ✕ ~ *officer* sous-officier *m* gradé.
non-com·mit·tal ['nɔnkə'mitl] diplomatique; qui n'engage à rien.

non·com·pli·ance ['nɔnkəm'plaiəns] refus *m* d'obéissance (à, with).

non com·pos men·tis 🏛 [nɔn 'kɔmpɔs 'mentis] aliéné, fou (fol *devant une voyelle ou un h muet*; folle *f*).

non·con·duc·tor ⚡ ['nɔnkən'dʌktə] inconducteur *m*; *phys.* non-conducteur *m*.

non·con·form·ist ['nɔnkən'fɔ:mist] non-conformiste *mf*; dissident(e *f*) *m*; **'non·con'form·i·ty** non-conformisme *m* (*a. eccl.*). [sable.]

non-creas·ing ['nɔn'kri:siŋ]infrois-

non-de·nom·i·na·tion·al ['nɔndinəmi'neiʃnl] laïque (*école*).

non·de·script ['nɔndiskript] 1. inclassable; 2. *fig.* personne *f ou* chose *f* indéfinissable.

none [nʌn] 1. aucun; pas de; 2. aucunement; ~ the less cependant, pourtant, quand même.

non·en·ti·ty [nɔ'nentiti] personne *f* insignifiante; *fig.* non-valeur *f*; nullité *f*.

non-es·sen·tial ['nɔni'senʃəl] 1. non essentiel(le *f*); 2. accessoire *m*.

non-ex·ist·ence ['nɔnig'zistəns] non-être *m*.

non-fic·tion ['nɔn'fikʃn] ouvrages *m/pl.* autres que les romans.

non-in·ter·ven·tion ['nɔnintə(:)-'venʃn] non-intervention *f*.

non-i·ron ['nɔn'aiən] ne pas repasser.

non-lad·der·ing ['nɔn'lædəriŋ] indémaillable.

non-ob·serv·ance ['nɔnəb'zə:vəns] inobservance *f*.

non-pa·reil ['nɔnpərel] 1. nonpareil(le *f*); 2. personne *f ou* chose *f* sans pareille; *typ.* nonpareille *f*.

non-par·ti·san [nɔn'pɑ:tizæn] impartial.

non-par·ty *pol.* ['nɔn'pɑ:ti] non partisan; impartial (-aux *m/pl.*).

non-pay·ment ['nɔn'peimənt] non-paiement *m*; défaut *m* de paiement.

non-per·form·ance 🏛 ['nɔnpə-'fɔ:məns] non-exécution *f*.

non-plus ['nɔn'plʌs] 1. embarras *m*, perplexité *f*; at a ~ à quia; 2. confondre, réduire à quia; ~sed désemparé; interdit.

non-prof·it-mak·ing ['nɔn'prɔfitmeikiŋ] sans but lucratif.

non-pro·lif·er·a·tion ['nɔnproulifə-'reiʃən] non-prolifération *f* (*des armes nucléaires*); ~ *treaty* traité *m* de non-prolifération.

non-res·i·dent ['nɔn'rezidənt] externe; forain; non-résident (*a. su./mf*).

non·sense ['nɔnsəns] absurdité *f*; bêtise *f*, -s *f/pl.*; **non·sen·si·cal** □ [.'sensikl] absurde; bête.

non-skid ['nɔn'skid] antidérapant.

non-smok·er ['nɔn'smoukə] non-fumeur *m*.

non-start·er ['nɔn'stɑ:tə] nonvaleur *f*; projet *m* sans avenir.

non-stick ['nɔn'stick] qui n'attache pas (*casserole etc.*).

non-stop ['nɔn'stɔp] 🚌, ✈ direct; sans arrêt; ✈ sans escale.

non·such ['nʌnsʌtʃ] personne *f ou* chose *f* sans pareille.

non·suit 🏛 ['nɔn'sju:t] débouté *m*, rejet *m* de la demande.

non-un·ion [nɔn'ju:njən] non-syndiqué (*ouvrier*).

noo·dle¹ ['nu:dl] F niais(e *f*) *m*.

noo·dle² [.] *usu.* ~s *pl.* nouilles *f/pl.*

nook [nuk] (re)coin *m*.

noon [nu:n] 1. (*a.* '~day, '~tide) midi *m*; 2. de midi.

noose [nu:s] 1. nœud *m* coulant; corde *f* (de potence); *fig.* piège *m*; 2. prendre au lacet; attraper au

nope *Am.* F [noup] non! [lasso.]

nor [nɔ:] *précédé de neither:* ni; *début de la phrase:* ne ... pas non plus; ~ do I (ni) moi non plus.

norm [nɔ:m] norme *f*; règle *f*; **'nor·mal** □ 1. normal (-aux *m/pl.*) (*a.* Å); Å perpendiculaire; ~ *school* école *f* normale; 2. condition *f* normale; Å normale *f*, perpendiculaire *f*; **'nor·mal·ize** rendre normal; régulariser. [2. Normand(e *f*) *m*.]

Nor·man ['nɔ:mən] 1. normand;

north [nɔ:θ] 1. *su.* nord *m*; 2. *adj.* du nord; septentrional (-aux *m/pl.*); '~·bound en direction du nord, allant vers le nord; '~-'east 1. nord-est *m*; 2. (*a.* '~·east·ern) du nord-est; **north·er·ly** ['~ðəli] du *ou* au nord; **north·ern** ['~ən] du nord; septentrional (-aux *m/pl.*); '**north·er** habitant(e *f*) *m* du nord; *Am.* ⌀ nordiste *mf*; '**north·ern·most** le plus au nord; **north·ing** ⚓ ['~θiŋ] chemin *m* nord; *astr.* mouvement *m* vers le nord; **north·ward** ['~wəd] 1. *adj.* au *ou* du nord; 2. *adv.* (*a.* **north·wards** ['~dz]) vers le nord.

notional

north...: '**~-west** 1. nord-ouest *m*;
♎ *a.* norois *m*; 2. (*a.* '**~-'west·ern**,
'**~-'west·er·ly**) (du) nord-ouest *inv*.
Nor·we·gian [nɔːˈwiːdʒən] 1. nor-
végien(ne *f*); 2. Norvégien(ne *f*) *m*.
nose [nouz] 1. nez *m* (*a.* = flair);
odorat *m*; *outil*: bec *m*; *tuyau*:
ajutage *m*; ✂ *balle*: pointe *f*; ♎
torpille: cône *m* de choc; 2. *v/t.* (*a.*
~ *out*) sentir, flairer; ~ *out* découvrir;
~ *one's way* s'avancer avec précau-
tions; *v/i.* chercher (qch., *after* [*ou
for*] *s.th.*); ~ *ahead of* aller un peu en
avant de (*qch.*); '**~·bag** musette *f*;
'**~·band** muserolle *f*; **nosed** au nez
...
nose...: '**~·dive** ✈ (vol *m*) piqué *m*;
'**~·gay** bouquet *m* de fleurs; '**~-
heav·y** ✈ lourd de l'avant.
no-show F [ˈnouˈʃou] personne qui
ne se présente pas à l'heure convenue.
nos·ing ⚠ [ˈnouzin] arête *f* (de
moulure); *marche d'escalier*: nez *m*.
nos·tal·gi·a [nɔsˈtældʒiə] nostalgie
f; **nos·tal·gic** [~dʒik] nostalgique.
nos·tril [ˈnɔstril] narine *f*; *cheval,
bœuf*: naseau *m*.
nos·trum [ˈnɔstrəm] panacée *f*;
remède *m* de charlatan.
nos·y [ˈnouzi] parfumé; *péj.* curieux
(-euse *f*); F fouinard, indiscret
(-ète *f*); ⚥ *Parker* indiscret *m*; F
fouinard *m*.
not [nɔt] (ne) pas, (ne) point.
no·ta·bil·i·ty [noutəˈbiliti] notabilité *f*; caractère *m* notable (*d'un
événement*); *see* **notable** 2; **no·ta·ble**
[ˈnoutəbl] 1. □ notable, insigne,
considérable; sensible; perceptible
(*quantité*); éminent (*personne*); 2.
personne: notable *m*, notabilité *f*;
'**no·ta·bly** 1. remarquablement;
2. notamment.
no·tar·i·al □ [nouˈteəriəl] de notaire; notarié (*document*); notarial
(-aux *m/pl.*) (*sceau*); **no·ta·ry**
[ˈnoutəri] (*a.* ~ *public*) notaire *m*.
no·ta·tion [nouˈteiʃn] *surt.* ♎, *a.* ♪
notation *f*.
notch [nɔtʃ] 1. encoche *f*; ⊕ cran*m*;
Am. défilé *m*, gorge *f*; 2. entailler,
encocher; denteler (*une roue*).
note [nout] 1. note *f* (*a.* ♪, ♩, *pol.*);
F ton *m* (*de la voix*); ♪ son *m*;
♩ *piano*: touche *f*; marque *f*, signe
m; *pol.* mémorandum *m*; ✝ billet
m, lettre *f*; *banque*: billet *m*; *texte*:

annotation *f*; renom *m*; *take ~s of*
prendre des notes de; 2. noter,
constater, remarquer; relever (*une
erreur*); faire attention à; (*a.* ~
down) inscrire, prendre note de;
'**~·book** carnet *m*; *sténographie*:
bloc-notes (*pl.* blocs-notes) *m*;
'**not·ed** distingué, éminent (*personne*); célèbre (par, *for*), connu
(pour, *for*) (*chose*); ~*ly* surtout; nettement; '**note·pa·per** papier *m* à
lettres; '**note·wor·thy** remarquable; digne d'attention.
noth·ing [ˈnʌθin] 1. rien (de *adj.*)
(*su./m.*); Ⓐ zéro *m*; néant *m*;
fig. bagatelle *f*; *for* ~ gratis; *good
for* ~ bon à rien, inutile; *bring to* ~
faire échouer; *come to* ~ ne pas
aboutir; *make* ~ *of* ne faire aucun
cas de; *I can make* ~ *of it* je n'y
comprends rien; 2. *adv.* aucunement; pas du tout; '**noth·ing·ness**
néant *m*; *fig.* nullité *f*.
no·tice [ˈnoutis] 1. avis *m*; avertissement *m*; convocation *f* (*d'une réunion*); ✝ délai *m*; *bourse*: terme *m*;
affiche *f*; écriteau *m*; annonce *f*,
journ. notice *f*; revue *f* (*d'un
ouvrage*); *fig.* attention *f*; congé *m*;
at short ~ à bref délai; *give* ~ *of departure* annoncer son départ; *give* ~
that prévenir que; *give s.o. a week's*
~ donner ses huit jours à q.; *take* ~
of faire attention à; *until further* ~
jusqu'à nouvel ordre; *without* ~ sans
avis préalable; 2. remarquer, observer; s'apercevoir de *ou* que; prendre
garde à; faire le compte rendu de (*un
ouvrage*); faire attention à; '**no·tice-
a·ble** □ sensible, perceptible; digne
d'attention; '**no·tice-board** écriteau *m*; porte-affiches *m/inv.*; panneau *m* indicateur.
no·ti·fi·a·ble ✚ [ˈnoutifaiəbl] dont la
déclaration est obligatoire (*maladie*);
no·ti·fi·ca·tion [~fiˈkeiʃn] avis *m*;
avertissement *f*; annonce *f*; déclaration *f*; notification *f*.
no·ti·fy [ˈnoutifai] annoncer; avertir; déclarer; aviser, notifier.
no·tion [ˈnouʃn] notion *f*, idée *f*;
pensée *f*; *fig.* caprice *m*; *Am.* ~*s pl.*
petites inventions *f/pl.* bon marché; (*petits*) articles *m/pl.* ingénieux; '**no·tion·al** □ spéculatif
(-ive *f*) (*connaissances etc.*); imaginaire; *surt. Am.* F capricieux (-euse
f); fantasque.

no·to·ri·e·ty [noutə'raiəti] notoriété
f; *personne*: notabilité *f*; **no·to·ri·ous** □ [nou'tɔːriəs]
connu; *péj.* d'une triste notoriété;
fameux (-euse *f*).

not·with·stand·ing [nɔtwiθ'stæn-
diŋ] **1.** *prp.* malgré, en dépit de;
2. *adv.* pourtant; tout de même;
3. *cj.* ~ *that* quoique (*sbj.*), bien
que (*sbj.*).

nought *surt.* Å [nɔːt] zéro *m*; F
rien *m*; *come to* ~ échouer, tomber à
l'eau.

noun *gramm.* [naun] nom *m*,
substantif *m*.

nour·ish ['nʌriʃ] nourrir (*a. fig.*);
alimenter; **'nour·ish·ing** nourrissant, nutritif (-ive *f*); **'nour·ish-
ment** nourriture *f*; alimentation *f*.

nov·el ['nɔvl] **1.** nouveau (-el *devant
une voyelle ou un h muet*; -elle *f*),
original (-aux *m/pl.*); **2.** roman *m*;
short ~ = **nov·el·ette** [nɔvə'let]
nouvelle *f*; **'nov·el·ist** romancier
(-ère *f*) *m*; **nov·el·ty** ['nɔvlti] nouveauté *f* (*a.* ✝).

No·vem·ber [no'vembə] novembre
m.

nov·ice ['nɔvis] novice *mf* (*a. eccl.*);
débutant(e *f*) *m*.

no·vi·ci·ate, no·vi·ti·ate [no'viʃiit]
noviciat *m* (*a. eccl.*); apprentissage
m.

now [nau] **1.** *adv.* maintenant; en ce
moment; tout de suite; *avec vbe.
passé*: alors; à ce moment-là; *just* ~
tout à l'heure; *before* ~ déjà; jusqu'ici; ~ *and again* de temps à
autre; ~ *and then* de temps en
temps; **2.** *cj.* (*a.* ~ *that*) maintenant
que; or; **3.** *su.* présent *m*.

now·a·day ['nauədei]d'aujourd'hui;
now·a·days ['~z] de nos jours.

no·way(s) F ['nouwei(z)] en aucune
façon.

no·where ['nouwɛə] nulle part.

no·wise ['nouwaiz] *see* noway(s).

nox·ious □ ['nɔkʃəs] nuisible.

noz·zle ['nɔzl] ⊕ ajutage *m*; jet
m.

nub [nʌb] (petit) morceau *m*; *Am.* F
essentiel *m* (*d'une affaire*).

nu·cle·ar ['njuːkliə] nucléaire; ~
deterrent force *f* de dissuasion nucléaire; ~ *disintegration* désintégration *f* nucléaire; ~ *energy* énergie *f*
nucléaire; ~ *physics* physique *f* nucléaire; ~ *pile* pile *f* nucléaire; ~ *power*

énergie *f* nucléaire; ~ *power plant*
centrale *f* (électro-)nucléaire; ~ *reactor* bouilleur *m* atomique; ~ *research*
recherches *f/pl.* nucléaires; ~ *submarine* sous-marin *m* atomique; ~ *warfare* guerre *f* nucléaire *ou* atomique;
~ *warhead* ogive *f* nucléaire; **nu·cle-
on** *phys.* ['~kliɔn] nucléon *m*; **nu-
cle·us** ['~kliəs], *pl.* -i [~ai] noyau
m.

nude [njuːd] **1.** nu; **2.** figure *f* nue;
peint. nu *m*; nudité *f*; *study from
the* ~ nu *m*.

nudge F [nʌdʒ] **1.** pousser (*q.*) du
coude; **2.** coup *m* de coude.

nud·ism ['njuːdizm] nudisme *m*;
'nud·ist nudiste *mf*; **'nu·di·ty**
nudité *f*; figure *f* nue.

nu·ga·to·ry ['njuːgətəri] futile, sans
valeur; inefficace.

nug·get ['nʌgit] pépite *f* (*d'or*).

nui·sance ['njuːsns] dommage *m*;
fig. personne: peste *f*, gêneur (-euse
f) *m*; *chose*: ennui *m*; *what a* ~!
quel ennui!; F quelle scie!; *commit
no* ~! défense de déposer des immondices!; défense d'uriner; *make
o.s.* (*ou be*) *a* ~ être assommant.

nuke *Am. sl.* [nuːk] **1.** arme *f* nucléaire; **2.** attaquer avec des armes
nucléaires.

null [nʌl] ⚥, *a. fig.* nul(le *f*); *fig.*
inefficace, insignifiant; ~ *and void*
nul et sans effet; **nul·li·fi·ca·tion**
annulation *f*, infirmation *f*; **nul·li-
fy** ['~ifai] annuler; nullifier; infirmer; **'nul·li·ty** nullité *f*, invalidité *f*; *fig.* homme *m* nul, non-
valeur *f*.

numb [nʌm] **1.** engourdi (par,
with); transi; **2.** engourdir (*a. fig.*).

num·ber ['nʌmbə] **1.** ⚥, *gramm.*,
personnes: nombre *m*; chiffre *m*
(*écrit*); numéro *m* (*de maison, auto,
journal, programme, etc.*); *poét.* ~s
pl. vers *m/pl.*; ♪ accords *m/pl.*;
2. compter; numéroter; ~ *among*,
~ *in*, ~ *with* (se) compter parmi;
'num·ber·less sans nombre; innombrable; **'num·ber·plate** *mot.*
plaque *f* matricule.

numb·ness ['nʌmnis] engourdissement *m*; *fig.* torpeur *f*.

nu·mer·a·ble ['njuːmərəbl] (dé-)
nombrable; **nu·mer·al 1.** numéral
(-aux *m/pl.*); **2.** nombre *m*, chiffre
m; nom *m* de nombre; ~s *pl.* numéraux *m/pl.*; **nu·mer·a·tion** numé-

ration *f*; **'nu·mer·a·tor** ⅍ numérateur *m* (*d'une fraction*).

nu·mer·i·cal □ [nju'merikl] numérique.

nu·mer·ous □ ['nju:mərəs] nombreux (-euse *f*); *vers*: cadencé; **'nu·mer·ous·ness** (grand) nombre *m*; abondance *f*.

nu·mis·mat·ic [nju:miz'mætik] (~ally) numismatique; **nu·mis'mat·ics** *usu. sg.* numismatique *f*; **nu·mis·ma·tist** [nju(:)'mizmətist] numismat(ist)e *m*.

num·skull F ['nʌmskʌl] nigaud(e *f*) *m*; idiot(e *f*) *m*.

nun [nʌn] religieuse *f*; *orn.* mésange *f* bleue, *a.* pigeon *m* nonnain.

nun·ci·a·ture *eccl.* ['nʌnʃiətʃə] nonciature *f*; **nun·ci·o** *eccl.* ['~ʃiou] nonce *m*.

nun·ner·y ['nʌnəri] couvent *m* (de religieuses).

nup·tial ['nʌpʃəl] **1.** nuptial (-aux *m/pl.*); **2.** ~s *pl.* noces *f/pl.*

nurse [nə:s] **1.** (*souv.* wet-~) nourrice *f*; bonne *f* d'enfants; garde-malade (*pl.* gardes-malades) *f*; *hôpital*: infirmière *f*; *at* ~ en nourrice; *put s.o. out to* ~ mettre q. en nourrice; **2.** allaiter (*un bébé*); soigner (*malade, plante, popularité, rhume*); entretenir (*un espoir, un sentiment*); mijoter (*un projet*); cultiver (*des électeurs, une relation, etc.*); **'~-maid** bonne *f* d'enfants.

nurs·er·y ['nə:sri] chambre *f* des enfants; garderie *f*; ✍ pépinière *f* (*a. fig.*); ~ *school* maternelle *f*; ~ **gov·ern·ess** gouvernante *f* (*pour jeunes enfants*); **'~·man** pépiniériste *m*; ~ **rhyme** chanson *f* de nourrice; poésie *f* enfantine.

nurs·ing ['nə:siŋ] allaitement *m*; soins *m/pl.*; profession *f* de garde-malade; ~ *home* maison *f* de santé *ou* de convalescence *ou* de repos *ou* de retraite; *Brit. a.* clinique *f* privée; ~ *bottle* biberon *m*.

nurs·ling ['nə:sliŋ] nourrisson *m*.

nur·ture ['nə:tʃə] **1.** nourriture *f*; aliments *m/pl.*; soins *m/pl.*, éducation *f*; **2.** nourrir (de, on) (*a. fig.*); élever; instruire.

nut [nʌt] **1.** noix *f*; ⊕ écrou *m*; *sl.* problème *m ou* personne *f* difficile; *sl.* boule *f* (= *tête*); ♩ *violon*: sillet *m*, *archet*: hausse *f*; *sl.* insensé(e *f*) *m*; ~s *pl.* charbon: gailletin *m*; **2.** *sl.* ~s toqué; *sl. that is* ~s *to* (*ou for*) *him* c'est un plaisir pour lui; *be* ~s on raffoler de; *sl. drive s.o.* ~s affoler q.; *go* ~s être toqué, déménager; **3.**: *go* ~*ting* aller aux noisettes.

nu·ta·tion [nju:'teiʃn] nutation *f*.

nut·crack·er ['nʌtkrækə] *usu.* (*a pair of*) ~s *pl.* (*des*) casse-noisettes *m/inv.*; **'nut-gall** noix *f* de galle; **nut·meg** ['~meg] (noix *f* de) muscade *f*.

nu·tri·ent ['nju:triənt] **1.** nourrissant, nutritif (-ive *f*); **2.** substance *f* nutritive; **'nu·tri·ment** nourriture *f*; aliments *m/pl.* nourrissants.

nu·tri·tion [nju:'triʃn] nutrition *f*; **nu'tri·tion·al** □ [~əl] alimentaire; nutritif (-ive *f*); ~ *value see nutritiousness*; **nu'tri·tious** □ nourrissant, nutritif (-ive *f*); **nu'tri·tious·ness** nutritivité *f*, valeur *f* nutritive.

nu·tri·tive □ ['nju:tritiv] *see nutritious*.

nut·shell ['nʌtʃel] coquille *f* de noix; *in a* ~ en peu de mots; **nut·ty** ['nʌti] abondant en noix *ou* en noisettes; ayant un goût de noisette; plein de saveur (*conte*); *sl.* entiché (de, on), timbré, un peu fou (fol *devant une voyelle ou un h muet*; folle *f*).

nuz·zle ['nʌzl] (contre, *against*) fouiller avec le groin (*cochon etc.*); fourrer son nez; *personne*: se blottir, se serrer.

ny·lon ['nailən] *tex.* nylon *m*; ~s *pl.* bas *m/pl.* nylon.

nymph [nimf] nymphe *f*.

O

O, o [ou] O *m*, o *m*.

o [ou] **1.** ♀ (= *nought*) zéro *m*; **2.**
int. O, ô, oh; ~ *for ...!* que ne
donnerais-je pas pour ...!

oaf [ouf] idiot(e *f*) *m*; lourdaud(e *f*)
m; **'oaf·ish** lourdaud.

oak [ouk] **1.** ♀ chêne *m*; *univ.* F
porte *f* extérieure; *see sport* 2; **2.** de
ou en chêne; '~-**ap·ple**, '~-**gall**
noix *f* de galle; '**oak·en** † de *ou*
en chêne; **oak·let** ['~lit], '**oak·ling**
chêneau *m*.

oa·kum ['oukəm] étoupe *f*.

oar [ɔ:] **1.** aviron *m*, rame *f*; *fig.*
rameur (-euse *f*) *m*; *fig.* put one's ~
in intervenir, s'en mêler; F *rest on
one's* ~*s* dormir sur ses lauriers;
2. *v/i.* ramer; *v/t.* faire avancer à la
rame; **oared** [ɔ:d] à rames; **oars·**
man ['ɔ:zmən] rameur *m*; '**oars·**
wom·an rameuse *f*.

o·a·sis [o'eisis], *pl.* -**ses** [~si:z]
oasis *f* (*a. fig.*).

oast [oust] séchoir *m* (à houblon).

oat [out] *usu.* ~*s pl.* avoine *f*; F *fig.*
feel one's ~*s* se sentir gaillard; *Am.*
a. se donner des airs; *sow one's wild*
~*s* faire des fredaines.

oath [ouθ], *pl.* **oaths** [ouðz]
serment *m*; *péj.* juron *m*, gros mot
m; *administer* (*ou tender*) *an* ~ *to*
faire prêter serment à, assermenter
(*q.*); *bind s.o. by* ~ lier par serment;
on ~ sous (la foi du) serment; *put
s.o. on his* ~ assermenter q.; *take
an* ~ prêter serment (*sur, on*); jurer
(*sur, on*; *de inf.*, *to inf.*).

oat·meal ['outmi:l] farine *f* d'a-
voine.

ob·du·ra·cy ['ɔbdjurəsi] opiniâtreté
f; inflexibilité *f*; **ob·du·rate** □
['~rit] obstiné; inflexible.

o·be·di·ence [o'bi:djəns] obéissance
f; *eccl.* obédience *f*; † *in* ~ *to*
conformément à; **o'be·di·ent** □
obéissant.

o·bei·sance [o'beisns] hommage *m*;
† révérence *f*; *do* (*ou make ou pay*) ~
(à, *to*) rendre hommage; prêter
obéissance (*au roi etc.*).

ob·e·lisk ['ɔbilisk] obélisque *m*; *typ.*
croix *f*, obèle *m*.

o·bese □ [o'bi:s] obèse; **o'bese·**
ness, **o'bes·i·ty** obésité *f*.

o·bey [o'bei] *v/t.* obéir à (*q.*, *un or-*
dre); *v/i.* obéir.

ob·fus·cate ['ɔbfʌskeit] *fig.* obscurcir; F griser.

o·bit·u·ar·y [o'bitjuəri] **1.** registre *m*
des morts; nécrologe *m*; **2.** nécrolo-
gique; *journ.* ~ *column* nécrologie *f*.

ob·ject 1. ['ɔbdʒikt] objet *m* (*a.*
fig.); chose *f*; *fig.* but *m*; *gramm.*
complément *m*, régime *m*; *salary
no* ~ les appointements impor-
tent peu; **2.** [əb'dʒekt] *v/t.* objecter
(*qch. à q.*, *s.th. to s.o.*); *v/i.* protester
(contre, *to*); ~ *to* (*gér.*) s'opposer à
(*inf.*); se refuser à (*inf.*); désapprouver (*inf.*); ~**-glass** *opt.* ['ɔbdʒikt-
glɑ:s] objectif *m*.

ob·jec·tion [əb'dʒekʃn] objection *f*;
fig. aversion *f*; *there is no* ~ (*to it*) il
n'y a aucun inconvénient; **ob'jec·**
tion·a·ble □ répréhensible; désagréable; choquant.

ob·jec·tive [əb'dʒektiv] **1.** □ objectif
(-ive *f*); **2.** objectif *m* (*a.* ✖, *opt.*);
but *m*; *gramm.* régime *m*; **ob'jec·**
tive·ness, **ob·jec'tiv·i·ty** objectivité *f*.

ob·ject...: '~-**lens** *opt.* objectif *m*;
'~-**less** □ sans but, sans objet; '~-
les·son leçon *f* de choses; *fig.* exemple *m*.

ob·jec·tor [əb'dʒektə] réclameur *m*;
contradicteur *m*; *see conscientious*.

ob·jur·gate ['ɔbdʒə:geit] accabler
(*q.*) de reproches; **ob·jur'ga·tion**
réprimande *f*; **ob'jur·ga·to·ry** [~
gətəri] objurgatoire.

ob·late □ ['ɔbleit] **1.** ♀ aplati (aux
pôles); **2.** *eccl.* oblat(e *f*) *m*; '**ob·**
late·ness ♀ aplatissement *m*.

ob·la·tion *eccl.* [o'bleiʃn] oblation *f*.

ob·li·ga·tion [ɔbli'geiʃn] obligation *f*
(*a.* ✝); devoir *m*; ✝ engagement *m*;
dette *f* de reconnaissance; *be under*
(*an*) ~ *to s.o.* avoir des obligations
envers q.; devoir de la reconnais-

sance à q.; *be under ~ to* (*inf.*) être dans l'obligation de (*inf.*), être tenu de (*inf.*); **ob·lig·a·to·ry** ['ˌɡətəri] obligatoire (à q., *on s.o.*); de rigueur.

o·blige [ə'blaidʒ] *v/t.* obliger (*a.* ⚖); astreindre; rendre service à (*q.*); ~ *the company with a song* avoir l'amabilité de chanter; *much ~d* bien reconnaissant; *v/i.* F ~ *with a song etc.* avoir l'amabilité de chanter *etc.*; *please ~ with an early reply* prière de bien vouloir répondre sous peu; **ob·li·gee** [ɔbli'dʒiː] ⚖ obligatoire *m*, créancier *m*; F obligé(e *f*) *m*; **o·blig·ing** □ [ə'blaidʒiŋ] obligeant, serviable, complaisant; **o·blig·ing·ness** obligeance *f*, complaisance *f*; **ob·li·gor** ⚖ [ɔbli'ɡɔː] obligé(e *f*) *m*.

ob·lique □ [ə'bliːk] ⚔, ♀, ♪, ⚓, ⚔, *anat.*, *astr.*, *gramm.* oblique; indirect (*discours, a. fig.*); de biais (*regard*); **ob·lique·ness**, **ob·liq·ui·ty** [ˌkwiti] obliquité *f*.

ob·lit·er·ate [o'blitəreit] effacer, faire disparaître; *fig.* passer l'éponge sur; ⚕, *anat.*, *poste:* oblitérer; **ob·lit·er·a·tion** effaçage *m*; rature *f*; ⚕, *anat.*, *timbre:* oblitération *f*.

ob·liv·i·on [o'bliviən] oubli *m*; *pol.* amnistie *f*; *fall (ou sink) into ~* tomber dans l'oubli; **ob·liv·i·ous** □ oublieux (-euse *f*); *be ~ of* oublier complètement; F ignorer tout à fait.

ob·long ['ɔblɔŋ] **1.** oblong(ue *f*); **2.** rectangle *m*.

ob·lo·quy ['ɔblɔkwi] blâme *m*, calomnie *f*; opprobre *m*, honte *f*.

ob·nox·ious □ [ɔb'nɔkʃəs] odieux (-euse *f*); désagréable; détesté (par, to); **ob'nox·ious·ness** caractère *m* odieux.

o·boe ♪ ['oubou] hautbois *m*; *personne:* hautboïste *mf*.

ob·scene □ [ɔb'siːn] obscène; *fig.* répugnant; **ob'scen·i·ty** [ˌiti] obscénité *f*; *langage:* grossièreté *f*.

ob·scur·ant [ɔb'skjuərənt] obscurantiste *mf*; **ob·scu·ra·tion** [ˌskjuˈreiʃn] obscurcissement *m*; *astr.* obscuration *f*, éclipse *f*; **ob·scure** [ɔb'skjuə] **1.** □ obscur (*a. fig.*); sombre; **2.** *v/t.* obscurcir (*a. fig.*); masquer (*la lumière*); *fig.* éclipser; **ob'scu·ri·ty** obscurité *f* (*a. fig.*).

ob·se·quies ['ɔbsikwiz] *pl.* obsèques *f/pl.*, funérailles *f/pl.*

ob·se·qui·ous □ [əb'siːkwiəs] obsé-

quieux (-euse *f*); **ob'se·qui·ous·ness** obséquiosité *f*, servilité *f*.

ob·serv·a·ble □ [əb'zɔːvəbl] visible; sensible; remarquable; **ob'serv·ance** *eccl.*, *dimanche, loi, ordre:* observance *f*; pratique *f*; **ob'serv·ant** □ observateur (-trice *f*) (de, of); attentif (-ive *f*) (à, of); **ob·ser·va·tion** [ɔbzɔːˈveiʃn] observation *f*; surveillance *f*; remarque *f*; *attr.* d'observation; ☒ ~ *car* wagon *m* d'observation; ⚕ ~ *ward* salle *f* des malades en observation; **ob·serv·a·to·ry** [əb'zɔːvətri] observatoire *m*; **ob'serve** *v/t.* observer (*a. fig.*); regarder; remarquer, apercevoir; dire; *v/i.* ~ *on* commenter (*qch.*); **ob'serv·er** observateur (-trice *f*) *m*.

ob·sess [əb'ses] obséder; ~*ed by* (*ou* with) obsédé par, hanté par; *en proie à*; **ob'ses·sion** obsession *f*.

ob·so·les·cence [ɔbsəˈlesns] vieillissement *m*; *biol.* atrophie *f*; **ob·so·les·cent** qui tombe en désuétude; *biol.* atrophié.

ob·so·lete ['ɔbsəliːt] désuet (-ète *f*); hors d'usage; démodé; *zo.* obsolète.

ob·sta·cle ['ɔbstəkl] obstacle *m*.

ob·ste·tri·cian [ɔbsteˈtriʃn] accoucheur *m*; **ob'stet·rics** [ˌriks] *usu. sg.* obstétrique *f*.

ob·sti·na·cy ['ɔbstinəsi] obstination *f*, opiniâtreté *f*; ⚕ persistance *f*; **ob·sti·nate** □ ['ˌnit] obstiné (*a.* ⚕), opiniâtre; acharné; rebelle (*fièvre*).

ob·strep·er·ous □ [əb'strepərəs] bruyant; rebelle; indiscipliné.

ob·struct [əb'strʌkt] *v/t.* obstruer (*a.* ⚕); encombrer; gêner; empêcher; **ob'struc·tion** ⊕ engorgement *m*; ⚕, *parl.* obstruction *f*; obstacle *m*; *fig.* empêchement *m*; encombrement *m*; **ob'struc·tive** □ ⚕ obstructif (-ive *f*); d'obstruction; *be ~ of* gêner.

ob·tain [əb'tein] *v/t.* obtenir, se procurer; gagner; *v/i.* régner, exister; **ob'tain·a·ble** procurable; trouvable; **ob'tain·ment** obtention *f*.

ob·trude [əb'truːd] (s')imposer (on, à); **ob'tru·sion** importunité *f*, intrusion *f*; **ob'tru·sive** □ [ˌsiv] importun; indiscret (-ète *f*).

ob·tu·rate ['ɔbtjuəreit] boucher, obturer; **'ob·tu·ra·tor** obturateur *m*.

ob·tuse □ [əb'tjuːs] ⚔, *angle, esprit, pointe:* obtus; *fig.* émoussé, sourd;

fig. stupide; **ob'tuse·ness** manque *m* de pointe; *fig.* stupidité *f.*

ob·verse ['ɔbvɜːs] obvers *m*; *médaille, monnaie:* face *f*; *fig.* opposé *m.*

ob·vi·ate ['ɔbvieit] *fig.* obvier à, éviter; prévenir.

ob·vi·ous □ ['ɔbviəs] évident, manifeste, clair; *fig.* voyant; **'ob·vi·ous·ness** évidence *f.*

oc·ca·sion [ə'keiʒn] **1.** occasion *f*, cause *f*; sujet *m*; besoin *m*; fois *f*; ~s *pl.* affaires *f/pl.*; on ~ de temps à autre; *on several* ~s à plusieurs reprises; *on all* ~s en toute occasion; *on the* ~ *of* à l'occasion de; *have no* ~ *for* n'avoir aucun sujet de; *rise to the* ~ être *ou* se montrer à la hauteur de la situation; **2.** occasionner, donner lieu à; **oc'ca·sion·al** □ ... de temps en temps, épars; ~ *furniture* meuble *m* volant.

oc·ci·dent *poét.* ['ɔksidənt] occident *m*, ouest *m*; **oc·ci·den·tal** □ [~-'dentl] occidental (-aux *m/pl.*); de l'ouest.

oc·cult □ [ɔ'kʌlt] occulte, secret (-ète *f*); **oc·cul'ta·tion** *astr.* occultation *f*; **oc·cult·ism** ['ɔkəltizm] occultisme *m*; **'oc·cult·ist** occultiste *mf*; **oc·cult·ness** [ɔ'kʌltnis] caractère *m* occulte.

oc·cu·pan·cy ['ɔkjupənsi] occupation *f*, habitation *f* (de, *of*); *emploi:* possession *f*; **'oc·cu·pant** *terre:* occupant(e *f*) *m*; *maison:* locataire *mf*; *emploi:* titulaire *mf*; **oc·cu'pa·tion** occupation *f* (*a.* ✗); emploi *m*, métier *m*, profession *f*; *be in* ~ *of* occuper; *employed in an* ~ employé; **oc·cu'pa·tion·al** de métier; professionnel(le *f*); ~ *disease* maladie *f* professionnelle; ~ *hazard* risque *m* du métier; ~ *therapy* thérapeutique *f* occupationnelle; **oc·cu·pi·er** ['~-paiə] *see* occupant; **oc·cu·py** ['~-pai] occuper (*q., qch., a.* ✗ *une ville*); habiter (*une maison*); remplir (*l'espace, le temps, un emploi*); occuper (*la place, le temps*); passer (*le temps*); ✗ s'emparer de (*un point stratégique*); garnir (*une place de guerre*); donner du travail à; ~ *o.s.* (*ou be occupied*) *with* (*ou in*) être occupé à, s'occuper à.

oc·cur [ə'kɜː] avoir lieu; arriver; se produire; se trouver; venir à l'esprit (à *q., to s.o.*); **oc·cur·rence** [ə'kʌrəns] événement *m*; occurrence *f*; *min.* venue *f.*

o·cean ['ouʃn] océan *m*; mer *f*; F ~s *pl.* of un tas *m* de; **'~·go·ing** ⚓ de haute mer (*bateau*); **o·ce·an·ic** [ouʃi'ænik] océanique; de l'océan.

o·chre *min.* ['oukə] ocre *f.*

o'clock [ə'klɔk]: *five* ~ cinq heures.

oc·ta·gon ['ɔktəgən] octogone *m*; **oc·tag·o·nal** [ɔk'tægənl] octogonal (-aux *m/pl.*).

oc·tane ♫ ['ɔktein] octane *m.*

oc·tave ♪ ['ɔktiv] octave *f*; **oc·ta·vo** [~'teivou] in-octavo *inv.* (*a. su./m*).

Oc·to·ber [ɔk'toubə] octobre *m.*

oc·to·ge·nar·i·an ['ɔktoudʒi'nɛəriən] octogénaire (*a. su./mf*).

oc·to·pus *zo.* ['ɔktəpəs] poulpe *m*; *surt.* pieuvre *f* (*a. fig.*).

oc·u·lar □ ['ɔkjulə] oculaire, des yeux, de l'œil; ~ *demonstration* démonstration *f* oculaire; ~*ly* oculairement, des yeux; **'oc·u·list** oculiste *m.*

odd □ [ɔd] impair (*nombre*); dépareillé; déparié (*de deux*); qui ne vont pas ensemble; *fig.* quelconque; *40* ~ une quarantaine; quelque quarante ...; *12 pounds* ~ 12 livres et quelques shillings; *there is still some* ~ *money* il reste encore quelque argent (de surplus); *at* ~ *times* par-ci par-là; *be* ~ *man* rester en surnombre; ~*ly enough* curieusement, chose curieuse; *see a.* odds; **'~·ball** *Am.* F drôle de type *m*; **Odd·fellows** ['ɔdfelouz] *pl.* une société de secours mutuels; **'odd·i·ty** singularité *f*, bizarrerie *f*; F original(e *f*) *m*; **'odd·ments** *pl.* restes *m/pl.*; ✝ fins *f/pl.* de série; fonds *m/pl.* de boutique; **odds** [ɔdz] *pl., a. sg.* chances *f/pl.*; avantage *m*; différence *f*; *courses:* cote *f*; *Am. a.* faveurs *f/pl.*; *at* ~ brouillé, en désaccord; ~ *and ends* bribes *f/pl.* et morceaux *m/pl.*; petits bouts *m/pl.*; *nourriture:* restes *m/pl.*; *sp. give s.o.* ~ concéder des points à q.; *what's the* ~? qu'est-ce que ça fait?; *it makes no* ~ ça ne fait rien; cela n'a pas d'importance; *the* ~ *are for* (*against*) *him* les chances sont pour (contre) lui.

ode [oud] ode *f.*

o·di·ous □ ['oudiəs] odieux (-euse *f*); détestable; répugnant; **o·di·um** ['oudiəm] détestation *f*; réprobation *f*; haine *f.*

o·dom·e·ter *mot.* [o'dɔmitə] odomètre *m*; compteur *m* enregistreur.

o·don·to·lo·gy ✵ [ɔdɔn'tɔlədʒi] odontologie *f*.

o·dor·if·er·ous □ [oudə'rifərəs], **'o·dor·ous** □ odorant; parfumé; *péj.* puant.

o·do(u)r ['oudə] parfum *m*; odeur *f* (*a. fig.*); *fig.* faveur *f*; **'o·do(u)r·less** sans odeur, inodore.

œconom... *see* econom...

œc·u·men·i·cal *eccl.* □ [i:kju:-'menikl] œcuménique; F universel(le *f*).

œ·de·ma ✵ [i:'di:mə] œdème *m*.

o'er [ɔə] *see* over.

œ·soph·a·gus *anat.* [i:'sɔfəgəs] œsophage *m*.

of [ɔv; əv] *prp. possession, dépendance*: de (*mon père*); *origine*: de (*bonne famille*); *cause*: de (*joie, faim, etc.*); *qualité, quantité, action, distance*: de; *lieu de bataille, etc.*: de; *titre de nobilité*: de; *matière*: de, en (*soie, or, etc.*); *titre universitaire*: en (*philosophie, droit, etc.*), ès (*lettres, sciences*); parmi, (d')entre (*un groupe*); *après certains verbes comme priver, ôter, etc.*: de; *génitif de description*: a man ~ honour un homme d'honneur; the city ~ London la cité de Londres; *génitif subjectif*: the love ~ a mother l'amour d'une mère; *génitif objectif*: the love ~ God l'amour de Dieu; a hatred ~ cruelty une haine de la cruauté; *article partitif*: a glass ~ wine un verre de vin; *pour of après verbe ou adjectif voir le verbe simple ou l'adjectif*; die ~ cancer mourir de cancer; enough ~ assez de; loved ~ all aimé de tous; north ~ Paris au nord de Paris; Duke ~ Kent Duc de Kent; get rid ~ se débarasser de; cheat s.o. ~ s.th. frustrer q. de qch.; rob s.o. ~ s.th. voler qch. à q.; think ~ penser à; *fig.* juger de; be afraid (ashamed) ~ avoir peur (honte) de; desirous (proud) ~ désireux (fier) de; it is very kind ~ you c'est très aimable à vous; the best ~ my friends le meilleur de mes amis; ~ late récemment; ~ old de jadis; the 2nd ~ May le 2 mai; it smells ~ roses cela sent les roses; the remedy ~ remedies le remède par excellence; this world ~ ours ce monde terrestre; he ~ all men lui entre tous; F ~ an evening le soir.

off [ɔ:f; ɔf] **1.** *adv. usu. avec verbe, voir le verbe simple*; ⚓ au large; 3 miles ~ à 3 milles de distance; 5 months ~ à 5 mois d'ici *ou* de là; ~ and on par intervalles; be ~ partir, s'en aller; *fig.* être fermé (*gaz etc.*); être coupé (*allumage etc.*); être épuisé (*plat*); être abandonné (*jeu*); être avancé (*viande etc.*); ne plus pondre (*poule*); be ~ with en avoir fini avec (*q.*); have one's shoes ~ avoir ôté ses souliers; be well (badly) ~ être dans l'aisance (dans la gêne *ou* misère, mal loti); **2.** *prp. usu.* de; *après certains verbes comme prendre, ôter, emprunter, etc.*: à; *distance*: éloigné de, écarté de; dégoûté de (*la nourriture*); ⚓ au large de; a street ~ the Strand une rue aboutissant au Strand; **3.** *adj.* de dehors; extérieur; droit (*Am.* gauche); *cheval*: de sous-verge; côté hors montoir (*cheval*); latéral (-aux *m/pl.*) (*rue*); subsidiaire (*importance*); ~ chance chance *f* douteuse; possibilité *f*; on the ~ chance au cas où; à tout hasard; dans le vague espoir (de *that*, of *gér.*); be (*ou* feel) ~ colo(u)r ne pas être en forme *ou* dans son assiette; ~ day jour *m* où l'on n'est pas en train; **4.** *su. cricket*: to the ~ en avant à droite; **5.** *int.* filez!; allez-vous-en!

of·fal ['ɔfal] déchets *m/pl.*, rebut *m*; ~s *pl. boucherie*: déchets *m/pl.* d'abattage; abats *m/pl.*

off...: '~·beat F excentrique; '~·cast **1.** rebut *m*; **2.** de rebut; '~·cen·tre, *Am.* '~·cen·ter décentré, désaxé, en porte-à-faux; ~·col·o(u)r scabreux (-euse *f*) (*histoire*).

off-du·ty hours ['ɔ:fdju:ti'auəz] *pl.* loisirs *m/pl.*, (heures *f/pl.* de) liberté *f*, congé *m*.

of·fence [ə'fens] offense *f*, faute *f*; sujet *m* de déplaisir; ⚖ crime *m*, délit *m*; minor ~ contravention *f*; no ~! pardonnez-moi!; je ne veux offenser personne!; give ~ offenser, froisser, blesser (q., to *s.o.*); take ~ se froisser (de, *at*).

of·fend [ə'fend] *v/t.* offenser, froisser, blesser; *v/i.* pécher (contre, *against*); violer (la loi, *against the law*); déplaire; **of'fend·er** délinquant(e *f*) *m*; coupable *mf*; offenseur *m*; pécheur (-eresse *f*) *m*; first ~ délinquant(e *f*) *m* primaire.

of·fense [ə'fens] *Am. see* offence.

of·fen·sive [ə'fensiv] **1.** ☐ offensif (-ive *f*); choquant, offensant; désagréable; **2.** offensive *f*.

of·fer ['ɔfə] **1.** offre *f*; demande *f* (*en mariage*); on ~ en vente; **2.** *v/t.* offrir (*qch., prix,* ✝, *occasion, etc.*); présenter (*spectacle, difficulté, excuses*); inviter (*un combat*); faire (*opposition, résistance, insulte*); avancer (*une opinion*); adresser (*des prières*); essayer (de, to); ~ *violence* faire violence (à, to); *v/i.* s'offrir, se présenter; **'of·fer·ing** action, chose: offre *f*; *eccl.* offrande *f*.

of·fer·to·ry *eccl.* ['ɔfətəri] oblation *f*; *argent*: (montant *m* de la) quête *f*.

off-hand F ['ɔːf'hænd] sans préparation; à première vue; cavalièrement; brusque(ment); improvisé; sans gêne.

of·fice ['ɔfis] service *m*; office *m* (*a. eccl.*); emploi *m*, charge *f*, fonctions *f/pl.*; dignité *f*; bureau *m*; ♀ ministère *m*; portefeuille *m*; good ~s *pl.* bons offices *m/pl.*; in ~ au pouvoir (*gouvernement, parti*); *Insurance* ♀ compagnie *f* d'assurance(s); *sl.* give s.o. the ~ avertir q.; F passer la consigne à q.; ~ *appliances* articles *m/pl.* de bureau; ~ *bearer* fonctionnaire *m*; ✝ membre *m* du comité *m* directeur; ~ *boy* garçon *m* de bureau; ~ *holder* employé(e *f*) *m* de l'État; ~ *hours* heures *f/pl.* de bureau.

of·fi·cer ['ɔfisə] fonctionnaire *m*; officier *m* (*a.* ✕); **'of·fi·cered** (by) commandé (par); sous le commandement (de).

of·fi·cial ☐ [ə'fiʃl] **1.** officiel(le *f*); titulaire; de service; *see officinal*; ~ *agency* agence *f*; *poste:* ~ *business* en franchise; service *m* de l'État; ~ *channel* filière *f*, voie *f* hiérarchique; ~ *clerk* employé *m*; fonctionnaire *m*; ~ *hours pl.* heures *f/pl.* de bureau; **2.** fonctionnaire *m*; employé *m*; **of·fi·cial·dom**, **of·fi·cial·ism** [~ʃəlizm] bureaucratie *f*, fonctionnarisme *m*.

of·fi·ci·ate [ə'fiʃieit] officier; *fig. a.* exercer les fonctions d'hôte.

of·fic·i·nal ⚕ [ɔfi'sainl] officinal (-aux *m/pl.*).

of·fi·cious ☐ [ə'fiʃəs] trop zélé; officieux (-euse *f*); empressé.

off·ing ⚓ ['ɔfiŋ] large *m*, pleine mer *f*; in the ~ au large, *fig.* en perspective; **'off·ish** F distant, réservé.

off...: '~**key** ♪ faux (fausse *f*); '~**peak** ~*charges pl.* tarif *m* réduit (aux heures creuses); ~ *hours pl.* heures *f/pl.* creuses; '~**print** tirage *m* à part; '~**put·ting** peu engageant, rebutant; répugnant; '~**scour·ings** *pl.*, '~**scum** rebut *m*; *fig.* lie *f*; '~**sea·son 1.** morte-saison *f*; **2.** hors-saison (*tarif etc.*); '~**set 1.** compensation *f*; ▲ saillie *f*; ▲ retrait *m* (*d'un mur*); ⊕ *tuyau:* double coude *m*; *piston:* rebord *m*; *typ.* maculage *m*; *phot.* offset *m*; *see* off-shoot; set-off; **2.** compenser; '~**shoot** rejeton *m*; F ramification *f*; '~**shore** côtier, littoral; '~**side** *sp.* hors jeu; '~**spring** descendants *m/pl.*; progéniture *f*; *fig.* produit *m*; '~**stage** *théâ.* dans la coulisse; *fig.* dans la vie privée; '~-**the-cuff** impromptu, au pied levé; '~-**the-peg** *cost.* de confection, prêt à porter; '~-**the-rec·ord** confidentiel(le *f*); '~**time** temps *m* (de) libre; loisirs *m/pl.*; ~-**white** blanc cassé *inv.*

of·ten ['ɔːfn], ✝, *poét.* ou mots composés **oft** [ɔːft] souvent, fréquemment. [maise *f*.]

o·gee ▲ ['oudʒiː] doucine *f*, ci-]
o·gi·val [ou'dʒaivəl] ogival (-aux *m/pl.*); en ogive; **o·give** ['oudʒaiv] ▲ ogive *f*.

o·gle ['ougl] lancer des œillades (à).

o·gre ['ougə] ogre *m*; **'o·gress** ogresse *f*.

oh [ou] O!, ô!

oil [ɔil] **1.** huile *f*; *sens restreint:* pétrole *m*; F *souv.* ~s *pl. see* ~-colo(u)r; ~ *dash-pot* frein *m* à huile; ~ (*level*) *gauge* jauge *f* de niveau d'huile; ~ *slick* nappe *f* de pétrole; **2.** graisser (*a. fig.*); ~ *up* (s')encrasser; '~**change** *mot.* vidange *m*; '~**cloth** toile *f* cirée; linoléum *m* imprimé; '~**col·o(u)r** couleur *f* à l'huile; '**oil·er** *personne:* graisseur *m*; *chose:* burette *f* de graissage; '**oil·field** gisement *m* ou champ *m* pétrolifère; '**oil·i·ness** état *m* ou aspect *m* graisseux; onctuosité *f* (*a. fig.*); '**oil-paint·ing** peinture *f* à l'huile; '**oil-pro·duc·ing** *coun·tries pl.* pays *m/pl.* producteurs de pétrole; **oil-rig** plate-forme *f* pétrolière; '**oil·skin** toile *f* cirée *ou* huilée; ~s *pl.* ciré *m*; cirage *m*; '**oil·y** ☐ huileux (-euse *f*); graisseux (-euse *f*); gras(se *f*) (*a. voix*); *fig.* onctueux (-euse *f*), mielleux (-euse *f*).

oint·ment ['ɔintmənt] onguent *m*, pommade *f*.

O.K., o·kay, o·keh ['ou'kei] **1.** parfait!; d'accord!; *écrit:* vu et approuvé; **2.** approuver; contresigner (*un ordre*).

old [ould] vieux (vieil *devant une voyelle ou un h muet*); vieille *f*; vieux *m/pl.*) (a. = expérimenté, rebattu, du temps ancien); ancien(ne *f*) (*devant su. = qui n'est plus en fonctions*); du temps ancien, de jadis; F ce cher ..., ce bon vieux ...; of ~ d'autrefois, de jadis; depuis longtemps; *in times of* ~ jadis, autrefois; *a friend of* ~ un vieux camarade; ~ *age* vieillesse *f*; *an* ~ *boy* un ancien élève; *surt. Am.* ♀ *Glory* la bannière étoilée; F *my* ~ *man* mon homme; F *my* ~ *woman* ma femme; '**~-age:** ~ *pension* retraite *f*, pension *f* vieillesse; ~ *pensioner* retraité(e *f*) *m*; '**old·en** † *ou poét.* (de) jadis; vieux (vieil *devant une voyelle ou un h muet*); vieille *f*; vieux *m/pl.*); '**old·'fash·ioned** démodé; à l'ancienne mode; '**old·ish** vieillot(te *f*); '**old·'maid·ish** de vieille fille; **old·ster** ['~stə] F vieillard(e *f*) *m*; **old wives' tale** conte *m* de bonne femme.

o·le·ag·i·nous [ouli'ædʒinəs] oléagineux (-euse *f*), huileux (-euse *f*).

ol·fac·to·ry *anat.* [ɔl'fæktəri] olfactif (-ive *f*).

ol·i·garch·y ['ɔligɑːki] oligarchie *f*.

o·li·o ['ouliou] F pot-pourri (*pl.* pots-pourris) *m*.

ol·ive ['ɔliv] **1.** ♀ olive *f*; *a. see* ~-*tree*; **2.** olive *adj./inv.*; '**~-branch** (rameau *m* d')olivier *m* (*a. fig.*); '**~-tree** olivier *m*.

O·lym·pi·ad [o'limpiæd] olympiade *f*.

O·lym·pi·an [o'limpiən] olympien (-ne *f*); de l'Olympe; **O'lym·pic games** *pl.* jeux *m/pl.* Olympiques.

om·buds·man ['ɔmbudzmən] médiateur *m*, protecteur *m* du citoyen.

om·e·let(te) ['ɔmlit] omelette *f*.

o·men ['oumen] présage *m*, augure *m*; **om·i·nous** □ ['ɔminəs] de mauvais augure.

o·mis·si·ble [o'misibl] négligeable; **o'mis·sion** omission *f*; négligence *f*; *fig.* oubli *m*; *eccl.* sin of ~ péché *m* ou faute *f* d'omission.

o·mit [o'mit] omettre (*qch.*; *de, to*); oublier (*de, to*); passer sous silence.

om·ni·bus ['ɔmnibəs] **1.** autobus *m*; **2.** embrassant (*des choses*) diverses; 🚂 ~ *train* train *m* omnibus.

om·nip·o·tence [ɔm'nipətəns] toute-puissance *f*; **om'nip·o·tent** tout-puissant (toute-puissante *f*).

om·ni·pres·ence ['ɔmni'prezəns] omniprésence *f*; '**om·ni'pres·ent** □ omniprésent.

om·nis·cience [ɔm'nisiəns] *eccl.* omniscience *f*; **om'nis·cient** □ omniscient.

om·niv·o·rous [ɔm'nivərəs] omnivore; *fig.* insatiable.

on [ɔn] **1.** *prp. usu.* sur; à (*la Bourse, cheval, l'arrivée de, pied, l'occasion de*); en (*vacances, route, perce, vente*); après; avec (*une pension, un salaire de*); de (*ce côté-ci*); pour; dans (*le train*); sous (*peine de*); *direction:* vers; ~ *the shore* sur le rivage; ~ *shore* à terre; ~ *the death of* à la mort de; ~ *examination* après considération; ~ *both sides* des deux côtés; ~ *all sides* de tous côtés; ~ *business* pour affaires; be ~ *a committee* faire partie d'un comité; ~ *Friday* vendredi; ~ *Fridays* les vendredi(s); ~ *the 5th of April* le 5 avril; ~ *the left (right)* à gauche (droite); *surt. Am.* get ~ *a train* monter en voiture; *turn one's back* ~ montrer le dos à (*q.*); ~ *these conditions* dans ces conditions; ~ *the model of* à l'imitation de; ~ *hearing it* lorsque je (*etc.*) l'entendis; *pour on après verbe, voir le verbe simple;* **2.** *adv.* (en) avant; *souv. ne se traduit pas* (*p.ex.* put ~ mettre) *ou s'exprime tout autrement* (*p.ex. théâ.* be ~ être en scène; *have one's shoes* ~ être chaussé *etc.*) *ou se traduit par l'idée verbale de* continuer (*qch.*; à *inf.*); *and so* ~ et ainsi de suite; ~ *and* ~ sans fin; ~ *to* sur, à; *from that day* ~ dès ce jour, à partir de ce jour; be ~ se trouver sur (*qch.*); faire partie de; se passer; être ouvert (*robinet, électricité*); *théâ.* être en scène; *sl.* be *a bit* ~ être quelque peu pompette (= *ivre*); F *what's* ~? qu'est-ce qui arrive?; *théâ.* qu'est-ce que qui joue?; **3.** *int.* en avant!, allez(-y)!

once [wʌns] **1.** *adv.* une (seule) fois; autrefois; jadis; *at* ~ tout de suite; sur-le-champ; à l'instant; *all at* ~ tout d'un coup, soudain; ~ *again* encore une fois, une fois de plus; ~

for all une fois pour toutes; *for* ~ pour une fois; ~ *in a while* (une fois) de temps en temps; *this* ~ cette fois-ci; ~ *more* une fois de plus, encore une fois; *contes etc.:* ~ *upon a time there was ...* il était une fois; **2.** *cj.* (*a.* ~ *that*) dès que; pour peu que.

once-o·ver *Am.* F ['wʌnsouvə]: *give s.o. a* ~ jeter un coup *m* d'œil rapide sur q.

on·com·ing ['ɔnkʌmiŋ] **1.** imminent; qui approche; ~ *traffic* circulation *f* en sens inverse; **2.** arrivée *f*; approche *f*.

one [wʌn] **1.** un(e *f*); unique, seul et même; celui *m* (celle *f*, ceux *m/pl.*); *pron. sujet indéfini:* on; *his* ~ *care* son seul souci; ~ *day* un jour; ~ *of these days* un de ces jours; ~ *Mr. Miller* un certain M. Miller, un nommé M.; *see any*~, *every*~, *no* 1; *give* ~'s *view* donner son avis; *a large dog and a little* ~ un grand chien et un petit; *for* ~ *thing* entre autres raisons, en premier lieu; **2.** un(e *f*) *m*; ~ (*o'clock*) une heure; *the little* ~*s* les petit(e)s; ~ *another* l'un(e) l'autre, les un(e)s les autres; *at* ~ d'accord; ~ *by* ~ *after another* un(e) à un(e), l'un(e) après l'autre; *it is all* ~ (*to me*) cela m'est égal; *I for* ~ *...* quant à moi, je ...; *for my part,* je ...; '~-'**horse** à un cheval; *fig. sl.* insignifiant; '**one·ness** unité *f*; identité *f*; accord *m*; '**one-night stand** *théâ.* soirée unique.

on·er·ous □ ['ɔnərəs] onéreux (-euse *f*); pénible.

one...: ~'**self** soi-même; *réfléchi:* se, *accentué:* soi; *by* ~ tout seul; '~-'**sid·ed** □ inégal (-aux *m/pl.*), injuste; asymétrique (*forme*); '~-'**time** ancien(ne *f*); '~-'**up·man·ship** art *m* de faire mieux que les autres; '~-'**way:** ~ *street* (rue *f* à) sens *m* unique; ~ *fare* (prix *m* du) billet *m* simple.

on·fall ['ɔnfɔ:l] assaut *m*.

on·go·ings ['ɔngouiŋz] *pl.* F manège *m*.

on·ion ['ʌnjən] oignon *m*.

on·look·er ['ɔnlukə] spectateur (-trice *f*) *m*.

on·ly ['ounli] **1.** *adj.* seul, unique; **2.** *adv.* seulement, ne ... que; rien que; ~ *yesterday* pas plus tard qu'hier; ~ *just* à peine; tout juste; ~ *think!* imaginez un peu!; **3.** *cj.* mais; ~ *that* si ce n'est *ou* était que.

on·rush ['ɔnrʌʃ] ruée *f*.

on·set ['ɔnset], **on·slaught** ['ɔnslɔ:t] assaut *m*; attaque *f* (*a. fig.*); *fig. at the onset* de prime abord.

on·shore ['ɔn'ʃɔ:] à terre; du large (*vent*).

o·nus ['ounəs] (*pas de pl.*) *fig.* responsabilité *f*, charge *f*.

on·ward ['ɔnwəd] **1.** *adj.* en avant, progressif (-ive *f*); **2.** *adv.* (*a.* **on·wards** ['~z]) en avant; plus loin.

oo·dles F ['u:dlz] *pl.* un tas *m* (de, of).

oof *sl.* [u:f] galette *f* (= *argent*).

oomph *sl.* [u:mf] énergie *f*, allant *m*, entrain *m*.

ooze [u:z] **1.** vase *f*; boue *f*; ⊕ jus(ée *f*) *m*; **2.** suinter; (*a.* ~ *out*) dégoutter; ~ *away* s'écouler, disparaître; *Am. sl.* ~ *out* (se dé)filer.

oo·zy □ ['u:zi] vaseux (-euse *f*); suintant.

o·pac·i·ty [o'pæsiti] opacité *f*; *fig. intelligence:* lourdeur *f*.

o·pal *min.* ['oupəl] opale *f*; **o·pal·es·cent** [~'lesnt] opalescent.

o·paque □ [ou'peik] opaque; *fig.* obtus, peu intelligent.

o·pen ['oupən] **1.** *adj.* *usu.* ouvert; plein (*air, campagne, mer*); grand (*air*); débouché (*bouteille*); courant (*compte*); non barré (*chèque*); nu (*feu*); public (-ique *f*) (*jugement*); haut (*mer*); défait (*paquet*); béant (*plaie*); discutable (*question*); déclaré (*rival*); manifeste (*sentiment*); franc(he *f*); doux (douce *f*) (*temps*); découvert (*voiture*); ~ *to* accessible à; exposé à; ~ *to conviction* accessible à la conviction; *in the* ~ *air* en plein air, au grand air; ⚒ ~*-cast*, ~*-cut* à ciel ouvert (*exploitation*); *in* ~ *court* en plein tribunal; *sp.* ~ *race* omnium *m*; *Am.* ~ *shop* atelier *m etc.* qui admet les ouvriers non-syndiqués; ⚹ *University* (Centre *m* de) Téléenseignement *m* universitaire; *leave o.s.* ~ *to* s'exposer à; **2.** *su. bring into the* ~ exposer au grand jour; **3.** *v/t. usu.* ouvrir; inaugurer; écarter; révéler, exposer; commencer, entamer; ~ *up* s'ouvrir; s'épanouir; s'étendre (*vue*); commencer; ~ *into* donner dans, communiquer avec; ~ *on to* donner sur, ouvrir sur; '~-'**air** en *ou* de plein air; '~-'**end(ed)** sans limite de durée; illimité; † flexible (*offre*); '**o·pen·er**

['oupnə] *personne:* ouvreur (-euse *f*) *m*; **'o·pen'hand·ed** libéral (-aux *m*/*pl*.); **'o·pen·ing 1.** ouverture *f*; inauguration *f*; commencement *m*, début *m*; trou *m*; éclaircie *f* (*dans les nuages*); *mur, forêt:* percée *f*; clairière *f* (*dans un bois*); **2.** d'ouverture, inaugural (-aux *m*/*pl*.); *théâ.* ~ **night pre·mière** *f*; ~ **time** heure *f* d'ouverture; **'o·pen'mind·ed** *fig.* impartial (-aux *m*/*pl*.); qui a l'esprit large; **'o·pen·'mouthed** bouche *f* bée; **o·pen·ness** ['oupnnis] aspect *m* découvert, situation *f* exposée; *fig.* franchise *f*; **'o·pen-plan** sans cloisons, à aire ouverte (*bureau etc.*); **'o·pen·work 1.** ouvrage *m* à jouré; (a)jours *m*/*pl*.; **2.** à jouré; à claire-voie.

op·er·a ['ɔpərə] opéra *m*.

op·er·a·ble ['ɔpərəbl] *&* opérable; praticable.

op·er·a...: '~·'**danc·er** danseur (-euse *f*) *m* d'opéra; ballerine *f*; '~·**glass(es** *pl*.) jumelle *f*, -s *f*/*pl*.; '~·**hat** (chapeau *m*) claque *m*; '~·**house** opéra *m*.

op·er·ate ['ɔpəreit] *v*/*t*. opérer, effectuer (*a. ✝, &, ⚔*); *✝* exploiter; *Am.* actionner; faire manœuvrer (*une machine*); gérer, diriger (*une entreprise*); *v*/*i*. *&* opérer (q., on s.o.); *Am.* fonctionner; *✝* faire des opérations, spéculer; entrer en vigueur, jouer; *be operating* fonctionner; **op·er·at·ic** [~'rætik] d'opéra; ~ **singer** chanteur (-euse *f*) *m* dramatique d'opéra; **op·er·at·ing** ['ɔpəreitiŋ] qui opère; *&* opérateur (*chirurgien*); d'exploitation; d'opération; ~ **expenses** *pl*. dépenses *f*/*pl*. courantes; ~ **instructions** *pl*. indications *f*/*pl*. du mode d'emploi; *&* ~ **room** (*ou* **theatre, theater**) salle *f* d'opération; **op·er·a·tion** fonctionnement *m*, action *f*; *&, ⚔, ✝* opération *f*; *be in* ~ fonctionner, jouer; *come into* ~ entrer en vigueur; **op·er·a·tion·al** d'opération; d'exploitation; **op·er·a·tive** ['~rətiv] **1.** □ actif (-ive *f*), opératif (-ive *f*); pratique; *fig.* essentiel(le *f*); *&* opératoire; **2.** ouvrier (-ère *f*) *m*; **op·er·a·tor** ['~reitə] opérateur (-trice *f*) *m* (*a. ⊕*); *&* opérateur *m* (*a. cin., a. ✝*); téléphoniste *mf*; *✝* joueur *m*; ouvrier (-ère *f*) *m*; *Am. mot.* conducteur *m*.

op·er·et·ta [ɔpə'retə] opérette *f*.

oph·thal·mi·a *&* [ɔf'θælmiə] ophtalmie *f*; **oph'thal·mic** ophtalmique; ~ **hospital** hôpital *m* ophtalmologique.

o·pi·ate *pharm.* **1.** ['oupiit] opiat *m*, opiacé *m*, narcotique *m*; **2.** ['~ieit] opiacer (*un médicament*).

o·pine [o'pain] *v*/*t*. être d'avis (que); *v*/*i*. opiner; **op·in·ion** [ə'pinjən] opinion *f*, avis *m*; *&* consultation *f*; ~ **poll** sondage *m* (d'opinion); *counsel's* ~ avis *m* motivé; *be of* ~ estimer, être d'avis (que, *that*); *in my* ~ à mon avis; **o'pin·ion·at·ed** [~eitid] opiniâtre; imbu de ses opinions.

o·pi·um *pharm.* ['oupjəm] opium *m*; ~ **addict** opiomane *mf*; ~ **den** fumerie *f* d'opium.

o·pos·sum *surt. Am.* [ə'pɔsəm] opossum *m*; sarigue *f*, *a. m*.

op·po·nent [ə'pounənt] **1.** adversaire *mf*; **2.** contraire *m*; anat. opposant.

op·por·tune □ ['ɔpətjuːn] opportun, commode; à propos; **'op·por·tun·ism** opportunisme *m*; **'op·por·tun·ist** opportuniste *mf*; **op·por·'tu·ni·ty** occasion *f* (favorable) (*pour inf. of gér., to inf.*); facilités *f*/*pl*. (de, for).

op·pose [ə'pouz] opposer (*deux choses*); s'opposer à (q., qch.); résister à (q., qch.); parler contre (*une proposition*); **op'posed** opposé, contraire, hostile; *be* ~ *to* être le rebours de; aller au contraire de; **op·po·site** ['ɔpəzit] **1.** *adj.* □ (*to*) opposé (à); en face (de); vis-à-vis (de); contraire (à); ~ **number** correspondant *m* en grade, F similaire *m*; **2.** *prp.* en face de, vis-à-vis de; **3.** *adv.* en face, vis-à-vis; **4.** *su.* opposé *m*; contre-pied *m*; **op·po'si·tion** opposition *f* (*a. parl., a. astr.*); résistance *f*; camp *m* adverse; *✝* concurrence *f*.

op·press [ə'pres] opprimer; *fig. a.* accabler, oppresser; **op·pres·sion** [ə'preʃn] oppression *f*; *fig.* accablement *m*; *fig.* abus *m* d'autorité; **op·'pres·sive** □ [~siv] oppressif (-ive *f*), tyrannique; *fig.* lourd (*temps*); **op'pres·sive·ness** caractère *m* oppressif; *fig. temps:* lourdeur *f*; **op'pres·sor** oppresseur *m*.

op·pro·bri·ous □ [ə'proubriəs] outrageant, injurieux (-euse *f*); **op·'pro·bri·um** [~briəm] opprobre *m*.

opt [ɔpt] opter (pour, *for*; entre, *between*).

op·tic ['ɔptik] optique, de l'œil; de vision; (*ou* '**op·ti·cal** □) optique; **op·ti·cian** [ɔp'tiʃn] opticien *m*; '**op·tics** *sg.* optique *f.*

op·ti·mism ['ɔptimizm] optimisme *m*; '**op·ti·mist** optimiste *mf*; **op·ti'mis·tic** (~*ally*) optimiste; ~*ally* avec optimisme; **op·ti·mize** ['~maiz] optimiser.

op·tion ['ɔpʃn] choix *m*, option *f*; faculté *f*; ✝ (marché *m* à) prime *f*; ~ *right* option *f*; '**op·tion·al** □ facultatif (-ive *f*).

op·u·lence ['ɔpjuləns] opulence *f*, richesse *f*; '**op·u·lent** □ opulent, très riche.

o·pus ['oupəs] opus *m*; *magnum* ~ œuvre *f* maîtresse.

or [ɔː] ou; *either* ... *or* ou ... ou; soit ... soit; ~ *else* ou bien; sinon.

or·a·cle ['ɔrəkl] oracle *m*; F *work the* ~ arriver à ses fins; faire agir certaines influences; **o·rac·u·lar** [ɔ'rækjulə] (en style) d'oracle; *fig.* équivoque, obscur.

o·ral □ ['ɔːrəl] oral (-aux *m/pl.*); buccal (-aux *m/pl.*).

or·ange ['ɔrindʒ] **1.** orange *f*; *arbre*: oranger *m*; *couleur*: orange *m*; orangé *m*; **2.** orangé; orange *adj./inv.*; **or·ange·ade** ['~eid] orangeade *f*; **or·ange·ry** ['~əri] orangerie *f.*

o·rate *co.* [ɔː'reit] pérorer; **o'ra·tion** allocution *f*, discours *m*; *co.*, *péj.* harangue *f*; **or·a·tor** ['ɔrətə] orateur *m*; **or·a·tor·i·cal** □ [ɔrə'tɔrikl] oratoire; ampoulé (*discours*); phraseur (-euse *f*) (*personne*); **or·a·to·ri·o** ♪ [~'tɔːriou] oratorio *m*; **or·a·to·ry** ['ɔrətəri] éloquence *f*; art *m* oratoire.

orb [ɔːb] orbe *m*; globe *m*; *poét.* astre *m*; **orbed** [ɔːbd; *usu. poét.* 'ɔːbid] rond, sphérique; **or·bic·u·lar** □ [ɔː'bikjulə], **or'bic·u·late** [~lit] orbiculaire, sphérique; **or·bit** [ɔːbit] *anat., a. astr.* orbite *f*; *put* (*go*) *into* ~ (se) placer sur son orbite.

or·chard ['ɔːtʃəd] verger *m*; '**or·chard·ing** fructiculture *f*; *Am.* terrains *m/pl.* aménagés en vergers.

or·ches·tra ♪ [ɔː'kistrə] orchestre *m*; ~ *pit* *théá.* fosse *f* d'orchestre; **or·ches·tral** [ɔː'kestrl] orchestral (-aux *m/pl.*); **or·ches·trate** ♪ [ɔː'kistreit] orchestrer, instrumenter.

or·chid ♀ ['ɔːkid] orchidée *f.*

or·dain [ɔː'dein] ordonner (*a. un diacre*); conférer les ordres à (*un prêtre*); fixer, destiner; prescrire.

or·deal [ɔː'diːl] épreuve *f*; *hist.* jugement *m* de Dieu, ordalie *f.*

or·der ['ɔːdə] **1.** ordre *m* (*a. moines, chevalerie, fig.,* ✝, △, ✕ [*de bataille*], ⚓ [*tactique*]); ✝ commande *f*; ordonnance *f* (*de paiement*); *parl.* rappel *m* à l'ordre; *admin.* arrêt(é) *m*; ✕, ⚓ consigne *f*; *poste:* mandat *m*; ⊕ état *m* de fonctionnement; instruction *f*; suite *f*, succession *f*; classe *f* (*sociale*); ✝ ~ *blank* (*ou form*) billet *m* de commande; ~ *book* carnet *m* de commandes; *by* ~ par ordre; ~ *of the day* ordre *m* du jour (*a. fig.*); *take* (*holy*) ~*s* prendre les ordres; *in* ~ dans les règles; *put in* ~ mettre en règle; *in* ~ *to* (*inf.*) pour (*inf.*), afin de (*inf.*); *in* ~ *that* pour que (*sbj.*), afin que (*sbj.*); *a. see in* ~ *to*; *on the* ~*s of* sur les ordres de; ✝ *be on* ~ être commandé; *make to* ~ faire sur commande; faire sur mesure (*un habit*); *parl. rise to* ~ se lever pour demander le rappel à l'ordre; *parl. standing* ~*s pl.* ordres *m/pl.* permanents; ✝, *pol.* règlement *m*, -s *m/pl.*; *to* (*the*) ~ *of* ✝ à l'ordre de (*q.*); **2.** (ar)ranger; ordonner; régler; prescrire; ✝ commander; ✕ ~ *arms!* reposez armes!; ~ *about* faire marcher (*q.*); ~ *s.o. down* (*up*) ordonner à q. de descendre (monter); '**or·der·er** ordonnateur (-trice *f*) *m*; '**or·der·li·ness** bon ordre *m*; discipline *f*; bonne conduite *f*; '**or·der·ly 1.** méthodique; réglé (*vie etc.*); discipliné (*foule etc.*); ✕ ~ *officer* officier *m* de service *ou* de semaine; ~ *room* salle *f* de rapport; **2.** ✕ planton *m*; (*medical*) ~ infirmier *m.*

or·di·nal ['ɔːdinl] ordinal (-aux *m/pl.*) (*a. su./m*).

or·di·nance ['ɔːdinəns] ordonnance *f*, décret *m*, règlement *m*; *eccl.* rite *m.*

or·di·nar·y ['ɔːdnri] **1.** □ ordinaire; coutumier (-ère *f*); *péj.* quelconque; ✝ ~ *debts pl.* dettes *f/pl.* compte; ⚓ ~ *seaman* matelot *m* de troisième classe; *see share 1*; **2.** *eccl.* ordinaire *m*; table *f* d'hôte; *Am.* auberge *f*; commun *m*; *in* ~ ordinaire; ⚓ en réserve (*navire*).

or·di·nate ♠ ['ɔːdnit] ordonnée *f.*

or·di·na·tion [ɔ:di'neiʃn] *eccl.* ordination *f*; arrangement *m*.

ord·nance ✕, ⚓ ['ɔ:dnəns] artillerie *f*; ✕ service *m* du matériel; ~ *map* carte *f* d'état-major; ~ *survey* service *m* cartographique.

or·dure ['ɔ:djuə] ordure *f*; immondice *f*.

ore [ɔ:] minerai *m*; *poét.* métal *m*.

or·gan ['ɔ:gən] ♪ orgue *m* (*f/pl.* -s); organe *m* (*ouïe, vue, etc., admin.,* a. = *journal*); bulletin *m*, porteparole *m/inv.*; **'~-grind·er** joueur *m* d'orgue de Barbarie; **or·gan·ic** [ɔ:'gænik] (*~ally*) organique; organisé (*êtres, croissance*); **or·gan·ism** ['ɔ:gənizm] organisme *m*; **'or·gan·ist** organiste *mf*; **or·gan·i·za·tion** [~nai'zeiʃn] organisation *f*; *pol.* organisme *m*; œuvre *f* (*de charité*); **'or·gan·ize** organiser; arranger; **~d** constitué; *biol., pol.* organisé; **'or·gan·iz·er** organisateur (-trice *f*) *m*.

or·gasm ['ɔ:gæzəm] orgasme *m*.

or·gy ['ɔ:dʒi] orgie *f* (a. *fig.*); *fig.* profusion *f*.

o·ri·el ⚙ ['ɔ:riəl] fenêtre *f* en saillie.

o·ri·ent ['ɔ:riənt] **1.** oriental (-aux *m/pl.*); de l'orient; **2.** orient *m* (a. = *éclat d'une perle*); *Am.* Asie *f*; **3.** ['~ent] orienter; **o·ri·en·tal** [~'entl] **1.** □ oriental (-aux *m/pl.*); d'Orient; **2.** Oriental(e *f*) *m*; indigène *mf* de l'Orient; **o·ri·en·tate** ['ɔ:rienteit] orienter; **o·ri·en·ta·tion** orientation *f*. [ture *f.*\

or·i·fice ['ɔrifis] orifice *m*, ouver-\

or·i·gin ['ɔridʒin] origine *f*, génèse*f*; provenance *f*.

o·rig·i·nal [ə'ridʒənl] **1.** □ originaire; premier (-ère *f*); original (-aux *m/pl.*) (*livre, style, idée, etc.*); inédit; *see share*; ~ *capital* capital *m* d'apport; ~ *sin* péché *m* original; **2.** original *m*; *personne*: original(e *f*) *m*; **o·rig·i·nal·i·ty** [~'næliti] originalité *f*.

o·rig·i·nate [ə'ridʒineit] *v/t.* faire naître, donner naissance à, être l'auteur de; *v/i.* (*from, in*) tirer son origine, dériver (de); avoir son origine (dans); **o·rig·i·na·tion** source *f*, origine *f*; naissance *f*; invention *f*; création *f*; **o·rig·i·na·tive** □ créateur (-trice *f*); **o·rig·i·na·tor** auteur *m*; initiateur (-trice *f*) *m*.

o·ri·ole *orn.* ['ɔ:rioul] loriot *m*.

or·mo·lu ['ɔ:molu:] or *m* moulu; similor *m*.

or·na·ment 1. ['ɔ:nəmənt] ornement *m* (a. *fig.*); parure *f*; **2.** ['~ment] orner, parer; agrémenter (*une robe*); **or·na'men·tal** ornemental (-aux *m/pl.*); d'ornement; d'agrément.

or·nate □ [ɔ:'neit] orné; *fig.* fleuri.

or·ni·tho·log·i·cal □ [ɔ:niθə'lɔdʒikl] ornithologique; **or·ni·thol·o·gist** [~'θɔlədʒist] ornithologue *mf*, -logiste *mf*; **or·ni'thol·o·gy** ornithologie *f*.

o·rog·ra·phy [ɔ'rɔgrəfi] orographie *f*.

o·ro·tund ['ɔrotʌnd] sonore.

or·phan ['ɔ:fən] **1.** orphelin(e *f*) *m*; **2.** (a. **'or·phaned**) orphelin(e *f*); **or·phan·age** ['~idʒ], **'or·phan·a·sy·lum** orphelinat *m*.

or·rer·y ['ɔrəri] planétaire *m*.

or·tho·dox □ ['ɔ:θədɔks] orthodoxe; *fig.* classique; bien pensant (*personne*); **'or·tho·dox·y** orthodoxie *f*.

or·tho·graph·ic, **or·tho·graph·i·cal** □ [ɔ:θə'græfik(l)] orthographique, d'orthographe; **or·thog·ra·phy** [ɔ:'θɔgrəfi] orthographe *f*; ⚙ coupe *f* perpendiculaire.

or·tho·pae·dic [ɔ:θo'pi:dik] (*~ally*) orthopédique; **or·tho'pae·dist** orthopédiste *mf*; **'or·tho·pae·dy** orthopédie *f*.

Os·car ['ɔskə] *surt. cin. Am.* oscar *m*; *p.ext.* récompense *f*.

os·cil·late ['ɔsileit] osciller (a. *fig.*); *fig.* hésiter, balancer; *mot.* oscillating axle essieu *m* orientable; **os·cil'la·tion** oscillation *f*; **os·cil·la·to·ry** ['~lətəri] oscillatoire; **os·cil·lo·graph** [ɔ'silougra:f] oscillographe *m*.

os·cu·late *co.* ['ɔskjuleit] s'embrasser.

o·sier ⚘ ['ouʒə] osier *m*.

os·prey ['ɔspri] *orn.* orfraie *f*; ✝ aigrette *f*.

os·se·ous ['ɔsiəs] osseux (-euse *f*); **os·si·fi·ca·tion** [ɔsifi'keiʃn] ossification *f*; **os·si·fy** ['~fai] (s')ossifier; **os·su·ar·y** ['ɔsjuəri] ossuaire *m*.

os·ten·si·ble □ [ɔs'tensəbl] prétendu.

os·ten·ta·tion [ɔsten'teiʃn] ostentation *f*; faste *m*; parade *f*; **os·ten-**

'ta·tious □ fastueux (-euse f); plein d'ostentation.

os·te·ol·o·gy anat. [ɔstiˈɔlədʒi] ostéologie f.

ost·ler [ˈɔslə] valet m d'écurie.

os·tra·cism [ˈɔstrəsizm] ostracisme m; os·tra·cize [ˈ‿saiz] bannir; ostraciser (a. fig.).

os·trich orn. [ˈɔstritʃ] autruche f.

oth·er [ˈʌðə] autre (than, from que); the ~ day l'autre jour, récemment; the ~ morning l'autre matin; every ~ day tous les deux jours; each ~ l'un(e) l'autre, les un(e)s les autres; somebody or ~ je ne sais qui; péj. quelque individu; '~·wise autrement.

o·ti·ose □ [ˈouʃious] superflu; oiseux (-euse f); o·ti·os·i·ty [ouʃiˈɔsiti] superfluité f.

ot·ter zo. [ˈɔtə] loutre f (a. peau).

Ot·to·man [ˈɔtəmən] 1. ottoman, turc (turque f); 2. Ottoman(e f) m; ⌢ divan m, ottomane f.

ought¹ [ɔːt] see aught.

ought² [‿] v/aux. (défectif): I ~ to (inf.) je dois ou devrais (inf.); you ~ to have done it vous auriez dû le faire.

ounce¹ [auns] once f (28,35 g); by the ~ à l'once; au poids.

ounce² zo. [‿] once f; léopard m des neiges.

our [ˈauə] notre, nos; ours [ˈauəz] le (la) nôtre, les nôtres; à nous; a ... of ~ un(e) de nos ...; our'self nous-même; réfléchi: nous (a. accentué); our'selves nous-mêmes; réfléchi: nous (a. accentué).

oust [aust] évincer; supplanter; déloger (d'un poste).

out [aut] 1. adv. (au, en) dehors; au clair, découvert; sorti; éteint; au bout, à la fin; be ~ être sorti; sortir; se tromper; être bas(se f) (marée); être démodé (vêtement); faire la grève, être en grève (ouvrier); être épanoui ou en fleur; être paru (livre); être éventé (secret); avoir fait son entrée dans le monde (jeune fille); être luxé (épaule etc.); être sur pied (troupes); être achevé ou à bout (patience, mois, etc.); pol. n'être plus au pouvoir; être connu ou publié (nouvelle etc.); sp. être hors jeu ou éliminé ou knock-out; avoir perdu connaissance; sl. be ~ for s.th. être à la recherche de qch.;

be ~ to (inf.) avoir entrepris de (inf.); avoir pour but de (inf.); be ~ with être fâché avec; hear s.th. ~ entendre qch. jusqu'au bout; and‿ complètement; ‿-and-‿ achevé, convaincu; ~ and about (de nouveau) sur pied; levé; ~ and away de beaucoup; see elbow; come ~ théá. débuter; débuter, faire son entrée dans le monde (jeune fille); have it ~ with vider une querelle avec (q.), s'expliquer avec (q.); voyage ~ aller m; way ~ sortie f; her Sunday ~ son dimanche de sortie f; upon him! fi de lui!; ~ with him! à la porte!; 2. su. typ. bourdon m; Am. F excuse f; parl. the ~s pl. l'opposition f; 3. adj. aller (match); exceptionel(le f) (taille); hors série; 4. prp. ~ of hors de, au ou en dehors de; par (la fenêtre); choix: parmi, d'entre; démuni de; drink ~ of boire dans (un verre), à (la bouteille); 3 ~ of 10 3 sur 10; ~ of respect par respect; see date² 1; laugh 2; money; 5. v/t. F rendre ivre mort; box. mettre knock-out.

out...: ~-and-'out·er sl. outrancier (-ère f) m; intransigeant(e f) m; chef-d'œuvre (pl. chefs-d'œuvre) m; ~'bal·ance l'emporter sur; ~'bid [irr. (bid)] renchérir sur; '~·board hors bord; extérieur; ~'brave braver; surpasser (q.) en bravoure; '~·break éruption f; début m; '~·build·ing bâtiment m extérieur; '~·burst explosion f, éruption f; '~·cast expulsé(e f) (a. su.); fig. réprouvé(e f) (a. su.); ~'class su·rclasser; '~·col·lege externe (étudiant[e]); '~·come issue f, conséquence f; '~·crop ⚒, géol. affleurement m; fig. épidémie f; '~·cry cri m; clameur f; ~'dat·ed vieilli, démodé; ~'dis·tance dépasser, distancer; ~'do [irr. (do)] surpasser; '~·door adj., '~·doors adv. au dehors; en plein air; au grand air.

out·er [ˈautə] extérieur; externe; '~·most le plus en dehors; extrême.

out...: ~'face dévisager (q.); faire baisser les yeux à (q.); '~·fall égout: déversoir m; rivière: embouchure f; '~·fit équipement m; trousse f; ⚓ armement m; habits: trousseau m; Am. équipe f d'ouvriers; ⚔ F compagnie f, bataillon m; '~·fit·ter fournisseur (-euse f) m; marchand *m* de confections; **~'flank** ⚔ déborder; **'~-flow** *gaz, eau, etc.*: dépense *f*; *égout*: décharge *f*; **~'go 1.** [*irr.* (go)] surpasser; dépasser; **2.** ['~] dépenses *f/pl.*; **'~-go·ing 1.** sortant; **2.** sortie *f*; dépenses *f/pl.*; **~'grow** [*irr.* (grow)] devenir plus grand que (*q.*); devenir trop grand pour (*qch.*); *fig.* se défaire de; **'~growth** excroissance *f*; conséquence *f* naturelle; **'~-house** dépendance *f*; appentis *m*; *Am.* water *m* extérieur.

out·ing ['autiŋ] promenade *f*; partie *f* de plaisir; excursion *f*, sortie *f*.

out...: **~'land·ish** baroque, bizarre; barbare (*langue*); retiré (*endroit*); **~'last** survivre à; **'~-law 1.** hors-la-loi *m/inv.*; proscrit(e *f*) *m*; **2.** proscrire; **'~-law·ry** proscription *f*; **'~-lay** dépenses *f/pl.*; frais *m/pl.*; **'~-let** sortie *f*, départ *m*; issue *f*; *tuyau*, *a.* ✝ débouché *m*; *fig.* issue *f*, déversoir *m*; **'~-line 1.** silhouette *f*; profil *m*; tracé *m*; *roman, pièce de théâ.*: canevas *m*; **2.** silhouetter; ébaucher; esquisser; **~d** dessiné, profilé (sur, *against*); **~'live** survivre à; **'~-look** guet *m*; vue *f*; perspective *f* (*a. fig.*); *pol.* horizon *m*; **'~-ly·ing** éloigné, écarté; ⚓ qui déborde (*appareil*); **~ma'nœu·vre** l'emporter sur (*q.*) en tactique; F déjouer; **~'march** devancer; **~'mod·ed** démodé; **'~-most** le plus en dehors; extrême; **'~-num·ber** surpasser en nombre; **'~-of-door**(s) see outdoor(s); **'~-of-the-'way** écarté (*lieu*); *fig.* insolite; **'~-of-'work pay** indemnité *f* de chômage; **~'pace** distancer; gagner de vitesse; **'~-pa·tient** malade *mf* qui va consulter à la clinique; **'~-post** poste *m* avancé; **'~-pour·ing** épanchement *m* (*a. fig.*); **'~-put** rendement *m*; *mine*: production *f*; ⊕ débit *m*; *ordinateur*: sortie *f*.

out·rage ['autreidʒ] **1.** atteinte *f*; outrage *m* (à on, *against*); attentat *m* (à, on); *fig.* indignité *f*; **2.** outrager, faire outrage à; violenter (*une femme*); *fig.* aller à l'encontre de; **out·ra·geous** □ immodéré; outrageux (-euse *f*); atroce.

out...: **~'reach** tendre la main plus loin que; *fig.* prendre de l'avance sur; **'~-re·lief** secours *m/pl.* à domicile; **~'ride** [*irr.* (ride)] dépasser ou devancer à cheval; ⚓ étaler (*une tempête*); **'~-rid·er** piqueur *m*; F avant-coureur *m*; **'~-rig·ger** ⚓ *prao*: balancier *m*; outrigger *m*; espar *m* en saillie; **~'right 1.** *adj.* ['autrait] à forfait; franc(he *f*); **2.** *adv.* [aut'rait] complètement; à forfait; sur le coup; carrément; **~'ri·val** surpasser; l'emporter sur (*q.*); **~'run** [*irr.* (run)] dépasser (*le but etc.*); distancer (*un concurrent*); *fig.* l'emporter sur; **'~-run·ner** see outrider; **~'sail** ⚓ dépasser (*un navire*); **~'set** commencement *m*, début *m*; **~'shine** [*irr.* (shine)] éclipser; surpasser en éclat; **'~-side 1.** *su.* extérieur *m*, dehors *m*; *autobus*: impériale *f*; *fig.* maximum *m*; at the ~ tout au plus; **2.** *adj.* extérieur; du dehors; de l'impériale (*d'un autobus*); du bout (*d'une place ou chaise*); maximum (*prix*); *foot.*: ~ right (left) ailier *m* droit (gauche); **3.** *adv.* (en) dehors; à l'extérieur; ~ of = **4.** *prp.* en dehors de; à l'extérieur de; hors de; **'~-sid·er** F étranger (-ère *f*) *m*; profane *mf*; **~'sit** [*irr.* (sit)] rester plus longtemps que; **~'size** taille *f* exceptionnelle; **'~-skirts** *pl.* ville: faubourgs *m/pl.*, banlieue *f*; *forêt*: lisière *f*; abords *m/pl.*; **~'smart** *Am.* F surpasser en finesse; déjouer; **~'spo·ken** □ carré; franc(he *f*); **~'stand·ing** saillant; marquant, *fig.* éminent; en suspens (*affaire*); ✝ dû (due *f*); échu (*intérêt*); **~'stay** rester plus longtemps que; ~ one's welcome lasser l'amabilité de ses hôtes; **~'step** *fig.* outrepasser; **~'stretch** étendre, déployer; **~'strip** dépasser, gagner de vitesse; *fig.* surpasser; **'~-turn** rendement *m* net; **~'val·ue** surpasser en valeur; **~'vote** obtenir une majorité sur; mettre (*q.*) en minorité; **'~-vot·er** électeur (-trice *f*) *m* qui ne réside pas dans la circonscription.

out·ward ['autwəd] **1.** *adj.* en dehors; extérieur, de dehors; d'aller (*billet*); ⚓ pour l'étranger; **2.** *adv.* (*usu.* **out·wards** ['~dz]) au dehors; vers l'extérieur; **'out·ward·ness** extériorité *f*; *fig.* objectivité *f*.

out...: **~'wear** [*irr.* (wear)] user complètement; durer plus longtemps que; se défaire de (*une habitude etc.*); ~'**weigh** dépasser en poids; *fig.* l'emporter sur; ~'**wit** déjouer les menées de; '~**work** ⚔ ouvrage *m* avancé; ⊕ travail (*pl. -aux*) *m* fait à domicile; '~**work·er** ouvrier (-ère *f*) *m* à domicile.

ou·zel orn. ['uːzl] merle *m*.

o·val ['ouvl] **1.** (en) ovale; **2.** ovale*m*.

o·va·ry ['ouvəri] anat., a. ⚕ ovaire *m*.

o·va·tion [ou'veiʃn] ovation *f*.

ov·en ['ʌvn] four *m*; ⊕ étuve *f*; ~ *cloth* poignée *f*; '~**proof** allant au four; '~**read·y** prêt à rôtir.

o·ver ['ouvə] **1.** *adv.* par-dessus (*qch.*); en plus; fini, achevé; à la renverse; *avec adj. ou adv.*: trop; *avec verbe:* sur-, trop; *avec su.*: excès *m* de; ~ *and above* en outre; (*all*) ~ *again* d'un bout à l'autre; de nouveau; ~ *against* vis-à-vis de; *all* ~ partout; ~ *and* ~ (*again*) maintes et maintes fois; à plusieurs reprises; *fifty times* ~ cinquante fois de suite; F *get s.th.* ~ (*and done*) *with* venir à bout de qch.; en finir avec qch.; *make* ~ transférer; *Am.* refaçonner; *read* ~ lire (*qch.*) en entier; parcourir; **2.** *prp.* sur, (par-)dessus; au-dessus de; au-delà de; *all* ~ *the town* partout dans la ville, dans toute la ville; ~ *night* pendant la nuit; ~ *a glass of wine* en prenant un verre de vin; ~ *the way* en face.

over...: '~**act** exagérer; '~**all** tablier *m* blouse; *école:* blouse *f*; sarrau (*pl. -s, -x*) *m*; ~*s pl.* salopette *f* (*a. d'enfant*); F bleus *m/pl.*; ~'**arch** former un arc au-dessus de (*qch.*); ~'**awe** intimider; ~'**bal·ance 1.** excédent *m*; **2.** (se) renverser; *v/t.* peser plus que; *v/i.* perdre l'équilibre (*personne*); ~'**bear** [*irr.* (*bear*)] l'emporter sur; ~'**bear·ing** arrogant; ~'**bid** [*irr.* (*bid*)] enchérir sur; '~**blown** trop épanoui; '~**board** ⚓ par-dessus bord; à la mer (*homme*); ~'**brim** déborder; '~**build** [*irr.* (*build*)] trop construire dans (*une localité*); ~'**burden** surcharger (de, *with*); '~**cast 1.** [*irr.* (*cast*)] obscurcir; ~ *a seam* faire un surjet; **2.** obscurci, couvert; ~ *seam* surjet *m*; ~**charge 1.** ['ouvə'tʃɑːdʒ] surcharger; survendre (*des marchandises*); faire payer (*qch.*) trop cher à (*q.*);

2. ['ouvətʃɑːdʒ] surcharge *f*; prix *m* surfait; ~'**cloud** (se) couvrir de nuages; (s')assombrir; '~**coat** pardessus *m*; ~'**come** [*irr.* (*come*)] vaincre; maîtriser; '~'**con·fi·dent** ☐ trop confiant; suffisant; ~'**crowd** trop remplir; ~'**do** [*irr.* (*do*)] outrer; charger (*un rôle*); *fig.* exagérer; *cuis.* trop cuire; ~**done** [ouvə'dʌn] outré, excessif (-ive *f*); F éreinté; exagéré; ['ouvə'dʌn] trop cuit; '~**dose** dose *f* trop forte *ou* excessive; ~'**draft** ✝ découvert *m*; ~'**draw** [*irr.* (*draw*)] charger, exagérer; ✝ mettre à découvert; ~'**dress** faire trop de toilette; (s')habiller avec trop de recherche; '~**drink** [*irr.* (*drink*)]: ~ *o.s.* se soûler; ~'**drive** *mot.* surmultiplication *f*; ~'**due** en retard (*a.* ⚙); ✝ arriéré, échu; '~**eat** [*irr.* (*eat*)]: ~ *o.s.* trop manger; ~'**es·ti·mate** surestimer; '~**ex·pose** phot. surexposer; '~**ex·po·sure** phot. surexposition *f*; '~**fa·tigue 1.** surmener; **2.** surmenage *m*; '~**feed** [*irr.* (*feed*)] *v/t.* suralimenter; *v/i.* trop manger; ~'**flow 1.** [ouvə'flou] [*irr.* (*flow*)] *v/t.* déborder de; inonder; *v/i.* déborder; **2.** ['ouvəflou] débordement *m*; inondation *f*; trop-plein *m*; '~**freight** surcharge *f*; '~**ground** (qui voyage) par voie de terre; ~'**grow** [*irr.* (*grow*)] (re)couvrir; envahir; '~**growth** surcroissance *f*; couverture *f* (*de ronces etc.*); ~'**hang 1.** [ouvə'hæŋ] [*irr.* (*hang*)] surplomber; faire saillie (au-dessus de qch., *s.th.*); **2.** ['ouvəhæŋ] saillie *f*; ~'**haul** examiner en détail; réparer; ~**head 1.** [ouvə'hed] *adv.* en haut; *works* ~! attention, travaux (en haut)!; **2.** ['ouvəhed] *adj.* ✝ général (-aux *m/pl.*) (*frais, dépenses, etc.*); ~ *railway* ⊕ pont *m* roulant; ⊕ chemin *m* de fer aérien; ⊕~ *wire* câble *m* aérien; **3.** *su.* ✝ ~*s pl.* frais *m/pl.* généraux; ~'**hear** [*irr.* (*hear*)] surprendre (*q., une conversation*); '~**heat** ⊕ surchauffer; ⊕ ~ *o.s.* s'échauffer; '~**house** *radio:* d'extérieur (*antenne*); ~'**in·dulge** montrer trop d'indulgence envers (*q.*), gâter (*q.*); céder trop facilement à (*un vice*); ~ *in* faire abus de (*qch.*); '~'**in·dul·gence** indulgence *f* excessive; ~'**is·sue** faire une surémission de (*billets de banque*); ~'**joy** ravir; *be* ~*ed a.* être aux anges, être au comble (de la joie); '~·**kill** ⚔ (capacité *f* de) surextermination *f*; ~·**land 1.** ['ouvəlænd] *adj.* qui voyage par voie de terre; **2.** [ouvə'lænd] *adv.* par voie de terre; ~·**lap** *v/t.* recouvrir (partiellement); dépasser; faire double emploi avec; *v/i.* (se) chevaucher; ~·**lay 1.** [ouvə'lei] [*irr.* (*lay*)] (re)couvrir (de, with); ⊕ mettre des hausses sur; **2.** ['ouvəlei]: ~ *mattress* matelas *m*; couvre-lit *m*; '~·**leaf** au verso; ~·**load 1.** ['ouvəloud] surcharge *f*; **2.** [ouvə'loud] surcharger; ~·**look** avoir vue sur; dominer; surveiller (*un travail*); *fig.* oublier; négliger; fermer les yeux sur; laisser passer; '~·**lord** suzerain *m*.

o·ver·ly ['ouvəli] trop, excessivement, à l'excès.

o·ver...: ~·**manned** ayant trop de personnel; ~·**man·tel** étagère *f* de cheminée; ~·**mas·ter** subjuguer; '~·**much** (par) trop; '~·**night 1.** (pendant) la nuit; jusqu'au lendemain; du jour au lendemain; **2.** d'une nuit; de nuit; *fig.* soudain; ~ *bag* sac *m* de voyage; ~ *stay* séjour *m* d'une nuit; ~ *stop* arrêt *m* pour la nuit; '~·**pay** [*irr.* (*pay*)] trop payer; surpayer; ~·**peo·pled** surpeuplé; '~·**play** exagérer; *fig.* ~ *one's hand* essayer de faire qch. au-dessus de ses moyens; '~·**plus** surplus *m*; ~·**pow·er** maîtriser; *fig.* accabler; '~·**pres·sure** suppression *f*; surmenage *m* (*de l'esprit*); '~·**print** *phot.* trop pousser; '~·**rate** surestimer; ~·**reach** dépasser; ~ *o.s.* être victime de sa propre fourberie; '~·**re·act** réagir excessivement *ou* trop vivement (à, to); ~·**ride** [*irr.* (*ride*)] outrepasser (*un ordre*); fouler aux pieds (*des droits*); surmener (*un cheval*); avoir plus d'importance que; ~·**rid·ing** primordial (-aux *m/pl.*); ~·**rule** décider contre; 🖉 annuler; rejeter; ~·**run** [*irr.* (*run*)] envahir; dépasser (*les bornes*); surmener (*une machine*); *typ.* reporter à la ligne *ou* page suivante; '~·**seas** d'outre-mer; à l'étranger; *adj. a.* étranger (-ère *f*); ~ *aid* aide *f* aux pays étrangers; ~ *trade* commerce *m* extérieur; ~·**see** [*irr.* (*see*)] surveiller; '~·**se·er** surveillant(e *f*) *m*; ⊕ chef *m* d'atelier; ~ *of the poor* directeur *m* du Bureau de bienfaisance; ~·**set** [*irr.* (*set*)] *v/t.* renverser; *fig.* bouleverser; *v/i.* se

renverser; '~·**sew** [*irr.* (*sew*)] surjeter; ~·**shad·ow** ombrager; éclipser (*q.*); '~·**shoe** galoche *f*; '~·**shoot** [*irr.* (*shoot*)] dépasser; dépeupler (*une chasse*); ~ *o.s.* aller trop loin; '~·**shot** à augets (*roue*); '~·**sight** oubli *m*; surveillance *f*; '~·**sim·pli·fi·ca·tion** simplisme *m*; '~·**sleep** [*irr.* (*sleep*)] (*a.* ~ *o.s.*) dormir trop longtemps; '~·**sleeve** fausse manche *f*; ~·**spill** excédent *m* (*surt.* de la population); ~·**spread** [*irr.* (*spread*)] couvrir (de, with); inonder (*qch.*); s'étendre sur; ~·**staffed** avec trop de personnel; '~·**state** exagérer; '~·**step** outrepasser; '~·**stock** constituer un cheptel trop important pour (*une ferme*); ✝ encombrer (*le marché*); ~·**strain 1.** ['ouvə'strein] surtendre; *fig.* surmener; **2.** ['ouvə'strein] tension *f* excessive; *fig.* surmenage *m*; ~·**strung** ['ouvə'strʌŋ] surexcité; ['ouvəstrʌŋ] oblique (*piano*); '~·**sub·scribe** ✝ surpasser (*une émission*); '~·**sup·ply** provision *f* excessive; excès *m*.

o·vert ['ouvə:t] patent, évident.

over...: ~·**take** [*irr.* (*take*)] dépasser (*qch.*); doubler (*une auto*); rattraper (*q.*); *fig.* arriver à, surprendre; '~·**tax** pressurer (*le peuple*); *fig.* trop exiger de (*q.*); surmener; ~·**throw 1.** [ouvə'θrou] [*irr.* (*throw*)] renverser (*a. fig.*); vaincre; **2.** ['ouvəθrou] renversement *m*; défaite *f* (*a. fig., a.* ⚔); '~·**time** heures *f/pl.* supplémentaires; '~·**tire** surmener; '~·**tone** ♪ harmonique *m*; *fig.* sous-entendu *m*, note *f*, nuance *f*, accent *m*; '~·**top** dépasser en hauteur; ~·**train** (s')épuiser par un entraînement trop sévère; '~·**trump** surcouper.

o·ver·ture ['ouvətjuə] ouverture *f* (*a.* ♪); offre *f*.

over...: ~·**turn 1.** ['ouvətə:n] renversement *m*; **2.** [ouvə'tə:n] (se) renverser; *mot.* (faire) capoter; ⚓ (faire) chavirer; '~·**val·ue** faire trop de cas de; ✝ surestimer; ~·**ween·ing** outrecuidant; ~·**weight 1.** ['ouvə-weit] *poids, bagages, etc.:* excédent *m*; **2.** [ouvə'weit] surcharger (de, with); ~·**whelm** accabler (*a. fig.*); submerger; combler; ~·**whelm·ing** □ accablant; écrasant; '~·**wise** prétentieux (-euse *f*); ~·**work 1.** ['ouvəwə:k] travail (*pl.* -aux) *m* en plus; ['ouvə'wə:k] *fig.* surmenage *m*; **2.** [~] [*irr.* (*work*)] (se) surmener; '~'**wrought** surmené; excédé de fatigue *etc.*; surexcité.

o·vi·form ['ouvifɔ:m] ovoïde, oviforme; **o·vip·a·rous** *biol.* [ou'vipərəs] ovipare.

owe [ou] devoir (*de l'argent, de l'obéissance, etc.*); *sp.* rendre (*des points*); ~ *s.o. a grudge* en vouloir à q.

ow·ing ['ouiŋ] dû (due *f*); ~ *to* par suite de; à cause de; *be* ~ *to* (pro-) venir de.

owl *orn.* [aul] hibou (*pl.* -x) *m*; chouette *f*; **owl·et** ['aulit] jeune hibou *m*; '**owl·ish** ☐ de hibou.

own [oun] **1.** propre; à moi (toi *etc.*); le mien (tien *etc.*); *my* ~ *self* moi-même; ~ *brother to* frère germain de (*q.*); **2.** *my* ~ le mien (la mienne *etc.*); *a house of one's* ~ une maison à soi; *come into one's* ~ entrer en possession de son bien; F *get one's* ~ *back* se venger, prendre sa revanche (sur, *on*); *hold one's* ~ tenir ferme; maintenir sa position; F *on one's* ~ (tout) seul; **3.** posséder; avoir; (*a.* ~ *to*) reconnaître; avouer; convenir de; F ~ *up* (*to*) faire l'aveu (de); avouer (*avoir fait qch.*).

own·er ['ounə] propriétaire *mf*; '~-'**driv·er** conducteur *m* propriétaire; '~**less** sans propriétaire; '**own·er·ship** (droit *m* de) propriété *f*; possession *f*.

ox [ɔks], *pl.* **ox·en** ['~ən] bœuf *m*.

ox·al·ic ac·id ⚗ [ɔk'sælik'æsid] acide *m* oxalique.

Ox·ford shoes ['ɔksfəd'ʃu:z] *pl.* souliers *m/pl.* de ville.

ox·i·da·tion [ɔksi'deiʃən] ⚗ oxydation *f*; *métall.* calcination *f*; **ox·ide** ⚗ ['ɔksaid] oxyde *m*; **ox·i·dize** ['ɔksidaiz] (s')oxyder; *v/t. métall.* calciner.

Ox·o·ni·an [ɔk'sounjən] **1.** oxonien (-ne *f*); **2.** membre *m* de l'Université d'Oxford. [la queue de bœuf.)

ox·tail soup ['ɔksteil'su:p] soupe *f* à ʃ

ox·y·a·cet·y·lene [ɔksiə'setili:n]: ~ *burner* (*ou lamp ou torch*) chalumeau *m* oxycétylénique, oxycoupeur *m*.

ox·y·gen ⚗ ['ɔksidʒən] oxygène *m*; **ox·y·gen·ate** [ɔk'sidʒineit] oxygéner, oxyder.

o·yer ⚖ ['ɔiə] audition *f*.

oys·ter ['ɔistə] huître *f*; *attr.* à huîtres, d'huître(s); '~-**bed** huîtrière *f*.

o·zone ⚗ ['ouzoun] ozone *m*.

P

P, p [piː] P *m*, p *m*; *mind one's Ps and Qs* se surveiller; faire bien attention.

pa F [pɑː] papa *m*.

pab·u·lum [ˈpæbjuləm]nourriture *f*.

pace [peis] **1.** pas *m* (*a. mesure*); vitesse *f*; allure *f*; *équitation*: amble *m*; *keep* ~ *with* marcher de pair avec; *put s.o. through his* ~*s* mettre q. à l'épreuve; *sp.* set the ~ donner l'allure; **2.** *v/t.* mesurer (*qch.*) au pas; arpenter; *sp.* entraîner (*q.*); *v/i.* marcher à pas mesurés; aller au pas; aller l'amble (*cheval*); **'pace-mak·er** *sp.* entraîneur *m*; meneur *m* de train; *🖤* stimulateur *m* cardiaque; **'pac·er** cheval *m* ambleur; *see* pace-maker.

pach·y·derm *zo.* [ˈpækidəːm] pachyderme *m*.

pa·cif·ic [pəˈsifik] (~*ally*) pacifique; paisible; ♀ *Ocean* l'océan *m* Pacifique, le Pacifique *m*; **pac·i·fi·ca·tion** [pæsifiˈkeiʃn] apaisement *m*; pacification *f*.

pac·i·fi·er [ˈpæsifaiə] pacificateur (-trice *f*) *m*; *Am.* sucette *f*; **'pac·i·fism** pacifisme *m*; **'pac·i·fist** pacifiste *mf*.

pac·i·fy [ˈpæsifai] pacifier (*la foule, un pays*); calmer, apaiser.

pack [pæk] **1.** paquet *m*; ballot *m*; bande *f*; ✂ paquetage *m*; *cartes*: jeu *m*, paquet *m*; ✂ enveloppement *m*; *sp. rugby*: pack *m*; *a* ~ *of nonsense* un tas *m* de sottises; ~ *animal* bête *f* de somme; *Am.* ~ *train* convoi *m* de bêtes de somme; **2.** *v/t.* tasser; remplir, bourrer; (*souv.* ~ *up*) emballer, empaqueter, envelopper (*a. 🖤*); (*a.* ~ *off*) envoyer (au lit, promener, *etc.*); F faire (*une malle*); conserver en boîtes (*la viande etc.*); *fig.* serrer, combler; ✂ garnir (*le piston, le gland*); *v/i.* (*usu.* ~ *up*) faire sa malle; plier bagage; F faire (*une malle*); ~ *s.o. off, send s.o.* ~*ing* envoyer q. à la balançoire; **'pack·age** empaquetage *m*, emballage *m*;

surt. *Am.* paquet *m*, colis *m*; *🖤* ~ *deal* marché *m ou* contrat *m* global; achat *m* forfaitaire; panier *m*; ~ *holiday* vacances *f/pl.* organisées; ~ *tour* voyage *m* organisé à prix forfaitaire; **'pack·er** emballeur *m*; *Am.* fabricant *m* de conserves en boîtes; **pack·et** [ˈ~it] paquet *m*; colis *m*; (*a.* ~*-boat*) paquebot *m*; **'pack·horse** cheval *m* de bât (*a. fig.*), sommier *m*.

pack·ing [ˈpækiŋ] emballage *m*; *viande etc.*: conservation *f*; tassement *m*; matière *f* pour emballage; ✂ garniture *f*; *attr.* d'emballage; **'~-box** 🖤 presse-étoupe *m/inv.*; ~ **house** *Am. usu.* fabrique *f* de conserves. [d'emballage; ficelle *f*.\]
pack·thread [ˈpækθred] fil *m*⟩

pact [pækt] pacte *m*, contrat *m*.

pad[1] *sl.* [pæd] (*a.* ~ *it*) aller à pied, trimarder.

pad[2] [~] **1.** bourrelet *m*, coussinet *m*; *ouate, encreur, etc.*: tampon *m*; bloc *m*; bloc-notes (*pl.* blocs-notes) *m*; *lapin etc.*: patte *f*; *doigt etc.*: pulpe *f*; *sp.* jambière *f*; **2.** rembourrer; ouater; *fig.* ~ *out* délayer; ajouter du remplissage à; ~*ded cell* cellule *f* matelassée; **'pad·ding** remplissage *m* (*a. fig.*); rembourrage *m*; ouate *f*; bourre *f*.

pad·dle [ˈpædl] **1.** aube *f*, palette *f*; *tortue etc.*: nageoire *f*; pagaie *f*; ⚓ roue *f* à aubes; **2.** pagayer; *fig.* barboter; patauger; *Am.* F fesser; **'~-box** ⚓ caisse *f* de roue; **'~-steam·er** ⚓ vapeur *m* à aubes; **'~-wheel** roue *f* à aubes.

pad·dock [ˈpædək] enclos *m* (*pour chevaux*); *sp.* paddock *m*, pesage *m*.

pad·dy[1] [ˈpædi] paddy *m* (= *riz non décortiqué*).

pad·dy[2] [~] F colère *f*.

pad·dy wag·on *Am. sl.* [ˈpædiwægən] panier *m* à salade.

pad·lock [ˈpædlɔk] cadenas *m*.

pa·gan [ˈpeigən] païen(ne *f*) (*a. su.*); **'pa·gan·ism** paganisme *m*.

page[1] [peidʒ] **1.** page *m* (*d'un roi etc.*); (*a.* ~*-boy*) *hôtel*: chasseur *m*, groom *m*; *Am.* huissier *m*; **2.** *Am.* envoyer chercher (*q.*) par un chasseur.

page² [∼] **1.** *livre*: page *f*; **2.** numéroter; paginer; *typ.* mettre en pages.

pag·eant ['pædʒənt] spectacle *m* historique; fête *f*; (*a.* '**pag·eant·ry**) pompe *f*; spectacle *m* pompeux.

pag·i·nate ['pædʒineit] *see* page² **2**; **pag·i·na·tion** pagination *f*; numérotage *m* (*des pages*).

paid [peid] *prét. et p.p. de* pay **2**.

pail [peil] seau *m*.

pail·lasse [pæl'jæs] paillasse *f*.

pain [pein] **1.** douleur *f*, souffrance *f*, peine *f* (*morale*); douleur *f* (*physique*); ∼s *pl.* douleurs *f/pl.*; *fig.* peine *f*; soins *m/pl.*; (up)on ∼ of sous peine de; F be a ∼ in the neck être casse-pieds; be in ∼ souffrir; be at ∼s (*of gér.*, to *inf.*), take ∼s (to *inf.*) prendre *ou* se donner de la peine (pour *inf.*); **2.** faire souffrir (*q.*); faire de la peine à (*q.*); **pain·ful** □ ['∼ful] douloureux (-euse *f*); *fig.* pénible; '**pain-kill·er** anodin *m*; '**pain·less** □ sans douleur; '**pains·tak·ing 1.** □ assidu; appliqué (*élève*); soigné (*travail*); **2.** application *f*; assiduité *f*.

paint [peint] **1.** peinture *f*; couleur *f*; *visage*: fard *m*; wet ∼! attention à la peinture!; **2.** peindre; (se) farder; *v/t.* peinturer; ✗, *co.* badigeonner; † *fig.* dépeindre; ∼ out effacer (au moyen d'une couche de peinture); *v/i.* faire de la peinture; '∼-brush pinceau *m*.

paint·er¹ ['peintə] (artiste-)peintre *m*; *a.* peintre en *m* bâtiments.

paint·er² ⚓ ['peintə] amarre *f*.

paint·ing ['peintiŋ] peinture *f*; tableau *m*; '**paint·ress** femme *f* peintre; '**paint·y** de peinture.

pair [pɛə] **1.** paire *f*; a ∼ of scissors une paire *f* de ciseaux; a carriage and ∼ une voiture *f* à deux chevaux; go up three ∼ of stairs monter trois étages; three ∼ front au troisième sur la rue; **2.** (s')apparier; *v/i.* faire la paire (avec, with); (*a.* ∼ off) s'en aller deux par deux.

pa·ja·mas *pl. usu. Am.* [pə'dʒɑːməz] *see* pyjamas.

pal *sl.* [pæl] **1.** camarade *mf*; *sl.* copain *m*, copine *f*; **2.** ∼ up se lier d'amitié (avec, with).

pal·ace ['pælis] palais *m*.

pal·at·a·ble □ ['pælətəbl] agréable

(au palais); '**pal·at·a·ble·ness** goût *m* agréable; caractère *m* agréable.

pal·a·tal ✗ ['pælətl] **1.** palatal (-aux *m/pl.*); **2.** *gramm.* palatale *f*.

pal·ate ['pælit] palais *m* (*a. fig.*); soft ∼ voile *m* du palais.

pa·la·tial □ [pə'leiʃəl] grandiose.

pa·lat·i·nate [pə'lætinit] palatinat *m*; the ♀ le Palatinat *m*.

pal·a·tine ['pælətain] palatin; Count ♀ comte *m* palatin.

pa·la·ver [pə'lɑːvə] **1.** palabre *f*, conférence *f*; *sl.* flagornerie *f*, *sl.* chichis *m/pl.*; **2.** palabrer.

pale¹ [peil] **1.** □ pâle (*a. couleur*), blême; ∼ blue bleu pâle; ∼ ale bière *f* blonde, pale-ale *m*; **2.** *v/t.* (faire) pâlir; *v/i.* pâlir, blêmir.

pale² [∼] pieu *m*; *fig.* limites *f/pl.*

pale-face ['peilfeis] visage pâle *mf*.

pale·ness ['peilnis] pâleur *f*.

Pal·es·tin·i·an [pæles'tiniən] palestinien(ne *f*).

pal·ette *peint.* ['pælit] palette *f*; '∼-knife couteau *m* à palette.

pal·frey ['pɔːlfri] palefroi *m*.

pal·ing ['peiliŋ] clôture *f* à claire-voie; palissade *f*.

pal·i·sade [pæli'seid] **1.** palissade *f*; **2.** palissader.

pall¹ [pɔːl] **1.** *eccl.* poêle *m*; *fig.* manteau *m*, voile *m*; **2.** couvrir d'un poêle.

pall² [∼] s'affadir; devenir insipide (pour *q.*, [up]on *s.o.*).

pal·la·di·um ⚗, *myth.* [pə'leidiəm] palladium *m*.

pal·let¹ ['pælit] paillasse *f*; grabat *m*.

pal·let² ⊕ [∼] cliquet *m*; *horloge etc.*: palette *f*.

pal·liasse [pæl'jæs] paillasse *f*.

pal·li·ate ['pælieit] pallier; atténuer; **pal·li·a·tion** palliation *f*; atténuation *f*; **pal·li·a·tive** ['pæliətiv] **1.** palliatif (-ive *f*); lénitif (-ive *f*); **2.** palliatif *m*; lénitif *m*; anodin *m*.

pal·lid □ ['pælid] décoloré; blafard (*lumière*); blême (*visage*); '**pal·lid·ness**, **pal·lor** ['pælə] pâleur *f*.

pal·ly F ['pæli]: be ∼ with s.o. être copain (copine *f*) avec q.

palm [pɑːm] **1.** *main*: paume *f*; *ancre*: oreille *f*; *bois de cerf*: empaumure *f*; ♀ *arbre*: palmier *m*; *branche*: palme *f*; *eccl.* rameau *m*; **2.** empalmer; cacher dans la main; ∼ off on s.o. F refiler (*qch.*) à q.; **pal·mar** ['pælmə] palmaire; **pal·mate**

['pælmit], **pal·mat·ed** ['⁓meitid] palmé; **pal·mer** ['pɑːmə] pèlerin *m*; **palm·is·try** ['⁓istri] chiromancie *f*; **'palm-oil** huile *f* de palme; *co. use* ⁓ *on s.o.* graisser la patte à q.; **Palm Sun·day** (dimanche *m* des) Rameaux *m/pl.*; **'palm-tree** palmier *m*; **'palm·y** F heureux (-euse *f*), florissant.

pal·pa·bil·i·ty [pælpə'biliti] palpabilité *f*; *fig.* évidence *f*; **'pal·pa·ble** □ palpable; *fig.* évident, manifeste; **'pal·pa·ble·ness** *see palpability.*

pal·pi·tate ['pælpiteit] palpiter; **pal·pi'ta·tion** palpitation *f*.

pal·sied ['pɔːlzid] paralysé, paralytique.

pal·sy ['pɔːlzi] 1. paralysie *f*; *fig.* évanouissement *m*; 2. paralyser.

pal·ter ['pɔːltə] (*with*) biaiser (avec); transiger (avec, sur).

pal·tri·ness ['pɔːltrinis] mesquinerie *f*; **'pal·try** □ mesquin, misérable.

pam·per ['pæmpə] choyer, dorloter.

pam·phlet ['pæmflit] brochure *f*; opuscule *m*; *péj.* pamphlet *m*; **pam·phlet·eer** [⁓'tiə] auteur *m* de brochures; *péj.* pamphlétaire *m*.

pan [pæn] 1. casserole *f*; *balance:* plateau *m*; 2. *Am.* F *v/t.* décrier, rabaisser; ⁓ *out* laver (*le gravier*); *v/i.* ⁓ *out* réussir.

pan... [⁓] pan-.

pan·a·ce·a [pænə'siə] panacée *f*; remède *m* universel.

pan·cake ['pænkeik] crêpe *f*; ✈ ⁓ *landing* descente *f* à plat.

pan·da ['pændə] panda *m*; *Brit.* ⁓ *car* voiture *f* pie (de la police); *Brit.* ⁓ *crossing passage m* pour piétons.

pan·de·mo·ni·um *fig.* [pændi'mouniəm] bruit *m* infernal.

pan·der ['pændə] 1. se prêter à (*un vice*); servir de proxénète à (*q.*); 2. entremetteur (-euse *f*) *m*.

pane [pein] vitre *f*, carreau *m*; ⊕ pan *m*.

pan·e·gyr·ic [pæni'dʒirik] panégyrique *m*; **pan·e'gyr·ist** panégyriste *m*.

pan·el ['pænl] 1. △ entre-deux *m/inv.*; panneau *m*; *porte:* placard *m*; *plafond:* caisson *m*; panneau *m* (*de lambris, de robe*); tableau *m* (t̳t̳ *du jury, a. mot. de manœuvre*); t̳t̳ le jury *m*; *peint.* panneau *m*; vantail (*pl.* -aux) *m*; ⁓ *discussion* réunion-débat *f* (*pl.* réunions-débats); ⁓ *doctor* médecin *m* conventionné; 2. diviser en *ou* recouvrir de panneaux; lambrisser (*un paroi*); **'pan·el·ist** membre *m* d'un jury; **'pan·el·(1)ing**, *a.* **'pan·el·work** lambris(sage *m*) *m/pl.*

pang [pæŋ] angoisse *f* subite; douleur *f*; *fig.* blessure *f*, tourments *m/pl.*; ⁓ *of hunger* tiraillement *m* d'estomac.

pan·han·dle ['pænhændl] 1. *Am. langue de terre d'un État, encaissée entre deux autres États*; 2. *Am.* F mendigoter; **'pan·han·dler** *Am.* F mendigot *m*.

pan·ic ['pænik] 1. de panique; 2. panique *f*; affolement *m*; 3. (s')affoler; remplir *ou* être pris de panique; **'pan·ick·y** F sujet à *ou* dicté par la panique; alarmiste; **'pan·ic-mon·ger** semeur (-euse *f*) *m* de panique.

pan·nier ['pæniə] panier *m*.

pan·ni·kin ['pænikin] écuelle *f ou* gobelet *m* en fer blanc.

pan·o·ply ['pænəpli] *fig.* panoplie *f*.

pan·o·ra·ma [pænə'rɑːmə] panorama *m*; **pan·o·ram·ic** [⁓'ræmik] (⁓ally) panoramique.

pan·sy ['pænzi] ⚥ pensée *f*; *sl.* homme *m* efféminé.

pant [pænt] haleter; panteler; chercher à reprendre haleine; palpiter (*cœur*); *fig.* ⁓ *for* (*ou after*) soupirer après; ⁓ *out* dire (*qch.*) en haletant.

Pan·ta·loon [pæntə'luːn] Pantalon *m*; ⁓s *pl.* pantalon *m* (*see pants*).

pan·tech·ni·con [pæn'teknikən] garde-meuble *m*; (*a.* ⁓ *van*) voiture *f* de déménagement.

pan·the·ism ['pænθiizm] panthéisme *m*; **pan·the·is·tic** (⁓ally) panthéiste.

pan·ther *zo.* ['pænθə] panthère *f*.

pant·ies *Am.* ['pæntiz] *pl.*: (*a pair of*) ⁓) (une) culotte *f* collante (*de femme*).   [panne *f*.]

pan·tile ['pæntail] tuile *f* flamande;⌡

pan·to·mime ['pæntəmaim] pantomime *f*; spectacle *m* traditionnel de Noël, fondé sur un conte de fée; **pan·to·mim·ic** [⁓'mimik] (⁓ally) pantomimique; de féerie.

pan·try ['pæntri] garde-manger *m/inv.*; dépense *f*; (*souv. butler's ou housemaid's* ⁓) office *f*.

pants *surt. Am.* F [pænts] *pl.*: (*a pair of*) ~ (un) pantalon *m*; (un) caleçon *m*; ~ *suit* tailleur-pantalon *m* (*pl.* tailleurs-pantalons).

pan·ty hose *Am.* ['pænti'houz] collant *m*.

pap [pæp] bouillie *f.*

pa·pa [pə'pɑ:] papa *m.*

pa·pa·cy ['peipəsi] papauté *f.*

pa·pal □ ['peipəl] papal (-aux *m/pl.*); du Pape.

pa·per ['peipə] 1. papier *m*; (*ou news~*) journal *m*; carte *f* (*d'épingles etc.*); document *m*; (*ou wall-~*) tenture *f*, papier *m* peint; étude *f*, mémoire *m*; *école:* composition *f*, épreuve *f*; † papier *m* négociable; billets *m/pl.* de banque; papiers-valeurs *m/pl.*; ~s *pl.* papiers *m/pl.*; journaux *m/pl.*; *pol.*, *a.* ᵗᵗ documents *m/pl.*; communiqués *m/pl.*; *read a* ~ on faire une conférence sur; 2. de papier; en carton; papetier (-ère *f*); à papier; ~ *war* guerre *f* de plume; 3. tapisser; *sl. théâ.* remplir de billets de faveur; '~·**back** livre *m* broché; '~·**bag** sac *m* de *ou* en papier; '~·**chase** rallye-paper *m*; '~·**clip** agrafe *f*, pince *f*; '~·**cred·it** † dettes *f/pl.* compte; '~·**fast·en·er** attache *f* métallique; '~·**hang·er** colleur *m* de papiers peints; '~·**hang·ings** *pl.* papier *m* peint, papiers *m/pl.* peints; '~·**mill** papeterie *f*; '~·**'stain·er** imprimeur *m* de papiers peints; '~·**thin** extrêmement fin; '~·**weight** presse-papiers *m/inv.*; '~·**work** écriture(s) *f(pl.)*; paperasserie *f*; **pa·per·y** ['~ri] semblable au papier; tout mince.

pa·pier mâ·ché ['pæpjei'mɑ:ʃei] carton-pâte (*pl.* cartons-pâtes) *m.*

pa·pil·la *anat.* [pə'pilə], *pl.* **-lae** [~li:] papille *f.*

pa·pist ['peipist] papiste *mf*; **pa·pis·tic, pa·pis·ti·cal** □ [pə'pistik(l)] *péj.* papiste; **pa·pis·try** ['peipistri] *péj.* papisme *m.*

pap·py ['pæpi] pâteux (-euse *f*); *fig.* flasque. [papyrus *m.*]

pa·py·rus [pə'paiərəs], *pl.* **-ri** [~rai]/

par [pɑ:] égalité *f*; pair *m* (*a.* †); *above,* (*below*) ~ au-dessus (*au-dessous*) du pair; *at* ~ au pair, à (la) parité; *be on a* ~ *with* être l'égal *ou* au niveau de; *put on a* ~ *with* mettre au même niveau que; *ne faire aucune distinction entre.*

par·a·ble ['pærəbl] parabole *f.*

pa·rab·o·la Å [pə'ræbələ] parabole *f*; **par·a·bol·ic, par·a·bol·i·cal** □ [pærə'bɔlik(l)] parabolique (*a.* Å).

par·a·chute ['pærəʃu:t] parachute *m*; ~ *jump* saut *m* en parachute; parachutage *m*; **'par·a·chut·ist** parachutiste *mf.*

pa·rade [pə'reid] 1. parade *m*; *fig.* étalage *m*; ✕ défilé *m*; ✕ exercice *m*; ✕ (*ou* ~*-ground*) place *f* d'armes; esplanade *f*; défilé *m* (*de mannequins*); *make a* ~ *of* faire parade de; 2. *v/t.* faire parade de; ✕ faire défiler; faire l'inspection de; *v/i.* défiler; parader (*pour, for*).

par·a·digm *gramm.* ['pærədaim] paradigme *m.*

par·a·dise ['pærədais] paradis *m.*

par·a·dis·i·ac [pærə'disiæk], **par·a·di·si·a·cal** □ [pærədi'saiəkəl] paradisiaque.

par·a·dox ['pærədɔks] paradoxe *m*; **par·a·dox·i·cal** □ paradoxal (-aux *m/pl.*).

par·af·fin ⚗ ['pærəfin] paraffine *f*; F pétrole *m* (*lampant*).

par·a·gon ['pærəgən] parangon *m*; modèle *m* (*a. fig.*).

par·a·graph ['pærəgrɑ:f] paragraphe *m*; alinéa *m*; *journal:* entrefilet *m*; *typ.* † pied *m* de mouche.

par·a·keet *orn.*['pærəki:t] perruche*f.*

par·al·lel ['pærəlel] 1. parallèle (à *to, with*); *fig.* pareil(le *f*), semblable; analogue; ~ *bars pl.* barres *f/pl.* parallèles; 2. *ligne, a. tranchée:* parallèle *f*; *géog.* parallèle *m*; *fig.* parallèle *m*, comparaison *f*, pareil(le *f*) *m*; cas *m* analogue; ⚡ *connect* (*ou join*) *in* ~ coupler en parallèle; *have no* ~ être sans pareil(le *f*); *without* ~ incomparable, sans égal (-aux *m/pl.*); 3. égaler (*qch.*); être égal (*ou* pareil) à (*qch.*); mettre (*deux choses*) en parallèle; ⚡ synchroniser; **'par·al·lel·ism** parallélisme *m*; **par·al'lel·o·gram** Å [~əgræm] parallélogramme *m.*

par·a·lyse ['pærəlaiz] paralyser (*a. fig.*); *fig.* transir; **pa·ral·y·sis** ⚗ [pə'rælisis] paralysie *f*; **par·a·lyt·ic** [pærə'litik] 1. (~*ally*) paralytique; 2. paralytique *mf.*

par·a·mil·i·tar·y ['pærə'militəri] paramilitaire.

par·a·mount ['pærəmaunt] 1. souverain, éminent; suprême (*impor-*

tance); be ~ (*to*) l'emporter (sur);
2. suzerain(e *f*) *m*; **'par·a·mount-cy** suzeraineté *f*; primauté *f*.

par·a·mour ['pærəmuə] amant(e *f*)
m; maîtresse *f*.

par·a·noi·a [pærə'nɔiə] paranoïa *f*;
par·a·noi·ac [~'nɔiək] paranoïque
mf.

par·a·pet ['pærəpit] ✕ parapet *m*;
pont: garde-corps *m/inv.*

par·a·pher·na·li·a [pærəfə'neiljə]
pl. F affaires *f/pl.*, bataclan *m*; attirail *m*, appareil *m*.

par·a·phrase ['pærəfreiz] **1.** paraphrase *f*; **2.** paraphraser, résumer.

par·a·ple·gi·a [pærə'pli:dʒə] para-
plégie *f*; **par·a·ple·gic** paraplégique
(*adj.*, *mf*).

par·a·site ['pærəsait] parasite *m*;
fig. écornifleur (-euse *f*) *m*; **par·a-
sit·ic, par·a·sit·i·cal** □ [~'sitik(l)]
parasite (de, on).

par·a·sol [pærə'sɔl] ombrelle *f*.

par·a·troop·er ✕ ['pærətru:pə]
parachutiste *m*; **par·a·troops** ['~-
tru:ps] *pl. les* parachutistes *m/pl.*

par·a·ty·phoid ✕ ['pærə'taifɔid] pa-
ratyphoïde *f*.

par·boil ['pɑ:bɔil] faire bouillir à
demi; *fig.* étourdir (*la viande*).

par·buck·le ⚓ ['pɑ:bʌkl] **1.** trévire
f; **2.** trévirer.

par·cel ['pɑ:sl] **1.** paquet *m*, colis *m*;
✝ lot *m*, envoi *m*; *péj.* tas *m*; parcelle *f* (*de terrain*); ~s office bureau
m de(s) messageries; **2.** empaqueter;
emballer; (*usu.* ~ out) parceler, lotir,
morceler (*un terrain*); ~ **post** service
m des colis postaux.

parch [pɑ:tʃ] (se des)sécher; *v/t.*
rôtir, griller; ~*ing heat* chaleur *f*
brûlante.

parch·ment['pɑ:tʃmənt] parchemin
m.

par·don ['pɑ:dn] **1.** pardon *m*; ⚖
grâce *f*; *eccl.* indulgence *f*; **2.** pardonner (qch. à q., s.o. s.th.); ⚖
faire grâce à; gracier; **'par·don·a-
ble** □ pardonnable; graciable;
'par·don·er *hist.* vendeur *m* d'in-
dulgences.

pare [pɛə] rogner (*les ongles etc.*);
peler (*une pomme etc.*); éplucher;
(*a.* ~ *away*, ~ *down*) *fig.* rogner.

par·ent ['pɛərənt] père *m*, mère *f*;
fig. mère *f*, source *f*; ~s *pl.* parents
m/pl., les père et mère; ~*teacher
association* association *f* des parents

d'élèves et des professeurs; **'par-
ent·age** naissance *f*, parentage *m*;
extraction *f*; **pa·ren·tal** □ [pə-
'rentl] paternel(le *f*).

pa·ren·the·sis [pə'renθisis], *pl.* -**ses**
[~si:z] parenthèse *f* (*a. typ.*); *fig.*
intervalle *m*; **pa'ren·the·size** mettre entre parenthèses (*a. typ.*); intercaler; **par·en·thet·ic, par·en·
thet·i·cal** □ [pærən'θetik(l)] entre
parenthèses.

par·ent·less ['pɛərəntlis] orphelin,
sans mère ni père.

par·get ['pɑ:dʒit] recouvrir (*un mur*)
d'une couche de plâtre; crépir.

pa·ri·ah ['pæriə] paria *m*, réprouvé
(-e *f*) *m*.

pa·ri·e·tal [pə'raiitl] pariétal (-aux
m/pl.); *anat.* ~ *bone* pariétal *m*.

par·ing ['pɛəriŋ] rognage *m*; épluchage *m*; ~s *pl.* rognures *f/pl.*; pe-
lures *f/pl.*; *métal:* cisaille *f*; ~*knife*
⊕ rognoir *m*; *souliers etc.:* tranchet
m.

par·ish ['pæriʃ] **1.** paroisse *f*; (*a.
civil* ~) commune *f*; *go on the* ~ tomber à la charge de la commune;
2. paroissial (-aux *m/pl.*); municipal
(-aux *m/pl.*); ~ *clerk* clerc *m* de paroisse; ~ *council* conseil *m* municipal; ~ *register* registre *m* paroissial;
pa·rish·ion·er [pə'riʃənə] parois-
sien(ne *f*) *m*; habitant(e *f*) *m* de la
commune.

Pa·ri·sian [pə'rizjən] **1.** parisien
(-ne *f*); de Paris; **2.** Parisien(ne *f*)
m.   [(*a. Bourse*).\

par·i·ty ['pæriti] égalité *f*; parité *f*\

park [pɑ:k] **1.** parc *m* (*a.* ✕); *chasse:*
réserve *f*; *château:* dépendances
f/pl.; *mot.* (parc *m* de) stationnement *m*; ~ *keeper* gardien(ne *f*) *m*
de parc; **2.** *v/t.* enfermer dans un
parc; ✕ mettre en parc; *mot.* parquer, garer; *v/i. mot.* stationner;
'park·ing *mot.* parcage *m*; *attr.* de
stationnement; ~ *brake* frein *m* à
main; ~ *fee* tarif *m ou* droit *m* de
stationnement; ~ *light* feu *m* de position; ~ *meter Am.* compteur *m* de
stationnement; ~ *place* parc *m ou*
endroit *m* de stationnement *m*; ~
space créneau *m*; ~ *ticket Am. parcage:* contravention *f*.

par·ka ['pɑ:kə] anorak *m*.

par·lance ['pɑ:ləns] langage *m*, parler *m*.

par·ley ['pɑ:li] **1.** conférence *f*; ✕

pourparlers *m/pl.*; **2.** *v/i.* entrer en pourparlers; parlementer; ⚔ entamer des négociations; *v/t.* co. parler.

par·lia·ment ['pɑːləmənt] parlement *m*; Chambres *f/pl.* (*en France*); **par·lia·men·tar·i·an** [ˌmenˈtɛəriən] parlementaire (*a. su./mf*); **par·lia·men·ta·ry** □ [ˌˈmentəri] parlementaire; législatif (-ive *f*); 🚌 ˷ *train* train *m* omnibus.

par·lo(u)r ['pɑːlə] petit salon *m*; *couvent:* parloir *m*; *Am.* salon *m* (*de coiffure etc.*), cabinet *m* (*de dentiste etc.*); *Am.* ˷ *car* 🚌 wagon-salon (*pl.* wagons-salons) *m*; 'ˋ-maid bonne *f*.

Par·me·san cheese [pɑːmiˈzænˈtʃiːz] parmesan *m*.

pa·ro·chi·al □ [pəˈroukjəl] *eccl.* paroissial (-aux *m/pl.*), de la paroisse; communal (-aux *m/pl.*); *fig.* de clocher, borné; ˷ *politics pl.* politique *f* de clocher.

par·o·dist ['pærədist] parodiste *mf*; pasticheur (-euse *f*) *m*; '**par·o·dy 1.** parodie *f*, pastiche *m*; *fig.* travestissement (-euse *f*) *m*; **2.** parodier, pasticher; *fig.* travestir.

pa·role [pəˈroul] **1.** ⚔ parole *f* (*d'honneur*); *put on* ˷ *see 3*; **2.** ⚖ *adj.* verbal (-aux *m/pl.*); **3.** ⚖ *surt. Am.* libérer sur parole *ou* conditionnellement.

par·ox·ysm ['pærəksizm] paroxysme *m*; F crise *f*; accès *m* (*de fureur*).

par·quet ['pɑːkei] parquet(age) *m*; *Am. théâ.* orchestre *m*; **par·quet·ed** ['ˌkitid] parqueté, en parquetage; '**par·quet·ry** parquetage *m*, parqueterie *f*.

par·ri·cid·al [pæriˈsaidl] parricide; '**par·ri·cide** parricide *m*; *personne:* parricide *mf*.

par·rot ['pærət] **1.** *orn.* perroquet *m*; **2.** répéter *ou* parler comme un perroquet.

par·ry *sp.* ['pæri] **1.** parade *f*; **2.** parer (*a. fig.*).

parse *gramm.* [pɑːz] faire l'analyse de.

par·si·mo·ni·ous □ [pɑːsiˈmounjəs] parcimonieux (-euse *f*); *péj.* pingre; **par·si·mo·ni·ous·ness**, **par·si·mo·ny** ['pɑːsiməni] parcimonie *f*; *péj.* pingrerie *f*.

pars·ley 🌿 ['pɑːsli] persil *m*.

pars·nip 🌿 ['pɑːsnip] panais *m*.

par·son ['pɑːsn] curé *m* (*catholique*); pasteur *m* (*protestant*); F ˷ *'s nose* croupion *m*; '**par·son·age** presbytère *m*; cure *f*.

part [pɑːt] **1.** *su.* partie *f* (*a. gramm., a.* ♪) (*de, of*); part *f* (*à, in*); *théâ., fig.* rôle *m*; *fig.* comédie *f*; *publication:* fascicule *m*, livraison *f*; ⊕ pièce *f*, organe *m*, élément *m*; parti *m*; ⚔ ˷ *s pl.* (*usu. private ou privy* ˷ *s pl.*) parties *f/pl.*; parages *m/pl.*, pays *m/pl.*, endroit *m*; facultés *f/pl.*; *gramm.* ˷ *s pl. of speech* parties *f/pl.* du discours; ˷ *and parcel of* partie *f* intégrante *f*; *a man of* ˷ *s* homme *m* bien doué; *have neither* ˷ *nor lot in* n'avoir aucune part dans; *in foreign* ˷ *s* à l'étranger *take s.o.'s* ˷ prendre parti pour q.; *take* ˷ *in s.th.* participer à qch., prendre part à qch.; *take in good (bad)* ˷ prendre en bonne (mauvaise) part; *for my (own)* ˷ pour ma part, pour ce qui est de moi, quant à moi; *for the most* ˷ pour la plupart; *in* ˷ en partie; partiellement; *do one's* ˷ faire son devoir; *on the* ˷ *of* de la part de; *on my* ˷ de ma part; **2.** *adv.* en partie, mi-, moitié ...; **3.** *v/t.* séparer (en deux); fendre; ˷ *one's hair* se faire une raie; ˷ *company* se séparer (*de, with*), *fig.* n'être plus d'accord (*avec, with*); *v/i.* se diviser; se quitter; se rompre; se séparer (*de, from*); ˷ *with* céder (*qch.*); se départir de; ⚖ aliéner; *fig.* dépenser (*de l'argent*).

par·take [pɑːˈteik] [*irr.* (*take*)] participer, prendre part (*à in, of*); ˷ *of* prendre (*un repas*); partager (*le repas*) (*de, with*); goûter (*un mets*); *fig.* tenir de; *eccl.* s'approcher de (*les sacrements*); **par·tak·er** participant(e *f*) *m* (*à, in*); partageant(e *f*) *m* (*de, in*).

par·terre ♪, *théâ.* [pɑːˈtɛə] parterre *m*.

par·tial □ ['pɑːʃl] partiel(le *f*), en partie; partial (-aux *m/pl.*) (*personne*); *be* ˷ *to* avoir un faible pour; **par·ti·al·i·ty** [pɑːʃiˈæliti] partialité *f* (*pour, envers for, to*); prédilection *f* (*pour, for*); injustice *f*.

par·tic·i·pant [pɑːˈtisipənt] participant(e *f*) *m* (*à, in*); **par·tic·i·pate** [ˌpeit] participer, prendre part (*à, in*); **par·tic·i·pa·tion** participation *f* (*à, in*); **par·ti·cip·i·al** □ *gramm.* [ˌˈsipiəl] participial (-aux *m/pl.*);

par·ti·ci·ple *gramm.* ['pɑ:tsipl]
participe *m*.

par·ti·cle ['pɑ:tikl] particule *f* (*a.
gramm.*); *métal*: paillette *f*; *fig.*
ombre *f*, trace *f*, grain *m*; *nobiliary*
~ particule *f* nobiliaire.

par·ti·col·oured ['pɑ:tikʌləd] mi-
parti; bigarré.

par·tic·u·lar [pə'tikjulə] **1.** □
particulier (-ère *f*); spécial (-aux
m/pl.); détaillé; méticuleux (-euse
f); pointilleux (-euse *f*); exigeant
(*sur about, as to*); délicat (*sur on,
about*); ~ly en particulier; **2.** détail
m, particularité *f*; ~s *pl.* détails
m/pl.; *in* ~ en particulier; par·tic·
u·lar·i·ty [~'læriti] particularité *f*;
méticulosité *f*; minutie *f*; **par'tic·
u·lar·ize** [~ləraiz] particulariser;
entrer dans les détails.

part·ing ['pɑ:tiŋ] séparation *f*; départ *m*; rupture *f*; *cheveux*: raie *f*;
~ *of the ways surt. fig.* carrefour *m*.

par·ti·san¹ *hist.* ['pɑ:tizn] pertui-
sane *f*.

par·ti·san² [pɑ:ti'zæn] **1.** partisan *m*
(*a.* ✕); **2.** de parti; sectaire; **par·ti·
'san·ship** esprit *m* de parti; partialité *f*; appartenance *f* à un parti.

par·ti·tion [pɑ:'tiʃn] **1.** partage *m*;
terre: morcellement *m*; cloison(nage
m) *f*; ~ *wall* paroi *f*, cloison *f*; mur
m de refend; **2.** morceler; démembrer; cloisonner (*une pièce*).

par·ti·tive *gramm.* ['pɑ:titiv] □ partitif (-ive *f*) (*a. su./m*).

part·ly ['pɑ:tli] en partie, partiellement.

part·ner ['pɑ:tnə] **1.** associé(e *f*) *m*
(*a.* ✝); *sp.* partenaire *mf*; danseur
(-euse *f*) *m*, cavalier *m*, dame *f*;
2. s'associer à, être associé à; *sp.*
être le partenaire de; *danse*: mener
(*une dame*); *be* ~ed *by s.o.* avoir q.
pour associé *etc.*; **'part·ner·ship**
association *f* (*a.* ✝); ✝ société *f*;
limited ~ société *f* en commandite;
enter into ~ *with* s'associer avec.

part...: '~-own·er copropriétaire
mf; '~-pay·ment versement *m* à
compte; acompte *m*.

par·tridge *orn.* ['pɑ:tridʒ] perdrix *f*.

part...: '~-song chant *m* à plusieurs
voix *ou* parties; '~-time chômage *m*
partiel; *attr.* pour une partie de la
journée *ou* de la semaine; ~ *school*
école *f* du soir; ~ *worker* employé(e

f) *m* à l'heure; travailleur (-euse *f*)
m pour une partie de la journée *etc.*;
have a ~ *job, work* ~ travailler à temps
partiel.

par·ty ['pɑ:ti] partie *f* (*de plaisir,
a.* ⚖); ⚖ personne *f*; *pol.* parti *m*;
soirée *f*; réception *f*; bande *f*,
groupe *m*; équipe *f*; ✕ détachement
m; *fig.* complice *mf*; F individu *m*,
monsieur *m*, dame *f*; *be a* ~ *to*
prendre part à; ~ *boss* chef *m* de
parti; ~ *line téléph.* poste *m* groupé;
Am. parl. directive *f* du parti;
follow the ~ *line parl.* observer (à
la lettre) les directives de son parti;
~ *liner Am. péj.* politicien *m* qui
observe à la lettre les directives de
son parti; ~ *meeting* (*ou* ~ *rally*) rassemblement *m* politique (*organisé
par un parti*); ~ *status* qualité *f* de
membre d'un parti politique; ~
ticket Am. liste *f* des candidats
(*d'un parti politique*); ~-*wall* mur *m*
mitoyen.

par·ve·nu ['pɑ:vənju:] parvenu *m*;
nouveau riche *m*.

pas·chal ['pɑ:skəl] pascal (-als, -aux
m/pl.); de Pâques *ou* Pâque.

pass [pɑ:s] **1.** *su. géog.* col *m*, défilé
m; ⚓, *sp.*, *escrime*, prestidigitation:
passe *f*; *univ.* mention *f* passable;
diplôme *m* sans spécialisation; *théâ.*
(*usu. free* ~) billet *m* de faveur;
🚋 carte *f* de circulation; coupe-file
m/inv.; **2.** *v/i.* passer (*de ... à ou
en, from ... to*); s'écouler, passer
(*temps*); disparaître; avoir lieu, arriver; avoir cours (*monnaie*); être
voté (*loi etc.*); être reçu (*à un examen*); *escrime, a. foot.* faire une
passe; *cartes*: passer (*parole*); être
approuvé (*action*); *bring to* ~
amener, faire arriver; *come to* ~
avoir lieu, arriver; ~ *as* passer pour;
~ *away* disparaître; trépasser (=
mourir); ~ *by* passer, défiler (devant); ~ *by the name of G.* être
connu sous le nom de G.; ~ *for*
passer pour; passer; devenir; ~ *into*
devenir; ~ *into law* passer en loi;
~ *off* disparaître; (se) passer; *surt.
Am.* passer pour (un) blanc (*nègre
à peau blanche*); ~ *on* continuer sa
route; passer (à, *to*); F trépasser;
~ *out* sortir; *sl.* s'évanouir; ~ *through
s.th.* passer par qch. (*a. fig.*); *fig.*
traverser (*une crise*); ~ *under s.o.'s
control* être soumis au contrôle *ou*

à la direction de q.; **3.** *v/t.* passer devant *ou* près de; dépasser; croiser; ne pas s'arrêter à; franchir (*le seuil, la frontière*); outrepasser (*les bornes*); surpasser (*q.*); rattraper (*q.*); *sp.* devancer; refiler (*de la fausse monnaie*); passer (*qch. en revue, le temps, l'été, sa main entre qch., d'un endroit à un autre*); laisser passer (*q.*); transmettre, faire circuler; subir (*une épreuve*) avec succès; réussir à, être reçu à (*un examen*); recevoir (*un candidat*); approuver (*une facture etc.*); voter (*une loi*); prononcer (*un jugement*); ~ one's hand over passer sa main sur; *the bill has not yet ~ed the house* le projet (de loi) n'a pas encore été adopté *ou* voté; ~ one's opinion upon dire *ou* émettre son opinion sur; ✝ ~ to account porter en compte; ~ water uriner, F faire de l'eau; ~ one's word donner sa parole; ~ by (*ou* over) s.th. franchir qch.; passer sur qch. (*a. fig.*); ~ off as faire passer pour; ~ on transmettre, (faire) passer; ~ round faire circuler; ~ a rope round s.th. passer une corde autour de qch.; ~ s.th. through s.th. passer qch. à travers qch.; ~ s.th. up monter qch., surt. Am. ~ up négliger; refuser; **'pass·a·ble** traversable; praticable (*chemin*); passable, assez bon; ayant cours (*monnaie*); **'pass·a·bly** passablement, assez; F plutôt.

pas·sage ['pæsidʒ] passage *m* (*a. d'un texte*); ruelle *f*, passage *m*; couloir *m*, corridor *m*; ⊕ conduit *m*; adoption *f* (*d'un projet de loi*); ♪ trait *m*; ~s *pl.* texte: morceaux *m/pl.*; *fig.* relations *f/pl.* intimes; ~ of (*ou* at) arms passe *f* d'armes; échange *m* de mots vifs; *bird of* ~ oiseau *m* passager; **'~-boat** paquebot *m*; **'~-mon·ey** prix *m* du passage *ou* de la traversée; **'~way** passage *m*, ruelle *f*; Am. couloir *m*, corridor *m*.

pass...: **'~-book** ✝ carnet *m* de banque; *mot.* carnet *m* de passage en douane; **'~-check** *théâ.* contremarque *f*.

pas·sen·ger ['pæsindʒə] ⚓, ⚙ passager (-ère *f*) *m*; voyageur (-euse *f*) *m*; ⚙ *coach* wagon *m* à voyageurs; **'~ train** ⚙ train *m* de voyageurs *ou* de grande vitesse.

passe-par·tout ['pæspa:'tu:] (clef *f*) passe-partout *m/inv.*; *phot.* bande *f* gommée.

pass·er-by ['pa:sə'bai], *pl.* **pass·ers-by** passant(e *f*) *m.*

pass·ing ['pɑ:siŋ] **1.** passage *m*; *oiseaux:* passe *f*; *mot.* doublement *m*; *loi:* adoption *f*; *fig.* mort *f*, trépas *m*; *in* ~ en passant; **2.** passant; passager (-ère *f*); éphémère; **'~-bell** glas *m*; **'pass·ing·ly** en passant; fugitivement.

pas·sion ['pæʃn] passion *f*, amour *m*; colère *f*; crise *f* (*de larmes*); ♀ Passion *f*; *be in a* ~ être furieux (-euse *f*); ⚕ *in* ~ dans la chaleur du moment; ♀ *Week* semaine *f* de la Passion; semaine *f* sainte; **pas·sion·ate** □ ['~ʃənit] passionné; véhément; **'pas·sion·ate·ness** passion *f*, ardeur *f*; véhémence *f*; **'pas·sion-flow·er** ♀ fleur *f* de la Passion, passiflore *f*; **'pas·sion·less** □ impassible; sans passion; **'pas·sion-play** mystère *m* de la Passion.

pas·sive □ ['pæsiv] **1.** passif (-ive *f*); ~ voice **2.** *gramm.* passif *m*; **'pas·sive·ness**, **pas·siv·i·ty** ['~-siviti] passivité *f*, inertie *f*.

pass-key ['pɑ:ski:] (clef *f*) passe-partout *m/inv.* [♀ agneau *m* pascal.)

Pass·o·ver [pɑ:souvə] Pâque *f*;)

pass·port ['pɑ:spɔ:t] passeport *m*.

pass·word ⚔ ['pɑ:swə:d] mot *m* de passe.

past [pɑ:st] **1.** *adj.* passé (*a. gramm.*); ancien(ne *f*) de jadis; *fig.* ~ *master* expert *m* (*dans, at*), maître *m* passé (*en, at; dans l'art de inf., at gér.*); *for some time* ~ depuis quelque temps; **2.** *adv. see verbe simple*; *rush* ~ passer en courant; **3.** *prp.* au-delà de; plus de; *half* ~ *two* deux heures et demie; *be* ~ *comprehension* être hors de toute compréhension; ~ *cure* inguérissable; ~ *endurance* insupportable; ~ *hope* perdu sans retour; *I would not put it* ~ *her* je ne l'en crois pas incapable; **4.** *su.* passé *m*.

paste [peist] **1.** pâte *f* (*a. cuis.*); colle *f*; faux brillants *m/pl.*; **2.** coller; *sl.* battre; **'~·board** planche *f* à pâte; carton *m*: *sl.* carte *f*; *attr.* de *ou* en carton.

pas·tel ['pæstəl] ♀ pastel *m*, guède *f*; *peint.* (crayon *m*) pastel *m*; **'pas·tel·(l)ist** pastelliste *mf*.

pas·tern *vét.* ['pæstə:n] paturon *m*; '~-joint boulet *m*.

pas·teur·ize ['pæstəraiz] pasteuriser; stériliser.

pas·tille [pæs'ti:l] pastille *f*.

pas·time ['pɑ:staim] passe-temps *m/inv.*; distraction *f*.

pas·tor ['pɑ:stə] pasteur *m*, ministre *m*; *Am.* prêtre *m*; '**pas·to·ral 1.** □ pastoral (-aux *m/pl.*); ~ *staff* bâton *m* pastoral; crosse *f*; **2.** poème *m* pastoral; *peint.* scène *f* pastorale; *poésie, a.* ♪ pastourelle *f*; *v/i.* paître. *eccl.* lettre *f* pastorale.

pas·try ['peistri] pâtisserie *f*; pâte *f* (*non cuite*); '~-cook pâtissier (-ère *f*) *m*.

pas·tur·age ['pɑ:stjuridʒ] pâturage *m*, pacage *m*.

pas·ture ['pɑ:stʃə] **1.** (lieu *m* de) pâture *f*; pré *m*; pâturage *m*; ~ *ground* lieu *m* de pâturage; **2.** *v/t.* (faire) paître; *v/i.* paître.

past·y 1. ['peisti] pâteux (-euse *f*); *fig.* terreux (-euse *f*) (*visage*); **2.** ['pæsti] pâté *m* (*sans terrine*).

pat [pæt] **1.** coup *m* léger; petite tape *f*; caresse *f*; *beurre*: rondelle *f*; **2.** tap(ot)er; caresser; **3.** apte; à propos (*a. adv.*); prêt; ~ *answer* réponse *f* toute prête; *answer* ~ répondre sur-le-champ; *have* (*ou know*) *s.th.* (*off*) ~ savoir qch. sur le bout du doigt.

patch [pætʃ] **1.** pièce *f*; *mot.* boudin *d'air*: pastille *f*, pneu: guêtre *f*; *couleur*: tache *f*; *fig.* pâté *m*; *légumes*: carré *m*; *terre*: parcelle *f*; ~ *pocket* cost. poche *f* appliquée; **2.** rapiécer, raccommoder; poser une pastille à; mettre une pièce à (*un pneu*); ~ *up* rapetasser; ⊕ rafistoler; *fig.* arranger, ajuster; '**patch·er** raccommodeur (-euse *f*) *m*; *fig.* rapetasseur (-euse *f*) *m*.

patch·ou·li ['pætʃuli] patchouli *m*.

patch·work ['pætʃwə:k] rapiéçage *m*; '**patch·y** inégal (-aux *m/pl.*) (*a. fig.*).

pate *sl.* [peit] tête *f*, caboche *f*.

pat·en *eccl.* ['pætən] patène *f*.

pat·ent 1. ['peitnt; ⚕, *Am.* 'pætnt] manifeste, patent; *letters* ~ ['pætnt] *pl.* lettres *f/pl.* patentes; ~ *article* article *m* breveté; ~ *fastener* bouton-pression (*pl.* boutons-pression) *m*; attache *f* à fermoir; ~ *fuel* boulets *m/pl.*, briquettes *f/pl.*; ~

leather cuir *m* verni; ~ *leather shoes* souliers *m/pl.* vernis; **2.** ['pætnt] brevet *m* d'invention; lettres *f/pl.* patentes; ⚕ ~ *pending* brevet *m* pendant; ~ *agent* agent *m* en brevets; ~ *office* bureau *m* des brevets; **3.** [~] faire breveter; **pat·ent·ee** [peitən'ti:] breveté *m*; concessionnaire *m* du brevet.

pa·ter·nal □ [pə'tə:nl] paternel(le *f*); **pa·ter·ni·ty** paternité *f*; *fig. a.* origine *f*.

path [pɑ:θ], *pl.* **paths** [pɑ:ðz] chemin *m*; sentier *m*; *jardin*: allée *f*; *fig.* route *f*; *sp.* piste *f*.

pa·thet·ic [pə'θetik] (~ally) pathétique; attendrissant.

path·less ['pɑ:θlis] sans chemin frayé.

path·o·log·i·cal □ [pæθə'lɔdʒikl] pathologique; **pa·thol·o·gist** [pə'θɔlədʒist] pathologiste *mf*; **pa·thol·o·gy** [pə'θɔlədʒi] pathologie *f*.

pa·thos ['peiθɔs] pathétique *m*.

path·way ['pɑ:θwei] sentier *m*; *rue*: trottoir *m*.

path·y ♣ *Am. co., a. péj.* ['pæθi] système *m* de traitement.

pa·tience ['peiʃns] patience *f*; *cartes*: réussite *f*, -s *f/pl.*; *be out of* ~ (*ou have no* ~) *with* être à bout de patience avec; '**pa·tient 1.** □ patient, endurant; *be* ~ *of* avoir de la patience avec; *fig.* savoir supporter (*qch.*); **2.** malade *mf*.

pa·ti·o *Am.* ['pætiou] patio *m*.

pa·tri·arch ['peitriɑ:k] patriarche *m*; **pa·tri·ar·chal** □ patriarcal (-aux *m/pl.*).

pa·tri·cian [pə'triʃn] patricien(ne *f*) *m* (*a. su.*).

pat·ri·mo·ny ['pætriməni] patrimoine *m*; *eccl.* biens-fonds *m/pl.*

pa·tri·ot ['pætriət] patriote *mf*; **pa·tri·ot·eer** *Am. sl.* [~'tiə] faux patriote *m*; **pa·tri·ot·ic** [~'ɔtik] (~ally) patriotique (*discours etc.*); patriote (*personne*); **pa·tri·ot·ism** ['~ətizm] patriotisme *m*.

pa·trol ✕ [pə'troul] **1.** patrouille *f*; ronde *f*; *police*: secteur *m*; *Am.* ~ *wagon* voiture *f* de police; F panier *m* à salade; **2.** *v/t.* faire la patrouille dans; *v/i.* patrouiller; '~·man *Am.* ['~mæn] patrouilleur *m*; agent *m* de police.

pa·tron ['peitrən] protecteur *m*; *eccl.* patron(ne *f*) *m*; ✝ client(e *f*) *m; charité:* patron *m;* **pa·tron·age** ['pætrənidʒ] protection *f;* patronage *m;* clientèle *f; eccl.* droit *m* de présentation; *péj.* air *m* protecteur; **pa·tron·ess** ['peitrənis] protectrice *f; charité:* patronnesse *f;* **pa·tron·ize** ['pætrənaiz] protéger; patronner; ⚓ accorder sa clientèle à; *péj.* traiter d'un air protecteur; **'pa·tron·iz·er** protecteur (-trice *f*) *m;* client(e *f*) *m.*

pat·ten ['pætn] socque *m.*

pat·ter ['pætə] **1.** sonner par petits coups; crépiter (*pluie etc.*); caqueter; *v/t.* bredouiller; parler tant bien que mal; **2.** petit bruit *m;* fouettement *m;* boniment *m.*

pat·tern ['pætən] **1.** modèle *m,* exemple *m (a. fig.);* type *m;* dessin *m;* patron *m (en papier);* échantillon *m; by ~ post* échantillon sans valeur; *télév.* test ~ mire *f;* **2.** modeler (sur *after, on*); **'~-mak·er** ⊕ modeleur *m* (-euse *f*) *m.*

pat·ty ['pæti] petit pâté *m;* bouchée *f* à la reine.

pau·ci·ty ['pɔːsiti] disette *f,* manque *m.*

Paul·ine ['pɔːlain] paulinien(ne *f*).

paunch [pɔːntʃ] panse *f,* ventre *m;* **'paunch·y** pansu.

pau·per ['pɔːpə] **1.** indigent(e *f*) *m;* pauvre(sse *f*) *m;* **2.** assisté, pauvre; **'pau·per·ism** paupérisme *m;* **'pau·per·ize** réduire à l'indigence.

pause [pɔːz] **1.** pause *f,* arrêt *m;* hésitation *f;* ♪ point *m* d'orgue; **2.** faire une pause; hésiter; s'arrêter (sur, [up]on).

pave [peiv] paver; *fig.* préparer; **'pave·ment** pavé *m;* dallage *m;* trottoir *m;* ~ *artist* artiste *mf* de trottoir.

pa·vil·ion [pə'viljən] pavillon *m.*

pav·ing-stone ['peiviŋstoun] pavé *m;* pierre *f* à paver.

pav·io(u)r ['peivjə] paveur *m;* dalleur *m;* carreleur *m.*

paw [pɔː] **1.** patte *f (sl. a. = main);* **2.** donner des coups de patte à; piaffer (*cheval*); F tripoter.

pawn[1] [pɔːn] *échecs:* pion *m; fig.* jouet *m.*

pawn[2] [~] **1.** gage *m; in (ou at)* ~ en gage; **2.** mettre en gage, engager; **'~-bro·ker** prêteur (-euse *f*) *m* sur gage(s); **pawn·ee** [~'niː] créancier (-ère *f*) *m* sur gage; **'pawn-**

er emprunteur (-euse *f*) *m* sur gage; **'pawn·shop** maison *f* de prêt; **'pawn-tick·et** reconnaissance *f* (de prêt sur gage).

pay [pei] **1.** salaire *m;* gages *m/pl.;* traitement *m;* ✕, ⚓ solde *f;* **2.** [*irr.*] *v/t.* payer; régler (*un compte*); acquitter (*des droits*); présenter (*ses respects à q.*); faire (*honneur à q., une visite à q.*); ~*-as-you-earn Am.* retenue *f* des impôts à la source; ~ *attention (ou heed) to* faire attention à; tenir compte de; ~ *away* dépenser; ⚓ laisser filer (*un câble*); ~ *down* payer comptant; ~ *in* donner (*qch.*) à l'encaissement; ~ *off* régler (*qch.*); rembourser (*un créancier*); congédier (*un employé*); ~ *out* payer, débourser; F se venger sur (*q.*); ⚓ (laisser) filer; ~ *up* se libérer de (*dettes*); rembourser intégralement; *v/i.* payer; rapporter; ~ *for* payer (*qch.*); rémunérer (*q., qch.*); *fig.* expier; **'pay·a·ble** payable (*a.* ✝); acquittable; ✕ exploitable; **'pay·day** jour *m* de paie; **pay-dirt** *Am.* alluvion *f* exploitable; *fig.* source *f* d'argent; **pay·ee** ✝ [~'iː] preneur (-euse *f*) *m;* porteur *m (d'un effet);* **'pay-en·ve·lope** sachet *m* de paie; **'pay·er** payant(e *f*) *m;* ✝ tiré *m,* accepteur *m;* **pay freeze** blocage *m* des salaires; **'pay·ing** payant; profitable; rémunérateur (-trice *f*); avantageux (-euse *f*); **'pay·ing-'in slip** bordereau *m* de versement; **'pay·load** charge *f* payante; ✈ poids *m* utile; **'pay·mas·ter** trésorier *m (a.* ✕); ⚓ commissaire *m;* **'pay·ment** paiement *m;* versement *m;* rémunération *f; additional* ~ supplément *m; on* ~ *of* moyennant paiement de.

pay...: '~*-off* règlement *m;* remboursement *m; Am.* F comble *m;* F bakchich *m;* '~*-of·fice* caisse *f,* guichet *m;* '~*-pack·et* sachet *m* de paie; '~*-roll* feuille *f* de paie; ~ *sta·tion Am.* téléphone *m* public.

pea ⚘ [piː] (petit) pois *m; attr.* pois; aux petits pois.

peace [piːs] paix *f;* tranquillité *f;* ordre *m;* traité *m* de paix; ~ *movement* mouvement *m* pacifiste; ~ *offering* cadeau *m* de réconciliation; ~ *pipe* calumet *m* de la paix; ~ *talks pl.* pourparlers *m/pl.* de paix; ~ *treaty* traité *m* de paix; *the (King's)* ~ l'ordre *m* public; *at* ~ en paix, paisible; *break* *the* ~ troubler l'ordre public; *keep the* ~ veiller à *ou* ne pas troubler l'ordre public; **'peace·a·ble** □ pacifique; en paix; paisible; **'peace-break·er** violateur (-trice *f*) *m* de l'ordre public; **peace·ful** □ ['~ful] paisible, tranquille; pacifique; **'peace-keep·ing force** forces *f/pl.* de maintien de la paix; **'peace·mak·er** conciliateur (-trice *f*) *m*; **'peace of·fi·cer** agent *m* de la sûreté.

peach¹ ♀ [pi:tʃ] pêche *f*; *arbre*: pêcher *m*; F vrai bijou *m*.

peach² *sl.* [~]: ~ *(up)on* moucharder; dénoncer.

pea-chick ['pi:tʃik] paonneau *m*.

peach·y ['pi:tʃi] velouté (*peau etc.*); *couleur*: fleur de pêcher *adj./inv.*; *sl.* épatant; délicieux (-euse *f*).

pea·cock ['pi:kɔk] paon *m*; **'pea-fowl** paon(ne *f*) *m*; **'pea·hen** paonne *f*.   [reuse *f*.\

pea-jack·et ⚓ ['pi:dʒækit] va-\

peak [pi:k] 1. pic *m*, cime *f*, sommet *m*; *casquette*: visière *f*; *attr.* de pic; de pointe; maximum; ~ *load* charge *f* maximum; ~ *power* débit *m* maximum; ~ *season* pleine saison *f*; 2. F dépérir; tomber en langueur; **peaked** [pi:kt] en pointe; ~ *cap* casquette *f* à visière; **'peak·y** F pâlot, malingre; hâve.

peal [pi:l] 1. carillon *m*; *tonnerre*: grondement *m*; retentissement *m*; ~ *of laughter* éclat *m* de rire; 2. *v/t.* sonner à toute volée; carillonner; *v/i.* carillonner; retentir; gronder (*tonnerre*).

pea·nut ['pi:nʌt] ♀ arachide *f*, 🌱 cacahouette *f*; *fig.* gnognote *f*; *Am. sl.* ~ *politics* politicailleries *f/pl.*

pear ♀ [pɛə] poire *f*; *arbre*: poirier *m*.

pearl [pə:l] 1. perle *f* (*a. fig.*); *typ.* parisienne *f*; *attr.* de perles; 2. perler; **'pearl·y** perlé, nacré.

pear-tree ['pɛətri:] poirier *m*.

peas·ant ['pezənt] 1. paysan(ne *f*) *m*; 2. campagnard; **'peas·ant·ry** paysannerie *f*; paysannat *m*.

pea-shoot·er ['pi:ʃu:tə] petite sarbacane *f* de poche.

pea-soup ['pi:su:p] potage *m* aux pois, potage *m* St.-Germain; **'pea-'soup·y** jaune et épais (*brouillard*).

peat [pi:t] tourbe *f*; **'~-moss** tourbière *f*.

peb·ble ['pebl] caillou (*pl.* -x) *m*; *plage*: galet *m*; agate *f*; **'peb·bly** cailouteux (-euse *f*); à galets (*plage*).

pec·ca·ble ['pekəbl] peccable; **pec·cant** ⚕ ['pekənt] peccant.

peck¹ [pek] (*approx.*) boisseau *m* (9,087 *litres*); *fig.* grande quantité *f*; *a* ~ *of* beaucoup de.

peck² [~] picoter (*qch., at s.th.*); picorer; ~ *at* chipoter (*un plat*); ~ *at one's food* manger son repas du bout des dents; **'peck·er** *sl.* courage *m*; nez *m*; **'peck·ish** F: *be* ~ avoir faim.

pec·to·ral ['pektərəl] pectoral (-aux *m/pl.*) (*a. su./m*).

pec·u·late ['pekjuleit] détourner des fonds; **pec·u·la·tion** détournement *m* de fonds; péculat *m*; **'pec·u·la·tor** dilapidateur *m* des deniers publics.

pe·cul·iar □ [pi'kju:ljə] bizarre, singulier (-ère *f*); étrange; particulier (-ère *f*); **pe·cu·li·ar·i·ty** [~li'æriti] particularité *f*; trait *m* distinctif; singularité *f*.

pe·cu·ni·ar·y [pi'kju:njəri] pécuniaire; d'argent.

ped·a·gog·ic, ped·a·gog·i·cal □ [pedə'gɔdʒik(l)] pédagogique; **ped·a'gog·ics** *usu. sg.* pédagogie *f*; **ped·a·gogue** ['~gɔg] pédagogue *m*; **ped·a·go·gy** ['~gi] pédagogie *f*.

ped·al ['pedl] 1. pédale *f*; 2. du pied; 3. *cycl.* pédaler; ♪ mettre la pédale.

ped·ant ['pedənt] pédant(e *f*) *m*; **pe·dan·tic** [pi'dæntik] (~*ally*) pédant(esque); **ped·ant·ry** ['pedəntri] pédantisme *m*.

ped·dle ['pedl] *v/t.* colporter; *v/i.* faire le colportage; **'ped·dling** colportage *m*; **'ped·dler** *Am.* see *pedlar.*

ped·es·tal ['pedistl] piédestal *m* (*a. fig.*); socle *m*.

pe·des·tri·an [pi'destriən] 1. pédestre; à pied; prosaïque; 2. piéton *m*; voyageur (-euse *f*) *m* à pied.

ped·i·cure ['pedikjuə] chirurgie *f* pédicure; *personne*: pédicure *mf*; **ped·i·cur·ist** ['~kjuərist] pédicure *mf*.

ped·i·gree ['pedigri:] 1. arbre *m* généalogique; généalogie *f*; 2. (*a.* **ped·i·greed** ['~d]) de race, de bonne souche.   [ton *m*.\

ped·i·ment △ ['pedimənt] fron-\

ped·lar ['pedlə] colporteur *m*; **'ped-lar·y** colportage *m*; marchandise *f* de balle.

pe·dom·e·ter [pi'dɔmitə] compte-pas *m/inv.*

pee F [pi:] faire pipi, pisser.

peek [pi:k] **1.** jeter un coup d'œil furtif (sur, *at*); **2.** coup *m* d'œil rapide *ou* furtif; **peek·a·boo** *Am.* ['pi:kəbu:] **1.** en dentelle; **2.** *Am.* cache-cache *m*.

peel [pi:l] **1.** pelure *f*; peau *f*; *citron*: zeste *m*; **2.** (*a. ~ off*) *v/t.* peler; se dépouiller de (*les vêtements*); *v/i.* peler; s'écailler; *sl.* se déshabiller.

peel·er *sl.* ['pi:lə] agent *m* de police; F flic *m*.

peel·ing ['pi:liŋ] épluchure *f*; *action*: épluchage *m*; (*a. ~ off*) écaillement *m*. [2. pépier.\
peep[1] *orn.* [pi:p] **1.** pépiement *m*;\
peep[2] [~] **1.** coup *m* d'œil rapide *ou* furtif; point *m* (*du jour*); **2.** regarder à la dérobée; jeter un coup *m* d'œil rapide (sur, *at*); *fig.* (*a. ~ out*) percer; se laisser entrevoir; **'peep·er** curieux (-euse *f*) *m*; indiscret (-ète *f*) *m*; *sl.* œil; **'peephole** judas *m*; **'peep·ing Tom** voyeur *m*; **'peep-show** optique *f*.

peer[1] [piə] risquer un coup d'œil; *~ at* scruter du regard; *~ into s.o.'s face* dévisager q.

peer[2] [~] pair *m*; **'peer·age** pairie *f*; pairs *m/pl.*; **'peer·ess** pairesse *f*; **'peer·less** □ sans pair; sans pareil(le *f*).

peeved F [pi:vd] irrité.

pee·vish □ ['pi:viʃ] irritable; maussade; **'pee·vish·ness** mauvaise humeur *f*; humeur *f* maussade.

peg [peg] **1.** cheville *f* (*a. ♪*); *toupie*: pointe *f*; *whisky*: doigt *m*; (*a. clothes-~*) vêtements: patère *f*; pince *f*; *fig.* take s.o. down a ~ or two remettre q. à sa place; be a ~ round in a square hole ne pas être dans son emploi; **2.** cheviller; (*a. ~ out*) piqueter (*une concession*); stabiliser, maintenir (*le prix, les gages, etc.*); F ~ away (*a. ~ along*) travailler ferme (à, *at*); *sl.* ~ out *sl.* casser sa pipe (= *mourir*).

peg-top ['pegtɔp] toupie *f*.

peign·oir ['peinwa:] peignoir *m*.

pe·jo·ra·tive ['pi:dʒərətiv] péjoratif (-ive *f*).

pe·kin·ese [pi:ki'ni:z] pékinois *m*.

pelf *péj.* [pelf] richesses *f/pl.*

pel·i·can *orn.* ['pelikən] pélican *m*.

pe·lisse [pe'li:s] pelisse *f*.

pel·let ['pelit] boulette *f*; *pharm.* pilule *f*; grain *m* de plomb.

pel·li·cle ['pelikl] pellicule *f*; membrane *f*.

pell-mell ['pel'mel] **1.** pêle-mêle; en désordre; **2.** confusion *f*.

pel·lu·cid [pe'lju:sid] transparent; clair.

pelt[1] ✝ [pelt] fourrure *f*, peau *f*.

pelt[2] [~] *pal* correspondant(e *f*) *m*; **2.** *v/t.* (*a. ~ at*) lancer (une volée de pierres) à; *v/i.* tomber à verse; F courir à toutes jambes; **2.** grêle *f*. [terie *f*.\
pelt·ry ['peltri] peaux *f/pl.*; pelle-\
pel·vis *anat.* ['pelvis] bassin *m*.

pen[1] [pen] **1.** plume *f*; *Brit.* ~ friend, *Am.* ~ *pal* correspondant(e *f*) *m*; ~ pusher gratte-papier *m/inv.*; **2.** écrire; composer.

pen[2] [~] **1.** enclos *m*; **2.** [*irr.*] parquer; (*usu. ~ up, ~ in*) renfermer.

pe·nal □ ['pi:nl] pénal (-aux *m/pl.*) (*loi, code*); qui entraîne une pénalité; ~ *servitude* travaux *m/pl.* forcés; **pe·nal·ize** ['~nəlaiz] sanctionner (*qch.*) d'une peine; *sp.* pénaliser; *fig.* punir; **pen·al·ty** ['penlti] peine *f*; pénalité *f* (*a. sp.*); *foot.* ~ area surface *f* de réparation; ~ kick penalty *m*; *under* ~ *of* sous peine de.

pen·ance ['penəns] pénitence *f*.

pen...: '~-and-'ink draw·ing dessin *m* à la plume; '~-case plumier *m*.

pence [pens] *pl. de* penny.

pen·cil ['pensl] **1.** crayon *m*; *sl.* pinceau *m*; *opt.* faisceau *m*; **2.** marquer (*ou* dessiner) au crayon; crayonner (*une lettre*); se faire (*les sourcils*) au crayon; **'pen·cil(l)ed** écrit *ou* tracé au crayon; *opt.* en faisceau lumineux; **'pen·cil-sharp·en·er** taille-crayon *m/inv.*

pend·ant ['pendənt] *collier*: pendentif *m*; *lustre*: pendeloque *f*; *tableau*: pendant *m*; ⚓ *drapeau*: flamme *f*; ◮ cul-de-lampe (*pl.* culs-de-lampe) *m*.

pend·ent [~] pendant; retombant.

pend·ing ['pendiŋ] **1.** *adj.* ⚖ pendant; en instance; **2.** *prp.* pendant; en attendant.

pen·du·lous ['pendjuləs] pendant; oscillant; **pen·du·lum** ['~ləm] pendule *m*, balancier *m*.

pen·e·tra·bil·i·ty [penitrə'biliti] pénétrabilité *f*; **pen·e·tra·ble** □ ['ᴗtrəbl] pénétrable; **pen·e·tra·li·a** F [peni'treiliə] *pl.* sanctuaire *m*; **pen·e·trate** ['ᴗtreit] *v/t.* percer; pénétrer (de, *with*) (*a. fig.*, *un secret etc.*); *v/i.* pénétrer (jusqu'à *to*, *as far as*); **pen·e'tra·tion** pénétration *f* (*a. fig.* = *perspicacité*); **'pen·e·tra·tive** □ pénétrant; perçant (*a. fig.*); ~ **effect** effet *m* marqué.

pen-feath·er ['penfeðə] penne *f*.

pen·guin *orn.* ['peŋgwin] pingouin *m*; manchot *m*.

pen·hold·er ['penhouldə] porte-plume *m/inv*.

pen·i·cil·lin *pharm.* [peni'silin] pénicilline *f*.

pen·in·su·la [pi'ninsjulə] presqu'île *f*; péninsule *f*; **pen'in·su·lar** péninsulaire.

pen·i·tence ['penitəns] pénitence *f*; contrition *f*; **'pen·i·tent 1.** □ pénitent, contrit; **2.** pénitent(e *f*) *m*); **pen·i·ten·tial** □ [ᴗ'tenʃl] pénitentiel(le *f*); de pénitent; **pen·i·ten·tia·ry** [ᴗ'tenʃəri] maison *f* de correction; *Am.* prison *f*; *eccl.* (*ou* ~ *priest*) pénitencier *m*.

pen·man ['penmən] écrivain *m*; auteur *m*; **'pen·man·ship** art *m* d'écrire; calligraphie *f*.

pen-name ['penneim] nom *m* de plume; *journ.* nom *m* de guerre.

pen·nant ['penənt] ⚓ flamme *f*; *surt. Am.* fanion *m* (*usu.* de championnat, *sp.*).

pen·ni·less □ ['penilis] sans ressources; sans le sou.

pen·non ['penən] ⚔ flamme *f*, banderole *f*; *sp.* fanion *m*.

pen·ny ['peni], *pl. valeur:* **pence** [pens], *pièces:* **pen·nies** penny *m* (¹/₁₀₀ *pound*); gros sou *m*; *Am.* cent *m*, F sou *m*; '~-**a-'lin·er** journaliste *m* à deux sous la ligne; écrivaillon *m*; '~-'**dread·ful** roman *m* à deux sous; feuilleton *m* à gros effets; '~-**in-the-'slot** automatique; ~ *machine* distributeur *m* automatique; '~·**wise** lésineur (-euse *f*); ~·**worth** ['penəθ] valeur *f* de deux sous; *fig.* miette *f*; *a* ~ *of tobacco* deux sous de tabac.

pen·sion 1. ['penʃn] pension *f*; retraite *f* de vieillesse; ⚔ (solde *f* de) retraite *f*; ~ *scheme* caisse *f* de retraite; ['pɑ̃:ŋsiɔ̃:ŋ] pension *f* de famille; **2.** ['penʃn] *usu.* ~ *off* mettre (*q.*) à la retraite; pensionner (*q.*); **pen·sion·ar·y** ['penʃənəri] '**pen·sion·er** titulaire *mf* d'une pension; pensionnaire *mf* (*de l'État*); ⚔ retraité *m*; invalide *m*; *be s.o.'s* ~ *péj.* être à la solde de q.

pen·sive □ ['pensiv] pensif (-ive *f*); songeur (-euse *f*); rêveur (-euse *f*); '**pen·sive·ness** air *m* pensif.

pent [pent] *prét. et p.p. de* pen² 2; ~-*up* contenu, refoulé (*colère etc.*).

pen·ta·gon ['pentəgən] pentagone *m*; *Am.* the ⚭ Ministère *m* de la Défense Nationale (*à Washington*); **pen·tag·o·nal** [ᴗ'tægənl] pentagonal (-aux *m/pl.*), pentagone.

pen·tath·lon *sp.* [pen'tæθlɔn] pentathlon *m*.

Pen·te·cost ['pentikɔst] la Pentecôte *f*; **pen·te'cos·tal** de la Pentecôte.

pent·house ['penthaus] appentis *m*; auvent *m*; *Am.* appartement *m* (*construit sur le toit d'un bâtiment élevé*).

pent-up ['pent'ʌp] enfermé; refoulé (*sentiment etc.*), réprimé.

pe·nul·ti·mate [pi'nʌltimit] pénultième, avant-dernier (-ière *f*).

pe·num·bra [pi'nʌmbrə] pénombre *f*.

pe·nu·ri·ous □ [pi'njuəriəs] pauvre; mesquin; parcimonieux (-euse *f*); **pe'nu·ri·ous·ness** avarice *f*; mesquinerie *f*.

pen·u·ry ['penjuri] pénurie *f*; indigence *f*; manque *m* (de, *of*).

pen-wip·er ['penwaipə] essuie-plume *m*.

pe·o·ny ⚘ ['piəni] pivoine *f*.

peo·ple ['pi:pl] **1.** *sg.* peuple *m*; nation *f*; *pl. coll.* peuple *m*, habitants *m/pl.*; *pol.* citoyens *m/pl.*; gens *m/pl.*; les gens *m/pl.*, on; ~ *pl. say* on dit; *English* ~ *pl.* des *ou* les Anglais *m/pl.*; *many* ~ *pl.* beaucoup de monde; F *my* ~ *pl.* mes parents *m/pl.*; ma famille *f*; *the* ~ *pl.* le grand public *m*, le peuple *m*; *pol.* ~'*s republic* république *f* populaire; **2.** peupler (de, *with*).

pep *Am. sl.* [pep] **1.** vigueur *f*, vitalité *f*; entrain *m*; F ~ *pill* excitant *m*; F ~ *talk* mots *m/pl.* d'encouragement; **2.** ~ *up* ragaillardir (*q.*); donner de l'entrain à (*qch.*).

pep·per ['pepə] **1.** poivre *m*; ~ *pot* poivrière *f*; **2.** poivrer; F cribler; '~-

and-'salt poivre et sel (*cheveux*); *cost.* marengo *inv.*; '~**corn** grain *m* de poivre; '~**mint** ♀ menthe *f* poivrée; (*a.* ~ *lozenge*) pastille *f* de menthe; '**pep·per·y** □ poivré; *fig.* irascible.

pep·tic ['peptik] gastrique, digestif (-ive *f*); ~ *ulcer* ulcère *m* de l'estomac.

per [pə:] par; suivant; d'après; par l'entremise de; ~ *cent* pour cent (⁰/₀).

per·ad·ven·ture [pərəd'ventʃə] **1.** peut-être; par hasard; **2.** doute *m*; *beyond* (*ou without*) ~ à n'en pas douter.

per·am·bu·late [pə'ræmbjuleit] se promener dans (*qch.*); parcourir (*qch.*); **per·am·bu·la·tion** promenade *f*; inspection *f*; **per·am·bu·la·tor** ['præmbjuleitə] voiture *f* d'enfant.

per·ceive [pə'si:v] (a)percevoir; s'apercevoir de; voir; comprendre.

per·cent·age [pə'sentidʒ] pourcentage *m*; proportion *f*; guelte *f*; tantième *m*, -s *m/pl.*

per·cep·ti·ble □ [pə'septəbl] perceptible; sensible; **per·cep·tion** perception *f*; sensibilité *f*; **per·'cep·tive** □ perceptif (-ive *f*); **per·cep·tive·ness**, **per·cep·tiv·i·ty** perceptivité *f*.

perch¹ *icht.* [pə:tʃ] perche *f*.

perch² [~] **1.** perche *f* (= 5,029 *m*); *oiseau:* perchoir *m*; F *fig.* trône *m*; *carrosse:* flèche *f*; **2.** (se) percher, (se) jucher; ~ed *fig.* perché; '**perch·er** *orn.* percheur *m*.

per·cip·i·ent [pə'sipiənt] **1.** percepteur (-trice *f*); conscient; **2.** sujet *m* télépathique.

per·co·late ['pə:kəleit] *v/t.* passer (*le café*); *v/i.* s'infiltrer; filtrer (*café*); '**per·co·la·tor** filtre *m*.

per·cus·sion [pə:'kʌʃn] choc *m*; percussion *f* (*a.* ♪); ~ *cap* capsule *f* de fulminate; ♪ ~ *instruments pl.* instruments *m/pl.* de *ou* à percussion; **per·cus·sive** [pə:'kʌsiv] percutant.

per·di·tion [pə:'diʃn] perte *f*, ruine *f*.

per·du(e) ⚔ [pə:'dju:] caché.

per·e·gri·nate ['perigrineit] voyager, pérégriner; **per·e·gri·na·tion** voyage *m*, pérégrination *f*.

per·emp·to·ri·ness [pə'remtərinis] intransigeance *f*; ton *m* ou caractère *m* absolu; **per·'emp·to·ry** □

péremptoire; décisif (-ive *f*); absolu; tranchant (*ton*).

per·en·ni·al [pə'renjəl] **1.** □ éternel (-le *f*); ♀ vivace, persistant; **2.** ♀ plante *f* vivace.

per·fect ['pə:fikt] **1.** □ parfait; achevé (*ouvrage*); complet (-ète *f*); ♪ juste; ♪ ~ *pitch* l'oreille *f* absolue; **2.** *gramm.* (*ou* ~ *tense*) parfait *m*; **3.** [pə'fekt] (par)achever; rendre parfait, parfaire; **per·fect·i·bil·i·ty** [~i'biliti] perfectibilité *f*; **per·'fect·i·ble** [~təbl] perfectible; **per·'fec·tion** perfection *f*, *a.* **per·'fect·ness** ['pə:fiktnis] achèvement *m*, accomplissement *m*; perfectionnement *m*; *fig.* be the ~ of ... être ... même.

per·fid·i·ous □ [pə'fidiəs] perfide; traître(sse *f*); **per·'fid·i·ous·ness**, **per·fi·dy** ['pə:fidi] perfidie *f*, traîtrise *f*.

per·fo·rate ['pə:fəreit] *v/t.* perforer, percer; *v/i.* pénétrer (dans, *into*); **per·fo·ra·tion** perforation *f* (*a. coll.*); percement *m*; (petit) trou *m*; '**per·fo·ra·tor** perforateur *m*; ⚒ perforatrice *f*.

per·force [pə'fɔ:s] forcément.

per·form [pə'fɔ:m] *v/t.* accomplir; célébrer (*un rite*); s'acquitter de (*un devoir*); exécuter (*un mouvement*, *a.* ♪ *un morceau*); ♪, *théâ.* jouer; *théâ.* représenter; *v/i.* jouer; ♪ ~ *on* jouer de; **per·'form·ance** exécution *f*; exploit *m*; *théâ.* représentation *f*; *sp.*, *mot.* performance *f*; *cin.* séance *f*; ⊕ fonctionnement *m*, marche *f*; **per·'form·er** artiste *mf*; *théâ.* acteur (-trice *f*) *m*; ♪ exécutant(e *f*) *m*; **per·'form·ing** savant (*animal*).

per·fume 1. ['pə:fju:m] parfum *m*; odeur *f*; **2.** [pə'fju:m] parfumer; **per·'fum·er** parfumeur (-euse *f*) *m*; **per·'fum·er·y** parfumerie *f*; parfums *m/pl.*

per·func·to·ry □ [pə'fʌŋktəri] superficiel(le *f*); peu zélé; négligent.

per·haps [pə'hæps; præps] peut-être.

per·i·car·di·um *anat.* [peri'ka:djəm] péricarde *m*.

per·i·gee *astr.* ['peridʒi:] périgée *m*.

per·il ['peril] **1.** péril *m*; danger *m*; *at my* ~ à mes risques et périls; **2.** mettre en péril; '**per·il·ous** □ périlleux (-euse *f*).

pe·ri·od ['piəriəd] période *f*; durée *f*; délai *m*; époque *f*, âge *m*; *école:*

leçon *f*; *rhétorique*: période *f*; *gramm.* point *m*; ✼ ⁓s *pl.* règles *f/pl.*; *a girl of the* ⁓ une jeune fille moderne; ⁓ *furniture* mobilier *m* de style; **per·i·od·ic** [⁓'ɔdik] périodique; **pe·ri'od·i·cal 1.** □ périodique; **2.** (publication *f*) périodique *m*.

per·i·pa·tet·ic [peripə'tetik] (⁓ally) F ambulant.

pe·riph·er·y [pə'rifəri] pourtour *m*.

pe·riph·ra·sis [pə'rifrəsis], *pl.* **-ses** [⁓si:z] périphrase *f*; circonlocution *f*; **per·i·phras·tic** [peri'fræstik] (⁓ally) périphrastique. [riscope *m*.]

per·i·scope ⚓, ⚔ ['periskoup] pé-]

per·ish ['periʃ] (faire) périr *ou* mourir; (se) détériorer; *be* ⁓*ed with* mourir de (*froid etc.*); **'per·ish·a·ble 1.** □ périssable; *fig.* éphémère; **2.** ⁓s *pl.* marchandises *f/pl.* périssables; **'per·ish·ing** □ transitoire; destructif (-ive *f*); F sacré.

per·i·style ['peristail] péristyle *m*.

per·i·to·ne·um *anat.* [peritou'ni:əm] péritoine *m*.

per·i·wig ['periwig] perruque *f*.

per·i·win·kle ['periwiŋkl] **1.** ♀ pervenche *f*; **2.** *zo.* bigorneau *m*.

per·jure ['pə:dʒə]: ⁓ *o.s.* se parjurer; **'per·jured** parjure; **'per·jur·er** parjure *mf*; **'per·ju·ry** parjure *m*; ⚖ faux témoignage *m*.

perk F [pə:k] **1.** (*usu.* ⁓ *up*) *v/i.* se ranimer; redresser la tête; *v/t.* redresser; requinquer (*q.*); **2.** *see* ⁓*y*; **perk·i·ness** ['⁓inis] air *m* alerte *ou* éveillé.

perks F [pə:ks] *pl. see perquisites*.

perk·y □ ['pə:ki] alerte, éveillé; désinvolte.

perm F [pə:m] (ondulation *f*) permanente *f*, indéfrisable *f*; *have a* ⁓ se faire faire une permanente.

per·ma·nence ['pə:mənəns] permanence *f*; stabilité *f*; **'per·ma·nen·cy** *see* permanence; emploi *m* permanent; **'per·ma·nent** □ permanent; fixe; inamovible (*place*); ⁓ *wave* ondulation *f* permanente; 🚂 ⁓ *way* voie *f* ferrée.

per·me·a·bil·i·ty [pə:miə'biliti] perméabilité *f*; **'per·me·a·ble** □ perméable; **per·me·ate** ['⁓mieit] *v/t.* filtrer à travers; *v/i.* pénétrer; s'infiltrer (dans *into, among*).

permed F [pə:md] ondulé; *have one's hair* ⁓ se faire faire une permanente.

per·mis·si·ble □ [pə'misəbl] permis, tolérable; **per·mis·sion** [⁓'miʃn] permission *f*; autorisation *f*; **per·mis·sive** □ [⁓'misiv] qui permet; facultatif (-ive *f*); permis.

per·mit 1. [pə'mit] (*a.* ⁓ *of*) permettre; souffrir; *weather* ⁓*ting* si le temps s'y prête; **2.** ['pə:mit] autorisation *f*, permis *m*; ⛴ passavant *m*.

per·ni·cious □ [pə:'niʃəs] pernicieux (-euse *f*); délétère.

per·nick·et·y F [pə'nikiti] pointilleux (-euse *f*); difficile.

per·o·ra·tion [perə'reiʃn] péroraison *f*.

per·ox·ide 🜄 [pə'rɔksaid] peroxyde *m*; ⁓ *of hydrogen* eau *f* oxygénée.

per·pen·dic·u·lar [pə:pən'dikjulə] **1.** □ vertical (-aux *m/pl.*); perpendiculaire (*a.* △ *style*); **2.** perpendiculaire *m*; aplomb *m*; fil *m* à plomb.

per·pe·trate ['pə:pitreit] perpétrer; commettre (F *a. un jeu de mots etc.*); **per·pe'tra·tion** perpétration *f*; péché *m*; **'per·pe·tra·tor** auteur *m*.

per·pet·u·al □ [pə'petjuəl] perpétuel(le *f*), éternel(le *f*); F sans fin; **per'pet·u·ate** [⁓eit] perpétuer; **per·pet·u'a·tion** perpétuation *f*; préservation *f*; **per·pe·tu·i·ty** [pə:pi'tjuiti] perpétuité *f*; rente *f* perpétuelle; *in* ⁓ à perpétuité.

per·plex [pə'pleks] embarrasser; troubler l'esprit de; **per'plexed** □ perplexe; confus; **per'plex·i·ty** perplexité *f*; embarras *m*; confusion *f*.

per·qui·sites ['pə:kwizits] *pl.* petits profits *m/pl.*; *sl.* gratte *f*.

per·se·cute ['pə:sikju:t] persécuter; *fig.* tourmenter; **per·se'cu·tion** persécution *f*; ⁓ *mania* délire *m* de (la) persécution; **per·se·cu·tor** ['⁓tə] persécuteur (-trice *f*) *m*.

per·se·ver·ance [pə:si'viərəns] persévérance *f*; constance *f*; **per·se·vere** [⁓'viə] persévérer (dans *in, with*; à *inf., in gér.*); **per·se'ver·ing** □ assidu (à, *in*), constant (dans, *in*).

Per·sian ['pə:ʃn] **1.** persan; de Perse; **2.** *ling.* persan *m*; Persan(e *f*) *m*.

per·sist [pə'sist] persister, s'obstiner (dans, *in*; à *inf.*, *in gér.*); **per·sist·ence, per·sist·en·cy** [pə'sistəns(i)] persistance *f*; obstination *f*; **per'sist·ent** □ persistant; continu.

per·son ['pə:sn] personne *f*; individu *m*; *théâ.* personnage *m*; *a* ~ quelqu'un(e); *no* ~ personne ... ne; *in* ~ en (propre) personne; *téléph.* ~*to*-~ *call* communication *f* (téléphonique) avec préavis; **'per·son·a·ble** bien de sa personne; beau (bel *devant une voyelle ou un h muet*; belle *f*); **'per·son·age** personnage *m* (*a. théâ.*); personnalité *f*; **'per·son·al 1.** □ personnel(le *f*) (*a. gramm.*); individuel(le *f*); particulier (-ère *f*); *be* ~ faire des personnalités; ⚖ ~ *property* (*ou estate*) *see personalty*; **2.** ~*s pl. Am.* F *journ.* chronique *f* mondaine; échos *m/pl.*; **per·son·al·i·ty** [~sə-'næliti] personnalité *f*, caractère *m* propre; **per·son·al·ty** ⚖ ['~snlti] biens *m/pl.* meubles; fortune *f* mobilière; **per·son·ate** ['~səneit] se faire passer pour; *théâ.* jouer; **per·son-'a·tion** usurpation *f* de nom *etc.*; *théâ.* représentation *f*; **per·son·i-fi·ca·tion** [~sɔnifi'keiʃn] personnification *f*; **per·son·i·fy** [~'sɔnifai] personnifier; **per·son·nel** [~sə'nel] personnel *m*.

per·spec·tive [pə'spektiv] **1.** □ perspectif (-ive *f*), en perspective; **2.** perspective *f*.

per·spi·ca·cious □ [pə:spi'keiʃəs] perspicace; **per·spi·cac·i·ty** [~'kæsiti] perspicacité *f*; **per·spi·cu-i·ty** [~'kjuiti] clarté *f*, netteté *f*; **per·spic·u·ous** [pə'spikjuəs] □ clair, lucide.

per·spi·ra·tion [pə:spə'reiʃn] transpiration *f*; sueur *f*; **per·spire** [pəs'paiə] transpirer; suer.

per·suade [pə'sweid] persuader (de, *of*; *que*, *that*; à q. de *inf. s.o. into gér.*, *s.o. to inf.*); convaincre; **per·suad·er** *sl.* éperon *m*; arrosage *m* (= *paiement illicite*).

per·sua·sion [pə'sweiʒən] persuasion *f*; religion *f*; F *co.* race *f*, genre *m*; *powers pl. of* ~ force *f* persuasive; art *m* de persuader.

per·sua·sive □ [pə'sweisiv] persuasif (-ive *f*); persuadant; **per'sua·sive·ness** (force *f* de) persuasion *f*.

pert □ [pə:t] effronté; mutin; *Am.* gaillard.

per·tain [pə:'tein] (*to*) appartenir (à); avoir rapport (à); être le propre (de).

per·ti·na·cious □ [pə:ti'neiʃəs] obstiné, entêté; **per·ti·nac·i·ty** [~'næ-siti] obstination *f*; opiniâtreté *f* (à, *in*).

per·ti·nence, per·ti·nen·cy ['pə:ti-nəns(i)] pertinence *f*; justesse *f*, à-propos *m*; **'per·ti·nent** □ pertinent, juste, à propos; ~ *to* ayant rapport à.

pert·ness ['pə:tnis] effronterie *f*.

per·turb [pə'tə:b] troubler; agiter; **per·tur·ba·tion** [pə:tə:'beiʃn] trouble *m*; agitation *f*; inquiétude *f*.

pe·ruke † [pə'ru:k] perruque *f*.

pe·rus·al [pə'ru:zl] lecture *f*; examen *m*; **pe·ruse** [pə'ru:z] lire attentivement; *fig.* examiner.

Pe·ru·vi·an [pə'ru:viən] **1.** péruvien (-ne *f*); ⚕ ~ *bark* quinquina *m*; **2.** Péruvien(ne *f*) *m*.

per·vade [pə:'veid] s'infiltrer dans; *fig.* animer; **per·va·sion** [~ʒn] infiltration *f*, pénétration *f*; **per·va·sive** [~siv] pénétrant.

per·verse □ [pə'və:s] pervers; méchant; revêche; contrariant; entêté dans le mal; ⚕ rebelle; **per'verse·ness** *see perversity*; **per'ver·sion** perversion *f*; *fig.* travestissement *m*; **per'ver·si·ty** perversité *f*; esprit *m* contraire; caractère *m* revêche; ⚕ dépravation *f*; **per'ver·sive** malsain, dépravant.

per·vert 1. [pə'və:t] pervertir; dépraver; fausser; détourner; **2.** ['pə:-və:t] apostat *m*; ⚕ perverti(e *f*) *m*; (*a. sexual* ~) inverti(e *f*) *m*; **per'vert·er** pervertisseur (-euse *f*) *m*.

per·vi·ous [pə'viəs] perméable (à, *to*); *fig.* accessible (à, *to*).

pes·ky □ *surt. Am.* F ['peski] maudit, sacré.

pes·sa·ry ['pesəri] passaire *m*.

pes·si·mism ['pesimizm] pessimisme *m*; **'pes·si·mist** pessimiste *mf*; **pes·si·mis·tic** (~*ally*) pessimiste.

pest [pest] animal *m* ou insecte *m* nuisible; *fig.* fléau *m*; peste *f*; ~ *control* lutte *f* antiparasitaire; **'pes·ter** importuner; tourmenter; *fig.* infester.

pest·i·cide ['pestisaid] pesticide *m*; insecticide *m*.

pes·tif·er·ous □ [pes'tifərəs] pestifère; nuisible; **pes·ti·lence** ['pesti-ləns] peste *f*; **'pes·ti·lent** *co.* assommant; **pes·ti·len·tial** □ [~'lenʃl] pestilentiel(le *f*); contagieux (-euse *f*); infecte.

pes·tle ['pesl] pilon *m*.

pet¹ [pet] accès *m* de mauvaise humeur; *in a* ~ de mauvaise humeur.

pet² [~] **1.** animal *m* favori; *fig.* enfant *mf* gâté(e), benjamin(e *f*) *m*, F chouchou(te *f*) *m*; **2.** favori(te *f*); de prédilection; ~ *dog* chien *m* favori *ou* de salon; ~ *name* diminutif *m*; ~ *subject* dada *m*; *co. it is my* ~ *aversion* il est mon cauchemar; **3.** choyer, F chouchouter; câliner; F (se) peloter; *Am.* F *petting party* réunion *f* intime (*entre jeunes gens des deux sexes*).

pet·al ⚕ ['petl] pétale *m*.

pe·tard [pi'tɑːd] † pétard *m* (*a. pyrotechnie*).

pe·ter F ['piːtə]: ~ *out* s'épuiser; disparaître; *mot.* s'arrêter.

pe·ti·tion [pi'tiʃn] **1.** pétition *f*; supplique *f*; requête *f*; *eccl.* prière *f*; ⚖ ~ *in bankruptcy* demande *f* d'ouverture de la faillite; ~ *for divorce* demande *f* en divorce; **2.** adresser une pétition *etc.* à; réclamer (qch. à q., s.o. for s.th.); **pe'ti·tion·er** solliciteur (-euse *f*) *m*; ⚖ requérant(e *f*) *m*.

pet·rel *orn.* ['petrəl] pétrel *m*; *stormy* ~ oiseau *m* des tempêtes; *fig.* émissaire *m* de discorde.

pet·ri·fac·tion [petri'fækʃn] pétrifaction *f*.

pet·ri·fy ['petrifai] (se) pétrifier.

pet·rol *mot. Brit.* ['petrəl] essence *f*; ~ *engine* moteur *m* à essence; ~ *station* poste *m* d'essence; ~ *tank* réservoir *m* à essence.

pe·tro·le·um [pi'trouljəm] pétrole *m*, huile *f* minérale *ou* de roche; ~ *jelly* vaseline *f*.

pe·trol·o·gy [pe'trɔlədʒi] pétrologie *f*.

pet·ti·coat ['petikout] jupon *m* (*a. fig.*), jupe *f* de dessous; *attr. fig.* de cotillons; ~ *government* régime *m* de cotillons.

pet·ti·fog·ger ['petifɔgə] avocassier *m*; chicanier *m*; **'pet·ti·fog·ging** chicanier (-ère *f*).

pet·ti·ness ['petinis] mesquinerie *f*, petitesse *f*.

pet·ting F ['petiŋ] pelotage *m*; *heavy* ~ pelotage *m* poussé.

pet·tish □ ['petiʃ] irritable; de mauvaise humeur; **'pet·tish·ness** irritabilité *f*; mauvaise humeur *f*.

pet·ty □ ['peti] insignifiant, petit; mesquin; ~ *bourgeoisie les petits*

bourgeois; ✝ ~ *cash* petite caisse *f*; ⚓ ~ *officer* contremaître *m*; ⚖ ~ *sessions pl.* session *f* de juges de paix.

pet·u·lance ['petjuləns] *see pettishness*; **pet·u·lant** ['~lənt] *see pettish*.

pew [pjuː] banc *m* d'église; *sl.* siège *m*, place *f*.

pe·wit *orn.* ['piːwit] vanneau *m* (huppé).

pew·ter ['pjuːtə] **1.** étain *m*, potin *m*; **2.** d'étain; **'pew·ter·er** potier *m* d'étain.

pha·e·ton ['feitn] phaéton *m*; *mot. Am.* torpédo *f*.

pha·lanx ['fælæŋks] phalange *f*.

phan·tasm ['fæntæzm] chimère *f*; ⚗ phantasme *m*; **phan·tas·ma·go·ri·a** [~məˈgɔːriə] fantasmagorie *f*.

phan·tom ['fæntəm] **1.** fantôme *m*, spectre *m*; **2.** fantôme.

Phar·i·sa·ic, Phar·i·sa·i·cal □ [færi'seiik(l)] pharisaïque.

Phar·i·see ['færisiː] pharisien *m* (*a. fig.*).

phar·ma·ceu·ti·cal □ [fɑːməˈsjuːtikl] pharmaceutique; **phar·ma'ceu·tics** *sg.* pharmacie *f*; **phar·ma·cist** ['fɑːməsist] pharmacien(ne *f*) *m*; **phar·ma·col·o·gy** [~'kɔlədʒi] pharmacologie *f*; **'phar·ma·cy** pharmacie *f*.

phar·ynx *anat.* ['færiŋks] pharynx *m*.

phase [feiz] phase *f*.

pheas·ant *orn.* ['feznt] faisan([d]e *f*) *m*; **'pheas·ant·ry** faisanderie *f*.

phe·nom·e·nal □ [fi'nɔminl] phénoménal (-aux *m/pl.*); *fig.* prodigieux (-euse *f*); **phe'nom·e·non** [~nən], *pl.* **-na** [~nə] phénomène *m* (*a. fig.*); *fig. personne*: prodige *m*.

phew [fjuː] pouf!; pouah! (*dégoût*).

phi·al ['faiəl] flacon *m*, fiole *f*.

Phi Be·ta Kap·pa *Am.* ['fai 'biːtə 'kæpə] *la plus ancienne association d'étudiants universitaires*.

phi·lan·der [fi'lændə] flirter; **phi'lan·der·er** coureur *m* de jupons.

phil·an·throp·ic [filən'θrɔpik] (~*ally*) philanthropique; philanthrope (*personne*); **phi·lan·thro·pist** [fi'lænθrəpist] philanthrope *mf*; **phi'lan·thro·py** philanthropie *f*.

phi·lat·e·list [fi'lætəlist] philatéliste *mf*; **phi'lat·e·ly** philatélie *f*.

phi·lip·pic [fi'lipik] philippique *f*.

Phi·lis·tine ['filistain] philistin *m* (*a. fig.*).

phil·o·log·i·cal □ [filə'lɔdʒikl] philologique; **phi·lol·o·gist** [fi'lɔlədʒist] philologue *mf*; **phi'lol·o·gy** philologie *f*.

phi·los·o·pher [fi'lɔsəfə] philosophe *mf*; ~s' stone pierre *f* philosophale; **phil·o·soph·ic, phil·o·soph·i·cal** □ [filə'sɔfik(l)] philosophique; **phi·los·o·phize** [fi'lɔsəfaiz] philosopher; **phi'los·o·phy** philosophie *f*; ~ of life conception *f* de la vie.

phil·tre, phil·ter ['filtə] philtre *m*.

phiz F *co.* [fiz] visage *m*, F binette *f*.

phle·bi·tis ✳ [fli'baitis] phlébite *f*.

phlegm [flem] flegme *m* (a. ✳), calme *m*; **phleg·mat·ic** [fleg'mætik] (~ally) flegmatique.

pho·bi·a ['foubiə] phobie *f*.

Phoe·ni·cian [fi'niʃiən] 1. phénicien(ne *f*) *m*; 2. *ling.* phénicien *m*; Phénicien(ne *f*) *m*.

ph(o)e·nix ['fi:niks] phénix *m*.

phone F [foun] *see telephone*; ~ call coup *m* de fil; **'~-in** *radio*, *télév.* programme *m* à ligne ouverte.

pho·net·ic [fo'netik] 1. (~ally) phonétique; ~ spelling écriture *f* phonétique. 2. ~s *pl.* phonétique *f*; **pho·ne·ti·cian** [founi'tiʃn] phonéticien *m*.

pho·no·graph ['founəgra:f] phonographe *m*; **pho·no·graph·ic** [~'græfik] (~ally) phonographique.

pho·nol·o·gy [fo'nɔlədʒi] phonologie *f*.

pho·n(e)y ['founi] 1. *Am. sl.* escroc *m*; 2. *Am.* F faux (fausse *f*); factice; en toc; ~ *flash* renseignement *m* inexact; nouvelle *f* inexacte; ~ *war* drôle de guerre.

phos·phate ✳ ['fɔsfeit] phosphate *m*.

phos·pho·resce [fɔsfə'res] être phosphorescent; **phos·pho'res·cent** phosphorescent; **phos·phor·ic** ✳ [~'fɔrik] phosphorique; **phos·pho·rous** ✳ ['~fərəs] phosphoreux (-euse *f*); **phos·pho·rus** ✳ ['~rəs] phosphore *m*.

pho·to F ['foutou] *see* ~*graph*; **'~-cop·i·er** machine *f* à photocopier, photocopieur *m*; **'~-cop·y** 1. photocopie *f*; 2. photocopier; **~-e'lec·tric cell** cellule *f* photoélectrique; **~-en·grav·ing** [~in'greiviŋ] photogravure *f* industrielle; **'~-fin·ish** décision *f* par photo, photo *f* à l'arrivée; **'~-flash** flash (*pl.* flashes) *m* (à ampoule);

~-gram·me·try [~'græmitri] photogrammétrie *f*.

pho·to·graph ['foutəgra:f] 1. photographie *f*; 2. photographier; prendre une photographie de; **pho·tog·ra·pher** [fə'tɔgrəfə] photographe *m*; **pho·to·graph·ic** [foutə'græfik] (~ally) photographique; ~ *library* archives *f/pl.* photographiques, photothèque *f*; **pho·tog·ra·phy** [fə'tɔgrəfi] photographie *f*; prise *f* de vues.

pho·to·gra·vure [foutəgrə'vjuə] photogravure *f*, héliogravure *f*; **pho·tom·e·ter** [fo'tɔmitə] photomètre *m*; **pho·to·play** ['foutəplei] film *m* dramatique; **pho·to·sen·si·tive** ['foutou'sensitiv] photosensible; **pho·to·stat** ['foutəstæt], **pho·to·stat·ic** [~'stætik]: ~ *copy* photocopie *f*; **pho·to·te·leg·ra·phy** [foutəti'legrəfi] téléphotographie *f*; **pho·to·type** ['~taip] phototype *m*.

phrase [freiz] 1. locution *f*; tour *m* de phrase; expression *f*; *gramm.* membre *m* de phrase; ♪ phrase *f*, période *f*; 2. exprimer (*une pensée*), rédiger; ♪ phraser; **'~-book** recueil *m* d'expressions; **'~-mon·ger** phraseur (-euse *f*) *m*; **phra·se·ol·o·gy** [~zi'ɔlədʒi] phraséologie *f*.

phre·net·ic [fri'netik] (~ally) affolé; frénétique.

phre·nol·o·gy [fri'nɔlədʒi] phrénologie *f*.

phthis·i·cal ['θaisikl] phtisique; **phthi·sis** ['~sis] phtisie *f*.

phut *sl.* [fʌt]: *go* ~ claquer.

phys·ic ['fizik] 1. médecine *f*; F drogues *f/pl.*; ~s *sg.* physique *f*; 2. *sl.* médicamenter (*q.*); **phys·i·cal** □ physique; corporel(le *f*); matériel(le *f*); ~ *condition* état *m* physique; ~ *culture* culture *f* physique; ~ *test* visite *f* médicale; **phy·si·cian** [fi'ziʃn] médecin *m*; **phys·i·cist** ['~sist] physicien(ne *f*) *m*.

phys·i·og·no·my [fizi'ɔnəmi] physionomie *f*; **phys·i·og·ra·phy** [~'ɔgrəfi] physiographie *f*; géographie *f* physique; **phys·i·ol·o·gy** [~'ɔlədʒi] physiologie *f*.

phys·i·o·ther·a·pist [fiziou'θerəpist] kinésithérapeute *mf*; **phys·i·o·ther·a·py** [~'θerəpi] kinésithérapie *f*.

phy·sique [fi'zi:k] physique *m*.

pi·an·ist ['pjænist; ♪ 'piənist] pianiste *mf*.

pi·a·no¹ ♪ ['pja:nou] *adv.* piano.

pi·an·o² ['pjænou; ♪ 'pja:nou] piano *m*; cottage ~ petit droit *m*; grand ~ piano *m* à queue.

pi·an·o·for·te [pjæno'fɔːti] see pi-ano².

pi·az·za [pi'ædzə] place *f*; Am. véranda *f*.

pi·broch ['piːbrɔk] pibroch *m* (= air de cornemuse).

pic·a·roon [pikə'ruːn] corsaire *m*.

pic·a·yune Am. [pikə'juːn] **1.** usu. fig. sou *m*; bagatelle *f*; **2.** mesquin.

pic·ca·nin·ny co. ['pikənini] **1.** négrillon(ne *f*) *m*; Am. F mioche *mf*; **2.** enfantin.

pick [pik] **1.** pic *m*, pioche *f*; ⚒ rivelaine *f*; (ou tooth~) cure-dent *m*; élite *f*, choix *m*; **2.** *v/t*. piocher (la terre); se curer (les dents); ronger (un os); plumer (la volaille); cueillir (une fleur, un fruit); trier (du minerai); effilocher (des chiffons); éplucher (de la laine); Am. jouer de (le banjo); crocheter (la serrure); choisir; F (a. ~ at) pignocher (sa nourriture); ~ one's way marcher avec précaution; ~ pockets voler à la tire; ~ a quarrel with chercher querelle à; see bone 1; crow 1; ~ out choisir; enlever; trouver; reconnaître; peint. échampir; *v/i.* picoter, picorer (oiseau); F manger du bout des dents; surt. Am. F ~ at (ou on) chercher noise à (q.); critiquer; ~ up *v/t*. prendre; ramasser; relever; (re)trouver; apprendre; aller chercher (q.); repérer (un avion); faire la connaissance de (q.); capter (⚡ le courant; un message); radio: avoir (un poste) *v/i.* se rétablir; mot. reprendre; ~-**a-back** ['ʌəbæk] sur le dos; '~-**axe** pioche *f*; **picked** choisi, de choix; '**pick·er** cueilleur (-euse *f*) *m* etc.; ⊕ machine *f* à éplucher.

pick·et ['pikit] **1.** piquet *m* (a. ✕, a. de grève); **2.** *v/t*. mettre (un cheval) au(x) piquet(s); palissader; ✕ détacher en grand-garde; ⊕ installer des piquets de grève; *v/i.* être gréviste en faction.

pick·ing ['pikiŋ] piochage *m* etc. (see pick); choix *m*; ~s *pl.* restes *m/pl.*, fig. sl. gratte *f*.

pick·le ['pikl] **1.** marinade *f*; saumure *f*; conserve *f* au vinaigre; F enfant *mf* terrible; F pétrin *m*; see mix; **2.** mariner, conserver; ~d herring hareng *m* salé.

pick...: '~-**lock** crochet *m*; personne: crocheteur *m* de serrures; '~-**me-up** F cordial *m*; remontant *m*; '~-**pock·et** voleur (-euse *f*) *m* à la tire; '~-**up 1.** ramassement *m*; chose *f* ramassée; phonographe: pick-up *m/inv.*; ✝ (ou ~ in prices) hausse *f*; Am. radio, télév. pick-up *m/inv.*; **2.** F hâtivement rassemblé (équipe, formation, etc.); improvisé; ~ dinner repas *m* fait de restes.

pick·y ['piki] difficile, délicat.

pic·nic ['piknik] **1.** pique-nique *m*; partie *f* de plaisir; dînette *f* sur l'herbe; **2.** faire un pique-nique; dîner sur l'herbe.

pic·to·ri·al [pik'tɔːriəl] **1.** □ en images; pittoresque; illustré; **2.** périodique *m* ou journal *m* illustré.

pic·ture ['piktʃə] **1.** tableau *m*; image *f*; peinture *f*; gravure *f*; portrait *m*; ~s *pl.* cinéma *m*; films *m/pl.*; attr. d'images; du cinéma; ~-palace cinéma *m*; ~ (post)card carte *f* postale illustrée; ~ puzzle rébus *m*; **2.** dépeindre; représenter; se figurer (qch.); s'imaginer (qch.); '~-**book** album *m*; livre *m* d'images; '~-**go·er** Brit. habitué(e *f*) *m* du cinéma.

pic·tur·esque □ [piktʃə'resk] pittoresque.

pidg·in Eng·lish ['pidʒin'iŋgliʃ] jargon *m* commercial anglo-chinois; fig. F petit nègre *m*.

pie¹ [pai] viande etc.: pâté *m*; fruits: tourte *f*; typ. pâte *f*, pâté *m*; see finger 1.   [fig. bigarré.]

pie² orn. [~] pie *f*; '~-**bald** pie;

piece [piːs] **1.** pièce *f* (a. théâ., échecs, monnaie, ✝); fragment *m*; morceau *m* (a. ♪); partie *f*; ~ of advice conseil *m*; ~ of jewellery bijou (pl. -x) *m*; ~ of news nouvelle *f*; by the ~ à la pièce *f*; in ~s en morceaux; of a ~ uniforme; all of a ~ tout d'une pièce; break (ou go) to ~s se désagréger; tomber en lambeaux (robe etc.); give s.o. a ~ of one's mind parler carrément à q.; take to ~s défaire; ⊕ démonter; **2.** raccommoder, rapiécer; ~ out rallonger; augmenter; ~ together joindre, unir; coordonner; ~ up raccommoder; '~-**goods** *pl.* marchandises *f/pl.* à la pièce; '~-**meal** pièce à pièce, peu à peu; '~-**work** travail (pl. -aux) *m* à la tâche.

pied [paid] mi-parti; bigarré.

pie-eyed *sl.* ['paiaid] soûl, rond, plein.

pie·plant *Am.* ['paiplɑːnt] rhubarbe *f*.

pier [piə] jetée *f*, digue *f*; quai *m*; △ pilastre *m*; pilier *m*; **'pier·age** ⚓ droits *m/pl.* de jetée.

pierce [piəs] *v/t.* percer (*a. fig.*); transpercer (*le cœur*); *v/i.* percer; *fig.* pénétrer; **'pierc·er** ⊕ perçoir *m*, poinçon *m*; **'pierc·ing** □ pénétrant (*a. fig.*).

pier-glass ['piəglɑːs] trumeau *m*.

pi·e·tism ['paiətizm] piétisme *m*.

pi·e·ty ['paiəti] piété *f*.

pif·fle *sl.* ['pifl] **1.** balivernes *f/pl.*; futilités *f/pl.*; **2.** dire des sottises.

pig [pig] **1.** porc *m*, cochon *m*; *métall.* gueuse *f* (*de fonte*); saumon *m* (*de plomb*); *buy a ~ in a poke* acheter chat en poche; **2.** cochonner; F vivre comme dans une étable.

pi·geon ['pidʒin] *zo.* pigeon *m*; F pigeon *m*, dupe *f*; *sl.* affaire *f*; **'~-hole 1.** case *f*; **2.** caser (*des papiers*); *admin.* classer; F faire rester dans les cartons; **'pi·geon·ry** colombier *m*.

pig·ger·y ['pigəri] porcherie *f*.

pig·gish □ ['pigiʃ] malpropre; entêté.

pig·head·ed ['pig'hedid] obstiné, têtu. [gueuse.\

pig-i·ron ['pigaiən] fonte *f* en\

pig·let ['piglit] petit cochon *m*.

pig·ment ['pigmənt] pigment *m*, colorant *m*.

pig·my *see* pygmy.

pig...: **'~-nut** gland *m* de terre; **'~-skin** peau *f* de porc; *Am. sl.* ballon *m* de football; **~-sty** ['~stai] porcherie *f*; *fig.* taudis *m*; **'~-tail** queue *f* (*de cheveux*); **'~-wash** pâtée *f* pour les porcs.

pike [paik] ⚔ pique *f*; *géog.* pic *m*; *icht.* brochet *m*; **'pik·er** *Am. sl.* boursicoteur *m*; lâcheur *m*; **'pike-staff**: *as plain as a ~* clair comme le jour.

pil·chard *icht.* ['piltʃəd] sardine *f*.

pile¹ [pail] **1.** tas *m*; ⚔ *armes*: faisceau *m*; △ masse *f*; édifice *m*; *fig.* fortune *f*; ⚡ pile *f* de Volta; *phys.* (*ou atomic ~*) pile *f* atomique; **2.** *v/i.* (*a. ~ up*) s'entasser, s'amonceler; *v/t.* (*a. ~ up*) entasser, empiler; amasser (*une fortune*); ⚔ ~

arms former les faisceaux; *fig.* ~ *it on* exagérer.

pile² [~] pieu *m*.

pile³ [~] *tex.* poil *m*.

pile-driv·er ⊕ ['paildraivə] sonnette *f*; **'pile-dwell·ing** habitation *f* lacustre *ou* sur pilotis.

piles ✻ [pailz] *pl.* hémorroïdes *f/pl.*

pile-up F ['pailʌp] carambolage *m ou* télescopage *m* (en série).

pil·fer ['pilfə] *v/t.* chiper; *v/i.* faire de petits vols.

pil·grim ['pilgrim] pèlerin(e *f*) *m*; ♀ *Père* ~ pèlerin; **'pil·grim·age** pèlerinage *m*.

pill [pil] pilule *f*; F personne *f* embêtante, casse-pieds *mf inv.*

pil·lage ['pilidʒ] **1.** pillage *m*; **2.** piller, saccager.

pil·lar ['pilə] pilier *m*, colonne *f*; **'~-box** boîte *f* aux lettres; borne *f* postale; **pil·lared** ['~ləd] à piliers, à colonnes; en pilier *etc.*

pil·lion ['piljən] coussinet *m* de cheval; *mot.* siège *m* arrière; *ride* ~ monter derrière.

pil·lo·ry ['piləri] **1.** pilori *m*; *in the* ~ au pilori; **2.** mettre au pilori; *fig.* exposer au ridicule.

pil·low ['pilou] **1.** oreiller *m*; coussin *m*; ⊕ coussinet *m*; **2.** reposer sa tête (sur, *on*); **'~-case**, ✝ **'~-slip** taie *f* d'oreiller.

pi·lot ['pailət] **1.** pilote *m* (*a.* ⚓, ✈); *fig.* guide *m*; ~ *instructor* professeur *m* de pilotage; ♀ *Officer* sous-lieutenant *m* aviateur; ~ *plant* installation *f* d'essai; ~ *project* projet *m* d'essai, projet-pilote *m* (*pl.* projets-pilotes); **2.** piloter; conduire; **'pi·lot·age** (frais *m/pl.* de) pilotage *m*; **'pi·lot-bal'loon** ballon *m* d'essai.

pil·ule ['pilju:l] petite pilule *f*.

pi·men·to [pi'mentou] piment *m*.

pimp [pimp] **1.** entremetteur (-euse *f*) *m*; **2.** exercer le métier de proxénète.

pim·ple ['pimpl] bouton *m*, bourgeon *m*; **'pim·pled**, **'pim·ply** boutonneux (-euse *f*); pustuleux (-euse *f*).

pin [pin] **1.** épingle *f*; ⊕ goupille *f*, cheville *f*; *jeu*: quille *f*; clou *m*; *cuis.* rouleau *m* (à pâte); *Am.* insigne *m* (*d'une association estudiantine etc.*); *~s pl. sl.* quilles *f/pl.* (= *jambes*). **2.** épingler; attacher avec des épingles; clouer; *sl. fig.*

pique

obliger (q.) à reconnaître les faits; (souv. ~ down) obliger (à, to); ~ one's hopes en mettre toutes ses espérances dans.

pin·a·fore ['pinəfɔ:] tablier m.

pin·ball ma·chine ['pinbɔ:lmə'ʃi:n] flipper m.

pin·cers ['pinsəz] pl.: (a pair of) ~ (une) pince f, (des) tenailles f/pl.

pinch [pintʃ] 1. pinçade f; tabac: prise f; sel etc.: pincée f; fig. morsure f; fig. besoin m; 2. v/t. pincer; gêner; sl. chiper (=voler); arrêter (q.); v/i. (se res)serrer; faire des petites économies; se priver; **pinched** étroit; gêné; fig. hâve.

pinch·beck ['pintʃbek] 1. ⊕ chrysocale m, similor m; fig. trompe-l'œil m/inv.; 2. d'occasion.

pinch·hit Am. ['pintʃhit] suppléer, remplacer (q., for s.o.).

pin·cush·ion ['pinkuʃin] pelote f à aiguilles.   [pin.\

pine¹ ⚭ [pain] pin m; bois m de\

pine² [~] languir (après, pour for); ~ away dépérir; mourir de langueur.

pine...: '~-**ap·ple** ⚭ ananas m; '~-**cone** pomme f de pin.

pin·er·y ['painəri] serre f à ananas; (a. 'pine·wood) pineraie f.

pin-feath·er ['pinfeðə] plume f naissante.

pin·fold ['pinfould] parc m (à moutons etc.); fourrière f.

ping [piŋ] cingler, fouetter.

ping-pong ['piŋpɔŋ] ping-pong m.

pin·ion ['pinjən] 1. aileron m; poét. aile f; (a. ~-feather) penne f; ⊕ pignon m; 2. rogner les ailes à; fig. lier les bras à.

pink¹ [piŋk] 1. ⚭ œillet m; couleur: rose m; chasse: rouge m; fig. modèle m; comble m; sl. in the ~ florissant, en parfaite santé; 2. v/t. teindre en rose; v/i. rougir.

pink² [~] toucher; denteler les bords de (une robe); fig. orner; ~ing shears pl. ciseaux m/pl. à denteler.

pink³ mot. [~] cliqueter.

pink·ish ['piŋkiʃ] rosâtre.

pin-mon·ey ['pinmʌni] argent m de poche (d'une femme ou jeune fille).

pin·nace ⚓ ['pinis] grand canot m, pinasse f.

pin·na·cle ['pinəkl] △ pinacle m; montagne: cime f; fig. faîte m, apogée m.

pin·nate ⚭ ['pinit] penné.

pi·noc(h)·le Am. ['pi:nʌkl] (sorte de) belote f.

pin...: '~-**point** localiser précisément; bien définir; mettre le doigt sur (un problème); '~-**prick** piqûre f d'épingle; '~-**stripe** tex. filet m.

pint [paint] pinte f (0,57, Am. 0,47 litre).

pin·tle ⊕ ['pintl] pivot m central; mot. cheville f ouvrière.

pin·to Am. ['pintou] 1. pl. -tos cheval m pie; 2. pie.

pin-up (**girl**) ['pinʌp('gə:l)] pin-up f/inv.; beauté f.

pi·o·neer [paiə'niə] 1. ✕, fig. pionnier m; fig. défricheur (-euse f) m; 2. frayer (le chemin).

pi·ous □ ['paiəs] pieux (-euse f); pie (œuvre).

pip¹ [pip] vét. pépie f; sl. have the ~ avoir le cafard.

pip² [~] fruit: pépin m; carte, dé, etc.: point m; ✕ grades: étoile f.

pip³ sl. [~] v/t. refuser (un candidat); vaincre; v/i. ~ out mourir.

pipe [paip] 1. tuyau m (a. gaz); tube m (a. anat.); pipe f (tabac, a. mesure de vin: 572,4 litres); ♪ chalumeau m; oiseau etc.: chant m; 2. canaliser; amener etc. par un pipe-line; jouer (un air); lisérer (une robe etc.); ⚓ siffler, donner un coup de sifflet; F ~ one's eye(s) pleurnicher; piped music musique f de fond enregistrée; '~-**clay** 1. terre f de pipe; blanc m de terre à pipe; 2. astiquer au blanc de terre à pipe; ~ **dream** fig. château m en Espagne; '~-**lay·er** poseur m de tuyaux; Am. pol. intrigant m; '~-**line** pipeline m; '**pip·er** joueur m de chalumeau etc.; F pay the ~ payer les violons.

pip·ing ['paipiŋ] 1. sifflant; heureux (-euse f) (époque); ~ hot tout chaud; 2. canalisation f; tuyauterie f; oiseaux: gazouillement m; robe: liserage m; cost. passepoil m.

pip·it orn. ['pipit] pipit m.

pip·kin ['pipkin] poêlon m.

pip·pin ⚭ ['pipin] reinette f; sl. it's a ~ il est remarquable.

pip·squeak F ['pipskwi:k] rien du tout mf (pl. riens du tout ou inv.).

pi·quan·cy ['pi:kənsi] (goût m) piquant m.

pi·quant □ ['pi:kənt] piquant.

pique [pi:k] 1. pique f, ressentiment

m; **2.** piquer; exciter (*la curiosité*); ~ *o.s. upon* se piquer de.

pi·ra·cy ['paiərəsi] piraterie *f*; contrefaçon *f* (*d'un livre*); plagiat *m*; **pi·rate** ['~rit] **1.** *homme ou navire*: pirate *m*; contrefacteur *m*; plagiaire *m*; radio ~, ~ *listener* auditeur (-trice *f*) *m* illicite; ~ *station* radio *f* pirate; **2.** pirater; contrefaire; plagier; **pi·rat·i·cal** □ [pai'rætikl] de pirate *etc.*

Pis·ces *astr.* ['paisi:z] les Poissons *m/pl.* [culture *f*.]

pis·ci·cul·ture ['pisikʌltʃə] pisci-)

pish [piʃ] bah!; pouah!

piss V [pis] **1.** pisse *f*, urine *f*; **2.** pisser, uriner; ~ *off!* fous le camp!; ~ed soûl, plein; *be* ~ed *off* en avoir marre, en avoir ras le bol.

pis·ta·chi·o [pi'stɑ:ʃiou] pistache *f*.

pis·til ♀ ['pistil] pistil *m*.

pis·tol ['pistl] pistolet *m*; '~-**whip** *Am.* F frapper d'un pistolet.

pis·ton ⊕ ['pistən] piston *m*; *pompe*: sabot *m*; ~ *displacement* cylindrée *f*; ~ *ring* segment *m* de piston; ~ *rod* tige *f* de piston; ~ *stroke* coup *m* de *ou* course *f* du piston.

pit [pit] **1.** fosse *f*, trou *m*; *anat.* creux *m*; *théâ.* parterre *m*; *Am.* bourse *f* de commerce, parquet *m*; *mot.* fosse *f*; mine *f* (*de charbon*); *petite vérole*: cicatrice *f*; piège *m* (*à animaux*); **2.** piquer, trouer; marquer; ✗ ensiler; ~ *against* mettre (*q.*) aux prises avec; ~ted *with smallpox* marqué de la petite vérole.

pit-(a-)pat ['pit(ə)'pæt] tic-tac.

pitch¹ [pitʃ] **1.** poix *f*; brai *m*; **2.** enduire de brai; ⚓ calfater.

pitch² [~] **1.** lancement *m*; ♪ *son*: hauteur *f*; *instrument*: diapason *m*; ⊕ pas *m*; *scie*: angle *m* des dents; ⚓ tangage *m*; ✝ *marché*: place *f*, *camelot*: place *f* habituelle; *cricket*: terrain *m*; *fig.* degré *m*; ~ *and toss* jeu *m* de pile ou face; **2.** *v/t.* lancer; mettre; paver (*la chaussée*); charger (*le foin etc.*); dresser (*une tente*); établir (*un camp*); poser (*une échelle*); ♪ ~ *higher* (*lower*) hausser (baisser) (*le ton*); ♪ jouer dans une clef donnée; *fig.* arrêter, déterminer; ~ed *battle* bataille *f* rangée; ~ *one's hope too high* viser trop haut; *v/i.* ✗ camper; tomber; ⚓ tanguer; ~ *upon* arrêter son choix sur; F ~ *into* taper sur; dire son fait à.

pitch·er¹ ['pitʃə] lanceur *m* (*de la balle*).

pitch·er² [~] cruche *f*; broc *m*.

pitch·fork ['pitʃfɔ:k] **1.** fourche *f* à foin *etc.*; ♪ diapason *m*; **2.** lancer avec la fourche; *fig.* bombarder (*q.* dans un poste, *s.o. into a job*).

pitch-pine ♀ ['pitʃpain] faux sapin *m*.

pitch·y ['pitʃi] poisseux (-euse *f*); noir comme poix.

pit-coal ✗ ['pitkoul] houille *f*.

pit·e·ous □ ['pitiəs] pitoyable, piteux (-euse *f*).

pit·fall ['pitfɔ:l] trappe *f*; piège *m*.

pith [piθ] moelle *f* (*a. fig.*); *orange*: peau *f* blanche; sève *f*, ardeur *f*.

pit-head ✗ ['pithed] carreau *m*.

pith·i·ness ['piθinis] concision *f*; '**pith·less** □ mou (mol *devant une voyelle ou un h muet*); molle *f*).

pith·y □ ['piθi] moelleux (-euse *f*); concis.

pit·i·a·ble □ ['pitiəbl] pitoyable.

pit·i·ful □ ['pitiful] compatissant; pitoyable; lamentable (*a. péj.*).

pit·i·less □ ['pitilis] impitoyable.

pit·man ['pitmən] mineur *m*; houilleur *m*.

pit-props ✗ ['pitprɔps] *pl.* bois *m* de soutènement.

pit·tance ['pitəns] maigre salaire *m*; gages *m/pl.* dérisoires; † aumône *f*.

pi·tu·i·tar·y *anat.* [pi'tju:itəri] pituitaire. [mine.)

pit·wood ✗ ['pitwud] bois *m* de)

pit·y ['piti] **1.** pitié *f*, compassion *f* (*de on, for*); *for* ~*'s sake!* par pitié!; *de grâce!*; *it is a* ~ c'est dommage; *it is a thousand pities* c'est mille fois *ou* bien dommage; **2.** plaindre; avoir pitié de; *I* ~ *him* il me fait pitié.

piv·ot ['pivət] **1.** ⊕, ✗ pivot *m*; ⊕ tourillon *m*; *fig.* axe *m*, pivot *m*; **2.** *v/i.* pivoter (*sur*, ~[up]on); *v/t.* faire pivoter; '**piv·o·tal** pivotal (-aux *m/pl.*); à pivot.

pix·ie ['piksi] lutin *m*; fée *f*.

pix·i·lat·ed *Am.* ['piksəleitid] loufoque; dingo *inv.*

pix·y ['piksi] *see* pixie.

pla·ca·bil·i·ty [pleikə'biliti] douceur *f*; '**pla·ca·ble** doux (douce *f*); facile à apaiser.

pla·card ['plækɑ:d] **1.** écriteau *m*, affiche *f*; **2.** afficher; couvrir (*qch.*) d'affiches.

pla·cate [plə'keit] apaiser, calmer.

place [pleis] **1.** lieu *m*, endroit *m*, localité *f*; station *f*; place *f*; rang *m*; emploi *m*, poste *m*, situation *f*; ~ of *delivery* destination *f*; ~ of *employment usu.* travail (*pl.* -aux) *m*, emploi *m*, bureau *m etc.*; *give* ~ *to* faire place à (*qch.*); *in* ~ en place; *in* ~ *of* au lieu de; *in his* ~ à sa place; *in the first* ~ d'abord; *out of* ~ déplacé; **2.** placer (*a. de l'argent*); (re)mettre; ✕ mettre en faction (*la sentinelle*); ✝ passer (*une commande*), mettre en vente; faire accepter (*un article à un éditeur etc.*); ~ *a child under s.o.'s care* mettre un enfant sous la garde de q.; ~ **mat** set *m*, napperon *m* individuel; **'~-name** nom *m* de lieu.

plac·id □ ['plæsid] calme; serein; **pla'cid·i·ty** calme *m*, tranquillité *f*.

plack·et ['plækit] fente *f* (*de jupe*).

pla·gi·a·rism ['pleidʒiərizm] plagiat *m*; **'pla·gi·a·rist** plagiaire *m*; démarqueur *m*; **'pla·gi·a·rize** plagier.

plague [pleig] **1.** peste *f*; fléau *m*; **2.** tourmenter, harceler; **'~-spot** *usu. fig.* foyer *m* d'infection.

pla·guy F ['pleigi] assommant; *adv.* rudement.

plaice *icht.* [pleis] plie *f*.

plaid [plæd] *tex.* tartan *m*; plaid *m* (écossais).

plain [plein] **1.** *adj.* □ évident, clair; simple; *tricot:* endroit *inv.*; lisse; carré, franc(he *f*); sans beauté; *cuis.* au naturel, bourgeois; *in* ~ *English* en bon anglais; ~ *chocolate* chocolat *m* à craquer; ~ *fare* cuisine *f* bourgeoise; ~ *knitting* tricot *m* à l'endroit; ~ *paper* papier *m* non réglé; ~ *sewing* couture *f* simple; **2.** *adv.* clairement; carrément; **3.** *su.* plaine *f*, *surt. Am. attr.* des champs; **'~-clothes man** agent *m* en civil; agent *m* de la sûreté; ~ **deal·ing 1.** franchise *f*, loyauté *f*; **2.** franc(he *f*) et loyal(e *f*); **'plain·ness** simplicité *f*; franchise *f*; clarté *f*; netteté *f*; manque *m* de beauté.

plaint ⚖ [pleint] plainte *f*; **plain·tiff** ⚖ ['~if] demandeur (-eresse *f*) *m*; **'plain·tive** □ plaintif (-ive *f*).

plait [plæt] **1.** *chevaux:* tresse *f*, natte *f*; *see* pleat 1; **2.** tresser; *see* pleat 2.

plan [plæn] **1.** plan *m*; projet *m*,

dessein *m*; levé *m* (*d'un terrain*); **2.** tracer le plan de; *fig.* projeter, se proposer (qch., s.th.; de *inf.*, to *inf.*); méditer; ~*ned economy* économie *f* planifiée; ~*ning board* conseil *m* de planification.

plane¹ [plein] **1.** uni; plat; égal (-aux *m*/*pl.*); **2.** ⚙ plan *m*; ✈ plan *m*, aile *f*; *fig.* niveau *m*; F avion *m*; ⊕ rabot *m*; *elevating (depressing)* ~ ✈ gouvernail *m* d'altitude (de profondeur); **3.** planer, dresser; aplanir; raboter; ✈ voyager en avion; planer.

plane² ♀ [~] (*a.* ~-*tree*) platane *m*.

plan·et *astr.* ['plænit] planète *f*.

plane-ta·ble *surv.* ['pleinteibl] planchette *f*.

plan·e·tar·i·um [plæni'tɛəriəm] planétaire *m*; **plan·e·tar·y** ['~təri] planétaire; terrestre; *fig.* errant.

plan·ish ⊕ ['plæniʃ] aplanir; polir.

plank [plæŋk] **1.** planche *f*; madrier *m*; *Am. parl.* point *m* d'un programme électoral; **2.** planchéier; couvrir de planches; *sl., Am.* F ~ *down (out)* payer, allonger (*l'argent*); ~ *bed* lit *m* de camp; couchette *f* en bois; **'plank·ing** planchéiage *m*; revêtement *m*.

plant [plɑ:nt] **1.** plante *f*; pose *f*; installation *f*; machines *f*/*pl.*; *sl.* coup *m* monté, escroquerie *f*; *Am. sl. a.* cachette *f*; **2.** planter (*a.* ✎, *a. fig.*); implanter (*une idée*) (dans l'esprit de q., *into s.o.'s mind*); loger; poser; enterrer (*des légumes*); F appliquer (*un coup de poing*); *sl.* monter (*un coup*) (contre, on); ~ *o.s.* se planter (devant, *in front of*).

plan·tain¹ ♀ ['plæntin] plantain *m*.

plan·tain² ♀ [~] banane *f* (*des Antilles*).

plan·ta·tion [plæn'teiʃn] plantation *f*; bosquet *m*; **plant·er** ['plɑ:ntə] planteur *m*; **'plant-louse** puceron *m*, aphis *m*. [~ plaque *f*.]

plaque [plɑ:k] plaque *f*; 🦷 *dental*)

plash¹ [plæʃ] **1.** clapotis *m*; flac *m*; flaque *f* d'eau; **2.** flac!; floc!; **3.** *v/t.* plonger en faisant flac; *v/i.* clapoter; faire flac.

plash² [~] entrelacer (*les branches d'une haie*).

plash·y ['plæʃi] bourbeux (-euse *f*); couvert de flaques d'eau.

plasm 1012

plasm, plas·ma *biol.* ['plæzm(ə)] (proto)plasma *m*.

plas·ter ['plɑːstə] **1.** *pharm.* emplâtre *m*; sparadrap *m*; ⊕ plâtre *m*; enduit *m*; (*usu.* ~ *of Paris*) plâtre *m* de moulage; ~ *cast* moulage *m* au plâtre; **2.** ✗ mettre un emplâtre sur; plâtrer; enduire; *fig.* recouvrir (de, *with*); '**plas·ter·er** plâtrier *m*.

plas·tic ['plæstik] **1.** (~ally) plastique; (*synthetic*) ~ *material* = **2.** (matière *f*) plastique *m*; **plas·ti·cine** ['~tisiːn] plasticine *f*; **plas·tic·i·ty** [~'tisiti] plasticité *f*.

plas·tron ['plæstrən] plastron *m*.

plat [plæt] *see* plait; plot¹.

plate [pleit] **1.** *usu.* plaque *f* (*a. mot., photo, radio, a. de porte*); *métal:* lame *f*; *typ.* cliché *m*; *livre:* planche *f*, gravure *f*; assiette *f*; *course:* coupe *f*; (*a.* ~ *iron*) tôle *f*; *Am. baseball:* point *m* de départ du batteur; limite *f* du batteur; (*a. dental* ~) dentier *m*; *radio:* anode *f*; ⊕ *machine:* plateau *m*; **2.** plaquer; métalliser; ✗ blinder; ⚓ border en acier *etc.*

pla·teau *géog.* ['plætou] plateau *m*.

plate-bas·ket ['pleitbɑːskit] ramasse-couverts *m/inv.*; **plate·ful** ['~ful] assiettée *f*.

plate...: '~-**glass** glace *f* de vitrage; '~-**hold·er** *phot.* châssis *m*; '~-**lay·er** ⛭ poseur *m* de rails; ouvrier *m* de la voie.

plat·en ['plætn] *typ.* platine *f*; *machine à écrire:* cylindre *m*.

plat·er ['pleitə] ⊕ plaqueur *m*; *sp.* cheval *m* à réclamer.

plat·form ['plætfɔːm] terrasse *f*; estrade *f*; *géog.* plate-forme (*pl. plates-formes*) *f*; ⛭ quai *m*, trottoir *m*; *Am. surt.* plate-forme (*pl. plates-formes*) *f* de wagon; *pol.* programme *m* (*Am. souv.* électoral).

plat·i·num *min.* ['plætinəm] platine *m*. [tude *f*.]

plat·i·tude *fig.* ['plætitjuːd] plati-⌋

pla·toon ✗ [plə'tuːn] section *f*.

plat·ter ['plætə] écuelle *f*.

plau·dit ['plɔːdit] *usu.* ~s *pl.* applaudissements *m/pl.*

plau·si·bil·i·ty [plɔːzə'biliti] plausibilité *f*; vraisemblance *f*.

plau·si·ble □ ['plɔːzəbl] plausible; vraisemblable; spécieux (-euse *f*).

play [plei] **1.** jeu *m* (*a.* ⊕, *lumière, amusement*); *théâ.* pièce *f*; spectacle *m*; ⊕ liberté *f*; ⊕ fonctionnement *m*; *fair (foul)* ~ jeu *m* loyal (déloyal); ~ *on words* jeu *m* de mots; calembour *m*; *bring into* ~ mettre en jeu *ou* en œuvre; *make great* ~ *with* attacher beaucoup d'importance à; souligner; **2.** *v/i.* jouer (*a. fig.*); s'amuser; folâtrer; ⊕ fonctionner librement, jouer; ~ *fast and loose* jouer double jeu avec; *sp.* ~ *at football (at cards)* jouer au football (aux cartes); ~ *for time* temporiser; *théâ.* ~ *to the gallery* jouer pour la galerie; F ~ *up to* flatter; ~ *upon* abuser de; agir sur; *v/t. sp.* jouer à; ♪ jouer de (*un instrument*); *théâ.* jouer (*un rôle*); *fig.* se conduire en; ~ *the deuce with* ruiner; faire un mal du diable à; ~ *down* minimiser; ~ *off* opposer (q. à q., s.o. *against* s.o.); ~*ed out* à bout de forces; épuisé; F ~ *up* chahuter (q.); '~·**act** *fig.* faire du théâtre, jouer la comédie; '~·**act·ing** *fig.* (pure) comédie *f*, cinéma *m*; '~-**back** lecture *f* sonore; play-back *m*; '~-**bill** affiche *f* de théâtre; '~-**book** *théâ.* recueil *m* de pièces; '~-**boy** viveur *m*; '**play·er** joueur (-euse *f*) *m*; acteur (-trice *f*) *m*; ♪ exécutant(*e f*) *m*; *sp.* équipier *m*; '**play·er-pi·an·o** piano *m* mécanique; '**play·fel·low** camarade *mf* de jeu; **play·ful** □ ['~ful] badin, enjoué; '**play·ful·ness** badinage *m*; enjouement *m*.

play...: '~-**go·er** amateur (-trice *f*) *m* du théâtre; '~-**ground** terrain *m* de jeu(x); cour *f* de récréation; '~-**house** théâtre *m*; *Am.* maison *f* de poupée.

play·ing...: '~-**card** carte *f* (à jouer); '~-**field** terrain *m* de jeu(x) *ou* de sports.

play...: '~-**mate** *see* playfellow; '~-**off** match *m* décisif (*après match nul*); '~-**pen** parc *m* pour bébés; '~-**thing** jouet *m*; '~-**wright** auteur *m* dramatique; '~-**writ·er** auteur *m* de pièces.

plea [pliː] ⚖ défense *f*; excuse *f*, prétexte *m*; F prière *f*; *make a* ~ alléguer; *on the* ~ *of* (*ou that*) sous prétexte de *ou* que.

plead [pliːd] *v/i.* plaider (pour, en faveur de *for*) (q., *qch.*); ~ *for mercy* demander grâce; *see* guilty; *v/t.* plaider; alléguer, invoquer (*une excuse*); prétexter (*qch.*);

'plead·a·ble plaidable; invocable; **'plead·er** ⚜ avocat *m*; défenseur *m*; **'plead·ing** ⚜ plaidoirie *f*; *fig.* intercession *f*; *special* ~ F argument *m* spécieux; ~s *pl.* dossier *m*; débats *m/pl.*

pleas·ant □ ['pleznt] agréable, charmant, doux (douce *f*); affable; **'pleas·ant·ness** charme *m*; affabilité *f*; **'pleas·ant·ry** plaisanterie *f*; gaieté *f*.

please [pli:z] *v/i.* plaire; être agréable; *if you* ~ s'il vous plaît; je vous en prie; ~ *come in!* veuillez entrer; *v/t.* plaire à, faire plaisir à; ~ *o.s.* agir à sa guise; *be* ~*d to do s.th.* faire qch. avec plaisir; *be* ~*d with* être (très) content de; **'pleased** content, satisfait.

pleas·ing □ ['pli:ziŋ] agréable, doux (douce *f*).

pleas·ur·a·ble □ ['pleʒərəbl] agréable.

pleas·ure ['pleʒə] **1.** plaisir *m*; volonté *f*; *attr.* d'agrément; ~ *boat* bateau *m* de plaisance; *at* ~ à volonté *f*; *give s.o.* ~ faire plaisir à q.; *take (a)* ~ éprouver du plaisir (à *inf.*, *in gér.*) prendre (du) plaisir (à qch. *in s.th.*); **2.** *v/i.* prendre plaisir (à *inf.*, *in gér.*); *v/t.* † faire plaisir à; **'~·ground** jardin *m* ou parc *m* d'agrément.

pleat [pli:t] **1.** pli *m*; *unpressed* ~*s pl.* plis *m/pl.* non repassés; **2.** plisser.

ple·be·ian [pli'bi:ən] **1.** du peuple; plébéien(ne *f*); **2.** plébéien(ne *f*) *m*.

pleb·i·scite ['plebisit] plébiscite *m*.

pledge [pledʒ] **1.** gage *m*, nantissement *m*; promesse *f*, vœu *m*; toast *m*; *put in* ~ engager; *take out of* ~ dégager; **2.** engager, mettre en gage; porter un toast à (*q.*); *he* ~*d himself* il promit, il engagea sa parole; **pledg·'ee** gagiste *m*; **'pledg·er** gageur *m*.

Ple·iad *ou pl.* **Ple·ia·des** ['plaiəd (-i:z)] Pléiade *f*.

ple·na·ry ['pli:nəri] complet (-ète *f*), entier (-ère *f*); plénier (-ère *f*).

plen·i·po·ten·ti·a·ry [plenipə'tenʃəri] plénipotentiaire (*a. su./m*).

plen·i·tude ['plenitju:d] plénitude *f*.

plen·te·ous □ *poét.* ['plentjəs] abondant; riche (en, *in*); **'plen·te·ous·ness** abondance *f*.

plen·ti·ful □ ['plentiful] abondant.

plen·ty ['plenti] **1.** abondance *f*; ~ *of* beaucoup de; en abondance; assez de; *horn of* ~ corne *f* d'abondance; **2.** F beaucoup de; *Am.* F très.

ple·o·nasm ['pli:ənæzm] pléonasme *m*.

pleth·o·ra ['pleθərə] pléthore *f*; *fig.* surabondance *f*; **ple·thor·ic** [ple'θɔrik] (~*ally*) pléthorique.

pleu·ri·sy ['pluərisi] pleurésie *f*.

pli·a·bil·i·ty [plaiə'biliti] souplesse *f*.

pli·a·ble □ ['plaiəbl] pliant; souple (*a. fig.*); *fig.* docile.

pli·an·cy ['plaiənsi] souplesse *f*.

pli·ant □ ['plaiənt] *see pliable*.

pli·ers ['plaiəz] *pl.*: (*a pair of*) ~ (une) pince *f*, (des) tenailles *f/pl.*

plight¹ [plait] **1.** engager (*sa foi, sa parole*); **2.** *poét.* engagement *m*.

plight² [~] condition *f*, état *m*.

plim·soll ['plimsəl] (chaussure *f* de) tennis *m*.

plinth △ [plinθ] socle *m*.

plod [plɔd] (*a.* ~ *along, on*) marcher lourdement *ou* péniblement; **'plod·ding** □ persévérant; lourd, pesant (*pas*).

plonk F [plɔŋk] vin *m* ordinaire, F pinard *m*.

plop [plɔp] **1.** flac (*a. su./m*); **2.** faire flac; tomber en faisant flac *ou* pouf.

plot¹ [plɔt] (parcelle *f ou* lot *m* de) terrain *m*.

plot² [~] **1.** complot *m*, conspiration *f*; action *f*, intrigue *f*, *roman etc.*: plan *m*; **2.** *v/t.* (*a.* ~ *down*) tracer; relever, dresser le plan de (*un terrain, un diagramme, etc.*); *péj.* combiner, comploter; *v/i.* comploter, conspirer; **'plot·ter** traceur *m*; conspirateur (-trice *f*) *m*.

plough [plau] **1.** charrue *f*; ⊕ guimbarde *f*; *astr. the* ♎ le Chariot; *univ. sl.* retoquage *m*; **2.** labourer; creuser (*un sillon*); *fig.* sillonner; *univ. sl. be* ~*ed* être refusé *ou* collé; **'~·man** laboureur *m*; **'~·share** soc *m* de charrue; **'~·tail** mancheron *m* de charrue.

plov·er ['plʌvə] *orn.* pluvier *m*; *a. cuis.* F vanneau *m*.

plow *surt. Am.* [plau] *see plough*.

ploy F [plɔi] stratagème *m*, truc *m*.

pluck [plʌk] **1.** arrachage *m*; *poulet etc.*: plumage *m*; *guitare*: pincement *m*; F courage *m*, cran *m*; **2.** arracher; plumer (*un poulet etc., a.*

fig.); épiler (*les sourcils*); détacher (de, *from*); pincer (*la guitare*); *univ. sl.* refuser, recaler; ~ *at* tirer; ~ *up courage* s'armer de courage.

pluck·y □ ['plʌki] courageux (-euse *f*); F crâne.

plug [plʌg] **1.** tampon *m* (⚙️ d'ouate); bouchon *m*; ⚡ fiche *f*; ⚡ prise *f*; *tabac*: chique *f*; *W.-C.*: chasse *f* d'eau; *W.-C.*: chaînette *f*; bouche *f* d'incendie; *radio Am.* publicité *f*; réclame *f*; *Am.* vieux cheval *m*; ~ *socket* douille *f*; prise *f*; **2.** *v/t.* boucher; tamponner; plomber (*une dent*); *sl.* flanquer un coup à; *Am.* F faire de la publicité en faveur de; ⚡ ~ *in* brancher; *v/i. sl.* ~ *away* turbiner (= *travailler dur*); **'plug-'ug·ly** *Am. sl.* pugiliste *m*; voyou *m*.

plum [plʌm] prune *f*; † raisin *m* sec; *fig.* morceau *m* de choix; *fig. la meilleure situation f*; † £ 100.000.

plum·age ['plu:midʒ] plumage *m*.

plumb [plʌm] **1.** d'aplomb; vertical (-aux *m/pl.*); droit; **2.** plomb *m*; ⚓ sonde *f*; aplomb *m*; **3.** *v/t.* sonder (*la mer*); plomber (*la canalisation*); vérifier l'aplomb de; *fig.* sonder; F installer les tuyaux dans (*une maison*); *v/i.* F être plombier; **plum·ba·go** [~'beigou] plombagine *f*; **plumb·er** ['~mə] plombier *m*; **plum·bic** ['~mbik] 🜍 plombique *f*; **plumb·ing** ['~miŋ] plomberie *f*; tuyauterie *f*; **'plumb-line** ⊕ fil *m* à plomb; ⚓ ligne *f* de sonde; **'plumb-rule** niveau *m* vertical.

plume [plu:m] **1.** panache *m*; *poét.* plume *f*; **2.** orner (*qch.*) de plumes; ~ *itself* se lisser les plumes (*oiseau*); ~ *o.s.* on se glorifier de.

plum·met ['plʌmit] plomb *m*; ⚓ sonde *f*.

plum·my F ['plʌmi] délicieux (-euse *f*); excellent.

plu·mose 🜍, *zo.* ['plu:mous] plumeux (-euse *f*).

plump¹ [plʌmp] **1.** rebondi, dodu, grassouillet(te *f*); **2.** rendre *ou* devenir dodu; engraisser.

plump² [~] **1.** *v/i.* tomber lourdement; *v/t.* flanquer; *parl.* donner tous ses votes (à, *for*); **2.** *su.* plouf *m*; **3.** F *adv.* plouf; avec un floc; carrément; **4.** F *adj.* □ catégorique.

plump·er ['plʌmpə] *sl.* gros men-

songe *m*; *parl.* vote *m* donné à un seul candidat; électeur *m* qui donne tous ses votes à un seul candidat.

plump·ness ['plʌmpnis] rondeur *f* (*a.* F *d'une réponse*), embonpoint *m*.

plum-pud·ding [plʌm'pudiŋ] plum-pudding *m*.

plum·y ['plu:mi] plumeux (-euse *f*); empanaché (*casque*).

plun·der ['plʌndə] **1.** pillage *m* (*d'une ville*); butin *m*; **2.** piller, dépouiller; **'plun·der·er** pillard *m*; pilleur *m*.

plunge [plʌndʒ] **1.** plongeon *m*; *cheval etc.*: course *f* précipitée; F risque *m*; F *make* (*ou* take) *the* ~ sauter le pas; **2.** *v/t.* plonger, immerger (dans, *in*[*to*]); *v/i.* plonger, s'enfoncer (dans, *into*); ruer (*cheval*); ⚓ tanguer; risquer de grosses sommes (*à la Bourse*).

plung·er ['plʌndʒə] plongeur *m*; *sl.* risque-tout *m/inv.*

plunk [plʌŋk] *v/t.* pincer (*la guitare etc.*); *v/i.* tomber raide; *Am.* F lancer, tirer (*sur, at*).

plu·per·fect *gramm.* ['plu:'pə:fikt] plus-que-parfait *m.*

plu·ral *gramm.* ['pluərəl] (*a.* ~ *number*) pluriel *m*; *in the* ~ au pluriel; **plu·ral·i·ty** [~'ræliti] pluralité *f*; cumul *m*; ~ *of wives* polygamie *f*.

plus [plʌs] **1.** *prp.* plus; **2.** *adj.* positif (-ive *f*); **3.** *su.* plus *m*; **~-fours** F ['~'fɔ:z] *pl.* culotte *f* de golf.

plush [plʌʃ] peluche *f*.

plush·y ['plʌʃi] pelucheux (-euse *f*).

plu·toc·ra·cy [plu:'tɔkrəsi] ploutocratie *f*; **plu·to·crat** ['~təkræt] ploutocrate *m*. [plutonium *m*.]

plu·to·ni·um 🜍 [plu:'touniəm]

plu·vi·al ['plu:viəl], **'plu·vi·ous** pluvial (-aux *m/pl.*); **plu·vi·om·e·ter** [~'ɔmitə] pluviomètre *m*.

ply [plai] **1.** pli *m* (*a. fig.*); *three-*~ laine *f* trois fils; *bois*: contre-plaqué *m* à trois épaisseurs; **2.** *v/t.* manier vigoureusement; exercer (*un métier*); faire courir (*l'aiguille*); presser (*q. de questions*); ~ *with drink* faire boire (*q.*) sans arrêt; *v/i.* faire le service; ~ *for hire* prendre des voyageurs.

ply-wood ['plaiwud] contre-plaqué *m.*

pneu·mat·ic [nju'mætik] **1.** (~*ally*) pneumatique; ~ *hammer* frappeur *m* pneumatique; ~ *post* tube *m* pneumatique; ~ *tire* = 2. pneu *m*.

pneu·mo·ni·a ☈ [nju'mounjə] pneumonie *f*.

poach[1] [poutʃ] braconner.

poach[2] [~] (*a.* ~ *up*) labourer (*la terre*).

poach[3] [~]: ~*ed eggs* œufs *m/pl.* pochés.

poach·er ['poutʃə] braconnier *m*.

PO Box [pi:'ou'bɔks] boîte *f* postale.

po·chette [po'ʃet] pochette *f*.

pock ☈ [pɔk] pustule *f*.

pock·et ['pɔkit] 1. poche *f* (*a. géol.*); *laine, houblon, a. géol. minerai:* sac *m*; ☈ trou *m* d'air; 2. mettre dans sa poche (*a. orgueil*); *péj.* chiper; refouler (*la colère*); avaler (*un affront*); *Am. pol.* ne pas signer, mettre un veto à (*une loi*); 3. de poche; ~ *calculator* calculatrice *f* de poche; ~ *edition* édition *f* de poche; ~ *lighter* briquet *m*; ~ *lamp* torche *f*; '~**·book** carnet *m* de poche, calepin *m*; *Am.* sac *m* à main; *Am.* livre *m* de poche; *surt. Am.* porte-billets *m/inv.*

pod [pɔd] 1. ♀ cosse *f*; *pois:* écale *f*; *sl.* ventre *m*; 2. *v/t.* écosser, écaler; *v/i.* former des cosses.

po·dag·ra ☈ [pə'dægrə] podagre *f*, goutte *f*.

podg·y F ['pɔdʒi] boulot(te *f*); rondelet(te *f*).

po·di·um ['poudiəm] podium *m*.

po·em ['pouim] poème *m*.

po·e·sy ['pouizi] poésie *f*.

po·et ['pouit] poète *m*; **po·et·as·ter** [~'tæstə] rimailleur *m*; '**po·et·ess** femme *f* poète, poétesse *f*; **po·et·ic, po·et·i·cal** [pou'etik(l)] poétique; **po'et·ics** *sg.* art *m* poétique; **po·et·ize** ['~itaiz] *v/i.* faire des vers; *v/t.* poétiser; '**po·et·ry** poésie *f*; vers *m/pl.*

poign·an·cy ['poinənsi] piquant *m*; âpreté *f*; *fig.* violence *f*; acuité *f*; '**poign·ant** □ piquant, âpre; *fig.* vif (vive *f*).

point [point] 1. point *m* (*a.* ♈, ♃, *astr., sp., typ., cartes, dés*); détail *m* (*a. fig.*); question *f* (*a. gramm.*); ⊕, *couteau, barbe, géog.* pointe *f*; extrémité *f*; aire *f* (*de vent*); *plume à écrire:* bec *m*; piquant *m* (*d'une plaisanterie*); *gramm.* point *m* (*de ponctuation*); ♃ (*a. decimal* ~) virgule *f*; *phys. thermomètre:* division *f*; *chien:* arrêt *m*; ⚡ contact *m*; ⚡ prise

f de courant; ⚓ quart *m*; *fig.* cas *m* (*de conscience*), point *m* (*d'honneur*); *fig.* caractère *m*; *see* ~*-lace*; ☈ ~*s pl.* aiguillage *m*; ~*s pl. chasse:* cors *m/pl.* (*cerf*); ~ *of view* point *m* de vue; *the* ~ *is that* ce dont il s'agit c'est que; *there is no* ~ *in* (*gér.*) il est inutile de (*inf.*); *make a* ~ faire ressortir un argument; *make a* ~ *of* ne pas manquer de (*inf.*); tenir à; *make the* ~ *that* faire remarquer que; *stretch a* ~ faire une concession; *in* ~ *of* sous le rapport de; *in* ~ *of fact* au *ou* en fait; *off* (*ou beyond*) *the* ~ hors de propos; *differ on many* ~*s* ne pas être d'accord sur des détails; *be on the* ~ *of* (*gér.*) être sur le point de (*inf.*); *win on* ~*s* gagner aux points; *to the* ~ à propos, bien dit; *stick to the* ~ ne pas s'écarter de la question; 2. *v/t.* marquer de points; aiguiser; *opt.* braquer (*une jumelle etc.*); △ jointoyer; (*souv.* ~ *out*) indiquer; inculquer (*la morale*); ~ *at* braquer (*une arme*) sur; *v/i. chasse:* tomber en arrêt; ~ *at* montrer du doigt; ~ *to* faire ressortir; marquer (*l'heure*); signaler; '~-**'blank** 1. *adj.* direct; net(te *f*) (*refus*); de but en blanc (*question*); 2. *adv.* à bout portant; *fig.* carrément; ~ *shot* coup *m* de feu à bout portant; '~-**du·ty** service *m* à poste fixe; *policeman on* ~ agent-vigie (*pl.* agents-vigies) *m*; '**point·ed** □ pointu, à pointe; *fig.* mordant, peu voilé; '**point·ed·ness** mordant *m*; caractère *m* peu voilé; '**point·er** aiguille *f*, index *m*; baguette *f*; *chasse:* chien *m* d'arrêt; F tuyau *m*; '**point·'lace** guipure *f*; '**point·less** émoussé; *fig.* sans sel; *fig.* inutile; '**points·man** ☈ aiguilleur *m*; '**point-to-'point race** course *f* au clocher.

poise [poiz] 1. équilibre *m*, aplomb *m*; port *m* (*du corps etc.*); 2. *v/t.* équilibrer, balancer; tenir (*la tête etc.*); *v/i.* (*a. be* ~*d*) être en équilibre.

poi·son ['poizn] 1. poison *m*; ~*-pen letter* lettre *f* anonyme venimeuse; 2. empoisonner; *fig.* corrompre; '**poi·son·er** empoisonneur (-euse *f*) *m*; '**poi·son·ous** □ toxique; vénimeux (-euse *f*) (*animal*); vénéneux (-euse *f*) (*plante*); *fig.* pernicieux (-euse *f*); F empoisonnant.

poke [pouk] 1. poussée *f*; coup *m* de

coude; **2.** *v/t.* pousser du coude *etc.*; (*a.* ~ **up**) attiser (*le feu*); fourrer (*a. fig.* son nez); passer, avancer (*la tête*); ~ *fun at* se moquer de; *v/i.* (*a.* ~ **about**) fouiller; fourrer (dans, *in*[to]).

pok·er¹ ['poukǝ] tisonnier *m.*

po·ker² [~] *cartes*: poker *m*; *fig.* ~-*face* visage *m* impassible.

pok·er-work ['poukǝwǝ:k] pyrogravure *f.*

pok·y ['pouki] misérable; mesquin.

po·lar ['poulǝ] polaire; du pôle; ~ *bear* ours *m* blanc; **po·lar·i·ty** *phys.* [po'læriti] polarité *f*; **po·lar·i·za·tion** *phys.* [poulǝrai'zeiʃn] polarisation *f*; *phot.* ~ *filter* filtre *m* de polarisation; **'po·lar·ize** *phys.* (se) polariser.

Pole¹ [poul] Polonais(e *f*) *m.*

pole² [~] *géog., astr., fig.* pôle *m*; ⚡ électrode *f.*

pole³ [~] **1.** perche *f* (*a. sp.*); mât *m*; hampe *f* (*de drapeau*); *voiture*: timon *m*; *mesure*: perche *f* (5,029 *m*); **2.** pousser *ou* conduire à la perche; '~-**ax(e)** ⚔ hache *f* d'armes; ⚓ hache *f* d'abordage; assommoir *m*; '~**cat** *zo.* putois *m*; *Am.* putois *m* d'Amérique; '~-**jump,** '~-**vault** saut *m* à la perche.

po·lem·ic [po'lemik] **1.** (*a.* **po'lem·i·cal** □) polémique; **2.** polémique *f*; **po'lem·ics** *sg.* polémique *f.*

pole-star ['poulsta:] (étoile *f*) polaire *f*; *fig.* point *m* de mire.

po·lice [pǝ'li:s] **1.** police *f*; *two* ~ deux agents *m/pl.* (de police); ~ *force* la police, *les* forces *f/pl.* de l'ordre; ~ *record* casier *m* judiciaire; **2.** policer; **po'lice·man** agent *m* de police; gardien *m* de la paix; **po'lice-of·fice** préfecture *f* de police; **po'lice-sta·tion** poste *m* de police; **po'lice-sur·veil·lance** surveillance *f* de police; **po'lice-trap** zone *f* de contrôle de vitesse.

pol·i·cy¹ ['polisi] politique *f*; diplomatique *f.*

pol·i·cy² [~] police *f*; *Am.* loterie *f* clandestine.

po·li·o(·my·e·li·tis) ['poliou(maiǝ-'laitis)] poliomyélite *f.*

Pol·ish¹ ['pouliʃ] polonais.

pol·ish² ['poliʃ] **1.** poli *m*; brillant *m*; *fig.* vernis *m*; *floor* ~ encaustique *f*; *boot* ~ cirage *m*; **2.** *v/t.* polir (*a. fig.*); brunir (*le métal*); cirer; F ~ *off* expé-

dier; ~ *up* polir; *v/i.* prendre bien le poli, la cire *etc.*; **'pol·ish·ing 1.** polissage *m*; cirage *m*; **2.** à polir.

po·lite □ [pǝ'lait] poli, courtois, civil; cultivé; **po'lite·ness** politesse *f.*

po·lit·ic □ ['politik] politique; adroit; *body* ~ corps *m* politique; **po·lit·i·cal** □ [pǝ'litikl] politique; ~ *science* sciences *f/pl.* politiques; ~ *scientist* politologue *mf*; **pol·i·ti·cian** [poli'tiʃn] homme *m* politique; *péj.* politicien *m*; **pol·i·tics** ['politiks] *pl., souv. sg.* politique *f.*

pol·i·ty ['politi] administration *f* politique; état *m*; régime *m.*

pol·ka-dot *Am. tex.* ['polkǝ'dot] pois *m.*

poll¹ [poul] **1.** *prov. ou co.* tête *f*; sommet *m*, haut *m*; vote *m* (par bulletins); scrutin *m*; *go to the* ~*s* prendre part au vote; se rendre aux urnes; **2.** *v/t.* † tondre; étêter (*un arbre*); réunir (*tant de voix*); *v/i.* voter (pour, *for*).

poll² [pol] perroquet *m*; *npr.* Tacquot *m.*

pol·lard ['polǝd] arbre *m* étêté; animal *m* sans cornes; *farine*: repasse *f.*

poll-book ['poulbuk] liste *f* électorale.

pol·len ⚘ ['polin] pollen *m.*

poll·ing...: '~-**booth** bureau *m* de scrutin; isoloir *m*; '~-**dis·trict** section *f* de vote; '~-**place,** '~-**sta·tion** poste *m* (de section de vote).

poll·ster ['poulstǝ] sondeur (-euse *f*) *m.*

poll-tax ['poultæks] capitation *f.*

pol·lut·ant [pǝ'lu:tǝnt] agent *m* de pollution; **pol·lute** [pǝ'lu:t] polluer; souiller; corrompre (*a. fig.*); profaner; **pol'lu·tion** pollution *f*; profanation *f.*

po·lo *sp.* ['poulou] polo *m*; ~ **neck** (chandail *m* à) col *m* roulé.

po·lo·ny [pǝ'louni] cervelas *m.*

pol·troon [pol'tru:n] poltron *m*; **pol'troon·er·y** poltronnerie *f.*

po·lyg·a·my [po'ligǝmi] polygamie *f*; **pol·y·glot** ['poliglot] polyglotte (*a. su./mf*); **pol·y·gon** ['~gǝn] polygone *m*; **po·lyg·o·nal** [po'ligǝnl] polygonal (-aux *m/pl.*); **pol·y·phon·ic** ♪ [~'fonik] polyphonique; **pol·yp** *zo.* ['~ip], **pol·y·pus** ⚕ ['~pǝs], *pl.* -**pi** [~pai] polype *m*; **pol·y·sty·rene** [poli'staiǝri:n] polystyrène *m*; **pol-**

y·syl·lab·ic ['pɔlisi'læbik] polysyl-lab(iqu)e; **pol·y·syl·la·ble** ['⌣silabl] polysyllabe *m*; **pol·y·tech·nic** [⌣'teknik] **1.** polytechnique; **2.** école *f* des arts et métiers; **pol·y·the·ism** ['⌣θiizm] polythéisme *m*; **pol·y·thene** ['⌣θi:n] polyéthylène *m*; ⌣ *bag* sac *m* en plastique.

po·made [pə'mɑ:d], **po·ma·tum** [pə'meitəm] pommade *f*.

pome·gran·ate ♀ ['pɔmgrænit] grenade *f*; *arbre:* grenadier *m*.

Pom·er·a·nian [pɔmə'reinjən] poméranien(ne *f*); ⌣ *(dog)* loulou *m* de Poméranie.

pom·mel ['pʌml] **1.** *épée, selle:* pommeau *m*; **2.** bourrer *(q.)* de coups.

pomp [pɔmp] pompe *f*, apparat *m*.

pom-pom ['pɔmpɔm] canon-revol-ver *(pl.* canons-revolvers) *m*.

pom·pos·i·ty [pɔm'pɔsiti] emphase *f*, suffisance *f*; **'pomp·ous** □ pompeux (-euse *f*); suffisant *(personne)*.

ponce *Brit. sl.* [pɔns] souteneur *m*, maquereau *m*; pédé *m*, tapette *f*.

pond [pɔnd] étang *m*; mare *f*; réservoir *m*; **'pond·age** accumulation *f* de l'eau; capacité *f*.

pon·der ['pɔndə] méditer (sur *on, over)*; **pon·der·a·bil·i·ty** [⌣rə'biliti] pondérabilité *f*; **'pon·der·a·ble** pondérable; **pon·der·os·i·ty** [⌣'rɔsiti] lourdeur *f (a. de style); fig.* importance *f*; **'pon·der·ous** □ lourd; massif (-ive *f*); laborieux (-euse *f*); *fig.* important; **'pon·der·ous·ness** *see* ponderosity.

pone *Am.* [poun] pain *m* de maïs.

pong *Brit. sl.* [pɔŋ] **1.** puanteur *f*; **2.** puer.

pon·iard ['pɔnjəd] **1.** poignard *m*; **2.** poignarder.

pon·tiff ['pɔntif] pontife *m*; prélat *m*; **pon·tif·i·cal** pontifical (-aux *m/pl.*); épiscopal (-aux *m/pl.*); **pon·tif·i·cate 1.** [⌣kit] pontificat *m*; **2.** [⌣keit] pontifier.

pon·toon ✗ [pɔn'tu:n] ponton *m*; **pon·toon-bridge** pont *m* de bateaux.

po·ny ['pouni] poney *m*; F *fig.* baudet *m; Am.* F traduction *f; sl.* 25 livres sterling; *Am.* F petit verre *m* d'alcool; *Am. attr.* petit; '⌣-'en·gine 🚂 locomotive *f* de manœuvre.

pooch *Am. sl.* [pu:tʃ] cabot *m*, chien *m*.

poo·dle ['pu:dl] caniche *mf*.

poof *Brit. sl.* [pu:f] tapette *f*, tante *f*.

pooh [pu:] bah!; peuh!

pooh-pooh [pu:'pu:] ridiculiser; faire peu de cas de *(qch.)*; faire fi de *(conseils etc.)*.

pool¹ [pu:l] flaque *f* d'eau; mare *f*; fontaine *f*.

pool² [⌣] **1.** cagnotte *f*; poule *f (a. billard);* concours *m* de pronostics; *(sorte de)* jeu *m* de billard; ✝ syndicat *m*; fonds *m/pl.* communs; *Brit.* the ⌣s les pronostics *m/pl.* (sur les matchs de football); *Am.* ⌣ *room* salle *f* de billard; *Am.* ⌣ *table* billard *m*; **2.** mettre en commun; ✝ mettre en syndicat.

poop ⚓ [pu:p] **1.** poupe *f*; dunette *f*; **2.** balayer la poupe de; embarquer par l'arrière; *Am.* ⌣ed exténué.

poor □ [puə] *usu.* pauvre; malheureux (-euse *f*); médiocre; de piètre qualité; maigre *(sol);* ⌣ *me!* pauvre de moi!; *make but a* ⌣ *shift's* accommoder mal de *(qch.); a* ⌣ *dinner* un mauvais dîner; ⌣ *health* santé *f* débile; '⌣-box tronc *m* pour les pauvres; '⌣-house asile *m* de pauvres; '⌣-law assistance *f* judiciaire; **'poor·ly 1.** *adj. prédicatif* souffrant; **2.** *adv.* pauvrement; **'poor·ness** pauvreté *f*, insuffisance *f*; infériorité *f*; **'poor-rate** taxe *f* des pauvres; **poor-'spir·it·ed** pusillanime.

pop¹ [pɔp] **1.** bruit *m* sec; F boisson *f* pétillante; limonade *f* gazeuse; **2.** *v/t.* crever; faire sauter; F mettre en gage; *Am.* faire éclater *(le maïs);* F fourrer vite; F ⌣ *the question* faire la demande en mariage; *v/i.* éclater, sauter; crever; ⌣ *in* entrer pour un instant *(chez q.);* ⌣ *up* se lever vivement; apparaître; **3.** inattendu; **4.** crac!; pan!

pop² F [⌣] concert *m* populaire; chanson *f* populaire.

pop³ *Am.* F [⌣] papa *m*; pépère *m*, pépé *m*.

pop·corn *usu. Am.* ['pɔpkɔ:n] maïs *m* grillé et éclaté.

pope [poup] pape *m*; Saint-Père *m*; **pope·dom** ['⌣dəm] papauté *f*; **pop·er·y** *péj.* ['⌣əri] papisme *m*.

pop-eyed ['pɔpaid] aux yeux en boules de loto.

pop·gun ['pɔpgʌn] pétoire *f*.

pop·in·jay *fig.* ['pɔpindʒei] fat *m*.

pop·ish □ *péj.* ['poupiʃ] papiste.

pop·lar ♀ ['pɔplə] peuplier *m*.

pop·lin *tex.* ['pɔplin] popeline *f*.

pop·per *surt. Brt.* ['pɔpə] bouton-pression *m* (*pl.* boutons-pression).

pop·pet ['pɔpit] ⚓ colombier *m*; ⊕ poupée *f*; *see* puppet.

pop·py ♀ ['pɔpi] pavot *m*; '**~·cock** *Am.* F fadaises *f/pl.*, bêtises *f/pl.*

pop·u·lace ['pɔpjuləs] peuple *m*; *péj.* populace *f*.

pop·u·lar □ ['pɔpjulə] populaire; du peuple; goûté du public; ♀ à la portée de tous; **pop·u·lar·i·ty** [~'læriti] popularité *f*; **pop·u·lar·ize** ['~ləraiz] populariser, vulgariser; rendre populaire; '**pop·u·lar·ly** populairement; communément.

pop·u·late ['pɔpjuleit] peupler; **pop·u·la·tion** population *f*; **~ explo·sion** explosion *f* démographique.

pop·u·lous □ ['pɔpjuləs] très peuplé; '**pop·u·lous·ness** densité *f* de (la) population.

por·ce·lain ['pɔːslin] porcelaine *f*.

porch [pɔːtʃ] porche *m*; portique *m*; *Am.* véranda *f*.

por·cu·pine *zo.* ['pɔːkjupain] porc-épic (*pl.* porcs-épics) *m*.

pore¹ [pɔː] pore *m*.

pore² [~] être plongé (dans *over*, *on*), méditer (qch. *over*, *on s.th.*).

pork [pɔːk] porc *m*; *Am.* F **~ barrel** fonds *m/pl.* publics; trésor *m* public; **~ butcher** charcutier *m*; **~ chop** côtelette *f* de porc; '**pork·er** goret *m*; porc *m*; '**pork·y 1.** F gras(se *f*), obèse; **2.** *Am.* F *see* porcupine.

por·nog·ra·phy [pɔː'nɔgrəfi] pornographie *f*.

po·ros·i·ty [pɔː'rɔsiti], **po·rous·ness** ['pɔːrəsnis] porosité *f*.

po·rous □ ['pɔːrəs] poreux (-euse *f*).

por·phy·ry *min.* ['pɔːfiri] porphyre *m*.

por·poise *zo.* ['pɔːpəs] marsouin *m*; phocène *f*.

por·ridge ['pɔridʒ] bouillie *f* d'avoine; **por·rin·ger** ['pɔrindʒə] écuelle *f*.

port¹ [pɔːt] port *m*; **~ of call** port d'escale; **~ of destination** port *m* de destination; **~ of transhipment** port *m* de transbordement.

port² ⚓ [~] sabord *m*.

port³ [~] **1.** ✕ présenter (*les armes*); **2.** maintien *m*, port *m*.

port⁴ ⚓ [~] **1.** côté *m*: bâbord *m*; **2.** *v/t.* mettre à bâbord; *v/i.* venir sur bâbord.

port⁵ [~] porto *m*.

port·a·ble ['pɔːtəbl] portatif (-ive *f*); mobile; **~ gramophone** (typewriter, radio) phonographe *m* (machine *f* à écrire, poste *m*) transportable; **~ railway** chemin *m* de fer à voie démontable.

por·tage ['pɔːtidʒ] portage *m*; *see* porterage.

por·tal ['pɔːtl] portail *m*; portique *m*; *fig.* (porte *f* d')entrée *f*; '**por·tal-to-'por·tal pay** paye *f* pour le temps d'aller de la porte (*de l'usine etc.*) à son travail et retour.

port·cul·lis ✕ *hist.* [pɔːt'kʌlis] herse *f*.

por·tend [pɔː'tend] présager.

por·tent ['pɔːtent] présage *m* de malheur; prodige *m*; **por'ten·tous** □ sinistre; de mauvais augure; prodigieux (-euse *f*); *co.* lugubre.

por·ter¹ ['pɔːtə] concierge *m*.

por·ter² [~] portefaix *m*; *hôtel:* garçon *m*; 🚂 porteur *m*; bière *f* brune; **por·ter·age** ['~ridʒ] (prix *m* de) transport *m*; factage *m*; '**por·ter-house** taverne *f*; *Am.* **~ steak** aloyau *m*, châteaubriant *m*.

port·fire ['pɔːtfaiə] boutefeu *m*; étoupille *f*.

port·fo·li·o [pɔːt'fouljou] serviette *f*; chemise *f* (*de carton*); portefeuille *m* (*d'un ministre*).

port·hole ⚓ ['pɔːthoul] sabord *m*.

por·ti·co △ ['pɔːtikou] portique *m*.

por·tion ['pɔːʃn] **1.** part *f*, partie *f*; portion *f*, *viande:* ration *f*; *gâteau:* quartier *m*; *terre:* lot *m*; *mariage:* dot *f*; *fig.* sort *m*; **2.** partager, répartir; doter; '**por·tion·less** sans dot.

port·li·ness ['pɔːtlinis] prestance *f*; embonpoint *m*; '**port·ly** majestueux (-euse *f*); corpulent.

port·man·teau [pɔːt'mæntou] valise *f*; *gramm.* **~ word** mot *m* fantaisiste (*fait de mots télescopés*).

por·trait ['pɔːtrit] portrait *m*; '**por·trait·ist** portraitiste *mf*; **por·trai·ture** ['~tʃə] portrait *m*; l'art *m* du portrait; *fig.* description *f*.

por·tray [pɔː'trei] (dé)peindre; décrire; **por'tray·al** peinture *f*, représentation *f*.

Por·tu·guese [pɔːtju'giːz] **1.** portugais; **2.** *ling.* portugais *m*; Portugais (-e *f*) *m*.

pose [pouz] **1.** pose *f*; **2.** *v/i.* se

poser; se faire passer (pour, *as*); *v/t.* poser (*une question*); énoncer; **'pos·er** question *f* embarrassante; F colle *f*.

posh *sl.* [pɔʃ] chic *inv. en genre*, chouette.

po·si·tion [pə'ziʃn] position *f* (*a. fig.*, ✕, *posture*); situation *f*; place *f*; emploi *m*; état *m*; *fig.* attitude *f*; *fig.* point *m* de vue; ✧ lieu *m*, point *m*; ⚓ poste *m*; ⁓ *light* feu *m* de position; *be in a* ⁓ *to do* être à même de faire.

pos·i·tive ['pɔzətiv] **1.** □ positif (-ive *f*); formel(le *f*); vrai; sûr, certain, convaincu; A⁀, ⚡, *phls.*, *phys.*, *phot.* positif (-ive *f*); **2.** positif *m*; **'pos·i·tive·ness** certitude *f*; ton *m* décisif.

pos·se ['pɔsi] troupe *f*, foule *f*; ⁓ **co·mi·ta·tus** [⁓ kɔmi'teitəs] détachement *m* de police.

pos·sess [pə'zes] avoir, posséder (*fig.* de, *with*); *fig.* pénétrer (de, *with*); ⁓*ed* possédé; *be* ⁓*ed of* posséder; ⁓ *o.s.* s'emparer de (*qch.*); **pos·ses·sion** [pə'zeʃn] possession *f* (*a. fig.*); jouissance *f* (de, *of*); colonie *f*; *in* ⁓ *of* en possession de; **pos·ses·sive** *gramm.* [pə'zesiv] **1.** □ possessif (-ive *f*); ⁓ *case* (cas *m*) possessif *m*; **2.** possessif *m*; **pos·'ses·sor** possesseur *m*; **pos'ses·so·ry** possessoire.

pos·set ['pɔsit] posset *m*.

pos·si·bil·i·ty [pɔsə'biliti] possibilité *f*; **'pos·si·ble 1.** possible; **2.** *sp.* maximum *m*; **'pos·si·bly** peut-être; *if I* ⁓ *can* s'il y a moyen; *how can I* ⁓ *do it?* comment pourrais-je le faire?; *I cannot* ⁓ *do it* il m'est impossible de le faire.

pos·sum F ['pɔsəm] *see* opossum.

post¹ [poust] **1.** poteau *m*; pieu *m*; **2.** (*usu.* ⁓ *up*) afficher, placarder.

post² [⁓] **1.** ✕ *sentinelle f.* : poste *m*, garnison *f*; † station *f* (de commerce); situation *f*, poste *m*; † malle-poste (*pl.* malles-poste) *f*; *poste*: courrier *m*, poste *f*; papier *m* écu; ✕ *at one's* ⁓ à son poste; *by* (*the*) ⁓ par la poste; ⁓ *last* ⁓ sonnerie *f* aux morts; retraite *f*; *Am.* ⁓ *exchange* magasin *m*, cantine *f*; **2.** *v/t.* ✕ poster, mettre en faction (*une sentinelle*); ⚓ nommer (*q. capitaine*); † (*souv.* ⁓ *up*) mettre au courant (*le grand-livre*); mettre à la poste; envoyer par la poste; F (*souv.* ⁓ *up ou keep s.o.* ⁓*ed*) mettre (*q.*) au courant, documenter (*q.*); *well* ⁓*ed* bien renseigné; † ⁓ *an entry* passer écriture d'un article; *v/i.* F aller un train de poste.

post·age ['poustidʒ] port *m*, affranchissement *m*; ... ⁓ ... pour frais d'envoi; ⁓ *due* surtaxe *f* postale; ⁓ **stamp** timbre-poste (*pl.* timbres-poste) *m*.

post·al □ ['poustəl] postal (-aux *m/pl.*); *Am.* ⁓ (*card*) carte *f* postale; ⁓ *cheque* chèque *m* postal; ⁓ *order* mandat-poste (*pl.* mandats-poste) *m*, mandat *m* postal; ♀ *Union* Union *f* postale.

post... : **'⁓·card** carte *f* postale; **'⁓·code** code *m* postal.

post·date ['poust'deit] postdater.

post·er ['poustə] affiche *f*; placard *m*.

pos·te·ri·or F [pɔs'tiəriə] **1.** □ postérieur (à, *to*); derrière *f*; **2.** (*a.* ⁓*s pl.*) postérieur *m*, derrière *m*.

pos·ter·i·ty [pɔs'teriti] postérité *f*.

pos·tern ['poustəːn] porte *f* de derrière.

post-free ['poust'friː] franco *inv.*

post-grad·u·ate ['poust'grædjuit] **1.** postscolaire; **2.** candidat *m* à un diplôme supérieur (*doctorat etc.*).

post-haste ['poust'heist] en toute hâte.

post·hu·mous □ ['pɔstjuməs] posthume.

pos·til·(l)ion [pɔs'tiljən] postillon *m*.

post... : **'⁓·man** facteur *m*; **'⁓·mark 1.** cachet *m* de la poste; timbre *m* (d'oblitération); **2.** timbrer; **'⁓·mas·ter** receveur *m* des postes; ♀ *General* ministre *m* des Postes et Télécommunications.

post·me·rid·i·an ['poustmə'ridiən] de l'après-midi, du soir; **post-mor·tem** ['⁓'mɔːtəm] **1.** après décès; **2.** (*a.* ⁓ *examination*) autopsie *f*; **post-o·bit** [⁓'ɔbit] exécutoire après le décès d'un tiers.

post... : **'⁓-of·fice**, *surt.* ⁓ *of·fice* bureau *m* de poste; *Am.* (*sorte de*) jeu *m* avec embrassades; *general* ⁓ bureau *m* central; ⁓ *box* boîte *f* postale; ⁓ *clerk* employé(e *f*) *m* des postes; ⁓ *counter* (*ou window*) guichet *m*; ⁓ *order* mandat *m* postal; ⁓ *savings-bank* caisse *f* d'épargne postale; **'⁓-paid** franco *inv.*, affranchi.

post·pone [poust'poun] ajourner,

remettre, renvoyer à plus tard; **post′pone·ment** ajournement *m*; remise *f* à plus tard.

post·pran·di·al □ *co.* [poust′præn-diəl] après dîner, après le repas.

post·script [′pousskript] post-scriptum *m*/*inv.* (*abbr.* P.-S.); postface *f* (*d'un livre*).

pos·tu·lant [′pɔstjulənt] postulant (-e *f*) *m*; **pos·tu·late 1.** [′⁓lit] postulat *m*; **2.** [′⁓leit] postuler (*a. v*/*i.*); poser (*qch.*) en postulat; **pos·tu′la·tion** sollicitation *f*; *phls.* supposition *f*, postulat *m*.

pos·ture [′pɔstʃə] **1.** posture *f*, *corps:* attitude *f*; position *f*; **2.** *v*/*t.* poser; *v*/*i.* prendre une pose; se poser en.

post-war [′poust′wɔ:] d'après-guerre.

po·sy¹ [′pouzi] devise *f*.

po·sy² [⁓] bouquet *m* (de fleurs).

pot [pɔt] **1.** pot *m*; marmite *f*; *sp.* coupe *f*; F *a* ⁓ *of money* des tas *m*/*pl.* d'argent; **2.** *v*/*t.* mettre en pot (*cuis. a. des plantes*); blouser (*au billard*); abattre (*du gibier*); *v*/*i.*: ⁓ *at* lâcher un coup de fusil à (*q.*); tirer sur.

po·ta·ble [′poutəbl] potable, buvable.

pot·ash 🜍 [′pɔtæʃ] potasse *f*.

po·tas·si·um 🜍 [pə′tæsiəm] potassium *m*.

po·ta·tion [pou′teiʃn] gorgée *f*; (*usu. pl.* ⁓s) libation *f*.

po·ta·to [pə′teitou], *pl.* **po′ta·toes** [⁓z] pomme *f* de terre; ⁓ *bug* doryphore *m*; *Am.* ⁓ *chips* pl., *Brit.* ⁓ *crisps* pl. pommes *f*/*pl.* chips; ⁓ *masher* presse-purée *m*/*inv.*; ⁓ *omelette* omelette *f* parmentière; *fig.* hot ⁓ sujet *m* brûlant, affaire *f* épineuse; *cuis.* mashed ⁓s purée *f* (de pommes de terre), pommes *f*/*pl.* mousseline.

pot...: ′⁓-**bel·ly** panse *f*; ′⁓-**boil·er** littérature *f* alimentaire; besognes *f*/*pl.* alimentaires; écrivain *m* etc. qui travaille pour faire bouillir sa marmite; ′⁓-**boy** garçon *m* de cabaret.

po·ten·cy [′poutənsi] puissance *f*; force *f*; ′**po·tent** □ puissant; fort; **po·ten·tate** [′⁓teit] potentat *m*; **po·ten·tial** [pə′tenʃl] **1.** latent, virtuel (-le *f*) potentiel(le *f*) (*a. phys.*); **2.** *gramm.* (*a.* ⁓ *mood*) potentiel *m*; *phys.* (*souv.* ⁓ *function*) fonction *f* potentielle; *p.ext.* rendement *m*

maximum; **po·ten·ti·al·i·ty** [⁓ʃi′æ-liti] potentialité *f*; potentiel *m* (*militaire etc.*); *fig.* promesse *f*.

poth·er [′pɔðə] **1.** nuage *m* de fumée etc.; confusion *f*; tumulte *m*; **2.** (se) tourmenter; *v*/*i.* faire des histoires (à propos de, *about*).

pot...: ′⁓-**herb** herbe *f* potagère; ′⁓-**hole** mot. nid-de-poule (*pl.* nids-de-poule) *m*; *géol.* marmite *f* torrentielle; ′⁓-**hol·er** spéléologue *mf*; ′⁓-**hook** crémaillère *f*; ⁓s *pl.* bâtons *m*/*pl.*; ′⁓-**house** cabaret *m*, taverne *f*.

po·tion [′pouʃn] potion *f*; 🜊 dose *f*.

pot-luck [′pɔt′lʌk]: *take* ⁓ *with s.o.* manger chez q. à la fortune du pot.

pot·ter¹ [′pɔtə] s'amuser (à, *at*); s'occuper en amateur (de, *at*); flâner.

pot·ter² [⁓] potier *m*; ⁓′s wheel tour *m* de potier; disque *m*; ′**pot·ter·y** poterie *f*.

pot·ty *sl.* [′pɔti] insignifiant; simple; toqué.

pouch [pautʃ] **1.** petit sac *m*; bourse *f*; *yeux:* poche *f*; blague *f*; *zo.* poche *f* ventrale; *singe:* abajoue *f*; **2.** *v*/*t.* empocher; faire bouffer (*une robe*); avaler (*un poisson*); *v*/*i.* bouffer; **pouched** à poche; à abajoue.

poul·ter·er [′poultərə] marchand *m* de volaille.

poul·tice 🜊 [′poultis] cataplasme *m*.

poul·try [′poultri] volaille *f*.

pounce¹ [pauns] **1.** (poudre *f* de) sandaraque *f*; ponce *f*; **2.** polir à la ponce; poncer (*a. un dessin*).

pounce² [⁓] **1.** *oiseau:* serre *f*; saut *m*; **2.** *v*/*t.* (ou ⁓ *upon*) *oiseau:* s'abattre sur (*sa proie*); *v*/*i.*: *fig.* ⁓ [*up*]on se jeter sur.

pound¹ [paund] livre *f* (*abr. lb.*) (453,6 g); ⁓ (*sterling*) livre *f* (sterling) (*abr.* £).

pound² [⁓] **1.** parc *m* (à moutons etc.); fourrière *f*; **2.** mettre en fourrière.

pound³ [⁓] *v*/*t.* broyer, piler; bourrer de coups de poing; ✗ pilonner; *sl. Bourse:* faire baisser (*les prix*); *v*/*i.*: ⁓ *along* avancer d'un pas lourd; ⁓ *away* frapper *ou* cogner dur (sur, *at*).

pound·age [′paundidʒ] remise *f* ou taux *m* de tant par livre.

pound·er [′paundə] de ... livres.

pour [pɔ:] *v*/*t.* (*a.* ⁓ *out*) verser; ⁓ *out* répandre; décharger (*son cœur*); *v*/*i.*

tomber à verse (*pluie*); sortir à flots *ou* en foule.

pout [paut] **1.** moue *f*; **2.** (*a.* ~ *the lips*) faire la moue; bouder.

pov·er·ty ['pɔvəti] pauvreté *f*; pénurie *f*.

pow·der ['paudə] **1.** poudre *f*; **2.** pulvériser; poudrer (*le visage*); saupoudrer (de, with); '~-**box** boîte *f* à poudre; ~ **keg** *fig.* poudrière *f*; '~-**puff** houpette *f* (à poudre); ~ **room** toilettes *f/pl.* pour dames; '**pow·der·y** poudreux (-euse *f*); friable.

pow·er ['pauə] *m* pouvoir (*a.* ⚡, *pol.* exécutif *etc.*); puissance *f* (*a.* ⊕, ⚕, *pol.* = *pays, influence*); vigueur *f*; ⚡ énergie *f* (*électrique*); aimant: force *f*; *admin.* autorité *f*; ⚡ mandat *m*; ⚡ quantité *f*, foule *f*; be in ~ être au pouvoir; Western ~s *pl. pol.* puissances *f/pl.* occidentales; '~-**as·sist·ed** ⊕ assisté; ~ **break** servofrein *m*; '~-**cur·rent** courant *m* à haute intensité; ~ **cut** ⚡ coupure *f* de courant; ~ **fail·ure** panne *f* de courant; **pow·er·ful** ['~ful] □ puissant, fort; '**pow·er·house** centrale *f* électrique; '**pow·er·less** impuissant; inefficace; '**pow·er line** ligne *f* à haute tension; '**pow·er-plant** groupe *m* générateur; *Am.* centrale *f* électrique; ~ **point** *Brit.* prise *f* de courant; ~ **saw** scie *f* à moteur; '**pow·er sta·tion** centrale *f* électrique; *long-distance* ~ centrale *f* interurbaine; ~ **steer·ing** servodirection *f*; ~ **strug·gle** *pol. etc.* lutte *f* pour le pouvoir.

pow·wow ['pau'wau] sorcier *m* guérisseur; *Am.* F conférence *f* (politique); palabre *f*.

pox V [pɔks] syphilis *f*.

pra(a)m ⚓ [prɑ:m] prame *f*.

prac·ti·ca·bil·i·ty [præktikə'biliti] praticabilité *f*; '**prac·ti·ca·ble** □ praticable; faisable; '**prac·ti·cal** pratique; appliqué (*science*); quasi; ~ *joke* mystification *f*; mauvais tour *m*; brimade *f*; attrape *f*; ~ *chemistry* chimie *f* appliquée; **prac·ti·cal·i·ty** ['~'kæliti] caractère *m* pratique; esprit *m* pratique; **prac·ti·cal·ly** ['~kli] pratiquement; en pratique; presque.

prac·tice ['præktis] **1.** pratique *f*; exercice *m* (*d'un métier*); habitude *f*, coutume *f*, usage *m*; *sp.* entraîne-

ment *m*; clientèle *f*; *usu.* ~s *pl.* menés *f/pl.*, intrigue *f*; be out of ~ avoir perdu l'habitude; *put into* ~ mettre en pratique *ou* en action; **2.** *Am. see* practise.

prac·tise [~] *v/t.* mettre en pratique *ou* en action; pratiquer; exercer (*une profession*); s'exercer (*au piano etc., sur la flûte*); entraîner (*q.*); *v/i.* exercer (*médecin*); *sp.*, ♪ s'exercer; répéter; ~ [up]on exploiter (*q.*), abuser de (*la faiblesse de q.*); '**prac·tised** expérimenté; versé (dans *at, in*).

prac·ti·tion·er [præk'tiʃnə] praticien *m*; *qqfois* médecin *m*; *general* ~ médecin *m* ordinaire, médecin *m* de médecine générale.

prag·mat·ic [præg'mætik] (~*ally*) pragmatique; (*souv.* **prag·mat·i·cal**) suffisant; dogmatique.

prai·rie *Am.* ['prɛəri] prairie *f*; savane *f*; *Am.* ~ *schooner* voiture *f* couverte (*des pionniers*).

praise [preiz] **1.** éloge *m*; louange *f*; **2.** louer, faire l'éloge de; F vanter. **praise·wor·thi·ness** ['preizwə:ðinis] caractère *m* estimable; mérite *m*; '**praise·wor·thy** □ digne d'éloges; méritoire.

pra·line ['prɑ:li:n] praline *f*.

pram F [præm] *see* perambulator.

prance [prɑ:ns] piaffer (*cheval*); se pavaner (*personne*); *fig.* trépigner (de, with).

pran·di·al □ ['prændiəl] *co.* de *ou* du dîner; de table.

prang ✕ *Brit. sl.* [præŋ] raid *m* sévère.

prank [præŋk] **1.** escapade *f*; tour *m*; **2.** (*a.* ~ *up*) parer (de, with).

prate [preit] **1.** riens *m/pl.*; jaserie *f*; **2.** dire des riens; jaser; '**prat·er** babillard(e *f*) *m*; '**prat·ing 1.** □ babillard, jaseur (-euse *f*); **2.** jaserie *f*.

prat·tle ['prætl] *see* prate.

prawn *zo.* [prɔ:n] crevette *f* rouge.

pray [prei] *v/i.* prier (q., to *s.o.*; de *inf.*, to *inf.*; pour q., for *s.o.*); ~ *for* *s.th.* prier Dieu qu'il (nous) accorde qch.; ~ je vous en prie, veuillez (*inf.*); ~ *for s.o.'s soul* prier pour l'âme de q.; *v/t.* prier, implorer; demander.

pray·er ['prɛə] prière *f*, oraison *f*; demande *f*; *souv.* ~s *pl.* dévotions *f/pl.*; Lord's ♀ oraison *f* dominicale;

prayer-book

pater *m*; Book of Common ♀ rituel *m* de l'Église anglicane; '~-book livre *m* de prières; **pray·er·ful** □ ['~ful] pieux (-euse *f*).

pre... [pri:; pri] pré-; avant; antérieur à.

preach [pri:tʃ] prêcher; '**preach·er** prédicateur (-trice *f*) *m*; '**preach·ing** prédication *f*, sermon *m*; '**preach·ment** *péj.* sermon *m*.

pre·am·ble [pri:'æmbl] préambule *m*.

preb·end *eccl.* ['prebənd] prébende *f*; '**pre·ben·dar·y** prébendier *m*, chanoine *m*.

pre·car·i·ous □ [pri'kɛəriəs] précaire, incertain; **pre'car·i·ous·ness** incertitude *f*; situation *f* précaire.

pre·cau·tion [pri'kɔːʃn] précaution *f*; **pre'cau·tion·ar·y** de précaution; d'avertissement.

pre·cede [pri'siːd] (faire) précéder; préfacer; *fig.* avoir le pas sur; '**pre·ced·ence, pre'ced·en·cy** [~dəns(i)] priorité *f*; préséance *f*; **prec·e·dent** ['presidənt] précédent *m* (*a.* ⚖).

pre·cen·tor *eccl.* [pri'sentə] premier chantre *m*; maître *m* de chapelle.

pre·cept ['pri:sept] précepte *m*; règle *f*; ⚖ mandat *m*; **pre·cep·tor** [pri'septə] précepteur *m*; **pre'cep·tress** [~tris] préceptrice *f*.

pre·cinct ['pri:siŋkt] enceinte *f*, enclos *m*; *surt. Am.* circonscription *f* électorale; *Am.* poste *m* de police d'une circonscription; *a.* ~s *pl.* pourtour *m*.

pre·cious ['preʃəs] 1. *adj.* □ précieux (-euse *f*); F *a. iro.* fameux (-euse *f*); 2. F *adv.* particulièrement, joliment; '**pre·cious·ness** haute valeur *f*.

prec·i·pice ['presipis] précipice *m*; **pre·cip·i·tance, pre·cip·i·tan·cy** [pri'sipitəns(i)] précipitation *f*; empressement *m*; **pre'cip·i·tate** 1. [~teit] *v/t.* précipiter (*a.* 🜄); accélérer; *météor.* condenser; *v/i.* se précipiter; 2. [~tit] □ précipité (🜄 *a. su./m*); fait à la hâte; irréfléchi; **pre·cip·i·ta·tion** [~'teiʃn] précipitation *f* (*a.* 🜄); **pre'cip·i·tous** □ à pic; escarpé; abrupt.

pré·cis ['preisiː], *pl.* -cis [~siːz] précis *m*, résumé *m*, abrégé *m*.

pre·cise □ [pri'sais] exact; précis; méticuleux (-euse *f*); ~ly! précisément!; **pre'cise·ness** précision *f*; méticulosité *f*.

pre·ci·sion [pri'siʒn] précision *f*; *attr.* de précision.

pre·clude [pri'kluːd] prévenir, empêcher; ~ *s.o.* from (*gér.*) mettre q. dans l'impossibilité de (*inf.*).

pre·co·cious □ [pri'kouʃəs] précoce; **pre'co·cious·ness, pre·coc·i·ty** [pri'kɔsiti] précocité *f*.

pre·con·ceive ['priːkən'siːv] préconcevoir; ~d préconçu (*idée*).

pre·con·cep·tion ['priːkən'sepʃn] préconception *f*; préjugé *m*.

pre·con·cert·ed ['priːkən'səːtid] convenu *ou* arrangé d'avance.

pre·con·di·tion ['priːkən'diʃn] condition *f* préliminaire.

pre·cool ⊕ ['priː'kuːl] préréfrigérer.

pre·cur·sor [pri'kəːsə] précurseur *m*, avant-coureur *m*; **pre'cur·so·ry** précurseur; préliminaire.

pre·date ['priː'deit] antidater; venir avant.

pred·a·to·ry ['predətəri] rapace; de proie (*bête*).

pre·de·cease ['priːdi'siːs] mourir avant (*q.*).

pre·de·ces·sor ['priːdisesə] prédécesseur *m*.

pre·des·ti·nate [priː'destineit] prédestiner; **pre·des·ti'na·tion** *eccl.* prédestination *f*; **pre'des·tined** prédestiné.

pre·de·ter·mine ['priːdi'təːmin] déterminer d'avance; *eccl.* préordonner. [cable.\]

pred·i·ca·ble ['predikəbl] prédi-\)

pre·dic·a·ment [pri'dikəmənt] *phls.* catégorie *f*; *fig.* situation *f* difficile.

pred·i·cate 1. ['predikeit] affirmer; 2. ['~kit] *gramm.* attribut *m*; *phls.* prédicat *m*; **pred·i·ca·tion** assertion *f*; **pred·i·ca·tive** [pri'dikətiv] □ affirmatif (-ive *f*); *gramm.* prédicatif (-ive *f*).

pre·dict [pri'dikt] prédire; **pre·dic·tion** [~'dikʃn] prédiction *f*.

pre·di·lec·tion [priːdi'lekʃn] prédilection *f* (pour, for).

pre·dis·pose ['priːdis'pouz] prédisposer (à, to); **pre·dis·po·si·tion** ['~dispə'ziʃn] prédisposition *f* (à, to).

pre·dom·i·nance [pri'dɔminəns] prédominance *f*; ascendant *m* (sur, over); **pre'dom·i·nant** □ prédominant; **pre'dom·i·nate** [~neit] prédominer; l'emporter par le nombre *etc.* (sur, over).

pre·em·i·nence [pri:'eminəns] prééminence *f*; primat *m*; **pre-'em·i·nent** □ prééminent; remarquable (par, *in*).

pre·emp·tion [pri:'empʃn] (droit *m* de) préemption *f*; **pre-'emp·tive** [~tiv] ✝ de préemption (*droit*); *fig.* préventif (-ive); ✕ ~ *first strike* attaque *f* préventive.

preen [pri:n] lisser (*les plumes*).

pre·en·gage [ˈpri:inˈgeidʒ] retenir *ou* engager d'avance; **'pre-en-'gage·ment** engagement *m* préalable.

pre-ex·ist [ˈpri:igˈzist] préexister; **'pre-ex'ist·ence** préexistence *f*; **'pre-ex'ist·ent** préexistant.

pre·fab [ˈpri:ˈfæb] **1.** préfabriqué; **2.** maison *f* préfabriquée; **'pre'fab·ri·cate** [~rikeit] préfabriquer.

pref·ace [ˈprefis] **1.** préface *f*; avant-propos *m/inv.*; **2.** préfacer; préluder à. [liminaire.\]

pref·a·to·ry □ [ˈprefətəri] pré-ʃ

pre·fect [ˈpri:fekt] préfet *m*; *école:* élève *mf* surveillant(e *f*).

pre·fer [priˈfə:] préférer (à, *to*), aimer mieux (que *sbj.*, *to inf.*); nommer (*q. à un emploi*); déposer (*une plainte*); intenter (*une action*); émettre (*une prétention*); *see share 1*; **pref·er·a·ble** □ [ˈprefərəbl] préférable (à, *to*); **'pref·er·a·bly** de préférence (à, *to*); préférablement; **'pref·er·ence** préférence *f* (pour, *for*); (*surt.* ✝) droit *m* de priorité; *douane:* tarif *m* de préférence; *see share 1*; **pref·er·en·tial** □ [~ˈrenʃl] préférentiel(le *f*); de préférence; **pref·er·en·tial·ly** de préférence; **pre·fer·ment** [priˈfə:mənt] avancement *m*; promotion *f*.

pre·fix 1. [ˈpri:fiks] préfixe *m*; titre *m*; **2.** [pri:ˈfiks] mettre comme introduction; *gramm.* préfixer.

preg·nan·cy [ˈpregnənsi] grossesse *f*; *animal:* gestation *f*; *fig.* grande portée *f*; fécondité *f*; **'preg·nant** □ ✳ enceinte (*femme*); gravide (*animal*); *fig.* gros(se *f*), fertile (en, *with*).

pre·heat ⊕ [ˈpri:ˈhi:t] réchauffer d'avance.

pre·hen·sile [priˈhensail] préhensile.

pre·his·tor·ic [ˈpri:hisˈtɔrik] préhistorique.

pre·ig·ni·tion *mot.* [ˈpri:igˈniʃn] auto-allumage *m*; allumage *m* prématuré.

pre·judge [ˈpri:ˈdʒʌdʒ] préjuger.

prej·u·dice [ˈpredʒudis] **1.** préjugé *m*, prévention *f*; préjudice *m*, dommage *m*; *without* ~ *to* réservation faite de; **2.** prévenir, prédisposer; porter préjudice à; ~*d* prévenu; à préjugés.

prej·u·di·cial □ [predʒuˈdiʃl] préjudiciable, nuisible (à, *to*).

prel·a·cy [ˈpreləsi] épiscopat *m*; prélats *m/pl.*

prel·ate [ˈprelit] prélat *m*.

pre·lec·tion [priˈlekʃn] conférence *f*; **pre'lec·tor** conférencier *m*; *univ.* maître *m* de conférences.

pre·lim·i·nar·y [priˈliminəri] **1.** □ préliminaire; préalable; **2.** prélude *m*; *preliminaries pl.* préliminaires *m/pl.*

prel·ude [ˈprelju:d] **1.** prélude *m* (*a.* ♪); **2.** *v/i.* ♪ préluder; *v/t.* précéder; préluder à.

pre·mar·i·tal [ˈpri:ˈmæritl] prématrimonial (-aux *m/pl.*), avant le mariage.

pre·ma·ture [preməˈtjuə] *fig.* prématuré; ~ *delivery* accouchement *m* avant terme; **pre·ma'ture·ness**, **pre·ma'tu·ri·ty** [~riti] *fig.* prématurité *f*.

pre·med·i·tate [pri:ˈmediteit] préméditer; **pre·med·i'ta·tion** préméditation *f*.

pre·mi·er [ˈpremjə] **1.** premier (-ère *f*); **2.** premier ministre *m*; président *m* du conseil; *Am.* ministre *m* des Affaires étrangères; **'pre·mi·er·ship** fonctions *f/pl.* de premier ministre; *Am.* Ministère *m* des Affaires étrangères.

prem·ise 1. [ˈpremis] prémisse *f*; ~*s pl.* local *m*; immeuble *m*, ⚡ intitulé *m*; *licensed* ~*s pl.* débit *m* de boissons; *on the* ~*s* sur les lieux; dans l'établissement; **2.** [pri:ˈmaiz] poser en prémisse; faire remarquer.

pre·mi·um [ˈpri:mjəm] prix *m*; prime *f* (*a.* ✝); indemnité *f*; *au début d'un bail:* droit *m*; ✝ agio *m*; *at a* ~ à prime.

pre·mo·ni·tion [pri:məˈniʃn] prémonition *f*; pressentiment *m*; **pre·mon·i·to·ry** □ [priˈmɔnitəri] prémonitoire; précurseur.

pre·na·tal [ˈpri:ˈneitl] prénatal (-als, -aux *m/pl.*).

pre·oc·cu·pan·cy [pri:ˈɔkjupənsi] *fig.* absorption *f* (par, *in*); **pre·oc-**

cu·pa·tion [priːɔkjuˈpeiʃn] préoccupation *f*; absorption *f* (par, with); souci *m*; préjugé *m*; **pre·oc·cu·pied** [ˌ ˈɔkjupaid] préoccupé; absorbé; **preˈoc·cu·py** [ˌpai] préoccuper, absorber; occuper par avance.

pre·or·dain [priːɔːˈdein] régler d'avance; préordonner.

prep F [prep] *see* preparation; *preparatory school*.

prep·a·ra·tion [prepəˈreiʃn] préparation *f*; préparatifs *m/pl.*; *école:* étude *f* (du soir); **pre·par·a·tive** [priˈpærətiv] *usu.* ~s *pl.* préparatifs *m/pl.*; **pre·par·a·to·ry** [ˌtəri] **1.** □ préparatoire; ~ *school* école *f* préparatoire; **2.** *adv.* ~ *to* préalablement à.

pre·pare [priˈpɛə] *v/t.* préparer; dresser; confectionner (*un mets*); *v/i.* se préparer, s'apprêter (à, for; à *inf.*, to *inf.*); **preˈpared** □ préparé; sur le qui-vive; ~ *for* prêt à (*qch.*) *ou* pour (*inf.*).

pre·pay [priːˈpei] [*irr.* (*pay*)] payer d'avance; affranchir (*une lettre*); **preˈpay·ment** paiement *m* d'avance; *lettre:* affranchissement *m*.

pre·pense □ [priˈpens] prémédité; *with malice* ~ avec intention criminelle.

pre·pon·der·ance [priˈpɔndərəns] prépondérance *f*; **preˈpon·der·ant** □ prépondérant; **preˈpon·der·ate** [ˌreit] peser davantage; *fig.* l'emporter (sur, over).

prep·o·si·tion *gramm.* [prepəˈziʃn] préposition *f*; **prep·oˈsi·tion·al** □ prépositionnel(le *f*).

pre·pos·sess [priːpəˈzes] imprégner, pénétrer (*l'esprit*) (de, with); prévenir (*q.*) (en faveur de, *in favour of*; contre, *against*); **pre·posˈsess·ing** □ prévenant; agréable; **preposˈses·sion** [ˌˈzeʃn] prévention *f*, préjugé *m*.

pre·pos·ter·ous [priˈpɔstərəs] absurde; déraisonnable; contraire au bon sens.

pre·puce *anat.* [ˈpriːpjuːs] prépuce *m*.

pre·req·ui·site [ˈpriːˈrekwizit] nécessité *f* préalable; condition *f* préalable.

pre·rog·a·tive [priˈrɔgətiv] prérogative *f*; privilège *m*.

pres·age [ˈpresidʒ] **1.** présage *m*;

pressentiment *m*; **2.** présager, annoncer; prédire.

pres·by·ter [ˈprezbitə] prêtre *m*; ancien *m*; **Pres·by·te·ri·an** [ˌ ˈtiəriən] **1.** presbytérien(ne *f*); **2.** Presbytérien(ne *f*) *m*; **pres·byter·y** [ˈ ˌtəri] △ sanctuaire *m*; *eccl.* presbytère *m*, consistoire *m*.

pre·sci·ence [ˈpresiəns] prescience *f*, prévision *f*; **ˈpre·sci·ent** prescient, prévoyant.

pre·scribe [prisˈkraib] *v/t.* prescrire, ordonner (*a.* ⚕); *v/i.:* ~ *for* prescrire à, ordonner à (*q.*); ⚕ indiquer un traitement pour (*q.*); ⚖ (*ou* ~ *to*) prescrire, acquérir (*un droit*) par prescription.

pre·script [ˈpriːskript] prescription *f*, précepte *m*; **pre·scrip·tion** [prisˈkripʃn] prescription *f* (*a.* ⚖); ordre *m*; ⚕ ordonnance *f*; ⚖ coutume *f*; droit *m* consacré par l'usage; *Brit.* ~ *charge* somme *f* fixe à payer lors de l'exécution d'une ordonnance; **preˈscrip·tive** □ consacré par l'usage; ordonnateur (-trice *f*).

pres·ence [ˈprezns] présence *f*; mine *f*, air *m*, maintien *m*; *in the* ~ *of* en présence de (*q.*); ~ *of mind* présence *f* d'esprit; **ˈ ~cham·ber** salle *f* d'audience.

pres·ent¹ [ˈpreznt] **1.** □ présent; actuel(le *f*); courant (*année etc.*); ~ *record holder* recordman *m* de l'heure; *gramm.* ~ *tense* (temps *m*) présent *m*; ~ *value* valeur *f* actuelle; ~! présent!; **2.** présent *m* (*a. gramm.*); temps *m* présent; ✝ *by the* ~, ⚖ *by these* ~s par la présente; *at* ~ à présent, actuellement; *for the* ~ pour le moment.

pre·sent² [priˈzent] présenter (*a. qch.* à *q.*, *s.o. with s.th.*); ˈdonner; offrir; faire cadeau de (*qch.*); ~ *o.s.* se présenter; s'offrir; ~ *one's compliments to s.o.* présenter ses compliments à q.

pres·ent³ [ˈpreznt] cadeau *m*; *make s.o. a* ~ *of s.th.* faire cadeau de qch. à q.

pre·sent·a·ble [priˈzentəbl] présentable; portable (*robe etc.*).

pres·en·ta·tion [prezənˈteiʃn] présentation *f*; ✝ remise *f*; *théâ.* (re)présentation *f*; souvenir *m*; ~ *copy* spécimen *m* gratuit; exemplaire *m* offert à titre d'hommage.

pres·ent-day ['prezntdei] d'aujourd'hui, actuel(le f).

pre·sen·ti·ment [pri'zentimənt] pressentiment m.

pres·ent·ly ['prezntli] bientôt; tout à l'heure; F actuellement.

pre·sent·ment [pri'zentmənt] see presentation; ⚖ déclaration f émanant du jury; théâ. représentation f.

pres·er·va·tion [prezə'veiʃn] conservation f; préservation f (de, from); maintien m; ~ of natural beauty préservation f des beautés de la nature; in good ~ en bon état de conservation f; **pre·serv·a·tive** [pri'zə:vətiv] 1. préservateur (-trice f); 2. préservatif m; antiseptique m.

pre·serve [pri'zə:v] 1. préserver, garantir (de, from); conserver; mettre en conserve; maintenir; garder (le silence, la chasse); ⚑ naturaliser; élever (du gibier) dans une réserve; 2. chasse f gardée; réserve f; poisson: vivier m; confiture f; **pre'serv·er** préservateur (-trice f) m; sauveur m; propriétaire m d'une chasse gardée ou d'un vivier; conservateur (-trice f) m; agent m de conservation.

pre·side [pri'zaid] présider (qch., à qch. over s.th.); occuper le fauteuil présidentiel; ~ over an assembly présider une assemblée.

pres·i·den·cy ['prezidənsi] présidence f; école: directorat m, rectorat m; **'pres·i·dent** président(e f) m; école: (di)recteur m; ✝ Am. directeur m général; **pres·i·den·tial** [ˌ~'denʃl] présidentiel(le f).

press [pres] 1. pression f (sur qch.); presse f (hydraulique, à copier, de journaux, fig. des affaires, a. typ.); typ. imprimerie f; 2. v/t. presser; appuyer sur; serrer (a. ✕); donner un coup de fer à (une robe etc.); fig. poursuivre (un avantage); forcer à accepter; réclamer (une dette, une réponse); imposer (une opinion); ~ the button appuyer sur le bouton; ~ the point that insister sur le fait que; be ~ed for time être très pressé ou à court de temps; v/i. se serrer, se presser; ~ for insister pour obtenir ou pour que (sbj.); ~ on presser le pas, forcer le pas, se dépêcher; ~ (up)on peser à (q.); ~ a·gen·cy agence f d'informa-

tions; ~ a·gent agent m de publicité; ~ bar·on magnat m de la presse; ~ but·ton bouton m à pression; gant: bouton m fermoir; ~ clip·ping see press cutting; ~ con·fer·ence conférence f de presse; ~ cor·rec·tor typ. correcteur m (-trice f); ~ cut·ting coupure f de journal; **'press·er** presse f (à viande); pressoir m (aux raisins); presseur (-euse f) m (personne); **'press-gal·le·ry** tribune f de la presse; **'press-gang**: F ~ s.o. into doing s.th. faire pression sur q. pour qu'il fasse qch.; **'press·ing** □ pressant; urgent, pressé; ~ lord see press baron; **'press·man** ⊕ presseur m; journaliste m; **'press-mark** bibliothèque: numéro m de classement; **press re·lease** communiqué m de presse; **'press-stud** boutonpression m (pl. boutons-pression), pression f; **'press-up**: do ~s faire des tractions ou des pompes; **pres·sure** ['preʃə] pression f (a. fig.); ⚡, ⚕ tension f; ~ group groupe m de pression; **pres·sure-cook·er** marmite f à pression; **'pres·sure-gauge** ⊕ manomètre m; **pres·sur·ize** ['ˌ~raiz] ✈ pressuriser; **'press-work** typ. impression f.

pres·ti·dig·i·ta·tion ['prestididʒi-'teiʃn] prestidigitation f.

pres·tige [pres'ti:ʒ] prestige m; crédit m; **pres·ti·gious** [ˌ~'tidʒəs] prestigieux.

pre·sum·a·ble □ [pri'zju:məbl] présumable (de la part de q., of s.o.); **pre'sum·ab·ly** [ˌ~i] probablement; **pre'sume** v/t. présumer, supporter; v/i. présumer; prendre des libertés; se permettre (de, to); prendre la liberté (de, to); ~ (up)on abuser de; se prévaloir de; **pre'sum·ed·ly** [ˌ~idli] probablement; **pre'sum·ing** □ présomptueux (-euse f); indiscret (-ète f).

pre·sump·tion [pri'zʌmpʃn] présomption f; arrogance f; préjugé m; qqfois conclusion f; **pre'sump·tive** □ par présomption; heir ~ héritier m présomptif; **pre'sump·tu·ous** □ [ˌ~tjuəs] présomptueux (-euse f), outrecuidant.

pre·sup·pose [pri:sə'pouz] présupposer; **pre·sup·po·si·tion** [pri:-sʌpə'ziʃn] présupposition f.

pre·tence, Am. **pre·tense** [pri-'tens] (faux) semblant m; prétexte *m*; prétention *f* (à, *to*); *false* ~ fraude *f*; faux semblant *m*.

pre·tend [pri'tend] feindre, simuler; prétendre (*inf.*, *to inf.*; à qch., *to s.th.*); faire semblant (de *inf.*, *to inf.*); **pre'tend·ed** □ feint, faux (fausse *f*); soi-disant (*personne*); prétendu; **pre'tend·er** simulateur (-trice *f*) *m*; prétendant *m* (*au trône*).

pre·ten·sion [pri'tenʃn] prétention *f*; droit *m*, titre *m*.

pre·ten·tious [pri'tenʃəs] prétentieux (-euse *f*); **pre'ten·tious·ness** prétention *f*.

pret·er·it(e) *gramm.* ['pretərit] prétérit *m*, passé *m*.

pre·ter·mis·sion [pri:tə'miʃn] omission *f*; interruption *f*.

pre·ter·mit [pri:tə'mit] omettre; interrompre; négliger (de *inf.*).

pre·ter·nat·u·ral □ [pri:tə'nætʃrəl] surnaturel(le *f*).

pre·text ['pri:tekst] prétexte *m*, excuse *f*.

pret·ti·ness ['pritinis] gentillesse *f* (*a. style*).

pret·ty ['priti] **1.** *adj.* □ joli, beau (bel *devant une voyelle ou un h muet*; belle *f*); gentil(le *f*); *my* ~! ma mignonne!; **2.** *adv.* assez, passablement; ~ *near* à peu près; ~ *close to perfect* presque parfait; ~ *much the same thing* à peu près la même chose; *a* ~ *large number* un assez grand nombre.

pre·vail [pri'veil] prédominer; régner; prévaloir (sur, *over*; contre, *against*); l'emporter (sur *over*, *against*); ~ (*up)on s.o. to* (*inf.*) amener *ou* déterminer q. à (*inf.*); **pre'vail·ing** □ courant; en vogue; dominant.

prev·a·lence ['prevələns] prédominance *f*; généralité *f*; fréquence *f*; **'prev·a·lent** □ (pré)dominant; répandu, général (-aux *m/pl.*).

pre·var·i·cate [pri'værikeit] équivoquer; mentir; **pre·var·i·ca·tion** équivoques *f/pl.*; mensonge *m*; **pre'var·i·ca·tor** barguigneur (-euse *f*) *m*; menteur (-euse *f*) *m*.

pre·vent [pri'vent] empêcher (de, *from*); mettre obstacle à (*qch.*); prévenir (*un malheur etc.*); **pre'vent·a·ble** évitable; **pre'vent·a·tive** [~tətiv] *see* preventive; **pre'vent·er** empêcheur (-euse *f*) *m*; ⚓ faux

étai *m*; **pre'ven·tion** empêchement *m*; protection *f* (contre, *of*); **pre'ven·tive 1.** □ préventif (-ive *f*); ~ *custody* détention *f* préventive; ~ *detention* emprisonnement *m* à titre préventif; ~ *medicine* médecine *f* préventive; **2.** empêchement *m*; médicament *m* préventif; mesure *f* préventive (contre, *of*).

pre·view ['pri:vju:] exhibition *f* préalable; *cin.* avant-première *f*.

pre·vi·ous □ ['pri:viəs] antérieur, antécédent (à, *to*); préalable; F trop pressé; ~ *conviction* condamnation *f* antérieure; ~ *to a.* avant; ~*ly* auparavant; préalablement.

pre·vi·sion [pri:'viʒn] prévision *f*.

pre·vo·ca·tion·al train·ing [pri:vo'keiʃnl'treiniŋ] enseignement *m* professionnel.

pre·war ['pri:'wɔ:] d'avant-guerre.

prey [prei] **1.** proie *f*; *beast* (*bird*) *of* ~ bête *f* (oiseau *m*) de proie; **2.:** ~ (*up)on* faire sa proie de; piller, ravager; *fig.* ronger.

price [prais] **1.** prix *m*; *course:* cote *f*; *bourse:* cours *m*; *at any* ~ coûte que coûte; **2.** mettre un prix à; estimer, évaluer; demander le prix de; ~ *s.o. out* chasser q. du marché en demandant des prix plus bas que celui-ci; ~ *o.s. out* (*of the market*) perdre un marché en demandant des prix trop élevés; ~ **brack·et** *see* price range; **pric·ey** F coûteux (-euse *f*), F cherot; **'price·less** inestimable; *sl.* impayable; **price range** éventeil *m ou* gamme *f* des prix; *within my* ~ dans mes prix; *in the medium* ~ dans les prix moyens; **price tick·et**, **price tag** étiquette *f* (de prix); *fig.* prix *m*; *have a heavy* ~ coûter cher.

prick [prik] **1.** piqûre *f*; *fig.* picoterie *f*; *conscience:* remords *m*; **2.** *v/t.* piquer; crever (*une ampoule*); ⚓ pointer (*une carte*); (*a.* ~ *out*) tracer un dessin en le piquant; ✗ ~ *out* repiquer; ~ *up one's ears* dresser l'oreille; *v/i.* picoter; fourmiller (*membre*); ~ *up* se dresser; **'prick·er** poinçon *m*, pointe *f*; **prick·le** ['~l] piquant *m*, épine *f*; **'prick·ly** épineux (-euse *f*); ✗ ~ *heat* bouton *m* de chaleur; ✿ ~ *pear* figuier *m ou* figue *f* de Barbarie.

pride [praid] **1.** orgueil *m*; *péj.* vanité *f*; faste *m*; *saison etc.:* apogée *m*; ~ *of place* priorité *f*;

take ~ *in* être fier (fière *f*) de; **2.:** ~ *o.s.* se piquer, se faire gloire, tirer vanité (de, [up]on).

pri·er ['praiə] curieux (-euse *f*) *m*.

priest [pri:st] prêtre *m*; '~·**craft** *péj.* cléricalisme *m*; intrigues *f/pl.* sacerdotales; '**priest·ess** prêtresse *f*; **priest·hood** ['~hud] le clergé *m*; sacerdoce *m*; '**priest·ly** sacerdotal (-aux *m/pl.*).

prig [prig] **1.** poseur *m* à la vertu; *sl.* chipeur (-euse *f*) *m*; **2.** *sl.* chiper; '**prig·gish** □ suffisant; collet monté *adj./inv.*

prim □ [prim] guindé, compassé; collet monté *adj./inv.* (*personne*).

pri·ma·cy ['praiməsi] primauté *f*; *eccl.* primatie *f*; **pri·ma·ri·ly** ['~rili] principalement; '**pri·ma·ry** □ principal (-aux *m/pl.*); primitif (-ive *f*); premier (-ère *f*) (*a. importance*); ♂, ♀, *astr.*, couleur, *école:* primaire; *Am.* ~ (meeting) élection *f* primaire directe; *see* share; **pri·mate** *eccl.* ['~mit] primat *m*.

prime [praim] **1.** □ premier (-ère *f*); de premier ordre; principal (-aux *m/pl.*); de surchoix (*viande*); ♀ cost prix *m* coûtant, prix *m* d'achat; ♀ Minister président *m* du Conseil; premier ministre *m*; ~ number nombre *m* premier; *radio, télév.* ~ time heure(s) *f(pl.)* d'écoute maximum; **2.** *fig.* perfection *f*; fleur *f* de l'âge; choix *m*; premiers jours *m/pl.*; *eccl.* prime *f*; **3.** *v/t.* amorcer (*une arme, un obus, une pompe*); *peint.* apprêter; *fig.* faire la leçon à; abreuver (*q. d'alcool*); *v/i.* ⊕ primer.

prim·er¹ ['praimə] premier cours *m* ou livre *m* de lecture; premiers éléments *m/pl.*; *typ.* ['primə]: great ~ gros romain *m*; corps 16; long ~ philosophie *f*; corps 10.

prim·er² ['praimə] amorceur *m*; apprêteur *m*; *peint.* couche *f* d'impression.

pri·me·val [prai'mi:vəl] primordial (-aux *m/pl.*).

prim·ing ['praimiŋ] *peint.* apprêtage *m*; couche *f* d'impression; ✗ amorce *f*; amorçage *m*.

prim·i·tive ['primitiv] **1.** □ primitif (-ive *f*), premier; rude, grossier (-ère *f*); **2.** *gramm.* mot *m* primitif; *peint.* primitif *m*; '**prim·i·tive·ness**

caractère *m* primitif; *peuple:* rudesse *f*.

prim·ness ['primnis] air *m* collet monté; *chambre etc.:* ordre *m* parfait.

pri·mo·gen·i·ture [praimo'dʒenitʃə] primogéniture *f*; droit *m* d'aînesse.

pri·mor·di·al □ [prai'mɔ:diəl] primordial (-aux *m/pl.*).

prim·rose ♀ ['primrouz] primevère *f* (à grandes fleurs); *fig.* ~ path chemin *m* de velours.

prince [prins] prince *m*; '**prince-like** princier (-ère *f*); '**prince·ly** princier (-ère *f*); royal (-aux *m/pl.*) (*a. fig.*); *fig.* magnifique; **prin·cess** [prin'ses; *devant npr.* 'prinses] princesse *f*.

prin·ci·pal ['prinsəpəl] **1.** □ principal (-aux *m/pl.*); en chef; premier (-ère *f*); *gramm.* ~ parts *pl.* temps *m/pl.* principaux (*du verbe.*); **2.** directeur *m*; chef *m*; patron *m*; ♀ employeur *m*; ⚖ *crime:* auteur *m*; ♀ capital *m*; *univ.* recteur *m*; **prin·ci·pal·i·ty** [prinsi'pæliti] principauté *f*.

prin·ci·ple ['prinsəpl] principe *m* (*a.* ♀); *in* ~ en principe; *on* ~ par principe; *on a* ~ d'après un principe.

prink ⨍ [priŋk] (s')attifer.

print [print] **1.** empreinte *f* (*digitale*); impression *f*; moule *m*; trace *f*; gravure *f*, estampe *f*; *typ.* matière *f* imprimée; caractères *m/pl.*; *phot.* copie *f*, épreuve *f*; ⊕ dessin; *usu. Am.* journal *m*; feuille *f* imprimée; ♀ *tex.* indienne *f*, cotonnade *f*; *out of* ~ épuisé; *in cold* ~ à la lecture, par écrit; *please* ~ écrire en lettres d'imprimerie; **2.** *v/t.* imprimer; marquer d'une empreinte; *phot.* tirer une épreuve de; *fig.* ~ *o.s.* se graver (dans, on); ~ed form imprimé *m*; ~ed matter imprimés *m/pl.*; *v/i.* être à l'impression; '**print·er** imprimeur *m*; ouvrier *m* typographe; ~'s devil apprenti *m* imprimeur; ~'s flower fleuron *m*; ~'s ink encre *f* d'impression.

print·ing ['printiŋ] impression *f*; *art:* imprimerie *f*; *phot.* tirage *m*; *attr.* à imprimer; d'impression; '~-**frame** châssis *m* (*positif*); '~-**ink** noir *m* d'imprimerie; '~-**of·fice** imprimerie *f*; '~-**pa·per** *phot.*

65*

papier *m* photographique; papier *m* sensible; '**~-press** presse *f* d'imprimerie.

print-out ['printaut] *ordinateur*: listage *m*.

pri·or ['praiə] 1. *adj.* préalable; antérieur (à, to); 2. *adv.*: ~ to antérieurement à; 3. *su. eccl.* prieur *m*; '**pri·or·ess** *eccl.* prieure *f*; **pri·or·i·ty** ['~riti] priorité *f* (sur, over); antériorité *f*; give s.th. (top) ~ donner la priorité (absolue) à qch.; have (ou take) ~ over s.th. avoir la priorité sur qch., primer qch.; get one's priorities right décider de ce qui est le plus important pour q.; *see* share; **pri·o·ry** *eccl.* ['~əri] prieuré *m*.

prism ['prizm] prisme *m*; ~ binoculars *pl.* jumelles *f/pl.* à prismes; **pris·mat·ic** [priz'mætik] (~ally) prismatique.

pris·on ['prizn] 1. prison *f*; 2. *poét.* emprisonner; '**pris·on·er** prisonnier (-ère *f*) *m*; ⚖ accusé(e *f*) *m*; prévenu(e *f*) *m*; détenu(e *f*) *m*; *fig.* be a ~ to être cloué à; take s.o. ~ faire q. prisonnier (-ère *f*); ~'s bars (ou base) (jeu *m* de) barres *f/pl.*

pris·sy *Am.* F ['prisi] chichiteux (-euse *f*).

pris·tine ['pristain] premier (-ère *f*), primitif (-ive *f*).

pri·va·cy ['praivəsi] intimité *f*; secret *m*; in the ~ of retiré dans.

pri·vate ['praivit] 1. □ privé; particulier (-ère *f*); personnel(le *f*); secret (-ète *f*); réservé; retiré (*endroit*); ~ company société *f* en nom collectif; ~ gentleman rentier *m*; *parl.* ~ member simple député *m*; ~ lessons *pl.* leçons *f/pl.* particulières; ~ theatricals comédie *f* de salon; ~ view *exposition*: avant-première *f*; ~ sale vente *f* à l'amiable; 2. ⚔ (*ou* soldier) simple soldat *m*; ~s *pl.* (*usu.* ~ parts *pl.*) parties *f/pl.* sexuelles; in ~ en séance privée; sans témoins; dans l'intimité; en famille.

pri·va·teer ⚓ [praivi'tiə] vaisseau, *a. personne*: corsaire *m*; **pri·va'teer·ing** course *f*; *attr.* de course.

pri·va·tion [prai'veiʃn] privation *f* (*a. fig.*).

pri·va·tive □ ['privətiv] négatif (-ive *f*); *gramm.* privatif (-ive *f*).

priv·et ♀ ['privit] troène *m*.

priv·i·lege ['privilidʒ] 1. privilège *m*, prérogative *f*; 2. privilégier (*q.*),

accorder le privilège à (*q.*) (de *inf.*, to *inf.*); ~d privilégié.

priv·i·ty ⚖ ['priviti] obligation *f*; lien *m* de droit.

priv·y ['privi] 1. □: ~ to instruit de; ⚖ intéressé dans, trempé dans; ♀ Council Conseil *m* privé; ♀ Councillor conseiller *m* privé; ~ parts *pl.* parties *f/pl.* sexuelles; ~ purse cassette *f* du roi; ♀ Seal petit Sceau *m*; Lord ♀ Seal Garde *m* du petit Sceau; 2. ⚖ partie *f* intéressée; complice *mf*; F lieux *m/pl.* d'aisance.

prize¹ [praiz] 1. prix *m*; *loterie*: lot *m*; ⚓ prise *f*, capture *f*; first ~ *loterie*: le gros lot; 2. couronné; médaillé; de prix; ⚓ de prise; ~ competition concours *m* pour un prix; 3. estimer, priser; ⚓ capturer.

prize² [~] 1. (*a.* ~ open) forcer avec un levier; 2. force *f* de levier.

prize...: '**~-fight·er** boxeur *m* professionnel; '**~-list** palmarès *m*; '**~-man**, '**~-win·ner** lauréat(e *f*) *m*; gagnant(e *f*) *m* du prix.

pro¹ [prou] pour; *see* con³.

pro² [~] professionnel(le *f*) *m*, F pro *mf*.

prob·a·bil·i·ty [prɔbə'biliti] probabilité *f*; '**prob·a·ble** □ probable.

pro·bate ⚖ ['proubit] homologation *f* (d'un testament).

pro·ba·tion [prə'beiʃn] épreuve *f*, stage *m*; *eccl.* probation *f*; ⚖ liberté *f* surveillée; on ~ en stage; ⚖ en liberté sous surveillance; **pro'ba·tion·ar·y**: ⚖ ~ period période *f* de liberté surveillée; **pro'ba·tion·er** stagiaire *mf*; *eccl.* novice *mf*; ⚖ condamné(e *f*) *m* mis(e *f*) en liberté sous surveillance.

pro·ba·tive ⚖ ['proubətiv] probant, probatoire.

probe ⚕ [proub] 1. sonde *f*, poinçon *m*; *surt. Am. parl., pol.* enquête *f*; 2. (*a.* ~ into) sonder; '**~-scis·sors** *pl.* (*sorte de*) ciseaux *m/pl.* de chirurgie, ciseaux *m/pl.* boutonnés.

prob·i·ty ['prɔbiti] probité *f*.

prob·lem ['prɔbləm] problème *m* (*a.* ♀); question *f*; ~ child enfant *mf* difficile; ~ play pièce *f* à thèse; **prob·lem·at·ic, prob·lem·at·i·cal** □ [~bli'mætik(l)] problématique; *fig.* douteux (-euse *f*).

pro·bos·cis *zo.* [prə'bɔsis] trompe *f*.

pro·ce·dur·al [prə'si:dʒərəl] de procédure; **pro'ce·dure** [ˌdʒə] procédure f; procédé m.

pro·ceed [prə'si:d] continuer son chemin; aller (a. fig.); marcher (a. fig.); continuer (qch., with s.th.); agir; se mettre (à inf., to inf.); se poursuivre; ⅍ poursuivre (q., against s.o.); univ. prendre le grade de; ~ from sortir de; ~ on one's journey poursuivre sa route; **pro-'ceed·ing** procédé m; façon f d'agir; ~s pl. ⅍ procès m, poursuites f/pl. judiciaires; société: transactions f/pl., débats m/pl.; cérémonie f, séance f; ⅍ take ~s against intenter un procès à; **pro-ceeds** ['prousi:dz] pl. produit m, montant m (de, from); net ~ produit m net.

pro·cess¹ [prə'ses] aller en procession.

proc·ess² ['prouses] **1.** processus m (a. anat.); procédé m; progrès m, marche f, cours m; méthode f; ⅍, a. anat. procès m; ⚕ réaction f, mode m (humide, sec); ⚑ proéminence f; in ~ en voie; en train; in ~ of construction en voie ou cours de construction; in the ~ of au cours de; **2.** ⊕ faire subir une opération à; apprêter; ~ into transformer en; **pro'cess·ing** ⊕ traitement m (d'une matière première).

pro·ces·sion [prə'seʃn] cortège m; défilé m; procession f.

pro·claim [prə'kleim] proclamer; déclarer (a. la guerre); publier (les bans); faire annoncer; fig. crier.

proc·la·ma·tion [prɔklə'meiʃn] proclamation f; déclaration f; publication f.

pro·cliv·i·ty [prə'kliviti] penchant m (à, to).

pro·cras·ti·nate [pro'kræstineit] remettre (qch.) à plus tard; temporiser; **pro·cras·ti'na·tion** remise f à plus tard; temporisation f.

pro·cre·ate ['proukrieit] engendrer; **pro·cre'a·tion** procréation f; **'pro-cre·a·tive** procréateur (-trice f).

proc·tor ['prɔktə] ⅍ procureur m (devant une cour); univ. censeur m; sl. ~'s (bull)dog appariteur m du censeur; **'proc·tor·ize** univ. réprimander; infliger une amende à.

pro·cum·bent [prou'kʌmbənt] couché sur le ventre; ⚑ rampant.

pro·cur·a·ble [prə'kjuərəbl] procurable.

proc·u·ra·tion [prɔkju'reiʃn] procuration f; ✝ commandement m; by ~ en vertu d'un commandement; **'proc·u·ra·tor** fondé m de pouvoir; procureur m.

pro·cure [prə'kjuə] v/t. obtenir; procurer (qch. à q. s.o. s.th., s.th. for s.o.); v/i. faire le métier de proxénète; **pro'cure·ment** obtention f; proxénétisme m; **pro-'cur·er** acquéreur (-euse f) m; entremetteur m; **pro'cur·ess** entremetteuse f, procureuse f.

prod [prɔd] **1.** coup m de coude etc.; fig. aiguillon m; **2.** pousser (du bout d'un bâton etc.); fig. aiguillonner.

prod·i·gal □ ['prɔdigəl] **1.** prodigue (de, of); the ♀ Son l'enfant prodigue; **2.** prodigue mf; **prod·i·gal·i·ty** [ˌ'gæliti] prodigalité f.

pro·di·gious □ [prə'didʒəs] prodigieux (-euse f); **prod·i·gy** ['prɔdidʒi] prodige m; fig. merveille f; (souv. infant ~) enfant m prodige.

prod·uce¹ ['prɔdju:s] champ: rendement m; produit m; coll. denrées f/pl., produits m/pl.

pro·duce² [prə'dju:s] produire; créer; ⅍, théâ. représenter; ⚡ engendrer (du courant); causer, provoquer; ⊕ fabriquer; théâ. mettre en scène; ⚓ prolonger; cin. éditer, diriger; **pro'duc·er** producteur (-trice f) m; théâ. metteur m en scène; cin. directeur m de productions; surt. Am. tenancier m d'un théâtre; gas-~ gazogène m; **pro'duc·i·ble** productible; **pro-'duc·ing** producteur (-trice f); productif (-ive f).

prod·uct ['prɔdəkt] produit m (a. ⚓), résultat m; **pro·duc·tion** [prə'dʌkʃn] production f (a. d'un livre); théâ. mise f en scène; ⅍, théâ. représentation f; ⊕ fabrication f, fabrique f; produit m, -s m/pl.; ⚓ prolongement m; be in good ~ être fabriqué en grand nombre; ⊕ flow ~ travail (pl. -aux) m à la chaîne; **pro'duc·tive** productif (-ive f), générateur (-trice f) (de, of); fécond (sol); en rapport (capital, arbre, usine, etc.); **pro'duc-tive·ness, pro·duc·tiv·i·ty** [prɔ-dʌk'tiviti] productivité f.   [prof m.]

prof Am. F [prɔf] professeur m, F ʃ

prof·a·na·tion [prɔfə'neiʃn] profanation *f*; **pro·fane** [prə'fein] **1.** □ profane; impie; blasphématoire; non initié; **2.** profaner; polluer; *fig.* violer; **pro·fan·i·ty** [prə'fæniti] impiété *f*; blasphème *m*, -s *m/pl.*

pro·fess [prə'fes] déclarer; professer (*la foi, école: un sujet*); faire profession de; exercer (*un métier*); prétendre; ~ *to be s.th.* passer pour qch.; **pro'fessed** □ prétendu; soidisant; *fig.* déclaré; *eccl.* profès (-esse *f*); **pro'fess·ed·ly** [~idli] de son propre aveu.

pro·fes·sion [prə'feʃn] profession *f*, métier *m*; déclaration *f*; **pro'fes·sion·al 1.** □ professionnel(le *f*); expert; du *ou* de métier; *the ~ classes* les membres *m/pl.* des professions libérales; **2.** expert *m*; *sp.* professionnel(le *f*) *m*; **pro'fes·sion·al·ism** [~əlizm] professionnalisme *m*.

pro·fes·sor [prə'fesə] professeur *m*; **pro'fes·sor·ship** professorat *m*; chaire *f*.

prof·fer ['prɔfə] **1.** offrir; **2.** offre *f*.

pro·fi·cien·cy [prə'fiʃənsi] compétence *f*, capacité *f* (en, *in*); **pro'fi·cient 1.** □ compétent; versé (dans *in, at*); **2.** expert *m* (en, *in*).

pro·file ['proufail] profil *m* (*a.* △); silhouette *f*; △ coupe *f* perpendiculaire.

prof·it ['prɔfit] **1.** profit *m*; avantage *m*; ✝ *souv.* ~*s pl.* bénéfice *m*; ✝ ~ *margin* marge *f* bénéficiaire; *excess* ~ *bénéfices* m/pl. extraordinaires; **2.** *v/t.* profiter à (*q.*); *v/i.:* ~ *by* profiter de; mettre (qch.) à profit; **prof·it·a·'bil·i·ty** rentabilité *f*; **'prof·it·a·ble** □ profitable; avantageux (-euse *f*); rémunérateur (-trice *f*), rentable; **'prof·it·a·ble·ness** nature *f* avantageuse; profit *m*, avantage *m*; **profit·eer** [~'tiə] **1.** faire des bénéfices excessifs; **2.** profiteur (-euse *f*) *m*, mercanti *m* (*surt. de guerre*); **prof·it·'eer·ing** mercantilisme *m*; **'prof·it·less** □ sans profit; **prof·it·shar·ing** ['~ʃɛəriŋ] participation *f* aux bénéfices.

prof·li·ga·cy ['prɔfligəsi] débauche *f*; prodigalité *f*; **prof·li·gate** ['~git] **1.** □ débauché, libertin; prodigue; **2.** débauché(e *f*) *m*, libertin(e *f*) *m*.

pro·found □ [prə'faund] profond (*a. fig.*); *fig.* absolu; **pro'found·ness**, **pro·fun·di·ty** [~'fʌnditi] profondeur *f* (*a. fig.*).

pro·fuse □ [prə'fjuːs] prodigue (de *in, of*); abondant, excessif (-ive *f*); **pro'fuse·ness**, **pro·fu·sion** [~'fjuːʒn] profusion *f*, abondance *f*.

prog *sl.* [prɔg] boustifaille *f*.

pro·gen·i·tor [prou'dʒenitə] aïeul *m*, ancêtre *m*; **pro'gen·i·tress** aïeule *f*; **prog·e·ny** ['prɔdʒini] progéniture *f*; descendants *m/pl.*; *fig.* conséquence *f*.

prog·no·sis ✻ [prɔg'nousis], *pl.* -ses [~siːz] pronostic *m*; *science:* prognose *f*.

prog·nos·tic [prɔg'nɔstik] **1.** pronostique; *be ~ of* prédire (qch.); **2.** pronostique *m*; symptôme *m*; **prog'nos·ti·cate** [~keit] pronostiquer; prédire; **prog·nos·ti·ca·tion** pronostication *f*.

pro·gram(me) ['prougræm] **1.** programme *m* (*a. traitement de l'information*); **2.** programmer; **'pro·gram·mer** *radio:* programmateur *m*; *traitement de l'information: personne:* programmeur (-euse *f*) *m*, *machine:* programmateur *m*; **'pro·gram·ming** *radio, traitement de l'information:* programmation *f*.

prog·ress[1] ['prougres] progrès *m*; avancement *m*; marche *f* (*a.* ✕); étapes *f/pl.* successives; *in ~* en cours (d'exécution).

pro·gress[2] [prə'gres] s'avancer; faire des progrès; **pro'gres·sion** [~ʃn] progression *f* (*a.* ♪); ♪ marche *f*; **pro'gress·ist** *pol.* progressiste (*a. su./mf*); **pro'gres·sive** □ progressif (-ive *f*); du progrès; *pol.* progressiste (*a. su./mf*).

pro·hib·it [prə'hibit] défendre, interdire (qch., s.th.; à q. de *inf., s.o. from gér.*); empêcher (q. de *inf., s.o. from gér.*); **pro·hi·bi·tion** [proui'biʃn] prohibition *f*, défense *f*; *Am.* régime *m* sec; **pro·hi'bi·tion·ist** prohibitionniste *mf*; *surt. Am.* partisan *m* du régime sec; **pro·hib·i·tive** □ [prə'hibitiv], **pro·hib·i·to·ry** □ [~təri] prohibitif (-ive *f*); *prohibitive duty* droits *m/pl.* prohibitifs.

proj·ect[1] ['prɔdʒekt] projet *m*.

pro·ject[2] [prə'dʒekt] *v/t.* projeter (*a.* ✕); lancer; avancer; ~ *o.s. into* se transporter dans; *v/i.* faire saillie;

pro·jec·tile [prə'dʒektail] projectile (*a. su./m*); **pro'jec·tion** ⚡, *cin.*, *lumière, cartes*: projection *f*; lancement *m*; ⚠ (partie *f* qui fait) saillie *f*; *fig.* image *f*; prolongement *m*; **pro'jec·tor** projecteur (-euse *f*) *m*; ✝ fondateur (-trice *f*) *m*; *opt.* projecteur *m*, appareil *m* de projection.

pro·le·tar·i·an [proule'tɛəriən] prolétaire (*a. su./mf*); prolétarien(ne *f*); **pro·le'tar·i·at(e)** [ˌ⁓riət] prolétariat *m*.

pro·lif·e·rate [prou'lifəreit] proliférer; se multiplier; **pro·lif·e'ra·tion** prolifération *f*; **pro·lif·ic** [prə'lifik] (⁓*ally*) prolifique; fécond (*in* of, *in*).

pro·lix □ ['prouliks] prolixe, diffus; **pro'lix·i·ty** prolixité *f*.

pro·logue, *Am. a.* **pro·log** ['proulɔg] prologue *m* (de, *to*).

pro·long [prə'lɔŋ] prolonger; ✝ proroger; ♩ allonger (*un coup d'archet*); **pro·lon·ga·tion** [proulɔŋ'geiʃn] prolongation *f*, prolongement *m*.

prom·e·nade [prɔmi'nɑːd] **1.** promenade *f*; esplanade *f*; *théâ.* promenoir *m*; **2.** *v/i.* se promener (dans, *in*); parader; *v/t.* promener (*q.*).

prom·i·nence ['prɔminəns] éminence *f*; importance *f*; protubérance *f*, saillie *f*; relief *m*; **'prom·i·nent** □ éminent; remarquable; saillant, prononcé.

prom·is·cu·i·ty [prɔmis'kjuːiti] promiscuité *f*; **pro·mis·cu·ous** □ [prə'miskjuəs] mêlé, confus; mixte; sans distinction de sexe; F dévergondé.

prom·ise ['prɔmis] **1.** promesse *f*; *fig.* espérance *f*; *of great* ⁓ plein de promesses, d'un grand avenir; **2.** *v/t.* promettre; *fig.* annoncer, laisser prévoir; F *I* ⁓ *you* je vous le promets; *v/i.* promettre; s'annoncer (*bien, mal*); **'prom·is·ing** □ plein de promesses, encourageant; **prom·is·so·ry** ['⁓səri] promissoire; ✝ ⁓ *note* billet *m* à ordre.

prom·on·to·ry ⚓, *géog.* ['prɔməntri] promontoire *m*.

pro·mote [prə'mout] promouvoir (*q.*); nommer (*q.*); *surt. Am. école*: faire passer; *parl.* prendre l'initiative de (*un projet de loi*); ✝ fonder, lancer (*une compagnie*); *surt. Am.* faire de la réclame pour (*un produit*); **pro'mot·er** instigateur (-trice *f*) *m*; ✝ fondateur *m*; monteur *m* (*d'affaires*); **pro'mo·tion** avancement *m*, promotion *f*; ✝ lancement *m* (*d'un article*); ✝ (*a. sales* ⁓) promotion *f* de la vente; ⁓ *prospects pl.* possibilités *f/pl.* d'avancement *ou* de développement.

prompt [prɔmpt] **1.** □ prompt; rapide; immédiat; **2.** promptement; **3.** inciter, pousser (à, *to*); suggérer (*qch. à. q.*, *s.o. to s.th.*); inspirer (*un sentiment*), donner (*une idée*); *théâ.* souffler; **4.** ✝ délai *m* de paiement; **'⁓-box** *théâ.* trou *m* du souffleur; **'prompt·er** instigateur (-trice *f*) *m*; *théâ.* souffleur (-euse *f*) *m*; **promp·ti·tude** [ˌ⁓itjuːd], **'prompt·ness** promptitude *f*, empressement *m*.

pro·mul·gate ['prɔmʌlgeit] promulguer (*une loi*); répandre; **pro·mul'ga·tion** *loi*: promulgation *f*; *idée*: dissémination *f*; proclamation *f*.

prone □ [proun] couché sur le ventre; en pente (*terrain*); escarpé; *fig.* ⁓ *to* porté à; prédisposé à; **'prone·ness** disposition *f* (à, *to*).

prong [prɔŋ] fourchon *m*, *fourche*: dent *f*; pointe *f*; *Am. rivière*: embranchement *m*; **pronged** à fourchons, à dents.

pro·nom·i·nal □ *gramm.* [prə'nɔminl] pronominal (-aux *m/pl.*).

pro·noun *gramm.* ['prounaun] pronom *m*.

pro·nounce [prə'nauns] *v/t.* déclarer; prononcer, articuler; *v/i.* prononcer (sur, *on*); se déclarer (pour, *in favour of*); **pro'nounced** □ prononcé; marqué; **pro'nounc·ed·ly** [ˌ⁓idli] de façon prononcée; **pro'nounce·ment** déclaration *f*.

pro·nounc·ing [prə'naunsiŋ] qui indique la prononciation.

pron·to *Am.* F ['prɔntou] sur-le-champ.

pro·nun·ci·a·tion [prənʌnsi'eiʃn] prononciation *f*.

proof [pruːf] **1.** preuve *f* (*a. fig., a.* ⚗ *alcool*); *typ., phot.* épreuve *f*; *a. see test 1*; confirmation *f*; *in* ⁓ *of* pour *ou* en preuve de; **2.** résistant (à *against, to*); à l'abri (de, *against*); **'⁓-read** *typ.* corriger les épreuves (de); **'⁓-read·er** *typ.* correcteur

(-trice *f*) *m*; '~-**sheet** *typ.* épreuve *f*;
'~-**spir·it** ⚓ trois-six *m*.

prop [prɔp] **1.** appui *m* (*a. fig.*);
théâ. sl. accessoire *m*; *Am. sl.* épingle *f* de cravate; **2.** (*ou ~ up*) appuyer, soutenir.

prop·a·gan·da [prɔpə'gændə] propagande *f*; **prop·a'gan·dist** propagandiste *mf*; **prop·a·gate** ['prɔpə-
geit] (se) propager (*a. fig.*); *fig.* (se)
répandre; **prop·a·ga·tion** propagation *f*; dissémination *f*; '**prop·a·
ga·tor** propagateur (-trice *f*) *m*; semeur (-euse *f*) *m*.

pro·pel [prə'pel] pousser en avant;
mouvoir (*une machine*); **pro'pel·
lant** propulseur *m*; **pro'pel·lent**
propulseur (*a. su./m*); propulsif
(-ive *f*); **pro'pel·ler** propulseur *m*;
⚓, ✈ hélice *f*; ~-*shaft* ⚓ arbre *m*
porte-hélice; ✈ arbre *m* à cardan;
mot. arbre *m* de transmission; **pro-
'pel·ling** moteur (-trice *f*); ~ *pencil*
porte-mine *m/inv.*

prop·er □ ['prɔpə] propre; (*souv.
après le su.*) proprement dit; particulier (-ère *f*) (à, *to*); juste, vrai;
convenable (à, *for*); comme il faut;
F parfait, dans toute l'acception
du mot; ~ *name* nom *m* propre;
'**prop·er·ty** (droit *m* de) propriété
f (*a. ♣, a. fig.*); biens *m/pl.*; immeuble *m*, -s *m/pl.*; *fig. a.* qualité *f*;
théâ. accessoire *m*; *théâ. properties
pl. a.* réserve *f* de décors *etc.*;
'**prop·er·ty tax** impôt *m* foncier.

proph·e·cy ['prɔfisi] prophétie *f*;
proph·e·sy ['~sai] *vt/i.* prophétiser;
v/t. a. prédire.

proph·et ['prɔfit] prophète *m*;
'**proph·et·ess** prophétesse *f*; **pro-
phet·ic, pro·phet·i·cal** □ [prɔ'fet-
ik(l)] prophétique.

pro·phy·lac·tic [prɔfi'læktik] (~*ally*)
prophylactique (*a. su./m*).

pro·pin·qui·ty [prə'piŋkwiti] proximité *f*; voisinage *m*; parenté *f*.

pro·pi·ti·ate [prə'piʃieit] apaiser;
rendre favorable; **pro·pi·ti·a·tion**
apaisement *m*; propitiation *f*; expiation *f*; **pro'pi·ti·a·tor** [~tə] pro-
pitiateur (-trice *f*) *m*; **pro'pi·ti·a·
to·ry** □ [~ʃiətəri] propitiatoire; expiatoire.

pro·pi·tious □ [prə'piʃəs] propice,
favorable; **pro'pi·tious·ness** na-

ture *f* propice *ou* favorable (*a.
fig.*).

pro·po·nent [prə'pounənt] parti-
san(e *f*) *m*, défenseur (-euse *f*) *m*.

pro·por·tion [prə'pɔ:ʃn] **1.** partie *f*;
part *f*; portion *f*; proportion *f* (*a.
△, A, ♪*); A proportionnalité *f*;
~*s pl.* dimensions *f/pl.*, proportions
f/pl.; **2.** proportionner (à, *to*); ⊕
déterminer les dimensions de; coter
(*un dessin*); **pro'por·tion·al 1.** □
proportionnel(le *f*); en proportion
(de, *to*); *see proportionate*; **2.** A proportionnelle *f*; **pro'por·tion·ate** □
[~it] proportionné (à, *to*).

pro·pos·al [prə'pouzəl] proposition
f, offre *f*; demande *f* en mariage;
projet *m*; **pro'pose** *v/t.* proposer;
suggérer; porter (*un toast*); ~ *s.o.'s
health* boire à la santé de q.,
porter un toast à q.; ~ *to o.s.* se
proposer; *v/i.* faire la demande en
mariage; demander sa main (à, *to*);
pro'pos·er proposeur (-euse *f*) *m*;
pro·po·si·tion [prɔpə'ziʃn] proposition *f* (*a. phls., A*); *sl.* affaire *f*.

pro·pound [prə'paund] (pro)poser
(*une question etc.*); exposer (*un programme*).

pro·pri·e·tar·y [prə'praiətəri] **1.** de
propriété; de propriétaire; privé;
possédant (*classe etc.*); ~ *article* spécialité *f*; **2.** (droit *m* de) propriété *f*;
pro'pri·e·tor propriétaire *mf*; pa-
tron(ne *f*) *m*; **pro'pri·e·tress** propriétaire *f*; patronne *f*; **pro'pri·e·
ty** propriété *f*, justesse *f*; bienséance *f*; *the proprieties pl.* les convenances *f/pl.*, la décence *f*.

pro·pul·sion [prə'pʌlʃn] propulsion *f*; **pro'pul·sive** [~siv] propulsif (-ive *f*); de propulsion.

pro·rate *Am.* [prou'reit] évaluer au
pro rata.

pro·ro·ga·tion *parl.* [prourə'geiʃn]
prorogation *f*; **pro·rogue** *parl.*
[prə'roug] proroger.

pro·sa·ic [prou'zeiik] (~*ally*) *fig.*
prosaïque (= *banal*).

pro·scribe [prou'skraib] proscrire.

pro·scrip·tion [prɔs'kripʃn] proscription *f*; interdiction *f*.

prose [prouz] **1.** prose *f*; **2.** en prose;
3. *v/t.* mettre en prose; *v/i.* F tenir
des discours ennuyeux.

pros·e·cute ['prɔsikju:t] poursuivre
(*a. en justice*); ⚖ intenter (*une
action*); exercer (*un métier*); effec-

tuer (*un voyage*); **pros·e·cu·tion**
continuation *f*; exercice *m*; ⚖
poursuites *f/pl*. (judiciaires); accusation *f*; *in ~ of* conformément à; ⚖
the ♀ le Ministère public; *witness
for the ~* témoin *m* à charge; **'pros-
e·cu·tor** ⚖ plaignant *m*; poursuivant *m*; *public ~* Ministère *m* public; procureur *m*.

pros·e·lyte *eccl*. ['prɔsilait] prosélyte
mf; **pros·e·lyt·ism** ['~litizm] pro-
sélytisme *m*; **'pros·e·lyt·ize** *v/t*.
convertir; *v/i*. faire des prosélytes.

pros·er ['prouzə] conteur *m* ennuyeux; F raseur *m*.

pros·o·dy ['prɔsədi] prosodie *f*,
métrique *f*.

pros·pect 1. ['prɔspekt] vue *f*; perspective *f* (*a. fig.*); paysage *m*; *~s pl*.
espérances *f/pl*., avenir *m*; ✝ *Am*.
client *m* possible; ⚒ prélèvement *m*
d'essai; *have in ~* avoir (*qch.*) en
vue; *hold out a ~ of* offrir des espérances de (*qch.*); **2.** [prɔs'pekt] ⚒
prospecter; *~ for* chercher; **pro-
'spec·tive** □ à venir; futur; *~ buyer*
client *m* éventuel; **pro'spec·tor** ⚒
chercheur *m* (*d'or*); **pro'spec·tus**
[~təs] prospectus *m*.

pros·per ['prɔspə] (faire) réussir;
v/t. prospérer; **pros·per·i·ty** [prɔs-
'periti] prospérité *f*; **pros·per·ous**
□ ['~pərəs] prospère, florissant; *fig*.
propice; favorable (*vent etc.*).

pros·tate *anat*. ['prɔsteit] (*a. ~ gland*)
prostate *f*.

pros·ti·tute ['prɔstitjuːt] **1.** prostituée *f*; *sl*. poule *f*; **2.** prostituer (*a.
fig.*); **pros·ti·tu·tion** prostitution *f*
(*a. fig.*).

pros·trate 1. ['prɔstreit] prosterné,
étendu; ⚒ prostré; *fig*. accablé,
abattu; **2.** [prɔs'treit] ⚒ abattre; *fig*.
~ o.s. se prosterner (*devant, before*);
pros'tra·tion prosternation *f*; ⚒
prostration *f*; *fig*. abattement *m*.

pros·y □ *fig*. ['prouzi] prosaïque;
verbeux (-euse *f*) (*personne*); ennuyeux (-euse *f*).

pro·tag·o·nist *théâ*., *a. fig*. [prou-
'tægənist] protagoniste *m*.

pro·tect [prə'tekt] protéger (*contre,
from*); abriter (*de, from*); ✝ faire
provision pour; **pro'tec·tion** protection *f*; défense *f*; sauvegarde *f*;
patronage *m*; abri *m*; **pro'tec·tion-
ist** protectionniste (*a. su./mf*); **pro-
'tec·tive** protecteur (-trice *f*); de

sûreté; *~ custody* détention *f* préventive; *~ duty* droit *m* protecteur;
pro'tec·tor protecteur *m* (*a*. ⊕);
fig. patron *m*; *-~* protège- *m*; **pro-
'tec·tor·ate** [~tərit] protectorat *m*;
pro'tec·to·ry asile *m* des enfants
abandonnés; **pro'tec·tress** protectrice *f*; *fig*. patronne *f*.

pro·te·in ⚗ ['proutiːn] protéine *f*.

pro·test 1. ['proutest] protestation *f*;
✝ protêt *m*; *in ~ against* pour protester contre; *enter (ou make) a ~*
élever des protestations, faire une
protestation; **2.** [prə'test] *v/t*. protester (*a*. ✝); *Am*. protester contre;
v/i. protester, réclamer (*contre,
against*).

Prot·es·tant ['prɔtistənt] protestant
(*a. su.*); **'Prot·es·tant·ism** protestantisme *m*.

prot·es·ta·tion [proutes'teiʃn] protestation *f*; **pro·test·er** [prə'testə]
protestateur (-trice *f*) *m*; protestataire *mf*; ✝ débiteur *m* qui a fait
protester un effet.

pro·to·col ['proutəkɔl] **1.** protocole
m; **2.** dresser un protocole.

pro·ton *phys*. ['proutɔn] proton
m.

pro·to·plasm *biol*. ['proutəplæzm]
protoplasme *m*, protoplasma *m*.

pro·to·type ['proutətaip] prototype
m, archétype *m*.

pro·tract [prə'trækt] prolonger;
traîner (*qch.*) en longueur; *surv*. relever (*un terrain*); **pro'trac·tion** prolongation *f*; *surv*. relevé *m*; **pro-
'trac·tor** ⚓ rapporteur *m*.

pro·trude [prə'truːd] *v/t*. faire sortir; *v/i*. faire saillie, s'avancer;
pro'tru·sion [~ʒn] saillie *f*; protubérance *f*.

pro·tu·ber·ance [prə'tjuːbərəns]
protubérance *f*; **pro'tu·ber·ant**
protubérant.

proud □ [praud] fier (fière *f*) (*de
of, to*); orgueilleux (-euse *f*); ⚒
fongueux (-euse *f*) (*chair*). ¡

prov·a·ble □ ['pruːvəbl] démontrable, prouvable; **prove** [pruːv] *v/t*.
prouver, démontrer; vérifier (*un
calcul*); ⊕ éprouver (*a. fig.*), essayer; *v/i*. se montrer, être, se
trouver; *~ true (false)* se révéler
comme étant vrai (faux).

prov·e·nance ['prɔvinəns] origine *f*,
provenance *f*.

prov·en·der ['prɔvində] *bêtes*: four-

rage *m*, provende *f*; F, *a. co.* nourriture *f*.

prov·erb ['prɔvəb] proverbe *m*; *be a*
~ être proverbial (-aux *m/pl.*); *péj.*
être d'une triste notoriété; *he is a* ~
for generosity sa générosité est
passée en proverbe; **pro·ver·bi·al**
□ [prə'və:biəl] proverbial (-aux
m/pl.).

pro·vide [prə'vaid] *v/t.* pourvoir,
fournir, munir (*q.*) (de, *with*); fournir (qch. à q., *s.o. with s.th.*); stipuler
(que, *that*); ~*d school* école *f* communale; *v/i.* venir en aide à q., *for
s.o.*); ~ *against* parer à; se pourvoir
contre; ~ *for* pourvoir aux besoins
de; prévoir; ✝ faire provision pour;
~*d that* pourvu que (*sbj.*); à condition que (*ind. ou sbj.*).

prov·i·dence ['prɔvidəns] prévoyance *f*; prudence *f*; providence *f* (*divine*); épargne *f*; **'prov·i·dent** □
prévoyant; économe; frugal (-aux
m/pl.); ~ *society* société *f* de prévoyance; **prov·i·den·tial** □ [~-
'denʃl] providentiel(le *f*); F heureux
(-euse *f*).

pro·vid·er [prə'vaidə] pourvoyeur
(-euse *f*) *m*; fournisseur (-euse *f*) *m*.
prov·ince ['prɔvins] province *f*; ✝,
a. fig. juridiction *f*, ressort *m*, compétence *f*.

pro·vin·cial [prə'vinʃl] **1.** provincial
(-aux *m/pl.*); de province; **2.** pro-
vincial(e *f*) *m*; *péj.* rustre *m*; **pro-
'vin·cial·ism** provincialisme *m*
(*souv. = locution provinciale*); esprit
m de clocher.

pro·vi·sion [prə'viʒn] **1.** disposition
f; fourniture *f*; ✝ réserve *f*, provision *f*; *fig.* stipulation *f*, clause *f*;
~*s pl.* comestibles *m/pl.*, vivres
m/pl.; *make* ~ *for* pourvoir aux besoins de; prévoir; pourvoir à; ~-
merchant marchand *m* de comestibles; **2.** approvisionner, ravitailler;
pro'vi·sion·al □ provisoire.

pro·vi·so [prə'vaizou] condition *f*;
with the ~ *that* à condition que;
pro'vi·so·ry [~zəri] conditionnel
(-le *f*); provisoire (*gouvernement
etc.*).

prov·o·ca·tion [prɔvə'keiʃn] provocation *f*; **pro·voc·a·tive** [prə'vɔkə-
tiv] **1.** provocateur (-trice *f*); provocant; **2.** stimulant *m*.

pro·voke [prə'vouk] provoquer, inciter (à, *to*); exaspérer, irriter; faire

naître, exciter; **pro'vok·ing** □
exaspérant, irritant, agaçant.

prov·ost ['prɔvəst] prévôt *m*; *écoss.*
maire *m*; *univ.* principal *m*; ✕ [prə-
'vou]: ~ *marshal* grand prévôt *m*.

prow ⚓ [prau] proue *f*.

prow·ess ['prauis] prouesse *f*, vaillance *f*; exploit *m*, -s *m/pl.*

prowl [praul] **1.** *v/i.* rôder (en quête
de proie); ~ rôder; **2.** action *f* de
rôder; *fig.* *be on the* ~ rôder; *Am.*
~ *car police*: voiture *f* de patrouille;
'prowl·er rôdeur (-euse *f*) *m*.

prox·i·mate □ ['prɔksimit] proche,
prochain, immédiat; approximatif
(-ive *f*); **prox'im·i·ty** proximité *f*;
in the ~ *of* à proximité de; **prox·
i·mo** ✝ ['~mou] (du mois) prochain.

prox·y ['prɔksi] procuration *f*;
mandat *m*, pouvoir *m*; *personne*:
mandataire *mf*, fondé *m* de pou-
voir(s); délégué(e *f*) *m*; *by* ~ par
procuration.

prude [pru:d] prude *f*; F bégueule
f.

pru·dence ['pru:dəns] prudence *f*,
sagesse *f*; **'pru·dent** □ prudent,
sage, judicieux (-euse *f*); **pru·den·
tial** □ [pru'denʃl] prudent; dicté
par la prudence.

prud·er·y ['pru:dəri] pruderie *f*; F
pudibonderie *f*; **'prud·ish** □
prude; F pudibond.

prune[1] [pru:n] pruneau *m*.

prune[2] [~] émonder (*un arbre*);
tailler (*un rosier etc.*); (*a.* ~ *away*,
off) élaguer (*a. fig.*).

prun·ing...: '~**-hook** émondoir *m*;
'~**-knife** serpette *f*.

pru·ri·ence, pru·ri·en·cy ['pruə-
riəns(i)] lasciveté *f*; curiosité *f* (de,
after); **'pru·ri·ent** □ lascif (-ive *f*).

Prus·sian ['prʌʃn] **1.** prussien(ne *f*);
~ *blue* bleu *m* de Prusse; **2.** Prussien
(-ne *f*) *m*.

prus·sic ac·id 🜍 ['prʌsik'æsid]
acide *m* prussique.

pry[1] [prai] fureter; fouiller; ~ *into*
chercher à pénétrer (*qch.*); F fourrer
le nez dans; **'pry·ing** □ curieux
(-euse *f*).

pry[2] [~] **1.**: ~ *open* forcer la serrure
de; forcer avec un levier; ~ *up* soulever à l'aide d'un levier; **2.** levier *m*.

psalm [sɑ:m] psaume *m*; **'psalm·
ist** psalmiste *m*; **psal·mody**
['sælmədi] psalmodie *f*.

Psal·ter [ˈsɔːltə] psautier *m*.

pse·phol·o·gy [pseˈfɔlədʒi] étude *f* des élections.

pseudo... [psju:dou] pseud(o)-; faux (fausse *f*); **pseu·do·nym** [ˈ⁓dənim] pseudonyme *m*; **pseu·don·y·mous** □ [⁓ˈdɔniməs] pseudonyme.

pshaw [pʃɔ:] peuh!; allons donc!

pso·ri·a·sis ⚕ [psɔˈraiəsis] psoriasis *m*.

psy·chi·a·trist [saiˈkaiətrist] psychiatre *m*; **psyˈchi·a·try** psychiatrie *f*.

psy·chic [ˈsaikik] **1.** (*ou* **ˈpsy·chi·cal** □) psychique; **2.** ⁓*s sg.* métapsychique *f*; métapsychisme *m*.

psy·cho·a·nal·y·sis [saikouəˈnæləsis] psychanalyse *f*; **psy·cho·an·a·lyst** [⁓ˈænəlist] psychanalyste *m*.

psy·cho·log·i·cal □ [saikəˈlɔdʒikl] psychologique; **psy·chol·o·gist** [saiˈkɔlədʒist] psychologue *m*; **psyˈchol·o·gy** psychologie *f*.

psy·cho·sis [saiˈkousis] psychose *f*.

pto·maine ⚕ [ˈtoumein] ptomaïne *f*.

pub F [pʌb] cabaret *m*; *sl.* bistrot *m*.

pu·ber·ty [ˈpjuːbəti] puberté *f*.

pu·bes·cence [pjuˈbesns] puberté *f*; ♀ pubescence *f*; **puˈbes·cent** pubère; ♀ pubescent; velu.

pub·lic [ˈpʌblik] **1.** □ public (-ique *f*); ⁓ **address system** (batterie *f* de) haut-parleurs *m/pl.*; ⁓ **enemy** ennemi *m* universel *ou* F public; ⚕ **Health** hygiène *f*, santé *f* publique; ⁓ **holiday** jour *m* férié; ⁓ **house** cabaret *m*; bistrot *m*; ⁓ **law** droit *m* public; ⁓ **library** bibliothèque *f* municipale *ou* communale; ⁓ **man** homme *m* public *ou* très en vue; ✝ ⁓ **relations** *pl.* relations *f/pl.* publiques; ⁓ **spirit** civisme *m*, patriotisme *m*; *see* **school, utility, works**; **2.** *sg., a. pl.* (grand) public *m*; F cabaret *m*; bistrot *m*; in ⁓ en public, publiquement; **pub·li·can** [ˈ⁓kən] aubergiste *m*; débitant *m* de boissons; *hist.* publicain *m*; **pub·liˈca·tion** publication *f*; apparition *f* (*d'un livre*); *loi:* promulgation *f*; ouvrage *m* (publié); *monthly* ⁓ revue *f* *etc.* mensuelle; **pub·li·cist** [ˈ⁓sist] publiciste *m*; journaliste *m*; **pub·licˈi·ty** [⁓ˈsiti] publicité *f*; réclame *f*; propagande *f*; service *m* de presse; ⁓ **agent** agent *m* de publicité; **pub·li·cize** [ˈ⁓saiz] faire connaître au public; **ˈpub·lic-ˈpri·vate** mixte (*éco-*

nomie); **ˈpub·lic-ˈspir·it·ed** □ dévoué au bien public, soucieux (-euse *f*) du bien public.

pub·lish [ˈpʌbliʃ] *usu.* publier; éditer; promulguer (*une loi*); révéler, répandre; **ˈpub·lish·er** éditeur *m*; libraire-éditeur (*pl.* libraires-éditeurs) *m*; *Am.* propriétaire *m* d'un journal; **ˈpub·lish·ing** publication *f*; mise *f* en vente; *attr.* d'édition; ⁓ **house** maison *f* d'édition.

puck [pʌk] puck *m*; lutin *m*; *hockey sur glace:* palet *m* en caoutchouc.

puck·er [ˈpʌkə] **1.** godet *m*, faux pli *m*; *visage:* ride *f*; F embarras *m*; **2.** *v/t.* froncer; faire goder; rider (*le visage*); *v/i.* (*a.* ⁓ up) se crisper; froncer, goder, grigner; se contracter. [cieux (-euse *f*).⧵

puck·ish □ [ˈpʌkiʃ] de lutin; malì⧵

pud·ding [ˈpudiŋ] pudding *m*, pouding *m*; *black* ⁓ boudin *m*; *white* ⁓ boudin *m* blanc.

pud·dle [ˈpʌdl] **1.** flaque *f* (d'eau); ⊕ braye *f* (d'argile); **2.** *v/t.* ⊕ corroyer (*l'argile, le fer*); puddler (*le fer*); damer (*la terre*); *v/i.* barboter; **ˈpud·dler** ⊕ brasseur *m* mécanique; *personne:* puddleur *m*; **ˈpud·dling-fur·nace** ⊕ four *m* à puddler.

pu·den·cy [ˈpjuːdənsi] pudicité *f*; **pu·den·da** [pjuːˈdendə] *pl.* parties *f/pl.* génitales; **ˈpu·dent** pudique.

pudg·y F [ˈpʌdʒi] boulot(te *f*).

pu·er·ile □ [ˈpjuːərail] puéril; *péj. a.* enfantin; **pu·er·il·i·ty** [⁓ˈriliti] puérilité *f*.

puff [pʌf] **1.** *air, respiration:* souffle *m*; *vapeur:* échappement *m* soudain; *fumée, tabac:* bouffée *f*; *robe:* bouillon *m*, manche: bouffant *m*; houppe(tte) *f* (*à poudre*); *fig.* (gâteau *m*) feuilleté *m*; tourtelet *m*; réclame *f*; F haleine *f*; **2.** *v/t.* lancer, émettre (*une bouffée de fumée etc.*); (*a.* ⁓ out, up) gonfler (*les joues etc.*); faire balloner (*une manche*); (*a.* ⁓ at) tirer sur (*une pipe*), fumer; (*a.* ⁓ up) vanter; ⁓ up augmenter (*le prix*); ⁓ed eyes yeux *m/pl.* gonflés; ⁓ed sleeve manche *f* bouffante; *v/i.* souffler, lancer des bouffées (*de fumée*); ⁓ out bouffer (*jupe*); **ˈpuff·er** ✝ renchérisseur *m*, allumeur *m*; ✝ réclamiste *m*; **ˈpuff·er·y** art *m* du puffisme; réclame *f* tapageuse; **puff·i·ness** [ˈ⁓inis] boursouflure *f*; **ˈpuff-**

ing † puffisme *m*; réclame *f* tapageuse; '**puff**-'**paste** pâte *f* feuilletée; '**puff·y** qui souffle par bouffées (*vent*); à l'haleine courte; gonflé; boursouflé; bouffant (*manche*).

pug[1] [pʌg] (*ou* ~-dog) carlin *m*; petit dogue *m*.

pug[2] ⊕ [~] corroyer (*a. un bassin*); pétrir (*l'argile*).

pu·gil·ism ['pju:dʒilizm] pugilat *m*, boxe *f*; '**pu·gil·ist** pugiliste *m*, boxeur *m*.

pug·na·cious [pʌg'neiʃəs] batailleur (-euse *f*); querelleur (-euse *f*); **pug·nac·i·ty** [~'næsiti] caractère *m* batailleur *ou* querelleur; attitude *f* batailleuse *ou* querelleuse.

pug-nose ['pʌgnouz] nez *m* troussé.

puis·ne ⚔ ['pju:ni] subalterne (*juge*).

puke *sl.* [pju:k] dégobiller (= *vomir*).

pule [pju:l] piauler, piailler.

pull [pul] **1.** (effort *m* de) traction *f*; tirage *m*; force *f* d'attraction (*d'un aimant*); *fig.* attrait *m*; *golf:* coup *m* tiré; *rame:* coup *m* d'aviron; *typ.* première épreuve *f*; F gorgée *f* (*de bière etc.*); *sl.* avantage *m*, *sl.* piston *m*; *sl.* ~ at the bottle coup *m* à même la bouteille; ~-fastener fermeture *f* éclair; **2.** *v/t.* tirer (*a. typ., a. sp. un cheval*); traîner; cueillir (*un fruit*); *fig.* attirer; ⚓ manier (*un aviron*); ⚓ ramer; ⚓ souquer; ~ the trigger presser la détente; F ~ one's weight y mettre du sien; ~ down faire descendre; baisser; démolir; ~ in retenir (*un cheval*); ~ off arracher; ôter; remporter (*un prix*); ~ through tirer (*q.*) d'affaire; ~ up (re)monter; relever; arracher (*une plante*); arrêter (*un cheval, une voiture, etc.*); *fig.* réprimander; *v/i.* tirer (*sur, at*); *mot.* peiner; ⚓ ramer; 🚂 ~ out sortir de la gare; partir; ~ through se tirer d'affaire; ~ up s'arrêter.

pul·let ['pulit] poulette *f*; fattened ~ poularde *f*.

pul·ley ⊕ ['puli] poulie *f*; set of ~s *pl.* palan *m*, moufle *f*.

Pull·man car 🚂 ['pulmən'ka:] voiture *f* Pullman; *Am.* wagon-salon (*pl.* wagons-salons) *m*.

pull...: '~-out **1.** supplément *m* détachable; **2.** détachable; rétractable; '~-o·ver pull-over *m*, F pull *m*; '~-'up arrêt *m*; auberge *f* (*etc. pour automobilistes*).

pul·mo·nar·y 🩺 ['pʌlmənəri] pulmonaire, des poumons; poitrinaire (*personne*).

pulp [pʌlp] **1.** dents etc.: pulpe *f*; fruits: chair *f*; ⊕ pâte *f* à papier; *Am.* (*a.* ~ magazine) revue *f* etc. à bon marché; **2.** réduire en pulpe *ou* pâte; mettre (*des livres*) au pilon.

pul·pit ['pulpit] chaire *f*.

pulp·y □ ['pʌlpi] pulpeux (-euse *f*), charnu; F flasque.

pul·sate [pʌl'seit] palpiter; vibrer; battre (*cœur*); **pul·sa·tile** ♪ ['~sətail] de percussion; **pul·sa·tion** pulsation *f*; battement *m*.

pulse[1] [pʌls] **1.** pouls *m*; battement *m*; **2.** palpiter; vibrer; battre.

pulse[2] [~] légumineuses *f/pl.*

pul·ver·i·za·tion [pʌlvərai'zeiʃn] pulvérisation *f*; '**pul·ver·ize** *v/t.* pulvériser; réduire en poudre; *fig.* démolir; atomiser; *v/i.* tomber en poussière; se vaporiser; '**pul·ver·iz·er** pulvérisateur *m*; vaporisateur *m*.

pum·ice ['pʌmis] (*a.* ~-stone) (pierre *f*) ponce *f*.

pum·mel ['pʌml] bourrer de coups de poings.

pump[1] [pʌmp] **1.** pompe *f*; *attr.* de pompe; **2.** *v/t.* pomper de l'eau; refouler (dans, *into*); F sonder (*q.*), faire parler (*q.*); *sl.* épuiser; *v/i.* pomper.

pump[2] [~] escarpin *m*; soulier *m* de bal.

pump·kin ♀ ['pʌmpkin] citrouille *f*; potiron *m*.

pump-room ['pʌmprum] station thermale: buvette *f*; Pavillon *m*.

pun [pʌn] **1.** jeu *m* de mots, calembour *m*; **2.** faire des jeux de mots etc.

Punch[1] [pʌntʃ] polichinelle *m*; guignol *m*; as pleased as ~ heureux (-euse *f*) comme un roi; ~ and Judy ['dʒu:di] show guignol *m*.

punch[2] ⊕ [~] **1.** pointeau *m*; chasse-clou *m*; perçoir *m*; poinçon *m* (*a.* 🔨); emporte-pièce *m/inv.*; **2.** percer; poinçonner; découper; estamper; ~ed card see punch card.

punch[3] F [~] **1.** coup *m* de poing; F force *f*; **2.** donner un coup de poing à; cogner sur; *Am.* conduire *ou* garder (*des bœufs*).

punch[4] [~] boisson: punch *m*.

punch[5] F [~] cheval, homme: trapu

m; *sl.* pull no ⁀es parler carrément; ne faire de quartier à personne.

punch card ['pʌntʃkɑːd] carte *f* perforée.

punch-drunk ['pʌntʃdrʌŋk] abruti (par les coups).

punch·er ['pʌntʃə] poinçonneur *m*; perceur *m*; estampeur *m*; *outil:* poinçonneuse *f*; découpeuse *f*; F pugiliste *m*; *Am.* cowboy *m*; **'punch(·ing)-ball** *boxe:* punching-ball *m*.

punch line ['pʌntʃlain] pointe *f* (*d'une plaisanterie*).

punch-up F ['pʌntʃʌp] bagarre *f*.

punc·til·i·o [pʌŋk'tiliou] point *m* d'étiquette; *see* punctiliousness.

punc·til·i·ous [pʌŋk'tiliəs] méticuleux (-euse *f*), pointilleux (-euse *f*); très soucieux (-euse *f*) du protocole; **punc'til·i·ous·ness** souci *m* du protocole; formalisme *m*; scrupule *m* des détails.

punc·tu·al □ ['pʌŋktjuəl] exact; **punc·tu·al·i·ty** [⁀'æliti] exactitude *f*, ponctualité *f*.

punc·tu·ate ['pʌŋktjueit] ponctuer (*a. fig.*); **punc·tu'a·tion** ponctuation *f*.

punc·ture ['pʌŋktʃə] 1. crevaison *f*; ⚕ ponction *f*; *mot. etc.* piqûre *f* de clou, crevaison *f*; 2. *v/t.* ⚕ ponctionner; *mot.* crever (*a. v/i.*).

pun·dit ['pʌndit] pandit *m*; F pontife *m*.

pun·gen·cy ['pʌndʒənsi] goût *m* piquant; odeur *f* piquante; *fig.* aigreur *f*; mordant *m*; saveur *f*; **'pun·gent** aigu (-uë *f*); poignant (*chagrin*); âcre (*odeur*); mordant (*paroles etc.*).

pu·ni·ness ['pjuːninis] chétiveté *f*.

pun·ish ['pʌniʃ] punir, châtier; F *fig.* taper dur sur (*q.*); ne pas épargner; **'pun·ish·a·ble** □ punissable; ⚖ délictueux (-euse *f*); **'pun·ish·er** punisseur (-euse *f*) *m*; **'pun·ish·ment** punition *f*; châtiment *m*.

pu·ni·tive ['pjuːnitiv] punitif (-ive *f*), répressif (-ive *f*).

punk *Am.* [pʌŋk] 1. amadou *m*; *fig.* sottises *f/pl.*; 2. mauvais, sans valeur. [lembours.\
pun·ster ['pʌnstə] faiseur *m* de ca-⌏
punt¹ ⚓ [pʌnt] 1. bateau *m* plat (*conduit à la perche*); bachot *m*; 2. conduire à la perche; transporter dans un bateau plat.

punt² [⁀] *turf:* parier; *cartes:* ponter.

pu·ny □ ['pjuːni] menu; mesquin; chétif (-ive *f*).　　[bas (des petits).\
pup [pʌp] 1. *see* puppy; 2. *zo.* mettre⌏
pu·pil ['pjuːpl] *anat.* pupille *f* (*a.* ⚖ *mf*); élève *mf*, écolier (-ère *f*) *m*; **pu·pil·(l)age** ['⁀pilidʒ] état *m* d'élève; ⚖ minorité *f*.

pup·pet ['pʌpit] marionnette *f*; *fig.* pantin *m*; **'⁀-show** théâtre *m* *ou* spectacle *m* de marionnettes.

pup·py ['pʌpi] jeune chien(ne *f*) *m*; *fig.* freluquet *m*.

pur·blind ['pəːblaind] presque aveugle; *fig.* obtus.

pur·chase ['pəːtʃəs] 1. achat *m*; emplette *f*; acquisition *f*; ⚙ force *f* mécanique; ⚙ prise *f*; ⚖ loyer *m*; *fig.* (point *m* d')appui *m*; make ⁀s faire des emplettes; *at twenty years'* ⁀ moyennant vingt années de loyer; *his life is not worth an hour's* ⁀ on ne lui donne(rait) pas une heure à vivre; ✝ ⁀ permit ordre *m* d'achat; 2. acheter, acquérir (*a. fig.*); ⚓ lever à l'aide du cabestan; **'pur·chas·er** acheteur (-euse *f*) *m*; ✝ preneur (-euse *f*) *m*.

pure □ [pjuə] pur; **'⁀-bred** *Am.* de race pure; **'pure·ness** pureté *f*.

pur·ga·tion *usu. fig.* [pəː'geiʃn] purgation *f* (*a.* ⚕); **pur·ga·tive** ['⁀gətiv] purgatif (-ive *f*) (*a. su./m*); **'pur·ga·to·ry** *eccl.* purgatoire *m* (*a. fig.*).

purge [pəːdʒ] 1. ⚕ purgatif *m*; purgation *f*; *pol.* épuration *f*; 2. *fig.* nettoyer; épurer; purger (de *of*, *from*) (*a.* ⚖); ⚖ faire amende honorable pour; *pol.* épurer, purger.

pu·ri·fi·ca·tion [pjuərifi'keiʃn] purification *f*; épuration *f*; **pu·ri·fi·er** ['⁀faiə] épurateur *m* (*de gaz etc.*); *personne:* purificateur (-trice *f*) *m*; **pu·ri·fy** ['⁀fai] purifier; ⚙, *a. fig.* épurer.

Pu·ri·tan ['pjuəritən] puritain(e *f*) (*a. su.*); **pu·ri·tan·ic** [⁀'tænik] (⁀ally) (de) puritain; **Pu·ri·tan·ism** ['⁀tənizm] puritanisme *m*.

pu·ri·ty ['pjuəriti] pureté *f* (*a. fig.*).

purl¹ [pəːl] cannetille *f* (*à broder*); picot *m* (*de dentelle*); (*a.* ⁀ *stitch*) maille *f* à l'envers.

purl² [⁀] 1. *ruisseau:* (*doux*) murmure *m*; 2. murmurer.

purl·er F ['pəːlə] chute *f* la tête la première; *sl.* billet *m* de parterre.

pur·lieus [ˈpəːljuːz] pl. bornes f/pl.; alentours m/pl.

pur·loin [pəːˈlɔin] détourner; voler; **purˈloin·er** détourneur m; voleur (-euse f) m; fig. plagiaire m.

pur·ple [ˈpəːpl] 1. violet(te f); 2. pourpre f; violet m; 3. (s')em-pourprer.

pur·port [ˈpəːpət] 1. sens m, signification f; portée f (d'un mot); 2. avoir la prétention (de inf., to inf.); † indiquer, vouloir dire.

pur·pose [ˈpəːpəs] 1. dessein m; but m, intention f; fin f; résolution f; for the ~ of pour; dans le but de; on ~ exprès, de propos délibéré; to the ~ à propos; to no ~ en vain, inutilement; novel with a ~ roman m à thèse; strenght of ~ détermination f; résolution f; 2. avoir l'intention (de inf., gér. ou to inf.), se proposer (qch., s.th.; de inf., gér. ou to inf.); '~-**built** construit spécialement; fonctionnalisé; **pur·pose·ful** □ [ˈ~ful] réfléchi; tenace, avisé (personne); **ˈpur·pose·less** □ inutile, sans but; **ˈpur·pose·ly** adv. à dessein; exprès.

purr [pəː] 1. ronronner (chat, moteur); 2. ronron m.

purse [pəːs] 1. bourse f, porte-monnaie m/inv.; fig. bourse f; sp. prix m (d'argent); public ~ Trésor m; finances f/pl. de l'État; 2. (souv. up) pincer (les lèvres); plisser (le front); froncer (les sourcils); '~-**proud** orgueilleux (-euse f) de sa fortune; **ˈpurs·er** ⚓ commissaire m; **ˈpurse-strings** pl.: hold the ~ tenir les cordons de la bourse.

pur·si·ness [ˈpəːsinis] peine f à respirer; essoufflement m.

purs·lane ♀ [ˈpəːslin] pourpier m.

pur·su·ance [pəˈsjuːəns] poursuite f; in ~ of par suite de, en vertu de, conformément à; **purˈsu·ant** □ : ~ to conformément à, par suite de.

pur·sue [pəˈsjuː] v/t. poursuivre; fig. rechercher (le plaisir); fig. courir après; suivre (le chemin, une ligne de conduite, une profession, etc.); v/i. suivre, continuer; ~ after poursuivre; **purˈsu·er** poursuivant(e f) m; **purˈsuit** [~ˈsjuːt] poursuite f; recherche f (de, of); occupation f; usu. ~s pl. travaux m/pl.; carrière f; qqfois passe-temps m/inv.; ~ plane chasseur m.

pur·sy¹ [ˈpəːsi] à l'haleine courte; gros(se f), corpulent.

pur·sy² [~] pincé (bouche, lèvres); riche; orgueilleux (-euse f) de sa fortune. [lent.]

pu·ru·lent □ ⚕ [ˈpjuərulənt] puru-]

pur·vey [pəːˈvei] v/t. fournir (des provisions); v/i. être (le) fournisseur (de, for); **purˈvey·ance** fourniture f de provisions; approvisionnement m; **purˈvey·or** fournisseur (-euse f) m (surt. de provisions).

pur·view [ˈpəːvjuː] portée f, limites f/pl.; ✝ statut: corps m. [boue f.]

pus ⚕ [pʌs] pus m; sanie f; abcès:]

push [puʃ] 1. poussée f, impulsion f; coup m; effort m; ✕ attaque f en masse; F énergie f; F hardiesse f; last ~ effort m suprême; sl. get the ~ se faire dégommer (= recevoir son congé); give s.o. the ~ flanquer q. à la porte; donner son congé à q.; 2. v/t. pousser; bousculer; appuyer sur (un bouton); enfoncer (dans, in[to]); pousser la vente de; importuner; (a. ~ through) faire accepter; faire passer (à travers, through); revendiquer (un droit); (a. ~ ahead ou forward ou on) (faire) avancer ou pousser (en avant); ~ s.th. (up)on s.o. imposer qch. à q.; ~ one's way se frayer un chemin (à travers, through); ~ed pressé; à court (d'argent, for money); fort embarrassé; v/i. avancer; pousser; ~ on se presser, se hâter; se remettre en route; ~ off ⚓ pousser au large; F fig. se mettre en route; '~-**ball** sp. (sorte de) jeu m de ballon; '~-**bike** bicyclette f; '~-**but·ton** ⚡ bouton m à pression; poussoir m; '~-**cart** charrette f à bras; '~-**chair** poussette f; **ˈpush·er** personne f qui pousse; arriviste mf; avion m à hélice propulsive; ⚙ Am. locomotive f de renfort; **push·ful** □ [ˈ~ful], **ˈpush·ing** □ débrouillard, entreprenant; péj. ambitieux (-euse f), trop accostant; **ˈpushˈoff** ⚓ poussée f au large; fig. impulsion f; **ˈpushˈo·ver** surt. Am. chose f facile à obtenir; tâche f facile à faire; victoire f facile; personne f crédule; a ~ la facilité même; be a ~ for ne pas pouvoir résister à; **ˈpush-up**: do ~s faire des tractions ou des pompes; **ˈpush·y** arriviste, qui se met trop en avant.

pu·sil·la·nim·i·ty [pjuːsiləˈnimiti]

pusillanimité *f*; **pu·sil·lan·i·mous** □ [ˌˈlænɪməs] pusillanime.

puss(·**y**) [ˈpus(i)] minet(te *f*) *m*; *fig.* coquine *f*; *fig.* chipie *f*; *Am. sl.* visage *m*; ♃ *bouleau*: chaton *m*; **'puss·y-foot** *Am.* F **1.** personne *f* furtive; fin Normand *m*; **2.** F aller furtivement; ne pas se compromettre.

pus·tule ⚕ [ˈpʌstjuːl] pustule *f*.

put [put] [*irr.*] **1.** *v/t.* mettre, poser (*a. une question*), placer; présenter (à, *to*); lancer (*un cheval*) (sur, *at*); exposer (*une condition, la situation, etc.*); exprimer; parler; estimer (à, *at*); ~ *it* s'exprimer; ~ *about* faire circuler, répandre; ⚓ virer de bord; F mettre (*q.*) en émoi, inquiéter; déranger; ~ *across* réussir dans (*une entreprise*); ~ *away* serrer; remiser (*son auto*); écarter; mettre de côté; *fig.* tuer; ~ *back* remettre; retarder (*une horloge, l'arrivée, etc.*); ~ *by* mettre de côté; mettre en réserve; ~ *down* (dé)poser; noter; supprimer; mettre fin à; fermer (*le parapluie*); juger; attribuer (à, *to*); inscrire (*q.* pour, *s.o. for*); débarquer (*les voyageurs*); ~ *forth* émettre; avancer; publier (*un livre etc.*); déployer, exercer; pousser (*des feuilles etc.*); ~ *forward* avancer (*l'heure, la montre, une opinion, etc.*); émettre; faire valoir (*une proposition, une théorie, etc.*); ~ *o.s. forward* se mettre en avant; s'imposer; se donner (pour, *as*); ~ *in* introduire dans; mettre, insérer dans (*un journal*); placer (*un mot*); ✍ planter; présenter (*un document, un témoin*; *a. q.* à *un examen*); ⚖ installer (*un huissier*); F faire (*des heures de travail*), passer (*le temps*); ~ *off* enlever, ôter, retirer (*un vêtement, le chapeau*); remettre (*un rendez-vous, l'heure, une tâche*); ajourner; renvoyer (*q.*); déconcerter, dérouter (*q.*); décourager (*q.*) (de, *from*); ~ *on* mettre (*a. la lumière, la vapeur, des vêtements*); prendre (*un air, du poids, de la vitesse*); gagner (*du poids*); ✝ augmenter (*le prix*); ajouter à; allumer (*le gaz etc.*); avancer (*la pendule*); *théâ.* monter (*une pièce*); confier (*une tâche*) (à *q.*, *to s.o.*); *école:* démander à (*un élève*) (de, *to*); 🚂 mettre en service; ajouter (*des voitures à un train*); *mot.* serrer (*le frein*);

sp. miser (*un pari*); *sp.* ~ *on* (*a score of*) *thirty* marquer trente points; F ~ *the screw on s.o.* forcer la main à q.; *he is* ~*ting it on* il fait l'important; il fait du chiqué; *fig.* ~ *it on thick* exagérer; flatter grossièrement; ~ *on airs* se donner des airs; ~ *s.o. on* (*gér.*) mettre q. à (*inf.*); ~ *out* mettre dehors; tendre (*la main*); étendre (*les bras*); tirer (*la langue*); sortir (*la tête*); mettre à l'eau (*un canot*); placer (*de l'argent*) (à intérêt, *to interest*); émettre (*un document etc.*); publier (*une revue etc.*); crever (l'œil à q., *s.o.'s eye*); éteindre (*le feu, le gaz, etc.*); lancer (*une histoire*); *fig.* déconcerter; *fig.* contrarier; *fig.* gêner; ~ *s.o. out* expulser q., chasser q. (de, *of*); ~ *out of action* mettre hors de combat; ⊕ détraquer; ~ *over* faire réussir; ~ *s.th. over on s.o.* faire accepter qch. à q.; ~ *through* téléph. mettre en communication (avec, *to*); F mener à bien; ~ *to* attacher; atteler (*un cheval*); ~ *s.o. to it* donner du mal à q.; contraindre q. (à, *to*); ~ *to expense* faire faire des dépenses à (*q.*); ~ *to death* mettre (*q.*) à mort; exécuter (*q.*); ~ *to the rack* (*ou torture*) mettre (*q.*) à la question *ou* torture; ~ *up* construire; ériger; installer; lever (*la fenêtre, une glace de wagon*); accrocher (*un tableau*); ouvrir (*le parapluie, a. qqfois la fenêtre*); augmenter, hausser (*le prix*); (faire) lever (*du gibier*); mettre (*en vente, aux enchères*); regainer (*l'épée*); relever (*les cheveux, le col*); afficher (*un avis*), coller (*une affiche*); poser (*le rideau*); fournir (*de l'argent*); faire, offrir (*une prière, une résistance*); proposer (*un candidat*); faire un paquet de (*sandwiches etc.*); loger (*q.*), donner à coucher à (*q.*); ✝ présenter (en, *in*); *sp.* F faire courir; *jeu:* se caver de; ~ *s.o. up to* mettre q. au courant de; inciter q. à; ~ *upon* en imposer à; ~ *it upon* laisser (à *q.*) le soin de; **2.** *v/i.* ⚓ ~ *in* entrer dans; faire escale dans (*un port*); ⚓ ~ *off* (*ou out ou to sea*) démarrer, pousser au large, quitter la côte *etc.*; ~ *up at* loger à *ou* chez (*q.*); descendre à *ou* chez (*q.*); ~ *up for* poser sa candidature à; ~ *up with* s'arranger de; tolérer; se résigner à; F ~ *upon* exploiter (*q.*); abuser de (*q.*); *be* ~ *upon* s'en laisser imposer.

pu·ta·tive [ˈpjuːtətiv] putatif (-ive f).

put·lock, put·log ⊕ [ˈpʌtlɔk; ˈ‿lɔg] boulin m.

put-on F [ˈpʌtɔn] 1. affecté, feint, simulé, faux (fausse f); 2. manière(s) f(pl.) affectée(s); mystification f, farce f.

pu·tre·fac·tion [pjuːtriˈfækʃn] putréfaction f; **pu·tre·fac·tive** putréfactif (-ive f); putride; de putréfaction.

pu·tre·fy [ˈpjuːtrifai] v/i. se putréfier; pourrir; ✍ suppurer; v/t. putréfier, pourrir.

pu·tres·cence [pjuːˈtresns] putrescence f; **pu·tres·cent** putrescent; en putréfaction.

pu·trid □ [ˈpjuːtrid] putride; en putréfaction; infect; sl. moche; **pu·trid·i·ty** pourriture f.

put·tee [ˈpʌti] bande f molletière.

put·ty [ˈpʌti] 1. (a. glaziers' ‿) mastic m (à vitres); (a. plasterers' ‿) pâte f de chaux; (a. jewellers' ‿) potée f (d'étain); 2. mastiquer.

put-up job [ˈpʌtʌpˈdʒɔb] coup m monté; affaire f machinée à l'avance.

puz·zle [ˈpʌzl] 1. énigme m; problème m; devinette f; picture ‿ rébus m; 2. v/t. intriguer; embarrasser; ‿ out débrouiller; déchiffrer; v/i. (souv. ‿ one's brains) se creuser la tête (pour comprendre qch., over

s.th.); ˈ‿-head·ed confus; ˈ‿-lock serrure f à combinaisons; cadenas m à secret; **ˈpuz·zler** question f embarrassante; F colle f.

pyg·m(a)e·an [pigˈmiːən] pygméen (-ne f); **pyg·my** [ˈpigmi] pygmée m; attr. pygméen(ne f). [m.]

py·ja·mas [pəˈdʒɑːməz] pl. pyjama⌋

py·lo·rus anat. [paiˈlɔːrəs] pylore m.

py·or·rh(o)e·a [paiəˈriə] pyorrhée f.

pyr·a·mid [ˈpirəmid] pyramide f; **py·ram·i·dal** □ [piˈræmidl] pyramidal (-aux m/pl.).

pyre [ˈpaiə] bûcher m (funéraire).

py·ret·ic [paiˈretik] pyrétique.

pyro... [ˈpairou] pyr(o)-; **py·rog·raphy** [paiˈrɔɡrəfi] pyrogravure f; **ˈpy·ro·scope** pyroscope m; **py·rotech·nic, py·ro·tech·ni·cal** [pairouˈteknik(l)] pyrotechnique; **py·ro·tech·nics** pl. pyrotechnique f; **py·ro·tech·nist** pyrotechnicien m; artificier m.

Pyr·rhic vic·to·ry [ˈpirikˈviktəri] victoire f à la Pyrrhus.

Py·thag·o·re·an [paiθæɡəˈriːən] 1. pythagoricien(ne f); de Pythagore; 2. pythagoricien m.

Pyth·i·an [ˈpiθiən] pythien(ne f).

py·thon [ˈpaiθən] python m.

pyx [piks] 1. eccl. ciboire m; 2. boîte f des monnaies destinées au contrôle; trial of the ‿ essai m des monnaies.

Q

Q, q [kju:] Q *m*, q *m*.

Q-boat ⚓ ['kju:bout] piège *m* à sous-marins.

quack¹ [kwæk] **1.** coin-coin *m*; **2.** crier, faire coin-coin.

quack² [~] **1.** charlatan *m*; † guérisseur *m*; **2.** de charlatan; **3.** F faire le charlatan; ~ *up* vanter; rafistoler (*qch. d'usagé*); **quack·er·y** ['~əri] charlatanisme *m*; hâblerie *f*.

quad [kwɔd] *see* quadrangle; quadrat.

quad·ra·ge·nar·i·an [kwɔdrədʒi-'nɛəriən] quadragénaire (*a. su./mf*).

quad·ran·gle ['kwɔdræŋgl] Å quadrilatère *m*; *école etc.*: cour *f*.

quad·rant ['kwɔdrənt] ⚓, ⊕ secteur *m*; Å quart *m* de cercle.

quad·ra·phon·ic [kwɔdrə'fɔnik] quadriphonique; *in* ~ *sound* en quadriphonie.

quad·rat *typ.* ['kwɔdrit] cadrat *m*; **quad·rat·ic** Å [kwɔ'drætik] **1.** du second degré; **2.** (*a.* ~ *equation*) équation *f* du second degré; **quad·ra·ture** ['kwɔdrətʃə] quadrature *f*.

quad·ren·ni·al □ [kwɔ'drenjəl] quadriennal (-aux *m/pl.*); qui a lieu tous les quatre ans.

quad·ri·lat·er·al Å [kwɔdri'lætərəl] **1.** quadrilatéral (-aux *m/pl.*); **2.** quadrilatère *m*.

qua·drille [kwə'dril] quadrille *m*.

quad·ri·par·tite [kwɔdri'pɑ:tait] quadripartite.

quad·ru·ped ['kwɔdruped] **1.** quadrupède *m*; **2.** (*a.* **quad·ru·pe·dal** [kwɔ'dru:pidl]) quadrupède; **quad·ru·ple** ['kwɔdrupl] **1.** □ quadruple; (*a.* ~ *to ou of*) au quadruple de; **2.** quadruple *m*; **3.** (se) quadrupler; **quad·ru·plet** ['~plit] quadruplé(e *f*) *m*; **quad·ru·pli·cate** [kwɔ'dru:plikit] **1.** quadruplé, quadruple; **2.** quatre exemplaires *m/pl.*; **3.** [~keit] quadrupler.

quaff *poét.* [kwɑ:f] boire à plein verre; ~ *off* vider d'un trait.

quag [kwæg] *see* ~*mire*; **'quag·gy**

marécageux (-euse *f*); **quag·mire** ['~maiə] marécage *m*; fondrière *f*; *fig.* embarras *m*.

quail¹ *orn.* [kweil] caille *f*.

quail² [~] fléchir, faiblir (devant, *before*).

quaint □ [kweint] bizarre; singulier (-ère *f*); pittoresque; **'quaint·ness** bizarrerie *f*; pittoresque *m*.

quake [kweik] trembler (de, *with*; pour, *for*); frémir (de, *with*).

Quak·er ['kweikə] quaker *m*; **'Quak·er·ism** quakerisme *m*.

qual·i·fi·ca·tion [kwɔlifi'keiʃn] titre *m* (à un emploi, for a post); aptitude *f*, capacité *f*; réserve *f*; **qual·i·fied** ['~faid] qui a les qualités requises *ou* titres requis; diplômé; compétent; autorisé; restreint, modéré; sous condition; **qual·i·fy** ['~fai] *v/t.* qualifier (*a. gramm.*) (de, *as*); rendre apte à; modifier; apporter des réserves à; couper (*une boisson*); *v/i.* se qualifier (pour, *for*), acquérir les titres requis *ou* connaissances requises; être reçu; ~*ing examination* examen *m* pour certificat d'aptitude; examen *m* d'entrée; **qual·i·ta·tive** □ ['~tətiv] qualitatif (-ive *f*); **'qual·i·ty** *usu.* qualité *f*; valeur *f*; pouvoir *m*; caractère *m*; *son:* timbre *m*.

qualm [kwɔ:m] nausée *f*; scrupule *m*, remords *m*; pressentiment *m* de malheur; hésitation *f*; **'qualm·ish** □ sujet(te *f*) aux nausées; mal à l'aise. [*m*; impasse *f*.]

quan·da·ry ['kwɔndəri] embarras)

quan·ti·ta·tive □ ['kwɔntitətiv] quantitatif (-ive *f*); **'quan·ti·ty** quantité *f* (*a.* Å, ♪, *prosodie*); somme *f*; *bill of quantities* devis *m*; Å *unknown* ~ inconnue *f* (*a. fig.*).

quan·tum ['kwɔntəm], *pl.* **-ta** [~tə] quantum *m*; part *f*; *phys.* ~ *theory* théorie *f* des quanta.

quar·an·tine ['kwɔrənti:n] **1.** quarantaine *f*; *place in* ~ = **2.** mettre en quarantaine.

quar·rel ['kwɔrəl] **1.** querelle *f*,

dispute *f*; **2.** se quereller, se disputer (avec, *with*; à propos de *about*, *over*); *fig.* se plaindre (de, *with*); **quar·rel·some** ['~səm] □ querelleur (-euse *f*), batailleur (-euse *f*).

quar·ry[1] ['kwɔri] **1.** carrière *f*; *fig.* mine *f*; **2.** *v/t.* extraire (*des pierres*) de la carrière; creuser une carrière dans; *v/i.* exploiter une carrière; *fig.* puiser (qch., *for s.th.*).

quar·ry[2] [~] *chasse:* proie *f*.

quar·ry·man ['kwɔrimən], *a.* **quar·ri·er** ['~iə] carrier *m*.

quart [kwɔːt] quart *m* (*de gallon*, = *approx. 1 litre*); *escrime:* [kɑːt] quarte *f*.

quar·tan ✻ ['kwɔːtn] (fièvre *f*) quarte.

quar·ter ['kwɔːtə] **1.** quart *m* (*a. cercle*, *heure*, *pomme*, *siècle*, *etc.*); terme *m* de loyer; région *f*, partie *f*; *ciel:* coin *m*; *Am.* quart *m* de dollar (*25 cents*); ⊘, *cuis.*, *lune*, *ville:* quartier *m*; ⚓ hanche *f*; ⚓ quart *m* de brasse; ⚓ (quart *m* d')aire *f* de vent; côté *m*, direction *f*; *orange:* tranche *f*; *mesure:* quart *m* (*de livre*), quarter *m* (*2,909 hl*); ✕, *a.fig.* cantonnement *m*, quartier *m*; *fig.* milieu *m*; ~s *pl.* appartements *m/pl.*; résidence *f*; ✕ quartier *m*, -s *m/pl.*; logement *m*; in this ~ ici, de ce côté-ci; from all ~s de toutes parts, de tous côtés; free ~s droit *m* au logement; **2.** diviser en quatre; équarrir (*un bœuf*); *hist.* écarteler (*un condamné*, *a.* ⊘); ✕ cantonner; be ~ed (up)on (*ou at*) loger chez; '~-day jour *m* du terme; '~-deck ⚓ plage *f* arrière; *coll.* officiers *m/pl.*; '**quar·ter·ly** [~li] trimestriel(le *f*); **2.** publication *f* trimestrielle; '**quar·ter·mas·ter** ✕ intendant *m* militaire; ⚓ second maître *m*; **quar·tern** ['~ən] quart *m* (*de pinte*); (*a.* ~ *loaf*) pain *m* de quatre livres.

quar·tet(te) ♪ [kwɔːˈtet] quatuor *m*.

quar·to ['kwɔːtou] in-quarto *m/inv.* (*a. adj.*).

quartz min. [kwɔːts] quarts *m*.

quash [kwɔʃ] ⚖ casser, annuler; *fig.* étouffer.

qua·si ['kwɑːzi] quasi-, presque.

qua·ter·na·ry ⚛, ⚙, *géol.* [kwəˈtəːnəri] quaternaire.

qua·ver ['kweivə] **1.** tremblement

m; ♪ croche *f*; ♪ trille *m*; **2.** chevroter, (*a.* ~ *out*) trembloter (*voix*); ♪ faire des trilles; '**qua·ver·y** tremblotant.

quay [kiː] quai *m*; **quay·age** ['~idʒ] droit *m*, -s *m/pl.* de quai; quais *m/pl.*

quea·si·ness ['kwiːzinis] malaise *f*; nausées *f/pl.*; scrupules *m/pl.* de conscience; '**quea·sy** □ sujet(te *f*) à des nausées; délicat (*estomac*); scrupuleux (-euse *f*); dégoûtant (*mets*); I feel ~ j'ai mal au cœur; F j'ai le cœur fade.

queen [kwiːn] **1.** reine *f*; *cartes:* dame *f*; *échecs:* dame *f*, reine *f*; *sl.* (*homosexuel*) tante *f*, tapette *f*; ~ *bee* reine *f*, abeille *f* mère; ~'s *metal* métal *m* blanc; ~'s-ware faïence *f* crème; **2.** *échecs: v/t.* damer; *v/i.* aller à dame; ~ *it* faire la reine; '**queen·like**, '**queen·ly** de reine, digne d'une reine; majestueux (-euse *f*).

queer [kwiə] **1.** bizarre; singulier (-ère *f*); étrange; suspect; F tout patraque (*malade*); **2.** *Am. sl.* homosexuel *m*; **3.** *vb.: sl.* ~ *the pitch for* contrecarrer (*q.*); faire échouer les projets de (*q.*).

quell *poét.* [kwel] apaiser; étouffer.

quench [kwentʃ] *fig.* apaiser (*la soif etc.*); étouffer, réprimer (*un désir*, *a.* ⚡); éteindre; '**quench·er** F boisson *f*, consommation *f*; '**quench·less** □ inextinguible; inassouvissable.

que·rist ['kwiərist] questionneur (-euse *f*) *m*.

quern [kwəːn] moulin *m* à bras.

quer·u·lous □ ['kwerʊləs] plaintif (-ive *f*); grognon(ne *f*).

que·ry ['kwiəri] **1.** reste à savoir (si, *if*); **2.** question *f*; *typ.* point *m* d'interrogation; **3.** *v/t.* mettre *ou* révoquer en doute; *v/i.* s'informer (si, *whether*).

quest [kwest] **1.** recherche *f*; *chasse:* quête *f*; in ~ *of* à la recherche de; en quête de; **2.** rechercher; *chasse:* quêter.

ques·tion ['kwestʃn] **1.** question *f*; (*mise en*) doute *m*; affaire *f*; sujet *m*; ~ *mark* point *m* d'interrogation; *radio*, *télév.* ~ *master* animateur *m*; *parl.* ~ *time* heure *f* réservée aux questions orales; *parl.* ~! au fait!; *beyond* (*all*) ~ sans aucun doute; incontestable(ment); in ~ en question, dont il s'agit; en doute; *come into* ~ arriver sur le tapis; *call in* ~ révoquer en doute; *beg the* ~ faire une pétition de principe, supposer vrai ce qui est en question; *the* ~ *is whether* il s'agit de savoir si; *that is out of the* ~ c'est impossible; *there is no* ~ il n'est pas question (de qch., of *s.th.*; que *sbj.*, of *ger.*); **2.** interroger; révoquer en doute; **'ques·tion·a·ble** □ contestable, discutable; *péj.* équivoque; **'ques·tion·a·ble·ness** caractère *m* douteux *ou* équivoque (de, of); **ques·tion·naire** [kwestiə'nɛə] questionnaire *m*; **'ques·tion·er** interrogateur (-trice *f*) *m*.

queue [kju:] **1.** queue *f* (*de personnes, de voitures, de cheveux, etc.*); **2.** (*usu.* ~ *up*) prendre la file (*voitures*); faire la queue; ~ *on* s'attacher à la queue.

quib·ble ['kwibl] **1.** chicane *f* (de mots), argutie *f*; † calembour *m*; **2.** *fig.* chicaner (sur les mots); **'quib·bler** chicaneur (-euse *f*) *m*; ergoteur (-euse *f*) *m*.

quick [kwik] **1.** vif (vive *f*) (*a. esprit, haie, œil*); fin (*oreille etc.*); † vivant; rapide, prompt; éveillé (*enfant, esprit, a. ♪*); ~ *to prompt* à; ✕ ~ *march* pas *m* cadencé *ou* accéléré; ~ *step* pas *m* rapide *ou* pressé; *double* ~ *step* pas *m* gymnastique; **2.** vif *m*, chair *f* vive; *the* ~ les vivants *m/pl.*; *to the* ~ jusqu'au vif; *fig.* au vif, au cœur; jusqu'à la moelle des os; *cut s.o. to the* ~ piquer q. au vif; **3.** *see* ~*ly*; **'~change ac·tor** acteur *m* à transformations rapides; **'quick·en** *v/t.* (r)animer; accélérer (*a. ♫*); presser; *v/i.* s'animer, se ranimer; devenir plus rapide; **'quick·fir·ing** ✕ à tir rapide; **'quick·fro·zen** surgelé; **quick·ie** F ['~i] chose *f* faite à la va-vite; **'quick·lime** chaux *f* vive; **'quick·ly** vite; vivement; rapidement; **'quick·match** mèche *f* d'artilleur; **'quick·mo·tion pic·ture** *cin.* accéléré *m*; **'quick·ness** vitesse *f*, rapidité *f*; vivacité *f*, promptitude *f* (*d'esprit*); finesse *f* (*d'oreille*); acuité *f* (*de vision*).

quick...: '~**·sand** sable *m* mouvant; lise *f*; '~**·set** ✓ *aubépine etc.*: bouture *f*; (*a.* ~ *hedge*) haie *f* vive; '~-'**sight·ed** aux yeux vifs; perspicace; '~**·sil·ver** *min.* vif-argent *m*

(*a. fig.*), mercure *m*; '~**-tem·pered** irascible; '~-'**wit·ted** éveillé; à l'esprit prompt; adroit.

quid[1] [kwid] *tabac:* chique *f*.

quid[2] *sl.* [~] livre *f* (sterling).

quid·di·ty ['kwiditi] *phls.* quiddité *f*, essence *f*; F chicane *f*.

quid·nunc F ['kwidnʌŋk] nouvelliste *mf*; curieux (-euse *f*) *m*.

quid pro quo ['kwid prou 'kwou] pareille *f*, équivalent *m*, compensation *f*.

qui·es·cence [kwai'esns] repos *m*; tranquillité *f*; **qui'es·cent** □ en repos; tranquille (*a. fig.*).

qui·et ['kwaiət] **1.** □ tranquille, calme; silencieux (-euse *f*); paisible; discret (-ète *f*) (*couleur etc.*); simple; voilé; **2.** repos *m*; tranquillité *f*; calme *m*; F *on the* ~ en douce; **3.** (s')apaiser; **'qui·et·en:** ~ *down* (s')apaiser; **'qui·et·ism** *eccl.* quiétisme *m*; **'qui·et·ist** quiétiste *mf*; **'qui·et·ness, qui·e·tude** ['~tju:d] tranquillité *f*, calme *m*; *fig.* sobriété *f*.   [grâce.]

qui·e·tus F [kwai'i:təs] coup *m* de∫

quill [kwil] **1.** *orn.* tuyau *m* (de plume); *porc-épic:* piquant *m*; (*a.* ~*-feather*) penne *f*; (*a.* ~ *pen*) plume *f* d'oie; **2.** tuyauter, rucher; '~**-driv·er** F gratte-papier *m/inv.*; **'quill·ing** tuyautage *m*; ruche *f*; **quill pen** plume *f* d'oie (*pour écrire*).

quilt [kwilt] **1.** édredon *m* piqué; **2.** piquer; ouater (*une robe*); **'quilt·ing** piquage *m*; piqué *m*.

quince ✿ [kwins] coing *m*; *arbre:* cognassier *m*.

qui·nine *pharm.* [kwi'ni:n; *Am.* 'kwainain] quinine *f*; ~ *wine* quinquina *m*.

quin·qua·ge·nar·i·an [kwiŋkwədʒi-'nɛəriən] quinquagénaire (*a. su./ mf*).

quin·quen·ni·al □ [kwiŋ'kwenjəl] quinquennal (-aux *m/pl.*).

quins F [kwinz] *pl.* quintuplés *m/pl.*

quin·sy ✿ ['kwinzi] esquinancie *f*.

quin·tal ['kwintl] quintal *m* (métrique).

quint·es·sence [kwin'tesns] quintessence *f*; F moelle *f* (*d'un livre*).

quin·tu·ple ['kwintjupl] **1.** quintuple (*a. su./m*); **2.** *vt/i.* quintupler; **quin·tu·plets** ['~plits] *pl.* quintuplés *m/pl.*

quip [kwip] mot *m* piquant; bon mot *m*; sarcasme *m*; raillerie *f*.

quire ['kwaiə] main *f* (*de papier*); in ~s en feuilles.

quirk [kwə:k] sarcasme *m*; bon mot *m*; repartie *f*; équivoque *f*; △ gorge *f*.

quis·ling *pol.* F ['kwizliŋ] collaborateur *m*.

quit [kwit] **1.** *v/t.* quitter; lâcher (*la prise*); déménager; *Am.* cesser; † récompenser; † ~ *o.s.* se comporter; *v/i. usu. Am.* démissionner; céder; **2.** quitte, libéré; débarrassé (de, of).

quite [kwait] tout à fait; entièrement; parfaitement; véritable; bien; ~ *a hero* un véritable *ou* vrai héros; F ~ *a* pas mal de; ~ (so)! (*ou that!*) parfaitement!; ~ *the go* le dernier cri; le grand chic.

quits [kwits] quitte (with, avec); *let's call it* ~ restons-en là; *we'll cry* ~ nous voilà quittes.

quit·tance ['kwitəns] acquit *m*; quittance *f*.

quit·ter *Am.* F ['kwitə] lâcheur (-euse *f*) *m*; *he is no* ~ *a.* il n'abandonne pas facilement la partie.

quiv·er[1] ['kwivə] **1.** tremblement *m*; frémissement *m*; frisson *m*; *paupière*: battement *m*; *cœur*: palpitation *f*; **2.** trembl(ot)er; tressaillir, frémir.

quiv·er[2] [~] carquois *m*.

quix·ot·ic [kwik'sɔtik] (~ally) de Don Quichotte; visionnaire; par trop chevaleresque.

quiz [kwiz] **1.** plaisanterie *f*, farce *f*; attrape *f*; *souv. Am.* F colle *f*, examen *m* oral; ~ *program(me)*, ~ *show* quiz *m*; **2.** railler; lorgner; *souv. Am.* examiner; poser des colles à; **'quiz·zi·cal** □ railleur (-euse *f*), moqueur (-euse *f*); risible.

quod *sl.* [kwɔd] boîte *f*, bloc *m* (= *prison*).

quoin [kɔin] pierre *f* d'angle; ⊕, *a. typ.* coin *m*.

quoit [kɔit] (*a. jeu:* ~s *sg.*) palet *m*.

quon·dam ['kwɔndæm] d'autrefois.

quo·rum *parl.* ['kwɔ:rəm] quorum *m*; nombre *m* suffisant; *be a* ~ être en nombre.

quo·ta ['kwoutə] quote-part *f*; contingent *m*.

quo·ta·tion [kwou'teiʃn] citation *f*; *typ.* cadrat *m* creux; ♥ cours *m*, prix *m*; *familiar* ~s *pl.* citations *f/pl.* très connues; **quo'ta·tion-marks** *pl.* guillemets *m/pl.*

quote [kwout] *v/t.* citer; *typ.* guillemeter; *à la Bourse:* coter (à, at); ♥ faire un prix (pour, for; à, to); *v/i.* citer; faire un prix (pour, for; à, to).

quoth † [kwouθ]: ~ *I* dis-je; ~ *he* dit-il.

quo·tid·i·an [kwɔ'tidiən] quotidien(ne *f*); de tous les jours; banal (-als *m/pl.*). [*m*.√

quo·tient ♣ ['kwouʃənt] quotient√

R

R, r [ɑ:] R *m*, r *m*.

rab·bet ⊕ ['ræbit] **1.** feuillure *f*, rainure *f*; **2.** faire une feuillure *ou* rainure à.

rab·bi ['ræbai] rabbin *m*; *titre*: rabbi *m*.

rab·bit ['ræbit] lapin *m*; Welsh ~ toast *m* au fromage fondu.

rab·ble ['ræbl] cohue *f*; the ~ la canaille *f*; '~-rous·er agitateur *m*; '~-rous·ing qui incite à la violence.

rab·id □ ['ræbid] féroce, acharné; *fig.* à outrance; *vét.* enragé (*chien etc.*); '**rab·id·ness** violence *f*; rage *f*.

ra·bies *vét.* ['reibi:z] rage *f*, hydrophobie *f*.

ra(c)·coon *zo.* [rə'ku:n] raton *m* laveur.

race¹ [reis] race *f*; lignée *f*; sang *m*; ~ riot bagarre *f* raciale.

race² [~] course *f* (*a. fig.*); *soleil*: cours *m*; *courant*: ras *m*; *fig.* carrière *f*; ~ against the clock course *f* contre la montre; ~s *pl.* course *f*, -s *f/pl.* (*de bateaux, de chevaux*); **2.** lutter de vitesse (avec, with); courir à toute vitesse; ⊕ s'emballer; battre la fièvre (*pouls*); *v/t.* ⊕ emballer à vide (*le moteur*); '~·course champ *m* de courses; piste *f*; '~-crew *course à l'aviron*: équipe *f* de canot.

race-ha·tred ['reis'heitrid] racisme *m*.

race·horse ['reishɔ:s] cheval *m* de course.

rac·er ['reisə] coureur (-euse *f*) *m*; cheval *m* de course; *mot.* coureur*m*; yacht *m* *ou* bicyclette *f* etc. de course.

ra·cial ['reiʃl] de (la) race; ~ discrimination discrimination *f* raciale; **ra·cial·ism** ['~ʃəlizm] racisme *m*.

rac·i·ness ['reisinis] verve *f*, piquant *m*; *vin etc.*: goût *m* de terroir.

rac·ing ['reisiŋ] courses *f/pl.*; *attr.* de course(s), de piste; ~ (bi)cyclist routier *m*; ~ motorist coureur *m*, racer *m*; ~ car automobile *f* de course.

ra·cism ['reisizəm] racisme *m*; '**ra·cist** raciste (*adj.*, *mf*).

rack¹ [ræk] **1.** *écurie, armes, etc.*: râtelier *m*; portemanteau *m*; ♪ classeur *m* (à musique); ⊕ crémaillère *f*; ✂ bomb ~ lance-bombes *m/inv.*; 🚊 luggage ~ porte-bagages *m/inv.*; filet *m* (à bagages); **2.** *hist.* faire subir le supplice du chevalet à; *fig.* tourmenter, torturer; extorquer (*un loyer*); pressurer (*un locataire*); étirer (*les peaux*); épuiser (*le sol*); détraquer (*une machine*); ~ one's brains se creuser la cervelle.

rack² [~] **1.** légers nuages *m/pl.* traînants; cumulus *m*; **2.** se traîner (*nuages*).

rack³ [~]: go to ~ and ruin tomber en ruine; se délabrer (*maison*).

rack⁴ [~] (*a.* ~ off) soutirer (*le vin etc.*).

rack·et¹ ['rækit] *tennis etc.*: raquette *f*; *jeu*: ~s *souv. sg.* la raquette *f*.

rack·et² [~] **1.** vacarme *m*, tapage *m*; *fig.* epreuve *f*; *fig.* dépenses *f/pl.*; gaieté *f*; F spécialité *f*; entreprise *f* (*de gangster*); chantage *m*; **2.** faire du tapage; *sl.* faire la noce; **rack·et·eer** *surt. Am. sl.* [~'tiə] gangster *m*; combinard *m*; bandit *m*; **rack·et·eer·ing** *surt. Am.* banditisme *m* au chantage; '**rack·et·y** tapageur (-euse *f*); *fig.* noceur (-euse *f*).

rack-rail·way ['ræk'reilwei] chemin *m* de fer à crémaillère.

rack-rent ['rækrent] **1.** loyer *m* exorbitant; **2.** imposer un loyer exorbitant à (*q.*).

rac·y □ ['reisi] qui sent le terroir (*vin*); vif (vive *f*), piquant (*personne*); *fig.* plein de verve; *fig.* savoureux (-euse *f*) (*histoire*); be ~ of the soil sentir le terroir.

rad *pol.* F [ræd] radical *m*.

ra·dar ['reidɑ:] radar *m*; ~ set (appareil *m* de) radar *m*.

rad·dle ['rædl] **1.** ocre *f* rouge; **2.** marquer à l'ocre; *fig.* farder.

ra·di·al □ ['reidjəl] ⊕, *a.* anat.

radial (-aux *m/pl.*); centrifuge (*force*); ⚕ du radium; ~ engine moteur *m* en étoile; ~ *tyre*, *Am.* ~ *tire* pneu *m* à carcasse radiale.

ra·di·ance, ra·di·an·cy ['reidjəns(i)] rayonnement *m*; splendeur *f*; '**ra·di·ant** □ rayonnant (*a. fig.*); radieux (-euse *f*) (*a. fig.*).

ra·di·ate 1. ['reidieit] *v/i.* rayonner; émettre des rayons; *v/t.* émettre; répandre; 2. ['ˎit] *zo. etc.* radié, rayonné; **ra·di·a·tion** rayonnement *m*; *radium etc.*: radiation *f*; **ra·di·a·tor** ['ˎeitə] radiateur *m* (*a. mot.*); ~ *mascot* bouchon *m* enjoliveur.

rad·i·cal ['rædikəl] 1. □ radical (-aux *m/pl.*) (*a. pol.*); fondamental (-aux *m/pl.*); Ⱥ ~ *sign* (signe *m*) radical *m*; 2. ⚕, Ⱥ, *gramm.* radical *m*; *pol.* radical(e *f*) *m/f*; '**rad·i·cal·ism** radicalisme *m*.

ra·di·o ['reidiou] 1. radio *f*, télégraphie *f* sans fil, T.S.F. *f*; ⚕ radiographie *f*; ⚕ radiologie *f*; (*a.* ~-*telegram*) radio *m*; ~ *drama* (*ou play*) pièce *f* radiophonique; ~ *engineer* ingénieur *m* radio; ~ *fan* sans-filiste *mf*; ~ *operator* (opérateur *m*) radio *m*; ~ *set* poste *m* (récepteur); ~ *studio* studio *m* d'émission; auditorium *m*; 2. envoyer (*qch.*) par la radio; radiotélégraphier; ⚕ radiographier; ⚕ traiter au radium; '~-**ac·tive** radioactif (-ive *f*); rayonnant (*matière*); ~ *waste* déchets *m/pl.* radioactifs; '~-**ac·tiv·i·ty** radio-activité *f*; **ra·di·o·gram** ['ˎgræm] radiogramme *m*; radiographie *f*; *a. abr. de* '**ra·di·o·**'**gram·o·phone** radiophono *m*; **ra·di·o·graph** ⚕ ['ˎgrɑːf] 1. radiographie *f*, radiogramme *m*; 2. radiographier; '**ra·di·o·lo·ca·tion** radiorepérage *m*; **ra·di·ol·o·gist** [reidi'ɔlədʒist] radiologue *mf*; **ra·di·ol·o·gy** *phys.* [reidi'ɔlədʒi] radiologie *f*; **ra·di·os·co·py** [ˎ'ɔskəpi] radioscopie *f*; '**ra·di·o·**'**tel·e·gram** radiotélégramme *m*; '**ra·di·o·**'**tel·e·scope** radiotélescope *m*; '**ra·di·o·**'**ther·a·py** ⚕ radiothérapie *f*.

rad·ish ⚕ ['rædiʃ] radis *m*.

ra·di·um ['reidjəm] radium *m*.

ra·di·us ['reidjəs], *pl.* ~**di·i** ['ˎdiai] Ⱥ, ⚕, *mot.*, *a. fig.* rayon *m*; *anat.* radius *m*; ⊕ *grue*: portée *f*; *fig. a.* circonscription *f*.   [(*air*).⟩

raff·ish ['ræfiʃ] bravache; canaille⟩

raf·fle ['ræfl] 1. *v/t.* mettre en tombola; *v/i.* prendre part à une tombola; prendre un billet (pour, *for*); 2. tombola *f*, loterie *f*.

raft [rɑːft] 1. radeau *m*; 2. transporter *etc.* sur un radeau; '**raft·er** (*a.* **rafts·man** ['ˎsmən]) flotteur *m*; △ chevron *m*.

rag[1] [ræg] chiffon *m*; lambeau *m*; *journ. péj.* feuille *f* de chou; ~*s pl.* haillons *m/pl.*, guenilles *f/pl.*; F *chew the* ~ tailler une bavette.

rag[2] *min.* [~] calcaire *m* oolithique.

rag[3] *sl.* [~] 1. *v/t.* chahuter; brimer; *v/i.* faire du chahut, chahuter; 2. brimade *f*; chahut *m*.

rag·a·muf·fin ['rægəmʌfin] gueux *m*; gamin *m* des rues; '**rag-and-**'**bone man** chiffonnier *m*; '**rag-bag** sac *m* aux chiffons; '**rag-book** livre *m* d'images sur toile.

rage [reidʒ] 1. rage *f*, fureur *f* (*a. du vent*), emportement *m*; manie *f* (de, *for*); *it is all the* ~ cela fait fureur, c'est le grand chic; 2. être furieux (-euse *f*) (*personne*); faire rage (*vent*); *fig.* tempêter (contre, *against*); sévir (*peste*).

rag-fair ['rægfɛə] marché *m* aux vieux habits; F marché *m* aux puces.

rag·ged □ ['rægid] déguenillé, en haillons (*personne*); en lambeaux, ébréché (*rocher*); désordonné (Ⅹ *feu*); déchiqueté (*contour*).

rag·man ['rægmən] chiffonnier *m*.

ra·gout ['rægu:] ragoût *m*.

rag...: '~-**tag** canaille *f*; '~-**time** ♩ musique *f* de jazz (nègre).

raid [reid] 1. descente *f* (*inattendue*) (Ⅹ, ⚓ raid *m*; *police:* rafle *f*; *bandits:* razzia *f*; 2. *v/i.* faire une descente *ou* une rafle *etc.*; *v/t. a.* marauder, razzier.

rail[1] [reil] 1. barre(au *m*) *f*; *chaise:* bâton *m*; *charrette:* ridelle *f*; (*a.* ~*s pl.*) palissade *f* (*en bois*), grille *f* (*en fer*); ⚙ rail *m*; F chemin *m* de fer, train *m*; ⚓ lisse *f*; ✝ ~*s pl.* les chemins *m/pl.* de fer; ~ *strike* grève *f* des cheminots; *get* (*ou run*) *off the* ~*s* dérailler (*a. fig.*); 2. (*a.* ~ *in ou off*) entourer d'une grille, griller, palissader; envoyer *ou* transporter par (le) chemin de fer.

rail[2] [~] crier, se répandre en invectives (contre *at*, *against*).

rail[3] *orn.* [~] râle *m*.

rail·er ['reilə] criailleur (-euse f) m; mauvaise langue f.

rail·ing ['reiliŋ] (a. ~s pl.) palissade f (en bois), grille f (en fer).

rail·ler·y ['reiləri] raillerie f.

rail-mo·tor ['reil'moutə] autorail m.

rail·road ['reilroud] **1.** surt. Am., (Brit. = **rail·way** ['reilwei]) chemin m de fer; ~ carriage voiture f, wagon m; **2.** v/t. pol. Am. faire voter avec vitesse; Am. sl. emprisonner après un jugement précipité.

rail·way·man ['reilweimən] employé m de chemin de fer, cheminot m.

rai·ment poét. ['reimənt] habillement m, vêtement m, -s m/pl.

rain [rein] **1.** pluie f; **2.** pleuvoir; '~·bow arc-en-ciel (pl. arcs-en-ciel) m; '~·coat imperméable m; '~·fall averse f; chute f de pluie; pluviosité f; ~·gauge ['~geidʒ] pluviomètre m; 'rain·i·ness ['~inis] pluviosité f; temps m pluvieux; 'rain-lack·ing dépourvu de pluie, sans pluie; sec (sèche f); 'rain·proof imperméable (a. su./m); 'rain·y □ pluvieux (-euse f); de pluie.

raise [reiz] (souv. ~ up) dresser, mettre debout; fig. exciter (la foule, le peuple); relever (courage, navire, store, tarif); lever (armée, bras, camp, gibier, impôt, siège, verre, yeux, etc.); (re)hausser (le prix); bâtir; élever (bétail, édifice, famille, prix, q., voix, etc.); ériger (une statue); cultiver (des plantes); produire (un sourire, de la vapeur, etc.); faire naître (une espérance); soulever (objection, peuple, poids, question); mettre sur pied (une armée); se procurer, emprunter (de l'argent); évoquer (un esprit, le souvenir); ressusciter (un mort); pousser (un cri); augmenter (le salaire); revendiquer (des droits); 'rais·er souleveur m; éleveur m.

rai·sin ['reizn] raisin m sec.

ra·ja(h) ['rɑːdʒə] rajah m.

rake¹ [reik] **1.** râteau m; (a. fire-~) fourgon m; **2.** v/t. (usu. ~ together) râteler, ratisser; gratter (la surface); fig. fouiller; (a. ~ up ou over) revenir sur; ✕, ⚓ enfiler; fig. dominer, embrasser du regard; ~ off (ou away) enlever au râteau; v/i. scruter, fouiller (pour trouver qch., for

s.th.); '~-off Am. sl. gratte f, ristourne f.

rake² ⚓ [~] **1.** inclinaison f; **2.** v/i. être incliné; v/t. incliner vers l'arrière.

rake³ [~] roué m, noceur m.

rak·ish¹ ⚓ etc. ['reikiʃ] élancé; en pente.   [bravache (air).\
rak·ish² □ [~] libertin, dissolu; fig.\

ral·ly¹ ['ræli] m; réunion f; sp. fig. retour m d'énergie; reprise f des forces ou ✕ en main; ✝ reprise f; tennis: échange m de balles; **2.** v/i. se rallier; se reprendre; se grouper; v/t. rassembler, réunir; ranimer.

ral·ly² [~] se gausser de (q.); railler (q.) (de, on).

ram [ræm] **1.** ✕, zo., astr. bélier m; ⊕ piston m plongeur; ⚓ éperon m; **2.** battre, tasser (le sol); heurter; mot. tamponner (une voiture); ⚓ éperonner; ~ up boucher (un trou); bourrer.

ram·ble ['ræmbl] **1.** promenade f, F balade f; **2.** errer à l'aventure; faire une excursion à pied; fig. parler sans suite; 'ram·bler excursionniste mf; promeneur m; fig. radoteur m; ⚘ rosier m grimpant; 'ram·bling **1.** □ vagabond; fig. décousu, sans suite; ⚘ grimpant, rampant; fig. tortueux (-euse f); **2.** vagabondage m; excursions f/pl. à pied; fig. radotages m/pl.

ram·i·fi·ca·tion [ræmifi'keiʃn] ramification f; **ram·i·fy** ['~fai] (se) ramifier.

ram·jet ['ræmdʒet] (a. ~ engine) statoréacteur m.

ram·mer ⊕ ['ræmə] pilon m.

ramp¹ sl. [ræmp] supercherie f.

ramp² [~] **1.** rampe f; pont m élévateur; **2.** v/t. construire (qch.) en rampe; v/i. ⚹ ramper; fig. rager; **ram'page** co. **1.** rager, tempêter; se conduire comme un fou furieux; **2.**: be on the ~ en avoir après tout le monde; 'ramp·an·cy violence f; exubérance f; fig. extension f; 'ramp·ant □ violent; exubérant; fig. effréné; ⚹, a. ⚹ rampant.

ram·part ['ræmpɑːt] rempart m.

ram·rod ['ræmrɔd] fusil: baguette f; straight as a ~ droit comme un i.

ram·shack·le ['ræmʃækl] délabré.

ran [ræn] prét. de run 1, 2.

ranch [rɑːntʃ; surt. Am. ræntʃ]

ferme *f ou* prairie *f* d'élevage; ranch *m*.

ran·cid □ ['rænsid] rance, ranci; **ran'cid·i·ty**, **'ran·cid·ness** rancidité *f*. [nier (-ère *f*).\]

ran·cor·ous □ ['ræŋkərəs] rancu-\]

ran·co(u)r ['ræŋkə] rancune *f*, ressentiment *m*.

ran·dom ['rændəm] 1.: *at* ~ au hasard; à l'aveuglette; 2. fait au hasard; de passage; ~ *sample* échantillon *m* prélevé au hasard; ~ *shot* coup *m* tiré au hasard; coup *m* perdu.

rand·y *sl.* ['rændi] excité, aguiché.

rang [ræŋ] *prét. de* ring[2] 2.

range [reindʒ] 1. rangée *f*; chaîne *f* (*de montagnes*); ⚭ assortiment *m*; série *f*; étendue *f*, portée *f* (*a. d'une arme à feu*); direction *f*; champ *m* libre; *sp.* distance *f*; *Am.* prairie *f*, fourneau *m* (de cuisine); (*a. shooting-*~) champ *m* de tir; *fig.* libre essor *m*; *fig.* variété *f*; *take the* ~ estimer *ou* régler le tir; 2. *v/t.* aligner, ranger; disposer; parcourir (*une région*); braquer (*un télescope*); ⚓ longer (*la côte*); *v/i.* errer, courir; s'étendre (*a. fig.*); varier; ✕ régler le tir; ~ *along* longer; ~ *over* parcourir; *canon:* avoir une portée (*de six milles, over six milles*); |~ *find·er* télémètre *m*; **'rang·er** † vagabond(e *f*) *m*; grand maître *m* des parcs royaux; *Indes:* garde-général (*pl.* gardes-généraux) *m* adjoint; ⚭s *pl.* gendarmes *m/pl.* à cheval; ✕ *Am.* soldats *m/pl.* de commando spécial.

rank[1] [ræŋk] 1. rang *m* (*social,* ✕, *a. fig.*); ligne *f*; classe *f*; ✕, ⚓ grade *m*; stationnement *m* (*pour taxis*); *the* ~s *pl.* (*ou and file*) les hommes *m/pl.* de) troupe *f*; *fig.* le commun *m* des hommes; *join the* ~s devenir soldat; entrer dans les rangs; *rise from the* ~s de simple soldat passer officier, sortir du rang; 2. *v/t.* ranger, compter; classer (avec, *with*); *v/i.* se ranger, être classé (avec, *with*; parmi, *among*); compter (parmi, *among*); occuper un rang (supérieur à, *above*); ~ *next to* occuper le premier rang après; ~ *as* avoir qualité de; compter pour.

rank[2] □ [~] luxuriant; exubérant (*plante*); riche, gras(se *f*) (*sol, terrain*); rance, fort, fétide; *fig. péj.* complet (-ète *f*), pur, parfait.

rank·er ✕ ['ræŋkə] simple soldat *m*; officier *m* sorti des rangs.

ran·kle *fig.* ['ræŋkl] rester sur le cœur (de q., *with s.o.*).

rank·ness ['ræŋknis] luxuriance *f*; odeur *f etc.* forte; *fig.* grossièreté *f*.

ran·sack ['rænsæk] fouiller (dans); saccager.

ran·som ['rænsəm] 1. rançon *f*; rachat *m* (*eccl., a. d'un captif*); 2. mettre à rançon, rançonner; racheter.

rant [rænt] 1. rodomontades *f/pl.*; 2. déclamer avec extravagance; F tempêter; **'rant·er** déclamateur (-trice *f*) *m*; énergumène *mf*.

ra·nun·cu·lus ♀ [rə'nʌŋkjuləs], *pl.* **-lus·es, -li** [~lai] renoncule *f*.

rap[1] [ræp] 1. petit coup *m* (sec); 2. frapper (à, *at*); *fig.* ~ *s.o.'s fingers* (*ou knuckles*) donner sur les doigts à q.; F remettre q. à sa place; ~ *out* lâcher; dire (*qch.*) d'un ton sec.

rap[2] *fig.* [~] sou *m*, liard *m*; *not care a* ~ s'en ficher.

ra·pa·cious □ [rə'peiʃəs] rapace; **ra·pac·i·ty** [rə'pæsiti] rapacité *f*.

rape[1] [reip] 1. rapt *m*; enlèvement *m*; ⚖ viol *m*; 2. ravir; ⚖ violer.

rape[2] ♀ [~] colza *m*; navette *f*; '~-oil huile *f* de colza *ou* de navette; '~-seed graine *f* de colza.

rap·id ['ræpid] 1. □ rapide; ~ *fire* feu *m* continu *ou* accéléré; 2. ~s *pl.* rapide *m*; **ra·pid·i·ty** [rə'piditi] rapidité *f*.

ra·pi·er ['reipjə] *escrime:* rapière *f*.

rap·ine *poét.* ['ræpain] rapine *f*.

rap·ist ['reipist] violeur *m*.

rap·proche·ment *pol.* [ræ'prɔʃmãːŋ] rapprochement *m*.

rapt *fig.* [ræpt] ravi, extasié (par *by*, *with*); absorbé (dans, *in*); profond.

rap·to·ri·al *zo.* [ræp'tɔːriəl] de proie.

rap·ture ['ræptʃə] (*a.* ~s *pl.*) extase *m*, ravissement *m*; *in* ~s ravi, enchanté; *go into* ~s s'extasier (sur, *over*); **'rap·tur·ous** □ d'extase, de ravissement; enthousiaste.

rare □ [reə] rare (*a. phys. etc., a. fig.*); F fameux (-euse *f*), riche; *surt. Am.* saignant (*bifteck*).

rare·bit ['reəbit]: *Welsh* ~ toast *m* au fromage fondu.

rar·e·fac·tion *phys.* [reəri'fækʃn] raréfaction *f*; **rar·e·fy** ['~fai] *v/t.* raréfier; affiner (*le goût*); subtiliser (*une idée*); *v/i.* se raréfier;

'**rare·ness**, '**rar·i·ty** rareté *f*; F excellence *f*.

ras·cal ['rɑːskəl] coquin(e *f*) *m* (*a. fig.*); fripon *m*; gredin *m*; **ras·cal·i·ty** [ˌˈkæliti] coquinerie *f*, gredinerie *f*; **ras·cal·ly** *adj. a. adv.* [ˈˌkəli] de coquin; méchant; retors; ignoble.

rase † [reiz] raser (*une ville etc.*).

rash[1] □ [ræʃ] irréfléchi, inconsidéré; téméraire; impétueux (-euse *f*).

rash[2] ⚕ [ˌ] éruption *f*.

rash·er ['ræʃə] tranche *f* de lard.

rash·ness ['ræʃnis] témérité *f*; étourderie *f*.

rasp [rɑːsp] **1.** râpe *f*; grincement *m*; **2.** *v/t.* râper; racler (*le gosier, une surface, etc.*); *v/i.* grincer, crisser.

rasp·ber·ry ♀ [ˈrɑːzbəri] framboise *f*; *sl.* get the ˌ se faire rabrouer.

rasp·er ['rɑːspə] râpeur (-euse *f*) *m*; râpe *f*.

rasp·ing ['rɑːspiŋ] râpage *m*; grincement *m*, ˌs *pl.* râpure *f*, -s *f/pl.*

rat [ræt] **1.** *zo.* rat *m*; *pol.* renégat *m*, transfuge *m*; *sl.* jaune *m*, faux frère *m*; *fig.* ˌ race foire *f* d'empoigne; smell a ˌ soupçonner anguille sous roche; **2.** attraper des rats; *pol.* tourner casaque; *sl.* faire le jaune; F ˌ on trahir (*q.*), vendre (*q.*).

rat·a·bil·i·ty [reitə'biliti] caractère *m* imposable; '**rat·a·ble** □ évaluable; imposable.

ratch ⊕ [rætʃ] encliquetage *m* à dents; *horloge:* cliquet *m.*

ratch·et ⊕ ['rætʃit] encliquetage *m* à dents; cliquet *m*; 'ˌ-**wheel** roue *f* à cliquet.

rate[1] [reit] **1.** quantité *f* proportionnelle; taux *m*; raison *f*, degré *m*; tarif *m*, cours *m*; droit *m*; prix *m*; impôt *m* local; taxe *f* municipale; *fig.* évaluation *f*; vitesse *f*, allure *f*, train *m*; † classe *f*, rang *m*; at the ˌ of au taux de, à raison de; sur le pied de; *mot.* à la vitesse de; ✝ at a cheap ˌ à un prix *ou* taux réduit; at any ˌ de toute façon, en tout cas; ✝ à n'importe quel prix; ˌ of exchange cours *m* du change; ˌ of interest taux *m* d'intérêt; ˌ of taxation taux *m* de l'imposition; ˌ of wages taux *m* du salaire; **2.** *v/t.* estimer; *Am.* mériter; considérer; classer (*a.* ⚓); taxer (à raison de, *at*); *v/i.* être classé.

rate[2] [ˌ] *v/t.* semoncer (de *for*, about); *v/i.* gronder, crier (contre, at).

rate-pay·er ['reitpeiə] contribuable *mf.*

rath·er ['rɑːðə] plutôt; quelque *ou* un peu; assez; pour mieux dire; F ˌ! bien sûr!, pour sûr!; I had (*ou* would) ˌ (*inf.*) j'aime mieux (*inf.*); I ˌ expected it je m'en doutais, je m'y attendais.

rat·i·fi·ca·tion [rætifi'keiʃn] ratification *f*; **rat·i·fy** ['ˌfai] ratifier, approuver.

rat·ing[1] ['reitiŋ] évaluation *f*; répartition *f* des impôts locaux; ⚓ classe *f* (*d'un homme*); ⚓ classement *m* (*d'un navire*); ⚓ matelot *m*; *télév.* (*a. popularity* ˌ) indice *m* de popularité, taux *m* d'écoute.

rat·ing[2] [ˌ] semonce *f.*

ra·tio ['reiʃiou] raison *f*, rapport *m.*

ra·tion ['ræʃn] **1.** ration *f*; ˌ card carte *f* alimentaire; (*a.* ˌ ticket) tickets *m/pl.* (*de pain etc.*); off the ˌ see ˌ-free; **2.** rationner; mettre (*q.*) à la ration.

ra·tion·al □ ['ræʃnəl] raisonnable; doué de raison; sensé; ♗ rationnel(le *f*) (*a. croyance*); **ra·tion·al·ism** ['ˌnəlizm] rationalisme *m*; '**ra·tion·al·ist** rationaliste (*a. su./mf*); **ra·tion·al·i·ty** [ˌ'næliti] rationalité *f*; faculté *f* de raisonner; **ra·tion·al·i·za·tion** ['ˌlai'zeiʃn] rationalisation *f* (*a.* ✝); '**ra·tion·al·ize** rationaliser; organiser de façon rationnelle.

ra·tion-free ['ræʃnfriː] sans tickets, en vente libre.   [rats *f.*)

rats·bane † ['rætsbein] mort-aux-)

rat-tat ['ræt'tæt] toc-toc *m.*

rat·ten ⊕ ['rætn] *v/t.* saboter; *v/i.* saboter l'outillage *ou* le matériel; '**rat·ten·ing** sabotage *m.*

rat·tle ['rætl] **1.** bruit *m*; *fusillade*: crépitement *m*; *machine à écrire*: tapotis *m*; crécelle *f*; *enfant*: hochet *m*; *fig.* caquetage *m*; ⚕ râle *m*; ˌs *pl. serpent*: sonnettes *f/pl.*; **2.** *v/i.* branler; crépiter; cliqueter; faire du bruit; ⚕ râler; *v/t.* faire sonner; faire cliqueter; agiter; F consterner; ˌ off (*ou* out) expédier; réciter rapidement; 'ˌ-**brained**, 'ˌ-**pat·ed** écervelé, étourdi; '**rat·tler** ⚓ klaxon *m* d'alarme; F coup *m* dur; *sl.* personne *f* *ou* chose *f* épatante; *Am. sl.* tramway *m*; *Am. sl.* tacot *m*; *Am.*

F = **'rat·tle·snake** serpent *m* à sonnettes; **'rat·tle·trap 1.** délabré; **2.** guimbarde *f*, tapecul *m*.

rat·tling ['rætliŋ] **1.** ☐ bruyant; crépitant; F vif (vive *f*); **2.** *adv.* rudement; *at a* ~ *pace* au grand trot, très rapidement.

rat·ty ['ræti] infesté de rats; en queue de rat (*natte*); *sl.* grincheux (-euse *f*); fâché.

rau·cous ☐ ['rɔ:kəs] rauque.

rav·age ['rævidʒ] **1.** ravage *m*, -s *m/pl.*, dévastation *f*; **2.** *v/t.* ravager, dévaster; *v/i.* faire des ravages.

rave [reiv] être en délire; *fig.* pester (contre, *at*); s'extasier (sur *about*, *of*).

rav·el ['rævl] *v/t.* embrouiller; (*a.* ~ *out*) effilocher; *v/i.* s'embrouiller, s'enchevêtrer; (*a.* ~ *out*) s'effilocher.

rav·en¹ ['reivn] (grand) corbeau *m*.

rav·en² ['rævn] **1.** *see ravin*; **2.** faire des ravages; chercher sa proie; être affamé (de, *for*); **'rav·en·ous** ☐ vorace; affamé; **'rav·en·ous·ness** voracité *f*; faim *f* de loup.

rav·in ['rævin] rapine *f*; butin *m*.

ra·vine [rə'vi:n] ravin *m*.

rav·ings *pl.* ['reiviŋz] délires *m/pl.*; paroles *f/pl.* incohérentes.

rav·ish ['ræviʃ] violer (*une femme*); *fig.* enchanter, ravir; † enlever de force, ravir; **'rav·ish·er** ravisseur *m*; **'rav·ish·ing** ☐ ravissant; **'rav·ish·ment** rapt *m*; enlèvement *m*; viol *m* (*d'une femme*); *fig.* ravissement *m*.

raw [rɔ:] **1.** cru (= *pas cuit*; *a. couleur, peau, histoire*); brut, premier (-ère *f*); vert (*cuir*); inexpérimenté (*personne*); âpre (*temps*); vif (vive *f*) (*plaie*); ~ *material* matériaux *m/pl.* bruts; matières *f/pl.* premières; F *he got a* ~ *deal* on le traita avec peu de générosité; **2.** vif *m*; endroit *m* sensible; **'~-boned** décharné; efflanqué (*cheval*); **'~-hide** cuir *m* vert; **'raw·ness** crudité *f*; écorchure *f*; *temps*: âpreté *f*; *fig.* inexpérience *f*.

ray¹ *icht.* [rei] raie *f*.

ray² [~] **1.** ♀, *phys., zo., etc.* rayon *m*; *fig.* lueur *f* (*d'espoir*); ☞ ~ *treatment* radiothérapie *f*; **2.** (*v/t.* faire) rayonner; **'~-less** sans rayons.

ray·on *tex.* ['reiɔn] rayonne *f*, soie *f* artificielle.

raze [reiz] (*a.* ~ *to the ground*) raser; ⚓ receper (*un mur*); *fig.* effacer.

ra·zor ['reizə] rasoir *m*; **'~-blade** lame *f* de rasoir; *be on the* ~'*s edge* être sur la corde raide; **'~-strop** cuir *m* à rasoir.

razz *Am. sl.* [ræz] **1.** ridicule *m*; **2.** taquiner, se moquer de, se payer la tête de.

raz·zi·a ['ræziə] *police:* razzia *f*.

raz·zle-daz·zle *sl.* ['ræzldæzl] bombe *f*, noce *f*; ivresse *f*; *usu. Am. sl.* fatras *m*.

re [ri:] ⚕ (en l')affaire; ✝ relativement à; *en-tête d'une lettre:* objet …

re... [~] re-, r-, ré-; de nouveau; à nouveau.

reach [ri:tʃ] **1.** extension *f* (*de la main*), *box.* allonge *f*; portée *f*; étendue *f* (*a. fig.*); partie *f* droite (*d'un fleuve*) entre deux coudes; *beyond* ~, *out of* ~ hors de portée; *within easy* ~ à proximité (de, *of*); tout près; à peu de distance; **2.** *v/i.* (*a.* ~ *out*) tendre la main (pour, *for*); s'étendre ([jusqu'] là, *to*); (*a.* ~ *to*) atteindre; *v/t.* arriver à, parvenir à; (*souv.* ~ *out*) (é)tendre; atteindre.

reach-me-down F ['ri:tʃmi'daun] costume *m* de confection, F décrochez-moi-ça *m/inv.*

re·act [ri'ækt] réagir (sur, *upon*; contre, *against*); réactionner (*prix*).

re·ac·tion [ri'ækʃn] réaction *f* (*a. ⚡, ⚗, physiol., pol.*); contrecoup *m*; **re'ac·tion·ar·y** *surt. pol.* **1.** réactionnaire; **2.** (*a.* **re'ac·tion·ist**) réactionnaire *mf.*

re·ac·tive ☐ [ri'æktiv] réactif (-ive *f*); de réaction (*a. pol.*); **re'ac·tor** *phys.* réacteur *m*; ⚡ bobine *f* de réactance.

read 1. [ri:d] [*irr.*] *v/t.* lire (*un livre, un thermomètre, etc.*); (*a.* ~ *up*) étudier; déchiffrer; *fig.* interpréter; ~ *off* lire sans hésiter; ~ *out* lire à haute voix; donner lecture (de); ~ *to* faire la lecture à (*q.*); *v/i.* lire; être conçu; marquer (*thermomètre*); ~ *for* préparer (*un examen*); ~ *like* faire l'effet de; ~ *well* se laisser lire; **2.** [red] *prét. et p.p.* de 1; **3.** [red] *adj.* instruit (en, *in*); versé (dans, *in*).

read·a·ble ☐ ['ri:dəbl] lisible.

read·er ['ri:də] lecteur (-trice *f*) *m* (*a. eccl.*); *typ.* correcteur *m* d'épreuves; lecteur *m* de manuscrits; *univ.*

maître *m* de conférences, chargé(e*f*)
m de cours; livre *m* de lecture;
'**read·er·ship** *journal etc.*: (nombre
m de) lecteurs *m/pl.*; *univ.* maîtrise *f*
de conférences; charge *f* de cours.

read·i·ly ['redili] *adv.* volontiers,
avec empressement; '**read·i·ness**
alacrité *f*, empressement *m*; bonne
volonté *f*; facilité *f*; ~ of mind (*ou*
wit) vivacité *f* d'esprit.

read·ing ['ri:diŋ] 1. lecture *f* (*a. d'un
instrument de précision*); *compteur:*
relevé *m*; observation *f*; cote *f*;
hauteur *f* (*barométrique*); interprétation *f*; leçon *f*, variante *f*; *parl.*
second ~ prise *f* en considération;
2. de lecture; ~ *matter* lecture(s) *f*
(*pl.*), de quoi lire.

re·ad·just ['ri:ə'dʒʌst] rajuster; remettre à point (*un instrument*); '**read'just·ment** rajustement *m*, rectification *f*; ⚓ régulation *f*.

re·ad·mis·sion ['ri:əd'miʃn] réadmission *f*.

re·ad·mit ['ri:əd'mit] réadmettre;
réintégrer; '**re·ad'mit·tance** réadmission *f*.

read·y ['redi] 1. *adj.* □ prêt (à *inf.*,
to *inf.*); sous la main; disposé, sur
le point (de *inf.*, to *inf.*); facile;
prompt (à, with); ✝ comptant (*argent*); ⚓ paré; ~ *reckoner* barème *m*
(de comptes); ✕ ~ *for action* prêt au
combat; ~ *for use* prêt à l'usage;
make (*ou get*) ~ (se) préparer;
(s')apprêter; 2. *adv.* tout, toute;
readier plus promptement; *readiest*
le plus promptement; 3. *su.*: *at
the* ~ paré à faire feu; '~-**made**
tout fait; de confection (*vêtement*);
'~-to-'**wear** prêt à porter.

re·af·firm ['ri:ə'fə:m] réaffirmer.

re·a·gent 🜋 [ri'eidʒənt] réactif *m*.

re·al □ [riəl] 1. vrai; véritable; réel
(-le *f*); ~ *property* (*ou estate*) propriété
f immobilière; biens-fonds *m/pl.*; 2.
surt. Am. F vraiment; très, F rudement, vachement; 3. *surt. Am.* F for ~
sérieusement, F pour de vrai; sérieux
(-euse *f*); '**re·al·ism** réalisme *m*;
re·al·is·tic (~ally) réaliste; ~ally avec
réalisme; **re·al·i·ty** [ri'æliti] réalité
f; réel *m*; *fig.* vérité *f*, réalisme *m*;
re·al·iz·a·ble □ ['riəlaizəbl] réalisable; imaginable; **re·al·i'za·tion**
réalisation *f* (*projet, a.* ✝ *placement*);
fig. perception *f*; idée *f*; ✝ conversion *f* en espèces; '**re·al·ize** réaliser

(*un projet, a.* ✝ *un placement*); concevoir nettement, bien comprendre;
se rendre compte de; rapporter (*un
prix*); ✝ convertir en espèces; gagner
(*une fortune*); '**re·al·ly** vraiment, en
effet; à vrai dire; réellement.

realm [relm] royaume *m*; *fig.* domaine *m*; *peer of the* ~ pair *m* du
Royaume.

re·al·tor *Am.* ['riəltə] agent *m* immobilier; courtier *m* en immeubles;
'**re·al·ty** 🜊 biens *m/pl.* immobiliers.

ream[1] [ri:m] *papier:* rame *f*; *papier
à lettres:* ramette *f*.

ream[2] ⊕ [~] fraiser (*un trou*); (*usu.
~ out*) aléser; '**ream·er** alésoir *m*.

re·an·i·mate [ri'ænimeit] ranimer;
re·an·i'ma·tion retour *m* à la vie;
fig. reprise *f* (*des affaires*).

reap [ri:p] moissonner (*le blé, un
champ*); (re)cueillir (*un fruit, a. fig.*);
fig. récolter; '**reap·er** moissonneuse *f*; *personne:* moissonneur
(-euse *f*) *m*; '**reap·ing** moisson *f*;
'**reap·ing-hook** faucille *f*.

re·ap·pear ['ri:ə'piə] reparaître;
'**re·ap'pear·ance** réapparition *f*;
théâ. rentrée *f*.

re·ap·pli·ca·tion ['ri:æpli'keiʃn]
nouvelle application *f*.

re·ap·point ['ri:ə'pɔint] réintégrer
(dans ses fonctions); renommer.

rear[1] [riə] *v/t.* élever; ériger; dresser; 🜩 cultiver; *v/i.* se dresser; se
cabrer (*cheval*).

rear[2] [~] 1. arrière *m* (*a.* ✕), derrière *m*; queue *f*; dernier rang *m*; ✕
arrière-garde *f*; *bring up the* ~ venir
en queue, ✕ fermer la marche; *at
the* ~ *of, in* (*the*) ~ *of* derrière, en
queue *f*; 2. (d')arrière; de derrière; dernier (-ère *f*); ~ *exit* sortie *f*
de derrière; *mot.* ~-*vision* (*ou* ~-*view*)
mirror rétroviseur *m*; ~ *wheel* roue *f*
arrière; *mot.* ~-*wheel drive* traction *f*
arrière; *mot.* ~ *window* glace *f* arrière;
'~-**'ad·mi·ral** ⚓ contre-amiral *m*;
'~-**guard** ✕ arrière-garde *f*; '~-
lamp *mot.* feu *m* arrière.

re·arm ['ri:'ɑ:m] réarmer; '**re·'ar-
ma·ment** [~məmənt] réarmement
m.   [*f*), de queue.\

rear·most ['riəmoust] dernier (-ère\

re·ar·range ['ri:ə'reindʒ] rarranger;
remettre en ordre.

rear·ward ['riəwəd] 1. *adj.* à l'arrière; en arrière; 2. *adv.* (*a.* '**rear-**

wards [~z]) à *ou* vers l'arrière; (par) derrière.

re·as·cend ['ri:ə'send] remonter.

rea·son ['ri:zn] **1.** raison *f*, cause *f*; motif *m*; bon sens *m*; *by* ~ *of* à cause de, en raison de; *for this* ~ pour cette raison; *listen to* ~ entendre raison; *it stands to* ~ *that* il est de toute évidence que; **2.** *v/i.* raisonner (sur, *about*); ~ *whether* discuter pour savoir si; *v/t.* (*a.* ~ *out*) arguer, déduire; ~ *away* prouver le contraire de (qch.) par le raisonnement; ~ *s.o. into* (*out of*) *doing s.th.* amener q. à (dissuader q. de) faire qch.; ~ed raisonné, logique; **'rea·son·a·ble** □ raisonnable (*a. fig.*); équitable; juste; bien fondé; **'rea·son·a·bly** raisonnablement; **'rea·son·er** raisonneur (-euse *f*) *m*; **'rea·son·ing** raisonnement *m*; dialectique *f*; *attr.* doué de raison.

re·as·sem·ble ['ri:ə'sembl] (se) rassembler; remonter (*une machine*).

re·as·sert ['ri:ə'sə:t] réaffirmer; insister.

re·as·sur·ance ['ri:ə'ʃuərəns] action *f* de rassurer; nouvelle affirmation *f*; *give s.o. a* ~ *about* rassurer q. sur; ✝ réassurer; **re·as·sure** ['~'ʃuə] tranquilliser (sur, *about*); ✝ réassurer.

re·bap·tize ['ri:'bæp'taiz] rebaptiser.

re·bate[1] ✝ ['ri:beit] rabais *m*, escompte *m*; remboursement *m*.

re·bate[2] ⊕ ['ræbit] **1.** feuillure *f*; **2.** faire une feuillure à; assembler (*deux planches*) à feuillure.

re·bel ['rebl] **1.** rebelle *mf*, insurgé(e *f*) *m*, révolté(e *f*) *m*; **2.** insurgé; *fig.* (*a.* **re·bel·lious** [ri'beljəs]) rebelle; **3.** [ri'bel] se révolter, se soulever (contre, *against*); **re'bel·lion** [~jən] rébellion *f*, révolte *f*.

re·birth ['ri:'bə:θ] renaissance *f*.

re·bound [ri'baund] **1.** rebondir; **2.** rebondissement *m*; *balle etc.*: ricochet *m*; *fig.* moment *m* de détente.

re·buff [ri'bʌf] **1.** échec *m*; refus *m*; **2.** repousser, rebuter.

re·build ['ri:'bild] [*irr.* (*build*)] rebâtir, reconstruire.

re·buke [ri'bju:k] **1.** réprimande *f*, blâme *m*; **2.** réprimander; reprocher (qch. à q., *s.o. for s.th.*).

re·bus ['ri:bəs] rébus *m*.

re·but [ri'bʌt] réfuter; repousser; **re'but·tal** réfutation *f*.

re·cal·ci·trant [ri'kælsitrənt] récalcitrant, rebelle.

re·call [ri'kɔ:l] **1.** rappel *m*; révocation *f*; rappel *m* d'un souvenir, évocation *f*; *total* ~ capacité *f* de se souvenir de tout détail; *théâ.* give *a.* ~ rappeler (*un acteur*); *beyond* (*ou past*) ~ irrémédiable; irrévocable; **2.** rappeler (*un ambassadeur etc.*; *fig.* qch. à q., *s.th. to s.o.*['*s mind*]); se rappeler, se souvenir de; revoir; retirer (*une parole*); rétracter, revenir sur (*une promesse*); ✝ annuler; révoquer (*un décret*, ✝ *un ordre*); ~ *that* se rappeler que; *until* ~ed jusqu'à nouvel ordre.

re·cant [ri'kænt] (se) rétracter; abjurer; **re·can·ta·tion** [ri:kæn'teiʃn] rétractation *f*, abjuration *f*.

re·cap[1] F ['ri:kæp] **1.** récapituler; résumer; **2.** récapitulation *f*; résumé *m*.

re·cap[2] [~] **1.** rechaper (*un pneu*); **2.** pneu *m* rechapé.

re·ca·pit·u·late [ri:kə'pitjuleit] récapituler; résumer; **'re·ca·pit·u'la·tion** récapitulation *f*; résumé *m*.

re·cap·ture ['ri:'kæptʃə] **1.** reprise *f*; **2.** reprendre; *fig.* revivre (*le passé*).

re·cast ['ri:'kɑ:st] **1.** [*irr.* (*cast*)] ⊕ refondre; remanier (*un roman etc.*); reconstruire; refaire le calcul de; *théâ.* faire une nouvelle distribution des rôles de; **2.** refonte *f*; nouveau calcul *m etc.*

re·cede [ri'si:d] s'éloigner, reculer (de, *from*); fuir (*front*); ⚔ se retirer (de, *from*); *fig.* ~ *from* abandonner (*une opinion*).

re·ceipt [ri'si:t] **1.** réception *f*; reçu *m*; accusé *m* de réception; ✝ récépissé *m*, quittance *f*; ✝ recette *f* (*a. cuis.*); **2.** acquitter.

re·ceiv·a·ble [ri'si:vəbl] recevable; ✝ à recevoir; **re'ceive** *v/t. usu.* recevoir; accepter; accueillir; essuyer (*un refus*), subir (*une défaite*); toucher (*un salaire*); *radio:* capter; ⚖ receler (*des objets volés*); ⚖ être condamné à; *v/i.* recevoir; **re'ceived** reçu; admis; ✝ *sur facture:* pour acquit; **re'ceiv·er** personne *f* qui reçoit; *lettre:* destinataire *mf*; *tél., téléph.* récepteur *m*; *radio:* poste *m* (récepteur); ✝ réceptionnaire *m*; (*a.* ~ *of stolen goods*) receleur (-euse *f*) *m*; ⚖ (*official* ~) administrateur *m* judiciaire, (*en France*) syndic *m* de faillite; ⚔, *phys.* récipient *m*, ballon *m*; *téléph.* lift the ~ décrocher; **re'ceiv·ing 1.** réception *f*; ⚖ recel *m*; **2.** récepteur (-trice *f*); ~ set poste *m* récepteur.

re·cen·cy ['ri:snsi] caractère *m* récent.

re·cen·sion [ri'senʃn] révision *f*; texte *m* révisé.

re·cent □ ['ri:snt] récent; de fraîche date; nouveau (-el *devant une voyelle ou un h muet*; -elle *f*; -eaux *m/pl.*); **'re·cent·ly** récemment, dernièrement; **'re·cent·ness** caractère *m* récent.

re·cep·ta·cle [ri'septəkl] récipient *m*; ♀ (*a. floral* ~) réceptacle *m* (*a. fig.*).

re·cep·tion [ri'sepʃn] réception *f* (*a. radio*); accueil *m*; acceptation *f* (*d'une théorie*); **re'cep·tion·ist** réceptionniste *mf*; **re'cep·tion-room** salle *f* de réception, salon *m*.

re·cep·tive □ [ri'septiv] réceptif (-ive *f*); sensible (à, *of*); **re·cep-'tiv·i·ty** réceptivité *f*.

re·cess [ri'ses] vacances *f/pl.* (*a.* ⚖, *a. parl.*); *Am. école:* récréation *f*; recoin *m*; enfoncement *m*; niche *f*; embrasure *f*; ~es *pl. fig.* replis *m/pl.*

re·ces·sion [ri'seʃn] retraite *f*, recul *m*; ✝ récession *f*; **re'ces·sion·al 1.** *eccl.* de sortie; *parl.* pendant les vacances; **2.** *eccl.* (*a.* ~ hymn) hymne *m* de sortie du clergé.

re·chris·ten ['ri:'krisn] rebaptiser.

rec·i·pe ['resipi] *cuis.* recette *f* (*a. fig.*); ✒ ordonnance *f*; *pharm.* formule *f*; ~ book livre *m* de cuisine.

re·cip·i·ent [ri'sipiənt] personne *f* qui reçoit; destinataire *mf*; ⚗ récipient *m*.

re·cip·ro·cal [ri'siprəkəl] **1.** □ réciproque (*a. gramm., phls., a.* ♈ *figure*); ♈ inverse (*fonction, raison*); mutuel(le *f*); **2.** ♈ réciproque *f*, inverse *m*; **re'cip·ro·cate** [~keit] *v/i.* retourner le compliment; ⊕ avoir un mouvement alternatif; *v/t.* échanger; répondre à; **re·cip·ro-'ca·tion** (action *f* de payer de) retour *m*; ⊕ va-et-vient *m/inv.*; **rec·i·proc·i·ty** [resi'prɔsiti] réciprocité *f*.

re·cit·al [ri'saitl] récit *m*, narration *f*; ⚖ exposé *m* (*des faits*); ♪ récital (*pl. -s*) *m*; audition *f*; **rec·i·ta·tion** [resi'teiʃn] récitation *f*; **rec·i·ta-**

tive ♪ [~tə'ti:v] récitatif *m*; **re·cite** [ri'sait] réciter (un poème); déclamer; énumérer; ⚖ exposer (*les faits*); **re'cit·er** récitateur (-trice *f*) *m*; livre *m* de récitations.

reck·less □ ['reklis] téméraire; ~ of insouciant de; **'reck·less·ness** témérité *f*, imprudence *f*; insouciance *f*.

reck·on ['rekn] *v/t.* compter (parmi among, with); calculer; juger; estimer; considérer (comme *for, as*); ~ up calculer, additionner; *v/i.* compter (sur, [up]on), calculer; ~ with faire rendre compte à; compter avec (*q., a. des difficultés etc.*); **'reck·on·er** calculateur (-trice *f*) *m*; barème *m*; **'reck·on·ing** compte *m*, calcul *m*; estimation *f*; ✝ règlement *m*; note *f*; addition *f*; *fig.* be out in (*ou of*) one's ~ s'être trompé dans son calcul; être loin de compte.

re·claim [ri'kleim] *fig.* tirer (de, from); corriger (*q.*), réformer (*q.*); civiliser; ramener (à, to); défricher, rendre cultivable, gagner sur l'eau (*du terrain*); assécher (*un marais*); ⊕ récupérer; régénérer(*l'huile etc.*); **re'claim·a·ble** corrigible (*personne*); amendable (*terrain*); asséchable (*marais*); ⊕ récupérable.

rec·la·ma·tion [reklə'meiʃn] réforme *f*; défrichement *m*, mise *f* en valeur; récupération *f*; réclamation *f*.

re·cline [ri'klain] *v/t.* reposer; coucher; *v/i.* être couché; se reposer; ~ upon s'étendre sur; *fig.* être appuyé sur; **re'clin·ing chair** confortable *m*; fauteuil *m*.

re·cluse [ri'klu:s] **1.** retiré du monde; reclus; **2.** reclus(e *f*) *m*; anachorète *m*; solitaire *mf*.

rec·og·ni·tion [rekəg'niʃn] reconnaissance *f*; **rec·og·niz·a·ble** □ ['~naizəbl] reconnaissable; **re·cog-ni·zance** ⚖ [ri'kɔgnizəns] caution *f* personnelle; engagement *m*; **rec-og·nize** ['rekəgnaiz] reconnaître (*a. fig.*) (à, by); saluer (*dans la rue*).

re·coil [ri'kɔil] **1.** se détendre; reculer (devant, from) (*personne, arme à feu*); *fig.* rejaillir (sur, on); **2.** rebondissement *m*; détente *f*; ✖ recul *m*; mouvement *m* de dégout.

re·coin [ri:'kɔin] refrapper.

rec·ol·lect 1. [rekə'lekt] se souvenir de; se rappeler (*qch.*); **2.** ['ri:kə-**

'lekt] réunir de nouveau; **rec·ol·lec·tion** [rekə'lekʃn] souvenir *m*, mémoire *f*; *fig.* recueillement *m* (de l'âme).

re·com·mence ['ri:kə'mens] recommencer.

rec·om·mend [rekə'mend] recommander; **rec·om'mend·a·ble** recommandable; **rec·om'men·da·tion** recommandation *f*; **rec·om·'mend·a·to·ry** [ˌ‿ətəri] de recommandation.

re·com·mis·sion ['ri:kə'miʃn] réarmer (un navire); réintégrer dans les cadres (un officier).

re·com·mit ['ri:kə'mit] *parl.* renvoyer à une commission; commettre de nouveau; ~ to prison renvoyer en prison.

rec·om·pense ['rekəmpens] **1.** récompense *f* (de, for); compensation *f* (de, for); dédommagement *m* (de, for); **2.** récompenser (q. de qch., s.o. for s.th.); réparer (un mal); dédommager (q. de qch., s.o. for s.th.).

re·com·pose ['ri:kəm'pouz] rarranger; calmer de nouveau; ♫ recomposer; ~ o.s. se disposer de nouveau à.

rec·on·cil·a·ble ['rekənsailəbl] conciliable, accordable (avec, with); **'rec·on·cile** réconcilier (avec with, to); faire accorder; faire accepter (qch. à q., s.o. to s.th.); ajuster (une querelle); ~ o.s. to se résigner à; **'rec·on·cil·er** réconciliateur (-trice *f*) *m*; **rec·on·cil·i·a·tion** [ˌ‿sili-'eiʃn] réconciliation *f*; conciliation *f* (d'opinions contraires).

rec·on·dite □ *fig.* [ri'kɔndait] abstrus; obscur.

re·con·di·tion ['ri:kən'diʃn] rénover, remettre à neuf.

rec·on·nais·sance ✕ [ri'kɔnisəns] reconnaissance *f*.

rec·on·noi·ter, rec·on·noi·tre ✕ [rekə'nɔitə] *v/t.* reconnaître; *v/i.* faire une reconnaissance.

rec·on·quer ['ri:'kɔŋkə] reconquérir; **'re'con·quest** ✕ [ˌ‿kwest] reprise *f*.

rec·on·sid·er ['ri:kən'sidə] examiner de nouveau; revoir; revenir sur (une décision); **'re'con·sid·er'a·tion** examen *m* de nouveau; révision *f*.

re·con·sti·tute ['ri:'kɔnstitjuːt] re-

constituer; **'re·con·sti'tu·tion** reconstitution *f*.

re·con·struct ['ri:kəns'trʌkt] reconstruire; reconstituer (un crime); **re·con'struc·tion** reconstruction *f*; crime: reconstitution *f*.

re·con·ver·sion ♱ ['ri:kən'vəːʃn] reconversion *f* (en industries de paix); **'re'con'vert** reconvertir; transformer.

rec·ord 1. ['rekɔːd] mémoire *m*; ⚖ enregistrement *m*; ⚖ feuille *f* d'audience; ⚖ procès-verbal *m* de témoignage; minute *f*; note *f*; dossier *m*; (a. police-~) casier *m* judiciaire; registre *m*; monument *m*; ♪ disque *m*, a. enregistrement *m*; *sp. etc.* record *m*; ~ breaker personne *f* ou chose *f* qui bat le record; ~ holder recordman (*pl.* -men) *m*, recordwoman (*pl.* -men) *f*; ~ time temps *m* record; it is left (ou stands) on ~ that il est rapporté que; place on ~ prendre acte de; consigner par écrit; beat (ou break) the ~ battre le record; set up (ou establish) a ~ établir un record; ⚻ Office les Archives *f/pl.*; surt. Am. off the ~ non officiel(le *f*); confidentiel(le *f*); on the ~ authentique; **2.** [ri'kɔːd] enregistrer; consigner par écrit; rapporter, relater; by ~ed delivery en recommandé; ~ing apparatus appareil *m* enregistreur; (a. tape-~er) magnétophone *m*; **re'cord·er** personne *f* qui enregistre; ⚖ (sorte de) juge *m* municipal (= avocat chargé de remplir certaines fonctions de juge); appareil *m* enregistreur; ♪ flûte *f* à bec.

re·count¹ [ri'kaunt] raconter.

re·count² ['ri:'kaunt] recompter.

re·coup [ri'kuːp] (se) dédommager; indemniser; ⚖ défalquer.

re·course [ri'kɔːs] recours *m*; expédient *m*; have ~ to avoir recours à, recourir à.

re·cov·er¹ [ri'kʌvə] *v/t.* retrouver; recouvrer (a. la santé); regagner; rentrer en possession de; reprendre (haleine); rattraper (de l'argent, le temps perdu); obtenir; ⊕ récupérer; be ~ed être remis (malade); *v/i.* guérir; (a. ~ o.s.) se remettre; ⚖ se faire dédommager (par q.).

re·cov·er² ['ri:'kʌvə] recouvrir; regarnir (un fauteuil).

re·cov·er·a·ble [ri'kʌvərəbl] recouvrable, récupérable; guérissable (personne); **re'cov·er·y** recouvrement *m*; ⊕ récupération *f*; rétablissement *m* (*a. fig.*), guérison *f*; ✝ reprise *f*; redressement *m* (*économique*); ⚖ obtention *f* (*de dommages-intérêts*); *mot*. ~ *vehicle* dépanneuse *f*.

rec·re·an·cy ['rekrɪənsi] lâcheté *f*; apostasie *f*; **'rec·re·ant 1.** □ lâche; infidèle, apostat; **2.** lâche *m*; renégat *m*.

re·cre·ate¹ ['ri:kri'eit] recréer.

rec·re·ate² ['rekrieit] *v/t.* divertir; *v/i.* (*a.* ~ *o.s.*) se divertir; **rec·re·'a·tion** récréation *f*, divertissement *m*; délassement *m*; ~ *centre* (*Am.* *center*) centre *m* de loisirs; ~ *ground* terrain *m* de jeux; *école:* cour *f* de récréation; **'rec·re·a·tive** divertissant, récréatif (-ive *f*).

re·crim·i·nate [ri'krimineit] récriminer; **re·crim·i·'na·tion** récrimination *f*.

re·cru·desce [ri:kru:'des] s'enflammer de nouveau (*plaie*); reprendre (*maladie, a. fig.*); **re·cru·'des·cence** recrudescence *f* (*a. fig.*).

re·cruit [ri'kru:t] **1.** recrue *f* (*a. fig.*); **2.** *v/t.* ✕ recruter (*a. pol.*); ✕ *hist.* racoler (*des hommes pour l'armée*); *fig.* apporter *ou* faire des recrues; *fig.* restaurer (*la santé*); *v/i.* faire des recrues; se remettre (*malade*); **re'cruit·ment** recrutement *m*; racolage *m*; *santé:* rétablissement *m*.

rec·tan·gle ['rektæŋgl] rectangle *m*; **rec'tan·gu·lar** □ [~gjulə] rectangulaire.

rec·ti·fi·a·ble ['rektifaiəbl] rectifiable; **rec·ti·fi·ca·tion** [~fi'keiʃn] rectification *f* (*a.* ⚗, ⚙, ⚡); ⚡ redressement *m*; **rec·ti·fi·er** ['~faiə] rectificateur (-trice *f*) *m*; ⚡ rectificateur *m*; ⚙, *radio:* redresseur *m*; **rec·ti·fy** ['~fai] rectifier (*a.* ⚗, ⚙); corriger (*a.* ⚗); ⚡, *radio:* redresser; **rec·ti·lin·e·al** [rekti'liniəl], **rec·ti·lin·e·ar** □ [~niə] rectiligne; **rec·ti·tude** ['~tju:d] rectitude *f*; *caractère:* droiture *f*.

rec·tor ['rektə] curé *m*; *univ.* recteur *m*; *écoss.* directeur *m* (*d'une école*); **rec·tor·ate** ['~rit], **'rec·tor·ship** rectorat *m*; **'rec·to·ry** presbytère *m*; cure *f*.

rec·tum *anat.* ['rektəm] rectum *m*.

re·cum·bent □ [ri'kʌmbənt] couché, étendu.

re·cu·per·ate [ri'kju:pəreit] *v/i.* se remettre, se rétablir; *v/t.* ⊕ récupérer; **re·cu·per·a·tion** rétablissement *m*; ⊕ récupération *f*; *power of* ~ = **re'cu·per·a·tive pow·er** [~rətiv 'pauə] pouvoir *m* de rétablissement.

re·cur [ri'kə:] revenir (*à la memoire, sur un sujet*); se renouveler; se reproduire (*a.* ⚗); ~ *to s.o.'s mind* revenir à la mémoire de q.; ⚗ ~*ring decimal* fraction *f* décimale périodique; **re·cur·rence** [ri'kʌrəns] renouvellement *m*, réapparition *f*; ⚕ récidive *f*; ~ *to* retour m à; **re'cur·rent** □ périodique (*a.* ⚕ *fièvre*); *anat.* récurrent.

re·curve [ri:'kə:v] (se) recourber.

re·cu·sant ['rekjuzənt] **1.** réfractaire (à, *against*); dissident; **2.** réfractaire *mf*; *eccl.* récusant(e *f*) *m*.

re·cy·cle [ri:'saikl] recycler, retraiter; **re'cy·cling** recyclage *m*, retraitement *m*.

red [red] **1.** rouge (*a. pol.*); roux (rousse *f*) (*cheveux, feuille*); ♀ *Cross* Croix-Rouge *f*; ♀ ~ *currant* groseille *f* rouge; *zo.* ~ *deer* cerf *m* commun; ⊕ ~ *heat* chaude *f* rouge; ~ *herring* hareng *m* saur; *fig. draw* ~ *herrings* brouiller la piste; *min.* ~ *lead* minium *m*; ~ *man see redskin*; *sl. paint the town* ~ faire la nouba, faire la bringue; **2.** rouge *m* (*a. pol. mf*); *billard:* bille *f* rouge; *surt. Am.* F sou *m* (*de bronze*); *see* ~ voir rouge; *Am.* F *be in the* ~ avoir débit en banque; F *in the* ~ en déficit.

re·dact [ri'dækt] rédiger, mettre au point; **re'dac·tion** rédaction *f*; mise *f* au point; révision *f*.

red·breast ['redbrest] (*souv. robin* ~) *see robin*; **'red·cap** 🎖 *Am.* porteur *m*; *Angl.* soldat *m* de la police militaire; **red·den** ['redn] *v/t./i.* rougir; *v/i.* roussir (*feuille*); rougeoyer (*ciel*); **'red·dish** rougeâtre; roussâtre; **red·dle** ['~l] ocre *f* rouge.

re·dec·o·rate ['ri:'dekəreit] peindre (et tapisser) à nouveau (*une chambre etc.*); **'re·dec·o'ra·tion** nouvelle décoration *f*; nouveau décor *m*.

re·deem [ri'di:m] racheter (*eccl., obligation, défaut, esclave, temps, etc.*); amortir (*une dette*); purger (*une hypothèque*); dégager, retirer (*une montre etc.*); honorer (*une traite*); libérer (*un esclave*); tenir (*une* *promesse*); F réparer (*le temps perdu*); *fig.* arracher (à, *from*); *fig.* ~ing feature qualité *f* qui rachète les défauts (*de q.*), le seul bon côté (*de q.*); **re'deem·a·ble** ✝ rachetable, amortissable; **Re'deem·er** Rédempteur *m*, Sauveur *m*.

re·de·liv·er ['ri:di'livə] remettre de nouveau (*une lettre*); répéter.

re·demp·tion [ri'dempʃn] *eccl.* rédemption *f*; *crime, esclave, etc.*, *a.* ✝: rachat *m*; ✝ amortissement *m*; dégagement *m*; purge *f*; **re'demp·tive** rédempteur (-trice *f*).

re·de·ploy ['ri:di:plɔi] réorganiser; ✕ redéployer; **re·de'ploy·ment** réorganisation *f*; ✕ redéploiement *m*.

re·de·vel·op ['ri:di'veləp] *urbanisme*: (re)mettre en valeur; **re·de'vel·op·ment** (re)mise *f* en valeur.

red...: '~faced rougeaud, rubicond; rougissant (*de colère, gêne etc.*); '~haired roux (rousse *f*), rouquin; '~hand·ed *fig.* catch s.o. (be caught) ~ prendre q. (être pris) en flagrant délit *ou* les mains dans le sac; '~head F rouquin(e *f*) *m*; '~head·ed F rouquin; '~hot (chauffé au) rouge; *fig.* ardent, enthousiaste; *fig.* tout chaud, (de) denière heure.

red·in·te·grate [re'dintigreit] rétablir (*qch.*) dans son intégrité; réintégrer (*q.*) dans ses possessions; **red·in·te'gra·tion** rétablissement *m* intégral; réintégration *f*.

re·di·rect ['ri:di'rekt] faire suivre, adresser de nouveau (*une lettre etc.*).

re·dis·cov·er ['ri:dis'kʌvə] retrouver; redécouvrir.

re·dis·trib·ute [ri:dis'tribju:t] redistribuer; répartir de nouveau.

red-let·ter day ['redletə'dei] jour *m* de fête; *fig.* jour *m* de bonheur.

red-light dis·trict *Am.* ['redlait-'distrikt] quartier *m* réservé *ou* malfamé.

red·ness ['rednis] rougeur *f*; *cheveux, feuille*: rousseur *f*.

re·do ['ri:'du:] [*irr.* (do)] refaire.

red·o·lence ['redoləns] odeur *f*; parfum *m*; **'red·o·lent** parfumé; qui a une forte odeur (de, *of*); *fig.* be ~ of sentir (*qch.*).

re·dou·ble [ri:'dʌbl] redoubler.

re·doubt ✕ [ri'daut] réduit *m*, redoute *f*; **re'doubt·a·ble** *poét.* redoutable.

re·dound [ri'daund]: ~ to contribuer à; résulter (*de qch.*) pour; ~ (up)on rejaillir sur.

re·draft ['ri:'drɑ:ft] **1.** nouvelle rédaction *f*; ✝ retraite *f*; **2.** (*ou* **re·draw** ['ri:'drɔ:] [*irr.* (draw)] rédiger; ✝ faire retraite (sur, *on*).

re·dress [ri'dres] **1.** redressement *m*; remède *m*; réforme *f*; réparation *f* (*a.* 🜨); **2.** redresser; réparer; rétablir (*l'équilibre*).

red...: '~skin Peau-Rouge (*pl.* Peaux-Rouges) *m*; '~start *orn.* rouge-queue (*pl.* rouges-queues) *m*; ~ tape ['~'teip], ~tap·ism ['~-'teipizm] bureaucratie *f*, F paperasserie *f*; '~'tap·ist bureaucrate *m*; paperassier (-ère *f*) *m*.

re·duce [ri'dju:s] *fig.* réduire (*a.* 🜁, 🜂, 🜃, ✕ *une ville*) (en, *to*); 🜁, *a. fig.* ramener (à, *to*); abaisser (🜄, *la tension, la température*); (ra)baisser, diminuer (*le prix*); affaiblir (*a. phot.*; *q.*); ✕ casser; amincir (*une planche*); ralentir (*la marche*); atténuer (*un contraste*); *fig.* ~ to ériger en; ~ to writing coucher *ou* consigner par écrit; **re'duc·i·ble** réductible (à, *to*); **re·duc·tion** [ri'dʌkʃn] réduction *f* (*a.* ✝, ✕ *une ville*, 🜄, 🜂); diminution *f*; ✕ rétrogradation *f* (*d'un sous-officier*), cassation *f*; ✝ rabais *m*; ✝ remise *f* (*sur, on*); baisse *f* (*de température*); rapetissement *m* (*d'un dessin etc.*); *phot.* atténuation *f*; 🜁 relaxation *f*.

re·dun·dance, re·dun·dan·cy [ri-'dʌndəns(i)] surplus *m*; surabondance *f*; **re'dun·dant** □ superflu; surabondant; *poét.* redondant.

re·du·pli·cate [ri'dju:plikeit] redoubler; répéter; **re·du·pli·ca·tion** redoublement *m*.

re·dye ['ri:'dai] (faire) reteindre.

re-ech·o [ri:'ekou] *v/t.* répéter; *v/i.* résonner.

reed [ri:d] roseau *m*; *poét.* chalumeau *m*; ♪ hautbois *etc.*: anche *f*.

re-ed·it ['ri:'edit] rééditer.

re-ed·u·ca·tion ['ri:edju'keiʃn] rééducation *f*.

reed·y ['ri:di] couvert de *ou* abondant en roseaux; grinçant (*voix*); nasillard (*timbre*).

reef¹ [ri:f] récif *m* (*de corail etc.*).

reef² ⚓ [~] **1.** ris *m*; ~knot nœud *m* plat; **2.** prendre un ris dans (*la voile*); rentrer (*le beaupré etc.*).

reef·er¹ ['ri:fə] veste *f* quartier-maître, caban *m*.

reef·er² *Am. sl.* [~] cigarette *f* à marijuana.

reek [ri:k] **1.** odeur *f* forte; atmos-phère *f* fétide; *écoss.* vapeur *f*; fumée *f*; **2.** exhaler une mauvaise odeur *ou* des vapeurs; *fig.* puer (qch., *of* s.th.); *écoss.* fumer; **'reek·y** enfumé.

reel [ri:l] **1.** *tex., papier, cin. a.* film ~: bobine *f*; *tél.* moulinet *m* (*a. canne à pêche*); *phot., a.* ⊕ rouleau *m*; *cin.* bande *f*; titubation *f*, chan-cellement *m*; *danse:* branle *m* écos-sais; **2.** *v/t.* bobiner; dévider; ~ *in* remonter; ~ *off* dévider; *fig.* réciter d'un trait; *v/i.* tournoyer; chanceler; tituber.

re·e·lect ['ri:i'lekt] réélire.

re·el·i·gi·ble ['ri:'elidʒəbl] rééligi-ble.

re·en·act ['ri:i'nækt] remettre en vigueur; *théâ.* reproduire.

re·en·gage ['ri:in'geidʒ] ✕ renga-ger; réintégrer (*un employé*); ren-grener (*une roue dentée*); *mot.* ~ *the clutch* rembrayer.

re·en·list✕['ri:in'list] (se) rengager.

re·en·ter ['ri:'entə] *v/t.* rentrer dans; ✝ inscrire de nouveau; *v/i.* rentrer; se présenter de nouveau (*à un examen*); **'re·'ent·er·ing, re-en-trant** [ri:'entrənt] rentrant; **'re·'en·try** rentrée *f*.

re·es·tab·lish ['ri:is'tæbliʃ] rétablir; **'re·es'tab·lish·ment** rétablisse-ment *m*.

reeve ⚓ [ri:v] [*irr.*] passer (*un cor-dage dans une poulie*).

re·ex·am·i·na·tion ['ri:igzæmi'nei-ʃn] nouvel examen *m ou* ⚖ interro-gatoire *m*; **'re·ex'am·ine** [~min] examiner *ou* ⚖ interroger de nou-veau.

re·ex·change ['ri:iks'tʃeindʒ] nou-vel échange *m*; ✝ rechange *m*; ✝ retraite *f*.

re·fec·tion [ri'fekʃn] rafraîchisse-ment *m*; **re'fec·to·ry** [~təri] réfec-toire *m*.

re·fer [ri'fə:] *v/t.* rapporter; ratta-cher (*a. une plante à sa famille*); soumettre (*à un tribunal*); s'en réfé-rer (à q. de qch., s.th. *to* s.o.); ren-voyer (q. à q., s.o. *to* s.o.); *fig.* attri-buer; *école:* ajourner (*un candidat*); ✝ refuser d'honorer (*un chèque*); *v/i.* (*to*) se rapporter (à); se repor-ter (à) (*un document*); se référer (à) (*une autorité*); faire allusion (à), faire mention (de); reparler (de); **ref'er·a·ble:** ~ *to* attribuable à; qui relève de; **ref·er·ee** [refə'ri:] **1.** répondant *m*; *sp.* arbitre *m*; ⚖ arbitre *m* expert; **2.** *sp.* arbitrer; **ref·er·ence** ['refrəns] renvoi *m*, ré-férence *f* (*à une autorité*); rapport *m*; mention *f*, allusion *f*; ⚖ compé-tence *f*; *cartographie:* point *m* coté; (*a.* foot-note ~) appel *m* de note; *typ.* (*ou* ~ mark) renvoi *m*; *accom-pagnant une demande d'emploi:* ré-férence *f*; *in* (*ou* with) ~ *to* comme suite à, me (*etc.*) référant à; *terms pl. of* ~ mandat *m*, compétence *f*; *work of* ~, ~ *book* ouvrage *m* à con-sulter; ~ *library* bibliothèque *f* de consultation sur place; ~ *number* cote *f*; ✝ numéro *m* de commande; ~ *point* point *m* de repère; *make* ~ *to* signaler, faire mention de.

ref·er·en·dum [refə'rendəm] (*a.* people's *ou* national ~) référendum *m*, plébiscite *m*.

re·fill ['ri:'fil] **1.** objet *m* de rempla-cement; pile *f ou* feuilles *f/pl. ou* mine *f* de rechange; **2.** *v/t.* remplir (de nouveau); *v/i.mot.* faire le plein.

re·fine [ri'fain] *v/t. fig.* épurer; raf-finer; *v/i.* se raffiner (*a.* ⊕, *a. fig.*); ~ (*up*)on renchérir sur; **re'fine-ment** (r)affinage *m*; *fig.* cruauté, goût, pensée: raffinement *m*; **re'fin-er** raffineur *m* (*a. fig.*); ⊕ affineur *m*; **re'fin·er·y** ⊕ (r)affinerie *f*; *fer:* finerie *f*.

re·fit ['ri:'fit] **1.** *v/t.* ⚓ radouber; réarmer; ⊕ rajuster; remonter (*une usine*); *v/i.* réparer ses avaries; réar-mer; **2.** (*a.* 're'fit·ment) ⚓ radoub *m*, réparation *f*; réarmement *m*; ⊕ rajustement *m*; remontage *m*.

re·flect [ri'flekt] *v/t.* réfléchir, re-fléter; renvoyer; *fig.* être le reflet de; *v/i.* ~ (*up*)on réfléchir sur *ou* à; méditer sur; *fig.* faire du tort à; *fig.* critiquer; **re'flec·tion** réflexion *f* (*a. fig.*); reflet *m* (*a. fig.*), image *f*; pensée *f*; blâme *m* (de, on); **re'flec-tive** □ réfléchissant; de réflexion; réfléchi (*esprit, personne*); **re'flec-tor** réflecteur *m*; *cycl. rear* ~ cata-dioptre *m*.

re·flex ['ri:fleks] **1.** reflété; réfléchi (*a.* ⚕); *physiol.* réflexe; *fig.* indi-rect; *physiol.* ~ *action* (mouvement *m*) réflexe *m*; *phot.* ~ *camera* (appareil *m*) reflex *m*; 2. reflet *m*; *physiol.* réflexe *m*; **re·flex·ive** □ [ri'fleksiv] réfléchi (*a.* gramm.).

ref·lu·ent ['refluənt] qui reflue.

re·flux ['ri:flʌks] reflux *m*; jusant *m* (*marée*).   [boisement *m*.]

re·for·est·a·tion ['ri:foris'teiʃn] re-)

re·form[1] [ri'fɔ:m] 1. réforme *f*; 2. (se) réformer, corriger; apporter des réformes à.

re·form[2] ['ri:'fɔ:m] (se) reformer.

ref·or·ma·tion [refə'meiʃn] réformation *f*; réforme *f* (*a. eccl.* 2); **re·form·a·to·ry** [ri'fɔ:mətəri] 1. de réforme; de correction; 2. maison *f* de correction; **re'formed** réformé (*a. eccl.*); **re'form·er** réformateur (-trice *f*) *m*; **re'form·ist** réformiste.

re·found [ri:'faund] refondre.

re·fract [ri'frækt] réfracter, briser (*un rayon de lumière*); ~*ing telescope* lunette *f* d'approche; **re'frac·tion** réfraction *f*; **re'frac·tive** *opt.* réfractif (-ive *f*); à réfraction; **re'frac·tor** *opt.* milieu *m* ou dispositif *m* réfringent; **re'frac·to·ri·ness** indocilité *f*; ⚕ *fièvre etc.*: opiniâtreté *f*; ♁ nature *f* réfractaire; **re'frac·to·ry** 1. □ réfractaire (*a.* ♁, ⊕ à l'épreuve du feu); indocile, récalcitrant; ⊕ rebelle (*minerai*); ⚕ opiniâtre (*fièvre etc.*); 2. ⊕ substance *f* réfractaire.

re·frain[1] [ri'frein] *v/t.* † refréner (*ses passions*); *v/i.* se retenir, s'abstenir (de, from).

re·frain[2] [~] refrain *m*.

re·fran·gi·ble *phys.* [ri'frændʒəbl] réfrangible.

re·fresh [ri'freʃ] (se) rafraîchir; (se) reposer; ranimer; **re'fresh·er** F rafraîchissement *m*; ⚖ honoraires *m/pl.* supplémentaires; **re'fresh·ment** rafraîchissement *m* (*a. cuis.*); délassement *m*; ~ *room* buffet *m*.

re·frig·er·ant [ri'fridʒərənt] ⚕, ⊕ réfrigérant (*a. su./m*); **re'frig·er·ate** [~reit] (se) réfrigérer; *v/t. a.* frigorifier; **re'frig·er·at·ing** réfrigérant, frigorifique; **re'frig·er·a·tion** réfrigération *f*, frigorification *f*; **re'frig·er·a·tor** réfrigérateur *m*, glacière *f*, chambre *f* frigorifique; ~ *van* wagon *m* frigorifique.

re·fu·el ✈, mot. [ri:'fjuəl] faire le plein (d'essence).

ref·uge ['refju:dʒ] refuge *m*, abri *m*; (lieu *m* d')asile *m*; *alp.* refuge *m*; *take* ~ *in* se réfugier dans (*a.* fig.); **ref·u·gee** [~'dʒi:] réfugié(e *f*) *m*.

re·ful·gence [ri'fʌldʒəns] splendeur *f*; **re'ful·gent** □ resplendissant.

re·fund [ri:'fʌnd] rembourser.

re·fur·bish ['ri:'fə:biʃ] remettre à neuf.   [neuf.]

re·fur·nish ['ri:'fə:niʃ] meubler de)

re·fus·al [ri'fju:zl] refus *m*; droit *m* de refuser.

re·fuse[1] [ri'fju:z] refuser; *sp.* refuser de sauter (*cheval*); repousser, rejeter.

ref·use[2] ['refju:s] 1. de rebut; à ordures; de décharge; ⊕ ~ *water* eaux *f/pl.* vannes; 2. rebut *m*; déchets *m/pl.*; ordures *f/pl.* (*a.* fig.).

ref·u·ta·ble □ ['refjutəbl] réfutable; **ref·u·ta·tion** réfutation *f*; **re·fute** [ri'fju:t] réfuter.

re·gain [ri'gein] regagner, reprendre.

re·gal □ ['ri:gəl] royal (-aux *m/pl.*).

re·gale [ri'geil] *v/t.* régaler (de, with); *v/i.* se régaler (de on, with).

re·ga·li·a [ri'geiljə] *pl.* insignes *m/pl.*; joyaux *m/pl.* de la Couronne.

re·gard [ri'gɑ:d] 1. † regard *m*; égard *m*; attention *f*; estime *f*, respect *m*; *have* ~ *to* tenir compte de; avoir égard à, faire attention à; *with* ~ *to* quant à; pour ce qui concerne; *with kind* ~*s* avec les sincères amitiés (de, from); 2. regarder (comme, as); prendre garde à; concerner; *as* ~*s* en ce qui concerne; **re'gard·ful** □ [~ful] plein d'égards (pour q., of s.o.); attentif (-ive *f*) (à, of), soigneux (-euse *f*) (de, of); **re'gard·ing** à l'égard de; quant à, en ce qui concerne; **re'gard·less** □ inattentif (-ive *f*) (à, of); peu soigneux (-euse *f*) (de, of); ~ *of* sans regarder à.

re·gat·ta [ri'gætə] régate *f*, -s *f/pl.*

re·ge·late ['ri:dʒəleit] se regeler.

re·gen·cy ['ri:dʒənsi] régence *f*.

re·gen·er·ate 1. [ri'dʒenəreit] (se) régénérer; 2. [~rit] régénéré; **re·gen·er·a·tion** régénération *f* (*a.* fig.); *fig.* amélioration *f*; ⊕ *huile*: épuration *f*; **re'gen·er·a·tive** [~rətiv] régénérateur (-trice *f*).

re·gent ['ri:dʒənt] 1. régent; 2. régent(e *f*) *m*; *Am.* membre *m* du

conseil d'administration; **'re·gent-
ship** régence *f.*
reg·i·cide ['redʒisaid] régicide *mf;
crime:* régicide *m.*
reg·i·men ['redʒimen] ✻, *gramm.,
etc.* régime *m.*
reg·i·ment ✕ **1.** ['redʒimənt] régiment *m; fig.* légion *f;* **2.** ['⁓ment]
enrégimenter; organiser; **reg·i-
'men·tal** ✕ de *ou* du régiment;
reg·i'men·tal·ly [⁓təli] par régiment; **reg·i'men·tals** ✕ [⁓tlz] *pl.*
(grand) uniforme *m;* **reg·i·men'tation** enrégimentation *f.*
re·gion ['riːdʒən] région *f; fig.* domaine *m;* **'re·gion·al** ☐ régional
(-aux *m/pl.*); *radio:* (*a.* ⁓ *station*)
poste *m* régional.
reg·is·ter ['redʒistə] **1.** registre *m*
(*a.* ♱, ♪, ⊕ *fourneau*); matricule *f;*
liste *f* (*électorale*); ⊕ *cheminée:*
rideau *m;* ⚓ lettre *f* de mer; ♪ *voix:*
étendue *f;* compteur *m* (*kilométrique*); ⁓ *office* bureau *m* d'enregistrement *ou* de l'état civil *ou* de placement; ⚓ *net* ⁓ *ton* tonne *f* de jauge
nette; **2.** *v/t.* enregistrer (*a. bagages,
a. Am. émotion*); inscrire; immatriculer (*une auto, un étudiant*); *thermomètre:* marquer (*les degrés*); ⊕
déposer (*une marque*), recommander
(*une lettre etc.*); *typ.* mettre en registre; *v/i.* ⊕ coïncider exactement;
typ. être en registre; s'inscrire (*personne*); **'reg·is·tered** enregistré,
inscrit, immatriculé; recommandé
(*lettre etc.*); ⁓ *design* modèle *m* déposé; ♱ ⁓ *share* (*ou Am. stock*)
action *f* nominative.
reg·is·trar [redʒis'traː] teneur *m* des
registres; officier *m* de l'état civil;
♱♱ greffier *m; univ.* secrétaire *m; get
married before the* ⁓ se marier ci-
vilement; **reg·is·tra·tion** [⁓'treiʃn]
enregistrement *m,* inscription *f;
auto etc.:* immatriculation *f; marque:*
dépôt *m;* ⁓ *fee* droit *m* d'inscription; *lettre etc.:* taxe *f* de recommandation; **'reg·is·try** enregistrement *m; admin.* greffe *m;* (*a.* ⁓ *office*) bureau *m* d'enregistrement *ou*
de l'état civil *ou* de placement; *servants'* ⁓ agence *f* de placement.
reg·nant ['regnənt] régnant.
re·gress 1. ['riːgres] retour *m* en
arrière; *fig.* déclin *m;* **2.** [ri'gres]
retourner en arrière, reculer; *biol.
etc.* rétrograder; **re·gres·sion** [ri-

'greʃn] rétrogression *f; biol.* régression *f;* ♀ rebroussement *m;* **re·gres-
sive** ☐ [ri'gresiv] régressif (-ive *f*).
re·gret [ri'gret] **1.** regret *m* (de *at,
for*); **2.** regretter (de *inf., gér. ou to
inf.*); **re'gret·ful** ☐ [⁓ful] plein de
regrets; ⁓*ly* avec *ou* à regret; **re-
'gret·ta·ble** ☐ regrettable; à regretter.
re·group ['riː'gruːp] (se) regrouper;
re'group·ment regroupement *m.*
reg·u·lar ['regjulə] **1.** ☐ régulier
(-ère *f*) (*a.* ✕, *eccl., etc.*); habituel
(-le *f*); ordinaire, normal (-aux
m/pl.); réglé; réglementaire, dans
les règles; *Am.* ⁓ *gas, Brit.* ⁓ *petrol*
essence *f* ordinaire; **2.** *eccl.* régulier
m, religieux *m;* ✕ soldat *m* de carrière; **reg·u·lar·i·ty** [⁓'læriti] régularité *f.*
reg·u·late ['regjuleit] régler (*a.* ⊕,
a. fig.); diriger; ⊕ ajuster; **'reg·u-
lat·ing** ⊕ régulateur (-trice *f*); ré-
glant; **reg·u'la·tion 1.** règlement
m; ⊕ réglage *m;* ✕ direction *f;*
2. réglementaire; d'ordonnance (*revolver*); **'reg·u·la·tive** ☐ régulateur (-trice *f*); **'reg·u·la·tor** régulateur (-trice *f*) *m;* ⊕ régulateur *m;*
⊕ ⁓ *lever* registre *m.*
re·gur·gi·tate [riː'gəːdʒiteit] *v/t.*
régurgiter, regorger; *v/i.* refluer,
regorger.
re·ha·bil·i·tate [riːə'biliteit] réhabiliter; **re·ha·bil·i'ta·tion** réhabilitation *f; finances:* assainissement *m.*
re·hash *fig.* ['riː'hæʃ] réchauffer.
re·hears·al [ri'həːsl] récit *m* détaillé;
♪, *théâ.* répétition *f;* **re·hearse**
[ri'həːs] énumérer; raconter (tout
au long); ♪, *théâ.* répéter.
re·heat ['riː'hiːt] réchauffer.
reign [rein] **1.** règne *m* (*a. fig.*); *in
the* ⁓ *of* sous le règne de; **2.** régner
(sur, over) (*a. fig.*).
re·im·burse ['riːim'bəːs] rembourser (*a.* ♱) (q. de qch., s.o. [for]
s.th.); **'re·im'burse·ment** remboursement *m.*
rein [rein] **1.** rêne *f;* guide *f; fig.
give* ⁓ *to* lâcher la bride à; **2.:** ⁓ *in
ou up ou back* retenir.
rein·deer *zo.* ['reindiə] renne *m.*
re·in·force [riːin'fɔːs] **1.** renforcer;
affermir (*la santé*); ⊕ ⁓*d concrete*
béton *m* armé; **2.** ⊕ armature *f;
canon:* renfort *m;* **'re·in'force-
ments** ✕ *pl.* renfort *m,* -s *m/pl.*

re·in·sert ['ri:in'sə:t] réinsérer; remettre en place.

re·in·stall ['ri:in'stɔ:l] réinstaller; **'re·in·stal(l)·ment** réinstallation *f*.

re·in·state ['ri:in'steit] réintégrer (*dans ses fonctions*); rétablir; **'re·in·state·ment** réintégration *f*; rétablissement *m*.

re·in·sur·ance ['ri:in'ʃuərəns] réassurance *f*; contre-assurance *f*; **re·in·sure** ['~'ʃuə] réassurer.

re·in·vest ['ri:in'vest] investir *etc.* de nouveau (*see invest*).

re·is·sue ['ri:'isju:; *surt. Am.* 'ri:'iʃu:] **1.** rééditer (*un livre*); ✝ émettre de nouveau; **2.** nouvelle édition *f ou* ✝ émission *f*.

re·it·er·ate [ri:'itəreit] réitérer, répéter; **re·it·er·a·tion** réitération *f*, répétition *f*.

re·ject [ri'dʒekt] rejeter; refuser; repousser; ⊕ mettre au rebut; **re·jec·tion** rejet *m*; refus *m*; repoussement *m*; **~s** *pl.* rebuts *m/pl.*, pièces *f/pl.* de rebut; **re'jec·tor cir·cuit** *radio*: filtre *m*.

re·joice [ri'dʒɔis] *v/t.* réjouir (*q.*); **~d** heureux (-euse *f*) (de *at, by*); *v/i.* se réjouir (de *at, in*); **re'joic·ing 1.** □ réjouissant; plein de joie (*personne*); **2.** (*souv.* ~s *pl.*) réjouissances *f/pl.*, fête *f*. } {réunir (à *to, with*).}

re·join¹ ['ri:'dʒɔin] (se) rejoindre,}

re·join² [ri'dʒɔin] répliquer; **re·'join·der** Ⰵ réplique *f*; repartie *f*.

re·ju·ve·nate [ri'dʒu:vineit] *vt/i.* rajeunir; **re·ju·ve·na·tion, re·ju·ve·nes·cence** ['~'nesns] rajeunissement *m*.

re·kin·dle ['ri:'kindl] (se) rallumer.

re·lapse [ri'læps] **1.** ⚕, *a. fig.* rechute *f*; **2.** retomber; ⚕ faire une rechute.

re·late [ri'leit] *v/t.* (ra)conter; rattacher (à *to, with*); *v/i.* se rapporter, avoir rapport (à *to*); **re'lat·ed** ayant rapport (à *to*); apparenté (à *to*) (*personne*); allié (à *to*); **~re'lat·er** conteur (-euse *f*) *m*, narrateur (-trice *f*) *m*.

re·la·tion [ri'leiʃn] récit *m*, relation *f*; rapport *m* (à *to, with*); parent(e *f*) *m*; **in ~ to** par rapport à; **re·'la·tion·ship** rapport *m*; lien *m*; relations *f/pl.*, rapports *m/pl.*; (liens *m/pl.* de) parenté *f*; *have a good ~ with s.o.* être en bons rapports avec q.; s'entendre bien avec q.

rel·a·tive ['relətiv] **1.** □ relatif (-ive *f*) (*a. gramm.*); qui se rapporte (à, *to*); **2.** *adv.*: ~ *to* au sujet de; **3.** *su. gramm.* pronom *m* relatif; **rel·a·tiv·i·ty** relativité *f*.

re·lax [ri'læks] *v/t.* relâcher; détendre; desserrer (*une étreinte*); mitiger (*un jugement etc.*); ⚕ enflammer (*la gorge*); ⚕ relâcher (*le ventre*); *v/i.* se relâcher; se détendre; diminuer; se délasser; **re·lax·a·tion** relâchement *m*; détente *f*, repos *m*, délassement *m*; mitigation *f*.

re·lay¹ [ri'lei] **1.** relais *m* (*a.* ⚡); ⚡ contacteur *m*; relève *f* (*d'ouvriers*); radiodiffusion *f* relayée; *sp.* ~-race course *f* de ou à relais; **2.** *radio*: relayer; ~ed by (ou from) en relais de.

re·lay² ['ri:'lei] poser de nouveau; remettre.

re·lease [ri'li:s] **1.** délivrance *f*; *fig.* libération *f*; élargissement *m*; ✝ mise *f* en vente; ✝ acquit *m*; *cin.* (*souv. first* ~) mise *f* en circulation; ⚖ relaxation *f* (*d'un prisonnier*); ⚖ cession *f* (*de terres*); ⊕ mise *f* en marche; ⊕ dégagement *m*; *phot.* déclencheur *m*; **2.** relâcher; libérer (de *from*); lâcher; renoncer à (*un droit*); faire la remise de (*une dette*); céder (*des terres*); ✝ mettre en vente; *cin.* mettre en circulation; émettre, dégager (*la fumée etc.*); ⊕, *phot.* déclencher; ⊕ décliquer; ⊕ mettre en marche.

rel·e·gate ['religeit] reléguer (à, *to*); renvoyer (à, *to*); bannir (*q.*); *sp.* be ~d être relégué (à la division inférieure); **rel·e·ga·tion** relégation *f*; mise *f* à l'écart; renvoi *m* (*sp. à la division inférieure*).

re·lent [ri'lent] s'adoucir; se laisser attendrir; **re'lent·less** □ implacable; impitoyable.

rel·e·vance, rel·e·van·cy ['relivəns(i)] pertinence *f*; applicabilité *f* (à, *to*); rapport *m* (avec, *to*); **'rel·e·vant** (à, *to*) pertinent; applicable; qui se rapporte.

re·li·a·bil·i·ty [rilaiə'biliti] sûreté *f*; véracité *f*; **re'li·a·ble** □ sûr; digne de foi (*source*) ou de confiance (*personne*).

re·li·ance [ri'laiəns] confiance *f*; place ~ on se fier à; **re'li·ant**: be ~ on compter sur; se fier à.

rel·ic ['relik] relique *f* (*a. eccl.*); *fig.*

vestige *m*; ⁓s *pl.* restes *m/pl.*; **rel·ict** † [ˈ⁓kt] veuve *f.*

re·lief [riˈliːf] soulagement *m*; décharge *f*; *détresse*: allégement *m*; ✕ *endroit*: délivrance *f*; *garde etc.*: relève *f*; ⚖ *tort*: réparation *f*, redressement *m*; secours *m* (*a*. aux pauvres), aide *f*; △ relief *m*; *fig.* agrément *m*; *fig.* détente *f*; ⊕ dégagement *m*; *be on* ⁓ être un pauvre assisté; *poor* ⁓ secours *m* aux pauvres; ⁓ *work* secours *m* aux sinistrés; ⁓ *works pl.* travaux *m/pl.* publics organisés pour aider les chômeurs; *in* ⁓ *against* découpé sur; qui se détache sur.

re·lieve [riˈliːv] soulager (*a*. △ *une poutre*); alléger (*la détresse*); secourir, aider (*les pauvres etc.*); ✕ dégager (*un endroit, a.* ⊕); ✕ relever (*les troupes etc.*); *peint. etc.* mettre en relief, donner du relief à; *fig.* faire ressortir; *cost.* agrémenter (*de with, by*); débarrasser (*de, of*); *fig.* tranquilliser (*l'esprit*), dissiper (*l'ennui*); F ⁓ *nature* faire ses besoins.

re·lie·vo [riˈliːvou] relief *m.*

re·li·gion [riˈlidʒən] religion *f.*

re·li·gious [riˈlidʒəs] religieux (-euse *f*) (*a. fig., a. eccl.*); dévot; pieux (-euse *f*); de piété; **re·li·gious·ness** piété *f*; F *fig.* religiosité *f.*

re·lin·quish [riˈliŋkwiʃ] renoncer à (*une idée, un projet, etc.*); abandonner; ⚖ délaisser; lâcher (*qch.*); **re·ˈlin·quish·ment** abandon *m* (*de, of*); renonciation *f* (à, *of*).   [*m.*]

rel·i·quar·y [ˈrelikwəri] reliquaire

rel·ish [ˈreliʃ] 1. goût *m*, saveur *f*; *fig.* attrait *m*; *cuis. piment*: soupçon *m*, pointe *f*; assaisonnement *m*; *with* ⁓ très volontiers; 2. *v/t.* relever le goût de; savourer, goûter; *fig.* trouver du plaisir à, avoir le goût de; *did you* ⁓ *your dinner?* votre dîner vous a-t-il plu?; *v/i.* sentir (*qch., of s.th.*), avoir un léger goût (*de, of*).

re·lo·cate [ˈriːlouˈkeit] transférer; déplacer; **ˈre·lo·ˈca·tion** transfert *m*, déplacement *m.*

re·luc·tance [riˈlʌktəns] répugnance *f* (à *inf.*, *to inf.*); *phys.* reluctance *f*; **reˈluc·tant** □ qui résiste; fait *ou* donné à contrecœur; *be* ⁓ *to* (*inf.*) être peu disposé à (*inf.*), hésiter à (*inf.*).

re·ly [riˈlai]: ⁓ (*up*)*on* compter sur, s'en rapporter à.

re·main [riˈmein] 1. rester; demeurer; persister; 2. ⁓s *pl.* restes *m/pl.*; vestiges *m/pl.*; **reˈmain·der** reste *m*, restant *m*; *livres*: solde *m* d'édition; ⚖ réversion *f* (sur, *to*).

re·make [ˈriːmeik] *film*: nouvelle version *f ou* réalisation *f*, remake *m.*

re·mand [riˈmɑːnd] 1. ⚖ renvoyer (*un prévenu*) à une autre audience; 2.: *on* ⁓ renvoyé à une autre audience; *prisoner on* ⁓ préventionnaire *mf.*

re·mark [riˈmɑːk] 1. remarque *f*; observation *f*; 2. *v/t.* remarquer, observer; faire la remarque (que, *that*); *v/i.* (sur, [*up*]*on*) faire des remarques; commenter; **reˈmark·a·ble** □ remarquable (par, *for*); frappant; singulier (-ère *f*); **reˈmark·a·ble·ness** ce qu'il y a de remarquable (dans, *of*); mérite *m.*

re·mar·ry [ˈriːˈmæri] *v/t.* se remarier à (*q.*); remarier (*des divorcés*); *v/i.* se remarier.

re·me·di·a·ble □ [riˈmiːdjəbl] réparable; remédiable; **reˈme·di·al** □ [riˈmiːdjəl] réparateur (-trice *f*); ✚ curatif (-ive *f*); ⁓ *teaching* cours *m/pl.* de rattrapage.

rem·e·dy [ˈremidi] 1. remède *m*; ⚖ réparation *f*; 2. porter remède à, remédier.

re·mem·ber [riˈmembə] se rappeler (*qch.*), se souvenir de (*qch.*); ne pas oublier (*a.* = *donner qch. à* [*q.*]); ⁓ *me to him!* dites-lui bien de choses de ma part!; rappelez-moi à son bon souvenir!; **reˈmem·brance** souvenir *m*, mémoire *f*; *give my kind* ⁓*s to him!* dites-lui bien des choses de ma part!

re·mind [riˈmaind] rappeler (qch. à q., *s.o. of s.th.*); ⁓ *o.s. that* se rappeler que; **reˈmind·er** mémento *m*; ✝ rappel *m* de compte.

rem·i·nisce [remiˈnis] remonter dans le passé, parler de *ou* évoquer ses souvenirs; **rem·i·nis·cence** [⁓ˈnisns] réminiscence *f*; souvenir *m*; **rem·iˈnis·cent** □ qui se souvient (de, *of*); *be* ⁓ *of* rappeler, faire penser à (*qch.*).

re·miss □ [riˈmis] négligent, insouciant; nonchalant; **reˈmis·si·ble** [⁓əbl] rémissible; **reˈmis·sion** [⁓ˈmiʃn] *dette, peine*: remise *f*; ✚, *eccl.* rémission *f*; *eccl.* pardon *m*;

relâchement *m*; **re'miss·ness** négligence *f*.

re·mit [ri'mit] *v/t.* remettre (*une dette, une peine,* ✝, *a. eccl.*); *eccl.* pardonner; relâcher; ⚖ renvoyer; *v/i.* diminuer d'intensité; *please* ~ prière de nous couvrir; **re'mit·tance** ✝ remise *f*; ✝ envoi *m* de fonds; **re·mit'tee** destinataire *mf*; **re'mit·tent** ⚕ rémittent; **re'mit·ter** ✝ remetteur (-euse *f*) *m*; envoyeur (-euse *f*) *m* (de fonds).

rem·nant ['remnənt] reste *m*, restant *m*; ✝ coupon *m* (*d'étoffe*); ~*s pl.* soldes *m/pl.*

re·mod·el [ri:'mɔdl] remodeler; remanier; ⊕ transformer.

re·mon·strance [ri'mɔnstrəns] remontrance *f*; **re'mon·strant 1.** de remontrance; qui proteste (*personne*); **2.** remontreur (-euse *f*) *m*; **re'mon·strate** [~streit] faire des représentations à q., *with s.o.*; au sujet de, [*up*]*on*); protester (que, *that*).

re·morse [ri'mɔ:s] remords *m* (pour, *for*; de, *at*); **re'morse·ful** □ [~ful] plein de remords; **re'morse·less** □ sans remords; impitoyable.

re·mote □ [ri'mout] écarté; éloigné; reculé; lointain; *fig.* vague; ~ **con·trol** ⊕ **1.** commande *f* à distance; **2.** télécommandé; **re'mote·ness** éloignement *m*; degré *m* éloigné; *fig.* faible degré (*de ressemblance*).

re·mount 1. [ri:'maunt] *v/t.* remonter (*a.* ⚔); *v/i.* remonter (*a.* à cheval); **2.** ⚔ ['ri:maunt] (cheval *m* de) remonte *f*; *army* ~*s pl.* chevaux *m/pl.* de troupe.

re·mov·a·ble [ri'mu:vəbl] détachable; extirpable (*mal*); transportable; révocable; **re'mov·al** [~əl] *tache etc.*: enlèvement *m*; *mot. pneu:* démontage *m*; ⚕ *pansement:* levée *f*; déplacement *m*; transport *m*; *fonctionnaire:* révocation *f*; *abus, mal:* suppression *f*; déménagement *m*; ~ **expenses** frais *m/pl.* de déplacement; ~ **service** entreprise *f* de déménagements; ~ **van** voiture *f* de déménagement; **re·move** [~'mu:v] **1.** *v/t.* enlever, ôter; écarter; chasser; déplacer; éloigner; révoquer (*un fonctionnaire*); assassiner; supprimer; ~ **furniture** déménager; *v/i.* se déplacer; déménager; **2.** distance *f*; degré *m*; *école anglaise:* classe *f*

intermédiaire; *école:* passage *m* à une classe supérieure; **re'mov·er** déménageur *m*; 🜄 dissolvant *m*; *pour taches:* détachant *m*; *pour vernis etc.:* décapant *m*.

re·mu·ner·ate [ri'mju:nəreit] rémunérer (de, *for*); **re·mu·ner'a·tion** rémunération *f*; **re'mu·ner·a·tive** □ [~rətiv] rémunérateur (-trice *f*).

ren·ais·sance [rə'neisəns] Renaissance *f*.

re·nal *anat.* ['ri:nl] des reins, rénal (-aux *m/pl.*).

re·nas·cence [ri'næsns] retour *m* à la vie; Renaissance *f*; **re'nas·cent** renaissant.

rend [rend] [*irr.*] déchirer; *fig. a.* fendre.

ren·der ['rendə] rendre (*a. compte, forteresse, grâce, hommage, service,* ♪ *phrase, a. = faire devenir*); faire (*honneur*); traduire (en, *into*); ✝ remettre (*un compte* à q., *s.o. an account*); 🔺 enduire (de, *with*); ♪ interpréter (*un morceau*); *cuis.* clarifier, fondre; **'ren·der·ing** ⚔ reddition *f*; ♪ interprétation *f*; traduction *f*; *cuis.* clarification *f*, fonte *f*; 🔺 enduit *m*.

ren·dez·vous ['rɔndivu:] rendez-vous *m*.

ren·di·tion [ren'diʃn] ⚔ reddition *f*; *Am.* interprétation *f*; traduction *f*.

ren·e·gade ['renigeid] renégat(e *f*) *m*.

re·new [ri'nju:] renouveler; **re·'new·al** [~əl] renouvellement *m*; remplacement *m*.

ren·net ['renit] présure *f*; *pomme:* reinette *f*.

re·nounce [ri'nauns] *v/t.* renoncer à, abandonner; répudier; *v/i. cartes:* renoncer.

ren·o·vate ['renoveit] renouveler; remettre à neuf; **ren·o'va·tion** renouvellement *m*; rénovation *f*; **'ren·o·va·tor** rénovateur (-trice *f*) *m*.

re·nown [ri'naun] renom(mée *f*) *m*; **re'nowned** (for) renommé (pour), célèbre (par).

rent¹ [rent] **1.** *prét. et p.p. de rend*; **2.** déchirure *f*; *terrain:* fissure *f*.

rent² [~] **1.** loyer *m*; location *f*; **2.** louer; affermer (*une terre*); **'rent·a·ble** qui peut se louer; affermable (*terre*); **'rent-a-'car** (*serv·ice*) location *f* de voitures; **'rent·al** (montant *m* du) loyer *m*; *Am.* location *f* (*d'une auto etc.*); ~ *value* valeur *f* locative; **'rent-charge** servitude *f* de rente (*à faire à un tiers*); **'rent·er** locataire *mf*; *cin.* distributeur *m*; **'rent'free 1.** *adj.* exempt de loyer; **2.** *adv.* sans payer de loyer.

re·num·ber [ri'nʌmbə] renuméroter, numéroter de nouveau; **re-'num·ber·ing** renumérotage *m*.

re·nun·ci·a·tion [rinʌnsi'eiʃn] (*of*) renoncement *m* (à); reniement *m* (de); ⚖ répudiation *f* (de).

re·oc·cu·pa·tion [riɔkju'peiʃn] réoccupation *f* (*d'un pays, d'un territoire, etc.*); **re'oc·cu·py** réoccuper (*un pays, un territoire, etc.*).

re·o·pen ['ri:'oupn] *v/t.* rouvrir; recommencer; *v/i.* se rouvrir (*plaie*); rentrer (*école*); *théâ.* rouvrir; **re'o·pen·ing** réouverture *f*.

re·or·ga·ni·za·tion ['ri:ɔ:gənai-'zeiʃn] réorganisation *f*; ⚕ assainissement *m*; **re'or·gan·ize** (se) réorganiser; ⚕ assainir.

rep ⚕ [rep] reps *m.* [*se*]; remballer. ⎫
re·pack ['ri:'pæk] refaire (*une vali-* ⎬
re·paint ['ri:'peint] repeindre. ⎭

re·pair¹ [ri'pɛə] **1.** réparation *f*; rétablissement *m* (*d'une maison etc.*); ⚓ radoub *m*; ~*s pl.* réparations *f/pl.*; réfection *f* (*d'une route*); ~ *kit* trousse *f* de réparation; ~ *man* réparateur *m*; ~ *shop* atelier *m* de réparations; (*damaged*) *beyond* ~ irréparable; *in* (*good*) ~ en bon état; *out of* ~ en mauvais état; *'road* ~*s* 'chantier' *m*; *under* ~ en réparation; **2.** réparer (*a. fig.*); raccommoder (*un vêtement*); remettre en état (*une machine*); ⚓ radouber; rétablir (*la santé*).

re·pair² [~] se rendre (à, *to*).

re·pa·ra·ble ['repərəbl] réparable; **rep·a'ra·tion** réparation *f* (*a. pol., a. fig.*); *pol. make* ~*s* réparer.

rep·ar·tee [repɑ:'ti:] repartie *f*, réplique *f* spirituelle; *be good at* ~ avoir la repartie; avoir la repartie facile; savoir répondre du tac au tac.

re·par·ti·tion [ri:pɑ:'tiʃn] répartition *f*; nouveau partage *m*.

re·pass ['ri:'pɑ:s] *v/i.* passer de nouveau; repasser; *v/i.* repasser (devant); *parl.* voter de nouveau.

re·past [ri'pɑ:st] repas *m.*

re·pa·tri·ate 1. [ri:'pætrieit] rapatrier; **2.** [~iit] rapatrié(e *f*) *m*; **'re·pa·tri'a·tion** rapatriement *m*.

re·pay [ri:'pei] [*irr.* (*pay*)] rembourser; récompenser; rendre (*de l'argent*); *fig.* se venger de; s'acquitter de (*de qch., s.th.*; envers q., *s.o.*); *fig.* payer (de, *with*); **re'pay·a·ble** remboursable; **re'pay·ment** remboursement *m*; récompense *f.*

re·peal [ri'pi:l] **1.** abrogation *f*; ⚖ annulation *f*; **2.** abroger; révoquer; annuler.

re·peat [ri'pi:t] **1.** *v/t.* répéter; réitérer; recommencer; ✝ ~ *an order* renouveler une commande (de qch., *for s.th.*); *v/i.* (*a.* ~ *o.s.*) se répéter; revenir (*nourriture*); être à répétition (*montre, fusil*); **2.** ♪ reprise *f*; renvoi *m*; ✝ (*souv.* ~ *order*) commande *f* renouvelée; **re'peat·ed** □ réitéré; **re'peat·er** rediseur (-euse *f*) *m*; ⚕ fraction *f* périodique; montre *f ou* fusil *m* à répétition; *tél.* répétiteur *m.*

re·pel [ri'pel] repousser (*a. fig.*); rebuter; inspirer de la répulsion à; **re'pel·lent** répulsif (-ive *f*).

re·pent [ri'pent] (*a.* ~ *of*) se repentir de.

re·pent·ance [ri'pentəns] repentir *m*; **re'pent·ant** repenti.

re·peo·ple ['ri:'pi:pl] repeupler.

re·per·cus·sion [ri:pə:'kʌʃn] répercussion *f* (*a. fig.*); contre-coup *m.*

rep·er·to·ry ♪, *théâ., a. fig.* ['repə-təri] répertoire *m.*

rep·e·ti·tion [repi'tiʃn] répétition *f*; recommencement *m*; *tél.* collationnement *m*; ♪ reprise *f*; ✝ ~ *order* commande *f* renouvelée.

re·pine [ri'pain] se chagriner, se plaindre (de, *at*); **re'pin·ing** □ mécontent; chagrin.

re·place [ri'pleis] replacer, remettre en place; remplacer (par, *by*); *téléph.* raccrocher (*le récepteur*); **re'place·ment** remise *f* en place; remplacement *m*; ⊕ pièce *f* de rechange.

re·plant ['ri:'plɑ:nt] replanter.

re·play *sp.* ['ri:'plei] match *m* rejoué.

re·plen·ish [ri'pleniʃ] remplir; se réapprovisionner (de, en *with*); **re'plen·ish·ment** remplissage *m*; ravitaillement *m.*

re·plete [ri'pli:t] rempli, plein (de, *with*); **re'ple·tion** réplétion *f*; *eat to* ~ manger jusqu'à satiété.

rep·li·ca ['replikə] *peint. etc.* réplique *f*, double *m* (*a. fig.*); *fig.* copie *f*.

rep·li·ca·tion [repli'keiʃn] ᴛᴌ réplique *f*; repartie *f*; *fig.* copie *f*; répercussion *f*.

re·ply [ri'plai] **1.** (à, to) répondre; répliquer (*a.* ᴛᴌ); **2.** réponse *f*; ᴛᴌ réplique *f*; ~ *postcard* carte *f* postale avec réponse payée.

re·port [ri'pɔːt] **1.** rapport *m* (sur, on); *journ.* reportage *m*; *école, a. météor.* bulletin *m*; *fig.* nouvelle *f*; rumeur *f*; *fusil:* coup *m*; réputation *f*; *école:* ~ *card* bulletin *m* (scolaire); **2.** *v/t.* rapporter (*a. parl.*); faire un rapport sur; faire le compte rendu de; dire; signaler; *v/i. journ.* faire des reportages; faire un rapport (sur, [up]on); (*a.* ~ *o.s.*) se présenter (à, devant to); *gramm.* ~*ed speech* discours *m ou* style *m* indirect; **re'port·er** journaliste *m*, reporter *m*.

re·pose [ri'pouz] **1.** repos *m*; sommeil *m*; calme *m*; **2.** *v/t.* reposer (*q., sa tête, etc.*); ~ *trust etc.* in mettre sa confiance *etc.* en; *v/i.* se reposer; dormir; se délasser; *fig.* reposer (sur, [up]on); **re·pos·i·to·ry** [ri'pɔzitəri] dépôt *m*, entrepôt *m*; dépositaire *mf* (*personne*); *fig.* répertoire *m*.

re·pos·sess ['riːpə'zes]: ~ *o.s.* of reprendre possession de (*qch.*).

rep·re·hend [repri'hend] blâmer, réprimander; **rep·re'hen·si·ble** □ répréhensible; **rep·re'hen·sion** réprimande *f*.

rep·re·sent [repri'zent] représenter (*a.* ♥, *a. théâ. une pièce*); *théâ.* jouer (*un personnage*); symboliser; signaler (qch. à q., *s.th.* to *s.o.*); **rep·re·sen'ta·tion** représentation *f* (*a.* ♥, ᴛᴌ, *pol., fig., théâ. pièce*); *théâ.* interprétation *f* (*d'un rôle*); *coll.* représentants *m/pl.*; *fig.* ~*s pl.* remontrance *f* courtoise; **rep·re'sent·a·tive** □ [~tətiv] **1.** représentatif (-ive *f*); *parl. a.* par députés; typique; *be* ~ of représenter (*qch.*); ~ of représentant (*qch.*); **2.** représentant(e *f*) *m*; *pol.* député *m*; *parl. Am. House of* ~*s* Chambre *f* des Représentants.

re·press [ri'pres] réprimer; retenir; étouffer; *psych.* refouler; **re·pres·sion** [ri'preʃn] (*a. psych. conscious* ~) répression *f*; *psych.* (*a. un-*

conscious ~) refoulement *m*; **re'pres·sive** □ répressif (-ive *f*), réprimant.

re·prieve [ri'priːv] **1.** surséance *f* (à, from); ᴛᴌ commutation *f* de la peine capitale; **2.** accorder un délai à; ᴛᴌ accorder une commutation de la peine capitale à (*q.*).

rep·ri·mand ['reprimɑːnd] **1.** réprimande *f*; ᴛᴌ blâme *m*; **2.** réprimander; ᴛᴌ blâmer publiquement.

re·print ['riːprint] **1.** réimprimer; **2.** nouveau tirage *m*; réimpression *f*.

re·pris·als [ri'praizls] *pl.* représailles *f/pl.*

re·proach [ri'proutʃ] **1.** reproche *m*, blâme *m*; **2.** reprocher (qch. à q., *s.o. with s.th.*); faire des reproches (à q. au sujet de qch., *s.o. with s.th.*); **re'proach·ful** □ [~ful] réprobateur (-trice *f*).

rep·ro·bate ['reprobeit] **1.** vil, bas(se *f*); **2.** *eccl.* réprouvé(e *f*) *m*; *F* vaurien *m*; **3.** réprouver; **rep·ro·ba·tion** réprobation *f*.

re·pro·cess ['riː'prouses] retraiter, recycler; ~*ing plant* usine *f* de retraitement *ou* de recyclage.

re·pro·duce [riːprə'djuːs] (se) reproduire; (se) multiplier; **re·pro·duc·tion** [~'dʌkʃn] reproduction *f* (*a. physiol., cin.,* ♥); copie *f*, imitation *f*; **re·pro'duc·tive** □ reproducteur (-trice *f*).

re·proof [ri'pruːf] reproche *m*, blâme *m*; réprimande *f*.

re·prov·al [ri'pruːvl] reproche *m*, blâme *m*; **re·prove** [~'pruːv] condamner; réprimander, reprendre.

rep·tile ['reptail] **1.** reptile *m* (*a. fig.*); *fig. a.* chien *m* couchant; **2.** rampant.

re·pub·lic [ri'pʌblik] république *f*; **re'pub·li·can** républicain (*a. su./mf*); **re'pub·li·can·ism** républicanisme *m*.

re·pub·li·ca·tion ['riːpʌbli'keiʃn] nouvelle publication *f*, *livre:* nouvelle édition *f*. [(*une loi*); rééditer.]

re·pub·lish ['riː'pʌbliʃ] republier)

re·pu·di·ate [ri'pjuːdieit] répudier (*femme, dette, doctrine, etc.*); **re·pu·di·a·tion** répudiation *f*; *dette:* reniement *m*.

re·pug·nance [ri'pʌgnəns] répugnance *f*, antipathie *f* (pour to, against); **re'pug·nant** □ répugnant (à, to)); incompatible (avec to, with); contraire (à to, with).

re·pulse [ri'pʌls] **1.** échec m; défaite f; rebuffade f; **2.** repousser (a. fig.); **re'pul·sion** phys., a. fig. répulsion f; fig. a. aversion f; **re'pul·sive** □ phys., a. fig. répulsif (-ive f); fig. froid, distant (personne).

re·pur·chase [ri:'pəːtʃəs] **1.** rachat m; ⚖ réméré m; **2.** racheter.

rep·u·ta·ble □ ['repjutəbl] honorable (personne, a. emploi); estimé; **rep·u·ta·tion** [ˌ'teiʃn] réputation f, renom m; **re·pute** [ri-'pjuːt] **1.** réputation f; by ~ de réputation; **2.** tenir pour; be ~d to be (ou as) passer pour; be well (ill) ~d avoir une belle (mauvaise) réputation; **re'put·ed** réputé; supposé; ⚖ putatif (-ive f); **re'put·ed·ly** suivant l'opinion commune.

re·quest [ri'kwest] **1.** demande f (a. ✝); requête f; recherche f; at s.o.'s ~ à ou sur la demande de q.; by ~ sur demande; facultatif (-ive f) (arrêt); in (great) ~ (très) recherché, demandé; ~ stop arrêt m facultatif; (musical) ~ programme disques m/pl. etc. ou programme m des auditeurs; **2.** demander (qch. à q., s.th. of s.o.; à q. de inf., s.o. to inf.); prier (q. de inf., s.o. to inf.).

re·qui·em ['rekwiem] requiem m/inv., messe f pour les morts.

re·quire [ri'kwaiə] exiger (qch. de q., s.th. of s.o.); réclamer (qch. à q., s.th. of s.o.); avoir besoin de (qch.); ~ (of) s.o. to (inf.) a. vouloir que q. (sbj.); **re'quired** exigé; voulu; **re'quire·ment** demande f; fig. exigence f; condition f requise.

req·ui·site ['rekwizit] **1.** requis (pour, to); nécessaire (à, to); voulu; **2.** condition f requise (pour, for); chose f nécessaire; toilet ~s pl. accessoires m/pl. de toilette; **req·ui·si·tion 1.** demande f; ✕ réquisition f; **2.** avoir recours à; ✕ réquisitionner; mettre (qch.) en réquisition; faire des réquisitions dans (un endroit).

re·quit·al [ri'kwaitl] récompense f; revanche f; **re'quite** [ˌ'kwait] récompenser; ~ s.o.'s love répondre à l'amour de q.

re·read ['riː'riːd] [irr. (read)] relire.

re·run 1. ['riː'rʌn] repasser, passer

(un film) de nouveau; **2.** ['riːrʌn] reprise f.

re·sale ['riː'seil] revente f; ~ price prix m de revente; ~ value valeur f à la revente.

re·scind [ri'sind] abroger (une loi); rétracter (un arrêt); annuler (un contrat, une décision, un vote, etc.); casser (un jugement).

re·scis·sion [ri'siʒn] rescision f, abrogation f etc., see rescind.

re·script ['riːskript] rescrit m; transcription f.

res·cue ['reskjuː] **1.** sauvetage m; secours m; délivrance f; ~ operation opérations f/pl. de sauvetage; ~ party équipe f de sauvetage ou de secours; come (ou go) to s.o.'s ~ venir en aide à q., aller à la rescousse de q.; **2.** sauver; secourir; porter secours à; délivrer; ~ s.o. from danger arracher q. à un danger; **'res·cu·er** sauveteur (-euse f) m; secoureur (-euse f) m; libérateur (-euse f) m.

re·search [ri'səːtʃ] recherche f (de for, after); recherches f/pl. (savantes); ~ establishment institut m de recherches (scientifiques etc.); marketing (motivation) ~ étude f du marché (de motivation); ~ work recherches f/pl.; ~ worker chercheur (-euse f) m; **re'search·er** chercheur (-euse f) m.

re·seat ['riː'siːt] (faire) rasseoir; remettre un fond à (une chaise); ⊕ roder le siège de.

re·se·da [ri'siːdə] réséda m.

re·sell ['riː'sel] [irr. (sell)] revendre; **'re'sell·er** revendeur (-euse f) m.

re·sem·blance [ri'zembləns] ressemblance f (à, avec to; entre, between); **re'sem·ble** [ˌbl] ressembler à.

re·sent [ri'zent] s'offenser de; être froissé de; **re'sent·ful** □ [ˌful] rancunier (-ère f); plein de ressentiment; froissé, irrité (de, of); **re'sent·ment** ressentiment m; rancune f.

res·er·va·tion [rezə'veiʃn] ⚖ réservation f; Am. terrain m réservé, réserves f/pl. indiennes; fig. a. places: réserve f; Am. place f retenue.

re·serve [ri'zəːv] **1.** usu. réserve f; terrain m réservé; restriction f; ~ price prix m minimum; in ~ en réserve; with certain ~s avec quelques réserves; 2. réserver; retenir (*une chambre, une place, etc.*); mettre (*qch.*) en réserve; **re'served** □ renfermé, réservé; *fig.* froid; ~ seat place *f* réservée.

re·serv·ist ✕ [ri'sə:vist] réserviste *m*.

res·er·voir ['rezəvwɑ:] réservoir *m* (*a. fig.*); (bassin *m* de) retenue *f*.

re·set ['ri:'set] [*irr.* (set)] remettre en place; ⊕ raffûter (*un outil*); *typ.* recomposer.

re·set·tle ['ri:'setl] (se) réinstaller; (se) rasseoir; se reposer (*vin*); **'re'set·tle·ment** nouvelle colonisation *f*; *vin etc.*: nouveau dépôt *m*.

re·ship ['ri:'ʃip] rembarquer; remonter (*l'hélice etc.*).

re·shuf·fle ['ri:'ʃʌfl] 1. rebattre (*des cartes*); *fig.* remanier; 2. nouveau battement *m*; *fig.* remaniement *m*.

re·side [ri'zaid] résider (à, at; dans, in) (*a. fig.*); demeurer; **res·i·dence** ['rezidəns] résidence *f*; demeure *f*; séjour *m*; maison *f*; habitation *f*; ~ permit permis *m ou* carte *f* de séjour; **'res·i·dent** 1. résidant, qui réside; à demeure (*maître d'école etc.*); en résidence; ✚ ~ physician interne *m*; 2. habitant(e *f*) *m*; (ministre) résident *m*; **res·i·den·tial** [~'denʃl] d'habitation; résidentiel(le *f*).

re·sid·u·al [ri'zidjuəl] résiduel(le *f*); **re'sid·u·ar·y** résiduaire; qui reste; ⚖ ~ legatee légataire *m* universel; **res·i·due** ['rezidju:] 🎵 residu *m*; reste *m*, -s *m/pl.*; ⚖ reliquat *m*; **re·sid·u·um** [ri'zidjuəm] *surt.* 🎵 résidu *m*; reste *m*.

re·sign [ri'zain] *v/t.* résigner; donner sa démission de (*son emploi*); abandonner; ~ o.s. to se résigner à; s'abandonner à; *v/i.* démissionner; **res·ig·na·tion** [rezig'neiʃn] démission *f*; abandon *m*; résignation *f* (à, to); **re·signed** □ [ri'zaind] résigné.

re·sil·i·ence [ri'ziliəns] ⊕ résilience *f*; *personne, a. peau*: élasticité *f*; rebondissement *m*; **re'sil·i·ent** rebondissant, élastique; *fig.* plein de ressort.

res·in ['rezin] 1. résine *f*; colophane *f*; 2. résiner; **'res·in·ous** résineux (-euse *f*).

re·sist [ri'zist] *v/t.* résister à (*qch., q.*); s'opposer à; repousser; *v/i.* résister; **re'sist·ance** résistance *f*

(*a. phys.*, ⚡) (à, to); **re'sist·ant** résistant; **re'sis·tor** ⚡ résistance *f*, rhéostat *m*.

re·sole ['ri:'soul] ressemeler.

re·sol·u·ble [ri'zɔljubl] qu'on peut résoudre; résoluble (*problème*); 🎵 décomposable.

res·o·lute □ ['rezəlu:t] résolu; ferme; **'res·o·lute·ness** résolution *f*.

res·o·lu·tion [rezə'lu:ʃn] 🎵, ♪, ♩, *parl., phys., fig.* résolution *f*; détermination *f*; *fig. a.* fermeté *f*.

re·solv·a·ble [ri'zɔlvəbl] résoluble; réductible.

re·solve [ri'zɔlv] 1. *v/t.* 🎵, ♩, ♫, *admin., fig.* résoudre; 🎵 décomposer; *personne*: se résoudre à (*qch.*); *fig.* dissiper (*un doute*); *parl.* the House ~s itself into a committee la Chambre se constitue en commission; *v/i.* (*a.* ~ o.s.) se résoudre; ~ (up)on se résoudre à; 2. résolution *f*; **re'solved** □ résolu, décidé.

res·o·nance ['reznəns] résonance *f*; **'res·o·nant** □ résonnant; sonore (*voix*).

re·sorp·tion *physiol.* [ri'sɔ:pʃn] résorption *f*.

re·sort [ri'zɔ:t] 1. recours *m*; ressource *f*; affluence *f*; lieu *m* de séjour; health ~ station *f* thermale; seaside ~ plage *f*; station *f* balnéaire; summer ~ station *f* d'été; in the last ~ en dernier ressort; en fin de compte; 2.: ~ to avoir recours à; fréquenter (*un lieu*); se rendre à (*un endroit*).

re·sound [ri'zaund] (faire) résonner, retentir (with, with).

re·source [ri'sɔ:s] ressource *f*; expédient *m*; distraction *f*; **re'source·ful** □ [~ful] fertile en ressources; F débrouillard.

re·spect [ris'pekt] 1. rapport *m* (à, to; de, of); égard *m*; respect *m* (pour, for); considération *f* (pour, envers for); ~s *pl.* hommages *m/pl.*; with ~ to quant à; en *ou* pour ce qui concerne; out of ~ for pour respect de; ✚ au compte de; pay one's ~s to présenter ses hommages à, rendre ses respects à (*q.*); 2. *v/t.* respecter honorer; avoir égard à; concerner, avoir rapport à; **re·spect·a·bil·i·ty** respectabilité *f*; ✚ *a.* solidité *f*; **re'spect·a·ble** □ respectable; convenable; honorable; passable; ✚

solide; **re'spect·ful** □ [ˌful] respectueux (-euse *f*) (envers, pour to[wards]); *Yours ˌly* je vous prie d'agréer mes salutations très respectueuses; **re'spect·ful·ness** respect *m*; **re'spect·ing** en ce qui concerne; touchant; quant à; **re'spec·tive** □ respectif (-ive *f*); *we went to our ˌ places* nous sommes allés chacun à notre place.

res·pi·ra·tion [respəˈreiʃn] respiration *f*.

res·pi·ra·tor [ˈrespəreitə] respirateur *m* (a. ✻); ✗ masque *m* à gaz; **re·spir·a·to·ry** [risˈpaiərətəri] respiratoire.

re·spire [risˈpaiə] respirer.

res·pite [ˈrespait] 1. ⚖ sursis *m*, délai *m*; répit *m*; 2. accorder un sursis à; remettre.

re·splend·ence, re·splend·en·cy [risˈplendəns(i)] splendeur *f*, éclat *m* (a. *fig.*); **re'splend·ent** □ resplendissant.

re·spond [risˈpɔnd] répondre (a. *fig.*); *eccl.* réciter les répons; ˌ to obéir à; être sensible à; **re'spond·ent** 1. ⚖ défendeur (-eresse *f*); ˌ to qui réagit à; 2. ⚖ défendeur (-eresse *f*) *m*; *cour de cassation:* intimé(e *f*) *m*.

re·sponse [risˈpɔns] réponse *f* (a. *fig.*), réplique *f*; *eccl.* répons *m*.

re·spon·si·bil·i·ty [risˌpɔnsəˈbiliti] responsabilité *f* (de for, of); ✝ solidité *f*; **re'spon·si·ble** responsable (de, for; envers, to); chargé (de, for); capable; qui comporte des responsabilités (*poste*); sérieux (-euse *f*) (*personne*); *be ˌ for* être maître de; être comptable de; être coupable de; **re'spon·sive** □ sensible (à, to); impressionnable; *be ˌ to* répondre à, obéir à.

rest¹ [rest] 1. repos *m* (a. *fig.*); sommeil *m*; *fig.* mort *f*; ♪ silence *m*; abri *m*; support *m*; ✚ ˌ cure cure *f* de repos; ˌ home maison *f* de repos; *Am.* ˌ room toilettes *f/pl.*; *at ˌ* en repos; *set at ˌ* calmer; régler; 2. *v/i.* se reposer; avoir *ou* prendre du repos; s'appuyer (sur, on); *fig. ˌ (up)on* reposer sur; peser sur (*q.*) (*responsabilité*); ˌ *with s.o. fig.* dépendre de (*q.*); *v/t.* (faire) reposer; appuyer; déposer (*un fardeau*).

rest² [ˌ] 1. reste *m*, restant *m*; *les autres m/pl.*; ✝ (fonds *m* de) réserve *f*; *for the ˌ* quant au reste; 2. rester, demeurer; ˌ *assured* être assuré (que, *that*).

re·state·ment [ˈriːˈsteitmənt] révision *f* (*d'un texte*); nouvel énoncé *m*.

res·tau·rant [ˈrestərɔ̃ːŋ] restaurant *m*.

rest·ing-place [ˈrestiŋpleis] abri *m*; (lieu *m* de) repos *m*; *last ˌ* dernière demeure *f*.

res·ti·tu·tion [restiˈtjuːʃn] restitution *f*; réintégration *f* (*du domicile conjugal*); *make ˌ of* restituer qch.

res·tive [ˈrestiv] nerveux (-euse *f*); rétif (-ive *f*) (*cheval,* F *personne*); **'res·tive·ness** humeur *f* rétive *ou* inquiète; nervosité *f*.

rest·less [ˈrestlis] sans repos; agité; inquiet (-ète *f*); **'rest·less·ness** agitation *f*; turbulence *f*; mouvement *m* incessant; nervosité *f*.

re·stock [ˈriːˈstɔk] ✝ réapprovisionner (en, with); repeupler (*un étang*).

res·to·ra·tion [restoˈreiʃn] restitution *f*; restauration *f* (*d'un bâtiment,* a. *pol.*); réintégration *f* (dans une fonction, to a post); **re·stor·a·tive** □ [risˈtɔrətiv] fortifiant (a. su./*m*); cordial (-aux *m/pl.*) (a. su./*m*).

re·store [risˈtɔː] restituer, rendre; restaurer; réintégrer; rétablir; ramener (à la vie, to life); ˌ *s.th. to its place* remettre qch. en place; ˌ *s.o. to liberty* rendre q. à la liberté; mettre q. en liberté; ˌ *to health* rétablir la santé de q.; **re'stor·er** restaurateur (-trice *f*) *m*; *meubles:* rénovateur *m*; *hair ˌ* régénérateur *m* des cheveux.

re·strain [risˈtrein] retenir, empêcher (de, from); refréner; contenir; **re'strained** tempéré; contenu (*colère*); sobre; **re'strain·ed·ly** [ˌidli] avec retenue *ou* contrainte; **re'straint** contrainte *f* (a. *fig.*); frein *m*; *fig.* réserve *f*; sobriété *f*; internement *m* (*d'un aliéné*).

re·strict [risˈtrikt] restreindre; réduire; **re'stric·tion** restriction *f*; réduction *f* (de of, on); **re'stric·tive** □ restrictif (-ive *f*).

re·sult [riˈzʌlt] 1. résultat *m*; aboutissement *m*; 2. résulter, provenir (de, from); ˌ *in* mener à, produire; avoir pour résultat; **re'sult·ant** 1. résultant; 2. ✗, *phys.* (force *f*) résultante *f*.

ré·su·mé ['rezju:mei] résumé m.
re·sume [ri'zju:m] reprendre, regagner; se remettre à; **re·sump·tion** [ri'zʌmpʃn] reprise f.
re·sur·gence [ri'sə:dʒəns] résurrection f; **re·sur·gent** qui resurgit.
res·ur·rect [rezə'rekt] vt/i. ressusciter; **res·ur·rec·tion** résurrection f; **res·ur·rec·tion·ist**, a. **res·ur·rec·tion man** déterreur m de cadavres.
re·sus·ci·tate [ri'sʌsiteit] vt/i. ressusciter; v/t. rappeler à la vie; v/i. revenir à la vie; **re·sus·ci·ta·tion** ressuscitation f.
re·tail ['ri:teil] 1. su. (vente f au) détail m; by ~ au détail; ~ *bookseller* libraire m; ~ *price* prix m de détail; 2. *adj.* au détail, de détail; 3. *adv.* au détail; 4. [ri:'teil] (se) vendre au détail; v/t. détailler; v/t. fig. colporter (*des nouvelles*); be ~ed se vendre au détail (à, *at*); **re·tail·er** marchand(e f) m au détail; fig. colporteur m.
re·tain [ri'tein] retenir (*un avocat, qch., fig. a. dans son souvenir*); maintenir (*en position*); conserver (*qch., coutume, faculté, etc.*); engager (*un domestique etc.*); **re·tain·er** hist. serviteur m, suivant m; (*usu. retaining fee*) avance f; honoraires m/pl. (*versés à un avocat pour retenir ses services*); old ~ vieux serviteur m.
re·take ['ri:'teik] [irr. (*take*)] reprendre; cin. tourner à nouveau.
re·tal·i·ate [ri'tælieit] v/t. user de représailles (envers, on); retourner (*une accusation*) (contre, *upon*); v/i. rendre la pareille (à, on); **re·tal·i·a·tion** représailles f/pl.; **re·tal·i·a·to·ry** [~iətəri] de représailles.
re·tard [ri'tɑ:d] v/t. retarder; v/i. tarder (*personne*); retarder (*chose*); mot. ~ed ignition retard m à l'allumage; ~ed *child* enfant m arriéré; **re·tar·da·tion** [ri:tɑ:'deiʃn] retard(ement) m; phys. retardation f; ♪ mesure: ralentissement m.
retch ♪ [ri:tʃ] avoir des haut-le-cœur.
re·tell ['ri:'tel] [irr. (*tell*)] répéter; raconter de nouveau.
re·ten·tion [ri'tenʃn] conservation f; maintien m; ♪, a. psych. rétention f; **re·ten·tive** □ gardeur (-euse f)

(de, of); fidèle, tenace (*mémoire*); anat. rétentif (-ive f); contentif (-ive f) (*bandage*).
re·think ['ri:'θiŋk] [irr. (*think*)] réfléchir encore sur; repenser à.
ret·i·cence ['retisəns] réticence f; fig. réserve f; **ret·i·cent** taciturne; réservé; peu communicatif (-ive f).
re·tic·u·late □ [ri'tikjulit], **re·tic·u·lat·ed** □ [~leitid] réticulé; réti-forme; **ret·i·cule** ['retikju:l] réticule m (a. opt.); sac m à main.
ret·i·na anat. ['retinə] rétine f.
ret·i·nue ['retinju:] suite f (*d'un noble*).
re·tire [ri'taiə] v/t. mettre à la retraite; ♱ retirer (*un effet*); v/i. se retirer (dans, to); s'éloigner; se coucher; se démettre; prendre sa retraite; ⚔ se replier; se retirer (de, *from*); **re·tired** □ retiré (*endroit, vie*); retraité; mis à la retraite; ~ *pay* pension f de retraite; **re·tire·ment** retraite f (a. ⚔); ♱ retrait m (*d'un effet*); ⚔ repliement m; sp. abandon m (de la partie); *early* ~ préretraite f; **re·tir·ing** □ sortant; réservé; farouche; ~ *pension* pension f de retraite.
re·tort [ri'tɔ:t] 1. réplique f, riposte f; 🜋 cornue f; 2. vt./i. répliquer, riposter; relancer (à, [up]on).
re·touch ['ri:'tʌtʃ] retoucher (a. phot.).
re·trace [ri'treis] retracer (*un dessin*); remonter à l'origine de; fig. ~ *one's steps* revenir sur ses pas.
re·tract [ri'trækt] (se) rétracter; vt./i. rentrer; ⊕ (se) contracter; ⚔ escamoter, rentrer; **re·tract·a·ble** zo. rétractile; ⚔ rentrant, escamotable; **re·trac·ta·tion** rétractation f; **re·trac·tion** retrait m; rétraction f (a. ✒); gramm. recul m.
re·train ['ri:'trein] (se) recycler.
re·trans·late ['ri:træns'leit] retraduire; **re·trans·la·tion** nouvelle traduction f.
re·trans·mit ['ri:trænz'mit] télév., a. radio: retransmettre.
re·tread ['ri:'tred] 1. rechaper (*un pneu*); 2. pneu m rechapé.
re·treat [ri'tri:t] 1. retraite f (a. ⚔, a. fig.); *glacier*: décrue f; fig. asile m; repaire m (*de brigands*); 2. v/t. ramener; v/i. se retirer, s'éloigner; ⚔ battre en retraite; box. etc. rompre.

re·trench [ri'trentʃ] v/t. restreindre; réformer; supprimer (un mot etc.); ✕ retrancher; v/i. faire des économies; restreindre sa dépense; **re'trench·ment** réduction f; économies f/pl.; suppression f; ✕ retranchement m.

re·tri·al ᵗᵗ ['riːtraiəl] procédure f de révision.

ret·ri·bu·tion [retri'bjuːʃn] châtiment m; **re·trib·u·tive** □ [ri-'tribjutiv] vengeur (-eresse f).

re·triev·a·ble [ri'triːvəbl] recouvrable (argent); réparable (erreur etc.); récupérable (matière etc.); **re'triev·al** recouvrement m; réparation f; récupération f; beyond (ou past) ~ irréparable, irrémédiable; (definitivement) perdu; **re·trieve** [ri'triːv] recouvrer; retrouver; rétablir; récupérer; arracher (à, from); réparer; chasse: rapporter; **re'triev·er** chasse: chien m rapporteur; race: retriever m.

retro- [retrou] rétro...; **~'ac·tive** rétroactif (-ive f); **~'cede** reculer; **~'ces·sion** recul m; mouvement m rétrograde; **~gra'da·tion** astr. rétrogradation f; biol. régression f; '**~grade 1.** rétrograde; **2.** rétrograder (a. fig.); fig. a. dégénérer.

ret·ro·gres·sion [retrou'greʃn] rétrogression f; fig. dégénérescence f; **ret·ro·spect** ['~spekt] coup m d'œil rétrospectif; consider in ~ jeter un coup d'œil rétrospectif sur; **ret·ro·spec·tion** examen m rétrospectif; **ret·ro·spec·tive** □ rétrospectif (-ive f) (vue etc.); vers l'arrière; ᵗᵗ à effet rétroactif (loi). **re·try** ᵗᵗ ['riː'trai] juger à nouveau (q., un procès).

re·turn [ri'təːn] **1.** retour m (a. ✍, ✝, marchandises, ⚠ mur); recrudescence f (a. ✍); ✝ circuit m de retour; parl. élection f; ✝ (souv. ~s pl.) recettes f/pl., rendement m, profit m; remboursement m (d'un capital); déclaration f (de revenu); Banque: situation f, bilan m; ✝ rapport m, relevé m (officiel); balle, son, etc.: renvoi m; ⊕ rappel m; ✝ ~s pl. rendus m/pl.; restitution f; fig. récompense f; fig. échangé m; ~s pl. relevé m; statistique f; attr. de retour; many happy ~s of the day mes meilleurs vœux pour votre anniversaire, joyeux anniversaire; in ~ en retour;

en échange (de, for); by ~ (of post) par retour de courrier; ~ match match m retour; ~ ticket billet m d'aller et retour; pay a ~ visit rendre une visite (à q.); **2.** v/i. revenir; rentrer; retourner; fig. ~ to revenir à (un sujet etc.); retomber dans (une habitude); v/t. rendre; renvoyer (accusation, balle, lumière); adresser (des remerciements); fig. répliquer, répondre (un bénéfice, a. admin.); faire une déclaration de (revenu); ᵗᵗ déclarer (q. coupable), rendre, prononcer (un verdict); parl. élire; cartes: rejouer; **re'turn·a·ble** restituable; **re'turn·er** personne f qui revient ou qui rend; **re·turn·ing of·fi·cer** directeur m du scrutin; deputy ~ scrutateur m.

re·un·ion ['riː'juːnjən] réunion f; assemblée f; **re·u·nite** ['riːjuː'nait] (se) réunir; (se) réconcilier.

rev mot. F [rev] **1.** tour m; **2.** (a. ~ up) (faire) s'emballer.

re·val·or·i·za·tion [riːvælərai'zeiʃn] revalorisation f; **re'val·or·ize** [~aiz] revaloriser; **re·val·u·a·tion** [~vælju'eiʃn] réévaluation f; réestimation f; **re·val·ue** [~'vælju:] réévaluer; réestimer.

re·vamp ⊕ ['riː'væmp] remplacer l'empeigne de (un soulier); Am. rafraîchir, renflouer.

re·veal [ri'viːl] révéler, découvrir; faire connaître ou voir; dévoiler (un mystère); **re'veal·ing** révélateur (-trice f).

re·veil·le ✕ [ri'væli] réveil m.

rev·el ['revl] **1.** réjouissances f/pl.; divertissement m, -s m/pl.; péj. orgie f; **2.** se divertir; faire bombance; se délecter (à, in).

rev·e·la·tion [revi'leiʃn] révélation f; bibl. ♀ l'Apocalypse f.

rev·el·(l)er ['revlə] noceur (-euse f) m; joyeux convive m; '**rev·el·ry** divertissements m/pl.; péj. orgie f.

re·venge [ri'vendʒ] **1.** vengeance f; jeux: revanche f; **2.** v/i. se venger (de qch., sur q. on); v/t. venger (q., qch.); ~ o.s. (ou be ~d) on se venger de (qch.) ou sur (q.); **re'venge·ful** □ [~ful] vindicatif (-ive f); vengeur (-eresse f); **re'venge·ful·ness** esprit m de vengeance; caractère m vindicatif; **re'veng·er** vengeur (-eresse f) m.

rev·e·nue ['revinju:] (a. ~s pl.) revenu m; rapport m; rentes f/pl.; ~ board (ou office) (bureau m de) perception f; ~ cutter cotre m de la douane; ~ officer employé m de la douane; ~ stamp timbre m fiscal.

re·ver·ber·ate [ri'və:bəreit] v/t. renvoyer (un son); réfléchir (la lumière etc.); v/i. résonner (son); réverbérer (chaleur, lumière); **re·ver·ber'a·tion** renvoi m; réverbération f; **re'ver·ber·a·tor** réflecteur m; **re'ver·ber·a·to·ry fur·nace** métall. (~ətəri) four m à réverbère.

re·vere [ri'viə] vénérer; **rev·er·ence** ['revərəns] 1. vénération f; révérence f; respect m (religieux); F Your ♀ monsieur l'abbé; co. saving your ~ sauf révérence; 2. révérer; **'rev·er·end** 1. vénérable; eccl. révérend; Right ♀ très révérend; 2. the Right ~ X le révérend m X.

rev·er·ent □ ['revərənt], **rev·er·en·tial** □ (~'renʃl) révérenciel(le f); plein de vénération.

rev·er·ie ['revəri] rêverie f.

re·ver·sal [ri'və:səl] renversement m (a. ⊕, a. opt.); revirement m (d'une opinion); ⚖ réforme f, annulation f; ⊕ ~ of stroke changement m de course; **re·verse** [~'və:s] 1. contraire m, inverse m; ✕, a. fig. revers m; mot. (a. ~ gear) marche f arrière; feuillet: verso m; in ~ en ordre inverse; en marche arrière; ✕ à revers; 2. □ contraire, inverse; ~ side tissu: envers m; 3. renverser (a. ✕); invertir (un ordre, a. phot.); cost. retourner; ⚖ réformer, révoquer; mot. a. v/i. faire (marche arrière); **re'vers·i·ble** réversible (procès); phot. inversible; à deux endroits (tissu); à double face (manteau); **re'vers·ing** ⊕ de renvoi.

re·ver·sion [ri'və:ʃn] ⚖ retour m (a. fig.), réversion f (a. biol.); substitution f; survivance f; phot. inversion f; in ~ grevé d'une réversion; réversible (rente); **re'ver·sion·ar·y** ⚖ de réversion; réversible; **re'ver·sion·er** ⚖ détenteur (-trice f) m d'un droit de réversion ou substitution.

re·vert [ri'və:t] (to) revenir (à) (a. ⚖, biol., fig.); a. biens: faire retour (à q.).

rev·er·y see reverie.

re·vet·ment ⊕ [ri'vetmənt] revêtement m.

re·view [ri'vju:] 1. ⚖ révision f; ✕, ⚓, périodique, fig.: revue f; examen m; compte rendu m; year under ~ année f de rapport; 2. v/t. ⚖ réviser; ✕, ⚓, fig. passer en revue; fig. revoir, examiner; faire le compte rendu de; v/i. faire de la critique littéraire etc.; **re'view·er** critique m (littéraire); ~'s copy exemplaire m de service de presse.

re·vile [ri'vail] injurier (q.).

re·vis·al [ri'vaizl] révision f.

re·vise [ri'vaiz] 1. revoir, relire (un livre etc.); corriger (des épreuves); réviser (une loi); 2. typ. épreuve f de révision; seconde f; **re'vis·er** réviseur m; typ. correcteur m.

re·vi·sion [ri'viʒn] révision f; **re'vi·sion·ism** (~izəm) révisionisme m.

re·vis·it ['ri:'vizit] visiter de nouveau.

re·vi·so·ry [ri'vaizəri] de révision.

re·vi·tal·ize ['ri:'vaitəlaiz] revivifier.

re·viv·al [ri'vaivl] ⚕ retour m des forces, retour m à la vie; reprise f des sens; théâ., a. ✝ reprise f; fig. renaissance f; renouveau m; **re·vive** [~'vaiv] v/t. ressusciter; rappeler à la vie; ranimer; réveiller; renouveler; v/i. reprendre connaissance; se ranimer; ✝ etc. reprendre; **re'viv·er** ressusciteur m; personne f qui ranime; F verre m (de cognac etc.); **re'viv·i·fy** (~'vivifai) revivifier.

rev·o·ca·ble □ ['revəkəbl] révocable; **rev·o·ca·tion** (~'keiʃn) révocation f; abrogation f.

re·voke [ri'vouk] v/t. révoquer; retirer; v/i. cartes: renoncer à faux.

re·volt [ri'voult] 1. révolte f; 2. v/i. se révolter (a. fig.), se soulever (contre against, from); v/t. fig. dégoûter; indigner (q.).

rev·o·lu·tion [revə'lu:ʃn] ⊕, pol., astr., fig. révolution f; ⊕ tour m; rotation f; ~s per minute tours m/pl. à la minute; **rev·o'lu·tion·ar·y** 1. révolutionnaire; 2. (a. **rev·o'lu·tion·ist**) révolutionnaire mf; **rev·o'lu·tion·ize** révolutionner.

re·volve [ri'vɔlv] v/i. tourner (sur, on; autour de, round); revenir (saisons); v/t. faire tourner; fig. ruminer, retourner; **re'volv·er** revolver m; **re'volv·ing** tournant; ~

stage scène *f* tournante; ~ *door* porte *f* tournante *ou* pivotante; ~ *pencil* porte-mine *m*/*inv.*

re·vue *théâ.* [ri'vjuː] revue *f.*

re·vul·sion [ri'vʌlʃn] *fig.* revirement *m* (*des sentiments*); nausée *f*; ⚕ révulsion *f*; **re'vul·sive** □ ⚕ révulsif (-ive *f*) (*a. su.*/*m*).

re·ward [ri'wɔːd] **1.** récompense *f*; **2.** récompenser, rémunérer (de, for); *fig.* payer (qch., *for* s.th.).

re·word [ˈriːˈwɔːd] rédiger à nouveau.

re·write [ˈriːˈrait] [*irr.* (write)] récrire; remanier, recomposer.

rhap·so·dist [ˈræpsədist] rhapsodiste *m*; **'rhap·so·dize** s'extasier (sur, over); **'rhap·so·dy** rhapsodie *f*; *fig.* transports *m*/*pl.*

rhe·o·stat ⚡ [ˈriːostæt] rhéostat *m.*

rhet·o·ric [ˈretərik] rhétorique *f* (*a. péj.*); éloquence *f*; **rhe·tor·i·cal** □ [riˈtɔrikl] de rhétorique; *péj.* ampoulé; **rhet·o·ri·cian** [retəˈriʃn] rhétoricien *m*; *hist.*,*a. péj.* rhéteur *m.*

rheu·mat·ic ⚕ [ruːˈmætik] (~ally) rhumatismal (-aux *m*/*pl.*); rhumatisant (*a. su.*/*mf*) (*personne*); **rheu'mat·ics** F *pl.*, **rheu·ma·tism** [ˈruːmətizm] rhumatisme *m.*

rhi·no[1] *sl.* [ˈrainou] galette *f* (= *argent*).

rhi·no[2] [~], **rhi·noc·er·os** *zo.* [raiˈnɔsərəs] rhinocéros *m.*

rhomb, rhom·bus ⚗ [ˈrɔm(bəs)], *pl.* **-bus·es, -bi** [~bai] losange *m*, † rhombe *m.*

rhu·barb ♧ [ˈruːbɑːb] rhubarbe *f.*

rhumb ⚓ [rʌm] rhumb *m.*

rhyme [raim] **1.** rime *f* (à, to); poésie *f*, vers *m*/*pl.*; *without* ~ *or reason* sans rime ni raison; **2.** (faire) rimer (avec, with); **'rhyme·less** □ sans rime; **'rhym·er, rhyme·ster** [ˈ~stə] versificateur *m*; *péj.* rimailleur *m.*

rhythm [riðm] rythme *m*; **'rhyth·mic, 'rhyth·mi·cal** □ rythmique, cadencé.

Ri·al·to *Am.* [riˈæltou] quartier *m* des théâtres (*de Broadway*).

rib [rib] **1.** côte *f*; ♧, △ nervure *f*; *parapluie*: baleine *f*; ~ *cage* cage *f* thoracique; **2.** garnir de côtes *ou* de nervures; *Am. sl.* taquiner (*q.*).

rib·ald [ˈribəld] **1.** paillard; licencieux (-euse *f*); **2.** paillard(e *f*) *m*;

homme *m* éhonté; **'rib·ald·ry** paillardises *f*/*pl.*; propos *m*/*pl.* grossiers.

rib·and ⊕ [ˈribənd] ruban *m.*

ribbed [ribd] ♧ à nervures (*a. plafond*); *tex.* à côtes.

rib·bon [ˈribən] ruban *m* (*a. décoration, machine à écrire*, ⊕ *etc.*); *ordre*: cordon *m*; bande *f*; ~*s pl.* lambeaux *m*/*pl.*; *sl.* guides *f*/*pl.*; ~ *building ou development* alignement *m* de maisons en bordure de route; ⊕ ~*work* travail (*pl.* -aux) *m* à la chaîne; **'rib·boned** orné de rubans; *zo.* rubané.

rice [rais] riz *m*; ~ *pudding* riz *m* au lait; *ground* ~ farine *f* de riz.

rich □ [ritʃ] riche (en, in) (*personne, terre, couleur, style, a. fig.*); fertile, gras(se *f*); somptueux (-euse *f*); de luxe; superbe; corsé (*vin*); ample, plein (*voix etc.*); F impayable, épatant; ~ *in meaning* significatif (-ive *f*); *gramm.* ayant beaucoup d'acceptions; ~ *milk* lait *m* non écrémé; **rich·es** [ˈ~iz] *pl.* richesses *f*/*pl.*; **'rich·ness** richesse *f*; abondance *f*; luxe *m*; *couleur*: éclat *m*; *voix*: ampleur *f.*

rick[1] ✧ [rik] **1.** meule *f* (*de foin*); **2.** mettre en meule(s).

rick[2] [~] *see* **wrick.**

rick·ets ⚕ [ˈrikits] *sg. ou pl.* rachitisme *m*; **'rick·et·y** rachitique; F branlant, bancal (*m*/*pl.* -als), chancelant.

rid [rid] [*irr.*] débarrasser (de, of); *get* ~ *of* se débarrasser de; ♧ éliminer; **'rid·dance** débarras *m*; *he is a good* ~ bon débarras!

rid·den [ˈridn] *p.p. de ride* 2; *gang*-~ infesté de gangsters; *family*-~ tyrannisé par sa famille.

rid·dle[1] [ˈridl] **1.** énigme *f* (*a. fig.*), devinette *f*; **2.** *v/t.* trouver la clef de; *v/i.* parler par énigmes; ~ *me* donnez-moi le mot de (*cette énigme*).

rid·dle[2] [~] **1.** crible *m*, claie *f*; **2.** cribler (*a. fig.*) (de, with); passer au crible.

rid·dling □ [ˈridliŋ] énigmatique.

ride [raid] **1.** promenade *f*; voyage *m*; course *f*; *autobus etc.*: trajet *m*; **2.** [*irr.*] *v/i.* se promener, aller (à cheval, en auto, à bicyclette); voyager; chevaucher; *fig.* voguer; remonter; ♧ ~ *at anchor* être mouillé; ~ *for a fall* aller en casse-cou; *fig.*

courir à un échec, aller au-devant de la défaite; *v/t.* monter (*un cheval etc.*); aller à (*une bicyclette etc.*); parcourir (*le pays*) (à cheval); diriger (*son cheval*); opprimer; voguer sur (*les vagues*); ∼ (*on*) *a bicycle* aller à bicyclette; ⚓ ∼ *out* étaler (*une tempête*); *fig.* surmonter (*une crise*); **'rid·er** cavalier (-ère *f*) *m*; *course:* jockey *m*; *cirque:* écuyer (-ère *f*) *m*; clause *f* additionnelle; annexe *f*; ⚖ exercice *m* d'application (*d'un théorème*); ⊕ cavalier *m*.

ridge [ridʒ] **1.** *montagne:* arête *f*, crête *f*; faîte *m* (*a.* △); *sable:* ride *f*; *rochers:* banc *m*; *coteaux:* chaîne *f*; ✗ billon *m*, butte *f*; **2.** *v/t.* △ enfaîter; ✗ disposer en billons; sillonner; *v/i.* former des crêtes; se rider; ∼ **way** route *f* des crêtes, chemin *m* de faîte.

rid·i·cule ['ridikjuːl] **1.** moquerie *f*, raillerie *f*; dérision *f*; ridicule *m*; **2.** se moquer de; ridiculiser; **ri-'dic·u·lous** [∼'juləs] ridicule; **ri-'dic·u·lous·ness** ridicule *m*.

rid·ing ['raidiŋ] **1.** équitation *f*; **2.** d'équitation; de cavalier (-ère *f*); '∼**-breech·es** *pl.* culotte *f* de cheval; '∼**-hab·it** *cost.* amazone *f*; ∼ **mas·ter** professeur *m* d'équitation; ∼ **school** manège *m*, école *f* d'équitation; ∼ **sta-ble(s** *pl.*) centre *m* d'équitation, manège *m*; écurie *f*; ∼ **whip** cravache *f*.

rife □ [raif] abondant (en, *with*); nombreux (-euse *f*); *be* ∼ régner; abonder (en, *with*).

riff-raff ['rifræf] canaille *f*.

ri·fle[1] ['raifl] piller.

ri·fle[2] [∼] **1.** fusil *m* (*rayé*); rayure *f* (*d'un fusil*); ✗ ∼*s pl.* fusiliers *m/pl.*; **2.** rayer (*un fusil*); '∼**·man** ✗ fusilier *m*; chasseur *m* à pied; ∼ **range** stand *m ou* champ *m* de tir; *within* ∼ à portée de fusil; ∼ **shot** coup *m* de fusil; *within* ∼ à portée de fusil.

ri·fling ⊕ ['raifliŋ] rayage *m*; *coll.* rayure *f*, -s *f/pl.* [fêlure *f*.]

rift [rift] fente *f*, fissure *f*; *fig.*

rig[1] F [rig] **1.** farce *f*; coup *m* monté; **2.** travailler (*le marché*); tripoter sur; truquer.

rig[2] [∼] **1.** ⚓ gréement *m*; F *fig.* équipement *m*; F toilette *f*; *Am.* F attelage *m*; **2.** (*a.* ∼ *out ou up*) gréer; F *fig.* accoutrer; ∼ *up* monter; '**rig-ger** ⚓ gréeur *m*; ⚡ monteur-régleur (*pl.* monteurs-régleurs) *m*;

'rig·ging ⚓ gréage *m*; ⚡ gréement *m*.

right [rait] **1.** □ droit (*a.* = *contraire de gauche*); bon(ne *f*); honnête; correct, exact, juste; bien placé; ⚓ ∼ *angle* angle *m* droit; *pol.* ∼ *wing* (aile *f*) droite *f*; *be* ∼ avoir raison; être à l'heure (*montre*); convenir (à, *for*); *be* ∼ *to* (*inf.*) avoir raison de (*inf.*); bien faire de (*inf.*); être fondé à (*inf.*); *all* ∼! entendu!; parfait!; très bien!; allez-y!; c'est bon!; *be on the* ∼ *side of* 40 avoir moins de 40 ans; *put* (*ou set*) ∼ ajuster; réparer; corriger; désabuser (*q.*); réconcilier (avec, *with*); **2.** *adv.* droit; tout ...; bien; fort, très; correctement; à droite; *dans un titre:* très; F *send to the* ∼*-about* envoyer promener (*q.*); ∼ *away* tout de suite; *sur-le-champ*; ∼ *in the middle* au beau milieu; ∼ *on* tout droit; **3.** *su.* droit *m*, titre *m*; bien *m*; justice *f*; côté *m* droit, droite *f* (*a. pol.*); *box.* coup *m* du droit; ∼ *of way* priorité *f*; *in his* (*ou her*) *own* ∼ de son propre chef; en propre; *the* ∼*s pl. of a story* la vraie histoire; *by* ∼(*s*) en toute justice; *by* ∼ *of* par droit de; à titre de; à cause de; *set* (*ou put*) *to* ∼*s* mettre en ordre; arranger; *on* (*ou to*) *the* ∼ à droite; **4.** *v/t.* redresser (*qch.*, *un tort*); rendre justice à; corriger; ⚓ (*v/i.* se) redresser; ∼*-an·gled* ⚓ [∼'æŋgld] à angle droit; rectangle (*triangle*); **right-eous** □ ['∼ʃəs] juste (*a.* = *justifié*); vertueux (-euse *f*); '**right-eous-ness** droiture *f*, vertu *f*; **right·ful** □ ['∼ful] légitime; équitable (*conduite*); '**right-hand** droite *ou* de droite; *mot.* ∼-*drive* conduite *f* à droite; *fig.* ∼ *man* le bras droit (*de q.*); '**right·'hand·ed** droitier (-ère *f*) (*personne*); ⊕ pour la main droite; à droite (*vis etc.*); '**right·ist** *pol.* **1.** homme *m* de droite; **2.** de droite; '**right·'mind·ed** bien pensant; '**right·ness** droiture *f*; décision *etc.:* justesse *f*; '**right·'wing** *pol.* de droite; '**right·'wing·er** *pol.* homme *m* de droite; *sp.* ailier *m* droit.

rig·id □ ['ridʒid] raide, rigide; *fig.* strict, sévère; **ri'gid·i·ty** raideur *f*, rigidité *f*; *fig.* sévérité *f*; intransigeance *f*.

rig·ma·role ['rigmərəul] discours *m* sans suite; F litanie *f*.

rig·or ✱ ['raigɔ:] frissons *m/pl.*; ∼ **mor·tis** [∼'mɔːtis] rigidité *f* cadavérique; **rig·or·ous** □ ['rigərəs] rigoureux (-euse f).

rig·o(u)r ['rigə] rigueur f, sévérité f; fig. austérité f; preuve: exactitude f; ~s pl. a. âpreté f du temps.

rile F [rail] agacer, exaspérer.

rill [ril] petit ruisseau m.

rim [rim] bord m; lunettes: monture f; roue: jante f.

rime¹ [raim] rime f.

rime² poét. [~] givre m, gelée f blanche; **'rim·y** couvert de givre; givré.

rind [raind] écorce f, peau f (a. d'un fruit); fromage: croûte f; lard: couenne f.

ring¹ [riŋ] **1.** anneau m; bague f; rond m (de serviette); ⊕ segment m; personnes: groupe m, cercle m; ✝ cartel m; cirque: arène f; box. ring m; lune: auréole f; ~ binder classeur m à anneaux; ~ road route f de ceinture; (boulevard m) périphérique m; **2.** boucler (un taureau); baguer (un pigeon); (usu. ~ in ou round ou about) entourer, encercler.

ring² [~] **1.** son(nerie f) m; tintement m; coup m de sonnette; F coup m de téléphone; **2.** [irr.] v/i. sonner; tinter (a. oreilles); (souv. ~ out) résonner, retentir (de, with); ~ again sonner de nouveau; téléph. ~ off raccrocher; the bell is ~ing on sonne; v/t. (faire) sonner; ~ the bell agiter la sonnette; fig. réussir le coup; ~ up sonner pour faire lever (qch.); téléph. donner un coup de téléphone à (q.); **'ring·er** sonneur m; **'ring·ing** □ qui résonne; retentissant; **'ring·lead·er** □ meneur m; chef m de bande; **ring·let** ['~lit] cheveux: boucle f; **'ring·worm** 🜏 teigne f tonsurante.

rink [riŋk] patinoire f; skating m.

rinse [rins] **1.** (souv. ~ out) rincer; **2.** = **'rins·ing** rinçage m; ~s pl. rinçure f, -s f/pl.

ri·ot ['raiət] **1.** émeute f, F bagarre f; fig. orgie f; ~ squad police f secours; run ~ pulluler; se déchaîner; **2.** provoquer une émeute; s'ameuter; faire du vacarme; fig. se livrer sans frein (à, in); **'ri·ot·er** émeutier m; séditieux m; fig. noceur m; **'ri·ot·ous** □ tumultueux (-euse f); séditieux (-euse f); tapageur (-euse f) (personne); dissolu (vie).

rip¹ [rip] **1.** déchirure f; fente f; ✂ ~ cord corde f de déchirure (d'un ballon), tirette f (d'un parachute); **2.** v/t. déchirer; fendre; ~ off arracher; sl. estamper; sl. voler, chiper; ~ up découdre; déchirer; v/i. se déchirer; se fendre; mot. F filer.

rip² F [~] mauvais garnement m; personne: gaillard m.

ri·par·i·an [rai'pɛəriən] riverain(e f) m, adj.

ripe □ [raip] mûr; fait (fromage); **'rip·en** vt/i. mûrir; **'ripe·ness** maturité f.

rip-off sl. ['ripɔf] estampage m; vol m.

ri·poste [ri'poust] **1.** escrime: riposte f (a. fig.); **2.** riposter.

rip·per ['ripə] fendoir m (pour ardoises); burin m à défoncer; scie f à refendre; sl. type m épatant; chose f épatante; **'rip·ping** □ sl. fameux (-euse f), épatant.

rip·ple ['ripl] **1.** ride f; cheveux: ondulation f; ruisseau: gazouillement m; murmure m; **2.** (se) rider; v/i. onduler; murmurer.

rise [raiz] **1.** eau, route: montée f; côte f; rampe f; terrain: éminence f; ascension f; hausse f (a. ✝, ♪); soleil, théâ. rideau: lever m; eaux: crue f; ▲ flèche f; prix etc.: augmentation f; emploi, rang: avancement m; fleuve, a. fig.: source f; give ~ to engendrer; provoquer; take (one's) ~ prendre sa source, avoir son origine (dans, in); **2.** [irr.] se lever (gibier, personne, soleil, etc.); se dresser (cheval, montagne, monument); se relever (personne); s'élever (bâtiment, terrain); monter (mer, terrain, à la surface, à un rang); lever (pain); se révolter, se soulever (contre, against); ressusciter (des morts); parl. s'ajourner; ✝ être à la hausse (a. baromètre); ✗ sortir (du rang); prendre sa source (dans, in; à, at); ~ to the occasion se montrer à la hauteur de la situation; ~ to the bait monter à la mouche; mordre; **ris·en** ['rizn] p.p. de rise 2; **'ris·er** ▲ contremarche f; early ~ personne f matinale.

ris·i·bil·i·ty [rizi'biliti] faculté f de rire; **'ris·i·ble** □ risible, dérisoire; ✝ rieur (-euse f) (personne).

ris·ing ['raiziŋ] **1.** lever m; chasse: envol m; prix, baromètre: hausse f;

eaux: crue *f*; soulèvement *m*, ameutement *m*; résurrection *f*; **2.** d'avenir; nouveau (-el *devant une voyelle ou un h muet*; -elle *f*; -eaux *m/pl.*); ~ *ground* élévation *f* de terrain.

risk [risk] **1.** risque *m* (*a.* ✝); péril *m*; *at the* ~ *of* (*gér.*) au risque de (*inf.*); *run a* (*ou the*) ~ courir un *ou* le risque; **2.** risquer; **'risk·y** □ hasardeux (-euse *f*); scabreux (-euse *f*).

ris·sole *cuis.* ['risoul] rissole *f*.

rite [rait] rite *m*; **rit·u·al** ['ritjuəl] **1.** □ rituel(le *f*); **2.** rites *m/pl.*; *livre*: rituel *m*.

ri·val ['raivl] **1.** rival(e *f*) *m*; émule *mf*; concurrent(e *f*) *m*; **2.** rival(e *f*, -aux *m/pl.*); ✝ concurrent; **3.** *vt/i.* rivaliser (avec); *v/t.* être l'émule de; **'ri·val·ry** rivalité *f*; concurrence *f*; émulation *f*.

rive [raiv] [*irr.*] (se) fendre.

riv·en ['rivn] *p.p. de* rive.

riv·er ['rivə] fleuve *m*; rivière *f*; *fig.* flot *m*; ~ *basin* bassin *m* fluvial; **'~·bank** rive *f*; **'~·bed** lit *m* de rivière; **'~·horse** hippopotame *m*; **'~·side** rive *f*; bord *m* de l'eau; *attr.* situé au bord de la rivière.

riv·et ['rivit] **1.** ⊕ rivet *m*; **2.** rive(te)r; *fig.* fixer, river (à, *to*; sur, [*up*]*on*); **'riv·et·ing** à river.

riv·u·let ['rivjulit] ruisseau *m*.

roach *icht.* [routʃ] gardon *m*.

road [roud] route *f*; rue *f*; chemin *m* (*a. fig.*); voie *f* (*a. fig.*); *Am. see* railroad 1; ~ *map* carte *f* routière; ~ *works* travaux *m/pl.*; *by* ~ par route; *en auto* (*personne*): ♣ *usu.* ~*s pl.* (*a.* '~·**stead**) rade *f*; *on the* ~ en route; F *hit the* ~ se mettre en route; **'~·house** relais *m*, hostellerie *f*; **'~ hog** *mot.* chauffard *m*; **'~·man**, **'~·mend·er** cantonnier *m*; **'~·race** course *f* sur route; **'~·sense** *surt. mot.* sens *m* pratique de la conduite sur route; **road·ster** ['~stə] cheval *m* de fatigue; *mot. etc.* voiture *f ou* bicyclette *f* de route; **'road·way** chaussée *f*; voie *f*; **'road·wor·thy** en état de marche (*voiture*).

roam [roum] *v/i.* errer, rôder; *v/t.* parcourir; **'roam·er** vagabond *m*; nomade *m*.

roan [roun] **1.** rouan(ne *f*); **2.** (*cheval m*) rouan *m*; vache *f* rouanne; ⊕ basane *f*.

roar [rɔː] **1.** *vt/i.* hurler, vociférer; *v/i.* rugir; mugir (*mer*, *taureau*);

tonner, gronder; ronfler (*auto*, *feu*); *v/t.* beugler (*un refrain*); **2.** hurlement *m*; rugissement *m*; éclat *m* (*de rires*); mugissement *m*; grondement *m*; **roar·ing** ['~riŋ] **1.** *see* roar 2; **2.** □ rugissant; mugissant; grondant; ✝ gros(se *f*); F superbe.

roast [roust] **1.** *v/t.* (faire) rôtir; *sl.* passer un savon à (*q.*); *v/i.* rôtir; *vt/i.* griller; **2.** rôti; ~ *beef* rôti *m* de bœuf, rosbif *m*; ~ *meat* viande *f* rôtie; *see rule* 2; **'roast·er** *personne*: rôtisseur (-euse *f*) *m*; *cuis.* rôtissoire *f*; volaille *f* à rôtir; **'roast·ing-jack** tournebroche *m*.

rob [rɔb] voler; **'rob·ber** voleur (-euse *f*) *m*; **'rob·ber·y** vol *m*.

robe [roub] **1.** robe *f* (*d'office*, *de cérémonie*, ⚖); vêtement *m*; maillot *m* anglais (*pour bébés*); ~*s pl.* robe *f*, -s *f/pl.*; *gentlemen of the* ~ gens *m/pl.* de robe; **2.** *v/t.* revêtir (*q.*) d'une robe (*ou univ.* de sa toge); *fig.* recouvrir; *v/i.* revêtir sa robe *ou* toge.

rob·in *orn.* ['rɔbin] rouge-gorge (*pl.* rouges-gorges) *m*.

ro·bot ['roubɔt] automate *m*; *attr.* automatique.

ro·bust □ [rə'bʌst] robuste; vigoureux (-euse *f*); **ro'bust·ness** nature *f ou* caractère *m* robuste; vigueur *f*.

rock¹ [rɔk] rocher *m*; roc *m*; roche *f*; *Am.* pierre *f*, diamant *m*; *get down to* ~ *bottom* être au plus bas; *toucher le fin fond*; ~*-crystal* cristal *m* de roche; ~*-salt* sel *m* gemme.

rock² [~] *v/t.* bercer; basculer; *v/i.* osciller; *vt/i.* balancer.

rock-bot·tom F ['rɔk'bɔtəm] le plus bas (*prix*).

rock·er ['rɔkə] berceau *etc.*: bascule *f*; *see rocking-chair*; *sl. be off one's* ~ être un peu toqué. [(rocaille).}

rock·er·y ['rɔkəri] jardin *m* de{

rock·et¹ ['rɔkit] **1.** fusée *f*; ~ *plane* avion-fusée (*pl.* avions-fusées) *m*; ~ *propulsion* propulsion *f* par fusée; **2.** passer en trombe; (*a.* ~ *up*) monter en flèche.

rock·et² ♀ [~] roquette *f*.

rock·et...: '~·**launch·ing site** base *f* de lancement (*de fusées*); '~·**pow·ered** propulsé par réaction.

rock...: '~·**fall** éboulement *m* de rocher; '~·**gar·den** jardin *m* de rocaille.

rock·ing... ['rɔkiŋ]: '**~-chair** rocking-chair m; '**~-horse** cheval m à bascule.

rock·y ['rɔki] rocailleux (-euse f); rocheux (-euse f); de roche.

ro·co·co [rə'koukou] rococo inv. (a. su./m).

rod [rɔd] verge f; baguette f; rideau, escalier: tringle f; ⊕ tige f; surv. mire f; mesure: perche f (5¹/₂ yards); Am. sl. revolver m, pistolet m; Black ♀ Huissier m de la Verge noire (haut fonctionnaire de la Chambre des Lords et de l'Ordre de la Jarretière).

rode [roud] prét. de ride 2.

ro·dent ['roudənt] rongeur m.

ro·de·o Am. [rou'deiou] rassemblement m du bétail; concours m d'équitation (des cowboys).

rod·o·mon·tade [rɔdəmɔn'teid] rodomontade f.

roe¹ [rou] (a. hard ~) œufs m/pl. (de poisson); soft ~ laite f, laitance f.

roe² [~] chevreuil m, chevrette f; '**~-buck** chevreuil m (mâle).

ro·ga·tion eccl. [rou'geiʃn] Rogation f; ♀ Sunday dimanche m des Rogations.

rogue [roug] fripon(ne f) m; coquin (-e f) m; éléphant: solitaire m; ~s' gallery musée m ou album m de portraits ou photos de criminels; '**ro·guer·y** fourberie f; coquinerie f; '**ro·guish** □ coquin; fripon(ne f) (a. fig.).

roist·er ['rɔistə] faire du tapage; '**roist·er·er** tapageur (-euse f) m; fêtard(e f) m.

role théâ. [roul] rôle m (a. fig.).

roll [roul] 1. ⊕, tex., étoffe, papier, tabac: rouleau m; ⊕ a. cylindre m; ✝ étoffe: pièce f; Am. billets: liasse f; typ., phot. bobine f; admin. contrôle m; beurre: coquille f; petit pain m; tambour, tonnerre: roulement m; ♣ (coup m de) roulis m; 2. v/t. rouler; cylindrer; ⊕ laminer; ~ out étendre (au rouleau); ~ up (en)rouler; ⊕ ~ed gold doublé m; v/i. rouler; couler (larmes); gronder (tonnerre); ♣ rouler, avoir du roulis; ~ up s'enrouler; F arriver; '**~-call** appel m (nominal) (a. ✕); '**roll·er** rouleau m; cylindre m; tex., papier: calandre f; ⊕ (usu. ~ bandage) bande f roulée; ♣ lame f de houle; Am. ~ coaster montagnes f/pl. russes; ~

towel essuie-mains m/inv. à rouleau; '**roll·er-skate** 1. patiner sur roulettes; 2. patin m à roulettes; '**roll·film** phot. pellicule f en bobine.

roll·ick ['rɔlik] faire la bombe; rigoler; '**rol·lick·ing** joyeux (-euse f); rigoleur (-euse f).

roll·ing ['rouliŋ] 1. roulant; ♣ houleux (-euse f); ondulé; ⊕ de laminage; 2. roulement m; ⊕ laminage m; ~pin rouleau m (à pâtisserie); ⊕~ mill usine f de laminage; laminoir m; typ. ~ press presse f à cylindres; '**~-stock** ▓ matériel m roulant.

roll...: '**~-neck** col m roulé; '**~-top desk** bureau m américain ou à cylindre.

ro·ly-po·ly ['rouli'pouli] 1. pouding m en rouleau aux confitures; 2. F boulot(te f).

Ro·man ['roumən] 1. romain; 2. Romain(e f) m; typ. (usu. ♀) (caractère m) romain m; ~-'**Cath·o·lic** catholique m/f, adj.

ro·mance [rə'mæns] 1. † roman m; conte m bleu; fig. fable f; ♪ romance f; fig. affaire f, amour m; romanesque m; ling. ♀ roman m, langue f romane; 2. fig. inventer à plaisir; 3. ling. ♀ roman; **ro'manc·er** † romancier (-ère f) m; brodeur (-euse f) m; menteur (-euse f) m.

Ro·man·esque [roumə'nesk] roman (a. su./m).

Ro·man·ic [rou'mænik] romain; ling. roman; surt. ~ peoples pl. Romains m/pl.

ro·man·tic [rə'mæntik] 1. (~ally) romantique; 2. (usu. **ro'man·ti·cist** [~tisist]) romantique m/f; **ro'man·ti·cism** romantisme m; idées f/pl. romanesques.

Ro·ma·ny ['roumæni] 1. romanichel(le f) m; ling. le romanichel; 2. de bohémien.

Rom·ish usu. péj. ['roumiʃ] catholique.

romp [rɔmp] 1. gambades f/pl.; enfant m/f turbulent(e f); gamine f; 2. s'ébattre; F ~ home gagner haut la main; '**romp·ers** pl. barboteuse f (pour enfants).

rönt·gen·ize ['rɔntgənaiz] radiographier.

rönt·gen·o·gram [rɔnt'genəgræm] radiogramme m; **rönt·gen·og·ra·phy** [~gə'nɔgrəfi] radiographie f;

rönt·gen·ol·o·gist [ˌˈɔlədʒist] radiographe *m*; **rönt·gen·ol·o·gy** [ˌˈdʒi] radiologie *f*; **rönt·gen·os·co·py** [ˌˈskəpi] radioscopie *f*.

rood [ruːd] crucifix *m*; *mesure*: quart *m* d'arpent (*10,117 ares*); **'~-screen** ⚠ jubé *m*.

roof [ruːf] **1.** toit(ure *f*) *m*; voûte *f*; *mot.* ~ **rack** galerie *f*; ~ **of the mouth** (dôme *m* du) palais *m*; **2.** (*souv.* ~ *in ou over*) recouvrir d'un toit; **'roof·ing** toiture *f*; pose *f* de la toiture; *attr.* de toits; ~ **felt** carton-pierre (*pl.* cartons-pierres) *m*.

rook[1] [ruk] **1.** *orn.* freux *m*; *fig.* escroc *m*; **2.** refaire (*q.*); filouter (son argent à q., s.o. of his money).

rook[2] [~] *échecs*: tour *f*.

rook·er·y ['rukəri] colonie *f* de freux; *fig.* colonie *f*, rookerie *f*.

rook·ie *sl.* ['ruki] ⚔ recrue *f*, bleu *m*; *fig.* débutant *m*.

room [rum] pièce *f*; salle *f*; (*a.* bed~) chambre *f*; place *f*, espace *m*; *fig.* lieu *m*; ~**s** *pl.* appartement *m*; ~ **and board** pension *f* (complète); *in my* ~ à ma place; *make* ~ faire place (à, *for*); **-roomed** [rumd] de ... pièces; **'room·er** *surt. Am.* sous-locataire *mf*; **'room·ing-house** *surt. Am.* hôtel *m* garni, maison *f* meublée; **'room-mate** compagnon *m* (compagne *f*) de chambre; **'room·y** □ spacieux (-euse *f*); ample.

roor·back *Am.* ['ruːrbæk] fausse nouvelle *f* (*répandue pour nuire à un parti politique*).

roost [ruːst] **1.** juchoir *m*, perchoir *m*; *see* rule 2; **2.** se jucher, se percher pour la nuit; **'roost·er** coq *m*.

root[1] [ruːt] **1.** racine *f* (*a.* ᴀ, *anat.*, *ling.*); *fig.* source *f*; ♪ base *f*; *take* ~, *strike* ~ prendre racine; ~*idea* idée *f* fondamentale; **2.** (s')enraciner; ~ *out* arracher; *fig.* extirper; **'root·ed** enraciné (*a. fig.*); *fig.* (*a.* ~ *in*) fondé sur.

root[2] [~] *v/t.* fouiller; (*a.* ~ *up*) trouver en fouillant; *fig.* ~ *out*, ~ *up* dénicher; *v/i.* fouiller avec le groin; *Am. sl.* ~ *for* appuyer; encourager par des cris; **'root·er** *Am. sl.* spectateur *m etc.* qui encourage par des cris; fanatique *mf* (de, *for*).

root·let ['ruːtlit] petite racine *f*.

rope [roup] **1.** corde *f* (*a. à pendre un criminel*); cordage *m*; câble *m* (métallique); *perles*: grand collier *m*; *sonnette*: cordon *m*; *Am. sl.* cigare *m* bon marché; *alp. on the* ~ en cordée; *alp.* ~ **team** cordée *f*; ⏸ *be at the end of one's* ~ être à *ou* au bout de ses ressources; *know the* ~*s* connaître son affaire; *show s.o. the* ~*s* mettre q. au courant; **2.** *v/t.* corder; (*usu.* ~ *in ou off ou out*) entourer de cordes; *Am.* prendre au lasso; *alp.* encorder; ~ *down* immobiliser au moyen d'une corde; *v/i.* devenir graisseux (-euse *f*); **'~-danc·er** funambule *mf*; **'~-lad·der** échelle *f* de corde; **'~-mak·er** cordier *m*; **'rop·er·y** corderie *f*; **'rope-walk** corderie *f*.

rop·i·ness ['roupinis] viscosité *f*; graisse *f*; **'rop·y** visqueux (-euse *f*); gras(se *f*), graisseux (-euse *f*).

ro·sa·ry ['rouzəri] *eccl.* rosaire *m*; chapelet *m*; ♪ roseraie *f*.

rose[1] [rouz] ♀ rose *f*; *couleur*: rose *m* (*a. adj.*); rosette *f* (*chapeau etc.*); ⚠, ⚙, *fenêtre*: rosace *f*; *arrosoir*: pomme *f*.

rose[2] [~] *prét. de* rise 2.

ro·se·ate ['rouziit] rosé.

rose ...: **'~-bud** bouton *m* de rose; **'~-bush** rosier *m*; **'~-col·o(u)red** rose, couleur de rose *inv.*; *see things* (*ou the world*) *through* ~ *glasses* (*ou spectacles*) voir tout *ou* la vie en rose; **'~-hip** gratte-cul *inv.*; **~·mar·y** ['rouzməri] romarin *m*.

ro·se·ry ['rouzəri] roseraie *f*.

ro·sette [rou'zet] rosette *f*; *ruban*: chou (*pl.* -x) *m*.

ros·in ['rozin] **1.** colophane *f*; **2.** frotter de colophane.

ros·ter ⚔ ['rɔstə] tableau *m* de service; liste *f*.

ros·trum ['rɔstrəm] tribune *f*.

ros·y □ ['rouzi] (de) rose; vermeil (-le *f*) (*teint*).

rot [rɔt] **1.** pourriture *f*; ⚕ carie *f*; *fig.* démoralisation *f*; *sl.* blague *f*; **2.** *v/t.* (faire) pourrir; *sl.* railler, blaguer (*q.*); gâcher (*un projet*); *v/i.* (se) pourrir; se décomposer.

ro·ta·ry ['routəri] rotatoire, rotatif (-ive *f*); ⊕ *de rotation*; ~ *press* rotative *f*; ⚡ ~ *switch* commutateur *m* rotatif; **ro·tate** [rou'teit] (faire) tourner; (faire) basculer; *v/t.* alterner (*les cultures*); **ro'ta·tion** rotation *f*; basculage *m*; *fig.* succession *f* tour à tour; *fig.* roulement *m*; ✔ ~ *of crops* assolement *m*; **ro-ta·to·ry** ['ˌtətəri] *see* rotary; ~ *door (ou gate)* porte *f* tournante; ~ *stage* plateau *m* tournant.

rote [rout] routine *f*; *by* ~ par cœur, mécaniquement.

ro·tor ['routə] ⊕, ⚓, ✈ hélicoptère: rotor *m*.

rot·ten □ ['rɒtn] pourri (*a. fig.*); gâté; ✿ carié; *sl.* moche, sale, mauvais; **'rot·ten·ness** (état *m* de) pourriture *f*.

rot·ter *sl.* ['rɒtə] sale type *m*.

ro·tund □ [rou'tʌnd] rond, arrondi; ampoulé (*style*); **ro'tun·da** △ [ˌdə] rotonde *f*; **ro'tun·di·ty** rondeur *f*; *style*: grandiloquence *f*.

rou·ble ['ruːbl] rouble *m*.

rouge [ruːʒ] 1. rouge *m*, fard *m*; 2. (se) farder; mettre du rouge.

rough [rʌf] 1. □ rude (*chemin, parler, peau, surface, vin, voix*); rêche, rugueux (-euse *f*) (*peau, surface, voix*); grossier (-ère *f*); dépoli (*verre*); inégal (-aux *m/pl.*) (*terrain*); brutal (-aux *m/pl.*), violent; fruste (*conduite, style*); agité (*mer*); âpre (*vin*); ⊕ brut; approximatif (-ive *f*); ~ *draft* brouillon *m*; ~ *and ready* exécuté grossièrement; *fig.* de fortune; *fig.* primitif (-ive *f*); sans façon (*personne*); *be* ~ *on s.o. évènement etc.*: être un coup dur pour q.; *be* ~ *with s.o.*, *give s.o. a* ~ *time (of it)* être dur ave q.; *cut up* ~ réagir avec violence; 2. état *m* brut; terrain *m* accidenté; *golf*: herbe *f* longue; *personne*: voyou *m*; 3. ébouriffer; (faire) aciérer les fers (*d'un cheval*); ~ *it* vivre à la dure; **'rough·age** détritus *m/pl.*; **'rough·cast 1.** ⊕ pièce *f* brute de fonderie; 2. △ crépi; ⊕ brut de fonte; 3. ⊕ crépir (*un mur*); *fig.* ébaucher (*un plan*); **'rough·en** rendre *ou* devenir rude *etc.*

rough...: ~**hewn** ['ˌ'hjuːn] taillé à coups de hache; dégrossi; *fig.* ébauché; ~**house** *sl.* chahut *m*; **'~house** *v/i.* chahuter; *v/t.* malmener; **'~neck** *Am. sl.* canaille *f*, voyou *m*; **'rough·ness** rudesse *f*; rugosité *f*; grossièreté *f*; **'rough·rid·er** dresseur *m* de chevaux; F casse-cou *m/inv.*; ✗ *hist.* cavalier *m* d'un corps irrégulier; **'rough·shod:** *ride* ~ *over* fouler (*q.*) aux pieds; traiter cavalièrement.

Rou·ma·nia(n) *see* Rumania(n).

round [raund] 1. □ rond (*a. fig.*); circulaire; plein; gros(se *f*) (*juron etc.*); voûté (*épaules*); ~ *game* jeu *m* en commun; ~ *hand* (écriture *f*) ronde *f*; ~ *trip* aller *m* et retour *m*; 2. *adv.* (tout) autour; (*souv.* ~ *about*) à l'entour; *all* ~ tout autour; tout à l'entour; *fig.* dans l'ensemble; sans exception; *all the year* ~ (pendant) toute l'année; *10 inches* ~ dix pouces de tour; 3. *prp.* (*souv.* ~ *about*) autour de; vers (*trois heures*); environ; *go* ~ *the shops* faire le tour des magasins; 4. *su.* cercle *m*, rond *m* (*a.* △); *cartes, tennis, voyage, etc.*: tour *m*; bière, facteur, médecin: tournée *f*; ✗ ronde *f* (*d'un officier*); *sp.* circuit *m*; *box.* round *m*; *fig.* train *m*; ✗ fusillade, *fig.* applaudissements: salve *f*; ✗ munitions: cartouche *f*; ♩ canon *m*; ✗ *100* ~*s* cent cartouches; 5. (s')arrondir; contourner (*une colline, un obstacle*); ⚓ doubler (*un cap*); ~ *off* arrondir; *fig.* achever; F ~ *on* dénoncer (*q.*); ~ *up* rassembler; rafler (*des voleurs*).

round·a·bout ['raundəbaut] 1. indirect, détourné; ~ *system (of traffic)* sens *m* giratoire; 2. détour *m*; clôture *f* circulaire; carrousel *m*; *mot.* F sens *m* gyro.

roun·del ['raundl] rondeau *m*; ♩ ronde *f*; **roun·de·lay** ['ˌdilei] chanson *f* à refrain; *danse*: ronde *f*.

round·ers ['raundəz] *pl.* balle *f* au camp; **'round·head** *hist.* tête *f* ronde; **'round·ish** presque rond; **'round·ness** rondeur *f*; **rounds·man** ['ˌzmən] livreur *m*; **'round-ta·ble con·fer·ence** réunion *f* paritaire; **'round-'up** rassemblement *m*; rafle *f* (*de voleurs etc.*).

roup *vét.* [ruːp] diphtérie *f* des poules.

rouse [rauz] *v/t.* (*a.* ~ *up*) (r)éveiller; faire lever (*le gibier*); susciter; mettre en colère; remuer; *v/i.* se réveiller; (*a.* ~ *o.s.*) se secouer; **'rous·ing** qui excite; enlevant (*discours*); chaleureux (-euse *f*) (*applaudissements*).

roust·a·bout *Am.* ['raustə'baut] débardeur *m*; manœuvre *m*.

rout[1] [raut] bande *f*; ⚖ attroupement *m*; *a. see* riot 1; † soirée *f*.

rout² [~] 1. ⚔ déroute *f*; débandade *f*; *put to* ~ = 2. mettre en déroute.
rout³ [~] *see* root².
route [ru:t; ⚔ raut] route *f* (*a.* ⚔); itinéraire *m*; '~**march** marche *f* d'entraînement.
rou·tine [ru:'ti:n] 1. routine *f*; ⚔, ⚓ emploi *m* du temps; *fig.* train-train *m* (journalier); 2. courant; ordinaire.
rove [rouv] *v/i.* rôder; vagabonder, errer; *v/t.* parcourir; '**rov·er** coureur *m*, vagabond *m*; éclaireur *m*.
row¹ [rou] rang *m* (*a.* théâ.), rangée *f*; file *f* (*de voitures*); ligne *f* (*de maisons etc.*); *Am.* a hard ~ to hoe une tâche *f* difficile.
row² [~] 1. ramer; faire du canotage; 2. promenade *f* en canot.
row³ F [rau] 1. vacarme *m*, tapage *m*; chahut *m*; dispute *f*, rixe *f*; F réprimande *f*; what's the ~? qu'est-ce qui se passe?; 2. *v/t.* semoncer (*q.*); *v/i.* se quereller (avec, with).
row·an ♀ ['rauən] sorbier *m* commun; '~**ber·ry** sorbe *f*.
row-boat ['roubout] bateau *m* à rames, canot *m*.
row·dy ['raudi] 1. chahuteur *m*; voyou *m*; 2. tapageur (-euse *f*).
row·el ['rauəl] 1. molette *f* (*d'éperon*); 2. éperonner.
row·er ['rouə] rameur (-euse *f*) *m*.
row·house *Am.* ['rouhaus] maison *f* attenante aux maisons voisines.
row·ing-boat ['rouiŋbout] *see* row-boat.
row·lock ⚓ ['rɔlək] tolet *m*, dame *f*.
roy·al ['rɔiəl] 1. □ royal (-aux *m/pl.*); *fig.* princier (-ère *f*); 2. ⚓ cacatois *m*; (*a.* ~ stag) cerf *m* à douze andouillers; F the ~s *pl.* la famille *f* royale; '**roy·al·ism** royalisme *m*; '**roy·al·ist** royaliste (*a.* su./*mf*); '**roy·al·ty** royauté *f*; personnage *m* royal; *royalties pl.* droits *m/pl.* d'auteur; redevance *f* (*à un inventeur*).
rub [rʌb] 1. frottement *m*; friction *f*; coup *m* de torchon; F there is the ~ c'est là le diable; 2. *v/t.* frotter; frictionner; ~ down frictionner; ⊕ adoucir; panser (*un cheval*); ~ in frictionner (*q.* à *qch.*); F don't ~ it in! n'insiste(z) pas!; ~ off enlever par le frottement; ~ out effacer; ~ up astiquer; faire reluire; rafraîchir sa mémoire de; *v/i.* (*personne:* se)

frotter (contre against, on); *fig.* ~ along (*ou* on *ou* through) se débrouiller.
rub-a-dub ['rʌbədʌb] *tambour:* rataplan *m*.
rub·ber ['rʌbə] caoutchouc *m*; gomme *f* à effacer; *personne:* frotteur (-euse *f*) *m*; ⊕ frottoir *m*; torchon *m*; ⊕ (*a.* ~ file) carreau *m*; *cartes:* robre *m*; *Am.* ~s *pl.* caoutchoucs *m/pl.*; *attr.* de *ou* en caoutchouc; à gomme (*arbre*); *Am. sl.* ~ check chèque *m* sans provision; ~ solution dissolution *f* de caoutchouc; '~**neck** *Am. sl.* 1. badaud(e *f*) *m*; touriste *mf*; 2. badauder; ~ **stamp** timbre *m* (en) caoutchouc; tampon *m*; *fig. Am.* F fonctionnaire *m* qui exécute aveuglément les ordres de ses supérieurs.
rub·bish ['rʌbiʃ] *Brit.* ordures *f/pl.*, immondices *f/pl.*, détritus *m/pl.*; ⊕ rebuts *m/pl.*; *fig.* fatras *m*; *fig.* camelote *f*; *fig.* bêtises *f/pl.*; *Brit.* ~ bin poubelle *f*; *Brit.* ~ chute vide-ordures *m/inv.*; *Brit.* ~ dump décharge *f*, dépotoir *m*; *Brit.* ~ heap monceau *m* de détritus, tas *m* d'ordures. '**rub·bish·y** sans valeur; de camelote.
rub·ble ['rʌbl] moellons *m/pl.* (bruts); (*a.* ~-work) moellonage *m*.
rube *Am. sl.* [ru:b] croquant *m*; nigaud *m*.
ru·be·fa·cient ஃ [ru:bi'feiʃjənt] rubéfiant (*a.* su./*m*).
ru·bi·cund ['ru:bikənd] rubicond, rougeaud.
ru·bric *typ.*, *eccl.* ['ru:brik] rubrique *f*; **ru·bri·cate** ['~keit] rubriquer.
ru·by ['ru:bi] 1. *min.* rubis *m*; couleur *f* de rubis; *typ.* corps *m* 5¹⁄₂; 2. rouge, vermeil(le *f*).
ruck [rʌk] *courses:* the ~ les coureurs *m/pl.*; *fig.* le commun *m* (du peuple); *cost.* fronçure *f*.
ruck(·le) ['rʌk(l)] (se) froisser; *v/i.* se rider; goder.
ruck·sack ['ruksæk] sac *m* à dos.
ruc·tion *sl.* ['rʌkʃn] bagarre *f*, scène *f*.
rud·der ⚓, *a.* ✈ ['rʌdə] gouvernail *m*.
rud·di·ness ['rʌdinis] rougeur *f*; coloration *f* du teint; **rud·dle** ['rʌdl] 1. ocre *f* rouge; 2. frotter d'ocre rouge; marquer *ou* passer (*qch.*) à l'ocre rouge; '**rud·dy** rouge; rougeâtre; coloré (*teint*); *sl.* sacré.

rude □ [ru:d] primitif (-ive *f*) (*dessin, outil, peuple, temps, etc.*); grossier (-ère *f*) (*langage, méthode, outil, personne*); rudimentaire; fruste (*style etc.*); *fig.* violent; mal élevé, impoli (*personne*); ⊕ brut (*minerai*); robuste (*santé*).

ru·di·ment biol. ['ru:dimənt] rudiment *m* (de, of) (*a. fig.*); ~s *pl. a.* éléments *m/pl.*; **ru·di·men·ta·ry** [~'mentəri] rudimentaire.

rue[1] ⚕ [ru:] rue *f*.

rue[2] [~] se repentir de, regretter amèrement.

rue·ful □ ['ru:ful] triste, lugubre; **'rue·ful·ness** tristesse *f*; air *m* triste ou lugubre; ton *m* triste.

ruff[1] [rʌf] fraise *f*, collerette *f*; *orn., zo.* collier *m*, cravate *f*; *orn.* pigeon *m* à cravate; *orn.* paon *m* de mer.

ruff[2] [~] *whist:* **1.** coupe *f*; **2.** couper (*avec un atout*).

ruf·fi·an ['rʌfjən] bandit *m*, apache *m*; F enfant: polisson *m*; **'ruf·fi·an·ly** de bandit, de brute; brutal (-aux *m/pl.*).

ruf·fle ['rʌfl] **1.** manchette *f* en dentelle; rides *f/pl.* (*sur l'eau*); *fig.* ennui *m*, agitation *f*; ~ *collar* fraise *f*; **2.** *v/t.* ébouriffer; agiter; hérisser (*les plumes*); irriter, froisser (*q.*); *cost.* rucher; plisser; froisser (*une robe*); *v/i.* s'ébouriffer; s'agiter; se hérisser (*oiseau*).

rug [rʌg] couverture *f*; (*a. floor* ~) carpette *f*; ⊕ descente *f* de lit.

Rug·by (**foot·ball**) ['rʌgbi ('futbɔ:l)] le rugby *m*.

rug·ged □ ['rʌgid] raboteux (-euse *f*) (*terrain, style*); rugueux (-euse *f*); rude (*traits, tempérament*); **'rug·ged·ness** nature *f* raboteuse; rudesse *f*.

ru·in ['ru:in] **1.** ruine *f*; *usu.* ~s *pl.* ruine *f*, -s *f/pl.*; *lay in* ~s détruire de fond en comble; **2.** ruiner; abîmer; gâcher; séduire (*une femme*); **ru·in·a·tion** F ruine *f*, perte *f*; **'ru·in·ous** □ délabré, en ruines; *fig.* ruineux (-euse *f*) (*dépenses etc.*).

rule [ru:l] **1.** règle *f* (*a. eccl.*); règlement *m*; (*a. standing* ~) règle *f* fixe; empire *m*, autorité *f*; ⚖ ordonnance *f*, décision *f*; ⊕ mètre *m*; *typ.* filet *m*; *as a* ~ en règle générale; ⚖ ~(s) *of court* directive *f* de procédure; décision *f* du tribunal;

mot. ~ *of the road* code *m* de la route; ⚓ règles *f/pl.* de route; ⚓ ~ *of three* règle *f* de trois; ~ *of thumb* méthode *f* empirique; procédé *m* mécanique; *make it a* ~ *se* faire une règle (de *inf.*, to *inf.*); *work to* ~ faire la grève du règlement; **2.** *v/t.* gouverner; (*a.* ~ *over*) régner sur; commander à; ⚖ décider, déclarer; régler (*du papier*); tracer à la règle (*une ligne*); ~ *the roost* (*ou roast*) être le maître; ~ *out* rayer; éliminer; *v/i.* régner; ✝ rester, se pratiquer (*prix*); **'rul·er** souverain(e *f*) *m*; règle *f*, mètre *m*; **'rul·ing 1.** *surt.* ⚖ ordonnance *f*, décision *f*; **2.** ✝ ~ *price* prix *m* du jour.

rum[1] [rʌm] rhum *m*; *Am.* spiritueux *m*.

rum[2] *sl.* [~] □ bizarre.

Ru·ma·nian [ru:'meinjən] **1.** roumain; **2.** *ling.* roumain *m*; Roumain(e *f*) *m*.

rum·ble[1] ['rʌmbl] **1.** roulement *m*; *tonnerre:* grondement *m*; grouillement *m*; *surt. mot.* siège *m* de derrière; (*Am.* ~-*seat*) spider *m*; *Am.* F bagarre *f* entre deux bandes d'adolescents; **2.** rouler; gronder (*tonnerre*); grouiller (*ventre*).

rum·ble[2] *sl.* [~] pénétrer les intentions de (*q.*) *ou* le secret de (*qch.*).

rum·bus·tious □ F [rʌm'bʌstiəs] exubérant.

ru·mi·nant ['ru:minənt] ruminant (*a. su./m*); **ru·mi·nate** ['~neit] ruminer (*a. fig.*); *fig. a.* méditer; **ru·mi'na·tion** rumination *f*; méditation *f*.

rum·mage ['rʌmidʒ] **1.** fouille *f*, recherches *f/pl.*; ✝ (*usu.* ~ *goods pl.*) choses *f/pl.* de rebut; ~ *sale* vente *f* d'objets usagés; **2.** *v/t.* (far)fouiller; *v/i.* fouiller (*pour trouver, for*). [Rhin.\

rum·mer ['rʌmə] verre *m* à vin du/

rum·my[1] *sl.* □ ['rʌmi] bizarre.

rum·my[2] [~] sorte de jeu de cartes.

ru·mo(u)r ['ru:mə] **1.** rumeur *f*, bruit *m*; **2.** répandre (*une nouvelle*); *it is* ~*ed* on bruit court que; **'~-mon·ger** colporteur *m* de faux bruits.

rump anat. [rʌmp] croupe *f*, *orn.* croupion *m* (*a.* F *co. d'un homme*); *cuis.* culotte *f* (*de bœuf*).

rum·ple ['rʌmpl] *v/t.* froisser, chiffonner; *fig.* contrarier, vexer.

rump·steak [ˈrʌmpsteik] romsteck *m*.

rum·pus F [ˈrʌmpəs] chahut *m*; fracas *m*; *Am*. ~ *room* salle *f* de jeux.

rum-run·ner *Am*. [ˈrʌmrʌnə] contrebandier *m* de spiritueux.

run [rʌn] **1.** [*irr.*] *v/i.* courir (*personne, animal, bruit, sp.*, ⚓, *fig.*, *etc.*); *mot*. aller, rouler, marcher (*a*. ⊕); ⚓ faire route; ⚓ faire la traversée; 🚌 faire le service (*entre Londres et la côte, between London and the coast*); ⊕ fonctionner, être en marche; ⊕ tourner (*roue*); remonter les rivières (*saumon*); (s'en)fuir; se sauver; s'écouler (*temps*); couler (*rivière, plume, a. couleur au lavage*); s'étendre (*encre, tache*); 🎵 suppurer (*ulcère*); *théâ.* tenir l'affiche, se jouer; se démailler (*bas*); *journ. Am.* paraître (*annonce*); ~ *across s.o.* rencontrer q. par hasard; ~ *after* courir après; ~ *away* s'enfuir; *fig.* enlever (q., *with s.o.*); ~ *down* descendre en courant; s'arrêter (*montre etc.*); *fig.* décliner; ~ *dry* se dessécher, s'épuiser; F ~ *for* courir après; *parl.* se porter candidat à *ou* pour; ~ *high* être gros(se *f*) (*mer*); s'échauffer (*sentiments*); *that* ~*s in the blood* (*ou family*) cela tient de famille; ~ *into* tomber dans; entrer en collision avec; rencontrer (q.) par hasard; s'élever à; ~ *low* s'abaisser; ~ *mad* perdre la tête; ~ *off* (s'en)fuir; ~ *on* continuer sa course; s'écouler (*temps*); suivre son cours; continuer à parler; ~ *out* sortir en courant; couler; s'épuiser; *I have* ~ *out of tobacco* je n'ai plus de tabac; ~ *over* parcourir; passer en revue; écraser (q.); ~ *short of* venir à bout de (*qch.*); ~ *through* traverser (en courant); parcourir du regard; dissiper (*une fortune*); ~ *to* se monter à, s'élever à; être de l'ordre de; F durer; F être suffisant pour (*inf.*); ~ *up* monter en courant; accourir; s'élever (*somme*); ~ *up to* s'élever à; ~ (*up*)*on* se ruer sur; rencontrer par hasard; ~ *with* ruisseler de; **2.** [*irr.*] *v/t.* courir (*une distance, une course*); mettre au galop (*un cheval*), *équit.* faire courir; chasser (*un renard*); diriger (*un navire, un train*) (sur, *to*); assurer le service de (*un navire, un autobus*); ⊕ faire fonc-

tionner; ⊕ couler, jeter (*du métal*); *fig.* entretenir (*une auto*); avoir (*une auto, la fièvre*); diriger (*affaire, ferme, hôtel, magasin, théâtre, etc.*); tenir (*hôtel, magasin, ménage*); éditer (*un journal etc.*); exploiter (*une usine*); (faire) passer; tracer (*une ligne*); 🎵 vendre; F appuyer (*un candidat*); ~ *down the blockade* forcer le blocus; *mot*. écraser (q.); ⚓ couler; *fig.* dénigrer, éreinter; F attraper, dépister; *be* ~ *down* être à plat; être épuisé; ~ *errands* faire des courses *ou* commissions; ~ *s.o. hard* presser q.; ~ *in mot. etc.* roder; F arrêter (*un criminel*), conduire au poste (de police); *mot*. s'emboutir contre; ~ *off* faire écouler (*un liquide*); réciter tout d'une haleine; faire (*qch.*) en moins de rien *ou* à la hâte; ~ *out* chasser; filer (*une corde*); ~ *over* passer sur le corps à, écraser (q.); parcourir (*un texte*); ~ *s.o. through* transpercer q.; ~ *up* hisser (*un pavillon*); faire monter (*le prix*); bâtir à la va-vite (*un bâtiment*); confectionner à la hâte (*une robe*); laisser grossir (*un compte*); laisser monter (*une dette*); **3.** action *f* de courir; course *f*; *mot*. tour *m*, promenade *f*; ⚓ traversée *f*; parcours *m*; 🚌 trajet *m*; ⊕ marche *f*; *fig.* cours *m*, marche *f*; suite *f*; *théâ.* durée *f*; ♪ roulade *f*; ⚔ ruée *f*, descente *f* (sur, [*up*]*on*); *Am*. petit ruisseau *m*; *surt. Am*. bas de dames; échelle *f*; ⚔ catégorie *f*; *cartes*: séquence *f*; *fig.* libre accès *m*; élan *m*; *the common* ~ le commun, l'ordinaire; *théâ.* a ~ *of 50 nights* 50 représentations; ~ (*up*)*on a bank* descente *f* sur une banque; *be in the* ~(*ning*) avoir des chances (d'arriver); *in the long* ~ à la longue, en fin de compte; *in the short* ~ ne songeant qu'au présent; *on the* ~ sans le temps de s'asseoir; en fuite.

run...: ~·a·bout *mot*. [ˈrʌnəbaut] voiturette *f*; (*a*. ~ *car*) petite auto *f*; ~·a·way [ˈrʌnəwei] fugitif (-ive *f*) *m*; cheval *m* emballé.

run-down 1. [rʌnˈdaun] épuisé; surmené; ruiné; délabré; **2.** F [ˈrʌndaun] compte *m* rendu minutieux.

rune [ruːn] rune *f*.

rung[1] [rʌŋ] *p.p.* de *ring*[2] 2.

rung² [ˌ] échelon m; échelle: traverse f.

run·ic [ˈruːnik] runique.

run-in F [ˈrʌnˈin] querelle f, altercation f.

run·let [ˈrʌnlit], **run·nel** [ˈrʌnl] ruisseau m; rigole f.

run·ner [ˈrʌnə] coureur (-euse f) m; ✕ courrier m; traîneau: patin m; lit, tiroir, etc.: coulisseau m; ♀ coulant m; ♀ traînée f (du fraisier); courses: partant m; ⊕ poulie f fixe; ⊕ roue f mobile; chariot m ou galet m de roulement; métall. jet m (de coulée); ~-up sp. [ˈˌˈʌp] bon second m; deuxième m.

run·ning [ˈrʌniŋ] 1. courant; two days ~ deux jours de suite; ✕ ~ fight combat m de retraite; ✕ ~ fire feu m roulant ou continu; ~ hand écriture f cursive; sp. ~ start départ m lancé; ~ stitch point m devant; 2. course f, -s f/pl.; 'ˌ~board mot., 🚂 marchepied m; ~ tablier m.

run-of-the-mill [rʌnəvðəˈmil] ordinaire; banal (-als m/pl.); médiocre.

runt [rʌnt] zo. bœuf m ou vache f de petite race; fig. nain m.

run-up [ˈrʌnʌp] période f préparatoire.

run·way [ˈrʌnwei] 🛬 piste f d'envol; chasse: coulée f; ⊕ chemin m de roulement.

ru·pee [ruːˈpiː] roupie f.

rup·ture [ˈrʌptʃə] 1. rupture f; 💊 a. hernie f; 2. (se) rompre; be ~d avoir une hernie.

ru·ral [ˌ] [ˈruərəl] rural (-aux m/pl.); champêtre; des champs; **'ru·ral·ize** v/t. rendre rural; v/i. vivre à la campagne.

rush¹ ♀ [rʌʃ] jonc m.

rush² [ˌ] 1. course f précipitée; élan m, bond m; hâte f; bouffée f (d'air); ✕ bond m; ✕, ✝ demande f considérable; torrent m (d'eau); ~ hours pl. heures f/pl. d'affluence; ✝ coup m de feu; ✝ ~ order commande f urgente; 2. v/i. se précipiter, s'élancer (sur, at); se jeter; ~ into extremes se porter aux dernières extrémités; ~ into print

publier à la légère; F ~ to conclusions conclure trop hâtivement; v/t. pousser etc. violemment; chasser; faire faire au galop; ✕ prendre d'assaut; fig. envahir; dépêcher (un travail); exécuter à la hâte ou d'urgence; sl. faire payer (qch. à q.); parl. ~ through faire passer à la hâte; **'rush·ing** □ tumultueux (-euse f).

rush·y [ˈrʌʃi] plein de joncs; fait de jonc.

rusk [rʌsk] biscotte f.

rus·set [ˈrʌsit] 1. roussâtre; 2. couleur f roussâtre; ✝ drap m de bure.

Rus·sia leath·er [ˈrʌʃəˈleðə] cuir m de Russie; **'Rus·sian 1.** russe; 2. ling. russe m; Russe mf.

rust [rʌst] 1. rouille f; 2. (se) rouiller (a. fig.).

rus·tic [ˈrʌstik] 1. (~ally) rustique; agreste; paysan(ne f); 2. paysan(ne f) m, campagnard(e f) m; rustaud(e f) m; **rus·ti·cate** [ˈˌkeit] v/t. univ. renvoyer pendant un temps; v/i. habiter la campagne; **rus·ti·ca·tion** vie f à la campagne; univ. renvoi m temporaire; **rus·tic·i·ty** [ˌˈtisiti] rusticité f.

rus·tle [ˈrʌsl] 1. (faire) bruire, froufrouter; v/t. a. froisser; Am. F ramasser, réunir; voler (du bétail); 2. bruissement m; frou-frou m; froissement m.

rust...: '~·less sans rouille; ✝ inoxydable; 'ˌ~ˈproof, '~-re·sist·ant antirouille; inoxydable; 'rust·y rouillé (a. fig.); couleur de rouille, rouilleux (-euse f).

rut¹ zo. [rʌt] 1. rut m; 2. être en rut.

rut² [ˌ] ornière f (a. fig.); fig. a. routine f.

ruth·less □ [ˈruːθlis] impitoyable; brutal (-aux m/pl.) (acte, vérité); **'ruth·less·ness** nature f ou caractère m impitoyable. [(chemin).]

rut·ted [ˈrʌtid] coupé d'ornières]

rut·ting zo. [ˈrʌtiŋ] du rut; en rut; ~ season saison f du rut.

rut·ty [ˈrʌti] coupé d'ornières (chemin).

rye [rai] ♀ seigle m; Am. sorte de whisky.

S

S, s [es] S *m*, s *m*.

sab·bath ['sæbəθ] *bibl.* sabbat *m*; *eccl.* dimanche *m*.

sab·bat·ic, sab·bat·i·cal □ [sə'bætik(l)] sabbatique; *univ.* sabbatical year année *f* de congé.

sa·ble ['seibl] **1.** *zo.* zibeline *f* (*a.* fourrure); noir *m*; ▨ sable *m*; **2.** noir; *poét.* de deuil.

sab·o·tage ['sæbəta:ʒ] **1.** sabotage *m*; **2.** saboter (*a. fig.*).

sa·bre ['seibə] **1.** sabre *m*; **2.** sabrer; **sa·bre·tache** ✕ ['sæbətæʃ] sabretache *f*.

sac·cha·rin(e) ⚗ ['sækərin] saccharine *f*; **sac·cha·rine** ['ˌ~rain] saccharin.

sac·er·do·tal □ [sæsə'doutl] sacerdotal (-aux *m/pl.*); de prêtre.

sack¹ [sæk] **1.** sac *m*; (*a.* ~ coat) vareuse *f* de sport, pardessus *m* sac; F get the ~ recevoir son congé; give s.o. the ~ donner son congé à q.; F hit the ~ se pieuter, aller au pieu (= se coucher); **2.** mettre en sac; F congédier (*q.*), mettre (*q.*) à pied.

sack² [ˌ~] **1.** sac *m*, pillage *m*; **2.** (*a.* put to ~) mettre à sac *ou* au pillage.

sack·cloth ['sækklɒθ], **'sack·ing** toile *f* à sacs; sackcloth and ashes le sac et la cendre; **sack·ful** ['ˌ~ful] plein sac *m*, sachée *f*.

sac·ra·ment *eccl.* ['sækrəmənt] sacrement *m*; **sac·ra·men·tal** □ [ˌ~'mentl] sacramentel(le *f*).

sa·cred □ ['seikrid] sacré; saint (*histoire*); religieux (-euse *f*) (*musique etc.*); **'sa·cred·ness** caractère *m* sacré; *serment:* inviolabilité *f*.

sac·ri·fice ['sækrifais] **1.** sacrifice *m*; ✝ at a ~ à perte; **2.** sacrifier; ✝ *a.* vendre à perte; **'sac·ri·fic·er** sacrificateur (-trice *f*) *m*.

sac·ri·fi·cial [sækri'fiʃl] sacrificatoire; ✝ à perte (*vente*).

sac·ri·lege ['sækrilidʒ] sacrilège *m*; **sac·ri·le·gious** □ [ˌ~'lidʒəs] sacrilège.

sa·crist ['seikrist], **sac·ris·tan** *eccl.* ['sækristən] sacristain *m*.

sac·ris·ty *eccl.* ['sækristi] sacristie *f*.

sad □ [sæd] triste; déplorable; malheureux (-euse *f*); cruel(le *f*); fâcheux (-euse *f*); terne (*couleur*).

sad·den ['sædn] (s')affliger; *v/t.* attrister.

sad·dle ['sædl] **1.** selle *f*; **2.** (*a.* ~ up) seller; *fig.* charger (q. de qch. *s.o.* with s.th., s.th. on s.o.); F encombler (de, with); '~-**backed** ensellé (*cheval*); '~-**bag** sacoche *f* de selle; '~-**cloth** tapis *m* de selle; housse *f* de cheval; '**sad·dler** sellier *m*; *Am.* cheval *m* de selle; **sad·dler·y** sellerie *f*.

sad·ism ['sædizm] sadisme *m*; '**sad·ist** sadique *mf*; **sa·dis·tic** [sæ'distik] sadique; ~*ally* avec sadisme.

sad·ness ['sædnis] tristesse *f*, mélancolie *f*.

sa·fa·ri [sə'fɑːri] expédition *f* de chasse.

safe [seif] **1.** □ en sûreté (contre, from), à l'abri (de, from); sûr; sans risque; hors de danger; ~ and sound sain et sauf; be on the ~ side être du bon côté; **2.** coffre-fort (*pl.* coffres-forts) *m*; ⚓ caisse *f* du bord; *cuis.* garde-manger *m/inv.*; ~ deposit dépôt *m* en coffre-fort; '~-**break·er, '~-crack·er** *Am.* crocheteur *m* de coffres-forts; '~-**con·duct** sauf-conduit *m*; '~-**guard** **1.** sauvegarde *f*; **2.** sauvegarder, protéger; ~*ing duty* tarif *m* de sauvegarde; '**safe·ness** sûreté *f*; sécurité *f*.

safe·ty ['seifti] **1.** sûreté *f*; sécurité *f*; **2.** de sûreté; ~ belt ceinture *f* de sécurité; *théâ.* ~ curtain rideau *m* de fer; ~ glass verre *m* Sécurit (*TM*); ~ island refuge *m*; ~ lamp lampe *f* de mineur; ~ match allumette de sûreté; ~ lock serrure *f* de sûreté; ~ pin épingle *f* de nourrice; ~ razor rasoir *m* de sûreté.

saf·fron ['sæfrən] **1.** safran *m* (*a.* couleur); **2.** safran *inv.*

sag [sæg] **1.** fléchir (a. ✝); s'affaisser; ⊕ pencher d'un côté; se relâcher (corde); pendre; **2.** affaissement m (a. ⊕); ♣ dérive f; ✝ baisse f.

sa·ga ['sɑːgə] saga f.

sa·ga·cious □ [sə'geiʃəs] sagace, avisé, rusé.

sa·gac·i·ty [sə'gæsiti] sagacité f.

sage¹ [seidʒ] **1.** □ sage, prudent; **2.** sage m.

sage² ⚘ [~] sauge f.

Sa·git·tar·i·us astr. [sædʒi'tɛəriəs] le Sagittaire m.

sa·go ['seigou] sagou m.

said [sed] prét. et p.p. de say 1.

sail [seil] **1.** voile f; coll. toile f; promenade f à voile; 10 ~ dix navires m/pl.; **2.** v/i. naviguer; faire route; partir; fig. planer, voler; v/t. naviguer sur; conduire (un vaisseau); '~-boat canot m à voiles; '~-cloth toile f à voile, canevas m; 'sail·er bateau: voilier m; 'sail·ing-ship, 'sail·ing-ves·sel voilier m; navire m à voiles; 'sail·or marin m; matelot m; cost. ~ blouse marinière f; ~'s knot nœud m régate; be a good (bad) ~ (ne pas) avoir le pied marin; 'sail-plane planeur m.

sain-foin ⚘ ['seinfɔin] sainfoin m; F éparcette f.

saint [seint; devant npr. sənt] **1.** saint(e f) m; the ~s pl. les fidèles m/pl. trépassés; **2.** v/t. canoniser; v/i. F ~ (it) faire le saint; 'saint·ed saint; 'saint·li·ness sainteté f; 'saint·ly adj. (de) saint.

sake [seik]: for the ~ of à cause de; pour l'amour de; dans l'intérêt de; for my ~ pour moi, pour me faire plaisir; for God's ~ pour l'amour de Dieu.

sal 🜍 [sæl] sel m; ~ ammoniac sel m ammoniac; ~ volatile sels m/pl. (volatils).

sal·a·ble ['seiləbl] vendable.

sa·la·cious □ [sə'leiʃəs] lubrique.

sal·ad ['sæləd] salade f.

sal·a·man·der ['sæləmændə] zo. salamandre f; cuis. couvercle m à braiser.

sa·la·me, sa·la·mi [sə'lɑːmi] salami m.

sal·a·ried ['sælərid] rétribué; aux appointements (personne); 'sal·a·ry **1.** traitement m, appointements m/pl.; **2.** payer des appointements

à; 'sal·a·ry-earn·er salarié(e f) m.

sale [seil] vente f (✝ de réclame); (a. public ~) vente f aux enchères; for (ou on) ~ en vente; à vendre; private ~ vente f à l'amiable; 'sale·a·ble vendable; de vente facile.

sale...: '~-note bordereau m de vente; '~-room salle f de(s) vente(s).

sales... [seilz]: ~ **clerk** Am. vendeur (-euse f) m; ~ **com·mis·sion** commission f (pour la vente); '~·man vendeur m; '~·girl, '~·wom·an vendeuse f; ~ **room** salle f des ventes; ~ **talk** Am. boniment m.

sa·li·ence ['seiliəns] projection f; saillie f; 'sa·li·ent □ saillant (a. fig.); en saillie; fig. frappant.

sa·line 1. ['seilain] salin (a. 🐟), salé; **2.** [sə'lain] salin m; 🜍 sel m purgatif.

sa·li·va [sə'laivə] salive f; **sal·i·var·y** ['sælivəri] salivaire; **sal·i·'va·tion** salivation f.

sal·low¹ ⚘ ['sælou] saule m.

sal·low² [~] jaunâtre, olivâtre; 'sal·low·ness teint: ton m jaunâtre.

sal·ly ['sæli] **1.** ⚔ sortie f; effort, esprit, etc.: saillie f; **2.** ⚔ (a. ~ out) faire une sortie; ~ forth (ou out) se mettre en route; '~-port ⚔ poterne f (de sortie).

sal·ma·gun·di [sælmə'gʌndi] salmigondis m; fig. méli-mélo (pl. mélis-mélos) m.

salm·on ['sæmən] **1.** saumon m (a. couleur); **2.** saumon inv.

sa·loon [sə'luːn] salon m (a. de paquebot); salle f; première classe f (en bateau); Am. cabaret m; **sa'loon-car** 🚂 wagon-salon (pl. wagons-salons) m; mot. (voiture f à) conduite f intérieure, limousine f.

salt [sɔːlt] sel m (a. fig.); fig. piquant m; old ~ loup m de mer (= vieux matelot); above (below) the ~ au haut (bas) bout de la table; **2.** salé (a. fig.); salin; salifère; **3.** saler; sl. ~ away mettre de côté, économiser.

sal·ta·tion [sæl'teiʃn] saltation f; biol. mutation f.

salt...: '~-cel·lar salière f; 'salt·ed F immunisé; fig. endurci; 'salt·er saleur (-euse f) m; saunier m; fabricant m de sel; 'salt-free sans sel; 'salt·ness salure f, salinité f; 'salt·pe·tre ['~-piːtə] salpêtre m, nitre m; 'salt-shak·er Am. salière f; 'salt·works saunerie *f*, saline *f*; **'salt·y** salé (*a. fig.*); de sel.

sa·lu·bri·ous □ [sə'lu:briəs] salubre, sain; sa'lu·bri·ty salubrité *f*; sal·u·tar·i·ness ['sæljutərinis] caractère *m* salutaire; 'sal·u·tar·y □ salutaire (à, to).

sal·u·ta·tion [sælju'teiʃn] salutation *f*; sa·lu·ta·to·ry [səl'ju:tətəri] de salutation; de bienvenue; sa·lute [sə'lu:t] 1. salut(ation *f*) *m*; *co.* baiser *m*; ✕, ♣ salut *m*; 2. saluer (a. ✕, ♣).

sal·vage ['sælvidʒ] 1. (indemnité *f* de) sauvetage *m*; objets *m/pl.* sauvés; 2. récupérer; ♣ effectuer le sauvetage de.

sal·va·tion [sæl'veiʃn] salut *m* (*a. fig.*); ♀ *Army* Armée *f* du Salut; sal'va·tion·ist salutiste *mf*.

salve¹ [sælv] sauver; effectuer le sauvetage de.

salve² [sɑːv] 1. *usu. fig.* baume *m*; 2. *usu. fig.* adoucir; calmer.

sal·ver ['sælvə] plateau *m*.

sal·vo ['sælvou], *pl.* -voes ['sælvouz] ✕ salve *f* (*a. fig.*); ✕ ~ release bombardement *m* en traînée; lâchage *m* par salves; sal'vor ♣ ['ʌvə] sauveteur *m*.

Sa·mar·i·tan [sə'mæritn] 1. samaritain; 2. Samaritain(e *f*) *m*.

sam·ba ['sæmbə] samba *f*.

same [seim]: *the* ~ le (la) même; *les mêmes pl.; all the* ~ tout de même; *it is all the* ~ *to me* ça m'est égal; *cela ne me fait rien;* 'same·ness identité *f* (avec, with); ressemblance *f* (à, with); monotonie *f*.   [maïs.]

samp *Am.* [sæmp] gruau *m* de]

sam·ple ['sɑːmpl] 1. *surt.* ♦ échantillon *m*; *sang, minerai, etc.*: prélèvement *m*; 2. échantillonner; *fig.* essayer, goûter; 'sam·pler modèle *m* de broderie; 'sam·pling échantillonnage *m*.

san·a·tive ['sænətiv] guérisseur (-euse *f*); san·a·to·ri·um [ʌ-'tɔːriəm] sanatorium *m*; *école:* infirmerie *f*; san·a·to·ry ['ʌtəri] guérisseur (-euse *f*), curatif (-ive *f*).

sanc·ti·fi·ca·tion [sæŋktifi'keiʃn] sanctification *f*; sanc·ti·fy ['ʌfai] sanctifier; consacrer; sanc·ti·mo·ni·ous □ [ʌ'mounjəs] bigot(te *f*), papelard; sanc·tion ['sæŋkʃn] 1. sanction *f*; autorisation *f*; 2. sanction-

ner; *fig.* approuver; sanc·ti·ty ['ʌtiti] sainteté *f*; caractère *m* sacré; sanc·tu·ar·y ['ʌtjuəri] sanctuaire *m*; asile *m*; sanc·tum ['ʌtəm] sanctuaire *m*; *fig.* F turne *f*.

sand [sænd] 1. sable *m*; *Am. sl.* cran *m*, étoffe *f*; *fig.* rope of ~ de vagues liens *m/pl.*; 2. sabler; répandre du sable sur.

san·dal¹ ['sændl] sandale *f*. [-s) *m*.\
san·dal² [ʌ] (*ou* ~-wood) santal (*pl.*]

sand...: '~·bag ✕ sac *m* à terre; *porte, fenêtre:* boudin *m*; '~·blast ⊕ jet *m* de sable; *appareil:* sableuse *f*; '~·glass sablier *m*; horloge *f* de sable; '~·pit tas *m* de sable (*pour enfants*); *carrière:* sablonnière *f*; '~·shoes espadrilles *f/pl.*

sand·wich ['sænwidʒ] 1. sandwich *m*; *Brit.* ~ *course* cours *m* intercalaire (de promotion professionnelle); 2. (*a.* ~ *in*) serrer; '~·man homme-sandwich (*pl.* hommes-sandwichs) *m*.

sand·y ['sændi] sabl(onn)eux (-euse *f*); sablé (*allée etc.*); blond roux (*cheveux*) *inv.*

sane [sein] sain d'esprit; sensé; sain (*jugement*).

San·for·ize *Am.* ['sænfəraiz] rendre irrétrécissable.

sang [sæŋ] *prét. de sing.*

san·gui·nar·y □ ['sæŋgwinəri] sanguinaire; altéré de sang; san·guine ['ʌgwin] sanguin; confiant, optimiste; d'un rouge sanguin; san·'guin·e·ous [ʌ'niəs] de sang; *see* sanguine.

san·i·tari·an [sæni'tɛəriən] hygiéniste (*a. su.*); san·i·tar·y □ ['ʌtəri] hygiénique (*a.* ⊕); sanitaire (*a.* ✕, ♣); ~ *towel, Am.* ~ *napkin* serviette *f* hygiénique.

san·i·ta·tion [sæni'teiʃn] hygiène *f*; système *m* sanitaire; salubrité *f* publique; 'san·i·ty santé *f* d'esprit; jugement *m* sain; bon sens *m*; modération *f*.

sank [sæŋk] *prét. de sink* 1.

San·skrit ['sænskrit] sanscrit *m*.

San·ta Claus [sæntə'klɔːz] Père *m* ou bonhomme *m* Noël.

sap¹ [sæp] ♀ sève *f* (*a. fig.*); *sl.* niais *m*.

sap² [ʌ] 1. ✕ sape *f*; F piocheur (-euse *f*) *m*; *sl.* boulot *m*; 2. *v/i.* saper; *sl.* piocher, bûcher; *v/t.* saper, miner (*a. fig.*).

sap·id ['sæpid] savoureux (-euse *f*); **sa·pid·i·ty** [sə'piditi] sapidité *f*.

sa·pi·ence *usu. iro.* ['seipjəns] sagesse *f*; **'sa·pi·ent** *usu. iro.* □ savant, sage.

sap·less ['sæplis] sans sève; sans vigueur (*personne*).

sap·ling ['sæpliŋ] jeune arbre *m*; *fig.* jeune homme *m*.

sap·o·na·ceous [sæpo'neiʃəs] saponacé; *fig.* onctueux (-euse *f*).

sap·per ✗ ['sæpə] sapeur *m*.

sap·phire *min.* ['sæfaiə] saphir *m*.

sap·pi·ness ['sæpinis] abondance *f* de sève.

sap·py ['sæpi] plein de sève (*a. fig.*); vert (*arbre*); *sl.* nigaud.

Sar·a·cen ['særəsn] Sarrasin(e *f*) *m*.

sar·casm ['sɑːkæzm] ironie *f*; sarcasme *m*; **sar'cas·tic, sar'cas·ti·cal** □ sarcastique, mordant.

sar·coph·a·gus [sɑː'kɔfəgəs], *pl.* -**gi** [.ʌdʒai] sarcophage *m*.

sar·dine *icht.* [sɑː'diːn] sardine *f*.

Sar·din·i·an [sɑː'dinjən] **1.** sarde; **2.** *ling.* sarde *m*; Sarde *mf*.

sar·don·ic [sɑː'dɔnik] (ʌally) sardonique (*rire*); ⚕ sardonien(ne *f*).

sar·to·ri·al [sɑː'tɔːriəl] de tailleur; vestimentaire.

sash¹ [sæʃ] châssis *m* (*de fenêtre à guillotine*).

sash² [ʌ] ceinture *f*; ✗ *a.* écharpe *f*.

sa·shay *Am.* F [sæ'ʃei] marcher d'un pas vif; danser.

sash-win·dow fenêtre *f* à guillotine.

sas·sy *Am.* ['sæsi] *see* saucy.

sat [sæt] *prét. et p.p. de* sit.

Sa·tan ['seitən] Satan *m*.

sa·tan·ic [sə'tænik] (ʌally) satanique, diabolique.

satch·el ['sætʃl] sacoche *f*; *école:* carton *m*.

sate [seit] *see* satiate.

sa·teen [sæ'tiːn] satinette *f*.

sat·el·lite ['sætəlait] satellite *m* (*a. fig.*); (*a.* ʌ *town*) ville *f* satellite; ʌ *country* pays *m* satellite.

sa·ti·ate ['seiʃieit] rassasier (de, with); **sa·ti·a·tion** rassasiement *m*; satiété *f*; **sa·ti·e·ty** [sə'taiəti] satiété *f*.

sat·in ['sætin] *tex.* satin *m*; **sat·i·net** ['sætinet], *usu.* **sat·i·nette** [ʌ'net] satinette *f*; *soie:* satinade *f*.

sat·ire ['sætaiə] satire *f* (contre, [up]on); **sa·tir·ic, sa·tir·i·cal** □

[sə'tirik(l)] satirique; ironique; **sat·i·rist** ['sætərist] satirique *m*; **'sat·i·rize** satiriser.

sat·is·fac·tion [sætis'fækʃn] satisfaction *f*, contentement *m* (de at, with); acquittement *m*, paiement *m*; *promesse:* exécution *f*; réparation *f* (*d'une offense*).

sat·is·fac·to·ri·ness [sætis'fæktərinis] caractère *m* satisfaisant; **sat·is·'fac·to·ry** □ satisfaisant; *eccl.* expiatoire.

sat·is·fied □ ['sætisfaid] satisfait, content (de, with; que, that); **sat·is·fy** ['ʌfai] satisfaire; contenter; payer, liquider (*une dette*); exécuter (*une promesse*); remplir (*une condition*); éclaircir (*un doute*).

sa·trap ['sætrəp] satrape *m*.

sat·u·rate ⌐m, *a. fig.* ['sætʃəreit] saturer (de, with); **sat·u·ra·tion** saturation *f*; imprégnation *f*; ʌ *point* point *m* de saturation.

Sat·ur·day ['sætədi] samedi *m*.

sat·ur·nine ['sætənain] taciturne, sombre.

sat·yr ['sætə] satyre *m*.

sauce [sɔːs] **1.** sauce *f*; *fig.* assaisonnement *m*; F impertinence *f*; **2.** assaisonner; F dire des impertinences à (*q.*); 'ʌ-**boat** saucière *f*; 'ʌ-**pan** casserole *f*; **'sauc·er** soucoupe *f*.

sau·ci·ness F ['sɔːsinis] impertinence *f*; chic *m* (*d'un chapeau*).

sau·cy □ F ['sɔːsi] gamin; effronté, impertinent; chic *inv. en genre*, coquet(te *f*).

sau·na ['sɔːnə] sauna *m* ou *f*.

saun·ter ['sɔːntə] **1.** flânerie *f*; promenade *f* (faite à loisir); **2.** flâner; se balader; **'saun·ter·er** flâneur (-euse *f*) *m*.

sau·ri·an *zo.* ['sɔːriən] saurien *m*.

sau·sage ['sɔsidʒ] saucisse *f*; saucisson *m*.

sav·age ['sævidʒ] **1.** □ sauvage; féroce; brutal (-aux *m/pl.*) (*coup*); F furieux (-euse *f*); **2.** sauvage *mf*; *fig.* barbare *mf*; **3.** attaquer, mordre (*chien*); **'sav·age·ness, 'sav·age·ry** sauvagerie *f*, barbarie *f*; férocité *f*.

sa·van·na(h) [sə'vænə] savane *f*.

save [seiv] **1.** *v/t.* sauver; économiser, épargner; gagner (*du temps*); mettre de côté; garder; éviter; *v/i.* faire des économies, économiser; **2.** *prp.* excepté, sauf; **3.** *cj.* ʌ *that* excepté que, hormis que; ~ *for* sauf; si ce n'était ...

sav·e·loy ['sævilɔi] cervelas *m*.

sav·er ['seivə] libérateur (-trice *f*) *m*; sauveteur *m*; ⊕ économiseur *m*; personne *f* économe.

sav·ing ['seiviŋ] **1.** □ économique; économe (*personne*); ⅍ ~ **clause** clause *f* de sauvegarde; réservation *f*; **2.** épargne *f*; *fig.* salut *m*; sauvetage *m*; ~**s** *pl.* économies *f/pl.*

sav·ings... ['seiviŋz]: ~ **ac·count** compte *m* d'épargne; '~-**bank** caisse *f* d'épargne; '~-**de·pos·it** dépôt *m* à la caisse d'épargne.

sav·io(u)r ['seivjə] sauveur *m*; *eccl.* the ⚲ le Sauveur *m*.

sa·vor·y ⚘ ['seivəri] sarriette *f*.

sa·vo(u)r ['seivə] **1.** saveur *f*; goût *m* (*a. fig.*); *fig.* trace *f*; **2.** *v/i. fig.* ~ *of* sentir (*qch.*), tenir de (*qch.*); *v/t. fig.* savourer; **sa·vo(u)r·i·ness** ['~rinis] saveur *f*, succulence *f*; **sa·vo(u)r·less** fade, insipide; sans saveur; '**sa·vo(u)r·y** □ savoureux (-euse *f*), succulent, appétissant; piquant, salé.

sa·voy [sə'vɔi] chou *m* frisé *ou* de Milan.

sav·vy *sl.* ['sævi] **1.** jugeote *f*; **2.** comprendre.

saw[1] [sɔ:] *prét.* de *see*.

saw[2] [~] adage *m*; dicton *m*.

saw[3] [~] **1.** scie *f*; **2.** [*irr.*] scier; '~-**buck** *Am. sl.* billet *m* de dix dollars; '~-**dust** sciure *f*; '~-**horse** chevalet *m* de scieur; '~-**mill** scierie *f*; **sawn** [sɔ:n] *p.p.* de *saw*[3] 2; **saw·yer** ['~jə] scieur *m* (de long).

Sax·on ['sæksn] **1.** saxon(ne *f*); **2.** *ling.* saxon *m*; Saxon(ne *f*) *m*.

sax·o·phone ♪ ['sæksəfoun] saxophone *m*.

say [sei] **1.** [*irr.*] dire; avouer; affirmer; réciter; ~ *no* refuser; ~ *grace* dire le bénédicité; ~ *mass* dire la messe; *that is to* ~ c'est-à-dire; *do you* ~ *so?* vous croyez?, vous trouvez?; *you don't* ~ *so!* pas possible!, vraiment!; *I* ~! dites donc!; pas possible!; *he is said to be rich* on dit qu'il est riche; on le dit riche; *no sooner said than done* sitôt dit, sitôt fait; **2.** dire *m*, mot *m*, parole *f*; *it is my* ~ *now* maintenant à moi la parole; *let him have his* ~ laissez-le parler; F *have a (no)* ~ *in s.th.* (ne pas) avoir voix au chapitre;

'**say·ing** dicton *m*, proverbe *m*; dit *m*; récitation *f*; *it goes without* ~ cela va sans dire.

scab [skæb] plaie: croûte *f*; *vét. etc.* gale *f*; *sl.* jaune *m*; *sl.* sale type *m*.

scab·bard ['skæbəd] épée: fourreau *m*; poignard: gaine *f*.

scab·by □ ['skæbi] croûteux (-euse *f*); galeux (-euse *f*); ⊕ dartreux (-euse *f*); *sl.* méprisable.

sca·bi·es ✧ ['skeibii:z] gale *f*.

sca·bi·ous ⚘ ['skeibiəs] scabieuse *f*.

sca·brous ['skeibrəs] rugueux (-euse *f*); scabreux (-euse *f*) (*conte etc.*).

scaf·fold ['skæfəld] ⅍ échafaud *m*; △ échafaudage *m*; '**scaf·fold·ing** échafaudage *m*; ~ *pole* écoperche *f*.

scald [skɔ:ld] **1.** échaudure *f*; **2.** (*a.* ~ *out*) échauder; faire chauffer (*le lait*) sans qu'il entre en ébullition.

scale[1] [skeil] **1.** ✧, *peau, poisson, reptile*; *a. de fer*: écaille *f*; ⊕, ✧ dartre *f*; ✧ *dents*: tartre *m*; **2.** *v/t.* écailler; ⊕ ~ piquer; ~ détarter (*a. dents*); ⊕ entartrer (= *incruster*); *v/i.* s'écailler; s'exfolier (*arbre*); se déplâtrer (*mur etc.*); ✧ se desquamer; ⊕ (*souv.* ~ *off*) s'entartrer.

scale[2] [~] **1.** plat(eau) *m*; (*a pair of*) ~*s pl.* (une) balance *f*; *astr.* Balance *f*; **2.** peser.

scale[3] [~] **1.** échelle *f*; ♪, ♩ gamme *f*; ♩ tarif *m*; *fig.* étendue *f*, envergure *f*; *on a large (small)* ~ en grand (petit); ~ *model* maquette *f*; *on a national* ~ à l'échelon national; **2.** escalader (*un mur etc.*); tracer (*q.*) à l'échelle; ~ *up (down)* augmenter (réduire) (*les gages etc.*) à l'échelle.

scaled [skeild] écaillé; écailleux (-euse *f*).

scale·less ['skeillis] sans écailles.

scal·ing-lad·der ['skeiliŋlædə] ✕ † échelle *f* d'escalade.

scal·lion ⚘ ['skæljən] ciboule *f*.

scal·lop ['skɔləp] **1.** *zo.* pétoncle *m*; *cuis.* coquille *f*; *cost.* feston *m*; dentelure *f*; **2.** découper, denteler; festonner; faire cuire en coquille(s).

scalp [skælp] **1.** épicrâne *m*; cuir *m* chevelu; *Peaux-Rouges*: scalpe *m*; **2.** scalper; ✧ ruginer.

scal·pel ✧ ['skælpəl] scalpel *m*.

scal·y [skeili] écailleux (-euse *f*); squameux (-euse *f*); *sl.* mesquin.

scamp [skæmp] **1.** vaurien *m*; *enfant*: coquin *m*; **2.** bâcler; '**scamp·er 1.** courir allègrement; ~ *off* détaler; 2. *fig.* course *f* folâtre *ou* rapide.

scan [skæn] *v/t.* scander (*des vers*); examiner, scruter; *v/i.* se scander.

scan·dal ['skændl] scandale *m*; honte *f*; médisance *f*; ⚖ diffamation *f*; **'scan·dal·ize** scandaliser; be ~d at (*ou* by) être choqué de *ou* scandalisé par; **'scan·dal·mon·ger** médisant(e *f*) *m*; cancanier (-ère *f*) *m*; **'scan·dal·ous** □ scandaleux (-euse *f*), infâme; honteux (-euse *f*); diffamatoire; **'scan·dal·ous·ness** infamie *f*; caractère *m* scandaleux *etc.*

Scan·di·na·vi·an [skændi'neivjən] 1. scandinave; 2. Scandinave *mf*.

scant [skænt] rare, insuffisant.

scant·i·ness ['skæntinis] rareté *f*, insuffisance *f*.

scant·ling ['skæntliŋ] volige *f*; bois *m* équarri; échantillon *m* (*de construction*); équarrissage *m*; *fig.* très petite quantité *f*.

scant·y □ ['skænti] rare, insuffisant, peu abondant; maigre.

scape·goat ['skeipgout] souffre-douleur *m/inv.*

scape·grace ['skeipgreis] polisson *m*; petit(e) écervelé(e) *m(f).*

scap·u·lar ['skæpjulə] 1. *anat.* scapulaire; 2. *eccl.* scapulaire *m.*

scar¹ [skɑ:] 1. cicatrice *f* (*a.* ♀, *a. fig.*); balafre *f* (*le long de la figure*); 2. *v/t.* balafrer; *v/i.* se cicatriser.

scar² [~] rocher *m* escarpé.

scar·ab *zo.* ['skærəb] scarabée *m.*

scarce [skɛəs] rare; peu abondant; F make o.s. ~ s'éclipser, déguerpir; **'scarce·ly** à peine; (ne) guère; **'scar·ci·ty** rareté *f*; manque *m*, disette *f* (de, *of*).

scare [skɛə] 1. effrayer; faire peur à (*q.*); épouvanter; ~d épouvanté; apeuré; be ~d (of) avoir peur (de); be ~d to death avoir une peur bleue; 2. panique *f*; **'~·crow** épouvantail *m* (*a. fig.*); **'~·head** *journ. Am.* manchette *f* sensationnelle; **'~·mon·ger** alarmiste *mf*; *sl.* paniquard *m.*

scarf¹ [skɑ:f]✕, *a. femme:* écharpe *f*; *homme:* cache-nez *m/inv.*; *soie:* foulard *m*; *eccl.* étole *f*; † cravate *f.*

scarf² ⊕ [~] 1. assemblage *m* à mi-bois; enture *f*; *métal:* chanfrein *m* de soudure; 2. ⚓ enter; ⊕ amorcer.

scarf...: **'~·pin** épingle *f* de cravate; **'~·skin** épiderme *m.*

scar·i·fi·ca·tion [skɛərifi'keiʃn] ⚕ scarification *f*; **scar·i·fy** ['~fai] scarifier (*a.* ✎); *fig.* éreinter (*un auteur*).   [scarlatine *f.*]

scar·la·ti·na [skɑ:lə'ti:nə] (fièvre *f*)]

scar·let ['skɑ:lit] écarlate (*a. su./f*); ~ fever (fièvre *f*) scarlatine *f*; ♀ ~ runner haricot *m* d'Espagne.

scarp [skɑ:p] 1. escarper; ~ed à pic; 2. escarpement *m*; versant *m* abrupt.

scarred [skɑ:d] balafré; portant des cicatrices.

scarves [skɑ:vz] *pl.* de scarf¹.

scar·y F ['skɛəri] timide; épouvantable.

scathe [skeið] *without* ~ indemne; **'scath·ing** *fig.* mordant, cinglant, caustique.

scat·ter ['skætə] (se) disperser, (s')éparpiller; (se) répandre; *v/t.* dissiper; ~ed *a.* épars, clairsemé; **'~·brain** écervelé(e *f*) *m*, étourdi(e *f*) *m.*

scav·enge ['skævindʒ] balayer, nettoyer; **'scav·en·ger** éboueur *m*, balayeur *m* (des rues); **'scav·eng·ing** balayage *m* (des rues); ébouage *m.*

sce·nar·i·o *cin., théâ.* [si'nɑ:riou] scénario *m*; **'~·writ·er,** *a.* **sce·nar·ist** ['si:nərist] scénariste *m.*

scene [si:n] scène *f* (*a. théâ.*); *fig. a.* théâtre *m*, lieu *m*; vue *f*, paysage *m*; spectacle *m*; see ~ry; ~s *pl.* coulisse *f*, ~s *f/pl.*; **'~·paint·er** peintre *m* de ou en décors; **scen·er·y** ['~əri] décors *m/pl.*, (mise *f* en) scène *f*; paysage *m*, vue *f.*

sce·nic, sce·ni·cal ['si:nik(l)] scénique; théâtral (-aux *m/pl.*) (*a. fig.*); scenic railway montagnes *f/pl.* russes; ~ road route *f* pittoresque.

scent [sent] 1. parfum *m*; odeur *f* (agréable); *chasse:* vent *m*; voie *f*, piste *f*; *chien:* flair *m*, nez *m*; 2. parfumer, embaumer; *chasse:* (*souv.* ~ out) flairer (*a. fig.*), sentir; **'scent·ed** parfumé (de, *with*); odorant; **'scent·less** inodore; sans odeur; *chasse:* sans fumet.

scep·tic ['skeptik] sceptique *mf*; **'scep·ti·cal** □ sceptique; be ~ about douter de; **scep·ti·cism** ['~sizm] scepticisme *m.*

scep·tre ['septə] sceptre *m.*

sched·ule ['ʃedju:l; *Am.* 'skedju:l] 1. inventaire *m*; cahier *m*; liste *f*;

scheme   1088

impôts: cédule *f*; ⚖ annexe *f*; *surt. Am.* horaire *m*; *surt. Am.* plan *m*; *on* ~ à l'heure; *fig.* selon les prévisions; **2.** inscrire sur l'inventaire *etc.*; ⚖ ajouter comme annexe; *Am.* dresser un plan de; *Am.* marquer sur l'horaire; *be* ~*d for* devoir arriver *ou* partir *etc.* à; ~*d flight* vol *m* de ligne, vol *m* régulier.

scheme [ski:m] **1.** plan *m*, projet *m*; arrangement *m*; *péj.* intrigue *f*; **2.** *v/t.* projeter; *v/i. péj.* intriguer (pour, *to*); comploter; combiner (de, *to*); '**schem·er** faiseur (-euse *f*) *m* de projets; *péj.* intrigant(e *f*) *m*.

schism ['sizm] schisme *m*; *fig.* division *f*; **schis·mat·ic** [siz'mætik] **1.** (*a.* **schis'mat·i·cal** □) schismatique; **2.** schismatique *mf*.

schist *min.* [ʃist] schiste *m*.

schol·ar ['skɔlə] élève *mf*; écolier (-ère *f*) *m*; érudit(e *f*) *m*; *univ.* boursier (-ère *f*) *m*; *he is an apt* ~ il apprend vite; '**schol·ar·ly** *adj.* savant; érudit; '**schol·ar·ship** érudition *f*, science *f*; *souv.* humanisme *m*; *univ.* bourse *f* (d'études).

scho·las·tic [skɔ'læstik] (~*ally*) scolaire; *fig.* pédant; *phls.* scolastique (*a. su./m*).

school[1] [sku:l] *see* **shoal**[1].

school[2] [~] **1.** école *f* (*a. fig. de pensée etc.*); académie *f*; *at* ~ à l'école; *grammar* ~ lycée *m*, collège *m*; *high* ~ *Angl.* lycée *m* (*souv.* de jeunes filles); *Am. et écoss.* collège *m*, école *f* secondaire; *primary* ~ école *f* primaire; *public* ~ *Angl.* grande école *f* d'enseignement secondaire; *Am. et écoss.* école *f* communale; *secondary modern* ~ collège *m* moderne; *technical* ~ école *f* des arts et métiers; *see a.* **board-**~; *put to* ~ envoyer à l'école; **2.** instruire; habituer; discipliner; '**~·boy** écolier *m*, élève *m*; '**~·fel·low**, '**~·mate** camarade *mf* de classe; '**~·girl** élève *f*, écolière *f*; '**school·ing** instruction *f*, éducation *f*.

school...: '**~·leav·er** jeune *mf* qui a terminé ses études scolaires; '**~·man** scolastique *m*; *Am.* professeur *m*; '**~·mas·ter** *école primaire*: instituteur *m*; *lycée, collège*: professeur *m*; '**~·mis·tress** institutrice *f*; *professeur m*; '**~·room** (salle *f* de) classe *f*.

schoon·er ['sku:nə] schooner *m*;

goélette *f*; *Am.* chope *f*, verre *m* de bière.

sci·at·i·ca ⚕ [sai'ætikə] sciatique *f*.

sci·ence ['saiəns] science *f*, -s *f/pl.* (*a.* † = *savoir*); '**~·fic·tion** science-fiction *f*.

sci·en·tif·ic [saiən'tifik] (~*ally*) scientifique; *box.* qui possède la science du combat; ~ *man* homme *m* de science.

sci·en·tist ['saiəntist] homme *m* de science; scientifique *mf*; ♀ *Am.* Scientiste *m* (chrétien).

scin·til·late ['sintileit] scintiller, étinceler; **scin·til'la·tion** scintillement *m*.

sci·on ['saiən] ✿ scion *m*; *fig.* rejeton *m*, descendant *m*.

scis·sion ['siʒn] cisaillage *m*; *fig.* scission *f*, division *f*; **scis·sors** ['sizəz] *pl.*: (*a pair of*) ~ (des) ciseaux *m/pl.*; '**scis·sor-tooth** *zo.* dent *f* carnassière.

scle·ro·sis ⚕ [skliə'rousis] sclérose *f*.

scoff [skɔf] **1.** sarcasme *m*; **2.** se moquer; ~ *at s.o.* railler q., se moquer de q.; '**scoff·er** moqueur (-euse *f*) *m*, gausseur (-euse *f*) *m*.

scold [skould] **1.** mégère *f*; **2.** gronder, crier (contre, *at*); '**scold·ing** réprimande *f*, semonce *f*.

scol·lop ['skɔləp] *see* **scallop**.

sconce[1] F [skɔns] tête *f*; jugeote *f*.

sconce[2] [~] bougeoir *m*; bobèche *f*; applique *f*; flambeau *m* (*de piano*).

sconce[3] *univ.* [~] mettre à l'amende.

scon(e) *cuis.* [skɔn] galette *f* au lait.

scoop [sku:p] **1.** pelle *f* à main; ⚓ épuisette *f*; ⊕, 🍴 cuiller *f*; ⚒ curette *f*; *sl.* rafle *f*, coup *m*; *sl.* (primeur *f* d'une) nouvelle *f* sensationnelle; **2.** (*usu.* ~ *out*) écoper (*l'eau*); excaver; évider; *sl.* publier une nouvelle à sensation avant (*un autre journal etc.*); *sl.* ~ *a large profit* faire une belle rafle.

scoot·er ['sku:tə] *enfants*: trottinette *f*, patinette *f*; *mot.* scooter *m*; motoscooter *m*.

scope [skoup] étendue *f*, portée *f*; liberté *f*, jeu *m*; espace *m*; but *m*; *have free* ~ avoir toute liberté (pour, *to*).

scorch [skɔːtʃ] *v/t.* roussir, brûler; *v/i.* F *mot.* brûler le pavé; '**scorch·er** F journée *f* torride; *mot.* chauffard *m*; *cycl.* cycliste *m* casse-cou.

score [skɔː] **1.** (en)coche *f*; *peau*:

éraflure *f*; (trait *m* de) repère *m*;
vingtaine *f*; *sp*. points *m/pl.*, total *m*;
foot. score *m*; *fig*. sujet *m*, point *m*,
raison *f*; ♪ partition *f*; *sl*. aubaine *f*,
coup *m* de fortune; *three* ~ soixante;
run up a ~ contracter une dette; *on
the* ~ *of* pour cause de; à titre de;
what's the ~? où en est le jeu?; *get
the* ~ faire le nombre de points
voulu; 2. *v/t*. entailler; (*a*. ~ *up*) inscrire, enregistrer; *sp*. compter,
marquer (*les points*); gagner (*une
partie, a. fig.*); remporter (*un succès*);
♪ noter (*un air*), orchestrer, arranger;
souligner (*une erreur, un passage*);
Am. F réprimander (*q.*), laver la tête
à (*q.*); ~ *out* rayer; *v/i*. gagner; *sp*., *a*.
cartes: faire *ou* marquer des points;
foot. enregistrer un but; *sl*. remporter un succès; *sl*. ~ *off* s.o. faire
pièce à q.; **'scor·er** *sp*. marqueur
(-euse *f*) *m* (*foot*. d'un but).

sco·ri·a ['skɔːriə], *pl*. **-ri·ae** ['~riː]
scorie *f*.

scorn [skɔːn] 1. mépris *m*, dédain *m*;
2. mépriser, dédaigner; **'scorn·er**
contempteur (-trice *f*) *m*; **scorn·ful**
□ ['~ful] méprisant.

Scor·pi·o *astr*. ['skɔːpiou] le Scorpion *m*.

scor·pi·on *zo*. ['skɔːpjən] scorpion
m.   [Scot *m*.]

Scot[1] [skɔt] Écossais(e *f*) *m*; *hist*.]

scot[2] [~] *hist*. écot *m*; compte *m*; ~ *and
lot* taxes *f/pl.* communales.

Scotch[1] [skɔtʃ] 1. écossais; 2. *ling*.
écossais *m*; F whisky *m*; *the* ~ *pl*.
les Écossais *m/pl*.

scotch[2] [~] 1. entaille *f*; *sp*. ligne *f* de
limite; 2. mettre hors de combat *ou*
hors d'état de nuire.

scotch[3] [~] 1. cale *f*; taquet *m* d'arrêt; 2. caler (*une roue*); *fig*. faire casser.

Scotch·man ['skɔtʃmən] Écossais *m*.

scot-free ['skɔt'friː] indemne.

Scots *ecoss*. [skɔts], **'Scots·man** *see
Scotch(man)*.

Scot·tish ['skɔtiʃ] écossais.

scoun·drel ['skaundrəl] scélérat *m*;
vaurien *m*; **'scoun·drel·ly** *adj*. scélérat, vil.

scour[1] ['skauə] nettoyer; frotter;
curer (*un fossé, un port*); décaper
(*une surface métallique*).

scour[2] [~] *v/i*. ~ *about* battre la campagne; *v/t*. parcourir; écumer (*les
mers*).

scourge [skəːdʒ] 1. fléau *m* (*a. fig.*);
eccl. discipline *f*; 2. fouetter; *fig*.
affliger.

scout[1] [skaut] 1. éclaireur *m*, avant-
coureur *m*; ⚔ reconnaissance *f*; ⚓
vedette *f*, croiseur *m*, éclaireur *m*; ✈
avion *m* de reconnaissance; *univ*.
garçon *m* de service; *Boy* ⚜s *pl*.
(boys-)scouts *m/pl.*; ⚔ ~ *party* reconnaissance *f*; 2. aller en reconnaissance.

scout[2] [~] repousser avec mépris.

scow ⚓ [skau] chaland *m*; (*a. ferry-*
~) toue *f*.

scowl [skaul] 1. air *m* renfrogné;
2. se renfrogner, F regarder noir.

scrab·ble ['skræbl] jouer des pieds
et des mains; chercher à quatre
pattes (*qch., for s.th.*); gratter çà et
là.

scrag [skræg] 1. *fig*. personne *f ou*
bête *f* décharnée; ~(-end) (*of mutton*) collet *m* (de mouton); 2. *sl*. garrotter; **scrag·gi·ness** ['~inis] maigreur *f*; **'scrag·gy** □ maigre, décharné.   [le camp!]

scram *Am. sl*. [skræm] fiche-moi]

scram·ble ['skræmbl] 1. monter *etc*.
à quatre pattes; se bousculer (pour
avoir qch., *for s.th.*); jouer des pieds
et des mains (*a. fig.*); ~*d eggs* *pl*.
œufs *m/pl*. brouillés; 2. marche *f
etc*. difficile; lutte *f*, mêlée *f*.

scrap [skræp] 1. petit morceau *m*;
bout *m*; *terrain*: parcelle *f* (*a. fig.*);
journal: coupure *f*; *pain, étoffe*:
bribe *f*; ⊕ déchets *m/pl.*; *sl*. rixe *f*,
querelle *f*; *box*. match (*pl*. match[e]s)
m; ~s *pl*. restes *m/pl.*; débris *m/pl.*;
péj. ~ *of paper* chiffon *m* de papier;
2. mettre au rebut; mettre hors
service; *fig*. mettre au rancart; **'~-
book** album *m* (de découpures).

scrape [skreip] 1. coup *m* de grattoir; grincement *m*; *fig*. mince
couche *f*; F embarras *m*, mauvais
pas *m*; 2. *v/t*. gratter, racler; écorcher (*la peau*); décrotter (*les souliers*); ~ *together* (*ou up*) amasser peu
à peu; ~ *acquaintance with* faire connaissance casuellement avec (*q.*); *v/i*.
gratter; s'érafler; grincer (*violon*);
'scrap·er grattoir *m*, racloir *m*;
souliers: décrottoir *m*; *personne*: ra-
cleur *m*; **'scrap·ing** raclage *m*; ~s
pl. raclures *f/pl.*; grattures *f/pl.*;
bribes *f/pl.*, restes *m/pl.*; *fig*. sous
m/pl. amassés un à un.

scrap...: '**~-heap** (tas *m* de) ferraille
f; *a. fig.* throw on the ~ mettre au
rancart, jeter au rebut; '**~-i-ron** ferraille *f*; débris *m/pl.* de fer; '**scrap-
py** F □ hétérogène; *fig.* décousu;
Am. a. batailleur (-euse *f*), querelleur (-euse *f*); '**scrap·yard** chantier
m de ferraille; *pour voitures:* cimetière *m* de voitures.

scratch [skrætʃ] **1.** coup *m* d'ongle
ou de griffe; égratignure *f*; gratte-
ment *m*; *surface polie:* rayure *f*; *sp.*
zéro *m*; *sp.* scratch *m*; *plume etc.:*
grincement *m*; come up to the ~ se
mettre en ligne; *fig.* se montrer à
la hauteur de l'occasion; **2.** improvisé; *sp.* mixte, sans homogénéité
(*équipe*); *parl.* par surprise; **3.** *v/t.*
gratter, égratigner; donner un coup
de griffe à; *sp.* scratcher; *sp.* décommander; ~ out rayer, biffer; gratter;
v/i. gratter; grincer; *sp.* déclarer
forfait; griffer (*chat*); '**scratch·y**
qui gratte, grinçant; inégal (-aux
m/pl.), peu assuré; *see scratch* 2.

scrawl [skrɔːl] **1.** griffonner; **2.** (*a.*
'**scrawl·ing**) griffonnage *m*.

scraw·ny *Am.* F ['skrɔːni] décharné.

scream [skriːm] **1.** cri *m* perçant;
F he is a ~ il est tordant; **2.** (*souv.* ~
out) pousser un cri perçant *ou*
d'angoisse; '**scream·ing** □ perçant; sifflant; criard (*personne, a.
couleur*); F tordant; à mourir de
rire; '**scream·y** F aigu(ë *f*); criard.

scree [skriː] éboulis *m*, pierraille *f*.

screech [skriːtʃ] *see scream*; '**~-owl**
orn. chouette *f* (*des clochers*).

screed [skriːd] longue liste *f*; longue
lettre *f*; jérémiade *f*.

screen [skriːn] **1.** ⚔, *phot.*, *cin.*, *radar,
a. meuble:* écran *m*; (*a.* draught-~)
paravent *m*; scrible *m*; sas *m*; *mot.*
rideaux *m/pl.* de côté; *fig.* rideau *m*;
on the ~ à l'écran; ~ advertising publicité *f* à l'écran; *phot.* focussing ~ verre
m dépoli; *cin.* ~ record film *m* de
reportage; *cin.* ~ test essai *m* à l'écran;
mot. ~ wiper essuie-glace *m*; **2.** abriter, protéger; ⚔ dérober (à, *from*);
voier (*le soleil etc.*); cacher; *cin.* mettre à l'écran; passer au crible; tamiser; *fig.* couvrir (*q.*); '**~-play** *cin.*
scénario *m*.

screw [skruː] **1.** vis *f*; tour *m* de vis;
tabac, papier, bonbons: cornet *m*;
fig. rigueur *f*; *sl.* paie *f*, salaire *m*,
appointements *m/pl.*; ⚓ hélice *f*; F
avare *m*; F he has a ~ loose il est
timbré *ou* *sl.* maboul; **2.** *v/t.* visser; *fig.* tordre; *fig.* opprimer; *fig.*
rappeler (*tout son courage*); *v/i.*
tourner; ~ round tordre (le cou, one's
head); ~ up visser; tortiller; plisser
(*les yeux*); pincer (*les lèvres*); ~ up
one's face faire une grimace; '**~-ball**
Am. sl. type *m* excentrique *ou*
dingo; '**~-driv·er** tournevis *m*; '**~-
jack** cric *m* (*menuisier:* à vis);
viole *f*; '**~-pro'pel·ler** hélice *f*; '**~-
steam·er** navire *m* à hélice.

scrib·ble ['skribl] **1.** griffonnage *m*;
écriture *f* illisible; **2.** *v/t.* griffonner;
~ over rendre illisible (*au moyen
du griffonnage*); *v/i.* F écrivailler;
'**scrib·bler** griffonneur (-euse *f*) *m*;
F écrivailleur (-euse *f*) *m*, gratte-
papier *m/inv.*

scribe [skraib] *bibl. ou co.* scribe *m*;
péj. plumitif *m*; ⊕ pointe *f* à tracer.

scrim·mage ['skrimidʒ] mêlée *f* (*a.
sp.*); escarmouche *f*.

scrimp [skrimp] **1.** *v/t.* être parcimonieux (-euse *f*) de, ménager
(-ère *f*) outre mesure; *v/i.* lésiner
sur tout; économiser outre mesure;
2. chiche (*personne*); (*a.* '**scrimp·y**)
insuffisant.

scrip † [skrip] titres *m/pl.*; certificat
m ou titre *m* provisoire.

script [skript] écriture *f*; manuscrit
m; *cin.* scénario *m*; ~s *pl. école etc.:*
copies *f/pl.* d'examen.

Scrip·tur·al ['skriptʃərəl] scriptural
(-aux *m/pl.*); biblique; **Scrip·ture**
['~tʃə] Écriture *f* sainte.

scrof·u·la ⚕ ['skrɔfjulə] scrofule *f*,
strume *f*; '**scrof·u·lous** □ scrofuleux (-euse *f*), strumeux (-euse *f*).

scroll [skroul] *papier:* rouleau *m*;
banderole *f* à inscription; *écriture:*
arabesque *f*; ⚛ spirale *f*; volute *f*
(*a. violon*).   [*m.*\

scro·tum *anat.* ['skroutəm] scrotum

scrounge [skraundʒ] chiper; écornifler (*un repas etc.*); ⚔ *sl.* récupérer.

scrub¹ [skrʌb] broussailles *f/pl.*;
arbuste *m* rabougri; F personne *f*
rabougrie.

scrub² [~] **1.** nettoyer; récurer;
2. *sp. Am.* équipe *f* numéro deux.

scrub·bing-brush ['skrʌbiŋbrʌʃ]
brosse *f* en chiendent *ou* de cuisine.

scrub·by ['skrʌbi] rabougri; insignifiant; couvert de broussailles.

scrub·wom·an *Am.* ['skrʌbwumən] femme *f* de ménage.

scruff of the neck ['skrʌfəvðə'nek] peau *f* de la nuque *ou* du cou.

scrum·mage ['skrʌmidʒ] mêlée *f* (*a. sp.*); escarmouche *f*.

scrump·tious *sl.* ['skrʌmpʃəs] exquis, épatant, délicieux (-euse *f*).

scrunch [skrʌntʃ] *v/t.* croquer; *v/i.* craquer.

scru·ple [skru:pl] **1.** scrupule *m* (*20 grains = 1,296 g*) (*a. = conscience*); make no ⁓ to (*inf.*) ne pas hésiter à (*inf.*); **2.** avoir des scrupules (à *inf.*, to *inf.*); ⊕ instruction *f*; '**scru·pu·lous** □ ['⁓ju-ləs] scrupuleux (-euse *f*) (sur *about*, *over*); *a.* méticuleux (-euse *f*) (*travail etc.*).

scru·ti·neer [skru:ti'niə] scrutateur *m*; '**scru·ti·nize** scruter; pointer (*des suffrages etc.*); '**scru·ti·ny** examen *m* minutieux *ou* attentif *ou* rigoureux; *suffrages*: vérification *f*.

scu·ba ['skju:bə] scaphandre *m* autonome; ⁓ **diving** plongée *f* sous-marine autonome.

scud [skʌd] **1.** fuite *f*, course *f* rapide; *nuages*: diablotins *m/pl.*; rafale *f*; embrun *m*; **2.** courir, fuir; ⚓ fuir devant le temps.

scuff [skʌf] *v/t.* effleurer; érafler; user; ⁓ up soulever; *v/i.* traîner les pieds; s'érafler (*cuir*).

scuf·fle ['skʌfl] **1.** rixe *f*, mêlée *f*; bagarre *f*; **2.** se bousculer; traîner les pieds.

scull ⚓ [skʌl] **1.** aviron *m* de couple; godille *f*; **2.** ramer en couple; godiller.

scul·ler·y ['skʌləri] arrière-cuisine *f*; ⁓*maid* laveuse *f* de vaisselle.

sculp·tor ['skʌlptə] sculpteur *m*.

sculp·ture ['skʌlptʃə] **1.** sculpture *f*; **2.** sculpter; orner de sculptures; '**sculp·tur·ing** sculpture *f*, sculptage *m*.

scum [skʌm] écume *f*; ⊕ scories *f/pl.*; *fig.* lie *f*, rebut *m*.

scup·per ⚓ ['skʌpə] dalot *m*.

scurf [skə:f] pellicules *f/pl.* (*du cuir chevelu*); ⊕ instruction *f*; '**scurf·y** □ pelliculeux (-euse *f*); ☞ ⁓ *affection* dartre *f*.

scur·ril·i·ty [skʌ'riliti] goujaterie *f*; grossièreté *f*; *action, personne:* bassesse *f*; '**scur·ril·ous** grossier (-ère *f*); bas(se *f*); ignoble.

scur·ry ['skʌri] **1.** *v/i.* se hâter; aller

à pas précipités; ⁓ through s.th. expédier qch.; **2.** débandade *f*; bousculade *f*.

scur·vy¹ ☞ ['skə:vi] scorbut *m*.

scur·vy² [⁓] vil(ain), bas(se *f*).

scut [skʌt] lapin, lièvre, etc.: couette *f*.

scutch·eon ['skʌtʃn] see escutcheon.

scut·tle¹ ['skʌtl] seau *m* à charbon.

scut·tle² [⁓] **1.** écoutillon *m*; hublot *m*; *mot.* bouclier *m* avant; *Am. toit etc.:* trappe *f*; **2.** saborder (*un navire*).

scut·tle³ [⁓] **1.** fuite *f*; *pol.* F lâchage *m*; **2.** décamper, filer; débouler; *pol.* F lâcher.

scythe ⚒ [saið] **1.** faux *f*; **2.** faucher.

sea [si:] mer *f*; *fig.* océan *m*; lame *f*, houle *f*; at ⁓ en mer; *fig.* dérouté; go to ⁓ se faire marin; *see* put 2; '⁓**board** littoral *m*; rivage *m*; '⁓**cap·tain** capitaine *m* de la marine; '⁓**far·ing** de mer; ⁓ *man* marin *m*; '⁓**food** *Am. a.* ⁓s *pl.* fruits *m/pl.* de mer (= *coquillages, crustacés et poissons*); '⁓**front** bord *m* de (la) mer; digue *f*, esplanade *f*; '⁓**go·ing** de haute mer; de long cours; maritime (*commerce*).

seal¹ *zo.* [si:l] phoque *m*.

seal² [⁓] **1.** *bouteille, distinction, a. lettre:* cachet *m*; *document:* sceau *m*; plomb *m*; ⊕ joint *m* étanche; great (*ou* broad) ⁓ grand sceau *m*; **2.** cacheter; sceller; (*a.* ⁓ up) fermer; *fig.* décider; *fig.* fixer; *fig.* ⁓ off boucher, fermer; ⁓ up fermer hermétiquement; ⁓ (with lead) plomber.

seal·er ⊕ ['si:lə] pince *f* à plomber.

sea-lev·el ['si:levl] niveau *m* de la mer.

seal·ing ['si:liŋ] scellage *m*; cachetage *m*; plombage *m*; fermeture *f*.

seal·ing-wax ['si:liŋwæks] cire *f* à cacheter.

seal·skin ['si:lskin] peau *f* de phoque; ✝ phoque *f*.

seam [si:m] **1.** couture *f* (*a. métall.*); ⊕ joint *m*; *géol.* couche *f*, veine *f*; *fig. visage:* ride *f*; *fig.* burst at the ⁓s craquer, crever; **2.** faire une couture à; ⊕ agrafer; couturer (*un visage*).

sea·man ['si:mən] marin *m*, matelot *m*; '**sea·man·ship** manœuvre *f*.

sea·mew ['si:mju:] mouette *f*, goéland *m*.

seam·less □ ['si:mlis] sans couture; ⊕ sans soudure.

seam·stress ['semstris] (ouvrière *f*) couturière *f*.

seam·y ['si:mi] qui montre les coutures; *fig.* ⁓ side dessous *m/pl.*, mauvais côté *m*.

sea...: '⁓·piece *peint.* marine *f*; '⁓·plane hydravion *m*; '⁓·port port *m* de mer; '⁓·pow·er *pol.* puissance *f* navale.

sear [siə] dessécher (*a. fig.*); faner (*les feuilles*); ✝ cautériser; *fig.* endurcir.

search [sɔːtʃ] **1.** recherche *f* (de, *for*); *admin.* visite *f*; *police:* perquisition *f*; fouille *f*; *in* ⁓ *of* à la recherche de; **2.** *v/t.* chercher dans (*qch.*); fouiller dans; visiter; ⚖ faire une perquisition dans; ✗ sonder; *fig.* scruter; ⁓ *out* dénicher; découvrir; *v/i.* faire des recherches; ⁓ *for* chercher (*qch.*); ⁓ *into* rechercher; '**search·er** (re)chercheur (-euse *f*) *m*; douanier *m*; ⚖ perquisiteur *m*; ✗ sonde *f*; '**search·ing** □ minutieux (-euse *f*); pénétrant (*regard, vent*); '**search·light** projection *f* électrique; ⚓ *etc.* projecteur *m*; '**search-war·rant** ⚖ ordre *m* de perquisition.

sea...: ⁓·scape ['si:skeip] *see* seapiece; '⁓·ser·pent serpent *m* de mer; '⁓·shore rivage *m*; côte *f*; plage *f*; '⁓·sick: be ⁓ avoir le mal de mer; '⁓·sick·ness mal *m* de mer; '⁓·side bord *m* de la mer; ⁓ resort plage *f*; bains *m/pl.* de mer; go to the ⁓ aller au bord de la mer.

sea·son ['si:zn] **1.** saison *f*; période *f*, temps *m*; époque *f*; *vét.* rut *m*; F abonnement *m*; *height of the* ⁓ (pleine) saison *f*; *in* (*good ou due*) ⁓ en temps voulu; *cherries are in* ⁓ c'est la saison des cerises; *out of* ⁓ hors de saison; *ne pas* (être) de saison; *for a* ⁓ pendant un *ou* quelque temps; *with the compliments of the* ⁓ meilleurs souhaits de nouvel an *etc.*; **2.** *v/t.* mûrir; dessécher (*le bois*); assaisonner (*a. fig.*), relever (de, *with*); *fig.* acclimater; *fig.* tempérer; *v/i.* se sécher (*bois*); mûrir; **sea·son·a·ble** □ de (la) saison; opportun; '**sea·son·a·ble·ness** opportunité *f*; **sea·son·al** □ ['si:znl] des saisons; ✝, ✿ saisonnier (-ère *f*); embauché pour les travaux de saison (*ouvrier*); '**sea·son·ing** dessèchement *m*; *cuis.* assaisonnement *m*,

condiment *m*; '**sea·son·'tick·et** carte *f* d'abonnement.

seat [si:t] **1.** siège *m* (*a.* ✗, ⊕); *théâ.*, *autobus:* place *f*; chaise *f*; banc *m*; (*a. country* ⁓) château *m*; *pantalon:* fond *m*; assiette *f* (*à cheval*); (*a. pilot's* ⁓) baquet *m*; ⁓ *of war* théâtre *m* de la guerre; **2.** (faire) asseoir; placer; fournir de chaises; poser; ⚙ caler; ⊕ faire reposer sur son siège; ⁓ *o.s.* s'asseoir; be ⁓ed être assis; avoir son siège (dans, *in*); '⁓·belt ceinture *f* de sécurité; '**seat·ed** assis; -**seat·er** surt. *mot.*, ✈: two-⁓ voiture *f* à deux places; appareil *m* biplace.

sea-ur·chin *zo.* ['si:ˈəːtʃin] oursin *m*; **sea·ward** ['⁓wəd] **1.** *adj.* qui porte au large; du large (*brise*); **2.** *adv.* (*a.* **sea·wards** ['⁓z]) vers le large *ou* la mer.

sea...: '⁓·weed ✿ algue *f*; varech *m*; '⁓·wor·thy navigable; qui tient la mer.

se·ba·ceous ✿ [si'beiʃəs] sébacé.

se·cant ⅄ ['si:kənt] **1.** sécant. **2.** sécante *f*.

séc·a·teur ✗ ['sekətəː] *usu.* (*a pair of*) ⁓s *pl.* (un) sécateur *m*.

se·cede [si'si:d] se séparer, faire scission (de, *from*); **se'ced·er** séparatiste *mf*; *eccl.* dissident(e *f*) *m*.

se·ces·sion [si'seʃn] scission *f*; sécession *f*; *eccl.* dissidence *f*; **se'ces·sion·ist** sécessioniste *mf*.

se·clude [si'kluːd] tenir éloigné; **se'clu·sion** [⁓ʒn] solitude *f*, isolement *m*.

sec·ond ['sekənd] **1.** □ second; deuxième; autre; *he is* ⁓ *to none* il ne le cède à personne (pour, *in*); on ⁓ *thoughts* toute réflexion faite; *the* ⁓ *of May* le deux Mai; *Charles the* ♀ Charles Deux; **2.** *temps:* seconde *f*; le (la) second(e *f*) *m ou* deuxième *mf*; *box.* second *m*; *duel:* témoin *m*; ✝ ⁓s *pl.* articles *m/pl.* de deuxième qualité; ✝ ⁓ *of exchange* seconde *f* de change; **3.** seconder; appuyer (*des débats, des troupes*); ✗ [si'kɔnd] mettre (*un officier*) en disponibilité; détacher; **sec·ond·ar·i·ness** ['sekəndərinis] caractère *m* secondaire *ou* peu important; '**sec·ond·ar·y** □ secondaire; auxiliaire; peu *ou* moins important; *see* school² 1; '**sec·ond·'best** numéro deux; deuxième; F *come off* ⁓ être battu; '**sec·ond·er**

parl. deuxième parrain *m; be the ~ of a motion* appuyer une proposition; **sec·ond-hand 1.** ['sekənd'hænd] d'occasion; *~ bookseller* bouquiniste *mf; ~ bookshop* librairie *f* d'occasion; **2.** ['sekəndhænd] aiguille *f* des secondes; trotteuse *f;* **'sec·ond·ly** en second lieu; deuxièmement; **'sec·ond·rate** inférieur(e *f*); de qualité inférieure; ✝ *~ quality* seconde qualité *f.*

se·cre·cy ['si:krisi] discrétion *f;* secret *m;* **se·cret** ['~krit] **1.** □ secret (-ète *f*); caché; retiré, isolé; discret (-ète *f*); **2.** secret *m; in ~* en secret; *be in the ~* être du *ou* dans le secret. [crétariat *m.*]

sec·re·tar·i·at(e) [sekri'tɛəriət] se-\ **sec·re·tar·y** ['sekrətri] secrétaire *mf;* dactylo *f;* ♀ *of State* ministre *m; Am.* ministre *m* des Affaires étrangères;* **'sec·re·tar·y·ship** secrétariat *m;* fonction *f* de secrétaire; *pol.* ministère *m.*

se·crete [si'kri:t] cacher; ✝ recéler; *physiol.* sécréter; **se'cre·tion** *physiol.* sécrétion *f;* ✝ recel *m;* **se'cre·tive** *fig.* réservé, F cachottier (-ère *f*).

sect [sekt] secte *f;* **sec·tar·i·an** [~'tɛəriən] sectaire (*a. su./m*).

sec·tion ['sekʃn] section *f (a.* ✻, ♀, △, ✕, *typ., zo.*); ✕ groupe *m* de combat; *microscope etc.:* lame *f* mince; △ coupe *f,* profil *m; typ.* paragraphe *m,* alinéa *m;* division *f;* tranche *f (a. d'oranges);* ▦ secteur *m, Am.* compartiment *m; Am. ville:* quartier *m;* **'sec·tion·al** □ de classe *ou* parti; en profil, en coupe; ⊕ démontable; ⊕ sectionnel(le *f*); **'sec·tion-mark** paragraphe *m.*

sec·tor ['sektə] ✕, ♀, ⊕, *admin., astr., cin.* secteur *m;* ♀ compas *m* de proportion.

sec·u·lar □ ['sekjulə] séculier (-ère *f*); laïque; très ancien(ne *f*); **sec·u·lar·i·ty** [~'læriti] mondanité *f;* laïcité *f; clergé:* sécularité *f;* **'sec·u·lar·ize** séculariser; laïciser (*une école*); désaffecter (*une église*).

se·cure [si'kjuə] **1.** □ sûr; assuré; en sûreté; à l'abri (de *against, from*); ferme; **2.** mettre en sûreté *ou* à l'abri (de *from, against*); assurer, fixer, retenir; se procurer; s'emparer de; garantir (*une dette*); nantir (*un prêteur*); ✕ fortifier.

se·cu·ri·ty [si'kjuəriti] sécurité *f;* sûreté *f;* solidité *f;* caution *f,* garantie *f; securities pl.* titres *m/pl.,* valeurs *f/pl.; public securities pl.* fonds *m/pl.* d'État; ♀ *Council* Conseil *m* de sécurité; ♀ *Forces* forces *f/pl.* de sécurité; *be a ~ risk* constituer un risque pour la sécurité, ne pas être sûr.

se·dan [si'dæn] (*voiture f* à) conduite intérieure, limousine *f; (a. ~ chair)* chaise *f* à porteur.

se·date □ [si'deit] (re)posé; calme; **se'date·ness** calme *m;* manière *f* posée.

se·da·tion ✻ [si'deiʃən] sédation *f.*

sed·a·tive *usu.* ✻ ['sedətiv] calmant (*a. su./m*).

sed·en·tar·i·ness ['sedntərinis] sédentarité *f;* vie *f* sédentaire; **'sed·en·tar·y** □ sédentaire (*emploi, oiseau, troupes, vie*); assis.

sedge [sedʒ] ♀ carex *m;* F joncs *m/pl.*

sed·i·ment ['sediment] sédiment *m; vin:* lie *f;* ⌃ résidu *m; géol.* atterrissement *m;* **sed·i·men·ta·ry** *géol.* [~'mentəri] sédimentaire.

se·di·tion [si'diʃn] sédition *f;* **se'di·tious** □ [~ʃəs] séditieux (-euse *f*).

se·duce [si'dju:s] séduire; **se'duc·er** séducteur (-trice *f*) *m;* **se·duc·tion** [~'dʌkʃn] séduction *f;* **se'duc·tive** □ séduisant.

sed·u·lous □ ['sedjuləs] assidu.

see¹ [si:] [*irr.*] *v/i.* voir; *fig.* comprendre; *I ~* je comprends; *~ about* s'occuper de (*qch.*); *~ through* pénétrer les intentions de (*q.*), pénétrer (*qch.*); *~ to* s'occuper de; veiller à; *v/t.* voir; s'assurer (que, *that*); visiter; accompagner; remarquer; consulter (*le médecin*); comprendre; *~ s.th. done* veiller à ce que qch. soit faite *ou* se fasse; *go to ~ s.o.* aller voir q.; rendre visite à q.; *~ s.o. home* accompagner q. chez lui; *~ off* reconduire, conduire (*un hôte, une visite à la gare etc.*); *~ out* accompagner (*q.*) jusqu'à la porte; mener (*qch.*) à bonne fin; *~ through* assister jusqu'au bout à (*qch.*); soutenir (*q.*) jusqu'au bout; *live to ~* vivre assez longtemps pour voir.

see² [~] évêché *m;* archevêché *m; Holy* ♀ Saint-Siège *m.*

seed [si:d] **1.** grain(e *f*) *m; coll., a. fig.* semence *f;* ✝ lignée *f; go (ou run) to ~* s'affricher (*terrain*); monter en graine (*plante*); *fig.* se décatir; **2.** *v/t.* semer; enlever la graine de (*un fruit*); *sp.* trier (*les joueurs*); ~ed *players* têtes *f/pl.* de série; *v/i.* venir à graine; monter en graine; s'égrener; '~·**bed** *see* seed-plot; **seed·i·ness** ['~inis] état *m* râpé *ou* misérable; F (état *m* de) malaise *f*; '**seed·ling** ✎ (jeune) plant *m*; '**seed-plot** ✎ germoir *m*; **seeds·man** ['~zmən] grainetier *m*; '**seed·y** râpé, usé; F indisposé, souffrant.

see·ing ['si:iŋ] **1.** *su.* vue *f*, vision *f*; *worth* ~ qui vaut la peine d'être vu; **2.** *cj.*: ~ *that* puisque, étant donné que.

seek [si:k] [*irr.*] (*a.* ~ *after, for*) (re)chercher; poursuivre; *be to* ~ *fig.* être peu clair; '**seek·er** chercheur (-euse *f*) *m*.

seem [si:m] sembler; paraître; '**seem·ing 1.** □ apparent; soidisant; **2.** apparence *f*; '**seem·li·ness** bienséance *f*, décence *f*; beauté *f*; '**seem·ly** convenable, agréable à voir.

seen [si:n] *p.p. de* see[1].

seep [si:p] (s'in)filtrer; suinter; '**seep·age** suintement *m*, infiltration *f*.

seer ['si:ə] voyant(e *f*) *m*, prophète *m*.

see·saw ['si:'sɔ:] **1.** bascule *f*; balançoire *f*; **2.** basculer; *fig.* balancer (*personne*).

seethe [si:ð] bouillonner; s'agiter (*a. fig.*); *fig.* grouiller (de, *with*).

seg·ment ['segmənt] ⚕ *etc.* segment *m*; *orange:* tranche *f*.

seg·re·gate ['segrigeit] (se) séparer; **seg·re·ga·tion** séparation *f*; *pol.* ségrégation *f*; **seg·re·ga·tion·ist** ségrégationniste *mf, adj.*

seine [sein] *filet:* seine *f*.

sei·sin ⚖ ['si:zin] saisine *f*.

seis·mic ['saizmik] sismique; **seis·mo·graph** ['saizməgra:f] sismographe *m*; **seis·mol·o·gy** [~'mɔlədʒi] sismologie *f*.

seize [si:z] *v/t.* saisir (*a.* = *comprendre*); s'emparer de; ⚓ amarrer (*des cordages*), velter (*un espar*); ⚖, *admin.* confisquer; *v/i.* ⊕ gripper; (se) caler; ~ *upon* saisir (*a. fig.*); '**seiz·ing** saisie *f*; empoignement *m*; ⊕ grippage *m*; ⚓ amarrage *m*; **sei·zure** ['~ʒə] saisie *f* (*a.* ⚖); 🔫 (attaque *f* d')apoplexie *f*.

sel·dom *adv.* ['seldəm] peu souvent, rarement.

se·lect [si'lekt] **1.** choisir; sélectionner; trier; **2.** choisi; d'élite; très fermé (*cercle*); **se'lec·tion** choix *m*; ♀, *zo.* sélection *f*; ♪ sélection *f* (sur, *from*; emprunté à q., *from* s.o.); morceaux *m/pl.* choisis (de, *from*); **se'lec·tive** □ de sélection; *radio:* sélecteur (-trice *f*); sélectif (-ive *f*); **se·lec·tiv·i·ty** [~'tiviti] *radio:* sélectivité *f*; **se'lect·man** *Am.* membre *m* du conseil municipal (*Nouvelle-Angleterre*); **se'lec·tor** *radio:* sélecteur *m*.

self [self] **1.** *pron.* même; ✝ *ou* F *see* myself; **2.** *adj.* automatique; de même; non mélangé; ♀ de couleur uniforme; **3.** *su.* (*pl.* **selves** [selvz]) personnalité *f*; moi *m*; *my poor* ~ ma pauvre (petite) personne *f*; '~-a'**base·ment** humiliation *f* de soi-même; '~-'**act·ing** automatique; '~-**ad'he·sive** auto-adhésif (-ive *f*); '~-**as'ser·tion** caractère *m* impérieux; autoritarisme *m*; '~-**as'ser·tive** impérieux (-euse *f*); autoritaire; '~-**as'sur·ance** confiance *f* en soi; assurance *f*; '~-**as'sured** sûr de soi; plein d'assurance; '~-'**cen·tred**, *Am.* '~-'**cen·tered** égocentrique; '~-**com'mand** maîtrise *f* de soi; sang-froid *m*; '~-**con'ceit** suffisance *f*, vanité *f*; '~-**con'ceit·ed** suffisant, vaniteux (-euse *f*); '~-**con·fi·dence** confiance *f* en soi; '~-**con·fi·dent** sûr de soi, plein de confiance en soi; '~-'**con·scious** gêné; contraint; '~-**con·tained** ['~kən'teind] indépendant; réservé (*personne*); ~ *country* pays *m* qui se suffit à lui-même; ~ *flat* appartement *m* indépendant; '~-**con'trol** maîtrise *f* de soi; possession *f* de soi-même; '~-**de'fence** défense *f* personnelle; *in* ~ en légitime défense; '~-**de'ni·al** abnégation *f* (de soi); '~-**de·ter·mi·'na·tion** libre disposition *f* de soi-même; '~-'**ed·u·cat·ed** autodidacte; '~-**es'teem** respect *m* de soi; '~-**ev·i·dent** évident en soi; '~-**ex'plan·a·to·ry** évident (en soi), qui s'explique de soi-même; '~-'**gov·ern·ing** autonome; '~-**im'port·ance** suffisance *f*, présomption *f*; '~-**im'port·ant** suffisant, présomptueux (-euse *f*); '~-**in·ter·est** intérêt *m* personnel; '**self·ish** □ égoïste,

intéressé; '**self·ish·ness** égoïsme *m*.
self...: '**~·less** altruiste, désintéressé;
'**~·'made**: ~ *man* fils *m* de ses
œuvres; parvenu *m*; '**~·o'pin·ion-
at·ed** entêté, opiniâtre; '**~·'pit·y**
apitoiement *m* sur soi-même; '**~-
'por·trait** autoportrait *m*; '**~·pos-
'sessed** calme, qui a du sang-froid;
'**~·pos'ses·sion** aplomb *m*, sang-
froid *m*; '**~·pre·ser'va·tion** conservation *f* de soi-même; '**~·pro'pelled**
autopropulsé; '**~·re'gard** respect *m*
de soi; '**~·re'li·ance** indépendance
f; '**~·re'li·ant** indépendant; '**~-
re'spect** respect *m* de soi; '**~-
re'spec·ting** qui se respecte; '**~-
'right·eous** pharisaïque; '**~·same**
poét. identique; '**~·'seek·ing** intéressé, égoïste; '**~·'serv·ice res·tau-
rant** restaurant *m* libre-service, self-
service *m*; '**~·'start·er** *mot.* (auto-)
démarreur *m*; '**~·suf'fi·cien·cy**
indépendance *f*; suffisance *f*; '**~-
'will** obstination *f*, opiniâtreté *f*; '**~-
'willed** obstiné, opiniâtre; '**~-
'wind·ing** (à remontage) automatique.

sell [sel] [*irr.*] **1.** *v/t.* vendre (*a. fig.*); F
tromper; *Am.* F convaincre, persua-
der; F ~ (*out*) vendre tout son stock de
(*qch*); † ~ *off* solder; liquider; ~ *up*
vendre (*q.*); *v/i.* se vendre; être en
vente; † ~ *off* (*ou* out) liquider; tout
vendre; **2.** F déception *f*; *sl.* blague *f*;
'**sell·er** vendeur (-euse *f*) *m*; † *good
etc.* ~ article *m* de bonne *etc.* vente;
best ~ livre *m* à (gros) succès, best-
seller *m*; '**sell·out** F succès *m* énorme, pièce *f etc.* pour laquelle tous les
billets sont vendus; trahison *f*; capitulation *f*.

selt·zer ['seltsə] (*a.* ~ *water*) eau *f* de
Seltz.

sel·vage, **sel·vedge** ['selvidʒ] *tex.*
lisière *f*; *géol.* salbande *f*.

se·man·tics [si'mæntiks] *sg.* sémantique *f*.

sem·a·phore ['seməfɔ:] **1.** sémaphore *m*; signal *m* à bras; **2.** transmettre par sémaphore *ou* par signaux à bras.

sem·blance ['sembləns] semblant
m, apparence *f*.

sem·i... [semi] semi-; demi-; à
moitié; mi-; '**~·breve** ♪ ronde *f*;
'**~·cir·cle** demi-cercle *m*; '**~·co·lon**
point-virgule (*pl.* points-virgules)
m; '**~·con'duc·tor** ⚡ semi-conduc-

teur *m*; '**~·'fi·nal** *sp.* demi-finale *f*;
'**~·man·u'fac·tured** semi-ouvré.

sem·i·nal ['si:minl] séminal (-aux
m/pl.); *fig.* embryonnaire.

sem·i·nar ['seminɑ:] *univ.* séminaire
m.

sem·i·nar·y ['seminəri] *fig.* pensionnat *m* (*de jeunes filles*); *eccl.* séminaire
m.

sem·i·of·fi·cial ['semiə'fiʃl] officieux (-euse *f*), semi-officiel(le *f*).

sem·i·prec·ious ['semi'preʃəs]: ~
stone pierre *f* fine *ou* sémi-précieuse.

sem·i·qua·ver ♪ ['semikweivə]
double croche *f*.

Sem·ite ['si:mait] Sémite *mf*; **Se-
mit·ic** [si'mitik] sémitique.

sem·i·tone ♪ ['semitoun] demi-ton
m, semi-ton *m*.   [voyelle *f*.\
sem·i·vow·el ['semi'vauəl] semi-\}
sem·o·li·na [semə'li:nə] semoule *f*.

sem·pi·ter·nal □ *poét.* [sempi-
'tə:nl] éternel(le *f*).

semp·stress ['sempstris] (ouvrière
f) couturière *f*.

sen·ate ['senit] sénat *m*; *univ.* conseil *m* de l'université.

sen·a·tor ['senətə] sénateur *m*; **sen-
a·to·ri·al** □ [ˌ'tɔ:riəl] sénatorial
(-aux *m/pl.*).

send [send] [*irr.*] *v/t.* envoyer; expédier; diriger (*un coup, une balle*);
remettre (*de l'argent*); rendre (*fou
etc.*); ~ *s.o.* (*gér.*) faire q. (*inf.*); *see
pack* 2; ~ *forth* envoyer (dehors);
répandre; émettre; lancer; ⚓ pousser; ~ *in* faire (r)entrer; envoyer; ~
in one's name se faire annoncer; ~
off expédier; faire partir; envoyer;
~ *up* faire monter (*a. fig.*); ~ *word to
s.o.* envoyer un mot à q.; *v/i.*: ~
for faire venir, envoyer chercher;
'**send·er** envoyer (-euse *f*) *m*;
lettre, télégramme: expéditeur (-trice
f) *m*; *tél.* transmetteur *m*; '**send-
'off** fête *f* d'adieu; *sl.* recommandation *f*, début *m*.

se·nile ['si:nail] sénile; **se·nil·i·ty**
[si'niliti] sénilité *f*.

sen·ior ['si:njə] **1.** aîné; plus âgé (que,
to); supérieur (à, to); premier (-ère *f*)
(*commis etc.*); ~ *citizens pl.* personnes
f/pl. âgées; † ~ *partner* associé *m*
principal; **2.** aîné(e *f*) *m*; le (la) plus
ancien(ne *f*) *m*; supérieur(e *f*) *m*;
Am. univ. étudiant(e *f*) *m* de quatrième année; *he is my ~ by a year, he
is a year my ~* il est mon aîné d'un an;

sen·ior·i·ty [si:ni'ɔriti] priorité *f* d'âge; *grade:* ancienneté *f.*

sen·sa·tion [sen'seiʃn] sensation *f (a. fig. = effet sensationnel);* sentiment *m,* impression *f;* **sen'sa·tion·al** □ sensationnel(le *f);* à sensation (*roman etc.*); **sen'sa·tion·al·ism** recherche *f* du sensationnel.

sense [sens] **1.** sens *m;* sentiment *m;* sensation *f;* intelligence *f;* signification *f;* ~ *of direction* sens *m* de l'orientation; ~ *of duty* sentiment *m* du devoir; ~ *of humo(u)r* (sens *m* de l')humour *m;* ~ *of time* notion *f* de l'heure; *common* (*ou good*) ~ sens *m* commun; bon sens *m;* *in one's* ~*s* sain d'esprit; *be out of one's* ~*s* avoir perdu le sens *ou* la tête; *bring s.o. to his* ~ remener q. à la raison; *make* ~ être compréhensible; *make* ~ *of* arriver à comprendre; *talk* ~ parler raison; **2.** sentir; *Am.* comprendre.

sense·less □ ['senslis] insensé, déraisonnable, stupide; sans connaissance, inanimé; **'sense·less·ness** stupidité *f,* absurdité *f;* insensibilité *f.*

sen·si·bil·i·ty [sensi'biliti] sensibilité *f* (à, *to*); conscience *f* (*de to, of*); ~ *to light* sensibilité *f* à la lumière.

sen·si·ble □ ['sensəbl] sensible, perceptible; appréciable; conscient (de, *of*); raisonnable, sensé; *fig.* pratique; *be* ~ *of* se rendre compte de (*qch.*); avoir conscience de (*qch.*); **'sen·si·ble·ness** bon sens *m;* intelligence *f;* raison *f.*

sen·si·tive □ ['sensitiv] sensible (à, *to*); susceptible; ombrageux (-euse *f*) (à l'endroit de, *with regard to*); ⁜ instable (*marché*); *phot.* sensible (*papier*), impressionnable (*plaque*); **'sen·si·tive·ness, sen·si·tiv·i·ty** [~'tiviti] sensibilité *f* (à, *to*).

sen·si·tize *phot.* ['sensitaiz] rendre sensible.

sen·so·ri·al [sen'sɔ:riəl], **sen·so·ry** ['~səri] sensoriel(le *f*); des sens.

sen·su·al □ ['sensjuəl] sensuel(le *f*); **'sen·su·al·ism** sensualité *f;* *phls.* sensualisme *m;* **'sen·su·al·ist** sensualiste *mf;* voluptueux (-euse *f*); **sen·su·al·i·ty** [~'æliti] sensualité *f.*

sen·su·ous □ ['sensjuəs] qui provient des sens; voluptueux (-euse*f*).

sent [sent] *prét. et p.p. de* send.

sen·tence ['sentəns] **1.** ⚖ jugement *m;* condamnation *f;* peine *f;* *gramm.* phrase *f;* *serve one's* ~ subir sa peine; *see life;* **2.** condamner (à, *to*).

sen·ten·tious [sen'tenʃəs] □ sentencieux (-euse *f*); **sen'ten·tious·ness** caractère *m ou* ton *m* sentencieux.

sen·tient ['senʃnt] sensible.

sen·ti·ment ['sentimənt] sentiment *m;* opinion *f;* sentimentalité *f;* toast *m;* *see* ~*ality;* **sen·ti·men·tal** □ [~'mentl] sentimental (-aux *m/pl.*); ~ *value* valeur *f* affective; **sen·ti·men·tal·i·ty** [~'tæliti] sentimentalité *f;* sensiblerie *f.*

sen·ti·nel ['sentinl], **sen·try** ['sentri] ⚔ sentinelle *f;* factionnaire *m.*

sen·try...: '~**box** guérite *f;* '~**go** faction *f.*

se·pal ♀ ['si:pəl] sépale *m.*

sep·a·ra·bil·i·ty [sepərə'biliti] séparabilité *f;* **'sep·a·ra·ble** □ séparable; **sep·a·rate 1.** □ ['seprit] séparé, détaché; indépendant; particulier (-ère *f*); ~ *property* biens *m/pl.* réservés; **2.** ['~əreit] (se) séparer; (se) détacher; (se) désunir; *v/t.:* ~*o.s. from* se séparer de; rompre avec; **sep·a·ra·tion** séparation *f* (d'avec q., *from s.o.*); *opt. etc.* écart *m;* **sep·a·ra·tist** ['~ərətist] *pol., a. eccl.* séparatiste *mf;* **sep·a·ra·tor** ['~reitə] séparateur *m;* classeur *m;* (*a. cream-*~) écrémeuse *f.*

se·pi·a *icht., a. peint.* ['si:pjə] sépia *f.*

se·poy ['si:pɔi] cipaye *m* (= *soldat de l'Inde anglaise*).

sep·sis ⚕ ['sepsis] septicémie *f;* putréfaction *f.*

Sep·tem·ber [sep'tembə] septembre *m.*

sep·ten·ni·al □ [sep'tenjəl] septennal (-aux *m/pl.*); ~*ly* tous les sept ans.

sep·tic ⚕ ['septik] septique.

sep·tu·a·ge·nar·i·an ['septjuedʒi-'nɛəriən] septuagénaire (*a. su.*).

se·pul·chral [si'pʌlkrəl] sépulcral (-aux *m/pl.*); **sep·ul·chre** *poét.* ['sepəlkə] **1.** sépulcre *m,* tombeau *m;* **2.** ensevelir; servir de tombe(au) à; **sep·ul·ture** ['sepəltʃə] sépulture *f.*

se·quel ['si:kwəl] suite *f;* *fig. a.* conséquence *f;* *in the* ~ par la suite.

se·quence ['si:kwəns] suite *f;* succession *f*; ordre *m*; ♪, *cartes, cin.*: séquence *f*; *cin*. F scène *f*; *gramm.* ⁓ *of tenses* concordance *f* des temps; **'se·quent** conséquent; consécutif (-ive *f*) (à [*up*]*on, to*); qui suit.

se·ques·ter [si'kwestə] *see* sequestrate; ⁓ *o.s.* se retirer (*de, from*); ⁓ed retiré, isolé; ⚖ en séquestre.

se·ques·trate ⚖ [si'kwestreit] séquestrer (*des biens*), mettre en séquestre; confisquer; **se·ques·tra·tion** [si:kwes'treiʃn] retraite *f*; confiscation *f*; ⚖ séquestration *f*; **'se·ques·tra·tor** ⚖ séquestre *m*.

se·quin ['si:kwin] paillette *f*.

se·quoi·a ♀ [si'kwɔiə] séquoia *m*.

se·ragl·io [se'rɑ:liou] sérail *m*.

ser·aph ['serəf], *pl. a.* -a·phim ['⁓fim] séraphin *m*; **se·raph·ic** [se'ræfik] (⁓ally) séraphique.

Serb [sə:b], **Ser·bi·an** ['⁓jən] **1.** serbe; **2.** *ling.* serbe *m*; Serbe *mf*.

sere *poét.* [siə] flétri, desséché.

ser·e·nade [seri'neid] **1.** ♪ sérénade *f*; **2.** donner une sérénade à.

se·rene □ [si'ri:n] serein, calme, paisible; *titre*: ♀ sérénissime; *Your* ♀ *Highness* votre Altesse *f* sérénissime; **se·ren·i·ty** [si'reniti] sérénité *f* (*a. titre*); calme *m*.

serf [sə:f] serf (serve *f*) *m*; **'serf·age**, **'serf·dom** servage *m*.

serge [sə:dʒ] serge *f*; *cotton* ⁓ sergé *m*.

ser·geant ✕ ['sɑ:dʒnt] sergent *m*; (*a. police* ⁓) brigadier *m*; **'⁓- 'ma·jor** ✕ adjudant *m*.

se·ri·al □ ['siəriəl] **1.** de série; en série; de reproduction en feuilleton (*droit*); ⁓ly en série, par série; en feuilleton; **2.** roman-feuilleton (*pl.* romans-feuilletons) *m*; **se·ri·al·ize** publier *ou* adapter en feuilleton *ou* épisodes (*un roman etc.*).

se·ries ['siəri:z] *sg., a. pl.* série *f*, suite *f* (*a.* ✍); ⚡ connect (*ou* join) in ⁓ grouper en série; ⁓ connexion montage *m* en série.

se·ri·ous □ ['siəriəs] sérieux (-euse *f*) (= *grave*; *réfléchi*; *sincère*; *gros, etc.*); be ⁓ ne pas plaisanter; **'se·rious·ness** gravité *f*; sérieux *m*.

ser·jeant *hist.* ['sɑ:dʒnt] (*a.* ⁓ *at law*) avocat *m* (supérieur); *Common* ♀ magistrat *m* de la corporation de Londres; *parl.* ♀-*at-arms* commandant *m* militaire du Parlement.

ser·mon ['sə:mən] sermon *m* (*a. fig.*); *catholique:* prône *m*, *protestant:* prêche *m*; **'ser·mon·ize** *v/i.* prêcher; *v/t.* chapitrer; faire la morale à.

se·rol·o·gy ⚕ [siə'rɔlədʒi] sérologie *f*.

se·rous ['siərəs] séreux (-euse *f*).

ser·pent ['sə:pənt] serpent *m*; **ser·pen·tine** ['⁓ain] **1.** serpentin; serpentant; tortueux (-euse *f*); **2.** *min.* serpentine *f*.

ser·rate ['serit], **ser·rat·ed** [se-'reitid] dentelé; denté (en scie); **ser·ra·tion** dent(el)ure *f*; *anat.* engrenure *f*.

ser·ried ['serid] serré.

se·rum ['siərəm] sérum *m*.

serv·ant ['sə:vənt] serviteur *m*; domestique *mf*; employé(e *f*) *m*; (*a.* ⁓*-girl ou* ⁓*-maid*) servante *f*, bonne *f*; *see* civil; ⁓s *pl.* domestiques *m/pl.*; personnel *m*; ⁓s' hall office *f*; salle *f* commune des domestiques.

serve [sə:v] **1.** *v/t.* servir (*a.* ✕, ⚓, *eccl., tennis,* [*a.* ⁓ *up*] *un mets*); être utile à; contenter; ⚓, *compagnie de gaz, etc.*: desservir, traiter (*q.*) (*bien ou mal*); subir, purger (*une peine*); ⚖ ⁓ *a writ on s.o.,* ⁓ *s.o. with a writ* délivrer une assignation à q.; (*it*) ⁓s *him right* cela lui apprendra; *see* sentence 1; ⁓ *out* distribuer (*qch.*); F faire payer (*qch.* à q., *s.o. s.th.*); *v/i.* servir (à, *for*; de, *as*); ✕ servir dans l'armée; ✕ faire la guerre (*sous, under*); être favorable (*temps*); ⁓ *at table* servir à table; ⁓ *on a jury* être du jury; **2.** *tennis:* service *m*; **'server** *tennis:* serveur (-euse *f* *m*); *eccl.* acolyte *m*.

serv·ice ['sə:vis] **1.** service *m* (*a.* ✕, ⚓, *domestique, mets, tennis, a. fig.*); eau, électricité, gaz: distribution *f*; entretien *m*; *mot.* entretien *m* et dépannage *m*; *fonctionnaire:* emploi *m*; disposition *f*; (*a. divine* ⁓) office *m*, *protestantisme:* service *m*, culte *m*; ⚓ *cordage:* fourrure *f*; ⚖ délivrance *f*, signification *f*; ⚓ *etc.* parcours *m*, ligne *f*; *fig.* utilité *f*; garniture *f* (*de toilette*); *the* (*army*) ⁓s *pl.* l'armée *f*; *public* ⁓s *pl.* services *m/pl.* publics; ✕ *Army* ♀ *Corps* service *m* de l'Intendance, F *le Train m*; *see* civil; be *at s.o.'s* ⁓ être à la disposition de q.; **2.** entretenir et réparer (*les automobiles etc.*); soigner l'entretien de; **'serv·ice·a·ble** □ utile, pratique; durable, avantageux (-euse *f*); en état de fonctionner; utilisable; serviable; **'service-a·ble·ness** utilité *f*; état *m* satisfaisant; solidité *f*.

serv·ice…: ~ **ar·e·a** *mot.* aire *f* de service; **'~-ball** *tennis*: balle *f* de service; ~ **charge** service *m*; **'~-line** *tennis*: ligne *f* de service *ou* fond; ~ **pipe** ⊕ branchement *m*; ~ **sta·tion** station-service (*pl.* stations-service) *f*; **'~-tree** ⚘ cormier *m*.

ser·vile □ ['sɔ:vail] servile (*a. fig.*); d'esclave; bas(se *f*) (*personne*); vil; **ser·vil·i·ty** [~'viliti] servilité *f* (*a. d'une personne*); bassesse *f*; *copie*: exactitude *f* trop étroite.

ser·vi·tude ['sɔ:vitju:d] servitude *f* (*a.* 🕮); asservissement *m*, esclavage *m*; *see* penal.

ses·a·me ⚘, *a. fig.* ['sesəmi] sésame *m*.

ses·qui·pe·da·li·an ['seskwipi'deiljən] sesquipédale *m*; *fig.* ampoulé, pédant (*personne*).

ses·sion ['seʃn] session *f* (*a.* 🕮); séance *f*; *univ.* année *f* universitaire; **be in** ~ siéger (*la montre, a.* ⊕); rérel-**a·ble·ness** utilité *f*; état *m* satis-**sion·al** de (la) session; annuel(le *f*).

set [set] **1.** [*irr.*] *v/t.* mettre (*a. le couvert*), poser (*a. un problème, une question*), placer; imposer (*une tâche*); régler (*la montre, a.* ⊕); mettre (*le réveille-matin*) (sur, *for*); dresser (*un piège*); donner (*un exemple*); fixer (*un jour, la mode*); planter; lancer (*un chien*) (contre *at, on*); ajuster; ⊕ redresser (*une lime*); affiler (*un outil*); affûter (*une scie*); monter (*une pierre précieuse*); *théâ. le décor*); déployer (*la voile*); mettre en plis (*les cheveux*); 🕮 remettre; ~ **laughing** provoquer les rires de q., faire rire q.; ~ **the fashion** lancer la mode; fixer *ou* mener la mode; ~ **sail** faire voile, prendre la mer; ~ **one's teeth** serrer les dents; ~ **against** animer *ou* prévenir contre; *see* apart; ~ **aside** mettre de côté; *fig.* rejeter, laisser de côté; écarter; 🕮 casser; ~ **at** defiance défier (*q.*); ~ **at ease** mettre à son aise; ~ **at liberty** mettre en liberté; ~ **at rest** calmer; décider (*une question*); ~ **store by** attacher grand prix à; ~ **down** (dé)poser; consigner par écrit; attribuer (à,

to); prendre (*q.*) (pour, *for*); ~ **forth** énoncer; exposer; formuler; ~ **off** compenser (par, *against*); faire ressortir, rehausser; faire partir (*une fusée*); ~ **on** inciter à attaquer; acharner (contre, *on*); lancer (contre, *on*); mettre (à *inf.*, to *inf.*); ~ **out** arranger, disposer; étaler; équiper (*q.*); orner (*q.*); mettre dehors; ~ **up** monter, dresser; fixer; relever; organiser; fonder; monter (*un magasin*); occasionner; afficher (*des prétentions*); mettre en avant; pousser (*une clameur*); rétablir (*la santé*); *typ.* ~ **up in type** composer; **2.** [*irr.*] *v/i.* se coucher (*soleil etc.*); (se) prendre; se figer (*gelée etc.*); prendre racine (*plante*); tomber (*robe etc.*); devenir fixe; 🕮 se nouer (*a. fruit*); souffler (*vent*); porter (*marée*); *chasse*: tomber en arrêt; ~ **about** se mettre à (*qch.*); attaquer (*q.*); ~ **forth** partir; ~ **forward** se mettre en route; ~ **in** commencer; ~ **off** se mettre en route; partir; ~ **out** se mettre en route; faire voile; partir; commencer à descendre (*marée*); ~ **to** se mettre au travail; F en venir aux coups; ~ **up** se poser (en, *as*); s'établir (qch., *as s.th.*); ~ **up for** poser pour; se donner des airs de; ~ **(up)on** attaquer; † se mettre à; **3.** fixe; résolu; pris; noué, immobile, assigné; prescrit; ~ **(up)on** déterminé à; résolu à; ~ **with** orné de; ~ **fair** (au) beau (fixe) (*baromètre*); **hard** ~ fort embarrassé; *peint. etc.* ~ **piece** pièce *f* montée; *théâ.* ferme *f*; ~ **speech** discours *m* étudié; **4.** ensemble *m*; collection *f*; série *f* (*a.* ✝); garniture *f* (*de boutons etc.*; *a. de toilette etc.*); porcelaine, linge: service *m*; *lingerie, pierres précieuses*: parure *f*; *casseroles etc.*: batterie *f*; *échecs, outils, etc.*: jeu *m*; coterie *f*, monde *m*, bande *f*; groupe *m* (*a.* ✝); *scie*: voie *f*; *cheveux*: mise *f* en plis; *radio*: poste *m*; ✎ plaçon *m*; *tennis*: set *m*; ⚓ *voiles*: orientation *f*; *poét. soleil*: coucher *m*; *fig.* attaque *f*; *théâ.* décor *m* (monté); (*a.* ~ scene) mise *f* en scène; ~ **of teeth** denture *f*; ~ **of false teeth** dentier *m*. **set·back** ['set'bæk] *fig.* échec *m*; ✝ recul *m*; mur *m* en retrait; **'set-'down** humiliation *f*; **'set-'off** contraste *m*; ✝ compensation *f*; 🕮 reconvention *f*; △ saillie *f*; *voyage*:

départ *m*; **'set-'square** ⚓ équerre *f* à dessin.

set·tee [se'ti:] canapé *m*.

set·ter ['setə] *typ.* compositeur *m*; poseur *m*; monteur *m etc.*; *see* set 1; *chasse*: chien *m* d'arrêt, setter *m*.

set·ting ['setiŋ] mise *f* (*a.* en musique, *to* music; *a. scie*: en voie; *cheveux*: en plis); arrangement *m* (*a.* ♪); ♪ ton *m*; *astr.* coucher *m*; monture *f* (*d'une pierre précieuse*); *spécimen*: montage *m*; *fig.* encadrement *m*; *théâ.* mise *f* en scène; *typ.* composition *f*; ⊕ calage *m*; ⊕ installation *f*; ⊕ *outil*: aiguisage *m*; *ciment, gelée*: prise *f*; ⚕ *os brisé*: recollement *m*; *fracture*: réduction *f*; **'~-lo·tion** *cheveux*: fixatif *m*.

set·tle ['setl] **1.** banc *m* à dossier; **2.** *v/t.* fixer; établir; installer; calmer (*un enfant*); régler (*un compte*); arranger (*une dispute*, ⚖ *un procès*); résoudre (*une question*); décider; ⚖ assigner (à, on); clarifier (*un liquide*); coloniser (*un pays*); *v/i.* (*souv.* ~ *down*) s'établir (*p.ex.* à Paris); se calmer (*enfant, passion*); (*a.* ~ *o.s.*) s'installer; se poser (*oiseau*); se tasser (*maison, sol*); ⚓ s'enfoncer; se remettre au beau (*temps*); (*a.* ~ *up*) s'acquitter (envers, with); se clarifier (*liquide*); se rasseoir (*vin*); se décider (pour, on); se ranger (*conduite, personne*); se mettre (à, to); *it is settling for a frost* le temps est à la gelée.

set·tled ['setld] sûr (*a. temps*); ⚓ établi (*temps, brise*); enraciné (*idée etc.*); rangé (*personne*); ✝ réglé; ✝ ~! pour acquit.

set·tle·ment ['setlmənt] établissement *m*; installation *f*; *sol etc.*: tassement *m*; arrangement *m*; *problème*: solution *f*; colonie *f*; ⚖ constitution *f* de rente (en faveur de, on); ⚖ contrat *m*; *fig.* accord *m*; ✝ règlement *m*; liquidation *f*; ✝ *for* ~ à terme.

set·tler ['setlə] colon *m*; F coup *m* décisif.

set·tling ['setliŋ] établissement *m etc.*; *see* settle 2; ✝ règlement *m*.

set...: '~-'to dispute *f*; lutte *f*; prise *f* de bec; '~-'up organisation *f*; *Am. sl.* affaire *f* bricolée (*surt. match de boxe*).

sev·en ['sevn] sept (*a. su./m*); **'sev·en·fold 1.** *adj.* septuple; **2.** *adv.* sept

fois autant; **sev·en·teen(th)** ['~-'ti:n(θ)] dix-sept(ième) (*a. su./m*); **sev·enth** ['~θ] **1.** □ septième; **2.** septième *m*, ♪ *f*; **sev·en·ti·eth** ['~tiiθ] soixante-dixième (*a. su./m*); **'sev·en·ty** soixante-dix (*a. su./m*).

sev·er ['sevə] (se) séparer, rompre; *v/t.* couper; désunir.

sev·er·al □ ['sevrəl] plusieurs; quelques; divers; séparé, différent; individuel(le) *f* (*surt.* ⚖); ⚖ joint *and* ~ solidaire; **'sev·er·al·ly** séparément; chacun à soi.

sev·er·ance ['sevərəns] séparation *f*; disjonction *f* (*a.* ⚖).

se·vere □ [si'viə] sévère (*beauté, personne, regard, style, etc.*); vif (vive *f*) (*douleur*); grave (*blessure, maladie*); intense, violent; rigoureux (-euse *f*) (*personne, sentence, climat, hiver, temps, etc.*); dur; **se·ver·i·ty** [~'veriti] sévérité *f*; violence *f*; gravité *f*; rigueur *f*.

sew [sou] [*irr.*] coudre; brocher (*un livre*); ~ *up* coudre; faire un point à (*une robe etc.*).

sew·age ['sju:idʒ] eaux *f/pl.* d'égouts; ~ *farm* champs *m/pl.* d'épandage.

sew·er¹ ['souə] couseur (-euse *f*) *m*; *livres*: brocheur (-euse *f*) *m*.

sew·er² ['sjuə] égout *m*; **'sew·er·age** système *m* d'égouts.

sew·ing ['souiŋ] couture *f*; *livres*: brochage *m*; ouvrage *m* à l'aiguille; *attr.* à coudre.

sewn [soun] *p.p. de* sew.

sex [seks] sexe *m*; *attr.* sexuel(le *f*); ~ *appeal* sex-appeal *m*; attrait *m*; ~ *education* enseignement *m* de la biologie humaine; F *have* ~ *with* coucher avec.

sex·a·ge·nar·i·an [seksədʒi'nɛəriən] sexagénaire (*a. su.*); **sex·en·ni·al** □ [sek'senjəl] sexennal (-aux *m/pl.*); **sex·tant** ['sekstənt] sextant *m*.

sex·ton ['sekstən] sacristain *m*; F fossoyeur *m*; F sonneur *m* (*du glas*).

sex·tu·ple ['sekstjupl] sextuple (*a. su./m*).

sex·u·al □ ['seksjuəl] sexuel(le *f*); ~ *desire* désir *m* sexuel; ~ *intercourse* rapports *m/pl.* sexuels; ~ *urge* instinct *m* sexuel, pulsion *f* sexuelle; **sex·u·al·i·ty** [~'æliti] sexualité *f*; **sex·y** F ['seksi] qui a du sex-appeal, F sexy *inv.*

shab·bi·ness ['ʃæbinis] état *m* râpé;

pauvreté f; mesquinerie f; **'shab-by** □ râpé, usé; pauvre; fig. mesquin, vilain; fig. parcimonieux (-euse f).

shack surt. Am. [ʃæk] cabane f.

shack·le ['ʃækl] **1.** fer m (fig. usu. ~s pl.), entraves f/pl., contrainte f; ⚓ maillon m (de chaîne); ⊕ maillon m de liaison; **2.** entraver (a. fig.); ⊕ maniller; ⚓ étalinguer (une an-\
shad icht. [ʃæd] alose f. [cre).⟨

shade [ʃeid] **1.** ombre f; fig. obscurité f; lampe: abat-jour m/inv.; yeux: garde-vue m/inv.; couleur, opinion: nuance f; teinte f; Am. fenêtre: store m; fig. soupçon m, nuance f; **2.** v/t. ombrager; obscurcir (a. fig.); fig. assombrir; voiler, masquer (la lumière); abriter (de, from); tex. etc. nuancer; peint. ombrer; dessin etc.: hachurer; ~ one's eyes with mettre (qch.) en abat-jour (sur les yeux); ~ away (ou off) estomper; v/i. (ou ~ off) se fondre (en, qqfois dans into); **shades** [ʃeidz] pl. F lunettes f/pl. de soleil.

shad·i·ness ['ʃeidinis] ombre f, ombrage m; F aspect m louche; réputation f louche.

shad·ow ['ʃædou] **1.** ombre f (a. fig.); peint., phot. noir m; see shade; police: filateur (-trice f) m; fig. mauvaise foi f; ~ boxing boxe f à vide; pol. Brit. ~ cabinet cabinet m fantôme; **2.** ombrager; tex. chiner; police: filer (q.); (usu. ~ forth, out) faire pressentir, symboliser; **'shad·ow·y** ombragé; obscur, ténébreux (-euse f); indécis, faible.

shad·y ['ʃeidi] ombragé, à l'ombre; frais (fraîche f); F louche; F be on the ~ side of forty avoir dépassé la quarantaine.

shaft [ʃɑːft] flèche f (a. fig.); manche m; lance: hampe f; poét. lumière: trait m; ⊕ arbre m; voitures: brancard m; ⚒ puits m.

shag [ʃæg] **1.** ⚱ peluche f; tabac m fort coupé fin; broussaille f; † poil m touffu; **2.** ébouriffer (les cheveux).

shag·gy ['ʃægi] ébouriffé (cheveux); touffu (barbe); en broussailles (sourcils); ⚱ poilu. [chagrin m.⟨

sha·green [ʃə'griːn] (peau f de)⟩
Shah [ʃɑː] s(c)hah m.

shake [ʃeik] **1.** [irr.] v/t. secouer; agiter; ébranler; fig. bouleverser; fig. effrayer; ~ down faire tomber (qch.) en secouant; tasser (qch.) en le secouant; Am. sl. ~ s.o. down for faire cracher (une somme) à q.; ~ hands serrer la main (à, with); ~ up secouer (a. F fig.); agiter; v/i. trembler (de, with; devant, at); chanceler; branler (tête); ♪ faire des trilles; ~ down s'habituer (à, [in]to); s'installer; **2.** secousse f; tremblement m (Am. de terre); ♪ trille m; hochement m (de tête); F rien m de temps; ~ of the hand see ~-hands; F no great ~s bien médiocre, bien peu de chose; '~-'down lit m improvisé; Am. sl. extorsion f; ⚓ Am. ~ cruise voyage m d'essai; '~-hands serrement m ou poignée f de main; **'shak·en 1.** p.p. de shake 1; **2.** secoué, ébranlé; **'shak·er** secoueur (-euse f) m; ⊕ secoueur m; shaker m; eccl. ♀ Trembleur (-euse f) m.

shake-up Am. F ['ʃeik'ʌp] remaniement m; chose f improvisée.

shak·i·ness ['ʃeikinis] manque m de solidité; tremblement m; voix: chevrotement m; **'shak·y** □ peu solide; chancelant; tremblant; fig. véreux (-euse f) (cas, compagnie, etc.).

shall [ʃæl] [irr.] v/aux. (défectif) usité pour former le fut.; qqfois je veux etc., je dois etc.; promesse, menace: se traduit par le fut.

shal·lot ♀ [ʃə'lɔt] échalote f.

shal·low ['ʃælou] **1.** peu profond; fig. superficiel(le f); **2.** bas-fond m; **3.** v/t. rendre ou v/i. devenir moins profond; **'shal·low·ness** peu m de profondeur; fig. superficialité f.

shalt † [ʃælt] 2e personne du sg. de shall.

sham [ʃæm] **1.** faux (fausse f), simulé; feint; **2.** feinte f, sl. chiqué m; personne: imposteur m; **3.** v/t. feindre, simuler; faire; v/i. faire semblant; jouer une comédie; ~ ill faire le malade.

sham·ble ['ʃæmbl] aller à pas traînants.

sham·bles ['ʃæmblz] sg. abattoir m; fig. scène f de carnage.

sham·bling □ ['ʃæmbliŋ] traînant.

shame [ʃeim] **1.** honte f; (for) ~! quelle honte!; vous n'avez pas honte!; cry ~ upon se récrier contre; put to ~ faire honte à; **2.** faire honte à; humilier; couvrir de honte.

shame·faced □ ['ʃeimfeist] honteux

(-euse *f*); embarrassé; **'shame-faced·ness** embarras *m*; timidité *f*.

shame·ful □ ['ʃeimful] honteux (-euse *f*); **'shame·ful·ness** honte *f*, indignité *f*.

shame·less □ ['ʃeimlis] sans honte, éhonté; **'shame·less·ness** effronterie *f*; immodestie *f*.

sham·my ['ʃæmi] (peau *f* de) chamois *m*.

sham·poo [ʃæm'pu:] **1.** (se) dégraisser (*les cheveux*); *v/t.* faire un shampooing à (*q.*); frictionner; **2.** *a.* = **sham'poo·ing** shampooing *m*; *dry* ~ friction *f*; ~ *and set* shampooing *m* (et) mise *f* en plis; *have a* ~ *and set* se faire faire un shampooing (et) mise en plis.

sham·rock ['ʃæmrɔk] ♣ trèfle *m* d'Irlande (*a. emblème national irlandais*).

shan·dy *Brit.* ['ʃændi] panaché *m*.

shang·hai ⚓ *sl.* [ʃæŋ'hai] embarquer un homme pour l'engager après l'avoir enivré.

shank [ʃæŋk] tige *f*; ⚓ verge *f* (*d'ancre*); queue *f* (*de bouton*); *cuis.* jarret *m* (*de bœuf*), manche *m* (*de gigot de mouton*); jambe *f*; *ride ♀'s mare* (*ou pony*) prendre le train onze; **~shanked**: *short-~* aux jambes courtes (*personne*).

shan't [ʃɑ:nt] = shall not.

shan·ty ['ʃænti] cabane *f*, hutte *f*.

shape [ʃeip] **1.** forme *f*; *cost.* coupe *f*; *personne*: taille *f*; *cuis.* moule *m*; crème *f*; *in bad* ~ en mauvais état; **2.** *v/t.* façonner, former; tailler; ajuster (à, *to*); ~ *one's course* ⚓ faire (une) route; *fig.* se diriger (vers, *for*); *v/i.* se développer; promettre; **shaped** façonné; en forme de; **'shape·less** informe; difforme; **'shape·li·ness** beauté *f* de forme; **'shape·ly** bien fait; beau (bel *devant une voyelle ou un h muet*); belle *f*; beaux *m/pl.*).

share [ʃɛə] **1.** part *f*, portion *f*; contribution *f*; ✝ action *f*, titre *m*, valeur *f*; *charrue*: soc *m*; ✝ *original* (*ou ordinary ou primary*) ~ action *f* ordinaire; ✝ *preference* (*ou preferred ou priority*) ~ action *f* privilégiée; *have a* ~ *in* avoir part à; *go* ~*s* partager (*qch.* avec *q.*, *in s.th. with s.o.*); ~ *and* ~ *alike* en partageant également; **2.** *v/t.* partager (entre, *among*[*st*]; avec, *with*); avoir part à

(*qch.*); *v/i.* prendre part (à, *in*), participer (à, *in*); **'~·crop·per** *Am.* métayer (-ère *f*) *m*; **'~·hold·er** ✝ actionnaire *mf*; **'shar·er** participant(e *f*) *m*.

shark [ʃɑ:k] **1.** *icht.* requin *m*; *fig. a.* escroc *m*; *Am. sl.* as *m* (= *expert*); **2.** *v/i.* écornifler.

sharp [ʃɑ:p] **1.** *adj.* □ tranchant (*couteau etc.*); aigu(ë *f*) (*pointe*); vif (vive *f*) (*froid*); *fig.* éveillé; *fig.* rusé; aigre (*fruit*); violent (*douleur*); vert (*vin, réprimande*); perçant (*cri, œil*); pénétrant (*regard*); fin (*oreille, esprit*); net(te *f*) (*profil*); piquant (*goût, sauce*); saillant (*angle*); raide (*pente*); prononcé (*courbe*); fort (*averse, gelée*); F élégant, chic *inv.* (*vêtement, voiture, personne etc.*); *péj.* peu honnête; ♩ dièse; ♩ C ~ do m dièse; **2.** *adv.* ♩ trop haut, en diésant; F ponctuellement; *look* ~! dépêchez-vous!; faites vite!; **3.** *su.* ♩ dièse *m*; F escroc *m*; *Am. sl.* as *m*; **'sharp·en** aiguiser (*a. fig. l'appétit*); tailler (*un crayon*); accentuer (*un trait, un contraste*); ♩ diéser; **sharp·en·er** fusil *m* (à aiguiser); taille-crayon *m/inv.*; **'sharp·er** escroc *m*; *cartes*: tricheur (-euse *f*) *m*; **'sharp-'eyed** à la vue perçante; à qui n'échappe rien; **'sharp·ness** tranchant *m*; pointe *f*; acuité *f*; violence *f*; acidité *f*; *fig.* rigueur *f*.

sharp...: **'~-'set** en grand appétit, affamé; *be* ~ *on* avoir un vif désir de; **'~-shoot·er** tirailleur *m*; **'~-'sight-ed** à la vue perçante; *fig.* perspicace; **'~-'wit·ted** éveillé.

shat·ter ['ʃætə] (se) fracasser; (se) briser (en éclats); *v/t.* détraquer (*les nerfs, la santé*); briser (*les espérances*); **'~·proof**: ~ *glass* verre *m* Sécurit (*TM*).

shave [ʃeiv] **1.** [*irr.*] *v/t.* raser; planer (*le bois*); friser, effleurer; *fig.* rogner; *v/i.* se raser; ~ *through* se faufiler entre (*les voitures etc.*); **2.** coup *m* à fleur de peau; *give s.o. a* ~ faire la barbe à q.; *have a* ~ se (faire) raser; *by a* ~ d'un iota; tout juste; *to have a close* (*ou narrow*) ~ l'échapper belle; **'shav·en** rasé; *a* ~ *head* une tête *f* rasée; **'shav·er** barbier *m*; rasoir *m* électrique; F *young* ~ gamin *m*.

Sha·vi·an ['ʃeivjən] de G.B. Shaw; à la G.B. Shaw.

shav·ing ['ʃeiviŋ] **1.** action *f* de (se) raser; ~s *pl.* bois: copeaux *m/pl.*; *métal:* rognures *f/pl.*; **2.** à barbe; ~ brush blaireau *m*; ~ cream crème *f* à raser; ~ mug plat *m* à barbe; ~ soap savon *m* à barbe; ~ stick bâton *m* de savon à barbe.

shawl [ʃɔ:l] châle *m*; fichu *m*.

shawm ♪ [ʃɔ:m] chalumeau *m*.

she [ʃi:] **1.** elle (*a. accentué*); **2.** femelle *f*; femme *f*; **she-** femelle *f* (*d'un animal*).

sheaf [ʃi:f] (*pl.* sheaves) blé: gerbe *f*; *papiers:* liasse *f*.

shear [ʃiə] **1.** [*irr.*] tondre; couper; *métall.* cisailler (*une tôle*); *fig.* dépouiller; **2.** (*a pair of*) ~s *pl.* (des) cisailles *f/pl.*; **'shear·ing** coupage *m*; *moutons:* tonte *f*; *drap:* tondage *m*; ~s *pl.* tontes *f/pl.* (*de laine*).

sheath [ʃi:θ] gaine *f* (*a.* ♀, *a. anat.*); *épée:* fourreau *m*; *phot.* châssis *m*; **sheathe** [ʃi:ð] mettre au fourreau; rengainer; ⊕, *a. fig.* revêtir, recouvrir (de, with); **'sheath·ing** ⊕ revêtement *m*; enveloppe *f*; chemise *f*; *câble:* gaine *f*.

sheave ⊕ [ʃi:v] rouet *m*; plateau *m* d'excentrique.

sheaves [ʃi:vz] *pl. de* sheaf.

she·bang *Am. sl.* [ʃə'bæŋ] hutte *f*; cabaret *m*, bar *m*; carriole *f*; *the whole* ~ tout le bazar.

she-bear ['ʃi:'bɛə] ourse *f*.

shed¹ [ʃed] [*irr.*] perdre (*ses feuilles, ses dents*); verser (*des larmes, du sang*); répandre (*du sang, de la lumière, a. fig.*); F ~ light on jeter le jour dans.

shed² [~] hangar *m*; ♪ tente *f* à marchandises.

shed·der ['ʃedə] personne *f* qui répand (*qch.*).

sheen [ʃi:n] *étoffe etc.:* brillant *m*; reflet *m*; chatoiement *m*; **'sheen·y** luisant, brillant.

sheep [ʃi:p] mouton *m*; brebis *f* (*a. fig.*); *coll.* moutons *m/pl.*; *fig.* ~'s eyes *pl.* yeux *m/pl.* doux; **'~-cot** *see* sheep-fold; **'~-dog** chien *m* de berger; **'~-fold** parc *m* à moutons; **'sheep·ish** □ timide; penaud; **'sheep·ish·ness** timidité *f*; air *m* penaud.

sheep...: '**~-man** *Am.* éleveur *m* de moutons; '**~-run** *see* sheep-walk; '**~·skin** peau *f* de mouton; *Am. sl.* diplôme *m*; (*a.* ~ leather) basane *f*;

'**~-walk** pâturage *m* pour moutons.

sheer¹ [ʃiə] **1.** *adj.* pur, vrai, véritable; à pic (*a. adv.*), escarpé, abrupt; **2.** *adv.* tout à fait; abruptement; à plomb.

sheer² [~] **1.** ♪ embarder; ~ off ♪ prendre le large; *fig.* s'écarter, s'éloigner; **2.** ♪ embardée *f*.

sheet [ʃi:t] **1.** *métal, papier, verre, etc.:* feuille *f*; *eau etc.:* nappe *f*; *neige:* couche *f*; *lit:* drap *m*; ♪ écoute *f*; ~ copper (iron) cuivre *m* (fer *m*) en feuilles; ~ glass verre *m* à vitres; ~ steel tôle *f* d'acier; **2.** couvrir d'un drap; *fig.* recouvrir; '**~-an·chor** ♪ ancre *f* de veille (*fig.* de salut); '**sheet·ing** *tex.* toile *f* pour draps; ⊕ tôles *f/pl.*; '**sheet-light·ning** éclairs *m/pl.* en nappe *ou* de chaleur.

sheik(h) [ʃeik] cheik *m*.

shelf [ʃelf] (*pl.* shelves) rayon *m*; planche *f*; *four, a. géog.:* plateau *m*; rebord *m*; écueil *m*; banc *m* de sable; ♱ ~ life durée *f* de conservation avant vente; *fig.* on the ~ au rancart; en passe de devenir vieille fille; *fig.* get on the ~ coiffer sainte Catherine (*femme*).

shell [ʃel] **1.** coquille *f* (*vide*); œuf: coque *f*; *huîtres:* écaille *f*; *homard etc.:* carapace *f*; *pois:* cosse *f*; ⊕ paroi *f*; *métall.* manteau *m*; ✕ obus *m*; classe *f* intermédiaire; cercueil *m*; *maison:* carcasse *f*; **2.** écaler; écosser; ✕ bombarder; *sl.* ~ out débourser; payer (*la note etc.*).

shel·lac [ʃe'læk] gomme *f* laque.

shell-cra·ter ['ʃelkreitə] cratère *m*, entonnoir *m*; **shelled** [ʃeld] à coquille *etc.*

shell...: '**~-fire** tir *m* à obus; '**~-fish** coquillage *m*; crustacé *m*; '**~-proof** à l'épreuve des obus; blindé; '**~-work** coquillages *m/pl.*

shel·ter ['ʃeltə] **1.** abri *m*; asile *m*; *fig.* protection *f*; in the (ou under) ~ of à l'abri de; **2.** *v/t.* abriter; donner asile à; *v/i.* (*a.* ~ o.s.) s'abriter; '**shel·ter·less** sans abri *etc.*

shelve¹ [ʃelv] garnir de rayons; mettre sur un rayon; *fig.* remettre, ajourner; *fig.* mettre au rancart, remiser (*q.*); F classer (*une question*).

shelve² [~] aller en pente douce.

shelves [ʃelvz] *pl. de* shelf.

shelv·ing ['ʃelviŋ] **1.** rayons *m/pl.*; **2.** en pente.

she·nan·i·gan *Am.* F [ʃi'nænigən] mystification *f.*

shep·herd ['ʃepəd] **1.** berger *m*; **2.** garder (*des moutons*); '**shep·herd·ess** bergère *f.*

sher·bet ['ʃɔ:bət] sorbet *m* (= *sorte de boisson à demi glacée*); (a. ~-powder) limonade *f* (sèche).

sher·iff ['ʃerif] *Angl.* chérif *m* (= *préfet*); *Am.* chef *m* de la police.

sher·ry ['ʃeri] vin *m* de Xérès, cherry *m.*

shew † [ʃou] *see* show 1.

shib·bo·leth *fig.* ['ʃibələθ] doctrine *f*; mot *m* d'ordre.

shield [ʃi:ld] **1.** bouclier *m*; *fig.* défense *f*; ⌧ écu *m*; **2.** protéger (contre *from*, *against*); '**shield·less** sans bouclier; *fig.* sans défense.

shift [ʃift] **1.** changement *m*; moyen *m*; expédient *m*; échappatoire *f*; ⊕ équipe *f*; ⊕ journée *f* (de travail); † chemise *f* (*de femme*); *make* ~ s'arranger (*pour inf.*, *to inf.*; *avec*, *with*); trouver moyen (de, *to*); *make* ~ *without* se passer de; *make* ~ *to live* arriver à vivre; **2.** *v/t.* changer (de place *etc.*); ⚓ changer (*une voile*); déplacer (a. ⚓ *la cargaison*); *v/i. Am. mot.* changer de vitesse; changer de place; bouger, se déplacer; changer (*scène*); tourner (*vent*); ⚓ se désarrimer (*cargaison*); F (a. ~ *for o.s.*) se débrouiller; '**shift·ing** ⌷ qui se déplace; mobile; ~ *sands pl.* sables *m/pl.* mouvants; '**shift·less** ⌷ sans ressources; peu débrouillard; *fig.* futile; '**shift·y** ⌷ sournois, peu franc(he *f*); fuyant (*yeux*); louche; † peu solide.

shil·ling ['ʃiliŋ] shilling *m*; *take the King's* ~ s'engager; *fig. cut s.o. off with a* ~ déshériter q.

shil·ly-shal·ly ['ʃiliʃæli] **1.** barguignage *m*; **2.** barguiner.

shim·mer ['ʃimə] miroiter, chatoyer.

shim·my¹ ['ʃimi] **1.** *danse:* shimmy *m*; **2.** osciller, vibrer.

shim·my² F [~] chemise *f* (de femme).

shin [ʃin] **1.** (*ou* ~-*bone*) tibia *m*; **2.** : ~ *up* grimper à.

shin·dy F ['ʃindi] chahut *m*, tapage *m*.

shine [ʃain] **1.** éclat *m*; brillant *m*; F *take the* ~ *out of s.o.* éclipser q.; *Am. sl. take a* ~ *to* s'enticher de; **2.** [*irr.*] *v/i.* briller (a. *fig.*); (re)luire; ~ *on*

éclairer; *v/t.* (a. ~ *up*) polir; cirer.

shin·er *sl.* ['ʃainə] pièce *f* d'or; œil *m* poché.

shin·gle¹ ['ʃiŋgl] **1.** ⚓ bardeau *m*; *cheveux:* coupe *f* à la garçonne; *Am.* petite enseigne *f*; **2.** couvrir de bardeaux; couper à la garçonne.

shin·gle² [~] galets *m/pl.*; plage *f* à galets.

shin·gles ⚕ ['ʃiŋglz] *pl.* zona *m*, F ceinture *f.*

shin·gly ['ʃiŋgli] couvert de galets.

shin·y ⌷ ['ʃaini] brillant, luisant.

ship [ʃip] **1.** (*usu. f*) navire *m*; vaisseau *m*; ~'*s company* équipage *m*; **2.** *v/t.* embarquer; ⚓ (*souv.* ~ *off*) mettre à bord, expédier; ⚓ mettre en place, monter; rentrer (*les avirons*); recruter (*des marins*); ~ *a sea* embarquer un coup de mer; *v/i.* s'embarquer; armer (sur, *on* [*board*]) (*marin*); '~·**board:** ⚓ *on* ~ à bord; '~·**build·er** constructeur *m* de navires; '~·**build·ing** construction *f* navale; '~-**ca·nal** canal *m* maritime; '~-'**chan·dler** fournisseur *m* de navires; '~-'**chan·dler·y** fournitures *f/pl.* de navires; '**ship·ment** embarquement *m*, mise *f* à bord; envoi *m* par mer; chargement *m* (= *choses embarquées*); '**ship·own·er** armateur *m*; '**ship·per** affréteur *m*; expéditeur *m*; '**ship·ping 1.** embarquement *m*; navires *m/pl.*; marine *f* marchande; **2.** d'embarquement; maritime; de navigation; d'expédition.

ship...: '~-**shape** bien tenu (a. *fig.*); en bon ordre; '~-**wreck 1.** naufrage *m*; **2.** *v/t.* faire naufrager; *v/i.* (a. *be* ~*ed*) faire naufrage; '~-**wrecked** naufragé; '~-**wright** charpentier *m* de navires; '~-**yard** chantier *m* de constructions navales.

shire ['ʃaiə; *mots composés* ʃiə] comté *m*; ~ *horse* cheval *m* de gros trait.

shirk [ʃə:k] *v/t.* se dérober à, négliger, esquiver; *v/i.* négliger son devoir; '**shirk·er** carotteur (-euse *f*) *m.*

shirt [ʃə:t] chemise *f* (*d'homme*, a. ⊕); (a. ~-*blouse*) chemisier *m*; *Am. sl. keep one's* ~ *on* ne pas se fâcher *ou* s'emballer; '**shirt·ing** ⚓ shirting *m* (*toile pour chemises*); '**shirt-sleeve 1.** manche *f* de chemise; **2.** en bras de chemise; *fig.* sans cérémonie; *surt. Am.* ~

diplomacy diplomatie *f* franche et honnête; **'shirt·y** *sl.* irritable.

shit ∨ [ʃit] **1.** merde *f*; **2.** chier.

shiv·er[1] [ʃivə] **1.** fragment *m*; *break to* ⁓*s* = **2.** (se) briser en éclats.

shiv·er[2] [⁓] **1.** frisson *m*; F *the* ⁓*s pl.* la tremblote *f*; *it gives me the* ⁓*s* ça me donne le frisson, ça me fait trembler; **2.** frissonner; grelotter; *have a* ⁓*ing fit* être pris de frissons; **'shiv·er·y** tremblant; fiévreux (-euse *f*).

shoal[1] [ʃoul] **1.** *poissons:* banc *m* voyageur; *fig.* multitude *f*; **2.** se réunir en *ou* aller par bancs.

shoal[2] [⁓] **1.** haut-fond (*pl.* hauts-fonds) *m*; **2.** diminuer de fond; **3.** (*a.* **'shoal·y**) plein de hauts-fonds.

shock[1] ⤳ [ʃɔk] moyette *f*.

shock[2] [⁓] **1.** choc *m* (*a.* ✱, ⊕, ✕); ✕ assaut *m*; secousse *f* (*a.* ⚡); coup *m*; *mot.* road ⁓*s pl.* cahots *m/pl.*; **2.** *fig.* choquer, scandaliser; bouleverser; offenser; ⁓*ed at* choqué de; scandalisé par.

shock[3] [⁓] ⁓ *of hair* tignasse *f*.

shock-ab·sorb·er *mot.* [ʃɔkəbsɔːbə] amortisseur *m* (de chocs); pare-chocs *m/inv.*

shock·er *sl.* [ʃɔkə] (*qqfois shilling* ⁓) roman *m* à gros effets.

shock·ing □ [ʃɔkiŋ] choquant; affreux (-euse *f*); abominable.

shock...: **'⁓·proof** anti-choc *inv.*; ⁓ **ther·a·py** thérapeutique *f* de choc; ⁓ **treat·ment** traitement *m* (de) choc; **electric** ⁓ traitement *m* par électrochocs; ⁓ **wave** onde *f* de choc.

shod [ʃɔd] *prét. et p.p. de shoe* 2.

shod·dy [ʃɔdi] **1.** *tex.* drap *m* de laine d'effilochage; *fig.* camelote *f*; pacotille *f*; **2.** d'effilochage; de camelote; de pacotille; *surt. Am.* ⁓ *aristocracy* parvenus *m/pl.*

shoe [ʃuː] **1.** chaussure *f*, soulier *m*; *cheval:* fer *m*; ⊕ sabot *m*; traîneau, *piston:* patin *m*; **2.** [irr.] chausser); ferrer; garnir d'un patin *etc.*; **'⁓·black** cireur *m* (de chaussures); **'⁓·black·ing** cirage *m ou* crème *f* pour chaussures; **'⁓·horn** chausse-pied *m*; corne *f*; **'⁓·lace** lacet *m*; **'⁓·mak·er** cordonnier *m*; ⁓ **pol·ish** cirage *m ou* crème pour chaussures; **'⁓·shine** cirage *m* (de chaussures); (*a.* ⁓ *boy*) cireur *m* (de chaussures);

'⁓·string *Am.* lacet *m*; *surt. Am.* F minces capitaux *m/pl.*

shone [ʃɔn] *prét. et p.p. de shine* 2.

shoo [ʃuː] chasser (*des oiseaux*).

shook [ʃuk] *prét. de shake* 1.

shoot [ʃuːt] **1.** *rivière:* rapide *m*; ⤳ rejeton *m*, pousse *f*; partie *f* de chasse; chasse *f* gardée; ✕ (concours *m* de) tir *m*; *tex.* duite *f*; ✕ couloir *m*; *fig.* jaillissement *m*; **2.** [irr.] *v/t.* tirer (*une arme à feu, les manchettes*); fusiller; tuer; chasser (*le gibier*); *fig.* passer rapidement sous (*un pont*); darder (*des rayons, fig. un regard*); décharger; (*a.* ⁓ *out*) ⚙ pousser; pousser (*le verrou*); *phot.* prendre un instantané de; tourner (*un film*); *sp.* marquer (*un but*); *sp.* shooter; *mot.* brûler (*les feux*); franchir (*un rapide*); *v/i.* tirer (sur, *at*); viser; *fig.* se précipiter, s'élancer; élancer (*douleur*); (*a.* ⁓ *forth*) pousser; ⁓ *ahead* aller rapidement en avant; ⁓ *ahead of* devancer (*q.*) rapidement.

shoot·er [ʃuːtə] tireur (-euse *f*) *m*; *sp.* marqueur *m* de but.

shoot·ing [ʃuːtiŋ] **1.** tir *m*; chasse *f*; fusillade *f*; **⁓·ground** (*ou* **⁓·range**) champ *m* de tir; *go* ⁓ aller à la chasse; ⁓ *of a film* prise *f* de vue; tournage *m*; **2.** lancinant (*douleur*); ⁓ *star* étoile *f* filante; **'⁓·box** pavillon *m* de chasse; muette *f*; **'⁓·brake** canadienne *f*.

shoot-out F [ʃuːtaut] échange *m* de coups de feu.

shop [ʃɔp] **1.** boutique *f*; magasin *m*; bureau *m* (*de tabac*); F métier *m*, affaires *f/pl.*; ⁓ *floor* les ouvriers *m/pl.*; *talk* ⁓ parler boutique; **2.** (*usu.* F *go* ⁓*ping*) faire des achats; **'⁓·keep·er** boutiquier (-ère *f*) *m*; marchand(e *f*) *m*; **'⁓·lift·er** voleur (-euse *f*) *m* à l'étalage; **'⁓·man** commis *m* de magasin; ⊕ homme *m* d'atelier; **'shop·ping** achats *m/pl.*; emplettes *f/pl.*; ⁓ *centre* quartier *m* commerçant; *Christmas* ⁓ emplettes *f/pl.* de Noël; **'shop·py** F qui sent la boutique; à l'esprit boutiquier.

shop...: **'⁓·soiled** ✝ défraîchi; **'⁓·stew·ard** délégué *m* (syndical) d'atelier; **'⁓·walk·er** chef *m* de rayon; inspecteur (-trice *f*) *m*; **'⁓·win·dow** vitrine *f*; devanture *f*.

shore[1] [ʃɔː] rivage *m*, bord *m*; côte *f*; ⚓ terre *f*; *on* ⁓ à terre.

shore[2] [∪] **1.** étai *m*, appui *m*; **2.**: ~ *up* étayer; buter.

shorn [ʃɔːn] *p.p. de shear* 1; *fig.* ~ *of* dépouillé de (*qch.*).

short [ʃɔːt] **1.** *adj.* court; de petite taille; bref (brève *f*); insuffisant; *fig.* brusque, cassant; *cuis.* croquant; aigre (*métal*); revêche (*fer*); *see circuit*; *Brit.* ~ *list* liste *f* des candidats sélectionnés; ~ *time* chômage *m* partiel; ~ *waves pl.* petites ondes *f/pl.*; *radio*: ondes *f/pl.* courtes; *by a* ~ *head turf*: de justesse; *fig.* tout juste; *nothing* ~ *of* ni plus ni moins (*ou fall*) ~ *of* rester au-dessous de (*qch.*); manquer à; ne pas être à la hauteur de (*q.*); ne pas atteindre; *fall* (*ou run*) ~ manquer; s'épuiser (*provisions*); *go* ~ *of* se priver de; **2.** *adv.* court; brusquement; ~ *of* sauf; à moins de; ~ *of London* à quelque distance de Londres; ~ *of lying* à moins de mentir; *cut* ~ couper la parole à (*q.*); *stop* ~ *of* s'arrêter au seuil de; ne pas aller jusqu'à; **3.** *su. gramm.* voyelle *f* brève; *cin.* court métrage *m*; ⚡ court-circuit (*pl.* courts-circuits) *m*; F ~ *pl.* culotte *f* de sport; short *m*; *in* ~ bref, en un mot; **4.** *v/t. see* ~*circuit*; '**short·age** manque *m*, insuffisance *f*; disette *f*; *admin.* crise *f*; ✝ déficit *m*.

short...: '~-**cake** sablé *m*; '~-'**change** tromper (*q.*) sur la monnaie; rouler (*q.*); '~-'**cir·cuit** ⚡ court-circuiter; ~-'**com·ing** défaut *m*, imperfection *f*; manque *m*; ~ *cut* chemin *m* de traverse; raccourci *m*; '~-'**dat·ed** ✝ à courte échéance; '**short·en** *v/t.* raccourcir; abréger; *v/i.* (se) raccourcir; se reserrer; diminuer; '**short·en·ing** raccourcissement *m*; abrègement *m*; *cuis.* matière *f* grasse.

short...: '~-'**fall** déficit *m*; '~-'**hand** sténographie *f*; ~ *writer* sténographe *mf*; '~-'**hand·ed** à court de personnel; '~-'**haul** à courte distance; '~-'**list** mettre (*q.*) sur la liste des candidats sélectionnés; '~-'**lived** qui vit peu de temps; passager (-ère *f*), éphémère *f*; '**short·ly** *adv.* brièvement; bientôt; brusquement; '**short·ness** brièveté *f*; *taille*: petitesse *f*; brusquerie *f*; manque *m*.

short...: '~-**range** à courte portée (*fusil etc.*); à court terme (*projet etc.*); à court rayon d'action (*avion etc.*); '~-**run** de courte durée; '~-

'**sight·ed** myope; *fig.* imprévoyant; '~-'**tem·pered** irascible; vif (vive *f*); '~-**term** ✝ à court terme; ~ *memory* mémoire *f* immediate; '~-'**time work·ing** chômage *m* partiel; '~-**wave** *radio*: sur ondes courtes; '~-'**wind·ed** à l'haleine courte.

shot[1] [ʃɔt] **1.** *prét. et p.p. de shoot* 2; **2.** chatoyant (*soie*).

shot[2] [∪] coup *m* (*a. fig., a. sp.*); *revolver*: coup *m* de feu; (*usu.* ~*pl.*) plomb *m*; F tireur (-euse *f*) *m*; chasseur *m*; *sp.* shot *m*; *phot.* prise *f* de vue; *cin.* plan *m*; ⚕ piqûre *f*; *sl.* alcool: goutte *f*; *fig.* essai *m*; *have a* ~ *at* essayer (*qch.*); F *not by a long* ~ tant s'en faut; pas à beaucoup près; *within* (*out of*) ~ à (hors de) portée; F *like a* ~ comme un trait; avec empressement; F *fig. big* ~ grosse légume *f* (= *personnage important*); *make a bad* ~ rater son coup; *fig.* deviner faux; '~-**gun** fusil *m* de chasse; F ~ *marriage* mariage *m* forcé; '~-**proof** à l'épreuve des balles; '~-**put** *sp.* lancer *m* du poids.

shot·ten her·ring ['ʃɔtn'heriŋ] hareng *m* guais.

should [ʃud] *prét. de shall* (*a. usité pour former le cond.*).

shoul·der ['ʃouldə] **1.** épaule *f*; ⊕ épaulement *m*; *give s.o. the cold* ~ battre froid à *q.*, tourner le dos à *q.*; *put one's* ~ *to the wheel* se mettre à l'œuvre; donner un coup d'épaule; *rub* ~*s with* s'associer avec, côtoyer; ~ *to* ~ côte à côte; **2.** pousser avec *ou* de l'épaule; mettre sur l'épaule; *fig.* endosser; ✕ porter (*l'arme*); '~-**bag** sac *m* à bandoulière; '~-**blade** *anat.* omoplate *f*; '~-**knot** nœud *m* d'épaule (*a.* ✕); '~-**strap** bretelle *f*; *dames, a.* ✕: patte *f* d'épaule; ✕ *uniforme*: attente *f*.

shout [ʃaut] **1.** cri *m*; clameur *f*; *rire*: éclat *m*; *sl. boisson*: tournée *f*; **2.** *v/i.* pousser des cris, crier; hurler (*de douleur*); *v/t.* ~ *down* huer (*q.*).

shove [ʃʌv] **1.** poussée *f*, coup *m* d'épaule; **2.** pousser; bousculer; fourrer (qch. dans qch., *s.th. in*[to] *s.th.*).

shov·el ['ʃʌvl] **1.** pelle *f*; **2.** pelleter; '~-**board** jeu *m* de galets.

show [ʃou] **1.** [*irr.*] *v/t.* montrer, faire voir; manifester; faire (*miséricorde à q.*); témoigner (de); laisser paraître; indiquer; représenter; *cin.* présenter; prouver; exposer (*des peintures, des raisons, etc.*); ~ *forth* proclamer; ~ *in* introduire; faire entrer; ~ *off* faire valoir *ou* ressortir; faire parade de; ~ *out* reconduire; ~ *up* faire monter; révéler; faire ressortir; démasquer; *v/i.* (*a.* ~ *up ou forth*) ressortir, se détacher; se montrer, se laisser voir; ~ *off* parader; se donner des airs; *sl.* faire de l'épate; **2.** spectacle *m*; étalage *m*; exposition *f*; concours *m*; mot. salon *m*; parade *f*, ostentation *f*; semblant *m*; *sl.* affaire *f*; ~ *of hands* vote *m* à mains levées; *dumb* ~ pantomime *f*; jeu *m* muet; on ~ exposé; *sl.* *run the* ~ diriger l'affaire; être le manitou de l'affaire; '**~·biz** F ['ʃoubiz], ~ **busi·ness** le monde *m ou* l'industrie *f* du spectacle; '**~·card** pancarte *f*; étiquette *f*; '**~·case** montre *f*, vitrine *f*; '**~·down** *cartes:* étalement *m* de son jeu; *fig.* mise *f* au jour de ses projets *etc.*; *come to a* ~ en venir au fait et au prendre.

show·er ['ʃauə] **1.** averse *f*; ondée *f*; grêle, neige: giboulée *f*; *fig.* volée *f*, pluie *f*; **2.** *v/t.* verser; *fig.* accabler (de, *with*), combler (de, *with*); *v/i.* pleuvoir; '**~·bath** ['~bɑ:θ] bain-douche (*pl.* bains-douches) *m*; douche *f*; '**show·er·y** de giboulées; pluvieux (-euse *f*).

show·i·ness ['ʃouinis] prétention *f*; ostentation *f*; '**show·man** montreur *m* de curiosités; forain *m*; F passé maître *m* pour la mise en scène; '**show·man·ship** art *m* de la mise *f* en scène; **shown** [ʃoun] *p.p. de* show 1; '**show·piece** pièce *f ou* objet *m* exemplaire, modèle *m* du genre; '**show·room** salon *m* d'exposition; '**show·win·dow** *surt. Am.* vitrine *f*; étalage *m*; devanture *f*; '**show·y** □ fastueux (-euse *f*); prétentieux (-euse *f*); voyant.

shrank [ʃræŋk] *prét. de* shrink.

shrap·nel ⚔ ['ʃræpnl] shrapnel *m*.

shred [ʃred] **1.** brin *m*; lambeau *m*; petit morceau *m*; *fig.* parcelle *f*, grain *m*; **2.** [*irr.*] déchirer en lambeaux *ou* en morceaux.

shrew [ʃru:] *zo.* (*a.* ~*-mouse*) musaraigne *f*; *personne:* mégère *f*, femme *f* criarde.

shrewd □ [ʃru:d] pénétrant, sagace; fin; *have a* ~ *idea* être porté à croire

(que, *that*); '**shrewd·ness** perspicacité *f*; pénétration *f*.

shrew·ish □ ['ʃru:iʃ] acariâtre.

shriek [ʃri:k] **1.** cri *m* perçant; éclat *m* (*de rire*); **2.** pousser un cri aigu.

shriev·al·ty ['ʃri:vəlti] fonctions *f/pl.* de shérif.

shrift [ʃrift]: *give short* ~ expédier vite.

shrill [ʃril] **1.** □ aigu(ë *f*), perçant; **2.** *v/i.* pousser un son aigu; *v/t.* (*a.* ~ *out*) chanter *ou* crier (*qch.*) d'une voix aiguë.

shrimp [ʃrimp] *zo.* crevette *f*; *fig.* petit bout *m* d'homme.

shrine [ʃrain] châsse *f*; reliquaire *m*; tombeau *m* (de saint[e]).

shrink [ʃriŋk] [*irr.*] *v/i.* se contracter; se rétrécir (*tissu*); se rapetisser; (*a.* ~*back*) reculer (devant qch., *from* s.th.; à *inf.*, *from gér.*); *v/t.* contracter (*un métal*); (faire) rétrécir (*un tissu*); ~ *with age* se tasser; '**shrink·age** rétrécissement *m*; contraction *f* (*a. cin.*); *fig.* diminution *f*.

shriv·el ['ʃrivl] (*a.* ~ *up*) (se) ratatiner; *fig.* (se) dessécher.

shroud¹ [ʃraud] **1.** linceul *m*; *fig.* voile *m*; ⊕ blindage *m*; ⊕ bandage *m*; **2.** ensevelir; *fig.* envelopper.

shroud² ⚓ [~] hauban *m*.

Shrove·tide ['ʃrouvtaid] jours *m/pl.* gras; **Shrove Tues·day** mardi *m* gras.

shrub [ʃrʌb] arbrisseau *m*; arbuste *m*; **shrub·ber·y** ['~əri] bosquet *m*; plantation *f* d'arbustes; '**shrub·by** ressemblant à un arbuste.

shrug [ʃrʌg] **1.** hausser (les épaules); **2.** haussement *m* d'épaules.

shrunk [ʃrʌŋk] *p.p. de* shrink; '**shrunk·en** *adj.* contracté; rétréci; ratatiné (*figure etc.*).

shud·der ['ʃʌdə] **1.** frissonner, frémir (de, *with*); **2.** frisson *m*, frémissement *m*.

shuf·fle ['ʃʌfl] **1.** *v/t.* traîner (*les pieds*); brouiller; battre (*les cartes*); ~ *away* faire disparaître (*qch.*); ~ *off* se débarrasser de; rejeter (*qch.*) (sur *upon, on, to*); ôter (*qch.*) à la hâte; *v/i.* traîner les pieds; avancer en traînant les pieds; *fig.* équivoquer, tergiverser; ~ *through* faire un travail bien que mal; **2.** pas *m/pl.* traînants; marche *f* traînante; *cartes:* battement *m*; *fig.* équivoca-

side-slip

tion *f*; faux-fuyant *m*; **'shuf·fler** personne *f* qui bat les cartes; *fig.* tergiversateur (-trice *f*) *m*; **'shuf·fling** □ traînant (*pas*); *fig.* équivoque; *fig.* tergiversateur (-trice *f*).

shun [ʃʌn] fuir, éviter.

shunt [ʃʌnt] **1.** 👥 garage *m*; 👥 changement *m* de voie; ⚡ shunt *m*; **2.** *v/t.* 👥 manœuvrer, garer; *fig.* détourner; ⚡ shunter; ~ *with care* défense de tamponner!; *v/i.* 👥 se garer; *fig.* s'esquiver; **'shunt·er** 👥 gareur *m*; *sl.* pousseur (-euse *f*) *m*; **'shunt·ing yard** 👥 chantier *m* de voies de garage et de triage.

shut [ʃʌt] [*irr.*] *v/t.* fermer; ~ *one's eyes to* fermer les yeux sur; *se refuser à*; ~ *down* fermer (*une usine*); couper (*la vapeur*); arrêter (*le moteur*); ~ *in* enfermer; entourer (de, *by*); *se* pincer (*le doigt*) dans; ~ *into* enfermer dans; ~ *out* exclure; ~ *up* enfermer; F faire taire (*q.*); ~ *up shop sl.* fermer boutique; *v/i.* (se) fermer; F ~ *up!* taisez-vous!, *sl.* la ferme!; **'~·down** fermeture *f*, chômage *m*; **~'out** *sp. Am.* victoire *f* écrasante; **'shut·ter** volet *m*; *phot.* obturateur *m*; *instantaneous* ~ obturateur *m* instantané; *phot.* ~ *speed* vitesse *f* d'obturation.

shut·tle [ʃʌtl] **1.** *tex.*, *a.* 👥 navette *f*; ~ *service* (service *m* de) navette *f*; ~ *train* train *m* qui fait la navette; **2.** faire la navette; **'~·cock** volant *m*.

shy¹ [ʃai] **1.** □ timide; farouche (*animal*); ombrageux (-euse *f*) (*cheval*); be (F *fight*) ~ *of* (*gér.*) hésiter à (*inf.*); *sl. I'm* ~ *ten pounds* il me manque dix livres; je suis en perte de dix livres; **2.** prendre ombrage (de, *at*) (*a. fig.*); faire un écart.

shy² F [~] **1.** lancer (*une pierre*); **2.** jet *m*; tentative *f* (pour faire qch., *at s.th.*); *have a* ~ *at* s'essayer à.

shy·ness ['ʃainis] timidité *f*.

shy·ster *sl.*, *surt. Am.* ['ʃaistə] homme *m* d'affaires véreux; avocassier *m*.

Si·a·mese [saiə'mi:z] **1.** siamois; **2.** *ling.* siamois *m*; Siamois(e *f*) *m*.

Si·be·ri·an [sai'biəriən] **1.** sibérien(ne *f*), de Sibérie; **2.** Sibérien(ne *f*) *m*.

sib·i·lant ['sibilənt] **1.** □ sifflant; ⚡ sibilant; **2.** *gramm.* sifflante *f*.

sib·ling ['siblin] frère *m*; sœur *f*.

sib·yl·line [si'bilain] sybillin.

Si·cil·ian [si'siljən] **1.** sicilien(ne *f*); **2.** Sicilien(ne *f*) *m*.

sick [sik] malade (de *of*, *with*); *fig.* las(se *f*), dégoûté (de, *of*); malsain; macabre; be ~ vomir; *fig.* be ~ (and tired) *of* (en) avoir assez de, F en avoir marre de; *feel* ~ avoir mal au cœur; go ~ se faire porter malade; **'~-bed** lit *m* de malade; **'~-cer·tif·i·cate** attestation *f* de médecin; **'sick·en** *v/i.* tomber malade; languir (*plante*); ~ se lasser (de qch., *of s.th.*); ~ *at* être écœuré à la vue de *ou* de voir; *v/t.* rendre malade; dégoûter; **'sick·fund** caisse *f* de maladie; **'~-in·sur·ance** assurance-maladie *f*.

sick·le ['sikl] faucille *f*.

sick-leave ['sikli:v] congé *m* de maladie; **'sick·li·ness** mauvaise santé *f*, état *m* maladif; pâleur *f*; *odeur etc.:* caractère *m* écœurant; *climat:* insalubrité *f*; **'sick·ly** maladif (-ive *f*); étiolé (*plante*); pâle; fade; écœurant (*odeur etc.*); malsain, insalubre (*climat*); **'sick·ness** maladie *f*; mal *m*; nausées *f/pl.*; *Brit.* ~ *benefit* prestations *f/pl.* d'assurance maladie; ~ *pay* indemnité *f* de maladie.

side [said] **1.** *usu.* côté *m*; flanc *m*; pente *f*; bord *m*; *sp.* camp *m*, équipe *f*; *pol. etc.* parti *m*; ~ *by* ~ côte à côte, ⚓ bord à bord; *fig.* en plus (de, *with*); ~ *by* ~ *with* à côté de; *at* (*ou by*) *s.o.'s* ~ à côté de q.; *Am* on the ~ par-dessus le marché; **2.** latéral (-aux *m/pl.*), de côté; secondaire; ~ *effect* effet *m* secondaire; ~ *street* rue *f* transversale; **3.** prendre parti (pour, *with*); se ranger du côté (de, *with*); **'~-arms** *pl.* ✖ armes *f/pl.* blanches; **'~-board** buffet *m*; *Brit.* ~s *pl.* = **'~-burns** *pl. Am.* favoris *m/pl.*, pattes *f/pl.*; **'~-car** *mot.* side-car *m*; **'sid·ed:** *four-*~ à quatre faces.

side...: **'~-face** profil *m*; *attr.* de profil; **'~-kick** *surt. Am.* F copain *m*, copine *f*; sous-fifre *m*; **'~-light** fenêtre *f* latérale; *mot.* feu *m* de côté; *fig.* aperçu *m* indirect; **'~-line** 👥 voie *f* secondaire; *fig.* occupation *f* secondaire; **'~-long 1.** *adv.* de côté; obliquement; **2.** *adj.* de côté, en coulisse (*a. fig.*); **'~-path** sentier *m* de côté; chemin *m* de traverse.

si·de·re·al *astr.* [sai'diəriəl] sidéral (-aux *m/pl.*).

side...: **'~-sad·dle** selle *f* de dame; **'~-slip** ✈ glisser sur l'aile; *mot.*, *a.*

cycl. déraper; '**~-split·ting** homérique (*rire*), F désopilant; '**~-step 1.** pas *m* de côté; **2.** *v/i.* faire un pas de côté; *v/t. fig.* éviter; '**~-stroke** nage *f* sur le côté; '**~-track 1.** 🚂 voie *f* secondaire *ou* de service; **2.** garer (*un train*); aiguiller (*un train*) sur une voie de service; *souv. Am. fig.* détourner; '**~-walk** *surt. Am.* trottoir *m*; **side·ward** ['saidwəd] **1.** *adj.* latéral (-aux *m/pl.*), de côté; **2.** *adv.* (a. **side·wards** ['~z], '**side·ways** ['~weiz], '**side·wise**) de côté.

sid·ing 🚂 ['saidiŋ] voie *f* de garage *ou* de service; embranchement *m*.

si·dle ['saidl] s'avancer *etc.* de guingois *ou* de côté.

siege [si:dʒ] siège *m*; *lay* ~ *to* assiéger.

sieve [siv] crible *m*; tamis *m*.

sift [sift] *v/t.* passer au crible *ou* au tamis; *fig.* examiner en détail; ~ *out fig.* démêler; *v/i. fig.* filtrer; '**sift·er** cribleur (-euse *f*) *m*; tamiseur (-euse *f*) *m*; crible *m*; tamis *m*.

sigh [sai] **1.** soupir *m*; **2.** soupirer (*pour, for*; *après, after*).

sight [sait] **1.** vue *f*; *fig.* spectacle *m*; portée *f* de la vue; visée *f*; bouton *m* de mire, guidon *m* (*d'une arme à feu*); 🔫 vue *f*; F beaucoup; *a* ~ *of* énormément de; *a* ~ *too big de* beaucoup trop grand; ~*s pl.* monuments *m/pl.*, curiosités *f/pl.* (*d'une ville*); beautés *f/pl.* naturelles; *second* ~ seconde vue *f*; voyance *f*; *at* (*ou* on) ~ à vue (a. 🎵, a. ♪); *du premier coup*; *by* ~ de vue; *catch* ~ *of* apercevoir, entrevoir; *lose* ~ *of* perdre de vue; *out of* ~ caché aux regards, hors de vue; *take* ~ viser; *within* ~ en vue, à portée de la vue; **2.** *v/t.* apercevoir; viser; pointer (*une arme à feu*); 🔫 voir (*un effet*); *v/i.* viser; '**sight·ed** à la vue; qui voit; '**sight·ing-line** ligne *f* de visée; '**sight·less** aveugle; '**sight·li·ness** beauté *f*, grâce *f*, charme *m*; '**sight·ly** charmant, avenant.

sight...: '**~-'read** [*irr.* (read)] ♪ jouer *ou* chanter à première vue; '**~-see·ing** visite *f* (de la ville); tourisme *m*; '**~-se·er** excursionniste *mf*; curieux (-euse *f*) *m*; '**~-sing·ing** ♪ chant *m* à vue.

sign [sain] **1.** signe *m*; réclame *f*; *auberge etc.*: enseigne *f*; *fig.* trace *f*; indice *m*; ~ *manual* signature *f*; seing *m*; *in* (*ou as a*) ~ *of* en signe de; **2.** *v/t.* signer; faire signe; *v/t.* signer; ~ *on v/t.* embaucher, engager; *v/i.* s'embaucher.

sig·nal ['signl] **1.** signal *m*; signe *m*; 🔀 *Brit.* ~*s pl.* sapeurs-télégraphistes *m/pl.*; *téléph.* *busy* ~ signal *m* de ligne occupée; **2.** □ insigne; remarquable; **3.** *vt/i.* signaler; *v/t.* donner un signal à; '**~-box** 🔀 cabine *f* à signaux *ou* d'aiguillage; **sig·nal·ize** ['~nəlaiz] signaler, marquer; *see signal 3*; '**sig·nal·man** signaleur *m*.

sig·na·to·ry ['signətəri] signataire (a. *su./mf*); ~ *powers pl.* to *an agreement* pays *m/pl.* *ou* puissances *f/pl.* signataires d'une convention *ou* d'un accord.

sig·na·ture ['signitʃə] 🎵, *typ.* signature *f*; *admin.* visa *m*; ♪ armature *f*, armure *f*; ~ *tune radio*: indicatif *m* musical.

sign·board ['sainbɔːd] *boutique etc.*: enseigne *f*; écriteau *m* indicateur; '**sign·er** signataire *mf*.

sig·net ['signit] sceau *m*, cachet *m*; '**~-ring** chevalière *f*; † anneau *m* à cachet.

sig·nif·i·cance, **sig·nif·i·can·cy** [sig'nifikəns(i)] signification *f*; importance *f*; **sig'nif·i·cant** □ significatif (-ive *f*); ~ *of* qui accuse *ou* trahit; **sig·ni·fi·ca·tion** signification *f*, sens *m*; **sig'nif·i·ca·tive** [~kətiv] significatif (-ive *f*) (*de, of*).

sig·ni·fy ['signifai] *v/t.* signifier; être (le) signe de; faire connaître; vouloir dire; *v/i.* importer; *it does not* ~ cela ne fait rien.

sign...: '**~-paint·er** peintre *m* d'enseignes; '**~-post** poteau *m* indicateur.

si·lence ['sailəns] **1.** silence *m*; ~! silence!, taisez-vous!; **2.** faire taire; réduire au silence; '**si·lenc·er** ⊕ amortisseur *m* de son; *mot.* pot *m* d'échappement.

si·lent □ ['sailənt] silencieux (-euse *f*); muet(te *f*) (a. *lettre*); *fig.* taciturne; ~ *film* film *m* muet; *surt. Am.* 🎬 ~ *partner* commanditaire *m*.

sil·hou·ette [silu'et] **1.** silhouette *f*; **2.**: *be* ~*d against* se silhouetter contre.

sil·i·cate 🜍 ['silikit] silicate *m*; **sil·i·cat·ed** ['~keitid] silicat(is)é; **si·li·ceous** [si'liʃəs] siliceux (-euse *f*); boueux (-euse *f*) (*sources*).

silk [silk] **1.** soie *f*; *p.ext.* fil *m* de soie, rayonne *f*; ⚡ conseiller *m* du roi; **2.** de soie; en soie; à soie; **'silk·en** de *ou* en soie; soyeux (-euse *f*); *fig.* mielleux (-euse *f*); *see* silky; **'silk·i·ness** nature *f* soyeuse; *fig.* *voix*: moelleux *m*; **'silk·'stock·ing** *Am.* distingué; **'silk·worm** ver *m* à soie; **'silk·y** □ soyeux (-euse *f*); *fig.* *péj.* mielleux (-euse *f*).

sill [sil] seuil *m*; rebord *m* (de fenêtre).

sil·li·ness ['silinis] sottise *f*.

sil·ly □ ['sili] sot(te *f*), niais, stupide; *journ.* ~ *season* l'époque *f* où la politique chôme.

si·lo ['sailou] silo *m*.

silt [silt] **1.** vase *f*, limon *m*; **2.** (*usu.* ~ *up*) *v/t.* envaser, ensabler; *v/i.* s'ensabler.

sil·ver ['silvə] **1.** argent *m*; argenterie *f*; pièce *f* *ou* pièces *f/pl.* d'argent; **2.** d'argent, en argent; *fig.* argenté; **3.** (*ou* ⊕ ~-*plate*) argenter (*a. fig.*); étamer (*un miroir*); **'sil·ver·y** argenté (*a. zo.*, *a.* ♀); d'argent; argentin (*ton, rire, voix*).

sim·i·lar □ ['similə] pareil(le *f*), semblable; ♀ *qqfois* similaire; **sim·i·lar·i·ty** [~'læriti] ressemblance *f*; similitude *f* (*a.* ♀).

sim·i·le ['simili] comparaison *f*, image *f*.

si·mil·i·tude [si'militju:d] similitude *f*, ressemblance *f*; allégorie *f*.

sim·mer ['simə] *v/i.* frémir; mijoter (*a. fig.*); *fig.* fermenter, être près d'éclater; *v/t.* faire mijoter.

Si·mon ['saimən] Simon *m*; F *the real* ~ *Pure* l'objet *m* authentique; la véritable personne *f*; F *simple* ~ nicodème *m*.

si·moom [si'mu:m] simoun *m*.

sim·per ['simpə] **1.** sourire *m* minaudier; **2.** minauder; faire des grimaces.

sim·ple □ ['simpl] simple; naïf (-ïve *f*); crédule; **'~-'heart·ed**, **'~-'mind·ed** simple, naïf (-ïve *f*), ingénu; **sim·ple·ton** ['~tən] nigaud(e *f*) *m*.

sim·plic·i·ty [sim'plisiti] candeur *f*; naïveté *f*; simplicité *f*; **sim·pli·fi·ca·tion** [~fi'keiʃn] simplification *f*; **sim·pli·fy** ['~fai] simplifier.

sim·ply ['simpli] *adv.* simplement *etc.*; *see* simple; absolument; uniquement.

sim·u·late ['simjuleit] simuler, feindre; se faire passer pour; **sim·u·'la·tion** simulation *f*, feinte *f*.

si·mul·ta·ne·i·ty [siməltə'niəti] simultanéité *f*.

si·mul·ta·ne·ous □ [siməl'teinjəs] simultané; qui arrive en même temps (que, *with*); **si·mul'ta·ne·ous·ness** simultanéité *f*.

sin [sin] **1.** péché *m*; **2.** pécher; *fig.* ~ *against* blesser (*qch.*).

since [sins] **1.** *prp.* depuis; **2.** *adv.* depuis; *long* ~ depuis *ou* il y a longtemps; *how long* ~? il y a combien de cela?; *a short time* ~ il y a peu de temps; **3.** *cj.* depuis que; puisque; que.

sin·cere □ [sin'siə] sincère; franc(he *f*); *yours* ~*ly* votre tout(e) dévoué(e *f*); cordialement à vous; **sin·cer·i·ty** [~'seriti] sincérité *f*, bonne foi *f*.

sine ♀ [sain] sinus *m*.

si·ne·cure ['sainikjuə] sinécure *f*.

sin·ew ['sinju:] tendon *m*; *cuis.* croquant *m*; *fig.* *usu.* ~*s* *pl.* nerf *m*, force *f*; **'sin·ew·y** musclé, nerveux (-euse *f*); *cuis.* tendineux (-euse *f*).

sin·ful □ ['sinful] pécheur (-eresse *f*); coupable; F scandaleux (-euse *f*); **'sin·ful·ness** culpabilité *f*; péché *m*.

sing [siŋ] [*irr.*] *v/t.* chanter (*fig.* = raconter, célébrer); célébrer; *v/i.* chanter (*bouilloire*); siffler (*vent etc.*); tinter, bourdonner (*oreilles*); *Am. sl.* se mettre à table, moucharder; F ~ *out* crier; F ~ *small* déchanter; se dégonfler, filer doux; ~ *another song* (*ou tune*) chanter une autre chanson; F changer de ton.

singe [sindʒ] brûler légèrement; roussir (*le drap*); *coiffeur*: brûler (*la pointe des cheveux*).

sing·er ['siŋə] chanteur (-euse *f*) *m*; *eccl.*, *a. poét.* chantre *m*; cantatrice *f* (*de profession*).

sing·ing ['siŋiŋ] chant *m*; ~-*bird* oiseau *m* chanteur.

sin·gle ['siŋgl] **1.** □ seul; simple; unique; individuel(le *f*); célibataire, pas marié; ✝ ~ *bill* billet *m* à ordre; ~ *combat* combat *m* singulier; *bookkeeping by* ~ *entry* comptabilité *f* en partie simple; *in* ~ *file* en file indienne; **2.** ⛓ aller *m* (simple); *théâ.* *etc.* place *f* séparée *ou* isolée; ♪ *disque*: 45 tours *m/inv.*; (*a.* ~ *game*) *tennis*: (partie *f*) simple *m*; **3.**

single-breasted

(*usu.* ~ *out*) choisir; distinguer; '~-'**breast·ed** droit (*veston etc.*); '~-'**en·gin·ed** ✕ à un moteur; '~-'**hand·ed** sans aide, seul; '~-'**heart·ed** □, '~-'**mind·ed** □ sincère, loyal (-aux *m/pl.*), honnête; '~-'**line** à voie unique; '**sin·gle·ness** sincérité *f*, honnêteté *f*; célibat *m*; unicité *f*; '**sin·gle-seat·er** ✕, *mot.* monoplace *m*; '**sin·gle·stick** canne *f*; **sin·glet** ✝ ['~lit] gilet *m* de corps; *sp.* maillot *m* fin; **sin·gle·ton** ['~tən] *cartes*: singleton *m*; '**sin·gle-'track** à une voie, à voie unique.

sing·song ['siŋsɔŋ] chant *m* monotone; *fig.* concert *m* improvisé.

sin·gu·lar ['siŋgjulə] **1.** □ seul; singulier (-ère *f*) (*a. gramm.*); remarquable, rare; bizarre; **2.** *gramm.* (*a.* ~ *number*) singulier *m*; **sin·gu·lar·i·ty** [~'læriti] singularité *f*.

Sin·ha·lese [sinhə'liːz] **1.** cingalais; **2.** *ling.* cingalais *m*; Cingalais(e *f*) *m*.

sin·is·ter □ ['sinistə] sinistre; menaçant; ⊘ sénestre.

sink [siŋk] **1.** [*irr.*] *v/i.* ⚓ sombrer; couler; descendre; s'enfoncer (dans, *into*); tomber (dans, *into*); se tasser (*édifice*); se renverser (*dans un fauteuil*); succomber, se plier (sous *beneath, under*); baisser; se serrer (*cœur*); *v/t.* enfoncer; baisser; ⚓ couler, faire sombrer; ✕ mouiller; creuser, foncer (*un puits*); amortir (*une dette*); placer (*de l'argent*); renoncer provisoirement à (*un nom*); supprimer (*une objection*); **2.** évier *m* (*de cuisine*); †, *a. fig.* cloaque *m*; '**sink·er** ✕ fonceur *m* de puits, puisatier *m*; *ligne de pêche*: plomb *m*; '**sink·ing** foncement *m*; ⚓ naufrage *m*, torpillage *m*; tassement *m*; *fig.* défaillance *f*; ✽ affaiblissement *m*; ~ *fund* caisse *f* d'amortissement.

sin·less ['sinlis] sans péché, pur.

sin·ner ['sinə] pécheur (-eresse *f*) *m*.

Sinn Fein ['ʃin'fein] (= *nous-mêmes*) *mouvement nationaliste irlandais*.

Sino... [sino] sino...

sin·u·os·i·ty [sinju'ɔsiti] sinuosité *f*; *route*: lacet *m*; '**sin·u·ous** □ sinueux (-euse *f*), tortueux (-euse *f*), onduleux (-euse *f*); agile (*personne*).

si·nus *anat.* ['sainəs] sinus *m*; **si·nus·i·tis** ✽ [~'saitis] sinusite *f*.

sip [sip] **1.** petite gorgée *f*, F goutte *f*; **2.** boire à petits coups, siroter.

si·phon ['saifən] **1.** siphon *m* (à eau de seltz); **2.** *v/t.* siphonner; *v/i.* se transvaser.

sir [sə:] monsieur (*pl.* messieurs) *m*; ♀ *titre de chevalerie, suivi du prénom:* Sir.

sire ['saiə] **1.** *poét.* père *m*; *titre donné à un souverain:* sire *m*; *zo.* père *m*, *souv.* étalon *m*; **2.** *zo.* engendrer.

si·ren ['saiərin] sirène *f* (*a.* = *trompe d'alarme*).

sir·loin ['sə:lɔin] aloyau *m*.

sis·kin *orn.* ['siskin] tarin *m*.

sis·sy *Am.* ['sisi] mollasson *m*.

sis·ter ['sistə] sœur *f* (*a. eccl.*); *eccl.* religieuse *f*; (*a. ward-*~) infirmière *f* en chef; ~ *of charity* (*ou mercy*) sœur *f* de Charité; **sis·ter·hood** ['~hud] communauté *f* religieuse; '**sis·ter-in-law** belle-sœur (*pl.* belles-sœurs) *f*; '**sis·ter·ly** de sœur.

sit [sit] [*irr.*] *v/i.* s'asseoir; être assis; siéger (*assemblée*); couver (*poule*); se présenter (à, *for*); poser (pour, *for*); ~ *down* s'asseoir; *fig.* ~ (*up*)*on s.o.* remettre q. à sa place; *sl.* moucher q.; ~ *up* veiller tard, se coucher tard; se redresser (*sur sa chaise*); F *make s.o.* ~ *up* étonner q.; *v/t.* asseoir; ~ *a horse well* se tenir bien à cheval; ~ *s.th. out* rester jusqu'à la fin de qch.; ~ *s.o. out* rester jusqu'après le départ de q.; '~-**down strike** grève *f* sur le tas.

site [sait] **1.** emplacement *m*; site *m*; terrain *m* à bâtir; **2.** situer, placer.

sit·ter ['sitə] personne *f* assise; personne *f* qui pose; *poule*: couveuse *f*; *Am. see* baby-sitter; *sl.* affaire *f* sûre.

sit·ting ['sitiŋ] séance *f*; ⚖ session *f*; '~-**room** petit salon *m*.

sit·u·at·ed ['sitjueitid] situé; *thus* ~ dans cette situation; ainsi situé; **sit·u·a·tion** situation *f*, position *f*; emploi *m*, place *f*.

six [siks] six (*a. su./m*); *be at* ~*es and sevens* être sens dessus dessous; manquer d'ensemble; *two and* ~ deux shillings *m/pl.* et six pence *m/pl.*; '~-**fold 1.** *adj.* sextuple; **2.** *adv.* six fois autant; **six·teen** ['~'ti:n] seize (*a. su./m*); '**six'teenth** [~θ] seizième (*a. su./m*); **sixth** [~θ] sixième (*a. su./m*); '**sixth·ly** sixièmement; **six·ti·eth** ['~tiiθ] soixantième (*a. su./m*); '**six·ty** soixante (*a. su./m*).

size[1] [saiz] **1.** grandeur *f*; grosseur *f*; *personne*: taille *f*; *papier etc.*: format *m*; *souliers etc.*: pointure *f*; *chemise*: encolure *f*; numéro *m*; **2.** classer par grosseur *etc.*; ~ *s.o. up* juger q., prendre la mesure de q.; *large-~d* de grande taille.

size[2] [~] **1.** colle *f*; *tex.* empois *m*; **2.** apprêter, (en)coller; *tex.* parer.

siz(e)·a·ble □ ['saizəbl] assez grand; d'une belle taille.

siz·zle ['sizl] grésillement *m*; *radio*: friture *f*.

skate[1] [skeit] *icht.* raie *f*.

skate[2] [~] **1.** patin *m*; (*ou roller-~*) patin *m* à roulettes; **2.** patiner (*a.* sur roulettes); '**skat·er** patineur (-euse *f*) *m*; '**skat·ing-rink** skating *m*; patinoire *f*.

ske·dad·dle F [ski'dædl] se sauver; décamper, filer.

skee·sicks *Am.* F ['ski:ziks] vaurien *m*.

skein [skein] *laine etc.*: écheveau *m*.

skel·e·ton ['skelitn] **1.** squelette *m*, *homme, bâtiment, etc.*: ossature *f*, charpente *f*; carcasse *f* (*a. d'un parapluie*); *roman etc.*: esquisse *f*; ✕ personnel *m* réduit; ✕ cadre *m*; *fig.* ~ *in the cupboard* (*Am.* closet) secret *m* honteux (de la famille); **2.** réduit; esquisse *f* de; ⊕ à clairevoie, à jour; ✕ *-cadre*; ~ *crew* équipage *m ou* personnel *m* réduit; ~ *key* passepartout *m/inv.*; *sl.* rossignol *m* (*de cambrioleur*); ~ *map* carte *f* muette.

skep·tic *Am.* ['skeptik] *see* sceptic.

sketch [sketʃ] **1.** esquisse *f*, croquis *m*; *théâ.* sketch *m*, saynète *f*; *fig.* aperçu *m*, plan *m*; **2.** esquisser; faire un *ou* des croquis de; '**sketch·y** □ imprécis; rudimentaire.

skew [skju:] (de) biais.

skew·er ['skuə] **1.** brochette *f*; **2.** brocheter.

ski [ʃi:] **1.** *pl.* **ski(s)** ski *m*; *attr.* de ski; à ski; ~ *platform* plate-forme *f* (*pl.* plates-formes) *f*; tremplin *m*; ~ *run* piste *f* de ski; **2.** faire du ski.

skid [skid] **1.** sabot *m ou* patin *m* d'enrayage; ✈ patin *m*; *mot.* dérapage *m*, embardée *f*; *mot.* ~ *mark* trace *f* de dérapage; **2.** *v/t.* ensaboter, enrayer; mettre sur traîneau; *v/i.* déraper, glisser; *mot.* faire une embardée; ✈ glisser sur l'aile; ~ *row*

Am. quartier *m* de(s) clochards; *be on* ~ être clochard.

ski·er ['ʃi:ə] skieur (-euse *f*) *m*.

skiff ⚓ [skif] esquif *m*; youyou *m* (*de bateau de commerce*); *canotage*: skiff *m*.

ski·ing ['ʃi:iŋ] ski *m*; '**ski-jump** tremplin *m* de ski; (*a.* '**ski·jump·ing**) saut *m* à skis; '**ski-lift** (re)monte-pente *m*.

skil(l)·ful □ ['skilful] adroit, habile; '**skil(l)·ful·ness, skill** [skil] adresse *f*, habileté *f*.

skilled [skild] habile; spécialisé (*ouvrier etc.*); expérimenté (*en at, in*).

skim [skim] **1.** *v/t.* (*souv.* ~ *off*) écumer; dégraisser (*la soupe*); écrémer (*le lait*); *fig.* effleurer (*la surface*); ~ *through* feuilleter, parcourir rapidement; *v/i.* glisser (*sur, over*); **2.**: ~ *milk* lait *m* écrémé; '**skim·mer** écumoire *f*; écrémoir *m*.

skimp [skimp] ménager outre mesure; mesurer (*qch. à q., s.o. in s.th.*); lésiner sur tout; F bâcler (*un ouvrage*); '**skimp·y** □ maigre, insuffisant; chiche, parcimonieux (-euse *f*) (*personne*).

skin [skin] **1.** peau *f* (*a. d'un animal, d'orange*); cuir *m*; pelure *f* (*de banane*); *café, lait, raisin*: pellicule *f*; *saucisson*: robe *f*; outre *f* (*à vin*); ⚓ *navire*: coque *f*, voile: chemise *f*; ⊕ *fonte*: croûte *f*; *by* (*ou with*) *the* ~ *of one's teeth* tout juste; à peine; *Am.* F *have got s.o. under one's* ~ ne pouvoir oublier *ou* se débarrasser de q.; **2.** *v/t.* écorcher; peler, éplucher (*un fruit*); *sl.* tondre (*q.*), dépouiller (*q.*) (*au jeu*); *keep one's eyes ~ned* avoir l'œil américain; F ~ *off* enlever (*les bas etc.*); *v/i.* (*a.* ~ *over*) se recouvrir de peau; '~-'**deep** à fleur de peau, peu profond; '~-'**dive** faire de la plongée sous-marine; '~-'**div·ing** plongée *f* sous-marine; '~-'**flick** *surt. Am. sl.* film *m* porno; '~-'**graft·ing** ✂ greffe *f* épidermique; '**skin·ner** écorcheur *m*; pelletier *m*; '**skin·ny** décharné, maigre; efflanqué (*cheval*); F chiche, avare.

skint *Brit. sl.* [skint] fauché, sans le rond.

skin·tight ['skintait] collant.

skip [skip] **1.** saut *m*; gambade *f*; ✕ benne *f*; **2.** *v/i.* sauter, gambader;

v/t. (*a.* ~ *over*) sauter (*qch.*); '**~-jack** poussah *m*; *zo.* scarabée *m* à ressort.

skip·per[1] ['skipə] sauteur (-euse *f*) *m.*

skip·per[2] [~] patron *m*, capitaine *m*; *sp.* chef *m* d'équipe.

skip·ping-rope ['skipiŋroup] corde *f* à sauter.

skir·mish ⚔ ['skə:miʃ] **1.** escarmouche *f*; **2.** escarmoucher; tirailler (contre, with); '**skir·mish·er** tirailleur *m.*

skirt [skə:t] **1.** *cost.* jupe *f*; *pardessus etc.*: pans *m/pl.*; *souv.* ~s *pl.* bord *m*; *forêt*: lisière *f*; **2.** *v/t.* border; *vt/i.* (*a.* ~ *along*), longer, contourner, côtoyer; '**skirt·ing-board** ⊕ plinthe *f*; bas *m* de lambris.

skit[1] [skit] *usu.* ~s *pl.* tas *m/pl.*

skit[2] [~] pièce *f* satirique; satire *f* (de, on); '**skit·tish** □ ombrageux (-euse *f*) (*cheval*); volage, capricieux (-euse *f*) (*personne*).

skit·tle ['skitl] quille *f*; *play* (*at*) ~s jouer aux quilles; '**~-al·ley** jeu *m* de quilles.

skive *Brit. sl.* [skaiv] tirer au flanc; **skiv·er** tire-au-flanc *mf/inv.*

skiv·vy F *péj.* ['skivi] bonniche *f* (= *bonne à tout faire*).

skul·dug·ger·y *Am.* F [skʌl'dʌgəri] fourberie *f*, ruse *f.*

skulk [skʌlk] se tenir caché; se cacher; rôder furtivement; '**skulk·er** carotteur (-euse *f*) *m.*

skull [skʌl] crâne *m.*

skunk [skʌŋk] *zo.* mouffette *f*; *fourrure*: skunks *m/pl.*; F mufle *m*; ladre *m.*

sky [skai] *souv.* skies *pl.* ciel (*pl.* cieux, ciels) *m*; '**~-'blue** bleu ciel *adj./inv.* (*a. su./m/inv.*); '**~-div·ing** parachutisme *m* en chute libre; '**~-lark 1.** *orn.* alouette *f* des champs; **2.** rigoler; '**~-light** jour *m* d'en haut; lucarne *f*; '**~-line** ligne *f* d'horizon; profil *m* (de l'horizon); ~ *advertising* publicité *f* dessinée en silhouette sur le ciel; '**~-rock·et** *Am.* F augmenter rapidement; monter en flèche (*prix*); '**~-scrap·er** gratte-ciel *m/inv.*; **sky·ward(s)** ['~wəd(z)] vers le ciel; '**sky-writ·ing** ✈ publicité *f* aérienne.

slab [slæb] *pierre*: dalle *f*; *ardoise*: table *f*; *métal, marbre, etc.*: plaque *f*; *chocolat*: tablette *f*; ⊕ *bois*: dosse *f.*

slack [slæk] **1.** lâche; faible (*a.* ✝);

négligent (*personne*); ✝ *a.* peu vif (vive *f*); ⚓ ~ *water*, ~ *tide* mer *f* étale; **2.** ⚓ *cable etc.*: mou *m*; ✝ accalmie *f*; ⊕ jeu *m*; ~s *pl.* pantalon *m*; **3.** *see* ~en; *see* slake; F flémarder; '**slack·en** (se) relâcher; (se) ralentir; diminuer (de); *v/t.* détendre; ⊕ donner du jeu à; *v/i.* devenir négligent; prendre du mou (*cordage, câble*); ✝ s'alanguir; '**slack·er** F paresseux (-euse *f*), F flémard(e *f*) *m*; ⚔ tireur *m* au flanc; '**slack·ness** relâchement *m*; négligence *f*; lenteur *f*; paresse *f*; ✝ stagnation *f.* [scoriacé.)

slag [slæg] scories *f/pl.*; '**slag·gy**)

slain [slein] *p.p. de* slay.

slake [sleik] étancher (*la soif*); éteindre (*le chaux*).

slam [slæm] **1.** *porte*: claquement *m*; *bridge*: chelem *m*; **2.** *v/t.* (faire) claquer; fermer avec violence; *v/i.* claquer.

slan·der ['sla:ndə] **1.** calomnie *f*; **2.** calomnier, diffamer; '**slan·der·er** calomniateur (-trice *f*) *m*; ⚖ diffamateur (-trice *f*) *m*; '**slan·der·ous** □ calomnieux (-euse *f*); ⚖ diffamatoire.

slang [slæŋ] **1.** argot *m*; **2.** F réprimander vivement; injurier; ~*ing match* prise *f* de bec; '**slang·y** □ argotier (-ère *f*), argotique.

slant [sla:nt] **1.** pente *f*, inclinaison *f*; biais *m*; *Am.* F point *m* de vue; **2.** *v/t.* incliner; *v/i.* (s')incliner, être en pente; être oblique; '**slant·ing** □ *adj.*, '**slant·wise** *adv.* en biais, de biais; oblique(ment *adv.*).

slap [slæp] **1.** coup *m*, tape *f*; claquement *m* (*d'un piston*); ~ *in the face* gifle *f*, soufflet *m*; *fig.* affront *m*; **2.** claquer; gifler; donner une tape à; **3.** pan!; '**~-bang** de but en blanc; '**~-dash** sans soin; à la six-quatre-deux; '**~-jack** *Am.* crêpe *f*; '**~-stick** *théâ.* batte *f* (d'Arlequin); ~ *comedy* pièce *f* etc. burlesque; arlequinades *f/pl.*; '**~-up** F fameux (-euse *f*), de premier ordre.

slash [slæʃ] **1.** balafre *f*; entaille *f*; *cost.* taillade *f*; **2.** *v/t.* balafrer; taillader; cingler (*a. fig.*); F éreinter (*un livre etc.*); *cost.* faire des taillades dans; F réduire (*le prix etc.*); *v/i.* frapper à droite et à gauche; cingler; '**slash·ing** □ cinglant (*a. fig.*); *fig. a.* mordant; *sl.* épatant.

slat [slæt] 1. *jalousie*: lame(lle) *f*; *lit*: traverse *f*; 2. battre, frapper sur.
slate [sleit] 1. ardoise *f*; *surt. Am.* liste *f* provisoire des candidats; 2. couvrir d'ardoises *ou* en ardoise; F tancer; F éreinter; be ~d for être un candidat sérieux à (*un poste*); '~-'**pen·cil** crayon *m* d'ardoise; '**slat·er** couvreur *m* (en ardoises).
slat·tern ['slætəːn] 1. souillon *f*; 2. (*a.* '**slat·tern·ly**) mal soigné (*femme*).
slat·y □ ['sleiti] ardoiseux (-euse *f*), schisteux (-euse *f*); ardoisé (*couleur*).
slaugh·ter ['slɔːtə] 1. *bêtes*: abattage *m*; *gibier*: abattis *m*; *fig.* massacre *m*, carnage *m*; 2. abattre; massacrer; '**slaugh·ter·er** abatteur *m*; *fig.* tueur *m*; '**slaugh·ter-house** abattoir *m*; '**slaugh·ter·ous** □ *poét.* meurtrier (-ère *f*).
Slav [slɑːv] 1. slave; 2. Slave *mf*.
slave [sleiv] 1. esclave *mf*; *attr.* d'esclaves, des esclaves; *a. fig.* ~ driver négrier *m*; 2. travailler comme un nègre; peiner.
slav·er¹ ['sleivə] négrier *m*; *personne*: marchand *m* d'esclaves.
slav·er² ['slævə] 1. bave *f*, salive *f*; 2. baver (sur, over).
slav·er·y ['sleivəri] esclavage *m*; *fig.* asservissement *m*.
slav·ey *sl.* ['slævi] bonniche *f*.
Slav·ic ['slɑːvik] 1. slave; 2. *ling.* slave *m*.
slav·ish □ ['sleiviʃ] servile, d'esclave; '**slav·ish·ness** servilité *f*.
slaw *Am.* [slɔː] salade *f* de choux.
slay *poét.* [slei] [*irr.*] tuer, mettre à mort; assassiner; '**slay·er** meurtrier (-ère *f*) *m*; tueur (-euse *f*) *m*; assassin *m*.
slea·zy ['sliːzi] usé; miteux (-euse *f*), minable.
sled [sled] *see* sledge¹.
sledge¹ [sledʒ] 1. traîneau *m*; 2. *v/t.* transporter en traîneau; *v/i.* aller en traîneau.
sledge² [~] (*a.* ~-hammer) marteau *m* de forgeron; masse *f* (*de pierres*).
sleek [sliːk] 1. □ lisse; luisant; *fig.* doucereux (-euse *f*), mielleux (-euse *f*); 2. lisser; planer; '**sleek·ness** luisant *m*; *fig.* douceur *f*, onctuosité *f*.
sleep [sliːp] 1. [*irr.*] *v/i.* dormir (*a. toupie*); coucher; ~ (up)on (*ou* over)

it remettre cela jusqu'au lendemain; consulter son chevet; *v/t.* coucher (*q.*); ~ the hours away passer les heures en dormant; ~ off faire passer (*une migraine*) en dormant; 2. sommeil *m*; go to ~ s'endormir; put (*ou* send) to ~ endormir; (faire) piquer (*un animal*); '**sleep·er** dormeur (-euse *f*) *m*; 🚋 wagon-lit (*pl.* wagons-lits) *m*; couchette *f*; be a light ~ avoir le sommeil léger; '**sleep·i·ness** assoupissement *m*.
sleep·ing ['sliːpiŋ]: ♀ Beauty Belle *f* au bois dormant; ♀ ~ partner commanditaire *m*; '~-bag sac *m* de couchage; '~-car, '~-'car·riage 🚋 wagon-lit (*pl.* wagons-lits) *m*; '~-draught narcotique *m*, somnifère *m*; ~ pill (*comprimé m*) somnifère *m*; '~-'sick·ness maladie *f* du sommeil.
sleep·less □ ['sliːplis] sans sommeil; *fig.* inlassable; '**sleep·less·ness** insomnie *f*.
sleep·walk·er ['sliːpwɔːkə] somnambule *mf*.
sleep·y □ ['sliːpi] somnolent; *fig.* endormi; blet(te *f*) (*fruit*); be ~ avoir sommeil; ~ sickness encéphalite *f* léthargique; '~-head F *fig.* endormi(e *f*) *m*.
sleet [sliːt] 1. neige *f* à moitié fondue; 2.: it is ~ing la pluie tourne à la neige; '**sleet·y** de pluie et de neige, de grésil.
sleeve [sliːv] 1. manche *f*; ⊕ fourreau *m*; *attr.* à manches; de manchette; ⊕ de manchon, à manchon; have something up one's ~ avoir qch. en réserve, avoir qch. dans son sac; laugh up (*ou* in) one's ~ rire sous cape; 2. mettre des manches à; **sleeved** à manches; '**sleeve·less** sans manches; '**sleeve-link** bouton *m* de manchette.
sleigh [slei] 1. traîneau *m*; 2. *v/t.* transporter en traîneau; *v/i.* aller en traîneau.
sleight [slait] (*usu.* ~ of hand) adresse *f*; prestidigitation *f*.
slen·der □ ['slendə] mince, ténu; svelte (*personne*); faible (*espoir*); maigre; modeste, exigu(ë *f*); '**slen·der·ness** minceur *f*; sveltesse *f*; faiblesse *f*; exiguïté *f*.
slept [slept] *prét. et p.p. de* sleep 1.
sleuth [sluːθ] (*a.* ~-hound) limier *m*, F détective *m*.
slew¹ [sluː] *prét. de* slay.

slew² [~] (a. ~ *round*) (faire) pivoter.
slice [slais] **1.** tranche *f*; tartine *f* (*de beurre etc.*); *fig.* part *f*; *cuis.* truelle *f* (à *poisson*); ~ *of luck* coup *m* de veine; **2.** découper en tranches; (a. ~ *off*) trancher, couper; *tennis*: choper; *golf*: faire dévier la balle à droite; **'slic·er** machine *f* à couper; coupe-jambon *m/inv.*
slick [slik] **1.** *adj.* (a. *adv.*) habile (-ment *adv.*), adroit(ement *adv.*); **2.** (a. ~ *paper*) *Am. sl.* magazine *m* de luxe.
slick·er *Am.* ['slikə] F escroc *m* (adroit); imperméable *m*.
slid [slid] *prét. et p.p. de slide 1.*
slide [slaid] **1.** [*irr.*] *v/i.* glisser (dans, into), couler; faire des glissades (*personne*); *let things* ~ laisser tout aller à vau-l'eau; *v/t.* faire glisser; **2.** glissade *f*; coulisse *f*; *cheveux*: barrette *f*; *phot.* châssis *m*; ⊕ glissoir *m*; projection *f*; **'slid·er** glisseur (-euse *f*) *m*; ⊕ coulisseau *m*; **'slide-rule** règle *f* à calcul.
slid·ing ['slaidiŋ] **1.** glissement *m*; **2.** glissant, coulant; *mot.* ~ *roof* toit *m* décapotable; ~ *rule* règle *f* à calcul; ~ *scale* échelle *f* mobile; ~ *seat* *mot.* siège *m* amovible; *canot*: banc *m* à glissières; ~ *table* table *f* à rallonges.
slight [slait] **1.** □ léger (-ère *f*); mince; frêle; svelte; peu important; insignifiant; **2.** affront *m*; manque *m* d'égards (pour, on); **3.** manquer d'égards pour; faire un affront à; **'slight·ing** □ de mépris; dédaigneux (-euse *f*); **'slight·ness** légèreté *f*; minceur *f*; insignifiance *f*.
slim [slim] **1.** □ svelte, mince, élancé; *sl.* mince, léger (-ère *f*); **2.** (s')amincir; *v/i.* suivre un régime amaigrissant; ~*ming line* ligne *f* qui amincit.
slime [slaim] limon *m*, vase *f*; *limace*: bave *f*; *liquide*: bitume *m*.
slim·i·ness ['slaiminis] état *m* vaseux *ou* boueux; *fig.* obséquiosité *f*.
slim·ness ['slimnis] sveltesse *f*.
slim·y □ ['slaimi] vaseux (-euse *f*), boueux (-euse *f*); *fig.* obséquieux (-euse *f*).
sling [sliŋ] **1.** fronde *f*; *barriques*: élingue *f*; suspenseur *m* (de *câble*); ⚕ écharpe *f*; **2.** [*irr.*] lancer (avec

une fronde); élinguer (*un fardeau*); F ~ *over* jeter sur; ~ *up* hisser.
slink [sliŋk] [*irr.*]: ~ *in* (out) entrer (sortir) furtivement; ~ *away* a. s'éclipser.
slip [slip] **1.** [*irr.*] *v/i.* glisser; couler (*nœud*); F aller (vite); (*souv.* ~ *away*) s'esquiver, *fig.* s'écouler; se tromper; *v/t.* glisser, couler; filer (*un câble*); s'échapper de; se dégager de; ~ *in v/t.* introduire; *v/i.* se faufiler, entrer discrètement; ~ *into* se glisser dans; ~ *on* enfiler, passer (*une robe etc.*); ~ *off* enlever, ôter (*une robe etc.*); **2.** glissade *f*; erreur *f*; écart *m* de conduite; faux pas *m*; *oreiller*: taie *f*; *chien*: laisse *f*; *géol.* éboulement *m*; (a. ~ *of paper*) feuille *f*, fiche *f*; ✿ bouture *f*; *fig.* rejeton *m*; *cost.* combinaison *f*; fond *m* de robe; ⚓ cale *f*; chantier *m*; ~*s pl. sp.* slip *m*; caleçon *m* de bain; *théâ.* coulisses *f/pl.*; F a ~ *of a girl* une jeune fille *f* fluette; ~ *of the pen* lapsus *m* calami; ~ *of the tongue* lapsus *m* linguae, faux pas *m*; *give s.o. the* ~ se dérober à q., planter q. là; **'~-knot** nœud *m* coulant; **'~-on** robe *f* etc. à enfiler; **'slip·per** pantoufle *f*; ⊕ patin *m*; **'slip·per·y** □ glissant; incertain; *fig.* matois; **slip·shod** ['~ʃɔd] en savates; *fig.* négligé, bâclé; **slip·slop** ['~'slɔp] bouillons *m/pl.*; lavasse *f*; *fig.* sensiblerie *f*; **slipt** *prét. et p.p. de slip 1;* **'slip-up** F gaffe *f*; contretemps *m*; fiasco *m*.
slit [slit] **1.** fente *f*; ajour *m*; *boîte aux lettres*: guichet *m*; incision *f*; **2.** [*irr.*] (se) fendre; *v/t.* éventrer; faire une incision dans.
slith·er F ['sliðə] *v/i.* glisser; *v/t.* traîner (*les pieds etc.*).
sliv·er ['slivə] **1.** tranche *f*; *bois*: éclat *m*; *tex.* ruban *m*; **2.** *v/t.* couper en tranches; établir les rubans de; *v/i.* éclater.
slob F [slɔb] rustaud *m*, goujat *m*.
slob·ber ['slɔbə] **1.** bave *f*; boue *f*; *fig.* sentimentalité *f* excessive; **2.** baver; *fig.* s'attendrir (sur, over); **'slob·ber·y** baveux (-euse *f*); négligé.
sloe ⚘ [slou] prunelle *f*; *arbre*: prunellier *m*.
slog F [slɔg] **1.** cogner; travailler avec acharnement; **2.** coup *m* violent; corvée *f*, *sl.* boulot *m*.
slo·gan ['slougən] *écoss.* cri *m* de

guerre (a. fig.); pol. mot m d'ordre; ✝ devise f; slogan m; **slo·gan·eer·ing** Am. F [slougə'niəriŋ] emploi m des mots d'ordre ou des cris de guerre. [aviso m.]

sloop ⚓ [slu:p] sloop m; marine:⌐

slop¹ [slɔp] **1.** gâchis m; ~s pl. lavasse f; eaux f/pl. ménagères; **2.** (a. ~ over) v/t. répandre; v/i. déborder; fig. faire de la sensiblerie.

slop² [~] blouse f; vêtements m/pl. de confection; hardes f/pl.; ⚓ frusques f/pl.

slop-ba·sin ['slɔpbeisn] bol m à rinçures (de thé).

slope [sloup] **1.** pente f, inclinaison f; talus m; montagne: versant m; **2.** v/t. couper en pente; taluter; ⊕ biseauter; ✕ ~ arms! l'arme sur l'épaule droite!; v/i. être en pente; incliner; aller en pente; sl. ~ off décamper, filer; '**slop·ing** □ en pente, incliné.

slop-pail ['slɔppeil] seau m de ménage; seau m de toilette; '**slop·py** □ fangeux (-euse f); encore mouillé; cost. mal ajusté, trop large; mou (mol devant une voyelle ou un h muet; molle f) (personne); fig. par trop sentimental (-aux m/pl.).

slop-shop ['slɔpʃɔp] magasin m de confections.

slosh F [slɔʃ] flanquer un coup; '**sloshed** F soûl, bourré.

slot [slɔt] chasse: erres f/pl.; fente f (d'un distributeur); ⊕ entaille f.

sloth [slouθ] paresse f; zo. paresseux m; **sloth·ful** ['~ful] paresseux (-euse f); indolent.

slot-ma·chine ['slɔtməʃi:n] chocolat, cigarettes: distributeur m automatique; jeu de hasard: appareil m à jetons.

slouch [slautʃ] **1.** v/i. manquer de tenue; traîner en marchant; (a. ~ about) rôder; v/t. rabattre le bord de (un chapeau); ~ed rabattu; mollasse (allure); aux épaules arrondies (personne); **2.** démarche f ou allure f mollasse; fainéant m; ~ hat chapeau m rabattu.

slough¹ [slau] bourbier m (a. fig.).

slough² [slʌf] **1.** zo. dépouille f; ⚕ escarre f; plaie: croûte f; **2.** v/i. se dépouiller; ⚕ se couvrir d'une escarre; ⚕ se détacher (croûte); v/t. jeter; fig. (a. ~ off) se dépouiller de.

slough·y ['slaui] bourbeux (-euse f).

Slo·vak ['slouvæk] **1.** ling. slovaque m; Slovaque mf; **2.** (ou **Slo·va·ki·an** [~iən]) slovaque.

slov·en ['slʌvn] souillon f; bousilleur (-euse f) m; '**slov·en·li·ness** négligence f; '**slov·en·ly** mal soigné, malpropre; négligent; débraillé (style, tenue); déhanché (allure).

slow [slou] □ lent (à of, to); en retard (pendule); lourd (esprit); 🚌 omnibus; petit (vitesse); ennuyeux (-euse f) (spectacle etc.); sp. qui ne rend pas; mot. ~ lane voie f pour véhicules lents; 🚂 ~ train train m omnibus; be ~ to (inf.) être lent à (inf.); my watch is ten minutes ~ ma montre retarde de dix minutes; **2.** adv. lentement; **3.** (souv. ~ down, up, off) v/t. ralentir; v/i. ralentir; diminuer de vitesse; '~-coach F lambin(e f) m; '~-match corde f à feu; '-'mo·tion pic·ture film m tourné au ralenti; '**slow·ness** lenteur f; montre: retard m; '**slow-worm** zo. orvet m.

sludge [slʌdʒ] fange f; ⊕ boue f; ✕ schlamm m.

slue [slu:] (a. ~ round) (faire) pivoter.

slug¹ [slʌg] lingot m (a. typ.); lino-type: ligne-bloc (pl. lignes-blocs) f.

slug² zo. [~] limace f.

slug³ Am. F [~] **1.** coup m (violent); coup m (de whisky etc.); **2.** cogner, frapper; ~ it out se rentrer dedans, se taper dessus.

slug·gard ['slʌgəd] paresseux (-euse f) m; fainéant(e f) m; '**slug·gish** □ paresseux (-euse f).

sluice [slu:s] **1.** écluse f; **2.** v/t. vanner; (a. ~ out) laisser échapper; laver à grande eau; v/i. ~ out couler à flots; '~-gate porte f d'écluse; '~-way canal m à vannes.

slum [slʌm] bas quartier m.

slum·ber ['slʌmbə] **1.** a. ~s pl. sommeil m; **2.** sommeiller, dormir; **slum·brous** ['~brəs], **slum·ber·ous** ['~bərəs] assoupi, somnolent.

slump [slʌmp] à la Bourse: **1.** baisse f soudaine; marasme m; F crise f; **2.** baisser tout à coup; s'effondrer.

slung [slʌŋ] prét. et p.p. de sling 2.

slunk [slʌŋk] prét. et p.p. de slink.

slur [slə:] **1.** tache f; fig. affront m, insulte f; mauvaise articulation f; ♪ liaison f; **2.** v/t. (a. ~ over) glisser sur; ♪ lier (deux notes), couler (un *passage*); bredouiller; *v/i.* s'estomper.

slush [slʌʃ] neige *f* à demi fondue; fange *f*; F lavasse *f*; F sensiblerie *f*; **'slush·y** détrempé par la neige; boueux (-euse *f*); F fadasse.

slut [slʌt] souillon *f*; F *co.* coquine *f*; **'slut·tish** malpropre.

sly □ [slai] sournois, rusé, matois; on the ~ en cachette; **'~·boots** F sournois(e *f*) *m*; espiègle *mf*; **'sly-ness** sournoiserie *f*, finesse *f*; espièglerie *f*.

smack[1] [smæk] **1.** léger goût *m*; soupçon *m* (*a. fig.*); *fig.* grain *m*; **2.**: ~ of avoir un goût de; sentir (*qch.*) (*a. fig.*).

smack[2] [~] **1.** *main*: claque *f*; *fouet*: claquement *m*; F gros baiser *m*; F essai *m*; **2.** *v/i.* claquer; *v/t.* faire claquer (*a. un baiser*); frapper, taper (avec, *with*); **3.** *int.* paf!, vlan!

smack[3] ⚓ [~] bateau *m* de pêche.

smack·er *Am. sl.* ['smækə] dollar *m*.

small [smɔ:l] **1.** *usu.* petit; de petite taille; faible (*pouls, ressources*); peu important; menu (*bétail, gibier, plomb*); court (*durée etc.*); léger (-ère *f*) (*progrès*); maigre (*récolte*); fluet(te *f*) (*voix*); bas(se *f*) (*carte*); *une* demi-mesure *f* de (*alcool*); *une* demi-tasse *f* de (*café*); make s.o. feel ~ humilier q., ravaler q.; ~ fry le menu fretin *m*; les gosses *m/pl.*; ~ game menu gibier *m*; ~ holder petit propriétaire *m*; ~ holding petite propriété *f*; in the ~ hours pl. fort avant dans la nuit; *surt. Am.* F *fig.* ~ potatoes bien peu de chose, insignifiant; ~ print les petits caractères *m/pl.*; l'important du bas de la page; † ~ wares pl. mercerie *f*; **2.** partie *f* mince; *charbon*: menu *m*; *jambe*: bas *m*; *anat.* ~ of the back creux *m* des reins; **'~·arms** pl. armes *f/pl.* portatives; **'small·ish** assez petit; **'small·ness** petitesse *f*; mesquinerie *f*; **'small·pox** ⚕ pl. petite vérole *f*; **small talk** banalités *f/pl.*; menus propos *m/pl.*; **'small-time** insignifiant, petit, piètre.

smalt ⊕ [smɔ:lt] smalt *m*; émail (pl. -aux) *m* de cobalt.

smarm·y F ['smɑːmi] mielleux (-euse *f*), flagorneur (-euse *f*).

smart [smɑːt] **1.** □ vif (vive *f*) (*allure, attaque, etc.*) (à *inf.*, in *gér.*); cuisant (*douleur etc.*); vert (*répri-*

mande); ⚔ chaud (*affaire*); habile, adroit; intelligent; éveillé, débrouillard; *péj.* malin (-igne *f*); bien entretenu, soigné; chic *inv.* en genre, élégant, coquet(te *f*); *Am.* ~ *aleck* finaud *m*; *un je sais* tout *m*; **2.** douleur *f* cuisante; **3.** cuire; souffrir (*personne*); you shall ~ for it il vous en cuira; **'smart·en** *v/t.* donner du chic à; *v/i.* prendre du chic; se faire beau; **'smart-mon·ey** pension *f* pour blessure; † forfait *m*; **'smart·ness** finesse *f*; intelligence *f*; élégance *f*, chic *m*; *esprit*: vivacité *f*.

smash [smæʃ] **1.** *v/t.* briser (en morceaux), (*souv.* ~ up) casser; *fig.* détruire; écraser (*a. tennis*); ~ *against* (*ou* on) heurter contre; *v/i.* se briser (contre *against*, on); éclater en morceaux; *fig.* échouer; † ~ (*a.* ~ up) faire faillite; **2.** mise *f* en morceaux; fracas *m*; collision *f*; 🚂 désastre *m*; † débâcle *f*, faillite *f*; *tennis*: smash *m*; F ~ hit succès *m* fou; all to ~ en miettes; **'~-and-'grab raid** vol *m* après bris de devanture; **'smash·er** *sl.* coup *m* écrasant; critique *f* mordante; **'smash·ing** écrasant; F formidable; **'smash-up** destruction *f* complète; collision *f*; † faillite *f*.

smat·ter·er ['smætərə] demi-savant *m*; **'smat·ter·ing** légère connaissance *f*.

smear [smiə] **1.** salir (de, *with*); barbouiller (de, *with*) (*a. une page écrite*); enduire (de graisse, *with grease*); **2.** tache *f*, macule *f*; ⚕ frottis *m* (*de sang*).

smell [smel] **1.** senteur *f*, parfum *m*; (*a. sense of* ~) odorat *m*; **2.** [*irr.*] *v/i.* sentir (*qch.*, of *s.th.*); avoir un parfum; *v/t.* sentir, flairer; (*a.* ~ at) sentir (*une fleur*). [smell 2.]

smelt[1] [smelt] *prét. et p.p. de* [smell 2.]

smelt[2] *icht.* [~] éperlan *m*.

smelt[3] [~] fondre; extraire par fusion; **'smelt·er** ⊕ fondeur *m*; métallurgiste *m*; **'smelt·ing-'fur-nace** fourneau *m* de fusion *ou* de fonte.

smile [smail] **1.** sourire *m*; **2.** sourire (à *at*, on). [souiller.]

smirch *poét.* [smə:tʃ] tacher; *fig.* [souiller.]

smirk [smə:k] **1.** minauder, mignarder; **2.** sourire *m* affecté; minauderie *f*.

smite [smait] [*irr.*] *poét. ou co.* frapper; abattre; ~ *upon* frapper sur; *fig.* frapper (*p.ex. l'oreille*).

smith [smiθ] forgeron *m*.

smith·er·eens F ['smiðə'ri:nz] *pl.* miettes *f/pl.*; morceaux *m/pl.*; *smash to* ~ briser en mille morceaux.

smith·y ['smiði] forge *f*.

smit·ten ['smitn] 1. *p.p. de smite*; 2. frappé, pris (*de, with*); *fig.* épris, amoureux (-euse *f*) (*de, with*).

smock [smɔk] 1. orner de smocks (= *fronces*); 2. (*ou* ~-*frock*) blouse *f*, sarrau *m*.

smog [smɔg] brouillard *m* enfumé.

smoke [smouk] 1. fumée *f*; F action *f* de fumer; F cigare *m*, cigarette *f*; ~-*consumer* (appareil *m*) fumivore *m*; *have a* ~ fumer; 2. *v/i.* fumer; *v/t.* fumer (*du jambon, du tabac*); enfumer (*une plante*); noircir de fumée (*le plafond etc.*); ⚒ enfumer; '~-**dried** fumé; '~-**hel·met** casque *m* à fumée; '**smoke·less** □ sans fumée; fumivore (*foyer*); '**smok·er** fumeur (-euse *f*) *m*; *see smoking-compartment*; '**smoke-screen** ⚔ rideau *m* de fumée; brume *f* artificielle; '**smoke·stack** 🚢, *a.* ⚓ cheminée *f*.

smok·ing ['smoukiŋ] 1. émission *f* de fumée; *jambon*: fumage *m*; *no* ~! défense *f* de fumer; 2. fumant; '~-**com·part·ment** 🚂 compartiment *m* de fumeurs, F fumeur *m*; '~-**con·cert** concert *m* où il est permis de fumer; '~-**room** fumoir *m*.

smok·y □ ['smouki] fumeux (-euse *f*); plein de fumée; noirci par la fumée.

smol·der *Am.* ['smouldə] *see smoulder.*

smooth [smu:ð] 1. □ lisse; uni; poli; calme (*mer*); doux (douce *f*); *fig.* doucereux (-euse *f*); *Am.* F chic *inv. en genre*; 2. (*souv.* ~ *out, down*) lisser (*a.* ~ *over, away*) aplanir (*le bois*; *fig.* une difficulté); calmer; adoucir (*une courbe*); ~ *down* (se) calmer, (s')apaiser; '**smooth·ing** lissage *m*; aplanissement *m*; 2. à repasser; '**smooth·ness** égalité *f*; douceur *f* (*fig.* feinte); calme *m*; '**smooth-tongued** mielleux (-euse *f*), enjôleur (-euse *f*).

smote [smout] *pret. de smite.*

smoth·er ['smʌðə] 1. fumée *f* épaisse; nuage *m* épais de poussière; 2. (*a.* ~ *up*) étouffer (*a. fig.*); *fig.* couvrir.

smoul·der ['smouldə] brûler lentement; *fig.* couver.

smudge [smʌdʒ] 1. *v/t.* souiller; barbouiller, maculer; *v/i.* baver (*plume*); s'estomper (*silhouette*); 2. tache *f*; encre: pâté *m*; '**smudg·y** □ taché; barbouillé; estompé (*silhouette*); illisible.

smug [smʌg] suffisant, satisfait de soi-même; glabre (*visage*).

smug·gle ['smʌgl] *v/t.* (faire) passer (*qch.*) en contrebande; *v/i.* faire la contrebande; '**smug·gler** contrebandier *m*; fraudeur *m*; '**smug·gling** contrebande *f*.

smut [smʌt] 1. noir *m*; flocon *m* ou tache *f* de suie; ♠ céréales: charbon *m*; *coll.* saletés *f/pl.*; 2. noircir, salir; *v/i.* ♠ être atteint du charbon.

smutch [smʌtʃ] 1. tacher; souiller; 2. tache *f*.

smut·ty □ ['smʌti] noirci; sale; *fig.* malpropre; ♠ piqué.

snack [snæk] casse-croûte *m/inv.*; F go ~*s* partager (qch. avec q., *in s.th. with s.o.*); '~-**bar** bar *m*, casse-croûte *m/inv.*

snaf·fle¹ ['snæfl] (*a.* ~-*bit*) filet *m*.

snaf·fle² *Angl. sl.* [~] chiper (= *voler*).

sna·fu *Am. sl.* ⚔ [snæ'fu:] 1. en désarroi; en pagaille; 2. pagaille *f*.

snag [snæg] *arbre, dent*: chicot *m*; saillie *f*, protubérance *f*; *fig.* obstacle *m*, F cheveu *m*, pépin *m*; *bas, robe*: accroc *m*; *Am.* chicot *m* submergé; souche *f* au ras d'eau; **snag·ged** ['~id], '**snag·gy** épineux (-euse *f*); semé d'obstacles submergés.

snail *zo.* [sneil] limaçon *m*; escargot *m* (comestible).

snake *zo.* [sneik] serpent *m*; '~-**weed** ♠ bistorte *f*.

snak·y □ ['sneiki] de serpent; infesté de serpents; *fig.* perfide; *fig.* serpentant (*chemin*).

snap [snæp] 1. coup *m* de dents ou de ciseaux ou de froid; coup *m* sec, claquement *m*; *fig.* énergie *f*, entrain *m*; *collier, valise*: fermoir *m*; *gant*: fermoir *m* pression; rupture *f* soudaine; *cartes*: (sorte de) jeu enfantin; *phot.* instantané *m*; *cuis.* croquet *m* au gingembre; *cold* ~

froid *m* soudain; **2.** *v/i.* happer; tâcher de saisir (q., qch. *at s.o.*, *at s.th.*); claquer (*dents, fouet, etc.*); se casser (avec un bruit sec); *fig.* ~ *at* saisir (*une occasion*); F ~ *at s.o.* parler à q. d'un ton sec; *Am.* F ~ *into* (*ou out of*) *it* secouez-vous!; grouillez-vous!; *v/t.* happer; saisir d'un coup de dents; faire claquer; casser, rompre; *phot.* prendre un instantané de, F prendre; F ~ *one's fingers at* narguer (q.); se moquer de; ~ *out* dire d'un ton sec; ~ *up* saisir (*a. fig.*); happer; enlever (vite); **3.** crac!; '~**·drag·on** ♀ gueule-de-loup (*pl.* gueules-de-loup) *f*; *a.* jeu qui consiste à happer des raisins secs dans du cognac flambant; '~**·fas·ten·er** gant, robe: fermoir (pression) *m*; '**snap·per** personne *f* hargneuse; '**snap·pish** □ hargneux (-euse *f*); irritable; '**snap·pish·ness** humeur *f* hargneuse; irritabilité *f*; mauvaise humeur *f*; '**snap·py** see *snappish*; F vif (vive *f*); F *make it* ~! dépêchez-vous!, *sl.* grouillez-vous!; '**snap·shot 1.** coup *m* lâché sans viser; *phot.* instantané *m*; **2.** prendre un instantané de.

snare [snɛə] **1.** piège *m*; lacet *m*; **2.** prendre au lacet *ou* au piège (*a. fig.*); attraper; '**snar·er** tendeur *m* de lacets.

snarl [snɑːl] **1.** *v/i.* grogner, gronder; *tex.* vriller; *Am.* s'emmêler; *v/t.* emmêler; **2.** grognement *m*, grondement *m*; *tex.* vrillage *m*; *Am.* enchevêtrement *m*; '~**·up** pagaïe (*f*); embouteillage *m* (*de voitures*).

snatch [snætʃ] **1.** mouvement *m* pour saisir; morceau *m*; courte période *f*; *by* ~*es* par boutades; par courts intervalles; **2.** saisir; se saisir de; empoigner; ~ *at* tâcher de saisir; arracher (qch. à q., *s.th. from s.o.*); ~ *up* saisir.

sneak [sniːk] **1.** *v/i.* se glisser furtivement (dans, *in[to]*; hors de, *out of*); *école:* moucharder (q., *on s.o.*); *v/t.* F chipper; **2.** pied *m* plat; *école:* mouchard *m*; '**sneak·ers** *pl. Am.* F (chaussures *m/pl.* de) tennis *m/pl.*; '**sneak·ing** □ furtif (-ive *f*); servile; dissimulé, inavoué; '**sneak-'thief** chapardeur (-euse *f*) *m*; '**sneak·y** F sournois.

sneer [snɪə] **1.** ricanement *m*, rire *m* moqueur; sarcasme *m*; **2.** ricaner; se moquer (de, *at*); dénigrer (qch., *at*

s.th.); '**sneer·er** moqueur (-euse *f*) *m*; '**sneer·ing** □ ricaneur (-euse *f*); sarcastique.

sneeze [sniːz] **1.** éternuer; **2.** éternuement *m*.

snib [snib] *porte:* loquet *m*; arrêt *m* de sûreté.

snick·er ['snikə] see *snigger*; hennir (*cheval*).

sniff [snif] **1.** *v/i.* renifler (sur, *at*); flairer (qch., [*at*] *s.th.*); *v/t.* renifler; humer; flairer; **2.** reniflement *m*; '**sniff·les** F ['sniflz] *pl.* petit rhume *m*; *have the* ~ être (légèrement) enrhumé; '**sniff·y** F malodorant; dédaigneux (-euse *f*); de mauvaise humeur.

snig·ger ['snigə] rire sous cape (de, *at*); ricaner tout bas.

snip [snip] **1.** coup *m* de ciseaux; petit bout *m*; petite entaille *f*; *sl.* certitude *f*; **2.** couper; détacher (*d'un coup de ciseaux*); poinçonner (*un billet*).

snipe [snaip] **1.** *orn.* bécassine *f*; *coll.* bécassines *f/pl.*; **2.** ⚔ tirailler contre; '**snip·er** ⚔ canardeur *m*.

snip·pets ['snipits] *pl.* bouts *m/pl.*; *livre:* extraits *m/pl.*; '**snip·py** F fragmentaire; hargneux (-euse *f*).

snitch *sl.* [snitʃ]: ~ *on s.o.* dénoncer q.

sniv·el ['snivl] avoir le nez qui coule; *fig.* pleurnicher; '**sniv·el·(l)ing** qui coule; morveux (-euse *f*) (*personne*); *fig.* pleurnicheur (-euse *f*).

snob [snɔb] snob *m*, parvenu(e *f*) *m*, poseur (-euse *f*) *m*; '**snob·ber·y** snobisme *m*, morgue *f*; '**snob·bish** □ poseur (-euse *f*); snob *adj./inv.*

snog F [snɔg] se peloter.

snoop *Am. sl.* [snuːp] **1.** *fig.* ~ *on* épier (q.); **2.** inquisiteur (-euse *f*) *m*; personne *f* indiscrète *ou* curieuse.

snoot·y *Am.* F ['snuːti] arrogant; suffisant.

snooze F [snuːz] **1.** petit somme *m*; **2.** sommeiller; faire un petit somme.

snore [snɔː] **1.** ronflement *m*; **2.** ronfler.

snort [snɔːt] **1.** reniflement *m* (*a. fig.* de dégoût*); ⊕ ronflement *m*; *cheval:* ébrouement *m*; **2.** renifler; s'ébrouer (*cheval*); *v/t.* grogner (*une réponse*).

snot *sl.* [snɔt] morve *f*; '**snot·ty** *sl.* morveux (-euse *f*); *fig.* maussade.

snout [snaut] museau *m*; *porc:* groin *m*.

snow [snou] **1.** neige *f*; *sl.* cocaïne *f*; **2.**

v/i. neiger; *v/t.* saupoudrer (de, with); *sl.* en imposer à (*q.*), impressionner (*q.*); *surt. Am.* F *fig.* be ~ed under être accablé (de, *with*); ~ed in (*ou* up) pris *ou* bloqué par la neige; '**~·ball 1.** boule *f* de neige; **2.** lancer des boules de neige; *fig.* faire boule de neige; '**~·drift** amas *m* de neige, congère *f*; '**~·drop** ♥ perce-neige *f/inv.*; '**~·gog·gles** *pl.* (*a pair of*) ~ (des) lunettes *f/pl.* d'alpiniste; **~·mo·bile** ['~məbi:l] autoneige *f*; '**~·plough**, *Am.* '**~·plow** chasse-neige *m/inv.*; '**~·white** blanc(he *f*) comme la neige; '**snow·y** □ neigeux (-euse *f*), de neige.

snub [snʌb] **1.** remettre (*q.*) à sa place; rembarrer; **2.** rebuffade *f*; mortification *f*; '**snub·ber** *mot.* amortisseur *m* à courroie; '**snub-nose** nez *m* retroussé; '**snub-nosed** (au nez) camus.

snuff [snʌf] **1.** *chandelle:* mouchure *f*; tabac *m* (à priser); F *up to* ~ dégourdi, à la coule; F *give s.o.* ~ laver la tête à q.; **2.** (*a. take* ~) priser; moucher; '**~·box** tabatière *f*; '**snuff·er** priseur (-euse *f*) *m*; (*a pair of*) ~s *pl.* (des) mouchettes *f/pl.*; **snuf·fle** ['~l] renifler; nasiller; ~ *at* flairer (*qch.*); '**snuff·y** au linge tacheté de tabac; au nez barbouillé de tabac; F *fig.* peu soigné.

snug □ [snʌg] confortable; bien au chaud; gentil(le *f*); ♣ paré; '**snug·ger·y** petite pièce *f* confortable; petit fumoir *m*; *sl.* turne *f*; **snug·gle** ['~l] (se) serrer; *v/i.* se pelotonner (contre *up to*, *into*); ~ *down* se blottir (dans, *in*).

so [sou] ainsi; par conséquent; si, tellement; donc; *I hope* ~ je l'espère bien; *are you tired?* ~ *I am* êtes-vous fatigué?; je le suis en effet; *you are tired,* ~ *am I* vous êtes fatigué, (et) moi aussi; *a mile or* ~ un mille à peu près; ~ *as to* pour *ou* afin de (*inf.*), pour *ou* afin que (*sbj.*); de sorte que (*sbj.*); de façon à (*inf.*); ~ *far* jusqu'ici; ~ *far as I know* autant que je sache.

soak [souk] **1.** *v/t.* tremper (dans, *in*); imbiber (de, *in*); F faire payer; ~ *up* (*ou in*) absorber; *v/i.* tremper, s'imbiber (dans, *into*); F boire comme une éponge; **2.** trempe *f*; F bain *m*; F ivrogne *m*, biberon(ne

f) *m*; F tombée *f*, *pluie:* arrosage *m*.

so-and-so ['souənsou] machin *m*, chose *m*; *Mr.* ♀ Monsieur *m* un tel.

soap [soup] **1.** savon *m*; F ~ *opera* mélodrame *m* radiodiffusé *ou* télévisé; *soft* ~ savon *m* vert; F flatterie *f*, flagornerie *f*; **2.** savonner; '**~·boil·er** chaudière *f* à savon; *personne:* savonnier (-ère *f*) *m*; '**~·box** caisse *f* à savon; ~ *orator* orateur *m* de carrefour; '**~·dish** plateau *m* à savon; '**~·suds** *pl.*, *a. sg.* eau *f* de savon; '**soap·y** □ savonneux (-euse *f*); qui sent le savon.

soar [sɔ:] prendre son essor; s'élever (*a. fig.*); ⚞ faire du vol à voile; '**soar·ing 1.** qui s'élève; plané (*vol*); **2.** essor *m*; hausse *f*; vol *m* plané.

sob [sɔb] **1.** sanglot *m*; **2.** sangloter.

so·ber ['soubə] **1.** □ sobre, modéré; grave; sérieux (-euse *f*); pas ivre; **2.** (*souv.* ~ *down*) (se) dégriser; '**so·ber·ness**, **so·bri·e·ty** [sou-'braiəti] sobriété *f*; sérieux *m*.

sob-stuff F ['sɔbstʌf] sensiblerie *f*, histoire *f* larmoyante.

so-called ['sou'kɔ:ld] prétendu, ce qu'on est convenu d'appeler.

soc·cer *sp.* ['sɔkə] football *m* association.

so·cia·bil·i·ty [souʃə'biliti] sociabilité *f*; '**so·cia·ble** □ **1.** sociable; *zo.* sociétaire; **2.** *véhicule:* sociable *m*; *meuble:* causeuse *f*; *Am.* soirée *f* amicale.

so·cial ['souʃl] **1.** □ social (-aux *m/pl.*); ~ *activities pl.* mondanités *f/pl.*; ~ *insurance* assurance *f ou* prévoyance *f* sociale; ~ *insurance stamp* timbre *m* de sécurité sociale; ~ *science* science *f* sociale; ~ *security* aide *f* sociale; *be on* ~ *security* recevoir l'aide sociale; ~ *services pl.* institutions *f/pl.* sociales; **2.** F soirée *f*; réunion *f*; '**so·cial·ism** socialisme *m*; '**so·cial·ist** socialiste (*a. su./mf*); **so·cial·ite** F ['souʃəlait] mondain(e *f*) *m*; '**so·cial·ize** rendre social; réunir en société; *pol.* socialiser.

so·ci·e·ty [sə'saiəti] société *f*; association *f*; beau monde *m*.

so·ci·o·log·i·cal □ [sousiə'lɔdʒikl] sociologique; **so·ci·ol·o·gist** [~-'ɔlədʒist] sociologue *m*; **so·ci·ol·o·gy** sociologie *f*.   [intérieure.\

sock[1] [sɔk] chaussette *f*; semelle *f]

sock[2] *sl.* [~] **1.** coup *m*, beigne *f*;

give s.o. ⁓(*s pl.*) = **2.** flanquer une beigne à (*q.*).

sock·dol·a·ger *Am. sl.* [sɔkˈdɔlədʒə] coup *m* violent, gnon *m*; argument *m* décisif.

sock·er F [ˈsɔkə] *see* soccer.

sock·et [ˈsɔkit] emboîture *f* (*a. os*); douille *f* (*a. ⚡*); *œil*: orbite *f*; *dent*: alvéole *m*; ⊕ godet *m*; ⚡ socle *m*; cavité *f*; *chandelle*: bobèche *f*.

so·cle [ˈsɔkl] socle *m*.

sod [sɔd] **1.** gazon *m*; motte *f*; *poét.* terre *f*; **2.** gazonner.

so·da ⚗ [ˈsoudə] soude *f*; '⁓**-foun-tain** siphon *m*; *Am.* bar *m*, débit *m f* (*de boissons non alcoolisées*).

sod·den [ˈsɔdn] détrempé; pâteux (-euse *f*) (*pain etc.*); (*trop long-temps*) bouilli; *fig.* abruti (*par la boisson*).

so·di·um ⚗ [ˈsoudjəm] sodium *m*; *attr.* de soude.

so·ev·er [souˈevə] que ce soi(en)t.

so·fa [ˈsoufə] canapé *m*.

sof·fit ⚿ [ˈsɔfit] soffite *m*; cintre *m*.

soft [sɔft] **1.** □ mou (mol *devant une consonne ou un h muet*; molle *f*); doux (douce *f*); tendre; flasque; *fig.* facile; F nigaud; F ⁓ *drink* boisson *f* non alcoolisée; F ⁓ *thing* une bonne affaire *f*; *see* soap; **2.** *adv.* douce-ment; sans bruit; **3.** F nigaud(e *f*) *m*; **soft·en** [ˈsɔfn] (s')amollir; (s')a-doucir (*a. couleurs, a.* ⊕ *acier*); (s')attendrir; (se) radoucir (*ton, voix, etc.*); *v/t.* atténuer (*des couleurs, la lumière, a. phot. les contours*); **soft·ness** [ˈsɔftnis] douceur *f* (*a. fig.*); *caractère*: mollesse *f*; F niaiserie *f*; '**soft-soap** F passer de la pommade à (*q.*), flatter; '**soft·spok·en** à la voix douce; '**soft·ware** logiciel *m*, soft-ware *m*; '**soft·y** F nigaud(e *f*) *m*, niais(e *f*) *m*.

sog·gy [ˈsɔgi] détrempé; lourd (*temps*); pâteux (-euse *f*).

soil[1] [sɔil] sol *m*, terre *f*, terroir *m*.

soil[2] [⁓] **1.** souillure *f*; tache *f*; **2.** (se) salir; *v/t.* souiller; '⁓**-pipe** descente *f* (*de W.-C.*).

so·journ [ˈsɔdʒəːn] **1.** séjour *m*; **2.** séjourner; '**so·journ·er** personne *f* de passage; hôte(sse *f*) *m*.

sol·ace [ˈsɔləs] **1.** consolation *f*; **2.** consoler.

so·lar [ˈsoulə] solaire; ⁓ *battery* bat-terie *f* solaire, photopile *f*; ⁓ *cell* cellule *f* photovoltaïque; ⁓ *eclipse*

éclipse *f* du soleil; *anat.* ⁓ *plexus* plexus *m* solaire; ⁓ *system* système *m* solaire, planétaire *m*.

sold [sould] *prét. et p.p. de* sell.

sol·der ⊕ [ˈsɔldə] **1.** soudure *f*; **2.** (res)souder; **sol·der·ing-i·ron** [ˈ⁓riŋaiən] fer *m* à souder.

sol·dier [ˈsould͡ʒə] **1.** soldat *m*; **2.** (*a. go* ⁓*ing*) faire le métier de soldat; '**sol·dier·like**, '**sol·dier·ly** de soldat; militaire; **sol·dier·ship** [ˈ⁓ʃip] aptitude *f* militaire; '**sol-dier·y** militaires *m/pl.*; *péj.* solda-tesque *f*.

sole[1] □ [soul] seul, unique; ⁓ *agent* agent *m* exclusif.

sole[2] [⁓] **1.** semelle *f*; *pied*: plante *f*; **2.** ressemeler.

sole[3] *icht.* [⁓] sole *f*.

sol·e·cism [ˈsɔlisizm] solécisme *m*; faute *f* de grammaire.

sol·emn □ [ˈsɔləm] solennel(le *f*); sérieux (-euse *f*); grave; **so·lem·ni-ty** [səˈlemniti] solennité *f* (*a.* = *fête*); gravité *f*; **sol·em·ni·za·tion** [sɔləmnaiˈzeiʃn] célébration *f*, so-lennisation *f*; '**sol·em·nize** célé-brer (*un mariage*); solenniser (*une fête*); rendre grave.

so·lic·it [səˈlisit] solliciter (qch. de q. s.o. *for* s.th., s.th. *from* s.o.); *prostituée*: raccrocher (*un homme*); **so·lic·i·ta·tion** sollicitation *f*; *votes*: brigue *f*; *prostituée*: racolage *m*; **so·lic·i·tor** ⚖ avoué *m*, *Brit.* solicitor *m*; *Am.* ✝ placier *m*; ♀ *General* conseiller *m* juridique de la Cou-ronne; **so·lic·it·ous** □ préoccupé (de, *about*); soucieux (-euse *f*) (de, of; de *inf.*, *to inf.*); be ⁓ *about* s'inquiéter de; be ⁓ *for* avoir (*qch.*) à cœur; **so·lic·i·tude** [⁓tjuːd] solli-citude *f*; souci *m*.

sol·id [ˈsɔlid] **1.** □ solide (*a. fig.*, ⚿ *angle*); plein (*acajou, mur, pneu, volume*); vif (vive *f*) (*pierre*); massif (-ive *f*) (*argent*); épais(se *f*); de volume (*mesures*); ⊕ solidaire (de, with); *fig.* bon(ne *f*); *fig.* ininter-rompu; *fig.* unanime; *surt. Am.* F *make o.s.* ⁓ *with* être bien avec, se mettre sur un bon pied avec; *a* ⁓ *hour* une bonne heure, une pleine heure; ⚿ *geometry* géométrie *f* dans l'espace; ⁓ *leather* cuir *m* à semelles; ⁓ *rubber* caoutchouc *m* plein; **2.** solide *m*; **sol·i·dar·i·ty** [⁓ˈdæriti] solidarité *f*; **so·lid·i·fy**

[⁓fai] (se) solidifier; *v/i.* se figer; **so'lid·i·ty** solidité *f*; ⁓ solidarité *f*.

so·lil·o·quize [sɔ'liləkwaiz] se parler à soi-même; faire un soliloque; **so'lil·o·quy** soliloque *m*, monologue *m*.

sol·i·taire [sɔli'tɛə] *diamant, a. jeu:* solitaire *m*; *cartes:* jeu *m* de patience; **sol·i·tar·y** □ ['⁓təri] solitaire, isolé; retiré; ⁓ *confinement* prison *f* cellulaire; **sol·i·tude** ['⁓tju:d] solitude *f*.

so·lo ['soulou] ♩ solo *m*; *cartes:* whist *m* de Gand; ✠ vol *m* solo; **'so·lo·ist** ♩ soliste *mf*.

sol·stice ['sɔlstis] solstice *m*.

sol·u·bil·i·ty [sɔlju'biliti] solubilité *f*; *problème:* résolubilité *f*; **sol·u·ble** ['sɔljubl] soluble; résoluble.

so·lu·tion [sə'lu:ʃn] solution *f* (*a.* ♠, ⚗, ⚕); ⊕ (dis)solution *f*.

solv·a·ble ['sɔlvəbl] soluble; ♠ *a.* résoluble; **solve** [sɔlv] résoudre; trouver la solution de; éclaircir (*un mystère etc.*); **sol·ven·cy** ['⁓vənsi] solvabilité *f*; **sol·vent 1.** dissolvant; ✝ solvable; **2.** (dis)solvant *m*.

som·ber, som·bre □ ['sɔmbə] sombre; morne.

some [sʌm, səm] **1.** *pron. indéf.* certains; quelques-uns, quelques-unes; un peu, en; *I need* ⁓ j'en ai besoin; **2.** *adj.* quelque, quelconque; un certain, une certaine; du, de la, des, quelques; ⁓ *bread* du pain; ⁓ *few* quelques-uns, quelques-unes; ⁓ *20 miles* une vingtaine de milles; *in* ⁓ *degree, to* ⁓ *extent* quelque peu; jusqu'à un certain point; *that was* ⁓ *meal!* c'était un chouette repas!; **3.** *adv.* quelque, environ; *sl.* pas mal; *he was annoyed* ⁓ il n'était pas mal fâché; **'⁓·bod·y, '⁓·one** quelqu'un; **'⁓·how** de façon *ou* d'autre; ⁓ *or other* d'une manière ou d'une autre.

som·er·sault ['sʌməsɔ:lt], **som·er·set** ['⁓set] *gymn.* saut *m* périlleux; culbute *f*; cabriole *f*; *turn* ⁓s faire le saut périlleux; faire des cabrioles.

some...: '⁓·thing ['sʌmθiŋ] quelque chose (*a. su./m*); *adv.* quelque peu; *that is* ⁓ c'est déjà quelque chose; ⁓ *like* en forme de; F un vrai ...; **'⁓·time 1.** *adv.* autrefois; jadis; **2.** *adj.* ancien(ne *f*) (*devant su.*); **⁓·times** ['⁓z] parfois, quelquefois;

'⁓·what quelque peu, un peu; assez; **'⁓·where** quelque part.

som·nam·bu·lism [sɔm'næmbjulizm] somnambulisme *m*, noctambulisme *m*; **som'nam·bu·list** somnambule *mf*, noctambule *mf*.

som·nif·er·ous □ [sɔm'nifərəs] somnifère, endormant.

som·no·lence ['sɔmnoləns] somnolence *f*, assoupissement *m*; **'som·no·lent** somnolent, assoupi.

son [sʌn] fils *m*.

so·nant *gramm.* ['sounənt] (consonne *f*) sonore.

so·na·ta ♩ [sə'nɑ:tə] sonate *f*.

song [sɔŋ] chant *m*; chanson *f*; *eccl.* cantique *m*; F *for a mere* (*ou an old*) ⁓ pour une bagatelle, pour rien; **'⁓·bird** oiseau *m* chanteur; **'⁓·book** recueil *m* de chansons; **'⁓·hit** succès *m*; **'song·ster** oiseau *m* chanteur; chanteur *m*; **'song·stress** chanteuse *f*.

son·ic ['sɔnik] sonique (*vitesse*); ⁓ *bang* (*ou boom*) bang *m ou* détonation *f* supersonique; ⁓ *barrier* mur *m* du son.

son-in-law ['sʌninlɔ:], *pl.* **sons-in·law** gendre *m*.

son·net ['sɔnit] sonnet *m*.

son·ny F ['sʌni] (mon) petit *m*.

so·nor·i·ty [sə'nɔriti] sonorité *f*; **so·no·rous** □ [sə'nɔ:rəs] sonore; **so'no·rous·ness** sonorité *f*.

soon [su:n] bientôt; tôt; vite; de bonne heure; *as* (*ou so*) ⁓ *as* dès que, aussitôt que; **'soon·er** plus tôt; plutôt; *no* ⁓ ... *than* à peine... que; *no* ⁓ *said than done* sitôt dit, sitôt fait.

soot [sut] **1.** suie *f*; **2.** couvrir de suie; calaminer (*les bougies*).

sooth [su:θ]: ✝ *in* ⁓ en vérité, vraiment; ⁓ *to say* à vrai dire; **soothe** [su:ð] calmer, apaiser; **sooth·say·er** ['su:θseiə] devin(eresse *f*) *m*.

soot·y □ ['suti] couvert de suie; (noir) de suie; fuligineux (-euse *f*).

sop [sɔp] **1.** morceau *m* (*de pain etc.*) trempé; *fig.* don *m* propitiatoire; **2.** tremper; ⁓ *up* éponger.

soph·ism ['sɔfizm] sophisme *m*.

soph·ist ['sɔfist] sophiste *m*; **so·phis·tic, so·phis·ti·cal** □ [sə'fistik(l)] sophist(iqu)e; captieux (-euse *f*) (*argument*); **so'phis·ti·cate** [⁓keit] sophistiquer; falsifier; **so'phis·ti·cat·ed** sophistiqué, falsifié; blasé; aux goûts compliqués; **soph·ist·ry** ['sɔfistri] sophistique *f*; sophistication *f*; sophismes *m/pl.* **soph·o·more** *Am.* ['sɔfəmɔː] étudiant(e *f*) *m* de seconde année.

so·po·rif·ic [soupə'rifik] (*∼ally*) soporifique (*a. su./m*), somnifère (*a. su./m*).

sop·ping ['sɔpiŋ] (*a. ∼ wet*) trempé; trempé jusqu'aux os (*personne*); **'sop·py** détrempé; *fig.* mou (*mol devant une voyelle ou un h muet*; molle *f*); F fadasse.

so·pran·o ♪ [sə'prɑːnou] soprano *m*.

sor·cer·er ['sɔːsərə] sorcier *m*; **'sor·cer·ess** sorcière *f*; **'sor·cer·y** sorcellerie *f*.

sor·did □ ['sɔːdid] sordide (*souv. fig. = sale, vil*); ✻ infect; **'sor·did·ness** sordidité *f*; saleté *f*; bassesse *f*.

sore [sɔː] **1.** □ douloureux (-euse *f*); irrité, enflammé; ulcéré; *fig.* cruel(le *f*); chagriné (*personne*), *Am.* F fâché; *∼ throat* mal *m* de gorge; **2.** plaie *f* (*a. fig.*); écorchure *f*; ulcère *m*; **'sore·head** *Am.* F *fig.* rouspéteur *m*; **'sore·ly** *adv.* gravement, vivement; **'sore·ness** sensibilité *f*; *fig.* chagrin *m*.

so·ror·i·ty [sə'rɔriti] communauté *f* religieuse; *univ. Am.* cercle *m* d'étudiantes.

sor·rel[1] ['sɔrəl] **1.** saure, alezan (*cheval*); **2.** alezan *m*.

sor·rel[2] ♀ [∼] oseille *f*.

sor·row ['sɔrou] **1.** douleur *f*, tristesse *f*, chagrin *m*; **2.** s'attrister, être affligé; **sor·row·ful** □ ['∼ful] triste, attristé; pénible.

sor·ry □ ['sɔri] désolé, fâché, peiné (*de to, at*); *fig.* misérable, pauvre; (*I am*) (*so*) *∼!* pardon!; *I am ∼ for you* je vous plains; *we are ∼ to say* nous regrettons d'avoir à dire... **sort** [sɔːt] **1.** sorte *f*, genre *m*, espèce *f*; classe *f*; façon *f*; *people of all ∼s* des gens de toutes sortes; *something of the ∼*, *that ∼ of thing* quelque chose de pareil(le *f*); *in some ∼* je l'aime; *out of ∼s* indisposé; de mauvaise humeur; F *he is a good ∼* c'est un brave type; (*a*) *∼ of peace* une paix telle quelle; **2.** trier, assortir; ✝ classifier, classer, lotir; *∼ out* séparer (de, d'avec *from*).

sor·tie ✕ ['sɔːtiː] sortie *f*.

sot [sɔt] ivrogne(sse *f*) *m*; *sl.* soû-

lard(e *f*) *m*; **sot·tish** □ ['sɔtiʃ] d'ivrogne; abruti par l'alcool.

sough [sau] **1.** murmure *m*, susurrement *m*; **2.** murmurer, susurrer.

sought [sɔːt] *prét. et p.p. de seek*; **'∼-'aft·er** recherché.

soul [soul] âme *f*; F *the ∼ of* le premier mobile (*d'une entreprise*); **'soul·less** □ sans âme; (*a.* **'soul-de·stroy·ing**) abrutissant.

sound[1] □ [saund] sain; en bon état; bon(ne *f*); *fig.*, *a.* ⚕ solide; droit; profond (*sommeil*); ✝ bon(ne *f*); ♱♱ valable, légal (*-aux m/pl.*).

sound[2] [∼] **1.** son *m*, bruit *m*; *phys.* acoustique *f*; *∼ barrier* mur *m* du son; *∼ effects pl.* bruitage *m*; *∼ film* film *m* sonore; *∼ wave* onde *f* sonore; **2.** *v/i.* (ré)sonner; retentir; paraître; avoir le son de; *v/t.* sonner; faire retentir; prononcer (*les R etc.*); chanter (*des louanges*); ✻ ausculter (*la poitrine*); ✕ *∼ the retreat* sonner la retraite.

sound[3] [∼] *géog.* détroit *m*; bras *m* de mer; *icht.* vessie *f* natatoire; *géog. the ♀ le Sund m*.

sound[4] [∼] **1.** ✻ sonde *f*; **2.** ✻ sonder (*a. fig.*, *a.* ⚓); *∼ s.o. out* sonder q. (*relativement à, about*).

sound·ing ⚓ ['saundiŋ] sondage *m*; *∼s pl.* sondes *f/pl.*, fonds *m/pl.*

sound(·ing)-board ['saund(iŋ)bɔːd] *chaire etc.:* abat-voix *m/inv.*; ♪ *orgue:* tamis *m*; *piano:* table *f* d'harmonie.

sound·less □ ['saundlis] muet(te *f*). **sound·ness** ['saundnis] bon état *m*; solidité *f* (*a. fig.*).

sound...: **'∼-proof 1.** insonorisé, insonore; **2.** insonoriser; **'∼-track** piste *f* ou bande *f* sonore.

soup[1] [suːp] potage *m*; soupe *f*.

soup[2] *Am. sl.* [∼] **1.** cheval-vapeur (*pl.* chevaux-vapeur) *m*; **2.** *∼ up* doper; *mot. ∼ed up engine* moteur *m* comprimé.

sour ['sauə] **1.** □ aigre, acide; vert (*fruit*); *fig.* revêche; aigre; acariâtre; **2.** *v/t.* aigrir (*a. fig.*); *v/i.* surir; (s')aigrir (*a. fig.*).

source [sɔːs] source *f*; *fig.* origine *f*; *∼ language* langue *f* de départ.

sour·dough *Am.* ['sauədou] vétéran *m* (*des placers d'Alaska*).

sour·ish □ ['sauəriʃ] aigrelet(te *f*); **'sour·ness** aigreur *f* (*a. fig.*); *fig.* humeur *f* revêche; **'sour·puss** ['sauəpus] grincheux (-euse *f*) *m*.

souse [saus] **1.** *v/t.* plonger; tremper (d'eau, *with water*); *cuis.* faire mariner; *v/i.* mariner; faire un plongeon; **~d** *sl.* ivre, F gris, parti; **2.** immersion *f*; plongon *m*; trempée *f*; *cuis.* marinade *f*; *Am.* ivrogne *m*; **3.** plouf!, floc!

south [sauθ] **1.** *su.* sud *m*; midi *m*; **2.** *adj.* du sud; méridional (-aux *m/pl.*); **3.** *adv.* au sud, vers le sud; **'~bound** en direction du Sud, allant vers le Sud.

south-east ['sauθ'i:st] **1.** sud-est *m*; **2.** (*a.* **south-'east-ern**) du sud-est.

south-er-ly ['sʌðəli], **south-ern** ['~ən] (du) sud; du midi; méridional (-aux *m/pl.*); **'south-ern-er** habitant(e *f*) *m* du sud; *Am.* ♀ sudiste *mf*.

south-ern-most ['sʌðənmoust] le plus au sud.

south-ing ['sauðiŋ] ♣ chemin *m* sud; *astr.* passage *m* au méridien.

south-paw *Am.* ['sauθpɔ:] *baseball*: gaucher *m*.

south-ward ['sauθwəd] **1.** *adj.* au ou du sud; **2.** *adv.* (*a.* **south-wards** ['~dz]) vers le sud.

south...: '~-'west **1.** *su.* sud-ouest *m*; **2.** *adv.* vers le sud-ouest; **3.** *adj.* (*a.* ~-'west-er-ly, ~-'west-ern) (du) sud-ouest; '~-'west-er (vent *m* du) sud-ouest; ♣ suroît *m* (= chapeau *impérméable*).

sou-ve-nir ['su:vəniə] souvenir *m*, mémento *m*.

sov-er-eign ['sɔvrin] **1.** □ souverain (*a. fig.*), suprême; **2.** souverain(e *f*) *m*; monarque *m*; monnaie anglaise: souverain *m* (= *pièce de 20 shillings*); **'sov-er-eign-ty** souveraineté *f*.

so-vi-et ['souviət] Soviet *m*; *attr.* soviétique.

sow¹ [sau] *zo.* truie *f*; ⊕ gueuse *f* des mères; (*a.* ~-channel) mère-gueuse (*pl.* mères-gueuses) *f*.

sow² [sou] [*irr.*] semer (*a.* with); ensemencer (*la terre*) (en blé, *with wheat*); **'sow-er** semeur (-euse *f*) *m* (*a. fig.*); **sown** [soun] *p.p. de* sow².

sox [sɔks] *pl. see* sock¹.

so-y(a) ♀ ['sɔi(ə)] (*a.* ~ bean) soya *m*.

spa [spɑ:] source *f* minérale; ville *f* d'eau.

space [speis] **1.** espace *m*, *typ. f*; intervalle *m* (*a. temps*); étendue *f*, surface *f*; F place *f*; **2.** (*a.* ~ out) espacer (*a. typ*); échelonner (*des*

troupes, des versements); **3.** spatial (-aux *m/pl.*), interplanétaire; ~ *flight* vol *m* spatial; vols *m/pl.* spatiaux; ~ *lab* laboratoire *m* spatial; ~ *shuttle* navette *f*; ~ *travel* voyages *m/pl.* spatiaux *ou* dans l'espace; ~ *weapons pl.* armes *f/pl.* spatiales; '~craft, '~ship vaisseau *m* spatial.

spa-cious □ ['speiʃəs] spacieux (-euse *f*), vaste; ample.

spade [speid] **1.** bêche *f*; *call a* ~ *a* ~ appeler les choses par leur nom; *usu.* ~s *pl.* cartes: pique *m*; **2.** bêcher; '~-work travaux *m/pl.* à la bêche *ou fig.* préliminaires.

span¹ [spæn] **1.** *main:* empan *m*; court espace *m* de temps; ⚓ portée *f*, largeur *f*; bras, ailes, *a.* ✈ envergure *f*; *Am.* paire *f*; **2.** franchir, enjamber; *fig.* embrasser; mesurer à l'empan.

span² [~] *prét. de* spin 1.

span-gle ['spæŋgl] **1.** paillette *f*; **2.** pailleter (de, *with*); *fig.* parsemer (de, *with*).

Span-iard ['spænjəd] Espagnol(e *f*) *m*.

span-iel ['spænjəl] épagneul *m*.

Span-ish ['spæniʃ] **1.** espagnol; d'Espagne; **2.** *ling.* espagnol *m*; *the* ~ *pl.* les Espagnols *m/pl.*

spank F [spæŋk] **1.** *v/t.* fesser; *v/i.* ~ *along* aller bon train; **2.** claque *f* sur le derrière; **'spank-er** ♣ brigantine *f*; **'spank-ing 1.** □ qui va bon train; vigoureux (-euse *f*); F de premier ordre; *sl.* épatant; **2.** F fessée *f*.

span-ner ⊕ ['spænə] clef *f* (à écrous); *fig.* throw a ~ in the works mettre des bâtons dans les roues.

spar¹ [spɑ:] ♣ espar *m*; ✈ longeron *m*.

spar² [~] faire mine de vouloir boxer (q., *at s.o.*); boxer amicalement; se battre (*coqs*); *fig.* argumenter (avec, *with*); *box.* ~*ring partner* sparring-partner *m*, partenaire *m* d'entraînement.

spar³ *min.* [~] spath *m*.

spare [speə] **1.** □ frugal (-aux *m/pl.*); maigre; sec (sèche *f*) (*personne*); disponible, de reste; de réserve, de rechange, de secours; ~ *hours* (heures *f/pl.* de) loisir *m*; ~ *room* chambre *f* d'ami; ~ *time* temps *m* disponible; **2.** ⊕ pièce *f* de rechange; **3.** *v/t.* épargner, ménager;

se passer de; prêter, donner; faire grâce à (*q.*); respecter; *enough and to* ~ plus qu'il n'en faut (de, *of*); *v/i.* épargner, faire des économies; **'spare·ness** minceur *f*; maigreur *f*; frugalité *f*; **spare·rib** *cuis.* ['~rib] côte *f* de porc.

spar·ing □ ['spɛəriŋ] ménager (-ère *f*) (de *in*, *of*); économe; frugal (-aux *m/pl.*); limité (*emploi*); **'spar·ing·ness** épargne *f*; frugalité *f*.

spark[1] [spɑːk] **1.** étincelle *f* (*a. fig.*); F ~s radiotélégraphiste *m*; **2.** *v/i.* émettre des étincelles; cracher (*dynamo*); *v/t.* faire éclater avec une étincelle électrique.

spark[2] [~] élégant *m*; beau cavalier *m*; joyeux compagnon *m*.

spark(·ing)-plug *mot.* ['spɑːk(iŋ)-plʌg] bougie *f*.

spar·kle ['spɑːkl] **1.** étincelle *f*; éclat *m*; *fig.* vivacité *f* d'esprit; **2.** étinceler, scintiller; chatoyer (*bijou*); pétiller (*esprit, feu, yeux, vin*); *sparkling wine* vin *m* mousseux; **spar·klet** ['~it] petite étincelle *f*; *eau de seltz*: sparklet *m*.

spar·row *orn.* ['spærou] moineau *m*, passereau *m*; **'~-hawk** *orn.* épervier *m*.

sparse □ [spɑːs] épars, clairsemé.

spasm ['spæzm] spasme *m*; *fig.* accès *m*; **spas·mod·ic, spas·mod·i·cal** □ [~'mɔdik(l)] spasmodique; involontaire; *fig.* par saccades; **spas·tic** ['spæstik] **1.** (~*ally*) spasmodique; **2.** paraplégique (spasmodique) *mf*.

spat[1] [spæt] *huîtres:* frai *m*.

spat[2] [~] guêtre *f* de ville.

spat[3] [~] *prét. et p.p.* de *spit*[2] 2.

spatch·cock ['spætʃkɔk] *cuis.* faire cuire à la crapaudine; *fig.* faire une intervention dans (*une dépêche*) (à la dernière minute).

spate [speit] crue *f*; *fig.* déluge *m*.

spa·tial □ ['speiʃl] spatial (-aux *m/pl.*).

spat·ter ['spætə] éclabousser (de, *with*); **spat·ter·dash** † ['~dæʃ] guêtre *f*.

spat·u·la ['spætjulə] spatule *f*; *cuis.* gâche *f*.

spav·in *vét.* ['spævin] éparvin *m*.

spawn [spɔːn] **1.** frai *m*, œufs *m/pl.*; *fig. usu. péj.* progéniture *f*; **2.** *v/i.* frayer; *péj.* se multiplier; naître (de,

from); *v/t. péj.* donner naissance à; **'spawn·er** poisson *m* qui fraye; **'spawn·ing** (acte *m ou* époque *f* du) frai *m*.

speak [spiːk] [*irr.*] *v/i.* parler (*a. fig.* = *retentir*); faire un discours; ♪ sonner; *téléph. Brown* ~*ing!* ici Brown!; ~ *out* parler à haute voix; parler franchement; ~ *to* parler à *ou* avec; ~ *up* parler plus fort *ou* haut; (*parlez*) plus fort!; *that* ~*s well for him* cela est tout à son honneur; ~ *well for* faire honneur à; *v/t.* dire (*qch.*); parler (*une langue*); exprimer; faire (*un éloge*); témoigner de; **'~-eas·y** *Am. sl.* bar *m* clandestin; **'speak·er** parleur (-euse *f*) *m*; interlocuteur (-trice *f*) *m*; orateur *m*; *radio:* haut-parleur *m*; *parl.* Président *m*.

speak·ing ['spiːkiŋ] parlant (*a. fig. portrait*); expressif (-ive *f*); *be on* ~ *terms with* se connaître assez pour se parler; **'~-trum·pet** porte-voix *m/inv.*

spear [spiə] **1.** lance *f*; *chasse:* épieu *m*; javelot *m*; *fig.* ~ *side* côté *m* paternel *ou* mâle; **2.** frapper *ou* tuer d'un coup de lance (*ou une bête:* d'épieu); **'~-head** pointe *f* de lance; *fig.* pointe *f*.

spec † *sl.* [spek] spéculation *f*.

spe·cial ['speʃl] **1.** □ spécial (-aux *m/pl.*); particulier (-ère *f*); *journ.* ~ *correspondent* envoyé(e *f*) *m* spécial(e); **2.** (*ou* ~ *constable*) agent *m* de police suppléant (= *citoyen assermenté*); (*ou* ~ *edition*) édition *f* spéciale; (*ou* ~ *train*) train *m* spécial; *Am. magasin:* ordre *m* exprès; *Am.* plat *m* du jour; *restaurant:* spécialité *f* de la maison; **spe·cial·ist** ['~ʃəlist] spécialiste *mf*; **spe·ci·al·i·ty** [speʃi'æliti] spécialité *f* (*a.* †); particularité *f*, caractéristique *f*; **spe·cial·ize** ['speʃəlaiz] *v/t.* particulariser; désigner *ou* adapter à un but spécial; *v/i.* se spécialiser (dans, *in*); *biol.* se différencier; **spe·cial·ty** ['~ʃlti] *see speciality*; *z*⁴ contrat *m* formel sous seing privé.

spe·cie ['spiːʃiː] monnaie *f* métallique; *espèces f/pl.* (sonnantes).

spe·cies ['spiːʃiːz] *sg. ou. pl.* espèce *f* (*a. eccl.*); genre *m*, sorte *f*.

spe·cif·ic [spi'sifik] **1.** (~*ally*) spécifique; précis; *phys.* ~ *gravity* pesan-

teur *f* spécifique; ⚙ ~ *performance*
contrat: exécution *f* intégrale; **2.** ⚗
spécifique *m* (contre, *for*).

spec·i·fi·ca·tion [spesifi'keiʃn] spécification *f*; △ cahier *m* des charges; ⚙ description *f* (*de brevet*);
spec·i·fy [ˈ⌣fai] spécifier, déterminer; préciser.

spec·i·men [ˈspesimin] exemple *m*,
spécimen *m*; échantillon *m*.

spe·cious □ [ˈspiːʃəs] spécieux
(-euse *f*); trompeur (-euse *f*);
ˈspe·cious·ness spéciosité *f*; apparence *f* trompeuse.

speck [spek] **1.** graine *f*; point *m*;
tache *f*; *fig.* brin *m*; **2.** moucheter,
tacheter; **speck·le** [ˈ⌣kl] **1.** moucheture *f*; *see* speck 1; **2.** *see* speck 2.

specs F [speks] *pl.* lunettes *f/pl.*

spec·ta·cle [ˈspektəkl] spectacle *m*;
(*a pair of*) ⌣s *pl.* (des) lunettes *f/pl.*;
ˈspec·ta·cled qui porte des lunettes; à lunettes.

spec·tac·u·lar □ [spek'tækjulə]
1. spectaculaire; impressionnant;
2. *Am.* F revue *f* à grand spectacle.

spec·ta·tor [spek'teitə] spectateur
(-trice *f*) *m*.

spec·tral □ [ˈspektrəl] spectral
(-aux *m/pl.*) (*a. opt.*); **spec·ter**,
Brit. **spec·tre** [ˈ⌣tə] fantôme *m*,
spectre *m*; **spec·trum** *opt.* [ˈ⌣trəm]
spectre *m*.

spec·u·late [ˈspekjuleit] spéculer
(*a.* ✝), méditer (sur, [*up*]on); ✝
a. jouer; **spe·cu'la·tion** spéculation *f* (*a.* ✝), méditation *f* (sur,
[*up*]on); entreprise *f* spéculative;
spec·u·la·tive □ [ˈ⌣lətiv] spéculatif
(-ive *f*) (*a.* ✝); contemplatif (-ive *f*);
théorique; **ˈspec·u·la·tor** penseur
m; ✝ spéculateur *m*; ✝ agioteur *m*.

spec·u·lum [ˈspekjuləm] ⚕ spécu-
lum *m*; *opt.* miroir *m*.

sped [sped] *prét. et p.p. de* speed 2.

speech [spiːtʃ] parole *f*, -s *f/pl.*;
langue *f*; discours *m*; ~ *defect* défaut
m d'élocution; **ˈ⌣·day** *école*: distribution *f* des prix; **speech·i·fy** *péj.*
[ˈ⌣ifai] pérorer, *sl.* laïusser; **ˈspeech-
less** □ muet(te *f*).

speed [spiːd] **1.** vitesse *f* (*a.* ⊕, *mot.*,
etc.); marche *f*; hâte *f*; ~ *control*
réglage *m* de la vitesse; ~ *trap* piège *m*
de police (pour contrôle de vitesse);
good ⌣! bonne chance!; **2.** [*irr.*] *v/i.* se
hâter, se presser; aller *etc.* vite; ✝ *a.*
poét. réussir; *no* ⌣*ing*! vitesse *f* limi-

tée!; *v/t.* hâter, accélérer; ✝ expédier, souhaiter le bon voyage à; ~ *up*
accélérer; *mot.* mettre en vitesse;
ˈ⌣·boat hors-bord *m/inv.*; **ˈ⌣·cop**
motard *m*; **ˈspeed·i·ness** rapidité *f*;
promptitude *f*; **speed lim·it** vitesse
f maxima; vitesse *f* limitée; **ˈspeed-
mer·chant** *mot.* chauffard *m*;
speed·om·e·ter *mot.* [spi'dɔmitə]
compteur *m*, indicateur *m* de vitesse;
ˈspeed·way *Am.* autostrade *f*; *Am.*
sp. (piste *f* d')autodrome *m*; **ˈspeed-
well** ♣ véronique *f*; **ˈspeed·y** □
rapide, prompt.

spell[1] [spel] temps *m*, période *f*;
⊕ tour *m* (de travail).

spell[2] [⌣] **1.** charme *m*, incantation *f*;
2. [*irr.*] épeler (*de vive voix*); écrire,
orthographier; *fig.* signifier; ~ *out*
lire péniblement; épeler; **ˈ⌣·bind-
er** *Am.* beau diseur *m*; **ˈ⌣·bound**
fig. fasciné, charmé; **ˈspell·er**: *he*
is a bad ⌣ il ne sait pas l'orthographe.

spell·ing [ˈspeliŋ] épellation *f*;
orthographe *f*; **ˈ⌣·bee** *surt. Am.*
concours *m* d'orthographe; **ˈ⌣·book**
syllabaire *m*.

spelt[1] [spelt] *prét. et p.p. de* spell[2] 2.

spelt[2] ♣ épeautre *m*.

spel·ter [ˈspeltə] zinc *m*.

spen·cer [ˈspensə] *cost.* spencer *m*.

spend [spend] [*irr.*] *v/t.* dépenser (*de*
l'argent) (en, à, pour on), *péj.* dissiper (pour, on); employer, passer
(*le temps*), *péj.* perdre; épuiser (*des*
forces); ~ *o.s.* s'épuiser; ⌣*ing money*
argent *m* de poche; *v/i.* dépenser de
l'argent; **ˈspend·er** personne *f* qui
dépense; *péj.* dépensier (-ère *f*) *m*.

spend·thrift [ˈspendθrift] dépensier (-ère *f*) *m* (*a. attr.*).

spent [spent] **1.** *prét. et p.p. de*
spend; **2.** épuisé (*personne, a.* 🏹
acide); mort (*balle*), vide (*cartouche*); écoulé (*jour*); apaisé
(*orage*).

sperm *physiol.* [spəːm] semence *f*
(*des mâles*); **sper·ma·ce·ti** [⌣əˈseti]
spermacéti *m*; blanc *m* de baleine;
sper·ma·to·zo·on *biol.* [⌣əto-
ˈzouɔn], *pl.* -zo·a [⌣əˈzouə] spermato-
zoïde *m*.

spew *sl.* [spjuː] *vt/i.* vomir.

sphere [sfiə] sphère *f* (*a. fig.* d'*activité*, d'*influence*, *etc.*); *fig.* domaine
m; *fig.* milieu *m*; **spher·i·cal** □
[ˈsferikl] sphérique, en forme de
sphère.

sphincter   1126

sphinc·ter *anat.* ['sfiŋktə] sphincter *m*, orbiculaire *m*.

spice [spais] **1.** épice *f*; *fig.* soupçon *m*, grain *m*, nuance *f*; **2.** épicer (*a. fig.*); **spic·er·y** ['⁓əri] épices *f/pl.* [épicé; *fig.* piquant *m*.\ **spic·i·ness** ['spaisinis] goût *m*∫ **spick and span** ['spikən'spæn] propre comme un sou neuf; tiré à quatre épingles (*personne*).

spic·y □ ['spaisi] épicé (*a. fig.*); aromatique; *fig.* piquant.

spi·der *zo.* ['spaidə] araignée *f*; ⁓'s web toile *f* d'araignée.

spiel *Am. sl.* [spi:l] discours *m*, allocution *f*; *sl.* laïus *m*.

spiff·y *sl.* ['spifi] élégant; pimpant.

spig·ot ['spigət] *tonneau:* fausset *m*; *robinet:* clef *f*.

spike [spaik] **1.** pointe *f*; *fil barbelé:* piquant *m*; clou *m* à large tête; ♀ *blé:* épi *m*; ♀ (*a. ⁓-lavender*) spic *m*; **2.** clouer; ⚔ enclouer (*un canon*); F *fig.* damer le pion à (*q.*); armer de pointes; **spike·nard** ['⁓nɑːd] nard *m* (indien); **spik·y** □ à pointe(s) aiguë(s); armé de pointes.

spill [spil] **1.** [*irr.*] *v/t.* répandre (*a. le sang*); renverser; F désarçonner (*un cavalier*); *Am.* dire; *v/i.* se répandre; s'écouler; **2.** F culbute *f*, chute *f* (*de cheval etc.*).

spill·way ['spilwei] passe-déversoir *m* (*pl.* passes-déversoirs) *f*.

spilt [spilt] *prét. et p.p. de spill 1*; *cry over ⁓ milk* lamenter ce qu'on ne pourrait changer.

spin [spin] **1.** [*irr.*] *v/t.* filer; faire tourner (*a. une toupie*); *fig.* raconter (*une histoire*); ⊕ centrifuger (*le métal*); *v/i.* tourner; (*a. ⁓ round*) tournoyer; ⚼ faire la vrille; ⁓ *along* filer; ⁓ (*a)round* se retourner vivement (*personne*); *send ⁓ ...ning* faire chanceler q.; **2.** tournoiement *m*, ⚼ vrille *f*; *cricket:* effet *m*; F *go for a ⁓* se balader en auto.

spin·ach ♀ ['spinidʒ] épinard *m*; *cuis.* épinards *m/pl.*

spi·nal ['spainl] vertébral (-aux *m/pl.*); ⁓ *column* colonne *f* vertébrale; ⁓ *cord* (*ou marrow*) moelle *f* épinière; ⁓ *curvature* déviation *f* de la colonne vertébrale.

spin·dle ['spindl] fuseau *m*; ⊕ arbre *m*; **spin·dly** long(ue *f*) et grêle.

spin·drift ['spindrift] *courant:* embruns *m/pl.*

spin-dry ['spindrai] essorer à la machine.

spine [spain] épine *f*; *homme:* épine *f* dorsale; *géog.* arête *f*; *livre:* dos *m*; **spine·less** sans épines; *fig.* mou (mol *devant une voyelle ou h muet;* molle *f*).

spin·ner ['spinə] fileur (-euse *f*) *m*; machine *f ou* métier *m* à filer.

spin·ney ['spini] bosquet *m*, petit bois *m*.

spin·ning...: ⁓**-jen·ny** ⊕ ['spiniŋ-'dʒeni] machine *f* à filer; **⁓-mill** filature *f*; **⁓-wheel** rouet *m*.

spin-off ['spinɔf] sous-produit *m*; avantage *m* supplémentaire.

spin·ster ['spinstə] fille *f* (non mariée); *p.ext.* vieille fille *f*; *admin.* célibataire *f*.

spin·y ['spaini] épineux (-euse *f*); ♀ spinifère.

spi·ra·cle ['spaiərəkl] évent *m*.

spi·rae·a ♀ [spai'riə] spirée *f*.

spi·ral ['spaiərəl] **1.** □ spiral (-aux *m/pl.*); spiralé; en spirale; spiroïdal (-aux *m/pl.*) (*mouvement*); en boudin (*ressort*); *zo.* cochléaire; **2.** spirale *f*, hélice *f*; tour *m ou* ⚼ montée *f etc.* en spirale; *fig. prix:* montée *f* en flèche; **3.** former une spirale; monter *ou* descendre en spirale.

spire ['spaiə] *église, arbre:* flèche *f*.

spir·it ['spirit] **1.** esprit *m*, âme *f*; *fig.* élan *m*, entrain *m*, ardeur *f*; courage *m*; alcool *m*; ⚗ *hist.* esprit *m*; *mot.* essence *f*; ⁓s *pl.* spiritueux *m/pl.*; liqueurs *f/pl.* fortes; *pharm.* alcoolat *m*; ⁓ *of wine* esprit *m* de vin; *in (high)* ⁓s en train; en verve; *in low* ⁓s abattu; accablé; tout triste; **2.**: ⁓ *away* enlever, faire disparaître; F escamoter; ⁓ *up* encourager.

spir·it·ed □ ['spiritid] animé, vif (vive *f*); plein d'entrain; fougueux (-euse *f*); *low-*⁓ abattu; **'spir·it·ed·ness** ardeur *f*, feu *m*; *cheval:* fougue *f*.

spir·it·ism ['spiritizm] *métapsychisme:* spiritisme *m*; **'spir·it·ist** spirite *mf* (*a. adj.*).

spir·it·less □ ['spiritlis] abattu; inanimé; sans vie (*a. fig.*); mou (mol *devant une voyelle ou un h muet;* molle *f*).

spir·it·u·al ['spiritjuəl] **1.** □ spirituel(le *f*); immatériel(le *f*); **2.** chant *m* religieux (*des nègres aux É.-U.*);

sponge

'**spir·it·u·al·ism** *phls.* spiritualisme *m*; *métapsychisme*: spiritisme *m*; **spir·it·u·al·i·ty** [~'æliti] spiritualité *f*; **spir·it·u·al·ize** ['~əlaiz] spiritualiser.

spir·it·u·ous ['spiritjuəs] spiritueux (-euse *f*), alcoolique.

spirt [spə:t] **1.** *v/t.* faire jaillir; *v/i.* jaillir, gicler; *see* spurt 1; **2.** (re)jaillissement *m*; jet *m*; *see* spurt 2.

spit¹ [spit] **1.** *cuis.* broche *f*; *géog.* langue *f* de sable, pointe *f* de terre; **2.** embrocher (*a. fig.*).

spit² [~] **1.** crachat *m*; salive *f*; F be the very ~ of s.o. être q. tout craché; **2.** [*irr.*] *v/i.* cracher (*a. chat, plume*); (*a.* ~ with rain) crachiner; ~ at (*ou* upon) cracher sur; *v/t.* (*a.* ~ out) cracher.

spit³ [~] profondeur *f* de fer de bêche; bêche *f* pleine.

spite [spait] **1.** dépit *m*, pique *f*; rancune *f*; in ~ of malgré; **2.** contrarier, vexer; **spite·ful** □ ['~ful] rancunier (-ère *f*); méchant; '**spite·ful·ness** rancune *f*; méchanceté *f*.

spit·fire ['spitfaiə] rageur (-euse *f*) *m*.

spit·tle ['spitl] salive *f*, crachat *m*.

spit·toon [spi'tu:n] crachoir *m*.

spiv *sl.* [spiv] parasite *m*; profiteur *m*.

splash [splæʃ] **1.** éclaboussement *m*; éclaboussure *f*; *vague*: clapotement *m*; *sl.* esbroufe *f*; F make a ~ faire sensation; **2.** *v/t.* éclabousser (de, with); tacher (de, with); *v/i.* jaillir; clapoter; barboter; cracher (*robinet*); '**~·board** garde-boue *m/inv.*; *métall.* parapluie *m*; plongeur *m* (de tête de bielle); '**~·down** amerissage *m*; '**splash-leath·er** pare-boue *m/inv.*; '**splash·y** □ bourbeux (-euse *f*); barbouillé (*dessin etc.*).

splay [splei] **1.** évasement *m*; **2.** évasé; tourné en dehors (*pied*); **3.** *v/t.* évaser; ⊕ chanfreiner; tourner en dehors; *v/i.* s'évaser.

splay·foot ['spleifut] pied *m* plat.

spleen [spli:n] *anat.* rate *f*; *fig.* spleen *m*, humeur *f* noire; **spleen·ful** ['~ful], '**spleen·y** atrabilaire; de mauvaise humeur.

splen·did □ ['splendid], **splen·dif·er·ous** [~'difərəs] splendide, magnifique; F épatant; **splen·do(u)r** ['~də] splendeur *f*; éclat *m*.

sple·net·ic [spli'netik] **1.** (*a.* sple·net·i·cal □ [~kl]) splénique (*a. ⚕*), atrabilaire; **2.** hypocondriaque *mf*.

splice [splais] **1.** ligature *f*; ⊕ enture *f* (*cricket: du manche de la batte*); **2.** ⊕ enter; *cin.* réparer; épisser; *sl.* marier.

splint ⚕ [splint] **1.** éclisse *f*; **2.** éclisser.

splin·ter ['splintə] **1.** éclat *m*; *os*: esquille *f*; **2.** *v/t.* briser; *v/i.* voler en éclats; se fendre; '**~·bone** *anat.* péroné *m*; '**splin·ter·less** se brisant sans éclats (*verre*).

split [split] **1.** fente *f*, fissure *f*; *fig.* scission *f*; F do the ~s faire le grand écart; **2.** fendu; **3.** [*irr.*] *v/t.* fendre; déchirer; partager; couper en deux; ~ hairs couper un cheveu en quatre; ~ one's sides with laughing se tordre de rire; ~ up fractionner; *v/i.* se fendre; éclater; *fig.* se diviser; *sl.* filer, ficher le camp (= s'en aller); *sl.* ~ on dénoncer (*q.*); F cafarder; '**split·ting** qui (se) fend; F fou (fol *devant une voyelle ou un h muet*; folle *f*), affreux (-euse *f*).

splotch [splɔtʃ] tache *f*.

splurge [splə:dʒ] *Am.* épate *f*; esbroufe *f*; grosse averse *f*.

splut·ter ['splʌtə] *see* sputter; *v/i.* bredouiller; cracher; ⚡ bafouiller (*moteur*).

spoil [spɔil] **1.** *souv.* ~s *pl.* butin *m* (*a. fig.*); *fig.* profit *m*; *surt. Am. pol.* ~s system octroi *m* des places à ses adhérents (*en arrivant au pouvoir*); **2.** [*irr.*] *v/t.* gâter (*a. un enfant*); piller; dépouiller (de, of); abîmer; couper (*l'appétit*); *v/i.* se gâter; s'altérer; ~ for a fight brûler du désir de se battre; '**spoil·er** spoliateur (-trice *f*) *m*; gâcheur (-euse *f*) *m*; **spoils·man** *Am. pol.* ['~zmən] chacal (*pl.* -s) *m*; '**spoil·sport** trouble-fête *mf/inv.*

spoilt [spɔilt] *prét. et p.p. de* spoil 2.

spoke¹ [spouk] *prét. de* speak.

spoke² [~] rayon *m*; *échelle*: échelon *m*; bâton *m* (*a. fig.*); ⚓ poignée *f*.

spo·ken ['spoukən] *p.p. de* speak.

spokes·man ['spouksmən] porte-parole *m/inv.*; orateur *m*.

spo·li·a·tion [spouli'eiʃn] spoliation *f*, dépouillement *m*; pillage *m*.

spon·dee ['spɔndi:] spondée *m*.

sponge [spʌndʒ] **1.** éponge *f*; *cuis.* pâte *f* molle; throw up the ~ box. jeter l'éponge; *fig.* abandonner (la partie); 2. *v/t.* nettoyer *ou* laver avec une éponge; ~ *up* éponger; *v/i.* vivre aux crochets (de q., *on s.o.*); F écornifler; **'~-bag** sac *m* de toilette; **'~-'cake** gâteau *m* de Savoie; baba *m* (*au rhum etc.*); **'spong·er** *fig.* écornifleur (-euse *f*) *m*; parasite *m*.

spon·gi·ness ['spʌndʒinis] spongiosité *f*; **'spon·gy** spongieux (-euse *f*).

spon·sor ['spɔnsə] 1. garant *m*, caution *f*; *eccl.*, *club:* parrain *m*, marraine *f*; be *a* ~ *to radio:* offrir (*un programme*); 2. être le garant de; prendre en charge; *radio:* offrir (*un programme*); financer; **spon·sor·ship** ['~ʃip] parrainage *m*.

spon·ta·ne·i·ty [spɔntə'niːiti] spontanéité *f*; **spon·ta·ne·ous** [~'teinjəs] spontané; volontaire; automatique; ♀ qui pousse à l'état sauvage; ~ *combustion* inflammation *f* spontanée; *auto-al*lumage *m*.

spoof F [spuːf] 1. mystification *f*; blague(s) *f*(*pl.*); 2. mystifier; raconter des blagues (à); faire marcher.

spook F [spuːk] 1. revenant *m*; 2. hanter; effrayer; **'spook·y** F de spectres, de revenants (*histoire*); qui donne le frisson; lugubre.

spool [spuːl] 1. bobine *f*; 2. bobiner.

spoon [spuːn] 1. cuiller *f*, cuillère *f*; F amoureux *m* d'une sentimentalité exagérée; *golf:* spoon *m*; *sl.* be ~s on avoir un béguin pour (*q.*); 2. manger *ou* ramasser *ou* servir *etc.* avec une cuiller; *sl.* faire le galant auprès de (*q.*); **'~-drift** embrun *m*; **'spoon·er·ism** contrepèterie *f*; **'spoon-feed** *fig.* mâcher la besogne à; **spoon·ful** ['~ful] cuillerée *f*; **'spoon-meat** aliment *m* liquide; **'spoon·y** □ F amoureux (-euse *f*) (de, on).

spo·rad·ic [spə'rædik] (~*ally*) *fig.* isolé, rare; ⚕, *zo.* sporadique.

spore ♀ [spɔː] spore *f*.

sport [spɔːt] 1. sport *m*; jeu *m*; divertissement *m*; *fig.* jouet *m*; *fig.* moquerie *f*; ♀, *biol.* type *m* anormal; *sl.* (*a. good* ~) chic type *m*; 2. *v/i.* jouer; se divertir; ♀, *biol.* produire une variété anormale (*of.*); F. porter; étaler; *univ. sl.* ~ *one's oak* défendre sa porte; s'enfermer à double porte; **'sport·ing** □ de sport; sportif (-ive *f*); amateur de la chasse; **'spor·tive** □ folâtre,

badin, enjoué; **sports-ground** ['~sgraund] terrain *m* de jeux; stade *m*; **sports·man** ['~smən] amateur *m* du sport, sportsman (*pl.* sportsmen) *m*; sportif *m*; chasseur *m*; **'sports·man·like** de sportsman; digne d'un sportsman; **'sports-wear** costume *m* de sport; **'sports·wom·an** femme *f* amateur du sport *ou* de la chasse *etc.*; sportive *f*.

spot [spɔt] 1. tache *f*; *cravate, étoffe:* pois *m*; endroit *m*, lieu *m*; *figure:* bouton *m*; *sl. vin:* goutte *f*, petit verre *m*; *théâ. etc.* projecteur *m*; *radio:* spot *m*; *Am.* F *ten* ~ billet *m* de dix dollars; ~ ~*s pl.* marchandises *f*/*pl.* payées comptant; F *a* ~ *of* un peu de; *on the* ~ sur place; *adv.* immédiatement; *be on the* ~ être là; arriver sur les lieux; 2. † (au) comptant, (du) disponible; fait au hasard; ~ *check* contrôle *m ou* vérification *f* fait(e) au hasard, sondage *m*; 3. *v/t.* tacher; tacheter, moucheter; F apercevoir; F repérer; F reconnaître; *v/i.* se tacher; F commencer à pleuvoir; **'~-check** contrôler au hasard *ou* à l'impoviste; **'spot·less** □ sans tache; immaculé; pur; **'spot·less·ness** netteté *f*; propreté *f*; pureté *f*; **'spot·light** *théâ.* projecteur *m*, spot *m*; *mot.* projecteur *m* orientable; *fig. in the* ~ en vedette; sous les feux de la rampe; **'spot-'on** *Brit.* F exact(ement), précis(ément), F en plein dans le mille; **'spot·ted** tacheté, moucheté; *tex.* à pois; *zo.* taché; ⚕ ~ *fever* méningite *f* cérébrospinale; **'spot·ter** ✈ avion *m* de réglage de tir; *personne:* observateur *m*; *Am.* détective *m* privé; *Am.* 🚂 inspecteur *m* en civil; **spot·ti·ness** ['~inis] caractère *m* tacheté *ou* boutonneux; **'spot·ty** moucheté, couvert de boutons (*figure*).

spouse [spauz] époux (-ouse *f*) *m*.

spout [spaut] 1. *théière etc.:* bec *m*; *arrosoir:* goulot *m*; *pompe:* jet *m*; ⚠ tuyau *m* de décharge; ⚠ gargouille *f*; gouttière *f*; 2. (faire) jaillir; *v/t.* F déclamer.

sprain [sprein] 1. entorse *f*, foulure *f*; 2. se fouler (la cheville, one's *ankle*).

sprang [spræŋ] *prét. de* spring 2.

sprat *icht.* [spræt] sprat *m*.

sprawl [sprɔːl] *v/i.* s'étendre, s'éta-

ler (*a. fig.*); ♥ traîner, ramper; *v/t.*
étendre (*les jambes*).

spray¹ [sprei] brin *m*, brindille *f*;
fleurs: branche *f*.

spray² [~] 1. poussière *f* d'eau; écume
f, embrun *m*; jet *m*; (*a. ~ can*) see ~er;
2. vaporiser (*un liquide*); arroser;
passer (*un arbre*) au vaporisateur;
'spray·er aérosol *m*, bombe *f*; atomiseur *m*, vaporisateur *m*; *foam* ~
extincteur *m* à mousse.

spread [spred] 1. [*irr.*] *v/t.* (*a. ~ out*)
étendre; tendre (*le filet*); répandre
(*un bruit, une nouvelle, une terreur*);
propager (*une maladie*); tartiner
(*une tranche de pain*); faire circuler,
faire connaître; ~ *the table* mettre
le couvert; *v/i.* s'étendre, s'étaler;
2. *prét. et p.p. de 1*; ⬛ ~ *eagle*
aigle *f* éployée; 3. étendue *f*; *ailes*:
envergure *f*; diffusion *f*, propagation *f*; *Am.* dessus *m* de lit; *sandwich etc.*: pâte *f*; *sl.* régal *m*, festin
m; **'~-ea·gle** F grandiloquent;
chauviniste; **'spread·er** étaleur
(-euse *f*) *m*; semeur (-euse *f*) *m*;
'spread·ing étendu; rameux (-euse
f) (*arbre*).

spree F [spri:] bombe *f*, noce *f*;
bringue *f*; *go on the* ~ faire la bringue *etc.*

sprig [sprig] 1. brin *m*, brindille *f*;
petite branche *f*; *fig.* rejeton *m*; ⊕
clou *m* (*de vitrier*); pointe *f* (de
Paris); 2.: ~ *on* (*ou down*) cheviller;
~ged à ramages (*tissu*).

spright·li·ness ['spraitlinis] vivacité *f*, sémillance *f*; **'spright·ly**
éveillé; vif (vive *f*).

spring [spriŋ] 1. saut *m*, bond *m*;
ressort *m*; *auto*: suspension *f*;
source *f* (*a. fig.*); *fig.* origine *f*;
saison: printemps *m*; 2. [*irr.*] *v/t.*
faire sauter; faire jouer (*un piège*);
suspendre (*l'auto*); munir de ressorts; franchir; (faire) lever (*le
gibier*); proposer *ou* présenter (*un
projet etc.*) à l'improviste, faire (*une
surprise*) (à q., [up]on s.o.); ⚓ ~ *a
leak* faire une voie d'eau; *v/i.*
sauter, bondir; jaillir, sourdre (de,
from); ♥ pousser; *fig.* sortir, descendre (de, *from*); ~ *up* sauter en l'air;
♥ pousser; se lever; se former (*idée*);
~ *into existence* naître, (ap)paraître;
'~-bal·ance balance *f ou* peson *m* à
ressort; **'~-board** tremplin *m*;
'~-bolt ⊕ verrou *m* à ressort; *serrure*:

pêne *m* coulant; **'~-'clean·ing** grand
nettoyage *m* de printemps.

springe [sprindʒ] *oiseaux*: lacet *m*;
lapins: collet *m*.

spring-gun ['spriŋgʌn] piège *m* à
fusil; **'spring·i·ness** élasticité *f*;
ressort *m*.

spring…: **'~-mat·tress** sommier *m*
élastique; **'~-tide** grande marée *f*;
poét. printemps *m*; **'~-time** printemps *m*; **'spring·y** □ élastique;
flexible; *fig.* moelleux (-euse *f*).

sprin·kle ['spriŋkl] *v/t.* (*with*, de)
répandre; arroser; *eccl.* asperger;
saupoudrer; *fig.* semer; *v/i.* tomber
en pluie fine; **'sprin·kler** arrosoir
m; extincteur *m* (*d'incendie*); *eccl.*
goupillon *m*; **'sprin·kling** aspersion *f*; légère couche *f*; *fig. a* ~ *of*
quelques bribes *f/pl.* de (*une science
etc.*).

sprint [sprint] 1. *sp.* course *f* de
vitesse, sprint *m*; 2. de vitesse;
3. faire une course de vitesse,
sprinter; **'sprint·er** *sp.* coureur
(-euse *f*) *m* de vitesse; sprinter *m*.

sprit ⚓ [sprit] livarde *f*.

sprite [sprait] lutin *m*, farfadet *m*;
esprit *m*.

sprock·et-wheel ⊕ ['sprɔkitwi:l]
pignon *m* de chaîne.

sprout [spraut] 1. (laisser) pousser;
2. ♥ pousse *f*; bourgeon *m*; *Brussels
~s pl.* choux *m/pl.* de Bruxelles.

spruce¹ □ [spru:s] soigné; pimpant.

spruce² ♥ [~] (*a. ~ fir*) sapin *m*,
épinette *f*.

sprung [sprʌŋ] *p.p. de* spring 2.

spry [sprai] vif (vive *f*), éveillé.

spud [spʌd] sarcloir *m*; *sl.* patate
f (= *pomme de terre*); F personne *f*
trapue.

spume *poét.* [spju:m] écume *f*;
'spu·mous, 'spum·y □ écumeux
(-euse *f*).

spun [spʌn] *prét. et p.p. de* spin 1.

spunk [spʌŋk] amadou *m*; *fig.* courage *m*; *Am.* irritation *f*.

spur [spə:] 1. éperon *m* (*a. géog.*, ♥,
†, ⚓); *coq, seigle*: ergot *m*; *fig.*
aiguillon *m*; *act on the* ~ *of the
moment* agir sous l'inspiration du
moment; *put* (*ou set*) ~*s to* éperonner, donner de l'éperon à (*un
cheval*); *fig.* stimuler; *win one's* ~*s* F
faire ses preuves; *hist.* gagner ses
éperons; ⊕ ~*-gear* engrenage *m*
droit; 2. *v/t.* (*a. ~ on*) éperonner;

spurge 1130

fig. aiguillonner, pousser; *v/i. poét.* aller au galop, piquer des deux.

spurge ♀ [spə:dʒ] euphorbe *f.*

spu·ri·ous □ ['spjuəriəs] faux (fausse *f*); '**spu·ri·ous·ness** fausseté *f.*

spurn [spə:n] repousser du pied; rejeter *ou* traiter avec mépris.

spurred [spə:d] éperonné; ergoté (*seigle, a. orn.*); ♀ calcarifère.

spurt [spə:t] **1.** (re)jaillir; *sp.* démarrer, faire un emballage; *see* spirt 1; **2.** effort *m* soudain; *sp.* effort *m* de vitesse, emballage *m*, rush *m*; *see* spirt 2.

sput·ter ['spʌtə] **1.** bredouillement *m*; *bois, feu*: pétillement *m*; **2.** *v/i.* bredouiller (*a.* qch. à q., *s.th.* at s.o.); cracher (*plume*); *v/t.* (*a.* ~ out) débiter en bredouillant.

spy [spai] **1.** espion(ne *f*) *m*; F mouchard *m*; **2.** *v/i.* espionner; *v/t.* apercevoir; ~ out explorer (*un terrain*); ~ (up)on s.o. épier, guetter q.; '~·**glass** lunette *f* d'approche; '~·**hole** *porte*: judas *m*; *rideau etc.*: trou *m.*

squab [skwɔb] boulot(te *f*) *m*; courtaud(e *f*) *m*; *orn.* pigeonneau *m* sans plumes; *Am. sl.* jeune fille: typesse *f*; *mot.* coussin *m*; ottomane *f*; pouf *m* (*a. adv.*).

squab·ble ['skwɔbl] **1.** querelle *f*, dispute *f*; *prise f* de bec; chamaille *f*; **2.** se chamailler (avec, *with*); '**squab·bler** chamaillard *m*; querelleur (-euse *f*) *m.*

squad [skwɔd] escouade *f*; peloton *m*; *police*: brigade *f*; *Am. sp.* équipe *f*; **squad·ron** ['~rən] ✕ escadron *m*; ✈ escadrille *f*; ⚓ escadre *f.*

squal·id □ ['skwɔlid] sordide, crasseux (-euse *f*).

squall¹ [skwɔ:l] **1.** cri *m* rauque; **2.** *vt/i.* brailler, crier.

squall² ⚓ [~] grain *m*, coup *m* de vent; '**squall·y** ⚓ à grains, à rafales (*temps*); orageux (-euse *f*).

squa·lor ['skwɔlə] misère *f*; caractère *m* sordide.

squa·mous ['skweiməs] squameux (-euse *f*).

squan·der ['skwɔndə] gaspiller; '~·**ma·ni·a** prodigalité *f.*

square [skwɛə] **1.** □ carré *m*; *fig.* honnête; en bon ordre; solide (*repas etc.*); catégorique (*refus*); ⊕ plat; ~ *measure* mesure *f* de sur-

face; ~ *mile* mille *m* carré; ⚹ *take a* ~ *root* extraire la racine carrée; ⚓ ~ *sail* voile *f* carrée; *Am.* F ~ *shooter* homme *m* loyal *ou* qui agit loyalement; ~ *with* (*ou* to) d'équerre avec; **2.** carré *m* (*a.* ⚹, ✕); carreau *m*; *échiquier etc.*: case *f*; *surv.* équerre *f*; place *f*; *Am.* bloc *m* de maisons; *silk* ~ foulard *m*; **3.** *v/t.* carrer; équarrir (*le bois, un bloc de marbre*); *fig.* accorder (avec, *with*); mettre en croix (*les vergues*); ✝ régler, balancer; *sl.* graisser la patte à (*q.*); F arranger; *v/i.* se carrer, se raccorder; *fig.* cadrer (avec, *with*); s'accorder (avec, *with*); '~-'**built** bâti en carré; aux épaules carrées (*personne*); '~-'**rigged** ⚓ gréé en carré; '~-**toes** *sg.* F pédant *m*; rigoriste *m* de l'ancienne mode.

squash¹ [skwɔʃ] **1.** écrasement *m*; F cohue *f*, presse *f*; *sp.* jeu *m* de balle au mur; *lemon* ~ citronnade *f*; **2.** (s')écraser; *fig.* (se) serrer.

squash² ♀ [~] gourde *f*; *Am.* courge *f.*

squat [skwɔt] **1.** accroupi; trapu; **2.** s'accroupir, se tapir; s'approprier une maison; '**squat·ter** *surt. Am. et Australie*: squatter *m.*

squaw [skwɔ:] femme *f* peau-rouge.

squawk [skwɔ:k] **1.** pousser des cris rauques; **2.** cri *m* rauque.

squeak [skwi:k] **1.** *v/i.* pousser des cris aigus; grincer; F *v/t.* crier d'une voix aiguë; **2.** cri *m* aigu; grincement *m*; '**squeak·y** □ criard; aigu(ë *f*).

squeal [skwi:l] pousser des cris aigus; F ~ *on* s.o. dénoncer q.; *see* squeak 1.

squeam·ish □ ['skwi:miʃ] sujet(te *f*) aux nausées; délicat, difficile, dégoûté; '**squeam·ish·ness** disposition *f* aux nausées; délicatesse *f.*

squee·gee ['skwi:'dʒi:] rabot *m* en caoutchouc; *phot.* raclette *f.*

squeez·a·ble ['skwi:zəbl] compressible, comprimable.

squeeze [skwi:z] **1.** *v/t.* serrer; presser; exercer une pression sur; *fig.* extorquer (à, *from*); ~ *into* faire entrer (de force); ~ *out* exprimer; *v/i.*: ~ *into* s'introduire dans; ~ *together* (*ou* up) se serrer; **2.** étreinte *f*, compression *f*; *main*: serrement *m*; F exaction *f*; '**squeez·er** machine *f* à compression; presse-citron *m/inv.*; F extorqueur *m.*

squelch F [skweltʃ] *v/t.* aplatir; réprimer; *v/i.* gicler; gargouiller.

squib [skwib] pétard *m*; *fig.* brocard *m.*

squid *zo.* [skwid] calmar *m.*

squif·fy *sl.* ['skwifi] gris, pompette.

squig·gle F ['skwigl] gribouillis *m.*

squill ♀ [skwil] scille *f.*

squint [skwint] **1.** loucher; **2.** strabisme *m*; regard *m* louche; F coup *m* d'œil.

squire ['skwaiə] **1.** propriétaire *m* terrien; seigneur *m* du village; *Am.* juge *m* de paix; *hist.* écuyer *m*; *co.* cavalier *m* servant; **2.** escorter (*une dame*).

squir(e)·arch·y ['skwaiərɑːki] corps *m* des propriétaires fonciers; tyrannie *f* terrienne.

squirm F [skwəːm] se tortiller; *fig.* se crisper (sous un reproche, *under a rebuke*).

squir·rel *zo.* ['skwirəl] écureuil *m*; (*a.* ~*fur*) petit-gris (*pl.* petits-gris) *m.*

squirt [skwəːt] **1.** seringue *f*; jet *m* (*d'eau etc.*); F petit fat *m*; **2.** (faire) jaillir; *v/i.* gicler.

squish F [skwiʃ] giclement *m.*

stab [stæb] **1.** coup *m* de poignard *ou* de couteau; **2.** *v/t.* poignarder; *v/i.* porter un coup de poignard *etc.* (à, at).

sta·bil·i·ty [stə'biliti] stabilité *f* (*a.* ✈); fermeté *f*, constance *f.*

sta·bi·li·za·tion [steibilai'zeiʃn] stabilisation *f* (*a.* ✈).

sta·bi·lize ['steibilaiz] stabiliser; **'sta·bi·liz·er** ✈ plan *m* fixe horizontal; ⚓ stabilisateur *m.*

sta·ble¹ □ ['steibl] stable; solide, fixe; ferme, constant.

sta·ble² [~] **1.** écurie *f*; **2.** mettre à l'écurie, mettre dans une écurie; **sta·ble·boy** palefrenier *m.*

sta·bling ['steibliŋ] logement *m* à l'écurie; *coll.* écuries *f/pl.*

stack [stæk] **1.** ✿ *foin etc.*: meule *f*, tas *m*, pile *f*; *cheminée:* souche *f*; ✕ faisceau *m*; 🚢 cheminée *f*; ~*s pl.* magasin *m* de livres; F ~*s pl.* un tas *m*; *Am.* F blow one's ~ sortir de ses gonds; se mettre en rogne; **2.** mettre en meule; *fig.* entasser; ✕ mettre en faisceaux.

sta·di·um *sp.* ['steidiəm], *pl.* **-di·a** ['~diə] stade *m.*

staff [stɑːf] **1.** bâton *m*; mât *m*; ♪ (*pl.*

staves [steivz]) portée *f*; ✕ état-major (*pl.* états-majors) *m*; ✝ personnel *m* (*école, univ.*: enseignant); *ecole:* ~ *room* salle *f* des professeurs; **2.** fournir de personnel.

stag [stæg] **1.** *zo.* cerf *m*; F homme *m* non accompagné d'une dame; ✝ loup *m*; **2.** ✝ acheter pour revendre à prime.

stage [steidʒ] **1.** estrade *f*; échafaudage *m*; *théâ.* scène *f*; *fig.* théâtre *m*; période *f*; étape *f*; phase *f*; (*a. landing-*~) débarcadère *m*; go on the ~ se faire acteur (-trice *f*); fare ~ *autobus etc.:* section *f* itinéraire; **2.** mettre sur la scène; monter; '~**box** loge *f* d'avant-scène; '~**coach** diligence *f*; ~ **di·rec·tion** indication *f* scénique; ~ **fright** trac *m*; ~ **hand** machiniste *m*; ~ **man·ag·er** régisseur *m*; '**stag·er** *old* ~ vieux routier *m*; '**stage-struck** fou (folle *f*) du théâtre; **stage whis·per** aparté *m*; '**stage·y** *see* stagy.

stag·ger ['stægə] **1.** *v/i.* chanceler, tituber; *fig.* hésiter; *v/t.* faire chanceler; ⊕ disposer en quinconce; étager; *fig.* échelonner; F confondre; **2.** chancellement *m*; allure *f* chancelante; ⊕ disposition *f* en quinconce; *fig.* échelonnement *m*; ~*s pl.* *vét.* *mouton:* lourd vertige *m*; *cheval:* vertigo *m*; F vertige *m*; '**stag·ger·ing** renversant.

stag·nan·cy ['stægnənsi] stagnation *f*; '**stag·nant** □ stagnant (*a.* ✝); ✝ en stagnation; dormant; **stag·nate** ['~neit] être *ou* devenir stagnant; croupir (*eau*); **stag·na·tion** stagnation *f*; ✝ *a.* marasme *m.*

stag·par·ty F ['stægpɑːti] réunion *f* d'hommes.

stag·y □ ['steidʒi] théâtral (-aux *m/pl.*).

staid □ [steid] posé, sérieux (-euse *f*); '**staid·ness** caractère *m ou* air *m* posé *ou* sérieux.

stain [stein] **1.** tache *f* (*a. fig.*); ⊕ couleur *f* (*pour bois*); **2.** *v/t.* tacher (*a. fig.*); ⊕ teindre, mettre en couleur; *v/i.* se tacher; se teindre; ~*ed glass* verre *m* de couleur; ~*ed glass (window)* vitrail (*pl.* -aux) *m*; '**stain·less** □ sans tache; immaculé; ⊕ inoxydable (*acier*); inrouillable.

stair [stɛə] marche *f*, degré *m*; ~*s pl.* escalier *m*; *flight of* ~*s pl.* (volée *f* d')escalier *m*; '~**-car·pet** tapis *m*

d'escalier; '**~·case** (cage *f* d')escalier
m; *moving* ~ escalier *m* roulant, escalator *m*; '**~-rod** tringle *f* d'escalier;
Am. '**~-way** *see* staircase.

stake [steik] **1.** pieu *m*; poteau *m*; *jeu*:
enjeu *m*; jeu *m* (*a. fig.*); bûcher *m*
(*d'un martyr*); ~s *pl. turf*: prix *m*/*pl.*;
surt. Am. pull up ~s partir, ficher le
camp; *be at* ~ être en jeu; *place*
one's ~ *on* parier sur; **2.** garnir de
ou soutenir avec des pieux; mettre
en jeu; jouer, parier; hasarder; ~
out (*ou off*) jalonner.

stale¹ □ [steil] **1.** vieux (vieil *devant*
une voyelle ou un h muet); vieille *f*;
vieux *m*/*pl.*); rassis (*pain etc.*); éventé (*bière etc.*); défraîchi (*article, nou-*
velle); vicié (*air*); de renfermé
(*odeur*); rance; usé, rebattu (*plaisan-*
terie etc.); **2.** *v/i.* s'éventer (*bière*);
perdre son intérêt.

stale² [~] **1.** uriner (*cheval etc.*);
2. urine *f*.

stale·mate ['steil'meit] **1.** *échecs*:
pat *m*; *fig.* impasse *f*; **2.** faire pat (*q.*).

stalk¹ [stɔːk] tige *f*; *chou*: trognon *m*;
verre: pied *m*.

stalk² [~] **1.** *v/i.* marcher à grandes
enjambées; se pavaner; chasser
sans chiens; *v/t.* traquer du affût;
2. chasse *f* à l'affût; '**stalk·er**
chasseur *m* à l'affût; '**stalk·ing-**
horse *fig.* masque *m*, prétexte *m*.

stall [stɔːl] **1.** *cheval*: stalle *f*; *bœuf*:
case *f*; *porc*: loge *f*; *marché*: étalage
m; *théâ.* fauteuil *m* d'orchestre; *eccl.*
stalle *f*; **2.** *v/t.* mettre à l'étable *ou*
l'écurie; *✶* mettre en perte de vitesse; *mot.* caler; *v/i. mot.* (se)
caler; *✶* s'engager; '**~-feed·ing**
nourrissage *m* à l'étable.

stal·lion ['stæljən] étalon *m*.

stal·wart ['stɔːlwət] **1.** □ robuste,
vigoureux (-euse *f*); *fig.* ferme;
2. *pol.* tenant *m*; partisan *m*.

sta·men ♀ ['steimen] étamine *f*;
stam·i·na ['stæminə] vigueur *f*,
résistance *f*.

stam·mer ['stæmə] **1.** bégayer, balbutier; **2.** bégaiement *m*; '**stam-**
mer·er bègue *mf*.

stamp [stæmp] **1.** battement *m*
(*a.* bruit *m*) de pied; ⊕ estampeuse
f; ⊕ emboutisseuse *f*; empreinte *f*
(*a. fig.*); *fig.* trempe *f*; timbre
(-poste) *m*; coin *m*; ✝ estampille *f*; ~
pad tampon *m* (encreur); *see* date-~;
2. *v/t.* frapper (du pied, *one's foot*);

estamper; ✝ estampiller; ✝ contrôler; marquer (*a. fig.*); timbrer (*un*
document); affranchir (*une lettre*); ~
on the memory (se) graver dans la
mémoire, imprimer sur l'esprit; ~
out étouffer; ⊕ découper à la presse;
v/i. frapper du pied; piétiner; '**~-**
al·bum album *m* de timbres-poste;
'**~-du·ty** droit *m* de timbre.

stam·pede [stæm'piːd] **1.** panique *f*;
débandade *f*; ruée *f*; **2.** *v/t.* mettre en
fuite; *v/i.* fuir en désordre; se précipiter (vers, sur *for*, *towards*).

stamp·er ['stæmpə] estampeuse *f*;
personne: timbreur (-euse *f*), estampeur (-euse *f*) *m*, frappeur (-euse *f*) *m*
de monnaie; '**stamp**(·**ing**)-**mill**
métall. (moulin *m* à) bocard(s *pl.*) *m*.

stanch [stɑːntʃ] **1.** étancher (*le sang*);
2. *adj. see* staunch 1; **stan·chion**
['stɑːnʃn] étançon *m*; colonnette *f* de
soutien.

stand [stænd] **1.** [*irr.*] *v/i.* se tenir
(debout); être; se trouver; rester;
se maintenir; se porter candidat;
(*usu.* ~ *still*) s'arrêter; se lever; ~
against s'adosser à; résister à, combattre; ~ *aside* se tenir à l'écart;
s'écarter; *fig.* se désister (*en faveur*
de q.); ~ *at* être à; marquer (*les*
degrés); ~ *back* se tenir en arrière;
(se) reculer; être écarté (de, *from*);
~ *by* se tenir prêt; *✶* se tenir paré;
✕ être consigné; se tenir à côté
de; *fig.* soutenir; *fig.* rester fidèle à;
radio: ne pas quitter l'écoute; ~ *for*
tenir lieu de; se présenter comme
candidat à; soutenir; vouloir dire;
représenter; F supporter, tolérer;
✶ in courir (vers, à *to*); ~ *in with*
s'associer à; ~ *off* se tenir éloigné
ou à l'écart; s'éloigner; ⊕ chômer; *✶* courir au large; avoir
le cap au large; ~ *off!* tenez-vous
à distance!; ~ *on* se tenir sur (*a.*
fig.); insister sur; ~ *out* être en
ou faire saillie, avancer; *fig.* se
détacher (sur, *against*); se profiler
(sur, *against*); se tenir à l'écart;
résister (à, *against*); tenir bon
(contre, *against*); insister (sur, *for*);
✶ se tenir au large; courir au large;
~ *over* rester en suspens; se pencher
sur; *Am.* F ~ *pat* tenir ferme, ne pas
en démordre; ~ *to* ne pas démordre
de, en tenir pour; s'en tenir à; *✶*
avoir le cap à; *see* reason 1; ✕ ~ *to!*
aux armes!; ~ *up* se lever; se dres-

ser; ~ *up for* soutenir, prendre le parti de; ~ *up to* résister à; ~ *upon* se tenir sur (*a. fig.*); insister sur; **2.** [*irr.*] *v/t.* poser, mettre; supporter, endurer; soutenir (*un combat, un choc, ✕ le feu*); *see* ground² 1; F ~ *s.o. a dinner* payer un dîner à q.; ~ *treat* régaler; **3.** position *f*, place *f*; station(nement *m*) *f*; estrade *f*, tribune *f*; étalage *m*; socle *m*, dessous *m*; *surt. Am.* barre *f* des témoins; arrêt *m*; (*a. wash-~*) lavabo *m*; *fig.* résistance *f*; *composés:* -~ porte- *m*; umbrella-~ porte-parapluies *m/inv.*; ✕ ~ *of arms* armement *m* (*d'un soldat*); *make a (ou* one's) ~ *against* s'opposer résolument à.

stand·ard ['stændəd] **1.** ✕ étendard *m*; ⚓ pavillon *m* (*a.* ♀); *mesure:* étalon *m*, type *m*; ⚑ échantillon *m*; modèle *m*, norme *f*; niveau *m* (*a. école, fig.*); qualité *f*; degré *m* (d'excellence); hauteur *f*; *or, argent, a.* ♫: titre *m*; *école primaire:* classe *f*; ⊕ pied *m*; ✔ arbre *m* de plein vent; *above ~* au-dessus de la moyenne; ~ *lamp* torchère *f*, lampadaire *m*; *the ~ is high* le niveau est élevé; ~ *of living* niveau *m* de vie; ~ *of value* prix *m* régulateur; **2.** standard *adj./inv.*; -étalon; type; classique; normal (-aux *m/pl.*); courant; ~-**gauge** ⛗ ['~geidʒ] voie *f* normale; **stan·ard·i·za·tion** ['~ai'zeiʃn] étalonnage *m*; unification *f*; ⊕, *cin.* standardisation *f*; ♫ titrage *m*; '**stand·ard·ize** étalonner, unifier; normaliser; ⊕, *cin.* standardiser; ♫ titrer.

stand-by ['stændbai] **1.** expédient *m*; réserve *f*; **2.** de réserve, de secours.

stand-ee *Am.* F [stæn'di:] spectateur (-trice *f*) *m* debout.

stand·er·by ['stændə'bai], *pl.* '**stand·ers-'by** spectateur (-trice *f*) *m*; assistant(e *f*) *m*, témoin *m*.

stand-in *cin.* ['stænd'in] doublure *f*.

stand·ing ['stændiŋ] **1.** ☐ debout *inv.*; dormant (*eau*); permanent; ordinaire; fixe; ~ *jump* saut *m* à pieds joints; *parl.* ~ *orders pl.* règlement *m*, -s *m/pl.*; **2.** position *f*, rang *m*; importance *f*; durée *f*; date *f*; *of long* ~ d'ancienne date; '~-**room** place *f*, -s *f/pl.* debout.

stand...: '~-**off** *Am.* raideur *f*, réserve *f*, morgue *f*; '~-'**off·ish** dis-

tant; raide; ~'**pat·ter** *Am. pol.* immobiliste *m*; '~-**pipe** réservoir *m* cylindrique; '~-**point** point *m* de vue; '~-**still** arrêt *m*; *be at a* ~ n'avancer plus; *come to a* ~ s'arrêter; '~-**up:** ~ *collar* col *m* droit; ~ *fight* bataille *f* rangée; combat *m* en règle.

stank [stæŋk] *prét. de* stink 2.

stan·nic ♫ ['stænik] stannique.

stan·za ['stænzə] strophe *f*, stance *f*.

sta·ple¹ ['steipl] **1.** matière *f* première; *fig.* fond *m*; produit *m* principal; marché *m* aux laines; **2.** principal (-aux *m/pl.*).

sta·ple² [~] crampon *m*, crampillon *m*; clou *m* à deux pointes; *serrure:* gâche *f*.

star [sta:] **1.** étoile *f* (*a. fig.*); astre *m*; *théâ.* vedette *f*; *Am.* ♫*s and Stripes pl.* bannière *f* étoilée; **2.** étoiler; marquer d'un astérisque; *théâ.* figurer en vedette, tenir le premier rôle; ~ (*it*) briller; *théâ.* figurer en vedette de la semaine *etc.*

star·board ⚓ ['sta:bəd] **1.** tribord *m*; **2.** *v/t.* mettre la barre à tribord; *v/i.* venir sur tribord.

starch [sta:tʃ] **1.** amidon *m*; *pâte:* empois *m*; *fig.* raideur *f*; **2.** empesé; *fig.* ~ed guindé, raide; '**starch·i·ness** manières *f/pl.* empesées, raideur *f*; '**starch·y** ☐ **1.** féculent; *fig.* guindé; **2.** (*ou* ~ *food*) féculent *m*.

star·dom ['sta:dəm] célébrité *f*; *rise to* ~ devenir une vedette.

stare [stɛə] **1.** regard *m* fixe; **2.** regarder fixement (*qch., at s.th.*); ouvrir de grands yeux; ~ *s.o. out* dévisager q.

star·fish *zo.* ['sta:fiʃ] étoile *f* de mer.

star·ing ☐ ['stɛəriŋ] fixe (*regard*); effrayé; criard.

stark [sta:k] raide; *poét.* fort; ~ *naked* tout nu; *nu comme un ver.*

star·ling¹ *orn.* ['sta:liŋ] étourneau *m*.

star·ling² [~] brise-glace *m/inv.*

star·lit ['sta:lit] étoilé.

star·ring *théâ.* ['sta:riŋ] présentant... (en vedette).

star·ry ['sta:ri] étoilé (*a.* ♀); *fig.* brillant; '~-**eyed** rêveur (-euse); extasié; peu réaliste.

star-span·gled ['sta:spæŋgld] constellé d'étoiles; *Am. Star-Spangled Banner* bannière *f* étoilée.

start [sta:t] **1.** départ *m* (*a. sp.*); commencement *m*; *sp.* envolée *f*; *sp.* avance *f*; *fig.* sursaut *m*, tres-

saillement *m*; get the ~ of s.o. devancer q.; *sp.* give s.o. *a* ~ donner
de l'avance à q.; laisser q. partir le
premier; **2.** *v/i.* partir, se mettre en
route; commencer (*a.* qch., on s.th.;
a. à *inf.*, on *gér.*); *mot.* démarrer; ✻
prendre son vol; *fig.* tressaillir,
(sur)sauter (de, *with*; à *at*, *with*);
faire un écart brusque (*cheval*);
jaillir (de, *from*) (*larmes*); ~ *up* se
lever brusquement; *v/t.* faire partir
(*a. le gibier*); mettre (*une machine*)
en marche; *sp.* donner le signal du
départ à; lever (*un lièvre*); lancer
(*une personne, une affaire, etc.*); commencer (*un travail, une lutte, etc.*);
entamer (*une conversation, un sujet,
etc.*); soulever (*une question*); ~ *s.o.*
(*gér.*) mettre q. à (*inf.*).

start·er ['stɑːtə] auteur *m*; *sp.* starter *m*; *sp.* partant *m* (= *concurrent*);
mot. etc. démarreur *m*; *fig.* lanceur
(-euse *f*) *m*.

start·ing ['stɑːtiŋ] **1.** départ *m*; commencement *m etc.*; **2.** de départ; de
début; initial; *sp.* ~ *block* bloc *m* de
départ; *sp.* ~ *line* ligne *f* de départ; ~
phase phase *f* initiale; ~ *place* (*ou
point*) point *m* de départ; ~ *salary*
salaire *m* initial *ou* de début.

star·tle ['stɑːtl] effrayer; **'star·tler** F
chose *f* sensationnelle; **'star·tling**
□ effrayant; étonnant.

star·va·tion [stɑːˈveiʃn] faim *f*; ✻
inanition *f*; *attr.* de famine; (*be on a*) ~
diet (suivre un) régime *m* draconien;
starve [stɑːv] (faire) mourir de
faim; *fig. v/t.* priver (de, *of*); **starveling** ['~liŋ] affamé(e *f*) (*a. su./mf*);
famélique (*a. su./mf*); *a.* de famine.

state [steit] **1.** état *m*, condition *f*;
pompe *f*, apparat *m*; *pol. usu.* ♀ État
m; *hist.* ♀s *pl.* états *m/pl.*, ordres
m/pl.; ~ *of life* rang *m*; *in* ~ en grand
apparat *ou* gala; *lie in* ~ être exposé
solennellement (*mort*); F *be in a* ~ être
très agité; **2.** d'État; national (-aux
m/pl.); d'apparat; *see department*; ~
funeral obsèques *f/pl.* nationales;
Am. ♀ *house* palais *m* du gouvernement; **3.** énoncer, déclarer, affirmer;
poser (*un problème*); fixer (*une date
etc.*); ✻ spécifier (*un compte*); **'stateless** sans patrie; **'state·li·ness** majesté *f*; grandeur *f*; **'state·ly** majestueux (-euse *f*); imposant; noble;
'state·ment déclaration *f*; exposition *f*, énoncé *m*; affirmation *f*; ✻

état *m* (de compte, *of account*); ✻
bilan *m*; **'state·room** salle *f* de réception; ♣ cabine *f* de luxe; **'state-
side** *Am.* aux *ou* des États-Unis; F *go*
~ rentrer.

states·man ['steitsmən] homme *m*
d'État; **'states·man·like** d'homme
d'État; F magistral (-aux *m/pl.*);
'states·man·ship science *f* du
gouvernement; politique *f*.

State(s') rights *Am.* ['steit(s)raits]
droits *m/pl.* fondamentaux des
États fédérés.

stat·ic ['stætik] statique; **'stat·ics**
pl. ou sg. phys. statique *f*; *pl. radio:*
parasites *m/pl.*

sta·tion ['steiʃn] **1.** position *f*, place
f; poste *m* (*a.* ✕, ♣, *radio*); *sauvetage etc.*: station *f*; ⚓, *zo.* habitat *m*;
🚂 gare *f*; *métro:* station *f*; rang *m*,
situation *f* sociale; **2.** placer; poster; **'sta·tion·ar·y** □ immobile;
stationnaire; fixe; ~ *engine* moteur
m fixe; **'sta·tion·er** papetier *m*; ♀s'
Hall Hôtel *m* de la Corporation des
libraires (*à Londres*); **'sta·tion·er·y**
papeterie *f*; **'sta·tion·mas·ter** □
chef *m* de gare; **sta·tion wag·on**
Am. mot. canadienne *f*.

sta·tis·ti·cal □ [stəˈtistikl] statistique; **stat·is·ti·cian** [stætisˈtiʃn]
statisticien(ne *f*) *m*; **sta·tis·tics**
[stəˈtistiks] *pl., comme science sg.*
statistique *f*.

stat·u·ar·y ['stætjuəri] **1.** statuaire;
2. statuaire *f*, art *m* statuaire; *personne:* statuaire *mf*; *coll.* statues
f/pl.; **stat·ue** ['~tjuː] statue *f*; **stat-
u·esque** □ [~tjuˈesk] plastique;
sculptural (-aux *m/pl.*); **stat·u·ette**
[~tjuˈet] statuette *f*.

stat·ure ['stætʃə] taille *f*; stature *f*.

sta·tus ['steitəs] statut *m* légal; situation *f*; état *m* (*a.* ✻); rang *m*; ~
seeker ambitieux (-euse *f*) *m*; ~ *symbol* marque *f* de standing.

stat·ute ['stætjuːt] loi *f*, ordonnance
f; ~*s pl.* statuts *m/pl.*; ~ *law* droit *m*
écrit; **'~·book** code *m* des lois.

stat·u·to·ry □ ['stætjutəri] établi
par la loi; statutaire.

staunch [stɔːntʃ] **1.** □ ferme; sûr;
dévoué; étanche (*navire*); **2.** étancher.

stave [steiv] **1.** douve *f*; bâton *m*;
strophe *f*; ♪ mesure *f*; **2.** [*irr.*] (*usu.*
~ *in*) défoncer, enfoncer; ~ *off* prévenir, parer à.

staves [steivz] *pl. de* staff 1.

stay [stei] 1. ⚓ *mât*: accore *m*, étai *m*; hauban *m*; *fig.* soutien *m*; séjour *m*; ⚖ suspension *f*; ⚖ sursis *m*; (*a pair of*) ⁓s *pl.* (un) corset *m*; 2. *v/t.* arrêter; remettre; étayer; ⁓ one's *stomach* tromper la faim; *v/i.* rester, demeurer; se tenir; séjourner; *sp.* soutenir l'allure; ⁓ *away* s'absenter; ⁓ *for* attendre; ⁓ *in* rester à *ou* garder la maison; ⁓ *put* rester en place; *sl.* ne plus changer; ⁓ *up* veiller; rester debout; ⁓*ing power* fond *m*, résistance *f*; '⁓**-at-home** casanier (-ère *f*) *m*; '**stay·er** *sp. personne*: stayer *m*; cheval *m* de longue haleine.

stead [sted] place *f*; *in his* ⁓ à sa place; *stand s.o. in good* ⁓ être fort utile à q.

stead·fast □ ['stedfəst] ferme, stable; solide; inébranlable; constant; '**stead·fast·ness** fermeté *f*, constance *f*.

stead·i·ness ['stedinis] persévérance *f*; ✝ stabilité *f*; *a. see* steadfastness.

stead·y ['stedi] 1. □ ferme; solide (*a.* ✝); constant; soutenu; sûr; régulier (-ère *f*); *walk a* ⁓ 2 *miles* aller deux bons milles; 2. *v/t.* (r)affermir; assurer; calmer; stabiliser; *v/i.* se raffermir; reprendre son aplomb *ou* équilibre; 3. *Am.* F ami(e *f*) *m* attitré(e *f*); 4. F *go* ⁓ sortir ensemble, être de bons amis; F *go* ⁓ *with s.o.* sortir avec q.

steak [steik] tranche *f*; bifteck *m*; *fillet* ⁓ tournedos *m*.

steal [sti:l] 1. [*irr.*] *v/t.* voler, dérober; (*a.* ⁓ *away*) séduire (le cœur de q., *s.o.'s heart*); ⁓ *a glance* jeter un coup d'œil furtif (à, *at*); ⁓ *a march on s.o.* devancer q.; *v/i.* marcher à pas furtifs; ⁓ *into* se faufiler dans; 2. *Am.* filouterie *f*; transaction *f* malhonnête.

stealth [stelθ] *by* ⁓ à la dérobée; furtivement; '**stealth·i·ness** caractère *m* furtif; '**stealth·y** □ furtif (-ive *f*).

steam [sti:m] 1. vapeur *f*; buée *f*; *let off* ⁓ ⊕ lâcher la vapeur; *fig.* donner libre cours à ses sentiments; dépenser son superflu d'énergie; 2. de *ou* à vapeur; 3. *v/i.* fumer; jeter de la vapeur; *v/t.* cuire à la vapeur; vaporiser (*du drap*); '⁓**-boil·er** chaudière *f* à vapeur; **steamed** couvert de buée (*fenêtre*); '**steam-en·gine** machine *f* à vapeur; '**steam·er** ⚓ vapeur *m*; *cuis.* marmite *f* à l'étuvée; '**steam·i·ness** *climat*: humidité *f*; '**steam-roll·er** rouleau *m* compresseur; **steam tug** ⚓ remorqueur *m* à vapeur; '**steam·y** □ couvert de buée (*fenêtre*); humide (*climat etc.*).

ste·a·rin ⚗ ['stiərin] stéarine *f*.

steed *poét.* [sti:d] destrier *m*.

steel [sti:l] 1. acier *m*; *poét.* épée *f*; *cuis.* affiloir *m*; 2. *v/t.* aciérer; ⁓**-works** *usu. sg.* aciérie *f*; ⁓ *engraving* gravure *f* sur acier; 3. aciérer; ⁓ *o.s.* s'endurcir; '⁓**-clad** revêtu d'acier; '**steel·y** *usu. fig.* d'acier; '**steel·yard** romaine *f*.

steep[1] [sti:p] 1. raide, escarpé; F fort, raide; incroyable; 2. *poét.* escarpement *m*.

steep[2] [⁓] 1. trempage *m*; mouillage *m*; 2. baigner, tremper; *fig.* ⁓ *o.s.* se noyer (dans, *in*).

steep·en *fig.* ['sti:pən] *vt/i.* augmenter.

stee·ple ['sti:pl] clocher *m*; '⁓**-chase** steeple(-chase) *m*.

steep·ness ['sti:pnis] raideur *f*; pente *f* rapide.

steer[1] [stiə] jeune bœuf *m*, bouvillon *m*; *Am.* bœuf *m*.

steer[2] [⁓] diriger, conduire; '**steer·a·ble** dirigeable.

steer·age ⚓ ['stiəridʒ] ✝ manœuvre *f* de la barre; entrepont *m*; troisième classe *f*; '⁓**-way** ⚓: *have good* ⁓ sentir la barre.

steer·ing... ['stiəriŋ]: '⁓**-arm** *mot.* levier *m* d'attaque de (la) direction; ⁓ **com·mit·tee** comité *m* d'organisation; '⁓**-wheel** ⚓ roue *f* du gouvernail; *mot.* volant *m*.

steers·man ⚓ ['stiəzmən] timonier *m*.

stein [stain] chope *f*, pot *m*.

stel·lar ['stelə] stellaire.

stem[1] [stem] 1. *plante, fleur*: tige *f*; *fruit*: queue *f*; *arbre*: souche *f*, tronc *m*; *bananes*: régime *m*; *verre*: pied *m*; *pipe*: tuyau *m*; *mot.*: radical *m*; 2. *v/t.* enlever les queues de; égrapper (*des raisins*); *v/i. Am.* être issu (de, *from*).

stem[2] [⁓] 1. ⚓ avant *m*; *poét.* proue *f*; 2. *v/t.* contenir, refouler; arrêter; résister à; *v/i. ski*: se ralentir en faisant un angle aigu; ∼(*ming*) *turn stemmbogen* m.

stench [stentʃ] odeur f infecte; puanteur f.

sten·cil ['stensl] **1.** patron m; *machine à écrire*: cliché m; **2.** peindre *etc.* au patron; polycopier.

ste·nog·ra·pher [ste'nɔgrəfə] sténographe *mf*; **sten·o·graph·ic** [stenəˈgræfik] (∼*ally*) sténographique; **ste·nog·ra·phy** [ste'nɔgrəfi] sténographie f.

step[1] [step] **1.** pas m (*a. fig.*); marche f (*a. autel*); échelon m; *auto etc.*: marchepied m; *maison*: seuil m; démarche f, mesure f; (*a pair ou set of*) ∼s *pl.*, (*a*) ∼-*ladder* (une) échelle f double, (un) escabeau m; *in* ∼ *with* au pas avec; **2.** *v/i.* faire un pas; marcher; ∼ *down* descendre; *fig.* donner sa démission, se retirer; ∼ *in* entrer; ∼ *on it!* *sl.* dépêchez-vous!; dégrouillez-vous!; ∼ *out* sortir; allonger le pas; *v/t.* (*a.* ∼ *off, out*) mesurer (*une distance*) au pas; ∼ *up* rehausser le niveau de; ⚡ survolter.

step[2] [∼] *mots composés*: beau- (belle f); '∼-**fa·ther** beau-père (*pl.* beaux-pères) m.

steppe [step] steppe f.

step·ping-stone ['stepiŋstoun] pierre f de gué (*dans une rivière*); *fig.* marchepied m; tremplin m.

ster·eo... ['steriə] stéréo...

ster·eo ['steriou] **1.** (*a.* ∼ *sound*) stéréophonie f, F stéréo f; (*a.* ∼ *set*) appareil m stéréo; phonographe m stéréo; *typ.* cliché m; **2.** stéréophonique, F stéréo *inv.*; ∼**scope** ['∼skoup] stéréoscope m; '∼-**type 1.** cliché m; **2.** stéréotyper.

ster·ile □ ['sterail] stérile; ⚕ acarpe; **ste·ril·i·ty** [∼'riliti] stérilité f; **ster·i·lize** ['∼rilaiz] stériliser.

ster·ling ['stə:liŋ] de bon aloi (*a. fig.*); ✝ sterling; *a pound* ∼ une livre sterling.

stern[1] □ [stə:n] sévère, dur; austère.

stern[2] ⚓ [∼] arrière m; derrière m.

stern·ness ['stə:nnis] sévérité f, dureté f; austérité f.

stern-post ⚓ ['stə:npoust] étambot m. [num m.)
ster·num *anat.* ['stə:nəm] ster-ʃ
steth·o·scope ⚕ ['steθəskoup] stéthoscope m.

ste·ve·dore ⚓ ['sti:vidɔ:] arrimeur m; entrepreneur m d'arrimage.

stew [stju:] **1.** *v/t.* fricasser, mettre en ragoût; faire une compote de (*fruit*); ∼*ed fruit* compote f; *v/i.* mijoter; cuire à la casserole; **2.** ragoût m; F émoi m.

stew·ard ['stjuəd] économe m; *maison*: maître m d'hôtel; ⚓ garçon m, steward m; *sp.*, *a. bal*: commissaire m; **'stew·ard·ess** ✈ hôtesse f de l'air; ⚓ stewardess f.

stew...: '∼-**pan**, '∼-**pot** casserole f; cocotte f.

stick[1] [stik] **1.** bâton m (*a. cire à cacheter*); canne f; baguette f; *vigne*: échalas m; *balai*: manche m; ✈ manche m à balai; ✈ *bombes*: chapelet m; *sp.* crosse f; *fig.* F type m; ∼s *pl.* du menu bois m; **2.** ⚘ ramer; mettre des tuteurs à.

stick[2] [∼] [*irr.*] *v/i.* se piquer; tenir (à, *to*); se coller; se coincer (*porte*); hésiter (devant, *at*); ∼ *at nothing* n'être retenu par rien; ∼ *out* faire saillie; F persister; F s'obstiner (à demander qch., *for s.th.*); ∼ *up* se dresser; F résister (à, *to*); *fig.* ∼ *to* persévérer dans; rester fidèle à; F ∼ *up for s.o.* prendre la défense de q.; *v/t.* piquer; attacher; fixer; coller; percer; ramer (*des pois*); *sl.* supporter (q.); ∼ *up* afficher; *sl.* attaquer à main armée; **'stick·er** couteau m; colleur m; *Am.* affiche f; **'stick·i·ness** viscosité f; **'stick·ing-plas·ter** sparadrap m; taffetas m anglais; **'stick-in-the-mud** F mal dégourdi; routinier (-ère f) m.

stick·le ['stikl] (se) disputer; **'stick·le·back** *icht.* épinoche f; **'stick·ler** rigoriste *mf* (à l'égard de, *for*).

stick-up ['stikʌp] F (*a.* ∼ *collar*) col m droit; *Am. sl.* bandit m.

stick·y □ ['stiki] collant; *fig.* pâteux (-euse f); *sl.* difficile; peu accommodant.

stiff □ [stif] **1.** raide, rigide; guindé, gêné; ferme; fort (*boisson*, *vent*); difficile; **2.** *sl.* cadavre m; *Am. sl.* nigaud m, bêta (-asse f) m; **'stiff·en** *v/t.* raidir (*a.* ⚡); renforcer; empeser (*un plastron*); lier (*une sauce*); corser (*une boisson*); *v/i.* (se) raidir; devenir ferme; **'stiff·en·er** renfort m; F verre m qui ravigote; **'stiff-'necked** *fig.* intraitable, obstiné.

sti·fle[1] *vét.* ['staifl] (affection f du) grasset m.

sti·fle[2] [∼] étouffer (*a. fig.*).

stig·ma ['stigmə] stigmate *m*; *fig. a.* flétrissure *f*; **'stig·ma·tize** marquer de stigmates; *fig.* stigmatiser.

stile [stail] échalier *m*, échalis *m*; ⊕ *porte etc.:* montant *m*.

sti·let·to [sti'letou] stylet *m*; *couture:* poinçon *m*; ~ *heel* talon *m* aiguille.

still¹ [stil] **1.** *adj.* tranquille; silencieux (-euse *f*); calme; ~ *wine* vin *m* non mousseux; **2.** *su. cin.* photographie *f*; **3.** *adv.* encore; **4.** *cj.* cependant, pourtant; encore; **5.** (se) calmer; *v/t.* tranquilliser, apaiser.

still² [~] alambic *m*; appareil *m* de distillation.

still...: '~**birth** enfant *mf* mort-né(e); mort *f* à la naissance; '~**born** mort-né(e *f*); '~**hunt** *Am.* traquer d'affût; '~**hunt·ing** *Am.* chasse *f* d'affût; ~ **life** nature *f* morte; **'still·ness** calme *m*; silence *m*.

still-room △ ['stilrum] office *f*.

still·y *poét.* ['stili] *adj.* calme, tranquille; **still·ly** [~] *adv.* silencieusement.

stilt [stilt] échasse *f*; **'stilt·ed** *fig.* guindé, tendu.

stim·u·lant ['stimjulənt] **1.** ✻ stimulant; **2.** ✻ surexcitant *m*; stimulant *m*; **stim·u·late** ['~leit] stimuler (*a.* ✻); *fig. a.* encourager (à *inf.*, to *inf.*); **stim·u'la·tion** stimulation *f*; **stim·u·la·tive** ['~lətiv] stimulateur (-trice *f*); **stim·u·lus** ['~ləs], *pl.* -**li** ['~lai] stimulant *m*, F aiguillon *m* (de, to); ✻ stimule *m*; *physiol.* stimulus *m*.

sting [stiŋ] **1.** *insecte:* aiguillon *m*; piqûre *f*; ♀ dard *m*; *fig.* pointe *f*, mordant *m*; **2.** [*irr.*] *v/t.* piquer (*fig.* au vif); *v/i.* cuire; *sl.* be stung for s.th. payer qch. à un prix exorbitant; **'sting·er** F coup *m* raide *ou* douloureux; **stin·gi·ness** ['stindʒinis] mesquinerie *f*, ladrerie *f*; **sting-(ing)-net·tle** ♀ ['stiŋ(iŋ)netl] ortie *f* brûlante; **stin·gy** □ ['stindʒi] mesquin, chiche.

stink [stiŋk] **1.** puanteur *f*; **2.** [*irr.*] *v/i.* puer (qch., of s.th.); *sl. a. fig.* ~ *of* trahir, accuser; *v/t.* enfumer (*un renard*); *fig.* sentir (qch.); **stink·er** F salaud *m*; salope *f*; vacherie *f*, saloperie *f*; lettre *f* d'engueulade.

stint [stint] **1.** restriction *f*; besogne *f* assignée; travail *m* exigé; **2.** imposer des restrictions à; priver (*q.*), être chiche de (*qch.*).

sti·pend ['staipend] traitement *m*

(*surt. eccl.*); **sti'pen·di·ar·y** [~jəri] **1.** appointé; **2.** *Angl.* juge *m* d'un tribunal de simple police.

stip·ple *peint.* ['stipl] pointiller.

stip·u·late ['stipjuleit] (*a.* ~ *for*) stipuler; convenir (de, for); **stip-u'la·tion** ⚖ stipulation *f*; condition *f*.

stir¹ [stə:] **1.** remuement *m*; mouvement *m* (*a. fig.*); *fig.* vie *f*; agitation *f*; **2.** *v/t.* remuer; tourner; agiter; *fig.* exciter; ~ *up* exciter; pousser; susciter; *v/i.* remuer, bouger.

stir² *sl.* [~] prison *f*.

stir·rup ['stirəp] étrier *m*.

stitch [stitʃ] **1.** point *m*, piqûre *f*; ✻ suture *f*; ✻ point *m* de côté; *he has not a dry* ~ *on him* il est complètement trempé; **2.** coudre; piquer (*le cuir, deux étoffes*); brocher (*un livre*); ✻ suturer.

stoat *zo.* [stout] hermine *f* (d'été).

stock [stɔk] **1.** *arbre:* tronc *m*; souche *f*; *outil:* manche *m*; *fusil:* fût *m*; *fig.* race *f*, famille *f*; ✻ ~-gilly-flower) matthiole *f*, giroflée *f* des jardins; ✕ col *m* droit; provision *f*; ✝ marchandises *f/pl.*, stock *m*; ✝ *a.* ~*s pl.* fonds *m/pl.*, valeurs *f/pl.*, *fig.* actions *f/pl.*; (*a. live* ~) bétail *m*, bestiaux *m/pl.*; (*a. dead* ~) matériel *m*; *cost.* cravate *f*, *eccl.* plastron *m* en soie noire; *cuis.* consommé *m*, bouillon *m*; ~*s pl. a. hist.* pilori *m*; ⚓ chantier *m*; ~ *building* ✝ stockage *m*; approvisionnement *m*; ~ *in hand* marchandises *f/pl.* en magasin; 🚂 *rolling* ~ matériel *m* roulant; *take* ~ *of* dresser l'inventaire de; *fig.* scruter, examiner attentivement; **2.** courant; de série; classique; consacré; *théâ.* ~ *company* troupe *f* à demeure; ~ *play* pièce *f* de *ou* du répertoire; **3.** *v/t.* (*a.* ~ *up*) approvisionner, fournir (de, with); ✝ avoir en magasin, tenir; *v/i.* se monter (en, with), s'approvisionner (de, with).

stock·ade [stɔ'keid] **1.** palissade *f*; *Am.* prison *f*; **2.** palissader.

stock...: '~**book** livre *m* de magasin; '~**breed·er** éleveur *m*; '~**brok·er** agent *m* de change; courtier *m* de bourse; ~ **ex·change** bourse *f* (des valeurs); '~**hold·er** actionnaire *mf*; porteur *m* de titres.

stock·i·net ['stɔkinet] tricot *m*.

stocking 1138

stock·ing ['stɔkiŋ] bas *m*; '~-**loom** métier *m* à bas.

stock·ist ✝ ['stɔkist] stockiste *m*.

stock...: '~-**job·ber** marchand *m* de titres; '~-**job·bing** courtage *m*; *péj.* agiotage *m*; '~-**pile** *vt/i.* stocker; amonceler; '~-**pot** pot-au-feu *m/inv.*; '~-'**still** (complètement) immobile; sans bouger; '~-**tak·ing** inventaire *m*; ~ **sale** solde *m* avant *ou* après inventaire; '**stock·y** trapu; ragot (*a. cheval*).

stodge *sl.* [stɔdʒ] se bourrer (*de nourriture*); '**stodg·y** □ lourd; qui bourre.

sto·gy, sto·gie *Am.* ['stougi] cigare *m* long et fort (à bouts coupés).

sto·ic ['stouik] stoïcien(ne *f*) (*a. su.*); stoïque; '**sto·i·cal** □ *fig.* stoïque.

stoke [stouk] charger; chauffer; '**stok·er** chauffeur *m*; chargeur *m*.

stole[1] [stoul] *cost.* écharpe *f*; étole *f* (*a. eccl.*).

stole[2] [~] *prét.*, '**sto·len** *p.p.* de **steal** 1.

stol·id □ ['stɔlid] impassible, lourd, lent; flegmatique; **sto·lid·i·ty** [~-'liditi] flegme *m*; impassibilité *f*.

stom·ach ['stʌmək] 1. estomac *m*; *fig.* appétit *m*; goût *m* (de, *for*); *euphémisme:* ventre *m*; 2. *fig.* supporter, tolérer, digérer; '~-**ache** mal *m* à l'estomac; **sto·mach·ic** [stou-'mækik] (~*ally*) stomachique (*a. su./m*); stomacal (-aux *m/pl.*).

stomp *Am.* [stɔmp] marcher à pas bruyants.

stone [stoun] 1. pierre *f*; *fruit:* noyau *m*; *a. mesure:* 6,348 *kg*; ✻ calcul *m*; 2. de *ou* en pierre; de *ou* en grès; 3. lapider; ôter les noyaux de (*un fruit*); '~-'**blind** complètement aveugle; '~-**coal** anthracite *m*.

stoned *sl.* [stound] soûl; drogué, F défonce.

stone...: '~-'**dead** raide mort; '~-'**deaf** complètement sourd; '~-**fruit** fruit *m* à noyau; '~-**ma·son** maçon *m*; '~-**pit** carrière *f* de pierre; '~-'**wall·ing** *fig.* jeu *m* prudent; *pol.* obstructionnisme *m*; '~-**ware** (poterie *f* de) grès *m*.

ston·i·ness ['stouninis] nature *f* pierreuse; *fig.* dureté *f*.

ston·y ['stouni] pierreux (-euse *f*); de pierre (*a. fig.*); *fig.* dur; F ~-**broke** à sec, sans le sou, fauché.

stood [stud] *prét. et p.p. de* **stand** 1, 2.

stooge *Am. sl.* [stu:dʒ] *théâ.* nègre *m*; *fig.* souffre-douleur *mf/inv.*

stool [stu:l] tabouret *m*; (*a. three-legged* ~) escabeau *m*; ✻ selle *f*; ♀ plante *f* mère; ♀ talle *f*; '~-**pi·geon** *surt. Am. sl.* mouchard *m*.

stoop [stu:p] 1. *v/i.* se pencher, se baisser; *fig.* s'abaisser, descendre ([jusqu'là, *to*); être voûté; *v/t.* incliner (*la tête*); 2. penchement *m* en avant; dos *m* voûté; *Am.* véranda *f*; *Am.* terrasse *f* surélevée.

stop [stɔp] 1. *v/t.* (*a.* ~ *up*) boucher; arrêter; bloquer (*un chèque; a. box., foot.*); retenir (*les gages*); plomber (*une dent*); étancher (*le sang*); *mot.* stopper; interrompre (*la circulation*); fermer, barrer (*la route etc.*); couper (*l'électricité, la respiration*); suspendre (*le paiement, une procédure*, ✗ *les permissions*); cesser; mettre fin à, supprimer; parer à (*un coup*); empêcher; ♪ presser (*une corde*), *flûte:* boucher (*des trous*); *gramm.* ponctuer; *v/i.* s'arrêter; cesser; rester, demeurer; attendre; descendre (à, *at*) (*un hôtel*); ~ **by**, ~ **in** faire une petite visite, s'arrêter un moment; ~ **off** faire étape; ~ **over** faire une halte, faire étape; 2. arrêt *m* (*a.* ⊕); halte *f*; interruption *f*; ⊕ butoir *m*; ⊕ crochet *m*; *porte:* butée *f*; *machine à écrire:* margeur *m*; ♪ jeu *m*, *orgue:* registre *m*, *clarinette:* clé *f*, *violon etc.:* barré *m*; *guitare:* touche *f*; *gramm.* (*a. full* ~) point *m*; *ling.* occlusive *f*; '~-**cock** ⊕ robinet *m* d'arrêt; '~-**gap** bouche-trou *m*; '~-**light** *Am.* feu *m* rouge; *auto:* stop *m*; '~-**off**, '~-**o·ver** *surt. Am.* court séjour *m*, courte visite *f*, étape *f*; faculté *f* d'arrêt; '**stop·page** obstruction *f* (*a.* ✻); arrêt *m*; *gages:* retenue *f*; *paiements etc.:* suspension *f*; *travail:* chômage *m*; *travail:* interruption *f*; ⊕ à-coup *m*; ⚡ ~ *of current* coupure *f* du courant; '**stop·per** 1. bouchon *m*; ⊕ taquet *m*; ✦ bosse *f*; 2. boucher; ✦ bosser; '**stop·ping** *dent:* plombage *m*; bouchon *m*; *a. see* stoppage; '**stop·ping train** ➔ train *m* omnibus; '**stop-press news** *pl.* informations *f/pl.* de dernière heure; '**stop-watch** *sp.* montre *f* à arrêt.

stor·age ['stɔ:ridʒ] emmagasinage *m*; entrepôts *m/pl.*; frais *m/pl.* d'entrepôt; ~ *battery* accumulateur *m*, F accu *m*.

store [stɔ:] **1.** (*fig.* bonne) provision *f*; *fig. a.* ~s *pl.* abondance *f*; *a.* ~s *pl.* magasin *m*; *fig.* fonds *m* (*de connaissances*); *fig.* prix *m*; *Am.* boutique *f*; ~s *pl.* entrepôt *m*; ✕, ⚓ magasin *m*; vivres *m*/*pl.*; in ~ en réserve; *be in* ~ *for* attendre (*q.*); *have in* ~ *for* ménager (*qch.*) à; *set great* ~ *by* faire grand cas de; **2.** (*a.* ~ *up*) amasser; emmagasiner; mettre en dépôt (*des meubles*); approvisionner (de, *with*); garnir (*la mémoire*); '~**house** magasin *m*, entrepôt *m*; *fig.* mine *f*; ✕ manutention *f*; '~**keep·er** garde-magasin (*pl.* gardes-magasin[s]) *m*; *Am.* boutiquier (-ère *f*) *m*, marchand(e *f*) *m*; '~**room** office *f*, *maison*: dépense *f*; ⚓ magasin *m*; ⊕ halle *f* de dépôt.

sto·rey(ed) *see* story²; storied².

sto·ried¹ ['stɔ:rid] historié; † célébré dans la légende *ou* histoire.

sto·ried² [~]: *four-*~ à quatre étages.

stork [stɔ:k] cigogne *f*.

storm [stɔ:m] **1.** orage *m*; tempête *f* (*a. fig.*); ✕ assaut *m*; *fig.* pluie *f*; *take by* ~ emporter (*a. fig.*), prendre d'assaut; **2.** *v/i.* se déchaîner; *fig.* tempêter; s'emporter (contre, *at*); *v/t.* ✕ livrer l'assaut à; prendre d'assaut; '**storm·y** □ tempétueux (-euse *f*); orageux (-euse *f*), d'orange; ~ *petrel* *orn.* pétrel *m*; *fig.* enfant *m* terrible.

sto·ry¹ ['stɔ:ri] histoire *f*, récit *m*; conte *m* (*a.* F = *mensonge*); pièce, *roman*: intrigue *f*; anecdote *f*; *short* ~ nouvelle *f*.

sto·ry² [~] étage *m*.

sto·ry-tell·er ['stɔ:ritelə] conteur (-euse *f*) *m*; F menteur (-euse *f*) *m*.

stout [staut] **1.** □ gros(se *f*); fort, vigoureux (-euse *f*); résolu, intrépide; solide; **2.** bière *f* brune forte; '~**heart·ed** vaillant; '**stout·ness** embonpoint *m*, corpulence *f*; *sp.* persévérance *f*.

stove [stouv] **1.** poêle *m*; ⊕ four *m*; ✍ serre *f* chaude; **2.** ⊕ étuver (*a. des vêtements*); ✍ élever en serre chaude; **3.** *prét. et p.p. de* stave 2; '~**pipe** tuyau *m* de poêle; *Am.* F cylindre *m*, chapeau *m* haut de forme.

stow [stou] ranger, serrer; ⚓ arrimer; '**stow·age** magasinage *m*; ⚓ (frais *m*/*pl.* d')arrimage *m*; '**stow·a·way** ⚓ passager *m* clandestin.

stra·bis·mus [strə'bisməs] strabisme *m*.

strad·dle ['strædl] *v/t.* se mettre à califourchon sur; enfourcher; ✕ être à cheval sur; écarter (*les jambes*); *v/i.* écarter les jambes; marcher *ou* se tenir les jambes écartées; *Am.* éviter de se compromettre.

strafe [strɑ:f] ✕ bombarder; F marmiter.

strag·gle ['strægl] marcher sans ordre; ✕ rester en arrière, traîner (*a.* ✍); *fig.* s'éparpiller; '**strag·gler** celui (celle *f*) *m* qui reste en arrière; ✕ traînard *m*; ⚓ retardataire *m*; '**strag·gling** □ épars, éparpillé.

straight [streit] **1.** *adj.* droit (*a. fig.*); d'aplomb; en ordre; *fig.* honnête; *Am.* sec (sèche *f*) (*whisky etc.*); *Am. pol.* bon teint, vrai; *put* ~ (r)ajuster; arranger, remettre de l'ordre dans; **2.** *su. the* ~ *turf*: la ligne droite; **3.** *adv.* droit; directement; ~ *ahead* tout droit; ~ *away*, ~ *off* immédiatement, aussitôt; tout de suite; du premier coup, d'emblée; ~ *on* tout droit; ~ *out* carrément, franchement; '**straight·en** redresser; ranger; ~ *out* mettre en ordre; arranger; **straight·for·ward** □ [~'fɔ:wəd] franc(he *f*); honnête; loyal (-aux *m*/*pl.*); '**straight·out** direct, franc(he *f*), droit; *Am.* F *a.* vrai, véritable, à cent pour cent.

strain¹ [strein] **1.** ⊕ tension *f* (de, *on*); effort *m*, fatigue *f*; ⊕ déformation *f*; *fig.* ton *m*, *discours*: sens *m*; *esprit*: surmenage *m*; entorse *f*; ♪ *usu.* ~s *pl.* accents *m*/*pl.*; *musique*: sons *m*/*pl.*; *put a great* ~ *on* beaucoup exiger de; mettre à l'épreuve; **2.** *v/t.* tendre; *fig.* forcer (*a.* ⊕), pousser trop loin; ⊕ déformer; ⊕ filtrer; *fig.* fatiguer; serrer; ✂ fouler, forcer; *cuis.* égoutter; *v/i.* faire un (grand) effort; peiner; tirer (sur, *at*); ⊕ déformer; ~ *after s.th.* faire tous ses efforts pour atteindre qch.

strain² [~] qualité *f* (héritée); tendance *f*; race *f*, lignée *f*.

strain·er ['streinə] ⊕ tendeur *m*; *cuis.* passoire *f*; tamis *m*; filtre *m*; (*a. tea-*~) passe-thé *m*/*inv.*

strait [streit] **1.** (*noms propres, géog.* ~s *pl.*) détroit *m*; ~s *pl.* embarras *m*, gêne *f*; **2.**: ~ *jacket* (*ou waistcoat*) camisole *f* de force; '**strait·en** † rétrécir; † resserrer; ~ed pauvre; in

~ed circumstances dans la gêne; **strait-laced** ['~leist] collet monté _inv._; prude; **'strait-ness** rigueur _f_; gêne _f_, besoin _m_; † étroitesse _f_.

strand¹ [strænd] **1.** plage _f_, rive _f_; **2.** _v/t._ jeter à la côte; _fig._ laisser (_q._) en plan; _~ed_ échoué; _fig._ à bout de ressources; _fig._ abandonné; _mot._ resté en panne; _v/i._ (s')échouer.

strand² [~] toron _m_, cordage; brin _m_; tissu, _a. fig._: fil _m_; cheveux: tresse _f_.

strange □ [streindʒ] étrange; singulier (-ère _f_); curieux (-euse _f_); inconnu; † étranger (-ère _f_); **'strange-ness** singularité _f_; étrangeté _f_; **'stran-ger** inconnu(e _f_) _m_; étranger (-ère _f_) _m_ (à, to); ⚖ tiers _m_.

stran-gle ['stræŋgl] étrangler (_a. la presse_); _fig._ étouffer; **'~-hold** _fig._ étau _m_; _have a ~ on s.o._ tenir q. par la gorge.

stran-gu-late ⚕ ['stræŋgjuleit] étrangler; **stran-gu-la-tion** étranglement _m_ (_a._ ⚕).

strap [stræp] **1.** courroie _f_; _cuir, toile_: bande _f_; _soulier_: barrette _f_; ⊕ _frein_: bande _f_; bride _f_; _soutien-gorge_: bretelle _f_; **2.** attacher ou lier avec une courroie; boucler (_une malle_); ⚕ mettre des bandelettes à, maintenir au moyen de bandages; bander; **'~-hang-er** F voyageur (-euse _f_) _m_ debout (_dans l'autobus etc._); **'strap-ping 1.** robuste, bien découplé; **2.** ⚕ emplâtre _m_ adhésif.

strat-a-gem ['strætidʒəm] ruse _f_ (de guerre), stratagème _m_.

stra-te-gic [strə'ti:dʒik] (_~ally_) stratégique; **strat-e-gist** ['strætidʒist] stratégiste _m_; stratège _m_; **'strat-e-gy** stratégie _f_.

strat-i-fy ['strætifai] (se) stratifier.

stra-to-cruis-er ['strætoukru:zə] avion _m_ stratosphérique.

strat-o-sphere _phys._ ['strætousfiə] stratosphère _f_.

stra-tum ['streitəm], _pl._ **-ta** ['~tə] _géol._ strate _f_; couche _f_ (_a. fig._); _fig._ étage _m_, rang _m_ social.

straw [strɔ:] **1.** paille _f_; chalumeau _m_; _fig._ brin _m_ d'herbe; _fig._ indication _f_; (_usu. ~ hat_) chapeau _m_ de paille; _surt. Am. ~ man_ homme _m_ de paille; F _I don't care a ~_ je m'en fiche; _the last ~_ le comble _m_; **2.** de paille; paille _adj./inv._ (_couleur_); _Am. pol. ~ vote_ vote _m_ d'essai; **'~-ber-ry** fraise _f_;

plante: fraisier _m_; **'straw-y** de paille; paille _adj./inv._, jaunâtre.

stray [strei] **1.** s'égarer, s'écarter (de, from); errer (_a. fig._); _fig._ sortir (d'un sujet, _from a subject_); **2.** (_a. ~ed_) égaré (_a. fig._), errant; **3.** bête _f_ perdue ou ⚖ épave; enfant _m_ abandonné; _~s pl. radio_: parasites _m/pl._; crachements _m/pl._; **'stray-er** égaré(e _f_) _m_.

streak [stri:k] **1.** raie _f_, bande _f_; _fig._ trace _f_; _aube_: lueur _f_; _Am._ F _talk a blue ~_ parler à n'en plus finir; **2.** rayer (de, with); **'streak-y** □ rayé, bariolé; en raies ou bandes; _tex._ vergé; entrelardé (_lard etc._).

stream [stri:m] **1.** cours _m_ d'eau, ruisseau _m_; courant _m_; torrent _m_ (_a. fig._); **2.** _v/i._ ruisseler, couler à flots (_a. yeux_); flotter (au vent) (_cheveux, drapeau, etc._); ~ in (out) entrer (sortir) à flots; _v/t._ verser à flots; laisser couler; ⚓ mouiller; **'stream-er** banderole _f_; _papier_: serpentin _m_; _journ._ manchette _f_; _météor._ ~s _pl._ lumière _f_ polaire; **stream-let** ['~lit] petit ruisseau _m_, ru _m_.

stream-line ['stri:mlain] **1.** fil _m_ de l'eau; courant _m_ naturel; _carrosserie_: ligne _f_ aérodynamique; **2.** (_a. stream-lined_) profilé, caréné, fuselé; **3.** _v/t._ caréner (_une auto etc._); _fig._ rénover, alléger.

street [stri:t] rue _f_ (_a. fig._); solidité _f_; _Am. ~ floor_ rez-de-chaussée _m/inv._; _the man in the ~_ l'homme _m_ moyen; F _not in the same ~ as_ ne pas de taille avec; **'~-car** _surt. Am._ tramway _m_; **'~-walk-er** fille _f_ de trottoir.

strength [streŋθ] force _f_ (_a. fig._); solidité _f_; _fig._ fermeté _f_; ⊕ résistance _f_; ✕, ⚓ effectif _m_, -s _m/pl._; contrôles _m/pl._; _on the ~ of_ sur la foi de, s'appuyant sur; de par; **'strength-en** _v/t._ affermir, renforcer; fortifier (_la santé_); _v/i._ s'affermir _etc._; (re)prendre des forces.

stren-u-ous □ ['strenjuəs] énergique, actif (-ive _f_); ardu (_travail_); tendu (_effort_); acharné (_lutte etc._); **'stren-u-ous-ness** ardeur _f_; acharnement _m_.

stress [stres] **1.** force _f_; insistance _f_; _circonstances_: pression _f_; _gramm._ accent _m_; appui _m_ de la voix (sur, on); violence _f_ (_du temps_); ⊕ tension _f_, effort _m_; _lay ~ (up)on_ insister sur, attacher de l'importance à; **2.** insister sur, appuyer sur; ⊕ faire travailler, fatiguer.

stretch [stretʃ] **1.** *v/t.* (*usu.* ~ *out*) tendre (*a. la main*); étendre; allonger; prolonger; déployer (*les ailes*); *fig.* exagérer; ~ *one's legs* se dégourdir les jambes; ~ *a point* faire une exception (en faveur de, *for*); ~ *words* forcer le sens des mots; *v/i.* (*souv.* ~ *out*) s'étendre; s'élargir; prêter (*étoffe*); *fig.* aller, suffire; **2.** étendue *f*; extension *f*; élasticité *f*; ~ tension *f*, effort *m*; *sl.* do a ~ faire de la prison; *at a* ~ (tout) d'un trait; sans arrêt; *on the* ~ tendu; **'stretch·er** ⊕ tendeur *m* (*a. pour chaussures*); brancard *m* (*pour malades*); *tente:* traverse *f*; ⚑ panneresse *f*.

strew [struː] [*irr.*] répandre, semer (de, *with*); **strewn** [struːn] *p.p. de* strew.   ['eitid] strié.\
stri·ate ['straiit], **stri·at·ed** [strai-]\
strick·en ['strikən] frappé, *fig.* accablé (de, *with*); (*well*) ~ *in years* chargé d'années.

strict [strikt] sévère, rigoureux (-euse *f*); précis, exact; ~*ly speaking* à proprement parler; **'strict·ness** rigueur *f*; exactitude *f*; **stric·ture** ['striktʃə] ⚕ rétrécissement *m*; *intestin:* étranglement *m*; *usu.* ~s *pl.* critique *f* (sur, *on*).

strid·den ['stridn] *p.p. de* stride 1.\
stride [straid] **1.** [*irr.*] *v/t.* enjamber; se tenir à califourchon sur; enfourcher (*un cheval*); *v/i.* marcher à grands pas; **2.** (grand) pas *m*; enjambée *f*; *get into one's* ~ prendre son allure normale; être lancé.

stri·dent □ ['straidnt] strident; ~*ly* stridemment.

strife [straif] conflit *m*, lutte *f*.

strike [straik] **1.** coup *m*; grève *f*; *Am.* F *fig.* rencontre *f*; coup *m* de veine; *Am. baseball:* coup *m* (du batteur); *ballot* référendum *m*; ~ *pay* salaire *m* de gréviste; *be on* ~ être en *ou* faire grève; *go on* ~ se mettre en grève, F débrayer; **2.** [*irr.*] *v/t.* frapper (*a. une médaille,* ♪, *a. fig.*) (de, *with*); heurter, cogner; porter (*un coup*); ⚓ rentrer (*le pavillon*); amener (*la voile*); plier (*une tente*); lever (*le camp*); former (*une commission*); faire (*le marché*); allumer (*une allumette*); faire jaillir (*une étincelle*); prendre (*une attitude, la moyenne, la racine*); toucher de (*la harpe*); sonner (*l'heu-*

re); bouturer (*une plante*); ⚓ donner sur (*les écueils*); *fig.* faire une impression sur; impressionner; rencontrer, découvrir, tomber sur; *fig.* paraître; ~ *a balance* établir une balance; dresser le bilan; ~ *oil* rencontrer le pétrole, *fig.* avoir du succès, trouver le filon; ~ *work* se mettre en grève; ~ *off* abattre; rayer; ~ *out* rayer; ouvrir (*une route*); ~ *up* commencer à jouer *ou* à chanter; lier (*une connaissance*); *v/i.* porter un coup, frapper (à, *at*); ⚓ (*ou* ~ [*the*] *bottom*) toucher le fond; ⚓, ✗ rentrer son pavillon; ⊕ se mettre en grève, F débrayer; sonner (l'heure); prendre feu (*allumette*); prendre racine; ~ *home* frapper juste; porter (*coup*); ~ *in* s'enfoncer; intervenir (*personne*); ~ *into* pénétrer dans; ♪ ~ *up* commencer à jouer *ou* à chanter; ~ *upon the ear* frapper l'oreille; **'~-break·er** briseur *m* de grève, F jaune *m*; **'strik·er** frappeur (-euse *f*) *m*; *pendule:* marteau *m*; *fusée:* rugueux *m*; *arme à feu:* percuteur *m*; ⊕ gréviste *mf*; *foot.* buteur *m*.

strik·ing □ ['straikiŋ] à sonnerie; *fig.* frappant; saillant; impressionnant.

string [striŋ] **1.** ficelle *f* (*a. fig.*); corde *f* (*a.* ♪, *arc, raquette*); cordon *m*; ♀ fibre *f*, filament *m*; *eccl., a.* oignons, outils: chapelet *m*; ♪ *fig.* condition *f*; *Am.* F prise *f*; *fig.* lisière *f*; *fig.* procession *f*, série *f*; F ♂ ligature *f*; ~ *of horses* écurie *f*; ~ *of pearls* collier *m*; ♪ ~s *pl.* instruments *m/pl.* à cordes; *have two* ~s *to one's bow* avoir deux cordes à son arc, avoir un pied dans deux chaussures; *pull the* ~s tirer les ficelles, tenir les fils; **2.** [*irr.*] bander (*un arc*); ficeler (*un paquet*); *fig.* (*a.* ~ *up*) tendre (*les nerfs*); enfiler (*des perles, a. fig.*); corder (*une raquette*); monter (*un violon*), monter les cordes de (*un piano*); effiler (*des haricots*); *Am. sl.* faire marcher (*q.*); F ~ *along v/t.* payer (*q.*) de promesses, faire marcher (*q.*); *v/i.* suivre; ~ *along with s.o.* suivre q., accompagner q.; venir *ou* aller avec q.; *fig.* se ranger à l'avis de q.; ~ *up* suspendre; ~ *s.o.* pendre q. haut et court; ~ *band* ♪ orchestre *m* à cordes; ~ *bean* *Am.* haricot *m* vert; **stringed** ♪ à cordes.

strin·gen·cy ['strindʒənsi] rigueur *f*; puissance *f*, force *f*; ✝ resserrement m; 'strin·gent □ rigoureux (-euse f), strict; convaincant; ⚓ serré (argent); tendu (marché).

string·y ['strini] filandreux (-euse f); visqueux (-euse f) (liquide).

strip [strip] **1.** v/t. dépouiller (de, of) (a. ⚡, a. fig.); ⚡, a.fig. dénuder (de, of); fig. dégarnir (une maison); ⊕ démonter (une machine); métall. démouler; ⚓ déshabiller, dégréer; (a. ~ off) ôter, enlever; v/i. F se déshabiller; sl. se mettre à poil; **2.** bande(lette) f.

stripe [straip] **1.** couleur: raie f; pantalon: bande f; ✗ galon m; (a. long-service ~) chevron m; **2.** rayer. [tout jeune homme m.]

strip·ling ['striplin] adolescent m,

strive [straiv] [irr.] s'efforcer (de, to; d'obtenir qch. after s.th., for s.th.); tâcher (de, to); lutter (contre, against); **striv·en** ['strivn] p.p. de strive.

strode [stroud] prét. de stride 1.

stroke [strouk] **1.** usu. coup m; ⚕ congestion f cérébrale, apoplexie f; ⊕ piston: course f; peint. coup m de pinceau; fig. retouche f; trait m (de plume, a. fig.); coup m (d'horloge); canotage: nage f, personne: chef m de nage; nage: brassée f; ~ of genius trait m de génie; ~ of luck coup m de bonheur; **2.** caresser; être chef de nage de (un canot); ~ 32 nager à 32 coups par minute.

stroll [stroul] **1.** v/i. flâner (se promener à l'aventure, F se balader); v/t. se promener dans (les rues); **2.** petit tour m; flânerie f; F balade f; 'stroll·er, 'stroll·ing ac·tor comédien(ne f) m ambulant(e f).

strong □ [stron] usu. fort (a. gramm.), solide; ferme (a. ⚓ marché); vif (vive f) (souvenir); bon(ne f) (mémoire); robuste (foi, santé); ardent (partisan); sérieux (-euse f) (candidat); énergique (mesure); accusé (trait); cartes: long(ue f) (couleur); see language; feel ~(ly) about attacher une grande importance à; F go it ~ dépasser les bornes; F going ~ vigoureux (-euse f) solide; 30 ~ au nombre de 30; '~-box coffre-fort (pl. coffres-forts) m; '~-hold forteresse f; fig. citadelle f; '~-'mind·ed à l'esprit décidé; '~-room chambre f blindée; cave f forte.

strop [strop] **1.** cuir m (à rasoir); ⚓ estrope f; **2.** repasser (un rasoir) sur le cuir.

stro·phe ['stroufi] strophe f.

strop·py Brit. F ['stropi] de mauvaise humeur.

strove [strouv] prét. de strive.

struck [strʌk] prét. et p.p. de strike 2.

struc·tur·al □ ['strʌktʃərəl] de structure, structural (-aux m/pl.); ⊕ de construction; **struc·ture** ['~tʃə] structure f; édifice m (a. fig.); péj. bâtisse f.

strug·gle ['strʌgl] **1.** lutter (contre, against; avec, with); se débattre; faire de grands efforts (pour, to); **2.** lutte f (a. fig.); combat m; 'strug·gler lutteur m.

strum [strʌm] tapoter (du piano); gratter (de la guitare etc.); fig. pianoter.

strum·pet poét., F ['strʌmpit] prostituée f; catin f.

strung [strʌŋ] prét. et p.p. de string 2.

strut [strʌt] **1.** v/i. se pavaner; v/t. ⊕ entretoiser; contreficher; **2.** démarche f fière; ⊕ entretoise f; arc-boutant (pl. arcs-boutants) m; ✗ pilier m, traverse f; 'strut·ting-piece ⊕ entretoise f, lierne f.

strych·nine ['strikni:n] strychnine f.

stub [stʌb] **1.** arbre: souche f; cigarette: bout m; Am. chèque: souche f, talon m; **2.** (usu. ~ up) arracher; essoucher (un champ); cogner (le pied); ~ out éteindre (une cigarette) en l'écrasant par le bout.

stub·ble ['stʌbl] chaume m.

stub·bly ['stʌbli] couvert de chaume; court et raide (barbe, cheveux).

stub·born □ ['stʌbən] obstiné, opiniâtre, entêté; rebelle, réfractaire; ingrat (sol, terre); 'stub·born·ness opiniâtreté f, entêtement m.

stub·by ['stʌbi] trapu (personne); tronqué (arbre etc.).

stuc·co ['stʌkou] **1.** stuc m; **2.** stuquer; recouvrir de stuc(age).

stuck [stʌk] prét. et p.p. de stick²; Am. F ~ on amoureux (-euse f) de (q.); F '~-'up hautain; prétentieux (-euse f).

stud¹ [stʌd] **1.** clou m à grosse tête; clou m (sur une robe, a. d'un passage clouté); chemise etc.: bouton m; foot.

crampon *m*; △ poteau *m*; **2.** clouter; orner (de, *with*); *fig.* parsemer (de, *with*).

stud² [◡] écurie *f*; (*a.* ~ *farm*) haras *m*; '~-**book** livre *m* d'origines, studbook *m*; '~-**horse** étalon *m*.

stud·ding △ ['stʌdiŋ] lattage *m*; lattis *m*.

stu·dent ['stju:dənt] étudiant(e *f*) *m*; boursier (-ère *f*) *m*; amateur *m* de livres; investigateur (-trice *f*) *m*; ~ **hostel** foyer *m* d'étudiants; '**student·ship** bourse *f* d'études.

stud·ied □ ['stʌdid] instruit (*personne*) (dans, *in*); étudié, recherché (*toilette etc.*); voulu, prémédité (*geste, insulte, etc.*).

stu·di·o ['stju:diou] atelier *m*; *radio:* studio *m*; ~ **couch** divan *m*.

stu·di·ous □ ['stju:djəs] appliqué, studieux (-euse *f*); attentif (-ive *f*) (à qch., *of s.th.*; à *inf.* of *gér.*, to *inf.*); soigneux (-euse *f*) (de *inf.*, to *inf.*); '**stu·di·ous·ness** amour *m* de l'étude; *fig.* attention *f*, zèle *m* (à *inf.*, in *gér.*).

stud·y ['stʌdi] **1.** étude *f* (*a.* ♪, *a.* peint.); cabinet *m* de travail; bureau *m*; soins *m/pl.*; *fig.* rêverie *f*; **2.** *v/i.* préparer (un examen, *for an examination*); étudier; *v/t.* étudier; observer; s'occuper de (*a. fig.*).

stuff [stʌf] **1.** matière *f*, substance *f*; étoffe *f* (*a. fig.*), tissu *m*; *péj.* camelote *f*; *fig.* F sottises *f/pl.*; **2.** *v/t.* bourrer (de, *with*); remplir (de, *with*); fourrer (dans, *into*); gaver; *cuis.* farcir; ~ *up* boucher; *Am. sl.* ~ed *shirt* collet *m* monté; *v/i.* manger avec excès; *fig. sl.* se les caler; '**stuff·ing** (rem)bourrage *m*; *oie etc.*: gavage *m*; *cuis.* farce *f*, farcissure *f*; matelassure *f* (*de crin*); ⊕ étoupe *f*; '**stuff·y** □ mal aéré; qui sent le renfermé; F collet monté *adj./inv.*; sans goût; F *Am.* fâché.

stul·ti·fi·ca·tion [stʌltifiˈkeiʃn] action *f* de rendre sans effet (*un décret etc.*) *ou* ridicule (*q.*); '**stul·ti·fy** ['~fai] infirmer, rendre nul *ou* vain *ou* sans effet; rendre ridicule.

stum·ble ['stʌmbl] **1.** trébuchement *m*, faux pas *m*; *cheval:* bronchade *f*; **2.** trébucher; faire un faux pas; broncher (*cheval*); se heurter (contre, *against*); hésiter (*en par-*

lant); '**stum·bling-block** *fig.* pierre *f* d'achoppement.

stump [stʌmp] **1.** tronçon *m*, souche *f*; *crayon, cigare:* bout *m*; *dessin:* estompe *f*; *dent:* chicot *m*; *cricket:* piquet *m*; moignon *m* (*d'un membre coupé*); F propagande *f* électorale; F ~s *pl.* quilles *f/pl.* (= *jambes*); ~ *speaker* (*ou orator*) orateur *m* de carrefour; orateur *m* de réunion électorale; **2.** *v/t. cricket:* mettre hors jeu en abattant le guichet avec la balle tenue à la main; F coller, embarrasser; *Am.* F défier; *sl.* ~ *up* cracher (= *payer*); ~ *the country* faire une tournée électorale; ~ed *for* embarrassé pour; *v/i.* clopiner; harangueur *m*; '**stump·y** □ écourté; trapu (*personne*).

stun [stʌn] étourdir; *fig.* abasourdir.

stung [stʌŋ] *prét. et p.p. de sting 2.*

stunk [stʌŋk] *prét. et p.p. de stink 2.*

stun·ner F ['stʌnə] type *m* épatant, chose *f* épatante; '**stun·ning** □ F épatant, étourdissant.

stunt¹ [stʌnt] **1.** tour *m* de force; F coup *m* d'épate; F nouvelle *f* sensationnelle; ⚔ acrobaties *f/pl.* aériennes, vol *m* de virtuosité; **2.** faire des acrobaties.

stunt² [◡] rabougrir; empêcher de croître; '**stunt·ed** rabougri; noué (*esprit*).

stupe ⚕ [stju:p] **1.** compresse *f* (pour fomentation); **2.** fomenter.

stu·pe·fac·tion [stju:piˈfækʃn] stupéfaction *f*; ahurissement *m*.

stu·pe·fy ['stju:pifai] *fig.* hébéter (par la douleur, *by grief*); stupéfier, abasourdir.

stu·pen·dous □ [stju:ˈpendəs] prodigieux (-euse *f*).

stu·pid □ ['stju:pid] stupide, sot(te *f*); F bête; insupportable; **stu·pid·i·ty** [stju:ˈpiditi] stupidité *f*; lourdeur *f* d'esprit; sottise *f*, bêtise *f*.

stu·por ['stju:pə] stupeur *f*.

stur·di·ness ['stə:dinis] vigueur *f*; résolution *f*; solidité *f*; '**stur·dy** □ vigoureux (-euse *f*); robuste; hardi.

stur·geon *icht.* ['stə:dʒən] esturgeon *m*.

stut·ter ['stʌtə] **1.** bégayer; **2.** bégaiement *m*; '**stut·ter·er** bègue *mf*.

sty¹ [stai] étable *f* (à porcs); porcherie *f*.

sty² [◡] *œil:* orgelet *m*.

style [stail] **1.** style *m* (*pour écrire,*

pour graver, △, ⚓, *cadran*, peint., a. = *manière*); façon f, manière f; cost. mode f; ton m, chic m; titre m; élégance f; ⚓ raison f sociale; *in* ~ *grand train*; *in the* ~ *of* dans le style *ou* goût de; ⚓ *under the* ~ *of* sous la raison de; **2.** appeler, dénommer; qualifier (q.) de.

styl·ist □ ['stailiʃ] élégant; chic *inv. en genre*; à la mode; **'styl·ish·ness** élégance f, chic m.

styl·ist ['stailist] styliste mf.

sty·lo F ['stailou], **sty·lo·graph** ['stailəgraːf], a. **sty·lo·graph·ic pen** [~'græfik'pen] stylographe m, F stylo m.

styp·tic ['stiptik] styptique (a. su./m), astringent (a. su./m).

sua·sion ['sweiʒn] persuasion f.

suave □ [sweiv] suave; affable; doux (douce f) (vin); péj. douce-reux (-euse f); **suav·i·ty** ['swaeviti] suavité f; douceur f; péj. politesse f mielleuse.

sub F [sʌb] abr. de subordinate 2; subscription; substitute 2; submarine.

sub...: usu. sous-; qqfois sub-; presque.

sub·ac·id ['sʌb'æsid] aigrelet(te f); fig. aigre-doux (-douce f).

sub·al·tern ['sʌbltən] **1.** subalterne (a. su./m); **2.** ✕ (sous-)lieutenant m.

sub·com·mit·tee ['sʌbkəmiti] sous-comité m; sous-commission f.

sub·con·scious □ ['sʌb'kɔnʃəs] subconscient (psych. a. su./m); ~ly inconsciemment.

sub·con·tract [sʌb'kɔntrækt] sous-traité m.

sub·cu·ta·ne·ous □ ['sʌbkju:'teinjəs] sous-cutané; ⚕ ~ *injection* injection f sous-cutanée.

sub·dean ['sʌb'di:n] sous-doyen m.

sub·di·vide ['sʌbdi'vaid] (se) subdiviser.

sub·di·vi·sion ['sʌbdiviʒn] subdivision f; sectionnement m; sous-division f; biol. sous-classe f; ⚓ section f.

sub·due [səb'dju:] subjuguer; dompter; maîtriser; réprimer; adoucir; baisser (la lumière).

sub·head(·ing) ['sʌbhed(iŋ)] sous-titre m.

sub·ja·cent [sʌb'dʒeisənt] sous-jacent, subjacent.

sub·ject ['sʌbdʒikt] **1.** *adj.* assujetti,

soumis; sujet(te f), exposé; porté (à, to); fig. ~ *to* passible de (droit, courtage); sous réserve de (une ratification); sauf; ~ *to a fee* (ou duty) sujet(te f) à une taxe *ou* à un droit; **2.** *adv.:* ~ *to* sous (la) réserve de; ~ *to change without notice* sauf modifications sans avis préalable; **3.** *su.* sujet(te f) m (d'un roi etc.); ⚓, ♪, gramm., conversation, peint. tableau: sujet m; (a. ~-matter) livre etc.: sujet m, thème m; question f; ⚕ malade mf; matière f; lettre: contenu m; peint. paysage: motif m; contrat réel, méditation: objet m; **4.** *v/t.* [səb'dʒekt] assujettir, subjuguer; ~ *to* soumettre à (un examen etc.); exposer à (un danger etc.);

sub·jec·tion sujétion f; asservissement m; **sub·jec·tive** □ [sʌb'dʒektiv] subjectif (-ive f).

sub·join ['sʌb'dʒɔin] adjoindre, ajouter.

sub·ju·gate ['sʌbdʒugeit] subjuguer; **sub·ju·ga·tion** subjugation f, assujettissement m.

sub·junc·tive gramm. [səb'dʒʌŋktiv] (a. ~ *mood*) subjonctif m; *in the* ~ au subjonctif.

sub·lease ['sʌb'li:s], **sub·let** ['~'let] [irr. (let)] donner *ou* prendre en sous-location *ou* à sous-ferme; sous-louer.

sub·li·mate ♒ **1.** ['sʌblimit] sublimé m; **2.** ['~meit] sublimer; **sub·li·ma·tion** sublimation f (a. psych.); **sub·lime** [sə'blaim] **1.** □ sublime; **2.:** *the* ~ le sublime m; **3.** ♒ (se) sublimer; v/t. fig. idéaliser; **sub·lim·i·nal** [səb'liminəl] □ subliminal (-aux m/pl.); ~ *advertising* publicité f insidieuse; **sub·lim·i·ty** [sə'blimiti] sublimité f.

sub·ma·chine gun ['sʌbmə'ʃi:n-'gʌn] mitraillette f.

sub·ma·rine ['sʌbməri:n] sous-marin (a. ⚓ su./m).

sub·merge [səb'mə:dʒ] v/t. submerger; noyer, inonder; v/i. plonger; **sub·mers·i·bil·i·ty** [səbmə:sə-'biliti] caractère m submersible; **sub·mer·sion** submersion f, plongée f.

sub·mis·sion [səb'miʃn] soumission f (a. fig.), résignation f (à, to); ⚖ plaidoirie f; thèse f; **sub·mis·sive** □ [~'misiv] soumis (air etc.); docile (personne).

sub·mit [sʌb'mit] v/t. soumettre; présenter; poser en thèse (que, that); v/i. (a. ~ o.s.) se soumettre (à, to); fig. se résigner (à, to); s'astreindre (à la discipline, to discipline).

sub·nor·mal [səb'nɔ:məl] au-dessous de la normale; faible d'esprit, arriéré.

sub·or·di·nate 1. □ [sə'bɔ:dnit] subordonné; inférieur; secondaire; gramm. ~ clause proposition f subordonnée; **2.** [~] subalterne mf, subordonné(e f) m; **3.** [~'bɔ:dineit] subordonner (à, to); **sub·or·di·na·tion** subordination f (à, to); soumission f (à, to).

sub·orn ⚖ [sʌ'bɔ:n] suborner, séduire; **sub·or·na·tion** subornation f, corruption f.

sub·p(o)e·na ⚖ [səb'pi:nə] **1.** assignation f; **2.** assigner, faire une assignation à.

sub·scribe [səb'skraib] v/t. souscrire (un nom, une obligation, etc.; pour une somme, a sum); v/i. souscrire (à, to, for; pour une somme, for a sum; a. à une opinion, to an opinion); s'abonner (à, to) (un journal); **sub·'scrib·er** signataire mf (de, to); fig. adhérent(e f) m; souscripteur m, cotisant m; journal, a. téléph. abonné(e f) m.

sub·scrip·tion [səb'skripʃn] souscription f; fig. adhésion f; société, club, etc.: cotisation f; journal: abonnement m.

sub·se·quence ['sʌbsikwəns] conséquence f; postériorité f; **'sub·sequent** □ conséquent, ultérieur; postérieur, consécutif (-ive f) (à, to); ~ly plus tard; postérieurement (à, to); par la suite.

sub·serve [səb'sə:v] favoriser, aider à; **sub'ser·vi·ence** [~viəns] soumission f; utilité f; servilité f; **sub'ser·vi·ent** □ servile, obséquieux (-euse f); utile; subordonné.

sub·side [səb'said] baisser; s'affaisser, se tasser (sol, maison); s'apaiser, tomber (orage, fièvre, etc.); F se taire; ~ into se changer en; **sub·sid·i·ary** [~'sidjəri] **1.** □ subsidiaire (à, to), auxiliaire; ~ company filiale f; **2.** filiale f; **sub·si·dize** ['sʌbsidaiz] subventionner; primer (une industrie); fournir des subsides à;

'sub·si·dy subvention f; industrie: prime f.

sub·sist [səb'sist] v/i. subsister; persister; vivre (de on, by); v/t. entretenir; **sub'sist·ence** existence f; subsistance f; ~ money acompte m.

sub·soil ['sʌbsɔil] sous-sol m.

sub·son·ic [səb'sɔnik] subsonique.

sub·stance ['sʌbstəns] substance f (a. eccl., a. fig.), matière f; fig. essentiel m, fond m; corps m, solidité f; fortune f, biens m/pl.

sub·stan·dard [səb'stændəd] de qualité inférieure; au-dessous de la moyenne.

sub·stan·tial □ [səb'stænʃl] substantiel(le f), réel(le f); solide; riche; considérable (somme, prix, etc.); **sub·stan·ti·al·i·ty** [~ʃi'æliti] solidité f; phls. substantialité f.

sub·stan·ti·ate [səb'stænʃieit] justifier, établir, prouver.

sub·stan·ti·val □ gramm. [sʌbstən'taivl] substantival (-aux m/pl.); **'sub·stan·tive 1.** □ réel(le f), autonome, indépendant; positif (-ive f) (droit); formel(le f) (résolution); gramm. substantival (-aux m/pl.); **2.** gramm. substantif m, nom m.

sub·sti·tute ['sʌbstitju:t] **1.** v/t. substituer (à, for); remplacer (par, by); v/i. ~ for s. o. remplacer q., suppléer q.; **2.** personne: remplaçant(e f) m (a. sp.), suppléant(e f) m; nourriture etc.: succédané m, factice m; **sub·sti'tu·tion** substitution f, remplacement m; ⚖ subrogation f; créance: novation f.

sub·stra·tum ['sʌb'strɑ:təm], pl. **-ta** ['~tə] couche f inférieure; souscouche f; phls. substrat(um) m; fig. fond m.

sub·struc·ture ['sʌbstrʌktʃə] édifice: fondement m; route, pont roulant: infrastructure f.

sub·ten·ant ['sʌb'tenənt] sous-locataire mf.   [fuge m.]

sub·ter·fuge ['sʌbtəfju:dʒ] subter-]

sub·ter·ra·ne·an □ [sʌbtə'reinjən] souterrain.

sub·til·ize ['sʌtilaiz] v/t. subtiliser; raffiner (son style), péj. alambiquer; v/i. subtiliser, raffiner.

sub·ti·tle ['sʌbtaitl] livre, cin.: soustitre m.

sub·tle □ ['sʌtl] subtil, fin; raffiné;

rusé, astucieux (-euse f); 'sub·tle-
ty subtilité f; finesse f; ruse f.
sub·tract [səb'trækt] soustraire;
sub'trac·tion soustraction f.
sub·urb ['sʌbə:b] faubourg m; in the
~s dans la ou en banlieue; sub·ur-
ban [sə'bə:bən] de banlieue (a.
péj.); suburbain; Sub·ur·bi·a F
[sə'bə:biə] la banlieue.
sub·ven·tion [səb'venʃn] subvention
f; industrie: prime f; octroi m d'une
subvention.
sub·ver·sion [sʌb'və:ʃn] subversion
f; sub'ver·sive [~siv] subversif
(-ve f) (de, of). [vertir.\]
sub·vert [sʌb'və:t] renverser, sub-]
sub·way ['sʌbwei] (passage m ou
couloir m) souterrain m; Am. métro
m; chemin m de fer souterrain.
sub-ze·ro ['sʌb'ziərou] au-dessous
de zéro.
suc·ceed [sək'si:d] v/t. succéder (à q.,
à qch., [to] s.o., s.th.); suivre; v/i.
réussir; arriver, aboutir; ~ to
prendre la succession ou la suite
de; hériter de (biens etc.); in ~
(gér.) il réussit ou parvient à (inf.).
suc·cess [sək'ses] succès m, réussite
f; (bonne) chance f; he was a great
~ il a eu un grand succès; suc'cessful □ [~ful] heureux (-euse f),
réussi; couronné de succès; be ~
réussir; avoir du succès; suc·ces-
sion [~'seʃn] succession f, suite f;
récoltes: rotation f; héritage m;
lignée f, descendants m/pl.; ~ to the
throne avènement m; in ~ successivement, tour à tour; ~ duty droits
m/pl. de succession; suc'ces·sive
[~siv] □ successif (-ive f),consécutif
(-ive f); suc'ces·sor successeur m
(de of, to); ~ to the throne successeur m à la couronne.
suc·cinct □ [sək'siŋkt] succint, concis.
suc·co·ry ♀ ['sʌkəri] chicorée f.
suc·co·tash Am. ['sʌkətæʃ] purée f
de maïs et de fèves.
suc·co(u)r ['sʌkə] 1. secours m, aide
f; ✗ renforts m/pl.; 2. secourir;
aider, venir en aide à, venir à l'aide
de; ✗ renforcer.
suc·cu·lence ['sʌkjuləns] succulence
f; 'suc·cu·lent □ succulent (a.
fig.).
suc·cumb [sə'kʌm] succomber,
céder.
such [sʌtʃ] 1. adj. tel(le f); pareil(le

f); semblable; ~ a man un tel
homme; see another; there is no ~
thing cela n'existe pas; no ~ thing!
il n'en est rien!; ~ as tel que; ~ and
~ tel et tel; F ~ a naughty dog un
chien si méchant; ~ is life c'est la
vie; 2. pron. tel(le f); ceux (celles
f/pl.) m/pl.; 'such·like de ce genre,
de la sorte.
suck [sʌk] 1. (v/t. a. ~ out) sucer;
2. action f de sucer; pompe: succion
f; give ~ donner la tétée ou le sein;
'suck·er suceur (-euse f) m; ⊕
pompe: piston m; ♀ arbre: surgeon
m, plante: rejeton m; Am. blanc-bec
(pl. blancs-becs) m; niais m; 'sucking à la mamelle (enfant); qui tette
(animal); ~ pig cochon m de lait;
suck·le ['~l] allaiter, nourrir; donner le sein à; 'suck·ling allaitement
m; nourrisson m.
suc·tion ['sʌkʃn] 1. succion f; aspiration f; 2. aspirant, d'aspiration; à
succion; ~-cleaner (ou sweeper) aspirateur m.
sud·den □ ['sʌdn] soudain, brusque; on a ~, (all) of a ~ soudain,
tout à coup; 'sud·den·ness soudaineté f; brusquerie f.
su·dor·if·ic [sju:də'rifik] sudorifique (a. su./m).
suds [sʌdz] pl. eau f de savon; lessive f; 'suds·y Am. plein ou couvert d'eau de savon.
sue [sju:] v/t. poursuivre; (usu. ~
out) obtenir à la suite d'une requête; v/i. solliciter (de q., to s.o.;
qch., for s.th.); demander (qch., for
s.th.).
suède [sweid] (peau f de) suède m;
chaussures: daim m.
su·et ['sjuit] graisse f de rognon ou
de bœuf; 'su·et·y graisseux (-euse
f).
suf·fer ['sʌfə] v/i. souffrir (de,
from); être affligé (de, from); v/t.
souffrir, éprouver; subir (une peine,
une défaite, une dépréciation); ressentir (une douleur); tolérer, supporter; 'suf·fer·ance tolérance f;
on ~ par tolérance; 'suf·fer·er victime f; ✚ malade mf; 'suf·fer·ing
souffrance f.
suf·fice [sə'fais] v/i. suffire (à, to);
v/t. suffire à.
suf·fi·cien·cy [sə'fiʃənsi] suffisance
f; quantité f suffisante; a ~ of
money l'aisance f; suf'fi·cient □

assez de; suffisant; *I am not ~ of a naturalist* je ne suis pas assez naturaliste.

suf·fix *gramm.* ['sʌfiks] **1.** suffixer; **2.** suffixe *m.*

suf·fo·cate ['sʌfəkeit] *vt/i.* étouffer, suffoquer; **suf·fo·ca·tion** suffocation *f*; étouffement *m*; **'suf·fo·ca·tive** □ qui suffoque; suffocant.

suf·fra·gan *eccl.* ['sʌfrəgən] *évêque:* suffragant *m*; **'suf·frage** suffrage *m*; (droit *m* de) vote *m*; voix *f*; **suf·fra·gette** [ʌ.ə'dʒet] suffragette *f*; **suf·fra·gist** ['ʌ.dʒist] partisan *m* du droit de vote (*surt.* des femmes).

suf·fuse [sə'fju:z] inonder; se répandre sur; **suf·fu·sion** [ʌ.ʒn] épanchement *m*; rougeur *f*; ✽ suffusion *f*.

su·gar ['ʃugə] **1.** sucre *m*; **2.** sucrer; saupoudrer (*un gâteau*) de sucre; **'~-ba·sin,** *Am.* '~-bowl sucrier *m*; **'~-cane** canne *f* à sucre; **'~-coat** revêtir de sucre; *fig.* sucrer; **'~-free** sans sucre; **'~-loaf** pain *m* de sucre; **'~-lump** morceau *m* de sucre; **'~-plum** dragée *f*, bonbon *m*; **'sug·ar·y** sucré (*a. fig.*); *fig.* mielleux (-euse *f*).

sug·gest [sə'dʒest] suggérer (*a.* ✽, *a. psych.*); proposer; inspirer; évoquer, donner l'idée de *ou* que; insinuer; **sug'ges·tion** suggestion *f*; conseil *m*; *fig.* trace *f*, nuance *f*. **sug·ges·tive** □ [sə'dʒestiv] suggestif (-ive *f*); évocateur (-trice *f*); *péj.* grivois; *be ~ of s.th.* évoquer qch.; **sug'ges·tive·ness** caractère *m* suggestif.

su·i·cid·al □ [sjui'saidl] de suicide; *~ maniac* suicidomane *mf*; **su·i·cide** ['~said] **1.** suicide *m*; *personne:* suicidé(e *f*) *m*; **2.** *Am.* se suicider.

suit [sju:t] **1.** requête *f*; demande *f*; (*a. ~ of clothes*) *homme:* complet *m*; *femme:* ensemble *m*; *cartes:* couleur *f*; ⚖ procès *m*; *fig. follow ~* en faire autant; **2.** *v/t.* adapter, accommoder (à to, with); convenir à, aller à; être l'affaire de; être fait pour; être apte à; accommoder (*q.*); *~ed* fait (pour to, for); satisfait; *be ~ed* avoir trouvé (*qch.*) qui convient; être satisfait; *v/i.* aller, convenir; **suit·a'bil·i·ty** convenance *f*; accord *m*; aptitude *f* (à, for); **'suit·a·ble** □ convenable, qui convient; bon, adapté (à to, for); **'suit·a·ble·ness** *see* suitability;

'suit·case mallette *f*, valise *f*; **suite** [swi:t] *prince, a.* ♪: suite *f*; *pièces:* appartement *m*; ameublement *m*; ensemble *m*; *salon:* mobilier *m*; *bedroom ~* chambre *f* à coucher; **suit·ing** ✝ ['sju:tiŋ] tissu *m* *ou* étoffe *f* pour complets; **'suit·or** soupirant *m*; ⚖ plaideur (-euse *f*) *m*.

sulk [sʌlk] **1.** (*a. be in the ~s*) bouder; faire la mine; **2.** *~s pl.* (*ou* '**sulk·i·ness**) bouderie *f*; **'sulk·y 1.** □ boudeur (-euse *f*), maussade; **2.** *sp.* sulky *m.*

sul·lage ['sʌlidʒ] eaux *f/pl.* d'égout; limon *m*; ⊕ scories *f/pl.*

sul·len □ ['sʌlən] maussade, morose (*personne*); morne, lugubre (*chose*); obstiné (*silence*); rétif (-ive *f*).

sul·phate ⚗ ['sʌlfeit] sulfate *m*; **sul·phide** ⚗ ['sʌlfaid] sulfure *m*; **sul·phon·a·mide** [ʌ'fɔnəmaid] sulfamide *m.*

sul·phur ⚗ ['sʌlfə] **1.** soufre *m*; **2.** soufrer; **sul·phu·re·ous** [sʌl'fjuəriəs] sulfureux (-euse *f*); **sul·phu·ret·ted hy·dro·gen** ['ʌ'fjuretid 'haidridʒən] hydrogène *m* sulfuré, sulfure *m* d'hydrogène; **sul·phu·ric** [ʌ'fjuərik] sulfurique, F vitriolique; *~ acid* acide *m* sulfurique; **'sul·phu·rize** ⊕ sulfurer (*un métal*); soufrer (*la laine*).

sul·tan ['sʌltən] sultan *m*; **sul·tan·a** [sʌl'tɑ:nə] sultane *f*; [sə'l'tɑ:nə] (*a. ~ raisin*) raisin *m* sec.

sul·tri·ness ['sʌltrinis] lourdeur *f*; **sul·try** □ ['sʌltri] étouffant, lourd; *fig.* chaud; *fig.* épicé.

sum [sʌm] **1.** somme *f*, total *m*; *fig.* fond *m*, essence *f*; F problème *m*; F *~s pl.* calcul *m*; **2.** (*usu. ~ up*) additionner, faire la somme de; *fig.* résumer, récapituler.

sum·ma·rize ['sʌməraiz] résumer; **'sum·ma·ry 1.** □ sommaire (*a.* ⚖); succint; en peu de mots; récapitulatif (-ive *f*); **2.** résumé *m*, sommaire *m*; récapitulation *f.*

sum·mer¹ ['sʌmə] **1.** été *m*; *~-house* pavillon *m*, kiosque *m* de jardin; *~ resort* station *f* estivale; **2.** *vt/i.* estiver; *v/i. a.* passer l'été.

sum·mer² △ [~] poutre *f* de plancher; poitrail *m*; linteau *m* de baie.

sum·mer·like ['sʌməlaik], **'summer·ly, 'sum·mer·y** d'été; estival (-aux *m/pl.*).

sum·mit ['sʌmit] sommet *m* (*a. pol.*),

faîte *m* (*a. fig.*); cime *f*; *fig.* comble *m*; ~ *conference* conférence *f* au sommet.

sum·mon ['sʌmən] appeler; convoquer; sommer (ⲧⲧ de comparaître); *fig.* (*usu.* ~ *up*) faire appel à; **'sum·mon·er** convocateur *m*; † huissier *m*; **sum·mons** ['~z] appel *m*; ⲧⲧ citation *f*, assignation *f*; ⲧ convocation *f*; ✕ ~ *to surrender* sommation *f*.

sump *mot.* [sʌmp] (fond *m* de) carter *m*.

sump·ter ['sʌmptə] (*usu.* ~-*horse*, ~-*mule*) cheval *m* ou mulet *m* de somme.

sump·tu·ar·y ['sʌmptjuəri] somptuaire.

sump·tu·ous □ ['sʌmptjuəs] somptueux (-euse *f*), fastueux (-euse *f*); **'sump·tu·ous·ness** faste *m*; richesse *f*; somptuosité *f*.

sun [sʌn] **1.** soleil *m*; **2.** du *ou* au *ou* de soleil, par le soleil; **3.** *v/t.* exposer au soleil; ~ *o.s.* se chauffer au soleil; prendre le soleil; **'~·baked** brûlé par le soleil; **~·beam** ['sʌnbi:m] rayon *m* de soleil.

sun·burn ['sʌnbə:n] hâle *m*; ⲧ coup *m* de soleil; **'sun·burnt** basané, brûlé par le soleil.

sun·dae *Am.* ['sʌnd(e)i] glace *f* aux fruits.

Sun·day ['sʌndi] dimanche *m*.

sun·der *poét.* ['sʌndə] (se) séparer; *v/t.* fendre en deux.

sun·di·al ['sʌndaiəl] cadran *m* solaire, gnomon *m*.

sun·down ['sʌndaun] coucher *m* du soleil; *Am.* occident *m*; *Am.* chapeau *m* à larges bords; **'sun·down·er** petit verre *m* pris au coucher du soleil.

sun·dry ['sʌndri] **1.** divers; **2.** *sundries pl. surt.* ⲧ articles *m/pl.* divers; frais *m/pl.* divers.

sung [sʌŋ] † *prét. et p.p. de sing.*

sun...: **'~-glass·es** *pl.* (*a. a pair of* ~) (des) lunettes *f/pl.* fumées *ou* solaires; **'~·'hel·met** casque *m* colonial.

sunk [sʌŋk] *p.p., a. prét. de sink 1.*

sunk·en ['sʌŋkən] sombré; *fig.* creux (creuse *f*) (*joues, yeux*); ⊕ enterré.

sun·lamp *cin.* ['sʌnlæmp] grand réflecteur *m*.

sun·lit ['sʌnlit] ensoleillé; éclairé par le soleil.

sun·ni·ness ['sʌninis] caractère *m*

ensoleillé; *fig.* gaieté *f*; **'sun·ny** □ ensoleillé; de soleil; *fig.* rayonnant; *fig.* heureux (-euse *f*).

sun...: **'~·rise** lever *m* du soleil; **'~·room** solarium *m*; **'~·set** coucher *m* du soleil; **'~·shade** ombrelle *f*; ⊕, *a. mot.* pare-soleil *m/inv.*; **'~·shine** (lumière *f* du) soleil *m*; *mot.* ~ *roof* toit *m* découvrable *ou* ouvrant; **'~·shin·y** ensoleillé, de soleil; **'~·spot** *astr.* tache *f* solaire; **'~·stroke** ⲧ coup *m* de soleil; insolation *f*; **'~·up** lever *m* du soleil.

sup [sʌp] *v/i.* souper (de *off, on*); *v/t.* donner à souper à (*q.*).

su·per¹ ['sju:pə] **1.** *théâ., a. cin.* F figurant(e *f*) *m*; **2.** F *mesure:* carré; ⲧ surfin.

su·per-² [~] super-; plus que; sus-.

su·per...: **~·a'bound** surabonder (de, en *in*, *with*); foisonner (en *in*, *with*); **~·a'bun·dant** □ surabondant; **~·ly** surabondamment; **~·add** surajouter; **~·an·nu·ate** ['~rænjueit] mettre à la retraite; *fig.* mettre au rancart; **~·d** suranné; démodé; en retraite (*personne*); **~·an·nu'a·tion** mise *f* en retraite; ~ *fund* caisse *f* des retraites.

su·perb □ [sju:'pə:b] superbe, magnifique.

su·per·car·go ⚓ ['sju:pəka:gou] subrécargue *m*; **'su·per·charg·er** *mot.* (sur)compresseur *m*; **su·per·cil·i·ous** □ [~'siliəs] hautain, dédaigneux (-euse *f*); **su·per'cil·i·ous·ness** hauteur *f*; arrogance *f*; **su·per·'dread·nought** super-dreadnought *m* (= *grand cuirassé*); **su·per·er·o·ga·tion** ['~rero'geiʃn] surérogation *f*; **su·per·e·rog·a·to·ry** □ ['~re'rogətəri] surérogatoire; **su·per·fi·cial** □ [~'fiʃl] superficiel(le *f*); **su·per·fi·ci·al·i·ty** [~fiʃi'æliti] superficialité *f*; **su·per·fi·ci·es** [~'fiʃi:z] superficie *f*; **'su·per'fine** superfin; ⲧ surfin; *fig.* raffiné; **su·per·flu·i·ty** [~'fluiti] superfluité *f*; embarras *m* (de, of); **su·per·flu·ous** □ [sju:'pə:fluəs] superflu; **su·per'heat** ⊕ surchauffer; **su·per·het** ['~'het] *radio:* super-hétérodyne *m*.

su·per...: **~·hu·man** □ [~'hju:mən] surhumain; **~·in·duce** ['~rin'dju:s] surajouter (à, *up]on*); superposer (sur, *[up]on*); **~·in·tend** [~prin'tend] surveiller, diriger; présider à; **~·in-**

'**tend·ence** direction *f*, surveillance *f*; ~**in'tend·ent 1.** surveillant(e *f*) *m*; directeur (-trice *f*) *m*; **2.** surveillant.

su·pe·ri·or [sjuːˈpiəriə] **1.** □ supérieur (à, *to*); *fig.* arrogant, de supériorité; *fig.* au-dessus (de, *to*); **2.** supérieur(e *f*) *m* (*a. eccl.*); (*Lady*) ♀ mère *f* abbesse; **su·pe·ri·or·i·ty** [~ˈɔriti] supériorité *f*.

su·per·la·tive [sjuːˈpəːlətiv] **1.** □ suprême; F *a. gramm.* superlatif (-ive *f*); **2.** *gramm.* (a. ~ degree) superlatif *m*; '**su·per·man** surhomme *m*; '**su·per·mar·ket** supermarché *m*; '**su·per'nat·u·ral** □ surnaturel (-le *f*); **su·per·nu·mer·ar·y** [~ˈnjuːmərəri] **1.** surnuméraire (*a. su./m*); **2.** *théâ.* figurant(e *f*) *m*; '**su·per'pose** superposer (à, [*up*]*on*); '**su·per·po'si·tion** superposition *f*; *géol.* disposition *f* en couches; stratification *f*; '**su·per'pow·er** *pol.* superpuissance *f*; '**su·per'scribe** mettre une inscription sur; mettre l'adresse sur; **su·per'scrip·tion** inscription *f*; adresse *f*; **su·per·sede** [~ˈsiːd] remplacer; *fig.* démonter; *fig.* supplanter; **su·per'ses·sion** remplacement *m*; évincement *m*; **su·per·son·ic** *phys.* [~ˈsɔnik] ultra-sonore; supersonique; **su·per·sti·tion** [~ˈstiʃn] superstition *f*; **su·per·'sti·tious** □ [~ʃəs] superstitieux (-euse *f*); **su·per·struc·ture** [ˈsuːprʌktʃə] superstructure *f*; **su·per·vene** [~ˈviːn] survenir; arriver (à la suite de, [*up*]*on*); **su·per·ven·tion** [~ˈvenʃn] survenance *f*, survenue *f*; **su·per·vise** [ˈ~vaiz] surveiller, diriger; **su·per·vi·sion** [~ˈviʒn] surveillance *f*; direction *f*; **su·per·vi·sor** [ˈ~vaizə] surveillant(e *f*) *m*; directeur (-trice *f*) *m*.

su·pine 1. *gramm.* [ˈsjuːpain] supin *m*; **2.** □ [~ˈpain] couché *ou* étendu sur le dos; *fig.* indolent; mou (mol *devant une voyelle ou un h muet*; molle *f*); nonchalant; **su·'pine·ness** indolence *f*, mollesse *f*, inertie *f*.

sup·per [ˈsʌpə] souper *m*; *the* (*Lord's*) ♀ la Cène *f*.

sup·plant [səˈplɑːnt] supplanter; remplacer; évincer (*q.*); F dégommer.

sup·ple [ˈsʌpl] **1.** □ souple; complaisant; **2.** assouplir.

sup·ple·ment 1. [ˈsʌplimənt] supplément *m*; annexe *f*, appendice *m*; **2.** [ˈ~ment] ajouter à, compléter; **sup·ple'men·tal** □, **sup·ple'men·ta·ry** supplémentaire (de, *to*); additionnel(le *f*) (à, *to*); ~ *benefit* allocation *f* supplémentaire; ✝ ~ *order* commande *f* renouvelée; *take a* ~ *ticket* prendre un billet supplémentaire.

sup·ple·ness [ˈsʌplnis] souplesse *f* (*a. fig.*); *fig.* complaisance *f*.

sup·pli·ant [ˈsʌpliənt] **1.** □ suppliant; de supplication; **2.** suppliant(e *f*) *m*.

sup·pli·cate [ˈsʌplikeit] supplier (pour obtenir, *for*; de *inf.*, *to inf.*); prier avec instance; **sup·pli·ca·tion** supplication *f*; supplique *f*; **sup·pli·ca·to·ry** [ˈ~kətəri] supplicatoire, de supplication.

sup·pli·er [səˈplaiə] fournisseur (-euse *f*) *m* (*a.* ✝); pourvoyeur (-euse *f*) *m*.

sup·ply [səˈplai] **1.** fournir, approvisionner, munir (de, *with*); combler (*une lacune*); réparer (*une omission*); remplir; répondre à (*un besoin*); remplacer (*q.*); **2.** fourniture *f*; approvisionnement *m*; ravitaillement *m* (*a. en munitions*); provision *f*; service *m* de (*gaz etc.*); ✝ offre *f*; *usu.* supplies *pl.* ✝ fournitures *f*/*pl.*; *parl.* budget *m*; crédits *m*/*pl.*; ✕ vivres *m*/*pl.*; approvisionnements *m*/*pl.*; ravitaillement *m* en munitions; *be in short* ~ manquer; *on* ~ par intérim; ~ *teacher* (professeur *mf*) suppléant(e *f*) *m*; *parl.* Committee of ♀ commission *f* du budget.

sup·port [səˈpɔːt] **1.** appui *m*, soutien *m* (*a.* ⊕, *a. fig.*); ⊕ soutènement *m*; maintien *m*, entretien *m*; ressources *f*/*pl.*; ✕ (troupes *f*/*pl.* de) soutien *m*; **2.** appuyer (*a. fig.*); soutenir (*a. parl. une motion, a. théâ. un rôle*); maintenir; entretenir; subvenir aux besoins de (*une famille*); venir à l'appui de (*une opinion etc.*); tolérer (*une injure*); entourer (*un président etc.*); *théâ.* donner la réplique à (*le premier rôle*); seconder; *théâ.* ~*ing part* rôle *m* secondaire; *cin.* ~*ing programme* film *m ou* -s *m*/*pl.* d'importance secondaire; △ ~*ing wall* mur *m* d'appui; **sup'port·a·ble** □ tolérable, sup-

portable; soutenable (*opinion*); **sup·**
'port·er adhérent(e *f*) *m*; partisan
(-e *f*) *m*; *sp.* supporter *m*; défenseur
m (*d'une opinion*); ☑ support *m*;
appareil: soutien *m*.

sup·pose [sə'pouz] supposer, s'imaginer; croire; *he is ⌐d to* (*inf.*) il
est censé (*inf.*); ⌐ (*that*), *supposing*
(*that*) admettons que (*sbj.*), supposé
que (*sbj.*); F ⌐ *we do so* eh bien!
et puis après?; *he is rich, I* ⌐ je
suppose qu'il est riche.

sup·posed ☐ [sə'pouzd] supposé,
prétendu; soi-disant; **sup'pos·ed·**
ly [⌐idli] probablement.

sup·po·si·tion [sʌpə'ziʃn] supposition *f*; hypothèse *f*; **sup·pos·i·ti·**
tious ☐ [səpozi'tiʃəs] faux (fausse
f), supposé; **sup'pos·i·to·ry** ☞
[⌐təri] suppositoire *m*.

sup·press [sə'pres] supprimer; réprimer; **sup·pres·sion** [sə'preʃn]
suppression *f*; répression *f*; étouffement *m*; **sup·pres·sive** ☐ [sə'pre-
siv] suppressif (-ive *f*), répressif
(-ive *f*); **sup'pres·sor** personne *f*
qui supprime *ou* réprime; *radio*:
grille *f* de freinage; *télév.* antiparasite *m*.

sup·pu·rate ['sʌpjureit] suppurer;
sup·pu'ra·tion suppuration *f*.

su·prem·a·cy [sju'preməsi] suprématie *f* (*sur, over*); **su·preme** ☐
[sju'pri:m] suprême (*a. poét. heure*);
souverain.

sur·charge 1. [sə:'tʃɑ:dʒ] surcharger
(*de, with*); *a. un timbre-poste*); surtaxer; **2.** ['⌐] surcharge *f* (*a. timbre-
poste*); charge *f* excessive; *lettre*:
surtaxe *f*.

surd ⅄ [sə:d] **1.** incommensurable;
irrationnel(le *f*); **2.** quantité *f* incommensurable; racine *f* irration-
nelle.

sure ☐ [ʃuə] sûr, certain; *to be ⌐!*,
F ⌐ *enough!, Am.* ⌐! vraiment!, en
effet!, bien sûr; *Am.* F ⌐ *fire* infaillible; absolument sûr; *Am.* F ⌐ *thing!*
bien sûr!; mais oui!; *it's a* ⌐ *thing*
c'est une certitude, c'est sûr et certain; *I'm* ⌐ *I don't know* je ne sais
vraiment pas; *he is* ⌐ *to return* il
reviendra sûrement *ou* à coup sûr;
make ⌐ s'assurer (*de, of*); prendre les
dispositions nécessaires (pour *inf.*, *to
inf.*); *be* ⌐ *to write* ne manquez pas
d'écrire; **'sure·ly** assurément; certainement; **'sure·ness** sûreté *f*; cer-

titude *f*; **'sure·ty** caution *f*, garant(e
f) *m*; † garantie *f*.

surf [sə:f] **1.** ressac *m*; brisants *m/pl.*;
2. (*a. ⌐ride, go ⌐ing*) surfer, faire du
surfing; ⌐ *board* planche *f* de surf.

sur·face ['sə:fis] **1.** surface *f*; *fig.*
dehors *m*; ✈ (*up lifting*) ⌐
aile *f* voilure; ✈ *control* ⌐ gouverne *f*;
2. *v/i.* revenir en *ou* faire surface;
'⌐·man 🚂 cheminot *m*.

sur·feit [sə:'fit] **1.** excès *m*, surabondance *f*; *fig.* dégoût *m*; **2.** (se) gorger (*de on, with*) (*a. fig.*).

surf·rid·ing [sə:'fraidiŋ] *sp.* planking *m*; sport *m* de l'aquaplane.

surge [sə:dʒ] **1.** houle *f*; vague *f* (*a.
∮ de courant*); lame *f* de fond; **2.** se
soulever; être *ou* devenir houleux;
fig. se répandre en flots.

sur·geon ['sə:dʒən] chirurgien(ne *f*)
m; ⚓, ⚔ médecin *m* (militaire);
sur·ger·y ['sə:dʒəri] chirurgie *f*;
médecine *f* opératoire; *endroit*: cabinet *m* de consultation; dispensaire *m*.

sur·gi·cal ☐ ['sə:dʒikl] chirurgical
(-aux *m/pl.*), de chirurgie.

sur·li·ness ['sə:linis] maussaderie *f*;
caractère *m* hargneux; air *m* bourru;
'sur·ly ☐ maussade; hargneux
(-euse *f*); bourru.

sur·mise 1. ['sə:maiz] conjecture *f*,
supposition *f*; **2.** [⌐'maiz] conjecturer; soupçonner.

sur·mount [sə:'maunt] surmonter
(*a. fig.*); *fig.* triompher de (*qch.*);
⌐ed by (*ou* with) surmonté *ou* couronné de; **sur'mount·a·ble** surmontable.

sur·name ['sə:neim] **1.** nom *m* (de
famille); **2.** donner un nom de famille à; ⌐d surnommé.

sur·pass *fig.* [sə:'pɑ:s] surpasser;
dépasser; **sur'pass·ing** ☐ sans
égal (-aux *m/pl.*); prééminent.

sur·plice *eccl.* ['sə:pləs] surplis *m*.

sur·plus ['sə:pləs] **1.** surplus *m*, excédent *m*; **2.** d'excédent; surplus
de; **'sur·plus·age** *see surplus 1*;
surabondance *f*; ⚖ redondance
f.

sur·prise [sə'praiz] **1.** surprise *f*;
étonnement *m*; ⚔ coup *m* de main;
take by ⌐ prendre au dépourvu, surprendre; **2.** à l'improviste; **3.** étonner; surprendre (*a.* ⚔); **sur'pris·**
ing ☐ étonnant, surprenant.

sur·re·al·ism [sə'riəlizm] *art:* surréalisme *m*; **sur're·al·ist** surréaliste (*a. su./mf*).

sur·ren·der [sə'rendə] **1.** ✕ reddition *f*; abandon *m*; **2.** *v/t.* abandonner (*a. fig.*); ✕ rendre; *v/i.* (*a. ⁓ o.s.*) se rendre.

sur·rep·ti·tious □ [sʌrəp'tiʃəs] clandestin, subreptice.

sur·ro·gate ['sʌrəgit] suppléant(e *f*) *m*; ⁝⁙, *eccl.* subrogé(e *f*) *m*.

sur·round [sə'raund] entourer (*a.* ✕); cerner; investir (*une ville*); **sur'round·ing 1.** environnant, d'alentour; **2.** *⁓s pl.* environnement *m*; milieu *m*; entourage *m*.

sur·tax ['sɜː'tæks] surtaxe *f*.

sur·veil·lance [sɜː'veiləns] surveillance *f*.

sur·vey 1. [sɜː'vei] contempler, promener ses regards sur; examiner attentivement; *surv.* arpenter (*un terrain*); faire le levé du plan de; **2.** ['sɜː'vei] vue *f* générale, aperçu *m*; étude *f* (*de la situation*); inspection *f*, visite *f*; *surv. terrain*: arpentage *m*; levé *m* (des plans); **sur'vey·or** arpenteur *m*, géomètre *m* expert; *admin.* inspecteur (-trice *f*) *m*; contrôleur (-euse *f*) *m*.

sur·viv·al [sɜː'vaivl] survivance *f*; restant *m*; ⁝⁙ survie *f*; **sur·vive** [⁓'vaiv] *v/t.* survivre à; *v/i.* survivre; demeurer en vie; subsister; **sur'vi·vor** survivant(e *f*) *m*.

sus·cep·ti·bil·i·ty [səseptə'biliti] prédisposition *f* (à, to), susceptibilité *f*; *souv.* susceptibilities *pl.* sensibilité *f*; **sus'cep·ti·ble** □, **sus'cep·tive** sensible, prédisposé (à of, to); *be ⁓ of* se prêter à (*qch.*); être susceptible de.

sus·pect 1. [səs'pekt] soupçonner; avoir idée (que, that); se douter de (*qch.*); **2.** ['sʌspekt] suspect(e *f*) *m*; **3.** [⁓] (*a. ⁓ed*) suspect.

sus·pend [səs'pend] pendre; suspendre (*fonctionnaire, jugement, paiements, poursuite, travail, etc.*); cesser; ✕ mettre (*un officier*) en non-activité; *parl.* exclure temporairement; ⁝⁙ surseoir à (*un jugement*); *sp.* exécuter (*un joueur*), mettre (*un jockey*) à pied; *⁓ed* suspendu; interrompu; *⁓ed animation* syncope *f*; *fig.* suspens *m*; **sus'pend·er** suspensoir *m*; *surt. Am. ⁓s pl.* bretelles *f/pl.*; jarretelles *f/pl*; fixe-chaussettes *m/inv.*

sus·pense [səs'pens] suspens *m*; incertitude *f*; *in ⁓* pendant(e *f*); ✝ *⁓ account* compte *m* d'ordre; **sus·pen·sion** [⁓'penʃn] suspension *f*; ⁝⁙ jugement: surséance *f*; *parl.* député: exclusion *f* temporaire; *sp.* exécution *f*; mise *f* à pied (*d'un jockey*); *⁓-bridge* pont *m* suspendu; *⁓ railway* chemin *m* de fer suspendu; **sus'pen·sive** □ suspensif (-ive *f*); **sus·pen·so·ry** [⁓'pensəri] **1.** suspensif (-ive *f*); **2.** *anat.* suspenseur *m*; *⁂ ⁓ bandage* suspensoir *m*.

sus·pi·cion [səs'piʃn] soupçon *m* (*a. fig.*); *fig.* sourire: ébauche *f*.

sus·pi·cious □ [səs'piʃəs] suspect; équivoque; louche; méfiant; **sus'pi·cious·ness** caractère *m* suspect *etc.*; méfiance *f*.

sus·tain [səs'tein] *usu.* soutenir (*a. fig.*); entretenir (*la vie*); appuyer (*des témoignages*); essuyer (*une perte*); **sus'tain·a·ble** soutenable; **sus'tained** soutenu, nourri (*a. fig.*); continu.

sus·te·nance ['sʌstinəns] sustentation *f*; subsistance *f*; nourriture *f*.

sut·ler ['sʌtlə] ✕ cantinier (-ère *f*) *m*; *sl.* mercanti *m*.

su·ture ['sjuːtʃə] **1.** ♀, ⁂, *anat.* suture *f*; **2.** suturer.

su·ze·rain ['suːzərein] suzerain *m*; **'su·ze·rain·ty** suzeraineté *f*.

swab [swɔb] **1.** torchon *m*; ⚓ faubert *m*; ⁂ tampon *m* d'ouate; ⁂ prélèvement *m* (dans, of); *sl.* andouille *f*; *sl.* ⚓ marin *m* d'eau douce; **2.** (*a. ⁓ down*) nettoyer; ⚓ fauberter.

swad·dle ['swɔdl] **1.** emmailloter (de, with); *swaddling clothes pl.* maillot *m*; F *fig.* langes *m/pl.*; **2.** lange *m*; bande *f*.

swag·ger ['swægə] **1.** crâner, se pavaner, se donner des airs; fanfaronner; **2.** F ultra-chic *inv. en genre*; élégant; **3.** air *m* avantageux; rodomontades *f/pl.*; '*⁓-cane* ✕ jonc *m* d'officier; jonc *m* de tenue de sortie.

swain [swein] ✝ berger *m*; *poét.*, *a. co.* soupirant *m*.

swal·low¹ *orn.* ['swɔlou] hirondelle *f*.

swal·low² [⁓] **1.** gosier *m*; gorgée *f*; **2.** *v/t.* avaler (*a. fig. une histoire, un affront*); gober (*une huître, a. fig.* [*qqfois ⁓ up*] *une histoire*); *fig.*

ravaler (*ses paroles*); mettre dans sa poche (*son orgueil*); *v/i.* avaler.

swam [swæm] *prét. de swim 1.*

swamp [swɔmp] **1.** marais *m*, marécage *m*; **2.** inonder (*a. fig.*); ⚓ remplir d'eau, submerger; *fig.* déborder (de, *with*); écraser; **'swamp·y** marécageux (-euse *f*).

swan [swɔn] cygne *m*.

swank *sl.* [swæŋk] **1.** prétention *f*, épate *f*; **2.** prétentieux (-euse *f*); snob *adj./inv.*; **3.** crâner, faire de l'épate.

swan-neck ['swɔnnek] ⊕ cou *m* de cygne; ⚓ *gui*: aiguillot *m*; **swan-ner·y** ['⁓əri] endroit *m* où on élève des cygnes; **'swan-song** chant *m* du cygne (*a. fig.*).

swap F [swɔp] troquer, échanger.

sward [swɔːd] gazon *m*; pelouse *f*.

swarm¹ [swɔːm] **1.** essaim *m*; *sauterelles*: vol *m*; *fig.* foule *f*, troupe *f*; **2.** essaimer; *fig.* fourmiller (de, *with*).

swarm² [⁓] (*usu.* ⁓ *up*) escalader; monter à.

swarth·i·ness ['swɔːθinis] teint *m* basané; **'swarth·y** □ basané, noiraud, brun.

swash [swɔʃ] **1.** *v/i.* clapoter; *v/t.* clapoter contre; faire jaillir; **2.** clapotis *m*, *vagues*: clapotage *m*; **⁓-buck·ler** ['⁓bʌklə] rodomont *m*, fanfaron *m*.

swas·ti·ka ['swɔstikə] svastika *m*; croix *f* gammée.

swat [swɔt] **1.** frapper; écraser (*une mouche*); **2.** coup *m*.

swath ✎ [swɔːθ] andain *m*, fauchée *f*.

swathe [sweið] **1.** bandage *m*, bande *f*; *see swath*; **2.** emmailloter, envelopper; rouler.

sway [swei] **1.** balancement *m*; oscillation *f*; *mot.* roulis *m*; empire *m*, domination *f*; **2.** *v/t.* balancer; influencer; gouverner; *v/i.* osciller, se balancer; *fig.* incliner, pencher.

swear [swɛə] **1.** [*irr.*] *v/i.* jurer (qch., by s.th.); prêter serment; sacrer, blasphémer; ⁓ *to* attester (*qch.*) sous serment; ⁓ *at* maudire; *fig.* ⁓ *by* se fier à; *v/t.* jurer (de, *to*); faire (*un serment*); faire jurer (*q.*); ⁓ *s.o.* faire prêter serment à q.; *be sworn* (*in*) prêter serment; ⁓ *off* jurer de renoncer à; **2.** F (*a.* ⁓-*word*) juron *m*.

sweat [swet] **1.** sueur *f*, transpira-

tion *f*; ⊕ ressuage *m*; *sl.* corvée *f*; ✕ F *old* ⁓ vieux troupier *m*; *by the* ⁓ *of one's brow* à la sueur de son front; **2.** [*irr.*] *v/i.* suer, transpirer; *v/t.* (faire) suer; ✎ faire transpirer; exploiter (*un ouvrier*); ⊕ souder (*un câble*) à l'étain; **'sweat·ed** fait à la sueur des ouvriers (-ères *f*); **'sweat·er** chandail *m*; tricot *m*; F pull *m*; **⁓·'shirt** sweat-shirt *m*; **'⁓·shop** atelier *m* où les ouvriers sont exploités; **'sweat·y** en sueur; imprégné de sueur; d'une chaleur humide.

Swede [swiːd] Suédois(e *f*) *m*; ✐ ♀ navet *m* de Suède, chou-navet *m* (*pl.* choux-navets) *m*.

Swedish ['swiːdiʃ] **1.** suédois; **2.** *ling.* suédois *m*; *the* ⁓ *pl.* les Suédois *m/pl.*

sweep [swiːp] **1.** [*irr.*] *v/t.* balayer (*une pièce, a. fig. une robe, les mers, etc.*); *fig.* parcourir; *fig.* (*souv. avec adv.*) entraîner; ramoner (*la cheminée*); *fig.* effleurer (*les cordes d'une harpe*); ✕ enfiler; *fig.* embrasser du regard; tracer (*une courbe*); *v/i.* s'étaler, s'étendre; *fig.* (*usu. avec adv.*) avancer rapidement; envahir, parcourir; entrer *etc.* d'un air majestueux; ⁓ *for mines* draguer des mines; ⁓ *in* entrer vivement ou majestueusement; **2.** coup *m* de balai *ou* de pinceau *ou* de faux; geste *m* large; mouvement *m* circulaire; courbe *f*; ligne *f* ininterrompue; *fig.* mouvement *m* majestueux; ♪ *harpe*: effleurement *m*; *mot.* virage *m*; *fleuve*: course *f* rapide; *maison*: allée *f*; *télév.* balayage *m*; étendue *f*, envergure *f*; ✕ *etc.* portée *f* (*a. fig.*); ⊕ zone *f* de jeu; *formes d'un navire*: courbure *f*; *colline*: versant *m*; ramoneur *m* (*de cheminées*); *embarcation etc.*: aviron *m* de queue; *pompe etc.*: balancier *m*; F sweepstake *m*; *make a clean* ⁓ faire table rase (de, *of*); *jeu*: faire rafle; *fig. at one* ⁓ d'un seul coup; **'sweep·er** balayeur *m* (*de rues*); *machine*: balayeuse *f*; **'sweep·ing 1.** □ rapide; entier (-ère *f*); par trop absolu (*affirmation*); allongé, élancé (*lignes*); **2.** ⁓*s pl.* ordures *f/pl.*, balayures *f/pl.*; **sweep·stake** ['⁓steik] sweepstake *m*, poule *f*.

sweet [swiːt] **1.** □ doux (douce *f*); sucré; mélodieux (-euse *f*); gen-

til(le *f*) (*personne*); odorant; agréable; sain (*haleine, sol, etc.*); ~ *oil*
huile *f* douce; *souv.* huile *f* d'olive;
♀ ~ *pea* pois *m* de senteur; ♀
~-*william* œillet *m* de poète; *have*
a ~ *tooth* aimer les douceurs;
2. chérie *f*; bonbon *m*; *cuis.* entre-
mets *m* (sucré); ~s *pl.* confiseries
f/pl.; friandises *f/pl.*; *fig.* délices
f/pl.; '~•**bread** ris *m* de veau *ou*
qqfois d'agneau; '**sweet•en** sucrer;
adoucir (*a. fig.*); assainir (*l'air, le sol,*
etc.); '**sweet•en•er** édulcorant *m*;
fig. pot-de-vin *m* (*pl.* pots-de-vin);
'**sweet•heart** bien-aimé(e *f*) *m*;
chéri(e *f*) *m*; '**sweet•ish** assez doux
(douce *f*); '**sweet•meat** bonbon *m*;
~s *pl.* confiserie *f*, sucreries *f/pl.*;
'**sweet•ness** douceur *f* (*a. fig.*); *fig.*
gentillesse *f*; *air etc.*: fraîcheur *f*;
'**sweet•shop** confiserie *f*.

swell [swel] 1. [*irr.*] *v/i.* se gonfler
(*a. voiles*); s'enfler (*a. fig.* jusqu'à
devenir qch., *into* s.th.); grossir;
se soulever (*mer*); *fig.* augmenter;
v/t. gonfler, enfler; augmenter;
2. F élégant, chic *inv.* en genre; *sl.*
bath; 3. bosse *f*; *terrain*: ondulation *f*; gonflement *m*; ♪ *orgue*: soufflet *m*, crescendo *m* (et diminuendo
m); ♫ houle *f*; F élégant(e *f*) *m*;
the ~s *pl.* le gratin *m*; '**swell•ing** 1.
enflure *f*; tumeur *f*; gonflement *m*;
vagues: soulèvement *m*; *mot. etc.*
hernie *f*; 2. □ qui s'enfle *ou* se
gonfle; enflé, gonflé; boursouflé
(*style*).　　　　　　　　　　　[nage.)
swel•ter ['sweltə] étouffer; être en)
swept [swept] *prét. et p.p. de*
sweep 1.
swerve [swə:v] *v/i.* faire un écart;
mot. faire une embardée; dévier;
foot. crocheter; *v/t.* faire écarter;
mot. faire faire une embardée; faire
dévier (*la balle*).
swift [swift] 1. □ rapide; prompt;
2. *orn.* martinet *m*; '**swift•ness**
vitesse *f*; promptitude *f*.
swig F [swig] 1. gorgée *f*; grand
coup *m*; 2. boire à grands coups;
lamper.
swill [swil] 1. lavage *m* à grande
eau; pâtée *f* pour les porcs; F *péj.*
rinçure *f*, mauvaise boisson *f*;
2. *v/t.* laver à grande eau; *v/i.*
avaler; boire comme une éponge.
swim [swim] 1. [*irr.*] *v/i.* nager;
être inondé (de, *with*); *my head* ~s

la tête me tourne; *v/t.* traverser à
la nage; faire (*une distance etc.*) à la
nage; faire nager (*un cheval*); 2. action *f* de nager; *be in the* ~ être à la
page; être lancé.
swim•ming ['swimiŋ] 1. nage *f*;
natation *f*; 2. □ de natation; ~*ly* F
à merveille; ~ *pool* piscine *f*; ~ *trunks*
pl. (*a pair of* ~ *trunks* un) caleçon de
bain.
swim•suit ['swimsju:t] maillot *m* (de
bain).
swin•dle ['swindl] 1. *v/t.* escroquer
(qch. à q., *s.o. out of* s.th.); *v/i.* faire
de l'escroquerie; 2. escroquerie *f*,
filouterie *f*; '**swin•dler** escroc *m*,
filou *m*; *sl.* floueur (-euse *f*) *m*.
swine *poét., zo., fig. péj.* [swain], *pl.*
swine cochon *m*; *sl.* salaud *m*;
'**swine•herd** porcher *m*.
swing [swiŋ] 1. [*irr.*] *v/i.* se balancer,
osciller, tournoyer, pivoter; ♫
éviter (*sur l'ancre*); être pendu; ✕
faire une conversion (vers, to); ~
along avancer en scandant le pas;
~ *into motion* se mettre en mouvement; ~ *to* se refermer (*porte*); *v/t.*
(faire) balancer, faire osciller; faire
pivoter; pendre; brandir; 2. balancement *m*; coup *m* balancé; va-et-
vient *m/inv.*; balançoire *f* (*d'enfant*); mouvement *m* rythmé; ♫
évitage *m*; *fig.* entrain *m*, marche *f*;
♪, *a.* box. swing *m*; *in full* ~ en
pleine marche; ~ **bridge** pont *m*
tournant; ~ **door** porte *f* battante,
porte *f* à bascule.
swinge•ing □ F ['swindʒiŋ] énorme;
écrasant.
swing•ing □ F ['swiŋiŋ] balançant,
oscillant; à bascule; *fig.* cadencé; *fig.*
entraînant; *Am.* ~ *door see swing door*;
♫ ~ *temperature* température *f* variable.
swin•gle ⊕ ['swiŋgl] 1. teiller,
écanguer (*le lin, le chanvre*);
2. écang *m*; '~•**tree** palonnier *m*.
swin•ish □ ['swainiʃ] de cochon,
bestial (-aux *m/pl.*).
swipe [swaip] 1. frapper à toute
volée; F donner une taloche à; *Am.*
sl. chiper; 2. F taloche *f*; ~s *pl.*
petite bière *f*, bibine *f*.
swirl [swə:l] 1. (faire) tournoyer *ou*
tourbillonner; 2. remous *m*; tour-
billon(nement) *m*.
swish [swiʃ] 1. *v/i.* bruire; siffler;
v/t. fouetter; faire siffler; 2. bruis-

sement *m*; sifflement *m*; frou(-)frou *m*; **3.** F chic *inv. en genre*, élégant.

Swiss [swis] **1.** suisse; **2.** Suisse(sse *f*) *m*; the ~ *pl.* les Suisses *m/pl.*

switch [switʃ] **1.** badine *f*; houssine *f* (*a. de cavalier*); 🚂 aiguille *f*; ⚡ interrupteur *m*, commutateur *m*; *cheveux:* postiche *m*; **2.** cingler; housser; 🚂 aiguiller (*a. fig.*); manœuvrer (*un train*); ⚡ (*souv. ~ over*) commuter (*le courant*); ⚡ ~ on (*off*) allumer (éteindre); '~**back** montagnes *f/pl.* russes; '~**board** panneau *m ou* tableau *m* de distribution; *telephone* ~ standard *m* téléphonique; '~**box** caisson *m* d'interrupteur, boîte *f* de distribution; '~**le·ver** 🚂 levier *m* d'aiguille.

swiv·el ⊕ ['swivl] émerillon *m*; pivot *m*; *attr.* tournant, pivotant; à pivot.

swol·len ['swouln] *p.p. de swell 1.*

swoon [swu:n] **1.** évanouissement *m*; ⚕ syncope *f*; **2.** s'évanouir.

swoop [swu:p] **1.** (*usu.* ~ *down*) s'abattre, foncer (*sur*, [*up*]*on*); **2.** descente *f* rapide; attaque *f* inattendue.

swop F [swɔp] troquer.

sword [sɔ:d] épée *f*; *cavalry* ~ sabre *m* de cavalerie; '~**cane** canne *f* à épée; '~**knot** dragonne *f*.

swords·man ['sɔ:dzmən] épéiste *m*, escrimeur *m*, F lame *f*; '**swords-man·ship** escrime *f*.

swore [swɔ:] *prét. de swear 1.*

sworn [swɔ:n] *p.p. de swear 1*; ⚖ juré, assermenté.

swot *école sl.* [swɔt] **1.** travail *m* intense, *sl.* turbin *m*; *personne:* bûcheur (-euse *f*) *m*; **2.** bûcher, piocher, potasser.

swum [swʌm] *p.p. de swim 1.*

swung [swʌŋ] *prét. et p.p. de swing 1.*

syb·a·rite ['sibərait] sybarite (*a. su./mf*).

syc·o·phant ['sikəfənt] sycophante *m*; flagorneur (-euse *f*) *m*; adulateur (-trice *f*) *m*; **syc·o·phan·tic** [sikə'fæntik] (~*ally*) adulateur (-trice *f*); ~*ally* bassement.

syl·lab·ic [si'læbik] (~*ally*) syllabique; **syl·la·ble** ['siləbl] syllabe *f*.

syl·la·bus ['siləbəs] *cours, études:* programme *m*; *eccl.* syllabus *m*.

syl·lo·gism *phls.* ['silədʒizm] syllogisme *m*.

sylph [silf] sylphe *m*; sylphide *f* (*a. fig.*).

sym·bi·o·sis *biol.* [simbai'ousis] symbiose *f*.

sym·bol ['simbəl] symbole *m* (*a.* Å); signe *m*; attribut *m*; **sym·bol·ic**, **sym·bol·i·cal** □ [~'bɔlik(l)] symbolique; **sym·bol·ism** ['~bəlizm] symbolisme *m*; '**sym·bol·ize** symboliser.

sym·met·ri·cal □ [si'metrikl] symétrique; **sym·me·try** ['simitri] symétrie *f*.

sym·pa·thet·ic [simpə'θetik] (~*ally*) sympathique (*a. nerf, encre*); de sympathie; compatissant; bien disposé; ~ *strike* grève *f* de solidarité; **sym·pa·thize** ['~θaiz] sympathiser (*avec, with*); compatir (*à, with*); s'associer (*à, with*); **sym·pa·thy** ['~θi] sympathie *f*; compassion *f*; *in* ~ par solidarité (*grève*); par contre-coup (*hausse de prix*); *letter of* ~ lettre *f* de condoléances.

sym·phon·ic ♪ [sim'fɔnik] symphonique; **sym·pho·ny** ♪ ['simfəni] symphonie *f*.

symp·tom ['simptəm] symptôme *m*; indice *m*; **symp·to·mat·ic** [~'mætik] (~*ally*) symptomatique; qui est un symptôme (*de, of*); *be* ~ *of* caractériser (*qch.*).

syn·a·gogue ['sinəgɔg] synagogue *f*.

sync(h) F [siŋk] synchronisation *f*; synchronisme *m*; *out of* ~ mal synchronisé, pas en synchronisme.

syn·chro·mesh gear *mot.* ['sinkromeʃ'giə] boîte *f* de vitesses synchronisée.

syn·chro·nism ['siŋkrənizm] synchronisme *m*; ⚡ *in* ~ en phase; *télév. irregular* ~ drapeau *m*; '**syn·chro·nize** *v/i.* marquer la même heure; arriver simultanément; *v/t.* synchroniser (*a. cin.*); ⚡ coupler en phase; *cin.* repérer; '**syn·chro·nous** □ synchrone; ⚡ en phase.

syn·co·pate ['siŋkəpeit] syncoper; **syn·co·pe** ⚕, ♪, *a. gramm.* ['~pi] syncope *f*.

syn·dic ['sindik] syndic *m*; **syn·di·cate 1.** ['~kit] syndicat *m*; conseil *m* de syndics; **2.** ['~keit] (se) syndiquer; '**syn·di·cat·ed** publié simultanément dans plusieurs journaux.

syn·drome ['sindroum] syndrome *m*.

syn·od *eccl.* ['sinəd] synode *m*, concile *m*; **syn·od·al** ['ˎdl], **syn·od·ic**, **syn·od·i·cal** □ *eccl.* [si'nɔdik(l)] synodal (-aux *m*/*pl.*).

syn·o·nym ['sinənim] synonyme *m*; **syn·on·y·mous** □ [si'nɔniməs] synonyme (de, *with*).

syn·op·sis [si'nɔpsis], *pl.* -**ses** [ˎsi:z] résumé *m*, abrégé *m*; tableau *m* synoptique; *bibl.* synopse *f*; *école*: aide-mémoire *m*/*inv.*

syn·op·tic, **syn·op·ti·cal** □ [si-'nɔptik(l)] synoptique.

syn·tac·tic, **syn·tac·ti·cal** □ *gramm.* [sin'tæktik(l)] syntaxique; **syn·tax** *gramm.* ['sintæks] syntaxe *f*.

syn·the·sis ['sinθisis], *pl.* -**ses** ['ˎsi:z] synthèse *f*; **syn·the·size** ⊕ ['ˎsaiz] synthétiser; faire la synthèse de.

syn·thet·ic, **syn·thet·i·cal** □ [sin-'θetik(l)] synthétique; de synthèse.

syn·to·nize ['sintənaiz] *radio*: syntoniser, accorder; **syn·to·ny** ['ˎni] syntonie *f*, accord *m*.

syph·i·lis ⚕ ['sifilis] syphilis *f*.

syph·i·lit·ic ⚕ [sifi'litik] syphilitique.

sy·phon ['saifən] *see* siphon.

Syr·i·an ['siriən] **1.** syrien(ne *f*); **2.** Syrien(ne *f*) *m*.

sy·rin·ga ♀ [si'riŋgə] seringa(t) *m*; jasmin *m* en arbre.

syr·inge ['sirindʒ] **1.** seringue *f*; **2.** seringuer; ⚕ laver avec une seringue.

syr·up ['sirəp] sirop *m*.

sys·tem ['sistim] système *m*; *pol.* régime *m*; méthode *f*; **sys·tem·at·ic** [ˎ'mætik] (ˎally) systématique, méthodique.

T

T, t [ti:] T *m*, t *m*; F to *a* T à merveille.

tab [tæb] patte *f*; étiquette *f*; cordon de soulier: ferret *m*; manteau etc.: attache *f*; *fichier*: touche *f*; ✂ patte *f* du collet; *Am.* pick up the ~ payer (la note); F keep ~(s) on ne pas perdre (*q.*) de vue.

tab·ard hist. ['tæbəd] tabar(d) *m*.

tab·by ['tæbi] **1.** soie *f* moirée; (*usu.* ~ cat) chat *m* tigré; F chatte *f*; F vieille chipie *f*; **2.** tex. de ou en tabis; rayé.

tab·er·nac·le ['tæbənækl] tabernacle *m*; *Am.* temple *m*.

ta·ble ['teibl] **1.** table *f* (*a.* fig. = bonne chère; *a.* ⚕); ⊕ plaque *f*; ⊕ banc *m* (*d'une machine à percer*); ⊕ table *f* de multiplication; occasional ~ guéridon *m*; nest of ~s table *f* gigogne; ~ of contents table *f* des matières; turn the ~s renverser les rôles; reprendre l'avantage (sur, on); **2.** mettre sur la table; *p.ext.* parl. saisir la Chambre de (*un projet de loi*); *Am.* ajourner (*usu.* un projet de loi); '~-**cloth** nappe *f*; '~-**lin·en** linge *m* de table; ~ **nap·kin** serviette *f*; '~-**spoon** cuiller (cuillère) *f* à bouche ou à soupe.

tab·let ['tæblit] tablette *f* (*de chocolat*, ⚕, *pharm.*, *pour écrire, etc.*); plaque *f*; *savon*: pain *m*; *pharm.* comprimé *m*.

table...: ~ **ten·nis** ping-pong *m*; '~-**top** dessus *m* de table; '~-**ware** vaisselle *f*; ~ **wine** vin *m* de table.

tab·loid ['tæbloid] *pharm.* comprimé *m*; pastille *f*; petit journal *m* qui vise à la sensation.

ta·boo [tə'bu:] **1.** tabou; F interdit; **2.** tabou *m*; **3.** tabouer; F interdire.

tab·u·lar □ ['tæbjulə] tabulaire; disposé en lamelles; **tab·u·late** ['~leit] disposer en forme de tables ou tableaux; classifier.

tac·it □ ['tæsit] tacite; **tac·i·turn** □ ['~təːn] taciturne; **tac·i·tur·ni·ty** taciturnité *f*.

tack [tæk] **1.** petit clou *m*; pointe *f*;

(*a.* tin ~) semence *f*; couture: point *m* de bâti; ⚓ bord(ée *f*) *m* (en louvoyant); fig. voie *f*; tactique *f*; on the wrong ~ sur la mauvaise voie; fourvoyé; **2.** *v/t.* clouer; faufiler (*un vêtement*); fig. attacher, annexer (à to, on); *v/i.* ⚓ louvoyer; virer (*a.* fig.).

tack·le ['tækl] **1.** appareil *m*, ustensiles *m/pl.*; ⚓ apparaux *m/pl.*, palan *m*; ⊕ appareil *m* de levage; *sp.* arrêt *m*; **2.** saisir à bras-le-corps; essayer, entreprendre; *sp.* plaquer.

tack·y ['tæki] collant; *Am.* F minable.

tact [tækt] tact *m*, savoir-faire *m/inv.*; **tact·ful** □ ['~ful] (plein) de tact.

tac·ti·cal □ ✕ ['tæktikl] tactique; **tac·ti·cian** [~'tiʃn] tacticien *m*; **tac·tics** *pl. ou sg.* ['~iks] tactique *f*.

tac·tile ['tæktail] tactile.

tact·less □ ['tæktlis] dépourvu de tact.

tad·pole zo. ['tædpoul] têtard *m*.

taf·fe·ta ['tæfitə] taffetas *m*.

taf·fy ['tæfi] caramel *m* au beurre; *Am.* F flagornerie *f*.

tag [tæg] **1.** morceau *m* qui pend, bout *m*; étiquette *f*, attache *f*; ferret *m*; fig. cliché *m*; **2.** ferrer; fig. attacher (à on, to); *Am.* attacher une fiche à; F ~ along suivre, traîner derrière.

tag-rag ['tægræg]: ~ (and bobtail) canaille *f*.

tail [teil] **1.** queue *f* (*a.* de jupe, *a.* fig. d'une classe, *etc.*); F chemise: pan *m*; (*usu.* ~s *pl.*) monnaie: pile *f*; page: pied *m*; charrue: manche *f*; voiture: arrière *m*; ✈ empennage *m*; adhérents *m/pl.* (*d'un parti*); F ~s *pl.* habit *m* à queue; fig. ~s up en train; de bonne humeur; ✈ ~ unit empennage *m*; **2.** *v/t.* mettre une queue à; fig. être ou se mettre à la queue de; couper la queue à (*un animal*); enlever les queues de (*les groseilles etc.*); *Am.* F filer (*q.*); *v/i.* suivre de près; ~ off s'espacer; s'allonger; s'éteindre (*voix*); '~-**back** bouchon *m* (de voitures), retenue *f*; '~·**board** layon *m*; '~-'**coat** habit *m* à queue; **tailed** à queue; *zo.* caudifère; '~-'**gate** *mot.* **1.** hayon *m* arrière; **2.** coller (*voiture*); '**tail·less** sans queue; '**tail·light** *mot.* feu *m* arrière *ou* rouge.

tai·lor ['teilə] **1.** tailleur *m*; **2.** *v/t.* faire (*un complet etc.*); habiller (*q.*); *well* ~*ed* bien habillé (*personne*); '~-**made 1.** tailleur (*vêtement*); **2.** (*a.* ~ *suit*) tailleur *m*.

tail...: '~-**piece** *typ.* cul-de-lampe (*pl.* culs-de-lampe) *m*; vignette *f*; '~-**pipe** *mot.* tuyau *m* d'échappement; ~ **plane** ✈ plan *m* fixe; ~ **skid** ✈ béquille *f*; ~ **wind** vent *m* arrière.

taint [teint] **1.** tache *f*; infection *f*, corruption *f*; trace *f*; tare *f* héréditaire; **2.** *v/t.* infecter; (se) corrompre; (se) gâter.

take [teik] **1.** [*irr.*] *v/t.* prendre (*a. livraison, maladie, nourriture, poison, repas, temps; a. bien ou mal*); saisir; s'emparer de; emprunter (à, *from*); conduire, (em)mener (à, *to*); louer (*une maison, une voiture*); faire (*phot., promenade, repas, vœu, voyage, etc.*); produire (*un effet*); tirer (*une épreuve*); passer (*un examen*); tourner (*un film*); acheter régulièrement (*un journal*); franchir (*un obstacle*); profiter de, saisir (*une occasion*); attraper (*un poisson etc.*); remporter (*le prix*); F comprendre, F tenir, prendre (pour, *for*); *the devil* ~ *it!* que le diable l'emporte!; *I* ~ *it that* je suppose que; ~ *air* se faire connaître; se répandre (*nouvelle*); ~ *the air* prendre l'air; ✈ s'envoler, prendre son vol; ~ (*a deep*) *breath* respirer (profondément); ~ *comfort* se consoler; ~ *compassion* avoir compassion *ou* pitié (de, *on*); ~ *counsel* prendre conseil (de, *with*); ~ *a drive* faire une promenade (en auto); ~ *fire* prendre feu; ~ *in hand* entreprendre; ~ *a hedge* franchir une haie; ~ *hold of* s'emparer de, saisir; ~ *an oath* prêter serment; ~ *offence* se froisser (de, *at*); ~ *pity on* prendre pitié de; ~ *place* avoir lieu; se passer; ~ *rest* se donner du repos; ~ *a rest* se reposer; ⚒ faire la pause; ~ *a seat* s'asseoir; ~ *ship* (s')embarquer; ~ *a view of* envisager (*qch.*), avoir une opinion de; ~ *a walk* faire une promenade; ~ *my*

word for it croyez-m'en; ~ *s.o. about* faire visiter (*qch.*) à q.; ~ *down* démonter (*une machine etc.*); descendre (*qch.*); avaler; prendre note de, écrire; ~ *for* prendre pour; ~ *from* prendre, enlever à; ~ *in* faire entrer (*q.*); acheter régulièrement (*un journal*); recevoir (*un locataire etc.*); recueillir (*un réfugié etc.*); accepter (*un travail*); comprendre; F tromper; F rouler; ~ *in sail* diminuer de voile(s); ~ *off* enlever; quitter (*ses vêtements*); emmener (*q.*); rabattre (*sur un prix*); supprimer (*un train*); F imiter, singer; ~ *on* entreprendre; accepter; engager; prendre; ~ *out* sortir (*qch.*); arracher (*une dent*); ôter (*une tache*); faire sortir (*q.*), emmener (*un enfant*) en promenade; retirer (*ses bagages*); contracter (*une assurance*); obtenir (*un brevet*); F ~ *it out of* se venger de (*q.*); épuiser (*q.*); ~ *to pieces* démonter (*une machine*); défaire; *fig.* démolir; ~ *up* relever (*a. un défi*); ramasser; prendre (*les armes*); embrasser (*une carrière*); ✝ honorer (*un effet*), lever (*une prime*); occuper (*une place*); fixer (*sa résidence*); *cost.* raccourcir; 🚗 embarquer; absorber (*de l'eau, le temps*); adopter (*une idée*); faire (*une promenade, un saut, un prisonnier*); ~ *upon o.s.* prendre sur soi(de,*to*);*see consideration; decision; effect* 1; *exercise* 1; *heart; liberty; note* 1; *notice* 1; *rise* 1; **2.** [*irr.*] *v/i.* prendre; réussir; avoir du succès; *phot. he* ~*s well* il est photogénique; il fait un bel effet sur une photographie; ~ *after* tenir de; ressembler à; ~ *from* diminuer (*qch.*); ~ *off* prendre son élan *ou* son essor; ✈ s'envoler; décoller; F ~ *on* laisser éclater son chagrin; avoir du succès *ou* de la vogue; F ~ *on with* s'embaucher chez; ~ *over* prendre le pouvoir; assumer la responsabilité; ~ *to* s'adonner à; prendre goût à; prendre (*la fuite*); prendre (*q.*) en amitié; ~ *to* (*gér.*) se mettre à (*inf.*); ~ *up with* se lier d'amitié avec; s'associer à; *that won't* ~ *with me* ça ne prend pas avec moi; **3.** action *f* de prendre; prise *f*; *cin.* prise *f* de vues.

take...: '~-**a·way 1.** à emporter; **2.** restaurant *m* qui vend des repas à

emporter; '~-'**home pay** gages *m/pl.*
nets; salaire *m* net; '~-'**in** F attrape *f;*
leurre *m;* '**tak·en** *p.p.* de take 1, 2; *be*
~ être pris; *be* ~ *with* être épris de; *be* ~
ill tomber malade; F *be* ~ *in* se laisser
attraper; *be* ~ *up with* être occupé de,
être tout à; '**take**'**off** caricature *f;*
élan *m;* ✈ décollage *m;* '**tak·er**
preneur (-euse *f*) *m; pari:* tenant *m.*

tak·ing ['teikiŋ] **1.** □ F attrayant,
charmant; **2.** prise *f;* † état *m* nerveux; ✝ ~s *pl.* recettes *f/pl.*

talc *min.* [tælk] talc *m.*

tale [teil] conte *m,* récit *m,* histoire *f;*
tell ~s (*out of school*) rapporter; trahir
un secret; '~-**bear·er** ['~-bɛərə] rapporteur (-euse *f*) *m;* mauvaise langue
f.

tal·ent ['tælənt] talent *m;* aptitude *f;*
don *m;* ~ *scout* (*ou spotter*) dénicheur
(-euse *f*) *m* de futures vedettes; '**tal-**
ent·ed doué; de talent.

ta·les ⚖ ['teili:z] *sg.* jurés *m/pl.* sup-
pléants.

tal·is·man ['tælizmən] talisman *m.*

talk [tɔ:k] **1.** conversation *f;* causerie
f; discours *m;* bruit *m;* bavardage *m;*
2. parler (de *of, about*); causer (avec,
to); bavarder; ~ *back* répondre d'une
manière impertinente, répliquer; ~
down faire taire, réduire (*q.*) au silence; ~ *down to* s.o. parler à q. avec
condescence; '**talk·a·tive** □ ['~ətiv]
bavard; causeur (-euse *f*); '**talk·ee-**
talk·ee F ['tɔ:ki'tɔ:ki] pur bavardage
m; † jargon *m* petit-nègre; '**talk·er**
causeur (-euse *f*) *m,* parleur (-euse *f*)
m; **talk·ie** F ['~i] film *m* parlant *ou*
parlé; '**talk·ing** conversation *f;* bavardage *m;* **talk·ing-to** F ['~tu:]
semonce *f.*

tall [tɔ:l] grand, de haute taille;
haut, élevé (*bâtiment etc.*); *sl.* ~
order grosse affaire *f;* demande *f*
exagérée; *sl.* ~ *story,* Am. a. ~ *tale*
histoire *f* dure à avaler; F craque *f;*
'**tall·boy** commode *f;* '**tall·ness**
grandeur *f;* hauteur *f,* grande
taille *f.*

tal·low ['tælou] suif *m;* '**tal·low·y**
suiffeux (-euse *f*); *fig.* terreux
(-euse *f*) (*teint etc.*).

tal·ly ['tæli] **1.** taille *f;* pointage *m*
(de, *of*); étiquette *f* (*plantes etc.*);
contre-partie *f;* **2.** s'accorder (avec,
with).

tal·ly-ho ['tæli'hou] *chasse:* **1.** taïaut!; **2.** taïaut *m;* **3.** crier taïaut.

tal·on *orn.* ['tælən] serre *f;* griffe *f.*

ta·lus[1] ['teiləs] talus *m* (*a. géol.*).

ta·lus[2] *anat.* [~] astragale *m.*

tam·a·ble ['teiməbl] apprivoisable.

tam·a·rind ⚘ ['tæmərind] (fruit *m*
du) tamarinier *m.*

tam·bour ['tæmbuə] **1.** *usu.* tambour *m;* ♪ grosse caisse *f;* **2.** broder
au tambour; **tam·bou·rine** ♪
[~bə'ri:n] tambour *m* de basque;
sans grelots: tambourin *m.*

tame [teim] **1.** □ apprivoisé;
domestique; soumis, dompté (*per-*
sonne); fade, insipide (*style*);
2. apprivoiser; domestiquer; dompter; '**tame·ness** docilité *f,* soumission *f;* fadeur *f;* '**tam·er** dompteur
(-euse *f*) *m;* apprivoiseur (-euse *f*)
m.

Tam·ma·ny Am. ['tæməni] parti *m*
démocrate de New York.

tam-o'-shan·ter [tæmə'ʃæntə] béret *m* écossais.

tamp [tæmp] ⚒ bourrer; ⊕ refouler; damer.

tam·per ['tæmpə]: ~ *with* toucher
à; se mêler à; falsifier (*un registre*);
suborner (*un témoin*); altérer (*un*
document).

tam·pon ⚕ ['tæmpən] tampon *m.*

tan [tæn] **1.** tan *m;* couleur *f* du
tan; (*a. sun* ~) brunissage *m;*
2. tanné; (*a. adj./inv.*); jaune (*sou-*
lier); **3.** *v/t.* tanner; *fig.* bronzer (*le*
teint); rosser (*q.*).

tan·dem ['tændem] tandem *m;* ⚡ ~
connexion accouplement *m* en série;
drive ~ conduire en tandem; *cycl.* se
promener en tandem; *in* ~ en collaboration, en tandem.

tang[1] [tæŋ] soie *f* (*d'un ciseau,*
couteau, etc.); *fig.* goût *m* vif; épice
etc.: montant *m; air marin:* salure *f.*

tang[2] [~] **1.** son *m* aigu; tintement
m; **2.** (faire) retentir; rendre un
son aigu.

tan·gent ⚓ ['tændʒənt] tangente *f;*
go (*ou fly*) *off at a* ~ changer brusquement de sujet, s'échapper par la
tangente; **tan·gen·tial** □ ⚓ [~-
'dʒenʃl] tangentiel(le *f*); de tan-
gence (*point*).

tan·gi·bil·i·ty [tændʒi'biliti] tangi-
bilité *f,* réalité *f;* **tan·gi·ble** □
['tændʒəbl] tangible, palpable; *fig.*
réel(le *f*).

tan·gle ['tæŋgl] **1.** enchevêtrement
m; nœud *m;* *fig.* embarras *m;*

2. (s')embrouiller, emmêler; F ~ *with s.o.* se disputer avec q., avoir une prise de bec avec q.; se colleter avec q.; *be* ~*d with s.th.* se trouver impliqué dans qch.

tan·go ['tæŋgou] tango *m* (*danse*).

tank [tæŋk] 1. réservoir *m* (*a.* ⊕); *phot.* cuve *f*; ✕ char *m* d'assaut; ~ *car* (*ou truck*) camion-citerne (*pl.* camions-citernes) *m*; 🚋 wagon-citerne (*pl.* wagons-citernes) *m*; 2. faire le plein d'essence; *Am. sl.* s'alcooliser; '**tank·age** capacité *f* d'un réservoir.

tank·ard ['tæŋkəd] pot *m* (*surt. de ou à bière*); *en étain:* chope *f*.

tank·er ⚓ ['tæŋkə] pétrolier *m*.

tan·ner¹ ['tænə] tanneur *m*.

tan·ner² *sl.* [~] (pièce *f* de) six pence.

tan·ner·y ['tænəri] tannerie *f*.

tan·nic ac·id 🜍 ['tænik'æsid] acide *m* tannique.

tan·nin 🜍 ['tænin] tan(n)in *m*.

tan·noy (*TM*) *Brit.* ['tænɔi] système *m* de haut-parleurs.

tan·ta·lize ['tæntəlaiz] tourmenter.

tan·ta·mount ['tæntəmaunt] équivalent (à, to).

tan·trum F ['tæntrəm] accès *m* de colère.

tap¹ [tæp] 1. tape *f*, petit coup *m*; 2. taper, toucher, frapper doucement.

tap² [~] 1. *fût:* fausset *m*; *eau:* robinet *m*; F *boisson f*, *usu.* bière *f*; ⊕ taraud *m*; *Brit.* ~ *water* eau *f* du robinet; F *see* ~*room;* *on* ~ en perce; 2. percer; mettre en perce; ⚡ ~ *the wire(s)* faire une prise sur un fil télégraphique; *téléph.* capter un message télégraphique.   [claquettes.)

tap-dance ['tæpdɑːns] danse *f* à)

tape [teip] ruban *m*; *sp.* bande *f* d'arrivée; *tél.* bande *f* du récepteur; *fig.* red ~ bureaucratie *f*, paperasserie *f*; '~-**meas·ure** mètre *m* à ruban; centimètre *m*; '~-**re·cord** enregistrer sur bande; '~-**re·cord·er** magnétophone *m*; '~-**re·cord·ing** enregistrement *m* sur magnétophone.

ta·per [teipə] 1. bougie *f* filée; *eccl.* cierge *m*; ⊕ cône *m*; 2. *adj.* effilé; ⊕ conique; 3. *v/i.* s'effiler; diminuer; ~*ing see* ~ 2; *v/t.* effiler; tailler en pointe.

tap·es·tried ['tæpistrid] tendu de tapisseries; tapissé; '**tap·es·try** tapisserie *f*.

tape·worm ['teipwəːm] ver *m* solitaire.

tap·pet ⊕ ['tæpit] came *f*; taquet *m*.

tap·room ['tæprum] buvette *f*, estaminet *m*.

tap-root 🌿 ['tæpruːt] pivot *m*.

taps *Am.* ✕ [tæps] *pl.* extinction *f* des feux.

tap·ster ['tæpstə] cabaretier *m*; garçon *m* de cabaret.

tar [tɑː] 1. goudron *m*; F *Jack* ⚓ mathurin *m*; 2. goudronner.

ta·ran·tu·la *zo.* [tə'ræntjulə] tarentule *f*.

tar·board ['tɑːbɔːd] carton *m* bitumé.

tar·di·ness ['tɑːdinis] lenteur *f*; *Am.* retard *m*; '**tar·dy** □ lent; peu empressé; tardif (-ive *f*); *Am.* en retard.

tare¹ 🌿 [tɛə] (*usu.* ~*s pl.*) vesce *f*.

tare² ✝ [~] 1. tare *f*; 2. tarer.

tar·get ['tɑːgit] cible *f*; but *m*, objectif *m* (*a. fig.*); *fig.* butte *f*; ~ *date* date *f* limite; ~ *language* langue *f* d'arrivée; ~ *practice* tir *m* à la cible.

tar·iff ['tærif] tarif *m* (*souv.* douanier).

tarn [tɑːn] laquet *m*.

tar·nish ['tɑːniʃ] 1. *v/t.* ⊕ ternir (*a. fig.*); *v/i.* se ternir; se dédorer (*dorure*); 2. ternissure *f*.

tar·pau·lin [tɑː'pɔːlin] ⚓ toile *f* goudronnée; bâche *f*; ⚓ prélart *m*.

tar·ra·gon ['tærəgən] estragon *m*.

tar·ry¹ *poét.* ['tæri] tarder; attendre; rester.   [*f*).\

tar·ry² ['tɑːri] goudronneux (-euse)

tart [tɑːt] 1. □ âpre, aigre; *fig.* mordant; 2. tourte *f*; tarte *f*; *sl.* poule *f* (= *prostituée*).

tar·tan ['tɑːtən] tartan *m*; ⚓ tartane *f*; ~ *plaid* plaid *m* en tartan.

Tar·tar¹ ['tɑːtə] Tartare *m*; *fig.* homme *m* intraitable; *femme:* mégère *f*; *catch a* ~ trouver son maître.

tar·tar² 🜍 [~] tartre *m* (*a. dent.*).

task [tɑːsk] 1. tâche *f*; besogne *f*, ouvrage *m*; *école:* devoir *m*; *take to* ~ réprimander (pour avoir fait, *for having done*); 2. assigner une tâche à; ⚓ mettre à l'épreuve (*les bordages etc.*); ~ **force** ✕ *Am.* détachement *m* spécial des forces de terre, de l'air et de mer; '~-**mas·ter** surveillant *m*; chef *m* de corvée; *fig.* tyran *m*.

tas·sel ['tæsl] **1.** gland *m*, houppe *f*; **2.** garnir de glands *etc.*

taste [teist] **1.** goût *m* (de *of, for*; pour, *for*); *fig. a.* prédilection *f* (pour, *for*); to ~ à volonté, selon son goût; *season to* ~ goûtez et rectifiez l'assaisonnement; **2.** *v/t.* goûter (*a. fig.*); déguster; *v/i.* sentir (qch., *of* s.th.); **3.** avoir un goût (de, *of*); **taste·ful** □ ['~ful] de bon goût; élégant; de goût (*personne*).

taste·less □ ['teistlis] sans goût, insipide, fade; **'taste·less·ness** insipidité *f*; manque *m* de goût.

tas·ter ['teistə] dégustateur (-trice *f*) *m* (de *thé, vins, etc.*).

tast·y □ F ['teisti] savoureux (-euse *f*).

tat[1] [tæt] *see* tit[1].

tat[2] [~] *couture*: faire de la frivolité.

ta-ta ['tæ'tɑ:] *enf., a. co.* au revoir!

tat·ter ['tætə] lambeau *m*, loque *f*; **tat·ter·de·mal·ion** [~də'meiljən] loqueteux (-euse *f*) *m*; **tat·tered** ['~əd] en lambeaux; déguenillé (*personne*).

tat·tle ['tætl] **1.** bavarder, babiller; *péj.* cancaner; **2.** bavardage *m*; *péj.* cancans *m/pl.*; **'tat·tler** bavard(e*f*) *m*; *péj.* cancanier (-ère *f*) *m*.

tat·too[1] [tə'tu:] **1.** ✕ retraite *f* du soir; *fig. beat the devil's* ~ tambouriner (*sur la table*); **2.** *fig.* tambouriner.

tat·too[2] [~] **1.** *v/t.* tatouer; **2.** tatouage *m*.

tat·ty F ['tæti] défraîchi, miteux (-euse *f*).

taught [tɔ:t] *prét. et p.p. de* teach.

taunt [tɔ:nt] **1.** reproche *m*; brocard *m*; sarcasme *m*; **2.** accabler de sarcasmes; reprocher (qch. à q., *s.o. with* s.th.); **'taunt·ing** □ de sarcasme, sarcastique.

Tau·rus *astr.* ['tɔ:rəs] le Taureau.

taut ⚓ [tɔ:t] raide, tendu; étarque (*voile*); **'taut·en** (se) raidir; (s')étarquer (*voile*).

tav·ern ['tævən] taverne *f*, cabaret *m*.

taw[1] ⊕ [tɔ:] mégir.

taw[2] [~] grosse bille *f* de verre.

taw·dri·ness ['tɔ:drinis] clinquant *m*, faux brillant *m*; **'taw·dry** □ d'un mauvais goût; voyant.

taw·ny ['tɔ:ni] fauve; basané (*teint*).

tax [tæks] **1.** impôt *m* (sur, *on*), contribution *f*; droit *m*, taxe *f* (sur, *on*); *fig.* charge *f* (à, *on*), fardeau *m*; ~ allowances *pl.* sommes *f/pl.* déductibles; ~ *bracket* catégorie *f* d'imposition; ~ *dodger*, ~ *evader* fraudeur (-euse*f*) *m* fiscal(e); ~ *evasion* fraude *f* fiscale; ~ *haven* refuge *m* fiscal; ~ *relief* allègement *m* fiscal; ~ *return* déclaration *f* d'impôts; **2.** taxer; frapper d'un impôt; *fig.* mettre à l'épreuve; ✝ taxer (*les dépens, q. de* qch., *a. fig.*); reprocher (qch. à q., *s.o. with* s.th.); ~ *s.o. with* s.th. *a.* accuser q. de qch.; **'tax·a·ble** □ imposable; **tax·a·tion** imposition *f*; prélèvement *m* fiscal; impôts *m/pl.*; *surt.* ✝ taxation *f*; **'tax col·lec·tor** percepteur *m* des contributions (*directes*); receveur *m*; **'tax-de·duct·i·ble** déductible (de l'impôt); **'tax-'free** exempt d'impôts.

tax·i ['tæksi] **1.** (*ou* ~-*cab*) taxi *m*; **2.** aller en taxi; ✈ rouler sur le sol; hydroplaner; **'~-danc·er**, **'~-girl** *Am.* entraîneuse*f*; **'~-driv·er** chauffeur *m* de taxi; **'~-me·ter** taximètre *m*; **'~-rank**, **'~-stand** station *f* de taxis.

tax·pay·er ['tækspeiə] contribuable *mf*.

tea [ti:] thé *m*; goûter *m*, five-o'clock *m*; *high* (*ou* *meat*) ~ repas *m* à la fourchette; **'~-bag** sachet *m* de thé; ~ *break* pause-thé *f* (*pl.* pauses-thé); **'~-cad·dy** *see* caddy.

teach [ti:tʃ] [*irr.*] enseigner; apprendre (qch. à q., *s.o.* s.th.; à *inf.*, to *inf.*); **'teach·a·ble** □ enseignable; à l'intelligence ouverte (*personne*); **'teach·er** instituteur (-trice *f*) *m*; maître(sse *f*) *m*; professeur *mf*; **'teach·er-'train·ing col·lege** école *f* normale; **'teach·ing** *école*: enseignement *m*; *phls. etc.* doctrine *f*.

tea...: **'~-co·sy** couvre-théière *m*; **'~-cup** tasse *f* à thé; *fig. storm in a* ~ tempête *f* dans un verre d'eau; **'~-gown** déshabillé *m*, robe *f* d'intérieur.

teak ♣ [ti:k] (bois *m* de) te(c)k *m*.

team [ti:m] attelage *m*; *surt. sp.* équipe *f*; *by a* ~ effort tous ensemble; **'~-spir·it** esprit *m* d'équipe; **team·ster** ['~stə] conducteur *m* (d'*attelage*); charretier *m*; **'team-work** ⊕, *sp.* travail *m* d'équipe, jeu *m* d'ensemble; *fig.* collaboration *f*.

tea·pot ['ti:pɔt] théière *f*.

tear[1] [tɛə] **1.** [*irr.*] *v/t.* déchirer; arracher (*les cheveux*); *v/i.* se déchirer; F *avec adv. ou prp.* aller *etc.* à toute vitesse; **2.** déchirure *f*; *see wear2.*

tear² [tiə] larme *f*; '~·**drop** larme *f*.

tear·ful □ ['tiəful] larmoyant, en pleurs.

tear-gas ['tiə'gæs] gaz *m* lacrymogène.

tear·ing ['tɛəriŋ] *fig.* rapide; déchirant.

tear·jerk·er F ['tiədʒə:kə] film *ou* histoire *etc.* larmoyant(e).

tear·less □ ['tiəlis] sans larmes, sec (*œil*).

tear-off cal·en·dar ['tɛərɔf 'kælində] éphéméride *f*.

tease [ti:z] **1.** démêler (*de la laine*); carder (*la laine etc.*); effil(och)er (*un tissu*); *fig.* taquiner; **2.** F taquin(e *f*) *m*; **tea·sel** ['~l] ♀ cardère *f*; ⊕ carde *f*; '**teas·er** F *fig.* colle *f* (= *problème difficile*).

teat [ti:t] bout *m* de sein; mamelon *m*; *vache*: tette *f*; *biberon*: tétine *f*; ⊕ *vis*: téton *m*.

tea... '~·**things** *pl.* F service *m* à thé; '~·**time** l'heure *f* du thé; ~ **tow·el** *Brit.* torchon *m* à vaisselle; ~ **tray** plateau *m* (à thé); ~ **trol·ley**, ~ **wag·on** table *f* roulante; ~ **urn** fontaine *f* à thé.

tech·nic ['teknik] (*a.* ~s *pl. ou sg.*) *see* technique; '**tech·ni·cal** □ technique; ✕ spécial (-aux *m/pl.*); 🏛 de procédure; professionnel(le *f*); ~ *hitch* incident *m* technique; **tech·ni·cal·i·ty** [~'kæliti] détail *m ou* terme *m* technique; considération *f* d'ordre technique; **tech·ni·cian** [tek'niʃn] technicien *m*.

tech·ni·col·or ['teknikʌlə] **1.** en couleurs; **2.** film *m* en couleurs; *cin.* technicolor *m*.

tech·nique [tek'ni:k] technique *f*; mécanique *f*.

tech·nol·o·gy [tek'nɔlədʒi] technologie *f*; *school of* ~ école *f* de technologie, école *f* technique.

tech·y ['tetʃi] *see* testy.

ted·der ['tedə] faneuse *f*; *personne*: faneur (-euse *f*) *m*.

te·di·ous □ ['ti:djəs] ennuyeux (-euse *f*); fatigant; assommant; '**te·di·ous·ness** ennui *m*; manque *m* d'intérêt.

te·di·um ['ti:diəm] ennui *m*.

tee [ti:] **1.** *sp.* curling: but *m*; golf:

dé *m*, tee *m*; **2.**: ~ *off* jouer sa balle; placer la balle sur le dé.

teem [ti:m] (*with*) abonder (en), fourmiller (de).

teen-ag·er ['ti:neidʒə] adolescent(e *f*) *m* (*entre 13 et 19 ans*).

teens [ti:nz] *pl.* années *f/pl.* entre 13 et 19 ans; adolescence *f*; *in one's* ~ n'ayant pas encore vingt ans.

teen·(s)y [ti:n(z)i], **teen·(s)y-ween-(s)y** ['ti:n(z)i'wi:n(z)i] tout petit, minuscule.   [celer.)

tee·ter F ['ti:tə] se balancer; chan-)

teeth [ti:θ] *pl. de* tooth.

teethe [ti:ð] faire ses dents; **teeth-ing** ['~iŋ] dentition *f*.

tee·to·tal [ti:'toutl] antialcoolique; qui ne prend pas de boissons alcooliques; **tee·to·tal·(l)er** néphaliste *mf*; abstinent(e *f*) *m*.

tee·to·tum ['ti:tou'tʌm] toton *m*.

tel·e·com·mu·ni·ca·tions ['telikəmju:ni'keiʃənz] *pl.* télécommunication *f*.

tel·e·course *Am.* ['telikɔ:s] cours *m* (de leçons) télévisé.

tel·e·gram ['teligræm] télégramme *m*, dépêche *f*.

tel·e·graph ['teligrɑ:f] **1.** télégraphe *m*; ⚓ transmetteur *m* d'ordres; **2.** télégraphique; de télégramme; **3.** télégraphier, envoyer un télégramme; **tel·e·graph·ic** [~'græfik] (~ally) télégraphique (*a. style*); **te·leg·ra·phist** [ti'legrəfist] télégraphiste *mf*; **te·leg·ra·phy** télégraphie *f*.

tel·e·phone ['telifoun] **1.** téléphone *m*; ~ *book* (*ou directory*) annuaire *m* (des téléphones); ~ *booth* (*ou box*) cabine *f* téléphonique; ~ *call* appel *m* téléphonique, F coup de fil; ~ *charges pl.* taxe *f* téléphonique; ~ *kiosk* cabine *f* téléphonique; ~ *line* ligne *f* téléphonique; ~ *number* numéro *m* de téléphone; ~ *subcriber* abonné(e *f*) *m* au téléphone; *at the* ~ au téléphone; *by* ~ par téléphone; *on the* ~ téléphoniquement; par téléphone; *be on the* ~ avoir le téléphone; être à l'appareil; **2.** téléphoner (à q., [*to*] s.o.); **tel·e·phon·ic** [~'fɔnik] (~ally) téléphonique; **te·leph·o·nist** [ti'lefənist] téléphoniste *mf*; standardiste *mf*; **te·leph·o·ny** téléphonie *f*.

tel·e·pho·to *phot.* ['teli'foutou] téléphotographie *f*; ~ *lens* téléobjectif *m*.

tel·e·print·er ['teliprintə] téléscripteur *m*.

tel·e·scope ['teliskoup] 1. *opt.* télescope *m*; lunette *f*; 2. (se) télescoper; **tel·e·scop·ic** [~'kɔpik] télescopique; à coulisse (*échelle etc.*); *phot.* ~ lens téléobjectif *m*; ~ sight lunette *f* de visée.

tel·e·type ['teli'taip] télétype *m*; *postes*: télex *m*.

tel·e·view·er ['telivju:ə] téléspectateur (-trice *f*) *m*.

tel·e·vise ['telivaiz] téléviser; **tel·e·vi·sion** ['~viʒn] télévision *f*; ~ set appareil *m* de télévision; ~ channel chaîne *f* de télévision.

tel·ex ['teleks] 1. télex *m*; 2. envoyer (*un message*) par télex.

tell [tel] [*irr.*] *v/t.* dire; raconter; apprendre; exprimer; savoir; reconnaître (à, *by*); compter; annoncer; ~ s.o. to do s.th. dire *ou* ordonner à q. de faire qch.; *I have been told that* on m'a dit que; j'ai appris que; *fig.* ~ a story en dire long; ~ off désigner (pour qch., *for* s.th.); F dire son fait à (*q.*); rembarrer (*q.*); *Am. sl.* ~ *the world* faire savoir partout; publier à son de trompe; produire son effet; porter; ~ *of (ou about)* annoncer, révéler, accuser; ~ *on* se faire sentir à, influer sur; peser sur; *sl.* cafarder; dénoncer (*q.*); '**tell·er** raconteur (-euse *f*) *m*; *parl. etc.* scrutateur *m*; *banque*: caissier *m*; '**tell·ing** □ efficace; impressionnant; qui porte; '**tell·ing-off**: F *give s.o. a* ~ gronder q., passer un savon à q.; '**tell·tale** ['~teil] 1. indicateur (-trice *f*); révélateur (-trice *f*); *fig.* qui en dit long; 2. rapporteur (-euse *f*) *m*; *école*: cafard(e *f*) *m*; ⊕ indicateur *m*; ~ clock horloge *f* enregistreuse.

tel·pher ['telfə] ⊕ de téléphérage; ~ line téléphérique *m*; ligne *f* de téléphérage.

te·mer·i·ty [ti'meriti] témérité *f*, audace *f*.

temp F [temp] intérimaire *mf*.

tem·per ['tempə] 1. tempérer; modérer; *fig.* retenir; ♪ accorder par tempérament; broyer (*les couleurs, le mortier, l'encre, etc.*); donner la trempe à (*l'acier*); adoucir (*le métal*); 2. ⊕ trempe *f*; *métall.* coefficient *m* de dureté; humeur *f*; colère *f*; caractère *m*, tempérament *m*; *lose one's* ~ se mettre en colère; perdre son sang-froid; s'emporter; **tem·**

per·a·ment ['~rəmənt] tempérament *m* (*a.* ♪); humeur *f*; **tem·per·a·men·tal** □ [~'mentl] du tempérament; capricieux (-euse *f*) (*personne*); '**tem·per·ance** 1. tempérance *f*, modération *f*; antialcoolisme *m*; 2. antialcoolique (*hôtel*); '**tem·per·ate** □ ['~rit] tempéré (*climat, a.* ♪); sobre (*personne*); modéré; **tem·per·a·ture** ['tempritʃə] température *f*; ~ *chart* feuille *f* de température; **tem·pered** ['tempəd]: *bad-*~ de mauvaise humeur.

tem·pest ['tempist] tempête *f*, tourmente *f*; **tem·pes·tu·ous** □ [~'pestjuəs] de tempête; fougueux (-euse *f*), turbulent (*personne*); orageux (-euse *f*) (*réunion etc.*).

Tem·plar ['templə] *hist.* templier *m*; *univ.* étudiant(e *f*) *m* en droit du *Temple* (*à Londres*).

tem·ple¹ ['templ] temple *m*; ⌾ *deux écoles de droit* (= *Inns of Court*) à *Londres*.

tem·ple² *anat.* [~] tempe *f*.

tem·po·ral □ ['tempərəl] temporel (-le *f*); **tem·po·ral·i·ties** [~'rælitiz] *pl.* possessions *f*/*pl.* *ou* revenus *m*/*pl.* ecclésiastiques; **tem·po·rar·i·ness** ['~pərərinis] caractère *m* temporaire *ou* provisoire; '**tem·po·rar·y** □ temporaire, provisoire; momentané; passager (-ère *f*); ~ *bridge* pont *m* provisoire; ~ *work* situation *f* intérimaire; '**tem·po·rize** temporiser; ~ *with* transiger provisoirement avec (*q.*).

tempt [tempt] tenter; induire (q. à *inf.*, *s.o. to inf.*); **temp·ta·tion** tentation *f*; '**tempt·er** tentateur *m*; '**tempt·ing** □ tentant; séduisant, attrayant; '**tempt·ress** tentatrice *f*.

ten [ten] dix (*a. su./m*).

ten·a·ble ['tenəbl] tenable; *fig.* soutenable.

te·na·cious □ [ti'neiʃəs] tenace; attaché (à, *of*); obstiné, opiniâtre; **te·nac·i·ty** [ti'næsiti] ténacité *f*; sûreté *f* (*de la mémoire*); attachement *m* (à, *of*); obstination *f*.

ten·an·cy ['tenənsi] location *f*.

ten·ant ['tenənt] 1. locataire *mf*; *fig.* habitant(e *f*) *m*; pensionnaire *mf*; ~ *right* droits *m*/*pl.* du tenancier; 2. habiter comme locataire; occuper; '**ten·ant·ry** locataires *m*/*pl.*; fermiers *m*/*pl.*

terminal

tench *icht.* [tenʃ] tanche *f.*

tend¹ [tend] **1.** tendre, se diriger (vers, *towards*); tourner; *fig.* pencher (vers, *towards*), tirer (sur, *to*); tendre (à, *to*); être susceptible (de *inf.*, to *inf.*); être enclin (à, *to*); ~ *from* s'écarter de.

tend² [~] soigner (*un malade*); garder (*les bêtes*); surveiller (*une machine etc.*); *Am.* tenir (*une boutique*); '**tend·ance** † soin *m*; serviteurs *m/pl.*

tend·en·cy ['tendənsi] tendance *f*, disposition *f*, penchant *m* (à, *to*); **ten·den·tious** [~'denʃəs] tendanciel(le *f*), tendancieux (-euse *f*); à tendance (*livre*).

ten·der¹ □ ['tendə] *usu.* tendre; sensible (*au toucher*); délicat (*sujet*); affectueux (-euse *f*) (*lettre*); jeune; soigneux (-euse *f*) (de, *of*); *of* ~ *years* en bas âge.

ten·der² [~] **1.** offre *f* (*de paiement etc.*); *contrat*: soumission *f*; *legal* ~ cours *m* légal; **2.** offrir; ✝ soumissionner ([pour], *for*); présenter.

ten·der³ [~] gardien *m*; 🚂, ⚓ tender *m*; ⚓ bateau *m* annexe; *bar-*~ garçon *m* de comptoir.

ten·der·foot *Am.* F ['tendəfut] nouveau débarqué *m*; cow-boy *m* d'opérette; **ten·der·ize** attendrir (*viande*); **ten·der·loin** [ˈ~lɔin] *surt. Am.* filet *m*; *Am.* quartier *m* malfamé; '**ten·der·ness** tendresse *f*; sensibilité *f*; *fig.* douceur *f*; *cuis.* tendreté *f.*

ten·don *anat.* ['tendən] tendon *m.*

ten·dril ⊕ ['tendril] vrille *f.*

ten·e·ment ['tenimənt] † habitation *f*; appartement *m*; ⚖️ fonds *m* de terre; tenure *f*; ~ *house* maison *f* de rapport.

ten·et ['tiːnet] doctrine *f*, principe *m.*

ten·fold ['tenfould] **1.** *adj.* décuple; **2.** *adv.* dix fois (autant).

ten·nis ['tenis] tennis *m*; '~-**court** terrain *m* de tennis, court *m.*

ten·on ⊕ ['tenən] tenon *m*; '~-**saw** ⊕ scie *f* à tenon.

ten·or ['tenə] cours *m*, progrès *m*; teneur *f*; sens *m* général; ♪ ténor *m.*

tense¹ *gramm.* [tens] temps *m.*

tense² □ [~] tendu (*a. fig.*); raide; '**tense·ness** tension *f* (*a. fig.*); **ten·sile** ['tensail] extensible; de tension, de traction; ~ *strength* résistance *f* à la tension; **ten·sion** [ˈ~ʃn] tension *f*; ⚡ *high* ~ circuit *m* de haute tension; ~ *test* essai *m* de traction.

tent¹ [tent] tente *f.*

tent² ⚕ [~] mèche *f.*

ten·ta·cle *zo.* ['tentəkl] tentacule *m*; cir(r)e *m.*

ten·ta·tive ['tentətiv] **1.** □ expérimental (-aux *m/pl.*); sujet(te *f*) à révision; hésitant; ~*ly* à titre d'essai; **2.** tentative *f*, essai *m.*

ten·ter *tex.* ['tentə] élargisseur *m*; '~·**hook** crochet *m*; *fig.* be *on* ~*s* être sur des charbons ardents.

tenth [tenθ] **1.** dixième; **2.** dixième *m*, ♪ *f*; *eccl.* dîme *f*; '**tenth·ly** en dixième lieu.

tent-peg ['tentpeg] piquet *m* de tente.

ten·u·i·ty [te'njuiti] *usu.* ténuité *f*; finesse *f*; faiblesse *f*; **ten·u·ous** □ ['tenjuəs] ténu; effilé; mince; grêle (*voix*); raréfié (*gaz*).

ten·ure ['tenjuə] tenure *f*; (période *f* de) jouissance *f*; *office etc.*: occupation *f.*

tep·id □ ['tepid] tiède; dégourdi (*eau*); **te'pid·i·ty**, '**tep·id·ness** tiédeur *f.*

ter·cen·te·nar·y [təːsen'tiːnəri], **ter·cen·ten·ni·al** [~'tenjəl] tricentenaire (*a. su./m*).

ter·gi·ver·sa·tion [təːdʒivəˈseiʃn] tergiversation *f.*

term [təːm] **1.** temps *m*, durée *f*, limite *f*; terme *m* (*a.* ⚖️, *phls.*, *ling.*); *ling. a.* mot *m*, expression *f*; ⚖️ session *f*; *univ.*, *école*: trimestre *m*; ✝ échéance *f*; délai *m* (*de congé, du droit d'auteur, de paiement, etc.*); *beginning of* ~ rentrée *f*; ~*s pl.* conditions *f/pl.*, termes *m/pl.*; prix *m/pl.*; relations *f/pl.*, rapports *m/pl.*; ⚖️ énoncé *m* (*d'un problème*); *in* ~*s of* en fonction de; *be on good* (*bad*) ~*s* être bien (mal) (avec, *with*); *come to* (*ou make*) ~*s with* s'arranger, prendre un arrangement avec; ✂ partiser; **2.** appeler, nommer; qualifier (de *qch.*, *s.th.*).

ter·ma·gant ['təːməgənt] **1.** □ revêche, acariâtre; **2.** mégère *f*; dragon *m* (= *femme*).

ter·mi·na·ble □ ['təːminəbl] terminable; résiliable (*contrat*); '**ter·mi·nal 1.** □ extrême; dernier (-ère *f*); final; *école*: trimestriel(le *f*); terminal (-aux *m/pl.*); ~*ly* par trimestre;

2. bout *m*; borne *f*; *gramm.* terminaison *f*; Am. terminus *m*; *ordinateur:* terminal *m*; **ter·mi·nate** ['⌣neit] (se) terminer; finir; **ter·mi·na·tion** fin *f*, conclusion *f*; terminaison *f* (*a. gramm.*); extinction *f*.

ter·mi·nol·o·gy [tə:mi'nɔlədʒi] terminologie *f*.

ter·mi·nus ['tə:minəs], *pl.* **-ni** [⌣nai] terminus *m*, tête *f* de ligne (*a.*).

ter·mite *zo.* ['tə:mait] termite *m*.

tern *orn.* [tə:n] sterne *f*, hirondelle *f* de mer.

ter·na·ry ['tə:nəri] ternaire.

ter·race ['terəs] terrasse *f*; rangée *f* de maisons; **'ter·raced** en terrasse; en rangée (*maisons*).

ter·rain ['terein] terrain *m*.

ter·rene □ [te'ri:n] terreux (-euse *f*); terrestre. [tre.]

ter·res·tri·al □ [ti'restriəl] terres-]

ter·ri·ble □ ['terəbl] terrible; affreux (-euse *f*); **'ter·ri·ble·ness** horreur *f*.

ter·ri·er *zo.* ['teriə] terrier *m*.

ter·rif·ic [tə'rifik] (⌣*ally*) épouvantable; terrible; colossal (-aux *m/pl.*); **ter·ri·fy** ['terifai] *v/t.* épouvanter, terrifier.

ter·ri·to·ri·al [teri'tɔ:riəl] **1.** □ territorial (-aux *m/pl.*); terrien(ne *f*), foncier (-ère *f*); ⌣ waters eaux *f/pl.* territoriales; ♀ Army (*ou* F Force) territoriale *f*; **2.** territorial *m*; **ter·ri·to·ry** ['⌣təri] territoire *m*; *Am.* ♀ territoire *m* des É.-U.

ter·ror ['terə] terreur *f* (*a. fig.*), effroi *m*, épouvante *f*; **'ter·ror·ism** terrorisme *m*; **'ter·ror·ist** terroriste *mf*; **'ter·ror·ize** terroriser.

ter·ry·(·cloth) ['teri(klɔθ)] tissu *m* éponge.

terse □ [tə:s] concis; net(te *f*); **'terse·ness** concision *f*.

ter·tian ['tə:ʃn] (fièvre *f*) tierce; **ter·ti·ar·y** ['⌣ʃəri] tertiaire.

tes·sel·lat·ed ['tesileitid] en mosaïque (*pavé*).

test [test] **1.** épreuve *f*, essai *m* (*a.*); *psych.*, ⊕ test *m*; réactif *m* (de, *for*); examen *m*; *fig.* épreuve *f*, critérium *m*; *put to the* ⌣ mettre à l'épreuve *ou* l'essai; **2.** *v/t.* éprouver, mettre à l'épreuve; examiner; essayer; *v/i.* faire la réaction (de, *for*).

tes·ta·ceous *zo.* [tes'teiʃəs] testacé.

tes·ta·ment *bibl.*, †, ['testəmənt] testament *m*; **tes·ta·men·ta·ry** [⌣'mentəri] testamentaire.

tes·ta·tor [tes'teitə] testateur *m*.

tes·ta·trix [tes'teitriks] testatrice *f*.

test...: ⌣ **ban** (**treat·y**) (traité *m* d')interdiction *f* d'essais nucléaires; ⌣ **case** cas *m* qui fait jurisprudence, précédent *m*; ⌣ **drive** *mot.* essai sur *ou* de route; '⌣**drive** faire un essai de route à (*une voiture*).

test·er ['testə] essayeur (-euse *f*) *m*; vérificateur (-trice *f*) *m*; *outil:* vérificateur *m*.

tes·ti·cle *anat.* ['testikl] testicule *m*.

tes·ti·fi·er ['testifaiə] témoin *m* (de, *to*); **tes·ti·fy** ['⌣fai] *v/t.* témoigner (*a. fig.*); déposer; *v/i.* attester (qch., *to s.th.*), témoigner (de, *to*).

tes·ti·mo·ni·al [testi'mounjəl] certificat *m*, attestation *f*; recommandation *f*; témoignage *m* d'estime; **tes·ti·mo·ny** ['⌣məni] témoignage *m* (de, *to*); *témoin:* déposition *f*.

tes·ti·ness ['testinis] irritabilité *f*.

test...: '⌣**pa·per** papier *m* réactif; *école:* composition *f*, épreuve *f*; '⌣**pi·lot** pilote *m* d'essai; '⌣**print** *phot.* épreuve *f* témoin; ⌣ **run** course *f* d'essai; essai *m* (de bon fonctionnement); '⌣**tube** éprouvette *f*; ⌣ *baby* bébé-éprouvette *m* (*pl.* bébés-éprouvettes).

tes·ty □ ['testi], **tetch·y** □ ['tetʃi] irascible, irritable; bilieux (-euse *f*).

teth·er ['teðə] **1.** attache *f*, longe *f*; *fig.* ressources *f/pl.*; **2.** mettre au piquet, attacher.

tet·ra·gon ['tetrəgən] quadrilatère *m*; **te·trag·o·nal** [⌣'trægənl] tétragone.

tet·ter ['tetə] dartre *f*.

Teu·ton ['tju:tən] Teuton(ne *f*) *m*; **Teu·ton·ic** [⌣'tɔnik] teuton(ne *f*), teutonique; ⌣ *Order* l'ordre *m* Teutonique.

text [tekst] texte *m*; *fig.* sujet *m*; *typ.* ⌣ *hand* grosse (écriture) *f*; '⌣**book** manuel *m*, livre *m* de classe.

tex·tile ['tekstail] **1.** textile; **2.** ⌣*s pl.* tissus *m/pl.*; textiles *m/pl.*

tex·tu·al □ ['tekstjuəl] textuel(le *f*).

tex·ture ['tekstʃə] texture *f* (*a. fig.*); tissu *m*; *bois*, *peau:* grain *m*.

tha·lid·o·mide [θə'lidəmaid] thalidomide *f*; ⌣ *baby*, ⌣ *child* (bébé *m*) victime *f* de la thalidomide.

than [ðæn; ðən] *après comp.* que; *devant nombres:* de.

thank [θæŋk] **1.** remercier (de *inf.*, for *gér.*); ~ you merci; I will ~ you for je vous saurais bien gré de (*me donner etc.*); *iro.* ~ you for nothing merci de rien; **2.** ~s *pl.* remerciements *m/pl.*; ~s to grâce à; **thank·ful** □ ['~ful] reconnaissant; **'thank·less** □ ingrat; **thanks·giv·ing** [~s'giviŋ] action *f* de grâce(s); *surt. Am.* ♀ (*Day*) le jour *m* d'action de grâces (*le dernier jeudi de novembre*); **'thank·wor·thy** † digne de reconnaissance.

that [ðæt] **1.** *cj.* [*usu.* ðət] que; **2.** *pron. dém.* (*pl.* those) celui-là (*pl.* ceux-là), celle-là (*pl.* celles-là); celui (*pl.* ceux), celle (*pl.* celles); cela, F ça; ce; so ~'s ~! et voilà!; and ... at ~ et encore ..., et ... par-dessus le marché; with ~ là-dessus; **3.** *pron. rel.* [a. ðət] qui, que; lequel, laquelle, lesquels, lesquelles; **4.** *adj.* ce (cet *devant une voyelle ou un h muet*; *pl.* ces), cette (*pl.* ces); ce (cet, cette, *pl.* ces) ...-là; **5.** *adv.* F (aus)si, ~ far si loin.

thatch [θætʃ] **1.** chaume *m*; **2.** couvrir de chaume.

thaw [θɔ:] **1.** dégel *m*; **2.** *v/i.* fondre (*neige etc.*); *v/t.* décongeler (*de la viande*); *mot.* dégeler (*le radiateur*).

the [ði:; *devant une voyelle* ði, *devant une consonne* ðə] **1.** *art.* le, la, les; **2.** *adv.* ~ richer he is ~ more arrogant he seems plus il est riche, plus il semble arrogant.

the·a·tre, *Am.* **the·a·ter** ['θiətə] théâtre *m* (*a. fig.*); **the·at·ric, the·at·ri·cal** □ [θi'ætrik(l)] théâtral (-aux *m/pl.*) (*a. fig.*); spectaculaire; d'acteur(s); **the'at·ri·cals** [~klz] *pl.* (*usu. amateur* ~) spectacle *m* d'amateurs, comédie *f* de société.

thee *bibl., poét.* [ði:] *accusatif:* te; *datif:* toi.

theft [θeft] vol *m*.

their [ðɛə] leur, leurs; **theirs** [~z] le (la) leur, les leurs; à eux, à elles.

the·ism ['θi:izm] théisme *m*.

them [ðem; ðəm] *accusatif:* les; *datif:* leur; à eux, à elles.

theme [θi:m] thème *m* (*a. ♪, a. gramm.*); sujet *m*; *gramm.* radical (-aux *pl.*) *m*; *école:* dissertation *f*, *Am.* thème *m*; ~ **song** leitmotiv (*pl.* -ve) *m*.

them·selves [ðəm'selvz] eux-mêmes, elles-mêmes; *réfléchi:* se.

then [ðen] **1.** *adv.* alors; en ce temps-là; puis; ensuite; aussi; d'ailleurs; every now and ~ de temps en temps; de temps à autre; there and ~ sur-le-champ; now ~ allons, voyons; **2.** *cj.* donc, alors, en ce cas; **3.** *adj.* de ce temps-là, d'alors.

thence *poét.* [ðens] par conséquent; *temps:* dès lors; '~forth *poét.* depuis ce temps-là; dès lors, à partir de ce jour.

the·oc·ra·cy [θi'ɔkrəsi] théocratie *f*; **the·o·crat·ic** [θio'krætik] (~ally) théocratique.

the·o·lo·gi·an [θiə'loudʒjən] théologien *m*; **the·o·log·i·cal** [~'lɔdʒikl] théologique; **the·ol·o·gy** [θi'ɔlədʒi] théologie *f*.

the·o·rem ['θiərəm] théorème *m*; **the·o·ret·ic, the·o·ret·i·cal** □ [~'retik(l)] théorique; **'the·o·rist** théoricien(ne *f*) *m*; théoriste *mf*; **'the·o·rize** théoriser; **'the·o·ry** théorie *f*.

the·os·o·phy [θi'ɔsəfi] théosophie *f*.

ther·a·peu·tics [θerə'pju:tiks] *usu. sg.* thérapeutique *f*; **'ther·a·py** thérapie *f*; *see occupational*; **'ther·a·pist** thérapeute *mf*; mental~ psycho-thérapeute *m*.

there [ðɛə] **1.** *adv.* là; y; là-bas; F ce, cette, ces, cettes ...-là; the man ~ cet homme-là; ~ is, ~ are il y a; ~'s a good fellow! vous serez bien gentil!; ~ you are! vous voilà!; ça y est!; **2.** *int.* voilà!

there...: '~a·bout(s) près de là, par là; à peu près; ~'aft·er après cela, ensuite; '~'by par là, de cette façon; '~fore donc, par conséquent; aussi (*avec inversion*); ~'in là-dedans; à cet égard, en cela; ~'of en; de cela; '~up'on là-dessus; ~'with avec cela.

ther·mal □ ['θə:məl] thermal (-aux *m/pl.*); *phys. a.* thermique, calorifique; ~ value pouvoir *m* calorifique; **ther·mic** ['~mik] (~ally) thermique; **therm·i·on·ic** [~mi'ɔnik]: ~ valve *radio:* lampe *f* thermoïonique.

ther·mo·e·lec·tric cou·ple *phys.* ['θə:moi'lektrik 'kʌpl] élément *m* thermo-électrique; **ther·mom·e·ter** [θə'mɔmitə] thermomètre *m*; **ther·mo·met·ric, ther·mo·met·ri·cal** □ [θə:mə'metrik(l)] thermométrique; **ther·mo·nu·cle·ar** *phys.* ['·'nju:kliə] thermonucléaire; **ther·mo·pile** *phys.* ['·mopail] thermopile *f*; **Ther·mos** ['·mɔs] (*ou* ~ *flask*, ~ *bottle*) bouteille *f* Thermos; **ther·mo·stat** ['·mostæt] thermostat *m*.

the·sau·rus [θiˈsɔ:rəs], *pl.* -**ri** [~rai] thésaurus *m*; trésor *m*.

these [ði:z] *pl. de this* 1, 2; ~ *three years* depuis trois ans; *in* ~ *days* à notre époque.

the·sis ['θi:sis], *pl.* -**ses** [~si:z] thèse *f*, dissertation *f*.

they [ðei] ils, *accentué*: eux; elles (*a. accentué*); *a.* on; ~ *who* ceux *ou* celles qui.

thick [θik] 1. □ *usu.* épais(se *f*) (*brouillard, liquide, etc.*); dense (*brouillard, foule*); abondant, dru (*cheveux*); trouble (*eau, vin*); crème (*potage*); empâté (*voix*); serré (*foule*); profond (*ténèbres*); F (*souv. as* ~ *as thieves*) très lié, intime; ~ *with* très lié avec; *sl. that's a bit* ~! ça c'est un peu fort!; 2. partie *f* épaisse; gras *m*; fort *m*; *in the* ~ *of* au plus fort de; au beau milieu de; '**thick·en** *v/t.* épaissir; *cuis.* lier; *v/i.* s'épaissir; se lier; se compliquer; s'échauffer; **thick·et** ['~it] fourré *m*, bosquet *m*; '**thick-'head·ed** lourdaud; obtus; '**thick·ness** épaisseur *f* (*a.* ⊕); grosseur *f*; abondance *f*; état *m* trouble; empâtement *m*; ✝ couche *f*; '**thick-'set** ⚓ dru; épais(se *f*); trapu (*personne*); '**thick-'skinned** *fig.* peu sensible.

thief [θi:f], *pl.* **thieves** [θi:vz] voleur (-euse *f*) *m*; F moucheron *m* (*de chandelle*); **thieve** [θi:v] voler; **thiev·er·y** ['~vəri] vol(erie *f*) *m*.

thiev·ish □ ['θi:viʃ] voleur (-euse *f*); '**thiev·ish·ness** habitude *f* du vol; penchant *m* au vol.

thigh [θai] cuisse *f*; '~**·bone** fémur *m*.

thill [θil] limon *m*, brancard *m*.

thim·ble ['θimbl] dé *m*; ⊕ bague *f*; ⚓ cosse *f*; **thim·ble·ful** ['~ful] plein un dé (de, *of*); **thim·ble·rig** ['~rig] F *vt/i.* frauder.

thin [θin] 1. □ *usu.* mince; peu épais (-se *f*); maigre; pauvre (*sol etc.*); clair (*liquide, tissu*); grêle (*voix*); ténu; rare, clairsemé; sans corps (*vin*); *fig.* peu convaincant; *théâ. a* ~ *house* un auditoire peu nombreux; 2. *v/t.* amincir; diminuer; (*a.* ~ *out*) éclaircir; *cuis.* délayer;

v/i. s'amincir, maigrir; s'éclaircir.

thine *bibl., poét.* [ðain] le tien, la tienne, les tiens, les tiennes; à toi.

thing [θiŋ] chose *f*, objet *m*, affaire *f*; être *m* (= *personne*); ~*s pl.* effets *m/pl.*; vêtements *f/pl.*; affaires *f/pl.*; choses *f/pl.*; F *be the* ~ être l'usage *ou* correct *ou* ce qu'il faut; F *know a* ~ *or two* être malin (-igne *f*); *en savoir plus d'un(e)*; *above all* ~*s* avant tout; ~*s are going better* les affaires vont mieux.

thing·um(·a)·bob F ['θiŋəm(i)bɔb], **thing·um·my** F ['~əmi] chose *m*; truc *m*.

think [θiŋk] [*irr.*] *v/i.* penser; réfléchir (sur *about, over*); compter (*inf., to inf.*); s'attendre (à *inf., to inf.*); ~*of* penser à, envisager; penser (*bien, mal*) de; considérer; ~*of* (*gér.*) penser à (*inf.*); *v/t.* croire; penser; s'imaginer; juger, trouver; tenir pour; ~ *much etc. of* avoir une bonne *etc.* opinion de; ~ *out* imaginer (*qch.*); arriver à la solution de (*qch.*); ~ *s.th. over* réfléchir sur qch.; '**think·a·ble** concevable; '**think·er** penseur (-euse *f*) *m*; '**think·ing** pensant; qui pense.

thin·ness ['θinnis] minceur *f*; peu d'épaisseur; légèreté *f*; maigreur *f*.

third [θə:d] 1. troisième; *date, roi:* trois; *surt. Am.* F ~ *degree passage m* à tabac; troisième degré *m*; *the* ♀ *World* le Tiers-Monde; 2. tiers *m*; troisième *mf*; ♪ tierce *f*; '**third·ly** en troisième lieu; '**third-'par·ty in·sur·ance** assurance *f* aux tiers; '**third-'rate** de qualité très inférieure.

thirst [θə:st] 1. soif *f* (*a. fig.*); 2. avoir soif (de *for, after*); '**thirst·y** □ altéré (de, *for*) (*a. fig.*); desséché (*sol*); F *it is* ~ *work* cela vous sèche le gosier.

thir·teen ['θə:'ti:n] treize; '**thir·teenth** [~θ] treizième; **thir·ti·eth** ['~tiiθ] trentième; '**thir·ty** trente.

this [ðis] 1. *pron. dém.* (*pl.* these) celui-ci (*pl.* ceux-ci), celle-ci (*pl.* celles-ci); celui (*pl.* ceux), celle (*pl.* celles); ceci; ce; 2. *adj. dém.* (*pl.* these) ce (cet *devant une voyelle ou un h muet*; *pl.* ces), cette (*pl.* ces); ce (cet, cette, *pl.* ces) ...-ci; *in this country* chez nous; ~ *day week* aujourd'hui en huit; 3. *adv.* F comme ceci; ~ *big* grand comme ça.

this·tle ♀ ['θisl] chardon *m.*

thith·er *poét.* ['ðiðə] là; y.

thole ⚓ [θoul] (*a.* ~*-pin*) tolet *m.*

thong [θɔŋ] lanière *f* (*souv. de fouet*).

tho·rax *anat., zo.* ['θɔːræks] thorax *m.*

thorn ♀ [θɔːn] épine *f*; '**thorn·y** épineux (-euse *f*) (*a. fig.*); ♀ spinifère.

thor·ough □ ['θʌrə] complet (-ète *f*); profond; minutieux (-euse *f*); parfait; vrai; achevé (*coquin*); ~ly *a.* tout à fait; '~-'**bass** ♩ basse *f* continue; '~-**bred 1.** pur sang *inv.*; de race; **2.** cheval *m* pur sang; chien *m etc.* de race; '~-**fare** voie *f* de communication; passage *m*; '~-**go·ing** achevé; consciencieux (-euse *f*); '**thor·ough·ness** perfection *f*; sincérité *f*; '**thor·ough-paced** achevé; parfait; enragé.

those [ðouz] **1.** *pl. de that; are ~ your parents?* sont-ce là vos parents?; **2.** *adj.* ces (...-là).

thou *bibl., poét.* [ðau] tu, *accentué:* toi.

though [ðou] quoique, bien que (*sbj.*); F (*usu. à la fin de la phrase*) pourtant, cependant; *int.* vraiment!; *as* ~ comme si.

thought [θɔːt] **1.** *prét. et p.p. de think*; **2.** pensée *f*; idée *f*; souci *m*; intention *f*; *give* ~ *to* penser à; *on second* ~*s* réflexion faite; *take* ~ *for* songer à.

thought·ful □ ['θɔːtful] pensif (-ive *f*); rêveur (-euse *f*); réfléchi; soucieux (-euse *f*) (de, of); prévenant (pour, of); '**thought·ful·ness** méditation *f*; prévenance *f*, égards *m/pl.*; souci *m.*

thought·less □ ['θɔːtlis] étourdi, irréfléchi, négligent (de, of); '**thought·less·ness** irréflexion *f*; inattention *f*; insouciance *f*; négligence *f.*

thought-read·ing ['θɔːtriːdiŋ] lecture *f* de pensée.

thou·sand ['θauzənd] **1.** mille; *dates a.* mil; **2.** mille *m/inv.*; millier *m*; '**thou·sandth** ['~zənθ] millième (*a. su./m*).

thrall *poét.* [θrɔːl] esclave *m* (de of, to); *a.* = **thral(l)·dom** ['θrɔːldəm] esclavage *m*; asservissement *m* (*a. fig.*).

thrash [θræʃ] *v/t.* battre; rosser; *sl.* vaincre; ~ *out* débattre; *v/i.* battre, clapoter; ⚓ vibrer; ⚓ se frayer un chemin; ⚓ bourlinguer; *see* thresh; '**thrash·ing** battage *m*; rossée *f*; F défaite *f*; *see* threshing.

thread [θred] **1.** fil *m* (*a. fig.*); filament *m*; ⊕ *vis:* filet *m*; **2.** enfiler; *fig.* s'insinuer, se faufiler; ⊕ fileter; '~-**bare** râpé; *fig.* usé; '**thread·y** fibreux (-euse *f*); plein de fils; ténu (*voix*).

threat [θret] menace *f*; '**threat·en** *vt/i.* menacer (de qch., [with] s.th.).

three [θriː] trois (*a. su./m*); '~-'**col·o(u)r** trichrome; '~-**fold** triple; ~-**pence** ['θrepəns] pièce *f* de trois pence; '~-**pen·ny** coûtant trois pence; *fig.* mesquin; ~-**phase cur·rent** ⚡ ['θriːfeiz'kʌrənt] courant *m* triphasé; '~-**piece** en trois pièces; ~ *suit* trois-pièces *m/inv.*; '~-'**score** soixante; '~-'**valve receiv·er** *radio:* poste *m* à trois lampes.

thresh [θreʃ] battre (*le blé*); *see* thrash; *fig.* ~ *out* discuter (*une question*) à fond.

thresh·ing ['θreʃiŋ] battage *m*; '~-**floor** aire *f*; '~-**ma·chine** batteuse *f*, machine *f* à battre.

thresh·old ['θreʃhould] seuil *m.*

threw [θruː] *prét. de throw* 1.

thrice † [θrais] trois fois.

thrift(·i·ness) ['θrift(inis)] économie *f*, épargne *f*; ♀ statice *m*; '**thrift·less** □ prodigue; imprévoyant; '**thrift·y** □ économe, ménager (-ère *f*); *poét., a. Am.* florissant.

thrill [θril] **1.** (*v/t.* faire) frissonner, frémir (de, with); *v/t. fig.* troubler; émotionner; **2.** frisson *m*; vive émotion *f*; '**thrill·er** F roman *m* sensationnel; pièce *f* à gros effets; '**thrill·ing** saisissant, émouvant; sensationnel(le *f*).

thrive [θraiv] [*irr.*] se développer; réussir; *fig.* prospérer; **thriv·en** ['θrivn] *p.p. de* thrive; **thriv·ing** □ ['θraiviŋ] vigoureux (-euse *f*); florissant.

throat [θrout] gorge *f* (*a. géog.*); ⚓ ancre: collet *m*; ⊕ rabot: lumière *f*; *fourneau:* gueulard *m*; *clear one's* ~ s'éclaircir le gosier; '**throat·y** □ guttural (-aux *m/pl.*).

throb [θrɔb] **1.** battre (*cœur etc.*);

lanciner (*doigt*); **2.** battement *m*, pulsation *f*; ⊕ vrombissement *m*.

throe [θrou] convulsion *f*; ~*s* *pl.* douleurs *f/pl.*; affres *f/pl.*; *fig.* tourments *m/pl.*

throm·bo·sis ✍ [θrɔm'bousis] thrombose *f*.

throne [θroun] **1.** trône *m*; **2.** *v/t.* mettre sur le trône; *v/i.* trôner.

throng [θrɔŋ] **1.** foule *f*; cohue *f*; presse *f*; **2.** *v/i.* se presser, affluer; *v/t.* encombrer; presser.

throt·tle ['θrɔtl] **1.** étrangler (*a.* ⊕ le moteur etc.); ⊕ mettre (*une machine*) au ralenti; **2.** = '~-**valve** soupape *f* de réglage; étrangleur *m*.

through [θru:] **1.** *prp.* à travers; au travers de; au moyen de, par; à cause de; pendant (*un temps*); **2.** *adj.* direct (*train, vol etc.*); *Am.* ~ street rue *f* prioritaire; ~ *traffic* transit *m*; ~'**out 1.** *prp.* d'un bout à l'autre de; dans tout; pendant tout (*un temps*); **2.** *adv.* partout; d'un bout à l'autre; '~-**way** *see* thruway.

throve [θrouv] *prét.* de thrive.

throw [θrou] **1.** [*irr.*] *v/t. usu.* jeter (*a. fig.*); lancer; projeter (*de l'eau, une image, etc.*); désarçonner (*un cavalier*); *tex.* jeter, tordre (*la soie*); tournasser (*un pot*); envoyer (*un baiser*); rejeter (*une faute*); *zo.* mettre bas (*des petits*); *Am.* ~ terrasser (*un adversaire*); ~ *away* (re)jeter; gaspiller; ne pas profiter de; ~ *in* jeter dedans; ajouter; placer (*un mot*); ~ *off* jeter; ôter (*un vêtement*); se défaire de; se dépouiller de; *fig.* dépister; ~ *out* jeter dehors; émettre; *fig.* faire ressortir; *fig.* lancer (*une insinuation etc.*); *surt. parl.* rejeter; ⊕ désaccoupler; ~ *over* abandonner; ⊕ renverser (*un levier*); ~ *up* jeter en l'air; lever; abandonner (*un poste*); vomir; construire à la hâte; ~ *up the cards* donner gagné à q.; *see* sponge 1; *v/i. zo.* mettre bas des petits; jeter les dés; ~ *off fig.* débuter; ~ *up* vomir; **2.** jet *m*; coup *m*; coup *m* de dé; ⊕ déviation *f*, écart *m*; '~-'**back** *surt. biol.* régression *f*; **thrown** [θroun] *p.p.* de throw 1; '**throw**-'**off** *chasse:* lancé *m*; *p.ext.* mise *f* en train.

thru *Am.* [θru:] *see* through.

thrum¹ [θrʌm] *tex.* penne *f*, -s *f/pl.*; bout *m*, -s *m/pl.*; ⚓ ~*s pl.* lardage *m*.

thrum² [~] (*a.* ~ *on*) tapoter (*le piano*); pincer de (*la guitare*).

thrush¹ *orn.* [θrʌʃ] grive *f*.

thrush² [~] ✍ aphtes *m/pl.*; *vét.* teigne *f*.

thrust [θrʌst] **1.** poussée *f* (*a.* ⊕); ✕ *a. fig.* assaut *m*; *escrime:* botte *f*; coup *m* de pointe (*d'épée*); **2.** [*irr.*] *vi/t.* pousser; *v/i.* porter un coup (à, at); ~ *o.s. into* s'enfoncer dans; ~ *out* mettre dehors, chasser; tirer (*sa langue*); ~ *s.th. upon s.o.* forcer q. à accepter qch.; imposer qch. à q.; ~ *o.s. upon s.o.* s'imposer à.

thru·way *Am.* ['θru:wei] autoroute *f* (à péage); rue *f* prioritaire.

thud [θʌd] **1.** résonner sourdement; tomber *etc.* avec un bruit sourd; **2.** bruit *m* sourd; son *m* mat.

thug [θʌg] thug *m*; *fig.* bandit *m*.

thumb [θʌm] **1.** pouce *m*; *Tom* ♀ le petit Poucet *m*; **2.** feuilleter (*un livre*); manier; *Am.* ~ *one's nose* faire un pied de nez (à q., *to s.o.*); ~ *a lift* (*ou a ride*) faire de l'auto-stop; arrêter une voiture (pour se faire emmener); ~ *in·dex* onglets *m/pl.* (d'un livre); '~-**nail** ongle *m* du pouce; ~ *sketch* petit croquis *m* (hâtif); '~-**print** marque *f* de pouce; '~-**screw** *torture:* poucettes *f/pl.*; ⊕ vis *f* ailée; '~-**stall** poucier *m*; ✍ doigtier *m* pour pouce, F pouce *m*; '~-**tack** *Am.* punaise *f*.

thump [θʌmp] **1.** coup *m* de poing; bruit *m* sourd; **2.** *v/t.* cogner (sur, on), donner un coup de poing à; *v/i.* sonner sourdement; battre fort (*cœur*); '**thump·er** *sl.* chose *f* énorme; *sl.* mensonge *m*; '**thump·ing** *sl.* colossal (-aux *m/pl.*).

thun·der ['θʌndə] **1.** tonnerre *m* (*a. fig.*); F *steal s.o.'s* ~ anticiper q.; **2.** tonner; '~-**bolt** foudre *f* (*poét. a. m*); '~-**clap** coup *m* de tonnerre *ou fig.* de foudre; '~-**cloud** nuage *m* orageux; '~-**head** partie *f* supérieure d'un cumulus; *fig.* menace *f*; '**thun·der·ing** *sl.* **1.** *adj.* colossal (-aux *m/pl.*), formidable; **2.** *adv.* joliment, rudement; '**thun·der·ous** □ orageux (-euse *f*); *fig.* menaçant; à tout rompre; de tonnerre (*bruit etc.*); '**thun·der·storm** orage *m*; '**thun·der·struck** foudroyé, abasourdi; '**thun·der·y** orageux (-euse *f*).

Thurs·day ['θə:zdi] jeudi *m*.

thus [ðʌs] ainsi; de cette manière; donc.

thwack [θwæk] see whack.

thwart [θwɔːt] **1.** contrarier; frustrer, déjouer; **2.** ♣ banc *m* de nage.

thy *bibl.*, *poét.* [ðai] ton, ta, tes.

thyme ♀ [taim] thym *m*.

thy·roid *anat.* ['θairɔid] **1.** thyroïde; ~ **extract** extrait *m* thyroïde; ~ **gland** = **1.** glande *f* thyroïde.

thy·self *bibl.*, *poét.* [ðai'self] toi-même; *réfléchi*: te.

ti·a·ra [ti'ɑːrə] tiare *f*.

tib·i·a *anat.* ['tibiə], *pl.* **-ae** [~iː] tibia *m*.

tic ✚ [tik] tic *m*.

tick¹ *zo.* [tik] tique *f*.

tick² [~] toile *f* à matelas.

tick³ F [~]: on ~ à crédit.

tick⁴ [~] **1.** tic-tac *m/inv.*; F instant *m*, moment *m*; marque *f*; to the ~ à l'heure sonnante; **2.** *v/i.* faire tic-tac; battre; *mot.* ~ over tourner au ralenti; *v/t.* pointer, faire une marque à; ~ off pointer; vérifier; *sl.* rembarrer (*q.*).

tick·er ['tikə] téléscripteur *m*; télé-imprimeur *m*; F tocante (= *montre*); F palpitant *m* (= *cœur*); '~**tape** bande *f* de téléscripteur; serpentin *m*.

tick·et ['tikit] **1.** ✿ *théâ.*, *loterie*: billet *m*; *métro*, *consigne*, *place réservée*, *etc.*: ticket *m*; coupon *m*; (*a. price-*~) étiquette *f*; bon *m* (*de soupe*); *mot.* *Am.* F contravention *f*; *parl.* *Am.* liste *f* des candidats; F programme *m*; F the ~ ce qu'il faut, correct; ~ of leave (bulletin *m* de) libération *f* conditionnelle; on ~ of leave libéré conditionellement; **2.** étiqueter, marquer; ~ **a·gen·cy** agence *f* de voyages; *théâ.* etc. agence *f* de spectacles; '~**col·lec·tor** ✿ contrôleur *m* des billets; '~**in·spec·tor** *autobus*: contrôleur *m*; '~**of·fice**, '~**win·dow** *surt.* *Am.* guichet *m*; '~**punch** poinçon *m* de contrôleur.

tick·ing ['tikiŋ] toile *f* à matelas.

tick·le ['tikl] chatouiller; *fig.* amuser; flatter; **tick·ler** (*ou* ~ *coil*) *radio*: bobine *f* de réaction; '**tick·lish** □ chatouilleux (-euse *f*); délicat; *fig.* susceptible (*personne*).

tid·al □ ['taidl] de marée; à marée; ~ **wave** raz *m* de marée; flot *m* de la marée; *fig.* vague *f*.

tid·bit *Am.* ['tidbit] see titbit.

tide [taid] **1.** marée *f*; *fig.* vague *f*; ♣ flot *m*; low (*high*) ~ marée *f* basse (haute); *fig.* fortune *f*; † saison *f*, temps *m*; turn of the ~ étale *m*; *fig.* tournure *f* (*des affaires*); **2.** porter (par la marée); *fig.* ~ over venir à bout de; s'en tirer; ~ *s.o.* over dépanner q., aider q. à s'en tirer, tirer q. d'embarras; '~**mark** ligne *f* de marée haute; F ligne crasse (*au cou*, *dans une baignoire etc.*).

ti·di·ness ['taidinis] (bon) ordre *m*; propreté *f*; *habillement*: bonne tenue *f*.

ti·dings *pl.* ou *sg.* ['taidiŋz] nouvelle *f*, -s *f/pl.*

ti·dy ['taidi] **1.** bien rangé; bien tenu, *fig.* passable, F joli; **2.** voile *m* (*sur un fauteuil etc.*); récipient *m* (*pour peignures*); corbeille *f* (*à ordures*); **3.** (*a.* ~ *up*) ranger; mettre de l'ordre dans, arranger (*une chambre etc.*).

tie [tai] **1.** lien *m* (*a. fig.*); attache *f*; (*a.* neck-~) cravate *f*; nœud *m*; ♩ liaison *f*; ♣ chaîne *f*, ancre *f*; *fig.* entrave *f*; *soulier*: cordon *m*; *sp.* match *m* à égalité, partie *f* nulle; *sp.* match *m* de championnat; *parl.* nombre *m* égal de suffrages; **2.** *v/t.* lier; nouer (*la cravate*); ficeler; ♣ chaîner; *v/i.* sp. être à égalité; ~ down *fig.* assujettir (à *une condition* etc., to); asservir (*q.*) (à, to); ~ up attacher; ficeler; ♣ amarrer; *fig.* immobiliser; F marier; *Am.* gêner.

tier [tiə] rangée *f*; étage *m*; *théâ.* balcon *m*.

tierce [tiəs] *escrime*, *cartes*: tierce *f*.

tie-up ['tai'ʌp] cordon *m*; association *f*; impasse *f*; *surt.* *Am.* grève *f*; *Am.* arrêt *m* (*de la circulation etc.*).

tiff [tif] **1.** petite querelle *f*; boutade *f*; **2.** bouder.

tif·fin ['tifin] *anglo-indien*: déjeuner *m* (de midi).

ti·ger ['taigə] tigre *m*; *fig.* as *m*; *fig.* homme *m* féroce; *Am.* F three cheers and a ~! trois hourras et encore un hourra!; '**ti·ger·ish** □ *fig.* cruel(le *f*); féroce; de tigre.

tight □ [tait] serré, tendu, raide; collant, étroit, juste (*vêtements*); bien fermé, imperméable; resserré, rare (*argent*); F ivre, gris; F *fig.* it was a ~ place (*ou* squeeze) on tenait tout juste; *it was a ~ squeeze to get through* il y avait à peine la place de passer; *hold ~* tenir serré; *in a ~ corner* en mauvaise passe; *in a ~ squeeze* dans l'embarras; **'tight·en** *v/t.* (res)serrer (*sa ceinture, une vis*); retendre (*une courroie*); tendre, remonter (*un ressort*); *v/i.* se (res)serrer; se bander (*ressort*); **'~·'fist·ed** F dur à la détente; **'~·laced** serré dans son corset; *fig.* collet monté *inv.*, prude; **'~·lipped** qui ne desserre pas les lèvres, taciturne; à l'air pincé; **'tight·ness** tension *f*; raideur *f*; étroitesse *f*; **'tight-rope** corde *f* tendue; **tights** [~s] *pl. théâ.* maillot *m*; **'tight-wad** *Am. sl.* grippe-sou *m*; pingre *m*.

ti·gress ['taigris] tigresse *f*.

tile [tail[**1.** *toit:* tuile *f*; *plancher:* carreau *m*; *sl.* chapeau *m*; **2.** couvrir de tuiles; carreler; **'~·lay·er,** **'til·er** couvreur *m*; carreleur *m*.

till¹ [til] tiroir-caisse (*pl.* tiroirs-caisses) *m*; caisse *f*.

till² [~] **1.** *prp.* jusqu'(à); **2.** *cj.* jusqu'à ce que (*sbj.*).

till³ [~] labourer; cultiver; **'till·age** labour(age) *m*; (agri)culture *f*; terre *f* en labour.

till·er ['tilə] barre *f* franche.

tilt¹ [tilt] bâche *f*, banne *f*; tendelet *m*.

tilt² [~] **1.** pente *f*, inclinaison *f*; † tournoi *m*; † coup *m* de lance; *fig.* coup *m* de patte, attaque *f*; *full ~* tête baissée; *on the ~* incliné, penché; **2.** *v/t.* pencher, incliner; *v/i.* pencher, s'incliner; courir une lance (contre, *at*); *fig.* donner un coup de patte (à, *at*); *~ against* attaquer; *~ up* basculer; **'tilt·ing** incliné, penché; à bascule.

tilth *poét.* [tilᵗ] *see* tillage.

tim·ber ['timbə] **1.** bois *m* (*d'œuvre, de charpente, de construction*); *piece of ~* poutre *f*; couple *m*; *Am. fig.* qualité *f*; **2.** boiser; *~ed* en bois; boisé (*terrain*); **'~·line** limite *f* de la végétation arborescente; **'~·work** charpente *f*; construction *f* en bois; **'~·yard** chantier *m*.

time [taim] **1.** temps *m*; fois *f*; heure *f*; moment *m*; saison *f*; époque *f*; terme *m*; *gymn. etc.:* pas *m*; ♪ mesure *f*, tempo *m*; *~, gentlemen, please!* on ferme!; *~ and again* à maintes reprises; *at ~s* de temps en temps; parfois; *at a (ou at the same)*

~ à la fois; at the same ~ en même temps; *before (one's) ~* en avance; prématurément; *behind (one's) ~* en retard; *behind the ~s* arriéré; *by that ~* à l'heure qu'il était; à ce moment-là; alors; *for the ~ being* pour le moment; provisoirement; actuellement; *have a good ~* s'amuser (bien); *in ~* à temps, à l'heure; *in good ~* de bonne heure; *see* mean² 1; *on ~* à temps, à l'heure; *out of ~* mal à propos; à contre-temps (*a.* ♪); *beat (the) ~* battre la mesure; *see* keep 2; **2.** *v/t.* faire (qch.) à propos; fixer l'heure de; choisir le moment de; régler (sur, *by*); *sp.* chronométrer; calculer la durée de; (*a.* take the ~ of) mesurer le temps de; *the train is ~d to leave at 7* le train doit partir à 7 heures; *v/i.* faire coïncider (avec *with*, to); **'~·and-'mo·tion stud·y** ✝ étude *f* des cadences; **'~·bar·gain** ✝ marché *m* à terme; *~* **bomb** bombe *f* à retardement; **'~·clock** enregistreur *m* de temps; **'~·con·sum·ing** qui prend beaucoup de temps; **'~·ex·po·sure** *phot.* pose *f*; **'~·hon·o(u)red** séculaire, vénérable; **'~·keep·er** chronomètre *m*, *surt.* montre *f*; *see* timer; contrôleur *m* (de présence); *~* **lag** retard *m*; **'~·'lim·it** limite *f* de temps; délai *m*; durée *f*; **'time·ly** opportun, à propos; **'time-out** *Am.* pause *f*; **'time-piece** pendule *f*; montre *f*; **'tim·er** chronométreur *m*.

time...: **~·serv·er** ['taimsə:və] opportuniste *mf*; **'~·sheet** feuille *f* de présence; semainier *m*; **'~·'sig·nal** *surt. radio:* signal *m* horaire; **'~·ta·ble** horaire *m*; ⚑ indicateur *m*; *école:* emploi *m* du temps; *~* **zone** fuseau *m* horaire.

tim·id □ ['timid] timide, peureux (-euse *f*); **ti·mid·i·ty** [ti'miditi] timidité *f*.

tim·ing ['taimiŋ] ⊕ *mot.* réglage *m*; *sp.* chronométrage *m*; *fig.* choix *m* du moment.

tim·or·ous □ ['timərəs] *see* timid.

tin [tin] **1.** étain *m*; fer-blanc (*pl.* fers-blancs) *m*; boîte *f* (*de conserves*); bidon *m* (*à essence*); *sl.* galette *f* (= argent); *Brit. ~ opener* ouvre-boîtes *m/inv.*; **2.** en ou d'étain; en fer-blanc; de plomb (*soldat*); *fig. péj.* en toc; *~ can* boîte *f* (en fer-blanc); F *~ god* (faux) idole *m*; F ~ hat casque *m*; 3. étamer; mettre en boîtes; ~ned meat viande *f* de conserve; F ~ned music musique *f* enregistrée.

tinc·ture ['tiŋktʃə] 1. teinte *f*; ⌀, *pharm.*, *a. fig.* teinture *f*; 2. teindre, colorer.

tin·der ['tində] amadou *m*.

tine [tain] dent *f*; fourchon *m*; *zo.* cor *m*, branche *f*.

tin·foil ['tin'fɔil] feuille *f* d'étain; papier *m* (d')étain.

ting F [tiŋ] *see* tinkle.

tinge [tindʒ] 1. teinte *f*; nuance *f* (*a. fig.*); 2. teinter (*a. fig.*), colorer (de, with); be ~d with avoir une teinte de.

tin·gle ['tiŋgl] tinter; picoter; cuire; *fig.* avoir grande envie (de *inf.*, to *inf.*).

tink·er ['tiŋkə] 1. chaudronnier *m*; 2. *v/t.* rafistoler; *v/i.* bricoler (dans, about); ~ at rafistoler; ~ up faire des réparations de fortune; ~ with retaper.

tin·kle ['tiŋkl] 1. (faire) tinter; 2. tintement *m*; F coup *m* de téléphone.

tin·man ['tinmən] étameur *m*; ferblantier *m*; '**tin·ny** métallique (*son*); '**tin·o·pen·er** ouvre-boîtes *m/inv.*; '**tin·plate** fer-blanc (*pl.* fers-blancs) *m*; ferblanterie *f*.

tin·sel ['tinsl] 1. lamé *m*, paillettes *f/pl.*; clinquant *m* (*a. fig.*); *fig. a.* faux éclat *m*; 2. de paillettes; *fig.* de clinquant, faux (fausse *f*); 3. garnir de paillettes; clinquanter; *fig.* donner un faux éclat à.

tin·smith ['tinsmiθ] *see* tinman.

tint [tint] 1. teinte *f*, nuance *f*; *peint.* ton *m*; 2. teinter, colorer; ~ed paper papier *m* teinté.

tin·tack ['tintæk] broquette *f*; ~s *pl.* semence *f*.

tin·tin·nab·u·la·tion ['tintinæbju-'leiʃn] tintement *m*.

tin·ware ['tinwɛə] ferblanterie *f*.

ti·ny □ ['taini] tout petit.

tip [tip] 1. pointe *f*; *cigarette:* bout *m*; extrémité *f*; F pourboire *m*; F tuyau *m*; pente *f*; F coup *m* léger; give s.th. a ~ faire pencher qch.; 2. *v/t.* mettre un bout à; ferrer, embouter (*une canne*); *fig.* dorer; F donner un pourboire à (*q.*); F (*a.* ~ off) tuyauter, avertir (*q.*); ~ over renverser; *v/i.* se renverser; '~-

cart tombereau *m* à bascule; '~·cat bâtonnet *m* (*sorte de jeu d'enfants*); '~-off tuyau *m*.

tip·pet ['tipit] pèlerine *f*; écharpe *f* en fourrure.

tip·ple ['tipl] 1. se livrer à la boisson; F lever le coude; 2. boisson *f*; '**tip·pler** ivrogne *m*; buveur (-euse *f*) *m*.

tip·si·ness ['tipsinis] ivresse *f*.

tip·staff ['tipstɑːf] huissier *m*.

tip·ster ['tipstə] tuyauteur *m*.

tip·sy □ ['tipsi] gris, ivre; F pompette.

tip·toe ['tiptou]: on ~ sur la pointe des pieds.

tip·top F ['tip'tɔp] 1. le plus haut point *m*; 2. de premier ordre; extra; F chic *inv.*

tip-up seat ['tipʌp'siːt] strapontin *m*.

ti·rade [tai'reid] tirade *f*, diatribe *f*.

tire[1] ['taiə] pneu(matique) *m*.

tire[2] [~] (se) lasser, ennuyer (de of, with).

tired □ ['taiəd] fatigué (*fig.* de, of); '**tired·ness** lassitude *f*, fatigue *f*.

tire·less □ ['taiəlis] infatigable.

tire·some □ ['taiəsəm] ennuyeux (-euse *f*); F exaspérant.

tire-valve ['taiəvælv] valve *f* de pneumatique.

ti·ro ['taiərou] novice *mf*.

tis·sue ['tisju:] tissu *m*; étoffe *f*; '~·**pa·per** papier *m* de soie; † papier *m* pelure.

tit[1] [tit]: ~ for tat à bon chat bon rat; un prêté pour un rendu.

tit[2] *Am.* [~] *see* teat.

tit[3] *orn.* [~] mésange *f*.

Ti·tan ['taitən] Titan *m*; '**Ti·tan·ess** femme *f* titanesque; **ti·ta·nic** [~'tænik] (~ally) titanique, titanesque; géant.

tit·bit ['titbit] friandise *f*; bon morceau *m*; *fig.* quelque chose de piquant.

tithe [taið] 1. dîme *f*; *usu. fig.* dixième *m*; 2. payer la dîme sur; dîmer sur.

tit·il·late ['titileit] chatouiller; **tit·il·la·tion** chatouillement *m*.

tit·i·vate F ['titiveit] (se) faire beau (belle *f*).

ti·tle ['taitl] 1. titre *m*; nom *m*; ⚖ droit *m* (à, to); 2. intituler (*un livre*); titrer (*un film*); '~-**deed** ⚖ titre *m* de propriété; acte *m*; '~-**hold·er** *surt. sp. record, coupe:* détenteur (-trice *f*) *m*; *championnat:* tenant(e *f*) *m*; ~ **role** *théâ.* rôle *m* principal.

tit·mouse *orn.* ['titmaus], *pl.* -**mice** [∼mais] mésange *f.*

ti·trate ⚗ ['taitreit] titrer, doser; **ti'tra·tion** dosage *m*; analyse *f* volumétrique.

tits V [tits] nénés *m/pl.* (= *seins*).

tit·ter ['titə] **1.** avoir un petit rire étouffé; **2.** rire *m* étouffé.

tit·tle ['titl] point *m*; *fig.* la moindre partie; *to a* ∼ trait pour trait; '∼-**tat·tle 1.** cancans *m/pl.*; bavardage *m*; **2.** cancaner; bavarder.

tit·tup ['titəp] F aller au petit galop.

tit·u·lar □ ['titjulə] titulaire, nominal (-aux *m/pl.*).

to [tu:; tu; tə] **1.** *prp. usu.* à; *direction:* à; vers (*Paris, la maison*); en (*France*); chez (*moi, ma tante*); *sentiment:* envers, pour (*q.*); *distance:* jusqu'à; *parenté, hérédité:* de; *pour indiquer le datif:* à; ∼ *my father* à mon père; ∼ *me accentué:* à moi, *inaccentué:* me; *it happened* ∼ *me* cela m'arriva; ∼ *the United States* aux États-Unis; ∼ *Japan* au Japon; *I bet 10* ∼ *1* je parie 10 contre 1; *the train (road)* ∼ *London* le train (la route) de Londres; *a quarter (ten)* ∼ *six* six heures moins le quart (dix); *alive* ∼ sensible à (*qch.*); *cousin* ∼ *cousin* (e *f*) de; *heir* ∼ héritier (-ère *f*) de; *secretary* ∼ secrétaire de; *here's* ∼ *you!* à votre santé!, F à la vôtre!; **2.** *adv.* [tu:]: ∼ *and fro* de long en large; *go* ∼ *and fro* aller et venir; *come* ∼ revenir à soi; *pull the door* ∼ fermer la porte; **3.** *pour indiquer l'inf.:* ∼ *take* prendre; *I am going* ∼ (*inf.*) je vais (*inf.*); *souvent on supprime l'inf.:* *I worked hard, I had* ∼ (sc. *work hard*) je travaillais dûr, il le fallut bien; *avec inf.*, *remplaçant une proposition subordonnée:* *I weep* ∼ *think of it* quand j'y pense, je pleure.

toad *zo.* [toud] crapaud *m*; '∼-**stool** champignon *m* vénéneux.

toad·y ['toudi] **1.** sycophante *m*, flagorneur (-euse *f*) *m*; **2.** lécher les bottes à (*q.*); flagorner (*q.*); '**toad·y·ism** flagornerie *f.* [venues *f/pl.*]

to-and-fro F ['tu:ən'frou] allées et)

toast [toust] **1.** toast *m* (*a. fig.*); pain *m* grillé; **2.** griller, rôtir; *fig.* chauffer; *fig.* porter un toast à.

to·bac·co [tə'bækou] tabac *m*; **to·'bac·co·nist** [∼kənist] marchand *m* de tabac.

to·bog·gan [tə'bɔgən] **1.** toboggan *m*; luge *f* (suisse); **2.** faire du toboggan.

to·by ['toubi] (*ou* ∼ *jug*) pot *m* à bière (de fantaisie); ∼ *collar* collerette *f* plissée.

to·co *sl.* ['toukou] châtiment *m* corporel; raclée *f.*

toc·sin ['tɔksin] tocsin *m.*

tod F [tɔd]: *on one's* ∼ tout(e) seul(e).

to·day [tə'dei] aujourd'hui.

tod·dle ['tɔdl] **1.** marcher à petits pas; trottiner; F ∼ *off* se trotter; **2.** F pas *m/pl.* chancelants (*d'un petit enfant*); F balade *f*; '**tod·dler** tout(e) petit(e) enfant *m*(*f*).

tod·dy ['tɔdi] grog *m* chaud.

to-do F [tə'du:] affaire *f*; scène *f*; façons *f/pl.*

toe [tou] **1.** *anat.* doigt *m* de pied; orteil *m*; *chaussettes:* bout *m*; **2.** botter (*a. sp.*); mettre un bout à (*un soulier*); ∼ *the line* s'aligner; *fig.* ∼ *the (party) line* obéir (aux ordres de son parti); s'aligner (avec son parti).

-toed [toud]: *three* ∼ à trois orteils.

toff *sl.* [tɔf] rupin(e *f*) *m*; dandy *m.*

tof·fee, tof·fy ['tɔfi] caramel *m* au beurre; '**tof·fee-nosed** F bêcheur (-euse *f*).

to·geth·er [tə'geðə] ensemble; en même temps; ∼ *with* avec; *all* ∼ tous ensemble.

tog·ger·y F ['tɔgəri] nippes *f/pl.*, frusques *f/pl.*

tog·gle ['tɔgl] **1.** ⚓ cabillot *m*; ⊕ clef *f*; ⚡ ∼ *switch* interrupteur *m* à bascule; **2.** ⚓ fixer avec *ou* munir d'un cabillot.

togs *sl.* [tɔgz] *pl.* nippes *f/pl.*, frusques *f/pl.*

toil [tɔil] **1.** travail (*pl.* -aux) *m*, peine *f*; **2.** travailler (dur); '**toil·er** travailleur (-euse *f*) *m.*

toi·let ['tɔilit] toilette *f*; ✚ détersion *f*; *les cabinets m/pl.*; *make one's* ∼ faire sa toilette; '∼-**bag** trousse *f* de toilette; '∼-**pa·per** papier *m* hygiénique; '∼-**set** garniture *f* de toilette; '∼-**ta·ble** table *f* de toilette.

toils [tɔilz] *pl.* filet *m*, lacs *m*, *a. m/pl.* (*a. fig.*).

toil·some □ ['tɔilsəm] fatigant.

toil-worn ['tɔilwɔ:n] usé par le travail; marqué par la fatigue (*visage*).

to·ken ['toukən] signe *m*, marque *f*; jeton *m*; bon *m* (*de livres*); ∼ *money* monnaie *f* fiduciaire; ~ *payment* paiement *m* symbolique; ~ *strike* grève *f* d'avertissement; *in* ~ *of* en signe *ou* témoignage de.

told [tould] *prét. et p.p. de* tell; *all* ~ tout compris; tout compte fait.

tol·er·a·ble □ ['tɔlərəbl] supportable, tolérable; assez bon(ne *f*); **'tol·er·ance** tolérance *f* (*a.* ⚙, ⊕); **'tol·er·ant** □ tolérant (à l'égard de, *of*); **tol·er·ate** ['⁓reit] tolérer, supporter; **tol·er·a·tion** tolérance *f*.

toll¹ [toul] droit *m* de passage; *marché:* droit *m* de place; *téléph.* (*a.* ~-*call*) conversation *f* interurbaine; ~ *of the road* la mortalité *f* sur routes; *take* ~ *of* faire payer le droit de passage à; *fig.* retrancher une bonne partie de; ~ *bar,* ~ *gate* barrière *f* (de péage); ~ *road* route *f* à péage.

toll² [~] 1. tintement *m; souv.* glas *m;* 2. tinter; sonner (*souv.* le glas).

tom [tɔm] mâle *m* (*animal*); ~ *cat* matou *m.*

tom·a·hawk ['tɔməhɔːk] 1. hache *f* de guerre, tomahawk *m;* 2. assommer; frapper avec un tomahawk.

to·ma·to ⚛ [tə'mɑːtou; *Am.* tə-'meitou], *pl.* -**toes** [⁓touz] tomate *f.*

tomb [tuːm] tombe(au *m*) *f;* ~*stone* pierre *f* tombale.

tom·boy ['tɔmbɔi] fillette *f* d'allures garçonnières; garçon *m* manqué.

tome [toum] tome *m,* livre *m.*

tom·fool ['tɔm'fuːl] 1. niais *m; attr.* insensé; stupide; 2. faire *ou* dire des sottises; **tom'fool·er·y** niaiserie *f,* -s *f/pl.*

tom·my *sl.* ['tɔmi] simple soldat *m* *anglais;* mangeaille *f,* ~-*gun* mitraillette *f;* ~ *rot* bêtises *f/pl.*

to·mor·row [tə'mɔrou] demain; ~ *week* de demain en huit.

tom·tom ['tɔmtɔm] tam-tam *m.*

ton [tʌn] tonne *f;* F ~*s pl.* tas *m/pl.*

to·nal·i·ty ♪, *a. peint.* [to'næliti] tonalité *f.*

tone [toun] 1. ton *m* (*a. ling.,* ♪, *peint.,fig.*); son *m;* accent *m;* voix *f; fig.* atmosphère *f;* ⚙ tonicité *f;* *out of* ~ désaccordé; 2. *v/t.* teinter; ♪ accorder; *peint.* adoucir les tons de; *phot.* virer; *v/i.* s'harmoniser (*avec, with*); *phot.* virer; ~ *down* s'adoucir.

tongs [tɔŋz] *pl.:* (*a pair of*) ~ (des)

pincettes *f/pl.;* ⊕ (des) tenailles *f/pl.*

tongue [tʌŋ] *usu.* langue *f* (*a. fig., ling.*); *soulier, bois, hautbois:* languette *f; cloche:* battant *m; give* ~ donner de la voix, aboyer (*chien*); *hold one's* ~ se taire; *speak with one's* ~ *in one's cheek* parler ironiquement; blaguer; **'tongue·less** sans langue; *fig.* muet(te *f*); **tongue·tied** qui a la langue liée; *fig.* interdit; muet(te *f*).

ton·ic ['tɔnik] 1. (~*ally*) ♪, ⚙, *gramm.* tonique; ♪ ~ *chord* accord *m* naturel; 2. ♪ tonique *f;* ⚙ tonique *m,* réconfortant *m.*

to·night [tə'nait] ce soir; cette nuit.

ton·ing so·lu·tion *phot.* ['touniŋ sə'luːʃn] (bain *m* de) virage *m.*

ton·nage ⚓ ['tʌnidʒ] tonnage *m,* jauge *f; hist.* droit *m* de tonnage.

-ton·ner ⚓ ['tʌnə]: *four-hundred* ~ vaisseau *m* de quatre cent tonneaux.

ton·sil *anat.* ['tɔnsl] amygdale *f;* **ton·sil·li·tis** [⁓si'laitis] amygdalite *f,* inflammation *f* des amygdales.

ton·sure ['tɔnʃə] 1. tonsure *f;* 2. tonsurer.

ton·y *Am. sl.* ['touni] chic, élégant.

too [tuː] (par) trop; aussi; d'ailleurs.

took [tuk] *prét. de* take 1, 2.

tool [tuːl] 1. outil *m;* ustensile *m;* instrument *m* (*a. fig.*); 2. ciseler (*le cuir, un livre*); bretteler (*une pierre*); ⊕ travailler; **'~-kit** sac *m* à outils; *mot.* sacoche *f;* **~ shed** cabane *f* à outils.

toot [tuːt] 1. sonner; *mot.* (*a.* ~ *the horn*) corner; klaxonner; 2. cornement *m;* coup *m* de klaxon.

tooth [tuːθ] (*pl.* **teeth**) dent *f;* **'~-ache** mal *m* de dents; **'~-brush** brosse *f* à dents; **toothed** [~θt] à ... dents; aux dents ...; ⊕ denté; **'tooth·ing** ⊕ *scie:* taille *f* des dents; *roue:* dents *f/pl.;* **'tooth·less** □ sans dents; **'tooth-paste** (pâte *f*) dentifrice *m;* **'tooth·pick** curedent *m.*

tooth·some □ ['tuːθsəm] savoureux (-euse *f*); **'tooth·some·ness** succulence *f;* goût *m* agréable.

too·tle ['tuːtl] flûter; *mot.* corner; F ~ *along* aller son petit bonhomme de chemin.

toot·sie, toot·sy F ['tu(ː)tsi] peton *m* (*pied*); *surt. Am.* nana *f* (= *fille*); *surt. Am.* chéri(e *f*) *m.*

top¹ [tɔp] **1.** sommet *m*, cime *f*; *tête*: haut *m*; *arbre*, *toit*: faîte *m*; *maison*: toit *m*; *page*: tête *f*; *eau*, *terre*: surface *f*; *cheminée*, *table*, *soulier*: dessus *m*; *table*: haut bout *m*; *bas*, *botte*: revers *m*; *boîte*: couvercle *m*; *autobus etc.*: impériale *f*; *fig.* chef *m*, tête *f* (*de rang*); *fig.* comble *m*; *mot. Am.* capote *f*; ⚓ hune *f*; *at the* ~ (*of*) au sommet (de), en haut (de); *at the* ~ *of one's speed* à toutes jambes, à toute vitesse; *at the* ~ *of one's voice* à pleine gorge, (*crier*) de toutes ses forces; *on* ~ sur le dessus; en haut; *on* ~ *of* sur, en haut de; *et aussi*, immédiatement après; F *blow one'* ~ sortir de ses gonds; **2.** supérieur; d'en haut; *the* ~ *floor* le plus haut étage; ~ *speed* vitesse maximum; *plafond m*; ~ *coat* pardessus *m*, manteau *m*; *the* ~ *earners pl.* les gros salaires; *sl.* ~ *banana* la personne la plus importante; *sl.* *be* ~ *dog* être celui qui commande; **3.** surmonter, couronner; dépasser, surpasser; atteindre le sommet de; être à la tête de (*une classe*, *une liste*, *etc.*); ✔ écimer (*un arbre*); pincer (*l'extrémité d'une plante*); *golf*: topper; F ~ *up*, ~ *off* remplir.

top² [~] toupie *f*.

to·paz *min.* ['toupæz] topaze *f*.

top-boots ['tɔp'buːts] *pl.* bottes *f/pl.* à revers.

to·pee ['toupi] casque *m* colonial.

top·er ['toupə] ivrogne *m*.

top…: '~**flight** F de premier ordre; ~**gal·lant** ⚓ [~'gælənt; ⚓ tə-'gælənt] **1.** de perroquet; **2.** (*ou* ~ *sail*) voile *f* de perroquet; '~**hat** *chapeau*: haut-de-forme (*pl.* hauts-de-forme) *m*; '~-**heav·y** trop lourd du haut; ⚓ jaloux (-se *f*); '~-**hole** *sl.* excellent, épatant.

top·ic ['tɔpik] sujet *m*, thème *m*; question *f*; matière *f*; '**top·i·cal** □ topique, local (-aux *m/pl.*) (*a.* ⚕); d'actualité.

top·knot ['tɔpnɔt] chignon *m*; *orn.* huppe *f*.

top·less ['tɔplis] en monokini; aux seins nus, torse nu.

top…: '~**mast** mât *m* de hune; '~**most** le plus haut *ou* élevé; '~**notch** F de premier ordre.

to·pog·ra·pher [tə'pɔgrəfə] topographe *m*; **top·o·graph·ic**, **top·o-graph·i·cal** □ [tɔpə'græfik(l)] topographique; **to·pog·ra·phy** [tə-'pɔgrəfi] topographie *f*; anatomie *f* topographique.

top·per *sl.* ['tɔpə] type *m* épatant; *see* *tophat*; '**top·ping** F excellent, chouette, chic.

top·ple ['tɔpl] (*usu.* ~ *over ou down*) (faire) écrouler, dégringoler.

tops *sl.* [tɔps] **1.** fantastique, le (la *f*) meilleur(e); **2.** *be the* ~ être champion.

top·sail ⚓ ['tɔpsl] hunier *m*.

top-se·cret ['tɔp'siːkrət] ultra-secret (-ète *f*).

top·sy·tur·vy □ ['tɔpsi'təːvi] sens dessus dessous; en désarroi.

tor [tɔː] pic *m*, massif *m* de roche.

torch [tɔːtʃ] torche *f*, flambeau *m*; *electric* ~ lampe *f* électrique de poche; torche *f* électrique; ~ *battery* pile *f*; *Am.* ~ *song* chanson *f* d'amour non partagé; '~-**light** lumière *f* de(s) torches; ~ *procession* défilé *m* aux flambeaux.

tore [tɔː] *prét. de tear¹* 1.

tor·ment 1. ['tɔːmənt] tourment *m*, torture *f*, supplice *m*; **2.** [tɔː'ment] tourmenter, torturer; harceler; *fig.* taquiner; **tor'men·tor** tourmenteur (-euse *f*) *m*; harceleur (-euse *f*) *m*.

torn [tɔːn] *p.p. de tear¹* 1.

tor·na·do [tɔː'neidou], *pl.* -**does** [~douz] tornade *f*; ouragan *m* (*a. fig.*).

tor·pe·do [tɔː'piːdou], *pl.* -**does** [~douz] **1.** ⚓, ✖, *icht.* torpille *f*; *Am. sl.* homme *m* de main; **2.** ⚓ torpiller (*a. fig. un projet*); ~**boat** ⚓ torpilleur *m*.

tor·pid □ ['tɔːpid] inerte, engourdi (*a. fig.*), torpide; *fig.* lent, léthargique; **tor'pid·i·ty**, '**tor·pid·ness**, **tor·por** ['tɔːpə] engourdissement *m*, torpeur *f*; *fig.* léthargie *f*.

torque ⊕ [tɔːk] moment *m* de torsion.

tor·rent ['tɔrənt] torrent *m* (*a. fig.*); *fig.* déluge *m*; *in* ~*s* à torrents; **tor·ren·tial** □ [tɔ'renʃl] torrentiel(le *f*).

tor·rid ['tɔrid] torride.

tor·sion ['tɔːʃn] torsion *f*; '**tor·sion·al** de torsion.

tort ⚖ [tɔːt] acte *m* dommageable; préjudice *m*.

tor·toise *zo.* ['tɔːtəs] tortue *f*;

~-shell ['~təʃel] écaille f (de tortue).

tor·tu·os·i·ty [tɔːtju'ɔsiti] tortuosité f; **'tor·tu·ous** □ tortueux (-euse f); sinueux (-euse f); tortu (esprit); Å gauche (courbe).

tor·ture ['tɔːtʃə] **1.** torture f, question f; supplice m; **2.** mettre (q.) à la question; torturer; **'tor·tur·er** bourreau m; harceleur m.

To·ry ['tɔːri] tory m (membre du parti conservateur anglais) (a. adj.); **'To·ry·ism** torysme m.

tosh sl. [tɔʃ] bêtises f/pl.

toss [tɔs] **1.** jet m, coup m; mouvement m (de tête) dédaigneux; équit. chute f de cheval; (a. ~up) coup m de pile ou face; it is a ~-up les chances sont égales; win the ~ gagner (à pile ou face); **2.** v/t. agiter, (a. ~ about) secouer; démonter (un cavalier); ~ aside jeter de côté; lancer; faner (le foin); cuis. sauter; (a. ~ up) lancer en l'air; ~ (up) a coin jouer à pile ou face; hocher (la tête); ~ off (ou down) avaler d'un trait (du vin etc.)); Å ~ the oars mâter les avirons; v/i. s'agiter; tanguer (navire); être ballotté; ~ (up) choisir à pile ou face (qch., for s.th.).

tot¹ F [tɔt] tout(e) petit(e) enfant mf; petit verre m.

tot² F [~] **1.** addition f; **2.**: ~ up v/t. additionner; v/i. s'élever (à, to).

to·tal ['toutl] **1.** □ total (-aux m/pl.); entier (-ère f); complet (-ète f); **2.** total m, montant m; grand ~ total m global, somme f globale; **3.** v/t. additionner; v/i. s'élever (à, up to); **to·tal·i·tar·i·an** [toutæli-'tɛəriən] totalitaire; **to·tal·i·tar·i·an·ism** totalitarisme m; **to'tal·i·ty** totalité f; **to·tal·i·za·tor** ['~təlaizeitə] totalisateur m; **to·tal·ize** ['~aiz] totaliser, additionner.

tote Am. [tout] (trans)porter.

tot·ter ['tɔtə] chanceler (a. fig.); tituber (ivrogne); **'tot·ter·ing** □, **'tot·ter·y** chancelant; titubant (ivrogne).

touch [tʌtʃ] **1.** v/t. toucher (de, with); émouvoir; effleurer (une surface, ♪ les cordes de la harpe); trinquer (des verres); toucher à (= déranger); fig. atteindre; F taper (de, for); rehausser (un dessin); ~ one's hat saluer (q., to s.o.); porter la main à son chapeau; F a bit (ou a

little) ~ed un peu toqué; sl. ~ s.o. for a pound taper q. d'une livre; ~ off ébaucher; faire partir (une mine); ~ up rafraîchir; repolir; phot. faire des retouches à; v/i. se toucher, être en contact; Å ~ at toucher à; faire escale à; ~ on toucher (qch.) (= traiter, mentionner); **2.** toucher m (♪, a. sens); contact m; attouchement m; léger coup m; cuis., maladie, etc.: soupçon m; peint. (coup m de) pinceau m; sp., peint. touche f; dactylographe: frappe f; fig. nuance f, pointe f; ~ of bronchitis pointe f de bronchite; get in(to) ~ (avec, with) se mettre en communication, prendre contact; **'~-and-'go** **1.** affaire f hasardeuse; it is ~ ça reste en balance; **2.** très incertain; hasardeux (-euse f); **'~-down** ✈ atterrissage m; amerrissage m; **'~-hole** canon: lumière f; **'touch·i·ness** susceptibilité f; **'touch·ing 1.** □ touchant, émouvant; **2.** prp. touchant, concernant; **'touch-line** foot. ligne f de touche; **'touch·stone** pierre f de touche (a. fig.); **touch-type** taper au toucher; **'touch·y** □ susceptible; see testy.

tough [tʌf] **1.** dur, résistant; fig. fort; rude; inflexible (personne); Am. dur; brutal (-aux m/pl.); de bandit; **2.** surt. Am. apache m, bandit m; **'tough·en** vt/i. durcir; (s')endurcir (personne); **'tough·ness** dureté f; résistance f (à la fatigue); fig. difficulté f.

tour [tuə] **1.** tour m; excursion f; tournée f; ~ operator organisateur m de voyage; **2.** faire le tour de; voyager; visiter en touriste; **'tour·ing** en tournée; de touristes; mot. ~ car voiture f de tourisme; **'tour·ism** tourisme m; **'tour·ist** touriste mf; voyageur (-euse f) m; ~ agency office ou bureau bureau m de tourisme; ~ industry tourisme m; ~ season la saison f; ~ ticket billet m circulaire.

tour·na·ment ['tuənəmənt], **tour·ney** ['~ni] tournoi m.

tou·sle ['tauzl] houspiller; chiffonner (une femme, une robe); ébouriffer (les cheveux).

tout [taut] **1.** pisteur m; racoleur m; (a. racing ~) tout m; **2.**: ~ for pister, racoler; Am. solliciter.

tow¹ Å [tou] **1.** (câble m de) remorque f; ~ car voiture f remorqueuse; take *in* ~ prendre à la remorque; 2. remorquer; haler (*un chaland*).

tow² [~] étoupe *f* (blanche).

tow·age ⚓ ['touidʒ] remorquage *m*; *chaland*: halage *m*.

to·ward(s) [tə'wɔːd(z)] vers, du côté de; *sentiment*: pour, envers.

tow·el ['tauəl] 1. serviette *f*; essuie-mains *m*/*inv*.; 2. frotter avec une serviette; *sl*. donner une raclée à (*q*.); '~**-horse**, '~**-rack** porte-serviettes *m*/*inv*.

tow·er ['tauə] 1. tour *f*; ⊕ pylône *m*; *église*: clocher *m*; *fig. a* ~ *of strength* un puissant appui; *Brit*. ~ *block* immeuble-tour *m* (*pl*. immeubles-tours); 2. (*a*. ~ *over*) dominer; monter très haut; '**tow·ered** surmonté *ou* flanqué d'une tour *ou* de tours; '**tow·er·ing** □ très élevé, qui domine; *fig*. violent, sans bornes.

tow(·ing)... ['tou(iŋ)]: '~**-line** (câble *m* de) remorque *f*; '~**-path** chemin *m ou* banquette *f* de halage; ~ **truck** dépanneuse *f*.

town [taun] 1. ville *f*; cité *f*; *county* ~ chef-lieu (*pl*. chefs-lieux) *m*; 2. municipal (-aux *m*/*pl*.); de la ville; à la ville; ~ *clerk* secrétaire *m* de mairie; ~ *council* conseil *m* municipal; ~ *hall* hôtel *m* de ville; mairie *f*; *surt. Am.* (*Nouvelle-Angleterre*): ~ *meeting* réunion *f* des électeurs de la ville; '~**-'plan·ning** urbanisation *f*; ~**scape** ['~skeip] panorama *m* de la ville.

towns·folk ['taunzfouk] *pl*., '**towns-peo·ple** *pl*. citadins *m*/*pl*.; bourgeois *m*/*pl*.; concitoyens *m*/*pl*.

town·ship ['taunʃip] commune *f*.

towns·man ['taunzmən] citadin *m*; bourgeois *m* (*a. univ*.); (*ou fellow* ~) concitoyen *m*.

tow-rope ⚓ ['touroup] (câble *m* de) remorque *f*; *chaland*: corde *f* de halage.

tox·ic, tox·i·cal □ ['tɔksik(l)] toxique; intoxicant; '**tox·in** toxine *f*.

toy [tɔi] 1. jouet *m*; F joujou(x *pl*.) *m*; *attr*. d'enfant; de jouets; tout petit; pour rire; 2. jouer, s'amuser (avec, *with*); *fig*. faire (*qch*.) en amateur; '~**-book** livre *m* d'images; '~**-box** boîte *f* à joujoux; '~**-shop** magasin *m* de jouets.

trace¹ [treis] 1. trace *f*; vestige *m* (*a. fig*.); *fig*. ombre *f*; 2. tracer (*a. un plan*); calquer (*un dessin*); *fig*. es-

quisser; suivre la piste de; suivre à la trace; recouvrer; retrouver les vestiges de; suivre (*un chemin*); ~ *back* faire remonter (à, *to*); ~ *out* tracer; esquisser; *surv*. faire le tracé de; ~ *to* (faire) remonter à.

trace² [~] trait *m*; ~**-horse** cheval *m* de renfort.

trace·a·ble □ ['treisəbl] que l'on peut tracer *ou* décalquer; facile à suivre; '**trac·er**: *radio-active* ~ traceur *m* radio-actif; ~ *bullet* balle *f* traçante; '**trac·er·y** ⚛ réseau *m*; tympan *m* (*de fenêtre gothique*).

tra·che·a ⚕ [trə'kiːə] trachée-artère (*pl*. trachées-artères) *f*.

trac·ing ['treisiŋ] tracé *m*; traçage *m*; calquage *m*; calque *m*; '~**-pa·per** papier *m* à calquer.

track [træk] 1. trace *f*; piste *f* (*a. sp*., *chasse*, ⊕); voie *f* (*a*. 🚂, *chasse*); sentier *m*; chemin *m* (*a*. ⊕); *tracteur*: chenille *f*; *Am*. 🚂 rail *m*; *surt. Am.* ~*athletics pl*. l'athlétisme *m* (sur piste); la course, le saut, et le lancement du poids; ~ *events pl*. épreuves *f*/*pl*. d'athlétisme; 2. *v*/*t*. suivre à la trace *ou* à la piste; traquer (*un malfaiteur*); ~ *down* (*ou out*) dépister; retrouver les traces de; *v*/*i*. être en alignement; '~**-and-'field sports** *pl*. l'athlétisme (sur piste); '**track·er** *usu. chasse*: traqueur *m*; '**track·less** sans traces; sans chemin; ⊕ sans rails, sans voie.

tract¹ [trækt] étendue *f*; région *f*; *anat*. appareil *m*.

tract² [~] brochure *f*.

trac·ta·bil·i·ty [træktə'biliti], '**trac-ta·ble·ness** docilité *f*; humeur *f* traitable; '**trac·ta·ble** □ docile, traitable.

trac·tion ['træk[n] traction *f*; ~*engine* machine *f* routière; remorqueur *m*; '**trac·tive** tractif (-ive *f*); de traction; '**trac·tor** ⊕ tracteur *m*; *caterpillar* ~ autochenille *f*; *Am*. ~*trailer* tracteur *m* à remorque.

trade [treid] 1. commerce *m*, affaires *f*/*pl*.; métier *m*, emploi *m*; état *m*; *Am*. marché *m*, vente *f* en reprise; *Board of* ♀ Ministère *m* du Commerce; *free* ~ libre échange *m*; *do a good* ~ faire de bonnes affaires, vendre beaucoup; 2. *v*/*i*. faire des affaires (avec, *with*); faire le commerce (de, *in*), trafiquer (en, *in*); ~ *in* échanger (contre, *for*); donner (*une vieille voi-*

ture) en reprise; *v/t.* échanger (contre, *for*); '**~-fair** ♀ foire *f*; '**~-'in** reprise; objet *m* donné en reprise; ~ *price* (*value*) prix *m* (valeur *f*) à la reprise; *take s.th. as a* ~ prendre qch. en reprise; '**~-mark** marque *f* de fabrique; *souv.* marque *f* déposée; ~ **name** raison *f* de commerce; nom *m* commercial, appellation *f* (*d'un article*); ~ **price** prix *m* marchand; '**trad·er** commerçant(e *f*) *m*, négociant(e *f*) *m*; marchand(e *f*) *m*; **trade re·la·tions** *pl.* relations *f/pl.* commerciales; '**trade school** école *f* industrielle; '**trades·man** marchand *m*; fournisseur *m*; *prov.* artisan *m*; '**trades·peo·ple** *pl.* commerçants *m/pl.*

trade(s)...: ~ **un·ion** syndicat *m* ouvrier; **~-'un·ion·ism** syndicalisme *m*; mouvement *m* syndical; **~-'un·ion·ist** 1. syndiqué(e *f*) *m*; 2. syndical (-aux *m/pl.*).

trade...: ~ **war** guerre *f* économique; ~ **wind** (vent *m*) alizé *m*.

trad·ing ['treidiŋ] de commerce, commercial (-aux *m/pl.*); commerçant (*ville*).

tra·di·tion [trə'diʃn] tradition *f* (*a.* 🕆); **tra'di·tion·al** □, **tra'di·tion·ar·y** □ traditionnel(le *f*); de tradition.

traf·fic ['træfik] 1. commerce *m*, trafic *m* (de, in) (*a. péj.*); *rue*: circulation *f*; ~ *census* recensement *m* de la circulation; ~ *jam* embouteillage *m*; ~ *lights pl.* feux *m/pl.* (de circulation); ~ *news pl.* radioguidage *m*; ~ *sign* poteau *m* de signalisation; ~ *warden* contractuel(le *f*) *m*; 2. *v/i.* trafiquer; faire le commerce (de, in); *v/t. usu. péj.* trafiquer de; ~ *away* vendre; **traf·fi·ca·tor** *mot.* ['træfikeitə] flèche *f* mobile; '**traf·fick·er** trafiquant *m* (de, en in) (*a. péj.*).

tra·ge·di·an [trə'dʒiːdjən] (auteur *m*) tragique *m*; *théá.* tragédien(ne *f*) *m*; **trag·e·dy** ['trædʒidi] tragédie *f* (*a. fig.*); *fig.* drame *m*.

trag·ic, **trag·i·cal** □ ['trædʒik(l)] tragique (*a. fig.*).

trag·i·com·e·dy ['trædʒi'kɔmidi] tragi-comédie *f*; '**trag·i'com·ic** (~ally) tragi-comique.

trail [treil] 1. *fig.* traînée *f*; sillon *m*; queue *f*; *chasse:* voie *f*, piste *f*; sentier *m*; 2. *v/t.* traîner; *chasse:* suivre à la piste, traquer (*a. un criminel*);

F suivre; *v/i.* traîner; se traîner (*personne*); ♀ grimper; ramper; ~ **blazer** *Am.* pionnier *m*; précurseur *m*; '**trail·er** ♀ plante *f* grimpante *ou* rampante; *chasse:* traqueur *m*; *véhicule:* remorque *f*; baladeuse *f*; *mot. Am.* roulotte *f*; *cin.* film-annonce *m*.

train [trein] 1. suite *f*, cortège *m*; train *m* (*a.* 🚂); *animaux, bateaux, wagons:* file *f*; *poudre:* traînée *f*; *cost.* queue *f*; *fig.* chaîne *f*; ✕ rame *f* (*de bennes, a. du Métro*); *by* ~ par le train; *in* ~ en train; *set in* ~ mettre en train; ~ *journey* voyage *m* en *ou* par chemin de fer; 2. *v/t.* former; dresser (*un animal*); élever (*un enfant*); diriger (*une plante*); *sp.* entraîner; braquer (*une arme à feu*); *v/i.* s'exercer; *sp.* s'entraîner; *F* ~ (*it*) voyager en *ou* par chemin de fer; '**~-ac·ci·dent**, '**~-dis·as·ter** accident *m* de chemin de fer; **train'ee** apprenti *m*; *box.* poulain *m*; '**train·er** dresseur *m* (*d'animaux*); *sp.* entraîneur *m*; '**train·'fer·ry** bac *m* transbordeur.

train·ing ['treiniŋ] éducation *f*; ✕ dressage *m* (*a. d'animaux*); *sp.* entraînement *m*; ~ *of horses* manège *m*; *physical* ~ éducation *f* physique; *go into light* ~ effectuer un léger entraînement; '**~-col·lege** école *f* normale; '**~-ship** navire-école (*pl.* navires-écoles) *m*.

train-oil ['treinɔil] huile *f* de baleine.

trait [treit] trait *m* (*de caractère etc.*).

trai·tor ['treitə] traître *m*; '**trai·tor·ous** □ traître(sse *f*).

trai·tress ['treitris] traîtresse *f*.

tra·jec·to·ry *phys.* ['trædʒiktəri] trajectoire *f*.

tram [træm] *see* ~-*car*, ~*way*; '**~-car** (voiture *f* de) tramway *m*.

tram·mel ['træml] 1. ⚓ tramail *m*; *fig.* ~s *pl.* entraves *f/pl.*; 2. entraver, empêtrer (de, with).

tramp [træmp] 1. promenade *f* à pied; pas *m* lourd, bruit *m* des pas; *personne:* vagabond *m*, chemineau *m*; ⚓ (*souv. ocean* ~) cargo *m* sans ligne régulière; *F on the* ~ sur le trimard; *be on the* ~ courir les routes; 2. *v/i.* marcher lourdement; voyager à pied; *v/t.* battre (*le pavé*); courir (*le pays*); **tram·ple** ['~l] piétiner, fouler (*qch.*) aux pieds.

tram·way ['træmwei] (voie *f* de) tramway *m*.

trance [trɑːns] transe *f*; extase *f*.

tran·ny *sl.* ['træni] transistor *m*.

tran·quil □ ['træŋkwil] tranquille, calme; **tran'quil·(l)i·ty** tranquillité *f*, calme *m*; **tran·quil·(l)i·za·tion** [ˌlaiˈzeiʃn] apaisement *m*; **'tran·quil·(l)ize** calmer, apaiser; **'tran·quil·(l)iz·er** ⚕ tranquillisant *m*.

trans·act [trænˈzækt] négocier; ~ *business* faire des affaires; **trans'ac·tion** conduite *f*; opération *f*; affaire *f*; *pl. péj.* commerce *m*; comptes-rendus *m/pl.* (des séances); **trans'ac·tor** négociateur (-trice *f*) *m*.

trans·al·pine ['trænzˈælpain] transalpin.

trans·at·lan·tic ['trænzətˈlæntik] transatlantique.

tran·scend [trænˈsend] outrepasser; dépasser; surpasser (*q.*); **tran'scend·ence, tran'scend·en·cy** [~dəns(i)] transcendance *f* (*a. phls*); **tran'scend·ent** □ transcendant; *a.* = **tran·scen·den·tal** □ [~ˈdentl] Å transcendant; *phls.* transcendantal (-aux *m/pl.*); F vague.

tran·scribe [trænsˈkraib] transcrire (*a.* ♪); traduire (*des notes sténographiques*); *radio*: enregistrer.

tran·script ['trænskript] copie *f*, transcription *f*; traduction *f* (*de notes sténographiques*); **tran'scrip·tion** transcription *f* (*a.* ♪); *radio*: enregistrement *m*; *see a.* transcript.

tran·sept Δ ['trænsept] transept *m*.

trans·fer 1. [trænsˈfəː] *v/t.* transférer; transporter; ⚖ transmettre, céder; (dé)calquer (*un dessin, une image*); *banque*: virer (*une somme*); *comptabilité*: contre-passer, ristourner; 🚌 déclasser; *v/i.* changer de train *etc.*; **2.** ['trænsfə] transport *m*; ⚖ transmission *f*, acte *m* de cession; ✝ transfert *m*; déclassement *m* (🚌 de voyageurs); ⚖ mutation *f* (*de biens*); *banque*: virement *m*; ristourne *f*; décalque *m*; ~*-picture* décalcomanie *f*; ✝ ~ *ticket* transfert *m*; *Am.* billet *m* de correspondance; **trans'fer·a·ble** transmissible, cessible; **trans·fer·ee** ⚖, ✝ [~fəˈriː] cessionnaire *mf*; **trans·fer·ence** ['~fərəns] transfèrement *m*;

psych. transfert *m* affectif; **'trans·fer·or** ⚖ cédant(e *f*) *m*.

trans·fig·u·ra·tion [trænsfigjuəˈreiʃn] transfiguration *f*; **trans·fig·ure** [~ˈfigə] transfigurer.

trans·fix [trænsˈfiks] transpercer; *fig.* ~*ed* cloué au sol (par, *with*).

trans·form [trænsˈfɔːm] transformer, convertir (en, *into*); **trans·for·ma·tion** [~fəˈmeiʃn] transformation *f*; conversion *f*; *fig.* métamorphose *f*; faux toupet *m*; **trans·form·er** ⚡ [~ˈfɔːmə] transformateur *m*.

trans·fuse [trænsˈfjuːz] transfuser (*a.* ⚕ *du sang*); ⚕ faire une transfusion de sang à (*un malade*); *fig.* pénétrer (de, *with*); *fig.* inspirer (qch. à q., *s.o. with s.th.*); **trans'fu·sion** [~ʒn] transfusion *f* (*surt.* ⚕ *de sang*).

trans·gress [trænsˈgres] *v/t.* transgresser, violer, enfreindre; *v/i.* pécher; **trans·gres·sion** [~ˈgreʃn] transgression *f*; péché *m*, faute *f*; **trans·gres·sor** [~ˈgresə] transgresseur *m*; pécheur (-eresse *f*) *m*.

tran·ship(·ment) [trænˈʃip(mənt)] *see* transship(ment).

tran·sience, tran·sien·cy ['trænziəns(i)] caractère *m* passager; courte durée *f*.

tran·sient ['trænziənt] **1.** passager (-ère *f*), transitoire; éphémère; momentané; ♪ de transition; **2.** *Am.* voyageur *m ou* client *m* de passage; ~ *camp* camp *m* de passage; **'tran·sient·ness** caractère *m* passager; courte durée *f*.

tran·sis·tor [trænˈsistə] transistor *m*; **tran'sis·tor·ize** [~raiz] transistoriser.

trans·it ['trænsit] passage *m*.

tran·si·tion [trænˈsiʒn] transition *f*; passage *m*; **tran'si·tion·al** □ de transition; transitionnel(le *f*).

tran·si·tive □ *gramm.* ['trænsitiv] transitif (-ive *f*).

tran·si·to·ri·ness ['trænsitərinis] caractère *m* transitoire *ou* passager; courte durée *f*; **'tran·si·to·ry** □ transitoire, passager (-ère *f*); de courte durée.

trans·lat·a·ble [trænsˈleitəbl] traduisible; **trans·late** [~ˈleit] traduire (*un livre etc.*); déchiffrer; *fig.* prendre pour; convertir (en, *into*); transférer (*un évêque*); **trans'la-**

1179

tion traduction *f*; déchiffrement *m*; *école*: version *f*; *eccl.* translation *f*; **trans'la·tor** traducteur (-trice *f*) *m*.

trans·lu·cence, trans·lu·cen·cy [trænz'luːsns(i)] translucidité *f*; **trans'lu·cent** translucide; *fig.* clair.

trans·ma·rine [trænzmə'riːn] d'outre-mer.

trans·mi·grant ['trænzmigrənt] émigrant *m* de passage; **trans·mi·grate** ['trænzmaigreit] transmigrer (*a. fig.*); **trans·mi·gra·tion** transmigration *f* (*a. des âmes*); *fig.* métempsycose *f*.

trans·mis·si·ble [trænz'misəbl] transmissible; **trans·mis·sion** [~'miʃn] transmission *f* (*a.* ⊕, *biol.*, *phys.*, *radio*); *radio a.* émission *f*.

trans·mit [trænz'mit] transmettre (*a. biol.*, *phys.*, *radio*); ⚡ transporter (*la force*); *radio a.* émettre; communiquer (*un mouvement*); **trans·mit·ter** celui (celle *f*) *m* qui transmet; *tél.* transmetteur *m*; *radio:* (poste *m*) émetteur *m*; **trans·mit·ting** transmetteur (-trice *f*); *radio:* émetteur (-trice *f*); d'émission; ~ **station** poste *m* émetteur.

trans·mog·ri·fy F [trænz'mɔgrifai] transformer (en, *into*).

trans·mut·a·ble □ [trænz'mjuːtəbl] transmu(t)able (en, *into*); **trans·mu·ta·tion** transmutation *f*; ⚛ mutation *f*; **trans·mute** [~'mjuːt] transformer, convertir (en, *into*).

trans·o·ce·an·ic ['trænzouʃi'ænik] transocéanien(ne *f*).

tran·som ⊕ ['trænsəm] traverse *f*; meneau *m* horizontal; *surt. Am.* vasistas *m*.

trans·par·en·cy [træns'pɛərənsi] transparence *f*; limpidité *f*; *phot.* diapositif *m*; **trans·par·ent** □ transparent; limpide; *fig.* évident.

tran·spi·ra·tion [trænspi'reiʃn] transpiration *f* (*a. fig.*); **tran·spire** [~'paiə] transpirer (*a. fig.*); V se passer.

trans·plant [træns'plɑːnt] transplanter; **trans·plan·ta·tion** transplantation *f*.

trans·port 1. [træns'pɔːt] transporter (*a. fig.*); *fig.* enlever; **2.** ['trænspɔːt] transport *m* (*a. fig.*); *coll.* ⚔ charrois *m/pl.*; *road* ~ transport *m* routier; ~ *undertaking* (*ou firm*) entreprise *f* de transport; *Minister*

of ⚔ ministre *m* des transports; *in* ~s transporté (*de joie, de colère*); **trans'port·a·ble** transportable; **trans·por·ta·tion** transport *m*; déportation *f* (*d'un criminel*); ⚔ *Am.* billet *m*.

trans·pose [træns'pouz] transposer (*a.* ♪); **trans·po·si·tion** [~pə'ziʃn] transposition *f*; ⚛ permutation *f*.

trans·ship ⚓, ⚔ [træns'ʃip] *v/t.* transborder; *v/i.* changer de vaisseau; **trans·ship·ment** transbordement *m*.

tran·sub·stan·ti·ate [trænsəb'stænʃieit] transsubstantier; **tran·sub·stan·ti·a·tion** transsubstantiation *f*.

tran·sude *physiol.* [træn'sjuːd] *vt/i.* transsuder.

trans·ver·sal [trænz'vəːsl] **1.** □ transversal (-aux *m/pl.*); **2.** ⚛ transversale *f*; *anat.* transversal *m*; **trans·verse** ['~vəːs] transversal (-aux *m/pl.*); en travers; ~ *section* section *f* transversale; ⊕ ~ *strength* résistance *f* à la flexion.

trans·ves·tite [træns'vestait] travesti(e *f*) *m*.

trap[1] [træp] **1.** piège *m* (*a. fig.*); trappe *f* (*a. théâ.*, *a. de colombier*); *sp.* ball-trap *m* (*pour pigeons artificiels*); boîte *f* de lancement (*pour pigeons vivants*); ⊕ collecteur *m* (*d'eau etc.*); *see* ~*door*; F carriole *f*; **2.** prendre au piège (*a. fig.*); *foot.* bloquer; ⊕ mettre un collecteur dans.

trap[2] *min.* [~] trapp *m*.

trap·door *théâ.* ['træp'dɔː] trappe *f*; abattant *m*.

trapes F [treips] se balader (dans).

tra·peze [trə'piːz] *cirque:* trapèze *m*; **tra·pe·zi·um** ⚛ [~ziəm] trapèze *m*; **trap·e·zoid** ⚛ ['træpizɔid] quadrilatère *m* irrégulier.

trap·per ['træpə] piégeur *m*; *Am.* trappeur *m*.

trap·pings ['træpiŋz] *pl. cheval:* harnachement *m*; caparaçon *m*; *fig.* apparat *m*.

trap·py F ['træpi] plein de traquenards.

traps F [træps] *pl.* effets *m/pl.* (personnels).

trash [træʃ] *surt. Am.* ordures *f/pl.*; déchets *m/pl.*; rebut *m*; camelote *f*; *fig.* sottises *f/pl.*; vauriens *m/pl.*; *Am.* ~ *can* poubelle *f*; **trash·y** □ sans valeur, de rebut, de camelote.

trau·ma [ˈtrɔːmə] trauma *m*; **trau·mat·ic** [~ˈmætik] traumatique; ~ *experience* traumatisme *m*.

trav·el [ˈtrævl] **1.** *v/i.* voyager; faire des voyages; ✝ être voyageur de commerce, représenter une maison de commerce; *fig.* se propager, se répandre; ⊕ se déplacer; F aller à toute vitesse; *v/t.* parcourir; faire (*une distance*); **2.** voyage *m*, -s *m/pl.*; ⊕ parcours *m*; ~ *agency*, ~ *agent's*, ~ *bureau* bureau *m* de voyages; ~ *allowance* indemnité *f* de déplacement; **ˈtrav·el(l)ed** qui a beaucoup voyagé; **ˈtrav·el·(l)er** voyageur (-euse *f*) *m*; ✝ commis *m* voyageur; ⊕ grue *f* roulante; pont *m* roulant; ~*'s cheque* chèque *m* de voyage; **ˈtrav·el·(l)ing** voyageur (-euse *f*); ambulant; de voyage; ⊕ roulant; ~ *salesman* représentant *m ou* voyageur *m* de commerce.

trav·e·log(ue) *Am.* [ˈtrævəloug] conférence *f* avec projections décrivant un voyage.

trav·erse [ˈtrævəːs] **1.** traversée *f* (*a. alp.*); passage *m* à travers ✕, *alp.* traverse *f*; ⚔ dénégation *f*; ✕ pare-éclats *m/inv.*; ⊕ chariot *m* de tour: translation *f* latérale; **2.** *v/t.* traverser (*a. fig.*), passer à travers; *fig.* passer en revue; *fig.* contrarier; ⚔ nier; ✕ pointer en direction (*un canon*); *v/i. alp.* prendre une traverse.

trav·es·ty [ˈtrævisti] **1.** parodie *f*; *fig. péj.* travestissement *m*; **2.** parodier; travestir.

trawl ⚓ [trɔːl] **1.** chalut *m*; câble *m* balayeur; **2.** pêcher au chalut; **ˈtrawl·er** *personne, a. bateau*: chalutier *m*.

tray [trei] plateau *m*; cuvette *f*; *malle, caisse*: compartiment *m*.

treach·er·ous □ [ˈtretʃərəs] traître (-sse *f*) (*a. fig.*); déloyal (-aux *m/pl.*); perfide; **ˈtreach·er·ous·ness**, **ˈtreach·er·y** perfidie *f*, trahison *f*; caractère *m* dangereux (*de la glace*).

trea·cle [ˈtriːkl] mélasse *f*.

tread [tred] **1.** [*irr.*] *v/i.* marcher, aller, avancer (sur, [up]on); *v/t.* marcher sur; fouler; ✝ danser; *coq:* côcher; ~ *water* nager debout; **2.** pas *m*; bruit *m* des pas; *coq:* accouplement *m*; *escalier:* marche *f*; *soulier, roue:* semelle *f*; **trea·dle** [ˈ~l] **1.** pédale *f*; **2.** *v/i.* pédaler; **ˈtread·mill** ✝ moulin *m* de discipline; *fig.* besogne *f* ingrate.

trea·son [ˈtriːzn] trahison *f*; **ˈtrea·son·a·ble** □ traître(sse *f*); de trahison.

treas·ure [ˈtreʒə] **1.** trésor *m*; ~*s of the soil* richesses *f/pl.* du (sous-)sol; ~ *hunt* chasse *f* au trésor; ⚒ ~ *trove* trésor *m*; **2.** priser; (*usu.* ~ *up*) conserver précieusement; **ˈtreas·ur·er** trésorier (-ère *f*) *m*; économe *m*.

treas·ur·y [ˈtreʒəri] trésorerie *f*; caisse *f* centrale; Trésor *m* public; *Am.* ♀ *Department* ministère *m* des Finances; *parl.* ♀ *Bench* banc *m* ministériel; ~ *bill* billet *m* du Trésor; ~ *bond* bon *m* du Trésor; ~ *note* coupure *f* émise par le Trésor.

treat [triːt] **1.** *v/t.* traiter; régaler (*q.*); payer à voir à; *v/i.* traiter (de, *of*; avec *q.* pour avoir qch., *with s.o. for s.th.*); **2.** régal (*s pl.*) *m*, festin *m*, plaisir *m*; F *it is my* ~ c'est moi qui régale, c'est ma tournée; *see stand* **2**; **ˈtreat·er** négociateur (-trice *f*) *m*; celui (celle *f*) *m* qui paye à boire; **trea·tise** [ˈ~iz] traité *m*; **ˈtreat·ment** traitement *m*; **ˈtrea·ty** traité *m*; convention *f*; contrat *m*; *be in* ~ *with* être en pourparlers avec; ~ *port* port *m* ouvert au commerce étranger.

tre·ble [ˈtrebl] **1.** □ triple; ♪ de soprano; ♪ ~ *clef* clef *f* de sol; **2.** triple *m*; ♪ dessus *m*; *personne, voix:* soprano *m*; **3.** *adv.* trois fois autant; ~ *v/t/i.* tripler.

tree [triː] **1.** arbre *m*; *souliers:* embauchoir *m*; poutre *f*; *see family* **2**; F *up a* ~ dans le pétrin; **2.** (forcer à) se réfugier dans un arbre; F réduire à quia.

tre·foil ♣, △ [ˈtrefɔil] trèfle *m*.

trek [trek] *Afrique du Sud:* **1.** voyager en chariot (à bœufs); F faire route; **2.** (étape *f* d'un) voyage *m* en chariot.

trel·lis [ˈtrelis] **1.** treillis *m*; ⚹ treille *f*; **2.** treillisser (*une fenêtre*); ⚹ échalasser (*une vigne*).

trem·ble [ˈtrembl] **1.** trembler (devant, *at*; de, *with*); **2.** trembl(ot)ement *m*.

tre·men·dous □ [triˈmendəs] épouvantable, terrible; F énorme, immense.

trem·or [ˈtremə] tremblement *m*, [frémissement *m*.]

1181

tricolo(u)r

trem·u·lous □ ['tremjuləs] trembl(ot)ant; frémissant; **'trem·u·lous·ness** tremblotement *m*; timidité *f*.

trench [trentʃ] **1.** tranchée *f* (*a.* ✕); fossé *m*; **~ warfare** guerre *f* de tranchées; **2.** *v/t.* creuser une tranchée *ou* un fossé dans; ✔ défoncer (*un terrain*); planter (*le céleri*) dans une rigole; *v/i.* ✕ creuser des tranchées; empiéter (sur, [up]on); *fig.* friser; **'trench·ant** □ tranchant (*surt. fig.*); *fig.* incisif (-ive *f*); **trench coat** (manteau *m*) imperméable *m*.

trench·er ['trentʃə] tranchoir *m*; *fig.* table *f*; **~ cap** toque *f* universitaire.

trench...: **'~-jack·et** blouson *m*; **'~-plough**, *Am.* **'~-plow 1.** rigoleuse *f*; **2.** rigoler.

trend [trend] **1.** direction *f*; *fig.* cours *m*; *fig.* marche *f*, tendance *f*; **2.** tendre, se diriger (vers, to [-wards]); **'~-set·ter** lanceur (-euse *f*) *m* de modes; personne *f* qui donne le ton; **'trend·y** F à la (dernière) mode, dernier cri; dans le vent; *the trendies pl.* les gens *m/pl.* dans le vent.

tre·pan [tri'pæn] **1.** ✚ trépan *m*; **2.** ✚, *a.* ⊕ trépaner.

trep·i·da·tion [trepi'deiʃn] trépidation *f*; émoi *m*.

tres·pass ['trespəs] **1.** transgression *f*; délit *m*; ⚖ violation *f* (*des droits de q.*); *eccl.* offense *f*; F empiétement *m* (sur, [up]on); abus *m* (de, [up]on); **2.** violer *ou* enfreindre les droits; empiéter sans autorisation sur la propriété de q.; **~ against** violer, enfreindre (*les droits etc.*); *fig.* **~ (up)on** empiéter sur, abuser de; **'tres·pass·er** violateur *m* des droits d'autrui; intrus(e *f*) *m*; **~s will be prosecuted** défense d'entrer sous peine d'amende.

tress [tres] tresse *f*, boucle *f* (*de cheveux*).

tres·tle ['tresl] tréteau *m*, chevalet *m*; **~-bridge** pont *m* de chevalets; ponton *m* à chevalets.

trey [trei] *cartes, a. dés:* trois *m*.

tri·ad ['traiəd] triade *f*; *phls., eccl.* unité *f* composée de trois personnes; ♪ accord *m* en tierce; ♒ élément *m* trivalent.

tri·al ['traiəl] essai *m*, épreuve *f* (de, of); *fig.* adversité *f*, épreuve *f*; ⚖ procès *m*, cause *f*, jugement *m*; **~**

marriage mariage *m* à l'essai; *sp.* **~ match** match *m* de sélection; **~ offer** offre *f* à l'essai; **~ period** période *f* d'essai; **on ~** à l'essai; ⚖ en jugement; *prisoner on* **~** prévenu(e *f*) *m*; **~ of strength** essai *m* de force; **bring to ~** mettre en jugement; **give s.th. a ~** faire l'essai de qch.; **send s.o. for ~** renvoyer q. en jugement; ⚖ **stand ~** comparaître devant le tribunal; passer en jugement, être jugé (pour, for).

tri·an·gle ['traiæŋgl] triangle *m* (*a.* ♪); **tri·an·gu·lar** □ [~'æŋgjulə] triangulaire; en triangle; **tri·an·gu·late** *surv.* [~leit] trianguler.

trib·al □ ['traibl] de tribu; qui appartient à la tribu; tribal; **tribe** [traib] tribu *f* (*a. zo.*); ♀, *zo.* classe *f*, genre *m*; *péj.* clan *m*; **'tribes·man** ['~zmən] membre *m* d'une *ou* de la tribu.

tri·bu·nal [trai'bju:nl] tribunal (-aux *pl.*) *m*; cour *f* (de justice); **trib·une** ['tribju:n] tribun *m*; tribune *f* (*d'orateur*).

trib·u·tar·y ['tribjutəri] **1.** □ tributaire; **2.** tributaire *m* (*a. géog.*); *géog.* affluent *m*; **trib·ute** ['~bju:t] tribut *m*; *fig.* hommage *m*; (*a. floral* **~**) couronne *f*.

tri·car ['traika:] tricar *m*.

trice [trais]: **in a ~** en un clin d'œil.

tri·chi·na *zo.* [tri'kainə], *pl.* **-nae** [~ni:] trichine *f*.

trick [trik] **1.** tour *m*; tour *m* d'adresse; ruse *f*; truc *m*; espièglerie *f*; habitude *f*; *cartes:* levée *f*; **~ film** film *m* à truquages; **2.** duper, attraper; **~ into** (*gér.*) amener par ruse à (*inf.*); **~ s.o. out of s.th.** escroquer qch. à q.; *fig.* **~ out** (*ou* **up**) attifer (de in, with); **'trick·er, 'trick·ster** ['~stə] escroc *m*, fourbe *m*; **'trick·er·y** fourberie *f*, tromperie *f*; **'trick·ish** □ trompeur (-euse *f*), fourbe; compliqué.

trick·le ['trikl] **1.** couler goutte à goutte; suinter; F *fig.* se répandre peu à peu; passer un à un; **2.** filet *m* (d'eau); quelques gouttes *f/pl.*; petits groupes *m/pl.* (d'hommes etc.).

trick·si·ness ['triksinis] humeur *f* capricieuse; espièglerie *f*; **'trick·sy** □ capricieux (-euse *f*); espiègle; **= 'trick·y** □ astucieux (-euse *f*); F délicat, compliqué.

tri·col·o(u)r ['trikələ] **1.** tricolore; **2.** drapeau *m* tricolore.

tri·cy·cle ['traisikl] tricycle *m*.

tri·dent ['traidənt] trident *m* (*a.* Ⓐ).

tri·en·ni·al □ [trai'enjəl] trisannuel (-le *f*); triennal (-aux *m*/*pl*.), qui dure trois ans.

tri·er ['traiə] juge *m*; F celui (celle *f*) *m* qui ne se laisse pas décourager.

tri·fle ['traifl] 1. bagatelle *f*; *fig.* un tout petit peu *m*; *cuis.* charlotte *f* russe; 2. *v/i.* jouer, badiner (avec, *with*); *v/t.* ~ *away* gaspiller (*son argent*); '**tri·fler** personne *f* frivole; amuseur (-euse *f*) *m*.

tri·fling ['traifliŋ] 1. manque *m* de sérieux; badinage *m*; futilités *f*/*pl.*; 2. □ insignifiant; léger (-ère *f*); '**tri·fling·ness** insignifiance *f*.

trig¹ [trig] 1. caler; enrayer; 2. cale *f*; sabot *m* d'enrayage.

trig² [~] soigné; net(te *f*).

trig·ger ['trigə] poussoir *m* à ressort; *arme à feu*: détente *f*; *phot.* déclencheur *m*; '~-'**hap·py** prêt à tirer pour un rien; *fig.* prêt à déclencher la guerre pour un rien.

trig·o·no·met·ric, trig·o·no·met·ri·cal □ Ⓐ [trigənə'metrik(l)] trigonométrique; **trig·o·nom·e·try** [~'ɔmitri] trigonométrie *f*.

tri·lat·er·al □ Ⓐ ['trai'lætərəl] trilatéral (-aux *m*/*pl.*).

tril·by ['trilbi] chapeau *m* mou.

tri·lin·gual □ ['trai'liŋgwəl] trilingue.

trill [tril] 1. trille *m*; *oiseau*: chant *m* perlé; R *m* roulé; 2. *v/t.* triller; rouler (*les R*); *v/i.* faire des trilles; perler son chant (*oiseau*).

tril·lion ['triljən] trillion *m*; *Am.* billion *m*.

tril·o·gy ['trilədʒi] trilogie *f*.

trim [trim] 1. □ en bon ordre; soigné; coquet(te *f*); bien tourné; ⚓ bien voilé; étarque (*voile*); 2. bon ordre *m*; parfait état *m*; ⚓ assiette *f*, arrimage *m*; *voiles*: orientation *f*; ⚡ équilibrage *m*; *cheveux*: coupe *f*; *just a* ~! simplement rafraîchir!; 3. *v/t.* mettre en ordre; arranger (*a. une lampe*); (*a.* ~ *up*) rafraîchir (*la barbe, les cheveux*); *cost.* garnir (de, *with*); tailler, tondre (*une haie etc.*); orner (de, *with*); F plumer (*q.*); *cuis.* parer (*la viande*); ⚓ redresser (*un navire*), orienter (*les voiles*); *v/i. fig.* tergiverser, nager entre deux eaux;

'**trim·mer** garnisseur (-euse *f*) *m*; ⊕ *personne*: pareur (-euse *f*) *m*; ⊕ machine *f* à trancher; ⚓ arrimeur *m*; *pol.* opportuniste *m*; *coal-*~ soutier *m*; '**trim·ming** ornement *m*; taille *f*; *usu.* ~*s pl.* passementerie *f*; *cuis.* garniture *f*; ⊕ rognures *f*/*pl.*; '**trim·ness** air *m* soigné *ou* coquet; élégance *f*.

tri·mo·tor ['traimoutə] trimoteur *m*; '**tri·mo·tored** trimoteur.

Trin·i·ty ['triniti] Trinité *f*.

trin·ket ['triŋkit] petit bijou *m*, colifichet *m*; bibelot *m*; ~*s pl.* affiquets *m*/*pl.*; *péj.* camelote *f*.

tri·o ♪ ['tri:ou] trio *m*.

trip [trip] 1. excursion *f*, voyage *m* d'agrément; randonnée *f*; *fig.* faux pas *m*; croc-en-jambe (*pl.* crocs-en-jambe) *m*; ⊕ déclic *m*; déclenche *f*; ⊕ ~ *dog* (*ou pin*) déclic *m*; 2. *v/i.* trébucher; faire un faux pas (*a. fig.*); ~ *along* aller d'un pas léger; *catch s.o.* ~*ping* prendre q. en défaut; *v/t.* (*usu.* ~ *up*) donner un croc-en-jambe à; faire trébucher (*q.*); surprendre (*un témoin etc.*) en contradiction.

tri·par·tite ['trai'pɑ:tait] tripartite; triple; trilatéral (-aux *m*/*pl.*).

tripe [traip] *cuis.* tripe *f*, -s *f*/*pl.*; *sl.* bêtises *f*/*pl.*, fatras *m*.

tri·phase ⚡ ['trai'feiz] triphasé (*courant*).

tri·ple □ ['tripl] triple; *sp.* ~ *jump* triple saut *m*.

tri·plet ['triplit] trio *m*; *prosodie*: tercet *m*; ♪, ♫ triplet *m*; ♪ triolet *m*.

tri·plex ['tripleks] se brisant sans éclats (*verre*), triplex (*TM*).

trip·li·cate 1. ['triplikit] triplé; triple (*a. su./m*); 2. ['~keit] tripler; rédiger en triple exemplaire.

tri·pod ['traipɔd] trépied *m*; pied *m* (à trois branches).

tri·pos ['traipɔs] examen *m* supérieur (*pour honours à Cambridge*).

trip·per F ['tripə] excursionniste *mf*; '**trip·ping** 1. □ léger (-ère *f*) (*pas*), leste; 2. pas *m* léger; faux pas *m*; ⊕ déclenchement *m*.

tri·sect [trai'sekt] diviser *ou* couper en trois.

tris·yl·lab·ic ['traisi'læbik] (~*ally*) trisyllab(iqu)e; **tri·syl·la·ble** ['~'si-ləbl] trisyllabe *m*.

trite □ [trait] banal (-als *ou* -aux *m*/*pl.*); rebattu.

trit·u·rate ['tritjureit] triturer.

tri·umph ['traiəmf] **1.** triomphe *m* (*a. fig.*) (sur, over); **2.** triompher (*a. fig.*) (de, over); **tri·um·phal** [ˌ⁓ˈʌm-fəl] de triomphe, triomphal (-aux *m/pl.*); ~ *arch* arc *m* de triomphe; ~ *procession* cortège *m* triomphal; **tri'um·phant** □ triomphant.

tri·une ['traijuːn] d'une unité triple.

triv·et ['trivit] trépied *m* (*pour bouilloire etc.*); *F as right as a* ~ en excellente santé; en parfait état.

triv·i·al □ ['trivial] insignifiant, sans importance; frivole (*personne*); banal (-als *ou* -aux *m/pl.*); † de tous les jours; **triv·i·al·i·ty** [ˌ⁓ˈæliti] insignifiance *f*; banalité *f*.

tro·chee ['trouki:] trochée *m*.

trod [trɔd] *prét.*, **trod·den** ['⁓n] *p.p. de* tread *1*.

trog·lo·dyte ['trɔglədait] troglodyte *m*.

Tro·jan ['troudʒn] **1.** de Troie; troyen(ne *f*); **2.** Troyen(ne *f*) *m*; *F like a* ~ en vaillant homme; (*travailler*) comme un nègre.

troll [troul] pêcher à la cuiller.

trol·l(e)y ['trɔli] **1.** 🚋 chariot *m* à bagages; fardier *m*; diable *m*; ⊕ moufle *mf*; chariot *m* (*de pont roulant*); ⚡ trolley *m*; (*a. dinner* ~) serveuse *f*; *Am.* (*a.* ~ *car*) tramway *m* à trolley; **2.** charrier; **'⁓-bus** trolleybus *m*.

trol·lop *péj.* ['trɔləp] **1.** souillon *f*; traînée *f*; **2.** rôder; traîner la savate.   [bone *m*.\

trom·bone ♩ [trɔmˈboun] trom-\

troop [truːp] **1.** troupe *f*, bande *f*; foule *f*; peloton *m* (*de cavalerie*); **2.** s'assembler; ~ *along* avancer en foule; ~ *away*, ~ *off* partir en bande; ✕ ~*ing the* colo(u)r(s) parade *f* du drapeau; **'⁓-car·ri·er** ✈ avion *m* de transport; ⚓ transport *m*; **'troop·er** cavalier *m*; soldat *m ou* F cheval *m* de cavalerie; *Am.* membre *m* de la police montée; ⚓ transport *m*; *péj.* old ~ soudard *m*; **'troop-horse** cheval *m* de cavalerie.

trope [troup] trope *m*.

tro·phy ['troufi] trophée *m*; *sp. a.* coupe *f*.

trop·ic ['trɔpik] **1.** tropique *m*; **2.** *a.* **'trop·i·cal** □ tropique; tropical (-aux *m/pl.*).

trot [trɔt] **1.** trot *m*; *F* petit(e) enfant *m(f)*; *Am. sl. école:* traduction *f*

juxtalinéaire; **2.** (faire) trotter; *F* ~ *out* sortir; présenter.

trot·ter ['trɔtə] trotteur (-euse *f*) *m*; ~*s pl.* pieds *m/pl.* de cochon; *F co.* pieds *m/pl.*

trou·ble ['trʌbl] **1.** trouble *m* (*a.* ⚕, ⊕); peine *f*; chagrin *m*; ennui *m*; inquiétude *f*; ⊕ conflits *m/pl.*; difficultés *f/pl.*; ~ *spot* point *m* de conflit, foyer *m* de troubles; *be in* ~ avoir des ennuis; avoir des soucis (d'argent); *look for* ~ se préparer des ennuis; *make* ~ semer la discorde; *take* (*the*) ~ se donner de la peine (de, to); se déranger (pour, to); **2.** *v/t.* affliger, chagriner (de, with); inquiéter; déranger; ennuyer; donner de la peine à; *may I* ~ *you for the salt?* voudriez-vous bien me passer le sel?; *v/i.* F se déranger; **'⁓·man, '⁓·shoot·er** *Am.* F dépanneur *m*; **trou·ble·some** □ ['⁓səm] ennuyeux (-euse *f*); gênant.

trough [trɔf] auge *f*; (*a. drinking* ~) abreuvoir *m*; pétrin *m* (*pour le pain*); caniveau *m*; ⚗ cuve(tte) *f*; ⚡, *phys.*, *a. fig.* creux *m*; *météor.* dépression *f*.

trounce F [trauns] rosser (*q.*).

troupe [truːp] *théâ. etc.:* troupe *f*.

trou·sered ['trauzəd] portant un pantalon; **'trou·ser·ing** étoffe *f* pour pantalon(s); **trou·sers** ['⁓z] *pl.* (*a pair of* ~ un) pantalon *m*; **trou·ser suit** tailleur-pantalon *m* (*pl.* tailleurs-pantalons).

trous·seau ['truːsou] trousseau *m*.

trout *icht.* [traut] truite *f*.

tro·ver ⚖ ['trouvə] appropriation *f* (*d'une chose perdue*); *action of* ~ action *f* en restitution.

trow·el ['trauəl] truelle *f*; ⚘ déplantoir *m*.

troy (**weight**) [trɔi(weit)] poids *m* troy (*pour peser de l'or etc.*).

tru·an·cy ['truːənsi] absence *f* de l'école sans permission; **'tru·ant 1.** absent; *fig.* vagabond; **2.** absent *m*; *fig.* vagabond *m*; *play* ~ faire l'école buissonnière; *fig.* vagabonder.

truce [truːs] trêve *f* (*a. fig.*) (de, to); *political* ~ trêve *f* (*des partis*).

truck[1] [trʌk] **1.** *surt. Am.* camion *m*; chariot *m* (à bagages); 🚋 wagon *m* (à marchandises); (*a. bogie-*~) boggie *m*; ~ *driver* camionneur *m*, routier *m*; ~ *stop* relais *m* des routiers; ~ *trailer* remorque *f*; **2.** transporter par camion, camionner.

truck

trucktruck# truck   1184

truck² [~] **1.** *vt/i.* troquer; *v/i.* ~ *in* faire le commerce de, trafiquer en; **2.** troc *m*, échange *m*; (*usu.* ~ *system*) paiement *m* des ouvriers en nature; *fig.* relations *f/pl.*; *péj.* camelote *f*; *Am.* légumes *m/pl.*; *attr.* maraîcher (-ère *f*); *Am.* ~ *farm* jardin *m* maraîcher.

truck·le¹ ['trʌkl] s'abaisser, ramper (devant, to).

truck·le² [~] poulie *f*; † *meuble*: roulette *f*; **~-bed** grabat *m*, lit *m* de fortune.

truck·man ['trʌkmən] camionneur *m*, routier *m*.

truc·u·lence, truc·u·len·cy ['trʌk-juləns(i)] férocité *f*; **'truc·u·lent** □ féroce, farouche; brutal (-aux *m/pl.*).

trudge [trʌdʒ] marcher lourdement *ou* péniblement.

true [tru:] (*adv.* truly) vrai; véritable; sincère, fidèle, honnête; exact; d'aplomb, juste; *be* ~ *of* en être de même pour; *it is* ~ il est vrai (que, that); c'est vrai; *come* ~ se réaliser; ~ *to life* (*ou* nature) tout à fait naturel; pris sur le vif; vécu (*roman*); *prove* ~ se vérifier; se réaliser; **'~-blue** *fig.* loyal (-aux *m/pl.*), fidèle; **'~-bred** pur sang *inv.*; de bonne race; **'~-love** bien-aimé(e *f*) *m*; **'true·ness** vérité *f*; sincérité *f*; justesse *f*.

truf·fle ['trʌfl] truffe *f*.

tru·ism ['tru:izm] truisme *m*, axiome *m*.

tru·ly ['tru:li] vraiment, véritablement, justement, sincèrement; loyalement; *yours* ~ agréez, Monsieur (Madame), l'expression de mes sentiments les plus distingués.

trump [trʌmp] **1.** *cartes*: atout *m*; F brave garçon (fille *f*) *m*; **2.** *v/i.* jouer atout; *v/t.* couper (*une carte*); ~ *up* forger, inventer; **trump·er·y** ['~əri] friperie *f*, camelote *f*; farce *f*; *attr.* de camelote; ridicule.

trum·pet ['trʌmpit] **1.** trompette *f* (*a.* ♫, ✗, orgues); ✗ *personne*: trompette *m*; ♫ cornet *m* acoustique; *see* ear-~, speaking-~; **2.** *v/i.* sonner de la trompette; barrir (*éléphant*); *v/t. fig.* (*a.* ~ *forth*) proclamer, publier à son de trompe; **'trum·pet·er** ♪, *orn.* trompette *m*.

trun·cate ['trʌŋkeit] tronquer; **trun'ca·tion** troncature *f*.

trun·cheon ['trʌnʃn] bâton *m* (*d'un agent de police*); casse-tête *m/inv.*, matraque *f*.

trun·dle ['trʌndl] **1.** roulette *f* (*pour meubles*); **2.** (faire) rouler; *v/t.* passer.

trunk [trʌŋk] tronc *m* (*d'arbre, a. de corps*); torse *m*; *éléphant*: trompe *f*; malle *f*; *Am.* ~s *pl.* caleçon *m* de bain; slip *m*; *téléph.* ~s, please! l'inter, s.v.p.; *see* ~-line; **'~-call** *téléph.* communication *f* interurbaine; ~ **ex·change** *téléph.* (service *m*) interurbain *m*; **'~-line** ⚑ grande ligne *f*; *téléph.* ligne *f* interurbaine; **'~-road** route *f* nationale.

trun·nion ⊕ ['trʌnjən] tourillon *m*.

truss [trʌs] **1.** botte *f*; *fleurs*: touffe *f*; ⚕ bandage *m* herniaire; △ armature *f*; ferme *f*; cintre *m*; **2.** mettre en bottes; lier; trousser (*une poule*); △ renforcer; **'~-bridge** ⊕ pont *m* à poutres en treillis métallique.

trust [trʌst] **1.** confiance *f* (en, in); espérance *f*, espoir *m*; charge *f*, responsabilité *f*; † fidéicommis *m*; † trust *m*, syndicat *m*; ~ *company institution de gestion*: trust-company *f*; *in* ~ par fidéicommis; en dépôt; *on* ~ en dépôt; † à crédit; *position of* ~ poste *m* de confiance; **2.** *v/t.* se fier à; mettre sa confiance en; confier (qch. à q. s.o. with s.th., s.th. to s.o.); † F faire crédit à (de qch., with s.th.); *fig.* espérer (que, that); ~ *s.o. to do s.th.* se fier à q. pour qu'il fasse qch.; *v/i.* se fier (à in, to); se confier (en in, to).

trus·tee [trʌs'ti:] dépositaire *m*, consignataire *m*; †, admin. administrateur *m*; ⚖ fidéicommissaire *m*, fiduciaire *m*; curateur (-trice *f*) *m*; ~ *securities pl.* (*ou* stock) valeurs *f/pl.* de tout repos; **trus'tee·ship** fidéicommis *m*; curatelle *f*, administration *f*; *pol.* tutelle *f*.   [confiant.\

trust·ful □ ['trʌstful], **'trust·ing** □⟩ **trust·wor·thi·ness** ['trʌstwə:ðinis] loyauté *f*, fidélité *f*; crédibilité *f* (*d'une nouvelle*); **'trust·wor·thy** digne de confiance, loyal (-aux *m/pl.*); digne de foi.

truth [tru:θ, *pl.* ~ðz] vérité *f*; véracité *f*; *home* ~s *pl.* vérités *f/pl.* bien senties; ~ *to life* fidélité *f*, exactitude *f*.

truth·ful □ ['truːθful] vrai; véridique; fidèle; **'truth·ful·ness** véracité *f*, fidélité *f*.

try [trai] **1.** *v/t.* essayer (de, to); tâcher (de, to); fatiguer (*les yeux*); *fig.* vexer; ⚖ juger, mettre en jugement, *Am.* plaider (*une cause*); éprouver, mettre à l'épreuve; ⊕ vérifier; *cuis.* goûter (*un mets*); ~ on essayer (*une robe etc.*); ~ one's hand at s'essayer à; *v/i.* faire un effort; essayer; ~ *for* tâcher d'obtenir (*qch.*); se porter candidat pour; F ~ *and read!* essayez de lire!; **2.** essai *m* (*a.* rugby); tentative *f*; have a ~ essayer; faire un effort; **'try·ing** □ difficile, vexant, ennuyeux (-euse *f*); **'try·on** ballon *m* d'essai; tentative *f* de déception, F de bluff; **'try·'out** essai *m* à fond; *sp.* (jeu d')essai *m*; **try-sail** ⚓ ['traisl] voile *f* goélette.

tryst *écos.* [traist] **1.** rendez-vous *m*; **2.** donner rendez-vous à (*q.*).

Tsar [zɑː] tsar *m*, czar *m*.

T-square ['tiːskweə] équerre *f* en T.

tub [tʌb] **1.** cuve *f*, baquet *m*; tonneau *m*; (*a.* bath-~) tub *m*; F bain *m*; ⚒ benne *f*; F *co.* coque *f*, baille *f*; F *co.* ventre *m*, panse *f*; **2.** *v/t.* encaisser (*une plante*); ⚒ boiser (*un puits*); donner un tub à; *v/i.* prendre un tub; s'exercer dans un canot d'entraînement; **'tub·by** rond comme un tonneau.

tube [tjuːb] tube *m* (*a. radio*), tuyau *m*; *mot.* chambre *f* à air; F métro *m*, chemin *m* de fer souterrain (*à Londres*); **'tube·less** sans chambre à air (*pneu*).

tu·ber ♀ ['tjuːbə] tubercule *m*; truffe *f*; **tu·ber·cle** *anat.*, *zo.*, *a.* ⚕ ['tjuːbəːkl] tubercule *m*; **tu·ber·cu·lo·sis** ⚕ [tjuːbəːkjuˈlousis] tuberculose *f*; **tu·ber·cu·lous** ⚕ tuberculeux (-euse *f*); **tu·ber·ous** ♀ ['tjuːbərəs] tubéreux (-euse *f*).

tub·ing ['tjuːbiŋ] tuyautage *m*; tuyau *m* en caoutchouc.

tub-thump·er ['tʌbθʌmpə] orateur *m* démagogue.

tu·bu·lar □ ['tjuːbjulə] tubulaire.

tuck [tʌk] **1.** petit pli *m*, rempli *m*; *sl.* mangeaille *f*; **2.** remplier; serrer; (*avec adv. ou prp.*) mettre; ~ *up* relever, retrousser; border (*q.*) (*dans son lit.*).

tuck·er ['tʌkə] **1.** *sl.* (*Australie*)

mangeaille *f*; **2.** *Am.* F fatiguer, lasser.

Tues·day ['tjuːzdi] mardi *m*; *Shrove* ~ mardi *m* gras.

tu·fa *min.* ['tjuːfə], **tuff** [tʌf] tuf *m* calcaire *ou* volcanique.

tuft [tʌft] herbe, cheveux, plumes: touffe *f*; oiseau, laine: houppe *f*; brosse: loquet *m*; cheveux: toupet *m*; **'~-hunt·er** sycophante *m*; **'tuft·y** □ touffu.

tug [tʌg] **1.** secousse *f*; saccade *f*; ⚓ remorqueur *m*; *fig.* effort *m*; *sp.* ~ *of war* lutte *f* à la corde (de traction); *fig.* course *f* au poteau; **2.** tirer (sur, at); ⚓ remorquer; *fig.* se mettre en peine; **'~-boat** remorqueur *m*.

tu·i·tion [tjuˈiʃn] instruction *f*.

tu·lip ♀ ['tjuːlip] tulipe *f*.

tulle [tjuːl] tulle *m*.

tum·ble ['tʌmbl] **1.** *v/i.* tomber; faire la culbute; *v/t.* bouleverser; déranger; chiffonner; **2.** chute *f*; culbute *f*; désordre *m*; **'~-down** en ruines, délabré; croulant; **'~-'drier** séchoir *m* (à linge) à air chaud; **'tum·bler** acrobate *mf*, jongleur *m*; *orn.* culbutant *m*; verre *m* sans pied; ⊕ gorge *f*, serrure: arrêt *m*; *arme à feu*: noix *f* (*de platine*).

tum·brel ['tʌmbrəl], **tum·bril** ['~bril] tombereau *m*.

tu·mid □ ['tjuːmid] ✿ enflé, gonflé; *zo.* protubérant; *fig.* boursouflé; **tuˈmid·i·ty** enflure *f* (*a. fig.*).

tum·my F ['tʌmi] estomac *m*, ventre *m*; bedaine *f*.

tu·mo(u)r ✿ ['tjuːmə] tumeur *f*.

tu·mult ['tjuːmʌlt] tumulte *m* (*a. fig.*); fracas *m*; *fig.* trouble *m*, émoi *m*; **tu·mul·tu·ous** □ [tjuˈmʌltjuəs] tumultueux (-euse *f*); orageux (-euse *f*).

tun [tʌn] **1.** tonneau *m*, fût *m*; cuve *f* (*de fermentation*); **2.** mettre en tonneaux.

tu·na *icht.* ['tjuːnə] thon *m*.

tune [tjuːn] **1.** ♪ air *m*; harmonie *f*; accord *m*; *fig.* ton *m*; *fig.* humeur *f*; *in* ~ d'accord; *fig.* en bon accord (avec, with); *out of* ~ désaccordé, faux (fausse *f*); *fig.* en désaccord (avec, with); F *to the* ~ *of £ 100* pour la somme de 100 livres; à la cadence de 100 livres; *fig. change one's* ~ changer de ton; **2.** accorder; *fig.* incliner; ~ *in radio*: accorder (sur, to), capter (un poste, *to a station*); ~ **out** *radio*: éliminer; ~ **up** ♪ *v/i.* s'accorder; *v/t. fig. mot.*, *a*. ⊕ mettre au point; *fig.* (se) tonifier; *v/t.* ♪ accorder; **tune·ful** □ ['~ful] mélodieux (-euse *f*), harmonieux (-euse *f*); **'tune·less** □ discordant; **'tun·er** ♪ accordeur *m*; *radio*: syntonisateur *m*.

tung·sten ⚗ ['tʌŋstən] tungstène *m*.

tu·nic *cost.*, ✕, *anat.*, *eccl.*, *a.* ⚕ ['tjuːnik] tunique *f*.

tun·ing...: **'~-coil** *radio*: bobine *f* syntonisatrice; **self** *f* d'accord; **'~-fork** ♪ diapason *m*.

tun·nel ['tʌnl] **1.** tunnel *m* (*a.* 🚗); ✕ galerie *f* à flanc de coteau; **2.** percer un tunnel (à travers, dans, sous).

tun·ny *icht.* ['tʌni] thon *m*.

tun·y F ['tjuːni] mélodieux (-euse *f*).

tur·ban ['təːbən] turban *m*.

tur·bid ['təːbid] trouble (*a. fig.*); bourbeux (-euse *f*); confus; **'tur·bid·ness** état *m* trouble; turbidité *f*.

tur·bine ⊕ ['təːbain] turbine *f*; **'~-'pow·ered** à turbines.

tur·bo-prop ['təːbou'prɔp] à turbopropulseur (*avion*); **tur·bo·su·per·charg·er** ['təːbou'sjupətʃɑːdʒə] turbocompresseur *m* de suralimentation.

tur·bot *icht.* ['təːbət] turbot *m*.

tur·bu·lence ['təːbjuləns] turbulence *f*; tumulte *m*; indiscipline *f*; **'tur·bu·lent** □ turbulent; orageux (-euse *f*); à remous (*vent*); insubordonné.

turd V [təːd] merde *f*; salaud *m*, salope *f*.

tu·reen [təˈriːn] soupière *f*; saucière *f*.

turf [təːf] **1.** gazon *m*; pelouse *f*; tourbe *f*; turf *m*, courses *f/pl.* de chevaux; *sl.* ~ **out** flanquer (*q.*) dehors; **turf·ite** ['~ait] turfiste *m*; **'turf·y** gazonné, couvert de gazon; tourbeux (-euse *f*); F du turf.

tur·gid □ ['təːdʒid] enflé, gonflé; *fig.* boursouflé; **tur'gid·i·ty** enflure *f* (*a. fig.*).

Turk [təːk] Turc (Turque *f*) *m*; *fig.* tyran *m*; homme *m* indiscipliné.

tur·key ['təːki]: ♀ *carpet* tapis *m* d'Orient *ou* de Turquie; *orn.* dindon *m*, dinde *f*; *cuis.* dindonneau *m*; *théâ.*, *cin.* *Am. sl.* navet *m*; *sl.* *talk* ~ ne pas ménager ses mots.

Turk·ish ['təːkiʃ] turc (turque *f*), de Turquie; ~ *bath* bain *m* turc; ~ *delight* rahat-lokoum *m*; ~ *towel* serviette-éponge (*pl.* serviettes-éponges) *f*.

tur·moil ['təːmɔil] trouble *m*, agitation *f*, tumulte *m*.

turn [təːn] **1.** *v/t.* tourner; faire tourner; retourner; rendre; changer, transformer (en, *into*); traduire (en anglais, *into English*); diriger; ⊕ tourner, façonner au tour; *fig.* tourner (*une phrase, des vers, etc.*); F *he has* ~*ed* (*ou is* ~*ed* [*of*]) 50 il a passé la cinquantaine; il a 50 ans passés; ~ *colo(u)r* pâlir *ou* rougir; changer de couleur; ~ *a corner* tourner un coin; ~ *the enemy's flanks* tourner le flanc de l'ennemi; *he can* ~ *his hand to anything* c'est un homme à toute main; F ~ *tail* prendre la fuite; ~ *s.o.'s argument against himself* rétorquer un argument contre q.; ~ *aside* détourner; écarter; ~ *away* détourner; *théâ.* refuser; ~ *down* rabattre; retourner (*une carte*); corner (*une page*); baisser (*le gaz etc.*); faire (*la couverture d'un lit*), ouvrir (*le lit*); F refuser (*une invitation etc.*); ~ *in* tourner en dedans; replier (*le bord*); F quitter (*un emploi*); renvoyer; 🚂 garer (*des wagons*); fermer (*l'eau, le gaz*); ~ *off* (*on*) fermer, (ouvrir) (*un robinet*); ~ *out* faire sortir; mettre dehors; vider (*les poches etc.*); nettoyer à fond; fabriquer, produire (*des marchandises*); éteindre, couper (*le gaz*); ~ *over* renverser; feuilleter, tourner (*les pages*); *fig.* transférer, remettre; 🌱 retourner (*le sol*); ⚓ faire; ~ *over a new leaf* revenir de ses erreurs; ~ *up* retourner (*a. des cartes, a.* ✎); relever (*un col, un pantalon*); retrousser (*les manches*); donner (*tout le gaz etc.*); remonter (*une mèche*); chercher, trouver (*dans le dictionnaire etc.*); F ~ *one's nose at* faire le dédaigneux devant; renifler sur; **2.** *v/i.* tourner; se (re)tourner; se diriger; se transformer (en, *into*); changer (*marée, temps*); tourner (*au froid etc.*); se faire, devenir (*chrétien, soldat, etc.*); se colorer en (*rouge etc.*); prendre

une teinte (*bleue etc.*); (*a. ~ sour*)
tourner (*lait*); ~ *about* se (re)tourner;
✂ faire demi-tour; ~ *away* se détourner (*de, from*); ~ *back* rebrousser chemin; regarder en arrière;
faire demi-tour; ~ *in* se tourner en
dedans; F se coucher; *his toes* ~ *in*
il a les pieds tournés en dedans;
~ *off* prendre (*à gauche, à droite*);
bifurquer; faire le coin avec; ~ *on*
se retourner contre, attaquer; *see*
~ *upon*; ~ *out* sortir; se tourner
en dehors (*pieds*); se mettre en
grève; tourner (*mal, bien*); aboutir;
devenir; se passer; arriver; se
trouver; se mettre (*à la pluie, au
beau, etc.*); F se lever, sortir du lit;
✂ sortir; ~ *over* se (re)tourner; *mot.
etc.* capoter; se renverser; ~ *round*
tourner; tournoyer; ~ *to* se mettre
à; tourner à; devenir; F ~ *to* (*adv.*)
se mettre au travail; ~ *up* se relever;
se retrousser (*nez*); arriver; se présenter; ~ *upon* rouler sur (*a. fig.*);
attaquer; **3.** *su.* tour *m* (*de corde, de
jeu, de danse*) *jeu; théâ.*; *a. = promenade,
a. = disposition d'esprit*); roue: révolution *f*; changement *m* de
direction, *mot.* virage *m*, ⚓ giration
f; *chemin*: tournant *m*; *typ.* caractère *m* retourné; fin *f* (*du mois*);
allure *f*, tournure *f* (*des affaires*);
disposition *f* (*pour, for*); *théâ.*
numéro *m*; *fig.* choc *m*, coup *m*;
crise *f*; *fig.* service *m*; *fig.* but *m*;
at every ~ à tout propos, à tout
moment; *by* (*ou in* ~s) à tour de
rôle, tour à tour; *in my* ~ à mon
tour; *it is my* ~ c'est à moi (*de, to*);
take a ~ faire un tour; *take a* ~ *at
s.th.* faire qch. à son tour; *take
one's* ~ prendre son tour; *take* ~s
alterner (*pour inf. at, in gér.*); *to a* ~
à point; *a friendly* ~ un service *m*
d'ami; *do s.o. a good* ~ rendre un
service à q.; *does it serve your* ~? est-ce
que cela fera votre affaire?; '~-**a-
bout** demi-tour *m*; '~-**buck·le** ⊕
lanterne *f* de serrage; '~-**coat** renégat
m; apostat(e *f*) *m*; '~-**down 1.** refus
m; (tendance *f* à la) baisse *f*; **2.** à
rabattre; ~ *collar* col *m* rabattu;
'**turn·er** tourneur *m*; '**turn·er·y**
travail (*pl.* -aux) *m* au tour, tournage
m; articles *m/pl.* tournés; atelier *m* de
tourneur.

turn·ing ['tə:niŋ] action *f* de tourner;
giration *f*; changement *m* de direc-

tion; *mot.* virage *m*; tournant *m* (*du
chemin*); retournage *m* (*d'un vêtement*); *typ.* blocage *m*; ⊕ tournage *m*;
'~-**lathe** ⊕ tour *m*; '~-**point** *fig.*
moment *m* critique, point *m* décisif.

tur·nip ♥ ['tə:nip] navet *m*.

turn·key ['tə:nki:]　　　porte-clefs
m/inv.; geôlier *m*; *admin.* fontainier
m; '**turn-off** *Am.* sortie *f* (*d'autoroute*); embranchement *m*; '**turn-
out** tenue *f*, uniforme *m*; équipage
m; assemblée *f*, assistance *f*, gens
m/pl.; grève *f*; ♦ production *f*, produits *m/pl.*; ⚙ aiguillage *m*; voie *f* de
garage; changement *m* de voie;
'**turn·o·ver** chausson *m* (*aux pommes etc.*); ♦ chiffre *m* d'affaires; ~ *tax*
impôt *m* sur le chiffre d'affaires;
'**turn·pike** (route *f* à) barrière *f*
de péage; tourniquet *m* d'entrée;
'**turn·screw** tournevis *m*; '**turnspit** tournebroche *m*; ⊕ ~ *lathe* tour *m*
tourniquet *m* (*d'entrée*); '**turn·ta-
ble** ⚙ plaque *f* tournante; *phonographe*: tourne-disque *m*, plateau *m*;
'**turn·up 1.** pliant (*lit.*); à bords
relevés; **2.** *pantalon*: revers *m*; F rixe
f, bagarre *f*; F affaire *f* de chance.

tur·pen·tine ⚚ ['tə:pəntain] térébenthine *f*.

tur·pi·tude ['tə:pitju:d] turpitude *f*.

tur·quoise *min.* ['tə:kwɑ:z] turquoise *f*.

tur·ret ['tʌrit] tourelle *f* (*a.* ✂, ⚓,
⊕); *a.* revolver *m*; ⊕ ~ *lathe* tour *m*
à revolver; '**tur·ret·ed** surmonté
ou garni de tourelles; *zo.* turriculé
(*conque*).

tur·tle[1] *zo.* ['tə:tl] tortue *f* de mer;
turn ~ chavirer; *canot, mot.*: capoter.

tur·tle[2] *orn.* [~] (*usu.* ~-*dove*)
tourterelle *f*, tourtereau *m*.

tur·tle·neck *surt. Am.* ['tə:tlnek]
(pullover *m* à) col *m* roulé.

Tus·can ['tʌskən] **1.** toscan; **2.** *ling.*
toscan *m*; Toscan(e *f*) *m*.

tusk [tʌsk] *éléphant*: défense *f*; ~s
pl. sanglier: broches *f/pl.*

tus·sle ['tʌsl] **1.** mêlée *f*, lutte *f*; *fig.*
passe *f* d'armes; **2.** lutter.

tus·sock ['tʌsək] touffe *f* d'herbe.

tut [tʌt] allons donc!; zut!

tu·te·lage ['tju:tilidʒ] tutelle *f*.

tu·te·lar·y ['tju:tiləri] tutélaire *f*.

tu·tor ['tju:tə] (*a. private* ~) précepteur (-trice *f*) *m*; *école, univ.*
directeur (-trice *f*) *m* d'études;
univ. a. répétiteur (-trice *f*) *m*; *Am.*

univ. chargé *m* de cours; 🔲 tuteur (-trice *f*) *m*; **2.** instruire; donner des leçons particulières à; diriger les études de; **tu·to·ri·al** [tju-'tɔːriəl] **1.** d'instruction; de répétiteur *etc.*; **2.** cours *m* individuel; travaux *m/pl.* pratiques; **tu·tor·ship** ['tjuːtəʃip] emploi *m* de répétiteur *etc.*; *private* ~ préceptorat *m*.

tux·e·do *Am.* [tʌk'siːdou] smoking *m*.

twad·dle ['twɔdl] **1.** fadaises *f/pl.*, sottises *f/pl.*; **2.** dire des sottises.

twang [twæŋ] **1.** bruit *m* sec; (*usu. nasal* ~) accent *m* nasillard; **2.** (faire) résonner; nasiller (*personne*).

tweak [twiːk] pincer.

tweed [twiːd] cheviote *f* écossaise; tweed *m* (=*étoffe de laine*).

'tween [twiːn] *see* between.

tween·y ['twiːni] (*a.* ~ *maid*) *see* between-maid.

tweez·ers ['twiːzəz] *pl.*: (*a pair of*) ~ (une) petite pince *f*; (des) pinces *f/pl.* à épiler.

twelfth [twelfθ] douzième (*a. su./mf*; *a.* 🔲 ~ *su./m*); 🔲-*cake* galette *f* des Rois; '🔲-*night* veille *f* des Rois.

twelve [twelv] douze (*a. su./m*); ~ *o'clock* midi *m*; minuit *m*; ~-*fold* ['~fould] douze fois autant.

twen·ti·eth ['twentiiθ] vingtième (*a. su./mf*; *a.* 🔲 *su./m*).

twen·ty ['twenti] vingt (*a. su./m*); ~-*fold* ['~fould] **1.** *adj.* vingtuple; **2.** *adv.* vingt fois autant.

twerp *sl.* [twəːp] cruche *f* (= *imbécile*).

twice [twais] deux fois; ~ *as much* deux fois autant; ~ *as many books* deux fois plus de livres.

twid·dle ['twidl] **1.** jouer (avec); *v/t.* tripoter (*qch.*); **2.** enjolivure *f*; ornement *m*.

twig¹ [twig] brindille *f*; *hydroscopie:* baguette *f* (*de coudrier*).

twig² *sl.* [~] observer (*q.*); comprendre, saisir (*qch.*).

twi·light ['twailait] **1.** crépuscule *m* (*a. fig.*); **2.** crépusculaire, du crépuscule; 🔲 ~ *sleep* demi-sommeil *m* provoqué.

twin [twin] **1.** jumeau (-elle *f*); jumelé; géminé; ~ *beds pl.* lits *m/pl.* jumeaux; **2.** jumeau (-elle *f*) *m*; ~-*en·gined* 🔲 ['~endʒind] bimoteur; '🔲-*jet* biréacteur *m*.

twine [twain] **1.** ficelle *f*; fil *m*

retors; *fig.* sinuosité *f*, repli *m*; **2.** *v/t.* tordre, tortiller; entrelacer (*les doigts etc.*); *fig.* entourer (de, *with*); (en)rouler (autour de *about, round*); *v/i.* (*a.* ~ *o.s.*) se tordre, se tortiller, s'enrouler; serpenter.

twinge [twindʒ] élancement *m*; légère atteinte *f*; *fig.* remords *m* (*de conscience*).

twin·kle ['twiŋkl] **1.** scintiller, étinceler; pétiller (*feu, a. fig. de, with*); **2.** (*a.* '**twin·kling**) scintillement *m*, clignotement *m*; *in a* ~ (*ou the twinkling of an eye*) en un clin d'œil.

twirl [twəːl] **1.** tournoiement *m*; *moustache:* tortillement *m*; pirouette *f*; *fumée:* volute *f*; enjolivure *f*; **2.** (faire) tourn(oy)er; '**twirl·ing-stick** *cuis.* agitateur *m*.

twist [twist] **1.** (*film*) retors *m*; torsion *f*; *chemin:* coude *m*; *soie:* tordage *m*; *cheveux:* torsade *f*; *tabac:* carotte *f*, rouleau *m*; *papier:* papillote *f*; contorsion *f* (*du visage*); *sp.* tour *m* de poignet; *mot. cornet:* spire *f*; *fig.* déformation *f*; *fig.* tournure *f*, prédisposition *f* (*de l'esprit*); *fig.* repli *m* (*du serpent*); F appétit *m*; **2.** *v/t.* tordre (*a. le visage, le bras, etc.*), tortiller; *tex.* retordre; torquer (*le tabac*); entortiller; enrouler; dénaturer, fausser; donner de l'effet à (*une balle*); *v/i.* se tordre, se tortiller; *fig.* tourner, serpenter; '**twist·er** tordeur (-euse *f*) *m*; *tex.* retordeur (-euse *f*) *m*; *sp.* balle *f* qui a de l'effet; *sl.* ficelle *f* (= *ricaneur*); *Am.* tornade *f*, ouragan *m*.

twit¹ [twit]: ~ *s.o. with s.th.* railler q. de qch.; reprocher qch. à q.

twit² *sl.* [~] idiot(e *f*) *m*.

twitch [twitʃ] **1.** *v/t.* tirer brusquement; *v/i.* se crisper, se contracter (de, *with*); **2.** saccade *f*, coup *m* sec; contraction *f*, tic *m* (*de visage*); *see* twinge; *vét.* serre-nez *m/inv.*

twit·ter ['twitə] **1.** gazouiller; **2.** gazouillement *m*; *be in a* ~ être agité *ou* en émoi.

two [tuː] deux (*a. su./m*); *in* ~ en deux; *fig. put* ~ *and* ~ *together* tirer ses conclusions; raisonner juste; '🔲-*bit* *Am.* F sans importance, infime; bon marché; '🔲-*edged* à deux tranchants (*a. fig.*); '🔲-'*faced* hypocrite; '🔲-*fist·ed* costaud; '🔲-*fold* double; '🔲-*hand·ed* à deux mains; ambidextre;

qui se joue à deux; '~-'**job man** F cumulard *m*; ~·**pence** ['tʌpəns] deux pence *m*; ~·**pen·ny** ['tʌpni] à *ou* de deux pence; *fig.* de quatre sous; '~-**phase** ⚡ biphasé, diphasé; '~-**pin plug** ⚡ fiche *f* à deux broches; '~-**ply** à deux brins (*cordage*); à deux épaisseurs (*contre-plaqué*); '~-'**seat·er** *mot.* voiture *f* à deux places; '~-**some** couple *m*; jeu *m ou* partie *f* à deux; '~-'**step** two-step *m* (*danse*); '~-'**sto·rey** à deux étages; '~-'**stroke** *mot.* à deux temps; '~-'**time** tromper, tricher; '~-'**valve re·ceiv·er** *radio*: poste *m* à deux lampes; '~-**way** ⊕ à deux voies; ⚡ ~ *adapter* bouchon *m* de raccord.

ty·coon *Am.* F [tai'ku:n] chef *m* de l'industrie; baron *m* de l'industrie.

tyke [taik] vilain chien *m*; rustre *m*.

tym·pa·num *anat.*, *a.* △ ['timpə- nəm], *pl.* -na [~nə] tympan *m*.

type [taip] **1.** type *m*; genre *m*; modèle *m*; *typ.* caractère *m*, type *m*, *coll.* caractères *m*/*pl.*; *typ.* in ~ com- posé; ~ *area* surface *f* imprimée; *true to* ~ conforme au type ances- tral; *typ.* set in ~ composer; **2.** = ~*write*; '~-'**found·er** fondeur *m* typographe; '~-**script** manuscrit *m* dactylographié; '~-**set·ter** *typ.* compositeur *m*; '~-**write** [*irr.* (*write*)] écrire à la machine; F taper (à la machine); '~-**writ·er** machine *f* à écrire; † dactylographe *mf*, F dactylo *mf*; ~ *ribbon* ruban *m* encreur.

ty·phoid 🖈 ['taifɔid] **1.** typhoïde; ~ *fever* = **2.** (fièvre *f*) typhoïde *f*.

ty·phoon *météor.* [tai'fu:n] typhon *m*.

ty·phus 🖈 ['taifəs] typhus *m*.

typ·i·cal □ ['tipikl] typique; carac- téristique (de, of); *it's* ~ *of him* c'est bien lui; **typ·i·fy** ['~fai] être caractéristique de; être le type de (*l'officier militaire*); symboliser.

typ·ing ['taipiŋ] dactylo(graphie) *f*; ~ *pool* bureau *m* des dactylos, F dactylo *f*; *be good at* ~ taper bien (à la machine); **typ·ist** ['taipist] dactylo- graphe *mf*, F dactylo *mf*; *shorthand* ~ sténodactylographe *mf*, F sténodac- tylo *mf*.

ty·pog·ra·pher [tai'pɔgrəfə] typo- graphe *m*, F typo *m*; **ty·po·graph- ic, ty·po·graph·i·cal** □ [~pə- 'græfik(l)] typographique; **ty·pog- ra·phy** [~'pɔgrəfi] typographie *f*.

ty·ran·nic, ty·ran·ni·cal □ [ti- 'rænik(l)] tyrannique; **ty'ran·ni- cide** [~said] *personne*: tyrannicide *mf*; *crime*: tyrannicide *m*; **tyr·an- nize** ['tirənaiz] faire le tyran; ~ *over* tyranniser (*q.*); '**tyr·an·nous** □ tyrannique; *fig.* violent; '**tyr- an·ny** tyrannie *f*.

ty·rant ['taiərənt] tyran *m* (*a. orn.*).

tyre ['taiə] see tire¹.

ty·ro ['taiərou] see tiro.

Tyr·o·lese [tirə'li:z] **1.** tyrolien(ne *f*); **2.** Tyrolien(ne *f*) *m*.

Tzar [za:] see Tsar.

U

U, u [juː] U *m*, u *m*.

u·biq·ui·tous □ [juˈbikwitəs] qui se trouve *ou* que l'on rencontre partout; **u'biq·ui·ty** ubiquité *f*.

ud·der [ˈʌdə] mamelle *f*.

ugh [uh; əːh] brrr!

ug·li·fy F [ˈʌɡlifai] enlaidir.

ug·li·ness [ˈʌɡlinis] laideur *f*.

ug·ly □ [ˈʌɡli] laid; vilain (*blessure, aspect, etc.*); mauvais (*temps*).

U·krain·i·an [juːˈkreinjən] 1. ukrainien(ne *f*); 2. Ukrainien(ne *f*) *m*.

u·ku·le·le ♪ [juːkəˈleili] ukulélé *m*.

ul·cer ⚕ [ˈʌlsə] ulcère *m*; **ul·cer·ate** [ˈ‿reit] (s')ulcérer; **ul·cer·'a·tion** ulcération *f*; **ˈul·cer·ous** ulcéreux (-euse *f*).

ul·lage ✝ [ˈʌlidʒ] coulage *m*; *douanes:* manquant *m*.

ul·na *anat.* [ˈʌlnə], *pl.* ‿nae [‿niː] cubitus *m*.

ul·ster [ˈʌlstə] *manteau:* ulster *m*.

ul·te·ri·or □ [ʌlˈtiəriə] ultérieur; *fig.* caché, secret (-ète *f*); ‿ *motive* arrière-pensée *f*; motif *m* secret.

ul·ti·mate □ [ˈʌltimit] final (-als *m/pl.*); dernier (-ère *f*); fondamental (-aux *m/pl.*); *phys.* ‿ *stress* résistance *f* de rupture; ‿*ly* en fin de compte, à la fin.

ul·ti·ma·tum [ʌltiˈmeitəm], *pl. a.* ‿ta [‿tə] ultimatum *m*. [dernier.]

ul·ti·mo ✝ [ˈʌltimou] du mois]

ultra- [ʌltrə] extrêmement; **ˈ‿ˈfash·ion·a·ble** ultra-chic; **ˈ‿-high fre·quen·cy** *radio:* très haute fréquence; **‿ˈma·rine** 1. d'outremer; 2. ♒, *peint.* (bleu *m* d')outremer *m/inv.*; **‿ˈmon·tane** *eccl., pol.* [‿ˈmɔntein] ultramontain(e *f*) (*a. su.*); **ˈ‿-ˈred** infrarouge; **ˈ‿-ˈshort wave** onde *f* ultracourte; **ˈ‿-ˈvi·o·let** ultraviolet(te *f*).

ul·u·late [ˈjuːljuleit] ululer; hurler.

um·bel ♀ [ˈʌmbl] ombelle *f*.

um·ber *min., peint.* [ˈʌmbə] terre *f* d'ombre; *couleur:* ombre *f*.

um·bil·i·cal □ [ʌmˈbilikl; ⚕ ‿laikl] ombilical (-aux *m/pl.*); ‿ *cord* cordon *m* ombilical.

um·brage [ˈʌmbridʒ] ressentiment *m*; ombrage *m* (*a. poét.*); **um·bra·geous** □ [‿ˈbreidʒəs] ombragé; ombrageux (-euse *f*) (*a. fig.*).

um·brel·la [ʌmˈbrelə] parapluie *m*; *pol.* compromis *m*; ✕ protection *f*; ‿ *organization* organisation *f* de tête; ‿ *stand* porte-parapluies *m/inv.*

um·pire [ˈʌmpaiə] 1. arbitre *m*; 2. *v/t.* arbitrer; *v/i.* servir d'arbitre.

ump·teen [ˈʌmtiːn], **ˈump·ty** F je ne sais combien.

un- [ʌn] non; in-; dé(s)-; ne ... pas; peu; sans.

un·a·bashed [ˈʌnəˈbæʃt] sans se déconcerter; aucunement ébranlé.

un·a·ble [ʌnˈeibl] incapable (de, to); impuissant (à, to).

un·a·bridged [ˈʌnəˈbridʒd] non abrégé; intégral (-aux *m/pl.*).

un·ac·cent·ed [ˈʌnækˈsentid] inaccentué; *gramm.* atone.

un·ac·cept·a·ble [ˈʌnəkˈseptəbl] inacceptable.

un·ac·com·mo·dat·ing [ˈʌnəˈkɔmədeitiŋ] peu commode; peu accommodant (*personne*).

un·ac·count·a·ble □ [ˈʌnəˈkauntəbl] inexplicable; bizarre.

un·ac·cus·tomed [ˈʌnəˈkʌstəmd] inaccoutumé (à, to) (*a. personne*); peu habitué (à, to) (*personne*).

un·ac·knowl·edged [ˈʌnəkˈnɔlidʒd] non avoué; demeuré sans réponse (*lettre*).

un·ac·quaint·ed [ˈʌnəˈkweintid]: *be ‿ with* ne pas connaître (*q.*); ignorer (*qch.*).

un·a·dorned [ˈʌnədɔːnd] sans ornements, naturel(le *f*); *fig.* sans fard.

un·a·dul·ter·at·ed □ [ˈʌnəˈdʌltəreitid] pur, sans mélange.

un·ad·vis·a·ble □ [ˈʌnədˈvaizəbl] imprudent; peu sage; **ˈun·ad·ˈvised** □ [*adv.* ‿zidli] imprudent; sans prendre conseil.

un·af·fect·ed □ [ˈʌnəˈfektid] qui n'est pas atteint; *fig.* sincère; sans affectation *ou* pose.

un·aid·ed [ˈʌnˈeidid] sans aide;

(tout) seul; inassisté (*pauvre*); nu (*œil*).

un·al·loyed [ˈʌnəˈlɔid] sans alliage; *fig.* pur, sans mélange.

un·al·ter·a·ble □ [ʌnˈɔːltərəbl] invariable, immuable.

un·am·big·u·ous □ [ˈʌnæmˈbigjuəs] non équivoque, sans ambiguïté.

un·am·bi·tious □ [ˈʌnæmˈbiʃəs] sans prétention; sans ambition (*personne*).

un·a·me·na·ble [ˈʌnəˈmiːnəbl] rebelle, réfractaire (à, to).

un·a·mi·a·ble □ [ʌnˈeimjəbl] peu aimable.

u·na·nim·i·ty [juːnəˈnimiti] unanimité *f*; **u·nan·i·mous** □ [juˈnæniməs] unanime.

un·an·swer·a·ble [ʌnˈɑːnsərəbl] sans réplique; incontestable.

un·ap·palled [ˈʌnəˈpɔːld] peu effrayé.   [sans appel.〕

un·ap·peal·a·ble ᵗᵗ [ˈʌnəˈpiːləbl]〕

un·ap·peas·a·ble □ [ˈʌnəˈpiːzəbl] insatiable; implacable.

un·ap·proach·a·ble □ [ˈʌnəˈproutʃəbl] inaccessible; inabordable (*a. personne*); *fig.* incomparable.

un·ap·pro·pri·at·ed [ˈʌnəˈprouprieitid] disponible; libre.

un·apt □ [ˈʌnˈæpt] peu juste; mal approprié; inapte (à, for), peu disposé (à *inf.*, to *inf.*); be ~ to (*inf.*) avoir beaucoup de mal à (*inf.*).

un·a·shamed □ [ˈʌnəˈʃeimd]; *adv.* ~midli] sans honte ou pudeur.

un·asked [ˈʌnˈɑːskt] non invité; spontané(ment *adv.*).

un·as·sail·a·ble □ [ˈʌnəˈseiləbl] inattaquable; irréfutable.

un·as·sist·ed □ [ˈʌnəˈsistid] tout seul, sans aide.

un·as·sum·ing [ˈʌnəˈsjuːmiŋ] sans prétentions; modeste.

un·at·tached [ˈʌnəˈtætʃt] non attaché; indépendant (de, to); *univ.* qui ne dépend d'aucun collège; ✕ en disponibilité; isolé; ᵗᵗ sans propriétaire.

un·at·tain·a·ble □ [ˈʌnəˈteinəbl] inaccessible (de, by).

un·at·tend·ed [ˈʌnəˈtendid] seul; sans escorte; dépourvu (de, by); (*usu.* ~ to) négligé.

un·at·trac·tive □ [ˈʌnəˈtræktiv] peu attrayant; peu sympathique (*personne*).

un·au·thor·ized [ˈʌnˈɔːθəraizd] sans autorisation; illicite; *admin.* sans mandat.

un·a·vail·a·ble [ˈʌnəˈveiləbl] non disponible; inutilisable; **un·a·vail·ing** □ vain; inutile.

un·a·void·a·ble □ [ˈʌnəˈvɔidəbl] inévitable.

un·a·ware [ˈʌnəˈwɛə] ignorant; be ~ ignorer (qch., of s.th.; que, that); **un·a·wares** au dépourvu; sans s'en rendre compte.

un·backed [ˈʌnˈbækt] *fig.* sans appui; non endossé (*a.* ✝); *turf:* sur lequel personne n'a parié.

un·bal·ance [ˈʌnˈbæləns] défaut *m* d'équilibrage; balourd *m*; **un·bal·anced** mal équilibré (*a. fig.*); ⊕ non compensé; ✝ non soldé; *phys.* en équilibre instable.

un·bap·tized [ˈʌnbæpˈtaizd] non baptisé.

un·bar [ˈʌnˈbɑː] débarrer, *fig.* ouvrir; dessaisir (*un sabord*).

un·bear·a·ble □ [ʌnˈbɛərəbl] insupportable, intolérable.

un·beat·en [ˈʌnˈbiːtn] invaincu; non frayé (*chemin*).

un·be·com·ing □ [ˈʌnbiˈkʌmiŋ] peu seyant (*robe*); peu convenable; déplacé (chez q. of, to, for).

un·be·friend·ed [ˈʌnbiˈfrendid] sans amis; délaissé.

un·be·known [ˈʌnbiˈnoun] **1.** *adj.* inconnu (de, to); **2.** *adv.* à l'insu (de q., to s.o.).

un·be·lief [ˈʌnbiˈliːf] incrédulité *f*; *eccl.* incroyance *f*; **un·be·liev·a·ble** □ incroyable; **un·be·liev·er** incrédule *mf*; *eccl.* incroyant(e *f*) *m*; **un·be·liev·ing** □ incrédule.

un·be·loved [ˈʌnbiˈlʌvd] peu aimé.

un·bend [ˈʌnˈbend] [*irr.* (bend)] *v/t.* détendre (*a. fig.*); redresser (*q., a.* ⊕); *v/i.* se détendre; *fig.* se déraidir; se détordre (*ressort*); se redresser; se déplier (*jambe*); **un·bend·ing** □ inflexible; *fig. a.* raide.

un·bi·as(s)ed □ [ˈʌnˈbaiəst] *fig.* impartial (-aux *m/pl.*), sans parti pris.

un·bid, un·bid·den [ˈʌnˈbid(n)] non invité; spontané.

un·bind [ˈʌnˈbaind] [*irr.* (bind)] dénouer (*les cheveux*); délier (*a. fig.*).

un·bleached *tex.* [ˈʌnˈbliːtʃt] écru.

un·blem·ished [ʌnˈblemiʃt] sans tache (*a. fig.*).

un·blush·ing □ [ʌnˈblʌʃiŋ] qui ne rougit pas; sans vergogne.

un·bolt [ˈʌnˈboult] déverrouiller; dévisser (*un rail etc.*); '**un'bolt·ed** déverrouillé; ⊕ déboulonné; dévissé (*rail*); non bluté (*farine*).

un·born [ˈʌnˈbɔːn] à naître; qui n'est pas encore né; *fig.* futur.

un·bos·om [ʌnˈbuzm] révéler; ∼ *o.s.* ouvrir son cœur (à q., *to s.o.*).

un·bound [ˈʌnˈbaund] délié; dénoué (*cheveux*); broché (*livre*).

un·bound·ed □ [ʌnˈbaundid] sans bornes; illimité; démesuré (*ambition etc.*).

un·bowed [ˈʌnˈbaud] invaincu.

un·brace [ˈʌnˈbreis] défaire; détendre (*les nerfs*); énerver (*q.*).

un·break·a·ble [ˈʌnˈbreikəbl] incassable.

un·bri·dled [ʌnˈbraidld] débridé (*a. fig.*); sans bride; *fig.* déchaîné.

un·bro·ken [ʌnˈbroukn] intact; non brisé; inviolé (*record*); imbattu (*record*); non dressé (*cheval*); *fig.* insoumis.

un·buck·le [ʌnˈbʌkl] déboucler.

un·bur·den [ˈʌnˈbəːdn] décharger; *fig.* alléger; ∼ *o.s.* (*ou one's heart*) se délester (le cœur).

un·bur·ied [ˈʌnˈberid] déterré; sans sépulture.

un·busi·ness·like [ˈʌnˈbiznislaik] peu commerçant; *fig.* irrégulier (-ère *f*).

un·but·ton [ˈʌnˈbʌtn] déboutonner.

un·called [ʌnˈkɔːld] non appelé (*a.* †); **un'called-for** injustifié; déplacé (*remarque*); spontané.

un·can·ny □ [ʌnˈkæni] sinistre; mystérieux (-euse *f*).

un·cared-for [ˈʌnˈkɛədfɔː] mal *ou* peu soigné; abandonné; négligé (*air*).

un·ceas·ing □ [ʌnˈsiːsiŋ] incessant; continu; soutenu.

un·cer·e·mo·ni·ous □ [ˈʌnseriˈmounjəs] peu cérémonieux (-euse *f*); sans gêne (*personne*).

un·cer·tain □ [ʌnˈsəːtn] incertain; douteux (-euse *f*); irrésolu; peu sûr; be ∼ ne pas savoir au juste (si, *whether*); **un'cer·tain·ty** incertitude *f*.   [donner libre cours à.]

un·chain [ˈʌnˈtʃein] déchaîner; *fig.*⟩

un·chal·lenge·a·ble [ˈʌnˈtʃælindʒəbl] incontestable; **un'chal·lenged** incontesté.

un·change·a·ble □ [ʌnˈtʃeindʒəbl], **un'chang·ing** □ immuable, invariable; éternel(le *f*).

un·char·i·ta·ble □ [ʌnˈtʃæritəbl] peu charitable.

un·chaste □ [ʌnˈtʃeist] impudique; **un·chas·ti·ty** [ʌnˈtʃæstiti] impudicité *f*; infidélité *f* (*d'une femme*).

un·checked [ˈʌnˈtʃekt] libre(ment *adv.*); † non vérifié.

un·chris·tian □ [ˈʌnˈkristjən] peu chrétien(ne *f*); païen(ne *f*).

un·civ·il □ [ˈʌnˈsivl] impoli; **un'civ·i·lized** [∼vilaizd] barbare, incivilisé.

un·claimed [ˈʌnˈkleimd] non réclamé; épave (*chien etc.*); de rebut (*lettre*).

un·clasp [ˈʌnˈklɑːsp] défaire, dégrafer; (se) desserrer (*poing*); laisser échapper.

un·clas·si·fied [ˈʌnˈklæsifaid] non classé; non secret (-ète) (*information*).

un·cle [ˈʌŋkl] oncle *m*; *sl.* at my ∼'s chez ma tante, au clou.

un·clean □ [ˈʌnˈkliːn] sale; *fig.*, *eccl.* immonde, impur.

un·clench [ˈʌnˈklentʃ] (se) desserrer.

un·cloak [ˈʌnˈklouk] ôter le manteau de; *fig.* dévoiler.

un·close [ˈʌnˈklouz] (s')ouvrir.

un·clothe [ˈʌnˈklouð] (se) déshabiller.   [nuage; clair (*a. fig.*).⟩

un·cloud·ed [ˈʌnˈklaudid] sans⟩

un·coil [ˈʌnˈkɔil] (se) dérouler.

un·col·lect·ed [ˈʌnkəˈlektid] non recueilli; *fig.* confus.

un·col·o·(u)red [ˈʌnˈkʌləd] non coloré; incolore; *fig.* non influencé.

un·come·ly [ˈʌnˈkʌmli] peu gracieux (-euse *f*).

un·com·fort·a·ble □ [ʌnˈkʌmfətəbl] peu confortable; désagréable; peu à son aise (*personne*).

un·com·mon □ [ʌnˈkɔmən] (*a.* F *adv.*) peu commun; singulier (-ère *f*); rare.

un·com·mu·ni·ca·tive [ˈʌnkəˈmjuː-nikeitiv] réservé, taciturne; peu communicatif (-ive *f*).

un·com·plain·ing □ [ˈʌnkəmˈplein-iŋ] patient; sans plainte; **un'com·plain·ing·ness** patience *f*, résignation *f*.

un·com·pro·mis·ing □ [ˈʌnˈkɔm-prəmaiziŋ] intransigeant; sans compromis; *fig.* raide; absolu.

un·con·cern [ˈʌnkənˈsəːn] indifférence *f*; insouciance *f*; **un·con·**

'cerned □ [*adv.* ~idli] insouciant; indifférent (à, *about*); étranger (-ère *f*) (à *with*, in).

un·con·di·tion·al □ ['ʌnkən'diʃnl] absolu; sans réserve.

un·con·fined □ ['ʌnkən'faind] illimité, sans bornes; libre.

un·con·firmed ['ʌnkən'fəːmd] non confirmé *ou* avéré; *eccl.* qui n'a pas reçu la confirmation.

un·con·gen·ial ['ʌnkən'dʒiːnjəl] peu agréable; peu favorable; peu sympathique (*personne*).

un·con·nect·ed □ ['ʌnkə'nektid] sans lien *ou* rapport; décousu (*idées*).

un·con·quer·a·ble □ [ʌn'kɔŋkərəbl] invincible; *fig.* insurmontable.

un·con·sci·en·tious □ ['ʌnkɔnʃi-'enʃəs] peu consciencieux (-euse *f*).

un·con·scion·a·ble □ [ʌn'kɔnʃənəbl] peu scrupuleux (-euse *f*); déraisonnable (*a. fig.*); exorbitant.

un·con·scious □ [ʌn'kɔnʃəs] **1.** inconscient; sans connaissance (= *évanoui*); be ~ of ne pas avoir conscience de; **2.** *psych.* the ~ l'inconscient *m*; un'con·scious·ness inconscience *f*; évanouissement *m*.

un·con·sid·ered ['ʌnkən'sidəd] irréfléchi, inconsidéré; sans valeur.

un·con·sti·tu·tion·al □ ['ʌnkɔnsti-'tjuːʃənl] in-, anticonstitutionnel(le *f*).

un·con·strained □ ['ʌnkən'streind] sans contrainte; aisé.

un·con·test·ed □ ['ʌnkən'testid] incontesté; *pol.* qui n'est pas disputé.

un·con·tra·dict·ed ['ʌnkɔntrə'diktid] non contredit.

un·con·trol·la·ble □ [ʌnkən'trouləbl] ingouvernable; irrésistible; absolu.

un·con·ven·tion·al □ ['ʌnkən-'venʃnl] qui va à l'encontre des conventions; original (-aux *m/pl.*).

un·con·vert·ed ['ʌnkən'vəːtid] inconverti (*a. eccl.*); ✝ *a.* non converti.

un·con·vinced ['ʌnkən'vinst] sceptique (à l'égard de, *of*).

un·cork ['ʌn'kɔːk] déboucher.

un·cor·rupt·ed □ ['ʌnkə'rʌptid] intègre; incorrompu. [comptable.)

un·count·a·ble ['ʌn'kauntəbl] in-)

un·cou·ple ['ʌn'kʌpl] découpler.

un·couth □ [ʌn'kuːθ] grossier (-ère *f*), rude; gauche, agreste.

un·cov·er [ʌn'kʌvə] découvrir (⚔, *a.* une partie du corps); démasquer.

un·crit·i·cal □ ['ʌn'kritikl] sans discernement; peu difficile.

un·crowned ['ʌn'kraund] non couronné; découronné.

un·crush·a·ble *tex.* [ʌn'krʌʃəbl] infroissable.

unc·tion ['ʌŋkʃn] onction *f* (*a. fig.*); *poét.* onguent *m*; *eccl.* extreme ~ extrême-onction *f*; unc·tu·ous □ ['ʌŋktjuəs] onctueux (-euse *f*) (*a. fig.*); graisseux (-euse *f*); *péj.* patelin.

un·cul·ti·vat·ed ['ʌn'kʌltiveitid] inculte; en friche (*terre*); *fig.* sans culture; ⚘ à l'état sauvage.

un·cured ['ʌn'kjuəd] ⚕ non guéri; *cuis.* frais (*hareng*).

un·curl ['ʌn'kəːl] (se) défriser (*cheveux*); (se) dérouler.

un·cut ['ʌn'kʌt] intact; sur pied (*blé etc.*); non coupé (*haie, livre*); non rogné (*livre*).

un·dam·aged ['ʌn'dæmidʒd] en bon état.

un·damped ['ʌn'dæmpt] sec (sèche *f*); *fig.* non découragé.

un·dat·ed ['ʌn'deitid] sans date.

un·daunt·ed □ [ʌn'dɔːntid] intrépide; non intimidé.

un·de·ceive ['ʌndi'siːv] désabuser (de, *of*); dessiller les yeux à (*q.*).

un·de·cid·ed □ ['ʌndi'saidid] indécis.

un·de·ci·pher·a·ble ['ʌndi'saifərəbl] indéchiffrable.

un·de·fend·ed ['ʌndi'fendid] sans protection.

un·de·filed ['ʌndi'faild] sans tache, pur.

un·de·fined □ ['ʌndi'faind]; *adv.* ~nidli] non défini; vague.

un·de·mon·stra·tive □ ['ʌndi'mɔnstrətiv] réservé.

un·de·ni·a·ble □ ['ʌndi'naiəbl] incontestable; qu'on ne peut nier.

un·de·nom·i·na·tion·al □ ['ʌndinɔmi'neiʃənl] non confessionnel(le *f*); laïque (*école*).

un·der ['ʌndə] **1.** *adv.* (au-)dessous; en *ou* dans la soumission; **2.** *prp.* sous; au-dessous de; *from* ~ sous; de dessous; ~ *sentence of* condamné à; **3.** *mots composés*: trop peu; insuffisamment; inférieur; sous-; '~·**age** mineur; de mineurs; '~·**bid** [*irr.* (*bid*)] demander moins cher que; '~⁓'**bred** mal élevé; qui n'a pas de race (*cheval*); '~⁓**brush** broussailles *f/pl.*; sousbois *m*; '~⁓**carriage**, '~⁓**cart** 🚂 train *m* d'atterrissage; '~⁓**cloth·ing** linge *m* de corps; lingerie *f* (*pour dames*); '~⁓**cur·rent** courant *m* de fond *ou* sous-marin; *fig.* fond *m*; '~⁓**cut** [*irr.* (*cut*)] vendre moins cher que; '~⁓**de'vel·oped** sous-développé; '~⁓**dog** perdant *m*; *fig.* the ⁓(*s pl.*) les opprimés *m/pl.*; '~⁓**done** pas assez cuit; saignant (*viande*); '~⁓**dress** (s')habiller trop simplement; '~⁓**em'ploy·ment** sous-emploi *m*; '~⁓**es·ti·mate** sous-estimer; '~⁓**ex'pose** sous-exposer; '~⁓**fed** mal nourri; '~⁓**feed·ing** sous-alimentation *f*; '~⁓**felt** assise *f* de feutre; '~⁓**foot** sous les pieds; '~⁓**gar·ments** *pl.* sous-vêtements *m/pl.*; '~⁓**go** [*irr.* (*go*)] subir; supporter; '~⁓**grad·u·ate** *univ.* étudiant(e *f*) *m*; '~⁓**ground** 1. souterrain; sous terre; ⁓ *engineering* construction *f* souterraine; ⁓ *mouvement* mouvement *m* clandestin; ✗ résistance *f*; ⁓ *water* eaux *f/pl.* souterraines; ⁓ *railway* = 2. métro *m*; chemin *m* de fer souterrain; '~⁓**growth** broussailles *f/pl.*; '~⁓**hand** clandestin; sournois (*a. personne*); ⁓ *service tennis*: service *m* par en dessous; '~⁓**hung** 🐟 prognathe; coulissant (*porte*); ~⁓**lay** 1. [ˌʌndə'lei] [*irr.* (*lay*)]: ⁓ *s.th. with s.th.* mettre qch. sous qch.; 2. ['ʌndəlei] assise *f* de feutre; *géol.* inclinaison *f*; '~⁓**let** [*irr.* (*let*)] sous-louer; louer à trop bas prix; ⚓ sous-fréter; ~⁓**lie** [*irr.* (*lie*)] être en dessous *ou* au-dessous *ou fig.* à la base de; ~⁓**line** 1. [ˌʌndə'lain] souligner; 2. ['ʌndəlain] légende *f* (*d'une illustration*).

un·der·ling [ˈʌndəliŋ] subordonné (-e *f*) *m*; sous-ordre *m*; **un·der·manned** [ˈˌʌ'mænd] à court de personnel *ou* ⚓ d'équipage; '**un·der·'men·tioned** (cité) ci-dessous; **un·der'mine** miner, saper (*a. fig.*); '**un·der·most** 1. *adj.* le (la) plus bas(se *f*); le plus en dessous; 2. *adv.* en dessous; **un·der'neath** [ˌ⁓'niːθ] 1. *prp.* au-dessous de, sous; 2. *adv.* au-dessous; par-dessous.

under...: '~⁓**nour·ished** mal nourri; '~⁓**pants** *pl.* (*a pair of* ⁓ un) caleçon *ou* slip; '~⁓**pass** *Am.* passage *m* souterrain; '~⁓**pay** [*irr.* (*pay*)] rétribuer mal; ~⁓**pin** ⊕ étayer (*un mur*); *fig.* soutenir; ~⁓**pin·ning** ⊕ étayage *m*; étais *m/pl.*; soutènement *m*; '~⁓**play** minimiser; ⁓ *one's hand* dissimuler ses intentions, cacher son jeu; '~⁓**plot** intrigue *f* secondaire; '~⁓**print** *phot.* tirer (*une épreuve*) trop claire; '~⁓**priv·i·leged** déshérité (*a. su.*); ~⁓**rate** sous-estimer; mésestimer; ~⁓**score** souligner; '~⁓**sec·re·tar·y** sous-secrétaire *mf*; '~⁓**sell** ✝ [*irr.*(*sell*)] vendre moins cher que (*q.*); vendre (*qch.*) au-dessous de sa valeur; '~⁓**shot** en dessous, à aubes (*roue*); '~⁓**signed** soussigné(e *f*) *m*; '~⁓**sized** trop petit; rabougri; ~⁓**slung** *mot.* à châssis surbaissé; ~⁓**staffed** à court de personnel; ~⁓**stand** [*irr.* (*stand*)] comprendre (*a. fig.*); s'entendre à; se rendre compte de; *gramm.* sous-entendre; *fig. a.* écouter bien; *make o.s. understood* se faire comprendre; *it is understood that* il est (bien) entendu que; *that is understood* cela va sans dire; *an understood thing* chose *f* convenue; ~⁓**stand·a·ble** compréhensible; ~⁓**stand·ing** 1. entendement *m*, compréhension *f*; entente *f*, accord *m*; *on the* ⁓ *that* à condition que; 2. intelligent; '~⁓**state** rester au-dessous de la vérité; amoindrir (*les faits*); '~⁓**state·ment** affirmation *f* qui reste au-dessous de la vérité; amoindrissement *m* (*des faits*).

under...: '~⁓**strap·per** *see underling*; '~⁓**stud·y** *théâ.* 1. doublure *f*; 2. doubler; ~⁓**take** [*irr.* (*take*)] entreprendre; se charger de; ⁓ *that* F promettre que; '~⁓**tak·er** entrepreneur *m* de pompes funèbres; '~⁓**tak·ing** [ˌʌndə'teikiŋ] entreprise *f* (*a.* ✝); promesse *f*; '~⁓**tak·ing** ['ʌndəteikiŋ] entreprise *f* de pompes funèbres; '~⁓**ten·ant** sous-locataire *mf*; '~⁓**the-coun·ter** clandestin(ement); '~⁓**tone** *fig.* fond *m*; *in an* ⁓ à demi-voix, à voix basse; '~⁓**val·ue** sous-estimer; mésestimer; '~⁓**wear** linge *m* de corps; lingerie *f* (*pour dames*); '~⁓**weight** manque *m* de poids; '~⁓**wood** broussailles *f/pl.*; sous-bois *m*; '~⁓**world** les enfers *m/pl.*; les bas-fonds *m/pl.* de la société; '~⁓**write** ✝ [*irr.*(*write*)] souscrire (*une émission, un risque*); garantir; '~⁓**writ·er** assureur *m*; membre *m* d'un syndicat de garantie.

un·de·served □ [ˈʌndiˈzəːvd; adv. ~vidli] immérité; injuste; **'un·de·'serv·ing** peu méritoire; sans mérite (personne).

un·de·signed □ [ˈʌndiˈzaind; adv. ~nidli] imprévu; involontaire.

un·de·sir·a·ble □ [ˈʌndiˈzaiərəbl] peu désirable; indésirable (a. su./mf).

un·de·terred [ˈʌndiˈtəːd] aucunement découragé.

un·de·vel·oped [ˈʌndiˈveləpt] non développé; inexploité (terrain).

un·de·vi·a·ting □ [ʌnˈdiːvieitiŋ] constant; droit.

un·di·gest·ed [ˈʌndiˈdʒestid] mal digéré.

un·dig·ni·fied □ [ʌnˈdignifaid] qui manque de dignité; peu digne.

un·dis·cerned □ [ˈʌndiˈsəːnd] inaperçu; **'un·dis·'cern·ing** sans discernement.

un·dis·charged [ˈʌndisˈtʃɑːdʒd] inaccompli (tâche etc.); inacquitté (dette); non réhabilité (failli).

un·dis·ci·plined [ʌnˈdisiplind] indiscipliné.

un·dis·crim·i·nat·ing □ [ˈʌndisˈkrimineitiŋ] sans discernement.

un·dis·guised □ [ˈʌndisˈgaizd] non déguisé; franc(he f).

un·dis·posed [ˈʌndisˈpouzd] peu disposé (à, to); (usu. ~of) qui reste; † non vendu.

un·dis·put·ed □ [ˈʌndisˈpjuːtid] incontesté.

un·dis·turbed □ [ˈʌndisˈtəːbd] tranquille; calme; non dérangé.

un·di·vid·ed □ [ˈʌndiˈvaidid] indivisé; non partagé; tout.

un·do [ˈʌnˈduː] [irr. (do)] défaire (= ouvrir); dénouer; annuler; réparer (un mal); † ruiner; † tuer; **'un·'do·ing** action f de défaire etc.; ruine f, perte f; **un·done** [ˈʌnˈdʌn] défait etc.; inachevé; non accompli; he is ~ c'en est fait de lui; come ~ se défaire.　　　[table; incontestable.]

un·doubt·ed □ [ʌnˈdautid] indubi-

un·dreamt-of [ʌnˈdremtɔv] inattendu; inimaginé.

un·dress [ˈʌnˈdres] 1. (se) déshabiller ou dévêtir; 2. déshabillé m, négligé m; ✕ petite tenue f; **'un·'dressed** déshabillé; en déshabillé; brut (pierre); inapprêté (cuir etc.); non pansé (blessure); cuis. non garni ou habillé.

un·due [ˈʌnˈdjuː] (adv. unduly) inexigible; † non échu; injuste; exagéré; illégitime.

un·du·late [ˈʌndjuleit] vt/i. onduler; v/i. ondoyer; **'un·du·'lat·ing** □ ondulé; vallonné (terrain); **un·du·'la·tion** ondulation f; pli m de terrain; **un·du·la·to·ry** [ˈ~lətəri] ondulatoire; ondulé.

un·dy·ing □ [ʌnˈdaiiŋ] immortel(le f); éternel(le f).

un·earned [ˈʌnˈəːnd] immérité; ~ income rente f, -s f/pl.

un·earth [ˈʌnˈəːθ] déterrer; chasse: faire sortir de son trou; fig. découvrir, F dénicher; **un·'earth·ly** sublime; surnaturel(le f); F abominable.

un·eas·i·ness [ʌnˈiːzinis] gêne f; inquiétude f; **un·'eas·y** □ gêné; mal à l'aise; inquiet (-ète f) (au sujet de, about).

un·eat·a·ble [ˈʌnˈiːtəbl] immangeable.

un·e·co·nom·ic, un·e·co·nom·i·cal □ [ˈʌniːkəˈnɔmik(l)] non économique; non rémunérateur (-trice f) (travail etc.).

un·ed·u·cat·ed [ˈʌnˈedjukeitid] sans éducation; ignorant; vulgaire (langage).

un·em·bar·rassed [ˈʌnimˈbærəst] peu gêné, désinvolte.

un·e·mo·tion·al □ [ˈʌniˈmouʃnl] peu émotif (-ive f); peu impressionnable.

un·em·ployed [ˈʌnimˈplɔid] 1. désœuvré, inoccupé; sans travail; ✕ en non-activité; † inemployé; 2.: the ~ pl. les chômeurs m/pl.; Welfare Work for the ♀ assistance f sociale contre le chômage; **'un·em·'ploy·ment** chômage m; manque m de travail; ~ benefit secours m de chômage; allocation f de chômage.

un·end·ing □ [ˈʌnˈendiŋ] sans fin; interminable; éternel(le f).

un·en·dur·a·ble [ˈʌninˈdjuərəbl] insupportable.

un·en·gaged [ˈʌninˈgeidʒd] libre; disponible; non fiancé.

un-English [ˈʌnˈiŋgliʃ] peu anglais.

un·en·light·ened fig. [ˈʌninˈlaitnd] non éclairé.

un·en·ter·pris·ing [ˈʌnˈentəpraiziŋ] peu entreprenant.

un·en·vi·a·ble □ [ˈʌnˈenviəbl] peu enviable.

un·e·qual □ [ˈʌnˈiːkwəl] inégal (-aux m/pl.); irrégulier (-ère f); ~ to au-dessous de; be ~ to (inf.) ne pas être de taille à (inf.); **un'e·qual(l)ed** sans égal (-aux m/pl.); sans pareil(le f).

un·e·qui·vo·cal □ [ˈʌniˈkwivəkl] clair; franc(he f); sans équivoque.

un·err·ing □ [ˈʌnˈəːriŋ] infaillible.

un·es·sen·tial □ [ˈʌniˈsenʃl] non essentiel(le f); accessoire.

un·e·ven □ [ˈʌnˈiːvn] inégal (-aux m/pl.) (a. humeur, souffle); accidenté (terrain); raboteux (-euse f) (chemin); rugueux (-euse f); impair (nombre); irrégulier (-ère f).

un·e·vent·ful □ [ˈʌniˈventful] calme; sans incidents.

un·ex·am·pled [ˈʌnigˈzaːmpld] unique; sans pareil(le f).

un·ex·cep·tion·a·ble □ [ˈʌnikˈsepʃənəbl] irréprochable; irrécusable (témoignage).

un·ex·cep·tion·al [ˈʌnikˈsepʃənl] ordinaire, banal (-als m/pl.), qui ne sort pas de l'ordinaire.

un·ex·pect·ed □ [ˈʌniksˈpektid] imprévu; inattendu.

un·ex·plored [ˈʌniksˈplɔːd] encore inconnu; ⚕ insondé.

un·ex·posed phot. [ˈʌniksˈpouzd] vierge.

un·ex·pressed [ˈʌniksˈprest] inexprimé; sousentendu (a. gramm.).

un·fad·ing □ [ʌnˈfeidiŋ] bon teint inv.; fig. impérissable.

un·fail·ing □ [ʌnˈfeiliŋ] sûr, infaillible; qui ne se dément jamais; inépuisable.

un·fair □ [ˈʌnˈfɛə] inéquitable; injuste, partial (-aux m/pl.) (personne); déloyal (-aux m/pl.) (jeu etc.); **un'fair·ness** injustice f; partialité f; déloyauté f.

un·faith·ful □ [ˈʌnˈfeiθful] infidèle; inexact; déloyal (-aux m/pl.) (envers, to); **un'faith·ful·ness** infidélité f.   [me; assuré.\
un·fal·ter·ing □ [ʌnˈfɔːltəriŋ] fer-\
un·fa·mil·iar [ˈʌnfəˈmiljə] étranger (-ère f); peu connu ou familier (-ère f).

un·fash·ion·a·ble □ [ˈʌnˈfæʃnəbl] démodé.

un·fas·ten [ˈʌnˈfaːsn] délier; détacher; ouvrir; défaire.

un·fath·om·a·ble □ [ʌnˈfæðəməbl] insondable.

un·fa·vo(u)r·a·ble □ [ˈʌnˈfeivərəbl] défavorable.

un·feel·ing □ [ʌnˈfiːliŋ] insensible.

un·feigned □ [ʌnˈfeind; adv. ~nidli] sincère, réel(le f), vrai.

un·felt [ˈʌnˈfelt] insensible.

un·fer·ment·ed [ˈʌnfəˈmentid] non fermenté.

un·fet·ter [ˈʌnˈfetə] désenchaîner; briser les fers de; fig. affranchir.

un·fil·i·al □ [ˈʌnˈfiljəl] indigne d'un fils.

un·fin·ished [ˈʌnˈfiniʃt] inachevé; imparfait; ⊕ brut.

un·fit 1. □ [ˈʌnˈfit] peu propre, qui ne convient pas (à inf., to inf.; à qch., for s.th.); inapte (à, for); **2.** [ʌnˈfit] rendre inapte ou impropre (à, for); **un'fit·ness** inaptitude f; mauvaise santé f; **un'fit·ted** (to, for) impropre (à); incapable (de); indigne (de).

un·fix [ˈʌnˈfiks] (se) détacher, défaire; **un'fixed** mobile; instable (personne); flottant; phot. non fixé.

un·flag·ging □ [ʌnˈflægiŋ] infatigable; soutenu (intérêt).

un·flat·ter·ing □ [ˈʌnˈflætəriŋ] peu flatteur (-euse f) (pour, to).

un·fledged [ˈʌnˈfledʒd] sans plumes; fig. sans expérience.

un·flinch·ing □ [ʌnˈflintʃiŋ] ferme, qui ne bronche pas; stoïque; impassible.

un·fold [ˈʌnˈfould] (se) déployer; (se) dérouler; v/t. [~ˈfould] révéler; développer.

un·forced □ [ˈʌnˈfɔːst; adv. ~sidli] libre; volontaire; naturel(le f).

un·fore·see·a·ble [ˈʌnfɔːˈsiːəbl] imprévisible.

un·fore·seen [ˈʌnfɔːˈsiːn] imprévu, inattendu.

un·for·get·ta·ble □ [ˈʌnfəˈgetəbl] inoubliable.

un·for·giv·a·ble [ˈʌnfəˈgivəbl] impardonnable; **un'for·giv·ing** implacable; rancunier (-ère f).

un·for·got·ten [ˈʌnfəˈgɔtn] inoublié.

un·for·ti·fied [ˈʌnˈfɔːtifaid] sans défenses; ouvert (ville etc.).

un·for·tu·nate [ʌnˈfɔːtʃənit] **1.** □ malheureux (-euse f) (a. su.); défavorable; **~ly** malheureusement, par malheur.

un·found·ed □ [ˈʌnˈfaundid] sans fondement; gratuit; non fondé.

un·fre·quent·ed [ˈʌnfriˈkwentid] peu fréquenté.

un·friend·ly [ˈʌnˈfrendli] inamical (-aux *m/pl.*); hostile.

un·fruit·ful □ [ˈʌnˈfruːtful] infécond (*arbre*); improductif (-ive *f*).

un·ful·filled [ˈʌnfulˈfild] inaccompli; inassouvi (*désir*); inexaucé (*vœu*).

un·furl [ʌnˈfɔːl] (se) déferler (*voile, drapeau*); (se) dérouler; (se) déplier.

un·fur·nished [ˈʌnˈfɔːniʃt] dégarni; dépourvu (de, *with*); non meublé (*appartement etc.*).

un·gain·li·ness [ʌnˈgeinlinis] gaucherie *f*; air *m* gauche; **un·gain·ly** gauche; dégingandé (*marche*).

un·gear ⊕ [ˈʌnˈgiə] débrayer.

un·gen·er·ous □ [ˈʌnˈdʒenərəs] peu généreux (-euse *f*); ingrat (*sol*).

un·gen·tle □ [ˈʌnˈdʒentl] rude, dur.

un·gen·tle·man·ly [ʌnˈdʒentlmənli] mal élevé; impoli.

un·glazed [ˈʌnˈgleizd] sans vitres; non glacé (*papier*).

un·gloved [ˈʌnˈglʌvd] déganté.

un·god·li·ness [ʌnˈgɔdlinis] impiété *f*; **un·god·ly** □ impie; F abominable.

un·gov·ern·a·ble □ [ʌnˈgʌvənəbl] irrésistible; effréné; ingouvernable (*enfant, pays*); **un·gov·erned** effréné; sans gouvernement (*pays, peuple*); désordonné.

un·grace·ful □ [ˈʌnˈgreisful] gauche; disgracieux (-euse *f*).

un·gra·cious □ [ˈʌnˈgreiʃəs] désagréable; peu aimable (*personne*); peu cordial (-aux *m/pl.*) (*accueil etc.*).

un·grate·ful □ [ʌnˈgreitful] ingrat; peu reconnaissant.

un·ground·ed [ˈʌnˈgraundid] sans fondement; ⚡ non (relié) à la terre.

un·grudg·ing □ [ˈʌnˈgrʌdʒiŋ] accordé de bon cœur; généreux (-euse *f*).   [(-aux *m/pl.*); onguéal.\
un·gual *anat.* [ˈʌŋgwəl] unguéal⌡

un·guard·ed □ [ˈʌnˈgɑːdid] non gardé; sans garde; sans défense (*ville*); ⊕ sans dispositif protecteur; *fig.* imprudent.

un·guent [ˈʌŋgwənt] onguent *m*.

un·guid·ed □ [ˈʌnˈgaidid] sans guide.

un·gu·late [ˈʌŋgjuleit] (*ou* ~ *animal*) ongulé *m*.

un·hal·lowed [ʌnˈhæloud] profane; imbéni; *fig.* impie.

un·ham·pered [ˈʌnˈhæmpəd] libre.

un·hand·some □ [ʌnˈhænsəm] laid (*action*); vilain.

un·hand·y □ [ʌnˈhændi] incommode; maladroit, gauche (*personne*).

un·hap·pi·ness [ʌnˈhæpinis] chagrin *m*; inopportunité *f*; **un·hap·py** □ triste, malheureux (-euse *f*); *fig.* peu heureux (-euse *f*).

un·harmed [ˈʌnˈhɑːmd] sain et sauf (-ve *f*).

un·har·ness [ˈʌnˈhɑːnis] dételer.

un·health·y □ [ʌnˈhelθi] malsain (*a. fig.*); maladif (-ive *f*) (*personne*).

un·heard [ˈʌnˈhɔːd] non entendu; ~of [ʌnˈhɔːdɔv] inouï; inconnu.

un·heed·ed [ˈʌnˈhiːdid] négligé; inaperçu.

un·hes·i·tat·ing □ [ʌnˈheziteitiŋ] ferme, résolu; prompt.

un·hinge [ʌnˈhindʒ] enlever (*une porte*) de ses gonds; *fig.* déranger, détraquer.

un·his·tor·i·cal □ [ˈʌnhisˈtɔrikl] contraire à l'histoire; légendaire.

un·ho·ly [ʌnˈhouli] profane; impie (*personne*); F invraisemblable.

un·hon·o(u)red [ˈʌnˈɔnəd] qui n'est pas honoré; dédaigné; † impayé (*chèque etc.*).

un·hook [ˈʌnˈhuk] (se) décrocher; (se) dégrafer.

un·hoped-for [ʌnˈhouptfɔː] inespéré; inattendu; **un·hope·ful** [~ful] peu optimiste; désespérant.

un·horse [ˈʌnˈhɔːs] désarçonner; dételer (*une voiture*).

un·house [ˈʌnˈhauz] déloger; laisser sans abri.

un·hurt [ˈʌnˈhɔːt] intact; sans blessure (*personne*); indemne.

u·ni·corn [ˈjuːnikɔːn] licorne *f*.

un·i·den·ti·fied [ˈʌnaiˈdentifaid] non identifié; ~ *flying object* objet *m* volant non identifié.

u·ni·fi·ca·tion [juːnifiˈkeiʃn] unification *f*.

u·ni·form [ˈjuːnifɔːm] 1. □ uniforme; constant; ~ *price* prix *m* unique; 2. uniforme *m*; ⚔ *a.* habit *m* d'ordonnance; 3. vêtir d'un uniforme; ~d en uniforme; **u·ni·form-**

i·ty uniformité *f*; régularité *f*; *eccl.* conformisme *m*.

u·ni·fy ['ju:nifai] unifier.

u·ni·lat·er·al ['ju:ni'lætərəl] unilatéral (-aux *m/pl.*).

un·im·ag·i·na·ble □ [ʌni'mædʒinəbl] inconcevable; '**un·im·ag·i·na·tive** □ [ˌ~nətiv] prosaïque.

un·im·paired ['ʌnim'pɛəd] intact; non diminué; non affaibli.

un·im·peach·a·ble □ [ʌnim'pi:tʃəbl] inattaquable; irréprochable (*conduite*).

un·im·por·tant □ ['ʌnim'pɔ:tənt] sans importance; insignifiant.

un·im·proved ['ʌnim'pru:vd] non amélioré; ✓, *fig.* inculte.

un·in·flu·enced ['ʌn'influənst] libre de toute prévention; non influencé.

un·in·formed ['ʌnin'fɔ:md] ignorant; non averti.

un·in·hab·it·a·ble ['ʌnin'hæbitəbl] inhabitable; '**un·in·hab·it·ed** inhabité; désert.

un·in·jured ['ʌn'indʒəd] intact; sain et sauf (-ve *f*) (*personne*); indemne.

un·in·struct·ed ['ʌnin'strʌktid] ignorant; sans instruction.

un·in·tel·li·gi·bil·i·ty ['ʌnintelidʒə'biliti] inintelligibilité *f*; '**un·in·tel·li·gi·ble** inintelligible.

un·in·ten·tion·al □ ['ʌnin'tenʃənl] involontaire; non voulu.

un·in·ter·est·ing □ ['ʌn'intristiŋ] sans intérêt; peu intéressant.

un·in·ter·rupt·ed □ ['ʌnintə'rʌptid] ininterrompu; ~ *working-hours* heures *f/pl.* de travail d'affilée.

un·in·vit·ed ['ʌnin'vaitid] sans être invité; intrus; '**un·in'vit·ing** □ peu attrayant.

un·ion ['ju:njən] union *f* (*a.* ⊕, *pol. etc.*); réunion *f*; *pol.* syndicat *m*; association *f*; asile *m* des pauvres; *fig.* concorde *f*; ⚓ soudure *f*; ⊕ raccord *m*; ♀ *Jack* pavillon *m* britannique; *member* syndiqué(e *f*) *m*; ~ *shop* atelier *m* d'ouvriers syndiqués; ~ *suit Am.* combinaison *f*; '**un·ion·ism** *pol. etc.* unionisme *m*; syndicalisme *m*; '**un·ion·ist** *pol. etc.* unioniste *mf*; syndiqué(e *f*) *m*; syndicaliste *mf*.

u·nique [ju:'ni:k] **1.** □ unique; seul en son genre; **2.** chose *f* unique.

u·ni·son ♪, *a. fig.* ['ju:nizn] unisson *m*; in ~ à l'unisson (de, *with*); *fig.* de concert (avec, *with*).

u·nit ['ju:nit] unité *f* (*a.* ✕, ♀, ✚, *mesure*); élément *m*; ⊕ bloc *m*; **U·ni·tar·i·an** [ju:ni'tɛəriən] **1.** unita(i)rien(ne *f*) *m*; unitaire *mf*; **2.** = **u·ni·tar·y** ['ˌ~təri] unitaire; **u·nite** [ju:'nait] (s')unir; (se)réunir; (se) joindre (à, *with*); ♀d *Kingdom* Royaume-Uni *m*; ♀d *Nations Organisation* Organisation *f* des Nations Unies; ♀d *States pl.* États-Unis *m/pl.* (d'Amérique); **u·ni·ty** ['ˌ~niti] unité *f*.

u·ni·ver·sal □ [ju:ni'və:səl] universel(le *f*); ~ *legatee* légataire *m* universel; ⊕ ~ *joint* joint *m* brisé *ou* de cardan; ~ *language* langue *f* universelle; ♀ *Postal Union* Union *f* Postale Universelle; ~ *suffrage* suffrage *m* universel; **u·ni·ver·sal·i·ty** [ˌ~'sæliti] universalité *f*; **u·ni·verse** ['ˌ~və:s] univers *m*; **u·ni·ver·si·ty** [ˌ~'və:siti] université *f*.

un·just □ ['ʌn'dʒʌst] injuste (avec, envers, pour *to*); **un·jus·ti·fi·a·ble** □ [ʌn'dʒʌstifaiəbl] injustifiable; inexcusable.

un·kempt ['ʌn'kempt] mal peigné; *fig.* mal *ou* peu soigné; mal tenu.

un·kind □ [ʌn'kaind] dur, cruel (-le *f*); peu aimable.

un·knot ['ʌn'nɔt] dénouer.

un·know·ing □ ['ʌn'nouiŋ] ignorant; inconscient (de, *of*); '**un·known 1.** inconnu (de, à *to*); *adv.* ~ *to me* à mon insu; **2.** inconnu *m*; *personne:* inconnu(e *f*) *m*; ♀ inconnue *f*.

un·lace ['ʌn'leis] délacer, défaire.

un·lade ['ʌn'leid] [*irr.* (*lade*)] décharger (*a.* ⚓); *fig.* délester.

un·la·dy·like ['ʌn'leidilaik] peu distingué; vulgaire.

un·laid ['ʌn'leid] détordu (*câble*); non posé (*tapis*); non mis (*couvert*, *table*). [regretté.\

un·la·ment·ed ['ʌnlə'mentid] non\

un·latch ['ʌn'lætʃ] lever le loquet de; ouvrir.

un·law·ful □ ['ʌn'lɔ:ful] illégal (-aux *m/pl.*); contraire à la loi; illicite; *p.ext.* illégitime.

un·learn ['ʌn'lə:n] désapprendre; '**un'learn·ed** □ [ˌ~id] ignorant; illettré; peu versé (dans, *in*).

un·leash ['ʌn'li:ʃ] découpler, lâcher; *fig.* déchaîner; détacher.

un·leav·ened ['ʌn'levnd] sans levain, azyme.

un·less [ən'les] **1.** *cj.* à moins que (*sbj.*); à moins de (*inf.*); si … ne … pas; **2.** *prp.* sauf, excepté.

un·let·tered ['ʌn'letəd] illettré.

un·li·censed ['ʌn'laisənst] non autorisé; sans brevet.

un·like □ ['ʌn'laik] différent (de q., [to]) *s.o.*); dissemblable; à la différence de; **un·like·li·hood** improbabilité *f*; **un·like·ly** invraisemblable, improbable.

un·lim·it·ed [ʌn'limitid] illimité; sans bornes (*a. fig.*).

un·link ['ʌn'liŋk] défaire, détacher; ~ *hands* se lâcher.

un·load ['ʌn'loud] décharger (*un bateau, une voiture, une cargaison*; *a.* une arme à feu; *a. phot.*); † se décharger de; *fig.* ~ *one's heart* épancher son cœur, se soulager.

un·lock ['ʌn'lɔk] ouvrir; tourner la clef dans; débloquer (*une roue*); *mot.* déverrouiller (*la direction*).

un·looked-for [ʌn'luktfɔ:] imprévu; inattendu. [faire.]

un·loose(n) ['ʌn'lu:s(n)] lâcher; dé-

un·lov·a·ble ['ʌn'lʌvəbl] peu aimable *ou* sympathique; **'un·love·ly** sans charme; laid; **'un·lov·ing** □ froid; peu affectueux (-euse *f*).

un·luck·y □ [ʌn'lʌki] malheureux (-euse *f*).

un·make ['ʌn'meik] [*irr.* (*make*)] défaire (*qch.*, *un roi*, *etc.*); perdre (*q.*), causer la ruine de (*q.*).

un·man ['ʌn'mæn] amollir (*une nation*); attendrir; *fig.* décourager.

un·man·age·a·ble □ [ʌn'mænidʒ-əbl] intraitable; indocile; difficile à manier; difficile à diriger (*entreprise*).

un·man·ly ['ʌn'mænli] efféminé; indigne d'un homme.

un·man·ner·ly [ʌn'mænəli] sans savoir-vivre; impoli, mal élevé.

un·mar·ried ['ʌn'mærid] célibataire; non marié.

un·mask ['ʌn'mɑ:sk] (se) démasquer; *v/t. fig.* dévoiler.

un·matched ['ʌn'mætʃt] incomparable; désassorti.

un·mean·ing □ [ʌn'mi:niŋ] vide de sens; **un·meant** ['ʌn'ment] involontaire; fait sans intention.

un·meas·ured [ʌn'meʒəd] non mesuré; *fig.* infini.

un·men·tion·a·ble [ʌn'menʃnəbl] **1.** dont il ne faut pas parler; qu'il ne faut pas prononcer; **2.** *the* ~*s pl.* le pantalon *m.*

un·mer·ci·ful □ [ʌn'mə:siful] impitoyable.

un·mer·it·ed ['ʌn'meritid] immérité.

un·mind·ful □ [ʌn'maindful] négligent (*personne*); ~ *of* oublieux (-euse *f*) de; sans penser à.

un·mis·tak·a·ble □ [ʌnmis'teik-əbl] clair; qui ne prête à aucune erreur; facilement reconnaissable.

un·mit·i·gat·ed [ʌn'mitigeitid] non mitigé; *fig.* parfait; véritable.

un·mo·lest·ed ['ʌnmo'lestid] sans être molesté; sans empêchement.

un·moor ['ʌn'muə] dé(sa)marrer; désaffourcher.

un·mort·gaged ['ʌn'mɔ:gidʒd] libre d'hypothèques.

un·mount·ed ['ʌn'mauntid] non monté; non serti (*pierre précieuse*); non encadré (*photo etc.*); ✕ à pied.

un·moved □ ['ʌn'mu:vd] toujours en place; *fig.* impassible.

un·mu·si·cal □ ['ʌn'mju:zikl] peu mélodieux (-euse *f*); peu musical (-aux *m/pl.*); qui n'aime pas la musique (*personne*).

un·muz·zle ['ʌn'mʌzl] démuseler (*a. fig.*); ~*d a.* sans muselière.

un·named ['ʌn'neimd] anonyme.

un·nat·u·ral □ [ʌn'nætʃrl] non naturel(le *f*); anormal (-aux *m/pl.*); forcé; dénaturé (*père etc.*).

un·nec·es·sar·y □ [ʌn'nesisəri] superflu.

un·neigh·bo(u)r·ly [ʌn'neibəli] de mauvais voisin; peu obligeant.

un·nerve [ʌn'nə:v] effrayer; faire perdre son courage (*etc.*) à (*q.*).

un·no·ticed ['ʌn'noutist] inaperçu.

un·num·bered ['ʌn'nʌmbəd] non numéroté; *poét.* innombrable.

un·ob·jec·tion·a·ble □ ['ʌnəb-'dʒekʃnəbl] irréprochable.

un·ob·serv·ant □ ['ʌnəb'zə:vənt] peu observateur (-trice *f*); *be* ~ *of* ne pas faire attention à; faire peu de cas de; **'un·ob'served** □ inaperçu, inobservé.

un·ob·tru·sive □ ['ʌnəb'tru:siv] modeste; discret (-ète *f*).

un·oc·cu·pied ['ʌn'ɔkjupaid] inoccupé; oisif (-ive *f*); inhabité; libre.

un·of·fend·ing ['ʌnə'fendiŋ] innocent.

un·of·fi·cial ☐ ['ʌnə'fiʃl] officieux (-euse f); non confirmé.

un·op·posed ['ʌnə'pouzd] sans opposition; pol. unique (candidat).

un·os·ten·ta·tious ☐ ['ʌnɔstən-'teiʃəs] simple; modeste; sans faste.

un·pack ['ʌn'pæk] déballer; défaire (v/i. sa valise etc.).

un·paid ['ʌn'peid] impayé; sans traitement; ✝ non acquitté; non affranchi (lettre).

un·pal·at·a·ble [ʌn'pælətəbl] désagréable (au goût, a. fig.).

un·par·al·leled ['ʌn'pærəleld] incomparable; sans égal (-aux m/pl.); sans précédent.

un·par·don·a·ble ☐ [ʌn'pɑ:dnəbl] impardonnable.

un·par·lia·men·ta·ry ☐ ['ʌnpɑ:lə-'mentəri] antiparlementaire; F grossier (-ère f).

un·pa·tri·ot·ic ['ʌnpætri'ɔtik] (~ally) peu patriotique; peu patriote (personne).

un·paved ['ʌn'peivd] non pavé.

un·peo·ple ['ʌn'pi:pl] dépeupler.

un·per·ceived ['ʌnpə'si:vd] inaperçu; non ressenti.

un·per·formed ['ʌnpə'fɔ:md] inexécuté (a. ♪); ♪, théâ. non joué.

un·phil·o·soph·i·cal ☐ ['ʌnfilə-'sɔfikl] peu philosophique.

un·picked ['ʌn'pikt] non trié; non cueilli (fruit).

un·pin ['ʌn'pin] enlever les épingles de; défaire; ⊕ dégoupiller.

un·pit·ied ['ʌn'pitid] sans être plaint; que personne ne plaint.

un·placed ['ʌn'pleist] sans place; turf: non placé; non classé.

un·pleas·ant ☐ [ʌn'pleznt] désagréable; fâcheux (-euse f); **un'pleas·ant·ness** caractère m désagréable; fig. ennui m.

un·plumbed ['ʌn'plʌmd] insondé.

un·po·et·ic, un·po·et·i·cal ☐ ['ʌn-pou'etik(l)] peu poétique.

un·po·lished ['ʌn'pɔliʃt] non poli; non verni; fig. fruste.

un·pol·lut·ed ['ʌnpə'lu:tid] impollué; pur.

un·pop·u·lar ☐ ['ʌn'pɔpjulə] impopulaire; mal vu; **un·pop·u·lar·i·ty** ['~'læriti] impopularité f.

un·prac·ti·cal ☐ ['ʌn'præktikl] impraticable; peu pratique (personne);

un·prac·ticed, un·prac·tised [~-tist] (in) inexercé (à, dans); peu versé (dans).

un·prec·e·dent·ed ☐ [ʌn'presi-dəntid] sans précédent; inouï.

un·prej·u·diced ☐ ['ʌn'predʒudist] sans préjugé; impartial (-aux m/pl.).

un·pre·med·i·tat·ed ☐ ['ʌnpri-'mediteitid] impromptu; spontané; ✝✝ non prémédité.

un·pre·pared ☐ ['ʌnpri'pɛəd; adv. ~ridli] non préparé; au dépourvu; improvisé (discours).

un·pre·pos·sess·ing ['ʌnpri:pə-'zesiŋ] peu engageant.

un·pre·sent·a·ble ['ʌnpri'zentəbl] peu présentable.

un·pre·tend·ing ☐ ['ʌnpri'tendiŋ], **'un·pre'ten·tious** ☐ sans prétention.

un·prin·ci·pled ['ʌn'prinsəpld] sans principes; improbe.

un·pro·duc·tive ☐ ['ʌnprə'dʌktiv] improductif (-ive f); stérile; ✝ dormant (capital); be ~ of ne pas produire (qch.).

un·pro·fes·sion·al ☐ ['ʌnprə'feʃənl] contraire aux usages du métier; sp. amateur.

un·prof·it·a·ble ☐ [ʌn'prɔfitəbl] improfitable; inutile; ingrat; **un-'prof·it·a·ble·ness** inutilité f.

un·prom·is·ing ☐ ['ʌn'prɔmisin] qui promet peu; qui s'annonce mal (temps).

un·pro·nounce·a·ble ☐ ['ʌnprə-'naunsəbl] imprononçable.

un·pro·pi·tious ☐ ['ʌnprə'piʃəs] impropice; peu favorable (à, to).

un·pro·tect·ed ☐ ['ʌnprə'tektid] sans défense; ⊕ exposé.

un·proved ['ʌn'pru:vd] non prouvé.

un·pro·vid·ed ['ʌnprə'vaidid] non fourni; dépourvu (de, with); **'un-pro'vid·ed-for** imprévu; non pourvu; (laissé) sans ressources (personne).

un·pro·voked ☐ ['ʌnprə'voukt] non provoqué; gratuit.

un·pub·lished ['ʌn'pʌbliʃt] non publié; inédit.

un·punc·tual ☐ ['ʌn'pʌŋktjuəl] inexact; en retard; **un·punc·tu·al·i·ty** ['~'æliti] inexactitude f.

un·pun·ished ['ʌn'pʌniʃt] impuni; go ~ rester impuni; échapper à la punition (personne).

un·qual·i·fied ☐ [ʌn'kwɔlifaid] incompétent; sans diplôme; *fig.* absolu, sans réserve; F achevé, fieffé (*menteur etc.*).

un·quench·a·ble ☐ [ʌn'kwentʃəbl] inextinguible; *fig.* inassouvissable.

un·ques·tion·a·ble ☐ [ʌn'kwestʃən-əbl] incontestable; indiscutable; **un'ques·tioned** incontesté; indiscuté; **un'ques·tion·ing** ☐ *fig.* aveugle.

un·quote [ʌn'kwout] fermer les guillemets; **un'quot·ed** *Bourse:* non coté.

un·rav·el [ʌn'rævl] (s')effiler; (se) défaire; (s')éclaircir; *v/t.* dénouer (*une intrigue*).

un·read [ʌn'red] non lu; illettré (*personne*); **un·read·a·ble** [ʌn-'riːdəbl] illisible.

un·read·i·ness [ʌn'redinis] manque *m* de préparation *ou* promptitude; **'un'read·y** ☐: *be* ~ ne pas être prêt *ou* prompt, être peu disposé (à qch., *for* s.th.; à *inf.*, *to inf.*); *attr.* hésitant.

un·re·al ☐ [ʌn'riəl] irréel(le *f*); **un·re·al·is·tic** [ʌnriə'listik] peu réaliste; peu pratique.

un·rea·son [ʌn'riːzn] déraison *f*; **un'rea·son·a·ble** ☐ déraisonnable; exorbitant; indu; *a.* exigeant (*personne*).

un·re·claimed [ʌnri'kleimd] non réformé; indéfriché (*terrain*).

un·rec·og·niz·a·ble ☐ [ʌn'rekəg-naizəbl] méconnaissable; **'un'rec·og·nized** non reconnu; méconnu (*génie etc.*).   [réconcilié.]

un·rec·on·ciled [ʌn'rekənsaild] ir-⟩

un·re·cord·ed [ʌnri'kɔːdid] non enregistré (*a.* ♪).

un·re·deemed ☐ [ʌnri'diːmd] non racheté *ou* récompensé (par, *by*); inaccompli (*promesse*); ✝ non remboursé *ou* amorti.

un·re·dressed [ʌnri'drest] non redressé.

un·reel [ʌn'riːl] (se) découler.

un·re·fined [ʌnri'faind] non raffiné; brut; *fig.* grossier (-ère *f*); fruste.

un·re·formed [ʌnri'fɔːmd] non réformé; qui ne s'est pas corrigé.

un·re·gard·ed [ʌnri'gɑːdid] négligé; **'un're'gard·ful** [~ful] (*of*) négligent (de); peu soigneux (-euse *f*) (de); inattentif (-ive *f*) (à).

un·reg·is·tered [ʌn'redʒistəd] non enregistré, non inscrit; non déposé (*marque*); non recommandé (*lettre*).

un·re·gret·ted [ʌnri'gretid] (*mourir*) sans laisser de regrets.

un·re·lat·ed [ʌnri'leitid] sans rapport (avec, *to*); non apparenté (*personne*).

un·re·lent·ing ☐ [ʌnri'lentiŋ] implacable; acharné.

un·re·li·a·ble [ʌnri'laiəbl] sur lequel on ne peut pas compter.

un·re·lieved ☐ [ʌnri'liːvd] non soulagé; sans secours; monotone.

un·re·mit·ting ☐ [ʌnri'mitiŋ] ininterrompu; soutenu.

un·re·mu·ner·a·tive ☐ [ʌnri'mjuː-nərətiv] peu rémunérateur (-trice *f*).

un·re·pealed [ʌnri'piːld] irrévoqué; encore en vigueur; non abrogé.

un·re·pent·ed [ʌnri'pentid] non regretté.

un·re·quit·ed [ʌnri'kwaitid] non récompensé; non partagé (*sentiment*).

un·re·sent·ed [ʌnri'zentid] dont on ne se froisse pas.

un·re·served ☐ [ʌnri'zəːvd; *adv.* ~vidli] sans réserve; franc(he *f*); entier (-ère *f*); non réservé (*place*).

un·re·sist·ing ☐ [ʌnri'zistiŋ] docile; qui ne résiste pas; mou (mol *devant une voyelle ou un h muet*; molle *f*); souple.

un·re·spon·sive [ʌnris'pɔnsiv] froid; peu sensible (à, *to*).

un·rest [ʌn'rest] inquiétude *f*; malaise *m*; *pol.* agitation *f*; *pol. etc.* mécontentement *m*.

un·re·strained ☐ [ʌnris'treind] non restreint; effréné; immodéré.

un·re·strict·ed ☐ [ʌnris'triktid] absolu; sans restriction.

un·re·vealed [ʌnri'viːld] non divulgué; caché.

un·re·ward·ed [ʌnri'wɔːdid] sans récompense; non récompensé.

un·rhymed [ʌn'raimd] sans rime(s); ~ *verse* vers *m/pl.* blancs.

un·rid·dle [ʌn'ridl] résoudre.

un·rig ⚓ [ʌn'rig] dégréer; dégarnir.

un·right·eous ☐ [ʌn'raitʃəs] impie; injuste.

un·rip [ʌn'rip] découdre; ouvrir en déchirant.

un·ripe [ʌn'raip] vert; *fig.* pas encore mûr.

un·ri·val(l)ed [ʌn'raivəld] sans pareil(le f); incomparable.

un·roll [ʌn'roul] (se) dérouler.

un·rope alp. ['ʌn'roup] détacher la corde.

un·ruf·fled ['ʌn'rʌfld] calme (personne, mer); serein (a. personne).

un·ruled ['ʌn'ru:ld] non gouverné; fig. sans frein; sans lignes (papier).

un·rul·y [ʌn'ru:li] indiscipliné, mutin; fig. déréglé; fougueux (-euse f) (cheval).

un·sad·dle ['ʌn'sædl] desseller (un cheval); désarçonner (un cavalier).

un·safe ['ʌn'seif] dangereux (-euse f); † véreux (-euse f).

un·said ['ʌn'sed] non prononcé; leave ~ passer sous silence.

un·sal·a·ried ['ʌn'sælərid] non rémunéré.

un·sal(e)·a·ble ['ʌn'seiləbl] invendable.

un·sanc·tioned ['ʌn'sæŋkʃnd] non autorisé; non ratifié.

un·san·i·tar·y ['ʌn'sænitəri] non hygiénique; insalubre.

un·sat·is·fac·to·ry □ ['ʌnsætis-'fæktəri], **'un'sat·is·fy·ing** □ [~-faiiŋ] peu satisfaisant; défectueux (-euse f).

un·sa·vo(u)r·y □ ['ʌn'seivəri] désagréable; fig. répugnant; vilain.

un·say ['ʌn'sei] [irr. (say)] rétracter, se dédire de.

un·scathed ['ʌn'skeiðd] indemne; sans dommage ou blessure.

un·schooled ['ʌn'sku:ld] illettré; spontané; peu habitué (à, to).

un·sci·en·tif·ic ['ʌnsaiən'tifik] (~ally) peu ou non scientifique.

un·screw ['ʌn'skru:] (se) dévisser.

un·scru·pu·lous □ [ʌn'skru:pjuləs] sans scrupules.

un·seal ['ʌn'si:l] décacheter (une lettre); fig. dessiller (les yeux à q., s.o.'s eyes).

un·search·a·ble □ [ʌn'sə:tʃəbl] inscrutable.

un·sea·son·a·ble □ [ʌn'si:znəbl] hors de saison; fig. inopportun; ~ weather temps m qui n'est pas de saison; **'un'sea·soned** vert (bois); cuis. non assaisonné; fig. non acclimaté.

un·seat ['ʌn'si:t] désarçonner (un cavalier); parl. faire perdre son siège à; invalider; **'un'seat·ed** sans chaise; parl. non réélu.

un·sea·wor·thy ⚓ ['ʌn'si:wə:ði] incapable de tenir la mer; 🚢 innavigable.

un·see·ing fig. ['ʌn'si:iŋ] aveugle.

un·seem·li·ness [ʌn'si:mlinis] inconvenance f; **un'seem·ly** adj. inconvenant; peu convenable.

un·seen ['ʌn'si:n] 1. inaperçu, invisible; 2. l'autre monde m; le surnaturel m; école: (a. ~ translation) version f à livre ouvert.

un·self·ish □ ['ʌn'selfiʃ] sans égoïsme; désintéressé; dévoué.

un·sen·ti·men·tal ['ʌnsenti'mentl] peu sentimental (-aux m/pl.).

un·serv·ice·a·ble □ ['ʌn'sə:visəbl] inutilisable; peu pratique.

un·set·tle ['ʌn'setl] déranger; troubler le repos de (q.); ébranler (les convictions); **'un'set·tled** dérangé; troublé (pays etc.); variable (temps); incertain; inquiet (-ète f) (esprit); † non réglé, impayé; indécis (question, esprit); sans domicile fixe; non colonisé (pays).

un·shack·le [ʌn'ʃækl] ôter les fers à; ⚓ détalinguer (l'ancre).

un·shak(e)·a·ble [ʌn'ʃeikəbl] inébranlable.

un·shak·en ['ʌn'ʃeikn] ferme; constant.

un·shape·ly ['ʌn'ʃeipli] difforme; informe.

un·shav·en ['ʌn'ʃeivn] non rasé.

un·sheathe ['ʌn'ʃi:ð] dégainer.

un·ship ['ʌn'ʃip] décharger (a. F fig.).

un·shod ['ʌn'ʃɔd] nu-pieds adj./inv.; sans fers, déferré (cheval).

un·shorn ['ʌn'ʃɔ:n] non tondu; poét. non coupé, non rasé.

un·shrink·a·ble tex. ['ʌn'ʃriŋkəbl] irrétrécissable; **'un'shrink·ing** □ qui ne bronche pas.

un·sight·ed ['ʌn'saitid] inaperçu; sans hausse (arme à feu); **un'sight·ly** laid.

un·signed ['ʌn'saind] sans signature.

un·sized ['ʌn'saizd] sans colle (papier).

un·skil(l)·ful □ ['ʌn'skilful] inhabile (à at, in); **'un'skilled** inexpérimenté (à, in); ~ work main-d'œuvre (pl. mains-d'œuvre) f non spécialisée; ~ worker manœuvre m.

un·skimmed ['ʌn'skimd] non écrémé.

un·so·cia·ble [ʌn'souʃəbl] farouche; sauvage; un'so·cial [-ʃl] insocial (-aux m/pl.); a. see unsociable.

un·sold [ʌn'sould] invendu.

un·sol·dier·ly [ʌn'souldʒəli] adj. peu militaire.

un·so·lic·it·ed [ʌnsə'lisitid] spontané; non sollicité.

un·solv·a·ble [ʌn'sɔlvəbl] insoluble; 'un'solved non résolu.

un·so·phis·ti·cat·ed [ʌnsə'fistikeitid] pur; non adultéré; candide, ingénu (personne).

un·sought [ʌn'sɔ:t] 1. adj. non (re)cherché; 2. adv. spontanément.

un·sound □ [ʌn'saund] peu solide; véreux (-euse f); malsain (personne); taré (cheval); gâté (pomme etc.); défectueux (-euse f); faux (fausse f) (opinion, doctrine, etc.); of ~ mind non sain d'esprit.

un·spar·ing □ [ʌn'spɛəriŋ] libéral (-aux m/pl.); prodigue (de of, in); impitoyable (pour q., of s.o.).

un·speak·a·ble □ [ʌn'spi:kəbl] indicible; inexprimable; F fig. ignoble.

un·spec·i·fied [ʌn'spesifaid] non spécifié.   [fig. inépuisé.⎫
un·spent [ʌn'spent] non dépensé;⎰

un·spo·ken [ʌn'spoukn] non dit; (a. 'un'spo·ken-of) dont on ne fait pas mention.

un·sports·man·like [ʌn'spɔ:tsmənlaik] indigne d'un sportsman; peu loyal (-aux m/pl.).

un·spot·ted [ʌn'spɔtid] non tacheté; fig. sans tache.

un·sta·ble □ [ʌn'steibl] instable; peu sûr; inconstant; ✝ peu solide.

un·stamped [ʌn'stæmpt] non estampé (papier); sans timbre, non affranchi (lettre).

un·stead·y □ [ʌn'stedi] peu stable; peu solide; irrésolu; chancelant (pas); mal assuré (voix); fig. déréglé (personne); irrégulier (-ère f).

un·stint·ed [ʌn'stintid] abondant; à discrétion.

un·stitch [ʌn'stitʃ] découdre.

un·stop [ʌn'stɔp] déboucher.

un·strained [ʌn'streind] non filtré (liquide); non tendu (corde etc.); fig. non forcé, naturel (le f).

un·stressed [ʌn'strest] inaccentué; gramm. atone.

un·string [ʌn'striŋ] [irr. (string)] déficeler; détraquer (les nerfs); dé-(sen)filer (des perles etc.).

un·stud·ied [ʌn'stʌdid] naturel(le f); ignorant (de, in).

un·sub·mis·sive □ [ʌnsəb'misiv] insoumis, indocile.

un·sub·stan·tial □ [ʌnsəb'stænʃl] insubstantiel(le f); immatériel(le f); sans substance; chimérique.

un·suc·cess·ful □ [ʌnsək'sesful] non réussi; qui n'a pas réussi (personne); pol. non élu.

un·suit·a·ble □ [ʌn'sju:təbl] impropre (à for, to); déplacé; mal assorti (mariage); peu fait (pour for, to) (personne); 'un'suit·ed (for, to) mal adapté (à); peu fait (pour) (personne).

un·sul·lied [ʌn'sʌlid] immaculé.

un·sure [ʌn'ʃuə] peu sûr; peu solide.

un·sus·pect·ed [ʌnsəs'pektid] insoupçonné (de, by); non suspect; 'un·sus'pect·ing qui ne se doute de rien; sans soupçons; sans défiance.

un·sus·pi·cious □ [ʌnsəs'piʃəs] qui ne suscite pas de soupçons; be ~ of ne pas se douter de.

un·swerv·ing □ [ʌn'swə:viŋ] constant.

un·sworn [ʌn'swɔ:n] qui n'a pas prêté serment.

un·taint·ed □ [ʌn'teintid] pur, non corrompu (a. fig.); fig. sans tache (réputation).

un·tam(e)·a·ble [ʌn'teiməbl] inapprivoisable; fig. indomptable; 'un'tamed inapprivoisé; fig. indompté.

un·tar·nished [ʌn'tɑ:niʃt] non terni (a. fig.); sans tache.

un·tast·ed [ʌn'teistid] non goûté.

un·taught [ʌn'tɔ:t] illettré (personne); naturel(le f); non enseigné.

un·taxed [ʌn'tækst] exempt(é) d'impôts ou de taxes.

un·teach·a·ble [ʌn'ti:tʃəbl] incapable d'apprendre (personne); non enseignable (chose).

un·tem·pered [ʌn'tempəd] ⊕ détrempé; fig. non adouci (de, with).

un·ten·a·ble [ʌn'tenəbl] intenable (position); insoutenable (opinion etc.).

un·ten·ant·ed [ʌn'tenəntid] inoccupé; vide; sans locataire.

un·thank·ful □ [ʌn'θæŋkful] ingrat.

un·think·a·ble [ʌn'θiŋkəbl] inconcevable; **un'think·ing** □ irréfléchi; étourdi.

un·thought ['ʌn'θɔːt], **un'thought-of** oublié; imprévu (*événement*).

un·thread ['ʌn'θred] dé(sen)filer; *fig.* trouver la sortie de.

un·thrift·y □ ['ʌn'θrifti] dépensier (-ère *f*); malvenant (*arbre*).

un·ti·dy □ [ʌn'taidi] en désordre; négligé; mal peigné (*cheveux*).

un·tie ['ʌn'tai] dénouer; délier (*q., qch., un nœud*).

un·til [ən'til] **1.** *prp.* jusqu'à; **2.** *cj.* jusqu'à ce que; jusqu'au moment où.

un·tilled ['ʌntild] inculte; en friche.

un·time·ly [ʌn'taimli] prématuré; inopportun; mal à propos.

un·tir·ing □ [ʌn'taiəriŋ] infatigable.

un·to ['ʌntu] *see* 1.

un·told ['ʌn'tould] non raconté (*incident etc.*); non computé; *fig.* immense.

un·touched ['ʌn'tʌtʃt] non manié; *fig.* intact; *fig.* indifférent; *phot.* non retouché.

un·trained ['ʌn'treind] inexpérimenté; inexpert; non dressé (*chien etc.*); non formé.

un·trans·fer·a·ble □ ['ʌntræns'fəːrəbl] intransférable; strictement personnel(le *f*) (*billet*); ⚖ inaliénable.

un·trans·lat·a·ble □ ['ʌntræns'leitəbl] intraduisible.

un·trav·el(l)ed ['ʌn'trævld] inexploré; qui n'a jamais voyagé (*personne*).

un·tried ['ʌn'traid] inessayé; jamais mis à l'épreuve; ⚖ pas encore jugé (*cause*); pas encore passé en jugement (*détenu*).

un·trimmed ['ʌn'trimd] non arrangé; non taillé (*haie*); ⊕, *a. cuis.* non paré; sans garniture (*robe etc.*).

un·trod·den ['ʌn'trɔdn] non frayé; inexploré.

un·trou·bled ['ʌn'trʌbld] non troublé; calme.

un·true □ ['ʌn'truː] faux (fausse *f*); infidèle (*personne*).

un·trust·wor·thy □ ['ʌn'trʌstwəːði] douteux (-euse *f*); faux (fausse *f*).

un·truth ['ʌn'truːθ] fausseté *f*; mensonge *m*.

un·tu·tored ['ʌn'tjuːtəd] illettré; naturel(le *f*).

un·twine ['ʌn'twain], **un·twist** ['ʌn'twist] (se) détordre, détortiller.

un·used ['ʌn'juːzd] inutilisé; neuf (neuve *f*); ['ʌn'juːst] peu habitué (à, *to*); **un·u·su·al** □ [ʌn'juːʒuəl] extraordinaire; peu commun.

un·ut·ter·a·ble □ [ʌn'ʌtərəbl] indicible; imprononçable (*mot*).

un·val·ued ['ʌn'væljuːd] non *ou* peu estimé (*personne*).

un·var·ied [ʌn'vɛərid] peu varié; uniforme.

un·var·nished ['ʌn'vɑːniʃt] non verni; *fig.* simple.

un·var·y·ing □ [ʌn'vɛəriiŋ] invariable.

un·veil ['ʌn'veil] (se) dévoiler.

un·versed ['ʌn'vəːst] ignorant (de, *in*); peu versé (dans, *in*).

un·voiced ['ʌn'vɔist] non exprimé; *gramm.* sourd (*consonne etc.*), muet(te *f*).

un·vouched ['ʌn'vautʃt], *usu.* **un·vouched-for** [ʌn'vautʃtfɔː] non garanti.

un·want·ed ['ʌn'wɔntid] non voulu; superflu.

un·war·i·ness [ʌn'wɛərinis] imprudence *f*.

un·war·rant·a·ble □ [ʌn'wɔrəntəbl] inexcusable; **'un'war·rant·ed** injustifié; sans garantie.

un·war·y □ ['ʌn'wɛəri] imprudent.

un·wa·tered ['ʌn'wɔːtəd] sans eau; non arrosé (*jardin*); non dilué (*capital*).　　　[tant; inébranlable.\
un·wa·ver·ing [ʌn'weivəriŋ] cons-⌡

un·wea·ry·ing □ [ʌn'wiəriiŋ] infatigable.

un·wel·come [ʌn'welkəm] importun; *fig.* fâcheux (-euse *f*).

un·well ['ʌn'wel] indisposé.

un·whole·some ['ʌn'houlsəm] malsain (*a. fig.*); insalubre.

un·wield·y □ [ʌn'wiːldi] peu maniable; encombrant (*colis*).

un·will·ing □ ['ʌn'wiliŋ] rétif (-ive *f*); fait *etc.* à contre-cœur; be ~ to (*inf.*) ne pas vouloir (*inf.*); be ~ for s.th. to be done ne pas vouloir que qch. soit faite.

un·wind ['ʌn'waind] [*irr.* (*wind*)] (se) dérouler; ⚓ *vt/i.* dévirer.

un·wis·dom ['ʌn'wizdəm] imprudence *f*; stupidité *f*; **un·wise** □ ['ʌn'waiz] imprudent; peu sage.

un·wished ['ʌn'wiʃt], *usu.* **un·wished-for** [ʌn'wiʃtfɔː] peu désiré.

un·wit·ting □ [ʌn'witiŋ] inconscient.

un·wom·an·ly [ʌnˈwumənli] peu digne d'une femme.

un·wont·ed □ [ʌnˈwountid] inaccoutumé (à *inf.*, *to inf.*); insolite.

un·work·a·ble [ˈʌnˈwɔːkəbl] impraticable; ⚓ immaniable; ⊕ rebelle; inexploitable.

un·wor·thy □ [ʌnˈwɔːði] indigne.

un·wound·ed [ˈʌnˈwuːndid] non blessé; sans blessure.

un·wrap [ˈʌnˈræp] enlever l'enveloppe de; défaire (*un paquet*).

un·wrin·kle [ˈʌnˈriŋkl] (se) dérider.

un·writ·ten [ˈʌnˈritn] non écrit; coutumier (-ère *f*), oral (-aux *m/pl.*) (*droit*); blanc(he *f*) (*page*).

un·wrought [ˈʌnˈrɔːt] non travaillé; brut.

un·yield·ing □ [ʌnˈjiːldiŋ] qui ne cède pas; ferme.

un·yoke [ˈʌnˈjouk] dételer; découpler.

un·zip [ˈʌnˈzip] ouvrir la fermeture éclair de.

up [ʌp] **1.** *adv.* vers le haut; en montant; haut; en haut; en dessus; en l'air; debout; levé (*a. soleil etc.*); fini (*temps*); fermé (*fenêtre etc.*); ouvert (*fenêtre à guillotine, stores, etc.*); *Am.* baseball: à la batte; *sl.* be hard ∼ être fauché (= *être à court d'argent*); be ∼ against a task être aux prises avec une tâche; ∼ to jusque, jusqu'à; *see* date² 1; be ∼ to s.th. être à la hauteur de qch.; être capable de qch.; être occupé à faire qch.; *it is* ∼ *to me to* (*inf.*) c'est à moi de (*inf.*); *see* mark² 1; *what are you* ∼ *to there?* qu'est-ce que vous faites *ou* mijotez?; *sl. what's* ∼? qu'est-ce qu'il y a?; qu'est-ce qui se passe?; ∼ *with* au niveau de; *it's all* ∼ *with him* c'en est fait de lui; *sl.* il est fichu; **2.** *int.* en haut!; **3.** *prp.* au haut de; sans *ou* vers le haut de; ∼ *the hill* en montant *ou* en haut de la colline; **4.** *adj.* ∼ *train* train *m* en direction de la capitale; F train *m* de retour; **5.** *su.:* *Am.* F on the ∼ and ∼ honnête, en règle, loyal (-aux *m/pl.*); en bonne voie, en train de monter *ou* de s'améliorer; ∼*s pl.* and downs pl. ondulations *f/pl.*; *fig.* vicissitudes *f/pl.* (*de la vie*); **6.** F *v/i.* se lever; *v/t.* (*a.* ∼ *with*) lever.

up-and-com·ing *Am.* F [ˈʌpənˈkʌmiŋ] ambitieux (-euse *f*); qui promet; qui a de l'avenir.

up·beat ♩ [ˈʌpbiːt] levé *m*.

up·braid [ʌpˈbreid] reprocher (qch. à q., s.o. *with ou for s.th.*).

up·bring·ing [ˈʌpbriŋiŋ] éducation *f*.

up·cast [ˈʌpkɑːst] relèvement *m*; ⚒ (*a.* ∼ shaft) puits *m* de retour.

up·com·ing *Am.* [ˈʌpkʌmiŋ] imminent.

up·coun·try 1. [ˈʌpˈkʌntri] *adj.* de l'intérieur du pays; **2.** *adv.* [ʌpˈkʌntri] à l'intérieur du pays.

up·cur·rent ⚡ [ˈʌpkʌrənt] courant *m* d'air ascendant.

up·date [ʌpˈdeit] mettre à jour; moderniser.

up·end [ʌpˈend] mettre debout; *fig.* renverser (*l'adversaire etc.*).

up·grade [ˈʌpgreid] montée *f*; on the ∼ *fig.* en bonne voie; ✝ à la hausse.

up·heav·al [ʌpˈhiːvl] *géol.* soulèvement *m*; *fig.* bouleversement *m*, agitation *f*.

up·hill [ˈʌpˈhil] montant; *fig.* ardu.

up·hold [ʌpˈhould] [*irr.* (hold)] soutenir, maintenir; **up·hold·er** partisan(e *f*) *m*.

up·hol·ster [ʌpˈhoulstə] tapisser, couvrir (*un meuble*) (de *in*, with); garnir (*une pièce*); **up·hol·ster·er** tapissier *m*; **up·hol·ster·y** tapisserie *f* d'ameublement; *meuble*: capitonnage *m*; *mot.* garniture *f*; *métier*: tapisserie *f*.

up·keep [ˈʌpkiːp] (frais *m/pl.* d')entretien *m*.

up·land [ˈʌplənd] **1.** *usu.* ∼s *pl.* hautes terres *f/pl.*; **2.** des montagnes.

up·lift 1. [ʌpˈlift] soulever; élever (*a. fig.*); **2.** [ˈʌplift] élévation *f* (*a. fig.*); *géol.* soulèvement *m*; ✝ reprise *f*.

up·on [əˈpɔn] *see* on.

up·per [ˈʌpə] **1.** plus haut; supérieur; the ∼ class(es *pl.*) la haute société; F the ∼ crust le gratin; get the ∼ hand (of) prendre le dessus (sur); get the ∼ hand of a. avoir raison de, venir à bout de; have the ∼ hand avoir le dessus; the ∼ ten (thousand) la haute société; **2.** *usu.* ∼s *pl.* empeignes *f/pl.*; *bottes:* tiges *f/pl.*; '∼-'case let·ter *typ.* majuscule *m*; '∼-'class aristocratique; '∼-'cut *box.* uppercut *m*; '∼-most le plus haut; principal.

up·pish □ [ˈʌpiʃ] arrogant.

up·pi·ty *Am.* F [ˈʌpiti] suffisant; arrogant.
up·raise [ʌpˈreiz] (sou)lever, élever.
up·rear [ʌpˈriə] dresser.
up·right 1. □ [ˈʌpˈrait] vertical (-aux *m/pl.*); droit (*a. fig.*); debout; *fig.* [ˈʌprait] juste, intègre; **2.** [∼] montant *m*; piano *m* droit; *out of* ∼ hors d'aplomb.
up·ris·ing [ʌpˈraiziŋ] lever *m*; insurrection *f.*
up·roar [ˈʌprɔː] *fig.* tapage *m*, vacarme *m*; tumulte *m*; **up·roar·i·ous** □ tumultueux (-euse *f*); tapageur (-euse *f*).   [(racher.)
up·root [ʌpˈruːt] déraciner; ar)
up·set [ʌpˈset] **1.** [*irr.* (set)] renverser; bouleverser (*a. fig.*); déranger; *fig.* mettre (*q.*) en émoi; ∼ *in-disposer*, déranger; ⊕ refouler; **2.**: ∼ *price* mise *f* à prix, prix *m* de départ; **3.** renversement *m*; bouleversement *m*; désordre *m.*
up·shot [ˈʌpʃɔt] résultat *m*, dénouement *m*; *in the* ∼ à la fin.
up·side *adv.* [ˈʌpsaid]: ∼ *down* sens dessus dessous; à l'envers; *fig.* en désordre; *turn* ∼ *down* renverser; *fig.* bouleverser.
up·stage F [ˈʌpˈsteidʒ] **1.** orgueilleux (-euse *f*), arrogant, hautain; **2.** éclipser (*q.*); remettre (*q.*) à sa place.
up·stairs [ˈʌpˈstɛəz] **1.** *adv.* en haut; jusqu'au haut; **2.** *adj.* d'en haut.
up·start [ˈʌpstɑːt] **1.** parvenu(e *f*) *m*; **2.** se lever brusquement.
up·state *Am.* [ˈʌpˈsteit] région *f* éloignée; *surt.* État *m* de New-York.
up·stream [ˈʌpˈstriːm] **1.** *adv.* en amont; en remontant le courant; **2.** *adj.* d'amont.   [*m.*)
up·stroke [ˈʌpstrouk] *écriture*: délié)
up·surge [ˈʌpsɔːdʒ] soulèvement *m*; accès *m* (*de colère etc.*); poussée *f.*
up·swing [ˈʌpˈswiŋ] essor *m*; montée *f.*
up·take [ˈʌpteik] entendement *m*; F *be slow* (*quick*) *in* (*ou on*) *the* ∼ avoir la compréhension difficile (facile), saisir mal (vite).
up·throw [ˈʌpθrou] rejet *m* en haut.
up·tight F [ˈʌptait] crispé, tendu; nerveux (-euse *f*).
up-to-date [ˈʌptəˈdeit] moderne; au courant; à jour; à la page.
up-to-the-min·ute [ˈʌptədðəˈminit] le (la *f*) plus moderne; très récent; de dernière heure, dernier (-ière *f*).

up·town [ˈʌpˈtaun] **1.** *adv. Am.* dans le quartier résidentiel de la ville; **2.** *adj.* du quartier bourgeois.
up·turn [ʌpˈtɔːn] **1.** lever; retourner; **2.** *Am.* reprise *f* des affaires.
up·ward [ˈʌpwəd] **1.** *adj.* montant; vers le haut; **2.** *adv.* (*ou* **up·wards** [ˈ∼z]) de bas en haut; vers le haut; en dessus, au-dessus; ∼ *of* plus de.
u·ra·ni·um [juəˈreinjəm] uranium *m.*
ur·ban [ˈɔːbən] urbain; **ur·bane** [ɔːˈbein] courtois, poli; **ur·ban·i·ty** [ɔːˈbæniti] urbanité *f*; courtoisie *f*; politesse *f*; **ur·ban·i·za·tion** [ɔːbənaiˈzeiʃn] aménagement *m* des agglomérations urbaines; **ˈur·ban·ize** urbaniser.
ur·chin [ˈɔːtʃin] gamin *m*; gosse *mf.*
urge [ɔːdʒ] **1.** pousser (*q.* à *inf.*, *s.o. to inf.*); (*souv.* ∼ *on*) encourager; hâter; *fig.* insister sur; mettre en avant; recommander (*qch.* à *q.*, *s.th. on s.o.*); **2.** impulsion *f*; forte envie *f*; **ur·gen·cy** [ˈ∼ənsi] urgence *f*; besoin *m* pressant; **ˈur·gent** □ urgent, pressant; *be* ∼ *with s.o. to* (*inf.*) insister pour que q. (*sbj.*).
u·ric [ˈjuərik] urique.
u·ri·nal [ˈjuərinl] urinoir *m*; ⚕ urinal *m*; **ˈu·ri·nar·y** urinaire; **u·ri·nate** [ˈ∼neit] uriner; **u·rine** [ˈ∼rin] urine *f.*
urn [ɔːn] urne *f*; (*usu. tea-*∼) samovar *m.*
us [ʌs; əs] *accusatif, datif*: nous.
us·a·ble [ˈjuːzəbl] utilisable.
us·age [ˈjuːzidʒ] usage *m* (♱ de commerce); coutume *f*; emploi *m*; traitement *m.*
us·ance ♱ [ˈjuːzəns] usance *f*; *bill at* ∼ effet *m* à usance.
use 1. [juːs] emploi *m* (*a.* ⚙); usage *m*; *fig.*, *a.* ⚖ jouissance *f*; coutume *f*, habitude *f*; utilité *f*; service *m*; *be of* ∼ être utile (à *for, to*); *it is* (*of*) *no* ∼ (*gér.*, *to inf.*) il est inutile (que *sbj.*); inutile (de *inf.*); *have no* ∼ *for* ne savoir que faire de (*qch.*); F ne pas pouvoir voir (*q.*); *put s.th. to* ∼ profiter de qch.; *faire bon* (*mauvais*) *usage de qch.*; **2.** [juːz] employer; se servir de; ∼ *up* user, épuiser; *I* ∼ *d* [ˈjuːs(t)] *to do* je faisais; j'avais l'habitude de faire; **used** [ˈjuːst] habitué (à, *to*); [ˈjuːzd] usé, usagé; usité; *a.* sale (*linge*); ∼

car auto *f* d'occasion; **useful** □ [ˈjuːsful] utile (*a.* ⊕); pratique; ~ *capacity*, ~ *efficiency* rendement *m ou* effet *m* utile; ~ *load* charge *f* utile; **ˈuseˈfulˈness** utilité *f*; **ˈuseˈless** □ inutile, inefficace; vain; **usˈer** [ˈjuːzə] usager (-ère *f*) *m*.

ushˈer [ˈʌʃə] **1.** huissier *m*; introducteur *m*; ⚖ audiencier *m*; *péj.* sous-maître *m*; maître *m* d'étude; **2.** (*usu.* ~ *in*) faire entrer, introduire; **usher·ette** *cin.* [~ˈret] ouvreuse *f*.

uˈsuˈal □ [ˈjuːʒuəl] ordinaire; habituel(le *f*); ~ *in* (*the*) *trade* d'usage dans le métier.

uˈsuˈfruct ⚖ [ˈjuːsjufrʌkt] usufruit *m*; **uˈsuˈfrucˈtuˈarˈy** [~juəri] **1.** usufruitier (-ère *f*) *m*; **2.** *adj.* usufructuaire (*droit*).

uˈsuˈrer [ˈjuːʒərə] usurier *m*; **uˈsuˈriˈous** □ [juːˈzjuəriəs] usuraire; usurier (-ère *f*) (*personne*).

uˈsurp [juːˈzɔːp] *v/i.* usurper (sur *from*, *on*); *v/t.* voler (à, *from*); **uˈsurˈpaˈtion** usurpation *f*; **uˈsurpˈing** □ usurpateur (-trice *f*).

uˈsuˈry [ˈjuːʒuri] usure *f*.

uˈtenˈsil [juːˈtensl] ustensil *m*; outil *m*; ~*s pl.* articles *m/pl.*, ustensiles *m/pl.*

uˈterˈine [ˈjuːtərain] utérin; ~ *brother* frère *m* utérin *ou* de mère; **uˈterˈus** *anat.* [ˈ~rəs], *pl.* **uˈterˈi** [ˈ~tərai] utérus *m*, matrice *f*.

uˈtilˈiˈtarˈiˈan [juːtiliˈtɛəriən] utilitaire (*a. su./mf*); **uˈtilˈiˈty 1.** utilité *f*; *public* ~ (entreprise *f* de) service *m* public; **2.** à toutes fins (*chariot etc.*).

uˈtiˈliˈzaˈtion [juːtilaiˈzeiʃn] utilisation *f*; exploitation *f*; emploi *m*; **ˈuˈtiˈlize** utiliser, se servir de; tirer parti de, profiter de.

utˈmost [ˈʌtmoust] **1.** extrême; **2.** dernier degré *m*.

Uˈtoˈpiˈan [juːˈtoupjən] **1.** d'utopie; **2.** utopiste *mf*; idéaliste *mf*.

uˈtriˈcle *biol.* [ˈjuːtrikl] utricule *m*.

utˈter [ˈʌtə] **1.** □ *fig.* absolu; extrême; complet (-ète *f*); **2.** dire, exprimer; pousser (*un gémissement etc.*); émettre (*de la monnaie*); **ˈutterˈance** expression *f*; émission *f*; prononciation *f*; ~*s pl.* propos *m/pl.*; *give* ~ *to* exprimer; **ˈutˈterˈer** diseur (-euse *f*) *m*; débiteur (-euse *f*) *m* (*de nouvelles etc.*); émetteur *m* (*de monnaie*); **utˈterˈmost** [ˈ~moust] extrême; dernier (~ère *f*).

U-turn [ˈjuːtɜːn] *mot.* demi-tour *m*; *fig.* revirement *m*, volte-face *f/inv.*; *mot.* 'no ~*s*' 'défense de faire demi-tour'.

uˈvuˈla *anat.* [ˈjuːvjulə] luette *f*; uvule *f*; **uˈvuˈlar** [~] uvulaire; ~ *R R m* vélaire.

uxˈoˈriˈous [ʌkˈsɔːriəs] (extrêmement) dévoué à sa femme (*mari*).

V

V, v [viː] V *m*, v *m*.

va·can·cy [ˈveikənsi] vide *m*; vacance *f*, poste *m* vacant; chambre *f* à louer; espace *m* vide; ~ **for** on cherche (*employé etc.*); **no** *vacancies* travail: pas d'embauche; *hotel*: complet; *gaze into* ~ regarder dans l'espace; **va·cant** □ [ˈ~kənt] vacant, libre; hébété (*air*); inoccupé (*esprit*).

va·cate [vəˈkeit] quitter (*un emploi, un hôtel, un siège, etc.*); évacuer (*un appartement*); laisser libre; *v/i.* *Am. sl.* ficher le camp; **va·ca·tion** **1.** *école, a. Am.:* vacances *f/pl.*; ⚖ vacations *f/pl.*; **2.** *surt. Am.* prendre des *ou* être en vacances; **va·ca·tion·ist** *Am.* vacancier *m*; estivant(e *f*) *m*.

vac·ci·nate [ˈvæksineit] vacciner; **vac·ci·na·tion** vaccination *f*; **vac·ci·na·tor** vaccinateur *m*; **vac·cine** [ˈ~siːn] **1.** vaccinal (-aux *m/pl.*); ~ *matter* = **2.** vaccin *m*.

vac·il·late [ˈvæsileit] vaciller; hésiter; **vac·il·la·tion** vacillation *f*; hésitation *f*.

va·cu·i·ty [væˈkjuiti] vacuité *f*; vide *m* (*a. fig.*); **vac·u·ous** □ [ˈ~kjuəs] vide; *fig. usu.* bête; **vac·u·um** [ˈ~əm] *phys.* **1.** vide *m*, vacuum *m*; ~ *brake* frein *m* à vide; ~ *cleaner* aspirateur *m*; ~ *flask*, ~ *bottle* (bouteille *f*) Thermos *f*; ~ *tube* tube *m* à vide; *radio*: audion *m*; **2.** F nettoyer à l'aspirateur; **vac·u·um-packed** emballé sous vide.

va·de-me·cum [ˈveidiˈmiːkəm] vade-mecum *m/inv.*

vag·a·bond [ˈvægəbənd] **1.** vagabond, errant; **2.** chemineau *m*; vagabond(e *f*) *m*; F vaurien *m*; **vag·a·bond·age** [ˈ~bɔndidʒ] vagabondage *m*.

va·gar·y [ˈveigəri] caprice *m*; fantaisie *f*.

va·gi·na *anat.* [vəˈdʒainə] vagin *m*.

va·gran·cy [ˈveigrənsi] vie *f* de vagabond; ⚖ vagabondage *m*; **va·grant 1.** errant, vagabond (*a. fig.*); **2.** *see* vagabond 2.

vague □ [veig] vague; imprécis; estompé; indécis; *be* ~ ne rien préciser (*personne*).

vain □ [vein] vain; fier (-ère *f*) (*de, of*); inutile; mensonger (-ère *f*); vaniteux (-euse *f*); *in* ~ en vain; *do s.th. in* ~ avoir beau faire qch.; ~**glo·ri·ous** □ [~ˈglɔːriəs] vaniteux (-euse *f*); ~**glo·ry** vaine gloire *f*.

val·ance [ˈvæləns] frange *f ou* tour *m* de lit.

vale [veil] *poét.*, *a.* dans les noms propres: vallée *f*, vallon *m*.

val·e·dic·tion [væliˈdikʃn] adieu *m*, -x *m/pl.*; **val·e·dic·to·ry** [~təri] **1.** d'adieu; **2.** discours *m* d'adieu.

va·lence ⚗ [ˈveiləns] valence *f*.

val·en·tine [ˈvæləntain] carte *f* de salutations (envoyée à la Saint-valentin) (*le 14 février*); *fig. personne*: valentin(e *f*) *m*, amour *m*.

va·le·ri·an ⚘ [vəˈliəriən] valériane *f*.

val·et [ˈvælit] **1.** valet *m* de chambre; **2.** servir (*q.*) comme valet de chambre; remettre (*un costume*) en état.

val·e·tu·di·nar·i·an [ˈvælitjuːdiˈnɛəriən] valétudinaire (*a. su./mf*).

val·iant □ [ˈvæljənt] vaillant.

val·id □ [ˈvælid] valable, valide; bon (pour, *for*); irréfutable; **val·i·date** [ˈ~deit] rendre valable, valider; **va·lid·i·ty** [vəˈliditi] validité *f*; justesse *f* (*d'un argument*).

val·ley [ˈvæli] vallée *f*; vallon *m*; △ cornière *f*.

val·or·i·za·tion [væləraiˈzeiʃn] valorisation *f*; **val·or·ize** valoriser.

val·or·ous □ *poét.* [ˈvælərəs] vaillant.

val·o(u)r *poét.* [ˈvælə] vaillance *f*.

val·u·a·ble [ˈvæljuəbl] **1.** □ précieux (-euse *f*); **2.** ~s *pl.* objets *m/pl.* de valeur.

val·u·a·tion [væljuˈeiʃn] évaluation *f*; valeur *f* estimée; inventaire *m*; **val·u·a·tor** estimateur *m*.

val·ue [ˈvælju:] **1.** valeur *f*; prix *m* (*a. fig.*); ~ *judgement* jugement *m* de valeur; ✝ *get good* ~ (for one's money) en avoir pour son argent; **2.** évaluer;

estimer, priser (*a. fig.*); **'val·ue·less** sans valeur; **'val·u·er** estimateur (-euse *f*) *m*; expert *m*; commissaire-priseur *m* (*pl.* commissaires-priseurs).

valve [vælv] soupape *f*; *mot. pneu.* valve *f*; *anat.* valvule *f*; *radio:* lampe *f*; *radio:* ~ amplifier, amplifying ~ lampe *f* amplificatrice; ~ set poste *m* à lampes.

va·moose *Am. sl.* [vəˈmuːs] filer; ficher le camp; décamper.

vamp¹ [væmp] **1.** *souliers:* empeigne *f*; ♪ accompagnement *m* improvisé; **2.** *v/t.* remonter (*un soulier*); mettre une empeigne à; *v/i.* ♪ improviser; tapoter au piano.

vamp² F [~] **1.** vamp *f*; femme *f* fatale; flirteuse *f*; **2.** *v/t.* ensorceler; enjôler; *v/i.* flirter.

vam·pire [ˈvæmpaiə] vampire *m*.

van¹ [væn] fourgon *m* (de déménagement *etc.*); 🚃 wagon *m*; fourgon *m* à bagages.

van² ✕ *ou fig.* [~] avant-garde *f*.

Van·dal [ˈvændl] **1.** vandale *m*; **2.** (*a.* **Van·dal·ic** [~ˈdælik]) vandalique; **van·dal·ism** [ˈ~dəlizm] vandalisme *m*; **van·dal·ize** [ˈ~dəlaiz] saccager, mutiler.

van·dyke [vænˈdaik] barbe *f* à la Van Dyck; pointe *f* (*de col à la Van Dyck*); *attr.* ♀ à la Van Dyck.

vane [vein] (*a.* weather-~, wind-~) girouette *f*; ⊕ ailette *f*; *radio:* lamette *f*; *surv.* viseur *m* (*de compas*).

van·guard ✕ [ˈvænɡɑːd] (tête *f* d')avant-garde *f*.

va·nil·la ♀ [vəˈnilə] vanille *f*.

van·ish [ˈvæniʃ] disparaître; s'évanouir; ~ing cream crème *f* de jour.

van·i·ty [ˈvæniti] vanité *f*; orgueil *m*; ~ bag sac(oche *f*) *m* de dame; ~ case pochette-poudrier *f*.

van·quish *poét.* [ˈvæŋkwiʃ] vaincre; triompher de.

van·tage [ˈvɑːntidʒ] *tennis:* avantage *m*; **'~-ground** position *f* avantageuse. [(*conversation*).]

vap·id □ [ˈvæpid] insipide; fade}

va·po(u)r·ize [ˈveipəraiz] (se) vaporiser; (se) pulvériser; **'va·po(u)r·iz·er** ⊕ vaporisateur *m* (*a.* 🖉).

va·por·ous □ [ˈveipərəs] vaporeux (-euse *f*) (*a. fig.*); *fig.* vague, nuageux (-euse *f*).

va·po(u)r [ˈveipə] **1.** vapeur *f* (*a. fig.*); ~ bath bain *m* de vapeur; ~ trail

traînée *f* de condensation; **2.** s'évaporer; *fig.* débiter des fadaises; **'va·po(u)r·y** *see* vaporous.

var·i·a·bil·i·ty [vɛəriəˈbiliti] variabilité *f*, inconstance *f*; **'var·i·a·ble** □ variable, inconstant; **'var·i·ance** variation *f*; divergence *f*; discorde *f*; be at ~ être en désaccord; avoir un différend; set at ~ mettre en désaccord; **'var·i·ant 1.** différent (de, *from*); **2.** variante *f*; **var·i'a·tion** variation *f* (*a.* ♪); changement *m*; différence *f*, écart *m*; ⊕ ~ of load fluctuation *f* de charge.

var·i·cose 🖉 [ˈværikous] variqueux (-euse *f*); ~ vein varice *f*.

var·ied □ [ˈvɛərid] varié, divers; **var·i·e·gate** [ˈ~riɡeit] varier; barioler; **'var·i·e·gat·ed** varié, bariolé, bigarré; ♀ *etc.* panaché; **var·i·e·'ga·tion** diversité *f* de couleurs; ♀ panachure *f*; **va·ri·e·ty** [vəˈraiəti] diversité *f*, variété *f* (*a. biol.*); 🌱 assortiment *m*; *théâ.* F music-hall *m*; ~ show attractions *f/pl.*; (spectacle *m* de) music-hall *m*; ~ theatre théâtre *m* de variétés.

va·ri·o·la 🖉 [vəˈraiələ] variole *f*.

var·i·ous □ [ˈvɛəriəs] varié, divers; différent; plusieurs.

var·mint [ˈvɑːmint] *sl.* petit polisson *m*; *chasse:* renard *m*; vermine *f*.

var·nish [ˈvɑːniʃ] **1.** vernis *m* (*a. fig.*); vernissage *m*; **2.** vernir; vernisser; *fig.* farder, glisser sur.

var·si·ty F [ˈvɑːsiti] université *f*.

var·y [ˈvɛəri] *v/t.* (faire) varier; diversifier; ♪ varier (*un air*); *v/i.* varier, changer; être variable; s'écarter (de, *from*).

vas·cu·lar ♀, *anat.* [ˈvæskjulə] vasculaire.

vase [vɑːz] vase *m*.

vas·sal [ˈvæsl] vassal (-aux *m/pl.*) (*a. su.*); **'vas·sal·age** vassalité *f*, vasselage *m*; *fig.* sujétion *f*.

vast □ [vɑːst] vaste, immense; **'vast·ness** immensité *f*; vaste étendue *f*.

vat [væt] **1.** cuve *f*; (*petit*) cuveau *m*; bain *m*; **2.** mettre en cuve; encuver.

vat·ted [ˈvætid] mis en cuve (*vin etc.*); en fût (*vin*).

vault¹ [vɔːlt] **1.** voûte *f* (*a. fig.*); *banque:* souterrain *m*; cave *f* (à *vin*); tombeau *m* (*de famille etc.*); **2.** (se) voûter.

vault² [.] **1.** *v/i.* sauter; *v/t.* (*ou* ~ *over*) sauter (*qch.*); **2.** saut *m.*

vault·ing △ ['vɔːltiŋ] (construction *f* de) voûtes *f/pl.*

vault-horse ['vɔːltiŋhɔːs] *gymn.* cheval *m* de bois.

vaunt *poét.* [vɔːnt] **1.** (se) vanter (de); **2.** vanterie *f*; **'vaunt·ing** □ vantard. [de veau.)

veal [viːl] veau *m*; *roast* ~ rôti *m*)

ve·dette ✗ [vi'det] vedette *f.*

veer [viə] **1.** (faire) virer; *v/i.* tourner; **2.** (*a.* ~ *round*) changement *m* de direction.

veg F *Brit.* [vedʒ] légume(s) *m* (*pl.*).

veg·e·ta·ble ['vedʒitəbl] **1.** végétal (-aux *m/pl.*); ~ *garden* (jardin *m*) potager *m*; ~ *soup* soupe *f* de légumes; **2.** légume *m*; ♀ végétal (*pl.* -aux) *m*; **veg·e·tar·i·an** [~'tɛəriən] végétarien(ne *f*) (*a. su.*); **veg·e·tate** ['~teit] végéter; **veg·e·ta·tion** végétation *f*; **veg·e·ta·tive** □ ['~tətiv] végétatif (-ive *f*).

ve·he·mence ['viːiməns] véhémence *f*; impétuosité *f*; **'ve·he·ment** □ véhément; passionné; violent.

ve·hi·cle ['viːikl] voiture *f*; véhicule *m* (*a. fig., pharm., peint.*); *pharm.* excipient *m*; **ve·hi·cu·lar** □ [vi'hikjulə] des voitures; véhiculaire (*a. langue*).

veil [veil] **1.** voile *m* (*a. fig.*); *phot.* voile *m* faible; **2.** (se) voiler (*a. fig.*); *v/t. fig. a.* cacher; **'veil·ing** action *f* de voiler; *phot.* voile *m* faible; voile *m*, -s *m/pl.* (*a.* ✝).

vein [vein] veine *f* (*a. fig.*) (de *inf.*, for *gér.*); ♀ nervure *f* (*a. d'aile*); *in the same* ~ dans le même esprit; **veined** veiné; ♀ nervuré; **'vein·ing** veinage *m*; veines *f/pl.*; ♀ nervures *f/pl.*

vel·le·i·ty [ve'liːiti] velléité *f.*

vel·lum ['veləm] vélin *m*; ~ *paper* papier *m* vélin.

ve·loc·i·ty [vi'lɔsiti] vitesse *f.*

vel·vet ['velvit] **1.** velours *m*; *bois de cerf*: peau *f* velue; F *fig.* on ~ sur le velours; **2.** de velours; velouté; **vel·vet·een** [~'tiːn] velours *m* de coton; ~s *pl.* pantalon *m* en velours de chasse; **'vel·vet·y** velouté.

ve·nal ['viːnl] vénal (-aux *m/pl.*); mercenaire; **ve·nal·i·ty** [viː'næliti] vénalité *f.*

vend [vend] vendre; **'vend·er,** **'ven·dor** vendeur (-euse *f*) *m*; marchand(e *f*) *m*; **'vend·i·ble** vendable; **'vend·ing ma·chine** distributeur *m* (automatique).

ve·neer [vi'niə] **1.** (bois *m* de) placage *m*; F vernis *m*, masque *m*; **2.** plaquer; *fig.* cacher (*qch.*) sous un vernis.

ven·er·a·ble □ ['venərəbl] vénérable; **ven·er·ate** ['~reit] vénérer; **ven·er·a·tion** vénération *f*; **'ven·er·a·tor** vénérateur (-trice *f*) *m.*

ve·ne·re·al [vi'niəriəl] vénérien(ne *f*); ~ *disease* maladie *f* vénérienne.

Ve·ne·tian [vi'niːʃn] **1.** de Venise; vénitien(ne *f*); ~ *blind* jalousie *f*; **2.** Vénitien(ne *f*) *m.*

venge·ance ['vendʒəns] vengeance *f*; F *with a* (*ou for*) ~ pas d'erreur!; pour de bon!; furieusement.

venge·ful □ ['vendʒful] vengeur (-eresse *f*).

ve·ni·al □ ['viːnjəl] pardonnable; véniel(le *f*) (*péché*).

ven·i·son ['venzn] venaison *f.*

ven·om ['venəm] venin *m* (*souv. fig.*); **'ven·om·ous** □ venimeux (-euse *f*) (*animal, a. fig.*); vénéneux (-euse *f*) (*plante*).

ve·nous ['viːnəs] veineux (-euse *f*).

vent [vent] **1.** trou *m*, orifice *m*, passage *m*; soupirail (-aux *pl.*) *m*; *orn., icht.* ouverture *f* anale; *give* ~ *to* donner libre cours à (*sa colère etc.*); *find* ~ s'échapper (en, in); **2.** *fig.* décharger, épancher (sur, on).

ven·ti·late ['ventileit] ventiler; aérer; *fig.* faire connaître, agiter (*une question*); **ven·ti·la·tion** aération *f*; ventilation *f*, aérage *m* (*a.* ✿); *fig.* mise *f* en discussion publique; **'ven·ti·la·tor** ventilateur *m*; soupirail (-aux *pl.*) *m*; *porte, fenêtre:* vasistas *m.*

vent-peg ['ventpeg] fausset *m.*

ven·tral ✿, *zo.* ['ventrəl] ventral (-aux *m/pl.*).

ven·tri·cle *anat.* ['ventrikl] ventricule *m.*

ven·tril·o·quist [ven'triləkwist] ventriloque *mf*; **ven'tril·o·quize** [~kwaiz] faire de la ventriloquie.

ven·ture ['ventʃə] **1.** risque *m*; aventure *f*; entreprise *f*; ✝ opération *f*, affaire *f*; *at a* ~ au hasard; **2.** *v/t.* risquer, hasarder; *v/i.:* ~ *to* (*inf.*) se risquer à (*inf.*), oser (*inf.*); *I* ~ *to say* je me permets de dire; ~ (*up*)*on* s'aventurer dans (*un endroit*);

ven·ture·some □ ['⌣səm], **'ven-tur·ous** □ risqué, hasardeux (-euse *f*); aventureux (-euse *f*) (*personne*).

ven·ue ['venjuː] ⚖ lieu *m* du jugement; *fig.* scène *f*; F rendez-vous *m*.

ve·ra·cious □ [vəˈreiʃəs] véridique; **ve·rac·i·ty** [⌣ˈræsiti] véracité *f*.

verb *gramm.* [vəːb] verbe *m*; **'ver·bal** □ verbal (-aux *m*/*pl.*); de mots; littéral (-aux *m*/*pl.*); (*ou* **ver·ba·tim** [⌣ˈbeitim]) mot pour mot; **'ver·bal·ize** verbaliser, rendre par des mots; **ver·bi·age** ['⌣biidʒ] verbiage *m*; **ver·bose** □ [⌣ˈbous] verbeux (-euse *f*), prolixe; **ver·bos·i·ty** [⌣ˈbɔsiti] verbosité *f*, prolixité *f*.

ver·dan·cy ['vəːdənsi] verdure *f*; F *fig.* inexpérience *f*; **'ver·dant** □ vert; F *fig.* inexpérimenté.

ver·dict ['vəːdikt] ⚖ verdict *m* (*du jury*); *fig.* jugement *m* (sur, *on*); *bring in* (*ou return*) *a* ⌣ (*of guilty etc.*) rendre un verdict (de culpabilité *etc.*).

ver·di·gris ['vəːdigris] vert-de-gris *m*.

ver·dure ['vəːdʒə] verdure *f*.

verge[1] [vəːdʒ] *eccl.* verge *f*.

verge[2] [⌣] **1.** *usu. fig.* bord *m*; seuil *m*; *on the* ⌣ au seuil (de, *of*); à deux doigts (de, *of*); sur le point (de *inf.*, *of gér.*); **2.** baisser; approcher (de, *towards*); ⌣ (*up*)*on* côtoyer (*qch.*); friser; être voisin de, toucher à.

ver·i·fi·a·ble ['verifaiəbl] vérifiable; facile à vérifier; **ver·i·fi·ca·tion** [⌣fiˈkeiʃn] vérification *f*, contrôle *m*; ⚖ confirmation *f*; **ver·i·fy** ['⌣fai] prouver; confirmer; contrôler, vérifier; **ver·i·si·mil·i·tude** [⌣siˈmilitjuːd] vraisemblance *f*; **'ver·i·ta·ble** □ véritable; **'ver·i·ty** vérité *f*.

ver·juice *usu. fig.* ['vəːdʒuːs] verjus *m*.

ver·mi·cel·li [vəːmiˈseli] vermicelle *m*; **ver·mi·cide** *pharm.* ['⌣said] vermicide *m*; **ver·mic·u·lar** [⌣ˈmikjulə] vermiculaire; vermoulu; **ver·mi·form** ['⌣fɔːm] vermiforme; **ver·mi·fuge** *pharm.* ['⌣fjuːdʒ] vermifuge *m*.

ver·mil·ion [vəˈmiljən] **1.** vermillon *m*; **2.** vermeil(le *f*); (de) vermillon *adj.*/*inv.*

ver·min ['vəːmin] vermine *f* (*a. fig.*); *chasse:* bêtes *f*/*pl.* puantes; **'⌣·kill·er** *personne:* preneur *m* de vermine; insecticide *m*; mort-aux-rats *f*; **'ver·min·ous** couvert de vermine; 🞄 vermineux (-euse *f*).

ver·m(o)uth ['vəːməθ] vermouth *m*.

ver·nac·u·lar □ [vəˈnækjulə] **1.** indigène; du pays; vulgaire (*langue*); **2.** langue *f* du pays; idiome *m* national; langue *f* vulgaire; langage *m* (*d'un métier*).

ver·nal ['vəːnl] printanier (-ère *f*); 🞄, *astr.* vernal (-aux *m*/*pl.*).

ver·ni·er ['vəːnjə] 🞄, *surv.* vernier *m*; ⊕ ⌣ *cal(l)iper* jauge *f* micrométrique.

ver·sa·tile □ ['vəːsətail] aux talents variés; souple; 🞄, *zo.* versatile; **ver·sa·til·i·ty** [⌣ˈtiliti] souplesse *f*; 🞄, *zo.* versatilité *f*; adaptation *f*.

verse [vəːs] vers *m*; strophe *f*; *coll.* vers *m*/*pl.*, poésie *f*; ♩ *motet:* solo *m*; **versed** versé (en, dans *in*).

ver·si·fi·ca·tion [vəːsifiˈkeiʃn] versification *f*; métrique *f* (*d'un auteur*); **ver·si·fy** ['⌣fai] *vt*/*i.* versifier; *v*/*t.* mettre (*qch.*) en vers; *v*/*i.* faire des vers.

ver·sion ['vəːʃn] version *f*; traduction *f*.

ver·so ['vəːsou] verso *m*.

ver·sus *surt.* ⚖ ['vəːsəs] contre.

vert F *eccl.* [vəːt] se convertir.

ver·te·bra *anat.* ['vəːtibrə], *pl.* -**brae** [⌣briː] vertèbre *f*; **ver·te·bral** ['⌣brəl] vertébral (-aux *m*/*pl.*); **ver·te·brate** ['⌣brit] **1.** vertébré; ⌣ *animal* = **2.** vertébré *m*.

ver·tex ['vəːteks], *pl. usu.* -**ti·ces** [⌣tisiːz] sommet *m*; *astr.* zénith *m*; **'ver·ti·cal 1.** □ vertical (-aux *m*/*pl.*); à pic (*falaise*); 🞄 ⌣ *angles* angles *m*/*pl.* opposés par le sommet; ⌣ *takeoff aircraft* avion *m* à décollage vertical; **2.** verticale *f*; *astr.* vertical *m*.

ver·tig·i·nous □ [vəːˈtidʒinəs] vertigineux (-euse *f*); **ver·ti·go** ['⌣tigou] vertige *m*.

verve [vɛəv] verve *f*.

ver·y ['veri] **1.** *adv.* très; fort; bien; *the* ⌣ *best* tout ce qu'il y a de mieux; **2.** *adj.* vrai, véritable, ... même; *the* ⌣ *same* le (la *etc.*) ... même(s *pl.*); *in the* ⌣ *act* sur le fait; *to the* ⌣ *bone* jusqu'aux os; jusqu'à l'os même; *the* ⌣ *thing* ce qu'il faut; *the* ⌣ *thought* la seule pensée; *the* ⌣ *stones* les pierres mêmes; *the veriest baby* (même) le plus petit enfant; *the veriest rascal* le plus parfait coquin; *radio*: ~ high frequency très haute fréquence *f*.

ves·i·ca·to·ry ['vesikeitəri] vésicatoire (*a. su./m*); **ves·i·cle** ['~kl] vésicule *f*; *géol.* vacuole *f*.

ves·pers *eccl.* ['vespəz] *pl.* vêpres *f/pl.*

ves·sel ['vesl] vaisseau *m* (*a.* ♀, *anat., fig.*); ⚓ *a.* navire *m*, bâtiment *m*.

vest [vest] **1.** gilet *m*; ✝ gilet *m* de dessous; *sp.* maillot *m*; **2.** *v/t.* *usu. fig.* revêtir, investir (de, *with*); assigner (qch. à q., *s.th. in s.o.*); *v/i.* être dévolu (à q., *in s.o.*); ~ed rights *pl.* droits *m/pl.* acquis.

ves·ta ['vestə] (*a.* ~ *match*, *wax* ~) allumette-bougie (*pl.* allumettes-bougies) *f*; *astr.* ♀ vesta *f*.

ves·tal ['vestl] **1.** de(s) vestale(s); **2.** vestale *f*.

ves·ti·bule ['vestibjuːl] vestibule *m* (*a. anat.*); salle *f* des pas perdus; ⚑ *surt. Am.* soufflet *m* (*entre deux wagons*); ~ *train* train *m* à soufflets.

ves·tige ['vestidʒ] vestige *m*, trace *f*; **ves'tig·i·al** à l'état rudimentaire.

vest·ment ['vestmənt] vêtement *m* (*a. eccl.*). [dimensions.)

vest·pock·et ['vest'pɔkit] de petites)

ves·try ['vestri] *eccl.* sacristie *f*; (réunion *f* du) conseil *m* d'administration de la paroisse; salle *f* de patronage; '~man marguillier *m*.

ves·ture *poét.* ['vestʃə] **1.** vêtement *m*; **2.** revêtir.

vet [vet] **1.** vétérinaire *m*; *Am.* ancien combattant *m*; **2.** traiter (*un animal*); *fig.* examiner médicalement; revoir, corriger; *fig.* mettre au point.

vetch ♣ [vetʃ] vesce *f*.

vet·er·an ['vetərən] **1.** expérimenté; ancien(ne *f*); de(s) vétéran(s); vieux (vieil *devant une voyelle ou un h muet*, vieille *f*); *mot.* ~ *car* vétéran *m*; **2.** vétéran *m*; ancien *m*; ancien combattant *m*.

vet·er·i·nar·i·an *Am.* [vetəri'nɛəriən] vétérinaire *mf*; **vet·er·i·nar·y** ['vetərinəri] **1.** vétérinaire; ~ *surgeon* = **2.** vétérinaire *m*.

ve·to ['viːtou] **1.** *pl.* -toes [~touz] veto *m*; *put a* (*ou one's*) ~ (*up*)*on* = **2.** mettre son veto à.

vex [veks] vexer (*a.* ⚖); fâcher, contrarier; **vex'a·tion** vexation *f*; tourment *m*; désagrément *m*; dépit *m*; **vex'a·tious** □ ennuyeux (-euse *f*); fâcheux (-euse *f*); ⚖ vexatoire; **'vexed** □ fâché, vexé (de qch., *at s.th.*; contre q., *with s.o.*); ~ *question* question *f* très débattue; **'vex·ing** □ agaçant; ennuyeux (-euse *f*).

vi·a ['vaiə] par; *poste*: voie.

vi·a·ble *biol.* ['vaiəbl] viable.

vi·a·duct ['vaiədʌkt] viaduc *m*.

vi·al ['vaiəl] fiole *f*.

vi·ands *poét.* ['vaiəndz] *pl.* aliments *m/pl.*

vi·at·i·cum *eccl.* [vai'ætikəm] viatique *m*.

vibes F [vaibz] *sg.* ♪ vibraphone *m*; *pl.* vibrations *f/pl.*

vi·brant ['vaibrənt] vibrant; *fig.* palpitant (de, *with*).

vi·bra·phone ♪ ['vaibrəfoun] vibraphone *m*.

vi·brate [vai'breit] (faire) vibrer *ou* osciller; **vi'bra·tion** vibration *f*; **vi·bra·to·ry** ['~brətəri] vibratoire.

vi·car *eccl.* ['vikə] curé *m*; ~ *general* vicaire *m* général; **'vic·ar·age** presbytère *m*; cure *f*; **vi·car·i·ous** □ [vai'kɛəriəs] délégué; fait *ou* souffert pour *ou* par un autre.

vice[1] [vais] vice *m*; *fig.* défaut *m*.

vice[2] ⊕ [~] étau *m*.

vice[3] **1.** ['vaisi] *prp.* à la place de; **2.** [vais] *adj.* vice-; sous-; '~'ad·mi·ral vice-amiral *m*; '~'chair·man vice-président(e *f*) *m*; '~-'chan·cel·lor vice-chancelier *m*; *univ.* recteur *m*; '~-'con·sul vice-consul *m*; ~ge·rent ['~'dʒerənt] représentant *m*; '~-'pres·i·dent vice-président(e *f*) *m*; '~-'re·gal de *ou* du vice-roi; ~ *reine* ['~'rein] vice-reine *f*; ~roy ['~rɔi] vice-roi *m*.

vi·ce ver·sa ['vaisi'vəːsə] vice versa, réciproquement.

vic·i·nage ['visinidʒ], **vi'cin·i·ty** environs *m/pl.* (de, *of*); proximité *f* (de *to*, *with*); *in the* ~ *of* 40 environ 40.

vi·cious □ ['viʃəs] vicieux (-euse *f*); dépravé (*a. personne*); *fig.* méchant (*a. cheval*); *phls.* ~ *circle* cercle *m* vicieux; argument *m* circulaire.

vi·cis·si·tude [vi'sisitjuːd] *usu.* ~s *pl.* vicissitudes *f/pl.*

vic·tim ['viktim] victime *f*; **'vic·tim·ize** prendre comme victime; ✖, *pol.* exercer des représailles contre; *fig.* duper.

vic·tor ['viktə] vainqueur *m*; **Vic·to·ri·an** *hist.* [vik'tɔ:riən] victorien (-ne *f*) (*a. su.*); **vic·to·ri·ous** □ victorieux (-euse *f*); de victoire; **vic·to·ry** ['ʌtəri] victoire *f*.

vict·ual ['vitl] **1.** (s')approvisionner; ✗, ⚓ (se) ravitailler; *v/i.* F bâfrer (= *manger*); **2.** *usu.* ~s *pl.* provisions *f/pl.*..; vivres *m/pl.*; **vict·ual·(l)er** ['vitlə] fournisseur *m* de vivres; *licensed* ~ débitant *m* de boissons.

vi·de ['vaidi] voir.

vi·de·li·cet [vi'di:liset] (*abr. viz.*) à savoir; c'est-à-dire.

vid·e·o ['vidiou] **1.** vidéo *f*; *Am.* F télévision *f*; **2.** vidéo *inv.*; ~ **cart·ridge**, ~ **cas·sette** vidéo(-)cassette *f*; ~ **disc** vidéo(-)disque *m*; '~**phone** vidéophone *m*; ~ **re·cord·er** magnétoscope *m*; ~ **tape** bande *f* vidéo; '~ **tape** enregistrer sur bande *f* vidéo, magnétoscoper; '~**tel·e·phone** vidéotéléphone *m*.

vie [vai] le disputer (à, *with*); rivaliser (avec, *with*).

Vi·en·nese [vie'ni:z] **1.** viennois *m*; **2.** Viennois(e *f*) *m*.

view [vju:] **1.** vue *f*, coup *m* d'œil; regard *m*; scène *f*; perspective *f*; aperçu *m*; *fig.* intention *f*; *fig.* idée *f*, opinion *f*, avis *m*; *field of* ~ champ *m*; *at first* ~ à première vue; *in* ~ en vue, sous les regards; *in* ~ *of* en vue de; *fig.* en raison *ou* considération de; étant donné; *in my* ~ à mon avis; *on* ~ exposé; ouvert au public; *on the long* ~ à la longue, envisageant les choses de loin; *out of* ~ hors de vue; caché aux regards; *with a* ~ *to* (*gér.*), *with the* ~ *of* (*gér.*) dans le but de (*inf.*), en vue de (*inf.*); dans l'intention de (*inf.*); *have in* ~ avoir en vue; *keep in* ~ ne pas perdre de vue; **2.** regarder (*a. télév.*); contempler; voir; apercevoir; *fig.* envisager; '**view·er** (*télév.*) télé)spectateur (-trice *f*) *m*; '**view-find·er** *phot.* viseur *m*; '**view·phone** vidéophone *m*; '**view·point** point *m* de vue; belvédère *m* (*dans le paysage*); '**view·y** □ F visionnaire.

vig·il ['vidʒil] veille *f*; *eccl.* vigile *f*; '**vig·i·lance** vigilance *f*; ~ *com·mittee Am.* comité *m* de surveillance (*des mœurs ou de l'ordre*); '**vig·i·lant** □ vigilant, éveillé; **vig·i·lan·te** *Am.* [ʌ'lænti] membre *m* du comité de surveillance.

vi·gnette [vi'njet] **1.** *typ.* vignette *f*; *phot.* cache *m* dégradé; **2.** *phot.* dégrader (*un portrait etc.*).

vig·or·ous □ ['vigərəs] vigoureux (-euse *f*), robuste; *phot.* à contrastes, corsé (*couleur*); '**vig·o(u)r** vigueur *f* (*a. fig.*); énergie *f*; ♪ brio *m*.

vile □ [vail] vil; infâme; F sale.

vil·i·fi·ca·tion [vilifi'keiʃn] dénigrement *m*, détraction *f*; **vil·i·fy** ['ʌfai] diffamer, dénigrer; médire de (*q.*).

vil·la ['vilə] villa *f*, maison *f* de campagne.

vil·lage ['vilidʒ] village *m*; '**vil·lag·er** villageois(e *f*) *m*.

vil·lain ['vilən] scélérat *m*; bandit *m*; misérable *m*; F *a. co.* coquin(e *f*) *m*; '**vil·lain·ous** □ infâme, vil; scélérat; F sale; '**vil·lain·y** infamie *f*; vilenie *f*.

vil·lein *hist.* ['vilin] vilain *m*; serf *m*.

vim F [vim] énergie *f*, vigueur *f*.

vin·di·cate ['vindikeit] défendre (contre, *from*); justifier; revendiquer (*ses droits*); **vin·di·ca·tion** défense *f*; revendication *f*; **vin·di·ca·to·ry** □ ['ʌkeitəri] vindicatif (-ive *f*); vengeur (-eresse *f*).

vin·dic·tive □ [vin'diktiv] vindicatif (-ive *f*); *a.* rancunier (-ère *f*) (*personne*).

vine [vain] vigne *f*; *houblon etc.*: sarment *m*; *Am.* plante *f* grimpante; '~**dres·ser** vigneron(ne *f*) *m*; **vin·e·gar** ['vinigə] **1.** vinaigre *m*; **2.** vinaigrer; '**vine-grow·er** viticulteur *m*; vigneron(ne *f*) *m*; '**vine-grow·ing** viticulture *f*; *attr.* vignoble; '**vine-louse** phylloxéra *m*; **vine·yard** ['vinjəd] vigne *f*; clos *m* de vigne; vignoble *m*.

vi·nous ['vainəs] vineux (-euse *f*); F ivrogne.

vin·tage ['vintidʒ] vendange *f*; cru *m*; *fig.* modèle *m*; ~ *year* grande année *f*; '**vin·tag·er** vendangeur (-euse *f*) *m*.

vi·o·la¹ ♪ [vi'oulə] alto *m*.

vi·o·la² ♀ ['vaiələ] pensée *f*.

vi·o·la·ble □ ['vaiələbl] qui peut être violé.

vi·o·late ['vaiəleit] violer (*un serment, une femme*); outrager (*une femme*); profaner (*une église*); **vi·o·la·tion** violation *f*; viol *m* (*d'une* *femme*); profanation *f*; **'vi·o·la·tor** violateur (-trice *f*) *m*.

vi·o·lence ['vaiələns] violence *f*; do (*ou offer*) ~ to faire violence à; **'vi·o·lent** □ violent; vif (vive *f*); criard (*couleur*).

vi·o·let ['vaiəlit] **1.** ♀ violette *f*; *couleur*: violet *m*; **2.** violet(te *f*).

vi·o·lin ♩ [vaiə'lin] violon *m*; **'vi·o·lin·ist** violoniste *mf*.

vi·o·lon·cel·list ♩ [vaiələn'tʃelist] violoncelliste *mf*; **vi·o·lon·cel·lo** [~lou] violoncelle *m*.

vi·per *zo.* ['vaipə] vipère *f* (*a. fig.*); ⌀ guivre (-aux *m/pl.*); **vi·per·ine** ['~rain], **vi·per·ous** □ ['~rəs] *usu. fig.* vipérin.

vi·ra·go [vi'rɑːgou] vrai gendarme *m*; mégère *f*.

vir·gin ['vəːdʒin] **1.** vierge *f*; **2.** vierge (*a.* ⊕, *a. fig.*); = **'vir·gin·al** □ virginal (-aux *m/pl.*); de vierge; **Vir·gin·ia** [və'dʒinjə] (*ou* ~ tobacco) tabac *m* de Virginie, virginie *f*; ~ creeper vigne *f* vierge; **vir·gin·i·ty** [və'dʒiniti] virginité *f*.

Vir·go *astr.* ['vəːgou] la Vierge.

vir·ile ['virail] viril, mâle; **vi·ril·i·ty** [vi'riliti] virilité *f*.

vir·tu [vəː'tuː] goût *m* des objets d'art; *article of* ~ objet *m* d'art; **vir·tu·al** □ ['~tjuəl] de fait; véritable; ⊕ virtuel(le *f*); **vir·tue** ['~tjuː] vertu *f*; *fig.* qualité *f*; avantage *m*; efficacité *f*; propriété *f*; *in* (*ou by*) ~ of en raison *ou* vertu de; **vir·tu·os·i·ty** [~tju-'ɔsiti] ♩ *etc.* virtuosité *f*; **vir·tu·o·so** [~'ouzou] *surt.* ♩ virtuose *mf*; amateur *m* des arts; amateur *m* de curiosités *etc.*; **'vir·tu·ous** □ vertueux (-euse *f*).

vir·u·lence ['viruləns] virulence *f*; *fig.* venin *m*; **'vir·u·lent** □ virulent (*a. fig.*); *fig. a.* venimeux (-euse *f*).

vi·rus ⚕ ['vaiərəs] virus *m*; *fig.* poison *m*.

vi·sa ['viːzə] *see* visé.

vis·age *poét.* ['vizidʒ] visage *m*.

vis·cer·a ['visərə] *pl.* viscères *m/pl.*

vis·cid □ ['visid] *see* viscous.

vis·cose ⚗ ['viskous] viscose *f*; ~ silk soie *f* artificielle; **vis·cos·i·ty** [~'kɔsiti] viscosité *f*.

vis·count ['vaikaunt] vicomte *m*; **'vis·count·ess** vicomtesse *f*.

vis·cous □ ['viskəs] visqueux (-euse *f*); gluant; pâteux (-euse *f*).

vi·sé ['viːzei] **1.** visa *m*; **2.** apposer un visa à (*un passeport*); viser.

vis·i·bil·i·ty [vizi'biliti] visibilité *f*; *good* ~ vue *f* dégagée; **vis·i·ble** □ ['vizəbl] visible; *fig.* évident; *be* ~ se montrer (*chose*); être visible (*personne*).

vi·sion ['viʒn] vision *f*, vue *f*; *fig.* pénétration *f*; imagination *f*; fantôme *m*, apparition *f*. **vi·sion·ar·y** ['viʒnəri] chimérique; rêveur (-euse *f*) (*personne*) (*a. su./mf*); visionnaire (*a. su./mf*).

vis·it ['vizit] **1.** *v/t.* faire (une) visite à, rendre visite à; aller voir; visiter (*un endroit*); ♱ passer chez; *fig.* causer avec; ~ *s.th. on* faire retomber qch. sur (*q.*); *v/i.* faire des visites; *Am.* F causer (avec, with); **2.** visite *f*; **'vis·it·ant** visiteur (-euse *f*) *m*; apparition *f*; *orn.* oiseau *m* de passage; **vis·it·a·tion** visite *f*; tournée *f* d'inspection; *fig.* affliction *f*; calamité *f*; apparition *f*; **vis·it·a·to·ri·al** [~tə'tɔːriəl] de visite; d'inspection; **'vis·it·ing** en visite; de visite; ~ *card* carte *f* de visite; ~ *hours* heures *f/pl.* de visite; *sp.* ~ *team* les visiteurs *m/pl.*; **'vis·i·tor** visiteur (-euse *f*) *m* (de, to); *hôtel:* client(e *f*) *m*; *admin.* inspecteur *m*; *they have* ~s ils ont du monde; ~s' *book* livre *m ou* registre *m* des voyageurs.

vi·sor ['vaizə] visière *f* (*de casque, Am. de casquette*); *mot.* pare-soleil *m/inv.*

vis·ta ['vistə] perspective *f* (*a. fig.*); *forêt:* éclaircie *f*.

vis·u·al □ ['vizjuəl] visuel(le *f*); *anat.* optique; **'vis·u·al·ize** se représenter (*qch.*), se faire une image de (*qch.*).

vi·tal □ ['vaitl] **1.** vital (-aux *m/pl.*); essentiel(le *f*); mortel(le *f*) (*blessure*); ~ *parts pl.* = **2.** ~s *pl.* organes *m/pl.* vitaux; **vi·tal·i·ty** [~'tæliti] vitalité *f*; vie *f*, vigueur *f*; **vi·tal·ize** ['~təlaiz] vivifier, animer.

vi·ta·min ['vitəmin], **vi·ta·mine** ['~miːn] vitamine *f*; **vi·ta·mi·nized** ['~minaizd] enrichi de vitamines.

vi·ti·ate ['viʃieit] vicier (*a.* 🜄); corrompre; gâter.

vit·i·cul·ture ['vitikʌltʃə] viticulture *f*.

vit·re·ous □ ['vitriəs] vitreux (-euse *f*); *♪, a. anat.* vitré.

vit·ri·fac·tion [vitri'fækʃn] vitrification *f*; **vit·ri·fy** ['ˏfai] (se) vitrifier.

vit·ri·ol ⚗ ['vitriəl] vitriol *m*; **vit·ri·ol·ic** [vitri'ɔlik] ⚗ vitriolique; *fig.* mordant.

vi·tu·per·ate [vi'tju:pəreit] injurier; outrager, insulter, vilipender; **vi·tu·per·a·tion** injures *f/pl.*; invectives *f/pl.*; **vi·tu·per·a·tive** □ [ˏreitiv] injurieux (-euse *f*); mal embouché.

Vi·tus ['vaitəs]: ⚕ St. ˏ's dance chorée *f*; danse *f* de Saint-Guy.

vi·va (vo·ce) ['vaivə ('vousi)] **1.** *adv.* de vive voix; **2.** *adj.* oral (-aux *m/pl.*); **3.** *su.* oral *m*.

vi·va·cious □ [vi'veiʃəs] animé, enjoué; vif (vive *f*); **vi·vac·i·ty** [ˏ'væsiti] vivacité *f*; verve *f*; enjouement *m*.

viv·id □ ['vivid] vif (vive *f*); éclatant, frappant; **'viv·id·ness** éclat *m*.

viv·i·fy ['vivifai] (s')animer; **vi·vip·a·rous** □ [ˏ'vipərəs] vivipare; **viv·i·sec·tion** [ˏ'sekʃn] vivisection *f*.

vix·en ['viksn] renarde *f*; F mégère *f*.

vi·zor ['vaizə] *see* visor.

vo·cab·u·lar·y [və'kæbjuləri] vocabulaire *m*; glossaire *m*.

vo·cal □ ['voukl] vocal (-aux *m/pl.*) (♪, *son, prière*); sonore, bruyant; doué de voix; *gramm.* voisé; sonore; *anat.* ˏ c(h)ords *pl.* cordes *ou* bandes *f/pl.* vocales; ˏ *part* partie *f* chantée; **'vo·cal·ist** chanteur *m*; cantatrice *f*; **'vo·cal·ize** *v/t.* chanter; *gramm.* voiser, sonoriser; *v/i.* vocaliser; F chanter; **'vo·cal·ly** *adv.* à l'aide du chant; oralement.

vo·ca·tion [vou'keiʃn] vocation *f* (*a. au sacerdoce etc.*); profession *f*, métier *m*; **vo'ca·tion·al** □ professionnel(le *f*); ˏ *guidance* orientation *f* professionnelle.

voc·a·tive *gramm.* ['vɔkətiv] (*a.* ˏ *case*) vocatif *m*.

vo·cif·er·ate [vou'sifəreit] *v/t./i.* vociférer, crier (contre, *against*); **vo·cif·er·a·tion** (*a.* ˏs *pl.*) vociférations *f/pl.*; cri *m*, -s *m/pl.*; **vo·'cif·er·ous** □ vociférant, bruyant.

vogue [voug] vogue *f*, mode *f*.

voice [vɔis] **1.** voix *f*; *gramm.* *active* ˏ actif *m*; *passive* ˏ passif *m*; *in* (*good*) ˏ en voix; *give* ˏ *to* exprimer (*qch.*); **2.** exprimer, énoncer; *gramm.* voiser, sonoriser; ♪ harmoniser; **voiced** *gramm.* voisé, sonore; *low-*ˏ à voix basse; **'voice·less** □ *surt. gramm.* sans voix, sourd.

void [vɔid] **1.** vide; ⚖ nul(le *f*); ˏ *of* dépourvu *ou* libre de, sans; **2.** vide *m*; **3.** ⚖ annuler, résilier; **'void·ness** vide *m*; ⚖ nullité *f*.

vol·a·tile ⚗ ['vɔlətail] volatil; *fig.* gai; *fig.* volage; **vol·a·til·i·ty** [ˏ'tiliti] ⚗ volatilité *f*; *fig.* inconstance *f*; **'vol·a·til·ize** (se) volatiliser.

vol·can·ic [vɔl'kænik] (ˏally) volcanique (*a. fig.*); **vol·ca·no** [ˏ'keinou], *pl.* -noes [ˏnouz] volcan *m*.

vole *zo.* [voul] campagnol *m*.

vo·li·tion [vou'liʃn] volonté *f*, volition *f*; *on one's own* ˏ de son propre gré.

vol·ley ['vɔli] **1.** volée *f*, salve *f* (*a. fig.*); *pierres, coups:* grêle *f*; *tennis:* volée *f*; **2.** *v/t.* lancer une volée *ou* grêle de; (*usu.* ˏ *out*) lâcher une bordée de; *reprendre* (*la balle*) de volée; *v/i.* partir ensemble (*canons*); *fig.* tonner; **'vol·ley-ball** *sp.* volley-ball *m*.

vol·plane ✈ ['vɔl'plein] **1.** vol *m* plané; **2.** planer; descendre en vol plané.

volt ⚡ [voult] volt *m*; **'volt·age** ⚡ voltage *m*, tension *f*; **vol·ta·ic** ⚡ [vɔl'teiik] voltaïque.

volte-face *fig.* ['vɔlt'fɑ:s] volte-face *f/inv.*; changement *m* d'opinion.

volt·me·ter ⚡ ['voultmi:tə] voltmètre *m*.

vol·u·bil·i·ty [vɔlju'biliti] volubilité *f*; **vol·u·ble** □ ['ˏbl] facile; grand parleur; coulant.

vol·ume ['vɔljum] livre *m*; volume *m* (*a. phys., voix, fig., etc.*); *fig. a.* ampleur *f*; ˏ *of sound radio:* volume *m*; ˏ *control*, ˏ *regulator* volume-contrôle *m*; **vo·lu·mi·nous** □ [və'lju:minəs] volumineux (-euse *f*).

vol·un·tar·y □ ['vɔləntəri] **1.** volontaire (*a. physiol.*); spontané; **2.** ♪ prélude *m*; improvisation *f*; **vol-**

un·teer [ˌ'tiə] **1.** volontaire *m*; *attr.* de volontaires; **2.** *v/i.* s'offrir; ✕ s'engager comme volontaire; *v/t.* offrir spontanément.

vo·lup·tu·ar·y [vəˈlʌptjuəri] voluptueux (-euse *f*) *m*; **vo·lup·tu·ous** □ sensuel(le *f*); voluptueux (-euse *f*); **vo·lup·tu·ous·ness** sensualité *f*.

vo·lute △ [vəˈljuːt] volute *f*; **vo·lut·ed** voluté; à volutes.

vom·it [ˈvɔmit] **1.** *vt/i.* vomir (*a. fig.*); *v/t.* rendre; **2.** vomissement *m*; matières *f/pl.* vomies.

voo·doo [ˈvuːduː] **1.** vaudou *m*; **2.** envoûter.

vo·ra·cious □ [vəˈreiʃəs] vorace, dévorant; **vo·ra·cious·ness**, **vo·rac·i·ty** [vɔˈræsiti] voracité *f*.

vor·tex [ˈvɔːteks], *pl. usu.* **-ti·ces** [ˌtisiːz] tourbillon (*a. fig.*).

vo·ta·ry [ˈvoutəri] dévot(e *f*) *m* (à, of); adorateur (-trice *f*) *m* (de, of); *fig.* suppôt *m* (de, of).

vote [vout] **1.** vote *m*; scrutin *m*; voix *f*; droit *m* de vote(r), suffrage *m*; *parl.* crédit *m*; résolution *f*; ~ *of* (*no*) *confidence* vote *m* de confiance (défiance); *cast a* ~ donner sa voix *ou* son vote; *put to the* ~ procéder au scrutin; mettre (*qch.*) aux voix; *take a* ~ procéder au scrutin; **2.** *v/t.* voter; F déclarer; *v/i.* voter; donner sa voix (pour, for); F être d'avis (de *inf.*, for *gér.*); être en faveur (de qch. for s.th.); F ~ *that* proposer que; **'vot·er** votant(e *f*) *m*; électeur (-trice *f*) *m*.

vot·ing [ˈvoutiŋ] vote *m*, scrutin *m*; ~ *booth* isoloir *m*; ~ *box* urne *f* de scrutin; ~ *machine* machine *f* pour

enregistrer les votes; ~ *paper* bulletin *m* de vote.

vo·tive [ˈvoutiv] votif (-ive *f*).

vouch [vautʃ] *v/t.* garantir, affirmer; *v/i.* répondre (de, for); ~ *that* affirmer que; **'vouch·er** pièce *f* justificative; ✝ bon *m*; ✝ fiche *f*; *théâ. etc.* contremarque *f*; *personne*: garant(e *f*) *m*; **vouch'safe** *v/t.* accorder; *v/i.*: ~ *to* (*inf.*) daigner (*inf.*). [**2.** *v/t.* vouer, jurer.\

vow [vau] **1.** vœu *m*; serment *m*;\
vow·el [ˈvauəl] voyelle *f*.

voy·age [ˈvɔidʒ] **1.** voyage *m* (sur mer; ✈ *Am.* par air); traversée *f*; **2.** *v/i.* voyager (sur *ou* par mer); *v/t.* parcourir (*la mer*).

vul·can·ite [ˈvʌlkənait] vulcanite *f*, caoutchouc *m* vulcanisé; **vul·can·i'za·tion** ⊕ vulcanisation *f*; **'vul·can·ize** ⊕ (se) vulcaniser.

vul·gar [ˈvʌlgə] **1.** □ du peuple; vulgaire (*a. péj.*); commun; ~ *tongue* langue *f* vulgaire; **2.** *the* ~ le vulgaire *m*; le commun *m* des hommes; **'vul·gar·ism** vulgarisme *m*; (*usu.* **vul·gar·i·ty** [ˌˈgæriti]) vulgarité *f*, trivialité *f*; **'vul·gar·ize** vulgariser.

vul·ner·a·bil·i·ty [vʌlnərəˈbiliti] vulnérabilité *f*; **'vul·ner·a·ble** □ vulnérable; ~ *spot fig.* défaut *m* dans la cuirasse; **'vul·ner·ar·y** vulnéraire (*a. su./m*).

vul·pine [ˈvʌlpain] de renard; qui a rapport au renard; *fig.* rusé.

vul·ture *orn.* [ˈvʌltʃə] vautour *m*; **vul·tur·ine** [ˌtʃurain] de(s) vautour(s). [lité *f*.\

vy·ing [ˈvaiiŋ] **1.** *p.pr. de* vie; **2.** riva-\

W

W, w ['dʌblju:] W *m*, w *m*.

wab·ble ['wɔbl] *see* wobble.

wack·y *Am. sl.* ['wæki] fou (fol *devant une voyelle ou un h muet*; folle *f*); toqué.

wad [wɔd] **1.** *ouate etc.:* tampon *m*, pelote *f*; ✗ *cartouche etc.:* bourre *f*; *surt. Am. F billets de banque:* liasse *f*; **2.** ouater; cotonner; bourrer (*une arme à feu*); *Am.* rouler en liasse; **'wad·ding** ouate *f*; bourre *f*; ouatage *m*.

wad·dle ['wɔdl] se dandiner.

wade [weid] *v/i.* marcher dans l'eau; *fig.* (s')avancer péniblement; *v/t.* (faire) passer à gué; **'wad·er** (*oiseau m*) échassier *m*; ~s *pl.* grandes bottes *f/pl.* imperméables.

wa·fer [weifə] **1.** gaufrette *f*; pain *m* à cacheter; *eccl. consecrated* ~ hostie *f*; **2.** apposer un cachet à.

waf·fle ['wɔfl] gaufre *f* (américaine).

waft [wɑ:ft] **1.** *v/t.* porter; faire avancer; *v/i.* flotter dans l'air; **2.** souffle *m*.

wag¹ [wæg] **1.** agiter, remuer (*le bras, la queue, etc.*) ~ one's tongue jacasser; **2.** agitation *f*; hochement *m* (*de la tête*).

wag² [~] moqueur (-euse *f*) *m*; blagueur *m*; *sl.* play ~ faire l'école buissonnière.

wage [weidʒ] **1.:** ~ war faire la guerre (à on, against); **2.** *souv.* ~s *pl.* salaire *m*, paye *f*; gages *m/pl.*; ~(s) claim, ~ demands revendication(s) *f(pl.)* de salaire(s); ~ dispute conflit *m* salarial; ~ earner salarié(e *f*) *m*; soutien *m* de (la) famille; ~ increase augmentation *f* de salaire(s); ~ packet enveloppe *f* de paye; ~ scale échelle *f* des salaires; ~ slip fiche *f* de paye; ~(s) sheet feuille *f* des salaires.

wa·ger *poét.* ['weidʒə] **1.** pari *m*, gageure *f*; **2.** parier, gager (sur, on).

wag·ger·y ['wægəri] facétie *f*, -s *f/pl.*, plaisanterie *f*; **'wag·gish** □ plaisant, espiègle, blagueur (-euse *f*).

wag·gle F ['wægl] *see* wag¹ 1; **'wag·gly** F qui branle; serpentant.

wag·(g)on ['wægən] charrette *f*; camion *m*; ✗ fourgon *m*; 🚃 wagon *m* (découvert); *Am. F* be (go) on the ~ s'abstenir de boissons alcooliques; **'wag·(g)on·er** roulier *m*; camionneur *m*; **wag·(g)on·ette** [~'net] wagonnette *f*.

wag·tail *orn.* ['wægteil] bergeronnette *f*.

waif [weif] ⚖, *a. fig.* épave *f*; ~s and strays enfants *m/pl.* abandonnés; épaves *f/pl.*

wail [weil] **1.** plainte *f*; gémissement *m*; **2.** *v/t.* lamenter sur, pleurer; *v/i.* gémir, se lamenter.

wain *poét.* [wein] *see* wag(g)on; *astr.* Charles's ♀, the ♀ le Chariot *m*.

wain·scot ['weinskət] **1.** lambris *m*; *salle:* boiserie *f*; **2.** lambrisser, boiser (de, with).

waist [weist] taille *f*, ceinture *f*; ⚓ embelle *f*; **'~-belt** ceinturon *m*; **~·coat** ['weiskout] gilet *m*; **'~'deep** jusqu'à la ceinture; **'waist·ed** *cost.* cintré; high-~ (low-~) à taille haute (basse); slim-~ qui a la taille fine, à la taille fine; **'~-line** taille *f*; ligne *f*.

wait [weit] **1.** *v/i.* attendre; (*souv.* ~ at table) servir; F~ about faire le pied de grue; ~ for attendre (qch., q.); ~ (up)on servir (q.); être aux ordres de (q.); être à la conséquence de (qch.); keep s.o. ~ing faire attendre q.; ~ and see attendre voir; ~ in line faire la queue; play a ~ing game attendre son heure; *v/t.* attendre; différer (*un repas*) (jusqu'à l'arrivée de q., for s.o.); **2.** attente *f*; ~s *pl.* chanteurs *m/pl.* de noëls; have a long ~ devoir attendre longtemps; be in ~ être à l'affût (de, for); **'wait·er** *restaurant:* garçon *m*; *fig.* plateau *m*.

wait·ing ['weitiŋ] attente *f*; service *m*; in ~ de service; ~ list liste *f* d'attente; ~ room salle *f* d'attente; antichambre *f*.

wait·ress ['weitris] fille *f* de service; ~! mademoiselle!

waive [weiv] ne pas insister sur, ⚖ renoncer à; **'waiv·er** ⚖ abandon *m*.

wake¹ [weik] ⚓ sillage *m* (*a. fig.*); *fig.* suite *f*; ⚞ remous *m* d'air.

wake² [~] **1.** [*irr.*] *v/i.* veiller; (*fig.* ~ *up*) se réveiller, s'éveiller; *v/t.* réveiller; ~ *a corpse* veiller un mort; **2.** veillée *f* de corps; fête *f* annuelle; **wake·ful** □ ['~ful] éveillé; sans sommeil; **'wak·en** (se) réveiller; (s')éveiller (*a. fig.*).

wale [weil] marque *f*; ⊕ *drap*: côté *f*; *palplanches*: moise *f*; ⚓ platbord (*pl.* plats-bords) *m*.

walk [wɔ:k] **1.** *v/i.* marcher, se promener; aller à pied; cheminer; aller au pas (*cheval*); revenir (*spectre*); ~ *about* se promener, circuler; *sl.* ~ *into* se heurter à (*qch.*); *Am.* ~ *out* se mettre en grève; *Am.* F ~ *out on* laisser *ou* planter la (*q.*); *v/t.* faire marcher; courir (*les rues*); faire (*une distance*); conduire *ou* mettre un cheval au pas; ~ *the hospitals* faire les hôpitaux; assister aux leçons cliniques; ✕ ~ *the rounds* faire sa faction; ~ *s.o. off* emmener q.; **2.** marche *f*; promenade *f*; tour(née *f*) *m*; allée *f*, avenue *f*; démarche *f*; pas *m*; ~ *of life* position *f* sociale; métier *m*; **'~·a·bout** *go on a* ~ prendre un bain de foule; **'~·a·way** *surt. Am.* victoire *f* facile; **'walk·er** marcheur (-euse *f*) *m*; piéton *m*; *sp.* amateur *m* du footing; *be a good* ~ être bon marcheur; **'walk·er·on** *sl.* figurant(e *f*) *m*.

walk·ie-talk·ie ['wɔ:ki'tɔ:ki] appareil *m* d'émission et réception radiophonique, walkie-talkie *m*.

walk·ing ['wɔ:kiŋ] **1.** marche *f*; promenade *f* à pied; *sp.* footing *m*; **2.** ambulant; de marche; *Am.* F ~ *papers pl.* congé *m*; ~ *tour* excursion *f* à pied; **'~-stick** canne *f*.

walk...: **'~-out** *Am.* grève *f*; **'~-o·ver** *sp.* walk-over *m*; *fig.* victoire *f* facile; **'~-up** *Am.* sans ascenseur (*appartement*).

wall [wɔ:l] **1.** mur *m*; muraille *f*; (*a. side*~) paroi *f* (*a.* ⊕); *give s.o. the* ~ donner à q. le haut du pavé; *fig. go to the* ~ être ruiné *ou* mis à l'écart; **2.** entourer de murs; murer; *fig.* emmurer; ~ *up* murer.

wal·la·by *zo.* ['wɔləbi] petit kangourou *m*, wallaby *m*.   [sacoche *f*.\

wal·let ['wɔlit] portefeuille *m*; sac *m*,\

wall...: **'~-eye** *vét.* œil *m* vairon; **'~-'eyed** *vét.* vairon; qui louche, à strabisme divergent; **'~-flow·er** ♀ giroflée *f* (jaune); *fig. be a* ~ faire tapisserie; **'~-fruit** fruit *m* d'espalier; **'~-map** carte *f* murale.

Wal·loon [wɔ'lu:n] **1.** wallon(ne *f*); **2.** *ling.* wallon *m*; Wallon(ne *f*) *m*.

wal·lop F ['wɔləp] **1.** rosser (*q.*), tanner le cuir à (*q.*); **2.** gros coup *m*; *sl.* bière *f*; **'wal·lop·ing** F énorme.

wal·low ['wɔlou] **1.** se vautrer; *fig.* se plonger (*dans, in*), nager (*dans, in*); **2.** fange *f*; *chasse*: souille *f*; *have a* ~ se vautrer.

wall...: **'~-pa·per** papier *m* peint *ou* à tapisser; **'~-sock·et** ⚡ prise *f* de courant; **'~-to-wall car·pet(ing)** moquette *f*.

wal·nut ♀ ['wɔ:lnʌt] noix *f*; *arbre*: noyer *m*; (*bois m de*) noyer *m*.

wal·rus *zo.* ['wɔ:lrəs] morse *m*.

waltz [wɔ:ls] **1.** valse *f*; **2.** valser.

wan □ [wɔn] blême, pâle; blafard.

wand [wɔnd] baguette *f*; bâton *m* (*de commandement*); verge *f* (*d'huissier*).

wan·der ['wɔndə] errer; (*a.* ~ *about*) se promener au hasard, aller à l'aventure; *fig.* s'écarter (de, *from*); *fig.* divaguer (*personne*); **'wan·der·er** vagabond(e *f*) *m*; **'wan·der·ing 1.** □ errant; vagabond (*a. fig.*); *fig.* distrait; **2.** vagabondage *m*; ⚕ délire *m*; *fig.* rêverie *f*; **'wan·der·lust** envie *f* de voyager.

wane [wein] **1.** décroître (*lune*); *fig.* s'affaiblir; **2.** déclin *m*; *on the* ~ sur *ou* à son déclin.

wan·gle *sl.* ['wæŋgl] employer le système D; carotter (*qch.*); **'wan·gler** carotteur (-euse *f*) *m*.

wan·ness ['wɔnnis] pâleur *f*.

want [wɔnt] **1.** manque *m*, défaut *m* (de, *of*); besoin *m*; gêne *f*; *for* ~ *of* faute de; *Am.* ~ *ad* demande *f* d'emploi (*dans les petites annonces*); **2.** *v/i. be* ~*ing* faire défaut, manquer (*chose*); *be* ~*ing* manquer (de, *in*) (*personne*); *be* ~*ing to* ne pas être à la hauteur de (*une tâche etc.*); *he does not* ~ *for* talent les talents ne lui font pas défaut; *v/t.* vouloir, désirer; manquer de; avoir besoin de; falloir; *it* ~*s five minutes of eight o'clock* il est huit heures moins cinq; ~*s two days to* il y a encore deux jours à; *he* ~*s energy* il manque d'énergie; *you* ~ *to be careful* il faut faire attention; ~ *s.o.* *to* (*inf.*) vouloir que q. (*sbj.*); ~ed recherché (par la police).

wan·ton ['wɒntən] **1.** □ impudique; licencieux (-euse *f*); folâtre; *poét.* luxuriant; gratuit; **2.** voluptueux (-euse *f*) *m*; femme *f* impudique; **3.** folâtrer; '**wan·ton·ness** libertinage *m*; gaieté *f* de cœur.

war [wɔː] **1.** guerre *f*; *attr.* de guerre; guerrier (-ère *f*); ~ *of nerves* guerre *f* des nerfs; *at* ~ en guerre (avec, contre *with*); *make* ~ faire la guerre (à, contre [*up*]on); **2.** *poét.* lutter; mener une campagne; *fig.* faire la guerre (à, *against*).

war·ble ['wɔːbl] **1.** *vt/i.* chanter (en gazouillant); *v/i.* gazouiller; **2.** gazouillement *m*; *ruisseau*: murmure *m*; '**war·bler** oiseau *m* chanteur; fauvette *f*.   [gle de guerre.\]

war-blind·ed ['wɔːblaindid] aveu-⌋

ward [wɔːd] **1.** garde *f*; † tutelle *f*; *personne*: pupille *mf*; *escrime*: garde *f*, parade *f*; quartier *m* (*d'une prison*); salle *f* (*d'hôpital*); *admin.* arrondissement *m*; circonscription *f* électorale; ~s *pl.* dents *f*/*pl.*, bouterolles *f*/*pl.* (*d'une clef*); *casual* ~ asile *m* de nuit; *in* ~ en tutelle; *sous la tutelle* (de, to); *Am.* F *pol.* ~ *heeler* politicien *m* à la manque; **2.** faire entrer (*à l'hôpital etc.*); ~ *off* écarter; '**ward·en** directeur (-trice *f*) *m*; recteur *m*; '**ward·er** gardien *m* de prison; '**ward·robe** garderobe *f*; *meuble*: armoire *f*; ~ *dealer* marchand(e *f*) *m* de toilette; ~ *trunk* malle-armoire (*pl.* malles-armoires) *f*; '**ward·room** ⚓ carré *m* des officiers; '**ward·ship** tutelle *f*.

ware [wɛə] marchandise *f*; ustensiles *m*/*pl.*

ware·house 1. ['wɛəhaus] entrepôt *m*; magasin *m*; **2.** ['~hauz] emmagasiner; *douane*: entreposer; ~·**man** ['~hausmən] emmagasineur *m*; *douane*: entreposeur *m*; garçon *m* de magasin; *Italian* ~ épicier *m*.

war...: '~-**fare** la guerre *f*; '~-**grave** sépulture *f* militaire; '~-**head** torpille *etc.*: cône *m* (de charge).

war·i·ness ['wɛərinis] circonspection *f*; prudence *f*; défiance *f*.

war...: '~-**like** guerrier (-ère *f*); martial (-aux *m*/*pl.*); '~-**loan** emprunt *m* de guerre.

warm [wɔːm] **1.** □ chaud (*a. fig.*); *fig.* chaleureux (-euse *f*), vif (vive *f*); F riche; *be* ~ avoir chaud (*personne*); être chaud (*chose*); **2.** F action *f* de (se) chauffer; **3.** *v/t.* chauffer; *fig.* (r)échauffer; *sl.* flanquer une tripotée à; ~ *up* (ré)chauffer; *v/i.* (*a.* ~ *up*) s'échauffer, se (ré)chauffer; s'animer; ~ *to* se sentir attiré vers (*q.*); '~-'**heart·ed** affectueux (-euse *f*), chaleureux (-euse *f*); '**warm·ing** *sl.* rossée *f*.

war-mon·ger ['wɔːmʌŋgə] belliciste *m*; '**war-mon·ger·ing**, '**war-mon·ger·y** propagande *f* de guerre.

warmth [wɔːmθ] chaleur *f*.

warm-up ['wɔːmʌp] mise *f* en train.

warn [wɔːn] avertir (de *of*, *against*); prévenir; (*ou* ~ *off*) détourner; conseiller (de *inf.*, *to inf.*); alerter; '**warn·ing** avertissement *m*; avis *m*; *turf*: exécution *f*; congé *m* (*d'un employé etc.*); alerte *f*; *take* ~ *from* profiter de l'exemple de; tirer une leçon de.

warp [wɔːp] **1.** *tex.* chaîne *f*; *tapisserie*: lisse *f*; ⚓ amarre *f*; voilure *f* (*d'une planche*); *fig.* perversion *f*; **2.** *v/i.* se voiler (*bois*); ⚓ (*usu.* ~ *out*) déhaler; *v/t.* (faire) voiler, déverser (*du bois etc.*); ✈ gauchir (*les ailes*); *tex.* ourdir (*une étoffe*), empeigner (*un métier*); ⚓ haler, touer; *fig.* fausser (*les sens*); pervertir (*l'esprit*).

warp...: '~-**paint** peinture *f* de guerre (*des Peaux-Rouges*); F *fig.* grande tenue *f*; gros maquillage *m*; '~-**path** (*be on the* ~ être sur le) sentier *m* de la guerre.

warp·ing ✈ ['wɔːpiŋ] gauchissement *m* des ailes.

war...: '~-**plane** avion *m* de guerre; '~-**prof·it·eer** mercanti *m* de guerre.

war·rant ['wɒrənt] **1.** garantie *f*; *fig.* garant *m*; justification *f*; ⚖ mandat *m*; pouvoir *m*; ✕ feuille *f* (de route); ✕ ordonnance *f* (*de paiement*); ✝ warrant *m*; ~ (*of apprehension*) mandat *m* d'amener; ~ *of arrest* mandat *m* d'arrêt; **2.** garantir (*a.* ✝); certifier; attester; répondre de (*qch.*); justifier; '**war·rant·a·ble** □ légitime; justifiable; que l'on peut garantir; *chasse*: courable; '**war·rant·ed** garanti; **war·ran·tee** ⚖ [~'tiː] receveur (-euse *f*) *m* d'une garantie; '**war·rant-of·fi·cer** ⚓

premier maître *m*; ✕ sous-officier *m* breveté; **war·ran·tor** ⚖ ['⁀tɔ:] répondant *m*; **'war·ran·ty** garantie *f*; autorisation *f*.

war·ren ['wɔrin] garenne *f*, lapinière *f*.

war·ri·or ['wɔriə] guerrier *m*; *the Unknown* ♀ le Soldat inconnu.

war·ship ['wɔ:ʃip] vaisseau *m* de guerre.

wart [wɔːt] verrue *f*; ♀ excroissance *f*; **'wart·y** verruqueux (-euse *f*).

war...: '⁀time temps *m* de guerre.

war·y □ ['wɛəri] circonspect, prudent; défiant; précautionneux (-euse *f*).

was [wɔz; wəz] *prét. de* be; *he* ⁀ *to have come* il devait venir.

wash [wɔʃ] **1.** *v/t.* laver; blanchir (*le linge*); *fig.* baigner; ⁀ed out délavé, décoloré; F flapi; ⁀ up faire la vaisselle; ⚓ rejeter sur le rivage; *sl.* ⁀ed up fini, fichu; *v/i.* se laver; ⁀ *against the cliff* baigner la falaise; ⚓ ⁀ *over* balayer (*le pont*); **2.** lessive *f*, blanchissage *m*; toilette *f*; remous *m*; ⚓ sillage *m*; 🎣 souffle *m* (*de l'hélice*); *peint.* lavis *m*; (*a.* colo[u]r ⁀) badigeon *m*; *péj.* lavasse *f*; 🎣, *pharm., vét.* lotion *f*; **'wash·a·ble** lavable; **'wash(-)and(-)wear** 'ne pas repasser'; **'wash-ba·sin** cuvette *f*, lavabo *m*; **'wash-cloth** torchon *m*; **'washed-'out** F épuisé, F lessivé; **'washed-'up** F fichu, ruiné; épuisé, F lessivé.

wash·er ['wɔʃə] laveur (-euse *f*) *m*; *machine:* laveuse *f*; ⊕ cylindre *m* à laver; '⁀·wom·an blanchisseuse *f*.

wash·i·ness F ['wɔʃinis] fadeur *f*, insipidité *f*.

wash·ing ['wɔʃiŋ] **1.** lavage *m*; ablution *f*; lessive *f*, blanchissage *m*; ⊕ lavée *f* (*de laine, de minerai*); ⁀s *pl.* produits *m/pl.* de lavage; ⊕ chantier *m* de lavage; **2.** de lessive; ⁀ *machine* machine *f* à laver; ⁀ *powder* lessive *f*; '⁀-silk soie *f* lavable; '⁀-'up (lavage *m* de la) vaisselle *f*; ⁀ *basin* cuvette *f*; ⁀ *water* eau *f* de vaisselle; *do the* ⁀ faire la vaisselle.

wash...: '⁀-'out *sl.* fiasco *m*; ratage *m*; raté(e) *f* (*personne*); '⁀-rag *surt. Am.* lavette *f*, gant *m* de toilette; '⁀-stand lavabo *m*; **'wash·y** délavé (*couleur*); *fig.* fade, insipide.

wasp [wɔsp] guêpe *f*; **'wasp·ish** □

méchant (*a. fig.*); acerbe; acariâtre (*femme*).

wast·age ['weistidʒ] déperdition *f*, perte *f*; gaspillage *m*; *coll.* déchets *m/pl.*

waste [weist] **1.** désert, inculte; perdu (*temps*); ⊕ de rebut; *lay* ⁀ dévaster, ravager; ⁀ *heat* chaleur *f* perdue; ⁀ *paper* vieux papiers *m/pl.*; papier *m* de rebut; ⁀ *products pl.* déchets *m/pl.*; ⁀ *steam* vapeur *f* perdue; ⁀ *water* eaux *f/pl.* ménagères; ⊕ eaux-vannes *f/pl.*; **2.** perte *f*; gaspillage *m*; rebut *m*; déchet *m*; région *f* inculte; *go* (*ou run*) *to* ⁀ se perdre, se dissiper; s'affricher (*terrain*); **3.** *v/t.* user, consumer, gaspiller; perdre (*son temps*); *v/i.* se perdre; s'user; maigrir (*malade*); **waste·ful** □ ['⁀ful] gaspilleur (-euse *f*); prodigue; inutile; ruineux (-euse *f*); **'waste·land** terre *f* en friche; **'waste-pa·per bas·ket** corbeille *f* à papier; **'waste·pipe** trop-plein *m*; *baignoire:* écoulement *m*; **'wast·er** gaspilleur (-euse *f*) *m*; *see* wastrel.

wast·rel ['weistrəl] vaurien *m*; mauvais sujet *m*.

watch [wɔtʃ] **1.** garde *f*; † veille *f*; † *personne:* garde *m*; ⚓ quart *m*; montre *f*; *be on the* ⁀ *for* épier, guetter; *être à l'affût de*; ♀ *Committee* comité *m* municipal qui veille au maintien de l'ordre; **2.** *v/i.* veiller (*sur, over*); ⁀ *for* attendre (*q., qch.*); guetter (*q.*); *v/t.* veiller sur, regarder; assister à; guetter (*l'occasion*); '⁀·boat ⚓ (bateau *m*) patrouilleur *m*; '⁀-brace·let montre-bracelet (*pl.* montres-bracelets) *f*; '⁀-case boîte *f* de montre; '⁀·dog chien *m* de garde; **'watch·er** veilleur (-euse *f*) *m*; observateur (-trice *f*) *m*; **watch·ful** □ ['⁀ful] vigilant, attentif (-ive *f*).

watch...: '⁀-mak·er horloger *m*; '⁀-man gardien *m*; veilleur *m* (*de nuit*); '⁀-tow·er tour *f* de guet; '⁀-word *pol. etc.* mot *m* d'ordre.

wa·ter ['wɔːtə] **1.** eau *f*; ⁀ *supply* (provision *f* d')eau *f*; service *m* des eaux; *high* (*low*) ⁀ marée *f* haute (basse); *by* ⁀ en bateau, par eau; *drink* (*ou take*) *the* ⁀s prendre les eaux; *of the first* ⁀ de première eau (*diamant*); *fig.* de premier ordre; F *be in hot* ⁀ être dans le pétrin; avoir des ennuis; F *be in low* ⁀ être dans la gêne; **2.** *v/t.* arroser (*terre, route, plante, région*); abreuver (*les bêtes*); *fig.* atténuer, affaiblir; (*souv. ~ down*) mouiller, diluer; ⊕ alimenter en eau (*une machine*); *tex.* moirer; *v/i.* pleurer (*yeux*); faire provision d'eau; s'abreuver (*bêtes*); ⊕, ⚓, *mot.* faire de l'eau; *make s.o.'s mouth ~* faire venir l'eau à la bouche de q.; '**~·blis·ter** ⚕ cloque *f*; '**~·borne** flottant; transporté par voie d'eau; **~ can·non** lance-eau *m/inv.*; '**~·cart** arroseuse *f* (*dans les rues*); '**~·clos·et** (*usu. écrit* W.C.) cabinets *m/pl.*, F waters *m/pl.*; '**~·col·o(u)r** aquarelle *f*; couleur *f* à l'eau; '**~·cooled** refroidi à eau; '**~·cool·ing** refroidissement *m* à eau; '**~·course** cours *m* d'eau; conduit *m*; conduite *f* d'eau; '**~·cress** ♀ cresson *m* (de fontaine); '**~·fall** chute *f* d'eau; '**~·fowl** gibier *m*, *coll.* **~s** *m/pl.* d'eau; '**~·front** *surt. Am.* quai *m*, bord *m* de l'eau; '**~·gauge** ⊕ hydromètre *m*; (indicateur *m* de) niveau *m* d'eau; '**~·hose** tuyau *m* d'arrosage; *qqfois* manche *f* à feu; '**wa·ter·i·ness** aquosité *f*; ⚕ sérosité *f*; *fig.* fadeur *f*.

wa·ter·ing ['wɔːtəriŋ] arrosage *m*; irrigation *f*; abreuvage *m* (*des bêtes*); '**~·can**, '**~·pot** arrosoir *m*; '**~·place** abreuvoir *m*; ville *f* d'eau; plage *f*, bains *m/pl.* de mer.

wa·ter...: '**~·jack·et** ⊕ chemise *f* d'eau; '**~·lev·el** niveau *m* d'eau (*a.* ⊕); '**~·lil·y** ♀ nénuphar *m*; '**~·logged** imbibé d'eau; ⚓ plein d'eau; '**~·main** conduite *f* (principale) d'eau; '**~·man** batelier *m*, marinier *m*; '**~·mark** niveau *m* des eaux; ⚓ laisse *f*; *papier*: filigrane *m*; '**~·part·ing** ligne *f* de partage des eaux; '**~·pipe** conduite *f* d'eau; '**~·plane** hydravion *m*; **~ pol·lu·tion** pollution *f* de l'eau; '**~·po·lo** water-polo *m*; '**~·pow·er** force *f* ou énergie *f* hydraulique; **~ station** centrale *f* hydraulique; '**~·proof 1.** imperméable (*a. su./m*); **2.** rendre imperméable; caoutchouter; '**~·re'pel·lent wool** laine *f* cirée; '**~·shed** *see* waterparting; *p. ext.* bassin *m*; '**~·side 1.** riverain; **2.** bord *m* de l'eau; '**~·spout** descente *f* d'eau; gouttière *f*; *météor.* trombe *f*; '**~·ta·ble** niveau *m* hydrostatique; '**~·tap** robinet *m*; '**~·tight** étanche; *fig.* sans échappatoire, inattaquable; *fig. in* **~** *compart-*

ments séparé(s) par des cloisons étanches; '**~·wave 1.** *cheveux*: mise *f* en plis; **2.** mettre (*les cheveux*) en plis; '**~·way** voie *f* d'eau; ⚓ gouttière *f*; '**~·works** *usu. sg.* usine *f* de distribution d'eau; '**wa·ter·y** aqueux (-euse *f*); larmoyant (*yeux*); *fig.* noyé *ou* plein d'eau; *fig.* peu épais (-se *f*).

watt ⚡ [wɔt] watt *m*.

wat·tle ['wɔtl] **1.** clayonnage *m*; claie *f*; *dindon*: caroncule *f*; **2.** clayonner; tresser (*l'osier*).

waul [wɔːl] miauler.

wave [weiv] **1.** vague *f* (*a. fig.*); *phys.* onde *f*; *cheveux*: ondulation *f*; geste *m*, signe *m* (de la main); **2.** *v/t.* agiter; brandir; onduler (*les cheveux*); faire signe de (*la main*); **~** *s.o. aside* écarter q. d'un geste; *v/i.* s'agiter; flotter; onduler; faire signe (à q., *to s.o.*); '**~·length** ⚡ *radio*: longueur *f* d'onde; F *fig.* *be on the same* **~** être sur la même longueur d'onde(s); '**~·me·ter** ondemètre *m*.

wa·ver ['weivə] hésiter; vaciller (*a. fig.*); ✗ *etc.* fléchir.

wave...: '**~·range** *radio*: gamme *f* de longueur d'onde; '**~·trap** *radio*: ondemètre *m* d'absorption.

wav·y ['weivi] onduleux (-euse *f*); ondulé; tremblé (*ligne*).

wax¹ [wæks] **1.** cire *f*; *oreilles*: cérumen *m*; **~** *candle* bougie *f* de cire; *eccl.* cierge *m*; **~** *doll* poupée *f* de cire; **2.** cirer; mettre (*le cuir*) en cire; empoisser (*le fil*).

wax² [~] croître (*lune*); *co. devant adj.*: devenir.

wax·en ['wæksn] de *ou* en cire; *fig. a.* cireux (-euse *f*); '**wax·work** figure *f* de cire; **~s** *pl.*, **~** *show* figures *f/pl.* de cire; '**wax·y** □ cireux (-euse *f*).

way [wei] **1.** chemin *m*, route *f*, voie *f*; direction *f*, côté *m*; façon *f*, manière *f*; genre *m*; moyen *m*; marche *f*; progrès *m*; état *m*; habitude *f*; idée *f*, guise *f*; **~** *in* entrée *f*; **~** *out* sortie *f*; *admin.* **~s** and means voies *f/pl.* et moyens *m/pl.*; *parl.* Committee of **⚥**s and Means Commission *f* du Budget; *right of* **~** ⚖ servitude *f* ou droit *m* de passage; *surt. mot.* priorité *f* de passage; *this* **~** par ici; *in some* (*ou a*) **~** en quelque sorte; *in no* **~** ne ... aucunement *ou* d'aucune façon; *go a great* (*ou some*) **~** *towards* (*gér.*), *go a long* (*ou some*) **~** *to* (inf.) contribuer de beaucoup ou quelque peu à (inf.); by the ~ en passant, à propos; by ~ of par la voie de; en guise de, à titre de; by ~ of excuse en guise d'excuse; on the (ou one's) ~ en route (pour, to); chemin faisant; out of the ~ écarté, isolé; fig. peu ordinaire; under ~ en marche (a. ⚓); give ~ céder, lâcher pied; faire place; have one's ~ agir à sa guise; if I had my ~ si on me laissait faire; have a ~ with se faire bien voir de (q.); lead the ~ marcher en tête; montrer le chemin; see make 1; pay one's ~ joindre les deux bouts; se suffire; see one's ~ to juger possible de; trouver moyen de; Am. ~ station petite gare f; Am. ~ train train m omnibus; 2. adv. Am. loin; là-bas; '~-bill feuille f de route; lettre f de voiture; '~-far-er voyageur (-euse f) m; '~lay [irr. (lay)] guetter (au passage); '~-leave droit m de passage ou de survol; '~-side 1. bord m de la route; by the ~ au bord de la route; 2. au bord de la route, en bordure de route.

way-ward □ ['weiwəd] capricieux (-euse f); entêté, rebelle; 'way-ward-ness entêtement m; caractère m difficile.

we [wi:; wi] nous (a. accentué).

weak □ [wi:k] faible; léger (-ère f) (thé); 'weak-en (s')affaiblir; 'weak-ling personne f faible; 'weak-ly 1. adj. faible; 2. adv. faiblement; sans résolution; 'weak-'mind-ed faible d'esprit; qui manque de résolution; 'weak-ness faiblesse f.

weal[1] [wi:l] 1. bien(-être) m.

weal[2] [~] marque f.

wealth [welθ] richesse f, -s f/pl.; fig. abondance f; 'wealth-y □ riche, opulent.

wean [wi:n] sevrer (un enfant); fig. détourner (q.) (de from, of).

weap-on ['wepən] arme f; 'weap-on-less sans armes, désarmé; 'weap-on-ry armes f/pl.; armement(s) m (pl.).

wear [wɛə] [irr.] 1. v/t. porter (un vêtement etc.); (a. ~ away, down, off, out) user, effacer; épuiser, lasser (la patience); v/i. faire bon usage; se conserver (bien etc.) (personne); ~ away s'user, s'effacer; passer; ~ off disparaître (a. fig.), s'effacer; ~ on s'écouler (temps);

s'avancer; ~ out s'user; s'épuiser; 2. usage m; mode f; vêtements m/pl.; fatigue f; (a. ~ and tear) usure f; gentlemen's ~ vêtements m/pl. pour hommes; for hard ~ d'un bon usage; be the ~ être à la mode ou de mise; the worse for ~ usé; there is plenty of ~ in it y et il est encore portable; 'wear-a-ble portable (vêtement).

wea-ri-ness ['wiərinis] fatigue f; lassitude f; fig. dégoût m.

wea-ri-some □ ['wiərisəm] ennuyeux (-euse f); fig. ingrat, F assommant; 'wea-ri-some-ness ennui m.

wea-ry ['wiəri] 1. □ las(se f), fatigué (de, with); fig. dégoûté (de, of); fatigant, fastidieux (-euse f); 2. (se) lasser, fatiguer.

wea-sel zo. ['wi:zl] belette f.

weath-er ['weðə] 1. temps m; see permit 1; 2. météorologique; ⚓ du côté du vent, au vent; 3. v/t. altérer (par les intempéries); ⚓ passer au vent de; doubler (un cap); (a. ~ out) étaler (une tempête etc.), fig. survivre à; ~ed altéré par le temps ou les intempéries; v/i. s'altérer; prendre la patine (cuivre etc.); '~-beat-en battu par les tempêtes; basané (figure etc.); '~-board fenêtre: reverseau m; toit etc.: planche f à recouvrement; '~-board-ing planches f/pl. à recouvrement; '~-bound retenu par le mauvais temps; '~-bu-reau bureau m météorologique; '~-chart carte f météorologique; '~-cock girouette f; '~-fore-cast bulletin m météorologique; prévisions f/pl. du temps; '~-proof, '~-tight imperméable; étanche; '~-sta-tion station f météorologique; '~-strip bourrelet m étanche; mot. gouttière f d'étanchéité; '~-vane girouette f; '~-worn rongé par les intempéries.

weave [wi:v] 1. [irr.] tisser; fig. tramer; 2. armure f; tissage m; 'weav-er tisserand(e f) m; 'weav-ing tissage m; entrelacement m; route: zigzags m/pl.; attr. à tisser.

wea-zen ['wi:zn] ratatiné, desséché.

web [web] tissu m (a. fig.); toile f (d'araignée); orn. plume: lame f; pattes: palmure f; ⊕ rouleau m (d'étoffe, de papier); **webbed** palmé, membrané; 'web-bing (toile f

1223

well-balanced

à) sangles *f/pl.*; **'web-foot·ed** palmipède, aux pieds palmés.

wed [wed] *v/t.* épouser, se marier avec (*q.*); marier (*un couple*); *fig.* unir (à *to, with*); *v/i.* se marier; **'wed·ded** conjugal (-aux *m/pl.*); marié; **'wed·ding 1.** mariage *m*; noce *f*, -s *f/pl.*; **2.** de noce(s); de mariage; nuptial (-aux *m/pl.*); ~ *an-niversary* anniversaire *m* de mariage; ~ *ring* alliance *f*.

wedge [wedʒ] **1.** coin *m*; *fig.* the thin end of the ~ le premier pas, un pied de pris; **2.** coincer; (*a.* ~ *in*) enclaver, insérer; **'~-shaped** en forme de coin; cunéiforme (*caractères, os*).

wed·lock ['wedlɔk] mariage *m*.

Wednes·day ['wenzdi] mercredi *m*.

wee *écoss.,* F [wi:] (tout) petit.

weed [wi:d] **1.** mauvaise herbe *f*; F tabac *m*; F personne *f* étique; **2.** sarcler; (*a.* ~ *up, out*) arracher les mauvaises herbes; *fig.* éliminer; **'weed·er** sarcleur (-euse *f*) *m*; *outil:* sarcloir *m*; extirpateur *m*.

weeds [wi:dz] *pl.* (*usu. widow's* ~) (vêtements *m/pl.* de) deuil *m*.

weed·y ['wi:di] plein de mauvaises herbes; F *fig.* étique; maigre.

week [wi:k] semaine *f*; *short working* ~ semaine *f* courte; *by the* ~ à la semaine; *this day* ~ d'aujourd'hui en huit; **'~-day** jour *m* de semaine; jour *m* ouvrable; **'~-'end 1.** fin *f* de semaine; week-end *m*; ~ *ticket* billet *m* valable du samedi au lundi; **2.** passer le week-end; **'~-'end·er** touriste *mf* de fin de semaine; **'week·ly 1.** hebdomadaire; **2.** (*a.* ~ *paper*) hebdomadaire *m*.

wee·ny F ['wi:ni] tout petit, minuscule.

weep [wi:p] [*irr.*] pleurer (de *joie etc.,* for; *qch.* for, over *s.th.*); verser des larmes; **'weep·er** pleureur (-euse *f*) *m*; ~s *pl.* manchettes *f/pl.* de deuil; **'weep·ing 1.** qui pleure; humide; ⚘ ~ *willow* saule *m* pleureur; **2.** larmes *f/pl.*, pleurs *m/pl.*

wee·vil ['wi:vil] charançon *m* (*du blé etc.*).

weft [weft] *tex.* trame *f*; *fig.* traînée *f* (*d'un nuage etc.*).

weigh [wei] **1.** *v/t.* peser (*a. fig.* le *pour et le contre*); *fig.* (*a.* ~ *up*) jauger; ⚓ ~ *anchor* lever l'ancre; ~ *down* peser plus que; ~*ed down* sur-

chargé, *fig.* accablé (de, *with*); *v/i.* peser (*a. fig.*); *fig.* avoir du poids (pour, *with*); ~ (*up*)*on* peser (lourd) sur; **2.** ⚓ *get under* ~ (*ou way*) se mettre en route; **'weigh·a·ble** pesable; **'weigh·bridge** (pont *m* à) bascule *f*; **'weigh·er** peseur (-euse *f*) *m*; **'weigh·ing-ma·chine** bascule *f*; appareil *m* de pesage.

weight [weit] **1.** poids *m*; pesanteur *f*, lourdeur *f*; force *f* (*d'un coup*); *fig.* importance *f*; *fig.* carry great ~ avoir beaucoup d'influence; avoir de l'autorité; *sp. putting the* ~ lancement *m* du poids; **2.** alourdir; attacher un poids à; *fig.* affecter d'un coefficient; **'weight·i·ness** pesanteur *f*; *fig.* importance *f*; **'weight·less** qui ne pèse rien; en état d'apesanteur; **'weight·less-ness** apesanteur *f*; **'weight·y** □ pesant, lourd; grave; sérieux (-euse *f*).

weir [wiə] barrage *m*; *étang:* déversoir *m*.

weird [wiəd] étrange; mystérieux (-euse *f*); F singulier (-ère *f*).

wel·come ['welkəm] **1.** □ bienvenu; agréable; *you are* ~ *to* (*inf.*) libre à vous de (*inf.*); *you are* ~ *to it* c'est à votre service; *iro.* grand bien vous fasse!; (*you are*) ~! soyez le bienvenu!; il n'y a pas de quoi!; **2.** bienvenue *f*; **3.** souhaiter la bienvenue à; accueillir (*a. fig.*).

weld ⊕ [weld] **1.** (se) souder; (se) corroyer (*acier*); ~ *into* fondre en; **2.** (*a.* ~*ing seam*) (joint *m* de) soudure *f*; **'weld·ing** ⊕ soudage *m*, soudure *f*; *attr.* soudant; à souder.

wel·fare ['welfeə] bien-être *m*; ~ *centre* dispensaire *m*; ~ *work* assistance *f* sociale; ~ *worker* assistant (-e *f*) *m* social(e).

well[1] [wel] **1.** puits *m*; *fig.* source *f*; ⊕ *haut fourneau:* creuset *m*; (*a. ink-*~) encrier *m*; *ascenseur:* cage *f*; *hôtel:* cour *f*; **2.** jaillir, sourdre.

well[2] [~] **1.** *adv.* bien; *see as* 1; ~ *off* aisé, riche; bien fourni (de, *for*); *be* ~ *past* fifty avoir largement dépassé la cinquantaine; *beat s.o.* ~ battre q. à plate couture; **2.** *adj. préd.* en bonne santé; bien; *I am not* ~ je ne me porte pas bien; *all's well* tout va bien; **3.** *int.* eh bien!; F ça alors!; **'~-ad'vised** sage; bien avisé (*personne*); **'~-'bal·anced**

well-being

(bien) equilibré; '~-'be·ing bien-êt-re *m*; '~-'born de bonne famille; bien né; '~-'bred bien élevé; '~-dis'posed bien disposé (envers, to[*wards*]); '~-'fa·vo(u)red beau (bel *devant une voyelle ou un h muet*; belle *f*); de bonne mine; '~-in-'formed bien renseigné.

Wel·ling·tons ['weliŋtənz] *pl.* bottes *f/pl.* en caoutchouc.

well...: '~-in'ten·tioned bien inten-tionné; '~-'judged bien calculé; judicieux (-euse *f*); '~-'knit bien bâti; solide; '~-'made de coupe soi-gnée (*habit*); bien découplé; '~-'man·nered bien élevé; '~-'mean-ing bien intentionné; '~-'meant fait avec de bonnes intentions; amical (-aux *m/pl.*) (*conseil etc.*); '~-'nigh presque; '~-'off bien *inv.*; (a. ~ for money) aisé, (bien) nanti; '~-pre-'served bien conservé; '~-'read let-tré, érudit; instruit; cultivé; '~-'spok·en qui soigne son élocution; cultivé; '~-'thought-of (bien) con-sidéré; estimé; '~-'timed opportun, à propos; bien calculé; ~-to-do aisé; prospère; ~ turned *fig.* bien tourné; '~-'wish·er ami(e *f*) *m* sin-cère, partisan *m*; '~-'worn usé; *fig.* rebattu.

Welsh[1] [welʃ] **1.** gallois; **2.** *ling.* gallois *m*; the ~ les Gallois *m/pl.*

welsh[2] [~] *turf*: décamper avec les enjeux des parieurs; '**welsh·er** bookmaker *m* marron; *p.ext.* escroc *m*.

Welsh...: '~-man Gallois *m*; '~-wom·an Galloise *f*.

welt [welt] **1.** ⊕ *semelle*: trépointe *f*; *chaussette, gant*: bordure *f*; couvre-joint *m*; **2.** mettre des trépointes à (*des souliers*); border; F rosser; ~ed à trépointes (*soulier*).

wel·ter ['weltə] **1.** se rouler, se vautrer; *fig.* ~ *in* nager dans (*son sang etc.*); **2.** désordre *m*; '~-weight box. poids *m* mi-moyen.

wen ⚕ [wen] kyste *m* sébacé; F goitre *m*.

wench [wentʃ] jeune fille *f* ou femme *f*.

wend [wend]: ~ *one's way* (vers, to) diriger ses pas; se diriger.

went went *prét.* de go 1.

wept [wept] *prét. et p.p. de* weep.

were [wə:; wə] *prét. et sbj. prét. de* be.

west [west] **1.** *su.* ouest *m*; **2.** *adj.* de

l'ouest; occidental (-aux *m/pl.*); **3.** *adv.* à *ou* vers l'ouest; *sl.* go ~ casser sa pipe (= *mourir*); '~-'bound en direc-tion de l'ouest; allant vers l'ouest.

west·er·ly ['westəli] de *ou* à l'ouest; **west·ern** ['westən] **1.** de l'ouest; occidental (-aux *m/pl.*); **2.** *see* westerner; *Am.* ♀ film *m* ou roman *m* de cowboys; western *m*; '**west-ern·er** occidental(e *f*) *m*; habi-tant(e *f*) *m* de l'ouest; '**west·ern-most** le plus à l'ouest.

west·ing ⚓ ['westiŋ] route *f* vers l'ouest; départ *m* pour l'ouest.

west·ward ['westwəd] **1.** *adj.* à *ou* de l'ouest; **2.** *adv.* (*a.* **west·wards** ['~dz]) vers l'ouest.

wet [wet] **1.** mouillé; humide; *Am.* qui permet la vente de l'alcool; *see blanket* 1; ⚡ ~ *cell* pile *f* à l'élément humide; ⊕ ~ *process* voie *f* humide; ~ *steam* vapeur *f* mouillée; ~ *through* trempé (jusqu'aux os); F *with a* ~ *finger* à souhait; **2.** pluie *f*; humidité *f*; **3.** [*irr.*] mouiller; tremper; F pleu-voir; F arroser (*une affaire*); ~ *through* tremper (jusqu'aux os).

wet·back *Am. sl.* ['wetbæk] immi-grant *m* mexicain illégal.

weth·er ['weðə] bélier *m* châtré.

wet-nurse ['wetnə:s] nourrice *f*.

whack F [wæk] **1.** battre; **2.** coup *m*; claque *f*; (grand) morceau *m*; *have* (*ou take*) *a* ~ *at* (*gér.*) essayer de (*inf.*); '**whack·er** F chose *f* ou personne *f* énorme; gros mensonge *m*; '**whack·ing** F **1.** rossée *f*, fessée *f*; **2.** colossal (-aux *m/pl.*).

whale [weil] baleine *f*; F *a* ~ *of a castle* un château magnifique; F *a* ~ *at* un as à; '~-bone baleine *f*; '~-fish·er, '~-man, *usu.* '**whal·er** baleinier *m*; '**whale-oil** huile *f* de baleine.

whal·ing ['weiliŋ] pêche *f* à la baleine.

whang F [wæŋ] **1.** coup *m* retentis-sant; **2.** retentir.

wharf [wɔ:f] **1.** (*pl. a.* **wharves** [wɔ:vz]) quai *m*; entrepôt *m* (*pour marchandises*); **2.** débarquer; dé-poser sur le quai; **wharf·age** ['~idʒ] débarquement *m*; mise *f* en entre-pôt; quayage *m*; **wharf·in·ger** ['~indʒə] propriétaire *m* d'un quai.

what [wɔt] **1.** *pron. interr.* que, quoi; qu'est-ce qui; qu'est-ce que; ~ *about...?* et ...?; ~ *about* (*gér.*)? que pensez-vous de (*inf.*)?; ~ *for?* pourquoi donc?; ~ of it? et alors?; ~ if ...? et si ...?; ~ though ...? qu'importe que (sbj.)?; F ~-d'ye-call-him (-her, -it, -'em), ~'s-his-name (-her-name, -its-name), Am. ~-is-it machin m, chose mf; ~ next? et ensuite?; iro. par exemple!; et quoi encore?; 2. pron. rel. ce qui, ce que; know ~'s ~ en savoir long; savoir son monde; and ~ not et ainsi de suite; ~ with ... ~ with ... entre ... et ...; 3. adj. interr. quel, quelle, quels, quelles; ~ time is it? quelle heure est-il?; ~ a blessing! quel bonheur!; ~ impudence! quelle audace!, F quel toupet!; (of) ~ use is it? à quoi sert-il (de, inf., to inf.)?; 4. adj. rel. que, qui; ~ money I had l'argent dont je disposais; 'what-not éta-gère f; what(·so)'ev·er 1. pron. tout ce qui, tout ce que, quoi qui (sbj.), quoi que (sbj.); 2. adj. quel-que ... qui ou que (sbj.); aucun; quelconque.

wheat ♀ [wi:t] blé m; 'wheat·en de blé, de froment.

whee·dle ['wi:dl] cajoler; ~ s.o. into (gér.) amener q. à (inf.) à force de cajoleries; ~ money out of s.o. soutirer de l'argent à q.

wheel [wi:l] 1. roue f; (a. steering-~) volant m; Am. F bicyclette f; ⊕ (a. grinding-~) meule f; see potter²; ⚓ barre f; ✗ conversion f; 2. v/t. rouler, tourner; promener; v/i. tourn(oy)er; se retourner (personne); ✗ faire une conversion; Am. aller à bicyclette; '~·bar·row brouette f; ~ base ⊕ empattement m; ~ chair fauteuil m roulant; 'wheeled à roues; roulant; 'wheel·ing and 'deal·ing F affaires f/pl. louches, manigances f/pl.; 'wheel·man F cycliste m; 'wheel-spi·der ⊕ croisillon m (de roue); 'wheel-wright charron m.

wheeze [wi:z] 1. v/i. siffler; respirer péniblement; corner (cheval); v/t. F seriner (un air); 2. sifflement m, respiration f asthmatique; cheval: cornage m; théâ. sl. trouvaille f; sl. truc m; 'wheez·y □ asthmatique; cornard (cheval).

whelp [welp] 1. see puppy; petit m (d'un fauve); 2. mettre bas.

when [wen] 1. adv. quand?; 2. cj. quand, lorsque; et alors; (le jour) où; (un jour) que.

whence [wens] d'où.

when(·so)·ev·er [wen(so)'evə] cha-que fois que, toutes les fois que; quand.

where [wɛə] 1. adv. où?; 2. cj. (là) où; ~·a·bout ['wɛərə'baut] 1. où (donc); 2. (usu. '~·a·bouts [~s]): the ~ of le lieu m où (q., qch.) se trouve; ~'as puisque, vu que, attendu que; tandis que, alors que; ⚖ considé-rant que; ~'at sur ou à ou de quoi; ~'by par où; par quoi; par lequel (etc.); '~·fore 1. adv. pourquoi?; 2. cj. c'est pourquoi; ~'in en quoi; où; dans lequel (etc.); ~'of dont, de quoi; duquel etc.; ~'on où; sur quoi; sur lequel (etc.); ~·so'ev·er partout où; ~·up'on sur quoi; sur lequel (etc.); wher'ev·er partout où; where-with·al 1. [wɛəwi'ðɔ:l] avec quoi; avec lequel (etc.); 2. F ['~] nécessaire m; moyens m/pl.; fonds m/pl.

wher·ry ['weri] bachot m; esquif m.

whet [wet] 1. aiguiser, affiler; fig. stimuler; 2. affilage m; fig. stimu-lation f; F stimulant m; petit verre m.

wheth·er ['weðə] si; ~ ... or no que ... (sbj.) ou non.

whet·stone ['wetstoun] pierre f à aiguiser. [fichtre!]

whew [hwu:] ouf!; int. par surprise:

whey [wei] petit lait m.

which [witʃ] 1. pron. interr. lequel, laquelle, lesquels, lesquelles; 2. pron. rel. qui, que; all ~ toutes choses qui ou que; in (by) ~ en (par) quoi; 3. adj. interr. quel, quelle, quels, quelles; 4. adj. rel. lequel, laquelle, lesquels, lesquelles; ~'ev·er 1. pron. rel. celui qui, celui que; n'importe lequel (etc.); 2. adj. le ... que, n'importe quel (etc.); quelque ... que (sbj.).

whiff [wif] 1. air, fumée, vent: bouffée f; petit cigare m; ⚓ skiff m; 2. émettre des bouffées (v/t. de fumée etc.).

whif·fle-tree ⊕ ['wifltri:] palon-nier m.

Whig hist. Brit. [wig] 1. whig m (membre d'un parti libéral); 2. des whigs; whig (parti); 'Whig·gism whiggisme m.

while [wail] 1. temps m; espace m; for a ~ pendant quelque temps; F be worth ~ valoir la peine; 2. (usu.

whilst

~ *away*) faire passer, tuer (*le temps*); **3.** (*a.* **whilst** [wailst]) pendant que, tandis que, en (*gér.*).

whim [wim] caprice *m*; lubie *f*; ⊕ triqueballe *m*.

whim·per ['wimpə] **1.** *v/i.* pleurnicher; pousser des petits cris plaintifs (*chien*); *v/t.* dire (*qch.*) en pleurnichant; **2.** pleurnicherie *f*; plainte *f*; petit cri *m* plaintif.

whim·si·cal □ ['wimzikl] bizarre; capricieux (-euse *f*) (*personne*); fantasque; **whim·si·cal·i·ty** [~'kæliti], **whim·si·cal·ness** ['~klnis] bizarrerie *f*; caractère *m* fantasque. **whim·s(e)y** ['wimzi] caprice *m*; boutade *f*.

whin ♭ [win] ajonc *m*.

whine [wain] **1.** *v/i.* se plaindre; gémir; *v/t.* dire (*qch.*) d'un ton dolent; **2.** plainte *f*; cri *m* dolent.

whin·ny ['wini] hennir.

whip [wip] **1.** *v/t.* fouetter (*q., qch., de la crème*); *fig.* corriger; *fig. pluie*: cingler (*le visage etc.*); *fig. surt. Am.* vaincre; battre (*des œufs*); *cost.* surjeter; ⚓ surlier (*un cordage*); *avec adv. ou prp.*: mouvoir (*qch.*) vivement *ou* brusquement; ~ *away* chasser à coups de fouet; ~ enlever vivement (à, *from*); *parl.* ~ *in* appeler; ~ *off* chasser; enlever (*qch.*) vivement; ~ *on* faire avancer à coups de fouet; *cost.* attacher à points roulés; ~ *up* stimuler; saisir vivement; *parl.* faire passer un appel urgent à (*q.*); *cuis.* ~*ped cream* crème *f* Chantilly; *v/i.* fouetter; ~ *round* se retourner vivement; **2.** fouet *m*; cocher *m*; *parl.* chef *m* de file; *parl.* appel *m* aux membres du parti; '~-**cord** mèche *f* de fouet; corde *f* à fouet; '~-'**hand** main *f* droite (*du cocher*); *have the* ~ *of* avoir la haute main sur (*q.*).

whip·per ['wipə] fouetteur (-euse *f*) *m*; '~-'**in** *chasse*: piqueur *m*; *parl.* chef *m* de file; '~-**snap·per** freluquet *m*; moucheron *m*.

whip·pet *zo.* ['wipit] *lévrier de course*: whippet *m*; ⚔ char *m* léger.

whip·ping ['wipiŋ] fouettage *m*; fouettement *m*; fouettée *f*; '~-**boy** F tête *f* de Turc; '~-**top** *jouet*: sabot *m*.

whip-round *Brit.* F ['wipraund]: *have a* ~ faire une collecte.

whip-saw ⊕ ['wipsɔ:] scie *f* à chantourner, scie *f* de long.

whirl [wə:l] **1.** (faire) tournoyer; *v/i.* tourbillonner; **2.** tourbillon(nement) *m*; **whirl·i·gig** ['~igig] tourniquet *m*; manège *m* de chevaux de bois; *fig.* tourbillon *m* (*d'eau*); '**whirl·pool** tourbillon *m*; gouffre *m*; **whirl·wind** ['~wind] trombe *f*, tourbillon *m* (*de vent*); **whirl·y·bird** ['~i'bə:d] *Am.* F helicoptère *m*, F banane *f*.

whir(r) [wə:] **1.** tourner en ronronnant; vrombir; siffler; **2.** bruissement *m* (*des ailes*); ronflement *m*; vrombissement *m*; sifflement *m*.

whisk [wisk] **1.** époussette *f*; verge(tte) *f*; *cuis.* fouet *m*; **2.** *v/t.* épousseter; agiter; *cuis.* fouetter, battre; ~ *away* enlever d'un geste rapide; *v/i.* aller comme un trait *ou* à toute vitesse; '**whisk·er** *zo.* moustache *f*; *usu.* (*a pair of*) ~*s pl.* (des) favoris *m/pl.*

whis·k(e)y ['wiski] whisky *m*.

whis·per ['wispə] **1.** *vt/i.* chuchoter; *v/i.* parler bas; murmurer; susurrer; **2.** chuchotement *m*; *fig.* bruit *m*; '**whis·per·er** chuchoteur (-euse *f*) *m*.

whist[1] [wist] chut!

whist[2] [~] *jeu de cartes*: whist *m*.

whis·tle ['wisl] **1.** siffler; **2.** sifflement *m*; sifflet *m*; F gorge *f*; '~-**stop** *Am.* petite station *f*.

whit[1] *poét.* [wit] brin *m*; *not a* ~ ne ... aucunement.

Whit[2] [~] de la Pentecôte.

white [wait] **1.** blanc(he *f*); blême, pâle; F pur, innocent; *Am.* loyal (-aux *m/pl.*); ⚒ ~ *arms pl.* armes *f/pl.* blanches; ⊕ ~ *bronze* métal *m* blanc; ~ *coffee* café *m* crème *ou* au lait; ~ *heat* chaude *f ou* chaleur *f* blanche; ~ *lead* blanc *m* de plomb; ~ *lie* mensonge *m* innocent; ~ *meat* viande *f* blanche; ✝ ~ *sale* exposition *f* de blanc; ~ *war* guerre *f* économique; *Am.* ~ *way* rue *f* commerçante éclairée à giorno; **2.** blanc *m*; couleur *f* blanche; *typ.* ligne *f* de blanc; '~-**bait** *icht.* blanchaille *f*; ~ *book* *pol.* livre *m* blanc; '**white-col·lar** d'employé de bureau; ~ *job* emploi *m* dans un bureau; ~ *worker* col *m* blanc; '~-'**hot** chauffé à blanc; '~-**liv·ered** pusillanime; '**whit·en** *v/t.* blanchir (*a. fig.*); blanchir à la chaux; ⊕ étamer (*du métal*); *v/i.* blanchir;

pâlir (*personne*); '**whit·en·er** blanchisseur *m*; '**white·ness** blancheur
f; pâleur *f*; '**whit·en·ing** blanchiment *m*; *cheveux*: blanchissement *m*;
métal: étamage *m*.

white...: '**~smith** ferblantier *m*;
serrurier *m*; '**~wash 1.** blanc *m* de
chaux; badigeon *m* blanc; **2.** blanchir à la chaux; *fig.* blanchir; '**~-
wash·er** badigeonneur *m*; *fig.*
apologiste *m*.

whith·er *poét.* ['wiðə] où.

whit·ing ['waitiŋ] blanc *m* d'Espagne; *icht.* merlan *m*.

whit·ish ['waitiʃ] blanchâtre.

whit·low ['witlou] panaris *m*.

Whit·sun ['witsn] de la Pentecôte;
~day ['wit'sʌndi] dimanche *m* de
la Pentecôte; **~tide** ['witsntaid]
(fête *f* de) la Pentecôte *f*.

whit·tle ['witl] amenuiser; *fig.* ~
away (*ou down*) rogner, réduire
petit à petit.   [brun; *fig.* terne.\
whit·y-brown ['waiti'braun] gris-\

whiz(z) [wiz] **1.** siffler; ~ *past*
passer à toute vitesse; **2.** sifflement
m.

who [hu:] **1.** *pron. interr.* qui (est-ce
qui); quelle personne; lequel, laquelle, lesquels, lesquelles; Who's
Who le Bottin mondain (=*annuaire
des notabilités*); **2.** *pron. rel.* [*a.* hu]
qui; lequel, laquelle, lesquels, lesquelles; celui (celle, ceux *pl.*) qui.

whoa [wou] ho!

who·dun·(n)it *sl.* [hu:'dʌnit] roman
m ou film *m* policier.

who·ev·er [hu:'evə] celui qui; quiconque; qui que (*sbj.*).

whole [houl] **1.** □ entier (-ère *f*);
complet (-ète *f*); tout (tous *m/pl.*);
Am. F made out of ~ *cloth* inventé
de toutes pièces; *Am. sl.* go the ~
hog aller jusqu'au bout; *pol.*
~hogger jusqu'au-boutiste *m*; ~
milk lait *m* entier; **2.** tout *m*,
ensemble *m*; the ~ *of London* le tout
Londres; (up)on the ~ à tout
prendre; somme toute; '**~bound**
relié pleine peau; '**~-heart·ed** □
sincère, qui vient du cœur; '**~-
length** (*a.* ~ *portrait*) portrait *m*
en pied; '**~-meal** complet (-ète *f*)
(*pain*); '**~sale 1.** (*usu.* ~ *trade*)
(vente *f* en) gros *m*; **2.** en gros; de
gros; F *fig.* en masse; '**~-sal·er**
grossiste *mf*; **whole·some** □ ['~-
səm] sain, salubre; '**whole-time**

de toute la journée; pour toute la
semaine.

whol·ly ['houli] *adv.* tout à fait,
complètement; intégralement.

whom [hu:m; hum] *accusatif de* who.

whoop [hu:p] **1.** houp *m/inv.*; cri *m*;
🎗 quinte *f*; **2.** pousser des houp *ou*
cris; *Am. sl.* ~ *it up* for faire de
la réclame pour, louer jusqu'aux
astres; **whoop·ee** *Am.* F ['wupi:]
bombe *f*, noce *f*; *make* ~ faire la
bombe; faire du chahut; **whoop·
ing-cough** 🎗 ['hu:piŋkɔf] coqueluche *f*.

whop *sl.* [wɔp] rosser; battre;
'**whop·per** *sl.* personne *f ou* chose
f énorme; *surt.* gros mensonge *m*;
'**whop·ping** *sl.* colossal (-aux
m/pl.), énorme.

whore V [hɔ:] prostituée *f*, putain *f*.

whorl [wə:l] ⊕ *fuseau*: volant *m*; ♀
verticille *m*; *zo.* volute *f*.

whor·tle·ber·ry ♀ ['wə:tlberi] airelle *f*; *red* ~ airelle *f* rouge.

whose [hu:z] *génitif de* who; **who-
so·ev·er** [hu:sou'evə] celui qui;
quiconque; qui que (*sbj.*).

why [wai] **1.** pourquoi?; pour quelle
raison?; ~ *so?* pourquoi cela?;
2. tiens!; eh bien!; vraiment.

wick [wik] mèche *f*.

wick·ed □ ['wikid] mauvais, méchant; *co.* fripon(ne *f*); '**wick·ed-
ness** méchanceté *f*.

wick·er ['wikə] en *ou* d'osier; ~ *basket* panier *m* d'osier; ~ *chair* fauteuil *m* en osier; ~ *furniture* meubles
m/pl. en osier; '**~work 1.** vannerie
f; **2.** *see* wicker.

wick·et ['wikit] guichet *m* (*a.
cricket*); barrière *f* (*d'un jardin*).

wide [waid] **1.** *adj.* (*a.* □) large;
étendu, ample, vaste; répandu
(*influence*); grand (*différence etc.*);
loin (de, *of*); *cricket*: écarté; *3 feet
~ large de 3 pieds*; **2.** *adv.* loin; à
de grands intervalles; largement; ~
awake tout éveillé; '**~-an·gle** *phot.*:
~ *lense* (objectif *m*) grand angulaire *m*; **~-a·wake** F **1.** ['waidə'weik]
averti, malin (-igne *f*); **2.** ['waidə-
weik] chapeau *m* (en feutre) à larges
bords; **wid·en** ['waidn] (s')élargir;
(s')agrandir; '**wide·ness** largeur *f*;
'**wide-'o·pen** grand ouvert; écarté
(*jambes*); *Am. sl.* qui manque de
discipline *ou* fermeté; '**wide·
spread** répandu.

wid·ow ['widou] veuve *f*; **'wid-owed** veuf (veuve *f*); *fig.* privé (de, of); **'wid·ow·er** veuf *m*; **wid·ow-hood** ['ˏhud] veuvage *m*.

width [widθ] largeur *f*; ampleur *f*.

wield *poét.* [wi:ld] manier (*l'épée, la plume*); tenir (*le sceptre*); *fig.* exercer (*le contrôle etc.*).

wife [waif] (*pl.* **wives**) femme *f*; épouse *f*; **'wife·ly** d'épouse.

wig¹ [wig] perruque *f*; postiche *m*; *attr.* à perruque; de perruques.

wig² F [ˏ] **1.** (*ou* **'wig·ging**) verte semonce *f*; **2.** laver la tête à (*q.*).

wig·gle ['wigl] agiter, remuer.

wight *co.* [wait] personne *f*, individu *m*.

wig·wam ['wigwæm] wigwam *m*.

wild [waild] **1.** □ sauvage; *p.ext.* insensé, fou (fol *devant une voyelle ou un h muet*; folle *f*); orageux (-euse *f*); effaré (*air, yeux*); *run* ~ courir en liberté; vagabonder; se dissiper; ♀ retourner à l'état sauvage; s'étendre de tous côtés; ~ *talk* propos *m/pl.* en l'air; *fig.* ~ *for* (*ou about*) passionné pour (*qch.*); **2.** (*ou* ~*s pl.*) *see* wilderness; **'wild·cat 1.** *zo.* chat *m* sauvage; *Am.* entreprise *f* risquée; *surt. Am.* (*ou* **'wild·cat·ing**) forage *m* dans un champ (*de pétrole*) non encore exploré; **2.** *fig.* risqué; hors horaire (*train*); illégal (-aux *m/pl.*); ~ *strike* grève *f* sauvage; **wil·der·ness** ['wildənis] désert *m*; pays *m* inculte; **wild·fire** ['waildfaiə]: *like* ~ comme l'éclair; **'wild-goose chase** *fig.* poursuite *f* vaine; **'wild·ing** ♀ plante *f* sauvage; **'wild·ness** état *m* sauvage; férocité *f*; folie *f*; air *m* égaré.

wile [wail] **1.** artifice *m*; *usu.* ~*s pl.* ruses *f/pl.*; **2.** séduire; ~ *away see* while 2.

wil·ful □ ['wilful] obstiné, entêté.

wil·i·ness ['wailinis] astuce *f*.

will [wil] **1.** volonté *f*; gré *m*; testament *m*; *at* ~ à volonté; *at one's own free* ~ selon son bon plaisir; *with a* ~ de bon cœur; **2.** [*irr.*] *v/aux.* (*défectif*) usité pour former le fut.; *he* ~ *come* il viendra; il viendra avec plaisir; il veut bien venir; *I* ~ *do it* je le ferai; je veux bien le faire; **3.** *prét. et. p.p.* **willed** *v/t.* † *Dieu, souverain:* vouloir, ordonner (*qch.*); ⚖ léguer; **willed**

disposé (à *inf.*, *to inf.*); *strong-*~ de forte volonté.

will·ing □ ['wiliŋ] de bonne volonté; bien disposé, prêt (à, *to*); *I am* ~ *to believe* je veux bien croire; ~*ly adv.* volontiers; de bon cœur; **'will·ing·ness** bonne volonté *f*; empressement *m*; complaisance *f*.

will-o'-the-wisp ['wiləðwisp] feu *m* follet.

wil·low ['wilou] ♀ saule *m*; F *cricket:* batte *f*; ⊕ effilocheuse *f*; **'~-herb** ♀ épilobe *m* à épi, F osier *m* fleuri; **'wil·low·y** couvert *ou* bordé de saules; *fig.* svelte, souple, élancé.

will·pow·er ['wilpauə] volonté *f*.

wil·ly-nil·ly ['wili'nili] bon gré mal gré.

wilt¹ † [wilt] *2me personne du sg. de* will 2.

wilt² [~] (se) flétrir; *v/i.* se faner; *fig.* languir; *sl.* se dégonfler.

Wil·ton car·pet ['wiltn'ka:pit] tapis *m* Wilton (= *tapis de haute laine*).

wily □ ['waili] astucieux (-euse *f*), rusé.

wim·ple ['wimpl] guimpe *f* (*de religieuse*).

win [win] **1.** [*irr.*] *v/t.* gagner; remporter (*un prix, une victoire*); acquérir; ⚒ *sl.* récupérer; amener (*q.*) (à *inf.*, *to inf.*); ~ *s.o. over* attirer *q.* à son parti; convertir *q.*; *v/i.* gagner; remporter la victoire; ~ *through* parvenir (à, *to*); **2.** *sp.* victoire *f*.

wince [wins] **1.** faire une grimace de douleur; sourciller; **2.** crispation *f*.

winch [wintʃ] manivelle *f*; treuil *m* (*de hissage*).

wind¹ [wind, *poét. a.* waind] **1.** vent *m* (*a.* ⚛); *fig.* haleine *f*, souffle *m*; ♪ *instruments m/pl.* à vent; *be in the* ~ se préparer; *have a long* ~ avoir du souffle; *fig. throw to the* ~*s* abandonner; F *raise the* ~ se procurer de l'argent; *sl. get the* ~ *up* avoir la frousse; *it's an ill* ~ *that blows nobody good* à quelque chose malheur est bon; **2.** *chasse:* flairer (*le gibier*); faire perdre le souffle à (*q.*); essouffler; *be* ~*ed* être à bout de souffle; ♪ [waind] sonner du cor.

wind² [waind] [*irr.*] *v/t.* tourner; enrouler; ~ *up* remonter (*un horloge, un ressort etc.*); *fig.* terminer, finir; † liquider; clôturer (*un compte*); *v/i.* tourner; (*a. ~ o.s., ~ one's way*) serpenter; *fig. ~ up* se terminer; s'achever.

wind... [wind]: '**~·bag** *péj.* moulin *m* à paroles; '**~·bound** ⚓ retardé par le vent; retenu par le vent; '**~·cheat·er** *cost.* anorak *m*; '**~·fall** fruit *m* abattu par le vent; *fig.* aubaine *f*; '**~·gauge** indicateur *m* de pression du vent; '**wind·i·ness** temps *m* venteux; F verbosité *f*; *sl.* frousse *f*.

wind·ing ['waindiŋ] **1.** mouvement *m ou* cours *m* sinueux; replis *m/pl.*; *tex.* bobinage *m*; ⚡ enroulement *m*; ⊕ gauchissement *m*; **2.** □ sinueux (-euse *f*); qui serpente; *~ staircase* (*ou stairs pl.*) escalier *m* tournant; '**~-sheet** linceul *m*; '**~-'up** remontage *m*; *fig.* fin *f*; ✝ liquidation *f*.

wind·in·stru·ment ♪ ['windinstrumənt] instrument *m* à vent.

wind·jam·mer ['winddʒæmə] ⚓ *sl.* voilier *m*.   [guindeau *m*.\

wind·lass ['windləs] ⊕ treuil *m*; ⚓/

wind·mill ['windmil] moulin *m* à vent; *~ plane* autogire *m*.

win·dow ['windou] fenêtre *f*; ✝ vitrine *f*, devanture *f*; *mot. etc.* glace *f*; *théâ. etc.* guichet *m*; *~ display* étalage *m*; *~ goods* articles *m/pl.* en devanture; '**~-dress·ing** art *m* de l'étalage; arrangement *m* de la vitrine; *fig.* façade *f*, camouflage *m*, trompe-l'œil *m/inv.*, décor *m* de théâtre; '**win·dowed** à fenêtre(s).

win·dow...: '**~·en·ve·lope** enveloppe *f* à fenêtre; '**~-frame** châssis *m* de fenêtre; '**~-shade** *Am.* store *m*; '**~-shop** = *go ~ping* faire du lèche-vitrines; '**~-shut·ter** volet *m*; '**~-sill** rebord *m* de fenêtre.

wind... [wind]: '**~-pipe** *anat.* trachée-artère (*pl.* trachées-artères) *f*; '**~-screen**, *Am.* '**~-shield** pare-brise *m/inv.*; *~ wiper* essuie-glace *m*; '**~-tun·nel** ✈ tunnel *m* aérodynamique.

wind·ward ['windwəd] **1.** au vent; **2.** côté *m* au vent.

wind·y □ ['windi] venteux (-euse *f*) (*a.* ✈); exposé au vent; *fig.* vain; *sl.* qui a le trac.

wine [wain] vin *m*; '**~-grow·er** viticulteur *m*; vigneron *m*; '**~-mer·chant** négociant *m* en vins; '**~-press** pressoir *m*; '**~-vault** cave *f*, caveau *m*.

wing [wiŋ] **1.** aile *f* (*a. fig.*, ✗, ⚓, ✈, ⚡, ⚙, *mot.*, *sp.*); vol *m*, essor *m*; F *co.* bras *m*; *foot. personne:* ailier *m*; *porte:* battant *m*; ⊕ oreille *f* (*d'un écrou*); *~s pl.* coulisse *f*; *take ~* s'envoler; *prendre son vol*; *be on the ~* voler; *fig.* partir; **2.** *v/t.* empenner; voler; blesser à l'aile *ou fig.* au bras; *v/i.* voler; '**~-case**, '**~-sheath** *zo.* élytre *m*; '**~-chair** fauteuil *m* à oreillettes; **winged** [~d] ailé; blessé à l'aile *ou* au bras; *~ word* parole *f* ailée; '**wing·span**, '**wing·spread** envergure *f*.

wink [wiŋk] **1.** clignement *m* d'œil; clin *m* d'œil; F *not get a ~ of sleep* ne pas fermer l'œil de toute la nuit; F *tip s.o. the ~* faire signe de l'œil à q.; prévenir q.; **2.** *v/i.* cligner les yeux; clignoter (*lumière*); *v/t.* cligner de (*l'œil*); signifier (*qch.*) par un clin d'œil; *~ at* cligner de l'œil à (*q.*); fermer les yeux sur (*qch.*).

win·ner ['winə] gagnant(e *f*) *m*; *sp.* vainqueur *m* (=*homme ou femme*).

win·ning ['winiŋ] **1.** □ gagnant; *fig.* engageant; **2.**: *~s pl.* gains *m/pl.* (*au jeu etc.*); '**~-post** *sp.* poteau *m* d'arrivée.

win·now ['winou] vanner (*le grain*); *fig.* examiner minutieusement.

win·ter ['wintə] **1.** hiver *m*; *~ sports pl.* sports *m/pl.* d'hiver; **2.** hiverner; **win·ter·ize** ['~təraiz] préparer pour l'hiver; **win·try** ['wintri] d'hiver; *fig.* glacial (-als *m/pl.*).

wipe [waip] **1.** essuyer; nettoyer; *~ off* essuyer, enlever; liquider (*une dette*); *~ out* essuyer; *fig.* effacer; exterminer; **2.** coup *m* de torchon *etc.*; F taloche *f* (= *coup*); '**wip·er** essuyeur (-euse *f*) *m*; torchon *m*.

wire ['waiə] **1.** fil *m* (de fer); *Am.* F dépêche *f*; *attr.* en *ou* de fil de fer; **2.** *v/t.* munir d'un fil métallique; ⚡ équiper (*une maison*); (*a. v/i.*) *tél.* télégraphier; '**~-drawn** tréfilé (*métal*); trait (*or etc.*); '**~-gauge** ⊕ jauge *f* pour fils métalliques; '**~-haired** à poil dur (*chien*); '**wire·less** **1.** □ sans fil; de T.S.F., de radio; *on the ~* à la radio; *~ control* radioguidage *m*; *~* (*message ou telegram*) radiogramme *m*; *~* (*telegraphy*) radiotélégraphie *f*; *télégraphie f sans fil*; (*air*) *~ operator* sans-filiste *mf*; opérateur *m* de T.S.F.; *~ pirate radio:* auditeur *m* illicite; *~*

(set) poste *m* (de radio); ~ station poste *m* émetteur; **2.** radiotélégraphier; **'wire-'net·ting** treillis *m* métallique; grillage *m*; **'wire-'pull·er** *fig.* intrigant(e *f*) *m*; **'wire-'tap·ping** *téléph.* mise *f* sur écoute.

wir·ing ['waiəriŋ] grillage *m* métallique; ⚡ câblage *m*; pose *f* des fils; *radio:* montage *m*; ⚡ croisillonnage *m*; ⚡ ~ *diagram* plan *m* de pose; **'wir·y** □ raide (*cheveux*); sec (sèche *f*) et nerveux (-euse *f*) (*personne*).

wis·dom ['wizdəm] sagesse *f*; ~ tooth dent *f* de sagesse.

wise[1] □ [waiz] sage; prudent; ~ crack *Am.* F bon mot *m*, saillie *f*; *Am. sl.* ~ *guy* finaud *m*, monsieur *m* je-sais-tout; *Am.* put *s.o.* ~ mettre q. à la page; avertir q. (de *to*, on).

wise[2] † [~] façon *f*; guise *f*.

wise·a·cre ['waizeikə] prétendu sage *m*; pédant(e *f*) *m*; **'wise-crack** *Am.* F faire de l'esprit.

wish [wiʃ] **1.** vouloir, désirer; souhaiter; ~ *s.o. joy* féliciter q. (de, of); ~ *for* désirer, vouloir, souhaiter (*qch.*); ~ *s.o. well* (*ill*) vouloir du bien (mal) à q.; **2.** vœu *m*, souhait *m*; désir *m*; *good* ~*es pl.* souhaits *m/pl.*, meilleurs vœux *m/pl.*; **wish·ful** □ ['~ful] désireux (-euse *f*) (de of, to); **'wish(·ing)-bone** *volaille:* lunette *f*.

wish-wash F ['wiʃwɔʃ] lavasse *f*; **'wish·y-wash·y** F fade, insipide.

wisp [wisp] bouchon *m* (*de paille*); mèche *f* folle (*de cheveux*).

wist·ful □ ['wistful] pensif (-ive *f*) d'envie; désenchanté.

wit [wit] **1.** (*a.* ~*s pl.*) esprit *m*; ~*s pl.* raison *f*, intelligence *f*; *personne:* homme *m* ou femme *f* d'esprit; *be at one's* ~*'s end* ne plus savoir que faire; *have one's* ~*s about one* avoir toute sa présence d'esprit; *live by one's* ~*s* vivre d'expédients ou d'industrie; *be out of one's* ~*s* avoir perdu la raison; **2.**: *to* ~ à savoir; c'est-à-dire.

witch [witʃ] sorcière *f*; *fig.* jeune charmeuse *f*; **'~·craft**, **'witch·er·y** sorcellerie *f*; *fig.* magie *f*; **'witch-hunt** *pol. Am. fig.* chasse *f* aux sorcières.

with [wið] avec; de; à; par; malgré; *sl.* ~ *it* dans le vent; *it is just so* ~ *me* il en va de même pour moi.

with·al † [wi'ðɔ:l] **1.** *adv.* aussi, de plus; **2.** *prp.* avec *etc.*

with·draw [wið'drɔ:] [*irr.* (draw)] (se) retirer (de, from); **with'draw·al** retraite *f*; rappel *m*; ✗ repli(ement) *m*; retrait *m* (d'argent).

withe [wiθ] brin *m* ou branche *f* d'osier.

with·er ['wiðə] (*souv.* ~ *up*, *away*) (se) flétrir; (se) dessécher; *v/i.* dépérir (*personne*); **'with·er·ing** □ *fig.* foudroyant, écrasant.

with·ers ['wiðəz] *pl.* garrot *m*.

with·hold [wið'hould] [*irr.* (hold)] retenir, empêcher (q. de *inf.*, *s.o.* from *gér.*); cacher, refuser (à q., from *s.o.*); *Am.* ~*ing tax* retenue *f* ou impôt *m* retenu à la source; **with'in** *poét.* **1.** *adv.* à l'intérieur, au dedans; à la maison; from ~ de l'intérieur; **2.** *prp.* à l'intérieur de, en dedans de; ~ *doors* à la maison; ~ *10 minutes* en moins de dix minutes; ~ *a mile* à moins d'un mille (de, of); dans un rayon d'un mille; ~ *call* (*ou hearing*) à (la) portée de la voix ou d'oreille; ~ *sight* en vue; **with'out 1.** *adv. poét.* à l'extérieur, au dehors; from ~ de l'extérieur, du dehors; **2.** *prp.* sans; *poét.* en dehors de; **with'stand** [*irr.* (stand)] résister à; supporter.

with·y ['wiði] *see* withe.

wit·less □ ['witlis] sot(te *f*) faible d'esprit; sans intelligence.

wit·ling *péj.* ['witliŋ] petit *ou iro.* bel esprit *m*.

wit·ness ['witnis] **1.** témoignage *m*; *personne:* témoin *m*; *bear* ~ témoigner, porter témoignage (de *to*, of); *in* ~ *of* en témoignage de; **2.** *v/t.* être témoin de; assister à; attester (*un acte etc.*); témoigner de; *v/i.* témoigner; ~ *for* (*against*) témoigner en faveur de (contre); **'~-box**, *Am.* ~ *stand* barre *f* des témoins.

wit·ted ['witid] *quick-*~ à l'esprit vif; **wit·ti·cism** ['~tisizm] trait *m* d'esprit, bon mot *m*; **'wit·ti·ness** esprit *m*; **'wit·ting·ly** à dessein; en connaissance de cause; **'wit·ty** □ spirituel(le *f*).

wives [waivz] *pl. de* wife.

wiz *Am. sl.* [wiz], **wiz·ard** ['~əd] **1.** sorcier *m*, magicien *m*; **2.** *fig. sl.* magnifique; **wiz·ard·ry** sorcellerie *f*, magie *f*.

wiz·en(·ed) ['wizn(d)] tatatiné; parcheminé (*visage etc.*).

wo(a) [wou] ho!

woad ♀,⊕ [woud] guède *f*.

wob·ble ['wɔbl] ballotter; trembler; chevroter (*voix*); ⊕ branler; *mot.* *wheel that* ~s roue *f* dévoyée.

woe *poét. ou co.* [wou] chagrin *m*; malheur *m*; ~ *is me!* pauvre de moi!; '~-**be·gone** triste, désolé; **woe·ful** □ *poét. ou co.* ['~ful] triste, affligé; de malheur; '**woe·ful·ness** tristesse *f*; malheur *m*.

wog *sl.* [wɔg] métèque *m*.

woke [wouk] *prét. et p.p. de* wake² 1.

wold [would] plaine *f* vallonnée.

wolf [wulf] 1. (*pl.* wolves) *zo.* loup *m*; *sl.* coureur *m* de cotillons, tombeur *m* de femmes; ~ *call*, ~ *whistle* sifflement *m* admiratif (*au passage d'une femme attractive*); *cry* ~ crier au loup; 2. F dévorer; '**wolf·ish** □ de loup; F *fig.* rapace.

wolf·ram *min.* ['wulfrəm] wolfram *m*; tungstène *m*.

wolves [wulvz] *pl. de* wolf 1.

wom·an ['wumən] (*pl.* women) femme *f*; young ~ jeune femme *f ou* fille *f*; ~'s (*ou* women's) *rights pl.* droits *m/pl.* de la femme; *attr.* femme ...; de femme(s); ~ *doctor* femme *f* médecin; ~ *student* étudiante *f*; '~-**hat·er** misogyne *m*; **wom·an·hood** ['~hud] état *m* de femme; *coll.* les femmes *f/pl.*; *reach* ~ devenir femme; '**wom·an·ish** □ féminin; efféminé (*homme*); '**wom·an·kind** les femmes *f/pl.*; '**wom·an·like** 1. *adj.* de femme; 2. *adv.* en femme; '**wom·an·ly** féminin.

womb [wu:m] *anat.* matrice *f*; *fig.* sein *m*.

wom·en ['wimin] *pl. de* woman; *votes pl.* for ~ suffrage *m* féminin; ~'s *lib* movement *m* de libération de la femme; ~'s *rights pl.* droits *m/pl.* de la femme; *sp.* ~'s *team* équipe *f* féminine; ~'s *single tennis*: simple *m* dames; **wom·en·folk** ['~fouk] *pl.*, '**wom·en·kind** les femmes *f/pl.* (*surt. d'une famille*).

won [wʌn] *prét. et p.p. de* win 1.

won·der ['wʌndə] 1. merveille *f*, prodige *m*; étonnement *m*; 2. s'étonner, s'émerveiller (de, *at*); se demander (si *whether*, *if*); **won·der·ful** □ ['~ful] merveilleux (-euse *f*), étonnant; admirable; '**won·der·ing** 1. □ émerveillé, étonné; 2. étonnement *m*; '**won·der-struck** émer-

veillé; '**won·der-work·er** faiseur (-euse *f*) *m* de prodiges.

won·drous □ *poét.* ['wʌndrəs] merveilleux (-euse *f*), étonnant.

wonk·y *sl.* ['wɔŋki] patraque (= *branlant*).

won't [wount] = will not.

wont [wount] 1. *préd.* habitué; be ~ *to* (*inf.*) avoir l'habitude de (*inf.*); 2. coutume *f*, habitude *f*; '**wont·ed** accoutumé.

woo [wu:] faire la cour à; courtiser (*a. fig.*); solliciter (de *inf.*, *to inf.*).

wood [wud] bois *m*; fût *m*, tonneau *m*; ♪ bois *m/pl.*; *sp.* ~s *pl.* boules *f/pl.*; F *touch* ~! touchez du bois!; 2. *attr. souv.* des bois; '~·**bine**, *a.* ~·**bind** ♀ ['~bain(d)] chèvrefeuille *m* des bois; *Am.* vigne *f* vierge; '~-**carv·ing** sculpture *f* sur bois; '~-**cock** *orn.* (*pl. usu.* ~) bécasse *f*; '~·**craft** connaissance *f* de la chasse à courre *ou* de la forêt; '~·**cut** gravure *f* sur bois; '~-**cut·ter** bûcheron *m*; graveur *m* sur bois; '**wood·ed** boisé; '**wood·en** en bois; de bois (*a. fig.*); *fig.* raide; '**wood-en·grav·er** graveur *m* sur bois; '**wood-en·grav·ing** gravure *f* sur bois (=*objet et art*); '**wood·i·ness** caractère *m* ligneux.

wood...: '~·**land** 1. bois *m*, pays *m* boisé; 2. sylvestre; des bois; '~·**lark** *orn.* alouette *f* des bois; '~·**louse** *zo.* cloporte *m*; '~·**man** garde *m* forestier; bûcheron *m*; † trappeur *m*; '~·**peck·er** *orn.* pic *m*; '~·**pile** tas *m* de bois; '~-**pulp** pâte *f* de bois; '~-**ruff** ♀ aspérule *f* odorante; '~-**shav·ings** *pl.* copeaux *m/pl.* de bois; '~-**shed** bûcher *m*; ~-**wind** ♪ ['~wind] (*ou* ~ *instruments pl.*) bois *m/pl.*; '~-**work** (*surt.* △) boiserie *f*, charpente *f*; menuiserie *f*; travail (*pl.* -aux) *m* du bois; '~-**work·ing ma·chine** machine *f* à bois; '**wood·y** boisé; couvert de bois; des bois; sylvestre; ♀ ligneux (-euse *f*); *fig.* sourd, mat; '**wood·yard** chantier *m* (de bois à brûler).

woo·er ['wu:ə] prétendant *m*.

woof [wu:f] *see* weft.

wool [wul] laine *f* (*fig. co.* = *cheveux crépus*); *dyed in the* ~ teint en laine; *fig.* convaincu; *pur* sang *adj./inv.*; '~-**gath·er·ing** 1. F rêvasserie *f*; *go* ~ avoir l'esprit absent, être distrait; 2. distrait; '**wool·(l)en** 1. de laine;

2.: ~s pl. laines f/pl.; draps m/pl.; tissus m/pl. de laine; **'wool·(1)y 1.** laineux (-euse f); de laine; cotonneux (-euse f) (fruit); peint. flou; fig. mou (mol devant une voyelle ou un h muet; molle f); fig. imprécis (idée); **2.** woollies pl. (vêtements m/pl. en) tricot m; lainages m/pl.

wool...: '~sack parl. siège m du ou dignité f de Lord Chancelier; '~stapler négociant m en laine; '~work tapisserie f.

wop Am. sl. [wɔp] immigrant(e f) m italien(ne); Italien(ne f) m.

word [wɜːd] **1.** usu. mot m; parole f (a. fig.); ordre m; ✕ mot m d'ordre; ~s pl. paroles f/pl.; fig. termes m/pl.; opéra: livret m; chanson: paroles f/pl.; gramm. ~ order ordre des mots; ~ processing traitement des mots; by ~ of mouth de vive voix; eat one's ~s se rétracter; have ~s se disputer (avec, with); leave ~ that faire dire que; send (bring) s.o. ~ of s.th. faire (venir) dire qch. à q.; be as good as one's ~ tenir sa parole; take s.o. at his ~ prendre q. au mot; **2.** rédiger; formuler par écrit; ~ed as follows ainsi conçu; '~book vocabulaire m, lexique m; 'word·iness verbosité f; 'word·ing rédaction f; langage m, termes m/pl.; 'word·'per·fect théâ. qui connaît parfaitement son rôle (école: sa leçon); 'word-split·ting ergotage m.

word·y □ ['wɜːdi] verbeux (-euse f), diffus.

wore [wɔː] prét. de wear 1.

work [wɜːk] **1.** travail m; tâche f, besogne f; ouvrage m (a. littérature, couture, etc.); emploi m; œuvre f; ⊕ ~s usu. sg. usine f, atelier m; horloge: mouvement m; public ~s pl. travaux m/pl. publics; ~ of art œuvre f d'art; ~s pl. of Keats l'œuvre m de Keats; at ~ au travail; en marche; fig. en jeu; be in ~ avoir du travail; be out of ~ chômer, être sans travail; make sad ~ of s'acquitter peu brillamment de; make short ~ of expédier (qch.); put s.o. out of ~ priver q. de travail; set to ~ se mettre au travail; set s.o. to ~ faire travailler q.; ~s council comité m de directeurs et de délégués syndicaux; **2.** [irr.] v/i. travailler; fonctionner, aller (machine); fig. réussir; se crisper (bouche); ~ at travailler (à); ~ out

sortir peu à peu; s'élever (à, at); aboutir; v/t. faire travailler; faire fonctionner ou marcher (une machine); diriger (un projet); opérer, amener; broder (un dessin etc.); ouvrer (du métal); façonner (du bois); faire (un calcul); résoudre (un problème); exploiter (une mine); ~ mischief semer le mal ou la discorde; ~ off se dégager de; cuver (sa colère); ✝ écouler (un stock); ~ one's way se frayer un chemin; ~ out mener à bien; élaborer, développer; résoudre; ~ up développer; se faire (une clientèle); exciter, émouvoir; élaborer (une idée, un sujet); phot. retoucher; préparer.

work·a·ble □ ['wɜːkəbl] réalisable (projet); ouvrable (bois etc.); exploitable (mine); 'work·a·day de tous les jours; fig. prosaïque; **work·a·hol·ic** F ['wɜːkəˈhɔlik] bourreau m de travail; 'work·bench établi m; 'work·day jour m ouvrable; 'work·er travailleur (-euse f) m; ouvrier (-ère f) m; ~s pl. classes f/pl. laborieuses; ouvriers m/pl.; social ~ assistante f sociale; 'work·force main-d'œuvre f, les ouvriers m/pl.; 'work·house hospice m, asile m des pauvres; Am. maison f de correction; 'work·ing **1.** fonctionnement m; manœuvre f; exploitation f; ~s pl. mécanisme m; **2.** qui travaille; qui fonctionne; de travail; in ~ order en état de service; ~ association (ou co-operation) groupe m de travailleurs; ✝ ~ capital capital m d'exploitation; ~ class classe f ouvrière; ~ committee (ou party) commission f d'enquête; ~ condition état m de fonctionnement; ~ day jour m ouvrable; journée f; ~ expenses pl. frais m/pl. généraux; ~ process mode m d'opération; ~ student étudiant m qui travaille pour gagner sa vie.

work·man ['wɜːkmən] ouvrier m, artisan m; '~·like bien travaillé, bien fait; compétent; 'work·man·ship exécution f; fini m; construction f; travail (pl. -aux) m.

work...: '~-out Am. F ['wɜːkaut] usu. sp. entraînement m (préliminaire); '~-shop atelier m; ~ place établi m; '~-'shy 1. qui renâcle à la besogne; paresseux (-euse f); 2. fainéant m; ~-to-'rule grève f du zèle; '~-wom·an ouvrière f.

world [wə:ld] monde *m*; *fig. a ~ of* beaucoup de; *in the ~* au monde; *what in the ~?* que diable?; *bring (come) into the ~* mettre (venir) au monde; *be for all the ~ like* avoir exactement l'air de (*qch., inf.*); *a ~ too wide* de beaucoup trop large; *think the ~ of* avoir une très haute opinion de; *man of the ~* homme *m* qui connaît la vie; mondain *m*; *~ champion* champion *m* du monde; *~ championship* championnat *m* du monde; *~ record* record *m* mondial; *~ record holder* recordman *m* du monde; *Am. ~ series baseball*: matches *m/pl.* entre les champions de deux ligues professionnelles; **'world·li·ness** mondanité *f*; **'world·ling** mondain(e *f*) *m*.

world·ly ['wə:ldli] du monde, de ce monde; mondain; *~ innocence* candeur *f*; naïveté *f*; *~ wisdom* sagesse *f* du siècle; '~-'wise qui connaît la vie.

world...: '~-pow·er *pol.* puissance *f* mondiale; '~-'wide universel(le *f*); mondial (-aux *m/pl.*).

worm [wə:m] **1.** ver *m* (*a. fig.*); ⊕ *alambic:* serpentin *m*; vis *f* sans fin; ⊕ spirale *f*; **2.:** *~ a secret out of s.o.* tirer un secret de q.; *~ o.s.* se glisser; *fig.* s'insinuer (dans, *into*); '~-drive ⊕ transmission *f* par vis sans fin; '~-eat·en rongé des vers; vermoulu (*bois*); '~-gear ⊕ engrenage *m* à vis sans fin; (*ou* '~-wheel) ⊕ roue *f* hélicoïdale; '~-wood armoise *f* amère; *fig.* be *~* to n'être qu'absinthe pour (*q.*); **'worm·y** plein de vers.

worn [wɔ:n] *p.p. de wear 1*; '~-'out usé; râpé (*vêtement*); épuisé (*personne*).

wor·ri·ment F ['wʌrimənt] souci *m*; **wor·rit** V ['wʌrit] (se) tourmenter, (se) tracasser; **'wor·ry 1.** *fig.* tourmenter, (se) tracasser, (s')inquiéter; *v/t.* harceler, piller (*des moutons*); **2.** ennui *m*, souci *m*, tracasserie *f*.

worse [wə:s] **1.** *adj.* pire; plus mauvais; ⚕ plus malade; *adv.* pis; plus mal; (*all*) *the ~ adv.* encore pis; *adj.* (encore) pire; *~ luck!* tant pis!; *he is none the ~ for it* il ne s'en trouve pas plus mal; **2.** quelque chose *m* de pire; le pire; *from bad to ~* de mal en pis; **'wors·en** empirer; (s')aggraver.

wor·ship ['wə:ʃip] **1.** culte *m*, adoration *f*; *your ♀* monsieur le maire *ou* juge; *place of ~* église *f*; *religion protestante:* temple *m*; **2.** adorer; **wor·ship·ful** □ ['~ful] *titre:* honorable; **'wor·ship·(p)er** adorateur (-trice *f*) *m*; *eccl.* fidèle *mf*.

worst [wə:st] **1.** *adj.* (le) pire; (le) plus mauvais; **2.** *adv.* (le) pis, (le) plus mal; **3.** *su.* le pire *m*; *at (the) ~* au pire; en tout cas; *do your ~!* faites du pis que vous pourrez!; *get the ~ of it* avoir le dessous; *if the ~ comes to the ~* en mettant les choses au pis; **4.** *v/t.* vaincre, battre.

wor·sted ['wustid] laine *f* peignée; (*a. ~ yarn*) laine *f* à tricoter; tissu *m* de laine peignée; *~ stockings pl.* bas *m/pl.* en laine peignée.

wort[1] ⚘ [wə:t] plante *f*, herbe *f*.

wort[2] [~] moût *m* (*de bière*).

worth [wə:θ] **1.** valant; *he is ~ a million £* il est riche d'un million de livres; *~ reading* qui mérite d'être lu; **2.** valeur *f*; **wor·thi·ness** ['~ðinis] mérite *m*; **'worth·less** □ ['~θlis] sans valeur, de nulle valeur; **'worth-'while** F be *~* valoir la peine; **wor·thy** □ ['wə:ði] **1.** digne (de, *of*); de mérite; **2.** personnage *m* (éminent).

would [wud] *prét. de will 2* (*a. usité pour former le cond.*).

would-be F ['wudbi:] prétendu; soidisant; affecté; *~ buyer* acheteur *m* éventuel; personne *f* qui voudrait acheter; *~ painter* personne *f* qui cherche à se faire peindre; *~ poet* poète *m* à la manque; *~ wit* prétendu bel esprit *m*; *~ worker* personne *f* qui voudrait avoir du travail.

wouldn't ['wudnt] = *would not*.

wound[1] [wu:nd] **1.** blessure *f* (*a. fig.*); plaie *f*; **2.** blesser (*a. fig.*).

wound[2] [waund] *prét. et p.p. de wind*[2]. [*p.p. de weave 1.*]

wove [wouv] *prét.,* **wo·ven** ['~vn]

wow *Am.* [wau] *théâ. sl.* grand succès *m*; *p.ext.* chose *f* épatante.

wrack[1] ⚘ [ræk] varech *m*.

wrack[2] [~] *see rack*[3].

wraith [reiθ] apparition *f*.

wran·gle ['ræŋgl] **1.** se chamailler, se disputer, se quereller; **2.** dispute *f*, querelle *f*, chamaille(rie) *f*; **'wran·gler** querelleur (-euse *f*) *m*, chamailleur (-euse *f*) *m*; *Am.* (*a. horse ~*) cowboy *m*.

wrap [ræp] **1.** *v/t.* (*souv.* ~ *up*) envelopper (de, *in*) (*a. fig.*); *fig.* be ~*ped up*
in être plongé dans; *v/i.* ~ *up* s'envelopper (dans, *in*); **2.** couverture *f*;
p.ext. pardessus *m*, châle *m*; manteau *m*; **'wrap·per** couverture *f*;
documents: chemise *f*; papier *m*
d'emballage; *cigare*: robe *f*; *cost.*
robe *f* de chambre; (*ou postal* ~)
bande *f*; **'wrap·ping** enveloppe
(-ment *m*) *f*; (*a.* ~ *paper*) papier *m*
d'emballage; **'wrap·up** *Am.* F résumé *m*.

wrath *poét. ou co.* [rɔ:θ] colère *f*;
courroux *m*; **wrath·ful** □ ['~ful]
courroucé; irrité.

wreak [ri:k] assouvir (*sa haine, sa
colère, sa vengeance*) (sur, [*up*]on).

wreath [ri:θ], *pl.* **wreaths** [~ðz]
fleurs: couronne *f*, guirlande *f*; (*a.
artificial* ~) couronne *f* de perles;
spirale *f*, volute *f* (*de fumée*); *écoss.*
amoncellement *m* (*de neige*);
wreathe [ri:ð] [*irr.*] *v/t.* couronner;
enguirlander; tresser (*des fleurs
etc.*); *v/i.* tourbillonner; s'enrouler.

wreck [rek] **1.** ⚓ naufrage *m* (*a.
fig.*); *fig.* ruine *f*; navire *m* naufragé;
2. causer le naufrage de; faire dérailler (*un train*); *fig.* faire échouer;
⚓ be ~ed faire naufrage; **'wreck·
age** débris *m/pl.*; *fig.* naufrage *m*;
wrecked naufragé; *fig.* ruiné;
'wreck·er démolisseur *m* (*a. de bâtiments*); ⚓ sauveteur *m* (*d'épaves*);
mot. Am. dépanneuse *f*, camion-grue
m (*pl.* camions-grues); *Am.* marchand *m* de voitures délabrées; † ⚓
pilleur *m* d'épaves; **'wreck·ing** démolition *f*; *Am.* ~ *company* entreprise
f de démolitions; *mot.* ~ *service* (service de) dépannage *m*.

wren *orn.* [ren] roitelet *m*.

wrench [rentʃ] **1.** tordre; arracher
(violemment) (à, *from*); forcer (*l'é-
paule, le sens*); ⊕ *open* forcer (*un couvercle etc.*); ~ *out* arracher; **2.** mouvement *m ou* effort *m* de torsion;
effort *m* violent; *fig.* déchirement *m*
de cœur; *fig.* violente douleur *f*; ⊕
clef *f* à écrous.

wrest [rest] arracher (à, *from*); fausser (*le sens*); **wres·tle** ['resl] **1.** *v/i.*
lutter; *v/t.* lutter avec *ou* contre;
2. (*ou* **'wres·tling**) lutte *f*; **'wres·
tler** lutteur *m*.

wretch [retʃ] malheureux (-euse *f*)
m; infortuné(e *f*) *m*; scélérat(e *f*) *m*;

co. fripon(ne *f*) *m*; type *m*; poor ~
pauvre diable *m*.

wretch·ed □ ['retʃid] misérable;
malheureux (-euse *f*); lamentable;
F diable de ..., sacré; **'wretch·ed·
ness** malheur *m*; misère *f*.

wrick [rik] **1.** fouler (*une cheville*);
~ *one's neck* se donner le torticolis;
2. ⚕ effort *m*; ~ *in the neck* torticolis
m.

wrig·gle ['rigl] (se) tortiller, (s')agi-
ter, (se) remuer; ~ *out of* se tirer
de.

wright [rait] *mots composés:* ouvrier
m, artisan *m*.

wring [riŋ] [*irr.*] **1.** tordre (*les mains,
le linge, le cou à une volaille*); étreindre (*la main de q.*); déchirer (*le
cœur*); ~ *s.th. from s.o.* arracher
qch. à q.; ~*ing wet* mouillé à tordre;
trempé jusqu'aux os (*personne*);
2. torsion *f*; **'wring·er**, **'wring·ing-
ma·chine** essoreuse *f*.

wrin·kle[1] ['riŋkl] **1.** *figure, eau:* ride
f; *robe:* pli *m*; rugosité *f*; **2.** (se)
rider; (se) froisser.

wrin·kle[2] F [~] tuyau *m*; bonne idée
f; ruse *f*.

wrist [rist] poignet *m*; ~ *watch* montre-
tre-bracelet (*pl.* montres-bracelets)
f; **'wrist·band** poignet *m*, manchette *f*; (*ou* **wrist·let** ['ristlit])
bracelet *m*; *sp.* bracelet *m* de force;
~*s pl.* menottes *f/pl.*; ~ *watch see
wrist watch.*

writ [rit] mandat *m*, ordonnance *f*;
acte *m* judiciaire; assignation *f*;
Holy ⚹ Écriture *f* sainte; ~ *for an
election* ordonnance *f* de procéder à
une élection; ⚹ ~ *of attachment*
ordre *m* de saisie; ~ *of execution*
exécutoire *m*.

write [rait] [*irr.*] *v/t.* écrire; rédiger
(*un article*); ~ *down* coucher par
écrit; noter; inscrire (*un nom*); ~ *off*
écrire (*une lettre etc.*) d'un trait;
† défalquer (*une dette*), réduire (*un
capital*); ~ *out* transcrire; écrire en
toutes lettres; remplir (*un chèque*);
~ *up* rédiger; écrire; prôner;
ajouter à; mettre au courant; *v/i.*
écrire; être écrivain; ~ *for* faire venir, commander; ~ *off* écrire à
(*q.*); F *nothing to* ~ *home about* rien
d'étonnant; **'~-off** annulation *f* par
écrit.

writ·er ['raitə] écrivain *m*; auteur
m; femme *f* écrivain *ou* auteur;

écoss. ~ *to the signet* notaire *m*; ~'s *cramp* (*ou palsy*) crampe *f* des écrivains.

write-up *Am.* F ['rait'ʌp] éloge *m* exagéré; compte *m* rendu.

writhe [raið] se tordre; se crisper.

writ·ing ['raitiŋ] écriture *f*; écrit *m*; ouvrage *m* littéraire; art *m* d'écrire; métier *m* d'écrivain; *attr.* d'écriture; à écrire; *in* ~ par écrit; ~ *desk* bureau *m*, secrétaire *m*; ~ *pad* sous-main *m* (*pl.* sous-mains); bloc-notes (*pl.* blocs-notes); ~ *paper* papier *m* à écrire *ou* à lettres. [(fait par) écrit.]

writ·ten ['ritn] 1. *p.p. de* write; 2.

wrong [rɔŋ] 1. □ mauvais; faux (fausse *f*); inexact; erroné; *be* ~ être faux; être mal (*de inf.*, *to inf.*); ne pas être à l'heure (*montre*); avoir tort (*personne*); *go* ~ se tromper (*a.* de chemin; *fig.* tomber dans le vice; ⊕ se détraquer; *there is something* ~ il y a quelque chose qui ne va pas *ou* qui cloche; F *what's* ~

with him? qu'est-ce qu'il a?; *on the* ~ *side of sixty* qui a dépassé la soixantaine; 2. mal *m*; tort *m*; ⚖ dommage *m*; *be in the* ~ avoir tort, être dans son tort; *put s.o. in the* ~ mettre q. dans son tort; 3. faire tort à; être injuste envers; '~'do·er méchant *m*; ⚖ délinquant(e *f*) *m*; '~'do·ing mal *m*; méfaits *m/pl.*; ⚖ infraction *f* à la loi; **wrong·ful** □ ['~ful] injuste; injustifié; préjudiciable; illégal (-aux *m/pl.*); '**wrong-'head·ed** (qui a l'esprit) pervers; '**wrong·ness** erreur *f*; inexactitude *f*; mal *m*.

wrote [rout] *prét. de* write.

wroth *poét.* [rouθ] courroucé.

wrought [rɔːt] *prét. et p.p. de* work 2; ~ *goods* produits *m/pl.* ouvrés; articles *m/pl.* apprêtés; ⊕ ~ *iron* fer *m* forgé *ou* ouvré.

wrung [rʌŋ] *prét. et p.p. de* wring 1.

wry □ [rai] tordu; de travers; *pull a* ~ *face* faire la grimace.

X

X, x [eks] X *m*, x *m*; ⅄, *a. fig.* X X *m* (= *l'inconnue*); x(-*certificate*) *film* film *m* interdit aux moins de 18 ans.

xen·o·pho·bi·a [zenəˈfoubiə] xéno- phobie *f* [phie *f.*⟩

xe·rog·ra·phy [ziəˈrɔgrəfi] xérogra-⟩

xe·rox (*TM*) [ˈziərɔks] **1.** photocopie *f*; **2.** photocopier.

X·mas F [ˈeksməs, ˈkrisməs] Noël *m*; *see a.* Christmas.

X-ray [ˈeksˈrei] **1.**: ⁓s *pl.* rayons *m/pl.* X; **2.** radiologique; **3.** radiographier.

xy·log·ra·pher [zaiˈlɔgrəfə] xylo- graphe *m* (= *graveur sur bois*); **xy·lo·graph·ic, xy·lo·graph·i·cal** [⁓ləˈgræfik(l)] xylographique; **xy·log·ra·phy** [⁓ˈlɔgrəfi] xylographie *f* (= *gravure sur bois*).

xy·lo·phone ♪ [ˈzailəfoun] xylopho- ne *m*.

Y

Y, y [wai] Y *m*, y *m*.

yacht ⚓ [jɔt] **1.** yacht *m*; **2.** faire du yachting; **'yacht·er, yachts·man** ['ᴗsmən] yachtman (*pl.* yachtmen) *m*; **'yacht·ing** yachting *m*; *attr.* en yacht; de yachtman.

ya·hoo [jəˈhu:] F brute *f*; *Am. sl.* petzouille *m*.

yam ♀ [jæm] igname *f*.

yank¹ [jæŋk] **1.** *v/t.* tirer (d'un coup sec); arracher; *v/i.* se mouvoir brusquement; **2.** coup *m* sec; secousse *f*.

Yank² *sl.* [ᴗ] *see* Yankee.

Yan·kee F ['jæŋki] Yankee *m*; Américain(e *f*) *m* (*des É.-U.*); ᴗ Doodle *chanson populaire des É.-U.*

yap [jæp] **1.** japper; F criailler; **2.** jappement *m*; *sl.* gueule *f*; *sl.* fadaises *f/pl.*; *sl.* rustre *m*.

yard¹ [jɑ:d] *mesure:* yard *m* (= 0,914 *m*); ⚓ vergue *f*; ⳨ ᴗ goods *pl.* étoffes *f/pl.*, nouveautés *f/pl.*; mercerie *f*.

yard² [ᴗ] cour *f*; chantier *m* (*de travail*); dépôt *m* (*de charbon, a.* ⳨); (*ou railway* ᴗ) gare *f* de triage.

yard...: '**ᴗ·arm** ⚓ bout *m* de vergue; '**ᴗ·man** manœuvre *m* de chantier; garçon *m* d'écurie; ⳨ gareur *m* de trains; '**ᴗ·stick** yard *m*; *fig.* étalon *m*; *fig.* aune *f*.

yarn [jɑ:n] **1.** *tex.* fil(é) *m*; ⚓ fil *m* de caret; *spin a* ᴗ débiter une histoire *ou* des histoires. [achillée *f*.\]

yar·row ♀ ['jærou] mille-feuille *f*,\]

yaw [jɔ:] ⚓ faire des embardées; ✈ faire un mouvement de lacet.

yawl ⚓ [jɔ:l] yole *f*.

yawn [jɔ:n] **1.** bâiller; **2.** bâillement *m*.

ye † *ou poét. ou co.* [ji:] vous.

yea † *ou prov.* [jei] **1.** oui; voire; **2.** oui *m*.

year [jə:] an *m*; année *f*; ᴗ *of grace* an(née *f*) *m* de grâce; *he bears his* ᴗ*s well* il porte bien son âge; '**ᴗ·book** annuaire *m*, almanach *m*; **year·ling** ['jə:liŋ] animal *m* d'un an; '**year·long** qui dure un an, d'un an;

'**year·ly 1.** *adj.* annuel(le *f*); **2.** *adv.* tous les ans; une fois par an.

yearn [jə:n] languir (pour, *for*; après, *after*); brûler (de *inf.*, *to inf.*); '**yearn·ing 1.** envie *f* (de, *for*); désir *m* ardent; **2.** □ ardent; plein d'envie.

yeast [ji:st] levure *f*; levain *m* (*a. fig.*); '**yeast·y** □ de levure; écumant (*mer etc.*); *fig.* enflé (*style*); emphatique (*personne*).

yegg(·man) *Am. sl.* ['jeg(mən)] cambrioleur *m*.

yell [jel] **1.** *vt/i.* hurler; *v/i.* crier à tue-tête; **2.** hurlement *m*; cri *m* aigu.

yel·low ['jelou] **1.** jaune *m*; F lâche, poltron(ne *f*); F sensationel(le *f*), à sensation, à effet; ⊕ ᴗ *brass* cuivre *m* jaune, laiton *m*; *Am.* ᴗ dog roquet *m*; *fig.* sale type *m*; *attr.* contraire aux règlements syndicaux; ᴗ *fever*, F ᴗ *Jack* fièvre *f* jaune; *zo.* ᴗ *jacket* petite guêpe *f*; ᴗ *jaundice* jaunisse *f*, ictère *m*; *téléph.* ᴗ *pages pl.* pages *f/pl.* jaunes; ᴗ *press* presse *f* sensationelle, journaux *m/pl.* à sensation; **2.** jaune *m*; **3.** *vt/i.* jaunir; *ᴗed* jauni; '**ᴗ·back** livre *m* broché; roman *m* bon marché; '**ᴗ-(h)am·mer** *orn.* bruant *m* jaune; '**yel·low·ish** jaunâtre.

yelp [jelp] **1.** jappement *m*; **2.** japper.

yen *Am. sl.* [jen] désir *m* (ardent).

yeo·man ['joumən] yeoman (*pl.* yeomen) *m*, franc tenancier *m*; petit propriétaire *m*; ⚓ *Am.* sous-officier *m* aux écritures; ✕ ᴗ *of the guard* soldat *m* de la Garde du corps; '**yeo·man·ry** francs tenanciers *m/pl.*; ✕ garde *f* montée.

yep *Am.* F [jep] oui.

yes [jes] **1.** oui; **2.** oui *m*; ᴗ**·man** *sl.* ['ᴗmæn] flagorneur *m*; béni-oui-oui *m*.

yes·ter·day ['jestədi] hier (*a. su./m*); '**yes·ter·year** l'an *m* dernier.

yet [jet] **1.** *adv.* encore; jusqu'ici; jusque-là; déjà; malgré tout; *as* ᴗ jusqu'à présent; *not* ᴗ pas encore; **2.** *cj.* (et) cependant; tout de même.

yew ♣ [ju:] if *m*; *attr.* en bois d'if.

Yid·dish ['jidiʃ] yiddish *m*, *adj.*

yield [ji:ld] **1.** *v/t.* rendre; donner; produire; céder (*un terrain*, *une ville, etc.*); rapporter (*a.* ♣ *un profit*); *v/i.* surt. ✗ rendre; céder (à *to*, *beneath*); se rendre (*personne*); **2.** rapport *m*; rendement *m*; production *f*; *planche etc.*: fléchissement *m*; **'yield·ing** □ peu résistant; mou (mol *devant une voyelle ou un h muet*; molle *f*); *fig.* accommodant (*personne*).

yip *Am.* F [jip] aboyer; rouspéter.

yo·del, yo·dle ['joudl] **1.** ioulement *m*; tyrolienne *f*; **2.** iouler; chanter à la tyrolienne.

yo·ga ['jougə] yoga *m*.   [yaourt *m*.\
yog·hourt, yog·(h)urt ['jɔgət]∫\
yo·ho [jou'hou] oh, hisse!

yoicks! [jɔiks] taïaut!

yoke [jouk] **1.** joug *m* (*a. fig.*); couple *f* (*de bœufs*); palanche *f* (*pour seaux*); *cost.* empiècement *m*; **2.** accoupler; atteler; *fig.* unir (à, *to*); '**~-fel·low** compagnon (compagne *f*) *m* de travail; F époux (-ouse *f*) *m*.

yo·kel F ['joukl] rustre *m*.

yolk [jouk] jaune *m* (d'œuf); suint *m* (*de laines*).

yon † *ou poét.* [jɔn], **yon·der** *poét.* ['~də] **1.** *adj.* ce (cette *f*, ces *pl.*) -là; **2.** *adv.* là-bas.

yore [jɔ:]: of ~ (d')autrefois.

you [ju:] **1.** tu; *accentué et datif*: toi; *accusatif*: te; *a.* on; **2.** vous.

young [jʌŋ] **1.** jeune; petit (*animal*); fils; *fig.* peu avancé (*nuit etc.*); **2.** jeunesse *f*, jeunes gens *m/pl.*; with ~ pleine *f* (*animal*); '**young·ish** assez jeune; **young·ster** F ['jʌŋstə] jeune homme *m*; petit(e *f*) *m*.

your [jɔ:; jə] **1.** ton, ta, tes; **2.** votre, vos; **yours** **1.** le tien, la tienne, les tiens, les tiennes; à toi; **2.** le (la) vôtre, les vôtres; à vous; **your'self** toi-même; *réfléchi*: te, *accentué*: toi; **your'selves** *pl.* [~'selvz] vous-mêmes; *réfléchi*: vous (*a. accentué*).

youth [ju:θ] jeunesse *f*; *coll.* jeunes gens *m/pl.*; (*pl.* **youths** [ju:ðz]) jeune homme *m*, adolescent *m*; ~ hostel auberge *f* de la jeunesse); **youth·ful** ['~ful] jeune; de jeunesse; '**youth·ful·ness** (air *m* de) jeunesse *f*.

Yu·go·slav ['ju:gou'slɑ:v] **1.** yougoslave; **2.** *ling.* yougoslave *m*; Yougoslave *mf*.

Yule *poét.* [ju:l] Noël *usu. f*; ~ log bûche *f* de Noël.

Z

Z, z [zed; *Am.* zi:] Z *m*, z *m*.

za·ny [ˈzeini] 1. bouffon *m*; 2. burlesque; loufoque.

zap *sl.* [zæp] 1. *v/t.* descendre (*q.*); agresser, assommer; (*a.* ~ *up*) faire à la hâte; *v/i.* filer (à toute allure); 2. vigueur *f*, énergie *f*, entrain *m*.

zeal [zi:l] zèle *m*; **zeal·ot** [ˈzelət] zélateur (-trice *f*) *m* (*a. eccl.*) (de, *for*); **ˈzeal·ot·ry** fanatisme *m*; *eccl.* zélotisme *m*; **ˈzeal·ous** □ zélé; zélateur (-trice *f*) (de, *for*); plein de zèle (pour, *for*); fanatique.

ze·bra *zo.* [ˈzi:brə] zèbre *m*; ~ *crossing* passage *m* clouté.

ze·bu *zo.* [ˈzi:bu:] zébu *m*, bœuf *m* à bosse.

ze·nith [ˈzeniθ] zénith *m*; *fig. a.* apogée *m*.

zeph·yr [ˈzefə] zéphyr *m*; ✝ laine *f* zéphire; *sp.* maillot *m*.

ze·ro [ˈziərou] 1. zéro *m* (*a. fig.*); 2. zéro *inv.*, nul(le *f*); ~ *growth* croissance *f* zéro; ~ *hour* ✕ l'heure *f* H; *fig.* le moment décisif; ~ *option* option *f* zéro; ✕ ~ *point* point *m* zéro, *a. fig.* origine *f*; 3. ~ *in on* ✕ régler le tir sur; *fig.* diriger son attention sur; *fig.* piquer droit sur.

zest [zest] 1. ✝ zeste *m*; saveur *f*, goût *m*; enthousiasme *m* (pour, *for*); élan *m*; verve *f*; ~ *for life* entrain *m*; 2. épicer.

zig·zag [ˈzigzæg] 1. zigzag *m*; 2. en zigzag; en lacets; 3. zigzaguer, faire des zigzags.

zinc [ziŋk] 1. *min.* zinc *m*; 2. zinguer.

zi·on [ˈzaiən] Sion *m*; **ˈzi·on·ism** sionisme *m*; **ˈzi·on·ist** sioniste (*a. su./mf*).

zip [zip] 1. sifflement *m*; F énergie *f*, allant *m*, vigueur *f*; (*a.* ~ *fastener*) fermeture *f* éclair *inv.* (*TM*) *ou* à glissière; *Am.* ~ *code* code *m* postal; 2. siffler; fermer; **ˈzip·per** 1. fermeture *f* éclair *inv.* (*TM*) *ou* à glissière; 2. fermer (avec une fermeture éclair); **ˈzip·py** F plein d'allant, vif (vive *f*); dynamique.

zith·er ♪ [ˈziθə] cithare *f*.

zo·di·ac *astr.* [ˈzoudiæk] zodiaque *m*; **zo·di·a·cal** [zouˈdaiəkl] zodiacal (-aux *m/pl.*).

zon·al □ [ˈzounl] zonal (-aux *m/pl.*); **zone** [zoun] zone *f*; ⚚ couche *f* (annuelle); *fig.* ceinture *f*.

zoo F [zu:] zoo *m* (= *jardin zoologique*).

zo·o·log·i·cal □ [zouəˈlɔdʒikl] zoologique; ~ *gar·den(s* pl.) [zuˈlɔdʒiklˈgɑːdn(z)] jardin *m* zoologique, F zoo *m*; **zo·ol·o·gist** [zouˈɔlədʒist] zoologiste *m*; **zoˈol·o·gy** zoologie *f*.

zoom *sl.* [zu:m] 1. ✈ monter en chandelle; filer (à toute allure); vrombir, bourdonner; *fig.* (*a.* ~ *up*) monter en flèche; 2. ✈ (montée *f* en) chandelle *f*; vrombissement *m*, bourdonnement *m*; *phot.* (*a.* ~ *lens*) zoom *m*.

zoot suit *Am.* [ˈzuːt ˈsjuːt] complet *m* zazou.

Zu·lu [ˈzuːluː] zoulou *m*; femme *f* zoulou. [tique.]

zy·mot·ic *biol.* [zaiˈmɔtik] zymo-∫

Proper names with pronunciation and explanation

Noms propres avec leur prononciation et notes explicatives

A

Ab·er·deen [æbə'di:n] *ville d'Écosse.*
A·bra·ham ['eibrəhæm] Abraham *m.*
Ab·ys·sin·i·a [æbi'sinjə] l'Abyssinie *f* (*ancien nom d'Éthiopie*).
A·chil·les [ə'kili:z] Achille *m* (*héros grec*).
Ad·am ['ædəm] Adam *m.*
Ad·di·son ['ædisn] *auteur anglais.*
Ad·e·laide ['ædəleid] Adélaïde *f*; ['ᴗlid] Adélaïde (*ville d'Australie*).
A·den ['eidn] *ville et port d'Arabie.*
Ad·i·ron·dacks [ædi'rɔndæks] *région montagneuse de l'État de New York* (*É.-U.*).
Ad·olf ['ædɔlf], **A·dol·phus** [ə'dɔlfəs] Adolphe *m.*
A·dri·at·ic (Sea) [eidri'ætik('si:)] (*mer f*) Adriatique *f.*
Ae·sop ['i:sɔp] Ésope *m* (*fabuliste grec*).
Af·ghan·i·stan [æf'gænistæn] l'Afghanistan *m.*
Af·ri·ca ['æfrikə] l'Afrique *f.*
Ag·a·tha ['ægəθə] Agathe *f.*
Al·a·bam·a [ælə'ba:mə; *Am.* ælə'bæmə] *État des É.-U.*
A·las·ka [ə'læskə] *État des É.-U.*
Al·ba·ni·a [æl'beinjə] l'Albanie *f.*
Al·ba·ny ['ɔːlbəni] *capitale de l'État de New York* (*É.-U.*).
Al·bert ['ælbət] Albert *m.*
Al·ber·ta [æl'bəːtə] *province du Canada.*
Al·bi·on *poét.* ['ælbjən] Albion *f,* la Grande-Bretagne *f.*
Al·der·ney ['ɔːldəni] Aurigny *f* (*île Anglo-Normande*).
Al·ex·an·der [ælig'zɑːndə] Alexandre *m.*

Al·ex·an·dra [ælig'zɑːndrə] Alexandra *f.*
Al·fred ['ælfrid] Alfred *m.*
Al·ge·ri·a [æl'dʒiəriə] l'Algérie *f.*
Al·ger·non ['ældʒənən] *prénom masculin.*
Al·giers [æl'dʒiəz] Alger *m.*
Al·ice ['ælis] Alice *f.*
Al·le·ghe·ny ['æligeini] *chaîne de montagnes des É.-U.; rivière des É.-U.*
Al·len ['ælin] Alain *m.*
Alps [ælps] *pl. les* Alpes *f/pl.*
Al·sace [æl'sæs] l'Alsace *f.*
A·me·lia [ə'mi:ljə] Amélie *f.*
A·mer·i·ca [ə'merikə] l'Amérique *f.*
A·my ['eimi] Aimée *f.*
An·chor·age ['æŋkəridʒ] *ville de l'Alaska* (*É.-U.*).
An·des ['ændi:z] *pl. la* Cordillère *f* des Andes, *les* Andes *f/pl.*
An·dor·ra [æn'dɔrə] Andorre *f.*
An·drew ['ændru:] André *m.*
An·gle·sey ['æŋglsi] *comté du Pays de Galles.*
An·nap·o·lis [ə'næpəlis] *capitale du Maryland* (*É.-U.*), *école navale.*
Ann(e) [æn] Anne *f.*
An·tho·ny ['æntəni] Antoine *m.*
An·til·les [æn'tili:z] *pl. les* Antilles *f/pl.* (*archipel entre l'Amérique du Nord et l'Amérique du Sud*).
An·to·ni·a [æn'tounjə] Antoinette *f.*
An·to·ny ['æntəni] Antoine *m.*
Ap·en·nines ['æpinainz] *pl. les* Apennins *m/pl.*
Ap·pa·lach·i·ans [æpə'leitʃiənz] *les* Appalaches *m/pl.*
Ar·chi·bald ['ɑːtʃibəld] Archambaud *m.*
Ar·chi·me·des [ɑːki'miːdiːz] Archimède *m* (*savant grec*).

Ar·den ['ɑ:dn] *nom de famille anglais.*
Ar·gen·ti·na [ɑ:'dʒən'ti:nə], **the Ar·gen·tine** [ði'ɑ:dʒəntain] l'Argentine *f.*
Ar·gyll(·shire) [ɑ:'gail(ʃiə)] *comté d'Écosse.*
Ar·is·tot·le ['ærɪstɔtl] Aristote *m (philosophe grec).*
Ar·i·zo·na [æri'zounə] *État des É.-U.*
Ar·kan·sas ['ɑ:kənsɔ:] *État des É.-U.; fleuve des É.-U.*
Ar·ling·ton ['ɑ:liŋtən] *cimetière national des É.-U. près de Washington.*
Ar·thur ['ɑ:θə] Arthur *m*; *King* ~ le roi Arthur (*ou* Artus).
As·cot ['æskət] *ville et champ de courses d'Angleterre.*
A·sia ['eiʃə] l'Asie *f*; ~ *Minor* l'Asie *f* Mineure.
Ath·ens ['æθinz] Athènes *f.*
At·kins ['ætkinz]: *Tommy* ~ *sobriquet du soldat britannique.*
At·lan·tic [ət'læntik] *m* l'Atlantique *m.*
Auck·land ['ɔ:klənd] *ville et port de la Nouvelle-Zélande.*
Au·drey ['ɔ:dri] *prénom féminin.*
Au·gus·tus [ɔ:'gʌstəs] Auguste *m.*
Aus·ten ['ɔ:stin] *femme écrivain anglaise.*
Aus·tin [~] *capitale du Texas (É.-U.).*
Aus·tra·lia [ɔ:s'treiljə] l'Australie *f.*
Aus·tri·a ['ɔ:striə] l'Autriche *f.*
A·von ['eivən] *rivière d'Angleterre.*
Ax·min·ster ['æksminstə] *ville d'Angleterre.*
Ayr [ɛə] *ville d'Écosse*; *a.* **Ayr·shire** ['~ʃiə] *comté d'Écosse.*
A·zores [ə'zɔ:z] *pl. les* Açores *f/pl.*

B

Bac·chus *myth.* ['bækəs] Bacchus *m (dieu grec du vin).*
Ba·con ['beikən] *homme d'État et philosophe anglais.*
Ba·den-Pow·ell ['beidn'pouel] *fondateur du scoutisme.*
Ba·ha·mas [bə'hɑ:məz] *pl. les* Bahamas *f/pl. (archipel de l'Atlantique).*
Bai·le A·tha Cli·ath [blɔ:'kli:] *nom gaélique de Dublin.*
Bald·win ['bɔ:ldwin] Baudouin *m.*
Bal·mor·al [bæl'mɔrəl] *château royal en Écosse.*
Bal·ti·more ['bɔ:ltimɔ:] *ville et port des É.-U.*

Bar·thol·o·mew [bɑ:'θɔləmju:] Barthélemy *m.*
Bath [bɑ:θ] *station thermale d'Angleterre.*
Ba·ton Rouge ['bætn'ru:ʒ] *capitale de la Louisiane (É.-U.).*
Ba·var·ia [bə'vɛəriə] la Bavière *f.*
Bea·cons·field ['bi:kənzfi:ld] *titre de noblesse de Disraeli.*
Beards·ley ['biədzli] *dessinateur et illustrateur anglais.*
Beck·ett ['bekit] *poète et dramaturge irlandais.*
Beck·y ['beki] *diminutif de Rebecca.*
Bed·ford ['bedfəd] *ville d'Angleterre*; *a.* **Bed·ford·shire** ['~ʃiə] *comté d'Angleterre.*
Bel·fast ['belfɑ:st] *capitale de l'Irlande du Nord.*
Bel·gium ['beldʒəm] la Belgique *f.*
Bel·grade [bel'greid] *capitale de la Yougoslavie.*
Bel·gra·vi·a [bel'greivjə] *quartier résidentiel de Londres.*
Ben [ben] *diminutif de Benjamin.*
Ben·e·dict ['benidikt; 'benit] Benoît *m.*
Ben·gal [beŋ'gɔ:l] le Bengale *m.*
Ben·ja·min ['bendʒəmin] Benjamin *m.*
Ben Ne·vis [ben'ni:vis] *point culminant de la Grande-Bretagne.*
Berke·ley ['bɑ:kli] *philosophe irlandais*; ['bə:kli] *ville des É.-U. (Californie).*
Berk·shire ['bɑ:kʃiə] *comté d'Angleterre*; ~ **Hills** ['bə:kʃiə'hilz] *pl. chaîne de montagnes du Massachusetts (É.-U.).*
Ber·lin [bə:'lin] Berlin.
Ber·mu·das [bə:'mju:dəz] *pl. les* Bermudes *f/pl. (archipel de l'Atlantique).*
Ber·nard ['bə:nəd] Bernard *m.*
Bern(e) [bə:n] Berne.
Ber·tha ['bə:θə] Berthe *f.*
Ber·trand ['bə:trənd] Bertram *m.*
Ber·yl ['beril] *prénom féminin.*
Bess, Bes·sy ['bes(i)], **Bet·s(e)y** ['betsi], **Bet·ty** ['beti] Babette *f.*
Bill, Bil·ly ['bil(i)] *diminutif de William.*
Bir·ken·head ['bə:kənhed] *port et ville industrielle d'Angleterre.*
Bir·ming·ham ['bə:miŋəm] *ville industrielle d'Angleterre*; ['~hæm] *ville des É.-U. (Alabama).*

1242

Bis·kay ['biskei]: *the Bay of* ~ le golfe *m* de Gascogne.

Blooms·bur·y ['blu:mzbri] *quartier d'artistes de Londres.*

Bob [bɔb] *diminutif de Robert.*

Bo·he·mia [bəu'hi:mjə] la Bohême *f.*

Boi·se ['bɔisi] *capitale de l'Idaho* (É.-U.).

Bol·eyn ['bulin]: Anne ~ Anne Boleyn *(femme de Henri VIII d'Angleterre).*

Bo·liv·i·a [bə'liviə] la Bolivie *f.*

Bom·bay [bɔm'bei] *ville et port de l'Inde.*

Bonn [bɔn] *capitale de la République fédérale d'Allemagne.*

Bos·ton ['bɔstən] *capitale du Massachusetts* (É.-U.).

Bourne·mouth ['bɔ:nməθ] *station balnéaire d'Angleterre.*

Brad·ford ['brædfəd] *ville industrielle d'Angleterre.*

Bra·zil [brə'zil] le Brésil *m.*

Breck·nock(·shire) ['breknɔk(ʃiə)] *comté du Pays de Galles.*

Bri·an ['braiən] *prénom masculin.*

Bridg·et ['bridʒit] Brigitte *f.*

Brigh·ton ['braitn] *station balnéaire d'Angleterre.*

Bris·tol ['bristl] *ville et port d'Angleterre.*

Bri·tan·ni·a *poét.* [bri'tænjə] la Grande-Bretagne *f.*

Brit·ta·ny ['britəni] la Bretagne *f.*

Brit·ten ['britn] *compositeur anglais.*

Broad·way ['brɔ:dwei] *rue principale de New York* (É.-U.).

Brontë ['brɔnti] *nom de trois femmes de lettres anglaises.*

Brook·lyn ['bruklin] *quartier de New York* (É.-U.).

Brus·sels ['brʌslz] Bruxelles.

Bu·cha·rest ['bju:kərest] Bucarest.

Buck [bʌk] *femme écrivain américaine.*

Buck·ing·ham ['bʌkiŋəm] *comté d'Angleterre;* ~ *Palace palais des rois de Grande-Bretagne;* **Buck·ing·ham·shire** ['bʌkiŋəmʃiə] *see* Buckingham.

Bu·da·pest ['bju:də'pest] *capitale de la Hongrie.*

Bud·dha ['budə] Bouddha.

Bul·gar·i·a [bʌl'gɛəriə] la Bulgarie *f.*

Bul·wer ['bulwə] *auteur anglais.*

Bur·ma ['bə:mə] la Birmanie *f.*

Burns [bə:nz] *poète écossais.*

By·ron ['baiərən] *poète anglais.*

C

Cae·sar ['si:zə] (Jules) César *m* (*général et dictateur romain*).

Cai·ro ['kaiərou] Le Caire *m.*

Cal·cut·ta [kæl'kʌtə] *capitale de l'État de Bengale-Occidental.*

Cal·i·for·nia [kæli'fɔ:njə] la Californie *f* (*État des É.-U.*).

Cam·bridge ['keimbridʒ] *ville universitaire anglaise; ville des É.-U.* (*Massachusetts*), *siège de l'université Harvard; a.* **Cam·bridge·shire** ['~ʃiə] *comté d'Angleterre.*

Camp·bell ['kæmbl] *nom de famille.*

Can·a·da ['kænədə] le Canada *m.*

Ca·nar·y Is·lands [kə'nɛəri'ailəndz] *les* îles *f/pl.* Canaries, *les* Canaries *f/pl.*

Can·ber·ra ['kænbərə] *capitale de l'Australie.*

Can·ter·bur·y ['kæntəbəri] Cantorbéry *f* (*ville d'Angleterre*).

Cape Town, Cape·town ['keiptaun] le Cap *m.*

Ca·pote [kə'pouti] *écrivain américain.*

Car·diff ['ka:dif] *capitale du Pays de Galles.*

Car·di·gan(·shire) ['ka:digən(ʃiə)] *comté du Pays de Galles.*

Car·lisle [ka:'lail] *ville d'Angleterre.*

Car·lyle [ka:'lail] *auteur anglais.*

Car·mar·then(·shire) [kə'ma:ðən (-ʃiə)] *comté du Pays de Galles.*

Car·nar·von(·shire) [kə'na:vən(-ʃiə)] *comté du Pays de Galles.*

Car·neg·ie ['ka:negi] *industriel américain.*

Car·o·li·na [kærə'lainə]: (North ~, South ~) la Caroline *f* (du Nord, du Sud) (*États des É.-U.*).

Car·o·line ['kærəlain] Caroline *f.*

Car·pa·thi·ans [ka:'peiθjənz] *pl. les* Karpates *f/pl.*

Car·rie ['kæri] *diminutif de Caroline.*

Cath·e·rine ['kæθərin] Catherine *f.*

Cau·ca·sus ['kɔ:kəsəs] Caucase *m.*

Cec·il ['sesl; 'sisl] *prénom masculin.*

Ce·cil·i·a [si'siljə], **Cec·i·ly** ['sisili] Cécile *f.*

Cey·lon [si'lɔn] Ceylan *m.*

Cham·ber·lain ['tʃeimbəlin] *nom de plusieurs hommes d'État britanniques.*

Chan·nel ['tʃænl]: *the English* ~ la Manche *f.*

Char·ing Cross ['tʃæriŋ'krɔs] *carrefour de Londres.*

Charles [tʃa:lz] Charles *m.*

Charles·ton ['tʃɑːlstən] *capitale de la Virginie Occidentale (É.-U.).*

Char·lotte ['ʃɑːlət] *Charlotte f.*

Chat·ham ['tʃætəm] *ville et port d'Angleterre.*

Chau·cer ['tʃɔːsə] *poète anglais.*

Chel·sea ['tʃelsi] *quartier de Londres.*

Chesh·ire ['tʃeʃə] *comté d'Angleterre.*

Ches·ter·field ['tʃestəfiːld] *ville industrielle d'Angleterre.*

Chev·i·ot Hills ['tʃeviət'hilz] *pl. chaîne de montagnes qui sépare l'Écosse de l'Angleterre.*

Chi·ca·go [ʃi'kɑːgou; *Am. souv.* ʃi-'kɔːgou] *ville des États de la Prairie (É.-U.).*

Chil·e, Chil·i ['tʃili] *le Chili m.*

Chi·na ['tʃainə] *la Chine f.*

Chlo·e ['klɔui] *prénom féminin.*

Chris·ti·na [kris'tiːnə] *Christine f.*

Chris·to·pher ['kristəfə] *Christophe m.*

Chrys·ler ['kraislə] *industriel américain.*

Church·ill ['tʃəːtʃil] *homme d'État britannique.*

Cin·cin·nat·i [sinsi'næti] *ville des É.-U.*

Cis·sie ['sisi] *diminutif de Cecilia.*

Clar·a ['klɛərə], **Clare** [klɛə] *Claire f.*

Clar·en·don ['klærəndən] *nom de plusieurs hommes d'État britanniques.*

Cle·o·pa·tra [kliə'pætrə] *Cléopâtre f. (reine d'Égypte).*

Cleve·land ['kliːvlənd] *ville industrielle et port des É.-U.*

Clive [klaiv] *général qui fonda la puissance britannique dans l'Inde.*

Clyde [klaid] *fleuve d'Écosse.*

Cole·ridge ['koulridʒ] *poète anglais.*

Col·in ['kɔlin] *prénom masculin.*

Co·lom·bi·a [kə'lɔmbiə] *la Colombie f.*

Col·o·ra·do [kɔlə'rɑːdou] *État des É.-U.; nom de deux fleuves des É.-U.*

Co·lum·bi·a [kə'lʌmbiə] *fleuve des É.-U.; district fédéral des É.-U. (capitale Washington); capitale de la Caroline du Sud (É.-U.).*

Con·cord ['kɔŋkəd] *capitale du New Hampshire (É.-U.).*

Con·nacht ['kɔnət], **Con·naught** ['kɔnɔːt] *province de la République d'Irlande.*

Con·nect·i·cut [kə'netikət] *fleuve des É.-U.; État des É.-U.*

Con·stance ['kɔnstəns] *Constance mf.*

Coo·per ['kuːpə] *auteur américain.*

Co·pen·ha·gen [koupn'heign] *Copenhague.*

Cor·dil·le·ras [kɔ:di'ljɛərəz] *pl. see* Andes.

Cor·ne·lia [kɔː'niːljə] *Cornélie f.*

Corn·wall ['kɔːnwəl] *la Cornouailles f (comté d'Angleterre).*

Cos·ta Ri·ca ['kɔstə'riːkə] *le Costa Rica m.*

Cov·ent Gar·den ['kɔvənt'gɑːdn] *l'opéra de Londres.*

Cov·en·try ['kɔvəntri] *ville industrielle d'Angleterre.*

Craig [kreig] *prénom.*

Crete [kriːt] *la Crète f.*

Cri·me·a [krai'miə] *la Crimée f.*

Crom·well ['krɔmwəl] *homme d'État anglais.*

Croy·don ['krɔidn] *ancien aéroport de Londres.*

Cu·ba ['kjuːbə] *(île f de) Cuba m.*

Cum·ber·land ['kʌmbələnd] *comté d'Angleterre.*

Cu·pid *myth.* ['kjuːpid] *Cupidon m (dieu romain de l'Amour).*

Cyn·thi·a ['sinθiə] *prénom féminin.*

Cy·prus ['saiprəs] *Chypre f.*

Cy·rus ['sairəs] *Cyrus m.*

Czech·o·Slo·va·ki·a ['tʃekouslou-'vækiə] *la Tchécoslovaquie f.*

D

Da·ko·ta [də'koutə]: *(North ~, South ~)* le Dakota m (du Nord, du Sud) *(États de É.-U.).*

Dan·iel ['dænjəl] *Daniel m.*

Dan·ube ['dænjuːb] *le Danube m.*

Daph·ne ['dæfni] *Daphné f.*

Dar·da·nelles [dɑ:də'nelz] *pl. les Dardanelles f/pl.*

Dar·jee·ling [dɑː'dʒiːliŋ] *ville de l'Inde.*

Dart·moor ['dɑ:tmuə] *massif cristallin d'Angleterre; prison.*

Dar·win ['dɑ:win] *naturaliste anglais.*

Da·vid ['deivid] *David m.*

Dee [diː] *fleuve d'Angleterre et d'Écosse.*

De·foe [di'fou] *auteur anglais.*

Deir·dre ['diədri] *prénom féminin.*

Del·a·ware ['deləwɛə] *fleuve des É.-U.; État des É.-U.*

Den·bigh(·shire) ['denbi(ʃiə)] *comté du Pays de Galles.*

Den·mark ['denmɑːk] *le Danemark m.*

Den·ver ['denvə] *capitale du Colorado* (*É.-U.*).

Der·by(·shire) ['dɑːbi(ʃiə)] *comté d'Angleterre.*

Des Moines [dəˈmɔin] *capitale de l'Iowa* (*É.-U.*).

De·troit [diˈtrɔit] *ville industrielle des É.-U.*

De Va·le·ra [dəvəˈliərə] *homme d'État irlandais.*

Dev·on(·shire) ['devn(ʃiə)] *comté d'Angleterre.*

Dew·ey ['djuːi] *philosophe américain.*

Di·an·a [daiˈænə] Diane *f.*

Dick [dik] *diminutif de Richard.*

Dick·ens ['dikinz] *auteur anglais.*

Dick·in·son ['dikinsn] *femme poète américaine.*

Dis·rae·li [dizˈreili] *homme d'État britannique.*

Dol·ly ['dɔli] *diminutif de Dorothy.*

Do·min·i·can Re·pub·lic [dəˈminikən riˈpʌblik] *la* République *f* Dominicaine.

Don·ald ['dɔnld] *prénom masculin.*

Don Quix·ote [dɔnˈkwiksət] Don Quichotte *m.*

Dor·o·the·a [dɔrəˈθiə], **Dor·o·thy** ['dɔrəθi] Dorothée *f.*

Dor·set(·shire) ['dɔːsit(ʃiə)] *comté d'Angleterre.*

Dos Pas·sos [dəsˈpæsəs] *écrivain américain.*

Doug [dʌg] *diminutif de Douglas.*

Doug·las ['dʌgləs] *puissante famille écossaise; prénom masculin.*

Do·ver ['douvə] Douvres (*port d'Angleterre, sur la Manche*); *capitale du Delaware* (*É.-U.*).

Down·ing Street ['dauniŋˈstriːt] *rue de Londres, résidence officielle du premier ministre.*

Drei·ser ['draisə] *auteur américain.*

Dry·den ['draidn] *poète anglais.*

Dub·lin ['dʌblin] *capitale de la République d'Irlande.*

Du·luth [dəˈluːθ] *ville des É.-U.* (*Minnesota*).

Dun·kirk [dʌnˈkəːk] Dunkerque *m.*

Dur·ham ['dʌrəm] *comté d'Angleterre.*

E

Ec·ua·dor [ekwəˈdɔː] Équateur *m.*

Ed·die ['edi] *diminutif de Edmund, Edward.*

E·den ['iːdn] Eden *m*, le paradis *m* terrestre.

Ed·in·burgh ['edinbərə] Édimbourg.

Ed·i·son ['edisn] *inventeur américain.*

Ed·mund ['edmənd] Edmond *m.*

Ed·ward ['edwəd] Édouard *m.*

E·gypt ['iːdʒipt] l'Égypte *f.*

Ei·leen ['ailiːn] *prénom féminin.*

Ei·re ['ɛərə] *ancien nom de la République d'Irlande.*

Ei·sen·how·er ['aizənhauə] *général et 34ᵉ président des É.-U.*

E·laine [iˈlein] *prénom féminin.*

El·ea·nor ['elinə] Eléonore *f.*

E·li·as [iˈlaiəs] Élie *m.*

El·i·nor ['elinə] Eléonore *f.*

El·i·ot ['eljət] *femme écrivain anglaise; poète anglais, né aux É.-U.*

E·li·za [iˈlaizə] *diminutif de Elizabeth.*

E·liz·a·beth [iˈlizəbəθ] Elisabeth *f.*

El·lis Is·land ['elisˈailənd] *île de la baie de New York* (*É.-U.*).

El Sal·va·dor [elˈsælvədɔː] El Salvador *m.*

Em·er·son ['eməsn] *philosophie et poète américain.*

Em·i·ly ['emili] Émilie *f.*

Eng·land ['iŋglənd] l'Angleterre *f.*

E·noch ['iːnɔk] Énoch *m.*

Ep·som ['epsəm] *ville d'Angleterre, célèbre course de chevaux.*

E·rie ['iəri]: Lake ~ le lac *m* Érie (*un des cinq grands lacs de l'Amérique du Nord*).

Er·nest ['əːnist] Ernest *m.*

Es·sex ['esiks] *comté d'Angleterre.*

Eth·el ['eθl] *prénom féminin.*

E·thi·o·pi·a [iːθiˈoupjə] l'Éthiopie *f.*

E·ton ['iːtn] *collège et ville d'Angleterre.*

Eu·clid ['juːklid] Euclide (*mathématicien grec*).

Eu·gene ['juːdʒiːn] Eugène *m.*

Eu·ge·ni·a [juːˈdʒiːniə] Eugénie *f.*

Eu·phra·tes [juːˈfreitiːz] l'Euphrate *m.*

Eu·rope ['juərəp] l'Europe *f.*

Eus·tace ['juːstəs] Eustache *m.*

Ev·ans ['evənz] *nom de famille anglais et gallois.*

Eve [iːv] Ève *f.*

Ev·e·lyn ['iːvlin] Éveline *f.*

F

Falk·land Is·lands ['fɔːkləndˈailəndz] *pl. les* îles *f/pl.* Falkland (*archipel de l'Atlantique*).

Faulk·ner ['fɔːknə] *auteur américain.*

Fawkes [fɔːks] *nom de famille anglais; chef de la Conspiration des Poudres (1605).*

Fe·li·ci·a [fi'lisiə] *prénom féminin.*

Fe·lix ['fiːliks] *Félix m.*

Fin·land ['finlənd] *la Finlande f.*

Fitz·ger·ald [fits'dʒerəld] *nom de famille.*

Flan·ders ['flɑːndəz] *la Flandre f.*

Flint·shire ['flintʃiə] *comté du Pays de Galles.*

Flor·ence ['flɔrəns] *Florence f (prénom).*

Flor·i·da ['flɔridə] *la Floride f (État des É.-U.).*

Flush·ing ['flʌʃiŋ] *Flessingue.*

Folke·stone ['foukstən] *ville et port d'Angleterre sur la Manche.*

Ford [fɔːd] *industriel américain.*

France [frɑːns] *la France f.*

Fran·ces ['frɑːnsis] *Françoise f.*

Fran·cis [~] *François m.*

Frank·fort ['fræŋkfət] *capitale du Kentucky (É.-U.).*

Frank·lin ['fræŋklin] *homme d'État et auteur américain.*

Fred(·dy) ['fred(i)] *diminutif de Alfred, Frederic(k).*

Fred·er·ic(k) ['fredrik] *Frédéric m.*

Ful·bright ['fulbrait] *homme politique américain.*

Ful·ton ['fultən] *inventeur américain.*

G

Gains·bor·ough ['geinzbərə] *peintre anglais.*

Gals·wor·thy ['gælzwəːði] *auteur anglais.*

Gan·ges ['gændʒiːz] *le Gange m.*

Gaul [gɔːl] *la Gaule f.*

Ge·ne·va [dʒi'niːvə] *Genève.*

Geof·frey ['dʒefri] *Geoffroi m.*

George [dʒɔːdʒ] *Georges m.*

Geor·gia ['dʒɔːdʒiə] *la Georgie f (État des É.-U.).*

Ger·ald ['dʒerəld] *Gérard m.*

Ger·al·dine ['dʒerəldiːn] *prénom féminin.*

Ger·ma·ny ['dʒəːməni] *l'Allemagne f.*

Gersh·win ['gəːʃwin] *compositeur américain.*

Ger·trude ['gəːtruːd] *Gertrude f.*

Get·tys·burg ['getizbəːg] *ville des É.-U.*

Gha·na ['gɑːnə] *le Ghana m.*

Gi·bral·tar [dʒi'brɔːltə] *Gibraltar m.*

Giles [dʒailz] *Gilles m.*

Gill [gil] *Julie f.*

Glad·ys ['glædis] *prénom féminin.*

Glad·stone ['glædstən] *homme d'État britannique.*

Gla·mor·gan(·shire) [glə'mɔːgən (-ʃiə)] *comté du Pays de Galles.*

Glas·gow ['glɑːsgou] *ville et port d'Écosse.*

Glouces·ter ['glɒstə] *ville d'Angleterre; a. **Glouces·ter·shire** ['~ʃiə] comté d'Angleterre.*

Gold·smith ['gouldsmiθ] *auteur anglais.*

Gor·don ['gɔːdn] *nom de famille anglais.*

Go·tham ['gɔtəm] *village d'Angleterre.*

Gra·ham ['greiəm] *nom de famille et prénom masculin anglais.*

Grand Can·yon [grænd'kænjən] *nom des gorges du Colorado (É.-U.).*

Great Brit·ain ['greit'britən] *la Grande-Bretagne f.*

Great Di·vide ['greitdi'vaid] *les montagnes Rocheuses (É.-U.).*

Greece [griːs] *la Grèce f.*

Greene [griːn] *auteur anglais.*

Green·land ['griːnlənd] *le Groenland m.*

Green·wich ['grinidʒ] *faubourg de Londres;~ Village quartier d'artistes de New York.*

Greg·o·ry ['gregəri] *Grégoire m.*

Gros·ve·nor ['grouvnə] *place et rue de Londres.*

Gua·te·ma·la [gwæti'mɑːlə] *le Guatemala m.*

Guern·sey ['gəːnzi] *Guernesey f (île Anglo-Normande).*

Gui·a·na [gi'ɑːnə] *la Guyane f.*

Guin·ea ['gini] *la Guinée f.*

Guin·ness ['ginis; gi'nes] *nom de famille, surt. irlandais.*

Guy [gai] *Gui m, Guy m.*

Gwen·do·len, Gwen·do·lyn ['gwendəlin] *prénom féminin.*

H

Hai·ti ['heiti] *la Haïti f.*

Hague [heig] *the ~ La Haye.*

Hal·i·fax ['hælifæks] *ville du Canada et d'Angleterre.*

Ham·il·ton ['hæmiltən] *nom de famille anglais.*

Hamp·shire ['hæmpʃiə] *comté d'Angleterre.*

Hamp·stead ['hæmpstid] *faubourg de Londres.*

Han·o·ver ['hænəvə] *Hanovre m.*

Har·lem ['hɑːləm] *quartier de New York, habité surtout par des noirs.*

Har·ri·et ['hæriət] *Henriette f.*

Har·ris·burg ['hærisbəːg] *capitale de la Pennsylvanie (É.-U.).*

Har·row ['hærou] *collège et ville d'Angleterre.*

Har·ry ['hæri] *diminutif de Henry.*

Har·vard U·ni·ver·si·ty ['hɑːvəd juːni'vəːsiti] *université américaine.*

Har·wich ['hæridʒ] *ville et port d'Angleterre.*

Has·tings ['heistiŋz] *ville d'Angleterre; homme d'État, gouverneur de l'Inde anglaise.*

Ha·wai·i [hɑː'waii] *pl. les Hawaii f/pl. (archipel de la Polynésie, État des É.-U.).*

Heb·ri·des ['hebridiːz] *pl. les Hébrides f/pl. (îles d'Écosse).*

Hel·en ['helin] *Hélène f.*

Hel·sin·ki ['helsiŋki] *capitale de la Finlande.*

Hem·ing·way ['hemiŋwei] *auteur américain.*

Hen·ley ['henli] *ville d'Angleterre sur la Tamise; régates célèbres.*

Hen·ry ['henri] *Henri m.*

Her·cu·les ['həːkjuliːz] *Hercule m.*

Her·e·ford(·shire) ['herifəd(ʃiə)] *comté d'Angleterre.*

Hert·ford(·shire) ['hɑːfəd(ʃiə)] *comté d'Angleterre.*

Hil·a·ry ['hiləri] *Hilaire f.*

Hi·ma·la·ya [himə'leiə] *l'Himalaya m.*

Hin·du·stan [hindu'stæn] *l'Hindoustan m.*

Ho·garth ['hougɑːθ] *peintre anglais.*

Hol·born ['houbən] *quartier de Londres.*

Hol·land ['hɔlənd] *la Hollande f.*

Hol·ly·wood ['hɔliwud] *centre de l'industrie cinématographique américaine.*

Home [hjuːm]: *Sir Alec Douglas-~ homme politique anglais.*

Ho·mer ['houmə] *Homère m (poète grec).*

Hon·du·ras [hɔn'djuərəs] *le Honduras m.*

Ho·no·lu·lu [hɔnə'luːlu] *capitale des Hawaii (É.-U.).*

Hoo·ver ['huːvə] *31ᵉ président des É.-U.*

Hous·ton ['(h)juːstən] *ville des É.-U. (Texas).*

Hud·son ['hʌdsn] *fleuve des É.-U., avec New York à l'embouchure; vaste golfe au nord de l'Amérique.*

Hugh [hjuː] *Hugues m.*

Hughes [hjuːz] *nom de famille.*

Hull [hʌl] *ville et port d'Angleterre.*

Hume [hjuːm] *philosophe anglais.*

Hum·phr(e)y ['hʌmfri] *prénom masculin.*

Hun·ga·ry ['hʌŋgəri] *la Hongrie f.*

Hun·ting·don(·shire) ['hʌntiŋdən (-ʃiə)] *comté d'Angleterre.*

Hu·ron ['hjuərən]: *Lake ~ le lac m Huron (un des cinq grands lacs de l'Amérique du Nord).*

Hux·ley ['hʌksli] *naturaliste anglais; zoologiste anglais; auteur anglais.*

Hyde Park ['haid'pɑːk] *Parc de Londres.*

I

I·an ['iːən, iən] *Jean m.*

Ice·land ['aislənd] *l'Islande f.*

I·da·ho ['aidəhou] *État des É.-U.*

I·dle·wild ['aidlwaild] *ancien nom de Kennedy Airport.*

Il·li·nois [ili'nɔi(z)] *rivière des É.-U.; État des É.-U.*

In·di·a ['indjə] *l'Inde f.*

In·di·an·a [indi'ænə] *État des É.-U.*

In·di·an Ocean ['indjən'ouʃən] *océan m Indien.*

In·dies ['indiz] *pl.: the (East, West) ~ les Indes f/pl. (orientales, occidentales).*

In·dus ['indəs] *l'Indus m.*

I·o·wa ['aiouə] *État des É.-U.*

I·rak, I·raq [i'rɑːk] *l'Irak m, l'Iraq m.*

I·ran [iə'rɑːn] *l'Iran m.*

Ire·land ['aiələnd] *l'Irlande f.*

I·re·ne [ai'riːni; 'airiːn] *Irène f.*

I·ris ['aiəris] *prénom féminin.*

Ir·ving ['əːviŋ] *auteur américain.*

I·saac ['aizək] *Isaac m.*

Is·a·bel ['izəbəl] *Isabelle f.*

Isle of Man [ailəv'mæn] *Isle f de*

Man (*île de la mer d'Irlande*).
Is·ra·el ['izreiəl] l'Israël *m.*
It·a·ly ['itəli] l'Italie *f.*
I·vy ['aivi] *prénom féminin.*

J

Jack [dʒæk] Jean(not) *m* (*see Jack au dictionnaire*).
Ja·mai·ca [dʒə'meikə] la Jamaïque *f.*
James [dʒeimz] Jacques *m.*
Jane [dʒein] Jeanne *f.*
Ja·net ['dʒænit] Jeanette *f.*
Ja·pan [dʒə'pæn] le Japon *m.*
Jean [dʒi:n] Jeanne *f.*
Jef·fer·son ['dʒefəsn] 3e président des É.-U., auteur de la Déclaration d'Indépendance; ~ City capitale du Missouri (É.-U.).
Jen·ny ['dʒeni] Jeanneton *f*, Jeannette *f.*
Jer·e·my ['dʒerimi] Jérémie *m.*
Jer·sey ['dʒə:zi] *île Anglo-Normande;* ~ City ville des É.-U.
Je·ru·sa·lem [dʒə'ru:sələm] Jérusalem.
Jes·si·ca ['dʒesikə] Jessica *f.*
Je·sus (Christ) ['dʒi:zəs ('kraist)] Jésus(-Christ) *m.*
Jill [dʒil] Julie *f*; *Jack and* ~ Jeannot et Colette.
Jim(·my) ['dʒim(i)] *diminutif de James.*
Joan [dʒoun] Jeanne *f.*
Joc·e·lin(e), Joc·e·lyn ['dʒɔslin] *prénom féminin.*
Jo(e) [dʒou] *diminutif de Joseph.*
John [dʒɔn] Jean *m.*
John·ny ['dʒɔni] Jeannot *m.*
John·son ['dʒɔnsn] 36e président des É.-U.; auteur anglais.
Jo·nah ['dʒounə] Jonas *m.*
Jon·a·than ['dʒɔnəθən] Jonathas *m.*
Jor·dan ['dʒɔ:dn] la Jordanie *f.*
Jo·seph ['dʒouzif] Joseph *m.*
Josh·u·a ['dʒɔʃwə] Josué *m.*
Joyce [dʒɔis] *écrivain irlandais.*
Ju·go·sla·vi·a ['ju:gou'slɑ:viə] la Yougoslavie *f.*
Jul·ia ['dʒu:ljə], **Ju·li·et** ['~t] Julie(tte) *f.*
Jul·ian ['dʒu:liən] *prénom masculin.*
Jul·ius ['dʒu:ljəs] Jules *m.*
Ju·neau ['dʒu:nou] *capitale de l'Alaska (É.-U.).*

K

Kam·pu·che·a [kæmpu'tʃiə] Cambodge *m.*
Kan·sas ['kænzəs] *rivière des É.-U.;* État des É.-U.
Kash·mir [kæʃ'miə] le Cachemire *m* (*ancien État de l'Inde*).
Kate [keit] *diminutif de Catherine, Katharine, Katherine, Kathleen.*
Kath·a·rine, Kath·er·ine ['kæθərin] Catherine *f.*
Kath·leen ['kæθli:n] Catherine *f.*
Keats [ki:ts] *poète anglais.*
Keith [ki:θ] *prénom masculin.*
Ken·ne·dy ['kenidi] 35e président des É.-U.; Cape ~ cap de la côte de Floride (lancement d'engins téléguidés et de satellites artificiels); ~ airport aéroport international de New York.
Ken·neth ['keniθ] *prénom masculin.*
Ken·sing·ton ['kenziŋtən] *quartier de Londres.*
Kent [kent] *comté d'Angleterre.*
Ken·tuck·y [ken'tʌki] *rivière des É.-U.;* État des É.-U.
Ken·ya ['ki:njə; 'kenjə] le Kenya *m.*
Kip·ling ['kipliŋ] *poète anglais.*
Kit·ty ['kiti] *diminutif de Catherine.*
Klon·dike ['klɔndaik] *rivière et région du Canada.*
Knox [nɔks] *réformateur écossais.*
Krem·lin ['kremlin] le Kremlin *m.*
Ku·wait [ku'weit] Koweït *m.*

L

Lab·ra·dor ['læbrədɔ:] *péninsule de l'Amérique du Nord.*
Lan·ca·shire ['læŋkəʃiə] *comté d'Angleterre.*
Lan·cas·ter ['læŋkəstə] Lancastre *f* (*ville d'Angleterre; ville des É.-U.*); *see Lancashire.*
Lau·rence, Law·rence ['lɔ:rəns] Laurent *m.*
Leb·a·non ['lebənən] le Liban *m.*
Leeds [li:dz] *ville industrielle d'Angleterre.*
Leg·horn ['leg'hɔ:n] Livourne.
Leices·ter ['lestə] *ville d'Angleterre;* a. **Leices·ter·shire** ['~ʃiə] *comté d'Angleterre.*
Leigh [li:; lai] *ville industrielle d'Angleterre; nom de famille anglais.*
Leix [li:ʃ] *comté d'Irlande.*

Le·man ['lemən]: *Lake* ~ le lac *m* Léman.

Leon·ard ['lenəd] Léonard *m*.

Les·lie ['lezli] *prénom masculin*.

Lew·is ['luːis] Louis *m*; *auteur américain*; *poète anglais*.

Lil·i·an ['liliən] *prénom féminin*.

Lim·er·ick ['limərik] *comté d'Irlande*.

Lin·coln ['liŋkən] *16ᵉ président des É.-U.; capitale du Nébraska (É.-U.); ville d'Angleterre; a.* **Lin·coln·shire** ['~ʃiə] *comté d'Angleterre*.

Li·o·nel ['laiənl] *prénom masculin*.

Lis·bon ['lizbən] Lisbonne *f*.

Lit·tle Rock ['litl'rɔk] *capitale de l'Arkansas (É.-U.)*.

Liv·er·pool ['livəpuːl] *ville industrielle et port d'Angleterre*.

Liz·zie ['lizi] Lisette *f*.

Lloyd [lɔid] *prénom masculin*.

Locke [lɔk] *philosophe anglais*.

Lon·don ['lʌndən] Londres.

Long·fel·low ['lɔŋfelou] *poète américain*.

Lor·raine [lɔ'rein] la Lorraine *f*.

Los An·ge·les [lɔs'ændʒiliːz; *Am. a.* 'æŋgələs] *ville et port des É.-U.*

Lou·i·sa [luːˈiːzə] Louise *f*.

Lou·i·si·an·a [luːiːziˈænə] la Louisiane *f (État des É.-U.)*.

Lu·cia ['luːsiə] Lucie *f*.

Lu·cius ['luːsiəs] Lucien *m*.

Lu·cy ['luːsi] Lucie *f*.

Luke [luːk] Luc *m*.

Lux·em·b(o)urg ['lʌksəmbəːg] Luxembourg *m*.

Lyd·i·a ['lidiə] Lydie *f*.

M

Mab [mæb] *reine des fées*.

Ma·bel ['meibl] *prénom féminin*.

Ma·cau·lay [məˈkɔːli] *historien et homme politique anglais; femme écrivain anglaise*.

Mac·Don·ald [məkˈdɔnld] *homme d'État britannique*.

Mac·Gee [məˈgiː] *nom de famille*.

Mac·ken·zie [məˈkenzi] *fleuve du Canada*.

Ma·dei·ra [məˈdiərə] Madère *f*.

Madge [mædʒ] Margot *f*.

Mad·i·son ['mædisn] *4ᵉ président des É.-U.; capitale du Wisconsin (É.-U.)*.

Ma·dras [məˈdrɑːs] *ville et port de l'Inde*.

Ma·drid [məˈdrid] *capitale de l'Espagne*.

Mag·da·len ['mægdəlin] Madeleine *f*.

Mag·gie ['mægi] Margot *f*.

Ma·hom·et [meˈhɔmit] Mahomet *m*.

Maine [mein] *État des É.-U.*

Ma·lay·sia [məˈleiʒə]: *the Federation of* ~ la Fédération *f* de Malaisie.

Mal·colm ['mælkəm] *prénom masculin*.

Mal·ta ['mɔːltə] Malte *f*.

Man·ches·ter ['mæntʃistə] *ville industrielle d'Angleterre*.

Man·hat·tan [mænˈhætn] *île et quartier de New York (É.-U.)*.

Man·i·to·ba [mæniˈtoubə] *province du Canada*.

Mar·ga·ret ['mɑːgərit] Marguerite *f*.

Mar·jo·rie ['mɑːdʒəri] *prénom féminin*.

Mark [mɑːk] Marc *m*.

Marl·bor·ough ['mɔːlbərə] *général anglais*.

Mar·tha ['mɑːθə] Marthe *f*.

Mar·y ['mɛəri] Marie *f*.

Mar·y·land ['mɛərilænd; *Am.* 'merilənd] *État des É.-U.*

Mas·sa·chu·setts [mæsəˈtʃuːsets] *État des É.-U.*

Ma(t)·thew ['mæθjuː] Mat(t)hieu *m*.

Maud [mɔːd] Mathilde *f*.

Maugham [mɔːm] *auteur anglais*.

Mau·reen [mɔˈriːn] *prénom féminin*.

Mau·rice ['mɔris] Maurice *m*.

May [mei] Mariette *f*, Manon *f*.

Meath [miːð, miːθ] *comté d'Irlande*.

Mel·bourne ['melbən] *ville et port d'Australie*.

Mel·ville ['melvil] *auteur américain*.

Mer·e·dith ['merədiθ] *auteur anglais*.

Mer·i·on·eth(·shire) [meriˈɔniθ (-ʃiə)] *comté du Pays de Galles*.

Mex·i·co ['meksikou] le Mexique *m*.

Mi·am·i [maiˈæmi] *station balnéaire de la Floride (É.-U.)*.

Mi·chael ['maikl] Michel *m*.

Mich·i·gan ['miʃigən] *État des É.-U.; Lake* ~ le lac *m* Michigan (*un des cinq grands lacs de l'Amérique du Nord*).

Mid·dle·sex ['midlseks] *comté d'Angleterre*.

Mid·west ['mid'west] *les États m/pl. de la Prairie (É.-U.)*.

Mil·dred ['mildrid] *prénom féminin*.

Mil·li·cent ['milisnt] *prénom féminin*.

Mil·ton ['miltən] *poète anglais.*
Mil·wau·kee [mil'wɔ:ki:] *ville des É.-U.*
Min·ne·ap·o·lis [mini'æpəlis] *ville des É.-U.*
Min·ne·so·ta [mini'soutə] *État des É.-U.*
Mis·sis·sip·pi [misi'sipi] *État des É.-U.; fleuve des E.-U.*
Mis·sou·ri [mi'suəri; *Am.* mi'zuəri] *rivière des É.-U.; État des É.-U.*
Mitch·ell ['mitʃl] *prénom; nom de famille.*
Mo·ham·med [mou'hæmed] *Mohammed m; islam: Mahomet m.*
Moll [mɔl] *Mariette f, Manon f.*
Mo·na·co ['mɔnəkou] *Monaco m.*
Mon·mouth(·shire) ['mʌnməθ(ʃiə)] *comté de' Angleterre.*
Mon·roe [mən'rou] *5e président des É.-U.*
Mon·tan·a [mɔn'tænə] *État des É.-U.*
Mont·gom·er·y [mənt'gʌməri] *maréchal britannique;* a. **Mont'gomer·y·shire** [~ʃiə] *comté du Pays de Galles.*
Mont·re·al [mɔntri'ɔ:l] *Montréal m (ville du Canada).*
Moore [muə] *sculpteur anglais.*
Mo·roc·co [mə'rɔkou] *le Maroc m.*
Mos·cow ['mɔskou] *Moscou.*
Mu·ri·el ['mjuəriəl] *prénom féminin.*
Mur·ray ['mʌri] *fleuve d'Australie.*
My·ra ['maiərə] *prénom féminin.*

N

Nan·cy ['nænsi] *Nanette f, Annette f.*
Na·ples ['neiplz] *Naples.*
Na·tal [nə'tæl] *le Natal m.*
Ne·bras·ka [ni'bræskə] *État des É.-U.*
Neil(l) [ni:l] *prénom; nom de famille.*
Nell, Nel·ly ['nel(i)] *diminutif de Eleanor, Helen.*
Nel·son ['nelsn] *amiral britannique.*
Ne·pal [ni'pɔ:l] *le Népal m.*
Neth·er·lands ['neðələndz] *pl. les Pays-Bas m/pl.*
Ne·vad·a [ne'vɑ:də] *État des É.-U.*
New Bruns·wick [nju:'brʌnzwik] *province du Canada.*
New·cas·tle ['nju:kɑ:sl] *ville et port d'Angleterre.*
New Del·hi ['nju:'deli] *capitale de l'Inde.*
New Eng·land ['nju:'iŋglənd] *la*

Nouvelle-Angleterre *f (États des É.-U.).*
New·found·land [nju:'faundlənd; *surt.* ⚓ nju:fənd'lænd] *Terre-Neuve f (province du Canada).*
New Hamp·shire [nju:'hæmpʃiə] *État des É.-U.*
New Jer·sey [nju:'dʒɔ:zi] *État des É.-U.*
New Guin·ea [nju:'gini] *la Nouvelle-Guinée f.*
New Mex·i·co [nju:'meksikou] *le Nouveau-Mexique m (État des É.-U.).*
New Or·le·ans [nju:'ɔ:liənz] *la Nouvelle-Orléans f (ville des É.-U.).*
New·ton ['nju:tn] *physicien et philosophe anglais.*
New York ['nju:'jɔ:k] *New York f (ville des É.-U.); New York m (État des É.-U.).*
New Zea·land [nju:'zi:lənd] *la Nouvelle-Zélande f.*
Ni·ag·a·ra [nai'ægərə] *le Niagara m (rivière de l'Amérique du Nord, unissant les lacs Erie et Ontario).*
Nich·o·las ['nikələs] *Nicolas m.*
Ni·ger ['naidʒə] *le Niger m.*
Ni·ge·ri·a [nai'dʒiəriə] *le (ou la) Nigeria m(f).*
Nile [nail] *le Nil m.*
Nix·on ['niksn] *37e président des É.-U.*
No·el ['nouəl] *prénom masculin.*
Nor·folk ['nɔ:fək] *comté d'Angleterre; ville et port des É.-U.*
North·amp·ton [nɔ:'θæmptən] *ville d'Angleterre;* a. **North'amp·ton·shire** [~ʃiə] *comté d'Angleterre.*
North·ern Ire·land [nɔ:ðən'aiə-lænd] *l'Irlande du Nord.*
North Sea ['nɔ:θ'si:] *mer f du Nord.*
North·um·ber·land [nɔ:'θʌmbə-lənd] *comté d'Angleterre.*
Nor·way ['nɔ:wei] *la Norvège f.*
Not·ting·ham ['nɔtiŋəm] *ville d'Angleterre;* a. **Not·ting·ham·shire** ['~ʃiə] *comté d'Angleterre.*
No·va Sco·tia ['nouvə'skouʃə] *la Nouvelle-Écosse f (province du Canada).*

O

Oak Ridge ['ouk'ridʒ] *ville des É.-U.; centre de recherches nucléaires.*
O'Ca·sey [ou'keisi] *dramaturge irlandais.*

O·ce·an·i·a [ouʃi'einiə] l'Océanie f.
O'Fla·her·ty [ou'flæ(h)əti] écrivain irlandais.
O'Har·a [əu'hɑːrə] nom de famille.
O.Hen·ry [əu'henri] écrivain américain.
O·hi·o [ou'haiou] rivière des É.-U.; État des É.-U.
O·kla·ho·ma [ouklə'houmə] État des É.-U.; ~ City capitale de l'Oklahoma (É.-U.).
Ol·i·ver ['ɔlivə] Olivier m.
O·liv·i·a [o'liviə] Olivia f, Olivie f.
O·ma·ha ['ouməhɑː] ville des É.-U.
O'Neill [ou'niːl] auteur américain.
On·tar·i·o [ɔn'tɛəriou] province du Canada; Lake ~ le lac m Ontario (un des cinq grands lacs de l'Amérique du Nord).
Or·ange ['ɔrindʒ] l'Orange m (fleuve de l'Afrique australe).
Or·e·gon ['ɔrigən] État des É.-U.
Ork·ney Is·lands ['ɔːkni'ailəndz] pl. les Orcades f/pl. (comté d'Écosse).
Or·well ['ɔːwəl] auteur anglais.
Os·borne ['ɔzbən] auteur anglais.
Os·lo ['ɔzlou] capitale de la Norvège.
Ost·end [ɔs'tend] Ostende f.
O'Sul·li·van [əu'sʌlivən] nom de famille.
Ot·ta·wa ['ɔtəwə] capitale du Canada.
Ouse [uːz] nom de deux rivières d'Angleterre.
Ox·ford ['ɔksfəd] ville universitaire d'Angleterre; a. **Ox·ford·shire** ['~ʃiə] comté d'Angleterre.
O·zark Moun·tains ['ouzɑː'k'mauntinz] pl. les Ozark m/pl. (massif des É.-U.).

P

Pa·cif·ic [pə'sifik] le Pacifique m.
Pad·dy ['pædi] diminutif de Patrick; sobriquet de l'Irlandais.
Pak·i·stan [pɑːkis'tɑːn] le Pakistan m.
Pall Mall ['pel'mel] rue des Londres.
Palm Beach ['pɑːm'biːtʃ] station balnéaire de la Floride (É.-U.).
Pal·mer ['pɑː(l)mə] nom de famille.
Pan·a·ma [pænə'mɑː, 'pænəmɑː] le Panama m.
Par·a·guay ['pærəgwai] le Paraguay m.
Par·is ['pæris] Paris m.
Pa·tri·cia [pə'triʃə] prénom féminin.

Pat·rick ['pætrik] Patrice m, Patrick m (patron de l'Irlande).
Paul [pɔːl] Paul m.
Pau·line [pɔː'liːn; '~] Pauline f.
Pearl Har·bor ['pəːl'hɑːbə] port des îles Hawaii.
Peg(·gy) ['peg(i)] Margot m.
Pe·kin(g) ['piːkin (~kin)] Pékin.
Pem·broke(·shire) ['pembruk(ʃiə)] comté du Pays de Galles.
Penn·syl·va·nia [pensil'veinjə] la Pennsylvanie f (État des É.-U.).
Per·cy ['pəːsi] prénom masculin.
Pe·ru [pə'ruː] le Pérou m.
Pe·ter ['piːtə] Pierre m.
Phil·a·del·phi·a [filə'delfjə] Philadelphie f (ville des É.-U.).
Phil·ip ['filip] Philippe m.
Phil·ip·pines ['filipiːnz] pl. archipel de la mer de Chine.
Phoe·be ['fiːbi] prénom féminin.
Phoe·nix ['fiːniks] capitale de l'Arizona (É.-U).
Pic·ca·dil·ly [pikə'dili] rue de Londres.
Pierce [piəs] prénom: nom de famille.
Pin·ter ['pintə] dramatiste anglais.
Pitts·burgh ['pitsbəːg] ville des É.-U.
Pla·to ['pleitou] Platon m (philosophe grec).
Plym·outh ['pliməθ] ville et port d'Angleterre; ville des É.-U.
Poe [pou] auteur américain.
Po·land ['poulənd] la Pologne f.
Poll [pɔl] Mariette f, Manon f.
Port·land ['pɔːtlənd] ville et port des É.-U. (Maine); ville des É.-U. (Oregon).
Ports·mouth ['pɔːtsməθ] ville et port d'Angleterre.
Por·tu·gal ['pɔːtugəl] le Portugal m.
Po·to·mac [pə'toumæk] fleuve des É.-U.
Pow·ell ['pauəl] nom de famille; prénom.
Prague [prɑːg] capitale de la Tchécoslovaquie.
Prus·sia ['prʌʃə] la Prusse f.
Pul·itz·er ['pulitsə] journaliste américain.
Pun·jab [pʌn'dʒɑːb] le Pendjab m.
Pur·cell ['pəːsl] compositeur anglais.

Q

Que·bec [kwi'bek] Québec m (ville et province du Canada).

Queens [kwiːnz] *quartier de New York.*
Quin·c(e)y [ˈkwinsi] *nom de famille; prénom.*

R

Ra·chel [ˈreitʃəl] Rachel *f.*
Rad·nor(·shire) [ˈrædnə(ʃiə)] *comté du Pays de Galles.*
Rae [rei] *prénom.*
Ra·leigh [ˈrɔːli; ˈrɑːli; ˈræli] *navigateur anglais; capitale de la Caroline du Nord (É.-U.).*
Ralph [reif; rælf] Raoul *m.*
Ra·wal·pin·di [rɔːlˈpindi] *capitale du Pakistan.*
Ray [rei] *prénom.*
Ray·mond [ˈreimənd] Raymond *m.*
Read·ing [ˈrediŋ] *ville industrielle d'Angleterre; ville des É.-U.*
Rea·gan [ˈregən] *40e président des É.-U.*
Re·bec·ca [riˈbekə] Rébecca *f.*
Reg·i·nald [ˈredʒinld] Renaud *m.*
Rey·kja·vik [ˈreikjəviːk] *capitale de l'Islande.*
Rhine [rain] *le Rhin m.*
Rhode Is·land [roudˈailənd] *État des É.-U.*
Rhodes [roudz] Rhodes *f.*
Rho·de·sia [rouˈdiːziə] *la Rhodésie f.*
Rich·ard [ˈritʃəd] Richard *m.*
Rich·mond [ˈritʃmənd] *capitale de la Virginie (É.-U.); district de New York; faubourg de Londres.*
Rob·ert [ˈrɔbət] Robert *m.*
Rob·in [ˈrɔbin] *diminutif de Robert.*
Rock·e·fel·ler [ˈrɔkifelə] *industriel américain.*
Rock·y Moun·tains [ˈrɔkiˈmauntinz] *les* (montagnes *f/pl.*) Rocheuses *f/pl.*
Rog·er [ˈrɔdʒə] Roger *m.*
Rome [roum] Rome *f.*
Roo·se·velt [*Am.* ˈrouzəvelt; *angl. usu.* ˈruːsvelt] *nom de deux présidents des É.-U.*
Rud·yard [ˈrʌdjəd] *prénom masculin.*
Rug·by [ˈrʌgbi] *collège et ville d'Angleterre.*
Ru·ma·ni·a [ruːˈmeinjə] *la Roumanie f.*
Rus·sel [ˈrʌsl] *nom de famille anglais.*
Rus·sia [ˈrʌʃə] *la Russie f.*
Rut·land(·shire) [ˈrʌtlənd(ʃiə)] *comté de'Angleterre.*

S

Sac·ra·men·to [sækrəˈmentou] *capitale de la Californie (É.-U.).*
Salis·bur·y [ˈsɔːlzbəri] *ville d'Angleterre.*
Sal·ly [ˈsæli] *diminutif de Sarah.*
Salt Lake Cit·y [ˈsɔːltˈleikˈsiti] *capitale de l'Utah (É.-U.).*
Sam [sæm] *diminutif de Samuel;* Uncle ~ *les États-Unis; sobriquet de l'Américain.*
Sam·u·el [ˈsæmjuəl] Samuel *m.*
San Fran·cis·co [sænfrənˈsiskou] *ville et port des É.-U.*
San Ma·ri·no [sænməˈriːnou] Saint-Marin *m.*
Sar·ah [ˈsɛərə] Sarah *f.*
Sas·katch·e·wan [səsˈkætʃiwən] *rivière et province du Canada.*
Sau·di A·ra·bi·a [sɑˈudiəˈreibjə] l'Arabie *f* Saoudite.
Say·ers [ˈseiəz] *femme écrivain anglaise.*
Scan·di·na·vi·a [skændiˈneivjə] *la* Scandinavie *f.*
Sche·nec·ta·dy [skiˈnektədi] *ville des É.-U.*
Scot·land [ˈskɔtlənd] l'Écosse *f;* ~ Yard *siège de la police londonienne.*
Sean [ʃɔːn] Jean *m.*
Scott [skɔt] *nom de famille et prénom anglais; auteur anglais.*
Se·at·tle [siˈætl] *ville et port des É.-U.*
Sev·ern [ˈsevəːn] *fleuve d'Angleterre.*
Sey·mour [ˈsiːmɔː, ˈseimɔː] *prénom; nom de famille.*
Shake·speare [ˈʃeikspiə] *poète anglais.*
Shaw [ʃɔː] *auteur anglo-irlandais.*
Shef·field [ˈʃefiːld] *ville industrielle d'Angleterre.*
Shei·la [ˈʃiːlə] *prénom féminin.*
Shel·ley [ˈʃeli] *poète anglais.*
Shir·ley [ˈʃəːli] *prénom féminin.*
Sher·lock [ˈʃəːlɔk] *prénom masculin.*
Shet·land Is·lands [ˈʃetləndˈailəndz] *pl. les îles f/pl.* (de) Shetland *(comté d'Écosse).*
Shrop·shire [ˈʃrɔpʃiə] *comté d'Angleterre.*
Sib·yl [ˈsibil] Sibylle *f.*
Sic·i·ly [ˈsisili] *la* Sicile *f.*
Sid·ney [ˈsidni] *prénom et nom de famille anglais.*
Sin·clair [ˈsinklɛə] *prénom masculin; auteur américain.*

Sin·ga·pore [siŋgə'pɔ:] Singapour *f*.

Sing-Sing ['siŋsiŋ] *prison de l'État de New York (É.-U.)*.

Snow·don ['snoudn] *montagne du Pays de Galles*.

So·fia ['soufjə] Sofia, *capitale de la Bulgarie*.

Sol·o·mon ['sɔləmən] Salomon *m*.

Som·er·set(·shire) ['sʌməsit(ʃiə)] *comté d'Angleterre*.

So·phi·a [so'faiə], **So·phy** ['soufi] Sophie *f*.

Sou·dan [su:'dæn] *see Sudan*.

South·amp·ton [sau'θæmtən] *ville et port d'Angleterre*.

South·wark ['sʌðək; 'sauθwək] *quartier de Londres*.

Spain [spein] l'Espagne *f*.

Staf·ford(·shire) ['stæfəd(ʃiə)] *comté d'Angleterre*.

Stat·en Is·land [stætn'ailənd] *quartier de New York (situé dans une île)*.

Stein·beck ['stainbek] *auteur américain*.

Ste·phen, Ste·ven ['sti:vn] Stéphan *m*.

Ste·ven·son ['sti:vnsn] *auteur anglais*.

Stew·art ['st(j)u:ət] *prénom masculin; nom de famille*.

St. Law·rence [snt'lɔ:rəns] *le* Saint-Laurent *m*.

St. Lou·is [snt'lu:is] *ville des É.-U.*

Stock·holm ['stɔkhoum] Stockholm, *capitale de la Suède*.

Strat·ford on A·von ['strætfədɔn-'eivən] *patrie de Shakespeare*.

Stu·art ['stjuət] *famille royale d'Écosse et d'Angleterre*.

Su·dan [su(:)'dɑ:n] *le* Soudan *m*.

Sue [sju:, su:] Suzanne *f*.

Su·ez ['su:iz] Suez *m*.

Suf·folk ['sʌfək] *comté d'Angleterre*.

Su·pe·ri·or [sju:'piəriə]: Lake ∼ *le* lac *m* Supérieur *(un des cinq grands lacs de l'Amérique du Nord)*.

Sur·rey ['sʌri] *comté d'Angleterre*.

Su·san ['su:zn] Suzanne *f*.

Sus·que·han·na [sʌskwə'hænə] *fleuve des É.-U.*

Sus·sex ['sʌsiks] *comté d'Angleterre*.

Swan·sea ['swɔnzi] *ville et port du Pays de Galles*.

Swe·den ['swi:dn] la Suède *f*.

Swift [swift] *auteur irlandais*.

Swit·zer·land ['switsələnd] la Suisse *f*.

Syd·ney ['sidni] *capitale de la Nouvelle-Galles du Sud (Australie)*.

Synge [siŋ] *poète et dramaturge irlandais*.

Syr·i·a ['siriə] la Syrie *f*.

T

Ta·hi·ti [tɑ:'hi:ti] Tahiti *f*.

Tal·la·has·see [tælə'hæsi] *capitale de la Floride (É.-U.)*.

Tan·gier [tæn'dʒiə] Tanger *f*.

Tay·lor ['teilə] *nom de famille*.

Ted(·dy) ['ted(i)] *diminutif de* Edward, Edmund, Theodore.

Ten·nes·see [tene'si:] *rivière des É.-U.; État des É.-U.*

Ten·ny·son ['tenisn] *poète anglais*.

Ter·ence ['terəns] *prénom masculin*.

Tex·as ['teksəs] *État des É.-U.*

Thack·er·ay ['θækəri] *auteur anglais*.

Thames [temz] *la* Tamise *f*.

The·o·dore ['θiədɔ:] Théodore *m*.

The·re·sa [ti'ri:zə] Thérèse *f*.

Thom·as ['tɔməs] Thomas *m*.

Tho·reau ['θɔ:rou] *philosophe américain*.

Ti·gris ['taigris] *le* Tigre *m*.

Tim [tim] *diminutif de* Timothy.

Tim·o·thy ['timəθi] Timothée *m*.

Ti·ra·na [ti'rɑ:nə] *capitale de l'Albanie*.

To·bi·as [tə'baiəs] Tobie *m*.

To·by ['toubi] *diminutif de* Tobias.

To·kyo ['toukjou] Tokyo.

Tol·kien ['tɔlki:n] *écrivain et philologue anglais*.

Tom(·my) ['tɔm(i)] *diminutif de* Thomas.

To·pe·ka [to'pi:kə] *capitale du Kansas (É.-U.)*.

To·ron·to [tə'rɔntou] *ville du Canada*.

Tow·er ['tauə]: the ∼ of London la Tour de Londres.

Tra·fal·gar [trə'fælgə] *cap de la côte d'Espagne*.

Trent [trent] *rivière d'Angleterre*.

Trol·lope ['trɔləp] *auteur anglais*.

Tru·man ['tru:mən] *33ᵉ président des É.-U.*

Tu·dor ['tju:də] *famille royale anglaise*.

Tu·ni·si·a [tju:'niziə] la Tunisie *f*.

Tur·key ['tə:ki] la Turquie *f*.

Twain [twein] *auteur américain*.

U

Ul·ster ['ʌlstə] l'Ulster m (*province d'Irlande*).
U·nit·ed Ar·ab Re·pub·lic [juː-'naitid'ærəbri'pʌblik] République f arabe unie.
U·nit·ed States of A·mer·i·ca [juː'naitid'steitsəvə'merikə] les États-Unis m/pl. d'Amérique.
Up·dike ['ʌpdaik] écrivain américain.
U·ri·ah [juə'raiə] prénom masculin.
U·ru·guay ['urugwai] l'Uruguay m.
U·tah ['juːtɑː] État des É.-U.

V

Val·en·tine ['væləntain] Valentin m; Valentine f.
Van·cou·ver [væn'kuːvə] ville et port du Canada.
Vat·i·can ['vætikən] le Vatican m.
Vaux·hall ['vɔksˈhɔːl] district de Londres.
Ven·e·zue·la [vene'zweilə] le Venezuela m.
Ven·ice ['venis] Venise f.
Ver·mont [vəːˈmɔnt] État des É.-U.
Ver·non ['vəːnən] prénom masculin.
Vic·to·ri·a [vik'tɔːriə] Victoire f.
Vi·en·na [vi'enə] Vienne f.
Vir·gin·ia [və'dʒinjə] la Virginie f (État des É.-U.).
Vi·tus ['vaitəs] Guy m, Gui m.
Viv·i·an ['viviən] Vivien m; Vivienne f.

W

Wa·bash ['wɔːbæʃ] rivière des É.-U.
Wales [weilz] le Pays m de Galles.
Wal·lace ['wɔləs] auteur anglais; auteur américain.
Wall Street ['wɔːlstriːt] rue de New York; siège de la Bourse.
Wal·pole ['wɔːlpoul] nom de deux écrivains anglais.
Wal·ter ['wɔːltə] Gauthier m.
War·hol ['wɑːhɔːl, 'wɑːhoul] artiste pop américain.
War·saw ['wɔːsɔː] Varsovie.
War·wick(·shire) ['wɔrik(ʃiə)] comté d'Angleterre.
Wash·ing·ton ['wɔʃiŋtən] 1er président des É.-U.; État des É.-U.; capitale et siège du gouvernement des É.-U.

Wa·ter·loo [wɔːtəˈluː] commune de Belgique.
Watt [wɔt] inventeur anglais.
Waugh [wɔː] écrivain anglais.
Wayne [wein] nom de famille; acteur américain.
Wedg·wood ['wedʒwud] céramiste anglais.
Wel·ling·ton ['weliŋtən] général et homme d'État anglais; capitale de la Nouvelle-Zélande.
Wells [welz] auteur anglais.
West·min·ster ['westminstə] quartier de Londres, siège du parlement britannique.
West·mor·land ['westmələnd] comté d'Angleterre.
West Vir·gin·ia ['westvə'dʒinjə] la Virginie Occidentale f (État des É.-U.).
Whit·acker, Whit·a·ker ['witəkə] nom de famille.
White·hall ['wait'hɔːl] rue de Londres, quartier des Ministères.
White House ['wait'haus] la Maison-Blanche f (résidence du président des É.-U. à Washington).
Wight [wait]: Isle of ~ île anglaise de la Manche.
Wilde [waild] écrivain et poète anglais.
Will [wil], **Wil·liam** ['wiljəm] Guillaume m.
Wil·son ['wilsn] homme politique britannique; 28e président des É.-U.
Wilt·shire ['wiltʃiə] comté d'Angleterre.
Wim·ble·don ['wimbldən] faubourg de Londres (championnat international de tennis).
Win·ni·peg ['winipeg] ville du Canada.
Win·ston ['winstən] prénom masculin.
Wis·con·sin [wis'kɔnsin] rivière des É.-U.; État des É.-U.
Wolfe [wulf] auteur américain.
Wol·sey ['wulzi] cardinal et homme d'État anglais.
Woolf [wulf] femme écrivain anglaise.
Worces·ter ['wustə] ville industrielle d'Angleterre et des É.-U.; a. **Worces·ter·shire** ['~ʃiə] comté d'Angleterre.
Words·worth ['wəːdzwə(ː)θ] poète anglais.
Wren [ren] architecte anglais.
Wright [rait] nom de famille; nom de

deux pionniers de l'aviation américains.

Wyc·lif(fe) [ˈwiklif] *réformateur religieux anglais.*

Wy·o·ming [waiˈoumiŋ] *État des É.-U.*

York [jɔːk] *ville d'Angleterre;* a.
York·shire [ˈ↷ʃiə] *comté d'Angleterre.*

Yo·sem·i·te [jouˈsemiti] *parc national des É.-U.*

Yu·go·sla·vi·a [ˈjuːgouˈslɑːviə] *la Yougoslavie f.*

Y

Yale U·ni·ver·si·ty [ˈjeiljuːniˈvəːsiti] *université américaine.*

Yeats [jeits] *poète irlandais.*

Yel·low·stone [ˈjeloustoun] *rivière des É.-U.; parc national.*

Yem·en [ˈjemən] *le Yémen m.*

Z

Zach·a·ri·ah [zækəˈraiə], **Zach·a·ry** [ˈzækəri] *Zacharie m.*

Zam·be·zi [zæmˈbiːzi] *le Zambèze m.*

Zim·ba·bwe [zimˈbɑːbwi] *Zimbabwe m.*

Zoe [ˈzoui] *Zoë f.*

Common British
and American Abbreviations

Abréviations usuelles, britanniques et américaines

A

a *acre* acre *f.*

A.A. *anti-aircraft* A.A., antiaérien; *Brit. Automobile Association* Automobile Club *m*; *Alcoholics Anonymous.*

A.A.A. *Brit. Amateur Athletic Association* Association *f* d'athlétisme amateur; *Am. American Automobile Association* Automobile Club *m* américaine.

A.B. *able-bodied seaman* matelot *m* (de deuxième classe); *see* B.A.

abbr. *abbreviated* abrégé; *abbreviation* abréviation *f.*

abr. *abridged* abrégé; *abridg(e)ment* abrégé *m*; réduction *f.*

A.B.C. *American Broadcasting Company* radiodiffusion-télévision *f* américaine.

A.B.M. *anti-ballistic missile* missile *m* anti-balistique.

a/c *account (current)* C.C., compte *m* (courant).

A.C. *alternating current* C.A., courant *m* alternatif.

acc(t). *account* compte *m*, note *f.*

A.D. *Anno Domini (latin = in the year of our Lord)* après J.-C., en l'an du Seigneur *ou* de grâce.

A.D.A. *Brit. Atom Development Administration* Commission *f* pour le développement de l'énergie atomique.

Adm. *Admiral* amiral *m*; *admiralty* amirauté *f.*

advt. *advertisement* annonce *f.*

AEC *Atomic Energy Commission* CEA, Commission *f* de l'énergie atomique.

A.E.F. *American Expeditionary Forces* corps *m* expéditionnaire américain.

AFL-CIO *American Federation of Labor & Congress of Industrial Organizations (fédération américaine du travail).*

A.F.N. *American Forces Network (radiodiffusion-télévison des forces armées américaines).*

AIDS *acquired immunity deficiency syndrome* S.I.D.A., syndrome *m* immuno-déficitaire acquis.

Ala. *Alabama (État des É.-U.).*

Alas. *Alaska (État des É.-U.).*

Am. *America* Amérique *f*; *American* américain.

a.m. *ante meridiem (latin = before noon)* avant midi.

A.M. *amplitude modulation* modulation *f* d'amplitude; *see* M.A.

A/P *account purchase* achat *m* porté sur un compte courant.

A.P. *Associated Press (agence d'informations américaine).*

A.P.O. *Am. Army Post Office* poste *f* aux armées.

A.R.C. *American Red Cross* Croix-Rouge *f* américaine.

Ariz. *Arizona (État des É.-U.).*

Ark. *Arkansas (État des É.-U).*

A.R.P. *air-raid precautions* D.A., défense *f* aérienne.

arr. *arrival* arrivée *f.*

A/S *account sales* compte *m* de vente.

ASA *American Standards Association* association *f* américaine de normalisation.

av. *average* moyenne *f*; avaries *f/pl.*

avdp. *avoirdupois* poids *m* du commerce.

A.W.O.L. *Am. absent without leave* absent sans permission.

B

b. *born* né(e *f*).

BA *British Airways (compagnie aérienne britannique).*

B.A. *Bachelor of Arts (approx.)* L. ès L., licencié(e *f*) *m* ès lettres.

B.A.O.R. *British Army of the Rhine* armée *f* britannique du Rhin.

Bart. *Baronet* Baronet *m (titre de noblesse).*

B.B.C. *British Broadcasting Corporation* radiodiffusion-télévision *f* britannique.

bbl. *barrel* tonneau *m*.

B.C. *before Christ* av. J.-C., avant Jésus-Christ.

B.D. *Bachelor of Divinity (approx.)* licencié(e *f*) *m* en théologie.

B.E. *Bachelor of Education (approx.)* licencié(e *f*) *m* en pédagogie; *Bachelor of Engineering (approx.)* ingénieur *m* diplômé.

B/E *Bill of Exchange* lettre *f* de change.

B.E.A. *British European Airways (compagnie aérienne britannique).*

Beds. *Bedfordshire (comté d'Angleterre).*

Benelux ['bene¹l ks] *Belgium, Netherlands, Luxemburg* Bénélux *m*, Belgique-Nederland-Luxembourg.

Berks. *Berkshire (comté d'Angleterre).*

b/f *brought forward* à reporter; report *m*.

B.F.A. *British Football Association* association *f* britannique du football.

B.F.N. *British Forces Network (radiodiffusion-télévision des forces armées britanniques).*

bl. *barrel* tonneau *m*.

B.L. *Bachelor of Law (approx.)* bachelier (-ère *f*) *m* en droit.

B/L *bill of lading* connaissement *m* (maritime).

bls. *bales* balles *f/pl.*, ballots *m/pl.*; *barrels* tonneaux *m/pl.*

B.M. *Bachelor of Medicine (approx.)* bachelier (-ère *f*) *m* en médecine.

B.M.A. *British Medical Association* association *f* médicale britannique.

B/O *Branch Office* filiale *f*.

B.O.A.C. *British Overseas Airways Corporation (compagnie aérienne britannique).*

bot. *bought* acheté; *bottle* bouteille *f*.

B.O.T. *Brit. Board of Trade* Ministère *m* du Commerce.

B.R. *British Railways (réseau national du chemin de fer britannique).*

B/R *bills receivable* effets *m/pl.* à recevoir.

B.R.C.S. *British Red Cross Society* Croix-Rouge *f* britannique.

Br(it). *Britain* la Grande-Bretagne *f*; *British* britannique.

Bros. *brothers* frères *m/pl. (dans un nom de société).*

B/S *bill of sale* acte *m (ou* contrat *m)* de vente; *Am.* facture *f*; bulletin *m* de livraison.

B.Sc. *Bachelor of Science (approx.)* L. ès Sc., licencié(e *f*) *m* ès sciences naturelles.

B.Sc.Econ. *Bachelor of Economic Science (approx.)* licencié(e *f*) *m* en économie politique.

bsh., bu. *bushel* boisseau *m*.

Bucks. *Buckinghamshire (comté d'Angleterre).*

B.U.P. *British United Press (agence d'informations britannique).*

bus(h). *bushel(s)* boisseau(x *pl.*) *m*.

C

c. *cent(s)* cent(s *pl.*) *m*; *circa* environ; *cubic* cubique, au cube; *century* siècle *m*.

C. *thermomètre:* Celsius, centigrade C, Celsius, cgr, centigrade.

C.A. *Brit. chartered accountant* expert *m* comptable.

C/A *current account* C.C., compte *m* courant.

c.a.d. *cash against documents* paiement *m* contre documents.

Cal(if). *California (État des É.-U).*

Cambs. *Cambridgeshire (comté d'Angleterre).*

Can. *Canada* Canada *m*; *Canadian* canadien.

Capt. *Captain* capitaine *m*.

C.B. *(a.* **C/B)** *cash book* livre *m* de caisse; *Companion of the Bath* Compagnon *m* de l'ordre du Bain; *Confinement to barracks* consigné au quartier.

C.B.C. *Canadian Broadcasting Corporation* radiodiffusion-télévision *f* canadienne.

C.B.I. *Confederation of British Industry* confédération *f* des industries britanniques.

C.C. *Brit. County Council* Conseil *m* de

Comté; *continuous current* C.C., courant *m* continu.

C.E. *Church of England* Église *f* Anglicane; *Civil Engineer* ingénieur *m* civil.

cert. *certificate* certificat *m*.

CET *Central European Time* H.E.C., heure *f* de l'Europe Centrale.

cf. *confer* Cf., conférez.

ch. *chain* (*approx.*) double décamètre *m*; *chapter* chapitre *m*.

Ches. *Cheshire* (*comté d'Angleterre*).

CIA *Am. Central Intelligence Agency* S.C.E., service *m* contre-espionnage.

C.I.D. *Brit. Criminal Investigation Department* (*police judiciaire*).

c.i.f. *cost, insurance, freight* C.A.F., coût, assurance, fret.

C. in C., CINC *Commander-in-Chief* commandant *m* en chef.

cl. *class* classe *f*.

Co. *Company* compagnie *f*, société *f*; *county* comté *m*.

C.O. *Commanding Officer* officier *m* commandant.

c/o *care of* aux bons soins de, chez.

C.O.D., c.o.d. *cash* (*Am. a. collect*) *on delivery* RB, (envoi *m*) contre remboursement.

Col. *Colorado* (*État des É.-U.*); *Colonel* Col., colonel *m*.

Colo. *Colorado* (*État des É.-U.*).

Conn. *Connecticut* (*État des É.-U.*).

Cons. *Conservative* conservateur *m*.

Corn. *Cornwall* (*comté d'Angleterre*).

Corp. *corporation* compagnie *f* (commerciale); *Corporal* caporal *m*.

cp. *compare* comparer.

C.P. *Canadian Press* (*agence d'informations canadienne*).

C.P.A. *Am. Certified Public Accountant* expert *m* comptable.

ct(s). *cent(s)* cent(s *pl.*) *m*.

cu(b). *cubic* cubique, au cube.

Cum(b). *Cumberland* (*comté d'Angleterre*).

c.w.o. *cash with order* payable à la commande.

cwt. *hundredweight* quintal *m*.

D

d. *penny, pence* (*pièce de monnaie britannique*); *died* m., mort.

D.A. *deposit account* compte *m* de dépôts; *Am. District Attorney approx.* procureur *m* de la République.

D.A.R. *Am. Daughters of the American Revolution* Filles *f/pl.* de la révolution américaine (*union patriotique féminine*).

D.B. *Day Book* (livre *m*) journal *m*.

D.C. *direct current* courant *m* continu; *District of Columbia* (*district fédéral des É.-U., capitale Washington*).

D.C.L. *Doctor of Civil Law* Docteur *m* en droit civil.

d-d *damned* s..., sacré ...!

D.D. *Doctor of Divinity* Docteur *m* en théologie.

DDD *Am. direct distance dialing* service *m* automatique interurbain.

DDT *dichloro-diphenyl-trichloroethane* D.D.T., dichlorodiphényltrichloréthane *m* (*insecticide*).

dec. *deceased* déc(édé).

Del. *Delaware* (*État des É.-U.*).

dep. *departure* depart *m*.

dept. *department* dép., département *m*.

Derby. *Derbyshire* (*comté d'Angleterre*).

Devon. *Devonshire* (*comté d'Angleterre*).

dft. *draft* traite *f*.

disc. *discount* escompte *m*.

div. *dividend* div., dividende *m*.

D.I.Y. *do-it-yourself* de bricolage (*magasin etc.*).

D.J. *disc jockey*.

do. *ditto* do., dito.

doc. *document* document *m*.

Dors. *Dorsetshire* (*comté d'Angleterre*).

doz. *dozen(s)* Dzne, douzaine(s *pl.*) *f*.

d/p *documents against payment* documents *m/pl.* contre paiement.

dpt. *department* dép., département *m*.

dr. *dra(ch)m* (*poids*); *drawer* tireur *m*.

Dr. *Doctor* Dr, docteur *m*; *debtor* débiteur *m*.

d.s., d/s *days after sight* traite: jours *m/pl.* de vue.

Dur(h). *Durhamshire* (*comté d'Angleterre*).

dwt. *pennyweight* (*poids*).

dz. *dozen(s)* Dzne, douzain(s *pl.*) *f*.

E

E. *east* E., est *m*; *eastern* (de l')est; *English* anglais.

E. & O.E. *errors and omissions excepted* S.E. ou O., sauf erreur ou omission.

E.C. *East Central* (*district postal de Londres*).

ECE *Economic Commission for Europe* CEE, Commission *f* économique pour l'Europe.

ECOSOC *Economic and Social Council* CES, Conseil *m* Économique et Social.

ECSC *European Coal and Steel Community* CECA, Communauté *f* européenne du charbon et de l'acier.

Ed., ed. *edition* édition *f*; *editor* éditeur *m*.

EDP *electronic data processing* informatique *f*.

EE., E./E. *errors excepted* sauf erreur.

EEC *European Economic Community* CEE, Communauté *f* économique européenne.

EFTA *European Free Trade Association* AELE, Association *f* européenne de libre échange.

e.g. *exempli gratia* (*latin = for instance*) p.ex., par exemple.

EMA *European Monetary Agreement* A.M.E., Accord *m* monétaire européen.

enc(l). *enclosure(s)* pièce(s *pl.*) *f* jointe(s).

Eng(l). *England* l'Angleterre *f*; *English* anglais.

EPU *European Payments Union* UEP, Union *f* européenne de paiements.

Esq. *Esquire* Monsieur *m* (*titre de politesse*).

ESRO *European Space-Research Organization* Organisation *f* européenne de recherches spatiales.

Ess. *Essex* (*comté d'Angleterre*).

E.T.A. *estimated time of arrival* heure *f* probable d'arrivée.

etc., &c. *et cetera, and so on* etc., et cætera, et ainsi de suite.

E.T.D. *estimated time of departure* heure *f* probable de départ.

EUCOM *Am. European Command* commandement *m* des troupes en Europe.

EURATOM *European Atomic Energy Community* EURATOM, Communauté *f* européenne de l'énergie atomique.

exam. *examination* examen *m*.

excl. *exclusive, excluding* non compris.

ex div. *ex dividend* ex D., ex-dividende.

ex int. *ex interest* sans intérêt.

F

f. *fathom* brasse *f*; *feminine* f., féminin; *foot* (*feet*) pied(s *pl.*) *m*; *following* suivant.

F. *thermomètre: Fahrenheit* F, Fahrenheit; *Fellow* agrégé(e *f*) *m*, membre *m* (*d'une société savante*).

F.A. *Football Association* Association *f* du football.

f.a.a. *free of all average* franc de toute avarie.

Fahr. *thermomètre: Fahrenheit* F, Fahrenheit.

FAO *Food and Agriculture Organization* OAA, Organisation *f* pour l'alimentation et l'agriculture.

f.a.s. *free alongside ship* F.A.S., franco à quai.

FBI *Federal Bureau of Investigation* (*service du département de la Justice des É.-U. qui est à la charge de la police fédérale*).

F.B.I. *Federation of British Industries* fédération *f* des industries britanniques.

F.C.C. *Am. Federal Communications Commission* Comité *m* fédéral des communications.

fig. *figure(s)* figure(s) *f*/(*pl.*).

Fla. *Florida* (*État des É.-U.*).

fm. *fathom* brasse *f*.

F.M. *frequency modulation* F.M., fréquence *f* modulée, modulation *f* de fréquence.

F.O. *Foreign Office* Ministère *m* britannique des Affaires étrangères.

f.o.b. *free on board* F.A.B., franco à bord.

fo(l). *folio* folio *m*, feuillet *m*.

f.o.q. *free on quay* F.O.Q., franco à quai.

f.o.r. *free on rail* F.O.R., franco sur rail.

f.o.t. *free on truck* F.O.T., franco en wagon.

f.o.w. *free on waggon* F.O.W., franco en wagon.

F.P. *fire-plug* bouche *f* d'incendie; *freezing point* point *m* de congélation.

fr. *franc(s)* franc(s) *m*/(*pl.*).

Fr. *France* la France *f*; *French* français.

Fri. *Friday* vendredi *m*.

ft. *foot* (*feet*) pied(s *pl.*) *m*.

FTC *Am. Federal Trade Commission* commission *f* du commerce fédéral.

fur. *furlong* (*mesure*).

G

g. *gauge* mesure-étalon *f*; ✂ écartement *m*; *gramme* gr., gramme *m*; *guinea* guinée *f* (*unité monétaire anglaise*); *grain* grain *m* (*poids*).

G *Am. cin. general audiences* pour tout le monde.

Ga. *Georgia* (*État des É.-U.*).

G.A. *General Agent* agent *m* d'affaires; *General Assembly* assemblée *f* générale.

gal. *gallon* gallon *m*.

GATT *General Agreement on Tariffs and Trade* Accord *m* Général sur les Tarifs Douaniers et le Commerce.

G.B. *Great Britain* la Grande-Bretagne *f*.

G.B.S. *George Bernard Shaw*.

G.C.B. (*Knight*) *Grand Cross of the Bath* (Chevalier *m*) Grand-croix *f* de l'ordre du Bain.

GCE *Brit. General Certificate of Education* Certificat *m* général d'éducation.

GDR *German Democratic Republic* RDA, République *f* démocratique allemande.

gen. *generally* généralement.

Gen. *General* Gal, général *m*.

GFR *German Federal Republic* RFA, République *f* fédérale d'Allemagne.

gi. *gill* gill *m*.

G.I. *government issue* fourni par le gouvernement; *fig. le* soldat américain.

gl. *gill* gill *m*.

G.L.C. *Greater London Council* (*conseil municipal de Londres*).

Glos. *Gloucestershire* (*comté d'Angleterre*).

G.M.T. *Greenwich mean time* T.U., temps universel.

GNP *gross national product* PNB, produit *m* national brut.

gns. *guineas* guinées *f/pl.* (*unité monétaire anglaise*).

G.O.P. *Am. Grand Old Party* (*le parti républicain*).

Gov(t). *Government* gouvernement *m*.

G.P. *general practitioner* médecin *m* de médecine générale.

G.P.O. *General Post Office* bureau *m* central des postes.

gr. *grain* grain *m* (*poids*); *gross* brut; grosse *f*.

gr.wt. *gross weight* poids *m* brut.

gs. *guineas* guinées *f/pl.* (*unité monétaire anglaise*).

Gt.Br. *Great Britain* la Grande-Bretagne *f*.

guar. *guaranteed* avec garantie.

H

h. *hour(s)* h., heure(s *pl.*) *f*.

Hants. *Hampshire* (*comté d'Angleterre*).

H.B.M. *His* (*Her*) *Britannic Majesty* Sa Majesté *f* britannique.

H.C. *House of Commons* Chambre *f* des Communes.

H.C.J. *Brit. High Court of Justice* Haute Cour *f* de Justice.

H.E. *high explosive* explosif *m* puissant; très explosif; *His Excellency* Son Excellence *f*.

Heref. *Herefordshire* (*comté d'Angleterre*).

Herts. *Hertfordshire* (*comté d'Angleterre*).

hf. *half* demi.

H.F. *high frequency* H.F., haute fréquence *f*.

HGV *Brit. heavy goods vehicle* poids lourds *m*.

hhd. *hogshead* fût *m*.

H.I. *Hawaiian Islands* les Hawaii *f/pl.* (*État des É.-U.*).

H.L. *House of Lords* Chambre *f* des Lords.

H.M. *His* (*Her*) *Majesty* S.M., Sa Majesté *f*.

H.M.S. *His* (*Her*) *Majesty's Service* service *m* de Sa Majesté (*marque des administrations nationales, surt. pour la franchise postale*); *His* (*Her*) *Majesty's Ship* le navire *m* de guerre ...

H.O. *Head Office* bureau *m or* siège *m* central, agence *f* centrale; *Home Office* Ministère *m* britannique de l'Intérieur.

Hon. *Honorary* honoraire; *Honourable* l'honorable (*titre de politesse ou de noblesse*).

H.P., h.p. *horse-power* ch, c.v., cheval-vapeur *m*; *high pressure* haute pression *f*; *hire purchase* achat *m or* vente *f* à tempérament.

H.Q., Hq. *Headquarters* quartier *m* général, état-major *m*.

H.R. *Am. House of Representatives* Chambre *f* des Représentants.

H.R.H. *His (Her) Royal Highness* S.A.R., Son Altesse *f* Royale.
hrs. *hours* heures *f/pl.*
H.T., h.t. *high tension* haute tension *f.*
ht *height* hauteur *f.*
Hunts. *Huntingdonshire (comté d'Angleterre).*

I

I. *Island, Isle* île *f; Idaho (État des É.-U.).*
Ia. *Iowa (État des É.-U.).*
IAAF *International Amateur Athletic Federation* FIAA, Fédération *f* internationale d'athlétisme amateur.
IATA *International Air Transport Association* Association *f* internationale des transports aériens.
I.B. *Invoice Book* livre *m* des achats.
ib(id). *ibidem (latin = in the same place)* ibid., ibidem.
IC *integrated circuit* circuit *m* intégré.
ICAO *International Civil Aviation Organization* OACI, Organisation *f* de l'aviation civile internationale.
I.C.B.M. *intercontinental ballistic missile* missile *m* balistique intercontinental.
ICFTU *International Confederation of Free Trade Unions* CISL, Confédération *f* internationale des syndicats libres.
ICPO *International Criminal Police Organization* OIPC, INTERPOL, Organisation *f* internationale de police criminelle.
ICRC *International Committee of the Red Cross* CICR, Comité *m* international de la Croix-Rouge.
id. *idem (latin = the same author ou word)* id., idem.
I.D. *Intelligence Department* service *m* des renseignements.
Id(a). *Idaho (État des É.-U.).*
ID card *identification or identity card* carte *f* d'identité.
i.e. *id est (latin = that is to say)* c.-à-d., c'est-à-dire.
IFT *International Federation of Translators* FIT, Fédération *f* internationale des traducteurs.
I.H.P., i.h.p. *indicated horse-power* chevaux *m/pl.* indiqués.
Ill. *Illinois (État des É.-U.).*
ILO *International Labo(u)r Organization* OIT, Organisation *f* internationale du travail.
IMF *International Monetary Fund* FMI, Fonds *m* monétaire international.
in. *inch(es)* pouce(s *pl.*) *m.*
Inc. *Incorporated* associés *m/pl. (après un nom de société), Am.* S.A., société *f* anonyme; *inclosure* pièce *f* jointe.
incl. *inclusive, including* inclusivement; y compris; ... compris.
incog. *incognito* incognito.
Ind. *Indiana (État des É.-U.).*
ins. *inches* pouces *m/pl.*
I.N.S. *International News Service* agence *f* d'informations internationale.
inst. *instant* c*t*, courant, de ce mois.
IOC *International Olympic Committee* CIO, Comité *m* international olympique.
I.of.M. *Isle of Man (île anglaise).*
I.of.W. *Isle of Wight (île anglaise).*
I.O.U. *I owe you* reconnaissance *f* de dette.
IPA *International Phonetic Association* API, Association *f* phonétique internationale.
I.Q. *intelligence quotient* quotient *m* intellectuel.
Ir. *Ireland* l'Irlande *f; Irish* irlandais.
I.R.A. *Irish Republican Army* Armée *f* républicaine d'Irlande.
IRC *International Red Cross* CRI, Croix-Rouge *f* internationale.
IRO *International Refugee Organization* OIR, Organisation *f* internationale pour les refugiés.
ISBN *international standard book number* ISBN.
ISO *International Organization for Standardization* OIN, Organisation *f* internationale de normalisation.
ITO *International Trade Organization* OIC, Organisation *f* internationale du commerce.
IUS *International Union of Students* UIE, Union *f* internationale des étudiants.
IUSY *International Union of Socialist Youth* UIJS, Union *f* internationale de la jeunesse socialiste.
IVS(P.) *International Voluntary Service (for peace)* SCI, Service *m* civil international (pour la paix).
I.W.W. *Industrial Workers of the World* Confédération *f* mondiale des ouvriers industriels.
IYHF *International Youth Hostel Fede-*

ration FIAJ, Fédération *f* internationale des auberges de la jeunesse.

J

J. *judge* juge *m*; *justice* justice *f*; juge *m*.
J.C. *Jesus Christ* J.-C., Jésus-Christ.
J.I.B. *Brit. Joint Intelligence Bureau* (service de renseignements et de sécurité).
J.P. *Justice of the Peace* juge *m* de paix.
Jr. *junior* (*latin = the younger*) cadet; fils; jeune.
Jun(r). *junior* (*latin = the younger*) cadet; fils.

K

Kan(s). *Kansas* (État des É.-U.).
K.C. *Knight Commander* Chevalier *m* Commandeur; *Brit. King's Counsel* conseiller *m* du Roi (approx. avocat général).
K.C.B. *Knight Commander of the Bath* Chevalier *m* Commandeur de l'ordre du Bain.
kg. *kilogramme* kg, kilogramme *m*.
K.G.B. *Russian secret police* (police secrète russe).
K.K.K. *Ku Klux Klan* (association secrète de l'Amérique du Nord hostile aux Noirs).
km. *kilometre* km, kilomètre *m*.
k.o., KO *knock(ed) out* K.-O., knockout.
k.v. *kilovolt* kV, kilovolt *m*.
k.w. *kilowatt* kW, kilowatt *m*.
Ky. *Kentucky* (État des É.-U.).

L

l. *left* gauche; *line* ligne *f*; *vers m*; *link* (mesure); *litre* l, litre *m*.
£ *pound sterling* livre *f* sterling (unité monétaire britannique).
La. *Louisiana* (État des É.-U.).
LA *Los Angeles* (ville des É.-U.).
Lancs. *Lancashire* (comté d'Angleterre).
lat. *latitude* lat., latitude *f*.
lb. *pound* livre *f* (poids).
L.C. *letter of credit* lettre *f* de crédit.
l.c. *loco citato* (latin = at the place cited) loc. cit., loco citato.
L.C.J. *Lord Chief Justice* président *m* du Tribunal du Banc de la Reine.

Leics. *Leicestershire* (comté d'Angleterre).
Lincs. *Lincolnshire* (comté d'Angleterre).
ll. *lines* v.v., vers *m/pl.*, ll., lignes *f/pl.*
LL.D. *legum doctor* (latin = Doctor of Laws) Docteur *m* en Droit.
LMT *local mean time* heure *f* locale.
loc.cit. *loco citato* (latin = at the place cited) loc. cit., loco citato.
L of N *League of Nations* SDN, Société *f* des Nations.
lon(g). *longitude* longitude *f*.
l.p. *low pressure* BP, basse pression *f*.
L.P. *Labour Party* Parti *m* Travailliste.
LP *long-playing record*, *long-player* (disque *m*) microsillon *m*.
LSD *lysergic acid diethylamide* diéthylamide *m* de l'acide lysergique (hallucinogène).
L.S.S. *Life Saving Service* service *m* américain de sauvetage.
Lt. *Lieutenant* Lt, Lieut., lieutenant *m*.
L.T., l.t. *low tension* BT, basse tension *f*.
Lt.-Col. *Lieutenant-Colonel* Lt-Col., lieutenant-colonel *m*.
Ltd. *limited* à responsabilité limitée (après un nom de société).
Lt.-Gen. *Lieutenant-General* général *m* de corps d'armée.

M

m *minim* (mesure).
m. *masculin* m., masculin; *metre* m, mètre *m*; *mile* mille *m*; *minute* mn, minute *f*.
M.A. *Master of Arts* Maître *m* ès Arts; diplômé(e *f*) *m* d'études supérieures.
Maj. *Major* commandant *m*.
Maj.-Gen. *Major-General* général *m* de brigade.
Man. *Manitoba* (État des É.-U.).
Mass. *Massachusetts* (État des É.-U.).
M.C. *Master of Ceremonies* maître *m* des cérémonies; *Am. Member of Congress* membre *m* du Congrès.
MCH *Maternal and Child Health* PMI, Protection *f* maternelle et infantile.
M.D. *medicinae doctor* (latin = Doctor of Medicine) Docteur *m* en Médecine; *Managing Director* Président *m* directeur général.
Md. *Maryland* (État des É.-U.).
Me. *Maine* (État des É.-U.).
mg. *milligramme* mg, milligramme *m*.

mi. *mile* mille *m.*
MI 5 (6) *Military Intelligence, section five (six) (service contre-espionnage).*
Mich. *Michigan (État des É.-U.).*
min. *minute(s)* mn, minute(s) *f/(pl.);* *minimum* minimum *m.*
Minn. *Minnesota (État des É.-U.).*
Miss. *Mississippi (État des É.-U.).*
mm. *millimetre* mm, millimètre *m.*
Mo. *Missouri (État des É.-U.).*
M.O. *money order* mandat-poste *m;* *mail order* achat *m or* vente *f* par correspondence.
Mon. *Monday* lundi *m.*
Mont. *Montana (État des É.-U.).*
MP, M.P. *Member of Parliament* membre *m* de la Chambre des Communes; *Military Police* P.M., police *f* militaire.
m.p.g. *miles per gallon approx.* litres au cent (kilomètres).
m.p.h. *miles per hour* milles *m/pl.* à l'heure *(vitesse horaire).*
Mr. *Mister* M., Monsieur *m.*
Mrs. *Mistress* Mᵐᵉ, Madame *f.*
MS. *manuscript* ms, manuscrit *m.*
Ms. [miz] = *Miss or Mrs.* Madame.
M.S. *motorship* M/S, navire *m* à moteur Diesel.
MSA *Mutual Security Agency* organisation *f* américaine de sécurité mutuelle.
MSS *manuscripts* mss, manuscrits *m/pl.*
mt. *megaton* mégatonne *f.*
Mt. *Mount* mont *m.*

N

N. *north* N., nord *m; northern* (du) nord.
N.A.A.F.I. *Navy, Army and Air Force Institutes (cantines organisées à l'intention des troupes britanniques).*
NASA *Am. National Aeronautics and Space Administration* administration *f* des questions aéronautiques et spatiales.
NATO *North Atlantic Treaty Organization* OTAN, Organisation *f* du traité de l'Atlantique Nord.
n.b., N.B. *nota bene (latin* = *note well)* N.B., notez bien.
N.B.C. *National Broadcasting Corporation (radiodiffusion-télévision américaine).*
N.C. *North Carolina (État des É.-U.).*

N.C.B. *Brit. National Coal Board* Office *m* national du charbon.
n.d. *no date* s.d., sans date.
N.D(ak). *North Dakota (État des É.-U.).*
N.E. *northeast* N.E., nord-est *m; northeastern* (du) nord-est.
Neb(r). *Nebraska (État des É.-U.).*
Nev. *Nevada (État des É.-U.).*
N.F., n/f. *no funds* défaut *m* de provision.
N.H. *New Hampshire (État des É.-U.).*
N.H.S. *Brit. National Health Service (service de santé national; sécurité sociale).*
N.J. *New Jersey (État des É.-U.).*
N.M(ex). *New Mexico (État des É.-U.).*
No. *(a. no.) numero* Nº, nº, numéro *m; number* nombre *m; north* N., nord *m.*
Norf. *Norfolk (comté d'Angleterre).*
Northants. *Northamptonshire (comté d'Angleterre).*
Northumb. *Northumberland (comté d'Angleterre).*
Notts. *Nottinghamshire (comté d'Angleterre).*
n.p. or d. *no place or date* s.l.n.d., sans lieu ni date.
N.S.P.C.A. *Brit. National Society for the Prevention of Cruelty to animals* S.P.A., Société *f* protectrice des animaux.
N.S.P.C.C. *National Society for the Prevention of Cruelty to Children* Société *f* nationale protectrice des enfants.
Nt.wt. *net weight* poids *m* net.
N.U.M. *Brit. National Union of Mineworkers* Syndicat *m* national des mineurs.
N.W. *northwest* N.O., N.W., nord-ouest; *northwestern* (du) nordouest.
N.Y. *New York (État des É.-U.).*
N.Y.C. *New York City* ville *f* de New York.
N.Z. *New Zealand* la Nouvelle-Zélande *f.*

O

O. *Ohio (État des É.-U.); order* ordre *m.*
o/a *on account* P.C., Pour-compte.
OAP *old-age-pensioner* retraité(e *f*) *m.*
O.A.S. *Organization of American States* O.E.A., Organisation *f* des États américains.
ob. *obiit (latin* = *died)* décédé.

OECD *Organization for Economic Co-operation and Development* OCED, Organisation *f* de coopération économique et de développement.

OEEC *Organization for European Economic Cooperation* OECE, Organisation *f* éuropéenne de coopération économique.

O.H. *on hand* en magasin.

O.H.M.S. *On His (Her) Majesty's Service* (pour le) service *m* de Sa Majesté (*marque des administrations nationales, surt. pour la franchise postale*).

O.K. (*peut-être de*) *all correct* très bien, d'accord.

Okla. *Oklahoma* (*État des É.-U.*).

O.N.A. *Overseas News Agency* (*agence d'informations américaine*).

O.N.S. *Overseas News Service* (*agence d'informations britannique*).

OPEC *Organization of Petroleum Exporting Countries* OPEP, Organisation *f* des pays exportateurs de pétrole.

o.r. *owner's risk* aux risques et périls du propriétaire.

Ore(g). *Oregon* (*État des É.-U.*).

Oxon. *Oxfordshire* (*comté d'Angleterre*).

oz. *ounce(s)* once(s *pl.*) *f*.

P

p (*new*) *penny*, (*new*) *pence* (*pièce de monnaie britannique*).

p. *page* page *f*; *part* partie *f*.

p.a. *per annum* (*latin = yearly*) par an.

Pa. *Pennsylvania* (*État des É.-U.*).

P.A. *public address* (*system*) sonorisation *f*; *personal assistant* assistant(e *f*) *m* personnel(le).

Panam *Pan American Airways* (*compagnie aérienne américaine*).

par. *paragraph* paragraphe *m*, alinéa *m*.

P.A.Y.E. *Brit. pay as you earn* impôt *m* retenu à la source.

P.C. *post-card* carte *f* postale; *police constable* gardien *m* de la paix, policeman *m*; *Personal Computer* ordinateur *m* personnel.

p.c. *per cent* P.C., pour-cent.

p/c *price current* P.C., prix *m* courant.

pd *paid* payé.

P.D. *Police Department* police *f*; *a.* **p.d.** *per diem* (*latin = by the day*) par jour.

P.E.N. *usu.* **PEN Club** *Poets, Playwrights, Editors, Essayists and Novelists* Union *f* internationale PEN (*fédération internationale d'écrivains*).

Penn(a). *Pennsylvania* (*État des É.-U.*).

per pro(c). *per procurationem* (*latin = by proxy*) par procuration.

P.f.c. *Am. private first class* caporal *m*.

PG *cin. parental guidance* (*suggested*) (*contient des scènes qui nécessitent l'explication des parents*).

Ph.D. *Philosophiae Doctor* (*latin = Doctor of Philosophy*) Docteur *m* en Philosophie.

pk. *peck* (*mesure*).

P./L. *profit and loss* profits et pertes.

PLC *public limited company* S.A., société *f* anonyme.

PLO *Palestine Liberation Organization* O.L.P., Organisation *f* de libération de la Palestine.

p.m. *post meridiem* (*latin = after noon*) de l'après-midi.

P.M. *Prime Minister* Premier ministre.

P.O. *Post Office* bureau *m* de poste; (*a.* **p.o.**) *postal order* mandat-poste *m*.

P.O.B. *Post Office Box* boîte *f* postale.

p.o.d. *pay on delivery* contre remboursement.

P.O.O. *Post Office Order* mandat-poste *m*.

P.O.S.B. *Post Office Savings Bank* caisse *f* d'épargne postale.

P.O.W. *Prisoner of War* P.G., prisonnier *m* de guerre.

p.p. *per procurationem* (*latin = by proxy*) par procuration.

P.R. *public relations* relations *f/pl.* publiques.

Pres. *President* président(e *f*) *m*.

Prof. *Professor* professeur *m*.

prox. *proximo* (*latin = next month*) du mois prochain.

P.S. *postscript* P.-S., post-scriptum *m*; *Passenger Steamer* paquebot *m*.

pt. *pint* pinte *f*.

P.T.A. *Parent-Teacher Association* Association *f* professeurs-parents.

Pte. *Private* soldat *m* de 1ère *ou* de 2ème classe.

P.T.O., p.t.o. *please turn over* T.S.V.P., tournez, s'il vous plaît.

PVC *polyvinyl chloride* chlorure *f* de polyvinyle.

Pvt. *Private* soldat *m* de 1ère *ou* de 2ème classe.

P.W. *Prisoner of War* P.G., prisonnier *m* de guerre.

PX *Post Exchange* (*cantines de l'armée américaine*).

Q

q. *query* question *f.*

Q.C. *Brit. Queen's Counsel* conseiller *m* de la Reine (*approx. avocat général*).

qr. *quarter* quarter *m.*

qt. *quart* (*approx.*) litre *m.*

qu. *query* question *f.*

quot. *quotation* cours *m.*

qy. *query* question *f.*

R

R *Am. cin. restricted* (*les mineurs doivent être accompagnés de leurs parents*).

R. *River* rivière *f*; fl., fleuve *m*; *Road* r., rue *f*; *thermomètre:* Réaumur R, Réaumur.

r. *right* dr., droit, à droite.

R.A. *Royal Academy* Académie *f* royale.

R.A.C. *Brit. Royal Automobile Club* Automobile Club *m* royal.

RADWAR *Am. radiological warfare* guerre *f* atomique.

R.A.F. *Royal Air Force* armée *f* de l'air britannique.

R.C. *Red Cross* C.R., Croix-Rouge *f*; *Roman Catholic* catholique.

rd. *rod* (*mesure*).

Rd. *Road* r., rue *f.*

recd. *received* reçu.

ref(c). (*In*) *reference* (*to*) faisant suite à; mention *f.*

regd. *registered* déposé; *poste:* recommandé.

reg.tn. *register(ed) tonnage* tonnage *m* enregistré.

res. *residence* résidence *f*; *research* recherche(s) *f*/(*pl.*).

resp. *respective(ly)* respectif (respectivement).

ret. *retired* retraité, à la retraite.

Rev. *Reverend* Révd., Révérend.

R.I. *Rhode Island* (*État des É.-U.*).

R.L.O. *Brit. Returned Letter Office* retour *m* à l'envoyeur.

rm *room* pièce *f*, chambre *f.*

R.N. *Royal Navy* Marine *f* britannique.

R.P. *reply* paid R.P., réponse *f* payée.

r.p.m. *revolutions per minute* t.p.m., tours *m*/*pl.* par minute.

R.R. *Am. Railroad* ch.d.f., chemin *m* de fer.

R.S. *Brit. Royal Society* Société *f* royale.

R.S.V.P. répondez s'il vous plaît.

Rt.Hon. *Right Honourable* le très honorable.

Ry. *Brit. Railway* Ch.d.f., chemin *m* de fer.

S

S. *South* S., sud *m*; *Southern* (du) sud.

s. *second* s, seconde *f*; *shilling* shilling *m.*

S.A. *South Africa* l'Afrique *f* du Sud; *South America* l'Amérique *f* du Sud; *Salvation Army* Armée *f* du Salut.

SACEUR *Supreme Allied Commander Europe* Commandant *m* Suprême des Forces Alliées en Europe.

SACLANT *Supreme Allied Commander Atlantic* Commandant *m* Suprême des Forces Alliées de l'Atlantique.

s.a.e. *stamped addressed envelope* enveloppe *f* munie de timbre et d'adresse.

Salop. *Shropshire* (*comté d'Angleterre*).

Sask. *Saskatchewan* (*province du Canada*).

S.B. *Sales Book* livre *m* de(s) vente(s).

S.C. *South Carolina* (*État des É.-U.*); *Security Council* Conseil *m* de Sécurité.

S.D(ak). *South Dakota* (*État des É.-U.*).

S.E. *Southeast* S.E., sud-est *m*; *southeastern* (du) sud-est; *Stock Exchange* Bourse *f.*

SEATO *South East Asia* (*Collective Defense*) *Treaty Organisation* O.T.A.S.E., Organisation *f* du traité de (défense collective pour) l'Asie du Sud-Est.

sec. *second* s, seconde *f.*

Sec. *Secretary* secrétaire *m*; ministre *m.*

SF *science fiction* science-fiction *f.*

SG *Secretary General* SG, Secrétaire *m* général.

sen(r). *senior* (*latin* = *the elder*) aîné, père.

S(er)gt. *Sergeant* Sgt, sergent *m.*

sh. *shilling* shilling *m*; ✝ *share* action *f.*

SHAPE *Supreme Headquarters Allied Powers Europe* Quartiers *m*/*pl.* Généraux des Forces Alliées en Europe.

S.M. *Sergeant-Major* Sergent-major *m.*

S.N. *shipping note* note *f* d'expédition.
Soc. *society* société *f*, association *f*; *Socialist* socialiste (*a. su.*).
Som(s). *Somersetshire* (*comté d'Angleterre*).
SOS *S.O.S.* (*signal de détresse*).
sov. *sovereign* souverain *m* (*pièce de monnaie britannique*).
sp.gr. *specific gravity* gravité *f* spécifique.
S.P.Q.R. *small profits, quick returns* à petits bénéfices, vente rapide.
sq. *square* ... carré.
Sq. *Square* place *f*.
Sr. *senior* (*latin = the elder*) aîné, père.
S.R.N. *Brit. State Registered Nurse* infirmière *f* diplômée d'État.
S.S. *steamship* S/S, navire *m* à vapeur.
st. *stone* (*poids*).
St. *Saint* St(*e f*); *saint*(*e f*); *Street* r., rue *f*; *Station* gare *f*.
Sta. *station* gare *f*.
Staffs. *Staffordshire* (*comté d'Angleterre*).
S.T.D. *Brit. subscriber trunk dialling service* m automatique interurbain.
St. Ex. *Stock Exchange* Bourse *f*.
stg. *sterling* sterling *m* (*unité monétaire britannique*).
sub. *substitute* succédané *m*.
Suff. *Suffolk* (*comté d'Angleterre*).
Sun. *Sunday* dimanche *m*.
suppl. *supplement* supplément *m*.
Suss. *Sussex* (*comté d'Angleterre*).
S.W. *southwest* S.-O., sud-ouest; *southwestern* (du) sud-ouest.
Sy. *Surrey* (*comté d'Angleterre*).

T

t. *ton* tonne *f*.
TB *tuberculosis* TB, tuberculose *f*.
TC *Trusteeship Council of the United Nations* Conseil *m* de tutelle des Nations Unies.
T.D. *Treasury Department* Ministère *m* américain des Finances.
tel. *telephone* téléphone *m*.
Tenn. *Tennessee* (*État des É.-U.*).
Tex. *Texas* (*État des É.-U.*).
tgm. *telegram* télégramme *m*.
T.G.W.U. *Brit. Transport General Workers' Union* Confédération *f* des employés d'entreprises de transport.
Thur(s). *Thursday* jeudi *m*.
T.M.O. *telegraph money order* mandat *m* télégraphique.

tn *ton*(*s*) tonne(*s*) *f*/(*pl.*).
TNT *trinitrotoluene* trinitrotoluène *m*.
T.O. *Telegraph (Telephone) Office* bureau *m* télégraphique (téléphonique).
t.o. *turnover* chiffre *m* d'affaires.
T.P.O. *Travelling Post Office* poste *f* ambulante.
TT *teetotal*(*ler*) abstinent (*a. su.*).
T.U. *Trade(s) Union(s)* syndicat(*s pl.*) *m* ouvrier(*s*).
T.U.C. *Brit. Trade(s) Union Congress* (*approx.*) C.G.T., Confédération *f* générale du travail.
Tue(s). *Tuesday* mardi *m*.
TV. *television* T.V., télévision *f*.
T.V.A. *Tennessee Valley Authority* (*organisation pour l'exploitation de la vallée de la rivière Tennessee*).
T.W.A. *Trans World Airlines* (*compagnie aérienne américaine*).

U

U *Brit. cin. universal* pour tout le monde.
UFO *unidentified flying object* OVNI *m*, objet *m* volant non identifié.
U.H.F. *ultra-high frequency* UHF, ultra haute fréquence *f*.
U.K. *United Kingdom* Royaume-Uni *m*.
ult. *ultimo* (*latin = last day of the month*) dernier, du mois dernier.
UMW *Am. United Mine Workers* Syndicat *m* des mineurs.
U.N. *United Nations* Nations *f/pl.* Unies.
UNESCO *United Nations Educational, Scientific, and Cultural Organization* UNESCO, Organisation *f* des Nations Unies pour l'Éducation, la Science et la Culture.
UNICEF *United Nations International Children's Emergency Fund* FISE, Fonds *m* International de Secours aux Enfants.
UNO *United Nations Organization* O.N.U., Organisation *f* des Nations Unies.
U.N.S.C. *United Nations Security Council* Conseil *m* de Sécurité des Nations Unies.
UPI *United Press International* (*agence d'informations américaine*).
U.S.(A.) *United States (of America)* É.-U., États-Unis *m/pl.* (d'Amérique).

USAF(E) *United States Air Force (Europe)* armée *f* de l'air des É.-U. (en Europe).

U.S.S.R. *Union of Socialist Soviet Republics* U.R.S.S., Union *f* des Républiques Socialistes Soviétiques.

Ut. *Utah* (*État des É.-U.*).

V

v. *verse* v., vers *m*, verset *m*; *versus* (*latin = against*) contre; *vide* (*latin = see*) v., voir, voyez.

V *volt* V, volt *m*.

Va. *Virginia* (*État des É.-U.*).

V.A.T. *value-added tax* T.V.A., taxe *f* à la valeur ajoutée.

V.D. *venereal disease* M.V., maladie *f* vénérienne.

VHF *very high frequency* OTC, onde *f* très courte.

V.I.P. *very important person* personnage *m* important.

Vis. *viscount(ess)* vicomte(sse *f*) *m*.

viz. *videlicet* (*latin = namely*) à savoir; c.-à-d., c'est-à-dire.

vol. *volume* t., tome *m*, vol., volume *m*.

vols. *volumes* tomes *m/pl.*, volumes *m/pl.*

V.P., V.Pres. *Vice-President* vice-président(e *f*) *m*.

V.S. *veterinary surgeon* vétérinaire *m*.

V.S.O.P. *very superior old pale* (*cognac de qualité supérieure*).

Vt. *Vermont* (*État des É.-U.*).

V.T.O.(L.) *vertical take-off (and landing) (aircraft)* A.D.A.V., avion *m* à décollage et atterrissage vertical.

v.v *vice versa* (*latin = conversely*) vice versa, réciproquement.

W

W *watt* W, watt *m*.

W. *west* O., W., ouest *m*; *western* (de l')ouest.

War. *Warwickshire* (*comté d'Angleterre*).

Wash. *Washington* (*État des É.-U.*).

W.C. *West Central* (*district postal de Londres*); *water-closet* W.-C., water-closet *m*.

WCC *World Council of Churches* COE, Conseil *m* œcuménique des églises.

Wed(s). *Wednesday* mercredi *m*.

WFPA *World Federation for the Protection of Animals* FMPA, Fédération *f* mondiale pour la protection des animaux.

WFTU *World Federation of Trade Unions* F.S.M., Fédération *f* syndicale mondiale.

WHO *World Health Organization* OMS, Organisation *f* mondiale de la Santé.

W. I. *West Indies* Indes *f/pl.* occidentales.

Wilts. *Wiltshire* (*comté d'Angleterre*).

Wis. *Wisconsin* (*État des É.-U.*).

wk *week* semaine *f*.

wkly *weekly* hebdomadaire; par semaine.

wks *weeks* semaines *f/pl.*

W/L., w.l. *wave length* longueur *f* d'onde.

w/o *without* sans.

W.O.M.A.N. *World Organization of Mothers of All Nations* Organisation *f* mondiale des mères de famille.

Worcs. *Worcestershire* (*comté d'Angleterre*).

W.P. *weather permitting* si le temps le permet.

W.S.R. *World Students' Relief* service *m* international de secours aux étudiants.

W/T *wireless telegraphy (telephony)* T.S.F., Télégraphie *f* (Téléphonie *f*) sans Fil.

wt. *weight* poids *m*.

W. Va. *West Virginia* (*État des É.-U.*).

WW *World War* guerre *f* mondiale.

Wyo. *Wyoming* (*État des É.-U.*).

X

X *cin. adults only* interdit aux mineurs.

x.-d. *ex dividend* ex D., ex-dividende.

x.-i. *ex interest* sans intérêt.

Xmas *Christmas* Noël *f*.

Xn *christian* chrétien.

Xroads *cross roads* carrefour *m*.

Xt. *Christ* le Christ, Jésus-Christ *m*.

Y

yd. *yard(s)* yard(s *pl.*) *m*.

YMCA *Young Men's Christian Association* UCJG, Union *f* chrétienne de jeunes gens.

Yorks. *Yorkshire* (*comté d'Angleterre*).

yr(s.) *year(s)* an(s) *m/(pl.)*.

YWCA *Young Women's Christian Association* Union *f* chrétienne féminine.

Numerals

Nombres

Cardinal Numbers — Nombres cardinaux

0 nought, zero, cipher *zéro*	50 fifty *cinquante*
1 one *un, une*	60 sixty *soixante*
2 two *deux*	70 seventy *soixante-dix*
3 three *trois*	71 seventy-one *soixante et onze*
4 four *quatre*	72 seventy-two *soixante-douze*
5 five *cinq*	80 eighty *quatre-vingts*
6 six *six*	81 eighty-one *quatre-vingt-un*
7 seven *sept*	90 ninety *quatre-vingt-dix*
8 eight *huit*	91 ninety-one *quatre-vingt-onze*
9 nine *neuf*	100 a *ou* one hundred *cent*
10 ten *dix*	101 one hundred and one *cent un*
11 eleven *onze*	200 two hundred *deux cents*
12 twelve *douze*	211 two hundred and eleven *deux*
13 thirteen *treize*	*cent onze*
14 fourteen *quatorze*	1000 a *ou* one thousand *mille*
15 fifteen *quinze*	1001 one thousand and one *mille un*
16 sixteen *seize*	1100 eleven hundred *onze cents*
17 seventeen *dix-sept*	1967 nineteen hundred and sixty-
18 eighteen *dix-huit*	seven *dix-neuf cent soixante-*
19 nineteen *dix-neuf*	*sept*
20 twenty *vingt*	2000 two thousand *deux mille*
21 twenty-one *vingt et un*	1 000 000 a *ou* one million *un million*
22 twenty-two *vingt-deux*	2 000 000 two million *deux millions*
30 thirty *trente*	1 000 000 000 a *ou* one milliard, *Am.*
40 forty *quarante*	one billion *un milliard*

Ordinal Numbers — Nombres ordinaux

1. first *le premier, la première*	17. seventeenth *dix-septième*
2. second *le ou la deuxième, le second,*	18. eighteenth *dix-huitième*
la seconde	19. nineteenth *dix-neuvième*
3. third *troisième*	20. twentieth *vingtième*
4. fourth *quatrième*	21. twenty-first *vingt et unième*
5. fifth *cinquième*	22. twenty-second *vingt-deuxième*
6. sixth *sixième*	30. thirtieth *trentième*
7. seventh *septième*	31. thirty-first *trente et unième*
8. eighth *huitième*	40. fortieth *quarantième*
9. ninth *neuvième*	41. forty-first *quarante et unième*
10. tenth *dixième*	50. fiftieth *cinquantième*
11. eleventh *onzième*	51. fifty-first *cinquante et unième*
12. twelfth *douzième*	60. sixtieth *soixantième*
13. thirteenth *treizième*	61. sixty-first *soixante et unième*
14. fourteenth *quatorzième*	70. seventieth *soixante-dixième*
15. fifteenth *quinzième*	71. seventy-first *soixante et on-*
16. sixteenth *seizième*	*zième*

72. seventy-second *soixante-douzième*
80. eightieth *quatre-vingtième*
81. eighty-first *quatre-vingt-unième*
90. ninetieth *quatre-vingt-dixième*

91. ninety-first *quatre-vingt-onzième*
100. (one) hundredth *centième*
101. hundred and first *cent unième*
200. two-hundredth *deux centième*
1000. (one) thousandth *millième*

Fractions — Fractions

½ one half *(un) demi*; (the) half *la moitié*
1½ one and a half *un et demi*
⅓ one third *un tiers*
⅔ two thirds *deux tiers*
¼ one quarter *un quart*
¾ three quarters *(les) trois quarts*

⅕ one fifth *un cinquième*
⅝ five eights *(les) cinq huitièmes*
⁹⁄₁₀ nine tenths *(les) neuf dixièmes*
0.45 point four five *zéro, virgule, quarante-cinq*
17.38 seventeen point three eight *dix-sept, virgule, trente-huit*

British and American weights and measures

Mesures britanniques et américaines

Linear Measures — Mesures de longueur

1 inch (in.)
= 2,54 cm
1 foot (ft.)
= 12 inches = 30,48 cm
1 yard (yd.)
= 3 feet = 91,44 cm
1 link (l.)
= 7.92 inches = 20,12 cm

1 rod (rd.), pole *ou* **perch (p.)**
= 25 links = 5,03 m
1 chain (ch.)
= 4 rods = 20,12 m
1 furlong (fur.)
= 10 chains = 201,17 m
1 (statute) mile (mi.)
= 8 furlongs = 1609,34 m

Nautical Measures — Mesures nautiques

1 fathom (fm.)
= 6 feet = 1,83 m
1 cable's length
= 100 fathoms = 183 m

Am. 120 fathoms
= 219 m
1 nautical mile (n.m.)
= 10 cables' length = 1852 m

Square Measures — Mesures de surface

1 square inch (sq. in.)
= 6,45 cm²
1 square foot (sq. ft.)
= 144 square inches
= 929,03 cm²
1 square yard (sq. yd.)
= 9 square feet = 0,836 m²

1 square rod (sq. rd.)
= 30.25 square yards = 25,29 m²
1 rood (ro.)
= 40 square rods = 10,12 ares
1 acre (a.)
= 4 rods = 40,47 ares
1 square mile (sq. mi.)
= 640 acres = 2,59 km²

Cubic Measures — Mesures de volume

1 cubic inch (cu. in.)
= 16,387 cm³
1 cubic foot (cu. ft.)
= 1728 cubic inches
= 0,028 m³

1 cubic yard (cu. yd.)
= 27 cubic feet = 0,765 m³
1 register ton (reg. tn.)
= 100 cubic feet
= 2,832 m³

British Measures of Capacity — Mesures de capacité britanniques

1 gill (gi., gl.)
= 0,142 l
1 pint (pt.)
= 4 gills = 0,568 l

1 quart (qt.)
= 2 pints = 1,136 l
1 gallon (gal.)
= 4 quarts = 4,546 l

1 **peck (pk.)**
= 2 gallons = 9,092 l
1 **bushel (bu., bsh.)**
= 4 pecks = 36,36 l

1 **quarter (qr.)**
= 8 bushels = 290,94 l
1 **barrel (bbl., bl.)**
= 36 gallons = 1,636 hl

U.S. Measures of Capacity — Mesures de capacité américaines

1 **dry pint**
= 0,550 l
1 **dry quart**
= 2 dry pints = 1,1 l
1 **peck**
= 8 dry quarts = 8,81 l
1 **bushel**
= 4 pecks = 35,24 l
1 **liquid gill**
= 0,118 l

1 **liquid pint**
= 4 liquid gills = 0,473 l
1 **liquid quart**
= 2 liquid pints = 0,946 l
1 **gallon**
= 4 liquid quarts = 3,785 l
1 **barrel**
= 31.50 gallons = 119 l
1 **barrel petroleum**
= 42 gallons = 158,97 l

Apothecaries' Fluid Measures — Mesures pharmaceutiques

1 **minim (min., m.)**
= 0,0006 dl
1 **fluid drachm,** *Am.* **dram (dr. fl.)**
= 60 minims = 0,0355 dl

1 **fluid ounce (oz. fl.)**
= 8 fluid drachms = 0,284 dl
1 **pint (pt.)**
Brit. = 20 fluid ounces = 0,586 l
Am. = 16 fluid ounces = 0,473 l

Avoirdupois Weight – Poids (système avoirdupois)

1 **grain (gr.)**
= 0,0684 g
1 **drachm,** *Am.* **dram (dr. av.)**
= 27.34 grains = 1,77 g
1 **ounce (oz. av.)**
= 16 drachms = 28,35 g
1 **pound (lb. av.)**
= 16 ounces = 0,453 kg
1 **stone (st.)**
= 14 pounds = 6,35 kg
1 **quarter (qr.)**

Brit. = 28 pounds = 12,70 kg
Am. = 25 pounds = 11,34 kg
1 **hundredweight (cwt.)**
Brit. = 112 pounds = 50,80 kg
Am. = 100 pounds = 45,36 kg
1 **long ton (tn. l.)**
Brit. = 20 hundredweights
= 1016 kg
1 **short ton (tn. sh.)**
Am. = 20 hundredweights
= 907,18 kg

Troy and Apothecaries' Weight –
Poids (système troy) et poids pharmaceutiques

1 **grain (gr.)**
= 0,0684 g
1 **scruple (s. ap.)**
= 20 grains = 1,296 g
1 **pennyweight (dwt.)**
= 24 grains = 1,555 g

1 **drachm,** *Am.* **dram (dr. t., dr. ap.)**
= 3 scruples = 3,888 g
1 **ounce (oz. ap.)**
= 8 drachms = 31,104 g
1 **pound (lb. t., lb. ap.)**
= 12 ounces = 0,373 kg

Conjugations of English verbs
Conjugaisons des verbes anglais

a) Conjugaison régulière faible

L'actif du présent de l'indicatif a la forme de l'infinitif. La 3e personne du singulier se termine par ...s. Après une consonne sonore, cet s se sonorise; p.ex. *he sends* [sendz]; après une consonne sourde, il est sourd; p.ex. *he paints* [peints]; après une sifflante, suivie d'un e muet ou non, elle se termine par ...es, prononcé [iz]; p.ex. *he catches* ['kætʃiz], *wishes* ['wiʃiz], *passes* ['pɑːsiz], *judges* ['dʒʌdʒiz], *rises* ['raiziz]. Les verbes terminés par ...o précédé d'une consonne la forment en ...es, prononcé [z]; p.ex. *he goes* [gouz].

Le prétérit et le participe passé se forment en ajoutant ...ed, ou, après e, ...d seulement, à l'infinitif; p.ex. *fetched* [fetʃt], mais *agreed* [ə'griːd], *judged* [dʒʌdʒd]. La terminaison ...ed se prononce [d] après un radical sonore; p.ex. *arrived* [ə'raivd], *judged* [dʒʌdʒd]. Ajoutée à la fin d'un radical sourd, elle se prononce [t]; p.ex. *liked* [laikt]. Après les verbes se terminant par ...d, ...de, ...t et ...te cet ...ed se prononce [id]; p.ex. *mended* ['mendid], *glided* ['glaidid], *painted* ['peintid], *hated* ['heitid].

La terminaison du participe présent et du gérondif se rend par ...ing. Les verbes terminés par ...ie les forment en ...ying; p.ex. *lie* [lai]: *lying* ['laiiŋ].

Les verbes terminés par ...y précédé d'une consonne transforment cet y en i et prennent les terminaisons ...es, ...ed; devant ...ing, y reste inchangé; p.ex. *try* [trai]: *he tries* [traiz], *he tried* [traid], mais *trying* ['traiiŋ].

Un e muet à la fin d'un verbe tombe devant ...ed ou ...ing; p.ex. *loved* [lʌvd], *loving* ['lʌviŋ]. Des cas exceptionnels sont *dyeing* ['daiiŋ] de *dye* [dai] et *shoeing* ['ʃuːiŋ] de *shoe* [ʃuː]. Pour des raisons phonétiques *singe* [sindʒ] a *singeing* ['sindʒiŋ] comme participe présent.

Les verbes terminés par une consonne simple précédée d'une seule voyelle accentuée, ou les verbes terminés par r simple, précédé d'une seule voyelle longue, redoublent leur consonne finale devant les terminaisons ...ed et ...ing; p.ex.

to lob [lɔb]	lobbed [lɔbd]	lobbing ['lɔbiŋ]
to wed [wed]	wedded ['wedid]	wedding ['wediŋ]
to beg [beg]	begged [begd]	begging ['begiŋ]
to step [step]	stepped [stept]	stepping ['stepiŋ]
to quit [kwit]	quitted ['kwitid]	quitting ['kwitiŋ]
to compel [kəm'pel]	compelled [kəm'peld]	compelling [kəm'peliŋ]
to bar [bɑː]	barred [bɑːd]	barring ['bɑːriŋ]
to stir [stəː]	stirred [stəːd]	stirring ['stəːriŋ]

Dans les verbes terminés par **...l** ou **...p**, précédé d'une seule voyelle simple, inaccentuée, le redouble-ment se fait si l'on écrit le mot à l'anglaise, et ne se fait pas générale-ment si on l'écrit à l'américaine:

to travel ['trævl] *travelled* ['trævld] *travelling* ['trævliŋ]
to worship ['wɔːʃip] *worshipped* ['wɔːʃipt] *worshipping* ['wɔːʃipiŋ]

Les verbes terminés par **...c** transforment ce **c** en **ck** devant **...ed** et **...ing**; p.ex. *to traffic* ['træfik] *trafficked* ['træfikt] *trafficking* ['træfikiŋ].

Le subjonctif présent a la même forme que l'indicatif, à l'exception de la 3e personne du singulier qui ne prend pas d's. Au prétérit il correspond à l'indicatif.

Les temps composés se forment à l'aide de l'auxiliaire *to have,* plus le participe passé.

Le passif se forme à l'aide de l'auxiliaire *to be,* plus le participe passé.

b) Liste des verbes forts et des verbes faibles irréguliers

La première forme en caractère gras indique le présent (*present*); après le premier tiret, on trouve le passé simple (*preterite*), après le deuxième tiret, le participe passé (*past participle*).

abide - abode - abode
arise - arose - arisen
awake - awoke - awoke, awaked

be (am, is, are) - was (were) - been
bear - bore - borne *porté,* born *né*
beat - beat - beaten, beat
become - became - become
beget - begot - begotten
begin - began - begun
belay - belayed, belaid - belayed, belaid
bend - bent - bent
bereave - bereaved, bereft - bereaved, bereft
beseech - besought - besought
bestead - besteaded - bested, bestead
bestrew - bestrewed - bestrewed, bestrewn
bestride - bestrode - bestridden
bet - bet, betted - bet, betted
bid - bade, bid - bidden, bid
bind - bound - bound
bite - bit - bitten
bleed - bled - bled
blow - blew - blown
break - broke - broken
breed - bred - bred
bring - brought - brought

build - built - built
burn - burnt, burned - burnt, burned
burst - burst - burst
buy - bought - bought

can - could
cast - cast - cast
catch - caught - caught
chide - chid - chid, chidden
choose - chose - chosen
cleave - clove, cleft - cloven, cleft
cling - clung - clung
clothe - clothed, *poét.* clad - clothed, *poét.* clad
come - came - come
cost - cost - cost
creep - crept - crept
cut - cut - cut

dare - dared, durst - dared
deal - dealt - dealt
dig - dug - dug
do - did - done
draw - drew - drawn
dream - dreamt, dreamed - dreamt, dreamed
drink - drank - drunk
drive - drove - driven
dwell - dwelt - dwelt

eat - ate -eaten

fall - fell - fallen
feed - fed - fed
feel - felt - felt
fight - fought - fought
find - found - found
flee - fled - fled
fling - flung - flung
fly - flew - flown
forbear - forbore - forborne
forbid - forbad(e) - forbidden
forget - forgot - forgotten
forgive - forgave - forgiven
forsake - forsook - forsaken
freeze - froze - frozen

geld - gelded, gelt - gelded, gelt
get - got - got
gild - gilded, gilt - gilded, gilt
gird - girded, girt - girded, girt
give - gave - given
go - went - gone
grave - graved - graved, graven
grind - ground - ground
grow - grew - grown

hang - hung, hanged - hung, hanged
have (has) - had - had
hear - heard - heard
heave - heaved, ♧ hove - heaved, ♧ hove
hew - hewed - hewed, hewn
hide - hid - hidden, hid
hit - hit - hit
hold - held - held
hurt - hurt - hurt

keep - kept - kept
kneel - knelt, kneeled - knelt, kneeled
knit - knitted, knit - knitted, knit
know - knew - known

lade - laded - laded, laden
lay - laid - laid
lead - led - led
lean - leaned, leant - leaned, leant
leap - leaped, leapt - leaped, leapt
learn - learned, learnt - learned, learnt
leave - left - left
lend - lent - lent

let - let - let
lie - lay - lain
light - lighted, lit - lighted, lit
lose - lost - lost

make - made - made
may - might
mean - meant - meant
meet - met - met
mow - mowed - mowed, mown
must - must

ought

pay - paid - paid
pen - penned, pent - penned, pent
put - put - put

read - read - read
rend - rent - rent
rid - ridded, rid - rid, ridded
ride - rode - ridden
ring - rang - rung
rise - rose - risen
rive - rived - riven
run - ran - run

saw - sawed - sawn, sawed
say - said - said
see - saw - seen
seek - sought - sought
sell - sold - sold
send - sent - sent
set - set - set
sew - sewed - sewed, sewn
shake - shook - shaken
shall - should
shave - shaved - shaved, shaven
shear - sheared - shorn
shed - shed - shed
shine - shone - shone
shoe - shod - shod
shoot - shot - shot
show - showed - shown
shred - shredded - shredded, shred
shrink - sharnk - shrunk
shut - shut - shut
sing - sang - sung
sink - sank - sunk
sit - sat - sat
slay - slew - slain
sleep - slept - slept
slide - slid - slid

sling - slung - slung
slink - slunk - slunk
slit - slit - slit
smell - smelt, smelled - smelt, smelled
smite - smote - smitten
sow - sowed - sown, sowed
speak - spoke - spoken
speed - sped, ⊕ speeded - sped, ⊕ speeded
spell - spelt, spelled - spelt, spelled
spend - spent - spent
spill - spilt, spilled - spilt, spilled
spin - spun, span - spun
spit - spat - spat
split - split - split
spoil - spoiled, spoilt - spoiled, spoilt
spread - spread - spread
spring - sprang - sprung
stand - stood - stood
stave - staved, stove - staved, stove
steal - stole - stolen
stick - stuck - stuck
sting - stung - stung
stink - stunk, stank - stunk
strew - strewed - (have) strewed, (be) strewn
stride - strode - stridden
strike - struck - struck

string - strung - strung
strive - strove - striven
swear - swore - sworn
sweep - swept - swept
swell - swelled - swollen
swim - swam - swum
swing - swung - swung
take - took - taken
teach - taught - taught
tear - tore - torn
tell - told - told
think - thought - thought
thrive - throve - thriven
throw - threw - thrown
thrust - thrust - thrust
tread - trod - trodden
wake - woke, waked - waked, woke(n)
wear - wore - worn
weave - wove - woven
weep - wept - wept
wet - wetted, wet - wetted, wet
will - would
win - won - won
wind - wound - wound
work - worked, *surt.* ⊕ wrought - worked, *surt.* ⊕ wrought
wring - wrung - wrung
write - wrote - written

Temperature Conversion Tables
Tables de conversion des températures

1. FROM $-273\,°C$ **TO** $+1000\,°C$
1. DE $-273\,°C$ À $+1000\,°C$

Celsius °C	Kelvin K	Fahrenheit °F	Réaumur °R
1000	1273	1832	800
950	1223	1742	760
900	1173	1652	720
850	1123	1562	680
800	1073	1472	640
750	1023	1382	600
700	973	1292	560
650	923	1202	520
600	873	1112	480
550	823	1022	440
500	773	932	400
450	723	842	360
400	673	752	320
350	623	662	280
300	573	572	240
250	523	482	200
200	473	392	160
150	423	302	120
100	373	212	80
95	368	203	76
90	363	194	72
85	358	185	68
80	353	176	64
75	348	167	60
70	343	158	56
65	338	149	52
60	333	140	48
55	328	131	44
50	323	122	40
45	318	113	36
40	313	104	32
35	308	95	28
30	303	86	24
25	298	77	20
20	293	68	16
15	288	59	12
10	283	50	8
+ 5	278	41	+ 4
0	273.15	32	0
− 5	268	23	− 4
− 10	263	14	− 8

Celsius °C	Kelvin K	Fahrenheit °F	Réaumur °R
− 15	258	+ 5	− 12
− 17.8	255.4	0	− 14.2
− 20	253	− 4	− 16
− 25	248	− 13	− 20
− 30	243	− 22	− 24
− 35	238	− 31	− 28
− 40	233	− 40	− 32
− 45	228	− 49	− 36
− 50	223	− 58	− 40
− 100	173	− 148	− 80
− 150	123	− 238	− 120
− 200	73	− 328	− 160
− 250	23	− 418	− 200
− 273.15	0	− 459.4	− 218.4

2. CLINICAL THERMOMETER
2. THERMOMÈTRE MÉDICAL

Celsius °C	Fahrenheit °F	Réaumur °R
42.0	107.6	33.6
41.8	107.2	33.4
41.6	106.9	33.3
41.4	106.5	33.1
41.2	106.2	33.0
41.0	105.8	32.8
40.8	105.4	32.6
40.6	105.1	32.5
40.4	104.7	32.3
40.2	104.4	32.2
40.0	104.0	32.0
39.8	103.6	31.8
39.6	103.3	31.7
39.4	102.9	31.5
39.2	102.6	31.4
39.0	102.2	31.2
38.8	101.8	31.0
38.6	101.5	30.9
38.4	101.1	30.7
38.2	100.8	30.6
38.0	100.4	30.4
37.8	100.0	30.2
37.6	99.7	30.1
37.4	99.3	29.9
37.2	99.0	29.8
37.0	98.6	29.6
36.8	98.2	29.4
36.6	97.9	29.3

3. RULES FOR CONVERTING TEMPERATURES
3. FORMULES DE CONVERSION DES TEMPÉRATURES

	Celsius	*Kelvin*
$x\,°C$	–	$= x + 273.15\,K$
$x\,K$	$= x - 273.15\,°C$	–
$x\,°F$	$= \frac{5}{9}(x - 32)\,°C$	$= \frac{5}{9}(x - 32) + 273.15\,K$
$x\,°R$	$= \frac{5}{4}x\,°C$	$= \left(\frac{5}{4}x\right) + 273.15\,K$
	Fahrenheit	*Réaumur*
$x\,°C$	$= \frac{9}{5}x + 32\,°F$	$= \left(\frac{4}{5}x\right)\,°R$
$x\,K$	$= \frac{9}{5}(x - 273.15) + 32\,°F$	$= \frac{4}{5}(x - 273.15)\,°R$
$x\,°F$	–	$= \frac{4}{9}(x - 32)\,°R$
$x\,°R$	$= \left(\frac{9}{4}x\right) + 32\,°F$	–

Phonetic Alphabets

Codes d'épellation

	Français	Anglais britannique	Anglais américain	International	Aviation civile
A	Anatole	Andrew	Abel	Amsterdam	Alfa
B	Berthe	Benjamin	Baker	Baltimore	Bravo
C	Célestin	Charlie	Charlie	Casablanca	Charlie
D	Désiré	David	Dog	Danemark	Delta
E	Eugène	Edward	Easy	Edison	Echo
É	Émile	—	—	—	—
F	François	Frederick	Fox	Florida	Foxtrot
G	Gaston	George	George	Gallipoli	Golf
H	Henri	Harry	How	Havana	Hotel
I	Irma	Isaac	Item	Italia	India
J	Joseph	Jack	Jig	Jerusalem	Juliett
K	Kléber	King	King	Kilogramme	Kilo
L	Louis	Lucy	Love	Liverpool	Lima
M	Marcel	Mary	Mike	Madagaskar	Mike
N	Nicolas	Nellie	Nan	New York	November
O	Oscar	Oliver	Oboe	Oslo	Oscar
P	Pierre	Peter	Peter	Paris	Papa
Q	Quintal	Queenie	Queen	Québec	Quebec
R	Raoul	Robert	Roger	Roma	Romeo
S	Suzanne	Sugar	Sugar	Santiago	Sierra
T	Thérèse	Tommy	Tare	Tripoli	Tango
U	Ursule	Uncle	Uncle	Upsala	Uniform
V	Victor	Victor	Victor	Valencia	Victor
W	William	William	William	Washington	Whiskey
X	Xavier	Xmas	X	Xanthippe	X-Ray
Y	Yvonne	Yellow	Yoke	Yokohama	Yankee
Z	Zoé	Zebra	Zebra	Zürich	Zulu